William Collins' dream of knowledge for all began with the publication of his first book in 1819. A self educated mill worker, he not only enriched millions of lives, but also founded a flourishing publishing house. Today, staying true to this spirit, Collins books are packed with inspiration, innovation, and practical expertise. They place you at the centre of a world of possibility and give you exactly what you need to explore it.

Language is the key to this exploration, and at the heart of Collins Dictionaries is language as it is really used. New words, phrases, and meanings spring up every day, and all of them are captured and analysed by the Collins Word Web. Constantly updated, and with over 2.5 billion entries, this living language resource is unique to our dictionaries.

Words are tools for life. And a Collins Dictionary makes them work for you.

Collins. Do more.

SCRABBLE

BRAND Crossword Game

Collins

HarperCollins Publishers
Westerhill Road
Bishopbriggs
Glasgow
G64 2QT

First Edition 2009

Reprint 10 9 8 7 6 5 4 3 2

© HarperCollins Publishers 2009

Collins Complete Scrabble Companion
ISBN 978-0-00-733196-3

Collins Ultimate Scrabble Word List
ISBN 978-0-00-733769-9
ISBN 978-0-00-787741-6 (WHS Edition)

www.collinslanguage.com

A catalogue record for this book is available from
the British Library

Typeset by Thomas Callan

Printed and bound at Thomson Press (India) Ltd

Acknowledgements
We would like to thank those authors and
publishers who kindly gave permission for
copyright material to be used in the Collins
Word Web. We would also like to thank Times
Newspapers Ltd for providing valuable data.

EDITORIAL STAFF

SCRABBLE® CONSULTANTS
Allan Simmons
Darryl Francis

EDITORS
Katharine Coates
Kay Cullen
Justin Crozier
Susan Gillespie
Lorna Gilmour
Alice Grandison
Penny Hands
Andrew Holmes
Helen Hucker
Cordelia Lilly
Cormac McKeown
Mike Munro
Elspeth Summers

COMPUTING SUPPORT
Thomas Callan

CORPUS RESEARCH
Nigel Rochford

FOR THE PUBLISHERS
Lucy Cooper
Elaine Higgleton

Contents

Introduction

This book is the most comprehensive SCRABBLE® reference, comprising the game's complete word list together with definitions for words of up to nine letters. As such, this book is an invaluable tool for any competitive or club player, as well as the ultimate authority for settling disputes between those who play with their friends and family.

A staggering 268,000 words are listed in this book – representing an exhaustive list of every valid play in **SCRABBLE®**. The book is divided into two sections: Section 1 contains every word of between two and nine letters, with either a definition or a cross reference to a defined root word at each entry, while Section 2 contains words of ten to fifteen letters, without definitions. In any SCRABBLE® game, most words will be between two and nine letters, with longer words being formed only very rarely. Therefore, while this book lists every word that could conceivably be played on the SCRABBLE® board, the main focus is on words that players are likely to have the opportunity to form from the seven letters on their rack and the words that are placed on the board during the game.

Section 1 thus allows every **SCRABBLE®** player, whether a beginner or veteran, access to the definitions of all the most useful words in **SCRABBLE®**, enabling them to learn words by meaning rather than simply as combinations of letters. For many players definitions are the key to remembering words, and to using them in **SCRABBLE®**, and the ability to check meanings, inflections, and variant spellings will add interest to most social games.

Definitions in Section 1 are succinct and practical. In many cases, only a single definition is given, and in general only those parts of speech necessary for existing inflections are included. Cross-referred words include noun plurals, verb inflections, the comparative and superlative forms of adjectives, and variant spellings. Adjectives formed with obvious suffixes, such as -*like* and -*less*, are also cross-referred to the root word when the meaning is easily deduced.

Section 2 contains all of the longer words permissible in **SCRABBLE®**, from ten to fifteen letters in length. Most of these words will only rarely appear on the board, due to their length, which is why definitions are not provided. The main function of this section of the book is to act as an indisputable authority when such longer words are played. Players may also wish to explore ways in which they can 'build' on words on the board by consulting Section 2. By exploring the ways in which shorter words can be combined with common suffixes such as -*man*, -*woman*, -*like*, -*less*, -*ness*, and -*lessness*, and the prefixes such as *non*-, *un*-, *over*-, and *under*-, the keen **SCRABBLE®** player can add an extra dimension to his or her game.

There is also a supplementary section, *A Quick Guide to Scrabble*, in the centre of this book. This section is new to this edition and includes expert advice on the best words for using up the J, Q, X, and Z tiles, tactics to help you outwit your opponent, and advice on how to achieve higher scores.

Unlike a conventional dictionary, every word in each section is listed in strict alphabetical order, regardless of the relationship between words. Thus there may be several, or many, words between the singular form of a noun and its plural. This strict alphabetization allows rapid checking of words – which is particularly important during **SCRABBLE®** tournaments.

Collins would also like to give warm thanks to Darryl Francis and Allan Simmons for their enormous contribution to the word list in this dictionary. They worked tirelessly with the editorial team to get this right. Any errors – and all the definitions in this book – are the responsibility of the publisher.

Using this book

This book includes all playable words of two to nine letters in length, in one straight alphabetical list. These words are either defined or cross-referred. Cross-referred words include noun plurals, verb inflections, the comparative and superlative forms of adjectives, and variant spellings. Adjectives formed with obvious suffixes, such as -like and -less are also cross-referred to the root word.

In this book, only a single definition is given for each part of speech, and in general only those parts of speech necessary for existing inflections are included. Some definitions have been sourced from Collins English Dictionary, Complete and Unabridged, and other definitions have been written specially for this dictionary. While we have shortened many of the Collins English Dictionary definitions for the purpose of this book, they are fuller than the others.

Word order   this book is in strict alphabetical order.

Offensive terms   there may be words in this book that most or some players
                      might consider derogatory, offensive, or even taboo.

Accents   as English language SCRABBLE® tiles are not accented, no
                      accents are shown in this book.

Main entry words   printed in bold, blue capitals, eg:
                          AA

                      All entry words, in one alphabetical sequence, eg:
                          AA
                          AAH
                          AAHED
                          AAL
                          AALI

| **Parts of Speech** | shown in italics as an abbreviation, eg: |
| | AA *n* |

When more than one part of speech is given, the change of part of speech is shown after an arrow, eg:

    ABANDON *vb* desert or leave
    ▷ *n* lack of inhibition

Cross-references   noun plurals, verb inflections, comparatives and superlatives, and derivatives are all cross-referred to their root form:

    ABASH *vb* cause or feel ill
        at ease, embarrassed, or
        confused
    ...
    ABASHES > ABASH
    ABASHING > ABASH
    ABASHLESS > ABASH
    ABASHMENT > ABASH

Variant forms   variant forms and synonyms are cross-referred to the most commonly-used form of a word, eg:

    CAFTAN *same as* > KAFTAN

noun plurals, verb inflections, comparitives, superlatives, and derivatives of the variant form are all cross-referred to the root form of that particular variant, eg

    CAFTAN *same as* > KAFTAN
    ...
    CAFTANS > CAFTAN

Phrases   when a word is most comonly used in a phrase, the phrase is given in italics and defined, eg:

    BANGALORE as in *bangalore*
        torpedo explosive device in
        a long metal tube, used to
        blow gaps in barbed-wire
        barriers

Addendum

The following words are also eligible for SCRABBLE®:
ARCHEAN

ASHRAF	PIRNIES	PREDIALS	PULVINULE
CANAPES	PISCINES	PREDIED	PUZEL
COURIERED	PLANARIAS	PREDIES	PUZELS
EDITIONED	PLATONICS	PREDYING	PYEING
GRICED	PLINKINGS	PREFARD	PYGALS
HUNNISH	PLUMPIE	PREHIRING	PYONERS
JAMMINGS	PODAL	PREJUDIZE	PYONINGS
JONGS	PODDIER	PRELIVES	PYROSISES
KLETT	PODDIEST	PREMIXT	RANCOURED
KLETTS	POLTFEET	PRESSFULS	RECLADDED
LINELESS	PONCEAUX	PRESSORS	RECLADS
LIPAEMIAS	PONKED	PREZES	RHEOPHILE
MAASES	PONKING	PRIMATALS	SADDOES
MATCHPLAY	PONTIE	PRINCESSE	SENSI
MIRANDISE	PONTILES	PROPINE	SENSIS
NATIS	POSTALS	PROPINED	SMUDGINGS
OUS	POUFF	PROPINES	SNIDED
PEEKABO	POWTERED	PROPINING	SNIDING
PEEKABOS	POWTERING	PROWESSED	SPOOFINGS
PEREGALS	PRACTICS	PROYNED	STETSON
PERFINGS	PRAEDIALS	PROYNING	STETSONS
PERIBOLI	PRAIRIED	PRYSED	TAPUED
PEROXO	PRATFELL	PRYSES	TAPUING
PHILAMOT	PRATTED	PRYSING	TEXTED
PHILAMOTS	PRATTING	PSHAWED	TEXTING
PHYCOCYAN	PRATTS	PSHAWING	TOGGERED
PINKERS	PRAYINGLY	PSOASES	TOGGERING
PINKIER	PREADOPT	PTYXISES	UNCOES
PINKIEST	PREADOPTS	PUBISES	
PINTADAS	PRECIEUX	PUDDENING	

Aa

AA *n* volcanic rock consisting of angular blocks of lava with a very rough surface

AAH *vb* exclaim in pleasure or surprise

AAHED > AAH

AAHING > AAH

AAHS > AAH

AAL *n* Asian shrub or tree

AALII *n* bushy sapindaceous shrub, *Dodonaea viscosa*, of Australia, Hawaii, Africa, and tropical America, having small greenish flowers and sticky foliage

AALIIS > AALII

AALS > AAL

AARDVARK *n* S African anteater with long ears and snout

AARDVARKS > AARDVARK

AARDWOLF *n* nocturnal mammal, *Proteles cristatus*, that inhabits the plains of southern Africa and feeds on termites and insect larvae: family *Hyaenidae* (hyenas), order *Carnivora* (carnivores)

AARGH *interj* cry of pain

AARRGH *interj* cry of pain

AARRGHH *interj* cry of pain

AARTI *n* Hindu ceremony in which lights with wicks soaked in ghee are lit and offered up to one or more deities

AARTIS > AARTI

AAS > AA

AASVOGEL *n* South African bird of prey

AASVOGELS > AASVOGEL

AB *n* abdominal muscle

ABA *n* type of cloth from Syria, made of goat hair or camel hair

ABAC *n* mathematical diagram

ABACA *n* Philippine plant, *Musa textilis*, related to the banana: family *Musaceae*. Its leafstalks are the source of Manila hemp

ABACAS > ABACA

ABACI > ABACUS

ABACK *adv* towards the back; backwards

ABACS > ABAC

ABACTINAL *adj* (of organisms showing radial symmetry) situated away from or opposite to the mouth

ABACTOR *n* cattle thief

ABACTORS > ABACTOR

ABACUS *n* beads on a wire frame, used for doing calculations

ABACUSES > ABACUS

ABAFT *adv* closer to the rear of (a ship) ▷ *adj* closer to the stern of a ship

ABAKA *n* abaca

ABAKAS > ABAKA

ABALONE *n* edible sea creature with a shell lined with mother of pearl

ABALONES > ABALONE

ABAMP *same as* > ABAMPERE

ABAMPERE *n* cgs unit of current in the electromagnetic system

ABAMPERES > ABAMPERE

ABAMPS > ABAMP

ABAND *vb* abandon

ABANDED > ABAND

ABANDING > ABAND

ABANDON *vb* desert or leave (one's wife, children, etc) ▷ *n* lack of inhibition

ABANDONED *adj* deserted

ABANDONEE *n* person to whom something is formally relinquished, esp an insurer having the right to salvage a wreck

ABANDONER > ABANDON

ABANDONS > ABANDON

ABANDS > ABAND

ABAPICAL *adj* away from or opposite the apex

ABAS > ABA

ABASE *vb* humiliate or degrade (oneself)

ABASED > ABASE

ABASEDLY > ABASE

ABASEMENT > ABASE

ABASER > ABASE

ABASERS > ABASE

ABASES > ABASE

ABASH *vb* cause to feel ill at ease, embarrassed, or confused

ABASHED *adj* embarrassed and ashamed

ABASHEDLY > ABASHED

ABASHES > ABASH

ABASHING > ABASH

ABASHLESS > ABASH

ABASHMENT > ABASH

ABASIA *n* disorder affecting ability to walk

ABASIAS > ABASIA

ABASING > ABASE

ABASK *adv* in pleasant warmth

ABATABLE > ABATE

ABATE *vb* make or become less strong

ABATED > ABATE

ABATEMENT *n* diminution or alleviation

ABATER > ABATE

ABATERS > ABATE

ABATES > ABATE

ABATING > ABATE

ABATIS *n* rampart of felled trees bound together, placed with their branches outwards

ABATISES > ABATIS

ABATOR *n* person who effects an abatement

ABATORS > ABATOR

ABATTIS *same as* > ABATIS

ABATTISES > ABATTIS

ABATTOIR *n* place where animals are killed for food

ABATTOIRS > ABATTOIR

ABATTU *adj* dejected

ABATURE *n* trail left by hunted stag

ABATURES > ABATURE

ABAXIAL *adj* facing away from the axis, as the surface of a leaf

ABAXILE *adj* away from the axis

ABAYA *n* Arab outer garment

ABAYAS > ABAYA

ABB *n* yarn used in weaving

ABBA *n* title for a bishop in the Coptic Church

ABBACIES > ABBACY

ABBACY *n* office or jurisdiction of an abbot or abbess

ABBAS > ABBA

ABBATIAL *adj* of or relating to an abbot, abbess, or abbey

ABBE *n* French abbot

ABBED *adj* displaying well-developed abdominal muscles

ABBES > ABBE

ABBESS *n* nun in charge of a convent

ABBESSES > ABBESS

ABBEY *n* dwelling place of, or a church belonging to, a community of monks or nuns

ABBEYS > ABBEY

ABBOT *n* head of an abbey of monks

ABBOTCIES > ABBOT

ABBOTCY > ABBOT

ABBOTS > ABBOT

ABBOTSHIP > ABBOT

ABBS > ABB

ABCEE *n* alphabet

ABCEES > ABCEE

ABCOULOMB *n* cgs unit of electric charge in the electromagnetic system

ABDABS *n* highly nervous state

ABDICABLE > ABDICATE

ABDICANT > ABDICATE

ABDICATE *vb* give up (the throne or a responsibility)

ABDICATED > ABDICATE

ABDICATES > ABDICATE

ABDICATOR > ABDICATE

ABDOMEN *n* part of the body containing the stomach and intestines

ABDOMENS > ABDOMEN

ABDOMINA > ABDOMEN

ABDOMINAL > ABDOMEN

ABDUCE *vb* abduct

ABDUCED > ABDUCE

ABDUCENS as in *abducens nerve* either of the sixth pair of cranial nerves, which supply the lateral rectus muscle of the eye

ABDUCENT *adj* (of a muscle) abducting

ABDUCES > ABDUCE

ABDUCING > ABDUCE

ABDUCT *vb* carry off, kidnap

ABDUCTED > ABDUCT

ABDUCTEE > ABDUCT

ABDUCTEES > ABDUCT
ABDUCTING > ABDUCT
ABDUCTION n act of taking someone away by force or cunning
ABDUCTOR > ABDUCT
ABDUCTORS > ABDUCT
ABDUCTS > ABDUCT
ABEAM adj at right angles to the length of a ship or aircraft
ABEAR vb bear or behave
ABEARING > ABEAR
ABEARS > ABEAR
ABED adv in bed
ABEGGING adj in the act of begging for money etc
ABEIGH adv aloof
ABELE n white poplar tree
ABELES > ABELE
ABELIA n garden plant with pink or white flowers
ABELIAN > ABELIA
ABELIAS > ABELIA
ABELMOSK n tropical bushy malvaceous plant, Hibiscus abelmoschus, cultivated for its yellow-and-crimson flowers and for its musk-scented seeds, which yield an oil used in perfumery
ABELMOSKS > ABELMOSK
ABERNETHY n crisp unleavened biscuit
ABERRANCE > ABERRANT
ABERRANCY > ABERRANT
ABERRANT adj showing aberration ▷ n person whose behaviour is considered to be aberrant
ABERRANTS > ABERRANT
ABERRATE vb deviate from what is normal or correct
ABERRATED > ABERRATE
ABERRATES > ABERRATE
ABESSIVE n grammatical case indicating absence
ABESSIVES > ABESSIVE
ABET vb help or encourage in wrongdoing
ABETMENT > ABET
ABETMENTS > ABET
ABETS > ABET
ABETTAL > ABET
ABETTALS > ABET
ABETTED > ABET
ABETTER > ABET
ABETTERS > ABET
ABETTING > ABET
ABETTOR > ABET
ABETTORS > ABET
ABEYANCE n state of being suspended or put aside temporarily
ABEYANCES > ABEYANCE
ABEYANCY n abeyance
ABEYANT > ABEYANCE
ABFARAD n cgs unit of capacitance in the electromagnetic system
ABFARADS > ABFARAD
ABHENRIES > ABHENRY
ABHENRY n cgs unit of inductance in the electromagnetic system
ABHENRYS > ABHENRY
ABHOR vb detest utterly

ABHORRED > ABHOR
ABHORRENT adj hateful, loathsome
ABHORRER > ABHOR
ABHORRERS > ABHOR
ABHORRING > ABHOR
ABHORS > ABHOR
ABID > ABIDE
ABIDANCE > ABIDE
ABIDANCES > ABIDE
ABIDDEN > ABIDE
ABIDE vb endure, put up with
ABIDED > ABIDE
ABIDER > ABIDE
ABIDERS > ABIDE
ABIDES > ABIDE
ABIDING adj lasting ▷ n action of one who abides
ABIDINGLY > ABIDING
ABIDINGS > ABIDING
ABIES n fir tree
ABIETIC adj pertaining to fir trees
ABIGAIL n maid for a lady
ABIGAILS > ABIGAIL
ABILITIES > ABILITY
ABILITY n competence, power
ABIOGENIC adj abiogenetic
ABIOSES > ABIOSIS
ABIOSIS n absence of life
ABIOTIC > ABIOSIS
ABJECT adj utterly miserable ▷ vb throw down
ABJECTED > ABJECT
ABJECTING > ABJECT
ABJECTION > ABJECT
ABJECTLY > ABJECT
ABJECTS > ABJECT
ABJOINT vb cut off
ABJOINTED > ABJOINT
ABJOINTS > ABJOINT
ABJURE vb deny or renounce on oath
ABJURED > ABJURE
ABJURER > ABJURE
ABJURERS > ABJURE
ABJURES > ABJURE
ABJURING > ABJURE
ABLATE vb remove by ablation
ABLATED > ABLATE
ABLATES > ABLATE
ABLATING > ABLATE
ABLATION n surgical removal of an organ or part
ABLATIONS > ABLATION
ABLATIVAL > ABLATIVE
ABLATIVE n case of nouns in Latin and other languages, indicating source, agent, or instrument of action ▷ adj (in certain inflected languages such as Latin) denoting a case of nouns, pronouns, and adjectives indicating the agent in passive sentences or the instrument, manner, or place of the action described by the verb
ABLATIVES > ABLATIVE
ABLATOR n heat shield of a space vehicle, which melts

or wears away during re-entry into the earth's atmosphere
ABLATORS > ABLATOR
ABLAUT n vowel gradation, esp in Indo-European languages
ABLAUTS > ABLAUT
ABLAZE adj burning fiercely ▷ adv on fire
ABLE adj capable, competent ▷ vb enable
ABLED adj having a range of physical powers as specified
ABLEGATE n papal envoy
ABLEGATES > ABLEGATE
ABLEISM n discrimination against disabled or handicapped people
ABLEISMS > ABLEISM
ABLEIST > ABLEISM
ABLEISTS > ABLEISM
ABLER > ABLE
ABLES > ABLE
ABLEST > ABLE
ABLET n freshwater fish
ABLETS > ABLET
ABLING > ABLE
ABLINGS adv possibly
ABLINS adv Scots word meaning perhaps
ABLOOM adj in flower
ABLOW adj blooming
ABLUENT n substance used for cleansing
ABLUENTS > ABLUENT
ABLUSH adj blushing
ABLUTED adj washed thoroughly
ABLUTION n ritual washing of a priest's hands or of sacred vessels
ABLUTIONS > ABLUTION
ABLY adv competently or skilfully
ABMHO n unit of electrical conductance
ABMHOS > ABMHO
ABNEGATE vb deny to oneself
ABNEGATED > ABNEGATE
ABNEGATES > ABNEGATE
ABNEGATOR > ABNEGATE
ABNORMAL adj not normal or usual ▷ n abnormal person or thing
ABNORMALS > ABNORMAL
ABNORMITY > ABNORMAL
ABNORMOUS > ABNORMAL
ABO offensive name for > ABORIGINE
ABOARD adv on, in, onto, or into (a ship, train, or plane) ▷ adj on, in, onto, or into (a ship, plane, or train)
ABODE n home, dwelling ▷ vb forebode
ABODED > ABODE
ABODEMENT > ABODE
ABODES > ABODE
ABODING > ABODE
ABOHM n cgs unit of resistance in the electromagnetic system: equivalent to 10$^{=9}$ohm
ABOHMS > ABOHM

ABOIDEAU n dyke with a sluicegate that allows flood water to drain but keeps the sea water out
ABOIDEAUS > ABOIDEAU
ABOIDEAUX > ABOIDEAU
ABOIL adj boiling
ABOITEAU same as > ABOIDEAU
ABOITEAUS > ABOITEAU
ABOITEAUX > ABOITEAU
ABOLISH vb do away with
ABOLISHED > ABOLISH
ABOLISHER > ABOLISH
ABOLISHES > ABOLISH
ABOLITION n act of abolishing or the state of being abolished
ABOLLA n Roman cloak
ABOLLAE > ABOLLA
ABOLLAS > ABOLLA
ABOMA n South American snake
ABOMAS > ABOMA
ABOMASA > ABOMASUM
ABOMASAL > ABOMASUM
ABOMASI > ABOMASUS
ABOMASUM n fourth and last compartment of the stomach of ruminants, which receives and digests food from the psalterium and passes it on to the small intestine
ABOMASUS n abomasum
ABOMINATE vb dislike intensely
ABONDANCE same as > ABUNDANCE
ABOON Scots word for > ABOVE
ABORAL adj away from or opposite the mouth
ABORALLY > ABORAL
ABORD vb accost
ABORDED > ABORD
ABORDING > ABORD
ABORDS > ABORD
ABORE > ABEAR
ABORIGEN n aborigine
ABORIGENS > ABORIGEN
ABORIGIN n aborigine
ABORIGINE n original inhabitant of a country or region, esp Australia
ABORIGINS > ABORIGIN
ABORNE adj Shakespearean form of auburn
ABORNING > ABEAR
ABORT vb have an abortion or perform an abortion on ▷ n premature termination or failure of (a space flight, military operation, etc)
ABORTED > ABORT
ABORTEE n woman having an abortion
ABORTEES > ABORTEE
ABORTER > ABORT
ABORTERS > ABORT
ABORTING > ABORT
ABORTION n operation to end a pregnancy
ABORTIONS > ABORTION
ABORTIVE adj unsuccessful
ABORTS > ABORT
ABORTUARY n place where

abortions are carried out

ABORTUS *n* aborted fetus

ABORTUSES > ABORTUS

ABOS > ABO

ABOUGHT > ABY

ABOULIA *same as* > ABULIA

ABOULIAS > ABOULIA

ABOULIC > ABOULIA

ABOUND *vb* be plentiful

ABOUNDED > ABOUND

ABOUNDING > ABOUND

ABOUNDS > ABOUND

ABOUT *adv* nearly, approximately

ABOUTS *prep* about

ABOVE *adv* over or higher (than) ⊳ *n* something that is or appears above

ABOVES > ABOVE

ABRACHIA *n* condition of having no arms

ABRACHIAS > ABRACHIA

ABRADABLE > ABRADE

ABRADANT > ABRADE

ABRADANTS > ABRADE

ABRADE *vb* scrape away or wear down by friction

ABRADED > ABRADE

ABRADER > ABRADE

ABRADERS > ABRADE

ABRADES > ABRADE

ABRADING > ABRADE

ABRAID *vb* awake

ABRAIDED > ABRAID

ABRAIDING > ABRAID

ABRAIDS > ABRAID

ABRAM *adj* auburn

ABRASAX *same as* > ABRAXAS

ABRASAXES > ABRASAX

ABRASION *n* scraped area on the skin

ABRASIONS > ABRASION

ABRASIVE *adj* harsh and unpleasant in manner ⊳ *n* substance for cleaning or polishing by rubbing

ABRASIVES > ABRASIVE

ABRAXAS *n* ancient charm composed of Greek letters: originally believed to have magical powers and inscribed on amulets, etc, but from the second century AD personified by Gnostics as a deity, the source of divine emanations

ABRAXASES > ABRAXAS

ABRAY *vb* awake

ABRAYED > ABRAY

ABRAYING > ABRAY

ABRAYS > ABRAY

ABRAZO *n* embrace

ABRAZOS > ABRAZO

ABREACT *vb* alleviate (emotional tension) through abreaction

ABREACTED > ABREACT

ABREACTS > ABREACT

ABREAST *adj* side by side

ABREGE *n* abridgment

ABREGES > ABREGE

ABRI *n* shelter or place of refuge, esp in wartime

ABRICOCK *n* apricot

ABRICOCKS > ABRICOCK

ABRIDGE *vb* shorten by

using fewer words

ABRIDGED > ABRIDGE

ABRIDGER > ABRIDGE

ABRIDGERS > ABRIDGE

ABRIDGES > ABRIDGE

ABRIDGING > ABRIDGE

ABRIM *adj* full to the brim

ABRIN *n* poisonous compound

ABRINS > ABRIN

ABRIS > ABRI

ABROACH *adj* (of a cask, barrel, etc) tapped

ABROAD *adv* in a foreign country ⊳ *adj* (of news, rumours, etc) in general circulation ⊳ *n* foreign place

ABROADS > ABROAD

ABROGABLE *adj* able to be abrogated

ABROGATE *vb* cancel (a law or agreement) formally

ABROGATED > ABROGATE

ABROGATES > ABROGATE

ABROGATOR > ABROGATE

ABROOKE *vb* bear or tolerate

ABROOKED > ABROOKE

ABROOKES > ABROOKE

ABROOKING > ABROOKE

ABROSIA *n* condition involving refusal to eat

ABROSIAS > ABROSIA

ABRUPT *adj* sudden, unexpected ⊳ *n* abyss

ABRUPTER > ABRUPT

ABRUPTEST > ABRUPT

ABRUPTION *n* breaking off of a part or parts from a mass

ABRUPTLY > ABRUPT

ABRUPTS > ABRUPT

ABS > AB

ABSCESS *n* inflamed swelling containing pus ⊳ *vb* form a swelling containing pus

ABSCESSED > ABSCESS

ABSCESSES > ABSCESS

ABSCIND *vb* cut off

ABSCINDED > ABSCIND

ABSCINDS > ABSCIND

ABSCISE *vb* separate or be separated by abscission

ABSCISED > ABSCISE

ABSCISES > ABSCISE

ABSCISIN *n* plant hormone

ABSCISING > ABSCISE

ABSCISINS > ABSCISIN

ABSCISS *n* cutting off

ABSCISSA *n* cutting off

ABSCISSAE > ABSCISSA

ABSCISSAS > ABSCISSA

ABSCISSE *n* cutting off

ABSCISSES > ABSCISSE

ABSCISSIN *n* plant hormone

ABSCOND *vb* leave secretly

ABSCONDED > ABSCOND

ABSCONDER > ABSCOND

ABSCONDS > ABSCOND

ABSEIL *vb* go down a steep drop by a rope fastened at the top and tied around one's body ⊳ *n* instance of abseiling

ABSEILED > ABSEIL

ABSEILING > ABSEIL

ABSEILS > ABSEIL

ABSENCE *n* being away

ABSENCES > ABSENCE

ABSENT *adj* not present ⊳ *vb* stay away

ABSENTED > ABSENT

ABSENTEE *n* person who should be present but is not

ABSENTEES > ABSENTEE

ABSENTER > ABSENT

ABSENTERS > ABSENT

ABSENTING > ABSENT

ABSENTLY *adv* in an absent-minded or preoccupied manner

ABSENTS > ABSENT

ABSEY *n* alphabet

ABSEYS > ABSEY

ABSINTH *same as* > ABSINTHE

ABSINTHE *n* strong green aniseed-flavoured liqueur

ABSINTHES > ABSINTHE

ABSINTHS > ABSINTH

ABSIT *n* overnight leave from college

ABSITS > ABSIT

ABSOLUTE *adj* complete, perfect ⊳ *n* something that is absolute

ABSOLUTER > ABSOLUTE

ABSOLUTES > ABSOLUTE

ABSOLVE *vb* declare to be free from blame or sin

ABSOLVED > ABSOLVE

ABSOLVENT *n* something that absolves

ABSOLVER > ABSOLVE

ABSOLVERS > ABSOLVE

ABSOLVES > ABSOLVE

ABSOLVING > ABSOLVE

ABSONANT *adj* unnatural and unreasonable

ABSORB *vb* soak up (a liquid)

ABSORBANT *n* absorbent substance

ABSORBATE *n* absorbed substance

ABSORBED *adj* engrossed

ABSORBENT *adj* able to absorb liquid ⊳ *n* substance that absorbs

ABSORBER *n* person or thing that absorbs

ABSORBERS > ABSORBER

ABSORBING *adj* occupying one's interest or attention

ABSORBS > ABSORB

ABSTAIN *vb* choose not to do something

ABSTAINED > ABSTAIN

ABSTAINER > ABSTAIN

ABSTAINS > ABSTAIN

ABSTERGE *vb* cleanse

ABSTERGED > ABSTERGE

ABSTERGES > ABSTERGE

ABSTINENT *adj* refraining from a certain activity

ABSTRACT *adj* existing as a quality or idea rather than a material object ⊳ *n* summary ⊳ *vb* summarize

ABSTRACTS > ABSTRACT

ABSTRICT *vb* release

ABSTRICTS > ABSTRICT

ABSTRUSE *adj* not easy to

understand

ABSTRUSER > ABSTRUSE

ABSURD *adj* incongruous or ridiculous ⊳ *n* conception of the world, esp in Existentialist thought, as neither designed nor predictable but irrational and meaningless

ABSURDER > ABSURD

ABSURDEST > ABSURD

ABSURDISM *n* belief that life is meaningless

ABSURDIST > ABSURDISM

ABSURDITY > ABSURD

ABSURDLY > ABSURD

ABSURDS > ABSURD

ABTHANE *n* ancient Scottish church territory

ABTHANES > ABTHANE

ABUBBLE *adj* bubbling

ABUILDING *adj* being built

ABULIA *n* pathological inability to take decisions

ABULIAS > ABULIA

ABULIC > ABULIA

ABUNA *n* male head of Ethiopian family

ABUNAS > ABUNA

ABUNDANCE *n* copious supply

ABUNDANCY *n* abundance

ABUNDANT *adj* plentiful

ABUNE *Scots word for* > ABOVE

ABURST *adj* bursting

ABUSABLE > ABUSE

ABUSAGE *n* wrong use

ABUSAGES > ABUSAGE

ABUSE *vb* use wrongly ⊳ *n* prolonged ill-treatment

ABUSED > ABUSE

ABUSER > ABUSE

ABUSERS > ABUSE

ABUSES > ABUSE

ABUSING > ABUSE

ABUSION *n* wrong use or deception

ABUSIONS > ABUSION

ABUSIVE *adj* rude or insulting

ABUSIVELY > ABUSIVE

ABUT *vb* be next to or touching

ABUTILON *n* any shrub or herbaceous plant of the malvaceous genus *Abutilon*, such as the flowering maple, that have showy white, yellow, or red flowers

ABUTILONS > ABUTILON

ABUTMENT *n* construction that supports the end of a bridge

ABUTMENTS > ABUTMENT

ABUTS > ABUT

ABUTTAL *same as* > ABUTMENT

ABUTTALS > ABUTTAL

ABUTTED > ABUT

ABUTTER *n* owner of adjoining property

ABUTTERS > ABUTTER

ABUTTING > ABUT

ABUZZ *adj* noisy, busy with activity etc

a

ABVOLT *n* cgs unit of potential difference in the electromagnetic system

ABVOLTS > ABVOLT

ABWATT *n* cgs unit of power in the electromagnetic system, equal to the power dissipated when a current of 1 abampere flows across a potential difference of 1 abvolt: equivalent to 10⁻⁷watt

ABWATTS > ABWATT

ABY *vb* pay the penalty for

ABYE *same as* > ABY

ABYEING > ABYE

ABYES > ABYE

ABYING > ABY

ABYS > ABY

ABYSM *archaic word for* > ABYSS

ABYSMAL *adj* extremely bad, awful

ABYSMALLY > ABYSMAL

ABYSMS > ABYSM

ABYSS *n* very deep hole or chasm

ABYSSAL *adj* of or belonging to the ocean depths, esp below 2000 metres (6500 feet)

ABYSSES > ABYSS

ACACIA *n* tree or shrub with yellow or white flowers

ACACIAS > ACACIA

ACADEME *n* place of learning

ACADEMES > ACADEME

ACADEMIA *n* academic world

ACADEMIAS > ACADEMIA

ACADEMIC *adj* of an academy or university ▷ *n* lecturer or researcher at a university

ACADEMICS > ACADEMIC

ACADEMIES > ACADEMY

ACADEMISM *n* adherence to rules and traditions in art, literature, etc

ACADEMIST > ACADEMY

ACADEMY *n* society to advance arts or sciences

ACAI *n* berry found in Brazilian rainforest

ACAIS > ACAI

ACAJOU *n* type of mahogany used by cabinet-makers in France

ACAJOUS > ACAJOU

ACALCULIA *n* inability to make simple mathematical calculations

ACALEPH *n* any of the coelenterates of the former taxonomic group *Acalephae*, which included the jellyfishes

ACALEPHAE > ACALEPH

ACALEPHAN > ACALEPH

ACALEPHE *n* acaleph

ACALEPHES > ACALEPHE

ACALEPHS > ACALEPH

ACANTH *n* acanthus

ACANTHA *n* thorn or prickle

ACANTHAE > ACANTHA

ACANTHAS > ACANTHA

ACANTHI > ACANTHUS

ACANTHIN *n* organic chemical used in medicine

ACANTHINE *adj* of or resembling an acanthus

ACANTHINS > ACANTHIN

ACANTHOID *adj* resembling a spine

ACANTHOUS *adj* of an acanthus

ACANTHS > ACANTH

ACANTHUS *n* prickly plant

ACAPNIA *n* lack of carbon dioxide

ACAPNIAS > ACAPNIA

ACARBOSE *n* diabetes medicine

ACARBOSES > ACARBOSE

ACARI > ACARUS

ACARIAN > ACARUS

ACARIASES > ACARIASIS

ACARIASIS *n* infestation of the hair follicles and skin with acarids, esp mites

ACARICIDE *n* any drug or formulation for killing acarids

ACARID *n* any of the small arachnids of the order *Acarina* (or *Acari*), which includes the ticks and mites ▷ *adj* of or relating to the order *Acarina*

ACARIDAN *same as* > ACARID

ACARIDANS > ACARIDAN

ACARIDEAN > ACARID

ACARIDIAN > ACARID

ACARIDS > ACARID

ACARINE *n* acarid

ACARINES > ACARINE

ACAROID *adj* resembling a mite or tick

ACAROLOGY *n* study of mites and ticks

ACARPOUS *adj* (of plants) producing no fruit

ACARUS *n* any of the free-living mites of the widely distributed genus *Acarus*, several of which, esp *A. siro*, are serious pests of stored flour, grain, etc

ACATER *n* buyer of provisions

ACATERS > ACATER

ACATES *n* provisions

ACATOUR *n* buyer of provisions

ACATOURS > ACATOUR

ACAUDAL *adj* having no tail

ACAUDATE *same as* > ACAUDAL

ACAULINE *adj* having no stem

ACAULOSE *same as* > ACAULINE

ACAULOUS *adj* having a short stem or no stem

ACCA *n* academic

ACCABLE *adj* dejected or beaten

ACCAS > ACCA

ACCEDE *vb* consent or agree (to)

ACCEDED > ACCEDE

ACCEDENCE > ACCEDE

ACCEDER > ACCEDE

ACCEDERS > ACCEDE

ACCEDES > ACCEDE

ACCEDING > ACCEDE

ACCEND *vb* set alight

ACCENDED > ACCEND

ACCENDING > ACCEND

ACCENDS > ACCEND

ACCENSION > ACCEND

ACCENT *n* distinctive style of pronunciation of a local, national, or social group ▷ *vb* place emphasis on

ACCENTED > ACCENT

ACCENTING > ACCENT

ACCENTOR *n* any small sparrow-like songbird of the genus *Prunella*, family *Prunellidae*, which inhabit mainly mountainous regions of Europe and Asia

ACCENTORS > ACCENTOR

ACCENTS > ACCENT

ACCENTUAL *adj* of, relating to, or having accents

ACCEPT *vb* receive willingly

ACCEPTANT *adj* receiving willingly

ACCEPTED *adj* generally approved

ACCEPTEE *n* person who has been accepted

ACCEPTEES > ACCEPTEE

ACCEPTER > ACCEPT

ACCEPTERS > ACCEPT

ACCEPTING > ACCEPT

ACCEPTIVE *adj* ready to accept

ACCEPTOR *n* person or organization on which a draft or bill of exchange is drawn after liability has been accepted, usually by signature

ACCEPTORS > ACCEPTOR

ACCEPTS > ACCEPT

ACCESS *n* means of or right to approach or enter ▷ *vb* obtain (data) from a computer

ACCESSARY *same as* > ACCESSORY

ACCESSED > ACCESS

ACCESSES > ACCESS

ACCESSING > ACCESS

ACCESSION *n* taking up of an office or position ▷ *vb* make a record of (additions to a collection)

ACCESSORY *n* supplementary part or object ▷ *adj* supplementary

ACCIDENCE *n* inflectional morphology

ACCIDENT *n* mishap, often causing injury

ACCIDENTS > ACCIDENT

ACCIDIA *same as* > ACCIDIE

ACCIDIAS > ACCIDIA

ACCIDIE *n* spiritual sloth

ACCIDIES > ACCIDIE

ACCINGE *vb* put a belt around

ACCINGED > ACCINGE

ACCINGES > ACCINGE

ACCINGING > ACCINGE

ACCIPITER *n* any hawk of the genus *Accipiter*, typically having short rounded wings and a long tail

ACCITE *vb* summon

ACCITED > ACCITE

ACCITES > ACCITE

ACCITING > ACCITE

ACCLAIM *vb* applaud, praise ▷ *n* enthusiastic approval

ACCLAIMED > ACCLAIM

ACCLAIMER > ACCLAIM

ACCLAIMS > ACCLAIM

ACCLIMATE *vb* adapt or become accustomed to a new climate or environment

ACCLIVITY *n* upward slope, esp of the ground

ACCLIVOUS > ACCLIVITY

ACCLOY *vb* choke or clog

ACCLOYED > ACCLOY

ACCLOYING > ACCLOY

ACCLOYS > ACCLOY

ACCOAST *vb* accost

ACCOASTED > ACCOAST

ACCOASTS > ACCOAST

ACCOIED > ACCOY

ACCOIL *n* welcome ▷ *vb* gather together

ACCOILS > ACCOIL

ACCOLADE *n* award or praise ▷ *vb* give an award or praise

ACCOLADED > ACCOLADE

ACCOLADES > ACCOLADE

ACCOMPANY *vb* go along with

ACCOMPT *vb* account

ACCOMPTED > ACCOMPT

ACCOMPTS > ACCOMPT

ACCORAGE *vb* encourage

ACCORAGED > ACCORAGE

ACCORAGES > ACCORAGE

ACCORD *n* agreement, harmony ▷ *vb* fit in with

ACCORDANT *adj* in conformity or harmony

ACCORDED > ACCORD

ACCORDER > ACCORD

ACCORDERS > ACCORD

ACCORDING *adj* in proportion

ACCORDION *n* portable musical instrument played by moving the two sides apart and together, and pressing a keyboard or buttons to produce the notes

ACCORDS > ACCORD

ACCOST *vb* approach and speak to, often aggressively ▷ *n* greeting

ACCOSTED > ACCOST

ACCOSTING > ACCOST

ACCOSTS > ACCOST

ACCOUNT *n* report, description ▷ *vb* judge to be

ACCOUNTED > ACCOUNT

ACCOUNTS > ACCOUNT

ACCOURAGE *vb* encourage

ACCOURT *vb* entertain

ACCOURTED > ACCOURT

ACCOURTS > ACCOURT

ACCOUTER *same as* > ACCOUTRE

ACCOUTERS > ACCOUTER

ACCOUTRE vb provide with equipment or dress, esp military

ACCOUTRED > ACCOUTRE

ACCOUTRES > ACCOUTRE

ACCOY vb soothe

ACCOYED > ACCOY

ACCOYING > ACCOY

ACCOYLD > ACCOIL

ACCOYS > ACCOY

ACCREDIT vb give official recognition to

ACCREDITS > ACCREDIT

ACCRETE vb grow or cause to grow together

ACCRETED > ACCRETE

ACCRETES > ACCRETE

ACCRETING > ACCRETE

ACCRETION n gradual growth

ACCRETIVE > ACCRETION

ACCREW vb accrue

ACCREWED > ACCREW

ACCREWING > ACCREW

ACCREWS > ACCREW

ACCROIDES n red alcohol-soluble resin

ACCRUABLE > ACCRUE

ACCRUAL n act of accruing

ACCRUALS > ACCRUAL

ACCRUE vb increase gradually

ACCRUED > ACCRUE

ACCRUES > ACCRUE

ACCRUING > ACCRUE

ACCUMBENT adj (of plant parts and plants) lying against some other part or thing

ACCURACY n faithful representation of the truth

ACCURATE adj exact, correct

ACCURSE vb curse

ACCURSED adj under a curse

ACCURSES > ACCURSE

ACCURSING > ACCURSE

ACCURST same as > ACCURSED

ACCUSABLE > ACCUSE

ACCUSABLY > ACCUSE

ACCUSAL n accusation

ACCUSALS > ACCUSAL

ACCUSANT n person who accuses

ACCUSANTS > ACCUSANT

ACCUSE vb charge with wrongdoing

ACCUSED n person or people accused of a crime in a court

ACCUSER > ACCUSE

ACCUSERS > ACCUSE

ACCUSES > ACCUSE

ACCUSING > ACCUSE

ACCUSTOM vb make used to

ACCUSTOMS > ACCUSTOM

ACE n playing card with one symbol on it ▷ adj excellent ▷ vb serve an ace in racquet sports

ACED > ACE

ACEDIA same as > ACCIDIE

ACEDIAS > ACEDIA

ACELDAMA n place with ill feeling

ACELDAMAS > ACELDAMA

ACELLULAR adj not made up of or containing cells

ACENTRIC adj without a centre ▷ n acentric chromosome or fragment

ACEPHALIC n having no head or one that is reduced and indistinct, as certain insect larvae

ACEQUIA n irrigation ditch

ACEQUIAS > ACEQUIA

ACER n any tree or shrub of the genus Acer, often cultivated for their brightly coloured foliage

ACERATE same as > ACERATED

ACERATED adj having sharp points

ACERB adj bitter

ACERBATE vb embitter or exasperate

ACERBATED > ACERBATE

ACERBATES > ACERBATE

ACERBER > ACERB

ACERBEST > ACERB

ACERBIC adj harsh or bitter

ACERBITY n bitter speech or temper

ACEROLA n cherry-like fruit

ACEROLAS > ACEROLA

ACEROSE adj shaped like a needle, as pine leaves

ACEROUS same as > ACEROSE

ACERS > ACER

ACERVATE adj growing in heaps or clusters

ACERVULI > ACERVULUS

ACERVULUS n spore-producing part of plant

ACES > ACE

ACESCENCE > ACESCENT

ACESCENCY > ACESCENT

ACESCENT adj slightly sour or turning sour ▷ n something that is turning sour

ACESCENTS > ACESCENT

ACETA > ACETUM

ACETABULA n deep cuplike cavities on the side of the hipbones that receive the head of the thighbone

ACETAL n 1,1-diethoxyethane

ACETALS > ACETAL

ACETAMID same as > ACETAMIDE

ACETAMIDE n white or colourless soluble deliquescent crystalline compound

ACETAMIDS > ACETAMID

ACETATE n salt or ester of acetic acid

ACETATED adj combined with acetic acid

ACETATES > ACETATE

ACETIC adj of or involving vinegar

ACETIFIED > ACETIFY

ACETIFIER > ACETIFY

ACETIFIES > ACETIFY

ACETIFY vb become or cause to become acetic acid or vinegar

ACETIN n type of acetate

ACETINS > ACETIN

ACETONE n colourless liquid used as a solvent

ACETONES > ACETONE

ACETONIC > ACETONE

ACETOSE same as > ACETOUS

ACETOUS adj containing, producing, or resembling acetic acid or vinegar

ACETOXYL n medicine used to treat acne

ACETOXYLS > ACETOXYL

ACETUM n solution that has dilute acetic acid as solvent

ACETYL n of, consisting of, or containing the monovalent group CH_3CO-

ACETYLATE vb introduce an acetyl group into (a chemical compound)

ACETYLENE n colourless flammable gas used in welding metals

ACETYLIC > ACETYL

ACETYLIDE n any of a class of carbides in which the carbon is present as a diatomic divalent ion (C_2^{2-}). They are formally derivatives of acetylene

ACETYLS > ACETYL

ACH interj Scots expression of surprise

ACHAENIA > ACHAENIUM

ACHAENIUM n achene

ACHAGE n pain

ACHAGES > ACHAGE

ACHALASIA n failure of the cardiac sphincter of the oesophagus to relax, resulting in difficulty in swallowing

ACHARNE adj furiously violent

ACHARYA n prominent religious teacher and spiritual guide

ACHARYAS > ACHARYA

ACHATES same as > ACATES

ACHE n dull continuous pain ▷ vb be in or cause continuous dull pain

ACHED > ACHE

ACHENE n dry one-seeded indehiscent fruit with the seed distinct from the fruit wall. It may be smooth, as in the buttercup, or feathery, as in clematis

ACHENES > ACHENE

ACHENIA > ACHENIUM

ACHENIAL > ACHENE

ACHENIUM n achene

ACHENIUMS > ACHENIUM

ACHES > ACHE

ACHIER > ACHY

ACHIEST > ACHY

ACHIEVE vb gain by hard work or ability

ACHIEVED > ACHIEVE

ACHIEVER > ACHIEVE

ACHIEVERS > ACHIEVE

ACHIEVES > ACHIEVE

ACHIEVING > ACHIEVE

ACHILLEA n any plant of the N temperate genus Achillea, with white, yellow, or purple flowers, some species of which are widely grown as garden plants: family Asteraceae (composites)

ACHILLEAS > ACHILLEA

ACHIMENES n any plant of the tropical S American tuberous-rooted perennial genus Achimenes, with showy red, blue, or white tubular flowers, some of which are grown as greenhouse plants: family Gesneriaceae

ACHINESS > ACHY

ACHING > ACHE

ACHINGLY > ACHE

ACHINGS > ACHE

ACHIOTE n annatto

ACHIOTES > ACHIOTE

ACHIRAL adj of a tuber producing arrowroot

ACHKAN n man's coat in India

ACHKANS > ACHKAN

ACHOLIA n condition involving lack of bile secretion

ACHOLIAS > ACHOLIA

ACHOO interj sound of a sneeze

ACHROMAT n lens designed to bring light of two chosen wavelengths to the same focal point, thus reducing chromatic aberration

ACHROMATS > ACHROMAT

ACHROMIC adj colourless

ACHROMOUS same as > ACHROMIC

ACHY adj affected by a continuous dull pain

ACICULA n needle-shaped part, such as a spine, prickle, or crystal

ACICULAE > ACICULA

ACICULAR > ACICULA

ACICULAS > ACICULA

ACICULATE adj having aciculae

ACICULUM n needle-like bristle that provides internal support for the appendages (chaetae) of some polychaete worms

ACICULUMS > ACICULUM

ACID n one of a class of compounds, corrosive and sour when dissolved in water, that combine with a base to form a salt ▷ adj containing acid

ACIDEMIA n abnormally high level of acid in blood

ACIDEMIAS > ACIDEMIA

ACIDER > ACID

ACIDEST > ACID

ACIDFREAK n person taking LSD regularly

ACIDHEAD n person who uses LSD

ACIDHEADS > ACIDHEAD

ACIDIC adj containing acid

ACIDIER > ACID

ACIDIEST > ACID

ACIDIFIED > ACIDIFY

a

ACIDIFIER > ACIDIFY
ACIDIFIES > ACIDIFY
ACIDIFY vb convert into acid
ACIDITIES > ACIDITY
ACIDITY n quality of being acid
ACIDLY > ACID
ACIDNESS > ACID
ACIDOPHIL adj (of cells or cell contents) easily stained by acid dyes ▷ n acidophil organism
ACIDOSES > ACIDOSIS
ACIDOSIS n condition characterized by an abnormal increase in the acidity of the blood and extracellular fluids
ACIDOTIC > ACIDOSIS
ACIDS > ACID
ACIDULATE vb make slightly acid or sour
ACIDULENT same as > ACIDULOUS
ACIDULOUS adj rather sour
ACIDURIA n abnormally high level of acid in urine
ACIDURIAS > ACIDURIA
ACIDY > ACID
ACIERAGE n iron-plating of metal
ACIERAGES > ACIERAGE
ACIERATE vb change (iron) into steel
ACIERATED > ACIERATE
ACIERATES > ACIERATE
ACIFORM adj shaped like a needle
ACINAR adj of small sacs
ACING > ACE
ACINI > ACINUS
ACINIC > ACINUS
ACINIFORM adj shaped like a bunch of grapes
ACINOSE > ACINUS
ACINOUS > ACINUS
ACINUS n any of the terminal saclike portions of a compound gland
ACKEE n sapindaceous tree, Blighia sapida, native to tropical Africa and cultivated in the Caribbean for its fruit, edible when cooked
ACKEES > ACKEE
ACKER same as > ACCA
ACKERS > ACKER
ACKNEW > ACKNOW
ACKNOW vb recognize
ACKNOWING > ACKNOW
ACKNOWN > ACKNOW
ACKNOWNE adj aware
ACKNOWS > ACKNOW
ACLINIC adj unbending
ACMATIC adj highest or ultimate
ACME n highest point of achievement or excellence
ACMES > ACME
ACMIC same as > ACMATIC
ACMITE n chemical with pyramid-shaped crystals
ACMITES > ACMITE
ACNE n pimply skin disease
ACNED adj marked by acne

ACNES > ACNE
ACNODAL > ACNODE
ACNODE n point whose coordinates satisfy the equation of a curve although it does not lie on the curve
ACNODES > ACNODE
ACOCK adv cocked
ACOELOUS adj not having a stomach
ACOEMETI n order of monks
ACOLD adj feeling cold
ACOLUTHIC adj of an afterimage
ACOLYTE n follower or attendant
ACOLYTES > ACOLYTE
ACOLYTH n acolyte
ACOLYTHS > ACOLYTH
ACONITE n poisonous plant with hoodlike flowers
ACONITES > ACONITE
ACONITIC > ACONITE
ACONITINE n poison made from aconite
ACONITUM same as > ACONITE
ACONITUMS > ACONITUM
ACORN n nut of the oak tree
ACORNED adj covered with acorns
ACORNS > ACORN
ACOSMISM n belief that no world exists outside the mind
ACOSMISMS > ACOSMISM
ACOSMIST > ACOSMISM
ACOSMISTS > ACOSMISM
ACOUCHI n any of several South American rodents of the genus Myoprocta, closely related to the agoutis but much smaller, with a white-tipped tail: family Dasyproctidae
ACOUCHIES > ACOUCHY
ACOUCHIS > ACOUCHI
ACOUCHY same as > ACOUCHI
ACOUSTIC adj of sound and hearing
ACOUSTICS n science of sounds
ACQUAINT vb make familiar, inform
ACQUAINTS > ACQUAINT
ACQUEST n something acquired
ACQUESTS > ACQUEST
ACQUIESCE vb agree to what someone wants
ACQUIGHT vb acquit
ACQUIGHTS > ACQUIGHT
ACQUIRAL > ACQUIRE
ACQUIRALS > ACQUIRE
ACQUIRE vb gain, get
ACQUIRED > ACQUIRE
ACQUIREE n one who acquires
ACQUIREES > ACQUIREE
ACQUIRER > ACQUIRE
ACQUIRERS > ACQUIRE
ACQUIRES > ACQUIRE
ACQUIRING > ACQUIRE
ACQUIST n acquisition
ACQUISTS > ACQUIST
ACQUIT vb pronounce

(someone) innocent
ACQUITE vb acquit
ACQUITES > ACQUITE
ACQUITING > ACQUITE
ACQUITS > ACQUIT
ACQUITTAL n deliverance and release of a person appearing before a court on a charge of crime, as by a finding of not guilty
ACQUITTED > ACQUIT
ACQUITTER > ACQUIT
ACRASIA n lack of willpower
ACRASIAS > ACRASIA
ACRASIN n chemical produced by slime moulds
ACRASINS > ACRASIN
ACRATIC > ACRASIA
ACRAWL adv crawling
ACRE n measure of land, 4840 square yards (4046.86 square metres)
ACREAGE n land area in acres ▷ adj of or relating to a large allotment of land, esp in a rural area
ACREAGES > ACREAGE
ACRED adj having acres of land
ACRES > ACRE
ACRID adj pungent, bitter
ACRIDER > ACRID
ACRIDEST > ACRID
ACRIDIN n acridine
ACRIDINE n colourless crystalline solid
ACRIDINES > ACRIDINE
ACRIDINS > ACRIDIN
ACRIDITY > ACRID
ACRIDLY > ACRID
ACRIDNESS > ACRID
ACRIMONY n bitterness and resentment felt about something
ACRITARCH n type of fossil
ACRITICAL adj not critical
ACROBAT n person skilled in gymnastic feats requiring agility and balance
ACROBATIC > ACROBAT
ACROBATS > ACROBAT
ACRODONT adj (of the teeth of some reptiles) having no roots and being fused at the base to the margin of the jawbones ▷ n acrodont reptile
ACRODONTS > ACRODONT
ACRODROME adj (of the veins of a leaf) running parallel to the edges of the leaf and fusing at the tip
ACROGEN n any flowerless plant, such as a fern or moss, in which growth occurs from the tip of the main stem
ACROGENIC > ACROGEN
ACROGENS > ACROGEN
ACROLECT n most correct form of language
ACROLECTS > ACROLECT
ACROLEIN n colourless or yellowish flammable poisonous pungent liquid
ACROLEINS > ACROLEIN
ACROLITH n (esp in ancient

Greek sculpture) a wooden, often draped figure with only the head, hands, and feet in stone
ACROLITHS > ACROLITH
ACROMIA > ACROMION
ACROMIAL > ACROMION
ACROMION n outermost edge of the spine of the shoulder blade
ACRONIC adj acronical
ACRONICAL adj occurring at sunset
ACRONYCAL same as > ACRONICAL
ACRONYM n word formed from the initial letters of other words, such as NASA
ACRONYMIC > ACRONYM
ACRONYMS > ACRONYM
ACROPETAL adj (of leaves and flowers) produced in order from the base upwards so that the youngest are at the apex
ACROPHOBE n person afraid of heights
ACROPHONY n use of symbols to represent sounds
ACROPOLIS n citadel of an ancient Greek city
ACROSOMAL > ACROSOME
ACROSOME n structure at the tip of a sperm cell
ACROSOMES > ACROSOME
ACROSPIRE n first shoot developing from the plumule of a germinating grain seed
ACROSS adv from side to side (of)
ACROSTIC n lines of writing in which the first or last letters of each line spell a word or saying
ACROSTICS > ACROSTIC
ACROTER n plinth bearing a statue, etc, at either end or at the apex of a pediment
ACROTERIA n acroters
ACROTERS > ACROTER
ACROTIC adj of a surface
ACROTISM n absence of pulse
ACROTISMS > ACROTISM
ACRYLATE n chemical compound in plastics and resins
ACRYLATES > ACRYLATE
ACRYLIC adj (synthetic fibre, paint, etc) made from acrylic acid ▷ n man-made fibre used for clothes and blankets
ACRYLICS > ACRYLIC
ACRYLYL n type of monovalent group
ACRYLYLS > ACRYLYL
ACT n thing done ▷ vb do something
ACTA n minutes of meeting
ACTABLE > ACT
ACTANT n (in valency grammar) a noun phrase functioning as the agent of the main verb of a sentence

ACTANTS > ACTANT

ACTED > ACT

ACTIN n protein that participates in many kinds of cell movement, including muscle contraction, during which it interacts with filaments of a second protein, myosin

ACTINAL adj of or denoting the oral part of a radiate animal, such as a jellyfish, sea anemone, or sponge, from which the rays, tentacles, or arms grow

ACTINALLY > ACTINAL

ACTING n art of an actor ▷ adj temporarily performing the duties of

ACTINGS > ACTING

ACTINIA n any sea anemone of the genus *Actinia*, which are common in rock pools

ACTINIAE > ACTINIA

ACTINIAN n sea-anemone

ACTINIANS > ACTINIAN

ACTINIAS > ACTINIA

ACTINIC adj (of radiation) producing a photochemical effect

ACTINIDE n member of the actinide series

ACTINIDES > ACTINIDE

ACTINISM > ACTINIC

ACTINISMS > ACTINIC

ACTINIUM n radioactive chemical element

ACTINIUMS > ACTINIUM

ACTINOID adj having a radiate form, as a sea anemone or starfish ▷ n member of the actinide series

ACTINOIDS > ACTINOID

ACTINON same as > ACTINIDE

ACTINONS > ACTINON

ACTINOPOD n any protozoan of the phylum *Actinopoda*, such as a radiolarian or a heliozoan, having stiff radiating cytoplasmic projections

ACTINS > ACTIN

ACTION n process of doing something ▷ vb put into effect

ACTIONED > ACTION

ACTIONER n film with a fast-moving plot, usually containing scenes of violence

ACTIONERS > ACTIONER

ACTIONING > ACTION

ACTIONIST n activist

ACTIONS > ACTION

ACTIVATE vb make active

ACTIVATED > ACTIVATE

ACTIVATES > ACTIVATE

ACTIVATOR > ACTIVATE

ACTIVE adj moving, working ▷ n active form of a verb

ACTIVELY > ACTIVE

ACTIVES > ACTIVE

ACTIVISE same as > ACTIVIZE

ACTIVISED same as > ACTIVISE

ACTIVISES same as > ACTIVISE

ACTIVISM n policy of taking direct and often militant action to achieve an end, esp a political or social one

ACTIVISMS > ACTIVISM

ACTIVIST > ACTIVISM

ACTIVISTS > ACTIVISM

ACTIVITY n state of being active

ACTIVIZE vb make active

ACTIVIZED > ACTIVIZE

ACTIVIZES > ACTIVIZE

ACTON n jacket or jerkin, originally of quilted cotton, worn under a coat of mail

ACTONS > ACTON

ACTOR n person who acts in a play, film, etc

ACTORISH > ACTOR

ACTORLY adj of or relating to an actor

ACTORS > ACTOR

ACTRESS n woman who acts in a play, film, broadcast, etc

ACTRESSES > ACTRESS

ACTRESSY adj exaggerated and affected in manner

ACTS > ACT

ACTUAL adj existing in reality

ACTUALISE same as > ACTUALIZE

ACTUALIST n person dealing in hard fact

ACTUALITE n humorous word for truth

ACTUALITY n reality

ACTUALIZE vb make actual or real

ACTUALLY adv really, indeed

ACTUALS pl n commercial commodities that can be bought and used

ACTUARIAL > ACTUARY

ACTUARIES > ACTUARY

ACTUARY n statistician who calculates insurance risks

ACTUATE vb start up (a device)

ACTUATED > ACTUATE

ACTUATES > ACTUATE

ACTUATING > ACTUATE

ACTUATION > ACTUATE

ACTUATOR > ACTUATE

ACTUATORS > ACTUATE

ACTURE n action

ACTURES > ACTURE

ACUATE adj sharply pointed

ACUITIES > ACUITY

ACUITY n keenness of vision or thought

ACULEATE adj cutting

ACULEATED same as > ACULEATE

ACULEI > ACULEUS

ACULEUS n prickle or spine, such as the thorn of a rose

ACUMEN n ability to make good judgments

ACUMENS > ACUMEN

ACUMINATE adj narrowing to a sharp point, as some

types of leaf ▷ vb make pointed or sharp

ACUMINOUS > ACUMEN

ACUPOINT n any of the specific points on the body where a needle is inserted in acupuncture or pressure is applied in acupressure

ACUPOINTS > ACUPOINT

ACUSHLA n Irish endearment

ACUSHLAS > ACUSHLA

ACUTANCE n physical rather than subjective measure of the sharpness of a photographic image

ACUTANCES > ACUTANCE

ACUTE adj severe ▷ n accent (´) over a letter to indicate the quality or length of its sound, as in café

ACUTELY > ACUTE

ACUTENESS > ACUTE

ACUTER > ACUTE

ACUTES > ACUTE

ACUTEST > ACUTE

ACYCLIC adj not cyclic

ACYCLOVIR n drug used against herpes

ACYL n member of the monovalent group of atoms RCO-

ACYLATE vb introduce an acyl group into a compound

ACYLATED > ACYLATE

ACYLATES > ACYLATE

ACYLATING > ACYLATE

ACYLATION n introduction into a chemical compound of an acyl group

ACYLOIN n organic chemical compound

ACYLOINS > ACYLOIN

ACYLS > ACYL

AD n advertisement

ADAGE n wise saying, proverb

ADAGES > ADAGE

ADAGIAL > ADAGE

ADAGIO adv (piece to be played) slowly and gracefully ▷ n movement or piece to be performed slowly

ADAGIOS > ADAGIO

ADAMANCE n being adamant

ADAMANCES > ADAMANCE

ADAMANCY n being adamant

ADAMANT adj unshakable in determination or purpose ▷ n any extremely hard or apparently unbreakable substance

ADAMANTLY > ADAMANT

ADAMANTS > ADAMANT

ADAMSITE n yellow poisonous crystalline solid that readily sublimes

ADAMSITES > ADAMSITE

ADAPT vb alter for new use or new conditions

ADAPTABLE > ADAPT

ADAPTED > ADAPT

ADAPTER same as > ADAPTOR

ADAPTERS > ADAPTER

ADAPTING > ADAPT

ADAPTION n adaptation

ADAPTIONS > ADAPTION

ADAPTIVE > ADAPT

ADAPTOGEN n any of various natural substances used in herbal medicine to normalize and regulate the systems of the body

ADAPTOR n device for connecting several electrical appliances to a single socket

ADAPTORS > ADAPTOR

ADAPTS > ADAPT

ADAW vb subdue

ADAWED > ADAW

ADAWING > ADAW

ADAWS > ADAW

ADAXIAL adj facing towards the axis, as the surface of a leaf that faces the stem

ADAYS adv daily

ADD vb combine (numbers or quantities)

ADDABLE > ADD

ADDAX n large light-coloured antelope, *Addax nasomaculatus*, having ribbed loosely spiralled horns and inhabiting desert regions in N Africa: family *Bovidae*, order *Artiodactyla*

ADDAXES > ADDAX

ADDEBTED adj indebted

ADDED > ADD

ADDEDLY > ADD

ADDEEM vb adjudge

ADDEEMED > ADDEEM

ADDEEMING > ADDEEM

ADDEEMS > ADDEEM

ADDEND n any of a set of numbers that is to be added

ADDENDA > ADDENDUM

ADDENDS > ADDEND

ADDENDUM n addition

ADDENDUMS > ADDENDUM

ADDER n small poisonous snake

ADDERS > ADDER

ADDERWORT n plant of the dock family

ADDIBLE adj addable

ADDICT n person who is unable to stop taking drugs ▷ vb cause (someone or oneself) to become dependent (on something, esp a narcotic drug)

ADDICTED > ADDICT

ADDICTING > ADDICT

ADDICTION n condition of being abnormally dependent on some habit, esp compulsive dependency on narcotic drugs

ADDICTIVE adj causing addiction

ADDICTS > ADDICT

ADDIES > ADDY

ADDING n act or instance of addition ▷ adj of, for, or relating to addition

ADDIO interj farewell ▷ n

cry of addio
ADDIOS > ADDIO
ADDITION n adding
ADDITIONS > ADDITION
ADDITIVE n something added, esp to a foodstuff, to improve it or prevent deterioration ▷ adj characterized or produced by addition
ADDITIVES > ADDITIVE
ADDITORY adj adding to something
ADDLE vb make or become confused or muddled ▷ adj indicating a confused or muddled state
ADDLED > ADDLE
ADDLEMENT > ADDLE
ADDLES > ADDLE
ADDLING > ADDLE
ADDOOM vb adjudge
ADDOOMED > ADDOOM
ADDOOMING > ADDOOM
ADDOOMS > ADDOOM
ADDORSED adj back to back
ADDRESS n place where a person lives ▷ vb mark the destination, as on an envelope
ADDRESSED > ADDRESS
ADDRESSEE n person addressed
ADDRESSER > ADDRESS
ADDRESSES > ADDRESS
ADDRESSOR > ADDRESS
ADDREST > ADDRESS
ADDS > ADD
ADDUCE vb mention something as evidence or proof
ADDUCED > ADDUCE
ADDUCENT > ADDUCE
ADDUCER > ADDUCE
ADDUCERS > ADDUCE
ADDUCES > ADDUCE
ADDUCIBLE > ADDUCE
ADDUCING > ADDUCE
ADDUCT vb (of a muscle) to draw or pull (a leg, arm, etc) towards the median axis of the body ▷ n compound formed by direct combination of two or more different compounds or elements
ADDUCTED > ADDUCT
ADDUCTING > ADDUCT
ADDUCTION > ADDUCT
ADDUCTIVE > ADDUCE
ADDUCTOR n muscle that adducts
ADDUCTORS > ADDUCTOR
ADDUCTS > ADDUCT
ADDY n e-mail address
ADEEM vb cancel
ADEEMED > ADEEM
ADEEMING > ADEEM
ADEEMS > ADEEM
ADEMPTION n failure of a specific legacy, as by a testator disposing of the subject matter in his lifetime
ADENINE n purine base present in tissues of all living organisms as a

constituent of the nucleic acids DNA and RNA and of certain coenzymes
ADENINES > ADENINE
ADENITIS n inflammation of a gland or lymph node
ADENOID adj of or resembling a gland
ADENOIDAL adj having a nasal voice caused by swollen adenoids
ADENOIDS pl n tissue at the back of the throat
ADENOMA n tumour, usually benign, occurring in glandular tissue
ADENOMAS > ADENOMA
ADENOMATA > ADENOMA
ADENOSES > ADENOSIS
ADENOSINE n nucleoside formed by the condensation of adenine and ribose
ADENOSIS n disease of glands
ADENYL n enzyme
ADENYLIC as in adenylic acid nucleotide consisting of adenine, ribose or deoxyribose, and a phosphate group
ADENYLS > ADENYL
ADEPT n very skilful (person) ▷ adj proficient in something requiring skill
ADEPTER > ADEPT
ADEPTEST > ADEPT
ADEPTLY > ADEPT
ADEPTNESS > ADEPT
ADEPTS > ADEPT
ADEQUACY > ADEQUATE
ADEQUATE adj sufficient, enough
ADERMIN n vitamin
ADERMINS > ADERMIN
ADESPOTA n anonymous writings
ADESSIVE n grammatical case denoting place
ADESSIVES > ADESSIVE
ADHAN n call to prayer
ADHANS > ADHAN
ADHARMA n wickedness
ADHARMAS > ADHARMA
ADHERABLE > ADHERE
ADHERE vb stick (to)
ADHERED > ADHERE
ADHERENCE > ADHERE
ADHEREND n something attached by adhesive
ADHERENDS > ADHEREND
ADHERENT n devotee, follower ▷ adj sticking or attached
ADHERENTS > ADHERENT
ADHERER > ADHERE
ADHERERS > ADHERE
ADHERES > ADHERE
ADHERING > ADHERE
ADHESION n sticking (to)
ADHESIONS > ADHESION
ADHESIVE n substance used to stick things together ▷ adj able to stick to things
ADHESIVES > ADHESIVE
ADHIBIT vb administer or apply

ADHIBITED > ADHIBIT
ADHIBITS > ADHIBIT
ADHOCRACY n management that responds to urgent problems rather than planning to avoid them
ADIABATIC adj (of a thermodynamic process) taking place without loss or gain of heat ▷ n curve or surface on a graph representing the changes in two or more characteristics (such as pressure and volume) of a system undergoing an adiabatic process
ADIAPHORA n matters of indifference
ADIEU n goodbye
ADIEUS > ADIEU
ADIEUX > ADIEU
ADIOS sentence substitute Spanish for goodbye
ADIPIC as in adipic acid colourless crystalline solid used in the preparation of nylon
ADIPOCERE n waxlike fatty substance formed during the decomposition of corpses
ADIPOCYTE n fat cell that accumulates and stores fats
ADIPOSE adj of or containing fat ▷ n animal fat
ADIPOSES > ADIPOSIS
ADIPOSIS n obesity
ADIPOSITY > ADIPOSE
ADIPOUS adj made of fat
ADIPSIA n complete lack of thirst
ADIPSIAS > ADIPSIA
ADIT n almost horizontal shaft into a mine, for access or drainage
ADITS > ADIT
ADJACENCE > ADJACENT
ADJACENCY > ADJACENT
ADJACENT adj near or next (to) ▷ n side lying between a specified angle and a right angle in a right-angled triangle
ADJACENTS > ADJACENT
ADJECTIVE n word that adds information about a noun or pronoun ▷ adj additional or dependent
ADJIGO n yam plant, Dioscorea hastifolia, native to SW Australia that has edible tubers
ADJIGOS > ADJIGO
ADJOIN vb be next to
ADJOINED > ADJOIN
ADJOINING adj being in contact
ADJOINS > ADJOIN
ADJOINT n type of mathematical matrix
ADJOINTS > ADJOINT
ADJOURN vb close (a court) at the end of a session
ADJOURNED > ADJOURN

ADJOURNS > ADJOURN
ADJUDGE vb declare (to be)
ADJUDGED > ADJUDGE
ADJUDGES > ADJUDGE
ADJUDGING > ADJUDGE
ADJUNCT n something incidental added to something else
ADJUNCTLY > ADJUNCT
ADJUNCTS > ADJUNCT
ADJURE vb command (to do)
ADJURED > ADJURE
ADJURER > ADJURE
ADJURERS > ADJURE
ADJURES > ADJURE
ADJURING > ADJURE
ADJUROR > ADJURE
ADJURORS > ADJURE
ADJUST vb adapt to new conditions
ADJUSTED > ADJUST
ADJUSTER > ADJUST
ADJUSTERS > ADJUST
ADJUSTING > ADJUST
ADJUSTIVE > ADJUST
ADJUSTOR > ADJUST
ADJUSTORS > ADJUST
ADJUSTS > ADJUST
ADJUTAGE n nozzle
ADJUTAGES > ADJUTAGE
ADJUTANCY > ADJUTANT
ADJUTANT n army officer in charge of routine administration
ADJUTANTS > ADJUTANT
ADJUVANCY > ADJUVANT
ADJUVANT adj aiding or assisting ▷ n something that aids or assists
ADJUVANTS > ADJUVANT
ADLAND n advertising industry and the people who work in it
ADLANDS > ADLAND
ADMAN n man who works in advertising
ADMASS n mass advertising
ADMASSES > ADMASS
ADMEASURE vb measure out (land, etc) as a share
ADMEN > ADMAN
ADMIN n administration
ADMINICLE n something contributing to prove a point without itself being complete proof
ADMINS > ADMIN
ADMIRABLE adj deserving or inspiring admiration
ADMIRABLY > ADMIRABLE
ADMIRAL n highest naval rank
ADMIRALS > ADMIRAL
ADMIRALTY n office or jurisdiction of an admiral
ADMIRANCE n admiration
ADMIRE vb regard with esteem and approval
ADMIRED > ADMIRE
ADMIRER > ADMIRE
ADMIRERS > ADMIRE
ADMIRES > ADMIRE
ADMIRING > ADMIRE
ADMISSION n permission to enter
ADMISSIVE > ADMISSION
ADMIT vb confess,

a

acknowledge
ADMITS > ADMIT
ADMITTED > ADMIT
ADMITTEE *n* one who admits
ADMITTEES > ADMITTEE
ADMITTER > ADMIT
ADMITTERS > ADMIT
ADMITTING > ADMIT
ADMIX *vb* mix or blend
ADMIXED > ADMIX
ADMIXES > ADMIX
ADMIXING > ADMIX
ADMIXT > ADMIX
ADMIXTURE *n* mixture
ADMONISH *vb* reprove sternly
ADMONITOR > ADMONISH
ADNASCENT *adj* growing with something else
ADNATE *adj* growing closely attached to an adjacent part or organ
ADNATION > ADNATE
ADNATIONS > ADNATE
ADNEXA *pl n* organs adjoining the uterus
ADNEXAL > ADNEXA
ADNOMINAL *n* word modifying a noun ▷ *adj* of or relating to an adnoun
ADNOUN *n* adjective used as a noun
ADNOUNS > ADNOUN
ADO *n* fuss, trouble
ADOBE *n* sun-dried brick
ADOBELIKE > ADOBE
ADOBES > ADOBE
ADOBO *n* Philippine dish
ADOBOS > ADOBO
ADONIS *n* beautiful young man
ADONISE *vb* adorn
ADONISED > ADONISE
ADONISES > ADONISE
ADONISING > ADONISE
ADONIZE *vb* adorn
ADONIZED > ADONIZE
ADONIZES > ADONIZE
ADONIZING > ADONIZE
ADOORS *adv* at the door
ADOPT *vb* take (someone else's child) as one's own
ADOPTABLE > ADOPT
ADOPTED *adj* having been adopted
ADOPTEE *n* one who has been adopted
ADOPTEES > ADOPTEE
ADOPTER *n* person who adopts
ADOPTERS > ADOPTER
ADOPTING > ADOPT
ADOPTION > ADOPT
ADOPTIONS > ADOPT
ADOPTIOUS *adj* adopted
ADOPTIVE *adj* related by adoption
ADOPTS > ADOPT
ADORABLE *adj* very attractive
ADORABLY > ADORABLE
ADORATION *n* deep love or esteem
ADORE *vb* love intensely
ADORED > ADORE
ADORER > ADORE

ADORERS > ADORE
ADORES > ADORE
ADORING > ADORE
ADORINGLY > ADORE
ADORN *vb* decorate, embellish
ADORNED > ADORN
ADORNER > ADORN
ADORNERS > ADORN
ADORNING > ADORN
ADORNMENT > ADORN
ADORNS > ADORN
ADOS > ADO
ADOWN *adv* down
ADOZE *adv* asleep
ADPRESS *vb* press together
ADPRESSED > ADPRESS
ADPRESSES > ADPRESS
ADRAD *adj* afraid
ADREAD *vb* dread
ADREADED > ADREAD
ADREADING > ADREAD
ADREADS > ADREAD
ADRED *adj* filled with dread
ADRENAL *adj* near the kidneys ▷ *n* adrenal gland
ADRENALIN *n* hormone secreted by the adrenal glands in response to stress
ADRENALLY > ADRENAL
ADRENALS > ADRENAL
ADRIFT *adv* drifting
ADROIT *adj* quick and skilful
ADROITER > ADROIT
ADROITEST > ADROIT
ADROITLY > ADROIT
ADRY *adj* dry
ADS > AD
ADSCRIPT *n* serf
ADSCRIPTS > ADSCRIPT
ADSORB *vb* (of a gas or vapour) condense and form a thin film on a surface
ADSORBATE *n* substance that has been or is to be adsorbed on a surface
ADSORBED > ADSORB
ADSORBENT *adj* capable of adsorption ▷ *n* material, such as activated charcoal, on which adsorption can occur
ADSORBER > ADSORB
ADSORBERS > ADSORB
ADSORBING > ADSORB
ADSORBS > ADSORB
ADSUKI *same as* > ADZUKI
ADSUKIS > ADSUKI
ADSUM *sentence substitute* I am present
ADUKI *same as* > ADZUKI
ADUKIS > ADUKI
ADULARIA *n* white or colourless glassy variety of orthoclase
ADULARIAS > ADULARIA
ADULATE *vb* flatter or praise obsequiously
ADULATED > ADULATE
ADULATES > ADULATE
ADULATING > ADULATE
ADULATION *n* uncritical admiration
ADULATOR > ADULATE
ADULATORS > ADULATE
ADULATORY *adj* expressing praise, esp obsequiously

ADULT *adj* fully grown, mature ▷ *n* adult person or animal
ADULTERER *n* person who has committed adultery
ADULTERY *n* sexual unfaithfulness of a husband or wife
ADULTHOOD > ADULT
ADULTLIKE > ADULT
ADULTLY > ADULT
ADULTNESS > ADULT
ADULTRESS *n* US word for a female adulterer
ADULTS > ADULT
ADUMBRAL *adj* shadowy
ADUMBRATE *vb* outline
ADUNC *adj* hooked
ADUNCATE *adj* hooked
ADUNCATED *adj* hooked
ADUNCITY *n* quality of being hooked
ADUNCOUS *adj* hooked
ADUST *vb* dry up or darken by heat
ADUSTED > ADUST
ADUSTING > ADUST
ADUSTS > ADUST
ADVANCE *vb* go or bring forward ▷ *n* forward movement ▷ *adj* done or happening before an event
ADVANCED *adj* at a late stage in development
ADVANCER > ADVANCE
ADVANCERS > ADVANCE
ADVANCES > ADVANCE
ADVANCING > ADVANCE
ADVANTAGE *n* more favourable position or state
ADVECT *vb* move horizontally in air
ADVECTED > ADVECT
ADVECTING > ADVECT
ADVECTION *n* transferring of heat in a horizontal stream of gas
ADVECTIVE > ADVECTION
ADVECTS > ADVECT
ADVENE *vb* add as extra
ADVENED > ADVENE
ADVENES > ADVENE
ADVENING > ADVENE
ADVENT *n* arrival
ADVENTIVE *adj* (of a species) introduced to a new area and not yet established there ▷ *n* such a plant or animal
ADVENTS > ADVENT
ADVENTURE *n* exciting and risky undertaking or exploit ▷ *vb* take a risk or put at risk
ADVERB *n* word that adds information about a verb, adjective, or other adverb
ADVERBIAL *n* word or group of words playing the grammatical role of an adverb, such as *in the rain* in the sentence *I'm singing in the rain* ▷ *adj* of or relating to an adverb or adverbial
ADVERBS > ADVERB
ADVERSARY *n* opponent or

enemy
ADVERSE *adj* unfavourable
ADVERSELY > ADVERSE
ADVERSER > ADVERSE
ADVERSEST > ADVERSE
ADVERSITY *n* very difficult or hard circumstances
ADVERT *n* advertisement . ▷ *vb* draw attention (to)
ADVERTED > ADVERT
ADVERTENT *adj* heedful
ADVERTING > ADVERT
ADVERTISE *vb* present or praise (goods or services) to the public in order to encourage sales
ADVERTIZE *same as* > ADVERTISE
ADVERTS > ADVERT
ADVEW *vb* look at
ADVEWED > ADVEW
ADVEWING > ADVEW
ADVEWS > ADVEW
ADVICE *n* recommendation as to what to do
ADVICEFUL > ADVICE
ADVICES > ADVICE
ADVISABLE *adj* prudent, sensible
ADVISABLY > ADVISABLE
ADVISE *vb* offer advice to
ADVISED *adj* considered, thought-out
ADVISEDLY > ADVISED
ADVISEE *n* person receiving advice
ADVISEES > ADVISEE
ADVISER *n* person who offers advice, e.g. on careers to students or school pupils
ADVISERS > ADVISER
ADVISES > ADVISE
ADVISING > ADVISE
ADVISINGS > ADVISE
ADVISOR *same as* > ADVISER
ADVISORS > ADVISOR
ADVISORY *adj* giving advice ▷ *n* statement giving advice or a warning
ADVOCAAT *n* liqueur with a raw egg base
ADVOCAATS > ADVOCAAT
ADVOCACY *n* active support of a cause or course of action
ADVOCATE *vb* propose or recommend ▷ *n* person who publicly supports a cause
ADVOCATED > ADVOCATE
ADVOCATES > ADVOCATE
ADVOCATOR *n* person who advocates
ADVOUTRER *n* adulterer
ADVOUTRY *n* adultery
ADVOWSON *n* right of presentation to a vacant benefice
ADVOWSONS > ADVOWSON
ADWARD *vb* award
ADWARDED > ADWARD
ADWARDING > ADWARD
ADWARDS > ADWARD
ADWARE *n* type of computer software that collects information about a user's

browsing patterns in order to display relevant advertisements in his or her Web browser

ADWARES > ADWARE

ADWOMAN *n* woman working in advertising

ADWOMEN > ADWOMAN

ADYNAMIA *n* loss of vital power or strength, esp as the result of illness

ADYNAMIAS > ADYNAMIA

ADYNAMIC > ADYNAMIA

ADYTA > ADYTUM

ADYTUM *n* most sacred place of worship in an ancient temple from which the laity was prohibited

ADZ *same as* > ADZE

ADZE *n* tool with an arched blade at right angles to the handle ▷ *vb* use an adze

ADZED > ADZE

ADZES > ADZE

ADZING > ADZE

ADZUKI *n* leguminous plant, *Phaseolus angularis*, that has yellow flowers and pods containing edible brown seeds and is widely cultivated as a food crop in China and Japan

ADZUKIS > ADZUKI

AE *determiner* one

AECIA > AECIUM

AECIAL > AECIUM

AECIDIA > AECIDIUM

AECIDIAL > AECIDIUM

AECIDIUM *same as* > AECIUM

AECIUM *n* globular or cup-shaped structure in some rust fungi in which aeciospores are produced

AEDES *n* any mosquito of the genus *Aedes* (formerly *Stegomyia*) of tropical and subtropical regions, esp *A. aegypti*, which transmits yellow fever and dengue

AEDICULE *n* opening such as a door or a window, framed by columns on either side, and a pediment above

AEDICULES > AEDICULE

AEDILE *n* magistrate of ancient Rome in charge of public works, games, buildings, and roads

AEDILES > AEDILE

AEDINE *adj* of a species of mosquito

AEFALD *adj* single

AEFAULD *adj* single

AEGIRINE *n* green mineral

AEGIRINES > AEGIRINE

AEGIRITE *n* green mineral

AEGIRITES > AEGIRITE

AEGIS *n* sponsorship, protection

AEGISES > AEGIS

AEGLOGUE *n* eclogue

AEGLOGUES > AEGLOGUE

AEGROTAT *n* (in British and certain other universities, and, sometimes, schools) a certificate allowing

a candidate to pass an examination although he has missed all or part of it through illness

AEGROTATS > AEGROTAT

AEMULE *vb* emulate

AEMULED > AEMULE

AEMULES > AEMULE

AEMULING > AEMULE

AENEOUS *adj* brass-coloured or greenish-gold

AENEUS *n* aquarium fish

AEOLIAN *adj* of or relating to the wind

AEOLIPILE *n* device illustrating the reactive forces of a gas jet: usually a spherical vessel mounted so as to rotate and equipped with angled exit pipes from which steam within it escapes

AEOLIPYLE > AEOLIPILE

AEON *n* immeasurably long period of time

AEONIAN *adj* everlasting

AEONIC > AEON

AEONS > AEON

AEPYORNIS *n* any of the large extinct flightless birds of the genus *Aepyornis*, remains of which have been found in Madagascar

AEQUORIN *n* type of protein

AEQUORINS > AEQUORIN

AERATE *vb* put gas into (a liquid), as when making a fizzy drink

AERATED > AERATE

AERATES > AERATE

AERATING > AERATE

AERATION > AERATE

AERATIONS > AERATE

AERATOR > AERATE

AERATORS > AERATE

AERIAL *adj* in, from, or operating in the air ▷ *n* metal pole, wire, etc, for receiving or transmitting radio or TV signals

AERIALIST *n* trapeze artist or tightrope walker

AERIALITY > AERIAL

AERIALLY > AERIAL

AERIALS > AERIAL

AERIE *a variant spelling (esp US) of* > EYRIE

AERIED *adj* in a very high place

AERIER > AERY

AERIES > AERIE

AERIEST > AERY

AERIFIED > AERIFY

AERIFIES > AERIFY

AERIFORM *adj* having the form of air

AERIFY *vb* change or cause to change into a gas

AERIFYING > AERIFY

AERILY > AERY

AERO *n* of or relating to aircraft or aeronautics

AEROBAT *n* person who does stunt flying

AEROBATIC *adj* pertaining to stunt flying

AEROBATS > AEROBAT

AEROBE *n* organism that requires oxygen to survive

AEROBES > AEROBE

AEROBIA > AEROBIUM

AEROBIC *adj* designed for or relating to aerobics

AEROBICS *n* exercises designed to increase the amount of oxygen in the blood

AEROBIONT *n* organism needing oxygen to live

AEROBIUM *same as* > AEROBE

AEROBOMB *n* bomb dropped from aircraft

AEROBOMBS > AEROBOMB

AEROBRAKE *vb* use airbrakes to slow aircraft

AEROBUS *n* type of monorail

AEROBUSES > AEROBUS

AERODART *n* metal arrow dropped from an aircraft as a weapon

AERODARTS > AERODART

AERODROME *n* small airport

AERODUCT *n* air duct

AERODUCTS > AERODUCT

AERODYNE *n* any heavier-than-air machine, such as an aircraft, that derives the greater part of its lift from aerodynamic forces

AERODYNES > AERODYNE

AEROFOIL *n* part of an aircraft, such as the wing, designed to give lift

AEROFOILS > AEROFOIL

AEROGEL *n* colloid that has a continuous solid phase containing dispersed gas

AEROGELS > AEROGEL

AEROGRAM *n* airmail letter on a single sheet of paper that seals to form an envelope

AEROGRAMS > AEROGRAM

AEROGRAPH *n* airborne instrument recording meteorological conditions

AEROLITE *n* stony meteorite consisting of silicate minerals

AEROLITES > AEROLITE

AEROLITH *n* meteorite

AEROLITHS > AEROLITH

AEROLITIC > AEROLITE

AEROLOGIC > AEROLOGY

AEROLOGY *n* study of the atmosphere, particularly its upper layers

AEROMANCY *n* using weather observation to foretell the future

AEROMETER *n* instrument for determining the mass or density of a gas, esp air

AEROMETRY *n* branch of physics concerned with the mechanical properties of gases, esp air

AEROMOTOR *n* aircraft engine

AERONAUT *n* person who flies in a lighter-than-air craft, esp the pilot or navigator

AERONAUTS > AERONAUT

AERONOMER *n* scientist studying atmosphere

AERONOMIC > AERONOMY

AERONOMY *n* science of the earth's upper atmosphere

AEROPAUSE *n* region of the upper atmosphere above which aircraft cannot fly

AEROPHAGY *n* spasmodic swallowing of air

AEROPHOBE *n* person suffering from aerophobia

AEROPHONE *n* wind instrument

AEROPHORE *n* device for playing a wind instrument

AEROPHYTE *another name for* > EPIPHYTE

AEROPLANE *n* powered flying vehicle with fixed wings

AEROPULSE *n* type of jet engine

AEROS > AERO

AEROSAT *n* communications satellite

AEROSATS > AEROSAT

AEROSCOPE *n* device for observing the atmosphere

AEROSHELL *n* parachute used to slow spacecraft

AEROSOL *n* pressurized can from which a substance can be dispensed as a fine spray

AEROSOLS > AEROSOL

AEROSPACE *n* earth's atmosphere and space beyond ▷ *adj* of rockets or space vehicles

AEROSTAT *n* lighter-than-air craft, such as a balloon

AEROSTATS > AEROSTAT

AEROTAXES > AEROTAXIS

AEROTAXIS *n* movement away from or towards oxygen

AEROTONE *n* bath incorporating air jets for massage

AEROTONES > AEROTONE

AEROTRAIN *n* train driven by a jet engine

AERUGO *(esp of old bronze) another name for* > VERDIGRIS

AERUGOS > AERUGO

AERY *adj* lofty, insubstantial, or visionary

AESC *n* rune

AESCES > AESC

AESCULIN *n* chemical in horse-chestnut bark

AESCULINS > AESCULIN

AESIR *n* chief of the Norse gods

AESTHESES > AESTHESIS

AESTHESIA *n* normal ability to experience sensation, perception, or sensitivity

AESTHESIS *variant of* > ESTHESIS

AESTHETE *n* person who has or affects an extravagant love of art

AESTHETES > AESTHETE

AESTHETIC *adj* relating to

the appreciation of art and beauty ▷ *n* principle or set of principles relating to the appreciation of art and beauty

AESTIVAL *adj* of or occurring in summer

AESTIVATE *vb* pass the summer

AETHER *same as* > ETHER

AETHEREAL *a variant spelling of* > ETHEREAL

AETHERIC > AETHER

AETHERS > AETHER

AETIOLOGY *n* philosophy or study of causation

AFALD *adj* single

AFAR *adv* at, from, or to a great distance ▷ *n* great distance

AFARA *n* African tree

AFARAS > AFARA

AFARS > AFAR

AFAWLD *adj* single

AFEAR *vb* frighten

AFEARD *an archaic or dialect word for* > AFRAID

AFEARED *same as* > AFEARD

AFEARING > AFEAR

AFEARS > AFEAR

AFEBRILE *adj* without fever

AFF *adv* off

AFFABLE *adj* friendly and easy to talk to

AFFABLY > AFFABLE

AFFAIR *n* event or happening

AFFAIRE *n* love affair

AFFAIRES > AFFAIRE

AFFAIRS *pl n* personal or business interests

AFFEAR *vb* frighten

AFFEARD > AFFEAR

AFFEARE *vb* frighten

AFFEARED > AFFEAR

AFFEARES > AFFEARE

AFFEARING > AFFEAR

AFFEARS > AFFEAR

AFFECT *vb* act on, influence ▷ *n* emotion associated with an idea or set of ideas

AFFECTED *adj* displaying affectation

AFFECTER > AFFECT

AFFECTERS > AFFECT

AFFECTING *adj* arousing feelings of pity

AFFECTION *n* fondness or love

AFFECTIVE *adj* relating to affects

AFFECTS > AFFECT

AFFEER *vb* assess

AFFEERED > AFFEER

AFFEERING > AFFEER

AFFEERS > AFFEER

AFFERENT *adj* bringing or directing inwards to a part or an organ of the body, esp towards the brain or spinal cord ▷ *n* nerve that conveys impulses towards an organ of the body

AFFERENTS > AFFERENT

AFFIANCE *vb* bind (a person or oneself) in a promise of marriage ▷ *n* solemn

pledge, esp a marriage contract

AFFIANCED > AFFIANCE

AFFIANCES > AFFIANCE

AFFIANT *n* person who makes an affidavit

AFFIANTS > AFFIANT

AFFICHE *n* poster or advertisement, esp one drawn by an artist, as for the opening of an exhibition

AFFICHES > AFFICHE

AFFIDAVIT *n* written statement made on oath

AFFIED > AFFY

AFFIES > AFFY

AFFILIATE *vb* (of a group) link up with a larger group ▷ *n* person or organization that is affiliated with another

AFFINAL > AFFINE

AFFINE *adj* of, characterizing, or involving transformations which preserve collinearity, esp in classical geometry, those of translation, rotation and reflection in an axis ▷ *n* relation by marriage

AFFINED *adj* closely related

AFFINELY > AFFINE

AFFINES > AFFINE

AFFINITY *n* close connection or liking

AFFIRM *vb* declare to be true

AFFIRMANT > AFFIRM

AFFIRMED > AFFIRM

AFFIRMER > AFFIRM

AFFIRMERS > AFFIRM

AFFIRMING > AFFIRM

AFFIRMS > AFFIRM

AFFIX *vb* attach or fasten ▷ *n* word or syllable added to a word to change its meaning

AFFIXABLE > AFFIRM

AFFIXAL > AFFIX

AFFIXED > AFFIX

AFFIXER > AFFIX

AFFIXERS > AFFIX

AFFIXES > AFFIX

AFFIXIAL > AFFIX

AFFIXING > AFFIX

AFFIXMENT > AFFIX

AFFIXTURE > AFFIX

AFFLATED *adj* inspired

AFFLATION *n* inspiration

AFFLATUS *n* impulse of creative power or inspiration, esp in poetry, considered to be of divine origin

AFFLICT *vb* give pain or grief to

AFFLICTED > AFFLICT

AFFLICTER *n* one who afflicts

AFFLICTS > AFFLICT

AFFLUENCE *n* wealth

AFFLUENCY *n* affluence

AFFLUENT *adj* having plenty of money ▷ *n* tributary stream

AFFLUENTS > AFFLUENT

AFFLUENZA *n* guilt or lack

of motivation experienced by people who have made or inherited large amounts of money

AFFLUX *n* flowing towards a point

AFFLUXES > AFFLUX

AFFLUXION *n* flow towards something

AFFOORD *vb* consent

AFFOORDED > AFFOORD

AFFOORDS > AFFOORD

AFFORCE *vb* strengthen

AFFORCED > AFFORCE

AFFORCES > AFFORCE

AFFORCING > AFFORCE

AFFORD *vb* have enough money to buy

AFFORDED > AFFORD

AFFORDING > AFFORD

AFFORDS > AFFORD

AFFOREST *vb* plant trees on

AFFORESTS > AFFOREST

AFFRAP *vb* strike

AFFRAPPED > AFFRAP

AFFRAPS > AFFRAP

AFFRAY *n* noisy fight, brawl ▷ *vb* frighten

AFFRAYED > AFFRAY

AFFRAYER > AFFRAY

AFFRAYERS > AFFRAY

AFFRAYING > AFFRAY

AFFRAYS > AFFRAY

AFFRENDED *adj* brought back into friendship

AFFRET *n* furious attack

AFFRETS > AFFRET

AFFRICATE *n* composite speech sound consisting of a stop and a fricative articulated at the same point, such as the sound written *ch*, as in *chair*.

AFFRIGHT *vb* frighten ▷ *n* sudden terror

AFFRIGHTS > AFFRIGHT

AFFRONT *n* insult ▷ *vb* hurt someone's pride or dignity

AFFRONTE *adj* facing

AFFRONTED > AFFRONT

AFFRONTEE *adj* facing

AFFRONTS > AFFRONT

AFFUSION *n* baptizing of a person by pouring water onto his head

AFFUSIONS > AFFUSION

AFFY *vb* trust

AFFYDE > AFFY

AFFYING > AFFY

AFGHAN *n* type of biscuit

AFGHANI *n* standard monetary unit of Afghanistan, divided into 100 puli

AFGHANIS > AFGHANI

AFGHANS > AFGHAN

AFIELD *adj* away from one's usual surroundings or home

AFIRE *adj* on fire

AFLAJ *n* Arabian irrigation channel

AFLAME *adj* burning

AFLATOXIN *n* toxin produced by the fungus *Aspergillus flavus* growing on peanuts, maize, etc,

causing liver disease (esp cancer) in man

AFLOAT *adj* floating ▷ *adv* floating

AFLUTTER *adv* in or into a nervous or excited state

AFOOT *adj* happening, in operation ▷ *adv* happening

AFORE *adv* before

AFOREHAND *adv* beforehand

AFORESAID *adj* referred to previously

AFORETIME *adv* formerly

AFOUL *adj* in or into a state of difficulty, confusion, or conflict (with)

AFRAID *adj* frightened

AFREET *n* powerful evil demon or giant monster

AFREETS > AFREET

AFRESH *adv* again, anew

AFRIT *same as* > AFREET

AFRITS > AFRIT

AFRO *n* bush-like frizzy hairstyle

AFRONT *adv* in front

AFROS > AFRO

AFT *adv* at or towards the rear of a ship or aircraft ▷ *adj* at or towards the rear of a ship or aircraft

AFTER *adv* at a later time

AFTERBODY *n* any discarded part that continues to trail a satellite, rocket, etc, in orbit

AFTERCARE *n* support given to a person discharged from a hospital or prison

AFTERCLAP *n* unexpected consequence

AFTERDAMP *n* poisonous gas formed after the explosion of firedamp in a coal mine

AFTERDECK *n* unprotected deck behind the bridge of a ship

AFTEREYE *vb* gaze at someone or something that has passed

AFTEREYED > AFTEREYE

AFTEREYES > AFTEREYE

AFTERGAME *n* second game that follows another

AFTERGLOW *n* glow left after a source of light has gone

AFTERHEAT *n* heat generated in a nuclear reactor after it has been shut down, produced by residual radioactivity in the fuel elements

AFTERINGS *n* last of the milk drawn in milking

AFTERLIFE *n* life after death

AFTERMATH *n* results of an event considered together

AFTERMOST *adj* closer or closest to the rear or (in a vessel) the stern

AFTERNOON *n* time between noon and evening

AFTERPAIN *n* pain that comes after a while

AFTERPEAK *n* space behind

a

the aftermost bulkhead, often used for storage

AFTERS n sweet course of a meal

AFTERSHOW n party held after a public performance of a play or film

AFTERSUN n moisturizing lotion applied to the skin to soothe sunburn and avoid peeling

AFTERSUNS > AFTERSUN

AFTERTAX adj after tax has been paid

AFTERTIME n later period

AFTERWARD adv after an earlier event or time

AFTERWORD n epilogue or postscript in a book, etc

AFTMOST adj furthest towards rear

AFTOSA n foot-and-mouth disease

AFTOSAS > AFTOSA

AG n agriculture

AGA n title of respect, often used with the title of a senior position

AGACANT adj irritating

AGACANTE adj irritating

AGACERIE n coquetry

AGACERIES > AGACERIE

AGAIN adv once more

AGAINST prep in opposition or contrast to

AGALACTIA n absence or failure of secretion of milk

AGALLOCH another name for > EAGLEWOOD

AGALLOCHS > AGALLOCH

AGALWOOD n eaglewood

AGALWOODS > AGALWOOD

AGAMA n any small terrestrial lizard of the genus Agama, which inhabit warm regions of the Old World: family Agamidae

AGAMAS > AGAMA

AGAMETE n reproductive cell, such as the merozoite of some protozoans, that develops into a new form without fertilization

AGAMETES > AGAMETE

AGAMI n South American bird

AGAMIC adj asexual

AGAMID same as > AGAMA

AGAMIDS > AGAMID

AGAMIS > AGAMI

AGAMOGONY n asexual reproduction in protozoans that is characterized by multiple fission

AGAMOID n lizard of the agamid type

AGAMOIDS > AGAMOID

AGAMONT another name for > SCHIZONT

AGAMONTS > AGAMONT

AGAMOUS adj without sex

AGAPAE > AGAPE

AGAPAI > AGAPE

AGAPE adj (of the mouth) wide open ▷ n love feast among the early Christians

AGAPEIC > AGAPE

AGAPES > AGAPE

AGAR n jelly-like substance obtained from seaweed and used as a thickener in food

AGARIC n fungus with gills on the underside of the cap, such as a mushroom

AGARICS > AGARIC

AGAROSE n gel used in chemistry

AGAROSES > AGAROSE

AGARS > AGAR

AGAS > AGA

AGAST adj aghast

AGATE n semiprecious form of quartz with striped colouring ▷ adv on the way

AGATES > AGATE

AGATEWARE n ceramic ware made to resemble agate or marble

AGATISE same as > AGATIZE

AGATISED same as > AGATISE

AGATISES same as > AGATISE

AGATISING same as > AGATISE

AGATIZE vb turn into agate

AGATIZED > AGATIZE

AGATIZES > AGATIZE

AGATIZING > AGATIZE

AGATOID adj like agate

AGAVE n tropical American plant with tall flower stalks and thick leaves

AGAVES > AGAVE

AGAZE adj gazing at something

AGAZED adj amazed

AGE n length of time a person or thing has existed ▷ vb make or grow old

AGED adj old

AGEDLY > AGED

AGEDNESS > AGED

AGEE adj awry, crooked, or ajar ▷ adv awry

AGEING n fact or process of growing old ▷ adj becoming or appearing older

AGEINGS > AGEING

AGEISM n discrimination against people on the grounds of age

AGEISMS > AGEISM

AGEIST > AGEISM

AGEISTS > AGEISM

AGELAST n someone who never laughs

AGELASTIC > AGELAST

AGELASTS > AGELAST

AGELESS adj apparently never growing old

AGELESSLY > AGELESS

AGELONG adj lasting for a very long time

AGEMATE n person the same age as another person

AGEMATES > AGEMATE

AGEN archaic form of > AGAIN

AGENCIES > AGENCY

AGENCY n organization providing a service

AGENDA n list of things to

be dealt with, esp at a meeting

AGENDAS same as > AGENDA

AGENDUM same as > AGENDA

AGENDUMS same as > AGENDA

AGENE n chemical used to whiten flour

AGENES > AGENE

AGENESES > AGENESIS

AGENESIA n imperfect development

AGENESIAS > AGENESIA

AGENESIS n (of an animal or plant) imperfect development

AGENETIC > AGENESIS

AGENISE same as > AGENIZE

AGENISED > AGENISE

AGENISES > AGENISE

AGENISING > AGENISE

AGENIZE vb whiten using agene

AGENIZED > AGENIZE

AGENIZES > AGENIZE

AGENIZING > AGENIZE

AGENT n person acting on behalf of another ▷ vb act as an agent

AGENTED > AGENT

AGENTIAL > AGENT

AGENTING > AGENT

AGENTINGS > AGENT

AGENTIVAL adj of the performer of an action

AGENTIVE adj (in some inflected languages) denoting a case of nouns, etc, indicating the agent described by the verb ▷ n agentive case

AGENTIVES > AGENTIVE

AGENTRIES > AGENTRY

AGENTRY n acting as agent

AGENTS > AGENT

AGER n something that ages

AGERATUM n any tropical American plant of the genus Ageratum, such as A. houstonianum and A. conyzoides, which have thick clusters of purplish-blue flowers

AGERATUMS > AGERATUM

AGERS > AGER

AGES > AGE

AGEUSIA n lack of the sense of taste

AGEUSIAS > AGEUSIA

AGGADA n explanation in Jewish literature

AGGADAH same as > AGGADA

AGGADAHS > AGGADAH

AGGADAS > AGGADA

AGGADIC adj of aggada

AGGADOT > AGGADA

AGGADOTH > AGGADA

AGGER n earthwork or mound forming a rampart, esp in a Roman military camp

AGGERS adj aggressive

AGGIE n American agricultural student

AGGIES > AGGIE

AGGRACE vb add grace to

AGGRACED > AGGRACE

AGGRACES > AGGRACE

AGGRACING > AGGRACE

AGGRADE vb build up the level of (any land surface) by the deposition of sediment

AGGRADED > AGGRADE

AGGRADES > AGGRADE

AGGRADING > AGGRADE

AGGRATE vb gratify

AGGRATED > AGGRATE

AGGRATES > AGGRATE

AGGRATING > AGGRATE

AGGRAVATE vb make worse

AGGREGATE n total ▷ adj gathered into a mass ▷ vb combine into a whole

AGGRESS vb attack first or begin a quarrel

AGGRESSED > AGGRESS

AGGRESSES > AGGRESS

AGGRESSOR n person or body that engages in aggressive behaviour

AGGRI adj of African beads

AGGRIEVE vb grieve

AGGRIEVED adj upset and angry

AGGRIEVES > AGGRIEVE

AGGRO n aggressive behaviour

AGGROS > AGGRO

AGGRY adj of African beads

AGHA same as > AGA

AGHAS > AGHA

AGHAST adj overcome with amazement or horror

AGILA n eaglewood

AGILAS > AGILA

AGILE adj nimble, quick-moving

AGILELY > AGILE

AGILENESS > AGILE

AGILER > AGILE

AGILEST > AGILE

AGILITIES > AGILE

AGILITY > AGILE

AGIN prep against, opposed to

AGING same as > AGEING

AGINGS > AGING

AGINNER n someone who is against something

AGINNERS > AGINNER

AGIO n difference between the nominal and actual values of a currency

AGIOS > AGIO

AGIOTAGE n business of exchanging currencies

AGIOTAGES > AGIOTAGE

AGISM same as > AGEISM

AGISMS > AGISM

AGIST vb care for and feed (cattle or horses) for payment

AGISTED > AGIST

AGISTER n person who grazes cattle for money

AGISTERS > AGISTER

AGISTING > AGIST

AGISTMENT > AGEISM

AGISTOR n person who grazes cattle for money

AGISTORS > AGISTOR

AGISTS > AGIST

AGITA n acid indigestion

AGITABLE > AGITATE**

AGITANS as in *paralysis agitans* Parkinson's disease
AGITAS > AGITA
AGITATE *vb* disturb or excite
AGITATED *adj* anxious or worried > AGITATE
AGITATES > AGITATE
AGITATING > AGITATE
AGITATION *n* state of excitement, disturbance, or worry
AGITATIVE > AGITATE
AGITATO *adv* (to be performed) in an agitated manner
AGITATOR *n* person who agitates for or against a cause, etc
AGITATORS > AGITATOR
AGITPOP *n* use of pop music to promote political propaganda
AGITPOPS > AGITPOP
AGITPROP *n* political agitation and propaganda
AGITPROPS > AGITPROP
AGLARE *adj* glaring
AGLEAM *adj* glowing
AGLEE *same as* > AGLEY
AGLET *n* metal sheath or tag at the end of a shoelace, ribbon, etc
AGLETS > AGLET
AGLEY *adj* awry
AGLIMMER *adj* glimmering
AGLITTER *adj* sparkling, glittering
AGLOO *same as* > AGLU
AGLOOS > AGLOO
AGLOSSAL > AGLOSSIA
AGLOSSATE > AGLOSSIA
AGLOSSIA *n* congenital absence of the tongue
AGLOSSIAS > AGLOSSIA
AGLOW *adj* glowing
AGLU *n* breathing hole made in ice by a seal
AGLUS > AGLU
AGLY *Scots word for* > WRONG
AGLYCON *n* chemical compound
AGLYCONE *n* chemical compound
AGLYCONES > AGLYCONE
AGLYCONS > AGLYCON
AGMA *n* symbol used to represent a velar nasal consonant
AGMAS > AGMA
AGMINATE *adj* gathered or clustered together
AGNAIL *another name for* > HANGNAIL
AGNAILS > AGNAIL
AGNAME *n* name additional to first name and surname
AGNAMED *adj* having an agname
AGNAMES > AGNAME
AGNATE *adj* related by descent from a common male ancestor ▷ *n* male or female descendant by male links from a common male ancestor
AGNATES > AGNATE

AGNATHAN *n* any jawless eel-like aquatic vertebrate of the superclass *Agnatha*, which includes the lampreys and hagfishes ▷ *adj* of, relating to, or belonging to the superclass *Agnatha*
AGNATHANS > AGNATHAN
AGNATHOUS *adj* (esp of lampreys and hagfishes) lacking jaws
AGNATIC > AGNATE
AGNATICAL > AGNATE
AGNATION > AGNATE
AGNATIONS > AGNATE
AGNISE *vb* acknowledge
AGNISED > AGNISE
AGNISES > AGNISE
AGNISING > AGNISE
AGNIZE *vb* acknowledge
AGNIZED > AGNIZE
AGNIZES > AGNIZE
AGNIZING > AGNIZE
AGNOMEN *n* fourth name or second cognomen occasionally acquired by an ancient Roman
AGNOMENS > AGNOMEN
AGNOMINA > AGNOMEN
AGNOMINAL > AGNOMEN
AGNOSIA *n* loss or diminution of the power to recognize familiar objects or people, usually as a result of brain damage
AGNOSIAS > AGNOSIA
AGNOSIC > AGNOSIA
AGNOSTIC *n* person who believes that it is impossible to know whether God exists ▷ *adj* of agnostics
AGNOSTICS > AGNOSTIC
AGO *adv* in the past
AGOG *adj* eager or curious
AGOGE *n* ancient Greek tempo
AGOGES > AGOGE
AGOGIC *n* musical accent
AGOGICS > AGOGIC
AGOING *adj* moving
AGON *n* (in ancient Greece) a festival at which competitors contended for prizes. Among the best known were the Olympic, Pythian, Nemean, and Isthmian Games
AGONAL *adj* of agony
AGONE *an archaic word for* > AGO
AGONES > AGON
AGONIC *adj* forming no angle
AGONIES > AGONY
AGONISE *same as* > AGONIZE
AGONISED > AGONISE
AGONISES > AGONISE
AGONISING > AGONISE
AGONIST *n* any muscle that is opposed in action by another muscle
AGONISTES *n* person suffering inner struggle
AGONISTIC *adj* striving for effect

AGONISTS > AGONIST
AGONIZE *vb* worry greatly
AGONIZED > AGONIZE
AGONIZES > AGONIZE
AGONIZING > AGONIZE
AGONS > AGON
AGONY *n* extreme physical or mental pain
AGOOD *adv* seriously or earnestly
AGORA *n* marketplace in Athens, used for popular meetings, or any similar place of assembly in ancient Greece
AGORAE > AGORA
AGORAS > AGORA
AGOROT > AGORA
AGOROTH *n* agorot
AGOUTA *n* Haitian rodent
AGOUTAS > AGOUTA
AGOUTI *n* any hystricomorph rodent of the genus *Dasyprocta*, of Central and South America and the Caribbean: family *Dasyproctidae*. Agoutis are agile and long-legged, with hooflike claws, and are valued for their meat
AGOUTIES > AGOUTI
AGOUTIS > AGOUTI
AGOUTY *n* agouti
AGRAFE *same as* > AGRAFFE
AGRAFES > AGRAFE
AGRAFFE *n* fastening consisting of a loop and hook, formerly used in armour and clothing
AGRAFFES > AGRAFFE
AGRAPHA > AGRAPHON
AGRAPHIA *n* loss of the ability to write, resulting from a brain lesion
AGRAPHIAS > AGRAPHIA
AGRAPHIC > AGRAPHIA
AGRAPHON *n* saying of Jesus not in Gospels
AGRARIAN *adj* of land or agriculture ▷ *n* person who favours the redistribution of landed property
AGRARIANS > AGRARIAN
AGRASTE > AGGRACE
AGRAVIC *adj* of zero gravity
AGREE *vb* be of the same opinion
AGREEABLE *adj* pleasant and enjoyable
AGREEABLY > AGREEABLE
AGREED *adj* determined by common consent
AGREEING > AGREE
AGREES > AGREE
AGREGE *n* winner in examination for university teaching post
AGREGES > AGREGE
AGREMENS *n* amenities
AGREMENT *n* diplomatic approval of a country
AGREMENTS *n* amenities
AGRESTAL *adj* (of uncultivated plants such as weeds) growing on

cultivated land
AGRESTIAL *adj* agrestal
AGRESTIC *adj* rural
AGRIA *n* appearance of pustules
AGRIAS > AGRIA
AGRIMONY *n* yellow-flowered plant with bitter-tasting fruits
AGRIN *adv* grinning
AGRIOLOGY *n* study of primitive peoples
AGRISE *vb* fill with fear
AGRISED > AGRISE
AGRISES > AGRISE
AGRISING > AGRISE
AGRIZE *vb* fill with fear
AGRIZED > AGRIZE
AGRIZES > AGRIZE
AGRIZING > AGRIZE
AGRODOLCE *n* Italian sweet-and-sour sauce
AGROLOGIC > AGROLOGY
AGROLOGY *n* scientific study of soils and their potential productivity
AGRONOMIC > AGRONOMY
AGRONOMY *n* science of soil management and crop production
AGROUND *adv* onto the bottom of shallow water ▷ *adj* on or onto the ground or bottom, as in shallow water
AGRYPNIA *n* inability to sleep
AGRYPNIAS > AGRYPNIA
AGRYZE *vb* fill with fear
AGRYZED > AGRYZE
AGRYZES > AGRYZE
AGRYZING > AGRYZE
AGS > AG
AGTERSKOT *n* final payment to a farmer for crops
AGUACATE *n* avocado
AGUACATES > AGUACATE
AGUE *n* periodic fever with shivering
AGUED *adj* suffering from fever
AGUELIKE > AGUE
AGUES > AGUE
AGUEWEED *n* North American gentianaceous plant, *Gentiana quinquefolia*, that has clusters of pale blue-violet or white flowers
AGUEWEEDS > AGUEWEED
AGUISE *vb* dress
AGUISED > AGUISE
AGUISES > AGUISE
AGUISH > AGUE
AGUISHLY > AGUE
AGUISING > AGUISE
AGUIZE *vb* dress
AGUIZED > AGUIZE
AGUIZES > AGUIZE
AGUIZING > AGUIZE
AGUTI *n* agouti
AGUTIS > AGUTI
AH *vb* say ah
AHA *interj* exclamation expressing triumph, surprise, etc, according to the intonation of the speaker

AHCHOO *interj* sound made by someone sneezing
AHEAD *adv* in front
AHEAP *adv* in a heap
AHED > AH
AHEIGHT *adv* at height
AHEM *interj* clearing of the throat in order to attract attention
AHEMERAL *adj* not constituting a full 24-hour day
AHENT *adv* behind
AHI *n* yellowfin tuna
AHIGH *adv* at height
AHIMSA *n* (in Hindu, Buddhist, and Jainist philosophy) the law of reverence for, and nonviolence to, every form of life
AHIMSAS > AHIMSA
AHIND *adv* behind
AHING > AH
AHINT *adv* behind
AHIS > AHI
AHISTORIC *adj* not related to history; not historical
AHOLD *n* holding
AHOLDS > AHOLD
AHORSE *adv* on horseback
AHOY *interj* hail used to call a ship
AHS > AH
AHULL *adv* with sails furled
AHUNGERED *adj* very hungry
AHUNGRY *adj* very hungry
AHURU *n* small pink cod, *Auchenoceros punctatus*, of SW Pacific waters
AHURUHURU *same as* > AHURU
AI *n* shaggy-coated slow-moving animal of South America
AIA *n* female servant in East
AIAS > AIA
AIBLINS *Scots word for* > PERHAPS
AID *n* (give) assistance or support ▷ *vb* help financially or in other ways
AIDANCE *n* help
AIDANCES > AIDANCE
AIDANT *adj* helping
AIDE *n* assistant
AIDED > AID
AIDER > AID
AIDERS > AID
AIDES > AIDE
AIDFUL *adj* helpful
AIDING > AID
AIDLESS *adj* without help
AIDMAN *n* military medical assistant
AIDMEN > AIDMAN
AIDOI *adj* of the genitals
AIDOS *Greek word for* > SHAME
AIDS > AID
AIERIES > AIERY
AIERY *n* eyrie
AIGA *n* Māori word for family
AIGAS > AIGA
AIGLET *same as* > AGLET
AIGLETS > AIGLET

AIGRET *same as* > AIGRETTE
AIGRETS > AIGRET
AIGRETTE *n* long plume worn on hats or as a headdress, esp one of long egret feathers
AIGRETTES > AIGRETTE
AIGUILLE *n* rock mass or mountain peak shaped like a needle
AIGUILLES > AIGUILLE
AIKIDO *n* Japanese system of self-defence employing similar principles to judo, but including blows from the hands and feet
AIKIDOS > AIKIDO
AIKONA *interj* South African expression meaning no
AIL *vb* trouble, afflict
AILANTHIC > AILANTHUS
AILANTHUS *n* E Asian simaroubaceous deciduous tree, *Ailanthus altissima*, planted in Europe and North America, having pinnate leaves, small greenish flowers, and winged fruits
AILANTO *n* Asian tree
AILANTOS > AILANTO
AILED > AIL
AILERON *n* movable flap on an aircraft wing which controls rolling
AILERONS > AILERON
AILETTE *n* shoulder armour
AILETTES > AILETTE
AILING *adj* sickly
AILMENT *n* illness
AILMENTS > AILMENT
AILS > AIL
AIM *vb* point (a weapon or missile) or direct (a blow or remark) at a target ▷ *n* aiming
AIMED > AIM
AIMER > AIM
AIMERS > AIM
AIMFUL *adj* with purpose or intention
AIMFULLY > AIMFUL
AIMING > AIM
AIMLESS *adj* having no purpose
AIMLESSLY > AIMLESS
AIMS > AIM
AIN *variant of* > AYIN
AINE *adj* French word for elder (male)
AINEE *adj* French word for elder (female)
AINGA *n* Māori word for village
AINGAS > AINGA
AINS > AIN
AINSELL *n* Scots word meaning own self
AINSELLS > AINSELL
AIOLI *n* garlic mayonnaise
AIOLIS > AIOLI
AIR *n* mixture of gases forming the earth's atmosphere ▷ *vb* make known publicly
AIRBAG *n* safety device in a car, consisting of a bag that

inflates automatically in an accident to protect the driver or passenger
AIRBAGS > AIRBAG
AIRBASE *n* centre from which military aircraft operate
AIRBASES > AIRBASE
AIRBOAT *n* shallow-draught boat powered by an aeroplane engine on a raised structure for use in swamps
AIRBOATS > AIRBOAT
AIRBORNE *adj* carried by air
AIRBOUND *adj* heading into the air
AIRBRICK *n* brick with holes in it, put into the wall of a building for ventilation
AIRBRICKS > AIRBRICK
AIRBRUSH *n* atomizer that sprays paint by compressed air ▷ *vb* paint using an airbrush
AIRBURST *n* explosion of a bomb, shell, etc, in the air
AIRBURSTS > AIRBURST
AIRBUS *n* commercial passenger aircraft
AIRBUSES > AIRBUS
AIRBUSSES > AIRBUS
AIRCHECK *n* recording of a radio broadcast
AIRCHECKS > AIRCHECK
AIRCOACH *n* bus travelling to and from an airport
AIRCRAFT *n* any machine that flies, such as an aeroplane
AIRCREW *n* crew of an aircraft
AIRCREWS > AIRCREW
AIRDATE *n* date of a programme broadcast
AIRDATES > AIRDATE
AIRDRAWN *adj* imaginary
AIRDROME *same as* > AERODROME
AIRDROMES > AIRDROME
AIRDROP *n* delivery of supplies, troops, etc, from an aircraft by parachute ▷ *vb* deliver (supplies, etc) by an airdrop
AIRDROPS > AIRDROP
AIRED > AIR
AIRER *n* device on which clothes are hung to dry
AIRERS > AIRER
AIREST > AIR
AIRFARE *n* money for an aircraft ticket
AIRFARES > AIRFARE
AIRFIELD *n* place where aircraft can land and take off
AIRFIELDS > AIRFIELD
AIRFLOW *n* flow of air in a wind tunnel or past a moving aircraft, car, train, etc
AIRFLOWS > AIRFLOW
AIRFOIL *same as* > AEROFOIL
AIRFOILS > AIRFOIL
AIRFRAME *n* body of an aircraft, excluding its

engines
AIRFRAMES > AIRFRAME
AIRGAP *n* gap between parts in an electrical machine
AIRGAPS > AIRGAP
AIRGLOW *n* faint light from the upper atmosphere in the night sky, esp in low latitudes
AIRGLOWS > AIRGLOW
AIRGRAPH *n* photographic reduction of a letter for sending airmail
AIRGRAPHS > AIRGRAPH
AIRHEAD *n* person who is stupid or incapable of serious thought
AIRHEADED > AIRHEAD
AIRHEADS > AIRHEAD
AIRHOLE *n* hole that allows the passage of air
AIRHOLES > AIRHOLE
AIRIER > AIRY
AIRIEST > AIRY
AIRILY *adv* in a light-hearted and casual manner
AIRINESS *n* quality or condition of being fresh, light, or breezy
AIRING *n* exposure to air for drying or ventilation
AIRINGS > AIRING
AIRLESS *adj* stuffy
AIRLIFT *n* transport of troops or cargo by aircraft when other routes are blocked ▷ *vb* transport by airlift
AIRLIFTED > AIRLIFT
AIRLIFTS > AIRLIFT
AIRLIKE > AIR
AIRLINE *n* company providing scheduled flights for passengers and cargo
AIRLINER *n* large passenger aircraft
AIRLINERS > AIRLINER
AIRLINES > AIRLINE
AIRLOCK *n* air bubble blocking the flow of liquid in a pipe
AIRLOCKS > AIRLOCK
AIRMAIL *n* system of sending mail by aircraft ▷ *adj* of, used for, or concerned with airmail ▷ *vb* send by airmail
AIRMAILED > AIRMAIL
AIRMAILS > AIRMAIL
AIRMAN *n* member of the air force
AIRMEN > AIRMAN
AIRMOBILE *adj* using aircraft as transport
AIRN *Scots word for* > IRON
AIRNED > AIRN
AIRNING > AIRN
AIRNS > AIRN
AIRPARK *n* car park at airport
AIRPARKS > AIRPARK
AIRPLANE *same as* > AEROPLANE
AIRPLANES > AIRPLANE
AIRPLAY *n* broadcast performances of a record

a

on radio

AIRPLAYS > AIRPLAY

AIRPORT *n* airfield for civilian aircraft, with facilities for aircraft maintenance and passengers

AIRPORTS > AIRPORT

AIRPOST *n* system of delivering mail by air

AIRPOSTS > AIRPOST

AIRPOWER *n* strength of a nation's air force

AIRPOWERS > AIRPOWER

AIRPROOF *vb* make something airtight

AIRPROOFS > AIRPROOF

AIRS *pl n* manners put on to impress people

AIRSCAPE *n* picture or view of sky

AIRSCAPES > AIRSCAPE

AIRSCREW *n* aircraft propeller

AIRSCREWS > AIRSCREW

AIRSHAFT *n* shaft for ventilation

AIRSHAFTS > AIRSHAFT

AIRSHED *n* air over a particular geographical area

AIRSHEDS > AIRSHED

AIRSHIP *n* lighter-than-air self-propelled aircraft

AIRSHIPS > AIRSHIP

AIRSHOT *n* (in golf) shot that misses the ball completely, but counts as a stroke

AIRSHOTS > AIRSHOT

AIRSHOW *n* occasion when an air base is open to the public and a flying display and, usually, static exhibitions are held

AIRSHOWS > AIRSHOW

AIRSICK *adj* nauseated from travelling in an aircraft

AIRSIDE *n* part of an airport nearest the aircraft

AIRSIDES > AIRSIDE

AIRSPACE *n* atmosphere above a country, regarded as its territory

AIRSPACES > AIRSPACE

AIRSPEED *n* speed of an aircraft relative to the air in which it moves

AIRSPEEDS > AIRSPEED

AIRSTOP *n* helicopter landing-place

AIRSTOPS > AIRSTOP

AIRSTREAM *n* wind, esp at a high altitude

AIRSTRIKE *n* attack by military aircraft

AIRSTRIP *n* cleared area where aircraft can take off and land

AIRSTRIPS > AIRSTRIP

AIRT *n* direction or point of the compass, esp the direction of the wind ▷ *vb* direct

AIRTED > AIRT

AIRTH *same as* > AIRT

AIRTHED > AIRTH

AIRTHING > AIRTH

AIRTHS > AIRTH

AIRTIGHT *adj* sealed so that air cannot enter

AIRTIME *n* time allocated to a particular programme, topic, or type of material on radio or television

AIRTIMES > AIRTIME

AIRTING > AIRT

AIRTS > AIRT

AIRWARD *adj* into air

AIRWARDS *adv* into air

AIRWAVE *n* radio wave used in radio and television broadcasting

AIRWAVES > AIRWAVE

AIRWAY *n* air route used regularly by aircraft

AIRWAYS > AIRWAY

AIRWISE *adv* towards the air

AIRWOMAN > AIRMAN

AIRWOMEN > AIRMAN

AIRWORTHY *adj* (of aircraft) fit to fly

AIRY *adj* well-ventilated

AIS > AI

AISLE *n* passageway separating seating areas in a church, theatre, etc, or row of shelves in a supermarket

AISLED > AISLE

AISLELESS > AISLE

AISLES > AISLE

AISLEWAY *n* aisle

AISLEWAYS > AISLEWAY

AISLING *Irish word for* > DREAM

AISLINGS > AISLING

AIT *n* islet, esp in a river

AITCH *n* letter *h* or the sound represented by it

AITCHBONE *n* cut of beef from the rump bone

AITCHES > AITCH

AITS > AIT

AITU *n* half-human half-divine being

AITUS > AITU

AIVER *n* a working horse

AIVERS > AIVER

AIZLE *n* Scots word for hot ashes

AIZLES > AIZLE

AJAR *adv* (of a door) partly open ▷ *adj* not in harmony

AJEE *same as* > AGEE

AJIVA *n* Jainist term for non-living thing

AJIVAS > AJIVA

AJOWAN *n* plant related to caraway

AJOWANS > AJOWAN

AJUGA *n* garden plant

AJUGAS > AJUGA

AJUTAGE *n* nozzle

AJUTAGES > AJUTAGE

AJWAN *n* plant related to caraway

AJWANS > AJWAN

AKA *n* vine, *Metrosideros scandens*, found in New Zealand

AKARYOTE *n* cell without a nucleus

AKARYOTES > AKARYOTE

AKARYOTIC > AKARYOTE

AKATEA *n* vine with white flowers, *Metrosideros diffusa*, found in New Zealand

AKATHISIA *n* inability to sit still because of uncontrollable movement caused by reaction to drugs

AKE *vb* old spelling of ache

AKEAKE *n* New Zealand tree

AKEAKES > AKEAKE

AKED > AKE

AKEDAH *n* binding of Isaac in Bible

AKEDAHS > AKEDAH

AKEE *same as* > ACKEE

AKEES > AKEE

AKELA *n* adult leader of a pack of Cub Scouts

AKELAS > AKELA

AKENE *same as* > ACHENE

AKENES > AKENE

AKENIAL > ACHENE

AKES > AKE

AKHARA *n* (in India) gymnasium

AKHARAS > AKHARA

AKIMBO as in *with arms akimbo* with hands on hips and elbows projecting outwards

AKIN *adj* related by blood

AKINESES > AKINESIS

AKINESIA *n* loss of power to move

AKINESIAS > AKINESIA

AKINESIS *n* loss of power to move

AKINETIC > AKINESIA

AKING > AKE

AKIRAHO *n* small New Zealand shrub, *Olearia paniculata*, with white flowers

AKITA *n* large powerfully-built dog of a Japanese breed with erect ears, a typically white coat, and a large full tail carried curled over its back

AKITAS > AKITA

AKKAS *slang word for* > MONEY

AKOLUTHOS *n* leader of Byzantine Varangian Guard

AKRASIA *n* weakness of will

AKRASIAS > AKRASIA

AKRATIC > AKRASIA

AKVAVIT *same as* > AQUAVIT

AKVAVITS > AKVAVIT

AL *same as* > AAL

ALA *n* wing or flat winglike process or structure, such as a part of some bones and cartilages

ALAAP *n* part of raga in Indian music

ALAAPS > ALAAP

ALABAMINE *old name for* > ASTATINE

ALABASTER *n* soft white translucent stone ▷ *adj* of or resembling alabaster

ALACHLOR *n* type of herbicide

ALACHLORS > ALACHLOR

ALACK *archaic or poetic word for* > ALAS

ALACKADAY *same as* > ALACK

ALACRITY *n* speed, eagerness

ALAE > ALA

ALAIMENT *old spelling of* > ALLAYMENT

ALAIMENTS > ALAIMENT

ALALAGMOI > ALALAGMOS

ALALAGMOS *n* ancient Greek war cry

ALALIA *n* complete inability to speak

ALALIAS > ALALIA

ALAMEDA *n* public walk or promenade lined with trees, often poplars

ALAMEDAS > ALAMEDA

ALAMO *n* poplar tree

ALAMODE *n* soft light silk used for shawls and dresses, esp in the 19th century

ALAMODES > ALAMODE

ALAMORT *adj* exhausted and downcast

ALAMOS > ALAMO

ALAN *n* member of ancient European nomadic people

ALAND *vb* come onto land

ALANDS > ALAND

ALANE *Scots word for* > ALONE

ALANG *n* type of grass in Malaysia

ALANGS > ALANG

ALANIN *n* alanine

ALANINE *n* nonessential aliphatic amino acid that occurs in many proteins

ALANINES > ALANINE

ALANINS > ALANIN

ALANNAH *interj* my child: used as a term of address or endearment ▷ *n* cry of alannah

ALANNAHS > ALANNAH

ALANS > ALAN

ALANT *n* flowering plant used in herbal medicine

ALANTS > ALANT

ALANYL *n* chemical found in proteins

ALANYLS > ALANYL

ALAP *n* Indian vocal music without words

ALAPA *n* part of raga in Indian music

ALAPAS > ALAPA

ALAPS > ALAP

ALAR *adj* relating to, resembling, or having wings or alae

ALARM *n* sudden fear caused by awareness of danger ▷ *vb* fill with fear

ALARMABLE > ALARMABLE

ALARMED > ALARM

ALARMEDLY > ALARM

ALARMING > ALARM

ALARMISM > ALARMIST

ALARMISMS > ALARMIST

ALARMIST *n* person who alarms others needlessly

▷ *adj* causing needless alarm
ALARMISTS > ALARMIST
ALARMS > ALARM
ALARUM *n* alarm, esp a call to arms ▷ *vb* raise the alarm
ALARUMED > ALARUM
ALARUMING > ALARUM
ALARUMS > ALARUM
ALARY *adj* of, relating to, or shaped like wings
ALAS *adv* unfortunately, regrettably
ALASKA *n* dessert made of cake and ice cream
ALASKAS > ALASKA
ALASTOR *n* avenging demon
ALASTORS > ALASTOR
ALASTRIM *n* form of smallpox
ALASTRIMS > ALASTRIM
ALATE *adj* having wings or winglike extensions ▷ *n* winged insect
ALATED *adj* having wings
ALATES > ALATE
ALATION *n* state of having wings
ALATIONS > ALATION
ALAY *vb* allay
ALAYED > ALAY
ALAYING > ALAY
ALAYS > ALAY
ALB *n* long white robe worn by a Christian priest
ALBA *n* song of lament
ALBACORE *n* tuna found in warm seas, eaten for food
ALBACORES > ALBACORE
ALBARELLI > ALBARELLO
ALBARELLO *n* jar for drugs
ALBAS > ALBA
ALBATA *n* variety of German silver consisting of nickel, copper, and zinc
ALBATAS > ALBATA
ALBATROSS *n* large sea bird with very long wings
ALBE *old word for* > ALBEIT
ALBEDO *n* ratio of the intensity of light reflected from an object, such as a planet, to that of the light it receives from the sun
ALBEDOES > ALBEDO
ALBEDOS > ALBEDO
ALBEE *archaic form of* > ALBEIT
ALBEIT *conj* even though
ALBERGHI > ALBERGO
ALBERGO *n* Italian word for inn
ALBERT *n* kind of watch chain usually attached to a waistcoat
ALBERTITE *n* black solid variety of bitumen that has a conchoidal fracture and occurs in veins in oil-bearing strata
ALBERTS > ALBERT
ALBESCENT *adj* shading into, growing, or becoming white
ALBESPINE *old name for* > HAWTHORN

ALBESPYNE *old name for* > HAWTHORN
ALBICORE *n* species of tunny
ALBICORES > ALBICORE
ALBINAL > ALBINO
ALBINESS *n* female albino
ALBINIC > ALBINO
ALBINISM > ALBINO
ALBINISMS > ALBINO
ALBINO *n* person or animal with white skin and hair and pink eyes
ALBINOISM > ALBINO
ALBINOS > ALBINO
ALBINOTIC > ALBINO
ALBITE *n* colourless, milky-white, yellow, pink, green, or black mineral
ALBITES > ALBITE
ALBITIC > ALBITE
ALBITICAL > ALBITE
ALBITISE *vb* turn into albite
ALBITISED > ALBITISE
ALBITISES > ALBITISE
ALBITIZE *vb* turn into albite
ALBITIZED > ALBITIZE
ALBITIZES > ALBITIZE
ALBIZIA *n* mimosa
ALBIZIAS > ALBIZIA
ALBIZZIA *n* mimosa
ALBIZZIAS > ALBIZZIA
ALBRICIAS *interj* Spanish expression of welcome
ALBS > ALB
ALBUGO *n* opacity of the cornea
ALBUGOS > ALBUGO
ALBUM *n* book with blank pages for keeping photographs or stamps in
ALBUMEN *same as* > ALBUMIN *n* egg white
ALBUMENS > ALBUMEN
ALBUMIN *n* protein found in blood plasma, egg white, milk, and muscle
ALBUMINS > ALBUMIN
ALBUMOSE *the US name for* > PROTEOSE
ALBUMOSES > ALBUMOSE
ALBUMS > ALBUM
ALBURNOUS > ALBURNUM
ALBURNUM *former name for* > SAPWOOD
ALBURNUMS > ALBURNUM
ALBUTEROL *n* drug used to treat lung diseases
ALCADE *same as* > ALCALDE
ALCADES > ALCADE
ALCAHEST *same as* > ALKAHEST
ALCAHESTS > ALCAHEST
ALCAIC *n* verse consisting of strophes with four tetrametric lines
ALCAICS > ALCAIC
ALCAIDE *n* commander of a fortress or castle
ALCAIDES > ALCAIDE
ALCALDE *n* (in Spain and Spanish America) the mayor or chief magistrate in a town
ALCALDES > ALCALDE

ALCARRAZA *n* Spanish water container
ALCATRAS *n* pelican
ALCAYDE *n* alcaide
ALCAYDES > ALCAYDE
ALCAZAR *n* any of various palaces or fortresses built in Spain by the Moors
ALCAZARS > ALCAZAR
ALCHEMIC > ALCHEMY
ALCHEMIES > ALCHEMY
ALCHEMISE *same as* > ALCHEMIZE
ALCHEMIST *n* person who practises alchemy
ALCHEMIZE *vb* alter (an element, metal, etc) by alchemy
ALCHEMY *n* medieval form of chemistry concerned with trying to turn base metals into gold and to find the elixir of life
ALCHERA *n* (in the mythology of Australian Aboriginal peoples) mythical Golden Age of the past
ALCHERAS > ALCHERA
ALCHYMIES > ALCHYMY
ALCHYMY *old spelling of* > ALCHEMY
ALCID *n* bird of the auk family
ALCIDINE *adj* of, relating to, or belonging to the *Alcidae*, a family of sea birds including the auks, guillemots, puffins, and related forms
ALCIDS > ALCID
ALCO *same as* > ALKO
ALCOHOL *n* colourless flammable liquid present in intoxicating drinks
ALCOHOLIC *adj* of alcohol ▷ *n* person addicted to alcohol
ALCOHOLS > ALCOHOL
ALCOLOCK *n* breath-alcohol ignition-interlock device, which is fitted to the ignition in certain motor vehicles. The driver must blow into a tube and, if his or her breath contains too much alcohol, a lock is activated to prevent the vehicle starting
ALCOLOCKS > ALCOLOCK
ALCOOL *n* form of pure grain spirit distilled in Quebec
ALCOOLS > ALCOOL
ALCOPOP *n* alcoholic drink that tastes like a soft drink
ALCOPOPS > ALCOPOP
ALCORZA *n* Spanish sweet
ALCORZAS > ALCORZA
ALCOS > ALCO
ALCOVE *n* recess in the wall of a room
ALCOVED *adj* with or in an alcove
ALCOVES > ALCOVE
ALDEA *n* Spanish village
ALDEAS > ALDEA
ALDEHYDE *n* one of a group

of chemical compounds derived from alcohol by oxidation
ALDEHYDES > ALDEHYDE
ALDEHYDIC > ALDEHYDE
ALDER *n* tree related to the birch
ALDERFLY *n* insect with large broad-based hind wings, which produces aquatic larvae
ALDERMAN *n* formerly, senior member of a local council
ALDERMEN > ALDERMAN
ALDERN *adj* made of alder wood
ALDERS > ALDER
ALDICARB *n* crystalline compound used as a pesticide
ALDICARBS > ALDICARB
ALDOL *n* colourless or yellowish oily liquid
ALDOLASE *n* enzyme present in the body
ALDOLASES > ALDOLASE
ALDOLS > ALDOL
ALDOSE *n* sugar that contains the aldehyde group or is a hemiacetal
ALDOSES > ALDOSE
ALDOXIME *n* oxime formed by reaction between hydroxylamine and an aldehyde
ALDOXIMES > ALDOXIME
ALDRIN *n* brown to white poisonous crystalline solid
ALDRINS > ALDRIN
ALE *n* kind of beer
ALEATORIC *same as* > ALEATORY
ALEATORY *adj* dependent on chance
ALEBENCH *n* bench at alehouse
ALEC *same as* > ALECK
ALECITHAL *adj* (of an ovum) having little or no yolk
ALECK *n* irritatingly oversmart person
ALECKS > ALECK
ALECOST *another name for* > COSTMARY
ALECOSTS > ALECOST
ALECS > ALEC
ALECTRYON *n* New Zealand tree
ALEE *adj* on or towards the lee
ALEF *n* first letter of Hebrew alphabet
ALEFS > ALEF
ALEFT *adv* at or to left
ALEGAR *n* malt vinegar
ALEGARS > ALEGAR
ALEGGE *vb* alleviate
ALEGGED > ALEGGE
ALEGGES > ALEGGE
ALEGGING > ALEGGE
ALEHOUSE *n* public house
ALEHOUSES > ALEHOUSE
ALEMBIC *n* anything that distils or purifies, esp an obsolete vessel used for distillation

ALEMBICS > ALEMBIC
ALEMBROTH n mercury compound in alchemy
ALENCON n elaborate lace worked on a hexagonal mesh
ALENCONS > ALENCON
ALENGTH adv at length
ALEPH n first letter in the Hebrew alphabet
ALEPHS > ALEPH
ALEPINE n type of cloth
ALEPINES > ALEPINE
ALERCE n wood of the sandarac tree
ALERCES > ALERCE
ALERION n eagle in heraldry
ALERIONS > ALERION
ALERT adj watchful, attentive ▷ n warning of danger ▷ vb warn of danger
ALERTED > ALERT
ALERTER > ALERT
ALERTEST > ALERT
ALERTING > ALERT
ALERTLY > ALERT
ALERTNESS > ALERT
ALERTS > ALERT
ALES > ALE
ALETHIC adj of or relating to such philosophical concepts as truth, necessity, possibility, contingency, etc
ALEURON n outer protein-rich layer of certain seeds, esp of cereal grains
ALEURONE same as > ALEURON
ALEURONES > ALEURONE
ALEURONIC > ALEURON
ALEURONS > ALEURON
ALEVIN n young fish, esp a young salmon or trout
ALEVINS > ALEVIN
ALEW n cry to call hunting hounds
ALEWASHED adj showing effects of beer drinking
ALEWIFE n North American fish
ALEWIVES > ALEWIFE
ALEWS > ALEW
ALEXANDER n cocktail made with creme de cacao
ALEXIA n disorder of the central nervous system characterized by impaired ability to read
ALEXIAS > ALEXIA
ALEXIC > ALEXIA
ALEXIN n complement
ALEXINE same as > ALEXIN
ALEXINES > ALEXINE
ALEXINIC > ALEXIN
ALEXINS > ALEXIN
ALEYE vb allay
ALEYED > ALEYE
ALEYES > ALEYE
ALEYING > ALEYE
ALF n uncultivated Australian
ALFA n type of grass
ALFAKI n expert in Muslim law
ALFAKIS > ALFAKI

ALFALFA n kind of plant used to feed livestock
ALFALFAS > ALFALFA
ALFAQUI n expert in Muslim law
ALFAQUIN n expert in Muslim law
ALFAQUINS > ALFAQUIN
ALFAQUIS > ALFAQUI
ALFAS > ALFA
ALFERECES > ALFEREZ
ALFEREZ n Spanish standard-bearer
ALFILARIA n plant with finely divided leaves and small pink or purplish flowers
ALFILERIA same as > ALFILARIA
ALFORJA n saddlebag made of leather or canvas
ALFORJAS > ALFORJA
ALFREDO adj cooked with a cheese and egg sauce
ALFRESCO adj in the open air ▷ adv in the open air
ALFS > ALF
ALGA n unicellular or multicellular organism formerly classified as a plant
ALGAE > ALGA
ALGAECIDE n substance for killing algae
ALGAL > ALGA
ALGAROBA same as > ALGARROBA
ALGAROBAS > ALGAROBA
ALGARROBA n edible pod of these trees
ALGARROBO n carob
ALGAS > ALGA
ALGATE adv anyway
ALGATES adv anyway
ALGEBRA n branch of mathematics using symbols to represent numbers
ALGEBRAIC adj of or relating to algebra
ALGEBRAS > ALGEBRA
ALGERINE n soft striped woollen cloth
ALGERINES > ALGERINE
ALGESES > ALGESIS
ALGESIA n capacity to feel pain
ALGESIAS > ALGESIA
ALGESIC > ALGESIA
ALGESIS n feeling of pain
ALGETIC > ALGESIA
ALGICIDAL > ALGICIDE
ALGICIDE n any substance that kills algae
ALGICIDES > ALGICIDE
ALGID adj chilly or cold
ALGIDITY > ALGID
ALGIDNESS > ALGID
ALGIN n gelatinous solution obtained as a by-product in the extraction of iodine from seaweed
ALGINATE n salt or ester of alginic acid
ALGINATES > ALGINATE
ALGINIC as in alginic acid, powdery substance

extracted from kelp
ALGINS > ALGIN
ALGOID adj resembling or relating to algae
ALGOLOGY n branch of biology concerned with the study of algae
ALGOMETER n instrument for measuring sensitivity to pressure or to pain
ALGOMETRY > ALGOMETER
ALGOR n chill
ALGORISM n Arabic or decimal system of counting
ALGORISMS > ALGORISM
ALGORITHM n logical arithmetical or computational procedure for solving a problem
ALGORS > ALGOR
ALGUACIL n Spanish law officer
ALGUACILS > ALGUACIL
ALGUAZIL n Spanish law officer
ALGUAZILS > ALGUAZIL
ALGUM n type of wood mentioned in Bible
ALGUMS > ALGUM
ALIAS adv also known as ▷ n false name
ALIASES > ALIAS
ALIASING n error in a vision or sound signal arising from limitations in the system that generates or processes the signal
ALIASINGS > ALIASING
ALIBI n plea of being somewhere else when a crime was committed ▷ vb provide someone with an alibi
ALIBIED > ALIBI
ALIBIES > ALIBI
ALIBIING > ALIBI
ALIBIS > ALIBI
ALIBLE adj nourishing
ALICANT n wine from Alicante in Spain
ALICANTS > ALICANT
ALICYCLIC adj (of an organic compound) having aliphatic properties, in spite of the presence of a ring of carbon atoms
ALIDAD same as > ALIDADE
ALIDADE n surveying instrument used in plane-tabling for drawing lines of sight on a distant object and taking angular measurements
ALIDADES > ALIDADE
ALIDADS > ALIDAD
ALIEN adj foreign ▷ n foreigner ▷ vb transfer (property, etc) to another
ALIENABLE adj able to be transferred to another owner
ALIENAGE > ALIEN
ALIENAGES > ALIEN
ALIENATE vb cause to become hostile
ALIENATED > ALIENATE
ALIENATES > ALIENATE

ALIENATOR > ALIENATE
ALIENED > ALIEN
ALIENEE n person to whom a transfer of property is made
ALIENEES > ALIENEE
ALIENER > ALIEN
ALIENERS > ALIEN
ALIENING > ALIEN
ALIENISM n study and treatment of mental illness
ALIENISMS > ALIENISM
ALIENIST n psychiatrist who specializes in the legal aspects of mental illness
ALIENISTS > ALIENIST
ALIENLY > ALIEN
ALIENNESS > ALIEN
ALIENOR n person who transfers property to another
ALIENORS > ALIENOR
ALIENS > ALIEN
ALIF n first letter of Arabic alphabet
ALIFORM adj wing-shaped
ALIFS > ALIF
ALIGARTA n alligator
ALIGARTAS > ALIGARTA
ALIGHT vb step out of (a vehicle) ▷ adj on fire ▷ adv on fire
ALIGHTED > ALIGHT
ALIGHTING > ALIGHT
ALIGHTS > ALIGHT
ALIGN vb bring (a person or group) into agreement with the policy of another
ALIGNED > ALIGN
ALIGNER > ALIGN
ALIGNERS > ALIGN
ALIGNING > ALIGN
ALIGNMENT n arrangement in a straight line
ALIGNS > ALIGN
ALIKE adj like, similar ▷ adv in the same way
ALIKENESS > ALIKE
ALIMENT n something that nourishes or sustains the body or mind ▷ vb support or sustain
ALIMENTAL > ALIMENT
ALIMENTED > ALIMENT
ALIMENTS > ALIMENT
ALIMONIED adj provided with alimony
ALIMONIES > ALIMONY
ALIMONY n allowance paid under a court order to a separated or divorced spouse
ALINE a rare spelling of > ALIGN
ALINED > ALINE
ALINEMENT > ALINE
ALINER > ALINE
ALINERS > ALINE
ALINES > ALINE
ALINING > ALINE
ALIPED n animal, like the bat, whose toes are joined by a membrane that serves as a wing ▷ adj (of bats and similar animals) having the digits connected by a winglike membrane

ALIPEDS > ALIPED

ALIPHATIC adj (of an organic compound) having an open chain structure

ALIQUANT adj denoting or belonging to a number that is not an exact divisor of a given number

ALIQUOT adj of or denoting an exact divisor of a number ▷ n exact divisor

ALIQUOTS > ALIQUOT

ALISMA n marsh plant

ALISMAS > ALISMA

ALISON same as > ALYSSUM

ALISONS > ALISON

ALIST adj leaning over

ALIT rare past tense and past participle of > ALIGHT

ALITERACY > ALITERATE

ALITERATE n person who is able to read but disinclined to do so ▷ adj of or relating to aliterates

ALIUNDE adj from a source extrinsic to the matter, document, or instrument under consideration

ALIVE adj living, in existence

ALIVENESS > ALIVE

ALIYA n immigration to Holy Land

ALIYAH n immigration to the Holy Land

ALIYAHS > ALIYAH

ALIYAS > ALIYA

ALIYOS n remission of sin in Jewish faith

ALIYOT > ALIYAH

ALIYOTH > ALIYAH

ALIZARI n madder from Middle East

ALIZARIN n brownish-yellow powder or orange-red crystalline solid

ALIZARINE n alizarin

ALIZARINS > ALIZARIN

ALIZARIS > ALIZARI

ALKAHEST n hypothetical universal solvent sought by alchemists

ALKAHESTS > ALKAHEST

ALKALI n substance which combines with acid and neutralizes it to form a salt

ALKALIC adj (of igneous rocks) containing large amounts of alkalis, esp sodium and potassium

ALKALIES > ALKALI

ALKALIFY vb make or become alkaline

ALKALIN adj leaning over

ALKALINE adj having the properties of or containing an alkali

ALKALIS > ALKALI

ALKALISE same as > ALKALIZE

ALKALISED > ALKALISE

ALKALISER > ALKALISE

ALKALISES > ALKALISE

ALKALIZE vb make alkaline

ALKALIZED > ALKALIZE

ALKALIZER > ALKALIZE

ALKALIZES > ALKALIZE

ALKALOID n any of a group of organic compounds containing nitrogen

ALKALOIDS > ALKALOID

ALKALOSES > ALKALOSIS

ALKALOSIS n abnormal increase in the alkalinity of the blood and extracellular fluids

ALKALOTIC > ALKALOSIS

ALKANE n any saturated hydrocarbon with the general formula $C n H_2 n+2$

ALKANES > ALKANE

ALKANET n European boraginaceous plant, *Alkanna tinctoria*, the roots of which yield a red dye

ALKANETS > ALKANET

ALKANNIN same as > ALKANET

ALKANNINS > ALKANNIN

ALKENE n type of unsaturated hydrocarbon

ALKENES > ALKENE

ALKIE same as > ALKY

ALKIES > ALKY

ALKINE n alkyne

ALKINES > ALKINE

ALKO n heavy drinker or alcoholic

ALKOS > ALKO

ALKOXIDE n chemical compound containing oxygen

ALKOXIDES > ALKOXIDE

ALKOXY adj of type of chemical compound containing oxygen

ALKY n heavy drinker or alcoholic

ALKYD n synthetic resin

ALKYDS > ALKYD

ALKYL n of, consisting of, or containing the monovalent group $C n H_2 n+1$

ALKYLATE vb add alkyl group to a compound

ALKYLATED > ALKYLATE

ALKYLATES > ALKYLATE

ALKYLIC > ALKYL

ALKYLS > ALKYL

ALKYNE n any unsaturated aliphatic hydrocarbon

ALKYNES > ALKYNE

ALL adj whole quantity or number (of) ▷ adv wholly, entirely ▷ n entire being, effort, or property

ALLANITE n rare black or brown mineral

ALLANITES > ALLANITE

ALLANTOIC > ALLANTOIS

ALLANTOID adj relating to or resembling the allantois

ALLANTOIN n chemical used in cosmetics

ALLANTOIS n membranous sac growing out of the ventral surface of the hind gut of embryonic reptiles, birds, and mammals. It combines with the chorion to form the mammalian placenta

ALLATIVE n word in grammatical case denoting movement towards

ALLATIVES > ALLATIVE

ALLAY vb reduce (fear or anger)

ALLAYED > ALLAY

ALLAYER > ALLAY

ALLAYERS > ALLAY

ALLAYING > ALLAY

ALLAYINGS > ALLAY

ALLAYMENT n mitigation

ALLAYS > ALLAY

ALLCOMERS n everyone who comes

ALLEDGE vb allege

ALLEDGED > ALLEDGE

ALLEDGES > ALLEDGE

ALLEDGING > ALLEDGE

ALLEE n avenue

ALLEES > ALLEE

ALLEGE vb state without proof

ALLEGED adj stated but not proved

ALLEGEDLY adv reportedly

ALLEGER > ALLEGE

ALLEGERS > ALLEGE

ALLEGES > ALLEGE

ALLEGGE vb alleviate

ALLEGGED > ALLEGGE

ALLEGGES > ALLEGGE

ALLEGGING > ALLEGGE

ALLEGIANT n loyalty

ALLEGING > ALLEGE

ALLEGORIC adj used in, containing, or characteristic of allegory

ALLEGORY n story with an underlying meaning as well as the literal one

ALLEGRO adv (piece to be played) in a brisk lively manner ▷ n piece or passage to be performed in a brisk lively manner

ALLEGROS > ALLEGRO

ALLEL n form of gene

ALLELE n any of two or more genes that are responsible for alternative characteristics, such as smooth or wrinkled seeds in peas

ALLELES > ALLELE

ALLELIC > ALLELE

ALLELISM > ALLELE

ALLELISMS > ALLELE

ALLELS > ALLEL

ALLELUIA n song of praise to God

ALLELUIAH interj alleluia

ALLELUIAS > ALLELUIA

ALLEMANDE n first movement of the classical suite, composed in a moderate tempo in a time signature of four-four

ALLENARLY adv solely

ALLERGEN n substance capable of causing an allergic reaction

ALLERGENS > ALLERGEN

ALLERGIC adj having or caused by an allergy ▷ n person suffering from an allergy

ALLERGICS > ALLERGIC

ALLERGIES > ALLERGY

ALLERGIN n allergen

ALLERGINS > ALLERGIN

ALLERGIST n physician skilled in the diagnosis and treatment of diseases or conditions caused by allergy

ALLERGY n extreme sensitivity to a substance, which causes the body to react to it

ALLERION n eagle in heraldry

ALLERIONS > ALLERION

ALLETHRIN n clear viscous amber-coloured liquid

ALLEVIANT n medical treatment that reduces pain but does not cure the underlying problem

ALLEVIATE vb lessen (pain or suffering)

ALLEY n narrow street or path

ALLEYCAT n homeless cat that roams in back streets

ALLEYCATS > ALLEYCAT

ALLEYED adj having alleys

ALLEYS > ALLEY

ALLEYWAY n narrow passage with buildings or walls on both sides

ALLEYWAYS > ALLEYWAY

ALLHEAL n any of several plants reputed to have healing powers, such as selfheal and valerian

ALLHEALS > ALLHEAL

ALLIABLE adj able to form an alliance

ALLIANCE n state of being allied

ALLIANCES > ALLIANCE

ALLICE n species of fish

ALLICES > ALLICE

ALLICHOLY n melancholy

ALLICIN n chemical found in garlic

ALLICINS > ALLICIN

ALLIED adj joined, as by treaty, agreement, or marriage

ALLIES > ALLY

ALLIGARTA n alligator

ALLIGATE vb join together

ALLIGATED > ALLIGATE

ALLIGATES > ALLIGATE

ALLIGATOR n reptile of the crocodile family, found in the southern US and China

ALLIS n species of fish

ALLISES > ALLIS

ALLIUM n any plant of the genus *Allium*, such as the onion, garlic, shallot, leek, or chive: family *Alliaceae*

ALLIUMS > ALLIUM

ALLNESS n being all

ALLNESSES > ALLNESS

ALLNIGHT adj lasting all night

ALLOBAR n form of element

ALLOBARS > ALLOBAR

ALLOCABLE > ALLOCATE

ALLOCARPY n production of fruit through cross-fertilization

ALLOCATE vb assign to someone or for a particular purpose

ALLOCATED > ALLOCATE

ALLOCATES > ALLOCATE

ALLOCATOR > ALLOCATE

ALLOD same as > ALLODIUM

ALLODIA > ALLODIUM

ALLODIAL adj (of land) held as an allodium

ALLODIUM n lands held in absolute ownership, free from such obligations as rent or services due to an overlord

ALLODIUMS > ALLODIUM

ALLODS > ALLOD

ALLOGAMY n cross-fertilization in flowering plants

ALLOGENIC adj having different genes

ALLOGRAFT n tissue graft from a donor genetically unrelated to the recipient

ALLOGRAPH n document written by a person who is not a party to it

ALLOMERIC adj of similar crystalline structure

ALLOMETRY n study of the growth of part of an organism in relation to the growth of the entire organism

ALLOMONE n chemical substance secreted externally by certain animals, such as insects, affecting the behaviour or physiology of another species detrimentally

ALLOMONES > ALLOMONE

ALLOMORPH n any of the phonological representations of a single morpheme

ALLONGE n paper extension to bill of exchange

ALLONGES > ALLONGE

ALLONS interj French word meaning let's go

ALLONYM n name, often one of historical significance or that of another person, assumed by a person, esp an author

ALLONYMS > ALLONYM

ALLOPATH n person who practises or is skilled in allopathy

ALLOPATHS > ALLOPATH

ALLOPATHY n orthodox method of treating disease, by using drugs that produce an effect opposite to the effect of the disease being treated, as contrasted with homeopathy

ALLOPATRY n condition of taking place or existing in areas that are geographically separated from one another

ALLOPHANE n variously coloured amorphous mineral consisting of hydrated aluminium silicate and occurring in cracks in some sedimentary rocks

ALLOPHONE n any of several speech sounds that are regarded as contextual or environmental variants of the same phoneme

ALLOPLASM n part of the cytoplasm that is specialized to form cilia, flagella, and similar structures

ALLOSAUR n any large carnivorous bipedal dinosaur common in North America in late Jurassic times

ALLOSAURS > ALLOSAUR

ALLOSTERY n condition of an enzyme in which the structure and activity of the enzyme are modified by the binding of a metabolic molecule

ALLOT vb assign as a share or for a particular purpose

ALLOTMENT n distribution

ALLOTROPE n any of two or more physical forms in which an element can exist

ALLOTROPY n existence of an element in two or more physical forms

ALLOTS > ALLOT

ALLOTTED > ALLOT

ALLOTTEE n person to whom something is allotted

ALLOTTEES > ALLOTTEE

ALLOTTER n person who allots

ALLOTTERS > ALLOTTER

ALLOTTERY n something allotted

ALLOTTING > ALLOT

ALLOTYPE n additional type specimen selected because of differences from the original type specimen, such as opposite sex or morphological details

ALLOTYPES > ALLOTYPE

ALLOTYPIC > ALLOTYPE

ALLOTYPY n existence of allotypes

ALLOVER n fabric completely covered with a pattern

ALLOVERS > ALLOVER

ALLOW vb permit

ALLOWABLE adj permissible

ALLOWABLY > ALLOWABLE

ALLOWANCE n amount of money given at regular intervals

ALLOWED > ALLOW

ALLOWEDLY adv by general admission or agreement

ALLOWING > ALLOW

ALLOWS > ALLOW

ALLOXAN n chemical found in uric acid

ALLOXANS > ALLOXAN

ALLOY n mixture of two or more metals ▷ vb mix (metals)

ALLOYED > ALLOY

ALLOYING > ALLOY

ALLOYS > ALLOY

ALLOZYME n any one of a number of different structural forms of the same enzyme encoded by a different allele

ALLOZYMES > ALLOZYME

ALLS > ALL

ALLSEED n any of several plants that produce many seeds, such as knotgrass

ALLSEEDS > ALLSEED

ALLSORTS n assorted sweets

ALLSPICE n spice made from the berries of a tropical American tree

ALLSPICES > ALLSPICE

ALLUDE vb refer indirectly to

ALLUDED > ALLUDE

ALLUDES > ALLUDE

ALLUDING > ALLUDE

ALLURE n attractiveness ▷ vb entice or attract

ALLURED > ALLURE

ALLURER > ALLURE

ALLURERS > ALLURE

ALLURES > ALLURE

ALLURING adj extremely attractive

ALLUSION n indirect reference

ALLUSIONS > ALLUSION

ALLUSIVE adj containing or full of allusions

ALLUVIA > ALLUVIUM

ALLUVIAL adj of or relating to alluvium ▷ n soil consisting of alluvium

ALLUVIALS > ALLUVIAL

ALLUVION n wash of the sea or of a river

ALLUVIONS > ALLUVION

ALLUVIUM n fertile soil deposited by flowing water

ALLUVIUMS > ALLUVIUM

ALLY vb unite or be united, esp formally, as by treaty, confederation, or marriage ▷ n country, person, or group allied with another

ALLYING > ALLY

ALLYL n of, consisting of, or containing the monovalent group CH_2:$CHCH_2^-$

ALLYLIC > ALLYL

ALLYLS > ALLYL

ALLYOU pron all of you

ALMA n Egyptian dancing girl

ALMAGEST n medieval treatise concerning alchemy or astrology

ALMAGESTS > ALMAGEST

ALMAH n Egyptian dancing girl

ALMAHS > ALMAH

ALMAIN n German dance

ALMAINS > ALMAIN

ALMANAC n yearly calendar with detailed information on anniversaries, phases of the moon, etc

ALMANACK same as > ALMANAC

ALMANACKS > ALMANACK

ALMANACS > ALMANAC

ALMANDINE n deep violet-red garnet

ALMANDITE n form of garnet

ALMAS > ALMA

ALME n Egyptian dancing girl

ALMEH n Egyptian dancing girl

ALMEHS > ALMEH

ALMEMAR n (in Ashkenazic usage) the raised platform in a synagogue on which the reading desk stands

ALMEMARS > ALMEMAR

ALMERIES > ALMERY

ALMERY n cupboard for church vessels

ALMES > ALME

ALMIGHTY adj all-powerful ▷ adv extremely

ALMIRAH n cupboard

ALMIRAHS > ALMIRAH

ALMNER n almoner

ALMNERS > ALMONER

ALMOND n edible oval-shaped nut which grows on a small tree

ALMONDS > ALMOND

ALMONDY > ALMOND

ALMONER n formerly, a hospital social worker

ALMONERS > ALMONER

ALMONRIES > ALMONRY

ALMONRY n house of an almoner, usually the place where alms were given

ALMOST adv very nearly

ALMOUS Scots word for > ALMS

ALMS pl n gifts to the poor

ALMSGIVER n one who gives alms

ALMSHOUSE n (formerly) a house, financed by charity, which offered accommodation to the poor

ALMSMAN n person who gives or receives alms

ALMSMEN > ALMSMAN

ALMSWOMAN n woman who gives or receives alms

ALMSWOMEN > ALMSWOMAN

ALMUCE n fur-lined hood or cape formerly worn by members of certain religious orders, more recently by canons of France

ALMUCES > ALMUCE

ALMUD n Spanish unit of measure

ALMUDE n Spanish unit of measure

ALMUDES > ALMUDE

ALMUDS > ALMUD

ALMUG n type of wood mentioned in Bible

ALMUGS > ALMUG

ALNAGE n measurement in ells

ALNAGER n inspector of

a

cloth

ALNAGERS > ALNAGER

ALNAGES > ALNAGE

ALNICO n alloy of various metals including iron, nickel, and cobalt

ALNICOS > ALNICO

ALOCASIA n any of various tropical plants of the genus *Alocasia*

ALOCASIAS > ALOCASIA

ALOD n feudal estate with no superior

ALODIA > ALODIUM

ALODIAL > ALODIUM

ALODIUM *same as*
> ALLODIUM

ALODIUMS > ALODIUM

ALODS > ALOD

ALOE n plant with fleshy spiny leaves

ALOED *adj* containing aloes

ALOES *another name for*
> EAGLEWOOD

ALOETIC > ALOE

ALOETICS > ALOE

ALOFT *adv* in the air ▷ *adj* in or into a high or higher place

ALOGIA n inability to speak

ALOGIAS > ALOGIA

ALOGICAL *adj* without logic

ALOHA a Hawaiian word for
> HELLO

ALOHAS > ALOHA

ALOIN n bitter crystalline compound derived from various species of aloe: used as a laxative and flavouring agent

ALOINS > ALOIN

ALONE *adv* without anyone or anything else

ALONELY > ALONE

ALONENESS > ALONE

ALONG *adv* forward

ALONGSIDE *adv* beside (something)

ALONGST *adv* along

ALOOF *adj* distant or haughty in manner

ALOOFLY > ALOOF

ALOOFNESS > ALOOF

ALOPECIA n loss of hair

ALOPECIAS > ALOPECIA

ALOPECIC > ALOPECIA

ALOPECOID > ALOPECIA

ALOUD *adv* in an audible voice ▷ *adj* in a normal voice

ALOW *adj* in or into the lower rigging of a vessel, near the deck

ALOWE Scots word for
> ABLAZE

ALP n high mountain

ALPACA n Peruvian llama

ALPACAS > ALPACA

ALPACCA *same as* > ALPACA

ALPACCAS > ALPACCA

ALPARGATA n Spanish sandal

ALPEEN n Irish cudgel

ALPEENS > ALPEEN

ALPENGLOW n reddish light on the summits of snow-covered mountain peaks at sunset or sunrise

ALPENHORN *same as*
> ALPHORN

ALPHA n first letter in the Greek alphabet

ALPHABET n set of letters used in writing a language

ALPHABETS > ALPHABET

ALPHAS > ALPHA

ALPHASORT *vb* arrange in alphabetical order

ALPHORN n wind instrument used in the Swiss Alps, consisting of a very long tube of wood or bark with a cornet-like mouthpiece

ALPHORNS > ALPHORN

ALPHOSIS n absence of skin pigmentation, as in albinism

ALPHYL n univalent radical

ALPHYLS > ALPHYL

ALPINE *adj* of high mountains ▷ *n* mountain plant

ALPINELY > ALPINE

ALPINES > ALPINE

ALPINISM > ALPINIST

ALPINISMS > ALPINIST

ALPINIST n mountain climber

ALPINISTS > ALPINIST

ALPS > ALP

ALREADY *adv* before the present time

ALRIGHT *adj* all right

ALS > AL

ALSIKE n clover native to Europe and Asia

ALSIKES > ALSIKE

ALSO *adv* in addition, too

ALSOON *same as* > ALSOONE

ALSOONE *adv* as soon

ALT n octave directly above the treble staff

ALTAR n table used for Communion in Christian churches

ALTARAGE n donations placed on altar for priest

ALTARAGES > ALTARAGE

ALTARS > ALTAR

ALTARWISE *adv* in the position of an altar

ALTER *vb* make or become different

ALTERABLE > ALTER

ALTERABLY > ALTER

ALTERANT n alternative

ALTERANTS > ALTERANT

ALTERCATE *vb* argue, esp heatedly

ALTERED > ALTER

ALTERER > ALTER

ALTERERS > ALTER

ALTERING > ALTER

ALTERITY n quality of being different

ALTERN *adj* alternate

ALTERNANT *adj* alternating

ALTERNAT n practice of deciding precedence by lot

ALTERNATE *vb* (cause to) occur by turns ▷ *adj* occurring by turns ▷ *n* person who substitutes for another in his absence

ALTERNATS > ALTERNAT

ALTERNE n neighbouring but different plant group

ALTERNES > ALTERNE

ALTERS > ALTER

ALTESSE n French word for highness

ALTESSES > ALTESSE

ALTEZA n Spanish word for highness

ALTEZAS > ALTEZA

ALTEZZA n Italian word for highness

ALTEZZAS > ALTEZZA

ALTHAEA n plant such as the hollyhock, having tall spikes of showy white, yellow, or red flowers

ALTHAEAS > ALTHAEA

ALTHEA *same as* > ALTHAEA

ALTHEAS > ALTHEA

ALTHO *conj* short form of although

ALTHORN n valved brass musical instrument belonging to the saxhorn or flügelhorn families

ALTHORNS > ALTHORN

ALTHOUGH *conj* despite the fact that; even though

ALTIGRAPH n instrument that measures altitude

ALTIMETER n instrument that measures altitude

ALTIMETRY n science of measuring altitudes, as with an altimeter

ALTIPLANO n high plateau

ALTISSIMO *adj* (of music) very high in pitch

ALTITUDE n height above sea level

ALTITUDES > ALTITUDE

ALTO n (singer with) the highest adult male voice ▷ *adj* denoting such an instrument, singer, or voice

ALTOIST n person who plays the alto saxophone

ALTOISTS > ALTOIST

ALTOS > ALTO

ALTRICES *pl n* altricial birds

ALTRICIAL *adj* (of the young of some species of birds after hatching) naked, blind, and dependent on the parents for food ▷ *n* altricial bird, such as a pigeon

ALTRUISM n unselfish concern for the welfare of others

ALTRUISMS > ALTRUISM

ALTRUIST > ALTRUISM

ALTRUISTS > ALTRUISM

ALTS > ALT

ALUDEL n pear-shaped vessel, open at both ends, formerly used with similar vessels for collecting condensates, esp of subliming mercury

ALUDELS > ALUDEL

ALULA n tuft of feathers attached to the first digit of a bird

ALULAE > ALULA

ALULAR > ALULA

ALUM n double sulphate of aluminium and potassium

ALUMIN n aluminium oxide

ALUMINA n aluminium oxide

ALUMINAS > ALUMINA

ALUMINATE n salt of the ortho or meta acid forms of aluminium hydroxide

ALUMINE n French word for alumina

ALUMINES > ALUMINE

ALUMINIC *adj* of aluminium

ALUMINISE *same as*
> ALUMINIZE

ALUMINIUM n light silvery-white metal that does not rust

ALUMINIZE *vb* cover with aluminium

ALUMINOUS *adj* resembling aluminium

ALUMINS > ALUMIN

ALUMINUM *same as*
> ALUMINIUM

ALUMINUMS > ALUMINUM

ALUMISH *adj* like alum

ALUMIUM old name for
> ALUMINIUM

ALUMIUMS > ALUMINUM

ALUMNA n female graduate of a school, college, etc

ALUMNAE > ALUMNA

ALUMNI > ALUMNUS

ALUMNUS n graduate of a college

ALUMROOT n North American plants having small white, reddish, or green bell-shaped flowers and astringent roots

ALUMROOTS > ALUMROOT

ALUMS > ALUM

ALUMSTONE *same as*
> ALUNITE

ALUNITE n white, grey, or reddish mineral

ALUNITES > ALUNITE

ALURE n area behind battlements

ALURES > ALURE

ALVEARIES > ALVEARY

ALVEARY n beehive

ALVEATED *adj* with vaults like beehive

ALVEOLAR *adj* of, relating to, or resembling an alveolus ▷ *n* alveolar consonant, such as the speech sounds written t, d, and s in English

ALVEOLARS > ALVEOLAR

ALVEOLATE *adj* having many alveoli

ALVEOLE n alveolus

ALVEOLES > ALVEOLE

ALVEOLI > ALVEOLUS

ALVEOLUS n any small pit, cavity, or saclike dilation, such as a honeycomb cell, a tooth socket, or the tiny air sacs in the lungs

ALVINE *adj* of or relating to the intestines or belly

ALWAY *same as* > ALWAYS

ALWAYS *adv* at all times

ALYSSUM n garden plant

a

with small yellow or white flowers

ALYSSUMS > ALYSSUM

AM *see* > BE

AMA *n* vessel for water

AMABILE *adj* sweet

AMADAVAT *same as* > AVADAVAT

AMADAVATS > AMADAVAT

AMADODA *pl n* grown men

AMADOU *n* spongy substance made from certain fungi, such as *Polyporus* (or *Fomes*) *fomentarius* and related species, used as tinder to light fires, in medicine to stop bleeding, and, esp formerly, by anglers to dry off dry flies between casts

AMADOUS > AMADOU

AMAH *n* (in the East, formerly) a nurse or maidservant

AMAHS > AMAH

AMAIN *adv* with great strength, speed, or haste

AMALGAM *n* blend or combination

AMALGAMS > AMALGAM

AMANDINE *n* protein found in almonds

AMANDINES > AMANDINE

AMANDLA *n* political slogan calling for power to the Black population

AMANDLAS > AMANDLA

AMANITA *n* type of fungus

AMANITAS > AMANITA

AMANITIN *n* poison from amanita

AMANITINS > AMANITIN

AMARACUS *n* marjoram

AMARANT *n* amaranth

AMARANTH *n* imaginary flower that never fades

AMARANTHS > AMARANTH

AMARANTIN *n* protein

AMARANTS > AMARANT

AMARELLE *n* variety of sour cherry that has pale red fruit and colourless juice

AMARELLES > AMARELLE

AMARETTI > AMARETTO

AMARETTO *n* Italian liqueur with a flavour of almonds

AMARETTOS > AMARETTO

AMARNA *adj* pertaining to the reign of the Pharaoh Akhenaton

AMARONE *n* strong dry red Italian wine

AMARONES > AMARONE

AMARYLLID *n* plant of the amaryllis family

AMARYLLIS *n* lily-like plant with large red, pink, or white flowers

AMAS > AMA

AMASS *vb* collect or accumulate

AMASSABLE > AMASS

AMASSED > AMASS

AMASSER > AMASS

AMASSERS > AMASS

AMASSES > AMASS

AMASSING > AMASS

AMASSMENT > AMASS

AMATE *vb* match

AMATED > AMATE

AMATES > AMATE

AMATEUR *n* person who engages in a sport or activity as a pastime rather than as a profession ▷ *adj* not professional

AMATEURS > AMATEUR

AMATING > AMATE

AMATION *n* lovemaking

AMATIONS > AMATION

AMATIVE *a rare word for* > AMOROUS

AMATIVELY > AMATIVE

AMATOL *n* explosive mixture of ammonium nitrate and TNT, used in shells and bombs

AMATOLS > AMATOL

AMATORIAL *same as* > AMATORY

AMATORIAN > AMATORY

AMATORY *adj* relating to romantic or sexual love

AMAUROSES > AMAUROSIS

AMAUROSIS *n* blindness, esp when occurring without observable damage to the eye

AMAUROTIC > AMAUROSIS

AMAUT *n* hood on an Inuit woman's parka for carrying a child

AMAUTS > AMAUT

AMAZE *vb* surprise greatly, astound

AMAZED > AMAZE

AMAZEDLY > AMAZE

AMAZEMENT *n* incredulity or great astonishment

AMAZES > AMAZE

AMAZING *adj* causing wonder or astonishment

AMAZINGLY > AMAZING

AMAZON *n* any tall, strong, or aggressive woman

AMAZONIAN > AMAZON

AMAZONITE *n* green variety of microcline used as a gemstone

AMAZONS > AMAZON

AMBACH *same as* > AMBATCH

AMBACHES > AMBACH

AMBAGE *n* ambiguity

AMBAGES > AMBAGE

AMBAGIOUS > AMBAGE

AMBAN *n* Chinese official

AMBANS > AMBAN

AMBARI *same as* > AMBARY

AMBARIES > AMBARY

AMBARIS > AMBARI

AMBARY *n* tropical Asian malvaceous plant, *Hibiscus cannabinus*, that yields a fibre similar to jute

AMBASSAGE *n* embassy

AMBASSIES > AMBASSY

AMBASSY *n* embassy

AMBATCH *n* tree or shrub of the Nile Valley, *Aeschynomene elaphroxylon*, valued for its light-coloured pithlike wood

AMBATCHES > AMBATCH

AMBEER *n* saliva coloured by tobacco juice

AMBEERS > AMBEER

AMBER *n* clear yellowish fossil resin ▷ *adj* brownish-yellow

AMBERED *adj* fixed in amber

AMBERGRIS *n* waxy substance secreted by the sperm whale, used in making perfumes

AMBERIES > AMBERY

AMBERINA *n* type of glassware

AMBERINAS > AMBERINA

AMBERITE *n* powder like amber

AMBERITES > AMBERITE

AMBERJACK *n* any of several large carangid fishes of the genus *Seriola*, esp *S. dumerili*, with golden markings when young, occurring in tropical and subtropical Atlantic waters

AMBEROID *n* synthetic amber made by compressing pieces of amber and other resins together at a high temperature

AMBEROIDS > AMBEROID

AMBEROUS *adj* like amber

AMBERS > AMBER

AMBERY *adj* like amber

AMBIANCE *same as* > AMBIENCE

AMBIANCES > AMBIANCE

AMBIENCE *n* atmosphere of a place

AMBIENCES > AMBIENCE

AMBIENT *adj* surrounding ▷ *n* ambient music

AMBIENTS > AMBIENT

AMBIGUITY *n* possibility of interpreting an expression in more than one way

AMBIGUOUS *adj* having more than one possible meaning

AMBIPOLAR *adj* (of plasmas and semiconductors) involving both positive and negative charge carriers

AMBIT *n* limits or boundary

AMBITION *n* desire for success

AMBITIONS > AMBITION

AMBITIOUS *adj* having a strong desire for success

AMBITS > AMBIT

AMBITTY *adj* crystalline and brittle

AMBIVERT *n* person who is intermediate between an extrovert and an introvert

AMBIVERTS > AMBIVERT

AMBLE *vb* walk at a leisurely pace ▷ *n* leisurely walk or pace

AMBLED > AMBLE

AMBLER > AMBLE

AMBLERS > AMBLE

AMBLES > AMBLE

AMBLING *n* walking at a leisurely pace

AMBLINGS > AMBLING

AMBLYOPIA *n* impaired vision with no discernible damage to the eye or optic

nerve

AMBLYOPIC > AMBLYOPIA

AMBO *n* either of two raised pulpits from which the gospels and epistles were read in early Christian churches

AMBOINA *same as* > AMBOYNA

AMBOINAS > AMBOINA

AMBONES > AMBO

AMBOS > AMBO

AMBOYNA *n* mottled curly-grained wood of an Indonesian leguminous tree, *Pterocarpus indicus*, used in making furniture

AMBOYNAS > AMBOYNA

AMBRIES > AMBRY

AMBROID *same as* > AMBEROID

AMBROIDS > AMBROID

AMBROSIA *n* anything delightful to taste or smell

AMBROSIAL > AMBROSIA

AMBROSIAN > AMBROSIA

AMBROSIAS > AMBROSIA

AMBROTYPE *n* early type of glass negative that could be made to appear as a positive by backing it with black varnish or paper

AMBRY *n* recessed cupboard in the wall of a church near the altar, used to store sacred vessels, etc

AMBSACE *n* double ace, the lowest throw at dice

AMBSACES > AMBSACE

AMBULACRA *n* radial bands on the ventral surface of echinoderms, such as the starfish and sea urchin, on which the tube feet are situated

AMBULANCE *n* motor vehicle designed to carry sick or injured people

AMBULANT *adj* moving about from place to place

AMBULANTS > AMBULANT

AMBULATE *vb* wander about or move from one place to another

AMBULATED > AMBULATE

AMBULATES > AMBULATE

AMBULATOR *n* person who walks

AMBULETTE *n* motor vehicle designed for transporting ill or handicapped people

AMBUSCADE *n* ambush ▷ *vb* ambush or lie in ambush

AMBUSCADO *n* ambuscade

AMBUSH *n* act of waiting in a concealed position to make a surprise attack ▷ *vb* attack from a concealed position

AMBUSHED > AMBUSH

AMBUSHER > AMBUSH

AMBUSHERS > AMBUSH

AMBUSHES > AMBUSH

AMBUSHING > AMBUSH

AMEARST *old form of* > AMERCE

AMEBA *same as* > AMOEBA

a

a

AMEBAE > AMEBA
AMEBAN > AMEBA
AMEBAS > AMEBA
AMEBEAN *same as*
> AMOEBEAN
AMEBIASES > AMEBIASIS
AMEBIASIS *n* disease
caused by amoeba
AMEBIC > AMEBA
AMEBOCYTE *n* any cell
having properties similar
to an amoeba, such as
shape, mobility, and ability
to engulf particles
AMEBOID *same as*
> AMOEBOID
AMEER *n* (formerly) the ruler
of Afghanistan
AMEERATE *n* country ruled
by an ameer
AMEERATES > AMEERATE
AMEERS > AMEER
AMEIOSES > AMEIOSIS
AMEIOSIS *n* absence of
pairing of chromosomes
during meiosis
AMELCORN *n* variety of
wheat
AMELCORNS > AMELCORN
AMELIA *n* congenital
absence of arms or legs
AMELIAS > AMELIA
AMEN *n* term used at the
end of a prayer or religious
statement ▷ *vb* say amen
AMENABLE *adj* likely or
willing to cooperate
AMENABLY > AMENABLE
AMENAGE *vb* tame
AMENAGED > AMENAGE
AMENAGES > AMENAGE
AMENAGING > AMENAGE
AMENAUNCE *n* person's
bearing
AMEND *vb* make small
changes to correct or
improve (something)
AMENDABLE > AMEND
AMENDE *n* public apology
and reparation made to
satisfy the honour of the
person wronged
AMENDED > AMEND
AMENDER > AMEND
AMENDERS > AMEND
AMENDES > AMENDE
AMENDING > AMEND
AMENDMENT *n* improvement
or correction
AMENDS *n* recompense or
compensation given or
gained for some injury,
insult, etc
AMENE *adj* pleasant
AMENED > AMEN
AMENING > AMEN
AMENITIES > AMENITY
AMENITY *n* useful or
enjoyable feature
AMENS > AMEN
AMENT *n* mentally deficient
person
AMENTA > AMENTUM
AMENTAL > AMENTUM
AMENTIA *n* severe mental
deficiency, usually
congenital

AMENTIAS > AMENTIA
AMENTS > AMENT
AMENTUM *same as* > AMENT
AMERCE *vb* punish by a fine
AMERCED > AMERCE
AMERCER > AMERCE
AMERCERS > AMERCE
AMERCES > AMERCE
AMERCING > AMERCE
AMERICIUM *n* white
metallic element artificially
produced from plutonium
AMESACE *same as* > AMBSACE
AMESACES > AMESACE
AMETHYST *n* bluish-violet
variety of quartz used as a
gemstone ▷ *adj* purple or
violet
AMETHYSTS > AMETHYST
AMETROPIA *n* loss of
ability to focus images
on the retina, caused by
an imperfection in the
refractive function of the
eye
AMETROPIC > AMETROPIA
AMI *n* male friend
AMIA *n* species of fish
AMIABLE *adj* friendly,
pleasant-natured
AMIABLY > AMIABLE
AMIANTHUS *n* any of the fine
silky varieties of asbestos
AMIANTUS *n* amianthus
AMIAS > AMIA
AMICABLE *adj* friendly
AMICABLY > AMICABLE
AMICE *n* rectangular piece
of white linen worn by
priests around the neck
and shoulders under the
alb or, formerly, on the
head
AMICES > AMICE
AMICI > AMICUS
AMICUS *n* Latin for friend
AMID *prep* in the middle
of, among ▷ *n* same as
> AMIDE
AMIDASE *n* enzyme
AMIDASES > AMIDASE
AMIDE *n* any organic
compound containing the
group —$CONH_2$
AMIDES > AMIDE
AMIDIC > AMIDE
AMIDIN *n* form of starch
AMIDINE *n* crystalline
compound
AMIDINES > AMIDINE
AMIDINS > AMIDIN
AMIDMOST *adv* in the middle
AMIDO *adj* containing amide
AMIDOGEN *n* chemical
compound derived from
ammonia
AMIDOGENS > AMIDOGEN
AMIDOL *n* chemical used in
developing photographs
AMIDOLS > AMIDOL
AMIDONE *n* pain-killing drug
AMIDONES > AMIDONE
AMIDS *same as* > AMID
AMIDSHIP *adj* in the middle
of a ship
AMIDSHIPS *adv* at or
towards the middle of

a ship ▷ *adj* at, near, or
towards the centre of a
vessel
AMIDST *same as* > AMID
AMIE *n* female friend
AMIES > AMIE
AMIGA *n* Spanish female
friend
AMIGAS > AMIGA
AMIGO *n* friend
AMIGOS > AMIGO
AMILDAR *n* manager in India
AMILDARS > AMILDAR
AMIN *same as* > AMINE
AMINE *n* organic base
formed by replacing one
or more of the hydrogen
atoms of ammonia by
organic groups
AMINES > AMINE
AMINIC > AMINE
AMINITIES > AMINITY
AMINITY *n* amenity
AMINO *n* of, consisting of,
or containing the group of
atoms -NH_2
AMINS > AMIN
AMIR *n* (formerly) the ruler
of Afghanistan
AMIRATE > AMIR
AMIRATES > AMIR
AMIRS > AMIR
AMIS > AMI
AMISES > AMI
AMISS *adv* wrongly, badly
▷ *adj* wrong, faulty ▷ *n* evil
deed
AMISSES > AMISS
AMISSIBLE *adj* likely to be
lost
AMISSING *adj* missing
AMITIES > AMITY
AMITOSES > AMITOSIS
AMITOSIS *n* unusual form
of cell division in which the
nucleus and cytoplasm
divide by constriction
without the formation of
chromosomes
AMITOTIC > AMITOSIS
AMITROLE *n* pesticide
AMITROLES > AMITROLE
AMITY *n* friendship
AMLA *n* species of Indian
tree
AMLAS > AMLA
AMMAN *same as* > AMTMAN
AMMANS > AMMAN
AMMETER *n* instrument for
measuring electric current
AMMETERS > AMMETER
AMMINE *n* compound that
has molecules containing
one or more ammonia
molecules bound to
another molecule, group,
or atom by coordinate
bonds
AMMINES > AMMINE
AMMINO *adj* containing
ammonia molecules
AMMIRAL *old word for*
> ADMIRAL
AMMIRALS > AMMIRAL
AMMO *n* ammunition
AMMOCETE *n* ammocoete
AMMOCETES > AMMOCETE

AMMOCOETE *n* larva
of primitive jawless
vertebrates, such as the
lamprey, that lives buried
in mud and feeds on
microorganisms
AMMON *n* Asian wild sheep
AMMONAL *n* explosive made
by mixing TNT, ammonium
nitrate, and aluminium
powder
AMMONALS > AMMONAL
AMMONATE *same as*
> AMMINE
AMMONATES > AMMONATE
AMMONIA *n* strong-smelling
alkaline gas containing
hydrogen and nitrogen
AMMONIAC *n* strong-
smelling gum resin
obtained from the stems of
the N Asian umbelliferous
plant *Dorema ammoniacum*
and formerly used as an
expectorant, stimulant,
perfume, and in porcelain
cement
AMMONIACS > AMMONIAC
AMMONIAS > AMMONIA
AMMONIATE *vb* unite or treat
with ammonia
AMMONIC *adj* of or
concerned with ammonia
or ammonium compounds
AMMONICAL > AMMONIC
AMMONIFY *vb* treat or
impregnate with ammonia
or a compound of
ammonia
AMMONITE *n* fossilized spiral
shell of an extinct sea
creature
AMMONITES > AMMONITE
AMMONITIC > AMMONITE
AMMONIUM *n* type of
monovalent chemical
group
AMMONIUMS > AMMONIUM
AMMONO *adj* using ammonia
AMMONOID *n* type of fossil
AMMONOIDS > AMMONOID
AMMONS > AMMON
AMMOS > AMMO
AMNESIA *n* loss of memory
AMNESIAC > AMNESIA
AMNESIACS > AMNESIA
AMNESIAS > AMNESIA
AMNESIC > AMNESIA
AMNESICS > AMNESIA
AMNESTIC *adj* relating to
amnesia
AMNESTIED > AMNESTY
AMNESTIES > AMNESTY
AMNESTY *n* general pardon
for offences against a
government ▷ *vb* overlook
or forget (an offence)
AMNIA > AMNION
AMNIC *adj* relating to
amnion
AMNIO *n* amniocentesis
AMNION *n* innermost of two
membranes enclosing an
embryo
AMNIONIC > AMNION
AMNIONS > AMNION
AMNIOS > AMNIO

AMNIOTE n any vertebrate animal, such as a reptile, bird, or mammal, that possesses an amnion, chorion, and allantois during embryonic development

AMNIOTES > AMNIOTE

AMNIOTIC adj of or relating to the amnion

AMNIOTOMY n breaking of the membrane surrounding a fetus to induce labour

AMOEBA n microscopic single-celled animal able to change its shape

AMOEBAE > AMOEBA

AMOEBAEAN adj of or relating to lines of verse dialogue that answer each other alternately

AMOEBAN > AMOEBA

AMOEBAS > AMOEBA

AMOEBEAN same as > AMOEBAEAN

AMOEBIC > AMOEBA

AMOEBOID adj of, related to, or resembling amoebae

AMOK n state of murderous frenzy, originally observed among Malays

AMOKS > AMOK

AMOKURA n white pelagian bird, *Paethon rubricauda*, of tropical latitudes in the Indian and Pacific oceans, with a red beak and long red tail feathers

AMOLE n American plant

AMOLES > AMOLE

AMOMUM n plant of ginger family

AMOMUMS > AMOMUM

AMONG prep in the midst of

AMONGST same as > AMONG

AMOOVE vb stir someone's emotions

AMOOVED > AMOOVE

AMOOVES > AMOOVE

AMOOVING > AMOOVE

AMORAL adj without moral standards

AMORALISM > AMORAL

AMORALIST > AMORAL

AMORALITY > AMORAL

AMORALLY > AMORAL

AMORANCE n condition of being in love

AMORANCES > AMORANCE

AMORANT > AMORANCE

AMORCE n small percussion cap

AMORCES > AMORCE

AMORET n sweetheart

AMORETS > AMORET

AMORETTI > AMORETTO

AMORETTO n (esp in painting) a small chubby naked boy representing a cupid

AMORETTOS > AMORETTO

AMORINI > AMORINO

AMORINO same as > AMORETTO

AMORISM > AMORIST

AMORISMS > AMORIST

AMORIST n lover or a writer about love

AMORISTIC > AMORIST

AMORISTS > AMORIST

AMORNINGS adv each morning

AMOROSA n lover

AMOROSAS > AMOROSA

AMOROSITY n quality of being amorous

AMOROSO adv (to be played) lovingly ▷ n rich sweetened sherry of a dark colour

AMOROSOS > AMOROSO

AMOROUS adj feeling, showing, or relating to sexual love

AMOROUSLY > AMOROUS

AMORPHISM > AMORPHOUS

AMORPHOUS adj without distinct shape

AMORT adj in low spirits

AMORTISE same as > AMORTIZE

AMORTISED > AMORTISE

AMORTISES > AMORTISE

AMORTIZE vb pay off (a debt) gradually by periodic transfers to a sinking fund

AMORTIZED > AMORTIZE

AMORTIZES > AMORTIZE

AMOSITE n form of asbestos

AMOSITES > AMOSITE

AMOTION n act of removing

AMOTIONS > AMOTION

AMOUNT n extent or quantity ▷ vb be equal or add up to

AMOUNTED > AMOUNT

AMOUNTING > AMOUNT

AMOUNTS > AMOUNT

AMOUR n (secret) love affair

AMOURETTE n minor love affair

AMOURS > AMOUR

AMOVE vb stir someone's emotions

AMOVED > AMOVE

AMOVES > AMOVE

AMOVING > AMOVE

AMOWT same as > AMAUT

AMOWTS > AMOWT

AMP n ampere ▷ vb excite or become excited

AMPASSIES > AMPASSY

AMPASSY n ampersand

AMPED > AMP

AMPERAGE n strength of an electric current measured in amperes

AMPERAGES > AMPERAGE

AMPERE n basic unit of electric current

AMPERES > AMPERE

AMPERSAND n character (&), meaning and

AMPERZAND n ampersand

AMPHIBIA n class of amphibians

AMPHIBIAN n animal that lives on land but breeds in water ▷ adj of, relating to, or belonging to the class *Amphibia*

AMPHIBOLE n any of a large group of minerals consisting of the silicates of calcium, iron, magnesium, sodium, and aluminium

AMPHIBOLY n ambiguity of expression, esp where due to a grammatical construction

AMPHIGORY n piece of nonsensical writing in verse or, less commonly, prose

AMPHIOXI > AMPHIOXUS

AMPHIOXUS another name for the > LANCELET

AMPHIPATH adj of or relating to a molecule that possesses both hydrophobic and hydrophilic elements

AMPHIPOD n any marine or freshwater crustacean of the order *Amphipoda*, such as the sand hoppers, in which the body is laterally compressed: subclass *Malacostraca* ▷ adj of, relating to, or belonging to the *Amphipoda*

AMPHIPODS > AMPHIPOD

AMPHOLYTE n electrolyte that can be acid or base

AMPHORA n two-handled ancient Greek or Roman jar

AMPHORAE > AMPHORA

AMPHORAL > AMPHORA

AMPHORAS > AMPHORA

AMPHORIC adj resembling the sound produced by blowing into a bottle. Amphoric breath sounds are heard through a stethoscope placed over a cavity in the lung

AMPING > AMP

AMPLE adj more than sufficient

AMPLENESS > AMPLE

AMPLER > AMPLE

AMPLEST > AMPLE

AMPLEXUS n mating in amphibians

AMPLIDYNE n magnetic amplifier

AMPLIFIED > AMPLIFY

AMPLIFIER n device used to amplify a current or sound signal

AMPLIFIES > AMPLIFY

AMPLIFY vb increase the strength of (a current or sound signal)

AMPLITUDE n greatness of extent

AMPLOSOME n stocky body type

AMPLY adv fully or generously

AMPOULE n small sealed glass vessel containing liquid for injection

AMPOULES > AMPOULE

AMPS > AMP

AMPUL n ampoule

AMPULE same as > AMPOULE

AMPULES > AMPULE

AMPULLA n dilated end part of certain tubes in the body

AMPULLAE > AMPULLA

AMPULLAR > AMPULLA

AMPULLARY > AMPULLA

AMPULS > AMPUL

AMPUTATE vb cut off (a limb or part of a limb) for medical reasons

AMPUTATED > AMPUTATE

AMPUTATES > AMPUTATE

AMPUTATOR > AMPUTATE

AMPUTEE n person who has had a limb amputated

AMPUTEES > AMPUTEE

AMREETA same as > AMRITA

AMREETAS > AMREETA

AMRIT n sanctified solution of sugar and water used in the Amrit Ceremony

AMRITA n ambrosia of the gods that bestows immortality

AMRITAS > AMRITA

AMRITS > AMRIT

AMSINCKIA n Californian herb

AMTMAN n magistrate in parts of Europe

AMTMANS > AMTMAN

AMTRAC n amphibious tracked vehicle

AMTRACK n amphibious tracked vehicle

AMTRACKS > AMTRACK

AMTRACS > AMTRAC

AMU n unit of mass

AMUCK same as > AMOK

AMUCKS > AMUCK

AMULET n something carried or worn as a protection against evil

AMULETIC > AMULET

AMULETS > AMULET

AMUS > AMU

AMUSABLE adj capable of being amused

AMUSE vb cause to laugh or smile

AMUSEABLE same as > AMUSABLE

AMUSED > AMUSE

AMUSEDLY > AMUSE

AMUSEMENT n state of being amused

AMUSER > AMUSE

AMUSERS > AMUSE

AMUSES > AMUSE

AMUSETTE n type of light cannon

AMUSETTES > AMUSETTE

AMUSIA n inability to recognize musical tones

AMUSIAS > AMUSIA

AMUSING adj mildly entertaining

AMUSINGLY > AMUSING

AMUSIVE adj deceptive

AMYGDAL n almond

AMYGDALA n almond-shaped part, such as a tonsil or a lobe of the cerebellum

AMYGDALAE > AMYGDALA

AMYGDALAS > AMYGDALA

AMYGDALE n vesicle in a volcanic rock, formed from a bubble of escaping gas, that has become filled with light-coloured minerals, such as quartz and calcite

AMYGDALES > AMYGDALE

AMYGDALIN n white soluble bitter-tasting crystalline glycoside extracted from bitter almonds

AMYGDALS > AMYGDAL

AMYGDULE same as > AMYGDALE

AMYGDULES > AMYGDULE

AMYL n of, consisting of, or containing any of eight isomeric forms of the monovalent group C_5H_{11}-

AMYLASE n enzyme, present in saliva, that helps to change starch into sugar

AMYLASES > AMYLASE

AMYLENE another name (no longer in technical usage) for > PENTENE

AMYLENES > AMYLENE

AMYLIC adj of or derived from amyl

AMYLOGEN n soluble part of starch

AMYLOGENS > AMYLOGEN

AMYLOID n complex protein resembling starch, deposited in tissues in some degenerative diseases ▷ adj starchlike

AMYLOIDAL > AMYLOID

AMYLOIDS > AMYLOID

AMYLOPSIN n enzyme of the pancreatic juice that converts starch into sugar

AMYLOSE n minor component (about 20 per cent) of starch, consisting of long unbranched chains of glucose units. It is soluble in water and gives an intense blue colour with iodine

AMYLOSES > AMYLOSE

AMYLS > AMYL

AMYLUM another name for > STARCH

AMYLUMS > AMYLUM

AMYOTONIA another name for > MYOTONIA

AMYTAL n barbiturate

AMYTALS > AMYTAL

AN adj form of a used before vowels, and sometimes before 'h'

ANA adv (of ingredients in a prescription) in equal quantities ▷ n collection of reminiscences, sketches, etc, of or about a person or place

ANABAENA n any freshwater alga of the genus Anabaena, sometimes occurring in drinking water, giving it a fishy taste and smell

ANABAENAS > ANABAENA

ANABANTID n any of various spiny-finned fishes constituting the family Anabantidae and including the fighting fish, climbing perch, and gourami ▷ adj of, relating to, or belonging to the family Anabantidae

ANABAS n type of fish

ANABASES > ANABASIS

ANABASIS n march of Cyrus the Younger and his Greek mercenaries from Sardis to Cunaxa in Babylonia in 401 BC

ANABATIC adj (of air currents) rising upwards, esp up slopes

ANABIOSES > ANABIOSIS

ANABIOSIS n ability to return to life after apparent death

ANABIOTIC > ANABIOSIS

ANABLEPS n any of various cyprinodont fishes constituting the genus Anableps, which includes the four-eyed fishes

ANABOLIC adj of or relating to anabolism

ANABOLISM n metabolic process in which body tissues are synthesized from food

ANABOLITE n product of anabolism

ANABRANCH n stream that leaves a river and enters it again further downstream

ANACHARIS n water plant

ANACLINAL adj (of valleys and similar formations) progressing in a direction opposite to the dip of the surrounding rock strata

ANACLISES > ANACLITIC

ANACLISIS > ANACLITIC

ANACLITIC adj of or relating to relationships that are characterized by the strong dependence of one person on others or another

ANACONDA n large S American snake which kills by constriction

ANACONDAS > ANACONDA

ANACRUSES > ANACRUSIS

ANACRUSIS n one or more unstressed syllables at the beginning of a line of verse

ANADEM n garland for the head

ANADEMS > ANADEM

ANAEMIA n deficiency in the number of red blood cells

ANAEMIAS > ANAEMIA

ANAEMIC adj having anaemia

ANAEROBE n organism that does not require oxygen

ANAEROBES > ANAEROBE

ANAEROBIA same as > ANAEROBES

ANAEROBIC adj not requiring oxygen

ANAGLYPH n stereoscopic picture consisting of two images of the same object, taken from slightly different angles

ANAGLYPHS > ANAGLYPH

ANAGLYPHY > ANAGLYPH

ANAGOGE n allegorical or spiritual interpretation,

esp of sacred works such as the Bible

ANAGOGES > ANAGOGE

ANAGOGIC > ANAGOGE

ANAGOGIES > ANAGOGY

ANAGOGY same as > ANAGOGE

ANAGRAM n word or phrase made by rearranging the letters of another word or phrase

ANAGRAMS > ANAGRAM

ANAL adj of the anus

ANALCIME same as > ANALCITE

ANALCIMES > ANALCIME

ANALCIMIC > ANALCIME

ANALCITE n white, grey, or colourless zeolite mineral

ANALCITES > ANALCITE

ANALECTA same as > ANALECTS

ANALECTIC > ANALECTS

ANALECTS pl n selected literary passages from one or more works

ANALEMMA n graduated scale shaped like a figure of eight that indicates the daily declination of the sun

ANALEMMAS > ANALEMMA

ANALEPTIC adj (of a drug, etc) stimulating the central nervous system ▷ n any drug, such as doxapram, that stimulates the central nervous system

ANALGESIA n absence of pain

ANALGESIC adj (drug) relieving pain ▷ n drug that relieves pain

ANALGETIC n painkilling drug

ANALGIA same as > ANALGESIA

ANALGIAS > ANALGIA

ANALITIES > ANALITY

ANALITY n quality of being psychologically anal

ANALLY > ANAL

ANALOG same as > ANALOGUE

ANALOGA > ANALOGON

ANALOGIC > ANALOGY

ANALOGIES > ANALOGY

ANALOGISE same as > ANALOGIZE

ANALOGISM > ANALOGIZE

ANALOGIST > ANALOGY

ANALOGIZE vb use analogy

ANALOGON n analogue

ANALOGONS > ANALOGON

ANALOGOUS adj similar in some respects

ANALOGS > ANALOG

ANALOGUE n something that is similar in some respects to something else ▷ adj displaying information by means of a dial

ANALOGUES > ANALOGUE

ANALOGY n similarity in some respects

ANALYSAND n any person who is undergoing psychoanalysis

ANALYSE vb make an analysis of (something)

ANALYSED > ANALYSE

ANALYSER > ANALYSE

ANALYSERS > ANALYSE

ANALYSES > ANALYSIS

ANALYSING > ANALYSE

ANALYSIS n separation of a whole into its parts for study and interpretation

ANALYST n person skilled in analysis

ANALYSTS > ANALYST

ANALYTE n substance that is being analyzed

ANALYTES > ANALYTE

ANALYTIC adj relating to analysis ▷ n analytical logic

ANALYTICS > ANALYTIC

ANALYZE same as > ANALYSE

ANALYZED > ANALYZE

ANALYZER > ANALYZE

ANALYZERS > ANALYZE

ANALYZES > ANALYZE

ANALYZING > ANALYZE

ANAMNESES > ANAMNESIS

ANAMNESIS n ability to recall past events

ANAMNIOTE n any vertebrate animal, such as a fish or amphibian, that lacks an amnion, chorion, and allantois during embryonic development

ANAN interj expression of failure to understand

ANANA n pineapple

ANANAS n plant related to the pineapple

ANANASES > ANANAS

ANANDROUS adj (of flowers) having no stamens

ANANKE n unalterable necessity

ANANKES > ANANKE

ANANTHOUS adj (of higher plants) having no flowers

ANAPAEST n metrical foot of three syllables, the first two short, the last long

ANAPAESTS > ANAPAEST

ANAPEST same as > ANAPAEST

ANAPESTIC > ANAPEST

ANAPESTS > ANAPEST

ANAPHASE n third stage of mitosis, during which the chromatids separate and migrate towards opposite ends of the spindle

ANAPHASES > ANAPHASE

ANAPHASIC > ANAPHASE

ANAPHOR n word referring back to a previous word

ANAPHORA n use of a word such as a pronoun that has the same reference as a word previously used in the same discourse

ANAPHORAL > ANAPHORA

ANAPHORAS > ANAPHORA

ANAPHORIC adj of or relating to anaphorism

ANAPHORS > ANAPHOR

ANAPLASIA n reversion of plant or animal cells to a simpler less differentiated form

ANAPLASTY *n* plastic surgery

ANAPTYXES > ANAPTYXIS

ANAPTYXIS *n* insertion of a short vowel between consonants in order to make a word more easily pronounceable

ANARCH *n* instigator or personification of anarchy

ANARCHAL > ANARCHY

ANARCHIAL > ANARCHY

ANARCHIC > ANARCHY

ANARCHIES > ANARCHY

ANARCHISE *vb* make anarchic

ANARCHISM *n* doctrine advocating the abolition of government

ANARCHIST *n* person who advocates the abolition of government

ANARCHIZE *vb* make anarchic

ANARCHS > ANARCH

ANARCHY *n* lawlessness and disorder

ANARTHRIA *n* loss of the ability to speak coherently

ANARTHRIC > ANARTHRIA

ANAS > ANA

ANASARCA *n* generalized accumulation of serous fluid within the subcutaneous connective tissue, resulting in oedema

ANASARCAS > ANASARCA

ANASTASES > ANASTASIS

ANASTASIS *n* Christ's harrowing of hell

ANASTATIC > ANASTASIS

ANATA *n* (in Theravada Buddhism) the belief that since all things are constantly changing, there can be no such thing as a permanent, unchanging self

ANATAS > ANATA

ANATASE *n* rare blue or black mineral

ANATASES > ANATASE

ANATHEMA *n* detested person or thing

ANATHEMAS > ANATHEMA

ANATMAN *same as* > ANATA

ANATMANS > ANATMAN

ANATOMIC > ANATOMY

ANATOMIES > ANATOMY

ANATOMISE *same as* > ANATOMIZE

ANATOMIST *n* expert in anatomy

ANATOMIZE *vb* dissect (an animal or plant)

ANATOMY *n* science of the structure of the body

ANATOXIN *n* bacterial toxin used in inoculation

ANATOXINS > ANATOXIN

ANATROPY *n* (of a plant ovule) condition of being inverted during development by a bending of the stalk (funicule) attaching it to the carpule

ANATTA *n* annatto

ANATTAS > ANATTA

ANATTO *same as* > ANNATTO

ANATTOS > ANATTO

ANAXIAL *adj* asymmetrical

ANBURIES > ANBURY

ANBURY *n* soft spongy tumour occurring in horses and oxen

ANCE *dialect form of* > ONCE

ANCESTOR *n* person from whom one is descended

ANCESTORS > ANCESTOR

ANCESTRAL *adj* of or inherited from ancestors ▷ *n* relation that holds between *x* and *y* if there is a chain of instances of a given relation leading from *x* to *y*

ANCESTRY *n* lineage or descent

ANCHO *n* chili pepper

ANCHOR *n* heavy hooked device attached to a boat by a cable and dropped overboard to fasten the ship to the sea bottom ▷ *vb* fasten with or as if with an anchor

ANCHORAGE *n* place where boats can be anchored

ANCHORED > ANCHOR

ANCHORESS > ANCHORITE

ANCHORET *n* achorite

ANCHORETS > ANCHORET

ANCHORING > ANCHOR

ANCHORITE *n* religious recluse

ANCHORMAN *n* broadcaster in a central studio who links up and presents items from outside camera units and other studios

ANCHORMEN > ANCHORMAN

ANCHORS *pl n* brakes of a motor vehicle

ANCHOS > ANCHOS

ANCHOVETA *n* small anchovy, *Cetengraulis mysticetus*, of the American Pacific, used as bait by tuna fishermen

ANCHOVIES > ANCHOVY

ANCHOVY *n* small strong-tasting fish

ANCHUSA *n* any Eurasian plant of the boraginaceous genus *Anchusa*, having rough hairy stems and leaves and blue flowers

ANCHUSAS > ANCHUSA

ANCHUSIN *same as* > ALKANET

ANCHUSINS > ANCHUSIN

ANCHYLOSE *same as* > ANKYLOSE

ANCIENT *adj* dating from very long ago ▷ *n* member of a civilized nation in the ancient world, esp a Greek, Roman, or Hebrew

ANCIENTER > ANCIENT

ANCIENTLY *adv* in ancient times

ANCIENTRY *n* quality of being ancient

ANCIENTS > ANCIENT

ANCILE *n* mythical Roman shield

ANCILIA > ANCILE

ANCILLA *n* Latin word for servant

ANCILLAE > ANCILLA

ANCILLARY *adj* supporting the main work of an organization ▷ *n* subsidiary or auxiliary thing or person

ANCILLAS > ANCILLA

ANCIPITAL *adj* flattened and having two edges

ANCLE *old spelling of* > ANKLE

ANCLES > ANCLE

ANCOME *n* inflammation

ANCOMES > ANCOME

ANCON *n* projecting bracket or console supporting a cornice

ANCONAL > ANCON

ANCONE *same as* > ANCON

ANCONEAL > ANCON

ANCONES > ANCONE

ANCONOID > ANCON

ANCORA *adv* Italian for encore

ANCRESS *n* female anchorite

ANCRESSES > ANCRESS

AND *n* additional matter or problem

ANDANTE *adv* (piece to be played) moderately slowly ▷ *n* passage or piece to be performed moderately slowly

ANDANTES > ANDANTE

ANDANTINI > ANDANTINO

ANDANTINO *adv* slightly faster or slower than andante ▷ *n* passage or piece to be performed in this way

ANDESINE *n* feldspar mineral of the plagioclase series

ANDESINES > ANDESINE

ANDESITE *n* fine-grained tan or grey volcanic rock

ANDESITES > ANDESITE

ANDESITIC > ANDESITE

ANDESYTE *n* andesite

ANDESYTES > ANDESYTE

ANDIRON *n* iron stand for supporting logs in a fireplace

ANDIRONS > ANDIRON

ANDOUILLE *n* spicy smoked pork sausage with a blackish skin

ANDRADITE *n* yellow, green, or brownish-black garnet

ANDRO *n* type of sex hormone

ANDROECIA *n* stamens of flowering plants collectively

ANDROGEN *n* any of several steroids, produced as hormones by the testes or made synthetically, that promote development of male sexual organs and male secondary sexual characteristics

ANDROGENS > ANDROGEN

ANDROGYNE *n* person having both male and female sexual characteristics and genital tissues

ANDROGYNY *n* condition of having male and female characteristics

ANDROID *n* robot resembling a human ▷ *adj* resembling a human being

ANDROIDS > ANDROID

ANDROLOGY *n* branch of medicine concerned with diseases and conditions specific to men

ANDROMEDA *n* type of shrub

ANDROS > ANDRO

ANDS > AND

ANDVILE *old form of* > ANVIL

ANDVILES > ANDVILE

ANE *Scots word for* > ONE

ANEAR *adv* nearly ▷ *vb* approach

ANEARED > ANEAR

ANEARING > ANEAR

ANEARS > ANEAR

ANEATH *Scots word for* > BENEATH

ANECDOTA *n* unpublished writings

ANECDOTAL *adj* containing or consisting exclusively of anecdotes rather than connected discourse or research conducted under controlled conditions

ANECDOTE *n* short amusing account of an incident

ANECDOTES > ANECDOTE

ANECDOTIC > ANECDOTE

ANECDYSES > ANECDYSIS

ANECDYSIS *n* period between moults in arthropods

ANECHOIC *adj* having a low degree of reverberation of sound

ANELACE *same as* > ANLACE

ANELACES > ANELACE

ANELASTIC *adj* not elastic

ANELE *vb* anoint, esp to give extreme unction to

ANELED > ANELE

ANELES > ANELE

ANELING > ANELE

ANEMIA *n* anaemia

ANEMIAS > ANEMIA

ANEMIC *same as* > ANAEMIC

ANEMOGRAM *n* record produced by anemograph

ANEMOLOGY *n* study of winds

ANEMONE *n* plant with white, purple, or red flowers

ANEMONES > ANEMONE

ANEMOSES > ANEMOSIS

ANEMOSIS *n* cracking in timber caused by wind affecting growing tree

ANENST *dialect word for* > AGAINST

ANENT *prep* lying against

ANERGIA *n* anergy

ANERGIAS > ANERGIA

ANERGIC > ANERGY

a

ANERGIES > ANERGY

ANERGY n lack of energy

ANERLY Scots word for > ONLY

ANEROID adj not containing a liquid ▷ n barometer that does not contain liquid

ANEROIDS > ANEROID

ANES > ANE

ANESTRA > ANESTRUS

ANESTRI > ANESTRUS

ANESTROUS > ANESTRUS

ANESTRUM n anestrus

ANESTRUS same as > ANOESTRUS

ANETHOL n substance derived from oil of anise

ANETHOLE n white water-soluble crystalline substance with a liquorice-like odour

ANETHOLES > ANETHOLE

ANETHOLS > ANETHOL

ANETIC adj medically soothing

ANEUPLOID adj (of polyploid cells or organisms) having a chromosome number that is not an exact multiple of the haploid number ▷ n cell or individual of this type

ANEURIN a less common name for > THIAMINE

ANEURINS > ANEURIN

ANEURISM same as > ANEURYSM

ANEURISMS > ANEURISM

ANEURYSM n permanent swelling of a blood vessel

ANEURYSMS > ANEURYSM

ANEW adv once more

ANGA n a part in Indian music

ANGAKOK n Inuit shaman

ANGAKOKS > ANGAKOK

ANGARIA n species of shellfish

ANGARIAS > ANGARIA

ANGARIES > ANGARY

ANGARY n right of a belligerent state to use the property of a neutral state or to destroy it if necessary, subject to payment of full compensation to the owners

ANGAS > ANGA

ANGASHORE n miserable person given to complaining

ANGEKKOK n Inuit shaman

ANGEKKOKS > ANGEKKOK

ANGEKOK n Inuit shaman

ANGEKOKS > ANGEKOK

ANGEL n spiritual being believed to be an attendant or messenger of God ▷ vb provide financial support for

ANGELED > ANGEL

ANGELFISH n South American aquarium fish with large fins

ANGELHOOD n state of being an angel

ANGELIC adj very kind, pure, or beautiful

ANGELICA n aromatic plant

ANGELICAL same as > ANGELIC

ANGELICAS > ANGELICA

ANGELING > ANGEL

ANGELS > ANGEL

ANGELUS n series of prayers recited in the morning, at midday, and in the evening, commemorating the Annunciation and Incarnation

ANGELUSES > ANGELUS

ANGER n fierce displeasure or extreme annoyance ▷ vb make (someone) angry

ANGERED > ANGER

ANGERING > ANGER

ANGERLESS > ANGER

ANGERLY adv old form of angrily

ANGERS > ANGER

ANGICO n South American tree

ANGICOS > ANGICO

ANGINA n heart disorder causing sudden severe chest pains

ANGINAL > ANGINA

ANGINAS > ANGINA

ANGINOSE > ANGINA

ANGINOUS > ANGINA

ANGIOGRAM n X-ray picture obtained by angiography

ANGIOLOGY n branch of medical science concerned with the blood vessels and the lymphatic system

ANGIOMA n tumour consisting of a mass of blood vessels or lymphatic vessels

ANGIOMAS > ANGIOMA

ANGIOMATA > ANGIOMA

ANGKLUNG n Asian musical instrument

ANGKLUNGS > ANGKLUNG

ANGLE n space between or shape formed by two lines or surfaces that meet ▷ vb bend or place (something) at an angle

ANGLED > ANGLE

ANGLEDUG n earthworm

ANGLEDUGS > ANGLEDUG

ANGLEPOD n American wild flower

ANGLEPODS > ANGLEPOD

ANGLER n person who fishes with a hook and line

ANGLERS > ANGLER

ANGLES > ANGLE

ANGLESITE n white or grey secondary mineral

ANGLEWISE > ANGLE

ANGLEWORM n earthworm used as bait by anglers

ANGLICE adv in English

ANGLICISE same as > ANGLICIZE

ANGLICISM n word, phrase, or idiom peculiar to the English language, esp as spoken in England

ANGLICIST n expert in or student of English literature or language

ANGLICIZE vb make or become English in outlook, form, etc

ANGLIFIED > ANGLIFY

ANGLIFIES > ANGLIFY

ANGLIFY same as > ANGLICIZE

ANGLING n art or sport of fishing with a hook and line

ANGLINGS > ANGLING

ANGLIST same as > ANGLICIST

ANGLISTS > ANGLIST

ANGLO n White inhabitant of the US not of Latin extraction

ANGLOPHIL n person having admiration for England or the English

ANGLOS > ANGLO

ANGOLA same as > ANGORA

ANGOPHORA n Australian tree related to the eucalyptus

ANGORA n variety of goat, cat, or rabbit with long silky hair

ANGORAS > ANGORA

ANGOSTURA n bitter aromatic bark

ANGRIER > ANGRY

ANGRIES > ANGRY

ANGRIEST > ANGRY

ANGRILY > ANGRY

ANGRINESS > ANGRY

ANGRY adj full of anger ▷ n angry person

ANGST n feeling of anxiety

ANGSTIER > ANGSTY

ANGSTIEST > ANGSTY

ANGSTROM n unit of length used to measure wavelengths

ANGSTROMS > ANGSTROM

ANGSTS > ANGST

ANGSTY adj displaying or feeling angst, esp in a self-conscious manner

ANGUIFORM adj shaped like a snake

ANGUINE adj of, relating to, or similar to a snake

ANGUIPED adj having snakes for legs

ANGUIPEDE adj having snakes for legs

ANGUISH n great mental pain ▷ vb afflict or be afflicted with anguish

ANGUISHED adj feeling or showing great mental pain

ANGUISHES > ANGUISH

ANGULAR adj (of a person) lean and bony

ANGULARLY > ANGULAR

ANGULATE adj having angles or an angular shape ▷ vb make or become angular

ANGULATED > ANGULATE

ANGULATES > ANGULATE

ANGULOSE adj having angles

ANGULOUS adj having angles

ANHEDONIA n inability to feel pleasure

ANHEDONIC > ANHEDONIA

ANHEDRAL n downward inclination of an aircraft wing in relation to the lateral axis

ANHINGA n type of bird

ANHINGAS > ANHINGA

ANHUNGRED adj very hungry

ANHYDRASE n enzyme that catalyzes the removal of water

ANHYDRIDE n substance that combines with water to form an acid

ANHYDRITE n colourless or greyish-white mineral found in sedimentary rocks

ANHYDROUS adj containing no water

ANI n any of several gregarious tropical American birds of the genus Crotophaga: family Cuculidae (cuckoos). They have a black plumage, long square-tipped tail, and heavily hooked bill

ANICCA n (in Theravada Buddhism) the belief that all things, including the self, are impermanent and constantly changing: the first of the three basic characteristics of existence

ANICCAS > ANICCA

ANICONIC adj (of images of deities, symbols, etc) not portrayed in a human or animal form

ANICONISM > ANICONIC

ANICONIST > ANICONIC

ANICUT n dam in India

ANICUTS > ANICUT

ANIDROSES > ANIDROSIS

ANIDROSIS n absence of sweating

ANIGH adv near

ANIGHT adv at night

ANIL n West Indian shrub, from which indigo is obtained

ANILE adj of or like a feeble old woman

ANILIN n aniline

ANILINE n colourless oily liquid obtained from coal tar and used for making dyes, plastics, and explosives

ANILINES > ANILINE

ANILINGUS n sexual stimulation involving oral contact with the anus

ANILINS > ANILIN

ANILITIES > ANILE

ANILITY > ANILE

ANILS > ANIL

ANIMA n feminine principle as present in the male unconscious

ANIMACIES > ANIMACY

ANIMACY n state of being animate

ANIMAL n living creature with specialized sense organs and capable of voluntary motion, esp one other than a human being

▷ *adj* of animals

ANIMALIAN > ANIMAL

ANIMALIC > ANIMAL

ANIMALIER *n* painter or sculptor of animal subjects, esp a member of a group of early 19th-century French sculptors who specialized in realistic figures of animals, usually in bronze

ANIMALISE *same as* > ANIMALIZE

ANIMALISM *n* preoccupation with physical matters

ANIMALIST > ANIMALISM

ANIMALITY *n* animal instincts of human beings

ANIMALIZE *vb* make (a person) brutal or sensual

ANIMALLY *adv* physically

ANIMALS > ANIMAL

ANIMAS > ANIMA

ANIMATE *vb* give life to ▷ *adj* having life

ANIMATED *adj* interesting and lively

ANIMATELY > ANIMATE

ANIMATER *same as* > ANIMATOR

ANIMATERS > ANIMATER

ANIMATES > ANIMATE

ANIMATIC *n* animated film sequence

ANIMATICS > ANIMATIC

ANIMATING > ANIMATE

ANIMATION *n* technique of making cartoon films

ANIMATISM *n* belief that inanimate objects have consciousness

ANIMATIST > ANIMATISM

ANIMATO *adv* (to be performed) in a lively manner

ANIMATOR *n* person who makes animated cartoons

ANIMATORS > ANIMATOR

ANIME *n* type of Japanese animated film with themes and styles similar to manga comics

ANIMES > ANIME

ANIMI > ANIMUS

ANIMIS > ANIMI

ANIMISM *n* belief that natural objects possess souls

ANIMISMS > ANIMISM

ANIMIST > ANIMISM

ANIMISTIC > ANIMISM

ANIMISTS > ANIMISM

ANIMOSITY *n* hostility, hatred

ANIMUS *n* hatred, animosity

ANIMUSES > ANIMUS

ANION *n* ion with negative charge

ANIONIC > ANION

ANIONS > ANION

ANIS > ANI

ANISE *n* plant with liquorice-flavoured seeds

ANISEED *n* liquorice-flavoured seeds of the anise plant

ANISEEDS > ANISEED

ANISES > ANISE

ANISETTE *n* liquorice-flavoured liqueur made from aniseed

ANISETTES > ANISETTE

ANISIC > ANISE

ANISOGAMY *n* type of sexual reproduction in which the gametes are dissimilar, either in size alone or in size and form

ANISOLE *n* colourless pleasant-smelling liquid used as a solvent

ANISOLES > ANISOLE

ANKER *n* old liquid measure for wine

ANKERITE *n* greyish to brown mineral that resembles dolomite

ANKERITES > ANKERITE

ANKERS > ANKER

ANKH *n* T-shaped cross with a loop on the top, which symbolized eternal life in ancient Egypt

ANKHS > ANKH

ANKLE *n* joint between the foot and leg ▷ *vb* move

ANKLEBONE *the nontechnical name for* > TALUS

ANKLED > ANKLE

ANKLES > ANKLE

ANKLET *n* ornamental chain worn round the ankle

ANKLETS > ANKLET

ANKLING > ANKLE

ANKLONG *n* Asian musical instrument

ANKLONGS > ANKLONG

ANKLUNG *n* Asian musical instrument

ANKLUNGS > ANKLUNG

ANKUS *n* stick used, esp in India, for goading elephants

ANKUSES > ANKUS

ANKUSH *n* Indian weapon

ANKUSHES > ANKUSH

ANKYLOSE *vb* (of bones in a joint, etc) to fuse or stiffen by ankylosis

ANKYLOSED > ANKYLOSE

ANKYLOSES > ANKYLOSE

ANKYLOSIS *n* abnormal immobility of a joint, caused by a fibrous growth

ANKYLOTIC > ANKYLOSIS

ANLACE *n* medieval short dagger with a broad tapering blade

ANLACES > ANLACE

ANLAGE *n* organ or part in the earliest stage of development

ANLAGEN > ANLAGE

ANLAGES > ANLAGE

ANLAS *same as* > ANLACE

ANLASES > ANLAS

ANN *n* old Scots word for a widow's pension

ANNA *n* former Indian coin worth one sixteenth of a rupee

ANNAL *n* recorded events of one year

ANNALISE *vb* record in annals

ANNALISED > ANNALISE

ANNALISES > ANNALISE

ANNALIST > ANNAL

ANNALISTS > ANNAL

ANNALIZE *vb* record in annals

ANNALIZED > ANNALIZE

ANNALIZES > ANNALIZE

ANNALS > ANNAL

ANNAS > ANNA

ANNAT *n* singular of annates

ANNATES *pl n* first year's revenue of a see, an abbacy, or a minor benefice, paid to the pope

ANNATS > ANNAT

ANNATTA *n* annatto

ANNATTAS > ANNATTA

ANNATTO *n* small tropical American tree, *Bixa orellana*, having red or pinkish flowers and pulpy seeds that yield a dye

ANNATTOS > ANNATTO

ANNEAL *vb* toughen (metal or glass) by heating and slow cooling ▷ *n* act of annealing

ANNEALED > ANNEAL

ANNEALER > ANNEAL

ANNEALERS > ANNEAL

ANNEALING > ANNEAL

ANNEALS > ANNEAL

ANNECTENT *adj* connecting

ANNELID *n* worm with a segmented body, such as an earthworm ▷ *adj* of, relating to, or belonging to the *Annelida*

ANNELIDAN > ANNELID

ANNELIDS > ANNELID

ANNEX *vb* seize (territory)

ANNEXABLE > ANNEX

ANNEXE *n* extension to a building

ANNEXED > ANNEX

ANNEXES > ANNEXE

ANNEXING > ANNEX

ANNEXION *n* old form of annexation

ANNEXIONS > ANNEXION

ANNEXMENT > ANNEX

ANNEXURE *n* something that is added

ANNEXURES > ANNEXURE

ANNICUT *n* dam in India

ANNICUTS > ANNICUT

ANNO *adv* Latin for in the year

ANNONA *n* American tree or shrub

ANNONAS > ANNONA

ANNOTATE *vb* add notes to (a written work)

ANNOTATED > ANNOTATE

ANNOTATES > ANNOTATE

ANNOTATOR > ANNOTATE

ANNOUNCE *vb* make known publicly

ANNOUNCED > ANNOUNCE

ANNOUNCER *n* person who introduces radio or television programmes

ANNOUNCES > ANNOUNCE

ANNOY *vb* irritate or displease

ANNOYANCE *n* feeling of being annoyed

ANNOYED > ANNOY

ANNOYER > ANNOY

ANNOYERS > ANNOY

ANNOYING *adj* causing irritation or displeasure

ANNOYS > ANNOY

ANNS > ANN

ANNUAL *adj* happening once a year ▷ *n* plant that completes its life cycle in a year

ANNUALISE *same as* > ANNUALIZE

ANNUALIZE *vb* calculate (a rate) for or as if for a year

ANNUALLY > ANNUAL

ANNUALS > ANNUAL

ANNUITANT *n* person in receipt of or entitled to an annuity

ANNUITIES > ANNUITY

ANNUITY *n* fixed sum paid every year

ANNUL *vb* declare (something, esp a marriage) invalid

ANNULAR *adj* ring-shaped ▷ *n* ring finger

ANNULARLY > ANNULAR

ANNULARS > ANNULAR

ANNULATE *adj* having, composed of, or marked with rings ▷ *n* annelid

ANNULATED > ANNULATE

ANNULATES > ANNULATE

ANNULET *n* moulding in the form of a ring, as at the top of a column adjoining the capital

ANNULETS > ANNULET

ANNULI > ANNULUS

ANNULLED > ANNUL

ANNULLING > ANNUL

ANNULMENT *n* formal declaration that a contract or marriage is invalid

ANNULOSE *adj* (of earthworms, crustaceans, and similar animals) having a body formed of a series of rings

ANNULS > ANNUL

ANNULUS *n* area between two concentric circles

ANNULUSES > ANNULUS

ANOA *n* type of small cattle

ANOAS > ANOA

ANOBIID *n* any type of beetle

ANOBIIDS > ANOBIID

ANODAL > ANODE

ANODALLY > ANODE

ANODE *n* positive electrode in a battery, valve, etc

ANODES > ANODE

ANODIC > ANODE

ANODISE *same as* > ANODIZE

ANODISED > ANODISE

ANODISES > ANODISE

ANODISING > ANODISE

ANODIZE *vb* coat (metal) with a protective oxide film by electrolysis

ANODIZED > ANODIZE

ANODIZES > ANODIZE

a

ANODIZING > ANODIZE

ANODONTIA n congenital absence of teeth

ANODYNE n something that relieves pain or distress ▷ adj relieving pain or distress

ANODYNES > ANODYNE

ANODYNIC > ANODYNE

ANOESES > ANOESIS

ANOESIS n feeling without understanding

ANOESTRA > ANOESTRUS

ANOESTRI > ANOESTRUS

ANOESTRUM > ANOESTRUS

ANOESTRUS n period of sexual inactivity between two periods of oestrus in many mammals

ANOETIC > ANOESIS

ANOINT vb smear with oil as a sign of consecration

ANOINTED > ANOINT

ANOINTER > ANOINT

ANOINTERS > ANOINT

ANOINTING > ANOINT

ANOINTS > ANOINT

ANOLE n type of lizard

ANOLES > ANOLE

ANOLYTE n part of electrolyte around anode

ANOLYTES > ANOLYTE

ANOMALIES > ANOMALY

ANOMALOUS adj different from the normal or usual order or type

ANOMALY n something that deviates from the normal, irregularity

ANOMIC > ANOMIE

ANOMIE n lack of social or moral standards

ANOMIES > ANOMIE

ANOMY same as > ANOMIE

ANON adv in a short time, soon

ANONYM n anonymous person or publication

ANONYMA n promiscuous woman

ANONYMAS > ANONYMA

ANONYMISE same as > ANONYMIZE

ANONYMITY > ANONYMOUS

ANONYMIZE vb organize in a way that preserves anonymity

ANONYMOUS adj by someone whose name is unknown or withheld

ANONYMS > ANONYM

ANOOPSIA n squint in which the eye turns upwards

ANOOPSIAS > ANOOPSIA

ANOPHELES n any of various mosquitoes constituting the genus *Anopheles*, some species of which transmit the malaria parasite to man

ANOPIA n inability to see

ANOPIAS > ANOPIA

ANOPSIA n squint in which the eye turns upwards

ANOPSIAS > ANOPSIA

ANORAK n light waterproof hooded jacket

ANORAKS > ANORAK

ANORECTAL adj of the anus and rectum

ANORECTIC > ANOREXIA

ANORETIC n anorectic

ANORETICS > ANORETIC

ANOREXIA n psychological disorder characterized by fear of becoming fat and refusal to eat

ANOREXIAS > ANOREXIA

ANOREXIC > ANOREXIA

ANOREXICS > ANOREXIA

ANOREXIES > ANOREXY

ANOREXY old name for > ANOREXIA

ANORTHIC another word for > TRICLINIC

ANORTHITE n white to greyish-white or reddish-white mineral

ANOSMATIC > ANOSMIA

ANOSMIA n loss of the sense of smell, usually as the result of a lesion of the olfactory nerve, disease in another organ or part, or obstruction of the nasal passages

ANOSMIAS > ANOSMIA

ANOSMIC > ANOSMIA

ANOTHER adj one more

ANOUGH adj enough

ANOUROUS adj having no tail

ANOVULANT n drug preventing ovulation

ANOVULAR adj without ovulation

ANOW adj old form of enough

ANOXAEMIA n deficiency in the amount of oxygen in the arterial blood

ANOXAEMIC > ANOXAEMIA

ANOXEMIA same as > ANOXAEMIA

ANOXEMIAS > ANOXEMIA

ANOXEMIC > ANOXEMIA

ANOXIA n lack or absence of oxygen

ANOXIAS > ANOXIA

ANOXIC > ANOXIA

ANSA n either end of Saturn's rings

ANSAE > ANSA

ANSATE adj having a handle or handle-like part

ANSATED adj ansate

ANSERINE adj of or resembling a goose ▷ n chemical compound

ANSERINES > ANSERINE

ANSEROUS same as > ANSERINE

ANSWER n reply to a question, request, letter, etc ▷ vb give an answer (to)

ANSWERED > ANSWER

ANSWERER > ANSWER

ANSWERERS > ANSWER

ANSWERING > ANSWER

ANSWERS > ANSWER

ANT n small insect living in highly-organized colonies

ANTA n pilaster attached to the end of a side wall or sometimes to the side of a doorway

ANTACID n substance that counteracts acidity, esp in the stomach ▷ adj having the properties of this substance

ANTACIDS > ANTACID

ANTAE > ANTA

ANTALGIC n pain-relieving drug

ANTALGICS > ANTALGIC

ANTALKALI n substance that neutralizes alkalis

ANTAR old word for > CAVE

ANTARA n South American panpipes

ANTARAS > ANTARA

ANTARCTIC adj relating to Antarctica

ANTARS > ANTAR

ANTAS > ANTA

ANTBEAR n aardvark

ANTBEARS > ANTBEAR

ANTBIRD n any of various dull-coloured South American passerine birds that typically feed on ants

ANTBIRDS > ANTBIRD

ANTE n player's stake in poker ▷ vb place (one's stake) in poker

ANTEATER n mammal which feeds on ants by means of a long snout

ANTEATERS > ANTEATER

ANTECEDE vb go before, as in time, order, etc

ANTECEDED > ANTECEDE

ANTECEDES > ANTECEDE

ANTECHOIR n part of a church in front of the choir, usually enclosed by screens, tombs, etc

ANTED > ANTE

ANTEDATE vb precede in time ▷ n earlier date

ANTEDATED > ANTEDATE

ANTEDATES > ANTEDATE

ANTEED > ANTE

ANTEFIX n carved ornament at the eaves of a roof to hide the joint between the tiles

ANTEFIXA > ANTEFIX

ANTEFIXAE > ANTEFIX

ANTEFIXAL > ANTEFIX

ANTEFIXES > ANTEFIX

ANTEING > ANTE

ANTELOPE n deerlike mammal with long legs and horns

ANTELOPES > ANTELOPE

ANTELUCAN adj before daylight

ANTENATAL adj during pregnancy, before birth ▷ n examination during pregnancy

ANTENATI n people born before certain date

ANTENNA n insect's feeler

ANTENNAE > ANTENNA

ANTENNAL > ANTENNA

ANTENNARY > ANTENNA

ANTENNAS > ANTENNA

ANTENNULE n one of a pair of small mobile appendages on the heads of crustaceans in front of the antennae, usually having a sensory function

ANTEPAST n appetizer

ANTEPASTS > ANTEPAST

ANTERIOR adj the front

ANTEROOM n small room leading into a larger one, often used as a waiting room

ANTEROOMS > ANTEROOM

ANTES > ANTE

ANTETYPE n earlier form

ANTETYPES > ANTETYPE

ANTEVERT vb displace (an organ or part) by tilting it forward

ANTEVERTS > ANTEVERT

ANTHELIA > ANTHELION

ANTHELION n faint halo sometimes seen in polar or high altitude regions around the shadow of an object cast onto a thick cloud bank or fog

ANTHELIX n prominent curved fold of cartilage just inside the outer rim of the external ear

ANTHEM n song of loyalty, esp to a country ▷ vb provide with an anthem

ANTHEMED > ANTHEM

ANTHEMIA > ANTHEMION

ANTHEMIC > ANTHEM

ANTHEMING > ANTHEM

ANTHEMION n floral design, used esp in ancient Greek and Roman architecture and decoration, usually consisting of honeysuckle, lotus, or palmette leaf motifs

ANTHEMS > ANTHEM

ANTHER n part of a flower's stamen containing pollen

ANTHERAL > ANTHER

ANTHERID n antheridium

ANTHERIDS > ANTHERID

ANTHERS > ANTHER

ANTHESES > ANTHESIS

ANTHESIS n time when a flower becomes sexually functional

ANTHILL n mound of soil, leaves, etc, near the entrance of an ants' nest, carried and deposited there by the ants while constructing the nest

ANTHILLS > ANTHILL

ANTHOCARP n fruit developing from many flowers

ANTHOCYAN n any of a class of water-soluble glycosidic pigments

ANTHODIA > ANTHODIUM

ANTHODIUM another name for > CAPITULUM

ANTHOID adj resembling a flower

ANTHOLOGY n collection of poems or other literary pieces by various authors

ANTHOTAXY n arrangement

of flowers on a stem or parts on a flower

ANTHOZOAN *n* any of the solitary or colonial sessile marine coelenterates of the class *Anthozoa*, including the corals, sea anemones, and sea pens, in which the body is in the form of a polyp ▷ *adj* of or relating to the class *Anthozoa*

ANTHOZOIC > ANTHOZOAN

ANTHRACES > ANTHRAX

ANTHRACIC *adj* of anthrax

ANTHRAX *n* dangerous disease of cattle and sheep, communicable to humans

ANTHRAXES > ANTHRAX

ANTHROPIC *adj* of or relating to human beings

ANTHURIUM *n* any of various tropical American aroid plants constituting the genus *Anthurium*, many of which are cultivated as house plants for their showy foliage and their flowers, which are borne in a long-stalked spike surrounded by a flaring heart-shaped white or red bract

ANTI *adj* opposed (to) ▷ *n* opponent of a party, policy, or attitude

ANTIABUSE *adj* designed to prevent abuse

ANTIACNE *adj* inhibiting the development of acne

ANTIAGING *adj* resisting the effects of ageing

ANTIAIR *adj* countering attack by aircraft or missile

ANTIALIEN *adj* designed to prevent foreign animal or plant species from becoming established

ANTIAR *another name for* > UPAS

ANTIARIN *n* poison derived from antiar

ANTIARINS > ANTIARIN

ANTIARMOR *adj* designed or equipped to combat armoured vehicles

ANTIARS > ANTIAR

ANTIATOM *n* atom composed of antiparticles, in which the nucleus contains antiprotons with orbiting positrons

ANTIATOMS > ANTIATOM

ANTIAUXIN *n* substance acting against auxin

ANTIBIAS *adj* countering bias

ANTIBLACK *adj* hostile to black people

ANTIBODY *n* protein produced in the blood, which destroys bacteria

ANTIBOSS *adj* acting against bosses

ANTIBUG *adj* acting against computer bugs

ANTIBUSER *n* person who

opposes the policy of transporting students to faraway schools to achieve racial balance

ANTIC *n* actor in a ludicrous or grotesque part ▷ *adj* fantastic

ANTICAL *adj* (of the position of plant parts) in front of or above another part

ANTICALLY > ANTICAL

ANTICAR *n* opposed to cars

ANTICHLOR *n* substance used to remove chlorine from a material after bleaching or to neutralize the chlorine present

ANTICISE *same as* > ANTICIZE

ANTICISED > ANTICISE

ANTICISES > ANTICISE

ANTICITY *adj* opposed to cities

ANTICIVIC *adj* opposed to citizenship

ANTICIZE *vb* play absurdly

ANTICIZED > ANTICIZE

ANTICIZES > ANTICIZE

ANTICK *vb* perform antics

ANTICKE *adj* old form of antique

ANTICKED > ANTICK

ANTICKING > ANTICK

ANTICKS > ANTICK

ANTICLINE *n* fold of rock raised up into a broad arch so that the strata slope down on both sides

ANTICLING *adj* acting against clinging

ANTICLY *adv* grotesquely

ANTICODON *n* element of RNA

ANTICOLD *adj* preventing or fighting the common cold

ANTICOUS *adj* on the part of a flower furthest from the stem

ANTICRACK *adj* protecting a computer against unauthorized access

ANTICRIME *adj* preventing or fighting crime

ANTICS *pl n* absurd acts or postures

ANTICULT *n* organisation that is opposed to religious cults

ANTICULTS > ANTICULT

ANTIDORA *n* bread used in Russian Orthodox Communion

ANTIDOTAL > ANTIDOTE

ANTIDOTE *n* substance that counteracts a poison ▷ *vb* counteract with an antidote

ANTIDOTED > ANTIDOTE

ANTIDOTES > ANTIDOTE

ANTIDRAFT *adj* opposed to conscription

ANTIDRUG *adj* intended to discourage illegal drug use

ANTIDUNE *n* sand hill or inclined bedding plane that forms a steep slope against the direction of a fast-

flowing current

ANTIDUNES > ANTIDUNE

ANTIELITE *adj* opposed to elitism

ANTIENT *old spelling of* > ANCIENT

ANTIENTS > ANTIENT

ANTIFAT *adj* acting to remove or prevent fat

ANTIFLU *adj* acting against influenza

ANTIFOAM *adj* allowing gas to escape rather than form foam

ANTIFOG *adj* preventing the buildup of moisture on a surface

ANTIFRAUD *adj* acting against fraud

ANTIFUR *adj* opposed to the wearing of fur garments

ANTIGANG *adj* designed to restrict the activities of criminal gangs

ANTIGAY *adj* hostile to homosexuals

ANTIGEN *n* substance causing the blood to produce antibodies

ANTIGENE *n* antigen

ANTIGENES > ANTIGENE

ANTIGENIC > ANTIGEN

ANTIGENS > ANTIGEN

ANTIGLARE *adj* cutting down glare

ANTIGRAFT *adj* designed to reduce corruption

ANTIGUN *adj* opposed to the possession of guns

ANTIHELIX *same as* > ANTHELIX

ANTIHERO *n* central character in a book, film, etc, who lacks the traditional heroic virtues

ANTIHUMAN *adj* inhuman

ANTIJAM *adj* preventing jamming

ANTIKING *n* rival to an established king

ANTIKINGS > ANTIKING

ANTIKNOCK *n* substance added to motor fuel to reduce knocking in the engine caused by too rapid combustion

ANTILABOR *adj* opposed to labor interests

ANTILEAK *adj* preventing leaks

ANTILEFT *adj* opposed to the left wing in politics

ANTILIFE *adj* in favour of abortion

ANTILIFER *n* person in favour of abortion

ANTILOCK *adj* designed to prevent overbraking

ANTILOG *n* number whose logarithm to a given base is a given number

ANTILOGS > ANTILOG

ANTILOGY *n* contradiction in terms

ANTIMACHO *adj* opposed to macho attitudes

ANTIMALE *adj* opposed to

men

ANTIMAN *adj* opposed to men

ANTIMASK *n* interlude in a masque

ANTIMASKS > ANTIMASK

ANTIMERE *n* part or organ of a bilaterally or radially symmetrical organism that corresponds to a similar structure on the other side of the axis, such as the right or left limb of a four-legged animal

ANTIMERES > ANTIMERE

ANTIMERIC > ANTIMERE

ANTIMINE *adj* designed to counteract landmines

ANTIMONIC *adj* of or containing antimony in the pentavalent state

ANTIMONY *n* brittle silvery-white metallic element

ANTIMONYL *n* of, consisting of, or containing the monovalent group SbO-

ANTIMUON *n* antiparticle of a muon

ANTIMUONS > ANTIMUON

ANTIMUSIC *n* music intended to overthrow traditional conventions and expectations

ANTIMYCIN *n* antibiotic drug

ANTING *n* placing or rubbing of ants by birds on their feathers. The body fluids of the ants are thought to repel parasites

ANTINGS > ANTING

ANTINODAL > ANTINODE

ANTINODE *n* point at which the amplitude of one of the two kinds of displacement in a standing wave has maximum value. Generally the other kind of displacement has its minimum value at this point

ANTINODES > ANTINODE

ANTINOISE *n* sound generated so that it is out of phase with a noise, such as that made by an engine, in order to reduce the noise level by interference

ANTINOME *n* opposite

ANTINOMES > ANTINOME

ANTINOMIC > ANTINOMY

ANTINOMY *n* contradiction between two laws or principles that are reasonable in themselves

ANTINOVEL *n* type of prose fiction in which conventional elements of the novel are rejected

ANTINUKE *same as* > ANTINUKER

ANTINUKER *n* person who is opposed to nuclear weapons or energy

ANTINUKES > ANTINUKE

ANTIPAPAL *adj* opposed to the pope

ANTIPARTY *adj* opposed to a political party

ANTIPASTI > ANTIPASTO

ANTIPASTO *n* appetizer in an Italian meal

ANTIPATHY *n* dislike, hostility

ANTIPHON *n* hymn sung in alternate parts by two groups of singers

ANTIPHONS > ANTIPHON

ANTIPHONY *n* antiphonal singing of a musical composition by two choirs

ANTIPILL *adj* opposed to the use of the contraceptive pill

ANTIPODAL *adj* of or relating to diametrically opposite points on the earth's surface

ANTIPODE *n* exact or direct opposite

ANTIPODES *pl n* any two places diametrically opposite one another on the earth's surface

ANTIPOLAR > ANTIPOLE

ANTIPOLE *n* opposite pole

ANTIPOLES > ANTIPOLE

ANTIPOPE *n* pope set up in opposition to the one chosen by church laws

ANTIPOPES > ANTIPOPE

ANTIPORN *adj* opposed to pornography

ANTIPOT *adj* opposed to illegal use of marijuana

ANTIPRESS *adj* hostile to the news media

ANTIPYIC *n* drug acting against suppuration

ANTIPYICS > ANTIPYIC

ANTIQUARK *n* antiparticle of a quark

ANTIQUARY *n* student or collector of antiques or ancient works of art

ANTIQUATE *vb* make obsolete or old-fashioned

ANTIQUE *n* object of an earlier period, valued for its beauty, workmanship, or age ▷ *adj* made in an earlier period ▷ *vb* give an antique appearance to

ANTIQUED > ANTIQUE

ANTIQUELY > ANTIQUE

ANTIQUER *n* collector of antiques

ANTIQUERS > ANTIQUE

ANTIQUES > ANTIQUE

ANTIQUEY *adj* having the appearance of an antique

ANTIQUING > ANTIQUE

ANTIQUITY *n* great age

ANTIRADAR *adj* preventing detection by radar

ANTIRAPE *adj* protecting against rape

ANTIRED *adj* of a particular colour of antiquark

ANTIRIOT *adj* (of police officers, equipment, measures, etc) designed for or engaged in the control of crowds

ANTIROCK *adj* designed to prevent a vehicle from rocking

ANTIROLL *adj* designed to prevent a vehicle from tilting

ANTIROYAL *adj* opposed to the monarchy

ANTIRUST *adj* (of a product or procedure) effective against rust ▷ *n* substance or device that prevents rust

ANTIRUSTS > ANTIRUST

ANTIS > ANTI

ANTISAG *adj* preventing sagging

ANTISCIAN *n* person living on other side of equator

ANTISENSE *adj* acting in opposite way to RNA

ANTISERA > ANTISERUM

ANTISERUM *n* blood serum containing antibodies used to treat or provide immunity to a disease

ANTISEX *adj* opposed to sexual activity

ANTISHARK *adj* protecting against sharks

ANTISHIP *adj* designed for attacking ships

ANTISHOCK *n* one of a pair of walking poles designed to reduce stress on the knees

ANTISKID *adj* intended to prevent skidding

ANTISLEEP *adj* acting to prevent sleep

ANTISLIP *adj* acting to prevent slipping

ANTISMOG *adj* reducing smog

ANTISMOKE *adj* preventing smoke

ANTISMUT *adj* opposed to obscene material

ANTISNOB *n* person opposed to snobbery

ANTISNOBS > ANTISNOB

ANTISOLAR *adj* opposite to the sun

ANTISPAM *adj* intended to prevent spam

ANTISPAST *n* group of four syllables in poetic metre

ANTISTAT *n* substance preventing static electricity

ANTISTATE *adj* opposed to state authority

ANTISTATS > ANTISTAT

ANTISTICK *adj* preventing things from sticking to a surface

ANTISTORY *n* story without a plot

ANTISTYLE *n* style that rejects traditional aesthetics

ANTITANK *adj* (of weapons) designed to destroy military tanks

ANTITAX *adj* opposed to taxation

ANTITHEFT *adj* (of a device, campaign, system, etc) designed to prevent theft

ANTITHET *n* example of antithesis

ANTITHETS > ANTITHET

ANTITOXIC > ANTITOXIN

ANTITOXIN *n* (serum containing) an antibody that acts against a toxin

ANTITRADE *n* wind blowing in the opposite direction to a trade wind

ANTITRAGI *n* cartilaginous projections of the external ear opposite the tragus

ANTITRUST *adj* (of laws) opposing business monopolies ▷ *n* regulating or opposing trusts, monopolies, cartels, or similar organizations, esp in order to prevent unfair competition

ANTITUMOR *adj* acting against tumours

ANTITYPAL > ANTITYPE

ANTITYPE *n* person or thing that is foreshadowed or represented by a type or symbol, esp a character or event in the New Testament prefigured in the Old Testament

ANTITYPES > ANTITYPE

ANTITYPIC > ANTITYPE

ANTIULCER *adj* used to treat ulcers

ANTIUNION *adj* opposed to union

ANTIURBAN *adj* opposed to city life

ANTIVENIN *n* antitoxin that counteracts a specific venom, esp snake venom

ANTIVENOM *n* venom antidote

ANTIVIRAL *adj* inhibiting the growth of viruses ▷ *n* any antiviral drug: used to treat diseases caused by viruses, such as herpes infections and AIDS

ANTIVIRUS *adj* relating to software designed to protect computer files from viruses ▷ *n* such a piece of software

ANTIWAR *adj* opposed to war

ANTIWEAR *adj* preventing wear

ANTIWEED *adj* killing or preventing weeds

ANTIWHITE *adj* hostile to white people

ANTIWOMAN *adj* hostile to women

ANTIWORLD *n* hypothetical or supposed world or universe composed of antimatter

ANTLER *n* branched horn of a male deer

ANTLERED *adj* having antlers

ANTLERS > ANTLER

ANTLIA *n* butterfly proboscis

ANTLIAE > ANTLIA

ANTLIATE *adj* relating to antlia

ANTLIKE *adj* of or like an ant or ants

ANTLION *n* any of various neuropterous insects of the family *Myrmeleontidae*, which typically resemble dragonflies and are most common in tropical regions

ANTLIONS > ANTLION

ANTONYM *n* word that means the opposite of another

ANTONYMIC > ANTONYM

ANTONYMS > ANTONYM

ANTONYMY *n* use of antonyms

ANTRA > ANTRUM

ANTRAL > ANTRUM

ANTRE *n* cavern or cave

ANTRES > ANTRE

ANTRORSE *adj* directed or pointing upwards or forwards

ANTRUM *n* natural cavity, esp in a bone

ANTRUMS > ANTRUM

ANTS > ANT

ANTSIER > ANTSY

ANTSIEST > ANTSY

ANTSINESS > ANTSY

ANTSY *adj* restless, nervous, and impatient

ANTWACKIE *adj* old-fashioned

ANUCLEATE *adj* without a nucleus

ANURAL *adj* without a tail

ANURAN *n* any of the vertebrates of the order *Anura* (or *Salientia*), characterized by absence of a tail and very long hind legs specialized for hopping: class *Amphibia* (amphibians). The group includes the frogs and toads ▷ *adj* of, relating to, or belonging to the order *Anura*

ANURANS > ANURAN

ANURESES > ANURESIS

ANURESIS *n* inability to urinate even though urine is formed by the kidneys and retained in the urinary bladder

ANURETIC > ANURESIS

ANURIA *n* complete suppression of urine formation, often as the result of a kidney disorder

ANURIAS > ANURIA

ANURIC > ANURIA

ANUROUS *adj* lacking a tail

ANUS *n* opening at the end of the alimentary canal, through which faeces are discharged

ANUSES > ANUS

ANVIL *n* heavy iron block on which metals are hammered into particular shapes ▷ *vb* forge on an anvil

ANVILED > ANVIL

ANVILING > ANVIL

ANVILLED > ANVIL

ANVILLING > ANVIL

ANVILS > ANVIL

ANVILTOP n type of stormcloud formation

ANVILTOPS > ANVILTOP

ANXIETIES > ANXIETY

ANXIETY n state of being anxious

ANXIOUS adj worried and tense

ANXIOUSLY > ANXIOUS

ANY adj one or some, no matter which ▷ adv at all

ANYBODIES > ANYBODY

ANYBODY n any person at random

ANYHOW adv anyway

ANYMORE adv at present

ANYON n (in mathematics) projective representation of a Lie group

ANYONE pron any person ▷ n any person at random

ANYONES > ANYONE

ANYONS > ANYON

ANYPLACE adv in, at, or to any unspecified place

ANYROAD a northern English dialect word for > ANYWAY

ANYTHING pron any object, event, or action whatever ▷ n any thing at random

ANYTHINGS > ANYTHING

ANYTIME adv at any time

ANYWAY adv at any rate, nevertheless

ANYWAYS nonstandard word for > ANYWAY

ANYWHEN adv at any time

ANYWHERE adv in, at, or to any place

ANYWHERES nonstandard word for > ANYWHERE

ANYWISE adv in any way or manner

ANZIANI n Italian word for councillors

AORIST n tense of the verb in classical Greek and in certain other inflected languages, indicating past action without reference to whether the action involved was momentary or continuous

AORISTIC > AORIST

AORISTS > AORIST

AORTA n main artery of the body, carrying oxygen-rich blood from the heart

AORTAE > AORTA

AORTAL > AORTA

AORTAS > AORTA

AORTIC > AORTA

AORTITIS n inflammation of the aorta

AOUDAD n wild mountain sheep, Ammotragus lervia, of N Africa, having horns curved in a semicircle and long hair covering the neck and forelegs

AOUDADS > AOUDAD

APACE adv swiftly

APACHE n Parisian gangster or ruffian

APACHES > APACHE

APADANA n ancient Persian palace hall

APADANAS > APADANA

APAGE interj Greek word meaning go away

APAGOGE n reduction to absurdity

APAGOGES > APAGOGE

APAGOGIC > APAGOGE

APAID > APAY

APANAGE same as > APPANAGE

APANAGED adj having apanage

APANAGES > APANAGE

APAREJO n kind of packsaddle made of stuffed leather cushions

APAREJOS > APAREJO

APART adv to pieces or in pieces

APARTHEID n former official government policy of racial segregation in S Africa

APARTMENT n room in a building

APARTNESS > APART

APATETIC adj of or relating to coloration that disguises and protects an animal

APATHATON old word for > EPITHET

APATHETIC adj having or showing little or no emotion

APATHIES > APATHY

APATHY n lack of interest or enthusiasm

APATITE n pale green to purple mineral, found in igneous rocks

APATITES > APATITE

APATOSAUR n long-necked dinosaur

APAY vb old word meaning satisfy

APAYD > APAY

APAYING > APAY

APAYS > APAY

APE n tailless monkey such as the chimpanzee or gorilla ▷ vb imitate

APEAK adj in a vertical or almost vertical position

APED > APE

APEDOM n state of being an ape

APEDOMS > APEDOM

APEEK adv nautical word meaning vertically

APEHOOD n state of being ape

APEHOODS > APEHOOD

APELIKE > APE

APEMAN n extinct primate thought to have been the forerunner of true humans

APEMEN > APEMAN

APEPSIA n digestive disorder

APEPSIAS > APEPSIA

APEPSIES > APEPSY

APEPSY n apepsia

APER n person who apes

APERCU n outline

APERCUS > APERCU

APERIENT adj having a mild laxative effect ▷ n mild laxative

APERIENTS > APERIENT

APERIES > APERY

APERIODIC adj not periodic

APERITIF n alcoholic drink taken before a meal

APERITIFS > APERITIF

APERITIVE n laxative

APERS > APER

APERT adj open

APERTNESS > APERT

APERTURAL > APERTURE

APERTURE n opening or hole

APERTURED adj having an aperture

APERTURES > APERTURE

APERY n imitative behaviour

APES > APE

APETALIES > APETALOUS

APETALOUS adj (of flowering plants) having no petals

APETALY > APETALOUS

APEX n highest point

APEXES > APEX

APGAR as in apgar score system for determining the condition of an infant at birth

APHAGIA n refusal or inability to swallow

APHAGIAS > APHAGIA

APHAKIA n absence of the lens of an eye, congenital or otherwise

APHAKIAS > APHAKIA

APHANITE n any fine-grained rock, such as a basalt, containing minerals that cannot be distinguished with the naked eye

APHANITES > APHANITE

APHANITIC > APHANITE

APHASIA n disorder of the central nervous system that affects the ability to speak and understand words

APHASIAC > APHASIA

APHASIACS > APHASIA

APHASIAS > APHASIA

APHASIC > APHASIA

APHASICS > APHASIA

APHELIA > APHELION

APHELIAN > APHELION

APHELION n point of a planet's orbit that is farthest from the sun

APHELIONS > APHELION

APHERESES > APHERESIS

APHERESIS n omission of a letter or syllable at the beginning of a word

APHERETIC > APHERESIS

APHESES > APHESIS

APHESIS n gradual disappearance of an unstressed vowel at the beginning of a word, as in squire from esquire

APHETIC > APHESIS

APHETISE vb lose a vowel at the beginning of a word

APHETISED > APHETISE

APHETISES > APHETISE

APHETIZE vb lose a vowel at the beginning of a word

APHETIZED > APHETIZE

APHETIZES > APHETIZE

APHICIDE n substance for killing aphids

APHICIDES > APHICIDE

APHID n small insect which sucks the sap from plants

APHIDES > APHIS

APHIDIAN > APHID

APHIDIANS > APHID

APHIDIOUS > APHID

APHIDS > APHID

APHIS n any of various aphids constituting the genus Aphis, such as the blackfly

APHOLATE n type of pesticide

APHOLATES > APHOLATE

APHONIA n loss of the voice caused by damage to the vocal tract

APHONIAS > APHONIA

APHONIC adj affected with aphonia ▷ n person affected with aphonia

APHONICS > APHONIC

APHONIES > APHONY

APHONOUS > APHONIA

APHONY same as > APHONIA

APHORISE same as > APHORIZE

APHORISED > APHORISE

APHORISER > APHORISE

APHORISES > APHORISE

APHORISM n short clever saying expressing a general truth

APHORISMS > APHORISM

APHORIST > APHORISM

APHORISTS > APHORISM

APHORIZE vb write or speak in aphorisms

APHORIZED > APHORIZE

APHORIZER > APHORIZE

APHORIZES > APHORIZE

APHOTIC adj characterized by or growing in the absence of light

APHRODITE n North American butterfly

APHTHA n small ulceration on a mucous membrane, as in thrush, caused by a fungal infection

APHTHAE > APHTHA

APHTHOUS > APHTHA

APHYLLIES > APHYLLOUS

APHYLLOUS adj (of plants) having no leaves

APHYLLY > APHYLLOUS

APIACEOUS adj parsley-like

APIAN adj of, relating to, or resembling bees

APIARIAN adj of or relating to the breeding and care of bees ▷ n apiarist

APIARIANS > APIARIAN

APIARIES > APIARY

APIARIST n beekeeper

APIARISTS > APIARIST

APIARY n place where bees

are kept

APICAL adj of, at, or being an apex ▷ n sound made with the tip of the tongue

APICALLY > APICAL

APICALS > APICAL

APICES plural of > APEX

APICIAN adj of fine or dainty food

APICULATE adj (of leaves) ending in a short sharp point

APICULI > APICULUS

APICULUS n short sharp point

APIECE adv each

APIMANIA n extreme enthusiasm for bees

APIMANIAS > APIMANIA

APING > APE

APIOL n substance formerly used to assist menstruation

APIOLOGY n study of bees

APIOLS > APIOL

APISH adj stupid or foolish

APISHLY > APISH

APISHNESS > APISH

APISM n behaviour like an ape

APISMS > APISM

APIVOROUS adj eating bees

APLANAT n aplanatic lens

APLANATIC adj (of a lens or mirror) free from spherical aberration

APLANATS > APLANAT

APLANETIC adj (esp of some algal and fungal spores) nonmotile or lacking a motile stage

APLASIA n congenital absence or abnormal development of an organ or part

APLASIAS > APLASIA

APLASTIC adj relating to or characterized by aplasia

APLENTY adv in plenty

APLITE n light-coloured fine-grained acid igneous rock with a sugary texture, consisting of quartz and feldspars

APLITES > APLITE

APLITIC > APLITE

APLOMB n calm self-possession

APLOMBS > APLOMB

APLUSTRE n stern ornament on an ancient Greek ship

APLUSTRES > APLUSTRE

APNEA same as > APNOEA

APNEAL > APNEA

APNEAS > APNEA

APNEIC > APNEA

APNEUSES > APNEUSIS

APNEUSIS n protracted gasping inhalation followed by short inefficient exhalation, which can cause asphyxia

APNEUSTIC adj of or relating to apneusis

APNOEA n temporary inability to breathe

APNOEAL > APNOEA

APNOEAS > APNOEA

APNOEIC > APNOEA

APO n type of protein

APOAPSES > APOAPSIS

APOAPSIS n point in an orbit furthest from the object orbited

APOCARP n apocarpous gynoecium or fruit

APOCARPS > APOCARP

APOCARPY n presence of many carpels

APOCOPATE vb omit the final sound or sounds of (a word)

APOCOPE n omission of the final sound or sounds of a word

APOCOPES > APOCOPE

APOCOPIC > APOCOPE

APOCRINE adj denoting a type of glandular secretion in which part of the secreting cell is lost with the secretion, as in mammary glands

APOCRYPHA n writings or statements of uncertain authority

APOD n animal without feet

APODAL adj (of snakes, eels, etc) without feet

APODE n animal without feet

APODES > APODE

APODICTIC adj unquestionably true by virtue of demonstration

APODOSES > APODOSIS

APODOSIS n consequent of a conditional statement, as the game will be cancelled in if it rains the game will be cancelled

APODOUS same as > APODAL

APODS > APOD

APOENZYME n protein component that together with a coenzyme forms an enzyme

APOGAEIC > APOGEE

APOGAMIC > APOGAMY

APOGAMIES > APOGAMY

APOGAMOUS > APOGAMY

APOGAMY n type of reproduction, occurring in some ferns, in which the sporophyte develops from the gametophyte without fusion of gametes

APOGEAL > APOGEE

APOGEAN > APOGEE

APOGEE n point of the moon's or a satellite's orbit that is farthest from the earth

APOGEES > APOGEE

APOGEIC > APOGEE

APOGRAPH n exact copy

APOGRAPHS > APOGRAPH

APOLLO n strikingly handsome youth

APOLLOS > APOLLO

APOLOG same as > APOLOGUE

APOLOGAL > APOLOGUE

APOLOGIA n formal written defence of a cause

APOLOGIAE > APOLOGIA

APOLOGIAS > APOLOGIA

APOLOGIES > APOLOGY

APOLOGISE same as > APOLOGIZE

APOLOGIST n person who formally defends a cause

APOLOGIZE vb make an apology

APOLOGS > APOLOG

APOLOGUE n allegory or moral fable

APOLOGUES > APOLOGUE

APOLOGY n expression of regret for wrongdoing

APOLUNE n point in a lunar orbit when a spacecraft is at its greatest distance from the moon

APOLUNES > APOLUNE

APOMICT n organism, esp a plant, produced by apomixis

APOMICTIC > APOMIXIS

APOMICTS > APOMICT

APOMIXES > APOMIXIS

APOMIXIS n (esp in plants) any of several types of asexual reproduction, such as parthenogenesis and apogamy, in which fertilization does not take place

APOOP adv on the poop deck

APOPHASES > APOPHASIS

APOPHASIS n device of mentioning a subject by stating that it will not be mentioned

APOPHATIC adj of theology that says God is indescribable

APOPHONY n change in the quality of vowels

APOPHYGE n outward curve at each end of the shaft of a column, adjoining the base or capital

APOPHYGES > APOPHYGE

APOPHYSES > APOPHYSIS

APOPHYSIS n process, outgrowth, or swelling from part of an animal or plant

APOPLAST n nonprotoplasmic component of a plant, including the cell walls and intercellular material

APOPLASTS > APOPLAST

APOPLEX vb afflict with apoplexy

APOPLEXED > APOPLEX

APOPLEXES > APOPLEX

APOPLEXY n stroke

APOPTOSES > APOPTOSIS

APOPTOSIS n programmed death of some of an organism's cells as part of its natural growth and development

APOPTOTIC > APOPTOSIS

APORETIC > APORIA

APORIA n doubt, real or professed, about what to do or say

APORIAS > APORIA

APORT adj on or towards the port side

APOS > APO

APOSITIA n unwillingness to eat

APOSITIAS > APOSITIA

APOSITIC > APOSITIA

APOSPORIC > APOSPORY

APOSPORY n development of the gametophyte from the sporophyte without the formation of spores

APOSTACY same as > APOSTASY

APOSTASY n abandonment of one's religious faith or other belief

APOSTATE n person who has abandoned his or her religion, political party, or cause ▷ adj guilty of apostasy

APOSTATES > APOSTATE

APOSTATIC > APOSTATE

APOSTIL n marginal note

APOSTILLE n apostil

APOSTILS > APOSTIL

APOSTLE n one of the twelve disciples chosen by Christ to preach his gospel

APOSTLES > APOSTLE

APOSTOLIC adj of or relating to the Apostles or their teachings

APOTHECE n obsolete word for shop

APOTHECES > APOTHECE

APOTHECIA n cup-shaped structures that contain the asci, esp in lichens

APOTHEGM n short cryptic remark containing some general or generally accepted truth; maxim

APOTHEGMS > APOTHEGM

APOTHEM n perpendicular line or distance from the centre of a regular polygon to any of its sides

APOTHEMS > APOTHEM

APOZEM n medicine dissolved in water

APOZEMS > APOZEM

APP n application program

APPAID > APPAY

APPAIR vb old form of impair

APPAIRED > APPAIR

APPAIRING > APPAIR

APPAIRS > APPAIR

APPAL vb dismay, terrify

APPALL same as > APPAL

APPALLED > APPALL

APPALLING adj dreadful, terrible

APPALLS > APPALL

APPALOOSA n North American horse breed

APPALS > APPAL

APPALTI > APPALTO

APPALTO n Italian word for contact

APPANAGE n land or other provision granted by a king for the support of a member of the royal family, esp a younger son

APPANAGED *adj* having appanage

APPANAGES > APPANAGE

APPARAT *n* Communist Party organization in the former Soviet Union and other states

APPARATS > APPARAT

APPARATUS *n* equipment for a particular purpose

APPAREL *n* clothing ▷ *vb* clothe, adorn, etc

APPARELED > APPAREL

APPARELS > APPAREL

APPARENCY *old word for* > APPARENT

APPARENT *adj* readily seen, obvious ▷ *n* heir apparent

APPARENTS > APPARENT

APPARITOR *n* officer who summons witnesses and executes the orders of an ecclesiastical and (formerly) a civil court

APPAY *old word for* > SATISFY

APPAYD > APPAY

APPAYING > APPAY

APPAYS > APPAY

APPEACH *old word for* > ACCUSE

APPEACHED > APPEACH

APPEACHES > APPEACH

APPEAL *vb* make an earnest request ▷ *n* earnest request

APPEALED > APPEAL

APPEALER > APPEAL

APPEALERS > APPEAL

APPEALING *adj* attractive or pleasing

APPEALS > APPEAL

APPEAR *vb* become visible or present

APPEARED > APPEAR

APPEARER > APPEAR

APPEARERS > APPEAR

APPEARING > APPEAR

APPEARS > APPEAR

APPEASE *vb* pacify (a person) by yielding to his or her demands

APPEASED > APPEASE

APPEASER > APPEASE

APPEASERS > APPEASE

APPEASES > APPEASE

APPEASING > APPEASE

APPEL *n* stamp of the foot, used to warn of one's intent to attack

APPELLANT *n* person who makes an appeal to a higher court

APPELLATE *adj* of appeals

APPELLEE *n* person who is accused or appealed against

APPELLEES > APPELLEE

APPELLOR *n* person initiating a law case

APPELLORS > APPELLOR

APPELS > APPEL

APPEND *vb* join on, add

APPENDAGE *n* thing joined on or added

APPENDANT *adj* attached, affixed, or added ▷ *n*

person or thing attached or added

APPENDED > APPEND

APPENDENT *same as* > APPENDANT

APPENDING > APPEND

APPENDIX *n* separate additional material at the end of a book

APPENDS > APPEND

APPERIL *old word for* > PERIL

APPERILL *old word for* > PERIL

APPERILLS > APPERILL

APPERILS > APPERIL

APPERTAIN *vb* belong to

APPESTAT *n* neural control centre within the hypothalamus of the brain that regulates the sense of hunger and satiety

APPESTATS > APPESTAT

APPETENCE *n* craving or desire

APPETENCY *same as* > APPETENCE

APPETENT *adj* eager

APPETIBLE *adj* old word meaning desirable

APPETISE *vb* stimulate the appetite

APPETISED > APPETISE

APPETISER *same as* > APPETIZER

APPETISES > APPETISE

APPETITE *n* desire for food or drink

APPETITES > APPETITE

APPETIZE *vb* stimulate the appetite

APPETIZED > APPETIZE

APPETIZER *n* thing eaten or drunk to stimulate the appetite

APPETIZES > APPETIZE

APPLAUD *vb* show approval of by clapping one's hands

APPLAUDED > APPLAUD

APPLAUDER > APPLAUD

APPLAUDS > APPLAUD

APPLAUSE *n* approval shown by clapping one's hands

APPLAUSES > APPLAUSE

APPLE *n* round firm fleshy fruit that grows on trees

APPLECART *n* cart used to carry apples

APPLEJACK *n* brandy made from apples

APPLES > APPLE

APPLET *n* computing program that runs within a page on the World Wide Web

APPLETS > APPLET

APPLEY *adj* resembling or tasting like an apple

APPLIABLE *adj* applicable

APPLIANCE *n* device with a specific function

APPLICANT *n* person who applies for something

APPLICATE *adj* applied practicably

APPLIED *adj* (of a skill, science, etc) put to

practical use

APPLIER > APPLY

APPLIERS > APPLY

APPLIES > APPLY

APPLIQUE *n* decoration or trimming of one material sewn or otherwise fixed onto another ▷ *vb* sew or fix (a decoration) on as an appliqué

APPLIQUED > APPLIQUE

APPLIQUES > APPLIQUE

APPLY *vb* make a formal request

APPLYING > APPLY

APPOINT *vb* assign to a job or position

APPOINTED > APPOINT

APPOINTEE *n* person who is appointed

APPOINTER > APPOINT

APPOINTOR *n* person to whom a power to nominate persons to take property is given by deed or will

APPOINTS > APPOINT

APPORT *n* production of objects by apparently supernatural means at a spiritualists' seance

APPORTION *vb* divide out in shares

APPORTS > APPORT

APPOSABLE *adj* capable of being apposed or brought into apposition

APPOSE *vb* place side by side or near to each other

APPOSED > APPOSE

APPOSER > APPOSE

APPOSERS > APPOSE

APPOSES > APPOSE

APPOSING > APPOSE

APPOSITE *adj* suitable, apt

APPRAISAL *n* assessment of the worth or quality of a person or thing

APPRAISE *vb* estimate the value or quality of

APPRAISED > APPRAISE

APPRAISEE *n* person being appraised

APPRAISER > APPRAISE

APPRAISES > APPRAISE

APPREHEND *vb* arrest and take into custody

APPRESS *vb* press together

APPRESSED > APPRESS

APPRESSES > APPRESS

APPRISE *vb* make aware (of)

APPRISED > APPRISE

APPRISER > APPRISE

APPRISERS > APPRISE

APPRISES > APPRISE

APPRISING > APPRISE

APPRIZE *same as* > APPRISE

APPRIZED > APPRIZE

APPRIZER > APPRIZE

APPRIZERS > APPRIZE

APPRIZES > APPRIZE

APPRIZING > APPRIZE

APPRO *n* approval

APPROACH *vb* come near or nearer (to) ▷ *n* approaching or means of

approaching

APPROBATE *vb* accept as valid

APPROOF *old word for* > TRIAL

APPROOFS > APPROOF

APPROS > APPRO

APPROVAL *n* consent

APPROVALS > APPROVAL

APPROVE *vb* consider good or right

APPROVED > APPROVE

APPROVER > APPROVE

APPROVERS > APPROVE

APPROVES > APPROVE

APPROVING > APPROVE

APPS > APP

APPUI *n* support

APPUIED > APPUY

APPUIS > APPUI

APPULSE *n* very close approach of two celestial bodies so that they are in conjunction but no eclipse or occultation occurs

APPULSES > APPULSE

APPULSIVE > APPULSE

APPUY *vb* support

APPUYED > APPUY

APPUYING > APPUY

APPUYS > APPUY

APRACTIC > APRAXIA

APRAXIA *n* disorder of the central nervous system caused by brain damage and characterized by impaired ability to carry out purposeful muscular movements

APRAXIAS > APRAXIA

APRAXIC > APRAXIA

APRES *prep* French word for after

APRICATE *vb* bask in sun

APRICATED > APRICATE

APRICATES > APRICATE

APRICOCK *old word for* > APRICOT

APRICOCKS > APRICOT

APRICOT *n* yellowish-orange juicy fruit like a small peach ▷ *adj* yellowish-orange

APRICOTS > APRICOT

APRIORISM *n* philosophical doctrine that there may be genuine knowledge independent of experience

APRIORIST > APRIORISM

APRIORITY *n* condition of being innate in the mind

APRON *n* garment worn over the front of the body to protect the clothes ▷ *vb* equip with an apron

APRONED > APRON

APRONFUL *n* amount held in an apron

APRONFULS > APRONFUL

APRONING > APRON

APRONLIKE > APRON

APRONS > APRON

APROPOS *adv* appropriate(ly)

APROTIC *adj* (of solvents) neither accepting nor donating hydrogen ions

APSARAS *n* Hindu water

sprite

APSARASES > APSARAS

APSE *n* arched or domed recess, esp in a church

APSES > APSE

APSIDAL > APSIS

APSIDES > APSIS

APSIDIOLE *n* small arch

APSIS *n* either of two points lying at the extremities of the elliptical orbit of a planet or satellite

APSO *n* Tibetan terrier

APSOS > APSO

APT *adj* having a specified tendency ▷ *vb* be fitting

APTED > APT

APTER > APT

APTERAL *adj* (esp of a classical temple) not having columns at the sides

APTERIA > APTERIUM

APTERISM > APTEROUS

APTERISMS > APTEROUS

APTERIUM *n* bare patch on the skin of a bird

APTEROUS *adj* (of insects) without wings, as silverfish and springtails

APTERYX *n* kiwi (the bird)

APTERYXES > APTERYX

APTEST > APT

APTING > APT

APTITUDE *n* natural ability

APTITUDES > APTITUDE

APTLY > APT

APTNESS > APT

APTNESSES > APT

APTOTE *n* noun without inflections

APTOTES > APTOTE

APTOTIC > APTOTE

APTS > APT

APYRASE *n* enzyme

APYRASES > APYRASE

APYRETIC > APYREXIA

APYREXIA *n* absence of fever

APYREXIAS > APYREXIA

AQUA *n* water

AQUABATIC *adj* of gymnastic feats in water

AQUABOARD *n* board used to ride on water

AQUACADE *same as* > AQUASHOW

AQUACADES > AQUACADE

AQUADROME *n* venue for water sports

AQUAE > AQUA

AQUAFARM *vb* cultivate fish or shellfish

AQUAFARMS > AQUAFARM

AQUAFER *n* aquifer

AQUAFERS > AQUAFER

AQUALUNG *n* mouthpiece attached to air cylinders, worn for underwater swimming

AQUALUNGS > AQUALUNG

AQUANAUT *n* person who lives and works underwater

AQUANAUTS > AQUANAUT

AQUAPHOBE *n* person afraid of water

AQUAPLANE *n* board on which a person stands to be towed by a motorboat ▷ *vb* ride on an aquaplane

AQUAPORIN *n* any one of a group of proteins in cell membranes that allow the passage of water across the membrane

AQUARELLE *n* method of watercolour painting in transparent washes

AQUARIA > AQUARIUM

AQUARIAL *adj* > AQUARIUM

AQUARIAN *n* person who keeps an aquarium

AQUARIANS > AQUARIAN

AQUARIIST *n* old form of > AQUARIST

AQUARIST *n* curator of an aquarium

AQUARISTS > AQUARIST

AQUARIUM *n* tank in which fish and other underwater creatures are kept

AQUARIUMS > AQUARIUM

AQUAROBIC *adj* pertaining to exercises performed standing up in a swimming pool

AQUAS > AQUA

AQUASHOW *n* exhibition of swimming and diving, often accompanied by music

AQUASHOWS > AQUASHOW

AQUATIC *adj* living in or near water ▷ *n* marine or freshwater animal or plant

AQUATICS *pl n* water sports

AQUATINT *n* print like a watercolour, produced by etching copper ▷ *vb* etch (a block, etc) in aquatint

AQUATINTA *n* aquatint

AQUATINTS > AQUATINT

AQUATONE *n* fitness exercise in water

AQUATONES > AQUATONE

AQUAVIT *n* grain- or potato-based spirit from the Scandinavian countries, flavoured with aromatic seeds and spices, esp caraway

AQUAVITS > AQUAVIT

AQUEDUCT *n* structure carrying water across a valley or river

AQUEDUCTS > AQUEDUCT

AQUEOUS *adj* of, like, or containing water

AQUEOUSLY > AQUEOUS

AQUIFER *n* deposit of rock, such as sandstone, containing water that can be used to supply wells

AQUIFERS > AQUIFER

AQUILEGIA *another name for* > COLUMBINE

AQUILINE *adj* (of a nose) curved like an eagle's beak

AQUILON *n* name for the north wind

AQUILONS > AQUILON

AQUIVER *adv* quivering

AR *n* letter R

ARAARA *another name for* > TREVALLY

ARAARAS > ARAARA

ARABA *n* Asian carriage

ARABAS > ARABA

ARABESK *same as* > ARABESQUE

ARABESKS > ARABESK

ARABESQUE *n* ballet position in which one leg is raised behind and the arms are extended ▷ *adj* designating, of, or decorated in this style

ARABIC *as in gum arabic* gum exuded by certain acacia trees

ARABICA *n* high-quality coffee bean

ARABICAS > ARABICA

ARABICISE *same as* > ARABICIZE

ARABICIZE *vb* make or become Arabic

ARABILITY *n* suitability of land for growing crops

ARABIN *n* essence of gum arabic

ARABINOSE *n* pentose sugar in plant gums

ARABINS > ARABIN

ARABIS *n* any plant of the annual or perennial genus *Arabis*, some of which form low-growing mats with downy grey foliage and white flowers: family *Brassicaceae* (crucifers)

ARABISE *vb* make or become Arab

ARABISED > ARABISE

ARABISES > ARABISE

ARABISING > ARABISE

ARABIZE *vb* make or become Arab

ARABIZED > ARABIZE

ARABIZES > ARABIZE

ARABIZING > ARABIZE

ARABLE *adj* suitable for growing crops on ▷ *n* arable land or farming

ARABLES > ARABLE

ARACEOUS *same as* > AROID

ARACHIS *n* Brazilian plant

ARACHISES > ARACHIS

ARACHNID *n* eight-legged invertebrate, such as a spider, scorpion, tick, or mite

ARACHNIDS > ARACHNID

ARACHNOID *n* middle of the three membranes that cover the brain and spinal cord ▷ *adj* of or relating to the middle of the three meninges

ARAGONITE *n* generally white or grey mineral, found in sedimentary rocks

ARAISE *vb* old form of raise

ARAISED > ARAISE

ARAISES > ARAISE

ARAISING > ARAISE

ARAK *same as* > ARRACK

ARAKS > ARAK

ARALIA *n* any plant of the genus *Aralia* of trees,

shrubs, and herbaceous plants. The greenhouse and house plant generally known as aralia is *Schefflera elegantissima* of a related genus, grown for its decorative evergreen foliage: family *Araliaceae*

ARALIAS > ARALIA

ARAME *n* Japanese edible seaweed

ARAMES > ARAME

ARAMID *n* synthetic fibre

ARAMIDS > ARAMID

ARANEID *n* any of numerous arachnids constituting the order *Araneae* (or *Araneida*), which comprises the spiders

ARANEIDAN > ARANEID

ARANEIDS > ARANEID

ARANEOUS *adj* like a spider's web

ARAPAIMA *n* very large primitive freshwater teleost fish that occurs in tropical S America

ARAPAIMAS > ARAPAIMA

ARAPONGA *n* South American bird with a bell-like call

ARAPONGAS > ARAPONGA

ARAPUNGA *n* South American bird with a bell-like call

ARAPUNGAS > ARAPUNGA

ARAR *n* African tree

ARAROBA *n* Brazilian leguminous tree, *Andira araroba*

ARAROBAS > ARAROBA

ARARS > ARAR

ARAUCARIA *n* any tree of the coniferous genus *Araucaria* of South America, Australia, and Polynesia, such as the monkey puzzle and bunya-bunya

ARAYSE *vb* old form of raise

ARAYSED > ARAYSE

ARAYSES > ARAYSE

ARAYSING > ARAYSE

ARB *short for* > ARBITRAGE

ARBA *n* Asian carriage

ARBALEST *n* large medieval crossbow, usually cocked by mechanical means

ARBALESTS > ARBALEST

ARBALIST *same as* > ARBALEST

ARBALISTS > ARBALIST

ARBAS > ARBA

ARBELEST *n* arbalest

ARBELESTS > ARBELEST

ARBITER *n* person empowered to judge in a dispute

ARBITERS > ARBITER

ARBITRAGE *n* purchase of currencies, securities, or commodities in one market for immediate resale in others in order to profit from unequal prices

ARBITRAL *adj* of or relating to arbitration

ARBITRARY *adj* based on

personal choice or chance, rather than reason

ARBITRATE *vb* settle (a dispute) by arbitration

ARBITRESS *n* female arbitrator

ARBITRIUM *n* power to decide

ARBLAST *n* arbalest

ARBLASTER > ARBLAST

ARBLASTS > ARBLAST

ARBOR *n* revolving shaft or axle in a machine

ARBOREAL *adj* of or living in trees

ARBORED *n* having arbors

ARBOREOUS *adj* thickly wooded

ARBORES > ARBOR

ARBORET *n* old name for an area planted with shrubs

ARBORETA > ARBORETUM

ARBORETS > ARBORET

ARBORETUM *n* place where rare trees or shrubs are cultivated

ARBORIO as in *arborio* rice variety of round-grain rice used for making risotto

ARBORISE *same as* > ARBORIZE

ARBORISED > ARBORISE

ARBORISES > ARBORISE

ARBORIST *n* specialist in the cultivation of trees

ARBORISTS > ARBORIST

ARBORIZE *vb* give or take on a treelike branched appearance

ARBORIZED > ARBORIZE

ARBORIZES > ARBORIZE

ARBOROUS *adj* of trees

ARBORS > ARBOR

ARBOUR *n* glade sheltered by trees

ARBOURED *adj* having arbours

ARBOURS > ARBOUR

ARBOVIRAL > ARBOVIRUS

ARBOVIRUS *n* any one of a group of viruses that cause such diseases as encephalitis and dengue and are transmitted to humans by arthropods, esp insects and ticks

ARBS > ARB

ARBUSCLE *n* small tree

ARBUSCLES > ARBUSCLE

ARBUTE *old name for* > ARBUTUS

ARBUTEAN > ARBUTUS

ARBUTES > ARBUTE

ARBUTUS *n* evergreen shrub with strawberry-like berries

ARBUTUSES > ARBUTUS

ARC *n* part of a circle or other curve ▷ *vb* form an arc

ARCADE *n* covered passageway lined with shops ▷ *vb* provide with an arcade

ARCADED > ARCADE

ARCADES > ARCADE

ARCADIA *n* traditional

idealized rural setting

ARCADIAN *n* person who leads a rural life

ARCADIANS > ARCADIAN

ARCADIAS > ARCADIA

ARCADING > ARCADE

ARCADINGS > ARCADE

ARCANA *n* either of the two divisions of a pack of tarot cards

ARCANAS > ARCANA

ARCANE *adj* mysterious and secret

ARCANELY > ARCANE

ARCANIST *n* person with secret knowledge

ARCANISTS > ARCANIST

ARCANUM *n* profound secret or mystery known only to initiates

ARCANUMS > ARCANUM

ARCATURE *n* small-scale arcade

ARCATURES > ARCATURE

ARCCOS *same as* > ARCCOSINE

ARCCOSES > ARCCOS

ARCCOSINE *n* trigonometric function

ARCED > ARC

ARCH *n* curved structure supporting a bridge or roof ▷ *vb* (cause to) form an arch ▷ *adj* superior, knowing

ARCHAEA *n* order of prokaryotic microorganisms

ARCHAEAL > ARCHAEAN

ARCHAEAN *n* type of microorganism

ARCHAEANS > ARCHAEAN

ARCHAEI > ARCHAEUS

ARCHAEON *same as* > ARCHAEAN

ARCHAEUS *n* spirit believed to inhabit a living thing

ARCHAIC *adj* ancient

ARCHAICAL *same as* > ARCHAIC

ARCHAISE *same as* > ARCHAIZE

ARCHAISED > ARCHAISE

ARCHAISER > ARCHAISE

ARCHAISES > ARCHAISE

ARCHAISM *n* archaic word or phrase

ARCHAISMS > ARCHAISM

ARCHAIST > ARCHAISM

ARCHAISTS > ARCHAISM

ARCHAIZE *vb* give an archaic appearance or character to, as by the use of archaisms

ARCHAIZED > ARCHAIZE

ARCHAIZER > ARCHAIZE

ARCHAIZES > ARCHAIZE

ARCHANGEL *n* chief angel

ARCHDUCAL *adj* of or relating to an archduke, archduchess, or archduchy

ARCHDUCHY *n* territory of an archduke or archduchess

ARCHDUKE *n* duke of specially high rank

ARCHDUKES > ARCHDUKE

ARCHEAN > ARCHAEAN

ARCHED *adj* provided with or spanned by an arch or arches

ARCHEI > ARCHEUS

ARCHENEMY *n* chief enemy

ARCHER *n* person who shoots with a bow and arrow

ARCHERESS *n* female archer

ARCHERIES > ARCHERY

ARCHERS > ARCHER

ARCHERY *n* art or sport of shooting with a bow and arrow

ARCHES > ARCH

ARCHEST > ARCH

ARCHETYPE *n* perfect specimen

ARCHEUS *n* spirit believed to inhabit a living thing

ARCHFIEND *n* the chief of fiends or devils

ARCHFOE *n* chief enemy

ARCHFOES > ARCHFOE

ARCHICARP *n* female reproductive structure in ascomycetous fungi that consists of a cell or hypha and develops into the ascogonium

ARCHIL *a variant spelling of* > ORCHIL

ARCHILOWE *n* treat given in return

ARCHILS > ARCHIL

ARCHIMAGE *n* great magician or wizard

ARCHINE *n* Russian unit of length equal to about 71 cm

ARCHINES > ARCHINE

ARCHING > ARCH

ARCHINGS > ARCH

ARCHITECT *n* person qualified to design and supervise the construction of buildings

ARCHITYPE *n* primitive original from which others derive

ARCHIVAL > ARCHIVE

ARCHIVE *n* collection of records or documents ▷ *vb* store (documents, data, etc) in an archive or other repository

ARCHIVED > ARCHIVE

ARCHIVES > ARCHIVE

ARCHIVING > ARCHIVE

ARCHIVIST *n* person in charge of archives

ARCHIVOLT *n* moulding around an arch, sometimes decorated

ARCHLET *n* small arch

ARCHLETS > ARCHLET

ARCHLUTE *n* old bass lute

ARCHLUTES > ARCHLUTE

ARCHLY > ARCH

ARCHNESS > ARCH

ARCHOLOGY *n* study of the origins of things

ARCHON *n* (in ancient Athens) one of the nine chief magistrates

ARCHONS > ARCHON

ARCHONTIC > ARCHON

ARCHOSAUR *n* early type of

dinosaur

ARCHRIVAL *n* chief rival

ARCHWAY *n* passageway under an arch

ARCHWAYS > ARCHWAY

ARCHWISE *adv* like an arch

ARCIFORM *adj* shaped like an arch

ARCING > ARC

ARCINGS > ARC

ARCKED > ARC

ARCKING > ARC

ARCKINGS > ARC

ARCMIN *n* 1/60 of a degree of an angle

ARCMINS > ARCMIN

ARCO *adv* musical direction meaning with bow

ARCOGRAPH *n* instrument used for drawing arcs without using a central point

ARCOLOGY *n* architecture blending buildings with the natural environment

ARCS > ARC

ARCSEC *n* 1/3600 of a degree of an angle

ARCSECOND *n* unit used in astronomy

ARCSECS > ARCSEC

ARCSIN *same as* > ARCSINE

ARCSINE *n* trigonometrical function

ARCSINES > ARCSINE

ARCSINS > ARCSIN

ARCTAN *n* trignometrical function

ARCTANS > ARCTAN

ARCTIC *adj* very cold ▷ *n* high waterproof overshoe with buckles

ARCTICS > ARCTIC

ARCTIID *n* any moth of the family *Arctiidae*, which includes the footman, ermine, and tiger moths

ARCTIIDS > ARCTIID

ARCTOID *adj* like a bear

ARCTOPHIL *n* arctophile

ARCUATE *adj* shaped or bent like an arc or bow

ARCUATED *same as* > ARCUATE

ARCUATELY > ARCUATE

ARCUATION *n* use of arches or vaults in buildings

ARCUS *n* circle around the cornea of the eye

ARCUSES > ARCUS

ARD *n* primitive plough

ARDEB *n* unit of dry measure used in Egypt and other Middle Eastern countries. In Egypt it is approximately equal to 0.195 cubic metres

ARDEBS > ARDEB

ARDENCIES > ARDENT

ARDENCY > ARDENT

ARDENT *adj* passionate

ARDENTLY > ARDENT

ARDOR *same as* > ARDOUR

ARDORS > ARDOR

ARDOUR *n* passion

ARDOURS > ARDOUR

ARDRI *n* Irish high king

ARDRIGH *n* Irish high king

Section 1: Words between 2 and 9 letters in length

a

ARDRIGHS > ARDRIGH
ARDRIS > ARDRI
ARDS > ARD
ARDUOUS *adj* hard to accomplish, strenuous
ARDUOUSLY > ARDUOUS
ARE *n* unit of measure, 100 square metres ▷ *vb* used as the singular form with *you*
AREA *n* part or region
AREACH *vb* old form of reach
AREACHED > AREACH
AREACHES > AREACH
AREACHING > AREACH
AREAD *vb* old word meaning declare
AREADING > AREAD
AREADS > AREAD
AREAE > AREA
AREAL > AREA
AREALLY > AREA
AREAR *n* old form of arrear
AREAS > AREA
AREAWAY *n* passageway between parts of a building or between different buildings
AREAWAYS > AREAWAY
ARECA *n* any of various tall palms of the genus *Areca*, which are native to SE Asia and have white flowers and orange or red egg-shaped nuts
ARECAS > ARECA
ARECOLINE *n* drug derived from betel nut
ARED > AREAD
AREDD > AREAD
AREDE *vb* old word meaning declare
AREDES > AREDE
AREDING > AREDE
AREFIED > AREFY
AREFIES > AREFY
AREFY *vb* dry up
AREFYING > AREFY
AREG *a plural of* > ERG
AREIC *adj* relating to area
ARENA *n* seated enclosure for sports events
ARENAS > ARENA
ARENATION *n* use of hot sand as a medical poultice
ARENE *n* aromatic hydrocarbon
ARENES > ARENE
ARENITE *n* any arenaceous rock
ARENITES > ARENITE
ARENITIC > ARENITE
ARENOSE *adj* sandy
ARENOUS *adj* sandy
AREOLA *n* small circular area, such as the coloured ring around the human nipple
AREOLAE > AREOLA
AREOLAR > AREOLA
AREOLAS > AREOLA
AREOLATE > AREOLA
AREOLATED *adj* areolate
AREOLE *n* space outlined on a surface, such as an area between veins on a leaf or on an insect's wing

AREOLES > AREOLE
AREOLOGY *n* study of the planet Mars
AREOMETER *n* instrument for measuring the density of liquids
AREOSTYLE *n* building with widely-spaced columns
AREPA *n* Colombian cornmeal cake
AREPAS > AREPA
ARERE *adv* old word meaning backwards
ARES > ARE
ARET *vb* old word meaning entrust
ARETE *n* sharp ridge separating two cirques or glacial valleys in mountainous regions
ARETES > ARETE
ARETHUSA *n* North American orchid, *Arethusa bulbosa*, having one long narrow leaf and one rose-purple flower fringed with yellow
ARETHUSAS > ARETHUSA
ARETS > ARET
ARETT *vb* old word meaning entrust
ARETTED > ARETT
ARETTING > ARETT
ARETTS > ARETT
AREW *adv* old word meaning in a row
ARF *n* barking sound
ARFS > ARF
ARGAL *same as* > ARGALI
ARGALA *n* Indian stork
ARGALAS > ARGALA
ARGALI *n* wild sheep, *Ovis ammon*, inhabiting semidesert regions in central Asia: family *Bovidae*, order *Artiodactyla*. It is the largest of the sheep, having massive horns in the male, which may almost form a circle
ARGALIS > ARGALI
ARGALS > ARGAL
ARGAN *n* Moroccan tree
ARGAND *n* lamp with a hollow circular wick
ARGANDS > ARGAND
ARGANS > ARGAN
ARGEMONE *n* prickly poppy
ARGEMONES > ARGEMONE
ARGENT *n* silver
ARGENTAL *adj* of or containing silver
ARGENTIC *adj* of or containing silver in the divalent or trivalent state
ARGENTINE *adj* of, relating to, or resembling silver ▷ *n* type of small silver fish
ARGENTITE *n* dark grey mineral that consists of silver sulphide, usually in cubic crystalline forms, and occurs in veins, often with native silver. It is found esp in Mexico, Nevada, and Saxony and is an important source of silver. Formula:

Ag_2S
ARGENTOUS *adj* of or containing silver in the monovalent state
ARGENTS > ARGENT
ARGENTUM *an obsolete name for* > SILVER
ARGENTUMS > ARGENTUM
ARGHAN *n* agave plant
ARGHANS > ARGHAN
ARGIL *n* clay, esp potters' clay
ARGILLITE *n* any argillaceous rock, esp a hardened mudstone
ARGILS > ARGIL
ARGINASE *n* type of enzyme
ARGINASES > ARGINASE
ARGININE *n* essential amino acid of plant and animal proteins, necessary for nutrition and for the production of excretory urea
ARGININES > ARGININE
ARGLE *vb* quarrel
ARGLED > ARGLE
ARGLES > ARGLE
ARGLING > ARGLE
ARGOL *n* crude potassium hydrogentartrate, deposited as a crust on the sides of wine vats
ARGOLS > ARGOL
ARGON *n* inert gas found in the air
ARGONAUT *n* paper nautilus
ARGONAUTS > ARGONAUT
ARGONON *n* inert gas
ARGONONS > ARGONON
ARGONS > ARGON
ARGOSIES > ARGOSY
ARGOSY *n* large merchant ship
ARGOT *n* slang or jargon
ARGOTIC > ARGOT
ARGOTS > ARGOT
ARGUABLE *adj* capable of being disputed
ARGUABLY *adv* it can be argued that
ARGUE *vb* try to prove by giving reasons
ARGUED > ARGUE
ARGUER > ARGUE
ARGUERS > ARGUE
ARGUES > ARGUE
ARGUFIED > ARGUFY
ARGUFIER > ARGUFY
ARGUFIERS > ARGUFY
ARGUFIES > ARGUFY
ARGUFY *vb* argue or quarrel, esp over something trivial
ARGUFYING > ARGUFY
ARGUING > ARGUE
ARGULI > ARGULUS
ARGULUS *n* parasite on fish
ARGUMENT *n* quarrel
ARGUMENTA *n* appeals to reason
ARGUMENTS > ARGUMENT
ARGUS *n* any of various brown butterflies
ARGUSES > ARGUS
ARGUTE *adj* shrill or keen
ARGUTELY > ARGUTE
ARGYLE *adj* made of knitted

or woven material with a diamond-shaped pattern of two or more colours ▷ *n* sock made of this
ARGYLES > ARGYLE
ARGYLL *n* sock with diamond pattern
ARGYLLS > ARGYLL
ARGYRIA *n* staining of skin by exposure to silver
ARGYRIAS > ARGYRIA
ARGYRITE *n* mineral containing silver sulphide
ARGYRITES > ARGYRITE
ARHAT *n* Buddhist, esp a monk who has achieved enlightenment and at death passes to nirvana
ARHATS > ARHAT
ARHATSHIP > ARHAT
ARHYTHMIA *n* irregular heartbeat
ARHYTHMIC > ARHYTHMIA
ARIA *n* elaborate song for solo voice, esp one from an opera
ARIARY *n* currency of Madagascar
ARIAS > ARIA
ARID *adj* parched, dry
ARIDER > ARID
ARIDEST > ARID
ARIDITIES > ARID
ARIDITY > ARID
ARIDLY > ARID
ARIDNESS > ARID
ARIEL *n* Arabian gazelle, *Gazella arabica* (or *dama*)
ARIELS > ARIEL
ARIETTA *n* short relatively uncomplicated aria
ARIETTAS > ARIETTA
ARIETTE *same as* > ARIETTA
ARIETTES > ARIETTE
ARIGHT *adv* rightly
ARIKI *n* first-born male or female in a notable family
ARIL *n* appendage on certain seeds, such as those of the yew and nutmeg, developed from or near the funicle of the ovule and often brightly coloured and fleshy
ARILED *adj* having an aril
ARILLARY *adj* having an aril
ARILLATE > ARILLATED
ARILLATED *adj* having an aril
ARILLI > ARILLUS
ARILLODE *n* structure in certain seeds that resembles an aril but is developed from the micropyle of the ovule
ARILLODES > ARILLODE
ARILLOID *adj* of or like an aril
ARILLUS *n* aril
ARILS > ARIL
ARIOSE *adj* songlike
ARIOSI > ARIOSO
ARIOSO *n* recitative with the lyrical quality of an aria
ARIOSOS > ARIOSO
ARIOT *adv* riotously
ARIPPLE *adv* in ripples

ARIS *n* Cockney slang for buttocks
ARISE *vb* come about
ARISEN > ARISE
ARISES > ARISE
ARISH *n* field that has been mown
ARISHES > ARISH
ARISING > ARISE
ARISTA *n* stiff bristle such as the awn of some grasses and cereals
ARISTAE > ARISTA
ARISTAS > ARISTA
ARISTATE > ARISTA
ARISTO *n* aristocrat
ARISTOS > ARISTO
ARISTOTLE *n* bottle
ARK *n* boat built by Noah, which survived the Flood ▷ *vb* place in an ark
ARKED > ARK
ARKING > ARK
ARKITE *n* passenger in ark
ARKITES > ARKITE
ARKOSE *n* sandstone consisting of grains of feldspar and quartz cemented by a mixture of quartz and clay minerals
ARKOSES > ARKOSE
ARKOSIC > ARKOSE
ARKS > ARK
ARLE *vb* make downpayment
ARLED > ARLE
ARLES > ARLE
ARLING > ARLE
ARM *n* either of the upper limbs from the shoulder to the wrist ▷ *vb* supply with weapons
ARMADA *n* large number of warships
ARMADAS > ARMADA
ARMADILLO *n* small S American mammal covered in strong bony plates
ARMAGNAC *n* dry brown brandy
ARMAGNACS > ARMAGNAC
ARMAMENT *n* military weapons
ARMAMENTS > ARMAMENT
ARMATURE *n* revolving structure in an electric motor or generator, wound with coils carrying the current
ARMATURED > ARMATURE
ARMATURES > ARMATURE
ARMBAND *n* band of material worn round the arm, such as one bearing an identifying mark, etc, or a black one indicating mourning
ARMBANDS > ARMBAND
ARMCHAIR *n* upholstered chair with side supports for the arms ▷ *adj* taking no active part
ARMCHAIRS > ARMCHAIR
ARMED *adj* equipped with or supported by arms, armour, etc

ARMER > ARM
ARMERS > ARM
ARMET *n* close-fitting medieval visored helmet with a neck guard
ARMETS > ARMET
ARMFUL *n* as much as can be held in the arms
ARMFULS > ARMFUL
ARMGAUNT *adj* word in Shakespeare of uncertain meaning
ARMHOLE *n* opening in a garment through which the arm passes
ARMHOLES > ARMHOLE
ARMIES > ARMY
ARMIGER *n* person entitled to bear heraldic arms, such as a sovereign or nobleman
ARMIGERAL > ARMIGER
ARMIGERO *n* armiger
ARMIGEROS > ARMIGERO
ARMIGERS > ARMIGER
ARMIL *n* bracelet
ARMILLA *n* bracelet
ARMILLAE > ARMILLA
ARMILLARY *adj* of or relating to bracelets
ARMILLAS > ARMILLA
ARMILS > ARMIL
ARMING *n* act of taking arms or providing with arms
ARMINGS > ARMING
ARMISTICE *n* agreed suspension of fighting
ARMLESS > ARM
ARMLET *n* band worn round the arm
ARMLETS > ARMLET
ARMLIKE > ARM
ARMLOAD *n* amount carried in the arms
ARMLOADS > ARMLOAD
ARMLOCK *vb* grip someone's arms
ARMLOCKED > ARMLOCK
ARMLOCKS > ARMLOCK
ARMOIRE *n* large cabinet, originally used for storing weapons
ARMOIRES > ARMOIRE
ARMONICA *n* glass harmonica
ARMONICAS > ARMONICA
ARMOR *same as* > ARMOUR
ARMORED *same as* > ARMOURED
ARMORER *same as* > ARMOURER
ARMORERS > ARMORER
ARMORIAL *adj* of or relating to heraldry or heraldic arms ▷ *n* book of coats of arms
ARMORIALS > ARMORIAL
ARMORIES > ARMORY
ARMORING > ARMOR
ARMORIST *n* heraldry expert
ARMORISTS > ARMORIST
ARMORLESS > ARMOR
ARMORS > ARMOR
ARMORY *same as* > ARMOURY
ARMOUR *n* metal clothing formerly worn to protect the body in battle ▷ *vb* equip or cover with armour
ARMOURED *adj* having a

protective covering
ARMOURER *n* maker, repairer, or keeper of arms or armour
ARMOURERS > ARMOURER
ARMOURIES > ARMOURY
ARMOURING > ARMOUR
ARMOURS > ARMOUR
ARMOURY *n* place where weapons are stored
ARMOZEEN *n* material used for clerical gowns
ARMOZEENS > ARMOZEEN
ARMOZINE *n* material used for clerical gowns
ARMOZINES > ARMOZINE
ARMPIT *n* hollow under the arm at the shoulder
ARMPITS > ARMPIT
ARMREST *n* part of a chair or sofa that supports the arm
ARMRESTS > ARMREST
ARMS > ARM
ARMSFUL > ARMFUL
ARMURE *n* silk or wool fabric with a small cobbled pattern
ARMURES > ARMURE
ARMY *n* military land forces of a nation
ARMYWORM *n* caterpillar of a widely distributed noctuid moth
ARMYWORMS > ARMYWORM
ARNA *n* Indian water buffalo
ARNAS > ARNA
ARNATTO *n* annatto
ARNATTOS > ARNATTO
ARNICA *n* any N temperate or arctic plant of the genus *Arnica*, typically having yellow flowers: family *Asteraceae* (composites)
ARNICAS > ARNICA
ARNOTTO *n* annatto
ARNOTTOS > ARNOTTO
ARNUT *n* plant with edible tubers
ARNUTS > ARNUT
AROBA *n* Asian carriage
AROBAS > AROBA
AROHA *n* love, compassion, or affection
AROHAS > AROHA
AROID *adj* of, relating to, or belonging to the *Araceae*, a family of plants having small flowers massed on a spadix surrounded by a large petaloid spathe. The family includes arum, calla, and anthurium ▷ *n* any plant of the *Araceae*
AROIDS > AROID
AROINT *vb* drive away
AROINTED > AROINT
AROINTING > AROINT
AROINTS > AROINT
AROLLA *n* European pine tree
AROLLAS > AROLLA
AROMA *n* pleasant smell
AROMAS > AROMA
AROMATASE *n* enzyme involved in the production of oestrogen
AROMATIC *adj* having a

distinctive pleasant smell ▷ *n* something, such as a plant or drug, that gives off a fragrant smell
AROMATICS > AROMATIC
AROMATISE *same as* > AROMATIZE
AROMATIZE *vb* make aromatic
AROSE *past tense of* > ARISE
AROUND *adv* on all sides (of)
AROUSABLE > AROUSE
AROUSAL > AROUSE
AROUSALS > AROUSE
AROUSE *vb* stimulate, make active
AROUSED > AROUSE
AROUSER > AROUSE
AROUSERS > AROUSE
AROUSES > AROUSE
AROUSING > AROUSE
AROW *adv* in a row
AROYNT *vb* old word meaning to drive away
AROYNTED > AROYNT
AROYNTING > AROYNT
AROYNTS > AROYNT
ARPA *n* website concerned with structure of the internet
ARPAS > ARPA
ARPEGGIO *n* notes of a chord played or sung in quick succession
ARPEGGIOS > ARPEGGIO
ARPEN *n* old French measure of land
ARPENS > ARPEN
ARPENT *n* former French unit of length equal to 190 feet (approximately 58 metres)
ARPENTS > ARPENT
ARPILLERA *n* Peruvian wall-hanging
ARQUEBUS *n* portable long-barrelled gun dating from the 15th century
ARRACACHA *n* S American plant
ARRACK *n* alcoholic drink distilled from grain or rice
ARRACKS > ARRACK
ARRAH *interj* Irish exclamation
ARRAIGN *vb* bring (a prisoner) before a court to answer a charge
ARRAIGNED > ARRAIGN
ARRAIGNER > ARRAIGN
ARRAIGNS > ARRAIGN
ARRANGE *vb* plan
ARRANGED > ARRANGE
ARRANGER > ARRANGE
ARRANGERS > ARRANGE
ARRANGES > ARRANGE
ARRANGING > ARRANGE
ARRANT *adj* utter, downright
ARRANTLY > ARRANT
ARRAS *n* tapestry wall-hanging
ARRASED *adj* having an arras
ARRASENE *n* material used in embroidery
ARRASENES > ARRASENE
ARRASES > ARRAS

Section 1: Words between 2 and 9 letters in length

a

ARRAUGHT > AREACH

ARRAY *n* impressive display or collection ▷ *vb* arrange in order

ARRAYAL > ARRAY

ARRAYALS > ARRAY

ARRAYED > ARRAY

ARRAYER > ARRAY

ARRAYERS > ARRAY

ARRAYING > ARRAY

ARRAYMENT *n* act of arraying

ARRAYS > ARRAY

ARREAR *n* singular of arrears

ARREARAGE *same as* > ARREARS

ARREARS *pl n* money owed

ARRECT *adj* pricked up

ARREEDE *vb* old word meaning declare

ARREEDES > ARREEDE

ARREEDING > ARREEDE

ARREST *vb* take (a person) into custody ▷ *n* act of taking a person into custody

ARRESTANT *n* substance that stops a chemical reaction

ARRESTED > ARREST

ARRESTEE *n* arrested person

ARRESTEES > ARRESTEE

ARRESTER *n* person who arrests

ARRESTERS > ARRESTER

ARRESTING *adj* attracting attention, striking

ARRESTIVE *adj* making something stop

ARRESTOR *n* person or thing that arrests

ARRESTORS > ARRESTOR

ARRESTS > ARREST

ARRET *n* judicial decision

ARRETS > ARRET

ARRHIZAL *adj* without roots

ARRIAGE *n* Scottish feudal service

ARRIAGES > ARRIAGE

ARRIBA *interj* exclamation of pleasure or approval

ARRIDE *vb* old word meaning gratify

ARRIDED > ARRIDE

ARRIDES > ARRIDE

ARRIDING > ARRIDE

ARRIERE *adj* French word meaning old-fashioned

ARRIERO *n* Spanish word for mule driver

ARRIEROS > ARRIERO

ARRIS *n* sharp edge at the meeting of two surfaces at an angle with one another, as at two adjacent sides of a stone block

ARRISES > ARRIS

ARRISH *n* corn stubble

ARRISHES > ARRISH

ARRIVAL *n* arriving

ARRIVALS > ARRIVAL

ARRIVANCE *n* old word meaning people who have arrived

ARRIVANCY *n* arrivance

ARRIVE *vb* reach a place or destination

ARRIVED > ARRIVE

ARRIVER > ARRIVE

ARRIVERS > ARRIVE

ARRIVES > ARRIVE

ARRIVING > ARRIVE

ARRIVISME *n* unscrupulous ambition

ARRIVISTE *n* person who is unscrupulously ambitious

ARROBA *n* unit of weight used in some Spanish-speaking countries

ARROBAS > ARROBA

ARROGANCE > ARROGANT

ARROGANCY > ARROGANT

ARROGANT *adj* proud and overbearing

ARROGATE *vb* claim or seize without justification

ARROGATED > ARROGATE

ARROGATES > ARROGATE

ARROGATOR > ARROGATE

ARROW *n* pointed shaft shot from a bow

ARROWED *adj* having an arrow pattern

ARROWHEAD *n* pointed tip of an arrow

ARROWING > ARROW

ARROWLESS > ARROW

ARROWLIKE > ARROW

ARROWROOT *n* nutritious starch obtained from the root of a W Indian plant

ARROWS > ARROW

ARROWWOOD *n* any of various trees or shrubs, esp certain viburnums, having long straight tough stems formerly used by North American Indians to make arrows

ARROWWORM *n* any small marine invertebrate of the genus *Sagitta*, having an elongated transparent body with fins and prehensile oral bristles

ARROWY *adj* like an arrow

ARROYO *n* steep-sided stream bed that is usually dry except after heavy rain

ARROYOS > ARROYO

ARS > AR

ARSE *n* buttocks or anus ▷ *vb* play the fool

ARSED > ARSE

ARSEHOLE *n* anus

ARSEHOLES > ARSEHOLE

ARSENAL *n* place where arms and ammunition are made or stored

ARSENALS > ARSENAL

ARSENATE *n* salt or ester of arsenic acid

ARSENATES > ARSENATE

ARSENIATE *n* arsenate

ARSENIC *n* toxic grey element ▷ *adj* of or containing arsenic

ARSENICAL *adj* of or containing arsenic ▷ *n* drug or insecticide containing arsenic

ARSENICS > ARSENIC

ARSENIDE *n* compound in which arsenic is the most

electronegative element

ARSENIDES > ARSENIDE

ARSENIOUS *adj* of or containing arsenic in the trivalent state

ARSENITE *n* salt or ester of arsenous acid, esp a salt containing the ion $A_5O_3{}^{3-}$

ARSENITES > ARSENITE

ARSENO *adj* containing arsenic

ARSENOUS *same as* > ARSENIOUS

ARSES > ARSIS

ARSEY *adj* aggressive, irritable, or argumentative

ARSHEEN *n* old measure of length in Russia

ARSHEENS > ARSHEEN

ARSHIN *n* old measure of length in Russia

ARSHINE *n* old measure of length in Russia

ARSHINES > ARSHINE

ARSHINS > ARSHIN

ARSIER > ARSY

ARSIEST > ARSY

ARSINE *n* colourless poisonous gas used in the manufacture of organic compounds, to dope transistors, and as a military poisonous gas

ARSINES > ARSINE

ARSING > ARSE

ARSINO *adj* containing arsine

ARSIS *n* (in classical prosody) the long syllable or part on which the ictus falls in a metrical foot

ARSON *n* crime of intentionally setting property on fire

ARSONIST > ARSON

ARSONISTS > ARSON

ARSONITE *n* person committing arson

ARSONITES > ARSONITE

ARSONOUS *adj* of arson

ARSONS > ARSON

ARSY *same as* > ARSEY

ART *n* creation of works of beauty, esp paintings or sculpture

ARTAL *a plural of* > ROTL

ARTEFACT *n* something made by human beings

ARTEFACTS > ARTEFACT

ARTEL *n* (in the former Soviet Union) a cooperative union or organization, esp of producers, such as peasants

ARTELS > ARTEL

ARTEMISIA *n* any herbaceous perennial plant of the genus *Artemisia*, of the N hemisphere, such as mugwort, sagebrush, and wormwood: family *Asteraceae* (composites)

ARTERIAL *adj* of an artery ▷ *n* major road

ARTERIALS > ARTERIAL

ARTERIES > ARTERY

ARTERIOLE *n* any of the

small subdivisions of an artery that form thin-walled vessels ending in capillaries

ARTERITIS *n* inflammation of an artery

ARTERY *n* one of the tubes carrying blood from the heart

ARTESIAN as in *artesian well* well sunk through impermeable strata receiving water from an area at a higher altitude than that of the well

ARTFUL *adj* cunning, wily

ARTFULLY > ARTFUL

ARTHRITIC > ARTHRITIS

ARTHRITIS *n* painful inflammation of a joint or joints

ARTHRODIA *n* joint

ARTHROPOD *n* animal, such as a spider or insect, with jointed limbs and a segmented body

ARTHROSES > ARTHROSIS

ARTHROSIS *n* disease of joint

ARTI *n* ritual performed in homes and temples in which incense and light is offered to a deity

ARTIC *n* articulated vehicle

ARTICHOKE *n* flower head of a thistle-like plant, cooked as a vegetable

ARTICLE *n* written piece in a magazine or newspaper ▷ *vb* bind by a written contract

ARTICLED > ARTICLE

ARTICLES > ARTICLE

ARTICLING > ARTICLE

ARTICS > ARTIC

ARTICULAR *adj* of or relating to joints

ARTIER > ARTY

ARTIES > ARTY

ARTIEST > ARTY

ARTIFACT *same as* > ARTEFACT

ARTIFACTS > ARTIFACT

ARTIFICE *n* clever trick

ARTIFICER *n* craftsman

ARTIFICES > ARTIFICE

ARTILLERY *n* large-calibre guns

ARTILY > ARTY

ARTINESS > ARTY

ARTIS > ARTI

ARTISAN *n* skilled worker, craftsman

ARTISANAL > ARTISAN

ARTISANS > ARTISAN

ARTIST *n* person who produces works of art, esp paintings or sculpture

ARTISTE *n* professional entertainer such as a singer or dancer

ARTISTES > ARTISTE

ARTISTIC *adj* of or characteristic of art or artists

ARTISTRY *n* artistic skill

ARTISTS > ARTIST

Section 1: Words between 2 and 9 letters in length

ARTLESS *adj* free from deceit or cunning
ARTLESSLY > ARTLESS
ARTS > ART
ARTSIER > ARTSY
ARTSIES > ARTSY
ARTSIEST > ARTSY
ARTSINESS > ARTSY
ARTSMAN old word for > CRAFTSMAN
ARTSMEN > ARTSMAN
ARTSY *adj* interested in the arts ▷ *n* person interested in the arts
ARTWORK *n* all the photographs and illustrations in a publication
ARTWORKS > ARTWORK
ARTY *adj* having an affected interest in art ▷ *n* person interested in art
ARUGOLA *n* salad plant
ARUGOLAS > ARUGOLA
ARUGULA another name for > ROCKET
ARUGULAS > ARUGULA
ARUHE *n* edible root of a fern
ARUM *n* any plant of the ariod genus *Arum*
ARUMS > ARUM
ARUSPEX variant spelling of > HARUSPEX
ARUSPICES > ARUSPEX
ARVAL *adj* of ploughed land
ARVICOLE *n* water rat
ARVICOLES > ARVICOLE
ARVO *n* afternoon
ARVOS > ARVO
ARY dialect form of > ANY
ARYBALLOS *n* ancient Greek flask
ARYL *n* of, consisting of, or containing an aromatic group
ARYLS > ARYL
ARYTENOID *adj* denoting either of two small cartilages of the larynx that are attached to the vocal cords ▷ *n* arytenoid cartilage or muscle
ARYTHMIA *n* any variation
ARYTHMIAS > ARYTHMIA
ARYTHMIC > ARYTHMIA
AS *adv* used to indicate amount or extent in comparisons ▷ *n* ancient Roman unit of weight
ASAFETIDA *n* bitter resin with an unpleasant onion-like smell
ASANA *n* any of various postures in yoga
ASANAS > ASANA
ASAR > AS
ASARUM *n* dried strong-scented root of the wild ginger plant: a flavouring agent and source of an aromatic oil used in perfumery, formerly used in medicine
ASARUMS > ASARUM
ASBESTIC > ASBESTOS
ASBESTINE > ASBESTOS
ASBESTOS *n* fibrous mineral

which does not burn
ASBESTOUS > ASBESTOS
ASBESTUS *n* asbestos
ASCARED *adj* afraid
ASCARID *n* any parasitic nematode worm of the family *Ascaridae*, such as the common roundworm of man and pigs
ASCARIDES > ASCARID
ASCARIDS > ASCARID
ASCARIS *n* ascarid
ASCAUNT *adv* old word meaning slantwise
ASCEND *vb* go or move up
ASCENDANT *adj* dominant or influential
ASCENDED > ASCEND
ASCENDENT same as > ASCENDANT
ASCENDER *n* part of certain lower-case letters, such as b or h, that extends above the body of the letter
ASCENDERS > ASCENDER
ASCENDEUR *n* metal grip that is threaded on a rope and can be alternately tightened and slackened as an aid to climbing the rope: used attached to slings for the feet and waist
ASCENDING *adj* moving upwards
ASCENDS > ASCEND
ASCENSION *n* act of ascending
ASCENSIVE *adj* moving upwards
ASCENT *n* ascending
ASCENTS > ASCENT
ASCERTAIN *vb* find out definitely
ASCESES > ASCESIS
ASCESIS *n* exercise of self-discipline
ASCETIC *adj* (person) abstaining from worldly pleasures and comforts ▷ *n* person who abstains from worldly comforts and pleasures
ASCETICAL ascetic
ASCETICS > ASCETIC
ASCI > ASCUS
ASCIAN *n* person living in the tropics
ASCIANS > ASCIAN
ASCIDIA > ASCIDIUM
ASCIDIAN *n* any minute marine invertebrate animal of the class *Ascidiacea*, such as the sea squirt, the adults of which are degenerate and sedentary
ASCIDIANS > ASCIDIAN
ASCIDIATE > ASCIDIUM
ASCIDIUM *n* part of a plant that is shaped like a pitcher, such as the modified leaf of the pitcher plant
ASCITES *n* accumulation of serous fluid in the peritoneal cavity
ASCITIC > ASCITES
ASCITICAL > ASCITES

ASCLEPIAD *n* Greek verse form
ASCLEPIAS *n* any plant of the perennial mostly tuberous genus *Asclepias*; some are grown as garden or greenhouse plants for their showy orange-scarlet or purple flowers: family *Asclepiadaceae*
ASCOCARP *n* (in some ascomycetous fungi) a globular structure containing the asci
ASCOCARPS > ASCOCARP
ASCOGONIA *n* female reproductive bodies in some fungi
ASCONCE *adv* old form of askance
ASCORBATE *n* salt of ascorbic acid
ASCORBIC as in ascorbic acid white crystalline vitamin present in plants, esp citrus fruits, tomatoes, and green vegetables
ASCOSPORE *n* one of the spores (usually eight in number) that are produced in an ascus
ASCOT *n* cravat with wide square ends, usually secured with an ornamental stud
ASCOTS > ASCOT
ASCRIBE *vb* attribute, as to a particular origin
ASCRIBED > ASCRIBE
ASCRIBES > ASCRIBE
ASCRIBING > ASCRIBE
ASCUS *n* saclike structure that produces (usually) eight ascospores during sexual reproduction in ascomycetous fungi such as yeasts and mildews
ASDIC an early form of > SONAR
ASDICS > ASDIC
ASEA *adv* towards the sea
ASEISMIC *adj* denoting a region free of earthquakes
ASEITIES > ASEITY
ASEITY *n* existence derived from itself, having no other source
ASEPALOUS *adj* (of a plant or flower) having no sepals
ASEPSES > ASEPSIS
ASEPSIS *n* aseptic condition
ASEPTATE *adj* not divided into cells or sections by septa
ASEPTIC *adj* free from harmful bacteria ▷ *n* aseptic substance
ASEPTICS > ASEPTIC
ASEXUAL *adj* without sex
ASEXUALLY > ASEXUAL
ASH *n* powdery substance left when something is burnt ▷ *vb* reduce to ashes
ASHAKE *adv* shaking
ASHAME *vb* make ashamed
ASHAMED *adj* feeling shame

ASHAMEDLY > ASHAMED
ASHAMES > ASHAME
ASHAMING > ASHAME
ASHCAKE *n* cornmeal bread
ASHCAKES > ASHCAKE
ASHCAN *n* large metal dustbin
ASHCANS > ASHCAN
ASHED > ASH
ASHEN *adj* pale with shock
ASHERIES > ASHERY
ASHERY *n* place where ashes are made
ASHES > ASH
ASHET *n* shallow oval dish or large plate
ASHETS > ASHET
ASHFALL *n* dropping of ash from a volcano
ASHFALLS > ASHFALL
ASHIER > ASHY
ASHIEST > ASHY
ASHINE *adv* old word meaning shining
ASHINESS > ASHY
ASHING > ASH
ASHIVER *adv* shivering
ASHKEY *n* winged fruit of the ash
ASHKEYS > ASHKEY
ASHLAR *n* square block of hewn stone used in building ▷ *vb* build with ashlars
ASHLARED > ASHLAR
ASHLARING > ASHLAR
ASHLARS > ASHLAR
ASHLER same as > ASHLAR
ASHLERED > ASHLER
ASHLERING > ASHLER
ASHLERS > ASHLER
ASHLESS > ASH
ASHMAN *n* man who shovels ashes
ASHMEN > ASHMAN
ASHORE *adv* towards or on land ▷ *adj* on land, having come from the water
ASHPLANT *n* walking stick made from an ash sapling
ASHPLANTS > ASHPLANT
ASHRAF > SHERIF
ASHRAM *n* religious retreat where a Hindu holy man lives
ASHRAMA *n* stage in Hindu spiritual life
ASHRAMAS > ASHRAMA
ASHRAMITE *n* person living in an ashram
ASHRAMS > ASHRAM
ASHTRAY *n* receptacle for tobacco ash and cigarette butts
ASHTRAYS > ASHTRAY
ASHY *adj* pale greyish
ASIAGO *n* either of two varieties (ripened or fresh) of a cow's-milk cheese produced in NE Italy
ASIAGOS > ASIAGO
ASIDE *adv* one side ▷ *n* remark not meant to be heard by everyone present
ASIDES > ASIDE
ASINICO *n* old Spanish word for fool

a

ASINICOS > ASINICO
ASININE adj stupid, idiotic
ASININELY > ASININE
ASININITY > ASININE
ASK vb say or write (something) in a form that requires an answer
ASKANCE adv with an oblique glance ▷ vb turn aside
ASKANCED > ASKANCE
ASKANCES > ASKANCE
ASKANCING > ASKANCE
ASKANT same as > ASKANCE
ASKANTED > ASKANT
ASKANTING > ASKANT
ASKANTS > ASKANT
ASKARI n (in East Africa) a soldier or policeman
ASKARIS > ASKARI
ASKED > ASK
ASKER > ASK
ASKERS > ASK
ASKESES > ASKESIS
ASKESIS n practice of self-discipline
ASKEW adj one side, crooked
ASKEWNESS > ASKEW
ASKING > ASK
ASKINGS > ASK
ASKLENT Scots word for > ASLANT
ASKOI > ASKOS
ASKOS n ancient Greek vase
ASKS > ASK
ASLAKE vb slake
ASLAKED > ASLAKE
ASLAKES > ASLAKE
ASLAKING > ASLAKE
ASLANT adv at a slant (to), slanting (across)
ASLEEP adj sleeping
ASLOPE adj sloping
ASLOSH adj awash
ASMEAR adj smeared
ASMOULDER adv old word meaning smouldering
ASOCIAL n person who avoids social contact
ASOCIALS > ASOCIAL
ASP n small poisonous snake
ASPARAGUS n plant whose shoots are cooked as a vegetable
ASPARKLE adv sparkling
ASPARTAME n artificial sweetener
ASPARTATE n enzyme found in blood
ASPARTIC as in aspartic acid nonessential amino acid that is a component of proteins and acts as a neurotransmitter
ASPECT n feature or element ▷ vb look at
ASPECTED > ASPECT
ASPECTING > ASPECT
ASPECTS > ASPECT
ASPECTUAL adj of or relating to grammatical aspect
ASPEN n kind of poplar tree ▷ adj trembling
ASPENS > ASPEN
ASPER n former Turkish

monetary unit, a silver coin, worth 1/120 of a piastre
ASPERATE adj (of plant parts) having a rough surface due to a covering of short stiff hairs ▷ vb make rough
ASPERATED > ASPERATE
ASPERATES > ASPERATE
ASPERGE vb sprinkle
ASPERGED > ASPERGE
ASPERGER > ASPERGE
ASPERGERS > ASPERGE
ASPERGES > ASPERGE
ASPERGILL n perforated instrument used to sprinkle holy water
ASPERGING > ASPERGE
ASPERITY n roughness of temper
ASPERMIA n failure to form or emit semen
ASPERMIAS > ASPERMIA
ASPEROUS same as > ASPERATE
ASPERS > ASPER
ASPERSE vb spread false rumours about
ASPERSED > ASPERSE
ASPERSER > ASPERSE
ASPERSERS > ASPERSE
ASPERSES > ASPERSE
ASPERSING > ASPERSE
ASPERSION n disparaging or malicious remark
ASPERSIVE > ASPERSE
ASPERSOIR n sprinkler for holy water
ASPERSOR > ASPERSE
ASPERSORS > ASPERSE
ASPERSORY n sprinkler for holy water
ASPHALT n black hard tarlike substance used for road surfaces etc ▷ vb cover with asphalt
ASPHALTED > ASPHALT
ASPHALTER n person who lays asphalt
ASPHALTIC > ASPHALT
ASPHALTS > ASPHALT
ASPHALTUM n asphalt
ASPHERIC adj not spherical
ASPHODEL n plant with clusters of yellow or white flowers
ASPHODELS > ASPHODEL
ASPHYXIA n suffocation
ASPHYXIAL > ASPHYXIA
ASPHYXIAS > ASPHYXIA
ASPHYXIES > ASPHYXY
ASPHYXY > ASPHYXIA
ASPIC n savoury jelly used to coat meat, eggs, fish, etc
ASPICK old word for > ASP
ASPICKS > ASPICK
ASPICS > ASPIC
ASPIDIA > ASPIDIUM
ASPIDIOID > ASPIDIUM
ASPIDIUM n variety of fern
ASPINE old word for > ASPEN
ASPINES > ASPINE
ASPIRANT n person who aspires ▷ adj aspiring or striving
ASPIRANTS > ASPIRANT

ASPIRATA n rough stop
ASPIRATAE > ASPIRATA
ASPIRATE vb pronounce with an h sound ▷ n h sound ▷ adj (of a stop) pronounced with a forceful and audible expulsion of breath
ASPIRATED > ASPIRATE
ASPIRATES > ASPIRATE
ASPIRATOR n device for removing fluids from a body cavity by suction
ASPIRE vb yearn (for), hope (to do or be)
ASPIRED > ASPIRE
ASPIRER > ASPIRE
ASPIRERS > ASPIRE
ASPIRES > ASPIRE
ASPIRIN n drug used to relieve pain and fever
ASPIRING > ASPIRE
ASPIRINS > ASPIRIN
ASPIS n horned viper
ASPISES > ASPIS
ASPISH adj like an asp
ASPLENIUM n type of fern
ASPORT vb old word meaning take away
ASPORTED > ASPORT
ASPORTING > ASPORT
ASPORTS > ASPORT
ASPOUT adv spouting
ASPRAWL adv sprawling
ASPREAD adv spreading
ASPRO n associate professor at an academic institution
ASPROS > ASPRO
ASPROUT adv sprouting
ASPS > ASP
ASQUAT adv squatting
ASQUINT adj with a glance from the corner of the eye, esp a furtive one
ASRAMA n stage in Hindu spiritual life
ASRAMAS > ASRAMA
ASS n donkey
ASSAGAI same as > ASSEGAI
ASSAGAIED > ASSAGAI
ASSAGAIS > ASSAGAI
ASSAI adv (usually preceded by a musical direction) very ▷ n any of several Brazilian palm trees of the genus Euterpe, esp E. edulis, that have small dark purple fleshy edible fruit
ASSAIL vb attack violently
ASSAILANT n person who attacks another, either physically or verbally
ASSAILED > ASSAIL
ASSAILER > ASSAIL
ASSAILERS > ASSAIL
ASSAILING > ASSAIL
ASSAILS > ASSAIL
ASSAIS > ASSAI
ASSAM n (in Malaysia) tamarind as used in cooking
ASSAMS > ASSAM
ASSART vb clear ground for cultivation
ASSARTED > ASSART
ASSARTING > ASSART
ASSARTS > ASSART

ASSASSIN n person who murders a prominent person
ASSASSINS > ASSASSIN
ASSAULT n violent attack ▷ vb attack violently
ASSAULTED > ASSAULT
ASSAULTER > ASSAULT
ASSAULTS > ASSAULT
ASSAY n analysis of a substance, esp a metal, to ascertain its purity ▷ vb make such an analysis
ASSAYABLE > ASSAY
ASSAYED > ASSAY
ASSAYER > ASSAY
ASSAYERS > ASSAY
ASSAYING > ASSAY
ASSAYINGS > ASSAY
ASSAYS > ASSAY
ASSEGAAI same as > ASSEGAI
ASSEGAAIS > ASSEGAI
ASSEGAI n slender spear used in S Africa ▷ vb spear with an assegai
ASSEGAIED > ASSEGAI
ASSEGAIS > ASSEGAI
ASSEMBLE vb collect or congregate
ASSEMBLED > ASSEMBLE
ASSEMBLER n person or thing that assembles
ASSEMBLES > ASSEMBLE
ASSEMBLY n assembled group
ASSENT n agreement or consent ▷ vb agree or consent
ASSENTED > ASSENT
ASSENTER n person supporting another's nomination
ASSENTERS > ASSENTER
ASSENTING > ASSENT
ASSENTIVE > ASSENT
ASSENTOR n any of the eight voters legally required to endorse the nomination of a candidate in a parliamentary or local election in addition to the nominator and seconder
ASSENTORS > ASSENTOR
ASSENTS > ASSENT
ASSERT vb declare forcefully
ASSERTED > ASSERT
ASSERTER > ASSERT
ASSERTERS > ASSERT
ASSERTING > ASSERT
ASSERTION n positive statement, usu made without evidence
ASSERTIVE adj confident and direct in dealing with others
ASSERTOR > ASSERT
ASSERTORS > ASSERT
ASSERTORY adj making affirmation
ASSERTS > ASSERT
ASSES > ASS
ASSESS vb judge the worth or importance of
ASSESSED > ASSESS
ASSESSES > ASSESS
ASSESSING > ASSESS
ASSESSOR n person who

values property for taxation or insurance purposes

ASSESSORS > ASSESSOR

ASSET *n* valuable or useful person or thing

ASSETLESS > ASSET

ASSETS > ASSET

ASSEVER *vb* old form of asseverate

ASSEVERED > ASSEVER

ASSEVERS > ASSEVER

ASSEZ *adv* (as part of a musical direction) fairly

ASSHOLE *same as* > ARSEHOLE

ASSHOLES > ASSHOLE

ASSIDUITY *n* constant and close application

ASSIDUOUS *adj* hard-working

ASSIEGE *vb* old form of besiege

ASSIEGED > ASSIEGE

ASSIEGES > ASSIEGE

ASSIEGING > ASSIEGE

ASSIENTO *n* slave trade treaty between Britain and Spain

ASSIENTOS > ASSIENTO

ASSIGN *vb* appoint (someone) to a job or task ▷ *n* person to whom property is assigned

ASSIGNAT *n* paper money issued by the Constituent Assembly in 1789, backed by the confiscated land of the Church and the émigrés

ASSIGNATS > ASSIGNAT

ASSIGNED > ASSIGN

ASSIGNEE *n* person to whom some right, interest, or property is transferred

ASSIGNEES > ASSIGNEE

ASSIGNER > ASSIGN

ASSIGNERS > ASSIGN

ASSIGNING > ASSIGN

ASSIGNOR *n* person who transfers or assigns property

ASSIGNORS > ASSIGNOR

ASSIGNS > ASSIGN

ASSIST *vb* give help or support ▷ *n* pass by a player which enables another player to score a goal

ASSISTANT *n* helper ▷ *adj* junior or deputy

ASSISTED > ASSIST

ASSISTER > ASSIST

ASSISTERS > ASSIST

ASSISTING > ASSIST

ASSISTIVE *adj* providing a means of reducing a physical impairment

ASSISTOR > ASSIST

ASSISTORS > ASSIST

ASSISTS > ASSIST

ASSIZE *n* sitting of a legislative assembly or administrative body

ASSIZED > ASSIZE

ASSIZER *n* weights and measures official

ASSIZERS > ASSIZER

ASSIZES > ASSIZE

ASSIZING > ASSIZE

ASSLIKE > ASS

ASSOCIATE *vb* connect in the mind ▷ *n* partner in business ▷ *adj* having partial rights or subordinate status

ASSOIL *vb* absolve

ASSOILED > ASSOIL

ASSOILING > ASSOIL

ASSOILS > ASSOIL

ASSOILZIE *vb* old Scots word meaning absolve

ASSONANCE *n* rhyming of vowel sounds but not consonants

ASSONANT > ASSONANCE

ASSONANTS > ASSONANCE

ASSONATE *vb* show assonance

ASSONATED > ASSONATE

ASSONATES > ASSONATE

ASSORT *vb* arrange or distribute into groups of the same type

ASSORTED *adj* consisting of various types mixed together

ASSORTER > ASSORT

ASSORTERS > ASSORT

ASSORTING > ASSORT

ASSORTIVE > ASSORT

ASSORTS > ASSORT

ASSOT *vb* old word meaning make infatuated

ASSOTS > ASSOT

ASSOTT *vb* besot

ASSOTTED > ASSOT

ASSOTTING > ASSOT

ASSUAGE *vb* relieve (pain, grief, thirst, etc)

ASSUAGED > ASSUAGE

ASSUAGER > ASSUAGE

ASSUAGERS > ASSUAGE

ASSUAGES > ASSUAGE

ASSUAGING > ASSUAGE

ASSUASIVE > ASSUAGE

ASSUETUDE *n* state of being accustomed

ASSUMABLE > ASSUME

ASSUMABLY > ASSUME

ASSUME *vb* take to be true without proof

ASSUMED *adj* false

ASSUMEDLY > ASSUME

ASSUMER > ASSUME

ASSUMERS > ASSUME

ASSUMES > ASSUME

ASSUMING *adj* expecting too much ▷ *n* action of one who assumes

ASSUMINGS > ASSUMING

ASSUMPSIT *n* (before 1875) an action to recover damages for breach of an express or implied contract or agreement that was not under seal

ASSURABLE > ASSURE

ASSURANCE *n* assuring or being assured

ASSURE *vb* promise or guarantee

ASSURED *adj* confident ▷ *n* beneficiary under a life assurance policy

ASSUREDLY > ASSURED

ASSUREDS > ASSURED

ASSURER > ASSURE

ASSURERS > ASSURE

ASSURES > ASSURE

ASSURGENT *adj* (of leaves, stems, etc) curving or growing upwards

ASSURING > ASSURE

ASSUROR > ASSURE

ASSURORS > ASSURE

ASSWAGE *old spelling of* > ASSUAGE

ASSWAGED > ASSWAGE

ASSWAGES > ASSWAGE

ASSWAGING > ASSWAGE

ASTABLE *adj* not stable

ASTARE *adv* staring

ASTART *old word for* > START

ASTARTED > ASTART

ASTARTING > ASTART

ASTARTS > ASTART

ASTASIA *n* inability to stand

ASTASIAS > ASTASIA

ASTATIC *adj* not static

ASTATIDE *n* binary compound of astatine with a more electropositive element

ASTATIDES > ASTATIDE

ASTATINE *n* radioactive nonmetallic element

ASTATINES > ASTATINE

ASTATKI *n* fuel derived from petroleum

ASTATKIS > ASTATKI

ASTEISM *n* use of irony

ASTEISMS > ASTEISM

ASTELIC > ASTELY

ASTELIES > ASTELY

ASTELY *n* lack of central cylinder in plants

ASTER *n* plant with daisy-like flowers

ASTERIA *n* gemstone with starlike light effect

ASTERIAS > ASTERIA

ASTERID *n* variety of flowering plant

ASTERIDS > ASTERID

ASTERISK *n* star-shaped symbol (*) used in printing or writing to indicate a footnote, etc ▷ *vb* mark with an asterisk

ASTERISKS > ASTERISK

ASTERISM *n* three asterisks arranged in a triangle to draw attention to the text that follows

ASTERISMS > ASTERISM

ASTERN *adv* at or towards the stern of a ship ▷ *adj* at or towards the stern of a ship

ASTERNAL *adj* not connected or joined to the sternum

ASTEROID *n* any of the small planets that orbit the sun between Mars and Jupiter ▷ *adj* of, relating to, or belonging to the class *Asteroidea*

ASTEROIDS > ASTEROID

ASTERS > ASTER

ASTERT *vb* start

ASTERTED > ASTERT

ASTERTING > ASTERT

ASTERTS > ASTERT

ASTHENIA *n* abnormal loss of strength

ASTHENIAS > ASTHENIA

ASTHENIC *adj* of, relating to, or having asthenia ▷ *n* person having long limbs and a small trunk

ASTHENICS > ASTHENIC

ASTHENIES > ASTHENY

ASTHENY *same as* > ASTHENIA

ASTHMA *n* illness causing difficulty in breathing

ASTHMAS > ASTHMA

ASTHMATIC *adj* of, relating to, or having asthma ▷ *n* person who has asthma

ASTHORE *n* Irish endearment

ASTHORES > ASTHORE

ASTICHOUS *adj* not arranged in rows

ASTIGMIA *n* defect of a lens resulting in the formation of distorted images

ASTIGMIAS > ASTIGMIA

ASTILBE *n* any perennial saxifragaceous plant of the genus *Astilbe* of E Asia and N America: cultivated for their ornamental spikes or panicles of pink or white flowers

ASTILBES > ASTILBE

ASTIR *adj* out of bed

ASTOMATAL *adj* having no stomata

ASTOMOUS *adj* having no mouth

ASTONE *vb* old form of > ASTONISH

ASTONED > ASTONE

ASTONES > ASTONE

ASTONIED *adj* stunned

ASTONIES > ASTONY

ASTONING > ASTONE

ASTONISH *vb* surprise greatly

ASTONY *vb* old form of > ASTONISH

ASTONYING > ASTONY

ASTOOP *adv* stooping

ASTOUND *vb* overwhelm with amazement

ASTOUNDED > ASTOUND

ASTOUNDS > ASTOUND

ASTRACHAN *same as* > ASTRAKHAN

ASTRADDLE *adj* with a leg on either side of something

ASTRAGAL *n* small convex moulding, usually with a semicircular cross section

ASTRAGALI *n* bones of the ankles that articulate with the leg bones to form ankle joints

ASTRAGALS > ASTRAGAL

ASTRAKHAN *n* dark curly fleece of lambs from Astrakhan in Russia

ASTRAL *adj* of stars ▷ *n* oil lamp

ASTRALLY > ASTRAL

a

ASTRALS > ASTRAL
ASTRAND adv on shore
ASTRANTIA n flowering plant
ASTRAY adv off the right path
ASTRICT vb bind, confine, or constrict
ASTRICTED > ASTRICT
ASTRICTS > ASTRICT
ASTRIDE adv with a leg on either side (of) ▷ adj with a leg on either side
ASTRINGE vb cause contraction
ASTRINGED > ASTRINGE
ASTRINGER n person who keeps goshawks
ASTRINGES > ASTRINGE
ASTROCYTE n any of the star-shaped cells in the tissue supporting the brain and spinal cord (neuroglia)
ASTRODOME n transparent dome on the top of an aircraft, through which observations can be made, esp of the stars
ASTROFELL n plant in Spenser's poetry
ASTROID n hypocycloid having four cusps
ASTROIDS > ASTROID
ASTROLABE n instrument formerly used to measure the altitude of stars and planets
ASTROLOGY n study of the alleged influence of the stars, planets, and moon on human affairs
ASTRONAUT n person trained for travelling in space
ASTRONOMY n scientific study of heavenly bodies
ASTROPHEL n plant in Spenser's poetry
ASTRUT adv old word meaning in a protruding way
ASTUCIOUS adj old form of astute
ASTUCITY n quality of being astute
ASTUN vb old form of astonish
ASTUNNED > ASTUN
ASTUNNING > ASTUN
ASTUNS > ASTUN
ASTUTE adj perceptive or shrewd
ASTUTELY > ASTUTE
ASTUTER > ASTUTE
ASTUTEST > ASTUTE
ASTYLAR adj without columns or pilasters
ASUDDEN adv old form of suddenly
ASUNDER adv into parts or pieces ▷ adj into parts or pieces
ASWARM adj filled, esp with moving things
ASWAY adv swaying
ASWIM adv floating
ASWING adv swinging

ASWIRL adv swirling
ASWOON adv swooning
ASYLA > ASYLUM
ASYLLABIC adj not functioning in the manner of a syllable
ASYLUM n refuge or sanctuary
ASYLUMS > ASYLUM
ASYMMETRY n lack of symmetry
ASYMPTOTE n straight line closely approached but never met by a curve
ASYNAPSES > ASYNAPSIS
ASYNAPSIS n failure of pairing of chromosomes at meiosis
ASYNDETA > ASYNDETON
ASYNDETIC adj (of a catalogue or index) without cross references
ASYNDETON n omission of a conjunction between the parts of a sentence
ASYNERGIA n lack of coordination between muscles or parts, as occurs in cerebellar disease
ASYNERGY same as > ASYNERGIA
ASYSTOLE n absence of heartbeat
ASYSTOLES > ASYSTOLE
ASYSTOLIC > ASYSTOLE
AT n Laotian monetary unit worth one hundredth of a kip
ATAATA n grazing marine gastropod
ATAATAS > ATAATA
ATABAL n N African drum
ATABALS > ATABAL
ATABEG n Turkish ruler
ATABEGS > ATABEG
ATABEK n Turkish ruler
ATABEKS > ATABEK
ATABRIN n drug formerly used for treating malaria
ATABRINE same as > ATABRIN
ATABRINES > ATABRINE
ATABRINS > ATABRIN
ATACAMITE n mineral containing copper
ATACTIC adj (of a polymer) having a random sequence of the stereochemical arrangement of groups on carbon atoms in the chain
ATAGHAN a variant of > YATAGHAN
ATAGHANS > ATAGHAN
ATALAYA n watchtower in Spain
ATALAYAS > ATALAYA
ATAMAN n elected leader of the Cossacks
ATAMANS > ATAMAN
ATAMASCO n N American lily
ATAMASCOS > ATAMASCO
ATAP n palm tree of S Asia
ATAPS > ATAP
ATARACTIC adj able to calm or tranquillize ▷ n ataractic drug
ATARAXIA n calmness or

peace of mind
ATARAXIAS > ATARAXIA
ATARAXIC same as > ATARACTIC
ATARAXICS > ATARAXIC
ATARAXIES > ATARAXY
ATARAXY same as > ATARAXIA
ATAVIC > ATAVISM
ATAVISM n recurrence of a trait present in distant ancestors
ATAVISMS > ATAVISM
ATAVIST > ATAVISM
ATAVISTIC adj of or relating to reversion to a former or more primitive type
ATAVISTS > ATAVISM
ATAXIA n lack of muscular coordination
ATAXIAS > ATAXIA
ATAXIC > ATAXIA
ATAXICS > ATAXIA
ATAXIES > ATAXY
ATAXY same as > ATAXIA
ATCHIEVE vb old form of > ACHIEVE
ATCHIEVED > ATCHIEVE
ATCHIEVES > ATCHIEVE
ATE past tense of > EAT
ATEBRIN n drug formerly used to treat malaria
ATEBRINS > ATEBRIN
ATECHNIC adj without technical ability
ATELIC adj of action without end
ATELIER n workshop, artist's studio
ATELIERS > ATELIER
ATEMOYA n tropical fruit tree
ATEMOYAS > ATEMOYA
ATEMPORAL adj not governed by time
ATENOLOL n type of beta-blocker
ATENOLOLS > ATENOLOL
ATES n shop selling confectionery
ATHAME n (in Wicca) witch's ceremonial knife, usually with a black handle, used in rituals rather than for cutting or carving
ATHAMES > ATHAME
ATHANASY n absence of death
ATHANOR n alchemist's furnace
ATHANORS > ATHANOR
ATHEISE vb speak atheistically
ATHEISED > ATHEISE
ATHEISES > ATHEISE
ATHEISING > ATHEISE
ATHEISM n belief that there is no God
ATHEISMS > ATHEISM
ATHEIST > ATHEISM
ATHEISTIC > ATHEISM
ATHEISTS > ATHEISM
ATHEIZE vb speak atheistically
ATHEIZED > ATHEIZE
ATHEIZES > ATHEIZE
ATHEIZING > ATHEIZE
ATHELING n (in Anglo-

Saxon England) a prince of any of the royal dynasties
ATHELINGS > ATHELING
ATHEMATIC adj not based on themes
ATHENAEUM n institution for the promotion of learning
ATHENEUM same as > ATHENAEUM
ATHENEUMS > ATHENEUM
ATHEOLOGY n opposition to theology
ATHEOUS adj without a belief in god
ATHERINE n small fish
ATHERINES > ATHERINE
ATHEROMA n fatty deposit on or within the inner lining of an artery, often causing an obstruction to the blood flow
ATHEROMAS > ATHEROMA
ATHETESES > ATHETESIS
ATHETESIS n dismissal of a text as not genuine
ATHETISE vb reject as not genuine
ATHETISED > ATHETISE
ATHETISES > ATHETISE
ATHETIZE vb reject as not genuine
ATHETIZED > ATHETIZE
ATHETIZES > ATHETIZE
ATHETOID > ATHETOSIS
ATHETOSES > ATHETOSIS
ATHETOSIC > ATHETOSIS
ATHETOSIS n condition characterized by uncontrolled rhythmic writhing movement, esp of fingers, hands, head, and tongue, caused by cerebral lesion
ATHETOTIC > ATHETOSIS
ATHIRST adj having an eager desire
ATHLETA n old form of > ATHLETE
ATHLETAS > ATHLETA
ATHLETE n person trained in or good at athletics
ATHLETES > ATHLETE
ATHLETIC adj physically fit or strong
ATHLETICS n track and field events
ATHODYD another name for > RAMJET
ATHODYDS > ATHODYD
ATHRILL adv feeling thrills
ATHROB adv throbbing
ATHROCYTE n cell able to store matter
ATHWART adv transversely
ATIGI n type of parka worn by the Inuit in Canada
ATIGIS > ATIGI
ATILT adj in a tilted or inclined position
ATIMIES > ATIMY
ATIMY n loss of honour
ATINGLE adv tingling
ATISHOO n sound of a sneeze
ATISHOOS > ATISHOO
ATLANTES > ATLAS
ATLAS n book of maps

ATLASES > ATLAS

ATLATL *n* Native American throwing stick

ATLATLS > ATLATL

ATMA *same as* > ATMAN

ATMAN *n* personal soul or self

ATMANS > ATMAN

ATMAS > ATMA

ATMOLOGY *n* study of aqueous vapour

ATMOLYSE *vb* separate gases by filtering

ATMOLYSED > ATMOLYSE

ATMOLYSES > ATMOLYSIS

ATMOLYSIS *n* method of separating gases that depends on their differential rates of diffusion through a porous substance

ATMOLYZE *vb* separate gases by filtering

ATMOLYZED > ATMOLYZE

ATMOLYZES > ATMOLYZE

ATMOMETER *n* instrument for measuring the rate of evaporation of water into the atmosphere

ATMOMETRY > ATMOMETER

ATOC *n* skunk

ATOCIA *n* inability to have children

ATOCIAS > ATOCIA

ATOCS > ATOC

ATOK *n* skunk

ATOKAL *adj* having no children

ATOKE *n* part of a worm

ATOKES > ATOKE

ATOKOUS *adj* having no children

ATOKS > ATOK

ATOLL *n* ring-shaped coral reef enclosing a lagoon

ATOLLS > ATOLL

ATOM *n* smallest unit of matter which can take part in a chemical reaction

ATOMIC *adj* of or using atomic bombs or atomic energy

ATOMICAL > ATOMIC

ATOMICITY *n* state of being made up of atoms

ATOMICS *n* science of atoms

ATOMIES > ATOMY

ATOMISE *same as* > ATOMIZE

ATOMISED > ATOMISE

ATOMISER *same as* > ATOMIZER

ATOMISERS > ATOMISER

ATOMISES > ATOMISE

ATOMISING > ATOMISE

ATOMISM *n* ancient philosophical theory that the ultimate constituents of the universe are atoms

ATOMISMS > ATOMISM

ATOMIST > ATOMISM

ATOMISTIC > ATOMISM

ATOMISTS > ATOMISM

ATOMIZE *vb* reduce to atoms or small particles

ATOMIZED > ATOMIZE

ATOMIZER *n* device for discharging a liquid in a fine

spray

ATOMIZERS > ATOMIZER

ATOMIZES > ATOMIZE

ATOMIZING > ATOMIZE

ATOMS > ATOM

ATOMY *n* atom or minute particle

ATONABLE > ATONE

ATONAL *adj* (of music) not written in an established key

ATONALISM > ATONAL

ATONALIST > ATONAL

ATONALITY *n* absence of or disregard for an established musical key in a composition

ATONALLY > ATONAL

ATONE *vb* make amends (for sin or wrongdoing)

ATONEABLE > ATONE

ATONED > ATONE

ATONEMENT *n* something done to make amends for wrongdoing

ATONER > ATONE

ATONERS > ATONE

ATONES > ATONE

ATONIA *n* lack of normal muscle tone

ATONIAS > ATONIA

ATONIC *adj* (of a syllable, word, etc) carrying no stress ▷ *n* unaccented or unstressed syllable, word, etc, such as *for* in *food for thought*

ATONICITY > ATONIC

ATONICS > ATONIC

ATONIES > ATONY

ATONING > ATONE

ATONINGLY > ATONE

ATONY *n* lack of normal tone or tension, as in muscles

ATOP *adv* on top

ATOPIC *adj* of or relating to hereditary hypersensitivity to certain allergens

ATOPIES > ATOPY

ATOPY *n* hereditary tendency to be hypersensitive to certain allergens

ATRAMENT *n* old word meaning black liquid

ATRAMENTS > ATRAMENT

ATRAZINE *n* white crystalline compound

ATRAZINES > ATRAZINE

ATREMBLE *adv* trembling

ATRESIA *n* absence of or unnatural narrowing of a body channel

ATRESIAS > ATRESIA

ATRESIC > ATRESIA

ATRETIC > ATRESIA

ATRIA > ATRIUM

ATRIAL > ATRIUM

ATRIP *adj* (of an anchor) no longer caught on the bottom

ATRIUM *n* upper chamber of either half of the heart

ATRIUMS > ATRIUM

ATROCIOUS *adj* extremely cruel or wicked

ATROCITY *n* wickedness

ATROPHIA *n* wasting disease

ATROPHIAS > ATROPHIA

ATROPHIC > ATROPHY

ATROPHIED > ATROPHY

ATROPHIES > ATROPHY

ATROPHY *n* wasting away of an organ or part ▷ *vb* (cause to) waste away

ATROPIA *n* atropine

ATROPIAS > ATROPIA

ATROPIN *same as* > ATROPINE

ATROPINE *n* poisonous alkaloid obtained from deadly nightshade

ATROPINES > ATROPINE

ATROPINS > ATROPIN

ATROPISM *n* condition caused by using belladonna

ATROPISMS > ATROPISM

ATROPOUS *adj* growing straight

ATT *n* old Siamese coin

ATTABOY *sentence substitute* expression of approval or exhortation

ATTACH *vb* join, fasten, or connect

ATTACHE *n* a specialist attached to a diplomatic mission

ATTACHED *adj* fond of

ATTACHER > ATTACH

ATTACHERS > ATTACH

ATTACHES > ATTACH

ATTACHING > ATTACH

ATTACK *vb* launch a physical assault (against) ▷ *n* act of attacking

ATTACKED > ATTACK

ATTACKER > ATTACK

ATTACKERS > ATTACK

ATTACKING > ATTACK

ATTACKMAN *n* attacking player in sport

ATTACKMEN > ATTACKMAN

ATTACKS > ATTACK

ATTAGIRL *humorous feminine version of* > ATTABOY

ATTAIN *vb* achieve or accomplish (a task or aim)

ATTAINDER *n* (formerly) the extinction of a person's civil rights resulting from a sentence of death or outlawry on conviction for treason or felony

ATTAINED > ATTAIN

ATTAINER > ATTAIN

ATTAINERS > ATTAIN

ATTAINING > ATTAIN

ATTAINS > ATTAIN

ATTAINT *vb* pass judgment of death or outlawry upon (a person) ▷ *n* dishonour

ATTAINTED > ATTAINT

ATTAINTS > ATTAINT

ATTAP *n* palm tree of South Asia

ATTAPS > ATTAP

ATTAR *n* fragrant oil made from roses

ATTARS > ATTAR

ATTASK *old word for* > CRITICIZE

ATTASKED > ATTASK

ATTASKING > ATTASK

ATTASKS > ATTASK

ATTASKT > ATTASK

ATTEMPER *vb* modify by blending

ATTEMPERS > ATTEMPER

ATTEMPT *vb* try, make an effort ▷ *n* effort or endeavour

ATTEMPTED > ATTEMPT

ATTEMPTER > ATTEMPT

ATTEMPTS > ATTEMPT

ATTEND *vb* be present at

ATTENDANT *n* person who assists, guides, or provides a service ▷ *adj* accompanying

ATTENDED > ATTEND

ATTENDEE *n* person who is present at a specified event

ATTENDEES > ATTENDEE

ATTENDER > ATTEND

ATTENDERS > ATTEND

ATTENDING > ATTEND

ATTENDS > ATTEND

ATTENT *old word for* > ATTENTION

ATTENTAT *n* attempt

ATTENTATS > ATTENTAT

ATTENTION *n* concentrated direction of the mind

ATTENTIVE *adj* giving attention

ATTENTS > ATTENT

ATTENUANT *adj* causing dilution or thinness, esp of the blood ▷ *n* attenuant drug or agent

ATTENUATE *vb* weaken or become weak ▷ *adj* diluted, weakened, slender, or reduced

ATTERCOP *n* spider

ATTERCOPS > ATTERCOP

ATTEST *vb* affirm the truth of, be proof of

ATTESTANT > ATTEST

ATTESTED *adj* (of cattle) certified to be free from a disease, such as tuberculosis

ATTESTER > ATTEST

ATTESTERS > ATTEST

ATTESTING > ATTEST

ATTESTOR > ATTEST

ATTESTORS > ATTEST

ATTESTS > ATTEST

ATTIC *n* space or room within the roof of a house

ATTICISE *same as* > ATTICIZE

ATTICISED > ATTICISE

ATTICISES > ATTICISE

ATTICISM *n* elegant, simple, and clear expression

ATTICISMS > ATTICISM

ATTICIST > ATTICISM

ATTICISTS > ATTICISM

ATTICIZE *vb* conform or adapt to the norms of Attica

ATTICIZED > ATTICIZE

ATTICIZES > ATTICIZE

ATTICS > ATTIC

ATTIRE *n* fine or formal clothes ▷ *vb* dress, esp in

a

fine elegant clothes

ATTIRED > ATTIRE

ATTIRES > ATTIRE

ATTIRING > ATTIRE

ATTIRINGS > ATTIRE

ATTITUDE *n* way of thinking and behaving

ATTITUDES > ATTITUDE

ATTOLASER *n* high-power laser capable of producing pulses with a duration measured in attoseconds

ATTOLLENS *adj* (of muscle) used to lift

ATTOLLENT *adj* muscle used in lifting

ATTONCE *adv* old word for at once

ATTONE *vb* old word meaning appease

ATTONES > ATTONE

ATTORN *vb* acknowledge a new owner of land as one's landlord

ATTORNED > ATTORN

ATTORNEY *n* person legally appointed to act for another

ATTORNEYS > ATTORNEY

ATTORNING > ATTORN

ATTORNS > ATTORN

ATTRACT *vb* arouse the interest or admiration of

ATTRACTED > ATTRACT

ATTRACTER > ATTRACT

ATTRACTOR > ATTRACT

ATTRACTS > ATTRACT

ATTRAHENS *adj* (of muscle) drawing towards

ATTRAHENT *adj* something that attracts

ATTRAP *vb* adorn

ATTRAPPED > ATTRAP

ATTRAPS > ATTRAP

ATTRIBUTE *vb* regard as belonging to or produced by ▷ *n* quality or feature representative of a person or thing

ATTRIST *vb* old word meaning to sadden

ATTRISTED > ATTRIST

ATTRISTS > ATTRIST

ATTRIT *vb* wear down or dispose of gradually

ATTRITE *vb* wear down

ATTRITED > ATTRITE

ATTRITES > ATTRITE

ATTRITING > ATTRITE

ATTRITION *n* constant wearing down to weaken or destroy

ATTRITIVE > ATTRITION

ATTRITS > ATTRIT

ATTRITTED > ATTRIT

ATTUENT *adj* carrying out attuition

ATTUITE *vb* perceive by attuition

ATTUITED > ATTUITE

ATTUITES > ATTUITE

ATTUITING > ATTUITE

ATTUITION *n* way of mentally perceiving something

ATTUITIVE > ATTUITION

ATTUNE *vb* adjust or

accustom (a person or thing)

ATTUNED > ATTUNE

ATTUNES > ATTUNE

ATTUNING > ATTUNE

ATUA *n* spirit or demon

ATUAS > ATUA

ATWAIN *adv* old word meaning into two parts

ATWEEL *Scots word for* > WELL

ATWEEN *an archaic or Scots word for* > BETWEEN

ATWITTER *adv* twittering

ATWIXT *old word for* > BETWEEN

ATYPIC *adj* not typical

ATYPICAL *adj* not typical

AUA *n* yellow-eye mullet

AUBADE *n* song or poem appropriate to or greeting the dawn

AUBADES > AUBADE

AUBERGE *n* inn or tavern

AUBERGES > AUBERGE

AUBERGINE *n* dark purple tropical fruit, cooked and eaten as a vegetable

AUBRETIA *same as* > AUBRIETIA

AUBRETIAS > AUBRETIA

AUBRIETA *same as* > AUBRIETIA

AUBRIETAS > AUBRIETA

AUBRIETIA *n* trailing plant with purple flowers

AUBURN *adj* (of hair) reddish-brown ▷ *n* moderate reddish-brown colour

AUBURNS > AUBURN

AUCEPS *n* old word meaning person who catches hawks

AUCEPSES > AUCEPS

AUCTION *n* public sale in which articles are sold to the highest bidder ▷ *vb* sell by auction

AUCTIONED > AUCTION

AUCTIONS > AUCTION

AUCTORIAL *adj* of or relating to an author

AUCUBA *n* Japanese laurel

AUCUBAS > AUCUBA

AUDACIOUS *adj* recklessly bold or daring

AUDACITY > AUDACIOUS

AUDAD *n* wild African sheep

AUDADS > AUDAD

AUDIAL *adj* of sound

AUDIBLE *adj* loud enough to be heard ▷ *n* change of playing tactics called by the quarterback when the offence is lined up at the line of scrimmage ▷ *vb* call an audible

AUDIBLED > AUDIBLE

AUDIBLES > AUDIBLE

AUDIBLING > AUDIBLE

AUDIBLY > AUDIBLE

AUDIENCE *n* group of spectators or listeners

AUDIENCES > AUDIENCE

AUDIENCIA *n* court in South America

AUDIENT *n* person who hears

AUDIENTS > AUDIENT

AUDILE *n* person who possesses a faculty for auditory imagery that is more distinct than his visual or other imagery ▷ *adj* of or relating to such a person

AUDILES > AUDILE

AUDING *n* practice of listening to try to understand

AUDINGS > AUDING

AUDIO *adj* of sound or hearing ▷ *n* of or relating to sound or hearing

AUDIOBOOK *n* recorded reading of a book

AUDIOGRAM *n* graphic record of the acuity of hearing of a person obtained by means of an audiometer

AUDIOLOGY *n* scientific study of hearing, often including the treatment of persons with hearing defects

AUDIOPHIL *n* audiophile

AUDIOS > AUDIO

AUDIOTAPE *n* tape for recording sound

AUDIPHONE *n* type of hearing aid consisting of a diaphragm that, when placed against the upper teeth, conveys sound vibrations to the inner ear

AUDIT *n* official examination of business accounts ▷ *vb* examine (business accounts) officially

AUDITABLE > AUDIT

AUDITED > AUDIT

AUDITEE *n* one who is audited

AUDITEES > AUDITEE

AUDITING > AUDIT

AUDITION *n* test of a performer's ability for a particular role or job ▷ *vb* test or be tested in an audition

AUDITIONS > AUDITION

AUDITIVE *n* person who learns primarily by listening

AUDITIVES > AUDITIVE

AUDITOR *n* person qualified to audit accounts

AUDITORIA *n* areas of concert halls, theatres, schools, etc, in which audiences sit

AUDITORS > AUDITOR

AUDITORY *adj* of or relating to hearing

AUDITRESS *n* female auditor

AUDITS > AUDIT

AUE *interj* Māori exclamation

AUF *old word for* > OAF

AUFGABE *n* word used in psychology to mean task

AUFGABES > AUFGABE

AUFS > AUF

AUGEND *n* number to which another number, the addend, is added

AUGENDS > AUGEND

AUGER *n* tool for boring holes

AUGERS > AUGER

AUGHT *adv* in any least part ▷ *n* less common word for 'nought' (zero)

AUGHTS > AUGHT

AUGITE *n* black or greenish-black mineral

AUGITES > AUGITE

AUGITIC > AUGITE

AUGMENT *vb* increase or enlarge ▷ *n* (in Greek and Sanskrit grammar) a vowel or diphthong prefixed to a verb to form a past tense

AUGMENTED > AUGMENT

AUGMENTER > AUGMENT

AUGMENTOR > AUGMENT

AUGMENTS > AUGMENT

AUGUR *vb* be a sign of (future events) ▷ *n* (in ancient Rome) a religious official who observed and interpreted omens and signs to help guide the making of public decisions

AUGURAL > AUGUR

AUGURED > AUGUR

AUGURER *old word for* > AUGUR

AUGURERS > AUGURER

AUGURIES > AUGURY

AUGURING > AUGUR

AUGURS > AUGUR

AUGURSHIP > AUGUR

AUGURY *n* foretelling of the future

AUGUST *same as* > AUGUSTE *adj* dignified and imposing

AUGUSTE *n* type of circus clown who usually wears battered ordinary clothes and is habitually maladroit or unlucky

AUGUSTER > AUGUST

AUGUSTES > AUGUSTE

AUGUSTEST > AUGUST

AUGUSTLY > AUGUST

AUGUSTS > AUGUST

AUK *n* northern sea bird with short wings and black-and-white plumage

AUKLET *n* any of various small auks of the genera *Aethia* and *Ptychoramphus*

AUKLETS > AUKLET

AUKS > AUK

AULA *n* hall

AULARIAN *n* Oxford University student belonging to hall

AULARIANS > AULARIAN

AULAS > AULA

AULD *a Scots word for* > OLD

AULDER > AULD

AULDEST > AULD

AULIC *adj* relating to a royal court

AULNAGE *n* measurement in ells

AULNAGER *n* inspector of

cloth

AULNAGERS > AULNAGER

AULNAGES > AULNAGE

AULOI > AULOS

AULOS *n* ancient Greek pipes

AUMAIL *old word for* > ENAMEL

AUMAILED > AUMAIL

AUMAILING > AUMAIL

AUMAILS > AUMAIL

AUMBRIES > AUMBRY

AUMBRY *same as* > AMBRY

AUMIL *n* manager in India

AUMILS > AUMIL

AUNE *n* old French measure of length

AUNES > AUNE

AUNT *n* father's or mother's sister

AUNTER *old word for* > ADVENTURE

AUNTERS > AUNTER

AUNTHOOD > AUNT

AUNTHOODS > AUNT

AUNTIE *n* aunt

AUNTIES > AUNTY

AUNTLIER > AUNTLY

AUNTLIEST > AUNTLY

AUNTLIKE > AUNT

AUNTLY *adj* of or like an aunt

AUNTS > AUNT

AUNTY *same as* > AUNTIE

AURA *n* distinctive air or quality of a person or thing

AURAE > AURA

AURAL *adj* of or using the ears or hearing

AURALITY > AURAL

AURALLY > AURAL

AURAR *plural of* > EYRIR

AURAS > AURA

AURATE *n* salt of auric acid

AURATED *adj* combined with auric acid

AURATES > AURATE

AUREATE *adj* covered with gold, gilded

AUREATELY > AUREATE

AUREI > AUREUS

AUREITIES > AUREITY

AUREITY *n* attributes of gold

AURELIA *n* large jellyfish

AURELIAN *n* person who studies butterflies and moths

AURELIANS > AURELIAN

AURELIAS > AURELIA

AUREOLA *same as* > AUREOLE

AUREOLAE > AUREOLA

AUREOLAS > AUREOLA

AUREOLE *n* halo

AUREOLED > AUREOLE

AUREOLES > AUREOLE

AUREOLING > AUREOLE

AURES > AURIS

AUREUS *n* gold coin of the Roman Empire

AURIC *adj* of or containing gold in the trivalent state

AURICLE *n* upper chamber of the heart

AURICLED > AURICLE

AURICLES > AURICLE

AURICULA *n* alpine primrose with leaves shaped like a bear's ear

AURICULAE > AURICULA

AURICULAR *adj* of, relating to, or received by the sense or organs of hearing ▷*n* auricular feather

AURICULAS > AURICULA

AURIFIED > AURIFY

AURIFIES > AURIFY

AURIFORM *adj* shaped like an ear

AURIFY *vb* turn into gold

AURIFYING > AURIFY

AURIS *n* medical word for ear

AURISCOPE *n* medical instrument for examinig the external ear

AURIST *a former name for* > AUDIOLOGY

AURISTS > AURIST

AUROCHS *n* recently extinct European wild ox

AUROCHSES > AUROCHS

AURORA *n* bands of light sometimes seen in the sky in polar regions

AURORAE > AURORA

AURORAL > AURORA

AURORALLY > AURORA

AURORAS > AURORA

AUROREAN *adj* of dawn

AUROUS *adj* of or containing gold, esp in the monovalent state

AURUM *n* gold

AURUMS > AURUM

AUSFORM *vb* temper steel

AUSFORMED > AUSFORM

AUSFORMS > AUSFORM

AUSLANDER *n* German word meaning foreigner

AUSPEX *same as* > AUGUR

AUSPICATE *vb* inaugurate with a ceremony intended to bring good fortune

AUSPICE *n* patronage or guidance

AUSPICES > AUSPICE

AUSTENITE *n* solid solution of carbon in face-centred-cubic gamma iron, usually existing above 723°C

AUSTERE *adj* stern or severe

AUSTERELY > AUSTERE

AUSTERER > AUSTERE

AUSTEREST > AUSTERE

AUSTERITY *n* state of being austere

AUSTRAL *adj* southern ▷*n* former monetary unit of Argentina equal to 100 centavos, replaced by the peso

AUSTRALES > AUSTRAL

AUSTRALIS *adj* Australian

AUSTRALS > AUSTRAL

AUSUBO *n* tropical tree

AUSUBOS > AUSUBO

AUTACOID *n* any natural internal secretion, esp one that exerts an effect similar to a drug

AUTACOIDS > AUTACOID

AUTARCH *n* absolute ruler

AUTARCHIC > AUTARCHY

AUTARCHS > AUTARCH

AUTARCHY *n* absolute power

or autocracy

AUTARKIC > AUTARKY

AUTARKIES > AUTARKY

AUTARKIST > AUTARKY

AUTARKY *n* policy of economic self-sufficiency

AUTECIOUS *adj* (of parasites, esp the rust fungi) completing the entire life cycle on a single species of host

AUTECISM > AUTECIOUS

AUTECISMS > AUTECIOUS

AUTEUR *n* director whose creative influence on a film is so great as to be considered its author

AUTEURISM > AUTEUR

AUTEURIST > AUTEUR

AUTEURS > AUTEUR

AUTHENTIC *adj* known to be real, genuine

AUTHOR *n* writer of a book etc ▷*vb* write or originate

AUTHORED > AUTHOR

AUTHORESS *n* female author

AUTHORIAL > AUTHOR

AUTHORING *n* creation of documents, esp multimedia documents

AUTHORISE *same as* > AUTHORIZE

AUTHORISH > AUTHOR

AUTHORISM *n* condition of being author

AUTHORITY *n* power to command or control others

AUTHORIZE *vb* give authority to

AUTHORS > AUTHOR

AUTISM *n* disorder characterized by lack of response to people and limited ability to communicate

AUTISMS > AUTISM

AUTIST *n* autistic person

AUTISTIC > AUTISM

AUTISTICS > AUTISM

AUTISTS > AUTIST

AUTO *n* automobile ▷*vb* travel in an automobile

AUTOBAHN *n* German motorway

AUTOBAHNS > AUTOBAHN

AUTOBUS *n* motor bus

AUTOBUSES > AUTOBUS

AUTOCADE *another name for* > MOTORCADE

AUTOCADES > AUTOCADE

AUTOCAR *n* motor car

AUTOCARP *n* fruit produced through self-fertilization

AUTOCARPS > AUTOCARP

AUTOCARS > AUTOCAR

AUTOCIDAL *adj* (of insect pest control) effected by the introduction of sterile or genetically altered individuals into the wild population

AUTOCLAVE *n* apparatus for sterilizing objects by steam under pressure ▷*vb* put in or subject to the action of an autoclave

AUTOCOID *n* hormone

AUTOCOIDS > AUTOCOID

AUTOCRACY *n* government by an autocrat

AUTOCRAT *n* ruler with absolute authority

AUTOCRATS > AUTOCRAT

AUTOCRIME *n* crime of stealing a car

AUTOCRINE *adj* relating to self-stimulation through production of a factor and its receptor

AUTOCROSS *n* motor-racing over a rough course

AUTOCUE *n* electronic television prompting device

AUTOCUES > AUTOCUE

AUTOCUTIE *n* young and attractive but inexperienced female television presenter

AUTOCYCLE *n* bicycle powered or assisted by a small engine

AUTODYNE *adj* denoting or relating to an electrical circuit in which the same elements and valves are used as oscillator and detector ▷*n* autodyne circuit

AUTODYNES > AUTODYNE

AUTOECISM *n* (of a parasite) completion of an entire lifecycle on a single species of host

AUTOED > AUTO

AUTOFLARE *n* automatic landing systen in aircraft

AUTOFOCUS *n* camera system in which the lens is focused automatically

AUTOGAMIC > AUTOGAMY

AUTOGAMY *n* self-fertilization in flowering plants

AUTOGENIC *adj* produced from within

AUTOGENY *n* hypothetical process by which living organisms first arose on earth from nonliving matter

AUTOGIRO *n* self-propelled aircraft resembling a helicopter but with an unpowered rotor

AUTOGIROS > AUTOGIRO

AUTOGRAFT *n* tissue graft obtained from one part of a patient's body for use on another part

AUTOGRAPH *n* handwritten signature of a (famous) person ▷*vb* write one's signature on or in

AUTOGUIDE *n* traffic information transmission system

AUTOGYRO *same as* > AUTOGIRO

AUTOGYROS > AUTOGYRO

AUTOHARP *n* zither-like musical instrument

AUTOHARPS > AUTOHARP

AUTOICOUS *adj* (of plants,

a

esp mosses) having male and female reproductive organs on the same plant
AUTOING > AUTO
AUTOLATRY n self-worship
AUTOLOGY n study of oneself
AUTOLYSE vb undergo or cause to undergo autolysis
AUTOLYSED > AUTOLYSE
AUTOLYSES > AUTOLYSE
AUTOLYSIN n any agent that produces autolysis
AUTOLYSIS n destruction of cells and tissues of an organism by enzymes produced by the cells themselves
AUTOLYTIC > AUTOLYSIS
AUTOLYZE same as > AUTOLYSE
AUTOLYZED > AUTOLYZE
AUTOLYZES > AUTOLYZE
AUTOMAKER n car manufacturer
AUTOMAN n car manufacturer
AUTOMAT n vending machine
AUTOMATA > AUTOMATON
AUTOMATE vb make (a manufacturing process) automatic
AUTOMATED > AUTOMATE
AUTOMATES > AUTOMATE
AUTOMATIC adj (of a device) operating mechanically by itself ▷ n self-loading firearm
AUTOMATON n robot
AUTOMATS > AUTOMAT
AUTOMEN > AUTOMAN
AUTOMETER n small device inserted in a photocopier to enable the process of copying to begin and to record the number of copies made
AUTONOMIC adj occurring involuntarily or spontaneously
AUTONOMY n self-government
AUTONYM n writing published under the real name of an author
AUTONYMS > AUTONYM
AUTOPEN n mechanical device used to produce imitation signatures
AUTOPENS > AUTOPEN
AUTOPHAGY n consumption of one's own tissue
AUTOPHOBY n reluctance to refer to oneself
AUTOPHONY n medical diagnosis by listening to vibration of one's own voice in patient
AUTOPHYTE n autotrophic plant, such as any green plant
AUTOPILOT n automatic pilot
AUTOPISTA n Spanish motorway
AUTOPOINT n point-to-point race in cars

AUTOPSIA n autopsy
AUTOPSIAS > AUTOPSIA
AUTOPSIC > AUTOPSY
AUTOPSIED > AUTOPSY
AUTOPSIES > AUTOPSY
AUTOPSIST > AUTOPSY
AUTOPSY n examination of a corpse to determine the cause of death
AUTOPTIC > AUTOPSY
AUTOPUT n motorway in the former Yugoslavia
AUTOPUTS > AUTOPUT
AUTOROUTE n French motorway
AUTOS > AUTO
AUTOSCOPY n hallucination in which one sees oneself
AUTOSOMAL > AUTOSOME
AUTOSOME n any chromosome that is not a sex chromosome
AUTOSOMES > AUTOSOME
AUTOSPORE n nonmotile algal spore that develops adult characteristics before being released
AUTOTELIC adj justifying itself
AUTOTIMER n device for turning a system on and off automatically at times predetermined by advance setting
AUTOTOMIC > AUTOTOMY
AUTOTOMY n casting off by an animal of a part of its body, to facilitate escape when attacked
AUTOTOXIC > AUTOTOXIN
AUTOTOXIN n any poison or toxin formed in the organism upon which it acts
AUTOTROPH n organism capable of manufacturing complex organic nutritive compounds from simple inorganic sources
AUTOTUNE n software package that automatically manipulates a recording of a vocal track until it is in tune regardless of whether or not the original performance was in tune
AUTOTUNES > AUTOTUNE
AUTOTYPE n photographic process for producing prints in black and white, using a carbon pigment ▷ vb process using autotype
AUTOTYPED > AUTOTYPE
AUTOTYPES > AUTOTYPE
AUTOTYPIC > AUTOTYPE
AUTOTYPY > AUTOTYPE
AUTOVAC n vacuum pump in a car petrol tank
AUTOVACS > AUTOVAC
AUTUMN n season between summer and winter
AUTUMNAL adj of, occurring in, or characteristic of autumn
AUTUMNS > AUTUMN

AUTUMNY adj like autumn
AUTUNITE n yellowish fluorescent radioactive mineral
AUTUNITES > AUTUNITE
AUXESES > AUXESIS
AUXESIS n growth in animal or plant tissues resulting from an increase in cell size without cell division
AUXETIC n something that promotes growth
AUXETICS > AUXETIC
AUXILIAR old word for > AUXILIARY
AUXILIARS > AUXILIAR
AUXILIARY adj secondary or supplementary ▷ n person or thing that supplements or supports
AUXIN n any of various plant hormones, such as indoleacetic acid, that promote growth and control fruit and flower development. Synthetic auxins are widely used in agriculture and horticulture
AUXINIC > AUXIN
AUXINS > AUXIN
AUXOCYTE n any cell undergoing meiosis, esp an oocyte or spermatocyte
AUXOCYTES > AUXOCYTE
AUXOMETER n instrument for measuring magnification
AUXOSPORE n diatom cell before its silicaceous cell wall is formed
AUXOTONIC adj (of muscle contraction) occurring against increasing force
AUXOTROPH n mutant strain of microorganism having nutritional requirements additional to those of the normal organism
AVA adv at all ▷ n Polynesian shrub
AVADAVAT n either of two Asian weaverbirds of the genus *Estrilda*, esp *E. amandava*, having a red plumage: often kept as cagebirds
AVADAVATS > AVADAVAT
AVAIL vb be of use or advantage (to) ▷ n use or advantage
AVAILABLE adj obtainable or accessible
AVAILABLY > AVAILABLE
AVAILE old word for > LOWER
AVAILED > AVAIL
AVAILES > AVAILE
AVAILFUL old word for > USEFUL
AVAILING > AVAIL
AVAILS > AVAIL
AVAL adj of a grandparent
AVALANCHE n mass of snow or ice falling down a mountain ▷ vb come down overwhelmingly

(upon)
AVALE old word for > LOWER
AVALED > AVALE
AVALES > AVALE
AVALING > AVALE
AVANT prep before
AVANTI interj forward!
AVANTIST n proponent of the avant-garde
AVANTISTS > AVANTIST
AVARICE n greed for wealth
AVARICES > AVARICE
AVAS > AVA
AVASCULAR adj (of certain tissues, such as cartilage) lacking blood vessels
AVAST sentence substitute stop! cease!
AVATAR n appearance of a god in animal or human form
AVATARS > AVATAR
AVAUNT sentence substitute go away! depart! ▷ vb go away; depart
AVAUNTED > AVAUNT
AVAUNTING > AVAUNT
AVAUNTS > AVAUNT
AVE n expression of welcome or farewell
AVEL a variant of > OVEL
AVELLAN adj of hazelnuts
AVELLANE adj of hazelnuts
AVELS > AVEL
AVENGE vb take revenge in retaliation for (harm done) or on behalf of (a person harmed)
AVENGED > AVENGE
AVENGEFUL > AVENGE
AVENGER > AVENGE
AVENGERS > AVENGE
AVENGES > AVENGE
AVENGING > AVENGE
AVENIR n future
AVENIRS > AVENIR
AVENS n any of several temperate or arctic rosaceous plants
AVENSES > AVENS
AVENTAIL n front flap of a helmet
AVENTAILE n avantail
AVENTAILS > AVENTAIL
AVENTRE old word for > THRUST
AVENTRED > AVENTRE
AVENTRES > AVENTRE
AVENTRING > AVENTRE
AVENTURE old form of > ADVENTURE
AVENTURES > AVENTURE
AVENTURIN n dark-coloured glass, usually green or brown, spangled with fine particles of gold, copper, or some other metal
AVENUE n wide street
AVENUES > AVENUE
AVER vb state to be true
AVERAGE n typical or normal amount or quality ▷ adj usual or typical ▷ vb calculate the average of
AVERAGED > AVERAGE
AVERAGELY > AVERAGE
AVERAGES > AVERAGE

AVERAGING > AVERAGE
AVERMENT > AVER
AVERMENTS > AVER
AVERRABLE > AVER
AVERRED > AVER
AVERRING > AVER
AVERS > AVER
AVERSE adj disinclined or unwilling
AVERSELY > AVERSE
AVERSION n strong dislike
AVERSIONS > AVERSION
AVERSIVE n tool or technique intended to repel animals etc
AVERSIVES > AVERSIVE
AVERT vb turn away
AVERTABLE > AVERT
AVERTED > AVERT
AVERTEDLY > AVERT
AVERTER > AVERT
AVERTERS > AVERT
AVERTIBLE > AVERT
AVERTING > AVERT
AVERTS > AVERT
AVES > AVE
AVGAS n aviation fuel
AVGASES > AVGAS
AVGASSES > AVGAS
AVIAN adj of or like a bird ▷n bird
AVIANISE same as > AVIANIZE
AVIANISED > AVIANISE
AVIANISES > AVIANISE
AVIANIZE vb modify microorganisms in a chicken embryo
AVIANIZED > AVIANIZE
AVIANIZES > AVIANIZE
AVIANS > AVIAN
AVIARIES > AVIARY
AVIARIST n person who keeps an aviary
AVIARISTS > AVIARIST
AVIARY n large cage or enclosure for birds
AVIATE vb pilot or fly in an aircraft
AVIATED > AVIATE
AVIATES > AVIATE
AVIATIC adj pertaining to aviation
AVIATING > AVIATE
AVIATION n art of flying aircraft
AVIATIONS > AVIATION
AVIATOR n pilot of an aircraft
AVIATORS > AVIATOR
AVIATRESS > AVIATOR
AVIATRICE > AVIATOR
AVIATRIX > AVIATOR
AVICULAR adj of small birds
AVID adj keen or enthusiastic
AVIDER > AVID
AVIDEST > AVID
AVIDIN n protein, found in egg-white, that combines with biotin to form a stable compound that cannot be absorbed, leading to a biotin deficiency in the consumer
AVIDINS > AVIDIN
AVIDITIES > AVIDITY

AVIDITY n quality or state of being avid
AVIDLY > AVID
AVIDNESS > AVID
AVIETTE n aeroplane driven by human strength
AVIETTES > AVIETTE
AVIFAUNA n all the birds in a particular region
AVIFAUNAE > AVIFAUNA
AVIFAUNAL > AVIFAUNA
AVIFAUNAS > AVIFAUNA
AVIFORM adj like a bird
AVIGATOR another word for > AVIATOR
AVIGATORS > AVIGATOR
AVINE adj of birds
AVION n aeroplane
AVIONIC > AVIONICS
AVIONICS n science and technology of electronics applied to aeronautics and astronautics
AVIONS > AVION
AVIRULENT adj (esp of bacteria) not virulent
AVISANDUM n consideration of a law case by a judge
AVISE old word for > ADVISE
AVISED > AVISE
AVISEMENT > AVISE
AVISES > AVISE
AVISING > AVISE
AVISO n boat carrying messages
AVISOS > AVISO
AVITAL adj of a grandfather
AVIZANDUM n judge's or court's decision to consider a case privately before giving judgment
AVIZE old word for > ADVISE
AVIZED > AVIZE
AVIZEFULL > AVIZE
AVIZES > AVIZE
AVIZING > AVIZE
AVO n Macao currency unit
AVOCADO n pear-shaped tropical fruit with a leathery green skin and yellowish-green flesh
AVOCADOES > AVOCADO
AVOCADOS > AVOCADO
AVOCATION n occupation
AVOCET n long-legged wading bird with a long slender upward-curving bill
AVOCETS > AVOCET
AVODIRE n African tree
AVODIRES > AVODIRE
AVOID vb prevent from happening
AVOIDABLE > AVOID
AVOIDABLY > AVOID
AVOIDANCE n act of keeping away from or preventing from happening
AVOIDANT adj (of behaviour) demonstrating a tendency to avoid intimacy or interaction with others
AVOIDED > AVOID
AVOIDER > AVOID
AVOIDERS > AVOID
AVOIDING > AVOID
AVOIDS > AVOID
AVOISION n nonpayment

of tax
AVOISIONS > AVOISION
AVOS > AVO
AVOSET n avocet
AVOSETS > AVOSET
AVOUCH vb vouch for
AVOUCHED > AVOUCH
AVOUCHER > AVOUCH
AVOUCHERS > AVOUCH
AVOUCHES > AVOUCH
AVOUCHING > AVOUCH
AVOURE old word for > AVOWAL
AVOURES > AVOURE
AVOUTERER old word for > ADULTERER
AVOUTRER old word for > ADULTERER
AVOUTRERS > AVOUTRER
AVOUTRIES > AVOUTRY
AVOUTRY old word for > ADULTERY
AVOW vb state or affirm
AVOWABLE > AVOW
AVOWABLY > AVOW
AVOWAL > AVOW
AVOWALS > AVOW
AVOWED > AVOW
AVOWEDLY > AVOW
AVOWER > AVOW
AVOWERS > AVOW
AVOWING > AVOW
AVOWRIES > AVOWRY
AVOWRY old word for > AVOWAL
AVOWS > AVOW
AVOYER n former Swiss magistrate
AVOYERS > AVOYER
AVRUGA n herring roe with a smoky flavour, sometimes used as a less expensive alternative to caviar
AVRUGAS > AVRUGA
AVULSE vb take away by force
AVULSED > AVULSE
AVULSES > AVULSE
AVULSING > AVULSE
AVULSION n forcible tearing away or separation of a bodily structure or part, either as the result of injury or as an intentional surgical procedure
AVULSIONS > AVULSION
AVUNCULAR adj (of a man) friendly, helpful, and caring towards someone younger
AVYZE old word for > ADVISE
AVYZED > AVYZE
AVYZES > AVYZE
AVYZING > AVYZE
AW variant of > ALL
AWA adv away
AWAIT vb wait for
AWAITED > AWAIT
AWAITER > AWAIT
AWAITERS > AWAIT
AWAITING > AWAIT
AWAITS > AWAIT
AWAKE vb emerge or rouse from sleep ▷adj not sleeping
AWAKED > AWAKE
AWAKEN vb awake
AWAKENED > AWAKEN

AWAKENER > AWAKEN
AWAKENERS > AWAKEN
AWAKENING n start of a feeling or awareness in someone
AWAKENS > AWAKEN
AWAKES > AWAKE
AWAKING > AWAKE
AWAKINGS > AWAKE
AWANTING adj missing
AWARD vb give (something, such as a prize) formally ▷n something awarded, such as a prize
AWARDABLE > AWARD
AWARDED > AWARD
AWARDEE > AWARD
AWARDEES > AWARD
AWARDER > AWARD
AWARDERS > AWARD
AWARDING > AWARD
AWARDS > AWARD
AWARE adj having knowledge, informed
AWARENESS > AWARE
AWARER > AWARE
AWAREST > AWARE
AWARN vb old form of warn
AWARNED > AWARN
AWARNING > AWARN
AWARNS > AWARN
AWASH adv washed over by water ▷adj washed over by water
AWATCH adv watching
AWATO n New Zealand caterpillar
AWAVE adv in waves
AWAY adv from a place ▷adj not present ▷n game played or won at an opponent's ground
AWAYDAY n day trip taken for pleasure
AWAYDAYS > AWAYDAY
AWAYES old word for > AWAY
AWAYNESS > AWAY
AWAYS > AWAY
AWDL n traditional Welsh poem
AWDLS > AWDL
AWE n wonder and respect mixed with dread ▷vb fill with awe
AWEARIED old word for > WEARY
AWEARY old form of > WEARY
AWEATHER adj towards the weather
AWED > AWE
AWEE adv for a short time
AWEEL interj Scots word meaning well
AWEIGH adj (of an anchor) no longer hooked onto the bottom
AWEING > AWE
AWELESS > AWE
AWES > AWE
AWESOME adj inspiring awe
AWESOMELY > AWESOME
AWESTRIKE vb inspire awe in
AWESTRUCK adj filled with awe
AWETO n New Zealand caterpillar

AWETOS > AWETO
AWFUL adj very bad or unpleasant ▷ adv very
AWFULLER > AWFUL
AWFULLEST > AWFUL
AWFULLY adv in an unpleasant way
AWFULNESS > AWFUL
AWHAPE old word for > AMAZE
AWHAPED > AWHAPE
AWHAPES > AWHAPE
AWHAPING > AWHAPE
AWHATO n New Zealand caterpillar
AWHEEL adv on wheels
AWHEELS same as > AWHEEL
AWHETO n New Zealand caterpillar
AWHILE adv for a brief time
AWHIRL adv whirling
AWING > AWE
AWKWARD adj clumsy or ungainly
AWKWARDER > AWKWARD
AWKWARDLY > AWKWARD
AWL n pointed tool for piercing wood, leather, etc
AWLBIRD n woodpecker
AWLBIRDS > AWLBIRD
AWLESS > AWE
AWLS > AWL
AWLWORT n small stemless aquatic plant, Subularia aquatica, of the N hemisphere, having slender sharp-pointed leaves and minute, often submerged, white flowers: family Brassicaceae (crucifers)
AWLWORTS > AWLWORT
AWMOUS Scots word for > ALMS
AWMRIE n cupboard for church vessels
AWMRIES > AWMRIE
AWMRY n cupboard for church vessels
AWN n any of the bristles growing from the flowering parts of certain grasses and cereals
AWNED > AWN
AWNER n machine for removing awns
AWNERS > AWNER
AWNIER > AWNY
AWNIEST > AWNY
AWNING n canvas roof supported by a frame to give protection against the weather
AWNINGED adj sheltered with awning
AWNINGS > AWNING
AWNLESS > AWN
AWNS > AWN
AWNY adj having awns
AWOKE past tense of > AWAKE
AWOKEN > AWAKE
AWOL n person who is absent without leave
AWOLS > AWOL
AWORK adv old word meaning at work
AWRACK adv in wrecked condition

AWRONG adv old word meaning wrongly
AWRY adj with a twist to one side, askew
AWSOME adj old form of awesome
AX same as > AXE
AXAL adj of an axis
AXE n tool with a sharp blade for felling trees or chopping wood ▷ vb dismiss (employees), restrict (expenditure), or terminate (a project)
AXEBIRD n nightjar of northern Queensland and New Guinea with a cry that sounds like a chopping axe
AXEBIRDS > AXEBIRD
AXED > AXE
AXEL n jump in which the skater takes off from the forward outside edge of one skate, makes one and a half, two and a half, or three and a half turns in the air, and lands on the backward outside edge of the other skate
AXELS > AXEL
AXEMAN n man who wields an axe, esp to cut down trees
AXEMEN > AXEMAN
AXENIC adj (of a biological culture or culture medium) free from other microorganisms
AXES > AXIS
AXIAL adj forming or of an axis
AXIALITY > AXIAL
AXIALLY > AXIAL
AXIL n angle where the stalk of a leaf joins a stem
AXILE adj of, relating to, or attached to the axis
AXILEMMA same as > AXOLEMMA
AXILEMMAS > AXILEMMA
AXILLA n area on the undersurface of a bird's wing corresponding to the armpit
AXILLAE > AXILLA
AXILLAR same as > AXILLARY
AXILLARS > AXILLAR
AXILLARY adj of, relating to, or near the armpit ▷ n one of the feathers growing from the axilla of a bird's wing
AXILLAS > AXILLA
AXILS > AXIL
AXING > AXE
AXINITE n crystalline substance
AXINITES > AXINITE
AXIOLOGY n theory of values, moral or aesthetic
AXIOM n generally accepted principle
AXIOMATIC adj containing axioms
AXIOMS > AXIOM
AXION n type of hypothetical elementary

particle
AXIONS > AXION
AXIS n (imaginary) line round which a body can rotate or about which an object or geometrical figure is symmetrical
AXISED adj having an axis
AXISES > AXIS
AXITE n type of gunpowder
AXITES > AXITE
AXLE n shaft on which a wheel or pair of wheels turns
AXLED adj having axle
AXLES > AXLE
AXLETREE n bar fixed across the underpart of a wagon or carriage that has rounded ends on which the wheels revolve
AXLETREES > AXLETREE
AXLIKE > AX
AXMAN same as > AXEMAN
AXMEN > AXMAN
AXOID n type of curve
AXOIDS > AXOID
AXOLEMMA n membrane that encloses the axon of a nerve cell
AXOLEMMAS > AXOLEMMA
AXOLOTL n aquatic salamander of central America
AXOLOTLS > AXOLOTL
AXON n long threadlike extension of a nerve cell that conducts nerve impulses from the cell body
AXONAL > AXON
AXONE same as > AXON
AXONEMAL > AXONEME
AXONEME n part of cell consisting of proteins
AXONEMES > AXONEME
AXONES > AXONE
AXONIC > AXON
AXONS > AXON
AXOPLASM n part of cell
AXOPLASMS > AXOPLASM
AXSEED n crown vetch
AXSEEDS > AXSEED
AY adv ever ▷ n expression of agreement
AYAH n (in parts of the former British Empire) a native maidservant or nursemaid
AYAHS > AYAH
AYAHUASCA n type of Brazilian plant
AYAHUASCO n South American vine
AYATOLLAH n Islamic religious leader in Iran
AYE n affirmative vote or voter ▷ adv always
AYELP adv yelping
AYENBITE old word for > REMORSE
AYENBITES > AYENBITE
AYES > AYE
AYGRE old word for > EAGER
AYIN n 16th letter in the Hebrew alphabet
AYINS > AYIN
AYONT adv beyond

AYRE old word for > AIR
AYRES > AYRE
AYRIE old word for > EYRIE
AYRIES > AYRIE
AYS > AY
AYU n small Japanese fish
AYURVEDA n ancient medical treatise on the art of healing and prolonging life
AYURVEDAS > AYURVEDA
AYURVEDIC > AYURVEDA
AYUS > AYU
AYWORD n old word meaning byword
AYWORDS > AYWORD
AZALEA n garden shrub grown for its showy flowers
AZALEAS > AZALEA
AZAN n call to prayer five times a day, usually by a muezzin from a minaret
AZANS > AZAN
AZEDARACH n astringent bark of the chinaberry tree, formerly used as an emetic and cathartic
AZEOTROPE n mixture of liquids that boils at a constant temperature, at a given pressure, without a change in composition
AZEOTROPY > AZEOTROPE
AZERTY n common European version of typewriter keyboard layout with the characters a, z, e, r, t, and y positioned on the top row of alphabetic characters at the left side of the keyboard
AZIDE n type of chemical compound
AZIDES > AZIDE
AZIDO adj containing an azide
AZIMUTH n arc of the sky between the zenith and the horizon
AZIMUTHAL > AZIMUTH
AZIMUTHS > AZIMUTH
AZINE n any organic compound having a six-membered ring containing at least one nitrogen atom
AZINES > AZINE
AZIONE n musical drama
AZIONES > AZIONE
AZLON n fibre made from protein
AZLONS > AZLON
AZO adj of, consisting of, or containing the divalent group -N:N-
AZOIC adj without life
AZOLE n organic five-membered ring compound containing one or more atoms in the ring, the number usually being specified by a prefix
AZOLES > AZOLE
AZOLLA n tropical water fern
AZOLLAS > AZOLLA
AZON n type of drawing

paper
AZONAL *adj* not divided into zones
AZONIC *adj* not confined to a zone
AZONS > AZON
AZOTAEMIA *a less common name for* > URAEMIA
AZOTAEMIC > AZOTAEMIA
AZOTE *an obsolete name for* > NITROGEN
AZOTED > AZOTE
AZOTEMIA *same as* > AZOTAEMIA
AZOTEMIAS > AZOTEMIA
AZOTEMIC > AZOTAEMIA
AZOTES > AZOTE
AZOTH *n* panacea

postulated by Paracelsus
AZOTHS > AZOTH
AZOTIC *adj* of, containing, or concerned with nitrogen
AZOTISE *same as* > AZOTIZE
AZOTISED > AZOTISE
AZOTISES > AZOTISE
AZOTISING > AZOTISE
AZOTIZE *vb* combine or treat with nitrogen or a nitrogen compound
AZOTIZED > AZOTIZE
AZOTIZES > AZOTIZE
AZOTIZING > AZOTIZE
AZOTOUS *adj* containing nitrogen
AZOTURIA *n* presence of excess nitrogen in urine

AZOTURIAS > AZOTURIA
AZUKI *same as* > ADZUKI
AZUKIS > AZUKI
AZULEJO *n* Spanish porcelain tile
AZULEJOS > AZULEJO
AZURE *n* (of) the colour of a clear blue sky ▷ *adj* deep blue
AZUREAN *adj* azure
AZURES > AZURE
AZURINE *n* blue dye
AZURINES > AZURINE
AZURITE *n* azure-blue mineral associated with copper deposits
AZURITES > AZURITE
AZURN *old word for* > AZURE

AZURY *adj* bluish
AZYGIES > AZYGY
AZYGOS *n* biological structure not in a pair
AZYGOSES > AZYGOS
AZYGOUS *adj* developing or occurring singly
AZYGY *n* state of not being joined in pair
AZYM *n* unleavened bread
AZYME *n* unleavened bread
AZYMES > AZYME
AZYMITE *n* member of a church using unleavened bread in the Eucharist
AZYMITES > AZYMITE
AZYMOUS *adj* unleavened
AZYMS > AZYM

a

Bb

BA *n* symbol for the soul in Ancient Egyptian religion
BAA *vb* make the characteristic bleating sound of a sheep ▷ *n* cry made by a sheep
BAAED > BAA
BAAING > BAA
BAAINGS > BAA
BAAL *n* any false god or idol
BAALEBOS *n* master of the house
BAALIM > BAAL
BAALISM > BAAL
BAALISMS > BAAL
BAALS > BAAL
BAAS *South African word for* > BOSS
BAASES > BAAS
BAASKAAP *same as* > BAASKAP
BAASKAAPS > BAASKAAP
BAASKAP *n* (in South Africa) control by Whites of non-Whites
BAASKAPS > BAASKAP
BAASSKAP *same as* > BAASKAP
BAASSKAPS > BAASSKAP
BABA *n* small cake of leavened dough, sometimes mixed with currants and usually soaked in rum
BABACO *n* greenish-yellow egg-shaped fruit
BABACOOTE *n* large lemur
BABACOS > BABACO
BABALAS *adj* drunk
BABAS > BABA
BABASSU *n* Brazilian palm tree, *Orbignya martiana* (or *O. speciosa*), having hard edible nuts that yield an oil used in making soap, margarine, etc
BABASSUS > BABASSU
BABBELAS *same as* > BABALAS
BABBITRY > BABBITT
BABBITT *vb* line (a bearing) or face (a surface) with Babbitt metal or a similar soft alloy
BABBITTED > BABBITT
BABBITTRY > BABBITT
BABBITTS > BABBITT

BABBLE *vb* talk excitedly or foolishly ▷ *n* muddled or foolish speech
BABBLED > BABBLE
BABBLER *n* person who babbles
BABBLERS > BABBLER
BABBLES > BABBLE
BABBLIER > BABBLE
BABBLIEST > BABBLE
BABBLING > BABBLE
BABBLINGS > BABBLE
BABBLY > BABBLE
BABE *n* baby
BABEL *n* confused mixture of noises or voices
BABELDOM > BABEL
BABELDOMS > BABEL
BABELISH > BABEL
BABELISM > BABEL
BABELISMS > BABEL
BABELS > BABEL
BABES > BABE
BABESIA *n* parasite causing infection in cattle
BABESIAS > BABESIA
BABICHE *n* thongs or lacings of rawhide
BABICHES > BABICHE
BABIED > BABY
BABIER > BABY
BABIES > BABY
BABIEST > BABY
BABIRUSA *n* wild pig, *Babyrousa babyrussa*, inhabiting marshy forests in Indonesia. It has an almost hairless wrinkled skin and enormous curved canine teeth
BABIRUSAS > BABIRUSA
BABIRUSSA *same as* > BABIRUSA
BABKA *n* cake
BABKAS > BABKA
BABLAH *n* type of acacia
BABLAHS > BABLAH
BABOO *same as* > BABU
BABOOL *n* type of acacia
BABOOLS > BABOOL
BABOON *n* large monkey with a pointed face and a long tail
BABOONERY *n* uncouth behaviour
BABOONISH *adj* uncouth
BABOONS > BABOON

BABOOS > BABOO
BABOOSH *same as* > BABOUCHE
BABOOSHES > BABOOSH
BABOUCHE *n* Middle-Eastern slipper
BABOUCHES > BABOUCHE
BABU *n* (in India) a title or form of address more or less equivalent to *Mr*, placed before a person's full name or after his first name
BABUCHE *same as* > BABOUCHE
BABUCHES > BABUCHE
BABUDOM > BABU
BABUDOMS > BABU
BABUISM > BABU
BABUISMS > BABU
BABUL *n* any of several leguminous trees of the genus *Acacia*, esp *A. arabica* of N Africa and India, which bear small yellow flowers and are a source of gum arabic, tannin, and hardwood
BABULS > BABUL
BABUS > BABU
BABUSHKA *n* headscarf tied under the chin, worn by Russian peasant women
BABUSHKAS > BABUSHKA
BABY *n* very young child or animal ▷ *adj* comparatively small of its type ▷ *vb* treat as a baby
BABYDOLL *n* woman's short nightdress
BABYDOLLS > BABYDOLL
BABYFOOD *n* puréed food for babies
BABYFOODS > BABYFOOD
BABYHOOD > BABY
BABYHOODS > BABY
BABYING > BABY
BABYISH > BABY
BABYISHLY > BABY
BABYPROOF *adj* safe for babies to handle ▷ *vb* make babyproof
BABYSAT > BABYSIT
BABYSIT *vb* look after a child in its parents' absence
BABYSITS > BABYSIT
BAC *n* baccalaureate
BACALAO *n* dried salt cod

BACALAOS > BACALAO
BACCA *n* berry
BACCAE > BACCA
BACCARA *same as* > BACCARAT
BACCARAS > BACCARA
BACCARAT *n* card game involving gambling
BACCARATS > BACCARAT
BACCARE *same as* > BACKARE
BACCAS > BACCA
BACCATE *adj* like a berry in form, texture, etc
BACCATED > BACCATE
BACCHANAL *n* follower of Bacchus ▷ *adj* of or relating to Bacchus
BACCHANT *n* priest or votary of Bacchus
BACCHANTE *n* priestess or female votary of Bacchus
BACCHANTS > BACCHANT
BACCHIAC > BACCHIUS
BACCHIAN *same as* > BACCHIC
BACCHIC *adj* riotously drunk
BACCHII > BACCHIUS
BACCHIUS *n* metrical foot of one short syllable followed by two long ones
BACCIES > BACCY
BACCIFORM *adj* shaped like a berry
BACCO *n* tobacco
BACCOES > BACCO
BACCOS > BACCO
BACCY *n* tobacco
BACH *same as* > BATCH
BACHA *n* Indian English word for young child
BACHARACH *n* German wine
BACHAS > BACHA
BACHCHA *n* Indian English word for young child
BACHCHAS > BACHCHA
BACHED > BACH
BACHELOR *n* unmarried man
BACHELORS > BACHELOR
BACHES > BACH
BACHING > BACH
BACHS > BACH
BACILLAR *same as* > BACILLARY
BACILLARY *adj* of or caused by bacilli
BACILLI > BACILLUS
BACILLUS *n* rod-shaped bacterium

BACK *n* rear part of the human body, from the neck to the pelvis ▷ *vb* (cause to) move backwards ▷ *adj* situated behind ▷ *adv* at, to, or towards the rear

BACKACHE *n* ache or pain in one's back

BACKACHES > BACKACHE

BACKARE *interj* instruction to keep one's distance; back off

BACKBAND *n* back support

BACKBANDS > BACKBAND

BACKBEAT *n* second and fourth beats in music written in even time or, in more complex time signatures, the last beat of the bar

BACKBEATS > BACKBEAT

BACKBENCH *n* lower-ranking seats in Parliament

BACKBEND *n* gymnastic exercise in which the trunk is bent backwards until the hands touch the floor

BACKBENDS > BACKBEND

BACKBIT > BACKBITE

BACKBITE *vb* talk spitefully about an absent person

BACKBITER > BACKBITE

BACKBITES > BACKBITE

BACKBLOCK *n* singular of backblock: bush or remote farming area

BACKBOARD *n* board that is placed behind something to form or support its back

BACKBOND *n* legal document

BACKBONDS > BACKBOND

BACKBONE *n* spinal column

BACKBONED > BACKBONE

BACKBONES > BACKBONE

BACKBURN *vb* clear (an area of bush) by creating a fire that burns in the opposite direction from the wind ▷ *n* act or result of backburning

BACKBURNS > BACKBURN

BACKCAST *n* backward casting of fishing rod

BACKCASTS > BACKCAST

BACKCHAT *n* impudent replies

BACKCHATS > BACKCHAT

BACKCHECK *vb* (in ice hockey) return from attack to defence

BACKCLOTH *n* painted curtain at the back of a stage set

BACKCOMB *vb* comb (the hair) towards the roots to give more bulk to a hairstyle

BACKCOMBS > BACKCOMB

BACKCOURT *n* part of the court between the service line and the baseline

BACKCROSS *vb* mate (a hybrid of the first generation) with one of its parents ▷ *n* offspring so produced

BACKDATE *vb* make (a document) effective from a date earlier than its completion

BACKDATED > BACKDATE

BACKDATES > BACKDATE

BACKDOOR *adj* secret, underhand, or obtained through influence

BACKDOWN *n* abandonment of an earlier claim

BACKDOWNS > BACKDOWN

BACKDRAFT *n* reverse movement of air

BACKDROP *vb* provide a backdrop to (something)

BACKDROPS > BACKDROP

BACKDROPT > BACKDROP

BACKED *adj* having a back or backing

BACKER *n* person who gives financial support

BACKERS > BACKER

BACKET *n* shallow box

BACKETS > BACKET

BACKFALL *n* fall onto the back

BACKFALLS > BACKFALL

BACKFIELD *n* quarterback and running backs in a team

BACKFILE *n* archives of a newspaper or magazine

BACKFILES > BACKFILE

BACKFILL *vb* refill an excavated trench, esp (in archaeology) at the end of an investigation ▷ *n* soil used to do this

BACKFILLS > BACKFILL

BACKFIRE *vb* (of a plan) fail to have the desired effect ▷ *n* (in an engine) explosion of unburnt gases in the exhaust system

BACKFIRED > BACKFIRE

BACKFIRES > BACKFIRE

BACKFISCH *n* young girl

BACKFIT *vb* overhaul nuclear power plant

BACKFITS > BACKFIT

BACKFLIP *n* backwards somersault

BACKFLIPS > BACKFLIP

BACKFLOW *n* reverse flow

BACKFLOWS > BACKFLOW

BACKHAND *n* stroke played with the back of the hand facing the direction of the stroke ▷ *adv* with a backhand stroke ▷ *vb* play (a shot) backhand

BACKHANDS > BACKHAND

BACKHAUL *vb* transmit data

BACKHAULS > BACKHAUL

BACKHOE *n* digger ▷ *vb* dig with a backhoe

BACKHOED > BACKHOE

BACKHOES > BACKHOE

BACKHOUSE *n* toilet

BACKIE *n* ride on the back of someone's bicycle

BACKIES > BACKIE

BACKING *n* support

BACKINGS > BACKING

BACKLAND *n* undeveloped land behind a property

BACKLANDS > BACKLAND

BACKLASH *n* sudden and adverse reaction ▷ *vb* create a sudden and adverse reaction

BACKLESS *adj* (of a dress) low-cut at the back

BACKLIFT *n* backward movement of bat

BACKLIFTS > BACKLIFT

BACKLIGHT *vb* illuminate (something) from behind

BACKLIST *n* publisher's previously published books that are still available ▷ *vb* put on a backlist

BACKLISTS > BACKLIST

BACKLIT *adj* illuminated from behind

BACKLOAD *n* load for lorry on return journey ▷ *vb* load a lorry for a return journey

BACKLOADS > BACKLOAD

BACKLOG *n* accumulation of things to be dealt with

BACKLOGS > BACKLOG

BACKLOT *n* area outside a film or television studio used for outdoor filming

BACKLOTS > BACKLOT

BACKMOST *adj* furthest back

BACKOUT *n* instance of withdrawing (from an agreement, etc)

BACKOUTS > BACKOUT

BACKPACK *n* large pack carried on the back ▷ *vb* go hiking with a backpack

BACKPACKS > BACKPACK

BACKPAY *n* pay received by an employee from an increase awarded retrospectively

BACKPAYS > BACKPAY

BACKPEDAL *vb* retract or modify a previous opinion, principle, etc

BACKPIECE *n* tattoo on the back

BACKRA *n* white person

BACKRAS > BACKRA

BACKREST *n* support for the back of something

BACKRESTS > BACKREST

BACKROOM *n* place where research or planning is done, esp secret research in wartime

BACKROOMS > BACKROOM

BACKRUSH *n* seaward return of wave

BACKS > BACK

BACKSAW *n* small handsaw stiffened along its upper edge by a metal section

BACKSAWS > BACKSAW

BACKSEAT *n* seat at the back, esp of a vehicle

BACKSEATS > BACKSEAT

BACKSET *n* reversal

BACKSETS > BACKSET

BACKSEY *n* sirloin

BACKSEYS > BACKSEY

BACKSHISH *same as* > BAKSHEESH

BACKSHORE *n* area of beach above high tide mark

BACKSIDE *n* buttocks

BACKSIDES > BACKSIDE

BACKSIGHT *n* sight of a rifle nearer the stock

BACKSLAP *vb* demonstrate effusive joviality

BACKSLAPS > BACKSLAP

BACKSLASH *n* slash which slopes to the left)

BACKSLID > BACKSLIDE

BACKSLIDE *vb* relapse into former bad habits

BACKSPACE *vb* move a typewriter carriage or computer cursor backwards ▷ *n* typewriter key that effects such a movements

BACKSPEER *same as* > BACKSPEIR

BACKSPEIR *vb* interrogate

BACKSPIN *n* backward spin given to a ball to reduce its speed at impact

BACKSPINS > BACKSPIN

BACKSTAB *vb* attack deceitfully

BACKSTABS > BACKSTAB

BACKSTAGE *adj* behind the stage in a theatre ▷ *adv* behind the stage in a theatre ▷ *n* area behind the stage in a theatre

BACKSTAIR *adj* underhand

BACKSTALL *n* backward flight of a kite

BACKSTAMP *n* mark stamped on the back of an envelope ▷ *vb* mark with a backstamp

BACKSTAY *n* stay leading aft from the upper part of a mast to the deck or stern

BACKSTAYS > BACKSTAY

BACKSTOP *n* screen or fence to prevent balls leaving the playing area ▷ *vb* provide with backing or support

BACKSTOPS > BACKSTOP

BACKSTORY *n* events assumed before a story begins

BACKSWEPT *adj* slanting backwards

BACKSWING *n* backward movement of a bat, etc

BACKSWORD *a* broad-bladed sword

BACKTRACK *vb* return by the same route by which one has come

BACKUP *n* support or reinforcement

BACKUPS > BACKUP

BACKVELD *n* (in South Africa) remote sparsely populated area

BACKVELDS > BACKVELD

BACKWARD *same as* > BACKWARDS

BACKWARDS *adv* towards the rear

BACKWASH *n* water washed backwards by the motion of a boat ▷ *vb* remove oil from (combed wool)

BACKWATER *n* isolated or backward place or condition ▷ *vb* reverse the

direction of a boat, esp to push the oars of a rowing boat
BACKWOOD > BACKWOODS
BACKWOODS *pl n* remote sparsely populated area
BACKWORD *n* act or an instance of failing to keep a promise or commitment
BACKWORDS > BACKWORD
BACKWORK *n* work carried out under the ground
BACKWORKS > BACKWORK
BACKWRAP *n* back support
BACKWRAPS > BACKWRAP
BACKYARD *n* yard at the back of a house, etc
BACKYARDS > BACKYARD
BACLAVA *same as* > BAKLAVA
BACLAVAS > BACLAVA
BACLOFEN *n* drug used to treat stroke victims
BACLOFENS > BACLOFEN
BACON *n* salted or smoked pig meat
BACONER *n* pig that weighs between 83 and 101 kg, from which bacon is cut
BACONERS > BACONER
BACONS > BACON
BACS > BAC
BACTERIA *pl n* large group of microorganisms
BACTERIAL > BACTERIA
BACTERIAN > BACTERIA
BACTERIAS > BACTERIA
BACTERIC > BACTERIA
BACTERIN *n* vaccine prepared from bacteria
BACTERINS > BACTERIN
BACTERISE *same as* > BACTERIZE
BACTERIUM singular form of > BACTERIA
BACTERIZE *vb* subject to bacterial action
BACTEROID *adj* resembling a bacterium ▷ *n* any rodlike bacterium of the genus *Bacteroides*, occurring in the gut of man and animals
BACULA > BACULUM
BACULINE *adj* relating to flogging
BACULITE *n* fossil
BACULITES > BACULITE
BACULUM *n* bony support in the penis of certain mammals, esp the carnivores
BACULUMS > BACULUM
BAD *adj* not good ▷ *n* unfortunate or unpleasant events collectively ▷ *adv* badly
BADASS *n* tough or aggressive person ▷ *adj* tough or aggressive
BADASSED > BADASS
BADASSES > BADASS
BADDER > BAD
BADDEST > BAD
BADDIE *n* bad character in a story, film, etc, esp an opponent of the hero
BADDIES > BADDY

BADDISH > BAD
BADDY *same as* > BADDIE
BADE > BID
BADGE *n* emblem worn to show membership, rank, etc ▷ *vb* put a badge on
BADGED > BADGE
BADGELESS > BADGE
BADGER *n* nocturnal burrowing mammal of Europe, Asia, and N America with a black and white head ▷ *vb* pester or harass
BADGERED > BADGER
BADGERING > BADGER
BADGERLY > BADGER
BADGERS > BADGER
BADGES > BADGE
BADGING > BADGE
BADINAGE *n* playful and witty conversation ▷ *vb* engage in badinage
BADINAGED > BADINAGE
BADINAGES > BADINAGE
BADINERIE *n* name given in the 18th century to a type of quick, light movement in a suite
BADIOUS *adj* chestnut; brownish-red
BADLAND > BADLANDS
BADLANDS *pl n* any deeply eroded barren area
BADLY *adv* poorly
BADMAN *n* hired gunman, outlaw, or criminal
BADMASH *n* evil-doer; hooligan ▷ *adj* naughty or bad
BADMASHES > BADMASH
BADMEN > BADMAN
BADMINTON *n* game played with rackets and a shuttlecock, which is hit back and forth over a high net
BADMOUTH *vb* speak unfavourably about (someone or something)
BADMOUTHS > BADMOUTH
BADNESS > BAD
BADNESSES > BAD
BADS > BAD
BAEL *n* spiny Indian rutaceous tree, *Aegle marmelos*
BAELS > BAEL
BAETYL *n* magical meteoric stone
BAETYLS > BAETYL
BAFF *vb* strike ground with golf club
BAFFED > BAFF
BAFFIES *pl n* slippers
BAFFING > BAFF
BAFFLE *vb* perplex or puzzle ▷ *n* device to limit or regulate the flow of fluid, light, or sound
BAFFLED > BAFFLE
BAFFLEGAB *n* insincere speech
BAFFLER > BAFFLE
BAFFLERS > BAFFLE
BAFFLES > BAFFLE
BAFFLING *adj* impossible to

understand
BAFFS > BAFF
BAFFY *n* golf club
BAFT *n* coarse fabric
BAFTS > BAFT
BAG *n* flexible container with an opening at one end ▷ *vb* put into a bag
BAGARRE *n* brawl
BAGARRES > BAGARRE
BAGASS *same as* > BAGASSE
BAGASSE *n* pulp remaining after the extraction of juice from sugar cane or similar plants: used as fuel and for making paper, etc
BAGASSES > BAGASSE
BAGATELLE *n* something of little value
BAGEL *n* hard ring-shaped bread roll
BAGELS > BAGEL
BAGFUL *n* amount (of something) that can be held in a bag
BAGFULS > BAGFUL
BAGGAGE *n* suitcases packed for a journey
BAGGAGES > BAGGAGE
BAGGED > BAG
BAGGER *n* person who packs groceries
BAGGERS > BAGGER
BAGGIE *n* plastic bag
BAGGIER > BAGGY
BAGGIES > BAGGY
BAGGIEST > BAGGY
BAGGILY > BAGGY
BAGGINESS > BAGGY
BAGGING > BAG
BAGGINGS > BAG
BAGGIT *n* unspawned salmon
BAGGITS > BAGGIT
BAGGY *same as* > BAGIE
BAGH *n* (in India and Pakistan) a garden
BAGHOUSE *n* dust-filtering chamber
BAGHOUSES > BAGHOUSE
BAGHS > BAGH
BAGIE *n* turnip
BAGIES > BAGIE
BAGLESS *adj* (esp of a vacuum cleaner) not containing a bag
BAGLIKE > BAG
BAGMAN *n* travelling salesman
BAGMEN > BAGMAN
BAGNETTE *variant of* > BAGUETTE
BAGNETTES > BAGNETTE
BAGNIO *n* brothel
BAGNIOS > BAGNIO
BAGPIPE *vb* play the bagpipes
BAGPIPED > BAGPIPE
BAGPIPER > BAGPIPES
BAGPIPERS > BAGPIPES
BAGPIPES *pl n* musical wind instrument with reed pipes and an inflatable bag
BAGPIPING > BAGPIPE
BAGS > BAG
BAGSFUL > BAGFUL
BAGUET *same as* > BAGUETTE

BAGUETS > BAGUET
BAGUETTE *n* narrow French stick loaf
BAGUETTES > BAGUETTE
BAGUIO *n* hurricane
BAGUIOS > BAGUIO
BAGWASH *n* laundry that washes clothes without drying or pressing them
BAGWASHES > BAGWASH
BAGWIG *n* 18th-century wig with hair pushed back into a bag
BAGWIGS > BAGWIG
BAGWORM *n* type of moth
BAGWORMS > BAGWORM
BAH *interj* expression of contempt or disgust
BAHADA *same as* > BAJADA
BAHADAS > BAHADA
BAHADUR *n* title formerly conferred by the British on distinguished Indians
BAHADURS > BAHADUR
BAHT *n* standard monetary unit of Thailand, divided into 100 satang
BAHTS > BAHT
BAHUT *n* decorative cabinet
BAHUTS > BAHUT
BAHUVRIHI *n* class of compound words consisting of two elements the first of which is a specific feature of the second
BAIDARKA *n* narrow hunting boat
BAIDARKAS > BAIDARKA
BAIGNOIRE *n* low-level theatre box
BAIL *n* money deposited with a court as security for a person's reappearance in court ▷ *vb* pay bail for (a person)
BAILABLE *adj* eligible for release on bail
BAILBOND *n* document in which a prisoner and one or more sureties guarantee that the prisoner will attend the court hearing of the charges against him if he is released on bail
BAILBONDS > BAILBOND
BAILED > BAIL
BAILEE *n* person to whom the possession of goods is transferred under a bailment
BAILEES > BAILEE
BAILER > BAIL
BAILERS > BAIL
BAILEY *n* outermost wall or court of a castle
BAILEYS > BAILEY
BAILIE *n* (in Scotland) a municipal magistrate
BAILIES > BAILIE
BAILIFF *n* sheriff's officer who serves writs and summonses
BAILIFFS > BAILIFF
BAILING > BAIL
BAILIWICK *n* area a person is interested in or operates

in

BAILLI n magistrate

BAILLIAGE n magistrate's area of authority

BAILLIE variant of > BAILIE

BAILLIES > BAILLIE

BAILLIS > BAILLI

BAILMENT n contractual delivery of goods in trust to a person for a specific purpose

BAILMENTS > BAILMENT

BAILOR n person who retains ownership of goods but entrusts possession of them to another under a bailment

BAILORS > BAILOR

BAILOUT n instance of helping (a person, organization, etc) out of a predicament

BAILOUTS > BAILOUT

BAILS > BAIL

BAILSMAN n one standing bail for another

BAILSMEN > BAILSMAN

BAININ n Irish collarless jacket made of white wool

BAININS > BAININ

BAINITE n mixture of iron and iron carbide found in incompletely hardened steels, produced when austenite is transformed at temperatures between the pearlite and martensite ranges

BAINITES > BAINITE

BAIRN n child

BAIRNISH > BAIRN

BAIRNLIER > BAIRN

BAIRNLIKE > BAIRN

BAIRNLY > BAIRN

BAIRNS > BAIRN

BAISEMAIN n kissing of the hand

BAIT n piece of food on a hook or in a trap to attract fish or animals ▷ vb put a piece of food on or in (a hook or trap)

BAITED > BAIT

BAITER > BAIT

BAITERS > BAIT

BAITFISH n small fish used as bait

BAITH adj both

BAITING > BAIT

BAITINGS > BAIT

BAITS > BAIT

BAIZA n Omani unit of currency

BAIZAS > BAIZA

BAIZE n woollen fabric used to cover billiard and card tables ▷ vb line or cover with such fabric

BAIZED > BAIZE

BAIZES > BAIZE

BAIZING > BAIZE

BAJADA n sloping surface formed from rock deposits

BAJADAS > BAJADA

BAJAN n freshman at Aberdeen University

BAJANS > BAJAN

BAJRA n Indian millet

BAJRAS > BAJRA

BAJREE variant of > BAJRA

BAJREES > BAJREE

BAJRI variant of > BAJRA

BAJRIS > BAJRI

BAJU n Malay jacket

BAJUS > BAJU

BAKE vb cook by dry heat as in an oven ▷ n party at which the main dish is baked

BAKEAPPLE n cloudberry

BAKEBOARD n board for bread-making

BAKED > BAKE

BAKEHOUSE same as > BAKERY

BAKELITE n tradename for any one of a class of thermosetting resins used as electric insulators and for making plastic ware, telephone receivers, etc

BAKELITES > BAKELITE

BAKEMEAT n pie

BAKEMEATS > BAKEMEAT

BAKEN > BAKE

BAKER n person whose business is to make or sell bread, cakes, etc

BAKERIES > BAKERY

BAKERS > BAKER

BAKERY n place where bread, cakes, etc are baked or sold

BAKES > BAKE

BAKESHOP n bakery

BAKESHOPS > BAKESHOP

BAKESTONE n flat stone in an oven

BAKEWARE n dishes for baking

BAKEWARES > BAKEWARE

BAKHSHISH same as > BAKSHEESH

BAKING n process of cooking bread, cakes, etc ▷ adj (esp of weather) very hot and dry

BAKINGS > BAKING

BAKKIE n small truck

BAKKIES > BAKKIE

BAKLAVA n rich cake of Middle Eastern origin consisting of thin layers of pastry filled with nuts and honey

BAKLAVAS > BAKLAVA

BAKLAWA same as > BAKLAVA

BAKLAWAS > BAKLAWA

BAKRA n White person, esp one from Britain ▷ adj (of people) White, esp British

BAKRAS > BAKRA

BAKSHEESH n (in some Eastern countries) money given as a tip ▷ vb give such money to (a person)

BAKSHISH same as > BAKSHEESH

BAL n balmoral

BALACLAVA n close-fitting woollen hood that covers the ears and neck, as originally worn by soldiers in the Crimean War

BALADIN n dancer

BALADINE n female dancer

BALADINES > BALADINE

BALADINS > BALADIN

BALALAIKA n guitar-like musical instrument with a triangular body

BALANCE n stability of mind or body ▷ vb weigh in a balance

BALANCED adj having weight equally distributed

BALANCER n person or thing that balances

BALANCERS > BALANCER

BALANCES > BALANCE

BALANCING > BALANCE

BALANITIS n inflammation of the glans penis, usually due to infection

BALAS n red variety of spinel, used as a gemstone

BALASES > BALAS

BALATA n tropical American sapotaceous tree, *Manilkara bidentata*, yielding a latex-like sap

BALATAS > BALATA

BALBOA n standard currency unit of Panama, divided into 100 centesimos

BALBOAS > BALBOA

BALCONET n small balcony

BALCONETS > BALCONET

BALCONIED > BALCONY

BALCONIES > BALCONY

BALCONY n platform on the outside of a building with a rail along the outer edge

BALD adj having little or no hair on the scalp ▷ vb make bald

BALDACHIN n richly ornamented silk and gold brocade

BALDAQUIN same as > BALDACHIN

BALDED > BALD

BALDER > BALD

BALDEST > BALD

BALDFACED same as > BALD

BALDHEAD n person with a bald head

BALDHEADS > BALDHEAD

BALDICOOT another name for > COOT

BALDIER > BALDY

BALDIES > BALDY

BALDIEST > BALDY

BALDING adj becoming bald

BALDISH > BALD

BALDLY > BALD

BALDMONEY another name for > SPIGNEL

BALDNESS > BALD

BALDPATE n person with a bald head

BALDPATED > BALDPATE

BALDPATES > BALDPATE

BALDRIC n wide silk sash or leather belt worn over the right shoulder to the left hip for carrying a sword, etc

BALDRICK same as > BALDRIC

BALDRICKS > BALDRICK

BALDRICS > BALDRIC

BALDS > BALD

BALDY adj bald ▷ n bald person

BALE same as > BAIL

BALECTION same as > BOLECTION

BALED > BALE

BALEEN n whalebone

BALEENS > BALEEN

BALEFIRE n bonfire

BALEFIRES > BALEFIRE

BALEFUL adj vindictive or menacing

BALEFULLY > BALEFUL

BALER > BAIL

BALERS > BAIL

BALES > BALE

BALING > BALE

BALISAUR n badger-like animal

BALISAURS > BALISAUR

BALISTA same as > BALLISTA

BALISTAE > BALISTA

BALISTAS > BALISTA

BALK vb stop short, esp suddenly or unexpectedly ▷ n roughly squared heavy timber beam

BALKANISE variant of > BALKANIZE

BALKANIZE vb divide (a territory) into small warring states

BALKED > BALK

BALKER > BALK

BALKERS > BALK

BALKIER > BALKY

BALKIEST > BALKY

BALKILY > BALKY

BALKINESS > BALKY

BALKING > BALK

BALKINGLY > BALK

BALKINGS > BALK

BALKLINE n line delimiting the balk area on a snooker table

BALKLINES > BALKLINE

BALKS > BALK

BALKY adj inclined to stop abruptly and unexpectedly

BALL n round or nearly round object, esp one used in games ▷ vb form into a ball

BALLABILE n part of ballet where all dancers perform

BALLABILI > BALLABILE

BALLAD n narrative poem or song ▷ vb sing or write a ballad

BALLADE n verse form consisting of three stanzas and an envoy, all ending with the same line

BALLADED > BALLAD

BALLADEER n singer of ballads ▷ vb perform as a balladeer

BALLADES > BALLADE

BALLADIC > BALLAD

BALLADIN same as > BALADIN

BALLADINE same as > BALADINE

BALLADING > BALLAD

BALLADINS > BALLADIN

BALLADIST > BALLAD

b

BALLADRY n ballad poetry or songs
BALLADS > BALLAD
BALLAN n species of fish
BALLANS > BALLAN
BALLANT vb write a ballad
BALLANTED > BALLANT
BALLANTS > BALLANT
BALLAST n substance, such as sand, used to stabilize a ship when it is not carrying cargo ▷ vb give stability or weight to
BALLASTED > BALLAST
BALLASTER > BALLAST
BALLASTS > BALLAST
BALLAT vb write a ballad
BALLATED > BALLAT
BALLATING > BALLAT
BALLATS > BALLAT
BALLCLAY n clay suitable for ceramics
BALLCLAYS > BALLCLAY
BALLCOCK n device for regulating the flow of a liquid into a tank, cistern, etc, consisting of a floating ball mounted at one end of an arm and a valve on the other end that opens and closes as the ball falls and rises
BALLCOCKS > BALLCOCK
BALLED > BALL
BALLER n ball-game player
BALLERINA n female ballet dancer
BALLERINE > BALLERINA
BALLERS > BALLER
BALLET n classical style of expressive dancing based on conventional steps
BALLETED > BALLAD
BALLETIC > BALLET
BALLETING > BALLAD
BALLETS > BALLET
BALLGAME n any game played with a ball
BALLGAMES > BALLGAME
BALLHAWK n skilled baseball player
BALLHAWKS > BALLHAWK
BALLIES > BALLY
BALLING > BALL
BALLINGS > BALL
BALLISTA n ancient catapult for hurling stones, etc
BALLISTAE > BALLISTA
BALLISTAS > BALLISTA
BALLISTIC adj of or relating to ballistics ▷ n the study of the flight of projectiles
BALLIUM same as > BAILEY
BALLIUMS > BALLIUM
BALLOCKS same as > BOLLOCKS
BALLON n light, graceful quality
BALLONET n air or gas compartment in a balloon or nonrigid airship, used to control buoyancy and shape
BALLONETS > BALLONET
BALLONNE n bouncing step

BALLONNES > BALLONNE
BALLONS > BALLON
BALLOON n inflatable rubber bag used as a plaything or decoration ▷ vb fly in a balloon
BALLOONED > BALLOON
BALLOONS > BALLOON
BALLOT n method of voting ▷ vb vote or ask for a vote from
BALLOTED > BALLOT
BALLOTEE > BALLOT
BALLOTEES > BALLOT
BALLOTER > BALLOT
BALLOTERS > BALLOT
BALLOTING > BALLOT
BALLOTINI n small glass beads
BALLOTS > BALLOT
BALLOW n heavy club
BALLOWS > BALLOW
BALLPARK n stadium used for baseball games
BALLPARKS > BALLPARK
BALLPOINT n pen with a tiny ball bearing as a writing point
BALLROOM n large hall for dancing
BALLROOMS > BALLROOM
BALLS pl n testicles
BALLSIER > BALLSY
BALLSIEST > BALLSY
BALLSY adj courageous and spirited
BALLUP n something botched or muddled
BALLUPS > BALLUP
BALLUTE n inflatable balloon parachute
BALLUTES > BALLUTE
BALLY another word for > BALLYHOO
BALLYARD n baseball ground
BALLYARDS > BALLYARD
BALLYHOO n exaggerated fuss ▷ vb advertise or publicize by sensational or blatant methods
BALLYHOOS > BALLYHOO
BALLYRAG same as > BULLYRAG
BALLYRAGS > BALLYRAG
BALM n aromatic substance used for healing and soothing ▷ vb apply balm to
BALMACAAN n man's knee-length loose flaring overcoat with raglan sleeves
BALMED > BALM
BALMIER > BALMY
BALMIEST > BALMY
BALMILY > BALMY
BALMINESS > BALMY
BALMING > BALM
BALMLIKE > BALM
BALMORAL n laced walking shoe
BALMORALS > BALMORAL
BALMS > BALM
BALMY adj (of weather) mild and pleasant
BALNEAL adj of or relating

to baths or bathing
BALNEARY same as > BALNEAL
BALONEY n foolish talk; nonsense
BALONEYS > BALONEY
BALOO n bear
BALOOS > BALOO
BALS > BAL
BALSA n very light wood from a tropical American tree
BALSAM n type of fragrant balm ▷ vb embalm
BALSAMED > BALSAM
BALSAMIC > BALSAM
BALSAMING > BALSAM
BALSAMS > BALSAM
BALSAMY > BALSAM
BALSAS > BALSA
BALSAWOOD same as > BALSA
BALTHASAR same as > BALTHAZAR
BALTHAZAR n wine bottle holding the equivalent of sixteen normal bottles (approximately 12 litres)
BALTI n spicy Indian dish served in a metal dish
BALTIS > BALTI
BALU same as > BALOO
BALUN n device for coupling two electrical circuit elements, such as an aerial and its feeder cable, where one is balanced and the other is unbalanced
BALUNS > BALUN
BALUS > BALU
BALUSTER n set of posts supporting a rail ▷ adj (of a shape) swelling at the base and rising in a concave curve to a narrow stem or neck
BALUSTERS > BALUSTER
BALZARINE n light fabric
BAM vb cheat
BAMBI n born-again middle-aged biker: an affluent middle-aged man who rides a powerful motorbike
BAMBINI > BAMBINO
BAMBINO n young child, esp an Italian one
BAMBINOS > BAMBINO
BAMBIS > BAMBI
BAMBOO n tall treelike tropical grass with hollow stems
BAMBOOS > BAMBOO
BAMBOOZLE vb cheat or mislead
BAMMED > BAM
BAMMER > BAM
BAMMERS > BAM
BAMMING > BAM
BAMPOT n fool
BAMPOTS > BAMPOT
BAMS > BAM
BAN vb prohibit or forbid officially ▷ n official prohibition
BANAK n tree of the genus Virola, of Central America: family Myristicaceae
BANAKS > BANAK

BANAL adj ordinary and unoriginal
BANALER > BANAL
BANALEST > BANAL
BANALISE > BANAL
BANALISED > BANAL
BANALISES > BANAL
BANALITY > BANAL
BANALIZE > BANAL
BANALIZED > BANAL
BANALIZES > BANAL
BANALLY > BANAL
BANANA n yellow crescent-shaped fruit
BANANAS adj crazy
BANAUSIAN > BANAUSIC
BANAUSIC adj merely mechanical
BANC as in in banc sitting as a full court
BANCO n call made in gambling games
BANCOS > BANCO
BANCS > BANC
BAND n group of musicians playing together ▷ vb unite
BANDA n African thatched hut
BANDAGE n piece of material used to cover a wound or wrap an injured limb ▷ vb cover with a bandage
BANDAGED > BANDAGE
BANDAGER > BANDAGE
BANDAGERS > BANDAGE
BANDAGES > BANDAGE
BANDAGING > BANDAGE
BANDAID n tradename for an adhesive plaster for cut
BANDALORE n old-fashioned type of yo-yo
BANDANA same as > BANDANNA
BANDANAS > BANDANA
BANDANNA n large brightly coloured handkerchief or neckerchief
BANDANNAS > BANDANNA
BANDAR n species of monkey
BANDARI n Indian English word for female monkey
BANDARIS > BANDARI
BANDARS > BANDAR
BANDAS > BANDA
BANDBOX n lightweight usually cylindrical box for hats
BANDBOXES > BANDBOX
BANDBRAKE n type of brake
BANDEAU n narrow ribbon worn round the head
BANDEAUS > BANDEAU
BANDEAUX > BANDEAU
BANDED > BAND
BANDELET n moulding round top of column
BANDELETS > BANDELET
BANDELIER same as > BANDOLEER
BANDER > BAND
BANDEROL same as > BANDEROLE
BANDEROLE n narrow flag usually with forked ends
BANDEROLS > BANDEROL
BANDERS > BAND

BANDH n (in India) a general strike

BANDHS > BANDH

BANDICOOT n ratlike Australian marsupial

BANDIED > BANDY

BANDIER > BANDY

BANDIES > BANDY

BANDIEST > BANDY

BANDINESS > BANDY

BANDING n practice of grouping schoolchildren according to ability to ensure a balanced intake at different levels of ability to secondary school

BANDINGS > BANDING

BANDIT n robber, esp a member of an armed gang

BANDITO n Mexican bandit

BANDITOS > BANDITO

BANDITRY > BANDIT

BANDITS > BANDIT

BANDITTI > BANDIT

BANDITTIS > BANDIT

BANDMATE n fellow member of band

BANDMATES > BANDMATE

BANDOBAST same as > BANDOBUST

BANDOBUST n (in India and Pakistan) an arrangement

BANDOG n ferocious dog

BANDOGS > BANDOG

BANDOLEER same as > BANDOLIER

BANDOLEON same as > BANDONEON

BANDOLERO n highwayman

BANDOLIER n shoulder belt for holding cartridges

BANDOLINE n glutinous hair dressing, used (esp formerly) to keep the hair in place

BANDONEON n type of square concertina, esp used in Argentina

BANDONION same as > BANDONEON

BANDOOK same as > BUNDOOK

BANDOOKS > BANDOOK

BANDORA same as > BANDORE

BANDORAS > BANDORA

BANDORE n 16th-century plucked musical instrument resembling a lute but larger and fitted with seven pairs of metal strings

BANDORES > BANDORE

BANDROL same as > BANDEROLE

BANDROLS > BANDROL

BANDS > BAND

BANDSAW n power saw with continuous blade

BANDSAWS > BANDSAW

BANDSHELL n bandstand concave at back

BANDSMAN n player in a musical band

BANDSMEN > BANDSMAN

BANDSTAND n roofed outdoor platform for a band

BANDSTER n binder of wheat sheaves

BANDSTERS > BANDSTER

BANDURA n type of lute

BANDURAS > BANDURA

BANDWAGON n type of wagon

BANDWIDTH n range of frequencies within a given waveband used for a particular transmission

BANDY adj having legs curved outwards at the knees ▷ vb exchange (words) in a heated manner

BANDYING > BANDY

BANDYINGS > BANDY

BANDYMAN n carriage or cart

BANDYMEN > BANDYMAN

BANE n person or thing that causes misery or distress ▷ vb cause harm or distress to (someone)

BANEBERRY n any ranunculaceous plant of the genus *Actaea*, esp *A. spicata*, which has small white flowers and red or white poisonous berries

BANED > BANE

BANEFUL adj destructive, poisonous, or fatal

BANEFULLY > BANEFUL

BANES > BANE

BANG vb make a short explosive noise

BANGALAY n myrtaceous Australian tree, *Eucalyptus botryoides*, valued for its hard red wood

BANGALAYS > BANGALAY

BANGALORE as in *bangalore torpedo* explosive device in a long metal tube, used to blow gaps in barbed-wire barriers

BANGALOW n Australian palm, *Archontophoenix cunninghamiana*, native to New South Wales and Queensland

BANGALOWS > BANGALOW

BANGED > BANG

BANGER n old decrepit car

BANGERS > BANGER

BANGING > BANG

BANGINGS > BANG

BANGKOK n type of straw hat

BANGKOKS > BANGKOK

BANGLE n bracelet worn round the arm or the ankle

BANGLED > BANGLE

BANGLES > BANGLE

BANGS > BANG

BANGSRING same as > BANXRING

BANGSTER n ruffian

BANGSTERS > BANGSTER

BANGTAIL n horse's tail cut straight across but not through the bone

BANGTAILS > BANGTAIL

BANI > BAN

BANIA same as > BANYAN

BANIAN same as > BANYAN

BANIANS > BANIAN

BANIAS > BANIA

BANING > BANE

BANISH vb send (someone) into exile

BANISHED > BANISH

BANISHER > BANISH

BANISHERS > BANISH

BANISHES > BANISH

BANISHING > BANISH

BANISTER same as > BANNISTER

BANISTERS pl n railing supported by posts on a staircase

BANJAX vb ruin; destroy

BANJAXED > BANJAX

BANJAXES > BANJAX

BANJAXING > BANJAX

BANJO n guitar-like musical instrument with a circular body

BANJOES > BANJO

BANJOIST > BANJO

BANJOISTS > BANJO

BANJOS > BANJO

BANJULELE n small banjo

BANK n institution offering services such as the safekeeping and lending of money ▷ vb deposit (cash or cheques) in a bank

BANKABLE adj likely to ensure financial success

BANKBOOK n book held by depositors at certain banks, in which the bank enters a record of deposits, withdrawals, and earned interest

BANKBOOKS > BANKBOOK

BANKCARD n card guaranteeing payment of cheque

BANKCARDS > BANKCARD

BANKED > BANK

BANKER n manager or owner of a bank

BANKERLY > BANKER

BANKERS > BANKER

BANKET n gold-bearing conglomerate found in South Africa

BANKETS > BANKET

BANKING same as > BANK

BANKINGS > BANK

BANKIT same as > BANQUETTE

BANKITS > BANKIT

BANKNOTE n piece of paper money

BANKNOTES > BANKNOTE

BANKROLL n roll of currency notes ▷ vb provide the capital for

BANKROLLS > BANKROLL

BANKRUPT n person declared by a court to be unable to pay his or her debts ▷ adj financially ruined ▷ vb make bankrupt

BANKRUPTS > BANKRUPT

BANKS > BANK

BANKSIA n Australian evergreen tree or shrub

BANKSIAS > BANKSIA

BANKSIDE n riverside

BANKSIDES > BANKSIDE

BANKSMAN n crane driver's helper, who signals instructions to the driver for the movement of the crane and its jib

BANKSMEN > BANKSMAN

BANLIEUE n suburb of a city

BANLIEUES > BANLIEUE

BANNABLE > BAN

BANNED > BAN

BANNER n long strip of cloth displaying a slogan, advertisement, etc ▷ vb (of a newspaper headline) to display (a story) prominently ▷ adj outstandingly successful

BANNERALL same as > BANDEROLE

BANNERED > BANNER

BANNERET n small banner

BANNERETS > BANNERET

BANNERING > BANNER

BANNEROL same as > BANDEROLE

BANNEROLS > BANNEROL

BANNERS > BANNER

BANNET n bonnet

BANNETS > BANNET

BANNING > BAN

BANNISTER same as > BANISTERS

BANNOCK n round flat cake made from oatmeal or barley

BANNOCKS > BANNOCK

BANNS pl n public declaration, esp in a church, of an intended marriage

BANOFFEE n filling for a pie, consisting of toffee and banana

BANOFFEES > BANOFFEE

BANOFFI same as > BANOFFEE

BANOFFIS > BANOFFI

BANQUET n elaborate formal dinner ▷ vb hold or take part in a banquet

BANQUETED > BANQUET

BANQUETER > BANQUET

BANQUETS > BANQUET

BANQUETTE n upholstered bench

BANS same as > BANNS

BANSELA same as > BONSELA

BANSELAS > BANSELA

BANSHEE n (in Irish folklore) female spirit whose wailing warns of a coming death

BANSHEES > BANSHEE

BANSHIE same as > BANSHEE

BANSHIES > BANSHIE

BANT n string ▷ vb tie with string

BANTAM n small breed of chicken

BANTAMS > BANTAM

BANTED > BANT

BANTENG n wild ox

BANTENGS > BANTENG

BANTER vb tease jokingly ▷ n teasing or joking conversation

BANTERED > BANTER

BANTERER > BANTER

BANTERERS > BANTER

BANTERING > BANTER
BANTERS > BANTER
BANTIES > BANTY
BANTING > BANT
BANTINGS > BANT
BANTLING *n* young child
BANTLINGS > BANTLING
BANTS > BANT
BANTU *n* offensive name for a person who speaks a Bantu language
BANTUS > BANTU
BANTY *n* bantam
BANXRING *n* tree-shrew
BANXRINGS > BANXRING
BANYAN *n* Indian tree whose branches grow down into the soil forming additional trunks
BANYANS > BANYAN
BANZAI *interj* patriotic cheer, battle cry, or salutation
BANZAIS > BANZAI
BAOBAB *n* African tree with a thick trunk and angular branches
BAOBABS > BAOBAB
BAP *n* large soft bread roll
BAPS > BAP
BAPTISE *same as* > BAPTIZE
BAPTISED > BAPTISE
BAPTISER > BAPTISE
BAPTISERS > BAPTISE
BAPTISES > BAPTISE
BAPTISIA *n* species of wild flower
BAPTISIAS > BAPTISIA
BAPTISING > BAPTISE
BAPTISM *n* Christian religious ceremony in which a person is immersed in or sprinkled with water as a sign of being cleansed from sin and accepted into the Church
BAPTISMAL > BAPTISM
BAPTISMS > BAPTISM
BAPTIST *n* one who baptizes
BAPTISTRY *n* part of a Christian church in which baptisms are carried out
BAPTISTS > BAPTIST
BAPTIZE *vb* perform baptism on
BAPTIZED > BAPTIZE
BAPTIZER > BAPTIZE
BAPTIZERS > BAPTIZE
BAPTIZES > BAPTIZE
BAPTIZING > BAPTIZE
BAPU *n* spiritual father
BAPUS > BAPU
BAR *n* rigid usually straight length of metal, wood, etc, that is longer than it is wide or thick, used esp as a barrier or as a structural or mechanical part ▷ *vb* fasten or secure with a bar
BARACAN *same as* > BARRACAN
BARACANS > BARACAN
BARACHOIS *n* (in the Atlantic Provinces of

Canada) a shallow lagoon formed by a sand bar
BARAGOUIN *n* incomprehensible language
BARASINGA *n* type of deer
BARATHEA *n* fabric made of silk and wool or cotton and rayon, used esp for coats
BARATHEAS > BARATHEA
BARATHRUM *n* abyss
BARAZA *n* place where public meetings are held
BARAZAS > BARAZA
BARB *n* cutting remark ▷ *vb* provide with a barb or barbs
BARBAL *adj* of a beard
BARBARIAN *n* member of a primitive or uncivilized people ▷ *adj* uncivilized or brutal
BARBARIC *adj* cruel or brutal
BARBARISE *same as* > BARBARIZE
BARBARISM *n* condition of being backward or ignorant
BARBARITY *n* state of being barbaric or barbarous
BARBARIZE *vb* make or become barbarous
BARBAROUS *adj* uncivilized
BARBASCO *n* S American plant
BARBASCOS > BARBASCO
BARBASTEL *n* insectivorous forest bat
BARBATE *adj* having tufts of long hairs
BARBATED > BARBATE
BARBE *n* Waldensian missionary
BARBECUE *n* grill on which food is cooked over hot charcoal, usu outdoors ▷ *vb* cook (food) on a barbecue
BARBECUED > BARBECUE
BARBECUER > BARBECUE
BARBECUES > BARBECUE
BARBED > BARB
BARBEL *n* long thin growth that hangs from the jaws of certain fishes, such as the carp
BARBELL *n* long metal rod to which heavy discs are attached at each end for weightlifting
BARBELLS > BARBELL
BARBELS > BARBEL
BARBEQUE *same as* > BARBECUE
BARBEQUED > BARBEQUE
BARBEQUES > BARBEQUE
BARBER *n* person who cuts men's hair and shaves beards ▷ *vb* cut the hair of
BARBERED > BARBER
BARBERING > BARBER
BARBERRY *n* shrub with orange or red berries
BARBERS > BARBER
BARBES > BARBE
BARBET *n* any small tropical brightly coloured bird of

the family *Capitonidae*, having short weak wings and a sharp stout bill with tuftlike feathers at its base: order *Piciformes* (woodpeckers, etc)
BARBETS > BARBET
BARBETTE *n* (formerly) an earthen platform inside a parapet, from which heavy guns could fire over the top
BARBETTES > BARBETTE
BARBICAN *n* walled defence to protect a gate or drawbridge of a fortification
BARBICANS > BARBICAN
BARBICEL *n* any of the minute hooks on the barbules of feathers that interlock with those of adjacent barbules
BARBICELS > BARBICEL
BARBIE *short for* > BARBECUE
BARBIES > BARBIE
BARBING > BARB
BARBITAL *same as* > BARBITONE
BARBITALS > BARBITAL
BARBITONE *n* long-acting barbiturate used medicinally, usually in the form of the sodium salt, as a sedative or hypnotic
BARBLESS > BARB
BARBOLA *n* small models of flowers, etc made from plastic paste
BARBOLAS > BARBOLA
BARBOTINE *n* clay used in making decorated pottery
BARBS > BARB
BARBULE *n* very small barb
BARBULES > BARBULE
BARBUT *n* open-faced helmet
BARBUTS > BARBUT
BARBWIRE *n* barbed wire
BARBWIRES > BARBWIRE
BARBY > BARBECUE
BARCA *n* boat
BARCAROLE *n* Venetian boat song
BARCAS > BARCA
BARCHAN *n* crescent-shaped shifting sand dune, convex on the windward side and steeper and concave on the leeward
BARCHANE *same as* > BARCHAN
BARCHANES > BARCHANE
BARCHANS > BARCHAN
BARD *n* poet ▷ *vb* place a piece of pork fat on
BARDASH *n* kept boy in a homosexual relationship
BARDASHES > BARDASH
BARDE *same as* > BARD
BARDED > BARDE
BARDES > BARDE
BARDIC > BARD
BARDIE *n* type of Australian grub
BARDIER > BARD
BARDIES > BARDIE

BARDIEST > BARD
BARDING > BARD
BARDISM > BARD
BARDISMS > BARD
BARDLING *n* inferior poet
BARDLINGS > BARDLING
BARDO *n* (in Tibetan Buddhism) the state of the soul between its death and its rebirth
BARDOS > BARDO
BARDS > BARD
BARDSHIP > BARD
BARDSHIPS > BARD
BARDY > BARD
BARE *adj* unclothed, naked ▷ *vb* uncover
BAREBACK *adv* (of horse-riding) without a saddle ▷ *vb* ride bareback
BAREBACKS > BAREBACK
BAREBOAT *n* boat chartered without crew, provisions, etc
BAREBOATS > BAREBOAT
BAREBONE *n* computer casing containing bare essentials
BAREBONED *adj* short of resources
BAREBONES > BAREBONE
BARED > BARE
BAREFACED *adj* shameless or obvious
BAREFIT > BAREFOOT
BAREFOOT *adv* with the feet uncovered
BAREGE *n* light silky gauze fabric made of wool ▷ *adj* made of such a fabric
BAREGES > BAREGE
BAREGINE *n* curative ingredient in thermal waters
BAREGINES > BAREGINE
BAREHAND *vb* handle with bare hands
BAREHANDS > BAREHAND
BAREHEAD *adv* with head unvovered
BARELY *adv* only just
BARENESS > BARE
BARER > BARE
BARES > BARE
BARESARK *another word for* > BERSERK
BARESARKS > BARESARK
BAREST > BARE
BARF *vb* vomit ▷ *n* act of vomiting
BARFED > BARF
BARFING > BARF
BARFLIES > BARFLY
BARFLY *n* person who frequents bars
BARFS > BARF
BARFUL *adj* presenting difficulties
BARGAIN *n* agreement establishing what each party will give, receive, or perform in a transaction ▷ *vb* negotiate the terms of an agreement
BARGAINED > BARGAIN
BARGAINER > BARGAIN
BARGAINS > BARGAIN

BARGANDER *same as* > BERGANDER

BARGE *n* flat-bottomed boat used to transport freight ▷ *vb* push violently

BARGED > BARGE

BARGEE *n* person in charge of a barge

BARGEES > BARGEE

BARGEESE > BARGOOSE

BARGELLO *n* zigzag tapestry stitch

BARGELLOS > BARGELLO

BARGEMAN *same as* > BARGEE

BARGEMEN > BARGEMAN

BARGEPOLE *n* long pole used to propel a barge

BARGES > BARGE

BARGEST *same as* > BARGHEST

BARGESTS > BARGEST

BARGHEST *n* mythical goblin in the shape of a dog

BARGHESTS > BARGHEST

BARGING > BARGE

BARGOON *Canadian word for* > BARGAIN

BARGOONS > BARGOON

BARGOOSE *n* type of goose; sheldrake

BARGUEST *same as* > BARGHEST

BARGUESTS > BARGUEST

BARHOP *vb* visit several bars in succession

BARHOPPED > BARHOP

BARHOPS > BARHOP

BARIATRIC *adj* of the treatment of obesity

BARIC *adj* of or containing barium

BARILLA *n* impure mixture of sodium carbonate and sodium sulphate obtained from the ashes of certain plants, such as the saltworts

BARILLAS > BARILLA

BARING > BARE

BARISH *adj* quite thinly covered

BARISTA *n* person who makes and sells coffee in a coffee bar

BARISTAS > BARISTA

BARITE *n* colourless or white mineral consisting of barium sulphate in orthorhombic crystalline form, occurring in sedimentary rocks and with sulphide ores: a source of barium.

BARITES > BARITE

BARITONAL > BARITONE

BARITONE *n* (singer with) the second lowest adult male voice ▷ *adj* relating to or denoting a baritone

BARITONES > BARITONE

BARIUM *n* soft white metallic element

BARIUMS > BARIUM

BARK *vb* (of a dog) make its typical loud abrupt cry

BARKAN *same as* > BARCHAN

BARKANS > BARKAN

BARKED > BARK

BARKEEP *n* barkeeper

BARKEEPER *another name (esp US) for* > BARTENDER

BARKEEPS > BARKEEP

BARKEN *vb* become dry with a bark-like outer layer

BARKENED > BARKEN

BARKENING > BARKEN

BARKENS > BARKEN

BARKER *n* person at a fairground who calls loudly to passers-by in order to attract customers

BARKERS > BARKER

BARKHAN *same as* > BARCHAN

BARKHANS > BARKHAN

BARKIER > BARKY

BARKIEST > BARKY

BARKING *adj* mad ▷ *adv* extremely

BARKLESS > BARK

BARKS > BARK

BARKY *adj* having the texture or appearance of bark

BARLEDUC *n* French preserve made of currants

BARLEDUCS > BARLEDUC

BARLESS > BAR

BARLEY *n* tall grasslike plant cultivated for grain ▷ *sentence substitute* cry for truce or respite from the rules of a game

BARLEYS > BARLEY

BARLOW *n* type of strong knife

BARLOWS > BARLOW

BARM *n* yeasty froth on fermenting malt liquors

BARMAID *n* woman who serves in a pub

BARMAIDS > BARMAID

BARMAN *same as* > BARTENDER

BARMBRACK *n* loaf of bread with currants in it

BARMEN > BARMAN

BARMIE *same as* > BARMY

BARMIER > BARMY

BARMIEST > BARMY

BARMINESS > BARMY

BARMKIN *n* protective wall around castle

BARMKINS > BARMKIN

BARMS > BARM

BARMY *adj* insane

BARN *n* large building on a farm used for storing grain ▷ *vb* keep in a barn

BARNACLE *n* shellfish that lives attached to rocks, ship bottoms, etc

BARNACLED > BARNACLE

BARNACLES > BARNACLE

BARNBRACK *same as* > BARMBRACK

BARNED > BARN

BARNET *n* hair

BARNETS > BARNET

BARNEY *n* noisy fight or argument ▷ *vb* argue or quarrel

BARNEYED > BARNEY

BARNEYING > BARNEY

BARNEYS > BARNEY

BARNIER > BARNY

BARNIEST > BARNY

BARNING > BARN

BARNLIKE > BARN

BARNS > BARN

BARNSTORM *vb* tour rural districts putting on shows or making speeches in a political campaign

BARNY *adj* reminiscent of a barn

BARNYARD *n* yard adjoining a barn

BARNYARDS > BARNYARD

BAROCCO *same as* > BAROQUE

BAROCCOS > BAROCCO

BAROCK *same as* > BAROQUE

BAROCKS > BAROCK

BAROGRAM *n* record of atmospheric pressure traced by a barograph or similar instrument

BAROGRAMS > BAROGRAM

BAROGRAPH *n* barometer that automatically keeps a record of changes in atmospheric pressure

BAROLO *n* red Italian wine

BAROLOS > BAROLO

BAROMETER *n* instrument for measuring atmospheric pressure

BAROMETRY > BAROMETER

BAROMETZ *n* fern whose woolly rhizoma resemble a lamb

BARON *n* member of the lowest rank of nobility

BARONAGE *n* barons collectively

BARONAGES > BARONAGE

BARONESS *n* woman holding the rank of baron

BARONET *n* commoner who holds the lowest hereditary British title

BARONETCY *n* rank, position, or patent of a baronet

BARONETS > BARONET

BARONG *n* broad-bladed cleaver-like knife used in the Philippines

BARONGS > BARONG

BARONIAL *adj* of, relating to, or befitting a baron or barons

BARONIES > BARONY

BARONNE *n* baroness

BARONNES > BARONNE

BARONS > BARON

BARONY *n* domain or rank of a baron

BAROPHILE > BAROPHILIC

BAROQUE *n* highly ornate style of art, architecture, or music from the late 16th to the early 18th century ▷ *adj* ornate in style

BAROQUELY > BAROQUE

BAROQUES > BAROQUE

BAROSAUR *n* large dinosaur

BAROSAURS > BAROSAUR

BAROSCOPE *n* any instrument for measuring atmospheric pressure, esp a manometer with one side open to the atmosphere

BAROSTAT *n* device for maintaining constant pressure, such as one used in an aircraft cabin

BAROSTATS > BAROSTAT

BAROUCHE *n* four-wheeled horse-drawn carriage, popular in the 19th century, having a retractable hood over the rear half, seats inside for two couples facing each other, and a driver's seat outside at the front

BAROUCHES > BAROUCHE

BARP *n* hillock or bank of stones

BARPERSON *n* person who serves in a pub: used esp in advertisements

BARPS > BARP

BARQUE *n* sailing ship, esp one with three masts

BARQUES > BARQUE

BARQUETTE *n* boat-shaped pastry shell

BARRA *n* barramundi

BARRABLE > BAR

BARRACAN *n* thick, strong fabric

BARRACANS > BARRACAN

BARRACE *n* record of teams entering a sports contest

BARRACES > BARRACE

BARRACK *vb* criticize loudly or shout against (a team or speaker)

BARRACKED > BARRACK

BARRACKER > BARRACK

BARRACKS *pl n* building used to accommodate military personnel

BARRACOON *n* (formerly) a temporary place of confinement for slaves or convicts, esp those awaiting transportation

BARRACUDA *n* tropical sea fish

BARRAGE *n* continuous delivery of questions, complaints, etc ▷ *vb* attack or confront with a barrage

BARRAGED > BARRAGE

BARRAGES > BARRAGE

BARRAGING > BARRAGE

BARRANCA *n* ravine or precipice

BARRANCAS > BARRANCA

BARRANCO *same as* > BARRANCA

BARRANCOS > BARRANCO

BARRAS > BARRA

BARRAT *n* fraudulent dealings

BARRATER *same as* > BARRATOR

BARRATERS > BARRATER

BARRATOR *n* person guilty of barratry

BARRATORS > BARRATOR

BARRATRY *n* (formerly) the vexatious stirring up of quarrels or bringing of lawsuits

b

BARRATS > BARRAT
BARRE *n* rail at hip height used for ballet practice ▷ *vb* execute guitar chords by laying the index finger over some or all of the strings so that the pitch of each stopped string is simultaneously raised ▷ *adv* by using the barré
BARRED > BAR
BARREED > BARRE
BARREFULL *same as* > BARFUL
BARREING > BARRE
BARREL *n* cylindrical container with rounded sides and flat ends ▷ *vb* put in a barrel
BARRELAGE > BARREL
BARRELED > BARREL
BARRELFUL *same as* > BARREL
BARRELING > BARREL
BARRELLED > BARREL
BARRELS > BARREL
BARREN *adj* (of a woman or female animal) incapable of producing offspring
BARRENER > BARREN
BARRENEST > BARREN
BARRENLY > BARREN
BARRENS *pl n* (in North America) a stretch of usually level land that is sparsely vegetated or barren
BARRES > BARRE
BARRET *n* small flat cap resembling a biretta
BARRETOR *n* quarrelsome person
BARRETORS > BARRETOR
BARRETRY *same as* > BARRATRY
BARRETS > BARRET
BARRETTE *n* clasp or pin for holding women's hair in place
BARRETTER *same as* > BARRETOR
BARRETTES > BARRETTE
BARRICADE *n* barrier, esp one erected hastily for defence ▷ *vb* erect a barricade across (an entrance)
BARRICADO *same as* > BARRICADE
BARRICO *n* small container for liquids
BARRICOES > BARRICO
BARRICOS > BARRICO
BARRIE *adj* very good
BARRIER *n* anything that prevents access, progress, or union ▷ *vb* create or form a barrier
BARRIERED > BARRIER
BARRIERS > BARRIER
BARRIES > BARRY
BARRIEST > BARRY
BARRING > BAR
BARRINGS > BAR
BARRIO *n* Spanish-speaking quarter in a town or city, esp in the US

BARRIOS > BARRIO
BARRISTER *n* lawyer qualified to plead in a higher court
BARRO *adj* embarrassing
BARROOM *n* room or building where alcoholic drinks are served over a counter
BARROOMS > BARROOM
BARROW *n* wheelbarrow
BARROWFUL *same as* > BARROW
BARROWS > BARROW
BARRULET *n* narrow band across heraldic shield
BARRULETS > BARRULET
BARRY *n* mistake or blunder
BARS > BAR
BARSTOOL *n* high stool in bar
BARSTOOLS > BARSTOOL
BARTEND *vb* serve drinks from a bar
BARTENDED > BARTEND
BARTENDER *n* man who serves in a bar
BARTENDS > BARTEND
BARTER *vb* trade (goods) in exchange for other goods ▷ *n* trade by the exchange of goods
BARTERED > BARTER
BARTERER > BARTER
BARTERERS > BARTER
BARTERING > BARTER
BARTERS > BARTER
BARTISAN *same as* > BARTIZAN
BARTISANS > BARTISAN
BARTIZAN *n* small turret projecting from a wall, parapet, or tower
BARTIZANS > BARTIZAN
BARTON *n* farmyard
BARTONS > BARTON
BARTSIA *n* type of semiparasitic plant
BARTSIAS > BARTSIA
BARWARE *n* glasses, etc used in a bar
BARWARES > BARWARE
BARWOOD *n* red wood from small African tree
BARWOODS > BARWOOD
BARYE *n* unit of pressure in the cgs system equal to one dyne per square centimetre. 1 barye is equivalent to 1 microbar
BARYES > BARYE
BARYON *n* elementary particle that has a mass greater than or equal to that of the proton
BARYONIC *adj* of or relating to a baryon
BARYONS > BARYON
BARYTA *same as* > BARITE
BARYTAS > BARYTA
BARYTE *same as* > BARYTA
BARYTES > BARYTE
BARYTIC > BARYTA
BARYTON *n* bass viol with sympathetic strings as well as its six main strings
BARYTONE *adj* having the last syllable unaccented

▷ *n* word in which the last syllable is unaccented
BARYTONES > BARYTONE
BARYTONS > BARYTON
BAS > BA
BASAL *adj* of, at, or constituting a base
BASALLY > BASAL
BASALT *n* dark volcanic rock
BASALTES *n* unglazed black stoneware
BASALTIC > BASALT
BASALTINE *n* type of mineral
BASALTS > BASALT
BASAN *n* sheepskin tanned in bark
BASANITE *n* black basaltic rock containing plagioclase, augite, olivine, and nepheline, leucite, or analcite, formerly used as a touchstone
BASANITES > BASANITE
BASANS > BASAN
BASCINET *same as* > BASINET
BASCINETS > BASCINET
BASCULE *n* drawbridge that operates by a counterbalanced weight
BASCULES > BASCULE
BASE *n* bottom or supporting part of anything ▷ *vb* use as a basis (for) ▷ *adj* dishonourable or immoral
BASEBALL *n* team game in which runs are scored by hitting a ball with a bat then running round four bases
BASEBALLS > BASEBALL
BASEBAND *n* transmission technique using a narrow range of frequencies that allows only one message to be telecommunicated at a time
BASEBANDS > BASEBAND
BASEBOARD *n* board functioning as the base of anything
BASEBORN *adj* born of humble parents
BASED > BASE
BASELARD *n* short sword
BASELARDS > BASELARD
BASELESS *adj* not based on fact
BASELINE *n* value or starting point on an imaginary scale with which other things are compared
BASELINER *n* tennis player who plays most of his or her shots from the back of the court
BASELINES > BASELINE
BASELY > BASE
BASEMAN *n* fielder positioned near a base
BASEMEN > BASEMAN
BASEMENT *n* partly or wholly underground storey of a building
BASEMENTS > BASEMENT
BASENESS > BASE

BASENJI *n* small smooth-haired breed of dog of African origin having a tightly curled tail and an inability to bark
BASENJIS > BASENJI
BASEPLATE *n* flat supporting plate or frame
BASER > BASE
BASES > BASIS
BASEST > BASE
BASH *vb* hit violently or forcefully ▷ *n* heavy blow
BASHAW *n* important or pompous person
BASHAWISM > BASHAW
BASHAWS > BASHAW
BASHED > BASH
BASHER > BASH
BASHERS > BASH
BASHES > BASH
BASHFUL *adj* shy or modest
BASHFULLY > BASHFUL
BASHING > BASH
BASHINGS > BASH
BASHLESS *adj* not ashamed
BASHLIK *n* Caucasian hood
BASHLIKS > BASHLIK
BASHLYK *same as* > BASHLIK
BASHLYKS > BASHLYK
BASHO *n* grand tournament in sumo wrestling
BASIC *adj* of or forming a base or basis ▷ *n* fundamental principle, fact, etc
BASICALLY *adv* in a fundamental or elementary manner
BASICITY *n* state of being a base
BASICS > BASIC
BASIDIA > BASIDIUM
BASIDIAL > BASIDIUM
BASIDIUM *n* structure, produced by basidiomycetous fungi after sexual reproduction, in which spores are formed at the tips of projecting slender stalks
BASIFIED > BASIFY
BASIFIER > BASIFY
BASIFIERS > BASIFY
BASIFIES > BASIFY
BASIFIXED *adj* (of an anther) attached to the filament by its base
BASIFUGAL *a less common word for* > ACROPETAL
BASIFY *vb* make basic
BASIFYING > BASIFY
BASIL *n* aromatic herb used in cooking
BASILAR *adj* of or situated at a base
BASILARY *same as* > BASILAR
BASILECT *n* debased dialect
BASILECTS > BASILECT
BASILIC > BASILICA
BASILICA *n* rectangular church with a rounded end and two aisles
BASILICAE > BASILICA
BASILICAL > BASILICA
BASILICAN > BASILICA
BASILICAS > BASILICA

BASILICON *n* healing ointment

BASILISK *n* legendary serpent said to kill by its breath or glance

BASILISKS > BASILISK

BASILS > BASIL

BASIN *n* round open container

BASINAL > BASIN

BASINED > BASIN

BASINET *n* close-fitting medieval helmet of light steel usually with a visor

BASINETS > BASINET

BASINFUL *n* amount a basin will hold

BASINFULS > BASINFUL

BASING > BASE

BASINLIKE > BASIN

BASINS > BASIN

BASION *n* (in anatomy) midpoint on the forward border of the foramen magnum

BASIONS > BASION

BASIPETAL *adj* (of leaves and flowers) produced in order from the apex downwards so that the youngest are at the base

BASIS *n* fundamental principles etc from which something is started or developed

BASK *vb* lie in or be exposed to something, esp pleasant warmth

BASKED > BASK

BASKET *n* container made of interwoven strips of wood or cane

BASKETFUL *n* as much as a basket will hold

BASKETRY *n* art or practice of making baskets

BASKETS > BASKET

BASKING > BASK

BASKS > BASK

BASMATI *n* variety of long-grain rice with slender aromatic grains, used for savoury dishes

BASMATIS > BASMATI

BASNET *same as* > BASINET

BASNETS > BASNET

BASOCHE *n* society of medieval French lawyers who performed comic plays

BASOCHES > BASOCHE

BASON *same as* > BASIN

BASONS > BASON

BASOPHIL *adj* (of cells or cell contents) easily stained by basic dyes ▷ *n* basophil cell, esp a leucocyte

BASOPHILE *same as* > BASOPHIL

BASOPHILS > BASOPHIL

BASQUE *n* tight-fitting bodice for women

BASQUED > BASQUE

BASQUES > BASQUE

BASQUINE *n* tight-fitting bodice

BASQUINES > BASQUINE

BASS *vb* speak or sing in a low pitch

BASSE *same as* > BASS

BASSED > BASS

BASSER > BASS

BASSES > BASS

BASSEST > BASS

BASSET *n* long low smooth-haired breed of hound with short strong legs and long ears ▷ *vb* outcrop

BASSETED > BASSET

BASSETING > BASSET

BASSETS > BASSET

BASSETT *same as* > BASSET

BASSETTED > BASSET

BASSETTS > BASSET

BASSI > BASSO

BASSIER > BASSY

BASSIEST > BASSY

BASSINET *n* wickerwork or wooden cradle or pram, usually hooded

BASSINETS > BASSINET

BASSING > BASS

BASSIST *n* player of a double bass, esp in a jazz band

BASSISTS > BASSIST

BASSLY > BASS

BASSNESS > BASS

BASSO *n* singer with a bass voice

BASSOON *n* low-pitched woodwind instrument

BASSOONS > BASSOON

BASSOS > BASSO

BASSWOOD *n* any of several North American linden trees, esp *Tilia americana*

BASSWOODS > BASSWOOD

BASSY *adj* manifesting strong bass tones

BAST *n* fibrous material obtained from the phloem of jute, hemp, flax, lime, etc, used for making rope, matting, etc

BASTA *interj* enough; stop

BASTARD *n* offensive term for an obnoxious or despicable person ▷ *adj* offensive term meaning illegitimate by birth

BASTARDLY > BASTARD

BASTARDRY *n* malicious or cruel behaviour

BASTARDS > BASTARD

BASTARDY *n* condition of being a bastard

BASTE *vb* moisten (meat) during cooking with hot fat

BASTED > BASTE

BASTER > BASTE

BASTERS > BASTE

BASTES > BASTE

BASTI *n* (in India) a slum inhabited by poor people

BASTIDE *n* small isolated house in France

BASTIDES > BASTIDE

BASTILE *same as* > BASTILLE

BASTILES > BASTILE

BASTILLE *n* prison

BASTILLES > BASTILLE

BASTINADE *same as* > BASTINADO

BASTINADO *n* punishment or torture by beating on the soles of the feet with a stick ▷ *vb* beat (a person) in this way

BASTING *n* loose temporary stitches

BASTINGS > BASTING

BASTION *n* projecting part of a fortification

BASTIONED > BASTION

BASTIONS > BASTION

BASTIS > BASTI

BASTLE *n* fortified house

BASTLES > BASTLE

BASTO *n* ace of clubs in certain card games

BASTOS > BASTO

BASTS > BAST

BASUCO *n* cocaine-based drug

BASUCOS > BASUCO

BAT *n* any of various types of club used to hit the ball in certain sports ▷ *vb* strike with or as if with a bat

BATABLE > BAT

BATATA *n* sweet potato

BATATAS > BATATA

BATAVIA *n* variety of lettuce with smooth pale green leaves

BATAVIAS > BATAVIA

BATBOY *n* boy who works at baseball game

BATBOYS > BATBOY

BATCH *n* group of people or things dealt with at the same time ▷ *vb* group (items) for efficient processing

BATCHED > BATCH

BATCHER > BATCH

BATCHERS > BATCH

BATCHES > BATCH

BATCHING > BATCH

BATCHINGS > BATCH

BATE *vb* (of hawks) to jump violently from a perch or the falconer's fist, often hanging from the leash while struggling to escape

BATEAU *n* light flat-bottomed boat used on rivers in Canada and the northern US

BATEAUX > BATEAU

BATED > BATE

BATELESS > BATE

BATELEUR *n* African crested bird of prey, *Terathopius ecaudatus*, with a short tail and long wings: subfamily *Circaetinae*, family *Accipitridae* (hawks, etc)

BATELEURS > BATELEUR

BATEMENT *n* reduction

BATEMENTS > BATEMENT

BATES > BATE

BATFISH *n* any angler of the family *Ogcocephalidae*, having a flattened scaleless body and moving on the sea floor by means of fleshy pectoral and pelvic fins

BATFISHES > BATFISH

BATFOWL *vb* catch birds by temporarily blinding them with light

BATFOWLED > BATFOWL

BATFOWLER > BATFOWL

BATFOWLS > BATFOWL

BATGIRL *n* girl who works at baseball games

BATGIRLS > BATGIRL

BATH *n* large container in which to wash the body ▷ *vb* wash in a bath

BATHCUBE *n* cube of soluble scented material for use in a bath

BATHCUBES > BATHCUBE

BATHE *vb* swim in open water for pleasure

BATHED > BATHE

BATHER > BATHE

BATHERS *pl n* swimming costume

BATHES > BATHE

BATHETIC *adj* containing or displaying bathos

BATHHOUSE *n* building containing baths, esp for public use

BATHING > BATHE

BATHLESS > BATH

BATHMAT *n* mat to stand on after a bath

BATHMATS > BATHMAT

BATHMIC > BATHMISM

BATHMISM *n* growth-force

BATHMISMS > BATHMISM

BATHOLITE *same as* > BATHOLITH

BATHOLITH *n* very large irregular-shaped mass of igneous rock, esp granite, formed from an intrusion of magma at great depth, esp one exposed after erosion of less resistant overlying rocks

BATHORSE *n* officer's packhorse

BATHORSES > BATHORSE

BATHOS *n* sudden ludicrous change in speech or writing from a serious subject to a trivial one

BATHOSES > BATHOS

BATHROBE *n* loose-fitting garment for wear before or after a bath or swimming

BATHROBES > BATHROBE

BATHROOM *n* room with a bath, sink, and usu a toilet

BATHROOMS > BATHROOM

BATHS > BATH

BATHTUB *n* bath, esp one not permanently fixed

BATHTUBS > BATHTUB

BATHWATER *n* used or unused water in a bathtub

BATHYAL *adj* denoting or relating to an ocean depth of between 200 and 2000 metres (about 100 and 1000 fathoms), corresponding to the continental slope

BATHYBIUS *n* gelatinous substance on seabed

BATHYLITE *same as* > BATHOLITH

b

b

BATHYLITH *same as* > BATHOLITH
BATIK *n* process of printing fabric using wax to cover areas not to be dyed ▷ *vb* treat material with this process
BATIKED > BATIK
BATIKING > BATIK
BATIKS > BATIK
BATING > BATE
BATISTE *n* fine plain-weave cotton fabric: used esp for shirts and dresses
BATISTES > BATISTE
BATLER *n* flat piece of wood for beating clothes, etc before washing
BATLERS > BATLER
BATLET *same as* > BATLER
BATLETS > BATLET
BATLIKE > BAT
BATMAN *n* officer's servant in the armed forces
BATMEN > BATMAN
BATOLOGY *n* study of brambles
BATON *n* thin stick used by the conductor of an orchestra ▷ *vb* carry or wave a baton
BATONED > BATON
BATONING > BATON
BATONS > BATON
BATOON *same as* > BATON
BATOONED > BATOON
BATOONING > BATOON
BATOONS > BATOON
BATRACHIA *n* group of amphibians including frogs and toads
BATS > BAT
BATSMAN *n* person who bats or specializes in batting
BATSMEN > BATSMAN
BATSWING *adj* in the form of the wing of a bat
BATSWOMAN > BATSMAN
BATSWOMEN > BATSMAN
BATT > BAT
BATTA *n* soldier's allowance
BATTALIA *n* arrangement of army prepared for battle
BATTALIAS > BATTALIA
BATTALION *n* army unit consisting of three or more companies
BATTAS > BATTA
BATTEAU *same as* > BATEAU
BATTEAUX > BATTEAU
BATTED > BAT
BATTEL *vb* make fertile
BATTELED > BATTEL
BATTELER > BATTEL
BATTELERS > BATTEL
BATTELING > BATTEL
BATTELLED > BATTEL
BATTELS > BATTEL
BATTEMENT *n* extension of one leg forwards, sideways, or backwards, either once or repeatedly
BATTEN *n* strip of wood fixed to something, esp to hold it in place ▷ *vb* strengthen or fasten with battens

BATTENED > BATTEN
BATTENER > BATTEN
BATTENERS > BATTEN
BATTENING > BATTEN
BATTENS > BATTEN
BATTER *vb* hit repeatedly ▷ *n* mixture of flour, eggs, and milk, used in cooking
BATTERED *adj* subjected to persistent physical violence, esp by a close relative living in the same house
BATTERER *n* person who batters someone
BATTERERS > BATTERER
BATTERIE *n* movement in ballet involving the legs beating together
BATTERIES > BATTERY
BATTERING *n* act or practice of battering someone
BATTERO *n* heavy club
BATTEROS > BATTERO
BATTERS > BATTER
BATTERY *n* device that produces electricity in a torch, radio, etc ▷ *adj* kept in series of cages for intensive rearing
BATTIER > BATTY
BATTIEST > BATTY
BATTIK *same as* > BATIK
BATTIKS > BATTIK
BATTILL *old spelling of* > BATTLE
BATTILLED > BATTILL
BATTILLS > BATTILL
BATTINESS > BATTY
BATTING > BAT
BATTINGS > BAT
BATTLE *n* fight between large armed forces ▷ *vb* struggle
BATTLEBUS *n* coach that transports politicians and their advisers round the country during an election campaign
BATTLED > BATTLE
BATTLER > BATTLE
BATTLERS > BATTLE
BATTLES > BATTLE
BATTLING > BATTLE
BATTOLOGY *n* unnecessary repetition of words
BATTS > BATT
BATTU *adj* (in ballet) involving a beating movement
BATTUE *n* beating of woodland or cover to force game to flee in the direction of hunters
BATTUES > BATTUE
BATTUTA *n* (in music) a beat
BATTUTAS > BATTUTA
BATTY *adj* eccentric or crazy
BATWING *adj* shaped like the wings of a bat, as a black tie, collar, etc
BATWOMAN *n* female servant in any of the armed forces
BATWOMEN > BATWOMAN
BAUBEE *same as* > BAWBEE
BAUBEES > BAUBEE
BAUBLE *n* trinket of little

value
BAUBLES > BAUBLE
BAUBLING > BAUBLE
BAUCHLE *vb* shuffle along
BAUCHLED > BAUCHLE
BAUCHLES > BAUCHLE
BAUCHLING > BAUCHLE
BAUD *n* unit used to measure the speed of transmission of electronic data
BAUDEKIN *old variant of* > BALDACHIN
BAUDEKINS > BAUDEKIN
BAUDRIC *same as* > BALDRIC
BAUDRICK *same as* > BALDRIC
BAUDRICKE *same as* > BALDRIC
BAUDRICKS > BAUDRICK
BAUDRICS > BAUDRIC
BAUDRONS *n* name for a cat
BAUDS > BAUD
BAUERA *n* small evergreen Australian shrub
BAUERAS > BAUERA
BAUHINIA *n* any climbing or shrubby leguminous plant of the genus *Bauhinia*, of tropical and warm regions, widely cultivated for ornament
BAUHINIAS > BAUHINIA
BAUK *same as* > BALK
BAUKED > BAUK
BAUKING > BAUK
BAUKS > BAUK
BAULK > BALK
BAULKED > BALK
BAULKER > BALK
BAULKERS > BALK
BAULKIER > BAULKY
BAULKIEST > BAULKY
BAULKILY > BALKY
BAULKING > BALK
BAULKS > BALK
BAULKY *same as* > BALKY
BAUR *n* humorous anecdote; joke
BAURS > BAUR
BAUSOND *adj* (of animal) dappled with white spots
BAUXITE *n* claylike substance that is the chief source of aluminium
BAUXITES > BAUXITE
BAUXITIC > BAUXITE
BAVARDAGE *n* chattering
BAVAROIS *n* cold dessert consisting of a rich custard set with gelatine and flavoured in various ways
BAVIN *n* impure limestone
BAVINS > BAVIN
BAWBEE *n* former Scottish silver coin
BAWBEES > BAWBEE
BAWBLE *same as* > BAUBLE
BAWBLES > BAWBLE
BAWCOCK *n* fine fellow
BAWCOCKS > BAWCOCK
BAWD *n* person who runs a brothel, esp a woman
BAWDIER > BAWDY
BAWDIES > BAWDY
BAWDIEST > BAWDY
BAWDILY > BAWDY
BAWDINESS > BAWDY

BAWDKIN *same as* > BALDACHIN
BAWDKINS > BAWDKIN
BAWDRIC *n* heavy belt to support sword
BAWDRICS > BAWDRIC
BAWDRIES > BAWDRY
BAWDRY *n* obscene talk or language
BAWDS > BAWD
BAWDY *adj* (of writing etc) containing humorous references to sex ▷ *n* obscenity or eroticism, esp in writing or drama
BAWL *vb* shout or weep noisily ▷ *n* loud shout or cry
BAWLED > BAWL
BAWLER > BAWL
BAWLERS > BAWL
BAWLEY *n* small fishing boat
BAWLEYS > BAWLEY
BAWLING > BAWL
BAWLINGS > BAWL
BAWLS > BAWL
BAWN *n* fortified enclosure
BAWNEEN *same as* > BAININ
BAWNEENS > BAWNEEN
BAWNS > BAWN
BAWR *same as* > BAUR
BAWRS > BAWR
BAWSUNT *adj* black and white in colour
BAWTIE *n* name for a dog
BAWTIES > BAWTIE
BAWTY *same as* > BAWTIE
BAXTER *old variant of* > BAKER
BAXTERS > BAXTER
BAY *n* wide semicircular indentation of a shoreline ▷ *vb* howl in deep tones
BAYADEER *same as* > BAYADERE
BAYADEERS > BAYADEER
BAYADERE *n* dancing girl, esp one serving in a Hindu temple ▷ *adj* (of fabric, etc) having horizontal stripes
BAYADERES > BAYADERE
BAYAMO *n* Cuban strong wind
BAYAMOS > BAYAMO
BAYARD *n* bay horse
BAYARDS > BAYARD
BAYBERRY *n* tropical American tree that yields an oil used in making bay rum
BAYE *vb* bathe
BAYED > BAY
BAYES > BAYE
BAYING > BAY
BAYLE *n* barrier
BAYLES > BAYLE
BAYMAN *n* fisherman
BAYMEN > BAYMAN
BAYONET *n* sharp blade that can be fixed to the end of a rifle ▷ *vb* stab with a bayonet
BAYONETED > BAYONET
BAYONETS > BAYONET
BAYOU *n* (in the southern US) a sluggish marshy tributary of a lake or river

BAYOUS > BAYOU

BAYS > BAY

BAYT *same as* > BATE

BAYTED > BAYT

BAYTING > BAYT

BAYTS > BAYT

BAYWOOD *n* light soft wood of a tropical American mahogany tree, *Swietenia macrophylla*, of the bay region of SE Mexico

BAYWOODS > BAYWOOD

BAYYAN *n* Islamic declaration

BAYYANS > BAYYAN

BAZAAR *n* sale in aid of charity

BAZAARS > BAZAAR

BAZAR *same as* > BAZAAR

BAZARS > BAZAR

BAZAZZ *same as* > PIZZAZZ

BAZAZZES > BAZAZZ

BAZILLION *same as* > GAZILLION

BAZOO *a US slang word for* > MOUTH

BAZOOKA *n* portable rocket launcher that fires an armour-piercing projectile

BAZOOKAS > BAZOOKA

BAZOOMS *pl n* woman's breasts

BAZOOS > BAZOO

BAZOUKI *same as* > BOUZOUKI

BAZOUKIS > BAZOUKI

BDELLIUM *n* any of several African or W Asian trees of the burseraceous genus *Commiphora* that yield a gum resin

BDELLIUMS > BDELLIUM

BE *vb* exist or live

BEACH *n* area of sand or pebbles on a shore ▷ *vb* run or haul (a boat) onto a beach

BEACHBALL *n* light ball for playing on beach

BEACHBOY *n* male lifeguard on beach

BEACHBOYS > BEACHBOY

BEACHCOMB *vb* collect objects, seashells, etc on seashore

BEACHED > BEACH

BEACHES > BEACH

BEACHGOER *n* person who goes to the beach

BEACHHEAD *n* beach captured by an attacking army on which troops can be landed

BEACHIER > BEACHY

BEACHIEST > BEACHY

BEACHING > BEACH

BEACHSIDE *adj* situated near a beach

BEACHWEAR *n* clothes suitable for the beach

BEACHY *adj* with gentle sandy slopes

BEACON *n* fire or light on a hill or tower, used as a warning ▷ *vb* guide or warn

BEACONED > BEACON

BEACONING > BEACON

BEACONS > BEACON

BEAD *n* small piece of plastic, wood, etc, pierced for threading on a string to form a necklace etc ▷ *vb* decorate with beads

BEADBLAST *n* jet of small glass beads blown from a nozzle under air or steam pressure ▷ *vb* clean or treat (a surface) with a beadblast

BEADED > BEAD

BEADER *n* person making things with beads

BEADERS > BEADER

BEADHOUSE *n* chapel

BEADIER > BEADY

BEADIEST > BEADY

BEADILY > BEADY

BEADINESS > BEADY

BEADING *n* strip of moulding used for edging furniture

BEADINGS > BEADING

BEADLE *n* (formerly) a minor parish official who acted as an usher

BEADLEDOM *n* petty officialdom

BEADLES > BEADLE

BEADLIKE > BEAD

BEADMAN *same as* > BEADSMAN

BEADMEN > BEADMAN

BEADROLL *n* list of persons for whom prayers are to be offered

BEADROLLS > BEADROLL

BEADS > BEAD

BEADSMAN *n* person who prays for another's soul, esp one paid or fed for doing so

BEADSMEN > BEADSMAN

BEADWORK *same as* > BEADING

BEADWORKS > BEADWORK

BEADY *adj* small, round, and glittering

BEAGLE *n* small hound with short legs and drooping ears ▷ *vb* hunt with beagles, normally on foot

BEAGLED > BEAGLE

BEAGLER *n* person who hunts with beagles

BEAGLERS > BEAGLER

BEAGLES > BEAGLE

BEAGLING > BEAGLE

BEAGLINGS > BEAGLE

BEAK *n* projecting horny jaws of a bird ▷ *vb* strike with the beak

BEAKED > BEAK

BEAKER *n* large drinking cup

BEAKERS > BEAKER

BEAKIER > BEAK

BEAKIEST > BEAK

BEAKLESS > BEAK

BEAKLIKE > BEAK

BEAKS > BEAK

BEAKY > BEAK

BEAM *n* broad smile ▷ *vb* smile broadly

BEAMED > BEAM

BEAMER *n* full-pitched ball bowled at the batsman's head

BEAMERS > BEAMER

BEAMIER > BEAM

BEAMIEST > BEAM

BEAMILY > BEAM

BEAMINESS > BEAM

BEAMING > BEAM

BEAMINGLY > BEAM

BEAMINGS > BEAM

BEAMISH *adj* smiling

BEAMISHLY > BEAMISH

BEAMLESS > BEAM

BEAMLET *n* small beam

BEAMLETS > BEAMLET

BEAMLIKE > BEAM

BEAMS > BEAM

BEAMY > BEAM

BEAN *n* seed or pod of various plants, eaten as a vegetable or used to make coffee etc ▷ *vb* strike on the head

BEANBAG *n* small cloth bag filled with dried beans and thrown in games

BEANBAGS > BEANBAG

BEANBALL *n* baseball intended to hit batter's head

BEANBALLS > BEANBALL

BEANED > BEAN

BEANERIES > BEANERY

BEANERY *n* cheap restaurant

BEANFEAST *n* any festive or merry occasion

BEANIE *n* close-fitting woollen hat

BEANIES > BEANY

BEANING > BEAN

BEANLIKE > BEAN

BEANO *n* celebration or party

BEANOS > BEANO

BEANPOLE *n* tall thin person

BEANPOLES > BEANPOLE

BEANS > BEAN

BEANSTALK *n* stem of a bean plant

BEANY *same as* > BEANIE

BEAR *vb* support or hold up (something) ▷ *n* any plantigrade mammal of the family *Ursidae*

BEARABLE *adj* endurable

BEARABLY > BEARABLE

BEARBERRY *n* type of shrub

BEARBINE *n* type of bindweed

BEARBINES > BEARBINE

BEARCAT *n* lesser panda

BEARCATS > BEARCAT

BEARD *n* hair growing on the lower parts of a man's face ▷ *vb* oppose boldly

BEARDED > BEARD

BEARDIE *n* another name for bearded loach

BEARDIER > BEARDY

BEARDIES > BEARDIE

BEARDIEST > BEARDY

BEARDING > BEARD

BEARDLESS *adj* without a beard

BEARDS > BEARD

BEARDY *adj* having a beard

BEARE *same as* > BEAR

BEARED > BEAR

BEARER *n* person who carries, presents, or upholds something

BEARERS > BEARER

BEARES > BEARE

BEARGRASS *n* North American plant

BEARHUG *n* wrestling hold in which the arms are locked tightly round an opponent's chest and arms

BEARHUGS > BEARHUG

BEARING > BEAR

BEARINGS > BEAR

BEARISH *adj* like a bear

BEARISHLY > BEARISH

BEARLIKE > BEAR

BEARNAISE *n* rich sauce made from egg yolks, lemon juice or wine vinegar, butter, shallots, herbs, and seasoning

BEARS > BEAR

BEARSKIN *n* tall fur helmet worn by some British soldiers

BEARSKINS > BEARSKIN

BEARWARD *n* bear keeper

BEARWARDS > BEARWARD

BEARWOOD *another name for* > CASCARA

BEARWOODS > BEARWOOD

BEAST *n* large wild animal

BEASTHOOD > BEAST

BEASTIE *n* small animal

BEASTIES > BEASTIE

BEASTILY > BESTIAL

BEASTINGS *same as* > BEESTINGS

BEASTLIER > BEASTLY

BEASTLIKE > BEAST

BEASTLY *adj* unpleasant or disagreeable ▷ *adv* extremely

BEASTS > BEAST

BEAT *vb* strike with or as if with a series of violent blows; dash or pound repeatedly (against) ▷ *n* stroke or blow ▷ *adj* totally exhausted

BEATABLE > BEAT

BEATBOX *n* drum machine

BEATBOXES > BEATBOX

BEATEN > BEAT

BEATER *n* device used for beating

BEATERS > BEATER

BEATH *vb* dry; heat

BEATHED > BEATH

BEATHING > BEATH

BEATHS > BEATH

BEATIER > BEATY

BEATIEST > BEATY

BEATIFIC *adj* displaying great happiness

BEATIFIED > BEATIFY

BEATIFIES > BEATIFY

BEATIFY *vb* declare (a dead person) to be among the blessed in heaven: the first step towards canonization

BEATING > BEAT

BEATINGS > BEAT

b

BEATITUDE n any of the blessings on the poor, meek, etc, in the Sermon on the Mount
BEATLESS > BEAT
BEATNIK n young person in the late 1950s who rebelled against conventional attitudes etc
BEATNIKS > BEATNIK
BEATS > BEAT
BEATY adj (of music) having a strong rhythm
BEAU n boyfriend or admirer
BEAUCOUP n large amount
BEAUCOUPS > BEAUCOUP
BEAUFET same as > BUFFET
BEAUFETS > BEAUFET
BEAUFFET same as > BUFFET
BEAUFFETS > BEAUFFET
BEAUFIN same as > BIFFIN
BEAUFINS > BEAUFIN
BEAUISH adj vain and showy
BEAUS > BEAU
BEAUT n person or thing that is outstanding or distinctive ▷ adj good or excellent ▷ interj exclamation of joy or pleasure
BEAUTEOUS adj beautiful
BEAUTIED > BEAUTY
BEAUTIES > BEAUTY
BEAUTIFUL adj very attractive to look at
BEAUTIFY vb make beautiful
BEAUTS > BEAUT
BEAUTY n combination of all the qualities of a person or thing that delight the senses and mind ▷ interj expression of approval or agreement ▷ vb make beautiful
BEAUTYING > BEAUTY
BEAUX > BEAU
BEAUXITE same as > BAUXITE
BEAUXITES > BEAUXITE
BEAVER n amphibious rodent with a big flat tail ▷ vb work steadily or assiduously
BEAVERED > BEAVER
BEAVERIES > BEAVERY
BEAVERING > BEAVER
BEAVERS > BEAVER
BEAVERY n place for keeping beavers
BEBEERINE n alkaloid, resembling quinine, obtained from the bark of the greenheart and other plants
BEBEERU n tropical American tree
BEBEERUS > BEBEERU
BEBLOOD vb stain with blood
BEBLOODED > BEBLOOD
BEBLOODS > BEBLOOD
BEBOP same as > BOP
BEBOPPED > BEBOP
BEBOPPER > BEBOP
BEBOPPERS > BEBOP
BEBOPPING > BEBOP

BEBOPS > BEBOP
BEBUNG n vibrato effect on clavichord
BEBUNGS > BEBUNG
BECALL vb use insulting words about someone
BECALLED > BECALL
BECALLING > BECALL
BECALLS > BECALL
BECALM vb make calm
BECALMED adj (of a sailing ship) motionless through lack of wind
BECALMING > BECALM
BECALMS > BECALM
BECAME > BECOME
BECAP vb put cap on
BECAPPED > BECAP
BECAPPING > BECAP
BECAPS > BECAP
BECARPET vb lay carpet on
BECARPETS > BECARPET
BECASSE n woodcock
BECASSES > BECASSE
BECAUSE conj on account of the fact that; on account of being; since
BECCACCIA n woodcock
BECCAFICO n any of various European songbirds, esp warblers of the genus Sylvia, eaten as a delicacy in Italy and other countries
BECHALK vb mark with chalk
BECHALKED > BECHALK
BECHALKS > BECHALK
BECHAMEL n thick white sauce flavoured with onion and seasoning
BECHAMELS > BECHAMEL
BECHANCE vb happen (to)
BECHANCED > BECHANCE
BECHANCES > BECHANCE
BECHARM vb delight
BECHARMED > BECHARM
BECHARMS > BECHARM
BECK n stream ▷ vb attract someone's attention by nodding or gesturing
BECKE same as > BEAK
BECKED > BECK
BECKES > BECKE
BECKET n clevis forming part of one end of a sheave, used for securing standing lines by means of a thimble
BECKETS > BECKET
BECKING > BECK
BECKON vb summon with a gesture ▷ n summoning gesture
BECKONED > BECKON
BECKONER > BECKON
BECKONERS > BECKON
BECKONING > BECKON
BECKONS > BECKON
BECKS > BECK
BECLAMOR vb clamour excessively
BECLAMORS > BECLAMOR
BECLASP vb embrace
BECLASPED > BECLASP
BECLASPS > BECLASP
BECLOAK vb dress in cloak
BECLOAKED > BECLOAK
BECLOAKS > BECLOAK

BECLOG vb put clogs on
BECLOGGED > BECLOG
BECLOGS > BECLOG
BECLOTHE vb put clothes on
BECLOTHED > BECLOTHE
BECLOTHES > BECLOTHE
BECLOUD vb cover or obscure with a cloud
BECLOUDED > BECLOUD
BECLOUDS > BECLOUD
BECLOWN vb clown around
BECLOWNED > BECLOWN
BECLOWNS > BECLOWN
BECOME vb come to be
BECOMES > BECOME
BECOMING adj attractive or pleasing ▷ n any process of change
BECOMINGS > BECOMING
BECOWARD vb make cowardly
BECOWARDS > BECOWARD
BECQUEREL n SI unit of activity of a radioactive source
BECRAWL vb crawl all over
BECRAWLED > BECRAWL
BECRAWLS > BECRAWL
BECRIME vb make someone guilty of a crime
BECRIMED > BECRIME
BECRIMES > BECRIME
BECRIMING > BECRIME
BECROWD vb crowd with something
BECROWDED > BECROWD
BECROWDS > BECROWD
BECRUST vb cover with crust
BECRUSTED > BECRUST
BECRUSTS > BECRUST
BECUDGEL vb arm with cudgel
BECUDGELS > BECUDGEL
BECURL vb curl
BECURLED > BECURL
BECURLING > BECURL
BECURLS > BECURL
BECURSE vb curse
BECURSED > BECURSE
BECURSES > BECURSE
BECURSING > BECURSE
BECURST > BECURSE
BED n piece of furniture on which to sleep ▷ vb plant in a bed
BEDABBLE vb dabble; moisten
BEDABBLED > BEDABBLE
BEDABBLES > BEDABBLE
BEDAD interj by God (oath)
BEDAGGLE vb soil by trailing through dirt
BEDAGGLED > BEDAGGLE
BEDAGGLES > BEDAGGLE
BEDAMN vb damn
BEDAMNED > BEDAMN
BEDAMNING > BEDAMN
BEDAMNS > BEDAMN
BEDARKEN vb make dark
BEDARKENS > BEDARKEN
BEDASH vb sprinkle with liquid
BEDASHED > BEDASH
BEDASHES > BEDASH
BEDASHING > BEDASH
BEDAUB vb smear with

something sticky or dirty
BEDAUBED > BEDAUB
BEDAUBING > BEDAUB
BEDAUBS > BEDAUB
BEDAWIN same as > BEDOUIN
BEDAWINS > BEDAWIN
BEDAZE vb daze
BEDAZED > BEDAZE
BEDAZES > BEDAZE
BEDAZING > BEDAZE
BEDAZZLE vb dazzle or confuse, as with brilliance
BEDAZZLED > BEDAZZLE
BEDAZZLES > BEDAZZLE
BEDBOARD n base of bed
BEDBOARDS > BEDBOARD
BEDBUG n small blood-sucking wingless insect that infests dirty houses
BEDBUGS > BEDBUG
BEDCHAIR n adjustable chair to support invalid in bed
BEDCHAIRS > BEDCHAIR
BEDCOVER n cover for bed
BEDCOVERS > BEDCOVER
BEDDABLE adj sexually attractive
BEDDED > BED
BEDDER n (at some universities) a college servant employed to keep students' rooms in order
BEDDERS > BEDDER
BEDDING > BED
BEDDINGS > BED
BEDE n prayer
BEDEAFEN vb deafen
BEDEAFENS > BEDEAFEN
BEDECK vb cover with decorations
BEDECKED > BEDECK
BEDECKING > BEDECK
BEDECKS > BEDECK
BEDEGUAR n growth found on rosebushes
BEDEGUARS > BEDEGUAR
BEDEHOUSE same as > BEADHOUSE
BEDEL archaic spellings of > BEADLE
BEDELL > BEADLE
BEDELLS > BEDELL
BEDELS > BEDEL
BEDELSHIP > BEDEL
BEDEMAN same as > BEADSMAN
BEDEMEN > BEDEMAN
BEDERAL same as > BEDRAL
BEDERALS > BEDERAL
BEDES > BEDE
BEDESMAN same as > BEADSMAN
BEDESMEN > BEDESMAN
BEDEVIL vb harass, confuse, or torment
BEDEVILED > BEDEVIL
BEDEVILS > BEDEVIL
BEDEW vb wet or cover with or as if with drops of dew
BEDEWED > BEDEW
BEDEWING > BEDEW
BEDEWS > BEDEW
BEDFAST an archaic word for > BEDRIDDEN
BEDFELLOW n temporary associate

BEDFRAME *n* framework of bed

BEDFRAMES > BEDFRAME

BEDGOWN *n* night dress

BEDGOWNS > BEDGOWN

BEDIAPER *vb* put a nappy on

BEDIAPERS > BEDIAPER

BEDIDE > BEDYE

BEDIGHT *vb* array or adorn ▷ *adj* adorned or bedecked

BEDIGHTED > BEDIGHT

BEDIGHTS > BEDIGHT

BEDIM *vb* make dim or obscure

BEDIMMED > BEDIM

BEDIMMING > BEDIM

BEDIMPLE *vb* form dimples in

BEDIMPLED > BEDIMPLE

BEDIMPLES > BEDIMPLE

BEDIMS > BEDIM

BEDIRTIED > BEDIRTY

BEDIRTIES > BEDIRTY

BEDIRTY *vb* make dirty

BEDIZEN *vb* dress or decorate gaudily or tastelessly

BEDIZENED > BEDIZEN

BEDIZENS > BEDIZEN

BEDLAM *n* noisy confused situation

BEDLAMISM > BEDLAM

BEDLAMITE *n* lunatic

BEDLAMP *n* bedside light

BEDLAMPS > BEDLAMP

BEDLAMS > BEDLAM

BEDLESS > BED

BEDLIKE *adj* like a bed

BEDMAKER *n* person who makes beds

BEDMAKERS > BEDMAKER

BEDMATE *n* person who shares a bed

BEDMATES > BEDMATE

BEDOTTED *adj* scattered; strewn

BEDOUIN *n* member of any of the nomadic tribes of Arabs inhabiting the deserts of Arabia, Jordan, and Syria, as well as parts of the Sahara

BEDOUINS > BEDOUIN

BEDPAN *n* shallow bowl used as a toilet by bedridden people

BEDPANS > BEDPAN

BEDPLATE *n* heavy metal platform or frame to which an engine or machine is attached

BEDPLATES > BEDPLATE

BEDPOST *n* vertical support on a bedstead

BEDPOSTS > BEDPOST

BEDQUILT *n* padded bed cover

BEDQUILTS > BEDQUILT

BEDRAGGLE *vb* make (hair, clothing, etc) limp, untidy, or dirty, as with rain or mud

BEDRAIL *n* rail or board along the side of a bed that connects the headboard with the footboard

BEDRAILS > BEDRAIL

BEDRAL *n* minor church official

BEDRALS > BEDRAL

BEDRAPE *vb* adorn

BEDRAPED > BEDRAPE

BEDRAPES > BEDRAPE

BEDRAPING > BEDRAPE

BEDRENCH *vb* drench

BEDRID *same as* > BEDRIDDEN

BEDRIDDEN *adj* confined to bed because of illness or old age

BEDRIGHT *n* rights expected in the marital bed

BEDRIGHTS > BEDRIGHT

BEDRIVEL *vb* drivel around

BEDRIVELS > BEDRIVEL

BEDROCK *n* solid rock beneath the surface soil

BEDROCKS > BEDROCK

BEDROLL *n* portable roll of bedding, such as a sleeping bag, used esp for sleeping in the open

BEDROLLS > BEDROLL

BEDROOM *n* room used for sleeping ▷ *adj* containing references to sex

BEDROOMED *adj* containing specified number of bedrooms

BEDROOMS > BEDROOM

BEDROP *vb* drop on

BEDROPPED > BEDROP

BEDROPS > BEDROP

BEDROPT > BEDROP

BEDRUG *vb* drug excessively

BEDRUGGED > BEDRUG

BEDRUGS > BEDRUG

BEDS > BED

BEDSHEET *n* sheet for bed

BEDSHEETS > BEDSHEET

BEDSIDE *n* area beside a bed ▷ *adj* placed at or near the side of the bed

BEDSIDES > BEDSIDE

BEDSIT *n* furnished sitting room with a bed

BEDSITS > BEDSIT

BEDSITTER *same as* > BEDSIT

BEDSOCKS *n* socks worn in bed

BEDSONIA *n* bacterium causing diseases such as trachoma

BEDSONIAS > BEDSONIA

BEDSORE *n* ulcer on the skin, caused by a lengthy period of lying in bed due to illness

BEDSORES > BEDSORE

BEDSPREAD *n* top cover on a bed

BEDSPRING *vb* spring supporting mattress on bed

BEDSTAND *n* bedside table

BEDSTANDS > BEDSTAND

BEDSTEAD *n* framework of a bed

BEDSTEADS > BEDSTEAD

BEDSTRAW *n* plant with small white or yellow flowers

BEDSTRAWS > BEDSTRAW

BEDTICK *n* case containing stuffing in mattress

BEDTICKS > BEDTICK

BEDTIME *n* time when one usually goes to bed

BEDTIMES > BEDTIME

BEDU *adj* relating to beduins

BEDUCK *vb* duck under water

BEDUCKED > BEDUCK

BEDUCKING > BEDUCK

BEDUCKS > BEDUCK

BEDUIN *variant of* > BEDOUIN

BEDUINS > BEDUIN

BEDUMB *vb* make dumb

BEDUMBED > BEDUMB

BEDUMBING > BEDUMB

BEDUMBS > BEDUMB

BEDUNCE *vb* cause to look or feel foolish

BEDUNCED > BEDUNCE

BEDUNCES > BEDUNCE

BEDUNCING > BEDUNCE

BEDUNG *vb* spread with dung

BEDUNGED > BEDUNG

BEDUNGING > BEDUNG

BEDUNGS > BEDUNG

BEDUST *vb* cover with dust

BEDUSTED > BEDUST

BEDUSTING > BEDUST

BEDUSTS > BEDUST

BEDWARD *adj* towards bed

BEDWARDS *adv* towards bed

BEDWARF *vb* hamper growth of

BEDWARFED > BEDWARF

BEDWARFS > BEDWARF

BEDWARMER *n* metal pan containing hot coals, formerly used to warm a bed

BEDWETTER *n* person who urinates in bed

BEDYDE > BEDYE

BEDYE *vb* dye

BEDYED > BEDYE

BEDYEING > BEDYE

BEDYES > BEDYE

BEE *n* insect that makes wax and honey

BEEBEE *n* air rifle

BEEBEES > BEEBEE

BEEBREAD *n* mixture of pollen and nectar prepared by worker bees and fed to the larvae

BEEBREADS > BEEBREAD

BEECH *n* tree with a smooth greyish bark

BEECHEN > BEECH

BEECHES > BEECH

BEECHIER > BEECH

BEECHIEST > BEECH

BEECHMAST *n* nuts of beech tree

BEECHNUT *n* small brown triangular edible nut of the beech tree

BEECHNUTS > BEECHNUT

BEECHWOOD *n* wood of beech tree

BEECHY > BEECH

BEEDI *n* Indian cigarette

BEEDIES > BEEDI

BEEF *n* flesh of a cow, bull, or ox ▷ *vb* complain

BEEFALO *n* cross between cow and buffalo

BEEFALOES > BEEFALO

BEEFALOS > BEEFALO

BEEFCAKE *n* musclemen as displayed in photographs

BEEFCAKES > BEEFCAKE

BEEFEATER *n* yeoman warder at the Tower of London

BEEFED > BEEF

BEEFIER > BEEFY

BEEFIEST > BEEFY

BEEFILY > BEEFY

BEEFINESS > BEEFY

BEEFING > BEEF

BEEFLESS > BEEF

BEEFS > BEEF

BEEFSTEAK *n* piece of beef that can be grilled, fried, etc, cut from any lean part of the animal

BEEFWOOD *n* any of various trees that produce very hard wood

BEEFWOODS > BEEFWOOD

BEEFY *adj* like beef

BEEGAH *same as* > BIGHA

BEEGAHS > BEEGAH

BEEHIVE *n* structure in which bees live

BEEHIVES > BEEHIVE

BEEKEEPER *n* person who keeps bees for their honey

BEELIKE > BEE

BEELINE *n* most direct route between two places ▷ *adj* make a beeline for (something)

BEELINED > BEELINE

BEELINES > BEELINE

BEELINING > BEELINE

BEEN > BE

BEENAH *n* understanding; insight

BEENAHS > BEENAH

BEENTO *n* person who has resided in Britain, esp during part of his education ▷ *adj* of, relating to, or characteristic of such a person

BEENTOS > BEENTO

BEEP *n* high-pitched sound, like that of a car horn ▷ *vb* (cause to) make this noise

BEEPED > BEEP

BEEPER > BEEP

BEEPERS > BEEP

BEEPING > BEEP

BEEPS > BEEP

BEER *n* alcoholic drink brewed from malt and hops

BEERAGE *n* brewing industry

BEERAGES > BEERAGE

BEERHALL *n* large public room where beer is consumed

BEERHALLS > BEERHALL

BEERIER > BEERY

BEERIEST > BEERY

BEERILY > BEERY

BEERINESS > BEERY

BEERS > BEER

BEERY *adj* smelling or

b

b

tasting of beer
BEES > BEE
BEESOME *same as* > BISSON
BEESTINGS *n* first milk secreted by the mammary glands of a cow or similar animal immediately after giving birth
BEESWAX *n* wax secreted by bees, used in polishes etc ▷ *vb* polish with such wax
BEESWAXED > BEESWAX
BEESWAXES > BEESWAX
BEESWING *n* light filmy crust of tartar that forms in port and some other wines after long keeping in the bottle
BEESWINGS > BEESWING
BEET *n* plant with an edible root and leaves ▷ *vb* improve or make better
BEETED > BEET
BEETFLIES > BEETFLY
BEETFLY *n* muscid fly, *Pegomyia hyoscyami* : a common pest of beets and mangel-wurzels
BEETING > BEET
BEETLE *n* insect with a hard wing cover on its back ▷ *adj* overhang or jut ▷ *vb* scuttle or scurry
BEETLED > BEETLE
BEETLER *n* one who operates a beetling machine
BEETLERS > BEETLER
BEETLES > BEETLE
BEETLING > BEETLE
BEETROOT *n* type of beet plant with a dark red root
BEETROOTS > BEETROOT
BEETS > BEET
BEEVES > BEEF
BEEYARD *n* place where bees are kept
BEEYARDS > BEEYARD
BEEZER *n* person or chap ▷ *adj* excellent
BEEZERS > BEEZER
BEFALL *vb* happen to (someone)
BEFALLEN > BEFALL
BEFALLING > BEFALL
BEFALLS > BEFALL
BEFANA *n* Italian gift-bearing good fairy
BEFANAS > BEFANA
BEFELD > BEFALL
BEFELL > BEFALL
BEFFANA *same as* > BEFANA
BEFFANAS > BEFFANA
BEFINGER *vb* mark by handling
BEFINGERS > BEFINGER
BEFINNED *adj* with fins
BEFIT *vb* be appropriate or suitable for
BEFITS > BEFIT
BEFITTED > BEFIT
BEFITTING > BEFIT
BEFLAG *vb* decorate with flags
BEFLAGGED > BEFLAG
BEFLAGS > BEFLAG
BEFLEA *vb* infect with fleas
BEFLEAED > BEFLEA

BEFLEAING > BEFLEA
BEFLEAS > BEFLEA
BEFLECK *vb* fleck
BEFLECKED > BEFLECK
BEFLECKS > BEFLECK
BEFLOWER *vb* decorate with flowers
BEFLOWERS > BEFLOWER
BEFLUM *vb* fool; deceive
BEFLUMMED > BEFLUM
BEFLUMS > BEFLUM
BEFOAM *vb* cover with foam
BEFOAMED > BEFOAM
BEFOAMING > BEFOAM
BEFOAMS > BEFOAM
BEFOG *vb* surround with fog
BEFOGGED > BEFOG
BEFOGGING > BEFOG
BEFOGS > BEFOG
BEFOOL *vb* make a fool of
BEFOOLED > BEFOOL
BEFOOLING > BEFOOL
BEFOOLS > BEFOOL
BEFORE *adv* indicating something earlier in time, in front of, or preferred to ▷ *prep* preceding in space or time
BEFORTUNE *vb* happen to
BEFOUL *vb* make dirty or foul
BEFOULED > BEFOUL
BEFOULER > BEFOUL
BEFOULERS > BEFOUL
BEFOULING > BEFOUL
BEFOULS > BEFOUL
BEFRET *vb* fret about something
BEFRETS > BEFRET
BEFRETTED > BEFRET
BEFRIEND *vb* become friends with
BEFRIENDS > BEFRIEND
BEFRINGE *vb* decorate with fringe
BEFRINGED > BEFRINGE
BEFRINGES > BEFRINGE
BEFUDDLE *vb* confuse, muddle, or perplex
BEFUDDLED > BEFUDDLE
BEFUDDLES > BEFUDDLE
BEG *vb* solicit (money, food, etc), esp in the street
BEGAD *interj* emphatic exclamation
BEGALL *vb* make sore by rubbing
BEGALLED > BEGALL
BEGALLING > BEGALL
BEGALLS > BEGALL
BEGAN > BEGIN
BEGAR *n* compulsory labour
BEGARS > BEGAR
BEGAT > BEGET
BEGAZE *vb* gaze about or around
BEGAZED > BEGAZE
BEGAZES > BEGAZE
BEGAZING > BEGAZE
BEGEM *vb* decorate with gems
BEGEMMED > BEGEM
BEGEMMING > BEGEM
BEGEMS > BEGEM
BEGET *vb* cause or create
BEGETS > BEGET
BEGETTER > BEGET

BEGETTERS > BEGET
BEGETTING > BEGET
BEGGAR *n* person who begs, esp one who lives by begging ▷ *vb* be beyond the resources of
BEGGARDOM > BEGGAR
BEGGARED > BEGGAR
BEGGARIES > BEGGARY
BEGGARING > BEGGAR
BEGGARLY *adj* meanly inadequate
BEGGARS > BEGGAR
BEGGARY *n* extreme poverty or need
BEGGED > BEG
BEGGING > BEG
BEGGINGLY > BEG
BEGGINGS > BEG
BEGHARD *n* member of a Christian brotherhood that was founded in Flanders in the 13th century and followed a life based on that of the Beguines
BEGHARDS > BEGHARD
BEGIFT *vb* give gift or gifts to
BEGIFTED > BEGIFT
BEGIFTING > BEGIFT
BEGIFTS > BEGIFT
BEGILD *vb* gild
BEGILDED > BEGILD
BEGILDING > BEGILD
BEGILDS > BEGILD
BEGILT > BEGILD
BEGIN *vb* start
BEGINNE *same as* > BEGINNING
BEGINNER *n* person who has just started learning to do something
BEGINNERS > BEGINNER
BEGINNES > BEGINNE
BEGINNING *n* start
BEGINS > BEGIN
BEGIRD *vb* surround
BEGIRDED > BEGIRD
BEGIRDING > BEGIRD
BEGIRDLE *vb* surround with girdle
BEGIRDLED > BEGIRDLE
BEGIRDLES > BEGIRDLE
BEGIRDS > BEGIRD
BEGIRT > BEGIRD
BEGLAD *vb* make glad
BEGLADDED > BEGLAD
BEGLADS > BEGLAD
BEGLAMOR *same as* > BEGLAMOUR
BEGLAMORS > BEGLAMOR
BEGLAMOUR *vb* glamourize
BEGLERBEG *n* governor in the Ottoman empire
BEGLOOM *vb* make gloomy
BEGLOOMED > BEGLOOM
BEGLOOMS > BEGLOOM
BEGNAW *vb* gnaw at
BEGNAWED > BEGNAW
BEGNAWING > BEGNAW
BEGNAWS > BEGNAW
BEGO *vb* harrass; beset
BEGOES > BEGO
BEGOGGLED *adj* wearing goggles
BEGOING > BEGO
BEGONE > BEGO

BEGONIA *n* tropical plant with waxy flowers
BEGONIAS > BEGONIA
BEGORAH *same as* > BEGORRA
BEGORED *adj* smear with gore
BEGORRA *interj* emphatic exclamation, regarded as a characteristic utterance of Irishmen
BEGORRAH *same as* > BEGORRA
BEGOT *past participle of* > BEGET
BEGOTTEN *past participle of* > BEGET
BEGRIM *same as* > BEGRIME
BEGRIME *vb* make dirty
BEGRIMED > BEGRIME
BEGRIMES > BEGRIME
BEGRIMING > BEGRIME
BEGRIMMED > BEGRIM
BEGRIMS > BEGRIM
BEGROAN *vb* groan at
BEGROANED > BEGROAN
BEGROANS > BEGROAN
BEGRUDGE *vb* envy (someone) the possession of something
BEGRUDGED > BEGRUDGE
BEGRUDGER > BEGRUDGE
BEGRUDGES > BEGRUDGE
BEGS > BEG
BEGUILE *vb* cheat or mislead
BEGUILED > BEGUILE
BEGUILER > BEGUILE
BEGUILERS > BEGUILE
BEGUILES > BEGUILE
BEGUILING *adj* charming, often in a deceptive way
BEGUIN *another name for* > BEGHARD
BEGUINAGE *n* convent for members of beguine sisterhood
BEGUINE *n* S American dance
BEGUINES > BEGUINE
BEGUINS > BEGUIN
BEGULF *vb* overwhelm
BEGULFED > BEGULF
BEGULFING > BEGULF
BEGULFS > BEGULF
BEGUM *n* Muslim woman of high rank
BEGUMS > BEGUM
BEGUN *past participle of* > BEGIN
BEGUNK *vb* delude; trick
BEGUNKED > BEGUNK
BEGUNKING > BEGUNK
BEGUNKS > BEGUNK
BEHALF *n* interest, part, benefit, or respect
BEHALVES > BEHALF
BEHAPPEN *vb* befall
BEHAPPENS > BEHAPPEN
BEHATTED *adj* wearing a hat
BEHAVE *vb* act or function in a particular way
BEHAVED > BEHAVE
BEHAVER > BEHAVE
BEHAVERS > BEHAVE
BEHAVES > BEHAVE
BEHAVING > BEHAVE
BEHAVIOR *same*

as > BEHAVIOUR

BEHAVIORS > BEHAVIOR

BEHAVIOUR *n* manner of behaving

BEHEAD *vb* remove the head from

BEHEADAL > BEHEAD

BEHEADALS > BEHEAD

BEHEADED > BEHEAD

BEHEADER > BEHEAD

BEHEADERS > BEHEAD

BEHEADING > BEHEAD

BEHEADS > BEHEAD

BEHELD > BEHOLD

BEHEMOTH *n* huge person or thing

BEHEMOTHS > BEHEMOTH

BEHEST *n* order or earnest request

BEHESTS > BEHEST

BEHIGHT *vb* entrust

BEHIGHTS > BEHIGHT

BEHIND *adv* indicating position to the rear, lateness, responsibility, etc ▷*n* buttocks ▷*prep* in or to a position further back than ▷*adj* in a position further back

BEHINDS > BEHIND

BEHOLD *vb* look (at)

BEHOLDEN *adj* indebted or obliged

BEHOLDER > BEHOLD

BEHOLDERS > BEHOLD

BEHOLDING > BEHOLD

BEHOLDS > BEHOLD

BEHOOF *n* advantage or profit

BEHOOFS > BEHOOF

BEHOOVE *same as* > BEHOVE

BEHOOVED > BEHOOVE

BEHOOVES > BEHOOVE

BEHOOVING > BEHOOVE

BEHOTE *same as* > BEHIGHT

BEHOTES > BEHOTE

BEHOTING > BEHOTE

BEHOVE *vb* be necessary or fitting for

BEHOVED > BEHOVE

BEHOVEFUL *adj* useful; of benefit

BEHOVELY *adj* useful

BEHOVES > BEHOVE

BEHOVING > BEHOVE

BEHOWL *vb* howl at

BEHOWLED > BEHOWL

BEHOWLING > BEHOWL

BEHOWLS > BEHOWL

BEIGE *adj* pale brown ▷*n* very light brown, sometimes with a yellowish tinge, similar to the colour of undyed wool

BEIGEL *same as* > BAGEL

BEIGELS > BEIGEL

BEIGES > BEIGE

BEIGNE *variant of* > BEIGNET

BEIGNES > BEIGNE

BEIGNET *n* square deep-fried pastry served hot and sprinkled with icing sugar

BEIGNETS > BEIGNET

BEIGY > BEIGE

BEIN *adj* financially comfortable

BEING > BE

BEINGLESS > BE

BEINGNESS > BE

BEINGS > BE

BEINKED *adj* daubed with ink

BEINNESS > BEIN

BEJABBERS *same as* > BEJABERS

BEJABERS *interj* by Jesus!

BEJADE *vb* jade; tire

BEJADED > BEJADE

BEJADES > BEJADE

BEJADING > BEJADE

BEJANT *same as* > BAJAN

BEJANTS > BEJANT

BEJEEBERS *same as* > BEJABERS

BEJEEZUS *same as* > BEJESUS

BEJESUIT *vb* convert to Jesuitism

BEJESUITS > BEJESUIT

BEJESUS *interj* exclamation of surprise

BEJEWEL *vb* decorate with or as if with jewels

BEJEWELED > BEJEWEL

BEJEWELS > BEJEWEL

BEJUMBLE *vb* jumble up

BEJUMBLED > BEJUMBLE

BEJUMBLES > BEJUMBLE

BEKAH *n* half shekel

BEKAHS > BEKAH

BEKISS *vb* smother with kisses

BEKISSED > BEKISS

BEKISSES > BEKISS

BEKISSING > BEKISS

BEKNAVE *vb* treat as knave

BEKNAVED > BEKNAVE

BEKNAVES > BEKNAVE

BEKNAVING > BEKNAVE

BEKNIGHT *vb* esteem

BEKNIGHTS > BEKNIGHT

BEKNOT *vb* tie knot or knots in

BEKNOTS > BEKNOT

BEKNOTTED > BEKNOT

BEKNOWN *adj* known about

BEL *n* unit for comparing two power levels or measuring the intensity of a sound, equal to 10 decibels

BELABOR *same as* > BELABOUR

BELABORED > BELABOR

BELABORS > BELABOR

BELABOUR *vb* attack verbally or physically

BELABOURS > BELABOUR

BELACE *vb* decorate with lace

BELACED > BELACE

BELACES > BELACE

BELACING > BELACE

BELADIED > BELADY

BELADIES > BELADY

BELADY *vb* call a lady

BELADYING > BELADY

BELAH *n* Australian casuarina tree, *Casuarina glauca*, yielding a useful timber

BELAHS > BELAH

BELAMIES > BELAMY

BELAMOURE *n* loved one

BELAMY *n* close friend

BELAR *same as* > BELAH

BELARS > BELAR

BELATE *vb* cause to be late

BELATED *adj* late or too late

BELATEDLY > BELATED

BELATES > BELATE

BELATING > BELATE

BELAUD *vb* praise highly

BELAUDED > BELAUD

BELAUDING > BELAUD

BELAUDS > BELAUD

BELAY *vb* secure a line to a pin or cleat ▷*n* attachment (of a climber) to a mountain by tying the rope off round a rock spike, piton, nut, etc, to safeguard the party in the event of a fall

BELAYED > BELAY

BELAYER > BELAY

BELAYERS > BELAY

BELAYING > BELAY

BELAYS > BELAY

BELCH *vb* expel wind from the stomach noisily through the mouth ▷*n* act of belching

BELCHED > BELCH

BELCHER > BELCH

BELCHERS > BELCH

BELCHES > BELCH

BELCHING > BELCH

BELDAM *n* old woman, esp an ugly or malicious one

BELDAME *same as* > BELDAM

BELDAMES > BELDAME

BELDAMS > BELDAM

BELEAGUER *vb* trouble persistently

BELEAP *vb* leap over

BELEAPED > BELEAP

BELEAPING > BELEAP

BELEAPS > BELEAP

BELEAPT > BELEAP

BELEE *vb* put on sheltered side

BELEED > BELEE

BELEEING > BELEE

BELEES > BELEE

BELEMNITE *n* any extinct marine cephalopod mollusc of the order *Belemnoidea*, related to the cuttlefish

BELEMNOID *adj* shaped like a dart

BELFRIED *adj* with a belfry

BELFRIES > BELFRY

BELFRY *n* part of a tower where bells are hung

BELGA *n* former Belgian monetary unit worth five francs

BELGARD *n* kind gaze

BELGARDS > BELGARD

BELGAS > BELGA

BELIE *vb* show to be untrue

BELIED > BELIE

BELIEF *n* faith or confidence

BELIEFS > BELIEF

BELIER > BELIE

BELIERS > BELIE

BELIES > BELIE

BELIEVE *vb* accept as true or real

BELIEVED > BELIEVE

BELIEVER > BELIEVE

BELIEVERS > BELIEVE

BELIEVES > BELIEVE

BELIEVING > BELIEVE

BELIKE *adv* perhaps

BELIQUOR *vb* cause to be drunk

BELIQUORS > BELIQUOR

BELITTLE *vb* treat as having little value or importance

BELITTLED > BELITTLE

BELITTLER > BELITTLE

BELITTLES > BELITTLE

BELIVE *adv* speedily

BELL *n* hollow, usu metal, cup-shaped instrument that emits a ringing sound when struck ▷*vb* utter (such a cry)

BELLBIND *n* bindweed-type climber

BELLBINDS > BELLBIND

BELLBIRD *n* Australasian bird with bell-like call

BELLBIRDS > BELLBIRD

BELLBOY *n* man or boy employed in a hotel, club, etc, to carry luggage and answer calls for service

BELLBOYS > BELLBOY

BELLCOTE *n* small roofed structure for bell

BELLCOTES > BELLCOTE

BELLE *n* beautiful woman, esp the most attractive woman at a function

BELLED > BELL

BELLEEK *n* kind of thin fragile porcelain with a lustrous glaze

BELLEEKS > BELLEEK

BELLES > BELLE

BELLETER *n* person who makes bells

BELLETERS > BELLETER

BELLHOP *same as* > BELLBOY

BELLHOPS > BELLHOP

BELLIBONE *n* beautiful and good woman

BELLICOSE *adj* warlike and aggressive

BELLIED > BELLY

BELLIES > BELLY

BELLING > BELL

BELLINGS > BELL

BELLMAN *n* man who rings a bell, esp (formerly) a town crier

BELLMEN > BELLMAN

BELLOCK *vb* shout

BELLOCKED > BELLOCK

BELLOCKS > BELLOCK

BELLOW *vb* make a low deep cry like that of a bull ▷*n* loud deep roar

BELLOWED > BELLOW

BELLOWER > BELLOW

BELLOWERS > BELLOW

BELLOWING > BELLOW

BELLOWS *pl n* instrument for pumping a stream of air into something

BELLPULL *n* handle, rope, or cord pulled to operate a doorbell or servant's bell

b

BELLPULLS > BELLPULL

BELLPUSH n button pressed to operate an electric bell

BELLS > BELL

BELLWORT n any plant of the North American liliaceous genus *Uvularia*, having slender bell-shaped yellow flowers

BELLWORTS > BELLWORT

BELLY n part of the body of a vertebrate which contains the intestines ▷ vb (cause to) swell out

BELLYACHE n pain in the abdomen ▷ vb complain repeatedly

BELLYBAND n strap around the belly of a draught animal, holding the shafts of a vehicle

BELLYFUL n more than one can tolerate

BELLYFULS > BELLYFUL

BELLYING > BELLY

BELLYINGS > BELLY

BELLYLIKE > BELLY

BELOMANCY n art of divination using arrows

BELON n type of oyster

BELONG vb be the property of

BELONGED > BELONG

BELONGER n native-born Caribbean

BELONGERS > BELONGER

BELONGING n secure relationship

BELONGS > BELONG

BELONS > BELON

BELOVE vb love

BELOVED adj dearly loved ▷ n person dearly loved

BELOVEDS > BELOVED

BELOVES > BELOVE

BELOVING > BELOVE

BELOW adv at or to a position lower than, under ▷ prep at or to a position lower than

BELOWS same as > BELLOWS

BELS > BEL

BELT n band of cloth, leather, etc, worn usu around the waist ▷ vb fasten with a belt

BELTED > BELT

BELTER n outstanding person or event

BELTERS > BELTER

BELTING n material used to make a belt or belts ▷ adj excellent

BELTINGS > BELTING

BELTLESS > BELT

BELTLINE n line separating car's windows from main body

BELTLINES > BELTLINE

BELTMAN n (formerly) the member of a beach life-saving team who swam out with a line attached to his belt

BELTMEN > BELTMAN

BELTS > BELT

BELTWAY n people and institutions located in the area bounded by the Washington Beltway, taken to be politically and socially out of touch with the rest of America and much given to political intrigue

BELTWAYS > BELTWAY

BELUGA n large white sturgeon of the Black and Caspian Seas, from which caviar and isinglass are obtained

BELUGAS > BELUGA

BELVEDERE n building designed and situated to look out on pleasant scenery

BELYING > BELIE

BEMA n speaker's platform in the assembly in ancient Athens

BEMAD vb cause to become mad

BEMADAM vb call a person madam

BEMADAMED > BEMADAM

BEMADAMS > BEMADAM

BEMADDED > BEMAD

BEMADDEN vb cause to become mad

BEMADDENS > BEMADDEN

BEMADDING > BEMAD

BEMADS > BEMAD

BEMAS > BEMA

BEMATA > BEMA

BEMAUL vb maul

BEMAULED > BEMAUL

BEMAULING > BEMAUL

BEMAULS > BEMAUL

BEMAZED adj amazed

BEMBEX n type of wasp

BEMBEXES > BEMBEX

BEMBIX same as > BEMBEX

BEMBIXES > BEMBIX

BEMEAN a less common word for > DEMEAN

BEMEANED > BEMEAN

BEMEANING > BEMEAN

BEMEANS > BEMEAN

BEMEANT > BEMEAN

BEMEDAL vb decorate with medals

BEMEDALED > BEMEDAL

BEMEDALS > BEMEDAL

BEMETE vb measure

BEMETED > BEMETE

BEMETES > BEMETE

BEMETING > BEMETE

BEMINGLE vb mingle

BEMINGLED > BEMINGLE

BEMINGLES > BEMINGLE

BEMIRE vb soil with or as if with mire

BEMIRED > BEMIRE

BEMIRES > BEMIRE

BEMIRING > BEMIRE

BEMIST vb cloud with mist

BEMISTED > BEMIST

BEMISTING > BEMIST

BEMISTS > BEMIST

BEMIX vb mix thoroughly

BEMIXED > BEMIX

BEMIXES > BEMIX

BEMIXING > BEMIX

BEMIXT > BEMIX

BEMOAN vb express sorrow or dissatisfaction about

BEMOANED > BEMOAN

BEMOANER > BEMOAN

BEMOANERS > BEMOAN

BEMOANING > BEMOAN

BEMOANS > BEMOAN

BEMOCK vb mock

BEMOCKED > BEMOCK

BEMOCKING > BEMOCK

BEMOCKS > BEMOCK

BEMOIL vb soil with mud

BEMOILED > BEMOIL

BEMOILING > BEMOIL

BEMOILS > BEMOIL

BEMONSTER vb treat as monster

BEMOUTH vb endow with mouth

BEMOUTHED > BEMOUTH

BEMOUTHS > BEMOUTH

BEMUD vb cover with mud

BEMUDDED > BEMUD

BEMUDDING > BEMUD

BEMUDDLE vb confound

BEMUDDLED > BEMUDDLE

BEMUDDLES > BEMUDDLE

BEMUDS > BEMUD

BEMUFFLE vb muffle up

BEMUFFLED > BEMUFFLE

BEMUFFLES > BEMUFFLE

BEMURMUR vb murmur at

BEMURMURS > BEMURMUR

BEMUSE vb confuse

BEMUSED adj puzzled or confused

BEMUSEDLY > BEMUSED

BEMUSES > BEMUSE

BEMUSING > BEMUSE

BEMUZZLE vb put muzzle on

BEMUZZLED > BEMUZZLE

BEMUZZLES > BEMUZZLE

BEN n mountain peak ▷ adv in ▷ adj inner

BENADRYL n tradename of an antihistamine drug used in sleeping tablets

BENADRYLS > BENADRYL

BENAME an archaic word for > NAME

BENAMED > BENAME

BENAMES > BENAME

BENAMING > BENAME

BENCH n long seat ▷ vb put a person on a bench

BENCHED > BENCH

BENCHER n member of the governing body of one of the Inns of Court, usually a judge or a Queen's Counsel

BENCHERS > BENCHER

BENCHES > BENCH

BENCHIER > BENCHY

BENCHIEST > BENCHY

BENCHING > BENCH

BENCHLAND n level ground at foot of mountains

BENCHLESS > BENCH

BENCHMARK n criterion by which to measure something ▷ vb measure or test against a benchmark

BENCHTOP adj for use at bench

BENCHY adj (of a hillside) hollowed out in benches

BEND vb (cause to) form a curve ▷ n curved part

BENDABLE > BEND

BENDAY vb (printing) reproduce using Benday technique

BENDAYED > BENDAY

BENDAYING > BENDAY

BENDAYS > BENDAY

BENDED > BEND

BENDEE same as > BENDY

BENDEES > BENDEE

BENDER n drinking bout

BENDERS > BENDER

BENDIER > BENDY

BENDIEST > BENDY

BENDING > BEND

BENDINGLY > BEND

BENDINGS > BEND

BENDLET n narrow diagonal stripe on heraldic shield

BENDLETS > BENDLET

BENDS > BEND

BENDWAYS same as > BENDWISE

BENDWISE adv diagonally

BENDY adj flexible or pliable ▷ n same as > OKRA

BENDYS > BENDY

BENE n blessing

BENEATH prep below ▷ adv below

BENEDICK n recently-married man

BENEDICKS > BENEDICK

BENEDICT n newly married man

BENEDICTS > BENEDICT

BENEDIGHT adj blessed

BENEFACT vb be benefactor to

BENEFACTS > BENEFACT

BENEFIC adj a rare word for beneficent

BENEFICE n church office providing its holder with an income ▷ vb provide with a benefice

BENEFICED > BENEFICE

BENEFICES > BENEFICE

BENEFIT n something that improves or promotes ▷ vb do or receive good

BENEFITED > BENEFIT

BENEFITER > BENEFIT

BENEFITS > BENEFIT

BENEMPT a past participle of > NAME

BENEMPTED > BENEMPT

BENES > BENE

BENET vb trap (something) in a net

BENETS > BENET

BENETTED > BENET

BENETTING > BENET

BENGALINE n heavy corded fabric, esp silk with woollen or cotton cord

BENI n sesame plant

BENIGHT vb shroud in darkness

BENIGHTED adj ignorant or uncultured

BENIGHTEN same as > BENIGHT

BENIGHTER > BENIGHT

BENIGHTS > BENIGHT

BENIGN *adj* showing kindliness
BENIGNANT *adj* kind or gracious
BENIGNER > BENIGN
BENIGNEST > BENIGN
BENIGNITY *n* kindliness
BENIGNLY > BENIGN
BENIS > BENI
BENISEED *n* sesame
BENISEEDS > BENISEED
BENISON *n* blessing, esp a spoken one
BENISONS > BENISON
BENITIER *n* basin for holy water
BENITIERS > BENITIER
BENJ *another word for* > BHANG
BENJAMIN *same as* > BENZOIN
BENJAMINS > BENJAMIN
BENJES > BENJ
BENNE *another name for* > SESAME
BENNES > BENNE
BENNET *n* Eurasian and N African rosaceous plant, *Geum urbanum*, with yellow flowers
BENNETS > BENNET
BENNI *n* sesame
BENNIES > BENNY
BENNIS > BENNI
BENNY *n* amphetamine tablet, esp benzedrine: a stimulant
BENOMYL *n* fungicide, derived from imidazole, used on cereal and fruit crops: suspected of being carcinogenic
BENOMYLS > BENOMYL
BENS > BEN
BENT *adj* not straight ▷ *n* personal inclination, propensity, or aptitude
BENTGRASS *n* variety of grass
BENTHAL > BENTHOS
BENTHIC > BENTHOS
BENTHOAL > BENTHON
BENTHON *same as* > BENTHOS
BENTHONIC > BENTHOS
BENTHONS > BENTHON
BENTHOS *n* animals and plants living at the bottom of a sea or lake
BENTHOSES > BENTHOS
BENTIER > BENTY
BENTIEST > BENTY
BENTO *n* thin lightweight box divided into compartments, which contain small separate dishes comprising a Japanese meal
BENTONITE *n* valuable clay, formed by the decomposition of volcanic ash, that swells as it absorbs water: used as a filler in the building, paper, and pharmaceutical industries
BENTOS > BENTO
BENTS > BENT

BENTWOOD *n* wood bent in moulds, used mainly for furniture ▷ *adj* made from such wood
BENTWOODS > BENTWOOD
BENTY *adj* covered with bentgrass
BENUMB *vb* make numb or powerless
BENUMBED > BENUMB
BENUMBING > BENUMB
BENUMBS > BENUMB
BENZAL *n* transparent crystalline substance
BENZALS > BENZAL
BENZENE *n* flammable poisonous liquid used as a solvent, insecticide, etc
BENZENES > BENZENE
BENZENOID *adj* similar to benzene
BENZIDIN *same as* > BENZIDINE
BENZIDINE *n* grey or reddish poisonous crystalline powder
BENZIDINS > BENZIDINE
BENZIL *n* yellow compound radical
BENZILS > BENZIL
BENZIN *same as* > BENZINE
BENZINE *n* volatile liquid used as a solvent
BENZINES > BENZINE
BENZINS > BENZIN
BENZOATE *n* any salt or ester of benzoic acid, containing the group $C_6H_5COO^-$ or the ion $C_6H_5COO^-$
BENZOATES > BENZOATE
BENZOIC *adj* of, containing, or derived from benzoic acid or benzoin
BENZOIN *n* gum resin containing benzoic acid, obtained from various trees of the genus *Styrax*, esp *S. benzoin* of Java and Sumatra, and used in ointments, perfume, etc
BENZOINS > BENZOIN
BENZOL *n* crude form of benzene, containing toluene, xylene, and other hydrocarbons, obtained from coal tar or coal gas and used as a fuel
BENZOLE *same as* > BENZOL
BENZOLES > BENZOLE
BENZOLINE *n* unpurified benzene
BENZOLS > BENZOL
BENZOYL *n* of, consisting of, or containing the monovalent group C_6H_5CO-
BENZOYLS > BENZOYL
BENZYL *n* of, consisting of, or containing the monovalent group $C_6H_5CH_2-$
BENZYLIC > BENZYL
BENZYLS > BENZYL
BEPAINT *vb* dye; paint
BEPAINTED > BEPAINT
BEPAINTS > BEPAINT
BEPAT *vb* pat

BEPATCHED *adj* mended with or covered in patches
BEPATS > BEPAT
BEPATTED > BEPAT
BEPATTING > BEPAT
BEPEARL *vb* decorate with pearls
BEPEARLED > BEPEARL
BEPEARLS > BEPEARL
BEPELT *vb* pelt energetically
BEPELTED > BEPELT
BEPELTING > BEPELT
BEPELTS > BEPELT
BEPEPPER *vb* shower with small missiles
BEPEPPERS > BEPEPPER
BEPESTER *vb* pester persistently
BEPESTERS > BEPESTER
BEPIMPLE *vb* form pimples on
BEPIMPLED > BEPIMPLE
BEPIMPLES > BEPIMPLE
BEPITIED > BEPITY
BEPITIES > BEPITY
BEPITY *vb* feel great pity for
BEPITYING > BEPITY
BEPLASTER *vb* cover in thick plaster
BEPLUMED *adj* decorated with feathers
BEPOMMEL *vb* beat vigorously
BEPOMMELS > BEPOMMEL
BEPOWDER *vb* cover with powder
BEPOWDERS > BEPOWDER
BEPRAISE *vb* praise highly
BEPRAISED > BEPRAISE
BEPRAISES > BEPRAISE
BEPROSE *vb* (of poetry) reduce to prose
BEPROSED > BEPROSE
BEPROSES > BEPROSE
BEPROSING > BEPROSE
BEPUFF *vb* puff up
BEPUFFED > BEPUFF
BEPUFFING > BEPUFF
BEPUFFS > BEPUFF
BEQUEATH *vb* dispose of (property) as in a will
BEQUEATHS > BEQUEATH
BEQUEST *n* legal gift of money or property by someone who has died
BEQUESTS > BEQUEST
BERAKE *vb* rake thoroughly
BERAKED > BERAKE
BERAKES > BERAKE
BERAKING > BERAKE
BERASCAL *vb* accuse of being rascal
BERASCALS > BERASCAL
BERATE *vb* scold harshly
BERATED > BERATE
BERATES > BERATE
BERATING > BERATE
BERAY *vb* soil; defile
BERAYED > BERAY
BERAYING > BERAY
BERAYS > BERAY
BERBERE *n* hot-tasting Ethiopian paste made from garlic, cayenne pepper, coriander, and other spices, often used in stews
BERBERES > BERBERE

BERBERIN *same as* > BERBERINE
BERBERINE *n* yellow bitter-tasting alkaloid obtained from barberry
BERBERINS > BERBERIN
BERBERIS *n* shrub with red berries
BERBICE as in *berbice chair* large armchair with long arms that can be folded inwards to act as leg rests
BERCEAU *n* arched trellis for climbing plants
BERCEAUX > BERCEAU
BERCEUSE *n* lullaby
BERCEUSES > BERCEUSE
BERDACHE *n* Native American transvestite
BERDACHES > BERDACHE
BERDASH *same as* > BERDACHE
BERDASHES > BERDASH
BERE *n* barley
BEREAVE *vb* deprive (of) something or someone valued, esp through death
BEREAVED *adj* having recently lost a close friend or relative through death
BEREAVEN > BEREAVE
BEREAVER > BEREAVE
BEREAVERS > BEREAVE
BEREAVES > BEREAVE
BEREAVING > BEREAVE
BEREFT *adj* deprived
BERES > BERE
BERET *n* round flat close-fitting brimless cap
BERETS > BERET
BERETTA *n* type of pistol
BERETTAS > BERETTA
BERG *n* iceberg
BERGAMA *n* type of Turkish rug
BERGAMAS > BERGAMA
BERGAMASK *n* person from Bergamo
BERGAMOT *n* small Asian tree, the fruit of which yields an oil used in perfumery
BERGAMOTS > BERGAMOT
BERGANDER *n* species of duck
BERGEN *n* large rucksack with a capacity of over 50 litres
BERGENIA *n* evergreen ground-covering plant
BERGENIAS > BERGENIA
BERGENS > BERGEN
BERGERE *n* type of French armchair
BERGERES > BERGERE
BERGFALL *n* avalanche
BERGFALLS > BERGFALL
BERGHAAN *same as* > BERGMEHL
BERGHAANS > BERGHAAN
BERGMEHL *n* light powdery variety of calcite
BERGMEHLS > BERGMEHL
BERGOMASK *same as* > BERGAMASK
BERGS > BERG
BERGYLT *n* large northern

b

b

marine food fish
BERGYLTS > BERGYLT
BERHYME vb mention in poetry
BERHYMED > BERHYME
BERHYMES > BERHYME
BERHYMING > BERHYME
BERIBERI n disease, endemic in E and S Asia, caused by dietary deficiency of thiamine (vitamin B₁). It affects the nerves to the limbs, producing pain, paralysis, and swelling
BERIBERIS > BERIBERI
BERIMBAU n Brazilian single-stringed bowed instrument, used to accompany capoeira
BERIMBAUS > BERIMBAU
BERIME same as > BERHYME
BERIMED > BERIME
BERIMES > BERIME
BERIMING > BERIME
BERINGED adj wearing a ring or rings
BERK n stupid person
BERKELIUM n radioactive element
BERKO adj berserk
BERKS > BERK
BERLEY n bait scattered on water to attract fish ▷ vb scatter (bait) on water
BERLEYED > BERLEY
BERLEYING > BERLEY
BERLEYS > BERLEY
BERLIN n fine wool yarn used for tapestry work, etc
BERLINE same as > BERLIN
BERLINES > BERLINE
BERLINS > BERLIN
BERM n narrow grass strip between the road and the footpath in a residential area ▷ vb create a berm
BERME same as > BERM
BERMED > BERM
BERMES > BERME
BERMING > BERM
BERMS > BERM
BERMUDAS pl n close-fitting shorts that come down to the knees
BERNICLE n barnacle goose: a N European goose that has a black-and-white head and body and grey wings
BERNICLES > BERNICLE
BEROB vb rob
BEROBBED > BEROB
BEROBBING > BEROB
BEROBED adj wearing a robe
BEROBS > BEROB
BEROUGED adj wearing rouge
BERRET same as > BERET
BERRETS > BERRET
BERRETTA same as > BIRETTA
BERRETTAS > BERRETTA
BERRIED > BERRY
BERRIES > BERRY
BERRIGAN n Australian tree, Pittosporum phylliraeoides, with hanging branches

BERRIGANS > BERRIGAN
BERRY n small soft stoneless fruit ▷ vb bear or produce berries
BERRYING > BERRY
BERRYINGS > BERRY
BERRYLESS > BERRY
BERRYLIKE > BERRY
BERSEEM n Mediterranean clover, Trifolium alexandrinum, grown as a forage crop and to improve the soil in the southwestern US and the Nile valley
BERSEEMS > BERSEEM
BERSERK adj frenziedly violent or destructive ▷ n member of a class of ancient Norse warriors who worked themselves into a frenzy before battle and fought with insane fury and courage
BERSERKER same as > BERSERK
BERSERKLY > BERSERK
BERSERKS > BERSERK
BERTH n bunk in a ship or train ▷ vb dock (a ship)
BERTHA n wide deep capelike collar, often of lace, usually to cover up a low neckline
BERTHAGE n place for mooring boats
BERTHAGES > BERTHAGE
BERTHAS > BERTHA
BERTHE n type of lace collar
BERTHED > BERTH
BERTHES > BERTHE
BERTHING > BERTH
BERTHS > BERTH
BERYL n hard transparent mineral
BERYLINE > BERYL
BERYLLIA n beryllium oxide
BERYLLIAS > BERYLLIA
BERYLLIUM n toxic silvery-white metallic element
BERYLS > BERYL
BES variant of > BETH
BESAINT vb give saint status to
BESAINTED > BESAINT
BESAINTS > BESAINT
BESANG > BESING
BESAT > BESIT
BESAW > BESEE
BESCATTER vb strew
BESCORCH vb scorch badly
BESCOUR vb scour thoroughly
BESCOURED > BESCOUR
BESCOURS > BESCOUR
BESCRAWL vb cover with scrawls
BESCRAWLS > BESCRAWL
BESCREEN vb conceal with screen
BESCREENS > BESCREEN
BESEE vb provide for; mind
BESEECH vb ask earnestly
BESEECHED > BESEECH
BESEECHER > BESEECH
BESEECHES > BESEECH
BESEEING > BESEE

BESEEKE same as > BESEECH
BESEEKES > BESEEKE
BESEEKING > BESEEKE
BESEEM vb be suitable for
BESEEMED > BESEEM
BESEEMING > BESEEM
BESEEMLY > BESEEM
BESEEMS > BESEEM
BESEEN > BESEE
BESEES > BESEE
BESES > BES
BESET vb trouble or harass constantly
BESETMENT > BESET
BESETS > BESET
BESETTER > BESET
BESETTERS > BESET
BESETTING adj tempting, harassing, or assailing
BESHADOW vb darken with shadow
BESHADOWS > BESHADOW
BESHAME vb cause to feel shame
BESHAMED > BESHAME
BESHAMES > BESHAME
BESHAMING > BESHAME
BESHINE vb illuminate
BESHINES > BESHINE
BESHINING > BESHINE
BESHIVER vb shatter
BESHIVERS > BESHIVER
BESHONE > BESHINE
BESHOUT vb shout about
BESHOUTED > BESHOUT
BESHOUTS > BESHOUT
BESHREW vb wish evil on
BESHREWED > BESHREW
BESHREWS > BESHREW
BESHROUD vb cover with a shroud
BESHROUDS > BESHROUD
BESIDE prep at, by, or to the side of
BESIDES prep in addition ▷ adv in addition
BESIEGE vb surround with military forces
BESIEGED > BESIEGE
BESIEGER > BESIEGE
BESIEGERS > BESIEGE
BESIEGES > BESIEGE
BESIEGING > BESIEGE
BESIGH vb sigh for
BESIGHED > BESIGH
BESIGHING > BESIGH
BESIGHS > BESIGH
BESING vb sing about joyfully
BESINGING > BESING
BESINGS > BESING
BESIT vb suit; fit
BESITS > BESIT
BESITTING > BESIT
BESLAVE vb treat as slave
BESLAVED > BESLAVE
BESLAVER vb fawn over
BESLAVERS > BESLAVER
BESLAVES > BESLAVE
BESLAVING > BESLAVE
BESLIME vb cover with slime
BESLIMED > BESLIME
BESLIMES > BESLIME
BESLIMING > BESLIME
BESLOBBER vb slobber over
BESLUBBER same

as > BESLOBBER
BESMEAR vb smear over
BESMEARED > BESMEAR
BESMEARER > BESMEAR
BESMEARS > BESMEAR
BESMILE vb smile on
BESMILED > BESMILE
BESMILES > BESMILE
BESMILING > BESMILE
BESMIRCH vb tarnish (someone's name or reputation)
BESMOKE vb blacken with smoke
BESMOKED > BESMOKE
BESMOKES > BESMOKE
BESMOKING > BESMOKE
BESMOOTH vb smooth
BESMOOTHS > BESMOOTH
BESMUDGE vb blacken
BESMUDGED > BESMUDGE
BESMUDGES > BESMUDGE
BESMUT vb blacken with smut
BESMUTCH same as > BESMIRCH
BESMUTS > BESMUT
BESMUTTED > BESMUT
BESNOW vb cover with snow
BESNOWED > BESNOW
BESNOWING > BESNOW
BESNOWS > BESNOW
BESOGNIO n worthless person
BESOGNIOS > BESOGNIO
BESOIN n need
BESOINS > BESOIN
BESOM n broom made of twigs ▷ vb sweep with a besom
BESOMED > BESOM
BESOMING > BESOM
BESOMS > BESOM
BESONIAN same as > BEZONIAN
BESONIANS > BESONIAN
BESOOTHE vb soothe
BESOOTHED > BESOOTHE
BESOOTHES > BESOOTHE
BESORT vb fit
BESORTED > BESORT
BESORTING > BESORT
BESORTS > BESORT
BESOT vb make stupid or muddled
BESOTS > BESOT
BESOTTED adj infatuated
BESOTTING > BESOT
BESOUGHT a past participle of > BESEECH
BESOULED adj having a soul
BESPAKE same as > BESPOKE
BESPANGLE vb cover or adorn with or as if with spangles
BESPAT > BESPIT
BESPATE > BESPIT
BESPATTER vb splash, e.g. with dirty water
BESPEAK vb indicate or suggest
BESPEAKS > BESPEAK
BESPECKLE vb mark with speckles
BESPED > BESPEED
BESPEED vb get on with (doing something)

BESPEEDS > BESPEED
BESPICE *vb* flavour with spices
BESPICED > BESPICE
BESPICES > BESPICE
BESPICING > BESPICE
BESPIT *vb* cover with spittle
BESPITS > BESPIT
BESPOKE *adj* (esp of a suit) made to the customer's specifications
BESPOKEN > BESPEAK
BESPORT *vb* amuse oneself
BESPORTED > BESPORT
BESPORTS > BESPORT
BESPOT *vb* mark with spots
BESPOTS > BESPOT
BESPOTTED > BESPOT
BESPOUSE *vb* marry
BESPOUSED > BESPOUSE
BESPOUSES > BESPOUSE
BESPOUT *vb* speak pretentiously
BESPOUTED > BESPOUT
BESPOUTS > BESPOUT
BESPREAD *vb* cover (a surface) with something
BESPREADS > BESPREAD
BESPRENT *adj* sprinkled over
BEST *adj* most excellent of a particular group etc ▷ *adv* in a manner surpassing all others ▷ *n* utmost effort ▷ *vb* defeat
BESTAD *same as* > BESTEAD
BESTADDE *same as* > BESTEAD
BESTAIN *vb* stain
BESTAINED > BESTAIN
BESTAINS > BESTAIN
BESTAR *vb* decorate with stars
BESTARRED > BESTAR
BESTARS > BESTAR
BESTEAD *vb* serve; assist
BESTEADED > BESTEAD
BESTEADS > BESTEAD
BESTED > BEST
BESTI *Indian English word for* > SHAME
BESTIAL *adj* brutal or savage
BESTIALLY > BESTIAL
BESTIALS > BESTIAL
BESTIARY *n* medieval collection of descriptions of animals
BESTICK *vb* cover with sharp points
BESTICKS > BESTICK
BESTILL *vb* cause to be still
BESTILLED > BESTILL
BESTILLS > BESTILL
BESTING > BEST
BESTIR *vb* cause (oneself) to become active
BESTIRRED > BESTIR
BESTIRS > BESTIR
BESTIS > BESTI
BESTORM *vb* assault
BESTORMED > BESTORM
BESTORMS > BESTORM
BESTOW *vb* present (a gift) or confer (an honour)
BESTOWAL > BESTOW

BESTOWALS > BESTOW
BESTOWED > BESTOW
BESTOWER > BESTOW
BESTOWERS > BESTOW
BESTOWING > BESTOW
BESTOWS > BESTOW
BESTREAK *vb* streak
BESTREAKS > BESTREAK
BESTREW *vb* scatter or lie scattered over (a surface)
BESTREWED > BESTREW
BESTREWN > BESTREW
BESTREWS > BESTREW
BESTRID > BESTRIDE
BESTRIDE *vb* have or put a leg on either side of
BESTRIDES > BESTRIDE
BESTRODE > BESTRIDE
BESTROW *same as* > BESTREW
BESTROWED > BESTROW
BESTROWN > BESTROW
BESTROWS > BESTROW
BESTS > BEST
BESTUCK > BESTICK
BESTUD *vb* set with, or as with studs
BESTUDDED > BESTUD
BESTUDS > BESTUD
BESUITED *adj* wearing a suit
BESUNG > BESING
BESWARM *vb* swarm over
BESWARMED > BESWARM
BESWARMS > BESWARM
BET *n* agreement between two parties that a sum of money or other stake will be paid by the loser to the party who correctly predicts the outcome of an event ▷ *vb* make or place a bet with (a person or persons)
BETA *n* second letter in the Greek alphabet, a consonant, transliterated as *b*
BETACISM *vb* type of speech impediment
BETACISMS > BETACISM
BETAINE *n* sweet-tasting alkaloid that occurs in the sugar beet
BETAINES > BETAINE
BETAKE *as in betake oneself go*
BETAKEN > BETAKE
BETAKES > BETAKE
BETAKING > BETAKE
BETAS > BETA
BETATOPIC *adj* (of atoms) differing in proton number by one, theoretically as a result of emission of a beta particle
BETATRON *n* type of particle accelerator for producing high-energy beams of electrons
BETATRONS > BETATRON
BETATTER *vb* make ragged
BETATTERS > BETATTER
BETAXED *adj* burdened with taxes
BETE *same as* > BEET
BETED > BETE
BETEEM *vb* accord

BETEEME *same as* > BETEEM
BETEEMED > BETEEM
BETEEMES > BETEEME
BETEEMING > BETEEM
BETEEMS > BETEEME
BETEL *n* Asian climbing plant, the leaves and nuts of which can be chewed
BETELNUT *n* seed of the betel palm, chewed with betel leaves and lime by people in S and SE Asia as a digestive stimulant and narcotic
BETELNUTS > BETELNUT
BETELS > BETEL
BETES > BETE
BETH *n* second letter of the Hebrew alphabet transliterated as *b*
BETHANK *vb* thank
BETHANKED > BETHANK
BETHANKIT *n* grace spoken before meal
BETHANKS > BETHANK
BETHEL *n* seaman's chapel
BETHELS > BETHEL
BETHESDA *n* church building of certain Christian denomintaions
BETHESDAS > BETHESDA
BETHINK *vb* cause (oneself) to consider or meditate
BETHINKS > BETHINK
BETHORN *vb* cover with thorns
BETHORNED > BETHORN
BETHORNS > BETHORN
BETHOUGHT > BETHINK
BETHRALL *vb* make slave of
BETHRALLS > BETHRALL
BETHS > BETH
BETHUMB *vb* (of books) wear by handling
BETHUMBED > BETHUMB
BETHUMBS > BETHUMB
BETHUMP *vb* thump hard
BETHUMPED > BETHUMP
BETHUMPS > BETHUMP
BETHWACK *vb* strike hard with flat object
BETHWACKS > BETHWACK
BETID > BETIDE
BETIDE *vb* happen (to)
BETIDED > BETIDE
BETIDES > BETIDE
BETIDING > BETIDE
BETIGHT > BETIDE
BETIME *vb* befall
BETIMED > BETIME
BETIMES > BETIME
BETIMING > BETIME
BETING > BETE
BETISE *n* folly or lack of perception
BETISES > BETISE
BETITLE *vb* give title to
BETITLED > BETITLE
BETITLES > BETITLE
BETITLING > BETITLE
BETOIL *vb* tire through hard work
BETOILED > BETOIL
BETOILING > BETOIL
BETOILS > BETOIL
BETOKEN *vb* indicate or signify

BETOKENED > BETOKEN
BETOKENS > BETOKEN
BETON *n* concrete
BETONIES > BETONY
BETONS > BETON
BETONY *n* North American plant
BETOOK *the past tense of* > BETAKE
BETOSS *vb* toss about
BETOSSED > BETOSS
BETOSSES > BETOSS
BETOSSING > BETOSS
BETRAY *vb* hand over or expose (one's nation, friend, etc) treacherously to an enemy
BETRAYAL > BETRAY
BETRAYALS > BETRAY
BETRAYED > BETRAY
BETRAYER > BETRAY
BETRAYERS > BETRAY
BETRAYING > BETRAY
BETRAYS > BETRAY
BETREAD *vb* tread over
BETREADS > BETREAD
BETRIM *vb* decorate
BETRIMMED > BETRIM
BETRIMS > BETRIM
BETROD > BETREAD
BETRODDEN > BETREAD
BETROTH *vb* promise to marry or to give in marriage
BETROTHAL *n* engagement to be married
BETROTHED *adj* engaged to be married ▷ *n* person to whom one is engaged
BETROTHS > BETROTH
BETS > BET
BETTA *n* fighting fish
BETTAS > BETTA
BETTED > BET
BETTER *adj* more excellent than others ▷ *adv* in a more excellent manner ▷ *pl n* one's superiors ▷ *vb* improve upon
BETTERED > BETTER
BETTERING > BETTER
BETTERS > BETTER
BETTIES > BETTY
BETTING > BET
BETTINGS > BET
BETTONG *n* short-nosed rat kangaroo
BETTONGS > BETTONG
BETTOR *n* person who bets
BETTORS > BETTOR
BETTY *n* type of short crowbar
BETUMBLED *adj* thrown into disorder
BETWEEN *adv* indicating position in the middle, alternatives, etc ▷ *prep* at a point intermediate to two other points in space, time, etc
BETWEENS > BETWEEN
BETWIXT *adv* between
BEUNCLED *adj* having many uncles
BEURRE *n* butter
BEURRES > BEURRE
BEVATRON *n* proton

b

synchrotron at the University of California
BEVATRONS > BEVATRON
BEVEL *n* slanting edge ▷ *vb* slope
BEVELED > BEVEL
BEVELER > BEVEL
BEVELERS > BEVEL
BEVELING > BEVEL
BEVELLED > BEVEL
BEVELLER > BEVEL
BEVELLERS > BEVEL
BEVELLING > BEVEL
BEVELMENT > BEVEL
BEVELS > BEVEL
BEVER *n* snack
BEVERAGE *n* drink
BEVERAGES > BEVERAGE
BEVERS > BEVER
BEVIES > BEVY
BEVOMIT *vb* vomit over
BEVOMITED > BEVOMIT
BEVOMITS > BEVOMIT
BEVOR *n* armour protecting lower part of face
BEVORS > BEVOR
BEVUE *n* careless error
BEVUES > BEVUE
BEVVIED > BEVVY
BEVVIES > BEVVY
BEVVY *n* alcoholic drink ▷ *vb* drink alcohol
BEVVYING > BEVVY
BEVY *n* flock or group
BEWAIL *vb* express great sorrow over
BEWAILED > BEWAIL
BEWAILER > BEWAIL
BEWAILERS > BEWAIL
BEWAILING > BEWAIL
BEWAILS > BEWAIL
BEWARE *vb* be on one's guard (against)
BEWARED > BEWARE
BEWARES > BEWARE
BEWARING > BEWARE
BEWEARIED > BEWEARY
BEWEARIES > BEWEARY
BEWEARY *vb* cause to be weary
BEWEEP *vb* express grief through weeping
BEWEEPING > BEWEEP
BEWEEPS > BEWEEP
BEWENT > BEGO
BEWEPT > BEWEEP
BEWET *vb* make wet
BEWETS > BEWET
BEWETTED > BEWET
BEWETTING > BEWET
BEWHORE *vb* treat as whore
BEWHORED > BEWHORE
BEWHORES > BEWHORE
BEWHORING > BEWHORE
BEWIG *vb* adorn with wig
BEWIGGED > BEWIG
BEWIGGING > BEWIG
BEWIGS > BEWIG
BEWILDER *vb* confuse utterly
BEWILDERS > BEWILDER
BEWINGED *adj* having wings
BEWITCH *vb* attract and fascinate
BEWITCHED > BEWITCH
BEWITCHER > BEWITCH
BEWITCHES > BEWITCH

BEWORM *vb* fill with worms
BEWORMED > BEWORM
BEWORMING > BEWORM
BEWORMS > BEWORM
BEWORRIED > BEWORRY
BEWORRIES > BEWORRY
BEWORRY *vb* beset with worry
BEWRAP *vb* wrap up
BEWRAPPED > BEWRAP
BEWRAPS > BEWRAP
BEWRAPT > BEWRAP
BEWRAY *an obsolete word for* > BETRAY
BEWRAYED > BEWRAY
BEWRAYER > BEWRAY
BEWRAYERS > BEWRAY
BEWRAYING > BEWRAY
BEWRAYS > BEWRAY
BEY *n* (in the Ottoman empire) a title given to senior officers, provincial governors, and certain other officials
BEYLIC *n* province ruled over by bey
BEYLICS > BEYLIC
BEYLIK *same as* > BEYLIC
BEYLIKS > BEYLIK
BEYOND *prep* at or to a point on the other side of ▷ *adv* at or to the far side of something ▷ *n* unknown, esp life after death
BEYONDS > BEYOND
BEYS > BEY
BEZ *n* part of deer's horn
BEZANT *n* medieval Byzantine gold coin
BEZANTS > BEZANT
BEZAZZ *another word for* > PIZZAZZ
BEZAZZES > BEZAZZ
BEZEL *n* sloping edge of a cutting tool
BEZELS > BEZEL
BEZES > BEZ
BEZIL *archaic word for* > ALCOHOLIC
BEZILS > BEZIL
BEZIQUE *n* card game for two or more players
BEZIQUES > BEZIQUE
BEZOAR *n* hard mass, such as a stone or hairball, in the stomach and intestines of animals, esp ruminants, and man: formerly thought to be an antidote to poisons
BEZOARDIC *adj* relating to bezoar
BEZOARS > BEZOAR
BEZONIAN *n* knave or rascal
BEZONIANS > BEZONIAN
BEZZANT *same as* > BEZANT
BEZZANTS > BEZZANT
BEZZAZZ > BEZAZZ
BEZZAZZES > BEZAZZ
BEZZLE *vb* drink to excess
BEZZLED > BEZZLE
BEZZLES > BEZZLE
BEZZLING > BEZZLE
BHAGEE *same as* > BHAJI
BHAGEES > BHAGEE
BHAJAN *n* singing of devotional songs and

hymns
BHAJANS > BHAJAN
BHAJEE *same as* > BHAJI
BHAJEES > BHAJEE
BHAJI *n* Indian deep-fried savoury of chopped vegetables in spiced batter
BHAJIS > BHAJI
BHAKTA *n* Hindu term for devotee of God
BHAKTAS > BHAKTA
BHAKTI *n* loving devotion to God leading to nirvana
BHAKTIS > BHAKTI
BHANG *n* preparation of Indian hemp used as a narcotic and intoxicant
BHANGRA *n* type of traditional Punjabi folk music combined with elements of Western pop music
BHANGRAS > BHANGRA
BHANGS > BHANG
BHARAL *n* wild Himalayan sheep, *Pseudois nayaur*, with a bluish-grey coat and round backward-curving horns
BHARALS > BHARAL
BHAT *n* currency of Thailand
BHAVAN *n* (in India) a large house or building
BHAVANS > BHAVAN
BHAWAN *same as* > BHAVAN
BHAWANS > BHAWAN
BHEESTIE *same as* > BHEESTY
BHEESTIES > BHEESTY
BHEESTY *same as* > BHISHTI
BHEL *same as* > BAEL
BHELS > BHEL
BHIKHU *n* fully ordained Buddhist monk
BHIKHUS > BHIKHU
BHIKKHUNI *n* fully ordained Buddhist nun
BHINDI *same as* > BINDHI
BHINDIS > BHINDI
BHISHTI *n* (formerly in India) a water-carrier
BHISHTIS > BHISHTI
BHISTEE *same as* > BHISHTI
BHISTEES > BHISTEE
BHISTI *same as* > BHISHTI
BHISTIE *same as* > BHISHTI
BHISTIES > BHISTIE
BHISTIS > BHISTI
BHOOT *same as* > BHUT
BHOOTS > BHOOT
BHUNA *n* Indian sauce
BHUNAS > BHUNA
BHUT *n* Hindu term for type of ghost
BHUTS > BHUT
BI *short for* > BISEXUAL
BIACETYL *adj* liquid with strong odour
BIACETYLS > BIACETYL
BIALI *same as* > BIALY
BIALIES > BIALY
BIALIS > BIALI
BIALY *n* type of bagel
BIALYS > BIALY
BIANNUAL *adj* occurring twice a year ▷ *n* something that happens

biannually
BIANNUALS > BIANNUAL
BIAS *n* mental tendency, esp prejudice ▷ *vb* cause to have a bias ▷ *adj* slanting obliquely ▷ *adv* obliquely
BIASED > BIAS
BIASEDLY > BIAS
BIASES > BIAS
BIASING > BIAS
BIASINGS > BIAS
BIASNESS > BIAS
BIASSED > BIAS
BIASSEDLY > BIAS
BIASSES > BIAS
BIASSING > BIAS
BIATHLETE *n* athlete taking part in biathlon
BIATHLON *n* contest in which skiers with rifles shoot at four targets along a 20-kilometre (12.5-mile) cross-country course
BIATHLONS > BIATHLON
BIAXAL *same as* > BIAXIAL
BIAXIAL *adj* (esp of a crystal) having two axes
BIAXIALLY > BIAXIAL
BIB *same as* > BIBCOCK
BIBACIOUS *adj* tending to drink to excess
BIBASIC *adj* with two bases
BIBATION *n* drinking to excess
BIBATIONS > BIBATION
BIBB *n* wooden support on a mast for the trestletrees
BIBBED > BIB
BIBBER *n* drinker
BIBBERIES > BIBBERY
BIBBERS > BIBBER
BIBBERY *n* drinking to excess
BIBBING > BIB
BIBBLE *n* pebble
BIBBLES > BIBBLE
BIBBS > BIBB
BIBCOCK *n* tap with a nozzle bent downwards
BIBCOCKS > BIBCOCK
BIBELOT *n* attractive or curious trinket
BIBELOTS > BIBELOT
BIBLE *n* any book containing the sacred writings of a religion
BIBLES > BIBLE
BIBLESS > BIB
BIBLICAL *adj* of, occurring in, or referring to the Bible
BIBLICISM *n* bible-learning
BIBLICIST > BIBLICISM
BIBLIKE > BIB
BIBLIOTIC *n* study of books
BIBLIST *same as* > BIBLICIST
BIBLISTS > BIBLIST
BIBS > BIB
BIBULOUS *adj* addicted to alcohol
BICAMERAL *adj* (of a legislature) consisting of two chambers
BICARB *n* bicarbonate of soda
BICARBS > BICARB
BICAUDAL *adj* having two

tails
BICCIES > BICCY
BICCY *n* biscuit
BICE *n* medium blue colour
BICENTRIC *adj* having two centres
BICEP *same as* > BICEPS
BICEPS *n* muscle with two origins, esp the muscle that flexes the forearm
BICEPSES > BICEPS
BICES > BICE
BICHORD *adj* having two strings for each note
BICHROME *adj* having two colours
BICIPITAL *adj* having two heads
BICKER *vb* argue over petty matters ▷ *n* petty squabble
BICKERED > BICKER
BICKERER > BICKER
BICKERERS > BICKER
BICKERING > BICKER
BICKERS > BICKER
BICKIE *short for* > BISCUIT
BICKIES > BICKIE
BICOASTAL *adj* relating to both the east and west coasts of the US
BICOLOR *same as* > BICOLOUR
BICOLORED *same as* > BICOLOUR
BICOLORS > BICOLOR
BICOLOUR *adj* two-coloured
BICOLOURS > BICOLOUR
BICONCAVE *adj* (of a lens) having concave faces on both sides
BICONVEX *adj* (of a lens) having convex faces on both sides
BICORN *adj* having two horns or hornlike parts
BICORNATE *same as* > BICORN
BICORNE *same as* > BICORN
BICORNES > BICORNE
BICORNS > BICORN
BICRON *n* billionth part of a metre
BICRONS > BICRON
BICUSPID *adj* having two points ▷ *n* bicuspid tooth
BICUSPIDS > BICUSPID
BICYCLE *n* vehicle with two wheels, one behind the other, pedalled by the rider ▷ *vb* ride a bicycle
BICYCLED > BICYCLE
BICYCLER > BICYCLE
BICYCLERS > BICYCLE
BICYCLES > BICYCLE
BICYCLIC *adj* of, forming, or formed by two circles, cycles, etc
BICYCLING > BICYCLE
BICYCLIST > BICYCLE
BID *vb* offer (an amount) in attempting to buy something, esp in competition with others as at an auction ▷ *n* offer of a specified amount, as at an auction

BIDARKA *n* canoe covered in animal skins, esp sealskin, used by the Inuit of Alaska
BIDARKAS > BIDARKA
BIDARKEE *same as* > BIDARKA
BIDARKEES > BIDARKEE
BIDDABLE *adj* obedient
BIDDABLY > BIDDABLE
BIDDEN > BID
BIDDER > BID
BIDDERS > BID
BIDDIES > BIDDY
BIDDING > BID
BIDDINGS > BID
BIDDY *n* woman, esp an old gossipy one
BIDE *vb* stay or continue
BIDED > BIDE
BIDENT *n* instrument with two prongs
BIDENTAL *n* sacred place where lightning has struck
BIDENTALS > BIDENTAL
BIDENTATE > BIDENT
BIDENTS > BIDENT
BIDER > BIDE
BIDERS > BIDE
BIDES > BIDE
BIDET *n* low basin for washing the genital area
BIDETS > BIDET
BIDI *same as* > BEEDI
BIDING > BIDE
BIDINGS > BIDE
BIDIS > BIDI
BIDON *n* oil drum
BIDONS > BIDON
BIDS > BID
BIELD *n* shelter ▷ *vb* shelter or take shelter
BIELDED > BIELD
BIELDIER > BIELDY
BIELDIEST > BIELDY
BIELDING > BIELD
BIELDS > BIELD
BIELDY *adj* sheltered
BIEN *adv* well
BIENNALE *n* event occurring every two years
BIENNALES > BIENNALE
BIENNIA > BIENNIUM
BIENNIAL *adj* occurring every two years ▷ *n* plant that completes its life cycle in two years
BIENNIALS > BIENNIAL
BIENNIUM *n* period of two years
BIENNIUMS > BIENNIUM
BIER *n* stand on which a corpse or coffin rests before burial
BIERS > BIER
BIESTINGS *same as* > BEESTINGS
BIFACE *n* prehistoric stone tool
BIFACES > BIFACE
BIFACIAL *adj* having two faces or surfaces
BIFARIOUS *adj* having parts arranged in two rows on either side of a central axis
BIFF *n* blow with the fist ▷ *vb* give (someone) such a blow

BIFFED > BIFF
BIFFER *n* someone, such as a sportsperson, who has a reputation for hitting hard
BIFFERS > BIFFER
BIFFIES > BIFFY
BIFFIN *n* variety of red cooking apple
BIFFING > BIFF
BIFFINS > BIFFIN
BIFFO *n* fighting or aggressive behaviour ▷ *adj* aggressive
BIFFOS > BIFFO
BIFFS > BIFF
BIFFY *n* outdoor toilet
BIFID *adj* divided into two by a cleft in the middle
BIFIDITY > BIFID
BIFIDLY > BIFID
BIFILAR *adj* having two parallel threads, as in the suspension of certain measuring instruments
BIFILARLY > BIFILAR
BIFLEX *adj* bent or flexed in two places
BIFOCAL *adj* having two different focuses
BIFOCALED *adj* wearing bifocals
BIFOCALS *pl n* spectacles with lenses permitting near and distant vision
BIFOLD *adj* that can be folded in two places
BIFOLIATE *adj* having only two leaves
BIFORATE *adj* having two openings, pores, or perforations
BIFORKED *adj* two-pronged
BIFORM *adj* having or combining the characteristics of two forms, as a centaur
BIFORMED *same as* > BIFORM
BIFTER *n* cannabis cigarette
BIFTERS > BIFTER
BIFURCATE *vb* fork into two branches ▷ *adj* forked into two branches
BIG *adj* of considerable size, height, number, or capacity ▷ *adv* on a grand scale ▷ *vb* build
BIGA *n* chariot drawn by two horses
BIGAE > BIGA
BIGAMIES > BIGAMY
BIGAMIST > BIGAMY
BIGAMISTS > BIGAMY
BIGAMOUS > BIGAMY
BIGAMY *n* crime of marrying a person while still legally married to someone else
BIGARADE *n* Seville orange
BIGARADES > BIGARADE
BIGAROON *same as* > BIGARREAU
BIGAROONS > BIGAROON
BIGARREAU *n* any of several heart-shaped varieties of sweet cherry that have firm flesh
BIGEMINAL *adj* double;

twinned
BIGEMINY *n* heart complaint
BIGENER *n* hybrid between individuals of different genera
BIGENERIC *adj* (of a hybrid plant) derived from parents of two different genera
BIGENERS > BIGENER
BIGEYE *n* any tropical or subtropical red marine percoid fish of the family *Priacanthidae*, having very large eyes and rough scales
BIGEYES > BIGEYE
BIGFEET > BIGFOOT
BIGFOOT *n* yeti ▷ *vb* throw one's weight around
BIGFOOTED > BIGFOOT
BIGFOOTS > BIGFOOT
BIGG *n* type of barley
BIGGED > BIG
BIGGER > BIG
BIGGEST > BIG
BIGGETY *same as* > BIGGITY
BIGGIE *n* something big or important
BIGGIES > BIGGIE
BIGGIN *n* plain close-fitting cap, often tying under the chin, worn in the Middle Ages and by children in the 17th century
BIGGING > BIG
BIGGINGS > BIG
BIGGINS > BIGGIN
BIGGISH > BIG
BIGGITY *adj* conceited
BIGGON *same as* > BIGGIN
BIGGONS > BIGGON
BIGGS > BIGG
BIGGY *same as* > BIGGIE
BIGHA *n* in India, unit for measuring land
BIGHAS > BIGHA
BIGHEAD *n* conceited person
BIGHEADED > BIGHEAD
BIGHEADS > BIGHEAD
BIGHORN *n* large wild sheep, *Ovis canadensis*, inhabiting mountainous regions in North America and NE Asia: family *Bovidae*, order *Artiodactyla*. The male has massive curved horns, and the species is well adapted for climbing and leaping
BIGHORNS > BIGHORN
BIGHT *n* long curved shoreline ▷ *vb* fasten or bind with a bight
BIGHTED > BIGHT
BIGHTING > BIGHT
BIGHTS > BIGHT
BIGLY > BIG
BIGMOUTH *n* noisy, indiscreet, or boastful person
BIGMOUTHS > BIGMOUTH
BIGNESS > BIG
BIGNESSES > BIG
BIGNONIA *n* any tropical American bignoniaceous climbing shrub of the genus *Bignonia* (or

b

Doxantha), cultivated for their trumpet-shaped yellow or reddish flowers

BIGNONIAS > BIGNONIA

BIGOS *n* Polish stew

BIGOSES > BIGOS

BIGOT *n* person who is intolerant, esp regarding religion or race

BIGOTED > BIGOT

BIGOTEDLY > BIGOT

BIGOTRIES > BIGOTRY

BIGOTRY *n* attitudes, behaviour, or way of thinking of a bigot

BIGOTS > BIGOT

BIGS > BIG

BIGSTICK *adj* of or relating to irresistible military strength

BIGTIME *adj* important

BIGUANIDE *n* any of a class of compounds some of which are used in the treatment of certain forms of diabetes

BIGWIG *n* important person

BIGWIGS > BIGWIG

BIHOURLY *adj* occurring every two hours

BIJECTION *n* mathematical function or mapping that is both an injection and a surjection and therefore has an inverse

BIJECTIVE *adj* (of a function, relation, etc) associating two sets in such a way that every member of each set is uniquely paired with a member of the other

BIJOU *adj* (of a house) small but elegant ▷ *n* something small and delicately worked

BIJOUS > BIJOU

BIJOUX > BIJOU

BIJUGATE *adj* (of compound leaves) having two pairs of leaflets

BIJUGOUS *same as* > BIJUGATE

BIJWONER *same as* > BYWONER

BIJWONERS > BIJWONER

BIKE *same as* > BICYCLE

BIKED > BIKE

BIKER *n* person who rides a motorcycle

BIKERS > BIKER

BIKES > BIKE

BIKEWAY *n* cycle lane

BIKEWAYS > BIKEWAY

BIKIE *n* member of a motorcycle gang

BIKIES > BIKIE

BIKING > BIKE

BIKINGS > BIKE

BIKINI *n* woman's brief two-piece swimming costume

BIKINIED > BIKINI

BIKINIS > BIKINI

BIKKIE *slang word for* > BISCUIT

BIKKIES > BIKKIE

BILABIAL *adj* of, relating to, or denoting a speech sound articulated using both lips ▷ *n* bilabial speech sound

BILABIALS > BILABIAL

BILABIATE *adj* divided into two lips

BILANDER *n* small two-masted cargo ship

BILANDERS > BILANDER

BILATERAL *adj* affecting or undertaken by two parties

BILAYER *n* part of cell membrane

BILAYERS > BILAYER

BILBERRY *n* bluish-black edible berry

BILBIES > BILBY

BILBO *n* (formerly) a sword with a marked temper and elasticity

BILBOA *same as* > BILBO

BILBOAS > BILBOA

BILBOES > BILBO

BILBOS > BILBO

BILBY *n* Australian marsupial with long pointed ears and grey fur

BILE *n* bitter yellow fluid secreted by the liver ▷ *vb* Scots word for > BOIL

BILECTION *same as* > BOLECTION

BILED > BILE

BILES > BILE

BILESTONE *another name for* > GALLSTONE

BILEVEL *n* hairstyle with two different lengths

BILEVELS > BILEVEL

BILGE *n* nonsense ▷ *vb* (of a vessel) to take in water at the bilge

BILGED > BILGE

BILGES > BILGE

BILGIER > BILGE

BILGIEST > BILGE

BILGING > BILGE

BILGY > BILGE

BILHARZIA *n* disease caused by infestation of the body with blood flukes

BILIAN *n* type of tree used for its wood

BILIANS > BILIAN

BILIARIES > BILIARY

BILIARY *adj* of bile, the ducts that convey bile, or the gall bladder ▷ *n* disease found in dogs

BILIMBI *n* type of fruit-bearing tree

BILIMBING *same as* > BILIMBI

BILIMBIS > BILIMBI

BILINEAR *adj* of or referring to two lines

BILING > BILE

BILINGUAL *adj* involving or using two languages ▷ *n* bilingual person

BILIOUS *adj* sick, nauseous

BILIOUSLY > BILIOUS

BILIRUBIN *n* orange-yellow pigment in the bile

BILITERAL *adj* relating to two letters

BILK *vb* cheat, esp by not paying ▷ *n* swindle or cheat

BILKED > BILK

BILKER > BILK

BILKERS > BILK

BILKING > BILK

BILKS > BILK

BILL *n* money owed for goods or services supplied ▷ *vb* to send or present an account for payment to (a person)

BILLABLE *adj* that can be charged to a client

BILLABONG *n* stagnant pool in an intermittent stream

BILLBOARD *n* large outdoor board for displaying advertisements

BILLBOOK *n* business record of bills received, paid, etc

BILLBOOKS > BILLBOOK

BILLBUG *n* type of weevil

BILLBUGS > BILLBUG

BILLED > BILL

BILLER *n* stem of a plant

BILLERS > BILLER

BILLET *vb* assign a lodging to (a soldier) ▷ *n* accommodation for a soldier in civil lodgings

BILLETED > BILLET

BILLETEE > BILLET

BILLETEES > BILLET

BILLETER > BILLET

BILLETERS > BILLET

BILLETING > BILLET

BILLETS > BILLET

BILLFISH *n* any of various fishes having elongated jaws, esp any fish of the family *Istiophoridae*, such as the spearfish and marlin

BILLFOLD *n* small folding case, usually of leather, for holding paper money, documents, etc

BILLFOLDS > BILLFOLD

BILLHEAD *n* printed form for making out bills

BILLHEADS > BILLHEAD

BILLHOOK *n* tool with a hooked blade, used for chopping etc

BILLHOOKS > BILLHOOK

BILLIARD *n* (modifier) of or relating to billiards

BILLIARDS *n* game played on a table with balls and a cue

BILLIE *same as* > BILLY

BILLIES > BILLY

BILLING *n* relative importance of a performer or act as reflected in the prominence given in programmes, advertisements, etc

BILLINGS > BILLING

BILLION *n* one thousand million ▷ *determiner* amounting to a billion

BILLIONS > BILLION

BILLIONTH > BILLION

BILLMAN *n* person who uses a billhook

BILLMEN > BILLMAN

BILLON *n* alloy consisting of gold or silver and a base metal, usually copper, used esp for coinage

BILLONS > BILLON

BILLOW *n* large sea wave ▷ *vb* rise up or swell out

BILLOWED > BILLOW

BILLOWIER > BILLOWY

BILLOWING > BILLOW

BILLOWS > BILLOW

BILLOWY *adj* full of or forming billows

BILLS > BILL

BILLY *n* metal can or pot for cooking on a camp fire

BILLYBOY *n* type of river barge

BILLYBOYS > BILLYBOY

BILLYCAN *same as* > BILLY

BILLYCANS > BILLYCAN

BILLYCOCK *n* any of several round-crowned brimmed hats of felt, such as the bowler

BILLYO *as in like billyo* phrase used to emphasize or intensify something

BILLYOH *same as* > BILLYO

BILLYOHS > BILLYOH

BILLYOS > BILLYO

BILOBAR *same as* > BILOBATE

BILOBATE *adj* divided into or having two lobes

BILOBATED *same as* > BILOBATE

BILOBED *same as* > BILOBATE

BILOBULAR *adj* having two lobules

BILOCULAR *adj* divided into two chambers or cavities

BILSTED *n* American gum tree

BILSTEDS > BILSTED

BILTONG *n* strips of dried meat

BILTONGS > BILTONG

BIMA *same as* > BEMA

BIMAH *same as* > BEMA

BIMAHS > BIMAH

BIMANAL *same as* > BIMANOUS

BIMANOUS *adj* (of man and the higher primates) having two hands distinct in form and function from the feet

BIMANUAL *adj* using or requiring both hands

BIMAS > BIMA

BIMBASHI *n* Turkish military official

BIMBASHIS > BIMBASHI

BIMBETTE *n* particularly unintelligent bimbo

BIMBETTES > BIMBETTE

BIMBLE *as in bimble box* type of dense Australian tree

BIMBO *n* attractive but empty-headed young person, esp a woman

BIMBOES > BIMBO

BIMBOS > BIMBO

BIMENSAL *adj* occurring

every two months

BIMESTER *n* period of two months

BIMESTERS > BIMESTER

BIMETAL *n* material made from two sheets of metal

BIMETALS > BIMETAL

BIMETHYL *another word for* > ETHANE

BIMETHYLS > BIMETHYL

BIMODAL *adj* having two modes

BIMONTHLY *adj* every two months ▷*adv* every two months ▷*n* periodical published every two months

BIMORPH *n* assembly of two piezoelectric crystals cemented together so that an applied voltage causes one to expand and the other to contract, converting electrical signals into mechanical energy. Conversely, bending can generate a voltage: used in loudspeakers, gramophone pick-ups, etc

BIMORPHS > BIMORPH

BIN *n* container for rubbish or for storing grain, coal, etc ▷*vb* put in a rubbish bin

BINAL *adj* twofold

BINARIES > BINARY

BINARISM *n* state of being binary

BINARISMS > BINARISM

BINARY *adj* composed of, relating to, or involving two ▷*n* something composed of two parts or things

BINATE *adj* occurring in two parts or in pairs

BINATELY > BINATE

BINAURAL *adj* relating to, having, or hearing with both ears

BIND *vb* make secure with or as if with a rope ▷*n* annoying situation

BINDABLE > BIND

BINDER *n* firm cover for holding loose sheets of paper together

BINDERIES > BINDERY

BINDERS > BINDER

BINDERY *n* bookbindery

BINDHI *same as* > BINDI

BINDHIS > BINDHI

BINDI *n* decorative dot worn in the middle of the forehead, esp by Hindu women

BINDING > BIND

BINDINGLY > BIND

BINDINGS > BIND

BINDIS > BINDI

BINDLE *n* small packet

BINDLES > BINDLE

BINDS > BIND

BINDWEED *n* plant that twines around a support

BINDWEEDS > BINDWEED

BINE *n* climbing or twining stem of any of various plants, such as the woodbine or bindweed

BINER *n* clip used by climbers

BINERS > BINER

BINERVATE *adj* having two nerves

BINES > BINE

BING *n* heap or pile, esp of spoil from a mine

BINGE *n* bout of excessive indulgence, esp in drink ▷*vb* indulge in a binge (esp of eating or drinking)

BINGED > BINGE

BINGEING > BINGE

BINGER *n* person who is addicted to crack cocaine

BINGERS > BINGER

BINGES > BINGE

BINGHI *n* Australian derogatory slang for an Aboriginal person

BINGHIS > BINGHI

BINGIES > BINGY

BINGING > BINGE

BINGLE *n* minor crash or upset, as in a car or on a surfboard ▷*vb* layer (hair)

BINGLED > BINGLE

BINGLES > BINGLE

BINGLING > BINGLE

BINGO *n* gambling game in which numbers are called out and covered by the players on their individual cards ▷*sentence substitute* cry by the winner of a game of bingo

BINGOES > BINGO

BINGOS > BINGO

BINGS > BING

BINGY *Australian slang for* > STOMACH

BINIOU *n* small high-pitched Breton bagpipe

BINIOUS > BINIOU

BINIT *n* (computing) early form of bit

BINITS > BINIT

BINK *n* ledge

BINKS > BINK

BINMAN *another name for* > DUSTMAN

BINMEN > BINMAN

BINNACLE *n* box holding a ship's compass

BINNACLES > BINNACLE

BINNED > BIN

BINNING > BIN

BINOCLE *n* binocular-style telescope

BINOCLES > BINOCLE

BINOCS > BINOCULAR

BINOCULAR *adj* involving both eyes

BINOMIAL *adj* consisting of two terms ▷*n* mathematical expression consisting of two terms, such as $3x + 2y$

BINOMIALS > BINOMIAL

BINOMINAL *adj* of or denoting the binomial nomenclature ▷*n* two-part taxonomic name

BINOVULAR *adj* relating to or derived from two different ova

BINS > BIN

BINT *n* derogatory term for a girl

BINTS > BINT

BINTURONG *n* arboreal SE Asian viverrine mammal, *Arctictis binturong*, closely related to the palm civets but larger and having long shaggy black hair

BINUCLEAR *adj* having two nuclei

BIO *short for* > BIOGRAPHY

BIOACTIVE *adj* able to interact with living system

BIOASSAY *n* method of determining the concentration, activity, or effect of a change to substance by testing its effect on a living organism and comparing this with the activity of an agreed standard ▷*vb* subject to a bioassay

BIOASSAYS > BIOASSAY

BIOBLAST *same as* > BIOPLAST

BIOBLASTS > BIOBLAST

BIOCENOSE *adj* living together in mutual dependence

BIOCHEMIC *adj* of or relating to chemical compounds, reactions, etc, occurring in living organisms

BIOCHIP *n* small glass or silicon plate containing an array of biochemical molecules or structures, used as a biosensor or in gene sequencing

BIOCHIPS > BIOCHIP

BIOCIDAL > BIOCIDE

BIOCIDE *n* substance used to destroy living things

BIOCIDES > BIOCIDE

BIOCLEAN *adj* free from harmful bacteria

BIOCYCLE *n* cycling of chemicals through the biosphere

BIOCYCLES > BIOCYCLE

BIODATA *n* information regarding an individual's education and work history, esp in the context of a selection process

BIODIESEL *n* biofuel intended for use in diesel engines

BIODOT *n* temperature-sensitive device stuck to the skin in order to monitor stress

BIODOTS > BIODOT

BIOETHIC > BIOETHICS

BIOETHICS *n* study of ethical problems arising from biological research and its applications in such fields as organ

transplantation, genetic engineering, or artificial insemination

BIOFACT *n* item of biological information

BIOFACTS > BIOFACT

BIOFILM *n* thin layer of living organisms

BIOFILMS > BIOFILM

BIOFOULER *n* animal that obstructs or pollutes the environment

BIOFUEL *n* gaseous, liquid, or solid substance of biological origin that is used as a fuel

BIOFUELED *adj* running on biofuel

BIOFUELS > BIOFUEL

BIOG *short form of* > BIOGRAPHY

BIOGAS *n* gaseous fuel produced by the fermentation of organic waste

BIOGASES > BIOGAS

BIOGASSES > BIOGAS

BIOGEN *n* hypothetical protein assumed to be the basis of the formation and functioning of body cells and tissues

BIOGENIC *adj* originating from a living organism

BIOGENIES > BIOGENY

BIOGENOUS > BIOGEN

BIOGENS > BIOGEN

BIOGENY *n* principle that a living organism must originate from a parent form similar to itself

BIOGRAPH *vb* write biography of

BIOGRAPHS > BIOGRAPH

BIOGRAPHY *n* account of a person's life by another person

BIOGS > BIOG

BIOHAZARD *n* material of biological origin that is hazardous to humans

BIOHERM *n* mound of material laid down by sedentary marine organisms, esp a coral reef

BIOHERMS > BIOHERM

BIOLOGIC *adj* of or relating to biology ▷*n* drug, such as a vaccine, that is derived from a living organism

BIOLOGICS > BIOLOGIC

BIOLOGIES > BIOLOGY

BIOLOGISM *n* explaining human behaviour through biology

BIOLOGIST > BIOLOGY

BIOLOGY *n* study of living organisms

BIOLYSES > BIOLYSIS

BIOLYSIS *n* death and dissolution of a living organism

BIOLYTIC > BIOLYSIS

BIOMARKER *n* substance, physiological characteristic, gene, etc that indicates, or may

b

indicate, the presence of disease, a physiological abnormality, or a psychological condition

BIOMASS *n* total number of living organisms in a given area

BIOMASSES > BIOMASS

BIOME *n* major ecological community, extending over a large area and usually characterized by a dominant vegetation

BIOMES > BIOME

BIOMETER *n* device for measuring natural radiation

BIOMETERS > BIOMETER

BIOMETRIC *adj* of any automated system using physiological or behavioural traits as a means of identification.

BIOMETRY *n* analysis of biological data using mathematical and statistical methods, especially for purposes of identification

BIOMINING *n* using plants, etc to collect precious metals for extraction

BIOMORPH *n* form or pattern resembling living thing

BIOMORPHS > BIOMORPH

BIONIC *adj* having a part of the body that is operated electronically

BIONICS *n* study of biological functions in order to develop electronic equipment that operates similarly

BIONOMIC > BIONOMICS

BIONOMICS *a less common name for* > ECOLOGY

BIONOMIES > BIONOMY

BIONOMIST > BIONOMICS

BIONOMY *n* laws of life

BIONT *n* living thing

BIONTIC > BIONT

BIONTS > BIONT

BIOPARENT *n* biological parent

BIOPHILIA *n* innate love for the natural world, supposed to be felt universally by humankind

BIOPHOR *n* hypothetical material particle

BIOPHORE *same as* > BIOPHOR

BIOPHORES > BIOPHORE

BIOPHORS > BIOPHOR

BIOPIC *n* film based on the life of a famous person

BIOPICS > BIOPIC

BIOPIRACY *n* use of wild plants by international companies to develop medicines, without recompensing the countries from which they are taken

BIOPIRATE > BIOPIRACY

BIOPLASM *n* living matter

BIOPLASMS > BIOPLASM

BIOPLAST *n* very small unit of bioplasm

BIOPLASTS > BIOPLAST

BIOPSIC > BIOPSY

BIOPSIED > BIOPSY

BIOPSIES > BIOPSY

BIOPSY *n* examination of tissue from a living body ▷ *vb* perform a biopsy on

BIOPSYING > BIOPSY

BIOPTIC > BIOPSY

BIOREGION *n* area in which climate and environment are consistent

BIORHYTHM *n* complex recurring pattern of physiological states, believed to affect physical, emotional, and mental states

BIOS > BIO

BIOSAFETY *n* precautions taken to control the cultivation and distribution of genetically modified crops and products

BIOSCOPE *n* kind of early film projector

BIOSCOPES > BIOSCOPE

BIOSCOPY *n* examination of a body to determine whether it is alive

BIOSENSOR *n* device used to monitor living systems

BIOSOCIAL *adj* relating to the interaction of biological and social elements

BIOSOLID *n* residue from treated sewage

BIOSOLIDS > BIOSOLID

BIOSPHERE *n* part of the earth's surface and atmosphere inhabited by living things

BIOSTABLE *adj* resistant to the effects of microorganisms

BIOSTATIC *adj* of or relating to the branch of biology that deals with the structure of organisms in relation to their function

BIOSTROME *n* rock layer consisting of a deposit of organic material, such as fossils

BIOTA *n* plant and animal life of a particular region or period

BIOTAS > BIOTA

BIOTECH *n* biotechnology

BIOTECHS > BIOTECH

BIOTERROR *n* use of biological weapons by terrorists

BIOTIC *adj* of or relating to living organisms ▷ *n* living organism

BIOTICAL *same as* > BIOTIC

BIOTICS > BIOTIC

BIOTIN *n* vitamin of the B complex, abundant in egg yolk and liver

BIOTINS > BIOTIN

BIOTITE *n* black or dark green mineral of the mica

group

BIOTITES > BIOTITE

BIOTITIC > BIOTITE

BIOTOPE *n* small area, such as the bark of a tree, that supports its own distinctive community

BIOTOPES > BIOTOPE

BIOTOXIN *n* toxic substance produced by a living organism

BIOTOXINS > BIOTOXIN

BIOTRON *n* climate-control chamber

BIOTRONS > BIOTRON

BIOTROPH *n* parasitic organism, esp a fungus

BIOTROPHS > BIOTROPH

BIOTURBED *adj* stirred by organisms

BIOTYPE *n* group of genetically identical plants within a species, produced by apomixis

BIOTYPES > BIOTYPE

BIOTYPIC > BIOTYPE

BIOVULAR *adj* (of twins) from two separate eggs

BIOWEAPON *n* living organism or a toxic product manufactured from it, used to kill or incapacitate

BIPACK *n* obsolete filming process

BIPACKS > BIPACK

BIPAROUS *adj* producing offspring in pairs

BIPARTED *adj* divided into two parts

BIPARTITE *adj* consisting of two parts

BIPARTY *adj* involving two parties

BIPED *n* animal with two feet ▷ *adj* having two feet

BIPEDAL *adj* having two feet

BIPEDALLY > BIPEDAL

BIPEDS > BIPED

BIPHASIC *adj* having two phases

BIPHENYL *n* white or colourless crystalline solid used as a heat-transfer agent

BIPHENYLS > BIPHENYL

BIPINNATE *adj* (of pinnate leaves) having the leaflets themselves divided into smaller leaflets

BIPLANE *n* aeroplane with two sets of wings, one above the other

BIPLANES > BIPLANE

BIPOD *n* two-legged support or stand

BIPODS > BIPOD

BIPOLAR *adj* having two poles

BIPRISM *n* prism having a highly obtuse angle to facilitate beam splitting

BIPRISMS > BIPRISM

BIPYRAMID *n* geometrical form consisting of two pyramids with a common polygonal base

BIRACIAL *adj* for, representing, or including members of two races, esp White and Black

BIRADIAL *adj* showing both bilateral and radial symmetry, as certain sea anemones

BIRADICAL *n* molecule with two centres

BIRAMOSE *same as* > BIRAMOUS

BIRAMOUS *adj* divided into two parts, as the appendages of crustaceans

BIRCH *n* tree with thin peeling bark ▷ *vb* flog with a birch

BIRCHBARK as in *birchbark biting* Native Canadian craft in which designs are bitten onto bark from birch trees

BIRCHED > BIRCH

BIRCHEN > BIRCH

BIRCHES > BIRCH

BIRCHING > BIRCH

BIRD *n* creature with feathers and wings, most types of which can fly ▷ *vb* hunt for birds

BIRDBATH *n* small basin or trough for birds to bathe in, usually in a garden

BIRDBATHS > BIRDBATH

BIRDBRAIN *n* stupid person

BIRDCAGE *n* wire or wicker cage in which captive birds are kept

BIRDCAGES > BIRDCAGE

BIRDCALL *n* characteristic call or song of a bird

BIRDCALLS > BIRDCALL

BIRDDOG *n* dog used or trained to retrieve game birds

BIRDDOGS > BIRDDOG

BIRDED > BIRD

BIRDER *n* birdwatcher

BIRDERS > BIRDER

BIRDFARM *n* place where birds are kept

BIRDFARMS > BIRDFARM

BIRDFEED *n* food for birds

BIRDFEEDS > BIRDFEED

BIRDHOUSE *n* small shelter or box for birds to nest in

BIRDIE *n* score of one stroke under par for a hole ▷ *vb* play (a hole) in one stroke under par

BIRDIED > BIRDIE

BIRDIEING > BIRDIE

BIRDIES > BIRDIE

BIRDING > BIRD

BIRDINGS > BIRD

BIRDLIFE *n* birds collectively

BIRDLIKE > BIRD

BIRDLIME *n* sticky substance smeared on twigs to catch small birds ▷ *vb* smear (twigs) with birdlime to catch (small birds)

BIRDLIMED > BIRDLIME

BIRDLIMES > BIRDLIME

BIRDMAN *n* man concerned with birds, such as a fowler or ornithologist
BIRDMEN > BIRDMAN
BIRDS > BIRD
BIRDSEED *n* mixture of various kinds of seeds for feeding cage birds
BIRDSEEDS > BIRDSEED
BIRDSEYE *n* type of primrose
BIRDSEYES > BIRDSEYE
BIRDSHOT *n* small pellets designed for shooting birds
BIRDSHOTS > BIRDSHOT
BIRDSONG *n* musical call of a bird or birds
BIRDSONGS > BIRDSONG
BIRDWATCH *vb* watch birds
BIRDWING *n* type of butterfly
BIRDWINGS > BIRDWING
BIREME *n* ancient galley having two banks of oars
BIREMES > BIREME
BIRETTA *n* stiff square cap worn by the Catholic clergy
BIRETTAS > BIRETTA
BIRIANI *same as* > BIRYANI
BIRIANIS > BIRIANI
BIRIYANI *same as* > BIRIANI
BIRIYANIS > BIRIYANI
BIRK *n* birch tree ▷ *adj* consisting or made of birch
BIRKEN *adj* relating to the birch tree
BIRKIE *n* spirited or lively person ▷ *adj* lively
BIRKIER > BIRKIE
BIRKIES > BIRKIE
BIRKIEST > BIRKIE
BIRKS > BIRK
BIRL *same as* > BURL
BIRLE *same as* > BURL
BIRLED > BIRL
BIRLER > BIRL
BIRLERS > BIRL
BIRLES > BIRLE
BIRLIEMAN *n* judge dealing with local law
BIRLIEMEN > BIRLIEMAN
BIRLING > BIRL
BIRLINGS > BIRL
BIRLINN *n* small Scottish book
BIRLINNS > BIRLINN
BIRLS > BIRL
BIRO *n* tradename of a kind of ballpoint pen
BIROS > BIRO
BIRR *vb* make or cause to make a whirring sound ▷ *n* whirring sound
BIRRED > BIRR
BIRRETTA *same as* > BIRETTA
BIRRETTAS > BIRRETTA
BIRRING > BIRR
BIRROTCH *n* Ethiopian monetary unit
BIRRS > BIRR
BIRSE *n* bristle
BIRSES > BIRSE
BIRSIER > BIRSY
BIRSIEST > BIRSY
BIRSLE *vb* roast
BIRSLED > BIRSLE
BIRSLES > BIRSLE

BIRSLING > BIRSLE
BIRSY *adj* bristly
BIRTH *n* process of bearing young ▷ *vb* give birth to
BIRTHDAY *n* anniversary of the day of one's birth
BIRTHDAYS > BIRTHDAY
BIRTHDOM *n* birthright
BIRTHDOMS > BIRTHDOM
BIRTHED > BIRTH
BIRTHING > BIRTH
BIRTHINGS > BIRTH
BIRTHMARK *n* blemish on the skin formed before birth
BIRTHNAME *n* name person was born with
BIRTHRATE *n* ratio of live births in a specified area, group, etc, to the population of that area, etc, usually expressed per 1000 population per year
BIRTHROOT *n* any of several North American plants of the genus *Trillium*, esp *T. erectum*, whose tuber-like roots were formerly used by the American Indians as an aid in childbirth: family *Trilliaceae*
BIRTHS > BIRTH
BIRTHWORT *n* any of several climbing plants of the genus *Aristolochia*, esp *A. clematitis* of Europe, once believed to ease childbirth: family *Aristolochiaceae*
BIRYANI *n* any of a variety of Indian dishes made with rice, highly flavoured and coloured with saffron or turmeric, mixed with meat or fish
BIRYANIS > BIRYANI
BIS *adv* twice ▷ *sentence substitute* encore! again!
BISCACHA *same as* > VISCACHA
BISCACHAS > BISCACHA
BISCOTTI > BISCOTTO
BISCOTTO *n* small Italian biscuit
BISCUIT *n* small flat dry sweet or plain cake ▷ *adj* pale brown
BISCUITS > BISCUIT
BISCUITY *adj* reminiscent of biscuit
BISE *n* cold dry northerly wind in Switzerland and the neighbouring parts of France and Italy, usually in the spring
BISECT *vb* divide into two equal parts
BISECTED > BISECT
BISECTING > BISECT
BISECTION > BISECT
BISECTOR *n* straight line or plane that bisects an angle
BISECTORS > BISECTOR
BISECTRIX *n* bisector of the angle between the optic axes of a crystal
BISECTS > BISECT
BISERIAL *adj* in two rows

BISERIATE *adj* (of plant parts, such as petals) arranged in two whorls, cycles, rows, or series
BISERRATE *adj* (of leaf margins, etc) having serrations that are themselves serrate
BISES > BISE
BISEXUAL *adj* sexually attracted to both men and women ▷ *n* bisexual person
BISEXUALS > BISEXUAL
BISH *n* mistake
BISHES > BISH
BISHOP *n* clergyman who governs a diocese ▷ *vb* make a bishop
BISHOPDOM *n* jurisdiction of bishop
BISHOPED > BISHOP
BISHOPESS > BISHOP
BISHOPING > BISHOP
BISHOPRIC *n* diocese or office of a bishop
BISHOPS > BISHOP
BISK *a less common spelling of* > BISQUE
BISKS > BISK
BISMAR *n* type of weighing scale
BISMARS > BISMAR
BISMILLAH *interj* in the name of Allah, a preface to all except one of the surahs of the Koran, used by Muslims as a blessing before eating or some other action
BISMUTH *n* pinkish-white metallic element
BISMUTHAL > BISMUTH
BISMUTHIC *adj* of or containing bismuth in the pentavalent state
BISMUTHS > BISMUTH
BISNAGA *n* type of cactus
BISNAGAS > BISNAGA
BISON *same as* > BUFFALO
BISONS > BISON
BISONTINE *adj* relating to bison
BISQUE *n* thick rich soup made from shellfish
BISQUES > BISQUE
BISSON *adj* blind
BIST *a form of the second person singular of* > BE
BISTABLE *adj* (of an electronic system) having two stable states ▷ *n* bistable system
BISTABLES > BISTABLE
BISTATE *adj* involving two states
BISTER *same as* > BESTIR
BISTERED > BISTER
BISTERS > BISTER
BISTORT *n* Eurasian polygonaceous plant, *Polygonum bistorta*, having leaf stipules fused to form a tube around the stem and a spike of small pink flowers
BISTORTS > BISTORT
BISTOURY *n* long surgical

knife with a narrow blade
BISTRE *n* transparent water-soluble brownish-yellow pigment made by boiling the soot of wood, used for pen and wash drawings
BISTRED > BISTRE
BISTRES > BISTRE
BISTRO *n* small restaurant
BISTROIC > BISTRO
BISTROS > BISTRO
BISULCATE *adj* marked by two grooves
BISULFATE *n* bisulphate
BISULFIDE *n* bisulphide
BISULFITE *n* bisulphite
BIT *n* small piece, portion, or quantity
BITABLE > BITE
BITCH *n* female dog, fox, or wolf ▷ *vb* complain or grumble
BITCHED > BITCH
BITCHEN *same as* > BITCHING
BITCHERY *n* spiteful talk
BITCHES > BITCH
BITCHFEST *n* malicious and spiteful discussion of people, events, etc
BITCHIER > BITCHY
BITCHIEST > BITCHY
BITCHILY > BITCHY
BITCHING *adj* wonderful or excellent
BITCHY *adj* spiteful or malicious
BITE *vb* grip, tear, or puncture the skin, as with the teeth or jaws ▷ *n* act of biting
BITEABLE > BITE
BITEPLATE *n* device used by dentists
BITER > BITE
BITERS > BITE
BITES > BITE
BITESIZE *adj* small enough to put in the mouth whole
BITEWING *n* dental x-ray film
BITEWINGS > BITEWING
BITING > BITE
BITINGLY > BITE
BITINGS > BITE
BITLESS *adj* without a bit
BITMAP *n* picture created by colour or shading on a visual display unit ▷ *vb* create a bitmap of
BITMAPPED > BITMAP
BITMAPS > BITMAP
BITO *n* African and Asian tree
BITONAL *adj* consisting of black and white tones
BITOS > BITO
BITOU as in *bitou bush* type of sprawling woody shrub
BITS > BIT
BITSER *n* mongrel dog
BITSERS > BITSER
BITSIER > BITSY
BITSIEST > BITSY
BITSTOCK *n* handle or stock of a tool into which a

drilling bit is fixed

BITSTOCKS > BITSTOCK

BITSTREAM n sequence of digital data

BITSY adj very small

BITT n one of a pair of strong posts on the deck of a ship for securing mooring and other lines ▷vb secure (a line) by means of a bitt

BITTACLE same as > BINNACLE

BITTACLES > BITTACLE

BITTE interj you're welcome

BITTED > BITT

BITTEN > BITE

BITTER adj having a sharp unpleasant taste ▷n beer with a slightly bitter taste ▷adv very ▷vb make or become bitter

BITTERED > BITTER

BITTERER > BITTER

BITTEREST > BITTER

BITTERING > BITTER

BITTERISH > BITTER

BITTERLY > BITTER

BITTERN n wading marsh bird with a booming call

BITTERNS > BITTERN

BITTERNUT n E North American hickory tree, Carya cordiformis, with thin-shelled nuts and bitter kernels

BITTERS pl n bitter-tasting spirits flavoured with plant extracts

BITTIE n small piece

BITTIER > BITTY

BITTIES > BITTIE

BITTIEST > BITTY

BITTINESS > BITTY

BITTING > BITT

BITTINGS > BITT

BITTOCK n small amount

BITTOCKS > BITTOCK

BITTOR n bittern

BITTORS > BITTOR

BITTOUR same as > BITTOR

BITTOURS > BITTOUR

BITTS > BITT

BITTUR same as > BITTOR

BITTURS > BITTUR

BITTY adj lacking unity, disjointed

BITUMED adj covered with bitumen

BITUMEN n black sticky substance obtained from tar or petrol

BITUMENS > BITUMEN

BIUNIQUE adj one-to-one correspondence

BIVALENCE n semantic principle that there are exactly two truth values, so that every meaningful statement is either true or false

BIVALENCY > BIVALENT

BIVALENT adj (of homologous chromosomes) associated together in pairs ▷n structure formed during meiosis consisting

of two homologous chromosomes associated together

BIVALENTS > BIVALENT

BIVALVATE same as > BIVALVE

BIVALVE adj (marine mollusc) with two hinged segments to its shell ▷n sea creature, such as an oyster or mussel, that has a shell consisting of two hinged valves and breathes through gills

BIVALVED > BIVALVE

BIVALVES > BIVALVE

BIVARIANT same as > BIVARIATE

BIVARIATE adj (of a distribution) involving two random variables, not necessarily independent of one another

BIVIA > BIVIUM

BIVINYL another word for > BUTADIENE

BIVINYLS > BIVINYL

BIVIOUS adj offering a choice of two different ways

BIVIUM n parting of ways

BIVOUAC n temporary camp in the open air ▷vb camp in a bivouac

BIVOUACKS > BIVOUAC

BIVOUACS > BIVOUAC

BIVVIED > BIVVY

BIVVIES > BIVVY

BIVVY n small tent or shelter ▷vb camp in a bivouac

BIVVYING > BIVVY

BIWEEKLY adv every two weeks ▷n periodical published every two weeks

BIYEARLY adv every two years

BIZ n business

BIZARRE adj odd or unusual ▷n bizarre thing

BIZARRELY > BIZARRE

BIZARRES > BIZARRE

BIZARRO n bizarre person

BIZARROS > BIZARRO

BIZAZZ same as > PIZAZZ

BIZAZZES > BIZAZZ

BIZCACHA same as > VISCACHA

BIZCACHAS > BIZCACHA

BIZE n dry, cold wind in France

BIZES > BIZE

BIZNAGA same as > BISNAGA

BIZNAGAS > BIZNAGA

BIZONAL > BIZONE

BIZONE n place comprising two zones

BIZONES > BIZONE

BIZZES > BIZ

BIZZIES > BIZZY

BIZZO n empty and irrelevant talk or ideas

BIZZOS > BIZZO

BIZZY n policeman

BLAB vb reveal (secrets) indiscreetly

BLABBED > BLAB

BLABBER vb talk without thinking ▷n person who blabs

BLABBERED > BLABBER

BLABBERS > BLABBER

BLABBING > BLAB

BLABBINGS > BLAB

BLABBY adj talking too much; indiscreet

BLABS > BLAB

BLACK adj of the darkest colour, like coal ▷n darkest colour ▷vb make black

BLACKBALL vb exclude from a group ▷n hard boiled sweet with black-and-white stripes

BLACKBAND n type of iron ore

BLACKBIRD n common European thrush ▷vb (formerly) to kidnap and sell into slavery

BLACKBODY n hypothetical body that would be capable of absorbing all the electromagnetic radiation falling on it

BLACKBOY n grass tree

BLACKBOYS > BLACKBOY

BLACKBUCK n Indian antelope, Antilope cervicapra, the male of which has spiral horns, a dark back, and a white belly

BLACKBUTT n Australian eucalyptus tree with hard wood used as timber

BLACKCAP n brownish-grey warbler, the male of which has a black crown

BLACKCAPS > BLACKCAP

BLACKCOCK n male of the black grouse

BLACKDAMP n air that is low in oxygen content and high in carbon dioxide as a result of an explosion in a mine

BLACKED > BLACK

BLACKEN vb make or become black

BLACKENED > BLACKEN

BLACKENER > BLACKEN

BLACKENS > BLACKEN

BLACKER > BLACK

BLACKEST > BLACK

BLACKFACE n performer made up to imitate a Black person

BLACKFIN n type of tuna

BLACKFINS > BLACKFIN

BLACKFISH n small dark Australian estuary fish

BLACKFLY n black aphid, Aphis fabae, that infests beans, sugar beet, and other plants

BLACKGAME n large N European grouse

BLACKGUM n US tree

BLACKGUMS > BLACKGUM

BLACKHEAD n black-tipped plug of fatty matter clogging a skin pore

BLACKING n preparation for giving a black finish to

shoes, metals, etc

BLACKINGS > BLACKING

BLACKISH > BLACK

BLACKJACK n pontoon or a similar card game ▷vb hit with or as if with a kind of truncheon

BLACKLAND n dark soil

BLACKLEAD another name for > GRAPHITE

BLACKLEG n person who continues to work during a strike ▷vb refuse to join a strike

BLACKLEGS > BLACKLEG

BLACKLIST n list of people or organizations considered untrustworthy etc ▷vb put on a blacklist

BLACKLY > BLACK

BLACKMAIL n act of attempting to extort money by threats ▷vb (attempt to) obtain money by blackmail

BLACKNESS > BLACK

BLACKOUT n extinguishing of all light as a precaution against an air attack

BLACKOUTS > BLACKOUT

BLACKPOLL n North American warbler, Dendroica striata, the male of which has a black-and-white head

BLACKS > BLACK

BLACKTAIL n variety of mule deer having a black tail

BLACKTOP n bituminous mixture used for paving

BLACKTOPS > BLACKTOP

BLACKWASH n wash for colouring a surface black

BLACKWOOD n tall Australian acacia tree, A. melanoxylon, having small clusters of flowers and curved pods and yielding highly valued black timber

BLAD same as > BLAUD

BLADDED > BLAD

BLADDER n sac in the body where urine is held

BLADDERED adj intoxicated

BLADDERS > BLADDER

BLADDERY > BLADDER

BLADDING > BLAD

BLADE n cutting edge of a weapon or tool

BLADED > BLADE

BLADELESS > BLADE

BLADELIKE > BLADE

BLADER n person skating with in-line skates

BLADERS > BLADER

BLADES > BLADE

BLADEWORK n rowing technique

BLADING n act or instance of skating with in-line skates

BLADINGS > BLADING

BLADS > BLAD

BLADY as in blady grass coarse leafy Australasian grass

BLAE *adj* bluish-grey

BLAEBERRY *another name for* > BILBERRY

BLAER > BLAE

BLAES *n* hardened clay or shale, esp when crushed and used to form the top layer of a sports pitch: bluish-grey or reddish in colour

BLAEST > BLAE

BLAFF *n* West Indian stew

BLAFFS > BLAFF

BLAG *vb* obtain by wheedling or cadging ▷ *n* robbery, esp with violence

BLAGGED > BLAG

BLAGGER > BLAG

BLAGGERS > BLAG

BLAGGING > BLAG

BLAGGINGS > BLAG

BLAGS > BLAG

BLAGUE *n* pretentious but empty talk

BLAGUER > BLAGUE

BLAGUERS > BLAGUE

BLAGUES > BLAGUE

BLAGUEUR *n* bluffer

BLAGUEURS > BLAGUEUR

BLAH *n* worthless or silly talk ▷ *adj* uninteresting ▷ *vb* talk nonsense or boringly

BLAHED > BLAH

BLAHING > BLAH

BLAHS > BLAH

BLAIN *n* blister, blotch, or sore on the skin

BLAINS > BLAIN

BLAISE *same as* > BLAES

BLAIZE *same as* > BLAES

BLAM *n* representation of the sound of a bullet being fired

BLAMABLE > BLAME

BLAMABLY > BLAME

BLAME *vb* consider (someone) responsible ▷ *n* responsibility for something that is wrong

BLAMEABLE > BLAME

BLAMEABLY > BLAME

BLAMED *euphemistic word for* > DAMNED

BLAMEFUL *adj* deserving blame

BLAMELESS *adj* free from blame

BLAMER > BLAME

BLAMERS > BLAME

BLAMES > BLAME

BLAMING > BLAME

BLAMS > BLAM

BLANCH *vb* become white or pale

BLANCHED > BLANCH

BLANCHER > BLANCH

BLANCHERS > BLANCH

BLANCHES > BLANCH

BLANCHING > BLANCH

BLANCO *n* whitening substance ▷ *vb* whiten (something) with blanco

BLANCOED > BLANCO

BLANCOING > BLANCO

BLANCOS > BLANCO

BLAND *adj* dull and uninteresting ▷ *n* bland thing

BLANDER > BLAND

BLANDEST > BLAND

BLANDISH *vb* persuade by mild flattery

BLANDLY > BLAND

BLANDNESS > BLAND

BLANDS > BLAND

BLANK *adj* not written on ▷ *n* empty space ▷ *vb* cross out, blot, or obscure

BLANKED > BLANK

BLANKER > BLANK

BLANKEST > BLANK

BLANKET *n* large thick cloth used as covering for a bed ▷ *adj* applying to a wide group of people, situations, conditions, etc ▷ *vb* cover as with a blanket

BLANKETED > BLANKET

BLANKETS > BLANKET

BLANKETY *adv* euphemism for any taboo word

BLANKIES > BLANKY

BLANKING > BLANK

BLANKINGS > BLANK

BLANKLY > BLANK

BLANKNESS > BLANK

BLANKS > BLANK

BLANKY *n* comfort blanket

BLANQUET *n* variety of pear

BLANQUETS > BLANQUET

BLARE *vb* sound loudly and harshly ▷ *n* loud harsh noise

BLARED > BLARE

BLARES > BLARE

BLARING > BLARE

BLARNEY *n* flattering talk ▷ *vb* cajole with flattery

BLARNEYED > BLARNEY

BLARNEYS > BLARNEY

BLART *vb* sound loudly and harshly

BLARTED > BLART

BLARTING > BLART

BLARTS > BLART

BLASE *adj* indifferent or bored through familiarity

BLASH *n* splash

BLASHES > BLASH

BLASHIER > BLASHY

BLASHIEST > BLASHY

BLASHY *adj* windy and rainy

BLASPHEME *vb* speak disrespectfully of (God or sacred things)

BLASPHEMY *n* behaviour or language that shows disrespect for God or sacred things

BLAST *n* explosion ▷ *vb* blow up (a rock etc) with explosives ▷ *interj* expression of annoyance

BLASTED *adv* extreme or extremely ▷ *adj* blighted or withered

BLASTEMA *n* mass of undifferentiated animal cells that will develop into an organ or tissue: present at the site of regeneration of a lost part

BLASTEMAL > BLASTEMA

BLASTEMAS > BLASTEMA

BLASTEMIC > BLASTEMA

BLASTER > BLAST

BLASTERS > BLAST

BLASTIE *n* ugly creature

BLASTIER > BLASTY

BLASTIES > BLASTIE

BLASTIEST > BLASTY

BLASTING *n* distortion of sound caused by overloading certain components of a radio system

BLASTINGS > BLASTING

BLASTMENT *n* something that frustrates one's plans

BLASTOFF *n* launching of a rocket

BLASTOFFS > BLASTOFF

BLASTOID *n* extinct echinoderm found in fossil form

BLASTOIDS > BLASTOID

BLASTOMA *n* tumour composed of embryonic tissue that has not yet developed a specialized function

BLASTOMAS > BLASTOMA

BLASTOPOR *n* opening of the archenteron in the gastrula that develops into the anus of some animals

BLASTS > BLAST

BLASTULA *n* early form of an animal embryo that develops from a morula, consisting of a sphere of cells with a central cavity

BLASTULAE > BLASTULA

BLASTULAR > BLASTULA

BLASTULAS > BLASTULA

BLASTY *adj* gusty

BLAT *vb* cry out or bleat like a sheep

BLATANCY > BLATANT

BLATANT *adj* glaringly obvious

BLATANTLY > BLATANT

BLATE *adj* shy; ill at ease

BLATER > BLATE

BLATEST > BLATE

BLATHER *vb* speak foolishly ▷ *n* foolish talk

BLATHERED > BLATHER

BLATHERER > BLATHER

BLATHERS > BLATHER

BLATS > BLAT

BLATT *n* newspaper

BLATTANT *same as* > BLATANT

BLATTED > BLAT

BLATTER *n, vb* prattle

BLATTERED > BLATTER

BLATTERS > BLATTER

BLATTING > BLAT

BLATTS > BLATT

BLAUBOK *n* South African antelope

BLAUBOKS > BLAUBOK

BLAUD *vb* slap

BLAUDED > BLAUD

BLAUDING > BLAUD

BLAUDS > BLAUD

BLAW *vb* blow

BLAWED > BLAW

BLAWING > BLAW

BLAWN > BLAW

BLAWORT *n* harebell

BLAWORTS > BLAWORT

BLAWS > BLAW

BLAY *n* small river fish

BLAYS > BLAY

BLAZE *n* strong fire or flame ▷ *vb* burn or shine brightly

BLAZED > BLAZE

BLAZER *n* lightweight jacket, often in the colours of a school etc

BLAZERED > BLAZER

BLAZERS > BLAZER

BLAZES *pl n* hell

BLAZING > BLAZE

BLAZINGLY > BLAZING

BLAZON *vb* proclaim publicly ▷ *n* coat of arms

BLAZONED > BLAZON

BLAZONER > BLAZON

BLAZONERS > BLAZON

BLAZONING > BLAZON

BLAZONRY *n* art or process of describing heraldic arms in proper form

BLAZONS > BLAZON

BLEACH *vb* make or become white or colourless ▷ *n* bleaching agent

BLEACHED > BLEACH

BLEACHER > BLEACH

BLEACHERS *pl n* tier of seats in a sports stadium, etc, that are unroofed and inexpensive

BLEACHERY *n* place where bleaching is carried out

BLEACHES > BLEACH

BLEACHING > BLEACH

BLEAK *adj* exposed and barren ▷ *n* any slender silvery European cyprinid fish of the genus *Alburnus*, esp *A. lucidus*, occurring in slow-flowing rivers

BLEAKER > BLEAK

BLEAKEST > BLEAK

BLEAKISH > BLEAK

BLEAKLY > BLEAK

BLEAKNESS > BLEAK

BLEAKS > BLEAK

BLEAKY *same as* > BLEAK

BLEAR *vb* make (eyes or sight) dim with or as if with tears ▷ *adj* bleary

BLEARED > BLEAR

BLEARER > BLEAR

BLEAREST > BLEAR

BLEAREYED *adj* with eyes blurred, as with old age or after waking

BLEARIER > BLEARY

BLEARIEST > BLEARY

BLEARILY > BLEARY

BLEARING > BLEAR

BLEARS > BLEAR

BLEARY *adj* with eyes dimmed, as by tears or tiredness

BLEAT *vb* (of a sheep, goat, or calf) utter its plaintive cry ▷ *n* cry of sheep, goats, and calves

BLEATED > BLEAT

BLEATER > BLEAT

BLEATERS > BLEAT

BLEATING > BLEAT
BLEATINGS > BLEAT
BLEATS > BLEAT
BLEB *n* fluid-filled blister on the skin
BLEBBIER > BLEB
BLEBBIEST > BLEB
BLEBBING *n* formation of bleb
BLEBBINGS > BLEB
BLEBBY > BLEB
BLEBS > BLEB
BLED > BLEED
BLEE *n* complexion; hue
BLEED *vb* lose or emit blood
BLEEDER *n* despicable person
BLEEDERS > BLEEDER
BLEEDING > BLEED
BLEEDINGS > BLEED
BLEEDS > BLEED
BLEEP *n* high-pitched signal or beep ▷ *vb* make such a noise
BLEEPED > BLEEP
BLEEPER *n* small portable radio receiver that makes a bleeping signal
BLEEPERS > BLEEPER
BLEEPING > BLEEP
BLEEPS > BLEEP
BLEES > BLEE
BLELLUM *n* babbler; blusterer
BLELLUMS > BLELLUM
BLEMISH *n* defect or stain ▷ *vb* spoil or tarnish
BLEMISHED > BLEMISH
BLEMISHER > BLEMISH
BLEMISHES > BLEMISH
BLENCH *vb* shy away, as in fear
BLENCHED > BLENCH
BLENCHER > BLENCH
BLENCHERS > BLENCH
BLENCHES > BLENCH
BLENCHING > BLENCH
BLEND *vb* mix or mingle (components or ingredients) ▷ *n* mixture
BLENDE *n* mineral consisting mainly of zinc sulphide
BLENDED > BLEND
BLENDER *n* electrical appliance for puréeing vegetables etc
BLENDERS > BLENDER
BLENDES > BLENDE
BLENDING > BLEND
BLENDINGS > BLEND
BLENDS > BLEND
BLENNIES > BLENNY
BLENNIOID *adj* of, relating to, or belonging to the *Blennioidea*, a large suborder of small mainly marine spiny-finned fishes having an elongated body with reduced pelvic fins. The group includes the blennies, butterfish, and gunnel ▷ *n* any fish belonging to the *Blennioidea*
BLENNY *n* small fish with a tapering scaleless body

BLENT *a past participle of* > BLEND
BLERT *n* foolish person
BLERTS > BLERT
BLESBOK *n* antelope, *Damaliscus dorcas* (or *albifrons*), of southern Africa. The coat is a deep reddish-brown with a white blaze between the eyes
BLESBOKS > BLESBOK
BLESBUCK *same as* > BLESBOK
BLESBUCKS > BLESBUCK
BLESS *vb* make holy by means of a religious rite
BLESSED > BLESS
BLESSEDER > BLESS
BLESSEDLY > BLESS
BLESSER > BLESS
BLESSERS > BLESS
BLESSES > BLESS
BLESSING > BLESS
BLESSINGS > BLESS
BLEST > BLESS
BLET *n* state of softness or decay in certain fruits, such as the medlar, brought about by overripening ▷ *vb* go soft
BLETHER *same as* > BLATHER
BLETHERED > BLETHER
BLETHERER > BLETHER
BLETHERS > BLETHER
BLETS > BLET
BLETTED > BLET
BLETTING > BLET
BLEUATRE *adj* blueish
BLEW > BLOW
BLEWART *same as* > BLAWORT
BLEWARTS > BLEWART
BLEWITS *n* edible saprotroph agaricaceous fungus, *Tricholoma saevum*, having a pale brown cap and bluish stalk
BLEWITSES > BLEWITS
BLEY *same as* > BLAY
BLEYS > BLEY
BLIGHT *n* person or thing that spoils or prevents growth ▷ *vb* cause to suffer a blight
BLIGHTED > BLIGHT
BLIGHTER *n* irritating person
BLIGHTERS > BLIGHTER
BLIGHTIES > BLIGHTY
BLIGHTING > BLIGHT
BLIGHTS > BLIGHT
BLIGHTY *n* home country; home leave
BLIKSEM *interj* South African expression of surprise
BLIMBING *same as* > BILIMBI
BLIMBINGS > BLIMBING
BLIMEY *interj* exclamation of surprise or annoyance
BLIMP *n* small airship
BLIMPISH *adj* complacent and reactionary
BLIMPS > BLIMP
BLIMY *same as* > BLIMEY
BLIN *Scots word for* > BLIND
BLIND *adj* unable to see

▷ *vb* deprive of sight ▷ *n* covering for a window
BLINDAGE *n* (esp formerly) a protective screen or structure, as over a trench
BLINDAGES > BLINDAGE
BLINDED > BLIND
BLINDER *same as* > BLIND
BLINDERS > BLIND
BLINDEST > BLIND
BLINDFISH *n* any of various small fishes, esp the cavefish, that have rudimentary or functionless eyes and occur in subterranean streams
BLINDFOLD *vb* prevent (a person) from seeing by covering the eyes ▷ *n* piece of cloth used to cover the eyes ▷ *adv* with the eyes covered by a cloth
BLINDGUT *same as* > CAECUM
BLINDGUTS > BLINDGUT
BLINDING *n* sand or grit spread over a road surface to fill up cracks ▷ *adj* making one blind or as if blind
BLINDINGS > BLINDING
BLINDLESS > BLIND
BLINDLY > BLIND
BLINDNESS > BLIND
BLINDS > BLIND
BLINDSIDE *vb* take (someone) by surprise
BLINDWORM *same as* > SLOWWORM
BLING *adj* flashy ▷ *n* ostentatious jewellery
BLINGER > BLING
BLINGEST > BLING
BLINGING *adj* flashy and expensive
BLINGLISH *n* spoken English mixed with Black slang
BLINGS > BLING
BLINI *pl n* Russian pancakes made of buckwheat flour and yeast
BLINIS *same as* > BLINI
BLINK *vb* close and immediately reopen (the eyes) ▷ *n* act of blinking
BLINKARD *n* something that twinkles
BLINKARDS > BLINKARD
BLINKED > BLINK
BLINKER *vb* provide (a horse) with blinkers ▷ *n* flashing light for sending messages, as a warning device, etc, such as a direction indicator on a road vehicle
BLINKERED *adj* considering only a narrow point of view
BLINKERS > BLIND
BLINKING *adv* extreme or extremely
BLINKS > BLINK
BLINNED > BLIN
BLINNING > BLIN
BLINS > BLIN
BLINTZ *n* thin pancake

folded over a filling usually of apple, cream cheese, or meat
BLINTZE *same as* > BLINTZ
BLINTZES > BLINTZE
BLINY *same as* > BLINI
BLIP *n* spot of light on a radar screen indicating the position of an object ▷ *vb* produce such a noise
BLIPPED > BLIP
BLIPPING > BLIP
BLIPS > BLIP
BLIPVERT *n* very short television advertisement
BLIPVERTS > BLIPVERT
BLISS *n* perfect happiness ▷ *vb* make or become perfectly happy
BLISSED > BLISS
BLISSES > BLISS
BLISSFUL *adj* serenely joyful or glad
BLISSING > BLISS
BLISSLESS > BLISS
BLIST *archaic form of* > BLESSED
BLISTER *n* small bubble on the skin ▷ *vb* (cause to) have blisters
BLISTERED > BLISTER
BLISTERS > BLISTER
BLISTERY > BLISTER
BLITE *n* type of herb
BLITES > BLITE
BLITHE *adj* casual and indifferent
BLITHEFUL *same as* > BLITHE
BLITHELY > BLITHE
BLITHER *same as* > BLETHER
BLITHERED > BLITHER
BLITHERS > BLITHER
BLITHEST > BLITHE
BLITZ *n* violent and sustained attack by aircraft ▷ *vb* attack suddenly and intensively
BLITZED > BLITZ
BLITZER > BLITZ
BLITZERS > BLITZ
BLITZES > BLITZ
BLITZING > BLITZ
BLIVE *same as* > BELIVE
BLIZZARD *n* blinding storm of wind and snow
BLIZZARDS > BLIZZARD
BLIZZARDY > BLIZZARD
BLOAT *vb* cause to swell, as with liquid or air ▷ *n* abnormal distention of the abdomen in cattle, sheep, etc, caused by accumulation of gas in the stomach
BLOATED *adj* swollen, as with a liquid, air, or wind
BLOATER *n* salted smoked herring
BLOATERS > BLOATER
BLOATING > BLOAT
BLOATINGS > BLOAT
BLOATS > BLOAT
BLOATWARE *n* software with more features than necessary
BLOB *n* soft mass or drop

▷ *vb* put blobs, as of ink or paint, on

BLOBBED > BLOB

BLOBBIER > BLOB

BLOBBIEST > BLOB

BLOBBING > BLOB

BLOBBY > BLOB

BLOBS > BLOB

BLOC *n* people or countries combined by a common interest

BLOCK *n* large solid piece of wood, stone, etc ▷ *vb* obstruct or impede by introducing an obstacle

BLOCKABLE > BLOCK

BLOCKADE *n* sealing off of a place to prevent the passage of goods ▷ *vb* impose a blockade on

BLOCKADED > BLOCKADE

BLOCKADER > BLOCKADE

BLOCKADES > BLOCKADE

BLOCKAGE *n* act of blocking or state of being blocked

BLOCKAGES > BLOCKAGE

BLOCKBUST *vb* (try to) bring about the sale of property at a bargain price by stirring up fears of racial change in an area

BLOCKED *adj* functionally impeded by amphetamine

BLOCKER *n* person or thing that blocks

BLOCKERS > BLOCKER

BLOCKHEAD *n* stupid person

BLOCKHOLE *n* lines marked near stumps on cricket pitch

BLOCKIE *n* owner of a small property, esp a farm

BLOCKIER > BLOCKY

BLOCKIES > BLOCKIE

BLOCKIEST > BLOCKY

BLOCKING *n* interruption of anode current in a valve because of the application of a high negative voltage to the grid

BLOCKINGS > BLOCKING

BLOCKISH *adj* lacking vivacity or imagination

BLOCKS > BLOCK

BLOCKWORK *n* wall-building style

BLOCKY *adj* like a block, esp in shape and solidity

BLOCS > BLOC

BLOG *n* journal written on-line and accessible to users of the internet

BLOGGER > BLOG

BLOGGERS > BLOG

BLOGGING > BLOG

BLOGGINGS > BLOG

BLOGS > BLOG

BLOKE *n* man

BLOKEDOM *n* state of being a bloke

BLOKEDOMS > BLOKEDOM

BLOKEISH *adj* denoting or exhibiting the characteristics believed typical of an ordinary man

BLOKES > BLOKE

BLOKEY *same as* > BLOKEISH

BLOKIER > BLOKEY

BLOKIEST > BLOKEY

BLOKISH *same as* > BLOKEISH

BLONCKET *adj* blue-grey

BLOND *adj* (of men's hair) of a light colour ▷ *n* person, esp a man, having light-coloured hair and skin

BLONDE *n* fair-haired (person) ▷ *adj* (of hair) fair

BLONDER > BLONDE

BLONDES > BLONDE

BLONDEST > BLONDE

BLONDINE *vb* dye hair blonde

BLONDINED > BLONDINE

BLONDINES > BLONDINE

BLONDING *n* act or an instance of dyeing hair blonde

BLONDINGS > BLONDING

BLONDISH > BLOND

BLONDNESS > BLOND

BLONDS > BLOND

BLOOD *n* red fluid that flows around the body ▷ *vb* initiate (a person) to war or hunting

BLOODBATH *n* massacre

BLOODED *adj* (of horses, cattle, etc) of good breeding

BLOODFIN *n* silvery red-finned South American freshwater fish, *Aphyocharax rubripinnis* : a popular aquarium fish: family *Characidae* (characins)

BLOODFINS > BLOODFIN

BLOODHEAT *n* normal human body temperature

BLOODIED > BLOODY

BLOODIER > BLOODY

BLOODIES > BLOODY

BLOODIEST > BLOODY

BLOODILY > BLOODY

BLOODING > BLOOD

BLOODINGS > BLOOD

BLOODLESS *adj* without blood or bloodshed

BLOODLIKE > BLOOD

BLOODLINE *n* all the members of a family group over generations, esp regarding characteristics common to that group

BLOODLUST *n* desire to see bloodshed

BLOODRED *adj* having a deep red colour

BLOODROOT *n* North American papaveraceous plant, *Sanguinaria canadensis*, having a single whitish flower and a fleshy red root that yields a red dye

BLOODS > BLOOD

BLOODSHED *n* slaughter or killing

BLOODSHOT *adj* (of an eye) inflamed

BLOODWOOD *n* any of several species of Australian eucalyptus that exude a red sap

BLOODWORM *n* red wormlike aquatic larva of the midge, *Chironomus plumosus*, which lives at the bottom of stagnant pools and ditches

BLOODWORT *n* plant with red dye in roots

BLOODY *adj* covered with blood ▷ *adv* extreme or extremely ▷ *vb* stain with blood

BLOODYING > BLOODY

BLOOEY *adj* out of order; faulty

BLOOIE *same as* > BLOOEY

BLOOM *n* blossom on a flowering plant ▷ *vb* (of flowers) open

BLOOMED *adj* (of a lens) coated with a thin film of magnesium fluoride or some other substance to reduce the amount of light lost by reflection

BLOOMER *n* stupid mistake

BLOOMERS *pl n* woman's baggy knickers

BLOOMERY *n* place in which malleable iron is produced directly from iron ore

BLOOMIER > BLOOMY

BLOOMIEST > BLOOMY

BLOOMING *adj* extreme or extremely

BLOOMLESS > BLOOM

BLOOMS > BLOOM

BLOOMY *adj* having a fine whitish coating on the surface, such as on the rind of a cheese

BLOOP *vb* (baseball) hit a ball into air beyond infield

BLOOPED > BLOOP

BLOOPER *n* stupid mistake

BLOOPERS > BLOOPER

BLOOPING > BLOOP

BLOOPS > BLOOP

BLOOSME *same as* > BLOSSOM

BLOOSMED > BLOOSME

BLOOSMES > BLOOSME

BLOOSMING > BLOOSME

BLOQUISTE *n* supporter of autonomy for Quebec

BLORE *n* strong blast of wind

BLORES > BLORE

BLOSSOM *n* flowers of a plant ▷ *vb* (of plants) flower

BLOSSOMED > BLOSSOM

BLOSSOMS > BLOSSOM

BLOSSOMY > BLOSSOM

BLOT *n* spot or stain ▷ *vb* cause a blemish in or on

BLOTCH *n* discoloured area or stain ▷ *vb* become or cause to become marked by such discoloration

BLOTCHED > BLOTCH

BLOTCHES > BLOTCH

BLOTCHIER > BLOTCHY

BLOTCHILY > BLOTCHY

BLOTCHING > BLOTCH

BLOTCHY *adj* covered in or marked by blotches

BLOTLESS > BLOT

BLOTS > BLOT

BLOTTED > BLOT

BLOTTER *n* sheet of blotting paper

BLOTTERS > BLOTTER

BLOTTIER > BLOTTY

BLOTTIEST > BLOTTY

BLOTTING *n* blot analysis

BLOTTINGS > BLOTTING

BLOTTO *adj* extremely drunk

BLOTTY *adj* covered in blots

BLOUBOK *same as* > BLAUBOK

BLOUBOKS > BLOUBOK

BLOUSE *n* woman's shirtlike garment ▷ *vb* hang or cause to hang in full loose folds

BLOUSED > BLOUSE

BLOUSES > BLOUSE

BLOUSIER > BLOUSY

BLOUSIEST > BLOUSY

BLOUSILY > BLOUSY

BLOUSING > BLOUSE

BLOUSON *n* short loose jacket with a tight waist

BLOUSONS > BLOUSON

BLOUSY *adj* loose; blouse-like

BLOVIATE *vb* discourse at length

BLOVIATED > BLOVIATE

BLOVIATES > BLOVIATE

BLOW *vb* (of air, the wind, etc) move ▷ *n* hard hit

BLOWBACK *n* escape to the rear of gases formed during the firing of a weapon or in a boiler, internal-combustion engine, etc

BLOWBACKS > BLOWBACK

BLOWBALL *n* dandelion seed head

BLOWBALLS > BLOWBALL

BLOWBY *n* leakage of gas past the piston of an engine at maximum pressure

BLOWBYS > BLOWBY

BLOWDOWN *n* accident in a nuclear reactor in which a cooling pipe bursts causing the loss of essential coolant

BLOWDOWNS > BLOWDOWN

BLOWED > BLOW

BLOWER *n* mechanical device, such as a fan, that blows

BLOWERS > BLOWER

BLOWFISH *a popular name for* > PUFFER

BLOWFLIES > BLOWFLY

BLOWFLY *n* fly that lays its eggs in meat

BLOWGUN *same as* > BLOWPIPE

BLOWGUNS > BLOWGUN

BLOWHARD *n* boastful person ▷ *adj* blustering or boastful

BLOWHARDS > BLOWHARD

BLOWHOLE *n* nostril of a whale

BLOWHOLES > BLOWHOLE

BLOWIE *n* bluebottle

BLOWIER > BLOWY

BLOWIES > BLOWIE

b

BLOWIEST > BLOWY
BLOWINESS > BLOWY
BLOWING > BLOW
BLOWJOB *slang term for* > FELLATIO
BLOWJOBS > BLOWJOB
BLOWKART *n* land vehicle with a sail
BLOWKARTS > BLOWKART
BLOWLAMP *another name for* > BLOWTORCH
BLOWLAMPS > BLOWLAMP
BLOWN > BLOW
BLOWOFF *n* discharge of a surplus fluid
BLOWOFFS > BLOWOFF
BLOWOUT *n* sudden loss of air in a tyre
BLOWOUTS > BLOWOUT
BLOWPIPE *n* long tube from which darts etc are shot by blowing
BLOWPIPES > BLOWPIPE
BLOWS > BLOW
BLOWSE *n* large, red-faced woman
BLOWSED *same as* > BLOWSY
BLOWSES > BLOWSE
BLOWSIER > BLOWSY
BLOWSIEST > BLOWSY
BLOWSILY > BLOWSY
BLOWSY *adj* fat, untidy, and red-faced
BLOWTORCH *n* small burner producing a very hot flame
BLOWTUBE *n* tube for blowing air or oxygen into a flame to intensify its heat
BLOWTUBES > BLOWTUBE
BLOWUP *n* fit of temper
BLOWUPS > BLOWUP
BLOWY *adj* windy
BLOWZE *variant of* > BLOWSE
BLOWZED *same as* > BLOWSY
BLOWZES > BLOWZE
BLOWZIER > BLOWZY
BLOWZIEST > BLOWZY
BLOWZILY > BLOWZY
BLOWZY *same as* > BLOWSY
BLUB *a slang word for* > BLUBBER
BLUBBED > BLUB
BLUBBER *n, vb* sob without restraint ▷ *adj* swollen or fleshy ▷ *n* fat of whales, seals, etc
BLUBBERED > BLUBBER
BLUBBERER > BLUBBER
BLUBBERS > BLUBBER
BLUBBERY *adj* of, containing, or like blubber
BLUBBING > BLUB
BLUBS > BLUB
BLUCHER *n* high shoe with laces over the tongue
BLUCHERS > BLUCHER
BLUDE *Scots form of* > BLOOD
BLUDES > BLUDE
BLUDGE *vb* evade work ▷ *n* easy task
BLUDGED > BLUDGE
BLUDGEON *n* short thick club ▷ *vb* hit with a bludgeon
BLUDGEONS > BLUDGEON
BLUDGER *n* person who scrounges
BLUDGERS > BLUDGER

BLUDGES > BLUDGE
BLUDGING > BLUDGE
BLUDIE *Scots form of* > BLOODY
BLUDIER > BLUDIE
BLUDIEST > BLUDIE
BLUDY *same as* > BLUDIE
BLUE *n* colour of a clear unclouded sky ▷ *adj* of the colour blue ▷ *vb* make or become blue
BLUEBACK *n* type of salmon
BLUEBACKS > BLUEBACK
BLUEBALL *n* type of European herb
BLUEBALLS > BLUEBALL
BLUEBEARD *n* any man who murders his wife or wives
BLUEBEAT *n* type of West Indian pop music of the 1960s
BLUEBEATS > BLUEBEAT
BLUEBELL *n* flower with blue bell-shaped flowers
BLUEBELLS > BLUEBELL
BLUEBERRY *n* very small blackish edible fruit that grows on a North American shrub
BLUEBILL *another name for* > SCAUP
BLUEBILLS > BLUEBILL
BLUEBIRD *n* North American songbird with a blue plumage
BLUEBIRDS > BLUEBIRD
BLUEBLOOD *n* royal or aristocratic person
BLUEBOOK *n* (in Britain) a government publication, usually the report of a commission
BLUEBOOKS > BLUEBOOK
BLUEBUCK *same as* > BLAUBOK
BLUEBUCKS > BLUEBUCK
BLUEBUSH *n* any of various blue-grey herbaceous Australian shrubs of the genus *Maireana*
BLUECAP *another name for* > BLUETIT
BLUECAPS > BLUECAP
BLUECOAT *n* person who wears blue uniform
BLUECOATS > BLUECOAT
BLUECURLS *n* North American plant
BLUED > BLUE
BLUEFIN *another name for* > TUNNY
BLUEFINS > BLUEFIN
BLUEFISH *n* bluish marine percoid food and game fish, *Pomatomus saltatrix*, related to the horse mackerel: family *Pomatomidae*
BLUEGILL *n* common North American freshwater sunfish, *Lepomis macrochirus*: an important food and game fish
BLUEGILLS > BLUEGILL
BLUEGOWN *n* in past, pauper, recipient of blue gown on King's birthday
BLUEGOWNS > BLUEGOWN

BLUEGRASS *n* any of several North American bluish-green grasses
BLUEGUM *n* tall fast-growing widely cultivated Australian myrtaceous tree, *Eucalyptus globulus*, having aromatic leaves containing a medicinal oil, bark that peels off in shreds, and hard timber
BLUEGUMS > BLUEGUM
BLUEHEAD *n* type of fish
BLUEHEADS > BLUEHEAD
BLUEING > BLUE
BLUEINGS > BLUE
BLUEISH *same as* > BLUISH
BLUEJACK *n* type of oak tree
BLUEJACKS > BLUEJACK
BLUEJAY *n* common North American jay, *Cyanocitta cristata*, having bright blue plumage with greyish-white underparts
BLUEJAYS > BLUEJAY
BLUEJEANS *n* blue denim jeans
BLUELINE *n* blue-toned photographic proof
BLUELINER *n* machine for making blueprints
BLUELINES > BLUELINE
BLUELY > BLUE
BLUENESS > BLUE
BLUENOSE *n* puritanical or prudish person
BLUENOSED > BLUENOSE
BLUENOSES > BLUENOSE
BLUEPOINT *n* type of small oyster
BLUEPRINT *n* photographic print of a plan ▷ *vb* make a blueprint of (a plan)
BLUER > BLUE
BLUES *pl n* type of music
BLUESHIFT *n* shift in the spectral lines of a stellar spectrum
BLUESIER > BLUES
BLUESIEST > BLUES
BLUESMAN *n* blues musician
BLUESMEN > BLUESMAN
BLUEST > BLUE
BLUESTEM *n* type of tall grass
BLUESTEMS > BLUESTEM
BLUESTONE *n* blue-grey sandstone containing much clay, used for building and paving
BLUESY > BLUES
BLUET *n* North American rubiaceous plant, *Houstonia caerulea*, with small four-petalled blue flowers
BLUETICK *n* fast-running dog
BLUETICKS > BLUETICK
BLUETIT *n* small European bird with a blue crown, wings, and tail and yellow underparts
BLUETITS > BLUETIT
BLUETS > BLUET
BLUETTE *n* short, brilliant piece of music

BLUETTES > BLUETTE
BLUEWEED *n* Eurasian boraginaceous weed, *Echium vulgare*, having blue flowers and pink buds
BLUEWEEDS > BLUEWEED
BLUEWING *n* type of duck
BLUEWINGS > BLUEWING
BLUEWOOD *n* type of Mexican shrub
BLUEWOODS > BLUEWOOD
BLUEY *adj* bluish ▷ *n* informal Australian word meaning blanket
BLUEYS > BLUEY
BLUFF *vb* pretend to be confident in order to influence (someone) ▷ *n* act of bluffing ▷ *adj* good-naturedly frank and hearty
BLUFFABLE > BLUFF
BLUFFED > BLUFF
BLUFFER > BLUFF
BLUFFERS > BLUFF
BLUFFEST > BLUFF
BLUFFING > BLUFF
BLUFFLY > BLUFF
BLUFFNESS > BLUFF
BLUFFS > BLUFF
BLUGGIER > BLUGGY
BLUGGIEST > BLUGGY
BLUGGY *same as* > BLOODY
BLUID *Scots word for* > BLOOD
BLUIDIER > BLUID
BLUIDIEST > BLUID
BLUIDS > BLUID
BLUIDY > BLUID
BLUIER > BLUEY
BLUIEST > BLUEY
BLUING > BLUE
BLUINGS > BLUE
BLUISH *adj* slightly blue
BLUME *Scots word for* > BLOOM
BLUMED > BLUME
BLUMES > BLUME
BLUMING > BLUME
BLUNDER *n* clumsy mistake ▷ *vb* make a blunder
BLUNDERED > BLUNDER
BLUNDERER > BLUNDER
BLUNDERS > BLUNDER
BLUNGE *vb* mix (clay or a similar substance) with water in order to form a suspension for use in ceramics
BLUNGED > BLUNGE
BLUNGER *n* large vat in which the contents, esp clay and water, are mixed by rotating arms
BLUNGERS > BLUNGER
BLUNGES > BLUNGE
BLUNGING > BLUNGE
BLUNK *vb* ruin; botch
BLUNKED > BLUNK
BLUNKER > BLUNK
BLUNKERS > BLUNK
BLUNKING > BLUNK
BLUNKS > BLUNK
BLUNT *adj* not having a sharp edge or point ▷ *vb* make less sharp ▷ *n* cannabis cigarette
BLUNTED > BLUNT

BLUNTER > BLUNT
BLUNTEST > BLUNT
BLUNTHEAD n frequent user of marijuana
BLUNTING > BLUNT
BLUNTISH > BLUNT
BLUNTLY > BLUNT
BLUNTNESS > BLUNT
BLUNTS > BLUNT
BLUR vb make or become vague or less distinct ▷ n something vague, hazy, or indistinct
BLURB n promotional description, as on the jacket of a book ▷ vb describe or recommend in a blurb
BLURBED > BLURB
BLURBING > BLURB
BLURBIST n writer of blurbs
BLURBISTS > BLURBIST
BLURBS > BLURB
BLURRED > BLUR
BLURREDLY > BLUR
BLURRIER > BLUR
BLURRIEST > BLUR
BLURRILY > BLUR
BLURRING > BLUR
BLURRY > BLUR
BLURS > BLUR
BLURT vb utter suddenly and involuntarily
BLURTED > BLURT
BLURTER > BLURT
BLURTERS > BLURT
BLURTING > BLURT
BLURTINGS > BLURT
BLURTS > BLURT
BLUSH vb become red in the face, esp from embarrassment or shame ▷ n reddening of the face
BLUSHED > BLUSH
BLUSHER n cosmetic for giving the cheeks a rosy colour
BLUSHERS > BLUSHER
BLUSHES > BLUSH
BLUSHET n modest young woman
BLUSHETS > BLUSHET
BLUSHFUL > BLUSH
BLUSHING > BLUSH
BLUSHINGS > BLUSH
BLUSHLESS > BLUSH
BLUSTER vb speak loudly or in a bullying way ▷ n empty threats or protests
BLUSTERED > BLUSTER
BLUSTERER > BLUSTER
BLUSTERS > BLUSTER
BLUSTERY > BLUSTER
BLUSTROUS adj inclined to bluster
BLUTWURST n blood sausage
BLYPE n piece of skin peeled off after sunburn
BLYPES > BLYPE
BO interj, n exclamation uttered to startle or surprise someone, esp a child in a game
BOA n large nonvenomous snake
BOAB short for > BAOBAB
BOABS > BOAB

BOAK same as > BOKE
BOAKED > BOAK
BOAKING > BOAK
BOAKS > BOAK
BOAR n uncastrated male pig
BOARD n long flat piece of sawn timber ▷ vb go aboard (a train, aeroplane, etc)
BOARDABLE > BOARD
BOARDED > BOARD
BOARDER n person who pays rent in return for accommodation in someone else's home
BOARDERS > BOARDER
BOARDING n act of embarking on an aircraft, train, ship, etc
BOARDINGS > BOARDING
BOARDLIKE > BOARD
BOARDMAN n man who carries a sandwich board
BOARDMEN > BOARDMAN
BOARDROOM n room where the board of a company meets
BOARDS > BOARD
BOARDWALK n promenade, esp along a beach, usually made of planks
BOARFISH n any of various spiny-finned marine teleost fishes of the genera Capros, Antigonia, etc, related to the dories, having a deep compressed body, a long snout, and large eyes
BOARHOUND n dog used to hunt boar
BOARISH adj coarse, cruel, or sensual
BOARISHLY > BOARISH
BOARS > BOAR
BOART same as > BORT
BOARTS > BOART
BOAS > BOA
BOAST vb speak too proudly about one's talents etc ▷ n bragging statement
BOASTED > BOAST
BOASTER > BOAST
BOASTERS > BOAST
BOASTFUL adj tending to boast
BOASTING > BOAST
BOASTINGS > BOAST
BOASTLESS > BOAST
BOASTS > BOAST
BOAT n small vehicle for travelling across water ▷ vb travel in a boat
BOATABLE adj able to be carried by boat
BOATBILL n nocturnal tropical American wading bird, Cochlearius cochlearius, similar to the night herons but with a broad flattened bill: family Ardeidae, order Ciconiiformes
BOATBILLS > BOATBILL
BOATED > BOAT
BOATEL n waterside hotel catering for boating people
BOATELS > BOATEL

BOATER n flat straw hat
BOATERS > BOATER
BOATFUL > BOAT
BOATFULS > BOAT
BOATHOOK n pole with a hook at one end, used aboard a vessel for fending off other vessels or obstacles or for catching a line or mooring buoy
BOATHOOKS > BOATHOOK
BOATHOUSE n shelter by the edge of a river, lake, etc, for housing boats
BOATIE n boating enthusiast
BOATIES > BOATIE
BOATING n rowing, sailing, or cruising in boats as a form of recreation
BOATINGS > BOATING
BOATLIFT n evacuation by boat
BOATLIFTS > BOATLIFT
BOATLIKE > BOAT
BOATLOAD n amount of cargo or number of people held by a boat or ship
BOATLOADS > BOATLOAD
BOATMAN n man who works on, hires out, or repairs boats
BOATMEN > BOATMAN
BOATNECK n wide open neck on garment
BOATNECKS > BOATNECK
BOATS > BOAT
BOATSMAN same as > BOATMAN
BOATSMEN > BOATSMAN
BOATSWAIN n petty officer on a merchant ship or a warrant officer on a warship who is responsible for the maintenance of the ship and its equipment
BOATTAIL n type of blackbird
BOATTAILS > BOATTAIL
BOATYARD n place where boats are kept, repaired, etc
BOATYARDS > BOATYARD
BOB vb move or cause to move up and down repeatedly, as while floating in water ▷ n short abrupt movement, as of the head
BOBA n type of Chinese tea
BOBAC same as > BOBAK
BOBACS > BOBAC
BOBAK n type of marmot
BOBAKS > BOBAK
BOBAS > BOBA
BOBBED > BOB
BOBBEJAAN n baboon
BOBBER n type of float for fishing
BOBBERIES > BOBBERY
BOBBERS > BOBBER
BOBBERY n mixed pack of hunting dogs, often not belonging to any of the hound breeds ▷ adj noisy or excitable
BOBBIES > BOBBY
BOBBIN n reel on which

thread is wound
BOBBINET n netted fabric of hexagonal mesh, made on a lace machine
BOBBINETS > BOBBINET
BOBBING > BOB
BOBBINS > BOBBIN
BOBBISH > CHEERY
BOBBITT vb sever the penis of
BOBBITTED > BOBBITT
BOBBITTS > BOBBITT
BOBBLE n small ball of material, usu for decoration ▷ vb (of a ball) to bounce erratically because of an uneven playing surface
BOBBLED > BOBBLE
BOBBLES > BOBBLE
BOBBLIER > BOBBLY
BOBBLIEST > BOBBLY
BOBBLING > BOBBLE
BOBBLY adj (of fabric) covered in small balls; worn
BOBBY n policeman
BOBBYSOCK n ankle-length sock worn esp by teenage girls
BOBBYSOX pl n bobbysocks
BOBCAT n North American feline mammal, Lynx rufus, closely related to but smaller than the lynx, having reddish-brown fur with dark spots or stripes, tufted ears, and a short tail
BOBCATS > BOBCAT
BOBECHE n candle drip-catcher
BOBECHES > BOBECHE
BOBFLOAT n small buoyant float, usually consisting of a quill stuck through a piece of cork
BOBFLOATS > BOBFLOAT
BOBLET n two-man bobsleigh
BOBLETS > BOBLET
BOBOL n fraud carried out by one or more persons with access to public funds in collusion with someone in a position of authority ▷ vb commit a bobol
BOBOLINK n American songbird, Dolichonyx oryzivorus, the male of which has a white back and black underparts in the breeding season: family Icteridae (American orioles)
BOBOLINKS > BOBOLINK
BOBOLLED > BOBOL
BOBOLLING > BOBOL
BOBOLS > BOBOL
BOBOTIE n dish of curried mince
BOBOTIES > BOBOTIE
BOBOWLER n large moth
BOBOWLERS > BOBOWLER
BOBS > BOB
BOBSLED same as > BOBSLEIGH
BOBSLEDS > BOBSLED
BOBSLEIGH n sledge for racing down an icy track

b

▷ *vb* ride on a bobsleigh

BOBSTAY *n* strong stay between a bowsprit and the stem of a vessel for holding down the bowsprit

BOBSTAYS > BOBSTAY

BOBTAIL *n* docked tail ▷ *adj* having the tail cut short ▷ *vb* dock the tail of

BOBTAILED > BOBTAIL

BOBTAILS > BOBTAIL

BOBWEIGHT *n* balance weight

BOBWHEEL *n* poetic device

BOBWHEELS > BOBWHEEL

BOBWHITE *n* brown North American quail, *Colinus virginianus*, the male of which has white markings on the head: a popular game bird

BOBWHITES > BOBWHITE

BOBWIG *n* type of short wig

BOBWIGS > BOBWIG

BOCACCIO *n* edible American fish

BOCACCIOS > BOCACCIO

BOCAGE *n* wooded countryside characteristic of northern France, with small irregular-shaped fields and many hedges and copses

BOCAGES > BOCAGE

BOCCA *n* mouth

BOCCAS > BOCCA

BOCCE *same as* > BOCCIE

BOCCES > BOCCE

BOCCI *same as* > BOCCIE

BOCCIA *same as* > BOCCIE

BOCCIAS > BOCCIA

BOCCIE *n* Italian version of bowls played on a lawn smaller than a bowling green

BOCCIES > BOCCIE

BOCCIS > BOCCI

BOCHE *n* derogatory slang for a German soldier

BOCHES > BOCHE

BOCK *a variant spelling of* > BOKE

BOCKED > BOCK

BOCKEDY *adj* (of a structure, piece of furniture, etc) unsteady

BOCKING > BOCK

BOCKS > BOCK

BOCONCINI *pl n* small pieces of mozzarella

BOD *n* person

BODACH *n* old man

BODACHS > BODACH

BODACIOUS *adj* impressive or remarkable

BODDLE *same as* > BODLE

BODDLES > BODDLE

BODE *vb* portend or presage

BODED > BODE

BODEFUL *adj* portentous

BODEGA *n* shop in a Spanish-speaking country that sells wine

BODEGAS > BODEGA

BODEGUERO *n* wine seller or grocer

BODEMENT > BODE

BODEMENTS > BODE

BODES > BODE

BODGE *vb* make a mess of

BODGED > BODGE

BODGER *adj* worthless or second-rate

BODGERS > BODGER

BODGES > BODGE

BODGIE *n* unruly or uncouth young man, esp in the 1950s ▷ *adj* inferior

BODGIER > BODGIE

BODGIES > BODGIE

BODGIEST > BODGIE

BODGING > BODGE

BODHRAN *n* shallow one-sided drum popular in Irish and Scottish folk music

BODHRANS > BODHRAN

BODICE *n* upper part of a dress

BODICES > BODICE

BODIED > BODY

BODIES > BODY

BODIKIN *n* little body

BODIKINS > BODIKIN

BODILESS *adj* having no body or substance

BODILY *adj* relating to the body ▷ *adv* by taking hold of the body

BODING > BODE

BODINGLY > BODE

BODINGS > BODE

BODKIN *n* blunt large-eyed needle

BODKINS > BODKIN

BODLE *n* small obsolete Scottish coin

BODLES > BODLE

BODRAG *n* enemy attack

BODRAGS > BODRAG

BODS > BOD

BODY *n* entire physical structure of an animal or human

BODYBOARD *n* surfboard that is shorter and blunter than the standard board and on which the surfer lies rather than stands

BODYCHECK *n* obstruction of another player ▷ *vb* deliver a bodycheck to (an opponent)

BODYGUARD *n* person or group of people employed to protect someone

BODYING > BODY

BODYLINE *n* (in cricket) fast bowling aimed at the batsman's body

BODYLINES > BODYLINE

BODYSHELL *n* external shell of a motor vehicle

BODYSUIT *n* one-piece undergarment for a baby

BODYSUITS > BODYSUIT

BODYSURF *vb* ride a wave by lying on it without a surfboard

BODYSURFS > BODYSURF

BODYWORK *n* outer shell of a motor vehicle

BODYWORKS > BODYWORK

BOEHMITE *n* grey, red, or brown mineral that consists of alumina in rhombic crystalline form and occurs in bauxite

BOEHMITES > BOEHMITE

BOEP *n* South African word for a big belly

BOEPS > BOEP

BOERBUL *n* crossbred mastiff used esp as a watchdog

BOERBULS > BOERBUL

BOEREWORS *n* spiced sausage

BOERTJIE *South African word for* > FRIEND

BOERTJIES > BOERTJIE

BOET *n* brother

BOETS > BOET

BOEUF *as in* *boeuf bourguignon* casserole of beef, vegetables, herbs, etc, cooked in red wine

BOFF *n* boffin ▷ *vb* hit

BOFFED > BOFF

BOFFIN *n* scientist or expert

BOFFING > BOFF

BOFFINS > BOFFIN

BOFFO *adj* very good

BOFFOLA *n* great success

BOFFOLAS > BOFFOLA

BOFFOS > BOFFO

BOFFS > BOFF

BOG *n* wet spongy ground ▷ *vb* mire or delay

BOGAN *n* youth who dresses and behaves rebelliously

BOGANS > BOGAN

BOGART *vb* monopolize or keep (something, esp a marijuana cigarette) to oneself selfishly

BOGARTED > BOGART

BOGARTING > BOGART

BOGARTS > BOGART

BOGBEAN *same as* > BUCKBEAN

BOGBEANS > BOGBEAN

BOGEY *n* evil or mischievous spirit ▷ *vb* play (a hole) in one stroke over par

BOGEYED > BOGEY

BOGEYING > BOGEY

BOGEYISM *n* demonization

BOGEYISMS > BOGEYISM

BOGEYMAN *n* frightening person, real or imaginary, used as a threat, esp to children

BOGEYMEN > BOGEYMAN

BOGEYS > BOGEY

BOGGARD *same as* > BOGGART

BOGGARDS > BOGGARD

BOGGART *n* ghost or poltergeist

BOGGARTS > BOGGART

BOGGED > BOG

BOGGER *n* lavatory

BOGGERS > BOGGER

BOGGIER > BOG

BOGGIEST > BOG

BOGGINESS > BOG

BOGGING > BOG

BOGGISH > BOG

BOGGLE *vb* be surprised, confused, or alarmed

BOGGLED > BOGGLE

BOGGLER > BOGGLE

BOGGLERS > BOGGLE

BOGGLES > BOGGLE

BOGGLING > BOGGLE

BOGGY > BOG

BOGIE *same as* > BOGEY

BOGIED > BOGIE

BOGIEING > BOGIE

BOGIES > BOGY

BOGLAND *n* area of wetland

BOGLANDS > BOGLAND

BOGLE *n* rhythmic dance performed to ragga music

BOGLES > BOGLE

BOGMAN *n* body of a person found preserved in a peat bog

BOGMEN > BOGMAN

BOGOAK *n* oak or other wood found preserved in peat bogs; bogwood

BOGOAKS > BOGOAK

BOGONG *n* large nocturnal Australian moth

BOGONGS > BOGONG

BOGS > BOG

BOGUS *adj* not genuine

BOGUSLY > BOGUS

BOGUSNESS > BOGUS

BOGWOOD *same as* > BOGOAK

BOGWOODS > BOGWOOD

BOGY *same as* > BOGEY

BOGYISM *same as* > BOGEYISM

BOGYISMS > BOGYISM

BOGYMAN *same as* > BOGEYMAN

BOGYMEN > BOGYMAN

BOH *same as* > BO

BOHEA *n* black Chinese tea, once regarded as the choicest, but now as an inferior grade

BOHEAS > BOHEA

BOHEMIA *n* area frequented by unconventional (esp creative) people

BOHEMIAN *adj* unconventional in lifestyle or appearance ▷ *n* person, esp an artist or writer, who lives an unconventional life

BOHEMIANS > BOHEMIAN

BOHEMIAS > BOHEMIA

BOHO *short for* > BOHEMIAN

BOHOS > BOHO

BOHRIUM *n* element artificially produced in minute quantities

BOHRIUMS > BOHRIUM

BOHS > BOH

BOHUNK *n* derogatory name for a labourer from east or central Europe

BOHUNKS > BOHUNK

BOI *n* lesbian who dresses like a boy

BOIL *vb* (cause to) change from a liquid to a vapour so quickly that bubbles are formed ▷ *n* state or action of boiling

BOILABLE > BOIL

BOILED > BOIL

BOILER *n* piece of equipment which provides hot water

BOILERIES > BOILERY

BOILERS > BOILER

BOILERY *n* place where water is boiled to extract salt

BOILING *adj* very hot ▷ *n* sweet

BOILINGLY > BOILING

BOILINGS > BOILING

BOILOFF *n* quantity of liquified gases lost in evaporation

BOILOFFS > BOILOFF

BOILOVER *n* surprising result in a sporting event, esp in a horse race

BOILOVERS > BOILOVER

BOILS > BOIL

BOING *vb* rebound making a noise

BOINGED > BOING

BOINGING > BOING

BOINGS > BOING

BOINK *same as* > BOING

BOINKED > BOINK

BOINKING > BOINK

BOINKS > BOINK

BOIS > BOI

BOISERIE *n* finely crafted wood-carving

BOISERIES > BOISERIE

BOITE *n* artist's portfolio

BOITES > BOITE

BOK *n* S African antelope

BOKE *vb* retch or vomit ▷ *n* retch

BOKED > BOKE

BOKES > BOKE

BOKING > BOKE

BOKO *slang word for* > NOSE

BOKOS > BOKO

BOKS > BOK

BOLA *n* missile used by gauchos and Indians of South America, consisting of two or more heavy balls on a cord. It is hurled at a running quarry, such as an ox or rhea, so as to entangle its legs

BOLAR *adj* relating to clay

BOLAS *same as* > BOLA

BOLASES > BOLAS

BOLD *adj* confident and fearless ▷ *n* boldface

BOLDEN *vb* make bold

BOLDENED > BOLDEN

BOLDENING > BOLDEN

BOLDENS > BOLDEN

BOLDER > BOLD

BOLDEST > BOLD

BOLDFACE *n* weight of type characterized by thick heavy lines ▷ *vb* print in boldface

BOLDFACED > BOLDFACE

BOLDFACES > BOLDFACE

BOLDLY > BOLD

BOLDNESS > BOLD

BOLDS > BOLD

BOLE *n* tree trunk

BOLECTION *n* stepped moulding covering and projecting beyond the joint between two members having surfaces at different levels

BOLERO *n* (music for)

traditional Spanish dance

BOLEROS > BOLERO

BOLES > BOLE

BOLETE *n* type of fungus

BOLETES > BOLETE

BOLETI > BOLETUS

BOLETUS *n* any saprotroph basidiomycetous fungus of the genus *Boletus*, having a brownish umbrella-shaped cap with spore-bearing tubes in the underside: family *Boletaceae*. Many species are edible

BOLETUSES > BOLETUS

BOLIDE *n* large exceptionally bright meteor that often explodes

BOLIDES > BOLIDE

BOLINE *n* (in Wicca) a knife, usually sickle-shaped and with a white handle, used for gathering herbs and carving symbols

BOLINES > BOLINE

BOLIVAR *n* standard monetary unit of Venezuela, equal to 100 céntimos

BOLIVARES > BOLIVAR

BOLIVARS > BOLIVAR

BOLIVIA *n* type of woollen fabric

BOLIVIANO *n* (until 1963 and from 1987) the standard monetary unit of Bolivia, equal to 100 centavos

BOLIVIAS > BOLIVIA

BOLIX *same as* > BOLLOCKS

BOLIXED > BOLIX

BOLIXES > BOLIX

BOLIXING > BOLIX

BOLL *n* rounded seed capsule of cotton, flax, etc ▷ *vb* form into a boll

BOLLARD *n* short thick post used to prevent the passage of motor vehicles

BOLLARDS > BOLLARD

BOLLED > BOLL

BOLLEN > BOLL

BOLLETRIE *n* type of W Indian tree

BOLLING > BOLL

BOLLIX *same as* > BOLLOCKS

BOLLIXED > BOLLIX

BOLLIXES > BOLLIX

BOLLIXING > BOLLIX

BOLLOCK *vb* rebuke severely

BOLLOCKED > BOLLOCK

BOLLOCKS *pl n* testicles ▷ *interj* exclamation of annoyance, disbelief, etc ▷ *vb* rebuke severely

BOLLOX *same as* > BOLLOCKS

BOLLOXED > BOLLOX

BOLLOXES > BOLLOX

BOLLOXING > BOLLOX

BOLLS > BOLL

BOLLWORM *n* any of various moth caterpillars that feed on and destroy cotton bolls

BOLLWORMS > BOLLWORM

BOLO *n* large single-edged knife, originating in the Philippines

BOLOGNA *n* type of sausage

BOLOGNAS > BOLOGNA

BOLOGRAPH *n* record made by a bolometer

BOLOMETER *n* sensitive instrument for measuring radiant energy by the increase in the resistance of an electrical conductor

BOLOMETRY > BOLOMETER

BOLONEY *a variant spelling of* > BALONEY

BOLONEYS > BOLONEY

BOLOS > BOLO

BOLSHEVIK *n* any political radical

BOLSHIE *adj* difficult or rebellious ▷ *n* any political radical

BOLSHIER > BOLSHIE

BOLSHIES > BOLSHY

BOLSHIEST > BOLSHIE

BOLSHY *same as* > BOLSHIE

BOLSON *n* desert valley surrounded by mountains, with a shallow lake at the centre

BOLSONS > BOLSON

BOLSTER *vb* support or strengthen ▷ *n* long narrow pillow

BOLSTERED > BOLSTER

BOLSTERER > BOLSTER

BOLSTERS > BOLSTER

BOLT *n* sliding metal bar for fastening a door etc ▷ *vb* run away suddenly

BOLTED > BOLT

BOLTER > BOLT

BOLTERS > BOLT

BOLTHEAD *n* glass receptacle used in chemistry

BOLTHEADS > BOLTHEAD

BOLTHOLE *n* place of escape from danger

BOLTHOLES > BOLTHOLE

BOLTING > BOLT

BOLTINGS > BOLT

BOLTLESS > BOLT

BOLTLIKE > BOLT

BOLTONIA *n* any North American plant of the genus *Boltonia*, having daisy-like flowers with white, violet, or pinkish rays: family *Compositae* (composites)

BOLTONIAS > BOLTONIA

BOLTROPE *n* rope sewn to the foot or luff of a sail to strengthen it

BOLTROPES > BOLTROPE

BOLTS > BOLT

BOLUS *same as* > BOLE

BOLUSES > BOLUS

BOMA *n* enclosure, esp a palisade or fence of thorn bush, set up to protect a camp, herd of animals, etc

BOMAS > BOMA

BOMB *n* container fitted with explosive material ▷ *vb* attack with bombs

BOMBABLE > BOMB

BOMBARD *vb* attack with heavy gunfire or bombs ▷ *n* ancient type of cannon

that threw stone balls

BOMBARDE *n* alto wind instrument similar to the oboe or medieval shawm, used mainly in Breton traditional music

BOMBARDED > BOMBARD

BOMBARDER > BOMBARD

BOMBARDES > BOMBARDE

BOMBARDON *n* brass instrument of the tuba type, similar to a sousaphone

BOMBARDS > BOMBARD

BOMBASINE *same as* > BOMBAZINE

BOMBAST *n* pompous language ▷ *vb* speak pompous language

BOMBASTED > BOMBAST

BOMBASTER > BOMBAST

BOMBASTIC > BOMBAST

BOMBASTS > BOMBAST

BOMBAX *n* type of S American tree

BOMBAXES > BOMBAX

BOMBAZINE *n* twill fabric, usually of silk and worsted, formerly worn dyed black for mourning

BOMBE *n* dessert of ice cream lined or filled with custard, cake crumbs, etc ▷ *adj* (of furniture) having a projecting swollen shape

BOMBED > BOMB

BOMBER *n* aircraft that drops bombs

BOMBERS > BOMBER

BOMBES > BOMBE

BOMBESIN *n* hormone found in brain

BOMBESINS > BOMBESIN

BOMBILATE *same as* > BOMBINATE

BOMBINATE *vb* make a buzzing noise

BOMBING > BOMB

BOMBINGS > BOMB

BOMBLET *n* small bomb

BOMBLETS > BOMBLET

BOMBLOAD *n* quantity of bombs carried at one time

BOMBLOADS > BOMBLOAD

BOMBO *n* inferior wine

BOMBORA *n* submerged reef

BOMBORAS > BOMBORA

BOMBOS > BOMBO

BOMBPROOF *adj* able to withstand the impact of a bomb

BOMBS > BOMB

BOMBSHELL *n* shocking or unwelcome surprise

BOMBSIGHT *n* mechanical or electronic device in an aircraft for aiming bombs

BOMBSITE *n* area where the buildings have been destroyed by bombs

BOMBSITES > BOMBSITE

BOMBYCID *n* any moth, including the silkworm moth, of the family *Bombycidae*, most of which occur in Africa and SE Asia ▷ *adj* of, relating

b

to, or belonging to the *Bombycidae*

BOMBYCIDS > BOMBYCID

BOMBYCOID *adj* of or like bombycids

BOMBYX *n* type of moth

BOMBYXES > BOMBYX

BOMMIE *n* outcrop of coral reef

BOMMIES > BOMMIE

BON *adj* good

BONA *n* goods

BONACI *n* type of fish

BONACIS > BONACI

BONAMANI > BONAMANO

BONAMANO *n* gratuity

BONAMIA *n* parasite

BONAMIAS > BONAMIA

BONANZA *n* sudden good luck or wealth

BONANZAS > BONANZA

BONASSUS *same as* > BONASUS

BONASUS *n* European bison

BONASUSES > BONASUS

BONBON *n* sweet

BONBONS > BONBON

BONCE *n* head

BONCES > BONCE

BOND *n* something that binds, fastens or holds together ▷ *vb* bind

BONDABLE > BOND

BONDAGE *n* slavery

BONDAGER > BONDAGE

BONDAGERS > BONDAGE

BONDAGES > BONDAGE

BONDED *adj* consisting of, secured by, or operating under a bond or bonds

BONDER *same as* > BONDSTONE

BONDERS > BONDER

BONDING *n* process by which individuals become emotionally attached to one another

BONDINGS > BONDING

BONDLESS > BOND

BONDMAID *n* unmarried female serf or slave

BONDMAIDS > BONDMAID

BONDMAN *same as* > BONDSMAN

BONDMEN > BONDMAN

BONDS > BOND

BONDSMAN *n* person bound by bond to act as surety for another

BONDSMEN > BONDSMAN

BONDSTONE *n* long stone or brick laid in a wall as a header

BONDUC *n* type of North American tree

BONDUCS > BONDUC

BONDWOMAN *n* female slave

BONDWOMEN > BONDWOMAN

BONE *n* any of the hard parts in the body that form the skeleton ▷ *vb* remove the bones from (meat for cooking etc)

BONEBLACK *n* black residue from the destructive distillation of bones, containing about 10 per

cent carbon and 80 per cent calcium phosphate, used as a decolorizing agent and pigment

BONED > BONE

BONEFISH *n* silvery marine clupeoid game fish, *Albula vulpes*, occurring in warm shallow waters: family *Albulidae*

BONEHEAD *n* stupid or obstinate person

BONEHEADS > BONEHEAD

BONELESS > BONE

BONEMEAL *n* product of dried and ground animal bones, used as a fertilizer or in stock feeds

BONEMEALS > BONEMEAL

BONER *n* blunder

BONERS > BONER

BONES > BONE

BONESET *n* any of various North American plants of the genus *Eupatorium*, esp *E. perfoliatum*, which has flat clusters of small white flowers: family *Asteraceae* (composites)

BONESETS > BONESET

BONEY *same as* > BONY

BONEYARD *an informal name for a* > CEMETERY

BONEYARDS > BONEYARD

BONEYER > BONEY

BONEYEST > BONEY

BONFIRE *n* large outdoor fire

BONFIRES > BONFIRE

BONG *n* deep reverberating sound, as of a large bell ▷ *vb* make a deep reverberating sound

BONGED > BONG

BONGING > BONG

BONGO *n* small drum played with the fingers

BONGOES > BONGO

BONGOIST *n* bongo player

BONGOISTS > BONGOIST

BONGOS > BONGO

BONGRACE *n* shade for face

BONGRACES > BONGRACE

BONGS > BONG

BONHAM *n* piglet

BONHAMS > BONHAM

BONHOMIE *n* cheerful friendliness

BONHOMIES > BONHOMIE

BONHOMMIE *same as* > BONHOMIE

BONHOMOUS *adj* exhibiting bonhomie

BONIATO *n* sweet potato

BONIATOS > BONIATO

BONIBELL *same as* > BONNIBELL

BONIBELLS > BONIBELL

BONIE *same as* > BONNY

BONIER > BONY

BONIEST > BONY

BONIFACE *n* pub landlord

BONIFACES > BONIFACE

BONILASSE *n* an attractive young woman

BONINESS > BONY

BONING > BONE

BONINGS > BONE

BONISM *n* doctrine that the world is good, although not the best of all possible worlds

BONISMS > BONISM

BONIST > BONISM

BONISTS > BONISM

BONITA *slang term for* > HEROIN

BONITAS > BONITA

BONITO *n* small tunny-like marine food fish

BONITOES > BONITO

BONITOS > BONITO

BONJOUR *interj* hello

BONK *vb* have sex with

BONKED > BONK

BONKERS *adj* crazy

BONKING > BONK

BONKINGS > BONK

BONKS > BONK

BONNE *n* housemaid or female servant

BONNES > BONNE

BONNET *n* metal cover over a vehicle's engine ▷ *vb* place a bonnet on

BONNETED > BONNET

BONNETING > BONNET

BONNETS > BONNET

BONNIBELL *n* beautiful girl

BONNIE *same as* > BONNY

BONNIER > BONNY

BONNIES > BONNY

BONNIEST > BONNY

BONNILY > BONNY

BONNINESS > BONNY

BONNOCK *n* thick oatmeal cake

BONNOCKS > BONNOCK

BONNY *adj* beautiful ▷ *adv* agreeably or well

BONOBO *n* anthropoid ape, *Pan paniscus*, of central W Africa: similar to the chimpanzee but much smaller and having a black face.

BONOBOS > BONOBO

BONSAI *n* ornamental miniature tree or shrub

BONSAIS > BONSAI

BONSELA *n* small gift of money

BONSELAS > BONSELA

BONSELLA *same as* > BONSELA

BONSELLAS > BONSELLA

BONSOIR *interj* good evening

BONSPELL *same as* > BONSPIEL

BONSPELLS > BONSPIEL

BONSPIEL *n* curling match

BONSPIELS > BONSPIEL

BONTEBOK *n* antelope, *Damaliscus pygargus* (or *dorcas*), of southern Africa, having a deep reddish-brown coat with a white blaze, tail, and rump patch

BONTEBOKS > BONTEBOK

BONUS *n* something given, paid, or received above what is due or expected

BONUSES > BONUS

BONXIE *n* great skua

BONXIES > BONXIE

BONY *adj* having many bones

BONZA *same as* > BONZER

BONZE *n* Chinese or Japanese Buddhist priest or monk

BONZER *adj* excellent

BONZES > BONZE

BOO *interj* shout of disapproval ▷ *vb* shout 'boo' to show disapproval

BOOB *n* foolish mistake ▷ *vb* make a foolish mistake ▷ *adj* of poor quality, similar to that provided in prison

BOOBED > BOOB

BOOBHEAD *n* repeat offender in a prison

BOOBHEADS > BOOBHEAD

BOOBIALLA *n* any of various trees or shrubs of the genus *Myoporum*, esp *M. insulare*

BOOBIE *same as* > BOOBY

BOOBIES > BOOBY

BOOBING > BOOB

BOOBIRD *n* person who boos

BOOBIRDS > BOOBIRD

BOOBISH > BOOBY

BOOBOISIE *n* group of people considered as (stupid

BOOBOO *n* blunder

BOOBOOK *n* small spotted Australian brown owl

BOOBOOKS > BOOBOOK

BOOBOOS > BOOBOO

BOOBS > BOOB

BOOBY *n* foolish person

BOOBYISH > BOOBY

BOOBYISM > BOOBY

BOOBYISMS > BOOBY

BOOCOO *same as* > BEAUCOUP

BOOCOOS > BOOCOO

BOODIE *n* type of kangaroo

BOODIED > BOODY

BOODIES > BOODY

BOODLE *n* money or valuables, esp when stolen, counterfeit, or used as a bribe ▷ *vb* give or receive money corruptly or illegally

BOODLED > BOODLE

BOODLER > BOODLE

BOODLERS > BOODLE

BOODLES > BOODLE

BOODLING > BOODLE

BOODY *vb* sulk

BOODYING > BOODY

BOOED > BOO

BOOFHEAD *n* stupid person

BOOFHEADS > BOOFHEAD

BOOFIER > BOOFY

BOOFIEST > BOOFY

BOOFY *adj* muscular and strong but stupid

BOOGER *n* dried mucus from the nose

BOOGERMAN *American form of* > BOGEYMAN

BOOGERMEN > BOOGERMAN

BOOGERS > BOOGER

BOOGEY *same as* > BOOGIE

BOOGEYED > BOOGEY

BOOGEYING > BOOGEY

BOOGEYMAN same as > BOGEYMAN

BOOGEYMEN > BOOGEYMAN

BOOGEYS > BOOGEY

BOOGIE vb dance to fast pop music ▷n session of dancing to pop music

BOOGIED > BOOGIE

BOOGIEING > BOOGIE

BOOGIEMAN same as > BOGEYMAN

BOOGIEMEN > BOOGIEMAN

BOOGIES > BOOGIE

BOOGY same as > BOOGIE

BOOGYING > BOOGY

BOOGYMAN same as > BOGEYMAN

BOOGYMEN > BOOGYMAN

BOOH same as > BOO

BOOHAI as in up the boohai thoroughly lost

BOOHAIS > BOOHAI

BOOHED > BOOH

BOOHING > BOOH

BOOHOO vb sob or pretend to sob noisily ▷n distressed or pretended sobbing

BOOHOOED > BOOHOO

BOOHOOING > BOOHOO

BOOHOOS > BOOHOO

BOOHS > BOOH

BOOING > BOO

BOOJUM n American tree

BOOJUMS > BOOJUM

BOOK n number of pages bound together between covers ▷vb reserve (a place, passage, etc) in advance

BOOKABLE > BOOK

BOOKCASE n piece of furniture containing shelves for books

BOOKCASES > BOOKCASE

BOOKED > BOOK

BOOKEND n one of a pair of usually ornamental supports for holding a row of books upright

BOOKENDS > BOOKEND

BOOKER > BOOK

BOOKERS > BOOK

BOOKFUL > BOOK

BOOKFULS > BOOK

BOOKIE short for > BOOKMAKER

BOOKIER > BOOKY

BOOKIES > BOOKIE

BOOKIEST > BOOKY

BOOKING n reservation, as of a table or seat

BOOKINGS > BOOKING

BOOKISH adj fond of reading

BOOKISHLY > BOOKISH

BOOKLAND n common land given to private owner

BOOKLANDS > BOOKLAND

BOOKLESS > BOOK

BOOKLET n thin book with paper covers

BOOKLETS > BOOKLET

BOOKLICE > BOOKLOUSE

BOOKLIGHT n small light that can be clipped onto a book for reading by

BOOKLORE n knowledge or

beliefs gleaned from books

BOOKLORES > BOOKLORE

BOOKLOUSE n wingless insect that feeds on bookbinding paste, etc

BOOKMAKER n person whose occupation is taking bets

BOOKMAN n learned person

BOOKMARK n a strip of material put between the pages of a book to mark a place ▷vb identify and store (a website) so that one can return to it quickly and easily

BOOKMARKS > BOOKMARK

BOOKMEN > BOOKMAN

BOOKOO same as > BOOCOO

BOOKOOS > BOOKOO

BOOKPLATE n label bearing the owner's name and an individual design or coat of arms, pasted into a book

BOOKRACK n rack for holding books

BOOKRACKS > BOOKRACK

BOOKREST n stand for supporting open book

BOOKRESTS > BOOKREST

BOOKS > BOOK

BOOKSHELF n shelf for books

BOOKSHOP n shop where books are sold

BOOKSHOPS > BOOKSHOP

BOOKSIE same as > BOOKSY

BOOKSIER > BOOKSY

BOOKSIEST > BOOKSY

BOOKSTALL n stall or stand where periodicals, newspapers, or books are sold

BOOKSTAND n support for open book

BOOKSTORE same as > BOOKSHOP

BOOKSY adj inclined to be bookish or literary

BOOKWORK n academic study

BOOKWORKS > BOOKWORK

BOOKWORM n person devoted to reading

BOOKWORMS > BOOKWORM

BOOKY adj bookish

BOOL n bowling bowl ▷vb play bowls

BOOLED > BOOL

BOOLING > BOOL

BOOLS > BOOL

BOOM vb make a loud deep echoing sound ▷n loud deep echoing sound

BOOMBOX n portable stereo system

BOOMBOXES > BOOMBOX

BOOMED > BOOM

BOOMER n large male kangaroo

BOOMERANG n curved wooden missile which can be made to return to the thrower ▷vb (of a plan) recoil unexpectedly

BOOMERS > BOOMER

BOOMIER > BOOMY

BOOMIEST > BOOMY

BOOMING > BOOM

BOOMINGLY > BOOM

BOOMINGS > BOOM

BOOMKIN n short boom projecting from the deck of a ship, used to secure the main-brace blocks or to extend the lower edge of the foresail

BOOMKINS > BOOMKIN

BOOMLET n small boom in business, birth rate, etc

BOOMLETS > BOOMLET

BOOMS > BOOM

BOOMSLANG n large greenish venomous tree-living snake of southern Africa

BOOMTOWN n town that is enjoying sudden prosperity or has grown rapidly

BOOMTOWNS > BOOMTOWN

BOOMY adj characterized by heavy bass sound

BOON n something extremely useful, helpful, or beneficial

BOONDOCK > BOONDOCKS

BOONDOCKS n remote rural area

BOONER n young working-class person from Canberra

BOONERS > BOONER

BOONG n offensive term for a Black person

BOONGA n offensive term for a Pacific Islander

BOONGARY n tree kangaroo of NE Queensland, Australia

BOONGAS

BOONGS > BOONG

BOONIES short form of > BOONDOCKS

BOONLESS > BOON

BOONS > BOON

BOOR n rude or insensitive person

BOORD obsolete spelling of > BOARD

BOORDE obsolete spelling of > BOARD

BOORDES > BOORDE

BOORDS > BOORD

BOORISH adj ill-mannered, clumsy, or insensitive

BOORISHLY > BOORISH

BOORKA same as > BURKA

BOORKAS > BOORKA

BOORS > BOOR

BOORTREE same as > BOURTREE

BOORTREES > BOORTREE

BOOS > BOO

BOOSE same as > BOOZE

BOOSED > BOOSE

BOOSES > BOOSE

BOOSHIT adj very good

BOOSING > BOOSE

BOOST n encouragement or help ▷vb improve

BOOSTED > BOOST

BOOSTER n small additional injection of a vaccine

BOOSTERS > BOOSTER

BOOSTING > BOOST

BOOSTS > BOOST

BOOT n outer covering for the foot that extends above

the ankle ▷vb kick

BOOTABLE > BOOT

BOOTBLACK another word for > SHOEBLACK

BOOTED adj wearing boots

BOOTEE n baby's soft shoe

BOOTEES > BOOTEE

BOOTERIES > BOOTERY

BOOTERY n shop where boots and shoes are sold

BOOTH n small partly enclosed cubicle

BOOTHOSE n stocking worn with boots

BOOTHS > BOOTH

BOOTIE n Royal Marine

BOOTIES > BOOTY

BOOTIKIN n small boot

BOOTIKINS > BOOTIKIN

BOOTING > BOOT

BOOTJACK n device that grips the heel of a boot to enable the foot to be withdrawn easily

BOOTJACKS > BOOTJACK

BOOTLACE n strong lace for fastening a boot

BOOTLACES > BOOTLACE

BOOTLAST n foot shape placed in boots or shoes to keep their shape

BOOTLASTS > BOOTLAST

BOOTLEG adj produced, distributed, or sold illicitly ▷vb make, carry, or sell (illicit goods) ▷n something made or sold illicitly, such as alcohol during Prohibition in the US

BOOTLEGS > BOOTLEG

BOOTLESS adj of little or no use

BOOTLICK vb seek favour by servile or ingratiating behaviour towards (someone, esp someone in authority)

BOOTLICKS > BOOTLICK

BOOTMAKER n person who makes boots and shoes

BOOTS > BOOT

BOOTSTRAP n leather or fabric loop on the back or side of a boot

BOOTY n valuable articles obtained as plunder

BOOZE n (consume) alcoholic drink ▷vb drink alcohol, esp in excess

BOOZED > BOOZE

BOOZER n person who is fond of drinking

BOOZERS > BOOZER

BOOZES > BOOZE

BOOZEY same as > BOOZY

BOOZIER > BOOZY

BOOZIEST > BOOZY

BOOZILY > BOOZY

BOOZINESS > BOOZY

BOOZING > BOOZE

BOOZINGS > BOOZE

BOOZY adj inclined to or involving excessive drinking of alcohol

BOP vb dance to pop music ▷n form of jazz with

b

complex rhythms and harmonies

BOPEEP *n* quick look; peek

BOPEEPS > BOPEEP

BOPPED > BOP

BOPPER > BOP

BOPPERS > BOP

BOPPING > BOP

BOPS > BOP

BOR *n* neighbour

BORA *n* Aboriginal ceremony

BORACES > BORAX

BORACHIO *n* pig's skin wine carrier

BORACHIOS > BORACHIO

BORACIC *same as* > BORIC

BORACITE *n* white mineral that forms salt deposits of magnesium borate

BORACITES > BORACITE

BORAGE *n* Mediterranean plant with star-shaped blue flowers

BORAGES > BORAGE

BORAK *n* rubbish

BORAKS > BORAK

BORAL *n* type of fine powder

BORALS > BORAL

BORANE *n* any compound of boron and hydrogen, used in the synthesis of other boron compounds and as high-energy fuels

BORANES > BORANE

BORAS > BORA

BORATE *n* salt or ester of boric acid. Salts of boric acid consist of BO_3 and BO_4 units linked together ▷ *vb* treat with borax, boric acid, or borate

BORATED > BORATE

BORATES > BORATE

BORATING > BORATE

BORAX *n* soluble white mineral occurring in alkaline soils and salt deposits

BORAXES > BORAX

BORAZON *n* extremely hard form of boron nitride

BORAZONS > BORAZON

BORD *obsolete spelling of* > BOARD

BORDAR *n* smallholder who held cottage in return for menial work

BORDARS > BORDAR

BORDE *obsolete spelling of* > BOARD

BORDEAUX *adj* any of several wines produced around Bordeaux

BORDEL *same as* > BORDELLO

BORDELLO *n* brothel

BORDELLOS > BORDELLO

BORDELS > BORDEL

BORDER *n* dividing line between political or geographical regions ▷ *vb* provide with a border

BORDEREAU *n* memorandum or invoice prepared for a company by an underwriter, containing a list of reinsured risks

BORDERED > BORDER

BORDERER *n* person who lives in a border area, esp the border between England and Scotland

BORDERERS > BORDERER

BORDERING > BORDER

BORDERS > BORDER

BORDES > BORDE

BORDS > BORD

BORDURE *n* outer edge of a shield, esp when decorated distinctively

BORDURES > BORDURE

BORE *vb* make (someone) weary by being dull

BOREAL *adj* of or relating to the north or the north wind

BOREALIS as in *aurora borealis* lights seen around the North Pole

BOREAS *n* name for the north wind

BOREASES > BOREAS

BORECOLE *another name for* > KALE

BORECOLES > BORECOLE

BORED > BORE

BOREDOM *n* state of being bored

BOREDOMS > BOREDOM

BOREE *same as* > MYALL

BOREEN *n* country lane or narrow road

BOREENS > BOREEN

BOREES > BOREE

BOREHOLE *n* hole driven into the ground to obtain geological information, release water, etc

BOREHOLES > BOREHOLE

BOREL *adj* unlearned

BORER *n* machine or hand tool for boring holes

BORERS > BORER

BORES > BEAR

BORESCOPE *n* long narrow device for inspection of, e.g. bore

BORESOME *adj* boring

BORGHETTO *n* settlement outside city walls

BORGO *n* small attractive medieval village

BORGOS > BORGO

BORIC *adj* of or containing boron

BORIDE *n* compound in which boron is the most electronegative element, esp a compound of boron and a metal

BORIDES > BORIDE

BORING *n* act or process of making or enlarging a hole ▷ *adj* dull

BORINGLY > BORING

BORINGS > BORING

BORK *vb* dismiss from job unfairly

BORKED > BORK

BORKING > BORK

BORKS > BORK

BORLOTTI as in *borlotti bean* variety of kidney bean

BORM *vb* smear with paint, oil, etc

BORMED > BORM

BORMING > BORM

BORMS > BORM

BORN *adj* possessing certain qualities from birth

BORNA as in *borna disease* viral disease found in mammals, esp horses

BORNE > BEAR

BORNEOL *n* white solid terpene alcohol

BORNEOLS > BORNEOL

BORNITE *n* mineral consisting of a sulphide of copper and iron that tarnishes to purple

BORNITES > BORNITE

BORNITIC > BORNITE

BORNYL as in *bornyl alcohol* white solid alcohol from a Malaysian tree

BORNYLS > BORNYL

BORON *n* element used in hardening steel

BORONIA *n* Australian aromatic flowering shrub

BORONIAS > BORONIA

BORONIC > BORON

BORONS > BORON

BOROUGH *n* town or district with its own council

BOROUGHS > BOROUGH

BORREL *adj* ignorant

BORRELIA *n* type of bacterium

BORRELIAS > BORRELIA

BORRELL *same as* > BORREL

BORROW *vb* obtain (something) temporarily

BORROWED > BORROW

BORROWER > BORROW

BORROWERS > BORROW

BORROWING > BORROW

BORROWS > BORROW

BORS > BOR

BORSCH *same as* > BORSCHT

BORSCHES > BORSCH

BORSCHT *n* Russian soup based on beetroot

BORSCHTS > BORSCHT

BORSHCH *same as* > BORSCHT

BORSHCHES > BORSHCH

BORSHT *same as* > BORSCHT

BORSHTS > BORSHT

BORSIC *n* strong light composite material of boron fibre and silicon carbide used in aviation

BORSICS > BORSIC

BORSTAL *n* (formerly in Britain) prison for young criminals

BORSTALL *same as* > BORSTAL

BORSTALLS > BORSTAL

BORSTALS > BORSTAL

BORT *n* inferior grade of diamond used for cutting and drilling or, in powdered form, as an industrial abrasive

BORTIER > BORT

BORTIEST > BORT

BORTS > BORT

BORTSCH *same as* > BORSCHT

BORTSCHES > BORTSCH

BORTY > BORT

BORTZ *same as* > BORT

BORTZES > BORTZ

BORZOI *n* tall dog with a long silky coat

BORZOIS > BORZOI

BOS > BO

BOSBERAAD *n* meeting in an isolated venue to break a political deadlock

BOSBOK *same as* > BUSHBUCK

BOSBOKS > BOSBOK

BOSCAGE *n* mass of trees and shrubs

BOSCAGES > BOSCAGE

BOSCHBOK *same as* > BUSHBUCK

BOSCHBOKS > BOSCHBOK

BOSCHE *same as* > BOCHE

BOSCHES > BOSCHE

BOSCHVARK *same as* > BUSHPIG

BOSCHVELD *same as* > BUSHVELD

BOSH *n* empty talk, nonsense

BOSHBOK *same as* > BUSHBUCK

BOSHBOKS > BOSHBOK

BOSHES > BOSH

BOSHTA *same as* > BOSHTER

BOSHTER *adj* excellent

BOSHVARK *same as* > BOSCHVARK

BOSHVARKS > BOSHVARK

BOSK *n* small wood of bushes and small trees

BOSKAGE *same as* > BOSCAGE

BOSKAGES > BOSKAGE

BOSKER *adj* excellent

BOSKET *n* clump of small trees or bushes

BOSKETS > BOSKET

BOSKIER > BOSKY

BOSKIEST > BOSKY

BOSKINESS > BOSKY

BOSKS > BOSK

BOSKY *adj* containing or consisting of bushes or thickets

BOSOM *n* chest of a person, esp the female breasts ▷ *adj* very dear ▷ *vb* embrace

BOSOMED > BOSOM

BOSOMIER > BOSOMY

BOSOMIEST > BOSOMY

BOSOMING > BOSOM

BOSOMS > BOSOM

BOSOMY *adj* (of a woman) having large breasts

BOSON *n* any of a group of elementary particles, such as a photon or pion, that has zero or integral spin and obeys the rules of Bose-Einstein statistics

BOSONIC > BOSON

BOSONS > BOSON

BOSQUE *same as* > BOSK

BOSQUES > BOSQUE

BOSQUET *same as* > BOSKET

BOSQUETS > BOSQUET

BOSS *n* raised knob or stud ▷ *vb* employ, supervise, or be in charge of ▷ *adj* excellent

BOSSBOY *n* Black African foreman of a gang of

workers

BOSSBOYS > BOSSBOY

BOSSDOM n bosses collectively

BOSSDOMS > BOSSDOM

BOSSED > BOSS

BOSSER > BOSS

BOSSES > BOSS

BOSSEST > BOSS

BOSSET n either of the rudimentary antlers found in young deer

BOSSETS > BOSSET

BOSSIER > BOSSY

BOSSIES > BOSSY

BOSSIEST > BOSSY

BOSSILY > BOSSY

BOSSINESS > BOSSY

BOSSING n act of shaping malleable metal, such as lead cladding, with mallets to fit a surface

BOSSISM n domination or the system of domination of political organizations by bosses

BOSSISMS > BOSSISM

BOSSY same as > BOSS

BOSTANGI n imperial Turkish guard

BOSTANGIS > BOSTANGI

BOSTHOON n boor

BOSTHOONS > BOSTHOON

BOSTON n card game for four, played with two packs

BOSTONS > BOSTON

BOSTRYX n phenomenon in which flowers develop on one side only

BOSTRYXES > BOSTRYX

BOSUN same as > BOATSWAIN

BOSUNS > BOSUN

BOT n larva of a botfly, which typically develops inside the body of a horse, sheep, or man

BOTA n leather container

BOTANIC same as > BOTANICAL

BOTANICA n botany

BOTANICAL adj of or relating to botany or plants ▷ n any drug or pesticide that is made from parts of a plant

BOTANICAS > BOTANICA

BOTANICS > BOTANIC

BOTANIES > BOTANY

BOTANISE same as > BOTANIZE

BOTANISED > BOTANISE

BOTANISER > BOTANIZE

BOTANISES > BOTANISE

BOTANIST > BOTANY

BOTANISTS > BOTANY

BOTANIZE vb collect or study plants

BOTANIZED > BOTANIZE

BOTANIZER > BOTANIZE

BOTANIZES > BOTANIZE

BOTANY n study of plants

BOTARGO n relish consisting of the roe of mullet or tunny, salted and pressed into rolls

BOTARGOES > BOTARGO

BOTARGOS > BOTARGO

BOTAS > BOTA

BOTCH vb spoil through clumsiness ▷ n badly done piece of work or repair

BOTCHED > BOTCH

BOTCHEDLY > BOTCH

BOTCHER > BOTCH

BOTCHERS > BOTCH

BOTCHERY n instance of botching

BOTCHES > BOTCH

BOTCHIER > BOTCHY

BOTCHIEST > BOTCHY

BOTCHILY > BOTCHY

BOTCHING > BOTCH

BOTCHINGS > BOTCH

BOTCHY adj clumsily done or made

BOTEL same as > BOATEL

BOTELS > BOTEL

BOTFLIES > BOTFLY

BOTFLY n any of various stout-bodied hairy dipterous flies of the families Oestridae and Gasterophilidae, the larvae of which are parasites of man, sheep, and horses

BOTH pron two considered together ▷ adj two considered together ▷ determiner two

BOTHAN n unlicensed drinking house

BOTHANS > BOTHAN

BOTHER vb take the time or trouble ▷ n trouble, fuss, or difficulty ▷ interj exclamation of slight annoyance

BOTHERED > BOTHER

BOTHERING > BOTHER

BOTHERS > BOTHER

BOTHIE same as > BOTHY

BOTHIES > BOTHY

BOTHOLE n hole made by the larva of the botfly

BOTHOLES > BOTHOLE

BOTHRIA > BOTHRIUM

BOTHRIUM n groove-shaped sucker on tapeworm

BOTHRIUMS > BOTHRIUM

BOTHY n hut used for temporary shelter

BOTHYMAN n man who lives in bothy

BOTHYMEN > BOTHYMAN

BOTNET n network of infected computers

BOTNETS > BOTNET

BOTONE adj having lobes at the ends

BOTONEE same as > BOTONE

BOTONNEE same as > BOTONE

BOTRYOID adj shaped like a bunch of grapes

BOTRYOSE same as > BOTRYOID

BOTRYTIS n any of a group of fungi of the genus Botrytis, several of which cause plant diseases

BOTS n digestive disease of horses and some other animals caused by the presence of botfly larvae in the stomach

BOTT same as > BOT

BOTTE n thrust or hit

BOTTED > BOT

BOTTEGA n workshop; studio

BOTTEGAS > BOTTEGA

BOTTES > BOTTE

BOTTIES > BOTTY

BOTTINE n light boot for women or children

BOTTINES > BOTTINE

BOTTING > BOT

BOTTLE n container for holding liquids ▷ vb put in a bottle

BOTTLED > BOTTLE

BOTTLEFUL same as > BOTTLE

BOTTLER n exceptional person or thing

BOTTLERS > BOTTLER

BOTTLES > BOTTLE

BOTTLING > BOTTLE

BOTTLINGS > BOTTLE

BOTTOM n lowest, deepest, or farthest removed part of a thing ▷ adj lowest or last ▷ vb provide with a bottom

BOTTOMED > BOTTOM

BOTTOMER n pit worker

BOTTOMERS > BOTTOMER

BOTTOMING n lowest level of foundation material for a road or other structure

BOTTOMRY n contract whereby the owner of a ship borrows money to enable the vessel to complete the voyage and pledges the ship as security for the loan

BOTTOMS > BOTTOM

BOTTOMSET as in bottomset bed fine sediment deposited at the front of a growing delta

BOTTONY same as > BOTONE

BOTTS > BOTT

BOTTY n diminutive for bottom

BOTULIN n potent toxin produced by the bacterium Clostridium botulinum in imperfectly preserved food, etc, causing botulism

BOTULINAL > BOTULIN

BOTULINS > BOTULIN

BOTULINUM n botulin-secreting bacterium

BOTULINUS n anaerobic bacterium, Clostridium botulinum, whose toxins (botulins) cause botulism: family Bacillaceae

BOTULISM n severe food poisoning

BOTULISMS > BOTULISM

BOUBOU n long flowing garment worn by men and women in Mali, Nigeria, Senegal, and some other parts of Africa

BOUBOUS > BOUBOU

BOUCHE n notch cut in top corner of shield

BOUCHEE n small pastry case filled with a savoury

mixture, served hot with cocktails or as an hors d'oeuvre

BOUCHEES > BOUCHEE

BOUCHES > BOUCHE

BOUCLE n looped yarn giving a knobbly effect ▷ adj of or designating such a yarn or fabric

BOUCLEE n support for a cue in billiards formed by doubling the first finger so that its tip is aligned with the thumb at its second joint, to form a loop through which the cue may slide

BOUCLEES > BOUCLEE

BOUCLES > BOUCLE

BOUDERIE n sulkiness

BOUDERIES > BOUDERIE

BOUDIN n French version of a black pudding

BOUDINS > BOUDIN

BOUDOIR n woman's bedroom or private sitting room

BOUDOIRS > BOUDOIR

BOUFFANT adj (of a hairstyle) having extra height through backcombing ▷ n bouffant hair style

BOUFFANTS > BOUFFANT

BOUFFE n type of light or satirical opera common in France during the 19th century

BOUFFES > BOUFFE

BOUGE vb move

BOUGED > BOUGE

BOUGES > BOUGE

BOUGET n budget

BOUGETS > BOUGET

BOUGH n large branch of a tree

BOUGHED > BOUGH

BOUGHLESS > BOUGH

BOUGHPOT n container for displaying boughs

BOUGHPOTS > BOUGHPOT

BOUGHS > BOUGH

BOUGHT > BUY

BOUGHTEN a dialect word for > BUY

BOUGHTS > BUY

BOUGIE n long slender semiflexible cylindrical instrument for inserting into body passages, such as the rectum or urethra, to dilate structures, introduce medication, etc

BOUGIES > BOUGIE

BOUGING > BOUGE

BOUILLI n stew

BOUILLIS > BOUILLI

BOUILLON n thin clear broth or stock

BOUILLONS > BOUILLON

BOUK n bulk; volume

BOUKS > BOUK

BOULDER n large rounded rock ▷ vb convert into boulders

BOULDERED > BOULDER

BOULDERER > BOULDER

Section 1: Words between 2 and 9 letters in length

b

BOULDERS > BOULDER
BOULDERY > BOULDER
BOULE same as > BOULLE
BOULES n game, popular in France, in which metal bowls are thrown to land as close as possible to a target ball
BOULEVARD n wide, usu tree-lined, street
BOULLE adj denoting or relating to a type of marquetry of patterned inlays of brass and tortoiseshell, occasionally with other metals such as pewter, much used on French furniture from the 17th century ▷ n something ornamented with such marquetry
BOULLES > BOULLE
BOULT same as > BOLT
BOULTED > BOULT
BOULTER > BOLT
BOULTERS > BOLT
BOULTING > BOULT
BOULTINGS > BOULT
BOULTS > BOULT
BOUN vb prepare to go out
BOUNCE vb (of a ball etc) rebound from an impact ▷ n act of rebounding
BOUNCED > BOUNCE
BOUNCER n person employed at a disco etc to remove unwanted people
BOUNCERS > BOUNCER
BOUNCES > BOUNCE
BOUNCIER > BOUNCY
BOUNCIEST > BOUNCY
BOUNCILY > BOUNCY
BOUNCING adj vigorous and robust
BOUNCY adj lively, exuberant, or self-confident
BOUND > BIND
BOUNDABLE > BIND
BOUNDARY n dividing line that indicates the farthest limit
BOUNDED adj (of a set) having a bound, esp where a measure is defined in terms of which all the elements of the set, or the differences between all pairs of members, are less than some value, or else all its members lie within some other well-defined set
BOUNDEN adj morally obligatory
BOUNDER n morally reprehensible person
BOUNDERS > BOUNDER
BOUNDING > BIND
BOUNDLESS adj unlimited
BOUNDNESS > BIND
BOUNDS pl n limit
BOUNED > BOUN
BOUNING > BOUN
BOUNS > BOUN
BOUNTEOUS adj giving freely
BOUNTIED > BOUNTY

BOUNTIES > BOUNTY
BOUNTIFUL adj plentiful
BOUNTREE another name for > BOUNTREE
BOUNTREES > BOURTREE
BOUNTY n generosity
BOUNTYHED n generosity
BOUQUET n bunch of flowers
BOUQUETS > BOUQUET
BOURASQUE n violent storm
BOURBON n whiskey made from maize
BOURBONS > BOURBON
BOURD n prank
BOURDER n prankster
BOURDERS > BOURDER
BOURDON n 16-foot organ stop of the stopped diapason type
BOURDONS > BOURDON
BOURDS > BOURD
BOURG n French market town, esp one beside a castle
BOURGEOIS n middle-class (person) ▷ adj characteristic of or comprising the middle class
BOURGEON same as > BURGEON
BOURGEONS > BOURGEON
BOURGS > BOURG
BOURKHA same as > BURKA
BOURKHAS same as > BOURKHA
BOURLAW same as > BYRLAW
BOURLAWS > BOURLAW
BOURN n (in S Britain) stream
BOURNE same as > BOURN
BOURNES > BOURNE
BOURNS > BOURN
BOURREE n traditional French dance in fast duple time
BOURREES > BOURREE
BOURRIDE n Mediterranean fish soup
BOURRIDES > BOURRIDE
BOURSE n stock exchange of continental Europe, esp Paris
BOURSES > BOURSE
BOURSIER n stock-exchange worker
BOURSIERS > BOURSIER
BOURSIN n tradename of a smooth white creamy cheese, often flavoured with garlic
BOURSINS > BOURSIN
BOURTREE n elder tree
BOURTREES > BOURTREE
BOUSE vb raise or haul with a tackle
BOUSED > BOUSE
BOUSES > BOUSE
BOUSIER > BOUSY
BOUSIEST > BOUSY
BOUSING > BOUSE
BOUSOUKI same as > BOUZOUKI
BOUSOUKIA > BOUSOUKI
BOUSOUKIS > BOUSOUKI
BOUSY adj drunken; boozy
BOUT n period of activity or

illness
BOUTADE n outburst
BOUTADES > BOUTADE
BOUTIQUE n small clothes shop
BOUTIQUES > BOUTIQUE
BOUTIQUEY adj typical of boutiques
BOUTON n knob-shaped contact between nerve fibres
BOUTONNE adj reserved or inhibited
BOUTONNEE same as > BOUTONNE
BOUTONS > BOUTON
BOUTS > BOUT
BOUVARDIA n flowering plant
BOUVIER n large powerful dog of a Belgian breed, having a rough shaggy coat: used esp for cattle herding and guarding
BOUVIERS > BOUVIER
BOUZOUKI n Greek stringed musical instrument
BOUZOUKIA > BOUZOUKI
BOUZOUKIS > BOUZOUKI
BOVATE n obsolete measure of land
BOVATES > BOVATE
BOVID adj of, relating to, or belonging to the Bovidae, a family of ruminant artiodactyl hollow-horned mammals including sheep, goats, cattle, antelopes, and buffalo ▷ n any bovid animal
BOVIDS > BOVID
BOVINE adj relating to cattle ▷ n any animal belonging to the Bovini
BOVINELY > BOVINE
BOVINES > BOVINE
BOVINITY > BOVINE
BOVVER n rowdiness, esp caused by gangs of teenage youths
BOVVERS > BOVVER
BOW vb lower (one's head) or bend (one's knee or body) as a sign of respect or shame ▷ n movement made when bowing
BOWAT n lamp
BOWATS > BOWAT
BOWBENT adj bent; bow-like
BOWED adj lowered, bent forward, or curved
BOWEL n intestine, esp the large intestine ▷ vb remove the bowels
BOWELED > BOWEL
BOWELING > BOWEL
BOWELLED > BOWEL
BOWELLESS > BOWEL
BOWELLING > BOWEL
BOWELS > BOWEL
BOWER n shady leafy shelter ▷ vb surround as with a bower
BOWERBIRD n songbird of Australia and New Guinea, the males of which build bower-like display grounds

to attract females
BOWERED > BOWER
BOWERIES > BOWER
BOWERING > BOWER
BOWERS > BOWER
BOWERY > BOWER
BOWES same as > BOUGH
BOWET same as > BOWAT
BOWETS > BOWET
BOWFIN n primitive North American freshwater bony fish, Amia calva, with an elongated body and a very long dorsal fin: family Amiidae
BOWFINS > BOWFIN
BOWFRONT adj having a front that curves outwards
BOWGET obsolete variant of > BUDGET
BOWGETS > BOWGET
BOWHEAD n large-mouthed arctic whale, Balaena mysticetus, that has become rare through overfishing but is now a protected species
BOWHEADS > BOWHEAD
BOWHUNTER n person hunting with bow and arrows
BOWIE as in bowie knife type of hunting knife
BOWING n technique of using the bow in playing a violin, viola, cello, or related instrument
BOWINGLY > BOWING
BOWINGS > BOWING
BOWKNOT n decorative knot usually having two loops and two loose ends
BOWKNOTS > BOWKNOT
BOWL n round container with an open top ▷ vb roll smoothly along the ground
BOWLDER same as > BOULDER
BOWLDERS > BOWLDER
BOWLED > BOWL
BOWLEG > BOWLEGS
BOWLEGGED adj having legs that curve outwards like a bow
BOWLEGS
BOWLER n player who sends (a ball) towards the batsman
BOWLERS > BOWLER
BOWLESS > BOW
BOWLFUL same as > BOWL
BOWLFULS > BOWLFUL
BOWLIKE > BOW
BOWLINE n line used to keep the sail taut against the wind
BOWLINES > BOWLINE
BOWLING n game in which bowls are rolled at a group of pins
BOWLINGS > BLOW
BOWLLIKE > BOWL
BOWLS n game played on a very smooth area of grass in which opponents roll biased wooden bowls as near a small bowl (the jack) as possible

BOWMAN *n* archer
BOWMEN > BOWMAN
BOWNE *same as* > BOUN
BOWNED > BOWNE
BOWNES > BOWNE
BOWNING > BOWNE
BOWPOT *same as* > BOUGHPOT
BOWPOTS > BOWPOT
BOWR *n* muscle
BOWRS > BOWR
BOWS > BOW
BOWSAW *n* saw with a thin blade in a bow-shaped frame
BOWSAWS > BOWSAW
BOWSE *same as* > BOUSE
BOWSED > BOWSE
BOWSER *n* tanker containing fuel for aircraft, military vehicles, etc
BOWSERS > BOWSER
BOWSES > BOWSE
BOWSEY *n* Irish word for mean person
BOWSEYS > BOWSEY
BOWSHOT *n* distance an arrow travels from the bow
BOWSHOTS > BOWSHOT
BOWSIE *n* low-class mean or obstreperous person
BOWSIES > BOWSIE
BOWSING > BOWSE
BOWSPRIT *n* spar projecting from the bow of a sailing ship
BOWSPRITS > BOWSPRIT
BOWSTRING *n* string of an archer's bow
BOWSTRUNG > BOWSTRING
BOWWOW *n* imitation of the bark of a dog ▷ *vb* make a noise like a dog
BOWWOWED > BOWWOW
BOWWOWING > BOWWOW
BOWWOWS > BOWWOW
BOWYANG *n* band worn round trouser leg below knee
BOWYANGS > BOWYANG
BOWYER *n* person who makes or sells archery bows
BOWYERS > BOWYER
BOX *n* container with a firm flat base and sides ▷ *vb* put into a box
BOXBALL *n* street ball game
BOXBALLS > BOXBALL
BOXBERRY *n* fruit of the partridgeberry or wintergreen
BOXBOARD *n* tough paperboard made from wood and wastepaper pulp: used for making boxes, etc
BOXBOARDS > BOXBOARD
BOXCAR *n* closed railway freight van
BOXCARS > BOXCAR
BOXED > BOX
BOXEN > BOX
BOXER *n* person who participates in the sport of boxing
BOXERCISE *n* system of sustained exercises

combining boxing movements with aerobic activities
BOXERS > BOXER
BOXES > BOX
BOXFISH *another name for* > TRUNKFISH
BOXFISHES > BOXFISH
BOXFUL *same as* > BOX
BOXFULS > BOX
BOXHAUL *vb* bring (a square-rigger) onto a new tack by backwinding the foresails and steering hard round
BOXHAULED > BOXHAUL
BOXHAULS > BOXHAUL
BOXIER > BOXY
BOXIEST > BOXY
BOXILY > BOXY
BOXINESS > BOXY
BOXING *n* sport of fighting with the fists
BOXINGS > BOXING
BOXKEEPER *n* person responsible for theatre boxes
BOXLIKE > BOX
BOXROOM *n* small room in which boxes, cases, etc may be stored
BOXROOMS > BOXROOM
BOXTHORN *n* matrimony vine
BOXTHORNS > BOXTHORN
BOXWALLAH *n* salesman
BOXWOOD *n* hard yellow wood of the box tree, used to make tool handles, etc
BOXWOODS > BOXWOOD
BOXY *adj* squarish or chunky
BOY *n* male child ▷ *vb* act the part of a boy in a play
BOYAR *n* member of an old order of Russian nobility, ranking immediately below the princes: abolished by Peter the Great
BOYARD *same as* > BOYAR
BOYARDS > BOYARD
BOYARISM > BOYAR
BOYARISMS > BOYAR
BOYARS > BOYAR
BOYAU *n* connecting trench
BOYAUX > BOYAU
BOYCHICK *same as* > BOYCHIK
BOYCHICKS > BOYCHICK
BOYCHIK *n* young boy
BOYCHIKS > BOYCHIK
BOYCOTT *vb* refuse to deal with (an organization or country) ▷ *n* instance of boycotting
BOYCOTTED > BOYCOTT
BOYCOTTER > BOYCOTT
BOYCOTTS > BOYCOTT
BOYED > BOY
BOYF *n* boyfriend
BOYFRIEND *n* male friend with whom a person is romantically or sexually involved
BOYFS > BOYF
BOYG *n* troll-like mythical creature
BOYGS > BOYG
BOYHOOD *n* state or time of

being a boy
BOYHOODS > BOYHOOD
BOYING > BOY
BOYISH *adj* of or like a boy in looks, behaviour, or character, esp when regarded as attractive or endearing
BOYISHLY > BOYISH
BOYLA *n* Australian Aboriginal word for magician
BOYLAS > BOYLA
BOYO *n* boy or young man: often used in direct address
BOYOS > BOYO
BOYS > BOY
BOYSIER > BOYSY
BOYSIEST > BOYSY
BOYSY *adj* suited to or typical of boys or young men
BOZO *n* man, esp a stupid one
BOZOS > BOZO
BOZZETTI > BOZZETTO
BOZZETTO *n* small sketch of planned work
BRA *same as* > BRASSIERE
BRAAI *vb* grill or roast (meat) over open coals
BRAAIED > BRAAI
BRAAIING > BRAAI
BRAAIS > BRAAI
BRAATA *n* small portion added to a purchase of food by a market vendor, to encourage the customer to return
BRAATAS *same as* > BRAATA
BRAATASES > BRAATAS
BRABBLE *rare word for* > SQUABBLE
BRABBLED > BRABBLE
BRABBLER > BRABBLE
BRABBLERS > BRABBLE
BRABBLES > BRABBLE
BRABBLING > BRABBLE
BRACCATE *adj* (of birds) having feathered legs
BRACCIA > BRACCIO
BRACCIO *n* former unit of measurement; length of man's arm
BRACE *n* object fastened to something to straighten or support it ▷ *vb* steady or prepare (oneself) for something unpleasant
BRACED > BRACE
BRACELET *n* ornamental chain or band for the wrist
BRACELETS *pl n* handcuffs
BRACER *n* person or thing that braces
BRACERO *n* Mexican World War II labourer
BRACEROS > BRACERO
BRACERS > BRACER
BRACES *pl n* pair of straps worn over the shoulders for holding up the trousers
BRACH *n* bitch hound
BRACHAH *n* blessing
BRACHAHS > BRACHAH
BRACHES > BRACH
BRACHET *same as* > BRACH

BRACHETS > BRACHET
BRACHIA > BRACHIUM
BRACHIAL *adj* of or relating to the arm or to an armlike part or structure ▷ *n* brachial part or structure
BRACHIALS > BRACHIAL
BRACHIATE *adj* having widely divergent paired branches ▷ *vb* (of some arboreal apes and monkeys) swing by the arms from one hold to the next
BRACHIUM *n* arm, esp the upper part
BRACHS > BRACH
BRACING *adj* refreshing and invigorating ▷ *n* system of braces used to strengthen or support
BRACINGLY > BRACING
BRACINGS > BRACING
BRACIOLA *n* Italian meat roulade
BRACIOLAS > BRACIOLA
BRACIOLE > BRACIOLA
BRACIOLES > BRACIOLE
BRACK *same as* > BARMBRACK
BRACKEN *n* large fern
BRACKENS > BRACKEN
BRACKET *n* pair of characters used to enclose a section of writing ▷ *vb* put in brackets
BRACKETED > BRACKET
BRACKETS > BRACKET
BRACKISH *adj* (of water) slightly salty
BRACKS > BRACK
BRACONID *n* type of fly with parasitic larva
BRACONIDS > BRACONID
BRACT *n* leaf at the base of a flower
BRACTEAL > BRACT
BRACTEATE *adj* (of a plant) having bracts ▷ *n* fine decorated dish or plate of precious metal
BRACTED > BRACT
BRACTEOLE *n* secondary bract subtending a flower within an inflorescence
BRACTLESS > BRACT
BRACTLET *variant of* > BRACTEOLE
BRACTLETS > BRACTLET
BRACTS > BRACT
BRAD *n* small tapered nail with a small head
BRADAWL *n* small boring tool
BRADAWLS > BRADAWL
BRADDED > BRAD
BRADDING > BRAD
BRADOON *same as* > BRIDOON
BRADOONS > BRADOON
BRADS > BRAD
BRAE *n* hill or slope
BRAEHEID *n* summit of a hill or slope
BRAEHEIDS > BRAEHEID
BRAES > BRAE
BRAG *vb* speak arrogantly and boastfully ▷ *n* boastful talk or behaviour
BRAGGART *n* person who

boasts loudly ▷ *adj* boastful

BRAGGARTS > BRAGGART

BRAGGED > BRAG

BRAGGER > BRAG

BRAGGERS > BRAG

BRAGGEST > BRAG

BRAGGIER > BRAGGY

BRAGGIEST > BRAGGY

BRAGGING > BRAG

BRAGGINGS > BRAG

BRAGGY *adj* boastful

BRAGLY > BRAG

BRAGS > BRAG

BRAHMA *n* heavy breed of domestic fowl with profusely feathered legs and feet

BRAHMAN *n* member of highest Hindu caste

BRAHMANI *n* woman of the highest Hindu caste

BRAHMANIS > BRAHMANI

BRAHMANS > BRAHMAN

BRAHMAS > BRAHMA

BRAHMIN *same as* > BRAHMAN

BRAHMINS > BRAHMIN

BRAID *vb* interweave (hair, thread, etc) ▷ *n* length of hair etc that has been braided ▷ *adj* broad ▷ *adv* broadly

BRAIDE *adj* given to deceit

BRAIDED *adj* (of a river or stream) flowing in several shallow interconnected channels separated by banks of deposited material

BRAIDER > BRAID

BRAIDERS > BRAID

BRAIDEST > BRAID

BRAIDING *n* braids collectively

BRAIDINGS > BRAIDING

BRAIDS > BRAID

BRAIL *n* one of several lines fastened to the leech of a fore-and-aft sail to aid in furling it ▷ *vb* furl (a fore-and-aft sail) using brails

BRAILED > BRAIL

BRAILING > BRAIL

BRAILLE *n* system of writing for the blind consisting of raised dots that can be interpreted by touch ▷ *vb* print or write using this method

BRAILLED > BRAILLE

BRAILLER *n* device for producing text in braille

BRAILLERS > BRAILLER

BRAILLES > BRAILLE

BRAILLING > BRAILLE

BRAILLIST *n* braille transcriber

BRAILS > BRAIL

BRAIN *n* soft mass of nervous tissue in the head ▷ *vb* hit (someone) hard on the head

BRAINBOX *n* skull

BRAINCASE *n* part of cranium that covers brain

BRAINDEAD *adj* having

suffered irreversible stoppage of breathing due to brain damage

BRAINED > BRAIN

BRAINFART *n* idea expressed without much previous thought

BRAINIAC *n* highly intelligent person

BRAINIACS > BRAINIAC

BRAINIER > BRAINY

BRAINIEST > BRAINY

BRAINILY > BRAINY

BRAINING > BRAIN

BRAINISH *adj* impulsive

BRAINLESS *adj* stupid

BRAINPAN *n* skull

BRAINPANS > BRAINPAN

BRAINS > BRAIN

BRAINSICK *adj* relating to or caused by insanity

BRAINSTEM *n* stalklike part of the brain consisting of the medulla oblongata, the midbrain, and the pons Varolii

BRAINWASH *vb* cause (a person) to alter his or her beliefs, esp by methods based on isolation, sleeplessness, etc

BRAINWAVE *n* sudden idea

BRAINY *adj* clever

BRAIRD *vb* appear as shoots

BRAIRDED > BRAIRD

BRAIRDING > BRAIRD

BRAIRDS > BRAIRD

BRAISE *vb* cook slowly in a covered pan with a little liquid

BRAISED > BRAISE

BRAISES > BRAISE

BRAISING > BRAISE

BRAIZE *same as* > BRAISE

BRAIZES > BRAIZE

BRAK *n* crossbred dog ▷ *adj* (of water) slightly salty

BRAKE *same as* > BRACKEN

BRAKEAGE > BRAKE

BRAKEAGES > BRAKE

BRAKED > BRAKE

BRAKELESS > BRAKE

BRAKEMAN *n* crew member of a goods or passenger train. His duties include controlling auxiliary braking power and inspecting the train

BRAKEMEN > BRAKEMAN

BRAKES > BRAKE

BRAKESMAN *n* pithead winch operator

BRAKESMEN > BRAKESMAN

BRAKIER > BRAKY

BRAKIEST > BRAKY

BRAKING > BRAKE

BRAKS > BRAK

BRAKY *adj* brambly

BRALESS > BRA

BRAMBLE *n* Scots word for blackberry

BRAMBLED > BRAMBLE

BRAMBLES > BRAMBLE

BRAMBLIER > BRAMBLE

BRAMBLING *n* Eurasian finch, *Fringilla montifringilla*, with a speckled head and

back and, in the male, a reddish brown breast and darker wings and tail

BRAMBLY > BRAMBLE

BRAME *n* powerful feeling of emotion

BRAMES > BRAME

BRAN *n* husks of cereal grain

BRANCARD *n* couch on shafts, carried between two horses

BRANCARDS > BRANCARD

BRANCH *n* secondary stem of a tree ▷ *vb* (of stems, roots, etc) divide, then develop in different directions

BRANCHED > BRANCH

BRANCHER *n* young bird learning to fly

BRANCHERS > BRANCHER

BRANCHERY *n* branches

BRANCHES > BRANCH

BRANCHIA *n* gill in aquatic animals

BRANCHIAE > BRANCHIA

BRANCHIAL *adj* of or relating to the gills of an aquatic animal, esp a fish

BRANCHIER > BRANCH

BRANCHING > BRANCH

BRANCHLET *n* small branch

BRANCHY > BRANCH

BRAND *n* particular product ▷ *vb* mark with a brand

BRANDADE *n* French puréed fish dish

BRANDADES > BRANDADE

BRANDED *adj* identifiable as being the product of a particular manufacturer or marketing company

BRANDER > BRAND

BRANDERED > BRAND

BRANDERS > BRAND

BRANDIED > BRANDY

BRANDIES > BRANDY

BRANDING > BRAND

BRANDINGS > BRAND

BRANDISE *n* three-legged metal stand for cooking pots

BRANDISES > BRANDISE

BRANDISH *vb* wave (a weapon etc) in a threatening way ▷ *n* threatening or defiant flourish

BRANDLESS > BRAND

BRANDLING *n* small red earthworm, *Eisenia foetida* (or *Helodrilus foetidus*), found in manure and used as bait by anglers

BRANDRETH *n* framework of bars used for cooking meat over fire

BRANDS > BRAND

BRANDY *n* alcoholic spirit distilled from wine ▷ *vb* give brandy to

BRANDYING > BRANDY

BRANGLE *vb* quarrel noisily

BRANGLED > BRANGLE

BRANGLES > BRANGLE

BRANGLING > BRANGLE

BRANK *vb* walk with

swaggering gait

BRANKED > BRANK

BRANKIER > BRANKY

BRANKIEST > BRANKY

BRANKING > BRANK

BRANKS *pl n* (formerly) iron bridle used to restrain scolding women

BRANKY *adj* ostentatious

BRANLE *n* old French country dance performed in a linked circle

BRANLES > BRANLE

BRANNED > BRAN

BRANNER *n* person or machine that treats metal with bran

BRANNERS > BRANNER

BRANNIER > BRANNY

BRANNIEST > BRANNY

BRANNIGAN *n* noisy quarrrel

BRANNING > BRAN

BRANNY *adj* having the appearance or texture of bran

BRANS > BRAN

BRANSLE *another word for* > BRANTLE

BRANSLES > BRANSLE

BRANT *n* small goose, *Branta bernicla*, that has a dark grey plumage and short neck and occurs in most northern coastal regions

BRANTAIL *n* singing bird with red tail

BRANTAILS > BRANTAIL

BRANTLE *n* French country dance

BRANTLES > BRANTLE

BRANTS > BRANT

BRAS > BRA

BRASCO *n* lavatory

BRASCOS > BRASCO

BRASERO *n* metal grid for burning coals

BRASEROS > BRASERO

BRASES > BRA

BRASH *adj* offensively loud, showy, or self-confident ▷ *n* loose rubbish, such as broken rock, hedge clippings, etc ▷ *vb* assault

BRASHED > BRASH

BRASHER > BRASH

BRASHES > BRASH

BRASHEST > BRASH

BRASHIER > BRASHY

BRASHIEST > BRASHY

BRASHING > BRASH

BRASHLY > BRASH

BRASHNESS > BRASH

BRASHY *adj* loosely fragmented

BRASIER *same as* > BRAZIER

BRASIERS > BRASIER

BRASIL *same as* > BRAZIL

BRASILEIN *same as* > BRAZILEIN

BRASILIN *same as* > BRAZILIN

BRASILINS > BRASILIN

BRASILS > BRASIL

BRASS *n* alloy of copper and zinc ▷ *vb* make irritated or annoyed

BRASSAGE *n* amount

charged by government for making coins

BRASSAGES > BRASSAGE

BRASSARD n identifying armband or badge

BRASSARDS > BRASSARD

BRASSART same as > BRASSARD

BRASSARTS > BRASSART

BRASSED > BRASS

BRASSERIE n restaurant serving drinks and cheap meals

BRASSES > BRASS

BRASSET same as > BRASSART

BRASSETS > BRASSET

BRASSICA n any plant of the cabbage and turnip family

BRASSICAS > BRASSICA

BRASSIE n former name for a club, a No. 2 wood, originally having a brass-plated sole and with a shallower face than a driver to give more loft

BRASSIER > BRASSY

BRASSIERE n bra

BRASSIES > BRASSIE

BRASSIEST > BRASSY

BRASSILY > BRASSY

BRASSING > BRASS

BRASSISH > BRASS

BRASSWARE n items made of brass

BRASSY same as > BRASSIE

BRAST same as > BURST

BRASTING > BRAST

BRASTS > BRAST

BRAT n unruly child

BRATCHET n hunting dog

BRATCHETS > BRATCHET

BRATLING n small badly-behaved child

BRATLINGS > BRATLING

BRATPACK n group of precocious and successful young actors, writers, etc

BRATPACKS > BRATPACK

BRATS > BRAT

BRATTICE n partition of wood or treated cloth used to control ventilation in a mine ▷ vb fit with a brattice

BRATTICED > BRATTICE

BRATTICES > BRATTICE

BRATTIER > BRAT

BRATTIEST > BRAT

BRATTISH same as > BRATTICE

BRATTLE vb make a rattling sound

BRATTLED > BRATTLE

BRATTLES > BRATTLE

BRATTLING > BRATTLE

BRATTY > BRAT

BRATWURST n type of small pork sausage

BRAUNCH old variant of > BRANCH

BRAUNCHED > BRAUNCH

BRAUNCHES > BRAUNCH

BRAUNITE n brown or black mineral

BRAUNITES > BRAUNITE

BRAVA n professional

assassin

BRAVADO n showy display of self-confidence ▷ vb behave with bravado

BRAVADOED > BRAVADO

BRAVADOES > BRAVADO

BRAVADOS > BRAVADO

BRAVAS > BRAVA

BRAVE adj having or showing courage, resolution, and daring ▷ n Native American warrior ▷ vb confront with resolution or courage

BRAVED > BRAVE

BRAVELY > BRAVE

BRAVENESS > BRAVE

BRAVER > BRAVE

BRAVERIES > BRAVE

BRAVERS > BRAVE

BRAVERY > BRAVE

BRAVES > BRAVE

BRAVEST > BRAVE

BRAVI > BRAVO

BRAVING > BRAVE

BRAVO interj well done! ▷ n cry of 'bravo' ▷ vb cry or shout 'bravo'

BRAVOED > BRAVO

BRAVOES > BRAVO

BRAVOING > BRAVO

BRAVOS > BRAVO

BRAVURA n display of boldness or daring

BRAVURAS > BRAVURA

BRAVURE > BRAVURA

BRAW adj fine or excellent, esp in appearance or dress ▷ pl n best clothes

BRAWER > BRAW

BRAWEST > BRAW

BRAWL n noisy fight ▷ vb fight noisily

BRAWLED > BRAWL

BRAWLER > BRAWL

BRAWLERS > BRAWL

BRAWLIE adj in good health

BRAWLIER > BRAWLIE

BRAWLIEST > BRAWLIE

BRAWLING > BRAWL

BRAWLINGS > BRAWL

BRAWLS > BRAWL

BRAWLY > BRAW

BRAWN n physical strength

BRAWNED > BRAWN

BRAWNIER > BRAWNY

BRAWNIEST > BRAWNY

BRAWNILY > BRAWNY

BRAWNS > BRAWN

BRAWNY adj muscular and strong

BRAWS n fine apparel

BRAXIES > BRAXY

BRAXY n acute and usually fatal bacterial disease of sheep characterized by high fever, coma, and inflammation of the fourth stomach, caused by infection with *Clostridium septicum*

BRAY vb (of a donkey) utter its loud harsh sound ▷ n donkey's loud harsh sound

BRAYED > BRAY

BRAYER > BRAY

BRAYERS > BRAY

BRAYING > BRAY

BRAYS > BRAY

BRAZA n Spanish unit of measurement

BRAZAS > BRAZA

BRAZE vb join (two metal surfaces) with brass ▷ n high-melting solder or alloy used in brazing

BRAZED > BRAZE

BRAZELESS > BRAZE

BRAZEN adj shameless and bold ▷ vb face and overcome boldly or shamelessly

BRAZENED > BRAZEN

BRAZENING > BRAZEN

BRAZENLY > BRAZEN

BRAZENRY adj audacity

BRAZENS > BRAZEN

BRAZER > BRAZE

BRAZERS > BRAZE

BRAZES > BRAZE

BRAZIER n portable container for burning charcoal or coal

BRAZIERS > BRAZIER

BRAZIERY > BRAZIER

BRAZIL n red wood obtained from various tropical leguminous trees of the genus *Caesalpinia*, such as *C. echinata* of America: used for cabinetwork

BRAZILEIN n red crystalline solid

BRAZILIN n pale yellow soluble crystalline solid

BRAZILINS > BRAZILIN

BRAZILS > BRAZIL

BRAZING > BRAZE

BREACH n breaking of a promise, obligation, etc ▷ vb break (a promise, law, etc)

BREACHED > BREACH

BREACHER > BREACH

BREACHERS > BREACH

BREACHES > BREACH

BREACHING > BREACH

BREAD n food made by baking a mixture of flour and water or milk ▷ vb cover (food) with breadcrumbs before cooking

BREADBOX n airtight container for bread, cakes, etc

BREADED > BREAD

BREADHEAD n person solely concerned with money

BREADING > BREAD

BREADLESS > BREAD

BREADLINE n queue of people waiting for free food given as charity

BREADNUT n moraceous tree, *Brosimum alicastrum*, of Central America and the Caribbean

BREADNUTS > BREADNUT

BREADROOM n place where bread is kept on ship

BREADROOT n leguminous plant, *Psoralea esculenta*,

of central North America, having an edible starchy root

BREADS > BREAD

BREADTH n extent of something from side to side

BREADTHS > BREADTH

BREADY adj having the appearance or texture of bread

BREAK > BRACKEN

BREAKABLE adj capable of being broken ▷ n fragile easily broken article

BREAKAGE n act or result of breaking

BREAKAGES > BREAKAGE

BREAKAWAY n (consisting of) a dissenting group who have left a larger unit ▷ adj dissenting ▷ vb leave hastily or escape

BREAKBACK adj backbreaking; arduous

BREAKBEAT n type of electronic dance music

BREAKBONE as in *breakbone fever* dengue

BREAKDOWN n act or instance of breaking down

BREAKER n large wave

BREAKERS > BREAKER

BREAKEVEN n the level of commercial activity at which the total cost and total revenue of a business enterprise are equal

BREAKFAST n first meal of the day ▷ vb eat breakfast

BREAKING > BRACKEN

BREAKINGS > BRACKEN

BREAKNECK adj fast and dangerous

BREAKOFF n act or an instance of breaking off or stopping

BREAKOFFS > BREAKOFF

BREAKOUT n escape, esp from prison or confinement

BREAKOUTS > BREAKOUT

BREAKS > BRACKEN

BREAKTIME n period of rest or recreation, esp at school

BREAKUP n separation or disintegration

BREAKUPS > BREAKUP

BREAKWALL n breakwater

BREAM n any of several Eurasian freshwater cyprinid fishes of the genus *Abramis*, esp *A. brama*, having a deep compressed body covered with silvery scales ▷ vb clean debris (from the bottom of a vessel)

BREAMED > BREAM

BREAMING > BREAM

BREAMS > BREAM

BREARE same as > BRIER

BREARES > BREARE

BREASKIT same as > BRISKET

BREASKITS > BREASKIT

BREAST n either of the (two soft fleshy milk-secreting glands on a woman's chest

▷ *vb* reach the summit of
BREASTED > BREAST
BREASTFED *adj* fed at mother's breast
BREASTING > BREAST
BREASTPIN *n* brooch worn on the breast, esp to close a garment
BREASTS > BREAST
BREATH *n* taking in and letting out of air during breathing
BREATHE *vb* take in oxygen and give out carbon dioxide
BREATHED *adj* relating to or denoting a speech sound for whose articulation the vocal cords are not made to vibrate
BREATHER *n* short rest
BREATHERS > BREATHER
BREATHES > BREATHE
BREATHFUL > BREATH
BREATHIER > BREATHY
BREATHILY > BREATHY
BREATHING *n* passage of air into and out of the lungs to supply the body with oxygen
BREATHS > BREATH
BREATHY *adj* (of the speaking voice) accompanied by an audible emission of breath
BRECCIA *n* rock consisting of angular fragments embedded in a finer matrix, formed by erosion, impact, volcanic activity, etc
BRECCIAL > BRECCIA
BRECCIAS > BRECCIA
BRECCIATE > BRECCIA
BRECHAM *n* straw horse-collar
BRECHAMS > BRECHAM
BRECHAN *same as* > BRECHAM
BRECHANS > BRECHAN
BRED > BREED ▷ *n* person who lives in a small remote place
BREDE *archaic spelling of* > BRAID
BREDED > BREDE
BREDES > BREDE
BREDIE *n* meat and vegetable stew
BREDIES > BREDIE
BREDING > BREDE
BREDS > BRED
BREE *n* broth, stock, or juice
BREECH *n* buttocks ▷ *vb* fit (a gun) with a breech
BREECHED > BREECH
BREECHES *pl n* trousers extending to just below the knee
BREECHING *n* strap of a harness that passes behind a horse's haunches
BREED *vb* produce new or improved strains of (domestic animals or plants) ▷ *n* group of animals etc within a (species that have certain clearly defined

characteristics
BREEDER *n* person who breeds plants or animals
BREEDERS > BREEDER
BREEDING > BREED
BREEDINGS > BREED
BREEDS > BREED
BREEKS *pl n* trousers
BREEM *same as* > BREME
BREENGE *vb* lunge forward ▷ *n* violent movement
BREENGED > BREENGE
BREENGES > BREENGE
BREENGING > BREENGE
BREER *another word for* > BRAIRD
BREERED > BREER
BREERING > BREER
BREERS > BREER
BREES > BREE
BREESE *same as* > BREEZE
BREESES > BREESE
BREEST > BREAST
BREESTS > BREAST
BREEZE *n* gentle wind ▷ *vb* move quickly or casually
BREEZED > BREEZE
BREEZES > BREEZE
BREEZEWAY *n* roofed passageway connecting two buildings, sometimes with the sides enclosed
BREEZIER > BREEZY
BREEZIEST > BREEZY
BREEZILY > BREEZY
BREEZING > BREEZE
BREEZY *adj* windy
BREGMA *n* point on the top (of the skull where the coronal and sagittal sutures meet: in infants this corresponds to the anterior fontanelle
BREGMATA > BREGMA
BREGMATE > BREGMA
BREGMATIC > BREGMA
BREHON *n* (formerly) judge in Ireland
BREHONS > BREHON
BREI *vb* speak with a uvular r, esp in Afrikaans
BREID *n* bread
BREIDS > BREID
BREIING > BREI
BREINGE *same as* > BREENGE
BREINGED > BREINGE
BREINGES > BREINGE
BREINGING > BREINGE
BREIS > BREI
BREIST *Scot word for* > BREAST
BREISTS > BREIST
BREKKIES > BREKKY
BREKKY *slang word for* > BREAKFAST
BRELOQUE *n* charm attached to watch chain
BRELOQUES > BRELOQUE
BREME *adj* well-known
BREN *n* type of machine gun
BRENNE *vb* burn
BRENNES > BRENNE
BRENNING > BREN
BRENS > BREN
BRENT *n* type of goose ▷ *adj* steep
BRENTER > BRENT

BRENTEST > BRENT
BRENTS > BRENT
BRER *n* brother: usually prefixed to a name
BRERE *same as* > BRIER
BRERES > BRERE
BRERS > BRER
BRETASCHE *another word for* > BRATTICE
BRETESSE *another word for* > BRATTICE
BRETESSES > BRETESSE
BRETHREN > BROTHER
BRETON *n* hat with an upturned brim and a rounded crown
BRETONS > BRETON
BRETTICE *same as* > BRATTICE
BRETTICED > BRETTICE
BRETTICES > BRETTICE
BREVE *n* accent (brevhere), placed over a vowel to indicate that it is short or is pronounced in a specified way
BREVES > BREVE
BREVET *n* document entitling a commissioned officer to hold temporarily a higher military rank without the appropriate pay and allowances ▷ *vb* promote by brevet
BREVETCY > BREVET
BREVETE *adj* patented
BREVETED > BREVET
BREVETING > BREVET
BREVETS > BREVET
BREVETTED > BREVET
BREVIARY *n* book of prayers to be recited daily by a Roman Catholic priest
BREVIATE *n* summary
BREVIATES > BREVIATE
BREVIER *n* (formerly) size of printer's type approximately equal to 8 point
BREVIERS > BREVIER
BREVIS *same as* > BREWIS
BREVISES > BREVIS
BREVITIES > BREVITY
BREVITY *n* shortness
BREW *vb* make (beer etc) by steeping, boiling, and fermentation ▷ *n* beverage produced by brewing
BREWAGE *n* product of brewing
BREWAGES > BREWAGE
BREWED > BREW
BREWER > BREW
BREWERIES > BREWERY
BREWERS > BREW
BREWERY *n* place where beer etc is brewed
BREWING *n* quantity of a beverage brewed at one time
BREWINGS > BREWING
BREWIS *n* bread soaked in broth, gravy, etc
BREWISES > BREWIS
BREWPUB *n* pub that incorporates a brewery on

its premises
BREWPUBS > BREWPUB
BREWS > BREW
BREWSKI *n* beer
BREWSKIES > BREWSKI
BREWSKIS > BREWSKI
BREWSTER *n* person, particularly a woman, who brews
BREWSTERS > BREWSTER
BREY *same as* > BREI
BREYED > BREY
BREYING > BREY
BREYS > BREY
BRIAR *n* ericaceous shrub, *Erica arborea*, of S Europe, having a hard woody root (briarroot)
BRIARD *n* medium-sized dog of an ancient French sheep-herding breed having a long rough coat of a single colour
BRIARDS > BRIARD
BRIARED > BRIAR
BRIARROOT *n* hard woody root of the briar, used for making tobacco pipes
BRIARS > BRIAR
BRIARWOOD *same as* > BRIARROOT
BRIARY > BRIAR
BRIBABLE > BRIBE
BRIBE *vb* offer or give something to someone to gain favour, influence, etc ▷ *n* something given or offered as a bribe
BRIBEABLE > BRIBE
BRIBED > BRIBE
BRIBEE *n* one who is bribed
BRIBEES > BRIBEE
BRIBER > BRIBE
BRIBERIES > BRIBERY
BRIBERS > BRIBE
BRIBERY *n* process of giving or taking bribes
BRIBES > BRIBE
BRIBING > BRIBE
BRICABRAC *n* miscellaneous small objects, esp furniture and curios, kept because they are ornamental or rare
BRICHT *Scot word for* > BRIGHT
BRICHTER > BRICHT
BRICHTEST > BRICHT
BRICK *n* (rectangular block of) baked clay used in building ▷ *vb* build, enclose, or fill with bricks
BRICKBAT *n* blunt criticism
BRICKBATS > BRICKBAT
BRICKCLAY *n* clay for making bricks
BRICKED > BRICK
BRICKEN *adj* made of brick
BRICKIE *n* bricklayer
BRICKIER > BRICKY
BRICKIES > BRICKIE
BRICKIEST > BRICKY
BRICKING > BRICK
BRICKINGS > BRICK
BRICKKILN *n* kiln for making bricks
BRICKLE *variant of* > BRITTLE

BRICKLES > BRICKLE
BRICKLIKE > BRICK
BRICKS > BRICK
BRICKWALL same as > BRICOLE
BRICKWORK n structure, such as a wall, built of bricks
BRICKY same as > BRICKIE
BRICKYARD n place in which bricks are made, stored, or sold
BRICOLAGE n jumbled effect produced by the close proximity of buildings from different periods and in different architectural styles
BRICOLE n shot in which the cue ball touches a cushion after striking the object ball and before touching another ball
BRICOLES > BRICOLE
BRIDAL adj of a bride or a wedding ▷n wedding or wedding feast
BRIDALLY > BRIDAL
BRIDALS > BRIDAL
BRIDE n woman who has just been or is about to be married
BRIDECAKE n wedding cake
BRIDED > BRIDE
BRIDEMAID n old form of bridesmaid
BRIDEMAN n bridegroom's attendant
BRIDEMEN > BRIDEMAN
BRIDES > BRIDE
BRIDESMAN same as > BRIDEMAN
BRIDESMEN > BRIDESMAN
BRIDEWELL n house of correction
BRIDGABLE > BRIDGE
BRIDGE n structure for crossing a river etc ▷vb build a bridge over (something)
BRIDGED > BRIDGE
BRIDGES > BRIDGE
BRIDGING n one or more timber struts fixed between floor or roof joists to stiffen the construction and distribute the loads
BRIDGINGS > BRIDGING
BRIDIE n semicircular pie containing meat and onions
BRIDIES > BRIDIE
BRIDING > BRIDE
BRIDLE n headgear for controlling a horse ▷vb show anger or indignation
BRIDLED > BRIDLE
BRIDLER > BRIDLE
BRIDLERS > BRIDLE
BRIDLES > BRIDLE
BRIDLEWAY n path for riding horses
BRIDLING > BRIDLE
BRIDOON n horse's bit: small snaffle used in double bridles
BRIDOONS > BRIDOON

BRIE same as > BREE
BRIEF adj short in duration ▷n condensed statement or written synopsis ▷vb give information and instructions to (a person)
BRIEFCASE n small flat case for carrying papers, books, etc
BRIEFED > BRIEF
BRIEFER > BRIEF
BRIEFERS > BRIEF
BRIEFEST > BRIEF
BRIEFING n meeting at which detailed information or instructions are given, as for military operations, etc
BRIEFINGS > BRIEFING
BRIEFLESS adj (said of a barrister) without clients
BRIEFLY > BRIEF
BRIEFNESS > BRIEF
BRIEFS pl n men's or women's underpants without legs
BRIER same as > BRIAR
BRIERED > BRIER
BRIERIER > BRIER
BRIERIEST > BRIER
BRIERROOT same as > BRIARROOT
BRIERS > BRIER
BRIERWOOD same as > BRIARROOT
BRIERY > BRIER
BRIES > BRIE
BRIG n two-masted square-rigged ship
BRIGADE n army unit smaller than a division ▷vb organize into a brigade
BRIGADED > BRIGADE
BRIGADES > BRIGADE
BRIGADIER n high-ranking army officer
BRIGADING > BRIGADE
BRIGALOW n type of acacia tree
BRIGALOWS > BRIGALOW
BRIGAND n bandit
BRIGANDRY > BRIGAND
BRIGANDS > BRIGAND
BRIGHT adj emitting or reflecting much light ▷adv brightly
BRIGHTEN vb make or become bright or brighter
BRIGHTENS > BRIGHTEN
BRIGHTER > BRIGHT
BRIGHTEST > BRIGHT
BRIGHTISH > BRIGHT
BRIGHTLY > BRIGHT
BRIGHTS pl n high beam of the headlights of a motor vehicle
BRIGS > BRIG
BRIGUE vb solicit
BRIGUED > BRIGUE
BRIGUES > BRIGUE
BRIGUING > BRIGUE
BRIGUINGS > BRIGUE
BRIK n Tunisian deep-fried spicy pastry filled with fish or meat and sometimes an egg
BRIKS > BRIK
BRILL n European food

fish, Scophthalmus rhombus, a flatfish similar to the turbot but lacking tubercles on the body: family Bothidae
BRILLER > BRILL
BRILLEST > BRILL
BRILLIANT adj shining with light ▷n popular circular cut for diamonds and other gemstones in the form of two many-faceted pyramids (the top one truncated) joined at their bases
BRILLO n tradename for a type of scouring pad impregnated with a detergent
BRILLOS > BRILLO
BRILLS > BRILL
BRIM n upper rim of a vessel ▷vb fill or be full to the brim
BRIMFUL adj completely filled with
BRIMFULL same as > BRIMFUL
BRIMFULLY > BRIMFUL
BRIMING n phosphorescence of sea
BRIMINGS > BRIMING
BRIMLESS > BRIM
BRIMMED > BRIM
BRIMMER n vessel, such as a glass or bowl, filled to the brim
BRIMMERS > BRIMMER
BRIMMING > BRIM
BRIMS > BRIM
BRIMSTONE n sulphur
BRIMSTONY > BRIMSTONE
BRIN n thread of silk from silkworm
BRINDED adj streaky or patchy
BRINDISI n song sung in celebration
BRINDISIS > BRINDISI
BRINDLE n brindled animal
BRINDLED adj brown or grey streaked with a darker colour
BRINDLES > BRINDLE
BRINE n salt water ▷vb soak in or treat with brine
BRINED > BRINE
BRINELESS > BRINE
BRINER > BRINE
BRINERS > BRINE
BRINES > BRINE
BRING vb carry, convey, or take to a designated place or person
BRINGDOWN n the decline from elation to depression, as when using drugs
BRINGER > BRING
BRINGERS > BRING
BRINGING > BRING
BRINGINGS > BRING
BRINGS > BRING
BRINIER > BRINY
BRINIES > BRINY
BRINIEST > BRINY
BRININESS > BRINY

BRINING > BRINE
BRINISH > BRINE
BRINJAL n dark purple tropical fruit, cooked and eaten as a vegetable
BRINJALS > BRINJAL
BRINJARRY n grain trader
BRINK n edge of a steep place
BRINKMAN n one who goes in for brinkmanship
BRINKMEN > BRINKMAN
BRINKS > BRINK
BRINNIES > BRINNY
BRINNY n stone, esp when thrown
BRINS > BRIN
BRINY adj very salty
BRIO n liveliness
BRIOCHE n soft roll or loaf made from a very light yeast dough, sometimes mixed with currants
BRIOCHES > BRIOCHE
BRIOLETTE n pear-shaped gem cut with long triangular facets
BRIONIES > BRIONY
BRIONY same as > BRYONY
BRIOS > BRIO
BRIQUET same as > BRIQUETTE
BRIQUETS > BRIQUET
BRIQUETTE n block of compressed coal dust ▷vb make into the form of a brick or bricks
BRIS n ritual circumcision of male babies, usually at eight days old, regarded as the formal entry of the child to the Jewish community
BRISANCE n shattering effect or power of an explosion or explosive
BRISANCES > BRISANCE
BRISANT > BRISANCE
BRISE n type of jump
BRISES > BRIS
BRISK adj lively and quick ▷vb enliven
BRISKED > BRISK
BRISKEN vb make or become more lively or brisk
BRISKENED > BRISKEN
BRISKENS > BRISKEN
BRISKER > BRISK
BRISKEST > BRISK
BRISKET n beef from the breast of a cow
BRISKETS > BRISKET
BRISKING > BRISK
BRISKISH > BRISK
BRISKLY > BRISK
BRISKNESS > BRISK
BRISKS > BRISK
BRISKY another word for > BRISK
BRISLING same as > SPRAT
BRISLINGS > BRISLING
BRISS same as > BRIS
BRISSES > BRIS
BRISTLE n short stiff hair ▷vb (cause to) stand up like bristles
BRISTLED > BRISTLE

b

BRISTLES > BRISTLE
BRISTLIER > BRISTLE
BRISTLING > BRISTLE
BRISTLY > BRISTLE
BRISTOL as in *bristol board* type of heavy cardboard
BRISTOLS *pl n* woman's breasts
BRISURE *n* mark of cadency in heraldry
BRISURES > BRISURE
BRIT *n* young of a herring, sprat, or similar fish
BRITANNIA *n* coin bearing figure of Britannia
BRITCHES *same as* > BREECHES
BRITH *same as* > BRIS
BRITHS > BRITH
BRITS > BRIT
BRITSCHKA *n* light open carriage
BRITSKA *same as* > BRITZKA
BRITSKAS > BRITSKA
BRITT *n* young herring or sprat
BRITTANIA *variant spelling of* > BRITANNIA
BRITTLE *adj* hard but easily broken ▷ *n* crunchy sweet made with treacle and nuts
BRITTLED > BRITTLE
BRITTLELY > BRITTLE
BRITTLER > BRITTLE
BRITTLES > BRITTLE
BRITTLEST > BRITTLE
BRITTLING > BRITTLE
BRITTLY > BRITTLE
BRITTS > BRITT
BRITZKA *n* long horse-drawn carriage with a folding top over the rear seat and a rear-facing front seat
BRITZKAS > BRITZKA
BRITZSKA *same as* > BRITZKA
BRITZSKAS > BRITZSKAS
BRIZE *same as* > BREEZE
BRIZES > BRIZE
BRO *n* family member
BROACH *vb* introduce (a topic) for discussion ▷ *n* spit for roasting meat
BROACHED > BROACH
BROACHER > BROACH
BROACHERS > BROACH
BROACHES > BROACH
BROACHING > BROACH
BROAD *adj* having great breadth or width ▷ *n* woman
BROADAX *same as* > BROADAXE
BROADAXE *n* broad-bladed axe
BROADAXES > BROADAXE
BROADBAND *n* telecommunication transmission technique using a wide range of frequencies
BROADBEAN *n* variety of bean
BROADBILL *n* any passerine bird of the family *Eurylaimidae*, of tropical Africa and Asia, having

bright plumage and a short wide bill
BROADBRIM *n* broad-brimmed hat, esp one worn by the Quakers in the 17th century
BROADCAST *n* programme or announcement on radio or television ▷ *vb* transmit (a programme or announcement) on radio or television ▷ *adj* dispersed over a wide area ▷ *adv* far and wide
BROADEN *vb* make or become broad or broader
BROADENED > BROADEN
BROADENER > BROADEN
BROADENS > BROADEN
BROADER > BROAD
BROADEST > BROAD
BROADISH > BROAD
BROADLEAF *n* any tobacco plant having broad leaves, used esp in making cigars
BROADLINE *n* company dealing in large volumes of cheap products
BROADLOOM *adj* of or designating carpets woven on a wide loom ▷ *n* of or designating carpets or carpeting woven on a wide loom to obviate the need for seams
BROADLY > BROAD
BROADNESS > BROAD
BROADS > BROAD
BROADSIDE *n* strong verbal or written attack ▷ *adv* with a broader side facing an object
BROADTAIL *n* highly valued black wavy fur obtained from the skins of newly born karakul lambs
BROADWAY *n* wide road
BROADWAYS > BROADWAY
BROADWISE *adv* rare form of breadthwise
BROCADE *n* rich fabric woven with a raised design ▷ *vb* weave with such a design
BROCADED > BROCADE
BROCADES > BROCADE
BROCADING > BROCADE
BROCAGE *another word for* > BROKERAGE
BROCAGES > BROCAGE
BROCARD *n* basic principle of civil law
BROCARDS > BROCARD
BROCATEL *n* heavy upholstery brocade
BROCATELS > BROCATEL
BROCCOLI *n* type of cabbage with greenish flower heads
BROCCOLIS > BROCCOLI
BROCH *n* (in Scotland) a circular dry-stone tower large enough to serve as a fortified home
BROCHAN *n* type of thin porridge
BROCHANS > BROCHAN

BROCHE *adj* woven with a raised design, as brocade
BROCHED > BROCHE
BROCHES > BROCHE
BROCHETTE *n* skewer used for holding pieces of meat or vegetables while grilling
BROCHING > BROCHE
BROCHO *same as* > BRACHAH
BROCHOS > BROCHO
BROCHS > BROCH
BROCHURE *n* booklet that contains information about a product or service
BROCHURES > BROCHURE
BROCK *n* badger
BROCKAGE *same as* > BROKERAGE
BROCKAGES > BROKERAGE
BROCKED *adj* having different colours
BROCKET *n* any small deer of the genus *Mazama*, of tropical America, having small unbranched antlers
BROCKETS > BROCKET
BROCKIT *same as* > BROCKED
BROCKRAM *another word for* > BRECCIA
BROCKRAMS > BROCKRAM
BROCKS > BROCK
BROCOLI *same as* > BROCCOLI
BROCOLIS > BROCOLI
BROD *vb* prod
BRODDED > BROD
BRODDING > BROD
BRODDLE *vb* poke or pierce (something)
BRODDLED > BRODDLE
BRODDLES > BRODDLE
BRODDLING > BRODDLE
BRODEKIN *another word for* > BUSKIN
BRODEKINS > BRODEKIN
BRODKIN *same as* > BRODEKIN
BRODKINS > BRODKIN
BRODS > BROD
BROEKIES *pl n* underpants
BROG *n* bradawl
BROGAN *n* heavy laced, usually ankle-high, work boot
BROGANS > BROGAN
BROGGED > BROG
BROGGING > BROG
BROGH *same as* > BROCH
BROGHS > BROGH
BROGS > BROG
BROGUE *n* sturdy walking shoe
BROGUEISH > BROGUE
BROGUERY > BROGUE
BROGUES > BROGUE
BROGUISH > BROGUE
BROIDER *archaic word for* > EMBROIDER
BROIDERED > BROIDER
BROIDERER > BROIDER
BROIDERS > BROIDER
BROIDERY *n* old form of embroidery
BROIL *vb* cook by direct heat under a grill ▷ *n* process of broiling
BROILED > BROIL

BROILER *n* young tender chicken for roasting
BROILERS > BROILER
BROILING > BROIL
BROILS > BROIL
BROKAGE *another word for* > BROKERAGE
BROKAGES > BROKAGE
BROKE *vb* negotiate or deal
BROKED > BROKE
BROKEN > BRACKEN
BROKENLY > BRACKEN
BROKER *n* agent who buys or sells goods, securities, etc ▷ *vb* act as a broker (in)
BROKERAGE *n* commission charged by a broker
BROKERED > BROKER
BROKERIES > BROKERY
BROKERING > BROKER
BROKERS > BROKER
BROKERY *n* work done by broker
BROKES > BROKE
BROKING > BROKE
BROKINGS > BROKE
BROLGA *n* large grey Australian crane with a trumpeting call
BROLGAS > BROLGA
BROLLIES > BROLLY
BROLLY *n* umbrella
BROMAL *n* yellowish oily synthetic liquid formerly used medicinally as a sedative and hypnotic
BROMALS > BROMAL
BROMATE *same as* > BROMINATE
BROMATED > BROMATE
BROMATES > BROMATE
BROMATING > BROMATE
BROME *n* type of grass
BROMELAIN *n* enzyme in pineapples
BROMELIA *n* type of plant
BROMELIAD *n* any plant of the tropical American family *Bromeliaceae*, typically epiphytes with a rosette of fleshy leaves. The family includes the pineapple and Spanish moss
BROMELIAS > BROMELIA
BROMELIN *n* protein-digesting enzyme found in pineapple and extracted for use in treating joint pain and inflammation, hay fever, and various other conditions
BROMELINS > BROMELIN
BROMEOSIN *another name for* > EOSIN
BROMES > BROME
BROMIC *adj* of or containing bromine in the trivalent or pentavalent state
BROMID *same as* > BROMIDE
BROMIDE *n* chemical compound used in medicine and photography
BROMIDES > BROMIDE
BROMIDIC *adj* ordinary
BROMIDS > BROMID
BROMIN *same as* > BROMINE

BROMINATE vb treat or react with bromine

BROMINE n dark red liquid element that gives off a pungent vapour

BROMINES > BROMINE

BROMINISM same as > BROMISM

BROMINS > BROMIN

BROMISE same as > BROMIZE

BROMISED > BROMIZE

BROMISES > BROMIZE

BROMISING > BROMIZE

BROMISM n poisoning caused by the excessive intake of bromine or compounds containing bromine

BROMISMS > BROMISM

BROMIZE vb treat with bromine

BROMIZED > BROMIZE

BROMIZES > BROMIZE

BROMIZING > BROMIZE

BROMMER n S African word for bluebottle

BROMMERS > BROMMER

BROMO n something that contains bromide

BROMOFORM n heavy colourless liquid substance with a sweetish taste

BROMOS > BROMO

BRONC same as > BRONCO

BRONCHI > BRONCHUS

BRONCHIA pl n bronchial tubes

BRONCHIAL adj of the bronchi

BRONCHIUM n medium-sized bronchial tube

BRONCHO same as > BRONCO

BRONCHOS > BRONCHO

BRONCHUS n either of the two branches of the windpipe

BRONCO n (in the US) wild or partially tamed pony

BRONCOS > BRONCO

BRONCS > BRONC

BROND n old form of brand

BRONDS > BROND

BRONDYRON n sword

BRONZE n alloy of copper and tin ▷ adj made of, or coloured like, bronze ▷ vb (esp of the skin) make or become brown

BRONZED > BRONZE

BRONZEN adj made of or the colour of bronze

BRONZER n cosmetic applied to the skin to simulate a sun tan

BRONZERS > BRONZER

BRONZES > BRONZE

BRONZIER > BRONZE

BRONZIEST > BRONZE

BRONZIFY vb cause to become colour of bronze

BRONZING n blue pigment producing a metallic lustre when ground into paint media at fairly high concentrations

BRONZINGS > BRONZING

BRONZITE n type of orthopyroxene often having a metallic or pearly sheen

BRONZITES > BRONZITE

BRONZY > BRONZE

BROO n brow of hill

BROOCH n ornament with a pin, worn fastened to clothes ▷ vb decorate with a brooch

BROOCHED > BROOCH

BROOCHES > BROOCH

BROOCHING > BROOCH

BROOD n number of birds produced at one hatching ▷ vb (of a bird) sit on or hatch eggs

BROODED > BROOD

BROODER n enclosure or other structure, usually heated, used for rearing young chickens or other fowl

BROODERS > BROODER

BROODIER > BROODY

BROODIEST > BROODY

BROODILY > BROODY

BROODING > BROOD

BROODINGS > BROOD

BROODLESS > BROOD

BROODMARE n mare for breeding

BROODS > BROOD

BROODY adj moody and sullen

BROOK n small stream ▷ vb bear or tolerate

BROOKABLE > BROOK

BROOKED > BROOK

BROOKIE n brook trout

BROOKIES > BROOKIE

BROOKING > BROOK

BROOKITE n reddish-brown to black mineral

BROOKITES > BROOKITE

BROOKLET n small brook

BROOKLETS > BROOKLET

BROOKLIKE > BROOK

BROOKLIME n either of two blue-flowered scrophulariaceous trailing plants, *Veronica americana* of North America or *V. beccabunga* of Europe and Asia, growing in moist places

BROOKS > BROOK

BROOKWEED n either of two white-flowered primulaceous plants, *Samolus valerandi* of Europe or *S. floribundus* of North America, growing in moist places

BROOL n low roar

BROOLS > BROOL

BROOM n long-handled sweeping brush ▷ vb sweep with a broom

BROOMBALL n type of ice hockey played with broom

BROOMCORN n variety of sorghum, *Sorghum vulgare technicum*, the long stiff flower stalks of which have been used for making brooms

BROOMED > BROOM

BROOMIER > BROOMY

BROOMIEST > BROOMY

BROOMING > BROOM

BROOMRAPE n any orobanchaceous plant of the genus *Orobanche*: brownish small-flowered leafless parasites on the roots of other plants, esp on legumes

BROOMS > BROOM

BROOMY adj covered with growth of broom

BROOS > BROO

BROOSE n race at country wedding

BROOSES > BROOSE

BROS > BRO

BROSE n oatmeal or pease porridge, sometimes with butter or fat added

BROSES > BROSE

BROSY adj smeared with porridge

BROTH n soup, usu containing vegetables

BROTHEL n house where men pay to have sex with prostitutes

BROTHELS > BROTHEL

BROTHER n boy or man with the same parents as another person ▷ interj exclamation of amazement, disgust, surprise, disappointment, etc ▷ vb treat someone like a brother

BROTHERED > BROTHER

BROTHERLY adj of or like a brother, esp in showing loyalty and affection ▷ adv in a brotherly way

BROTHERS > BROTHER

BROTHS > BROTH

BROTHY adj having appearance or texture of broth

BROUGH same as > BROCH

BROUGHAM n horse-drawn closed carriage with a raised open driver's seat in front

BROUGHAMS > BROUGHAM

BROUGHS > BROUGH

BROUGHT > BRING

BROUGHTA same as > BRAATA

BROUGHTAS same as > BRAATA

BROUHAHA n loud confused noise

BROUHAHAS > BROUHAHA

BROUZE same as > BROOSE

BROUZES > BROUZE

BROW n part of the face (from the eyes to the hairline

BROWALLIA n flowering plant

BROWBAND n strap of a horse's bridle that goes across the forehead

BROWBANDS > BROWBAND

BROWBEAT vb frighten (someone) with threats

BROWBEATS > BROWBEAT

BROWED adj having a brow

BROWLESS > BROW

BROWN n colour of earth or wood ▷ adj (of bread) made from wheatmeal or wholemeal flour ▷ vb make or become brown

BROWNED > BROWN

BROWNER > BROWN

BROWNEST > BROWN

BROWNIE n small square nutty chocolate cake

BROWNIER > BROWN

BROWNIES > BROWNIE

BROWNIEST > BROWN

BROWNING n substance used to darken gravies

BROWNINGS > BROWNING

BROWNISH > BROWN

BROWNNESS > BROWN

BROWNNOSE vb be abjectly subservient

BROWNOUT n dimming or reduction in the use of electric lights in a city, esp to conserve electric power or as a defensive precaution in wartime

BROWNOUTS > BROWNOUT

BROWNS > BROWN

BROWNY > BROWN

BROWRIDGE n ridge of bone over eyes

BROWS > BROW

BROWSABLE > BROWSE

BROWSE vb look through (a book or articles for sale) in a casual manner ▷ n instance of browsing

BROWSED > BROWSE

BROWSER n software package that enables a user to read hypertext, esp on the Internet

BROWSERS > BROWSER

BROWSES > BROWSE

BROWSIER > BROWSE

BROWSIEST > BROWSE

BROWSING > BROWSE

BROWSINGS > BROWSE

BROWST n brewing (of ale, tea)

BROWSTS > BROWST

BROWSY > BROWSE

BRR same as > BRRR

BRRR interj used to suggest shivering

BRU South African word for > FRIEND

BRUCELLA n type of bacterium

BRUCELLAE > BRUCELLA

BRUCELLAS > BRUCELLA

BRUCHID n type of beetle

BRUCHIDS > BRUCHID

BRUCIN same as > BRUCINE

BRUCINE n bitter poisonous alkaloid resembling strychnine

BRUCINES > BRUCINE

BRUCINS > BRUCIN

BRUCITE n white translucent mineral

BRUCITES > BRUCITE

BRUCKLE adj brittle

BRUGH n large house

BRUGHS > BRUGH**

b

BRUHAHA same as > BROUHAHA
BRUHAHAS > BRUHAHA
BRUILZIE same as > BRULZIE
BRUILZIES > BRUILZIE
BRUIN n name for a bear, used in children's tales, fables, etc
BRUINS > BRUIN
BRUISE n discoloured area on the skin caused by an injury ▷ vb cause a bruise on
BRUISED > BRUISE
BRUISER n strong tough person
BRUISERS > BRUISER
BRUISES > BRUISE
BRUISING adj causing bruises, as by a blow ▷ n bruise or bruises
BRUISINGS > BRUISING
BRUIT vb report ▷ n abnormal sound heard within the body during auscultation, esp a heart murmur
BRUITED > BRUIT
BRUITER > BRUIT
BRUITERS > BRUIT
BRUITING > BRUIT
BRUITS > BRUIT
BRULE n shortened form of the archaic word for a mixed-race person of Canadian Indian and White (usually French-Canadian) ancestry
BRULES > BRULE
BRULOT n coffee-based alcoholic drink, served flaming
BRULOTS > BRULOT
BRULYIE same as > BRULYIE
BRULYIES > BRULYIE
BRULZIE n noisy dispute
BRULZIES > BRULZIE
BRUMAL adj of, characteristic of, or relating to winter
BRUMBIES > BRUMBY
BRUMBY n wild horse
BRUME n heavy mist or fog
BRUMES > BRUME
BRUMMAGEM n something that is cheap and flashy, esp imitation jewellery
BRUMMER same as > BROMMER
BRUMMERS > BRUMMER
BRUMOUS > BRUME
BRUNCH n breakfast and lunch combined ▷ vb eat brunch
BRUNCHED > BRUNCH
BRUNCHER > BRUNCH
BRUNCHERS > BRUNCH
BRUNCHES > BRUNCH
BRUNCHING > BRUNCH
BRUNET adj dark brown
BRUNETS > BRUNET
BRUNETTE n girl or woman with dark brown hair ▷ adj dark brown
BRUNETTES > BRUNETTE
BRUNG > BRING
BRUNIZEM n prairie soil

BRUNIZEMS > BRUNIZEM
BRUNT n main force or shock of a blow, attack, etc ▷ vb suffer the main force or shock of a blow, attack, etc
BRUNTED > BRUNT
BRUNTING > BRUNT
BRUNTS > BRUNT
BRUS > BRU
BRUSH n device made of bristles, wires, etc used for cleaning, painting, etc ▷ vb clean, scrub, or paint with a brush
BRUSHBACK n (baseball) ball intended to hit the batter
BRUSHED adj treated with a brushing process to raise the nap and give a softer and warmer finish
BRUSHER > BRUSH
BRUSHERS > BRUSH
BRUSHES > BRUSH
BRUSHFIRE n fire in bushes and scrub
BRUSHIER > BRUSHY
BRUSHIEST > BRUSHY
BRUSHING > BRUSH
BRUSHINGS > BRUSH
BRUSHLAND n land characterized by patchy shrubs
BRUSHLESS > BRUSH
BRUSHLIKE > BRUSH
BRUSHMARK n indented lines sometimes left by the bristles of a brush on a painted surface
BRUSHOFF n an abrupt dismissal or rejection
BRUSHOFFS > BRUSHOFF
BRUSHUP n the act or an instance of tidying one's appearance
BRUSHUPS > BRUSHUP
BRUSHWOOD n cut or broken-off tree branches and twigs
BRUSHWORK n characteristic manner of applying paint with a brush
BRUSHY adj like a brush
BRUSK same as > BRUSQUE
BRUSKER > BRUSK
BRUSKEST > BRUSK
BRUSQUE adj blunt or curt in manner or speech
BRUSQUELY > BRUSQUE
BRUSQUER > BRUSQUE
BRUSQUEST > BRUSQUE
BRUSSEN adj bold
BRUST same as > BURST
BRUSTING > BRUST
BRUSTS > BRUST
BRUT adj (of champagne or sparkling wine) very dry ▷ n very dry champagne
BRUTAL adj cruel and vicious
BRUTALISE same as > BRUTALIZE
BRUTALISM n austere architectural style of the 1950s on, characterized by the use of exposed concrete and angular shapes
BRUTALIST > BRUTALISM
BRUTALITY > BRUTAL

BRUTALIZE vb make or become brutal
BRUTALLY > BRUTAL
BRUTE n brutal person ▷ adj wholly instinctive or physical, like an animal
BRUTED > BRUTE
BRUTELIKE > BRUTE
BRUTELY > BRUTE
BRUTENESS > BRUTE
BRUTER n diamond cutter
BRUTERS > BRUTER
BRUTES > BRUTE
BRUTIFIED > BRUTIFY
BRUTIFIES > BRUTIFY
BRUTIFY less common word for > BRUTALIZE
BRUTING n diamond cutting
BRUTINGS > BRUTING
BRUTISH adj of or like an animal
BRUTISHLY > BRUTISH
BRUTISM n stupidity; vulgarity
BRUTISMS > BRUTISM
BRUTS > BRUT
BRUX vb grind one's teeth
BRUXED > BRUX
BRUXES > BRUX
BRUXING > BRUX
BRUXISM n habit of grinding the teeth, esp unconsciously
BRUXISMS > BRUXISM
BRYOLOGY n branch of botany concerned with the study of bryophytes
BRYONIES > BRYONY
BRYONY n wild climbing hedge plant
BRYOPHYTE n any plant of the phyla Bryophyta (mosses), Hepatophyta (liverworts), or Anthocerophyta (hornworts), having stems and leaves but lacking true vascular tissue and roots and reproducing by spores
BRYOZOAN n any aquatic invertebrate animal of the phylum Bryozoa, forming colonies of polyps each having a ciliated feeding organ (lophophore) ▷ adj of, relating to, or belonging to the Bryozoa
BRYOZOANS > BRYOZOAN
BUAT same as > BOWAT
BUATS > BUAT
BUAZE n fibrous African plant
BUAZES > BUAZE
BUB n youngster
BUBA another name for > YAWS
BUBAL n any of various antelopes, esp an extinct N African variety of hartebeest
BUBALE n large antelope
BUBALES > BUBALE
BUBALINE adj (of antelopes) related to or resembling the bubal
BUBALIS same as > BUBAL
BUBALISES > BUBALIS

BUBALS > BUBAL
BUBAS > BUBA
BUBBA n ordinary American person
BUBBAS > BUBBA
BUBBIES > BUBBY
BUBBLE n ball of air in a liquid or solid ▷ vb form bubbles
BUBBLED > BUBBLE
BUBBLEGUM n type of chewing gum that can be blown into large bubbles
BUBBLER n drinking fountain in which the water is forced in a stream from a small vertical nozzle
BUBBLERS > BUBBLER
BUBBLES > BUBBLE
BUBBLIER > BUBBLY
BUBBLIES > BUBBLY
BUBBLIEST > BUBBLY
BUBBLING > BUBBLE
BUBBLY adj excited and lively ▷ n champagne
BUBBY n old word for woman's breast
BUBINGA n reddish-brown wood from African tree
BUBINGAS > BUBINGA
BUBKES n very small amount
BUBO n inflammation and swelling of a lymph node, esp in the armpit or groin
BUBOED > BUBO
BUBOES > BUBO
BUBONIC > BUBO
BUBS > BUB
BUBU same as > BOUBOU
BUBUKLE n red spot on skin
BUBUKLES > BUBUKLE
BUBUS > BUBU
BUCCAL adj of or relating to the cheek
BUCCALLY > BUCCAL
BUCCANEER n pirate ▷ vb be or act like a buccaneer
BUCCANIER same as > BUCCANEER
BUCCINA n curved Roman horn
BUCCINAS > BUCCINA
BUCELLAS n type of Portuguese white wine
BUCENTAUR n state barge of Venice from which the doge and other officials dropped a ring into the sea on Ascension Day to symbolize the ceremonial marriage of the state with the Adriatic
BUCHU n any of several S. African rutaceous shrubs of the genus Barosma, esp B. betulina, whose leaves are used as an antiseptic and diuretic
BUCHUS > BUCHU
BUCK n male of the goat, hare, kangaroo, rabbit, and reindeer ▷ vb (of a horse etc) jump with legs stiff and back arched
BUCKAROO n cowboy
BUCKAROOS > BUCKAROO

BUCKAYRO same as > BUCKAROO

BUCKAYROS > BUCKAYRO

BUCKBEAN n marsh plant, *Menyanthes trifoliata*, with white or pink flowers: family *Menyanthaceae*

BUCKBEANS > BUCKBEAN

BUCKBOARD n open four-wheeled horse-drawn carriage with the seat attached to a flexible board between the front and rear axles

BUCKBRUSH n American shrub

BUCKED > BUCK

BUCKEEN n (in Ireland) poor young man who aspires to the habits and dress of the wealthy

BUCKEENS > BUCKEEN

BUCKER > BUCK

BUCKEROO same as > BUCKAROO

BUCKEROOS > BUCKEROO

BUCKERS > BUCK

BUCKET vb open-topped roughly cylindrical container ▷vb rain heavily

BUCKETED > BUCKET

BUCKETFUL same as > BUCKET

BUCKETING > BUCKET

BUCKETS > BUCKET

BUCKEYE n any of several North American trees of the genus *Aesculus*, esp *A. glabra* (Ohio buckeye), having erect clusters of white or red flowers and prickly fruits: family *Hippocastanaceae*

BUCKEYES > BUCKEYE

BUCKHORN n horn from a buck, used for knife handles, etc

BUCKHORNS > BUCKHORN

BUCKHOUND n hound, smaller than a staghound, used for hunting the smaller breeds of deer, esp fallow deer

BUCKIE n whelk or its shell

BUCKIES > BUCKIE

BUCKING > BUCK

BUCKINGS > BUCK

BUCKISH > BUCK

BUCKISHLY > BUCK

BUCKLE n clasp for fastening a belt or strap ▷vb fasten or be fastened with a buckle

BUCKLED > BUCKLE

BUCKLER n small round shield worn on the forearm ▷vb defend

BUCKLERED > BUCKLER

BUCKLERS > BUCKLER

BUCKLES > BUCKLE

BUCKLING another name for > BLOATER

BUCKLINGS > BUCKLING

BUCKO n lively young fellow: often a term of address

BUCKOES > BUCKO

BUCKOS > BUCKO

BUCKRA n (used contemptuously by Black people, esp in the US) White man

BUCKRAKE n large rake attached to tractor

BUCKRAKES > BUCKRAKE

BUCKRAM n cotton or linen cloth stiffened with size, etc, used in lining or stiffening clothes, bookbinding, etc ▷vb stiffen with buckram

BUCKRAMED > BUCKRAM

BUCKRAMS > BUCKRAM

BUCKRAS > BUCKRA

BUCKS > BUCK

BUCKSAW n woodcutting saw having its blade set in a frame and tensioned by a turnbuckle across the back of the frame

BUCKSAWS > BUCKSAW

BUCKSHEE adj free

BUCKSHEES > BUCKSHEE

BUCKSHISH n tip, present or gift

BUCKSHOT n large lead pellets used for shooting game

BUCKSHOTS > BUCKSHOT

BUCKSKIN n skin of a male deer ▷adj greyish-yellow

BUCKSKINS pl n (in the US and Canada) breeches, shoes, or a suit of buckskin

BUCKSOM same as > BUXOM

BUCKTAIL n in fishing, fly with appearance of minnow

BUCKTAILS > BUCKTAIL

BUCKTEETH > BUCKTOOTH

BUCKTHORN n thorny shrub whose berries were formerly used as a purgative

BUCKTOOTH n projecting upper front tooth

BUCKU same as > BUCHU

BUCKUS > BUCKU

BUCKWHEAT n small black grain used for making flour

BUCKYBALL n ball-like polyhedral carbon molecule of the type found in buckminsterfullerene and other fullerenes

BUCKYTUBE n tube of carbon atoms structurally similar to buckminsterfullerene

BUCOLIC adj of the countryside or country life ▷n pastoral poem

BUCOLICAL > BUCOLIC

BUCOLICS > BUCOLIC

BUD n swelling on a plant that develops into a leaf or flower ▷vb produce buds

BUDA n derogatory Indian English word for an old man

BUDAS > BUDA

BUDDED > BUD

BUDDER > BUD

BUDDERS > BUD

BUDDHA n person who has achieved a state of perfect enlightenment

BUDDHAS > BUDDHA

BUDDIED > BUDDY

BUDDIER > BUDDY

BUDDIES > BUDDY

BUDDIEST > BUDDY

BUDDING > BUDDY

BUDDINGS > BUDDY

BUDDLE n sloping trough in which ore is washed ▷vb wash (ore) in a buddle

BUDDLED > BUDDLE

BUDDLEIA n shrub with long spikes of purple flowers

BUDDLEIAS > BUDDLEIA

BUDDLES > BUDDLE

BUDDLING > BUDDLE

BUDDY n friend ▷vb act as a friend to ▷adj friendly

BUDDYING > BUDDY

BUDGE vb move slightly ▷n lambskin dressed for the fur to be worn on the outer side

BUDGED > BUDGE

BUDGER > BUDGE

BUDGEREE adj good

BUDGERO same as > BUDGEROW

BUDGEROS > BUDGERO

BUDGEROW n barge use on Ganges

BUDGEROWS > BUDGEROW

BUDGERS > BUDGE

BUDGES > BUDGE

BUDGET n financial plan for a period of time ▷vb plan the expenditure of (money or time) ▷adj cheap

BUDGETARY > BUDGET

BUDGETED > BUDGET

BUDGETEER > BUDGET

BUDGETER > BUDGET

BUDGETERS > BUDGET

BUDGETING > BUDGET

BUDGETS > BUDGET

BUDGIE n short form of budgerigar

BUDGIES > BUDGIE

BUDGING > BUDGE

BUDI n derogatory Indian English word an for old woman

BUDIS > BUDI

BUDLESS > BUD

BUDLIKE > BUD

BUDMASH n badmash

BUDMASHES > BUDMASH

BUDO n combat and spirit in martial arts

BUDOS > BUDO

BUDS > BUD

BUDWORM n pest that eats tree leaves and buds

BUDWORMS > BUDWORM

BUFF n soft flexible undyed leather ▷adj dull yellowish-brown ▷vb clean or polish with soft material

BUFFA > BUFFO

BUFFABLE > BUFF

BUFFALO n member of the cattle tribe, *Syncerus caffer*, mostly found in game reserves in southern and eastern Africa and having upward-curving horns ▷vb confuse

BUFFALOED > BUFFALO

BUFFALOES > BUFFALO

BUFFALOS > BUFFALO

BUFFE > BUFFO

BUFFED > BUFF

BUFFEL as in *buffel grass* grass used for pasture in Africa, India, and Australia

BUFFER same as > BUFF

BUFFERED > BUFFER

BUFFERING > BUFFER

BUFFERS > BUFFER

BUFFEST > BUFF

BUFFET n counter where drinks and snacks are served ▷vb knock against or about

BUFFETED > BUFFET

BUFFETER > BUFFET

BUFFETERS > BUFFET

BUFFETING n response of an aircraft structure to buffet, esp an irregular oscillation of the tail

BUFFETS > BUFFET

BUFFI > BUFFO

BUFFIER > BUFFY

BUFFIEST > BUFFY

BUFFING > BUFF

BUFFINGS > BUFFING

BUFFO n (in Italian opera of the 18th century) comic part, esp one for a bass

BUFFOON n clown or fool

BUFFOONS > BUFFOON

BUFFOS > BUFFO

BUFFS > BUFF

BUFFY adj having appearance or texture of buff

BUFO n type of toad

BUFOS > BUFO

BUFOTALIN n principal poisonous substance in the skin and saliva of the common European toad

BUG n insect ▷vb irritate

BUGABOO n imaginary source of fear

BUGABOOS > BUGABOO

BUGBANE n any of several ranunculaceous plants of the genus *Cimicifuga*, esp *C. foetida* of Europe, whose flowers are reputed to repel insects

BUGBANES > BUGBANE

BUGBEAR n thing that causes obsessive anxiety

BUGBEARS > BUGBEAR

BUGEYE n oyster-dredging boat

BUGEYES > BUGEYE

BUGGAN n evil spirit

BUGGANE same as > BUGGAN

BUGGANES > BUGGANE

BUGGANS > BUGGAN

BUGGED > BUG

BUGGER n unpleasant or difficult person or thing ▷vb tire ▷interj exclamation of annoyance or disappointment

b

b

BUGGERED > BUGGER
BUGGERIES > BUGGERY
BUGGERING > BUGGER
BUGGERS > BUGGER
BUGGERY n anal intercourse
BUGGIER > BUGGY
BUGGIES > BUGGY
BUGGIEST > BUGGY
BUGGIN same as > BUGGAN
BUGGINESS > BUGGY
BUGGING > BUG
BUGGINGS > BUG
BUGGINS > BUGGIN
BUGGY n light horse-drawn carriage having two or four wheels ▷ adj infested with bugs
BUGHOUSE n offensive name for a mental hospital or asylum ▷ adj offensive word for insane
BUGHOUSES > BUGHOUSE
BUGLE n instrument like a small trumpet ▷ vb play or sound (on) a bugle
BUGLED > BUGLE
BUGLER > BUGLE
BUGLERS > BUGLE
BUGLES > BUGLE
BUGLET n small bugle
BUGLETS > BUGLET
BUGLEWEED same as > BUGLE
BUGLING > BUGLE
BUGLOSS n any of various hairy Eurasian boraginaceous plants of the genera Anchusa, Lycopsis, and Echium, esp L. arvensis, having clusters of blue flowers
BUGLOSSES > BUGLOSS
BUGONG same as > BOGONG
BUGONGS > BUGONG
BUGOUT n act of running away
BUGOUTS > BUGOUT
BUGS > BUG
BUGSEED n form of tumbleweed
BUGSEEDS > BUGSEED
BUGSHA same as > BUQSHA
BUGSHAS > BUGSHA
BUGWORT another name for > BUGBANE
BUGWORTS > BUGWORT
BUHL same as > BOULLE
BUHLS > BUHL
BUHLWORK n woodwork with decorative inlay
BUHLWORKS > BUHLWORK
BUHR > BURR
BUHRS > BURR
BUHRSTONE n hard tough rock containing silica, fossils, and cavities, formerly used as a grindstone
BUHUND n type of Norwegian dog
BUHUNDS > BUHUND
BUIBUI n piece of black cloth worn as a shawl by Muslim women, esp on the E African coast
BUIBUIS > BUIBUI
BUIK same as > BOOK
BUIKS > BUIK

BUILD vb make, construct, or form by joining parts or materials ▷ n shape of the body
BUILDABLE adj suitable for building on
BUILDDOWN n planned reduction
BUILDED > BUILD
BUILDER n person who constructs houses and other buildings
BUILDERS > BUILDER
BUILDING > BUILD
BUILDINGS > BUILD
BUILDS > BUILD
BUILDUP n gradual approach to a climax or critical point
BUILDUPS > BUILDUP
BUILT > BUILD
BUIRDLIER > BUIRDLY
BUIRDLY adj well-built
BUIST vb brand sheep with identification mark
BUISTED > BUIST
BUISTING > BUIST
BUISTS > BUIST
BUKE same as > BOOK
BUKES > BUKE
BUKKAKE n type of sexual practice
BUKKAKES > BUKKAKE
BUKSHEE n person in charge of paying wages
BUKSHEES > BUKSHEE
BUKSHI same as > BUKSHEE
BUKSHIS > BUKSHI
BULB n onion-shaped root which grows into a flower or plant ▷ vb form into the shape of a bulb
BULBAR adj of or relating to a bulb, esp the medulla oblongata
BULBED > BULB
BULBEL same as > BULBIL
BULBELS > BULBEL
BULBIL n small bulblike organ of vegetative reproduction growing in leaf axils or on flower stalks of plants such as the onion and tiger lily
BULBILS > BULBIL
BULBING > BULB
BULBLET n small bulb at base of main bulb
BULBLETS > BULBLET
BULBOSITY > BULBOUS
BULBOUS adj round and fat
BULBOUSLY > BULBOUS
BULBS > BULB
BULBUL n any songbird of the family Pycnonotidae of tropical Africa and Asia, having brown plumage and, in many species, a distinct crest
BULBULS > BULBUL
BULGE n swelling on a normally flat surface ▷ vb swell outwards
BULGED > BULGE
BULGER > BULGE
BULGERS > BULGE
BULGES > BULGE

BULGHUR same as > BULGUR
BULGHURS > BULGHUR
BULGIER > BULGE
BULGIEST > BULGE
BULGINE same as > BULLGINE
BULGINES > BULGINE
BULGINESS > BULGE
BULGING > BULGE
BULGINGLY > BULGE
BULGUR n kind of dried cracked wheat
BULGURS > BULGUR
BULGY > BULGE
BULIMIA n disorder characterized by compulsive overeating followed by vomiting
BULIMIAC > BULIMIA
BULIMIAS > BULIMIA
BULIMIC > BULIMIA
BULIMICS > BULIMIA
BULIMIES > BULIMIA
BULIMUS > BULIMIA
BULIMUSES > BULIMIA
BULIMY > BULIMIA
BULK n volume, size, or magnitude of something ▷ vb cohere or cause to cohere in a mass
BULKAGE > BULK
BULKAGES > BULK
BULKED > BULK
BULKER n ship that carries unpackaged cargo, usually consisting of a single dry commodity, such as coal or grain
BULKERS > BULKER
BULKHEAD n partition in a ship or aeroplane
BULKHEADS > BULKHEAD
BULKIER > BULKY
BULKIEST > BULKY
BULKILY > BULKY
BULKINESS > BULKY
BULKING n expansion of excavated material to a volume greater than that of the excavation from which it came
BULKS > BULK
BULKY adj very large and massive, esp so as to be unwieldy
BULL adj any male bovine animal, esp one that is sexually mature
BULLA n leaden seal affixed to a papal bull, having a representation of Saints Peter and Paul on one side and the name of the reigning pope on the other
BULLACE n small Eurasian rosaceous tree, Prunus domestica insititia (or P. insititia), of which the damson is the cultivated form
BULLACES > BULLACE
BULLAE > BULLA
BULLARIES > BULLARY
BULLARY n boilery for preparing salt
BULLATE adj puckered or blistered in appearance

BULLBAR singular form of > BULLBARS
BULLBARS n large protective metal grille on the front of some vehicles, esp four-wheel-drive vehicles
BULLBAT another name for > NIGHTHAWK
BULLBATS > BULLBAT
BULLBRIER n prickly Americaan vine
BULLDOG n thickset dog with a broad head and a muscular body
BULLDOGS > BULLDOG
BULLDOZE vb demolish or flatten with a bulldozer
BULLDOZED > BULLDOZE
BULLDOZER n powerful tractor for moving earth
BULLDOZES > BULLDOZE
BULLDUST n fine dust
BULLDUSTS > BULLDUST
BULLDYKE n mannish lesbian
BULLDYKES > BULLDYKE
BULLED > BULL
BULLER vb make bubbling sound
BULLERED > BULLER
BULLERING > BULLER
BULLERS > BULLER
BULLET n small piece of metal fired from a gun ▷ vb move extremely quickly
BULLETED > BULLET
BULLETIN n short official report or announcement ▷ vb make known by bulletin
BULLETING > BULLET
BULLETINS > BULLETIN
BULLETRIE n W Indian fruit tree
BULLETS > BULLET
BULLFIGHT n public show in which a matador kills a bull
BULLFINCH n common European songbird
BULLFROG n large American frog with a deep croak
BULLFROGS > BULLFROG
BULLGINE n steam locomotive
BULLGINES > BULLGINE
BULLHEAD n any of various small northern mainly marine scorpaenoid fishes of the family Cottidae that have a large head covered with bony plates and spines
BULLHEADS > BULLHEAD
BULLHORN n portable loudspeaker having a built-in amplifier and microphone
BULLHORNS > BULLHORN
BULLIED > BULLY
BULLIER > BULLY
BULLIES > BULLY
BULLIEST > BULLY
BULLING > BULL
BULLINGS > BULL
BULLION n gold or silver in the form of bars

BULLIONS > BULLION

BULLISH adj like a bull

BULLISHLY > BULLISH

BULLNECK n enlarged neck

BULLNECKS > BULLNECK

BULLNOSE n rounded exterior angle, as where two walls meet

BULLNOSES > BULLNOSE

BULLOCK n castrated bull ▷ vb work hard and long

BULLOCKED > BULLOCK

BULLOCKS > BULLOCK

BULLOCKY n driver of a team of bullocks

BULLOSA as in *epidermolysis bullosa* type of genetic skin disorder

BULLOUS adj blistered

BULLPEN n large cell where prisoners are confined together temporarily

BULLPENS > BULLPEN

BULLPOUT n type of fish

BULLPOUTS > BULLPOUT

BULLRING n arena for staging bullfights

BULLRINGS > BULLRING

BULLRUSH same as > BULRUSH

BULLS > BULL

BULLSHAT > BULLSHIT

BULLSHIT n exaggerated or foolish talk ▷ vb talk bullshit to

BULLSHITS > BULLSHIT

BULLSHOT n cocktail of vodka and beef stock

BULLSHOTS > BULLSHOT

BULLSNAKE n American burrowing snake

BULLWADDY n N Australian tree, *Macropteranthes kekwickii*, growing in dense thickets

BULLWEED n knapweed

BULLWEEDS > BULLWEED

BULLWHACK vb flog with short whip

BULLWHIP n long tapering heavy whip, esp one of plaited rawhide ▷ vb whip with a bullwhip

BULLWHIPS > BULLWHIP

BULLY n person who hurts, persecutes, or intimidates weaker people ▷ vb hurt, intimidate, or persecute (a weaker or smaller person), esp to make him do something ▷ adj dashing

BULLYBOY n ruffian or tough, esp a hired one

BULLYBOYS > BULLYBOY

BULLYING > BULLY

BULLYISM > BULLY

BULLYISMS > BULLY

BULLYRAG vb bully, esp by means of cruel practical jokes

BULLYRAGS > BULLYRAG

BULNBULN another name for > LYREBIRD

BULNBULNS > BULNBULN

BULRUSH n tall stiff reed

BULRUSHES > BULRUSH

BULRUSHY > BULRUSH

BULSE n purse or bag for diamonds

BULSES > BULSE

BULWADDEE > BULLWADDY

BULWADDY > BULLWADDY

BULWARK n wall used as a fortification ▷ vb defend or fortify with or as if with a bulwark

BULWARKED > BULWARK

BULWARKS > BULWARK

BUM n buttocks or anus ▷ vb get by begging ▷ adj of poor quality

BUMALO same as > BUMMALO

BUMALOTI same as > BUMMALOTI

BUMALOTIS > BUMALOTI

BUMBAG n small bag attached to a belt and worn round the waist

BUMBAGS > BUMBAG

BUMBAZE vb confuse; bewilder

BUMBAZED > BUMBAZE

BUMBAZES > BUMBAZE

BUMBAZING > BUMBAZE

BUMBLE vb speak, do, or move in a clumsy way ▷ n blunder or botch

BUMBLEBEE n large hairy bee

BUMBLED > BUMBLE

BUMBLEDOM n self-importance in a minor office

BUMBLER > BUMBLE

BUMBLERS > BUMBLE

BUMBLES > BUMBLE

BUMBLING > BUMBLE

BUMBLINGS > BUMBLE

BUMBO n drink with gin or rum, nutmeg, lemon juice, etc

BUMBOAT n any small boat used for ferrying supplies or goods for sale to a ship at anchor or at a mooring

BUMBOATS > BUMBOAT

BUMBOS > BUMBO

BUMELIA n thorny shrub

BUMELIAS > BUMELIA

BUMF n official documents or forms

BUMFLUFF n soft and fluffy growth of hair on the chin of an adolescent

BUMFLUFFS > BUMFLUFF

BUMFS > BUMF

BUMFUZZLE vb confuse

BUMKIN same as > BUMPKIN

BUMKINS > BUMKIN

BUMMALO n Bombay duck

BUMMALOS > BUMMALO

BUMMALOTI another word for > BUMMALO

BUMMAREE n dealer at Billingsgate fish market

BUMMAREES > BUMMAREE

BUMMED > BUM

BUMMEL n stroll

BUMMELS > STROLL

BUMMER n unpleasant or disappointing experience

BUMMERS > BUMMER

BUMMEST > BUM

BUMMING > BUM

BUMMLE *Scots* variant of > BUMBLE

BUMMLED > BUMMLE

BUMMLES > BUMMLE

BUMMLING > BUMMLE

BUMMOCK n submerged mass of ice projecting downwards

BUMMOCKS > BUMMOCK

BUMP vb knock or strike with a jolt ▷ n dull thud from an impact or collision

BUMPED > BUMP

BUMPER n bar on the front and back of a vehicle to protect against damage ▷ adj unusually large or abundant ▷ vb toast with a bumper

BUMPERED > BUMPER

BUMPERING > BUMPER

BUMPERS > BUMPER

BUMPH same as > BUMF

BUMPHS > BUMPH

BUMPIER > BUMPY

BUMPIEST > BUMPY

BUMPILY > BUMPY

BUMPINESS > BUMPY

BUMPING > BUMP

BUMPINGS > BUMP

BUMPKIN n awkward simple country person

BUMPKINLY > BUMPKIN

BUMPKINS > BUMPKIN

BUMPOLOGY n humorous word for phrenology

BUMPS > BUMP

BUMPTIOUS adj offensively self-assertive

BUMPY adj having an uneven surface

BUMS > BUM

BUMSTERS pl n trousers cut so that the top lies just above the cleft of the buttocks

BUMSUCKER n toady

BUN n small sweet bread roll or cake

BUNA n synthetic rubber formed by polymerizing butadiene or by copolymerizing it with such compounds as acrylonitrile or styrene

BUNAS > BUNA

BUNCE n windfall; boom ▷ vb charge someone too much money

BUNCED > BUNCE

BUNCES > BUNCE

BUNCH n number of things growing, fastened, or grouped together ▷ vb group or be grouped together in a bunch

BUNCHED > BUNCH

BUNCHES pl n hairstyle in which hair is tied into two sections on either side of the head at the back

BUNCHIER > BUNCHY

BUNCHIEST > BUNCHY

BUNCHILY > BUNCHY

BUNCHING > BUNCH

BUNCHINGS > BUNCH

BUNCHY adj composed of or resembling bunches

BUNCING > BUNCE

BUNCO n swindle, esp one by confidence tricksters ▷ vb swindle

BUNCOED > BUNCO

BUNCOING > BUNCO

BUNCOMBE same as > BUNKUM

BUNCOMBES > BUNCOMBE

BUNCOS > BUNCO

BUND n embankment or German federation ▷ vb form into an embankment

BUNDE > BUND

BUNDED > BUND

BUNDH same as > BANDH

BUNDHS > BUNDH

BUNDIED > BUNDY

BUNDIES > BUNDY

BUNDING > BUND

BUNDIST > BUND

BUNDISTS > BUND

BUNDLE n number of things gathered loosely together ▷ vb cause to go roughly or unceremoniously

BUNDLED > BUNDLE

BUNDLER > BUNDLE

BUNDLERS > BUNDLE

BUNDLES > BUNDLE

BUNDLING > BUNDLE

BUNDLINGS > BUNDLE

BUNDOBUST same as > BANDOBUST

BUNDOOK n rifle

BUNDOOKS > BUNDOOK

BUNDS > BUND

BUNDT n type of sweet cake

BUNDTS > BUNDT

BUNDU n largely uninhabited wild region far from towns

BUNDUS > BUNDU

BUNDWALL n concrete or earth wall surrounding a storage tank containing crude oil or its refined product, designed to hold the contents of the tank in the event of a rupture or leak

BUNDWALLS > BUNDWALL

BUNDY n time clock at work ▷ vb register arrival or departure from work on a time clock

BUNDYING > BUNDY

BUNFIGHT n tea party

BUNFIGHTS > BUNFIGHT

BUNG n stopper for a cask etc ▷ vb close with a bung

BUNGALOID n bungalow-type house

BUNGALOW n one-storey house

BUNGALOWS > BUNGALOW

BUNGED > BUNG

BUNGEE n strong elastic cable

BUNGEES > BUNGEE

BUNGER n firework

BUNGERS > BUNGER

BUNGEY same as > BUNGEE

BUNGEYS > BUNGEY

BUNGHOLE n hole in a cask or barrel through which liquid can be drained

BUNGHOLES > BUNGHOLE

BUNGIE *same as* > BUNGEE

BUNGIES > BUNGY

BUNGING > BUNG

BUNGLE *vb* spoil through incompetence ▷ *n* blunder or muddle

BUNGLED > BUNGLE

BUNGLER > BUNGLE

BUNGLERS > BUNGLE

BUNGLES > BUNGLE

BUNGLING > BUNGLE

BUNGLINGS > BUNGLE

BUNGS > BUNG

BUNGWALL *n* Australian fern, *Blechnum indicum*, having an edible rhizome

BUNGWALLS > BUNGWALL

BUNGY > BUNGEE

BUNIA *same as* > BUNNIA

BUNIAS > BUNIA

BUNION *n* inflamed swelling on the big toe

BUNIONS > BUNION

BUNJE *same as* > BUNGEE

BUNJEE *same as* > BUNGEE

BUNJEES > BUNJEE

BUNJES > BUNJE

BUNJIE *same as* > BUNGEE

BUNJIES > BUNJIE

BUNJY *same as* > BUNGEE

BUNK *n* narrow shelflike bed ▷ *vb* prepare to sleep

BUNKED > BUNK

BUNKER *n* sand-filled hollow forming an obstacle on a golf course ▷ *vb* drive (the ball) into a bunker

BUNKERED > BUNKER

BUNKERING > BUNKER

BUNKERS > BUNKER

BUNKHOUSE *n* (in the US and Canada) building containing the sleeping quarters of workers on a ranch

BUNKING > BUNK

BUNKMATE *n* person who sleeps in the same quarters as another

BUNKMATES > BUNKMATE

BUNKO *same as* > BUNCO

BUNKOED > BUNKO

BUNKOING > BUNKO

BUNKOS > BUNKO

BUNKS > BUNK

BUNKUM *n* nonsense

BUNKUMS > BUNKUM

BUNN *same as* > BUN

BUNNET *same as* > BONNET

BUNNETS > BUNNET

BUNNIA *n* Hindu shopkeeper

BUNNIAS > BUNNIA

BUNNIES > BUNNY

BUNNS > BUNN

BUNNY *n* child's word for a rabbit

BUNODONT *adj* (of the teeth of certain mammals) having cusps that are separate and rounded

BUNRAKU *n* Japanese form of puppet theatre in which the puppets are usually about four feet high, with moving features as well as

limbs and each puppet is manipulated by up to three puppeteers who remain onstage

BUNRAKUS > BUNRAKU

BUNS *pl n* buttocks

BUNSEN as in *bunsen burner* gas burner used in scientific labs

BUNSENS > BUNSEN

BUNT *vb* (of an animal) butt (something) with the head or horns ▷ *n* act or an instance of bunting

BUNTAL *n* straw obtained from leaves of the talipot palm

BUNTALS > BUNTAL

BUNTED > BUNT

BUNTER *n* batter who deliberately taps ball lightly

BUNTERS > BUNTER

BUNTIER > BUNT

BUNTIEST > BUNT

BUNTING *n* decorative flags

BUNTINGS > BUNTING

BUNTLINE *n* one of several lines fastened to the foot of a square sail for hauling it up to the yard when furling

BUNTLINES > BUNTLINE

BUNTS > BUNT

BUNTY > BUNT

BUNYA *n* tall dome-shaped Australian coniferous tree

BUNYAS > BUNYA

BUNYIP *n* legendary monster said to live in swamps and lakes

BUNYIPS > BUNYIP

BUOY *n* floating marker anchored in the sea ▷ *vb* prevent from sinking

BUOYAGE *n* system of buoys

BUOYAGES > BUOYAGE

BUOYANCE *same as* > BUOYANCY

BUOYANCES > BUOYANCE

BUOYANCY *n* ability to float in a liquid or to rise in a fluid

BUOYANT *adj* able to float

BUOYANTLY > BUOYANT

BUOYED > BUOY

BUOYING > BUOY

BUOYS > BUOY

BUPKES *same as* > BUBKES

BUPKUS *same as* > BUBKES

BUPLEVER *n* type of plant

BUPLEVERS > BUPLEVER

BUPPIE *n* affluent young Black person

BUPPIES > BUPPY

BUPPY *variant of* > BUPPIE

BUPRESTID *n* any beetle of the mainly tropical family *Buprestidae*, the adults of which are brilliantly coloured and the larvae of which bore into and cause damage to trees, roots, etc ▷ *adj* of, relating to, or belonging to the family *Buprestidae*

BUQSHA *n* former Yemeni coin

BUQSHAS > BUQSHA

BUR > BURR

BURA *same as* > BURAN

BURAN *n* blizzard, with the wind blowing from the north and reaching gale force

BURANS > BURAN

BURAS > BURA

BURB *n* suburb

BURBLE *vb* make a bubbling sound ▷ *n* bubbling or gurgling sound

BURBLED > BURBLE

BURBLER > BURBLE

BURBLERS > BURBLE

BURBLES > BURBLE

BURBLIER > BURBLY

BURBLIEST > BURBLY

BURBLING > BURBLE

BURBLINGS > BURBLE

BURBLY *adj* burbling

BURBOT *n* freshwater fish of the cod family that has barbels around its mouth

BURBOTS > BURBOT

BURBS > BURB

BURD *Scots form of* > BIRD

BURDASH *n* fringed sash worn over coat

BURDASHES > BURDASH

BURDEN *n* heavy load ▷ *vb* put a burden on

BURDENED > BURDEN

BURDENER > BURDEN

BURDENERS > BURDEN

BURDENING > BURDEN

BURDENOUS > BURDEN

BURDENS > BURDEN

BURDIE *Scots form of* > BIRDIE

BURDIES > BURDIE

BURDIZZO *n* surgical instrument used to castrate animals

BURDIZZOS > BURDIZZO

BURDOCK *n* weed with prickly burrs

BURDOCKS > BURDOCK

BURDS > BURD

BUREAU *n* office that provides a service

BUREAUS > BUREAU

BUREAUX > BUREAU

BURET *same as* > BURETTE

BURETS > BURET

BURETTE *n* glass tube for dispensing known volumes of fluids

BURETTES > BURETTE

BURG *n* fortified town

BURGAGE *n* (in England) tenure of land or tenement in a town or city, which originally involved a fixed money rent

BURGAGES > BURGAGE

BURGANET *same as* > BURGONET

BURGANETS > BURGANET

BURGEE *n* triangular or swallow-tailed flag flown from the mast of a merchant ship for identification and from the mast of a yacht to indicate its owner's membership of a particular yacht club

BURGEES > BURGEE

BURGEON *vb* develop or grow rapidly ▷ *n* bud of a plant

BURGEONED > BURGEON

BURGEONS > BURGEON

BURGER *n* hamburger

BURGERS > BURGER

BURGESS *n* (in England) citizen or freeman of a borough

BURGESSES > BURGESS

BURGH *n* Scottish borough

BURGHAL > BURGH

BURGHER *n* citizen

BURGHERS > BURGHER

BURGHS > BURGH

BURGHUL *same as* > BULGUR

BURGHULS > BURGHUL

BURGLAR *n* person who enters a building to commit a crime, esp theft ▷ *vb* burgle

BURGLARED > BURGLAR

BURGLARS > BURGLAR

BURGLARY *n* crime of entering a building as a trespasser to commit theft or another offence

BURGLE *vb* break into (a house, shop, etc)

BURGLED > BURGLE

BURGLES > BURGLE

BURGLING > BURGLE

BURGONET *n* light 16th-century helmet, usually made of steel, with hinged cheekpieces

BURGONETS > BURGONET

BURGOO *n* porridge

BURGOOS > BURGOO

BURGOUT *same as* > BURGOO

BURGOUTS > BURGOUT

BURGRAVE *n* military governor of a German town or castle, esp in the 12th and 13th centuries

BURGRAVES > BURGRAVE

BURGS > BURG

BURGUNDY *adj* dark-purplish red

BURHEL *same as* > BHARAL

BURHELS > BURHEL

BURIAL *n* burying of a dead body

BURIALS > BURIAL

BURIED > BURY

BURIER *n* person or thing that buries

BURIERS > BURIER

BURIES > BURY

BURIN *n* steel chisel used for engraving metal, wood, or marble

BURINIST > BURIN

BURINISTS > BURIN

BURINS > BURIN

BURITI *n* type of palm tree

BURITIS > BURITI

BURK *same as* > BERK

BURKA *same as* > BURQA

BURKAS > BURKA

BURKE *vb* murder in such a way as to leave no marks on the body, usually by suffocation

BURKED > BURKE

BURKER > BURKE

BURKERS > BURKE
BURKES > BURKE
BURKING > BURKE
BURKITE > BURKE
BURKITES > BURKE
BURKS > BURK
BURL *n* small knot or lump in wool ▷ *vb* remove the burls from (cloth)
BURLADERO *n* safe area for bull-fighter in bull ring
BURLAP *n* coarse fabric woven from jute, hemp, or the like
BURLAPS > BURLAP
BURLED > BURL
BURLER > BURL
BURLERS > BURL
BURLESK *same as* > BURLESQUE
BURLESKS > BURLESK
BURLESQUE *n* artistic work which satirizes a subject by caricature ▷ *adj* of or characteristic of a burlesque ▷ *vb* represent or imitate (a person or thing) in a ludicrous way
BURLETTA *n* type of comic opera
BURLETTAS > BURLETTA
BURLEY *same as* > BERLEY
BURLEYCUE *same as* > BURLESQUE
BURLEYED > BURLEY
BURLEYING > BURLEY
BURLEYS > BURLEY
BURLIER > BURLY
BURLIEST > BURLY
BURLILY > BURLY
BURLINESS > BURLY
BURLING > BURL
BURLS > BURL
BURLY *adj* (of a person) broad and strong
BURN *vb* be or set on fire ▷ *n* injury or mark caused by fire or exposure to heat
BURNABLE > BURN
BURNABLES > BURN
BURNED > BURN
BURNER *n* part of a stove or lamp that produces the flame
BURNERS > BURNER
BURNET *n* type of rose
BURNETS > BURNET
BURNIE *n* sideburn
BURNIES > BURNIE
BURNING > BURN
BURNINGLY > BURN
BURNINGS > BURN
BURNISH *vb* make smooth and shiny by rubbing ▷ *n* shiny finish
BURNISHED > BURNISH
BURNISHER > BURNISH
BURNISHES > BURNISH
BURNOOSE *same as* > BURNOUS
BURNOOSED > BURNOUS
BURNOOSES > BURNOOSE
BURNOUS *n* long circular cloak with a hood, worn esp by Arabs
BURNOUSE *same as* > BURNOUS

BURNOUSED > BURNOUS
BURNOUSES > BURNOUSE
BURNOUT *n* failure of a mechanical device from excessive heating
BURNOUTS > BURNOUT
BURNS > BURN
BURNSIDE *n* land along side of burn
BURNSIDES > BURNSIDE
BURNT > BURN
BUROO *n* government office from which unemployment benefit is distributed
BUROOS > BUROO
BURP *n* belch ▷ *vb* belch
BURPED > BURP
BURPEE *n* type of physical exercise movement
BURPEES > BURPEE
BURPING > BURP
BURPS > BURP
BURQA *n* long enveloping garment worn by Muslim women in public, covering all but the wearer's eyes
BURQAS > BURQA
BURR *n* small power-driven hand-operated rotary file, esp for removing burrs or for machining recesses ▷ *vb* form a rough edge on (a workpiece)
BURRAMYS *n* very rare mountain pigmy possum, *Burramys parvus*, of Australia. It is about the size of a rat and restricted in habitat to very high altitudes, mainly Mt Hotham, Victoria. Until 1966 it was known only as a fossil
BURRAWANG *n* Australian plant with fernlike leaves and an edible nut
BURRED > BURR
BURREL *same as* > BHARAL
BURRELL *variant of* > BHARAL
BURRELLS > BURRELL
BURRELS > BURREL
BURRER *n* person who removes burrs
BURRERS > BURRER
BURRHEL *same as* > BURREL
BURRHELS > BURRHEL
BURRIER > BURRY
BURRIEST > BURRY
BURRING > BURR
BURRITO *n* tortilla folded over a filling of minced beef, chicken, cheese, or beans
BURRITOS > BURRITO
BURRO *n* donkey, esp one used as a pack animal
BURROS > BURRO
BURROW *n* hole dug in the ground by a rabbit etc ▷ *vb* dig holes in the ground
BURROWED > BURROW
BURROWER > BURROW
BURROWERS > BURROW
BURROWING > BURROW
BURROWS > BURROW
BURRS > BURR
BURRSTONE *same*

as > BUHRSTONE
BURRY *adj* full of or covered in burs
BURS > BURR
BURSA *n* small fluid-filled sac that reduces friction between movable parts of the body, esp at joints
BURSAE > BURSA
BURSAL > BURSA
BURSAR *n* treasurer of a school, college, or university
BURSARIAL *adj* of, relating to, or paid by a bursar or bursary
BURSARIES > BURSARY
BURSARS > BURSAR
BURSARY *n* scholarship
BURSAS > BURSA
BURSATE > BURSA
BURSE *n* flat case used at Mass as a container for the corporal
BURSEED *n* type of plant
BURSEEDS > BURSEED
BURSERA *adj* of a type of gum tree
BURSES > BURSE
BURSICON *n* hormone, produced by the insect brain, that regulates processes associated with ecdysis, such as darkening of the cuticle
BURSICONS > BURSICON
BURSIFORM *adj* shaped like a pouch or sac
BURSITIS *n* inflammation of a bursa, esp one in the shoulder joint
BURST *vb* break or cause to break open or apart suddenly and noisily, esp from internal pressure ▷ *n* sudden breaking open or apart ▷ *adj* broken apart
BURSTED > BURST
BURSTEN > BURST
BURSTER > BURST
BURSTERS > BURST
BURSTING > BURST
BURSTONE *same*
as > BUHRSTONE
BURSTONES > BURSTONE
BURSTS > BURST
BURTHEN *archaic word for* > BURDEN
BURTHENED > BURTHEN
BURTHENS > BURTHEN
BURTON *n* type of hoisting tackle
BURTONS > BURTON
BURWEED *n* any of various plants that bear burs, such as the burdock
BURWEEDS > BURWEED
BURY *vb* place in a grave
BURYING > BURY
BUS *n* large motor vehicle for carrying passengers between stops ▷ *vb* travel by bus
BUSBAR *n* electrical conductor, maintained at a specific voltage and capable of carrying a

high current, usually used to make a common connection between several circuits in a system
BUSBARS > BUSBAR
BUSBIES > BUSBY
BUSBOY *n* waiter's assistant
BUSBOYS > BUSBOY
BUSBY *n* tall fur hat worn by some soldiers
BUSED > BUS
BUSERA *n* Ugandan alcoholic drink made from millet: sometimes mixed with honey
BUSERAS > BUSERA
BUSES > BUS
BUSGIRL *n* waiter's assistant
BUSGIRLS > BUSGIRL
BUSH *n* dense woody plant, smaller than a tree ▷ *vb* fit a bush to (a casing or bearing)
BUSHBABY *n* small African tree-living mammal with large eyes
BUSHBUCK *n* small nocturnal spiral-horned antelope, *Tragelaphus scriptus*, of the bush and tropical forest of Africa. Its coat is reddish-brown with a few white markings
BUSHBUCKS > BUSHBUCK
BUSHCRAFT *n* ability and experience in matters concerned with living in the bush
BUSHED *adj* extremely tired
BUSHEL *n* obsolete unit of measure equal to 8 gallons (36.4 litres) ▷ *vb* alter or mend (a garment)
BUSHELED > BUSHEL
BUSHELER > BUSHEL
BUSHELERS > BUSHEL
BUSHELING > BUSHEL
BUSHELLED > BUSHEL
BUSHELLER > BUSHEL
BUSHELMAN > BUSHEL
BUSHELMEN > BUSHEL
BUSHELS > BUSHEL
BUSHER > BUSH
BUSHERS > BUSH
BUSHES > BUSH
BUSHFIRE *n* uncontrolled fire in the bush
BUSHFIRES > BUSHFIRE
BUSHFLIES > BUSHFLY
BUSHFLY *n* any of various small black dipterous flies of Australia, esp *Musca vetustissima*, that breed in faeces and dung: family *Calliphoridae*
BUSHGOAT *n* S African antelope
BUSHGOATS > BUSHGOAT
BUSHIDO *n* feudal code of the Japanese samurai, stressing self-discipline, courage and loyalty
BUSHIDOS > BUSHIDO
BUSHIE *same as* > BUSHY
BUSHIER > BUSHY
BUSHIES > BUSHY

b

BUSHIEST > BUSHY
BUSHILY > BUSHY
BUSHINESS > BUSHY
BUSHING same as > BUSH
BUSHINGS > BUSHING
BUSHLAND n land characterized by natural vegetation
BUSHLANDS > BUSHLAND
BUSHLESS > BUSH
BUSHLIKE > BUSH
BUSHMAN n person who lives or travels in the bush
BUSHMEAT n meat taken from any animal native to African forests, including species that may be endangered or not usually eaten outside Africa
BUSHMEATS > BUSHMEAT
BUSHMEN > BUSHMAN
BUSHPIG n wild pig, *Potamochoerus porcus*, inhabiting forests in tropical Africa and Madagascar. It is brown or black, with pale markings on the face
BUSHPIGS > BUSHPIG
BUSHTIT n small grey active North American songbird
BUSHTITS > BUSHTIT
BUSHVELD n bushy countryside
BUSHVELDS > BUSHVELD
BUSHWA n nonsense
BUSHWAH same as > BUSHWA
BUSHWAHS > BUSHWAH
BUSHWALK vb hike through bushland
BUSHWALKS > BUSHWALK
BUSHWAS > BUSHWA
BUSHWHACK vb ambush
BUSHWOMAN > BUSHMAN
BUSHWOMEN > BUSHMAN
BUSHY adj (of hair) thick and shaggy ▷ n person who lives in the bush
BUSIED > BUSY
BUSIER > BUSY
BUSIES > BUSY
BUSIEST > BUSY
BUSILY adv in a busy manner
BUSINESS n purchase and sale of goods and services
BUSINESSY adj of, relating to, typical of, or suitable for the world of commercial or industrial business
BUSING > BUS
BUSINGS > BUS
BUSK vb act as a busker ▷ n strip of whalebone, wood, steel, etc, inserted into the front of a corset to stiffen it
BUSKED > BUSK
BUSKER > BUSK
BUSKERS > BUSK
BUSKET n bouquet
BUSKETS > BUSKET
BUSKIN n (formerly) sandal-like covering for the foot and leg, reaching the calf and usually laced
BUSKINED adj relating to tragedy

BUSKING > BUSK
BUSKINGS > BUSK
BUSKINS > BUSKIN
BUSKS > BUSK
BUSKY same as > BOSKY
BUSLOAD n number of people bus carries
BUSLOADS > BUSLOAD
BUSMAN n person who drives a bus
BUSMEN > BUSMAN
BUSS archaic or dialect word for > KISS
BUSSED > BUS
BUSSES > BUS
BUSSING > BUS
BUSSINGS > BUS
BUSSU n type of palm tree
BUSSUS > BUSSU
BUST n chest of a human being, esp a woman's bosom ▷ adj broken ▷ vb burst or break
BUSTARD n bird with long strong legs, a heavy body, a long neck, and speckled plumage
BUSTARDS > BUSTARD
BUSTED > BUST
BUSTEE same as > BASTI
BUSTEES > BUSTEE
BUSTER n person or thing destroying something as specified
BUSTERS > BUSTER
BUSTI same as > BASTI
BUSTIC n type of small American tree
BUSTICATE vb break
BUSTICS > BUSTIC
BUSTIER n close-fitting strapless women's top
BUSTIERS > BUSTIER
BUSTIEST > BUSTY
BUSTINESS > BUSTY
BUSTING > BUST
BUSTINGS > BUST
BUSTIS > BUSTI
BUSTLE vb hurry with a show of activity or energy ▷ n energetic and noisy activity
BUSTLED > BUSTLE
BUSTLER > BUSTLE
BUSTLERS > BUSTLE
BUSTLES > BUSTLE
BUSTLINE n shape or size of woman's bust
BUSTLINES > BUSTLINE
BUSTLING > BUSTLE
BUSTS > BUST
BUSTY adj (of a woman) having a prominent bust
BUSULFAN n drug used to treat cancer
BUSULFANS > BUSULFAN
BUSUUTI n long garment with short sleeves and a square neckline, worn by Ugandan women, esp in S Uganda
BUSUUTIS > BUSUUTI
BUSY adj actively employed ▷ vb keep (someone, esp oneself) busy
BUSYBODY n meddlesome or nosy person

BUSYING > BUSY
BUSYNESS > BUSY
BUSYWORK n unproductive work
BUSYWORKS > BUSYWORK
BUT prep except ▷ adv only ▷ n outer room of a two-roomed cottage: usually the kitchen
BUTADIENE n colourless easily liquefiable flammable gas
BUTANE n gas used for fuel
BUTANES > BUTANE
BUTANOL n colourless substance
BUTANOLS > BUTANOL
BUTANONE n colourless soluble flammable liquid used mainly as a solvent for resins
BUTANONES > BUTANONE
BUTCH adj markedly or aggressively masculine ▷ n lesbian who is noticeably masculine
BUTCHER n person who slaughters animals or sells their meat ▷ vb kill and prepare (animals) for meat
BUTCHERED > BUTCHER
BUTCHERER > BUTCHER
BUTCHERLY > BUTCHER
BUTCHERS > BUTCHER
BUTCHERY n senseless slaughter
BUTCHES > BUTCH
BUTCHEST > BUTCH
BUTCHING > BUTCH
BUTCHINGS > BUTCH
BUTCHNESS > BUTCH
BUTE n drug used illegally to dope horses
BUTENE n pungent colourless gas
BUTENES > BUTENE
BUTEO n type of American hawk
BUTEONINE adj of hawks
BUTEOS > BUTEO
BUTES > BUTE
BUTLE vb act as butler
BUTLED > BUTLE
BUTLER n chief male servant ▷ vb act as a butler
BUTLERAGE > BUTLER
BUTLERED > BUTLER
BUTLERIES > BUTLERY
BUTLERING > BUTLER
BUTLERS > BUTLER
BUTLERY n butler's room
BUTLES > BUTLE
BUTLING > BUTLE
BUTMENT same as > ABUTMENT
BUTMENTS > BUTMENT
BUTS > BUT
BUTSUDAN n (in Buddhism) small household altar
BUTSUDANS > BUTSUDAN
BUTT n thicker or blunt end of something, such as the end of the stock of a rifle ▷ vb strike or push with the head or horns
BUTTALS n abuttal
BUTTE n isolated steep flat-

topped hill
BUTTED > BUTT
BUTTER n edible fatty yellow solid made form cream ▷ vb put butter on
BUTTERBUR n plant of the Eurasian genus *Petasites* with fragrant whitish or purple flowers, woolly stems, and leaves formerly used to wrap butter: family *Asteraceae* (composites)
BUTTERCUP n small yellow flower
BUTTERED > BUTTER
BUTTERFAT n fatty substance of milk from which butter is made, consisting of a mixture of glycerides, mainly butyrin, olein, and palmitin
BUTTERFLY n insect with brightly coloured wings
BUTTERIER > BUTTERY
BUTTERIES > BUTTERY
BUTTERINE n artificial butter made partly from milk
BUTTERING > BUTTER
BUTTERNUT n walnut tree, *Juglans cinerea* of E North America
BUTTERS > BUTTER
BUTTERY n (in some universities) room in which food and drink are sold to students ▷ adj containing, like, or coated with butter
BUTTES > BUTTE
BUTTHEAD n stupid person
BUTTHEADS > BUTTHEAD
BUTTIES > BUTTY
BUTTING > BUTT
BUTTINSKI same as > BUTTINSKY
BUTTINSKY n busybody
BUTTLE vb act as butler
BUTTLED > BUTTLE
BUTTLES > BUTTLE
BUTTLING > BUTTLE
BUTTOCK n either of the two fleshy masses that form the human rump ▷ vb perform a kind of wrestling manoeuvre on a person
BUTTOCKED > BUTTOCK
BUTTOCKS > BUTTOCK
BUTTON n small disc or knob sewn to clothing, which can be passed through a slit in another piece of fabric to fasten them ▷ vb fasten with buttons
BUTTONED > BUTTON
BUTTONER > BUTTON
BUTTONERS > BUTTON
BUTTONING > BUTTON
BUTTONS n page boy
BUTTONY > BUTTON
BUTTRESS n structure to support a wall ▷ vb support with, or as if with, a buttress
BUTTS > BUTT
BUTTSTOCK n part of gun
BUTTY n sandwich
BUTTYMAN n offensive term

for a homosexual

BUTTYMEN > BUTTYMAN

BUTUT *n* Gambian monetary unit worth one hundredth of a dalasi

BUTUTS > BUTUT

BUTYL *adj* of or containing any of four isomeric forms of the group C_4H_9- ▷ *n* of, consisting of, or containing any of four isomeric forms of the group C_4H_9-

BUTYLATE *vb* introduce butyl into (compound)

BUTYLATED > BUTYLATE

BUTYLATES > BUTYLATE

BUTYLENE *same as* > BUTENE

BUTYLENES > BUTYLENE

BUTYLS > BUTYL

BUTYRAL *n* type of resin

BUTYRALS > BUTYRAL

BUTYRATE *n* any salt or ester of butyric acid

BUTYRATES > BUTYRATE

BUTYRIC as in *butyric acid* type of acid

BUTYRIN *n* colourless liquid ester or oil found in butter. It is formed from butyric acid and glycerine

BUTYRINS > BUTYRIN

BUTYROUS *adj* butyraceous

BUTYRYL *n* radical of butyric acid

BUTYRYLS > BUTYRYL

BUVETTE *n* roadside café

BUVETTES > BUVETTE

BUXOM *adj* (of a woman) healthily plump and full-bosomed

BUXOMER > BUXOM

BUXOMEST > BUXOM

BUXOMLY > BUXOM

BUXOMNESS > BUXOM

BUY *vb* acquire by paying money for ▷ *n* thing acquired through payment

BUYABLE > BUY

BUYABLES > BUY

BUYBACK *n* repurchase by a company of some or all of its shares from an investor, who acquired them by putting venture capital into the company when it was formed

BUYBACKS > BUYBACK

BUYER *n* customer

BUYERS > BUYER

BUYING > BUY

BUYOFF *n* purchase

BUYOFFS > BUYOFF

BUYOUT *n* purchase of a company, esp by its former management or staff

BUYOUTS > BUYOUT

BUYS > BUY

BUZKASHI *n* game played in Aghanistan, in which opposing teams of horsemen strive for possession of the headless carcass of a goat

BUZKASHIS > BUZKASHI

BUZUKI *same as* > BOUZOUKI

BUZUKIA > BUZUKI

BUZUKIS > BUZUKI

BUZZ *n* rapidly vibrating humming sound ▷ *vb* make a humming sound

BUZZARD *n* bird of prey of the hawk family

BUZZARDS > BUZZARD

BUZZCUT *n* very short haircut

BUZZCUTS > BUZZCUT

BUZZED > BUZZ

BUZZER *n* electronic device that produces a buzzing sound as a signal

BUZZERS > BUZZER

BUZZES > BUZZ

BUZZIER > BUZZY

BUZZIEST > BUZZY

BUZZING > BUZZ

BUZZINGLY > BUZZ

BUZZINGS > BUZZ

BUZZWIG *n* bushy wig

BUZZWIGS > BUZZWIG

BUZZWORD *n* word, often originating in a particular jargon, that becomes a vogue word in the community as a whole or among a particular group

BUZZWORDS > BUZZWORD

BUZZY *adj* making a buzzing sound

BWANA *n* (in E Africa) master, often used as a respectful form of address corresponding to *sir*

BWANAS > BWANA

BWAZI *same as* > BUAZE

BWAZIS > BWAZI

BY *prep* indicating the doer of an action, nearness, movement past, time before or during which, etc ▷ *adv* near ▷ *n* bye

BYCATCH *n* unwanted fish and other sea animals caught in a fishing net along with the desired kind of fish

BYCATCHES > BYCATCH

BYCOKET *n* former Italian high-crowned hat

BYCOKETS > BYCOKET

BYDE *same as* > BIDE

BYDED > BYDE

BYDES > BYDE

BYDING > BYDE

BYE *n* situation where a player or team wins a round by having no opponent ▷ *interj* goodbye ▷ *sentence substitute* goodbye

BYELAW *n* rule made by a local authority for the regulation of its affairs or management of the area it governs

BYELAWS > BYELAW

BYES > BYE

BYGONE *adj* past

BYGONES > BYGONE

BYKE > BICYCLE

BYKED > BICYCLE

BYKES > BICYCLE

BYKING > BICYCLE

BYLANDER *same as* > BILANDER

BYLANDERS > BYLANDER

BYLANE *n* side lane or alley off a road

BYLANES > BYLANE

BYLAW *n* rule made by a local authority

BYLAWS > BYLAW

BYLINE *n* line under the title of a newspaper or magazine article giving the author's name ▷ *vb* give a byline to

BYLINED > BYLINE

BYLINER > BYLINE

BYLINERS > BYLINE

BYLINES > BYLINE

BYLINING > BYLINE

BYLIVE *same as* > BELIVE

BYNAME *n* nickname

BYNAMES > BYNAME

BYNEMPT > BENAME

BYPASS *n* main road built to avoid a city ▷ *vb* go round or avoid

BYPASSED > BYPASS

BYPASSES > BYPASS

BYPASSING > BYPASS

BYPAST > BYPASS

BYPATH *n* little-used path or track, esp in the country

BYPATHS > BYPATH

BYPLACE *n* private place

BYPLACES > BYPLACE

BYPLAY *n* secondary action or talking carried on apart while the main action proceeds, esp in a play

BYPLAYS > BYPLAY

BYPRODUCT *n* secondary product

BYRE *n* shelter for cows

BYREMAN *n* man who works in byre

BYREMEN > BYREMAN

BYRES > BYRE

BYREWOMAN *n* woman who works in byre

BYREWOMEN > BYREWOMAN

BYRL *same as* > BIRL

BYRLADY *interj* short for By Our Lady

BYRLAKIN *interj* By Our Ladykin

BYRLAW *same as* > BYLAW

BYRLAWS > BYRLAW

BYRLED > BYRL

BYRLING > BYRL

BYRLS > BYRL

BYRNIE *n* archaic word for coat of mail

BYRNIES > BYRNIE

BYROAD *n* secondary or side road

BYROADS > BYROAD

BYROOM *n* private room

BYROOMS > BYROOM

BYS > BY

BYSSAL *adj* of mollusc's byssus

BYSSI > BYSSUS

BYSSINE *adj* made from flax

BYSSOID *adj* consisting of fine fibres

BYSSUS *n* mass of strong threads secreted by a sea mussel or similar mollusc that attaches the animal to a hard fixed surface

BYSSUSES > BYSSUS

BYSTANDER *n* person present but not involved

BYSTREET *n* obscure or secondary street

BYSTREETS > BYSTREET

BYTALK *n* trivial conversation

BYTALKS > BYTALK

BYTE *n* group of bits processed as one unit of data

BYTES > BYTE

BYTOWNITE *n* rare mineral

BYWAY *n* minor road

BYWAYS > BYWAY

BYWONER *n* poor tenant-farmer

BYWONERS > BYWONER

BYWORD *n* person or thing regarded as a perfect example of something

BYWORDS > BYWORD

BYWORK *n* work done outside usual working hours

BYWORKS > BYWORK

BYZANT *same as* > BEZANT

BYZANTINE *adj* of, characteristic of, or relating to Byzantium or the Byzantine Empire

BYZANTS > BYZANT

Cc

CAA *a Scot word for* > CALL
CAAED > CAA
CAAING > CAA
CAAS > CAA
CAATINGA *n* Brazilian semi-arid scrub forest
CAATINGAS > CAATINGA
CAB *n* taxi ▷ *vb* take a taxi
CABA *same as* > CABAS
CABAL *n* small group of political plotters ▷ *vb* form a cabal
CABALA *a variant spelling of* > KABBALAH
CABALAS > CABALA
CABALETTA *n* final section of an aria
CABALETTE > CABALETTA
CABALISM > CABALA
CABALISMS > CABALA
CABALIST > CABALA
CABALISTS > CABALA
CABALLED > CABAL
CABALLER > CABAL
CABALLERO *n* Spanish gentleman
CABALLERS > CABAL
CABALLINE *adj* pertaining to a horse
CABALLING > CABAL
CABALS > CABAL
CABANA *n* tent used as a dressing room by the sea
CABANAS > CABANA
CABARET *n* dancing and singing show in a nightclub
CABARETS > CABARET
CABAS *n* reticule
CABBAGE *n* vegetable with a large head of green leaves ▷ *vb* steal
CABBAGED > CABBAGE
CABBAGES > CABBAGE
CABBAGEY > CABBAGE
CABBAGING > CABBAGE
CABBAGY > CABBAGE
CABBALA *a variant spelling of* > KABBALAH
CABBALAH *same as* > CABBALA
CABBALAHS > CABBALA
CABBALAS > CABBALA
CABBALISM > CABBALA
CABBALIST > CABBALA
CABBED > CAB
CABBIE *n* taxi driver
CABBIES > CABBIE

CABBING > CAB
CABBY *same as* > CABBIE
CABDRIVER *n* taxi-driver
CABER *n* tree trunk tossed in competition at Highland games
CABERNET *n* type of grape, or the red wine made from it
CABERNETS > CABERNET
CABERS > CABER
CABESTRO *n* halter made from horsehair
CABESTROS > CABESTRO
CABEZON *n* large food fish, *Scorpaenichthys marmoratus*, of North American Pacific coastal waters, having greenish flesh: family *Cottidae* (bullheads and sea scorpions)
CABEZONE *same as* > CABEZON
CABEZONES > CABEZON
CABEZONS > CABEZON
CABILDO *n* Spanish municipal council
CABILDOS > CABILDO
CABIN *n* compartment in a ship or aircraft ▷ *vb* confine in a small space
CABINED > CABIN
CABINET *n* piece of furniture with drawers or shelves
CABINETRY *n* cabinetmaking
CABINETS > CABINET
CABINING > CABIN
CABINMATE *n* sharer of cabin
CABINS > CABIN
CABLE *n* strong thick rope; a wire or bundle of wires that conduct electricity ▷ *vb* send (someone) a message by cable
CABLECAST *n* broadcast on cable
CABLED > CABLE
CABLEGRAM *n* message sent by cable
CABLER *n* cable broadcasting company
CABLERS > CABLER
CABLES > CABLE
CABLET *n* small cable, esp a

cable-laid rope that has a circumference of less than 25 centimetres (ten inches)
CABLETS > CABLET
CABLEWAY *n* system for moving people or bulk materials in which suspended cars, buckets, etc, run on cables that extend between terminal towers
CABLEWAYS > CABLEWAY
CABLING > CABLE
CABLINGS > CABLE
CABMAN *n* driver of a cab
CABMEN > CABMAN
CABOB *vb* roast on a skewer
CABOBBED > CABOB
CABOBBING > CABOB
CABOBS > CABOB
CABOC *n* type of Scottish cheese
CABOCEER *n* in African history, indigenous representative appointed by his leader to deal with European slave traders
CABOCEERS > CABOCEER
CABOCHED *adj* in heraldry, with the face exposed, but neck concealed
CABOCHON *n* smooth domed gem, polished but unfaceted
CABOCHONS > CABOCHON
CABOCS > CABOC
CABOMBA *n* type of aquatic plant
CABOMBAS > CABOMBA
CABOODLE *n* lot, bunch, or group
CABOODLES > CABOODLE
CABOOSE *n* guard's van on a train
CABOOSES > CABOOSE
CABOSHED *same as* > CABOCHED
CABOTAGE *n* coastal navigation or shipping, esp within the borders of one country
CABOTAGES > CABOTAGE
CABOVER *adj* of or denoting a truck or lorry in which the cab is over the engine
CABRE *adj* heraldic term designating an animal

rearing
CABRESTA *variant of* > CABESTRO
CABRESTAS > CABRESTA
CABRESTO *variant of* > CABESTRO
CABRESTOS > CABRESTO
CABRETTA *n* soft leather obtained from the skins of certain South American or African sheep
CABRETTAS > CABRETTA
CABRIE *n* pronghorn antelope
CABRIES > CABRIE
CABRILLA *n* any of various serranid food fishes, esp *Epinephelus analogus*, occurring in warm seas around Florida and the Caribbean
CABRILLAS > CABRILLA
CABRIO *short for* > CABRIOLET
CABRIOLE *n* type of furniture leg, popular in the first half of the 18th century, in which an upper convex curve descends tapering to a concave curve
CABRIOLES > CABRIOLE
CABRIOLET *n* small horse-drawn carriage with a folding hood
CABRIOS > CABRIO
CABRIT *n* pronghorn antelope
CABRITS > CABRIT
CABS > CAB
CABSTAND *n* taxi-rank
CABSTANDS > CABSTAND
CACA *n* heroin
CACAFOGO *same as* > CACAFUEGO
CACAFOGOS > CACAFUEGO
CACAFUEGO *n* spitfire
CACAO *same as* > COCOA
CACAOS > COCOA
CACAS > CACA
CACHAEMIA *n* poisoned condition of the blood
CACHAEMIC > CACHAEMIA
CACHALOT *n* sperm whale
CACHALOTS > CACHALOT
CACHE *n* hidden store of weapons or treasure ▷ *vb* store in a cache

CACHECTIC > CACHEXIA

CACHED > CACHE

CACHEPOT n ornamental container for a flowerpot

CACHEPOTS > CACHEPOT

CACHES > CACHE

CACHET n prestige, distinction ▷ vb apply a commemorative design to an envelope, as a first-day cover

CACHETED > CACHET

CACHETING > CACHET

CACHETS > CACHET

CACHEXIA n generally weakened condition of body or mind resulting from any debilitating chronic disease

CACHEXIAS > CACHEXIA

CACHEXIC > CACHEXIA

CACHEXIES > CACHEXIA

CACHEXY same as > CACHEXIA

CACHING > CACHE

CACHOLONG n a type of opal

CACHOLOT same as > CACHALOT

CACHOLOTS > CACHALOT

CACHOU same as > CATECHU

CACHOUS > CATECHU

CACHUCHA n graceful Spanish solo dance in triple time

CACHUCHAS > CACHUCHA

CACIQUE n American Indian chief in a Spanish-speaking region

CACIQUES > CACIQUE

CACIQUISM n (esp in Spanish America) government by local political bosses

CACKIER > CACKY

CACKIEST > CACKY

CACKLE vb laugh shrilly ▷ n cackling noise

CACKLED > CACKLE

CACKLER > CACKLE

CACKLERS > CACKLE

CACKLES > CACKLE

CACKLING > CACKLE

CACKY adj of or like excrement

CACODEMON n evil spirit or devil

CACODOXY n heterodoxy

CACODYL n oily poisonous liquid with a strong garlic smell

CACODYLIC > CACODYL

CACODYLS > CACODYL

CACOEPIES > CACOEPY

CACOEPY n bad or mistaken pronunciation

CACOETHES n uncontrollable urge or desire, esp for something harmful

CACOETHIC > CACOETHES

CACOGENIC adj reducing the quality of a race

CACOLET n seat fitted to the back of a mule

CACOLETS > CACOLET

CACOLOGY n bad choice of words

CACOMIXL n carnivorous mammal

CACOMIXLE same as > CACOMIXL

CACOMIXLS > CACOMIXL

CACONYM n erroneous name

CACONYMS > CACONYM

CACONYMY > CACONYM

CACOON n large seed of the sword-bean

CACOONS > CACOON

CACOPHONY n harsh discordant sound

CACOTOPIA n dystopia, the opposite of utopia

CACTI > CACTUS

CACTIFORM adj cactus-like

CACTOID adj resembling a cactus

CACTUS n fleshy desert plant with spines but no leaves

CACTUSES > CACTUS

CACUMEN n apex

CACUMINA > CACUMEN

CACUMINAL adj relating to or denoting a consonant articulated with the tip of the tongue turned back towards the hard palate ▷ n consonant articulated in this manner

CAD n dishonourable man

CADAGA n eucalyptus tree, E. torelliana, of tropical and subtropical Australia, having a smooth green trunk

CADAGAS > CADAGA

CADAGI same as > CADAGA

CADAGIS > CADAGI

CADASTER n official register showing details of ownership, boundaries, and value of real property in a district, made for taxation purposes

CADASTERS > CADASTER

CADASTRAL > CADASTER

CADASTRE same as > CADASTER

CADASTRES > CADASTER

CADAVER n corpse

CADAVERIC > CADAVER

CADAVERS > CADAVER

CADDICE same as > CADDIS

CADDICES > CADDIS

CADDIE n person who carries a golfer's clubs ▷ vb act as a caddie

CADDIED > CADDIE

CADDIES > CADDIE

CADDIS n type of coarse woollen yarn, braid, or fabric

CADDISED adj trimmed with a type of ribbon

CADDISES > CADDIS

CADDISFLY n small fly

CADDISH > CAD

CADDISHLY > CAD

CADDY same as > CADDIE

CADDYING > CADDIE

CADDYSS same as > CADDIS

CADDYSSES > CADDIS

CADE n juniper tree ▷ adj (of a young animal) left by its mother and reared by humans, usually as a pet

CADEAU n present

CADEAUX > CADEAU

CADEE old form of > CADET

CADEES > CADEE

CADELLE n widely distributed beetle, Tenebroides mauritanicus, that feeds on flour, grain, and other stored foods: family Trogositidae

CADELLES > CADELLE

CADENCE n rise and fall in the pitch of the voice ▷ vb modulate musically

CADENCED > CADENCE

CADENCES > CADENCE

CADENCIES > CADENCY

CADENCING > CADENCE

CADENCY same as > CADENCE

CADENT adj having cadence

CADENTIAL > CADENCE

CADENZA n complex solo passage in a piece of music

CADENZAS > CADENZA

CADES > CADE

CADET n young person training for the armed forces or police

CADETS > CADET

CADETSHIP > CADET

CADGE vb get (something) by taking advantage of someone's generosity

CADGED > CADGE

CADGER n person who cadges

CADGERS > CADGER

CADGES > CADGE

CADGIER > CADGY

CADGIEST > CADGY

CADGING > CADGE

CADGY adj cheerful

CADI n judge in a Muslim community

CADIE n messenger

CADIES > CADIE

CADIS > CADI

CADMIC > CADMIUM

CADMIUM n bluish-white metallic element used in alloys

CADMIUMS > CADMIUM

CADRANS n instrument used in gemcutting

CADRANSES > CADRANS

CADRE n small group of people selected and trained to form the core of a political organization or military unit

CADRES > CADRE

CADS > CAD

CADUAC n windfall

CADUACS > CADUAC

CADUCEAN > CADUCEUS

CADUCEI > CADUCEUS

CADUCEUS n staff entwined with two serpents and bearing a pair of wings at the top, carried by Hermes (Mercury) as messenger of the gods

CADUCITY n perishableness

CADUCOUS adj (of parts of a plant or animal) shed during the life of the organism

CAECA > CAECUM

CAECAL > CAECUM

CAECALLY > CAECUM

CAECILIAN n any tropical limbless cylindrical amphibian of the order Apoda (or Gymnophiona), resembling earthworms and inhabiting moist soil

CAECITIS n inflammation of the caecum

CAECUM n pouch at the beginning of the large intestine

CAEOMA n aecium in some rust fungi that has no surrounding membrane

CAEOMAS > CAEOMA

CAERULE same as > CERULE

CAERULEAN same as > CERULEAN

CAESAR n any emperor, autocrat, dictator, or other powerful ruler

CAESAREAN n surgical incision through the abdominal and uterine walls in order to deliver a baby

CAESARIAN variant spelling of > CAESAREAN

CAESARISM another word for > IMPERIALISM

CAESARS > CAESAR

CAESE interj Shakespearean interjection

CAESIOUS adj having a waxy bluish-grey coating

CAESIUM n silvery-white metallic element used in photocells

CAESIUMS > CAESIUM

CAESTUS same as > CESTUS

CAESTUSES > CAESTUS

CAESURA n pause in a line of verse

CAESURAE > CAESURA

CAESURAL > CAESURA

CAESURAS > CAESURA

CAESURIC > CAESURA

CAFARD n feeling of severe depression

CAFARDS > CAFARD

CAFE n small or inexpensive restaurant serving light refreshments

CAFES > CAFE

CAFETERIA n self-service restaurant

CAFETIERE n kind of coffeepot in which boiling water is poured onto ground coffee and a plunger fitted with a metal filter is pressed down, forcing the grounds to the bottom

CAFETORIA variant of > CAFETERIA

CAFF n café

CAFFEIN same as > CAFFEINE

CAFFEINE n stimulant found in tea and coffee

CAFFEINES > CAFFEINE

CAFFEINIC adj of or containing caffeine

CAFFEINS > CAFFEINE
CAFFEISM n addiction to caffeine
CAFFEISMS > CAFFEISM
CAFFILA n caravan train
CAFFILAS > CAFFILA
CAFFS > CAFF
CAFILA same as > CAFFILA
CAFILAS > CAFILA
CAFTAN same as > KAFTAN
CAFTANED adj wearing caftan
CAFTANS > CAFTAN
CAG same as > CAGOULE
CAGANER n figure of a squatting defecating person, a traditional character in Catalan Christmas crèche scenes
CAGANERS > CAGANER
CAGE n enclosure of bars or wires, for keeping animals or birds ▷ vb confine in a cage
CAGEBIRD n bird habitually kept caged
CAGEBIRDS > CAGEBIRD
CAGED > CAGE
CAGEFUL n amount which fills a cage to capacity
CAGEFULS > CAGEFUL
CAGELIKE > CAGE
CAGELING n bird kept in a cage
CAGELINGS > CAGELING
CAGER n basketball player
CAGERS > CAGER
CAGES > CAGE
CAGEWORK n something constructed as if from the bars of a cage
CAGEWORKS > CAGEWORK
CAGEY adj reluctant to go into details
CAGEYNESS > CAGEY
CAGIER > CAGEY
CAGIEST > CAGEY
CAGILY > CAGEY
CAGINESS > CAGY
CAGING > CAGE
CAGMAG adj done shoddily ▷ vb chat idly
CAGMAGGED > CAGMAG
CAGMAGS > CAGMAG
CAGOT n member of a class of French outcasts
CAGOTS > CAGOT
CAGOUL same as > CAGOULE
CAGOULE n lightweight hooded waterproof jacket
CAGOULES > CAGOULE
CAGOULS > CAGOUL
CAGS > CAG
CAGY same as > CAGEY
CAGYNESS > CAGY
CAHIER n notebook
CAHIERS > CAHIER
CAHOOT n partnership
CAHOOTS > CAHOOT
CAHOW n Bermuda petrel
CAHOWS > CAHOW
CAID n Moroccan district administrator
CAIDS > CAID
CAILLACH same as > CAILLEACH
CAILLACHS > CAILLACH

CAILLE n quail
CAILLEACH n old woman
CAILLES > CAILLE
CAILLIACH same as > CAILLEACH
CAIMAC same as > CAIMACAM
CAIMACAM n Turkish governor of a sanjak
CAIMACAMS > CAIMACAM
CAIMACS > CAIMAC
CAIMAN same as > CAYMAN
CAIMANS > CAIMAN
CAIN n (in Scotland and Ireland) payment in kind, usually farm produce paid as rent
CAINS > CAIN
CAIQUE n long narrow light rowing skiff used on the Bosporus
CAIQUES > CAIQUE
CAIRD n travelling tinker
CAIRDS > CAIRD
CAIRN n mound of stones erected as a memorial or marker
CAIRNED adj marked by a cairn
CAIRNGORM n yellow or brownish quartz gemstone
CAIRNS > CAIRN
CAIRNY adj covered with cairns
CAISSON > COFFERDAM
CAISSONS > CAISSON
CAITIFF n cowardly or base person ▷ adj cowardly
CAITIFFS > CAITIFF
CAITIVE n captive
CAITIVES > CAITIVE
CAJAPUT same as > CAJUPUT
CAJAPUTS > CAJAPUT
CAJEPUT same as > CAJUPUT
CAJEPUTS > CAJEPUT
CAJOLE vb persuade by flattery
CAJOLED > CAJOLE
CAJOLER > CAJOLE
CAJOLERS > CAJOLE
CAJOLERY > CAJOLE
CAJOLES > CAJOLE
CAJOLING > CAJOLE
CAJON n Peruvian wooden box used as a drum
CAJONES > CAJON
CAJUN n music of the Cajun people, combining blues and European folk music
CAJUPUT n small myrtaceous tree or shrub, Melaleuca leucadendron, native to the East Indies and Australia, with whitish flowers and leaves
CAJUPUTS > CAJUPUT
CAKE n sweet food baked from a mixture of flour, eggs, etc ▷ vb form into a hardened mass or crust
CAKED > CAKE
CAKES > CAKE
CAKEWALK n dance based on a march with intricate steps, originally performed by African-Americans with the prize of a cake for the best performers ▷ vb

perform the cakewalk
CAKEWALKS > CAKEWALK
CAKEY > CAKE
CAKIER > CAKE
CAKIEST > CAKE
CAKINESS > CAKE
CAKING > CAKE
CAKINGS > CAKE
CAKY > CAKE
CALABASH n type of large round gourd
CALABAZA n variety of squash
CALABAZAS > CALABAZA
CALABOGUS n mixed drink containing rum, spruce beer, and molasses
CALABOOSE n prison
CALABRESE n kind of green sprouting broccoli
CALADIUM n any of various tropical plants of the aroid genus Caladium, which are widely cultivated as potted plants for their colourful variegated foliage
CALADIUMS > CALADIUM
CALALOO same as > CALALU
CALALOOS > CALALOO
CALALU n edible leaves of various plants, used as greens or in making thick soups
CALALUS > CALALU
CALAMANCO n glossy woollen fabric woven with a checked design that shows on one side only
CALAMAR n any member of the squid family
CALAMARI n squid cooked for eating, esp cut into rings and fried in batter
CALAMARIS > CALAMARI
CALAMARS > CALAMAR
CALAMARY variant of > CALAMARI
CALAMATA same as > KALAMATA
CALAMATAS > CALAMATA
CALAMI > CALAMUS
CALAMINE n pink powder consisting chiefly of zinc oxide, used in skin lotions and ointments ▷ vb apply calamine
CALAMINED > CALAMINE
CALAMINES > CALAMINE
CALAMINT n any aromatic Eurasian plant of the genus Satureja (or Calamintha), having clusters of purple or pink flowers: family Lamiaceae (labiates)
CALAMINTS > CALAMINT
CALAMITE n any extinct treelike plant of the genus Calamites, of Carboniferous times, related to the horsetails
CALAMITES > CALAMITE
CALAMITY n disaster
CALAMUS n any tropical Asian palm of the genus Calamus, some species of which are a source of rattan and canes

CALANDO adv (to be performed) with gradually decreasing tone and speed
CALANDRIA n cylindrical vessel through which vertical tubes pass, esp one forming part of an evaporator, heat exchanger, or nuclear reactor
CALANTHE n type of orchid
CALANTHES > CALANTHE
CALASH n horse-drawn carriage with low wheels and a folding top
CALASHES > CALASH
CALATHEA n South American perennial plant, many species of which are grown as greenhouse or house plants for their decorative variegated leaves
CALATHEAS > CALATHEA
CALATHI > CALATHUS
CALATHOS same as > CALATHUS
CALATHUS n vase-shaped basket represented in ancient Greek art, used as a symbol of fruitfulness
CALAVANCE n type of pulse
CALCANEA > CALCANEUS
CALCANEAL > CALCANEUS
CALCANEAN > CALCANEUS
CALCANEI > CALCANEUS
CALCANEUM same as > CALCANEUS
CALCANEUS n largest tarsal bone, forming the heel in man
CALCAR n spur or spurlike process, as on the leg of a bird or the corolla of a flower
CALCARATE > CALCAR
CALCARIA > CALCAR
CALCARINE > CALCAR
CALCARS > CALCAR
CALCEATE vb to shoe
CALCEATED > CALCEATE
CALCEATES > CALCEATE
CALCED adj wearing shoes
CALCEDONY n a microcrystalline often greyish form of quartz with crystals arranged in parallel fibres: a gemstone.
CALCES > CALX
CALCIC adj of, containing, or concerned with lime or calcium
CALCICOLE n any plant that thrives in lime-rich soils
CALCIFIC adj forming or causing to form lime or chalk
CALCIFIED > CALCIFY
CALCIFIES > CALCIFY
CALCIFUGE n any plant that thrives in acid soils but not in lime-rich soils
CALCIFY vb harden by the depositing of calcium salts
CALCIMINE n white or pale tinted wash for walls ▷ vb cover with calcimine

CALCINE vb oxidize (a substance) by heating

CALCINED > CALCINE

CALCINES > CALCINE

CALCINING > CALCINE

CALCITE n colourless or white form of calcium carbonate

CALCITES > CALCITE

CALCITIC > CALCITE

CALCIUM n silvery-white metallic element found in bones, teeth, limestone, and chalk

CALCIUMS > CALCIUM

CALCRETE another name for > CALICHE

CALCRETES > CALCRETE

CALCSPAR another name for > CALCITE

CALCSPARS > CALCSPAR

CALCTUFA another name for > TUFA

CALCTUFAS > CALCTUFA

CALCTUFF another name for > TUFA

CALCTUFFS > CALCTUFF

CALCULAR adj relating to calculus

CALCULARY adj relating to stone

CALCULATE vb solve or find out by a mathematical procedure or by reasoning

CALCULI > CALCULUS

CALCULOSE adj relating to calculi

CALCULOUS adj of or suffering from a stonelike accretion of minerals and salts found in ducts or hollow organs of the body

CALCULUS n branch of mathematics dealing with infinitesimal changes to a variable number or quantity

CALDARIA > CALDARIUM

CALDARIUM n (in ancient Rome) a room for taking hot baths

CALDERA n large basin-shaped crater at the top of a volcano, formed by the collapse or explosion of the cone

CALDERAS > CALDERA

CALDRON same as > CAULDRON

CALDRONS > CALDRON

CALECHE a variant of > CALASH

CALECHES > CALECHE

CALEFIED > CALEFY

CALEFIES > CALEFY

CALEFY vb to make warm

CALEFYING > CALEFY

CALEMBOUR n pun

CALENDAL > CALENDS

CALENDAR n chart showing a year divided up into months, weeks, and days ▷ vb enter in a calendar

CALENDARS > CALENDAR

CALENDER n machine in which paper or cloth is smoothed by passing it between rollers ▷ vb smooth in such a machine

CALENDERS > CALENDER

CALENDRER > CALENDER

CALENDRIC > CALENDAR

CALENDRY n place where calendering is carried out

CALENDS pl n first day of each month in the ancient Roman calendar

CALENDULA n marigold

CALENTURE n mild fever of tropical climates, similar in its symptoms to sunstroke

CALESA n horse-drawn buggy

CALESAS > CALESA

CALESCENT adj increasing in heat

CALF n young cow, bull, elephant, whale, or seal

CALFDOZER n small bulldozer

CALFLESS > CALF

CALFLICK another word for > COWLICK

CALFLICKS > CALFLICK

CALFLIKE > CALF

CALFS > CALF

CALFSKIN n fine leather made from the skin of a calf

CALFSKINS > CALFSKIN

CALIATOUR n red sandalwood

CALIBER same as > CALIBRE

CALIBERED > CALIBER

CALIBERS > CALIBER

CALIBRATE vb mark the scale or check the accuracy of (a measuring instrument)

CALIBRE n person's ability or worth

CALIBRED > CALIBRE

CALIBRES > CALIBRE

CALICES > CALIX

CALICHE n bed of sand or clay in arid regions cemented by calcium carbonate, sodium chloride, and other soluble minerals

CALICHES > CALICHE

CALICLE same as > CALYCLE

CALICLES > CALICLE

CALICO n white cotton fabric

CALICOES > CALICO

CALICOS > CALICO

CALICULAR > CALYCLE

CALID adj warm

CALIDITY > CALID

CALIF same as > CALIPH

CALIFATE same as > CALIPHATE

CALIFATES > CALIFATE

CALIFONT n gas water heater

CALIFONTS > CALIFONT

CALIFS > CALIF

CALIGO n speck on the cornea causing poor vision

CALIGOES > CALIGO

CALIGOS > CALIGO

CALIMA n Saharan dust-storm

CALIMAS > CALIMA

CALIOLOGY n the study of birds' nests

CALIPASH n greenish glutinous edible part of the turtle found next to the upper shell, considered a delicacy

CALIPEE n yellow glutinous edible part of the turtle found next to the lower shell, considered a delicacy

CALIPEES > CALIPEE

CALIPER same as > CALLIPER

CALIPERED > CALLIPER

CALIPERS > CALIPER

CALIPH n Muslim ruler

CALIPHAL > CALIPH

CALIPHATE n office, jurisdiction, or reign of a caliph

CALIPHS > CALIPH

CALISAYA n bark of any of several tropical trees of the rubiaceous genus Cinchona, esp C. calisaya, from which quinine is extracted

CALISAYAS > CALISAYA

CALIVER n type of musket

CALIVERS > CALIVER

CALIX n cup

CALK same as > CAULK

CALKED > CALK

CALKER > CALK

CALKERS > CALK

CALKIN > CALK

CALKING > CALK

CALKINGS > CALK

CALKINS > CALK

CALKS > CALK

CALL vb name ▷ n cry, shout

CALLA n any southern African plant of the aroid genus Zantedeschia, esp Z. aethiopica, which has a white funnel-shaped spathe enclosing a yellow spadix

CALLABLE adj (of a security) subject to redemption before maturity

CALLAIDES > CALLAIS

CALLAIS n green stone found as beads and ornaments in the late Neolithic and early Bronze Age of W Europe

CALLALOO n leafy green vegetable

CALLALOOS > CALLALOO

CALLAN same as > CALLANT

CALLANS > CALLAN

CALLANT n youth

CALLANTS > CALLANT

CALLAS > CALLA

CALLBACK n telephone call made in response to an earlier call

CALLBACKS > CALLBACK

CALLBOARD n notice board listing opportunities for performers

CALLBOY n person who notifies actors when it is time to go on stage

CALLBOYS > CALLBOY

CALLED > CALL

CALLEE n computer function being used

CALLEES > CALLEE

CALLER n person or thing that calls, esp a person who makes a brief visit ▷ adj (of food, esp fish) fresh

CALLERS > CALLER

CALLET n scold

CALLETS > CALLET

CALLID adj cunning

CALLIDITY > CALLID

CALLIGRAM n poem in which words are positioned so as to create a visual image of the subject on the page

CALLING n vocation, profession

CALLINGS > CALLING

CALLIOPE n steam organ

CALLIOPES > CALLIOPE

CALLIPASH same as > CALIPASH

CALLIPEE same as > CALIPEE

CALLIPEES > CALLIPEE

CALLIPER n metal splint for supporting the leg ▷ vb measure the dimensions of (an object) with callipers

CALLIPERS > CALLIPER

CALLOP n edible freshwater fish, Plectroplites ambiguus, of Australia, often golden or pale yellow in colour

CALLOPS > CALLOP

CALLOSE n carbohydrate, a polymer of glucose, found in plants, esp in the sieve tubes

CALLOSES > CALLOSE

CALLOSITY same as > CALLUS

CALLOUS adj showing no concern for other people's feelings ▷ vb make or become callous

CALLOUSED > CALLOUS

CALLOUSES > CALLOUS

CALLOUSLY > CALLOUS

CALLOW adj young and inexperienced ▷ n someone young and inexperienced

CALLOWER > CALLOW

CALLOWEST > CALLOW

CALLOWS > CALLOW

CALLS > CALL

CALLUNA n type of heather

CALLUNAS > CALLUNA

CALLUS n area of thick hardened skin ▷ vb produce or cause to produce a callus

CALLUSED > CALLUS

CALLUSES > CALLUS

CALLUSING > CALLUS

CALM adj not agitated or excited ▷ n peaceful state ▷ vb make or become calm

CALMANT n sedative

CALMANTS > CALMANT

CALMATIVE adj (of a remedy or agent) sedative ▷ n sedative remedy or drug

CALMED > CALM

CALMER > CALM

C

CALMEST > CALM
CALMIER > CALMY
CALMIEST > CALMY
CALMING > CALM
CALMINGLY > CALM
CALMINGS > CALM
CALMLY > CALM
CALMNESS > CALM
CALMS > CALM
CALMSTONE same as
  > CAMSTONE
CALMY adj tranquil
CALO n military servant
CALOMEL n colourless
  tasteless powder
CALOMELS > CALOMEL
CALORIC adj of heat or
  calories ▷n hypothetical
  elastic fluid formerly
  postulated as the
  embodiment of heat
CALORICS > CALORIC
CALORIE n unit of
  measurement for the
  energy value of food
CALORIES > CALORIE
CALORIFIC adj of calories
  or heat
CALORISE same as
  > CALORIZE
CALORISED > CALORISE
CALORISES > CALORISE
CALORIST n believer in
  caloric theory
CALORISTS > CALORIST
CALORIZE vb coat (a ferrous
  metal) by spraying with
  aluminium powder and
  then heating
CALORIZED > CALORIZE
CALORIZES > CALORIZE
CALORY same as > CALORIE
CALOS > CALO
CALOTTE n skullcap worn by
  Roman Catholic clergy
CALOTTES > CALOTTE
CALOTYPE n early
  photographic process
  invented by W. H. Fox
  Talbot, in which the image
  was produced on paper
  treated with silver iodide
  and developed by sodium
  thiosulphite
CALOTYPES > CALOTYPE
CALOYER n monk of the
  Greek Orthodox Church,
  esp of the Basilian Order
CALOYERS > CALOYER
CALP n type of limestone
CALPA n Hindu unit of time
CALPAC n large black
  brimless hat made of
  sheepskin or felt, worn by
  men in parts of the Near
  East
CALPACK same as > CALPAC
CALPACKS > CALPACK
CALPACS > CALPAC
CALPAIN n type of enzyme
CALPAINS > CALPAIN
CALPAS > CALPA
CALPS > CALP
CALQUE > CAULK
CALQUED > CALQUE
CALQUES > CALQUE
CALQUING > CALQUE

CALTHA n marsh marigold
CALTHAS > CALTHA
CALTHROP same as
  > CALTHROP
CALTHROPS > CALTROP
CALTRAP same as > CALTROP
CALTRAPS > CALTRAP
CALTROP n floating Asian
  plant
CALTROPS > CALTROP
CALUMBA n Mozambiquan
  root used for medicinal
  purposes
CALUMBAS > CALUMBA
CALUMET n peace pipe
CALUMETS > CALUMET
CALUMNIES > CALUMNY
CALUMNY n false or
  malicious statement
CALUTRON n device used for
  the separation of isotopes
CALUTRONS > CALUTRON
CALVADOS n type of apple
  brandy
CALVARIA n top part of the
  skull of vertebrates
CALVARIAL > CALVARIUM
CALVARIAN > CALVARIUM
CALVARIAS > CALVARIA
CALVARIES > CALVARY
CALVARIUM same as
  > CALVARIA
CALVARY n representation
  of Christ's crucifixion,
  usually sculptured and in
  the open air
CALVE vb give birth to a calf
CALVED > CALVE
CALVER vb prepare fish for
  cooking
CALVERED > CALVER
CALVERING > CALVER
CALVERS > CALVER
CALVES > CALF
CALVING > CALVE
CALVITIES n baldness
CALX n powdery metallic
  oxide formed when an ore
  or mineral is roasted
CALXES > CALX
CALYCATE > CALYX
CALYCEAL adj resembling
  a calyx
CALYCES > CALYX
CALYCINAL same as
  > CALYCINE
CALYCINE adj relating
  to, belonging to, or
  resembling a calyx
CALYCLE n cup-shaped
  structure, as in the coral
  skeleton
CALYCLED > CALYCLE
CALYCLES > CALYCLE
CALYCOID adj resembling
  a calyx
CALYCULAR > CALYCLE
CALYCULE n bracts
  surrounding the base of
  the calyx
CALYCULES > CALYCULE
CALYCULI > CALYCULUS
CALYCULUS same as
  > CALYCLE
CALYPSO n West Indian
  song with improvised
  topical lyrics

CALYPSOES > CALYPSO
CALYPSOS > CALYPSO
CALYPTER n alula
CALYPTERA same as
  > CALYPTRA
CALYPTERS > CALYPTER
CALYPTRA n membranous
  hood covering the spore-
  bearing capsule of mosses
  and liverworts
CALYPTRAS > CALYPTRA
CALYX n outer leaves that
  protect a flower bud
CALYXES > CALYX
CALZONE n folded pizza
  filled with cheese,
  tomatoes, etc
CALZONES > CALZONE
CALZONI > CALZONE
CAM n device that converts
  a circular motion to a
  to-and-fro motion ▷vb
  furnish (a machine) with
  a cam
CAMA n hybrid offspring of a
  camel and a llama
CAMAIEU n cameo
CAMAIEUX > CAMAIEU
CAMAIL n neck and
  shoulders covering of mail
  worn with and laced to the
  basinet
CAMAILED > CAMAIL
CAMAILS > CAMAIL
CAMAN n wooden stick used
  to hit the ball in shinty
CAMANACHD n shinty
CAMANS > CAMAN
CAMARILLA n group of
  confidential advisers, esp
  formerly, to the Spanish
  kings
CAMARON n shrimp
CAMARONS > CAMARON
CAMAS same as > CAMASS
CAMASES > CAMAS
CAMASH same as > CAMASS
CAMASHES > CAMASH
CAMASS n type of North
  American plant
CAMASSES > CAMASS
CAMBER n slight upward
  curve to the centre of a
  surface ▷vb form or be
  formed with a surface
  that curves upwards to its
  centre
CAMBERED > CAMBER
CAMBERING > CAMBER
CAMBERS > CAMBER
CAMBIA > CAMBIUM
CAMBIAL > CAMBIUM
CAMBIFORM > CAMBIUM
CAMBISM > CAMBIST
CAMBISMS > CAMBIST
CAMBIST n dealer or expert
  in foreign exchange
CAMBISTRY > CAMBIST
CAMBISTS > CAMBIST
CAMBIUM n meristem that
  increases the girth of stems
  and roots by producing
  additional xylem and
  phloem
CAMBIUMS > CAMBIUM
CAMBOGE n type of gum
  resin

CAMBOGES > CAMBOGE
CAMBOGIA another name for
  > GAMBOGE
CAMBOGIAS > CAMBOGIA
CAMBOOSE n cabin built as
  living quarters for a gang of
  lumbermen
CAMBOOSES > CAMBOOSE
CAMBREL a variant of
  > GAMBREL
CAMBRELS > CAMBREL
CAMBRIC n fine white linen
  fabric
CAMBRICS > CAMBRIC
CAMCORDER n combined
  portable video camera and
  recorder
CAME > COME
CAMEL n humped mammal
  that can survive long
  periods without food or
  water in desert regions
CAMELBACK n type of
  locomotive
CAMELEER n camel-driver
CAMELEERS > CAMELEER
CAMELEON same as
  > CHAMELEON
CAMELEONS > CAMELEON
CAMELHAIR n hair of camel
CAMELIA same as > CAMELLIA
CAMELIAS > CAMELIA
CAMELID adj of or relating
  to camels ▷n any animal
  of the camel family
CAMELIDS > CAMELID
CAMELINE n material made
  from camel hair
CAMELINES > CAMELINE
CAMELISH > CAMEL
CAMELLIA n evergreen
  ornamental shrub with
  white, pink, or red flowers
CAMELLIAS > CAMELLIA
CAMELLIKE > CAMEL
CAMELOID n member of the
  camel family
CAMELOIDS > CAMELOID
CAMELOT n supposedly
  idyllic period or age
CAMELOTS > CAMELOT
CAMELRIES > CAMELRY
CAMELRY n troops mounted
  on camels
CAMELS > CAMEL
CAMEO n brooch or ring with
  a profile head carved in
  relief ▷vb to appear in a
  brief role
CAMEOED > CAMEO
CAMEOING > CAMEO
CAMEOS > CAMEO
CAMERA n apparatus used
  for taking photographs or
  pictures for television or
  cinema
CAMERAE > CAMERA
CAMERAL adj of or relating
  to a judicial or legislative
  chamber
CAMERAMAN n man who
  operates a camera for
  television or cinema
CAMERAMEN > CAMERAMAN
CAMERAS > CAMERA
CAMERATED adj vaulted
CAMES obsolete form of

> CANVAS

CAMESE *same as* > CAMISE

CAMESES > CAMESE

CAMION *n* lorry, or, esp formerly, a large dray

CAMIONS > CAMION

CAMIS *n* light robe

CAMISA *n* smock

CAMISADE *same as* > CAMISADO

CAMISADES > CAMISADE

CAMISADO *n* (formerly) an attack made under cover of darkness

CAMISADOS > CAMISADO

CAMISAS > CAMISA

CAMISE *n* loose light shirt, smock, or tunic originally worn in the Middle Ages

CAMISES > CAMISE

CAMISIA *n* surplice

CAMISIAS > CAMISIA

CAMISOLE *n* woman's bodice-like garment

CAMISOLES > CAMISOLE

CAMLET *n* tough waterproof cloth

CAMLETS > CAMLET

CAMMED > CAM

CAMMIE *n* webcam award

CAMMIES > CAMMIE

CAMMING > CAM

CAMO short for camouflage

CAMOGIE *n* form of hurling played by women

CAMOGIES > CAMOGIE

CAMOMILE *n* aromatic plant, used to make herbal tea

CAMOMILES > CAMOMILE

CAMOODI *a Caribbean name for* > ANACONDA

CAMOODIS > CAMOODI

CAMORRA *n* secret criminal group

CAMORRAS > CAMORRA

CAMORRIST > CAMORRA

CAMOS > CAMO

CAMOTE *n* type of sweet potato

CAMOTES > CAMOTE

CAMOUFLET *n* type of bomb used in a seige to collapse an enemy's tunnel

CAMP *vb* stay in a camp ▷ *adj* effeminate or homosexual ▷ *adj* (place for) temporary lodgings consisting of tents, huts, or cabins

CAMPAGNA *same as* > CHAMPAIGN

CAMPAGNAS > CAMPAGNA

CAMPAGNE > CAMPAGNA

CAMPAIGN *n* series of coordinated activities designed to achieve a goal ▷ *vb* take part in a campaign

CAMPAIGNS > CAMPAIGN

CAMPANA *n* bell or bell shape

CAMPANAS > CAMPANA

CAMPANERO *n* South American bellbird

CAMPANILE *n* bell tower, usu one not attached to another building

CAMPANILI > CAMPANILE

CAMPANIST *n* expert on bells

CAMPANULA *n* plant with blue or white bell-shaped flowers

CAMPCRAFT *n* skills required when camping

CAMPEADOR *n* champion; term applied especially to El Cid

CAMPED > CAMP

CAMPER *n* person who lives or temporarily stays in a tent, cabin, etc

CAMPERS > CAMPER

CAMPESINO *n* Latin American rural peasant

CAMPEST > CAMP

CAMPFIRE *n* outdoor fire in a camp, esp one used for cooking or as a focal point for community events

CAMPFIRES > CAMPFIRE

CAMPHANE *n* one of the terpene hydrocarbons

CAMPHANES > CAMPHANE

CAMPHENE *n* colourless crystalline insoluble terpene

CAMPHENES > CAMPHENE

CAMPHINE *n* type of solvent

CAMPHINES > CAMPHINE

CAMPHIRE *an archaic name for* > HENNA

CAMPHIRES > CAMPHIRE

CAMPHOL *another word for* > BORNEOL

CAMPHOLS > CAMPHOL

CAMPHOR *n* aromatic crystalline substance used medicinally and in mothballs

CAMPHORIC > CAMPHOR

CAMPHORS > CAMPHOR

CAMPI > CAMPO

CAMPIER > CAMPY

CAMPIEST > CAMPY

CAMPILY > CAMPY

CAMPINESS > CAMPY

CAMPING > CAMP

CAMPINGS > CAMP

CAMPION *n* red, pink, or white wild flower

CAMPIONS > CAMPION

CAMPLE *vb* to argue

CAMPLED > CAMPLE

CAMPLES > CAMPLE

CAMPLING > CAMPLE

CAMPLY > CAMP

CAMPNESS > CAMP

CAMPO *n* level or undulating savanna country, esp in the uplands of Brazil

CAMPODEID *n* member of the Campodea genus of bristle-tails

CAMPONG *n* in Malaysia, a village

CAMPONGS > CAMPONG

CAMPOREE *n* local meeting or assembly of Scouts

CAMPOREES > CAMPOREE

CAMPOS > CAMPO

CAMPOUT *n* camping trip

CAMPOUTS > CAMPOUT

CAMPS > CAMP

CAMPSHIRT *n* short-sleeved shirt

CAMPSITE *n* area on which holiday makers may pitch a tent

CAMPSITES > CAMPSITE

CAMPSTOOL *n* folding stool

CAMPUS *n* grounds of a university or college ▷ *vb* to restrict a student to campus, as a punishment

CAMPUSED > CAMPUS

CAMPUSES > CAMPUS

CAMPUSING > CAMPUS

CAMPY *adj* effeminate

CAMS > CAM

CAMSHAFT *n* part of an engine consisting of a rod to which cams are fixed

CAMSHAFTS > CAMSHAFT

CAMSHO *adj* crooked

CAMSHOCH *same as* > CAMSHO

CAMSTAIRY *adj* perverse

CAMSTANE *same as* > CAMSTONE

CAMSTANES > CAMSTONE

CAMSTEARY *same as* > CAMSTAIRY

CAMSTONE *n* a limestone used for whitening stone doorsteps

CAMSTONES > CAMSTONE

CAMUS *n* type of loose robe

CAMUSES > CAMUS

CAMWOOD *n* W African leguminous tree, *Baphia nitida*, whose hard wood was formerly used in making a red dye

CAMWOODS > CAMWOOD

CAN *vb* be able to ▷ *n* metal container for food or liquids

CANADA *n* canada goose

CANADAS > CANADA

CANAIGRE *n* dock, *Rumex hymenosepalus*, of the southern US, the root of which yields a substance used in tanning

CANAIGRES > CANAIGRE

CANAILLE *n* masses or rabble

CANAILLES > CANAILLE

CANAKIN *same as* > CANNIKIN

CANAKINS > CANAKIN

CANAL *n* artificial waterway ▷ *vb* dig a canal through

CANALBOAT *n* boat made for canals

CANALED > CANAL

CANALING > CANAL

CANALISE *same as* > CANALIZE

CANALISED > CANALIZE

CANALISES > CANALIZE

CANALIZE *vb* give direction to

CANALIZED > CANALIZE

CANALIZES > CANALIZE

CANALLED > CANAL

CANALLER *n* canal boat worker

CANALLERS > CANALLER

CANALLING > CANAL

CANALS > CANAL

CANAPE *n* small piece of bread or toast with a savoury topping

CANAPES > CANAPE

CANARD *n* false report

CANARDS > CANARD

CANARIED > CANARY

CANARIES > CANARY

CANARY *n* small yellow songbird often kept as a pet ▷ *vb* perform a dance called the canary

CANARYING > CANARY

CANASTA *n* card game like rummy, played with two packs

CANASTAS > CANASTA

CANASTER *n* coarsely broken dried tobacco leaves

CANASTERS > CANASTER

CANBANK *n* container for receiving cans for recycling

CANBANKS > CANBANK

CANCAN *n* lively high-kicking dance performed by a female group

CANCANS > CANCAN

CANCEL *vb* stop (something that has been arranged) from taking place ▷ *n* new leaf or section of a book replacing a defective one, one containing errors, or one that has been omitted

CANCELED > CANCEL

CANCELEER *vb* (of a hawk) to turn in flight when a stoop fails, in order to re-attempt it

CANCELER > CANCEL

CANCELERS > CANCEL

CANCELIER *a variant of* > CANCELEER

CANCELING > CANCEL

CANCELLED > CANCEL

CANCELLER > CANCEL

CANCELLI *n* any lattice-like structures

CANCELS > CANCEL

CANCER *n* serious disease resulting from a malignant growth or tumour

CANCERATE *vb* to become cancerous

CANCERED *adj* affected by cancer

CANCEROUS > CANCER

CANCERS > CANCER

CANCHA *n* toasted maize

CANCHAS > CANCHA

CANCRINE *adj* crab-like

CANCROID *adj* resembling a cancerous growth ▷ *n* skin cancer, esp one of only moderate malignancy

CANCROIDS > CANCROID

CANDELA *n* unit of luminous intensity

CANDELAS > CANDELA

CANDENT *adj* emitting light as a result of being heated to a high temperature

CANDID *adj* honest and straightforward ▷ *n* unposed photograph

CANDIDA *n* yeastlike parasitic fungus which causes thrush

C

CANDIDACY > CANDIDATE

CANDIDAL > CANDIDA

CANDIDAS > CANDIDA

CANDIDATE n person seeking a job or position

CANDIDER > CANDID

CANDIDEST > CANDID

CANDIDLY > CANDID

CANDIDS > CANDID

CANDIE n South Indian unit of weight

CANDIED adj coated with sugar

CANDIES > CANDY

CANDLE n stick of wax enclosing a wick, which is burned to produce light ▷ vb test by holding up to a candle

CANDLED > CANDLE

CANDLELIT adj lit by the light of candles

CANDLENUT n euphorbiaceous tree, Aleurites mollucana, of tropical Asia and Polynesia

CANDLEPIN n bowling pin, as used in skittles, tenpin bowling, candlepins, etc

CANDLER > CANDLE

CANDLERS > CANDLE

CANDLES > CANDLE

CANDLING > CANDLE

CANDOCK n type of water lily, or horsetail

CANDOCKS > CANDOCK

CANDOR same as > CANDOUR

CANDORS > CANDOR

CANDOUR n honesty and straightforwardness

CANDOURS > CANDOUR

CANDY n sweet or sweets ▷ vb make sweet

CANDYGRAM n message accompanied by sweets

CANDYING > CANDY

CANDYTUFT n garden plant with clusters of white, pink, or purple flowers

CANE n stem of the bamboo or similar plant ▷ vb beat with a cane

CANEBRAKE n thicket of canes

CANED > CANE

CANEFRUIT n fruit, like the raspberry, which grows on woody-stemmed plants

CANEH n Hebrew unit of length

CANEHS > CANEH

CANELLA n fragrant cinnamon-like inner bark of a West Indian tree, Canella winterana (family Canellaceae) used as a spice and in medicine

CANELLAS > CANELLA

CANELLINI n white kidney bean

CANEPHOR n sculpted figure carrying a basket on its head

CANEPHORA same as > CANEPHOR

CANEPHORE same as > CANEPHOR

CANEPHORS > CANEPHOR

CANER > CANE

CANERS > CANE

CANES > CANE

CANESCENT adj white or greyish due to the presence of numerous short white hairs

CANEWARE n type of unglazed stoneware

CANEWARES > CANEWARE

CANFIELD n gambling game adapted from a type of patience

CANFIELDS > CANFIELD

CANFUL n amount a can will hold

CANFULS > CANFUL

CANG same as > CANGUE

CANGLE vb to wrangle

CANGLED > CANGLE

CANGLES > CANGLE

CANGLING > CANGLE

CANGS > CANG

CANGUE n (formerly in China) a large wooden collar worn by petty criminals as a punishment

CANGUES > CANGUE

CANICULAR adj of or relating to the star Sirius or its rising

CANID n animal of the dog family

CANIDS > CANID

CANIER > CANY

CANIEST > CANY

CANIKIN same as > CANNIKIN

CANIKINS > CANIKIN

CANINE adj of or like a dog ▷ n sharp pointed tooth between the incisors and the molars

CANINES > CANINE

CANING n beating with a cane as a punishment

CANINGS > CANING

CANINITY > CANINE

CANISTEL n Caribbean fruit

CANISTELS > CANISTEL

CANISTER n metal container ▷ vb to put into canisters

CANISTERS > CANISTER

CANITIES n grey hair

CANKER n ulceration, ulcerous disease ▷ vb infect or become infected with or as if with canker

CANKERED > CANKER

CANKERING > CANKER

CANKEROUS adj having cankers

CANKERS > CANKER

CANKERY adj like a canker

CANN vb direct a ship's steering

CANNA n any of various tropical plants constituting the genus Canna, having broad leaves and red or yellow showy flowers for which they are cultivated: family Cannaceae

CANNABIC > CANNABIS

CANNABIN n greenish-black poisonous resin obtained from the Indian hemp plant

CANNABINS > CANNABIN

CANNABIS n Asian plant with tough fibres

CANNACH n cotton grass

CANNACHS > CANNACH

CANNAE vb can not

CANNAS > CANNA

CANNED > CAN

CANNEL n type of dull coal

CANNELON n type of meat loaf

CANNELONI pl n pasta in the shape of tubes, which are usually stuffed

CANNELONS > CANNELON

CANNELS > CANNEL

CANNELURE n groove or fluting, esp one around the cylindrical part of a bullet

CANNER n person or organization whose job is to can foods

CANNERIES > CANNERY

CANNERS > CANNER

CANNERY n factory where food is canned

CANNIBAL n person who eats human flesh

CANNIBALS > CANNIBAL

CANNIE same as > CANNY

CANNIER > CANNY

CANNIEST > CANNY

CANNIKIN n small can, esp one used as a drinking vessel

CANNIKINS > CANNIKIN

CANNILY > CANNY

CANNINESS > CANNY

CANNING > CAN

CANNINGS > CAN

CANNISTER same as > CANISTER

CANNOLI n Sicilian pudding of pasta shells filled with sweetened ricotta

CANNOLIS > CANNOLI

CANNON n gun of large calibre ▷ vb to collide (with)

CANNONADE n continuous heavy gunfire ▷ vb attack (a target) with cannon

CANNONED > CANNON

CANNONEER n (formerly) a soldier who served and fired a cannon

CANNONIER same as > CANNONEER

CANNONING > CANNON

CANNONRY n volley of artillery fire

CANNONS > CANNON

CANNOT vb can not

CANNS > CANN

CANNULA n narrow tube for insertion into a bodily cavity, as for draining off fluid, introducing medication, etc

CANNULAE > CANNULA

CANNULAR adj shaped like a cannula

CANNULAS > CANNULA

CANNULATE vb insert a cannula into ▷ adj shaped like a cannula

CANNY adj shrewd, cautious ▷ adv quite

CANOE n light narrow open boat propelled by a paddle or paddles ▷ vb use a canoe

CANOEABLE > CANOE

CANOED > CANOE

CANOEING > CANOE

CANOEINGS > CANOE

CANOEIST > CANOE

CANOEISTS > CANOE

CANOER > CANOE

CANOERS > CANOE

CANOES > CANOE

CANOEWOOD n type of tree

CANOLA n cooking oil extracted from a variety of rapeseed developed in Canada

CANOLAS > CANOLA

CANON n priest serving in a cathedral

CANONESS n woman belonging to any one of several religious orders and living under a rule but not under a vow

CANONIC same as > CANONICAL

CANONICAL adj conforming with canon law

CANONISE same as > CANONIZE

CANONISED > CANONISE

CANONISER > CANONISE

CANONISES > CANONISE

CANONIST n specialist in canon law

CANONISTS > CANONIST

CANONIZE vb declare (a person) officially to be a saint

CANONIZED > CANONIZE

CANONIZER > CANONIZE

CANONIZES > CANONIZE

CANONRIES > CANONRY

CANONRY n office, benefice, or status of a canon

CANONS > CANON

CANOODLE vb kiss and cuddle

CANOODLED > CANOODLE

CANOODLER > CANOODLE

CANOODLES > CANOODLE

CANOPIC adj of ancient Egyptian vase

CANOPIED > CANOPY

CANOPIES > CANOPY

CANOPY n covering above a bed, door, etc ▷ vb cover with or as if with a canopy

CANOPYING > CANOPY

CANOROUS adj tuneful

CANS > CAN

CANSFUL > CANFUL

CANSO n love song

CANSOS > CANSO

CANST vb form of 'can' used with the pronoun thou or its relative form

CANSTICK n candlestick

CANSTICKS > CANSTICK

CANT n insincere talk ▷ vb use cant ▷ adj oblique

CANTABANK *n* itinerant singer

CANTABILE *adv* flowing and melodious ▷ *n* piece or passage performed in this way

CANTAL *n* French cheese

CANTALA *n* tropical American plant, *Agave cantala*, similar to the century plant: family *Agavaceae* (agaves)

CANTALAS > CANTALA

CANTALOUP *n* type of melon

CANTALS > CANTAL

CANTAR *variant form of* > KANTAR

CANTARS > CANTAR

CANTATA *n* musical work consisting of arias, duets, and choruses

CANTATAS > CANTATA

CANTATE *n* 98th psalm sung as a nonmetrical hymn

CANTATES > CANTATE

CANTDOG *same as* > CANTHOOK

CANTDOGS > CANTDOG

CANTED > CANT

CANTEEN *n* restaurant attached to a workplace or school

CANTEENS > CANTEEN

CANTER *vb* move at gait between trot and gallop

CANTERED > CANTER

CANTERING > CANTER

CANTERS > CANTER

CANTEST > CANT

CANTHAL > CANTHUS

CANTHARI > CANTHARUS

CANTHARID *n* any beetle of the family *Cantharidae*, having a soft elongated body

CANTHARIS *n* singular of plural noun, cantharides: a diuretic and urogenital stimulant or irritant prepared from the dried bodies of Spanish fly (family *Meloidae*, not *Cantharidae*), once thought to be an aphrodisiac

CANTHARUS *n* large two-handled pottery cup

CANTHI > CANTHUS

CANTHITIS *n* inflammation of canthus

CANTHOOK *n* wooden pole with a hook used for handling logs

CANTHOOKS > CANTHOOK

CANTHUS *n* inner or outer corner or angle of the eye, formed by the natural junction of the eyelids

CANTIC > CANT

CANTICLE *n* short hymn with words from the Bible

CANTICLES > CANTICLE

CANTICO *vb* to dance as part of an act of worship

CANTICOED > CANTICO

CANTICOS > CANTICO

CANTICOY *same as* > CANTICO

CANTICOYS > CANTICOY

CANTICUM *n* canticle

CANTICUMS > CANTICUM

CANTIER > CANTY

CANTIEST > CANTY

CANTILENA *n* smooth flowing style in the writing of vocal music

CANTILY > CANTY

CANTINA *n* bar or wine shop, esp in a Spanish-speaking country

CANTINAS > CANTINA

CANTINESS > CANTY

CANTING > CANT

CANTINGLY > CANT

CANTINGS > CANT

CANTION *n* song

CANTIONS > CANTION

CANTLE *n* back part of a saddle that slopes upwards ▷ *vb* to set up, or stand, on high

CANTLED > CANTLE

CANTLES > CANTLE

CANTLET *n* piece

CANTLETS > CANTLET

CANTLING > CANTLE

CANTO *same as* > CANTUS

CANTON *n* political division of a country, esp Switzerland ▷ *vb* divide into cantons

CANTONAL > CANTON

CANTONED > CANTON

CANTONING > CANTON

CANTONISE *vb* to divide into cantons

CANTONIZE *same as* > CANTONISE

CANTONS > CANTON

CANTOR *n* man employed to lead services in a synagogue

CANTORIAL *adj* of or relating to a precentor

CANTORIS *adj* (in antiphonal music) to be sung by the cantorial side of a choir

CANTORS > CANTOR

CANTOS > CANTO

CANTRAIP *n* witch's spell or charm

CANTRAIPS > CANTRAIP

CANTRAP *same as* > CANTRAIP

CANTRAPS > CANTRAP

CANTRED *n* district comprising a hundred villages

CANTREDS > CANTRED

CANTREF *same as* > CANTRED

CANTREFS > CANTREF

CANTRIP *n* magic spell ▷ *adj* (of an effect) produced by black magic

CANTRIPS > CANTRIP

CANTS > CANT

CANTUS *n* medieval form of church singing

CANTY *adj* lively

CANULA *same as* > CANNULA

CANULAE > CANULA

CANULAR *adj* shaped like a cannula

CANULAS > CANULA

CANULATE *same as*

> CANNULATE

CANULATED > CANULATE

CANULATES > CANULATE

CANVAS *n* heavy coarse cloth used for sails and tents, and for oil painting ▷ *vb* to cover with, or be applied to, canvas

CANVASED > CANVAS

CANVASER > CANVAS

CANVASERS > CANVAS

CANVASES > CANVAS

CANVASING > CANVAS

CANVASS *vb* try to get votes or support (from) ▷ *n* canvassing

CANVASSED > CANVASS

CANVASSER > CANVASS

CANVASSES > CANVASS

CANY *adj* cane-like

CANYON *n* deep narrow valley

CANYONEER *n* canyon explorer

CANYONING *n* sport of going down a canyon river by any of various means

CANYONS > CANYON

CANZONA *n* type of 16th- or 17th-century contrapuntal music, usually for keyboard, lute, or instrumental ensemble

CANZONAS > CANZONA

CANZONE *n* Provençal or Italian lyric, often in praise of love or beauty

CANZONES > CANZONE

CANZONET *n* short, cheery, or lively Italian song

CANZONETS > CANZONET

CANZONI > CANZONE

CAP *n* soft close-fitting covering for the head ▷ *vb* cover or top with something

CAPA *n* type of Spanish cloak

CAPABLE *adj* having the ability (for)

CAPABLER > CAPABLE

CAPABLEST > CAPABLE

CAPABLY > CAPABLE

CAPACIOUS *adj* roomy

CAPACITOR *n* device for storing electrical charge

CAPACITY *n* ability to contain, absorb, or hold ▷ *adj* of the maximum amount or number possible

CAPARISON *n* decorated covering for a horse or other animal, esp (formerly) for a warhorse ▷ *vb* put a caparison on

CAPAS > CAPA

CAPE *n* short cloak ▷ *vb* to cut and remove the hide of an animal

CAPED > CAPE

CAPELAN *another word for* > CAPELIN

CAPELANS > CAPELAN

CAPELET *n* small cape

CAPELETS > CAPELET

CAPELIN *n* small marine food fish, *Mallotus villosus*, occurring in northern and Arctic seas: family *Osmeridae* (smelts)

CAPELINE *n* cap-shaped bandage to cover the head or an amputation stump

CAPELINES > CAPELINE

CAPELINS > CAPELIN

CAPELLET *n* wen-like swelling on a horse

CAPELLETS > CAPELLET

CAPELLINE *same as* > CAPELINE

CAPELLINI *n* type of pasta

CAPER *n* high-spirited prank ▷ *vb* skip about

CAPERED > CAPER

CAPERER > CAPER

CAPERERS > CAPER

CAPERING > CAPER

CAPERS *pl n* pickled flower buds of a Mediterranean shrub used in sauces

CAPES > CAPE

CAPESKIN *n* soft leather obtained from the skins of a type of lamb or sheep having hairlike wool ▷ *adj* made of this leather

CAPESKINS > CAPESKIN

CAPEWORK *n* use of the cape by the matador in bullfighting

CAPEWORKS > CAPEWORK

CAPFUL *n* quantity held by a (usually bottle) cap

CAPFULS > CAPFUL

CAPH *n* letter of the Hebrew alphabet

CAPHS > CAPH

CAPI > CAPO

CAPIAS *n* (formerly) a writ directing a sheriff or other officer to arrest a named person

CAPIASES > CAPIAS

CAPILLARY *n* very fine blood vessel ▷ *adj* (of a tube) having a fine bore

CAPING > CAPE

CAPITA > CAPUT

CAPITAL *n* chief city of a country ▷ *adj* involving or punishable by death

CAPITALLY *adv* in an excellent manner

CAPITALS > CAPITAL

CAPITAN *another name for* > HOGFISH

CAPITANI > CAPITANO

CAPITANO *n* chief; captain

CAPITANOS > CAPITANO

CAPITANS > CAPITAN

CAPITATE *adj* shaped like a head, as certain flowers or inflorescences

CAPITATED *adj* having fixed upper limit

CAPITAYN *n* captain

CAPITAYNS > CAPITAYN

CAPITELLA *n* plural form of singular: capitellum, an enlarged knoblike structure at the end of a bone that forms an articulation with another

C

bone

CAPITOL *n* (in America) building housing the state legislature

CAPITOLS > CAPITOL

CAPITULA > CAPITULUM

CAPITULAR *adj* of or associated with a cathedral chapter ▷ *n* member of a cathedral chapter

CAPITULUM *n* racemose inflorescence in the form of a disc of sessile flowers, the youngest at the centre. It occurs in the daisy and related plants

CAPIZ *n* bivalve shell of a mollusc (*Placuna placenta*) found esp in the Philippines and having a smooth translucent shiny interior: used in jewellery, ornaments, lampshades, etc

CAPIZES > CAPIZ

CAPLE *n* horse

CAPLES > CAPLE

CAPLESS > CAP

CAPLET *n* medicinal tablet, usually oval in shape, coated in a soluble substance

CAPLETS > CAPLET

CAPLIN *same as* > CAPELIN

CAPLINS > CAPLIN

CAPMAKER > CAP

CAPMAKERS > CAP

CAPO *n* device fitted across the strings of a guitar or similar instrument so as to raise the pitch

CAPOCCHIA *n* fool

CAPOEIRA *n* combination of martial art and dance, which originated among African slaves in 19th-century Brazil

CAPOEIRAS > CAPOEIRA

CAPON *n* castrated cock fowl fattened for eating

CAPONATA *n* Sicilian antipasto relish

CAPONATAS > CAPONATA

CAPONIER *n* covered passageway built across a ditch as a military defence

CAPONIERE *same as* > CAPONIER

CAPONIERS > CAPONIER

CAPONISE *same as* > CAPONIZE

CAPONISED > CAPONISE

CAPONISES > CAPONISE

CAPONIZE *vb* make (a cock) into a capon

CAPONIZED > CAPONIZE

CAPONIZES > CAPONIZE

CAPONS > CAPON

CAPORAL *n* strong coarse dark tobacco

CAPORALS > CAPORAL

CAPOS > CAPO

CAPOT *n* winning of all the tricks by one player ▷ *vb* score a capot (against)

CAPOTASTO *same as* > CAPO

CAPOTE *n* long cloak or soldier's coat, usually with a hood

CAPOTES > CAPOTE

CAPOTS > CAPOT

CAPOTTED > CAPOT

CAPOTTING > CAPOT

CAPOUCH *same as* > CAPUCHE

CAPOUCHES > CAPOUCHE

CAPPED > CAP

CAPPER > CAP

CAPPERS > CAP

CAPPING > CAP

CAPPINGS > CAP

CAPRATE *n* any salt of capric acid

CAPRATES > CAPRATE

CAPRIC *adj* (of a type of acid) smelling of goats

CAPRICCI > CAPRICCIO

CAPRICCIO *n* lively piece composed freely and without adhering to the rules for any specific musical form

CAPRICE *same as* > CAPRICCIO

CAPRICES > CAPRICE

CAPRID *n* any member of the goat family

CAPRIDS > CAPRID

CAPRIFIED > CAPRIFY

CAPRIFIES > CAPRIFY

CAPRIFIG *n* wild variety of fig, *Ficus carica sylvestris*, of S Europe and SW Asia, used in the caprification of the edible fig

CAPRIFIGS > CAPRIFIG

CAPRIFOIL *variant of* > CAPRIFOLE

CAPRIFOLE *n* honeysuckle

CAPRIFORM *adj* goatlike

CAPRIFY *vb* induce figs to ripen

CAPRINE *adj* of or resembling a goat

CAPRIOLE *n* upward but not forward leap made by a horse ▷ *vb* perform a capriole

CAPRIOLED > CAPRIOLE

CAPRIOLES > CAPRIOLE

CAPRIS *pl n* women's tight-fitting trousers

CAPROATE *n* any salt of caproic acid

CAPROATES > CAPROATE

CAPROCK *n* layer of rock that overlies a salt dome

CAPROCKS > CAPROCK

CAPROIC as in *caproic acid* oily acid found in milk

CAPRYLATE *n* any salt of caprylic acid

CAPRYLIC *variant of* > CAPRIC

CAPS > CAP

CAPSAICIN *n* colourless crystalline bitter alkaloid

CAPSICIN *n* liquid or resin extracted from capsicum

CAPSICINS > CAPSICIN

CAPSICUM *n* kind of pepper used as a vegetable or as a spice

CAPSICUMS > CAPSICUM

CAPSID *n* outer protein coat of a mature virus

CAPSIDAL > CAPSID

CAPSIDS > CAPSID

CAPSIZAL > CAPSIZE

CAPSIZALS > CAPSIZE

CAPSIZE *vb* (of a boat) overturn accidentally

CAPSIZED > CAPSIZE

CAPSIZES > CAPSIZE

CAPSIZING > CAPSIZE

CAPSOMER *n* one of the units making up a viral capsid

CAPSOMERE *n* any of the protein units that together form the capsid of a virus

CAPSOMERS > CAPSOMER

CAPSTAN *n* rotating cylinder round which a ship's rope is wound

CAPSTANS > CAPSTAN

CAPSTONE *n* one of a set of slabs on the top of a wall, building, etc

CAPSTONES > CAPSTONE

CAPSULAR *adj* relating to a capsule

CAPSULARY *same as* > CAPSULAR

CAPSULATE *adj* within or formed into a capsule

CAPSULE *n* soluble gelatine case containing a dose of medicine ▷ *adj* very concise ▷ *vb* to contain within a capsule

CAPSULED > CAPSULE

CAPSULES > CAPSULE

CAPSULING > CAPSULE

CAPSULISE *same as* > CAPSULIZE

CAPSULIZE *vb* state (information) in a highly condensed form

CAPTAIN *n* commander of a ship or civil aircraft ▷ *vb* be captain of

CAPTAINCY > CAPTAIN

CAPTAINED > CAPTAIN

CAPTAINRY *n* condition or skill of being a captain

CAPTAINS > CAPTAIN

CAPTAN *n* type of fungicide

CAPTANS > CAPTAN

CAPTION *n* title or explanation accompanying an illustration ▷ *vb* provide with a caption

CAPTIONED > CAPTION

CAPTIONS > CAPTION

CAPTIOUS *adj* tending to make trivial criticisms

CAPTIVATE *vb* attract and hold the attention of

CAPTIVE *n* person kept in confinement ▷ *adj* kept in confinement ▷ *vb* to take prisoner

CAPTIVED > CAPTIVE

CAPTIVES > CAPTIVE

CAPTIVING > CAPTIVE

CAPTIVITY *n* state of being kept in confinement

CAPTOPRIL *n* drug used to treat high blood pressure and congestive heart failure

CAPTOR *n* person who captures a person or animal

CAPTORS > CAPTOR

CAPTURE *vb* take by force ▷ *n* capturing

CAPTURED > CAPTURE

CAPTURER > CAPTURE

CAPTURERS > CAPTURE

CAPTURES > CAPTURE

CAPTURING > CAPTURE

CAPUCCIO *n* hood

CAPUCCIOS > CAPUCCIO

CAPUCHE *n* large hood or cowl, esp that worn by Capuchin friars

CAPUCHED *adj* hooded

CAPUCHES > CAPUCHE

CAPUCHIN *n* S American monkey with thick hair on the top of its head

CAPUCHINS > CAPUCHIN

CAPUERA *variant of* > CAPOEIRA

CAPUERAS > CAPUERA

CAPUL *same as* > CAPLE

CAPULS > CAPUL

CAPUT *n* main or most prominent part of an organ or structure

CAPYBARA *n* very large S American rodent

CAPYBARAS > CAPYBARA

CAR *n* motor vehicle designed to carry a small number of people

CARABAO *n* water buffalo

CARABAOS > CARABAO

CARABID *n* any typically dark-coloured beetle of the family *Carabidae*, including the bombardier and other ground beetles. ▷ *adj* of, relating to, or belonging to the *Carabidae*

CARABIDS > CARABID

CARABIN *same as* > CARBINE

CARABINE > CARBINE

CARABINER *a variant spelling of* > KARABINER

CARABINES > CARABINE

CARABINS > CARABIN

CARACAL *n* lynx with reddish fur, which inhabits deserts of N Africa and S Asia

CARACALS > CARACAL

CARACARA *n* any of various large carrion-eating diurnal birds of prey of the genera *Caracara, Polyborus*, etc, of S North, Central, and South America, having long legs and naked faces: family *Falconidae* (falcons)

CARACARAS > CARACARA

CARACK *same as* > CARRACK

CARACKS > CARACK

CARACOL *same as* > CARACOLE

CARACOLE *n* half turn to the right or left ▷ *vb* execute a half turn to the right or left

CARACOLED > CARACOLE

CARACOLER > CARACOLE

CARACOLES > CARACOLE

CARACOLS > CARACOL

CARACT *n* sign or symbol

CARACTS > CARACT

CARACUL n black loosely curled fur obtained from the skins of newly born lambs of the karakul sheep

CARACULS > CARACUL

CARAFE n glass bottle for serving water or wine

CARAFES > CARAFE

CARAGANA n pea tree

CARAGANAS > CARAGANA

CARAGEEN same as > CARRAGEEN

CARAGEENS > CARAGEEN

CARAMBA n Spanish interjection similar to 'wow!'

CARAMBOLA n yellow edible star-shaped fruit that grows on a Brazilian tree

CARAMBOLE vb make a carom or carambola (shot in billiards)

CARAMEL n chewy sweet made from sugar and milk ▷ vb to turn into caramel

CARAMELS > CARAMEL

CARANGID n any marine percoid fish of the family *Carangidae*, having a compressed body and deeply forked tail. The group includes the jacks, horse mackerel, pompano, and pilot fish ▷ adj of, relating to, or belonging to the *Carangidae*

CARANGIDS > CARANGID

CARANGOID same as > CARANGID

CARANNA n gumlike substance

CARANNAS > CARANNA

CARAP n crabwood

CARAPACE n hard upper shell of tortoises and crustaceans

CARAPACED adj having carapace

CARAPACES > CARAPACE

CARAPAX n carapace

CARAPAXES > CARAPAX

CARAPS > CARAP

CARASSOW same as > CURASSOW

CARASSOWS > CARASSOW

CARAT n unit of weight of precious stones

CARATE n tropical disease

CARATES > CARATE

CARATS > CARAT

CARAUNA same as > CARANNA

CARAUNAS > CARAUNA

CARAVAN n large enclosed vehicle for living in, designed to be towed by a car or horse ▷ vb travel or have a holiday in a caravan

CARAVANCE same as > CALAVANCE

CARAVANED > CARAVAN

CARAVANER n person who holidays in a caravan

CARAVANS > CARAVAN

CARAVEL n two- or three-masted sailing ship, esp one with a broad beam, high poop deck, and lateen rig that was used by the Spanish and Portuguese in the 15th and 16th centuries

CARAVELLE variant of > CARAVEL

CARAVELS > CARAVEL

CARAWAY n plant whose seeds are used as a spice

CARAWAYS > CARAWAY

CARB n carbohydrate

CARBACHOL n carbamylcholine, a cholinergic agent

CARBAMATE n salt or ester of carbamic acid

CARBAMIC as in *carbamic acid* hypothetical compound known only in carbamate salts

CARBAMIDE another name for > UREA

CARBAMINO adj relating to the compound produced when carbon dioxide reacts with an amino group

CARBAMOYL same as > CARBAMYL

CARBAMYL n radical from carbamic acid

CARBAMYLS > CARBAMYL

CARBANION n negatively charged organic ion in which most of the negative charge is localized on a carbon atom

CARBARN n streetcar depot

CARBARNS > CARBARN

CARBARYL n organic compound of the carbamate group

CARBARYLS > CARBARYL

CARBAZOLE n colourless insoluble solid obtained from coal tar

CARBEEN n Australian eucalyptus tree, *E. tessellaris*, having drooping branches and grey bark

CARBEENS > CARBEEN

CARBENE n neutral divalent free radical, such as methylene: CH_2

CARBENES > CARBENE

CARBIDE n compound of carbon with a metal

CARBIDES > CARBIDE

CARBIES > CARBY

CARBINE n light automatic rifle

CARBINEER n (formerly) a soldier equipped with a carbine

CARBINES > CARBINE

CARBINIER same as > CARBINEER

CARBINOL another word for > CARABINOL

CARBINOLS > CARBINOL

CARBO n carbohydrate

CARBOLIC as in *carbolic acid* phenol, when it is used as a disinfectant

CARBOLICS > CARBOLIC

CARBOLISE same as > CARBOLIZE

CARBOLIZE another word for > PHENOLATE

CARBON n nonmetallic element occurring as charcoal, graphite, and diamond, found in all organic matter

CARBONADE n stew of beef and onions cooked in beer

CARBONADO n piece of meat, fish, etc, scored and grilled ▷ vb score and grill (meat, fish, etc)

CARBONARA n pasta sauce containing cream, bacon and cheese

CARBONATE n salt or ester of carbonic acid ▷ vb form or turn into a carbonate

CARBONIC adj containing carbon

CARBONISE same as > CARBONIZE

CARBONIUM as in *carbonium ion* type of positively charged organic ion

CARBONIZE vb turn into carbon as a result of heating

CARBONOUS > CARBON

CARBONS > CARBON

CARBONYL n of, consisting of, or containing the divalent group =CO

CARBONYLS > CARBONYL

CARBORA n former name for the koala

CARBORAS > CARBORA

CARBOS > CARBO

CARBOXYL as in *carboxyl group* functional group in organic acids

CARBOXYLS > CARBOXYL

CARBOY n large bottle with a protective casing

CARBOYED > CARBOY

CARBOYS > CARBOY

CARBS > CARB

CARBUNCLE n inflamed boil

CARBURATE same as > CARBURET

CARBURET vb combine or mix (a gas) with carbon or carbon compounds ▷ vb to combine with carbon

CARBURETS > CARBURET

CARBURISE > CARBONIZE

CARBURIZE same as > CARBONIZE

CARBY n short for carburettor

CARCAJOU a North American name for > WOLVERINE

CARCAJOUS > CARCAJOU

CARCAKE n (formerly, in Scotland) a cake traditionally made for Shrove Tuesday

CARCAKES > CARCAKE

CARCANET n jewelled collar or necklace

CARCANETS > CARCANET

CARCASE same as > CARCASS vb to make a carcase of

CARCASED > CARCASE

CARCASES > CARCASE

CARCASING > CARCASE

CARCASS n dead body of an animal ▷ vb to make a carcass of

CARCASSED > CARCASS

CARCASSES > CARCASS

CARCEL n French unit of light

CARCELS > CARCEL

CARCERAL adj relating to prison

CARCINOID n small serotonin-secreting tumour

CARCINOMA n malignant tumour

CARD n piece of thick stiff paper or cardboard used for identification, reference, or sending greetings or messages ▷ vb comb out fibres of wool or cotton before spinning

CARDAMINE n bittercress

CARDAMOM n spice obtained from the seeds of a tropical plant

CARDAMOMS > CARDAMOM

CARDAMON same as > CARDAMOM

CARDAMONS > CARDAMON

CARDAMUM same as > CARDAMOM

CARDAMUMS > CARDAMUM

CARDAN as in *cardan joint* type of universal joint

CARDBOARD n thin stiff board made from paper pulp ▷ adj without substance

CARDCASE n small case for holding business cards

CARDCASES > CARDCASE

CARDECU n old French coin (a quarter of a crown)

CARDECUE same as > CARDECU

CARDECUES > CARDECUE

CARDECUS > CARDECU

CARDED > CARD

CARDER > CARD

CARDERS > CARD

CARDI n cardigan

CARDIA n lower oesophageal sphincter

CARDIAC adj of the heart ▷ n person with a heart disorder

CARDIACAL > CARDIAC

CARDIACS > CARDIAC

CARDIAE > CARDIA

CARDIALGY n pain in or near the heart

CARDIAS > CARDIA

CARDIE short for > CARDIGAN

CARDIES > CARDIE

CARDIGAN n knitted jacket

CARDIGANS > CARDIGAN

CARDINAL n any of the high-ranking clergymen of the RC Church who elect the Pope and act as his counsellors ▷ adj fundamentally important

CARDINALS > CARDINAL

CARDING > CARD

CARDINGS > CARD

CARDIO adj exercising heart

CARDIOID n heart-shaped

c

curve generated by a fixed point on a circle as it rolls around another fixed circle of equal radius, *a*. Equation: $r = a(1 - \cos n)$, where *r* is the radius vector and *n* is the polar angle.

CARDIOIDS > CARDIOID

CARDIS > CARDI

CARDITIC > CARDITIS

CARDITIS *n* inflammation of the heart

CARDON *n* variety of cactus

CARDONS > CARDON

CARDOON *n* thistle-like S European plant, *Cynara cardunculus*, closely related to the artichoke, with spiny leaves, purple flowers, and a leafstalk that may be blanched and eaten: family *Asteraceae* (composites)

CARDOONS > CARDOON

CARDPHONE *n* public telephone operated by the insertion of a phonecard instead of coins

CARDPUNCH *n* device for putting data from a CPU onto punched cards

CARDS > CARD

CARDSHARP *n* professional card player who cheats

CARDUUS *n* thistle

CARDUUSES > CARDUUS

CARDY *same as* > CARDIE

CARE *vb* be concerned ▷ *n* careful attention, caution

CARED > CARE

CAREEN *vb* tilt over to one side

CAREENAGE > CAREEN

CAREENED > CAREEN

CAREENER > CAREEN

CAREENERS > CAREEN

CAREENING > CAREEN

CAREENS > CAREEN

CAREER *n* series of jobs in a profession or occupation that a person has through their life ▷ *vb* rush in an uncontrolled way ▷ *adj* having chosen to dedicate his or her life to a particular occupation

CAREERED > CAREER

CAREERER > CAREER

CAREERERS > CAREER

CAREERING > CAREER

CAREERISM > CAREERIST

CAREERIST *n* person who seeks advancement by any possible means

CAREERS > CAREER

CAREFREE *adj* without worry or responsibility

CAREFUL *adj* cautious in attitude or action

CAREFULLY > CAREFUL

CAREGIVER *same as* > CARER

CARELESS *adj* done or acting with insufficient attention

CARELINE *n* telephone service set up by a company or other organization to provide its customers or

clients with information about its products or services

CARELINES > CARELINE

CAREME *n* period of Lent

CAREMES > CAREME

CARER *n* person who looks after someone who is ill or old, often a relative

CARERS > CARER

CARES > CARE

CARESS *n* gentle affectionate touch or embrace ▷ *vb* touch gently and affectionately

CARESSED > CARESS

CARESSER > CARESS

CARESSERS > CARESS

CARESSES > CARESS

CARESSING > CARESS

CARESSIVE *adj* caressing

CARET *n* symbol indicating a place in written or printed matter where something is to be inserted

CARETAKE *vb* to work as a caretaker

CARETAKEN > CARETAKE

CARETAKER *n* person employed to look after a place ▷ *adj* performing the duties of an office temporarily

CARETAKES > CARETAKE

CARETOOK > CARETAKE

CARETS > CARET

CAREWORN *adj* showing signs of worry

CAREX *n* any member of the sedge family

CARFARE *n* fare that a passenger is charged for a ride on a bus, etc

CARFARES > CARFARE

CARFAX *n* place where principal roads or streets intersect, esp a place in a town where four roads meet

CARFAXES > CARFAX

CARFOX *same as* > CARFAX

CARFOXES > CARFOX

CARFUFFLE *a variant spelling of* > KERFUFFLE

CARFUL *n* maximum number of people a car will hold

CARFULS > CARFUL

CARGEESE > CARGOOSE

CARGO *n* goods carried by a ship, aircraft, etc ▷ *vb* to load

CARGOED > CARGO

CARGOES > CARGO

CARGOING > CARGO

CARGOOSE *n* crested grebe

CARGOS > CARGO

CARHOP *n* waiter or waitress at a drive-in restaurant ▷ *vb* work as a carhop

CARHOPPED > CARHOP

CARHOPS > CARHOP

CARIACOU *n* type of deer

CARIACOUS > CARIACOU

CARIAMA *another word for* > SERIEMA

CARIAMAS > CARIAMA

CARIBE *n* piranha

CARIBES > CARIBE

CARIBOU *n* large N American reindeer

CARIBOUS > CARIBOU

CARICES > CAREX

CARIED *adj* (of teeth) decayed

CARIERE *obsolete word for* > CAREER

CARIERES > CARIERE

CARIES *n* tooth decay

CARILLON *n* set of bells played by keyboard or mechanically ▷ *vb* play a carillon

CARILLONS > CARILLON

CARINA *n* keel-like part or ridge, as in the breastbone of birds or the fused lower petals of a leguminous flower

CARINAE > CARINA

CARINAL *adj* keel-like

CARINAS > CARINA

CARINATE *adj* having a keel or ridge

CARINATED *same as* > CARINATE

CARING *adj* feeling or showing care and compassion for other people ▷ *n* practice or profession of providing social or medical care

CARIOCA *n* Brazilian dance similar to the samba

CARIOCAS > CARIOCA

CARIOLE *n* small open two-wheeled horse-drawn vehicle

CARIOLES > CARIOLE

CARIOSE *same as* > CARIOUS

CARIOSITY > CARIOUS

CARIOUS *adj* (of teeth or bone) affected with caries

CARITAS *n* divine love; charity

CARITASES > CARITAS

CARITATES > CARITAS

CARJACK *vb* attack (a car driver) to rob them or to steal the car ▷ *vb* to steal a car, by force, from a person who is present

CARJACKED > CARJACK

CARJACKER > CARJACK

CARJACKS > CARJACK

CARJACOU *variation of* > CARIACOU

CARJACOUS > CARJACOU

CARK *vb* break down

CARKED > CARK

CARKING > CARK

CARKS > CARK

CARL *another word for* > CHURL

CARLE *same as* > CARL

CARLES > CARLE

CARLESS > CAR

CARLIN > CARLING

CARLINE *same as* > CARLING

CARLINES > CARLINE

CARLING *n* fore-and-aft beam in a vessel, used for supporting the deck, esp around a hatchway or

other opening

CARLINGS > CARLING

CARLINS > CARLING

CARLISH *adj* churlish

CARLOAD *n* amount that can be carried by a car

CARLOADS > CARLOAD

CARLOCK *n* type of Russian isinglass

CARLOCKS > CARLOCK

CARLOT *n* boor

CARLOTS > CARLOT

CARLS > CARL

CARMAKER *n* car manufacturing company

CARMAKERS > CARMAKER

CARMAN *n* man who drives a car or cart

CARMELITE *n* member of an order of mendicant friars

CARMEN > CARMAN

CARMINE *adj* vivid red ▷ *n* vivid red colour, sometimes with a purplish tinge

CARMINES > CARMINE

CARN *n* cairn

CARNAGE *n* extensive slaughter of people

CARNAGES > CARNAGE

CARNAHUBA *same as* > CARNAUBA

CARNAL *adj* of a sexual or sensual nature ▷ *vb* act in a carnal manner

CARNALISE *vb* to sensualise

CARNALISM > CARNALISE

CARNALIST > CARNALISE

CARNALITY > CARNAL

CARNALIZE *same as* > CARNALISE

CARNALLED > CARNAL

CARNALLY > CARNAL

CARNALS > CARNAL

CARNAROLI *n* variety of short-grain rice used for risotto

CARNATION *n* cultivated plant with fragrant white, pink, or red flowers

CARNAUBA *n* Brazilian fan palm, *Copernicia cerifera*

CARNAUBAS > CARNAUBA

CARNELIAN *n* reddish-yellow gemstone

CARNEOUS *adj* fleshy

CARNET *n* customs licence permitting motorists to take their cars across certain frontiers

CARNETS > CARNET

CARNEY *same as* > CARNY

CARNEYED > CARNEY

CARNEYING > CARNEY

CARNEYS > CARNEY

CARNIE *same as* > CARNY

CARNIED > CARNY

CARNIER > CARNY

CARNIES > CARNY

CARNIEST > CARNY

CARNIFEX *n* executioner

CARNIFIED > CARNIFY

CARNIFIES > CARNIFY

CARNIFY *vb* (esp of lung tissue, as the result of pneumonia) to be altered so as to resemble skeletal muscle

CARNITINE *n* type of white betaine

CARNIVAL *n* festive period with processions, music, and dancing in the street

CARNIVALS > CARNIVAL

CARNIVORA *n* members of a group of carnivorous mammals

CARNIVORE *n* meat-eating animal

CARNIVORY *n* state of being carnivore

CARNOSAUR *n* meat-eating dinosaur

CARNOSE *adj* fleshy

CARNOSITY *n* fleshy protrusion

CARNOTITE *n* radioactive yellow mineral

CARNS > CARN

CARNY *vb* coax or cajole or act in a wheedling manner ▷ *n* person who works in a carnival ▷ *adj* sly

CARNYING > CARNY

CAROACH *same as* > CAROCHE

CAROACHES > CAROACH

CAROB *n* pod of a Mediterranean tree, used as a chocolate substitute

CAROBS > CAROB

CAROCH *same as* > CAROCHE

CAROCHE *n* stately ceremonial carriage used in the 16th and 17th centuries

CAROCHES > CAROCHE

CAROL *n* joyful Christmas hymn ▷ *vb* sing carols

CAROLED > CAROL

CAROLER > CAROL

CAROLERS > CAROL

CAROLI > CAROLUS

CAROLING > CAROL

CAROLINGS > CAROL

CAROLLED > CAROL

CAROLLER > CAROL

CAROLLERS > CAROL

CAROLLING > CAROL

CAROLS > CAROL

CAROLUS *n* any of several coins struck in the reign of a king called Charles, esp an English gold coin from the reign of Charles I

CAROLUSES > CAROLUS

CAROM *n* shot in which the cue ball is caused to contact one object ball after another ▷ *vb* to carambole

CAROMED > CAROM

CAROMEL *vb* to turn into caramel

CAROMELS > CAROMEL

CAROMING > CAROM

CAROMS > CAROM

CAROTENE *n* any of four orange-red hydrocarbons, found in many plants, converted to vitamin A in the liver

CAROTENES > CAROTENE

CAROTID *n* either of the two arteries supplying blood to the head ▷ *adj* of either of these arteries

CAROTIDAL > CAROTID

CAROTIDS > CAROTID

CAROTIN *same as* > CAROTENE

CAROTINS > CAROTIN

CAROUSAL *n* merry drinking party

CAROUSALS > CAROUSAL

CAROUSE *vb* have a merry drinking party

CAROUSED > CAROUSE

CAROUSEL *n* revolving conveyor belt for luggage or photographic slides

CAROUSELS > CAROUSEL

CAROUSER > CAROUSE

CAROUSERS > CAROUSE

CAROUSES > CAROUSE

CAROUSING > CAROUSE

CARP *n* large freshwater fish ▷ *vb* complain, find fault

CARPACCIO *n* Italian dish of thin slices of raw meat or fish

CARPAL *n* wrist bone

CARPALE *same as* > CARPAL

CARPALES > CARPAL

CARPALIA > CARPAL

CARPALS > CARPAL

CARPARK *n* area or building reserved for parking cars

CARPARKS > CARPARK

CARPED > CARP

CARPEL *n* female reproductive organ of a flowering plant

CARPELS > CARPEL

CARPENTER *n* person who makes or repairs wooden structures ▷ *vb* do the work of a carpenter

CARPENTRY *n* skill or work of a carpenter

CARPER > CARP

CARPERS > CARP

CARPET *n* heavy fabric for covering floors ▷ *vb* cover with a carpet

CARPETBAG *n* travelling bag made of carpeting

CARPETED > CARPET

CARPETING *n* carpet material or carpets in general

CARPETS > CARPET

CARPI > CARPUS

CARPING *adj* tending to make petty complaints ▷ *n* petty complaint

CARPINGLY > CARPING

CARPINGS > CARPING

CARPOLOGY *n* branch of botany concerned with the study of fruits and seeds

CARPOOL *vb* (of a group of people) to share the use of a single car to travel to work or school

CARPOOLED > CARPOOL

CARPOOLER > CARPOOL

CARPOOLS > CARPOOL

CARPORT *n* shelter for a car, consisting of a roof supported by posts

CARPORTS > CARPORT

CARPS > CARP

CARPUS *n* set of eight bones of the wrist

CARR *n* area of bog or fen in which scrub, esp willow, has become established

CARRACK *n* galleon sailed in the Mediterranean as a merchantman in the 15th and 16th centuries

CARRACKS > CARRACK

CARRACT *same as* > CARRACK

CARRACTS > CARRACT

CARRAGEEN *n* edible red seaweed of North America and N Europe

CARRAT *same as* > CARAT

CARRATS > CARRAT

CARRAWAY *same as* > CARAWAY

CARRAWAYS > CARRAWAY

CARRECT *same as* > CARRACK

CARRECTS > CARRECT

CARREFOUR *n* public square, esp one at the intersection of several roads

CARREL *n* small individual study room or private desk, often in a library, where a student or researcher can work undisturbed

CARRELL *same as* > CARREL

CARRELLS > CARRELL

CARRELS > CARREL

CARRIAGE *n* one of the sections of a train for passengers

CARRIAGES > CARRIAGE

CARRICK *as in* *carrick bend* type of knot

CARRIED > CARRY

CARRIER *n* person or thing that carries something

CARRIERS > CARRIER

CARRIES > CARRY

CARRIOLE *same as* > CARIOLE

CARRIOLES > CARRIOLE

CARRION *n* dead and rotting flesh

CARRIONS > CARRION

CARRITCH *n* catechism

CARROCH *variant of* > CAROCHE

CARROCHES > CAROM

CARROM > CAROM

CARROMED > CAROM

CARROMING > CAROM

CARROMS > CAROM

CARRON *as in* *carron oil* ointment of limewater and linseed oil

CARRONADE *n* obsolete naval gun of short barrel and large bore

CARROT *n* long tapering orange root vegetable

CARROTIER > CARROTY

CARROTIN *n* carotene

CARROTINS > CARROTIN

CARROTS > CARROT

CARROTTOP *n* facetious term for a person with red hair

CARROTY *adj* (of hair) reddish-orange

CARROUSEL *a variant spelling of* > CAROUSEL

CARRS > CARR

CARRY *vb* take from one place to another

CARRYALL *n* light four-wheeled horse-drawn carriage usually designed to carry four passengers

CARRYALLS > CARRYALL

CARRYBACK *n* amount carried back in accounting

CARRYCOT *n* light portable bed for a baby, with handles and a hood

CARRYCOTS > CARRYCOT

CARRYING > CARRY

CARRYON *n* fuss or commotion

CARRYONS > CARRYON

CARRYOUT *n* hot cooked food bought in a shop for consumption elsewhere

CARRYOUTS > CARRYOUT

CARRYOVER *n* sum or balance carried forward in accounting

CARRYTALE *n* gossip

CARS > CAR

CARSE *n* riverside area of flat fertile alluvium

CARSES > CARSE

CARSEY *slang word for* > TOILET

CARSEYS > CARSEY

CARSICK *adj* nauseated from riding in a car

CART *n* open two-wheeled horse-drawn vehicle for carrying goods or passengers ▷ *vb* carry, usu with some effort

CARTA *n* charter

CARTABLE > CART

CARTAGE *n* process or cost of carting

CARTAGES > CARTAGE

CARTAS > CARTA

CARTE *n* fencing position

CARTED > CART

CARTEL *n* association of competing firms formed to fix prices

CARTELISE *same as* > CARTELIZE

CARTELISM > CARTEL

CARTELIST > CARTEL

CARTELIZE *vb* form or be formed into a cartel

CARTELS > CARTEL

CARTER > CART

CARTERS > CART

CARTES > CARTE

CARTFUL *n* amount a cart can hold

CARTFULS > CARTFUL

CARTHORSE *n* large heavily built horse

CARTILAGE *n* strong flexible tissue forming part of the skeleton

CARTING > CART

CARTLOAD *n* amount a cart can hold

CARTLOADS > CARTLOAD

CARTOGRAM *n* map showing statistical information in diagrammatic form

CARTOLOGY *n* theory of mapmaking

CARTON *n* container made

of cardboard or waxed paper ▷ vb enclose (goods) in a carton

CARTONAGE n material from which mummy masks and coffins were made

CARTONED > CARTON

CARTONING > CARTON

CARTONS > CARTON

CARTOON n humorous or satirical drawing ▷ vb to depict in a cartoon

CARTOONED > CARTOON

CARTOONS > CARTOON

CARTOONY > CARTOON

CARTOP adj designed to be transported on top of a vehicle

CARTOPPER n anything designed to be transported on top of a vehicle

CARTOUCH same as > CARTOUCHE

CARTOUCHE n ornamental tablet or panel in the form of a scroll

CARTRIDGE n casing containing an explosive charge and bullet for a gun

CARTROAD n road for carts to drive on

CARTROADS > CARTROAD

CARTS > CART

CARTULARY n collection of charters or records, esp relating to the title to an estate or monastery

CARTWAY n way by which carts travel

CARTWAYS > CARTWAY

CARTWHEEL n sideways somersault supported by the hands with legs outstretched ▷ vb to perform a cartwheel movement

CARUCAGE n tax due on a carucate

CARUCAGES > CARUCAGE

CARUCATE n area of land an oxen team could plough in a year

CARUCATES > CARUCATE

CARUNCLE n fleshy outgrowth on the heads of certain birds, such as a cock's comb

CARUNCLES > CARUNCLE

CARVACROL n aromatic phenol found in oregano

CARVE vb cut to form an object

CARVED > CARVE

CARVEL same as > CARAVEL

CARVELS > CARVEL

CARVEN an archaic or literary past participle of > CARVE

CARVER n carving knife

CARVERIES > CARVERY

CARVERS > CARVER

CARVERY n restaurant where customers pay a set price for unrestricted helpings of carved meat and other food

CARVES > CARVE

CARVIES > CARVY

CARVING n figure or design produced by carving stone or wood

CARVINGS > CARVING

CARVY n caraway seed

CARWASH n drive-through structure containing automated equipment for washing cars

CARWASHES > CARWASH

CARYATIC same as > CARYATID

CARYATID n supporting column in the shape of a female figure

CARYATIDS > CARYATID

CARYOPSES > CARYOPSIS

CARYOPSIS n dry seedlike fruit having the pericarp fused to the seed coat of the single seed: produced by the grasses

CARYOTIN variant of > KARYOTIN

CARYOTINS > CARYOTIN

CASA n house

CASABA n kind of winter muskmelon having a yellow rind and sweet juicy flesh

CASABAS > CASABA

CASAS > CASA

CASAVA same as > CASSAVA

CASAVAS > CASAVA

CASBAH n citadel of a N African city

CASBAHS > CASBAH

CASCABEL n knoblike protrusion on the rear part of the breech of an obsolete muzzle-loading cannon

CASCABELS > CASCABEL

CASCABLE same as > CASCABEL

CASCABLES > CASCABLE

CASCADE n waterfall ▷ vb flow or fall in a cascade

CASCADED > CASCADE

CASCADES > CASCADE

CASCADING > CASCADE

CASCADURA n Trinidadian fish

CASCARA n bark of a N American shrub, used as a laxative

CASCARAS > CASCARA

CASCHROM n wooden hand-plough

CASCHROMS > CASCHROM

CASCO n Argentinian homestead

CASCOS > CASCO

CASE n instance, example ▷ vb inspect (a building) with the intention of burgling it

CASEASE n proteolytic enzyme formed by certain bacteria that activates the solution of albumin and casein in milk and cheese

CASEASES > CASEASE

CASEATE vb undergo caseation

CASEATED > CASEATE

CASEATES > CASEATE

CASEATING > CASEATE

CASEATION n formation of cheese from casein during the coagulation of milk

CASEBOOK n book in which records of legal or medical cases are kept

CASEBOOKS > CASEBOOK

CASEBOUND another word for > HARDBACK

CASED > CASE

CASEFIED > CASEFY

CASEFIES > CASEFY

CASEFY vb make or become similar to cheese

CASEFYING > CASEFY

CASEIC adj relating to cheese

CASEIN n a phosphoprotein, precipitated from milk by the action of rennin, forming the basis of cheese: used in the manufacture of plastics and adhesives

CASEINATE n protein found in milk

CASEINS > CASEIN

CASELOAD n number of cases that someone like a doctor or social worker deals with at any one time

CASELOADS > CASELOAD

CASEMAKER n in bookbinding, machine that makes stiff covers for hardbacks

CASEMAN n in printing, a person who sets and corrects type

CASEMATE n armoured compartment in a ship or fortification in which guns are mounted

CASEMATED > CASEMATE

CASEMATES > CASEMATE

CASEMEN > CASEMAN

CASEMENT n window that is hinged on one side

CASEMENTS > CASEMENT

CASEOSE n peptide produced by the peptic digestion of casein

CASEOSES > CASEOSE

CASEOUS adj of or like cheese

CASERN n (formerly) a billet or accommodation for soldiers in a town

CASERNE same as > CASERN

CASERNES > CASERNE

CASERNS > CASERN

CASES > CASE

CASETTE variant of > CASSETTE

CASETTES > CASETTE

CASEWORK n social work based on close study of the personal histories and circumstances of individuals and families

CASEWORKS > CASEWORK

CASEWORM n caddis worm

CASEWORMS > CASEWORM

CASH n banknotes and coins ▷ adj of, for, or paid in cash ▷ vb obtain cash for

CASHABLE > CASH

CASHAW n winter squash

CASHAWS > CASHAW

CASHBACK n discount offered in return for immediate payment

CASHBACKS > CASHBACK

CASHBOOK n journal in which cash receipts and payments are recorded

CASHBOOKS > CASHBOOK

CASHBOX n box for holding cash

CASHBOXES > CASHBOX

CASHED > CASH

CASHES > CASH

CASHEW n edible kidney-shaped nut

CASHEWS > CASHEW

CASHIER n person responsible for handling cash in a bank, shop, etc ▷ vb dismiss with dishonour from the armed forces

CASHIERED > CASHIER

CASHIERER > CASHIER

CASHIERS > CASHIER

CASHING > CASH

CASHLESS adj functioning, operated, or performed without using coins or banknotes for money transactions but instead using credit cards or electronic transfer of funds

CASHMERE n fine soft wool obtained from goats

CASHMERES > CASHMERE

CASHOO n catechu

CASHOOS > CASHOO

CASHPOINT n cash dispenser

CASIMERE same as > CASSIMERE

CASIMERES > CASIMERE

CASIMIRE variant of > CASSIMERE

CASIMIRES > CASIMIRE

CASING n protective case, covering

CASINGS > CASING

CASINI > CASINO

CASINO n public building or room where gambling games are played

CASINOS > CASINO

CASITA n small house

CASITAS > CASITA

CASK n barrel used to hold alcoholic drink ▷ vb to put into a cask

CASKED > CASK

CASKET n small box for valuables ▷ vb to put into a casket

CASKETED > CASKET

CASKETING > CASKET

CASKETS > CASKET

CASKING > CASK

CASKS > CASK

CASKSTAND n frame on which a cask rests

CASKY adj (of wine) having a musty smell due to resting too long in the cask

CASQUE n helmet or a

helmet-like process or structure, as on the bill of most hornbills

CASQUED > CASQUE

CASQUES > CASQUE

CASSABA same as > CASABA

CASSABAS > CASSABA

CASSAREEP n juice of the bitter cassava root, boiled down to a syrup and used as a flavouring, esp in West Indian cookery

CASSATA n ice cream, originating in Italy, usually containing nuts and candied fruit

CASSATAS > CASSATA

CASSATION n (esp in France) annulment, as of a judicial decision by a higher court

CASSAVA n starch obtained from the roots of a tropical American plant, used to make tapioca

CASSAVAS > CASSAVA

CASSENA same as > CASSINA

CASSENAS > CASSENA

CASSENE same as > CASSINA

CASSENES > CASSENE

CASSEROLE n covered dish in which food is cooked slowly, usu in an oven ▷ vb cook in a casserole

CASSETTE n plastic container for magnetic tape

CASSETTES > CASSETTE

CASSIA n tropical plant whose pods yield a mild laxative

CASSIAS > CASSIA

CASSIMERE n woollen suiting cloth of plain or twill weave

CASSINA n American tree

CASSINAS > CASSINA

CASSINE same as > CASSINA

CASSINES > CASSINE

CASSINGLE n cassette single

CASSINO n card game for two to four players in which players pair cards from their hands with others exposed on the table

CASSINOS > CASSINO

CASSIS n blackcurrant cordial

CASSISES > CASSIS

CASSOCK n long tunic, usu black, worn by priests

CASSOCKED > CASSOCK

CASSOCKS > CASSOCK

CASSONADE n raw sugar

CASSONE n highly-decorated Italian dowry chest

CASSONES > CASSONE

CASSOULET n stew originating from France, made from haricot beans and goose, duck, pork, etc

CASSOWARY n large flightless bird of Australia and New Guinea

CASSPIR n armoured military vehicle

CASSPIRS > CASSPIR

CAST n actors in a play or film collectively ▷ vb select (an actor) to play a part in a play or film

CASTABLE adj able to be cast

CASTANET > CASTANETS

CASTANETS pl n musical instrument, used by Spanish dancers, consisting of curved pieces of hollow wood clicked together in the hand

CASTAWAY n shipwrecked person ▷ adj shipwrecked or put adrift ▷ vb cause (a ship, person, etc) to be shipwrecked or abandoned

CASTAWAYS > CASTAWAY

CASTE n any of the hereditary classes into which Hindu society is divided

CASTED adj having a caste

CASTEISM n belief in, and adherence to, the caste system

CASTEISMS > CASTEISM

CASTELESS adj having no caste

CASTELLA > CASTELLUM

CASTELLAN n keeper or governor of a castle

CASTELLUM n fort

CASTER n person or thing that casts

CASTERS > CASTER

CASTES > CASTE

CASTIGATE vb reprimand severely

CASTING > CAST

CASTINGS > CAST

CASTLE n large fortified building, often built as a ruler's residence ▷ vb (in chess) move (the king) two squares laterally on the first rank and place the nearest rook on the square passed over by the king

CASTLED adj like a castle in construction

CASTLES > CASTLE

CASTLING > CASTLE

CASTOCK n kale stalk

CASTOCKS > CASTOCK

CASTOFF n person or thing that has been discarded or abandoned

CASTOFFS > CASTOFF

CASTOR same as > CASTER

CASTOREUM n oil secreted from the beaver, used as bait by trappers

CASTORIES > CASTORY

CASTORS > CASTOR

CASTORY n dye derived from beaver pelts

CASTRAL adj relating to camps

CASTRATE vb remove the testicles of

CASTRATED > CASTRATE

CASTRATER > CASTRATE

CASTRATES > CASTRATE

CASTRATI > CASTRATO

CASTRATO n (in 17th- and 18th-century opera) a male singer whose testicles were removed before puberty, allowing the retention of a soprano or alto voice

CASTRATOR > CASTRATE

CASTRATOS > CASTRATO

CASTS > CAST

CASUAL adj careless, nonchalant ▷ n occasional worker

CASUALISE vb to make (a regular employee) into a casual worker

CASUALISM > CASUALISE

CASUALIZE same as > CASUALISE

CASUALLY > CASUAL

CASUALS > CASUAL

CASUALTY n person killed or injured in an accident or war

CASUARINA n Australian tree with jointed green branches

CASUIST n person, esp a theologian, who attempts to resolve moral dilemmas by the application of general rules and the careful distinction of special cases

CASUISTIC > CASUIST

CASUISTRY n reasoning that is misleading or oversubtle

CASUISTS > CASUIST

CASUS n event

CAT n small domesticated furry mammal ▷ vb flog with a cat-'o-nine-tails

CATABASES > CATABASIS

CATABASIS n descent or downward movement

CATABATIC > CATABASIS

CATABOLIC adj of a metabolic process in which complex molecules are broken down into simple ones with the release of energy

CATACLASM n breaking down

CATACLYSM n violent upheaval

CATACOMB n underground burial place, esp the galleries at Rome, consisting of tunnels with vaults or niches leading off them for tombs

CATACOMBS > CATACOMB

CATAFALCO n temporary raised platform on which a body lies in state before or during a funeral

CATALASE n enzyme that catalyses the decomposition of hydrogen peroxide

CATALASES > CATALASE

CATALATIC adj relating to catalase

CATALEPSY n trancelike state in which the body is rigid

CATALEXES > CATALEXIS

CATALEXIS n the state of lacking a syllable in the last foot of a line of poetry

CATALO same as > CATTALO

CATALOES > CATALO

CATALOG same as > CATALOGUE

CATALOGED > CATALOGUE

CATALOGER > CATALOGUE

CATALOGIC > CATALOG

CATALOGS > CATALOG

CATALOGUE n book containing details of items for sale ▷ vb enter (an item) in a catalogue

CATALOS > CATALO

CATALPA n tree of N America and Asia with bell-shaped whitish flowers

CATALPAS > CATALPA

CATALYSE vb speed up (a chemical reaction) by a catalyst

CATALYSED > CATALYSE

CATALYSER > CATALYSE

CATALYSES > CATALYSIS

CATALYSIS n acceleration of a chemical reaction by the action of a catalyst

CATALYST n substance that speeds up a chemical reaction without itself changing

CATALYSTS > CATALYST

CATALYTIC adj of or relating to catalysis

CATALYZE same as > CATALYSE

CATALYZED > CATALYZE

CATALYZER > CATALYZE

CATALYZES > CATALYZE

CATAMARAN n boat with twin parallel hulls

CATAMENIA another word for > MENSES

CATAMITE n boy kept as a homosexual partner

CATAMITES > CATAMITE

CATAMOUNT n any of various medium-sized felines, such as the puma or lynx

CATAPAN n governor in the Byzantine Empire

CATAPANS > CATAPAN

CATAPHORA n use of a word such as a pronoun that has the same reference as a word used subsequently in the same discourse

CATAPHYLL n simplified form of plant leaf, such as a scale leaf or cotyledon

CATAPLASM another name for > POULTICE

CATAPLEXY n sudden temporary paralysis, brought on by severe shock

CATAPULT n Y-shaped device with a loop of elastic, used by children for firing stones ▷ vb shoot forwards or upwards violently

CATAPULTS > CATAPULT

CATARACT *n* eye disease in which the lens becomes opaque

CATARACTS > CATARACT

CATARHINE *n* having a thin or narrow nose

CATARRH *n* excessive mucus in the nose and throat, during or following a cold

CATARRHAL > CATARRH

CATARRHS > CATARRH

CATASTA *n* platform on which slaves were presented for sale

CATASTAS > CATASTA

CATATONIA *n* form of schizophrenia characterized by stupor, with outbreaks of excitement

CATATONIC > CATATONIA

CATATONY *another word for* > CATATONIA

CATAWBA *n* type of red North American grape

CATAWBAS > CATAWBA

CATBIRD *n* any of several North American songbirds of the family *Mimidae* (mockingbirds), esp *Dumetella carolinensis*, whose call resembles the mewing of a cat

CATBIRDS > CATBIRD

CATBOAT *n* sailing vessel with a single mast, set well forward and often unstayed, and a large sail, usually rigged with a gaff

CATBOATS > CATBOAT

CATBRIER *n* greenbrier

CATBRIERS > CATBRIER

CATCALL *n* derisive whistle or cry ▷ *vb* utter such a call (at)

CATCALLED > CATCALL

CATCALLER > CATCALL

CATCALLS > CATCALL

CATCH *vb* seize, capture ▷ *n* device for fastening a door, window, etc

CATCHABLE > CATCH

CATCHALL *n* something designed to cover a variety of situations

CATCHALLS > CATCHALL

CATCHCRY *n* well-known much-used phrase, perhaps associated with a particular group

CATCHED *rarely used past tense of* > CATCH

CATCHEN *same as* > CATCH

CATCHER *n* person or thing that catches, esp in a game or sport

CATCHERS > CATCHER

CATCHES > CATCH

CATCHFLY *n* any of several caryophyllaceous plants of the genus *Silene* that have sticky calyxes and stems on which insects are sometimes trapped

CATCHIER > CATCHY

CATCHIEST > CATCHY

CATCHING > CATCH

CATCHINGS > CATCH

CATCHMENT *n* structure in which water is collected

CATCHPOLE *n* (in medieval England) a sheriff's officer who arrested debtors

CATCHPOLL *same as* > CATCHPOLE

CATCHT *same as* > CATCHED

CATCHUP *a variant spelling (esp US) of* > KETCHUP

CATCHUPS > CATCHUP

CATCHWEED *n* goosegrass

CATCHWORD *n* well-known and frequently used phrase

CATCHY *adj* (of a tune) pleasant and easily remembered

CATCLAW *n* type of shrub; black bead

CATCLAWS > CATCLAW

CATE *n* delicacy

CATECHIN *n* soluble yellow solid substance found in mahogany wood

CATECHINS > CATECHIN

CATECHISE *same as* > CATECHIZE

CATECHISM *n* instruction on the doctrine of a Christian Church in a series of questions and answers

CATECHIST > CATECHIZE

CATECHIZE *vb* instruct by using a catechism

CATECHOL *n* colourless crystalline phenol found in resins and lignins

CATECHOLS > CATECHOL

CATECHU *n* water-soluble astringent resinous substance obtained from any of certain tropical plants, esp the leguminous tree *Acacia catechu* of S Asia, and used in medicine, tanning, and dyeing

CATECHUS > CATECHU

CATEGORIC *adj* unqualified

CATEGORY *n* class, group

CATELOG *obsolete word for* > CATALOGUE

CATELOGS > CATELOG

CATENA *n* connected series, esp of patristic comments on the Bible

CATENAE > CATENA

CATENANE *n* type of chemical compound in which the molecules have two or more rings that are interlocked like the links of a chain

CATENANES > CATENANE

CATENARY *n* curve assumed by a heavy uniform flexible cord hanging freely from two points. When symmetrical about the *y*-axis and intersecting it at $y = a$, the equation is $y = a \cosh x / a$ ▷ *adj* of, resembling, relating to, or constructed using a catenary or suspended chain

CATENAS > CATENA

CATENATE *vb* arrange or be arranged in a series of chains or rings

CATENATED > CATENATE

CATENATES > CATENATE

CATENOID *n* geometrical surface generated by rotating a catenary about its axis

CATENOIDS > CATENOID

CATER *vb* provide what is needed or wanted, esp food or services

CATERAN *n* (formerly) a member of a band of brigands and marauders in the Scottish highlands

CATERANS > CATERAN

CATERED > CATER

CATERER *n* person whose job is to provide food for social events such as parties and weddings

CATERERS > CATERER

CATERESS *n* female caterer

CATERING *n* supplying of food for a social event

CATERINGS > CATERING

CATERS > CATER

CATERWAUL *n* wail, yowl ▷ *vb* make a yowling noise like a cat

CATES *pl n* choice dainty food

CATFACE *n* deformity of the surface of a tree trunk, caused by fire or disease

CATFACES > CATFACE

CATFACING *n* disorder that affects tomatoes, causing scarring of the fruit

CATFALL *n* line used as a tackle for hoisting an anchor to the cathead

CATFALLS > CATFALL

CATFIGHT *n* fight between two women

CATFIGHTS > CATFIGHT

CATFISH *n* fish with whisker-like barbels round the mouth

CATFISHES > CATFISH

CATGUT *n* strong cord used to string musical instruments and sports rackets

CATGUTS > CATGUT

CATHARISE *vb* to purify

CATHARIZE *same as* > CATHARISE

CATHARSES > CATHARSIS

CATHARSIS *n* relief of strong suppressed emotions

CATHARTIC *adj* causing catharsis ▷ *n* drug that causes catharsis

CATHEAD *n* fitting at the bow of a vessel for securing the anchor when raised

CATHEADS > CATHEAD

CATHECT *vb* to invest mental or emotional energy in

CATHECTED > CATHECT

CATHECTIC *adj* of or relating to cathexis

CATHECTS > CATHECT

CATHEDRA *n* bishop's throne

CATHEDRAE > CATHEDRA

CATHEDRAL *n* principal church of a diocese

CATHEDRAS > CATHEDRA

CATHEPSIN *n* proteolytic enzyme responsible for the autolysis of cells after death

CATHEPTIC > CATHEPSIN

CATHETER *n* tube inserted into a body cavity to drain fluid

CATHETERS > CATHETER

CATHETUS *n* straight line or radius perpendicular to another line or radius

CATHEXES > CATHEXIS

CATHEXIS *n* concentration of psychic energy on a single goal

CATHISMA *n* short hymn used as a response

CATHISMAS > CATHISMA

CATHODAL > CATHODE

CATHODE *n* negative electrode, by which electrons leave a circuit

CATHODES > CATHODE

CATHODIC > CATHODE

CATHOLE *n* hole in a ship through which ropes are passed

CATHOLES > CATHOLE

CATHOLIC *adj* (of tastes or interests) covering a wide range ▷ *n* member of the Roman Catholic Church

CATHOLICS > CATHOLIC

CATHOLYTE *same as* > CATOLYTE

CATHOOD *n* state of being a cat

CATHOODS > CATHOOD

CATHOUSE *a slang word for* > BROTHEL

CATHOUSES > CATHOUSE

CATION *n* positively charged ion

CATIONIC > CATION

CATIONS > CATION

CATJANG *n* tropical shrub

CATJANGS > CATJANG

CATKIN *n* drooping flower spike of certain trees

CATKINATE *adj* like catkin

CATKINS > CATKIN

CATLIKE > CAT

CATLIN *same as* > CATLING

CATLING *n* long double-edged surgical knife for amputations

CATLINGS > CATLING

CATLINS > CATLIN

CATMINT *n* Eurasian plant with scented leaves that attract cats

CATMINTS > CATMINT

CATNAP *vb* doze ▷ *n* short sleep or doze

CATNAPER > CATNAP

CATNAPERS > CATNAP

CATNAPPED > CATNAP

CATNAPPER > CATNAP

CATNAPS > CATNAP

CATNEP *same as* > CATMINT

CATNEPS > CATNEP

CATNIP same as > CATMINT

CATNIPS > CATMINT

CATOLYTE n part of the electrolyte that surrounds the cathode in an electrolytic cell

CATOLYTES > CATOLYTE

CATOPTRIC adj relating to reflection

CATRIGGED adj rigged like a catboat

CATS > CAT

CATSKIN n skin and/or fur of a cat

CATSKINS > CATSKIN

CATSPAW n person used by another as a tool

CATSPAWS > CATSPAW

CATSUIT n one-piece usually close-fitting trouser suit

CATSUITS > CATSUIT

CATSUP a variant (esp US) of > KETCHUP

CATSUPS > CATSUP

CATTABU n cross between common cattle and zebu

CATTABUS > CATTABU

CATTAIL n reed mace

CATTAILS > CATTAIL

CATTALO n hardy breed of cattle developed by crossing the American bison with domestic cattle

CATTALOES > CATTALO

CATTALOS > CATTALO

CATTED > CAT

CATTERIES > CATTERY

CATTERY n place where cats are bred or looked after

CATTIE same as > CATTY

CATTIER > CATTY

CATTIES > CATTY

CATTIEST > CATTY

CATTILY > CATTY

CATTINESS > CATTY

CATTING > CAT

CATTISH > CAT

CATTISHLY > CAT

CATTLE pl n domesticated cows and bulls

CATTLEMAN n person who breeds, rears, or tends cattle

CATTLEMEN > CATTLEMAN

CATTLEYA n any tropical American orchid of the genus Cattleya, cultivated for their purplish-pink or white showy flowers

CATTLEYAS > CATTLEYA

CATTY adj spiteful ▷ n unit of weight, used esp in China, equal to about one and a half pounds or about 0.67 kilogram

CATWALK n narrow pathway or platform

CATWALKS > CATWALK

CATWORKS n machinery on a drilling platform

CATWORM n active carnivorous polychaete worm, Nephthys hombergi, that is about 10cm (4in) long, having a pearly sheen to its body: often dug for bait

CATWORMS > CATWORM

CAUCHEMAR n nightmare

CAUCUS n local committee or faction of a political party ▷ vb hold a caucus

CAUCUSED > CAUCUS

CAUCUSES > CAUCUS

CAUCUSING > CAUCUS

CAUCUSSED > CAUCUS

CAUCUSSES > CAUCUS

CAUDA n area behind the anus of an animal

CAUDAD adv towards the tail or posterior part

CAUDAE > CAUDA

CAUDAL adj at or near an animal's tail

CAUDALLY > CAUDAL

CAUDATE adj having a tail or a tail-like appendage ▷ n lizard-like amphibian

CAUDATED same as > CAUDATE

CAUDATES > CAUDATE

CAUDATION > CAUDATE

CAUDEX n thickened persistent stem base of some herbaceous perennial plants

CAUDEXES > CAUDEX

CAUDICES > CAUDEX

CAUDICLE n stalk to which an orchid's pollen masses are attached

CAUDICLES > CAUDICLE

CAUDILLO n (in Spanish-speaking countries) a military or political leader

CAUDILLOS > CAUDILLO

CAUDLE n hot spiced wine drink made with gruel, formerly used medicinally ▷ vb make such a drink

CAUDLED > CAUDLE

CAUDLES > CAUDLE

CAUDLING > CAUDLE

CAUDRON Spenserian spelling of > CAULDRON

CAUDRONS > CAUDRON

CAUF n cage for holding live fish in the water

CAUGHT > CATCH

CAUK n type of barite

CAUKER n one who caulks

CAUKERS > CAUKER

CAUKS > CAUK

CAUL n membrane sometimes covering a child's head at birth

CAULD a Scot word for > COLD

CAULDER > CAULD

CAULDEST > CAULD

CAULDRIFE adj susceptible to cold

CAULDRON n large pot used for boiling

CAULDRONS > CAULDRON

CAULDS > CAULD

CAULES > CAULIS

CAULICLE n small stalk or stem

CAULICLES > CAULICLE

CAULICULI n plural form of singular cauliculus: another word for caulicle

CAULIFORM adj resembling a caulis

CAULINARY another word for > CAULINE

CAULINE adj relating to or growing from a plant stem

CAULIS n main stem of a plant

CAULK vb fill in (cracks) with paste etc

CAULKED > CAULK

CAULKER > CAULK

CAULKERS > CAULK

CAULKING > CAULK

CAULKINGS > CAULK

CAULKS > CAULK

CAULOME n plant's stem structure, considered as a whole

CAULOMES > CAULOME

CAULS > CAUL

CAUM same as > CAM

CAUMED > CAUM

CAUMING > CAUM

CAUMS > CAUM

CAUMSTONE same as > CAMSTONE

CAUP n type of quaich

CAUPS > CAUP

CAUSA n reason or cause

CAUSABLE > CAUSE

CAUSAE > CAUSA

CAUSAL adj of or being a cause ▷ n something that suggests a cause

CAUSALGIA n burning sensation along the course of a peripheral nerve together with local changes in the appearance of the skin

CAUSALGIC > CAUSALGIA

CAUSALITY n relationship of cause and effect

CAUSALLY > CAUSAL

CAUSALS > CAUSAL

CAUSATION n relationship of cause and effect

CAUSATIVE adj producing an effect ▷ n causative form or class of verbs

CAUSE n something that produces a particular effect ▷ vb be the cause of

CAUSED > CAUSE

CAUSELESS > CAUSE

CAUSEN old infinitive of > CAUSE

CAUSER > CAUSE

CAUSERIE n informal talk or conversational piece of writing

CAUSERIES > CAUSERIE

CAUSERS > CAUSE

CAUSES > CAUSE

CAUSEWAY n raised path or road across water or marshland

CAUSEWAYS > CAUSEWAY

CAUSEY n cobbled street ▷ vb cobble

CAUSEYED > CAUSEY

CAUSEYS > CAUSEY

CAUSING > CAUSE

CAUSTIC adj capable of burning by chemical action ▷ n caustic substance

CAUSTICAL > CAUSTIC

CAUSTICS > CAUSTIC

CAUTEL n craftiness

CAUTELOUS > CAUTEL

CAUTELS > CAUTEL

CAUTER n cauterising instrument

CAUTERANT same as > CAUTERY

CAUTERIES > CAUTERY

CAUTERISE same as > CAUTERIZE

CAUTERISM > CAUTERIZE

CAUTERIZE vb burn (a wound) with heat or a caustic agent to prevent infection

CAUTERS > CAUTER

CAUTERY n coagulation of blood or destruction of body tissue by cauterizing

CAUTION n care, esp in the face of danger ▷ vb warn, advise

CAUTIONED > CAUTION

CAUTIONER > CAUTION

CAUTIONRY n in Scots law, standing surety

CAUTIONS > CAUTION

CAUTIOUS adj showing caution

CAUVES > CAUF

CAVA n Spanish sparkling wine produced by a method similar to that used for champagne

CAVALCADE n procession of people on horseback or in cars

CAVALERO n cavalier

CAVALEROS > CAVALERO

CAVALETTI n bars supported on low stands used in dressage and horse jumping

CAVALIER adj showing haughty disregard ▷ n gallant gentleman

CAVALIERS > CAVALIER

CAVALLA n any of various tropical carangid fishes, such as Gnathanodon speciosus (golden cavalla)

CAVALLAS > CAVALLA

CAVALLIES > CAVALLY

CAVALLY same as > CAVALLA

CAVALRIES > CAVALRY

CAVALRY n part of the army orig. on horseback, but now often using fast armoured vehicles

CAVAS > CAVA

CAVASS n Turkish armed police officer

CAVASSES > CAVASS

CAVATINA n solo song resembling a simple aria

CAVATINAS > CAVATINA

CAVATINE > CAVATINA

CAVE n hollow in the side of a hill or cliff ▷ vb hollow out

CAVEAT n warning ▷ vb to introduce a caveat

CAVEATED > CAVEAT

CAVEATING > CAVEAT

CAVEATOR n person who

enters a caveat

CAVEATORS > CAVEATOR

CAVEATS > CAVEAT

CAVED > CAVE

CAVEFISH *n* any of various small freshwater cyprinodont fishes of the genera *Amblyopsis*, *Chologaster*, etc, living in subterranean and other waters in S North America

CAVEL *n* drawing of lots among miners for an easy and profitable place at the coalface

CAVELIKE *adj* resembling a cave

CAVELS > CAVEL

CAVEMAN *n* prehistoric cave dweller

CAVEMEN > CAVEMAN

CAVENDISH *n* tobacco that has been sweetened and pressed into moulds to form bars

CAVER > CAVING

CAVERN *n* large cave ▷ *vb* shut in or as if in a cavern

CAVERNED > CAVERN

CAVERNING > CAVERN

CAVERNOUS *adj* like a cavern in vastness, depth, or hollowness

CAVERNS > CAVERN

CAVERS > CAVING

CAVES > CAVE

CAVESSON *n* kind of hard noseband, used (esp formerly) in breaking a horse in

CAVESSONS > CAVESSON

CAVETTI > CAVETTO

CAVETTO *n* concave moulding, shaped to a quarter circle in cross section

CAVETTOS > CAVETTO

CAVIAR *n* salted sturgeon roe, regarded as a delicacy

CAVIARE *same as* > CAVIAR

CAVIARES > CAVIARE

CAVIARIE *same as* > CAVIAR

CAVIARIES > CAVIARY

CAVIARS > CAVIAR

CAVICORN *adj* (of sheep, goats, etc) having hollow horns as distinct from the solid antlers of deer ▷ *n* sheep, goats, etc with hollow horns as distinct from the solid antlers of deer

CAVICORNS > CAVICORN

CAVIE *n* hen coop

CAVIER *same as* > CAVIAR

CAVIERS > CAVIER

CAVIES > CAVY

CAVIL *vb* make petty objections ▷ *n* petty objection

CAVILED > CAVIL

CAVILER > CAVIL

CAVILERS > CAVIL

CAVILING > CAVIL

CAVILLED > CAVIL

CAVILLER > CAVIL

CAVILLERS > CAVIL

CAVILLING > CAVIL

CAVILS > CAVIL

CAVING *n* sport of exploring caves

CAVINGS > CAVING

CAVITARY *adj* containing cavities

CAVITATE *vb* to form cavities or bubbles

CAVITATED > CAVITATE

CAVITATES > CAVITATE

CAVITIED > CAVITY

CAVITIES > CAVITY

CAVITY *n* hollow space

CAVORT *vb* skip about

CAVORTED > CAVORT

CAVORTER > CAVORT

CAVORTERS > CAVORT

CAVORTING > CAVORT

CAVORTS > CAVORT

CAVY *n* any small South American hystricomorph rodent of the family *Caviidae*, esp any of the genus *Cavia*, having a thickset body and very small tail

CAW *n* cry of a crow, rook, or raven ▷ *vb* make this cry

CAWED > CAW

CAWING > CAW

CAWINGS > CAW

CAWK *same as* > CAUK

CAWKER *n* metal projection on a horse's shoe to prevent slipping

CAWKERS > CAWKER

CAWKS > CAWK

CAWS > CAW

CAXON *n* type of wig

CAXONS > CAXON

CAY *n* low island or bank composed of sand and coral fragments

CAYENNE *n* very hot condiment, bright red in colour, made from dried capsicums

CAYENNED *adj* seasoned with cayenne

CAYENNES > CAYENNE

CAYMAN *n* S American reptile similar to an alligator

CAYMANS > CAYMAN

CAYS > CAY

CAYUSE *n* small American Indian pony used by cowboys

CAYUSES > CAYUSE

CAZ *short for* > CASUAL

CAZIQUE *same as* > CACIQUE

CAZIQUES > CAZIQUE

CEANOTHUS *n* any shrub of the North American rhamnaceous genus *Ceanothus*: grown for their ornamental, often blue, flower clusters

CEAS *same as* > CAESE

CEASE *vb* bring or come to an end

CEASED > CEASE

CEASEFIRE *n* temporary truce

CEASELESS *adj* without stopping

CEASES > CEASE

CEASING > CEASE

CEASINGS > CEASE

CEAZE *obsolete spelling of* > SEIZE

CEAZED > CEAZE

CEAZES > CEAZE

CEAZING > CEAZE

CEBADILLA *same as* > SABADILLA

CEBID *n* any member of the Cebidae family of New World monkeys

CEBIDS > CEBID

CEBOID *same as* > CEBID

CEBOIDS > CEBOID

CECA > CECUM

CECAL > CECUM

CECALLY > CECUM

CECILS *n* fried meatballs

CECITIES > CECITY

CECITIS *n* inflammation of the c(a)ecum

CECITISES > CECITIS

CECITY *n* rare word for blindness

CECROPIA *n* large North American moth

CECROPIAS > CECROPIA

CECUM *same as* > CAECUM

CEDAR *n* evergreen coniferous tree ▷ *adj* made of the wood of a cedar tree

CEDARBIRD *n* type of waxwing

CEDARED *adj* covered with cedars

CEDARN *adj* relating to cedar

CEDARS > CEDAR

CEDARWOOD *n* wood of any of the cedar trees

CEDARY *adj* like cedar

CEDE *vb* surrender (territory or legal rights)

CEDED > CEDE

CEDER > CEDE

CEDERS > CEDE

CEDES > CEDE

CEDI *n* standard monetary unit of Ghana, divided into 100 pesewas

CEDILLA *n* character placed under a *c* in some languages, to show that it is pronounced s, not k

CEDILLAS > CEDILLA

CEDING > CEDE

CEDIS > CEDI

CEDRATE *n* citron

CEDRATES > CEDRATE

CEDRINE *adj* relating to cedar

CEDULA *n* form of identification in Spanish-speaking countries

CEDULAS > CEDULA

CEE *n* third letter of the alphabet

CEES > CEE

CEIBA *n* any bombacaceous tropical tree of the genus *Ceiba*, such as the silk-cotton tree

CEIBAS > CEIBA

CEIL *vb* line (a ceiling) with plaster, boarding, etc

CEILED > CEIL

CEILER > CEIL

CEILERS > CEIL

CEILI *variant spelling of* > CEILIDH

CEILIDH *n* informal social gathering for singing and dancing, esp in Scotland

CEILIDHS > CEILIDH

CEILING *n* inner upper surface of a room ▷ *vb* make a ceiling

CEILINGED > CEILING

CEILINGS > CEILING

CEILIS > CEILI

CEILS > CEIL

CEINTURE *n* belt

CEINTURES > CEINTURE

CEL *short for* > CELLULOID

CELADON *n* type of porcelain having a greyish-green glaze: mainly Chinese

CELADONS > CELADON

CELANDINE *n* wild plant with yellow flowers

CELEB *n* celebrity

CELEBRANT *n* person who performs a religious ceremony

CELEBRATE *vb* hold festivities to mark (a happy event, anniversary, etc)

CELEBRITY *n* famous person

CELEBS > CELEB

CELERIAC *n* variety of celery with a large turnip-like root

CELERIACS > CELERIAC

CELERIES > CELERY

CELERITY *n* swiftness

CELERY *n* vegetable with long green crisp edible stalks

CELESTA *n* instrument like a small piano in which key-operated hammers strike metal plates

CELESTAS > CELESTA

CELESTE *same as* > CELESTA

CELESTES > CELESTE

CELESTIAL *adj* heavenly, divine

CELESTINE *same as* > CELESTITE

CELESTITE *n* white, red, or blue mineral

CELIAC *same as* > COELIAC

CELIACS > CELIAC

CELIBACY > CELIBATE

CELIBATE *adj* unmarried or abstaining from sex, esp because of a religious vow of chastity ▷ *n* celibate person

CELIBATES > CELIBATE

CELIBATIC *adj* celibate

CELL *n* smallest unit of an organism that is able to function independently

CELLA *n* inner room of a classical temple, esp the room housing the statue of a deity

CELLAE > CELLA

CELLAR *n* underground room for storage ▷ *vb* store in a cellar

CELLARAGE *n* area of a cellar

CELLARED > CELLAR

CELLARER n monastic official responsible for food, drink, etc

CELLARERS > CELLARER

CELLARET n case, cabinet, or sideboard with compartments for holding wine bottles

CELLARETS > CELLARET

CELLARING > CELLAR

CELLARIST same as > CELLARER

CELLARMAN n person in charge of a cellar

CELLARMEN > CELLARMAN

CELLAROUS adj relating to a cellar

CELLARS > CELLAR

CELLARWAY n way into cellar

CELLBLOCK n group of prison cells

CELLED adj cellular

CELLI > CELLO

CELLING n formation of cells

CELLIST > CELLO

CELLISTS > CELLO

CELLMATE n person with whom a prisoner shares a prison cell

CELLMATES > CELLMATE

CELLO n large low-pitched instrument of the violin family

CELLOIDIN n nitrocellulose compound derived from pyroxylin, used in a solution of alcohol and ether for embedding specimens before cutting sections for microscopy

CELLOS > CELLO

CELLOSE n a disaccharide obtained by the hydrolysis of cellulose by cellulase.

CELLOSES > CELLOSE

CELLPHONE n portable telephone operated by cellular radio

CELLS > CELL

CELLULAR adj of or consisting of cells ▷ n cellular phone

CELLULARS > CELLULAR

CELLULASE n any enzyme that converts cellulose to the disaccharide cellobiose

CELLULE n very small cell

CELLULES > CELLULE

CELLULITE n fat deposits under the skin alleged to resist dieting

CELLULOID n kind of plastic used to make toys and, formerly, photographic film

CELLULOSE n main constituent of plant cell walls, used in making paper, plastics, etc

CELLULOUS > CELLULOSE

CELOM same as > COELOM

CELOMATA > CELOM

CELOMIC > CELOM

CELOMS > CELOM

CELOSIA same as > COCKSCOMB

CELOSIAS > CELOSIA

CELOTEX n tradename for a type of insulation board

CELOTEXES > CELOTEX

CELS > CEL

CELSITUDE n loftiness

CELT n stone or metal axelike instrument with a bevelled edge

CELTS > CELT

CEMBALI > CEMBALO

CEMBALIST > CEMBALO

CEMBALO n harpsichord

CEMBALOS > CEMBALO

CEMBRA n Swiss pine

CEMBRAS > CEMBRA

CEMENT n fine grey powder mixed with water and sand to make mortar or concrete ▷ vb join, bind, or cover with cement

CEMENTA > CEMENTUM

CEMENTED > CEMENT

CEMENTER > CEMENT

CEMENTERS > CEMENT

CEMENTING > CEMENT

CEMENTITE n hard brittle compound of iron and carbon

CEMENTS > CEMENT

CEMENTUM n thin bonelike tissue that covers the dentine in the root of a tooth

CEMENTUMS > CEMENTUM

CEMETERY n place where dead people are buried

CEMITARE obsolete spelling of > SCIMITAR

CEMITARES > CEMITARE

CENACLE n supper room, esp one on an upper floor

CENACLES > CENACLE

CENDRE adj ash-blond

CENOBITE same as > COENOBITE

CENOBITES > CENOBITE

CENOBITIC > CENOBITE

CENOTAPH n monument honouring soldiers who died in a war

CENOTAPHS > CENOTAPH

CENOTE n (esp in the Yucatán peninsula) a natural well formed by the collapse of an overlying limestone crust: often used as a sacrificial site by the Mayas

CENOTES > CENOTE

CENOZOIC adj of or relating to the most recent geologiacl era, characterized by the development and increase of the mammals

CENS n type of annual property rent

CENSE vb burn incense near or before (an altar, shrine, etc)

CENSED > CENSE

CENSER n container for burning incense

CENSERS > CENSER

CENSES > CENSE

CENSING > CENSE

CENSOR n person authorized to examine films, books, etc, to ban or cut anything considered obscene or objectionable ▷ vb ban or cut parts of (a film, book, etc)

CENSORED > CENSOR

CENSORIAL > CENSOR

CENSORIAN > CENSOR

CENSORING > CENSOR

CENSORS > CENSOR

CENSUAL > CENSUS

CENSURE n severe disapproval ▷ vb criticize severely

CENSURED > CENSURE

CENSURER > CENSURE

CENSURERS > CENSURE

CENSURES > CENSURE

CENSURING > CENSURE

CENSUS n official count of a population ▷ vb to conduct a census

CENSUSED > CENSUS

CENSUSES > CENSUS

CENSUSING > CENSUS

CENT n hundredth part of a monetary unit such as the dollar or euro

CENTAGE n rate per hundred

CENTAGES > CENTAGE

CENTAI > CENTAS

CENTAL n unit of weight equal to 100 pounds (45.3 kilograms)

CENTALS > CENTAL

CENTARE same as > CENTIARE

CENTARES > CENTARE

CENTAS n monetary unit of Lithuania, worth one hundredth of a litas

CENTAUR n mythical creature with the head, arms, and torso of a man, and the lower body and legs of a horse

CENTAUREA n any plant of the genus Centaurea, which includes the cornflower and knapweed

CENTAURIC adj integrating mind and body

CENTAURS > CENTAUR

CENTAURY n any Eurasian plant of the genus Centaurium, esp C. erythraea, having purplish-pink flowers and formerly believed to have medicinal properties: family Gentianaceae

CENTAVO n monetary unit worth one hundredth of the main unit of currency in Portugal and many Latin American countries

CENTAVOS > CENTAVO

CENTENARY n 100th anniversary or its celebration ▷ adj of or relating to a period of 100 years

CENTENIER n in Jersey, a local police officer

CENTER same as > CENTRE

CENTERED > CENTER

CENTERING same as > CENTRING

CENTERS > CENTER

CENTESES > CENTESIS

CENTESIMI > CENTESIMO

CENTESIMO n former monetary unit of Italy, San Marino, and the Vatican City worth one hundredth of a lira

CENTESIS n surgical puncturing of part of the body with a hollow needle, to extract fluid

CENTIARE n unit of area equal to one square metre

CENTIARES > CENTIARE

CENTIGRAM n one hundredth of a gram

CENTILE n one of 99 actual or notional values of a variable dividing its distribution into 100 groups with equal frequencies

CENTILES > CENTILE

CENTIME n monetary unit worth one hundredth of a franc

CENTIMES > CENTIME

CENTIMO n monetary unit of Costa Rica, Paraguay, Peru, and Venezuela. It is worth one hundredth of their respective standard currency units

CENTIMOS > CENTIMO

CENTINEL obsolete variant of > SENTINEL

CENTINELL obsolete variant of > SENTINEL

CENTINELS > CENTINEL

CENTIPEDE n small wormlike creature with many legs

CENTNER n unit of weight equivalent to 100 pounds (45.3 kilograms)

CENTNERS > CENTNER

CENTO n piece of writing, esp a poem, composed of quotations from other authors

CENTOIST n one who composes centos

CENTOISTS > CENTOIST

CENTONATE adj having many patches

CENTONEL obsolete variant of > SENTINEL

CENTONELL obsolete variant of > SENTINEL

CENTONELS > CENTONEL

CENTONES > CENTO

CENTONIST same as > CENTOIST

CENTOS > CENTO

CENTRA > CENTRUM

CENTRAL adj of, at, or forming the centre ▷ n workplace serving as a telecommunications facility

CENTRALER > CENTRAL

CENTRALLY > CENTRAL

CENTRALS > CENTRAL

CENTRE *n* middle point or part ▷ *vb* put in the centre of something

CENTRED *adj* mentally and emotionally confident, focused, and well-balanced

CENTREING *same as* > CENTRING

CENTRES > CENTRE

CENTRIC *adj* being central or having a centre

CENTRICAL *same as* > CENTRIC

CENTRIES > CENTRY

CENTRING *n* temporary structure, esp one made of timber, used to support an arch during construction

CENTRINGS > CENTRING

CENTRIOLE *n* either of two rodlike bodies in most animal cells that form the poles of the spindle during mitosis

CENTRISM > CENTRIST

CENTRISMS > CENTRIST

CENTRIST *n* person favouring political moderation

CENTRISTS > CENTRIST

CENTRODE *n* locus produced by plotting course of the instantaneous centre of two bodies in relative motion

CENTRODES > CENTRODE

CENTROID *n* centre of mass of an object of uniform density, esp of a geometric figure

CENTROIDS > CENTROID

CENTRUM *n* main part or body of a vertebra

CENTRUMS > CENTRUM

CENTRY *obsolete variant of* > SENTRY

CENTS > CENT

CENTU *n* Lithuanian money unit

CENTUM *adj* denoting or belonging to the Indo-European languages in which original velar stops (k) were not palatalized, namely languages of the Hellenic, Italic, Celtic, Germanic, Anatolian, and Tocharian branches ▷ *n* hundred

CENTUMS > CENTUM

CENTUMVIR *n* one of the Roman judges who sat in civil cases

CENTUPLE *n* one hundredfold

CENTUPLED > CENTUPLE

CENTUPLES > CENTUPLE

CENTURIAL *adj* of or relating to a Roman century

CENTURIES > CENTURY

CENTURION *n* (in ancient Rome) officer commanding 100 men

CENTURY *n* period of 100 years

CEORL *n* freeman of the lowest class in Anglo-Saxon England

CEORLISH > CEORL

CEORLS > CEORL

CEP *another name for* > PORCINO

CEPACEOUS *adj* having an onion-like smell or taste

CEPE *another spelling of* > CEP

CEPES > CEPE

CEPHALAD *adv* towards the head or anterior part

CEPHALATE *adj* possessing a head

CEPHALIC *adj* of or relating to the head ▷ *n* remedy for pains in the head

CEPHALICS > CEPHALIC

CEPHALIN *n* phospholipid, similar to lecithin, that occurs in the nerve tissue and brain

CEPHALINS > CEPHALIN

CEPHALOUS *adj* with a head

CEPHEID *n* type of variable star with a regular cycle of variations in luminosity

CEPHEIDS > CEPHEID

CEPS > CEP

CERACEOUS *adj* waxlike or waxy

CERAMAL *same as* > CERMET

CERAMALS > CERAMAL

CERAMIC *n* hard brittle material made by heating clay to a very high temperature ▷ *adj* made of ceramic

CERAMICS *n* art of producing ceramic objects

CERAMIDE *n* any of a class of biologically important compounds used as moisturizers in skin-care preparations

CERAMIDES > CERAMIDE

CERAMIST > CERAMICS

CERAMISTS > CERAMICS

CERASIN *n* meta-arabinic acid

CERASINS > CERASIN

CERASTES *n* any venomous snake of the genus *Cerastes*, esp the horned viper

CERASTIUM *n* mouse-eared chickweed

CERATE *n* hard ointment or medicated paste consisting of lard or oil mixed with wax or resin

CERATED *adj* (of certain birds, such as the falcon) having a cere

CERATES > CERATE

CERATIN *same as* > KERATIN

CERATINS > CERATIN

CERATITIS *same as* > KERATITIS

CERATODUS *n* any of various extinct lungfish constituting the genus *Ceratodus*, common in Cretaceous and Triassic times

CERATOID *adj* having the shape or texture of animal horn

CERBEREAN *adj* of or resembling Cerberus, the three-headed dog that guarded the entrance to Hades in Greek mythology

CERBERIAN *same as* > CERBEREAN

CERCAL *adj* of or relating to a tail

CERCARIA *n* one of the larval forms of trematode worms. It has a short forked tail and resembles an immature adult

CERCARIAE > CERCARIA

CERCARIAL > CERCARIA

CERCARIAN > CERCARIA

CERCARIAS > CERCARIA

CERCI > CERCUS

CERCIS *n* any tree or shrub of the leguminous genus *Cercis*, which includes the redbud and Judas tree

CERCISES > CERCIS

CERCUS *n* one of a pair of sensory appendages at the tip of the abdomen of some insects and other arthropods

CERE *n* soft waxy swelling, containing the nostrils, at the base of the upper beak of a parrot ▷ *vb* wrap (a corpse) in a cerecloth

CEREAL *n* grass plant with edible grain, such as oat or wheat

CEREALIST *n* expert in cereals

CEREALS > CEREAL

CEREBELLA *n* plural of singular cerebellum: one of the major divisions of the vertebrate brain

CEREBRA > CEREBRUM

CEREBRAL *same as* > CACUMINAL

CEREBRALS > CEREBRAL

CEREBRATE *vb* use the mind

CEREBRIC > CEREBRUM

CEREBROID > CEREBRUM

CEREBRUM *n* main part of the brain

CEREBRUMS > CEREBRUM

CERECLOTH *n* waxed waterproof cloth of a kind formerly used as a shroud

CERED > CERE

CEREMENT *n* any burial clothes

CEREMENTS > CEREMENT

CEREMONY *n* formal act or ritual

CEREOUS *adj* waxlike

CERES > CERE

CERESIN *n* white wax extracted from ozocerite

CERESINE *same as* > CERESIN

CERESINES > CERESINE

CERESINS > CERESIN

CEREUS *n* any tropical American cactus of the genus *Cereus*, esp C. *jamacaru* of N Brazil, which grows to a height of 13 metres (40 feet)

CEREUSES > CEREUS

CERGE *n* large altar candle

CERGES > CERGE

CERIA *n* ceric oxide

CERIAS > CERIA

CERIC *adj* of or containing cerium in the tetravalent state

CERING > CERE

CERIPH *same as* > SERIF

CERIPHS > CERIPH

CERISE *adj* cherry-red ▷ *n* moderate to dark red colour

CERISES > CERISE

CERITE *n* hydrous silicate of cerium

CERITES > CERITE

CERIUM *n* steel-grey metallic element

CERIUMS > CERIUM

CERMET *n* any of several materials consisting of a metal matrix with ceramic particles disseminated through it. They are hard and resistant to high temperatures

CERMETS > CERMET

CERNE *obsolete variant of* > ENCIRCLE

CERNED > CERNE

CERNES > CERNE

CERNING > CERNE

CERNUOUS *adj* (of some flowers or buds) drooping

CERO *n* large spiny-finned food fish, *Scomberomorus regalis*, of warm American coastal regions of the Atlantic: family *Scombridae* (mackerels, tunnies, etc)

CEROGRAPH *n* writing on wax

CEROMANCY *n* divination by interpreting significance of shapes formed when melted wax is dropped into water

CEROON *n* hide-covered bale

CEROONS > CEROON

CEROS > CERO

CEROTIC *as in cerotic acid* white insoluble odourless wax

CEROTYPE *n* process for preparing a printing plate by engraving a wax-coated copper plate and then using this as a mould for an electrotype

CEROTYPES > CEROTYPE

CEROUS *adj* of or containing cerium in the trivalent state

CERRIAL *adj* relating to the cerris

CERRIS *n* Turkey oak

CERRISES > CERRIS

CERT *n* certainty

CERTAIN *adj* positive and confident

CERTAINER > CERTAIN

CERTAINLY *adv* without doubt ▷ *sentence substitute*

by all means

CERTAINTY n state of being sure

CERTES adv with certainty

CERTIFIED > CERTIFY

CERTIFIER > CERTIFY

CERTIFIES > CERTIFY

CERTIFY vb confirm, attest to

CERTITUDE n confidence, certainty

CERTS > CERT

CERULE adj sky-blue

CERULEAN n deep blue colour ▷ n light shade of blue

CERULEANS > CERULEAN

CERULEIN n type of dyestuff

CERULEINS > CERULEIN

CERULEOUS adj sky-blue

CERUMEN n soft brownish-yellow wax secreted by glands in the auditory canal of the external ear

CERUMENS > CERUMEN

CERUSE n white lead

CERUSES > CERUSE

CERUSITE same as > CERUSSITE

CERUSITES > CERUSITE

CERUSSITE n usually white mineral, found in veins

CERVELAS n French garlicky pork sausage

CERVELAT n smoked sausage made from pork and beef

CERVELATS > CERVELAT

CERVEZA n Spanish word for beer

CERVEZAS > CERVEZA

CERVICAL adj of or relating to the neck or cervix

CERVICES > CERVIX

CERVICUM n flexible region between the prothorax and head in insects

CERVICUMS > CERVICUM

CERVID n any ruminant mammal of the family Cervidae, including the deer, characterized by the presence of antlers ▷ adj of, relating to, or belonging to the Cervidae

CERVIDS > CERVID

CERVINE adj resembling or relating to a deer

CERVIX n narrow entrance of the womb

CERVIXES > CERVIX

CESAREAN variant of > CAESAREAN

CESAREANS > CESAREAN

CESAREVNA n wife of a Russian tsar's eldest son

CESARIAN US variant of > CAESAREAN

CESARIANS > CESARIAN

CESIOUS same as > CAESIOUS

CESIUM same as > CAESIUM

CESIUMS > CESIUM

CESPITOSE adj growing in dense tufts

CESS n any of several special taxes, such as a land tax in Scotland ▷ vb tax or assess

for taxation

CESSATION n ceasing

CESSE obsolete variant of > CEASE

CESSED > CESS

CESSER n coming to an end of a term interest or annuity

CESSERS > CESSER

CESSES > CESS

CESSING > CESS

CESSION n ceding

CESSIONS > CESSION

CESSPIT same as > CESSPOOL

CESSPITS > CESSPIT

CESSPOOL n covered tank or pit for collecting and storing sewage or waste water

CESSPOOLS > CESSPOOL

CESTA n in jai alai, the basket used to throw and catch the pelota

CESTAS > CESTA

CESTI > CESTUS

CESTODE n any parasitic flatworm of the class Cestoda, which includes the tapeworms

CESTODES > CESTODE

CESTOI > CESTOS

CESTOID adj (esp of tapeworms and similar animals) ribbon-like in form ▷ n ribbon-like worm

CESTOIDS > CESTOID

CESTOS same as > CESTUS

CESTOSES > CESTOS

CESTUI n "the one (who)"; legal term, used in certain phrases, to designate a person

CESTUIS > CESTUI

CESTUS n girdle of Aphrodite (Venus) decorated to cause amorousness

CESTUSES > CESTUS

CESURA a variant spelling of > CAESURA

CESURAE > CESURA

CESURAL > CESURA

CESURAS > CESURA

CESURE same as > CAESURA

CESURES > CESURE

CETACEAN n fish-shaped sea mammal such as a whale or dolphin ▷ adj relating to these mammals

CETACEANS > CETACEAN

CETACEOUS same as > CETACEAN

CETANE n colourless liquid hydrocarbon, used as a solvent

CETANES > CETANE

CETE n group of badgers

CETERACH n scale-fern

CETERACHS > CETERACH

CETES > CETE

CETOLOGY n branch of zoology concerned with the study of whales (cetaceans)

CETRIMIDE n quaternary ammonium compound

used as a detergent

CETYL n univalent alcohol radical

CETYLS > CETYL

CETYWALL n valerian

CETYWALLS > CETYWALL

CEVADILLA same as > SABADILLA

CEVAPCICI n sausages made with beef and paprika

CEVICHE n Peruvian seafood dish

CEVICHES > CEVICHE

CEYLANITE same as > CEYLONITE

CEYLONITE n pleonaste

CH variant of > ICH

CHA n tea

CHABAZITE n pink, white, or colourless zeolite mineral

CHABLIS n dry white French wine

CHABOUK n type of whip

CHABOUKS > CHABOUK

CHABUK same as > CHABOUK

CHABUKS > CHABUK

CHACE obsolete variant of > CHASE

CHACED > CHACE

CHACES > CHACE

CHACHKA n cheap trinket

CHACHKAS > CHACHKA

CHACING > CHACE

CHACK vb to bite

CHACKED > CHACK

CHACKING > CHACK

CHACKS > CHACK

CHACMA n baboon, Papio (or Chaeropithecus) ursinus, having coarse greyish hair and occurring in southern and eastern Africa

CHACMAS > CHACMA

CHACO same as > SHAKO

CHACOES > CHACO

CHACONNE n musical form consisting of a set of variations on a repeated melodic bass line

CHACONNES > CHACONNE

CHACOS > CHACO

CHAD n small pieces removed during the punching of holes in punch cards, printer paper, etc

CHADAR same as > CHUDDAR

CHADARIM > CHEDER

CHADARS > CHADAR

CHADDAR same as > CHUDDAR

CHADDARS > CHADDAR

CHADDOR same as > CHUDDAR

CHADDORS > CHADDOR

CHADLESS adj (of a keypunch) not producing chads

CHADO n Japanese tea ceremony

CHADOR same as > CHUDDAR

CHADORS > CHADOR

CHADOS > CHADO

CHADRI n shroud which covers the body from head to foot, usually worn by females in Islamic countries

CHADS > CHAD

CHAEBOL n large, usually family-owned, business group in South Korea

CHAEBOLS > CHAEBOL

CHAETA n any of the chitinous bristles on the body of such annelids as the earthworm and the lugworm: used in locomotion

CHAETAE > CHAETA

CHAETAL > CHAETA

CHAETODON n butterfly fish

CHAETOPOD n any annelid worm of the classes Oligochaeta or Polychaeta

CHAFE vb make sore or worn by rubbing

CHAFED > CHAFE

CHAFER n large beetle

CHAFERS > CHAFER

CHAFES > CHAFE

CHAFF n grain husks ▷ vb tease good-naturedly

CHAFFED > CHAFF

CHAFFER vb haggle

CHAFFERED > CHAFFER

CHAFFERER > CHAFFER

CHAFFERS > CHAFFER

CHAFFERY n bargaining

CHAFFIER > CHAFF

CHAFFIEST > CHAFF

CHAFFINCH n small European songbird

CHAFFING > CHAFF

CHAFFINGS > CHAFF

CHAFFRON same as > CHAMFRON

CHAFFRONS > CHAFFRON

CHAFFS > CHAFF

CHAFFY > CHAFF

CHAFING > CHAFE

CHAFT n jaw

CHAFTS > CHAFT

CHAGAN n Mongolian royal or imperial title

CHAGANS > CHAGAN

CHAGRIN n annoyance and disappointment ▷ vb embarrass and annoy

CHAGRINED > CHAGRIN

CHAGRINS > CHAGRIN

CHAI n tea, esp as made in India with added spices

CHAIN n flexible length of connected metal links ▷ vb restrict or fasten with or as if with a chain

CHAINE adj (of a dance turn) producing a full rotation for every two steps taken ▷ vb produce a full rotation for every two steps taken

CHAINED > CHAIN

CHAINES > CHAINE

CHAINFALL n type of hoist

CHAINING > CHAIN

CHAINLESS adj having no chain

CHAINLET n small chain

CHAINLETS > CHAINLET

CHAINMAN n person who does the chaining in a survey

CHAINMEN > CHAINMAN

CHAINS > CHAIN

C

CHAINSAW n motor-driven saw with teeth linked in a continuous chain ▷ vb operate a chainsaw
CHAINSAWS > CHAINSAW
CHAINSHOT n cannon shot of two balls joined by a chain
CHAINWORK n work linked or looped in the manner of a chain
CHAIR n seat with a back, for one person ▷ vb preside over (a meeting)
CHAIRDAYS n old age
CHAIRED > CHAIR
CHAIRING > CHAIR
CHAIRLIFT n series of chairs suspended from a moving cable for carrying people up a slope
CHAIRMAN n person in charge of a company's board of directors or a meeting ▷ vb to act as chairman of
CHAIRMANS > CHAIRMAN
CHAIRMEN > CHAIRMAN
CHAIRS > CHAIR
CHAIS > CHAI
CHAISE n light horse-drawn carriage
CHAISES > CHAISE
CHAKALAKA n relish made from tomatoes, onions, and spices
CHAKRA n (in yoga) any of the seven major energy centres in the body
CHAKRAS > CHAKRA
CHAL n in Romany, person or fellow
CHALAH same as > CHALLAH
CHALAHS > CHALAH
CHALAN vb (in India) to cause an accused person to appear before a magistrate
CHALANED > CHALAN
CHALANING > CHALAN
CHALANS > CHALAN
CHALAZA n one of a pair of spiral threads of albumen holding the yolk of a bird's egg in position
CHALAZAE > CHALAZA
CHALAZAL > CHALAZA
CHALAZAS > CHALAZA
CHALAZIA > CHALAZION
CHALAZION n small cyst on the eyelid resulting from chronic inflammation of a meibomian gland
CHALCID n any tiny hymenopterous insect of the family *Chalcididae* and related families, whose larvae are parasites of other insects
CHALCIDS > CHALCID
CHALCOGEN n any of the elements oxygen, sulphur, selenium, tellurium, or polonium, of group 6A of the periodic table
CHALDER n former Scottish dry measure
CHALDERS > CHALDER

CHALDRON n unit of capacity equal to 36 bushels. Formerly used in the US for the measurement of solids, being equivalent to 1.268 cubic metres. Used in Britain for both solids and liquids, it is equivalent to 1.309 cubic metres
CHALDRONS > CHALDRON
CHALEH same as > CHALLAH
CHALEHS > CHALEH
CHALET n kind of Swiss wooden house with a steeply sloping roof
CHALETS > CHALET
CHALICE n large goblet
CHALICED adj (of plants) having cup-shaped flowers
CHALICES > CHALICE
CHALK n soft white rock consisting of calcium carbonate ▷ vb draw or mark with chalk
CHALKED > CHALK
CHALKFACE n work or art of teaching in a school
CHALKIER > CHALK
CHALKIEST > CHALK
CHALKING > CHALK
CHALKLIKE > CHALK
CHALKPIT n quarry for chalk
CHALKPITS > CHALKPIT
CHALKS > CHALK
CHALKY > CHALK
CHALLA same as > CHALLAH
CHALLAH n bread, usually in the form of a plaited loaf, traditionally eaten by Jews to celebrate the Sabbath
CHALLAHS > CHALLAH
CHALLAN same as > CHALAN
CHALLANED > CHALLAN
CHALLANS > CHALLAN
CHALLAS > CHALLA
CHALLENGE n demanding or stimulating situation ▷ vb issue a challenge to
CHALLIE same as > CHALLIS
CHALLIES > CHALLIE
CHALLIS n lightweight plain-weave fabric of wool, cotton, etc, usually with a printed design
CHALLISES > CHALLIS
CHALLOT > CHALLAH
CHALLOTH > CHALLAH
CHALLY same as > CHALLIS
CHALONE n any internal secretion that inhibits a physiological process or function
CHALONES > CHALONE
CHALONIC > CHALONE
CHALOT > CHALAH
CHALOTH > CHALAH
CHALS > CHAL
CHALUMEAU n early type of reed instrument, precursor of the clarinet
CHALUPA n Mexican dish
CHALUPAS > CHALUPA
CHALUTZ n member of an organization of immigrants to Israeli agricultural settlements
CHALUTZES > CHALUTZ

CHALUTZIM > CHALUTZ
CHALYBEAN adj (of steel) of superior quality
CHALYBITE another name for > SIDERITE
CHAM an archaic word for > KHAN
CHAMADE n (formerly) a signal by drum or trumpet inviting an enemy to a parley
CHAMADES > CHAMADE
CHAMBER n hall used for formal meetings ▷ vb act lasciviously
CHAMBERED > CHAMBER
CHAMBERER n lascivious person
CHAMBERS pl n judge's room for hearing private cases not taken in open court
CHAMBRAY n smooth light fabric of cotton, linen, etc, with white weft and a coloured warp
CHAMBRAYS > CHAMBRAY
CHAMBRE adj (of wine) at room temperature
CHAMELEON n small lizard that changes colour to blend in with its surroundings
CHAMELOT same as > CAMLET
CHAMELOTS > CHAMELOT
CHAMETZ n leavened food which may not be eaten during Passover
CHAMETZES > CHAMETZ
CHAMFER same as > CHASE
CHAMFERED > CHAMFER
CHAMFERER > CHAMFER
CHAMFERS > CHAMFER
CHAMFRAIN same as > CHAMFRON
CHAMFRON n piece of armour for a horse's head
CHAMFRONS > CHAMFRON
CHAMISA n American shrub
CHAMISAL n place overgrown with chamiso
CHAMISALS > CHAMISAL
CHAMISAS > CHAMISA
CHAMISE same as > CHAMISO
CHAMISES > CHAMISE
CHAMISO n fourwing saltbush
CHAMISOS > CHAMISO
CHAMLET same as > CAMLET
CHAMLETS > CHAMLET
CHAMMIED > CHAMMY
CHAMMIES > CHAMMY
CHAMMY same as > CHAMOIS
CHAMMYING > CHAMMY
CHAMOIS n small mountain antelope or a pice of leather from its skin, used for polishing ▷ vb polish with a chamois
CHAMOISED > CHAMOIS
CHAMOISES > CHAMOIS
CHAMOIX same as > CHAMOIS
CHAMOMILE same as > CAMOMILE
CHAMP vb chew noisily
CHAMPAC n magnoliaceous tree, *Michelia champaca,* of India and the East

Indies. Its fragrant yellow flowers yield an oil used in perfumes and its wood is used for furniture
CHAMPACA same as > CHAMPAC
CHAMPACAS > CHAMPACA
CHAMPACS > CHAMPAC
CHAMPAGNE n sparkling white French wine ▷ adj denoting a luxurious lifestyle
CHAMPAIGN n expanse of open level or gently undulating country
CHAMPAK same as > CHAMPAC
CHAMPAKS > CHAMPAK
CHAMPART n granting of land to a person, on condition that a portion of the crops will be given to the seller
CHAMPARTS > CHAMPART
CHAMPED > CHAMP
CHAMPER > CHAMP
CHAMPERS n champagne
CHAMPERTY n (formerly) an illegal bargain between a party to litigation and an outsider whereby the latter agrees to pay for the action and thereby share in any proceeds recovered
CHAMPING > CHAMP
CHAMPION n overall winner of a competition ▷ vb support ▷ adj excellent ▷ adv very well
CHAMPIONS > CHAMPION
CHAMPLEVE adj of or relating to a process of enamelling by which grooves are cut into a metal base and filled with enamel colours ▷ n object enamelled by this process
CHAMPS > CHAMP
CHAMPY adj (of earth) churned up (by cattle, for example)
CHAMS > CHAM
CHANCE n likelihood, probability ▷ vb risk, hazard
CHANCED > CHANCE
CHANCEFUL > CHANCE
CHANCEL n part of a church containing the altar and choir
CHANCELS > CHANCEL
CHANCER n unscrupulous or dishonest opportunist who is prepared to try any dubious scheme for making money or furthering his own ends
CHANCERS > CHANCER
CHANCERY n Lord Chancellor's court, now a division of the High Court of Justice
CHANCES > CHANCE
CHANCEY same as > CHANCY
CHANCIER > CHANCY
CHANCIEST > CHANCY
CHANCILY > CHANCY
CHANCING > CHANCE

CHANCRE n small hard growth which is the first sign of syphilis

CHANCRES > CHANCRE

CHANCROID n soft venereal ulcer, esp of the male genitals, caused by infection with the bacillus *Haemophilus ducreyi* ▷ adj relating to or resembling a chancroid or chancre

CHANCROUS > CHANCRE

CHANCY adj uncertain, risky

CHANDELLE n abrupt climbing turn almost to the point of stalling, in which an aircraft's momentum is used to increase its rate of climb ▷ vb carry out a chandelle

CHANDLER n dealer, esp in ships' supplies

CHANDLERS > CHANDLER

CHANDLERY n business, warehouse, or merchandise of a chandler

CHANFRON same as > CHAMFRON

CHANFRONS > CHANFRON

CHANG n loud discordant noise

CHANGA interj in Indian English, an expression of approval or agreement

CHANGE n becoming different ▷ vb make or become different

CHANGED > CHANGE

CHANGEFUL adj often changing

CHANGER > CHANGE

CHANGERS > CHANGE

CHANGES > CHANGE

CHANGEUP n type of baseball pitch

CHANGEUPS > CHANGEUP

CHANGING > CHANGE

CHANGS > CHANG

CHANK n shell of several types of sea conch, used to make bracelets

CHANKS > CHANK

CHANNEL n band of broadcasting frequencies ▷ vb direct or convey through a channel

CHANNELED > CHANNEL

CHANNELER > CHANNEL

CHANNELS > CHANNEL

CHANNER n gravel

CHANNERS > CHANNER

CHANOYO a variant of > CHADO

CHANOYOS > CHANOYO

CHANOYU same as > CHADO

CHANOYUS > CHADO

CHANSON n song

CHANSONS > CHANSON

CHANT vb utter or sing (a slogan or psalm) ▷ n rhythmic or repetitious slogan

CHANTABLE > CHANT

CHANTAGE n blackmail

CHANTAGES > CHANTAGE

CHANTED > CHANT

CHANTER n (on bagpipes) pipe on which the melody is played

CHANTERS > CHANTER

CHANTEUSE n female singer, esp in a nightclub or cabaret

CHANTEY the usual US spelling of > SHANTY

CHANTEYS > CHANTEY

CHANTIE n chamber pot

CHANTIES > CHANTY

CHANTILLY as in *chantilly lace* delicate ornamental lace

CHANTING > CHANT

CHANTOR same as > CHANTER

CHANTORS > CHANTOR

CHANTRESS n female chanter

CHANTRIES > CHANTRY

CHANTRY n endowment for the singing of Masses for the soul of the founder or others designated by him

CHANTS > CHANT

CHANTY same as > SHANTY

CHANUKIAH a variant spelling of > HANUKIAH

CHAO n Vietnamese rice porridge

CHAOLOGY n study of chaos theory

CHAORDIC adj combining elements of chaos and order

CHAOS n complete disorder or confusion

CHAOSES > CHAOS

CHAOTIC > CHAOS

CHAP n man or boy ▷ vb (of the skin) to make or become raw and cracked, esp by exposure to cold

CHAPARRAL n (in the southwestern US) a dense growth of shrubs and trees, esp evergreen oaks

CHAPATI n (in Indian cookery) flat thin unleavened bread

CHAPATIES > CHAPATI

CHAPATIS > CHAPATI

CHAPATTI same as > CHAPATI

CHAPATTIS > CHAPATTI

CHAPBOOK n book of popular ballads, stories, etc, formerly sold by chapmen or pedlars

CHAPBOOKS > CHAPBOOK

CHAPE n metal tip or trimming for a scabbard

CHAPEAU n hat

CHAPEAUS > CHAPEAU

CHAPEAUX > CHAPEAU

CHAPEL n place of worship with its own altar, within a church

CHAPELESS > CHAPE

CHAPELRY n district legally assigned to and served by an Anglican chapel

CHAPELS > CHAPEL

CHAPERON n (esp formerly) an older or married woman who accompanies or supervises a young unmarried woman on social occasions ▷ vb act as a chaperon to

CHAPERONE same as > CHAPERON

CHAPERONS > CHAPERON

CHAPES > CHAPE

CHAPESS n woman

CHAPESSES > CHAPESS

CHAPITER same as > CAPITAL

CHAPITERS > CHAPITER

CHAPKA same as > CZAPKA

CHAPKAS > CHAPKA

CHAPLAIN n clergyman attached to a chapel, military body, or institution

CHAPLAINS > CHAPLAIN

CHAPLESS adj lacking a lower jaw

CHAPLET n garland for the head ▷ vb create a garland

CHAPLETED > CHAPLET

CHAPLETS > CHAPLET

CHAPMAN n travelling pedlar

CHAPMEN > CHAPMAN

CHAPPAL n one of a pair of sandals, usually of leather, worn in India

CHAPPALS > CHAPPAL

CHAPPATI same as > CHAPATI

CHAPPATIS > CHAPPATI

CHAPPED > CHAP

CHAPPESS same as > CHAPESS

CHAPPIE n man or boy

CHAPPIER > CHAPPY

CHAPPIES > CHAPPIE

CHAPPIEST > CHAPPY

CHAPPING > CHAP

CHAPPY adj (of skin) chapped

CHAPRASSI n in India, during the British Empire, an office messenger

CHAPS > CHAP

CHAPSTICK n cylinder of a substance for preventing or soothing chapped lips

CHAPT adj chapped

CHAPTER n division of a book ▷ vb divide into chapters

CHAPTERAL > CHAPTER

CHAPTERED > CHAPTER

CHAPTERS > CHAPTER

CHAPTREL n capital of a pillar supporting an arch

CHAPTRELS > CHAPTREL

CHAQUETA n South American cowboy jacket

CHAQUETAS > CHAQUETA

CHAR vb blacken by partial burning ▷ n charwoman

CHARA n type of green freshwater algae

CHARABANC n coach for sightseeing

CHARACID same as > CHARACIN

CHARACIDS > CHARACIN

CHARACIN n any small carnivorous freshwater cyprinoid fish of the family *Characidae*, of Central and South America and Africa. They are similar to the carps but more brightly coloured

CHARACINS > CHARACIN

CHARACT n distinctive mark

CHARACTER n combination of qualities distinguishing a person, group, or place

CHARACTS > CHARACT

CHARADE n absurd pretence

CHARADES n game in which one team acts out each syllable of a word or phrase, which the other team has to guess

CHARANGA n type of orchestra used in performing traditional Cuban music

CHARANGAS > CHARANGA

CHARANGO n Andean ten-stringed mandolin

CHARANGOS > CHARANGO

CHARAS another name for > HASHISH

CHARASES > CHARAS

CHARBROIL vb to grill over charcoal

CHARCOAL n black substance formed by partially burning wood ▷ adj very dark grey ▷ vb write, draw, or blacken with charcoal

CHARCOALS > CHARCOAL

CHARCOALY > CHARCOAL

CHARD n variety of beet, *Beta vulgaris cicla*, with large succulent leaves and thick stalks, used as a vegetable

CHARDS > CHARD

CHARE same as > CHAR

CHARED > CHAR

CHARES > CHAR

CHARET obsolete variant of > CHARIOT

CHARETS > CHARET

CHARGE vb ask as a price ▷ n price charged

CHARGED > CHARGE

CHARGEFUL adj expensive

CHARGER n device for charging an accumulator

CHARGERS > CHARGER

CHARGES > CHARGE

CHARGING > CHARGE

CHARGRILL vb to grill over charcoal

CHARIDEE n jocular spelling of charity, as pronounced in a mid-Atlantic accent

CHARIDEES > CHARIDEE

CHARIER > CHARY

CHARIEST > CHARY

CHARILY adv cautiously

CHARINESS n state of being chary

CHARING > CHAR

CHARIOT n two-wheeled horse-drawn vehicle used in ancient times in wars and races ▷ vb to ride in a chariot

CHARIOTED > CHARIOT

CHARIOTS > CHARIOT

CHARISM same as > CHARISMA

CHARISMA n person's power to attract or influence people

CHARISMAS > CHARISMA
CHARISMS > CHARISM
CHARITIES > CHARITY
CHARITY n organization that gives help, such as money or food, to those in need
CHARIVARI n discordant mock serenade to newlyweds, made with pans, kettles, etc ▷ vb make such a serenade
CHARK vb to char
CHARKA same as > CHARKHA
CHARKAS > CHARKA
CHARKED > CHARK
CHARKHA n (in India) a spinning wheel, esp for cotton
CHARKHAS > CHARKHA
CHARKING > CHARK
CHARKS > CHARK
CHARLADY same as > CHARWOMAN
CHARLATAN n person who claims expertise that he or she does not have
CHARLEY as in charley horse muscle stiffness after strenuous exercise
CHARLEYS > CHARLEY
CHARLIE n fool
CHARLIER as in charlier shoe special light horseshoe
CHARLIES > CHARLIE
CHARLOCK n weed with hairy leaves and yellow flowers
CHARLOCKS > CHARLOCK
CHARLOTTE n dessert made with fruit and bread or cake crumbs
CHARM n attractive quality ▷ vb attract, delight
CHARMED adj delighted or fascinated
CHARMER n attractive person
CHARMERS > CHARMER
CHARMEUSE n trademark for a lightweight fabric with a satin-like finish
CHARMFUL adj highly charming or enchanting
CHARMING adj attractive
CHARMLESS adj devoid of charm
CHARMONIA pl n elementary particles containing an antiquark and a charm quark
CHARMS > CHARM
CHARNECO n type of sweet wine
CHARNECOS > CHARNECO
CHARNEL adj ghastly ▷ n ghastly thing
CHARNELS > CHARNEL
CHAROSET n dish of chopped fruit, nuts and wine, eaten at Passover
CHAROSETH same as > CHAROSET
CHAROSETS > CHAROSET
CHARPAI same as > CHARPOY
CHARPAIS > CHARPAI
CHARPIE n lint pieces used to make surgical dressings
CHARPIES > CHARPIE
CHARPOY n bedstead of woven webbing or hemp stretched on a wooden frame on four legs, common in India
CHARPOYS > CHARPOY
CHARQUI n meat, esp beef, cut into strips and dried
CHARQUID > CHARQUI
CHARQUIS > CHARQUI
CHARR same as > CHAR
CHARRED > CHAR
CHARRIER > CHARRY
CHARRIEST > CHARRY
CHARRING > CHAR
CHARRO n Mexican cowboy
CHARROS > CHARRO
CHARRS > CHARR
CHARRY adj of or relating to charcoal
CHARS > CHAR
CHART n graph, table, or diagram showing information ▷ vb plot the course of
CHARTA n charter
CHARTABLE > CHART
CHARTAS > CHARTA
CHARTED > CHART
CHARTER n document granting or demanding certain rights ▷ vb hire by charter
CHARTERED adj officially qualified to practise a profession
CHARTERER > CHARTER
CHARTERS > CHARTER
CHARTING > CHART
CHARTISM n historical reform movement in Britain
CHARTISMS > CHARTISM
CHARTIST n supporter of chartism
CHARTISTS > CHARTIST
CHARTLESS adj not mapped
CHARTS > CHART
CHARVER n derogatory term for a young woman
CHARVERS > CHARVER
CHARWOMAN n woman whose job is to clean other people's homes
CHARWOMEN > CHARWOMAN
CHARY adj wary, careful
CHAS > CHA
CHASE vb run after quickly in order to catch or drive away ▷ n chasing, pursuit
CHASEABLE > CHASE
CHASED > CHASE
CHASEPORT n porthole through which a chase gun is fired
CHASER n milder drink drunk after another stronger one
CHASERS > CHASER
CHASES > CHASE
CHASING > CHASE
CHASINGS > CHASE
CHASM n deep crack in the earth ▷ vb create a chasm
CHASMAL > CHASM

CHASMED > CHASM
CHASMIC > CHASM
CHASMIER > CHASMY
CHASMIEST > CHASMY
CHASMS > CHASM
CHASMY adj full of chasms
CHASSE n one of a series of gliding steps in ballet in which the same foot always leads ▷ vb perform either of these steps
CHASSED > CHASSE
CHASSEED > CHASSE
CHASSEING > CHASSE
CHASSEPOT n breech-loading bolt-action rifle formerly used by the French Army
CHASSES > CHASSE
CHASSEUR n member of a unit specially trained and equipped for swift deployment ▷ adj designating or cooked in a sauce consisting of white wine and mushrooms
CHASSEURS > CHASSEUR
CHASSIS n frame, wheels, and mechanical parts of a vehicle
CHASTE adj abstaining from sex outside marriage or altogether
CHASTELY > CHASTE
CHASTEN vb subdue by criticism
CHASTENED > CHASTEN
CHASTENER > CHASTEN
CHASTENS > CHASTEN
CHASTER > CHASTE
CHASTEST > CHASTE
CHASTISE vb scold severely
CHASTISED > CHASTISE
CHASTISER > CHASTISE
CHASTISES > CHASTISE
CHASTITY n state of being chaste
CHASUBLE n long sleeveless robe worn by a priest when celebrating Mass
CHASUBLES > CHASUBLE
CHAT n informal conversation ▷ vb have an informal conversation
CHATBOT n computer program in the form of a virtual e-mail correspondent that can reply to messages from computer users
CHATBOTS > CHATBOT
CHATCHKA variant of > TCHOTCHKE
CHATCHKAS > CHATCHKA
CHATCHKE same as > TCHOTCHKE
CHATCHKES > CHATCHKE
CHATEAU n French castle
CHATEAUS > CHATEAU
CHATEAUX > CHATEAU
CHATELAIN same as > CASTELLAN
CHATLINE n telephone service enabling callers to join in general conversation with each other

CHATLINES > CHATLINE
CHATON n in jewellery, a stone with a reflective metal foil backing
CHATONS > CHATON
CHATOYANT adj having changeable lustre ▷ n gemstone with a changeable lustre
CHATROOM n site on the Internet where users have group discussions by e-mail
CHATROOMS > CHATROOM
CHATS > CHAT
CHATTA n umbrella
CHATTAS > CHATTA
CHATTED > CHAT
CHATTEL n item of movable personal property
CHATTELS > CHATTEL
CHATTER vb speak quickly and continuously about unimportant things ▷ n idle talk
CHATTERED > CHATTER
CHATTERER same as > COTINGA
CHATTERS > CHATTER
CHATTERY > CHATTER
CHATTI n (in India) an earthenware pot
CHATTIER > CHATTY
CHATTIES > CHATTI
CHATTIEST > CHATTY
CHATTILY > CHATTY
CHATTING > CHAT
CHATTIS > CHATTI
CHATTY adj (of a person) fond of friendly, informal conversation
CHAUFE obsolete variant of > CHAFE
CHAUFED > CHAUFE
CHAUFER same as > CHAUFFER
CHAUFERS > CHAUFER
CHAUFES > CHAUFE
CHAUFF obsolete variant of > CHAFE
CHAUFFED > CHAUFF
CHAUFFER n small portable heater or stove
CHAUFFERS > CHAUFFER
CHAUFFEUR n person employed to drive a car for someone ▷ vb act as driver for (someone)
CHAUFFING > CHAUFF
CHAUFFS > CHAUFF
CHAUFING > CHAUFE
CHAUMER n chamber
CHAUMERS > CHAUMER
CHAUNCE archaic variant of > CHANCE
CHAUNCED > CHAUNCE
CHAUNCES > CHAUNCE
CHAUNCING > CHAUNCE
CHAUNGE archaic variant of > CHANGE
CHAUNGED > CHAUNGE
CHAUNGES > CHAUNGE
CHAUNGING > CHAUNGE
CHAUNT a less common variant of > CHANT
CHAUNTED > CHAUNT
CHAUNTER > CHAUNT

CHAUNTERS > CHAUNT
CHAUNTING > CHAUNT
CHAUNTRY *same as*
   > CHANTRY
CHAUNTS > CHAUNT
CHAUSSES *n* tight-fitting
   medieval garment covering
   the feet and legs, usually
   made of chain mail
CHAUSSURE *n* any type of
   footwear
CHAUVIN *n* chauvinist
CHAUVINS > CHAUVIN
CHAV *n* informal derogatory
   word for a young working-
   class person who wears
   casual sports clothes
CHAVE *vb* old dialect term
   for "I have"
CHAVENDER *n* chub
CHAVETTE *n* informal
   derogatory word for a
   young working-class
   female who wears casual
   sports clothes
CHAVETTES > CHAVETTE
CHAVISH > CHAV
CHAVS > CHAV
CHAW *vb* chew (tobacco),
   esp without swallowing
   it ▷ *n* something chewed,
   esp a plug of tobacco
CHAWBACON *n* bumpkin
CHAWDRON *n* entrails
CHAWDRONS > CHAWDRON
CHAWED > CHAW
CHAWER > CHAW
CHAWERS > CHAW
CHAWING > CHAW
CHAWK *n* jackdaw
CHAWKS > CHAWK
CHAWS > CHAW
CHAY *n* plant of the madder
   family
CHAYA *same as* > CHAY
CHAYAS > CHAYA
CHAYOTE *n* tropical
   American cucurbitaceous
   climbing plant, *Sechium
   edule*, that has edible pear-
   shaped fruit enclosing a
   single enormous seed
CHAYOTES > CHAYOTE
CHAYROOT *n* root of the chay
   plant
CHAYROOTS > CHAYROOT
CHAYS > CHAY
CHAZAN *same as* > CANTOR
CHAZANIM > CHAZAN
CHAZANS > CHAZAN
CHAZZAN *variant of*
   > CHAZAN
CHAZZANIM > CHAZZAN
CHAZZANS > CHAZZAN
CHAZZEN *same as* > CHAZZAN
CHAZZENIM > CHAZZEN
CHAZZENS > CHAZZEN
CHE *pron* dialectal form
   meaning "I"
CHEAP *adj* costing relatively
   little ▷ *adv* at very little
   cost ▷ *n* bargain ▷ *vb* take
   the cheapest option
CHEAPED > CHEAP
CHEAPEN *vb* lower the
   reputation of
CHEAPENED > CHEAPEN

CHEAPENER > CHEAPEN
CHEAPENS > CHEAPEN
CHEAPER > CHEAP
CHEAPEST > CHEAP
CHEAPIE *n* something
   inexpensive
CHEAPIES > CHEAPIE
CHEAPING > CHEAP
CHEAPISH > CHEAP
CHEAPJACK *n* person who
   sells cheap and shoddy
   goods ▷ *adj* shoddy or
   inferior
CHEAPLY > CHEAP
CHEAPNESS > CHEAP
CHEAPO *n* very cheap and
   possibly shoddy thing
CHEAPOS > CHEAPO
CHEAPS > CHEAP
CHEAPY *same as* > CHEAPIE
CHEAT *vb* act dishonestly
   to gain profit or advantage
   ▷ *n* person who cheats
CHEATABLE > CHEAT
CHEATED > CHEAT
CHEATER > CHEAT
CHEATERS > CHEAT
CHEATERY *n* cheating
CHEATING > CHEAT
CHEATINGS > CHEAT
CHEATS > CHEAT
CHEBEC *n* type of boat
CHEBECS > CHEBEC
CHECHAKO *same as*
   > CHEECHAKO
CHECHAKOS > CHECHAKO
CHECHAQUO *same as*
   > CHEECHAKO
CHECHIA *n* Berber skullcap
CHECHIAS > CHECHIA
CHECK *vb* examine or
   investigate ▷ *n* control
   designed to ensure
   accuracy
CHECKABLE > CHECK
CHECKBOOK *n* American
   word for chequebook
CHECKED > CHECK
CHECKER *same as* > CHEQUER
CHECKERED *same as*
   > CHEQUERED
CHECKERS *n* game for
   two players using a
   checkerboard and 12
   checkers each. The object
   is to jump over and capture
   the opponent's pieces
CHECKING > CHECK
CHECKLESS *adj* without
   check or restraint
CHECKLIST *vb* check items,
   facts, etc, against those in
   a list used for verification
CHECKMARK *vb* make a mark
   of approval or verification
CHECKMATE *n* winning
   position in which an
   opponent's king is under
   attack and unable to
   escape ▷ *vb* place the
   king of (one's opponent)
   in checkmate ▷ *interj*
   call made when placing
   an opponent's king in
   checkmate
CHECKOFF *n* procedure
   where an employer pays

   the employee's union dues
   straight from his or her
   salary
CHECKOFFS > CHECKOFF
CHECKOUT *n* counter in
   a supermarket, where
   customers pay
CHECKOUTS > CHECKOUT
CHECKRAIL *another word for*
   > GUARDRAIL
CHECKREIN *n* bearing rein
CHECKROOM *n* place at a
   railway station, airport,
   etc, where luggage may
   be left for a small charge
   with an attendant for
   safekeeping
CHECKROW *n* row of plants,
   esp corn, in which the
   spaces between adjacent
   plants are equal to those
   between adjacent rows to
   facilitate cultivation ▷ *vb*
   plant in checkrows
CHECKROWS > CHECKROW
CHECKS > CHECK
CHECKSUM *n* digit
   representing the number
   of bits of information
   transmitted, attached to
   the end of a message, to
   verify the integrity of data
CHECKSUMS > CHECKSUM
CHECKUP *n* thorough
   medical examination ▷ *vb*
   investigate or make an
   inquiry into (a person's
   character, evidence, etc),
   esp when suspicions have
   been aroused
CHECKUPS > CHECKUP
CHECKY *adj* having squares
   of alternating tinctures
   or furs
CHEDDAR *n* type of smooth
   hard yellow or whitish
   cheese
CHEDDARS > CHEDDAR
CHEDDARY > CHEDDAR
CHEDDITE *n* explosive made
   by mixing a powdered
   chlorate or perchlorate
   with a fatty substance,
   such as castor oil
CHEDDITES > CHEDDITE
CHEDER *n* (in Western
   countries) elementary
   religious education classes,
   usually outside normal
   school hours
CHEDERS > CHEDER
CHEDITE *same as*
   > CHEDDITE
CHEDITES > CHEDITE
CHEECHAKO *n* local name for
   a newcomer to Alaska
CHEEK *n* either side of the
   face below the eye ▷ *vb*
   speak impudently to
CHEEKBONE *n* bone at the
   top of the cheek, just below
   the eye
CHEEKED > CHEEK
CHEEKFUL *n* quantity that
   can be held in a cheek
CHEEKFULS > CHEEKFUL
CHEEKIER > CHEEKY

CHEEKIEST > CHEEKY
CHEEKILY > CHEEKY
CHEEKING > CHEEK
CHEEKLESS > CHEEK
CHEEKS > CHEEK
CHEEKY *adj* impudent,
   disrespectful
CHEEP *n* young bird's high-
   pitched cry ▷ *vb* utter a
   cheep
CHEEPED > CHEEP
CHEEPER > CHEEP
CHEEPERS > CHEEP
CHEEPING > CHEEP
CHEEPS > CHEEP
CHEER *vb* applaud or
   encourage with shouts
   ▷ *n* shout of applause or
   encouragement
CHEERED > CHEER
CHEERER > CHEER
CHEERERS > CHEER
CHEERFUL *adj* having a
   happy disposition
CHEERIER > CHEERY
CHEERIEST > CHEERY
CHEERILY > CHEERY
CHEERING > CHEER
CHEERIO *interj* goodbye ▷ *n*
   small red cocktail sausage
   ▷ *sentence substitute*
   farewell greeting
CHEERIOS > CHEERIO
CHEERLEAD *vb* to lead a
   crowd in formal cheers at
   sports events
CHEERLED > CHEERLEAD
CHEERLESS *adj* dreary,
   gloomy
CHEERLY *adv* cheerful or
   cheerfully
CHEERO *same as* > CHEERIO
CHEEROS > CHEERO
CHEERS *interj* drinking
   toast ▷ *sentence substitute*
   drinking toast
CHEERY *adj* cheerful
CHEESE *n* food made from
   coagulated milk curd ▷ *vb*
   stop
CHEESED > CHEESE
CHEESES > CHEESE
CHEESEVAT *n* in
   cheesemaking, vat in
   which curds are formed
   and cut
CHEESIER > CHEESY
CHEESIEST > CHEESY
CHEESILY > CHEESY
CHEESING > CHEESE
CHEESY *adj* like cheese
CHEETAH *n* large fast-
   running spotted African
   wild cat
CHEETAHS > CHEETAH
CHEEWINK *same as*
   > CHEWINK
CHEEWINKS > CHEEWINK
CHEF *n* cook in a restaurant
   ▷ *vb* to work as a chef
CHEFDOM *n* state or
   condition of being a chef
CHEFDOMS > CHEFDOM
CHEFED > CHEF
CHEFFED > CHEF
CHEFFING > CHEF
CHEFING > CHEF

CHEFS > CHEF
CHEGOE same as > CHIGGER
CHEGOES > CHIGGER
CHEILITIS n inflammation of the lip(s)
CHEKA n secret police set up in Russia in 1917
CHEKAS > CHEKA
CHEKIST n member of the cheka
CHEKISTS > CHEKIST
CHELA n disciple of a religious teacher
CHELAE > CHELA
CHELAS > CHELA
CHELASHIP > CHELA
CHELATE n coordination compound in which a metal atom or ion is bound to a ligand at two or more points on the ligand, so as to form a heterocyclic ring containing a metal atom ▷ adj of or possessing chelae ▷ vb form a chelate
CHELATED > CHELATE
CHELATES > CHELATE
CHELATING > CHELATE
CHELATION n process by which a chelate is formed
CHELATOR > CHELATE
CHELATORS > CHELATE
CHELICERA n one of a pair of appendages on the head of spiders and other arachnids: often modified as food-catching claws
CHELIFORM adj shaped like a chela
CHELIPED n (on a arthropod) either of two legs which each carry a claw
CHELIPEDS > CHELIPED
CHELLUP n noise
CHELLUPS > CHELLUP
CHELOID a variant spelling of > KELOID
CHELOIDAL > CHELOID
CHELOIDS > CHELOID
CHELONE n any plant of the hardy N American genus Chelone, grown for its white, rose, or purple flower spikes: family Scrophulariaceae
CHELONES > CHELONE
CHELONIAN n any reptile of the order Chelonia, including the tortoises and turtles, in which most of the body is enclosed in a protective bony capsule ▷ adj of, relating to, or belonging to the Chelonia
CHELP vb (esp of women or children) to chatter or speak out of turn
CHELPED > CHELP
CHELPING > CHELP
CHELPS > CHELP
CHEMIC vb to bleach ▷ n chemist
CHEMICAL n substance used in or resulting from a reaction involving changes to atoms or molecules

▷ adj of chemistry or chemicals
CHEMICALS > CHEMICAL
CHEMICKED > CHEMIC
CHEMICS > CHEMIC
CHEMISE n woman's loose-fitting slip
CHEMISES > CHEMISE
CHEMISM n chemical action
CHEMISMS > CHEMISM
CHEMISORB vb take up (a substance) by chemisorption
CHEMIST n shop selling medicines and cosmetics
CHEMISTRY n science of the composition, properties, and reactions of substances
CHEMISTS > CHEMIST
CHEMITYPE n process by which a relief impression is obtained from an engraving
CHEMITYPY > CHEMITYPE
CHEMMIES > CHEMMY
CHEMMY n gambling card game
CHEMO n short form of chemotherapy
CHEMOKINE n type of protein
CHEMOS > CHEMO
CHEMOSORB same as > CHEMISORB
CHEMOSTAT n apparatus for growing bacterial cultures at a constant rate by controlling the supply of nutrient medium
CHEMPADUK n evergreen moraceous tree, Artocarpus champeden (or A. integer), of Malaysia, similar to the jackfruit
CHEMURGIC > CHEMURGY
CHEMURGY n branch of chemistry concerned with the industrial use of organic raw materials, esp materials of agricultural origin
CHENAR n oriental plane tree
CHENARS > CHENAR
CHENET another word for > GENIP
CHENETS > CHENET
CHENILLE n (fabric of) thick tufty yarn
CHENILLES > CHENILLE
CHENIX n ancient measure, slightly more than a quart
CHENIXES > CHENIX
CHENOPOD n any flowering plant of the family Chenopodiaceae, which includes the beet, mangel-wurzel, spinach, and goosefoot
CHENOPODS > CHENOPOD
CHEONGSAM n straight dress, usually of silk or cotton, with a stand-up collar and a slit in one side of the skirt, worn by Chinese women
CHEQUE n written order to

one's bank to pay money from one's account
CHEQUER n piece used in Chinese chequers ▷ vb make irregular in colour or character
CHEQUERED adj marked by varied fortunes
CHEQUERS n game of draughts
CHEQUES > CHEQUE
CHEQUING as in chequing account (in Canada) account against which cheques can be drawn
CHEQUY same as > CHECKY
CHER adj dear or expensive
CHERALITE n rare phosphate-silicate of Thorium and Calcium
CHERE feminine variant of > CHER
CHERIMOYA n large tropical fruit with custardlike flesh
CHERISH vb cling to (an idea or feeling)
CHERISHED > CHERISH
CHERISHER > CHERISH
CHERISHES > CHERISH
CHERNOZEM n black soil, rich in humus and carbonates, in cool or temperate semiarid regions, as the grasslands of Russia
CHEROOT n cigar with both ends cut flat
CHEROOTS > CHEROOT
CHERRIED > CHERRY
CHERRIER > CHERRY
CHERRIES > CHERRY
CHERRIEST > CHERRY
CHERRY n small red or black fruit with a stone ▷ adj deep red ▷ vb to cheer
CHERRYING > CHERRY
CHERT n microcrystalline form of silica usually occurring as bands or layers of pebbles in sedimentary rock. Formula: SiO_2. Varieties include flint, lyddite (Lydian stone)
CHERTIER > CHERT
CHERTIEST > CHERT
CHERTS > CHERT
CHERTY > CHERT
CHERUB n angel, often represented as a winged child
CHERUBIC > CHERUB
CHERUBIM > CHERUB
CHERUBIMS > CHERUB
CHERUBIN n cherub ▷ adj cherubic
CHERUBINS > CHERUBIN
CHERUBS > CHERUB
CHERUP same as > CHIRRUP
CHERUPED > CHERUP
CHERUPING > CHERUP
CHERUPS > CHERUP
CHERVIL n aniseed-flavoured herb
CHERVILS > CHERVIL
CHESHIRE n breed of American pig
CHESHIRES > CHESHIRE
CHESIL n gravel or shingle

CHESILS > CHESIL
CHESNUT rare variant of > CHESTNUT
CHESNUTS > CHESNUT
CHESS n game for two players with 16 pieces each, played on a chequered board of 64 squares
CHESSEL n mould used in cheese-making
CHESSELS > CHESSEL
CHESSES > CHESS
CHESSMAN n piece used in chess
CHESSMEN > CHESSMAN
CHEST n front of the body, from neck to waist ▷ vb to hit with the chest, as with a ball in football
CHESTED > CHEST
CHESTFUL n amount a chest will hold
CHESTFULS > CHESTFUL
CHESTIER > CHESTY
CHESTIEST > CHESTY
CHESTILY > CHESTY
CHESTING > CHEST
CHESTNUT n reddish-brown edible nut ▷ adj (of hair or a horse) reddish-brown
CHESTNUTS > CHESTNUT
CHESTS > CHEST
CHESTY adj symptomatic of chest disease
CHETAH same as > CHEETAH
CHETAHS > CHETAH
CHETH same as > HETH
CHETHS > CHETH
CHETNIK n member of a Serbian nationalist paramilitary group
CHETNIKS > CHETNIK
CHETRUM n monetary unit in Bhutan
CHETRUMS > CHETRUM
CHEVAL as in cheval glass full-length mirror that can swivel
CHEVALET n bridge of a stringed musical instrument
CHEVALETS > CHEVALET
CHEVALIER n member of the French Legion of Honour
CHEVELURE n nebulous part of the tail of a comet
CHEVEN n chub
CHEVENS > CHEVEN
CHEVEREL n kid or goatskin leather
CHEVERELS > CHEVEREL
CHEVERIL same as > CHEVEREL
CHEVERILS > CHEVERIL
CHEVERON same as > CHEVRON
CHEVERONS > CHEVERON
CHEVERYE same as > CHIEFERY
CHEVERYES > CHEVERYE
CHEVET n semicircular or polygonal east end of a church, esp a French Gothic church, often with a number of attached apses
CHEVETS > CHEVET

CHEVIED > CHEVY
CHEVIES > CHEVY
CHEVILLE n peg of a stringed musical instrument
CHEVILLES > CHEVILLE
CHEVIN same as > CHEVEN
CHEVINS > CHEVIN
CHEVIOT n type of British sheep reared for its wool
CHEVIOTS > CHEVIOT
CHEVRE n any cheese made from goats' milk
CHEVRES > CHEVRE
CHEVRET n type of goats' cheese
CHEVRETS > CHEVRET
CHEVRETTE n skin of a young goat
CHEVRON n V-shaped pattern, esp on the sleeve of a military uniform to indicate rank ▷ vb make a chevron
CHEVRONED > CHEVRON
CHEVRONS > CHEVRON
CHEVRONY adj in heraldry, bearing chevrons
CHEVY same as > CHIVY
CHEVYING > CHEVY
CHEW vb grind (food) between the teeth ▷ n act of chewing
CHEWABLE > CHEW
CHEWED > CHEW
CHEWER > CHEW
CHEWERS > CHEW
CHEWET n type of meat pie
CHEWETS > CHEWET
CHEWIE n chewing gum
CHEWIER > CHEWY
CHEWIES > CHEWY
CHEWIEST > CHEWY
CHEWINESS > CHEWY
CHEWING > CHEW
CHEWINK n towhee
CHEWINKS > CHEWINK
CHEWS > CHEW
CHEWY adj requiring a lot of chewing ▷ n dog's rubber toy
CHEZ prep at the home of
CHI n 22nd letter of the Greek alphabet, a consonant, transliterated as ch or rarely kh
CHIA n plant of the mint family
CHIACK vb tease or banter ▷ n good-humoured banter
CHIACKED > CHIACK
CHIACKING > CHIACK
CHIACKS > CHIACK
CHIANTI n dry red Italian wine
CHIANTIS > CHIANT
CHIAO n Chinese coin equal to one tenth of one yuan
CHIAREZZA n (in music) clarity
CHIAREZZE > CHIAREZZA
CHIAS > CHIA
CHIASM same as > CHIASMA
CHIASMA n cross-shaped connection produced by the crossing over of pairing

chromosomes during meiosis
CHIASMAL > CHIASMA
CHIASMAS > CHIASMA
CHIASMATA > CHIASMA
CHIASMI > CHIASMUS
CHIASMIC > CHIASMA
CHIASMS > CHIASMA
CHIASMUS n reversal of the order of words in the second of two parallel phrases
CHIASTIC > CHIASMUS
CHIAUS same as > CHOUSE
CHIAUSED > CHIAUS
CHIAUSES > CHIAUS
CHIAUSING > CHIAUS
CHIB vb in Scots English, stab or slash with a sharp weapon ▷ n sharp weapon
CHIBBED > CHIB
CHIBBING > CHIB
CHIBOL n spring onion
CHIBOLS > CHIBOL
CHIBOUK n Turkish tobacco pipe with an extremely long stem
CHIBOUKS > CHIBOUK
CHIBOUQUE same as > CHIBOUK
CHIBS > CHIB
CHIC adj stylish, elegant ▷ n stylishness, elegance
CHICA n Spanish young girl
CHICALOTE n poppy, Argemone platyceras, of the southwestern US and Mexico with prickly leaves and white or yellow flowers
CHICANA n female chicano
CHICANAS > CHICANA
CHICANE n obstacle in a motor-racing circuit ▷ vb deceive or trick by chicanery
CHICANED > CHICANE
CHICANER > CHICANE
CHICANERS > CHICANE
CHICANERY n trickery, deception
CHICANES > CHICANE
CHICANING > CHICANE
CHICANO n American citizen of Mexican origin
CHICANOS > CHICANO
CHICAS > CHICA
CHICCORY a variant spelling of > CHICORY
CHICER > CHIC
CHICEST > CHIC
CHICH another word for > CHICKPEA
CHICHA n Andean drink made from fermented maize
CHICHAS > CHICHA
CHICHES > CHICKPEA
CHICHI adj affectedly pretty or stylish ▷ n quality of being affectedly pretty or stylish
CHICHIER > CHICHI
CHICHIEST > CHICHI
CHICHIS > CHICHI
CHICK n baby bird
CHICKADEE n small North American songbird

CHICKAREE n American red squirrel
CHICKEE n opensided, thatched building on stilts
CHICKEES > CHICKEE
CHICKEN n domestic fowl ▷ adj cowardly ▷ vb to lose one's nerve
CHICKENED > CHICKEN
CHICKENS > CHICKEN
CHICKLING n small chick
CHICKORY same as > CHICORY
CHICKPEA n edible yellow pealike seed
CHICKPEAS > CHICKPEA
CHICKS > CHICK
CHICKWEED n weed with small white flowers
CHICLE n gumlike substance obtained from the sapodilla
CHICLES > CHICLE
CHICLY > CHIC
CHICNESS > CHIC
CHICO n spiny chenopodiaceous shrub
CHICON same as > CHICORY
CHICONS > CHICON
CHICORIES > CHICORY
CHICORY n plant whose leaves are used in salads
CHICOS > CHICO
CHICS > CHIC
CHID > CHIDE
CHIDDEN > CHIDE
CHIDE vb rebuke, scold
CHIDED > CHIDE
CHIDER > CHIDE
CHIDERS > CHIDE
CHIDES > CHIDE
CHIDING > CHIDE
CHIDINGLY > CHIDE
CHIDINGS > CHIDE
CHIDLINGS n intestines of a pig prepared as a dish
CHIEF n head of a group of people ▷ adj most important
CHIEFDOM n any tribal social group led by a chief
CHIEFDOMS > CHIEFDOM
CHIEFER > CHIEF
CHIEFERY n lands belonging to a chief
CHIEFESS n female chief
CHIEFEST > CHIEF
CHIEFLESS adj lacking a chief
CHIEFLING n petty chief
CHIEFLY adv especially ▷ adj of or relating to a chief or chieftain
CHIEFRIES > CHIEFRY
CHIEFRY same as > CHIEFERY
CHIEFS > CHIEF
CHIEFSHIP n state of being a chief
CHIEFTAIN n leader of a tribe
CHIEL n young man
CHIELD same as > CHIEL
CHIELDS > CHIEL
CHIELS > CHIEL
CHIFFON n fine see-through fabric ▷ adj made of chiffon

CHIFFONS > CHIFFON
CHIFFONY > CHIFFON
CHIGETAI n variety of the Asiatic wild ass, Equus hemionus, of Mongolia
CHIGETAIS > CHIGETAI
CHIGGA n informal Australian derogatory word for a young working-class person from Hobart, Tasmania
CHIGGAS > CHIGGA
CHIGGER n parasitic larva of any of various free-living mites of the family Trombidiidae, which causes intense itching of human skin
CHIGGERS > CHIGGER
CHIGNON n knot of hair pinned up at the back of the head ▷ vb make a chignon
CHIGNONED > CHIGNON
CHIGNONS > CHIGNON
CHIGOE same as > CHIGGER
CHIGOES > CHIGOE
CHIGRE same as > CHIGGER
CHIGRES > CHIGRE
CHIHUAHUA n tiny short-haired dog
CHIK n slatted blind
CHIKARA n Indian seven-stringed musical instrument
CHIKARAS > CHIKARA
CHIKHOR same as > CHUKAR
CHIKHORS > CHIKHOR
CHIKOR same as > CHUKAR
CHIKORS > CHIKOR
CHIKS > CHIK
CHILBLAIN n inflammation of the fingers or toes, caused by exposure to cold
CHILD n young human being, boy or girl ▷ vb to give birth
CHILDBED n condition of giving birth to a child
CHILDBEDS > CHILDBED
CHILDCARE n care provided for children without homes (or with a seriously disturbed home life) by a local authority
CHILDE n young man of noble birth
CHILDED > CHILD
CHILDER dialect variant of > CHILDREN
CHILDES > CHILDE
CHILDHOOD n time or condition of being a child
CHILDING > CHILD
CHILDISH adj immature, silly
CHILDLESS > CHILD
CHILDLIER > CHILD
CHILDLIKE adj innocent, trustful
CHILDLY > CHILD
CHILDNESS n nature of a child
CHILDREN > CHILD
CHILDS > CHILD
CHILE a variant spelling of > CHILLI

CHILES > CHILE
CHILI *same as* > CHILLI
CHILIAD *n* group of one thousand
CHILIADAL > CHILIAD
CHILIADIC > CHILIAD
CHILIADS > CHILIAD
CHILIAGON *n* thousand-sided polygon
CHILIARCH *n* commander of a thousand men
CHILIASM *n* belief in the Second Coming of Christ
CHILIASMS > CHILIASM
CHILIAST > CHILIASM
CHILIASTS > CHILIASM
CHILIDOG *n* hot dog served with chilli sauce
CHILIDOGS > CHILIDOG
CHILIES > CHILI
CHILIOI *n* thousand
CHILIOIS > CHILIOI
CHILIS > CHILI
CHILL *n* feverish cold ▷ *vb* make (something) cool or cold ▷ *adj* unpleasantly cold
CHILLADA *n* spicy Mexican dish made of fried vegetables and pulses
CHILLADAS > CHILLADA
CHILLED > CHILL
CHILLER *n* cooling or refrigerating device
CHILLERS > CHILLER
CHILLEST > CHILL
CHILLI *n* small red or green hot-tasting capsicum pod, used in cooking
CHILLIER > CHILLY
CHILLIES > CHILLI
CHILLIEST > CHILLY
CHILLILY > CHILLY
CHILLING > CHILL
CHILLINGS > CHILL
CHILLIS > CHILLI
CHILLNESS > CHILL
CHILLS > CHILL
CHILLUM *n* short pipe, usually of clay, used esp for smoking cannabis
CHILLUMS > CHILLUM
CHILLY *adj* moderately cold
CHILOPOD *n* any arthropod of the class *Chilopoda*, which includes the centipedes
CHILOPODS > CHILOPOD
CHILTEPIN *n* variety of chilli pepper
CHIMAERA *same as* > CHIMERA
CHIMAERAS > CHIMAERA
CHIMAERIC > CHIMAERA
CHIMAR *same as* > CHIMERE
CHIMARS > CHIMAR
CHIMB *same as* > CHIME
CHIMBLEY *same as* > CHIMNEY
CHIMBLEYS > CHIMBLEY
CHIMBLIES > CHIMBLY
CHIMBLY *same as* > CHIMNEY
CHIMBS > CHIME
CHIME *n* musical ringing sound of a bell or clock ▷ *vb* make a musical ringing sound

CHIMED > CHIME
CHIMER > CHIME
CHIMERA *n* unrealistic hope or idea
CHIMERAS > CHIMERA
CHIMERE *n* sleeveless red or black gown, part of a bishop's formal dress though not a vestment
CHIMERES > CHIMERE
CHIMERIC > CHIMERA
CHIMERID *n* fish of the genus Chimaera
CHIMERIDS > CHIMERID
CHIMERISM *n* medical condition in which a person possesses two genetically distinct sets of cells
CHIMERS > CHIME
CHIMES > CHIME
CHIMING > CHIME
CHIMLA *same as* > CHIMNEY
CHIMLAS > CHIMLA
CHIMLEY *same as* > CHIMNEY
CHIMLEYS > CHIMLEY
CHIMNEY *n* hollow vertical structure for carrying away smoke from a fire ▷ *vb* to climb two vertical, parallel, chimney-like rock faces
CHIMNEYED > CHIMNEY
CHIMNEYS > CHIMNEY
CHIMO *interj* Inuit greeting and toast
CHIMP *n* chimpanzee
CHIMPS > CHIMP
CHIN *n* part of the face below the mouth ▷ *vb* hit someone in the chin
CHINA *n* fine earthenware or porcelain
CHINAMAN *n* in cricket, a ball bowled by a left-handed bowler to a right-handed batsman that spins from off to leg
CHINAMEN > CHINAMAN
CHINAMPA *n* in Mesoamerican agriculture, an artificially created island used for growing crops
CHINAMPAS > CHINAMPA
CHINAR *same as* > CHINAR
CHINAROOT *n* bristly greenbrier
CHINARS > CHENAR
CHINAS > CHINA
CHINAWARE *n* articles made of china, esp those made for domestic use
CHINBONE *n* front part of the mandible which forms the chin
CHINBONES > CHINBONE
CHINCAPIN *n* dwarf chestnut tree
CHINCH *another name for a* > BEDBUG
CHINCHES > CHINCH
CHINCHIER > CHINCHY
CHINCHY *adj* tightfisted
CHINCOUGH *n* whooping cough
CHINDIT *n* Allied soldier fighting behind the Japanese lines in Burma during World War II

CHINDITS > CHINDIT
CHINE *same as* > CHIME
CHINED > CHINE
CHINES > CHINE
CHINESE *adj* of or relating to China
CHINING > CHINE
CHINK *n* small narrow opening ▷ *vb* make a light ringing sound
CHINKAPIN *same as* > CHINCAPIN
CHINKARA *n* Indian gazelle
CHINKARAS > CHINKARA
CHINKED > CHINK
CHINKIE *n* offensive term for a (takeaway) meal of Chinese food
CHINKIER > CHINK
CHINKIES > CHINKIE
CHINKIEST > CHINK
CHINKING > CHINK
CHINKS > CHINK
CHINKY > CHINK
CHINLESS *adj* having a receding chin
CHINNED > CHIN
CHINNING > CHIN
CHINO *n* durable cotton twill cloth
CHINONE *n* benzoquinone
CHINONES > CHINONE
CHINOOK *n* warm dry southwesterly wind blowing down the eastern slopes of the Rocky Mountains
CHINOOKS > CHINOOK
CHINOS *pl n* trousers made of a kind of hard-wearing cotton
CHINOVNIK *n* Russian official or bureaucrat
CHINS > CHIN
CHINSTRAP *n* strap on a helmet which fastens under the chin
CHINTS *obsolete variant of* > CHINTZ
CHINTSES > CHINTS
CHINTZ *n* printed cotton fabric with a glazed finish
CHINTZES > CHINTZ
CHINTZIER > CHINTZY
CHINTZY *adj* of or covered with chintz
CHINWAG *n* chat
CHINWAGS > CHINWAG
CHIP *n* strip of potato, fried in deep fat ▷ *vb* break small pieces from
CHIPBOARD *n* thin board made of compressed wood particles
CHIPMUCK *another word for* > CHIPMUCK
CHIPMUCKS > CHIPMUK
CHIPMUNK *n* small squirrel-like N American rodent with a striped back
CHIPMUNKS > CHIPMUNK
CHIPOCHIA *same as* > CAPOCCHIA
CHIPOLATA *n* small sausage
CHIPOTLE *n* dried chilli pepper
CHIPOTLES > CHIPOTLE

CHIPPABLE > CHIP
CHIPPED > CHIP
CHIPPER *vb* chirp or chatter
CHIPPERED > CHIPPER
CHIPPERS > CHIPPER
CHIPPIE *same as* > CHIPPY
CHIPPIER > CHIPPY
CHIPPIES > CHIPPY
CHIPPIEST > CHIPPY
CHIPPING > CHIP
CHIPPINGS > CHIP
CHIPPY *n* fish-and-chip shop ▷ *adj* resentful or oversensitive about being perceived as inferior
CHIPS > CHIP
CHIPSET *n* highly integrated circuit on the motherboard of a computer that controls many of its data transfer functions
CHIPSETS > CHIPSET
CHIRAGRA *n* gout occurring in the hands
CHIRAGRAS > CHIRAGRA
CHIRAGRIC > CHIRAGRA
CHIRAL > CHIRALITY
CHIRALITY *n* configuration or handedness (left or right) of an asymmetric, optically active chemical compound
CHIRIMOYA *same as* > CHERIMOYA
CHIRK *vb* to creak, like a door ▷ *adj* spritely; high-spirited
CHIRKED > CHIRK
CHIRKER > CHIRK
CHIRKEST > CHIRK
CHIRKING > CHIRK
CHIRKS > CHIRK
CHIRL *vb* to warble
CHIRLED > CHIRL
CHIRLING > CHIRL
CHIRLS > CHIRL
CHIRM *n* chirping of birds ▷ *vb* (esp of a bird) to chirp
CHIRMED > CHIRM
CHIRMING > CHIRM
CHIRMS > CHIRM
CHIRO *n* an informal name for chiropractor
CHIROLOGY *n* palmistry
CHIRONOMY *n* art of hand movement in oratory or theatrical performance
CHIROPODY *n* treatment of the feet, esp the treatment of corns, verrucas, etc
CHIROPTER *n* type of bat
CHIROS > CHIRO
CHIRP *vb* (of a bird or insect) make a short high-pitched sound ▷ *n* chirping sound
CHIRPED > CHIRP
CHIRPER > CHIRP
CHIRPERS > CHIRP
CHIRPIER > CHIRPY
CHIRPIEST > CHIRPY
CHIRPILY > CHIRPY
CHIRPING > CHIRP
CHIRPS > CHIRP
CHIRPY *adj* lively and cheerful
CHIRR *vb* (esp of certain

insects, such as crickets) to make a shrill trilled sound ▷ *n* sound of chirring

CHIRRE *same as* > CHIRR

CHIRRED > CHIRR

CHIRREN *n* dialect form of children

CHIRRES > CHIRRE

CHIRRING > CHIRR

CHIRRS > CHIRR

CHIRRUP *vb* (of some birds) to chirp repeatedly ▷ *n* chirruping sound

CHIRRUPED > CHIRRUP

CHIRRUPER > CHIRRUP

CHIRRUPS > CHIRRUP

CHIRRUPY > CHIRRUP

CHIRT *vb* to squirt

CHIRTED > CHIRT

CHIRTING > CHIRT

CHIRTS > CHIRT

CHIRU *n* Tibetan antelope, *Pantholops hodgsoni*, having a dense woolly pinkish-brown fleece prized as the source of shahtoosh wool: now close to extinction due to illegal slaughter for its fleece

CHIRUS > CHIRU

CHIS > CHI

CHISEL *n* metal tool with a sharp end for shaping wood or stone ▷ *vb* carve or form with a chisel

CHISELED *same as* > CHISELLED

CHISELER > CHISEL

CHISELERS > CHISEL

CHISELING > CHISEL

CHISELLED *adj* finely or sharply formed

CHISELLER *n* person who uses a chisel

CHISELS > CHISEL

CHIT *n* short official note, such as a receipt ▷ *vb* to sprout

CHITAL *n* type of deer

CHITALS > CHITAL

CHITCHAT *n* chat, gossip ▷ *vb* gossip

CHITCHATS > CHITCHAT

CHITIN *n* tough substance forming the outer layer of the bodies of arthropods

CHITINOID > CHITIN

CHITINOUS > CHITIN

CHITINS > CHITIN

CHITLIN > CHITLINS

CHITLING > CHITLINGS

CHITLINGS *same as* > CHIDLINGS

CHITLINS *same as* > CHITTERLINGS

CHITON *n* (in ancient Greece and Rome) a loose woollen tunic worn knee length by men and full length by women

CHITONS > CHITON

CHITOSAN *n* polysaccharide derived from chitin

CHITOSANS > CHITOSAN

CHITS > CHIT

CHITTED > CHIT

CHITTER *vb* twitter or chirp

CHITTERED > CHITTER

CHITTERS > CHITTER

CHITTIER > CHIT

CHITTIES > CHITTY

CHITTIEST > CHIT

CHITTING > CHIT

CHITTY *same as* > CHIT *adj* childish

CHIV *n* knife ▷ *vb* stab (someone)

CHIVALRIC > CHIVALRY

CHIVALRY *n* courteous behaviour, esp by men towards women

CHIVAREE *same as* > CHARIVARI *vb* to perform a chivaree

CHIVAREED > CHIVAREE

CHIVAREES > CHIVAREE

CHIVARI *same as* > CHARIVARI

CHIVARIED > CHIVARI

CHIVARIES > CHIVARI

CHIVE *n* small Eurasian purple-flowered alliaceous plant, *Allium schoenoprasum*, whose long slender hollow leaves are used in cooking to flavour soups, stews, etc ▷ *vb* file or cut off

CHIVED > CHIVE

CHIVES *same as* > CHIVE

CHIVIED > CHIVY

CHIVIES > CHIVY

CHIVING > CHIVE

CHIVS > CHIV

CHIVVED > CHIV

CHIVVIED > CHIVVY

CHIVVIES > CHIVVY

CHIVVING > CHIV

CHIVVY *same as* > CHIVY

CHIVVYING > CHIVVY

CHIVY *vb* harass or nag ▷ *n* hunt

CHIVYING > CHIVY

CHIYOGAMI *n* type of highly decorated Japanese craft paper

CHIZ *n* cheat ▷ *vb* cheat

CHIZZ *same as* > CHIZ

CHIZZED > CHIZ

CHIZZES > CHIZ

CHIZZING > CHIZ

CHLAMYDES > CHLAMYS

CHLAMYDIA *n* any Gram-negative bacteria of the genus *Chlamydia*, responsible for some sexually transmitted diseases

CHLAMYS *n* woollen cloak worn by ancient Greek soldiers

CHLAMYSES > CHLAMYS

CHLOASMA *n* appearance on a person's skin, esp of the face, of patches of darker colour: associated with hormonal changes caused by liver disease or the use of oral contraceptives

CHLOASMAS > CHLOASMA

CHLORACNE *n* disfiguring skin disease that results from contact with or ingestion or inhalation

of certain chlorinated aromatic hydrocarbons

CHLORAL *n* colourless oily liquid with a pungent odour, made from chlorine and acetaldehyde and used in preparing chloral hydrate and DDT

CHLORALS > CHLORAL

CHLORATE *n* type of chemical salt

CHLORATES > CHLORATE

CHLORDAN *same as* > CHLORDANE

CHLORDANE *n* white insoluble toxic solid

CHLORDANS > CHLORDAN

CHLORELLA *n* any microscopic unicellular green alga of the genus *Chlorella*: some species are used in the preparation of human food

CHLORIC *adj* of or containing chlorine in the pentavalent state

CHLORID *n* type of chlorine compound

CHLORIDE *n* compound of chlorine and another substance

CHLORIDES > CHLORIDE

CHLORIDIC > CHLORIDE

CHLORIDS > CHLORID

CHLORIN *same as* > CHLORINE

CHLORINE *n* strong-smelling greenish-yellow gaseous element, used to disinfect water

CHLORINES > CHLORINE

CHLORINS > CHLORIN

CHLORITE *n* any of a group of green soft secondary minerals consisting of the hydrated silicates of aluminium, iron, and magnesium in monoclinic crystalline form: common in metamorphic rocks

CHLORITES > CHLORITE

CHLORITIC > CHLORITE

CHLOROSES > CHLOROSIS

CHLOROSIS *n* disorder, formerly common in adolescent girls, characterized by pale greenish-yellow skin, weakness, and palpitation and caused by insufficient iron in the body

CHLOROTIC > CHLOROSIS

CHLOROUS *adj* of or containing chlorine in the trivalent state

CHOANA *n* posterior nasal aperture

CHOANAE > CHOANA

CHOBDAR *n* in India and Nepal, king's macebearer or attendant

CHOBDARS > CHOBDAR

CHOC *short form of* > CHOCOLATE

CHOCCIER > CHOCCY

CHOCCIES > CHOCCY

CHOCCIEST > CHOCCY

CHOCCY *n* chocolate ▷ *adj* made of, tasting of, smelling of, or resembling chocolate

CHOCHO *same as* > CHAYOTE

CHOCHOS > CHOCHO

CHOCK *n* block or wedge used to prevent a heavy object from moving ▷ *vb* secure by a chock ▷ *adv* as closely or tightly as possible

CHOCKED > CHOCK

CHOCKER *adj* full up

CHOCKFUL *adj* filled to capacity

CHOCKFULL *variant of* > CHOCKFUL

CHOCKING > CHOCK

CHOCKO *same as* > CHOCO

CHOCKOS > CHOCKO

CHOCKS > CHOCK

CHOCO *n* member of the Australian army

CHOCOLATE *n* sweet food made from cacao seeds ▷ *adj* dark brown

CHOCOLATY > CHOCOLATE

CHOCOS > CHOCO

CHOCS > CHOC

CHOCTAW *n* turn from the inside edge of one skate to the outside edge of the other or vice versa

CHOCTAWS > CHOCTAW

CHODE > CHIDE

CHOENIX *same as* > CHENIX

CHOENIXES > CHOENIX

CHOG *n* core of a piece of fruit

CHOGS > CHOG

CHOICE *n* choosing ▷ *adj* of high quality

CHOICEFUL *adj* fickle

CHOICELY > CHOICE

CHOICER > CHOICE

CHOICES > CHOICE

CHOICEST > CHOICE

CHOIR *n* organized group of singers, esp in church ▷ *vb* to sing in chorus

CHOIRBOY *n* boy who sings in a church choir

CHOIRBOYS > CHOIRBOY

CHOIRED > CHOIR

CHOIRGIRL *n* girl who sings in a choir

CHOIRING > CHOIR

CHOIRLIKE > CHOIR

CHOIRMAN *n* man who sings in a choir

CHOIRMEN > CHOIRMAN

CHOIRS > CHOIR

CHOKE *vb* hinder or stop the breathing of (a person) by strangling or smothering ▷ *n* device controlling the amount of air that is mixed with the fuel in a petrol engine

CHOKEABLE > CHOKE

CHOKEBORE *n* shotgun bore that becomes narrower towards the muzzle so that the shot is not scattered

CHOKECOIL *n* type of electronic inductor

CHOKED *adj* disappointed or angry

CHOKEDAMP *another word for* > BLACKDAMP

CHOKEHOLD *n* act of holding a person's neck across the windpipe, esp from behind

CHOKER *n* tight-fitting necklace

CHOKERS > CHOKER

CHOKES > CHOKE

CHOKEY *n* a slang word for prison ▷ *adj* involving, caused by, or causing choking

CHOKEYS > CHOKEY

CHOKIDAR *n* in India, a gatekeeper

CHOKIDARS > CHOKIDAR

CHOKIER > CHOKEY

CHOKIES > CHOKEY

CHOKIEST > CHOKEY

CHOKING > CHOKE

CHOKINGLY > CHOKE

CHOKO *n* pear-shaped fruit of a tropical American vine, eaten as a vegetable

CHOKOS > CHOKO

CHOKRA *n* in India, a boy or young man

CHOKRAS > CHOKRA

CHOKRI *n* in India, a girl or young woman

CHOKRIS > CHOKRI

CHOKY *same as* > CHOKEY

CHOLA *n* Hispanic girl

CHOLAEMIA *n* toxic medical condition indicated by the presence of bile in the blood

CHOLAEMIC > CHOLAEMIA

CHOLAS > CHOLA

CHOLATE *n* salt of cholic acid

CHOLATES > CHOLATE

CHOLECYST *n* gall bladder

CHOLELITH *n* gallstone

CHOLEMIA *same as* > CHOLAEMIA

CHOLEMIAS > CHOLEMIA

CHOLENT *n* meal usually consisting of a stew of meat, potatoes, and pulses prepared before the Sabbath on Friday and left to cook until eaten for Sabbath lunch

CHOLENTS > CHOLENT

CHOLER *n* bad temper

CHOLERA *n* serious infectious disease causing severe vomiting and diarrhoea

CHOLERAIC > CHOLERA

CHOLERAS > CHOLERA

CHOLERIC *adj* bad-tempered

CHOLEROID > CHOLERA

CHOLERS > CHOLER

CHOLI *n* short-sleeved bodice, as worn by Indian women

CHOLIAMB *n* imperfect iambic trimeter, with a spondee as the last foot

CHOLIAMBS > CHOLIAMB

CHOLIC as in *cholic acid* crystalline acid found in bile

CHOLINE *n* colourless viscous soluble alkaline substance present in animal tissues, esp as a constituent of lecithin: used as a supplement to the diet of poultry and in medicine for preventing the accumulation of fat in the liver

CHOLINES > CHOLINE

CHOLIS > CHOLI

CHOLLA *n* any of several spiny cacti of the genus *Opuntia* that grow in the southwestern US and Mexico and have cylindrical stem segments

CHOLLAS > CHOLLA

CHOLLERS *pl n* jowls or cheeks

CHOLO *n* chicano gangster

CHOLOS > CHOLO

CHOLTRIES > CHOLTRY

CHOLTRY *n* caravanserai

CHOMETZ *same as* > CHAMETZ

CHOMETZES > CHOMETZ

CHOMMIE *n* (in informal South African English) friend

CHOMMIES > CHOMMIE

CHOMP *vb* chew noisily ▷ *n* act or sound of chewing in this manner

CHOMPED > CHOMP

CHOMPER > CHOMP

CHOMPERS > CHOMP

CHOMPING > CHOMP

CHOMPS > CHOMP

CHON *n* North and South Korean monetary unit worth one hundredth of a won

CHONDRAL *adj* of or relating to cartilage

CHONDRE *another word for* > CHONDRULE

CHONDRES > CHONDRE

CHONDRI > CHONDRUS

CHONDRIFY *vb* become or convert into cartilage

CHONDRIN *n* resilient translucent bluish-white substance that forms the matrix of cartilage

CHONDRINS > CHONDRIN

CHONDRITE *n* stony meteorite consisting mainly of silicate minerals in the form of chondrules

CHONDROID *adj* resembling cartilage

CHONDROMA *n* benign cartilaginous growth or neoplasm

CHONDRULE *n* one of the small spherical masses of mainly silicate minerals present in chondrites

CHONDRUS *n* cartilage

CHONS > CHON

CHOOF *vb* go away

CHOOFED > CHOOF

CHOOFING > CHOOF

CHOOFS > CHOOF

CHOOK *n* hen or chicken ▷ *vb*
make the sound of a hen of chicken

CHOOKED > CHOOK

CHOOKIE *same as* > CHOOK

CHOOKIES > CHOOK

CHOOKING > CHOOK

CHOOKS > CHOOK

CHOOM *n* Englishman

CHOOMS > CHOOM

CHOOSE *vb* select from a number of alternatives

CHOOSER > CHOOSE

CHOOSERS > CHOOSE

CHOOSES > CHOOSE

CHOOSEY *same as* > CHOOSY

CHOOSIER > CHOOSY

CHOOSIEST > CHOOSY

CHOOSING > CHOOSE

CHOOSY *adj* fussy, hard to please

CHOP *vb* cut with a blow from an axe or knife ▷ *n* cutting or sharp blow

CHOPHOUSE *n* restaurant specializing in steaks, grills, chops, etc

CHOPIN *same as* > CHOPINE

CHOPINE *n* sandal-like shoe on tall wooden or cork bases popular in the 18th century

CHOPINES > CHOPINE

CHOPINS > CHOPIN

CHOPLOGIC *n* person who uses excessively subtle or involved logic

CHOPPED > CHOP

CHOPPER *n* helicopter ▷ *vb* travel by helicopter

CHOPPERED > CHOPPER

CHOPPERS > CHOPPER

CHOPPIER > CHOPPY

CHOPPIEST > CHOPPY

CHOPPILY > CHOPPY

CHOPPING > CHOP

CHOPPINGS > CHOP

CHOPPY *adj* (of the sea) fairly rough

CHOPS > CHOP

CHOPSOCKY *n* genre of martial arts film

CHOPSTICK *n* one of a pair of thin sticks used as eating utensils

CHORAGI > CHORAGUS

CHORAGIC > CHORAGUS

CHORAGUS *n* leader of a chorus

CHORAL *adj* of a choir

CHORALE *n* slow stately hymn tune

CHORALES > CHORALE

CHORALIST *n* singer or composer of chorals

CHORALLY > CHORAL

CHORALS > CHORAL

CHORD *n* straight line joining two points on a curve ▷ *vb* provide (a melodic line) with chords

CHORDA *n* in anatomy, a cord

CHORDAE > CHORDA

CHORDAL > CHORDA

CHORDATE *n* any animal that has a long fibrous rod just above the gut to
support the body, such as the vertebrates ▷ *adj* of, relating to, or belonging to the *Chordata*

CHORDATES > CHORDATE

CHORDED > CHORD

CHORDEE *n* painful penile erection, a symptom of gonorrhoea

CHORDEES > CHORDEE

CHORDING *n* distribution of chords throughout a piece of harmony

CHORDINGS > CHORDING

CHORDS > CHORD

CHORDWISE *adv* in the direction of an aerofoil chord ▷ *adj* moving in this direction

CHORE *n* routine task ▷ *vb* to carry out chores

CHOREA *n* disorder of the nervous system characterized by uncontrollable brief jerky movements

CHOREAL > CHOREA

CHOREAS > CHOREA

CHOREATIC > CHOREA

CHORED > CHORE

CHOREE *n* trochee

CHOREES > CHOREE

CHOREGI > CHOREGUS

CHOREGIC > CHOREGUS

CHOREGUS *n* in ancient Greece, the producer/ financier of a dramatist's works

CHOREIC > CHOREA

CHOREMAN *n* handyman

CHOREMEN > CHOREMAN

CHOREOID *adj* resembling chorea

CHORES > CHORE

CHOREUS *same as* > CHOREE

CHOREUSES > CHOREUS

CHORIA > CHORION

CHORIAL > CHORION

CHORIAMB *n* metrical foot used in classical verse consisting of four syllables, two short ones between two long ones

CHORIAMBI > CHORIAMB

CHORIAMBS > CHORIAMB

CHORIC *adj* of, like, for, or in the manner of a chorus, esp of singing, dancing, or the speaking of verse

CHORINE *n* chorus girl

CHORINES > CHORINE

CHORING > CHORE

CHORIOID *same as* > CHOROID

CHORIOIDS > CHORIOID

CHORION *n* outer of two membranes that form a sac around the embryonic reptile, bird, or mammal

CHORIONIC > CHORION

CHORIONS > CHORION

CHORISES > CHORISIS

CHORISIS *n* multiplication of leaves etc by branching or splitting

CHORISM > CHORISIS

CHORISMS > CHORISIS

CHORIST n choir member
CHORISTER n singer in a choir
CHORISTS > CHORIST
CHORIZO n kind of highly seasoned pork sausage of Spain or Mexico
CHORIZONT n person who challenges the authorship of a work
CHORIZOS > CHORIZO
CHOROID adj resembling the chorion, esp in being vascular ▷ n brownish vascular membrane of the eyeball between the sclera and the retina
CHOROIDAL > CHOROID
CHOROIDS > CHOROID
CHOROLOGY n study of the causal relations between geographical phenomena occurring within a particular region
CHORRIE n dilapidated old car
CHORRIES > CHORRIE
CHORTEN n Buddhist shrine
CHORTENS > CHORTEN
CHORTLE vb chuckle in amusement ▷ n amused chuckle
CHORTLED > CHORTLE
CHORTLER > CHORTLE
CHORTLERS > CHORTLE
CHORTLES > CHORTLE
CHORTLING > CHORTLE
CHORUS n large choir ▷ vb sing or say together
CHORUSED > CHORUS
CHORUSES > CHORUS
CHORUSING > CHORUS
CHORUSSED > CHORUS
CHORUSSES > CHORUS
CHOSE > CHOOSE
CHOSEN > CHOOSE
CHOSES > CHOOSE
CHOTA adj (in British Empire Indian usage) small
CHOTT a variant spelling of > SHOTT
CHOTTS > CHOTT
CHOU n type of cabbage
CHOUGH n large black Eurasian and N African bird of the crow family
CHOUGHS > CHOUGH
CHOULTRY same as > CHOLTRY
CHOUNTER same as > CHUNTER
CHOUNTERS > CHOUNTER
CHOUSE vb to cheat
CHOUSED > CHOUSE
CHOUSER > CHOUSE
CHOUSERS > CHOUSE
CHOUSES > CHOUSE
CHOUSH n Turkish messenger
CHOUSHES > CHOUSH
CHOUSING > CHOUSE
CHOUT n blackmail
CHOUTS > CHOUT
CHOUX > CHOU
CHOW n thick-coated dog with a curled tail, orig. from China ▷ vb eat

CHOWCHOW same as > CHOW
CHOWCHOWS > CHOWCHOW
CHOWDER n thick soup containing clams or fish ▷ vb to make a chowder of
CHOWDERED > CHOWDER
CHOWDERS > CHOWDER
CHOWED > CHOW
CHOWHOUND n person who loves eating
CHOWING > CHOW
CHOWK n marketplace or market area
CHOWKIDAR same as > CHOKIDAR
CHOWKS > CHOWK
CHOWRI n fly-whisk
CHOWRIES > CHOWRI
CHOWRIS > CHOWRI
CHOWRY same as > CHOWRI
CHOWS > CHOW
CHOWSE same as > CHOUSE
CHOWSED > CHOWSE
CHOWSES > CHOWSE
CHOWSING > CHOWSE
CHOWTIME n mealtime
CHOWTIMES > CHOWTIME
CHRESARD n amount of water present in the soil that is available to plants
CHRESARDS > CHRESARD
CHRISM n consecrated oil used for anointing in some churches
CHRISMA > CHRISMON
CHRISMAL n chrism container
CHRISMALS > CHRISMAL
CHRISMON n monogram and symbol of Christ's name
CHRISMONS > CHRISMON
CHRISMS > CHRISM
CHRISOM same as > CHRISM
CHRISOMS > CHRISOM
CHRISTEN vb baptize
CHRISTENS > CHRISTEN
CHRISTIAN adj exhibiting kindness or goodness
CHRISTIE same as > CHRISTY
CHRISTIES > CHRISTIE
CHRISTOM same as > CHRISOM
CHRISTOMS > CHRISTOM
CHRISTY n skiing turn for stopping or changing direction quickly
CHROMA n attribute of a colour that enables an observer to judge how much chromatic colour it contains irrespective of achromatic colour present
CHROMAKEY n (in colour television) a special effect in which a coloured background can be eliminated and a different background substituted
CHROMAS > CHROMA
CHROMATE n any salt or ester of chromic acid
CHROMATES > CHROMATE
CHROMATIC adj of colour or colours
CHROMATID n either of the two strands into which

a chromosome divides during mitosis. They separate to form daughter chromosomes at anaphase
CHROMATIN n part of the nucleus of a cell that forms the chromosomes and can easily be dyed
CHROME n anything plated with chromium ▷ vb plate with chromium ▷ vb to chromium-plate ▷ adj of or having the appearance of chrome
CHROMED > CHROME
CHROMEL n nickel-based alloy containing about 10 per cent chromium, used in heating elements
CHROMELS > CHROMEL
CHROMENE n chemical compound
CHROMENES > CHROMENE
CHROMES > CHROME
CHROMIC adj of or containing chromium in the trivalent state
CHROMIDE n any member of the cichlid family of fish
CHROMIDES > CHROMIDE
CHROMIDIA n chromatins in cell cytoplasm
CHROMIER > CHROME
CHROMIEST > CHROMY
CHROMING > CHROME
CHROMINGS > CHROME
CHROMISE same as > CHROMIZE
CHROMISED > CHROMISE
CHROMISES > CHROMISE
CHROMITE n brownish-black mineral which is the only commercial source of chromium
CHROMITES > CHROMITE
CHROMIUM n grey metallic element used in steel alloys and for electroplating
CHROMIUMS > CHROMIUM
CHROMIZE vb chrome-plate
CHROMIZED > CHROMIZE
CHROMIZES > CHROMIZE
CHROMO n picture produced by the process of making coloured prints by lithography
CHROMOGEN n compound that forms coloured compounds on oxidation
CHROMOS > CHROMO
CHROMOUS adj of or containing chromium in the divalent state
CHROMY adj
CHROMYL n of, consisting of, or containing the divalent radical CrO_2
CHROMYLS > CHROMYL
CHRONAXIE n minimum time required for excitation of a nerve or muscle when the stimulus is double the minimum (threshold) necessary to elicit a basic response
CHRONAXY same as > CHRONAXIE

CHRONIC adj (of an illness) lasting a long time ▷ n chronically-ill patient
CHRONICAL > CHRONIC
CHRONICLE n record of events in order of occurrence ▷ vb record in or as if in a chronicle
CHRONICS > CHRONIC
CHRONON n unit of time equal to the time that a photon would take to traverse the diameter of an electron: about 10^{-24} seconds
CHRONONS > CHRONON
CHRYSALID adj of or relating to a chrysalis
CHRYSALIS n insect in the stage between larva and adult, when it is in a cocoon
CHRYSANTH n chrysanthemum
CHTHONIAN adj of or relating to the underworld
CHTHONIC same as > CHTHONIAN
CHUB n European freshwater fish of the carp family
CHUBASCO n in Mexico, a hurricane
CHUBASCOS > CHUBASCO
CHUBBIER > CHUBBY
CHUBBIEST > CHUBBY
CHUBBILY > CHUBBY
CHUBBY adj plump and round
CHUBS > CHUB
CHUCK vb throw ▷ n cut of beef from the neck to the shoulder
CHUCKED > CHUCK
CHUCKER n person who throws something
CHUCKERS > CHUCKER
CHUCKHOLE n pothole
CHUCKIE n small stone
CHUCKIES > CHUCKIE
CHUCKING > CHUCK
CHUCKLE vb laugh softly ▷ n soft laugh
CHUCKLED > CHUCKLE
CHUCKLER > CHUCKLE
CHUCKLERS > CHUCKLE
CHUCKLES > CHUCKLE
CHUCKLING > CHUCKLE
CHUCKS > CHUCK
CHUCKY same as > CHUCKIE
CHUDDAH same as > CHUDDAR
CHUDDAHS > CHUDDAH
CHUDDAR n large shawl or veil worn by Muslim or Hindu women that covers them from head to foot
CHUDDARS > CHUDDAR
CHUDDER same as > CHUDDAR
CHUDDERS > CHUDDER
CHUDDIES pl n underpants
CHUDDY n chewing gum
CHUFA n sedge, Cyperus esculentus, of warm regions of the Old World, with nutlike edible tubers
CHUFAS > CHUFA
CHUFF vb (of a steam engine) move while

Section 1: Words between 2 and 9 letters in length

making a puffing sound ▷ *n* puffing sound of or as if of a steam engine ▷ *adj* boorish

CHUFFED *adj* very pleased

CHUFFER > CHUFF

CHUFFEST > CHUFF

CHUFFIER > CHUFFY

CHUFFIEST > CHUFFY

CHUFFING > CHUFF

CHUFFS > CHUFF

CHUFFY *adj* boorish and surly

CHUG *n* short dull sound like the noise of an engine ▷ *vb* operate or move with this sound

CHUGALUG *vb* to gulp down a drink in one go

CHUGALUGS > CHUGALUG

CHUGGED > CHUG

CHUGGER > CHUG

CHUGGERS > CHUG

CHUGGING > CHUG

CHUGS > CHUG

CHUKAR *n* common Indian partridge, *Alectoris chukar* (or *graeca*), having red legs and bill and a black-barred sandy plumage

CHUKARS > CHUKAR

CHUKKA *n* period of play in polo

CHUKKAR *same as* > CHUKKA

CHUKKARS > CHUKKAR

CHUKKAS > CHUKKA

CHUKKER *same as* > CHUKKA

CHUKKERS > CHUKKER

CHUKOR *same as* > CHUKAR

CHUKORS > CHUKOR

CHUM *n* close friend ▷ *vb* be or become an intimate friend (of)

CHUMASH *n* printed book containing one of the Five Books of Moses

CHUMASHES > CHUMASH

CHUMLEY *same as* > CHIMNEY

CHUMLEYS > CHUMLEY

CHUMMAGE *n* formerly, fee paid by a prisoner for sole occupancy of a cell

CHUMMAGES > CHUMMAGE

CHUMMED > CHUM

CHUMMIER > CHUMMY

CHUMMIES > CHUMMY

CHUMMIEST > CHUMMY

CHUMMILY > CHUMMY

CHUMMING > CHUM

CHUMMY *adj* friendly ▷ *n* chum

CHUMP *n* stupid person ▷ *vb* chew noisily

CHUMPED > CHUMP

CHUMPING *n* collecting wood for bonfires on Guy Fawkes Day

CHUMPINGS > CHUMPING

CHUMPS > CHUMP

CHUMS > CHUM

CHUMSHIP *n* friendship

CHUMSHIPS > CHUMSHIP

CHUNDER *vb* vomit ▷ *n* vomit

CHUNDERED > CHUNDER

CHUNDERS > CHUNDER

CHUNK *n* thick solid piece

▷ *vb* to break up into chunks

CHUNKED > CHUNK

CHUNKIER > CHUNKY

CHUNKIEST > CHUNKY

CHUNKILY > CHUNKY

CHUNKING *n* grouping together of a number of items by the mind, after which they can be remembered as a single item, such as a word or a musical phrase

CHUNKINGS > CHUNKING

CHUNKS > CHUNK

CHUNKY *adj* (of a person) broad and heavy

CHUNNEL *n* rail tunnel beneath the English Channel, linking England and France

CHUNNELS > CHUNNEL

CHUNNER *same as* > CHUNTER

CHUNNERED > CHUNNER

CHUNNERS > CHUNNER

CHUNTER *vb* mutter or grumble incessantly in a meaningless fashion

CHUNTERED > CHUNTER

CHUNTERS > CHUNTER

CHUPATI *same as* > CHUPATTI

CHUPATIS > CHUPATI

CHUPATTI *variant spellings of* > CHAPATI

CHUPATTIS > CHUPATTI

CHUPATTY *same as* > CHUPATTI

CHUPPA *variant of* > CHUPPAH

CHUPPAH *n* canopy under which a marriage is performed

CHUPPAHS > CHUPPAH

CHUPPAS > CHUPPA

CHUPRASSY *same as* > CHAPRASSI

CHURCH *n* building for public Christian worship ▷ *vb* bring (someone, esp a woman after childbirth) to church for special ceremonies

CHURCHED > CHURCH

CHURCHES > CHURCH

CHURCHIER > CHURCHY

CHURCHING > CHURCH

CHURCHISM *n* adherence to the principles of an established church

CHURCHLY *adj* appropriate to, associated with, or suggestive of church life and customs

CHURCHMAN *n* clergyman

CHURCHMEN > CHURCHMAN

CHURCHWAY *n* way or road that leads to a church

CHURCHY *adj* like a church, church service, etc

CHURIDAR *as in churidar pyjamas* long tight-fitting trousers, worn by Indian men and women

CHURIDARS > CHURIDAR

CHURINGA *n* sacred amulet of the native Australians

CHURINGAS > CHURINGA

CHURL *n* surly ill-bred person

CHURLISH *adj* surly and rude

CHURLS > CHURL

CHURN *n* machine in which cream is shaken to make butter ▷ *vb* stir (cream) vigorously to make butter

CHURNED > CHURN

CHURNER > CHURN

CHURNERS > CHURN

CHURNING *n* quantity of butter churned at any one time

CHURNINGS > CHURNING

CHURNMILK *n* buttermilk

CHURNS > CHURN

CHURR *same as* > CHIRR

CHURRED > CHURR

CHURRING > CHURR

CHURRO *n* Spanish dough stick snack

CHURROS > CHURRO

CHURRS > CHURR

CHURRUS *n* hemp resin

CHURRUSES > CHURRUS

CHUSE *obsolete variant of* > CHOOSE

CHUSES > CHUSE

CHUSING > CHUSE

CHUT *interj* expression of surprise or annoyance ▷ *vb* make such an expression

CHUTE *n* steep slope down which things may be slid ▷ *vb* to descend by a chute

CHUTED > CHUTE

CHUTES > CHUTE

CHUTING > CHUTE

CHUTIST > CHUTE

CHUTISTS > CHUTE

CHUTNEE *same as* > CHUTNEY

CHUTNEES > CHUTNEE

CHUTNEY *n* pickle made from fruit, vinegar, spices, and sugar

CHUTNEYS > CHUTNEY

CHUTZPA *same as* > CHUTZPAH

CHUTZPAH *n* unashamed self-confidence

CHUTZPAHS > CHUTZPAH

CHUTZPAS > CHUTZPA

CHYACK *same as* > CHIACK

CHYACKED > CHYACK

CHYACKING > CHYACK

CHYACKS > CHYACK

CHYLDE *archaic word for* > CHILD

CHYLE *n* milky fluid formed in the small intestine during digestion

CHYLES > CHYLE

CHYLIFIED > CHYLIFY

CHYLIFIES > CHYLIFY

CHYLIFY *vb* to be turned into chyle

CHYLOUS > CHYLE

CHYLURIA *n* presence of chyle in urine

CHYLURIAS > CHYLURIA

CHYME *n* thick fluid mass of partially digested food that leaves the stomach

CHYMES > CHYME

CHYMIC *same as* > CHEMIC

CHYMICS > CHYMIC

CHYMIFIED > CHYMIFY

CHYMIFIES > CHYMIFY

CHYMIFY *vb* to form into chyme

CHYMIST *same as* > CHEMIST

CHYMISTRY *same as* > CHEMISTRY

CHYMISTS > CHYMIST

CHYMOSIN *another name for* > RENNIN

CHYMOSINS > CHYMOSIN

CHYMOUS > CHYME

CHYND *adj* chined

CHYPRE *n* perfume made from sandalwood

CHYPRES > CHYPRE

CHYTRID *n* variety of fungus

CHYTRIDS > CHYTRID

CIABATTA *n* type of bread made with olive oil

CIABATTAS > CIABATTA

CIABATTE > CIABATTA

CIAO *an informal word for* > HELLO

CIAOS > CIAO

CIBATION *n* feeding

CIBATIONS > CIBATION

CIBOL *same as* > CHIBOL

CIBOLS > CIBOL

CIBORIA > CIBORIUM

CIBORIUM *n* goblet-shaped lidded vessel used to hold consecrated wafers in Holy Communion

CIBOULE *same as* > CHIBOL

CIBOULES > CIBOULE

CICADA *n* large insect that makes a high-pitched drone

CICADAE > CICADA

CICADAS > CICADA

CICALA *same as* > CICADA

CICALAS > CICALA

CICALE > CICALA

CICATRICE *n* scar

CICATRISE *same as* > CICATRIZE

CICATRIX *n* scar

CICATRIZE *vb* (of a wound or defect in tissue) to close or be closed by scar formation

CICELIES > CICELY

CICELY *n* type of plant

CICERO *n* measure for type that is somewhat larger than the pica

CICERONE *n* person who guides and informs sightseers ▷ *vb* to act as a cicerone

CICERONED > CICERONE

CICERONES > CICERONE

CICERONI > CICERONE

CICEROS > CICERO

CICHLID *n* any tropical freshwater percoid fish of the family *Cichlidae*, which includes the mouthbrooders. Cichlids are popular aquarium fishes ▷ *adj* of, relating to, or belonging to the *Cichlidae*

CICHLIDAE *n* cichlids

CICHLIDS > CICHLID

CICHLOID > CICHLID

CICINNUS *n* scorpioid cyme

CICISBEI > CICISBEO

CICISBEO *n* escort or lover of a married woman, esp in 18th-century Italy

CICISBEOS > CICISBEO

CICLATON *n* rich material of silk and gold

CICLATONS > CICLATON

CICLATOUN *same as* > CICLATON

CICOREE *same as* > CHICORY

CICOREES > CICOREE

CICUTA *n* spotted hemlock

CICUTAS > CICUTA

CICUTINE *same as* > CONIINE

CICUTINES > CICUTINE

CID *n* leader

CIDARIS *n* sea urchin

CIDARISES > CIDARIS

CIDE *Shakespearean variant of* > DECIDE

CIDED > CIDE

CIDER *n* alcoholic drink made from fermented apple juice

CIDERKIN *n* weak type of cider

CIDERKINS > CIDERKIN

CIDERS > CIDER

CIDERY > CIDER

CIDES > CIDE

CIDING > CIDE

CIDS > CID

CIEL *same as* > CEIL

CIELED > CIEL

CIELING > CIEL

CIELINGS > CIEL

CIELS > CIEL

CIERGE *same as* > CERGE

CIERGES > CIERGE

CIG *same as* > CIGARETTE

CIGAR *n* roll of cured tobacco leaves for smoking

CIGARET *same as* > CIGARETTE

CIGARETS > CIGARET

CIGARETTE *n* thin roll of shredded tobacco in thin paper, for smoking

CIGARILLO *n* small cigar often only slightly larger than a cigarette

CIGARLIKE > CIGAR

CIGARS > CIGAR

CIGGIE *same as* > CIGARETTE

CIGGIES > CIGGIE

CIGGY > CIGARETTE

CIGS > CIG

CIGUATERA *n* food poisoning caused by a toxin in seafood

CILANTRO > CORIANDER

CILANTROS > CILANTRO

CILIA > CILIUM

CILIARY *adj* of or relating to cilia

CILIATE *adj* possessing or relating to cilia ▷ *n* protozoan of the phylum *Ciliophora*

CILIATED > CILIATE

CILIATELY > CILIATE

CILIATES > CILIATE

CILIATION > CILIATE

CILICE *n* haircloth fabric or garment

CILICES > CILICE

CILICIOUS *adj* made of hair

CILIOLATE *adj* covered with minute hairs, as some plants

CILIUM *n* short thread projecting from a cell, whose rhythmic beating causes movement

CILL *a variant spelling (used in the building industry)* for > SILL

CILLS > CILL

CIMAR *same as* > CYMAR

CIMARS > CIMAR

CIMBALOM *n* type of dulcimer, esp of Hungary

CIMBALOMS > CIMBALOM

CIMELIA *n* (especially, ecclesiastical) treasures

CIMEX *n* any of the heteropterous insects of the genus *Cimex*, esp the bedbug

CIMICES > CIMEX

CIMIER *n* crest of a helmet

CIMIERS > CIMIER

CIMINITE *n* type of igneous rock

CIMINITES > CIMINITE

CIMMERIAN *adj* very dark or gloomy

CIMOLITE *n* clayey, whitish mineral

CIMOLITES > CIMOLITE

CINCH *n* easy task ▷ *vb* fasten a girth around (a horse)

CINCHED > CINCH

CINCHES > CINCH

CINCHING > CINCH

CINCHINGS > CINCH

CINCHONA *same as* > CALISAYA

CINCHONAS > CINCHONA

CINCHONIC > CINCHONA

CINCINNUS *same as* > CICINNUS

CINCT *adj* encircled

CINCTURE *n* something, such as a belt or girdle, that goes around another thing ▷ *vb* to encircle

CINCTURED > CINCTURE

CINCTURES > CINCTURE

CINDER *n* piece of material that will not burn, left after burning coal ▷ *vb* burn to cinders

CINDERED > CINDER

CINDERING > CINDER

CINDEROUS > CINDER

CINDERS > CINDER

CINDERY > CINDER

CINE *as in cine camera* camera able to film moving pictures

CINEAST *same as* > CINEASTE

CINEASTE *n* enthusiast for films

CINEASTES > CINEASTE

CINEASTS > CINEAST

CINEMA *n* place for showing films

CINEMAS > CINEMA

CINEMATIC > CINEMA

CINEOL *n* colourless oily liquid with a camphor-like odour and a spicy taste

CINEOLE *same as* > CINEOL

CINEOLES > CINEOLE

CINEOLS > CINEOL

CINEPHILE *n* film enthusiast

CINEPLEX *n* (tradename for) a large cinema complex

CINERAMIC *adj* relating to a cinematic process producing widescreen images

CINERARIA *n* garden plant with daisy-like flowers

CINERARY *adj* of (someone's) ashes

CINERATOR *same as* > CREMATOR

CINEREA *n* grey matter of the brain and nervous system

CINEREAL *adj* ashy

CINEREAS > CINEREA

CINEREOUS *adj* of a greyish colour

CINERIN *n* either of two organic compounds used as insecticides

CINERINS > CINERIN

CINES > CINE

CINGULA > CINGULUM

CINGULAR *adj* ring-shaped

CINGULATE > CINGULUM

CINGULUM *n* girdle-like part, such as the ridge round the base of a tooth or the band of fibres connecting parts of the cerebrum

CINNABAR *n* heavy red mineral containing mercury

CINNABARS > CINNABAR

CINNAMIC > CINNAMON

CINNAMON *n* spice obtained from the bark of an Asian tree

CINNAMONS > CINNAMON

CINNAMONY > CINNAMON

CINNAMYL *n* univalent radical of cinnamic compounds

CINNAMYLS > CINNAMYL

CINQUAIN *n* stanza of five lines

CINQUAINS > CINQUAIN

CINQUE *n* number five in cards, dice, etc

CINQUES > CINQUE

CION *same as* > SCION

CIONS > CION

CIOPPINO *n* Italian rich fish stew

CIOPPINOS > CIOPPINO

CIPHER *n* system of secret writing ▷ *vb* put (a message) into secret writing

CIPHERED > CIPHER

CIPHERER > CIPHER

CIPHERERS > CIPHER

CIPHERING > CIPHER

CIPHERS > CIPHER

CIPHONIES > CIPHONY

CIPHONY *n* ciphered telephony; process of enciphering audio information, producing encrypted speech

CIPOLIN *n* Italian marble with alternating white and green streaks

CIPOLINS > CIPOLIN

CIPOLLINO *same as* > CIPOLIN

CIPPI > CIPPUS

CIPPUS *n* pillar bearing an inscription

CIRCA *prep* approximately, about

CIRCADIAN *adj* of biological processes that occur regularly at 24-hour intervals

CIRCAR *n* in India, part of a province

CIRCARS > CIRCAR

CIRCINATE *adj* (of part of a plant, such as a young fern) coiled so that the tip is at the centre

CIRCITER *prep* around, about

CIRCLE *n* perfectly round geometric figure, line, or shape ▷ *vb* move in a circle (round)

CIRCLED > CIRCLE

CIRCLER > CIRCLE

CIRCLERS > CIRCLE

CIRCLES > CIRCLE

CIRCLET *n* circular ornament worn on the head

CIRCLETS > CIRCLET

CIRCLING > CIRCLE

CIRCLINGS > CIRCLE

CIRCLIP *n* flat spring ring split at one point so that it can be sprung open, passed over a shaft or spindle, and allowed to close into a closely fitting annular recess to form a collar on the shaft. A similar design can be closed to pass into a bore and allowed to spring out into an annular recess to form a shoulder in the bore

CIRCLIPS > CIRCLIP

CIRCS *pl n* circumstances

CIRCUIT *n* complete route or course, esp a circular one ▷ *vb* make or travel in a circuit around (something)

CIRCUITAL > CIRCUIT

CIRCUITED > CIRCUIT

CIRCUITRY *n* electrical circuit(s)

CIRCUITS > CIRCUIT

CIRCUITY *n* (of speech, reasoning, etc) a roundabout or devious quality

CIRCULAR *adj* in the shape of a circle ▷ *n* letter for general distribution

CIRCULARS > CIRCULAR

CIRCULATE *vb* send, go, or

C

pass from place to place or person to person

CIRCUS *n* (performance given by) a travelling company of acrobats, clowns, performing animals, etc

CIRCUSES > CIRCUS

CIRCUSSY > CIRCUS

CIRCUSY > CIRCUS

CIRE *adj* (of fabric) treated with a heat or wax process to make it smooth ▷ *n* such a surface on a fabric

CIRES > CIRE

CIRL *n* bird belonging to the bunting family

CIRLS > CIRL

CIRQUE *n* steep-sided semicircular hollow found in mountainous areas

CIRQUES > CIRQUE

CIRRATE *adj* bearing or resembling cirri

CIRRHOSED > CIRRHOSIS

CIRRHOSES > CIRRHOSIS

CIRRHOSIS *n* serious liver disease, often caused by drinking too much alcohol

CIRRHOTIC > CIRRHOSIS

CIRRI > CIRRUS

CIRRIFORM *adj* cirrus-like

CIRRIPED *same as* > CIRRIPEDE

CIRRIPEDE *n* any marine crustacean of the subclass *Cirripedia*, including the barnacles, the adults of which are sessile or parasitic ▷ *adj* of, relating to, or belonging to the *Cirripedia*

CIRRIPEDS > CIRRIPED

CIRROSE *same as* > CIRRATE

CIRROUS *same as* > CIRRATE

CIRRUS *n* high wispy cloud

CIRSOID *adj* resembling a varix

CIS *adj* having two groups of atoms on the same side of a double bond

CISALPINE *adj* on this (the southern) side of the Alps, as viewed from Rome

CISCO *n* whitefish, esp the lake herring of cold deep lakes of North America

CISCOES > CISCO

CISCOS > CISCO

CISELEUR *n* person who is expert in ciselure

CISELEURS > CISELEUR

CISELURE *n* art or process of chasing metal

CISELURES > CISELURE

CISLUNAR *adj* of or relating to the space between the earth and the moon

CISPADANE *adj* on this (the southern) side of the River Po, as viewed from Rome

CISPLATIN *n* cytotoxic drug that acts by preventing DNA replication and hence cell division, used in the treatment of tumours, esp of the ovary and testis

CISSIER > CISSY

CISSIES > CISSY

CISSIEST > CISSY

CISSIFIED *another word for* > SISSY

CISSING *n* appearance of pinholes, craters, etc, in paintwork due to poor adhesion of the paint to the surface

CISSINGS > CISSING

CISSOID *n* geometric curve whose two branches meet in a cusp at the origin and are asymptotic to a line parallel to the *y*-axis

CISSOIDS > CISSOID

CISSUS *n* any plant of the climbing genus *Cissus*, some species of which, esp the kangaroo vine (C. *antarctica*) from Australia, are grown as greenhouse or house plants for their shiny green or mottled leaves: family *Vitaceae*

CISSUSES > CISSUS

CISSY *same as* > SISSY

CIST *n* wooden box for holding ritual objects used in ancient Rome and Greece ▷ *vb* make a cist

CISTED > CIST

CISTERN *n* water tank, esp one that holds water for flushing a toilet

CISTERNA *n* sac or partially closed space containing body fluid, esp lymph or cerebrospinal fluid

CISTERNAE > CISTERNA

CISTERNAL > CISTERN

CISTERNS > CISTERN

CISTIC *adj* cist-like

CISTRON *n* section of a chromosome that encodes a single polypeptide chain

CISTRONIC > CISTRON

CISTRONS > CISTRON

CISTS > CIST

CISTUS *n* any plant of the genus *Cistus*

CISTUSES > CISTUS

CISTVAEN *n* pre-Christian stone coffin or burial chamber

CISTVAENS > CISTVAEN

CIT *n* pejorative term for a town dweller

CITABLE > CITE

CITADEL *n* fortress in a city

CITADELS > CITADEL

CITAL *n* court summons

CITALS > CITAL

CITATION *n* commendation for bravery

CITATIONS > CITATION

CITATOR *n* legal publication listing cases and statutes, their history and current status

CITATORS > CITATOR

CITATORY > CITATION

CITE *vb* quote, refer to

CITEABLE > CITE

CITED > CITE

CITER > CITE

CITERS > CITE

CITES > CITE

CITESS *n* female cit

CITESSES > CITESS

CITHARA *n* stringed musical instrument of ancient Greece and elsewhere, similar to the lyre and played with a plectrum

CITHARAS > CITHARA

CITHARIST *n* player of the cithara

CITHER *same as* > CITTERN

CITHERN > CITTERN

CITHERNS > CITHERN

CITHERS > CITHER

CITHREN *same as* > CITHARA

CITHRENS > CITHREN

CITIED *adj* having cities

CITIES > CITY

CITIFIED > CITIFY

CITIFIES > CITIFY

CITIFY *vb* cause to conform to or adopt the customs, habits, or dress of city people

CITIFYING > CITIFY

CITIGRADE *adj* relating to (fast-moving) wolf spiders

CITING > CITE

CITIZEN *n* native or naturalized member of a state or nation

CITIZENLY > CITIZEN

CITIZENRY *n* citizens collectively

CITIZENS > CITIZEN

CITO *adv* swiftly

CITOLA *n* type of medieval stringed instrument

CITOLAS > CITOLA

CITOLE *a rare word for* > CITTERN

CITOLES > CITOLE

CITRAL *n* yellow volatile liquid with a lemon-like odour, found in oils of lemon grass, orange, and lemon and used in perfumery

CITRALS > CITRAL

CITRANGE *n* type of acidic and aromatic orange

CITRANGES > CITRANGE

CITRATE *n* any salt or ester of citric acid

CITRATED *adj* treated with a citrate

CITRATES > CITRATE

CITREOUS *adj* of a greenish-yellow colour

CITRIC *adj* of or derived from citrus fruits or citric acid

CITRIN *n* vitamin P

CITRINE *n* brownish-yellow variety of quartz: a gemstone

CITRINES > CITRINE

CITRININ *n* a mycotoxin

CITRININS > CITRININ

CITRINS > CITRIN

CITRON *n* lemon-like fruit of a small Asian tree

CITRONS > CITRON

CITROUS *same as* > CITRUS

CITRUS *n* any tree or

shrub of the tropical and subtropical rutaceous genus *Citrus*, which includes the orange, lemon, lime, grapefruit, citron, and calamondin ▷ *adj* of, relating to, or belonging to the genus *Citrus* or to the fruits of plants of this genus

CITRUSES > CITRUS

CITRUSSY *adj* having or resembling the taste or colour of a citrus fruit

CITRUSY *same as* > CITRUSSY

CITS > CIT

CITTERN *n* medieval stringed instrument resembling a lute but having wire strings and a flat back

CITTERNS > CITTERN

CITY *n* large or important town

CITYFIED > CITYFY

CITYFIES > CITYFY

CITYFY *same as* > CITIFY

CITYFYING > CITYFY

CITYSCAPE *n* urban landscape

CITYWARD *adv* towards a city

CITYWIDE *adj* occurring throughout a city

CIVE *same as* > CHIVE

CIVES > CIVE

CIVET *n* spotted catlike African mammal

CIVETLIKE > CIVET

CIVETS > CIVET

CIVIC *adj* of a city or citizens

CIVICALLY > CIVIC

CIVICISM *n* principle of civil government

CIVICISMS > CIVICISM

CIVICS *n* study of the rights and responsibilities of citizenship

CIVIE *same as* > CIVVY

CIVIES > CIVIE

CIVIL *adj* relating to the citizens of a state as opposed to the armed forces or the Church

CIVILIAN *adj* not belonging to the armed forces ▷ *n* person who is not a member of the armed forces or police

CIVILIANS > CIVILIAN

CIVILISE *same as* > CIVILIZE

CIVILISED *same as* > CIVILIZED

CIVILISER > CIVILISE

CIVILISES > CIVILISE

CIVILIST *n* civilian

CIVILISTS > CIVILIST

CIVILITY *n* polite or courteous behaviour

CIVILIZE *vb* refine or educate (a person)

CIVILIZED *adj* having a high state of culture and social development

CIVILIZER > CIVILIZE

CIVILIZES > CIVILIZE

CIVILLY > CIVIL

CIVILNESS > CIVIL

CIVISM n good citizenship

CIVISMS > CIVISM

CIVVIES > CIVVY

CIVVY n civilian

CIZERS archaic spelling of > SCISSORS

CLABBER vb to cover with mud

CLABBERED > CLABBER

CLABBERS > CLABBER

CLACH n stone

CLACHAN n small village

CLACHANS > CLACHAN

CLACHS > CLACH

CLACK n sound made by two hard objects striking each other ▷ vb make this sound

CLACKBOX n casing enclosing a clack

CLACKDISH n formerly, a dish carried by a beggar

CLACKED > CLACK

CLACKER n object that makes a clacking sound

CLACKERS > CLACKER

CLACKING > CLACK

CLACKS > CLACK

CLAD vb bond a metal to (another metal), esp to form a protective coat

CLADDAGH n Irish ring

CLADDAGHS > CLADDAGH

CLADDED adj covered with cladding

CLADDER > CLAD

CLADDERS > CLAD

CLADDIE another name for > KORARI

CLADDIES > CLADDIE

CLADDING > CLOTHE

CLADDINGS > CLOTHE

CLADE n group of organisms considered as having evolved from a common ancestor

CLADES > CLADE

CLADISM > CLADIST

CLADISMS > CLADIST

CLADIST n proponent of cladistics: a method of grouping animals that makes use of lines of descent rather than structural similarities

CLADISTIC > CLADIST

CLADISTS > CLADIST

CLADODE n flattened stem resembling and functioning as a leaf, as in butcher's-broom

CLADODES > CLADODE

CLADODIAL > CLADODE

CLADOGRAM n treelike diagram illustrating the development of a clade

CLADS > CLAD

CLAES Scots word for > CLOTHES

CLAFOUTI same as > CLAFOUTIS

CLAFOUTIS n French baked pudding

CLAG n sticky mud ▷ vb stick, as mud

CLAGGED > CLAG

CLAGGIER > CLAGGY

CLAGGIEST > CLAGGY

CLAGGING > CLAG

CLAGGY adj stickily clinging, as mud

CLAGS > CLAG

CLAIM vb assert as a fact ▷ n assertion that something is true

CLAIMABLE > CLAIM

CLAIMANT n person who makes a claim

CLAIMANTS > CLAIMANT

CLAIMED > CLAIM

CLAIMER > CLAIM

CLAIMERS > CLAIM

CLAIMING > CLAIM

CLAIMS > CLAIM

CLAM n edible shellfish with a hinged shell ▷ vb gather clams

CLAMANCY n urgency

CLAMANT adj noisy

CLAMANTLY > CLAMANT

CLAMBAKE n picnic, often by the sea, at which clams, etc, are baked

CLAMBAKES > CLAMBAKE

CLAMBE old variant of > CLIMB

CLAMBER vb climb awkwardly ▷ n climb performed in this manner

CLAMBERED > CLAMBER

CLAMBERER > CLAMBER

CLAMBERS > CLAMBER

CLAME archaic variant of > CLAIM

CLAMES > CLAIM

CLAMLIKE > CLAM

CLAMMED > CLAM

CLAMMER n person who gathers clams

CLAMMERS > CLAMMER

CLAMMIER > CLAMMY

CLAMMIEST > CLAMMY

CLAMMILY > CLAMMY

CLAMMING > CLAM

CLAMMY adj unpleasantly moist and sticky

CLAMOR same as > CLAMOUR

CLAMORED > CLAMOR

CLAMORER > CLAMOR

CLAMORERS > CLAMOR

CLAMORING > CLAMOR

CLAMOROUS > CLAMOR

CLAMORS > CLAMOR

CLAMOUR n loud protest ▷ vb make a loud noise or outcry

CLAMOURED > CLAMOUR

CLAMOURER > CLAMOUR

CLAMOURS > CLAMOUR

CLAMP n tool with movable jaws for holding things together tightly ▷ vb fasten with a clamp

CLAMPDOWN n sudden restrictive measure

CLAMPED > CLAMP

CLAMPER n spiked metal frame fastened to the sole of a shoe to prevent slipping on ice ▷ vb to tread heavily

CLAMPERED > CLAMPER

CLAMPERS > CLAMPER

CLAMPING > CLAMP

CLAMPS > CLAMP

CLAMS > CLAM

CLAMSHELL n dredging bucket that is hinged like the shell of a clam

CLAMWORM the US name for the > RAGWORM

CLAMWORMS > CLAMWORM

CLAN n group of families with a common ancestor, esp among Scottish Highlanders

CLANG vb make a loud ringing metallic sound ▷ n ringing metallic sound

CLANGBOX n device fitted to a jet-engine to change the direction of thrust

CLANGED > CLANG

CLANGER n obvious mistake

CLANGERS > CLANGER

CLANGING > CLANG

CLANGINGS > CLANG

CLANGOR same as > CLANGOUR

CLANGORED > CLANGOR

CLANGORS > CLANGOR

CLANGOUR n loud continuous clanging sound ▷ vb make or produce a loud resonant noise

CLANGOURS > CLANGOUR

CLANGS > CLANG

CLANK n harsh metallic sound ▷ vb make such a sound

CLANKED > CLANK

CLANKIER > CLANKY

CLANKIEST > CLANKY

CLANKING > CLANK

CLANKINGS > CLANK

CLANKS > CLANK

CLANKY adj making clanking sounds

CLANNISH adj (of a group) tending to exclude outsiders

CLANS > CLAN

CLANSHIP n association of families under the leadership of a chieftain

CLANSHIPS > CLANSHIP

CLANSMAN n man belonging to a clan

CLANSMEN > CLANSMAN

CLAP vb applaud by hitting the palms of one's hands sharply together ▷ n act or sound of clapping

CLAPBOARD n long thin timber board with one edge thicker than the other, used esp in the US and Canada in wood-frame construction by lapping each board over the one below ▷ vb cover with such boards

CLAPBREAD n type of cake made from oatmeal

CLAPDISH same as > CLACKDISH

CLAPNET n net that can be closed instantly by pulling a string

CLAPNETS > CLAPNET

CLAPPED > CLAP

CLAPPER n piece of metal inside a bell, which causes it to sound when struck against the side ▷ vb make a sound like a clapper

CLAPPERED > CLAPPER

CLAPPERS > CLAPPER

CLAPPING > CLAP

CLAPPINGS > CLAP

CLAPS > CLAP

CLAPT old inflection > CLAP

CLAPTRAP n foolish or pretentious talk

CLAPTRAPS > CLAPTRAP

CLAQUE n group of people hired to applaud

CLAQUER same as > CLAQUEUR

CLAQUERS > CLAQUER

CLAQUES > CLAQUE

CLAQUEUR n member of a claque

CLAQUEURS > CLAQUEUR

CLARAIN n one of the four major lithotypes of banded coal

CLARAINS > CLARAIN

CLARENCE n closed four-wheeled horse-drawn carriage, having a glass front

CLARENCES > CLARENCE

CLARENDON n style of boldface roman type

CLARET n dry red wine from Bordeaux ▷ adj purplish-red ▷ vb to drink claret

CLARETED > CLARET

CLARETING > CLARET

CLARETS > CLARET

CLARIES > CLARY

CLARIFIED > CLARIFY

CLARIFIER > CLARIFY

CLARIFIES > CLARIFY

CLARIFY vb make (a matter) clear and unambiguous

CLARINET n keyed woodwind instrument with a single reed

CLARINETS > CLARINET

CLARINI > CLARINO

CLARINO adj of or relating to a high passage for the trumpet in 18th-century music ▷ n high register of the trumpet

CLARINOS > CLARINO

CLARION n obsolete high-pitched trumpet ▷ adj clear and ringing ▷ vb proclaim loudly

CLARIONED > CLARION

CLARIONET same as > CLARINET

CLARIONS > CLARION

CLARITIES > CLARITY

CLARITY n clearness

CLARKIA n any North American onagraceous plant of the genus Clarkia: cultivated for their red, purple, or pink flowers

CLARKIAS > CLARKIA

CLARO n mild light-coloured

cigar
CLAROES > CLARO
CLAROS > CLARO
CLARSACH n Celtic harp of Scotland and Ireland
CLARSACHS > CLARSACH
CLART vb to dirty
CLARTED > CLART
CLARTHEAD n slow-witted or stupid person
CLARTIER > CLARTY
CLARTIEST > CLARTY
CLARTING > CLART
CLARTS pl n lumps of mud, esp on shoes
CLARTY adj dirty, esp covered in mud
CLARY n any of several European plants of the genus *Salvia*, having aromatic leaves and blue flowers: family *Lamiaceae* (labiates)
CLASH vb come into conflict ▷ n fight, argument
CLASHED > CLASH
CLASHER > CLASH
CLASHERS > CLASH
CLASHES > CLASH
CLASHING > CLASH
CLASHINGS > CLASH
CLASP n device for fastening things ▷ vb grasp or embrace firmly
CLASPED > CLASP
CLASPER > CLASP
CLASPERS pl n paired organ of male insects, used to clasp the female during copulation
CLASPING > CLASP
CLASPINGS > CLASP
CLASPS > CLASP
CLASPT old inflection of > CLASP
CLASS n group of people sharing a similar social position ▷ vb place in a class
CLASSABLE > CLASS
CLASSED > CLASS
CLASSER > CLASS
CLASSERS > CLASS
CLASSES > CLASSIS
CLASSIBLE adj able to be classed
CLASSIC adj being a typical example of something ▷ n author, artist, or work of art of recognized excellence
CLASSICAL adj of or in a restrained conservative style
CLASSICO adj (of Italian wines) coming from the centre of a specific wine-growing region
CLASSICS pl n the. a body of literature regarded as great or lasting, esp that of ancient Greece or Rome
CLASSIER > CLASSY
CLASSIEST > CLASSY
CLASSIFIC adj relating to classification
CLASSIFY vb divide into

groups with similar characteristics
CLASSILY > CLASSY
CLASSING > CLASS
CLASSINGS > CLASS
CLASSIS n governing body of elders or pastors
CLASSISM n belief that people from certain social or economic classes are superior to others
CLASSISMS > CLASSISM
CLASSIST > CLASSISM
CLASSISTS > CLASSISM
CLASSLESS adj not belonging to a class
CLASSMAN n graduate of Oxford University with a classed honours degree
CLASSMATE n friend or contemporary in the same class of a school
CLASSMEN > CLASSMAN
CLASSON n elementary atomic particle
CLASSONS > CLASSON
CLASSROOM n room in a school where lessons take place
CLASSWORK n school work done in class
CLASSY adj stylish and elegant
CLAST n fragment of a clastic rock
CLASTIC adj (of sedimentary rock, etc) composed of fragments of pre-existing rock that have been transported some distance from their points of origin ▷ n clast
CLASTICS > CLASTIC
CLASTS > CLAST
CLAT n irksome or troublesome task ▷ vb to scrape
CLATCH vb to move making a squelching sound
CLATCHED > CLATCH
CLATCHES > CLATCH
CLATCHING > CLATCH
CLATHRATE adj resembling a net or lattice ▷ n solid compound in which molecules of one substance are physically trapped in the crystal lattice of another
CLATS > CLAT
CLATTED > CLAT
CLATTER n (make) a rattling noise ▷ vb make a rattling noise, as when hard objects hit each other
CLATTERED > CLATTER
CLATTERER > CLATTER
CLATTERS > CLATTER
CLATTERY > CLATTER
CLATTING > CLAT
CLAUCHT vb to seize by force
CLAUCHTED > CLAUCHT
CLAUCHTS > CLAUCHT
CLAUGHT same as > CLAUCHT
CLAUGHTED > CLAUGHT
CLAUGHTS > CLAUGHT
CLAUSAL > CLAUSE

CLAUSE n section of a legal document
CLAUSES > CLAUSE
CLAUSTRA > CLAUSTRUM
CLAUSTRAL same as > CLOISTRAL
CLAUSTRUM n thin layer of gret matter in the brain
CLAUSULA n type of cadence in polyphony
CLAUSULAE > CLAUSULA
CLAUSULAR > CLAUSE
CLAUT same as > CLAT
CLAUTED > CLAUT
CLAUTING > CLAUT
CLAUTS > CLAUT
CLAVATE adj shaped like a club with the thicker end uppermost
CLAVATED same as > CLAVATE
CLAVATELY > CLAVATE
CLAVATION > CLAVATE
CLAVE n one of a pair of hardwood sticks struck together to make a hollow sound, esp to mark the beat of Latin-American dance music
CLAVECIN n harpsichord
CLAVECINS > CLAVECIN
CLAVER vb talk idly ▷ n idle talk
CLAVERED > CLAVER
CLAVERING > CLAVER
CLAVERS > CLAVER
CLAVES > CLAVE
CLAVI > CLAVUS
CLAVICLE n either of the two bones connecting the shoulder blades with the upper part of the breastbone
CLAVICLES > CLAVICLE
CLAVICORN n any beetle of the group *Clavicornia*, including the ladybirds, characterized by club-shaped antennae ▷ adj of, relating to, or belonging to the *Clavicornia*
CLAVICULA n clavicle
CLAVIE n tar-barrel traditionally set alight in Moray in Scotland on Hogmanay
CLAVIER n any keyboard instrument
CLAVIERS > CLAVIER
CLAVIES > CLAVIE
CLAVIFORM same as > CLAVATE
CLAVIGER n key- or club-bearer
CLAVIGERS > CLAVIGER
CLAVIS n key
CLAVULATE adj club-shaped
CLAVUS n corn on the toe
CLAW n sharp hooked nail of a bird or beast ▷ vb tear with claws or nails
CLAWBACK n recovery of a sum of money
CLAWBACKS > CLAWBACK
CLAWED > CLAW
CLAWER > CLAW
CLAWERS > CLAW

CLAWING > CLAW
CLAWLESS > CLAW
CLAWLIKE adj resembling a claw or claws
CLAWS > CLAW
CLAXON same as > KLAXON
CLAXONS > CLAXON
CLAY n fine-grained earth, soft when moist and hardening when baked, used to make bricks and pottery ▷ vb cover or mix with clay
CLAYBANK n dull brownish-orange colour
CLAYBANKS > CLAYBANK
CLAYED > CLAY
CLAYEY > CLAY
CLAYIER > CLAY
CLAYIEST > CLAY
CLAYING > CLAY
CLAYISH > CLAY
CLAYLIKE > CLAY
CLAYMORE n large two-edged sword formerly used by Scottish Highlanders
CLAYMORES > CLAYMORE
CLAYPAN n layer of stiff impervious clay situated just below the surface of the ground, which holds water after heavy rain
CLAYPANS > CLAYPAN
CLAYS > CLAY
CLAYSTONE n compact very fine-grained rock consisting of consolidated clay particles
CLAYTONIA n any low-growing North American succulent portulacaceous plant of the genus *Claytonia*
CLAYWARE n pottery
CLAYWARES > CLAYWARE
CLEAN adj free from dirt or impurities ▷ vb make (something) free from dirt ▷ adv completely
CLEANABLE > CLEAN
CLEANED > CLEAN
CLEANER n person or thing that removes dirt
CLEANERS > CLEANER
CLEANEST > CLEAN
CLEANING n act of cleaning something
CLEANINGS > CLEANING
CLEANLIER > CLEANLY
CLEANLILY > CLEANLY
CLEANLY adv easily or smoothly ▷ adj habitually clean or neat
CLEANNESS > CLEAN
CLEANS > CLEAN
CLEANSE vb make clean
CLEANSED > CLEANSE
CLEANSER n cleansing agent, such as a detergent
CLEANSERS > CLEANSER
CLEANSES > CLEANSE
CLEANSING > CLEANSE
CLEANSKIN n unbranded animal
CLEANUP n process of cleaning up or eliminating something
CLEANUPS > CLEANUP

CLEAR adj free from doubt or confusion ▷ adv in a clear or distinct manner ▷ vb make or become clear
CLEARABLE > CLEAR
CLEARAGE n clearance
CLEARAGES > CLEARAGE
CLEARANCE n clearing
CLEARCOLE n type of size containing whiting ▷ vb paint (a wall) with this size
CLEARCUT n act of felling all trees in area
CLEARCUTS > CLEARCUT
CLEARED > CLEAR
CLEARER > CLEAR
CLEARERS > CLEAR
CLEAREST > CLEAR
CLEAREYED adj having good judgment
CLEARING n treeless area in a wood
CLEARINGS > CLEARING
CLEARLY adv in a clear, distinct, or obvious manner
CLEARNESS > CLEAR
CLEARS > CLEAR
CLEARSKIN same as > CLEANSKIN
CLEARWAY n stretch of road on which motorists may stop in an emergency
CLEARWAYS > CLEARWAY
CLEARWEED n plant like nettle
CLEARWING n type of moth
CLEAT n wedge ▷ vb supply or support with a cleat or cleats
CLEATED > CLEAT
CLEATING > CLEAT
CLEATS > CLEAT
CLEAVABLE > CLEAVE
CLEAVAGE n space between a woman's breasts, as revealed by a low-cut dress
CLEAVAGES > CLEAVAGE
CLEAVE vb split apart ▷ n split
CLEAVED > CLEAVE
CLEAVER n butcher's heavy knife with a square blade
CLEAVERS n plant with small white flowers and sticky fruits
CLEAVES > CLEAVE
CLEAVING > CLEAVE
CLEAVINGS > CLEAVE
CLECHE adj (in heraldry) voided so that only a narrow border is visible
CLECK vb (of birds) to hatch ▷ n piece of gossip
CLECKED > CLECK
CLECKIER > CLECK
CLECKIEST > CLECK
CLECKING > CLECK
CLECKINGS > CLECK
CLECKS > CLECK
CLECKY > CLECK
CLEEK n large hook, such as one used to land fish ▷ vb to seize
CLEEKED > CLEEK
CLEEKING > CLEEK
CLEEKIT > CLEEK
CLEEKS > CLEEK

CLEEP same as > CLEPE
CLEEPED > CLEEP
CLEEPING > CLEEP
CLEEPS > CLEEP
CLEEVE n cliff
CLEEVES > CLEEVE
CLEF n symbol at the beginning of a stave to show the pitch
CLEFS > CLEF
CLEFT > CLEAVE
CLEFTED > CLEAVE
CLEFTING > CLEAVE
CLEFTS > CLEAVE
CLEG another name for a > HORSEFLY
CLEGS > CLEG
CLEIDOIC as in cleidoic egg egg of birds and insects
CLEIK same as > CLEEK
CLEIKS > CLEEK
CLEITHRAL adj covered with a roof
CLEM vb be hungry or cause to be hungry
CLEMATIS n climbing plant with large colourful flowers
CLEMENCY n kind or lenient treatment
CLEMENT adj (of weather) mild
CLEMENTLY > CLEMENT
CLEMMED > CLEM
CLEMMING > CLEM
CLEMS > CLEM
CLENCH vb close or squeeze (one's teeth or fist) tightly ▷ n firm grasp or grip
CLENCHED > CLENCH
CLENCHER > CLENCH
CLENCHERS > CLENCH
CLENCHES > CLENCH
CLENCHING > CLENCH
CLEOME n any herbaceous or shrubby plant of the mostly tropical capparidaceous genus Cleome, esp C. spinosa, cultivated for their clusters of white or purplish flowers with long stamens
CLEOMES > CLEOME
CLEOPATRA n yellow butterfly, Gonepteryx cleopatra, the male of which has its wings flushed with orange
CLEPE vb call by the name of
CLEPED > CLEPE
CLEPES > CLEPE
CLEPING > CLEPE
CLEPSYDRA n ancient device for measuring time by the flow of water or mercury through a small aperture
CLEPT > CLEPE
CLERGIES > CLERGY
CLERGY n priests and ministers as a group
CLERGYMAN n member of the clergy
CLERGYMEN > CLERGYMAN
CLERIC n member of the clergy
CLERICAL adj of clerks or office work

CLERICALS pl n distinctive dress of a clergyman
CLERICATE n clerical post
CLERICITY n condition of being a clergyman
CLERICS > CLERIC
CLERID n beetle that preys on other insects
CLERIDS > CLERID
CLERIHEW n form of comic or satiric verse, consisting of two couplets and containing the name of a well-known person
CLERIHEWS > CLERIHEW
CLERISIES > CLERISY
CLERISY n learned or educated people
CLERK n employee in an office, bank, or court who keeps records, files, and accounts ▷ vb work as a clerk
CLERKDOM > CLERK
CLERKDOMS > CLERK
CLERKED > CLERK
CLERKESS n female office clerk
CLERKING > CLERK
CLERKISH > CLERK
CLERKLIER > CLERKLY
CLERKLIKE adj acting in a scholarly manner
CLERKLING n young or inexperienced clerk
CLERKLY adj of or like a clerk ▷ adv in the manner of a clerk
CLERKS > CLERK
CLERKSHIP > CLERK
CLERUCH n settler in a cleruchy
CLERUCHIA same as > CLERUCHY
CLERUCHS > CLERUCH
CLERUCHY n (in the ancient world) a special type of Athenian colony, in which settlers retained their Athenian citizenship and the community remained a political dependency of Athens
CLEUCH same as > CLOUGH
CLEUCHS > CLEUCH
CLEUGH same as > CLOUGH
CLEUGHS > CLEUGH
CLEVE same as > CLEEVE
CLEVEITE n crystalline variety of the mineral uranitite
CLEVEITES > CLEVEITE
CLEVER adj intelligent, quick at learning
CLEVERER > CLEVER
CLEVEREST > CLEVER
CLEVERISH > CLEVER
CLEVERLY > CLEVER
CLEVES > CLEEVE
CLEVIS n U-shaped component of a shackle for attaching a drawbar to a plough or similar implement
CLEVISES > CLEVIS
CLEW n ball of thread, yarn, or twine ▷ vb coil or roll

into a ball
CLEWED > CLEW
CLEWING > CLEW
CLEWS > CLEW
CLIANTHUS n Australian or NZ plant with slender scarlet flowers
CLICHE n expression or idea that is no longer effective because of overuse ▷ vb use a cliché (in speech or writing)
CLICHED > CLICHE
CLICHEED > CLICHE
CLICHES > CLICHE
CLICK n short sharp sound ▷ vb make this sound
CLICKABLE adj (of a website) having links that can be accessed by clicking a computer mouse
CLICKED > CLICK
CLICKER > CLICK
CLICKERS > CLICK
CLICKET vb make a click
CLICKETED > CLICKET
CLICKETS > CLICKET
CLICKING > CLICK
CLICKINGS > CLICK
CLICKLESS > CLICK
CLICKS > CLICK
CLICKWRAP adj (of agreement) consented to by user clicking computer button
CLIED > CLY
CLIENT n person who uses the services of a professional person or company
CLIENTAGE same as > CLIENTELE
CLIENTAL > CLIENT
CLIENTELE n clients collectively
CLIENTS > CLIENT
CLIES > CLY
CLIFF n steep rock face, esp along the sea shore ▷ vb scale a cliff
CLIFFED > CLIFF
CLIFFHANG vb (of a serial or film) to end on a note of suspense
CLIFFHUNG > CLIFFHANG
CLIFFIER > CLIFF
CLIFFIEST > CLIFF
CLIFFLIKE > CLIFF
CLIFFS > CLIFF
CLIFFY > CLIFF
CLIFT same as > CLIFF
CLIFTED > CLIFF
CLIFTIER > CLIFF
CLIFTIEST > CLIFF
CLIFTS > CLIFF
CLIFTY > CLIFF
CLIMACTIC adj consisting of, involving, or causing a climax
CLIMATAL > CLIMATE
CLIMATE n typical weather conditions of an area ▷ vb acclimatize
CLIMATED > CLIMATE
CLIMATES > CLIMATE
CLIMATIC > CLIMATE
CLIMATING > CLIMATE

CLIMATISE *vb* in Australia, adapt or become accustomed to a new climate or environment

CLIMATIZE *same as* > CLIMATISE

CLIMATURE *n* clime

CLIMAX *n* most intense point of an experience, series of events, or story ▷ *vb* reach a climax

CLIMAXED > CLIMAX

CLIMAXES > CLIMAX

CLIMAXING > CLIMAX

CLIMB *vb* go up, ascend ▷ *n* climbing

CLIMBABLE > CLIMB

CLIMBDOWN *n* act of backing down from opinion

CLIMBED > CLIMB

CLIMBER *n* person or thing that climbs

CLIMBERS > CLIMBER

CLIMBING > CLIMB

CLIMBINGS > CLIMB

CLIMBS > CLIMB

CLIME *n* place or its climate

CLIMES > CLIME

CLINAL > CLINE

CLINALLY > CLINE

CLINAMEN *n* bias

CLINAMENS > CLINAMEN

CLINCH *vb* settle (an argument or agreement) decisively ▷ *n* movement in which one competitor holds on to the other to avoid punches

CLINCHED > CLINCH

CLINCHER *n* something decisive

CLINCHERS > CLINCHER

CLINCHES > CLINCH

CLINCHING > CLINCH

CLINE *n* continuous variation in form between members of a species having a wide variable geographical or ecological range

CLINES > CLINE

CLING *vb* hold tightly or stick closely ▷ *n* tendency of cotton fibres in a sample to stick to each other

CLINGED > CLING

CLINGER > CLING

CLINGERS > CLING

CLINGFILM *n* thin polythene material for wrapping food

CLINGFISH *n* any small marine teleost fish of the family *Gobiesocidae*, having a flattened elongated body with a sucking disc beneath the head for clinging to rocks, etc

CLINGIER > CLING

CLINGIEST > CLING

CLINGING > CLING

CLINGS > CLING

CLINGY > CLING

CLINIC *n* building where outpatients receive medical treatment or advice

CLINICAL *adj* of a clinic

CLINICIAN *n* physician, psychiatrist, etc, who specializes in clinical work as opposed to one engaged in laboratory or experimental studies

CLINICS > CLINIC

CLINIQUE *same as* > CLINIC

CLINIQUES > CLINIC

CLINK *n* (make) a light sharp metallic sound ▷ *vb* make a light sharp metallic sound

CLINKED > CLINK

CLINKER *n* fused coal left over in a fire or furnace ▷ *vb* form clinker during burning

CLINKERED > CLINKER

CLINKERS > CLINKER

CLINKING > CLINK

CLINKS > CLINK

CLINOAXES > CLINOAXIS

CLINOAXIS *n* in a monoclinic crystal, the lateral axis which forms an oblique angle with the vertical axis

CLINOSTAT *n* apparatus for studying tropisms in plants, usually a rotating disc to which the plant is attached so that it receives an equal stimulus on all sides

CLINQUANT *adj* glittering, esp with tinsel ▷ *n* tinsel or imitation gold leaf

CLINT *n* section of a limestone pavement separated from adjacent sections by solution fissures

CLINTONIA *n* any temperate liliaceous plant of the genus *Clintonia*, having white, greenish-yellow, or purplish flowers, broad ribbed leaves, and blue berries

CLINTS > CLINT

CLIP *vb* cut with shears or scissors ▷ *n* short extract of a film

CLIPART *n* large collection of simple drawings stored in a computer

CLIPARTS > CLIPART

CLIPBOARD *n* portable writing board with a clip at the top for holding paper

CLIPE *same as* > CLYPE

CLIPED > CLIPE

CLIPES > CLIPE

CLIPING > CLIPE

CLIPPABLE > CLIP

CLIPPED > CLIP

CLIPPER *n* fast commercial sailing ship

CLIPPERS *pl n* tool for clipping

CLIPPIE *n* bus conductress

CLIPPIES > CLIPPIE

CLIPPING > CLIP

CLIPPINGS > CLIP

CLIPS > CLIP

CLIPSHEAR *n* earwig

CLIPSHEET *n* sheet of paper with text printed on one side only

CLIPT *old inflection of* > CLIP

CLIQUE *n* small exclusive group ▷ *vb* to form a clique

CLIQUED > CLIQUE

CLIQUES > CLIQUE

CLIQUEY *adj* exclusive, confined to a small group

CLIQUIER > CLIQUEY

CLIQUIEST > CLIQUEY

CLIQUING > CLIQUE

CLIQUISH > CLIQUE

CLIQUISM > CLIQUE

CLIQUISMS > CLIQUE

CLIQUY *same as* > CLIQUEY

CLITELLA > CLITELLUM

CLITELLAR > CLITELLUM

CLITELLUM *n* thickened saddle-like region of epidermis in earthworms and leeches whose secretions bind copulating worms together and later form a cocoon around the eggs

CLITHRAL *same as* > CLEITHRAL

CLITIC *adj* (of a word) incapable of being stressed, usually pronounced as if part of the word that follows or precedes it: for example, in French, *me*, *te*, and *le* are clitic pronouns ▷ *n* clitic word

CLITICISE *same as* > CLITICIZE

CLITICIZE *vb* pronounce as part of following or preceding word

CLITICS > CLITIC

CLITORAL > CLITORIS

CLITORIC > CLITORIS

CLITORIS *n* small sexually sensitive organ at the front of the vulva

CLITTER *vb* to stridulate

CLITTERED > CLITTER

CLITTERS > CLITTER

CLIVERS *same as* > CLEAVERS

CLIVIA *n* plant belonging to the Amaryllid family

CLIVIAS > CLIVIA

CLOACA *n* cavity in most animals, except higher mammals, into which the alimentary canal and the genital and urinary ducts open

CLOACAE > CLOACA

CLOACAL > CLOACA

CLOACAS > CLOACA

CLOACINAL > CLOACA

CLOACITIS *n* inflammation of the cloaca in birds, including domestic fowl, and other animals with a common opening of the urinary and gastrointestinal tracts

CLOAK *n* loose sleeveless outer garment ▷ *vb* cover or conceal

CLOAKED > CLOAK

CLOAKING > CLOAK

CLOAKROOM *n* room where coats may be left temporarily

CLOAKS > CLOAK

CLOAM *adj* made of clay or earthenware ▷ *n* clay or earthenware pots, dishes, etc, collectively

CLOAMS > CLOAM

CLOBBER *vb* hit ▷ *n* belongings, esp clothes

CLOBBERED > CLOBBER

CLOBBERS > CLOBBER

CLOCHARD *n* tramp

CLOCHARDS > CLOCHARD

CLOCHE *n* cover to protect young plants

CLOCHES > CLOCHE

CLOCK *n* instrument for showing the time ▷ *vb* record (time) with a stopwatch

CLOCKED > CLOCK

CLOCKER > CLOCK

CLOCKERS > CLOCK

CLOCKING > CLOCK

CLOCKINGS > CLOCK

CLOCKLIKE > CLOCK

CLOCKS > CLOCK

CLOCKWISE *adj* in the direction in which the hands of a clock rotate

CLOCKWORK *n* mechanism similar to the kind in a clock, used in wind-up toys

CLOD *n* lump of earth ▷ *vb* pelt with clods

CLODDED > CLOD

CLODDIER > CLOD

CLODDIEST > CLOD

CLODDING > CLOD

CLODDISH > CLOD

CLODDY > CLOD

CLODLY > CLOD

CLODPATE *n* dull or stupid person

CLODPATED *adj* stupid

CLODPATES > CLODPATE

CLODPOLE *same as* > CLODPATE

CLODPOLES > CLODPOLE

CLODPOLL *same as* > CLODPATE

CLODPOLLS > CLODPOLL

CLODS > CLOD

CLOFF *n* cleft of a tree

CLOFFS > CLOFF

CLOG *vb* obstruct ▷ *n* wooden or wooden-soled shoe

CLOGDANCE *n* dance performed in clogs

CLOGGED > CLOG

CLOGGER *n* clogmaker

CLOGGERS > CLOGGER

CLOGGIER > CLOG

CLOGGIEST > CLOG

CLOGGILY > CLOG

CLOGGING > CLOG

CLOGGINGS > CLOG

CLOGGY > CLOG

CLOGS > CLOG

CLOISON *n* partition

CLOISONNE *n* design made by filling in a wire outline

with coloured enamel ▷ adj of, relating to, or made by cloisonné

CLOISONS > CLOISON

CLOISTER n covered pillared arcade, usu in a monastery ▷ vb confine or seclude in or as if in a monastery

CLOISTERS > CLOISTER

CLOISTRAL adj of, like, or characteristic of a cloister

CLOKE same as > CLOAK

CLOKED > CLOKE

CLOKES > CLOKE

CLOKING > CLOKE

CLOMB a past tense and past participle of > CLIMB

CLOMP same as > CLUMP

CLOMPED > CLOMP

CLOMPING > CLOMP

CLOMPS > CLOMP

CLON same as > CLONE

CLONAL > CLONE

CLONALLY > CLONE

CLONE n animal or plant produced artificially from the cells of another animal or plant, and identical to the original ▷ vb produce as a clone

CLONED > CLONE

CLONER > CLONE

CLONERS > CLONE

CLONES > CLONE

CLONIC > CLONUS

CLONICITY > CLONUS

CLONIDINE n antihypertensive drug

CLONING > CLONE

CLONINGS > CLONE

CLONISM n series of clonic spasms

CLONISMS > CLONISM

CLONK vb make a loud dull thud ▷ n loud thud

CLONKED > CLONK

CLONKING > CLONK

CLONKS > CLONK

CLONS > CLON

CLONUS n type of convulsion characterized by rapid contraction and relaxation of a muscle

CLONUSES > CLONUS

CLOOP n sound made when a cork is drawn from a bottle

CLOOPS > CLOOP

CLOOT n hoof

CLOOTS > CLOOT

CLOP vb make or move along with a sound as of a horse's hooves striking the ground ▷ n sound of this nature

CLOPPED > CLOP

CLOPPING > CLOP

CLOPS > CLOP

CLOQUE n fabric with an embossed surface

CLOQUES > CLOQUE

CLOSABLE > CLOSE

CLOSE vb shut ▷ n end, conclusion ▷ adj near ▷ adv closely, tightly ▷ n passageway leading to a

tenement building

CLOSEABLE > CLOSE

CLOSED > CLOSE

CLOSEDOWN n closure or stoppage of operations

CLOSEHEAD n entrance to a close

CLOSELY > CLOSE

CLOSENESS > CLOSE

CLOSEOUT n termination of an account on which the margin is exhausted

CLOSEOUTS > CLOSEOUT

CLOSER > CLOSE

CLOSERS > CLOSE

CLOSES > CLOSE

CLOSEST > CLOSE

CLOSET n cupboard ▷ adj private, secret ▷ vb shut (oneself) away in private

CLOSETED > CLOSET

CLOSETFUL n quantity that may be contained in a closet

CLOSETING > CLOSET

CLOSETS > CLOSET

CLOSEUP n photo taken close to subject

CLOSEUPS > CLOSEUP

CLOSING > CLOSE

CLOSINGS > CLOSE

CLOSURE n closing ▷ vb (in a deliberative body) to end (debate) by closure

CLOSURED > CLOSURE

CLOSURES > CLOSURE

CLOSURING > CLOSURE

CLOT n soft thick lump formed from liquid ▷ vb form soft thick lumps

CLOTBUR n burdock

CLOTBURS > CLOTBUR

CLOTE n burdock

CLOTES > CLOTE

CLOTH n (piece of) woven fabric

CLOTHE vb put clothes on

CLOTHED > CLOTHE

CLOTHES n garments

CLOTHIER n maker or seller of clothes or cloth

CLOTHIERS > CLOTHIER

CLOTHING > CLOTHE

CLOTHINGS > CLOTHE

CLOTHLIKE > CLOTH

CLOTHS > CLOTH

CLOTPOLL same as > CLODPOLL

CLOTPOLLS > CLOTPOLL

CLOTS > CLOT

CLOTTED > CLOT

CLOTTER vb to clot

CLOTTERED > CLOTTER

CLOTTERS > CLOTTER

CLOTTIER > CLOTTY

CLOTTIEST > CLOTTY

CLOTTING > CLOT

CLOTTINGS > CLOT

CLOTTISH > CLOT

CLOTTY adj full of clots

CLOTURE n closure in the US Senate ▷ vb end (debate) in the US Senate by cloture

CLOTURED > CLOTURE

CLOTURES > CLOTURE

CLOTURING > CLOTURE

CLOU n crux; focus

CLOUD n mass of condensed water vapour floating in the sky ▷ vb become cloudy

CLOUDAGE n mass of clouds

CLOUDAGES > CLOUDAGE

CLOUDED > CLOUD

CLOUDIER > CLOUDY

CLOUDIEST > CLOUDY

CLOUDILY > CLOUDY

CLOUDING > CLOUD

CLOUDINGS > CLOUD

CLOUDLAND n realm or fantasy or impractical notions

CLOUDLESS > CLOUD

CLOUDLET n small cloud

CLOUDLETS > CLOUDLET

CLOUDLIKE > CLOUD

CLOUDS > CLOUD

CLOUDTOWN n cloudland

CLOUDY adj having a lot of clouds

CLOUGH n gorge or narrow ravine

CLOUGHS > CLOUGH

CLOUR vb to thump or dent

CLOURED > CLOUR

CLOURING > CLOUR

CLOURS > CLOUR

CLOUS > CLOU

CLOUT n hard blow ▷ vb hit hard

CLOUTED > CLOUT

CLOUTER > CLOUT

CLOUTERLY adj clumsy

CLOUTERS > CLOUT

CLOUTING > CLOUT

CLOUTS > CLOUT

CLOVE n tropical evergreen myrtaceous tree

CLOVEN > CLEAVE

CLOVEPINK n carnation

CLOVER n plant with three-lobed leaves

CLOVERED adj covered with clover

CLOVERS > CLOVER

CLOVERY > CLOVER

CLOVES > CLOVE

CLOVIS as in clovis point flint projectile dating from the 10th millennium bc

CLOW n clove

CLOWDER n collective terms for a group of cats

CLOWDERS > CLOWDER

CLOWN n comic entertainer in a circus ▷ vb behave foolishly

CLOWNED > CLOWN

CLOWNERY > CLOWN

CLOWNING > CLOWN

CLOWNINGS > CLOWN

CLOWNISH > CLOWN

CLOWNS > CLOWN

CLOWS > CLOW

CLOY vb make weary or cause weariness through an excess of something initially pleasurable or sweet

CLOYE vb to claw

CLOYED > CLOY

CLOYES > CLOYE

CLOYING adj sickeningly sweet

CLOYINGLY > CLOYING

CLOYLESS adj not cloying

CLOYMENT n satiety

CLOYMENTS > CLOYMENT

CLOYS > CLOY

CLOYSOME adj cloying

CLOZAPINE n drug used to treat mental illness

CLOZE as in cloze test test of the ability to understand text

CLOZES > CLOZE

CLUB n association of people with common interests ▷ vb hit with a club

CLUBABLE same as > CLUBBABLE

CLUBBABLE adj suitable to be a member of a club

CLUBBED > CLUB

CLUBBER n person who regularly frequents nightclubs and similar establishments

CLUBBERS > CLUBBER

CLUBBIER > CLUBBY

CLUBBIEST > CLUBBY

CLUBBILY > CLUBBY

CLUBBING > CLUB

CLUBBINGS > CLUB

CLUBBISH adj clubby

CLUBBISM n advantage gained through membership of a club or clubs

CLUBBISMS > CLUBBISM

CLUBBIST > CLUBBISM

CLUBBISTS > CLUBBISM

CLUBBY adj sociable, esp effusively so

CLUBFACE n face of golf club

CLUBFACES > CLUBFACE

CLUBFEET > CLUBFOOT

CLUBFOOT n congenital deformity of the foot

CLUBHAND n congenital deformity of the hand

CLUBHANDS > CLUBHAND

CLUBHAUL vb force (a sailing vessel) onto a new tack, esp in an emergency

CLUBHAULS > CLUBHAUL

CLUBHEAD n head of golf club

CLUBHEADS > CLUBHEAD

CLUBHOUSE n premises of a sports or other club, esp a golf club

CLUBLAND n (in Britain) the area of London around St. James's, which contains most of the famous London clubs

CLUBLANDS > CLUBLAND

CLUBMAN n man who is an enthusiastic member of a club or clubs

CLUBMEN > CLUBMAN

CLUBROOM n room in which a club meets

CLUBROOMS > CLUBROOM

CLUBROOT n disease of cabbages

CLUBROOTS > CLUBROOT

CLUBRUSH n any rush of the genus Scirpus

CLUBS > CLUB
CLUBWOMAN n woman who is an enthusiastic member of a club or clubs
CLUBWOMEN > CLUBWOMAN
CLUCK n low clicking noise made by a hen ▷vb make this noise
CLUCKED > CLUCK
CLUCKIER > CLUCKY
CLUCKIEST > CLUCKY
CLUCKING > CLUCK
CLUCKS > CLUCK
CLUCKY adj wishing to have a baby
CLUDGIE n toilet
CLUDGIES > CLUDGIE
CLUE n something that helps to solve a mystery or puzzle ▷vb help solve a mystery or puzzle
CLUED > CLUE
CLUEING > CLUE
CLUELESS adj stupid
CLUES > CLUE
CLUING > CLUE
CLUMBER n type of thickset spaniel
CLUMBERS > CLUMBER
CLUMP n small group of things or people ▷vb walk heavily
CLUMPED > CLUMP
CLUMPER > CLUMP
CLUMPERS > CLUMP
CLUMPIER > CLUMP
CLUMPIEST > CLUMP
CLUMPING > CLUMP
CLUMPISH > CLUMP
CLUMPLIKE > CLUMP
CLUMPS > CLUMP
CLUMPY > CLUMP
CLUMSIER > CLUMSY
CLUMSIEST > CLUMSY
CLUMSILY > CLUMSY
CLUMSY adj lacking skill or physical coordination
CLUNCH n hardened clay
CLUNCHES > CLUNCH
CLUNG > CLING
CLUNK n dull metallic sound ▷vb make such a sound
CLUNKED > CLUNK
CLUNKER n dilapidated old car or other machine
CLUNKERS > CLUNKER
CLUNKIER > CLUNKY
CLUNKIEST > CLUNKY
CLUNKING > CLUNK
CLUNKS > CLUNK
CLUNKY adj making a clunking noise
CLUPEID n any widely distributed soft-finned teleost fish of the family Clupeidae, typically having oily flesh, and including the herrings, sardines, shad, etc ▷adj of, relating to, or belonging to the family Clupeidae
CLUPEIDS > CLUPEID
CLUPEOID adj of, relating to, or belonging to the Isospondyli (or Clupeiformes), a large order of soft-finned fishes, including

the herrings, salmon, and tarpon ▷n any fish belonging to the order Isospondyli
CLUPEOIDS > CLUPEOID
CLUSIA n tree of the tropical American genus Clusia
CLUSIAS > CLUSIA
CLUSTER n small close group ▷vb gather in clusters
CLUSTERED > CLUSTER
CLUSTERS > CLUSTER
CLUSTERY > CLUSTER
CLUTCH vb grasp tightly ▷n device enabling two revolving shafts to be connected and disconnected, esp in a motor vehicle
CLUTCHED > CLUTCH
CLUTCHES > CLUTCH
CLUTCHING > CLUTCH
CLUTCHY adj (of a person) tending to cling
CLUTTER vb scatter objects about (a place) untidily ▷n untidy mess
CLUTTERED > CLUTTER
CLUTTERS > CLUTTER
CLUTTERY adj full of clutter
CLY vb to steal or seize
CLYING > CLY
CLYPE vb tell tales ▷n person who tells tales
CLYPEAL > CLYPEUS
CLYPEATE > CLYPEUS
CLYPED > CLYPE
CLYPEI > CLYPEUS
CLYPES > CLYPE
CLYPEUS n cuticular plate on the head of some insects between the labrum and the frons
CLYPING > CLYPE
CLYSTER a former name for an > ENEMA
CLYSTERS > CLYSTER
CNEMIAL > CNEMIS
CNEMIDES > CNEMIS
CNEMIS n shin or tibia
CNIDA n nematocyst
CNIDAE > CNIDA
CNIDARIAN n any invertebrate of the phylum Cnidaria, which comprises the coelenterates ▷adj of, relating to, or belonging to the Cnidaria
COACH n long-distance bus ▷vb train, teach
COACHABLE adj capable of being coached
COACHDOG n Dalmatian dog
COACHDOGS > COACHDOG
COACHED > COACH
COACHEE n person who receives training from a coach, esp in business or office practice
COACHEES > COACHEE
COACHER > COACH
COACHERS > COACH
COACHES > COACH
COACHIES > COACHY
COACHING > COACH

COACHINGS > COACH
COACHLINE n decorative line on the bodywork of a vehicle
COACHLOAD n quantity that a coach can carry
COACHMAN n driver of a horse-drawn coach or carriage
COACHMEN > COACHMAN
COACHWHIP n whipsnake
COACHWOOD n Australian tree, Ceratopetalum apetalum, yielding light aromatic wood used for furniture, turnery, etc
COACHWORK n body of a car
COACHY n coachman
COACT vb to act together
COACTED > COACT
COACTING > COACT
COACTION n any relationship between organisms within a community
COACTIONS > COACTION
COACTIVE > COACTION
COACTOR > COACT
COACTORS > COACT
COACTS > COACT
COADAPTED adj adapted to one another
COADJUTOR n bishop appointed as assistant to a diocesan bishop
COADMIRE vb to admire together
COADMIRED > COADMIRE
COADMIRES > COADMIRE
COADMIT vb to admit together
COADMITS > COADMIT
COADUNATE same as > CONNATE
COAEVAL n contemporary
COAEVALS > COAEVAL
COAGENCY n joint agency
COAGENT > COAGENCY
COAGENTS > COAGENCY
COAGULA > COAGULUM
COAGULANT n substance causing coagulation
COAGULASE n any enzyme that causes coagulation of blood
COAGULATE vb change from a liquid to a semisolid mass ▷n solid or semisolid substance produced by coagulation
COAGULUM n any coagulated mass
COAGULUMS > COAGULUM
COAITA n spider monkey
COAITAS > COAITA
COAL n black rock consisting mainly of carbon, used as fuel ▷vb take in, or turn into coal
COALA same as > KOALA
COALAS > COALA
COALBALL n in coal, nodule containing petrified plant or animal remains
COALBALLS > COALBALL
COALBIN n bin for holding coal

COALBINS > COALBIN
COALBOX n box for holding coal
COALBOXES > COALBOX
COALED > COAL
COALER n ship, train, etc, used to carry or supply coal
COALERS > COALER
COALESCE vb come together, merge
COALESCED > COALESCE
COALESCES > COALESCE
COALFACE n exposed seam of coal in a mine
COALFACES > COALFACE
COALFIELD n area with coal under the ground
COALFISH n dark-coloured gadoid food fish, Pollachius virens, occurring in northern seas
COALHOLE n small coal cellar
COALHOLES > COALHOLE
COALHOUSE n shed or building for storing coal
COALIER > COAL
COALIEST > COAL
COALIFIED > COALIFY
COALIFIES > COALIFY
COALIFY vb to turn into coal
COALING > COAL
COALISE vb to form a coalition
COALISED > COALISE
COALISES > COALISE
COALISING > COALISE
COALITION n temporary alliance, esp between political parties
COALIZE same as > COALISE
COALIZED > COALIZE
COALIZES > COALIZE
COALIZING > COALIZE
COALLESS adj without coal
COALMAN n man who delivers coal
COALMEN > COALMAN
COALMINE n mine from which coal is extracted
COALMINER > COALMINE
COALMINES > COALMINE
COALPIT n pit from which coal is extracted
COALPITS > COALPIT
COALS > COAL
COALSACK n dark nebula near the constellation Cygnus
COALSACKS > COALSACK
COALSHED n shed in which coal is stored
COALSHEDS > COALSHED
COALTAR n black tar distilled from coal
COALTARS > COALTAR
COALY > COAL
COALYARD n yard in which coal is stored
COALYARDS > COALYARD
COAMING n raised frame round a ship's hatchway for keeping out water
COAMINGS > COAMING
COANCHOR vb to co-present a TV programme
COANCHORS > COANCHOR

COANNEX *vb* to annex with something else
COANNEXED > COANNEX
COANNEXES > COANNEX
COAPPEAR *vb* to appear jointly
COAPPEARS > COAPPEAR
COAPT *vb* to secure
COAPTED > COAPT
COAPTING > COAPT
COAPTS > COAPT
COARB *n* spiritual successor
COARBS > COARB
COARCTATE *adj* (of a pupa) enclosed in a hard barrel-shaped case (puparium), as in the housefly ▷ *vb* (esp of the aorta) to become narrower
COARSE *adj* rough in texture
COARSELY > COARSE
COARSEN *vb* make or become coarse
COARSENED > COARSEN
COARSENS > COARSEN
COARSER > COARSE
COARSEST > COARSE
COARSISH > COARSE
COASSIST *vb* to assist jointly
COASSISTS > COASSIST
COASSUME *vb* to assume jointly
COASSUMED > COASSUME
COASSUMES > COASSUME
COAST *n* place where the land meets the sea ▷ *vb* move by momentum, without the use of power
COASTAL > COAST
COASTALLY > COAST
COASTED > COAST
COASTER *n* small mat placed under a glass
COASTERS > COASTER
COASTING > COAST
COASTINGS > COAST
COASTLAND *n* land fringing a coast
COASTLINE *n* outline of a coast
COASTS > COAST
COASTWARD *adv* towards the coast
COASTWISE *adv* along the coast
COAT *n* outer garment with long sleeves ▷ *vb* cover with a layer
COATDRESS *n* garment that can be worn as a coat or a dress
COATE *same as* > QUOTE
COATED *adj* covered with an outer layer, film, etc
COATEE *n* short coat, esp for a baby
COATEES > COATEE
COATER *n* machine that applies a coating to something
COATERS > COATER
COATES > COATE
COATI *n* any omnivorous mammal of the genera *Nasua* and *Nasuella*, of Central and South America:

family *Procyonidae*, order *Carnivora* (carnivores). They are related to but larger than the raccoons, having a long flexible snout and a brindled coat
COATING *n* covering layer
COATINGS > COATING
COATIS > COATI
COATLESS *adj* without a coat
COATRACK *n* rack for hanging coats on
COATRACKS > COATRACK
COATROOM *n* cloakroom
COATROOMS > COATROOM
COATS > COAT
COATSTAND *n* stand for hanging coats on
COATTAIL *n* long tapering tail at the back of a man's tailored coat
COATTAILS > COATTAIL
COATTEND *vb* to attend jointly
COATTENDS > COATTEND
COATTEST *vb* to attest jointly
COATTESTS > COATTEST
COAUTHOR *n* person who shares the writing of a book, article, etc, with another ▷ *vb* be the joint author of (a book, article, etc)
COAUTHORS > COAUTHOR
COAX *vb* persuade gently
COAXAL *same as* > COAXIAL
COAXED > COAX
COAXER > COAX
COAXERS > COAX
COAXES > COAX
COAXIAL *adj* (of a cable) transmitting by means of two concentric conductors separated by an insulator
COAXIALLY > COAXIAL
COAXING > COAX
COAXINGLY > COAX
COB *n* stalk of an ear of maize ▷ *vb* beat, esp on the buttocks
COBAEA *n* any climbing shrub of the tropical American genus *Cobaea*, esp *C. scandens*, grown for its large trumpet-shaped purple or white flowers: family *Polemoniaceae*
COBAEAS > COBAEA
COBALAMIN *n* vitamin B12
COBALT *n* brittle silvery-white metallic element
COBALTIC *adj* of or containing cobalt, esp in the trivalent state
COBALTINE *same as* > COBALTITE
COBALTITE *n* rare silvery-white mineral
COBALTOUS *adj* of or containing cobalt in the divalent state
COBALTS > COBALT
COBB *same as* > COB
COBBED > COB
COBBER *n* friend

COBBERS > COBBER
COBBIER > COBBY
COBBIEST > COBBY
COBBING > COB
COBBLE *n* cobblestone ▷ *vb* pave (a road) with cobblestones
COBBLED > COBBLE
COBBLER *n* shoe mender
COBBLERS *pl n* nonsense ▷ *interj* exclamation of strong disagreement
COBBLERY *n* shoemaking or shoemending
COBBLES *pl n* coal in small rounded lumps
COBBLING > COBBLE
COBBLINGS > COBBLE
COBBS > COBB
COBBY *adj* short and stocky
COBIA *n* large dark-striped game fish of tropical and subtropical seas
COBIAS > COBIA
COBLE *n* small single-masted flat-bottomed fishing boat
COBLES > COBLE
COBLOAF *n* round loaf of bread
COBLOAVES > COBLOAF
COBNUT *another name for* > HAZELNUT
COBNUTS > COBNUT
COBRA *n* venomous hooded snake of Asia and Africa
COBRAS > COBRA
COBRIC > COBRA
COBRIFORM *adj* cobra-like
COBS > COB
COBURG *n* rounded loaf with a cross cut on the top
COBURGS > COBURG
COBWEB *n* spider's web
COBWEBBED > COBWEB
COBWEBBY > COBWEB
COBWEBS > COBWEB
COBZA *n* Romanian lute
COBZAS > COBZA
COCA *n* dried leaves of a S American shrub which contain cocaine
COCAIN *same as* > COCAINE
COCAINE *n* addictive drug used as a narcotic and as an anaesthetic
COCAINES > COCAINE
COCAINISE *same as* > COCAINIZE
COCAINISM *n* use of cocaine
COCAINIST *n* cocaine addict
COCAINIZE *vb* anaesthetize with cocaine
COCAINS > COCAIN
COCAPTAIN *vb* to captain jointly
COCAS > COCA
COCCAL > COCCUS
COCCI > COCCUS
COCCIC > COCCUS
COCCID *n* any homopterous insect of the superfamily *Coccoidea*, esp any of the family *Coccidae*, which includes the scale insects
COCCIDIA > COCCIDIUM

COCCIDIUM *n* any parasitic protozoan of the order *Coccidia*
COCCIDS > COCCID
COCCO *n* taro
COCCOID > COCCUS
COCCOIDAL > COCCUS
COCCOIDS > COCCUS
COCCOLITE *n* variety of pyroxene
COCCOLITH *n* any of the round calcareous plates in chalk formations: formed the outer layer of unicellular plankton
COCCOS > COCCO
COCCOUS > COCCUS
COCCUS *n* any spherical or nearly spherical bacterium, such as a staphylococcus
COCCYGEAL > COCCYX
COCCYGES > COCCYX
COCCYGIAN > COCCYX
COCCYX *n* bone at the base of the spinal column
COCCYXES > COCCYX
COCH *obsolete variant of* > COACH
COCHAIR *vb* to chair jointly
COCHAIRED > COCHAIR
COCHAIRS > COCHAIR
COCHES > COCH
COCHIN *n* large breed of domestic fowl
COCHINEAL *n* red dye obtained from a Mexican insect, used for food colouring
COCHINS > COCHIN
COCHLEA *n* spiral tube in the internal ear, which converts sound vibrations into nerve impulses
COCHLEAE > COCHLEA
COCHLEAR *adj* of or relating to the cochlea ▷ *n* spoonful
COCHLEARE *variant of* > COCHLEAR
COCHLEARS > COCHLEAR
COCHLEAS > COCHLEA
COCHLEATE *adj* shaped like a snail's shell
COCINERA *n* in Mexico, a female cook
COCINERAS > COCINERA
COCK *n* male bird, esp of domestic fowl ▷ *vb* draw back (the hammer of a gun) to firing position
COCKADE *n* feather or rosette worn on a hat as a badge
COCKADED > COCKADE
COCKADES > COCKADE
COCKAMAMY *adj* ridiculous or nonsensical
COCKAPOO *n* cross between a cocker spaniel and a poodle
COCKAPOOS > COCKAPOO
COCKATEEL *same as* > COCKATIEL
COCKATIEL *n* crested Australian parrot with a greyish-brown and yellow plumage

COCKATOO *n* crested parrot of Australia or the East Indies

COCKATOOS > COCKATOO

COCKBILL *vb* to tilt up one end of

COCKBILLS > COCKBILL

COCKBIRD *n* male bird

COCKBIRDS > COCKBIRD

COCKBOAT *n* any small boat

COCKBOATS > COCKBOAT

COCKCROW *n* daybreak

COCKCROWS > COCKCROW

COCKED > COCK

COCKER *n* devotee of cockfighting ▷ *vb* pamper or spoil by indulgence

COCKERED > COCKER

COCKEREL *n* young domestic cock

COCKERELS > COCKEREL

COCKERING > COCKER

COCKERS > COCKER

COCKET *n* document issued by a customs officer

COCKETS > COCKET

COCKEYE *n* eye affected with strabismus or one that squints

COCKEYED *adj* crooked, askew

COCKEYES > COCKEYE

COCKFIGHT *n* fight between two gamecocks fitted with sharp metal spurs

COCKHORSE *n* rocking horse

COCKIER > COCKY

COCKIES > COCKY

COCKIEST > COCKY

COCKILY > COCKY

COCKINESS *n* conceited self-assurance

COCKING > COCK

COCKISH *adj* wanton

COCKLE *n* edible shellfish ▷ *vb* fish for cockles

COCKLEBUR *n* any coarse weed of the genus *Xanthium*, having spiny burs: family *Asteraceae* (composites)

COCKLED > COCKLE

COCKLEERT *a Southwest English dialect variant of* > COCKCROW

COCKLEMAN *n* man who collects cockles

COCKLEMEN > COCKLEMAN

COCKLER *n* person employed to gather cockles

COCKLERS > COCKLER

COCKLES > COCKLE

COCKLIKE *adj* resembling a cock

COCKLING > COCKLE

COCKLOFT *n* small loft, garret, or attic

COCKLOFTS > COCKLOFT

COCKMATCH *n* cockfight

COCKNEY *n* native of London, esp of its East End ▷ *adj* characteristic of cockneys or their dialect

COCKNEYFY *vb* cause (one's speech, manners, etc) to fit the stereotyped idea of a cockney

COCKNEYS > COCKNEY

COCKNIFY *same as* > COCKNEYFY

COCKPIT *n* pilot's compartment in an aircraft

COCKPITS > COCKPIT

COCKROACH *n* beetle-like insect which is a household pest

COCKS > COCK

COCKSCOMB *n* comb of a domestic cock

COCKSFOOT *n* perennial Eurasian grass, *Dactylis glomerata*, cultivated as a pasture grass in North America and South Africa

COCKSHIES > COCKSHY

COCKSHOT *another name for* > COCKSHY

COCKSHOTS > COCKSHOT

COCKSHUT *n* dusk

COCKSHUTS > COCKSHUT

COCKSHY *n* target aimed at in throwing games

COCKSIER > COCKSY

COCKSIEST > COCKSY

COCKSPUR *n* spur on the leg of a cock

COCKSPURS > COCKSPUR

COCKSURE *adj* overconfident, arrogant

COCKSWAIN *same as* > COXSWAIN

COCKSY *adj* cocky

COCKTAIL *n* mixed alcoholic drink

COCKTAILS > COCKTAIL

COCKUP *n* something done badly ▷ *vb* ruin or spoil

COCKUPS > COCKUP

COCKY *adj* conceited and overconfident ▷ *n* farmer whose farm is regarded as small or of little account

COCO *n* coconut palm

COCOA *n* powder made from the seed of the cacao tree

COCOANUT *same as* > COCONUT

COCOANUTS > COCONUT

COCOAS > COCOA

COCOBOLA *n* type of rosewood

COCOBOLAS > COCOBOLA

COCOBOLO *same as* > COCOBOLA

COCOBOLOS > COCOBOLO

COCOMAT *n* mat made from coconut fibre

COCOMATS > COCOMAT

COCONUT *n* large hard fruit of a type of palm tree

COCONUTS > COCONUT

COCOON *n* silky protective covering of a silkworm ▷ *vb* wrap up tightly for protection

COCOONED > COCOON

COCOONERY *n* place where silkworms feed and make cocoons

COCOONING > COCOON

COCOONS > COCOON

COCOPAN *n* (in South Africa) a small wagon running on narrow-gauge railway lines

used in mines

COCOPANS > COCOPAN

COCOPLUM *n* tropical shrub, also known as icaco, or its fruit

COCOPLUMS > COCOPLUM

COCOS > COCO

COCOTTE *n* small fireproof dish in which individual portions of food are cooked

COCOTTES > COCOTTE

COCOUNSEL *vb* to counsel jointly

COCOYAM *n* either of two food plants of West Africa, the taro or the yantia, both of which have edible underground stems

COCOYAMS > COCOYAM

COCOZELLE *n* variety of squash

COCREATE *vb* to create jointly

COCREATED > COCREATE

COCREATES > COCREATE

COCREATOR > COCREATE

COCTILE *adj* made by exposing to heat

COCTION *n* boiling

COCTIONS > COCTION

COCULTURE *vb* to culture together

COCURATOR *n* joint curator

COCUSWOOD *n* wood from the tropical American leguminous tree *Brya ebenus*, used for inlaying, turnery, musical instruments, etc

COD *n* large food fish of the North Atlantic ▷ *adj* having the character of an imitation or parody ▷ *vb* make fun of

CODA *n* final part of a musical composition

CODABLE *adj* capable of being coded

CODAS > CODA

CODDED > COD

CODDER *n* cod fisherman or his boat

CODDERS > CODDER

CODDING > COD

CODDLE *vb* pamper, overprotect ▷ *n* stew made from ham and bacon scraps

CODDLED > CODDLE

CODDLER > CODDLE

CODDLERS > CODDLE

CODDLES > CODDLE

CODDLING > CODDLE

CODE *n* system of letters, symbols, or prearranged signals by which messages can be communicated secretly or briefly ▷ *vb* put into code

CODEBOOK *n* book containing the means to decipher a code

CODEBOOKS > CODEBOOK

CODEBTOR *n* fellow debtor

CODEBTORS > CODEBTOR

CODEC *n* set of equipment that encodes an analogue

speech or video signal into digital form for transmission purposes and at the receiving end decodes the digital signal into a form close to its original

CODECS > CODEC

CODED > CODE

CODEIA *n* codeine

CODEIAS > CODEIA

CODEIN *same as* > CODEINE

CODEINA *obsolete variant of* > CODEINE

CODEINAS > CODEINA

CODEINE *n* drug used as a painkiller

CODEINES > CODEINE

CODEINS > CODEIN

CODELESS *adj* lacking a code

CODEN *n* unique six-character code assigned to a publication for identification purposes

CODENAME *same as* > CODEWORD

CODENAMES > CODEWORD

CODENS > CODEN

CODER *n* person or thing that codes

CODERIVE *vb* to derive jointly

CODERIVED > CODERIVE

CODERIVES > CODERIVE

CODERS > CODER

CODES > CODE

CODESIGN *vb* to design jointly

CODESIGNS > CODESIGN

CODETTA *n* short coda

CODETTAS > CODETTA

CODEVELOP *vb* to develop jointly

CODEWORD *n* (esp in military use) a word used to identify a classified plan, operation, etc

CODEWORDS > CODEWORD

CODEX *n* volume of manuscripts of an ancient text

CODFISH *n* cod

CODFISHES > CODFISH

CODGER *n* old man

CODGERS > CODGER

CODICES > CODEX

CODICIL *n* addition to a will

CODICILS > CODICIL

CODIFIED > CODIFY

CODIFIER > CODIFY

CODIFIERS > CODIFY

CODIFIES > CODIFY

CODIFY *vb* organize (rules or procedures) systematically

CODIFYING > CODIFY

CODILLA *n* coarse tow of hemp and flax

CODILLAS > CODILLA

CODILLE *n* in the card game ombre, term indicating that the game is won

CODILLES > CODILLE

CODING > CODE

CODINGS > CODE

CODIRECT *vb* to direct jointly

CODIRECTS > CODIRECT

CODIST *n* codifier

CODISTS > CODIST

CODLIN *same as* > CODLING

CODLING *n* young cod

CODLINGS > CODLING

CODLINS > CODLIN

CODOLOGY *n* art or practice of bluffing or deception

CODOMAIN *n* set of values that a function is allowed to take

CODOMAINS > CODOMAIN

CODON *n* unit that consists of three adjacent bases on a DNA molecule and that determines the position of a specific amino acid in a protein molecule during protein synthesis

CODONS > CODON

CODPIECE *n* bag covering the male genitals, attached to the breeches

CODPIECES > CODPIECE

CODRIVE *vb* take alternate turns driving a car with another person

CODRIVEN > CODRIVE

CODRIVER *n* one of two drivers who take turns to drive a car

CODRIVERS > CODRIVER

CODRIVES > CODRIVE

CODRIVING > CODRIVE

CODROVE > CODRIVE

CODS > COD

COED *adj* educating both sexes together ▷ *n* school or college that educates both sexes together

COEDIT *vb* edit (a book, newspaper, etc) jointly

COEDITED > COEDIT

COEDITING > COEDIT

COEDITOR > COEDIT

COEDITORS > COEDIT

COEDITS > COEDIT

COEDS > COED

COEFFECT *n* secondary effect

COEFFECTS > COEFFECT

COEHORN *n* type of small artillery mortar

COEHORNS > COEHORN

COELIAC *adj* of or relating to the abdomen ▷ *n* person who has coeliac disease

COELIACS > COELIAC

COELOM *n* body cavity of many multicellular animals, situated in the mesoderm and containing the digestive tract and other visceral organs

COELOMATA *n* animals possessing a coelom

COELOMATE *adj* possessing a coelom

COELOME *same as* > COELOM

COELOMES > COELOME

COELOMIC > COELOM

COELOMS > COELOM

COELOSTAT *n* astronomical instrument consisting of a plane mirror mounted parallel to the earth's axis and rotated about this axis once every two days so that light from a celestial body, esp the sun, is reflected onto a second mirror, which reflects the beam into a telescope

COEMBODY *vb* to embody jointly

COEMPLOY *vb* to employ together

COEMPLOYS > COEMPLOY

COEMPT *vb* buy up something in its entirety

COEMPTED > COEMPT

COEMPTING > COEMPT

COEMPTION *n* buying up of the complete supply of a commodity

COEMPTS > COEMPT

COENACLE *same as* > CENACLE

COENACLES > COENACLE

COENACT *vb* to enact jointly

COENACTED > COENACT

COENACTS > COENACT

COENAMOR *vb* enamour jointly

COENAMORS > COENAMOR

COENDURE *vb* to endure together

COENDURED > COENDURE

COENDURES > COENDURE

COENOBIA > COENOBIUM

COENOBITE *n* member of a religious order in a monastic community

COENOBIUM *n* monastery or convent

COENOCYTE *n* mass of protoplasm containing many nuclei and enclosed by a cell wall: occurs in many fungi and some algae

COENOSARC *n* system of protoplasmic branches connecting the polyps of colonial organisms such as corals

COENURE *variant form of* > COENURUS

COENURES > COENURE

COENURI > COENURUS

COENURUS *n* encysted larval form of the tapeworm *Multiceps*, containing many encapsulated heads. In sheep it can cause the gid, and when eaten by dogs it develops into several adult forms

COENZYME *n* nonprotein organic molecule that forms a complex with certain enzymes and is essential for their activity

COENZYMES > COENZYME

COEQUAL *n* equal ▷ *adj* of the same size, rank, etc

COEQUALLY > COEQUAL

COEQUALS > COEQUAL

COEQUATE *vb* to equate together

COEQUATED > COEQUATE

COEQUATES > COEQUATE

COERCE *vb* compel, force

COERCED > COERCE

COERCER > COERCE

COERCERS > COERCE

COERCES > COERCE

COERCIBLE > COERCE

COERCIBLY > COERCE

COERCING > COERCE

COERCION *n* act or power of coercing

COERCIONS > COERCION

COERCIVE > COERCE

COERECT *vb* to erect together

COERECTED > COERECT

COERECTS > COERECT

COESITE *n* polymorph of silicon dioxide

COESITES > COESITE

COETERNAL *adj* existing together eternally

COEVAL *n* contemporary ▷ *adj* contemporary

COEVALITY > COEVAL

COEVALLY > COEVAL

COEVALS > COEVAL

COEVOLVE *vb* to evolve together

COEVOLVED > COEVOLVE

COEVOLVES > COEVOLVE

COEXERT *vb* to exert together

COEXERTED > COEXERT

COEXERTS > COEXERT

COEXIST *vb* exist together, esp peacefully despite differences

COEXISTED > COEXIST

COEXISTS > COEXIST

COEXTEND *vb* extend or cause to extend equally in space or time

COEXTENDS > COEXTEND

COFACTOR *n* number associated with an element in a square matrix, equal to the determinant of the matrix formed by removing the row and column in which the element appears from the given determinant

COFACTORS > COFACTOR

COFEATURE *vb* to feature together

COFF *vb* buy

COFFED > COFF

COFFEE *n* drink made from the roasted and ground seeds of a tropical shrub ▷ *adj* medium-brown

COFFEEPOT *n* pot in which coffee is brewed or served

COFFEES > COFFEE

COFFER *n* chest, esp for storing valuables ▷ *vb* store

COFFERDAM *n* watertight enclosure pumped dry to enable construction work to be done

COFFERED > COFFERDAM

COFFERING > COFFERDAM

COFFERS > COFFERDAM

COFFIN *n* box in which a corpse is buried or cremated ▷ *vb* place in or as in a coffin

COFFINED > COFFIN

COFFING > COFF

COFFINING > COFFIN

COFFINITE *n* uranium-bearing silicate mineral

COFFINS > COFFIN

COFFLE *n* (esp formerly) a line of slaves, beasts, etc, fastened together ▷ *vb* to fasten together in a coffle

COFFLED > COFFLE

COFFLES > COFFLE

COFFLING > COFFLE

COFFRET *n* small coffer

COFFRETS > COFFRET

COFFS > COFF

COFINANCE *vb* to finance jointly

COFOUND *vb* to found jointly

COFOUNDED > COFOUND

COFOUNDER > COFOUND

COFOUNDS > COFOUND

COFT > COFF

COG *n* one of the teeth on the rim of a gearwheel ▷ *vb* roll (cast-steel ingots) to convert them into blooms

COGENCE > COGENT

COGENCES > COGENT

COGENCIES > COGENT

COGENCY > COGENT

COGENER *n* congener

COGENERS > COGENER

COGENT *adj* forcefully convincing

COGENTLY > COGENT

COGGED > COG

COGGER *n* deceiver

COGGERS > COGGER

COGGIE *n* quaich or drinking cup

COGGIES > COGGIE

COGGING > COG

COGGINGS > COG

COGGLE *vb* wobble or rock

COGGLED > COGGLE

COGGLES > COGGLE

COGGLIER > COGGLE

COGGLIEST > COGGLE

COGGLING > COGGLE

COGGLY > COGGLE

COGIE *same as* > COGGIE

COGIES > COGIE

COGITABLE *adj* conceivable

COGITATE *vb* think deeply about

COGITATED > COGITATE

COGITATES > COGITATE

COGITATOR > COGITATE

COGITO *n* philosophical theory that one must exist because one is capable of thought

COGITOS > COGITO

COGNAC *n* French brandy

COGNACS > COGNAC

COGNATE *adj* derived from a common original form ▷ *n* cognate word or language

COGNATELY > COGNATE

COGNATES > COGNATE

COGNATION > COGNATE

COGNISANT *same as* > COGNIZANT

COGNISE *same as* > COGNIZE

COGNISED > COGNISE

COGNISER > COGNISE

COGNISERS > COGNISE

c

COGNISES > COGNISE
COGNISING > COGNISE
COGNITION n act or experience of knowing or acquiring knowledge
COGNITIVE adj of or relating to cognition
COGNIZANT adj aware
COGNIZE vb perceive, become aware of, or know
COGNIZED > COGNIZE
COGNIZER > COGNIZE
COGNIZERS > COGNIZE
COGNIZES > COGNIZE
COGNIZING > COGNIZE
COGNOMEN n nickname
COGNOMENS > COGNOMEN
COGNOMINA > COGNOMEN
COGNOSCE vb in Scots law, to give judgment upon
COGNOSCED > COGNOSCE
COGNOSCES > COGNOSCE
COGNOVIT n in law, a defendant's confession that the case against him is just
COGNOVITS > COGNOVIT
COGON n any of the coarse tropical grasses of the genus Imperata, esp I. cylindrica and I. exaltata of the Philippines, which are used for thatching
COGONS > COGON
COGS > COG
COGUE n wooden pail or drinking vessel
COGUES > COGUE
COGWAY n rack railway
COGWAYS > COGWAY
COGWHEEL same as > GEARWHEEL
COGWHEELS > COGWHEEL
COHAB n cohabitor
COHABIT vb live together as husband and wife without being married
COHABITED > COHABIT
COHABITEE > COHABIT
COHABITER > COHABIT
COHABITOR > COHABIT
COHABITS > COHABIT
COHABS > COHAB
COHEAD vb to head jointly
COHEADED > COHEAD
COHEADING > COHEAD
COHEADS > COHEAD
COHEIR n person who inherits jointly with others
COHEIRESS > COHEIR
COHEIRS > COHEIR
COHERE vb hold or stick together
COHERED > COHERE
COHERENCE n logical or natural connection or consistency
COHERENCY same as > COHERENCE
COHERENT adj logical and consistent
COHERER n electrical component formerly used to detect radio waves, consisting of a tube containing loosely packed metal particles. The waves

caused the particles to cohere, thereby changing the current through the circuit
COHERERS > COHERER
COHERES > COHERE
COHERING > COHERE
COHERITOR n coheir
COHESIBLE adj capable of cohesion
COHESION n sticking together
COHESIONS > COHESION
COHESIVE adj sticking together to form a whole
COHIBIT vb to restrain
COHIBITED > COHIBIT
COHIBITS > COHIBIT
COHO n Pacific salmon, Oncorhynchus kisutch
COHOBATE vb redistil (a distillate), esp by allowing it to mingle with the remaining matter
COHOBATED > COHOBATE
COHOBATES > COHOBATE
COHOE same as > COHO
COHOES > COHO
COHOG n quahog, an edible clam
COHOGS > COHOG
COHOLDER n joint holder
COHOLDERS > COHOLDER
COHORN same as > COEHORN
COHORNS > COEHORN
COHORT n band of associates
COHORTS > COHORT
COHOS > COHO
COHOSH n type of North American plant
COHOSHES > COHOSH
COHOST vb to host jointly
COHOSTED > COHOST
COHOSTESS vb (of a woman) to host jointly
COHOSTING > COHOST
COHOSTS > COHOST
COHOUSING n type of housing with some shared facilities
COHUNE n tropical American feather palm, Attalea (or Orbignya) cohune, whose large oily nuts yield an oil similar to coconut oil
COHUNES > COHUNE
COHYPONYM n word which is one of multiple hyponyms of another word
COIF vb arrange the hair of ▷ n close-fitting cap worn in the Middle Ages
COIFED adj wearing a coif
COIFFE vb to coiffure
COIFFED > COIF
COIFFES > COIFFE
COIFFEUR n hairdresser
COIFFEURS > COIFFEUR
COIFFEUSE > COIFFEUR
COIFFING > COIF
COIFFURE n hairstyle ▷ vb dress or arrange (the hair)
COIFFURED > COIFFURE
COIFFURES > COIFFURE
COIFING > COIF
COIFS > COIF

COIGN variant spelling of > QUOIN vb wedge
COIGNE same as > COIGN
COIGNED > COIGN
COIGNES > COIGNE
COIGNING > COIGN
COIGNS > COIGN
COIL vb wind in loops ▷ n something coiled
COILED > COIL
COILER > COIL
COILERS > COIL
COILING > COIL
COILS > COIL
COIN n piece of metal money ▷ vb invent (a word or phrase)
COINABLE > COIN
COINAGE n coins collectively
COINAGES > COINAGE
COINCIDE vb happen at the same time
COINCIDED > COINCIDE
COINCIDES > COINCIDE
COINED > COIN
COINER > COIN
COINERS > COIN
COINFECT vb infect at same time as other infection
COINFECTS > COINFECT
COINFER vb infer jointly
COINFERS > COINFER
COINHERE vb to inhere together
COINHERED > COINHERE
COINHERES > COINHERE
COINING > COIN
COININGS > COIN
COINMATE n fellow inmate
COINMATES > COINMATE
COINS > COIN
COINSURE vb insure jointly
COINSURED > COINSURE
COINSURER > COINSURE
COINSURES > COINSURE
COINTER vb to inter together
COINTERS > COINTER
COINTREAU n tradename for a French orange liqueur
COINVENT vb to invent jointly
COINVENTS > COINVENT
COIR n coconut fibre, used for matting
COIRS > COIR
COISTREL n knave
COISTRELS > COISTREL
COISTRIL same as > COISTREL
COISTRILS > COISTRIL
COIT n buttocks
COITAL > COITUS
COITALLY > COITUS
COITION same as > COITUS
COITIONAL > COITION
COITIONS > COITION
COITS > COIT
COITUS n sexual intercourse
COITUSES > COITUS
COJOIN vb to conjoin
COJOINED > COJOIN
COJOINING > COJOIN
COJOINS > COJOIN
COJONES pl n testicles
COKE n solid fuel left after

gas has been distilled from coal ▷ vb become or convert into coke
COKED > COKE
COKEHEAD n cocaine addict
COKEHEADS > COKEHEAD
COKELIKE > COKE
COKERNUT same as > COCONUT
COKERNUTS > COKERNUT
COKES n fool
COKESES > COKES
COKIER > COKY
COKIEST > COKY
COKING > COKE
COKULORIS n palette with irregular holes, placed between lighting and camera to prevent glare
COKY adj like coke
COL n high mountain pass
COLA n dark brown fizzy soft drink
COLANDER n perforated bowl for straining or rinsing foods
COLANDERS > COLANDER
COLAS > COLA
COLBIES > COLBY
COLBY n type of mild-tasting hard cheese
COLBYS > COLBY
COLCANNON n dish, originating in Ireland, of potatoes and cabbage or other greens boiled and mashed together
COLCHICA > COLCHICUM
COLCHICUM n any Eurasian liliaceous plant of the genus Colchicum, such as the autumn crocus
COLCOTHAR n finely powdered form of ferric oxide produced by heating ferric sulphate and used as a pigment and as jewellers' rouge
COLD adj lacking heat ▷ n lack of heat
COLDBLOOD n any heavy draught-horse
COLDCOCK vb to knock to the ground
COLDCOCKS > COLDCOCK
COLDER > COLD
COLDEST > COLD
COLDHOUSE n unheated greenhouse
COLDIE n cold can or bottle of beer
COLDIES > COLDIE
COLDISH > COLD
COLDLY > COLD
COLDNESS > COLD
COLDS > COLD
COLE same as > CABBAGE
COLEAD vb to lead together
COLEADER > COLEAD
COLEADERS > COLEAD
COLEADING > COLEAD
COLEADS > COLEAD
COLECTOMY n surgical removal of part or all of the colon
COLED > COLEAD
COLEOPTER n aircraft that

has an annular wing with the fuselage and engine on the centre line

COLES > COLE

COLESEED n common rape or cole

COLESEEDS > COLESEED

COLESLAW n salad dish of shredded raw cabbage in a dressing

COLESLAWS > COLESLAW

COLESSEE n joint lessee

COLESSEES > COLESSEE

COLESSOR n joint lessor

COLESSORS > COLESSOR

COLETIT n coal tit

COLETITS > COLETIT

COLEUS n any plant of the Old World genus *Coleus*: cultivated for their variegated leaves, typically marked with red, yellow, or white

COLEUSES > COLEUS

COLEWORT > CABBAGE

COLEWORTS > CABBAGE

COLEY same as > COALFISH

COLEYS > COLEY

COLIBRI n hummingbird

COLIBRIS > COLIBRI

COLIC n severe pains in the stomach and bowels

COLICIN n bacteriocidal protein

COLICINE n antibacterial protein

COLICINES > COLICINE

COLICINS > COLICIN

COLICKIER > COLICKY

COLICKY adj relating to or suffering from colic

COLICROOT n either of two North American liliaceous plants, *Aletris farinosa* or *A. aurea*, having tubular white or yellow flowers and a bitter root formerly used to relieve colic

COLICS > COLIC

COLICWEED n any of several plants of the genera *Dicentra* or *Corydalis*, such as the squirrel corn and Dutchman's-breeches: family *Fumariaceae*

COLIES > COLY

COLIFORM n type of bacteria of the intestinal tract

COLIFORMS > COLIFORM

COLIN n quail

COLINEAR same as > COLLINEAR

COLINS > COLIN

COLIPHAGE n bacteriophage

COLISEUM n large building, such as a stadium or theatre, used for entertainments, sports, etc

COLISEUMS > COLISEUM

COLISTIN n polymyxin antibiotic

COLISTINS > COLISTIN

COLITIC > COLITIS

COLITIS n inflammation of the colon

COLITISES > COLITIS

COLL vb to embrace

COLLAGE n art form in which various materials or objects are glued onto a surface ▷ vb to make a collage

COLLAGED > COLLAGE

COLLAGEN n protein found in cartilage and bone that yields gelatine when boiled

COLLAGENS > COLLAGEN

COLLAGES > COLLAGE

COLLAGING > COLLAGE

COLLAGIST > COLLAGE

COLLAPSAR n collapsed star, either a white dwarf, neutron star, or black hole

COLLAPSE vb fall down suddenly ▷ n collapsing

COLLAPSED > COLLAPSE

COLLAPSES > COLLAPSE

COLLAR n part of a garment round the neck ▷ vb seize, arrest

COLLARD n variety of the cabbage, *Brassica oleracea acephala*, having a crown of edible leaves

COLLARDS > COLLARD

COLLARED > COLLAR

COLLARET n small collar

COLLARETS > COLLARET

COLLARING > COLLAR

COLLARS > COLLAR

COLLATE vb gather together, examine, and put in order

COLLATED > COLLATE

COLLATES > COLLATE

COLLATING > COLLATE

COLLATION n collating

COLLATIVE adj involving collation

COLLATOR n person or machine that collates texts or manuscripts

COLLATORS > COLLATOR

COLLEAGUE n fellow worker, esp in a profession

COLLECT vb gather together ▷ n short prayer

COLLECTED adj calm and controlled

COLLECTOR n person who collects objects as a hobby

COLLECTS > COLLECT

COLLED > COLL

COLLEEN n girl

COLLEENS > COLLEEN

COLLEGE n place of higher education

COLLEGER n member of a college

COLLEGERS > COLLEGER

COLLEGES > COLLEGE

COLLEGIA > COLLEGIUM

COLLEGIAL adj of or relating to a college

COLLEGIAN n member of a college

COLLEGIUM n (in the former Soviet Union) a board in charge of a department

COLLET n (in a jewellery setting) a band or coronet-shaped claw that holds

an individual stone ▷ vb mount in a collet

COLLETED > COLLET

COLLETING > COLLET

COLLETS > COLLET

COLLICULI n plural form of singular colliculus: small elevation, as on the surface of the optic lobe of the brain

COLLIDE vb crash together violently

COLLIDED > COLLIDE

COLLIDER n particle accelerator in which beams of particles are made to collide

COLLIDERS > COLLIDER

COLLIDES > COLLIDE

COLLIDING > COLLIDE

COLLIE n silky-haired sheepdog

COLLIED > COLLY

COLLIER n coal miner

COLLIERS > COLLIER

COLLIERY n coal mine

COLLIES > COLLY

COLLIGATE vb connect or link together

COLLIMATE vb adjust the line of sight of (an optical instrument)

COLLINEAR adj lying on the same straight line

COLLING n embrace

COLLINGS > COLLING

COLLINS n tall fizzy iced drink made with gin, vodka, rum, etc, mixed with fruit juice, soda water, and sugar

COLLINSES > COLLINS

COLLINSIA n North American plant of the scrophulariaceous genus *Collinsia*, having blue, white, or purple flowers

COLLISION n violent crash between moving objects

COLLOCATE vb (of words) occur together regularly

COLLODION n colourless or yellow syrupy liquid that consists of a solution of pyroxylin in ether and alcohol: used in medicine and in the manufacture of photographic plates, lacquers, etc

COLLODIUM same as > COLLODION

COLLOGUE vb confer confidentially

COLLOGUED > COLLOGUE

COLLOGUES > COLLOGUE

COLLOID n suspension of particles in a solution ▷ adj of or relating to the gluelike translucent material found in certain degenerating tissues

COLLOIDAL adj of, denoting, or having the character of a colloid

COLLOIDS > COLLOID

COLLOP n small slice of meat

COLLOPS > COLLOP

COLLOQUE vb to converse

COLLOQUED > COLLOQUE

COLLOQUES > COLLOQUE

COLLOQUIA n plural form of singular colloquium: informal gathering

COLLOQUY n conversation or conference

COLLOTYPE n method of lithographic printing from a flat surface of hardened gelatine: used mainly for fine-detail reproduction in monochrome or colour

COLLOTYPY > COLLOTYPE

COLLS > COLL

COLLUDE vb act in collusion

COLLUDED > COLLUDE

COLLUDER > COLLUDE

COLLUDERS > COLLUDE

COLLUDES > COLLUDE

COLLUDING > COLLUDE

COLLUSION n secret or illegal cooperation

COLLUSIVE > COLLUSION

COLLUVIA > COLLUVIUM

COLLUVIAL > COLLUVIUM

COLLUVIES n offscourings

COLLUVIUM n mixture of rock fragments from the bases of cliffs

COLLY n soot or grime, such as coal dust ▷ vb begrime

COLLYING > COLLY

COLLYRIA > COLLYRIUM

COLLYRIUM a technical name for an > EYEWASH

COLOBI > COLOBUS

COLOBID > COLOBUS

COLOBOMA n structural defect of the eye, esp in the choroid, retina, or iris

COLOBOMAS > COLOBOMA

COLOBUS n any leaf-eating arboreal Old World monkey of the genus *Colobus*, of W and central Africa, having a slender body, long silky fur, long tail, and reduced or absent thumbs

COLOBUSES > COLOBUS

COLOCATE vb to locate together

COLOCATED > COLOCATE

COLOCATES > COLOCATE

COLOCYNTH n cucurbitaceous climbing plant, *Citrullus colocynthis*, of the Mediterranean region and Asia, having bitter-tasting fruit

COLOG n logarithm of the reciprocal of a number

COLOGNE n mild perfume

COLOGNED > COLOGNE

COLOGNES > COLOGNE

COLOGS > COLOG

COLOMBARD n grape used to make wine

COLON n punctuation mark (:); Costa Rican monetary unit

COLONE variant of > COLON

COLONEL n senior commissioned army or air-force officer

COLONELCY > COLONEL

COLONELS > COLONEL

COLONES > COLONE

COLONI > COLONUS

COLONIAL n inhabitant of a colony ▷ adj of or inhabiting a colony or colonies

COLONIALS > COLONIAL

COLONIC adj of or relating to the colon ▷ n irrigation of the colon by injecting large amounts of fluid high into the colon

COLONICS > COLONIC

COLONIES > COLONY

COLONISE same as > COLONIZE

COLONISED > COLONISE

COLONISER > COLONISE

COLONISES > COLONISE

COLONIST n settler in a colony

COLONISTS > COLONIST

COLONITIS same as > COLITIS

COLONIZE vb make into a colony

COLONIZED > COLONIZE

COLONIZER > COLONIZE

COLONIZES > COLONIZE

COLONNADE n row of columns

COLONS > COLON

COLONUS n ancient Roman farmer

COLONY n group of people who settle in a new country but remain under the rule of their homeland

COLOPHON n publisher's symbol on a book

COLOPHONS > COLOPHON

COLOPHONY another name for > ROSIN

COLOR same as > COLOUR

COLORABLE > COLOR

COLORABLY > COLOR

COLORADO adj (of a cigar) of middling colour and strength

COLORANT n any substance that imparts colour, such as a pigment, dye, or ink

COLORANTS > COLORANT

COLORBRED adj (of animals) bred for their colour

COLORCAST vb broadcast in colour

COLORED US spelling of > COLOURED

COLOREDS > COLORED

COLORER > COLOR

COLORERS > COLOR

COLORFAST adj variant of colourfast: (of a fabric) having a colour that does not run when washed

COLORFUL > COLOR

COLORIFIC adj producing, imparting, or relating to colour

COLORING > COLOUR

COLORINGS > COLOUR

COLORISE same as > COLOURIZE

COLORISED > COLORISE

COLORISER > COLORISE

COLORISES > COLORISE

COLORISM > COLOR

COLORISMS > COLOR

COLORIST > COLOR

COLORISTS > COLOR

COLORIZE same as > COLOURIZE

COLORIZED > COLOURIZE

COLORIZER > COLORIZE

COLORIZES > COLORIZE

COLORLESS > COLOR

COLORMAN same as > COLOURMAN

COLORMEN > COLORMAN

COLORS > COLOR

COLORWAY variant of > COLOURWAY

COLORWAYS > COLORWAY

COLORY same as > COLOURY

COLOSSAL adj very large

COLOSSEUM same as > COLISEUM

COLOSSI > COLOSSUS

COLOSSUS n huge statue

COLOSTOMY n operation to form an opening from the colon onto the surface of the body, for emptying the bowel

COLOSTRAL > COLOSTRUM

COLOSTRIC > COLOSTRUM

COLOSTRUM n thin milky secretion from the nipples that precedes and follows true lactation. It consists largely of serum and white blood cells

COLOTOMY n colonic incision

COLOUR n appearance of things as a result of reflecting light ▷ vb apply colour to

COLOURANT same as > COLORANT

COLOURED adj having colour ▷ n person who is not white

COLOUREDS > COLOURED

COLOURER > COLOUR

COLOURERS > COLOUR

COLOURFUL adj with bright or varied colours

COLOURING n application of colour

COLOURISE same as > COLOURIZE

COLOURIST n person who uses colour, esp an artist

COLOURIZE vb add colour electronically to (an old black-and-white film)

COLOURMAN n person who deals in paints

COLOURMEN > COLOURMAN

COLOURS > COLOUR

COLOURWAY n one of several different combinations of colours in which a given pattern is printed on fabrics, wallpapers, etc

COLOURY adj possessing colour

COLPITIS another name for > VAGINITIS

COLPOTOMY n surgical incision into the wall of the vagina

COLS > COL

COLT n young male horse ▷ vb to fool

COLTAN n metallic ore found esp in the E Congo, consisting of columbite and tantalite and used as a source of tantalum

COLTANS > COLTAN

COLTED > COLT

COLTER same as > COULTER

COLTERS > COULTER

COLTING > COLT

COLTISH adj inexperienced

COLTISHLY > COLTISH

COLTS > COLT

COLTSFOOT n weed with yellow flowers and heart-shaped leaves

COLTWOOD n plant mentioned in Spenser's Faerie Queene

COLTWOODS > COLTWOOD

COLUBRIAD n epic poem about a snake

COLUBRID n any snake of the family Colubridae, including many harmless snakes, such as the grass snake and whip snakes, and some venomous types ▷ adj of, relating to, or belonging to the Colubridae

COLUBRIDS > COLUBRID

COLUBRINE adj of or resembling a snake

COLUGO n flying lemur

COLUGOS > COLUGO

COLUMBARY n dovecote

COLUMBATE n niobate

COLUMBIC another word for > NIOBIC

COLUMBINE n garden flower with five petals ▷ adj of, relating to, or resembling a dove

COLUMBITE n black mineral occurring in coarse granite

COLUMBIUM the former name of > NIOBIUM

COLUMBOUS another word for > NIOBOUS

COLUMEL n in botany, the central column in a capsule

COLUMELLA n central part of the spore-producing body of some fungi and mosses

COLUMELS > COLUMEL

COLUMN n pillar ▷ vb create a column

COLUMNAL > COLUMN

COLUMNAR > COLUMN

COLUMNEA n flowering plant

COLUMNEAS > COLUMNEA

COLUMNED > COLUMN

COLUMNIST n journalist who writes a regular feature in a newspaper

COLUMNS > COLUMN

COLURE n either of two great circles on the celestial sphere, one of which passes through the celestial poles and the equinoxes and the other through the poles and the solstices

COLURES > COLURE

COLY n any of the arboreal birds of the genus Colius, family Coliidae, and order Coliiformes, of southern Africa. They have a soft hairlike plumage, crested head, and very long tail

COLZA n oilseed rape, a Eurasian plant with bright yellow flowers

COLZAS > COLZA

COMA n state of deep unconsciousness

COMADE > COMAKE

COMAE > COMA

COMAKE vb to make together

COMAKER > COMAKE

COMAKERS > COMAKE

COMAKES > COMAKE

COMAKING > COMAKE

COMAL > COMA

COMANAGE vb to manage jointly

COMANAGED > COMANAGE

COMANAGER > COMANAGE

COMANAGES > COMANAGE

COMARB same as > COARB

COMARBS > COMARB

COMART n covenant

COMARTS > COMART

COMAS > COMA

COMATE adj having tufts of hair ▷ n companion

COMATES > COMATE

COMATIC > COMA

COMATIK variant of > KOMATIK

COMATIKS > COMATIK

COMATOSE adj in a coma

COMATULA same as > COMATULID

COMATULAE > COMATULID

COMATULID n any of a group of crinoid echinoderms, including the feather stars, in which the adults are free-swimming

COMB n toothed implement for arranging the hair ▷ vb use a comb on

COMBAT vb fight, struggle ▷ n fight or struggle

COMBATANT n fighter ▷ adj fighting

COMBATED > COMBAT

COMBATER > COMBAT

COMBATERS > COMBAT

COMBATING > COMBAT

COMBATIVE adj eager or ready to fight, argue, etc

COMBATS > COMBAT

COMBATTED > COMBAT

COMBE same as > COMB

COMBED > COMB

COMBER n long curling wave

COMBERS > COMBER

COMBES > COMBE

COMBI n combination boiler

COMBIER > COMBY

COMBIES > COMBY

COMBIEST > COMBY

COMBINATE adj betrothed

COMBINE vb join together ▷ n association of people

or firms for a common purpose

COMBINED > COMBINE

COMBINEDS > COMBINE

COMBINER > COMBINE

COMBINERS > COMBINE

COMBINES > COMBINE

COMBING > COMB

COMBINGS *pl n* loose hair or fibres removed by combing, esp from animals

COMBINING > COMBINE

COMBIS > COMBI

COMBLE *n* apex; zenith

COMBLES > COMBLE

COMBLESS *adj* without a comb

COMBLIKE *adj* resembling a comb

COMBO *n* small group of jazz musicians

COMBOS > COMBO

COMBRETUM *n* any tree or shrub belonging to the genus Combretum

COMBS > COMB

COMBUST *adj* (of a star or planet) invisible for a period between 24 and 30 days each year due to its proximity to the sun ▷ *vb* burn

COMBUSTED > COMBUST

COMBUSTOR *n* combustion system of a jet engine or ramjet, comprising the combustion chamber, the fuel injection apparatus, and the igniter

COMBUSTS > COMBUST

COMBWISE *adv* in the manner of a comb

COMBY *adj* comb-like ▷ *n* combination boiler

COME *vb* move towards a place, arrive

COMEBACK *n* return to a former position ▷ *vb* return, esp to the memory

COMEBACKS > COMEBACK

COMEDDLE *vb* mix

COMEDDLED > COMEDDLE

COMEDDLES > COMEDDLE

COMEDIAN *n* entertainer who tells jokes

COMEDIANS > COMEDIAN

COMEDIC *adj* of or relating to comedy

COMEDIES > COMEDY

COMEDO *the technical name for* > BLACKHEAD

COMEDONES > COMEDO

COMEDOS > COMEDO

COMEDOWN *n* decline in status ▷ *vb* come to a place regarded as lower

COMEDOWNS > COMEDOWN

COMEDY *n* humorous play, film, or programme

COMELIER > COMELY

COMELIEST > COMELY

COMELILY > COMELY

COMELY *adj* nice-looking

COMEMBER *n* fellow member

COMEMBERS > COMEMBER

COMEOVER *n* person who has come from Britain to

the Isle of Man to settle

COMEOVERS > COMEOVER

COMER *n* person who comes

COMERS > COMER

COMES > COME

COMET *n* heavenly body with a long luminous tail

COMETARY > COMET

COMETH > COME

COMETHER *n* coaxing; allure

COMETHERS > COMETHER

COMETIC > COMET

COMETS > COMET

COMFIER > COMFY

COMFIEST > COMFY

COMFINESS > COMFY

COMFIT *n* sugar-coated sweet

COMFITS > COMFIT

COMFITURE *n* confiture

COMFORT *n* physical ease or wellbeing ▷ *vb* soothe, console

COMFORTED > COMFORT

COMFORTER *n* person or thing that comforts

COMFORTS > COMFORT

COMFREY *n* tall plant with bell-shaped flowers

COMFREYS > COMFREY

COMFY *adj* comfortable

COMIC *adj* humorous, funny ▷ *n* comedian

COMICAL *adj* amusing

COMICALLY > COMICAL

COMICE *n* kind of pear

COMICES > COMICE

COMICS > COMIC

COMING > COME

COMINGLE *same as* > COMMINGLE

COMINGLED > COMMINGLE

COMINGLES > COMINGLE

COMINGS > COME

COMIQUE *n* comic actor

COMIQUES > COMIQUE

COMITADJI *n* Balkan guerrilla fighter

COMITAL *adj* relating to a count or earl

COMITATUS *n* leader's retinue

COMITIA *n* ancient Roman assembly that elected officials and exercised judicial and legislative authority

COMITIAL > COMITIA

COMITIAS > COMITIA

COMITIES > COMITY

COMITY *n* friendly politeness, esp between different countries

COMIX *n* comic books in general

COMM as in *comm badge* small wearable badge-shaped radio transmitter and receiver

COMMA *n* punctuation mark (,)

COMMAND *vb* order ▷ *n* authoritative instruction that something must be done

COMMANDED > COMMAND

COMMANDER *n* military

officer in command of a group or operation

COMMANDO *n* (member of) a military unit trained for swift raids in enemy territory

COMMANDOS > COMMANDO

COMMANDS > COMMAND

COMMAS > COMMA

COMMATA > COMMA

COMMENCE *vb* begin

COMMENCED > COMMENCE

COMMENCER > COMMENCE

COMMENCES > COMMENCE

COMMEND *vb* praise

COMMENDAM *n* temporary holding of an ecclesiastical benefice

COMMENDED > COMMEND

COMMENDER > COMMEND

COMMENDS > COMMEND

COMMENSAL *adj* (of two different species of plant or animal) living in close association, such that one species benefits without harming the other ▷ *n* commensal plant or animal

COMMENT *n* remark ▷ *vb* make a comment

COMMENTED > COMMENT

COMMENTER > COMMENT

COMMENTOR > COMMENT

COMMENTS > COMMENT

COMMER *same as* > COMER

COMMERCE *n* buying and selling, trade ▷ *vb* to trade

COMMERCED > COMMERCE

COMMERCES > COMMERCE

COMMERE *n* female compere

COMMERES > COMMERE

COMMERGE *vb* to merge together

COMMERGED > COMMERGE

COMMERGES > COMMERGE

COMMERS > COMMER

COMMIE *adj* communist

COMMIES > COMMIE

COMMINATE *vb* to anathematise

COMMINGLE *vb* mix or be mixed

COMMINUTE *vb* break (a bone) into several small fragments

COMMIS *n* apprentice waiter or chef ▷ *adj* (of a waiter or chef) apprentice

COMMISSAR *n* (formerly) official responsible for political education in Communist countries

COMMIT *vb* perform (a crime or error)

COMMITS > COMMIT

COMMITTAL *n* act of committing or pledging

COMMITTED > COMMIT

COMMITTEE *n* group of people appointed to perform a specified service or function

COMMITTER > COMMIT

COMMIX *a rare word for* > MIX

COMMIXED > COMMIX

COMMIXES > COMMIX

COMMIXING > COMMIX

COMMIXT > COMMIX

COMMO *short for* > COMMUNIST

COMMODE *n* seat with a hinged flap concealing a chamber pot

COMMODES > COMMODE

COMMODIFY *vb* to make into a commodity

COMMODITY *n* something that can be bought or sold

COMMODO *same as* > COMODO

COMMODORE *n* senior commissioned officer in the navy

COMMON *adj* occurring often ▷ *n* area of grassy land belonging to a community ▷ *vb* sit at table with strangers

COMMONAGE *n* use of something, esp a pasture, in common with others

COMMONED > COMMON

COMMONER *n* person who does not belong to the nobility

COMMONERS > COMMONER

COMMONEST > COMMON

COMMONEY *n* playing marble of a common sort

COMMONEYS > COMMONEY

COMMONING > COMMON

COMMONLY *adv* usually

COMMONS *n* people not of noble birth viewed as forming a political order

COMMORANT *n* resident

COMMOS > COMMO

COMMOT *n* in medieval Wales, a division of land

COMMOTE *same as* > COMMOT

COMMOTES > COMMOTE

COMMOTION *n* noisy disturbance

COMMOTS > COMMOT

COMMOVE *vb* disturb

COMMOVED > COMMOVE

COMMOVES > COMMOVE

COMMOVING > COMMOVE

COMMS *pl n* communications

COMMUNAL *adj* shared

COMMUNARD *n* member of a commune

COMMUNE *n* group of people who live together and share everything ▷ *vb* feel very close (to)

COMMUNED > COMMUNE

COMMUNER > COMMUNE

COMMUNERS > COMMUNE

COMMUNES > COMMUNE

COMMUNING > COMMUNE

COMMUNION *n* sharing of thoughts or feelings

COMMUNISE *same as* > COMMUNIZE

COMMUNISM *n* belief that all property and means of production should be shared by the community

COMMUNIST *n* supporter of any form of communism ▷ *adj* of, characterized by, favouring, or relating to communism

COMMUNITY *n* all the people

living in one district

COMMUNIZE vb make (property) public

COMMUTATE vb reverse the direction of (an electric current)

COMMUTE vb travel daily to and from work ▷n journey made by commuting

COMMUTED > COMMUTE

COMMUTER n person who commutes to and from work

COMMUTERS > COMMUTER

COMMUTES > COMMUTE

COMMUTING > COMMUTE

COMMUTUAL adj mutual

COMMY same as > COMMIE

COMODO adv (to be performed) at a convenient relaxed speed

COMONOMER n monomer that, with another, constitutes a copolymer

COMORBID adj (of illness) happening at same time as other illness

COMOSE another word for > COMATE

COMOUS adj hairy

COMP n person who sets and corrects type ▷vb set or correct type

COMPACT adj closely packed ▷n small flat case containing a mirror and face powder ▷vb pack closely together

COMPACTED > COMPACT

COMPACTER > COMPACT

COMPACTLY > COMPACT

COMPACTOR n machine which compresses waste material for easier disposal

COMPACTS > COMPACT

COMPADRE n masculine friend

COMPADRES > COMPADRE

COMPAGE obsolete form of > COMPAGES

COMPAGES n structure or framework

COMPAND vb (of a transmitter signal) to compress before, and expand after, transmission

COMPANDED > COMPAND

COMPANDER n system for improving the signal-to-noise ratio of a signal at a transmitter or recorder by first compressing the volume range of the signal and then restoring it to its original amplitude level at the receiving or reproducing apparatus

COMPANDOR same as > COMPANDER

COMPANDS > COMPAND

COMPANIED > COMPANY

COMPANIES > COMPANY

COMPANING > COMPANY

COMPANION n person who associates with or accompanies someone ▷vb accompany or be a

companion to

COMPANY n business organization ▷vb associate or keep company with someone

COMPARE vb examine (things) and point out the resemblances or differences

COMPARED > COMPARE

COMPARER > COMPARE

COMPARERS > COMPARE

COMPARES > COMPARE

COMPARING > COMPARE

COMPART vb to divide into parts

COMPARTED > COMPART

COMPARTS > COMPART

COMPAS n rhythm in flamenco

COMPASS n instrument for showing direction, with a needle that points north ▷vb encircle or surround

COMPASSED > COMPASS

COMPASSES > COMPASS

COMPAST adj rounded

COMPEAR vb in Scots law, to appear in court

COMPEARED > COMPEAR

COMPEARS > COMPEAR

COMPED > COMPOSITOR

COMPEER n person of equal rank, status, or ability ▷vb to equal

COMPEERED > COMPEER

COMPEERS > COMPEER

COMPEL vb force (to be or do)

COMPELLED > COMPEL

COMPELLER > COMPEL

COMPELS > COMPEL

COMPEND n compendium

COMPENDIA n plural form of singular compendium: book containing a collection of useful hints

COMPENDS > COMPEND

COMPER n person who regularly enters competitions in newspapers, magazines, etc, esp competitions offering consumer goods as prizes

COMPERE n person who presents a stage, radio, or television show ▷vb be the compere of

COMPERED > COMPERE

COMPERES > COMPERE

COMPERING > COMPERE

COMPERS > COMPER

COMPESCE vb to curb

COMPESCED > COMPESCE

COMPESCES > COMPESCE

COMPETE vb try to win or achieve (a prize, profit, etc)

COMPETED > COMPETE

COMPETENT adj having the skill or knowledge to do something well

COMPETES > COMPETE

COMPETING > COMPETE

COMPILE vb collect and arrange (information), esp to make a book

COMPILED > COMPILE

COMPILER n person who compiles information

COMPILERS > COMPILER

COMPILES > COMPILE

COMPILING > COMPILE

COMPING > COMP

COMPINGS > COMP

COMPITAL adj pertaining to crossroads

COMPLAIN vb express resentment or displeasure

COMPLAINS > COMPLAIN

COMPLAINT n complaining

COMPLEAT an archaic spelling of > COMPLETE

COMPLECT vb interweave or entwine

COMPLECTS > COMPLECT

COMPLETE adj thorough, absolute ▷vb finish

COMPLETED > COMPLETE

COMPLETER > COMPLETE

COMPLETES > COMPLETE

COMPLEX adj made up of parts ▷n whole made up of parts ▷vb to form a complex

COMPLEXED > COMPLEX

COMPLEXER > COMPLEX

COMPLEXES > COMPLEX

COMPLEXLY > COMPLEX

COMPLEXUS n complex

COMPLIANT adj complying, obliging, or yielding

COMPLICE n associate or accomplice

COMPLICES > COMPLICE

COMPLICIT adj involved in a crime or questionable act

COMPLIED > COMPLY

COMPLIER > COMPLY

COMPLIERS > COMPLY

COMPLIES > COMPLY

COMPLIN same as > COMPLINE

COMPLINE n last service of the day in the Roman Catholic Church

COMPLINES > COMPLINE

COMPLINS > COMPLIN

COMPLISH vb accomplish

COMPLOT n plot or conspiracy ▷vb plot together

COMPLOTS > COMPLOT

COMPLUVIA n plural form of singular compluvium: an unroofed space over the atrium in a Roman house, though which rain fell and was collected

COMPLY vb act in accordance (with)

COMPLYING > COMPLY

COMPO n mixture of materials, such as mortar, plaster, etc ▷adj intended to last for several days

COMPONE same as > COMPONY

COMPONENT adj (being) part of a whole ▷n constituent part or feature of a whole

COMPONY adj made up of alternating metal and colour, colour and fur, or fur

and metal

COMPORT vb behave (oneself) in a specified way

COMPORTED > COMPORT

COMPORTS > COMPORT

COMPOS > COMPO

COMPOSE vb put together

COMPOSED adj calm

COMPOSER n person who writes music

COMPOSERS > COMPOSER

COMPOSES > COMPOSE

COMPOSING > COMPOSE

COMPOSITE adj made up of separate parts ▷n something composed of separate parts ▷vb merge related motions from local branches of (a political party, trade union, etc) so as to produce a manageable number of proposals for discussion at national level

COMPOST n decayed plants used as a fertilizer ▷vb make (vegetable matter) into compost

COMPOSTED > COMPOST

COMPOSTER n bin or other container used to turn garden waste into compost

COMPOSTS > COMPOST

COMPOSURE n calmness

COMPOT same as > COMPOTE

COMPOTE n fruit stewed with sugar

COMPOTES > COMPOTE

COMPOTIER n dish for holding compote

COMPOTS > COMPOT

COMPOUND adj (thing, esp chemical) made up of two or more combined parts or elements ▷vb combine or make by combining ▷n fenced enclosure containing buildings

COMPOUNDS > COMPOUND

COMPRADOR n (formerly in China and some other Asian countries) a native agent of a foreign enterprise

COMPRESS vb squeeze together ▷n pad applied to stop bleeding or cool inflammation

COMPRINT vb to print jointly

COMPRINTS > COMPRINT

COMPRISAL > COMPRISE

COMPRISE vb be made up of or make up

COMPRISED > COMPRISE

COMPRISES > COMPRISE

COMPRIZE same as > COMPRISE

COMPRIZED > COMPRIZE

COMPRIZES > COMPRIZE

COMPS > COMP

COMPT obsolete variant of > COUNT

COMPTABLE n countable

COMPTED > COMPT

COMPTER n formerly, a prison

COMPTERS > COMPT

COMPTIBLE *same as* > COMPTABLE
COMPTING > COUNT
COMPTROLL *obsolete variant of* > CONTROL
COMPTS > COUNT
COMPULSE *vb* to compel
COMPULSED > COMPULSE
COMPULSES > COMPULSE
COMPUTANT *n* calculator
COMPUTE *vb* calculate, esp using a computer ▷ *n* calculation
COMPUTED > COMPUTE
COMPUTER *n* electronic machine that stores and processes data
COMPUTERS > COMPUTER
COMPUTES > COMPUTE
COMPUTING *n* activity of using computers and writing programs for them ▷ *adj* of or relating to computers
COMPUTIST *n* one who computes
COMRADE *n* fellow member of a union or socialist political party
COMRADELY > COMRADE
COMRADERY *n* comradeship
COMRADES > COMRADE
COMS *pl n* one-piece woollen undergarment with longs sleeves and legs
COMSYMP *n* Communist Party sympathizer
COMSYMPS > COMSYMP
COMTE *n* European nobleman
COMTES > COMTE
COMUS *n* wild party
COMUSES > COMUS
CON *vb* deceive, swindle ▷ *n* convict ▷ *prep* with
CONACRE *n* farming land let for a season or for eleven months ▷ *vb* to let conacre
CONACRED > CONACRE
CONACRES > CONACRE
CONACRING > CONACRE
CONARIA > CONARIUM
CONARIAL > CONARIUM
CONARIUM *n* pineal gland
CONATION *n* element in psychological processes that tends towards activity or change and appears as desire, volition, and striving
CONATIONS > CONATION
CONATIVE *adj* denoting an aspect of verbs in some languages used to indicate the effort of the agent in performing the activity described by the verb
CONATUS *n* effort or striving of natural impulse
CONCAUSE *n* shared cause
CONCAUSES > CONCAUSE
CONCAVE *adj* curving inwards ▷ *vb* make concave
CONCAVED > CONCAVE
CONCAVELY > CONCAVE
CONCAVES > CONCAVE

CONCAVING > CONCAVE
CONCAVITY *n* state or quality of being concave
CONCEAL *vb* cover and hide
CONCEALED > CONCEAL
CONCEALER > CONCEAL
CONCEALS > CONCEAL
CONCEDE *vb* admit to be true
CONCEDED > CONCEDE
CONCEDER > CONCEDE
CONCEDERS > CONCEDE
CONCEDES > CONCEDE
CONCEDING > CONCEDE
CONCEDO *interj* I allow; I concede (a point)
CONCEIT *n* too high an opinion of oneself ▷ *vb* like or be able to bear (something, such as food or drink)
CONCEITED *adj* having an excessively high opinion of oneself
CONCEITS > CONCEIT
CONCEITY *adj* full of conceit
CONCEIVE *vb* imagine, think
CONCEIVED > CONCEIVE
CONCEIVER > CONCEIVE
CONCEIVES > CONCEIVE
CONCENT *n* concord, as of sounds, voices, etc
CONCENTER *same as* > CONCENTRE
CONCENTRE *vb* converge or cause to converge on a common centre
CONCENTS > CONCENT
CONCENTUS *n* vocal harmony
CONCEPT *n* abstract or general idea
CONCEPTI > CONCEPTUS
CONCEPTS > CONCEPT
CONCEPTUS *n* any product of conception, including the embryo, foetus and surrounding tissue
CONCERN *n* anxiety, worry ▷ *vb* worry (someone)
CONCERNED *adj* interested, involved
CONCERNS > CONCERN
CONCERT *n* musical entertainment
CONCERTED *adj* done together
CONCERTI > CONCERTO
CONCERTO *n* large-scale composition for a solo instrument and orchestra
CONCERTOS > CONCERTO
CONCERTS > CONCERT
CONCETTI > CONCETTO
CONCETTO *n* conceit, ingenious thought
CONCH *same as* > CONCHA
CONCHA *n* any bodily organ or part resembling a shell in shape, such as the external ear
CONCHAE > CONCHA
CONCHAL > CONCHA
CONCHAS > CONCHA
CONCHATE *adj* shell-shaped
CONCHE *vb* (in chocolate-making) to use a conche

(machine which mixes and smooths the chocolate mass)
CONCHED > CONCHE
CONCHES > CONCHE
CONCHIE *n* conscientious objector
CONCHIES > CONCHIE
CONCHING > CONCHE
CONCHITIS *n* inflammation of the outer ear
CONCHO *n* American metal ornament
CONCHOID *n* type of plane curve
CONCHOIDS > CONCHOID
CONCHOS > CONCHO
CONCHS > CONCH
CONCHY *same as* > CONCHIE
CONCIERGE *n* (in France) caretaker in a block of flats
CONCILIAR *adj* of, from, or by means of a council, esp an ecclesiastical one
CONCISE *adj* brief and to the point ▷ *vb* mutilate
CONCISED > CONCISE
CONCISELY > CONCISE
CONCISER > CONCISE
CONCISES > CONCISE
CONCISEST > CONCISE
CONCISING > CONCISE
CONCISION *n* quality of being concise
CONCLAVE *n* secret meeting
CONCLAVES > CONCLAVE
CONCLUDE *vb* decide by reasoning
CONCLUDED > CONCLUDE
CONCLUDER > CONCLUDE
CONCLUDES > CONCLUDE
CONCOCT *vb* make up (a story or plan)
CONCOCTED > CONCOCT
CONCOCTER > CONCOCT
CONCOCTOR > CONCOCT
CONCOCTS > CONCOCT
CONCOLOR *adj* of a single colour
CONCORD *n* state of peaceful agreement, harmony ▷ *vb* to agree
CONCORDAL > CONCORD
CONCORDAT *n* pact or treaty
CONCORDED > CONCORD
CONCORDS > CONCORD
CONCOURS *n* contest
CONCOURSE *n* large open public place where people can gather
CONCREATE *vb* to create at the same time
CONCRETE *n* mixture of cement, sand, stone, and water, used in building ▷ *vb* cover with concrete ▷ *adj* made of concrete
CONCRETED > CONCRETE
CONCRETES > CONCRETE
CONCREW *vb* to grow together
CONCREWED > CONCREW
CONCREWS > CONCREW
CONCUBINE *n* woman living in a man's house but not married to him and kept for his sexual pleasure

CONCUPIES > CONCUPY
CONCUPY *n* concupiscence
CONCUR *vb* agree
CONCURRED > CONCUR
CONCURS > CONCUR
CONCUSS *vb* injure (the brain) by a fall or blow
CONCUSSED > CONCUSS
CONCUSSES > CONCUSS
CONCYCLIC *adj* (of a set of geometric points) lying on a common circle
COND *old inflection of* > CON
CONDEMN *vb* express disapproval of
CONDEMNED > CONDEMN
CONDEMNER > CONDEMN
CONDEMNOR > CONDEMN
CONDEMNS > CONDEMN
CONDENSE *vb* make shorter
CONDENSED *adj* (of printers' type) narrower than usual for a particular height
CONDENSER *same as* > CAPACITOR
CONDENSES > CONDENSE
CONDER *n* person who directs the steering of a vessel
CONDERS > CONDER
CONDIDDLE *vb* to steal
CONDIE *n* culvert; tunnel
CONDIES > CONDIE
CONDIGN *adj* (esp of a punishment) fitting
CONDIGNLY > CONDIGN
CONDIMENT *n* seasoning for food, such as salt or pepper
CONDITION *n* particular state of being ▷ *vb* train or influence to behave in a particular way
CONDO *n* condominium
CONDOES > CONDO
CONDOLE *vb* express sympathy with someone in grief, pain, etc
CONDOLED > CONDOLE
CONDOLENT *adj* expressing sympathy with someone in grief
CONDOLER > CONDOLE
CONDOLERS > CONDOLE
CONDOLES > CONDOLE
CONDOLING > CONDOLE
CONDOM *n* rubber sheath worn on the penis or in the vagina during sexual intercourse to prevent conception or infection
CONDOMS > CONDOM
CONDONE *vb* overlook or forgive (wrongdoing)
CONDONED > CONDONE
CONDONER > CONDONE
CONDONERS > CONDONE
CONDONES > CONDONE
CONDONING > CONDONE
CONDOR *n* large vulture of S America
CONDORES > CONDOR
CONDORS > CONDOR
CONDOS > CONDO
CONDUCE *vb* lead or contribute (to a result)
CONDUCED > CONDUCE
CONDUCER > CONDUCE

CONDUCERS > CONDUCE
CONDUCES > CONDUCE
CONDUCING > CONDUCE
CONDUCIVE adj likely to lead (to)
CONDUCT n management of an activity ▷ vb carry out (a task)
CONDUCTED > CONDUCT
CONDUCTI > CONDUCTUS
CONDUCTOR n person who conducts musicians
CONDUCTS > CONDUCT
CONDUCTUS n medieval liturgical composition
CONDUIT n channel or tube for fluid or cables
CONDUITS > CONDUIT
CONDYLAR > CONDYLE
CONDYLE n rounded projection on the articulating end of a bone, such as the ball portion of a ball-and-socket joint
CONDYLES > CONDYLE
CONDYLOID adj of or resembling a condyle
CONDYLOMA n skin tumour near the anus or genital organs, esp as a result of syphilis
CONE n object with a circular base, tapering to a point ▷ vb shape like a cone or part of a cone
CONED > CONE
CONELRAD n US defence and information system for use in the event of air attack
CONELRADS > CONELRAD
CONENOSE n bloodsucking bug of the genus Triatoma
CONENOSES > CONENOSE
CONEPATE same as > CONEPATL
CONEPATES > CONEPATE
CONEPATL n skunk
CONEPATLS > CONEPATL
CONES > CONE
CONEY same as > CONY
CONEYS > CONEY
CONF n online forum
CONFAB n conversation ▷ vb converse
CONFABBED > CONFAB
CONFABS > CONFAB
CONFECT vb prepare by combining ingredients
CONFECTED > CONFECT
CONFECTS > CONFECT
CONFER vb discuss together
CONFEREE n person who takes part in a conference
CONFEREES > CONFEREE
CONFERRAL > CONFER
CONFERRED > CONFER
CONFERREE same as > CONFEREE
CONFERRER > CONFER
CONFERS > CONFER
CONFERVA n any of various threadlike green algae, esp any of the genus Tribonema, typically occurring in fresh water
CONFERVAE > CONFERVA
CONFERVAL > CONFERVA

CONFERVAS > CONFERVA
CONFESS vb admit (a fault or crime)
CONFESSED > CONFESS
CONFESSES > CONFESS
CONFESSOR n priest who hears confessions
CONFEST adj admitted
CONFESTLY adv confessedly
CONFETTI n small pieces of coloured paper thrown at weddings
CONFETTO n sweetmeat
CONFIDANT n person confided in
CONFIDE vb tell someone (a secret)
CONFIDED > CONFIDE
CONFIDENT adj sure, esp of oneself
CONFIDER > CONFIDE
CONFIDERS > CONFIDE
CONFIDES > CONFIDE
CONFIDING adj trusting
CONFIGURE vb to design or set up
CONFINE vb keep within bounds ▷ n limit
CONFINED adj enclosed or restricted
CONFINER > CONFINE
CONFINERS > CONFINE
CONFINES > CONFINE
CONFINING > CONFINE
CONFIRM vb prove to be true
CONFIRMED adj firmly established in a habit or condition
CONFIRMEE n person to whom a confirmation is made
CONFIRMER > CONFIRM
CONFIRMOR n person who makes a confirmation
CONFIRMS > CONFIRM
CONFISEUR n confectioner
CONFIT n preserve
CONFITEOR n Catholic prayer asking for forgiveness
CONFITS > CONFIT
CONFITURE n confection, preserve of fruit, etc
CONFIX vb to fasten
CONFIXED > CONFIX
CONFIXES > CONFIX
CONFIXING > CONFIX
CONFLATE vb combine or blend into a whole
CONFLATED > CONFLATE
CONFLATES > CONFLATE
CONFLICT n disagreement ▷ vb be incompatible
CONFLICTS > CONFLICT
CONFLUENT adj flowing together or merging ▷ n stream that flows into another, usually of approximately equal size
CONFLUX n merging or folowing togther, especially of rivers
CONFLUXES > CONFLUX
CONFOCAL adj having a common focus or common foci
CONFORM vb comply with

accepted standards or customs
CONFORMAL adj (of a transformation) preserving the angles of the depicted surface
CONFORMED > CONFORM
CONFORMER > CONFORM
CONFORMS > CONFORM
CONFOUND vb astound, bewilder
CONFOUNDS > CONFOUND
CONFRERE n colleague
CONFRERES > CONFRERE
CONFRERIE n brotherhood
CONFRONT vb come face to face with
CONFRONTE adj in heraldry, (of two animals) face to face
CONFRONTS > CONFRONT
CONFS > CONF
CONFUSE vb mix up
CONFUSED adj lacking a clear understanding of something
CONFUSES > CONFUSE
CONFUSING adj causing bewilderment
CONFUSION n mistaking one person or thing for another
CONFUTE vb prove wrong
CONFUTED > CONFUTE
CONFUTER > CONFUTE
CONFUTERS > CONFUTE
CONFUTES > CONFUTE
CONFUTING > CONFUTE
CONGA n dance performed by a number of people in single file ▷ vb dance the conga
CONGAED > CONGA
CONGAING > CONGA
CONGAS > CONGA
CONGE n permission to depart or dismissal, esp when formal ▷ vb to take one's leave
CONGEAL vb (of a liquid) become thick and sticky
CONGEALED > CONGEAL
CONGEALER > CONGEAL
CONGEALS > CONGEAL
CONGED > CONGE
CONGEE same as > CONGE
CONGEED > CONGEE
CONGEEING > CONGEE
CONGEES > CONGEE
CONGEING > CONGE
CONGENER n member of a class, group, or other category, esp any animal of a specified genus
CONGENERS > CONGENER
CONGENIAL adj pleasant, agreeable
CONGENIC adj (of inbred animal cells) genetically identical except for a single gene locus
CONGER n large sea eel
CONGERIES n collection of objects or ideas
CONGERS > CONGER
CONGES > CONGE
CONGEST vb crowd or become crowded to excess

CONGESTED adj crowded to excess
CONGESTS > CONGEST
CONGIARY n Roman emperor's gift to the people or soldiers
CONGII > CONGIUS
CONGIUS n unit of liquid measure equal to 1 Imperial gallon
CONGLOBE vb to gather into a globe or ball
CONGLOBED > CONGLOBE
CONGLOBES > CONGLOBE
CONGO same as > CONGOU
CONGOES > CONGOU
CONGOS > CONGO
CONGOU n kind of black tea from China
CONGOUS > CONGOU
CONGRATS sentence substitute congratulations
CONGREE vb to agree
CONGREED > CONGREE
CONGREES > CONGREE
CONGREET vb (of two or more people) to greet one another
CONGREETS > CONGREET
CONGRESS n formal meeting for discussion
CONGRUE vb to agree
CONGRUED > CONGRUE
CONGRUENT adj similar, corresponding
CONGRUES > CONGRUE
CONGRUING > CONGRUE
CONGRUITY > CONGRUOUS
CONGRUOUS adj appropriate or in keeping
CONI > CONUS
CONIA same as > CONIINE
CONIAS > CONIINE
CONIC adj having the shape of a cone
CONICAL adj cone-shaped
CONICALLY > CONIC
CONICINE same as > CONIINE
CONICINES > CONICINE
CONICITY > CONICAL
CONICS n branch of geometry concerned with the parabola, ellipse, and hyperbola
CONIDIA > CONIDIUM
CONIDIAL > CONIDIUM
CONIDIAN > CONIDIUM
CONIDIUM n asexual spore formed at the tip of a specialized hypha (conidiophore) in fungi such as Penicillium
CONIES > CONY
CONIFER n cone-bearing tree, such as the fir or pine
CONIFERS > CONIFER
CONIFORM adj cone-shaped
CONIINE n colourless poisonous soluble liquid alkaloid found in hemlock
CONIINES > CONIINE
CONIMA n gum resin from the conium hemlock tree
CONIMAS > CONIMA
CONIN same as > CONIINE
CONINE same as > CONIINE

CONINES > CONINE
CONING > CONE
CONINS > CONIN
CONIOLOGY *a variant spelling of* > KONIOLOGY
CONIOSES > CONIOSIS
CONIOSIS *n* any disease or condition caused by dust inhalation
CONIUM *n* either of the two N temperate plants of the umbelliferous genus *Conium*, esp hemlock
CONIUMS > CONIUM
CONJECT *vb* to conjecture
CONJECTED > CONJECT
CONJECTS > CONJECT
CONJEE *vb* prepare as, or in, a conjee (a gruel of boiled rice and water)
CONJEED > CONJEE
CONJEEING > CONJEE
CONJEES > CONJEE
CONJOIN *vb* join or become joined
CONJOINED > CONJOIN
CONJOINER > CONJOIN
CONJOINS > CONJOIN
CONJOINT *adj* united, joint, or associated
CONJUGAL *adj* of marriage
CONJUGANT *n* either of a pair of organisms or gametes undergoing conjugation
CONJUGATE *vb* inflect (a verb) systematically
CONJUNCT *adj* joined ▷*n* one of the propositions or formulas in a conjunction
CONJUNCTS > CONJUNCT
CONJUNTO *n* style of Mexican music
CONJUNTOS > CONJUNTO
CONJURE *vb* perform tricks that appear to be magic
CONJURED > CONJURE
CONJURER *same as* > CONJUROR
CONJURERS > CONJUROR
CONJURES > CONJURE
CONJURIES > CONJURY
CONJURING *n* performance of tricks that appear to defy natural laws ▷*adj* denoting or relating to such tricks or entertainment
CONJUROR *n* person who performs magic tricks for people's entertainment
CONJURORS > CONJUROR
CONJURY *n* magic
CONK *n* nose ▷*vb* strike (someone) on the head or nose
CONKED > CONK
CONKER *n* nut of the horse chestnut
CONKERS *n* game played with conkers tied on strings
CONKIER > CONKY
CONKIEST > CONKY
CONKING > CONK
CONKS > CONK
CONKY *adj* affected by the timber disease, conk

CONN *same as* > CON
CONNATE *adj* existing in a person or thing from birth
CONNATELY > CONNATE
CONNATION *n* joining of similar parts or organs
CONNATURE *n* sharing a common nature or character
CONNE *same as* > CON
CONNECT *vb* join together
CONNECTED *adj* joined or linked together
CONNECTER > CONNECT
CONNECTOR > CONNECT
CONNECTS > CONNECT
CONNED > CON
CONNER *same as* > CONDER
CONNERS > CONNER
CONNES > CONNE
CONNEXION *n* act or state of connecting
CONNEXIVE *adj* connective
CONNING > CON
CONNINGS > CON
CONNIVE *vb* allow (wrongdoing) by ignoring it
CONNIVED > CONNIVE
CONNIVENT *adj* (of parts of plants and animals) touching without being fused, as some petals, insect wings, etc
CONNIVER > CONNIVE
CONNIVERS > CONNIVE
CONNIVERY *n* act of conniving
CONNIVES > CONNIVE
CONNIVING > CONNIVE
CONNOTATE *vb* to connote
CONNOTE *vb* (of a word, phrase, etc) to imply or suggest (associations or ideas) other than the literal meaning
CONNOTED > CONNOTE
CONNOTES > CONNOTE
CONNOTING > CONNOTE
CONNOTIVE *adj* act or state of connecting
CONNS > CONN
CONNUBIAL *adj* of marriage
CONODONT *n* any of various small Palaeozoic toothlike fossils derived from an extinct eel-like marine animal
CONODONTS > CONODONT
CONOID *n* geometric surface formed by rotating a parabola, ellipse, or hyperbola about one axis ▷*adj* conical, cone-shaped
CONOIDAL *same as* > CONOID
CONOIDIC > CONOID
CONOIDS > CONOID
CONOMINEE *n* joint nominee
CONQUER *vb* defeat
CONQUERED > CONQUER
CONQUERER *variant of* > CONQUEROR
CONQUEROR > CONQUER
CONQUERS > CONQUER
CONQUEST *n* conquering
CONQUESTS > CONQUEST
CONQUIAN *same as* > COONCAN

CONQUIANS > COONCAN
CONS > CON
CONSCIENT *adj* conscious
CONSCIOUS *adj* alert and awake ▷*n* conscious part of the mind
CONSCRIBE *vb* to enrol compulsorily
CONSCRIPT *n* person enrolled for compulsory military service ▷*vb* enrol (someone) for compulsory military service
CONSEIL *n* advice
CONSEILS > CONSEIL
CONSENSUS *n* general agreement
CONSENT *n* agreement, permission ▷*vb* permit, agree to
CONSENTED > CONSENT
CONSENTER > CONSENT
CONSENTS > CONSENT
CONSERVE *vb* protect from harm, decay, or loss ▷*n* jam containing large pieces of fruit
CONSERVED > CONSERVE
CONSERVER > CONSERVE
CONSERVES > CONSERVE
CONSIDER *vb* regard as
CONSIDERS > CONSIDER
CONSIGN *vb* put somewhere
CONSIGNED > CONSIGN
CONSIGNEE *n* person, agent, organization, etc, to which merchandise is consigned
CONSIGNER *same as* > CONSIGNOR
CONSIGNOR *n* person, enterprise, etc, that consigns goods
CONSIGNS > CONSIGN
CONSIST *vb* be composed (of)
CONSISTED > CONSIST
CONSISTS > CONSIST
CONSOCIES *n* natural community with a single dominant species
CONSOL *n* consolidated annuity, a British government bond
CONSOLATE *vb* to console
CONSOLE *vb* comfort in distress ▷*n* panel of controls for electronic equipment
CONSOLED > CONSOLE
CONSOLER > CONSOLE
CONSOLERS > CONSOLE
CONSOLES > CONSOLE
CONSOLING > CONSOLE
CONSOLS *pl n* irredeemable British government securities carrying annual interest rates of two and a half or four per cent
CONSOLUTE *adj* (of two or more liquids) mutually soluble in all proportions
CONSOMME *n* thin clear meat soup
CONSOMMES > CONSOMME
CONSONANT *n* speech sound made by partially or

completely blocking the breath stream, such as b or f ▷*adj* agreeing (with)
CONSONOUS *adj* harmonious
CONSORT *vb* keep company (with) ▷*n* husband or wife of a monarch
CONSORTED > CONSORT
CONSORTER > CONSORT
CONSORTIA *n* plural form of singular consortium: association of financiers, companies etc
CONSORTS > CONSORT
CONSPIRE *vb* plan a crime together in secret
CONSPIRED > CONSPIRE
CONSPIRER > CONSPIRE
CONSPIRES > CONSPIRE
CONSTABLE *n* police officer of the lowest rank
CONSTANCY *n* quality of having a resolute mind, purpose, or affection
CONSTANT *adj* continuous ▷*n* unvarying quantity
CONSTANTS > CONSTANT
CONSTATE *vb* to affirm
CONSTATED > CONSTATE
CONSTATES > CONSTATE
CONSTER *obsolete variant of* > CONSTRUE
CONSTERED > CONSTRUE
CONSTERS > CONSTRUE
CONSTRAIN *vb* compel, force
CONSTRICT *vb* make narrower by squeezing
CONSTRUAL *n* act of construing
CONSTRUCT *vb* build or put together ▷*n* complex idea resulting from the combination of simpler ideas
CONSTRUE *vb* interpret ▷*n* something that is construed, such as a piece of translation
CONSTRUED > CONSTRUE
CONSTRUER > CONSTRUE
CONSTRUES > CONSTRUE
CONSUL *n* official representing a state in a foreign country
CONSULAGE *n* duty paid by merchants for a consul's protection of their goods while abroad
CONSULAR *n* anyone of consular rank
CONSULARS > CONSULAR
CONSULATE *n* workplace or position of a consul
CONSULS > CONSUL
CONSULT *vb* go to for advice or information
CONSULTA *n* official planning meeting
CONSULTAS > CONSULTA
CONSULTED > CONSULT
CONSULTEE *n* person who is consulted
CONSULTER > CONSULT
CONSULTOR > CONSULT
CONSULTS > CONSULT
CONSUME *vb* eat or drink

CONSUMED > CONSUME

CONSUMER n person who buys goods or uses services

CONSUMERS > CONSUMER

CONSUMES > CONSUME

CONSUMING > CONSUME

CONSUMPT n quantity used up; consumption

CONSUMPTS > CONSUMPT

CONTACT n communicating ▷ vb get in touch with ▷ interj (formerly) a call made by the pilot to indicate that an aircraft's ignition is switched on and that the engine is ready for starting by swinging the propeller

CONTACTED > CONTACT

CONTACTEE n person contacted by aliens

CONTACTOR n type of switch for repeatedly opening and closing an electric circuit. Its operation can be mechanical, electromagnetic, or pneumatic

CONTACTS > CONTACT

CONTADINA n female Italian farmer

CONTADINE > CONTADINA

CONTADINI > CONTADINO

CONTADINO n Italian farmer

CONTAGIA > CONTAGIUM

CONTAGION n passing on of disease by contact

CONTAGIUM n specific virus or other direct cause of any infectious disease

CONTAIN vb hold or be capable of holding

CONTAINED > CONTAIN

CONTAINER n object used to hold or store things in

CONTAINS > CONTAIN

CONTANGO n (formerly, on the London Stock Exchange) postponement of payment for and delivery of stock from one account day to the next ▷ vb arrange such a postponement of payment (for)

CONTANGOS > CONTANGO

CONTE n tale or short story, esp of adventure

CONTECK n contention

CONTECKS > CONTECK

CONTEMN vb regard with contempt

CONTEMNED > CONTEMN

CONTEMNER > CONTEMN

CONTEMNOR > CONTEMN

CONTEMNS > CONTEMN

CONTEMPER vb to modify

CONTEMPO adj contemporary

CONTEMPT n dislike and disregard

CONTEMPTS > CONTEMPT

CONTEND vb deal with

CONTENDED > CONTEND

CONTENDER > CONTEND

CONTENDS > CONTEND

CONTENT n meaning or

substance of a piece of writing ▷ adj satisfied with things as they are ▷ vb make (someone) content

CONTENTED adj satisfied with one's situation or life

CONTENTLY > CONTENT

CONTENTS > CONTENT

CONTES > CONTE

CONTESSA n Italian countess

CONTESSAS > CONTESSA

CONTEST n competition or struggle ▷ vb dispute, object to

CONTESTED > CONTEST

CONTESTER > CONTEST

CONTESTS > CONTEST

CONTEXT n circumstances of an event or fact

CONTEXTS > CONTEXT

CONTICENT adj silent

CONTINENT n one of the earth's large masses of land ▷ adj able to control one's bladder and bowels

CONTINUA > CONTINUUM

CONTINUAL adj constant

CONTINUE vb (cause to) remain in a condition or place

CONTINUED > CONTINUE

CONTINUER > CONTINUE

CONTINUES > CONTINUE

CONTINUO n continuous bass part, usu played on a keyboard instrument

CONTINUOS > CONTINUO

CONTINUUM n continuous series

CONTLINE n space between the bilges of stowed casks

CONTLINES > CONTLINE

CONTO n former Portuguese monetary unit worth 1000 escudos

CONTORNO n in Italy, side dish of salad or vegetables

CONTORNOS > CONTORNO

CONTORT vb twist out of shape

CONTORTED adj twisted out of shape

CONTORTS > CONTORT

CONTOS > CONTO

CONTOUR n outline ▷ vb shape so as to form or follow the contour of something

CONTOURED > CONTOUR

CONTOURS > CONTOUR

CONTRA n counter-argument

CONTRACT n (document setting out) a formal agreement ▷ vb make a formal agreement (to do something)

CONTRACTS > CONTRACT

CONTRAIL n aeroplane's vapour trail

CONTRAILS > CONTRAIL

CONTRAIR adj contrary

CONTRALTI > CONTRALTO

CONTRALTO n (singer with) the lowest female voice ▷ adj of or denoting a

contralto

CONTRARY n complete opposite ▷ adj opposed, completely different ▷ adv in opposition

CONTRAS > CONTRA

CONTRAST n obvious difference ▷ vb compare in order to show differences

CONTRASTS > CONTRAST

CONTRASTY adj (of a photograph or subject) having sharp gradations in tone, esp between light and dark areas

CONTRAT old form of > CONTRACT

CONTRATE adj (of gears) having teeth set at a right angle to the axis

CONTRATS > CONTRAT

CONTRIST vb to make sad

CONTRISTS > CONTRIST

CONTRITE adj sorry and apologetic

CONTRIVE vb make happen

CONTRIVED adj planned or artificial

CONTRIVER > CONTRIVE

CONTRIVES > CONTRIVE

CONTROL n power to direct something ▷ vb have power over

CONTROLE adj officially registered

CONTROLS > CONTROL

CONTROUL obsolete variant of > CONTROL

CONTROULS > CONTROUL

CONTUMACY n obstinate disobedience

CONTUMELY n scornful or insulting treatment

CONTUND vb to pummel

CONTUNDED > CONTUND

CONTUNDS > CONTUND

CONTUSE vb injure (the body) without breaking the skin

CONTUSED > CONTUSE

CONTUSES > CONTUSE

CONTUSING > CONTUSE

CONTUSION n bruise

CONTUSIVE > CONTUSE

CONUNDRUM n riddle

CONURBAN adj relating to an urban region

CONURBIA n conurbations considered collectively

CONURBIAS > CONURBIA

CONURE n any of various small American parrots of the genus Aratinga and related genera

CONURES > CONURE

CONUS n any of several cone-shaped structures, such as the conus medullaris, the lower end of the spinal cord

CONVECT vb to circulate hot air by convection

CONVECTED > CONVECT

CONVECTOR n heater that gives out hot air

CONVECTS > CONVECT

CONVENE vb gather or

summon for a formal meeting

CONVENED > CONVENE

CONVENER n person who calls a meeting

CONVENERS > CONVENER

CONVENES > CONVENE

CONVENING > CONVENE

CONVENOR same as > CONVENER

CONVENORS > CONVENOR

CONVENT n building where nuns live ▷ vb to summon

CONVENTED > CONVENT

CONVENTS > CONVENT

CONVERGE vb meet or join

CONVERGED > CONVERGE

CONVERGES > CONVERGE

CONVERSE vb have a conversation ▷ n opposite or contrary ▷ adj reversed or opposite

CONVERSED > CONVERSE

CONVERSER > CONVERSE

CONVERSES > CONVERSE

CONVERSO n medieval Spanish Jew converting to Catholicism

CONVERSOS > CONVERSO

CONVERT vb change in form, character, or function ▷ n person who has converted to a different belief or religion

CONVERTED > CONVERT

CONVERTER n person or thing that converts

CONVERTOR same as > CONVERTER

CONVERTS > CONVERT

CONVEX adj curving outwards ▷ vb make convex

CONVEXED > CONVEX

CONVEXES > CONVEX

CONVEXING > CONVEX

CONVEXITY n state or quality of being convex

CONVEXLY > CONVEX

CONVEY vb communicate (information)

CONVEYAL n act or means of conveying

CONVEYALS > CONVEYAL

CONVEYED > CONVEY

CONVEYER same as > CONVEYOR

CONVEYERS > CONVEYER

CONVEYING > CONVEY

CONVEYOR n person or thing that conveys

CONVEYORS > CONVEYOR

CONVEYS > CONVEY

CONVICT vb declare guilty ▷ n person serving a prison sentence ▷ adj convicted

CONVICTED > CONVICT

CONVICTS > CONVICT

CONVINCE vb persuade by argument or evidence

CONVINCED > CONVINCE

CONVINCER > CONVINCE

CONVINCES > CONVINCE

CONVIVE vb to feast together

CONVIVED > CONVIVE

CONVIVES > CONVIVE

Section 1: Words between 2 and 9 letters in length

CONVIVIAL *adj* sociable, lively
CONVIVING > CONVIVE
CONVO *n* conversation
CONVOCATE *vb* to call together
CONVOKE *vb* call together
CONVOKED > CONVOKE
CONVOKER > CONVOKE
CONVOKERS > CONVOKE
CONVOKES > CONVOKE
CONVOKING > CONVOKE
CONVOLUTE *vb* form into a twisted, coiled, or rolled shape ▷ *adj* rolled longitudinally upon itself
CONVOLVE *vb* wind or roll together
CONVOLVED > CONVOLVE
CONVOLVES > CONVOLVE
CONVOS > CONVO
CONVOY *n* group of vehicles or ships travelling together ▷ *vb* escort while in transit
CONVOYED > CONVOY
CONVOYING > CONVOY
CONVOYS > CONVOY
CONVULSE *vb* (of part of the body) undergo violent spasms
CONVULSED > CONVULSE
CONVULSES > CONVULSE
CONY *n* rabbit
COO *vb* (of a dove or pigeon) make a soft murmuring sound ▷ *n* sound of cooing ▷ *interj* exclamation of surprise, awe, etc
COOCH *n* slang term for vagina
COOCHES > COOCH
COOCOO *old spelling of* > CUCKOO
COOED > COO
COOEE *interj* call to attract attention ▷ *vb* utter this call ▷ *n* calling distance
COOEED > COOEE
COOEEING > COOEE
COOEES > COOEE
COOER > COO
COOERS > COO
COOEY *same as* > COOEE
COOEYED > COOEY
COOEYING > COOEY
COOEYS > COOEY
COOF *n* simpleton
COOFS > COOF
COOING > COO
COOINGLY > COO
COOINGS > COO
COOK *vb* prepare (food) by heating ▷ *n* person who cooks food
COOKABLE > COOK
COOKBOOK *n* book containing recipes and instructions for cooking
COOKBOOKS > COOKBOOK
COOKED > COOK
COOKER *n* apparatus for cooking heated by gas or electricity
COOKERIES > COOKERY
COOKERS > COOKER
COOKERY *n* art of cooking
COOKEY *same as* > COOKIE

COOKEYS > COOKEY
COOKHOUSE *n* place for cooking, esp a camp kitchen
COOKIE *n* biscuit
COOKIES > COOKIE
COOKING > COOK
COOKINGS > COOK
COOKLESS *adj* devoid of a cook
COOKMAID *n* maid who assists a cook
COOKMAIDS > COOKMAID
COOKOFF *n* cookery competition
COOKOFFS > COOKOFF
COOKOUT *n* party where a meal is cooked and eaten out of doors
COOKOUTS > COOKOUT
COOKROOM *n* room in which food is cooked
COOKROOMS > COOKROOM
COOKS > COOK
COOKSHACK *n* makeshift building in which food is cooked
COOKSHOP *n* shop that sells cookery equipment
COOKSHOPS > COOKSHOP
COOKSTOVE *n* stove for cooking
COOKTOP *n* flat unit for cooking in saucepans or the top part of a stove
COOKTOPS > COOKTOP
COOKWARE *n* cooking utensils
COOKWARES > COOKWARE
COOKY *same as* > COOKIE
COOL *adj* moderately cold ▷ *vb* make or become cool ▷ *n* coolness
COOLABAH *n* Australian myrtaceous tree, *Eucalyptus microtheca*, that grows along rivers and has smooth bark and long narrow leaves
COOLABAHS > COOLABAH
COOLAMON *n* shallow dish of wood or bark, used for carrying water
COOLAMONS > COOLAMON
COOLANT *n* fluid used to cool machinery while it is working
COOLANTS > COOLANT
COOLDOWN *n* gentle stretching exercises after strenuous activity, to allow the heart rate gradually to return to normal
COOLDOWNS > COOLDOWN
COOLED > COOL
COOLER *n* container for making or keeping things cool
COOLERS > COOLER
COOLEST > COOL
COOLHOUSE *n* greenhouse in which a cool temperature is maintained
COOLIBAH *same as* > COOLABAH
COOLIBAHS > COOLIBAH
COOLIBAR *same as*

> COOLABAH
COOLIBARS > COOLIBAR
COOLIE *n* unskilled Oriental labourer
COOLIES > COOLIE
COOLING > COOL
COOLINGLY > COOL
COOLISH > COOL
COOLLY > COOL
COOLNESS > COOL
COOLS > COOL
COOLTH *n* coolness
COOLTHS > COOLTH
COOLY *same as* > COOLIE
COOM *n* waste material, such as dust from coal, grease from axles, etc ▷ *vb* to blacken
COOMB *same as* > COMB
COOMBE > COMB
COOMBES > COOMBE
COOMBS > COOMB
COOMED > COOM
COOMIER > COOMY
COOMIEST > COOMY
COOMING > COOM
COOMS > COOM
COOMY *adj* grimy
COON *n* raccoon
COONCAN *n* card game for two players, similar to rummy
COONCANS > COONCAN
COONDOG *n* dog trained to hunt raccoons
COONDOGS > COONDOG
COONHOUND *n* dog for hunting raccoons
COONS > COON
COONSKIN *n* pelt of a raccoon
COONSKINS > COONSKIN
COONTIE *n* evergreen plant, *Zamia floridana* of S Florida, related to the cycads and having large dark green leathery leaves: family *Zamiaceae*
COONTIES > COONTIE
COONTY *same as* > COONTIE
COOP *n* cage or pen for poultry ▷ *vb* confine in a restricted area
COOPED > COOP
COOPER *n* person who makes or repairs barrels ▷ *vb* make or mend (barrels, casks, etc)
COOPERAGE *n* craft, place of work, or products of a cooper
COOPERATE *vb* work or act together
COOPERED > COOPER
COOPERIES > COOPERY
COOPERING > COOPER
COOPERS > COOPER
COOPERY *same as* > COOPERAGE
COOPING > COOP
COOPS > COOP
COOPT *vb* add (someone) to a group by the agreement of the existing members
COOPTED > COOPT
COOPTING > COOPT
COOPTION > COOPT

COOPTIONS > COOPT
COOPTS > COOPT
COORDINAL *adj* (of animals or plants) belonging to the same order
COORIE *same as* > COURIE
COORIED > COORIE
COORIEING > COORIE
COORIES > COORIE
COOS > COO
COOSEN *same as* > COZEN
COOSENED > COOSEN
COOSENING > COOSEN
COOSENS > COOSEN
COOSER *n* stallion
COOSERS > COOSER
COOSIN *same as* > COZEN
COOSINED > COOSIN
COOSINING > COOSIN
COOSINS > COOSIN
COOST *Scots form of* > CAST
COOT *n* small black water bird
COOTCH *n* hiding place ▷ *vb* hide
COOTCHED > COOTCH
COOTCHES > COOTCH
COOTCHING > COOTCH
COOTER *n* type of freshwater turtle
COOTERS > COOTER
COOTIE > LOUSE
COOTIES > COOTIE
COOTIKIN *n* gaiter
COOTIKINS > COOTIKIN
COOTS > COOT
COOZE *n* US and Canadian taboo slang word for the female genitals
COOZES > COOZE
COP *same as* > COPPER
COPACETIC *adj* very good
COPAIBA *n* transparent yellowish viscous oleoresin obtained from certain tropical South American trees of the leguminous genus *Copaifera*: used in varnishes and ointments
COPAIBAS > COPAIBA
COPAIVA *same as* > COPAIBA
COPAIVAS > COPAIVA
COPAL *n* resin used in varnishes
COPALM *n* aromatic brown resin obtained from the sweet gum tree
COPALMS > COPALM
COPALS > COPAL
COPARCENY *n* form of joint ownership of property
COPARENT *n* fellow parent
COPARENTS > COPARENT
COPARTNER *n* partner or associate
COPASETIC *same as* > COPACETIC
COPASTOR *n* fellow pastor
COPASTORS > COPASTOR
COPATAINE *adj* (of a hat) high-crowned
COPATRIOT *n* fellow patriot
COPATRON *n* fellow patron
COPATRONS > COPATRON
COPAY *n* amount payable for treatment by person with medical insurance**

COPAYMENT *n* fee paid for medical insurance

COPAYS > COPAY

COPE *vb* deal successfully (with) ▷ *n* large ceremonial cloak worn by some Christian priests

COPECK *same as* > KOPECK

COPECKS > COPECK

COPED > COPE

COPEMATE *n* partner

COPEMATES > COPEMATE

COPEN *n* shade of blue

COPENS > COPEN

COPEPOD *n* any minute free-living or parasitic crustacean of the subclass *Copepoda* of marine and fresh waters: an important constituent of plankton ▷ *adj* of, relating to, or belonging to the *Copepoda*

COPEPODS > COPEPOD

COPER *n* horse-dealer ▷ *vb* to smuggle liquor to deep-sea fishermen

COPERED > COPER

COPERING > COPER

COPERS > COPER

COPES > COPE

COPESETIC *same as* > COPACETIC

COPESTONE *same as* > CAPSTONE

COPIED > COPY

COPIER *n* machine that copies

COPIERS > COPIER

COPIES > COPY

COPIHUE *n* Chilean bellflower

COPIHUES > COPIHUE

COPILOT *n* second pilot of an aircraft

COPILOTS > COPILOT

COPING *n* sloping top row of a wall

COPINGS > COPING

COPIOUS *adj* abundant, plentiful

COPIOUSLY > COPIOUS

COPITA *n* tulip-shaped sherry glass

COPITAS > COPITA

COPLANAR *adj* lying in the same plane

COPLOT *vb* plot together

COPLOTS > COPLOT

COPLOTTED > COPLOT

COPOLYMER *n* chemical compound of high molecular weight formed by uniting the molecules of two or more different compounds (monomers)

COPOUT *n* act of avoiding responsibility

COPOUTS > COPOUT

COPPED > COPPER

COPPER *n* soft reddish-brown metal ▷ *adj* reddish-brown ▷ *vb* coat or cover with copper

COPPERAH *same as* > COPRA

COPPERAHS > COPPERAH

COPPERAS *n* ferrous sulphate

COPPERED > COPPER

COPPERING > COPPER

COPPERISH *adj* copper-like

COPPERS > COPPER

COPPERY > COPPER

COPPICE *n* small group of trees growing close together ▷ *vb* trim back (trees or bushes) to form a coppice

COPPICED > COPPICE

COPPICES > COPPICE

COPPICING > COPPICE

COPPIES > COPPY

COPPIN *n* ball of thread

COPPING > COPPER

COPPINS > COPPIN

COPPLE *n* hill rising to a point

COPPLES > COPPLE

COPPRA *same as* > COPRA

COPPRAS > COPPRA

COPPY *n* small wooden stool

COPRA *n* dried oil-yielding kernel of the coconut

COPRAH *same as* > COPRA

COPRAHS > COPRAH

COPRAS > COPRA

COPREMIA *n* poisoning due to chronic constipation

COPREMIAS > COPREMIA

COPREMIC > COPREMIA

COPRESENT *vb* to present jointly

COPRINCE *n* fellow prince

COPRINCES > COPRINCE

COPRODUCE *vb* to produce jointly

COPRODUCT *n* joint product

COPROLITE *n* any of various rounded stony nodules thought to be the fossilized faeces of Palaeozic-Cenozoic vertebrates

COPROLITH *n* hard stony mass of dried faeces

COPROLOGY *n* preoccupation with excrement

COPROSMA *n* any shrub of the Australasian rubiaceous genus *Coprosma*: sometimes planted for ornament

COPROSMAS > COPROSMA

COPROZOIC *adj* (of animals) living in dung

COPS > COP

COPSE *same as* > COPPICE *vb* to trim back (trees) to form a copse

COPSED > COPSE

COPSES > COPSE

COPSEWOOD *n* brushwood

COPSHOP *n* police station

COPSHOPS > COPSHOP

COPSIER > COPSY

COPSIEST > COPSY

COPSING > COPSE

COPSY *adj* having copses

COPTER *n* helicopter

COPTERS > COPTER

COPUBLISH *vb* to publish jointly

COPULA *n* verb used to link the subject and complement of a sentence, e.g. *become* in *they become chums*

COPULAE > COPULA

COPULAR > COPULA

COPULAS > COPULA

COPULATE *vb* have sexual intercourse

COPULATED > COPULATE

COPULATES > COPULATE

COPURIFY *vb* to purify together

COPY *n* thing made to look exactly like another ▷ *vb* make a copy of

COPYABLE > COPY

COPYBOOK *n* book of specimens for imitation

COPYBOOKS > COPYBOOK

COPYBOY *n* formerly, in journalism, boy who carried copy and ran errands

COPYBOYS > COPYBOY

COPYCAT *n* person who imitates or copies someone ▷ *vb* to imitate with great attention to detail

COPYCATS > COPYCAT

COPYDESK *n* desk where newspaper copy is edited

COPYDESKS > COPYDESK

COPYEDIT *vb* prepare text for printing by styling, correcting, etc

COPYEDITS > COPYEDIT

COPYGIRL *n* female copyboy

COPYGIRLS > COPYGIRL

COPYGRAPH *n* process for copying type

COPYHOLD *n* tenure less than freehold of land in England evidenced by a copy of the Court roll

COPYHOLDS > COPYHOLD

COPYING > COPY

COPYISM *n* slavish copying

COPYISMS > COPYISM

COPYIST *n* person who makes written copies

COPYISTS > COPYIST

COPYLEFT *n* permission to use something free of charge

COPYLEFTS > COPYLEFT

COPYREAD *vb* subedit

COPYREADS > COPYREAD

COPYRIGHT *n* exclusive legal right to reproduce and control a book, work of art, etc ▷ *vb* take out a copyright on ▷ *adj* protected by copyright

COPYTAKER *n* (esp in a newspaper office) a person employed to type reports as journalists dictate them over the telephone

COQUET *vb* behave flirtatiously

COQUETRY *n* flirtation

COQUETS > COQUET

COQUETTE *n* woman who flirts

COQUETTED > COQUET

COQUETTES > COQUETTE

COQUILLA *n* type of South American nut

COQUILLAS > COQUILLA

COQUILLE *n* any dish, esp seafood, served in a scallop shell

COQUILLES > COQUILLE

COQUINA *n* soft limestone consisting of shells, corals, etc, that occurs in parts of the US

COQUINAS > COQUINA

COQUITO *n* Chilean palm tree, *Jubaea spectabilis*, yielding edible nuts and a syrup

COQUITOS > COQUITO

COR *interj* exclamation of surprise, amazement, or admiration

CORACLE *n* small round boat of wicker covered with skins

CORACLES > CORACLE

CORACOID *n* paired ventral bone of the pectoral girdle in vertebrates

CORACOIDS > CORACOID

CORAGGIO *interj* exhortation to hold one's nerve

CORAGGIOS > CORAGGIO

CORAL *n* hard substance formed from the skeletons of very small sea animals ▷ *adj* orange-pink

CORALLA > CORALLUM

CORALLINE *adj* of, relating to, or resembling coral ▷ *n* any of various red algae impregnated with calcium carbonate, esp any of the genus *Corallina*

CORALLITE *n* skeleton of a coral polyp

CORALLOID *same as* > CORALLINE

CORALLUM *n* skeleton of any zoophyte

CORALROOT *n* any N temperate leafless orchid of the genus *Corallorhiza*, with small yellow-green or purple flowers and branched roots resembling coral

CORALS > CORAL

CORALWORT *n* coralroot or toothwort

CORAM *prep* before, in the presence of

CORAMINE *n* drug which is a circulatory stimulant

CORAMINES > CORAMINE

CORANACH *same as* > CORONACH

CORANACHS > CORANACH

CORANTO *same as* > COURANTE

CORANTOES > CORANTO

CORANTOS > CORANTO

CORBAN *n* gift to God

CORBANS > CORBAN

CORBE *obsolete variant of* > CORBEL

CORBEAU *n* blackish green colour

CORBEAUS > CORBEAU

Section 1: Words between 2 and 9 letters in length

CORBEIL *n* carved ornament in the form of a basket of fruit, flowers, etc
CORBEILLE *same as* > CORBEIL
CORBEILS > CORBEIL
CORBEL *n* stone or timber support sticking out of a wall ▷ *vb* lay (a stone or brick) so that it forms a corbel
CORBELED > CORBEL
CORBELING *n* set of corbels stepped outwards, one above another
CORBELLED > CORBEL
CORBELS > CORBEL
CORBES > CORBE
CORBICULA *n* pollen basket
CORBIE *n* raven or crow
CORBIES > CORBIE
CORBINA *n* type of North American whiting
CORBINAS > CORBINA
CORBY *same as* > CORBIE
CORCASS *n* in Ireland, marshland
CORCASSES > CORCASS
CORD *n* thin rope or thick string ▷ *adj* (of fabric) ribbed ▷ *vb* bind or furnish with a cord or cords
CORDAGE *n* lines and rigging of a vessel
CORDAGES > CORDAGE
CORDATE *adj* heart-shaped
CORDATELY > CORDATE
CORDED *adj* tied or fastened with cord
CORDELLE *vb* to tow
CORDELLED > CORDELLE
CORDELLES > CORDELLE
CORDER > CORD
CORDERS > CORD
CORDGRASS *n* type of coarse grass
CORDIAL *adj* warm and friendly ▷ *n* drink with a fruit base
CORDIALLY > CORDIAL
CORDIALS > CORDIAL
CORDIFORM *adj* heart-shaped
CORDINER *n* shoemaker
CORDINERS > CORDINER
CORDING > CORD
CORDINGS > CORD
CORDITE *n* explosive used in guns and bombs
CORDITES > CORDITE
CORDLESS *adj* (of an electrical appliance) powered by an internal battery, so that there is no cable connecting the appliance itself to the electrical mains
CORDLIKE > CORD
CORDOBA *n* standard monetary unit of Nicaragua, divided into 100 centavos
CORDOBAS > CORDOBA
CORDON *n* chain of police, soldiers, etc, guarding an area ▷ *vb* put or form a cordon (around)

CORDONED > CORDON
CORDONING > CORDON
CORDONNET *n* type of thread
CORDONS > CORDON
CORDOTOMY *n* method of pain relief in which nerves are cut > CHORDOTOMY
CORDOVAN *n* fine leather now made principally from horsehide, isolated from the skin layers above and below it and tanned
CORDOVANS > CORDOVAN
CORDS *pl n* trousers made of corduroy
CORDUROY *n* cotton fabric with a velvety ribbed surface
CORDUROYS *pl n* trousers made of corduroy
CORDWAIN *an archaic name for* > CORDOVAN
CORDWAINS > CORDWAIN
CORDWOOD *n* wood that has been cut into lengths of four feet so that it can be stacked in cords
CORDWOODS > CORDWOOD
CORDYLINE *n* any tree of the genus Cordyline
CORE *n* central part of certain fruits, containing the seeds ▷ *vb* remove the core from
CORED > CORE
COREDEEM *vb* to redeem together
COREDEEMS > COREDEEM
COREGENT *n* joint regent
COREGENTS > COREGENT
COREIGN *vb* to reign jointly
COREIGNS > COREIGN
CORELATE *same as* > CORRELATE
CORELATED > CORELATE
CORELATES > CORELATE
CORELESS > CORE
CORELLA *n* white Australian cockatoo
CORELLAS > CORELLA
COREMIA > COREMIUM
COREMIUM *n* spore-producing organ of certain fungi
COREOPSIS *n* any plant of the genus Coreopsis, of America and tropical Africa, cultivated for their yellow, brown, or yellow-and-red daisy-like flowers: family Asteraceae (composites)
CORER > CORE
CORERS > CORE
CORES > CORE
COREY *n* slang word for the penis
COREYS > COREY
CORF *n* wagon or basket used formerly in mines
CORFHOUSE *n* shed used for curing salmon and storing nets
CORGI *n* short-legged sturdy dog
CORGIS > CORGI
CORIA > CORIUM

CORIANDER *n* plant grown for its aromatic seeds and leaves
CORIES > CORY
CORING > CORE
CORIOUS *adj* leathery
CORIUM *n* deep inner layer of the skin, beneath the epidermis, containing connective tissue, blood vessels, and fat
CORIUMS > CORIUM
CORIVAL *same as* > CORRIVAL
CORIVALRY > CORIVAL
CORIVALS > CORIVAL
CORIXID *n* type of water bug
CORIXIDS > CORIXID
CORK *n* thick light bark of a Mediterranean oak ▷ *vb* seal with a cork ▷ *adj* made of cork
CORKAGE *n* restaurant's charge for serving wine bought elsewhere
CORKAGES > CORKAGE
CORKBOARD *n* thin slab made of granules of cork, used as a floor or wall finish and as an insulator
CORKBORER *n* tool for cutting a hole in a stopper to insert a glass tube
CORKED *adj* (of wine) spoiled through having a decayed cork
CORKER *n* splendid or outstanding person or thing
CORKERS > CORKER
CORKIER > CORKY
CORKIEST > CORKY
CORKINESS > CORKY
CORKING *adj* excellent
CORKIR *n* lichen from which red or purple dye is made
CORKIRS > CORKIR
CORKLIKE > CORK
CORKS > CORK
CORKSCREW *n* spiral metal tool for pulling corks from bottles ▷ *adj* like a corkscrew in shape ▷ *vb* move in a spiral or zigzag course
CORKTREE *n* type of evergreen oak tree
CORKTREES > CORKTREE
CORKWING *n* greenish or bluish European fish of the wrasse family, Ctenolabrus melops
CORKWINGS > CORKWING
CORKWOOD *n* small tree, Leitneria floridana, of the southeastern US, having very lightweight porous wood: family Leitneriaceae
CORKWOODS > CORKWOOD
CORKY *same as* > CORKED
CORM *n* bulblike underground stem of certain plants
CORMEL *n* new small corm arising from the base of a fully developed one

CORMELS > CORMEL
CORMIDIA > CORMIDIUM
CORMIDIUM *n* iteration of the repeating zooid pattern in a siphosome
CORMLIKE *adj* resembling a corm
CORMOID *adj* like a corm
CORMORANT *n* large dark-coloured long-necked sea bird
CORMOUS > CORM
CORMS > CORM
CORMUS *n* corm
CORMUSES > CORMUS
CORN *n* cereal plant such as wheat or oats ▷ *vb* feed (animals) with corn, esp oats
CORNACRE *same as* > CONACRE
CORNACRES > CORNACRE
CORNAGE *n* rent fixed according to the number of horned cattle pastured
CORNAGES > CORNAGE
CORNBALL *n* person given to mawkish or unsophisticated behaviour
CORNBALLS > CORNBALL
CORNBORER *n* larva of the pyralid moth
CORNBRAID *vb* braid hair in cornrows
CORNBRASH *n* type of limestone which produces good soil for growing corn
CORNBREAD *n* bread made from maize meal
CORNCAKE *n* kind of cornmeal flatbread
CORNCAKES > CORNCAKE
CORNCOB *n* core of an ear of maize, to which the kernels are attached
CORNCOBS > CORNCOB
CORNCRAKE *n* brown Eurasian bird with a harsh cry
CORNCRIB *n* ventilated building for the storage of unhusked maize
CORNCRIBS > CORNCRIB
CORNEA *n* transparent membrane covering the eyeball
CORNEAE > CORNEA
CORNEAL > CORNEA
CORNEAS > CORNEA
CORNED *adj* (esp of beef) cooked and then preserved or pickled in salt or brine, now often canned
CORNEITIS *n* inflammation of cornea
CORNEL *n* any cornaceous plant of the genus Cornus, such as the dogwood and dwarf cornel
CORNELIAN *same as* > CARNELIAN
CORNELS > CORNEL
CORNEMUSE *n* French bagpipe
CORNEOUS *adj* horny
CORNER *n* area or angle where two converging

C

lines or surfaces meet ▷ vb force into a difficult or inescapable position
CORNERED > CORNER
CORNERING > CORNER
CORNERMAN n in baseball, first baseman
CORNERMEN > CORNERMAN
CORNERS > CORNER
CORNET same as > CORNETT
CORNETCY n commission or rank of a cornet
CORNETIST n person who plays the cornet
CORNETS > CORNET
CORNETT n musical instrument consisting of a straight or curved tube of wood or ivory having finger holes like a recorder and a cup-shaped mouthpiece like a trumpet
CORNETTI > CORNETTO
CORNETTO same as > CORNETT
CORNETTS > CORNETT
CORNFED adj fed on corn
CORNFIELD n field planted with cereal crops
CORNFLAG n gladiolus
CORNFLAGS > CORNFLAG
CORNFLAKE n singular form of plural cornflakes: toasted flakes made from cornmeal, sold as a breakfast cereal
CORNFLIES > CORNFLY
CORNFLOUR n fine maize flour
CORNFLY n small fly whose larvae cause swollen, gouty stems in cereal crops
CORNHUSK n outer protective covering of an ear of maize
CORNHUSKS > CORNHUSK
CORNI > CORNO
CORNICE n decorative moulding round the top of a wall ▷ vb furnish or decorate with or as if with a cornice
CORNICED > CORNICE
CORNICES > CORNICE
CORNICHE n coastal road, esp one built into the face of a cliff
CORNICHES > CORNICHE
CORNICHON n type of small gherkin
CORNICING > CORNICE
CORNICLE n wax-secreting organ on an aphid's abdomen
CORNICLES > CORNICLE
CORNICULA n plural form of singular corniculum: small horn
CORNIER > CORNY
CORNIEST > CORNY
CORNIFIC adj producing horns
CORNIFIED > CORNIFY
CORNIFIES > CORNIFY
CORNIFORM adj horn-shaped
CORNIFY vb turn soft tissue

hard
CORNILY > CORNY
CORNINESS > CORNY
CORNING > CORN
CORNIST n horn-player
CORNISTS > CORNIST
CORNLAND n land suitable for growing corn or grain
CORNLANDS > CORNLAND
CORNLOFT n loft for storing corn
CORNLOFTS > CORNLOFT
CORNMEAL n meal made from maize
CORNMEALS > CORNMEAL
CORNMILL n flour mill
CORNMILLS > CORNMILL
CORNMOTH n moth whose larvae feed on grain
CORNMOTHS > CORNMOTH
CORNO n French horn
CORNOPEAN n cornet (the brass musical instrument)
CORNPIPE n musical instrument made from a stalk of corn etc
CORNPIPES > CORNPIPE
CORNPONE n American corn bread
CORNPONES > CORNPONE
CORNRENT n rent paid in corn, rather than money
CORNRENTS > CORNRENT
CORNROW n hairstyle in which the hair is plaited in close parallel rows ▷ vb style the hair in a cornrow
CORNROWED > CORNROW
CORNROWS > CORNROW
CORNS > CORN
CORNSTALK n stalk or stem of corn
CORNSTONE n mottled green and red limestone
CORNU n part or structure resembling a horn or having a hornlike pattern, such as a cross section of the grey matter of the spinal cord
CORNUA > CORNU
CORNUAL > CORNU
CORNUS n any member of the genus Cornus, such as dogwood
CORNUSES > CORNUS
CORNUTE adj having or resembling cornua ▷ vb to make a cuckold of
CORNUTED same as > CORNUTE
CORNUTES > CORNUTE
CORNUTING > CORNUTE
CORNUTO n cuckold
CORNUTOS > CORNUTO
CORNWORM n cornmoth larva
CORNWORMS > CORNWORM
CORNY adj unoriginal or oversentimental
COROCORE same as > COROCORO
COROCORES > COROCORE
COROCORO n South Asian vessel fitted with outriggers
COROCOROS > COROCORO
CORODIES > CORODY

CORODY n (originally) the right of a lord to receive free quarters from his vassal
COROLLA n petals of a flower collectively
COROLLARY n idea, fact, or proposition which is the natural result of something else ▷ adj consequent or resultant
COROLLAS > COROLLA
COROLLATE adj having a corolla
COROLLINE adj relating to a corolla
CORONA n ring of light round the moon or sun
CORONACH n dirge or lamentation for the dead
CORONACHS > CORONACH
CORONAE > CORONA
CORONAL n circlet for the head ▷ adj of or relating to a corona or coronal
CORONALLY > CORONAL
CORONALS > CORONAL
CORONARY adj of the arteries surrounding the heart ▷ n coronary thrombosis
CORONAS > CORONA
CORONATE vb to crown
CORONATED > CORONATE
CORONATES > CORONATE
CORONEL n iron head of a tilting spear
CORONELS > CORONEL
CORONER n official responsible for the investigation of violent, sudden, or suspicious deaths
CORONERS > CORONER
CORONET n small crown
CORONETED adj wearing a coronet
CORONETS > CORONET
CORONIS n in Greek grammar, symbol placed over a contracted syllable
CORONISES > CORONIS
CORONIUM n highly-ionized iron and nickel seen as a green line in the solar coronal spectrum
CORONIUMS > CORONIUM
CORONOID adj crown-shaped
COROTATE vb to rotate together
COROTATED > COROTATE
COROTATES > COROTATE
COROZO n tropical American palm, Corozo oleifera, whose seeds yield a useful oil
COROZOS > COROZO
CORPORA > CORPUS
CORPORAL n noncommissioned officer in an army ▷ adj of the body
CORPORALE same as > CORPORAL
CORPORALS > CORPORAL
CORPORAS n communion cloth
CORPORATE adj of business corporations

CORPOREAL adj physical or tangible
CORPORIFY vb to embody
CORPOSANT n Saint Elmo's fire
CORPS n military unit with a specific function
CORPSE n dead body ▷ vb laugh or cause to laugh involuntarily or inopportunely while on stage
CORPSED > CORPSE
CORPSES > CORPSE
CORPSING > CORPSE
CORPSMAN n medical orderly or stretcher-bearer
CORPSMEN > CORPSMAN
CORPULENT adj fat or plump
CORPUS n collection of writings, esp by a single author
CORPUSCLE n red or white blood cell
CORPUSES > CORPUS
CORRADE vb (of rivers, streams, etc) to erode (land) by the abrasive action of rock particles
CORRADED > CORRADE
CORRADES > CORRADE
CORRADING > CORRADE
CORRAL n enclosure for cattle or horses ▷ vb put in a corral
CORRALLED > CORRAL
CORRALS > CORRAL
CORRASION n erosion of rocks caused by fragments transported over them by water, wind, or ice
CORRASIVE > CORRASION
CORREA n Australian evergreen shrub of the genus Correa, with large showy tubular flowers
CORREAS > CORREA
CORRECT adj free from error, true ▷ vb put right
CORRECTED > CORRECT
CORRECTER > CORRECT
CORRECTLY > CORRECT
CORRECTOR > CORRECT
CORRECTS > CORRECT
CORRELATE vb place or be placed in a mutual relationship ▷ n either of two things mutually related ▷ adj having a mutual, complementary, or reciprocal relationship
CORRIDA the Spanish word for > BULLFIGHT
CORRIDAS > CORRIDA
CORRIDOR n passage in a building or train
CORRIDORS > CORRIDOR
CORRIE same as > CIRQUE
CORRIES > CORRIE
CORRIGENT n corrective
CORRIVAL a rare word for > RIVAL vb to vie
CORRIVALS > CORRIVAL
CORRODANT > CORRODE
CORRODE vb eat or be eaten away by chemical action or rust

CORRODED > CORRODE
CORRODENT > CORRODE
CORRODER > CORRODE
CORRODERS > CORRODE
CORRODES > CORRODE
CORRODIES > CORRODY
CORRODING > CORRODE
CORRODY same as > CORODY
CORROSION n process by which something, esp a metal, is corroded
CORROSIVE adj (esp of acids or alkalis) capable of destroying solid materials ▷ n corrosive substance, such as a strong acid or alkali
CORRUGATE vb fold into alternate grooves and ridges ▷ adj folded into furrows and ridges
CORRUPT adj open to or involving bribery ▷ vb make corrupt
CORRUPTED > CORRUPT
CORRUPTER > CORRUPT
CORRUPTLY > CORRUPT
CORRUPTOR > CORRUPT
CORRUPTS > CORRUPT
CORS > COR
CORSAC n fox, Vulpes corsac, of central Asia
CORSACS > CORSAC
CORSAGE n small bouquet worn on the bodice of a dress
CORSAGES > CORSAGE
CORSAIR n pirate
CORSAIRS > CORSAIR
CORSE n corpse
CORSELET n one-piece undergarment combining a corset and bra
CORSELETS > CORSELET
CORSES > CORSE
CORSET n women's close-fitting undergarment worn to shape the torso ▷ vb dress or enclose in, or as in, a corset
CORSETED > CORSET
CORSETIER n man who makes and fits corsets
CORSETING > CORSET
CORSETRY n making of or dealing in corsets
CORSETS > CORSET
CORSEY n pavement or pathway
CORSEYS > CORSEY
CORSIVE n corroded
CORSIVES > CORSIVE
CORSLET same as > CORSELET
CORSLETED > CORSLET
CORSLETS > CORSLET
CORSNED n ordeal whereby an accused person had to eat a morsel of bread; swallowing it freely indicated innocence; choking, guilt
CORSNEDS > CORSNED
CORSO n promenade
CORSOS > CORSO
CORTEGE n funeral procession

CORTEGES > CORTEGE
CORTEX n outer layer of the brain or other internal organ
CORTEXES > CORTEX
CORTICAL > CORTEX
CORTICATE adj (of plants, seeds, etc) having a bark, husk, or rind
CORTICES > CORTEX
CORTICOID n steroid hormone
CORTICOSE adj consisting of or like bark
CORTILE n open, internal courtyard
CORTILI > CORTILE
CORTIN n adrenal cortex extract containing cortisone and other hormones
CORTINA n weblike part of certain mushrooms
CORTINAS > CORTINA
CORTINS > CORTIN
CORTISOL n principal glucocorticoid secreted by the adrenal cortex
CORTISOLS > CORTISOL
CORTISONE n steroid hormone used to treat various diseases
CORULER n joint ruler
CORULERS > CORULER
CORUNDUM n hard mineral used as an abrasive
CORUNDUMS > CORUNDUM
CORUSCANT adj giving off flashes of light
CORUSCATE vb sparkle
CORVEE n day's unpaid labour owed by a feudal vassal to his lord
CORVEES > CORVEE
CORVES > CORF
CORVET same as > CURVET
CORVETED > CORVET
CORVETING > CORVET
CORVETS > CORVET
CORVETTE n lightly armed escort warship ▷ vb to participate in social activities with fellow Corvette car enthusiasts
CORVETTED > CORVETTE
CORVETTES > CORVETTE
CORVID n any member of the crow family
CORVIDS > CORVID
CORVINA same as > CORBINA
CORVINAS > CORVINA
CORVINE adj of, relating to, or resembling a crow
CORVUS n type of ancient hook
CORVUSES > CORVUS
CORY n catfish belonging to the South American Corydoras genus
CORYBANT n wild attendant of the goddess Cybele
CORYBANTS > CORYBANT
CORYDALIS n any erect or climbing plant of the N temperate genus Corydalis, having finely-lobed leaves and spurred yellow or

pinkish flowers: family Fumariaceae
CORYLUS n hazel genus
CORYLUSES > CORYLUS
CORYMB n flat-topped flower cluster with the stems growing progressively shorter towards the centre ▷ vb be corymb-like
CORYMBED > CORYMB
CORYMBOSE > CORYMB
CORYMBOUS > CORYMB
CORYMBS > CORYMB
CORYPHAEI n plural form of singular coryphaeus: leader of the chorus
CORYPHE n coryphaeus
CORYPHEE n leading dancer of a corps de ballet
CORYPHEES > CORYPHEE
CORYPHENE n any fish of the genus Coryphaena
CORYPHES > CORYPHE
CORYZA n acute inflammation of the mucous membrane of the nose, with discharge of mucus
CORYZAL > CORYZA
CORYZAS > CORYZA
COS same as > COSINE
COSCRIPT vb to script jointly
COSCRIPTS > COSCRIPT
COSE vb get cosy
COSEC same as > COSECANT
COSECANT n (in trigonometry) the ratio of the length of the hypotenuse to that of the opposite side in a right-angled triangle
COSECANTS > COSECANT
COSECH n hyperbolic cosecant
COSECHS > COSECH
COSECS > COSEC
COSED > COSE
COSEISMAL adj of or designating points at which earthquake waves are felt at the same time ▷ n such a line on a map
COSEISMIC same as > COSEISMAL
COSES > COSE
COSET n mathematical set
COSETS > COSET
COSEY n tea cosy
COSEYS > COSEY
COSH n heavy blunt weapon ▷ vb hit with a cosh
COSHED > COSH
COSHER vb pamper or coddle
COSHERED > COSHER
COSHERER > COSHER
COSHERERS > COSHER
COSHERIES > COSHERY
COSHERING > COSHER
COSHERS > COSHER
COSHERY n Irish chief's right to lodge at his tenants' houses
COSHES > COSH
COSHING > COSH
COSIE same as > COSY

COSIED > COSY
COSIER n cobbler
COSIERS > COSIER
COSIES > COSY
COSIEST > COSY
COSIGN vb to sign jointly
COSIGNED > COSIGN
COSIGNER > COSIGN
COSIGNERS > COSIGN
COSIGNING > COSIGN
COSIGNS > COSIGN
COSILY > COSY
COSINE n (in trigonometry) ratio of the length of the adjacent side to that of the hypotenuse in a right-angled triangle
COSINES > COSINE
COSINESS > COSY
COSING > COSE
COSMEA n plant of the genus Cosmos
COSMEAS > COSMEA
COSMESES > COSMESIS
COSMESIS n aesthetic covering on a prosthesis to make it look more natural
COSMETIC n preparation used to improve the appearance of a person's skin ▷ adj improving the appearance only
COSMETICS > COSMETIC
COSMIC adj of the whole universe
COSMICAL > COSMIC
COSMID n segment of DNA
COSMIDS > COSMID
COSMIN same as > COSMINE
COSMINE n substance resembling dentine, forming the outer layer of cosmoid scales
COSMINES > COSMINE
COSMINS > COSMIN
COSMISM n Russian cultural and philosophical movement
COSMISMS > COSMISM
COSMIST > COSMISM
COSMISTS > COSMISM
COSMOCRAT n ruler of the world
COSMOGENY same as > COSMOGONY
COSMOGONY n study of the origin of the universe
COSMOID adj (of the scales of coelacanths and lungfish) consisting of two inner bony layers and an outer layer of cosmine
COSMOLINE n type of petroleum jelly
COSMOLOGY n study of the origin and nature of the universe
COSMONAUT n Russian name for an astronaut
COSMORAMA n lifelike display, using mirrors and lenses, which shows reflections of various views of parts of the world
COSMOS n universe
COSMOSES > COSMOS
COSMOTRON n large type of

particle accelerator

COSPHERED *adj* sharing the same sphere

COSPONSOR *vb* to sponsor jointly

COSS *another name for* > KOS

COSSACK *n* Slavonic warrior-peasant who served in the Russian cavalry under the tsars

COSSACKS > COSSACK

COSSES > COSS

COSSET *vb* pamper ▷ *n* any pet animal, esp a lamb

COSSETED > COSSET

COSSETING > COSSET

COSSETS > COSSET

COSSIE *n* informal name for a swimming costume

COSSIES > COSSIE

COST *n* amount of money, time, labour, etc, required for something ▷ *vb* have as its cost

COSTA *n* riblike part, such as the midrib of a plant leaf

COSTAE > COSTA

COSTAL *n* strengthening rib of an insect's wing

COSTALGIA *n* pain in the ribs

COSTALLY > COSTAL

COSTALS > COSTAL

COSTAR *n* actor who shares the billing with another ▷ *vb* share the billing with another actor

COSTARD *n* English variety of apple tree

COSTARDS > COSTARD

COSTARRED > COSTAR

COSTARS > COSTAR

COSTATE *adj* having ribs

COSTATED *same as* > COSTATE

COSTE *vb* to draw near

COSTEAN *vb* to mine for lodes

COSTEANED > COSTEAN

COSTEANS > COSTEAN

COSTED > COST

COSTER *n* person who sells fruit, vegetables etc from a barrow

COSTERS > COSTER

COSTES > COSTE

COSTING > COST

COSTIVE *adj* having or causing constipation

COSTIVELY > COSTIVE

COSTLESS > COST

COSTLIER > COSTLY

COSTLIEST > COSTLY

COSTLY *adj* expensive

COSTMARY *n* herbaceous plant, *Chrysanthemum balsamita*, native to Asia. Its fragrant leaves were used as a seasoning and to flavour ale: family *Asteraceae* (composites)

COSTOTOMY *n* surgical incision into a rib

COSTREL *n* flask, usually of earthenware or leather

COSTRELS > COSTREL

COSTS > COST

COSTUME *n* style of dress of a particular place or time, or for a particular activity ▷ *vb* provide with a costume

COSTUMED > COSTUME

COSTUMER *same as* > COSTUMIER

COSTUMERS > COSTUMIER

COSTUMERY *n* collective term for costumes

COSTUMES > COSTUME

COSTUMEY *adj* (stage) costume-like; unrealistic

COSTUMIER *n* maker or seller of costumes

COSTUMING > COSTUME

COSTUS *n* Himalayan herb with an aromatic root

COSTUSES > COSTUS

COSY *adj* warm and snug ▷ *n* cover for keeping things warm ▷ *vb* to make oneself snug and warm

COSYING > COSY

COT *n* baby's bed with high sides ▷ *vb* entangle or become entangled

COTAN *same as* > COTANGENT

COTANGENT *n* (in trigonometry) the ratio of the length of the adjacent side to that of the opposite side in a right-angled triangle

COTANS > COTANGENT

COTE > COT

COTEAU *n* hillside

COTEAUX > COTEAU

COTED > COT

COTELETTE *n* cutlet

COTELINE *n* kind of muslin

COTELINES > COTELINE

COTENANCY > COTENANT

COTENANT *n* person who holds property jointly or in common with others

COTENANTS > COTENANT

COTERIE *n* exclusive group, clique

COTERIES > COTERIE

COTES > COTE

COTH *n* hyperbolic cotangent

COTHS > COTH

COTHURN *same as* > COTHURNUS

COTHURNAL > COTHURNUS

COTHURNI > COTHURNUS

COTHURNS > COTHURNUS

COTHURNUS *n* buskin worn in ancient Greek tragedy

COTICULAR *adj* relating to whetstones

COTIDAL *adj* (of a line on a tidal chart) joining points at which high tide occurs simultaneously

COTILLION *n* French formation dance of the 18th century

COTILLON *same as* > COTILLION

COTILLONS > COTILLON

COTING > COT

COTINGA *n* any tropical American passerine bird

of the family *Cotingidae*, such as the umbrella bird and the cock-of-the-rock, having a broad slightly hooked bill

COTINGAS > COTINGA

COTININE *n* substance used to indicate presence of nicotine

COTININES > COTININE

COTISE *same as* > COTTISE

COTISED > COTISE

COTISES > COTISE

COTISING > COTISE

COTLAND *n* grounds that belong to a cotter

COTLANDS > COTLAND

COTQUEAN *n* coarse woman

COTQUEANS > COTQUEAN

COTRUSTEE *n* fellow trustee

COTS > COT

COTT *same as* > COT

COTTA *n* short form of surplice

COTTABUS *n* ancient Greek game involving throwing wine into a vessel

COTTAE > COTTA

COTTAGE *n* small house in the country ▷ *vb* engage in homosexual activity in a public lavatory

COTTAGED > COTTAGE

COTTAGER *n* person who lives in a cottage

COTTAGERS > COTTAGER

COTTAGES > COTTAGE

COTTAGEY *adj* resembling a cottage

COTTAGING *n* homosexual activity between men in a public lavatory

COTTAR *same as* > COTTER

COTTARS > COTTAR

COTTAS > COTTA

COTTED > COT

COTTER *n* pin or wedge used to secure machine parts ▷ *vb* secure (two parts) with a cotter

COTTERED > COTTER

COTTERING > COTTER

COTTERS > COTTER

COTTID *n* any fish of the scorpaenoid family *Cottidae*, typically possessing a large head, tapering body, and spiny fins, including the pogge, sea scorpion, bullhead, father lasher, and cottus

COTTIDS > COTTID

COTTIER *same as* > COTTER

COTTIERS > COTTIER

COTTING > COT

COTTISE *n* type of heraldic decoration ▷ *vb* (in heraldry) decorate with a cottise

COTTISED > COTTISE

COTTISES > COTTISE

COTTISING > COTTISE

COTTOID *adj* resembling a fish of the genus *Cottus*

COTTON *n* white downy fibre covering the seeds of a tropical plant ▷ *vb* take

a liking

COTTONADE *n* coarse fabric of cotton or mixed fibres, used for work clothes, etc

COTTONED > COTTON

COTTONING > COTTON

COTTONS > COTTON

COTTONY > COTTON

COTTOWN *Scots variant of* > COTTON

COTTOWNS > COTTON

COTTS > COTT

COTTUS *n* scorpaenoid fish of the family *Cottidae*; the type genus, having four yellowish knobs on its head

COTTUSES > COTTUS

COTURNIX *n* variety of quail

COTWAL *n* Indian police officer

COTWALS > COTWAL

COTYLAE > COTYLE

COTYLE *n* cuplike cavity

COTYLEDON *n* first leaf of a plant embryo

COTYLES > COTYLE

COTYLOID *adj* shaped like a cup ▷ *n* small bone forming part of the acetabular cavity in some mammals

COTYLOIDS > COTYLOID

COTYPE *n* additional type specimen from the same brood as the original type specimen

COTYPES > COTYPE

COUCAL *n* any ground-living bird of the genus *Centropus*, of Africa, S Asia, and Australia, having long strong legs: family *Cuculidae* (cuckoos)

COUCALS > COUCAL

COUCH *n* piece of upholstered furniture for seating more than one person ▷ *vb* express in a particular way

COUCHANT *adj* in a lying position

COUCHE *adj* in heraldry (of a shield), tilted

COUCHED > COUCH

COUCHEE *n* reception held late at night

COUCHEES > COUCHEE

COUCHER > COUCH

COUCHERS > COUCH

COUCHES > COUCH

COUCHETTE *n* bed converted from seats on a train or ship

COUCHING *n* method of embroidery in which the thread is caught down at intervals by another thread passed through the material from beneath

COUCHINGS > COUCHING

COUDE *adj* (of a reflecting telescope) having plane mirrors positioned to reflect light from the primary mirror along the axis onto a detector

COUGAN *n* drunk and rowdy person

Section 1: Words between 2 and 9 letters in length

COUGANS > COUGAN

COUGAR *n* puma

COUGARS > COUGAR

COUGH *vb* expel air from the lungs abruptly and noisily ▷ *n* act or sound of coughing

COUGHED > COUGH

COUGHER > COUGH

COUGHERS > COUGH

COUGHING > COUGH

COUGHINGS > COUGH

COUGHS > COUGH

COUGUAR *same as* > COUGAR

COUGUARS > COUGUAR

COULD > CAN

COULDEST *same as* > COULDST

COULDST *vb* form of 'could' used with the pronoun *thou* or its relative form

COULEE *n* flow of molten lava

COULEES > COULEE

COULIBIAC *n* Russian fish pie

COULIS *n* thin purée of vegetables or fruit, usually served as a sauce surrounding a dish

COULISSE *n* timber member grooved to take a sliding panel, such as a sluicegate, portcullis, or stage flat

COULISSES > COULISSE

COULOIR *n* deep gully on a mountain side, esp in the French Alps

COULOIRS > COULOIR

COULOMB *n* SI unit of electric charge

COULOMBIC > COULOMB

COULOMBS > COULOMB

COULTER *n* blade at the front of a ploughshare

COULTERS > COULTER

COUMARIC > COUMARIN

COUMARIN *n* white vanilla-scented crystalline ester, used in perfumes and flavourings and as an anticoagulant

COUMARINS > COUMARIN

COUMARONE *n* a colourless insoluble aromatic liquid obtained from coal tar and used in the manufacture of synthetic resins

COUMAROU *n* tonka bean tree, or its seed

COUMAROUS > COUMAROU

COUNCIL *n* group meeting for discussion or consultation ▷ *adj* of or by a council

COUNCILOR *n* member of a council

COUNCILS > COUNCIL

COUNSEL *n* advice or guidance ▷ *vb* give guidance to

COUNSELED > COUNSEL

COUNSELEE *n* one who is counselled

COUNSELOR *n* person who gives counsel

COUNSELS > COUNSEL

COUNT *vb* say numbers in order ▷ *n* counting

COUNTABLE *adj* capable of being counted

COUNTABLY > COUNTABLE

COUNTBACK *n* system of deciding the winner of a tied competition by comparing earlier points or scores

COUNTDOWN *n* counting backwards to zero of the seconds before an event ▷ *vb* count numbers backwards towards zero, esp in timing such a critical operation

COUNTED > COUNT

COUNTER *n* long flat surface in a bank or shop, on which business is transacted ▷ *vb* oppose, retaliate against ▷ *adv* in the opposite direction

COUNTERED > COUNTER

COUNTERS > COUNTER

COUNTESS *n* woman holding the rank of count or earl

COUNTIAN *n* dweller in a given county

COUNTIANS > COUNTIAN

COUNTIES > COUNTY

COUNTING > COUNT

COUNTLESS *adj* too many to count

COUNTLINE *n* (in confectionery marketing) a chocolate-based bar

COUNTRIES > COUNTRY

COUNTROL *obsolete variant of* > CONTROL

COUNTROLS > COUNTROL

COUNTRY *n* nation

COUNTS > COUNT

COUNTSHIP > COUNT

COUNTY *n* (in some countries) division of a country ▷ *adj* upper-class

COUP *n* successful action ▷ *vb* turn or fall over

COUPE *n* sports car with two doors and a sloping fixed roof

COUPED > COUP

COUPEE *n* (in dance) a forward movement on one leg, with the other slightly bent and raised

COUPEES > COUPEE

COUPER *n* dealer

COUPERS > COUPER

COUPES > COUPE

COUPING > COUP

COUPLE *n* two people who are married or romantically involved ▷ *vb* connect, associate

COUPLED > COUPLE

COUPLEDOM *n* state of living as a couple, esp when regarded as being interested in each other to the exclusion of the outside world

COUPLER *n* link or rod transmitting power between two rotating mechanisms or a rotating part and a reciprocating part

COUPLERS > COUPLER

COUPLES > COUPLE

COUPLET *n* two consecutive lines of verse, usu rhyming and of the same metre

COUPLETS > COUPLET

COUPLING *n* device for connecting things, such as railway carriages

COUPLINGS > COUPLING

COUPON *n* piece of paper entitling the holder to a discount or gift

COUPONING *n* in marketing, distribution or redemption of promotional coupons

COUPONS > COUPON

COUPS > COUP

COUPURE *n* entrenchment made by beseiged forces behind a breach in their defences

COUPURES > COUPURE

COUR *obsolete variant of* > COVER

COURAGE *n* ability to face danger or pain without fear

COURAGES > COURAGE

COURANT *n* courante ▷ *adj* (of an animal) running

COURANTE *n* old dance in quick triple time

COURANTES > COURANTE

COURANTO *same as* > COURANTE

COURANTOS > COURANTO

COURANTS > COURANT

COURB *vb* to bend

COURBARIL *n* tropical American leguminous tree, *Hymenaea courbaril*. Its wood is a useful timber and its gum is a source of copal

COURBED > COURB

COURBETTE *same as* > CURVET

COURBING > COURB

COURBS > COURB

COURD *obsolete variant of* > COVERED

COURE *obsolete variant of* > COVER

COURED > COURE

COURES > COURE

COURGETTE *n* type of small vegetable marrow

COURIE *vb* nestle or snuggle

COURIED > COURIE

COURIEING > COURIE

COURIER *n* person employed to look after holiday-makers ▷ *vb* send (a parcel, letter, etc) by courier

COURIERED > COURIER

COURIERS > COURIER

COURIES > COURIE

COURING > COUR

COURLAN *another name for* > LIMPKIN

COURLANS > COURLAN

COURS > COUR

COURSE *n* series of lessons or medical treatment ▷ *vb* (of liquid) run swiftly

COURSED > COURSE

COURSER *n* swift horse

COURSERS > COURSER

COURSES *another word for* > MENSES

COURSING *n* hunting with hounds trained to hunt game by sight

COURSINGS > COURSING

COURT *n* body which decides legal cases ▷ *vb* try to gain the love of

COURTED > COURT

COURTEOUS *adj* polite

COURTER *n* suitor

COURTERS > COURTER

COURTESAN *n* mistress or high-class prostitute

COURTESY *n* politeness, good manners

COURTEZAN *same as* > COURTESAN

COURTIER *n* attendant at a royal court

COURTIERS > COURTIER

COURTING > COURT

COURTINGS > COURT

COURTLET *n* small court

COURTLETS > COURTLET

COURTLIER > COURTLY

COURTLIKE *adj* courtly

COURTLING *n* fawning courtier

COURTLY *adj* ceremoniously polite

COURTROOM *n* room in which the sittings of a law court are held

COURTS > COURT

COURTSHIP *n* courting of an intended spouse or mate

COURTSIDE *n* in sport, area closest to the court

COURTYARD *n* paved space enclosed by buildings or walls

COUSCOUS *n* type of semolina used in North African cookery

COUSIN *n* child of one's uncle or aunt

COUSINAGE *n* kinship

COUSINLY > COUSIN

COUSINRY *n* collective term for cousins

COUSINS > COUSIN

COUTEAU *n* large two-edged knife used formerly as a weapon

COUTEAUX > COUTEAU

COUTER *n* armour designed to protect the elbow

COUTERS > COUTER

COUTH *adj* refined ▷ *n* refinement

COUTHER > COUTH

COUTHEST > COUTH

COUTHIE *adj* sociable

COUTHIER > COUTHIE

COUTHIEST > COUTHIE

COUTHS > COUTH

COUTHY *same as* > COUTHIE

COUTIL *n* type of tightly-woven twill cloth

COUTILLE same as > COUTIL

COUTILLES > COUTILLE

COUTILS > COUTIL

COUTURE n high-fashion designing and dressmaking ▷ adj relating to high fashion design and dress-making

COUTURES > COUTURE

COUTURIER n person who designs women's fashion clothes

COUVADE n custom in certain cultures of treating the husband of a woman giving birth as if he were bearing the child

COUVADES > COUVADE

COUVERT another word for > COVER

COUVERTS > COUVERT

COUZIN n South African word for a friend

COUZINS > COUZIN

COVALENCE same as > COVALENCY

COVALENCY n ability to form a bond in which two atoms share a pair of electrons

COVALENT > COVALENCY

COVARIANT n variant that varies leaving certain mathematical relationships it has with another variant (its covariant) unchanged

COVARIATE n statistical variable

COVARIED > COVARY

COVARIES > COVARY

COVARY vb vary together maintaining a certain mathematical relationship

COVARYING > COVARY

COVE n small bay or inlet ▷ vb form an architectural cove in

COVED > COVE

COVELET n small cove

COVELETS > COVELET

COVELLINE same as > COVELLITE

COVELLITE n indigo copper (blue sulphide of copper)

COVEN n meeting of witches

COVENANT n contract ▷ vb agree by a covenant

COVENANTS > COVENANT

COVENS > COVEN

COVENT same as > CONVENT

COVENTS > COVENT

COVER vb place something over, to protect or conceal ▷ n anything that covers

COVERABLE > COVER

COVERAGE n amount or extent covered

COVERAGES > COVERAGE

COVERALL n thing that covers something entirely

COVERALLS > COVERALL

COVERED > COVER

COVERER > COVER

COVERERS > COVER

COVERING another word for > COVER

COVERINGS > COVERING

COVERLESS > COVER

COVERLET n bed cover

COVERLETS > COVERLET

COVERLID same as > COVERLET

COVERLIDS > COVERLID

COVERS > COVER

COVERSED as in coversed sine obsolete function in trigonometry

COVERSINE n function in trigometry

COVERSLIP n very thin piece of glass placed over a specimen on a glass slide

COVERT adj concealed, secret ▷ n thicket giving shelter to game birds or animals

COVERTLY > COVERT

COVERTS > COVERT

COVERTURE n condition or status of a married woman considered as being under the protection and influence of her husband

COVERUP n concealment of a mistake, crime, etc

COVERUPS > COVERUP

COVES > COVE

COVET vb long to possess (what belongs to someone else)

COVETABLE > COVET

COVETED > COVET

COVETER > COVET

COVETERS > COVET

COVETING > COVET

COVETISE n covetousness

COVETISES > COVETISE

COVETOUS adj jealously longing to possess something

COVETS > COVET

COVEY n small flock of grouse or partridge

COVEYS > COVEY

COVIN n conspiracy between two or more persons to act to the detriment or injury of another

COVING same as > COVE

COVINGS > COVING

COVINOUS adj deceitful

COVINS > COVIN

COVYNE same as > COVIN

COVYNES > COVYNE

COW n mature female of cattle and of certain other mammals, such as the elephant or seal ▷ vb intimidate, subdue

COWAGE n tropical climbing leguminous plant, Stizolobium (or Mucuna) pruriens, whose bristly pods cause severe itching and stinging

COWAGES > COWAGE

COWAL n shallow lake or swampy depression supporting vegetation

COWALS > COWAL

COWAN n drystone waller

COWANS > COWAN

COWARD n person who lacks courage ▷ vb show (someone) up to be a coward

COWARDED > COWARD

COWARDICE n lack of courage

COWARDING > COWARD

COWARDLY adj of or characteristic of a coward

COWARDRY n cowardice

COWARDS > COWARD

COWBANE n any of several N temperate poisonous umbelliferous marsh plants of the genus Cicuta, esp C. virosa, having clusters of small white flowers

COWBANES > COWBANE

COWBELL n bell hung around a cow's neck

COWBELLS > COWBELL

COWBERRY n creeping ericaceous evergreen shrub, Vaccinium vitis-idaea, of N temperate and arctic regions, with pink or red flowers and edible slightly acid berries

COWBIND n any of various bryony plants, esp the white bryony

COWBINDS > COWBIND

COWBIRD n any of various American orioles of the genera Molothrus, Tangavius, etc, esp M. ater (common or brown-headed cowbird). They have a dark plumage and short bill

COWBIRDS > COWBIRD

COWBOY n (in the US) ranch worker who herds and tends cattle, usu on horseback ▷ vb work or behave as a cowboy

COWBOYED > COWBOY

COWBOYING > COWBOY

COWBOYS > COWBOY

COWED > COW

COWEDLY > COW

COWER vb cringe in fear

COWERED > COWER

COWERING > COWER

COWERS > COWER

COWFEEDER n dairyman

COWFISH n any trunkfish, such as Lactophrys quadricornis, having hornlike spines over the eyes

COWFISHES > COWFISH

COWFLAP n cow dung

COWFLAPS > COWFLAP

COWFLOP n foxglove

COWFLOPS > COWFLOP

COWGIRL n female cowboy

COWGIRLS > COWGIRL

COWGRASS n red clover

COWHAGE same as > COWAGE

COWHAGES > COWHAGE

COWHAND same as > COWBOY

COWHANDS > COWBOY

COWHEARD same as > COWHERD

COWHEARDS > COWHEARD

COWHEEL n heel of a cow, used as cooking ingredient

COWHEELS > COWHEEL

COWHERB n European caryophyllaceous plant, Saponaria vaccaria, having clusters of pink flowers: a weed in the US

COWHERBS > COWHERB

COWHERD n person employed to tend cattle

COWHERDS > COWHERD

COWHIDE n hide of a cow ▷ vb to lash with a cowhide whip

COWHIDED > COWHIDE

COWHIDES > COWHIDE

COWHIDING > COWHIDE

COWHOUSE n byre

COWHOUSES > COWHOUSE

COWIER > COWY

COWIEST > COWY

COWING > COW

COWINNER n joint winner

COWINNERS > COWINNER

COWISH adj cowardly

COWITCH another name for > COWAGE

COWITCHES > COWITCH

COWK vb retch or feel nauseated

COWKED > COWK

COWKING > COWK

COWKS > COWK

COWL same as > COWLING

COWLED adj wearing a cowl

COWLICK n tuft of hair over the forehead

COWLICKS > COWLICK

COWLING n cover on an engine

COWLINGS > COWLING

COWLS > COWL

COWLSTAFF n pole, used by two people, for carrying a vessel

COWMAN n man who owns cattle

COWMEN > COWMAN

COWORKER n fellow worker

COWORKERS > COWORKER

COWP same as > COUP

COWPAT n pool of cow dung

COWPATS > COWPAT

COWPEA n leguminous tropical climbing plant, Vigna sinensis, producing long pods containing edible pealike seeds: grown for animal fodder and sometimes as human food

COWPEAS > COWPEA

COWPED > COWP

COWPIE n cowpat

COWPIES > COWPIE

COWPING > COWP

COWPLOP n cow dung

COWPLOPS > COWPLOP

COWPOKE n cowboy

COWPOKES > COWPOKE

COWPOX n disease of cows, the virus of which is used in the smallpox vaccine

COWPOXES > COWPOX

COWPS > COWP

COWRIE n brightly-marked sea shell

COWRIES > COWRIE
COWRITE vb to write jointly
COWRITER > COWRITE
COWRITERS > COWRITE
COWRITES > COWRITE
COWRITING > COWRITE
COWRITTEN > COWRITE
COWROTE > COWRITE
COWRY same as > COWRIE
COWS > COW
COWSHED n byre
COWSHEDS > COWSHED
COWSKIN same as > COWHIDE
COWSKINS > COWSKIN
COWSLIP n small yellow
   wild European flower
COWSLIPS > COWSLIP
COWTREE n South American
   tree that produces latex
COWTREES > COWTREE
COWY adj cowlike
COX n coxswain ▷ vb act as
   cox of (a boat)
COXA n technical name for
   the hipbone or hip joint
COXAE > COXA
COXAL > COXA
COXALGIA n pain in the hip
   joint
COXALGIAS > COXALGIA
COXALGIC > COXALGIA
COXALGIES > COXALGIA
COXALGY same as > COXALGIA
COXCOMB same as
   > COCKSCOMB
COXCOMBIC > COXCOMB
COXCOMBRY n conceited
   arrogance or foppishness
COXCOMBS > COXCOMB
COXED > COX
COXES > COX
COXIER > COXY
COXIEST > COXY
COXINESS > COXY
COXING > COX
COXITIDES > COXITIS
COXITIS n inflammation of
   the hip joint
COXLESS > COX
COXSWAIN n person who
   steers a rowing boat
COXSWAINS > COXSWAIN
COXY adj cocky
COY adj affectedly shy or
   modest ▷ vb to caress
COYDOG n cross between a
   coyote and a dog
COYDOGS > COYDOG
COYED > COY
COYER > COY
COYEST > COY
COYING > COY
COYISH > COY
COYISHLY > COY
COYLY > COY
COYNESS > COY
COYNESSES > COY
COYOTE n prairie wolf of N
   America
COYOTES > COYOTE
COYOTILLO n thorny
   poisonous rhamnaceous
   shrub, Karwinskia
   humboldtiana of Mexico
   and the southwestern US,
   the berries of which cause
   paralysis

COYPOU same as > COYPU
COYPOUS > COYPOU
COYPU n beaver-like aquatic
   rodent native to S America,
   bred for its fur
COYPUS > COYPU
COYS > COY
COYSTREL same as
   > COISTREL
COYSTRELS > COYSTREL
COYSTRIL same as
   > COISTREL
COYSTRILS > COYSTRIL
COZ n %i%>archaic word
   for%/i%> > COUSIN
COZE vb to chat
COZED > COZE
COZEN vb cheat, trick
COZENAGE > COZEN
COZENAGES > COZEN
COZENED > COZEN
COZENER > COZEN
COZENERS > COZEN
COZENING > COZEN
COZENS > COZEN
COZES > COZE
COZEY n tea cosy
COZEYS > COZEY
COZIE same as > COZEY
COZIED > COSY
COZIER n cobbler
COZIERS > COZIER
COZIES > COZEY
COZIEST > COZY
COZILY > COZY
COZINESS > COZY
COZING > COZE
COZY same as > COSY vb to
   make oneself snug and
   warm
COZYING > COZY
COZZES > COZ
CRAAL vb to enclose in a
   craal (or kraal)
CRAALED > CRAAL
CRAALING > CRAAL
CRAALS > CRAAL
CRAB n edible shellfish
   with ten legs, the first pair
   modified into pincers
CRABAPPLE n tree bearing
   small sour apple-like fruit
CRABBED > CRAB
CRABBEDLY > CRAB
CRABBER n crab fisherman
CRABBERS > CRABBER
CRABBIER > CRABBY
CRABBIEST > CRABBY
CRABBILY > CRABBY
CRABBING > CRAB
CRABBY adj bad-tempered
CRABEATER n species of seal
CRABGRASS n type of coarse
   weedy grass
CRABLIKE adj resembling
   a crab
CRABMEAT n edible flesh of
   a crab
CRABMEATS > CRABMEAT
CRABS > CRAB
CRABSTICK n stick, cane, or
   cudgel made of crabapple
   wood
CRABWISE adv (of motion)
   sideways
CRABWOOD n tropical
   American meliaceous tree,

Carapa guianensis
CRABWOODS > CRABWOOD
CRACK vb break or split
   partially ▷ n sudden sharp
   noise ▷ adj first-rate,
   excellent
CRACKA n US derogatory
   word for a poor White
   person
CRACKAS > CRACKA
CRACKBACK n in American
   football, illegal blocking of
   an opponent
CRACKDOWN n severe
   disciplinary measures
CRACKED adj damaged by
   cracking ▷ n sharp noise
CRACKER n thin dry biscuit
CRACKERS adj insane
CRACKET n low stool, often
   one with three legs
CRACKETS > CRACKET
CRACKHEAD n person
   addicted to the drug crack
CRACKING adj very fast
CRACKINGS > CRACKING
CRACKJAW adj difficult to
   pronounce ▷ n word or
   phrase that is difficult to
   pronounce
CRACKJAWS > CRACKJAW
CRACKLE vb make small
   sharp popping noises ▷ n
   crackling sound
CRACKLED > CRACKLE
CRACKLES > CRACKLE
CRACKLIER > CRACKLY
CRACKLING n crackle
CRACKLY adj making a
   cracking sound
CRACKNEL n type of hard
   plain biscuit
CRACKNELS > CRACKNEL
CRACKPOT adj eccentric ▷ n
   eccentric person
CRACKPOTS > CRACKPOT
CRACKS > CRACK
CRACKSMAN n burglar, esp a
   safe-breaker
CRACKSMEN > CRACKSMAN
CRACKUP n physical or
   mental breakdown
CRACKUPS > CRACKUP
CRACKY adj full of cracks
CRACOWE n medieval shoe
   with a sharply pointed toe
CRACOWES > CRACOWE
CRADLE n baby's bed on
   rockers ▷ vb hold gently as
   if in a cradle
CRADLED > CRADLE
CRADLER > CRADLE
CRADLERS > CRADLE
CRADLES > CRADLE
CRADLING n framework of
   iron or wood, esp as used
   in the construction of a
   ceiling
CRADLINGS > CRADLING
CRAFT n occupation
   requiring skill with the
   hands ▷ vb make skilfully
CRAFTED > CRAFT
CRAFTER n person doing
   craftwork
CRAFTERS > CRAFTER
CRAFTIER > CRAFTY

CRAFTIEST > CRAFTY
CRAFTILY > CRAFTY
CRAFTING > CRAFT
CRAFTLESS adj guileless
CRAFTS > CRAFT
CRAFTSMAN n skilled worker
CRAFTSMEN > CRAFTSMAN
CRAFTWORK n handicraft
CRAFTY adj skilled in
   deception
CRAG n steep rugged rock
CRAGFAST adj stranded on
   a crag
CRAGGED same as > CRAGGY
CRAGGIER > CRAGGY
CRAGGIEST > CRAGGY
CRAGGILY > CRAGGY
CRAGGY adj having many
   crags
CRAGS > CRAG
CRAGSMAN n rock climber
CRAGSMEN > CRAGSMAN
CRAIC n Irish word meaning
   fun
CRAICS > CRAIC
CRAIG a Scot word for > CRAG
CRAIGS > CRAIG
CRAKE n bird of the rail
   family, such as the
   corncrake ▷ vb to boast
CRAKED > CRAKE
CRAKES > CRAKE
CRAKING > CRAKE
CRAM vb force into too
   small a space ▷ n act or
   condition of cramming
CRAMBE n any plant of the
   genus Crambe
CRAMBES > CRAMBE
CRAMBO n word game in
   which one team says a
   rhyme or rhyming line for
   a word or line given by the
   other team
CRAMBOES > CRAMBO
CRAMBOS > CRAMBO
CRAME n merchant's booth
   or stall
CRAMES > CRAME
CRAMESIES > CRAMESY
CRAMESY same as
   > CRAMOISY
CRAMMABLE adj able to be
   crammed or filled
CRAMMED > CRAM
CRAMMER n person or school
   that prepares pupils for an
   examination
CRAMMERS > CRAMMER
CRAMMING > CRAM
CRAMOISIE same as
   > CRAMOISY
CRAMOISY adj of a crimson
   colour ▷ n crimson cloth
CRAMP n painful muscular
   contraction ▷ vb affect
   with a cramp
CRAMPBARK n guelder rose
CRAMPED adj closed in
CRAMPER n spiked metal
   plate used as a brace for the
   feet in throwing the stone
CRAMPERS > CRAMPER
CRAMPET n cramp iron
CRAMPETS > CRAMPET
CRAMPFISH n electric ray
CRAMPIER > CRAMPY

CRAMPIEST > CRAMPY
CRAMPING > CRAMP
CRAMPIT same as > CRAMPET
CRAMPITS > CRAMPIT
CRAMPON n spiked plate strapped to a boot for climbing on ice ▷ vb climb using crampons
CRAMPONED > CRAMPON
CRAMPONS > CRAMPON
CRAMPOON same as > CRAMPON
CRAMPOONS > CRAMPOON
CRAMPS > CRAMP
CRAMPY adj affected with cramp
CRAMS > CRAM
CRAN n unit of capacity used for measuring fresh herring, equal to 37.5 gallons
CRANAGE n use of a crane
CRANAGES > CRANAGE
CRANBERRY n sour edible red berry
CRANCH vb to crunch
CRANCHED > CRANCH
CRANCHES > CRANCH
CRANCHING > CRANCH
CRANE n machine for lifting and moving heavy weights ▷ vb stretch (one's neck) to see something
CRANED > CRANE
CRANEFLY n fly with long legs, slender wings, and a narrow body
CRANES > CRANE
CRANIA > CRANIUM
CRANIAL adj of or relating to the skull
CRANIALLY > CRANIAL
CRANIATE adj having a skull or cranium ▷ n vertebrate
CRANIATES > CRANIATE
CRANING > CRANE
CRANIUM n skull
CRANIUMS > CRANIUM
CRANK n arm projecting at right angles from a shaft, for transmitting or converting motion ▷ vb turn with a crank ▷ adj (of a sailing vessel) easily keeled over by the wind
CRANKCASE n metal case that encloses the crankshaft in an internal-combustion engine
CRANKED > CRANK
CRANKER > CRANK
CRANKEST > CRANK
CRANKIER > CRANK
CRANKIEST > CRANK
CRANKILY > CRANK
CRANKING > CRANK
CRANKISH adj somewhat eccentric or bad-tempered
CRANKLE vb to bend or wind
CRANKLED > CRANKLE
CRANKLES > CRANKLE
CRANKLING > CRANKLE
CRANKLY adj vigorously
CRANKNESS n (of a vessel) liability to capsize
CRANKOUS adj fretful
CRANKPIN n short

cylindrical pin in a crankshaft, to which the connecting rod is attached
CRANKPINS > CRANKPIN
CRANKS > CRANK
CRANKY same as > CRANK
CRANNIED > CRANNY
CRANNIES > CRANNY
CRANNOG n ancient Celtic lake or bog dwelling dating from the late Bronze Age to the 16th century AD, often fortified and used as a refuge
CRANNOGE same as > CRANNOG
CRANNOGES > CRANNOGE
CRANNOGS > CRANNOG
CRANNY n narrow opening ▷ vb to become full of crannies
CRANNYING > CRANNY
CRANREUCH n hoarfrost
CRANS > CRAN
CRANTS n garland carried in front of a maiden's bier
CRANTSES > CRANTS
CRAP n rubbish, nonsense ▷ vb defecate
CRAPAUD n frog or toad
CRAPAUDS > CRAPAUD
CRAPE same as > CREPE
CRAPED > CRAPE
CRAPELIKE > CRAPE
CRAPES > CRAPE
CRAPIER > CRAPE
CRAPIEST > CRAPE
CRAPING > CRAPE
CRAPLE same as > GRAPPLE
CRAPLES > CRAPLE
CRAPOLA n rubbish
CRAPOLAS > CRAPOLA
CRAPPED > CRAP
CRAPPER n toilet
CRAPPERS > CRAPPER
CRAPPIE n N American freshwater fish)
CRAPPIER > CRAPPY
CRAPPIES > CRAPPIE
CRAPPIEST > CRAPPY
CRAPPING > CRAP
CRAPPY adj worthless, lousy
CRAPS > CRAP
CRAPSHOOT n dice game
CRAPULENT adj given to or resulting from excessive eating or drinking
CRAPULOUS same as > CRAPULENT
CRAPY > CRAPE
CRARE n type of trading vessel
CRARES > CRARE
CRASES > CRASIS
CRASH n collision involving a vehicle or vehicles ▷ vb (cause to) collide violently with a vehicle, a stationary object, or the ground ▷ adj requiring or using great effort in order to achieve results quickly
CRASHED > CRASH
CRASHER > CRASH
CRASHERS > CRASH
CRASHES > CRASH
CRASHING adj extreme

CRASHLAND n land an aircraft in an emergency causing damage
CRASHPAD n place to sleep or live temporarily
CRASHPADS > CRASHPAD
CRASIS n fusion or contraction of two adjacent vowels into one
CRASS adj stupid and insensitive
CRASSER > CRASS
CRASSEST > CRASS
CRASSLY > CRASS
CRASSNESS > CRASS
CRATCH n rack for holding fodder for cattle, etc
CRATCHES > CRATCH
CRATE n large wooden container for packing goods ▷ vb put in a crate
CRATED > CRATE
CRATEFUL > CRATE
CRATEFULS > CRATE
CRATER n bowl-shaped opening at the top of a volcano vb make or form craters
CRATERED > CRATER
CRATERING > CRATER
CRATERLET n small crater
CRATEROUS > CRATER
CRATERS > CRATER
CRATES > CRATE
CRATING > CRATE
CRATON n stable part of the earth's continental crust or lithosphere that has not been deformed significantly for many millions, even hundreds of millions, of years
CRATONIC > CRATON
CRATONS > CRATON
CRATUR n whisky or whiskey
CRATURS > CRATUR
CRAUNCH same as > CRUNCH
CRAUNCHED > CRAUNCH
CRAUNCHES > CRAUNCH
CRAUNCHY > CRAUNCH
CRAVAT n man's scarf worn like a tie ▷ vb wear a cravat
CRAVATS > CRAVAT
CRAVATTED > CRAVAT
CRAVE vb desire intensely
CRAVED > CRAVE
CRAVEN adj cowardly ▷ n coward ▷ vb to make cowardly
CRAVENED > CRAVEN
CRAVENING > CRAVEN
CRAVENLY > CRAVEN
CRAVENS > CRAVEN
CRAVER > CRAVE
CRAVERS > CRAVE
CRAVES > CRAVE
CRAVING n intense desire or longing
CRAVINGS > CRAVING
CRAW n pouchlike part of a bird's oesophagus
CRAWDAD n crayfish
CRAWDADDY n crayfish
CRAWDADS > CRAWDAD
CRAWFISH same as > CRAYFISH
CRAWL vb move on one's

hands and knees ▷ n crawling motion or pace
CRAWLED > CRAWL
CRAWLER n servile flatterer
CRAWLERS > CRAWLER
CRAWLIER > CRAWLY
CRAWLIEST > CRAWLY
CRAWLING n defect in freshly applied paint or varnish characterized by bare patches and ridging
CRAWLINGS > CRAWLING
CRAWLS > CRAWL
CRAWLWAY n in a mine, low passageway that can only be negotiated by crawling
CRAWLWAYS > CRAWLWAY
CRAWLY adj feeling or causing a sensation like creatures crawling on one's skin
CRAWS > CRAW
CRAY n crayfish
CRAYER same as > CRARE
CRAYERS > CRAYER
CRAYFISH n edible shellfish like a lobster
CRAYON n a stick or pencil of coloured wax or clay ▷ vb draw or colour with a crayon
CRAYONED > CRAYON
CRAYONER > CRAYON
CRAYONERS > CRAYON
CRAYONING > CRAYON
CRAYONIST > CRAYON
CRAYONS > CRAYON
CRAYS > CRAY
CRAYTHUR variant of > CRATUR
CRAYTHURS > CRAYTHUR
CRAZE n short-lived fashion or enthusiasm ▷ vb make mad
CRAZED adj wild and uncontrolled
CRAZES > CRAZE
CRAZIER > CRAZY
CRAZIES > CRAZY
CRAZIEST > CRAZY
CRAZILY > CRAZY
CRAZINESS > CRAZY
CRAZING > CRAZE
CRAZY adj ridiculous ▷ n crazy person ▷ n crazy person
CRAZYWEED n locoweed
CREACH same as > CREAGH
CREACHS > CREACH
CREAGH n foray
CREAGHS > CREAGH
CREAK n (make) a harsh squeaking sound ▷ vb make or move with a harsh squeaking sound
CREAKED > CREAK
CREAKIER > CREAK
CREAKIEST > CREAK
CREAKILY > CREAK
CREAKING > CREAK
CREAKS > CREAK
CREAKY > CREAK
CREAM n fatty part of milk ▷ adj yellowish-white ▷ vb beat to a creamy consistency
CREAMCUPS n Californian

papaveraceous plant, *Platystemon californicus*, with small cream-coloured or yellow flowers on long flower stalks

CREAMED > CREAM

CREAMER n powdered milk substitute for use in coffee

CREAMERS > CREAMER

CREAMERY n place where dairy products are made or sold

CREAMIER > CREAMY

CREAMIEST > CREAMY

CREAMILY > CREAMY

CREAMING > CREAM

CREAMLAID adj (of laid paper) cream-coloured and of a ribbed appearance

CREAMLIKE > CREAM

CREAMPUFF n puff pastry filled with cream

CREAMS > CREAM

CREAMWARE n type of earthenware with a deep cream body developed about 1720 and widely produced

CREAMWOVE adj (of wove paper) cream-coloured and even-surfaced

CREAMY adj resembling cream in colour, taste, or consistency

CREANCE n long light cord used in falconry

CREANCES > CREANCE

CREANT adj formative

CREASE n line made by folding or pressing ▷vb crush or line

CREASED > CREASE

CREASER > CREASE

CREASERS > CREASE

CREASES > CREASE

CREASIER > CREASE

CREASIEST > CREASE

CREASING > CREASE

CREASOTE same as > CREOSOTE

CREASOTED > CREASOTE

CREASOTES > CREASOTE

CREASY > CREASE

CREATABLE > CREATE

CREATE vb make, cause to exist

CREATED > CREATE

CREATES > CREATE

CREATIC adj relating to flesh or meat

CREATIN same as > CREATINE

CREATINE n important metabolite involved in many biochemical reactions and present in many types of living cells

CREATINES > CREATINE

CREATING > CREATE

CREATINS > CREATINE

CREATION n creating or being created

CREATIONS > CREATION

CREATIVE adj imaginative or inventive ▷n person who is creative professionally

CREATIVES > CREATIVE

CREATOR n person who creates

CREATORS > CREATOR

CREATRESS > CREATOR

CREATRIX > CREATOR

CREATURAL > CREATURE

CREATURE n animal, person, or other being

CREATURES > CREATURE

CRECHE n place where small children are looked after while their parents are working, shopping, etc

CRECHES > CRECHE

CRED n short for credibility

CREDAL > CREED

CREDENCE n belief in the truth or accuracy of a statement

CREDENCES > CREDENCE

CREDENDA > CREDENDUM

CREDENDUM n article of faith

CREDENT adj believing or believable

CREDENZA n type of small sideboard

CREDENZAS > CREDENZA

CREDIBLE adj believable

CREDIBLY > CREDIBLE

CREDIT n system of allowing customers to receive goods and pay later ▷vb enter as a credit in an account

CREDITED > CREDIT

CREDITING > CREDIT

CREDITOR n person to whom money is owed

CREDITORS > CREDITOR

CREDITS pl n list of people responsible for the production of a film, programme, or record

CREDO n creed

CREDOS > CREDO

CREDS > CRED

CREDULITY n willingness to believe something on little evidence

CREDULOUS adj too willing to believe

CREE vb to soften grain by boiling or soaking

CREED n statement or system of (Christian) beliefs or principles

CREEDAL > CREED

CREEDS > CREED

CREEING > CREE

CREEK n narrow inlet or bay

CREEKIER > CREEKY

CREEKIEST > CREEKY

CREEKS > CREEK

CREEKY adj abounding in creeks

CREEL n wicker basket used by anglers ▷vb to fish using creels

CREELED > CREEL

CREELING > CREEL

CREELS > CREEL

CREEP vb move quietly and cautiously ▷n creeping movement

CREEPAGE n imperceptible movement

CREEPAGES > CREEPAGE

CREEPED > CREEP

CREEPER n creeping plant ▷vb train a plant to creep

CREEPERED > CREEPER

CREEPERS > CREEPER

CREEPIE n low stool

CREEPIER > CREEPY

CREEPIES > CREEPIE

CREEPIEST > CREEPY

CREEPILY > CREEPY

CREEPING > CREEP

CREEPS > CREEP

CREEPY adj causing a feeling of fear or disgust

CREES > CREE

CREESE a rare spelling of > KRIS vb to stab with a creese (or kris)

CREESED > CREESE

CREESES > CREESE

CREESH vb to lubricate

CREESHED > CREESH

CREESHES > CREESH

CREESHIER > CREESHY

CREESHING > CREESH

CREESHY adj greasy

CREESING > CREESE

CREM n crematorium

CREMAINS n cremated remains of a body

CREMANT adj (of wine) moderately sparkling

CREMASTER n muscle which raises and lowers the scrotum

CREMATE vb burn (a corpse) to ash

CREMATED > CREMATE

CREMATES > CREMATE

CREMATING > CREMATE

CREMATION > CREMATE

CREMATOR n furnace for cremating corpses

CREMATORS > CREMATOR

CREMATORY adj of or relating to cremation or crematoriums

CREME n cream ▷adj (of a liqueur) rich and sweet

CREMES > CREME

CREMINI n variety of mushroom

CREMINIS > CREMINI

CREMOCARP n any fruit, such as anise or fennel, consisting of two united carpels

CREMONA same as > CROMORNA

CREMONAS > CREMONA

CREMOR n cream

CREMORNE n penis

CREMORNES > CREMORNE

CREMORS > CREMOR

CREMOSIN adj crimson

CREMS > CREM

CREMSIN same as > CREMOSIN

CRENA n cleft or notch

CRENAS > CRENA

CRENATE adj having a scalloped margin, as certain leaves

CRENATED same as > CRENATE

CRENATELY > CRENATE

CRENATION n any of the rounded teeth or the notches between them on a crenate structure

CRENATURE same as > CRENATION

CRENEL n any of a set of openings formed in the top of a wall or parapet and having slanting sides, as in a battlement ▷vb to crenelate

CRENELATE vb supply with battlements

CRENELED > CRENEL

CRENELING > CRENEL

CRENELLE same as > CRENEL

CRENELLED > CRENEL

CRENELLES > CRENELLE

CRENELS > CRENEL

CRENSHAW n variety of melon

CRENSHAWS > CRENSHAW

CRENULATE adj having a margin very finely notched with rounded projections, as certain leaves

CREODONT n any of a group of extinct Tertiary mammals some of which are thought to have been the ancestors of modern carnivores: order *Carnivora*

CREODONTS > CREODONT

CREOLE n language developed from a mixture of languages ▷adj of or relating to a creole

CREOLES > CREOLE

CREOLIAN n Creole

CREOLIANS > CREOLIAN

CREOLISE vb (of a pidgin language) to become the native language of a speech community

CREOLISED same as > CREOLIZED

CREOLISES > CREOLISE

CREOLIST n student of creole languages

CREOLISTS > CREOLIST

CREOLIZE same as > CREOLISE

CREOLIZED adj (of a language) incorporating a considerable range of features from one or more unrelated languages, as the result of contact between language communities

CREOLIZES > CREOLIZE

CREOPHAGY n act of eating meat

CREOSOL n colourless or pale yellow insoluble oily liquid with a smoky odour and a burning taste

CREOSOLS > CREOSOL

CREOSOTE n dark oily liquid made from coal tar and used for preserving wood ▷vb treat with creosote

CREOSOTED > CREOSOTE

CREOSOTES > CREOSOTE

CREOSOTIC > CREOSOTE

CREPANCE n injury to a horse's hind leg caused by

being struck by the shoe of the other hind foot

CREPANCES > CREPANCE

CREPE n fabric or rubber with a crinkled texture ▷ vb cover or drape with crepe ▷ vb to crimp or frizz

CREPED > CREPE

CREPERIE n eating establishment that specializes in pancakes

CREPERIES > CREPERIE

CREPES > CREPE

CREPEY same as > CREPY

CREPIER > CREPY

CREPIEST > CREPY

CREPINESS > CREPY

CREPING > CREPE

CREPITANT > CREPITATE

CREPITATE vb make a rattling or crackling sound

CREPITUS n crackling chest sound heard in pneumonia and other lung diseases

CREPOLINE n light silk material used in dressmaking

CREPON n thin material made of fine wool and/or silk

CREPONS > CREPON

CREPT > CREEP

CREPUSCLE n twilight

CREPY adj (esp of the skin) having a dry wrinkled appearance like crepe

CRESCENDI > CRESCENDO

CRESCENDO n gradual increase in loudness, esp in music ▷ adv gradually getting louder ▷ vb increase in loudness or force

CRESCENT n (curved shape of) the moon as seen in its first or last quarter ▷ adj crescent-shaped

CRESCENTS > CRESCENT

CRESCIVE adj increasing

CRESOL n aromatic compound derived from phenol, existing in three isomeric forms: found in coal tar and creosote and used in making synthetic resins and as an antiseptic and disinfectant

CRESOLS > CRESOL

CRESS n plant with strong-tasting leaves, used in salads

CRESSES > CRESS

CRESSET n metal basket mounted on a pole in which oil or pitch was burned for illumination

CRESSETS > CRESSET

CRESSY > CRESS

CREST n top of a mountain, hill, or wave ▷ vb come to or be at the top of

CRESTA as in *cresta run* high-speed tobogganing down a steep narrow passage of compacted snow and ice

CRESTAL > CREST

CRESTED > CREST

CRESTING same as > CREST

CRESTINGS > CREST

CRESTLESS > CREST

CRESTON n hogback

CRESTONS > CRESTON

CRESTS > CREST

CRESYL n tolyl

CRESYLIC adj of, concerned with, or containing creosote or cresol

CRESYLS > CRESYL

CRETIC n metrical foot consisting of three syllables, the first long, the second short, and the third long

CRETICS > CRETIC

CRETIN n stupid person

CRETINISE vb make (someone) a cretin

CRETINISM n condition arising from a deficiency of thyroid hormone, present from birth, characterized by dwarfism and mental retardation

CRETINIZE same as > CRETINISE

CRETINOID > CRETIN

CRETINOUS > CRETIN

CRETINS > CRETIN

CRETISM n lying

CRETISMS > CRETISM

CRETONNE n heavy printed cotton fabric used in furnishings

CRETONNES > CRETONNE

CREUTZER n former copper and silver coin of Germany or Austria

CREUTZERS > CREUTZER

CREVALLE n any fish of the family Carangidae

CREVALLES > CREVALLE

CREVASSE n deep open crack in a glacier ▷ vb make a break or fissure in (a dyke, wall, etc)

CREVASSED > CREVASSE

CREVASSES > CREVASSE

CREVETTE n shrimp

CREVETTES > CREVETTE

CREVICE n narrow crack or gap in rock

CREVICED > CREVICE

CREVICES > CREVICE

CREW n people who work on a ship or aircraft ▷ vb serve as a crew member (on)

CREWCUT n very short haircut

CREWCUTS > CREWCUT

CREWE n type of pot

CREWED > CREW

CREWEL n fine worsted yarn used in embroidery ▷ vb to embroider in crewel

CREWELIST > CREWEL

CREWELLED > CREWEL

CREWELS > CREWEL

CREWES > CREWE

CREWING > CREW

CREWLESS adj lacking a crew

CREWMAN n member of a ship's crew

CREWMATE n colleague on the crew of a boat or ship

CREWMATES > CREWMATE

CREWMEN > CREWMAN

CREWNECK n plain round neckline in sweaters

CREWNECKS > CREWNECK

CREWS > CREW

CRIANT adj garish

CRIB n piece of writing stolen from elsewhere ▷ vb copy (someone's work) dishonestly

CRIBBAGE n card game for two to four players

CRIBBAGES > CRIBBAGE

CRIBBED > CRIB

CRIBBER > CRIB

CRIBBERS > CRIB

CRIBBING > CRIB

CRIBBINGS > CRIB

CRIBBLE vb to sift

CRIBBLED > CRIBBLE

CRIBBLES > CRIBBLE

CRIBBLING > CRIBBLE

CRIBELLA > CRIBELLUM

CRIBELLAR > CRIBELLUM

CRIBELLUM n sievelike spinning organ in certain spiders that occurs between the spinnerets

CRIBLE adj dotted

CRIBRATE adj sievelike

CRIBROSE adj pierced with holes

CRIBROUS > CRIBROSE

CRIBS > CRIB

CRIBWORK > CRIB

CRIBWORKS > CRIBWORK

CRICETID n any member of the family Cricetidae, such as the hamster and vole

CRICETIDS > CRICETID

CRICK n muscle spasm or cramp in the back or neck ▷ vb cause a crick in

CRICKED > CRICK

CRICKET n outdoor game played with bats, a ball, and wickets by two teams of eleven ▷ vb play cricket

CRICKETED > CRICKET

CRICKETER > CRICKET

CRICKETS > CRICKET

CRICKEY same as > CRIKEY

CRICKING > CRICK

CRICKS > CRICK

CRICKY same as > CRIKEY

CRICOID adj of or relating to the ring-shaped lowermost cartilage of the larynx ▷ n this cartilage

CRICOIDS > CRICOID

CRIED > CRY

CRIER n (formerly) official who made public announcements

CRIERS > CRIER

CRIES > CRY

CRIKEY interj expression of surprise

CRIM short for > CRIMINAL

CRIME n unlawful act ▷ vb charge with a crime

CRIMED > CRIME

CRIMEFUL adj criminal

CRIMELESS adj innocent

CRIMEN n crime

CRIMES > CRIME

CRIMEWAVE n period of increased criminal activity

CRIMINA > CRIMEN

CRIMINAL n person guilty of a crime ▷ adj of crime

CRIMINALS > CRIMINAL

CRIMINATE vb charge with a crime

CRIMINE interj expression of surprise

CRIMING > CRIME

CRIMINI same as > CRIMINE

CRIMINIS n accomplice in crime

CRIMINOUS adj criminal

CRIMINY interj cry of surprise

CRIMMER a variant spelling of > KRIMMER

CRIMMERS > CRIMMER

CRIMP vb fold or press into ridges ▷ n act or result of crimping

CRIMPED > CRIMP

CRIMPER > CRIMP

CRIMPERS > CRIMP

CRIMPIER > CRIMP

CRIMPIEST > CRIMP

CRIMPING > CRIMP

CRIMPLE vb crumple, wrinkle, or curl

CRIMPLED > CRIMPLE

CRIMPLES > CRIMPLE

CRIMPLING > CRIMPLE

CRIMPS > CRIMP

CRIMPY > CRIMP

CRIMS > CRIM

CRIMSON adj deep purplish-red ▷ n deep or vivid red colour ▷ vb make or become crimson

CRIMSONED > CRIMSON

CRIMSONS > CRIMSON

CRINAL adj relating to the hair

CRINATE adj having hair

CRINATED same as > CRINATE

CRINE vb to shrivel

CRINED > CRINE

CRINES > CRINE

CRINGE vb flinch in fear ▷ n act of cringing

CRINGED > CRINGE

CRINGER > CRINGE

CRINGERS > CRINGE

CRINGES > CRINGE

CRINGING > CRINGE

CRINGINGS > CRINGE

CRINGLE n eye at the edge of a sail, usually formed from a thimble or grommet

CRINGLES > CRINGLE

CRINING > CRINE

CRINITE adj covered with soft hairs or tufts ▷ n sedimentary rock

CRINITES > CRINITE

CRINKLE n wrinkle, crease, or fold ▷ vb become slightly creased or folded

CRINKLED > CRINKLE

CRINKLES > CRINKLE

CRINKLIER > CRINKLY

CRINKLIES > CRINKLY

CRINKLING > CRINKLE

CRINKLY adj wrinkled ▷ n old person

CRINOID n any primitive echinoderm of the class *Crinoidea*, having delicate feathery arms radiating from a central disc. The group includes the free-swimming feather stars, the sessile sea lilies, and many stemmed fossil forms ▷ adj of, relating to, or belonging to the *Crinoidea*

CRINOIDAL > CRINOID

CRINOIDS > CRINOID

CRINOLINE n hooped petticoat

CRINOSE adj hairy

CRINUM n any plant of the mostly tropical amaryllidaceous genus *Crinum*, having straplike leaves and clusters of lily-like flowers

CRINUMS > CRINUM

CRIOLLO n native or inhabitant of Latin America of European descent, esp of Spanish descent ▷ adj of, relating to, or characteristic of a criollo or criollos

CRIOLLOS > CRIOLLO

CRIOS n multicoloured woven woollen belt traditionally worn by men in the Aran Islands

CRIOSES > CRIOS

CRIPE variant of > CRIPES

CRIPES interj expression of surprise

CRIPPLE n offensive word for a person who is lame or disabled ▷ vb make lame or disabled

CRIPPLED > CRIPPLE

CRIPPLER > CRIPPLE

CRIPPLERS > CRIPPLE

CRIPPLES > CRIPPLE

CRIPPLING adj damaging or injurious

CRIS variant of > KRIS

CRISE n crisis

CRISES > CRISIS

CRISIC adj relating to a crisis

CRISIS n crucial stage, turning point

CRISP adj fresh and firm ▷ n very thin slice of potato fried till crunchy ▷ vb make or become crisp

CRISPATE adj having a curled or waved appearance

CRISPATED same as > CRISPATE

CRISPED same as > CRISPATE

CRISPEN vb to make crisp

CRISPENED > CRISPEN

CRISPENS > CRISPEN

CRISPER n compartment in a refrigerator for storing salads, vegetables, etc, in order to keep them fresh

CRISPERS > CRISPER

CRISPEST > CRISP

CRISPHEAD n variety of lettuce

CRISPIER > CRISPY

CRISPIEST > CRISPY

CRISPILY > CRISPY

CRISPIN n cobbler

CRISPING > CRISP

CRISPINS > CRISPIN

CRISPLY > CRISP

CRISPNESS > CRISP

CRISPS > CRISP

CRISPY adj hard and crunchy

CRISSA > CRISSUM

CRISSAL > CRISSUM

CRISSUM n area or feathers surrounding the cloaca of a bird

CRISTA n structure resembling a ridge or crest, such as that formed by folding of the inner membrane of a mitochondrion

CRISTAE > CRISTA

CRISTATE > CRISTA

CRISTATE adj having a crest

CRISTATED same as > CRISTATE

CRIT abbreviation of > CRITICISM

CRITERIA > CRITERION

CRITERIAL > CRITERION

CRITERION n standard of judgment

CRITERIUM n type of bicycle race, involving many laps of a short course

CRITH n unit of weight for gases

CRITHS > CRITH

CRITIC n professional judge of any of the arts

CRITICAL adj very important or dangerous

CRITICISE same as > CRITICIZE

CRITICISM n fault-finding

CRITICIZE vb find fault with

CRITICS > CRITIC

CRITIQUE n critical essay ▷ vb to review critically

CRITIQUED > CRITIQUE

CRITIQUES > CRITIQUE

CRITS > CRIT

CRITTER a dialect word for > CREATURE

CRITTERS > CRITTER

CRITTUR same as > CRITTER

CRITTURS > CRITTUR

CRIVENS interj expression of surprise

CRIVVENS same as > CRIVENS

CROAK vb (of a frog or crow) give a low hoarse cry ▷ n low hoarse sound

CROAKED > CROAK

CROAKER n animal, bird, etc, that croaks

CROAKERS > CROAKER

CROAKIER > CROAK

CROAKIEST > CROAK

CROAKILY > CROAK

CROAKING > CROAK

CROAKINGS > CROAK

CROAKS > CROAK

CROAKY > CROAK

CROC short for > CROCODILE

CROCEATE adj saffron-coloured

CROCEIN n any one of a group of red or orange acid azo dyes

CROCEINE same as > CROCEIN

CROCEINES > CROCEIN

CROCEINS > CROCEIN

CROCEOUS adj saffron-coloured

CROCHE n knob at the top of a deer's horn

CROCHES > CROCHE

CROCHET vb make by looping and intertwining yarn with a hooked needle ▷ n work made in this way

CROCHETED > CROCHET

CROCHETER > CROCHET

CROCHETS > CROCHET

CROCI > CROCUS

CROCINE adj relating to the crocus

CROCK n earthenware pot or jar ▷ vb become or cause to become weak or disabled

CROCKED adj injured

CROCKERY n dishes

CROCKET n carved ornament in the form of a curled leaf or cusp, used in Gothic architecture

CROCKETED > CROCKET

CROCKETS > CROCKET

CROCKING > CROCK

CROCKPOT n tradename for a brand of slow cooker

CROCKPOTS > CROCKPOT

CROCKS > CROCK

CROCODILE n large amphibious tropical reptile

CROCOITE n rare orange secondary mineral

CROCOITES > CROCOITE

CROCOSMIA n any plant of the cormous S. African genus *Crocosmia*, including the plant known to gardeners as montbretia: family *Iridaceae*

CROCS > CROC

CROCUS n flowering plant

CROCUSES > CROCUS

CROFT n small farm worked by one family in Scotland

CROFTER n owner or tenant of a small farm, esp in Scotland or northern England

CROFTERS > CROFTER

CROFTING n system or occupation of working land in crofts

CROFTINGS > CROFTING

CROFTS > CROFT

CROG vb ride on a bicycle as a passenger

CROGGED > CROG

CROGGIES > CROGGY

CROGGING > CROG

CROGGY n ride on a bicycle as a passenger

CROGS > CROG

CROISSANT n rich flaky crescent-shaped roll

CROJIK n triangular sail

CROJIKS > CROJIK

CROKINOLE n board game popular in Canada in which players flick wooden discs

CROMACK same as > CRUMMOCK

CROMACKS > CROMACK

CROMB same as > CROME

CROMBEC n any African Old World warbler of the genus *Sylvietta*, having colourful plumage

CROMBECS > CROMBEC

CROMBED > CROMB

CROMBING > CROMB

CROMBS > CROMB

CROME n hook ▷ vb use a crome

CROMED > CROME

CROMES > CROME

CROMING > CROME

CROMLECH n circle of prehistoric standing stones

CROMLECHS > CROMLECH

CROMORNA n one of the reed stops in an organ

CROMORNAS > CROMORNA

CROMORNE variant of > CROMORNA

CROMORNES > CROMORNE

CRONE n witchlike old woman

CRONES > CRONE

CRONET n hair which grows over the top of a horse's hoof

CRONETS > CRONET

CRONIES > CRONY

CRONISH > CRONE

CRONK adj unfit

CRONKER > CRONK

CRONKEST > CRONK

CRONY n close friend

CRONYISM n practice of appointing friends to high-level, esp political, posts regardless of their suitability

CRONYISMS > CRONYISM

CROODLE vb to nestle close

CROODLED > CROODLE

CROODLES > CROODLE

CROODLING > CROODLE

CROOK n dishonest person ▷ vb bend or curve

CROOKBACK a rare word for > HUNCHBACK

CROOKED adj bent or twisted

CROOKEDER > CROOKED

CROOKEDLY > CROOKED

CROOKER > CROOK

CROOKERY n illegal or dishonest activity

CROOKEST > CROOK

CROOKING > CROOK

CROOKNECK n any type of summer squash

CROOKS > CROOK

CROOL vb spoil

CROOLED > CROOL

CROOLING > CROOL

CROOLS > CROOL

CROON vb sing, hum, or speak in a soft low tone ▷ n soft low singing or humming
CROONED > CROON
CROONER > CROON
CROONERS > CROON
CROONING > CROON
CROONINGS > CROON
CROONS > CROON
CROOVE n animal enclosure
CROOVES > CROOVE
CROP n cultivated plant ▷ vb cut very short
CROPBOUND n poultry disease causing a pendulous crop
CROPFUL n quantity that can be held in the craw
CROPFULL adj satiated
CROPFULS > CROPFUL
CROPLAND n land on which crops are grown
CROPLANDS > CROPLAND
CROPLESS adj without crops
CROPPED > CROP
CROPPER n person who cultivates or harvests a crop
CROPPERS > CROPPER
CROPPIE same as > CROPPY
CROPPIES > CROPPY
CROPPING > CROP
CROPPINGS > CROP
CROPPY n rebel in the Irish rising of 1798
CROPS > CROP
CROPSICK adj sick from excessive food or drink
CROQUANTE n crisp nut-filled chocolate or cake
CROQUET n game played on a lawn in which balls are hit through hoops ▷ vb drive away (another player's ball) by hitting one's own ball when the two are in contact
CROQUETED > CROQUET
CROQUETS > CROQUET
CROQUETTE n fried cake of potato, meat, or fish
CROQUIS n rough sketch
CRORE n (in Indian English) ten million
CRORES > CRORE
CROSIER n staff surmounted by a crook or cross, carried by bishops as a symbol of pastoral office ▷ vb bear or carry such a cross
CROSIERED > CROSIER
CROSIERS > CROSIER
CROSS vb move or go across (something) ▷ n structure, symbol, or mark of two intersecting lines ▷ adj angry, annoyed
CROSSABLE adj capable of being crossed
CROSSARM n in mining, horizontal bar on which a drill is mounted
CROSSARMS > CROSSARM
CROSSBAND vb to set the

grain of layers of wood at right angles to one another
CROSSBAR n horizontal bar across goalposts or on a bicycle ▷ vb provide with crossbars
CROSSBARS > CROSSBAR
CROSSBEAM n beam that spans from one support to another
CROSSBILL n finch that has a bill with crossed tips
CROSSBIT > CROSSBITE
CROSSBITE vb to trick
CROSSBOW n weapon consisting of a bow fixed across a wooden stock
CROSSBOWS > CROSSBOW
CROSSBRED adj bred from two different types of animal or plant ▷ n crossbred plant or animal, esp an animal resulting from a cross between two pure breeds
CROSSBUCK n US roadsign used at railroad crossings
CROSSCUT vb cut across ▷ adj cut across ▷ n transverse cut or course
CROSSCUTS > CROSSCUT
CROSSE n light staff with a triangular frame to which a network is attached, used in playing lacrosse
CROSSED > CROSS
CROSSER > CROSS
CROSSERS > CROSS
CROSSES > CROSS
CROSSEST > CROSS
CROSSETTE n in architecture, return in a corner of the architrave of a window or door
CROSSFALL n camber of a road
CROSSFIRE n gunfire crossing another line of fire
CROSSFISH n starfish
CROSSHAIR n one of two fine wires that cross in the focal plane of a gunsight or other optical instrument, used to define the line of sight
CROSSHEAD n subsection or paragraph heading printed within the body of the text
CROSSING n place where a street may be crossed safely
CROSSINGS > CROSSING
CROSSISH > CROSS
CROSSJACK n square sail on a ship's mizzenmast
CROSSLET n cross having a smaller cross near the end of each arm
CROSSLETS > CROSSLET
CROSSLY > CROSS
CROSSNESS > CROSS
CROSSOVER n place at which a crossing is made ▷ adj (of music, fashion, art, etc) combining two distinct styles
CROSSROAD n road that

crosses another road
CROSSRUFF n alternate trumping of each other's leads by two partners, or by declarer and dummy ▷ vb trump alternately in two hands of a partnership
CROSSTALK n rapid or witty talk
CROSSTIE n railway sleeper
CROSSTIED adj tied with ropes going across
CROSSTIES > CROSSTIE
CROSSTOWN adj going across town
CROSSTREE n either of a pair of wooden or metal braces on the head of a mast to support the topmast, etc
CROSSWALK n place marked where pedestrians may cross a road
CROSSWAY same as > CROSSROAD
CROSSWAYS same as > CROSSWISE
CROSSWIND n wind that blows at right angles to the direction of travel
CROSSWISE adv across ▷ adj across
CROSSWORD n puzzle in which the solver deduces words suggested by clues and writes them into a grid
CROSSWORT n herbaceous perennial Eurasian rubiaceous plant, Galium cruciata, with pale yellow flowers and whorls of hairy leaves
CROST > CROSS
CROSTINI > CROSTINO
CROSTINIS > CROSTINO
CROSTINO n piece of toasted bread served with a savoury topping
CROTAL n any of various lichens used in dyeing wool, esp for the manufacture of tweeds
CROTALA > CROTALUM
CROTALINE adj relating to rattlesnakes
CROTALISM n posoining due to ingestion of plants of the genus Crotalaria
CROTALS > CROTAL
CROTALUM n ancient castanet-like percussion instrument
CROTCH n part of the body between the tops of the legs ▷ vb have crotch (usu of a piece of clothing) removed
CROTCHED > CROTCH
CROTCHES > CROTCH
CROTCHET n musical note half the length of a minim
CROTCHETS > CROTCHET
CROTCHETY adj bad-tempered
CROTON n any shrub or tree of the chiefly tropical euphorbiaceous genus Croton, esp C. tiglium, the

seeds of which yield croton oil
CROTONBUG n species of cockroach
CROTONIC as in crotonic acid type of colourless acid
CROTONS > CROTON
CROTTLE same as > CROTAL
CROTTLES > CROTTLE
CROUCH vb bend low with the legs and body close ▷ n this position
CROUCHED > CROUCH
CROUCHES > CROUCH
CROUCHING > CROUCH
CROUP n throat disease of children, with a cough ▷ vb have croup
CROUPADE n leap by a horse, pulling the hind legs towards the belly
CROUPADES > CROUPADE
CROUPE same as > CROUP
CROUPED > CROUP
CROUPER obsolete variant of > CRUPPER
CROUPERS > CROUPER
CROUPES > CROUPE
CROUPIER n person who collects bets and pays out winnings at a gambling table in a casino
CROUPIERS > CROUPIER
CROUPIEST > CROUP
CROUPILY > CROUP
CROUPING > CROUP
CROUPON n type of highly-polished flexible leather
CROUPONS > CROUPON
CROUPOUS > CROUP
CROUPS > CROUP
CROUPY > CROUP
CROUSE adj lively, confident, or saucy
CROUSELY > CROUSE
CROUSTADE n pastry case in which food is served
CROUT n sauerkraut
CROUTE n small round of toasted bread on which a savoury mixture is served
CROUTES > CROUTE
CROUTON n small piece of fried or toasted bread served in soup
CROUTONS > CROUTON
CROUTS > CROUT
CROW n large black bird with a harsh call ▷ vb (of a cock) make a shrill squawking sound
CROWBAR n iron bar used as a lever ▷ vb use a crowbar to lever (something)
CROWBARS > CROWBAR
CROWBERRY n low-growing N temperate evergreen shrub, Empetrum nigrum, with small purplish flowers and black berry-like fruit: family Empetraceae
CROWBOOT n type of Inuit boot made of fur and leather
CROWBOOTS > CROWBOOT
CROWD n large group of people or things ▷ vb

gather together in large numbers

CROWDED > CROWD

CROWDEDLY > CROWD

CROWDER > CROWD

CROWDERS > CROWD

CROWDIE n porridge of meal and water

CROWDIES > CROWDIE

CROWDING > CROWD

CROWDS > CROWD

CROWDY same as > CROWDIE

CROWEA n Australian shrub of the genus *Crowea*, having pink flowers

CROWEAS > CROWEA

CROWED > CROW

CROWER > CROW

CROWERS > CROW

CROWFEET > CROWFOOT

CROWFOOT n type of plant

CROWFOOTS > CROWFOOT

CROWING > CROW

CROWINGLY > CROW

CROWN n monarch's headdress of gold and jewels ▷ vb put a crown on the head of (someone) to proclaim him or her monarch

CROWNED > CROWN

CROWNER n promotional label consisting of a shaped printed piece of card or paper attached to a product on display

CROWNERS > CROWNER

CROWNET n coronet

CROWNETS > CROWNET

CROWNING n stage of labour when the infant's head is passing through the vaginal opening

CROWNINGS > CROWNING

CROWNLAND n large administrative division of the former empire of Austria-Hungary

CROWNLESS > CROWN

CROWNLET n small crown

CROWNLETS > CROWNLET

CROWNS > CROWN

CROWNWORK n manufacture of artificial crowns for teeth

CROWS > CROW

CROWSFEET > CROWSFOOT

CROWSFOOT n wrinkle at side of eye

CROWSTEP n set of steps to the top of a gable on a building

CROWSTEPS > CROWSTEP

CROZE n recess cut at the end of a barrel or cask to receive the head

CROZER n machine which cuts grooves in cask staves

CROZERS > CROZER

CROZES > CROZE

CROZIER same as > CROSIER

CROZIERS > CROZIER

CROZZLED adj blackened or burnt at the edges

CRU n (in France) a vineyard, group of vineyards, or wine-producing region

CRUBEEN n pig's trotter

CRUBEENS > CRUBEEN

CRUCES > CRUX

CRUCIAL adj very important

CRUCIALLY > CRUCIAL

CRUCIAN n European cyprinid fish, *Carassius carassius*, with a dark-green back, a golden-yellow undersurface, and reddish dorsal and tail fins: an aquarium fish

CRUCIANS > CRUCIAN

CRUCIATE adj shaped or arranged like a cross

CRUCIBLE n pot in which metals are melted

CRUCIBLES > CRUCIBLE

CRUCIFER n any plant of the family Brassicaceae (formerly *Cruciferae*), having a corolla of four petals arranged like a cross and a fruit called a siliqua. The family includes the brassicas, mustard, cress, and wallflower

CRUCIFERS > CRUCIFER

CRUCIFIED > CRUCIFY

CRUCIFIER > CRUCIFY

CRUCIFIES > CRUCIFY

CRUCIFIX n model of Christ on the Cross

CRUCIFORM adj cross-shaped ▷ n geometric curve, shaped like a cross, that has four similar branches asymptotic to two mutually perpendicular pairs of lines. Equation: $x^2y^{2-}a^2x^{2-}a^2y^2 = 0$, where $x = y = \pm a$ are the four lines.

CRUCIFY vb put to death by fastening to a cross

CRUCK n one of a pair of curved wooden timbers supporting the end of the roof in certain types of building

CRUCKS > CRUCK

CRUD n sticky or encrusted substance ▷ interj expression of disgust, disappointment, etc ▷ vb cover with a sticky or encrusted substance

CRUDDED > CRUD

CRUDDIER > CRUDDY

CRUDDIEST > CRUDDY

CRUDDING > CRUD

CRUDDLE vb to curdle

CRUDDLED > CRUDDLE

CRUDDLES > CRUDDLE

CRUDDLING > CRUDDLE

CRUDDY adj dirty or unpleasant

CRUDE adj rough and simple ▷ n crude oil

CRUDELY > CRUDE

CRUDENESS > CRUDE

CRUDER > CRUDE

CRUDES > CRUDE

CRUDEST > CRUDE

CRUDITES pl n selection of raw vegetables often served with a variety of dips before a meal

CRUDITIES > CRUDE

CRUDITY > CRUDE

CRUDS > CRUD

CRUDY adj raw

CRUE obsolete variant of > CREW

CRUEL adj delighting in others' pain

CRUELER > CRUEL

CRUELEST > CRUEL

CRUELLER > CRUEL

CRUELLEST > CRUEL

CRUELLS same as > CRUELS

CRUELLY > CRUEL

CRUELNESS > CRUEL

CRUELS n disease of cattle and sheep, caused by infection with an *Actinobacillus lignieresii* and characterized by soft tissue lesions, esp of the tongue

CRUELTIES > CRUELTY

CRUELTY n deliberate infliction of pain or suffering

CRUES > CREW

CRUET n small container for salt, pepper, etc, at table

CRUETS > CRUET

CRUISE n sail for pleasure ▷ vb sail from place to place for pleasure

CRUISED > CRUISE

CRUISER n fast warship

CRUISERS > CRUISER

CRUISES > CRUISE

CRUISEWAY n canal used for recreational purposes

CRUISIE same as > CRUIZIE

CRUISIES > CRUISIE

CRUISING > CRUISE

CRUISINGS > CRUISE

CRUIVE n animal enclosure

CRUIVES > CRUIVE

CRUIZIE n oil lamp

CRUIZIES > CRUIZIE

CRULLER n light sweet ring-shaped cake, fried in deep fat

CRULLERS > CRULLER

CRUMB n small fragment of bread or other dry food ▷ vb prepare or cover (food) with breadcrumbs ▷ adj (esp of pie crusts) made with a mixture of biscuit crumbs, sugar, etc

CRUMBED > CRUMB

CRUMBER > CRUMB

CRUMBERS > CRUMB

CRUMBIER > CRUMBY

CRUMBIEST > CRUMBY

CRUMBING > CRUMB

CRUMBLE vb break into fragments ▷ n pudding of stewed fruit with a crumbly topping

CRUMBLED > CRUMBLE

CRUMBLES > CRUMBLE

CRUMBLIER > CRUMBLY

CRUMBLIES n elderly people

CRUMBLING > CRUMBLE

CRUMBLY adj easily crumbled or crumbling

CRUMBS interj expression of dismay or surprise

CRUMBUM n rogue

CRUMBUMS > CRUMBUM

CRUMBY adj full of crumbs

CRUMEN n deer's larmier or tear-pit

CRUMENAL n purse

CRUMENALS > CRUMENAL

CRUMENS > CRUMEN

CRUMHORN n medieval woodwind instrument of bass pitch, consisting of an almost cylindrical tube curving upwards and blown through a double reed covered by a pierced cap

CRUMHORNS > CRUMHORN

CRUMMACK same as > CRUMMOCK

CRUMMACKS > CRUMMACK

CRUMMIE n cow with a crumpled horn

CRUMMIER > CRUMMY

CRUMMIES > CRUMMY

CRUMMIEST > CRUMMY

CRUMMOCK n stick with a crooked head

CRUMMOCKS > CRUMMOCK

CRUMMY adj of poor quality ▷ n lorry that carries loggers to work from their camp

CRUMP vb thud or explode with a loud dull sound ▷ n crunching, thudding, or exploding noise ▷ adj crooked

CRUMPED > CRUMP

CRUMPER > CRUMP

CRUMPEST > CRUMP

CRUMPET n round soft yeast cake, eaten buttered

CRUMPETS > CRUMPET

CRUMPIER > CRUMPY

CRUMPIEST > CRUMPY

CRUMPING > CRUMP

CRUMPLE vb crush, crease ▷ n untidy crease or wrinkle

CRUMPLED > CRUMPLE

CRUMPLES > CRUMPLE

CRUMPLIER > CRUMPLE

CRUMPLING > CRUMPLE

CRUMPLY > CRUMPLE

CRUMPS > CRUMP

CRUMPY adj crisp

CRUNCH vb bite or chew with a noisy crushing sound ▷ n crunching sound

CRUNCHED > CRUNCH

CRUNCHER > CRUNCH

CRUNCHERS > CRUNCH

CRUNCHES > CRUNCH

CRUNCHIE n derogatory word for an Afrikaner

CRUNCHIER > CRUNCH

CRUNCHIES > CRUNCHIE

CRUNCHILY > CRUNCH

CRUNCHING > CRUNCH

CRUNCHY > CRUNCH

CRUNKLE Scots variant of > CRINKLE

CRUNKLED > CRUNKLE

CRUNKLES > CRUNKLE

CRUNKLING > CRUNKLE

CRUNODAL > CRUNODE

CRUNODE n point at which

two branches of a curve intersect, each branch having a distinct tangent

CRUNODES > CRUNODE

CRUOR *n* blood clot

CRUORES > CRUOR

CRUORS > CRUOR

CRUPPER *n* strap that passes from the back of a saddle under a horse's tail

CRUPPERS > CRUPPER

CRURA > CRUS

CRURAL *adj* of or relating to the leg or thigh

CRUS *n* leg, esp from the knee to the foot

CRUSADE *n* medieval Christian war to recover the Holy Land from the Muslims ▷ *vb* take part in a crusade

CRUSADED > CRUSADE

CRUSADER > CRUSADE

CRUSADERS > CRUSADE

CRUSADES > CRUSADE

CRUSADING > CRUSADE

CRUSADO *n* former gold or silver coin of Portugal bearing on its reverse the figure of a cross

CRUSADOES > CRUSADO

CRUSADOS > CRUSADO

CRUSE *n* small earthenware jug or pot

CRUSES > CRUSE

CRUSET *n* goldsmith's crucible

CRUSETS > CRUSET

CRUSH *vb* compress so as to injure, break, or crumple ▷ *n* dense crowd

CRUSHABLE > CRUSH

CRUSHED > CRUSH

CRUSHER > CRUSH

CRUSHERS > CRUSH

CRUSHES > CRUSH

CRUSHING > CRUSH

CRUSIAN *variant of* > CRUCIAN

CRUSIANS > CRUSIAN

CRUSIE *same as* > CRUIZIE

CRUSIES > CRUSIE

CRUSILY *adj* (in heraldry) strewn with crosses

CRUST *n* hard outer part of something, esp bread ▷ *vb* cover with or form a crust

CRUSTA *n* hard outer layer

CRUSTACEA *n* members of the Crustacea class of arthropods including the lobster

CRUSTAE > CRUSTA

CRUSTAL *adj* of or relating to the earth's crust

CRUSTATE *adj* covered with a crust

CRUSTATED *same as* > CRUSTATE

CRUSTED > CRUST

CRUSTIER > CRUSTY

CRUSTIES > CRUSTY

CRUSTIEST > CRUSTY

CRUSTILY > CRUSTY

CRUSTING > CRUST

CRUSTLESS *adj* lacking a crust

CRUSTOSE *adj* having a crustlike appearance

CRUSTS > CRUST

CRUSTY *adj* having a crust ▷ *n* dirty type of punk or hippy whose lifestyle involves travelling and squatting

CRUSY *same as* > CRUIZIE

CRUTCH *n* long sticklike support with a rest for the armpit, used by a lame person ▷ *vb* support or sustain (a person or thing) as with a crutch

CRUTCHED > CRUTCH

CRUTCHES > CRUTCH

CRUTCHING > CRUTCH

CRUVE *same as* > CRUIVE

CRUVES > CRUVE

CRUX *n* crucial or decisive point

CRUXES > CRUX

CRUZADO *same as* > CRUSADO

CRUZADOES > CRUZADO

CRUZADOS > CRUZADO

CRUZEIRO *n* former monetary unit of Brazil, replaced by the cruzeiro real

CRUZEIROS > CRUZEIRO

CRUZIE *same as* > CRUIZIE

CRUZIES > CRUZIE

CRWTH *n* ancient stringed instrument of Celtic origin similar to the cithara but bowed in later types

CRWTHS > CRWTH

CRY *vb* shed tears ▷ *n* fit of weeping

CRYBABIES > CRYBABY

CRYBABY *n* person, esp a child, who cries too readily

CRYING > CRY

CRYINGLY > CRY

CRYINGS > CRY

CRYOBANK *n* place for storing genetic material at low temperature

CRYOBANKS > CRYOBANK

CRYOCABLE *n* highly conducting electrical cable cooled with a refrigerant such as liquid nitrogen

CRYOGEN *n* substance used to produce low temperatures

CRYOGENIC *adj* of the branch of physics concerned with the production of very low temperatures

CRYOGENS > CRYOGEN

CRYOGENY *n* cryogenic science

CRYOLITE *n* white or colourless mineral

CRYOLITES > CRYOLITE

CRYOMETER *n* thermometer for measuring low temperatures

CRYOMETRY > CRYOMETER

CRYONIC > CRYONICS

CRYONICS *n* practice of freezing a human corpse in the hope of restoring it to life in the future

CRYOPHYTE *n* organism, esp an alga or moss, that grows on snow or ice

CRYOPROBE *n* supercooled instrument used in surgery

CRYOSCOPE *n* any instrument used to determine the freezing point of a substance

CRYOSCOPY *n* determination of freezing points, esp for the determination of molecular weights by measuring the lowering of the freezing point of a solvent when a known quantity of solute is added

CRYOSTAT *n* apparatus for maintaining a constant low temperature or a vessel in which a substance is stored at a low temperature

CRYOSTATS > CRYOSTAT

CRYOTRON *n* miniature switch working at the temperature of liquid helium and depending for its action on the production and destruction of superconducting properties in the conductor

CRYOTRONS > CRYOTRON

CRYPT *n* vault under a church, esp one used as a burial place

CRYPTADIA *n* things to be kept hidden

CRYPTAL > CRYPT

CRYPTIC *adj* obscure in meaning, secret

CRYPTICAL *same as* > CRYPTIC

CRYPTO *n* person who is a secret member of an organization or sect

CRYPTOGAM *n* plant that reproduces by spores not seeds

CRYPTON *n* krypton

CRYPTONS > CRYPTON

CRYPTONYM *n* code name

CRYPTOS > CRYPTO

CRYPTS > CRYPT

CRYSTAL *n* (single grain of) a symmetrically shaped solid formed naturally by some substances ▷ *adj* bright and clear

CRYSTALS > CRYSTAL

CSARDAS *n* type of Hungarian folk dance

CSARDASES > CSARDAS

CTENE *n* locomotor organ found in ctenophores (or comb jellies)

CTENES > CTENE

CTENIDIA > CTENIDIUM

CTENIDIUM *n* one of the comblike respiratory gills of molluscs

CTENIFORM *adj* comblike

CTENOID *adj* toothed like a comb, as the scales of perches

CUADRILLA *n* matador's

assistants in a bullfight

CUATRO *n* four-stringed guitar

CUATROS > CUATRO

CUB *n* young wild animal such as a bear or fox ▷ *adj* young or inexperienced ▷ *vb* give birth to cubs

CUBAGE *same as* > CUBATURE

CUBAGES > CUBATURE

CUBANE *n* rare octahedral hydrocarbon

CUBANELLE *n* variety of pepper

CUBANES > CUBANE

CUBATURE *n* determination of the cubic contents of something

CUBATURES > CUBATURE

CUBBED > CUB

CUBBIES > CUBBY

CUBBING > CUB

CUBBINGS > CUB

CUBBISH > CUB

CUBBISHLY > CUB

CUBBY *same as* > CUBBYHOLE

CUBBYHOLE *n* small enclosed space or room

CUBE *n* object with six equal square sides ▷ *vb* cut into cubes

CUBEB *n* SE Asian treelike piperaceous woody climbing plant, *Piper cubeba*, with brownish berries

CUBEBS > CUBEB

CUBED > CUBE

CUBER > CUBE

CUBERS > CUBE

CUBES > CUBE

CUBHOOD *n* state of being a cub

CUBHOODS > CUBHOOD

CUBIC *adj* having three dimensions ▷ *n* cubic equation, such as $x^3 + x + 2 = 0$

CUBICA *n* fine shalloon-like fabric

CUBICAL *adj* of or related to volume

CUBICALLY > CUBICAL

CUBICAS > CUBICA

CUBICITY *n* property of being cubelike

CUBICLE *n* enclosed part of a large room, screened for privacy

CUBICLES > CUBICLE

CUBICLY > CUBIC

CUBICS > CUBIC

CUBICULA > CUBICULUM

CUBICULUM *n* underground burial chamber in Imperial Rome, such as those found in the catacombs

CUBIFORM *adj* having the shape of a cube

CUBING > CUBE

CUBISM *n* style of art in which objects are represented by geometrical shapes

CUBISMS > CUBISM

CUBIST > CUBISM

CUBISTIC > CUBISM

CUBISTS > CUBISM

CUBIT n old measure of length based on the length of the forearm

CUBITAL adj of or relating to the forearm

CUBITI adj of elbow

CUBITS > CUBIT

CUBITUS n elbow

CUBITUSES > CUBITUS

CUBLESS adj having no cubs

CUBOID adj shaped like a cube ▷n geometric solid whose six faces are rectangles

CUBOIDAL same as > CUBOID

CUBOIDS > CUBOID

CUBS > CUB

CUCKING as in cucking stool stool to which suspected witches, etc, were tied and pelted or ducked into water as punishment

CUCKOLD n man whose wife has been unfaithful ▷vb be unfaithful to (one's husband)

CUCKOLDED > CUCKOLD

CUCKOLDLY adj possessing the qualities of a cuckold

CUCKOLDOM n state of being a cuckold

CUCKOLDRY > CUCKOLD

CUCKOLDS > CUCKOLD

CUCKOO n migratory bird with a characteristic two-note call, which lays its eggs in the nests of other birds ▷adj insane or foolish ▷interj imitation or representation of the call of a cuckoo ▷vb repeat over and over

CUCKOOED > CUCKOO

CUCKOOING > CUCKOO

CUCKOOS > CUCKOO

CUCULLATE adj shaped like a hood or having a hoodlike part

CUCUMBER n long green-skinned fleshy fruit used in salads

CUCUMBERS > CUCUMBER

CUCURBIT n any creeping flowering plant of the mainly tropical and subtropical family Cucurbitaceae, which includes the pumpkin, cucumber, squashes, and gourds

CUCURBITS > CUCURBIT

CUD n partially digested food which a ruminant brings back into its mouth to chew again

CUDBEAR another name for > ORCHIL

CUDBEARS > CUDBEAR

CUDDEN n young coalfish

CUDDENS > CUDDEN

CUDDIE same as > CUDDY

CUDDIES > CUDDY

CUDDIN same as > CUDDEN

CUDDINS > CUDDIN

CUDDLE n hug ▷vb hold (another person or thing) close or (of two people, etc) to hold each other close, as for affection, comfort, or warmth

CUDDLED > CUDDLE

CUDDLER > CUDDLE

CUDDLERS > CUDDLE

CUDDLES > CUDDLE

CUDDLIER > CUDDLE

CUDDLIEST > CUDDLE

CUDDLING > CUDDLE

CUDDLY > CUDDLE

CUDDY n small cabin in a boat

CUDGEL n short thick stick used as a weapon ▷vb use a cudgel

CUDGELED > CUDGEL

CUDGELER > CUDGEL

CUDGELERS > CUDGEL

CUDGELING > CUDGEL

CUDGELLED > CUDGEL

CUDGELLER > CUDGEL

CUDGELS > CUDGEL

CUDGERIE n large tropical rutaceous tree, Flindersia schottina, having light-coloured wood

CUDGERIES > CUDGERIE

CUDS > CUD

CUDWEED n any of various temperate woolly plants of the genus Gnaphalium, having clusters of whitish or yellow button-like flowers: family Asteraceae (composites)

CUDWEEDS > CUDWEED

CUE n signal to an actor or musician to begin speaking or playing ▷vb give a cue to

CUED > CUE

CUEING > CUE

CUEIST n snooker or billiards player

CUEISTS > CUEIST

CUES > CUE

CUESTA n long low ridge with a steep scarp slope and a gentle back slope, formed by the differential erosion of strata of differing hardness

CUESTAS > CUESTA

CUFF n end of a sleeve ▷vb hit with an open hand

CUFFED > CUFF

CUFFIN n man

CUFFING > CUFF

CUFFINS > CUFFIN

CUFFLE vb scuffle

CUFFLED > CUFFLE

CUFFLES > CUFFLE

CUFFLESS adj having no cuff(s)

CUFFLING > CUFFLE

CUFFLINK n detachable fastener for shirt cuff

CUFFLINKS > CUFFLINK

CUFFO adv free of charge

CUFFS > CUFF

CUFFUFFLE same as > KERFUFFLE

CUIF same as > COOF

CUIFS > CUIF

CUING > CUE

CUIRASS n piece of armour, of leather or metal covering the chest and back ▷vb equip with a cuirass

CUIRASSED > CUIRASS

CUIRASSES > CUIRASS

CUISH same as > CUISSE

CUISHES > CUISH

CUISINART n tradename for a type of food processor

CUISINE n style of cooking

CUISINES > CUISINE

CUISINIER n cook

CUISSE n piece of armour for the thigh

CUISSER same as > COOSER

CUISSERS > CUISSER

CUISSES > CUISSE

CUIT n ankle

CUITER vb to pamper

CUITERED > CUITER

CUITERING > CUITER

CUITERS > CUITER

CUITIKIN n gaiter

CUITIKINS > CUITIKIN

CUITS > CUIT

CUITTLE vb to wheedle

CUITTLED > CUITTLE

CUITTLES > CUITTLE

CUITTLING > CUITTLE

CUKE n cucumber

CUKES > CUKE

CULCH n mass of broken stones, shells, and gravel that forms the basis of an oyster bed

CULCHES > CULCH

CULCHIE n rough or unsophisticated country-dweller from outside Dublin

CULCHIES > CULCHIE

CULET n flat face at the bottom of a gem

CULETS > CULET

CULEX n any mosquito of the genus Culex, such as C. pipiens, the common mosquito

CULEXES > CULEX

CULICES > CULEX

CULICID n any dipterous insect of the family Culicidae, which comprises the mosquitoes ▷adj of, relating to, or belonging to the Culicidae

CULICIDS > CULICID

CULICINE n any member of the genus Culex containing mosquitoes

CULICINES > CULICINE

CULINARY adj of kitchens or cookery

CULL vb choose, gather ▷n culling

CULLAY n soapbark tree

CULLAYS > CULLAY

CULLED > CULL

CULLENDER same as > COLANDER

CULLER n person employed to cull animals

CULLERS > CULLER

CULLET n waste glass for melting down to be reused

CULLETS > CULLET

CULLIED > CULLY

CULLIES > CULLY

CULLING > CULL

CULLINGS > CULL

CULLION n rascal

CULLIONLY > CULLION

CULLIONS > CULLION

CULLIS same as > COULISSE

CULLISES > CULLIS

CULLS > CULL

CULLY n pal ▷vb to trick

CULLYING > CULLY

CULLYISM n state of being a dupe

CULLYISMS > CULLYISM

CULM n coal-mine waste ▷vb to form a culm or grass stem

CULMED > CULM

CULMEN n summit

CULMENS > CULMEN

CULMINANT adj highest or culminating

CULMINATE vb reach the highest point or climax

CULMING > CULM

CULMS > CULM

CULOTTE > CULOTTES

CULOTTES pl n women's knee-length trousers cut to look like a skirt

CULPA n act of neglect

CULPABLE adj deserving blame

CULPABLY > CULPABLE

CULPAE > CULPA

CULPATORY adj expressing blame

CULPRIT n person guilty of an offence or misdeed

CULPRITS > CULPRIT

CULT n specific system of worship ▷adj very popular among a limited group of people

CULTCH same as > CULTCH

CULTCHES > CULTCH

CULTER same as > COULTER

CULTERS > CULTER

CULTI > CULTUS

CULTIC adj of or relating to a religious cult

CULTIER > CULTY

CULTIEST > CULTY

CULTIGEN n species of plant that is known only as a cultivated form and did not originate from a wild type

CULTIGENS > CULTIGEN

CULTISH adj intended to appeal to a small group of fashionable people

CULTISHLY > CULTISH

CULTISM > CULT

CULTISMS > CULT

CULTIST > CULT

CULTISTS > CULT

CULTIVAR n variety of a plant that was produced from a natural species and is maintained by cultivation

CULTIVARS > CULTIVAR

CULTIVATE vb prepare (land) to grow crops

CULTLIKE adj resembling a cult

C

CULTRATE *adj* shaped like a knife blade

CULTRATED *same as* > CULTRATE

CULTS > CULT

CULTURAL *adj* of or relating to artistic or social pursuits or events considered to be valuable or enlightened

CULTURATI *n* people interested in cultural activities

CULTURE *n* ideas, customs, and art of a particular society ▷ *vb* grow (bacteria) for study

CULTURED *adj* showing good taste or manners

CULTURES > CULTURE

CULTURING > CULTURE

CULTURIST > CULTURE

CULTUS *another word for* > CULT

CULTUSES > CULTUS

CULTY *same as* > CULTISH

CULVER *an archaic or poetic name for* > PIGEON

CULVERIN *n* long-range medium to heavy cannon used during the 15th, 16th, and 17th centuries

CULVERINS > CULVERIN

CULVERS > CULVER

CULVERT *n* drain under a road or railway

CULVERTS > CULVERT

CUM *prep* with

CUMACEAN *n* any small malacostracan marine crustacean of the *Cumacea* family, mostly dwelling on the sea bed but sometimes found among the plankton ▷ *adj* of, relating to, or belonging to the *Cumacea*

CUMACEANS > CUMACEAN

CUMARIC > CUMARIN

CUMARIN *same as* > COUMARIN

CUMARINS > CUMARIN

CUMARONE *variant spelling of* > COUMARONE

CUMARONES > CUMARONE

CUMBENT *adj* lying down

CUMBER *vb* obstruct or hinder ▷ *n* hindrance or burden

CUMBERED > CUMBER

CUMBERER > CUMBER

CUMBERERS > CUMBER

CUMBERING > CUMBER

CUMBERS > CUMBER

CUMBIA *n* Colombian style of music

CUMBIAS > CUMBIA

CUMBRANCE *n* burden, obstacle, or hindrance

CUMBROUS *adj* awkward because of size, weight, or height

CUMBUNGI *n* any of various tall Australian marsh plants of the genus *Typha*

CUMBUNGIS > CUMBUNGI

CUMEC *n* unit of volumetric rate of flow

CUMECS > CUMEC

CUMIN *n* sweet-smelling seeds of a Mediterranean plant, used in cooking

CUMINS > CUMIN

CUMMER *n* gossip

CUMMERS > CUMMER

CUMMIN *same as* > CUMIN

CUMMINS > CUMMIN

CUMQUAT *same as* > KUMQUAT

CUMQUATS > CUMQUAT

CUMSHAW *n* (used, esp formerly, by beggars in Chinese ports) a present or tip

CUMSHAWS > CUMSHAW

CUMULATE *vb* accumulate ▷ *adj* heaped up

CUMULATED > CUMULATE

CUMULATES > CUMULATE

CUMULET *n* variety of domestic fancy pigeon, pure white or white with light red markings

CUMULETS > CUMULET

CUMULI > CUMULUS

CUMULOSE *adj* full of heaps

CUMULOUS *adj* resembling or consisting of cumulus clouds

CUMULUS *n* thick white or dark grey cloud

CUNABULA *n* cradle

CUNCTATOR *n* person in habit of being late

CUNDIES > CUNDY

CUNDUM *n* early form of condom

CUNDUMS > CUNDUM

CUNDY *n* sewer

CUNEAL *same as* > CUNEIFORM

CUNEATE *adj* wedge-shaped: cuneate leaves are attached at the narrow end

CUNEATED *same as* > CUNEATE

CUNEATELY > CUNEATE

CUNEATIC *adj* cuneiform

CUNEI > CUNEUS

CUNEIFORM *adj* (written in) an ancient system of writing using wedge-shaped characters ▷ *n* ancient system of writing using wedge-shaped characters

CUNETTE *n* small trench dug in the main ditch of a fortification

CUNETTES > CUNETTE

CUNEUS *n* small wedge-shaped area of the cerebral cortex

CUNIFORM *same as* > CUNIFORM

CUNIFORMS > CUNIFORM

CUNJEVOI *n* plant of tropical Asia and Australia with small flowers, cultivated for its edible rhizome

CUNJEVOIS > CUNJEVOI

CUNNER *n* fish of the wrasse family

CUNNERS > CUNNER

CUNNING *adj* clever at deceiving ▷ *n* cleverness at deceiving

CUNNINGER > CUNNING

CUNNINGLY > CUNNING

CUNNINGS > CUNNING

CUNT *n* taboo word for female genitals

CUNTS > CUNT

CUP *n* small bowl-shaped drinking container with a handle ▷ *vb* form (one's hands) into the shape of a cup

CUPBEARER *n* attendant who fills and serves wine cups, as in a royal household

CUPBOARD *n* piece of furniture or alcove with a door, for storage ▷ *vb* to store in a cupboard

CUPBOARDS > CUPBOARD

CUPCAKE *n* small cake baked in a cup-shaped foil or paper case

CUPCAKES > CUPCAKE

CUPEL *n* refractory pot in which gold or silver is refined ▷ *vb* refine (gold or silver) by means of cupellation

CUPELED > CUPEL

CUPELER > CUPEL

CUPELERS > CUPEL

CUPELING > CUPEL

CUPELLED > CUPEL

CUPELLER > CUPEL

CUPELLERS > CUPEL

CUPELLING > CUPEL

CUPELS > CUPEL

CUPFERRON *n* compound used in chemical analysis

CUPFUL *n* amount a cup will hold

CUPFULS > CUPFUL

CUPGALL *n* gall found on oakleaves

CUPGALLS > CUPGALL

CUPHEAD *n* type of bolt or rivet with a cup-shaped head

CUPHEADS > CUPHEAD

CUPID *n* figure representing the Roman god of love

CUPIDITY *n* greed for money or possessions

CUPIDS > CUPID

CUPLIKE > CUP

CUPMAN *n* drinking companion

CUPMEN > CUPMAN

CUPOLA *n* domed roof or ceiling ▷ *vb* to provide with a cupola

CUPOLAED > CUPOLA

CUPOLAING > CUPOLA

CUPOLAR > CUPOLA

CUPOLAS > CUPOLA

CUPOLATED > CUPOLA

CUPPA *n* cup of tea

CUPPAS > CUPPA

CUPPED > CUP

CUPPER *same as* > CUPPA

CUPPERS > CUPPER

CUPPIER > CUPPY

CUPPIEST > CUPPY

CUPPING > CUP

CUPPINGS > CUP

CUPPY *adj* cup-shaped

CUPREOUS *adj* of copper

CUPRESSUS *n* any tree of the genus *Cupressus*

CUPRIC *adj* of or containing copper in the divalent state

CUPRITE *n* red secondary mineral

CUPRITES > CUPRITE

CUPROUS *adj* of or containing copper in the monovalent state

CUPRUM *an obsolete name for* > COPPER

CUPRUMS > CUPRUM

CUPS > CUP

CUPSFUL > CUPFUL

CUPULA *n* dome-shaped structure, esp the sensory structure within the semicircular canals of the ear

CUPULAE > CUPULA

CUPULAR *same as* > CUPULATE

CUPULATE *adj* shaped like a small cup

CUPULE *n* cup-shaped part or structure, such as the cup around the base of an acorn

CUPULES > CUPULE

CUR *n* mongrel dog

CURABLE *adj* capable of being cured

CURABLY > CURABLE

CURACAO *n* orange-flavoured liqueur

CURACAOS > CURACAO

CURACIES > CURACY

CURACOA *same as* > CURACAO

CURACOAS > CURACOA

CURACY *n* work or position of a curate

CURAGH *same as* > CURRACH

CURAGHS > CURAGH

CURANDERA *n* female faith healer

CURANDERO *n* male faith healer

CURARA *same as* > CURARE

CURARAS > CURARA

CURARE *n* poisonous resin of a S American tree, used as a muscle relaxant in medicine

CURARES > CURARE

CURARI *same as* > CURARE

CURARINE *n* alkaloid extracted from curare, used as a muscle relaxant in surgery

CURARINES > CURARINE

CURARIS > CURARI

CURARISE *same as* > CURARIZE

CURARISED > CURARISE

CURARISES > CURARISE

CURARIZE *vb* paralyse or treat with curare

CURARIZED > CURARIZE

CURARIZES > CURARIZE

CURASSOW *n* gallinaceous ground-nesting bird with long legs and tails and, typically, a distinctive crest of curled feathers

CURASSOWS > CURASSOW

CURAT n cuirass

CURATE n clergyman who assists a parish priest ▷ vb be in charge of (an art exhibition or museum) ▷ vb to act as a curator

CURATED > CURATE

CURATES > CURATE

CURATING > CURATE

CURATIVE n something able to cure ▷ adj able to cure

CURATIVES > CURATIVE

CURATOR n person in charge of a museum or art gallery

CURATORS > CURATOR

CURATORY > CURATOR

CURATRIX n female curator

CURATS > CURAT

CURB n something that restrains ▷ vb control, restrain

CURBABLE adj capable of being restrained

CURBED > CURB

CURBER > CURB

CURBERS > CURB

CURBING the US spelling of > KERBING

CURBINGS > CURBING

CURBLESS adj having no restraint

CURBS > CURB

CURBSIDE n pavement

CURBSIDES > CURBSIDE

CURBSTONE the US spelling of > KERBSTONE

CURCH n woman's plain cap or kerchief

CURCHEF same as > CURCH

CURCHEFS > CURCHEF

CURCHES > CURCH

CURCULIO n type of American weevil

CURCULIOS > CURCULIO

CURCUMA n type of tropical Asian tuberous plant

CURCUMAS > CURCUMA

CURCUMIN n yellow dye derived from turmeric

CURCUMINE same as > CURCUMIN

CURCUMINS > CURCUMIN

CURD n coagulated milk, used to make cheese ▷ vb turn into or become curd

CURDED > CURD

CURDIER > CURD

CURDIEST > CURD

CURDINESS > CURD

CURDING > CURD

CURDLE vb turn into curd, coagulate

CURDLED > CURDLE

CURDLER > CURDLE

CURDLERS > CURDLE

CURDLES > CURDLE

CURDLING > CURDLE

CURDS > CURD

CURDY > CURD

CURE vb get rid of (an illness or problem) ▷ n (treatment causing) curing of an illness or person

CURED > CURE

CURELESS > CURE

CURER > CURE

CURERS > CURE

CURES > CURE

CURET same as > CURETTE

CURETS > CURET

CURETTAGE n process of using a curette

CURETTE n surgical instrument for scraping tissue from body cavities ▷ vb scrape with a curette

CURETTED > CURETTE

CURETTES > CURETTE

CURETTING > CURETTE

CURF n type of limestone

CURFEW n law ordering people to stay inside their homes after a specific time at night

CURFEWS > CURFEW

CURFS > CURF

CURFUFFLE vb make a kerfuffle

CURIA n papal court and government of the Roman Catholic Church

CURIAE > CURIA

CURIAL > CURIA

CURIALISM n ultramontanism

CURIALIST > CURIALISM

CURIAS > CURIA

CURIE n standard unit of radioactivity

CURIES > CURIE

CURIET n cuirass

CURIETS > CURIET

CURING > CURE

CURIO n rare or unusual object valued as a collector's item

CURIOS > CURIO

CURIOSA n curiosities

CURIOSITY n eagerness to know or find out

CURIOUS adj eager to learn or know

CURIOUSER > CURIOUS

CURIOUSLY > CURIOUS

CURITE n oxide of uranium and lead

CURITES > CURITE

CURIUM n radioactive element artificially produced from plutonium

CURIUMS > CURIUM

CURL n curved piece of hair ▷ vb make (hair) into curls or (of hair) grow in curls

CURLED > CURL

CURLER n pin or small tube for curling hair

CURLERS > CURLER

CURLEW n long-billed wading bird

CURLEWS > CURLEW

CURLI pl n curled hairlike processes on the surface of the bacterium Escherichia coli by means of which the bacterium adheres to and infects wounds

CURLICUE n ornamental curl or twist ▷ vb to curl or twist elaborately, as in curlicues

CURLICUED > CURLICUE

CURLICUES > CURLICUE

CURLIER > CURLY

CURLIES as in have by the short and curlies have completely in one's power

CURLIEST > CURLY

CURLILY > CURLY

CURLINESS > CURLY

CURLING n game like bowls, played with heavy stones on ice

CURLINGS > CURLING

CURLPAPER n strip of paper used to roll up and set a section of hair, usually wetted, into a curl

CURLS > CURL

CURLY adj tending to curl

CURLYCUE same as > CURLICUE

CURLYCUES > CURLYCUE

CURN n grain (of corn etc)

CURNEY same as > CURNY

CURNIER > CURNY

CURNIEST > CURNY

CURNS > CURN

CURNY adj granular

CURPEL same as > CRUPPER

CURPELS > CURPEL

CURR vb to purr

CURRACH a Scot or Irish name for > CORACLE

CURRACHS > CURRACH

CURRAGH same as > CURRACH

CURRAGHS > CURRAGH

CURRAJONG same as > KURRAJONG

CURRAN n black bun

CURRANS > CURRAN

CURRANT n small dried grape

CURRANTS > CURRANT

CURRANTY > CURRANT

CURRAWONG n Australian songbird

CURRED > CURR

CURREJONG same as > KURRAJONG

CURRENCY n money in use in a particular country

CURRENT adj of the immediate present ▷ n flow of water or air in one direction

CURRENTLY > CURRENT

CURRENTS > CURRENT

CURRICLE n two-wheeled open carriage drawn by two horses side by side

CURRICLES > CURRICLE

CURRICULA n plural form of singular curriculum: course of study in one subject at school or college

CURRIE same as > CURRY

CURRIED > CURRY

CURRIER n person who curries leather

CURRIERS > CURRIER

CURRIERY n trade, work, or place of occupation of a currier

CURRIES > CURRY

CURRIJONG same as > KURRAJONG

CURRING > CURR

CURRISH adj of or like a cur

CURRISHLY > CURRISH

CURRS > CURR

CURRY n Indian dish of meat or vegetables in a hot spicy sauce ▷ vb prepare (food) with curry powder

CURRYCOMB n ridged comb used for grooming horses

CURRYING > CURRY

CURRYINGS > CURRY

CURS > CUR

CURSAL > CURSUS

CURSE vb swear (at) ▷ n swearword

CURSED > CURSE

CURSEDER > CURSE

CURSEDEST > CURSE

CURSEDLY > CURSE

CURSENARY same as > CURSORARY

CURSER > CURSE

CURSERS > CURSE

CURSES > CURSE

CURSI > CURSUS

CURSING > CURSE

CURSINGS > CURSE

CURSITOR n clerk in the Court of Chancery

CURSITORS > CURSITOR

CURSITORY > CURSITOR

CURSIVE n (handwriting) done with joined letters ▷ adj of handwriting or print in which letters are joined in a flowing style

CURSIVELY > CURSIVE

CURSIVES > CURSIVE

CURSOR n movable point of light that shows a specific position on a visual display unit

CURSORARY adj cursory

CURSORES > CURSOR

CURSORIAL adj adapted for running

CURSORILY > CURSORY

CURSORS > CURSOR

CURSORY adj quick and superficial

CURST > CURSE

CURSTNESS n peevishness

CURSUS n Neolithic parallel earthworks

CURT adj brief and rather rude

CURTAIL vb cut short

CURTAILED > CURTAIL

CURTAILER > CURTAIL

CURTAILS > CURTAIL

CURTAIN n piece of cloth hung at a window or opening as a screen ▷ vb provide with curtains

CURTAINED > CURTAIN

CURTAINS pl n death or ruin

CURTAL adj cut short ▷ n animal whose tail has been docked

CURTALAX same as > CURTALAXE

CURTALAXE n cutlass

CURTALS > CURTAL

CURTANA n unpointed sword carried before an English sovereign at a coronation as an emblem of mercy

CURTANAS > CURTANA
CURTATE adj shortened
CURTATION > CURTATE
CURTAXE same as
  > CURTALAXE
CURTAXES > CURTAXE
CURTER > CURT
CURTESIES > CURTESY
CURTEST > CURT
CURTESY n widower's life
  interest in his wife's estate
CURTILAGE n enclosed
  area of land adjacent to a
  dwelling house
CURTLY > CURT
CURTNESS > CURT
CURTSEY same as > CURTSY
CURTSEYED > CURTSEY
CURTSEYS > CURTSEY
CURTSIED > CURTSY
CURTSIES > CURTSY
CURTSY n woman's gesture
  of respect made by bending
  the knees and bowing the
  head ▷ vb make a curtsy
CURTSYING > CURTSY
CURULE adj (in ancient
  Rome) of the highest rank,
  esp one entitled to use a
  curule chair
CURVATE adj curved
CURVATED same as
  > CURVATE
CURVATION > CURVATE
CURVATIVE adj having
  curved edges
CURVATURE n curved shape
CURVE n continuously
  bending line with no
  straight parts ▷ vb form or
  move in a curve
CURVEBALL n in baseball,
  a ball pitched in a curving
  path ▷ vb pitch a curveball
CURVED > CURVE
CURVEDLY > CURVE
CURVES > CURVE
CURVESOME adj curvaceous
CURVET n horse's low leap
  with all four feet off the
  ground ▷ vb make such
  a leap
CURVETED > CURVET
CURVETING > CURVET
CURVETS > CURVET
CURVETTED > CURVET
CURVEY same as > CURVY
CURVIER > CURVE
CURVIEST > CURVE
CURVIFORM adj having a
  curved form
CURVING > CURVE
CURVITAL adj relating to
  curvature
CURVITIES > CURVITY
CURVITY n curvedness
CURVY > CURVE
CUSCUS n large Australian
  nocturnal possum
CUSCUSES > CUSCUS
CUSEC n unit of flow equal
  to 1 cubic foot per second
CUSECS > CUSEC
CUSH n cushion
CUSHAT n wood pigeon
CUSHATS > CUSHAT
CUSHAW same as > CASHAW

CUSHAWS > CUSHAW
CUSHES > CUSH
CUSHIE same as > CUSHAT
CUSHIER > CUSHY
CUSHIES > CUSHIE
CUSHIEST > CUSHY
CUSHILY > CUSHY
CUSHINESS > CUSHY
CUSHION n bag filled with
  soft material, to make a
  seat more comfortable
  ▷ vb lessen the effects of
CUSHIONED > CUSHION
CUSHIONET n small cushion
CUSHIONS > CUSHION
CUSHIONY > CUSHION
CUSHTY interj exclamation
  of pleasure, agreement,
  approval, etc
CUSHY adj easy
CUSK n gadoid food fish,
  Brosmius brosme, of
  northern coastal waters,
  having a single long dorsal
  fin
CUSKS > CUSK
CUSP n pointed end, esp on
  a tooth
CUSPAL > CUSP
CUSPATE adj having a cusp
  or cusps
CUSPATED same as
  > CUSPATE
CUSPED same as > CUSPATE
CUSPID n tooth having one
  point
CUSPIDAL same as
  > CUSPIDATE
CUSPIDATE adj having a
  cusp or cusps
CUSPIDES > CUSPIS
CUSPIDOR another word (esp
  US) for > SPITTOON
CUSPIDORE same as
  > CUSPIDOR
CUSPIDORS > CUSPIDOR
CUSPIDS > CUSPID
CUSPIS n in anatomy,
  tapering structure
CUSPS > CUSP
CUSS n curse, oath ▷ vb
  swear (at)
CUSSED adj obstinate
CUSSEDLY > CUSSED
CUSSER same as > COOSER
CUSSERS > CUSSER
CUSSES > CUSS
CUSSING > CUSS
CUSSO n tree of the rose
  family
CUSSOS > CUSSO
CUSSWORD n swearword
CUSSWORDS > CUSSWORD
CUSTARD n sweet yellow
  sauce made from milk and
  eggs
CUSTARDS > CUSTARD
CUSTARDY > CUSTARD
CUSTOCK same as > CASTOCK
CUSTOCKS > CUSTOCK
CUSTODE n custodian
CUSTODES > CUSTODE
CUSTODIAL > CUSTODY
CUSTODIAN n person in
  charge of a public building
CUSTODIER n custodian
CUSTODIES > CUSTODY

CUSTODY n protective care
CUSTOM n long-established
  activity or action ▷ adj
  made to the specifications
  of an individual customer
CUSTOMARY adj usual ▷ n
  statement in writing
  of customary laws and
  practices
CUSTOMED adj accustomed
CUSTOMER n person who
  buys goods or services
CUSTOMERS > CUSTOMER
CUSTOMISE same as
  > CUSTOMIZE
CUSTOMIZE vb make
  (something) according to
  a customer's individual
  requirements
CUSTOMS n duty charged on
  imports or exports
CUSTOS n superior in the
  Franciscan religious order
CUSTREL n knave
CUSTRELS > CUSTREL
CUSTUMAL another word for
  > CUSTOMARY
CUSTUMALS > CUSTUMAL
CUSTUMARY n customary
CUT vb open up, penetrate,
  wound, or divide with a
  sharp instrument ▷ n act
  of cutting
CUTANEOUS adj of the skin
CUTAWAY adj (of a drawing
  or model) having part of
  the outside omitted to
  reveal the inside ▷ n man's
  coat cut diagonally from
  the front waist to the back
  of the knees
CUTAWAYS > CUTAWAY
CUTBACK n decrease or
  reduction ▷ vb shorten by
  cutting
CUTBACKS > CUTBACK
CUTBANK n steep banking at
  a bend in a river
CUTBANKS > CUTBANK
CUTCH same as > CATECHU
CUTCHA adj crude
CUTCHERRY n (formerly, in
  India) government offices
  and law courts collectively
CUTCHERY same as
  > CUTCHERRY
CUTCHES > CUTCH
CUTDOWN n decrease
CUTDOWNS > CUTDOWN
CUTE adj appealing or
  attractive
CUTELY > CUTE
CUTENESS > CUTE
CUTER > CUTE
CUTES > CUTIS
CUTESIE same as > CUTESY
CUTESIER > CUTESY
CUTESIEST > CUTESY
CUTEST > CUTE
CUTESY adj affectedly cute
  or coy
CUTEY same as > CUTIE
CUTEYS > CUTEY
CUTGLASS adj (of an accent)
  upper-class
CUTGRASS n any grass of the
  genus Leersia

CUTICLE n skin at the base
  of a fingernail or toenail
CUTICLES > CUTICLE
CUTICULA n cuticle
CUTICULAE > CUTICULA
CUTICULAR > CUTICLE
CUTIE n person regarded as
  appealing or attractive, esp
  a girl or woman
CUTIES > CUTIE
CUTIKIN same as > CUTIKIN
CUTIKINS > CUTIKIN
CUTIN n waxy waterproof
  substance, consisting
  of derivatives of fatty
  acids, that is the main
  constituent of the plant
  cuticle
CUTINISE same as
  > CUTINIZE
CUTINISED > CUTINISE
CUTINISES > CUTINISE
CUTINIZE vb become or
  cause to become covered
  or impregnated with cutin
CUTINIZED > CUTINIZE
CUTINIZES > CUTINIZE
CUTINS > CUTIN
CUTIS a technical name for the
  > SKIN
CUTISES > CUTIS
CUTLAS same as > CUTLASS
CUTLASES > CUTLAS
CUTLASS n curved one-
  edged sword formerly used
  by sailors
CUTLASSES > CUTLASS
CUTLER n maker of cutlery
CUTLERIES > CUTLERY
CUTLERS > CUTLER
CUTLERY n knives, forks,
  and spoons
CUTLET n small piece of
  meat like a chop
CUTLETS > CUTLET
CUTLINE n caption
CUTLINES > CUTLINE
CUTOFF n limit or
  termination
CUTOFFS > CUTOFF
CUTOUT n something that
  has been cut out from
  something else
CUTOUTS > CUTOUT
CUTOVER n transitional
  period in IT system
  changeover, during which
  old and new systems are
  working concurrently
CUTOVERS > CUTOVER
CUTPURSE n pickpocket
CUTPURSES > CUTPURSE
CUTS > CUT
CUTTABLE adj capable of
  being cut
CUTTAGE n propagation
  by using parts taken from
  growing plants
CUTTAGES > CUTTAGE
CUTTER n person or tool
  that cuts
CUTTERS > CUTTER
CUTTHROAT n person who
  cuts throats
CUTTIER > CUTTY
CUTTIES > CUTTY
CUTTIEST > CUTTY

CUTTING > CUT
CUTTINGLY > CUT
CUTTINGS > CUT
CUTTLE vb to whisper
CUTTLED > CUTTLE
CUTTLES > CUTTLE
CUTTLING > CUTTLE
CUTTO n large knife
CUTTOE same as > CUTTO
CUTTOES > CUTTO
CUTTY adj short or cut short
▷ n something cut short,
such as a spoon or short-
stemmed tobacco pipe
CUTUP n joker or prankster
CUTUPS > CUTUP
CUTWATER n forward part of
the stem of a vessel, which
cuts through the water
CUTWATERS > CUTWATER
CUTWORK n openwork
embroidery in which the
pattern is cut away from
the background
CUTWORKS > CUTWORK
CUTWORM n caterpillar of
various noctuid moths,
esp those of the genus
Argrotis, which is a pest of
young crop plants in North
America
CUTWORMS > CUTWORM
CUVEE n individual batch or
blend of wine
CUVEES > CUVEE
CUVETTE n shallow dish or
vessel for holding liquid
CUVETTES > CUVETTE
CUZ n cousin
CUZZES > CUZ
CWM same as > CIRQUE
CWMS > CWM
CWTCH vb be snuggled up
CWTCHED > CWTCH
CWTCHES > CWTCH
CWTCHING > CWTCH
CYAN n highly saturated
green-blue that is the
complementary colour
of red and forms, with
magenta and yellow, a set
of primary colours ▷ adj of
this colour
CYANAMID same as
> CYANAMIDE
CYANAMIDE n white or
colourless crystalline
soluble weak dibasic acid,
which can be hydrolysed
to urea
CYANAMIDS > CYANAMID
CYANATE n any salt or ester
of cyanic acid
CYANATES > CYANATE
CYANIC as in cyanic acid
colourless poisonous
volatile liquid acid
CYANID same as > CYANIDE
CYANIDE n extremely
poisonous chemical
compound ▷ vb treat with
cyanide
CYANIDED > CYANIDE
CYANIDES > CYANIDE
CYANIDING > CYANIDE
CYANIDS > CYANID
CYANIN same as > CYANINE

CYANINE n blue dye used
to extend the sensitivity of
photographic emulsions to
colours other than blue and
ultraviolet
CYANINES > CYANINE
CYANINS > CYANIN
CYANISE vb to turn into
cyanide
CYANISED > CYANISE
CYANISES > CYANISE
CYANISING > CYANISE
CYANITE a variant spelling of
> KYANITE
CYANITES > CYANITE
CYANITIC > CYANITE
CYANIZE same as > CYANISE
CYANIZED > CYANIZE
CYANIZES > CYANIZE
CYANIZING > CYANIZE
CYANO adj containing
cyanogen
CYANOGEN n poisonous
colourless flammable gas
CYANOGENS > CYANOGEN
CYANOSED adj affected by
cyanosis
CYANOSES > CYANOSIS
CYANOSIS n blueness of the
skin, caused by a deficiency
of oxygen in the blood
CYANOTIC > CYANOSIS
CYANOTYPE another name for
> BLUEPRINT
CYANS > CYAN
CYANURATE n chemical
derived from cyanide
CYANURET n cyanide
CYANURETS > CYANURET
CYATHI > CYATHUS
CYATHIA > CYATHIUM
CYATHIUM n inflorescence
of the type found on the
poinsettia
CYATHUS n ancient measure
of wine
CYBER adj involving
computers
CYBERCAFE n café equipped
with computer terminals
which customers can use
to access the internet
CYBERCAST same as
> WEBCAST
CYBERNATE vb control (a
manufacturing process)
with a servomechanism
or (of a process) to
be controlled by a
servomechanism
CYBERNAUT n person using
internet
CYBERPET n electronic
toy that simulates the
activities of a pet, requiring
the owner to feed,
discipline, and entertain it
CYBERPETS > CYBERPET
CYBERPORN n pornography
on Internet
CYBERPUNK n genre of
science fiction that
features rebellious
computer hackers and is
set in a dystopian society
integrated by computer
networks

CYBERSEX n exchanging
of sexual messages or
information via the
internet
CYBERWAR n information
warfare
CYBERWARS > CYBERWAR
CYBORG n (in science fiction)
a living being whose
powers are enhanced by
computer implants
CYBORGS > CYBORG
CYBRARIAN n person
in charge of computer
archives
CYBRID n cytoplasmic
hybrid (hybrid resulting
from the fusion of a
cytoplast and a whole cell)
CYBRIDS > CYBRID
CYCAD n any tropical or
subtropical gymnosperm
plant of the phylum
Cycadophyta, having an
unbranched stem with
fernlike leaves crowded at
the top
CYCADEOID n (now extinct)
plant with a woody stem
and tough leaves
CYCADS > CYCAD
CYCAS n palm tree of the
genus Cycas
CYCASES > CYCAS
CYCASIN n glucoside, toxic
to mammals, occurring in
cycads
CYCASINS > CYCASIN
CYCLAMATE n salt or ester
of cyclamic acid. Certain of
the salts have a very sweet
taste and were formerly
used as food additives and
sugar substitutes
CYCLAMEN n plant with red,
pink, or white flowers ▷ adj
of a dark reddish-purple
colour
CYCLAMENS > CYCLAMEN
CYCLASE n enzyme which
acts as a catalyst in the
formation of a cyclic
compound
CYCLASES > CYCLASE
CYCLE vb ride a bicycle ▷ n
bicycle
CYCLECAR n any light car
with an engine capacity of
1100cc or less
CYCLECARS > CYCLECAR
CYCLED > CYCLE
CYCLER same as > CYCLIST
CYCLERIES > CYCLERY
CYCLERS > CYCLIST
CYCLERY n business dealing
in bicycles and bicycle
accessories
CYCLES > CYCLE
CYCLEWAY n path or way
designed, and reserved for,
cyclists
CYCLEWAYS > CYCLEWAY
CYCLIC adj recurring or
revolving in cycles
CYCLICAL same as > CYCLIC
n short-term trend, of
which reversal is expected

CYCLICALS > CYCLIC
CYCLICISM > CYCLIC
CYCLICITY > CYCLIC
CYCLICLY > CYCLIC
CYCLIN n type of protein
CYCLING > CYCLE
CYCLINGS > CYCLE
CYCLINS > CYCLIN
CYCLISE same as > CYCLIZE
CYCLISED > CYCLISE
CYCLISES > CYCLISE
CYCLISING > CYCLISE
CYCLIST n person who
rides a bicycle
CYCLISTS > CYCLIST
CYCLITOL n alicyclic
compound
CYCLITOLS > CYCLITOL
CYCLIZE vb be cyclical
CYCLIZED > CYCLIZE
CYCLIZES > CYCLIZE
CYCLIZINE n drug used to
relieve the symptoms of
motion sickness
CYCLIZING > CYCLIZE
CYCLO n type of rickshaw
CYCLOGIRO n aircraft lifted
and propelled by pivoted
blades rotating parallel
to roughly horizontal
transverse axes
CYCLOID adj resembling
a circle ▷ n curve
described by a point on the
circumference of a circle
as the circle rolls along a
straight line
CYCLOIDAL > CYCLOID
CYCLOIDS > CYCLOID
CYCLOLITH n stone circle
CYCLONAL > CYCLONE
CYCLONE n violent wind
moving round a central
area
CYCLONES > CYCLONE
CYCLONIC > CYCLONE
CYCLONITE n white
crystalline insoluble
explosive prepared by the
action of nitric acid on
hexamethylenetetramine
CYCLOPEAN adj of or
relating to the Cyclops
CYCLOPES > CYCLOPS
CYCLOPIAN > CYCLOPS
CYCLOPIC > CYCLOPS
CYCLOPS n any copepod
of the genus Cyclops,
characterized by having
one eye
CYCLORAMA n large picture,
such as a battle scene,
on the interior wall of a
cylindrical room, designed
to appear in natural
perspective to a spectator
in the centre
CYCLOS > CYCLO
CYCLOSES > CYCLOSIS
CYCLOSIS n circulation
of cytoplasm or cell
organelles, such as
food vacuoles in some
protozoans
CYCLOTRON n apparatus
that accelerates charged
particles by means of a

strong vertical magnetic field

CYCLUS n cycle

CYCLUSES > CYCLUS

CYDER same as > CIDER

CYDERS > CYDER

CYESES > CYESIS

CYESIS the technical name for > PREGNANCY

CYGNET n young swan

CYGNETS > CYGNET

CYLICES > CYLIX

CYLINDER n solid or hollow body with straight sides and circular ends

CYLINDERS > CYLINDER

CYLINDRIC adj shaped like, or characteristic of a cylinder

CYLIX a variant of > KYLIX

CYMA n moulding with a double curve, part concave and part convex

CYMAE > CYMA

CYMAGRAPH same as > CYMOGRAPH

CYMAR n woman's short fur-trimmed jacket, popular in the 17th and 18th centuries

CYMARS > CYMAR

CYMAS > CYMA

CYMATIA > CYMATIUM

CYMATICS n theory and practice of a therapy whereby sound waves are directed at the body, with the aim of promoting health

CYMATIUM n top moulding of a classical cornice or entablature

CYMBAL n percussion instrument consisting of a brass plate which is struck against another or hit with a stick

CYMBALEER > CYMBAL

CYMBALER > CYMBAL

CYMBALERS > CYMBAL

CYMBALIST > CYMBAL

CYMBALO another name for > DULCIMER

CYMBALOES > CYMBALO

CYMBALOM same as > CIMBALOM

CYMBALOMS > CYMBALOM

CYMBALOS > CYMBALO

CYMBALS > CYMBAL

CYMBIDIA > CYMBIDIUM

CYMBIDIUM n any orchid of the genus Cymbidium

CYMBIFORM adj shaped like a boat

CYMBLING same as > CYMLING

CYMBLINGS > CYMLING

CYME n flower cluster which has a single flower on the end of each stem and of which the central flower blooms first

CYMENE n colourless insoluble liquid with an aromatic odour that exists in three isomeric forms

CYMENES > CYMENE

CYMES > CYME

CYMLIN same as > CYMLING

CYMLING n pattypan squash

CYMLINGS > CYMLING

CYMLINS > CYMLIN

CYMOGENE n mixture of volatile flammable hydrocarbons, mainly butane, obtained in the distillation of petroleum

CYMOGENES > CYMOGENE

CYMOGRAPH n instrument for tracing the outline of an architectural moulding

CYMOID adj resembling a cyme or cyma

CYMOL same as > CYMENE

CYMOLS > CYMOL

CYMOPHANE n yellow or green opalescent variety of chrysoberyl

CYMOSE adj having the characteristics of a cyme

CYMOSELY > CYMOSE

CYMOUS adj relating to a cyme

CYNANCHE n any disease characterised by inflammation and swelling of the throat

CYNANCHES > CYNANCHE

CYNEGETIC adj relating to hunting

CYNIC n person who believes that people always act selfishly ▷ adj of or relating to Sirius, the Dog Star

CYNICAL adj believing that people always act selfishly

CYNICALLY > CYNICAL

CYNICISM n attitude or beliefs of a cynic

CYNICISMS > CYNICISM

CYNICS > CYNIC

CYNODONT n carnivorous mammal-like reptile of the late Permian and Triassic periods, whose specialized teeth were well developed

CYNODONTS > CYNODONT

CYNOMOLGI n plural form of singular cynomolgus: type of monkey

CYNOSURAL > CYNOSURE

CYNOSURE n centre of attention

CYNOSURES > CYNOSURE

CYPHER same as > CIPHER

CYPHERED > CYPHER

CYPHERING > CYPHER

CYPHERS > CYPHER

CYPRES n legal doctrine stating that a testator's intentions should be carried out as closely as possible

CYPRESES > CYPRES

CYPRESS n evergreen tree with dark green leaves

CYPRESSES > CYPRESS

CYPRIAN n prostitute or dancer

CYPRIANS > CYPRIAN

CYPRID n cypris

CYPRIDES > CYPRIS

CYPRIDS > CYPRID

CYPRINE adj relating to carp

CYPRINID n any teleost fish of the mainly freshwater family Cyprinidae, typically having toothless jaws and cycloid scales and including such food and game fishes as the carp, tench, roach, rudd, and dace ▷ adj of, relating to, or belonging to the Cyprinidae

CYPRINIDS > CYPRINID

CYPRINOID adj of, relating to, or belonging to the Cyprinoidea, a large suborder of teleost fishes including the cyprinids, characins, electric eels, and loaches ▷ n any fish belonging to the %i%>Cyprinoidea%/i%>

CYPRIS n member of the genus Cypris (small bivalve freshwater crustaceans)

CYPRUS same as > CYPRESS

CYPRUSES > CYPRUS

CYPSELA n dry one-seeded fruit of the daisy and related plants, which resembles an achene but is surrounded by a calyx sheath

CYPSELAE > CYPSELA

CYST n (abnormal) sac in the body containing fluid or soft matter

CYSTEIN same as > CYSTEINE

CYSTEINE n sulphur-containing amino acid

CYSTEINES > CYSTEINE

CYSTEINIC > CYSTEINE

CYSTEINS > CYSTEINE

CYSTIC adj of, relating to, or resembling a cyst

CYSTID n cystidean

CYSTIDEAN n any echinoderm of the class Cystoidea, an extinct order of sea lilies

CYSTIDS > CYSTID

CYSTIFORM adj having the form of a cyst

CYSTINE n sulphur-containing amino acid

CYSTINES > CYSTINE

CYSTITIS n inflammation of the bladder

CYSTOCARP n reproductive body in red algae, developed after fertilization and consisting of filaments bearing carpospores

CYSTOCELE n hernia of the urinary bladder, esp one protruding into the vagina

CYSTOID adj resembling a cyst or bladder ▷ n tissue mass, such as a tumour, that resembles a cyst but lacks an outer membrane

CYSTOIDS > CYSTOID

CYSTOLITH n knoblike deposit of calcium carbonate in the epidermal cells of such plants as the stinging nettle

CYSTOTOMY n surgical incision into the gall bladder or urinary bladder

CYSTS > CYST

CYTASE n cellulose-dissolving enzyme

CYTASES > CYTASE

CYTASTER another word for > ASTER

CYTASTERS > CYTASTER

CYTE n biological cell

CYTES > CYTE

CYTIDINE n nucleoside formed by the condensation of cytosine and ribose

CYTIDINES > CYTIDINE

CYTIDYLIC as in cytidylic acid nucleotide that is found in DNA

CYTISI > CYTISUS

CYTISINE n poisonous alkaloid found in laburnum seeds

CYTISINES > CYTISINE

CYTISUS n any plant of the broom genus, Cytisus

CYTODE n mass of protoplasm without a nucleus

CYTODES > CYTODE

CYTOGENY n origin and development of plant cells

CYTOID adj resembling a cell

CYTOKINE n any of various proteins, secreted by cells, that carry signals to neighbouring cells. Cytokines include interferon

CYTOKINES > CYTOKINE

CYTOKININ n any of a group of plant hormones that promote cell division and retard ageing in plants

CYTOLOGIC > CYTOLOGY

CYTOLOGY n study of plant and animal cells

CYTOLYSES > CYTOLYSIS

CYTOLYSIN n substance that can partially or completely destroy animal cells

CYTOLYSIS n dissolution of cells, esp by the destruction of their membranes

CYTOLYTIC > CYTOLYSIS

CYTOMETER n glass slide used to count and measure blood cells

CYTOMETRY n counting of blood cells using a cytometer

CYTON n main part of a neuron

CYTONS > CYTON

CYTOPENIA n blood disorder where there is a deficiency in the blood cells

CYTOPLASM n protoplasm of a cell excluding the nucleus

CYTOPLAST n intact cytoplasm of a single cell

CYTOSINE n white crystalline pyrimidine occurring in nucleic acids

CYTOSINES > CYTOSINE

CYTOSOL n solution of proteins and metabolites inside a biological cell, in which the organelles are suspended

CYTOSOLIC > CYTOSOL

CYTOSOLS > CYTOSOL

CYTOSOME n body of a cell excluding its nucleus

CYTOSOMES > CYTOSOME

CYTOTAXES > CYTOTAXIS

CYTOTAXIS n movement of cells due to external stimulation

CYTOTOXIC adj poisonous to living cells: denoting certain drugs used in the treatment of leukaemia and other cancers

CYTOTOXIN n any substance that is poisonous to living cells

CZAPKA n leather and felt peaked military helmet of Polish origin

CZAPKAS > CZAPKA

CZAR same as > TSAR

CZARDAS n Hungarian national dance of alternating slow and fast sections

CZARDASES > CZARDAS

CZARDOM > CZAR

CZARDOMS > CZAR

CZAREVICH n son of a czar

CZAREVNA a variant spelling (esp US) of > TSAREVNA

CZAREVNAS > CZAREVNA

CZARINA variant spellings (esp US) of > TSARINA

CZARINAS > CZARINA

CZARISM a variant spelling (esp US) of > TSARISM

CZARISMS > CZARISM

CZARIST > CZARISM

CZARISTS > CZARISM

CZARITSA n Russian empress

CZARITSAS > CZARITSA

CZARITZA same as > CZARINA

CZARITZAS > CZARINA

CZARS > CZAR

C

Dd

DA *n* Burmese knife

DAB *vb* pat lightly ▷ *n* small amount of something soft or moist

DABBA *n* in Indian cookery, round metal box used to transport hot food

DABBAS > DABBA

DABBED > DAB

DABBER *n* pad used by printers for applying ink by hand

DABBERS > DABBER

DABBING > DAB

DABBITIES > DABBITY

DABBITY *n* temporary tattoo

DABBLE *vb* be involved in something superficially

DABBLED > DABBLE

DABBLER > DABBLE

DABBLERS > DABBLE

DABBLES > DABBLE

DABBLING > DABBLE

DABBLINGS > DABBLE

DABCHICK *n* any of several small grebes of the genera *Podiceps* and *Podilymbus*, such as *Podiceps ruficollis* of the Old World

DABCHICKS > DABCHICK

DABS > DAB

DABSTER *n* incompetent or amateurish worker

DABSTERS > DABSTER

DACE *n* small European freshwater fish

DACES > DACE

DACHA *n* country cottage in Russia

DACHAS > DACHA

DACHSHUND *n* dog with a long body and short legs

DACITE *n* volcanic rock

DACITES > DACITE

DACK *vb* remove the trousers from (someone) by force

DACKED > DACK

DACKER *vb* walk slowly

DACKERED > DACKER

DACKERING > DACKER

DACKERS > DACKER

DACKING > DACK

DACKS > DACK

DACOIT *n* (in India and Myanmar) a member of a

gang of armed robbers

DACOITAGE *n* robbery by armed gang

DACOITIES > DACOITY

DACOITS > DACOIT

DACOITY *n* (in India and Myanmar) robbery by an armed gang

DACQUOISE *n* cake with meringue layers

DACRON *n* US tradename for a synthetic polyester fibre or fabric characterized by lightness and crease resistance

DACRONS > DACRON

DACTYL *n* metrical foot of three syllables, one long followed by two short

DACTYLAR *adj* poetry term

DACTYLI > DACTYLUS

DACTYLIC *same as* > DACTYL

DACTYLICS > DACTYLIC

DACTYLIST *n* poet

DACTYLS > DACTYL

DACTYLUS *n* tip of a squid's tentacular club

DAD *n* father ▷ *vb* act or treat as a father

DADA *n* nihilistic artistic movement of the early 20th century

DADAH *n* illegal drugs

DADAHS > DADAH

DADAISM *same as* > DADA

DADAISMS > DADAISM

DADAIST > DADA

DADAISTIC > DADA

DADAISTS > DADA

DADAS > DADA

DADDED > DAD

DADDIES > DADDY

DADDING > DAD

DADDLE *vb* walk unsteadily

DADDLED > DADDLE

DADDLES > DADDLE

DADDLING > DADDLE

DADDOCK *n* core of a dead tree

DADDOCKS > DADDOCK

DADDY *n* father

DADGUM *mild form of* > DAMNED

DADO *n* lower part of an interior wall, below a rail, decorated differently from the upper part ▷ *vb*

provide with a dado

DADOED > DADO

DADOES > DADO

DADOING > DADO

DADOS > DADO

DADS > DAD

DAE *a Scot word for* > DO

DAEDAL *adj* skilful or intricate

DAEDALEAN *same as* > DAEDALIAN

DAEDALIAN *adj* of, relating to, or resembling the work of Daedalus, the Athenian architect and inventor of Greek mythology

DAEDALIC *same as* > DAEDALIAN

DAEING > DAE

DAEMON *same as* > DEMON

DAEMONES > DAEMON

DAEMONIC > DAEMON

DAEMONS > DAEMON

DAES > DAE

DAFF *vb* frolic

DAFFED > DAFF

DAFFIER > DAFFY

DAFFIES > DAFFY

DAFFIEST > DAFFY

DAFFILY > DAFFY

DAFFINESS > DAFFY

DAFFING > DAFF

DAFFINGS > DAFF

DAFFODIL *n* yellow trumpet-shaped flower that blooms in spring ▷ *adj* brilliant yellow

DAFFODILS > DAFFODIL

DAFFS > DAFF

DAFFY *another word for* > DAFT

DAFT *adj* foolish or crazy

DAFTAR *Indian word for* > OFFICE

DAFTARS > DAFTAR

DAFTER > DAFT

DAFTEST > DAFT

DAFTIE *n* foolish person

DAFTIES > DAFTIE

DAFTLY > DAFT

DAFTNESS > DAFT

DAG *n* character ▷ *vb* cut daglocks from sheep

DAGABA *n* shrine for Buddhist relics

DAGABAS > DAGABA

DAGGA *n* cannabis

DAGGAS > DAGGA

DAGGED > DAG

DAGGER > DAG

DAGGERED > DAG

DAGGERING > DAG

DAGGERS > DAG

DAGGIER > DAGGY

DAGGIEST > DAGGY

DAGGING > DAG

DAGGINGS > DAG

DAGGLE *vb* trail through water

DAGGLED > DAGGLE

DAGGLES > DAGGLE

DAGGLING > DAGGLE

DAGGY *adj* amusing

DAGLOCK *n* dung-caked lock of wool around the hindquarters of a sheep

DAGLOCKS > DAGLOCK

DAGO *n* offensive term for a member of a Latin race, esp a Spaniard or Portuguese

DAGOBA *n* dome-shaped shrine containing relics of the Buddha or a Buddhist saint

DAGOBAS > DAGOBA

DAGOES > DAGO

DAGOS > DAGO

DAGS > DAG

DAGWOOD *n* European shrub

DAGWOODS > DAGWOOD

DAH *n* long sound used in combination with the short sound dit, in the spoken representation of Morse and other telegraphic codes

DAHABEAH *n* houseboat used on the Nile

DAHABEAHS > DAHABEAH

DAHABEEAH *n* Egyptian houseboat

DAHABIAH *same as* > DAHABEAH

DAHABIAHS > DAHABIAH

DAHABIEH *n* Egyptian houseboat

DAHABIEHS > DAHABIEH

DAHABIYA *n* Egyptian houseboat

DAHABIYAH *n* Egyptian houseboat

DAHABIYAS > DAHABIYA

DAHABIYEH *n* Egyptian houseboat

DAHL *same as* > DHAL
DAHLIA *n* brightly coloured garden flower
DAHLIAS > DAHLIA
DAHLS > DAHL
DAHOON *n* evergreen shrub
DAHOONS > DAHOON
DAHS > DAH
DAIDLE *vb* waddle about
DAIDLED > DAIDLE
DAIDLES > DAIDLE
DAIDLING > DAIDLE
DAIDZEIN *n* type of protein
DAIDZEINS > DAIDZEIN
DAIKER *vb* walk slowly
DAIKERED > DAIKER
DAIKERING > DAIKER
DAIKERS > DAIKER
DAIKON *another name for* > MOOLI
DAIKONS > DAIKON
DAILIES > DAILY
DAILINESS > DAILY
DAILY *adj* occurring every day or every weekday ▷ *adv* every day ▷ *n* daily newspaper
DAILYNESS > DAILY
DAIMEN *adj* occasional
DAIMIO *same as* > DAIMYO
DAIMIOS > DAIMIO
DAIMOKU *n* Nichiren Buddhist chant
DAIMOKUS > DAIMOKU
DAIMON *same as* > DEMON
DAIMONES *pl n* disembodied souls
DAIMONIC > DAIMON
DAIMONS > DAIMON
DAIMYO *n* (in Japan) one of the territorial magnates who dominated much of the country from about the 11th to the 19th century
DAIMYOS > DAIMYO
DAINE *vb* condescend
DAINED > DAINE
DAINES > DAINE
DAINING > DAINE
DAINT *adj* dainty
DAINTIER > DAINTY
DAINTIES > DAINTY
DAINTIEST > DAINTY
DAINTILY > DAINTY
DAINTY *adj* delicate or elegant ▷ *n* small cake or sweet
DAIQUIRI *n* iced drink containing rum, lime juice, and sugar
DAIQUIRIS > DAIQUIRI
DAIRIES > DAIRY
DAIRY *n* place for the processing or sale of milk and its products ▷ *adj* of milk or its products
DAIRYING *n* business of producing, processing, and selling dairy products
DAIRYINGS > DAIRYING
DAIRYMAID *n* (formerly) woman employed to milk cows
DAIRYMAN *n* man employed to look after cows
DAIRYMEN > DAIRYMAN
DAIS *n* raised platform in a

hall, used by a speaker
DAISES > DAIS
DAISHIKI *n* upper garment
DAISHIKIS > DAISHIKI
DAISIED > DAISY
DAISIES > DAISY
DAISY *n* small wild flower with a yellow centre and white petals
DAK *n* system of mail delivery or passenger transport by relays of bearers or horses stationed at intervals along a route
DAKER *vb* walk slowly
DAKERED > DAKER
DAKERHEN *n* European bird
DAKERHENS > DAKERHEN
DAKERING > DAKER
DAKERS > DAKER
DAKOIT *same as* > DACOIT
DAKOITI *same as* > DAKOIT
DAKOITIES > DAKOIT
DAKOITIS > DAKOIT
DAKOITS > DAKOIT
DAKOITY *n* armed robbery
DAKS *an informal name for* > TROUSERS
DAL *same as* > DECALITRE
DALAPON *n* herbicide
DALAPONS > DALAPON
DALASI *n* standard monetary unit of The Gambia, divided into 100 bututs
DALASIS > DALASI
DALE *n* (esp in N England) valley
DALED *same as* > DALETH
DALEDH *n* letter of Hebrew alphabet
DALEDHS > DALEDH
DALEDS > DALED
DALES > DALE
DALESMAN *n* person living in a dale, esp in the dales of N England
DALESMEN > DALESMAN
DALETH *n* fourth letter of the Hebrew alphabet, transliterated as *d* or, when final, *dh*
DALETHS > DALETH
DALGYTE *another name for* > BILBY
DALGYTES > DALGYTE
DALI *n* type of tree
DALIS > DALI
DALLE > DALLES
DALLES *pl n* stretch of a river between high rock walls, with rapids and dangerous currents
DALLIANCE *n* flirtation
DALLIED > DALLY
DALLIER > DALLY
DALLIERS > DALLY
DALLIES > DALLY
DALLOP *n* semisolid lump
DALLOPS > DALLOP
DALLY *vb* waste time
DALLYING > DALLY
DALMAHOY *n* bushy wig
DALMAHOYS > DALMAHOY
DALMATIAN *n* breed of dog characterized by its striking spotted markings

DALMATIC *n* wide-sleeved tunic-like vestment open at the sides, worn by deacons and bishops
DALMATICS > DALMATIC
DALS > DAL
DALT *n* foster child
DALTON *n* atomic mass unit
DALTONIAN > DALTON
DALTONIC > DALTONISM
DALTONISM *n* colour blindness, esp the confusion of red and green
DALTONS > DALTON
DALTS > DALT
DAM *n* barrier built across a river to create a lake ▷ *vb* build a dam across (a river)
DAMAGE *vb* harm, spoil ▷ *n* harm to a person or thing
DAMAGED > DAMAGE
DAMAGER > DAMAGE
DAMAGERS > DAMAGE
DAMAGES *pl n* money awarded as compensation for injury or loss
DAMAGING > DAMAGE
DAMAN *n* esp the Syrian rock hyrax
DAMANS > DAMAN
DAMAR *same as* > DAMMAR
DAMARS > DAMAR
DAMASCENE *vb* ornament (metal, esp steel) by etching or by inlaying, usually with gold or silver ▷ *n* design or article produced by this process ▷ *adj* of or relating to this process
DAMASK *n* fabric with a pattern woven into it, used for tablecloths etc ▷ *vb* ornament (metal) by etching or inlaying, usually with gold or silver
DAMASKED > DAMASK
DAMASKEEN *vb* decorate metal
DAMASKIN *vb* decorate metal
DAMASKING > DAMASK
DAMASKINS > DAMASKIN
DAMASKS > DAMASK
DAMASQUIN *vb* decorate metal
DAMASSIN *n* patterned damask
DAMASSINS > DAMASSIN
DAMBOARD *n* draughtboard
DAMBOARDS > DAMBOARD
DAMBROD *n* draughtboard
DAMBRODS > DAMBROD
DAME *n* woman
DAMES > DAME
DAMEWORT *n* sweet-scented perennial plant with mauve or white flowers
DAMEWORTS > DAMEWORT
DAMFOOL *adj* foolish
DAMIANA *n* herbal medicine
DAMIANAS > DAMIANA
DAMMAR *n* any of various resins obtained from SE Asian trees used for varnishes, lacquers, bases for oil paints, etc

DAMMARS > DAMMAR
DAMME *interj* exclamation of surprise
DAMMED > DAM
DAMMER *same as* > DAMMAR
DAMMERS > DAMMER
DAMMING > DAM
DAMMIT *interj* exclamation of surprise
DAMN *interj* exclamation of annoyance ▷ *adj* extreme(ly) ▷ *vb* condemn as bad or worthless
DAMNABLE *adj* annoying
DAMNABLY *adv* in a detestable manner
DAMNATION *interj* exclamation of anger ▷ *n* eternal punishment
DAMNATORY *adj* threatening or occasioning condemnation
DAMNDEST *n* utmost
DAMNDESTS > DAMNDEST
DAMNED *adj* condemned to hell ▷ *adv* extreme or extremely
DAMNEDER > DAMNED
DAMNEDEST *n* utmost
DAMNER *n* person who damns
DAMNERS > DAMNER
DAMNIFIED > DAMNIFY
DAMNIFIES > DAMNIFY
DAMNIFY *vb* cause loss or damage to (a person)
DAMNING > DAMN
DAMNINGLY > DAMN
DAMNS > DAMN
DAMOISEL *same as* > DAMSEL
DAMOISELS > DAMOISEL
DAMOSEL *same as* > DAMSEL
DAMOSELS > DAMOSEL
DAMOZEL *same as* > DAMOISELLE
DAMOZELS > DAMOZEL
DAMP *adj* slightly wet ▷ *n* slight wetness, moisture ▷ *vb* make damp
DAMPED > DAMP
DAMPEN *vb* reduce the intensity of
DAMPENED > DAMPEN
DAMPENER > DAMPEN
DAMPENERS > DAMPEN
DAMPENING > DAMPEN
DAMPENS > DAMPEN
DAMPER *n* movable plate to regulate the draught in a fire
DAMPERS > DAMPER
DAMPEST > DAMP
DAMPIER > DAMPY
DAMPIEST > DAMPY
DAMPING *n* moistening or wetting
DAMPINGS > DAMPING
DAMPISH > DAMP
DAMPLY > DAMP
DAMPNESS > DAMP
DAMPS > DAMP
DAMPY *adj* damp
DAMS > DAM
DAMSEL *n* young woman
DAMSELFLY *n* any insect of the suborder *Zygoptera*, similar to but smaller than

dragonflies and usually resting with the wings closed over the back: order *Odonata*
DAMSELS > DAMSEL
DAMSON *n* small blue-black plumlike fruit
DAMSONS > DAMSON
DAN *n* in judo, any of the 10 black-belt grades of proficiency
DANAZOL *n* type of drug
DANAZOLS > DANAZOL
DANCE *vb* move the feet and body rhythmically in time to music ▷ *n* series of steps and movements in time to music
DANCEABLE > DANCE
DANCED > DANCE
DANCEHALL *n* style of dance-oriented reggae
DANCER > DANCE
DANCERS > DANCE
DANCES > DANCE
DANCETTE another name for > CHEVRON
DANCETTEE *adj* having a zigzag pattern
DANCETTES > DANCETTE
DANCETTY *adj* having a zigzag pattern
DANCEY *adj* of, relating to, or resembling dance music
DANCIER > DANCEY
DANCIEST > DANCEY
DANCING > DANCE
DANCINGS > DANCE
DANDELION *n* yellow-flowered wild plant
DANDER *n* stroll ▷ *vb* stroll
DANDERED > DANDER
DANDERING > DANDER
DANDERS > DANDER
DANDIACAL *adj* like a dandy
DANDIER > DANDY
DANDIES > DANDY
DANDIEST > DANDY
DANDIFIED > DANDIFY
DANDIFIES > DANDIFY
DANDIFY *vb* dress like or cause to resemble a dandy
DANDILY > DANDY
DANDIPRAT *n* small English coin minted in the 16th century
DANDLE *vb* move (a child) up and down on one's knee
DANDLED > DANDLE
DANDLER > DANDLE
DANDLERS > DANDLE
DANDLES > DANDLE
DANDLING > DANDLE
DANDRIFF same as > DANDRUFF
DANDRIFFS > DANDRIFF
DANDRUFF *n* loose scales of dry dead skin shed from the scalp
DANDRUFFS > DANDRUFF
DANDRUFFY > DANDRUFF
DANDY *n* man who is overconcerned with the elegance of his appearance ▷ *adj* very good
DANDYFUNK *n* ship's biscuit
DANDYISH > DANDY

DANDYISM > DANDY
DANDYISMS > DANDY
DANDYPRAT *n* English coin
DANEGELD *n* tax levied in Anglo-Saxon England to provide protection money for, or to finance forces to oppose, Viking invaders
DANEGELDS > DANEGELD
DANEGELT same as > DANEGELD
DANEGELTS > DANEGELT
DANELAGH same as > DANELAW
DANELAGHS > DANELAGH
DANELAW *n* Danish law and customs of northern, central, and eastern parts of Anglo-Saxon England
DANELAWS > DANELAW
DANEWEED *n* dwarf elder
DANEWEEDS > DANEWEED
DANEWORT *n* dwarf elder
DANEWORTS > DANEWORT
DANG a euphemistic word for > DAMN
DANGED > DANG
DANGER *n* possibility of being injured or killed ▷ *vb* in archaic usage, endanger
DANGERED > DANGER
DANGERING > DANGER
DANGEROUS *adj* likely or able to cause injury or harm
DANGERS > DANGER
DANGING > DANG
DANGLE *vb* hang loosely ▷ *n* act of dangling or something that dangles
DANGLED > DANGLE
DANGLER > DANGLE
DANGLERS > DANGLE
DANGLES > DANGLE
DANGLIER > DANGLE
DANGLIEST > DANGLE
DANGLING > DANGLE
DANGLINGS > DANGLE
DANGLY > DANGLE
DANGS > DANG
DANIO *n* any brightly coloured tropical freshwater cyprinid fish of the genus *Danio* and related genera: popular aquarium fishes
DANIOS > DANIO
DANISH *n* sweet pastry
DANISHES > DANISH
DANK *adj* unpleasantly damp and chilly ▷ *n* unpleasant damp and chilliness
DANKER > DANK
DANKEST > DANK
DANKISH > DANK
DANKLY > DANK
DANKNESS > DANK
DANKS > DANK
DANNEBROG *n* Danish flag
DANNIES > DANNY
DANNY *n* hand (used esp when addressing children)
DANS > DAN
DANSEUR *n* male ballet dancer
DANSEURS > DANSEUR
DANSEUSE *n* female ballet

dancer
DANSEUSES > DANSEUSE
DANT *vb* intimidate
DANTED > DANT
DANTHONIA *n* any of various grasses of the genus *Danthonia*, of N temperate regions and South America
DANTING > DANT
DANTON same as > DAUNTON
DANTONED > DANTON
DANTONING > DANTON
DANTONS > DANTON
DANTS > DANT
DAP *vb* fish with a natural or artificial fly on a floss silk line so that the wind makes the fly bob on and off the surface of the water
DAPHNE *n* any shrub of the Eurasian thymelaeaceous genus *Daphne*, such as the mezereon and spurge laurel: ornamentals with shiny evergreen leaves and clusters of small bell-shaped flowers
DAPHNES > DAPHNE
DAPHNIA *n* any water flea of the genus *Daphnia*, having a rounded body enclosed in a transparent shell and bearing branched swimming antennae
DAPHNIAS > DAPHNIA
DAPHNID *n* water flea
DAPHNIDS > DAPHNID
DAPPED > DAP
DAPPER *adj* (of a man) neat in appearance ▷ *n* fisherman or -woman who uses a bobbing bait
DAPPERER > DAPPER
DAPPEREST > DAPPER
DAPPERLY > DAPPER
DAPPERS > DAPPER
DAPPING > DAP
DAPPLE *vb* mark or become marked with spots or patches of a different colour ▷ *n* mottled or spotted markings ▷ *adj* marked with dapples or spots
DAPPLED > DAPPLE
DAPPLES > DAPPLE
DAPPLING > DAPPLE
DAPS > DAP
DAPSONE *n* antimicrobial drug used to treat leprosy and certain types of dermatitis
DAPSONES > DAPSONE
DAQUIRI *n* rum cocktail
DAQUIRIS > DAQUIRI
DARAF *n* unit of elastance equal to a reciprocal farad
DARAFS > DARAF
DARB *n* something excellent
DARBAR *n* hall in Sikh temple
DARBARS > DARBAR
DARBIES > HANDCUFFS
DARBS > DARB
DARCIES > DARCY
DARCY *n* unit expressing the permeability coefficient of rock

DARCYS > DARCY
DARE *vb* be courageous enough to try (to do something) ▷ *n* challenge to do something risky
DARED > DARE
DAREDEVIL *n* recklessly bold person ▷ *adj* recklessly bold or daring
DAREFUL *adj* daring
DARER > DARE
DARERS > DARE
DARES > DARE
DARESAY *vb* venture to say
DARG *n* day's work
DARGA *n* Muslim shrine
DARGAH *n* tomb of a Muslim saint
DARGAHS > DARGAH
DARGAS > DARGA
DARGLE *n* wooded hollow
DARGLES > DARGLE
DARGS > DARG
DARI *n* variety of sorghum
DARIC *n* gold coin of ancient Persia
DARICS > DARIC
DARING *adj* willing to take risks ▷ *n* courage to do dangerous things
DARINGLY > DARING
DARINGS > DARING
DARIOLE *n* small cup-shaped mould used for making individual sweet or savoury dishes
DARIOLES > DARIOLE
DARIS > DARI
DARK *adj* having little or no light ▷ *n* absence of light ▷ *vb* in archaic usage, darken
DARKED > DARK
DARKEN *vb* make or become dark or darker
DARKENED > DARKEN
DARKENER > DARKEN
DARKENERS > DARKEN
DARKENING > DARKEN
DARKENS > DARKEN
DARKER > DARK
DARKEST > DARK
DARKEY same as > DARKY
DARKEYS > DARKEY
DARKIE same as > DARKY
DARKIES > DARKY
DARKING > DARK
DARKISH > DARK
DARKLE *vb* grow dark
DARKLED > DARKLE
DARKLES > DARKLE
DARKLIER > DARK
DARKLIEST > DARK
DARKLING *adj* in the dark or night
DARKLINGS *adv* in darkness
DARKLY > DARK
DARKMANS *n* slang term for night-time
DARKNESS > DARK
DARKROOM *n* darkened room for processing photographic film
DARKROOMS > DARKROOM
DARKS > DARK
DARKSOME *adj* dark or darkish

DARKY n offensive word for a Black person

DARLING n much-loved person ▷ adj much-loved

DARLINGLY > DARLING

DARLINGS > DARLING

DARN vb mend (a garment) with a series of interwoven stitches ▷ n patch of darned work

DARNATION mild form of > DAMNATION

DARNDEST n utmost

DARNDESTS > DARNDEST

DARNED adj damned

DARNEDER > DARNED

DARNEDEST a euphemistic word for > DAMNEDEST

DARNEL n weed that grows in grain fields

DARNELS > DARNEL

DARNER > DARN

DARNERS > DARN

DARNING > DARN

DARNINGS > DARN

DARNS > DARN

DAROGHA n in India, manager

DAROGHAS > DAROGHA

DARRAIGN same as > DERAIGN

DARRAIGNE vb clear from guilt

DARRAIGNS > DARRAIGN

DARRAIN vb clear of guilt

DARRAINE vb clear of guilt

DARRAINED > DARRAINE

DARRAINES > DARRAINE

DARRAINS > DARRAIN

DARRAYN vb clear of guilt

DARRAYNED > DARRAYN

DARRAYNS > DARRAYN

DARRE vb dare

DARRED > DARRE

DARRES > DARRE

DARRING > DARRE

DARSHAN n Hindu blessing

DARSHANS > DARSHAN

DART n small narrow pointed missile that is thrown or shot, esp in the game of darts ▷ vb move or direct quickly and suddenly

DARTBOARD n circular board used as the target in the game of darts

DARTED > DART

DARTER n any aquatic bird of the genus Anhinga and family Anhingidae, of tropical and subtropical inland waters, having a long slender neck and bill: order Pelecaniformes (pelicans, cormorants, etc)

DARTERS > DARTER

DARTING > DART

DARTINGLY > DART

DARTLE vb move swiftly

DARTLED > DARTLE

DARTLES > DARTLE

DARTLING > DARTLE

DARTRE n skin disease

DARTRES > DARTRE

DARTROUS adj having a skin disease

DARTS n game in which darts are thrown at a dartboard

DARZI n tailor in India

DARZIS > DARZI

DAS > DA

DASH vb move quickly ▷ n sudden quick movement

DASHBOARD n instrument panel in a vehicle

DASHED > DASH

DASHEEN another name for > TARO

DASHEENS > DASHEEN

DASHEKI n upper garment

DASHEKIS > DASHEKI

DASHER n one of the boards surrounding an ice-hockey rink

DASHERS > DASHER

DASHES > DASH

DASHI n clear stock made from dried fish and kelp

DASHIER > DASHY

DASHIEST > DASHY

DASHIKI n large loose-fitting buttonless upper garment worn esp by Blacks in the US, Africa, and the Caribbean

DASHIKIS > DASHIKI

DASHING adj stylish and attractive

DASHINGLY > DASHING

DASHIS > DASHI

DASHPOT n device for damping vibrations

DASHPOTS > DASHPOT

DASHY adj showy

DASSIE n type of hoofed rodent-like animal

DASSIES > DASSIE

DASTARD n contemptible sneaking coward

DASTARDLY adj wicked and cowardly

DASTARDS > DASTARD

DASTARDY n cowardice

DASYMETER n device for measuring density of gases

DASYPOD n armadillo

DASYPODS > DASYPOD

DASYURE n small marsupial of Australia, New Guinea, and adjacent islands

DASYURES > DASYURE

DATA n information consisting of observations, measurements, or facts

DATABANK n store of a large amount of information, esp in a form that can be handled by a computer

DATABANKS > DATABANK

DATABASE n store of information in a form that can be easily handled by a computer ▷ vb put data into a database

DATABASED > DATABASE

DATABASES > DATABASE

DATABLE > DATE

DATABUS n computing term

DATABUSES > DATABUS

DATACARD n smart card

DATACARDS > DATACARD

DATACOMMS n computing term

DATAFLOW as in dataflow architecture means of arranging computer data processing in which operations are governed by the data present and the processing it requires rather than by a prewritten program that awaits data to be processed

DATAGLOVE n computing term

DATAL adj slow-witted ▷ n day labour

DATALLER n worker paid by the day

DATALLERS > DATALLER

DATALS > DATAL

DATARIA n Roman Catholic office

DATARIAS > DATARIA

DATARIES > DATARY

DATARY n head of the dataria, the papal office that assesses candidates for benefices reserved to the Holy See

DATCHA same as > DACHA

DATCHAS > DATCHA

DATE n specified day of the month ▷ vb mark with the date

DATEABLE > DATE

DATEBOOK n list of forthcoming events

DATEBOOKS > DATEBOOK

DATED adj old-fashioned

DATEDLY > DATED

DATEDNESS > DATED

DATELESS > DATE

DATELINE n information about the place and time a story was written, placed at the top of the article

DATELINED > DATELINE

DATELINES > DATELINE

DATER n person who dates

DATERS > DATER

DATES > DATE

DATING n any of several techniques, such as radioactive dating, dendrochronology, or varve dating, for establishing the age of rocks, palaeontological or archaeological specimens, etc

DATINGS > DATING

DATIVAL > DATIVE

DATIVE adj denoting a case of nouns, pronouns, and adjectives used to express the indirect object ▷ n this grammatical case

DATIVELY > DATIVE

DATIVES > DATIVE

DATO n chief of any of certain Muslim tribes in the Philippine Islands

DATOLITE n colourless mineral

DATOLITES > DATOLITE

DATOS > DATO

DATTO n Datsun car

DATTOS > DATTO

DATUM n single piece of information in the form of a fact or statistic

DATUMS > DATUM

DATURA n any of various chiefly Indian solanaceous plants of the genus Datura, such as the moonflower and thorn apple, having large trumpet-shaped flowers, prickly pods, and narcotic properties

DATURAS > DATURA

DATURIC > DATURA

DATURINE n poisonous alkaloid

DATURINES > DATURINE

DAUB vb smear or spread quickly or clumsily ▷ n crude or badly done painting

DAUBE n braised meat stew

DAUBED > DAUB

DAUBER > DAUB

DAUBERIES > DAUBERY

DAUBERS > DAUB

DAUBERY n act or an instance of daubing

DAUBES > DAUBE

DAUBIER > DAUB

DAUBIEST > DAUB

DAUBING > DAUB

DAUBINGLY > DAUB

DAUBINGS > DAUB

DAUBRIES > DAUBRY

DAUBRY n unskilful painting

DAUBS > DAUB

DAUBY > DAUB

DAUD n lump or chunk of something ▷ vb (in dialect) whack

DAUDED > DAUD

DAUDING > DAUD

DAUDS > DAUD

DAUGHTER n female child ▷ adj denoting a cell, chromosome, etc produced by the division of one of its own kind

DAUGHTERS > DAUGHTER

DAULT n foster child

DAULTS > DAULT

DAUNDER vb stroll

DAUNDERED > DAUNDER

DAUNDERS > DAUNDER

DAUNER vb stroll

DAUNERED > DAUNER

DAUNERING > DAUNER

DAUNERS > DAUNER

DAUNT vb intimidate

DAUNTED > DAUNT

DAUNTER > DAUNT

DAUNTERS > DAUNT

DAUNTING adj intimidating or worrying

DAUNTLESS adj fearless

DAUNTON vb dishearten

DAUNTONED > DAUNTON

DAUNTONS > DAUNTON

DAUNTS > DAUNT

DAUPHIN n (formerly) eldest son of the king of France

DAUPHINE n wife of a dauphin

DAUPHINES > DAUPHINE

DAUPHINS > DAUPHIN

DAUR a Scot word for > DARE

d

DAURED > DAUR
DAURING > DAUR
DAURS > DAUR
DAUT vb fondle
DAUTED > DAUT
DAUTIE n darling
DAUTIES > DAUTIE
DAUTING > DAUT
DAUTS > DAUT
DAVEN vb pray
DAVENED > DAVEN
DAVENING > DAVEN
DAVENPORT n small writing table with drawers
DAVENS > DAVEN
DAVIDIA n Chinese shrub
DAVIDIAS > DAVIDIA
DAVIES > DAVY
DAVIT n crane, usu one of a pair, at a ship's side, for lowering and hoisting a lifeboat
DAVITS > DAVIT
DAVY n miner's safety lamp
DAW n an archaic, dialect, or poetic name for a jackdaw ▷ vb old word for dawn
DAWAH n practice of educating non-Muslims about the message of Islam
DAWAHS > DAWAH
DAWBAKE n foolish or slow-witted person
DAWBAKES > DAWBAKE
DAWBRIES > DAWBRY
DAWBRY n unskilful painting
DAWCOCK n male jackdaw
DAWCOCKS > DAWCOCK
DAWD vb thump
DAWDED > DAWD
DAWDING > DAWD
DAWDLE vb walk slowly, lag behind
DAWDLED > DAWDLE
DAWDLER > DAWDLE
DAWDLERS > DAWDLE
DAWDLES > DAWDLE
DAWDLING > DAWDLE
DAWDS > DAWD
DAWED > DAW
DAWEN > DAW
DAWING > DAW
DAWISH > DAW
DAWK same as > DAK
DAWKS > DAWK
DAWN n daybreak ▷ vb begin to grow light
DAWNED > DAWN
DAWNER vb stroll
DAWNERED > DAWNER
DAWNERING > DAWNER
DAWNERS > DAWNER
DAWNEY adj (of a person) dull or slow
DAWNING > DAWN
DAWNINGS > DAWN
DAWNLIKE > DAWN
DAWNS > DAWN
DAWS > DAW
DAWSONITE n mineral
DAWT vb fondle
DAWTED > DAWT
DAWTIE n darling
DAWTIES > DAWTIE
DAWTING > DAWT
DAWTS > DAWT
DAY n period of 24 hours

DAYAN n senior rabbi, esp one who sits in a religious court
DAYANIM > DAYAN
DAYANS > DAYAN
DAYBED n narrow bed with a head piece and sometimes a foot piece and back, for day use
DAYBEDS > DAYBED
DAYBOOK n book in which the transactions of each day are recorded as they occur
DAYBOOKS > DAYBOOK
DAYBOY n boy who attends a boarding school daily, but returns home each evening
DAYBOYS > DAYBOY
DAYBREAK n time in the morning when light first appears
DAYBREAKS > DAYBREAK
DAYCARE n occupation, treatment, or supervision during the working day for people who might be at risk if left on their own, or whose usual carers need daytime relief
DAYCARES > DAYCARE
DAYCENTRE n building used for daycare or other welfare services
DAYCH vb thatch
DAYCHED > DAYCH
DAYCHES > DAYCH
DAYCHING > DAYCH
DAYDREAM n pleasant fantasy indulged in while awake ▷ vb indulge in idle fantasy
DAYDREAMS > DAYDREAM
DAYDREAMT > DAYDREAM
DAYDREAMY > DAYDREAM
DAYFLIES > DAYFLY
DAYFLOWER n any of various tropical and subtropical plants of the genus *Commelina*, having jointed creeping stems, narrow pointed leaves, and blue or purplish flowers which wilt quickly: family *Commelinaceae*
DAYFLY another name for > MAYFLY
DAYGLO n fluorescent colours
DAYGLOW n fluorescent colours
DAYGLOWS > DAYGLOW
DAYLIGHT n light from the sun
DAYLIGHTS pl n consciousness or wits
DAYLILIES > DAYLILY
DAYLILY n any of various plants having lily-like flowers that typically last only one day before being succeeded by others
DAYLIT > DAYLIGHT
DAYLONG adv lasting the entire day
DAYMARE n bad dream during the day

DAYMARES > DAYMARE
DAYMARK n navigation aid
DAYMARKS > DAYMARK
DAYNT adj dainty
DAYROOM n communal living room in a residential institution
DAYROOMS > DAYROOM
DAYS adv during the day, esp regularly
DAYSACK n rucksack
DAYSACKS > DAYSACK
DAYSHELL n thistle
DAYSHELLS > DAYSHELL
DAYSIDE n side of a planet nearest the sun
DAYSIDES > DAYSIDE
DAYSMAN n umpire
DAYSMEN > DAYSMAN
DAYSPRING a poetic word for > DAWN
DAYSTAR a poetic word for > SUN
DAYSTARS > DAYSTAR
DAYTALE n day labour
DAYTALER n worker paid by the day
DAYTALERS > DAYTALER
DAYTALES > DAYTALE
DAYTIME n time from sunrise to sunset
DAYTIMES > DAYTIME
DAYWORK n daytime work
DAYWORKER > DAYWORK
DAYWORKS > DAYWORK
DAZE vb stun, by a blow or shock ▷ n state of confusion or shock
DAZED > DAZE
DAZEDLY > DAZE
DAZEDNESS > DAZE
DAZER > DAZE
DAZERS > DAZE
DAZES > DAZE
DAZING > DAZE
DAZZLE vb impress greatly ▷ n bright light that dazzles
DAZZLED > DAZZLE
DAZZLER > DAZZLE
DAZZLERS > DAZZLE
DAZZLES > DAZZLE
DAZZLING > DAZZLE
DAZZLINGS > DAZZLING
DE prep of or from
DEACIDIFY vb removal acid from
DEACON n ordained minister ranking immediately below a priest ▷ vb make a deacon of
DEACONED > DEACON
DEACONESS n (in the early church and in some modern Churches) a female member of the laity with duties similar to those of a deacon
DEACONING > DEACON
DEACONRY n office or status of a deacon
DEACONS > DEACON
DEAD adj no longer alive ▷ n period during which coldness or darkness is most intense ▷ adv extremely ▷ vb in archaic

usage, die or kill
DEADBEAT n lazy useless person
DEADBEATS > DEADBEAT
DEADBOLT n bolt operated without a spring
DEADBOLTS > DEADBOLT
DEADBOY > DEADMAN
DEADBOYS > DEADBOY
DEADED > DEAD
DEADEN vb make less intense
DEADENED > DEADEN
DEADENER > DEADEN
DEADENERS > DEADEN
DEADENING > DEADEN
DEADENS > DEADEN
DEADER > DEAD
DEADERS > DEAD
DEADEST > DEAD
DEADEYE n either of a pair of disclike wooden blocks, supported by straps in grooves around them, between which a line is rove so as to draw them together to tighten a shroud
DEADEYES > DEADEYE
DEADFALL n type of trap, used esp for catching large animals, in which a heavy weight falls to crush the prey
DEADFALLS > DEADFALL
DEADHEAD n person who does not pay on a bus, at a game, etc ▷ vb cut off withered flowers from (a plant)
DEADHEADS > DEADHEAD
DEADHOUSE n mortuary
DEADING > DEAD
DEADLIER > DEADLY
DEADLIEST > DEADLY
DEADLIFT vb weightlifting term
DEADLIFTS > DEADLIFT
DEADLIGHT n bull's-eye let into the deck or hull of a vessel to admit light to a cabin
DEADLINE n time limit ▷ vb put a time limit on an action, decision, etc
DEADLINED > DEADLINE
DEADLINES > DEADLINE
DEADLOCK n point in a dispute at which no agreement can be reached ▷ vb bring or come to a deadlock
DEADLOCKS > DEADLOCK
DEADLY adj likely to cause death ▷ adv extremely
DEADMAN n heavy plate, wall, or block buried in the ground that acts as an anchor for a retaining wall, sheet pile, etc, by a tie connecting the two
DEADMEN > DEADMAN
DEADNESS > DEAD
DEADPAN adv showing no emotion or expression ▷ adj deliberately emotionless ▷ n deadpan

expression or manner
DEADPANS > DEADPAN
DEADS > DEAD
DEADSTOCK n farm equipment
DEADWOOD n dead trees or branches
DEADWOODS > DEADWOOD
DEAERATE vb remove air from
DEAERATED > DEAERATE
DEAERATES > DEAERATE
DEAERATOR > DEAERATE
DEAF adj unable to hear
DEAFBLIND adj unable to hear or see
DEAFEN vb make deaf, esp temporarily
DEAFENED > DEAFEN
DEAFENING n excessively loud
DEAFENS > DEAFEN
DEAFER > DEAF
DEAFEST > DEAF
DEAFISH > DEAF
DEAFLY > DEAF
DEAFNESS > DEAF
DEAIR vb reove air from
DEAIRED > DEAIR
DEAIRING > DEAIR
DEAIRS > DEAIR
DEAL n agreement or transaction ▷ vb inflict (a blow) on ▷ adj of fir or pine
DEALATE adj (of ants and other insects) having lost their wings, esp by biting or rubbing them off after mating ▷ n insect that has shed its wings
DEALATED same as > DEALATE
DEALATES > DEALATE
DEALATION > DEALATE
DEALBATE adj bleached
DEALER n person whose business involves buying and selling
DEALERS > DEALER
DEALFISH n long thin fish
DEALING > DEAL
DEALINGS pl n transactions or business relations
DEALS > DEAL
DEALT > DEAL
DEAMINASE n enzyme that breaks down amino compounds
DEAMINATE vb remove one or more amino groups from (a molecule)
DEAMINISE same as > DEAMINATE
DEAMINIZE same as > DEAMINATE
DEAN n chief administrative official of a college or university faculty ▷ vb punish (a student) by sending them to the dean
DEANED > DEAN
DEANER n shilling
DEANERIES > DEANERY
DEANERS > DEANER
DEANERY n office or residence of a dean
DEANING > DEAN

DEANS > DEAN
DEANSHIP > DEAN
DEANSHIPS > DEAN
DEAR n someone regarded with affection ▷ adj much-loved
DEARE vb harm
DEARED > DEARE
DEARER > DEAR
DEARES > DEARE
DEAREST > DEAR
DEARIE same as > DEARY
DEARIES > DEARY
DEARING > DEARE
DEARLING n darling
DEARLINGS > DEARLING
DEARLY adv very much
DEARN vb hide
DEARNESS > DEAR
DEARNFUL adj secret
DEARNLY > DEARN
DEARNS > DEARN
DEARS > DEAR
DEARTH n inadequate amount, scarcity
DEARTHS > DEARTH
DEARY n term of affection: now often sarcastic or facetious
DEASH vb remove ash from
DEASHED > DEASH
DEASHES > DEASH
DEASHING > DEASH
DEASIL adv in the direction of the apparent course of the sun ▷ n motion in this direction
DEASILS > DEASIL
DEASIUL n motion towards the sun
DEASIULS > DEASIUL
DEASOIL n motion towards the sun
DEASOILS > DEASOIL
DEATH n permanent end of life in a person or animal
DEATHBED n bed where a person is about to die or has just died
DEATHBEDS > DEATHBED
DEATHBLOW n thing or event that destroys hope
DEATHCUP n poisonous fungus
DEATHCUPS > DEATHCUP
DEATHFUL adj murderous
DEATHIER > DEATH
DEATHIEST > DEATH
DEATHLESS adj everlasting, because of fine qualities
DEATHLIER > DEATHLY
DEATHLIKE > DEATH
DEATHLY adv like death ▷ adj resembling death
DEATHS > DEATH
DEATHSMAN n executioner
DEATHSMEN > DEATHSMAN
DEATHTRAP n building, vehicle, etc, that is considered very unsafe
DEATHWARD adv heading towards death
DEATHY > DEATH
DEAVE vb deafen
DEAVED > DEAVE
DEAVES > DEAVE
DEAVING > DEAVE

DEAW n dew
DEAWIE > DEAW
DEAWS > DEAW
DEAWY > DEAW
DEB n debutante
DEBACLE n disastrous failure
DEBACLES > DEBACLE
DEBAG vb remove the trousers from (someone) by force
DEBAGGED > DEBAG
DEBAGGING > DEBAG
DEBAGS > DEBAG
DEBAR vb prevent, bar
DEBARK vb remove the bark from (a tree)
DEBARKED > DEBARK
DEBARKER > DEBARK
DEBARKERS > DEBARK
DEBARKING > DEBARK
DEBARKS > DEBARK
DEBARMENT > DEBAR
DEBARRASS vb relieve
DEBARRED > DEBAR
DEBARRING > DEBAR
DEBARS > DEBAR
DEBASE vb lower in value, quality, or character
DEBASED > DEBASE
DEBASER > DEBASE
DEBASERS > DEBASE
DEBASES > DEBASE
DEBASING > DEBASE
DEBATABLE adj not absolutely certain
DEBATABLY > DEBATABLE
DEBATE n discussion ▷ vb discuss formally
DEBATED > DEBATE
DEBATEFUL adj quarrelsome
DEBATER > DEBATE
DEBATERS > DEBATE
DEBATES > DEBATE
DEBATING > DEBATE
DEBAUCH vb make (someone) bad or corrupt, esp sexually ▷ n instance or period of extreme dissipation
DEBAUCHED > DEBAUCH
DEBAUCHEE n man who leads a life of reckless drinking, promiscuity, and self-indulgence
DEBAUCHER > DEBAUCH
DEBAUCHES > DEBAUCH
DEBBIER > DEBBY
DEBBIES > DEBBY
DEBBIEST > DEBBY
DEBBY n debutante ▷ adj of, or resembling a debutante
DEBE n tin
DEBEAK vb remove part of the beak of poultry to reduce the risk of such habits as feather-picking or cannibalism
DEBEAKED > DEBEAK
DEBEAKING > DEBEAK
DEBEAKS > DEBEAK
DEBEARD vb remove beard from mussel
DEBEARDED > DEBEARD
DEBEARDS > DEBEARD

DEBEL vb beat in war
DEBELLED > DEBEL
DEBELLING > DEBEL
DEBELS > DEBEL
DEBENTURE n long-term bond bearing fixed interest, issued by a company or a government agency
DEBES > DEBE
DEBILE adj lacking strength
DEBILITY n weakness, infirmity
DEBIT n acknowledgment of a sum owing by entry on the left side of an account ▷ vb charge (an account) with a debt
DEBITED > DEBIT
DEBITING > DEBIT
DEBITOR n person in debt
DEBITORS > DEBITOR
DEBITS > DEBIT
DEBONAIR adj (of a man) charming and refined
DEBONAIRE adj sauve and refined
DEBONE vb remove bones from
DEBONED > DEBONE
DEBONER > DEBONE
DEBONERS > DEBONE
DEBONES > DEBONE
DEBONING > DEBONE
DEBOSH vb debauch
DEBOSHED > DEBOSH
DEBOSHES > DEBOSH
DEBOSHING > DEBOSH
DEBOSS vb carve a design into
DEBOSSED > DEBOSS
DEBOSSES > DEBOSS
DEBOSSING > DEBOSS
DEBOUCH vb move out from a narrow place to a wider one ▷ n outlet or passage, as for the exit of troops
DEBOUCHE same as > DEBOUCH
DEBOUCHED > DEBOUCH
DEBOUCHES > DEBOUCH
DEBRIDE vb remove dead tissue from
DEBRIDED > DEBRIDE
DEBRIDES > DEBRIDE
DEBRIDING > DEBRIDE
DEBRIEF vb receive a report from (a soldier, diplomat, etc) after an event
DEBRIEFED > DEBRIEF
DEBRIEFER > DEBRIEF
DEBRIEFS > DEBRIEF
DEBRIS n fragments of something destroyed
DEBRUISE vb (in heraldry) overlay or partly cover
DEBRUISED > DEBRUISE
DEBRUISES > DEBRUISE
DEBS > DEB
DEBT n something owed, esp money
DEBTED adj in debt
DEBTEE n person owed a debt
DEBTEES > DEBTEE
DEBTLESS > DEBT
DEBTOR n person who owes money

d

DEBTORS > DEBTOR
DEBTS > DEBT
DEBUD *same as* > DISBUD
DEBUDDED > DEBUD
DEBUDDING > DEBUD
DEBUDS > DEBUD
DEBUG *vb* find and remove defects in (a computer program) ▷ *n* something, esp a computer program, that locates and removes defects in a device, system, etc
DEBUGGED > DEBUG
DEBUGGER > DEBUG
DEBUGGERS > DEBUG
DEBUGGING > DEBUG
DEBUGS > DEBUG
DEBUNK *vb* expose the falseness of
DEBUNKED > DEBUNK
DEBUNKER > DEBUNK
DEBUNKERS > DEBUNK
DEBUNKING > DEBUNK
DEBUNKS > DEBUNK
DEBURR *vb* remove burrs from (a workpiece)
DEBURRED > DEBURR
DEBURRING > DEBURR
DEBURRS > DEBURR
DEBUS *vb* unload (goods) or (esp of troops) to alight from a motor vehicle
DEBUSED > DEBUS
DEBUSES > DEBUS
DEBUSING > DEBUS
DEBUSSED > DEBUS
DEBUSSES > DEBUS
DEBUSSING > DEBUS
DEBUT *n* first public appearance of a performer ▷ *vb* make a debut
DEBUTANT *n* person who is making a first appearance in a particular capacity, such as a sportsperson playing in a first game for a team
DEBUTANTE *n* young upper-class woman being formally presented to society
DEBUTANTS > DEBUTANT
DEBUTED > DEBUT
DEBUTING > DEBUT
DEBUTS > DEBUT
DEBYE *n* unit of electric dipole moment
DEBYES > DEBYE
DECACHORD *n* instrument with ten strings
DECAD *n* ten years
DECADAL > DECADE
DECADE *n* period of ten years
DECADENCE *n* deterioration in morality or culture
DECADENCY *same as* > DECADENCE
DECADENT *adj* characterized by decay or decline, as in being self-indulgent or morally corrupt ▷ *n* decadent person
DECADENTS > DECADENT
DECADES > DECADE
DECADS > DECAD

DECAF *n* decaffeinated coffee ▷ *adj* decaffeinated
DECAFF *n* decaffeinated coffee
DECAFFS > DECAFF
DECAFS > DECAF
DECAGON *n* geometric figure with ten faces
DECAGONAL > DECAGON
DECAGONS > DECAGON
DECAGRAM *n* ten grams
DECAGRAMS > DECAGRAM
DECAHEDRA *n* plural form of singular decahedron: solid figure with ten plane faces
DECAL *vb* transfer (a design) by decalcomania
DECALCIFY *vb* remove calcium or lime from (bones, teeth, etc)
DECALED > DECAL
DECALING > DECAL
DECALITER *same as* > DECALITRE
DECALITRE *n* measure of volume equivalent to 10 litres
DECALLED > DECAL
DECALLING > DECAL
DECALOG *same as* > DECALOGUE
DECALOGS > DECALOG
DECALOGUE *n* Ten Commandments
DECALS > DECAL
DECAMETER *same as* > DECAMETRE
DECAMETRE *n* unit of length equal to ten metres
DECAMP *vb* depart secretly or suddenly
DECAMPED > DECAMP
DECAMPING > DECAMP
DECAMPS > DECAMP
DECANAL *adj* of or relating to a dean or deanery
DECANALLY > DECANAL
DECANE *n* liquid alkane hydrocarbon
DECANES > DECANE
DECANI *adv* be sung by the decanal side of a choir
DECANOIC *as in decanoic acid* white crystalline insoluble carboxylic acid with an unpleasant odour, used in perfumes and for making fruit flavours
DECANT *vb* pour (a liquid) from one container to another
DECANTATE *vb* decant
DECANTED > DECANT
DECANTER *n* stoppered bottle for wine or spirits
DECANTERS > DECANTER
DECANTING > DECANT
DECANTS > DECANT
DECAPOD *n* creature, such as a crab, with five pairs of walking limbs ▷ *adj* of, relating to, or belonging to these creatures
DECAPODAL > DECAPOD
DECAPODAN > DECAPOD
DECAPODS > DECAPOD
DECARB *vb* decoke

DECARBED > DECARB
DECARBING > DECARB
DECARBS > DECARB
DECARE *n* ten ares or 1000 square metres
DECARES > DECARE
DECASTERE *n* ten steres
DECASTICH *n* poem with ten lines
DECASTYLE *n* portico consisting of ten columns
DECATHLON *n* athletic contest with ten events
DECAUDATE *vb* remove the tail from
DECAY *vb* become weaker or more corrupt ▷ *n* process of decaying
DECAYABLE > DECAY
DECAYED > DECAY
DECAYER > DECAY
DECAYERS > DECAY
DECAYING > DECAY
DECAYLESS *adj* immortal
DECAYS > DECAY
DECCIE *n* decoration
DECCIES > DECCIE
DECEASE *n* death
DECEASED *adj* dead ▷ *n* dead person
DECEASES > DECEASE
DECEASING > DECEASE
DECEDENT *n* deceased person
DECEDENTS > DECEDENT
DECEIT *n* behaviour intended to deceive
DECEITFUL *adj* full of deceit
DECEITS > DECEIT
DECEIVE *vb* mislead by lying
DECEIVED > DECEIVE
DECEIVER > DECEIVE
DECEIVERS > DECEIVE
DECEIVES > DECEIVE
DECEIVING > DECEIVE
DECELERON *n* type of aileron
DECEMVIR *n* (in ancient Rome) a member of a board of ten magistrates, esp either of the two commissions established in 451 and 450 BC to revise the laws
DECEMVIRI > DECEMVIR
DECEMVIRS > DECEMVIR
DECENARY *adj* of or relating to a tithing
DECENCIES *pl n* generally accepted standards of good behaviour
DECENCY *n* conformity to the prevailing standards of what is right
DECENNARY *same as* > DECENARY
DECENNIA > DECENNIUM
DECENNIAL *adj* lasting for ten years ▷ *n* tenth anniversary or its celebration
DECENNIUM *a less common word for* > DECADE
DECENT *adj* (of a person) polite and morally acceptable
DECENTER *vb* put out of centre

DECENTERS > DECENTER
DECENTEST > DECENT
DECENTLY > DECENT
DECENTRE *vb* put out of centre
DECENTRED > DECENTRE
DECENTRES > DECENTRE
DECEPTION *n* deceiving
DECEPTIVE *adj* likely or designed to deceive
DECEPTORY *adj* deceiving
DECERN *vb* decree or adjudge
DECERNED > DECERN
DECERNING > DECERN
DECERNS > DECERN
DECERTIFY *vb* withdraw or remove a certificate or certification from (a person, organization, or country)
DECESSION *n* departure
DECHEANCE *n* forfeiting
DECIARE *n* one tenth of an are or 10 square metres
DECIARES > DECIARE
DECIBEL *n* unit for measuring the intensity of sound
DECIBELS > DECIBEL
DECIDABLE *adj* able to be decided
DECIDE *vb* (cause to) reach a decision
DECIDED *adj* unmistakable
DECIDEDLY > DECIDED
DECIDER *n* point, goal, game, etc, that determines who wins a match or championship
DECIDERS > DECIDER
DECIDES > DECIDE
DECIDING > DECIDE
DECIDUA *n* specialized mucous membrane that lines the uterus of some mammals during pregnancy: is shed, with the placenta, at parturition
DECIDUAE > DECIDUA
DECIDUAL > DECIDUA
DECIDUAS > DECIDUA
DECIDUATE > DECIDUA
DECIDUOUS *adj* (of a tree) shedding its leaves annually
DECIGRAM *n* tenth of a gram
DECIGRAMS > DECIGRAM
DECILE *n* one of nine actual or notional values of a variable dividing its distribution into ten groups with equal frequencies: the ninth decile is the value below which 90% of the population lie
DECILES > DECILE
DECILITER *same as* > DECILITRE
DECILITRE *n* measure of volume equivalent to one tenth of a litre
DECILLION *n* (in Britain, France, and Germany) the number represented as one followed by 60 zeros (10^{60})
DECIMAL *n* fraction written

in the form of a dot followed by one or more numbers ▷ *adj* relating to or using powers of ten

DECIMALLY > DECIMAL

DECIMALS > DECIMAL

DECIMATE *vb* destroy or kill a large proportion of

DECIMATED > DECIMATE

DECIMATES > DECIMATE

DECIMATOR > DECIMATE

DECIME *n* a former French coin

DECIMES > DECIME

DECIMETER *same as* > DECIMETRE

DECIMETRE *n* unit of length equal to one tenth of a metre

DECIPHER *vb* work out the meaning of (something illegible or in code)

DECIPHERS > DECIPHER

DECISION *n* judgment, conclusion, or resolution

DECISIONS > DECISION

DECISIVE *adj* having a definite influence

DECISORY *adj* deciding

DECISTERE *n* tenth of a stere

DECK *n* area of a ship that forms a floor dress or decorate)

DECKCHAIR *n* folding wooden and canvas chair designed for use outside

DECKED *adj* having a wooden deck or platform

DECKEL *same as* > DECKLE

DECKELS > DECKEL

DECKER > DECK

DECKERS > DECK

DECKHAND *n* seaman assigned various duties, such as mooring and cargo handling, on the deck of a ship

DECKHANDS > DECKHAND

DECKHOUSE *n* houselike cabin on the deck of a ship

DECKING *n* wooden platform in a garden

DECKINGS > DECKING

DECKLE *n* frame used to contain pulp on the mould in the making of handmade paper

DECKLED > DECKLE

DECKLES > DECKLE

DECKO *n* look ▷ *vb* have a look

DECKOED > DECKO

DECKOING > DECKO

DECKOS > DECKO

DECKS > DECK

DECLAIM *vb* speak loudly and dramatically

DECLAIMED > DECLAIM

DECLAIMER > DECLAIM

DECLAIMS > DECLAIM

DECLARANT *n* person who makes a declaration

DECLARE *vb* state firmly and forcefully

DECLARED > DECLARE

DECLARER *n* person who

declares

DECLARERS > DECLARER

DECLARES > DECLARE

DECLARING > DECLARE

DECLASS *vb* lower in social status or position

DECLASSE *adj* having lost social standing or status

DECLASSED > DECLASS

DECLASSEE *adj* (of a woman) having lost social standing or status

DECLASSES > DECLASS

DECLAW *vb* remove claws from

DECLAWED > DECLAW

DECLAWING > DECLAW

DECLAWS > DECLAW

DECLINAL *adj* bending down

DECLINANT *adj* heraldry term

DECLINATE *adj* (esp of plant parts) descending from the horizontal in a curve

DECLINE *vb* become smaller, weaker, or less important ▷ *n* gradual weakening or loss

DECLINED > DECLINE

DECLINER > DECLINE

DECLINERS > DECLINE

DECLINES > DECLINE

DECLINING > DECLINE

DECLINIST *n* person believing something is in decline

DECLIVITY *n* downward slope

DECLIVOUS *adj* steep

DECLUTCH *vb* disengage the clutch of a motor vehicle

DECLUTTER *vb* simplify or get rid of mess, disorder, complications, etc

DECO as in *art deco* style of art, jewellery, design, etc

DECOCT *vb* extract the essence from (a substance) by boiling

DECOCTED > DECOCT

DECOCTING > DECOCT

DECOCTION *n* extraction by boiling

DECOCTIVE > DECOCT

DECOCTS > DECOCT

DECOCTURE *n* substance obtained by decoction

DECODE *vb* convert from code into ordinary language

DECODED > DECODE

DECODER > DECODE

DECODERS > DECODE

DECODES > DECODE

DECODING > DECODE

DECOHERER *n* electrical device

DECOKE *same as* > DECARBONIZE

DECOKED > DECOKE

DECOKES > DECOKE

DECOKING > DECOKE

DECOLLATE *vb* separate (continuous stationery, etc) into individual forms

DECOLLETE *adj* (of a

woman's garment) low-cut ▷ *n* low-cut neckline

DECOLOR *vb* bleach

DECOLORED > DECOLOR

DECOLORS > DECOLOR

DECOLOUR *vb* deprive of colour, as by bleaching

DECOLOURS > DECOLOUR

DECOMMIT *vb* withdraw from a commitment or agreed course of action

DECOMMITS > DECOMMIT

DECOMPLEX *adj* repeatedly compound

DECOMPOSE *vb* be broken down through chemical or bacterial action

DECONGEST *vb* relieve congestion in

DECONTROL *vb* free of restraints or controls, esp government controls

DECOR *n* style in which a room or house is decorated

DECORATE *vb* make more attractive by adding something ornamental

DECORATED > DECORATE

DECORATES > DECORATE

DECORATOR *n* person whose profession is the painting and wallpapering of buildings

DECOROUS *adj* polite, calm, and sensible in behaviour

DECORS > DECOR

DECORUM *n* polite and socially correct behaviour

DECORUMS > DECORUM

DECOS > DECO

DECOUPAGE *n* art or process of decorating a surface with shapes or illustrations cut from paper, card, etc

DECOUPLE *vb* separate (joined or coupled subsystems) thereby enabling them to exist and operate separately

DECOUPLED > DECOUPLE

DECOUPLER > DECOUPLE

DECOUPLES > DECOUPLE

DECOY *n* person or thing used to lure someone into danger ▷ *vb* lure away by means of a trick

DECOYED > DECOY

DECOYER > DECOY

DECOYERS > DECOY

DECOYING > DECOY

DECOYS > DECOY

DECREASE *vb* make or become less ▷ *n* lessening, reduction

DECREASED > DECREASE

DECREASES > DECREASE

DECREE *n* law made by someone in authority ▷ *vb* order by decree

DECREED > DECREE

DECREEING > DECREE

DECREER > DECREE

DECREERS > DECREE

DECREES > DECREE

DECREET *n* final judgment or sentence of a court

DECREETS > DECREET

DECREMENT *n* act of decreasing

DECREPIT *adj* weakened or worn out by age or long use

DECRETAL *n* papal decree ▷ *adj* of or relating to a decretal or a decree

DECRETALS > DECRETAL

DECRETIST *n* law student

DECRETIVE *adj* of a decree

DECRETORY *adj* of a decree

DECREW *vb* decrease

DECREWED > DECREW

DECREWING > DECREW

DECREWS > DECREW

DECRIAL > DECRY

DECRIALS > DECRY

DECRIED > DECRY

DECRIER > DECRY

DECRIERS > DECRY

DECRIES > DECRY

DECROWN *vb* depose

DECROWNED > DECROWN

DECROWNS > DECROWN

DECRY *vb* express disapproval of

DECRYING > DECRY

DECRYPT *vb* decode (a message) with or without previous knowledge of its key

DECRYPTED > DECRYPT

DECRYPTS > DECRYPT

DECTET *n* ten musicians

DECTETS > DECTET

DECUBITAL > DECUBITUS

DECUBITI > DECUBITUS

DECUBITUS *n* posture adopted when lying down

DECUMAN *n* large wave

DECUMANS > DECUMAN

DECUMBENT *adj* lying down or lying flat

DECUPLE *vb* increase by ten times ▷ *n* amount ten times as large as a given reference ▷ *adj* increasing tenfold

DECUPLED > DECUPLE

DECUPLES > DECUPLE

DECUPLING > DECUPLE

DECURIA *n* group of ten

DECURIAS > DECURIA

DECURIES > DECURY

DECURION *n* local councillor

DECURIONS > DECURION

DECURRENT *adj* extending down the stem, esp (of a leaf) having the base of the blade extending down the stem as two wings

DECURSION *n* state of being decurrent

DECURSIVE *adj* extending downwards

DECURVE *vb* curve downards

DECURVED *adj* bent or curved downwards

DECURVES > DECURVE

DECURVING > DECURVE

DECURY *n* (in ancient Rome) a body of ten men

DECUSSATE *vb* cross or cause to cross in the form of the letter X ▷ *adj* in the form of the letter X

DEDAL *same as* > DAEDAL
DEDALIAN *adj* of Daedalus
DEDANS *n* open gallery at the server's end of the court
DEDICANT *n* person who dedicates
DEDICANTS > DEDICANT
DEDICATE *vb* commit (oneself or one's time) wholly to a special purpose or cause
DEDICATED *adj* devoted to a particular purpose or cause
DEDICATEE > DEDICATE
DEDICATES > DEDICATE
DEDICATOR > DEDICATE
DEDIMUS *n* legal term
DEDIMUSES > DEDIMUS
DEDUCE *vb* reach (a conclusion) by reasoning from evidence
DEDUCED > DEDUCE
DEDUCES > DEDUCE
DEDUCIBLE > DEDUCE
DEDUCIBLY > DEDUCE
DEDUCING > DEDUCE
DEDUCT *vb* subtract
DEDUCTED > DEDUCT
DEDUCTING > DEDUCT
DEDUCTION *n* deducting
DEDUCTIVE *adj* of or relating to deduction
DEDUCTS > DEDUCT
DEE *a Scot word for* > DIE
DEED *n* something that is done ▷ *vb* convey or transfer (property) by deed ▷ *adj* Scots form of dead
DEEDED > DEED
DEEDER > DEED
DEEDEST > DEED
DEEDFUL *adj* full of exploits
DEEDIER > DEEDY
DEEDIEST > DEEDY
DEEDILY > DEEDY
DEEDING > DEED
DEEDLESS *adj* without exploits
DEEDS > DEED
DEEDY *adj* hard-working
DEEING > DEE
DEEJAY *n* disc jockey ▷ *vb* work or act as a disc jockey
DEEJAYED > DEEJAY
DEEJAYING > DEEJAY
DEEJAYS > DEEJAY
DEEK *vb* look at
DEELY *as in deely boppers* hairband with two bobbing antennae-like attachments
DEEM *vb* consider, judge
DEEMED > DEEM
DEEMING > DEEM
DEEMS > DEEM
DEEMSTER *n* title of one of the two justices in the Isle of Man
DEEMSTERS > DEEMSTER
DEEN *n* din
DEENS > DEEN
DEEP *adj* extending or situated far down, inwards, backwards, or sideways ▷ *n* any deep place on land or under water

DEEPEN *vb* make or become deeper or more intense
DEEPENED > DEEPEN
DEEPENER > DEEPEN
DEEPENERS > DEEPEN
DEEPENING > DEEPEN
DEEPENS > DEEPEN
DEEPER > DEEP
DEEPEST > DEEP
DEEPFELT *adj* sincere
DEEPFROZE *vb* froze in a freezer
DEEPIE *n* 3D film
DEEPIES > DEEPIE
DEEPLY > DEEP
DEEPMOST *adj* deepest
DEEPNESS > DEEP
DEEPS > DEEP
DEEPWATER *adj* seagoing
DEER *n* large wild animal, the male of which has antlers
DEERBERRY *n* huckleberry
DEERE *adj* serious
DEERFLIES > DEERFLY
DEERFLY *n* insect related to the horsefly
DEERGRASS *n* perennial cyperaceous plant, *Trichophorum caespitosum*, that grows in dense tufts in peat bogs of temperate regions
DEERHORN *n* deer's antler
DEERHORNS > DEERHORN
DEERHOUND *n* very large rough-coated breed of dog of the greyhound type
DEERLET *n* ruminant mammal
DEERLETS > DEERLET
DEERLIKE *adj* like a deer
DEERS > DEER
DEERSKIN *n* hide of a deer
DEERSKINS > DEERSKIN
DEERWEED *n* forage plant
DEERWEEDS > DEERWEED
DEERYARD *n* gathering place for deer
DEERYARDS > DEERYARD
DEES > DEE
DEET *n* insect-repellent
DEETS > DEET
DEEV *n* mythical monster
DEEVE *vb* deafen
DEEVED > DEEVE
DEEVES > DEEVE
DEEVING > DEEVE
DEEVS > DEEV
DEEWAN *n* chief of a village in India
DEEWANS > DEEWAN
DEF *adj* very good
DEFACE *vb* deliberately spoil the appearance of
DEFACED > DEFACE
DEFACER > DEFACE
DEFACERS > DEFACE
DEFACES > DEFACE
DEFACING > DEFACE
DEFAECATE *same as* > DEFECATE
DEFALCATE *vb* make wrong use of funds entrusted to one
DEFAME *vb* attack the good reputation of

DEFAMED > DEFAME
DEFAMER > DEFAME
DEFAMERS > DEFAME
DEFAMES > DEFAME
DEFAMING > DEFAME
DEFAMINGS > DEFAME
DEFANG *vb* remove the fangs of
DEFANGED > DEFANG
DEFANGING > DEFANG
DEFANGS > DEFANG
DEFAST *adj* defaced
DEFASTE *adj* defaced
DEFAT *vb* remove fat from
DEFATS > DEFAT
DEFATTED > DEFAT
DEFATTING > DEFAT
DEFAULT *n* failure to do something ▷ *vb* fail to fulfil an obligation
DEFAULTED > DEFAULT
DEFAULTER *n* person who defaults
DEFAULTS > DEFAULT
DEFEAT *vb* win a victory over ▷ *n* defeating
DEFEATED > DEFEAT
DEFEATER > DEFEAT
DEFEATERS > DEFEAT
DEFEATING > DEFEAT
DEFEATISM *n* ready acceptance or expectation of defeat
DEFEATIST > DEFEATISM
DEFEATS > DEFEAT
DEFEATURE *vb* deform
DEFECATE *vb* discharge waste from the body through the anus
DEFECATED > DEFECATE
DEFECATES > DEFECATE
DEFECATOR > DEFECATE
DEFECT *n* imperfection, blemish ▷ *vb* desert one's cause or country to join the opposing forces
DEFECTED > DEFECT
DEFECTING > DEFECT
DEFECTION *n* act or an instance of defecting
DEFECTIVE *adj* imperfect, faulty
DEFECTOR > DEFECT
DEFECTORS > DEFECT
DEFECTS > DEFECT
DEFENCE *n* resistance against attack
DEFENCED > DEFENCE
DEFENCES > DEFENCE
DEFENCING > DEFENCE
DEFEND *vb* protect from harm or danger
DEFENDANT *n* person accused of a crime ▷ *adj* making a defence
DEFENDED > DEFEND
DEFENDER > DEFEND
DEFENDERS > DEFEND
DEFENDING > DEFEND
DEFENDS > DEFEND
DEFENSE *same as* > DEFENCE
DEFENSED > DEFENSE
DEFENSES > DEFENSE
DEFENSING > DEFENSE
DEFENSIVE *adj* intended for defence
DEFER *vb* delay (something)

until a future time
DEFERABLE > DEFER
DEFERENCE *n* polite and respectful behaviour
DEFERENT *adj* (esp of a bodily nerve, vessel, or duct) conveying an impulse, fluid, etc, outwards, down, or away ▷ *n* (in the Ptolemaic system) a circle centred on the earth around which the centre of the epicycle was thought to move
DEFERENTS > DEFERENT
DEFERMENT *n* act of deferring or putting off until another time
DEFERRAL *same as* > DEFERMENT
DEFERRALS > DEFERRAL
DEFERRED *adj* withheld over a certain period
DEFERRER > DEFER
DEFERRERS > DEFER
DEFERRING > DEFER
DEFERS > DEFER
DEFFER > DEF
DEFFEST > DEF
DEFFLY *archaic word meaning the same as* > DEFTLY
DEFFO *interj* definitely: an expression of agreement or consent
DEFI *n* challenge
DEFIANCE *n* open resistance or disobedience
DEFIANCES > DEFIANCE
DEFIANT *adj* marked by resistance or bold opposition, as to authority
DEFIANTLY > DEFIANT
DEFICIENT *adj* lacking some essential thing or quality
DEFICIT *n* amount by which a sum of money is too small
DEFICITS > DEFICIT
DEFIED > DEFY
DEFIER > DEFY
DEFIERS > DEFY
DEFIES > DEFY
DEFILADE *n* protection provided by obstacles against enemy crossfire from the rear, or observation ▷ *vb* provide protection for by defilade
DEFILADED > DEFILADE
DEFILADES > DEFILADE
DEFILE *vb* treat (something sacred or important) without respect ▷ *n* narrow valley or pass
DEFILED > DEFILE
DEFILER > DEFILE
DEFILERS > DEFILE
DEFILES > DEFILE
DEFILING > DEFILE
DEFINABLE > DEFINE
DEFINABLY > DEFINE
DEFINE *vb* state precisely the meaning of
DEFINED > DEFINE
DEFINER > DEFINE
DEFINERS > DEFINE

Section 1: Words between 2 and 9 letters in length

DEFINES > DEFINE

DEFINIENS n word or words used to define or give an account of the meaning of another word, as in a dictionary entry

DEFINING > DEFINE

DEFINITE adj firm, clear, and precise

DEFIS > DEFI

DEFLATE vb (cause to) collapse through the release of air

DEFLATED > DEFLATE

DEFLATER > DEFLATE

DEFLATERS > DEFLATE

DEFLATES > DEFLATE

DEFLATING > DEFLATE

DEFLATION n reduction in economic activity resulting in lower output and investment

DEFLATOR > DEFLATE

DEFLATORS > DEFLATE

DEFLEA vb remove fleas from

DEFLEAED > DEFLEA

DEFLEAING > DEFLEA

DEFLEAS > DEFLEA

DEFLECT vb (cause to) turn aside from a course

DEFLECTED > DEFLECT

DEFLECTOR > DEFLECT

DEFLECTS > DEFLECT

DEFLEX vb turn downwards

DEFLEXED > DEFLEX

DEFLEXES > DEFLEX

DEFLEXING > DEFLEX

DEFLEXION same as > DEFLECTION

DEFLEXURE n act of deflecting

DEFLORATE vb deflower

DEFLOWER vb deprive (a woman) of her virginity

DEFLOWERS > DEFLOWER

DEFLUENT adj running downwards

DEFLUXION n discharge

DEFOAM vb remove foam from

DEFOAMED > DEFOAM

DEFOAMER > DEFOAM

DEFOAMERS > DEFOAM

DEFOAMING > DEFOAM

DEFOAMS > DEFOAM

DEFOCUS vb put out of focus

DEFOCUSED > DEFOCUS

DEFOCUSES > DEFOCUS

DEFOG vb clear of vapour

DEFOGGED > DEFOG

DEFOGGER > DEFOG

DEFOGGERS > DEFOG

DEFOGGING > DEFOG

DEFOGS > DEFOG

DEFOLIANT n chemical sprayed or dusted onto trees to cause their leaves to fall, esp to remove cover from an enemy in warfare

DEFOLIATE vb deprive (a plant) of its leaves ▷ adj (of a plant) having shed its leaves

DEFORCE vb withhold (property, esp land) wrongfully or by force from the rightful owner

DEFORCED > DEFORCE

DEFORCER > DEFORCE

DEFORCERS > DEFORCE

DEFORCES > DEFORCE

DEFORCING > DEFORCE

DEFOREST vb clear of trees

DEFORESTS > DEFOREST

DEFORM vb put out of shape or spoil the appearance of

DEFORMED adj disfigured or misshapen

DEFORMER > DEFORM

DEFORMERS > DEFORM

DEFORMING > DEFORM

DEFORMITY n distortion of a body part

DEFORMS > DEFORM

DEFOUL vb defile

DEFOULED > DEFOUL

DEFOULING > DEFOUL

DEFOULS > DEFOUL

DEFRAG vb defragment

DEFRAGGED > DEFRAG

DEFRAGGER > DEFRAG

DEFRAGS > DEFRAG

DEFRAUD vb cheat out of money, property, etc

DEFRAUDED > DEFRAUD

DEFRAUDER > DEFRAUD

DEFRAUDS > DEFRAUD

DEFRAY vb provide money for (costs or expenses)

DEFRAYAL > DEFRAY

DEFRAYALS > DEFRAY

DEFRAYED > DEFRAY

DEFRAYER > DEFRAY

DEFRAYERS > DEFRAY

DEFRAYING > DEFRAY

DEFRAYS > DEFRAY

DEFREEZE vb defrost

DEFREEZES > DEFREEZE

DEFROCK vb deprive (a priest) of priestly status

DEFROCKED > DEFROCK

DEFROCKS > DEFROCK

DEFROST vb make or become free of ice

DEFROSTED > DEFROST

DEFROSTER n device by which the de-icing process of a refrigerator is accelerated, usually by circulating the refrigerant without the expansion process

DEFROSTS > DEFROST

DEFROZE > DEFREEZE

DEFROZEN > DEFREEZE

DEFT adj quick and skilful in movement

DEFTER > DEFT

DEFTEST > DEFT

DEFTLY > DEFT

DEFTNESS > DEFT

DEFUEL vb remove fuel from

DEFUELED > DEFUEL

DEFUELING > DEFUEL

DEFUELLED > DEFUEL

DEFUELS > DEFUEL

DEFUNCT adj no longer existing or operative ▷ n deceased person

DEFUNCTS > DEFUNCT

DEFUND vb stop funds to

DEFUNDED > DEFUND

DEFUNDING > DEFUND

DEFUNDS > DEFUND

DEFUSE vb remove the fuse of (an explosive device)

DEFUSED > DEFUSE

DEFUSER > DEFUSE

DEFUSERS > DEFUEL

DEFUSES > DEFUSE

DEFUSING > DEFUSE

DEFUZE same as > DEFUSE

DEFUZED > DEFUZE

DEFUZES > DEFUZE

DEFUZING > DEFUZE

DEFY vb resist openly and boldly

DEFYING > DEFY

DEG vb water (a plant, etc)

DEGAGE adj unconstrained in manner

DEGAME n tree of South and Central America

DEGAMES > DEGAME

DEGAMI same as > DEGAME

DEGAMIS > DEGAMI

DEGARNISH vb remove ornament from

DEGAS vb remove gas from (a container, vacuum tube, liquid, adsorbent, etc)

DEGASES > DEGAS

DEGASSED > DEGAS

DEGASSER > DEGAS

DEGASSERS > DEGAS

DEGASSES > DEGAS

DEGASSING > DEGAS

DEGAUSS same as > DEMAGNETIZE

DEGAUSSED > DEGAUSS

DEGAUSSER > DEGAUSS

DEGAUSSES > DEGAUSS

DEGEARING n process in which a company replaces some or all of its fixed-interest loan stock with ordinary shares

DEGENDER vb remove reference to gender from

DEGENDERS > DEGENDER

DEGERM vb remove germs from

DEGERMED > DEGERM

DEGERMING > DEGERM

DEGERMS > DEGERM

DEGGED > DEG

DEGGING > DEG

DEGLAZE vb dilute meat sediments in (a pan) in order to make a sauce or gravy

DEGLAZED > DEGLAZE

DEGLAZES > DEGLAZE

DEGLAZING > DEGLAZE

DEGOUT n disgust

DEGOUTS > DEGOUT

DEGRADE vb reduce to dishonour or disgrace

DEGRADED > DEGRADE

DEGRADER > DEGRADE

DEGRADERS > DEGRADE

DEGRADES > DEGRADE

DEGRADING adj causing humiliation

DEGRAS n emulsion used for dressing hides

DEGREASE vb remove grease from

DEGREASED > DEGREASE

DEGREASER > DEGREASE

DEGREASES > DEGREASE

DEGREE n stage in a scale of relative amount or intensity

DEGREED adj having a degree

DEGREES > DEGREE

DEGS > DEG

DEGUM vb remove gum from

DEGUMMED > DEGUM

DEGUMMING > DEGUM

DEGUMS > DEGUM

DEGUST vb taste, esp with care or relish

DEGUSTATE same as > DEGUST

DEGUSTED > DEGUST

DEGUSTING > DEGUST

DEGUSTS > DEGUST

DEHISCE vb (of the seed capsules of some plants) to burst open spontaneously

DEHISCED > DEHISCE

DEHISCENT adj (of fruits, anthers, etc) opening spontaneously to release seeds or pollen

DEHISCES > DEHISCE

DEHISCING > DEHISCE

DEHORN vb remove or prevent the growth of the horns of (cattle, sheep, or goats)

DEHORNED > DEHORN

DEHORNER > DEHORN

DEHORNERS > DEHORN

DEHORNING > DEHORN

DEHORNS > DEHORN

DEHORT vb dissuade

DEHORTED > DEHORT

DEHORTER > DEHORT

DEHORTERS > DEHORT

DEHORTING > DEHORT

DEHORTS > DEHORT

DEHYDRATE vb remove water from (food) to preserve it

DEI > DEUS

DEICE vb to free or be freed of ice

DEICED > DEICE

DEICER > DEICE

DEICERS > DEICE

DEICES > DEICE

DEICIDAL > DEICIDE

DEICIDE n act of killing a god

DEICIDES > DEICIDE

DEICING > DEICE

DEICTIC adj proving by direct argument

DEICTICS > DEICTIC

DEID a Scot word for > DEAD

DEIDER > DEID

DEIDEST > DEID

DEIDS > DEID

DEIF a Scot word for > DEAF

DEIFER > DEIF

DEIFEST > DEIF

DEIFIC adj making divine or exalting to the position of a god

DEIFICAL adj divine

DEIFIED > DEIFY

DEIFIER > DEIFY

DEIFIERS > DEIFY

DEIFIES > DEIFY

d

d

DEIFORM adj having the form or appearance of a god
DEIFY vb treat or worship as a god
DEIFYING > DEIFY
DEIGN vb agree (to do something), but as if doing someone a favour
DEIGNED > DEIGN
DEIGNING > DEIGN
DEIGNS > DEIGN
DEIL a Scot word for > DEVIL
DEILS > DEIL
DEINDEX vb cause to become no longer index-linked
DEINDEXED > DEINDEX
DEINDEXES > DEINDEX
DEINOSAUR n dinosaur
DEIONISE same as > DEIONIZE
DEIONISED > DEIONISE
DEIONISER > DEIONISE
DEIONISES > DEIONISE
DEIONIZE vb to remove ions from (water, etc), esp by ion exchange
DEIONIZED > DEIONIZE
DEIONIZER > DEIONIZE
DEIONIZES > DEIONIZE
DEIPAROUS adj giving birth to a god
DEISEAL n clockwise motion
DEISEALS > DEISEAL
DEISHEAL n clockwise motion
DEISHEALS > DEISHEAL
DEISM n belief in God but not in divine revelation
DEISMS > DEISM
DEIST > DEISM
DEISTIC > DEISM
DEISTICAL > DEISM
DEISTS > DEISM
DEITIES > DEITY
DEITY n god or goddess
DEIXES > DEIXIS
DEIXIS n use or reference of a deictic word
DEIXISES > DEIXIS
DEJECT vb have a depressing effect on ▷ adj downcast
DEJECTA pl n waste products excreted through the anus
DEJECTED adj unhappy
DEJECTING > DEJECT
DEJECTION n lowness of spirits
DEJECTORY adj causing dejection
DEJECTS > DEJECT
DEJEUNE n lunch
DEJEUNER n lunch
DEJEUNERS > DEJEUNER
DEJEUNES > DEJEUNE
DEKAGRAM n ten grams
DEKAGRAMS > DEKAGRAM
DEKALITER n ten litres
DEKALITRE n ten litres
DEKALOGY n series of ten related works
DEKAMETER n ten meters
DEKAMETRE n ten metres

DEKARE n unit of measurement equal to ten ares
DEKARES > DEKARE
DEKE vb (in ice hockey or box lacrosse) to draw (a defending player) out of position by faking a shot or movement ▷ n such a shot or movement
DEKED > DEKE
DEKEING > DEKE
DEKES > DEKE
DEKING > DEKE
DEKKO n look ▷ vb have a look
DEKKOED > DEKKO
DEKKOING > DEKKO
DEKKOS > DEKKO
DEL n differential operator
DELAINE n sheer wool or wool and cotton fabric
DELAINES > DELAINE
DELAPSE vb be inherited
DELAPSED > DELAPSE
DELAPSES > DELAPSE
DELAPSING > DELAPSE
DELAPSION n falling down
DELATE vb (formerly) to bring a charge against
DELATED > DELATE
DELATES > DELATE
DELATING > DELATE
DELATION > DELATE
DELATIONS > DELATE
DELATOR > DELATE
DELATORS > DELATE
DELAY vb put off to a later time ▷ n act of delaying
DELAYABLE > DELAY
DELAYED > DELAY
DELAYER > DELAY
DELAYERS > DELAY
DELAYING > DELAY
DELAYS > DELAY
DELE n sign indicating that typeset matter is to be deleted ▷ vb mark (matter to be deleted) with a dele
DELEAD vb remove lead from
DELEADED > DELEAD
DELEADING > DELEAD
DELEADS > DELEAD
DELEAVE vb separate copies
DELEAVED > DELEAVE
DELEAVES > DELEAVE
DELEAVING > DELEAVE
DELEBLE adj able to be deleted
DELECTATE vb delight
DELED > DELE
DELEGABLE > DELEGATE
DELEGACY n elected standing committee at some British universities
DELEGATE n person chosen to represent others, esp at a meeting ▷ vb entrust (duties or powers) to someone
DELEGATED > DELEGATE
DELEGATEE > DELEGATE
DELEGATES > DELEGATE
DELEGATOR > DELEGATE
DELEING > DELE
DELENDA pl n items for

deleting
DELES > DELE
DELETABLE > DELETE
DELETE vb remove (something written or printed)
DELETED > DELETE
DELETES > DELETE
DELETING > DELETE
DELETION n act of deleting or fact of being deleted
DELETIONS > DELETION
DELETIVE > DELETE
DELETORY > DELETE
DELF n kind of earthenware
DELFS > DELF
DELFT n tin-glazed earthenware, typically having blue designs on white
DELFTS > DELFT
DELFTWARE same as > DELFT
DELI n delicatessen
DELIBATE vb taste
DELIBATED > DELIBATE
DELIBATES > DELIBATE
DELIBLE adj able to be deleted
DELICACY n being delicate
DELICATE adj fine or subtle in quality or workmanship ▷ n delicacy
DELICATES > DELICATE
DELICE n delicacy
DELICES > DELICE
DELICIOUS adj very appealing to taste or smell
DELICT n wrongful act for which the person injured has the right to a civil remedy
DELICTS > DELICT
DELIGHT n (source of) great pleasure ▷ vb please greatly
DELIGHTED adj greatly pleased ▷ sentence substitute I should be delighted to!
DELIGHTER > DELIGHT
DELIGHTS > DELIGHT
DELIME vb remove lime from
DELIMED > DELIME
DELIMES > DELIME
DELIMING > DELIME
DELIMIT vb mark or lay down the limits of
DELIMITED > DELIMIT
DELIMITER > DELIMIT
DELIMITS > DELIMIT
DELINEATE vb show by drawing
DELIQUIUM n loss of consciousness
DELIRIA > DELIRIUM
DELIRIANT > DELIRIUM
DELIRIOUS adj suffering from delirium
DELIRIUM n state of excitement and mental confusion, often with hallucinations
DELIRIUMS > DELIRIUM
DELIS > DELI
DELISH adj delicious
DELIST vb remove from

a list
DELISTED > DELIST
DELISTING > DELIST
DELISTS > DELIST
DELIVER vb carry (goods etc) to a destination
DELIVERED > DELIVER
DELIVERER > DELIVER
DELIVERLY adv quickly
DELIVERS > DELIVER
DELIVERY n delivering
DELL n small wooded hollow
DELLIES > DELLY
DELLS > DELL
DELLY n delicatessen
DELO an informal word for > DELEGATE
DELOPE vb shoot into the air
DELOPED > DELOPE
DELOPES > DELOPE
DELOPING > DELOPE
DELOS > DELO
DELOUSE vb rid (a person or animal) of lice
DELOUSED > DELOUSE
DELOUSER > DELOUSE
DELOUSERS > DELOUSE
DELOUSES > DELOUSE
DELOUSING > DELOUSE
DELPH n kind of earthenware
DELPHIC adj obscure or ambiguous
DELPHIN n fatty substance from dolphin oil
DELPHINIA n plural form of singular delphinium: garden plant with blue, white or pink flowers
DELPHS > DELPH
DELS > DEL
DELT n deltoid muscle
DELTA n fourth letter in the Greek alphabet
DELTAIC > DELTA
DELTAS > DELTA
DELTIC > DELTA
DELTOID n thick muscle forming the rounded contour of the outer edge of the shoulder and acting to raise the arm ▷ adj shaped like a Greek capital delta
DELTOIDEI n deltoid
DELTOIDS > DELTOID
DELTS > DELT
DELUBRUM n shrine
DELUBRUMS > DELUBRUM
DELUDABLE > DELUDE
DELUDE vb deceive
DELUDED > DELUDE
DELUDER > DELUDE
DELUDERS > DELUDE
DELUDES > DELUDE
DELUDING > DELUDE
DELUGE n great flood ▷ vb flood
DELUGED > DELUGE
DELUGES > DELUGE
DELUGING > DELUGE
DELUNDUNG n spotted mammal
DELUSION n mistaken idea or belief
DELUSIONS > DELUSION

DELUSIVE > DELUSION
DELUSORY > DELUSION
DELUSTER vb remove the lustre from
DELUSTERS > DELUSTER
DELUXE adj rich, elegant, superior, or sumptuous
DELVE vb research deeply (for information)
DELVED > DELVE
DELVER > DELVE
DELVERS > DELVE
DELVES > DELVE
DELVING > DELVE
DEMAGOG same
as > DEMAGOGUE
DEMAGOGED > DEMAGOG
DEMAGOGIC adj of, characteristic of, relating to, or resembling a demagogue
DEMAGOGS > DEMAGOG
DEMAGOGUE n political agitator who appeals to the prejudice and passions of the mob
DEMAGOGY n demagoguery
DEMAIN n demesne
DEMAINE n demesne
DEMAINES > DEMAINE
DEMAINS > DEMAIN
DEMAN vb reduce the workforce of (a plant, industry, etc)
DEMAND vb request forcefully ▷n forceful request
DEMANDANT n (formerly) the plaintiff in an action relating to real property
DEMANDED > DEMAND
DEMANDER > DEMAND
DEMANDERS > DEMAND
DEMANDING adj requiring a lot of time or effort
DEMANDS > DEMAND
DEMANNED > DEMAN
DEMANNING > DEMAN
DEMANS > DEMAN
DEMANTOID n bright green variety of andradite garnet
DEMARCATE vb mark, fix, or draw the boundaries, limits, etc, of
DEMARCHE n move, step, or manoeuvre, esp in diplomatic affairs
DEMARCHES > DEMARCHE
DEMARK vb demarcate
DEMARKED > DEMARK
DEMARKET vb discourage consumers from buying (a particular product), either because it is faulty or because it could jeopardize the seller's reputation
DEMARKETS > DEMARKET
DEMARKING > DEMARK
DEMARKS > DEMARK
DEMAST vb remove the mast from
DEMASTED > DEMAST
DEMASTING > DEMAST
DEMASTS > DEMAST
DEMAYNE n demesne
DEMAYNES > DEMAYNE
DEME n (in preclassical

Greece) the territory inhabited by a tribe
DEMEAN vb lower (oneself) in dignity, status, or character
DEMEANE n demesne
DEMEANED > DEMEAN
DEMEANES n demesne
DEMEANING > DEMEAN
DEMEANOR same
as > DEMEANOUR
DEMEANORS > DEMEANOR
DEMEANOUR n way a person behaves
DEMEANS > DEMEAN
DEMENT vb deteriorate mentally, esp because of old age
DEMENTATE vb deteriorate mentally
DEMENTED adj mad
DEMENTI n denial
DEMENTIA n state of serious mental deterioration
DEMENTIAL > DEMENTIA
DEMENTIAS > DEMENTIA
DEMENTING > DEMENT
DEMENTIS > DEMENTI
DEMENTS > DEMENT
DEMERARA n brown crystallized cane sugar from the Caribbean and nearby countries
DEMERARAN adj from Demerara
DEMERARAS > DEMERARA
DEMERGE vb separate a company from another with which it was previously merged
DEMERGED > DEMERGE
DEMERGER n separation of two or more companies which have previously been merged
DEMERGERS > DEMERGER
DEMERGES > DEMERGE
DEMERGING > DEMERGE
DEMERIT n fault, disadvantage ▷vb deserve
DEMERITED > DEMERIT
DEMERITS > DEMERIT
DEMERSAL adj living or occurring on the bottom of a sea or a lake
DEMERSE vb immerse
DEMERSED > DEMERSE
DEMERSES > DEMERSE
DEMERSING > DEMERSE
DEMERSION > DEMERSE
DEMES > DEME
DEMESNE n land surrounding a house
DEMESNES > DEMESNE
DEMETON n insecticide
DEMETONS > DEMETON
DEMIC adj of population
DEMIES > DEMY
DEMIGOD n being who is part mortal, part god
DEMIGODS > DEMIGOD
DEMIJOHN n large bottle with a short neck, often encased in wicker
DEMIJOHNS > DEMIJOHN
DEMILUNE n outwork in front of a fort, shaped like a

crescent moon
DEMILUNES > DEMILUNE
DEMIMONDE n (esp in the 19th century) class of women considered to be outside respectable society because of promiscuity
DEMIPIQUE n low pique on a saddle
DEMIREP n woman of bad repute, esp a prostitute
DEMIREPS > DEMIREP
DEMISABLE > DEMISE
DEMISE n eventual failure (of something successful) ▷vb transfer for a limited period
DEMISED > DEMISE
DEMISES > DEMISE
DEMISING > DEMISE
DEMISS adj humble
DEMISSION n relinquishment of or abdication from an office, responsibility, etc
DEMISSIVE adj humble
DEMISSLY > DEMISS
DEMIST vb remove condensation from (a windscreen)
DEMISTED > DEMIST
DEMISTER n device incorporating a heater and/or blower used in a motor vehicle to free the windscreen of condensation
DEMISTERS > DEMISTER
DEMISTING > DEMIST
DEMISTS > DEMIST
DEMIT vb resign (an office, position, etc)
DEMITASSE n small cup used to serve coffee, esp after a meal
DEMITS > DEMIT
DEMITTED > DEMIT
DEMITTING > DEMIT
DEMIURGE n (in the philosophy of Plato) the creator of the universe
DEMIURGES > DEMIURGE
DEMIURGIC > DEMIURGE
DEMIURGUS n demiurge
DEMIVEG n person who eats poultry and fish, but no red meat ▷adj denoting a person who eats poultry and fish, but no red meat
DEMIVEGES > DEMIVEG
DEMIVOLT n half turn on the hind legs
DEMIVOLTE same
as > DEMIVOLT
DEMIVOLTS > DEMIVOLT
DEMIWORLD n demimonde
DEMO n demonstration, organized expression of public opinion ▷vb demonstrate
DEMOB vb demobilize ▷n (as modifier)
DEMOBBED > DEMOB
DEMOBBING > DEMOB
DEMOBS > DEMOB
DEMOCRACY n government by the people or their

elected representatives
DEMOCRAT n advocate of democracy
DEMOCRATS > DEMOCRAT
DEMOCRATY n democracy
DEMODE adj out of fashion
DEMODED adj out of fashion
DEMOED > DEMO
DEMOING > DEMO
DEMOLISH vb knock down or destroy (a building)
DEMOLOGY n demography
DEMON n evil spirit
DEMONESS n female demon
DEMONIAC adj appearing to be possessed by a devil ▷n person possessed by an evil spirit or demon
DEMONIACS > DEMONIAC
DEMONIAN adj of a demon
DEMONIC adj evil
DEMONICAL adj demonic
DEMONISE same
as > DEMONIZE
DEMONISED > DEMONISE
DEMONISES > DEMONISE
DEMONISM same
as > DEMONOLOGY
DEMONISMS > DEMONISM
DEMONIST > DEMONISM
DEMONISTS > DEMONISM
DEMONIZE vb make into a demon
DEMONIZED > DEMONIZE
DEMONIZES > DEMONIZE
DEMONRIES > DEMONRY
DEMONRY > DEMON
DEMONS > DEMON
DEMOS n people of a nation regarded as a political unit
DEMOSES > DEMOS
DEMOTE vb reduce in status or rank
DEMOTED > DEMOTE
DEMOTES > DEMOTE
DEMOTIC adj of the common people ▷n demotic script of ancient Egypt
DEMOTICS > DEMOTIC
DEMOTING > DEMOTE
DEMOTION > DEMOTE
DEMOTIONS > DEMOTE
DEMOTIST > DEMOTIC
DEMOTISTS > DEMOTIC
DEMOUNT vb remove (a motor, gun, etc) from its mounting or setting
DEMOUNTED > DEMOUNT
DEMOUNTS > DEMOUNT
DEMPSTER same
as > DEEMSTER
DEMPSTERS > DEMPSTER
DEMPT > DEEM
DEMULCENT adj soothing ▷n drug or agent that soothes the irritation of inflamed or injured skin surfaces
DEMULSIFY vb undergo or cause to undergo a process in which an emulsion is permanently broken down into its constituents
DEMUR vb raise objections or show reluctance ▷n act of demurring
DEMURE adj quiet, reserved,

and rather shy ▷ *vb* archaic for look demure ▷ *n* archaic for demure look

DEMURED > DEMURE

DEMURELY > DEMURE

DEMURER > DEMURE

DEMURES > DEMURE

DEMUREST > DEMURE

DEMURING > DEMURE

DEMURRAGE *n* delaying of a ship, railway wagon, etc, caused by the charterer's failure to load, unload, etc, before the time of scheduled departure

DEMURRAL *n* act of demurring

DEMURRALS > DEMURRAL

DEMURRED > DEMUR

DEMURRER *n* pleading that admits an opponent's point but denies that it is a relevant or valid argument

DEMURRERS > DEMURRER

DEMURRING > DEMUR

DEMURS > DEMUR

DEMY *n* size of printing paper, 17½ by 22½ inches (444.5 × 571.5 mm)

DEMYSHIP > DEMY

DEMYSHIPS > DEMY

DEMYSTIFY *vb* remove the mystery from

DEN *n* home of a wild animal ▷ *vb* live in or as if in a den

DENAR *n* standard monetary unit of Macedonia, divided into 100 deni

DENARI > DENAR

DENARIES > DENARIUS

DENARII > DENARIUS

DENARIUS *n* ancient Roman silver coin, often called a penny in translation

DENARS > DENAR

DENARY *adj* calculated by tens

DENATURE *vb* change the nature of

DENATURED > DENATURE

DENATURES > DENATURE

DENAY *vb* deny

DENAYED > DENAY

DENAYING > DENAY

DENAYS > DENAY

DENAZIFY *vb* free or declare (people, institutions, etc) freed from Nazi influence or ideology

DENDRIMER *n* chemical compound with treelike molecular structure

DENDRITE *n* any of the short branched threadlike extensions of a nerve cell, which conduct impulses towards the cell body

DENDRITES > DENDRITE

DENDRITIC > DENDRITE

DENDROID *adj* freely branching

DENDRON *same as* > DENDRITE

DENDRONS > DENDRON

DENE *n* narrow wooded valley

DENERVATE *vb* deprive (a tissue or organ) of its nerve supply

DENES > DENE

DENET *vb* remove from the Net Book Agreement

DENETS > DENET

DENETTED > DENET

DENETTING > DENET

DENGUE *n* viral disease transmitted by mosquitoes, characterized by headache, fever, pains in the joints, and a rash

DENGUES > DENGUE

DENI *n* monetary unit of the Former Yugoslav Republic of Macedonia, worth one hundredth of a denar

DENIABLE *adj* able to be denied

DENIABLY > DENIABLE

DENIAL *n* statement that something is not true

DENIALS > DENIAL

DENIED > DENY

DENIER *n* unit of weight used to measure the fineness of nylon or silk

DENIERS > DENIER

DENIES > DENY

DENIGRATE *vb* criticize unfairly

DENIM *n* hard-wearing cotton fabric, usu blue

DENIMED *adj* wearing denim

DENIMS *pl n* jeans or overalls made of denim

DENIS > DENI

DENITRATE *vb* undergo or cause to undergo a process in which a compound loses a nitro or nitrate group, nitrogen dioxide, or nitric acid

DENITRIFY *vb* undergo or cause to undergo loss or removal of nitrogen compounds or nitrogen

DENIZEN *n* inhabitant ▷ *vb* make a denizen

DENIZENED > DENIZEN

DENIZENS > DENIZEN

DENNED > DEN

DENNET *n* carriage for one horse

DENNETS > DENNET

DENNING > DEN

DENOMINAL *adj* formed from a noun

DENOTABLE > DENOTE

DENOTATE *vb* denote

DENOTATED > DENOTATE

DENOTATES > DENOTATE

DENOTE *vb* be a sign of

DENOTED > DENOTE

DENOTES > DENOTE

DENOTING > DENOTE

DENOTIVE > DENOTE

DENOUNCE *vb* speak vehemently against

DENOUNCED > DENOUNCE

DENOUNCER > DENOUNCE

DENOUNCES > DENOUNCE

DENS > DEN

DENSE *adj* closely packed

DENSELY > DENSE

DENSENESS > DENSE

DENSER > DENSE

DENSEST > DENSE

DENSIFIED > DENSIFY

DENSIFIER > DENSIFY

DENSIFIES > DENSIFY

DENSIFY *vb* make or become dense

DENSITIES > DENSITY

DENSITY *n* degree to which something is filled or occupied

DENT *n* hollow in the surface of something, made by hitting it ▷ *vb* make a dent in

DENTAL *adj* of teeth or dentistry ▷ *n* dental consonant

DENTALIA > DENTALIUM

DENTALITY *n* use of teeth in pronouncing words

DENTALIUM *n* any scaphopod mollusc of the genus *Dentalium*

DENTALLY > DENTAL

DENTALS > DENTAL

DENTARIA *n* botanical term

DENTARIAS > DENTARIA

DENTARIES > DENTARY

DENTARY *n* lower jawbone with teeth

DENTATE *adj* having teeth or teethlike notches

DENTATED *adj* having teeth

DENTATELY > DENTATE

DENTATION *n* state or condition of being dentate

DENTED > DENT

DENTEL *n* architectural term

DENTELLE *n* bookbinding term

DENTELLES > DENTELLE

DENTELS > DENTEL

DENTEX *n* large active predatory sparid fish, *Dentex dentex*, of Mediterranean and E Atlantic waters, having long sharp teeth and powerful jaws

DENTEXES > DENTEX

DENTICLE *n* small tooth or toothlike part, such as any of the placoid scales of sharks

DENTICLES > DENTICLE

DENTIFORM *adj* shaped like a tooth

DENTIL *n* one of a set of small square or rectangular blocks evenly spaced to form an ornamental row, usually under a classical cornice on a building, piece of furniture, etc

DENTILED > DENTIL

DENTILS > DENTIL

DENTIN *same as* > DENTINE

DENTINAL > DENTINE

DENTINE *n* hard dense tissue forming the bulk of a tooth

DENTINES > DENTINE

DENTING > DENT

DENTINS > DENTIN

DENTIST *n* person qualified to practise dentistry

DENTISTRY *n* branch of medicine concerned with the teeth and gums

DENTISTS > DENTIST

DENTITION *n* typical arrangement of teeth in a species

DENTOID *adj* resembling a tooth

DENTS > DENT

DENTULOUS *adj* having teeth

DENTURAL > DENTURE

DENTURE *n* false tooth

DENTURES > DENTURE

DENTURIST *n* person who makes dentures

DENUDATE *adj* denuded ▷ *vb* denude

DENUDATED > DENUDATE

DENUDATES > DENUDATE

DENUDE *vb* remove the covering or protection from

DENUDED > DENUDE

DENUDER > DENUDE

DENUDERS > DENUDE

DENUDES > DENUDE

DENUDING > DENUDE

DENY *vb* declare to be untrue

DENYING > DENY

DENYINGLY > DENY

DEODAND *n* (formerly) a thing that had caused a person's death and was forfeited to the crown for a charitable purpose: abolished 1862

DEODANDS > DEODAND

DEODAR *n* Himalayan cedar with drooping branches

DEODARA *same as* > DEODAR

DEODARAS > DEODARA

DEODARS > DEODAR

DEODATE *n* offering to God

DEODATES > DEODATE

DEODORANT *n* substance applied to the body to mask the smell of perspiration

DEODORISE *same as* > DEODORIZE

DEODORIZE *vb* remove or disguise the smell of

DEONTIC *adj* of or relating to such ethical concepts as obligation and permissibility

DEONTICS > DEONTIC

DEORBIT *vb* go out of orbit

DEORBITED > DEORBIT

DEORBITS > DEORBIT

DEOXIDATE *vb* remove oxygen atoms from

DEOXIDISE *same as* > DEOXIDIZE

DEOXIDIZE *vb* remove oxygen atoms from (a compound, molecule, etc)

DEOXY *adj* having less oxygen than a specified related compound

DEPAINT *vb* depict

DEPAINTED > DEPAINT

DEPAINTS > DEPAINT

DEPANNEUR *n* (in Quebec) a

convenience store

DEPART *vb* leave

DEPARTED *adj* dead

DEPARTEE > DEPART

DEPARTEES > DEPART

DEPARTER > DEPART

DEPARTERS > DEPART

DEPARTING > DEPART

DEPARTS > DEPART

DEPARTURE *n* act of departing

DEPASTURE *vb* graze or denude by grazing (a pasture, esp a meadow specially grown for the purpose)

DEPECHE *n* message

DEPECHES > DEPECHE

DEPEINCT *vb* paint

DEPEINCTS > DEPEINCT

DEPEND *vb* put trust (in)

DEPENDANT *same as* > DEPENDENT

DEPENDED > DEPEND

DEPENDENT *adj* depending on someone or something ▷ *n* element in a phrase or clause that is not the governor

DEPENDING > DEPEND

DEPENDS > DEPEND

DEPEOPLE *vb* reduce population

DEPEOPLED > DEPEOPLE

DEPEOPLES > DEPEOPLE

DEPERM *vb* demagnetize

DEPERMED > DEPERM

DEPERMING > DEPERM

DEPERMS > DEPERM

DEPICT *vb* produce a picture of

DEPICTED > DEPICT

DEPICTER > DEPICT

DEPICTERS > DEPICT

DEPICTING > DEPICT

DEPICTION > DEPICT

DEPICTIVE > DEPICT

DEPICTOR > DEPICT

DEPICTORS > DEPICT

DEPICTS > DEPICT

DEPICTURE *a less common word for* > DEPICT

DEPILATE *vb* remove the hair from

DEPILATED > DEPILATE

DEPILATES > DEPILATE

DEPILATOR > DEPILATE

DEPLANE *vb* disembark from an aeroplane

DEPLANED > DEPLANE

DEPLANES > DEPLANE

DEPLANING > DEPLANE

DEPLETE *vb* use up

DEPLETED > DEPLETE

DEPLETER > DEPLETE

DEPLETERS > DEPLETE

DEPLETES > DEPLETE

DEPLETING > DEPLETE

DEPLETION > DEPLETE

DEPLETIVE > DEPLETE

DEPLETORY > DEPLETE

DEPLORE *vb* condemn strongly

DEPLORED > DEPLORE

DEPLORER > DEPLORE

DEPLORERS > DEPLORE

DEPLORES > DEPLORE

DEPLORING > DEPLORE

DEPLOY *vb* organize (troops or resources) into a position ready for immediate action

DEPLOYED > DEPLOY

DEPLOYER > DEPLOY

DEPLOYERS > DEPLOY

DEPLOYING > DEPLOY

DEPLOYS > DEPLOY

DEPLUME *vb* deprive of feathers

DEPLUMED > DEPLUME

DEPLUMES > DEPLUME

DEPLUMING > DEPLUME

DEPOLISH *vb* remove the polish from

DEPONE *vb* declare (something) under oath

DEPONED > DEPONE

DEPONENT *n* person who makes a statement on oath ▷ *adj* (of a verb, esp in Latin) having the inflectional endings of a passive verb but the meaning of an active verb

DEPONENTS > DEPONENT

DEPONES > DEPONE

DEPONING > DEPONE

DEPORT *vb* remove forcibly from a country

DEPORTED > DEPORT

DEPORTEE *n* person deported or awaiting deportation

DEPORTEES > DEPORTEE

DEPORTER > DEPORT

DEPORTERS > DEPORT

DEPORTING > DEPORT

DEPORTS > DEPORT

DEPOSABLE > DEPOSE

DEPOSAL *another word for* > DEPOSITION

DEPOSALS > DEPOSAL

DEPOSE *vb* remove from an office or position of power

DEPOSED > DEPOSE

DEPOSER > DEPOSE

DEPOSERS > DEPOSE

DEPOSES > DEPOSE

DEPOSING > DEPOSE

DEPOSIT *vb* put down ▷ *n* sum of money paid into a bank account

DEPOSITED > DEPOSIT

DEPOSITOR *n* person who places or has money on deposit in a bank or similar organization

DEPOSITS > DEPOSIT

DEPOT *n* building where goods or vehicles are kept when not in use ▷ *adj* (of a drug or drug dose) designed for gradual release from the site of an injection so as to act over a long period

DEPOTS > DEPOT

DEPRAVE *vb* make morally bad

DEPRAVED *adj* morally bad

DEPRAVER > DEPRAVE

DEPRAVERS > DEPRAVE

DEPRAVES > DEPRAVE

DEPRAVING > DEPRAVE

DEPRAVITY *n* moral corruption

DEPRECATE *vb* express disapproval of

DEPREDATE *vb* plunder or destroy

DEPREHEND *vb* apprehend

DEPRENYL *n* drug combating effects of ageing

DEPRENYLS > DEPRENYL

DEPRESS *vb* make sad

DEPRESSED *adj* low in spirits

DEPRESSES > DEPRESS

DEPRESSOR *n* person or thing that depresses

DEPRIVAL > DEPRIVE

DEPRIVALS > DEPRIVE

DEPRIVE *vb* prevent from (having or enjoying)

DEPRIVED *adj* lacking adequate living conditions, education, etc

DEPRIVER > DEPRIVE

DEPRIVERS > DEPRIVE

DEPRIVES > DEPRIVE

DEPRIVING > DEPRIVE

DEPROGRAM *same as* > DEPROGRAMME

DEPSIDE *n* any ester formed by the condensation of the carboxyl group of one phenolic carboxylic acid with the hydroxyl group of another, found in plant cells

DEPSIDES > DEPSIDE

DEPTH *n* distance downwards, backwards, or inwards

DEPTHLESS *adj* immeasurably deep

DEPTHS > DEPTH

DEPURANT *same as* > DEPURATIVE

DEPURANTS > DEPURANT

DEPURATE *vb* cleanse or purify or to be cleansed or purified

DEPURATED > DEPURATE

DEPURATES > DEPURATE

DEPURATOR > DEPURATE

DEPUTABLE > DEPUTE

DEPUTE *vb* appoint (someone) to act on one's behalf ▷ *n* deputy

DEPUTED > DEPUTE

DEPUTES > DEPUTE

DEPUTIES > DEPUTY

DEPUTING > DEPUTE

DEPUTISE *same as* > DEPUTIZE

DEPUTISED > DEPUTISE

DEPUTISES > DEPUTISE

DEPUTIZE *vb* act as deputy

DEPUTIZED > DEPUTIZE

DEPUTIZES > DEPUTIZE

DEPUTY *n* person appointed to act on behalf of another

DERACINE *adj* uprooted

DERAIGN *vb* contest (a claim, suit, etc)

DERAIGNED > DERAIGN

DERAIGNS > DERAIGN

DERAIL *vb* cause (a train) to go off the rails ▷ *n* device designed to make rolling

stock or locomotives leave the rails to avoid a collision or accident

DERAILED > DERAIL

DERAILER *same as* > DERAIL

DERAILERS > DERAILER

DERAILING > DERAIL

DERAILS > DERAIL

DERANGE *vb* disturb the order or arrangement of

DERANGED > DERANGE

DERANGER > DERANGE

DERANGERS > DERANGE

DERANGES > DERANGE

DERANGING > DERANGE

DERAT *vb* remove rats from

DERATE *vb* assess the value of (some types of property, such as agricultural land) at a lower rate than others for local taxation

DERATED > DERATE

DERATES > DERATE

DERATING > DERATE

DERATINGS > DERATE

DERATION *vb* end rationing of (food, petrol, etc)

DERATIONS > DERATION

DERATS > DERAT

DERATTED > DERAT

DERATTING > DERAT

DERAY *vb* go mad

DERAYED > DERAY

DERAYING > DERAY

DERAYS > DERAY

DERBIES > DERBY

DERBY *n* bowler hat

DERE *vb* injure

DERED > DERE

DERELICT *adj* unused and falling into ruins ▷ *n* social outcast, vagrant

DERELICTS > DERELICT

DEREPRESS *vb* induce operation of gene

DERES > DERE

DERHAM *same as* > DIRHAM

DERHAMS > DERHAM

DERIDE *vb* treat with contempt or ridicule

DERIDED > DERIDE

DERIDER > DERIDE

DERIDERS > DERIDE

DERIDES > DERIDE

DERIDING > DERIDE

DERIG *vb* remove equipment, e.g. from stage set

DERIGGED > DERIG

DERIGGING > DERIG

DERIGS > DERIG

DERING > DERE

DERINGER *same as* > DERRINGER

DERINGERS > DERINGER

DERISIBLE *adj* subject to or deserving of derision

DERISION *n* act of deriding

DERISIONS > DERISION

DERISIVE *adj* mocking, scornful

DERISORY *adj* too small or inadequate to be considered seriously

DERIVABLE > DERIVE

DERIVABLY > DERIVE

DERIVATE *n* derivative

DERIVATES > DERIVATE
DERIVE *vb* take or develop (from)
DERIVED > DERIVE
DERIVER > DERIVE
DERIVERS > DERIVE
DERIVES > DERIVE
DERIVING > DERIVE
DERM *same as* > DERMA
DERMA *n* beef or fowl intestine used as a casing for certain dishes, esp kishke
DERMAL *adj* of or relating to the skin
DERMAS > DERMA
DERMATIC *adj* of skin
DERMATOID *adj* resembling skin
DERMATOME *n* surgical instrument for cutting thin slices of skin, esp for grafting
DERMESTID *n* any beetle of the family *Dermestidae*, whose members are destructive at both larval and adult stages to a wide range of stored organic materials such as wool, fur, feathers, and meat. They include the bacon (or larder), cabinet, carpet, leather, and museum beetles
DERMIC > DERMIS
DERMIS *another name for* > CORIUM
DERMISES > DERMIS
DERMOID *adj* of or resembling skin ▷ *n* congenital cystic tumour whose walls are lined with epithelium
DERMOIDS > DERMOID
DERMS > DERM
DERN *n* concealment
DERNFUL *adj* sorrowful
DERNIER *adj* last
DERNLY *adv* sorrowfully
DERNS > DERN
DERO *n* tramp or derelict
DEROGATE *vb* detract from ▷ *adj* debased or degraded
DEROGATED > DEROGATE
DEROGATES > DEROGATE
DEROS > DERO
DERRICK *n* simple crane ▷ *vb* raise or lower the jib of (a crane)
DERRICKED > DERRICK
DERRICKS > DERRICK
DERRIERE > BUTTOCK
DERRIERES > DERRIERE
DERRIES > DERRY
DERRINGER *n* small large-bored pistol
DERRIS *n* any East Indian leguminous woody climbing plant of the genus *Derris*, esp *D. elliptica*, whose roots yield the compound rotenone
DERRISES > DERRIS
DERRO *n* vagrant
DERROS > DERRO
DERRY *n* derelict house, esp

one used by tramps, drug addicts, etc
DERTH *same as* > DEARTH
DERTHS > DERTH
DERV *n* diesel oil, when used for road transport
DERVISH *n* member of a Muslim religious order noted for a frenzied whirling dance
DERVISHES > DERVISH
DERVS > DERV
DESALT *same as* > DESALINATE
DESALTED > DESALT
DESALTER > DESALT
DESALTERS > DESALT
DESALTING > DESALT
DESALTS > DESALT
DESAND *vb* remove sand from
DESANDED > DESAND
DESANDING > DESAND
DESANDS > DESAND
DESCALE *vb* remove a hard coating from inside (a kettle or pipe)
DESCALED > DESCALE
DESCALES > DESCALE
DESCALING > DESCALE
DESCANT *n* tune played or sung above a basic melody ▷ *adj* denoting the highest member in a family of musical instruments ▷ *vb* compose or perform a descant (for a piece of music)
DESCANTED > DESCANT
DESCANTER > DESCANT
DESCANTS > DESCANT
DESCEND *vb* move down (a slope etc)
DESCENDED > DESCEND
DESCENDER > DESCEND
DESCENDS > DESCEND
DESCENT *n* descending
DESCENTS > DESCENT
DESCHOOL *vb* separate education from the institution of school and operate through the pupil's life experience as opposed to a set curriculum
DESCHOOLS > DESCHOOL
DESCRIBE *vb* give an account of (something or someone) in words
DESCRIBED > DESCRIBE
DESCRIBER > DESCRIBE
DESCRIBES > DESCRIBE
DESCRIED > DESCRY
DESCRIER > DESCRY
DESCRIERS > DESCRY
DESCRIES > DESCRY
DESCRIVE *vb* describe
DESCRIVED > DESCRIVE
DESCRIVES > DESCRIVE
DESCRY *vb* catch sight of
DESCRYING > DESCRY
DESECRATE *vb* damage or insult (something sacred)
DESELECT *vb* refuse to select (an MP) for re-election
DESELECTS > DESELECT
DESERT *n* region with little

or no vegetation because of low rainfall ▷ *vb* abandon (a person or place) without intending to return
DESERTED > DESERT
DESERTER > DESERT
DESERTERS > DESERT
DESERTIC *adj* (of soil) developing in hot climates
DESERTIFY *vb* turn into desert
DESERTING > DESERT
DESERTION *n* act of deserting or abandoning or the state of being deserted or abandoned
DESERTS > DESERT
DESERVE *vb* be entitled to or worthy of
DESERVED > DESERVE
DESERVER > DESERVE
DESERVERS > DESERVE
DESERVES > DESERVE
DESERVING *adj* worthy of help, praise, or reward ▷ *n* merit or demerit
DESEX *same as* > DESEXUALIZE
DESEXED > DESEX
DESEXES > DESEX
DESEXING > DESEX
DESHI *same as* > DESI
DESI *adj* in Indian English, indigenous or local
DESICCANT *adj* desiccating or drying ▷ *n* substance, such as calcium oxide, that absorbs water and is used to remove moisture
DESICCATE *vb* remove most of the water from
DESIGN *vb* work out the structure or form of (something), by making a sketch or plans ▷ *n* preliminary drawing
DESIGNATE *vb* give a name to ▷ *adj* appointed but not yet in office
DESIGNED > DESIGN
DESIGNEE *n* person designated to do something
DESIGNEES > DESIGNEE
DESIGNER *n* person who draws up original sketches or plans from which things are made ▷ *adj* designed by a well-known designer
DESIGNERS > DESIGNER
DESIGNFUL *adj* scheming
DESIGNING *adj* cunning and scheming
DESIGNS > DESIGN
DESILVER *vb* remove silver from
DESILVERS > DESILVER
DESINE *same as* > DESIGN
DESINED > DESINE
DESINENCE *n* ending or termination, esp an inflectional ending of a word
DESINENT > DESINENCE
DESINES > DESINE
DESINING > DESINE
DESIPIENT *adj* foolish

DESIRABLE *adj* worth having ▷ *n* person or thing that is the object of desire
DESIRABLY > DESIRABLE
DESIRE *vb* want very much ▷ *n* wish, longing
DESIRED > DESIRE
DESIRER > DESIRE
DESIRERS > DESIRE
DESIRES > DESIRE
DESIRING > DESIRE
DESIROUS *adj* having a desire for
DESIST *vb* stop (doing something)
DESISTED > DESIST
DESISTING > DESIST
DESISTS > DESIST
DESK *n* piece of furniture with a writing surface and drawers
DESKBOUND *adj* engaged in or involving sedentary work, as at an office desk
DESKFAST *n* breakfast eaten at one's desk at work
DESKFASTS > DESKFAST
DESKILL *vb* mechanize or computerize (a job) thereby reducing the skill required to do it
DESKILLED > DESKILL
DESKILLS > DESKILL
DESKMAN *n* police officer in charge in police station
DESKMEN > DESKMAN
DESKNOTE *n* small computer
DESKNOTES > DESKNOTE
DESKS > DESK
DESKTOP *adj* (of a computer) small enough to use at a desk ▷ *n* denoting a computer system, esp for word processing, that is small enough to use at a desk
DESKTOPS > DESKTOP
DESMAN *n* either of two molelike amphibious mammals
DESMANS > DESMAN
DESMID *n* any freshwater green alga of the mainly unicellular family *Desmidioideae*, typically constricted into two symmetrical halves
DESMIDIAN > DESMID
DESMIDS > DESMID
DESMINE *n* type of mineral
DESMINES > DESMINE
DESMODIUM *n* type of plant
DESMOID *adj* resembling a tendon or ligament ▷ *n* very firm tumour of connective tissue
DESMOIDS > DESMOID
DESMOSOME *n* structure in the cell membranes of adjacent cells that binds them together
DESNOOD *vb* remove the snood of a turkey poult to reduce the risk of cannibalism
DESNOODED > DESNOOD

DESNOODS > DESNOOD
DESOEUVRE adj with nothing to do
DESOLATE adj uninhabited and bleak ▷ vb deprive of inhabitants
DESOLATED > DESOLATE
DESOLATER > DESOLATE
DESOLATES > DESOLATE
DESOLATOR > DESOLATE
DESORB vb change from an adsorbed state on a surface to a gaseous or liquid state
DESORBED > DESORB
DESORBING > DESORB
DESORBS > DESORB
DESOXY same as > DEOXY
DESPAIR n total loss of hope ▷ vb lose hope
DESPAIRED > DESPAIR
DESPAIRER n one who despairs
DESPAIRS > DESPAIR
DESPATCH same as > DISPATCH
DESPERADO n reckless person ready to commit any violent illegal act
DESPERATE adj in despair and reckless
DESPIGHT obsolete form of > DESPITE
DESPIGHTS > DESPIGHT
DESPISAL > DESPISE
DESPISALS > DESPISE
DESPISE vb regard with contempt
DESPISED > DESPISE
DESPISER > DESPISE
DESPISERS > DESPISE
DESPISES > DESPISE
DESPISING > DESPISE
DESPITE prep in spite of ▷ n contempt ▷ vb show contempt for
DESPITED > DESPITE
DESPITES > DESPITE
DESPITING > DESPITE
DESPOIL vb plunder
DESPOILED > DESPOIL
DESPOILER > DESPOIL
DESPOILS > DESPOIL
DESPOND vb lose heart or hope
DESPONDED > DESPOND
DESPONDS > DESPOND
DESPOT n person in power who acts unfairly or cruelly
DESPOTAT n despot's domain
DESPOTATE same as > DESPOTAT
DESPOTATS > DESPOTAT
DESPOTIC > DESPOT
DESPOTISM n unfair or cruel government or behaviour
DESPOTS > DESPOT
DESPUMATE vb clarify or purify (a liquid) by skimming a scum from its surface
DESSE n desk
DESSERT n sweet course served at the end of a meal
DESSERTS > DESSERT
DESSES > DESSE
DESTAIN vb remove stain

from
DESTAINED > DESTAIN
DESTAINS > DESTAIN
DESTEMPER same as > DISTEMPER
DESTINATE same as > DESTINE
DESTINE vb set apart or appoint (for a certain purpose or person, or to do something)
DESTINED adj certain to be or to do something
DESTINES > DESTINE
DESTINIES > DESTINY
DESTINING > DESTINE
DESTINY n future marked out for a person or thing
DESTITUTE adj having no money or possessions
DESTOCK vb (of a retailer) to reduce the amount of stock held or cease to stock certain products
DESTOCKED > DESTOCK
DESTOCKS > DESTOCK
DESTRIER an archaic word for > WARHORSE
DESTRIERS > DESTRIER
DESTROY vb ruin, demolish
DESTROYED > DESTROY
DESTROYER n small heavily armed warship
DESTROYS > DESTROY
DESTRUCT vb destroy (one's own missile or rocket) for safety ▷ n act of destructing ▷ adj designed to be capable of destroying itself or the object, system, or installation containing it
DESTRUCTO n person who causes havoc or destruction
DESTRUCTS > DESTRUCT
DESUETUDE n condition of not being in use
DESUGAR vb remove sugar from
DESUGARED > DESUGAR
DESUGARS > DESUGAR
DESULFUR same as > DESULPHUR
DESULFURS > DESULFUR
DESULPHUR vb remove sulphur from
DESULTORY adj jumping from one thing to another, disconnected
DESYATIN n Russian unit of area
DESYATINS > DESYATIN
DESYNE same as > DESIGN
DESYNED > DESYNE
DESYNES > DESYNE
DESYNING > DESYNE
DETACH vb disengage and separate
DETACHED adj (of a house) not joined to another house
DETACHER > DETACH
DETACHERS > DETACH
DETACHES > DETACH
DETACHING > DETACH
DETAIL n individual piece of information ▷ vb list fully

DETAILED adj having many details
DETAILER > DETAIL
DETAILERS > DETAIL
DETAILING > DETAIL
DETAILS > DETAIL
DETAIN vb delay (someone)
DETAINED > DETAIN
DETAINEE > DETAIN
DETAINEES > DETAIN
DETAINER n wrongful withholding of the property of another person
DETAINERS > DETAINER
DETAINING > DETAIN
DETAINS > DETAIN
DETASSEL vb remove top part of corn plant
DETASSELS > DETASSEL
DETECT vb notice
DETECTED > DETECT
DETECTER > DETECT
DETECTERS > DETECT
DETECTING > DETECT
DETECTION n act of noticing, discovering, or sensing something
DETECTIVE n police officer or private agent who investigates crime ▷ adj used in or serving for detection
DETECTOR n instrument used to find something
DETECTORS > DETECTOR
DETECTS > DETECT
DETENT n locking piece of a mechanism, often spring-loaded to check the movement of a wheel in one direction only
DETENTE n easing of tension between nations
DETENTES > DETENTE
DETENTION n imprisonment
DETENTIST n supporter of detente
DETENTS > DETENT
DETENU n prisoner
DETENUE n female prisoner
DETENUES > DETENUE
DETENUS > DETENU
DETER vb discourage (someone) from doing something by instilling fear or doubt
DETERGE vb wash or wipe away
DETERGED > DETERGE
DETERGENT n chemical substance for washing clothes or dishes ▷ adj having cleansing power
DETERGER n detergent
DETERGERS > DETERGER
DETERGES > DETERGE
DETERGING > DETERGE
DETERMENT > DETER
DETERMINE vb settle (an argument or a question) conclusively
DETERRED > DETER
DETERRENT n something that deters ▷ adj tending to deter
DETERRER > DETER

DETERRERS > DETERRER
DETERRING > DETER
DETERS > DETER
DETERSION n act of cleansing
DETERSIVE same as > DETERGENT
DETEST vb dislike intensely
DETESTED > DETEST
DETESTER > DETEST
DETESTERS > DETEST
DETESTING > DETEST
DETESTS > DETEST
DETHATCH vb remove dead grass from lawn
DETHRONE vb remove from a throne or position of power
DETHRONED > DETHRONE
DETHRONER > DETHRONE
DETHRONES > DETHRONE
DETICK vb remove ticks from
DETICKED > DETICK
DETICKER > DETICK
DETICKERS > DETICK
DETICKING > DETICK
DETICKS > DETICK
DETINUE n action brought by a plaintiff to recover goods wrongfully detained
DETINUES > DETINUE
DETONABLE adj that can be detonated
DETONATE vb explode
DETONATED > DETONATE
DETONATES > DETONATE
DETONATOR n small amount of explosive, or a device, used to set off an explosion
DETORSION > DETORT
DETORT vb pervert
DETORTED > DETORT
DETORTING > DETORT
DETORTION > DETORT
DETORTS > DETORT
DETOUR n route that is not the most direct one ▷ vb deviate or cause to deviate from a direct route or course of action
DETOURED > DETOUR
DETOURING > DETOUR
DETOURS > DETOUR
DETOX n treatment to rid the body of poisonous substances ▷ vb undergo treatment to rid the body of poisonous substances, esp alcohol and drugs
DETOXED > DETOX
DETOXES > DETOX
DETOXIFY vb remove poison from
DETOXING > DETOX
DETRACT vb make (something) seem less good
DETRACTED > DETRACT
DETRACTOR > DETRACT
DETRACTS > DETRACT
DETRAIN vb leave or cause to leave a railway train, as passengers, etc
DETRAINED > DETRAIN
DETRAINS > DETRAIN
DETRAQUE n insane person
DETRAQUEE n female insane

person
DETRAQUES > DETRAQUE
DETRIMENT *n* disadvantage or damage
DETRITAL > DETRITUS
DETRITION *n* act of rubbing or wearing away by friction
DETRITUS *n* loose mass of stones and silt worn away from rocks
DETRUDE *vb* force down or thrust away or out
DETRUDED > DETRUDE
DETRUDES > DETRUDE
DETRUDING > DETRUDE
DETRUSION > DETRUDE
DETUNE *vb* change pitch of (stringed instrument)
DETUNED > DETUNE
DETUNES > DETUNE
DETUNING > DETUNE
DEUCE *vb* score deuce in tennis ▷*n* score of forty all
DEUCED *adj* damned
DEUCEDLY > DEUCED
DEUCES > DEUCE
DEUCING > DEUCE
DEUDDARN *n* two-tiered Welsh dresser
DEUDDARNS > DEUDDARN
DEUS *n* god
DEUTERATE *vb* treat or combine with deuterium
DEUTERIC *adj* (of mineral) formed by metasomatic changes
DEUTERIDE *n* compound of deuterium with some other element. It is analogous to a hydride
DEUTERIUM *n* isotope of hydrogen twice as heavy as the normal atom
DEUTERON *n* nucleus of a deuterium atom, consisting of one proton and one neutron
DEUTERONS > DEUTERON
DEUTON *old form of* > DEUTERON
DEUTONS > DEUTON
DEUTZIA *n* shrub with clusters of pink or white flowers
DEUTZIAS > DEUTZIA
DEV *same as* > DEVA
DEVA *n* (in Hinduism and Buddhism) divine being or god
DEVALL *vb* stop
DEVALLED > DEVALL
DEVALLING > DEVALL
DEVALLS > DEVALL
DEVALUATE *same as* > DEVALUE
DEVALUE *vb* reduce the exchange value of (a currency)
DEVALUED > DEVALUE
DEVALUES > DEVALUE
DEVALUING > DEVALUE
DEVAS > DEVA
DEVASTATE *vb* destroy
DEVEIN *vb* remove vein from
DEVEINED > DEVEIN
DEVEINING > DEVEIN

DEVEINS > DEVEIN
DEVEL *same as* > DEVVEL
DEVELED > DEVEL
DEVELING > DEVEL
DEVELLED > DEVEL
DEVELLING > DEVEL
DEVELOP *vb* grow or bring to a later, more elaborate, or more advanced stage
DEVELOPE *old form of* > DEVELOP
DEVELOPED > DEVELOP
DEVELOPER *n* person who develops property
DEVELOPES > DEVELOPE
DEVELOPPE *n* ballet position
DEVELOPS > DEVELOP
DEVELS > DEVEL
DEVERBAL *n* word deriving from verb
DEVERBALS > DEVERBAL
DEVEST *variant spelling of* > DIVEST
DEVESTED > DEVEST
DEVESTING > DEVEST
DEVESTS > DEVEST
DEVIANCE *n* act or state of being deviant
DEVIANCES > DEVIANCE
DEVIANCY *same as* > DEVIANCE
DEVIANT *adj* (person) deviating from what is considered acceptable behaviour ▷*n* person whose behaviour deviates from what is considered to be acceptable
DEVIANTS > DEVIANT
DEVIATE *vb* differ from others in belief or thought
DEVIATED > DEVIATE
DEVIATES > DEVIATE
DEVIATING > DEVIATE
DEVIATION *n* act or result of deviating
DEVIATIVE *adj* tending to deviate
DEVIATOR > DEVIATE
DEVIATORS > DEVIATE
DEVIATORY > DEVIATE
DEVICE *n* machine or tool used for a specific task
DEVICEFUL *adj* full of devices
DEVICES > DEVICE
DEVIL *n* evil spirit ▷*vb* prepare (food) with a highly flavoured spiced mixture
DEVILDOM *n* domain of evil spirits
DEVILDOMS > DEVILDOM
DEVILED > DEVIL
DEVILESS *n* female devil
DEVILET *n* young devil
DEVILETS > DEVILET
DEVILFISH *n* manta fish
DEVILING > DEVIL
DEVILINGS > DEVIL
DEVILISH *adj* cruel or unpleasant ▷*adv* extremely
DEVILISM *n* doctrine of devil
DEVILISMS > DEVILISM
DEVILKIN *n* small devil

DEVILKINS > DEVILKIN
DEVILLED > DEVIL
DEVILLING > DEVIL
DEVILMENT *n* mischievous conduct
DEVILRIES > DEVILRY
DEVILRY *n* mischievousness
DEVILS > DEVIL
DEVILSHIP *n* character of devil
DEVILTRY *same as* > DEVILRY
DEVILWOOD *n* small US tree
DEVIOUS *adj* insincere and dishonest
DEVIOUSLY > DEVIOUS
DEVISABLE *adj* (of property, esp realty) capable of being transferred by will
DEVISAL *n* act of inventing, contriving, or devising
DEVISALS > DEVISAL
DEVISE *vb* work out (something) in one's mind ▷*n* disposition of property by will
DEVISED > DEVISE
DEVISEE *n* person to whom property, esp realty, is devised by will
DEVISEES > DEVISEE
DEVISER > DEVISE
DEVISERS > DEVISE
DEVISES > DEVISE
DEVISING > DEVISE
DEVISOR *n* person who devises property, esp realty, by will
DEVISORS > DEVISOR
DEVITRIFY *vb* change from a vitreous state to a crystalline state
DEVLING *n* young devil
DEVLINGS > DEVLING
DEVOICE *vb* make (a voiced speech sound) voiceless
DEVOICED > DEVOICE
DEVOICES > DEVOICE
DEVOICING > DEVOICE
DEVOID *adj* completely lacking (in)
DEVOIR *n* duty
DEVOIRS > DEVOIR
DEVOLVE *vb* pass (power or duties) or (of power or duties) be passed to a successor or substitute
DEVOLVED > DEVOLVE
DEVOLVES > DEVOLVE
DEVOLVING > DEVOLVE
DEVON *n* bland processed meat in sausage form, eaten cold in slices
DEVONIAN *adj* of, denoting, or formed in the fourth period of the Palaeozoic era, between the Silurian and Carboniferous periods
DEVONPORT *same as* > DAVENPORT
DEVONS > DEVON
DEVORE *n* velvet fabric with a raised pattern created by disintegrating some of the pile with chemicals
DEVORES > DEVORE
DEVOT *n* devotee

DEVOTE *vb* apply or dedicate to a particular purpose
DEVOTED *adj* showing loyalty or devotion
DEVOTEDLY > DEVOTED
DEVOTEE *n* person who is very enthusiastic about something
DEVOTEES > DEVOTEE
DEVOTES > DEVOTE
DEVOTING > DEVOTE
DEVOTION *n* strong affection for or loyalty to someone or something
DEVOTIONS > DEVOTION
DEVOTS > DEVOT
DEVOUR *vb* eat greedily
DEVOURED > DEVOUR
DEVOURER > DEVOUR
DEVOURERS > DEVOUR
DEVOURING > DEVOUR
DEVOURS > DEVOUR
DEVOUT *adj* deeply religious
DEVOUTER > DEVOUT
DEVOUTEST > DEVOUT
DEVOUTLY > DEVOUT
DEVS > DEV
DEVVEL *vb* strike with blow
DEVVELLED > DEVVEL
DEVVELS > DEVVEL
DEW *n* drops of water that form on the ground at night from vapour in the air ▷*vb* moisten with or as with dew
DEWAN *n* (formerly in India) the chief minister or finance minister of a state ruled by an Indian prince
DEWANI *n* post of dewan
DEWANIS > DEWANI
DEWANNIES > DEWANNY
DEWANNY *same as* > DEWANI
DEWANS > DEWAN
DEWAR *as in* dewar flask type of vacuum flask
DEWARS > DEWAR
DEWATER *vb* remove water from
DEWATERED > DEWATER
DEWATERER > DEWATER
DEWATERS > DEWATER
DEWAX *vb* remove wax from
DEWAXED > DEWAX
DEWAXES > DEWAX
DEWAXING > DEWAX
DEWBERRY *n* type of bramble with blue-black fruits
DEWCLAW *n* nonfunctional claw on a dog's leg
DEWCLAWED > DEWCLAW
DEWCLAWS > DEWCLAW
DEWDROP *n* drop of dew
DEWDROPS > DEWDROP
DEWED > DEW
DEWFALL *n* formation of dew
DEWFALLS > DEWFALL
DEWFULL *obsolete form of* > DUE
DEWIER > DEWY
DEWIEST > DEWY
DEWILY > DEWY
DEWINESS > DEWY
DEWING > DEW
DEWITT *vb* kill, esp hang unlawfully

DEWITTED > DEWITT
DEWITTING > DEWITT
DEWITTS > DEWITT
DEWLAP n loose fold of skin hanging under the throat in dogs, cattle, etc
DEWLAPPED > DEWLAP
DEWLAPS > DEWLAP
DEWLAPT > DEWLAP
DEWLESS > DEW
DEWOOL vb remove wool from
DEWOOLED > DEWOOL
DEWOOLING > DEWOOL
DEWOOLS > DEWOOL
DEWORM vb rid of worms
DEWORMED > DEWORM
DEWORMER > DEWORM
DEWORMERS > DEWORM
DEWORMING > DEWORM
DEWORMS > DEWORM
DEWPOINT n temperature at which water vapour in the air becomes saturated and water droplets begin to form
DEWPOINTS > DEWPOINT
DEWS > DEW
DEWY adj moist with or as with dew
DEX n dextroamphetamine
DEXES > DEX
DEXIE n pill containing dextroamphetamine
DEXIES > DEXIE
DEXTER adj of or on the right side of a shield, etc, from the bearer's point of view ▷ n small breed of red or black beef cattle, originally from Ireland
DEXTERITY n skill in using one's hands
DEXTEROUS adj possessing or done with dexterity
DEXTERS > DEXTER
DEXTRAL adj of, relating to, or located on the right side, esp of the body
DEXTRALLY > DEXTRAL
DEXTRAN n polysaccharide produced by the action of bacteria on sucrose: used as a substitute for plasma in blood transfusions
DEXTRANS > DEXTRAN
DEXTRIN n sticky substance obtained from starch, used as a thickening agent in food
DEXTRINE same as > DEXTRIN
DEXTRINES > DEXTRINE
DEXTRINS > DEXTRIN
DEXTRO adj dextrorotatory or rotating to the right
DEXTRORSE adj (of some climbing plants) growing upwards in a helix from left to right or anticlockwise
DEXTROSE n glucose occurring in fruit, honey, and the blood of animals
DEXTROSES > DEXTROSE
DEXTROUS same as > DEXTEROUS
DEXY same as > DEXIE

DEY n title given to commanders or (from 1710) governors of the Janissaries of Algiers (1671–1830)
DEYS > DEY
DEZINC vb remove zinc from
DEZINCED > DEZINC
DEZINCING > DEZINC
DEZINCKED > DEZINC
DEZINCS > DEZINC
DHAK n tropical Asian leguminous tree, Butea frondosa, that has bright red flowers and yields a red resin, used as an astringent
DHAKS > DHAK
DHAL n curry made from lentils or beans
DHALS > DHAL
DHAMMA variant of > DHARMA
DHAMMAS > DHAMMA
DHANSAK n any of a variety of Indian dishes consisting of meat or vegetables braised with water or stock and lentils
DHANSAKS > DHANSAK
DHARMA n moral law or behaviour
DHARMAS > DHARMA
DHARMIC > DHARMA
DHARMSALA n Indian hostel
DHARNA n (in India) a method of obtaining justice, as the payment of a debt, by sitting, fasting, at the door of the person from whom reparation is sought
DHARNAS > DHARNA
DHOBI n (in India, Malaya, East Africa, etc, esp formerly) a washerman
DHOBIS > DHOBI
DHOL n type of Indian drum
DHOLE n fierce canine mammal, Cuon alpinus, of the forests of central and SE Asia, having a reddish-brown coat and rounded ears: hunts in packs
DHOLES > DHOLE
DHOLL same as > DHAL
DHOLLS > DHOLL
DHOLS > DHOL
DHOOLIES > DHOOLY
DHOOLY same as > DOOLIE
DHOORA same as > DURRA
DHOORAS > DHOORA
DHOOTI same as > DHOTI
DHOOTIE same as > DHOTI
DHOOTIES > DHOOTIE
DHOOTIS > DHOOTI
DHOTI n long loincloth worn by men in India
DHOTIS > DHOTI
DHOURRA same as > DURRA
DHOURRAS > DHOURRA
DHOW n Arab sailing ship
DHOWS > DHOW
DHURNA same as > DHARNA
DHURNAS > DHURNA
DHURRA same as > DURRA
DHURRAS > DHURRA
DHURRIE same as > DURRIE
DHURRIES > DHURRIE
DHUTI same as > DHOTI
DHUTIS > DHUTI

DI > DEUS
DIABASE n altered dolerite
DIABASES > DIABASE
DIABASIC > DIABASE
DIABETES n disorder in which an abnormal amount of urine containing an excess of sugar is excreted
DIABETIC n person who has diabetes ▷ adj of or having diabetes
DIABETICS > DIABETIC
DIABLE n type of sauce
DIABLERIE n magic or witchcraft connected with devils
DIABLERY same as > DIABLERIE
DIABLES > DIABLE
DIABOLIC adj of the Devil
DIABOLISE same as > DIABOLIZE
DIABOLISM n witchcraft, devil worship
DIABOLIST > DIABOLISM
DIABOLIZE vb make (someone or something) diabolical
DIABOLO n game in which one throws and catches a spinning top on a cord fastened to two sticks held in the hands
DIABOLOGY n study of devils
DIABOLOS > DIABOLO
DIACETYL n aromatic compound
DIACETYLS > DIACETYL
DIACHRONY n change over time
DIACHYLON n acid or salt that contains two acidic hydrogen atoms
DIACHYLUM n plaster containing glycerin with lead salts
DIACID n lead plaster
DIACIDIC adj (of a base, such as calcium hydroxide $Ca(OH)_2$) capable of neutralizing two protons with one of its molecules
DIACIDS > DIACID
DIACODION n herbal remedy aiding sleep
DIACODIUM n syrup of poppies
DIACONAL adj of or associated with a deacon or the diaconate
DIACONATE n position or period of office of a deacon
DIACRITIC n sign above or below a character to indicate phonetic value or stress
DIACT n two-rayed
DIACTINAL adj having two pointed ends
DIACTINE adj two-rayed
DIACTINIC adj able to transmit photochemically active radiation
DIADEM n crown ▷ vb adorn or crown with or as with a diadem

DIADEMED > DIADEM
DIADEMING > DIADEM
DIADEMS > DIADEM
DIADOCHI pl n the six Macedonian generals who, after the death of Alexander the Great, fought for control of his empire
DIADOCHY n replacement of one element in a crystal by another
DIADROM n complete course of pendulum
DIADROMS > DIADROM
DIAERESES > DIAERESIS
DIAERESIS n mark (¨) placed over a vowel to show that it is pronounced separately from the preceding one, for example in Noël
DIAERETIC > DIAERESIS
DIAGLYPH n figure cut into stone
DIAGLYPHS > DIAGLYPH
DIAGNOSE vb determine by diagnosis
DIAGNOSED > DIAGNOSE
DIAGNOSES > DIAGNOSIS
DIAGNOSIS n discovery and identification of diseases from the examination of symptoms
DIAGONAL adj from corner to corner ▷ n diagonal line
DIAGONALS > DIAGONAL
DIAGRAM n sketch showing the form or workings of something ▷ vb show in or as if in a diagram
DIAGRAMED > DIAGRAM
DIAGRAMS > DIAGRAM
DIAGRAPH n device for enlarging or reducing maps, plans, etc
DIAGRAPHS > DIAGRAPH
DIAGRID n diagonal structure network
DIAGRIDS > DIAGRID
DIAL n face of a clock or watch ▷ vb operate the dial or buttons on a telephone in order to contact (a number)
DIALECT n form of a language spoken in a particular area
DIALECTAL > DIALECT
DIALECTIC n logical debate by question and answer to resolve differences between two views ▷ adj of or relating to logical disputation
DIALECTS > DIALECT
DIALED > DIAL
DIALER > DIAL
DIALERS > DIAL
DIALING > DIAL
DIALINGS > DIAL
DIALIST n dial-maker
DIALISTS > DIALIST
DIALLAGE n green or brownish-black variety of the mineral augite in the form of layers of platelike

crystals

DIALLAGES > DIALLAGE

DIALLAGIC > DIALLAGE

DIALLED > DIAL

DIALLEL n interbreeding among a group of parents

DIALLER > DIAL

DIALLERS > DIAL

DIALLING > DIAL

DIALLINGS > DIAL

DIALLIST same as > DIALIST

DIALLISTS > DIALLIST

DIALOG same as > DIALOGUE

DIALOGED > DIALOG

DIALOGER > DIALOG

DIALOGERS > DIALOG

DIALOGIC > DIALOGUE

DIALOGING > DIALOG

DIALOGISE same as > DIALOGIZE

DIALOGISM n deduction with one premise and a disjunctive conclusion

DIALOGIST n person who writes or takes part in a dialogue

DIALOGITE n carbonate mineral

DIALOGIZE vb carry on a dialogue

DIALOGS > DIALOG

DIALOGUE n conversation between two people, esp in a book, film, or play ▷ vb put into the form of a dialogue

DIALOGUED > DIALOGUE

DIALOGUER > DIALOGUE

DIALOGUES > DIALOGUE

DIALS > DIAL

DIALYSATE n liquid used in dialysis

DIALYSE vb separate by dialysis

DIALYSED > DIALYSE

DIALYSER n machine that performs dialysis, esp one that removes impurities from the blood of patients with malfunctioning kidneys

DIALYSERS > DIALYSER

DIALYSES > DIALYSIS

DIALYSING > DIALYSE

DIALYSIS n filtering of blood through a membrane to remove waste products

DIALYTIC > DIALYSIS

DIALYZATE same as > DIALYSATE

DIALYZE same as > DIALYSE

DIALYZED > DIALYZE

DIALYZER same as > DIALYSER

DIALYZERS > DIALYZER

DIALYZES > DIALYZE

DIALYZING > DIALYZE

DIAMAGNET n substance exhibiting diamagnetism

DIAMANTE adj decorated with artificial jewels or sequins ▷ n fabric so covered

DIAMANTES > DIAMANTE

DIAMETER n (length of) a straight line through the centre of a circle or sphere

DIAMETERS > DIAMETER

DIAMETRAL same as > DIAMETRIC

DIAMETRIC adj of a diameter

DIAMIDE n compound containing two amido groups

DIAMIDES > DIAMIDE

DIAMIN same as > DIAMIN

DIAMINE n any chemical compound containing two amino groups in its molecules

DIAMINES > DIAMINE

DIAMINS > DIAMIN

DIAMOND n exceptionally hard, usu colourless, precious stone ▷ adj (of an anniversary) the sixtieth ▷ vb stud or decorate with diamonds

DIAMONDED > DIAMOND

DIAMONDS > DIAMOND

DIAMYL adj with two amyl groups

DIANDRIES > DIANDRY

DIANDROUS adj (of some flowers or flowering plants) having two stamens

DIANDRY n practice of having two husbands

DIANODAL adj going through a node

DIANOETIC adj of or relating to thought, esp to discursive reasoning rather than intuition

DIANOIA n perception and experience regarded as lower modes of knowledge

DIANOIAS > DIANOIA

DIANTHUS n any Eurasian caryophyllaceous plant of the widely cultivated genus *Dianthus*, such as the carnation, pink, and sweet william

DIAPASE same as > DIAPASON

DIAPASES > DIAPASE

DIAPASON n either of two stops found throughout the range of a pipe organ

DIAPASONS > DIAPASON

DIAPAUSE vb undergo diapause ▷ n period of suspended development and growth accompanied by decreased metabolism in insects and some other animals. It is correlated with seasonal changes

DIAPAUSED > DIAPAUSE

DIAPAUSES > DIAPAUSE

DIAPENTE n (in classical Greece) the interval of a perfect fifth

DIAPENTES > DIAPENTE

DIAPER n nappy ▷ vb decorate with a geometric pattern

DIAPERED > DIAPER

DIAPERING > DIAPER

DIAPERS > DIAPER

DIAPHONE n set of all realizations of a given phoneme in a language

DIAPHONES > DIAPHONE

DIAPHONIC > DIAPHONY

DIAPHONY n style of two-part polyphonic singing

DIAPHRAGM n muscular partition that separates the abdominal cavity and chest cavity

DIAPHYSES > DIAPHYSIS

DIAPHYSIS n shaft of a long bone

DIAPIR n anticlinal fold in which the brittle overlying rock has been pierced by material, such as salt, from beneath

DIAPIRIC > DIAPIR

DIAPIRISM > DIAPIR

DIAPIRS > DIAPIR

DIAPSID n reptile with two holes in rear of skull

DIAPSIDS > DIAPSID

DIAPYESES > DIAPYESIS

DIAPYESIS n discharge of pus

DIAPYETIC > DIAPYESIS

DIARCH adj (of a vascular bundle) having two strands of xylem

DIARCHAL > DIARCHY

DIARCHIC > DIARCHY

DIARCHIES > DIARCHY

DIARCHY n government by two states, individuals, etc

DIARIAL > DIARY

DIARIAN > DIARY

DIARIES > DIARY

DIARISE same as > DIARIZE

DIARISED > DIARISE

DIARISES > DIARISE

DIARISING > DIARISE

DIARIST n person who writes a diary

DIARISTIC > DIARIST

DIARISTS > DIARIST

DIARIZE vb record in diary

DIARIZED > DIARIZE

DIARIZES > DIARIZE

DIARIZING > DIARIZE

DIARRHEA same as > DIARRHOEA

DIARRHEAL > DIARRHEA

DIARRHEAS > DIARRHEA

DIARRHEIC > DIARRHEA

DIARRHOEA n frequent discharge of abnormally liquid faeces

DIARY n (book for) a record of daily events, appointments, or observations

DIASCOPE n optical projector used to display transparencies

DIASCOPES > DIASCOPE

DIASPORA n dispersion or spreading, as of people originally belonging to one nation or having a common culture

DIASPORAS > DIASPORA

DIASPORE n white, yellowish, or grey mineral

DIASPORES > DIASPORE

DIASPORIC > DIASPORA

DIASTASE n enzyme that converts starch into sugar

DIASTASES > DIASTASIS

DIASTASIC > DIASTASE

DIASTASIS n separation of an epiphysis from the long bone to which it is normally attached without fracture of the bone

DIASTATIC > DIASTASIS

DIASTEM same as > DIASTEMA

DIASTEMA n abnormal space, fissure, or cleft in a bodily organ or part

DIASTEMAS > DIASTEMA

DIASTEMS > DIASTEM

DIASTER n stage in cell division at which the chromosomes are in two groups at the poles of the spindle before forming daughter nuclei

DIASTERS > DIASTER

DIASTOLE n dilation of the chambers of the heart

DIASTOLES > DIASTOLE

DIASTOLIC > DIASTOLE

DIASTRAL > DIASTER

DIASTYLE adj having columns about three diameters apart ▷ n diastyle building

DIASTYLES > DIASTYLE

DIATHERMY n local heating of the body tissues with an electric current for medical or surgical purposes

DIATHESES > DIATHESIS

DIATHESIS n hereditary or acquired susceptibility of the body to one or more diseases

DIATHETIC > DIATHESIS

DIATOM n microscopic unicellular alga

DIATOMIC adj containing two atoms

DIATOMIST n specialist in diatoms

DIATOMITE n soft very fine-grained whitish rock consisting of the siliceous remains of diatoms deposited in the ocean or in ponds or lakes. It is used as an absorbent, filtering medium, insulator, filler, etc

DIATOMS > DIATOM

DIATONIC adj of a regular major or minor scale

DIATRETUM n Roman glass bowl

DIATRIBE n bitter critical attack

DIATRIBES > DIATRIBE

DIATRON n circuit that uses diodes

DIATRONS > DIATRON

DIATROPIC adj relating to a type of response in plants to an external stimulus

DIAXON n bipolar cell

DIAXONS > DIAXON

DIAZEPAM n chemical compound used as a minor tranquillizer and muscle relaxant and to treat acute epilepsy

DIAZEPAMS > DIAZEPAM

DIAZEUXES > DIAZEUXIS

DIAZEUXIS n separation of two tetrachords by interval of a tone

DIAZIN same as > DIAZINE

DIAZINE n organic compound

DIAZINES > DIAZINE

DIAZINON n type of insecticide

DIAZINONS > DIAZINON

DIAZINS > DIAZIN

DIAZO adj of, or relating to the reproduction of documents using the bleaching action of ultraviolet radiation on diazonium salts ▷ n document produced by this method

DIAZOES > DIAZO

DIAZOLE n type of organic compound

DIAZOLES > DIAZOLE

DIAZONIUM n type of chemical group

DIAZOS > DIAZO

DIAZOTISE same as > DIAZOTIZE

DIAZOTIZE vb cause (an aryl amine) to react with nitrous acid to produce a diazonium salt

DIB vb fish by allowing the bait to bob and dip on the surface

DIBASIC adj (of an acid, such as sulphuric acid, H_2SO_4) containing two acidic hydrogen atoms

DIBBED > DIB

DIBBER same as > DIBBLE

DIBBERS > DIBBER

DIBBING > DIB

DIBBLE n small hand tool used to make holes in the ground for seeds or plants ▷ vb make a hole in (the ground) with a dibble

DIBBLED > DIBBLE

DIBBLER > DIBBLE

DIBBLERS > DIBBLE

DIBBLES > DIBBLE

DIBBLING > DIBBLE

DIBBS n money

DIBBUK variant spelling of > DYBBUK

DIBBUKIM > DIBBUK

DIBBUKKIM > DIBBUK

DIBBUKS > DIBBUK

DIBROMIDE n chemical compound that contains two bromine atoms per molecule

DIBS > DIB

DIBUTYL adj with two butyl groups

DICACIOUS adj teasing

DICACITY n playful teasing

DICACODYL n oily slightly water-soluble poisonous liquid with garlic-like odour

DICAMBA n type of weedkiller

DICAMBAS > DICAMBA

DICAST n (in ancient Athens) a juror in the popular courts chosen by lot from a list of citizens

DICASTERY another word for > CONGREGATION

DICASTIC > DICAST

DICASTS > DICAST

DICE n small cube each of whose sides has a different number of spots (1 to 6), used in games of chance ▷ vb cut (food) into small cubes

DICED > DICE

DICENTRA n any Asian or North American plant of the genus Dicentra, such as bleeding heart and Dutchman's-breeches, having finely divided leaves and ornamental clusters of drooping flowers: family Fumariaceae

DICENTRAS > DICENTRA

DICENTRIC n abnormal chromosome with two centromeres

DICER > DICE

DICERS > DICE

DICES > DICE

DICEY adj dangerous or risky

DICH interj archaic expression meaning "may it do"

DICHASIA > DICHASIUM

DICHASIAL > DICHASIUM

DICHASIUM n cymose inflorescence in which each branch bearing a flower gives rise to two other flowering branches, as in the stitchwort

DICHOGAMY n maturation of male and female parts of a flower at different times, preventing automatic self-pollination

DICHONDRA n creeping perennial herb

DICHOPTIC adj having the eyes distinctly separate

DICHORD n two-stringed musical instrument

DICHORDS > DICHORD

DICHOTIC adj relating to or involving the stimulation of each ear simultaneously by different sounds

DICHOTOMY n division into two opposed groups or parts

DICHROIC adj having or consisting of only two colours

DICHROISM n property of a uniaxial crystal, such as tourmaline, of showing a perceptible difference in colour when viewed along two different axes in transmitted white light

DICHROITE n grey or violet-blue dichroic material

DICHROMAT n person able to distinguish only two colours

DICHROMIC adj of or involving only two colours

DICHT vb wipe

DICHTED > DICHT

DICHTING > DICHT

DICHTS > DICHT

DICIER > DICEY

DICIEST > DICEY

DICING > DICE

DICINGS > DICE

DICK n penis ▷ vb penetrate with a penis

DICKED > DICK

DICKENS n euphemism for devil

DICKENSES > DICKENS

DICKER vb trade (goods) by bargaining ▷ n petty bargain or barter

DICKERED > DICKER

DICKERING > DICKER

DICKERS > DICKER

DICKEY same as > DICKY

DICKEYS > DICKEY

DICKHEAD n stupid or despicable man or boy

DICKHEADS > DICKHEAD

DICKIE same as > DICKY

DICKIER > DICKY

DICKIES > DICKY

DICKIEST > DICKY

DICKING > DICK

DICKS > DICK

DICKTIER > DICKTY

DICKTIEST > DICKTY

DICKTY same as > DICTY

DICKY n false shirt front ▷ adj shaky or weak

DICKYBIRD See > DICKY

DICLINIES > DICLINOUS

DICLINISM > DICLINOUS

DICLINOUS adj (of flowering plants) bearing unisexual flowers

DICLINY > DICLINOUS

DICOT n type of flowering plant

DICOTS > DICOT

DICOTYL n a type of flowering plant; dicotyledon

DICOTYLS > DICOTYL

DICROTAL same as > DICROTIC

DICROTIC adj having or relating to a double pulse for each heartbeat

DICROTISM > DICROTIC

DICROTOUS same as > DICROTIC

DICT vb dictate

DICTA > DICTUM

DICTATE vb say aloud for someone else to write down ▷ n authoritative command

DICTATED > DICTATE

DICTATES > DICTATE

DICTATING > DICTATE

DICTATION n act of dictating words to be taken down in writing

DICTATOR n ruler who has complete power

DICTATORS > DICTATOR

DICTATORY adj tending to dictate

DICTATRIX > DICTATOR

DICTATURE n dictatorship

DICTED > DICT

DICTIER > DICTY

DICTIEST > DICTY

DICTING > DICT

DICTION n manner of pronouncing words and sounds

DICTIONAL > DICTION

DICTIONS > DICTION

DICTS > DICT

DICTUM n formal statement

DICTUMS > DICTUM

DICTY adj conceited; snobbish

DICTYOGEN n plant with net-veined leaves

DICUMAROL n anticoagulant drug

DICYCLIC adj having the perianth arranged in two whorls

DICYCLIES > DICYCLIC

DICYCLY > DICYCLIC

DID > DO

DIDACT n instructive person

DIDACTIC adj intended to instruct

DIDACTICS n art or science of teaching

DIDACTS > DIDACT

DIDACTYL adj having only two toes on each foot ▷ n animal with only two toes on each foot

DIDACTYLS > DIDACTYL

DIDAKAI same as > DIDICOY

DIDAKAIS > DIDAKAI

DIDAKEI same as > DIDICOY

DIDAKEIS > DIDAKEI

DIDAPPER n small grebe

DIDAPPERS > DIDAPPER

DIDDER vb shake with fear

DIDDERED > DIDDER

DIDDERING > DIDDER

DIDDERS > DIDDER

DIDDICOY same as > DIDICOY

DIDDICOYS > DIDDICOY

DIDDIER > DIDDY

DIDDIES > DIDDY

DIDDIEST > DIDDY

DIDDLE vb swindle

DIDDLED > DIDDLE

DIDDLER > DIDDLE

DIDDLERS > DIDDLE

DIDDLES > DIDDLE

DIDDLEY n worthless amount

DIDDLEYS > DIDDLEY

DIDDLIES > DIDDLY

DIDDLING > DIDDLE

DIDDLY n worthless amount

DIDDY n female breast or nipple ▷ adj of or relating to a diddy

DIDELPHIC adj with two genital tubes or ovaries

DIDELPHID n marsupial

DIDICOI same as > DIDICOY

DIDICOIS > DIDICOI

DIDICOY n (in Britain) one of a group of caravan-dwelling roadside people who live like Gypsies but are not true Romanies

DIDICOYS > DIDICOY

DIDIE *same as* > DIDY

DIDIES > DIDY

DIDJERIDU *n* Australian Aboriginal wind instrument

DIDO *n* antic

DIDOES > DIDO

DIDOS > DIDO

DIDRACHM *n* two-drachma piece

DIDRACHMA *same as* > DIDRACHM

DIDRACHMS > DIDRACHM

DIDST *form of the past tense of* > DO

DIDY *n* woman's breast

DIDYMIUM *n* mixture of the metallic rare earths neodymium and praseodymium, once thought to be an element

DIDYMIUMS > DIDYMIUM

DIDYMOUS *adj* in pairs or in two parts

DIDYNAMY *n* (of stamens) being in two unequal pairs

DIE *vb* (of a person, animal, or plant) cease all biological activity permanently ▷ *n* shaped block used to cut or form metal

DIEB *n* N African jackal

DIEBACK *n* disease of trees and shrubs characterized by death of the young shoots, which spreads to the larger branches: caused by injury to the roots or attack by bacteria or fungi ▷ *vb* (of plants) to suffer from dieback

DIEBACKS > DIEBACK

DIEBS > DIEB

DIECIOUS *same as* > DIOECIOUS

DIED > DIE

DIEDRAL *same as* > DIHEDRAL

DIEDRALS > DIEDRAL

DIEDRE *n* large shallow groove or corner in a rock face

DIEDRES > DIEDRE

DIEGESES > DIEGESIS

DIEGESIS *n* utterance of fact

DIEHARD *n* person who resists change or who holds on to an outdated attitude

DIEHARDS > DIEHARD

DIEING > DIE

DIEL *n* 24-hour period

DIELDRIN *n* highly toxic insecticide

DIELDRINS > DIELDRIN

DIELYTRA *n* genus of herbaceous plants

DIELYTRAS > DIELYTRA

DIEMAKER *n* one who makes dies

DIEMAKERS > DIEMAKER

DIENE *n* hydrocarbon that contains two carbon-to-

carbon double bonds in its molecules

DIENES > DIENE

DIEOFF *n* process of dying in large numbers

DIEOFFS > DIEOFF

DIERESES > DIERESIS

DIERESIS *same as* > DIAERESIS

DIERETIC > DIERESIS

DIES > DIE

DIESEL *vb* drive diesel-fueled vehicle ▷ *n* diesel engine

DIESELED > DIESEL

DIESELING > DIESEL

DIESELISE *same as* > DIESELIZE

DIESELIZE *vb* be equipped with diesel engine

DIESELS > DIESEL

DIESES > DIESIS

DIESINKER *n* person who engraves dies

DIESIS *n* (in ancient Greek theory) any interval smaller than a whole tone, esp a semitone in the Pythagorean scale

DIESTER *n* synthetic lubricant

DIESTERS > DIESTER

DIESTOCK *n* device holding the dies used to cut an external screw thread

DIESTOCKS > DIESTOCK

DIESTROUS *same as* > DIOESTRUS

DIESTRUM *another word for* > DIESTROUS

DIESTRUMS > DIESTRUM

DIESTRUS *same as* > DIOESTRUS

DIET *n* food that a person or animal regularly eats ▷ *vb* follow a special diet so as to lose weight ▷ *adj* (of food) suitable for a weight-reduction diet

DIETARIAN *n* dieter

DIETARIES > DIETARY

DIETARILY > DIETARY

DIETARY *adj* of or relating to a diet ▷ *n* regulated diet

DIETED > DIET

DIETER > DIET

DIETERS > DIET

DIETETIC *adj* prepared for special dietary requirements

DIETETICS *n* study of diet and nutrition

DIETHER *n* chemical compound

DIETHERS > DIETHER

DIETHYL *as in diethyl ether same as* > ETHER

DIETHYLS > DIETHYL

DIETICIAN *n* person who specializes in dietetics

DIETINE *n* low-ranking diet

DIETINES > DIETINE

DIETING > DIET

DIETINGS > DIET

DIETIST *another word for* > DIETITIAN

DIETISTS > DIETIST

DIETITIAN *same as* > DIETICIAN

DIETS > DIET

DIF *same as* > DIFF

DIFF *shortening of* > DIFFERENCE

DIFFER *vb* be unlike

DIFFERED > DIFFER

DIFFERENT *adj* unlike

DIFFERING > DIFFER

DIFFERS > DIFFER

DIFFICILE *adj* difficult

DIFFICULT *adj* requiring effort or skill to do or understand

DIFFIDENT *adj* lacking self-confidence

DIFFLUENT *adj* flowing; not fixed

DIFFORM *adj* irregular in form

DIFFRACT *vb* cause to undergo diffraction

DIFFRACTS > DIFFRACT

DIFFS > DIFF

DIFFUSE *vb* spread over a wide area ▷ *adj* widely spread

DIFFUSED > DIFFUSE

DIFFUSELY > DIFFUSE

DIFFUSER *n* person or thing that diffuses

DIFFUSERS > DIFFUSER

DIFFUSES > DIFFUSE

DIFFUSING > DIFFUSE

DIFFUSION *n* act of diffusing or the fact of being diffused

DIFFUSIVE *adj* characterized by diffusion

DIFFUSOR *same as* > DIFFUSER

DIFFUSORS > DIFFUSOR

DIFS > DIF

DIG *vb* cut into, break up, and turn over or remove (earth), esp with a spade ▷ *n* digging

DIGAMIES > DIGAMY

DIGAMIST > DIGAMY

DIGAMISTS > DIGAMY

DIGAMMA *n* letter of the Greek alphabet that became obsolete before the classical period of the language.

DIGAMMAS > DIGAMMA

DIGAMOUS > DIGAMY

DIGAMY *n* second marriage contracted after the termination of the first by death or divorce

DIGASTRIC *adj* (of certain muscles) having two fleshy portions joined by a tendon ▷ *n* muscle of the mandible that assists in lowering the lower jaw

DIGENESES > DIGENESIS

DIGENESIS *n* ability to alternate sexual and asexual means of reproduction

DIGENETIC *adj* of or relating to digenesis

DIGERATI *pl n* people who earn large amounts of

money through internet-related business

DIGEST *vb* subject to a process of digestion ▷ *n* shortened version of a book, report, or article

DIGESTANT *same as* > DIGESTIVE

DIGESTED > DIGEST

DIGESTER *n* apparatus or vessel, such as an autoclave, in which digestion is carried out

DIGESTERS > DIGESTER

DIGESTIF *n* something, esp a drink, taken as an aid to digestion, either before or after a meal

DIGESTIFS > DIGESTIF

DIGESTING > DIGEST

DIGESTION *n* (body's system for) breaking down food into easily absorbed substances

DIGESTIVE *adj* relating to digestion

DIGESTOR *same as* > DIGESTER

DIGESTORS > DIGESTOR

DIGESTS > DIGEST

DIGGABLE *adj* that can be dug

DIGGED *a past tense of* > DIG

DIGGER *n* machine used for digging

DIGGERS > DIGGER

DIGGING > DIG

DIGGINGS *pl n* material that has been dug out

DIGHT *vb* adorn or equip, as for battle

DIGHTED > DIGHT

DIGHTING > DIGHT

DIGHTS > DIGHT

DIGICAM *n* digital camera

DIGICAMS > DIGICAM

DIGIT *n* finger or toe

DIGITAL *adj* displaying information as numbers rather than with hands and a dial ▷ *n* one of the keys on the manuals of an organ or on a piano, harpsichord, etc

DIGITALIN *n* poisonous amorphous crystalline mixture of glycosides extracted from digitalis leaves and formerly used in treating heart disease.

DIGITALIS *n* drug made from foxglove leaves, used as a heart stimulant

DIGITALLY > DIGITAL

DIGITALS > DIGITAL

DIGITATE *adj* (of leaves) having leaflets in the form of a spread hand

DIGITATED *same as* > DIGITATE

DIGITISE *same as* > DIGITIZE

DIGITISED > DIGITISE

DIGITISER > DIGITIZE

DIGITISES > DIGITISE

DIGITIZE *vb* transcribe (data) into a digital form for processing by a computer

DIGITIZED *adj* recorded or stored in digital form

DIGITIZER > DIGITIZE

DIGITIZES > DIGITIZE

DIGITONIN *n* type of glycoside

DIGITOXIN *same as* > DIGOXIN

DIGITRON *n* type of tube, for displaying information, having a common anode and several cathodes shaped in the form of characters, which can be lit by a glow discharge

DIGITRONS > DIGITRON

DIGITS > DIGIT

DIGITULE *n* any small finger-like process

DIGITULES > DIGITULE

DIGLOSSIA *n* existence in a language of a high, or socially prestigious, and a low, or everyday, form, as German and Swiss German in Switzerland

DIGLOSSIC > DIGLOSSIA

DIGLOT *n* bilingual book

DIGLOTS > DIGLOT

DIGLOTTIC > DIGLOT

DIGLYPH *n* ornament in Doric frieze with two grooves

DIGLYPHS > DIGLYPH

DIGNIFIED *adj* calm, impressive, and worthy of respect

DIGNIFIES > DIGNIFY

DIGNIFY *vb* add distinction to

DIGNITARY *n* person of high official position

DIGNITIES > DIGNITY

DIGNITY *n* serious, calm, and controlled behaviour or manner

DIGONAL *adj* of or relating to a symmetry operation in which the original figure is reconstructed after a 180° turn about an axis

DIGOXIN *n* glycoside extracted from the leaves of the woolly foxglove

DIGOXINS > DIGOXIN

DIGRAPH *n* two letters used to represent a single sound, such as gh in tough

DIGRAPHIC > DIGRAPH

DIGRAPHS > DIGRAPH

DIGRESS *vb* depart from the main subject in speech or writing

DIGRESSED > DIGRESS

DIGRESSER > DIGRESS

DIGRESSES > DIGRESS

DIGS > DIG

DIGYNIAN *adj* relating to plant class Digynia

DIGYNOUS *another word for* > DIGYNIAN

DIHEDRA > DIHEDRON

DIHEDRAL *adj* having or formed by two intersecting planes ▷ *n* figure formed by two intersecting planes

DIHEDRALS > DIHEDRAL

DIHEDRON *same as* > DIHEDRAL

DIHEDRONS > DIHEDRON

DIHYBRID *n* offspring of two individuals that differ with respect to two pairs of genes

DIHYBRIDS > DIHYBRID

DIHYDRIC *adj* (of an alcohol) containing two hydroxyl groups per molecule

DIKA *n* wild mango

DIKAS > DIKA

DIKAST *same as* > DICAST

DIKASTS > DIKAST

DIKDIK *n* small African antelope

DIKDIKS > DIKDIK

DIKE *same as* > DYKE

DIKED > DIKE

DIKER *n* builder of dikes

DIKERS > DIKER

DIKES > DIKE

DIKEY *adj* (of a lesbian) masculine

DIKIER > DIKEY

DIKIEST > DIKEY

DIKING > DIKE

DIKKOP *n* any of several brownish shore birds of the family *Burhinidae*, esp *Burhinus oedicnemus*, having a large head and eyes: order *Charadriiformes*

DIKKOPS > DIKKOP

DIKTAT *n* dictatorial decree

DIKTATS > DIKTAT

DILATABLE > DILATE

DILATABLY > DILATE

DILATANCY *n* phenomenon caused by the nature of the stacking or fitting together of particles or granules in a heterogeneous system, such as the solidification of certain sols under pressure, and the thixotropy of certain gels

DILATANT *adj* tending to dilate ▷ *n* something, such as a catheter, that causes dilation

DILATANTS > DILATANT

DILATATE *same as* > DILATE

DILATATOR *same as* > DILATOR

DILATE *vb* make or become wider or larger

DILATED > DILATE

DILATER *same as* > DILATOR

DILATERS > DILATER

DILATES > DILATE

DILATING > DILATE

DILATION > DILATE

DILATIONS > DILATE

DILATIVE > DILATE

DILATOR *n* something that dilates an object, esp a surgical instrument for dilating a bodily cavity

DILATORS > DILATOR

DILATORY *adj* tending or intended to waste time

DILDO *n* object used as a substitute for an erect penis

DILDOE *same as* > DILDO

DILDOES > DILDOE

DILDOS > DILDO

DILEMMA *n* situation offering a choice between two equally undesirable alternatives

DILEMMAS > DILEMMA

DILEMMIC > DILEMMA

DILIGENCE *n* steady and careful application

DILIGENT *adj* careful and persevering in carrying out duties

DILL *vb* flavour with dill ▷ *n* sweet-smelling herb

DILLED > DILL

DILLI *n* dilly bag; small bag, esp one made of plaited grass and used for carrying food

DILLIER > DILLY

DILLIES > DILLY

DILLIEST > DILLY

DILLING > DILL

DILLINGS > DILL

DILLIS > DILLI

DILLS > DILL

DILLY *adj* foolish ▷ *n* person or thing that is remarkable

DILTIAZEM *n* drug used to treat angina

DILUENT *adj* causing dilution or serving to dilute ▷ *n* substance used for or causing dilution

DILUENTS > DILUENT

DILUTABLE > DILUTE

DILUTE *vb* make (a liquid) less concentrated, esp by adding water ▷ *adj* (of a liquid) thin and watery

DILUTED > DILUTE

DILUTEE > DILUTE

DILUTEES > DILUTE

DILUTER > DILUTE

DILUTERS > DILUTE

DILUTES > DILUTE

DILUTING > DILUTE

DILUTION *n* act of diluting or state of being diluted

DILUTIONS > DILUTION

DILUTIVE *adj* having effect of decreasing earnings per share

DILUTOR *n* having diluting effect

DILUTORS > DILUTOR

DILUVIA > DILUVIUM

DILUVIAL *adj* of a flood, esp the great Flood described in the Old Testament

DILUVIAN *same as* > DILUVIAL

DILUVION *same as* > DILUVIUM

DILUVIONS > DILUVION

DILUVIUM *n* glacial drift

DILUVIUMS > DILUVIUM

DIM *adj* badly lit ▷ *vb* make or become dim

DIMBLE *n* wooded hollow; dingle

DIMBLES > DIMBLE

DIME *n* coin of the US and Canada, worth ten cents

DIMENSION *n* measurement of the size of something in a particular direction ▷ *vb* shape or cut to specified dimensions

DIMER *n* molecule made up of two identical molecules bonded together

DIMERIC *adj* of a dimer

DIMERISE *same as* > DIMERIZE

DIMERISED > DIMERISE

DIMERISES > DIMERISE

DIMERISM > DIMEROUS

DIMERISMS > DIMEROUS

DIMERIZE *vb* react or cause to react to form a dimer

DIMERIZED > DIMERIZE

DIMERIZES > DIMERIZE

DIMEROUS *adj* consisting of or divided into two segments, as the tarsi of some insects

DIMERS > DIMER

DIMES > DIME

DIMETER *n* line of verse consisting of two metrical feet or a verse written in this metre

DIMETERS > DIMETER

DIMETHYL *n* ethane

DIMETHYLS > DIMETHYL

DIMETRIC *adj* of, relating to, or shaped like a quadrilateral

DIMIDIATE *adj* divided in halves ▷ *vb* halve (two bearings) so that they can be represented on the same shield

DIMINISH *vb* make or become smaller, fewer, or less

DIMISSORY *adj* granting permission to be ordained

DIMITIES > DIMITY

DIMITY *n* light strong cotton fabric with woven stripes or squares

DIMLY > DIM

DIMMABLE *adj* that can be dimmed

DIMMED > DIM

DIMMER > DIM

DIMMERS > DIM

DIMMEST > DIM

DIMMING > DIM

DIMMISH > DIM

DIMNESS > DIM

DIMNESSES > DIM

DIMORPH *n* either of two forms of a substance that exhibits dimorphism

DIMORPHIC > DIMORPHISM

DIMORPHS > DIMORPH

DIMOUT *n* reduction of lighting

DIMOUTS > DIMOUT

DIMP *n* in Northern English dialect, a cigarette butt

DIMPLE *n* small natural dent, esp in the cheeks or chin ▷ *vb* produce dimples by smiling

DIMPLED > DIMPLE

DIMPLES > DIMPLE

DIMPLIER > DIMPLE

d

DIMPLIEST > DIMPLE
DIMPLING > DIMPLE
DIMPLY > DIMPLE
DIMPS > DIMP
DIMPSIES > DIMPSY
DIMPSY n twilight
DIMS > DIM
DIMWIT n stupid person
DIMWITS > DIMWIT
DIMWITTED > DIMWIT
DIMYARIAN adj with two adductor muscles
DIN n loud unpleasant confused noise ▷ vb instil (something) into someone by constant repetition
DINAR n monetary unit of various Balkan, Middle Eastern, and North African countries
DINARCHY same as > DIARCHY
DINARS > DINAR
DINDLE another word for > DINNLE
DINDLED > DINDLE
DINDLES > DINDLE
DINDLING > DINDLE
DINE vb eat dinner
DINED > DINE
DINER n person eating a meal
DINERIC adj of or concerned with the interface between immiscible liquids
DINERO n money
DINEROS > DINERO
DINERS > DINER
DINES > DINE
DINETTE n alcove or small area for use as a dining room
DINETTES > DINETTE
DINFUL adj noisy
DING n small dent in a vehicle ▷ vb ring or cause to ring, esp with tedious repetition
DINGBAT n any unnamed object, esp one used as a missile
DINGBATS > DINGBAT
DINGDONG n sound of a bell or bells ▷ vb make such a sound
DINGDONGS > DINGDONG
DINGE n dent ▷ vb make a dent in (something)
DINGED > DINGE
DINGER n (in baseball) home run
DINGERS > DINGER
DINGES n jocular word for something whose name is unknown or forgotten
DINGESES > DINGES
DINGEY same as > DINGHY
DINGEYS > DINGEY
DINGHIES > DINGHY
DINGHY n small boat, powered by sails, oars, or a motor
DINGIER > DINGY
DINGIES > DINGY
DINGIEST > DINGY
DINGILY > DINGY

DINGINESS > DINGY
DINGING > DINGE
DINGLE n small wooded hollow or valley
DINGLES > DINGLE
DINGO n Australian wild dog ▷ vb act in a cowardly manner
DINGOED > DINGO
DINGOES > DINGO
DINGOING > DINGO
DINGS > DING
DINGUS same as > DINGES
DINGUSES > DINGUS
DINGY adj lacking light
DINIC n remedy for vertigo
DINICS > DINIC
DINING > DINE
DINITRO adj containing two nitro groups
DINK adj neat or neatly dressed ▷ vb carry (a second person) on a horse, bicycle, etc ▷ n ball struck delicately
DINKED > DINK
DINKER > DINK
DINKEST > DINK
DINKEY n small locomotive
DINKEYS > DINKEY
DINKIE n affluent married childless person ▷ adj designed for or appealing to dinkies
DINKIER > DINKY
DINKIES > DINKIE
DINKIEST > DINKY
DINKING > DINK
DINKLY adj neat
DINKS > DINK
DINKUM n truth or genuineness
DINKUMS > DINKUM
DINKY adj small and neat
DINMONT n neutered sheep
DINMONTS > DINMONT
DINNA vb a Scots word for do not
DINNED > DIN
DINNER vb dine ▷ n main meal of the day, eaten either in the evening or at midday
DINNERED > DINNER
DINNERING > DINNER
DINNERS > DINNER
DINNING > DIN
DINNLE vb shake
DINNLED > DINNLE
DINNLES > DINNLE
DINNLING > DINNLE
DINO n dinosaur
DINOCERAS another name for a > UINTATHERE
DINOMANIA n strong interest in dinosaurs
DINOS > DINO
DINOSAUR n type of extinct prehistoric reptile, many of which were of gigantic size
DINOSAURS > DINOSAUR
DINOTHERE n any extinct late Tertiary elephant-like mammal of the genus Dinotherium (or Deinotherium), having a down-turned jaw with

tusks curving downwards and backwards
DINS > DIN
DINT variant of > DENT
DINTED > DINT
DINTING > DINT
DINTLESS > DINT
DINTS > DINT
DIOBOL n ancient Greek coin
DIOBOLON same as > DIOBOL
DIOBOLONS > DIOBOLON
DIOBOLS > DIOBOL
DIOCESAN adj of or relating to a diocese ▷ n bishop of a diocese
DIOCESANS > DIOCESAN
DIOCESE n district over which a bishop has control
DIOCESES > DIOCESE
DIODE n semiconductor device for converting alternating current to direct current
DIODES > DIODE
DIOECIES > DIOECY
DIOECIOUS adj (of plants) having the male and female reproductive organs on separate plants
DIOECISM > DIOECIOUS
DIOECISMS > DIOECIOUS
DIOECY n state of being dioecious
DIOESTRUS n period in mammal's oestral cycle
DIOICOUS same as > DIOECIOUS
DIOL n any of a class of alcohols that have two hydroxyl groups in each molecule
DIOLEFIN n type of polymer
DIOLEFINS > DIOLEFIN
DIOLS > DIOL
DIONYSIAC same as > DIONYSIAN
DIONYSIAN adj wild or orgiastic
DIOPSIDE n colourless or pale-green pyroxene mineral
DIOPSIDES > DIOPSIDE
DIOPSIDIC > DIOPSIDE
DIOPTASE n green glassy mineral
DIOPTASES > DIOPTASE
DIOPTER same as > DIOPTRE
DIOPTERS > DIOPTER
DIOPTRAL > DIOPTRE
DIOPTRATE adj (of compound eye) divided by transverse line
DIOPTRE n unit for measuring the refractive power of a lens
DIOPTRES > DIOPTRE
DIOPTRIC adj of or concerned with dioptrics
DIOPTRICS n branch of geometrical optics concerned with the formation of images by lenses
DIORAMA n miniature three-dimensional scene, in which models of figures

are seen against a three-dimensional background
DIORAMAS > DIORAMA
DIORAMIC > DIORAMA
DIORISM n definition; clarity
DIORISMS > DIORISM
DIORISTIC > DIORISM
DIORITE n dark coarse-grained igneous plutonic rock consisting of plagioclase feldspar and ferromagnesian minerals such as hornblende
DIORITES > DIORITE
DIORITIC > DIORITE
DIOSGENIN n yam-based substance used in hormone therapy
DIOTA n type of ancient vase
DIOTAS > DIOTA
DIOXAN n colourless insoluble toxic liquid made by heating ethanediol with sulphuric acid
DIOXANE same as > DIOXAN
DIOXANES > DIOXANE
DIOXANS > DIOXAN
DIOXID same as > DIOXIDE
DIOXIDE n oxide containing two oxygen atoms per molecule
DIOXIDES > DIOXIDE
DIOXIDS > DIOXID
DIOXIN n any of a number of mostly poisonous chemical by-products of the manufacture of certain herbicides and bactericides, esp the extremely toxic 2,3,7,8-tetrachlorodibenzo-para-dioxin
DIOXINS > DIOXIN
DIP vb plunge quickly or briefly into a liquid ▷ n dipping
DIPCHICK same as > DABCHICK
DIPCHICKS > DIPCHICK
DIPEPTIDE n compound consisting of two linked amino acids
DIPHASE adj of, having, or concerned with two phases
DIPHASIC same as > DIPHASE
DIPHENYL another name for > BIPHENYL
DIPHENYLS > DIPHENYL
DIPHONE n combination of two speech sounds
DIPHONES > DIPHONE
DIPHTHONG n union of two vowel sounds in a single compound sound
DIPHYSITE n belief in Christ having both divine and human natures
DIPLEGIA n paralysis of corresponding parts on both sides of the body
DIPLEGIAS > DIPLEGIA
DIPLEGIC > DIPLEGIA
DIPLEX adj (in

telecommunications) permitting the transmission of simultaneous signals in both directions

DIPLEXER *n* device that enables the simultaneous transmission of more than one signal

DIPLEXERS > DIPLEXER

DIPLOE *n* spongy bone separating the two layers of compact bone of the skull

DIPLOES > DIPLOE

DIPLOGEN *n* heavy hydrogen

DIPLOGENS > DIPLOGEN

DIPLOIC *adj* relating to diploe

DIPLOID *adj* denoting a cell or organism with pairs of homologous chromosomes ▷ *n* diploid cell or organism

DIPLOIDIC > DIPLOID

DIPLOIDS > DIPLOID

DIPLOIDY > DIPLOID

DIPLOMA *vb* bestow diploma on ▷ *n* qualification awarded by a college on successful completion of a course

DIPLOMACY *n* conduct of the relations between nations by peaceful means

DIPLOMAED > DIPLOMA

DIPLOMAS > DIPLOMA

DIPLOMAT *n* official engaged in diplomacy

DIPLOMATA > DIPLOMA

DIPLOMATE *n* any person who has been granted a diploma, esp a physician certified as a specialist

DIPLOMATS > DIPLOMAT

DIPLON *another name for* > DEUTERON

DIPLONEMA *a less common name for* > DIPLOTENE

DIPLONS > DIPLON

DIPLONT *n* animal or plant that has the diploid number of chromosomes in its somatic cells

DIPLONTIC > DIPLONT

DIPLONTS > DIPLONT

DIPLOPIA *n* visual defect in which a single object is seen in duplicate

DIPLOPIAS > DIPLOPIA

DIPLOPIC > DIPLOPIA

DIPLOPOD *n* any arthropod of the class *Diplopoda*, which includes the millipedes

DIPLOPODS > DIPLOPOD

DIPLOSES > DIPLOSIS

DIPLOSIS *n* doubling of the haploid number of chromosomes that occurs during fusion of gametes to form a diploid zygote

DIPLOTENE *n* fourth stage of the prophase of meiosis, during which the paired homologous

chromosomes separate except at the places where genetic exchange has occurred

DIPLOZOA *n* type of parasitic worm

DIPLOZOIC *adj* (of certain animals) bilaterally symmetrical

DIPLOZOON *n* type of parasitic worm

DIPNET *vb* fish using fishing net on pole

DIPNETS > DIPNET

DIPNETTED > DIPNET

DIPNOAN *adj* of, relating to, or belonging to the *Dipnoi*, a subclass of bony fishes comprising the lungfishes ▷ *nany lungfish*

DIPNOANS > DIPNOAN

DIPNOOUS *adj* having lungs and gills

DIPODIC > DIPODY

DIPODIES > DIPODY

DIPODY *n* metrical unit consisting of two feet

DIPOLAR > DIPOLE

DIPOLE *n* two equal but opposite electric charges or magnetic poles separated by a small distance

DIPOLES > DIPOLE

DIPPABLE > DIP

DIPPED > DIP

DIPPER *n* ladle used for dipping

DIPPERFUL *n* amount held by scoop

DIPPERS > DIPPER

DIPPIER > DIPPY

DIPPIEST > DIPPY

DIPPINESS > DIPPY

DIPPING > DIP

DIPPINGS > DIP

DIPPY *adj* odd, eccentric, or crazy

DIPROTIC *adj* having two hydrogen atoms

DIPS > DIP

DIPSADES > DIPSAS

DIPSAS *n* type of snake

DIPSHIT *n* stupid person

DIPSHITS > DIPSHIT

DIPSO *same as* > DIPSOMANIAC

DIPSOS > DIPSO

DIPSTICK *n* notched rod dipped into a container to measure the level of a liquid

DIPSTICKS > DIPSTICK

DIPT > DIP

DIPTERA *n* order of insects with two wings

DIPTERAL *adj* having a double row of columns

DIPTERAN *n* dipterous insect ▷ *adj* having two wings or winglike parts

DIPTERANS > DIPTERAN

DIPTERAS > DIPTERA

DIPTERIST *n* fly expert

DIPTEROI > DIPTEROS

DIPTERON *same as* > DIPTERAN

DIPTERONS > DIPTERON

DIPTEROS *n* Greek building

with double columns

DIPTEROUS *adj* having two wings or winglike parts

DIPTYCA *same as* > DIPTYCH

DIPTYCAS > DIPTYCA

DIPTYCH *n* painting on two hinged panels

DIPTYCHS > DIPTYCH

DIQUARK *n* low-energy configuration of two quarks attracted to one another by virtue of having antisymmetric colours and spins

DIQUARKS > DIQUARK

DIQUAT *n* type of herbicide

DIQUATS > DIQUAT

DIRAM *n* money unit of Tajikistan

DIRAMS > DIRAM

DIRDAM *same as* > DIRDUM

DIRDAMS > DIRDAM

DIRDUM *n* tumult

DIRDUMS > DIRDUM

DIRE *adj* disastrous, urgent, or terrible

DIRECT *adj* (of a route) shortest, straight ▷ *adv* in a direct manner ▷ *vb* lead and organize

DIRECTED *adj* (of a number, line, or angle) having either a positive or negative sign to distinguish measurement in one direction or orientation from that in the opposite direction or orientation

DIRECTER > DIRECT

DIRECTEST > DIRECT

DIRECTING > DIRECT

DIRECTION *n* course or line along which a person or thing moves, points, or lies

DIRECTIVE *n* instruction, order ▷ *adj* tending to direct

DIRECTLY *adv* in a direct manner

DIRECTOR *n* person or thing that directs or controls

DIRECTORS > DIRECTOR

DIRECTORY *n* book listing names, addresses, and telephone numbers ▷ *adj* directing

DIRECTRIX *n* fixed reference line, situated on the convex side of a conic section, that is used when defining or calculating its eccentricity

DIRECTS > DIRECT

DIREFUL *same as* > DIRE

DIREFULLY > DIREFUL

DIRELY > DIRE

DIREMPT *vb* separate with force

DIREMPTED > DIREMPT

DIREMPTS > DIREMPT

DIRENESS > DIRE

DIRER > DIRE

DIREST > DIRE

DIRGE *n* slow sad song of mourning

DIRGEFUL > DIRGE

DIRGELIKE > DIRGE

DIRGES > DIRGE

DIRHAM *n* standard monetary unit of Morocco, divided into 100 centimes

DIRHAMS > DIRHAM

DIRHEM *same as* > DIRHAM

DIRHEMS > DIRHEM

DIRIGE *n* dirge

DIRIGENT *adj* directing

DIRIGES > DIRIGE

DIRIGIBLE *adj* able to be steered ▷ *n* airship

DIRIGISM *same as* > DIRIGISME

DIRIGISME *n* control by the state of economic and social matters

DIRIGISMS > DIRIGISM

DIRIGISTE > DIRIGISME

DIRIMENT *adj* (of an impediment to marriage in canon law) totally invalidating

DIRK *n* dagger, formerly worn by Scottish Highlanders ▷ *vb* stab with a dirk

DIRKE *variant of same as* > DIRK

DIRKED > DIRK

DIRKES > DIRKE

DIRKING > DIRK

DIRKS > DIRK

DIRL *vb* tingle; vibrate

DIRLED > DIRL

DIRLING > DIRL

DIRLS > DIRL

DIRNDL *n* full gathered skirt originating from Tyrolean peasant wear

DIRNDLS > DIRNDL

DIRT *vb* soil ▷ *n* unclean substance, filth

DIRTBAG *n* filthy person

DIRTBAGS > DIRTBAG

DIRTED > DIRT

DIRTIED > DIRTY

DIRTIER > DIRTY

DIRTIES > DIRTY

DIRTIEST > DIRTY

DIRTILY > DIRTY

DIRTINESS > DIRTY

DIRTING > DIRT

DIRTS > DIRT

DIRTY *adj* covered or marked with dirt ▷ *vb* make dirty

DIRTYING > DIRTY

DIS *same as* > DISS

DISA *n* type of orchid

DISABLE *vb* make ineffective, unfit, or incapable

DISABLED *adj* lacking a physical power, such as the ability to walk

DISABLER > DISABLE

DISABLERS > DISABLE

DISABLES > DISABLE

DISABLING > DISABLE

DISABUSAL > DISABUSE

DISABUSE *vb* rid (someone) of a mistaken idea

DISABUSED > DISABUSE

DISABUSES > DISABUSE

DISACCORD *n* lack of agreement or harmony

▷*vb* be out of agreement

DISADORN *vb* deprive of ornamentation

DISADORNS > DISADORN

DISAFFECT *vb* cause to lose loyalty or affection

DISAFFIRM *vb* deny or contradict (a statement)

DISAGREE *vb* argue or have different opinions

DISAGREED > DISAGREE

DISAGREES > DISAGREE

DISALLIED > DISALLY

DISALLIES > DISALLY

DISALLOW *vb* reject as untrue or invalid

DISALLOWS > DISALLOW

DISALLY *vb* separate

DISANCHOR *vb* raise anchor of

DISANNEX *vb* disunite

DISANNUL *vb* cancel

DISANNULS > DISANNUL

DISANOINT *vb* invalidate anointment of

DISAPPEAR *vb* cease to be visible

DISAPPLY *vb* make (law) invalid

DISARM *vb* deprive of weapons

DISARMED > DISARM

DISARMER > DISARM

DISARMERS > DISARM

DISARMING *adj* removing hostility or suspicion

DISARMS > DISARM

DISARRAY *n* confusion and lack of discipline ▷*vb* throw into confusion

DISARRAYS > DISARRAY

DISAS > DISA

DISASTER *n* occurrence that causes great distress or destruction

DISASTERS > DISASTER

DISATTIRE *vb* remove clothes from

DISATTUNE *vb* render out of tune

DISAVOUCH *archaic form of* > DISAVOW

DISAVOW *vb* deny connection with or responsibility for

DISAVOWAL > DISAVOW

DISAVOWED > DISAVOW

DISAVOWER > DISAVOW

DISAVOWS > DISAVOW

DISBAND *vb* (cause to) cease to function as a group

DISBANDED > DISBAND

DISBANDS > DISBAND

DISBAR *vb* deprive (a barrister) of the right to practise

DISBARK *same as* > DISEMBARK

DISBARKED > DISBARK

DISBARKS > DISBARK

DISBARRED > DISBAR

DISBARS > DISBAR

DISBELIEF *n* refusal or reluctance to believe

DISBENCH *vb* remove from bench

DISBODIED *adj*

disembodied

DISBOSOM *vb* disclose

DISBOSOMS > DISBOSOM

DISBOUND *adj* unbound

DISBOWEL *vb* disembowel

DISBOWELS > DISBOWEL

DISBRANCH *vb* remove or cut a branch or branches from (a tree)

DISBUD *vb* remove superfluous buds, flowers, or shoots from (a plant, esp a fruit tree)

DISBUDDED > DISBUD

DISBUDS > DISBUD

DISBURDEN *vb* remove a load from (a person or animal)

DISBURSAL > DISBURSE

DISBURSE *vb* pay out

DISBURSED > DISBURSE

DISBURSER > DISBURSE

DISBURSES > DISBURSE

DISC *n* flat circular object ▷*vb* work (land) with a disc harrow

DISCAGE *vb* release from cage

DISCAGED > DISCAGE

DISCAGES > DISCAGE

DISCAGING > DISCAGE

DISCAL *adj* relating to or resembling a disc

DISCALCED *adj* barefooted: used to denote friars and nuns who wear sandals

DISCANDIE *same as* > DISCANDY

DISCANDY *vb* melt; dissolve

DISCANT *same as* > DESCANT

DISCANTED > DISCANT

DISCANTER > DISCANT

DISCANTS > DISCANT

DISCARD *vb* get rid of (something or someone) as useless or undesirable ▷*n* person or thing that has been cast aside

DISCARDED > DISCARD

DISCARDER > DISCARD

DISCARDS > DISCARD

DISCASE *vb* remove case from

DISCASED > DISCASE

DISCASES > DISCASE

DISCASING > DISCASE

DISCED > DISC

DISCEPT *vb* discuss

DISCEPTED > DISCEPT

DISCEPTS > DISCEPT

DISCERN *vb* see or be aware of (something) clearly

DISCERNED > DISCERN

DISCERNER > DISCERN

DISCERNS > DISCERN

DISCERP *vb* divide

DISCERPED > DISCERP

DISCERPS > DISCERP

DISCHARGE *vb* release, allow to go ▷*n* substance that comes out from a place

DISCHURCH *vb* deprive of church membership

DISCI > DISCUS

DISCIDE *vb* split

DISCIDED > DISCIDE

DISCIDES > DISCIDE

DISCIDING > DISCIDE

DISCIFORM *adj* disc-shaped

DISCINCT *adj* loosely dressed, without belt

DISCING > DISC

DISCIPLE *vb* teach ▷*n* follower of the doctrines of a teacher, esp Jesus Christ

DISCIPLED > DISCIPLE

DISCIPLES > DISCIPLE

DISCLAIM *vb* deny (responsibility for or knowledge of something)

DISCLAIMS > DISCLAIM

DISCLIKE > DISC

DISCLIMAX *n* climax community resulting from the activities of man or domestic animals in climatic and other conditions that would otherwise support a different type of community

DISCLOSE *vb* make known

DISCLOSED > DISCLOSE

DISCLOSER > DISCLOSE

DISCLOSES > DISCLOSE

DISCLOST > DISCLOSE

DISCO *vb* go to a disco ▷*n* nightclub where people dance to amplified pop records

DISCOBOLI *pl n* discus throwers

DISCOED > DISCO

DISCOER > DISCO

DISCOERS > DISCO

DISCOID *adj* like a disc ▷*n* dislike object

DISCOIDAL *adj* like a disc

DISCOIDS > DISCOID

DISCOING > DISCO

DISCOLOGY *n* study of gramophone records

DISCOLOR *same as* > DISCOLOUR

DISCOLORS > DISCOLOR

DISCOLOUR *vb* change in colour, fade

DISCOMFIT *vb* make uneasy or confused

DISCOMMON *vb* deprive (land) of the character and status of common, as by enclosure

DISCORD *n* lack of agreement or harmony between people ▷*vb* disagree

DISCORDED > DISCORD

DISCORDS > DISCORD

DISCOS > DISCO

DISCOUNT *vb* take no account of (something) because it is considered to be unreliable, prejudiced, or irrelevant ▷*n* deduction from the full price of something

DISCOUNTS > DISCOUNT

DISCOURE *vb* discover

DISCOURED > DISCOURE

DISCOURES > DISCOURE

DISCOURSE *n* conversation ▷*vb* speak or write (about)

at length

DISCOVER *vb* be the first to find or to find out about

DISCOVERS > DISCOVER

DISCOVERT *adj* (of a woman) not under the protection of a husband

DISCOVERY *n* discovering

DISCREDIT *vb* damage the reputation of ▷*n* damage to someone's reputation

DISCREET *adj* careful to avoid embarrassment, esp by keeping confidences secret

DISCRETE *adj* separate, distinct

DISCRETER > DISCRETE

DISCROWN *vb* deprive of a crown

DISCROWNS > DISCROWN

DISCS > DISC

DISCUMBER *vb* disencumber

DISCURE *old form of* > DISCOVER

DISCURED > DISCURE

DISCURES > DISCURE

DISCURING > DISCURE

DISCURSUS *n* discursive reasoning

DISCUS *n* heavy disc-shaped object thrown in sports competitions

DISCUSES > DISCUS

DISCUSS *vb* consider (something) by talking it over

DISCUSSED > DISCUSS

DISCUSSER > DISCUSS

DISCUSSES > DISCUSS

DISDAIN *n* feeling of superiority and dislike ▷*vb* refuse with disdain

DISDAINED > DISDAIN

DISDAINS > DISDAIN

DISEASE *vb* make uneasy ▷*n* illness, sickness

DISEASED *adj* having or affected with disease

DISEASES > DISEASE

DISEASING > DISEASE

DISEDGE *vb* render blunt

DISEDGED > DISEDGE

DISEDGES > DISEDGE

DISEDGING > DISEDGE

DISEMBARK *vb* get off a ship, aircraft, or bus

DISEMBODY *vb* free from the body or from physical form

DISEMPLOY *vb* dismiss from employment

DISENABLE *vb* cause to become incapable

DISENDOW *vb* take away an endowment from

DISENDOWS > DISENDOW

DISENGAGE *vb* release from a connection

DISENROL *vb* remove from register

DISENROLS > DISENROL

DISENTAIL *vb* free (an estate) from entail ▷*n* act of disentailing

DISENTOMB *vb* disinter

DISESTEEM *vb* think little of ▷*n* lack of esteem

DISEUR *same as* > DISEUSE
DISEURS > DISEUR
DISEUSE *n* (esp formerly) an actress who presents dramatic recitals, usually sung accompanied by music
DISEUSES > DISEUSE
DISFAME *n* discredit
DISFAMES > DISFAME
DISFAVOR *same as* > DISFAVOUR
DISFAVORS > DISFAVOR
DISFAVOUR *n* disapproval or dislike ▷ *vb* regard or treat with disapproval or dislike
DISFIGURE *vb* spoil the appearance of
DISFLESH *vb* reduce flesh of
DISFLUENT *adj* lacking fluency in speech
DISFOREST *same as* > DEFOREST
DISFORM *vb* change form of
DISFORMED > DISFORM
DISFORMS > DISFORM
DISFROCK *another word for* > UNFROCK
DISFROCKS > DISFROCK
DISGAVEL *vb* deprive of quality of gavelkind
DISGAVELS > DISGAVEL
DISGEST *vb* digest
DISGESTED > DISGEST
DISGESTS > DISGEST
DISGODDED *adj* deprived of religion
DISGORGE *vb* empty out, discharge
DISGORGED > DISGORGE
DISGORGER *n* thin notched metal implement for removing hooks from a fish
DISGORGES > DISGORGE
DISGOWN *vb* remove gown from
DISGOWNED > DISGOWN
DISGOWNS > DISGOWN
DISGRACE *n* condition of shame, loss of reputation, or dishonour ▷ *vb* bring shame upon (oneself or others)
DISGRACED > DISGRACE
DISGRACER > DISGRACE
DISGRACES > DISGRACE
DISGRADE *vb* degrade
DISGRADED > DISGRADE
DISGRADES > DISGRADE
DISGUISE *vb* change the appearance or manner in order to conceal the identity of (someone or something) ▷ *n* mask, costume, or manner that disguises
DISGUISED > DISGUISE
DISGUISER > DISGUISE
DISGUISES > DISGUISE
DISGUST *n* great loathing or distaste ▷ *vb* sicken, fill with loathing
DISGUSTED > DISGUST
DISGUSTS > DISGUST
DISH *n* shallow container used for holding or serving food ▷ *vb* put into a dish

DISHABIT *vb* dislodge
DISHABITS > DISHABIT
DISHABLE *obsolete form of* > DISABLE
DISHABLED > DISHABLE
DISHABLES > DISHABLE
DISHALLOW *vb* make unholy
DISHCLOTH *n* cloth for washing dishes
DISHCLOUT *same as* > DISHCLOTH
DISHDASHA *n* long-sleeved collarless white garment worn by some Muslim men
DISHED *adj* shaped like a dish
DISHELM *vb* remove helmet from
DISHELMED > DISHELM
DISHELMS > DISHELM
DISHERIT *vb* disinherit
DISHERITS > DISHERIT
DISHES > DISH
DISHEVEL *vb* disarrange (the hair or clothes) of (someone)
DISHEVELS > DISHEVEL
DISHFUL *n* the amount that a dish is able to hold
DISHFULS > DISHFUL
DISHIER > DISHY
DISHIEST > DISHY
DISHING > DISH
DISHINGS > DISH
DISHLIKE > DISH
DISHOME *vb* deprive of home
DISHOMED > DISHOME
DISHOMES > DISHOME
DISHOMING > DISHOME
DISHONEST *adj* not honest or fair
DISHONOR *same as* > DISHONOUR
DISHONORS > DISHONOR
DISHONOUR *vb* treat with disrespect ▷ *n* lack of respect
DISHORN *vb* remove horns from
DISHORNED > DISHORN
DISHORNS > DISHORN
DISHORSE *vb* dismount
DISHORSED > DISHORSE
DISHORSES > DISHORSE
DISHOUSE *vb* deprive of home
DISHOUSED > DISHOUSE
DISHOUSES > DISHOUSE
DISHPAN *n* large pan for washing dishes, pots, etc
DISHPANS > DISHPAN
DISHRAG *n* dishcloth
DISHRAGS > DISHRAG
DISHTOWEL *n* towel for drying dishes and kitchen utensils
DISHUMOUR *vb* upset; offend
DISHWARE *n* tableware
DISHWARES > DISHWARE
DISHWATER *n* water in which dishes and kitchen utensils are or have been washed
DISHY *adj* good-looking
DISILLUDE *vb* remove illusions from

DISIMMURE *vb* release
DISINFECT *vb* rid of harmful germs, chemically
DISINFEST *vb* rid of vermin
DISINFORM *vb* give wrong information
DISINHUME *vb* dig up
DISINTER *vb* dig up
DISINTERS > DISINTER
DISINURE *vb* render unaccustomed
DISINURED > DISINURE
DISINURES > DISINURE
DISINVEST *vb* remove investment (from)
DISINVITE *vb* retract invitation to
DISJASKIT *adj* fatigued
DISJECT *vb* break apart
DISJECTED > DISJECT
DISJECTS > DISJECT
DISJOIN *vb* disconnect or become disconnected
DISJOINED > DISJOIN
DISJOINS > DISJOIN
DISJOINT *vb* take apart or come apart at the joints ▷ *adj* (of two sets) having no members in common
DISJOINTS > DISJOINT
DISJUNCT *adj* not united or joined ▷ *n* one of the propositions or formulas in a disjunction
DISJUNCTS > DISJUNCT
DISJUNE *n* breakfast
DISJUNES > DISJUNE
DISK *same as* > DISC
DISKED > DISK
DISKETTE *n* floppy disk
DISKETTES > DISKETTE
DISKING > DISK
DISKLESS > DISK
DISKLIKE > DISK
DISKS > DISK
DISLEAF *vb* remove leaf or leaves from
DISLEAFED > DISLEAF
DISLEAFS > DISLEAF
DISLEAL *archaic form of* > DISLOYAL
DISLEAVE *variant of* > DISLEAF
DISLEAVED > DISLEAVE
DISLEAVES > DISLEAVE
DISLIKE *vb* consider unpleasant or disagreeable ▷ *n* feeling of not liking something or someone
DISLIKED > DISLIKE
DISLIKEN *vb* render dissimilar to
DISLIKENS > DISLIKEN
DISLIKER > DISLIKE
DISLIKERS > DISLIKE
DISLIKES > DISLIKE
DISLIKING > DISLIKE
DISLIMB *vb* remove limbs from
DISLIMBED > DISLIMB
DISLIMBS > DISLIMB
DISLIMN *vb* efface
DISLIMNED > DISLIMN
DISLIMNS > DISLIMN
DISLINK *vb* disunite
DISLINKED > DISLINK
DISLINKS > DISLINK

DISLOAD *vb* unload
DISLOADED > DISLOAD
DISLOADS > DISLOAD
DISLOCATE *vb* displace (a bone or joint) from its normal position
DISLODGE *vb* remove (something) from a previously fixed position
DISLODGED > DISLODGE
DISLODGES > DISLODGE
DISLOIGN *vb* put at a distance
DISLOIGNS > DISLOIGN
DISLOYAL *adj* not loyal, deserting one's allegiance
DISLUSTRE *vb* remove lustre from
DISMAL *adj* gloomy and depressing
DISMALER > DISMAL
DISMALEST > DISMAL
DISMALITY > DISMAL
DISMALLER > DISMAL
DISMALLY > DISMAL
DISMALS *pl n* gloomy state of mind
DISMAN *vb* remove men from
DISMANNED > DISMAN
DISMANS > DISMAN
DISMANTLE *vb* take apart piece by piece
DISMASK *vb* remove mask from
DISMASKED > DISMASK
DISMASKS > DISMASK
DISMAST *vb* break off the mast or masts of (a sailing vessel)
DISMASTED > DISMAST
DISMASTS > DISMAST
DISMAY *vb* fill with alarm or depression ▷ *n* alarm mixed with sadness
DISMAYD > DISMAY
DISMAYED > DISMAY
DISMAYFUL > DISMAY
DISMAYING > DISMAY
DISMAYL *vb* remove a coat of mail from
DISMAYLED > DISMAYL
DISMAYLS > DISMAYL
DISMAYS > DISMAY
DISME *old form of* > DIME
DISMEMBER *vb* remove the limbs of
DISMES > DISME
DISMISS *vb* remove (an employee) from a job ▷ *sentence substitute* order to end an activity or give permission to disperse
DISMISSAL *n* official notice of discharge from employment or service
DISMISSED > DISMISS
DISMISSES > DISMISS
DISMODED *adj* no longer fashionable
DISMOUNT *vb* get off a horse or bicycle ▷ *n* act of dismounting
DISMOUNTS > DISMOUNT
DISNEST *vb* remove from nest
DISNESTED > DISNEST

d

DISNESTS > DISNEST
DISOBEY vb neglect or refuse to obey
DISOBEYED > DISOBEY
DISOBEYER > DISOBEY
DISOBEYS > DISOBEY
DISOBLIGE vb disregard the desires of
DISODIUM n compound containing two sodium atoms
DISOMIC adj having an extra chromosome in the haploid state that is homologous to an existing chromosome in this set
DISOMIES > DISOMIC
DISOMY > DISOMIC
DISORBED adj thrown out of orbit
DISORDER n state of untidiness and disorganization ▷ vb upset the order of
DISORDERS > DISORDER
DISORIENT same as > DISORIENTATE
DISOWN vb deny any connection with (someone)
DISOWNED > DISOWN
DISOWNER > DISOWN
DISOWNERS > DISOWN
DISOWNING > DISOWN
DISOWNS > DISOWN
DISPACE vb move or travel about
DISPACED > DISPACE
DISPACES > DISPACE
DISPACING > DISPACE
DISPARAGE vb speak contemptuously of
DISPARATE adj completely different ▷ n unlike things or people
DISPARITY n inequality or difference
DISPARK vb release
DISPARKED > DISPARK
DISPARKS > DISPARK
DISPART vb separate
DISPARTED > DISPART
DISPARTS > DISPART
DISPATCH vb send off to a destination or to perform a task ▷ n official communication or report, sent in haste
DISPATHY obsolete spelling of > DYSPATHY
DISPAUPER vb state that someone is no longer a pauper
DISPEACE n absence of peace
DISPEACES > DISPEACE
DISPEL vb destroy or remove
DISPELLED > DISPEL
DISPELLER > DISPEL
DISPELS > DISPEL
DISPENCE same as > DISPENSE
DISPENCED > DISPENCE
DISPENCES > DISPENCE
DISPEND vb spend
DISPENDED > DISPEND

DISPENDS > DISPEND
DISPENSE vb distribute in portions
DISPENSED > DISPENSE
DISPENSER n device, such as a vending machine, that automatically dispenses a single item or a measured quantity
DISPENSES > DISPENSE
DISPEOPLE vb remove inhabitants from
DISPERSAL n act of dispersing or the condition of being dispersed
DISPERSE vb scatter over a wide area ▷ adj of or consisting of the particles in a colloid or suspension
DISPERSED > DISPERSE
DISPERSER > DISPERSE
DISPERSES > DISPERSE
DISPIRIT vb make downhearted
DISPIRITS > DISPIRIT
DISPLACE vb move from the usual location
DISPLACED > DISPLACE
DISPLACER > DISPLACE
DISPLACES > DISPLACE
DISPLANT vb displace
DISPLANTS > DISPLANT
DISPLAY vb make visible or noticeable ▷ n displaying
DISPLAYED > DISPLAY
DISPLAYER > DISPLAY
DISPLAYS > DISPLAY
DISPLE vb punish
DISPLED > DISPLE
DISPLES > DISPLE
DISPLING > DISPLE
DISPLODE obsolete word for > EXPLODE
DISPLODED > DISPLODE
DISPLODES > DISPLODE
DISPLUME vb remove feathers from
DISPLUMED > DISPLUME
DISPLUMES > DISPLUME
DISPONDEE n (poetry) double foot of two long syllables
DISPONE vb transfer ownership
DISPONED > DISPONE
DISPONEE vb person whom something is disponed to
DISPONEES > DISPONEE
DISPONER > DISPONE
DISPONERS > DISPONE
DISPONES > DISPONE
DISPONGE same as > DISPUNGE
DISPONGED > DISPONGE
DISPONGES > DISPONGE
DISPONING > DISPONE
DISPORT vb indulge (oneself) in pleasure ▷ n amusement
DISPORTED > DISPORT
DISPORTS > DISPORT
DISPOSAL n getting rid of something
DISPOSALS > DISPOSAL
DISPOSE vb place in a

certain order
DISPOSED adj willing or eager
DISPOSER > DISPOSE
DISPOSERS > DISPOSE
DISPOSES > DISPOSE
DISPOSING > DISPOSE
DISPOST vb remove from post
DISPOSTED > DISPOST
DISPOSTS > DISPOST
DISPOSURE a rare word for > DISPOSAL
DISPRAD old form of > DISPREAD
DISPRAISE vb express disapproval or condemnation of ▷ n disapproval, etc, expressed
DISPREAD vb spread out
DISPREADS > DISPREAD
DISPRED old spelling of > DISPREAD
DISPREDS > DISPRED
DISPRISON vb release from captivity
DISPRIZE vb scorn
DISPRIZED > DISPRIZE
DISPRIZES > DISPRIZE
DISPROFIT n loss
DISPROOF n facts that disprove something
DISPROOFS > DISPROOF
DISPROOVE vb disapprove of
DISPROVAL > DISPROVE
DISPROVE vb show (an assertion or claim) to be incorrect
DISPROVED > DISPROVE
DISPROVEN > DISPROVE
DISPROVER > DISPROVE
DISPROVES > DISPROVE
DISPUNGE vb expunge
DISPUNGED > DISPUNGE
DISPUNGES > DISPUNGE
DISPURSE another word for > DISBURSE
DISPURSED > DISPURSE
DISPURSES > DISPURSE
DISPURVEY vb strip of equipment, provisions, etc
DISPUTANT n person who argues ▷ adj engaged in argument
DISPUTE n disagreement, argument ▷ vb argue about (something)
DISPUTED > DISPUTE
DISPUTER > DISPUTE
DISPUTERS > DISPUTE
DISPUTES > DISPUTE
DISPUTING > DISPUTE
DISQUIET n feeling of anxiety ▷ vb make (someone) anxious ▷ adj uneasy or anxious
DISQUIETS > DISQUIET
DISRANK vb demote
DISRANKED > DISRANK
DISRANKS > DISRANK
DISRATE vb punish (an officer) by lowering in rank
DISRATED > DISRATE
DISRATES > DISRATE
DISRATING > DISRATE
DISREGARD vb give little or

no attention to ▷ n lack of attention or respect
DISRELISH vb have a feeling of aversion for ▷ n such a feeling
DISREPAIR n condition of being worn out or in poor working order
DISREPUTE n loss or lack of good reputation
DISROBE vb undress
DISROBED > DISROBE
DISROBER > DISROBE
DISROBERS > DISROBE
DISROBES > DISROBE
DISROBING > DISROBE
DISROOT vb uproot
DISROOTED > DISROOT
DISROOTS > DISROOT
DISRUPT vb interrupt the progress of
DISRUPTED > DISRUPT
DISRUPTER > DISRUPT
DISRUPTOR > DISRUPT
DISRUPTS > DISRUPT
DISS vb treat (a person) with contempt
DISSAVE vb spend savings
DISSAVED > DISSAVE
DISSAVES > DISSAVE
DISSAVING > DISSAVE
DISSEAT vb unseat
DISSEATED > DISSEAT
DISSEATS > DISSEAT
DISSECT vb cut open (a corpse) to examine it
DISSECTED adj in the form of narrow lobes or segments
DISSECTOR > DISSECT
DISSECTS > DISSECT
DISSED > DISS
DISSEISE vb deprive of seisin
DISSEISED > DISSEISE
DISSEISEE n person who is disseised
DISSEISES > DISSEISE
DISSEISIN n act of disseising or state of being disseised
DISSEISOR > DISSEISE
DISSEIZE same as > DISSEISE
DISSEIZED > DISSEIZE
DISSEIZEE n person who is disseized
DISSEIZES > DISSEIZE
DISSEIZIN same as > DISSEISIN
DISSEIZOR > DISSEIZE
DISSEMBLE vb conceal one's real motives or emotions by pretence
DISSEMBLY n dismantling
DISSENSUS n disagreement within group
DISSENT vb disagree ▷ n disagreement
DISSENTED > DISSENT
DISSENTER > DISSENT
DISSENTS > DISSENT
DISSERT n give or make a dissertation; dissertate
DISSERTED > DISSERT
DISSERTS > DISSERT
DISSERVE vb do a disservice

to

DISSERVED > DISSERVE

DISSERVES > DISSERVE

DISSES > DISS

DISSEVER vb break off or become broken off

DISSEVERS > DISSEVER

DISSHIVER vb break in pieces

DISSIDENT n person who disagrees with and criticizes the government ▷ adj disagreeing with the government

DISSIGHT n eyesore

DISSIGHTS > DISSIGHT

DISSIMILE n comparison using contrast

DISSING > DISS

DISSIPATE vb waste or squander

DISSOCIAL same as > DISSOCIABLE

DISSOLUTE adj leading an immoral life

DISSOLVE vb (cause to) become liquid ▷ n scene filmed or televised by dissolving

DISSOLVED > DISSOLVE

DISSOLVER > DISSOLVE

DISSOLVES > DISSOLVE

DISSONANT adj discordant

DISSUADE vb deter (someone) by persuasion from doing something

DISSUADED > DISSUADE

DISSUADER > DISSUADE

DISSUADES > DISSUADE

DISSUNDER vb separate

DISTAFF n rod on which wool etc is wound for spinning

DISTAFFS > DISTAFF

DISTAIN vb stain; tarnish

DISTAINED > DISTAIN

DISTAINS > DISTAIN

DISTAL adj (of a muscle, bone, limb, etc) situated farthest from the centre, median line, or point of attachment or origin

DISTALLY > DISTAL

DISTANCE n space between two points

DISTANCED > DISTANCE

DISTANCES > DISTANCE

DISTANT adj far apart

DISTANTLY > DISTANT

DISTASTE n dislike, disgust

DISTASTED > DISTASTE

DISTASTES > DISTASTE

DISTAVES > DISTAFF

DISTEMPER n highly contagious viral disease of dogs ▷ vb paint with distemper

DISTEND vb (of part of the body) swell

DISTENDED > DISTEND

DISTENDER > DISTEND

DISTENDS > DISTEND

DISTENT adj bloated; swollen

DISTHENE n bluish-green mineral

DISTHENES > DISTHENE

DISTHRONE vb remove from throne

DISTICH n unit of two verse lines

DISTICHAL > DISTICH

DISTICHS > DISTICH

DISTIL vb subject to or obtain by distillation

DISTILL same as > DISTIL

DISTILLED > DISTIL

DISTILLER n person or company that makes strong alcoholic drink, esp whisky

DISTILLS > DISTILL

DISTILS > DISTIL

DISTINCT adj not the same

DISTINGUE adj distinguished or noble

DISTOME n parasitic flatworm

DISTOMES > DISTOME

DISTORT vb misrepresent (the truth or facts)

DISTORTED > DISTORT

DISTORTER > DISTORT

DISTORTS > DISTORT

DISTRACT vb draw the attention of (a person) away from something

DISTRACTS > DISTRACT

DISTRAIL n trail made by aircraft flying through cloud

DISTRAILS > DISTRAIL

DISTRAIN vb seize (personal property) to enforce payment of a debt

DISTRAINS > DISTRAIN

DISTRAINT n act or process of distraining

DISTRAIT adj absent-minded or preoccupied

DISTRAITE feminine form of > DISTRAIT

DISTRESS n extreme unhappiness ▷ vb upset badly

DISTRICT n area of land regarded as an administrative or geographical unit ▷ vb divide into districts

DISTRICTS > DISTRICT

DISTRIX n splitting of the ends of hairs

DISTRIXES > DISTRIX

DISTRUST vb regard as untrustworthy ▷ n feeling of suspicion or doubt

DISTRUSTS > DISTRUST

DISTUNE vb cause to be out of tune

DISTUNED > DISTUNE

DISTUNES > DISTUNE

DISTUNING > DISTUNE

DISTURB vb intrude on

DISTURBED adj emotionally upset or maladjusted

DISTURBER > DISTURB

DISTURBS > DISTURB

DISTYLE n temple with two columns

DISTYLES > DISTYLE

DISULFATE n chemical compound containing two sulfate ions

DISULFID same as > DISULFIDE

DISULFIDE n compound of a base with two atoms of sulfur

DISULFIDS > DISULFID

DISUNION > DISUNITE

DISUNIONS > DISUNITE

DISUNITE vb cause disagreement among

DISUNITED > DISUNITE

DISUNITER > DISUNITE

DISUNITES > DISUNITE

DISUNITY n dissension or disagreement

DISUSAGE n disuse

DISUSAGES > DISUSAGE

DISUSE vb stop using ▷ n state of being no longer used

DISUSED adj no longer used

DISUSES > DISUSE

DISUSING > DISUSE

DISVALUE vb belittle

DISVALUED > DISVALUE

DISVALUES > DISVALUE

DISVOUCH vb dissociate oneself from

DISYOKE vb unyoke

DISYOKED > DISYOKE

DISYOKES > DISYOKE

DISYOKING > DISYOKE

DIT vb stop something happening ▷ n short sound used, in combination with the long sound dah, in the spoken representation of Morse and other telegraphic codes

DITA n apocynaceous shrub, Alstonia scholaris, of tropical Africa and Asia, having large shiny whorled leaves and medicinal bark

DITAL n key for raising pitch of lute string

DITALS > DITAL

DITAS > DITA

DITCH n narrow channel dug in the earth for drainage or irrigation ▷ vb abandon

DITCHED > DITCH

DITCHER > DITCH

DITCHERS > DITCH

DITCHES > DITCH

DITCHING > DITCH

DITCHLESS > DITCH

DITE vb set down in writing

DITED > DITE

DITES > DITE

DITHECAL adj having two thecae

DITHECOUS another word for > DITHECAL

DITHEISM n belief in two equal gods

DITHEISMS > DITHEISM

DITHEIST > DITHEISM

DITHEISTS > DITHEISM

DITHELETE n one believing that Christ had two wills

DITHELISM n belief that Christ had two wills

DITHER vb be uncertain or indecisive ▷ n state of

indecision or agitation

DITHERED > DITHER

DITHERER > DITHER

DITHERERS > DITHER

DITHERIER > DITHER

DITHERING > DITHER

DITHERS > DITHER

DITHERY > DITHER

DITHIOL n chemical compound

DITHYRAMB n (in ancient Greece) a passionate choral hymn in honour of Dionysus

DITING > DITE

DITOKOUS adj producing two eggs

DITONE n interval of two tones

DITONES > DITONE

DITROCHEE n double metrical foot

DITS > DIT

DITSIER > DITSY

DITSIEST > DITSY

DITSINESS > DITSY

DITSY same as > DITZY

DITT same as > DIT

DITTANDER n plant, Lepidium latifolium, of coastal regions of Europe, N Africa, and SW Asia, with clusters of small white flowers: family Brassicaceae (crucifers)

DITTANIES > DITTANY

DITTANY n aromatic Cretan plant, Origanum dictamnus, with pink drooping flowers: formerly credited with great medicinal properties: family Lamiaceae (labiates)

DITTAY n accusation; charge

DITTAYS > DITTAY

DITTED > DIT

DITTIED > DITTY

DITTIES > DITTY

DITTING > DIT

DITTIT > DIT

DITTO n same ▷ adv in the same way ▷ sentence substitute used to avoid repeating or to confirm agreement with an immediately preceding sentence ▷ vb copy

DITTOED > DITTO

DITTOING > DITTO

DITTOLOGY n interpretation in two ways

DITTOS > DITTO

DITTS > DITT

DITTY vb set to music ▷ n short simple poem or song

DITTYING > DITTY

DITZ n silly scatterbrained person

DITZES > DITZ

DITZIER > DITZY

DITZIEST > DITZY

DITZINESS > DITZY

DITZY adj silly and scatterbrained

DIURESES > DIURESIS

DIURESIS n excretion of an

unusually large quantity of urine

DIURETIC *n* drug that increases the flow of urine ▷ *adj* acting to increase the flow of urine

DIURETICS > DIURETIC

DIURNAL *adj* happening during the day or daily ▷ *n* service book containing all the canonical hours except matins

DIURNALLY > DIURNAL

DIURNALS > DIURNAL

DIURON *n* type of herbicide

DIURONS > DIURON

DIUTURNAL *adj* long-lasting

DIV *n* stupid or foolish person

DIVA *n* distinguished female singer

DIVAGATE *vb* digress or wander

DIVAGATED > DIVAGATE

DIVAGATES > DIVAGATE

DIVALENCE > DIVALENT

DIVALENCY > DIVALENT

DIVALENT *n* element that can unite with two atoms ▷ *adj* having two valencies or a valency of two

DIVALENTS > DIVALENT

DIVAN *n* low backless bed

DIVANS > DIVAN

DIVAS > DIVA

DIVE *vb* plunge headfirst into water ▷ *n* diving

DIVEBOMB *vb* bomb while making steep dives

DIVEBOMBS > DIVEBOMB

DIVED > DIVE

DIVELLENT *adj* separating

DIVER *n* person who works or explores underwater

DIVERGE *vb* separate and go in different directions

DIVERGED > DIVERGE

DIVERGENT *adj* diverging or causing divergence

DIVERGES > DIVERGE

DIVERGING > DIVERGE

DIVERS *adj* various ▷ *determiner* various

DIVERSE *vb* turn away ▷ *adj* having variety, assorted

DIVERSED > DIVERSE

DIVERSELY > DIVERSE

DIVERSES > DIVERSE

DIVERSIFY *vb* create different forms of

DIVERSING > DIVERSE

DIVERSION *n* official detour used by traffic when a main route is closed

DIVERSITY *n* quality of being different or varied

DIVERSLY > DIVERS

DIVERT *vb* change the direction of

DIVERTED > DIVERT

DIVERTER > DIVERT

DIVERTERS > DIVERT

DIVERTING > DIVERT

DIVERTIVE > DIVERT

DIVERTS > DIVERT

DIVES > DIVE

DIVEST *vb* strip (of clothes)

DIVESTED > DIVEST

DIVESTING > DIVEST

DIVESTS > DIVEST

DIVESTURE > DIVEST

DIVI *alternative spelling of* > DIVVY

DIVIDABLE > DIVIDE

DIVIDANT *adj* distinct

DIVIDE *vb* separate into parts ▷ *n* division, split

DIVIDED *adj* split

DIVIDEDLY > DIVIDED

DIVIDEND *n* sum of money representing part of the profit made, paid by a company to its shareholders

DIVIDENDS > DIVIDEND

DIVIDER *n* screen used to divide a room into separate areas

DIVIDERS *pl n* compasses with two pointed arms, used for measuring or dividing lines

DIVIDES > DIVIDE

DIVIDING > DIVIDE

DIVIDINGS > DIVIDE

DIVIDIVI *n* tropical tree

DIVIDIVIS > DIVIDIVI

DIVIDUAL *adj* divisible

DIVIDUOUS *adj* divided

DIVINABLE > DIVINE

DIVINATOR *n* diviner

DIVINE *adj* of God or a god ▷ *vb* discover (something) by intuition or guessing ▷ *n* priest who is learned in theology

DIVINED > DIVINE

DIVINELY > DIVINE

DIVINER > DIVINE

DIVINERS > DIVINE

DIVINES > DIVINE

DIVINEST > DIVINE

DIVING > DIVE

DIVINGS > DIVE

DIVINIFY *vb* give divine status to

DIVINING > DIVINE

DIVINISE *same as* > DIVINIZE

DIVINISED > DIVINISE

DIVINISES > DIVINISE

DIVINITY *n* study of religion

DIVINIZE *vb* make divine

DIVINIZED > DIVINIZE

DIVINIZES > DIVINIZE

DIVIS > DIVI

DIVISIBLE *adj* capable of being divided

DIVISIBLY > DIVISIBLE

DIVISIM *adv* separately

DIVISION *n* dividing, sharing out

DIVISIONS > DIVISION

DIVISIVE *adj* tending to cause disagreement

DIVISOR *n* number to be divided into another number

DIVISORS > DIVISOR

DIVORCE *n* legal ending of a marriage ▷ *vb* legally end one's marriage (to)

DIVORCED > DIVORCE

DIVORCEE *n* person who is divorced

DIVORCEES > DIVORCEE

DIVORCER > DIVORCE

DIVORCERS > DIVORCE

DIVORCES > DIVORCE

DIVORCING > DIVORCE

DIVORCIVE > DIVORCE

DIVOT *n* small piece of turf

DIVOTS > DIVOT

DIVS > DIV

DIVULGATE *vb* make publicly known

DIVULGE *vb* make known, disclose

DIVULGED > DIVULGE

DIVULGER > DIVULGE

DIVULGERS > DIVULGE

DIVULGES > DIVULGE

DIVULGING > DIVULGE

DIVULSE *vb* tear apart

DIVULSED > DIVULSE

DIVULSES > DIVULSE

DIVULSING > DIVULSE

DIVULSION *n* tearing or pulling apart

DIVULSIVE > DIVULSION

DIVVIED > DIVVY

DIVVIES > DIVVY

DIVVY *vb* divide and share ▷ *n* stupid person

DIVVYING > DIVVY

DIWAN *same as* > DEWAN

DIWANS > DIWAN

DIXI *interj* I have spoken

DIXIE *n* large metal pot for cooking, brewing tea, etc

DIXIES > DIXIE

DIXIT *n* statement

DIXITS > DIXIT

DIXY *same as* > DIXIE

DIZAIN *n* ten-line poem

DIZAINS > DIZAIN

DIZEN *archaic word for* > BEDIZEN

DIZENED > DIZEN

DIZENING > DIZEN

DIZENMENT > DIZEN

DIZENS > DIZEN

DIZYGOTIC *adj* developed from two separately fertilized eggs

DIZYGOUS *another word for* > DIZYGOTIC

DIZZARD *n* dunce

DIZZARDS > DIZZARD

DIZZIED > DIZZY

DIZZIER > DIZZY

DIZZIES > DIZZY

DIZZIEST > DIZZY

DIZZILY > DIZZY

DIZZINESS > DIZZY

DIZZY *adj* having or causing a whirling sensation ▷ *vb* make dizzy

DIZZYING > DIZZY

DJEBEL *a variant spelling of* > JEBEL

DJEBELS > DJEBEL

DJELLABA *n* kind of loose cloak with a hood, worn by men esp in North Africa and the Middle East

DJELLABAH *same as* > DJELLABA

DJELLABAS > DJELLABA

DJEMBE *n* W African drum

played by beating with the hand

DJEMBES > DJEMBE

DJIBBAH *same as* > JUBBAH

DJIBBAHS > DJIBBAH

DJIN *same as same as* > JINN

DJINN > DJINNI

DJINNI *same as* > JINNI

DJINNS > DJINN

DJINNY *same as same as* > JINNI

DJINS > DJIN

DO *vb* perform or complete (a deed or action) ▷ *n* party, celebration

DOAB *n* alluvial land between two converging rivers, esp the area between the Ganges and Jumna in N India

DOABLE *adj* capable of being done

DOABS > DOAB

DOAT *same as* > DOTE

DOATED > DOAT

DOATER > DOAT

DOATERS > DOAT

DOATING > DOAT

DOATINGS > DOAT

DOATS > DOAT

DOB *as in dob in* inform against or report

DOBBED > DOB

DOBBER *n* informant or traitor

DOBBERS > DOBBER

DOBBIE *same as* > DOBBY

DOBBIES > DOBBY

DOBBIN *n* name for a horse, esp a workhorse, often used in children's tales, etc

DOBBING > DOB

DOBBINS > DOBBIN

DOBBY *n* attachment to a loom, used in weaving small figures

DOBCHICK *same as* > DABCHICK

DOBCHICKS > DOBCHICK

DOBHASH *n* interpreter

DOBHASHES > DOBHASH

DOBIE *n* cannabis

DOBIES > DOBIE

DOBLA *n* medieval Spanish gold coin, probably worth 20 maravedis

DOBLAS > DOBLA

DOBLON *a variant spelling of* > DOUBLOON

DOBLONES > DOBLON

DOBLONS > DOBLON

DOBRA *n* standard monetary unit of São Tomé e Principe, divided into 100 cêntimos

DOBRAS > DOBRA

DOBRO *n* tradename for a type of acoustic guitar having a metal resonator built into the body

DOBROS > DOBRO

DOBS > DOB

DOBSON *n* larva of dobsonfly

DOBSONFLY *n* large North American insect

DOBSONS > DOBSON

DOBY *same as* > DOBIE

DOC *same as* > DOCTOR

DOME *n* rounded roof built on a circular base ▷*vb* cover with or as if with a dome

DOMED > DOME

DOMELIKE > DOME

DOMES > DOME

DOMESDAY *same as* > DOOMSDAY

DOMESDAYS > DOMESDAY

DOMESTIC *adj* of one's own country or a specific country ▷*n* person whose job is to do housework in someone else's house

DOMESTICS > DOMESTIC

DOMETT *n* wool and cotton cloth

DOMETTS > DOMETT

DOMIC *adj* dome-shaped

DOMICAL > DOME

DOMICALLY > DOME

DOMICIL *same as* > DOMICILE

DOMICILE *n* place where one lives ▷*vb* establish or be established in a dwelling place

DOMICILED > DOMICILE

DOMICILES > DOMICILE

DOMICILS > DOMICIL

DOMIER > DOMY

DOMIEST > DOMY

DOMINANCE *n* control

DOMINANCY > DOMINANCE

DOMINANT *adj* having authority or influence ▷*n* dominant allele or character

DOMINANTS > DOMINANT

DOMINATE *vb* control or govern

DOMINATED > DOMINATE

DOMINATES > DOMINATE

DOMINATOR > DOMINATE

DOMINE *n* clergyman

DOMINEE *n* minister of the Dutch Reformed Church

DOMINEER *vb* act with arrogance or tyranny

DOMINEERS > DOMINEER

DOMINEES > DOMINEE

DOMINES > DOMINE

DOMING > DOME

DOMINICAL *adj* of, relating to, or emanating from Jesus Christ as Lord

DOMINICK *n* breed of chicken

DOMINICKS > DOMINICK

DOMINIE *n* minister or clergyman: also used as a term of address

DOMINIES > DOMINIE

DOMINION *same as* > DOMINIUM

DOMINIONS *same as* > DOMINION

DOMINIQUE *n* type of chicken

DOMINIUM *n* ownership or right to possession of property, esp realty

DOMINIUMS > DOMINIUM

DOMINO *n* small rectangular block marked with dots, used in dominoes

DOMINOES *n* game in which dominoes with matching halves are laid together

DOMINOS > DOMINO

DOMS > DOM

DOMY *adj* having a dome or domes

DON *vb* put on (clothing) ▷*n* member of the teaching staff at a university or college

DONA *n* Spanish lady

DONAH *n* woman

DONAHS > DONAH

DONARIES > DONARY

DONARY *n* thing given for holy use

DONAS > DONA

DONATARY *n* recipient

DONATE *vb* give, esp to a charity or organization

DONATED > DONATE

DONATES > DONATE

DONATING > DONATE

DONATION *n* donating

DONATIONS > DONATION

DONATISM *n* doctrine and beliefs relating to a schismatic heretical Christian sect originating in N Africa in 311 AD

DONATISMS > DONATISM

DONATIVE *n* gift or donation ▷*adj* of or like a donation

DONATIVES > DONATIVE

DONATOR > DONATE

DONATORS > DONATE

DONATORY *n* recipient

DONDER *vb* beat (someone) up ▷*n* wretch

DONDERED > DONDER

DONDERING > DONDER

DONDERS > DONDER

DONE > DO

DONEE *n* person who receives a gift

DONEES > DONEE

DONENESS *n* extent to which something is cooked

DONER *as in doner kebab* grilled meat and salad served in pitta bread with chilli sauce

DONG *n* deep reverberating sound of a large bell ▷*vb* (of a bell) to make a deep reverberating sound

DONGA *n* steep-sided gully created by soil erosion

DONGAS > DONGA

DONGED > DONG

DONGING > DONG

DONGLE *n* electronic device that accompanies a software item to prevent the unauthorized copying of programs

DONGLES > DONGLE

DONGOLA *n* leather tanned using a particular method

DONGOLAS > DONGOLA

DONGS > DONG

DONING *n* act of giving blood

DONINGS > DONING

DONJON *n* heavily fortified central tower of a castle

DONJONS > DONJON

DONKEY *n* long-eared member of the horse family

DONKEYS > DONKEY

DONKO *n* tearoom or cafeteria in a factory, wharf area, etc

DONKOS > DONKO

DONNA *n* Italian lady

DONNARD *same as* > DONNERT

DONNART *same as* > DONNERT

DONNAS > DONNA

DONNAT *n* lazy person

DONNATS > DONNAT

DONNE *same as* > DONNEE

DONNED > DON

DONNEE *n* subject or theme

DONNEES > DONNEE

DONNERD *adj* stupid

DONNERED *same as* > DONNERT

DONNERT *adj* stunned

DONNES > DONNE

DONNICKER *n* toilet

DONNIES > DONNY

DONNIKER *same as* > DONNICKER

DONNIKERS > DONNIKER

DONNING > DON

DONNISH *adj* serious and academic

DONNISHLY > DONNISH

DONNISM *n* loftiness

DONNISMS > DONNISM

DONNOT *n* lazy person

DONNOTS > DONNOT

DONNY *same as* > DANNY

DONOR *n* person who gives blood or organs for use in the treatment of another person

DONORS > DONOR

DONORSHIP > DONOR

DONS > DON

DONSHIP *n* state or condition of being a don

DONSHIPS > DONSHIP

DONSIE *adj* rather unwell

DONSIER > DONSIE

DONSIEST > DONSIE

DONSY *same as* > DONSIE

DONUT *same as* > DOUGHNUT

DONUTS > DONUT

DONUTTED > DONUT

DONUTTING > DONUT

DONZEL *n* man of high birth

DONZELS > DONZEL

DOO *a Scot word for* > DOVE

DOOB *n* cannabis cigarette

DOOBIE *same as* > DOOB

DOOBIES > DOOBIE

DOOBS > DOOB

DOOCED *as in get dooced* be dismissed on account of indiscretions written in a blog or on a website

DOOCOT *n* dovecote

DOOCOTS > DOOCOT

DOODAD *same as* > DOODAH

DOODADS > DOODAD

DOODAH *n* unnamed thing, esp an object the name of which is unknown or uncertain

DOODAHS > DOODAH

DOODIES > DOODY

DOODLE *vb* scribble or draw aimlessly ▷*n* shape or picture drawn aimlessly

DOODLEBUG *n* diviner's rod

DOODLED > DOODLE

DOODLER > DOODLE

DOODLERS > DOODLE

DOODLES > DOODLE

DOODLING > DOODLE

DOODOO *n* excrement

DOODOOS > DOODOO

DOODY *same as* > DOODOO

DOOFER *n* thingamajig

DOOFERS > DOOFER

DOOFUS *n* slow-witted or stupid person

DOOFUSES > DOOFUS

DOOHICKEY *another name for* > DOODAH

DOOK *n* wooden plug driven into a wall to hold a nail, screw, etc ▷*vb* dip or plunge

DOOKED > DOOK

DOOKET *n* dovecote

DOOKETS > DOOKET

DOOKING > DOOK

DOOKS > DOOK

DOOL *n* boundary marker

DOOLALLY *adj* out of one's mind

DOOLAN *n* Roman Catholic

DOOLANS > DOOLAN

DOOLE *same as* > DOOL

DOOLEE *same as* > DOOLIE

DOOLEES > DOOLEE

DOOLES > DOOLE

DOOLIE *n* enclosed couch on poles for carrying passengers

DOOLIES > DOOLIE

DOOLS > DOOL

DOOLY *same as* > DOOLIE

DOOM *n* death or a terrible fate ▷*vb* destine or condemn to death or a terrible fate

DOOMED > DOOM

DOOMFUL > DOOM

DOOMFULLY > DOOM

DOOMIER > DOOMY

DOOMIEST > DOOMY

DOOMILY > DOOMY

DOOMING > DOOM

DOOMS > DOOM

DOOMSAYER *n* pessimist

DOOMSDAY *n* day on which the Last Judgment will occur

DOOMSDAYS > DOOMSDAY

DOOMSMAN *n* pessimist

DOOMSMEN > DOOMSMAN

DOOMSTER *n* person habitually given to predictions of impending disaster or doom

DOOMSTERS > DOOMSTER

DOOMWATCH *n* surveillance of the environment to warn of and prevent harm to it from human factors such as pollution or overpopulation

DOOMY *adj* despondent or pessimistic

DOON *same as* > DOWN

DOONA *n* large quilt used as a bed cover in place of the top sheet and blankets

DOONAS > DOONA

d

DOOR n hinged or sliding panel for closing the entrance to a building, room, etc

DOORBELL n device for visitors to announce presence at a door

DOORBELLS > DOORBELL

DOORCASE same as > DOORFRAME

DOORCASES > DOORCASE

DOORFRAME n frame that supports a door

DOORJAMB n vertical post forming one side of a door frame

DOORJAMBS > DOORJAMB

DOORKNOB n knob for opening and closing a door

DOORKNOBS > DOORKNOB

DOORKNOCK n fund-raising campaign for charity conducted by seeking donations from door to door

DOORLESS > DOOR

DOORMAN n man employed to be on duty at the entrance to a large public building

DOORMAT n mat for wiping dirt from shoes before going indoors

DOORMATS > DOORMAT

DOORMEN > DOORMAN

DOORN n thorn

DOORNAIL as in dead as a doornail dead beyond any doubt

DOORNAILS > DOORNAIL

DOORNS > DOORN

DOORPLATE n name-plate on door

DOORPOST same as > DOORJAMB

DOORPOSTS > DOORPOST

DOORS > DOOR

DOORSILL n horizontal member of wood, stone, etc, forming the bottom of a doorframe

DOORSILLS > DOORSILL

DOORSMAN n doorkeeper

DOORSMEN > DOORSMAN

DOORSTEP n step in front of a door

DOORSTEPS > DOORSTEP

DOORSTONE n stone of threshold

DOORSTOP n heavy object or one fixed to the floor, which prevents a door from closing or from striking a wall

DOORSTOPS > DOORSTOP

DOORWAY n opening into a building or room

DOORWAYS > DOORWAY

DOORWOMAN n female doorman

DOORWOMEN > DOORWOMAN

DOORYARD n yard in front of the front or back door of a house

DOORYARDS > DOORYARD

DOOS > DOO

DOOSRA n in cricket, a delivery, bowled by an off-spinner, that turns the opposite way from an off-break

DOOSRAS > DOOSRA

DOOWOP n style of singing in harmony

DOOWOPS > DOOWOP

DOOZER same as > DOOZY

DOOZERS > DOOZER

DOOZIE same as > DOOZY

DOOZIES > DOOZIE

DOOZY n something excellent

DOP vb curtsy ▷ n tot or small drink, usually alcoholic ▷ vb fail to reach the required standard in (an examination, course, etc)

DOPA n precursor to dopamine

DOPAMINE n chemical found in the brain that acts as a neurotransmitter

DOPAMINES > DOPAMINE

DOPANT n element or compound used to dope a semiconductor

DOPANTS > DOPANT

DOPAS > DOPA

DOPATTA n headscarf

DOPATTAS > DOPATTA

DOPE n illegal drug, usu cannabis ▷ vb give a drug to, esp in order to improve performance in a race ▷ adj excellent

DOPED > DOPE

DOPEHEAD n habitual drug user

DOPEHEADS > DOPEHEAD

DOPER n person who administers dope

DOPERS > DOPER

DOPES > DOPE

DOPESHEET n document giving information on horse races

DOPESTER n person who makes predictions, esp in sport or politics

DOPESTERS > DOPESTER

DOPEY adj half-asleep, drowsy

DOPEYNESS > DOPEY

DOPIAZA n Indian meat or fish dish cooked in onion sauce

DOPIAZAS > DOPIAZA

DOPIER > DOPY

DOPIEST > DOPY

DOPILY > DOPEY

DOPINESS > DOPEY

DOPING > DOPE

DOPINGS > DOPE

DOPPED > DOP

DOPPER n member of an Afrikaner church that practises a stict Calvinism

DOPPERS > DOPPER

DOPPIE n cartridge case

DOPPIES > DOPPIE

DOPPING > DOP

DOPPINGS > DOP

DOPPIO n double measure, esp of espresso coffee

DOPPIOS > DOPPIO

DOPS > DOP

DOPY same as > DOPEY

DOR n any European dung beetle of the genus Geotrupes and related genera, esp G. stercorarius, having a droning flight

DORAD n South American river fish

DORADO n large marine percoid fish

DORADOS > DORADO

DORADS > DORAD

DORB same as > DORBA

DORBA n stupid, inept, or clumsy person

DORBAS > DORBA

DORBEETLE same as > DOR

DORBS > DORB

DORBUG n type of beetle

DORBUGS > DORBUG

DORE n walleye fish

DOREE n type of fish

DOREES > DOREE

DORHAWK n nightjar

DORHAWKS > DORHAWK

DORIC adj rustic

DORIDOID n shell-less mollusc

DORIDOIDS > DORIDOID

DORIES > DORY

DORIS n woman

DORISE same as > DORIZE

DORISED > DORISE

DORISES > DORISE

DORISING > DORISE

DORIZE vb become Doric

DORIZED > DORIZE

DORIZES > DORIZE

DORIZING > DORIZE

DORK n stupid person

DORKIER > DORK

DORKIEST > DORK

DORKINESS > DORK

DORKS > DORK

DORKY > DORK

DORLACH n quiver of arrows

DORLACHS > DORLACH

DORM same as > DORMITORY

DORMANCY > DORMANT

DORMANT n supporting beam ▷ adj temporarily quiet, inactive, or not being used

DORMANTS > DORMANT

DORMER n window that sticks out from a sloping roof

DORMERED adj having dormer windows

DORMERS > DORMER

DORMICE > DORMOUSE

DORMIE adj (of a player or side) as many holes ahead of an opponent as there are still to play

DORMIENT adj dormant

DORMIN n hormone found in plants

DORMINS > DORMIN

DORMITION n Mary's assumption to heaven

DORMITIVE adj sleep-inducing

DORMITORY n large room, esp at a school, containing several beds ▷ adj (of a town or suburb) having many inhabitants who travel to work in a nearby city

DORMOUSE n small mouselike rodent with a furry tail

DORMS > DORM

DORMY same as > DORMIE

DORNECK same as > DORNICK

DORNECKS > DORNECK

DORNICK n heavy damask cloth, formerly used for vestments, curtains, etc

DORNICKS > DORNICK

DORNOCK n type of coarse fabric

DORNOCKS > DORNOCK

DORONICUM n any plant of the Eurasian and N African genus Doronicum, such as leopard's-bane, having yellow daisy-like flower heads: family Asteraceae (composites)

DORP n small town

DORPER n breed of sheep

DORPERS > DORPER

DORPS > DORP

DORR same as > DOR

DORRED > DOR

DORRING > DOR

DORRS > DORR

DORS > DOR

DORSA > DORSUM

DORSAD adj towards the back or dorsal aspect

DORSAL adj of or on the back ▷ n dorsal fin

DORSALLY > DORSAL

DORSALS > DORSAL

DORSE n type of small fish

DORSEL another word for > DOSSAL

DORSELS > DORSEL

DORSER n hanging tapestry

DORSERS > DORSER

DORSES > DORSE

DORSIFLEX adj bending towards the back

DORSUM n the back

DORT vb sulk

DORTED > DORT

DORTER n dormitory

DORTERS > DORTER

DORTIER > DORTY

DORTIEST > DORTY

DORTINESS > DORTY

DORTING > DORT

DORTOUR same as > DORTER

DORTOURS > DORTOUR

DORTS > DORT

DORTY adj haughty, or sullen

DORY n spiny-finned edible sea fish

DOS > DO

DOSAGE same as > DOSE

DOSAGES > DOSAGE

DOSE n specific quantity of a medicine taken at one time ▷ vb give a dose to

DOSED > DOSE

DOSEH n former Egyptian religious ceremony

DOSEHS > DOSEH

DOSEMETER same

as > DOSIMETER

DOSER > DOSE

DOSERS > DOSE

DOSES > DOSE

DOSH *n* money

DOSHES > DOSH

DOSIMETER *n* instrument for measuring the dose of X-rays or other radiation absorbed by matter or the intensity of a source of radiation

DOSIMETRY > DOSIMETER

DOSING > DOSE

DOSIOLOGY *n* study of doses

DOSOLOGY same *as* > DOSIOLOGY

DOSS *vb* sleep, esp in a dosshouse ▷ *n* bed, esp in a dosshouse

DOSSAL *n* ornamental hanging, placed at the back of an altar or at the sides of a chancel

DOSSALS > DOSSAL

DOSSED > DOSS

DOSSEL same as > DOSSAL

DOSSELS > DOSSEL

DOSSER *n* bag or basket for carrying objects on the back

DOSSERET *n* stone above column supporting an arch

DOSSERETS > DOSSERET

DOSSERS > DOSSER

DOSSES > DOSS

DOSSHOUSE *n* cheap lodging house for homeless people

DOSSIER *n* collection of documents about a subject or person

DOSSIERS > DOSSIER

DOSSIL *n* lint for dressing wound

DOSSILS > DOSSIL

DOSSING > DOSS

DOST *a singular form of the present tense (indicative mood) of* > DO

DOT *n* small round mark ▷ *vb* mark with a dot

DOTAGE *n* weakness as a result of old age

DOTAGES > DOTAGE

DOTAL > DOT

DOTANT *another word for* > DOTARD

DOTANTS > DOTANT

DOTARD *n* person who is feeble-minded through old age

DOTARDLY > DOTARD

DOTARDS > DOTARD

DOTATION *n* act of giving a dowry

DOTATIONS > DOTATION

DOTCOM *n* company that does most of its business on the Internet

DOTCOMMER *n* person who carries out business on the internet

DOTCOMS > DOTCOM

DOTE *vb* love to an excessive or foolish degree

DOTED > DOTE

DOTER > DOTE

DOTERS > DOTE

DOTES > DOTE

DOTH *a singular form of the present tense of* > DO

DOTIER > DOTY

DOTIEST > DOTY

DOTING > DOTE

DOTINGLY > DOTE

DOTINGS > DOTE

DOTISH *adj* foolish

DOTS > DOT

DOTTED > DOT

DOTTEL same as > DOTTLE

DOTTELS > DOTTEL

DOTTER > DOT

DOTTEREL *n* rare kind of plover

DOTTERELS > DOTTEREL

DOTTERS > DOT

DOTTIER > DOTTY

DOTTIEST > DOTTY

DOTTILY > DOTTY

DOTTINESS > DOTTY

DOTTING > DOT

DOTTLE *n* tobacco left in a pipe after smoking ▷ *adj* relating to dottle

DOTTLED *adj* foolish

DOTTLER > DOTTLE

DOTTLES > DOTTLE

DOTTLEST > DOTTLE

DOTTREL same *as* > DOTTEREL

DOTTRELS > DOTTREL

DOTTY *adj* rather eccentric

DOTY *adj* (of wood) rotten

DOUANE *n* customs house

DOUANES > DOUANE

DOUANIER *n* customs officer

DOUANIERS > DOUANIER

DOUAR same as > DUAR

DOUARS > DOUAR

DOUBLE *adj* as much again in number, amount, size, etc ▷ *adv* twice over ▷ *n* twice the number, amount, size, etc ▷ *vb* make or become twice as much or as many

DOUBLED > DOUBLE

DOUBLER > DOUBLE

DOUBLERS > DOUBLE

DOUBLES *n* game between two pairs of players

DOUBLET *n* man's close-fitting jacket, with or without sleeves

DOUBLETON *n* original holding of two cards only in a suit

DOUBLETS > DOUBLET

DOUBLING > DOUBLE

DOUBLINGS > DOUBLE

DOUBLOON *n* former Spanish gold coin

DOUBLOONS > DOUBLOON

DOUBLURE *n* decorative lining of vellum or leather, etc, on the inside of a book cover

DOUBLURES > DOUBLURE

DOUBLY *adv* in a greater degree, quantity, or measure

DOUBT *n* uncertainty about the truth, facts, or existence of something ▷ *vb* question the truth of

DOUBTABLE > DOUBT

DOUBTABLY > DOUBT

DOUBTED > DOUBT

DOUBTER > DOUBT

DOUBTERS > DOUBT

DOUBTFUL *adj* unlikely ▷ *n* person who is undecided or uncertain about an issue

DOUBTFULS > DOUBTFUL

DOUBTING > DOUBT

DOUBTINGS > DOUBT

DOUBTLESS *adv* probably or certainly ▷ *adj* certain

DOUBTS > DOUBT

DOUC *n* Old World monkey, *Pygathrix nemaeus*, of SE Asia, with a bright yellow face surrounded by tufts of reddish-brown fur, a white tail, and white hindquarters: one of the langurs

DOUCE *adj* quiet

DOUCELY > DOUCE

DOUCENESS > DOUCE

DOUCEPERE same *as* > DOUZEPER

DOUCER > DOUCE

DOUCEST > DOUCE

DOUCET *n* former flute-like instrument

DOUCETS > DOUCET

DOUCEUR *n* gratuity, tip, or bribe

DOUCEURS > DOUCEUR

DOUCHE *n* (instrument for applying) a stream of water directed onto or into the body for cleansing or medical purposes ▷ *vb* cleanse or treat by means of a douche

DOUCHEBAG *n* despicable person

DOUCHED > DOUCHE

DOUCHES > DOUCHE

DOUCHING > DOUCHE

DOUCINE *n* type of moulding for cornice

DOUCINES > DOUCINE

DOUCS > DOUC

DOUGH *n* thick mixture of flour and water or milk, used for making bread etc

DOUGHBOY *n* infantryman, esp in World War I

DOUGHBOYS > DOUGHBOY

DOUGHFACE *n* Northern Democrat who sided with the South in the American Civil War

DOUGHIER > DOUGHY

DOUGHIEST > DOUGHY

DOUGHLIKE > DOUGH

DOUGHNUT *n* small cake of sweetened dough fried in deep fat ▷ *vb* (of Members of Parliament) to surround (a speaker) during the televising of Parliament to give the impression that the chamber is crowded or the speaker is well supported

DOUGHNUTS > DOUGHNUT

DOUGHS > DOUGH

DOUGHT > DOW

DOUGHTIER > DOUGHTY

DOUGHTILY > DOUGHTY

DOUGHTY *adj* brave and determined

DOUGHY *adj* resembling dough in consistency, colour, etc

DOUK same as > DOOK

DOUKED > DOUK

DOUKING > DOUK

DOUKS > DOUK

DOULA *n* woman who is trained to provide support to women and their families during pregnancy, childbirth, and the period of time following the birth

DOULAS > DOULA

DOULEIA same as > DULIA

DOULEIAS > DOULEIA

DOUM as in *doum palm* variety of palm tree

DOUMA same as > DUMA

DOUMAS > DOUMA

DOUMS > DOUM

DOUN same as > DOWN

DOUP *n* bottom

DOUPIONI *n* type of fabric

DOUPIONIS > DOUPIONI

DOUPPIONI *n* type of silk yarn

DOUPS > DOUP

DOUR *adj* sullen and unfriendly

DOURA same as > DURRA

DOURAH same as > DURRA

DOURAHS > DOURAH

DOURAS > DOURA

DOURER > DOUR

DOUREST > DOUR

DOURINE *n* infectious venereal disease of horses characterized by swollen glands, inflamed genitals, and paralysis of the hindquarters, caused by the protozoan *Trypanosoma equiperdum* contracted during copulation

DOURINES > DOURINE

DOURLY > DOUR

DOURNESS > DOUR

DOUSE *vb* drench with water or other liquid ▷ *n* immersion

DOUSED > DOUSE

DOUSER > DOUSE

DOUSERS > DOUSE

DOUSES > DOUSE

DOUSING > DOUSE

DOUT *vb* extinguish

DOUTED > DOUT

DOUTER > DOUT

DOUTERS > DOUT

DOUTING > DOUT

DOUTS > DOUT

DOUX *adj* sweet

DOUZEPER *n* distinguished person

DOUZEPERS > DOUZEPER

DOVE *vb* be semi-conscious ▷ *n* bird with a heavy body, small head, and short legs

DOVECOT same *as* > DOVECOTE

DOVECOTE *n* structure for

housing pigeons
DOVECOTES > DOVECOTE
DOVECOTS > DOVECOT
DOVED > DOVE
DOVEISH *adj* dovelike
DOVEKEY *same as* > DOVEKIE
DOVEKEYS > DOVEKEY
DOVEKIE *n* small short-billed auk
DOVEKIES > DOVEKIE
DOVELET *n* small dove
DOVELETS > DOVELET
DOVELIKE > DOVE
DOVEN *vb* pray
DOVENED > DOVEN
DOVENING > DOVEN
DOVENS > DOVEN
DOVER *vb* doze ▷*n* doze
DOVERED > DOVER
DOVERING > DOVER
DOVERS > DOVER
DOVES > DOVE
DOVETAIL *n* joint containing wedge-shaped tenons ▷*vb* fit together neatly
DOVETAILS > DOVETAIL
DOVIE *Scots word for* > STUPID
DOVIER > DOVIE
DOVIEST > DOVIE
DOVING > DOVE
DOVISH > DOVE
DOW *vb* archaic word meaning be of worth
DOWABLE *adj* capable of being endowed
DOWAGER *n* widow possessing property or a title obtained from her husband
DOWAGERS > DOWAGER
DOWAR *same as* > DUAR
DOWARS > DOWAR
DOWD *n* woman who wears unfashionable clothes
DOWDIER > DOWDY
DOWDIES > DOWDY
DOWDIEST > DOWDY
DOWDILY > DOWDY
DOWDINESS > DOWDY
DOWDS > DOWD
DOWDY *adj* dull and old-fashioned ▷*n* dowdy woman
DOWDYISH > DOWDY
DOWDYISM > DOWD
DOWDYISMS > DOWD
DOWED > DOW
DOWEL *n* wooden or metal peg that fits into two corresponding holes to join two adjacent parts ▷*vb* join pieces of wood using dowels
DOWELED > DOWEL
DOWELING *n* joining of two pieces of wood using dowels
DOWELLED > DOWEL
DOWELLING *same as* > DOWELING
DOWELS > DOWEL
DOWER *n* life interest in a part of her husband's estate allotted to a widow by law ▷*vb* endow

DOWERED > DOWER
DOWERIES > DOWERY
DOWERING > DOWER
DOWERLESS > DOWER
DOWERS > DOWER
DOWERY *same as* > DOWRY
DOWF *adj* dull; listless
DOWFNESS > DOWF
DOWIE *adj* dull and dreary
DOWIER > DOWIE
DOWIEST > DOWIE
DOWING > DOW
DOWITCHER *n* either of two snipelike shore birds, *Limnodromus griseus* or *L. scolopaceus*, of arctic and subarctic North America: family *Scolopacidae* (sandpipers, etc), order *Charadriiformes*
DOWL *n* fluff
DOWLAS *n* coarse fabric
DOWLASES > DOWLAS
DOWLE *same as* > DOWL
DOWLES > DOWLE
DOWLIER > DOWLY
DOWLIEST > DOWLY
DOWLNE *obsolete form of* > DOWN
DOWLNES > DOWLNE
DOWLNEY > DOWLNE
DOWLS > DOWL
DOWLY *adj* dull
DOWN *adv* indicating movement to or position in a lower place ▷*adj* depressed, unhappy ▷*vb* drink quickly ▷*n* soft fine feathers
DOWNA *obsolete Scots form of* > CANNOT
DOWNBEAT *adj* gloomy ▷*n* first beat of a bar
DOWNBEATS > DOWNBEAT
DOWNBOW *n* (in music) a downward stroke of the bow across the strings
DOWNBOWS > DOWNBOW
DOWNBURST *n* very high-speed downward movement of turbulent air in a limited area for a short time. Near the ground it spreads out from its centre with high horizontal velocities
DOWNCAST *adj* sad, dejected ▷*n* ventilation shaft
DOWNCASTS > DOWNCAST
DOWNCOME *same as* > DOWNCOMER
DOWNCOMER *n* pipe that connects a cistern to a WC, wash basin, etc
DOWNCOMES > DOWNCOME
DOWNCOURT *adj* in far end a of court
DOWNDRAFT *n* downward air current
DOWNED > DOWN
DOWNER *n* barbiturate, tranquillizer, or narcotic
DOWNERS > DOWNER
DOWNFALL *same as* > DEADFALL
DOWNFALLS > DOWNFALL
DOWNFIELD *adj* at far end

of field
DOWNFLOW *n* something that flows down
DOWNFLOWS > DOWNFLOW
DOWNFORCE *n* force produced by air resistance plus gravity that increases the stability of an aircraft or motor vehicle by pressing it downwards
DOWNGRADE *vb* reduce in importance or value
DOWNHAUL *n* line for hauling down a sail or for increasing the tension at its luff
DOWNHAULS > DOWNHAUL
DOWNHILL *adj* going or sloping down ▷*adv* towards the bottom of a hill ▷*n* downward slope
DOWNHILLS > DOWNHILL
DOWNHOLE *adj* (in the oil industry) denoting any piece of equipment that is used in the well itself
DOWNIER > DOWNY
DOWNIEST > DOWNY
DOWNINESS > DOWNY
DOWNING > DOWN
DOWNLAND *same as* > DOWNS
DOWNLANDS > DOWNLAND
DOWNLESS > DOWN
DOWNLIGHT *n* lamp shining downwards
DOWNLIKE > DOWN
DOWNLINK *n* satellite transmission channel
DOWNLINKS > DOWNLINK
DOWNLOAD *vb* transfer (data) from the memory of one computer to that of another, especially over the Internet ▷*n* file transferred in such a way
DOWNLOADS > DOWNLOAD
DOWNMOST *adj* lowest
DOWNPIPE *n* pipe for carrying rainwater from a roof gutter to the ground or to a drain
DOWNPIPES > DOWNPIPE
DOWNPLAY *vb* play down
DOWNPLAYS > DOWNPLAY
DOWNPOUR *n* heavy fall of rain
DOWNPOURS > DOWNPOUR
DOWNRANGE *adv* in the direction of the intended flight path of a rocket or missile
DOWNRIGHT *adv* extreme(ly) ▷*adj* absolute
DOWNRIVER *adv* in direction of current
DOWNRUSH *n* instance of rushing down
DOWNS *pl n* low grassy hills, esp in S England
DOWNSCALE *vb* reduce in scale
DOWNSHIFT *vb* reduce work hours
DOWNSIDE *n* disadvantageous aspect of a situation
DOWNSIDES > DOWNSIDE

DOWNSIZE *vb* reduce the number of people employed by (a company)
DOWNSIZED > DOWNSIZE
DOWNSIZES > DOWNSIZE
DOWNSLIDE *n* downward trend
DOWNSLOPE *adv* towards the bottom of a slope
DOWNSPIN *n* sudden downturn
DOWNSPINS > DOWNSPIN
DOWNSPOUT *same as* > DOWNPIPE
DOWNSTAGE *adj* or at the front part of the stage ▷*adv* at or towards the front of the stage ▷*n* front half of the stage
DOWNSTAIR *adj* situated on lower floor
DOWNSTATE *adj* in, or relating to the part of the state away from large cities, esp the southern part ▷*adv* towards the southern part of a state ▷*n* southern part of a state
DOWNSWING *n* statistical downward trend in business activity, the death rate, etc
DOWNTHROW *n* state of throwing down or being thrown down
DOWNTICK *n* small decrease
DOWNTICKS > DOWNTICK
DOWNTIME *n* time during which a computer or other machine is not working
DOWNTIMES > DOWNTIME
DOWNTOWN *n* central or lower part of a city, esp the main commercial area ▷*adv* towards, to, or into this area ▷*adj* of, relating to, or situated in the downtown area
DOWNTOWNS > DOWNTOWN
DOWNTREND *n* downward trend
DOWNTROD *same as* > DOWNTRODDEN
DOWNTURN *n* drop in the success of an economy or a business
DOWNTURNS > DOWNTURN
DOWNWARD *same as* > DOWNWARDS
DOWNWARDS *adv* from a higher to a lower level, condition, or position
DOWNWASH *n* downward deflection of an airflow, esp one caused by an aircraft wing
DOWNWIND *adj* in the same direction towards which the wind is blowing
DOWNY *adj* covered with soft fine hair or feathers
DOWNZONE *vb* reduce density of housing in area
DOWNZONED > DOWNZONE
DOWNZONES > DOWNZONE
DOWP *same as* > DOUP
DOWPS > DOWP

DOWRIES > DOWRY
DOWRY n property brought by a woman to her husband at marriage
DOWS > DOW
DOWSABEL obsolete word for > SWEETHEART
DOWSABELS > DOWSABEL
DOWSE same as > DOUSE
DOWSED > DOWSE
DOWSER > DOWSE
DOWSERS > DOWSE
DOWSES > DOWSE
DOWSET same as > DOUCET
DOWSETS > DOWSET
DOWSING > DOWSE
DOWT n cigarette butt
DOWTS > DOWT
DOXASTIC adj of or relating to belief
DOXIE same as > DOXY
DOXIES > DOXY
DOXOLOGY n short hymn of praise to God
DOXY n opinion or doctrine, esp concerning religious matters
DOY n beloved person: used esp as an endearment
DOYEN n senior member of a group, profession, or society
DOYENNE > DOYEN
DOYENNES > DOYEN
DOYENS > DOYEN
DOYLEY same as > DOILY
DOYLEYS > DOYLEY
DOYLIES > DOYLY
DOYLY same as > DOILY
DOYS > DOY
DOZE vb sleep lightly or briefly ▷ n short sleep
DOZED adj (of timber or rubber) rotten or decayed
DOZEN vb stun
DOZENED > DOZEN
DOZENING > DOZEN
DOZENS > DOZEN
DOZENTH > DOZEN
DOZENTHS > DOZEN
DOZER > DOZE
DOZERS > DOZE
DOZES > DOZE
DOZIER > DOZY
DOZIEST > DOZY
DOZILY > DOZY
DOZINESS > DOZY
DOZING > DOZE
DOZINGS > DOZE
DOZY adj feeling sleepy
DRAB adj dull and dreary ▷ n light olive-brown colour ▷ vb consort with prostitutes
DRABBED > DRAB
DRABBER n one who frequents low women
DRABBERS > DRABBER
DRABBEST > DRAB
DRABBET n yellowish-brown fabric of coarse linen
DRABBETS > DRABBET
DRABBIER > DRABBY
DRABBIEST > DRABBY
DRABBING > DRAB
DRABBISH adj promiscuous
DRABBLE vb make or

become wet or dirty
DRABBLED > DRABBLE
DRABBLER n part fixed to bottom of sail
DRABBLERS > DRABBLER
DRABBLES > DRABBLE
DRABBLING > DRABBLE
DRABBY adj promiscuous
DRABETTE n type of rough linen fabric
DRABETTES > DRABETTE
DRABLER same as > DRABBLE
DRABLERS > DRABLER
DRABLY > DRAB
DRABNESS > DRAB
DRABS > DRAB
DRAC same as > DRACK
DRACAENA n any tropical plant of the genus Dracaena: some species are cultivated as house plants for their decorative foliage: family Agavaceae
DRACAENAS > DRACAENA
DRACENA same as > DRACAENA
DRACENAS > DRACENA
DRACHM same as > DRAM
DRACHMA n former monetary unit of Greece
DRACHMAE > DRACHMA
DRACHMAI > DRACHMA
DRACHMAS > DRACHMA
DRACHMS > DRACHM
DRACK adj (esp of a woman) unattractive
DRACO as in draco lizard flying lizard
DRACONE n large flexible cylindrical container towed by a ship, used for transporting liquids
DRACONES > DRACONE
DRACONIAN adj severe, harsh
DRACONIC same as > DRACONIAN
DRACONISM > DRACONIAN
DRACONTIC same as > DRACONIC
DRAD > DREAD
DRAFF n residue of husks after fermentation of the grain used in brewing, used as a food for cattle
DRAFFIER > DRAFF
DRAFFIEST > DRAFF
DRAFFISH adj worthless
DRAFFS > DRAFF
DRAFFY > DRAFF
DRAFT same as > DRAUGHT
DRAFTABLE > DRAFT
DRAFTED > DRAFT
DRAFTEE n conscript
DRAFTEES > DRAFTEE
DRAFTER > DRAFT
DRAFTERS > DRAFT
DRAFTIER > DRAFTY
DRAFTIEST > DRAFTY
DRAFTILY > DRAFTY
DRAFTING > DRAFT
DRAFTINGS > DRAFT
DRAFTS > DRAFT
DRAFTSMAN same as > DRAUGHTSMAN
DRAFTSMEN > DRAFTSMAN
DRAFTY same as > DRAUGHTY

DRAG vb pull with force, esp along the ground ▷ n person or thing that slows up progress
DRAGEE n sweet made of a nut, fruit, etc, coated with a hard sugar icing
DRAGEES > DRAGEE
DRAGGED > DRAG
DRAGGER > DRAG
DRAGGERS > DRAG
DRAGGIER > DRAGGY
DRAGGIEST > DRAGGY
DRAGGING > DRAG
DRAGGLE vb make or become wet or dirty by trailing on the ground
DRAGGLED > DRAGGLE
DRAGGLES > DRAGGLE
DRAGGLING > DRAGGLE
DRAGGY adj slow or boring
DRAGHOUND n hound used to follow an artificial trail of scent in a drag hunt
DRAGLINE same as > DRAGROPE
DRAGLINES > DRAGLINE
DRAGNET n net used to scour the bottom of a pond or river to search for something
DRAGNETS > DRAGNET
DRAGOMAN n (in some Middle Eastern countries) professional interpreter or guide
DRAGOMANS > DRAGOMAN
DRAGOMEN > DRAGOMAN
DRAGON n mythical fire-breathing monster like a huge lizard
DRAGONESS > DRAGON
DRAGONET n any small spiny-finned fish of the family Callionymidae, having a flat head and a slender tapering brightly coloured body and living at the bottom of shallow seas
DRAGONETS > DRAGONET
DRAGONFLY n brightly coloured insect with a long slender body and two pairs of wings
DRAGONISE same as > DRAGONIZE
DRAGONISH > DRAGON
DRAGONISM n vigilance
DRAGONIZE vb turn into dragon
DRAGONNE adj dragonlike
DRAGONS > DRAGON
DRAGOON n heavily armed cavalryman ▷ vb coerce, force
DRAGOONED > DRAGOON
DRAGOONS > DRAGOON
DRAGROPE n rope used to drag military equipment, esp artillery
DRAGROPES > DRAGROPE
DRAGS > DRAG
DRAGSMAN n carriage driver
DRAGSMEN > DRAGSMAN
DRAGSTER n car specially built or modified for drag racing

DRAGSTERS > DRAGSTER
DRAGSTRIP n track for drag racing
DRAIL n weighted hook used in trolling ▷ vb fish with a drail
DRAILED > DRAIL
DRAILING > DRAIL
DRAILS > DRAIL
DRAIN n pipe or channel that carries off water or sewage ▷ vb draw off or remove liquid from
DRAINABLE > DRAIN
DRAINAGE n system of drains
DRAINAGES > DRAINAGE
DRAINED > DRAIN
DRAINER n person or thing that drains
DRAINERS > DRAINER
DRAINING > DRAIN
DRAINPIPE > DOWNPIPE
DRAINS > DRAIN
DRAISENE same as > DRAISINE
DRAISENES > DRAISENE
DRAISINE n light rail vehicle
DRAISINES > DRAISINE
DRAKE n male duck
DRAKES > DRAKE
DRAM n small amount of a strong alcoholic drink, esp whisky ▷ vb drink a dram
DRAMA n serious play for theatre, television, or radio
DRAMADIES > DRAMEDY
DRAMADY same as > DRAMEDY
DRAMAS > DRAMA
DRAMATIC adj of or like drama
DRAMATICS n art of acting or producing plays
DRAMATISE same as > DRAMATIZE
DRAMATIST n person who writes plays
DRAMATIZE vb rewrite (a book) in the form of a play
DRAMATURG n literary adviser at a theatre
DRAMEDIES > DRAMEDY
DRAMEDY n television or film drama in which there are important elements of comedy
DRAMMACH n oatmeal mixed with cold water
DRAMMACHS > DRAMMACH
DRAMMED > DRAM
DRAMMING > DRAM
DRAMMOCK same as > DRAMMACH
DRAMMOCKS > DRAMMOCK
DRAMS > DRAM
DRAMSHOP n bar
DRAMSHOPS > DRAMSHOP
DRANGWAY n narrow lane
DRANGWAYS > DRANGWAY
DRANK > DRINK
DRANT vb drone
DRANTED > DRANT
DRANTING > DRANT
DRANTS > DRANT
DRAP a Scot word for > DROP
DRAPABLE > DRAPE
DRAPE vb cover with

material, usu in folds ▷ *n* piece of cloth hung at a window or opening as a screen

DRAPEABLE > DRAPE

DRAPED > DRAPE

DRAPER *n* person who sells fabrics and sewing materials

DRAPERIED > DRAPERY

DRAPERIES > DRAPERY

DRAPERS > DRAPER

DRAPERY *n* fabric or clothing arranged and draped

DRAPES *pl n* material hung at an opening or window to shut out light or to provide privacy

DRAPET *n* cloth

DRAPETS > DRAPET

DRAPEY *adj* hanging in loose folds

DRAPIER *n* draper

DRAPIERS > DRAPIER

DRAPING > DRAPE

DRAPPED > DRAP

DRAPPIE *n* little drop, esp a small amount of spirits

DRAPPIES > DRAPPIE

DRAPPING > DRAP

DRAPPY *n* drop (of liquid)

DRAPS > DRAP

DRASTIC *n* strong purgative ▷ *adj* strong and severe

DRASTICS > DRASTIC

DRAT *interj* exclamation of annoyance ▷ *vb* curse

DRATCHELL *n* low woman

DRATS > DRAT

DRATTED *adj* wretched

DRATTING > DRAT

DRAUGHT *vb* make preliminary plan ▷ *n* current of cold air, esp in an enclosed space ▷ *adj* (of an animal) used for pulling heavy loads

DRAUGHTED > DRAUGHT

DRAUGHTER > DRAUGHT

DRAUGHTS *n* game for two players using a draughtboard and 12 draughtsmen each

DRAUGHTY *adj* exposed to draughts of air

DRAUNT *same as* > DRANT

DRAUNTED > DRAUNT

DRAUNTING > DRAUNT

DRAUNTS > DRAUNT

DRAVE *archaic past of* > DRIVE

DRAW *vb* sketch (a figure, picture, etc) with a pencil or pen ▷ *n* raffle or lottery

DRAWABLE > DRAW

DRAWBACK *n* disadvantage ▷ *vb* move backwards

DRAWBACKS > DRAWBACK

DRAWBAR *n* strong metal bar on a tractor, locomotive, etc, bearing a hook or link and pin to attach a trailer, wagon, etc

DRAWBARS > DRAWBAR

DRAWBORE *n* hole bored through tenon

DRAWBORES > DRAWBORE

DRAWDOWN *n* decrease

DRAWDOWNS > DRAWDOWN

DRAWEE *n* person or organization on which a cheque or other order for payment is drawn

DRAWEES > DRAWEE

DRAWER *n* sliding box-shaped part of a piece of furniture, used for storage

DRAWERFUL *n* amount contained in drawer

DRAWERS *pl n* undergarment worn on the lower part of the body

DRAWING > DRAW

DRAWINGS > DRAW

DRAWKNIFE *n* woodcutting tool with two handles at right angles to the blade, used to shave wood

DRAWL *vb* speak slowly, with long vowel sounds ▷ *n* drawling manner of speech

DRAWLED > DRAWL

DRAWLER > DRAWL

DRAWLERS > DRAWL

DRAWLIER > DRAWL

DRAWLIEST > DRAWL

DRAWLING > DRAWL

DRAWLS > DRAWL

DRAWLY > DRAWL

DRAWN > DRAW

DRAWNWORK *n* type of ornamental needlework

DRAWPLATE *n* plate used to reduce the diameter of wire by drawing it through conical holes

DRAWS > DRAW

DRAWSHAVE *same as* > DRAWKNIFE

DRAWTUBE *n* tube, such as one of the component tubes of a telescope, fitting coaxially within another tube through which it can slide

DRAWTUBES > DRAWTUBE

DRAY *vb* pull using cart ▷ *n* low cart used for carrying heavy loads

DRAYAGE *n* act of transporting something a short distance by lorry or other vehicle

DRAYAGES > DRAYAGE

DRAYED > DRAY

DRAYHORSE *n* large powerful horse used for drawing a dray

DRAYING > DRAY

DRAYMAN *n* driver of a dray

DRAYMEN > DRAYMAN

DRAYS > DRAY

DRAZEL *n* low woman

DRAZELS > DRAZEL

DREAD *vb* anticipate with apprehension or fear ▷ *n* great fear ▷ *adj* awesome

DREADED > DREAD

DREADER > DREAD

DREADERS > DREAD

DREADFUL *n* cheap, often lurid or sensational book or magazine ▷ *adj* very disagreeable or shocking

DREADFULS > DREADFUL

DREADING > DREAD

DREADLESS > DREAD

DREADLOCK *n* Rastafarian hair braid

DREADLY > DREAD

DREADS > DREAD

DREAM *n* imagined series of events experienced in the mind while asleep ▷ *vb* see imaginary pictures in the mind while asleep ▷ *adj* ideal

DREAMBOAT *n* exceptionally attractive person or thing, esp a person of the opposite sex

DREAMED > DREAM

DREAMER *n* person who dreams habitually

DREAMERS > DREAMER

DREAMERY *n* dream world

DREAMFUL > DREAM

DREAMHOLE *n* light-admitting hole in a tower

DREAMIER > DREAMY

DREAMIEST > DREAMY

DREAMILY > DREAMY

DREAMING > DREAM

DREAMINGS > DREAM

DREAMLAND *n* ideal land existing in dreams or in the imagination

DREAMLESS > DREAM

DREAMLIKE > DREAM

DREAMS > DREAM

DREAMT > DREAM

DREAMTIME *n* time when the world was new and fresh

DREAMY *adj* vague or impractical

DREAR *same as* > DREARY

DREARE *obsolete form of* > DREAR

DREARER > DREAR

DREARES > DREARE

DREAREST > DREAR

DREARIER > DREARY

DREARIES > DREARY

DREARIEST > DREARY

DREARILY > DREARY

DREARING *n* sorrow

DREARINGS > DREARING

DREARS > DREAR

DREARY *adj* dull, boring ▷ *n* a dreary thing or person

DRECK *n* rubbish

DRECKIER > DRECK

DRECKIEST > DRECK

DRECKS > DRECK

DRECKSILL *n* doorstep

DRECKY > DRECK

DREDGE *vb* clear or search (a river bed or harbour) by removing silt or mud ▷ *n* machine used to scoop or suck up silt or mud from a river bed or harbour

DREDGED > DREDGE

DREDGER *same as* > DREDGE

DREDGERS > DREDGER

DREDGES > DREDGE

DREDGING > DREDGE

DREDGINGS > DREDGE

DREE *vb* endure

DREED > DREE

DREEING > DREE

DREES > DREE

DREG *n* small quantity

DREGGIER > DREGGY

DREGGIEST > DREGGY

DREGGISH *adj* foul

DREGGY *adj* like or full of dregs

DREGS *pl n* solid particles that settle at the bottom of some liquids

DREICH *adj* dreary

DREICHER > DREICH

DREICHEST > DREICH

DREIDEL *n* spinning top

DREIDELS > DREIDEL

DREIDL *same as* > DREIDEL

DREIDLS > DREIDL

DREIGH *same as* > DREICH

DREK *same as* > DRECK

DREKS > DREK

DRENCH *vb* make completely wet ▷ *n* act or an instance of drenching

DRENCHED > DRENCH

DRENCHER > DRENCH

DRENCHERS > DRENCH

DRENCHES > DRENCH

DRENCHING > DRENCH

DRENT > DRENCH

DREPANID *n* any moth of the superfamily *Drepanoidae* (family *Drepanidae*): it comprises the hook-tip moths

DREPANIDS > DREPANID

DREPANIUM *n* type of flower cluster

DRERE *obsolete form of* > DREAR

DRERES > DRERE

DRERIHEAD *n* obsolete word for dreary

DRESS *n* one-piece garment for a woman or girl, consisting of a skirt and bodice and sometimes sleeves ▷ *vb* put clothes on ▷ *adj* suitable for a formal occasion

DRESSAGE *n* training of a horse to perform manoeuvres in response to the rider's body signals

DRESSAGES > DRESSAGE

DRESSED > DRESS

DRESSER *n* piece of furniture with shelves and with cupboards, for storing or displaying dishes

DRESSERS > DRESSER

DRESSES > DRESS

DRESSIER > DRESSY

DRESSIEST > DRESSY

DRESSILY > DRESSY

DRESSING *n* sauce for salad

DRESSINGS *pl n* dressed stonework, mouldings, and carved ornaments used to form quoins, keystones, sills, and similar features

DRESSMADE > DRESSMAKE

DRESSMAKE *vb* make clothes

DRESSY *adj* (of clothes) elegant

DREST > DRESS

DREVILL *n* offensive person
DREVILLS > DREVILL
DREW > DRAW
DREY *n* squirrel's nest
DREYS > DREY
DRIB *vb* flow in drops
DRIBBED > DRIB
DRIBBER > DRIB
DRIBBERS > DRIB
DRIBBING > DRIB
DRIBBLE *vb* (allow to) flow in drops ▷ *n* small quantity of liquid falling in drops
DRIBBLED > DRIBBLE
DRIBBLER > DRIBBLE
DRIBBLERS > DRIBBLE
DRIBBLES > DRIBBLE
DRIBBLET *same as* > DRIBLET
DRIBBLETS > DRIBBLET
DRIBBLIER > DRIBBLE
DRIBBLING > DRIBBLE
DRIBBLY > DRIBBLE
DRIBLET *n* small amount
DRIBLETS > DRIBLET
DRIBS > DRIB
DRICE *n* pellets of frozen carbon dioxide
DRICES > DRICE
DRICKSIE *same as* > DRUXY
DRICKSIER > DRICKSIE
DRIED > DRY
DRIEGH *adj* tedious
DRIER > DRY
DRIERS > DRY
DRIES > DRY
DRIEST > DRY
DRIFT *vb* be carried along by currents of air or water ▷ *n* something piled up by the wind or current, such as a snowdrift
DRIFTAGE *n* act of drifting
DRIFTAGES > DRIFTAGE
DRIFTED > DRIFT
DRIFTER *n* person who moves aimlessly from place to place or job to job
DRIFTERS > DRIFTER
DRIFTIER > DRIFT
DRIFTIEST > DRIFT
DRIFTING > DRIFT
DRIFTLESS > DRIFT
DRIFTPIN *same as* > DRIFT
DRIFTPINS > DRIFTPIN
DRIFTS > DRIFT
DRIFTWOOD *n* wood floating on or washed ashore by the sea
DRIFTY > DRIFT
DRILL *n* tool or machine for boring holes ▷ *vb* bore a hole in (something) with or as if with a drill
DRILLABLE > DRILL
DRILLED > DRILL
DRILLER > DRILL
DRILLERS > DRILL
DRILLING *same as* > DRILL
DRILLINGS > DRILL
DRILLS > DRILL
DRILLSHIP *n* floating drilling platform
DRILY *adv* in a dry manner
DRINK *vb* swallow (a liquid) ▷ *n* (portion of) a liquid suitable for drinking
DRINKABLE > DRINK

DRINKABLY > DRINK
DRINKER *n* person who drinks, esp a person who drinks alcohol habitually
DRINKERS > DRINKER
DRINKING > DRINK
DRINKINGS > DRINK
DRINKS > DRINK
DRIP *vb* (let) fall in drops ▷ *n* falling of drops of liquid
DRIPLESS > DRIP
DRIPPED > DRIP
DRIPPER > DRIP
DRIPPERS > DRIP
DRIPPIER > DRIPPY
DRIPPIEST > DRIPPY
DRIPPILY > DRIPPY
DRIPPING > DRIP
DRIPPINGS > DRIP
DRIPPY *adj* mawkish, insipid, or inane
DRIPS > DRIP
DRIPSTONE *n* form of calcium carbonate existing in stalactites or stalagmites
DRIPT > DRIP
DRISHEEN *n* pudding made of sheep's intestines filled with meal and sheep's blood
DRISHEENS > DRISHEEN
DRIVABLE > DRIVE
DRIVE *vb* guide the movement of (a vehicle) ▷ *n* journey by car, van, etc
DRIVEABLE > DRIVE
DRIVEL *n* foolish talk ▷ *vb* speak foolishly
DRIVELED > DRIVEL
DRIVELER > DRIVEL
DRIVELERS > DRIVEL
DRIVELINE *n* transmission line from engine to wheels of vehicle
DRIVELING > DRIVEL
DRIVELLED > DRIVEL
DRIVELLER > DRIVEL
DRIVELS > DRIVEL
DRIVEN > DRIVE
DRIVER *n* person who drives a vehicle
DRIVERS > DRIVER
DRIVES > DRIVE
DRIVEWAY *n* path for vehicles connecting a building to a public road
DRIVEWAYS > DRIVEWAY
DRIVING > DRIVE
DRIVINGLY > DRIVE
DRIVINGS > DRIVE
DRIZZLE *n* very light rain ▷ *vb* rain lightly
DRIZZLED > DRIZZLE
DRIZZLES > DRIZZLE
DRIZZLIER > DRIZZLE
DRIZZLING > DRIZZLE
DRIZZLY > DRIZZLE
DROGER *n* W Indian boat
DROGERS > DROGER
DROGHER *same as* > DROGER
DROGHERS > DROGHER
DROGUE *n* any funnel-like device, esp one of canvas, used as a sea anchor
DROGUES > DROGUE
DROGUET *n* woollen fabric

DROGUETS > DROGUET
DROICH *n* dwarf
DROICHIER > DROICHY
DROICHS > DROICH
DROICHY *adj* dwarfish
DROID *same as* > ANDROID
DROIDS > DROID
DROIL *vb* carry out boring menial work
DROILED > DROIL
DROILING > DROIL
DROILS > DROIL
DROIT *n* legal or moral right or claim
DROITS > DROIT
DROLE *adj* amusing ▷ *n* scoundrel
DROLER > DROLE
DROLES > DROLE
DROLEST > DROLE
DROLL *vb* speak wittily ▷ *adj* quaintly amusing
DROLLED > DROLL
DROLLER > DROLL
DROLLERY *n* humour
DROLLEST > DROLL
DROLLING > DROLL
DROLLINGS > DROLL
DROLLISH *adj* somewhat droll
DROLLNESS > DROLL
DROLLS > DROLL
DROLLY > DROLL
DROME *n* informal word for > AERODROME
DROMEDARE *obsolete form of* > DROMEDARY
DROMEDARY *n* camel with a single hump
DROMES > DROME
DROMIC *adj* relating to running track
DROMICAL *same as* > DROMIC
DROMOI > DROMOS
DROMON *same as* > DROMOND
DROMOND *n* large swift sailing vessel of the 12th to 15th centuries
DROMONDS > DROMOND
DROMONS > DROMON
DROMOS *n* Greek passageway
DRONE *n* male bee ▷ *vb* make a monotonous low dull sound
DRONED > DRONE
DRONER > DRONE
DRONERS > DRONE
DRONES > DRONE
DRONGO *n* tropical songbird with a glossy black plumage, a forked tail, and a stout bill
DRONGOES > DRONGO
DRONGOS > DRONGO
DRONIER > DRONY
DRONIEST > DRONY
DRONING > DRONE
DRONINGLY > DRONE
DRONISH > DRONE
DRONISHLY > DRONE
DRONKLAP *n* South African word for a drunkard
DRONKLAPS > DRONKLAP
DRONY *adj* monotonous
DROOB *n* pathetic person
DROOBS > DROOB

DROOG *n* ruffian
DROOGISH > DROOG
DROOGS > DROOG
DROOK *same as* > DROUK
DROOKED > DROOK
DROOKING > DROOK
DROOKINGS > DROOK
DROOKIT *same as* > DROUKIT
DROOKS > DROOK
DROOL *vb* show excessive enthusiasm (for)
DROOLED > DROOL
DROOLIER > DROOLY
DROOLIEST > DROOLY
DROOLING > DROOL
DROOLS > DROOL
DROOLY *adj* tending to drool
DROOME *obsolete form of* > DRUM
DROOMES > DRUM
DROOP *vb* hang downwards loosely ▷ *n* act or state of drooping
DROOPED > DROOP
DROOPIER > DROOPY
DROOPIEST > DROOPY
DROOPILY > DROOPY
DROOPING > DROOP
DROOPS > DROOP
DROOPY *adj* hanging or sagging downwards
DROP *vb* (allow to) fall vertically ▷ *n* small quantity of liquid forming a round shape
DROPCLOTH *n* cloth spread on floor to catch drips while painting
DROPFLIES > DROPFLY
DROPFLY *n* (angling) artificial fly
DROPFORGE *vb* forge metal between two dies
DROPHEAD as in *drophead coupe* two-door car with a folding roof and sloping back
DROPHEADS > DROPHEAD
DROPKICK *n* (in certain ball games) a kick in which the ball is first dropped then kicked as it bounces from the ground
DROPKICKS > DROPKICK
DROPLET *n* very small drop of liquid
DROPLETS > DROPLET
DROPLIGHT *n* electric light that may be raised or lowered by means of a pulley or other mechanism
DROPOUT *n* person who rejects conventional society ▷ *vb* abandon or withdraw (from an institution or group)
DROPOUTS > DROPOUT
DROPPABLE > DROP
DROPPED > DROP
DROPPER *n* small tube with a rubber part at one end for drawing up and dispensing drops of liquid
DROPPERS > DROPPER
DROPPING > DROP
DROPPINGS *pl n* faeces of certain animals, such as

Section 1: Words between 2 and 9 letters in length

d

rabbits or birds
DROPPLE *n* trickle
DROPPLES > DROPPLE
DROPS > DROP
DROPSHOT *n* (in tennis) shot in which a softly returned ball just clears the net before falling abruptly
DROPSHOTS > DROPSHOT
DROPSICAL > DROPSY
DROPSIED > DROPSY
DROPSIES > DROPSY
DROPSONDE *n* radiosonde dropped by parachute
DROPSTONE *n* calcium carbonate in stalactites
DROPSY *n* illness in which watery fluid collects in the body
DROPT > DROP
DROPWISE *adv* in form of a drop
DROPWORT *See also* > MEADOWSWEET
DROPWORTS > DROPWORT
DROSERA *n* insectivorous plant
DROSERAS > DROSERA
DROSHKIES > DROSHKY
DROSHKY *n* open four-wheeled horse-drawn passenger carriage, formerly used in Russia
DROSKIES > DROSKY
DROSKY *same as* > DROSHKY
DROSS *n* scum formed on the surfaces of molten metals
DROSSES > DROSS
DROSSIER > DROSS
DROSSIEST > DROSS
DROSSY > DROSS
DROSTDIES > DROSTDY
DROSTDY *n* office of landdrost
DROSTDYS > DROSTDY
DROUGHT *n* prolonged shortage of rainfall
DROUGHTS > DROUGHT
DROUGHTY > DROUGHT
DROUK *vb* drench
DROUKED > DROUK
DROUKING > DROUK
DROUKINGS > DROUK
DROUKIT *adj* drenched
DROUKS > DROUK
DROUTH *same as* > DROUGHT
DROUTHIER > DROUTHY
DROUTHS > DROUTH
DROUTHY *adj* thirsty or dry
DROVE > DRIVE
DROVED > DRIVE
DROVER *n* person who drives sheep or cattle
DROVERS > DROVER
DROVES > DRIVE
DROVING > DRIVE
DROVINGS > DRIVE
DROW *n* sea fog
DROWN *vb* die or kill by immersion in liquid
DROWND *dialect form of* > DROWN
DROWNDED > DROWND
DROWNDING > DROWND
DROWNDS > DROWND
DROWNED > DROWN

DROWNER > DROWN
DROWNERS > DROWN
DROWNING > DROWN
DROWNINGS > DROWN
DROWNS > DROWN
DROWS > DROW
DROWSE *vb* be sleepy, dull, or sluggish ▷*n* state of being drowsy
DROWSED > DROWSE
DROWSES > DROWSE
DROWSIER > DROWSY
DROWSIEST > DROWSY
DROWSIHED *adj* old form of drowsy
DROWSILY > DROWSY
DROWSING > DROWSE
DROWSY *adj* feeling sleepy
DRUB *vb* beat as with a stick ▷*n* blow, as from a stick
DRUBBED > DRUB
DRUBBER > DRUB
DRUBBERS > DRUB
DRUBBING > DRUB
DRUBBINGS > DRUB
DRUBS > DRUB
DRUCKEN *adj* drunken
DRUDGE *n* person who works hard at uninteresting tasks ▷*vb* work at such tasks
DRUDGED > DRUDGE
DRUDGER > DRUDGE
DRUDGERS > DRUDGE
DRUDGERY *n* uninteresting work that must be done
DRUDGES > DRUDGE
DRUDGING > DRUDGE
DRUDGISM > DRUDGE
DRUDGISMS > DRUDGE
DRUG *n* substance used in the treatment or prevention of disease ▷*vb* give a drug to (a person or animal) to cause sleepiness or unconsciousness
DRUGGED > DRUG
DRUGGER *n* druggist
DRUGGERS > DRUGGER
DRUGGET *n* coarse fabric used as a protective floor-covering, etc
DRUGGETS > DRUGGET
DRUGGIE *n* drug addict
DRUGGIER > DRUG
DRUGGIES > DRUGGIE
DRUGGIEST > DRUG
DRUGGING > DRUG
DRUGGIST *n* pharmacist
DRUGGISTS > DRUGGIST
DRUGGY > DRUG
DRUGLORD *n* criminal who controls the distribution and sale of large quantities of illegal drugs
DRUGLORDS > DRUGLORD
DRUGMAKER *n* manufacturer of drugs
DRUGS > DRUG
DRUGSTORE *n* pharmacy where a wide range of goods are available
DRUID *n* member of an ancient order of priests in Gaul, Britain, and Ireland in the pre-Christian era
DRUIDESS > DRUID

DRUIDIC > DRUID
DRUIDICAL > DRUID
DRUIDISM > DRUID
DRUIDISMS > DRUID
DRUIDRIES > DRUID
DRUIDRY > DRUID
DRUIDS > DRUID
DRUM *n* percussion instrument sounded by striking a membrane stretched across the opening of a hollow cylinder ▷*vb* play (music) on a drum
DRUMBEAT *n* sound made by beating a drum
DRUMBEATS > DRUMBEAT
DRUMBLE *vb* be inactive
DRUMBLED > DRUMBLE
DRUMBLES > DRUMBLE
DRUMBLING > DRUMBLE
DRUMFIRE *n* heavy, rapid, and continuous gunfire, the sound of which resembles rapid drumbeats
DRUMFIRES > DRUMFIRE
DRUMFISH *n* one of several types of fish that make a drumming sound
DRUMHEAD *n* part of a drum that is struck
DRUMHEADS > DRUMHEAD
DRUMLIER > DRUMLY
DRUMLIEST > DRUMLY
DRUMLIKE > DRUM
DRUMLIN *n* streamlined mound of glacial drift, rounded or elongated in the direction of the original flow of ice
DRUMLINS > DRUMLIN
DRUMLY *adj* dismal; dreary
DRUMMED > DRUM
DRUMMER *n* person who plays a drum or drums
DRUMMERS > DRUMMER
DRUMMIES > DRUMMY
DRUMMING > DRUM
DRUMMOCK *same as* > DRAMMOCK
DRUMMOCKS > DRUMMOCK
DRUMMY *n* (in South Africa) drum majorette
DRUMROLL *n* continued repeated sound of drum
DRUMROLLS > DRUMROLL
DRUMS > DRUM
DRUMSTICK *n* stick used for playing a drum
DRUNK > DRINK
DRUNKARD *n* person who frequently gets drunk
DRUNKARDS > DRUNKARD
DRUNKEN *adj* drunk or frequently drunk
DRUNKENLY > DRUNKEN
DRUNKER > DRINK
DRUNKEST > DRINK
DRUNKS > DRINK
DRUPE *n* fleshy fruit with a stone, such as the peach or cherry
DRUPEL *same as* > DRUPELET
DRUPELET *n* small drupe, usually one of a number forming a compound fruit
DRUPELETS > DRUPELET

DRUPELS > DRUPEL
DRUPES > DRUPE
DRUSE *n* aggregate of small crystals within a cavity, esp those lining a cavity in a rock or mineral
DRUSES > DRUSE
DRUSIER > DRUSY
DRUSIEST > DRUSY
DRUSY *adj* made of tiny crystals
DRUTHERS *n* preference
DRUXIER > DRUXY
DRUXIEST > DRUXY
DRUXY *adj* (of wood) having decayed white spots
DRY *adj* lacking moisture ▷*vb* make or become dry
DRYABLE > DRY
DRYAD *n* wood nymph
DRYADES > DRYAD
DRYADIC > DRYAD
DRYADS > DRYAD
DRYASDUST *adj* boringly bookish
DRYBEAT *vb* beat severely
DRYBEATEN > DRYBEAT
DRYBEATS > DRYBEAT
DRYER > DRY
DRYERS > DRY
DRYEST > DRY
DRYING > DRY
DRYINGS > DRY
DRYISH *adj* fairly dry
DRYLAND *adj* of an arid area
DRYLOT *n* livestock enclosure
DRYLOTS > DRYLOT
DRYLY *same as* > DRILY
DRYMOUTH *n* condition of insufficient saliva
DRYMOUTHS > DRYMOUTH
DRYNESS > DRY
DRYNESSES > DRY
DRYPOINT *n* copper engraving technique using a hard steel needle
DRYPOINTS > DRYPOINT
DRYS > DRY
DRYSALTER *n* dealer in certain chemical products, such as dyestuffs and gums, and in dried, tinned, or salted foods and edible oils
DRYSTONE *adj* (of a wall) made without mortar
DRYWALL *n* wall built without mortar ▷*vb* build a wall without mortar
DRYWALLED > DRYWALL
DRYWALLS > DRYWALL
DRYWELL *n* type of sewage disposal system
DRYWELLS > DRYWELL
DSO *same as* > ZHO
DSOBO *same as* > ZOBO
DSOBOS > DSOBO
DSOMO *same as* > ZHOMO
DSOMOS > DSOMO
DSOS > DSO
DUAD *a rare word for* > PAIR
DUADS > DUAD
DUAL *adj* having two parts, functions, or aspects ▷*n* dual number ▷*vb* make (a road) into a dual

carriageway

DUALIN n explosive substance

DUALINS > DUALIN

DUALISE same as > DUALIZE

DUALISED > DUALISE

DUALISES > DUALISE

DUALISING > DUALISE

DUALISM n state of having or being believed to have two distinct parts or aspects

DUALISMS > DUALISM

DUALIST > DUALISM

DUALISTIC > DUALISM

DUALISTS > DUALISM

DUALITIES > DUALITY

DUALITY n state or quality of being two or in two parts

DUALIZE vb cause to have two parts

DUALIZED > DUALIZE

DUALIZES > DUALIZE

DUALIZING > DUALIZE

DUALLED > DUAL

DUALLING > DUAL

DUALLY > DUAL

DUALS > DUAL

DUAN n poem

DUANS > DUAN

DUAR n Arab camp

DUARCHIES > DUARCHY

DUARCHY same as > DIARCHY

DUARS > DUAR

DUATHLON n athletic contest in which each athlete competes in running and cycling events

DUATHLONS > DUATHLON

DUB vb give (a person or place) a name or nickname ▷ n style of reggae record production involving exaggeration of instrumental parts, echo, etc

DUBBED > DUB

DUBBER > DUB

DUBBERS > DUB

DUBBIN n thick grease applied to leather to soften and waterproof it

DUBBING > DUB

DUBBINGS > DUB

DUBBINS > DUBBIN

DUBBO adj stupid ▷ n stupid person

DUBBOS > DUBBO

DUBIETIES > DUBIETY

DUBIETY n state of being doubtful

DUBIOSITY same as > DUBIETY

DUBIOUS adj feeling or causing doubt

DUBIOUSLY > DUBIOUS

DUBITABLE adj open to doubt

DUBITABLY > DUBITABLE

DUBITANCY > DUBITATE

DUBITATE vb doubt

DUBITATED > DUBITATE

DUBITATES > DUBITATE

DUBNIUM n element produced in minute quantities by bombarding plutonium with high-

energy neon ions

DUBNIUMS > DUBNIUM

DUBONNET n dark purplish-red colour

DUBONNETS > DUBONNET

DUBS > DUB

DUCAL adj of a duke

DUCALLY > DUCAL

DUCAT n former European gold or silver coin

DUCATOON n former silver coin

DUCATOONS > DUCATOON

DUCATS > DUCAT

DUCDAME interj Shakespearean nonsense word

DUCE n leader

DUCES > DUCE

DUCHESS n woman who holds the rank of duke ▷ vb overwhelm with flattering attention

DUCHESSE n type of satin

DUCHESSED > DUCHESS

DUCHESSES > DUCHESS

DUCHIES > DUCHY

DUCHY n territory of a duke or duchess

DUCI > DUCE

DUCK n water bird with short legs, webbed feet, and a broad blunt bill ▷ vb move (the head or body) quickly downwards, to avoid being seen or to dodge a blow

DUCKBILL n duckbilled platypus

DUCKBILLS > DUCKBILL

DUCKBOARD n board or boards laid so as to form a floor or path over wet or muddy ground

DUCKED > DUCK

DUCKER > DUCK

DUCKERS > DUCK

DUCKFOOT as in duckfoot quote chevron-shaped quotation mark

DUCKIE same as > DUCKY

DUCKIER > DUCKY

DUCKIES > DUCKY

DUCKIEST > DUCKY

DUCKING > DUCK

DUCKINGS > DUCK

DUCKLING n baby duck

DUCKLINGS > DUCKLING

DUCKMOLE another word for > DUCKBILL

DUCKMOLES > DUCKMOLE

DUCKPIN n short bowling pin

DUCKPINS > DUCKPIN

DUCKS > DUCK

DUCKSHOVE vb evade responsibility

DUCKTAIL n Teddy boy's hairstyle

DUCKTAILS > DUCKTAIL

DUCKWALK vb walk in a squatting posture

DUCKWALKS > DUCKWALK

DUCKWEED n any of various small stemless aquatic plants of the family Lemnaceae, esp any of the

genus Lemna, that have rounded leaves and occur floating on still water in temperate regions

DUCKWEEDS > DUCKWEED

DUCKY n darling or dear: used as a term of endearment among women, but now often used in imitation of the supposed usage of homosexual men ▷ adj delightful

DUCT vb convey via a duct ▷ n tube, pipe, or channel through which liquid or gas is conveyed

DUCTAL > DUCT

DUCTED > DUCT

DUCTILE adj (of a metal) able to be shaped into sheets or wires

DUCTILELY > DUCTILE

DUCTILITY > DUCTILE

DUCTING > DUCT

DUCTINGS > DUCT

DUCTLESS > DUCT

DUCTS > DUCT

DUCTULE n small duct

DUCTULES > DUCTULE

DUCTWORK n system of ducts

DUCTWORKS > DUCTWORK

DUD n ineffectual person or thing ▷ adj bad or useless

DUDDER n door-to-door salesman

DUDDERIES > DUDDERY

DUDDERS > DUDDER

DUDDERY n place where old clothes are sold

DUDDIE adj ragged

DUDDIER > DUDDIE

DUDDIEST > DUDDIE

DUDDY same as > DUDDIE

DUDE vb dress fashionably ▷ n man

DUDED > DUDE

DUDEEN n clay pipe with a short stem

DUDEENS > DUDEEN

DUDES > DUDE

DUDGEON n anger or resentment

DUDGEONS > DUDGEON

DUDHEEN n type of pipe

DUDHEENS > DUDHEEN

DUDING > DUDE

DUDISH > DUDE

DUDISHLY > DUDE

DUDISM n being a dude

DUDISMS > DUDISM

DUDS > DUD

DUE vb supply with ▷ adj expected or scheduled to be present or arrive ▷ n something that is owed or required ▷ adv directly or exactly

DUECENTO n thirteenth century (in Italian art)

DUECENTOS > DUECENTO

DUED > DUE

DUEFUL adj proper

DUEL n formal fight with deadly weapons between two people, to settle a quarrel ▷ vb fight in a duel

DUELED > DUEL

DUELER > DUEL

DUELERS > DUEL

DUELING > DUEL

DUELIST > DUEL

DUELISTS > DUEL

DUELLED > DUEL

DUELLER > DUEL

DUELLERS > DUEL

DUELLI > DUELLO

DUELLING > DUEL

DUELLINGS > DUEL

DUELLIST > DUEL

DUELLISTS > DUEL

DUELLO n art of duelling

DUELLOS > DUELLO

DUELS > DUEL

DUELSOME adj given to duelling

DUENDE n Spanish goblin

DUENDES > DUENDE

DUENESS > DUE

DUENESSES > DUE

DUENNA n (esp in Spain) elderly woman acting as chaperone to a young woman

DUENNAS > DUENNA

DUES pl n membership fees paid to a club or organization

DUET n piece of music for two performers ▷ vb perform a duet

DUETED > DUET

DUETING > DUET

DUETS > DUET

DUETT same as > DUET

DUETTED > DUET

DUETTI > DUETTO

DUETTING > DUET

DUETTINO n simple duet

DUETTINOS > DUETTINO

DUETTIST > DUET

DUETTISTS > DUET

DUETTO same as > DUET

DUETTOS > DUETTO

DUETTS > DUETT

DUFF adj broken or useless ▷ vb change the appearance of or give a false appearance to (old or stolen goods) ▷ n rump or buttocks

DUFFED > DUFF

DUFFEL n heavy woollen cloth with a thick nap

DUFFELS > DUFFEL

DUFFER n dull or incompetent person

DUFFERDOM n condition of being a duffer

DUFFERISM same as > DUFFERDOM

DUFFERS > DUFFER

DUFFEST > DUFF

DUFFING > DUFF

DUFFINGS > DUFF

DUFFLE same as > DUFFEL

DUFFLES > DUFFLE

DUFFS > DUFF

DUFUS same as > DOOFUS

DUFUSES > DUFUS

DUG > DIG

DUGITE n medium-sized Australian venomous snake

DUGITES > DUGITE

DUGONG n whalelike mammal of tropical waters

DUGONGS > DUGONG

DUGOUT n (at a sports ground) covered bench where managers and substitutes sit

DUGOUTS > DUGOUT

DUGS > DIG

DUH interj ironic response to a question or statement, implying that the speaker is stupid or that the reply is obvious

DUHKHA same as > DUKKHA

DUHKHAS > DUHKHA

DUI > DUO

DUIKER n small African antelope

DUIKERBOK same as > DUIKER

DUIKERS > DUIKER

DUING > DUE

DUIT n former Dutch coin

DUITS > DUIT

DUKA n shop

DUKAS > DUKA

DUKE vb fight with fists ▷ n nobleman of the highest rank

DUKED > DUKE

DUKEDOM n title, rank, or position of a duke

DUKEDOMS > DUKEDOM

DUKELING n low-ranking duke

DUKELINGS > DUKELING

DUKERIES > DUKERY

DUKERY n duke's domain

DUKES pl n fists

DUKESHIP > DUKE

DUKESHIPS > DUKE

DUKING > DUKE

DUKKA n mix of ground roast nuts and spices, originating in Egypt, and used for sprinkling on meat or as a dip

DUKKAH same as > DUKKA

DUKKAHS > DUKKAH

DUKKAS > DUKKA

DUKKHA n (in Theravada Buddhism) the belief that all things are suffering, due to the desire to seek permanence or recognise the self when neither exist: one of the three basic characteristics of existence

DUKKHAS > DUKKHA

DULCAMARA n orange-fruited vine

DULCET adj (of a sound) soothing or pleasant ▷ n soft organ stop

DULCETLY > DULCET

DULCETS > DULCET

DULCIAN n precursor to the bassoon

DULCIANA n sweet-toned organ stop, controlling metal pipes of narrow scale

DULCIANAS > DULCIANA

DULCIANS > DULCIAN

DULCIFIED > DULCIFY

DULCIFIES > DULCIFY

DULCIFY vb make pleasant or agreeable

DULCIMER n tuned percussion instrument consisting of a set of strings stretched over a sounding board and struck with hammers

DULCIMERS > DULCIMER

DULCIMORE former name for > DULCIMER

DULCINEA n man's sweetheart

DULCINEAS > DULCINEA

DULCITE n sweet substance

DULCITES > DULCITE

DULCITOL another word for > DULCITE

DULCITOLS > DULCITOL

DULCITUDE n sweetness

DULCOSE another word for > DULCITE

DULCOSES > DULCOSE

DULE n suffering; misery

DULES > DULE

DULIA n veneration accorded to saints in the Roman Catholic and Eastern Churches, as contrasted with hyperdulia and latria

DULIAS > DULIA

DULL adj not interesting ▷ vb make or become dull

DULLARD n dull or stupid person

DULLARDS > DULLARD

DULLED > DULL

DULLER > DULL

DULLEST > DULL

DULLIER > DULL

DULLIEST > DULL

DULLING > DULL

DULLISH > DULL

DULLISHLY > DULL

DULLNESS > DULL

DULLS > DULL

DULLY > DULL

DULNESS > DULL

DULNESSES > DULL

DULOCRACY n rule by slaves

DULOSES > DULOSIS

DULOSIS n practice of some ants, in which one species forces members of a different species to do the work of the colony

DULOTIC > DULOSIS

DULSE n seaweed with large red edible fronds

DULSES > DULSE

DULY adv in a proper manner

DUMA n elective legislative assembly established by Tsar Nicholas II in 1905: overthrown by the Bolsheviks in 1917

DUMAIST n member of duma

DUMAISTS > DUMAIST

DUMAS > DUMA

DUMB vb silence ▷ adj lacking the power to speak

DUMBBELL n short bar with a heavy ball or disc at each end, used for physical exercise

DUMBBELLS > DUMBBELL

DUMBCANE n West Indian aroid plant

DUMBCANES > DUMBCANE

DUMBED > DUMB

DUMBER > DUMB

DUMBEST > DUMB

DUMBFOUND vb strike dumb with astonishment

DUMBHEAD n dunce

DUMBHEADS > DUMBHEAD

DUMBING > DUMB

DUMBLY > DUMB

DUMBNESS > DUMB

DUMBO n slow-witted unintelligent person

DUMBOS > DUMBO

DUMBS > DUMB

DUMBSHIT n taboo slang word for a stupid person

DUMBSHITS > DUMBSHIT

DUMDUM n soft-nosed bullet that expands on impact and causes serious wounds

DUMDUMS > DUMDUM

DUMELA sentence substitute hello

DUMFOUND same as > DUMBFOUND

DUMFOUNDS > DUMFOUND

DUMKA n Slavonic lyrical song

DUMKY > DUMKA

DUMMERER n person who pretends to be dumb

DUMMERERS > DUMMERER

DUMMIED > DUMMY

DUMMIER > DUMMY

DUMMIES > DUMMY

DUMMIEST > DUMMY

DUMMINESS > DUMMY

DUMMKOPF n stupid person

DUMMKOPFS > DUMMKOPF

DUMMY adj sham ▷ n figure representing the human form, used for displaying clothes etc ▷ adj imitation, substitute ▷ vb prepare a dummy of (a proposed book, page, etc)

DUMMYING > DUMMY

DUMOSE adj bushlike

DUMOSITY > DUMOSE

DUMOUS same as > DUMOSE

DUMP vb drop or let fall in a careless manner ▷ n place where waste materials are left

DUMPBIN n free-standing unit in a bookshop in which a particular publisher's books are displayed

DUMPBINS > DUMPBIN

DUMPCART n cart for dumping without handling

DUMPCARTS > DUMPCART

DUMPED > DUMP

DUMPER > DUMP

DUMPERS > DUMP

DUMPIER > DUMPY

DUMPIES > DUMPY

DUMPIEST > DUMPY

DUMPILY > DUMPY

DUMPINESS > DUMPY

DUMPING > DUMP

DUMPINGS > DUMP

DUMPISH same as > DUMPY

DUMPISHLY > DUMPISH

DUMPLE vb form into dumpling shape

DUMPLED > DUMPLE

DUMPLES > DUMPLE

DUMPLING n small ball of dough cooked and served with stew

DUMPLINGS > DUMPLING

DUMPS pl n state of melancholy or depression

DUMPSITE n location of dump

DUMPSITES > DUMPSITE

DUMPSTER n refuse skip

DUMPSTERS > DUMPSTER

DUMPTRUCK n lorry with a tipping container

DUMPY n dumpy person ▷ adj short and plump

DUN adj brownish-grey ▷ vb demand payment from (a debtor) ▷ n demand for payment

DUNAM n unit of area measurement

DUNAMS > DUNAM

DUNCE n person who is stupid or slow to learn

DUNCEDOM > DUNCE

DUNCEDOMS > DUNCE

DUNCELIKE > DUNCE

DUNCERIES > DUNCERY

DUNCERY n duncelike behaviour

DUNCES > DUNCE

DUNCH vb push against gently

DUNCHED > DUNCH

DUNCHES > DUNCH

DUNCHING > DUNCH

DUNCICAL adj duncelike

DUNCISH adj duncelike

DUNCISHLY > DUNCE

DUNDER n cane juice lees

DUNDERS > DUNDER

DUNE n mound or ridge of drifted sand

DUNELAND n land characterized by dunes

DUNELANDS > DUNELAND

DUNELIKE > DUNE

DUNES > DUNE

DUNG n faeces from animals such as cattle ▷ vb cover (ground) with manure

DUNGAREE n coarse cotton fabric used chiefly for work clothes, etc

DUNGAREED adj wearing dungarees

DUNGAREES > DUNGAREE

DUNGED > DUNG

DUNGEON vb hold captive in dungeon ▷ n underground prison cell

DUNGEONED > DUNGEON

DUNGEONER n jailer

DUNGEONS > DUNGEON

DUNGER n old decrepit car

DUNGERS > DUNGER

DUNGHILL n heap of dung

DUNGHILLS > DUNGHILL

DUNGIER > DUNG

DUNGIEST > DUNG

DUNGING > DUNG

DUNGMERE *n* cesspool
DUNGMERES > DUNGMERE
DUNGS > DUNG
DUNGY > DUNG
DUNITE *n* ultrabasic igneous rock consisting mainly of olivine
DUNITES > DUNITE
DUNITIC > DUNITE
DUNK *vb* dip (a biscuit or bread) in a drink or soup before eating it
DUNKED > DUNK
DUNKER > DUNK
DUNKERS > DUNK
DUNKING > DUNK
DUNKS > DUNK
DUNLIN *n* small sandpiper with a brown back found in northern regions
DUNLINS > DUNLIN
DUNNAGE *n* loose material used for packing cargo
DUNNAGES > DUNNAGE
DUNNAKIN *n* lavatory
DUNNAKINS > DUNNAKIN
DUNNART *n* mouselike insectivorous marsupial of the genus *Sminthopsis* of Australia and New Guinea
DUNNARTS > DUNNART
DUNNED > DUN
DUNNER > DUN
DUNNESS > DUN
DUNNESSES > DUN
DUNNEST > DUN
DUNNIER > DUNNY
DUNNIES > DUNNY
DUNNIEST > DUNNY
DUNNING > DUN
DUNNINGS > DUN
DUNNISH > DUN
DUNNITE *n* explosive containing ammonium picrate
DUNNITES > DUNNITE
DUNNO *vb* slang for don't know
DUNNOCK *n* hedge sparrow
DUNNOCKS > DUNNOCK
DUNNY *n* in Australia, toilet ▷ *adj* relating to dunny
DUNS > DUN
DUNSH *same as* > DUNCH
DUNSHED > DUNSH
DUNSHES > DUNSH
DUNSHING > DUNSH
DUNT *n* blow ▷ *vb* strike or hit
DUNTED > DUNT
DUNTING > DUNT
DUNTS > DUNT
DUO *same as* > DUET
DUOBINARY *adj* denoting a communications system for coding digital data in which three data bands are used, 0, +1, −1
DUODECIMO *n* book size resulting from folding a sheet of paper into twelve leaves
DUODENA > DUODENUM
DUODENAL > DUODENUM
DUODENARY *adj* of or relating to the number 12
DUODENUM *n* first part of the small intestine, just below the stomach
DUODENUMS > DUODENUM
DUOLOG *same as* > DUOLOGUE
DUOLOGS > DUOLOG
DUOLOGUE *n* (in drama) conversation between only two speakers
DUOLOGUES > DUOLOGUE
DUOMI > DUOMO
DUOMO *n* cathedral in Italy
DUOMOS > DUOMO
DUOPOLIES > DUOPOLY
DUOPOLY *n* situation in which control of a commodity or service in a particular market is vested in just two producers or suppliers
DUOPSONY *n* two rival buyers controlling sellers
DUOS > DUO
DUOTONE *n* process for producing halftone illustrations using two shades of a single colour or black and a colour
DUOTONES > DUOTONE
DUP *vb* open
DUPABLE > DUPE
DUPATTA *n* scarf worn in India
DUPATTAS > DUPATTA
DUPE *vb* deceive or cheat ▷ *n* person who is easily deceived
DUPED > DUPE
DUPER > DUPE
DUPERIES > DUPE
DUPERS > DUPE
DUPERY > DUPE
DUPES > DUPE
DUPING > DUPE
DUPION *n* silk fabric made from the threads of double cocoons
DUPIONS > DUPION
DUPLE *adj* having two beats in a bar
DUPLET *n* pair of electrons shared between two atoms in a covalent bond
DUPLETS > DUPLET
DUPLEX *vb* duplicate ▷ *n* apartment on two floors ▷ *adj* having two parts
DUPLEXED > DUPLEX
DUPLEXER *n* telecommunications system
DUPLEXERS > DUPLEXER
DUPLEXES > DUPLEX
DUPLEXING > DUPLEX
DUPLEXITY > DUPLEX
DUPLICAND *n* feu duty doubled
DUPLICATE *adj* copied exactly from an original ▷ *n* exact copy ▷ *vb* make an exact copy of
DUPLICITY *n* deceitful behaviour
DUPLIED > DUPLY
DUPLIES > DUPLY
DUPLY *vb* give a second reply
DUPLYING > DUPLY
DUPONDII > DUPONDIUS
DUPONDIUS *n* brass coin of ancient Rome worth half a sesterce
DUPPED > DUP
DUPPIES > DUPPY
DUPPING > DUP
DUPPY *n* spirit or ghost
DUPS > DUP
DURA *same as* > DURRA
DURABLE *adj* long-lasting
DURABLES *pl n* goods that require infrequent replacement
DURABLY > DURABLE
DURAL *n* alloy of aluminium and copper
DURALS > DURAL
DURALUMIN *n* light and strong aluminium alloy containing copper, silicon, magnesium, and manganese
DURAMEN *another name for* > HEARTWOOD
DURAMENS > DURAMEN
DURANCE *n* imprisonment
DURANCES > DURANCE
DURANT *n* tough, leathery cloth
DURANTS > DURANT
DURAS > DURA
DURATION *n* length of time that something lasts
DURATIONS > DURATION
DURATIVE *adj* denoting an aspect of verbs that includes the imperfective and the progressive ▷ *n* durative aspect of a verb
DURATIVES > DURATIVE
DURBAR *n* (formerly) the court of a native ruler or a governor in India
DURBARS > DURBAR
DURDUM *same as* > DIRDUM
DURDUMS > DURDUM
DURE *vb* endure
DURED > DURE
DUREFUL *adj* lasting
DURES > DURE
DURESS *n* compulsion by use of force or threats
DURESSE *same as* > DURESS
DURESSES > DURESS
DURGAH *same as* > DARGAH
DURGAHS > DURGAH
DURGAN *n* dwarf
DURGANS > DURGAN
DURGIER > DURGY
DURGIEST > DURGY
DURGY *adj* dwarflike
DURIAN *n* SE Asian bombacaceous tree, *Durio zibethinus*, having very large oval fruits with a hard spiny rind containing seeds surrounded by edible evil-smelling aril
DURIANS > DURIAN
DURICRUST *another name for* > CALICHE
DURING *prep* throughout or within the limit of (a period of time)
DURION *same as* > DURIAN
DURIONS > DURION
DURMAST *n* large Eurasian oak tree, *Quercus petraea*, with lobed leaves and sessile acorns
DURMASTS > DURMAST
DURN *vb* variant of > DARN
DURNDEST *same as* > DARNEDEST
DURNED > DURN
DURNEDER > DURN
DURNEDEST > DURN
DURNING > DURN
DURNS > DURN
DURO *n* silver peso of Spain or Spanish America
DUROC *n* breed of pig
DUROCS > DUROC
DUROMETER *n* instrument for measuring hardness
DUROS > DURO
DUROY *n* coarse woollen fabric
DUROYS > DUROY
DURR *same as* > DURRA
DURRA *n* Old World variety of sorghum, *Sorghum vulgare durra*, with erect hairy flower spikes and round seeds: cultivated for grain and fodder
DURRAS > DURRA
DURRIE *n* cotton carpet made in India, often in rectangular pieces fringed at the ends: sometimes used as a sofa cover, wall hanging, etc
DURRIES > DURRY
DURRS > DURR
DURRY *n* cigarette
DURST *a past tense of* > DARE
DURUKULI *n* S American monkey
DURUKULIS > DURUKULI
DURUM *n* variety of wheat, *Triticum durum*, with a high gluten content, cultivated mainly in the Mediterranean region, and used chiefly to make pastas
DURUMS > DURUM
DURZI *n* Indian tailor
DURZIS > DURZI
DUSH *vb* strike hard
DUSHED > DUSH
DUSHES > DUSH
DUSHING > DUSH
DUSK *n* time just before nightfall, when it is almost dark ▷ *adj* shady ▷ *vb* make or become dark
DUSKED > DUSK
DUSKEN *vb* grow dark
DUSKENED > DUSKEN
DUSKENING > DUSKEN
DUSKENS > DUSKEN
DUSKER > DUSK
DUSKEST > DUSK
DUSKIER > DUSKY
DUSKIEST > DUSKY
DUSKILY > DUSKY
DUSKINESS > DUSKY
DUSKING > DUSK
DUSKISH > DUSK
DUSKISHLY > DUSK
DUSKLY > DUSK
DUSKNESS > DUSK
DUSKS > DUSK

DUSKY *adj* dark in colour

DUST *n* small dry particles of earth, sand, or dirt ▷ *vb* remove dust from (furniture) by wiping

DUSTBIN *n* large container for household rubbish

DUSTBINS > DUSTBIN

DUSTCART *n* truck for collecting household rubbish

DUSTCARTS > DUSTCART

DUSTCOVER *same as* > DUSTSHEET

DUSTED > DUST

DUSTER *n* cloth used for dusting

DUSTERS > DUSTER

DUSTHEAP *n* accumulation of refuse

DUSTHEAPS > DUSTHEAP

DUSTIER > DUSTY

DUSTIEST > DUSTY

DUSTILY > DUSTY

DUSTINESS > DUSTY

DUSTING > DUST

DUSTINGS > DUST

DUSTLESS > DUST

DUSTLIKE > DUST

DUSTMAN *n* man whose job is to collect household rubbish

DUSTMEN > DUSTMAN

DUSTOFF *n* casualty evacuation helicopter

DUSTOFFS > DUSTOFF

DUSTPAN *n* short-handled shovel into which dust is swept from floors

DUSTPANS > DUSTPAN

DUSTPROOF *adj* repelling dust

DUSTRAG *n* cloth for dusting

DUSTRAGS > DUSTRAG

DUSTS > DUST

DUSTSHEET *n* large cloth cover to protect furniture from dust

DUSTSTORM *n* storm with whirling column of dust

DUSTUP *n* quarrel, fight, or argument

DUSTUPS > DUSTUP

DUSTY *adj* covered with dust

DUTCH *n* wife

DUTCHES > DUTCH

DUTCHMAN *n* piece of wood, metal, etc, used to repair or patch faulty workmanship

DUTCHMEN > DUTCHMAN

DUTEOUS *adj* dutiful or obedient

DUTEOUSLY > DUTEOUS

DUTIABLE *adj* (of goods) requiring payment of duty

DUTIED *adj* liable for duty

DUTIES > DUTY

DUTIFUL *adj* doing what is expected

DUTIFULLY > DUTIFUL

DUTY *n* work or a task performed as part of one's job

DUUMVIR *n* one of two coequal magistrates or officers

DUUMVIRAL > DUUMVIR

DUUMVIRI > DUUMVIR

DUUMVIRS > DUUMVIR

DUVET *same as* > DOONA

DUVETINE *same as* > DUVETYN

DUVETINES > DUVETINE

DUVETS > DUVET

DUVETYN *n* soft napped velvety fabric of cotton, silk, wool, or rayon

DUVETYNE *same as* > DUVETYN

DUVETYNES > DUVETYNE

DUVETYNS > DUVETYN

DUX *n* (in Scottish and certain other schools) the top pupil in a class or school

DUXELLES *n* paste of mushrooms and onions

DUXES > DUX

DUYKER *same as* > DUIKER

DUYKERS > DUYKER

DVANDVA *n* class of compound words consisting of two elements having a coordinate relationship as if connected by *and*

DVANDVAS > DVANDVA

DVORNIK *n* Russian doorkeeper

DVORNIKS > DVORNIK

DWAAL *n* state of absent-mindedness

DWAALS > DWAAL

DWALE *n* deadly nightshade

DWALES > DWALE

DWALM *vb* faint

DWALMED > DWALM

DWALMING > DWALM

DWALMS > DWALM

DWAM *n* stupor or daydream ▷ *vb* faint or fall ill

DWAMMED > DWAM

DWAMMING > DWAM

DWAMS > DWAM

DWANG *n* short piece of wood inserted in a timber-framed wall

DWANGS > DWANG

DWARF *adj* undersized ▷ *n* person who is smaller than average ▷ *adj* (of an animal or plant) much smaller than the usual size for the species ▷ *vb* cause (someone or something) to seem small by being much larger

DWARFED > DWARF

DWARFER > DWARF

DWARFEST > DWARF

DWARFING > DWARF

DWARFISH > DWARF

DWARFISM *n* condition of being a dwarf

DWARFISMS > DWARFISM

DWARFLIKE > DWARF

DWARFNESS > DWARF

DWARFS > DWARF

DWARVES > DWARF

DWAUM *same as* > DWAM

DWAUMED > DWAUM

DWAUMING > DWAUM

DWAUMS > DWAUM

DWEEB *n* stupid or uninteresting person

DWEEBIER > DWEEBY

DWEEBIEST > DWEEBY

DWEEBISH > DWEEB

DWEEBS > DWEEB

DWEEBY *adj* like or typical of a dweeb

DWELL *vb* live, reside ▷ *n* regular pause in the operation of a machine

DWELLED > DWELL

DWELLER > DWELL

DWELLERS > DWELL

DWELLING > DWELL

DWELLINGS > DWELL

DWELLS > DWELL

DWELT > DWELL

DWILE *n* floor cloth

DWILES > DWILE

DWINDLE *vb* grow less in size, strength, or number

DWINDLED > DWINDLE

DWINDLES > DWINDLE

DWINDLING > DWINDLE

DWINE *vb* languish

DWINED > DWINE

DWINES > DWINE

DWINING > DWINE

DYABLE > DYE

DYAD *n* operator that is the unspecified product of two vectors. It can operate on a vector to produce either a scalar or vector product

DYADIC *adj* of or relating to a dyad ▷ *n* sum of a particular number of dyads

DYADICS > DYADIC

DYADS > DYAD

DYARCHAL > DIARCHY

DYARCHIC > DYARCHY

DYARCHIES > DYARCHY

DYARCHY *same as* > DIARCHY

DYBBUK *n* (in the folklore of the cabala) the soul of a dead sinner that has transmigrated into the body of a living person

DYBBUKIM > DYBBUK

DYBBUKKIM > DYBBUK

DYBBUKS > DYBBUK

DYE *n* colouring substance ▷ *vb* colour (hair or fabric) by applying a dye

DYEABLE > DYE

DYED > DYE

DYEING > DYE

DYEINGS > DYE

DYELINE *same as* > DIAZO

DYELINES > DYELINE

DYER > DYE

DYERS > DYE

DYES > DYE

DYESTER *n* dyer

DYESTERS > DYESTER

DYESTUFF *n* substance that can be used as a dye or from which a dye can be obtained

DYESTUFFS > DYESTUFF

DYEWEED *n* plant that produces dye

DYEWEEDS > DYEWEED

DYEWOOD *n* any wood, such as brazil, from which dyes and pigments can be obtained

DYEWOODS > DYEWOOD

DYING > DIE

DYINGLY > DIE

DYINGNESS > DIE

DYINGS > DIE

DYKE *n* wall built to prevent flooding ▷ *vb* embankment or wall built to confine a river to a particular course

DYKED > DYKE

DYKES > DYKE

DYKEY *same as* > DIKEY

DYKIER > DYKEY

DYKIEST > DYKEY

DYKING > DYKE

DYNAMETER *n* instrument for determining the magnifying power of telescopes

DYNAMIC *adj* full of energy, ambition, and new ideas ▷ *n* energetic or driving force

DYNAMICAL *same as* > DYNAMIC

DYNAMICS *n* branch of mechanics concerned with the forces that change or produce the motions of bodies

DYNAMISE *same as* > DYNAMIZE

DYNAMISED > DYNAMISE

DYNAMISES > DYNAMISE

DYNAMISM *n* great energy and enthusiasm

DYNAMISMS > DYNAMISM

DYNAMIST > DYNAMISM

DYNAMISTS > DYNAMISM

DYNAMITE *n* explosive made of nitroglycerine ▷ *vb* blow (something) up with dynamite

DYNAMITED > DYNAMITE

DYNAMITER > DYNAMITE

DYNAMITES > DYNAMITE

DYNAMITIC > DYNAMITE

DYNAMIZE *vb* cause to be dynamic

DYNAMIZED > DYNAMIZE

DYNAMIZES > DYNAMIZE

DYNAMO *n* device for converting mechanical energy into electrical energy

DYNAMOS > DYNAMO

DYNAMOTOR *n* electrical machine having a single magnetic field and two independent armature windings of which one acts as a motor and the other a generator: used to convert direct current from a battery into alternating current

DYNAST *n* hereditary ruler

DYNASTIC > DYNASTY

DYNASTIES > DYNASTY

DYNASTS > DYNAST

DYNASTY *n* sequence of hereditary rulers

DYNATRON as in *dynatron oscillator* type of oscillator

DYNATRONS > DYNATRON

DYNE *n* cgs unit of force

DYNEIN *n* class of proteins

DYNEINS > DYNEIN

DYNEL *n* trade name for synthetic fibre

DYNELS > DYNEL

DYNES > DYNE

DYNODE *n* electrode onto which a beam of electrons can fall, causing the emission of a greater number of electrons by secondary emission. They are used in photomultipliers to amplify the signal

DYNODES > DYNODE

DYNORPHIN *n* drug used to treat cocaine addiction

DYSBINDIN *n* gene associated with schizophrenia

DYSCHROA *n* discolouration of skin

DYSCHROAS > DYSCHROA

DYSCHROIA *same as* > DYSCHROA

DYSCRASIA *n* any abnormal physiological condition, esp of the blood

DYSCRASIC > DYSCRASIA

DYSCRATIC > DYSCRASIA

DYSENTERY *n* infection of the intestine causing severe diarrhoea

DYSGENIC *adj* of, relating to, or contributing to a degeneration or deterioration in the fitness and quality of a race or strain

DYSGENICS *n* study of factors capable of reducing the quality of a race or strain, esp the human race

DYSLALIA *n* defective speech characteristic of those affected by aphasia

DYSLALIAS > DYSLALIA

DYSLECTIC > DYSLEXIA

DYSLEXIA *n* disorder causing impaired ability to read

DYSLEXIAS > DYSLEXIA

DYSLEXIC > DYSLEXIA

DYSLEXICS > DYSLEXIA

DYSLOGIES > DYSLOGY

DYSLOGY *n* uncomplimentary remarks

DYSMELIA *n* condition of missing or stunted limbs

DYSMELIAS > DYSMELIA

DYSMELIC > DYSMELIA

DYSODIL *n* yellow or green mineral

DYSODILE *same as* > DYSODIL

DYSODILES > DYSODILE

DYSODILS > DYSODIL

DYSODYLE *same as* > DYSODIL

DYSODYLES > DYSODYLE

DYSPATHY *n* dislike

DYSPEPSIA *n* indigestion

DYSPEPSY *same as* > DYSPEPSIA

DYSPEPTIC *adj* relating to or suffering from dyspepsia ▷ *n* person suffering from dyspepsia

DYSPHAGIA *n* difficulty in swallowing, caused by obstruction or spasm of the oesophagus

DYSPHAGIC > DYSPHAGIA

DYSPHAGY *same as* > DYSPHAGIA

DYSPHASIA *n* disorder of language caused by a brain lesion

DYSPHASIC > DYSPHASIA

DYSPHONIA *n* any impairment in the ability to speak normally, as from spasm or strain of the vocal cords

DYSPHONIC > DYSPHONIA

DYSPHORIA *n* feeling of being ill at ease

DYSPHORIC > DYSPHORIA

DYSPLASIA *n* abnormal development of an organ or part of the body, including congenital absence

DYSPNEA *same as* > DYSPNOEA

DYSPNEAL > DYSPNEA

DYSPNEAS > DYSPNEA

DYSPNEIC > DYSPNEA

DYSPNOEA *n* difficulty in breathing or in catching the breath

DYSPNOEAL > DYSPNOEA

DYSPNOEAS > DYSPNOEA

DYSPNOEIC > DYSPNOEA

DYSPNOIC > DYSPNOEA

DYSPRAXIA *n* impairment in the control of the motor system

DYSTAXIA *n* lack of muscular coordination resulting in shaky limb movements and unsteady gait

DYSTAXIAS > DYSTAXIA

DYSTECTIC *adj* difficult to fuse together

DYSTHESIA *n* unpleasant skin sensation

DYSTHETIC > DYSTHESIA

DYSTHYMIA *n* characteristics of the neurotic and introverted, including anxiety, depression, and compulsive behaviour

DYSTHYMIC > DYSTHYMIA

DYSTOCIA *n* abnormal, slow, or difficult childbirth, usually because of disordered or ineffective contractions of the uterus

DYSTOCIAL > DYSTOCIA

DYSTOCIAS > DYSTOCIA

DYSTONIA *n* neurological disorder, caused by disease of the basal ganglia, in which the muscles of the trunk, shoulders, and neck go into spasm, so that the head and limbs are held in unnatural positions

DYSTONIAS > DYSTONIA

DYSTONIC > DYSTONIA

DYSTOPIA *n* imaginary place where everything is as bad as it can be

DYSTOPIAN > DYSTOPIA

DYSTOPIAS > DYSTOPIA

DYSTROPHY *n* any of various bodily disorders, characterized by wasting of tissues

DYSURIA *n* difficult or painful urination

DYSURIAS > DYSURIA

DYSURIC > DYSURIA

DYSURIES > DYSURY

DYSURY *same as* > DYSURIA

DYTISCID *n* any carnivorous aquatic beetle of the family *Dytiscidae*, having large flattened back legs used for swimming ▷ *adj* of, relating to, or belonging to the *Dytiscidae*

DYTISCIDS > DYTISCID

DYVOUR *n* debtor

DYVOURIES > DYVOURY

DYVOURS > DYVOUR

DYVOURY *n* bankruptcy

DZEREN *n* Chinese yellow antelope

DZERENS > DZEREN

DZHO *same as* > ZHO

DZHOS > DZHO

DZIGGETAI *a variant of* > CHIGETAI

DZO *a variant spelling of* > ZO

DZOS > ZO

Ee

EA *n* river
EACH *pron* every (one) taken separately ▷ *determiner* every (one) of two or more considered individually ▷ *adv* for, to, or from each one
EACHWHERE *adv* everywhere
EADISH *n* aftermath
EADISHES > EADISH
EAGER *adj* showing or feeling great desire, keen ▷ *n* eagre
EAGERER > EAGER
EAGEREST > EAGER
EAGERLY > EAGER
EAGERNESS > EAGER
EAGERS > EAGER
EAGLE *n* bird of prey ▷ *vb* in golf, score two strokes under par for a hole
EAGLED > EAGLE
EAGLEHAWK *n* large Australian eagle
EAGLES > EAGLE
EAGLET *n* young eagle
EAGLETS > EAGLET
EAGLEWOOD *n* Asian thymelaeaceous tree with fragrant wood that yields a resin used as a perfume
EAGLING > EAGLE
EAGRE *n* tidal bore, esp of the Humber or Severn estuaries
EAGRES > EAGRE
EALDORMAN *n* official of Anglo-Saxon England, appointed by the king, who was responsible for law, order, and justice in his shire and for leading his local fyrd in battle
EALDORMEN > EALDORMAN
EALE *n* beast in Roman legend
EALES > EALE
EAN *vb* give birth
EANED > EAN
EANING > EAN
EANLING *n* newborn lamb
EANLINGS > EANLING
EANS > EAN
EAR *n* organ of hearing, esp the external part of it ▷ *vb* (of cereal plants) to develop such parts

EARACHE *n* pain in the ear
EARACHES > EARACHE
EARBALL *n* (in acupressure) a small ball kept in position in the ear and pressed when needed to relieve stress
EARBALLS > EARBALL
EARBASH *vb* talk incessantly
EARBASHED > EARBASH
EARBASHER > EARBASH
EARBASHES > EARBASH
EARBOB *n* earring
EARBOBS > EARBOB
EARBUD *n* small earphone
EARBUDS > EARBUD
EARCON *n* sound representing object or event
EARCONS > EARCON
EARD *vb* bury
EARDED > EARD
EARDING > EARD
EARDROP *n* pendant earring
EARDROPS *pl n* liquid medication for inserting into the external ear
EARDRUM *n* thin piece of skin inside the ear which enables one to hear sounds
EARDRUMS > EARDRUM
EARDS > EARD
EARED *adj* having an ear or ears
EARFLAP *n* either of two pieces of fabric or fur attached to a cap, which can be let down to keep the ears warm
EARFLAPS > EARFLAP
EARFUL *n* scolding or telling-off
EARFULS > EARFUL
EARING *n* line fastened to a corner of a sail for reefing
EARINGS > EARING
EARL *n* British nobleman ranking next below a marquess
EARLAP *same as* > EARFLAP
EARLAPS > EARLAP
EARLDOM *n* rank, title, or dignity of an earl or countess
EARLDOMS > EARLDOM
EARLESS > EAR
EARLIER > EARLY

EARLIES > EARLY
EARLIEST > EARLY
EARLIKE > EAR
EARLINESS > EARLY
EARLOBE *n* fleshy lower part of the outer ear
EARLOBES > EARLOBE
EARLOCK *n* curl of hair close to ear
EARLOCKS > EARLOCK
EARLS > EARL
EARLSHIP *n* title or position of earl
EARLSHIPS > EARLSHIP
EARLY *adv* before the expected or usual time ▷ *adj* occurring or arriving before the correct or expected time ▷ *n* something which is early
EARLYWOOD *n* light wood made by tree in spring
EARMARK *vb* set (something) aside for a specific purpose ▷ *n* distinguishing mark
EARMARKED > EARMARK
EARMARKS > EARMARK
EARMUFF *n* one of a pair of pads of fur or cloth, joined by a headband, for keeping the ears warm
EARMUFFS > EARMUFF
EARN *vb* obtain by work or merit
EARNED > EARN
EARNER > EARN
EARNERS > EARN
EARNEST *adj* serious and sincere ▷ *n* part payment given in advance, esp to confirm a contract
EARNESTLY > EARNEST
EARNESTS > EARNEST
EARNING > EARN
EARNINGS *pl n* money earned
EARNS > EARN
EARPHONE *n* receiver for a radio etc, held to or put in the ear
EARPHONES > EARPHONE
EARPICK *n* instrument for removing ear wax
EARPICKS > EARPICK
EARPIECE *n* earphone in a telephone receiver
EARPIECES > EARPIECE

EARPLUG *n* piece of soft material placed in the ear to keep out water or noise
EARPLUGS > EARPLUG
EARRING *n* ornament for the lobe of the ear
EARRINGED *adj* wearing earrings
EARRINGS > EARRING
EARS > EAR
EARSHOT *n* hearing range
EARSHOTS > EARSHOT
EARST *adv* first; previously
EARSTONE *n* calcium carbonate crystal in the ear
EARSTONES > EARSTONE
EARTH *n* planet that we live on ▷ *vb* connect (a circuit) to earth
EARTHBORN *adj* of earthly origin
EARTHED > EARTH
EARTHEN *adj* made of baked clay or earth
EARTHFALL *n* landslide
EARTHFAST *adj* method of building
EARTHFLAX *n* type of asbestos
EARTHIER > EARTHY
EARTHIEST > EARTHY
EARTHILY > EARTHY
EARTHING > EARTH
EARTHLIER > EARTHLY
EARTHLIES > EARTHLY
EARTHLIKE > EARTH
EARTHLING *n* (esp in poetry or science fiction) an inhabitant of the earth
EARTHLY *adj* conceivable or possible ▷ *n* a chance
EARTHMAN *n* (esp in science fiction) an inhabitant or native of the earth
EARTHMEN > EARTHMAN
EARTHNUT *n* perennial umbelliferous plant of Europe and Asia, with edible dark brown tubers
EARTHNUTS > EARTHNUT
EARTHPEA *n* peanut; groundnut
EARTHPEAS > EARTHPEA
EARTHRISE *n* rising of the earth above the lunar horizon, as seen from a spacecraft emerging from

the lunar farside
EARTHS > EARTH
EARTHSET n setting of the earth below the lunar horizon, as seen from a spacecraft emerging from the lunar farside
EARTHSETS > EARTHSET
EARTHSTAR n any of various basidiomycetous saprotrophic woodland fungi of the genus *Geastrum*, whose brown onion-shaped reproductive body splits into a star shape to release the spores
EARTHWARD adv towards the earth
EARTHWAX n ozocerite
EARTHWOLF n aardvark
EARTHWORK n fortification made of earth
EARTHWORM n worm which burrows in the soil
EARTHY adj coarse or crude
EARWAX nontechnical name for > CERUMEN
EARWAXES > EARWAX
EARWIG n small insect with a pincer-like tail ▷ vb eavesdrop
EARWIGGED > EARWIG
EARWIGGY > EARWIG
EARWIGS > EARWIG
EARWORM n irritatingly catchy tune
EARWORMS > EARWORM
EAS > EA
EASE n freedom from difficulty, discomfort, or worry ▷ vb give bodily or mental ease to
EASED > EASE
EASEFUL adj characterized by or bringing ease
EASEFULLY > EASEFUL
EASEL n frame to support an artist's canvas or a blackboard
EASELED adj mounted on easel
EASELESS > EASE
EASELS > EASEL
EASEMENT n right enjoyed by a landowner of making limited use of his neighbour's land, as by crossing it to reach his own property
EASEMENTS > EASEMENT
EASER > EASE
EASERS > EASE
EASES > EASE
EASIED > EASY
EASIER > EASY
EASIES > EASY
EASIEST > EASY
EASILY adv without difficulty
EASINESS n quality or condition of being easy to accomplish, do, obtain, etc
EASING > EASE
EASLE n hot ash
EASLES > EASLE
EASSEL adv easterly
EASSIL adv easterly

EAST n (direction towards) the part of the horizon where the sun rises ▷ adj in the east ▷ adv in, to, or towards the east ▷ vb move or turn east
EASTBOUND adj going towards the east
EASTED > EAST
EASTER n most important festival of the Christian Church, commemorating the Resurrection of Christ
EASTERLY adj of or in the east ▷ adv towards the east ▷ n wind from the east
EASTERN adj situated in or towards the east
EASTERNER n person from the east of a country or area
EASTERS > EASTER
EASTING n net distance eastwards made by a vessel moving towards the east
EASTINGS > EASTING
EASTLAND n land to east
EASTLIN adj easterly
EASTLING adj easterly
EASTLINGS adv eastward
EASTLINS adv eastward
EASTMOST adj furthest east
EASTS > EAST
EASTWARD same as > EASTWARDS
EASTWARDS adv towards the east
EASY adj not needing much work or effort ▷ vb stop rowing
EASYGOING adj relaxed in manner
EASYING > EASY
EAT vb take (food) into the mouth and swallow it
EATABLE adj fit or suitable for eating
EATABLES pl n food
EATAGE n grazing rights
EATAGES > EATAGE
EATCHE n adze
EATCHES > EATCHE
EATEN > EAT
EATER > EAT
EATERIE same as > EATERY
EATERIES > EATERY
EATERS > EAT
EATERY n restaurant or eating house
EATH adj easy
EATHE same as > EATH
EATHLY > EATH
EATING > EAT
EATINGS > EAT
EATS > EAT
EAU same as > EA
EAUS > EAU
EAUX > EAU
EAVE n overhanging edge of a roof
EAVED adj having eaves
EAVES > EAVE
EAVESDRIP n water dropping from eaves
EAVESDROP vb listen secretly to a private

conversation
EBAUCHE n rough sketch
EBAUCHES > EBAUCHE
EBAYER n any person who buys or sells using the internet auction site, eBay
EBAYERS > EBAYER
EBAYING n buying or selling using the internet auction site eBay
EBAYINGS > EBAYING
EBB vb (of tide water) flow back ▷ n flowing back of the tide
EBBED > EBB
EBBET n type of newt
EBBETS > EBBET
EBBING > EBB
EBBLESS > EBB
EBBS > EBB
EBBTIDE n ebbing tide
EBBTIDES > EBBTIDE
EBENEZER n chapel
EBENEZERS > EBENEZER
EBENISTE n cabinetmaker
EBENISTES > EBENISTE
EBIONISE same as > EBIONIZE
EBIONISED > EBIONISE
EBIONISES > EBIONISE
EBIONISM n doctrine that the poor shall be saved
EBIONISMS > EBIONISM
EBIONITIC > EBIONISM
EBIONIZE vb preach ebionism
EBIONIZED > EBIONIZE
EBIONIZES > EBIONIZE
EBON poetic word for > EBONY
EBONICS n dialect used by African-Americans
EBONIES > EBONY
EBONISE same as > EBONIZE
EBONISED > EBONISE
EBONISES > EBONISE
EBONISING > EBONISE
EBONIST n carver of ebony
EBONISTS > EBONIST
EBONITE another name for > VULCANITE
EBONITES > EBONITE
EBONIZE vb stain or otherwise finish in imitation of ebony
EBONIZED > EBONIZE
EBONIZES > EBONIZE
EBONIZING > EBONIZE
EBONS > EBON
EBONY n hard black wood ▷ adj deep black
EBOOK n book in electronic form
EBOOKS > EBOOK
EBRIATE adj drunk
EBRIATED > EBRIATE
EBRIETIES > EBRIETY
EBRIETY n drunkenness
EBRILLADE n jerk on rein, when horse refuses to turn
EBRIOSE adj drunk
EBRIOSITY > EBRIOSE
EBULLIENT adj full of enthusiasm or excitement
EBURNEAN adj made of ivory
EBURNEOUS adj like ivory
ECAD n organism whose form has been affected by

its environment
ECADS > ECAD
ECARINATE adj having no carina or keel
ECARTE n card game for two, played with 32 cards and king high
ECARTES > ECARTE
ECAUDATE adj tailless
ECBOLE n digression
ECBOLES > ECBOLE
ECBOLIC adj hastening labour or abortion ▷ n drug or agent that hastens labour or abortion
ECBOLICS > ECBOLIC
ECCE interj behold
ECCENTRIC adj odd or unconventional ▷ n eccentric person
ECCLESIA n (in formal Church usage) a congregation
ECCLESIAE > ECCLESIA
ECCLESIAL adj ecclesiastical
ECCO interj look there
ECCRINE adj of or denoting glands that secrete externally, esp the numerous sweat glands on the human body
ECCRISES > ECCRISIS
ECCRISIS n excrement
ECCRITIC n purgative
ECCRITICS > ECCRITIC
ECDEMIC adj not indigenous or endemic
ECDYSES > ECDYSIS
ECDYSIAL > ECDYSIS
ECDYSIAST facetious word for > STRIPPER
ECDYSIS n periodic shedding of the cuticle in insects and other arthropods or the outer epidermal layer in reptiles
ECDYSON > ECDYSONE
ECDYSONE n hormone secreted by the prothoracic gland of insects that controls ecdysis and stimulates metamorphosis
ECDYSONES > ECDYSONE
ECDYSONS > ECDYSON
ECESIC > ECESIS
ECESIS n establishment of a plant in a new environment
ECESISES > ECESIS
ECH same as > ECHE
ECHAPPE n leap in ballet
ECHAPPES > ECHAPPE
ECHARD n water that is present in the soil but cannot be absorbed or otherwise utilized by plants
ECHARDS > ECHARD
ECHE vb eke out
ECHED > ECHE
ECHELLE n ladder; scale
ECHELLES > ECHELLE
ECHELON n level of power or responsibility ▷ vb assemble in echelon
ECHELONED > ECHELON

e

e

ECHELONS > ECHELON

ECHES > ECHE

ECHEVERIA n any of various tropical American crassulaceous plants of the genus Echeveria, cultivated for their colourful foliage

ECHIDNA n Australian spiny egg-laying mammal

ECHIDNAE > ECHIDNA

ECHIDNAS > ECHIDNA

ECHIDNINE n snake poison

ECHINACEA n either of the two N American plants of the genus Echinacea, having flower heads with purple rays and black centres: family Compositae (composites)

ECHINATE adj covered with spines, bristles, or bristle-like outgrowths

ECHINATED same as > ECHINATE

ECHING > ECHE

ECHINI > ECHINUS

ECHINOID n any of the echinoderms constituting the class Echinoidea, typically having a rigid ovoid body. The class includes the sea urchins and sand dollars ▷ adj of or belonging to this class

ECHINOIDS > ECHINOID

ECHINUS n ovolo moulding between the shaft and the abacus of a Doric column

ECHINUSES > ECHINUS

ECHIUM n any plant of the Eurasian and African genus Echium

ECHIUMS > ECHIUM

ECHIUROID n marine worm

ECHO n repetition of sounds by reflection of sound waves off a surface ▷ vb repeat or be repeated as an echo

ECHOED > ECHO

ECHOER > ECHO

ECHOERS > ECHO

ECHOES > ECHO

ECHOEY > ECHO

ECHOGRAM n record made by echography

ECHOGRAMS > ECHOGRAM

ECHOIC adj characteristic of or resembling an echo

ECHOING > ECHO

ECHOISE same as > ECHOIZE

ECHOISED > ECHOISE

ECHOISES > ECHOISE

ECHOISING > ECHOISE

ECHOISM n onomatopoeia as a source of word formation

ECHOISMS > ECHOISM

ECHOIST > ECHOISM

ECHOISTS > ECHOISM

ECHOIZE vb repeat like echo

ECHOIZED > ECHOIZE

ECHOIZES > ECHOIZE

ECHOIZING > ECHOIZE

ECHOLALIA n tendency to repeat mechanically words just spoken by

another person: can occur in cases of brain damage, mental retardation, and schizophrenia

ECHOLALIC > ECHOLALIA

ECHOLESS > ECHO

ECHOS > ECHO

ECHOVIRUS n any of a group of viruses that can cause symptoms of mild meningitis, the common cold, or infections of the intestinal and respiratory tracts

ECHT adj real

ECLAIR n finger-shaped pastry filled with cream and covered with chocolate

ECLAIRS > ECLAIR

ECLAMPSIA n serious condition that can develop towards the end of a pregnancy, causing high blood pressure, swelling, and convulsions

ECLAMPSY same as > ECLAMPSIA

ECLAMPTIC > ECLAMPSIA

ECLAT n brilliant success

ECLATS > ECLAT

ECLECTIC adj selecting from various styles, ideas, or sources ▷ n person who takes an eclectic approach

ECLECTICS > ECLECTIC

ECLIPSE n temporary obscuring of one star or planet by another ▷ vb surpass or outclass

ECLIPSED > ECLIPSE

ECLIPSER > ECLIPSE

ECLIPSERS > ECLIPSE

ECLIPSES > ECLIPSIS

ECLIPSING > ECLIPSE

ECLIPSIS same as > ELLIPSIS

ECLIPTIC n apparent path of the sun ▷ adj of or relating to an eclipse

ECLIPTICS > ECLIPTIC

ECLOGITE n rare coarse-grained basic rock consisting principally of garnet and pyroxene. Quartz, feldspar, etc, may also be present. It is thought to originate by metamorphism or igneous crystallization at extremely high pressure

ECLOGITES > ECLOGITE

ECLOGUE n pastoral or idyllic poem, usually in the form of a conversation or soliloquy

ECLOGUES > ECLOGUE

ECLOSE vb emerge

ECLOSED > ECLOSE

ECLOSES > ECLOSE

ECLOSING > ECLOSE

ECLOSION n emergence of an insect larva from the egg or an adult from the pupal case

ECLOSIONS > ECLOSION

ECO n ecology activist

ECOCIDAL > ECOCIDE

ECOCIDE n total destruction of an area of the natural environment, esp by human agency

ECOCIDES > ECOCIDE

ECOD same as > EGAD

ECOFREAK n environmentalist

ECOFREAKS > ECOFREAK

ECOLOGIC > ECOLOGY

ECOLOGIES > ECOLOGY

ECOLOGIST > ECOLOGY

ECOLOGY n study of the relationships between living things and their environment

ECOMMERCE n business transactions conducted on the internet

ECONOBOX n fuel efficient utility vehicle

ECONOMIC adj of economics

ECONOMICS n social science concerned with the production and consumption of goods and services

ECONOMIES > ECONOMY

ECONOMISE same as > ECONOMIZE

ECONOMISM n political theory that regards economics as the main factor in society, ignoring or reducing to simplistic economic terms other factors such as culture, nationality, etc

ECONOMIST n specialist in economics

ECONOMIZE vb reduce expense or waste

ECONOMY n system of interrelationship of money, industry, and employment in a country ▷ adj denoting a class of air travel that is cheaper than first-class

ECONUT n environmentalist

ECONUTS > ECONUT

ECOPHOBIA n fear of home

ECORCHE n anatomical figure without the skin, so that the muscular structure is visible

ECORCHES > ECORCHE

ECOREGION n area defined by its environmental conditions, esp climate, landforms, and soil characteristics

ECOS > ECO

ECOSPHERE n planetary ecosystem, consisting of all living organisms and their environment

ECOSSAISE n lively dance in two-four time

ECOSTATE adj with no ribs or nerves

ECOSYSTEM n system involving interactions between a community and its environment

ECOTAGE n sabotage for ecological motives

ECOTAGES > ECOTAGE

ECOTONAL > ECOTONE

ECOTONE n zone between two major ecological communities

ECOTONES > ECOTONE

ECOTOUR n holiday taking care not to damage environment

ECOTOURS > ECOTOUR

ECOTOXIC adj harmful to animals, plants or the environment

ECOTYPE n group of organisms within a species that is adapted to particular environmental conditions and therefore exhibits behavioural, structural, or physiological differences from other members of the species

ECOTYPES > ECOTYPE

ECOTYPIC > ECOTYPE

ECRASEUR n surgical device consisting of a heavy wire loop placed around a part to be removed and tightened until it cuts through

ECRASEURS > ECRASEUR

ECRITOIRE n writing desk with compartments and drawers

ECRU adj pale creamy-brown ▷ n greyish-yellow to a light greyish colour

ECRUS > ECRU

ECSTASES > ECSTASIS

ECSTASIED > ECSTASY

ECSTASIES > ECSTASY

ECSTASIS same as > ECSTASY

ECSTASISE same as > ECSTASIZE

ECSTASIZE vb make or become ecstatic

ECSTASY n state of intense delight

ECSTATIC adj in a trancelike state of great rapture or delight ▷ n person who has periods of intense trancelike joy

ECSTATICS pl n fits of delight or rapture

ECTASES > ECTASIS

ECTASIA n distension or dilation of a duct, vessel, or hollow viscus

ECTASIAS > ECTASIA

ECTASIS same as > ECTASIA

ECTATIC > ECTASIA

ECTHYMA n local inflammation of the skin characterized by flat ulcerating pustules

ECTHYMAS > ECTHYMA

ECTHYMATA > ECTHYMA

ECTOBLAST same as > EPIBLAST

ECTOCRINE n substance that is released by an organism into the external environment and influences the development, behaviour, etc, of members of the same or different species

ECTODERM n outer germ layer of an animal embryo, which gives rise to epidermis and nervous tissue

ECTODERMS > ECTODERM

ECTOGENIC adj capable of developing outside the host

ECTOGENY n (of bacteria, etc) development outside the host

ECTOMERE n any of the blastomeres that later develop into ectoderm

ECTOMERES > ECTOMERE

ECTOMERIC > ECTOMERE

ECTOMORPH n person with a thin body build: said to be correlated with cerebrotonia

ECTOPHYTE n parasitic plant that lives on the surface of its host

ECTOPIA n congenital displacement or abnormal positioning of an organ or part

ECTOPIAS > ECTOPIA

ECTOPIC > ECTOPIA

ECTOPIES > ECTOPY

ECTOPLASM n substance that supposedly is emitted from the body of a medium during a trance

ECTOPROCT another word for > BRYOZOAN

ECTOPY same as > ECTOPIA

ECTOSARC n ectoplasm of an amoeba or any other protozoan

ECTOSARCS > ECTOSARC

ECTOTHERM n animal whose body temperature is determined by ambient temperature

ECTOZOA > ECTOZOON

ECTOZOAN same as > ECTOZOON

ECTOZOANS > ECTOZOAN

ECTOZOIC > ECTOZOON

ECTOZOON n parasitic organism that lives on the outside of its host

ECTROPIC > ECTROPION

ECTROPION n condition in which the eyelid turns over exposing some of the inner lid

ECTROPIUM same as > ECTROPION

ECTYPAL > ECTYPE

ECTYPE n copy as distinguished from a prototype

ECTYPES > ECTYPE

ECU n any of various former French gold or silver coins

ECUELLE n covered soup bowl with handles

ECUELLES > ECUELLE

ECUMENIC adj tending to promote unity among Churches

ECUMENICS > ECUMENIC

ECUMENISM n aim of unity among Christian churches

throughout the world

ECUMENIST > ECUMENISM

ECURIE n team of motor-racing cars

ECURIES > ECURIE

ECUS > ECU

ECZEMA n skin disease causing intense itching

ECZEMAS > ECZEMA

ED n editor

EDACIOUS adj devoted to eating

EDACITIES > EDACIOUS

EDACITY > EDACIOUS

EDAPHIC adj of or relating to the physical and chemical conditions of the soil, esp in relation to the plant and animal life it supports

EDDIED > EDDY

EDDIES > EDDY

EDDISH n pasture grass

EDDISHES > EDDISH

EDDO same as > TARO

EDDOES > EDDO

EDDY n circular movement of air, water, etc ▷ vb move with a circular motion

EDDYING > EDDY

EDELWEISS n alpine plant with white flowers

EDEMA same as > OEDEMA

EDEMAS > EDEMA

EDEMATA > EDEMA

EDEMATOSE > EDEMA

EDEMATOUS > EDEMA

EDENIC adj delightful, like the Garden of Eden

EDENTAL adj having few or no teeth

EDENTATE n mammal with few or no teeth, such as an armadillo or a sloth ▷ adj denoting such a mammal

EDENTATES > EDENTATE

EDGE n border or line where something ends or begins ▷ vb provide an edge or border for

EDGEBONE n aitchbone

EDGEBONES > EDGEBONE

EDGED > EDGE

EDGELESS > EDGE

EDGER > EDGE

EDGERS > EDGE

EDGES > EDGE

EDGEWAYS adv with the edge forwards or uppermost

EDGEWISE same as > EDGEWAYS

EDGIER > EDGY

EDGIEST > EDGY

EDGILY > EDGY

EDGINESS > EDGY

EDGING n anything placed along an edge to finish it ▷ adj relating to or used for making an edge

EDGINGS > EDGING

EDGY adj nervous or irritable

EDH n character of the runic alphabet used to represent the voiced dental fricative as in then, mother, bathe

EDHS > EDH

EDIBILITY > EDIBLE

EDIBLE adj fit to be eaten

EDIBLES pl n articles fit to eat

EDICT n order issued by an authority

EDICTAL > EDICT

EDICTALLY > EDICT

EDICTS > EDICT

EDIFICE n large building

EDIFICES > EDIFICE

EDIFICIAL > EDIFICE

EDIFIED > EDIFY

EDIFIER > EDIFY

EDIFIERS > EDIFY

EDIFIES > EDIFY

EDIFY vb improve morally by instruction

EDIFYING > EDIFY

EDILE variant spelling of > AEDILE

EDILES > EDILE

EDIT vb prepare (a book, film, etc) for publication or broadcast ▷ n act of editing

EDITABLE > EDIT

EDITED > EDIT

EDITING > EDIT

EDITINGS > EDIT

EDITION n number of copies of a new publication printed at one time ▷ vb produce multiple copies of (an original work of art)

EDITIONED > EDITION

EDITIONS > EDITION

EDITOR n person who edits

EDITORIAL n newspaper article stating the opinion of the editor ▷ adj of editing or editors

EDITORS > EDITOR

EDITRESS n female editor

EDITRICES > EDITRIX

EDITRIX n female editor

EDITRIXES > EDITRIX

EDITS > EDIT

EDS > ED

EDUCABLE adj capable of being trained or educated ▷ n mentally retarded person who is capable of being educated

EDUCABLES > EDUCABLE

EDUCATE vb teach

EDUCATED adj having an education, esp a good one

EDUCATES > EDUCATE

EDUCATING > EDUCATE

EDUCATION n process of acquiring knowledge and understanding

EDUCATIVE adj educating

EDUCATOR n person who educates

EDUCATORS > EDUCATOR

EDUCATORY adj educative or educational

EDUCE vb evolve or develop, esp from a latent or potential state

EDUCED > EDUCE

EDUCEMENT > EDUCE

EDUCES > EDUCE

EDUCIBLE > EDUCE

EDUCING > EDUCE

EDUCT n substance

separated from another substance without chemical change

EDUCTION n something educed

EDUCTIONS > EDUCTION

EDUCTIVE > EDUCE

EDUCTOR > EDUCE

EDUCTORS > EDUCE

EDUCTS > EDUCT

EDUSKUNTA n Finnish parliament

EE Scots word for > EYE

EECH same as > ECHE

EECHED > EECH

EECHES > EECH

EECHING > EECH

EEJIT Scots and Irish word for > IDIOT

EEJITS > EEJIT

EEK interj indicating shock or fright

EEL n snakelike fish

EELFARE n young eel

EELFARES > EELFARE

EELGRASS n any of several perennial submerged marine plants of the genus Zostera, esp Z. marina, having grasslike leaves: family Zosteraceae

EELIER > EEL

EELIEST > EEL

EELLIKE adj resembling an eel

EELPOUT n marine eel-like blennioid fish

EELPOUTS > EELPOUT

EELS > EEL

EELWORM n any of various nematode worms, esp the wheatworm and the vinegar eel

EELWORMS > EELWORM

EELWRACK n grasslike plant growing in seawater

EELWRACKS > EELWRACK

EELY > EEL

EEN > EE

EERIE adj uncannily frightening or disturbing

EERIER > EERIE

EERIEST > EERIE

EERILY > EERIE

EERINESS > EERIE

EERY same as > EERIE

EEVEN n evening

EEVENS > EEVEN

EEVN n evening

EEVNING n evening

EEVNINGS > EEVNING

EEVNS > EEVN

EF n sixth letter of Roman alphabet

EFF vb say the word 'fuck'

EFFABLE adj capable of being expressed in words

EFFACE vb remove by rubbing

EFFACED > EFFACE

EFFACER > EFFACE

EFFACERS > EFFACE

EFFACES > EFFACE

EFFACING > EFFACE

EFFECT n change or result caused by someone or something ▷ vb cause to happen, accomplish

EFFECTED > EFFECT

EFFECTER > EFFECT

EFFECTERS > EFFECT

EFFECTING > EFFECT

EFFECTIVE adj producing a desired result ▷ n serviceman who is equipped and prepared for action

EFFECTOR n nerve ending that terminates in a muscle or gland and provides neural stimulation causing contraction or secretion

EFFECTORS > EFFECTOR

EFFECTS pl n personal belongings

EFFECTUAL adj producing the intended result

EFFED > EFF

EFFEIR vb suit

EFFEIRED > EFFEIR

EFFEIRING > EFFEIR

EFFEIRS > EFFEIR

EFFENDI n (in the Ottoman Empire) a title of respect used to address men of learning or social standing

EFFENDIS > EFFENDI

EFFERE same as > EFFEIR

EFFERED > EFFERE

EFFERENCE > EFFERENT

EFFERENT adj carrying or conducting outwards from a part or an organ of the body, esp from the brain or spinal cord ▷ n nerve that carries impulses outwards from the brain or spinal cord

EFFERENTS > EFFERENT

EFFERES > EFFERE

EFFERING > EFFERE

EFFETE adj powerless, feeble

EFFETELY > EFFETE

EFFICACY n quality of being successful in producing an intended result

EFFICIENT adj functioning effectively with little waste of effort

EFFIERCE vb archaic word meaning make fierce

EFFIERCED > EFFIERCE

EFFIERCES > EFFIERCE

EFFIGIAL > EFFIGY

EFFIGIES > EFFIGY

EFFIGY n image or likeness of a person

EFFING > EFF

EFFINGS > EFF

EFFLUENCE n act or process of flowing out

EFFLUENT n liquid discharged as waste ▷ adj flowing out or forth

EFFLUENTS > EFFLUENT

EFFLUVIA > EFFLUVIUM

EFFLUVIAL > EFFLUVIUM

EFFLUVIUM n unpleasant smell, as of decaying matter or gaseous waste

EFFLUX same as > EFFLUENCE

EFFLUXES > EFFLUX

EFFLUXION same as > EFFLUX

EFFORCE vb force

EFFORCED > EFFORCE

EFFORCES > EFFORCE

EFFORCING > EFFORCE

EFFORT n physical or mental exertion

EFFORTFUL > EFFORT

EFFORTS > EFFORT

EFFRAIDE same as > AFRAID

EFFRAY same as > AFFRAY

EFFRAYS > EFFRAY

EFFS > EFF

EFFULGE vb radiate

EFFULGED > EFFULGE

EFFULGENT adj radiant

EFFULGES > EFFULGE

EFFULGING > EFFULGE

EFFUSE vb pour or flow out ▷ adj (esp of an inflorescence) spreading out loosely

EFFUSED > EFFUSE

EFFUSES > EFFUSE

EFFUSING > EFFUSE

EFFUSION n unrestrained outburst

EFFUSIONS > EFFUSION

EFFUSIVE adj openly emotional, demonstrative

EFS > EF

EFT n dialect or archaic name for a newt ▷ adv again

EFTEST adj nearest at hand

EFTS > EFT

EFTSOON > EFTSOONS

EFTSOONS adv soon afterwards

EGAD n mild oath or expression of surprise

EGADS > EGAD

EGAL adj equal

EGALITE n equality

EGALITES > EGALITY

EGALITIES > EGALITY

EGALITY n equality

EGALLY > EGAL

EGAREMENT n confusion

EGENCE n need

EGENCES > EGENCE

EGENCIES > EGENCY

EGENCY same as > EGENCE

EGER same as > EAGRE

EGERS > EGER

EGEST vb excrete (waste material)

EGESTA pl n anything egested, as waste material from the body

EGESTED > EGEST

EGESTING > EGEST

EGESTION > EGEST

EGESTIONS > EGEST

EGESTIVE > EGEST

EGESTS > EGEST

EGG n oval or round object laid by the females of birds and other creatures, containing a developing embryo ▷ vb urge or incite, esp to daring or foolish acts

EGGAR same as > EGGER

EGGARS > EGGAR

EGGBEATER n kitchen utensil for beating eggs, whipping cream, etc

EGGCUP n cup for holding a boiled egg

EGGCUPS > EGGCUP

EGGED > EGG

EGGER n any of various widely distributed moths having brown bodies and wings

EGGERIES > EGGERY

EGGERS > EGGER

EGGERY n place where eggs are laid

EGGFRUIT n fruit of eggplant

EGGFRUITS > EGGFRUIT

EGGHEAD n intellectual person

EGGHEADED > EGGHEAD

EGGHEADS > EGGHEAD

EGGIER > EGGY

EGGIEST > EGGY

EGGING > EGG

EGGLER n egg dealer: sometimes itinerant

EGGLERS > EGGLER

EGGLESS > EGG

EGGMASS n intelligentsia

EGGMASSES > EGGMASS

EGGNOG n drink made of raw eggs, milk, sugar, spice, and brandy or rum

EGGNOGS > EGGNOG

EGGPLANT n dark purple tropical fruit, cooked and eaten as a vegetable

EGGPLANTS > EGGPLANT

EGGS > EGG

EGGSHELL n hard covering round the egg of a bird or animal ▷ adj (of paint) having a very slight sheen

EGGSHELLS > EGGSHELL

EGGWASH n beaten egg for brushing on pastry

EGGWASHES > EGGWASH

EGGWHISK same as > EGGBEATER

EGGWHISKS > EGGWHISK

EGGY adj soaked in or tasting of egg

EGIS rare spelling of > AEGIS

EGISES > EGIS

EGLANTINE n Eurasian rose

EGLATERE archaic name for > EGLANTINE

EGLATERES > EGLATERE

EGLOMISE n gilding

EGMA mispronunciation of > ENIGMA

EGMAS > EGMA

EGO n conscious mind of an individual

EGOISM n excessive concern for one's own interests

EGOISMS > EGOISM

EGOIST n person who is preoccupied with his own interests

EGOISTIC > EGOIST

EGOISTS > EGOIST

EGOITIES > EGOITY

EGOITY n essence of the ego

EGOLESS adj without an ego

EGOMANIA n obsessive concern with fulfilling one's own needs and desires, regardless of the effect on other people

EGOMANIAC > EGOMANIA

EGOMANIAS > EGOMANIA

EGOS > EGO

EGOTHEISM n making god of oneself

EGOTISE same as > EGOTIZE

EGOTISED > EGOTISE

EGOTISES > EGOTISE

EGOTISING > EGOTISE

EGOTISM n concern only for one's own interests and feelings

EGOTISMS > EGOTISM

EGOTIST n conceited boastful person

EGOTISTIC > EGOTIST

EGOTISTS > EGOTIST

EGOTIZE vb talk or write in self-important way

EGOTIZED > EGOTIZE

EGOTIZES > EGOTIZE

EGOTIZING > EGOTIZE

EGREGIOUS adj outstandingly bad

EGRESS same as > EMERSION

EGRESSED > EGRESS

EGRESSES > EGRESS

EGRESSING > EGRESS

EGRESSION same as > EGRESS

EGRET n lesser white heron

EGRETS > EGRET

EGYPTIAN n type of typeface

EGYPTIANS > EGYPTIAN

EH interj exclamation of surprise or inquiry, or to seek confirmation of a statement or question ▷ vb say 'eh'

EHED > EH

EHING > EH

EHS > EH

EIDE adj enhanced integrated drive electronics

EIDENT adj diligent

EIDER n Arctic duck

EIDERDOWN n quilt (orig. stuffed with eider feathers)

EIDERS > EIDER

EIDETIC adj (of visual, or sometimes auditory, images) exceptionally vivid and allowing detailed recall of something previously perceived ▷ n person with eidetic ability

EIDETICS > EIDETIC

EIDOGRAPH n device for copying drawings

EIDOLA > EIDOLON

EIDOLIC > EIDOLON

EIDOLON n unsubstantial image

EIDOLONS > EIDOLON

EIDOS n intellectual character of a culture or a social group

EIGENMODE n characteristic vibration pattern

EIGENTONE n characteristic acoustic resonance frequency of a system

EIGHT n one more than seven ▷ adj amounting to

eight

EIGHTBALL *n* black ball in pool

EIGHTEEN *n* eight and ten ▷ *adj* amounting to eighteen ▷ *determiner* amounting to eighteen

EIGHTEENS > EIGHTEEN

EIGHTFOIL *n* eight leaved flower shape in heraldry

EIGHTFOLD *adj* having eight times as many or as much ▷ *adv* by eight times as many or as much

EIGHTFOOT *adj* measuring eight feet

EIGHTH *n* (of) number eight in a series ▷ *adj* coming after the seventh and before the ninth in numbering or counting order, position, time, etc ▷ *adv* after the seventh person, position, event, etc

EIGHTHLY *same as* > EIGHTH

EIGHTHS > EIGHTH

EIGHTIES > EIGHTY

EIGHTIETH *n* one of 80 approximately equal parts of something

EIGHTS > EIGHT

EIGHTSMAN *n* member of an eight-man team

EIGHTSMEN > EIGHTSMAN

EIGHTSOME *n* group of eight people

EIGHTVO *another word for* > OCTAVO

EIGHTVOS > EIGHTVO

EIGHTY *n* eight times ten ▷ *adj* amounting to eighty ▷ *determiner* amounting to eighty

EIGNE *adj* firstborn

EIK *variant form of* > EKE

EIKED > EIK

EIKING > EIK

EIKON *variant spelling of* > ICON

EIKONES > EIKON

EIKONS > EIKON

EIKS > EIK

EILD *n* old age

EILDING *n* fuel

EILDINGS > EILDING

EILDS > EILD

EINA *interj* exclamation of pain

EINE *pl n* eyes

EINKORN *n* variety of wheat of Greece and SW Asia

EINKORNS > EINKORN

EINSTEIN *n* scientific genius

EINSTEINS > EINSTEIN

EIRACK *n* young hen

EIRACKS > EIRACK

EIRENIC *variant spelling of* > IRENIC

EIRENICAL *same as* > IRENIC

EIRENICON *n* proposition that attempts to harmonize conflicting viewpoints

EISEGESES > EISEGESIS

EISEGESIS *n* interpretation of a text, esp a biblical text,

using one's own ideas

EISEL *n* vinegar

EISELL *same as* > EISEL

EISELLS > EISELL

EISELS > EISEL

EISH *interj* South African exclamation expressive of surprise, agreement, disapproval, etc

EISWEIN *n* wine made from grapes frozen on the vine

EISWEINS > EISWEIN

EITHER *pron* one or the other (of two) ▷ *adv* likewise ▷ *determiner* one or the other (of two)

EJACULATE *vb* eject (semen)

EJECT *vb* force out, expel

EJECTA *pl n* matter thrown out of a crater by an erupting volcano or during a meteorite impact

EJECTABLE > EJECT

EJECTED > EJECT

EJECTING > EJECT

EJECTION > EJECT

EJECTIONS > EJECT

EJECTIVE *adj* relating to or causing ejection ▷ *n* ejective consonant

EJECTIVES > EJECTIVE

EJECTMENT *n* (formerly) an action brought by a wrongfully dispossessed owner seeking to recover possession of his land

EJECTOR *n* person or thing that ejects

EJECTORS > EJECTOR

EJECTS > EJECT

EKE *vb* increase, enlarge, or lengthen

EKED > EKE

EKES > EKE

EKING > EKE

EKISTIC > EKISTICS

EKISTICAL > EKISTICS

EKISTICS *n* science or study of human settlements

EKKA *n* type of one-horse carriage

EKKAS > EKKA

EKLOGITE *same as* > ECLOGITE

EKLOGITES > EKLOGITE

EKPHRASES > EKPHRASIS

EKPHRASIS *n* description of a visual work of art

EKPWELE *n* former monetary unit of Equatorial Guinea

EKPWELES > EKPWELE

EKTEXINE *n* in pollen and spores, the outer of the two layers that make up the exine

EKTEXINES > EKTEXINE

EKUELE *same as* > EKPWELE

EL *n* American elevated railway

ELABORATE *adj* with a lot of fine detail ▷ *vb* expand upon

ELAEOLITE *n* nephelite

ELAIN *same as* > TRIOLEIN

ELAINS > ELAIN

ELAIOSOME *n* oil-rich body on seeds or fruits that attracts ants, which act as dispersal agents

ELAN *n* style and vigour

ELANCE *vb* throw a lance

ELANCED > ELANCE

ELANCES > ELANCE

ELANCING > ELANCE

ELAND *n* large antelope of southern Africa

ELANDS > ELAND

ELANET *n* bird of prey

ELANETS > ELANET

ELANS > ELAN

ELAPHINE *adj* of or like a red deer

ELAPID *n* any venomous snake of the mostly tropical family *Elapidae*

ELAPIDS > ELAPID

ELAPINE *adj* of or like an elapid

ELAPSE *vb* (of time) pass by

ELAPSED > ELAPSE

ELAPSES > ELAPSE

ELAPSING > ELAPSE

ELASTANCE *n* reciprocal of capacitance

ELASTANE *n* synthetic fibre that is able to return to its original shape after being stretched

ELASTANES > ELASTANE

ELASTASE *n* enzyme that digests elastin

ELASTASES > ELASTASE

ELASTIC *adj* resuming normal shape after distortion ▷ *n* tape or fabric containing interwoven strands of flexible rubber

ELASTICS > ELASTIC

ELASTIN *n* fibrous scleroprotein constituting the major part of elastic tissue, such as the walls of arteries

ELASTINS > ELASTIN

ELASTOMER *n* any material, such as natural or synthetic rubber, that is able to resume its original shape when a deforming force is removed

ELATE *vb* fill with high spirits, exhilaration, pride or optimism

ELATED *adj* extremely happy and excited

ELATEDLY > ELATED

ELATER *n* elaterid beetle

ELATERID *n* any of the beetles constituting the widely distributed family *Elateridae* (click beetles)

ELATERIDS > ELATERID

ELATERIN *n* white crystalline substance found in elaterium, used as a purgative

ELATERINS > ELATERIN

ELATERITE *n* dark brown naturally occurring bitumen resembling rubber

ELATERIUM *n* greenish sediment prepared from the juice of the squirting cucumber, used as a purgative

ELATERS > ELATER

ELATES > ELATE

ELATING > ELATE

ELATION *n* feeling of great happiness and excitement

ELATIONS > ELATION

ELATIVE *adj* (in the grammar of Finnish and other languages) denoting a case of nouns expressing a relation of motion or direction, usually translated by the English prepositions *out of* or *away from* ▷ *n* elative case

ELATIVES > ELATIVE

ELBOW *n* joint between the upper arm and the forearm ▷ *vb* shove or strike with the elbow

ELBOWED > ELBOW

ELBOWING > ELBOW

ELBOWROOM *n* sufficient scope to move or function

ELBOWS > ELBOW

ELCHEE *n* ambassador

ELCHEES > ELCHEE

ELCHI *same as* > ELCHEE

ELCHIS > ELCHI

ELD *n* old age

ELDER *adj* older ▷ *n* older person

ELDERCARE *n* care of elderly

ELDERLIES > ELDERLY

ELDERLY *adj* (fairly) old

ELDERS > ELDER

ELDERSHIP > ELDER

ELDEST *adj* oldest

ELDIN *n* fuel

ELDING *same as* > ELDIN

ELDINGS > ELDING

ELDINS > ELDIN

ELDORADO *n* place of great riches or fabulous opportunity

ELDORADOS > ELDORADO

ELDRESS *n* woman elder

ELDRESSES > ELDRESS

ELDRICH *same as* > ELDRITCH

ELDRITCH *adj* weird, uncanny

ELDS > ELD

ELECT *vb* choose by voting ▷ *adj* appointed but not yet in office

ELECTABLE > ELECT

ELECTED > ELECT

ELECTEE *n* someone who is elected

ELECTEES > ELECTEE

ELECTING > ELECT

ELECTION *n* choosing of representatives by voting

ELECTIONS > ELECTION

ELECTIVE *adj* chosen by election ▷ *n* optional course or hospital placement undertaken by a medical student

ELECTIVES > ELECTIVE

ELECTOR *n* someone who has the right to vote in an

e

election

ELECTORAL *adj* of or relating to elections

ELECTORS > ELECTOR

ELECTRESS *n* female elector

ELECTRET *n* permanently polarized dielectric material

ELECTRETS > ELECTRET

ELECTRIC *adj* produced by, transmitting, or powered by electricity ▷ *n* electric train, car, etc

ELECTRICS > ELECTRIC

ELECTRIFY *vb* adapt for operation by electric power

ELECTRISE *same as* > ELECTRIZE

ELECTRIZE *vb* electrify

ELECTRO *vb* (in printing) make a metallic copy of a page

ELECTRODE *n* conductor through which an electric current enters or leaves a battery, vacuum tube, etc

ELECTROED > ELECTRO

ELECTRON *n* elementary particle in all atoms that has a negative electrical charge

ELECTRONS > ELECTRON

ELECTROS > ELECTRO

ELECTRUM *n* alloy of gold (55–88 per cent) and silver used for jewellery and ornaments

ELECTRUMS > ELECTRUM

ELECTS > ELECT

ELECTUARY *n* paste taken orally, containing a drug mixed with syrup or honey

ELEDOISIN *n* substance extracted from the salivary glands of a small octopus for medical applications

ELEGANCE *n* dignified grace in appearance, movement, or behaviour

ELEGANCES > ELEGANCE

ELEGANCY *same as* > ELEGANCE

ELEGANT *adj* pleasing or graceful in dress, style, or design

ELEGANTLY > ELEGANT

ELEGIAC *adj* mournful or plaintive ▷ *n* elegiac couplet or stanza

ELEGIACAL > ELEGIAC

ELEGIACS > ELEGIAC

ELEGIAST *n* writer of elegies

ELEGIASTS > ELEGIAST

ELEGIES > ELEGY

ELEGISE *same as* > ELEGIZE

ELEGISED > ELEGISE

ELEGISES > ELEGISE

ELEGISING > ELEGISE

ELEGIST > ELEGIZE

ELEGISTS > ELEGIZE

ELEGIT *n* writ delivering debtor's property to plaintiff

ELEGITS > ELEGIT

ELEGIZE *vb* compose an elegy or elegies (in memory

of)

ELEGIZED > ELEGIZE

ELEGIZES > ELEGIZE

ELEGIZING > ELEGIZE

ELEGY *n* mournful poem, esp a lament for the dead

ELEMENT *n* component part

ELEMENTAL *adj* of primitive natural forces or passions ▷ *n* spirit or force that is said to appear in physical form

ELEMENTS > ELEMENT

ELEMI *n* any of various fragrant resins obtained from tropical trees, esp trees of the family *Burseraceae*: used in making varnishes, ointments, inks, etc

ELEMIS > ELEMI

ELENCH *n* refutation in logic

ELENCHI > ELENCHUS

ELENCHIC > ELENCHUS

ELENCHS > ELENCH

ELENCHTIC *same as* > ELENCTIC

ELENCHUS *n* refutation of an argument by proving the contrary of its conclusion, esp syllogistically

ELENCTIC *adj* refuting an argument by proving the falsehood of its conclusion

ELEOPTENE *n* liquid part of a volatile oil

ELEPHANT *n* huge four-footed thick-skinned animal with ivory tusks and a long trunk

ELEPHANTS *adj* in Australia, a slang word for drunk

ELEUTHERI *pl n* secret society

ELEVATE *vb* raise in rank or status

ELEVATED *adj* higher than normal ▷ *n* railway that runs on an elevated structure

ELEVATEDS > ELEVATED

ELEVATES > ELEVATE

ELEVATING > ELEVATE

ELEVATION *n* raising

ELEVATOR *n* lift for carrying people

ELEVATORS > ELEVATOR

ELEVATORY > ELEVATE

ELEVEN *n* one more than ten ▷ *adj* amounting to eleven ▷ *determiner* amounting to eleven

ELEVENS > ELEVEN

ELEVENSES *n* mid-morning snack

ELEVENTH *n* (of) number eleven in a series ▷ *adj* coming after the tenth in numbering or counting order, position, time, etc

ELEVENTHS > ELEVENTH

ELEVON *n* aircraft control surface that combines the functions of an elevator and aileron, usually fitted to tailless or delta-wing aircraft

ELEVONS > ELEVON

ELF *n* (in folklore) small mischievous fairy ▷ *vb* entangle (esp hair)

ELFED > ELF

ELFHOOD > ELF

ELFHOODS > ELF

ELFIN *adj* small and delicate ▷ *n* young elf

ELFING > ELF

ELFINS > ELFIN

ELFISH *adj* of, relating to, or like an elf or elves ▷ *n* supposed language of elves

ELFISHLY > ELFISH

ELFLAND *another name for* > FAIRYLAND

ELFLANDS > ELFLAND

ELFLIKE > ELF

ELFLOCK *n* lock of hair, fancifully regarded as having been tangled by the elves

ELFLOCKS > ELFLOCK

ELFS > ELF

ELHI *adj* informal word for or relating to elementary high school

ELIAD *n* glance

ELIADS > ELIAD

ELICHE *n* pasta in the form of spirals

ELICHES > ELICHE

ELICIT *vb* bring about (a response or reaction)

ELICITED > ELICIT

ELICITING > ELICIT

ELICITOR > ELICIT

ELICITORS > ELICIT

ELICITS > ELICIT

ELIDE *vb* omit (a vowel or syllable) from a spoken word

ELIDED > ELIDE

ELIDES > ELIDE

ELIDIBLE > ELIDE

ELIDING > ELIDE

ELIGIBLE *adj* meeting the requirements or qualifications needed ▷ *n* eligible person or thing

ELIGIBLES > ELIGIBLE

ELIGIBLY > ELIGIBLE

ELIMINANT > ELIMINATE

ELIMINATE *vb* get rid of

ELINT *n* electronic intelligence

ELINTS > ELINT

ELISION *n* omission of a syllable or vowel from a spoken word

ELISIONS > ELISION

ELITE *n* most powerful, rich, or gifted members of a group ▷ *adj* of, relating to, or suitable for an elite

ELITES > ELITE

ELITISM *n* belief that society should be governed by a small group of superior people

ELITISMS > ELITISM

ELITIST > ELITISM

ELITISTS > ELITISM

ELIXIR *n* imaginary liquid that can prolong life or turn base metals into gold

ELIXIRS > ELIXIR

ELK *n* large deer of N Europe and Asia

ELKHOUND *n* powerful breed of dog of the spitz type with a thick grey coat and tightly curled tail

ELKHOUNDS > ELKHOUND

ELKS > ELK

ELL *n* obsolete unit of length equal to approximately 45 inches

ELLAGIC *adj* of an acid derived from gallnuts

ELLIPSE *n* oval shape

ELLIPSES > ELLIPSIS

ELLIPSIS *n* omission of letters or words in a sentence

ELLIPSOID *n* surface whose plane sections are ellipses or circles

ELLIPTIC *adj* relating to or having the shape of an ellipse

ELLOPS *same as* > ELOPS

ELLOPSES > ELLOPS

ELLS > ELL

ELLWAND *n* stick for measuring lengths

ELLWANDS > ELLWAND

ELM *n* tree with serrated leaves

ELMEN *adj* of or relating to elm trees

ELMIER > ELMY

ELMIEST > ELMY

ELMS > ELM

ELMWOOD *n* wood from an elm tree

ELMWOODS > ELMWOOD

ELMY *adj* of or relating to elm trees

ELOCUTE *vb* speak as if practising elocution

ELOCUTED > ELOCUTE

ELOCUTES > ELOCUTE

ELOCUTING > ELOCUTE

ELOCUTION *n* art of speaking clearly in public

ELOCUTORY > ELOCUTION

ELODEA *n* type of American plant

ELODEAS > ELODEA

ELOGE *same as* > EULOGY

ELOGES > ELOGE

ELOGIES > ELOGY

ELOGIST > ELOGY

ELOGISTS > ELOGY

ELOGIUM *same as* > EULOGY

ELOGIUMS > ELOGIUM

ELOGY *same as* > EULOGY

ELOIGN *vb* remove (oneself, one's property, etc) to a distant place

ELOIGNED > ELOIGN

ELOIGNER > ELOIGN

ELOIGNERS > ELOIGN

ELOIGNING > ELOIGN

ELOIGNS > ELOIGN

ELOIN *same as* > ELOIGN

ELOINED > ELOIN

ELOINER > ELOIGN

ELOINERS > ELOIGN

ELOINING > ELOIN

ELOINMENT > ELOIGN

ELOINS > ELOIN

ELONGATE *vb* make or become longer ▷ *adj* long and narrow
ELONGATED > ELONGATE
ELONGATES > ELONGATE
ELOPE *vb* (of two people) run away secretly to get married
ELOPED > ELOPE
ELOPEMENT > ELOPE
ELOPER > ELOPE
ELOPERS > ELOPE
ELOPES > ELOPE
ELOPING > ELOPE
ELOPS *n* type of fish
ELOPSES > ELOPS
ELOQUENCE *n* fluent powerful use of language
ELOQUENT *adj* (of speech or writing) fluent and persuasive
ELPEE *n* LP, long-playing record
ELPEES > ELPEE
ELS > EL
ELSE *adv* in addition or more
ELSEWHERE *adv* in or to another place
ELSEWISE *adv* otherwise
ELSHIN *n* cobbler's awl
ELSHINS > ELSHIN
ELSIN *variant of* > ELSHIN
ELSINS > ELSIN
ELT *n* young female pig
ELTCHI *variant of* > ELCHEE
ELTCHIS > ELTCHI
ELTS > ELT
ELUANT *same as* > ELUENT
ELUANTS > ELUANT
ELUATE *n* solution of adsorbed material in the eluent obtained during the process of elution
ELUATES > ELUATE
ELUCIDATE *vb* make (something difficult) clear
ELUDE *vb* escape from by cleverness or quickness
ELUDED > ELUDE
ELUDER > ELUDE
ELUDERS > ELUDE
ELUDES > ELUDE
ELUDIBLE *adj* able to be eluded
ELUDING > ELUDE
ELUENT *n* solvent used for eluting
ELUENTS > ELUENT
ELUSION > ELUDE
ELUSIONS > ELUDE
ELUSIVE *adj* difficult to catch or remember
ELUSIVELY > ELUSIVE
ELUSORY *adj* avoiding the issue
ELUTE *vb* wash out (a substance) by the action of a solvent, as in chromatography
ELUTED > ELUTE
ELUTES > ELUTE
ELUTING > ELUTE
ELUTION > ELUTE
ELUTIONS > ELUTE
ELUTOR > ELUTE
ELUTORS > ELUTE

ELUTRIATE *vb* purify or separate (a substance or mixture) by washing and straining or decanting
ELUVIA > ELUVIUM
ELUVIAL > ELUVIUM
ELUVIATE *vb* remove material suspended in water in a layer of soil by the action of rainfall
ELUVIATED > ELUVIATE
ELUVIATES > ELUVIATE
ELUVIUM *n* mass of sand, silt, etc: a product of the erosion of rocks that has remained in its place of origin
ELUVIUMS > ELUVIUM
ELVAN *n* type of rock
ELVANITE *variant of* > ELVAN
ELVANITES > ELVANITE
ELVANS > ELVAN
ELVER *n* young eel
ELVERS > ELVER
ELVES > ELF
ELVISH *same as* > ELFISH
ELVISHLY > ELVISH
ELYSIAN *adj* delightful, blissful
ELYTRA > ELYTRUM
ELYTRAL > ELYTRON
ELYTROID > ELYTRON
ELYTRON *n* either of the horny front wings of beetles and some other insects, which cover and protect the hind wings
ELYTROUS > ELYTRON
ELYTRUM *same as* > ELYTRON
EM *n* square of a body of any size of type, used as a unit of measurement
EMACIATE *vb* become or cause to become abnormally thin
EMACIATED *adj* abnormally thin
EMACIATES > EMACIATE
EMACS *n* powerful computer program used for creating and editing text
EMACSEN > EMACS
EMAIL *n* electronic mail ▷ *vb* send a message by electronic mail
EMAILED > EMAIL
EMAILING > EMAIL
EMAILS > EMAIL
EMANANT > EMANATE
EMANATE *vb* issue, proceed from a source
EMANATED > EMANATE
EMANATES > EMANATE
EMANATING > EMANATE
EMANATION *n* act or instance of emanating
EMANATIST > EMANATE
EMANATIVE > EMANATE
EMANATOR > EMANATE
EMANATORS > EMANATE
EMANATORY > EMANATE
EMBACE *variant of* > EMBASE
EMBACES > EMBACE
EMBACING > EMBACE
EMBAIL *vb* enclose in a circle
EMBAILED > EMBAIL
EMBAILING > EMBAIL

EMBAILS > EMBAIL
EMBALE *vb* bind
EMBALED > EMBALE
EMBALES > EMBALE
EMBALING > EMBALE
EMBALL *vb* enclose in a circle
EMBALLED > EMBALL
EMBALLING > EMBALL
EMBALLS > EMBALL
EMBALM *vb* preserve (a corpse) from decay by the use of chemicals etc
EMBALMED > EMBALM
EMBALMER > EMBALM
EMBALMERS > EMBALM
EMBALMING > EMBALM
EMBALMS > EMBALM
EMBANK *vb* protect, enclose, or confine (a waterway, road, etc) with an embankment
EMBANKED > EMBANK
EMBANKER > EMBANK
EMBANKERS > EMBANK
EMBANKING > EMBANK
EMBANKS > EMBANK
EMBAR *vb* close in with bars
EMBARGO *n* order by a government prohibiting trade with a country ▷ *vb* put an embargo on
EMBARGOED > EMBARGO
EMBARGOES > EMBARGO
EMBARK *vb* board a ship or aircraft
EMBARKED > EMBARK
EMBARKING > EMBARK
EMBARKS > EMBARK
EMBARRASS *vb* cause to feel self-conscious or ashamed
EMBARRED > EMBAR
EMBARRING > EMBAR
EMBARS > EMBAR
EMBASE *vb* degrade or debase
EMBASED > EMBASE
EMBASES > EMBASE
EMBASING > EMBASE
EMBASSADE *n* embassy
EMBASSAGE *n* work of an embassy
EMBASSIES > EMBASSY
EMBASSY *n* offices or official residence of an ambassador
EMBASTE > EMBASE
EMBATHE *vb* bathe with water
EMBATHED > EMBATHE
EMBATHES > EMBATHE
EMBATHING > EMBATHE
EMBATTLE *vb* deploy (troops) for battle
EMBATTLED *adj* having a lot of difficulties
EMBATTLES > EMBATTLE
EMBAY *vb* form into a bay
EMBAYED > EMBAY
EMBAYING > EMBAY
EMBAYLD > EMBAIL
EMBAYMENT *n* shape resembling a bay
EMBAYS > EMBAY
EMBED *vb* fix firmly in something solid ▷ *n* journalist accompanying an active military unit

EMBEDDED > EMBED
EMBEDDING *n* practice of assigning or being assigned a journalist to accompany an active military unit
EMBEDMENT > EMBED
EMBEDS > EMBED
EMBELLISH *vb* decorate
EMBER *n* glowing piece of wood or coal in a dying fire
EMBERS > EMBER
EMBEZZLE *vb* steal money that has been entrusted to one
EMBEZZLED > EMBEZZLE
EMBEZZLER > EMBEZZLE
EMBEZZLES > EMBEZZLE
EMBITTER *vb* make (a person) resentful or bitter
EMBITTERS > EMBITTER
EMBLAZE *vb* cause to light up
EMBLAZED > EMBLAZE
EMBLAZER > EMBLAZE
EMBLAZERS > EMBLAZE
EMBLAZES > EMBLAZE
EMBLAZING > EMBLAZE
EMBLAZON *vb* decorate with bright colours
EMBLAZONS > EMBLAZON
EMBLEM *n* object or design that symbolizes a quality, type, or group ▷ *vb* represent or signify
EMBLEMA *n* mosaic decoration
EMBLEMATA > EMBLEMA
EMBLEMED > EMBLEM
EMBLEMING > EMBLEM
EMBLEMISE *same as* > EMBLEMIZE
EMBLEMIZE *vb* function as an emblem of
EMBLEMS > EMBLEM
EMBLIC *n* type of Indian tree
EMBLICS > EMBLIC
EMBLOOM *vb* adorn with blooms
EMBLOOMED > EMBLOOM
EMBLOOMS > EMBLOOM
EMBLOSSOM *vb* adorn with blossom
EMBODIED > EMBODY
EMBODIER > EMBODY
EMBODIERS > EMBODY
EMBODIES > EMBODY
EMBODY *vb* be an example or expression of
EMBODYING > EMBODY
EMBOG *vb* sink down into a bog
EMBOGGED > EMBOG
EMBOGGING > EMBOG
EMBOGS > EMBOG
EMBOGUE *vb* go out through a narrow channel or passage
EMBOGUED > EMBOGUE
EMBOGUES > EMBOGUE
EMBOGUING > EMBOGUE
EMBOIL *vb* enrage or be enraged
EMBOILED > EMBOIL
EMBOILING > EMBOIL
EMBOILS > EMBOIL
EMBOLDEN *vb* encourage (someone)

e

EMBOLDENS > EMBOLDEN
EMBOLI > EMBOLUS
EMBOLIC *adj* of or relating to an embolus or embolism
EMBOLIES > EMBOLY
EMBOLISE *same as* > EMBOLIZE
EMBOLISED > EMBOLISE
EMBOLISES > EMBOLISE
EMBOLISM *n* blocking of a blood vessel by a blood clot or air bubble
EMBOLISMS > EMBOLISM
EMBOLIZE *vb* cause embolism in (a blood vessel)
EMBOLIZED > EMBOLIZE
EMBOLIZES > EMBOLIZE
EMBOLUS *n* material, such as a blood clot, that blocks a blood vessel
EMBOLUSES > EMBOLUS
EMBOLY *n* infolding of the outer layer of cells of an organism or part of an organism so as to form a pocket in the surface
EMBORDER *vb* edge or border
EMBORDERS > EMBORDER
EMBOSCATA *n* sudden attack or raid
EMBOSK *vb* hide or cover
EMBOSKED > EMBOSK
EMBOSKING > EMBOSK
EMBOSKS > EMBOSK
EMBOSOM *vb* enclose or envelop, esp protectively
EMBOSOMED > EMBOSOM
EMBOSOMS > EMBOSOM
EMBOSS *vb* mould or carve a decoration on (a surface) so that it stands out from the surface
EMBOSSED *adj* (of a design or pattern) standing out from a surface
EMBOSSER > EMBOSS
EMBOSSERS > EMBOSS
EMBOSSES > EMBOSS
EMBOSSING > EMBOSS
EMBOST > EMBOSS
EMBOUND *vb* surround or encircle
EMBOUNDED > EMBOUND
EMBOUNDS > EMBOUND
EMBOW *vb* design or create (a structure) in the form of an arch or vault
EMBOWED > EMBOW
EMBOWEL *vb* bury or embed deeply
EMBOWELED > EMBOWEL
EMBOWELS > EMBOWEL
EMBOWER *vb* enclose in or as in a bower
EMBOWERED > EMBOWER
EMBOWERS > EMBOWER
EMBOWING > EMBOW
EMBOWMENT > EMBOW
EMBOWS > EMBOW
EMBOX *vb* put in a box
EMBOXED > EMBOX
EMBOXES > EMBOX
EMBOXING > EMBOX
EMBRACE *vb* clasp in the arms, hug ▷ *n* act of embracing

EMBRACED > EMBRACE
EMBRACEOR *n* person guilty of embracery
EMBRACER > EMBRACE
EMBRACERS > EMBRACE
EMBRACERY *n* offence of attempting by corrupt means to influence a jury or juror, as by bribery or threats
EMBRACES > EMBRACE
EMBRACING > EMBRACE
EMBRACIVE > EMBRACE
EMBRAID *vb* braid or interweave
EMBRAIDED > EMBRAID
EMBRAIDS > EMBRAID
EMBRANGLE *vb* confuse or entangle
EMBRASOR *n* one who embraces
EMBRASORS > EMBRASOR
EMBRASURE *n* door or window having splayed sides so that the opening is larger on the inside
EMBRAVE *vb* adorn or decorate
EMBRAVED > EMBRAVE
EMBRAVES > EMBRAVE
EMBRAVING > EMBRAVE
EMBRAZURE *variant of* > EMBRASURE
EMBREAD *vb* braid
EMBREADED > EMBREAD
EMBREADS > EMBREAD
EMBREATHE *vb* breathe in air
EMBRITTLE *vb* become brittle
EMBROCATE *vb* apply a liniment or lotion to (a part of the body)
EMBROGLIO *same as* > IMBROGLIO
EMBROIDER *vb* decorate with needlework
EMBROIL *vb* involve (a person) in problems
EMBROILED > EMBROIL
EMBROILER > EMBROIL
EMBROILS > EMBROIL
EMBROWN *vb* make or become brown
EMBROWNED > EMBROWN
EMBROWNS > EMBROWN
EMBRUE *variant spelling of* > IMBRUE
EMBRUED > EMBRUE
EMBRUES > EMBRUE
EMBRUING > EMBRUE
EMBRUTE *variant of* > IMBRUTE
EMBRUTED > EMBRUTE
EMBRUTES > EMBRUTE
EMBRUTING > EMBRUTE
EMBRYO *n* unborn creature in the early stages of development
EMBRYOID > EMBRYO
EMBRYOIDS > EMBRYO
EMBRYON *variant of* > EMBRYO
EMBRYONAL *same as* > EMBRYONIC
EMBRYONIC *adj* at an early stage
EMBRYONS > EMBRYON

EMBRYOS > EMBRYO
EMBRYOTIC *variant of* > EMBRYONIC
EMBUS *vb* cause (troops) to board or (of troops) to board a transport vehicle
EMBUSED > EMBUS
EMBUSES > EMBUS
EMBUSIED > EMBUSY
EMBUSIES > EMBUSY
EMBUSING > EMBUS
EMBUSQUE *n* man who avoids military conscription by obtaining a government job
EMBUSQUES > EMBUSQUE
EMBUSSED > EMBUS
EMBUSSES > EMBUS
EMBUSSING > EMBUS
EMBUSY *vb* keep occupied
EMBUSYING > EMBUSY
EMCEE *n* master of ceremonies ▷ *vb* act as master of ceremonies (for or at)
EMCEED > EMCEE
EMCEEING > EMCEE
EMCEES > EMCEE
EMDASH *n* long dash in punctuation
EMDASHES > EMDASH
EME *n* uncle
EMEER *variant of* > EMIR
EMEERATE *variant of* > EMIRATE
EMEERATES > EMEERATE
EMEERS > EMEER
EMEND *vb* remove errors from
EMENDABLE > EMEND
EMENDALS *pl n* funds put aside for repairs
EMENDATE *vb* make corrections
EMENDATED > EMENDATE
EMENDATES > EMENDATE
EMENDATOR *n* one who emends a text
EMENDED > EMEND
EMENDER > EMEND
EMENDERS > EMEND
EMENDING > EMEND
EMENDS > EMEND
EMERALD *n* bright green precious stone ▷ *adj* bright green
EMERALDS > EMERALD
EMERAUDE *archaic variant of* > EMERALD
EMERAUDES > EMERAUDE
EMERGE *vb* come into view
EMERGED > EMERGE
EMERGENCE *n* act or process of emerging
EMERGENCY *n* sudden unforeseen occurrence needing immediate action
EMERGENT *adj* coming into being or notice ▷ *n* aquatic plant with stem and leaves above the water
EMERGENTS > EMERGENT
EMERGES > EMERGE
EMERGING > EMERGE
EMERIED > EMERY
EMERIES > EMERY
EMERITA *adj* retired, but

retaining an honorary title ▷ *n* woman who is retired, but retains an honorary title
EMERITAE > EMERITA
EMERITAS > EMERITA
EMERITI > EMERITUS
EMERITUS *adj* retired, but retaining an honorary title ▷ *n* man who is retired, but retains an honorary title
EMEROD *n* haemorrhoid
EMERODS > EMEROD
EMEROID *variant of* > EMEROD
EMEROIDS > EMEROID
EMERSED *adj* (of the leaves or stems of aquatic plants) protruding above the surface of the water
EMERSION *n* act or an instance of emerging
EMERSIONS > EMERSION
EMERY *n* hard mineral used for smoothing and polishing ▷ *vb* apply emery to
EMERYING > EMERY
EMES > EME
EMESES > EMESIS
EMESIS *technical name for* > VOMITING
EMETIC *n* substance that causes vomiting ▷ *adj* causing vomiting
EMETICAL *same as* > EMETIC
EMETICS > EMETIC
EMETIN *same as* > EMETINE
EMETINE *n* white bitter poisonous alkaloid
EMETINES > EMETINE
EMETINS > EMETIN
EMEU *variant of* > EMU
EMEUS > EMEU
EMEUTE *n* uprising or rebellion
EMEUTES > EMEUTE
EMIC *adj* of or relating to a significant linguistic unit
EMICANT > EMICATE
EMICATE *vb* twinkle
EMICATED > EMICATE
EMICATES > EMICATE
EMICATING > EMICATE
EMICATION > EMICATE
EMICTION *n* passing of urine
EMICTIONS > EMICTION
EMICTORY > EMICTION
EMIGRANT *n* person who leaves one place or country, esp a native country, to settle in another
EMIGRANTS > EMIGRANT
EMIGRATE *vb* go and settle in another country
EMIGRATED > EMIGRATE
EMIGRATES > EMIGRATE
EMIGRE *n* someone who has left his native country for political reasons
EMIGRES > EMIGRE
EMINENCE *n* position of superiority or fame
EMINENCES > EMINENCE
EMINENCY *same as* > EMINENCE

EMINENT *adj* distinguished, well-known

EMINENTLY > EMINENT

EMIR *n* Muslim ruler

EMIRATE *n* emir's country

EMIRATES > EMIRATE

EMIRS > EMIR

EMISSARY *n* agent sent on a mission by a government ▷ *adj* (of veins) draining blood from sinuses in the dura mater to veins outside the skull

EMISSILE *adj* able to be emitted

EMISSION *n* act of giving out heat, light, a smell, etc

EMISSIONS > EMISSION

EMISSIVE > EMISSION

EMIT *vb* give out

EMITS > EMIT

EMITTANCE > EMIT

EMITTED > EMIT

EMITTER *n* person or thing that emits

EMITTERS > EMITTER

EMITTING > EMIT

EMLETS as in *blood-drop emlets* Chilean plant with red-spotted yellow flowers

EMMA *n* former communications code for the letter A

EMMARBLE *vb* decorate with marble

EMMARBLED > EMMARBLE

EMMARBLES > EMMARBLE

EMMAS > EMMA

EMMER *n* variety of wheat grown in mountainous parts of Europe

EMMERS > EMMER

EMMESH *variant of* > ENMESH

EMMESHED > EMMESH

EMMESHES > EMMESH

EMMESHING > EMMESH

EMMET *n* tourist or holiday-maker

EMMETROPE *n* person whose vision is normal

EMMETS > EMMET

EMMEW *vb* restrict

EMMEWED > EMMEW

EMMEWING > EMMEW

EMMEWS > EMMEW

EMMOVE *vb* cause emotion in

EMMOVED > EMMOVE

EMMOVES > EMMOVE

EMMOVING > EMMOVE

EMMY *n* (in the US) one of the gold-plated statuettes awarded annually for outstanding television performances and productions

EMMYS > EMMY

EMO *n* type of music combining hard rock with emotional lyrics

EMODIN *n* type of chemical compound

EMODINS > EMODIN

EMOLLIATE *vb* make soft or smooth

EMOLLIENT *adj* softening, soothing ▷ *n* substance which softens or soothes

the skin

EMOLUMENT *n* fees or wages from employment

EMONG *variant of* > AMONG

EMONGES *variant of* > AMONG

EMONGEST *variant of* > AMONGST

EMONGST *variant of* > AMONGST

EMOS > EMO

EMOTE *vb* display exaggerated emotion, as if acting

EMOTED > EMOTE

EMOTER > EMOTE

EMOTERS > EMOTE

EMOTES > EMOTE

EMOTICON *n* any of several combinations of symbols used in electronic mail and text messaging to indicate the state of mind of the writer, such as :-) to express happiness

EMOTICONS > EMOTICON

EMOTING > EMOTE

EMOTION *n* strong feeling

EMOTIONAL *adj* readily affected by or appealing to the emotions

EMOTIONS > EMOTION

EMOTIVE *adj* tending to arouse emotion

EMOTIVELY > EMOTIVE

EMOTIVISM *n* theory that moral utterances do not have a truth value but express the feelings of the speaker, so that *murder is wrong* is equivalent to *down with murder*

EMOTIVITY > EMOTIVE

EMOVE *vb* cause to feel emotion

EMOVED > EMOVE

EMOVES > EMOVE

EMOVING > EMOVE

EMPACKET *vb* wrap up

EMPACKETS > EMPACKET

EMPAESTIC *adj* embossed

EMPAIRE *variant of* > IMPAIR

EMPAIRED > EMPAIRE

EMPAIRES > EMPAIRE

EMPAIRING > EMPAIRE

EMPALE *less common spelling of* > IMPALE

EMPALED > EMPALE

EMPALER > EMPALE

EMPALERS > EMPALE

EMPALES > EMPALE

EMPALING > EMPALE

EMPANADA *n* Spanish meat-filled pastry

EMPANADAS > EMPANADA

EMPANEL *vb* enter on a list (names of persons to be summoned for jury service)

EMPANELED > EMPANEL

EMPANELS > EMPANEL

EMPANOPLY *vb* put armour on

EMPARE *variant of* > IMPAIR

EMPARED > EMPARE

EMPARES > EMPARE

EMPARING > EMPARE

EMPARL *variant of* > IMPARL

EMPARLED > EMPARL

EMPARLING > EMPARL

EMPARLS > EMPARL

EMPART *variant of* > IMPART

EMPARTED > EMPART

EMPARTING > EMPART

EMPARTS > EMPART

EMPATHIC *adj* of or relating to empathy

EMPATHIES > EMPATHY

EMPATHISE *same as* > EMPATHIZE

EMPATHIST > EMPATHY

EMPATHIZE *vb* sense and understand someone else's feelings as if they were one's own

EMPATHY *n* ability to understand someone else's feelings as if they were one's own

EMPATRON *vb* treat in the manner of a patron

EMPATRONS > EMPATRON

EMPAYRE *variant of* > IMPAIR

EMPAYRED > EMPAYRE

EMPAYRES > EMPAYRE

EMPAYRING > EMPAYRE

EMPEACH *variant of* > IMPEACH

EMPEACHED > EMPEACH

EMPEACHES > EMPEACH

EMPENNAGE *n* rear part of an aircraft, comprising the fin, rudder, and tailplane

EMPEOPLE *vb* bring people into

EMPEOPLED > EMPEOPLE

EMPEOPLES > EMPEOPLE

EMPERCE *variant of* > EMPIERCE

EMPERCED > EMPERCE

EMPERCES > EMPERCE

EMPERCING > EMPERCE

EMPERIES > EMPERY

EMPERISE *variant of* > EMPERIZE

EMPERISED > EMPERISE

EMPERISES > EMPERISE

EMPERISH *vb* damage or harm

EMPERIZE *vb* act like an emperor

EMPERIZED > EMPERIZE

EMPERIZES > EMPERIZE

EMPEROR *n* ruler of an empire

EMPERORS > EMPEROR

EMPERY *n* dominion or power

EMPHASES > EMPHASIS

EMPHASIS *n* special importance or significance

EMPHASISE *same as* > EMPHASIZE

EMPHASIZE *vb* give emphasis or prominence to

EMPHATIC *adj* showing emphasis ▷ *n* emphatic consonant, as used in Arabic

EMPHATICS > EMPHATIC

EMPHLYSES > EMPHLYSIS

EMPHLYSIS *n* outbreak of blisters on the body

EMPHYSEMA *n* condition in which the air sacs of the lungs are grossly enlarged,

causing breathlessness

EMPIERCE *vb* pierce or cut

EMPIERCED > EMPIERCE

EMPIERCES > EMPIERCE

EMPIGHT *adj* attached or positioned

EMPIRE *n* group of territories under the rule of one state or person

EMPIRES > EMPIRE

EMPIRIC *n* person who relies on empirical methods

EMPIRICAL *adj* relying on experiment or experience, not on theory ▷ *n* posterior probability of an event derived on the basis of its observed frequency in a sample

EMPIRICS > EMPIRIC

EMPLACE *vb* put in place or position

EMPLACED > EMPLACE

EMPLACES > EMPLACE

EMPLACING > EMPLACE

EMPLANE *vb* board or put on board an aeroplane

EMPLANED > EMPLANE

EMPLANES > EMPLANE

EMPLANING > EMPLANE

EMPLASTER *vb* cover with plaster

EMPLASTIC *adj* sticky

EMPLEACH *variant of* > IMPLEACH

EMPLECTON *n* type of masonry filled with rubbish

EMPLECTUM *variant of* > EMPLECTON

EMPLONGE *variant of* > IMPLUNGE

EMPLONGED > EMPLONGE

EMPLONGES > EMPLONGE

EMPLOY *vb* engage or make use of the services of (a person) in return for money ▷ *n* state of being employed

EMPLOYE *same as* > EMPLOYEE

EMPLOYED > EMPLOY

EMPLOYEE *n* person who is hired to work for someone in return for payment

EMPLOYEES > EMPLOYEE

EMPLOYER *n* person or organization that employs someone

EMPLOYERS > EMPLOYER

EMPLOYES > EMPLOYE

EMPLOYING > EMPLOY

EMPLOYS > EMPLOY

EMPLUME *vb* put a plume on

EMPLUMED > EMPLUME

EMPLUMES > EMPLUME

EMPLUMING > EMPLUME

EMPOISON *vb* embitter or corrupt

EMPOISONS > EMPOISON

EMPOLDER *variant spelling of* > IMPOLDER

EMPOLDERS > EMPOLDER

EMPORIA > EMPORIUM

EMPORIUM *n* large general shop

EMPORIUMS > EMPORIUM

EMPOWER *vb* enable,

authorize
EMPOWERED > EMPOWER
EMPOWERS > EMPOWER
EMPRESS *n* woman who rules an empire
EMPRESSE *adj* keen; zealous
EMPRESSES > EMPRESS
EMPRISE *n* chivalrous or daring enterprise
EMPRISES > EMPRISE
EMPRIZE *variant of* > EMPRISE
EMPRIZES > EMPRIZE
EMPT *vb* empty
EMPTED > EMPT
EMPTIABLE > EMPTY
EMPTIED > EMPTY
EMPTIER > EMPTY
EMPTIERS > EMPTY
EMPTIES > EMPTY
EMPTIEST > EMPTY
EMPTILY > EMPTY
EMPTINESS > EMPTY
EMPTING > EMPT
EMPTINGS *variant of* > EMPTINS
EMPTINS *pl n* liquid leavening agent made from potatoes
EMPTION *n* process of buying something
EMPTIONAL > EMPTION
EMPTIONS > EMPTION
EMPTS > EMPT
EMPTY *adj* containing nothing ▷ *vb* make or become empty ▷ *n* empty container, esp a bottle
EMPTYING > EMPTY
EMPTYINGS > EMPTY
EMPTYSES > EMPTYSIS
EMPTYSIS *n* act of spitting up blood
EMPURPLE *vb* make or become purple
EMPURPLED > EMPURPLE
EMPURPLES > EMPURPLE
EMPUSA *n* goblin in Greek mythology
EMPUSAS > EMPUSA
EMPUSE *variant of* > EMPUSA
EMPUSES > EMPUSE
EMPYEMA *n* collection of pus in a body cavity, esp in the chest
EMPYEMAS > EMPYEMA
EMPYEMATA > EMPYEMA
EMPYEMIC > EMPYEMA
EMPYESES > EMPYESIS
EMPYESIS *n* pus-filled boil on the skin
EMPYREAL *variant of* > EMPYREAN
EMPYREAN *n* heavens or sky ▷ *adj* of or relating to the sky or the heavens
EMPYREANS > EMPYREAN
EMPYREUMA *n* smell and taste associated with burning vegetable and animal matter
EMS > EM
EMU *n* large Australian flightless bird with long legs
EMULATE *vb* attempt to equal or surpass by

imitating
EMULATED > EMULATE
EMULATES > EMULATE
EMULATING > EMULATE
EMULATION *n* act of emulating or imitating
EMULATIVE > EMULATE
EMULATOR > EMULATE
EMULATORS > EMULATE
EMULE *variant of* > EMULATE
EMULED > EMULE
EMULES > EMULE
EMULGE *vb* remove liquid from
EMULGED > EMULGE
EMULGENCE > EMULGE
EMULGENT > EMULGE
EMULGES > EMULGE
EMULGING > EMULGE
EMULING > EMULE
EMULOUS *adj* desiring or aiming to equal or surpass another
EMULOUSLY > EMULOUS
EMULSIBLE > EMULSIFY
EMULSIFY *vb* (of two liquids) join together
EMULSIN *n* enzyme that is found in almonds
EMULSINS > EMULSIN
EMULSION *n* light-sensitive coating on photographic film ▷ *vb* paint with emulsion paint
EMULSIONS > EMULSION
EMULSIVE > EMULSION
EMULSOID *n* sol with a liquid disperse phase
EMULSOIDS > EMULSOID
EMULSOR *n* device that emulsifies
EMULSORS > EMULSOR
EMUNCTION > EMUNCTORY
EMUNCTORY *adj* of or relating to a bodily organ or duct having an excretory function ▷ *n* excretory organ or duct, such as a skin pore
EMUNGE *vb* clean or clear out
EMUNGED > EMUNGE
EMUNGES > EMUNGE
EMUNGING > EMUNGE
EMURE *variant of* > IMMURE
EMURED > EMURE
EMURES > EMURE
EMURING > EMURE
EMUS > EMU
EMYD *n* freshwater tortoise or terrapin
EMYDE *same as* > EMYD
EMYDES > EMYDE
EMYDS > EMYD
EMYS *n* freshwater tortoise or terrapin
EN *n* unit of measurement, half the width of an em
ENABLE *vb* provide (a person) with the means, opportunity, or authority (to do something)
ENABLED > ENABLE
ENABLER > ENABLE
ENABLERS > ENABLE
ENABLES > ENABLE
ENABLING > ENABLE
ENACT *vb* establish by law

ENACTABLE > ENACT
ENACTED > ENACT
ENACTING > ENACT
ENACTION > ENACT
ENACTIONS > ENACT
ENACTIVE > ENACT
ENACTMENT > ENACT
ENACTOR > ENACT
ENACTORS > ENACT
ENACTORY > ENACT
ENACTS > ENACT
ENACTURE > ENACT
ENACTURES > ENACT
ENALAPRIL *n* ACE inhibitor used to treat high blood pressure and congestive heart failure
ENALLAGE *n* act of using one grammatical form in the place of another
ENALLAGES > ENALLAGE
ENAMEL *n* glasslike coating applied to metal etc to preserve the surface ▷ *vb* cover with enamel
ENAMELED > ENAMEL
ENAMELER > ENAMEL
ENAMELERS > ENAMEL
ENAMELING > ENAMEL
ENAMELIST > ENAMEL
ENAMELLED > ENAMEL
ENAMELLER > ENAMEL
ENAMELS > ENAMEL
ENAMINE *n* type of unsaturated compound
ENAMINES > ENAMINE
ENAMOR *same as* > ENAMOUR
ENAMORADO *n* beloved one, lover
ENAMORED *same as* > ENAMOURED
ENAMORING > ENAMOR
ENAMORS > ENAMOR
ENAMOUR *vb* inspire with love
ENAMOURED *adj* inspired with love
ENAMOURS > ENAMOUR
ENARCH *variant of* > INARCH
ENARCHED > ENARCH
ENARCHES > ENARCH
ENARCHING > ENARCH
ENARM *vb* provide with arms
ENARMED > ENARM
ENARMING > ENARM
ENARMS > ENARM
ENATE *adj* growing out or outwards ▷ *n* relative on the mother's side
ENATES > ENATE
ENATIC *adj* related on one's mother's side
ENATION > ENATE
ENATIONS > ENATE
ENAUNTER *conj* in case that
ENCAENIA *n* festival of dedication or commemoration
ENCAENIAS > ENCAENIA
ENCAGE *vb* confine in or as in a cage
ENCAGED > ENCAGE
ENCAGES > ENCAGE
ENCAGING > ENCAGE
ENCALM *vb* becalm, settle
ENCALMED > ENCALM
ENCALMING > ENCALM

ENCALMS > ENCALM
ENCAMP *vb* set up in a camp
ENCAMPED > ENCAMP
ENCAMPING > ENCAMP
ENCAMPS > ENCAMP
ENCANTHIS *n* tumour of the eye
ENCAPSULE *vb* enclose or be enclosed in or as if in a capsule
ENCARPUS *n* decoration of fruit or flowers on a frieze
ENCASE *vb* enclose or cover completely
ENCASED > ENCASE
ENCASES > ENCASE
ENCASH *vb* exchange (a cheque) for cash
ENCASHED > ENCASH
ENCASHES > ENCASH
ENCASHING > ENCASH
ENCASING > ENCASE
ENCASTRE *adj* (of a beam) fixed at the ends
ENCAUSTIC *adj* decorated by any process involving burning in colours, esp by inlaying coloured clays and baking or by fusing wax colours to the surface ▷ *n* process of burning in colours
ENCAVE *variant of* > INCAVE
ENCAVED > ENCAVE
ENCAVES > ENCAVE
ENCAVING > ENCAVE
ENCEINTE *n* boundary wall enclosing a defended area
ENCEINTES > ENCEINTE
ENCEPHALA *n* brains
ENCHAFE *vb* heat up
ENCHAFED > ENCHAFE
ENCHAFES > ENCHAFE
ENCHAFING > ENCHAFE
ENCHAIN *vb* bind with chains
ENCHAINED > ENCHAIN
ENCHAINS > ENCHAIN
ENCHANT *vb* delight and fascinate
ENCHANTED > ENCHANT
ENCHANTER > ENCHANT
ENCHANTS > ENCHANT
ENCHARGE *vb* give into the custody of
ENCHARGED > ENCHARGE
ENCHARGES > ENCHARGE
ENCHARM *vb* enchant
ENCHARMED > ENCHARM
ENCHARMS > ENCHARM
ENCHASE *less common word for* > CHASE
ENCHASED > ENCHASE
ENCHASER > ENCHASE
ENCHASERS > ENCHASE
ENCHASES > ENCHASE
ENCHASING > ENCHASE
ENCHEASON *n* reason
ENCHEER *vb* cheer up
ENCHEERED > ENCHEER
ENCHEERS > ENCHEER
ENCHILADA *n* Mexican dish of a tortilla filled with meat, served with chilli sauce
ENCHORIAL *adj* of or used in a particular country:

Section 1: Words between 2 and 9 letters in length

used esp of the popular (demotic) writing of the ancient Egyptians

ENCHORIC *same as* > ENCHORIAL

ENCIERRO *n* Spanish bull run

ENCIERROS > ENCIERRO

ENCINA *n* type of oak

ENCINAL > ENCINA

ENCINAS > ENCINA

ENCIPHER *vb* convert (a message, document, etc) from plain text into code or cipher

ENCIPHERS > ENCIPHER

ENCIRCLE *vb* form a circle around

ENCIRCLED > ENCIRCLE

ENCIRCLES > ENCIRCLE

ENCLASP *vb* clasp

ENCLASPED > ENCLASP

ENCLASPS > ENCLASP

ENCLAVE *n* part of a country entirely surrounded by foreign territory ▷ *vb* hold in an enclave

ENCLAVED > ENCLAVE

ENCLAVES > ENCLAVE

ENCLAVING > ENCLAVE

ENCLISES > ENCLISIS

ENCLISIS *n* state of being enclitic

ENCLITIC *adj* denoting or relating to a monosyllabic word or form that is treated as a suffix of the preceding word, as Latin *-que* in *populusque* ▷ *n* enclitic word or linguistic form

ENCLITICS > ENCLITIC

ENCLOSE *vb* surround completely

ENCLOSED > ENCLOSE

ENCLOSER > ENCLOSE

ENCLOSERS > ENCLOSE

ENCLOSES > ENCLOSE

ENCLOSING > ENCLOSE

ENCLOSURE *n* area of land enclosed by a fence, wall, or hedge

ENCLOTHE *vb* clothe

ENCLOTHED > ENCLOTHE

ENCLOTHES > ENCLOTHE

ENCLOUD *vb* hide with clouds

ENCLOUDED > ENCLOUD

ENCLOUDS > ENCLOUD

ENCODABLE > ENCODE

ENCODE *vb* convert (a message) into code

ENCODED > ENCODE

ENCODER > ENCODE

ENCODERS > ENCODE

ENCODES > ENCODE

ENCODING > ENCODE

ENCOLOUR *vb* give a colour to

ENCOLOURS > ENCOLOUR

ENCOLPION *n* religious symbol worn on the breast

ENCOLPIUM *variant of* > ENCOLPION

ENCOLURE *n* mane of a horse

ENCOLURES > ENCOLURE

ENCOMIA > ENCOMIUM

ENCOMIAST *n* person who speaks or writes an encomium

ENCOMION *variant of* > ENCOMIUM

ENCOMIUM *n* formal expression of praise

ENCOMIUMS > ENCOMIUM

ENCOMPASS *vb* surround

ENCORE *interj* again, once more ▷ *n* extra performance due to enthusiastic demand ▷ *vb* demand an extra or repeated performance of (a work, piece of music, etc) by (a performer)

ENCORED > ENCORE

ENCORES > ENCORE

ENCORING > ENCORE

ENCOUNTER *vb* meet unexpectedly ▷ *n* unexpected meeting

ENCOURAGE *vb* inspire with confidence

ENCRADLE *vb* put in a cradle

ENCRADLED > ENCRADLE

ENCRADLES > ENCRADLE

ENCRATIES > ENCRATY

ENCRATY *n* control of one's desires, actions, etc

ENCREASE *variant form of* > INCREASE

ENCREASED > ENCREASE

ENCREASES > ENCREASE

ENCRIMSON *vb* make crimson

ENCRINAL > ENCRINITE

ENCRINIC > ENCRINITE

ENCRINITE *n* sedimentary rock formed almost exclusively from the skeletal plates of crinoids

ENCROACH *vb* intrude gradually on a person's rights or land

ENCRUST *vb* cover with a layer of something

ENCRUSTED > ENCRUST

ENCRUSTS > ENCRUST

ENCRYPT *vb* put (a message) into code

ENCRYPTED > ENCRYPT

ENCRYPTS > ENCRYPT

ENCUMBER *vb* hinder or impede

ENCUMBERS > ENCUMBER

ENCURTAIN *vb* cover or surround with curtains

ENCYCLIC *n* letter sent by the Pope to all bishops

ENCYCLICS > ENCYCLIC

ENCYST *vb* enclose or become enclosed by a cyst, thick membrane, or shell

ENCYSTED > ENCYST

ENCYSTING > ENCYST

ENCYSTS > ENCYST

END *n* furthest point or part ▷ *vb* bring or come to a finish

ENDAMAGE *vb* cause injury to

ENDAMAGED > ENDAMAGE

ENDAMAGES > ENDAMAGE

ENDAMEBA *same as* > ENDAMOEBA

ENDAMEBAE > ENDAMEBA

ENDAMEBAS > ENDAMEBA

ENDAMEBIC > ENDAMEBA

ENDAMOEBA *same as* > ENTAMOEBA

ENDANGER *vb* put in danger

ENDANGERS > ENDANGER

ENDARCH *adj* (of a xylem strand) having the first-formed xylem internal to that formed later

ENDARCHY *n* state of being endarch

ENDART *variant of* > INDART

ENDARTED > ENDART

ENDARTING > ENDART

ENDARTS > ENDART

ENDASH *n* short dash in punctuation

ENDASHES > ENDASH

ENDBRAIN *n* part of the brain

ENDBRAINS > ENDBRAIN

ENDEAR *vb* cause to be liked

ENDEARED > ENDEAR

ENDEARING *adj* giving rise to love or esteem

ENDEARS > ENDEAR

ENDEAVOR *same as* > ENDEAVOUR

ENDEAVORS > ENDEAVOR

ENDEAVOUR *vb* try ▷ *n* effort

ENDECAGON *n* figure with eleven sides

ENDED > END

ENDEICTIC > ENDEIXIS

ENDEIXES > ENDEIXIS

ENDEIXIS *n* sign or mark

ENDEMIAL *same as* > ENDEMIC

ENDEMIC *adj* present within a localized area or peculiar to a particular group of people ▷ *n* endemic disease or plant

ENDEMICAL *adj* endemic

ENDEMICS > ENDEMIC

ENDEMISM > ENDEMIC

ENDEMISMS > ENDEMIC

ENDENIZEN *vb* make a denizen

ENDER > END

ENDERMIC *adj* (of a medicine) acting by absorption through the skin

ENDERON *variant of* > ANDIRON

ENDERONS > ENDERON

ENDERS > END

ENDEW *variant of* > ENDUE

ENDEWED > ENDEW

ENDEWING > ENDEW

ENDEWS > ENDEW

ENDEXINE *n* inner layer of an exine

ENDEXINES > ENDEXINE

ENDGAME *n* closing stage of a game of chess, in which only a few pieces are left on the board

ENDGAMES > ENDGAME

ENDING *n* last part or conclusion of something

ENDINGS > ENDING

ENDIRON *variant of* > ANDIRON

ENDIRONS > ENDIRON

ENDITE *variant of* > INDICT

ENDITED > ENDITE

ENDITES > ENDITE

ENDITING > ENDITE

ENDIVE *n* curly-leaved plant used in salads

ENDIVES > ENDIVE

ENDLANG *variant of* > ENDLONG

ENDLEAF *n* endpaper in a book

ENDLEAFS > ENDLEAF

ENDLEAVES > ENDLEAF

ENDLESS *adj* having no end

ENDLESSLY > ENDLESS

ENDLONG *adv* lengthways or on end

ENDMOST *adj* nearest the end

ENDNOTE *n* note at the end of a section of writing

ENDNOTES > ENDNOTE

ENDOBLAST *less common name for* > ENDODERM

ENDOCARP *n* inner, usually woody, layer of the pericarp of a fruit, such as the stone of a peach or cherry

ENDOCARPS > ENDOCARP

ENDOCAST *n* cast made of the inside of a cranial cavity to show the size and shape of a brain

ENDOCASTS > ENDOCAST

ENDOCRINE *adj* relating to the glands which secrete hormones directly into the bloodstream ▷ *n* endocrine gland

ENDOCYTIC *adj* involving absorption of cells

ENDODERM *n* inner germ layer of an animal embryo, which gives rise to the lining of the digestive and respiratory tracts

ENDODERMS > ENDODERM

ENDODYNE *same as* > AUTODYNE

ENDOERGIC *adj* (of a nuclear reaction) occurring with absorption of energy, as opposed to *exoergic*

ENDOGAMIC > ENDOGAMY

ENDOGAMY *n* marriage within one's own tribe or similar unit

ENDOGEN *n* plant that increases in size by internal growth

ENDOGENIC > ENDOGEN

ENDOGENS > ENDOGEN

ENDOGENY *n* development by internal growth

ENDOLYMPH *n* fluid that fills the membranous labyrinth of the internal ear

ENDOMIXES > ENDOMIXIS

ENDOMIXIS *n* reorganization of certain nuclei with some protozoa

ENDOMORPH *n* person with a fat and heavy body build: said to be correlated with viscerotonia

ENDOPHAGY *n* cannibalism

within the same group or tribe

ENDOPHYTE n fungus, or occasionally an alga or other organism, that lives within a plant

ENDOPLASM n inner cytoplasm in some cells, esp protozoa, which is more granular and fluid than the outer cytoplasm

ENDOPOD n inner branch of a two-branched crustacean

ENDOPODS > ENDOPOD

ENDOPROCT n small animal living in water

ENDORPHIN n chemical occurring in the brain, which has a similar effect to morphine

ENDORSE vb give approval to

ENDORSED > ENDORSE

ENDORSEE n person in whose favour a negotiable instrument is endorsed

ENDORSEES > ENDORSEE

ENDORSER > ENDORSE

ENDORSERS > ENDORSE

ENDORSES > ENDORSE

ENDORSING > ENDORSE

ENDORSIVE > ENDORSE

ENDORSOR > ENDORSE

ENDORSORS > ENDORSE

ENDOSARC same as > ENDOPLASM

ENDOSARCS > ENDOSARC

ENDOSCOPE n long slender medical instrument used for examining the interior of hollow organs including the lung, stomach, bladder and bowel

ENDOSCOPY > ENDOSCOPE

ENDOSMOS same as > ENDOSMOSE

ENDOSMOSE n osmosis in which water enters a cell or organism from the surrounding solution

ENDOSOME n sac within a biological cell

ENDOSOMES > ENDOSOME

ENDOSPERM n tissue within the seed of a flowering plant that surrounds and nourishes the developing embryo

ENDOSPORE n small asexual spore produced by some bacteria and algae

ENDOSS vb endorse

ENDOSSED > ENDOSS

ENDOSSES > ENDOSS

ENDOSSING > ENDOSS

ENDOSTEA > ENDOSTEUM

ENDOSTEAL > ENDOSTEUM

ENDOSTEUM n highly vascular membrane lining the marrow cavity of long bones, such as the femur and humerus

ENDOSTYLE n groove or fold in the pharynx of various chordates

ENDOTHERM n animal with warm blood

ENDOTOXIC > ENDOTOXIN

ENDOTOXIN n toxin contained within the protoplasm of an organism, esp a bacterium, and liberated only at death

ENDOW vb provide permanent income for

ENDOWED > ENDOW

ENDOWER > ENDOW

ENDOWERS > ENDOW

ENDOWING > ENDOW

ENDOWMENT n money given to an institution, such as a hospital

ENDOWS > ENDOW

ENDOZOA > ENDOZOON

ENDOZOIC adj (of a plant) living within an animal

ENDOZOON variant of > ENTOZOON

ENDPAPER n either of two leaves at the front and back of a book pasted to the inside of the cover

ENDPAPERS > ENDPAPER

ENDPLATE n any usually flat platelike structure at the end of something

ENDPLATES > ENDPLATE

ENDPLAY n way of playing the last few tricks in a hand so that an opponent is forced to make a particular lead ▷ vb force (an opponent) to make a particular lead near the end of a hand

ENDPLAYED > ENDPLAY

ENDPLAYS > ENDPLAY

ENDPOINT n point at which anything is complete

ENDPOINTS > ENDPOINT

ENDRIN n type of insecticide

ENDRINS > ENDRIN

ENDS > END

ENDSHIP n small village

ENDSHIPS > ENDSHIP

ENDUE vb invest or provide, as with some quality or trait

ENDUED > ENDUE

ENDUES > ENDUE

ENDUING > ENDUE

ENDUNGEON vb put in a dungeon

ENDURABLE > ENDURE

ENDURABLY > ENDURE

ENDURANCE n act or power of enduring

ENDURE vb bear (hardship) patiently

ENDURED > ENDURE

ENDURER > ENDURE

ENDURERS > ENDURE

ENDURES > ENDURE

ENDURING adj long-lasting

ENDURO n long-distance race for vehicles, intended to test endurance

ENDUROS > ENDURO

ENDWAYS adv having the end forwards or upwards ▷ adj vertical or upright

ENDWISE same as > ENDWAYS

ENDYSES > ENDYSIS

ENDYSIS n formation of new layers of integument

after ecdysis

ENE variant of > EVEN

ENEMA n medicine injected into the rectum to empty the bowels

ENEMAS > ENEMA

ENEMATA > ENEMA

ENEMIES > ENEMY

ENEMY n hostile person or nation, opponent ▷ adj of or belonging to an enemy

ENERGETIC adj having or showing energy and enthusiasm

ENERGIC > ENERGY

ENERGID n nucleus and the cytoplasm associated with it in a syncytium

ENERGIDS > ENERGID

ENERGIES > ENERGY

ENERGISE same as > ENERGIZE

ENERGISED > ENERGISE

ENERGISER > ENERGISE

ENERGISES > ENERGISE

ENERGIZE vb give vigour to

ENERGIZED > ENERGIZE

ENERGIZER > ENERGIZE

ENERGIZES > ENERGIZE

ENERGUMEN n person thought to be possessed by an evil spirit

ENERGY n capacity for intense activity

ENERVATE vb deprive of strength or vitality ▷ adj deprived of strength or vitality

ENERVATED > ENERVATE

ENERVATES > ENERVATE

ENERVATOR > ENERVATE

ENERVE vb enervate

ENERVED > ENERVE

ENERVES > ENERVE

ENERVING > ENERVE

ENES > ENE

ENEW vb force a bird into water

ENEWED > ENEW

ENEWING > ENEW

ENEWS > ENEW

ENFACE vb write, print, or stamp (something) on the face of (a document)

ENFACED > ENFACE

ENFACES > ENFACE

ENFACING > ENFACE

ENFANT n French child

ENFANTS > ENFANT

ENFEEBLE vb weaken

ENFEEBLED > ENFEEBLE

ENFEEBLER > ENFEEBLE

ENFEEBLES > ENFEEBLE

ENFELON vb infuriate

ENFELONED > ENFELON

ENFELONS > ENFELON

ENFEOFF vb invest (a person) with possession of a freehold estate in land

ENFEOFFED > ENFEOFF

ENFEOFFS > ENFEOFF

ENFESTED adj made bitter

ENFETTER vb fetter

ENFETTERS > ENFETTER

ENFEVER vb make feverish

ENFEVERED > ENFEVER

ENFEVERS > ENFEVER

ENFIERCE vb make ferocious

ENFIERCED > ENFIERCE

ENFIERCES > ENFIERCE

ENFILADE n burst of gunfire sweeping from end to end along a line of troops ▷ vb attack with an enfilade

ENFILADED > ENFILADE

ENFILADES > ENFILADE

ENFILED adj passed through

ENFIRE vb set alight

ENFIRED > ENFIRE

ENFIRES > ENFIRE

ENFIRING > ENFIRE

ENFIX variant of > INFIX

ENFIXED > ENFIX

ENFIXES > ENFIX

ENFIXING > ENFIX

ENFLAME variant of > INFLAME

ENFLAMED > ENFLAME

ENFLAMES > ENFLAME

ENFLAMING > ENFLAME

ENFLESH vb make flesh

ENFLESHED > ENFLESH

ENFLESHES > ENFLESH

ENFLOWER vb put flowers on

ENFLOWERS > ENFLOWER

ENFOLD vb cover by wrapping something around

ENFOLDED > ENFOLD

ENFOLDER > ENFOLD

ENFOLDERS > ENFOLD

ENFOLDING > ENFOLD

ENFOLDS > ENFOLD

ENFORCE vb impose obedience (to a law etc)

ENFORCED > ENFORCE

ENFORCER > ENFORCE

ENFORCERS > ENFORCE

ENFORCES > ENFORCE

ENFORCING > ENFORCE

ENFOREST vb make into a forest

ENFORESTS > ENFOREST

ENFORM variant of > INFORM

ENFORMED > ENFORM

ENFORMING > ENFORM

ENFORMS > ENFORM

ENFRAME vb put inside a frame

ENFRAMED > ENFRAME

ENFRAMES > ENFRAME

ENFRAMING > ENFRAME

ENFREE vb release, make free

ENFREED > ENFREE

ENFREEDOM variant of > ENFREE

ENFREEING > ENFREE

ENFREES > ENFREE

ENFREEZE vb freeze

ENFREEZES > ENFREEZE

ENFROSEN > ENFREEZE

ENFROZE > ENFREEZE

ENFROZEN > ENFREEZE

ENG another name for > AGMA

ENGAGE vb take part, participate ▷ adj (of a writer or artist, esp a man) morally or politically committed to some ideology

ENGAGED adj pledged to be

married
ENGAGEDLY > ENGAGED
ENGAGEE *adj* (of a female writer or artist) morally or politically committed to some ideology
ENGAGER > ENGAGE
ENGAGERS > ENGAGE
ENGAGES > ENGAGE
ENGAGING *adj* charming
ENGAOL *vb* put into gaol
ENGAOLED > ENGAOL
ENGAOLING > ENGAOL
ENGAOLS > ENGAOL
ENGARLAND *vb* cover with garlands
ENGENDER *vb* produce, cause to occur
ENGENDERS > ENGENDER
ENGENDURE > ENGENDER
ENGILD *vb* cover with or as if with gold
ENGILDED > ENGILD
ENGILDING > ENGILD
ENGILDS > ENGILD
ENGILT > ENGILD
ENGINE *n* any machine which converts energy into mechanical work ▷ *vb* put an engine in
ENGINED > ENGINE
ENGINEER *n* person trained in any branch of engineering ▷ *vb* plan in a clever manner
ENGINEERS > ENGINEER
ENGINER > ENGINE
ENGINERS > ENGINE
ENGINERY *n* collection or assembly of engines
ENGINES > ENGINE
ENGINING > ENGINE
ENGINOUS *adj* ingenious or clever
ENGIRD *vb* surround
ENGIRDED > ENGIRD
ENGIRDING > ENGIRD
ENGIRDLE *variant of* > ENGIRD
ENGIRDLED > ENGIRDLE
ENGIRDLES > ENGIRDLE
ENGIRDS > ENGIRD
ENGIRT > ENGIRD
ENGISCOPE *variant of* > ENGYSCOPE
ENGLACIAL *adj* embedded in, carried by, or running through a glacier
ENGLISH *vb* put a spinning movement on a billiard ball
ENGLISHED > ENGLISH
ENGLISHES > ENGLISH
ENGLOBE *vb* surround as if in a globe
ENGLOBED > ENGLOBE
ENGLOBES > ENGLOBE
ENGLOBING > ENGLOBE
ENGLOOM *vb* make dull or dismal
ENGLOOMED > ENGLOOM
ENGLOOMS > ENGLOOM
ENGLUT *vb* devour ravenously
ENGLUTS > ENGLUT
ENGLUTTED > ENGLUT
ENGOBE *n* liquid put on pottery before glazing

ENGOBES > ENGOBE
ENGORE *vb* pierce or wound
ENGORED > ENGORE
ENGORES > ENGORE
ENGORGE *vb* clog with blood
ENGORGED > ENGORGE
ENGORGES > ENGORGE
ENGORGING > ENGORGE
ENGORING > ENGORE
ENGOULED *adj* (in heraldry) with ends coming from the mouths of animals
ENGOUMENT *n* obsessive liking
ENGRACE *vb* give grace to
ENGRACED > ENGRACE
ENGRACES > ENGRACE
ENGRACING > ENGRACE
ENGRAFF *variant of* > ENGRAFT
ENGRAFFED > ENGRAFF
ENGRAFFS > ENGRAFF
ENGRAFT *vb* graft (a shoot, bud, etc) onto a stock
ENGRAFTED > ENGRAFT
ENGRAFTS > ENGRAFT
ENGRAIL *vb* decorate or mark (the edge of) (a coin) with small carved notches
ENGRAILED > ENGRAIL
ENGRAILS > ENGRAIL
ENGRAIN *variant spelling of* > INGRAIN
ENGRAINED > ENGRAIN
ENGRAINER > ENGRAIN
ENGRAINS > ENGRAIN
ENGRAM *n* physical basis of an individual memory in the brain
ENGRAMMA *variant of* > ENGRAM
ENGRAMMAS > ENGRAMMA
ENGRAMME *variant of* > ENGRAM
ENGRAMMES > ENGRAMME
ENGRAMMIC > ENGRAM
ENGRAMS > ENGRAM
ENGRASP *vb* grasp or seize
ENGRASPED > ENGRASP
ENGRASPS > ENGRASP
ENGRAVE *vb* carve (a design) onto a hard surface
ENGRAVED > ENGRAVE
ENGRAVEN > ENGRAVE
ENGRAVER > ENGRAVE
ENGRAVERS > ENGRAVE
ENGRAVERY > ENGRAVE
ENGRAVES > ENGRAVE
ENGRAVING *n* print made from an engraved plate
ENGRENAGE *n* act of putting into gear
ENGRIEVE *vb* grieve
ENGRIEVED > ENGRIEVE
ENGRIEVES > ENGRIEVE
ENGROOVE *vb* put a groove in
ENGROOVED > ENGROOVE
ENGROOVES > ENGROOVE
ENGROSS *vb* occupy the attention of (a person) completely
ENGROSSED > ENGROSS
ENGROSSER > ENGROSS
ENGROSSES > ENGROSS
ENGS > ENG
ENGUARD *vb* protect or defend

ENGUARDED > ENGUARD
ENGUARDS > ENGUARD
ENGULF *vb* cover or surround completely
ENGULFED > ENGULF
ENGULFING > ENGULF
ENGULFS > ENGULF
ENGULPH *variant of* > ENGULF
ENGULPHED > ENGULPH
ENGULPHS > ENGULPH
ENGYSCOPE *n* microscope
ENHALO *vb* surround with or as if with a halo
ENHALOED > ENHALO
ENHALOES > ENHALO
ENHALOING > ENHALO
ENHALOS > ENHALO
ENHANCE *vb* increase in quality, value, or attractiveness
ENHANCED > ENHANCE
ENHANCER > ENHANCE
ENHANCERS > ENHANCE
ENHANCES > ENHANCE
ENHANCING > ENHANCE
ENHANCIVE > ENHANCE
ENHEARSE *variant of* > INHEARSE
ENHEARSED > ENHEARSE
ENHEARSES > ENHEARSE
ENHEARTEN *vb* give heart to, encourage
ENHUNGER *vb* cause to be hungry
ENHUNGERS > ENHUNGER
ENHYDRITE *n* type of mineral
ENHYDROS *n* piece of chalcedony that contains water
ENHYDROUS > ENHYDROS
ENIAC *n* early type of computer built in the 1940s
ENIACS > ENIAC
ENIGMA *n* puzzling thing or person
ENIGMAS > ENIGMA
ENIGMATA > ENIGMA
ENIGMATIC > ENIGMA
ENISLE *vb* put on or make into an island
ENISLED > ENISLE
ENISLES > ENISLE
ENISLING > ENISLE
ENJAMB *vb* (of a line of verse) run over into the next line
ENJAMBED > ENJAMB
ENJAMBING > ENJAMB
ENJAMBS > ENJAMB
ENJOIN *vb* order (someone) to do something
ENJOINDER *n* order
ENJOINED > ENJOIN
ENJOINER > ENJOIN
ENJOINERS > ENJOIN
ENJOINING > ENJOIN
ENJOINS > ENJOIN
ENJOY *vb* take joy in
ENJOYABLE > ENJOY
ENJOYABLY > ENJOY
ENJOYED > ENJOY
ENJOYER > ENJOY
ENJOYERS > ENJOY
ENJOYING > ENJOY
ENJOYMENT *n* act or condition of receiving

pleasure from something
ENJOYS > ENJOY
ENKERNEL *vb* put inside a kernel
ENKERNELS > ENKERNEL
ENKINDLE *vb* set on fire
ENKINDLED > ENKINDLE
ENKINDLER > ENKINDLE
ENKINDLES > ENKINDLE
ENLACE *vb* bind or encircle with or as with laces
ENLACED > ENLACE
ENLACES > ENLACE
ENLACING > ENLACE
ENLARD *vb* put lard on
ENLARDED > ENLARD
ENLARDING > ENLARD
ENLARDS > ENLARD
ENLARGE *vb* make or grow larger
ENLARGED > ENLARGE
ENLARGEN *variant of* > ENLARGE
ENLARGENS > ENLARGEN
ENLARGER *n* optical instrument for making enlarged photographic prints in which a negative is brightly illuminated and its enlarged image is focused onto a sheet of sensitized paper
ENLARGERS > ENLARGER
ENLARGES > ENLARGE
ENLARGING > ENLARGE
ENLEVE *adj* having been abducted
ENLIGHT *vb* light up
ENLIGHTED > ENLIGHT
ENLIGHTEN *vb* give information to
ENLIGHTS > ENLIGHT
ENLINK *vb* link together
ENLINKED > ENLINK
ENLINKING > ENLINK
ENLINKS > ENLINK
ENLIST *vb* enter the armed forces
ENLISTED > ENLIST
ENLISTEE > ENLIST
ENLISTEES > ENLIST
ENLISTER > ENLIST
ENLISTERS > ENLIST
ENLISTING > ENLIST
ENLISTS > ENLIST
ENLIT > ENLIGHT
ENLIVEN *vb* make lively or cheerful
ENLIVENED > ENLIVEN
ENLIVENER > ENLIVEN
ENLIVENS > ENLIVEN
ENLOCK *vb* lock or secure
ENLOCKED > ENLOCK
ENLOCKING > ENLOCK
ENLOCKS > ENLOCK
ENLUMINE *vb* illuminate
ENLUMINED > ENLUMINE
ENLUMINES > ENLUMINE
ENMESH *vb* catch or involve in or as if in a net or snare
ENMESHED > ENMESH
ENMESHES > ENMESH
ENMESHING > ENMESH
ENMEW *variant of* > EMMEW
ENMEWED > ENMEW
ENMEWING > ENMEW
ENMEWS > ENMEW

ENMITIES > ENMITY
ENMITY n ill will, hatred
ENMOSSED adj having a covering of moss
ENMOVE variant of > EMMOVE
ENMOVED > ENMOVE
ENMOVES > ENMOVE
ENMOVING > ENMOVE
ENNAGE n total number of ens in a piece of matter to be set in type
ENNAGES > ENNAGE
ENNEAD n group or series of nine
ENNEADIC > ENNEAD
ENNEADS > ENNEAD
ENNEAGON another name for > NONAGON
ENNEAGONS > ENNEAGON
ENNOBLE vb make noble, elevate
ENNOBLED > ENNOBLE
ENNOBLER > ENNOBLE
ENNOBLERS > ENNOBLE
ENNOBLES > ENNOBLE
ENNOBLING > ENNOBLE
ENNOG n back alley
ENNOGS > ENNOG
ENNUI n boredom, dissatisfaction ▷ vb bore
ENNUIED > ENNUI
ENNUIS > ENNUI
ENNUYE adj bored
ENNUYED > ENNUI
ENNUYEE same as > ENNUYE
ENNUYING > ENNUI
ENODAL adj having no nodes
ENOKI variant of > ENOKITAKE
ENOKIDAKE variant of > ENOKITAKE
ENOKIS > ENOKI
ENOKITAKE n Japanese mushroom
ENOL n any organic compound containing the group -CH:CO-, often existing in chemical equilibrium with the corresponding keto form
ENOLASE n type of enzyme
ENOLASES > ENOLASE
ENOLIC > ENOL
ENOLOGIES > ENOLOGY
ENOLOGIST n wine expert
ENOLOGY usual US spelling of > OENOLOGY
ENOLS > ENOL
ENOMOTIES > ENOMOTY
ENOMOTY n division of the Spartan army in ancient Greece
ENOPHILE n lover of wine
ENOPHILES > ENOPHILE
ENORM variant of > ENORMOUS
ENORMITY n great wickedness
ENORMOUS adj very big, vast
ENOSES > ENOSIS
ENOSIS n union of Greece and Cyprus
ENOSISES > ENOSIS
ENOUGH adj as much or as many as necessary ▷ n sufficient quantity ▷ adv sufficiently

ENOUGHS > ENOUGH
ENOUNCE vb enunciate
ENOUNCED > ENOUNCE
ENOUNCES > ENOUNCE
ENOUNCING > ENOUNCE
ENOW archaic word for > ENOUGH
ENOWS > ENOW
ENPLANE vb board an aircraft
ENPLANED > ENPLANE
ENPLANES > ENPLANE
ENPLANING > ENPLANE
ENPRINT n standard photographic print produced from a negative
ENPRINTS > ENPRINT
ENQUIRE same as > INQUIRE
ENQUIRED > ENQUIRE
ENQUIRER > ENQUIRE
ENQUIRERS > ENQUIRE
ENQUIRES > ENQUIRE
ENQUIRIES > ENQUIRE
ENQUIRING > ENQUIRE
ENQUIRY > ENQUIRE
ENRACE vb bring in a race of people
ENRACED > ENRACE
ENRACES > ENRACE
ENRACING > ENRACE
ENRAGE vb make extremely angry
ENRAGED > ENRAGE
ENRAGEDLY > ENRAGE
ENRAGES > ENRAGE
ENRAGING > ENRAGE
ENRANCKLE vb upset, make irate
ENRANGE vb arrange, organize
ENRANGED > ENRANGE
ENRANGES > ENRANGE
ENRANGING > ENRANGE
ENRANK vb put in a row
ENRANKED > ENRANK
ENRANKING > ENRANK
ENRANKS > ENRANK
ENRAPT > ENRAPTURE
ENRAPTURE vb fill with delight
ENRAUNGE variant of > ENRANGE
ENRAUNGED > ENRAUNGE
ENRAUNGES > ENRAUNGE
ENRAVISH vb enchant
ENRHEUM vb pass a cold on to
ENRHEUMED > ENRHEUM
ENRHEUMS > ENRHEUM
ENRICH vb improve in quality
ENRICHED > ENRICH
ENRICHER > ENRICH
ENRICHERS > ENRICH
ENRICHES > ENRICH
ENRICHING > ENRICH
ENRIDGED adj ridged
ENRING vb put a ring round
ENRINGED > ENRING
ENRINGING > ENRING
ENRINGS > ENRING
ENRIVEN adj ripped
ENROBE vb dress in or as if in a robe
ENROBED > ENROBE
ENROBER > ENROBE
ENROBERS > ENROBE

ENROBES > ENROBE
ENROBING > ENROBE
ENROL vb (cause to) become a member
ENROLL same as > ENROL
ENROLLED > ENROLL
ENROLLEE > ENROL
ENROLLEES > ENROL
ENROLLER > ENROL
ENROLLERS > ENROL
ENROLLING > ENROLL
ENROLLS > ENROLL
ENROLMENT n act of enrolling or state of being enrolled
ENROLS > ENROL
ENROOT vb establish (plants) by fixing their roots in the earth
ENROOTED > ENROOT
ENROOTING > ENROOT
ENROOTS > ENROOT
ENROUGH vb roughen
ENROUGHED > ENROUGH
ENROUGHS > ENROUGH
ENROUND vb encircle
ENROUNDED > ENROUND
ENROUNDS > ENROUND
ENS n being or existence in the most general abstract sense
ENSAMPLE n example ▷ vb make an example
ENSAMPLED > ENSAMPLE
ENSAMPLES > ENSAMPLE
ENSATE adj shaped like a sword
ENSCONCE vb settle firmly or comfortably
ENSCONCED > ENSCONCE
ENSCONCES > ENSCONCE
ENSCROLL variant of > INSCROLL
ENSCROLLS > ENSCROLL
ENSEAL vb seal up
ENSEALED > ENSEAL
ENSEALING > ENSEAL
ENSEALS > ENSEAL
ENSEAM vb put a seam on
ENSEAMED > ENSEAM
ENSEAMING > ENSEAM
ENSEAMS > ENSEAM
ENSEAR vb dry
ENSEARED > ENSEAR
ENSEARING > ENSEAR
ENSEARS > ENSEAR
ENSEMBLE n all the parts of something taken together ▷ adv all together or at once ▷ adj (of a film or play) involving several separate but often interrelated story lines
ENSEMBLES > ENSEMBLE
ENSERF vb enslave
ENSERFED > ENSERF
ENSERFING > ENSERF
ENSERFS > ENSERF
ENSEW variant of > ENSUE
ENSEWED > ENSEW
ENSEWING > ENSEW
ENSEWS > ENSEW
ENSHEATH variant of > INSHEATHE
ENSHEATHE variant of > INSHEATHE
ENSHEATHS > ENSHEATH

ENSHELL variant of > INSHELL
ENSHELLED > ENSHELL
ENSHELLS > ENSHELL
ENSHELTER vb shelter
ENSHIELD vb protect
ENSHIELDS > ENSHIELD
ENSHRINE vb cherish or treasure
ENSHRINED > ENSHRINE
ENSHRINEE > ENSHRINE
ENSHRINES > ENSHRINE
ENSHROUD vb cover or hide as with a shroud
ENSHROUDS > ENSHROUD
ENSIFORM adj shaped like a sword blade
ENSIGN n naval flag ▷ vb mark with a sign
ENSIGNCY > ENSIGN
ENSIGNED > ENSIGN
ENSIGNING > ENSIGN
ENSIGNS > ENSIGN
ENSILAGE n process of ensiling green fodder ▷ vb make into silage
ENSILAGED > ENSILAGE
ENSILAGES > ENSILAGE
ENSILE vb store and preserve (green fodder) in an enclosed pit or silo
ENSILED > ENSILE
ENSILES > ENSILE
ENSILING > ENSILE
ENSKIED > ENSKY
ENSKIES > ENSKY
ENSKY vb put in the sky
ENSKYED > ENSKY
ENSKYING > ENSKY
ENSLAVE vb make a slave of (someone)
ENSLAVED > ENSLAVE
ENSLAVER > ENSLAVE
ENSLAVERS > ENSLAVE
ENSLAVES > ENSLAVE
ENSLAVING > ENSLAVE
ENSNARE vb catch in or as if in a snare
ENSNARED > ENSNARE
ENSNARER > ENSNARE
ENSNARERS > ENSNARE
ENSNARES > ENSNARE
ENSNARING > ENSNARE
ENSNARL vb become tangled in
ENSNARLED > ENSNARL
ENSNARLS > ENSNARL
ENSORCEL vb enchant
ENSORCELL variant of > ENSORCEL
ENSORCELS > ENSORCEL
ENSOUL vb endow with a soul
ENSOULED > ENSOUL
ENSOULING > ENSOUL
ENSOULS > ENSOUL
ENSPHERE vb enclose in or as if in a sphere
ENSPHERED > ENSPHERE
ENSPHERES > ENSPHERE
ENSTAMP vb imprint with a stamp
ENSTAMPED > ENSTAMP
ENSTAMPS > ENSTAMP
ENSTATITE n grey, green, yellow, or brown pyroxene mineral consisting of

magnesium silicate in orthorhombic crystalline form

ENSTEEP *vb* soak in water
ENSTEEPED > ENSTEEP
ENSTEEPS > ENSTEEP
ENSTYLE *vb* give a name to
ENSTYLED > ENSTYLE
ENSTYLES > ENSTYLE
ENSTYLING > ENSTYLE
ENSUE *vb* come next, result
ENSUED > ENSUE
ENSUES > ENSUE
ENSUING *adj* following subsequently or in order
ENSURE *vb* make certain or sure
ENSURED > ENSURE
ENSURER > ENSURE
ENSURERS > ENSURE
ENSURES > ENSURE
ENSURING > ENSURE
ENSWATHE *vb* bind or wrap
ENSWATHED > ENSWATHE
ENSWATHES > ENSWATHE
ENSWEEP *vb* sweep across
ENSWEEPS > ENSWEEP
ENSWEPT > ENSWEEP
ENTAIL *vb* bring about or impose inevitably ▷ *n* restriction imposed by entailing an estate
ENTAILED > ENTAIL
ENTAILER > ENTAIL
ENTAILERS > ENTAIL
ENTAILING > ENTAIL
ENTAILS > ENTAIL
ENTAME *vb* make tame
ENTAMEBA *same as* > ENTAMOEBA
ENTAMEBAE > ENTAMEBA
ENTAMEBAS > ENTAMEBA
ENTAMED > ENTAME
ENTAMES > ENTAME
ENTAMING > ENTAME
ENTAMOEBA *n* parasitic amoeba that lives in the intestines of man and causes amoebic dysentery
ENTANGLE *vb* catch or involve in or as if in a tangle
ENTANGLED > ENTANGLE
ENTANGLER > ENTANGLE
ENTANGLES > ENTANGLE
ENTASES > ENTASIS
ENTASIA *same as* > ENTASIS
ENTASIAS > ENTASIA
ENTASIS *n* slightly convex curve given to the shaft of a column, pier, or similar structure, to correct the illusion of concavity produced by a straight shaft
ENTASTIC *adj* (of a disease) characterized by spasms
ENTAYLE *variant of* > ENTAIL
ENTAYLED > ENTAYLE
ENTAYLES > ENTAYLE
ENTAYLING > ENTAYLE
ENTELECHY *n* (in the philosophy of Aristotle) actuality as opposed to potentiality
ENTELLUS *n* langur of S Asia
ENTENDER *vb* make more tender

ENTENDERS > ENTENDER
ENTENTE *n* friendly understanding between nations
ENTENTES > ENTENTE
ENTER *vb* come or go in
ENTERA > ENTERON
ENTERABLE > ENTER
ENTERAL *same as* > ENTERIC
ENTERALLY > ENTERIC
ENTERATE *adj* with an intestine separate from the outer wall of the body
ENTERED > ENTER
ENTERER > ENTER
ENTERERS > ENTER
ENTERIC *adj* intestinal ▷ *n* infectious disease of the intestines
ENTERICS > ENTERIC
ENTERING > ENTER
ENTERINGS > ENTER
ENTERITIS *n* inflammation of the intestine, causing diarrhoea
ENTERON *n* alimentary canal, esp of an embryo or a coelenterate
ENTERONS > ENTERON
ENTERS > ENTER
ENTERTAIN *vb* amuse
ENTERTAKE *vb* entertain
ENTERTOOK > ENTERTAKE
ENTETE *adj* obsessed
ENTETEE *variant of* > ENTETE
ENTHALPY *n* thermodynamic property of a system equal to the sum of its internal energy and the product of its pressure and volume
ENTHETIC *adj* (esp of infectious diseases) introduced into the body from without
ENTHRAL *vb* hold the attention of
ENTHRALL *same as* > ENTHRAL
ENTHRALLS > ENTHRALL
ENTHRALS > ENTHRAL
ENTHRONE *vb* place (someone) on a throne
ENTHRONED > ENTHRONE
ENTHRONES > ENTHRONE
ENTHUSE *vb* (cause to) show enthusiasm
ENTHUSED > ENTHUSE
ENTHUSES > ENTHUSE
ENTHUSING > ENTHUSE
ENTHYMEME *n* incomplete syllogism, in which one or more premises are unexpressed as their truth is considered to be self-evident
ENTIA > ENS
ENTICE *vb* attract by exciting hope or desire, tempt
ENTICED > ENTICE
ENTICER > ENTICE
ENTICERS > ENTICE
ENTICES > ENTICE
ENTICING > ENTICE
ENTICINGS > ENTICE
ENTIRE *adj* including every

detail, part, or aspect of something ▷ *n* state of being entire
ENTIRELY *adv* without reservation or exception
ENTIRES > ENTIRE
ENTIRETY *n* state of being entire or whole
ENTITIES > ENTITY
ENTITLE *vb* give a right to
ENTITLED > ENTITLE
ENTITLES > ENTITLE
ENTITLING > ENTITLE
ENTITY *n* separate distinct thing
ENTOBLAST *less common name for* > ENDODERM
ENTODERM *same as* > ENDODERM
ENTODERMS > ENTODERM
ENTOIL *archaic word for* > ENSNARE
ENTOILED > ENTOIL
ENTOILING > ENTOIL
ENTOILS > ENTOIL
ENTOMB *vb* place (a corpse) in a tomb
ENTOMBED > ENTOMB
ENTOMBING > ENTOMB
ENTOMBS > ENTOMB
ENTOMIC *adj* denoting or relating to insects
ENTOPHYTE *variant of* > ENDOPHYTE
ENTOPIC *adj* situated in its normal place or position
ENTOPROCT *n* type of marine animal
ENTOPTIC *adj* (of visual sensation) resulting from structures within the eye itself
ENTOPTICS *n* study of entoptic visions
ENTOTIC *adj* of or relating to the inner ear
ENTOURAGE *n* group of people who assist an important person
ENTOZOA > ENTOZOON
ENTOZOAL > ENTOZOON
ENTOZOAN *same as* > ENTOZOON
ENTOZOANS > ENTOZOAN
ENTOZOIC *adj* of or relating to an entozoon
ENTOZOON *n* internal parasite
ENTRAIL *vb* twist or entangle
ENTRAILED > ENTRAIL
ENTRAILS *pl n* intestines
ENTRAIN *vb* board or put aboard a train
ENTRAINED > ENTRAIN
ENTRAINER > ENTRAIN
ENTRAINS > ENTRAIN
ENTRALL *variant of* > ENTRAILS
ENTRALLES *variant of* > ENTRAILS
ENTRAMMEL *vb* hamper or obstruct by entangling
ENTRANCE *n* way into a place ▷ *vb* delight ▷ *adj* necessary in order to enter something

ENTRANCED > ENTRANCE
ENTRANCES > ENTRANCE
ENTRANT *n* person who enters a university, contest, etc
ENTRANTS > ENTRANT
ENTRAP *vb* trick into difficulty etc
ENTRAPPED > ENTRAP
ENTRAPPER > ENTRAP
ENTRAPS > ENTRAP
ENTREAT *vb* ask earnestly
ENTREATED > ENTREAT
ENTREATS > ENTREAT
ENTREATY *n* earnest request
ENTRECHAT *n* leap in ballet during which the dancer repeatedly crosses his feet or beats them together
ENTRECOTE *n* beefsteak cut from between the ribs
ENTREE *n* dish served before a main course
ENTREES > ENTREE
ENTREMES *variant of* > ENTREMETS
ENTREMETS *n* dessert
ENTRENCH *vb* establish firmly
ENTREPOT *n* warehouse for commercial goods
ENTREPOTS > ENTREPOT
ENTRESOL *another name for* > MEZZANINE
ENTRESOLS > ENTRESOL
ENTREZ *interj* enter
ENTRIES > ENTRY
ENTRISM *variant of* > ENTRYISM
ENTRISMS > ENTRISM
ENTRIST > ENTRYISM
ENTRISTS > ENTRYISM
ENTROLD *adj* surrounded
ENTROPIC > ENTROPY
ENTROPIES > ENTROPY
ENTROPION *n* turning inwards of the edge of the eyelid
ENTROPIUM *variant of* > ENTROPION
ENTROPY *n* lack of organization
ENTRUST *vb* put into the care or protection of
ENTRUSTED > ENTRUST
ENTRUSTS > ENTRUST
ENTRY *n* entrance ▷ *adj* necessary in order to enter something
ENTRYISM *n* policy or practice of members of a particular political group joining an existing political party with the intention of changing its principles and policies, instead of forming a new party
ENTRYISMS > ENTRYISM
ENTRYIST > ENTRYISM
ENTRYISTS > ENTRYISM
ENTRYWAY *n* entrance passage
ENTRYWAYS > ENTRYWAY
ENTWINE *vb* twist together or around
ENTWINED > ENTWINE

e

ENTWINES > ENTWINE

ENTWINING > ENTWINE

ENTWIST *vb* twist together or around

ENTWISTED > ENTWIST

ENTWISTS > ENTWIST

ENUCLEATE *vb* remove the nucleus from (a cell) ▷ *adj* (of cells) deprived of their nuclei

ENUF *common intentional literary misspelling of* > ENOUGH

ENUMERATE *vb* name one by one

ENUNCIATE *vb* pronounce clearly

ENURE *variant spelling of* > INURE

ENURED > ENURE

ENUREMENT > ENURE

ENURES > ENURE

ENURESES > ENURESIS

ENURESIS *n* involuntary discharge of urine, esp during sleep

ENURETIC > ENURESIS

ENURETICS > ENURESIS

ENURING > ENURE

ENVASSAL *vb* make a vassal of

ENVASSALS > ENVASSAL

ENVAULT *vb* enclose in a vault; entomb

ENVAULTED > ENVAULT

ENVAULTS > ENVAULT

ENVEIGLE *same as* > INVEIGLE

ENVEIGLED > ENVEIGLE

ENVEIGLES > ENVEIGLE

ENVELOP *vb* wrap up, enclose

ENVELOPE *n* folded gummed paper cover for a letter

ENVELOPED > ENVELOP

ENVELOPER > ENVELOP

ENVELOPES > ENVELOPE

ENVELOPS > ENVELOP

ENVENOM *vb* fill or impregnate with venom

ENVENOMED > ENVENOM

ENVENOMS > ENVENOM

ENVERMEIL *vb* dye vermilion

ENVIABLE *adj* arousing envy, fortunate

ENVIABLY > ENVIABLE

ENVIED > ENVY

ENVIER > ENVY

ENVIERS > ENVY

ENVIES > ENVY

ENVIOUS *adj* full of envy

ENVIOUSLY > ENVIOUS

ENVIRO *n* environmentalist

ENVIRON *vb* encircle or surround

ENVIRONED > ENVIRON

ENVIRONS *pl n* surrounding area, esp of a town

ENVIROS > ENVIRO

ENVISAGE *vb* conceive of as a possibility

ENVISAGED > ENVISAGE

ENVISAGES > ENVISAGE

ENVISION *vb* conceive of as a possibility, esp in the future

ENVISIONS > ENVISION

ENVOI *same as* > ENVOY

ENVOIS > ENVOI

ENVOY *n* messenger

ENVOYS > ENVOY

ENVOYSHIP > ENVOY

ENVY *n* feeling of discontent aroused by another's good fortune ▷ *vb* grudge (another's good fortune, success, or qualities)

ENVYING > ENVY

ENVYINGLY > ENVY

ENVYINGS > ENVY

ENWALL *vb* wall in

ENWALLED > ENWALL

ENWALLING > ENWALL

ENWALLOW *vb* sink or plunge

ENWALLOWS > ENWALLOW

ENWALLS > ENWALL

ENWHEEL *archaic word for* > ENCIRCLE

ENWHEELED > ENWHEEL

ENWHEELS > ENWHEEL

ENWIND *vb* wind or coil around

ENWINDING > ENWIND

ENWINDS > ENWIND

ENWOMB *vb* enclose in or as if in a womb

ENWOMBED > ENWOMB

ENWOMBING > ENWOMB

ENWOMBS > ENWOMB

ENWOUND > ENWIND

ENWRAP *vb* wrap or cover up

ENWRAPPED > ENWRAP

ENWRAPS > ENWRAP

ENWREATH *vb* surround or encircle with or as with a wreath or wreaths

ENWREATHE *same as* > ENWREATH

ENWREATHS > ENWREATH

ENZIAN *n* gentian violet

ENZIANS > ENZIAN

ENZONE *vb* enclose in a zone

ENZONED > ENZONE

ENZONES > ENZONE

ENZONING > ENZONE

ENZOOTIC *adj* (of diseases) affecting animals within a limited region ▷ *n* enzootic disease

ENZOOTICS > ENZOOTIC

ENZYM *same as* > ENZYME

ENZYMATIC > ENZYME

ENZYME *n* any of a group of complex proteins that act as catalysts in specific biochemical reactions

ENZYMES > ENZYME

ENZYMIC > ENZYME

ENZYMS > ENZYM

EOAN *adj* of or relating to the dawn

EOBIONT *n* hypothetical chemical precursor of a living cell

EOBIONTS > EOBIONT

EOCENE *adj* of, denoting, or formed in the second epoch of the Tertiary period

EOHIPPUS *n* earliest horse: an extinct Eocene dog-sized animal of the genus with four-toed forelegs, three-toed hindlegs, and teeth specialized for browsing

EOLIAN *adj* of or relating to the wind

EOLIENNE *n* type of fine cloth

EOLIENNES > EOLIENNE

EOLIPILE *variant of* > AEOLIPILE

EOLIPILES > EOLIPILE

EOLITH *n* stone, usually crudely broken, used as a primitive tool in Eolithic times

EOLITHIC > EOLITH

EOLITHS > EOLITH

EOLOPILE *variant of* > AEOLIPILE

EOLOPILES > EOLOPILE

EON *n* longest division of geological time, comprising two or more eras

EONIAN *adj* of or relating to an eon

EONISM *n* adoption of female dress and behaviour by a male

EONISMS > EONISM

EONS > EON

EORL *n* Anglo-Saxon nobleman

EORLS > EORL

EOSIN *n* red crystalline water-insoluble derivative of fluorescein

EOSINE *same as* > EOSIN

EOSINES > EOSINE

EOSINIC > EOSIN

EOSINS > EOSIN

EOTHEN *adv* from the East

EPACRID *n* type of heath-like plant

EPACRIDS > EPACRID

EPACRIS *n* genus of the epacrids

EPACRISES > EPACRIS

EPACT *n* difference in time, about 11 days, between the solar year and the lunar year

EPACTS > EPACT

EPAENETIC *adj* eulogistic

EPAGOGE *n* inductive reasoning

EPAGOGES > EPAGOGE

EPAGOGIC > EPAGOGE

EPANODOS *n* return to main theme after a digression

EPARCH *n* bishop or metropolitan in charge of an eparchy

EPARCHATE *same as* > EPARCHY

EPARCHIAL > EPARCHY

EPARCHIES > EPARCHY

EPARCHS > EPARCH

EPARCHY *n* diocese of the Eastern Christian Church

EPATANT *adj* startling or shocking, esp through being unconventional

EPAULE *n* shoulder of a fortification

EPAULES > EPAULE

EPAULET *same as* > EPAULETTE

EPAULETS > EPAULET

EPAULETTE *n* shoulder ornament on a uniform

EPAXIAL *adj* above the axis

EPAZOTE *n* type of herb

EPAZOTES > EPAZOTE

EPEDAPHIC *adj* of or relating to atmospheric conditions

EPEE *n* straight-bladed sword used in fencing

EPEEIST *n* one who uses or specializes in using an epee

EPEEISTS > EPEEIST

EPEES > EPEE

EPEIRA *same as* > EPEIRID

EPEIRAS > EPEIRA

EPEIRIC *adj* in, of, or relating to a continent

EPEIRID *n* type of spider

EPEIRIDS > EPEIRID

EPENDYMA *n* membrane lining the ventricles of the brain and the central canal of the spinal cord

EPENDYMAL > EPENDYMA

EPENDYMAS > EPENDYMA

EPEOLATRY *n* worship of words

EPERDU *adj* distracted

EPERDUE *adj* distracted

EPERGNE *n* ornamental centrepiece for a table: a stand with holders for sweetmeats, fruit, flowers, etc

EPERGNES > EPERGNE

EPHA *same as* > EPHAH

EPHAH *n* Hebrew unit of dry measure equal to approximately one bushel or about 33 litres

EPHAHS > EPHAH

EPHAS > EPHA

EPHEBE *n* (in ancient Greece) youth about to enter full citizenship, esp one undergoing military training

EPHEBES > EPHEBE

EPHEBI > EPHEBE

EPHEBIC > EPHEBE

EPHEBOI > EPHEBOS

EPHEBOS *same as* > EPHEBE

EPHEBUS *same as* > EPHEBE

EPHEDRA *n* gymnosperm shrub of warm regions of America and Eurasia

EPHEDRAS > EPHEDRA

EPHEDRIN *same as* > EPHEDRINE

EPHEDRINE *n* alkaloid used for treatment of asthma and hay fever

EPHEDRINS > EPHEDRIN

EPHELIDES > EPHELIS

EPHELIS *n* freckle

EPHEMERA *n* something transitory or short-lived

EPHEMERAE > EPHEMERA

EPHEMERAL *adj* short-lived ▷ *n* short-lived organism, such as the mayfly

EPHEMERAS > EPHEMERA

EPHEMERID *n* mayfly

EPHEMERIS *n* table giving

the future positions of a planet, comet, or satellite

EPHEMERON > EPHEMERA

EPHIALTES *n* incubus

EPHOD *n* embroidered vestment believed to resemble an apron with shoulder straps, worn by priests in ancient Israel

EPHODS > EPHOD

EPHOR *n* (in ancient Greece) one of a board of senior magistrates in any of several Dorian states, esp the five Spartan ephors, who were elected by the vote of all full citizens and who wielded effective power

EPHORAL > EPHOR

EPHORALTY > EPHOR

EPHORATE > EPHOR

EPHORATES > EPHOR

EPHORI > EPHOR

EPHORS > EPHOR

EPIBIOSES > EPIBIOSIS

EPIBIOSIS *n* any relationship between two organisms in which one grows on the other but is not parasitic on it

EPIBIOTIC > EPIBIOSIS

EPIBLAST *n* outermost layer of an embryo, which becomes the ectoderm at gastrulation

EPIBLASTS > EPIBLAST

EPIBLEM *n* outermost cell layer of a root

EPIBLEMS > EPIBLEM

EPIBOLIC > EPIBOLY

EPIBOLIES > EPIBOLY

EPIBOLY *n* process that occurs during gastrulation in vertebrates, in which cells on one side of the blastula grow over and surround the remaining cells and yolk and eventually form the ectoderm

EPIC *n* long poem, book, or film about heroic events or actions ▷ *adj* very impressive or ambitious

EPICAL > EPIC

EPICALLY > EPIC

EPICALYX *n* series of small sepal-like bracts forming an outer calyx beneath the true calyx in some flowers

EPICANTHI *n* folds of skin extending vertically over the inner angles of the eyes

EPICARDIA *n* layers of pericardia in direct contact with the heart

EPICARP *n* outermost layer of the pericarp of fruits: forms the skin of a peach or grape

EPICARPS > EPICARP

EPICEDE *same as* > EPICEDIUM

EPICEDES > EPICEDE

EPICEDIA > EPICEDIUM

EPICEDIAL > EPICEDIUM

EPICEDIAN > EPICEDIUM

EPICEDIUM *n* funeral ode

EPICENE *adj* having the characteristics of both sexes; hermaphroditic ▷ *n* epicene person or creature

EPICENES > EPICENE

EPICENISM > EPICENE

EPICENTER *same as* > EPICENTRE

EPICENTRA *n* epicentres

EPICENTRE *n* point on the earth's surface immediately above the origin of an earthquake

EPICIER *n* grocer

EPICIERS > EPICIER

EPICISM *n* style or trope characteristic of epics

EPICISMS > EPIC

EPICIST *n* writer of epics

EPICISTS > EPIC

EPICLESES > EPICLESIS

EPICLESIS *n* invocation of the Holy Spirit to consecrate the bread and wine of the Eucharist

EPICLIKE *adj* resembling or reminiscent of an epic

EPICOTYL *n* part of an embryo plant stem above the cotyledons but beneath the terminal bud

EPICOTYLS > EPICOTYL

EPICRANIA *n* tissue covering the cranium

EPICRISES > EPICRISIS

EPICRISIS *n* secondary crisis occurring in the course of a disease

EPICRITIC *adj* (of certain nerve fibres of the skin) serving to perceive and distinguish fine variations of temperature or touch

EPICS > EPIC

EPICURE *n* person who enjoys good food and drink

EPICUREAN *adj* devoted to sensual pleasures, esp food and drink ▷ *n* epicure

EPICURES > EPICURE

EPICURISE *same as* > EPICURIZE

EPICURISM > EPICURE

EPICURIZE *vb* act as an epicure

EPICYCLE *n* (in the Ptolemaic system) a small circle, around which a planet was thought to revolve

EPICYCLES > EPICYCLE

EPICYCLIC > EPICYCLE

EPIDEMIC *n* widespread occurrence of a disease ▷ *adj* (esp of a disease) affecting many people in an area

EPIDEMICS > EPIDEMIC

EPIDERM *same as* > EPIDERMIS

EPIDERMAL > EPIDERMIS

EPIDERMIC > EPIDERMIS

EPIDERMIS *n* outer layer of the skin

EPIDERMS > EPIDERM

EPIDICTIC *adj* designed to display something, esp the skill of the speaker in rhetoric

EPIDOSITE *n* rock formed of quartz and epidote

EPIDOTE *n* green mineral consisting of hydrated calcium iron aluminium silicate in monoclinic crystalline form: common in metamorphic rocks

EPIDOTES > EPIDOTE

EPIDOTIC > EPIDOTE

EPIDURAL *n* spinal anaesthetic injected to relieve pain during childbirth ▷ *adj* on or over the outermost membrane covering the brain and spinal cord

EPIDURALS > EPIDURAL

EPIFAUNA *n* animals that live on the surface of the seabed

EPIFAUNAE > EPIFAUNA

EPIFAUNAL > EPIFAUNA

EPIFAUNAS > EPIFAUNA

EPIFOCAL *adj* situated or occurring at an epicentre

EPIGAEAL *same as* > EPIGEAL

EPIGAEAN *same as* > EPIGEAL

EPIGAEOUS *same as* > EPIGEAL

EPIGAMIC *adj* attractive to the opposite sex

EPIGEAL *adj* of or relating to seed germination in which the cotyledons appear above the ground because of the growth of the hypocotyl

EPIGEAN *same as* > EPIGEAL

EPIGEIC *same as* > EPIGEAL

EPIGENE *adj* formed or taking place at or near the surface of the earth

EPIGENIC *adj* pertaining to the theory of the gradual development of the embryo

EPIGENIST *n* one who studies or espouses the theory of the gradual development of the embryo

EPIGENOUS *adj* growing on the surface, esp the upper surface, of an organism or part

EPIGEOUS *same as* > EPIGEAL

EPIGON *same as* > EPIGONE

EPIGONE *n* inferior follower or imitator

EPIGONES > EPIGONE

EPIGONI > EPIGONE

EPIGONIC > EPIGONE

EPIGONISM > EPIGONE

EPIGONOUS > EPIGONE

EPIGONS > EPIGON

EPIGONUS *same as* > EPIGONE

EPIGRAM *n* short witty remark or poem

EPIGRAMS > EPIGRAM

EPIGRAPH *n* quotation at the start of a book

EPIGRAPHS > EPIGRAPH

EPIGRAPHY *n* study of ancient inscriptions

EPIGYNIES > EPIGYNOUS

EPIGYNOUS *adj* (of flowers) having the receptacle enclosing and fused with the gynoecium so that the other floral parts arise above it

EPIGYNY > EPIGYNOUS

EPILATE *vb* remove hair from

EPILATED > EPILATE

EPILATES > EPILATE

EPILATING > EPILATE

EPILATION > EPILATE

EPILATOR *n* electrical appliance consisting of a metal spiral head that rotates at high speed, plucking unwanted hair

EPILATORS > EPILATOR

EPILEPSY *n* disorder of the nervous system causing loss of consciousness and sometimes convulsions

EPILEPTIC *adj* of or having epilepsy ▷ *n* person who has epilepsy

EPILIMNIA *n* upper layers of water in lakes

EPILITHIC *adj* (of plants) growing on the surface of rock

EPILOBIUM *n* willow-herb

EPILOG *same as* > EPILOGUE

EPILOGIC > EPILOGUE

EPILOGISE *same as* > EPILOGIZE

EPILOGIST > EPILOGUE

EPILOGIZE *vb* write or deliver epilogues

EPILOGS > EPILOG

EPILOGUE *n* short speech or poem at the end of a literary work, esp a play

EPILOGUED *adj* followed by an epilogue

EPILOGUES > EPILOGUE

EPIMER *n* isomer

EPIMERASE *n* enzyme that interconverts epimers

EPIMERE *n* dorsal part of the mesoderm of a vertebrate embryo, consisting of a series of segments

EPIMERES > EPIMERE

EPIMERIC > EPIMERISM

EPIMERISM *n* optical isomerism in which isomers can form about asymmetric atoms within the molecule

EPIMERS > EPIMER

EPIMYSIA > EPIMYSIUM

EPIMYSIUM *n* sheath of connective tissue that encloses a skeletal muscle

EPINAOI > EPINAOS

EPINAOS *n* rear vestibule

EPINASTIC > EPINASTY

EPINASTY *n* increased growth of the upper surface of a plant part, such as a leaf, resulting in a downward bending of the part

EPINEURAL *adj* outside a nerve trunk

EPINEURIA *n* sheaths of connective tissue around bundles of nerve fibres

EPINICIAN > EPINICION

EPINICION *n* victory song

EPINIKIAN > EPINICION

EPINIKION *same as* > EPINICION

EPINOSIC *adj* unhealthy

EPIPHANIC > EPIPHANY

EPIPHANY *n* moment of great or sudden revelation

EPIPHRAGM *n* disc of calcium phosphate and mucilage secreted by snails over the aperture of their shells before hibernation

EPIPHYSES > EPIPHYSIS

EPIPHYSIS *n* end of a long bone, initially separated from the shaft (diaphysis) by a section of cartilage that eventually ossifies so that the two portions fuse together

EPIPHYTAL > EPIPHYTE

EPIPHYTE *n* plant that grows on another plant but is not parasitic on it

EPIPHYTES > EPIPHYTE

EPIPHYTIC > EPIPHYTE

EPIPLOIC > EPIPLOON

EPIPLOON *n* greater omentum

EPIPLOONS > EPIPLOON

EPIPOLIC > EPIPOLISM

EPIPOLISM *n* fluorescence

EPIROGENY *n* formation and submergence of continents by broad, relatively slow, displacements of the earth's crust

EPIRRHEMA *n* address in Greek comedy

EPISCIA *n* creeping plant

EPISCIAS > EPISCIA

EPISCOPAL *adj* of or governed by bishops

EPISCOPE *n* optical device that projects an enlarged image of an opaque object, such as a printed page or photographic print, onto a screen by means of reflected light

EPISCOPES > EPISCOPE

EPISCOPY *n* area overseen

EPISEMON *n* emblem

EPISEMONS > EPISEMON

EPISODAL *same as* > EPISODIC

EPISODE *n* incident in a series of incidents

EPISODES > EPISODE

EPISODIAL *same as* > EPISODIC

EPISODIC *adj* occurring at irregular intervals

EPISOMAL > EPISOME

EPISOME *n* unit of genetic material (DNA) in bacteria, such as a plasmid, that

can either replicate independently or can be integrated into the host chromosome

EPISOMES > EPISOME

EPISPERM *n* protective outer layer of certain seeds

EPISPERMS > EPISPERM

EPISPORE *n* outer layer of certain spores

EPISPORES > EPISPORE

EPISTASES > EPISTASIS

EPISTASIS *n* scum on the surface of a liquid, esp on an old specimen of urine

EPISTASY *same as* > EPISTASIS

EPISTATIC > EPISTASIS

EPISTAXES > EPISTAXIS

EPISTAXIS *technical name for* > NOSEBLEED

EPISTEMIC *adj* of or relating to knowledge or epistemology

EPISTERNA *n* parts of the sternums of mammals

EPISTLE *n* letter, esp of an apostle ▷ *vb* preface

EPISTLED > EPISTLE

EPISTLER *n* writer of an epistle or epistles

EPISTLERS > EPISTLER

EPISTLES > EPISTLE

EPISTLING > EPISTLE

EPISTOLER *same as* > EPISTLER

EPISTOLET *n* short letter

EPISTOLIC > EPISTLE

EPISTOME *n* area between the mouth and antennae of crustaceans

EPISTOMES > EPISTOME

EPISTYLE *n* lowest part of an entablature that bears on the columns

EPISTYLES > EPISTYLE

EPITAPH *n* commemorative inscription on a tomb ▷ *vb* compose an epitaph

EPITAPHED > EPITAPH

EPITAPHER > EPITAPH

EPITAPHIC > EPITAPH

EPITAPHS > EPITAPH

EPITASES > EPITASIS

EPITASIS *n* (in classical drama) part of a play in which the main action develops

EPITAXES > EPITAXIS

EPITAXIAL > EPITAXY

EPITAXIC > EPITAXY

EPITAXIES > EPITAXY

EPITAXIS *same as* > EPITAXY

EPITAXY *n* growth of a thin layer on the surface of a crystal so that the layer has the same structure as the underlying crystal

EPITHECA *n* outer and older layer of the cell wall of a diatom

EPITHECAE > EPITHECA

EPITHELIA *n* animal tissues consisting of one or more layers of closely packed cells covering the external and internal surfaces of

the body

EPITHEM *n* external topical application

EPITHEMA > EPITHEM

EPITHEMS > EPITHEM

EPITHESES > EPITHESIS

EPITHESIS *n* addition of a letter to the end of a word, so that its sense does not change

EPITHET *n* descriptive word or name ▷ *vb* name

EPITHETED > EPITHET

EPITHETIC > EPITHET

EPITHETON *same as* > EPITHET

EPITHETS > EPITHET

EPITOME *n* typical example

EPITOMES > EPITOME

EPITOMIC > EPITOME

EPITOMISE *same as* > EPITOMIZE

EPITOMIST > EPITOMIZE

EPITOMIZE *vb* be the epitome of

EPITONIC *adj* undergoing too great a strain

EPITOPE *n* site on an antigen at which a specific antibody becomes attached

EPITOPES > EPITOPE

EPITRITE *n* metrical foot with three long syllables and one short one

EPITRITES > EPITRITE

EPIZEUXES > EPIZEUXIS

EPIZEUXIS *n* deliberate repetition of a word

EPIZOA > EPIZOON

EPIZOAN *same as* > EPIZOON

EPIZOANS > EPIZOAN

EPIZOIC *adj* (of an animal or plant) growing or living on the exterior of a living animal

EPIZOISM > EPIZOIC

EPIZOISMS > EPIZOIC

EPIZOITE *n* organism that lives on an animal but is not parasitic on it

EPIZOITES > EPIZOITE

EPIZOON *n* animal, such as a parasite, that lives on the body of another animal

EPIZOOTIC *adj* (of a disease) suddenly and temporarily affecting a large number of animals over a large area ▷ *n* epizootic disease

EPIZOOTY *n* animal disease

EPOCH *n* period of notable events

EPOCHA *same as* > EPOCH

EPOCHAL > EPOCH

EPOCHALLY > EPOCH

EPOCHAS > EPOCHA

EPOCHS > EPOCH

EPODE *n* part of a lyric ode that follows the strophe and the antistrophe

EPODES > EPODE

EPODIC > EPODE

EPONYM *n* name, esp a place name, derived from the name of a real or mythical

person, as for example *Constantinople* from *Constantine I*

EPONYMIC > EPONYM

EPONYMIES > EPONYMY

EPONYMOUS *adj* after whom a book, play, etc is named

EPONYMS > EPONYM

EPONYMY *n* derivation of names of places, etc, from those of persons

EPOPEE *n* epic poem

EPOPEES > EPOPEE

EPOPOEIA *same as* > EPOPEE

EPOPOEIAS > EPOPOEIA

EPOPT *n* one initiated into mysteries

EPOPTS > EPOPT

EPOS *n* body of poetry in which the tradition of a people is conveyed, esp a group of poems concerned with a common epic theme

EPOSES > EPOS

EPOXIDE *n* compound containing an oxygen atom joined to two different groups that are themselves joined to other groups

EPOXIDES > EPOXIDE

EPOXIDISE *same as* > EPOXIDIZE

EPOXIDIZE *vb* form an epoxide

EPOXIED > EPOXY

EPOXIES > EPOXY

EPOXY *adj* of or containing an oxygen atom joined to two different groups that are themselves joined to other groups ▷ *n* epoxy resin ▷ *vb* glue with epoxy resin

EPOXYED > EPOXY

EPOXYING > EPOXY

EPRIS *adj* enamoured

EPRISE *feminine form of* > EPRIS

EPROM *n* type of computer memory

EPROMS > EPROM

EPSILON *n* fifth letter of the Greek alphabet, a short vowel, transliterated as *e*

EPSILONIC *adj* of or relating to an arbitrary small quantity

EPSILONS > EPSILON

EPSOMITE *n* sulphate of magnesium

EPSOMITES > EPSOMITE

EPUISE *adj* exhausted

EPUISEE *feminine form of* > EPUISE

EPULARY *adj* of or relating to feasting

EPULATION *n* feasting

EPULIDES > EPULIS

EPULIS *n* swelling of the gum, usually as a result of fibrous hyperplasia

EPULISES > EPULIS

EPULOTIC *n* scarring

EPULOTICS > EPULOTIC

EPURATE *vb* purify

EPURATED > EPURATE

EPURATES > EPURATE

EPURATING > EPURATE
EPURATION > EPURATE
EPYLLIA > EPYLLION
EPYLLION *n* miniature epic
EPYLLIONS > EPYLLION
EQUABLE *adj* even-tempered
EQUABLY > EQUABLE
EQUAL *adj* identical in size, quantity, degree, etc ▷ *n* person or thing equal to another ▷ *vb* be equal to
EQUALED > EQUAL
EQUALI *pl n* pieces for a group of instruments of the same kind
EQUALING > EQUAL
EQUALISE *same as* > EQUALIZE
EQUALISED > EQUALISE
EQUALISER *same as* > EQUALIZER
EQUALISES > EQUALISE
EQUALITY *n* state of being equal
EQUALIZE *vb* make or become equal
EQUALIZED > EQUALIZE
EQUALIZER *n* person or thing that equalizes, esp a device to counterbalance opposing forces
EQUALIZES > EQUALIZE
EQUALLED > EQUAL
EQUALLING > EQUAL
EQUALLY > EQUAL
EQUALNESS *n* equality
EQUALS > EQUAL
EQUANT *n* circle in which a planet was formerly believed to move
EQUANTS > EQUANT
EQUATABLE > EQUATE
EQUATE *vb* make or regard as equivalent
EQUATED > EQUATE
EQUATES > EQUATE
EQUATING > EQUATE
EQUATION *n* mathematical statement that two expressions are equal
EQUATIONS > EQUATION
EQUATOR *n* imaginary circle round the earth, equidistant from the poles
EQUATORS > EQUATOR
EQUERRIES > EQUERRY
EQUERRY *n* officer who acts as an attendant to a member of a royal family
EQUID *n* any animal of the horse family
EQUIDS > EQUID
EQUIMOLAL *adj* having an equal number of moles
EQUIMOLAR *same as* > EQUIMOLAL
EQUINAL *same as* > EQUINE
EQUINE *adj* of or like a horse ▷ *n* any animal of the horse family
EQUINELY > EQUINE
EQUINES > EQUINE
EQUINIA *n* glanders
EQUINIAS > EQUINIA
EQUINITY *n* horse-like nature

EQUINOX *n* time of year when day and night are of equal length
EQUINOXES > EQUINOX
EQUIP *vb* provide with supplies, components, etc
EQUIPAGE *n* horse-drawn carriage, esp one elegantly equipped and attended by liveried footmen ▷ *vb* equip
EQUIPAGED > EQUIPAGE
EQUIPAGES > EQUIPAGE
EQUIPE *n* (esp in motor racing) team
EQUIPES > EQUIPE
EQUIPMENT *n* set of tools or devices used for a particular purpose
EQUIPOISE *n* perfect balance ▷ *vb* offset or balance in weight or force
EQUIPPED > EQUIP
EQUIPPER > EQUIP
EQUIPPERS > EQUIP
EQUIPPING > EQUIP
EQUIPS > EQUIP
EQUISETA > EQUISETUM
EQUISETIC > EQUISETUM
EQUISETUM *n* tracheophyte plant of the genus *Equisetum*
EQUITABLE *adj* fair and reasonable
EQUITABLY > EQUITABLE
EQUITANT *adj* (of a leaf) having the base folded around the stem so that it overlaps the leaf above and opposite
EQUITES *pl n* cavalry
EQUITIES > EQUITY
EQUITY *n* fairness
EQUIVALVE *adj* equipped with identical valves
EQUIVOCAL *adj* ambiguous
EQUIVOKE *same as* > EQUIVOQUE
EQUIVOKES > EQUIVOKE
EQUIVOQUE *n* play on words
ER *interj* sound made when hesitating in speech
ERA *n* period of time considered as distinctive
ERADIATE *less common word for* > RADIATE
ERADIATED > ERADIATE
ERADIATES > ERADIATE
ERADICANT > ERADICATE
ERADICATE *vb* destroy completely
ERAS > ERA
ERASABLE > ERASE
ERASE *vb* destroy all traces of
ERASED > ERASE
ERASEMENT > ERASE
ERASER *n* object for erasing something written
ERASERS > ERASER
ERASES > ERASE
ERASING > ERASE
ERASION *n* act of erasing
ERASIONS > ERASION
ERASURE *n* erasing
ERASURES > ERASURE
ERATHEM *n* stratum of rocks

representing a specific geological era
ERATHEMS > ERATHEM
ERBIA *n* oxide of erbium
ERBIAS > ERBIA
ERBIUM *n* metallic element of the lanthanide series
ERBIUMS > ERBIUM
ERE *prep* before ▷ *vb* plough
ERECT *vb* build ▷ *adj* upright
ERECTABLE > ERECT
ERECTED > ERECT
ERECTER *same as* > ERECTOR
ERECTERS > ERECTER
ERECTILE *adj* capable of becoming erect from sexual excitement
ERECTING > ERECT
ERECTION *n* act of erecting or the state of being erected
ERECTIONS > ERECTION
ERECTIVE *adj* producing erections
ERECTLY > ERECT
ERECTNESS > ERECT
ERECTOR *n* any muscle that raises a part or makes it erect
ERECTORS > ERECTOR
ERECTS > ERECT
ERED > ERE
ERELONG *adv* before long
EREMIC *adj* of or relating to deserts
EREMITAL > EREMITE
EREMITE *n* Christian hermit
EREMITES > EREMITE
EREMITIC > EREMITE
EREMITISH > EREMITE
EREMITISM > EREMITE
EREMURI > EREMURUS
EREMURUS *n* type of herb
ERENOW *adv* long before the present
EREPSIN *n* mixture of proteolytic enzymes secreted by the small intestine
EREPSINS > EREPSIN
ERES > ERE
ERETHIC > ERETHISM
ERETHISM *n* abnormally high degree of irritability or sensitivity in any part of the body
ERETHISMS > ERETHISM
ERETHITIC > ERETHISM
EREV *n* day before
EREVS > EREV
EREWHILE *adv* short time ago
EREWHILES *same as* > EREWHILE
ERF *n* plot of land, usually urban, marked off for building purposes
ERG *same as* > ERGOMETER
ERGASTIC *adj* consisting of the non-living by-products of protoplasmic activity
ERGATANER *n* wingless male ant
ERGATE *n* worker ant
ERGATES > ERGATE

ERGATIVE *adj* denoting a type of verb that takes the same noun as either direct object or as subject, with equivalent meaning. Thus, "fuse" is an ergative verb: "He fused the lights" and "The lights fused" have equivalent meaning ▷ *n* ergative verb
ERGATIVES > ERGATIVE
ERGATOID > ERGATE
ERGO *same as* > ERGOMETER
ERGODIC *adj* of or relating to the probability that any state will recur
ERGOGENIC *adj* giving energy
ERGOGRAM *n* tracing produced by an ergograph
ERGOGRAMS > ERGOGRAM
ERGOGRAPH *n* instrument that measures and records the amount of work a muscle does during contraction, its rate of fatigue, etc
ERGOMANIA *n* excessive desire to work
ERGOMETER *n* dynamometer
ERGOMETRY *n* measurement of work done
ERGON *n* work
ERGONOMIC *adj* designed to minimize effort
ERGONS > ERGON
ERGOS > ERGO
ERGOT *n* fungal disease of cereal
ERGOTIC > ERGOT
ERGOTISE *same as* > ERGOTIZE
ERGOTISED > ERGOTISE
ERGOTISES > ERGOTISE
ERGOTISM *n* ergot poisoning, producing either burning pains and eventually gangrene in the limbs or itching skin and convulsions
ERGOTISMS > ERGOTISM
ERGOTIZE *vb* inflict ergotism upon
ERGOTIZED > ERGOTIZE
ERGOTIZES > ERGOTIZE
ERGOTS > ERGOT
ERGS > ERG
ERIACH *same as* > ERIC
ERIACHS > ERIACH
ERIC *n* (in old Irish law) fine paid by a murderer to the family of his victim
ERICA *n* genus of plants including heathers
ERICAS > ERICA
ERICK *same as* > ERIC
ERICKS > ERICK
ERICOID *adj* (of leaves) small and tough, resembling those of heather
ERICS > ERIC
ERIGERON *n* any plant of the genus *Erigeron*
ERIGERONS > ERIGERON
ERING > ERE

e

ERINGO *same as* > ERYNGO
ERINGOES > ERINGO
ERINGOS > ERINGO
ERINITE *n* arsenate of copper
ERINITES > ERINITE
ERINUS *n* any plant of the scrophulariaceous genus *Erinus*
ERINUSES > ERINUS
ERIOMETER *n* device for measuring the diameters of minute particles or fibres
ERIONITE *n* common form of zeolite
ERIONITES > ERIONITE
ERIOPHYID *n* type of mite
ERISTIC *adj* of, relating, or given to controversy or logical disputation, esp for its own sake ▷ *n* person who engages in logical disputes
ERISTICAL *same as* > ERISTIC
ERISTICS > ERISTIC
ERK *n* aircraftman or naval rating
ERKS > ERK
ERLANG *n* unit of traffic intensity in a telephone system equal to the intensity for a specific period when the average number of simultaneous calls is unity
ERLANGS > ERLANG
ERLKING *n* malevolent spirit who carries off children
ERLKINGS > ERLKING
ERMELIN *n* ermine
ERMELINS > ERMELIN
ERMINE *n* stoat in northern regions, where it has a white winter coat with a black-tipped tail
ERMINED *adj* clad in the fur of the ermine
ERMINES > ERMINE
ERN *archaic variant of* > EARN
ERNE *n* fish-eating (European) sea eagle
ERNED > ERN
ERNES > ERNE
ERNING > ERN
ERNS > ERN
ERODABLE > ERODE
ERODE *vb* wear away
ERODED > ERODE
ERODENT > ERODE
ERODENTS > ERODE
ERODES > ERODE
ERODIBLE > ERODE
ERODING > ERODE
ERODIUM *n* type of geranium
ERODIUMS > ERODIUM
EROGENIC *same as* > EROGENOUS
EROGENOUS *adj* sensitive to sexual stimulation
EROS *n* lust
EROSE *adj* jagged or uneven, as though gnawed or bitten
EROSELY > EROSE

EROSES > EROS
EROSIBLE *adj* able to be eroded
EROSION *n* wearing away of rocks or soil by the action of water, ice, or wind
EROSIONAL > EROSION
EROSIONS > EROSION
EROSIVE > EROSION
EROSIVITY > EROSION
EROSTRATE *adj* without a beak
EROTEMA *n* rhetorical question
EROTEMAS > EROTEMA
EROTEME *same as* > EROTEMA
EROTEMES > EROTEME
EROTESES > EROTESIS
EROTESIS *same as* > EROTEMA
EROTETIC *adj* pertaining to a rhetorical question
EROTIC *adj* relating to sexual pleasure or desire ▷ *n* person who has strong sexual desires or is especially responsive to sexual stimulation
EROTICA *n* sexual literature or art
EROTICAL *adj* erotic
EROTICISE *same as* > EROTICIZE
EROTICISM *n* erotic quality or nature
EROTICIST > EROTICISM
EROTICIZE *vb* regard or present in a sexual way
EROTICS > EROTIC
EROTISE *same as* > EROTIZE
EROTISED > EROTISE
EROTISES > EROTISE
EROTISING > EROTISE
EROTISM *same as* > EROTICISM
EROTISMS > EROTISM
EROTIZE *vb* make erotic
EROTIZED > EROTIZE
EROTIZES > EROTIZE
EROTIZING > EROTIZE
EROTOLOGY *n* study of erotic stimuli and sexual behaviour
ERR *vb* make a mistake
ERRABLE *adj* capable of making a mistake
ERRANCIES > ERRANCY
ERRANCY *n* state or an instance of erring or a tendency to err
ERRAND *n* short trip to do something for someone
ERRANDS > ERRAND
ERRANT *adj* behaving in a manner considered to be unacceptable ▷ *n* knight-errant
ERRANTLY > ERRANT
ERRANTRY *n* way of life of a knight errant
ERRANTS > ERRANT
ERRATA > ERRATUM
ERRATAS *informal variant of* > ERRATA
ERRATIC *adj* irregular or unpredictable ▷ *n* rock that has been transported

by glacial action
ERRATICAL *adj* erratic
ERRATICS > ERRATIC
ERRATUM *n* error in writing or printing
ERRED > ERR
ERRHINE *adj* causing nasal secretion ▷ *n* errhine drug or agent
ERRHINES > ERRHINE
ERRING > ERR
ERRINGLY > ERR
ERRINGS > ERR
ERRONEOUS *adj* incorrect, mistaken
ERROR *n* mistake, inaccuracy, or misjudgment
ERRORIST *n* one who makes errors
ERRORISTS > ERRORIST
ERRORLESS > ERROR
ERRORS > ERROR
ERRS > ERR
ERS *same as* > ERVIL
ERSATZ *adj* made in imitation ▷ *n* ersatz substance or article
ERSATZES > ERSATZ
ERSES > ERS
ERST *adv* long ago
ERSTWHILE *adj* former ▷ *adv* formerly
ERUCIC *as in* *erucic acid* crystalline fatty acid derived from rapeseed, mustard seed and wallflower seed
ERUCIFORM *adj* resembling a caterpillar
ERUCT *vb* belch
ERUCTATE *same as* > ERUCT
ERUCTATES > ERUCTATE
ERUCTED > ERUCT
ERUCTING > ERUCT
ERUCTS > ERUCT
ERUDITE *adj* having great academic knowledge ▷ *n* erudite person
ERUDITELY > ERUDITE
ERUDITES > ERUDITE
ERUDITION > ERUDITE
ERUGO *n* verdigris
ERUGOS > ERUGO
ERUMPENT *adj* bursting out or (esp of plant parts) developing as though bursting through an overlying structure
ERUPT *vb* eject (steam, water, or volcanic material) violently
ERUPTED > ERUPT
ERUPTIBLE > ERUPT
ERUPTING > ERUPT
ERUPTION > ERUPT
ERUPTIONS > ERUPT
ERUPTIVE *adj* erupting or tending to erupt ▷ *n* type of volcanic rock
ERUPTIVES > ERUPTIVE
ERUPTS > ERUPT
ERUV *n* area, circumscribed by a symbolic line, within which certain activities forbidden to Orthodox

Jews on the Sabbath are permitted
ERUVIM > ERUV
ERUVIN > ERUV
ERUVS > ERUV
ERVALENTA *n* health food made from lentil and barley flour
ERVEN > ERF
ERVIL *n* type of vetch
ERVILS > ERVIL
ERYNGIUM *n* any plant of the temperate and subtropical perennial umbelliferous genus *Eryngium*
ERYNGIUMS > ERYNGIUM
ERYNGO *n* any umbelliferous plant of the genus *Eryngium*
ERYNGOES > ERYNGO
ERYNGOS > ERYNGO
ERYTHEMA *n* patchy inflammation of the skin
ERYTHEMAL > ERYTHEMA
ERYTHEMAS > ERYTHEMA
ERYTHEMIC > ERYTHEMA
ERYTHRINA *n* tropical tree with red flowers
ERYTHRISM *n* abnormal red coloration, as in plumage or hair
ERYTHRITE *n* sweet crystalline compound extacted from certain algae and lichens
ERYTHROID *adj* red or reddish
ERYTHRON *n* red blood cells and their related tissues
ERYTHRONS > ERYTHRON
ES *n* letter S
ESCALADE *n* assault by the use of ladders, esp on a fortification ▷ *vb* gain access to (a place) by the use of ladders
ESCALADED > ESCALADE
ESCALADER > ESCALADE
ESCALADES > ESCALADE
ESCALADO *n* escalade
ESCALATE *vb* increase in extent or intensity
ESCALATED > ESCALATE
ESCALATES > ESCALATE
ESCALATOR *n* moving staircase
ESCALIER *n* staircase
ESCALIERS > ESCALIER
ESCALLOP *another word for* > SCALLOP
ESCALLOPS > ESCALLOP
ESCALOP *another word for* > SCALLOP
ESCALOPE *n* thin slice of meat, esp veal
ESCALOPED > ESCALOP
ESCALOPES > ESCALOPE
ESCALOPS > ESCALOP
ESCAPABLE > ESCAPE
ESCAPADE *n* mischievous adventure
ESCAPADES > ESCAPADE
ESCAPADO *n* escaped criminal
ESCAPE *vb* get free (of) ▷ *n* act of escaping
ESCAPED > ESCAPE
ESCAPEE *n* person who has

escaped
ESCAPEES > ESCAPEE
ESCAPER > ESCAPE
ESCAPERS > ESCAPE
ESCAPES > ESCAPE
ESCAPING > ESCAPE
ESCAPISM *n* taking refuge in fantasy to avoid unpleasant reality
ESCAPISMS > ESCAPISM
ESCAPIST > ESCAPISM
ESCAPISTS > ESCAPISM
ESCAR *same as* > ESKER
ESCARGOT *n* variety of edible snail, usually eaten with a sauce made of melted butter and garlic
ESCARGOTS > ESCARGOT
ESCAROLE *n* variety of endive with broad leaves, used in salads
ESCAROLES > ESCAROLE
ESCARP *n* inner side of the ditch separating besiegers and besieged ▷ *vb* make into a slope
ESCARPED > ESCARP
ESCARPING > ESCARP
ESCARPS > ESCARP
ESCARS > ESCAR
ESCHALOT *another name for a* > SHALLOT
ESCHALOTS > ESCHALOT
ESCHAR *n* dry scab or slough, esp one following a burn or cauterization of the skin
ESCHARS > ESCHAR
ESCHEAT *n* private possessions that become state property in the absence of an heir ▷ *vb* attain such property
ESCHEATED > ESCHEAT
ESCHEATOR > ESCHEAT
ESCHEATS > ESCHEAT
ESCHEW *vb* abstain from, avoid
ESCHEWAL > ESCHEW
ESCHEWALS > ESCHEW
ESCHEWED > ESCHEW
ESCHEWER > ESCHEW
ESCHEWERS > ESCHEW
ESCHEWING > ESCHEW
ESCHEWS > ESCHEW
ESCLANDRE *n* scandal or notoriety
ESCOLAR *n* slender spiny-finned fish
ESCOLARS > ESCOLAR
ESCOPETTE *n* carbine
ESCORT *n* people or vehicles accompanying another person for protection or as an honour ▷ *vb* act as an escort to
ESCORTAGE > ESCORT
ESCORTED > ESCORT
ESCORTING > ESCORT
ESCORTS > ESCORT
ESCOT *vb* maintain
ESCOTED > ESCOT
ESCOTING > ESCOT
ESCOTS > ESCOT
ESCOTTED > ESCOT
ESCOTTING > ESCOT
ESCRIBANO *n* clerk

ESCRIBE *vb* draw (a circle) so that it is tangential to one side of a triangle and to the other two sides produced
ESCRIBED > ESCRIBE
ESCRIBES > ESCRIBE
ESCRIBING > ESCRIBE
ESCROC *n* conman
ESCROCS > ESCROC
ESCROL *same as* > ESCROLL
ESCROLL *n* scroll
ESCROLLS > ESCROLL
ESCROLS > ESCROL
ESCROW *n* money, goods, or a written document, such as a contract bond, delivered to a third party and held by him pending fulfilment of some condition ▷ *vb* place (money, a document, etc) in escrow
ESCROWED > ESCROW
ESCROWING > ESCROW
ESCROWS > ESCROW
ESCUAGE (*in medieval Europe*) *another word for* > SCUTAGE
ESCUAGES > ESCUAGE
ESCUDO *n* former monetary unit of Portugal
ESCUDOS > ESCUDO
ESCULENT *adj* edible ▷ *n* any edible substance
ESCULENTS > ESCULENT
ESEMPLASY *n* unification
ESERINE *n* crystalline alkaloid
ESERINES > ESERINE
ESES > ES
ESILE *n* vinegar
ESILES > ESILE
ESKAR *same as* > ESKER
ESKARS > ESKAR
ESKER *n* long winding ridge of gravel, sand, etc, originally deposited by a meltwater stream running under a glacier
ESKERS > ESKER
ESKIES > ESKY
ESKY *n* portable insulated container for keeping food and drink cool
ESLOIN *same as* > ELOIGN
ESLOINED > ESLOIN
ESLOINING > ESLOIN
ESLOINS > ESLOIN
ESLOYNE *same as* > ELOIGN
ESLOYNED > ESLOYNE
ESLOYNES > ESLOYNE
ESLOYNING > ESLOYNE
ESNE *n* household slave
ESNECIES > ESNECY
ESNECY *n* right of the eldest daughter to make the first choice when dividing inheritance
ESNES > ESNE
ESOPHAGI > ESOPHAGUS
ESOPHAGUS *n* part of the alimentary canal between the pharynx and the stomach
ESOTERIC *adj* understood by only a small number of people with special

knowledge
ESOTERICA *pl n* esoteric things
ESOTERIES > ESOTERIC
ESOTERISM > ESOTERIC
ESOTERY > ESOTERIC
ESOTROPIA *n* condition in which eye turns inwards
ESOTROPIC > ESOTROPIA
ESPADA *n* sword
ESPADAS > ESPADA
ESPAGNOLE *n* tomato and sherry sauce
ESPALIER *n* shrub or fruit tree trained to grow flat ▷ *vb* train (a plant) on an espalier
ESPALIERS > ESPALIER
ESPANOL *n* Spanish person
ESPANOLES > ESPANOL
ESPARTO *n* grass of S Europe and N Africa used for making rope etc
ESPARTOS > ESPARTO
ESPECIAL *adj* special
ESPERANCE *n* hope or expectation
ESPIAL *n* act or fact of being seen or discovered
ESPIALS > ESPIAL
ESPIED > ESPY
ESPIEGLE *adj* playful
ESPIER > ESPY
ESPIERS > ESPY
ESPIES > ESPY
ESPIONAGE *n* spying
ESPLANADE *n* wide open road used as a public promenade
ESPOUSAL *n* adoption or support
ESPOUSALS > ESPOUSAL
ESPOUSE *vb* adopt or give support to (a cause etc)
ESPOUSED > ESPOUSE
ESPOUSER > ESPOUSE
ESPOUSERS > ESPOUSE
ESPOUSES > ESPOUSE
ESPOUSING > ESPOUSE
ESPRESSO *n* strong coffee made by forcing steam or boiling water through ground coffee beans
ESPRESSOS > ESPRESSO
ESPRIT *n* spirit, liveliness, or wit
ESPRITS > ESPRIT
ESPUMOSO *n* sparkling wine
ESPUMOSOS > ESPUMOSO
ESPY *vb* catch sight of
ESPYING > ESPY
ESQUIRE *n* courtesy title placed after a man's name ▷ *vb* escort
ESQUIRED > ESQUIRE
ESQUIRES > ESQUIRE
ESQUIRESS *feminine form of* > ESQUIRE
ESQUIRING > ESQUIRE
ESQUISSE *n* sketch
ESQUISSES > ESQUISSE
ESS *n* letter S
ESSAY *n* short literary composition ▷ *vb* attempt
ESSAYED > ESSAY
ESSAYER > ESSAY
ESSAYERS > ESSAY

ESSAYETTE *n* short essay
ESSAYING > ESSAY
ESSAYISH > ESSAY
ESSAYIST *n* person who writes essays
ESSAYISTS > ESSAYIST
ESSAYS > ESSAY
ESSE *n* existence
ESSENCE *n* most important feature of a thing which determines its identity
ESSENCES > ESSENCE
ESSENTIAL *adj* vitally important ▷ *n* something fundamental or indispensable
ESSES > ESS
ESSIVE *n* grammatical case
ESSIVES > ESSIVE
ESSOIN *n* excuse
ESSOINER > ESSOIN
ESSOINERS > ESSOIN
ESSOINS > ESSOIN
ESSONITE *variant spelling of* > HESSONITE
ESSONITES > ESSONITE
ESSOYNE *same as* > ESSOIN
ESSOYNES > ESSOYNE
EST *n* treatment intended to help people towards psychological growth, in which they spend many hours in large groups, deprived of food and water and hectored by stewards
ESTABLISH *vb* set up on a permanent basis
ESTACADE *n* defensive arrangement of stakes
ESTACADES > ESTACADE
ESTAFETTE *n* mounted courier
ESTAMINET *n* small café, bar, or bistro, esp a shabby one
ESTANCIA *n* (*in Spanish America*) a large estate or cattle ranch
ESTANCIAS > ESTANCIA
ESTATE *n* landed property ▷ *vb* provide with an estate
ESTATED > ESTATE
ESTATES > ESTATE
ESTATING > ESTATE
ESTEEM *n* high regard ▷ *vb* think highly of
ESTEEMED > ESTEEM
ESTEEMING > ESTEEM
ESTEEMS > ESTEEM
ESTER *n* compound produced by the reaction between an acid and an alcohol
ESTERASE *n* any of a group of enzymes that hydrolyse esters into alcohols and acids
ESTERASES > ESTERASE
ESTERIFY *vb* change or cause to change into an ester
ESTERS > ESTER
ESTHESES > ESTHESIS
ESTHESIA *US spelling of* > AESTHESIA
ESTHESIAS > ESTHESIA
ESTHESIS *n* esthesia

ESTHETE *US spelling of* > AESTHETE
ESTHETES > ESTHETE
ESTHETIC > ESTHETE
ESTHETICS > ESTHETE
ESTIMABLE *adj* worthy of respect
ESTIMABLY > ESTIMABLE
ESTIMATE *vb* calculate roughly ▷ *n* approximate calculation
ESTIMATED > ESTIMATE
ESTIMATES > ESTIMATE
ESTIMATOR *n* person or thing that estimates
ESTIVAL *usual US spelling of* > AESTIVAL
ESTIVATE *usual US spelling of* > AESTIVATE
ESTIVATED > ESTIVATE
ESTIVATES > ESTIVATE
ESTIVATOR > ESTIVATE
ESTOC *n* short stabbing sword
ESTOCS > ESTOC
ESTOILE *n* heraldic star with wavy points
ESTOILES > ESTOILE
ESTOP *vb* preclude by estoppel
ESTOPPAGE > ESTOP
ESTOPPED > ESTOP
ESTOPPEL *n* rule of evidence whereby a person is precluded from denying the truth of a statement of facts he has previously asserted
ESTOPPELS > ESTOPPEL
ESTOPPING > ESTOP
ESTOPS > ESTOP
ESTOVER *same as* > ESTOVERS
ESTOVERS *pl n* right allowed by law to tenants of land to cut timber, esp for fuel and repairs
ESTRADE *n* dais or raised platform
ESTRADES > ESTRADE
ESTRADIOL *n* most potent estrogenic hormone secreted by the mammalian ovary
ESTRAGON *another name for* > TARRAGON
ESTRAGONS > ESTRAGON
ESTRAL *US spelling of* > OESTRAL
ESTRANGE *vb* separate and live apart from (one's spouse)
ESTRANGED *adj* no longer living with one's spouse
ESTRANGER > ESTRANGE
ESTRANGES > ESTRANGE
ESTRAPADE *n* attempt by a horse to throw its rider
ESTRAY *n* stray domestic animal of unknown ownership ▷ *vb* stray
ESTRAYED > ESTRAY
ESTRAYING > ESTRAY
ESTRAYS > ESTRAY
ESTREAT *n* true copy of or extract from a court record ▷ *vb* enforce (a

recognizance that has been forfeited) by sending an extract of the court record to the proper authority
ESTREATED > ESTREAT
ESTREATS > ESTREAT
ESTREPE *vb* lay waste
ESTREPED > ESTREPE
ESTREPES > ESTREPE
ESTREPING > ESTREPE
ESTRICH *n* ostrich
ESTRICHES > ESTRICH
ESTRIDGE *n* ostrich
ESTRIDGES > ESTRIDGE
ESTRILDID *n* weaver finch
ESTRIN *US spelling of* > OESTRIN
ESTRINS > ESTRIN
ESTRIOL *usual US spelling of* > OESTRIOL
ESTRIOLS > ESTRIOL
ESTRO *n* poetic inspiration
ESTROGEN *usual US spelling of* > OESTROGEN
ESTROGENS > ESTROGEN
ESTRONE *usual US spelling of* > OESTRONE
ESTRONES > ESTRONE
ESTROS > ESTRO
ESTROUS > ESTRUS
ESTRUAL > ESTRUS
ESTRUM *usual US spelling of* > OESTRUM
ESTRUMS > ESTRUM
ESTRUS *usual US spelling of* > OESTRUS
ESTRUSES > ESTRUS
ESTS > EST
ESTUARIAL > ESTUARY
ESTUARIAN > ESTUARY
ESTUARIES > ESTUARY
ESTUARINE *adj* formed or deposited in an estuary
ESTUARY *n* mouth of a river
ESURIENCE > ESURIENT
ESURIENCY > ESURIENT
ESURIENT *adj* greedy
ET *dialect past tense of* > EAT
ETA *n* seventh letter in the Greek alphabet, a long vowel sound
ETACISM *n* pronunciation of eta as a long vowel sound
ETACISMS > ETACISM
ETAERIO *n* aggregate fruit, as one consisting of drupes (raspberry) or achenes (traveller's joy)
ETAERIOS > ETAERIO
ETAGE *n* floor in a multi-storey building
ETAGERE *n* stand with open shelves for displaying ornaments, etc
ETAGERES > ETAGERE
ETAGES > ETAGE
ETALAGE *n* display
ETALAGES > ETALAGE
ETALON *n* device used in spectroscopy to measure wavelengths by interference effects produced by multiple reflections between parallel half-silvered glass or quartz plates
ETALONS > ETALON

ETAMIN *same as* > ETAMINE
ETAMINE *n* cotton or worsted fabric of loose weave, used for clothing, curtains, etc
ETAMINES > ETAMINE
ETAMINS > ETAMIN
ETAPE *n* public storehouse
ETAPES > ETAPE
ETAS > ETA
ETAT *n* state
ETATISM *same as* > ETATISME
ETATISME *n* authoritarian control by the state
ETATISMES > ETATISME
ETATISMS > ETATISM
ETATIST > ETATISME
ETATISTE > ETATISME
ETATISTES > ETATISME
ETATS > ETAT
ETCETERA *n* number of other items
ETCETERAS *pl n* miscellaneous extra things or people
ETCH *vb* wear away or cut the surface of (metal, glass, etc) with acid
ETCHANT *n* any acid or corrosive used for etching
ETCHANTS > ETCHANT
ETCHED > ETCH
ETCHER > ETCH
ETCHERS > ETCH
ETCHES > ETCH
ETCHING *n* picture printed from an etched metal plate
ETCHINGS > ETCHING
ETEN *n* giant
ETENS > ETEN
ETERNAL *adj* without beginning or end ▷ *n* eternal thing
ETERNALLY > ETERNAL
ETERNALS > ETERNAL
ETERNE *archaic or poetic word for* > ETERNAL
ETERNISE *same as* > ETERNIZE
ETERNISED > ETERNISE
ETERNISES > ETERNISE
ETERNITY *n* infinite time
ETERNIZE *vb* make eternal
ETERNIZED > ETERNIZE
ETERNIZES > ETERNIZE
ETESIAN *adj* (of NW winds) recurring annually in the summer in the E Mediterranean ▷ *n* etesian wind
ETESIANS > ETESIAN
ETH *same as* > EDH
ETHAL *n* cetyl alcohol
ETHALS > ETHAL
ETHANAL *n* colourless volatile pungent liquid
ETHANALS > ETHANAL
ETHANE *n* odourless flammable gas obtained from natural gas and petroleum
ETHANES > ETHANE
ETHANOATE *same as* > ACETATE
ETHANOIC as in *ethanoic acid* acetic acid

ETHANOL *same as* > ALCOHOL
ETHANOLS > ETHANOL
ETHANOYL *n* substance consisting of or containing the monovalent group CH_3CO-
ETHANOYLS > ETHANOYL
ETHE *adj* easy
ETHENE *same as* > ETHYLENE
ETHENES > ETHENE
ETHEPHON *n* synthetic plant-growth regulator
ETHEPHONS > ETHEPHON
ETHER *n* colourless sweet-smelling liquid used as an anaesthetic
ETHERCAP *n* spider
ETHERCAPS > ETHERCAP
ETHEREAL *adj* extremely delicate
ETHEREOUS *same as* > ETHEREAL
ETHERIAL *same as* > ETHEREAL
ETHERIC > ETHER
ETHERICAL > ETHER
ETHERIFY *vb* change (a compound, such as an alcohol) into an ether
ETHERION *n* gas formerly believed to exist in air
ETHERIONS > ETHERION
ETHERISE *same as* > ETHERIZE
ETHERISED > ETHERISE
ETHERISER > ETHERISE
ETHERISES > ETHERISE
ETHERISH > ETHER
ETHERISM *n* addiction to ether
ETHERISMS > ETHERISM
ETHERIST > ETHERISM
ETHERISTS > ETHERISM
ETHERIZE *vb* subject (a person) to the anaesthetic influence of ether fumes
ETHERIZED > ETHERIZE
ETHERIZER > ETHERIZE
ETHERIZES > ETHERIZE
ETHERS > ETHER
ETHIC *n* moral principle
ETHICAL *adj* of or based on a system of moral beliefs about right and wrong ▷ *n* drug available only by prescription
ETHICALLY > ETHICAL
ETHICALS > ETHICAL
ETHICIAN > ETHICS
ETHICIANS > ETHICS
ETHICISE *same as* > ETHICIZE
ETHICISED > ETHICISE
ETHICISES > ETHICISE
ETHICISM > ETHICS
ETHICISMS > ETHICS
ETHICIST > ETHICS
ETHICISTS > ETHICS
ETHICIZE *vb* make or consider as ethical
ETHICIZED > ETHICIZE
ETHICIZES > ETHICIZE
ETHICS *n* code of behaviour
ETHINYL *same as* > ETHYNYL
ETHINYLS > ETHINYL
ETHION *n* type of pesticide
ETHIONINE *n* type of amino

acid

ETHIONS > ETHION

ETHIOPS n dark-coloured chemical compound

ETHIOPSES > ETHIOPS

ETHMOID adj denoting or relating to a bone of the skull that forms part of the eye socket and the nasal cavity ▷ n ethmoid bone

ETHMOIDAL same as > ETHMOID

ETHMOIDS > ETHMOID

ETHNARCH n ruler of a people or province, as in parts of the Roman and Byzantine Empires

ETHNARCHS > ETHNARCH

ETHNARCHY > ETHNARCH

ETHNIC adj relating to a people or group that shares a culture, religion, or language ▷ n member of an ethnic group, esp a minority group

ETHNICAL same as > ETHNIC

ETHNICISM n paganism

ETHNICITY > ETHNIC

ETHNICS > ETHNIC

ETHNOCIDE n extermination of a race

ETHNOGENY n branch of ethnology that deals with the origin of races or peoples

ETHNOLOGY n study of human races

ETHNONYM n name of ethnic group

ETHNONYMS > ETHNONYM

ETHNOS n ethnic group

ETHNOSES > ETHNOS

ETHOGRAM n description of animal's behaviour

ETHOGRAMS > ETHOGRAM

ETHOLOGIC > ETHOLOGY

ETHOLOGY n study of the behaviour of animals in their normal environment

ETHONONE another name for > KETENE

ETHONONES > ETHONONE

ETHOS n distinctive spirit and attitudes of a people, culture, etc

ETHOSES > ETHOS

ETHOXIDE n any of a class of saltlike compounds

ETHOXIDES > ETHOXIDE

ETHOXIES > ETHOXY

ETHOXY > ETHOXYL

ETHOXYL n univalent radical

ETHOXYLS > ETHOXYL

ETHS > ETH

ETHYL adj type of chemical hydrocarbon group

ETHYLATE same as > ETHOXIDE

ETHYLATED > ETHYLATE

ETHYLATES > ETHYLATE

ETHYLENE n poisonous gas used as an anaesthetic and as fuel

ETHYLENES > ETHYLENE

ETHYLENIC > ETHYLENE

ETHYLIC > ETHYL

ETHYLS > ETHYL

ETHYNE another name for > ACETYLENE

ETHYNES > ETHYNE

ETHYNYL n univalent radical

ETHYNYLS > ETHYNYL

ETIC adj (in linguistics) of or relating to items analyzed without consideration of their structural function

ETIOLATE vb become pale and weak

ETIOLATED > ETIOLATE

ETIOLATES > ETIOLATE

ETIOLIN n yellow pigment

ETIOLINS > ETIOLIN

ETIOLOGIC > ETIOLOGY

ETIOLOGY n study of the causes of diseases

ETIQUETTE n conventional code of conduct

ETNA n container used to heat liquids

ETNAS > ETNA

ETOILE n star

ETOILES > ETOILE

ETOUFFEE n spicy Cajun stew

ETOUFFEES > ETOUFFEE

ETOURDI adj foolish

ETOURDIE feminine form of > ETOURDI

ETRANGER n foreigner

ETRANGERE feminine form of > ETRANGER

ETRANGERS > ETRANGER

ETRENNE n New Year's gift

ETRENNES > ETRENNE

ETRIER n short portable ladder or set of webbing loops that can be attached to a karabiner or fifi hook

ETRIERS > ETRIER

ETTERCAP n spider

ETTERCAPS > ETTERCAP

ETTIN n giant

ETTINS > ETTIN

ETTLE vb intend

ETTLED > ETTLE

ETTLES > ETTLE

ETTLING > ETTLE

ETUDE n short musical composition for a solo instrument, esp intended as a technical exercise

ETUDES > ETUDE

ETUI n small usually ornamented case for holding needles, cosmetics, or other small articles

ETUIS > ETUI

ETWEE same as > ETUI

ETWEES > ETUI

ETYMA > ETYMON

ETYMIC > ETYMON

ETYMOLOGY n study of the sources and development of words

ETYMON n form of a word or morpheme, usually the earliest recorded form or a reconstructed form, from which another word or morpheme is derived: the etymon of English "ewe" is Indo-European "owi"

ETYMONS > ETYMON

ETYPIC n unable to conform to type

ETYPICAL same as > ETYPIC

EUCAIN same as > EUCAINE

EUCAINE n crystalline optically active substance formerly used as a local anaesthetic

EUCAINES > EUCAINE

EUCAINS > EUCAIN

EUCALYPT n myrtaceous tree

EUCALYPTI n eucalypts

EUCALYPTS > EUCALYPT

EUCARYON same as > EUKARYOTE

EUCARYONS > EUCARYON

EUCARYOT same as > EUKARYOTE

EUCARYOTE same as > EUKARYOTE

EUCARYOTS > EUCARYOT

EUCHARIS n any amaryllidaceous plant of the South American genus Eucharis, cultivated for their large white fragrant flowers

EUCHLORIC > EUCHLORIN

EUCHLORIN n explosive gaseous mixture of chlorine and chlorine dioxide

EUCHOLOGY n prayer formulary

EUCHRE n US and Canadian card game similar to écarté for two to four players, using a poker pack with joker ▷ vb prevent (a player) from making his contracted tricks

EUCHRED > EUCHRE

EUCHRES > EUCHRE

EUCHRING > EUCHRE

EUCLASE n brittle green gem

EUCLASES > EUCLASE

EUCLIDEAN adj of or relating to Euclid (Greek mathematician of Alexandria, 3rd century BC), esp his system of geometry

EUCLIDIAN same as > EUCLIDEAN

EUCRITE n type of stony meteorite

EUCRITES > EUCRITE

EUCRITIC > EUCRITE

EUCRYPHIA n any tree or shrub of the mostly evergreen genus Eucryphia, native to Australia and S America, having leaves of a dark lustrous green and white flowers: family Eucryphiaceae

EUCYCLIC adj (of plants) having the same number of leaves in each whorl

EUDAEMON same as > EUDEMON

EUDAEMONS > EUDAEMON

EUDAEMONY same as > EUDEMONIA

EUDAIMON same

as > EUDAEMON

EUDAIMONS > EUDAIMON

EUDEMON n benevolent spirit or demon

EUDEMONIA n happiness, esp (in the philosophy of Aristotle) that resulting from a rational active life

EUDEMONIC > EUDEMONIA

EUDEMONS > EUDEMON

EUDIALYTE n brownish-red mineral

EUGARIE another name for > PIPI

EUGARIES > EUGARIE

EUGE interj well done!

EUGENIA n plant of the clove family

EUGENIAS > EUGENIA

EUGENIC > EUGENICS

EUGENICAL > EUGENICS

EUGENICS n study of methods of improving the human race

EUGENISM > EUGENICS

EUGENISMS > EUGENICS

EUGENIST > EUGENICS

EUGENISTS > EUGENICS

EUGENOL n colourless or pale yellow oily liquid substance with a spicy taste and an odour of cloves, used in perfumery

EUGENOLS > EUGENOL

EUGH archaic form of > YEW

EUGHEN archaic form of > YEW

EUGHS > EUGH

EUGLENA n any freshwater unicellular organism of the genus Euglena, moving by means of flagella and typically having holophytic nutrition. It has been variously regarded as an alga or a protozoan but is now usually classified as a protoctist (phylum Euglenophyta)

EUGLENAS > EUGLENA

EUGLENID same as > EUGLENA

EUGLENIDS > EUGLENID

EUGLENOID > EUGLENA

EUK vb itch

EUKARYON same as > EUKARYOTE

EUKARYONS > EUKARYON

EUKARYOT same as > EUKARYOTE

EUKARYOTE n any member of the Eukarya, a domain of organisms having cells each with a distinct nucleus within which the genetic material is contained

EUKARYOTS > EUKARYOT

EUKED > EUK

EUKING > EUK

EUKS > EUK

EULACHAN same as > EULACHON

EULACHANS > EULACHAN

EULACHON n salmonoid food fish

EULACHONS > EULACHON

EULOGIA n blessed bread

e

distributed to members of the congregation after the liturgy, esp to those who have not communed

EULOGIAE > EULOGIA

EULOGIAS > EULOGIA

EULOGIES > EULOGY

EULOGISE same as > EULOGIZE

EULOGISED > EULOGISE

EULOGISER > EULOGISE

EULOGISES > EULOGISE

EULOGIST > EULOGIZE

EULOGISTS > EULOGIZE

EULOGIUM same as > EULOGY

EULOGIUMS > EULOGIUM

EULOGISE vb praise (a person or thing) highly in speech or writing

EULOGIZED > EULOGIZE

EULOGIZER > EULOGIZE

EULOGIZES > EULOGIZE

EULOGY n speech or writing in praise of a person

EUMELANIN n dark melanin

EUMERISM n collection of similar parts

EUMERISMS > EUMERISM

EUMONG same as > EUMUNG

EUMONGS > EUMONG

EUMUNG n any of various Australian acacias

EUMUNGS > EUMUNG

EUNUCH n castrated man, esp (formerly) a guard in a harem

EUNUCHISE same as > EUNUCHIZE

EUNUCHISM > EUNUCH

EUNUCHIZE vb castrate

EUNUCHOID n one suffering from deficient sexual development

EUNUCHS > EUNUCH

EUOI n cry of Bacchic frenzy

EUONYMIN n extract derived from the bark of the eunonymus

EUONYMINS > EUONYMIN

EUONYMUS n any tree or shrub of the N temperate genus *Euonymus*

EUOUAE n cry of Bacchic frenzy

EUOUAES > EUOUAE

EUPAD n antiseptic powder

EUPADS > EUPAD

EUPATRID n (in ancient Greece) hereditary noble or landowner

EUPATRIDS > EUPATRID

EUPEPSIA n good digestion

EUPEPSIAS > EUPEPSIA

EUPEPSIES > EUPEPSY

EUPEPSY same as > EUPEPSIA

EUPEPTIC > EUPEPSIA

EUPHAUSID n small pelagic shrimplike crustacean

EUPHEMISE same as > EUPHEMIZE

EUPHEMISM n inoffensive word or phrase substituted for one considered offensive or upsetting

EUPHEMIST > EUPHEMISM

EUPHEMIZE vb speak in euphemisms or refer to by

means of a euphemism

EUPHENIC n of or pertaining to biological improvement

EUPHENICS n science of biological improvement

EUPHOBIA n fear of good news

EUPHOBIAS > EUPHOBIA

EUPHON n glass harmonica

EUPHONIA same as > EUPHONY

EUPHONIAS > EUPHONIA

EUPHONIC adj denoting or relating to euphony

EUPHONIES > EUPHONY

EUPHONISE same as > EUPHONIZE

EUPHONISM n use of pleasant-sounding words

EUPHONIUM n brass musical instrument, tenor tuba

EUPHONIZE vb make pleasant to hear

EUPHONS > EUPHON

EUPHONY n pleasing sound

EUPHORBIA n any plant of the genus *Euphorbia*

EUPHORIA n sense of elation

EUPHORIAS > EUPHORIA

EUPHORIC > EUPHORIA

EUPHORIES > EUPHORY

EUPHORY same as > EUPHORIA

EUPHOTIC adj denoting or relating to the uppermost part of a sea or lake down to about 100 metres depth, which receives enough light to enable photosynthesis to take place

EUPHRASY same as > EYEBRIGHT

EUPHROE n wooden block with holes through which the lines of a crowfoot are rove

EUPHROES > EUPHROE

EUPHUISE same as > EUPHUIZE

EUPHUISED > EUPHUISE

EUPHUISES > EUPHUISE

EUPHUISM n artificial prose style of the Elizabethan period, marked by extreme use of antithesis, alliteration, and extended similes and allusions

EUPHUISMS > EUPHUISM

EUPHUIST > EUPHUISM

EUPHUISTS > EUPHUISM

EUPHUIZE vb write in euphuism

EUPHUIZED > EUPHUIZE

EUPHUIZES > EUPHUIZE

EUPLASTIC adj healing quickly and well

EUPLOID adj having chromosomes present in an exact multiple of the haploid number ▷ n euploid cell or individual

EUPLOIDS > EUPLOID

EUPLOIDY > EUPLOID

EUPNEA same as > EUPNOEA

EUPNEAS > EUPNEA

EUPNEIC > EUPNOEA

EUPNOEA n normal relaxed breathing

EUPNOEAS > EUPNOEA

EUPNOEIC > EUPNOEA

EUREKA n exclamation of triumph at finding something

EUREKAS > EUREKA

EURHYTHMY n rhythmic movement

EURIPI > EURIPUS

EURIPUS n strait or channel with a strong current or tide

EURIPUSES > EURIPUS

EURO n unit of the single currency of the European Union

EUROBOND n bond issued in a eurocurrency

EUROBONDS > EUROBOND

EUROCRAT n member, esp a senior member, of the administration of the European Union

EUROCRATS > EUROCRAT

EUROCREEP n gradual introduction of the euro into use in Britain

EUROKIES > EUROKY

EUROKOUS > EUROKY

EUROKY n ability of an organism to live under different conditions

EURONOTE n form of euro-commercial paper consisting of short-term negotiable bearer notes

EURONOTES > EURONOTE

EUROPHILE n person who admires Europe, Europeans, or the European Union

EUROPIUM n silvery-white element of the lanthanide series

EUROPIUMS > EUROPIUM

EUROS > EURO

EURYBATH n organism that can live at different depths underwater

EURYBATHS > EURYBATH

EURYOKIES > EURYOKY

EURYOKOUS > EURYOKY

EURYOKY same as > EUROKY

EURYTHERM n organism that can tolerate widely differing temperatures

EURYTHMIC adj having a pleasing and harmonious rhythm, order, or structure

EURYTHMY > EURYTHMICS

EURYTOPIC adj (of a species) able to tolerate a wide range of environments

EUSOCIAL adj using division of labour

EUSOL n solution of eupad in water

EUSOLS > EUSOL

EUSTACIES > EUSTATIC

EUSTACY > EUSTATIC

EUSTASIES > EUSTATIC

EUSTASY > EUSTATIC

EUSTATIC adj denoting or relating to worldwide changes in sea level,

caused by the melting of ice sheets, movements of the ocean floor, sedimentation, etc

EUSTELE n central cylinder of a seed plant

EUSTELES > EUSTELE

EUSTYLE n building with columns optimally spaced

EUSTYLES > EUSTYLE

EUTAXIA n condition of being easily melted

EUTAXIAS > EUTAXIA

EUTAXIES > EUTAXY

EUTAXITE n banded volcanic rock

EUTAXITES > EUTAXITE

EUTAXITIC > EUTAXITE

EUTAXY n good order

EUTECTIC adj (of a mixture of substances, esp an alloy) having the lowest freezing point of all possible mixtures of the substances ▷ n eutectic mixture

EUTECTICS > EUTECTIC

EUTECTOID n mixture of substances similar to a eutectic, but forming two or three constituents from a solid instead of from a melt ▷ adj concerned with or suitable for eutectoid mixtures

EUTEXIA same as > EUTAXIA

EUTEXIAS > EUTEXIA

EUTHANASY n the act of killing someone painlessly

EUTHANISE same as > EUTHANIZE

EUTHANIZE vb put (someone, esp one suffering from a terminal illness) to death painlessly

EUTHENICS n study of the control of the environment, esp with a view to improving the health and living standards of the human race

EUTHENIST > EUTHENICS

EUTHERIAN adj of, relating to, or belonging to the *Eutheria*, a subclass of mammals all of which have a placenta and reach an advanced state of development before birth ▷ n any eutherian mammal

EUTHYMIA n pleasant state of mind

EUTHYMIAS > EUTHYMIA

EUTHYROID n condition of having thyroid glands that function normally

EUTRAPELY n conversational skill

EUTROPHIC adj (of lakes and similar habitats) rich in organic and mineral nutrients and supporting an abundant plant life, which in the process of decaying depletes the oxygen supply for animal life

EUTROPHY > EUTROPHIC

EUTROPIC > EUTROPY
EUTROPIES > EUTROPY
EUTROPOUS > EUTROPY
EUTROPY n regular variation of the crystalline structure of a series of compounds according to atomic number
EUXENITE n rare brownish-black mineral containing erbium, cerium, uranium, columbium, and yttrium
EUXENITES > EUXENITE
EVACUANT adj serving to promote excretion, esp of the bowels ▷ n evacuant agent
EVACUANTS > EVACUANT
EVACUATE vb send (someone) away from a place of danger
EVACUATED > EVACUATE
EVACUATES > EVACUATE
EVACUATOR > EVACUATE
EVACUEE n person evacuated from a place of danger, esp in wartime
EVACUEES > EVACUEE
EVADABLE > EVADE
EVADE vb get away from or avoid
EVADED > EVADE
EVADER > EVADE
EVADERS > EVADE
EVADES > EVADE
EVADIBLE > EVADE
EVADING > EVADE
EVADINGLY > EVADE
EVAGATION n digression
EVAGINATE vb turn (an organ or part) inside out
EVALUABLE > EVALUATE
EVALUATE vb find or judge the value of
EVALUATED > EVALUATE
EVALUATES > EVALUATE
EVALUATOR > EVALUATE
EVANESCE vb fade gradually from sight
EVANESCED > EVANESCE
EVANESCES > EVANESCE
EVANGEL n gospel of Christianity
EVANGELIC adj of, based upon, or following from the gospels
EVANGELS > EVANGEL
EVANGELY n gospel
EVANISH poetic word for > VANISH
EVANISHED > EVANISH
EVANISHES > EVANISH
EVANITION > EVANISH
EVAPORATE vb change from a liquid or solid to a vapour
EVAPORITE n any sedimentary rock, such as rock salt, gypsum, or anhydrite, formed by evaporation of former seas or salt-water lakes
EVASIBLE > EVASION
EVASION n act of evading something, esp a duty or responsibility, by cunning or illegal means
EVASIONAL > EVASION

EVASIONS > EVASION
EVASIVE adj not straightforward
EVASIVELY > EVASIVE
EVE n evening or day before some special event
EVECTION n irregularity in the moon's motion caused by perturbations of the sun and planets
EVECTIONS > EVECTION
EVEJAR n nightjar
EVEJARS > EVEJAR
EVEN adj flat or smooth ▷ adv equally ▷ vb make even ▷ n eve
EVENED > EVEN
EVENEMENT n event
EVENER > EVEN
EVENERS > EVEN
EVENEST > EVEN
EVENFALL n early evening
EVENFALLS > EVENFALL
EVENING n end of the day or early part of the night ▷ adj of or in the evening
EVENINGS adv in the evening, esp regularly
EVENLY > EVEN
EVENNESS > EVEN
EVENS adv (of a bet) winning the same as the amount staked if successful
EVENSONG n evening prayer
EVENSONGS > EVENSONG
EVENT n anything that takes place ▷ vb take part or ride (a horse) in eventing
EVENTED > EVENT
EVENTER > EVENTING
EVENTERS > EVENTING
EVENTFUL adj full of exciting incidents
EVENTIDE n evening
EVENTIDES > EVENTIDE
EVENTING n riding competitions, usu involving cross-country, jumping, and dressage
EVENTINGS > EVENTING
EVENTLESS > EVENT
EVENTRATE vb open the belly of
EVENTS > EVENT
EVENTUAL adj ultimate
EVENTUATE vb result ultimately (in)
EVER adv at any time
EVERGLADE n large area of submerged marshland
EVERGREEN adj (tree or shrub) having leaves throughout the year ▷ n evergreen tree or shrub
EVERMORE adv for all time to come
EVERNET n hypothetical form of internet that is continuously accessible using a wide variety of devices
EVERNETS > EVERNET
EVERSIBLE > EVERT
EVERSION > EVERT
EVERSIONS > EVERT
EVERT vb turn (an eyelid, the intestines, or some

other bodily part) outwards or inside out
EVERTED > EVERT
EVERTING > EVERT
EVERTOR n any muscle that turns a part outwards
EVERTORS > EVERTOR
EVERTS > EVERT
EVERWHERE adv to or in all parts or places
EVERWHICH dialect version of > WHICHEVER
EVERY adj each without exception
EVERYBODY pron every person
EVERYDAY adj usual or ordinary ▷ n ordinary day
EVERYDAYS > EVERYDAY
EVERYMAN n ordinary person; common man
EVERYMEN > EVERYMAN
EVERYONE pron every person
EVERYWAY adv in every way
EVERYWHEN adv to or in all parts or places
EVES > EVE
EVET n eft
EVETS > EVET
EVHOE interj cry of Bacchic frenzy
EVICT vb legally expel (someone) from his or her home
EVICTED > EVICT
EVICTEE > EVICT
EVICTEES > EVICT
EVICTING > EVICT
EVICTION > EVICT
EVICTIONS > EVICT
EVICTOR > EVICT
EVICTORS > EVICT
EVICTS > EVICT
EVIDENCE n ground for belief ▷ vb demonstrate, prove
EVIDENCED > EVIDENCE
EVIDENCES > EVIDENCE
EVIDENT adj easily seen or understood ▷ n item of evidence
EVIDENTLY adv without question
EVIDENTS > EVIDENT
EVIL n wickedness ▷ adj harmful ▷ adv in an evil manner
EVILDOER n wicked person
EVILDOERS > EVILDOER
EVILDOING > EVILDOER
EVILER > EVIL
EVILEST > EVIL
EVILLER > EVIL
EVILLEST > EVIL
EVILLY > EVIL
EVILNESS > EVIL
EVILS > EVIL
EVINCE vb make evident
EVINCED > EVINCE
EVINCES > EVINCE
EVINCIBLE > EVINCE
EVINCIBLY > EVINCE
EVINCING > EVINCE
EVINCIVE > EVINCE
EVIRATE vb castrate
EVIRATED > EVIRATE

EVIRATES > EVIRATE
EVIRATING > EVIRATE
EVITABLE adj able to be avoided
EVITATE archaic word for > AVOID
EVITATED > EVITATE
EVITATES > EVITATE
EVITATING > EVITATE
EVITATION > EVITATE
EVITE archaic word for > AVOID
EVITED > EVITE
EVITERNAL adj eternal
EVITES > EVITE
EVITING > EVITE
EVO informal word for > EVENING
EVOCABLE > EVOKE
EVOCATE vb evoke
EVOCATED > EVOCATE
EVOCATES > EVOCATE
EVOCATING > EVOCATE
EVOCATION n act of evoking
EVOCATIVE adj tending or serving to evoke
EVOCATOR n person or thing that evokes
EVOCATORS > EVOCATOR
EVOCATORY adj evocative
EVOE interj cry of Bacchic frenzy
EVOHE interj cry of Bacchic frenzy
EVOKE vb call or summon up (a memory, feeling, etc)
EVOKED > EVOKE
EVOKER > EVOKE
EVOKERS > EVOKE
EVOKES > EVOKE
EVOKING > EVOKE
EVOLUE n (in the African former colonies of Belgium and France) African person educated according to European principles
EVOLUES > EVOLUE
EVOLUTE n geometric curve that describes the locus of the centres of curvature of another curve ▷ adj having the margins rolled outwards ▷ vb evolve
EVOLUTED > EVOLUTE
EVOLUTES > EVOLUTE
EVOLUTING > EVOLUTE
EVOLUTION n gradual change in the characteristics of living things over successive generations, esp to a more complex form
EVOLUTIVE adj relating to, tending to, or promoting evolution
EVOLVABLE > EVOLVE
EVOLVE vb develop gradually
EVOLVED > EVOLVE
EVOLVENT adj evolving
EVOLVER > EVOLVE
EVOLVERS > EVOLVE
EVOLVES > EVOLVE
EVOLVING > EVOLVE
EVONYMUS same as > EUONYMUS
EVOS > EVO

e

EVOVAE n cry of Bacchic frenzy

EVOVAES > EVOVAE

EVULGATE vb make public

EVULGATED > EVULGATE

EVULGATES > EVULGATE

EVULSE vb extract by force

EVULSED > EVULSE

EVULSES > EVULSE

EVULSING > EVULSE

EVULSION n act of extracting by force

EVULSIONS > EVULSION

EVZONE n soldier in an elite Greek infantry regiment

EVZONES > EVZONE

EWE n female sheep

EWER n large jug with a wide mouth

EWERS > EWER

EWES > EWE

EWEST Scots word for > NEAR

EWFTES Spenserian plural of > EFT

EWGHEN archaic form of > YEW

EWHOW interj expression of pity or regret

EWK vb itch

EWKED > EWK

EWKING > EWK

EWKS > EWK

EWT archaic form of > NEWT

EWTS > EWT

EX prep not including ▷ vb cross out or delete

EXABYTE n very large unit of computer memory

EXABYTES > EXABYTE

EXACT adj correct and complete in every detail ▷ vb demand (payment or obedience)

EXACTA n horse-racing bet in which the first and second horses must be named in the correct order

EXACTABLE > EXACT

EXACTAS > EXACTA

EXACTED > EXACT

EXACTER > EXACT

EXACTERS > EXACT

EXACTEST > EXACT

EXACTING adj making rigorous or excessive demands

EXACTION n act of obtaining or demanding money as a right

EXACTIONS > EXACTION

EXACTLY adv precisely, in every respect ▷ interj just so! precisely!

EXACTMENT n condition of being exact

EXACTNESS > EXACT

EXACTOR > EXACT

EXACTORS > EXACT

EXACTRESS > EXACT

EXACTS > EXACT

EXACUM n any plant of the annual or perennial tropical genus Exacum; some are grown as greenhouse biennials for their bluish-purple platter-shaped flowers: family Gentianaceae

EXACUMS > EXACUM

EXAHERTZ n very large unit of frequency

EXALT vb praise highly

EXALTED adj high or elevated in rank, position, dignity, etc

EXALTEDLY > EXALTED

EXALTER > EXALT

EXALTERS > EXALT

EXALTING > EXALT

EXALTS > EXALT

EXAM n examination

EXAMEN n examination of conscience, usually made daily by Jesuits and others

EXAMENS > EXAMEN

EXAMINANT n examiner

EXAMINATE n examinee

EXAMINE vb look at closely

EXAMINED > EXAMINE

EXAMINEE n person who sits an exam

EXAMINEES > EXAMINEE

EXAMINER > EXAMINE

EXAMINERS > EXAMINE

EXAMINES > EXAMINE

EXAMINING > EXAMINE

EXAMPLAR archaic form of > EXEMPLAR

EXAMPLARS > EXAMPLAR

EXAMPLE n specimen typical of its group

EXAMPLED > EXAMPLE

EXAMPLES > EXAMPLE

EXAMPLING > EXAMPLE

EXAMS > EXAM

EXANIMATE adj lacking life

EXANTHEM same as > EXANTHEMA

EXANTHEMA n skin eruption or rash occurring as a symptom in a disease such as measles or scarlet fever

EXANTHEMS > EXANTHEM

EXAPTED adj biologically adapted

EXAPTIVE adj involving biological adaptation

EXARATE adj (of the pupa of such insects as ants and bees) having legs, wings, antennae, etc, free and movable

EXARATION n writing

EXARCH n head of certain autonomous Orthodox Christian Churches, such as that of Bulgaria and Cyprus ▷ adj (of a xylem strand) having the first-formed xylem external to that formed later

EXARCHAL > EXARCH

EXARCHATE n office, rank, or jurisdiction of an exarch

EXARCHIES > EXARCHY

EXARCHIST n supporter of an exarch

EXARCHS > EXARCH

EXARCHY same as > EXARCHATE

EXCAMB vb exchange

EXCAMBED > EXCAMB

EXCAMBING > EXCAMB

EXCAMBION n exchange, esp of land

EXCAMBIUM same as > EXCAMBION

EXCAMBS > EXCAMB

EXCARNATE vb remove flesh from

EXCAUDATE adj having no tail or tail-like process

EXCAVATE vb unearth buried objects from (a piece of land) methodically to learn about the past

EXCAVATED > EXCAVATE

EXCAVATES > EXCAVATE

EXCAVATOR n large machine used for digging

EXCEED vb be greater than

EXCEEDED > EXCEED

EXCEEDER > EXCEED

EXCEEDERS > EXCEED

EXCEEDING adj very great

EXCEEDS > EXCEED

EXCEL vb be superior to

EXCELLED > EXCEL

EXCELLENT adj exceptionally good

EXCELLING > EXCEL

EXCELS > EXCEL

EXCELSIOR n excellent: used as a motto and as a trademark for various products, esp in the US for fine wood shavings used for packing breakable objects

EXCENTRIC same as > ECCENTRIC

EXCEPT prep other than, not including ▷ vb leave out; omit; exclude

EXCEPTANT n person taking exception

EXCEPTED > EXCEPT

EXCEPTING prep except

EXCEPTION n excepting

EXCEPTIVE adj relating to or forming an exception

EXCEPTOR > EXCEPT

EXCEPTORS > EXCEPT

EXCEPTS > EXCEPT

EXCERPT n passage taken from a book, speech, etc ▷ vb take a passage from a book, speech, etc

EXCERPTA > EXCERPTUM

EXCERPTED > EXCERPT

EXCERPTER > EXCERPT

EXCERPTOR > EXCERPT

EXCERPTS > EXCERPT

EXCERPTUM n excerpt

EXCESS n state or act of exceeding the permitted limits ▷ vb make (a position) redundant

EXCESSED > EXCESS

EXCESSES > EXCESS

EXCESSING > EXCESS

EXCESSIVE adj exceeding the normal or permitted extents or limits

EXCHANGE vb give or receive (something) in return for something else ▷ n act of exchanging

EXCHANGED > EXCHANGE

EXCHANGER n person or thing that exchanges

EXCHANGES > EXCHANGE

EXCHEAT same as > ESCHEAT

EXCHEATS > EXCHEAT

EXCHEQUER n (in Britain and certain other countries) accounting department of the Treasury, responsible for receiving and issuing funds

EXCIDE vb cut out

EXCIDED > EXCIDE

EXCIDES > EXCIDE

EXCIDING > EXCIDE

EXCIMER n excited dimer formed by the association of excited and unexcited molecules, which would remain dissociated in the ground state

EXCIMERS > EXCIMER

EXCIPIENT n substance, such as sugar or gum, used to prepare a drug or drugs in a form suitable for administration

EXCIPLE n part of a lichen

EXCIPLES > EXCIPLE

EXCISABLE > EXCISE

EXCISE n tax on goods produced for the home market ▷ vb cut out or away

EXCISED > EXCISE

EXCISEMAN n (formerly) a government agent who collected excise and prevented smuggling

EXCISEMEN > EXCISEMAN

EXCISES > EXCISE

EXCISING > EXCISE

EXCISION > EXCISE

EXCISIONS > EXCISE

EXCITABLE adj easily excited

EXCITABLY > EXCITABLE

EXCITANCY n ability to excite

EXCITANT adj able to excite or stimulate ▷ n something, such as a drug or other agent, able to excite

EXCITANTS > EXCITANT

EXCITE vb arouse to strong emotion

EXCITED adj emotionally aroused, esp to pleasure or agitation

EXCITEDLY > EXCITED

EXCITER n person or thing that excites

EXCITERS > EXCITER

EXCITES > EXCITE

EXCITING adj causing excitement

EXCITON n mobile neutral entity in a crystalline solid consisting of an excited electron bound to the hole produced by its excitation

EXCITONIC > EXCITON

EXCITONS > EXCITON

EXCITOR n nerve that, when stimulated, causes increased activity in the organ or part it supplies

EXCITORS > EXCITOR

EXCLAIM vb speak suddenly,

cry out

EXCLAIMED > EXCLAIM

EXCLAIMER > EXCLAIM

EXCLAIMS > EXCLAIM

EXCLAVE *n* part of a country entirely surrounded by foreign territory: viewed from the position of the home country

EXCLAVES > EXCLAVE

EXCLOSURE *n* area of land, esp in a forest, fenced round to keep out unwanted animals

EXCLUDE *vb* keep out, leave out

EXCLUDED > EXCLUDE

EXCLUDEE > EXCLUDE

EXCLUDEES > EXCLUDE

EXCLUDER > EXCLUDE

EXCLUDERS > EXCLUDE

EXCLUDES > EXCLUDE

EXCLUDING *prep* excepting

EXCLUSION *n* act or an instance of excluding or the state of being excluded

EXCLUSIVE *adj* excluding everything else ▷ *n* story reported in only one newspaper

EXCLUSORY > EXCLUDE

EXCORIATE *vb* censure severely

EXCREMENT *n* waste matter discharged from the body

EXCRETA *n* excrement

EXCRETAL > EXCRETA

EXCRETE *vb* discharge (waste matter) from the body

EXCRETED > EXCRETE

EXCRETER > EXCRETE

EXCRETERS > EXCRETE

EXCRETES > EXCRETE

EXCRETING > EXCRETE

EXCRETION > EXCRETE

EXCRETIVE > EXCRETE

EXCRETORY > EXCRETE

EXCUBANT *adj* keeping guard

EXCUDIT *sentence substitute* (named person) made this

EXCULPATE *vb* free from blame or guilt

EXCURRENT *adj* having an outward flow, as certain pores in sponges, ducts, etc

EXCURSE *vb* wander

EXCURSED > EXCURSE

EXCURSES > EXCURSE

EXCURSING > EXCURSE

EXCURSION *n* short journey, esp for pleasure

EXCURSIVE *adj* tending to digress

EXCURSUS *n* incidental digression from the main topic under discussion or from the main story in a narrative

EXCUSABLE > EXCUSE

EXCUSABLY > EXCUSE

EXCUSAL > EXCUSE

EXCUSALS > EXCUSE

EXCUSE *n* explanation offered to justify (a fault etc) ▷ *vb* put forward a

reason or justification for (a fault etc)

EXCUSED > EXCUSE

EXCUSER > EXCUSE

EXCUSERS > EXCUSE

EXCUSES > EXCUSE

EXCUSING > EXCUSE

EXCUSIVE *adj* excusing

EXEAT *n* leave of absence from school or some other institution

EXEATS > EXEAT

EXEC *n* executive

EXECRABLE *adj* of very poor quality

EXECRABLY > EXECRABLE

EXECRATE *vb* feel and express loathing and hatred of (someone or something)

EXECRATED > EXECRATE

EXECRATES > EXECRATE

EXECRATOR > EXECRATE

EXECS > EXEC

EXECUTANT *n* performer, esp of musical works

EXECUTARY *n* person whose job comprises tasks appropriate to a middle-management executive as well as those traditionally carried out by a secretary

EXECUTE *vb* put (a condemned person) to death

EXECUTED > EXECUTE

EXECUTER > EXECUTE

EXECUTERS > EXECUTE

EXECUTES > EXECUTE

EXECUTING > EXECUTE

EXECUTION *n* act of executing

EXECUTIVE *n* person or group in an administrative position ▷ *adj* having the function of carrying out plans, orders, laws, etc

EXECUTOR *n* person appointed to perform the instructions of a will

EXECUTORS > EXECUTOR

EXECUTORY *adj* (of a law, agreement, etc) coming into operation at a future date

EXECUTRIX *n* female executor

EXECUTRY *n* condition of being an executor

EXED > EX

EXEDRA *n* building, room, portico, or apse containing a continuous bench, used in ancient Greece and Rome for holding discussions

EXEDRAE > EXEDRA

EXEEM *same as* > EXEME

EXEEMED > EXEEM

EXEEMING > EXEEM

EXEEMS > EXEEM

EXEGESES > EXEGESIS

EXEGESIS *n* explanation of a text, esp of the Bible

EXEGETE *n* person who practises exegesis

EXEGETES > EXEGETE

EXEGETIC *adj* of or relating to exegesis

EXEGETICS *n* scientific study of exegesis and exegetical methods

EXEGETIST *same as* > EXEGETE

EXEME *vb* set free

EXEMED > EXEME

EXEMES > EXEME

EXEMING > EXEME

EXEMPLA > EXEMPLUM

EXEMPLAR *n* person or thing to be copied, model

EXEMPLARS > EXEMPLAR

EXEMPLARY *adj* being a good example

EXEMPLE *same as* > EXAMPLE

EXEMPLES > EXEMPLE

EXEMPLIFY *vb* show an example of

EXEMPLUM *n* anecdote that supports a moral point or sustains an argument, used esp in medieval sermons

EXEMPT *adj* not subject to an obligation etc ▷ *vb* release from an obligation etc ▷ *n* person who is exempt from an obligation, tax, etc

EXEMPTED > EXEMPT

EXEMPTING > EXEMPT

EXEMPTION > EXEMPT

EXEMPTIVE > EXEMPT

EXEMPTS > EXEMPT

EXEQUATUR *n* official authorization issued by a host country to a consular agent, permitting him to perform his official duties

EXEQUIAL > EXEQUY

EXEQUIES > EXEQUY

EXEQUY *n* funeral rite

EXERCISE *n* activity to train the body or mind ▷ *vb* make use of

EXERCISED > EXERCISE

EXERCISER *n* device with springs or elasticated cords for muscular exercise

EXERCISES > EXERCISE

EXERCYCLE *n* exercise bicycle

EXERGONIC *adj* (of a biochemical reaction) producing energy and therefore occurring spontaneously

EXERGUAL > EXERGUE

EXERGUE *n* space on the reverse of a coin or medal below the central design, often containing the date, place of minting, etc

EXERGUES > EXERGUE

EXERT *vb* use (influence, authority, etc) forcefully or effectively

EXERTED > EXERT

EXERTING > EXERT

EXERTION > EXERT

EXERTIONS > EXERT

EXERTIVE > EXERT

EXERTS > EXERT

EXES > EX

EXEUNT *vb* (they) go out

EXFOLIANT *n* cosmetic removing dead skin

EXFOLIATE *vb* peel in scales or layers

EXHALABLE > EXHALE

EXHALANT *adj* emitting a vapour or liquid ▷ *n* organ or vessel that emits a vapour or liquid

EXHALANTS > EXHALANT

EXHALE *vb* breathe out

EXHALED > EXHALE

EXHALENT *same as* > EXHALANT

EXHALENTS > EXHALENT

EXHALES > EXHALE

EXHALING > EXHALE

EXHAUST *vb* tire out ▷ *n* gases ejected from an engine as waste products

EXHAUSTED > EXHAUST

EXHAUSTER > EXHAUST

EXHAUSTS > EXHAUST

EXHEDRA *same as* > EXEDRA

EXHEDRAE > EXHEDRA

EXHIBIT *vb* display to the public ▷ *n* object exhibited to the public

EXHIBITED > EXHIBIT

EXHIBITER > EXHIBIT

EXHIBITOR *n* person or thing that exhibits

EXHIBITS > EXHIBIT

EXHORT *vb* urge earnestly

EXHORTED > EXHORT

EXHORTER > EXHORT

EXHORTERS > EXHORT

EXHORTING > EXHORT

EXHORTS > EXHORT

EXHUMATE *same as* > EXHUME

EXHUMATED > EXHUMATE

EXHUMATES > EXHUMATE

EXHUME *vb* dig up (something buried, esp a corpse)

EXHUMED > EXHUME

EXHUMER > EXHUME

EXHUMERS > EXHUME

EXHUMES > EXHUME

EXHUMING > EXHUME

EXIES *n* hysterics

EXIGEANT *adj* exacting

EXIGEANTE *same as* > EXIGEANT

EXIGENCE *same as* > EXIGENCY

EXIGENCES > EXIGENCE

EXIGENCY *n* urgent demand or need

EXIGENT *adj* urgent ▷ *n* emergency

EXIGENTLY > EXIGENT

EXIGENTS > EXIGENT

EXIGIBLE *adj* liable to be exacted or required

EXIGUITY > EXIGUOUS

EXIGUOUS *adj* scanty or meagre

EXILABLE > EXILE

EXILE *n* prolonged, usu enforced, absence from one's country ▷ *vb* expel from one's country

EXILED > EXILE

EXILEMENT *same as* > EXILE

EXILER > EXILE
EXILERS > EXILE
EXILES > EXILE
EXILIAN > EXILE
EXILIC > EXILE
EXILING > EXILE
EXILITIES > EXILITY
EXILITY n poverty or
   meagreness
EXIMIOUS adj select and
   distinguished
EXINE n outermost coat of
   a pollen grain or a spore
EXINES > EXINE
EXING > EX
EXIST vb have being or
   reality
EXISTED > EXIST
EXISTENCE n fact or state
   of being real, live, or actual
EXISTENT adj in existence
   ▷ n person or a thing that
   exists
EXISTENTS > EXISTENT
EXISTING > EXIST
EXISTS > EXIST
EXIT n way out ▷ vb go out
EXITANCE n measure of the
   ability of a surface to emit
   radiation
EXITANCES > EXITANCE
EXITED > EXIT
EXITING > EXIT
EXITLESS > EXIT
EXITS > EXIT
EXO informal word
   for > EXCELLENT
EXOCARP same as > EPICARP
EXOCARPS > EXOCARP
EXOCRINE adj relating
   to a gland, such as the
   sweat gland, that secretes
   externally through a duct
   ▷ n exocrine gland
EXOCRINES > EXOCRINE
EXOCYCLIC adj (of a sea
   urchin) having the anus
   situated outside the apical
   disc
EXOCYTIC adj outside
   biological cell
EXOCYTOSE vb secrete
   substance from within cell
EXODE n exodus
EXODERM same
   as > ECTODERM
EXODERMAL > EXODERM
EXODERMIS same
   as > ECTODERM
EXODERMS > EXODERM
EXODES > EXODE
EXODIC > EXODE
EXODIST > EXODUS
EXODISTS > EXODUS
EXODOI > EXODOS
EXODONTIA n branch of
   dental surgery concerned
   with the extraction of teeth
EXODOS n processional song
   performed at the end of
   a play
EXODUS n departure of a
   large number of people
EXODUSES > EXODUS
EXOENZYME n extracellular
   enzyme
EXOERGIC adj (of a nuclear

reaction) occurring with
   evolution of energy
EXOGAMIC > EXOGAMY
EXOGAMIES > EXOGAMY
EXOGAMOUS > EXOGAMY
EXOGAMY n custom or an
   act of marrying a person
   belonging to another tribe,
   clan, or similar social unit
EXOGEN n plant with a stem
   that develops through the
   growth of new layers on its
   outside
EXOGENISM > EXOGENOUS
EXOGENOUS adj having an
   external origin
EXOGENS > EXOGEN
EXOMION same as > EXOMIS
EXOMIONS > EXOMION
EXOMIS n sleeveless jacket
EXOMISES > EXOMIS
EXON n one of the four
   officers who command the
   Yeomen of the Guard
EXONERATE vb free from
   blame or a criminal charge
EXONIC > EXON
EXONS > EXON
EXONUMIA n objects of
   interest to numismatists
   that are not coins, such as
   medals and tokens
EXONUMIST n collector of
   medals and tokens
EXONYM n name given to a
   place by foreigners
EXONYMS > EXONYM
EXOPHAGY n (among
   cannibals) custom of
   eating only members of
   other tribes
EXOPHORIC adj denoting or
   relating to a pronoun such
   as "I" or "you", the meaning
   of which is determined
   by reference outside the
   discourse rather than by
   a preceding or following
   expression
EXOPLANET n planet that
   orbits a star in a solar
   system other than that of
   Earth
EXOPLASM another name
   for > ECTOPLASM
EXOPLASMS > EXOPLASM
EXOPOD same
   as > EXOPODITE
EXOPODITE n outer
   projection on the hind legs
   of some crustaceans
EXOPODS > EXOPOD
EXORABLE adj able to be
   persuaded or moved by
   pleading
EXORATION n plea
EXORCISE same
   as > EXORCIZE
EXORCISED > EXORCISE
EXORCISER > EXORCISE
EXORCISES > EXORCISE
EXORCISM > EXORCIZE
EXORCISMS > EXORCIZE
EXORCIST > EXORCIZE
EXORCISTS > EXORCIZE
EXORCIZE vb expel (evil
   spirits) by prayers and

religious rites
EXORCIZED > EXORCIZE
EXORCIZER > EXORCIZE
EXORCIZES > EXORCIZE
EXORDIA > EXORDIUM
EXORDIAL > EXORDIUM
EXORDIUM n introductory
   part or beginning, esp of an
   oration or discourse
EXORDIUMS > EXORDIUM
EXOSMIC > EXOSMOSIS
EXOSMOSE same
   as > EXOSMOSIS
EXOSMOSES > EXOSMOSIS
EXOSMOSIS n osmosis in
   which water flows from a
   cell or organism into the
   surrounding solution
EXOSMOTIC > EXOSMOSIS
EXOSPHERE n outermost
   layer of the earth's
   atmosphere
EXOSPORAL > EXOSPORE
EXOSPORE n outer layer of
   the spores of some algae
   and fungi
EXOSPORES > EXOSPORE
EXOSPORIA n exospores
EXOSTOSES > EXOSTOSIS
EXOSTOSIS n abnormal
   bony outgrowth from the
   surface of a bone
EXOTERIC adj intelligible to
   or intended for more than a
   select or initiated minority
EXOTIC adj having a strange
   allure or beauty ▷ n non-
   native plant
EXOTICA pl n (collection of)
   exotic objects
EXOTICISM > EXOTIC
EXOTICIST > EXOTIC
EXOTICS > EXOTIC
EXOTISM > EXOTIC
EXOTISMS > EXOTIC
EXOTOXIC > EXOTOXIN
EXOTOXIN n toxin produced
   by a microorganism
   and secreted into the
   surrounding medium
EXOTOXINS > EXOTOXIN
EXOTROPIA n condition in
   which eye turns outwards
EXOTROPIC > EXOTROPIA
EXPAND vb make or become
   larger
EXPANDED adj (of printer's
   type) wider than usual for a
   particular height
EXPANDER n device for
   exercising and developing
   the muscles of the body
EXPANDERS > EXPANDER
EXPANDING > EXPAND
EXPANDOR same
   as > EXPANDER
EXPANDORS > EXPANDOR
EXPANDS > EXPAND
EXPANSE n uninterrupted
   wide area
EXPANSES > EXPANSE
EXPANSILE adj able to
   expand or cause expansion
EXPANSION n act of
   expanding
EXPANSIVE adj wide or
   extensive

EXPAT n short for
EXPATIATE vb speak or
   write at great length (on)
EXPATS > EXPAT
EXPECT vb regard as
   probable
EXPECTANT adj expecting
   or hopeful ▷ n person who
   expects something
EXPECTED > EXPECT
EXPECTER n person who
   expects
EXPECTERS > EXPECTER
EXPECTING adj pregnant
EXPECTS > EXPECT
EXPEDIENT n something
   that achieves a particular
   purpose ▷ adj suitable
   to the circumstances,
   appropriate
EXPEDITE vb hasten
   the progress of ▷ adj
   unimpeded or prompt
EXPEDITED > EXPEDITE
EXPEDITER n person who
   expedites something,
   esp a person employed
   in an industry to ensure
   that work on each job
   progresses efficiently
EXPEDITES > EXPEDITE
EXPEDITOR same
   as > EXPEDITER
EXPEL vb drive out with
   force
EXPELLANT adj forcing out
   or having the capacity to
   force out ▷ n medicine
   used to expel undesirable
   substances or organisms
   from the body, esp worms
   from the digestive tract
EXPELLED > EXPEL
EXPELLEE > EXPEL
EXPELLEES > EXPEL
EXPELLENT same
   as > EXPELLANT
EXPELLER > EXPEL
EXPELLERS pl n residue
   remaining after an oilseed
   has been crushed to expel
   the oil, used for animal
   fodder
EXPELLING > EXPEL
EXPELS > EXPEL
EXPEND vb spend, use up
EXPENDED > EXPEND
EXPENDER > EXPEND
EXPENDERS > EXPEND
EXPENDING > EXPEND
EXPENDS > EXPEND
EXPENSE n cost
EXPENSED > EXPENSE
EXPENSES > EXPENSE
EXPENSING > EXPENSE
EXPENSIVE adj high-priced
EXPERT n person with
   extensive skill or
   knowledge in a particular
   field ▷ adj skilful or
   knowledgeable ▷ vb
   experience
EXPERTED > EXPERT
EXPERTING > EXPERT
EXPERTISE same
   as > EXPERTIZE
EXPERTISM > EXPERTIZE

EXPERTIZE *vb* act as an expert or give an expert opinion (on)

EXPERTLY > EXPERT

EXPERTS > EXPERT

EXPIABLE *adj* capable of being expiated or atoned for

EXPIATE *vb* make amends for

EXPIATED > EXPIATE

EXPIATES > EXPIATE

EXPIATING > EXPIATE

EXPIATION *n* act, process, or a means of expiating

EXPIATOR > EXPIATE

EXPIATORS > EXPIATE

EXPIATORY *adj* capable of making expiation

EXPIRABLE > EXPIRE

EXPIRANT *n* one who expires

EXPIRANTS > EXPIRANT

EXPIRE *vb* finish or run out

EXPIRED > EXPIRE

EXPIRER > EXPIRE

EXPIRERS > EXPIRE

EXPIRES > EXPIRE

EXPIRIES > EXPIRY

EXPIRING > EXPIRE

EXPIRY *n* end, esp of a contract period

EXPISCATE *vb* find; fish out

EXPLAIN *vb* make clear and intelligible

EXPLAINED > EXPLAIN

EXPLAINER > EXPLAIN

EXPLAINS > EXPLAIN

EXPLANT *vb* transfer (living tissue) from its natural site to a new site or to a culture medium ▷ *n* piece of tissue treated in this way

EXPLANTED > EXPLANT

EXPLANTS > EXPLANT

EXPLETIVE *n* swearword ▷ *adj* expressing no particular meaning, esp when filling out a line of verse

EXPLETORY *adj* expletive

EXPLICATE *vb* explain

EXPLICIT *adj* precisely and clearly expressed ▷ *n* word used to indicate the end of a book

EXPLICITS > EXPLICIT

EXPLODE *vb* burst with great violence, blow up

EXPLODED > EXPLODE

EXPLODER > EXPLODE

EXPLODERS > EXPLODE

EXPLODES > EXPLODE

EXPLODING > EXPLODE

EXPLOIT *vb* take advantage of for one's own purposes ▷ *n* notable feat or deed

EXPLOITED > EXPLOIT

EXPLOITER > EXPLOIT

EXPLOITS > EXPLOIT

EXPLORE *vb* investigate

EXPLORED > EXPLORE

EXPLORER > EXPLORE

EXPLORERS > EXPLORE

EXPLORES > EXPLORE

EXPLORING > EXPLORE

EXPLOSION *n* exploding

EXPLOSIVE *adj* tending to explode ▷ *n* substance that causes explosions

EXPO *n* exposition, large public exhibition

EXPONENT *n* person who advocates an idea, cause, etc ▷ *adj* offering a declaration, explanation, or interpretation

EXPONENTS > EXPONENT

EXPONIBLE *adj* able to be explained

EXPORT *n* selling or shipping of goods to a foreign country ▷ *vb* sell or ship (goods) to a foreign country

EXPORTED > EXPORT

EXPORTER > EXPORT

EXPORTERS > EXPORT

EXPORTING > EXPORT

EXPORTS > EXPORT

EXPOS > EXPO

EXPOSABLE > EXPOSE

EXPOSAL > EXPOSE

EXPOSALS > EXPOSE

EXPOSE *vb* uncover or reveal ▷ *n* bringing of a crime, scandal, etc to public notice

EXPOSED *adj* not concealed

EXPOSER > EXPOSE

EXPOSERS > EXPOSE

EXPOSES > EXPOSE

EXPOSING > EXPOSE

EXPOSIT *vb* state

EXPOSITED > EXPOSIT

EXPOSITOR *n* person who expounds

EXPOSITS > EXPOSIT

EXPOSTURE *n* exposure

EXPOSURE *n* exposing

EXPOSURES > EXPOSURE

EXPOUND *vb* explain in detail

EXPOUNDED > EXPOUND

EXPOUNDER > EXPOUND

EXPOUNDS > EXPOUND

EXPRESS *vb* put into words ▷ *adj* explicitly stated ▷ *n* fast train or bus stopping at only a few stations ▷ *adv* by express delivery

EXPRESSED > EXPRESS

EXPRESSER > EXPRESS

EXPRESSES > EXPRESS

EXPRESSLY *adv* definitely

EXPRESSO *variant of* > ESPRESSO

EXPRESSOS > EXPRESSO

EXPUGN *vb* storm

EXPUGNED > EXPUGN

EXPUGNING > EXPUGN

EXPUGNS > EXPUGN

EXPULSE *vb* expel

EXPULSED > EXPULSE

EXPULSES > EXPULSE

EXPULSING > EXPULSE

EXPULSION *n* act of expelling or the fact of being expelled

EXPULSIVE *adj* tending or serving to expel

EXPUNCT *vb* expunge

EXPUNCTED > EXPUNCT

EXPUNCTS > EXPUNCT

EXPUNGE *vb* delete, erase, blot out

EXPUNGED > EXPUNGE

EXPUNGER > EXPUNGE

EXPUNGERS > EXPUNGE

EXPUNGES > EXPUNGE

EXPUNGING > EXPUNGE

EXPURGATE *vb* remove objectionable parts from (a book etc)

EXPURGE *vb* purge

EXPURGED > EXPURGE

EXPURGES > EXPURGE

EXPURGING > EXPURGE

EXQUISITE *adj* of extreme beauty or delicacy ▷ *n* dandy

EXSCIND *vb* cut off or out

EXSCINDED > EXSCIND

EXSCINDS > EXSCIND

EXSECANT *n* trigonometric function

EXSECANTS > EXSECANT

EXSECT *vb* cut out

EXSECTED > EXSECT

EXSECTING > EXSECT

EXSECTION > EXSECT

EXSECTS > EXSECT

EXSERT *vb* thrust out ▷ *adj* protruded, stretched out, or (esp of stamens) projecting beyond the corolla of a flower

EXSERTED > EXSERT

EXSERTILE > EXSERT

EXSERTING > EXSERT

EXSERTION > EXSERT

EXSERTS > EXSERT

EXSICCANT > EXSICCATE

EXSICCATE *vb* dry up

EXSTROPHY *n* congenital eversion of a hollow organ, esp the urinary bladder

EXSUCCOUS *adj* without sap or juice

EXTANT *adj* still existing

EXTASIES > EXTASY

EXTASY *same as* > ECSTASY

EXTATIC *same as* > ECSTATIC

EXTEMPORE *adj* without planning or preparation ▷ *adv* without planning or preparation

EXTEND *vb* draw out or be drawn out, stretch

EXTENDANT *adj* (in heraldry) with wings spread

EXTENDED *same as* > EXPANDED

EXTENDER *n* person or thing that extends

EXTENDERS > EXTENDER

EXTENDING > EXTEND

EXTENDS > EXTEND

EXTENSE *adj* extensive

EXTENSILE *adj* capable of being extended

EXTENSION *n* room or rooms added to an existing building ▷ *adj* denoting something that can be extended or that extends another object

EXTENSITY *n* that part of sensory perception relating to the spatial aspect of objects

EXTENSIVE *adj* having a large extent, widespread

EXTENSOR *n* muscle that extends a part of the body

EXTENSORS > EXTENSOR

EXTENT *n* range over which something extends, area

EXTENTS > EXTENT

EXTENUATE *vb* make (an offence or fault) less blameworthy

EXTERIOR *n* part or surface on the outside ▷ *adj* of, on, or coming from the outside

EXTERIORS > EXTERIOR

EXTERMINE *vb* exterminate

EXTERN *n* person, such as a physician at a hospital, who has an official connection with an institution but does not reside in it

EXTERNAL *adj* of, situated on, or coming from the outside ▷ *n* external circumstance or aspect, esp one that is superficial or inessential

EXTERNALS > EXTERNAL

EXTERNAT *n* day school

EXTERNATS > EXTERNAT

EXTERNE *same as* > EXTERN

EXTERNES > EXTERNE

EXTERNS > EXTERN

EXTINCT *adj* having died out ▷ *vb* extinguish

EXTINCTED > EXTINCT

EXTINCTS > EXTINCT

EXTINE *same as* > EXINE

EXTINES > EXTINE

EXTIRP *vb* extirpate

EXTIRPATE *vb* destroy utterly

EXTIRPED > EXTIRP

EXTIRPING > EXTIRP

EXTIRPS > EXTIRP

EXTOL *vb* praise highly

EXTOLD *archaic past participle of* > EXTOL

EXTOLL *same as* > EXTOL

EXTOLLED > EXTOLL

EXTOLLER > EXTOL

EXTOLLERS > EXTOL

EXTOLLING > EXTOLL

EXTOLLS > EXTOLL

EXTOLMENT > EXTOL

EXTOLS > EXTOL

EXTORSIVE *adj* intended or tending to extort

EXTORT *vb* get (something) by force or threats

EXTORTED > EXTORT

EXTORTER > EXTORT

EXTORTERS > EXTORT

EXTORTING > EXTORT

EXTORTION *n* act of securing money, favours, etc by intimidation or violence

EXTORTIVE > EXTORT

EXTORTS > EXTORT

EXTRA *adj* more than is usual, expected or needed ▷ *n* additional person or thing ▷ *adv* unusually or exceptionally

EXTRABOLD *n* very bold typeface

EXTRACT vb pull out by force ▷ n something extracted, such as a passage from a book etc
EXTRACTED > EXTRACT
EXTRACTOR n person or thing that extracts
EXTRACTS > EXTRACT
EXTRADITE vb send (an accused person) back to his or her own country for trial
EXTRADOS n outer curve or surface of an arch or vault
EXTRAIT n extracts
EXTRAITS > EXTRAIT
EXTRALITY n diplomatic immunity
EXTRANET n intranet that is modified to allow outsiders access to it, esp one belonging to a business that allows access to customers
EXTRANETS > EXTRANET
EXTRAPOSE vb move (a word or words) to the end of a clause or sentence
EXTRAS > EXTRA
EXTRAUGHT old past participle of > EXTRACT
EXTRAVERT same as > EXTROVERT
EXTREAT n extraction
EXTREATS > EXTREAT
EXTREMA > EXTREMUM
EXTREMAL n clause in a recursive definition that specifies that no items other than those generated by the stated rules fall within the definition, as in 1 is an integer, if n is an integer so is n+1, and nothing else is
EXTREMALS > EXTREMAL
EXTREME adj of a high or the highest degree or intensity ▷ n either of the two limits of a scale or range
EXTREMELY > EXTREME
EXTREMER > EXTREME
EXTREMES > EXTREME
EXTREMEST > EXTREME
EXTREMISM > EXTREMIST
EXTREMIST n person who favours immoderate methods ▷ adj holding extreme opinions
EXTREMITY n farthest point
EXTREMUM n extreme point
EXTRICATE vb free from complication or difficulty
EXTRINSIC adj not contained or included within
EXTRORSAL same as > EXTRORSE
EXTRORSE adj turned or opening outwards or away from the axis
EXTROVERT adj lively and outgoing ▷ n extrovert person
EXTRUDE vb squeeze or force out
EXTRUDED > EXTRUDE
EXTRUDER > EXTRUDE

EXTRUDERS > EXTRUDE
EXTRUDES > EXTRUDE
EXTRUDING > EXTRUDE
EXTRUSION n act or process of extruding
EXTRUSIVE adj tending to extrude
EXTRUSORY > EXTRUDE
EXTUBATE vb remove tube from hollow organ
EXTUBATED > EXTUBATE
EXTUBATES > EXTUBATE
EXUBERANT adj high-spirited
EXUBERATE vb be exuberant
EXUDATE same as > EXUDATION
EXUDATES > EXUDATE
EXUDATION n act of exuding or oozing out
EXUDATIVE > EXUDATION
EXUDE vb (of a liquid or smell) seep or flow out slowly and steadily
EXUDED > EXUDE
EXUDES > EXUDE
EXUDING > EXUDE
EXUL n exile
EXULS > EXUL
EXULT vb be joyful or jubilant
EXULTANCE > EXULTANT
EXULTANCY > EXULTANT
EXULTANT adj elated or jubilant, esp because of triumph or success
EXULTED > EXULT
EXULTING > EXULT
EXULTS > EXULT
EXURB n residential area beyond suburbs
EXURBAN > EXURBIA
EXURBIA n region outside the suburbs of a city, consisting of residential areas that are occupied predominantly by rich commuters
EXURBIAS > EXURBIA
EXURBS > EXURB
EXUVIA n cast-off exoskeleton of animal
EXUVIAE > EXUVIA
EXUVIAL > EXUVIA
EXUVIATE vb shed (a skin or similar outer covering)
EXUVIATED > EXUVIATE
EXUVIATES > EXUVIATE
EXUVIUM n cast-off exoskeleton of animal
EYALET n province of Ottoman Empire
EYALETS > EYALET
EYAS n nestling hawk or falcon, esp one reared for training in falconry
EYASES > EYAS
EYASS same as > EYAS
EYASSES > EYASS
EYE n organ of sight ▷ vb look at carefully or warily
EYEABLE adj pleasant to look at
EYEBALL n ball-shaped part of the eye ▷ vb eye
EYEBALLED > EYEBALL
EYEBALLS > EYEBALL

EYEBANK n place in which corneas are stored for use in corneal grafts
EYEBANKS > EYEBANK
EYEBAR n bar with flattened ends with holes for connecting pins
EYEBARS > EYEBAR
EYEBATH same as > EYECUP
EYEBATHS > EYEBATH
EYEBEAM n glance
EYEBEAMS > EYEBEAM
EYEBLACK another name for > MASCARA
EYEBLACKS > EYEBLACK
EYEBLINK n very small amount of time
EYEBLINKS > EYEBLINK
EYEBOLT n threaded bolt, the head of which is formed into a ring or eye for lifting, pulling, or securing
EYEBOLTS > EYEBOLT
EYEBRIGHT n any scrophulariaceous annual plant of the genus Euphrasia, esp E. nemorosa, having small white-and-purple two-lipped flowers: formerly used in the treatment of eye disorders
EYEBROW n line of hair on the bony ridge above the eye ▷ vb equip with artificial eyebrows
EYEBROWED > EYEBROW
EYEBROWS > EYEBROW
EYECUP same as > EYEBATH
EYECUPS > EYECUP
EYED > EYE
EYEDNESS > EYE
EYEDROPS n medicine applied to the eyes in drops
EYEFOLD n fold of skin above eye
EYEFOLDS > EYEFOLD
EYEFUL n view
EYEFULS > EYEFUL
EYEGLASS n lens for aiding defective vision
EYEHOLE n hole through which something, such as a rope, hook, or bar, is passed
EYEHOLES > EYEHOLE
EYEHOOK n hook attached to a ring at the extremity of a rope or chain
EYEHOOKS > EYEHOOK
EYEING > EYE
EYELASH n short hair that grows out from the eyelid
EYELASHES > EYELASH
EYELESS > EYE
EYELET n small hole for a lace or cord to be passed through ▷ vb supply with an eyelet or eyelets
EYELETED > EYELET
EYELETEER n small bodkin or other pointed tool for making eyelet holes
EYELETING > EYELET
EYELETS > EYELET
EYELETTED > EYELET
EYELEVEL adj level with a person's eyes

EYELIAD same as > OEILLADE
EYELIADS > EYELIAD
EYELID n fold of skin that covers the eye when it is closed
EYELIDS > EYELID
EYELIFT n cosmetic surgery for eyes
EYELIFTS > EYELIFT
EYELIKE > EYE
EYELINER n cosmetic used to outline the eyes
EYELINERS > EYELINER
EYEN pl n eyes
EYEOPENER n something surprising
EYEPIECE n lens in a microscope, telescope, etc, into which the person using it looks
EYEPIECES > EYEPIECE
EYEPOINT n position of a lens at which the sharpest image is obtained
EYEPOINTS > EYEPOINT
EYEPOPPER n something that excites the eye
EYER n someone who eyes
EYERS > EYER
EYES > EYE
EYESHADE n opaque or tinted translucent visor, worn on the head like a cap to protect the eyes from glare
EYESHADES > EYESHADE
EYESHADOW n coloured cosmetic put around the eyes so as to enhance their colour or shape
EYESHINE n reflection of light from animal eye at night
EYESHINES > EYESHINE
EYESHOT n range of vision
EYESHOTS > EYESHOT
EYESIGHT n ability to see
EYESIGHTS > EYESIGHT
EYESOME adj attractive
EYESORE n ugly object
EYESORES > EYESORE
EYESPOT n small area of light-sensitive pigment in some protozoans, algae, and other simple organisms
EYESPOTS > EYESPOT
EYESTALK n movable stalk bearing a compound eye at its tip: occurs in crustaceans and some molluscs
EYESTALKS > EYESTALK
EYESTONE n device for removing foreign body from eye
EYESTONES > EYESTONE
EYESTRAIN n fatigue or irritation of the eyes, caused by tiredness or a failure to wear glasses
EYETEETH > EYETOOTH
EYETOOTH n either of the two canine teeth in the upper jaw
EYEWASH n nonsense
EYEWASHES > EYEWASH

EYEWATER *n* lotion for the eyes

EYEWATERS > EYEWATER

EYEWEAR *n* spectacles; glasses

EYEWINK *n* wink of the eye; instant

EYEWINKS > EYEWINK

EYING > EYE

EYLIAD *same as* > OEILLADE

EYLIADS > EYLIAD

EYNE *poetic plural of* > EYE

EYOT *n* island

EYOTS > EYOT

EYRA *n* reddish-brown variety of the jaguarondi

EYRAS > EYRA

EYRE *n* any of the circuit courts held in each shire from 1176 until the late 13th century

EYRES > EYRE

EYRIE *n* nest of an eagle

EYRIES > EYRIE

EYRIR *n* Icelandic monetary unit worth one hundredth of a krona

EYRY *same as* > EYRIE

e

Ff

f

FA *same as* > FAH

FAA *Scot word for* > FALL

FAAING > FAA

FAAN > FAA

FAAS > FAA

FAB *adj* excellent ▷ *n* excellent thing

FABACEOUS *less common term for* > LEGUMINOUS

FABBER > FAB

FABBEST > FAB

FABLE *n* story with a moral ▷ *vb* relate or tell (fables)

FABLED *adj* made famous in legend

FABLER > FABLE

FABLERS > FABLE

FABLES > FABLE

FABLIAU *n* comic usually ribald verse tale, of a kind popular in France in the 12th and 13th centuries

FABLIAUX > FABLIAU

FABLING > FABLE

FABLINGS > FABLE

FABRIC *n* knitted or woven cloth

FABRICANT *n* manufacturer

FABRICATE *vb* make up (a story or lie)

FABRICKED *adj* built

FABRICS > FABRIC

FABS > FAB

FABULAR *adj* relating to fables

FABULATE *vb* make up fables

FABULATED > FABULATE

FABULATES > FABULATE

FABULATOR > FABULATE

FABULISE *vb* make up fables

FABULISED > FABULISE

FABULISES > FABULISE

FABULIST *n* person who invents or recounts fables

FABULISTS > FABULIST

FABULIZE *vb* make up fables

FABULIZED > FABULIZE

FABULIZES > FABULIZE

FABULOUS *adj* excellent

FABURDEN *n* early form of counterpoint

FABURDENS > FABURDEN

FACADE *n* front of a building

FACADES > FACADE

FACE *n* front of the head ▷ *vb* look or turn towards

FACEABLE > FACE

FACEBAR *n* wrestling hold in which a wrestler stretches the skin on his opponent's face backwards

FACEBARS > FACEBAR

FACECLOTH *n* small piece of cloth used to wash the face and hands

FACED > FACE

FACEDOWN *vb* confront and force (someone or something) to back down

FACEDOWNS > FACEDOWN

FACELESS *adj* impersonal, anonymous

FACELIFT *n* cosmetic surgery for the face

FACELIFTS > FACELIFT

FACEMAIL *n* computer program which uses an electronically generated face to deliver messages on screen

FACEMAILS > FACEMAIL

FACEMAN *n* miner who works at the coalface

FACEMASK *n* protective mask for the face

FACEMASKS > FACEMASK

FACEMEN > FACEMAN

FACEPLATE *n* perforated circular metal plate that can be attached to the headstock of a lathe in order to hold flat or irregularly shaped workpieces

FACEPRINT *n* digitally recorded representation of a person's face that can be used for security purposes because it is as individual as a fingerprint

FACER *n* difficulty or problem

FACERS > FACER

FACES > FACE

FACET *n* aspect ▷ *vb* cut facets in (a gemstone)

FACETE *adj* witty and humorous

FACETED > FACET

FACETELY > FACETE

FACETIAE *pl n* humorous or witty sayings

FACETING > FACET

FACETIOUS *adj* funny or trying to be funny, esp at inappropriate times

FACETS > FACET

FACETTED > FACET

FACETTING > FACET

FACEUP *adj* with the face or surface exposed

FACIA *same as* > FASCIA

FACIAE > FACIA

FACIAL *adj* of or relating to the face ▷ *n* beauty treatment for the face

FACIALLY > FACIAL

FACIALS > FACIAL

FACIAS > FACIA

FACIEND *n* multiplicand

FACIENDS > FACIEND

FACIES *n* general form and appearance of an individual or a group of plants or animals

FACILE *adj* (of a remark, argument, etc) superficial and showing lack of real thought

FACILELY > FACILE

FACILITY *n* skill

FACING *n* lining or covering for decoration or reinforcement

FACINGS > FACING

FACONNE *adj* denoting a fabric with the design woven in ▷ *n* such a fabric

FACONNES > FACONNE

FACSIMILE *n* exact copy ▷ *vb* make an exact copy of

FACT *n* event or thing known to have happened or existed

FACTFUL > FACT

FACTICE *n* soft rubbery material made by reacting sulphur or sulphur chloride with vegetable oil

FACTICES > FACTICE

FACTICITY *n* philosophical process

FACTION *n* (dissenting) minority group within a larger body

FACTIONAL > FACTION

FACTIONS > FACTION

FACTIOUS *adj* of or producing factions

FACTIS *variant of* > FACTICE

FACTISES > FACTIS

FACTITIVE *adj* denoting a verb taking a direct object as well as a noun in apposition, as for example *elect* in *They elected John president*, where *John* is the direct object and *president* is the complement

FACTIVE *adj* (of a linguistic context) giving rise to the presupposition that a sentence occurring in that context is true, as *John regrets that Mary did not attend*

FACTOID *n* piece of unreliable information believed to be true because of the way it is presented or repeated in print

FACTOIDAL > FACTOID

FACTOIDS > FACTOID

FACTOR *n* element contributing to a result ▷ *vb* engage in the business of a factor

FACTORAGE *n* commission payable to a factor

FACTORED > FACTOR

FACTORIAL *n* product of all the integers from one to a given number ▷ *adj* of factorials or factors

FACTORIES > FACTORY

FACTORING *n* business of a factor

FACTORISE *same as* > FACTORIZE

FACTORIZE *vb* calculate the factors of (a number)

FACTORS > FACTOR

FACTORY *n* building where goods are manufactured

FACTOTUM *n* person employed to do all sorts of work

FACTOTUMS > FACTOTUM

FACTS > FACT

FACTSHEET *n* printed sheet containing information relating to items covered in a television or radio programme

FACTUAL *adj* concerning

facts rather than opinions or theories

FACTUALLY > FACTUAL

FACTUM n something done, deed

FACTUMS > FACTUM

FACTURE n construction

FACTURES > FACTURE

FACULA n any of the bright areas on the sun's surface, usually appearing just before a sunspot and subject to the same 11-year cycle

FACULAE > FACULA

FACULAR > FACULA

FACULTIES > FACULTY

FACULTY n physical or mental ability

FACUNDITY n eloquence, fluency of speech

FAD n short-lived fashion

FADABLE > FADE

FADAISE n silly remark

FADAISES > FADAISE

FADDIER > FADDY

FADDIEST > FADDY

FADDINESS n excessive fussiness

FADDISH > FAD

FADDISHLY > FAD

FADDISM > FAD

FADDISMS > FAD

FADDIST > FAD

FADDISTS > FAD

FADDLE vb mess around, toy with

FADDLED > FADDLE

FADDLES > FADDLE

FADDLING > FADDLE

FADDY adj unreasonably fussy, particularly about food

FADE vb (cause to) lose brightness, colour, or strength ▷ n act or an instance of fading

FADEAWAY n fading to the point of disappearance

FADEAWAYS > FADEAWAY

FADED > FADE

FADEDLY > FADE

FADEDNESS > FADE

FADEIN n gradual appearance of image on film

FADEINS > FADEIN

FADELESS adj not subject to fading

FADEOUT n gradual disappearance of image on film

FADEOUTS > FADEOUT

FADER > FADE

FADERS > FADE

FADES > FADE

FADEUR n blandness, insipidity

FADEURS > FADEUR

FADGE vb agree ▷ n package of wool in a wool-bale that weighs less than 100 kilograms

FADGED > FADGE

FADGES > FADGE

FADGING > FADGE

FADIER > FADY

FADIEST > FADY

FADING n variation in the strength of received radio signals due to variations in the conditions of the transmission medium

FADINGS > FADING

FADLIKE > FAD

FADO n type of melancholy Portuguese folk song

FADOMETER n instrument used to determine the resistance to fading of a pigment or dye

FADOS > FADO

FADS > FAD

FADY adj faded

FAE Scot word for > FROM

FAECAL adj of, relating to, or consisting of faeces

FAECES pl n waste matter discharged from the anus

FAENA n matador's final series of passes with sword and cape before the kill

FAENAS > FAENA

FAERIE n land of fairies

FAERIES > FAERY

FAERY same as > FAERIE

FAFF vb dither or fuss

FAFFED > FAFF

FAFFING > FAFF

FAFFS > FAFF

FAG same as > FAGGOT

FAGACEOUS adj of, relating to, or belonging to the Fagaceae, a family of trees, including beech, oak, and chestnut, whose fruit is partly or wholly enclosed in a husk (cupule)

FAGGED > FAG

FAGGERIES > FAGGERY

FAGGERY n offensive term for homosexuality

FAGGIER > FAG

FAGGIEST > FAG

FAGGING > FAG

FAGGINGS > FAG

FAGGOT n ball of chopped liver, herbs, and bread ▷ vb collect into a bundle or bundles

FAGGOTED > FAGGOT

FAGGOTING n decorative needlework done by tying vertical threads together in bundles

FAGGOTRY n offensive term for homosexuality

FAGGOTS > FAGGOT

FAGGOTY > FAGGOT

FAGGY > FAG

FAGIN n criminal

FAGINS > FAGIN

FAGOT same as > FAGGOT

FAGOTED > FAGOT

FAGOTER > FAGOT

FAGOTERS > FAGOT

FAGOTING same as > FAGGOTING

FAGOTINGS > FAGOTING

FAGOTS > FAGOT

FAGOTTI > FAGOTTO

FAGOTTIST n bassoon player

FAGOTTO n bassoon

FAGS > FAG

FAH n (in tonic sol-fa) fourth

degree of any major scale

FAHLBAND n thin bed of schistose rock impregnated with metallic sulphides

FAHLBANDS > FAHLBAND

FAHLERZ n copper ore

FAHLERZES > FAHLERZ

FAHLORE n copper ore

FAHLORES > FAHLORE

FAHS > FAH

FAIBLE variant of > FOIBLE

FAIBLES > FAIBLE

FAIENCE n tin-glazed earthenware

FAIENCES > FAIENCE

FAIK vb grasp

FAIKED > FAIK

FAIKES > FAIK

FAIKING > FAIK

FAIKS > FAIK

FAIL vb be unsuccessful ▷ n instance of not passing an exam or test

FAILED > FAIL

FAILING n weak point ▷ prep in the absence of

FAILINGLY > FAILING

FAILINGS > FAILING

FAILLE n soft light ribbed fabric of silk, rayon, or taffeta

FAILLES > FAILLE

FAILS > FAIL

FAILURE n act or instance of failing

FAILURES > FAILURE

FAIN adv gladly ▷ adj willing or eager

FAINE variant of > FAIN

FAINEANCE > FAINEANT

FAINEANCY > FAINEANT

FAINEANT n lazy person ▷ adj indolent

FAINEANTS > FAINEANT

FAINED > FAIN

FAINER > FAIN

FAINES > FAINE

FAINEST > FAIN

FAINING > FAIN

FAINITES interj cry for truce or respite from the rules of a game

FAINLY > FAIN

FAINNE n small ring-shaped metal badge worn by advocates of the Irish language

FAINNES > FAINNE

FAINNESS > FAIN

FAINS same as > FAINITES

FAINT adj lacking clarity, brightness, or volume ▷ vb lose consciousness temporarily ▷ n temporary loss of consciousness

FAINTED > FAINT

FAINTER > FAINT

FAINTERS > FAINT

FAINTEST > FAINT

FAINTIER > FAINTY

FAINTIEST > FAINTY

FAINTING > FAINT

FAINTINGS > FAINT

FAINTISH > FAINT

FAINTLY > FAINT

FAINTNESS > FAINT

FAINTS > FAINT

FAINTY > FAINT

FAIR adj unbiased and reasonable ▷ adv fairly ▷ n travelling entertainment with sideshows, rides, and amusements ▷ vb join together so as to form a smooth or regular shape or surface

FAIRED > FAIR

FAIRER > FAIR

FAIREST > FAIR

FAIRFACED adj (of brickwork) having a neat smooth unplastered surface

FAIRGOER n person attending fair

FAIRGOERS > FAIRGOER

FAIRIES > FAIRY

FAIRILY > FAIRY

FAIRING n curved metal structure fitted round part of a car, aircraft, etc to reduce drag

FAIRINGS > FAIRING

FAIRISH adj moderately good, well, etc

FAIRISHLY > FAIRISH

FAIRLEAD n block or ring through which a line is rove to keep it clear of obstructions, prevent chafing, or maintain it at an angle

FAIRLEADS > FAIRLEAD

FAIRLY adv moderately

FAIRNESS > FAIR

FAIRS > FAIR

FAIRWAY n smooth area between the tee and the green

FAIRWAYS > FAIRWAY

FAIRY n imaginary small creature with magic powers

FAIRYDOM > FAIRY

FAIRYDOMS > FAIRY

FAIRYHOOD > FAIRY

FAIRYISM > FAIRY

FAIRYISMS > FAIRY

FAIRYLAND n imaginary place where fairies live

FAIRYLIKE > FAIRY

FAIRYTALE n story about fairies or other mythical or magical beings, esp one of traditional origin told to children

FAITH n strong belief, esp without proof

FAITHCURE n healing through prayer

FAITHED adj having faith or a faith

FAITHER Scot word for > FATHER

FAITHERS > FAITHER

FAITHFUL adj loyal

FAITHFULS > FAITHFUL

FAITHING n practising a faith

FAITHLESS adj disloyal or dishonest

FAITHS > FAITH

FAITOR n traitor, impostor

FAITORS > FAITOR

f

Section 1: Words between 2 and 9 letters in length

FAITOUR n impostor
FAITOURS > FAITOUR
FAIX n faith
FAJITA > FAJITAS
FAJITAS pl n Mexican dish of soft tortillas wrapped around fried strips of meat or vegetables
FAKE vb cause something not genuine to appear real or more valuable by fraud ▷ n person, thing, or act that is not genuine ▷ adj not genuine
FAKED > FAKE
FAKEER same as > FAKIR
FAKEERS > FAKEER
FAKEMENT n something false, counterfeit
FAKEMENTS > FAKEMENT
FAKER > FAKE
FAKERIES > FAKE
FAKERS > FAKE
FAKERY > FAKE
FAKES > FAKE
FAKEY n skateboarding term
FAKING > FAKE
FAKIR n Muslim who spurns worldly possessions
FAKIRISM > FAKIR
FAKIRISMS > FAKIR
FAKIRS > FAKIR
FALAFEL n ball or cake of ground spiced chickpeas, deep-fried and often served with pitta bread
FALAFELS > FALAFEL
FALAJ n water channel
FALANGISM > FALANGIST
FALANGIST n member of the Fascist movement founded in Spain in 1933
FALBALA n gathered flounce, frill, or ruffle
FALBALAS > FALBALA
FALCADE n movement of a horse
FALCADES > FALCADE
FALCATE adj shaped like a sickle
FALCATED > FALCATE
FALCATION > FALCATE
FALCES > FALX
FALCHION n short and slightly curved medieval sword broader towards the point
FALCHIONS > FALCHION
FALCIFORM same as > FALCATE
FALCON n small bird of prey
FALCONER n person who breeds or trains hawks or who follows the sport of falconry
FALCONERS > FALCONER
FALCONET n any of various small falcons, esp any of the Asiatic genus Microhierax
FALCONETS > FALCONET
FALCONINE adj of, relating to, or resembling a falcon
FALCONOID n chemical thought to resist cancer
FALCONRY n art of training falcons

FALCONS > FALCON
FALCULA n sharp curved claw, esp of a bird
FALCULAE > FALCULA
FALCULAS > FALCULA
FALCULATE > FALCULA
FALDAGE n feudal right
FALDAGES > FALDAGE
FALDERAL n showy but worthless trifle
FALDERALS > FALDERAL
FALDEROL same as > FALDERAL
FALDEROLS > FALDEROL
FALDETTA n Maltese woman's garment with a stiffened hood
FALDETTAS > FALDETTA
FALDSTOOL n backless seat, sometimes capable of being folded, used by bishops and certain other prelates
FALL vb drop from a higher to a lower place through the force of gravity ▷ n falling
FALLACIES > FALLACY
FALLACY n false belief
FALLAL n showy ornament, trinket, or article of dress
FALLALERY > FALLAL
FALLALS > FALLAL
FALLAWAY n friendship that has been withdrawn
FALLAWAYS > FALLAWAY
FALLBACK n something that recedes or retreats
FALLBACKS > FALLBACK
FALLBOARD n cover for piano keyboard
FALLEN > FALL
FALLER n any device that falls or operates machinery by falling, as in a spinning machine
FALLERS > FALLER
FALLFISH n large North American freshwater cyprinid fish, Semotilus corporalis, resembling the chub
FALLIBLE adj (of a person) liable to make mistakes
FALLIBLY > FALLIBLE
FALLING > FALL
FALLINGS > FALL
FALLOFF n decline or drop
FALLOFFS > FALLOFF
FALLOUT n radioactive particles spread as a result of a nuclear explosion ▷ vb disagree and quarrel ▷ sentence substitute order to leave a parade or disciplinary formation
FALLOUTS > FALLOUT
FALLOW adj (of land) ploughed but left unseeded to regain fertility ▷ n land treated in this way ▷ vb leave (land) unseeded after ploughing and harrowing it
FALLOWED > FALLOW
FALLOWER > FALLOW
FALLOWEST > FALLOW
FALLOWING > FALLOW
FALLOWS > FALLOW

FALLS > FALL
FALSE adj not true or correct ▷ adv in a false or dishonest manner ▷ vb falsify
FALSED > FALSE
FALSEFACE n mask
FALSEHOOD n quality of being untrue
FALSELY > FALSE
FALSENESS > FALSE
FALSER > FALSE
FALSERS n colloquial term for false teeth
FALSES > FALSE
FALSEST > FALSE
FALSETTO n voice pitched higher than one's natural range
FALSETTOS > FALSETTO
FALSEWORK n framework supporting something under construction
FALSIE n pad used to enlarge breast shape
FALSIES > FALSIE
FALSIFIED > FALSIFY
FALSIFIER > FALSIFY
FALSIFIES > FALSIFY
FALSIFY vb alter fraudulently
FALSING > FALSE
FALSISH > FALSE
FALSISM > FALSE
FALSISMS > FALSE
FALSITIES > FALSITY
FALSITY n state of being false
FALTBOAT n collapsible boat made of waterproof material stretched over a light framework
FALTBOATS > FALTBOAT
FALTER vb be hesitant, weak, or unsure ▷ n uncertainty or hesitancy in speech or action
FALTERED > FALTER
FALTERER > FALTER
FALTERERS > FALTER
FALTERING > FALTER
FALTERS > FALTER
FALX n sickle-shaped anatomical structure
FAME n state of being widely known or recognized ▷ vb make known or famous
FAMED > FAME
FAMELESS > FAME
FAMES > FAME
FAMILIAL adj of or relating to the family
FAMILIAR adj well-known ▷ n demon supposed to attend a witch
FAMILIARS n attendant demons
FAMILIES > FAMILY
FAMILISM n practice of a mystical Christian religious sect of the 16th and 17th centuries based upon love
FAMILISMS > FAMILISM
FAMILLE n type of Chinese porcelain
FAMILLES > FAMILLE
FAMILY n group of parents and their children ▷ adj

suitable for parents and children together
FAMINE n severe shortage of food
FAMINES > FAMINE
FAMING > FAME
FAMISH vb be or make very hungry or weak
FAMISHED adj very hungry
FAMISHES > FAMISH
FAMISHING > FAMISH
FAMOUS adj very well-known ▷ vb make famous
FAMOUSED > FAMOUS
FAMOUSES > FAMOUS
FAMOUSING > FAMOUS
FAMOUSLY adv excellently
FAMULI > FAMULUS
FAMULUS n (formerly) the attendant of a sorcerer or scholar
FAMULUSES > FAMULUS
FAN n hand-held or mechanical object used to create a current of air for ventilation or cooling ▷ vb blow or cool with a fan
FANAL n lighthouse
FANALS > FANAL
FANATIC n person who is excessively enthusiastic about something ▷ adj excessively enthusiastic
FANATICAL adj surpassing what is normal or accepted in enthusiasm for or belief in something
FANATICS > FANATIC
FANBASE n body of admirers of a particular pop singer, sports team, etc
FANBASES > FANBASE
FANCIABLE adj sexually attractive
FANCIED adj imaginary
FANCIER n person who is interested in and often breeds plants or animals
FANCIERS > FANCIER
FANCIES > FANCY
FANCIEST > FANCY
FANCIFIED > FANCIFY
FANCIFIES > FANCIFY
FANCIFUL adj not based on fact
FANCIFY vb make more beautiful
FANCILESS > FANCY
FANCILY > FANCY
FANCINESS > FANCY
FANCY adj elaborate, not plain ▷ n sudden irrational liking or desire ▷ vb be sexually attracted to
FANCYING > FANCY
FANCYWORK n ornamental needlework
FAND vb try
FANDANGLE n elaborate ornament
FANDANGO n lively Spanish dance
FANDANGOS > FANDANGO
FANDED > FAND
FANDING > FAND
FANDOM n collectively, the fans of a sport, pastime or person

FANDOMS > FANDOM

FANDS > FAND

FANE n temple or shrine

FANEGA n Spanish unit of measurement

FANEGADA n Spanish unit of land area

FANEGADAS > FANEGADA

FANEGAS > FANEGA

FANES > FANE

FANFARADE n fanfare

FANFARE n short loud tune played on brass instruments ▷ vb perform a fanfare

FANFARED > FANFARE

FANFARES > FANFARE

FANFARING > FANFARE

FANFARON n braggart

FANFARONA n gold chain

FANFARONS > FANFARON

FANFIC n fiction written around previously established characters invented by other authors

FANFICS > FANFIC

FANFOLD vb fold (paper) like a fan

FANFOLDED > FANFOLD

FANFOLDS > FANFOLD

FANG n snake's tooth which injects poison ▷ vb seize

FANGA same as > FANEGA

FANGAS > FANGA

FANGED > FANG

FANGING > FANG

FANGLE vb fashion

FANGLED > FANGLE

FANGLES > FANGLE

FANGLESS > FANG

FANGLIKE > FANG

FANGLING > FANGLE

FANGO n mud from thermal springs in Italy, used in the treatment of rheumatic disease

FANGOS > FANGO

FANGS > FANG

FANION n small flag used by surveyors to mark stations

FANIONS > FANION

FANJET same as > TURBOFAN

FANJETS > FANJET

FANK n sheep pen

FANKLE vb entangle ▷ n tangle

FANKLED > FANKLE

FANKLES > FANKLE

FANKLING > FANKLE

FANKS > FANK

FANLIGHT n semicircular window over a door or window

FANLIGHTS > FANLIGHT

FANLIKE > FAN

FANNED > FAN

FANNEL n ecclesiastical vestment

FANNELL variant of > FANNEL

FANNELLS > FANNELL

FANNELS > FANNEL

FANNER > FAN

FANNERS > FAN

FANNIES > FANNY

FANNING > FAN

FANNINGS > FAN

FANNY n taboo word for female genitals

FANO same as > FANON

FANON n collar-shaped vestment worn by the pope when celebrating mass

FANONS > FANON

FANOS > FANO

FANS > FAN

FANTAD n nervous, agitated state

FANTADS > FANTAD

FANTAIL n small New Zealand bird with a tail like a fan

FANTAILED adj having a tail like a fan

FANTAILS > FANTAIL

FANTASIA n musical composition of an improvised nature

FANTASIAS > FANTASIA

FANTASIE same as > FANTASY

FANTASIED > FANTASY

FANTASIES > FANTASY

FANTASISE same as > FANTASIZE

FANTASIST n person who indulges in fantasies

FANTASIZE vb indulge in daydreams

FANTASM archaic spelling of > PHANTASM

FANTASMAL > FANTASM

FANTASMIC > FANTASM

FANTASMS > FANTASM

FANTASQUE n fantasy

FANTAST n dreamer or visionary

FANTASTIC adj very good ▷ n person who dresses or behaves eccentrically

FANTASTRY n condition of being fantastic

FANTASTS > FANTAST

FANTASY n far-fetched notion ▷ adj of a competition in which a participant selects players for an imaginary, ideal team and points are awarded according to the actual performances of the chosen players ▷ vb fantasize

FANTEEG n nervous, agitated state

FANTEEGS > FANTEEG

FANTIGUE variant of > FANTEEG

FANTIGUES > FANTIGUE

FANTOD n crotchety or faddish behaviour

FANTODS > FANTOD

FANTOM archaic spelling of > PHANTOM

FANTOMS > FANTOM

FANTOOSH adj pretentious

FANUM n temple

FANUMS > FANUM

FANWISE adj like a fan

FANWORT n aquatic plant

FANWORTS > FANWORT

FANZINE n magazine produced by fans of a specific interest, soccer club, etc, for fellow fans

FANZINES > FANZINE

FAP adj drunk

FAQIR same as > FAKIR

FAQIRS > FAQIR

FAQUIR variant of > FAQIR

FAQUIRS > FAQUIR

FAR adv at, to, or from a great distance ▷ adj remote in space or time ▷ vb go far

FARAD n unit of electrical capacitance

FARADAIC same as > FARADIC

FARADAY n quantity of electricity, used in electrochemical calculations

FARADAYS > FARADAY

FARADIC adj of or concerned with an intermittent asymmetric alternating current such as that induced in the secondary winding of an induction coil

FARADISE same as > FARADIZE

FARADISED > FARADISE

FARADISER > FARADISE

FARADISES > FARADISE

FARADISM n therapeutic use of faradic currents

FARADISMS > FARADISM

FARADIZE vb treat (an organ or part) with faradic currents

FARADIZED > FARADIZE

FARADIZER > FARADIZE

FARADIZES > FARADIZE

FARADS > FARAD

FARAND n manner, fashion

FARANDINE n silk and wool cloth

FARANDOLE n lively dance in six-eight or four-four time from Provence

FARAWAY adj very distant

FARAWAYS same as > FARAWAY

FARCE n boisterous comedy ▷ vb enliven (a speech, etc) with jokes

FARCED > FARCE

FARCEMEAT > FORCEMEAT

FARCER same as > FARCEUR

FARCERS > FARCER

FARCES > FARCE

FARCEUR n writer of or performer in farces

FARCEURS > FARCEUR

FARCEUSE n female farceur

FARCEUSES > FARCEUSE

FARCI adj (of food) stuffed

FARCICAL adj ludicrous

FARCIE same as > FARCI

FARCIED adj afflicted with farcy

FARCIES > FARCY

FARCIFIED > FARCIFY

FARCIFIES > FARCIFY

FARCIFY vb turn into a farce

FARCIN n equine disease

FARCING > FARCE

FARCINGS > FARCE

FARCINS > FARCIN

FARCY n form of glanders in which lymph vessels near the skin become thickened, with skin lesions and abscess-forming nodules, caused by a bacterium, Burkholderia mallei

FARD n paint for the face, esp white paint ▷ vb paint (the face) with fard

FARDAGE n material laid beneath or between cargo

FARDAGES > FARDAGE

FARDED > FARD

FARDEL n bundle or burden

FARDELS > FARDEL

FARDEN n farthing

FARDENS > FARDEN

FARDING > FARD

FARDINGS > FARD

FARDS > FARD

FARE n charge for a passenger's journey ▷ vb get on (as specified)

FAREBOX n box where money for bus fares is placed

FAREBOXES > FAREBOX

FARED > FARE

FARER > FARE

FARERS > FARE

FARES > FARE

FAREWELL interj goodbye ▷ n act of saying goodbye and leaving ▷ vb say goodbye ▷ adj parting or closing ▷ sentence substitute goodbye

FAREWELLS > FAREWELL

FARFAL same as > FELAFEL

FARFALLE n pasta in bow shapes

FARFALS > FARFAL

FARFEL same as > FELAFEL

FARFELS > FARFEL

FARFET adj far-fetched

FARINA n flour or meal made from any kind of cereal grain

FARINAS > FARINA

FARING > FARE

FARINHA n cassava meal

FARINHAS > FARINHA

FARINOSE adj similar to or yielding farina

FARL n thin cake of oatmeal, often triangular in shape

FARLE same as > FARL

FARLES > FARLE

FARLS > FARL

FARM n area of land for growing crops or rearing livestock ▷ vb cultivate (land)

FARMABLE > FARM

FARMED adj (of fish or game) reared on a farm rather than caught in the wild

FARMER n person who owns or runs a farm

FARMERESS n female farmer

FARMERIES > FARMERY

FARMERS > FARMER

FARMERY n farm buildings

FARMHAND n person who is hired to work on a farm

FARMHANDS > FARMHAND

FARMHOUSE n house attached to a farm

FARMING n business or skill of agriculture

FARMINGS > FARMING

FARMLAND *n* land that is used for or suitable for farming

FARMLANDS > FARMLAND

FARMOST > FAR

FARMS > FARM

FARMSTEAD *n* farm and its buildings

FARMWIFE *n* woman who works on a farm

FARMWIVES > FARMWIFE

FARMWORK *n* tasks carried out on a farm

FARMWORKS > FARMWORK

FARMYARD *n* small area of land enclosed by or around the farm buildings

FARMYARDS > FARMYARD

FARNARKEL *vb* spend time or act in a careless or inconsequential manner

FARNESOL *n* colourless aromatic sesquiterpene alcohol found in many essential oils and used in the form of its derivatives in perfumery

FARNESOLS > FARNESOL

FARNESS > FAR

FARNESSES > FAR

FARO *n* gambling game in which players bet against the dealer on what cards he will turn up

FAROLITO *n* votive candle

FAROLITOS > FAROLITO

FAROS > FARO

FAROUCHE *adj* sullen or shy

FARRAGO *n* jumbled mixture of things

FARRAGOES > FARRAGO

FARRAGOS > FARRAGO

FARRAND *variant of* > FARAND

FARRANT *variant of* > FARAND

FARRED > FAR

FARREN *n* allotted ground

FARRENS > FARREN

FARRIER *n* person who shoes horses

FARRIERS > FARRIER

FARRIERY *n* art, work, or establishment of a farrier

FARRING > FAR

FARROW *n* litter of piglets ▷ *vb* (of a sow) give birth ▷ *adj* (of a cow) not calving in a given year

FARROWED > FARROW

FARROWING > FARROW

FARROWS > FARROW

FARRUCA *n* flamenco dance performed by men

FARRUCAS > FARRUCA

FARS > FAR

FARSE *vb* insert into

FARSED > FARSE

FARSEEING *adj* having shrewd judgment

FARSES > FARSE

FARSIDE *n* part of the Moon facing away from the Earth

FARSIDES > FARSIDE

FARSING > FARSE

FART *n* emission of gas from the anus ▷ *vb* emit gas from the anus

FARTED > FART

FARTHEL *same as* > FARL

FARTHELS > FARTHEL

FARTHER > FAR

FARTHEST > FAR

FARTHING *n* former British coin equivalent to a quarter of a penny

FARTHINGS > FARTHING

FARTING > FART

FARTLEK *n* in sport, another name for interval training

FARTLEKS > FARTLEK

FARTS > FART

FAS > FA

FASCES *pl n* (in ancient Rome) a bundle of rods containing an axe with its blade pointing out

FASCI > FASCIO

FASCIA *n* outer surface of a dashboard

FASCIAE > FASCIA

FASCIAL > FASCIA

FASCIAS > FASCIA

FASCIATE *adj* (of stems and branches) abnormally flattened due to coalescence

FASCIATED *same as* > FASCIATE

FASCICLE *same as* > FASCICULE

FASCICLED *adj* in instalments

FASCICLES > FASCICLE

FASCICULE *n* one part of a printed work that is published in instalments

FASCICULI > FASCICULE

FASCIITIS *n* inflammation of the fascia of a muscle

FASCINATE *vb* attract and interest strongly

FASCINE *n* bundle of long sticks used for filling in ditches and in the construction of embankments, roads, fortifications, etc

FASCINES > FASCINE

FASCIO *n* political group

FASCIOLA *n* band

FASCIOLAS > FASCIOLA

FASCIOLE *n* band

FASCIOLES > FASCIOLE

FASCIS > FASCI

FASCISM *n* right-wing totalitarian political system characterized by state control and extreme nationalism

FASCISMI > FASCISMO

FASCISMO *Italian word for* > FASCISM

FASCISMS > FASCISM

FASCIST *n* adherent or practitioner of fascism ▷ *adj* characteristic of or relating to fascism

FASCISTA *Italian word for* > FASCIST

FASCISTI > FASCISTA

FASCISTIC > FASCIST

FASCISTS > FASCIST

FASCITIS *same as* > FASCIITIS

FASH *n* worry ▷ *vb* trouble

FASHED > FASH

FASHERIES > FASHERY

FASHERY *n* difficulty, trouble

FASHES > FASH

FASHING > FASH

FASHION *n* style in clothes, hairstyle, etc, popular at a particular time ▷ *vb* form or make into a particular shape

FASHIONED > FASHION

FASHIONER > FASHION

FASHIONS > FASHION

FASHIONY *adj* of or relating to fashion

FASHIOUS *adj* troublesome

FAST *adj* (capable of) acting or moving quickly ▷ *adv* quickly ▷ *vb* go without food, esp for religious reasons ▷ *n* period of fasting

FASTBACK *n* car having a back that forms one continuous slope from roof to rear

FASTBACKS > FASTBACK

FASTBALL *n* ball pitched at the pitcher's top speed

FASTBALLS > FASTBALL

FASTED > FAST

FASTEN *vb* make or become firmly fixed or joined

FASTENED > FASTEN

FASTENER > FASTEN

FASTENERS > FASTEN

FASTENING *n* something that fastens something, such as a clasp or lock

FASTENS > FASTEN

FASTER > FAST

FASTERS > FAST

FASTEST > FAST

FASTI *n* in ancient Rome, days when business could legally be carried out

FASTIE *n* deceitful act

FASTIES > FASTIE

FASTIGIUM *n* highest point

FASTING > FAST

FASTINGS > FAST

FASTISH > FAST

FASTLY > FAST

FASTNESS *n* fortress, safe place

FASTS > FAST

FASTUOUS *adj* arrogant

FAT *adj* having excess flesh on the body ▷ *n* extra flesh on the body

FATAL *adj* causing death or ruin

FATALISM *n* belief that all events are predetermined and people are powerless to change their destinies

FATALISMS > FATALISM

FATALIST > FATALISM

FATALISTS > FATALISM

FATALITY *n* death caused by an accident or disaster

FATALLY *adv* resulting in death or disaster

FATALNESS > FATAL

FATBACK *n* fat, usually salted, from the upper part of a side of pork

FATBACKS > FATBACK

FATBIRD *n* nocturnal bird

FATBIRDS > FATBIRD

FATE *n* power supposed to predetermine events ▷ *vb* predetermine

FATED *adj* destined

FATEFUL *adj* having important, usu disastrous, consequences

FATEFULLY > FATEFUL

FATES > FATE

FATHEAD *n* stupid person

FATHEADED *adj* stupid

FATHEADS > FATHEAD

FATHER *n* male parent ▷ *vb* be the father of (offspring)

FATHERED > FATHER

FATHERING > FATHER

FATHERLY *adj* kind or protective, like a father

FATHERS > FATHER

FATHOM *n* unit of length, used in navigation, equal to six feet (1.83 metres) ▷ *vb* understand

FATHOMED > FATHOM

FATHOMER > FATHOM

FATHOMERS > FATHOM

FATHOMING > FATHOM

FATHOMS > FATHOM

FATIDIC *adj* prophetic

FATIDICAL *same as* > FATIDIC

FATIGABLE > FATIGUE

FATIGATE *vb* fatigue

FATIGATED > FATIGATE

FATIGATES > FATIGATE

FATIGUE *n* extreme physical or mental tiredness ▷ *vb* tire out

FATIGUED > FATIGUE

FATIGUES > FATIGUE

FATIGUING > FATIGUE

FATING > FATE

FATISCENT > FATISCENCE

FATLESS > FAT

FATLIKE > FAT

FATLING *n* young farm animal fattened for killing

FATLINGS > FATLING

FATLY > FAT

FATNESS > FAT

FATNESSES > FAT

FATS > FAT

FATSIA *n* any shrub of the araliaceous genus *Fatsia*, esp *F. japonica*, with large deeply palmate leaves and umbels of white flowers

FATSIAS > FATSIA

FATSO *n* fat person: used as an insulting or disparaging term of address

FATSOES > FATSO

FATSOS > FATSO

FATSTOCK *n* livestock fattened and ready for market

FATSTOCKS > FATSTOCK

FATTED > FAT

FATTEN *vb* (cause to) become fat

FATTENED > FATTEN

FATTENER > FATTEN

FATTENERS > FATTEN

FATTENING > FATTEN

FATTENS > FATTEN

FATTER > FAT
FATTEST > FAT
FATTIER > FATTY
FATTIES > FATTY
FATTIEST > FATTY
FATTILY > FATTY
FATTINESS > FATTY
FATTING > FAT
FATTISH > FAT
FATTISM n discrimination on the basis of weight, esp prejudice against those considered to be overweight
FATTISMS > FATTISM
FATTIST > FATTISM
FATTISTS > FATTISM
FATTRELS n ends of ribbon
FATTY adj containing fat ▷ n fat person
FATUITIES > FATUITY
FATUITOUS > FATUITY
FATUITY n foolish thoughtlessness
FATUOUS adj foolish
FATUOUSLY > FATUOUS
FATWA n religious decree issued by a Muslim leader ▷ vb issue a fatwa
FATWAED > FATWA
FATWAH same as > FATWA
FATWAHED > FATWAH
FATWAHING > FATWAH
FATWAHS > FATWAH
FATWAING > FATWA
FATWAS > FATWA
FATWOOD n wood used for kindling
FATWOODS > FATWOOD
FAUBOURG n suburb or quarter, esp of a French city
FAUBOURGS > FAUBOURG
FAUCAL adj of or relating to the fauces
FAUCALS > FAUCAL
FAUCES n area between the cavity of the mouth and the pharynx, including the surrounding tissues
FAUCET n tap
FAUCETS > FAUCET
FAUCHION n short sword
FAUCHIONS > FAUCHION
FAUCHON variant of > FAUCHION
FAUCHONS > FAUCHON
FAUCIAL same as > FAUCAL
FAUGH interj exclamation of disgust, scorn, etc
FAULCHION variant of > FAUCHION
FAULD n piece of armour
FAULDS > FAULD
FAULT n responsibility for something wrong ▷ vb criticize or blame
FAULTED > FAULT
FAULTFUL > FAULT
FAULTIER > FAULTY
FAULTIEST > FAULTY
FAULTILY > FAULTY
FAULTING > FAULT
FAULTLESS adj without fault
FAULTS > FAULT
FAULTY adj badly designed or not working properly
FAUN n (in Roman legend)

creature with a human face and torso and a goat's horns and legs
FAUNA n animals of a given place or time
FAUNAE > FAUNA
FAUNAL > FAUNA
FAUNALLY > FAUNA
FAUNAS > FAUNA
FAUNIST > FAUNA
FAUNISTIC > FAUNA
FAUNISTS > FAUNA
FAUNLIKE > FAUN
FAUNS > FAUN
FAUNULA n fauna of a small single environment
FAUNULAE > FAUNULA
FAUNULE same as > FAUNULA
FAUNULES > FAUNULE
FAUR Scot word for > FAR
FAURD adj favoured
FAURER > FAUR
FAUREST > FAUR
FAUSTIAN adj of or relating to Faust, esp reminiscent of his bargain with the devil
FAUT Scot word for > FAULT
FAUTED > FAUT
FAUTEUIL n armchair, the sides of which are not upholstered
FAUTEUILS > FAUTEUIL
FAUTING > FAUT
FAUTOR n patron
FAUTORS > FAUTOR
FAUTS > FAUT
FAUVE adj of the style of the Fauve art movement
FAUVES > FAUVE
FAUVETTE n singing bird, warbler
FAUVETTES > FAUVETTE
FAUVISM > FAUVE
FAUVISMS > FAUVISM
FAUVIST n artist following the Fauve style of painting
FAUVISTS > FAUVIST
FAUX adj false
FAVA n type of bean
FAVAS > FAVA
FAVE short for > FAVOURITE
FAVEL n dun-coloured horse
FAVELA n (in Brazil) a shanty or shantytown
FAVELAS > FAVELA
FAVELL variant of > FAVEL
FAVELLA n group of spores
FAVELLAS > FAVELLA
FAVEOLATE adj pitted with cell-like cavities
FAVER > FAVE
FAVES > FAVE
FAVEST > FAVE
FAVISM n type of anaemia
FAVISMS > FAVISM
FAVONIAN adj of or relating to the west wind
FAVOR same as > FAVOUR
FAVORABLE same as > FAVOURABLE
FAVORABLY > FAVOURABLE
FAVORED > FAVOR
FAVORER > FAVOUR
FAVORERS > FAVOUR
FAVORING > FAVOR
FAVORITE same as > FAVOURITE

FAVORITES > FAVORITE
FAVORLESS > FAVOR
FAVORS same as > FAVOURS
FAVOSE same as > FAVEOLATE
FAVOUR n approving attitude ▷ vb prefer
FAVOURED > FAVOUR
FAVOURER > FAVOUR
FAVOURERS > FAVOUR
FAVOURING > FAVOUR
FAVOURITE adj most liked ▷ n preferred person or thing
FAVOURS pl n sexual intimacy, as when consented to by a woman
FAVOUS adj resembling honeycomb
FAVRILE n type of iridescent glass
FAVRILES > FAVRILE
FAVUS n infectious fungal skin disease of man and some domestic animals, characterized by formation of a honeycomb-like mass of roundish dry cup-shaped crusts
FAVUSES > FAVUS
FAW n gypsy
FAWN n young deer ▷ adj light yellowish-brown ▷ vb seek attention from (someone) by insincere flattery
FAWNED > FAWN
FAWNER > FAWN
FAWNERS > FAWN
FAWNIER > FAWNY
FAWNIEST > FAWNY
FAWNING > FAWN
FAWNINGLY > FAWN
FAWNINGS > FAWN
FAWNLIKE > FAWN
FAWNS > FAWN
FAWNY adj of a fawn colour
FAWS > FAW
FAX n electronic system for sending facsimiles of documents by telephone ▷ vb send (a document) by this system
FAXED > FAX
FAXES > FAX
FAXING > FAX
FAY n fairy or sprite ▷ adj of or resembling a fay ▷ vb fit or be fitted closely or tightly
FAYALITE n rare brown or black mineral
FAYALITES > FAYALITE
FAYED > FAY
FAYENCE variant of > FAIENCE
FAYENCES > FAYENCE
FAYER > FAY
FAYEST > FAY
FAYING > FAY
FAYNE vb pretend
FAYNED > FAYNE
FAYNES > FAYNE
FAYNING > FAYNE
FAYRE pseudo-archaic spelling of > FAIR
FAYRES > FAYRE
FAYS > FAY
FAZE vb disconcert or

fluster
FAZED adj worried or disconcerted
FAZENDA n large estate or ranch
FAZENDAS > FAZENDA
FAZES > FAZE
FAZING > FAZE
FE same as > FEE
FEAGUE vb whip or beat
FEAGUED > FEAGUE
FEAGUES > FEAGUE
FEAGUING > FEAGUE
FEAL vb conceal
FEALED > FEAL
FEALING > FEAL
FEALS > FEAL
FEALTIES > FEALTY
FEALTY n (in feudal society) subordinate's loyalty to his ruler or lord
FEAR n distress or alarm caused by impending danger or pain ▷ vb be afraid of (something or someone)
FEARE n companion, spouse
FEARED > FEAR
FEARER > FEAR
FEARERS > FEAR
FEARES > FEARE
FEARFUL adj feeling fear
FEARFULLY adv in a fearful manner
FEARING > FEAR
FEARLESS > FEAR
FEARS > FEAR
FEARSOME adj terrifying
FEASANCE n performance of an act
FEASANCES > FEASANCE
FEASE vb perform an act
FEASED > FEASE
FEASES > FEASE
FEASIBLE adj able to be done, possible
FEASIBLY > FEASIBLE
FEASING > FEASE
FEAST n lavish meal ▷ vb eat a feast
FEASTED > FEAST
FEASTER > FEAST
FEASTERS > FEAST
FEASTFUL adj festive
FEASTING > FEAST
FEASTINGS > FEAST
FEASTLESS > FEAST
FEASTS > FEAST
FEAT n remarkable, skilful, or daring action
FEATED > FEAT
FEATEOUS adj neat
FEATER > FEAT
FEATEST > FEAT
FEATHER n one of the barbed shafts forming the plumage of birds ▷ vb fit or cover with feathers
FEATHERED > FEATHER
FEATHERS > FEATHER
FEATHERY > FEATHER
FEATING > FEAT
FEATLIER > FEAT
FEATLIEST > FEAT
FEATLY > FEAT
FEATOUS variant of > FEATEOUS

f

FEATS > FEAT
FEATUOUS variant of > FEATEOUS
FEATURE n part of the face, such as the eyes ▷ vb have as a feature or be a feature in
FEATURED adj having features as specified
FEATURELY adj handsome
FEATURES > FEATURE
FEATURING > FEATURE
FEAZE same as > FEEZE
FEAZED > FEAZE
FEAZES > FEAZE
FEAZING > FEAZE
FEBLESSE n feebleness
FEBLESSES > FEBLESSE
FEBRICITY n condition of having a fever
FEBRICULA n slight transient fever
FEBRICULE variant of > FEBRICULA
FEBRIFIC adj causing or having a fever
FEBRIFUGE n any drug or agent for reducing fever ▷ adj serving to reduce fever
FEBRILE adj very active and nervous
FEBRILITY > FEBRILE
FECAL same as > FAECAL
FECES same as > FAECES
FECHT Scot word for > FIGHT
FECHTER > FECHT
FECHTERS > FECHT
FECHTING > FECHT
FECHTS > FECHT
FECIAL adj heraldic
FECIALS > FECIAL
FECIT (he or she) made it: used formerly on works of art next to the artist's name
FECK vb euphemism for 'fuck'
FECKED > FECK
FECKIN same as > FECKING
FECKING > FECK
FECKLESS adj ineffectual or irresponsible
FECKLY > FECK
FECKS > FECK
FECULA n starch obtained by washing the crushed parts of plants, such as the potato
FECULAE > FECULA
FECULAS > FECULA
FECULENCE > FECULENT
FECULENCY > FECULENT
FECULENT adj filthy, scummy, muddy, or foul
FECUND adj fertile
FECUNDATE vb make fruitful
FECUNDITY n fertility
FED n FBI agent
FEDARIE n accomplice
FEDARIES > FEDARIE
FEDAYEE n (in Arab states) a commando, esp one fighting against Israel
FEDAYEEN > FEDAYEE
FEDELINI n type of pasta
FEDELINIS > FEDELINI
FEDERACY n alliance

FEDERAL adj of a system in which power is divided between one central government and several regional governments ▷ n supporter of federal union or federation
FEDERALLY > FEDERAL
FEDERALS > FEDERAL
FEDERARIE variant of > FEDARIE
FEDERARY variant of > FEDARIE
FEDERATE vb unite in a federation ▷ adj federal
FEDERATED > FEDERATE
FEDERATES > FEDERATE
FEDERATOR > FEDERATE
FEDEX vb send by FedEx
FEDEXED > FEDEX
FEDEXES > FEDEX
FEDEXING > FEDEX
FEDORA n man's soft hat with a brim
FEDORAS > FEDORA
FEDS > FEE
FEE n charge paid to be allowed to do something ▷ vb pay a fee to
FEEB n contemptible person
FEEBLE adj lacking physical or mental power ▷ vb make feeble
FEEBLED > FEEBLE
FEEBLER > FEEBLE
FEEBLES > FEEBLE
FEEBLEST > FEEBLE
FEEBLING > FEEBLE
FEEBLISH > FEEBLE
FEEBLY > FEEBLE
FEEBS > FEEB
FEED vb give food to ▷ n act of feeding
FEEDABLE > FEE
FEEDBACK n information received in response to something done ▷ adv return (part of the output of a system) to its input
FEEDBACKS > FEEDBACK
FEEDBAG n any bag in which feed for livestock is sacked
FEEDBAGS > FEEDBAG
FEEDBOX trough, manger
FEEDBOXES > FEEDBOX
FEEDER n baby's bib
FEEDERS > FEEDER
FEEDGRAIN n cereal grown to feed livestock
FEEDHOLE n small hole through which cable etc is inserted
FEEDHOLES > FEEDHOLE
FEEDING > FEED
FEEDINGS > FEED
FEEDLOT n area or building where livestock are fattened rapidly for market
FEEDLOTS > FEEDLOT
FEEDS > FEED
FEEDSTOCK n main raw material used in the manufacture of a product
FEEDSTUFF n any material used as a food, esp for animals
FEEDWATER n water,

previously purified to prevent scale deposit or corrosion, that is fed to boilers for steam generation
FEEDYARD n place where cattle are kept and fed
FEEDYARDS > FEEDYARD
FEEING > FEE
FEEL vb have a physical or emotional sensation of ▷ n act of feeling
FEELBAD n something inducing depression
FEELBADS > FEELBAD
FEELER n organ of touch in some animals
FEELERS > FEELER
FEELESS > FEE
FEELGOOD adj causing or characterized by a feeling of self-satisfaction
FEELGOODS > FEELGOOD
FEELING > FEEL
FEELINGLY > FEEL
FEELINGS > FEEL
FEELS > FEEL
FEEN n in Irish dialect, an informal word for 'man'
FEENS > FEEN
FEER vb make a furrow
FEERED > FEER
FEERIE n fairyland
FEERIES > FEERIE
FEERIN n furrow
FEERING > FEER
FEERINGS > FEER
FEERINS > FEERIN
FEERS > FEER
FEES > FEE
FEESE vb perturb
FEESED > FEESE
FEESES > FEESE
FEESING > FEESE
FEET > FOOT
FEETFIRST adv with the feet coming first
FEETLESS > FOOT
FEEZE vb beat ▷ n rush
FEEZED > FEEZE
FEEZES > FEEZE
FEEZING > FEEZE
FEG same as > FIG
FEGARIES > FEGARY
FEGARY variant of > VAGARY
FEGS > FEG
FEH n Hebrew coin
FEHM n medieval German court
FEHME > FEHM
FEHMIC > FEHM
FEHS > FEH
FEIGN vb pretend
FEIGNED > FEIGN
FEIGNEDLY > FEIGN
FEIGNER > FEIGN
FEIGNERS > FEIGN
FEIGNING > FEIGN
FEIGNINGS > FEIGN
FEIGNS > FEIGN
FEIJOA n evergreen myrtaceous shrub of S America
FEIJOAS > FEIJOA
FEINT n sham attack or blow meant to distract an opponent ▷ vb make a feint ▷ adj printing term

meaning ruled with faint lines
FEINTED > FEINT
FEINTER > FEINT
FEINTEST > FEINT
FEINTING > FEINT
FEINTS pl n leavings of the second distillation of Scotch malt whisky
FEIRIE adj nimble
FEIS n Irish music and dance festival
FEISEANNA > FEIS
FEIST n small aggressive dog
FEISTIER > FEISTY
FEISTIEST > FEISTY
FEISTILY > FEISTY
FEISTS > FEIST
FEISTY adj showing courage or spirit
FELAFEL same as > FALAFEL
FELAFELS > FELAFEL
FELDGRAU n ordinary German soldier (from uniform colour)
FELDGRAUS > FELDGRAU
FELDSCHAR same as > FELDSHER
FELDSCHER same as > FELDSHER
FELDSHER n (in Russia) a medical doctor's assistant
FELDSHERS > FELDSHER
FELDSPAR n hard mineral that is the main constituent of igneous rocks
FELDSPARS > FELDSPAR
FELDSPATH variant of > FELDSPAR
FELICIA n type of African herb
FELICIAS > FELICIA
FELICIFIC adj making or tending to make happy
FELICITER > FELICITY
FELICITY n happiness
FELID n any animal belonging to the family Felidae; a cat
FELIDS > FELID
FELINE adj of cats ▷ n member of the cat family
FELINELY > FELINE
FELINES > FELINE
FELINITY > FELINE
FELL vb cut or knock down ▷ adj cruel or deadly
FELLA nonstandard variant of > FELLOW
FELLABLE > FALL
FELLAH n peasant in Arab countries
FELLAHEEN > FELLAH
FELLAHIN > FELLAH
FELLAHS > FELLAH
FELLAS > FELLA
FELLATE vb perform fellatio on (a person)
FELLATED > FELLATE
FELLATES > FELLATE
FELLATING > FELLATE
FELLATIO n sexual activity in which the penis is stimulated by the partner's mouth
FELLATION same

as > FELLATIO

FELLATIOS > FELLATIO

FELLATOR > FELLATIO

FELLATORS > FELLATIO

FELLATRIX > FELLATIO

FELLED > FELL

FELLER *n* person or thing that fells

FELLERS > FELLER

FELLEST > FELL

FELLIES > FELLY

FELLING > FELL

FELLNESS > FELL

FELLOE *n* (segment of) the rim of a wheel

FELLOES > FELLOE

FELLOW *n* man or boy ▷ *adj* in the same group or condition

FELLOWED > FELLOW

FELLOWING > FELLOW

FELLOWLY *adj* friendly, companionable

FELLOWMAN *n* companion

FELLOWMEN > FELLOWMAN

FELLOWS > FELLOW

FELLS > FELL

FELLY *same as* > FELLOE

FELON *n* (formerly) person guilty of a felony ▷ *adj* evil

FELONIES > FELONY

FELONIOUS *adj* of, involving, or constituting a felony

FELONOUS *adj* wicked

FELONRIES > FELONRY

FELONRY *n* felons collectively

FELONS > FELON

FELONY *n* serious crime

FELSIC *adj* relating to igneous rock

FELSITE *n* any fine-grained igneous rock consisting essentially of quartz and feldspar

FELSITES > FELSITE

FELSITIC > FELSITE

FELSPAR *same as* > FELDSPAR

FELSPARS > FELSPAR

FELSTONE *same as* > FELSITE

FELSTONES > FELSTONE

FELT *n* matted fabric ▷ *vb* become matted

FELTED > FELT

FELTER *vb* mat together

FELTERED > FELTER

FELTERING > FELTER

FELTERS > FELTER

FELTIER > FELT

FELTIEST > FELT

FELTING *n* felted material

FELTINGS > FELTING

FELTLIKE > FEEL

FELTS > FELT

FELTY > FELT

FELUCCA *n* narrow lateen-rigged vessel of the Mediterranean

FELUCCAS > FELUCCA

FELWORT *n* biennial gentianaceous plant, *Gentianella amarella*, of Europe and SW China, having purple flowers and rosettes of leaves

FELWORTS > FELWORT

FEM *n* passive homosexual

FEMAL *adj* effeminate ▷ *n* effeminate person

FEMALE *adj* of the sex which bears offspring ▷ *n* female person or animal

FEMALES > FEMALE

FEMALITY > FEMALE

FEMALS > FEMAL

FEME *n* woman or wife

FEMERALL *n* ventilator or smoke outlet on a roof

FEMERALLS > FEMERALL

FEMES > FEME

FEMETARY *variant of* > FUMITORY

FEMINACY *n* feminine character

FEMINAL *adj* feminine, female

FEMINAZI *n* militant feminist

FEMINAZIS > FEMINAZI

FEMINEITY *n* quality of being feminine

FEMINIE *n* women collectively

FEMININE *adj* having qualities traditionally regarded as suitable for, or typical of, women ▷ *n* short for feminine noun

FEMININES > FEMININE

FEMINISE *same as* > FEMINIZE

FEMINISED > FEMINISE

FEMINISES > FEMINISE

FEMINISM *n* advocacy of equal rights for women

FEMINISMS > FEMINISM

FEMINIST *n* person who advocates equal rights for women ▷ *adj* of, relating to, or advocating feminism

FEMINISTS > FEMINIST

FEMINITY > FEMINAL

FEMINIZE *vb* make or become feminine

FEMINIZED > FEMINIZE

FEMINIZES > FEMINIZE

FEMITER *variant of* > FUMITORY

FEMITERS > FEMITER

FEMME *n* woman or wife

FEMMES > FEMME

FEMMIER > FEMMY

FEMMIEST > FEMMY

FEMMY *adj* markedly or exaggeratedly feminine in appearance, manner, etc

FEMORA > FEMUR

FEMORAL *adj* of the thigh

FEMS > FEM

FEMUR *n* thighbone

FEMURS > FEMUR

FEN *n* low-lying flat marshy land

FENAGLE *variant of* > FINAGLE

FENAGLED > FENAGLE

FENAGLES > FENAGLE

FENAGLING > FENAGLE

FENCE *n* barrier of posts linked by wire or wood, enclosing an area ▷ *vb* enclose with or as if with a fence

FENCED > FENCE

FENCELESS > FENCE

FENCELIKE > FENCE

FENCER *n* person who fights with a sword, esp one who practises the art of fencing

FENCEROW *n* uncultivated land flanking a fence

FENCEROWS > FENCEROW

FENCERS > FENCER

FENCES > FENCE

FENCIBLE *n* (formerly) a person who undertook military service in immediate defence of his homeland only

FENCIBLES > FENCIBLE

FENCING *n* sport of fighting with swords

FENCINGS > FENCING

FEND *vb* give support (to someone, esp oneself) ▷ *n* shift or effort

FENDED > FEND

FENDER *n* low metal frame in front of a fireplace

FENDERED *adj* having a fender

FENDERS > FENDER

FENDIER > FENDY

FENDIEST > FENDY

FENDING > FEND

FENDS > FEND

FENDY *adj* thrifty

FENESTRA *n* small opening in or between bones, esp one of the openings between the middle and inner ears

FENESTRAE > FENESTRA

FENESTRAL > FENESTRA

FENESTRAS > FENESTRA

FENI *n* Goan alcoholic drink

FENIS > FENI

FENITAR *variant of* > FUMITORY

FENITARS > FENITAR

FENKS *n* whale blubber

FENLAND > FEN

FENLANDS > FEN

FENMAN > FEN

FENMEN > FEN

FENNEC *n* very small nocturnal fox, *Fennecus zerda*, inhabiting deserts of N Africa and Arabia, having pale fur and enormous ears

FENNECS > FENNEC

FENNEL *n* fragrant plant whose seeds, leaves, and root are used in cookery

FENNELS > FENNEL

FENNIER > FENNY

FENNIES > FENNY

FENNIEST > FENNY

FENNISH > FEN

FENNY *adj* boggy or marshy ▷ *n* feni

FENS > FEN

FENT *n* piece of waste fabric

FENTANYL *n* narcotic drug used in medicine to relieve pain

FENTANYLS > FENTANYL

FENTHION *n* type of pesticide

FENTHIONS > FENTHION

FENTS > FENT

FENUGREEK *n* Mediterranean plant grown for its heavily scented seeds

FENURON *n* type of herbicide

FENURONS > FENURON

FEOD *same as* > FEUD

FEODAL > FEOD

FEODARIES > FEOD

FEODARY > FEOD

FEODS > FEOD

FEOFF *same as* > FIEF

FEOFFED > FEOFF

FEOFFEE *n* (in feudal society) a vassal granted a fief by his lord

FEOFFEES > FEOFFEE

FEOFFER > FEOFF

FEOFFERS > FEOFF

FEOFFING > FEOFF

FEOFFMENT *n* (in medieval Europe) a lord's act of granting a fief to his man

FEOFFOR > FEOFF

FEOFFORS > FEOFF

FEOFFS > FEOFF

FER *same as* > FAR

FERACIOUS *adj* fruitful

FERACITY > FERACIOUS

FERAL *adj* wild ▷ *n* person who displays such tendencies and appearance

FERALISED *same as* > FERALIZED

FERALIZED *adj* once domesticated, but now wild

FERALS > FERAL

FERBAM *n* black slightly water-soluble fluffy powder used as a fungicide

FERBAMS > FERBAM

FERE *n* companion ▷ *adj* fierce

FERER > FERE

FERES > FERE

FEREST > FERE

FERETORY *n* shrine, usually portable, for a saint's relics

FERIA *n* weekday, other than Saturday, on which no feast occurs

FERIAE > FERIA

FERIAL *adj* of or relating to a feria

FERIAS > FERIA

FERINE *same as* > FERAL

FERITIES > FERAL

FERITY > FERAL

FERLIE *same as* > FERLY

FERLIED > FERLY

FERLIER > FERLY

FERLIES > FERLY

FERLIEST > FERLY

FERLY *adj* wonderful ▷ *n* wonder ▷ *vb* wonder

FERLYING > FERLY

FERM *variant of* > FARM

FERMATA *another word for* > PAUSE

FERMATAS > FERMATA

FERMATE > FERMATA

FERMENT *n* any agent that causes fermentation ▷ *vb* (cause to) undergo fermentation

FERMENTED > FERMENT

FERMENTER > FERMENT

FERMENTOR > FERMENT

FERMENTS > FERMENT

FERMI n unit of length used in nuclear physics equal to 10^{-15} metre

FERMION n any of a group of elementary particles, such as a nucleon, that has half-integral spin and obeys Fermi-Dirac statistics

FERMIONIC > FERMION

FERMIONS > FERMION

FERMIS > FERMI

FERMIUM n element artificially produced by neutron bombardment of plutonium

FERMIUMS > FERMIUM

FERMS > FERM

FERN n flowerless plant with fine fronds

FERNBIRD n small brown and white New Zealand swamp bird, *Bowdleria punctata*, with a fernlike tail

FERNBIRDS > FERNBIRD

FERNERIES > FERNERY

FERNERY n place where ferns are grown

FERNIER > FERN

FERNIEST > FERN

FERNING n production of a fern-like pattern

FERNINGS > FERNING

FERNINST same as > FORNENST

FERNLESS > FERN

FERNLIKE > FERN

FERNS > FERN

FERNSHAW n fern thicket

FERNSHAWS > FERNSHAW

FERNTICLE variant of > FERNTICKLE

FERNY > FERN

FEROCIOUS adj savagely fierce or cruel

FEROCITY > FEROCIOUS

FERRATE n type of salt

FERRATES > FERRATE

FERREL variant of > FERRULE

FERRELED > FERREL

FERRELING > FERREL

FERRELLED > FERREL

FERRELS > FERREL

FERREOUS adj containing or resembling iron

FERRET n tamed polecat used to catch rabbits or rats ▷ vb hunt with ferrets

FERRETED > FERRET

FERRETER > FERRET

FERRETERS > FERRET

FERRETING > FERRET

FERRETS > FERRET

FERRETY > FERRET

FERRIAGE n transportation by ferry

FERRIAGES > FERRIAGE

FERRIC adj of or containing iron

FERRIED > FERRY

FERRIES > FERRY

FERRITE n any of a group of ferromagnetic highly resistive ceramic compounds

FERRITES > FERRITE

FERRITIC > FERRITE

FERRITIN n protein that contains iron and plays a

part in the storage of iron in the body. It occurs in the liver and spleen

FERRITINS > FERRITIN

FERROCENE n reddish-orange insoluble crystalline compound

FERROTYPE n photographic print produced directly in a camera by exposing a sheet of iron or tin coated with a sensitized enamel

FERROUS adj of or containing iron in the divalent state

FERRUGO n disease affecting plants

FERRUGOS > FERRUGO

FERRULE n metal cap to strengthen the end of a stick ▷ vb equip (a stick, etc) with a ferrule

FERRULED > FERRULE

FERRULES > FERRULE

FERRULING > FERRULE

FERRUM Latin word for > IRON

FERRUMS > FERRUM

FERRY n boat for transporting people and vehicles ▷ vb carry by ferry

FERRYBOAT same as > FERRY

FERRYING > FERRY

FERRYMAN n someone who provides a ferry service

FERRYMEN > FERRYMAN

FERTIGATE vb fertilize and irrigate at the same time

FERTILE adj capable of producing young, crops, or vegetation

FERTILELY > FERTILE

FERTILER > FERTILE

FERTILEST > FERTILE

FERTILISE same as > FERTILIZE

FERTILITY n ability to produce offspring, esp abundantly

FERTILIZE vb provide (an animal or plant) with sperm or pollen to bring about fertilization

FERULA n any large umbelliferous plant of the Mediterranean genus *Ferula*, having thick stems and dissected leaves: cultivated as the source of several strongly-scented gum resins, such as galbanum

FERULAE > FERULA

FERULAS > FERULA

FERULE same as > FERRULE

FERULED > FERULE

FERULES > FERULE

FERULING > FERULE

FERVENCY another word for > FERVOUR

FERVENT adj intensely passionate and sincere

FERVENTER > FERVENT

FERVENTLY > FERVENT

FERVID same as > FERVENT

FERVIDER > FERVID

FERVIDEST > FERVID

FERVIDITY > FERVID

FERVIDLY > FERVID

FERVOR same as > FERVOUR

FERVOROUS > FERVOUR

FERVORS > FERVOR

FERVOUR n intensity of feeling

FERVOURS > FERVOUR

FES > FE

FESCUE n pasture and lawn grass with stiff narrow leaves

FESCUES > FESCUE

FESS same as > FESSE

FESSE n ordinary consisting of a horizontal band across a shield, conventionally occupying a third of its length and being wider than a bar

FESSED > FESS

FESSES > FESSE

FESSING > FESS

FESSWISE adv in heraldry, with a horizontal band across the shield

FEST n event at which the emphasis is on a particular activity

FESTA n festival

FESTAL adj festive ▷ n festivity

FESTALLY > FESTAL

FESTALS > FESTAL

FESTAS > FESTA

FESTER vb grow worse and increasingly hostile ▷ n small ulcer or sore containing pus

FESTERED > FESTER

FESTERING > FESTER

FESTERS > FESTER

FESTIER > FESTY

FESTIEST > FESTY

FESTILOGY n treatise about church festivals

FESTINATE vb hurry

FESTIVAL n organized series of special events or performances

FESTIVALS > FESTIVAL

FESTIVE adj of or like a celebration

FESTIVELY > FESTIVE

FESTIVITY n happy celebration

FESTIVOUS > FESTIVE

FESTOLOGY variant of > FESTILOGY

FESTOON vb hang decorations in loops ▷ n decorative chain of flowers or ribbons suspended in loops

FESTOONED > FESTOON

FESTOONS > FESTOON

FESTS > FEST

FESTY adj dirty

FET vb fetch

FETA n white salty Greek cheese

FETAL adj of, relating to, or resembling a fetus

FETAS > FETA

FETATION n state of pregnancy

FETATIONS > FETATION

FETCH vb go after and bring back ▷ n ghost or apparition of a living

person

FETCHED > FETCH

FETCHER n person or animal that fetches

FETCHERS > FETCHER

FETCHES > FETCH

FETCHING adj attractive

FETE n gala, bazaar, etc, usu held outdoors ▷ vb honour or entertain regally

FETED > FETE

FETERITA n type of sorghum

FETERITAS > FETERITA

FETES > FETE

FETIAL n (in ancient Rome) any of the 20 priestly heralds involved in declarations of war and in peace negotiations ▷ adj of or relating to the fetiales

FETIALES > FETIAL

FETIALIS n priest in ancient Rome

FETIALS > FETIAL

FETICH same as > FETISH

FETICHE variant of > FETICH

FETICHES > FETICH

FETICHISE variant of > FETICHIZE

FETICHISM same as > FETISHISM

FETICHIST > FETISHISM

FETICHIZE vb be excessively or irrationally devoted to an object, activity, etc

FETICIDAL > FETICIDE

FETICIDE n destruction of a fetus in the uterus

FETICIDES > FETICIDE

FETID adj stinking

FETIDER > FETID

FETIDEST > FETID

FETIDITY > FETID

FETIDLY > FETID

FETIDNESS > FETID

FETING > FETE

FETISH n form of behaviour in which sexual pleasure is derived from looking at or handling an inanimate object

FETISHES > FETISH

FETISHISE same as > FETISHIZE

FETISHISM n condition in which the handling of an inanimate object or a specific part of the body other than the sexual organs is a source of sexual satisfaction

FETISHIST > FETISHISM

FETISHIZE vb be excessively or irrationally devoted to (an object, activity, etc)

FETLOCK n projection behind and above a horse's hoof

FETLOCKED adj having fetlocks

FETLOCKS > FETLOCK

FETOLOGY n branch of medicine concerned with the fetus in the uterus

FETOR n offensive stale or

putrid odour

FETORS > FETOR

FETOSCOPE n fibreoptic instrument that can be passed through the abdomen of a pregnant woman to enable examination of the fetus and withdrawal of blood for sampling in prenatal diagnosis

FETOSCOPY > FETOSCOPE

FETS > FET

FETT variant of > FET

FETTA variant of > FETA

FETTAS > FETTA

FETTED > FET

FETTER n chain or shackle for the foot ▷vb restrict

FETTERED > FETTER

FETTERER > FETTER

FETTERERS > FETTER

FETTERING > FETTER

FETTERS > FETTER

FETTING > FET

FETTLE same as > FETTLING

FETTLED > FETTLE

FETTLER n person employed to maintain railway tracks

FETTLERS > FETTLER

FETTLES > FETTLE

FETTLING n refractory material used to line the hearth of puddling furnaces

FETTLINGS > FETTLING

FETTS > FETT

FETTUCINE n type of pasta in the form of narrow ribbons

FETTUCINI same as > FETTUCINE

FETUS n embryo of a mammal in the later stages of development

FETUSES > FETUS

FETWA variant of > FATWA

FETWAS > FETWA

FEU n (in Scotland) right of use of land in return for a fixed annual payment

FEUAR n tenant of a feu

FEUARS > FEUAR

FEUD n long bitter hostility between two people or groups ▷vb carry on a feud

FEUDAL adj of or like feudalism

FEUDALISE same as > FEUDALIZE

FEUDALISM n medieval system in which people held land from a lord, and in return worked and fought for him

FEUDALIST > FEUDALISM

FEUDALITY n state or quality of being feudal

FEUDALIZE vb make feudal

FEUDALLY > FEUDAL

FEUDARIES > FEUDARY

FEUDARY n holder of land through feudal right

FEUDATORY n person holding a fief ▷adj relating to or characteristic of the relationship between lord and vassal

FEUDED > FEUD

FEUDING > FEUD

FEUDINGS > FEUD

FEUDIST n person who takes part in a feud or quarrel

FEUDISTS > FEUDIST

FEUDS > FEUD

FEUED > FEU

FEUILLETE n puff pastry

FEUING > FEU

FEUS > FEU

FEUTRE vb place in a resting position

FEUTRED > FEUTRE

FEUTRES > FEUTRE

FEUTRING > FEUTRE

FEVER n (illness causing) high body temperature ▷vb affect with or as if with fever

FEVERED > FEVER

FEVERFEW n bushy European strong-scented perennial plant, *Tanacetum parthenium*, with white flower heads, formerly used medicinally: family *Asteraceae* (composites)

FEVERFEWS > FEVERFEW

FEVERING > FEVER

FEVERISH adj suffering from fever

FEVERLESS > FEVER

FEVEROUS same as > FEVERISH

FEVERROOT n American wild plant

FEVERS > FEVER

FEVERWEED n plant thought to be medicinal

FEVERWORT n any of several plants considered to have medicinal properties, such as horse gentian and boneset

FEW adj not many

FEWER > FEW

FEWEST > FEW

FEWMET variant of > FUMET

FEWMETS > FEWMET

FEWNESS > FEW

FEWNESSES > FEW

FEWTER variant of > FEUTRE

FEWTERED > FEUTRE

FEWTERING > FEUTRE

FEWTERS > FEUTRE

FEWTRILS n trifles, trivia

FEY adj whimsically strange ▷vb clean out

FEYED > FEY

FEYER > FEY

FEYEST > FEY

FEYING > FEY

FEYLY > FEY

FEYNESS > FEY

FEYNESSES > FEY

FEYS > FEY

FEZ n brimless tasselled cap, orig. from Turkey

FEZES > FEZ

FEZZED adj wearing a fez

FEZZES > FEZ

FEZZY > FEZ

FIACRE n small four-wheeled horse-drawn carriage, usually with a folding roof

FIACRES > FIACRE

FIANCE n man engaged to be married

FIANCEE n woman who is engaged to be married

FIANCEES > FIANCEE

FIANCES > FIANCE

FIAR n property owner

FIARS n legally fixed price of corn

FIASCHI > FIASCO

FIASCO n ridiculous or humiliating failure

FIASCOES > FIASCO

FIASCOS > FIASCO

FIAT n arbitrary order ▷vb issue a fiat

FIATED > FIAT

FIATING > FIAT

FIATS > FIAT

FIAUNT n fiat

FIAUNTS > FIAUNT

FIB n trivial lie ▷vb tell a lie

FIBBED > FIB

FIBBER > FIB

FIBBERIES > FIB

FIBBERS > FIB

FIBBERY > FIB

FIBBING > FIB

FIBER same as > FIBRE

FIBERED > FIBRE

FIBERFILL same as > FIBREFILL

FIBERISE same as > FIBERIZE

FIBERISED > FIBERISE

FIBERISES > FIBERISE

FIBERIZE vb break into fibres

FIBERIZED > FIBERIZE

FIBERIZES > FIBERIZE

FIBERLESS > FIBRE

FIBERLIKE > FIBER

FIBERS > FIBER

FIBRANNE n synthetic fabric

FIBRANNES > FIBRANNE

FIBRE n thread that can be spun into yarn

FIBRED > FIBRE

FIBREFILL n synthetic fibre used as a filling for pillows, quilted materials, etc

FIBRELESS > FIBRE

FIBRES > FIBRE

FIBRIFORM adj having the form of a fibre or fibres

FIBRIL n small fibre

FIBRILAR > FIBRIL

FIBRILLA same as > FIBRIL

FIBRILLAE > FIBRILLA

FIBRILLAR > FIBRIL

FIBRILLIN n kind of protein

FIBRILS > FIBRIL

FIBRIN n white insoluble elastic protein formed when blood clots

FIBRINOID > FIBRIN

FIBRINOUS adj of, containing, or resembling fibrin

FIBRINS > FIBRIN

FIBRO n mixture of cement and asbestos fibre, used in sheets for building

FIBROCYTE n type of fibroblast

FIBROID adj (of structures or tissues) containing or resembling fibres ▷n benign tumour composed of fibrous connective tissue

FIBROIDS > FIBROID

FIBROIN n tough elastic protein that is the principal component of spiders' webs and raw silk

FIBROINS > FIBROIN

FIBROLINE n type of yarn

FIBROLITE n trademark name for a type of building board containing asbestos and cement

FIBROMA n benign tumour derived from fibrous connective tissue

FIBROMAS > FIBROMA

FIBROMATA > FIBROMA

FIBROS > FIBRO

FIBROSE vb become fibrous

FIBROSED > FIBROSE

FIBROSES > FIBROSE

FIBROSING > FIBROSE

FIBROSIS n formation of an abnormal amount of fibrous tissue

FIBROTIC > FIBROSIS

FIBROUS adj consisting of, containing, or resembling fibres

FIBROUSLY > FIBROUS

FIBS > FIB

FIBSTER n fibber

FIBSTERS > FIBSTER

FIBULA n slender outer bone of the lower leg

FIBULAE > FIBULA

FIBULAR > FIBULA

FIBULAS > FIBULA

FICE n small aggressive dog

FICES > FICE

FICHE n sheet of film for storing publications in miniaturized form

FICHES > FICHE

FICHU n woman's shawl or scarf of some light material, worn esp in the 18th century

FICHUS > FICHU

FICIN n enzyme

FICINS > FICIN

FICKLE adj changeable, inconstant ▷vb puzzle

FICKLED > FICKLE

FICKLER > FICKLE

FICKLES > FICKLE

FICKLEST > FICKLE

FICKLING > FICKLE

FICKLY > FICKLE

FICO n worthless trifle

FICOES > FICO

FICOS > FICO

FICTILE adj moulded or capable of being moulded from clay

FICTION n literary works of the imagination, such as novels

FICTIONAL > FICTION

FICTIONS > FICTION

FICTIVE adj of, relating to, or able to create fiction

FICTIVELY > FICTIVE

FICTOR n sculptor

f

FICTORS > FICTOR

FICUS n any plant of the genus *Ficus*, which includes the edible fig and several greenhouse and house plants

FICUSES > FICUS

FID n spike for separating strands of rope in splicing

FIDDIOUS vb treat someone as Coriolanus, in the eponymous play, dealt with Aufidius

FIDDLE n violin ▷ vb play the violin

FIDDLED > FIDDLE

FIDDLER n person who plays the fiddle

FIDDLERS > FIDDLER

FIDDLES > FIDDLE

FIDDLEY n vertical space above a vessel's engine room extending into its stack

FIDDLEYS > FIDDLEY

FIDDLIER > FIDDLY

FIDDLIEST > FIDDLY

FIDDLING adj trivial

FIDDLY adj awkward to do or use

FIDEISM n theological doctrine that religious truth is a matter of faith and cannot be established by reason

FIDEISMS > FIDEISM

FIDEIST > FIDEISM

FIDEISTIC > FIDEISM

FIDEISTS > FIDEISM

FIDELISMO n belief in, adherence to, or advocacy of the principles of Fidel Castro, the Cuban Communist statesman (born 1927)

FIDELISTA n advocate of fidelism; a fidelist

FIDELITY n faithfulness

FIDGE obsolete word for > FIDGET

FIDGED > FIDGE

FIDGES > FIDGE

FIDGET vb move about restlessly ▷ n person who fidgets

FIDGETED > FIDGET

FIDGETER > FIDGET

FIDGETERS > FIDGET

FIDGETIER > FIDGET

FIDGETING > FIDGET

FIDGETS > FIDGET

FIDGETY > FIDGET

FIDGING > FIDGE

FIDIBUS n spill for lighting a candle or pipe

FIDIBUSES > FIDIBUS

FIDO n generic term for a dog

FIDOS > FIDO

FIDS > FID

FIDUCIAL adj used as a standard of reference or measurement

FIDUCIARY n person bound to act for someone else's benefit, as a trustee ▷ adj of a trust or trustee

FIE interj exclamation of disapproval

FIEF n land granted by a lord in return for war service

FIEFDOM n (in Feudal Europe) the property owned by a lord

FIEFDOMS > FIEFDOM

FIEFS > FIEF

FIELD n piece of land, usu enclosed with a fence or hedge, and used for pasture or growing crops ▷ vb stop, catch, or return (the ball) as a fielder

FIELDED > FIELD

FIELDER n (in certain sports) player whose task is to field the ball

FIELDERS > FIELDER

FIELDFARE n type of large Old World thrush

FIELDING > FIELD

FIELDINGS > FIELD

FIELDMICE pl n nocturnal mice

FIELDS > FIELD

FIELDSMAN n fielder

FIELDSMEN > FIELDSMAN

FIELDVOLE n small rodent

FIELDWARD adv towards a field or fields

FIELDWORK n investigation made in the field as opposed to the classroom or the laboratory

FIEND n evil spirit

FIENDISH adj of or like a fiend

FIENDLIKE > FIEND

FIENDS > FIEND

FIENT n fiend

FIENTS > FIENT

FIER same as > FERE

FIERCE adj wild or aggressive

FIERCELY > FIERCE

FIERCER > FIERCE

FIERCEST > FIERCE

FIERE > FERE

FIERES > FERE

FIERIER > FIERY

FIERIEST > FIERY

FIERILY > FIERY

FIERINESS > FIERY

FIERS > FIER

FIERY adj consisting of or like fire

FIEST > FIE

FIESTA n religious festival, carnival

FIESTAS > FIESTA

FIFE n small high-pitched flute ▷ vb play (music) on a fife

FIFED > FIFE

FIFER > FIFE

FIFERS > FIFE

FIFES > FIFE

FIFI n type of mountaineering hook

FIFING > FIFE

FIFTEEN n five and ten ▷ adj amounting to fifteen ▷ determiner amounting to fifteen

FIFTEENER n fifteen-syllable line of poetry

FIFTEENS > FIFTEEN

FIFTEENTH adj coming after the fourteenth in order, position, time, etc Often written: 15th ▷ n one of 15 equal or nearly equal parts of something

FIFTH n (of) number five in a series ▷ adj of or being number five in a series ▷ adv after the fourth person, position, event, etc

FIFTHLY same as > FIFTH

FIFTHS > FIFTH

FIFTIES > FIFTY

FIFTIETH adj being the ordinal number of *fifty* in order, position, time, etc Often written: 50th ▷ n one of 50 equal or approximately equal parts of something

FIFTIETHS > FIFTIETH

FIFTY n five times ten ▷ adj amounting to fifty ▷ determiner amounting to fifty

FIFTYISH > FIFTY

FIG n soft pear-shaped fruit ▷ vb dress (up) or rig (out)

FIGEATER n large beetle

FIGEATERS > FIGEATER

FIGGED > FIG

FIGGERIES > FIGGERY

FIGGERY n adornment, ornament

FIGGING > FIG

FIGHT vb struggle (against) in battle or physical combat ▷ n aggressive conflict between two (groups of) people

FIGHTABLE > FIGHT

FIGHTBACK n act or campaign of resistance

FIGHTER n boxer

FIGHTERS > FIGHTER

FIGHTING > FIGHT

FIGHTINGS > FIGHT

FIGHTS > FIGHT

FIGJAM n very conceited person

FIGJAMS > FIGJAM

FIGMENT n fantastic notion, invention, or fabrication

FIGMENTS > FIGMENT

FIGO variant of > FICO

FIGOS > FIGO

FIGS > FIG

FIGULINE adj of or resembling clay ▷ n article made of clay

FIGULINES > FIGULINE

FIGURABLE > FIGURE

FIGURAL adj composed of or relating to human or animal figures

FIGURALLY > FIGURAL

FIGURANT n ballet dancer who does group work but no solo roles

FIGURANTE n female figurant

FIGURANTS > FIGURANT

FIGURATE adj exhibiting or produced by figuration

FIGURE n numerical symbol ▷ vb calculate (sums or amounts)

FIGURED adj decorated with a design

FIGUREDLY > FIGURED

FIGURER > FIGURE

FIGURERS > FIGURE

FIGURES > FIGURE

FIGURINE n statuette

FIGURINES > FIGURINE

FIGURING > FIGURE

FIGURIST n user of numbers

FIGURISTS > FIGURIST

FIGWORT n any scrophulariaceous plant of the N temperate genus *Scrophularia*, having square stems and small brown or greenish flowers

FIGWORTS > FIGWORT

FIKE vb fidget

FIKED > FIKE

FIKERIES > FIKERY

FIKERY n fuss

FIKES > FIKE

FIKIER > FIKY

FIKIEST > FIKY

FIKING > FIKE

FIKISH adj fussy

FIKY adj fussy

FIL same as > FILS

FILA > FILUM

FILABEG variant of > FILIBEG

FILABEGS > FILABEG

FILACEOUS adj made of threads

FILACER n formerly, English legal officer

FILACERS > FILACER

FILAGREE same as > FILIGREE

FILAGREED > FILAGREE

FILAGREES > FILAGREE

FILAMENT n fine wire in a light bulb that gives out light

FILAMENTS > FILAMENT

FILANDER n species of kangaroo

FILANDERS > FILANDER

FILAR adj of thread

FILAREE n type of storksbill, a weed

FILAREES > FILAREE

FILARIA n any parasitic nematode worm of the family *Filariidae*, living in the blood and tissues of vertebrates and transmitted by insects: the cause of filariasis

FILARIAE > FILARIA

FILARIAL > FILARIA

FILARIAN > FILARIA

FILARIAS > FILARIA

FILARIID adj of or relating to a family of threadlike roundworms

FILARIIDS > FILARIID

FILASSE n vegetable fibre such as jute

FILASSES > FILASSE

FILATORY n machine for making threads

FILATURE n act or process of spinning silk, etc, into threads

FILATURES > FILATURE

FILAZER *variant of* > FILACER

FILAZERS > FILAZER

FILBERD *variant of* > FILBERT

FILBERDS > FILBERD

FILBERT *n* hazelnut

FILBERTS > FILBERT

FILCH *vb* steal (small amounts)

FILCHED > FILCH

FILCHER > FILCH

FILCHERS > FILCH

FILCHES > FILCH

FILCHING > FILCH

FILCHINGS > FILCH

FILE *n* box or folder used to keep documents in order ▷ *vb* place (a document) in a file

FILEABLE > FILE

FILECARD *n* type of brush with sharp steel bristles, used for cleaning the teeth of a file

FILECARDS > FILECARD

FILED > FILE

FILEFISH *n* any tropical triggerfish, such as *Alutera scripta*, having a narrow compressed body and a very long dorsal spine

FILEMOT *n* type of brown colour

FILEMOTS > FILEMOT

FILENAME *n* arrangement of characters that enables a computer system to permit the user to have access to a particular file

FILENAMES > FILENAME

FILER > FILE

FILERS > FILE

FILES > FILE

FILET *variant of* > FILLET

FILETED > FILET

FILETING > FILET

FILETS > FILET

FILFOT *variant of* > FYLFOT

FILFOTS > FILFOT

FILIAL *adj* of or befitting a son or daughter

FILIALLY > FILIAL

FILIATE *vb* fix judicially the paternity of (a child, esp one born out of wedlock)

FILIATED > FILIATE

FILIATES > FILIATE

FILIATING > FILIATE

FILIATION *n* line of descent

FILIBEG *n* kilt worn by Scottish Highlanders

FILIBEGS > FILIBEG

FILICIDAL > FILICIDE

FILICIDE *n* act of killing one's own son or daughter

FILICIDES > FILICIDE

FILIFORM *adj* having the form of a thread

FILIGRAIN *n* filigree

FILIGRANE *variant of* > FILIGRAIN

FILIGREE *n* delicate ornamental work of gold or silver wire ▷ *adj* made of filigree ▷ *vb* decorate with or as if with filigree

FILIGREED > FILIGREE

FILIGREES > FILIGREE

FILING > FILE

FILINGS *pl n* shavings removed by a file

FILIOQUE *n* theological term found in the Nicene Creed

FILIOQUES > FILIOQUE

FILISTER *same as* > FILLISTER

FILISTERS > FILISTER

FILL *vb* make or become full

FILLABLE > FILL

FILLAGREE *same as* > FILIGREE

FILLE *n* girl

FILLED > FILL

FILLER *n* substance that fills a gap or increases bulk

FILLERS > FILLER

FILLES > FILLE

FILLESTER *same as* > FILLISTER

FILLET *n* boneless piece of meat or fish ▷ *vb* remove the bones from

FILLETED > FILLET

FILLETING > FILLET

FILLETS > FILLET

FILLIBEG *same as* > FILIBEG

FILLIBEGS > FILLIBEG

FILLIES > FILLY

FILLING *n* substance that fills a gap or cavity, esp in a tooth ▷ *adj* (of food) substantial and satisfying

FILLINGS > FILLING

FILLIP *n* something that adds stimulation or enjoyment ▷ *vb* stimulate or excite

FILLIPED > FILLIP

FILLIPEEN *n* philopoena

FILLIPING > FILLIP

FILLIPS > FILLIP

FILLISTER *n* adjustable plane for cutting rabbets, grooves, etc

FILLO *variant of* > FILO

FILLOS > FILLO

FILLS > FILL

FILLY *n* young female horse

FILM *n* sequence of images projected on a screen, creating the illusion of movement ▷ *vb* photograph with a movie or video camera ▷ *adj* connected with films or the cinema

FILMABLE > FILM

FILMCARD *n* cinema loyalty card

FILMCARDS > FILMCARD

FILMDOM *n* cinema industry

FILMDOMS > FILMDOM

FILMED > FILM

FILMER *n* film-maker

FILMERS > FILMER

FILMGOER *n* person who goes regularly to the cinema

FILMGOERS > FILMGOER

FILMGOING > FILMGOER

FILMI *adj* in Indian English, of or relating to the Indian film industry or Indian films

FILMIC *adj* of or suggestive of films or the cinema

FILMIER > FILMY

FILMIEST > FILMY

FILMILY > FILMY

FILMINESS > FILMY

FILMING > FILM

FILMIS > FILMI

FILMISH > FILM

FILMLAND *n* cinema industry

FILMLANDS > FILMLAND

FILMLESS > FILM

FILMLIKE > FILM

FILMMAKER *n* person who makes films

FILMS > FILM

FILMSET *vb* set (type matter) by filmsetting

FILMSETS > FILMSET

FILMSTRIP *n* strip of film composed of different images projected separately as slides

FILMY *adj* very thin, delicate

FILO *n* type of flaky Greek pastry in very thin sheets

FILOPLUME *n* any of the hairlike feathers that lack vanes and occur between the contour feathers

FILOPODIA *n* plural form of singular filopodium: ectoplasmic pseudopodium

FILOS > FILO

FILOSE *adj* resembling or possessing a thread or threadlike process

FILOSELLE *n* soft silk thread, used esp for embroidery

FILOVIRUS *n* any member of a family of viruses that includes the agents responsible for Ebola virus disease and Marburg disease

FILS *n* fractional monetary unit of Bahrain, Iraq, Jordan, and Kuwait, worth one thousandth of a dinar

FILTER *n* material or device permitting fluid to pass but retaining solid particles ▷ *vb* remove impurities from (a substance) with a filter

FILTERED > FILTER

FILTERER > FILTER

FILTERERS > FILTER

FILTERING > FILTER

FILTERS > FILTER

FILTH *n* disgusting dirt

FILTHIER > FILTHY

FILTHIEST > FILTHY

FILTHILY > FILTHY

FILTHS > FILTH

FILTHY *adj* characterized by or full of filth ▷ *adv* extremely

FILTRABLE *adj* capable of being filtered

FILTRATE *n* filtered gas or liquid ▷ *vb* remove impurities with a filter

FILTRATED > FILTRATE

FILTRATES > FILTRATE

FILUM *n* any threadlike structure or part

FIMBLE *n* male plant of the hemp, which matures before the female plant

FIMBLES > FIMBLE

FIMBRIA *n* fringe or fringelike margin or border, esp at the opening of the Fallopian tubes

FIMBRIAE > FIMBRIA

FIMBRIAL > FIMBRIA

FIMBRIATE *adj* having a fringed margin, as some petals, antennae, etc

FIN *n* any of the firm appendages that are the organs of locomotion and balance in fishes and some other aquatic mammals ▷ *vb* provide with fins

FINABLE *adj* liable to a fine

FINAGLE *vb* get or achieve by craftiness or trickery

FINAGLED > FINAGLE

FINAGLER > FINAGLE

FINAGLERS > FINAGLE

FINAGLES > FINAGLE

FINAGLING > FINAGLE

FINAL *adj* at the end ▷ *n* deciding contest between winners of previous rounds in a competition

FINALE *n* concluding part of a dramatic performance or musical work

FINALES > FINALE

FINALIS *n* musical finishing note

FINALISE *same as* > FINALIZE

FINALISED > FINALISE

FINALISER > FINALISE

FINALISES > FINALISE

FINALISM *n* doctrine that final causes determine the course of all events

FINALISMS > FINALISM

FINALIST *n* competitor in a final

FINALISTS > FINALIST

FINALITY *n* condition or quality of being final or settled

FINALIZE *vb* put into final form

FINALIZED > FINALIZE

FINALIZER > FINALIZE

FINALIZES > FINALIZE

FINALLY *adv* after a long delay

FINALS *pl n* deciding part of a competition

FINANCE *vb* provide or obtain funds for ▷ *n* system of money, credit, and investment

FINANCED > FINANCE

FINANCES > FINANCE

FINANCIAL *adj* of or relating to finance, finances, or people who manage money

FINANCIER *n* person involved in large-scale financial business

FINANCING > FINANCE

Section 1: Words between 2 and 9 letters in length

FINBACK *another name for* > RORQUAL

FINBACKS > FINBACK

FINCA *n* Spanish villa

FINCAS > FINCA

FINCH *n* small songbird with a short strong beak

FINCHED *adj* with streaks or spots on the back

FINCHES > FINCH

FIND *vb* discover by chance ▷ *n* person or thing found, esp when valuable

FINDABLE > FIND

FINDER *n* small telescope fitted to a larger one

FINDERS > FINDER

FINDING > FIND

FINDINGS > FIND

FINDRAM *variant of* > FINNAN

FINDRAMS > FINDRAM

FINDS > FIND

FINE *adj* very good ▷ *n* payment imposed as a penalty ▷ *vb* impose a fine on

FINEABLE *same as* > FINABLE

FINED > FINE

FINEER *variant of* > VENEER

FINEERED > FINEER

FINEERING > FINEER

FINEERS > FINEER

FINEISH > FINE

FINELESS > FINE

FINELY *adv* into small pieces

FINENESS *n* state or quality of being fine

FINER > FINE

FINERIES > FINERY

FINERS > FINE

FINERY *n* showy clothing

FINES > FINE

FINESPUN *adj* spun or drawn out to a fine thread

FINESSE *n* delicate skill ▷ *vb* bring about with finesse

FINESSED > FINESSE

FINESSER > FINESSE

FINESSERS > FINESSE

FINESSES > FINESSE

FINESSING > FINESSE

FINEST > FINE

FINFISH *n* fish with fins, as opposed to shellfish

FINFISHES > FINFISH

FINFOOT *n* any aquatic bird of the tropical and subtropical family *Heliornithidae*, having broadly lobed toes, a long slender head and neck, and pale brown plumage: order *Gruiformes* (cranes, rails etc)

FINFOOTS > FINFOOT

FINGAN *variant of* > FINJAN

FINGANS > FINGAN

FINGER *n* one of the four long jointed parts of the hand ▷ *vb* touch or handle with the fingers

FINGERED *adj* marked or dirtied by handling

FINGERER > FINGER

FINGERERS > FINGER

FINGERING *n* technique of using the fingers in playing

a musical instrument

FINGERS > FINGER

FINGERTIP *n* end joint or tip of a finger

FINI *n* end; finish

FINIAL *n* ornament at the apex of a gable or spire

FINIALED *adj* having a finial or finials

FINIALS > FINIAL

FINICAL *another word for* > FINICKY

FINICALLY > FINICAL

FINICKETY *adj* fussy or tricky

FINICKIER > FINICKY

FINICKIN *variant of* > FINICKY

FINICKING *same as* > FINICKY

FINICKY *adj* excessively particular, fussy

FINIKIN *variant of* > FINICKY

FINIKING *variant of* > FINICKY

FINING *n* process of removing undissolved gas bubbles from molten glass

FININGS > FINING

FINIS > FINI

FINISES > FINIS

FINISH *vb* bring to an end, stop ▷ *n* end, last part

FINISHED *adj* perfected

FINISHER *n* craftsman who carries out the final tasks in a manufacturing process

FINISHERS > FINISHER

FINISHES > FINISH

FINISHING *n* act or skill of goal scoring

FINITE *adj* having limits in space, time, or size

FINITELY > FINITE

FINITES > FINITE

FINITISM *n* view that only those entities may be admitted to mathematics that can be constructed in a finite number of steps, and only those propositions entertained whose truth can be proved in a finite number of steps

FINITISMS > FINITISM

FINITO *adj* finished

FINITUDE > FINITE

FINITUDES > FINITE

FINJAN *n* small, handleless coffee cup

FINJANS > FINJAN

FINK *n* strikebreaker ▷ *vb* inform (on someone), as to the police

FINKED > FINK

FINKING > FINK

FINKS > FINK

FINLESS > FIN

FINLIKE > FIN

FINMARK *n* monetary unit of Finland

FINMARKS > FINMARK

FINNAC *variant of* > FINNOCK

FINNACK *variant of* > FINNOCK

FINNACKS > FINNACK

FINNACS > FINNAC

FINNAN *n* smoked haddock

FINNANS > FINNAN

FINNED > FIN

FINNER *another name for* > RORQUAL

FINNERS > FINNER

FINNESKO *n* reindeer-skin boot

FINNICKY *variant of* > FINICKY

FINNIER > FINNY

FINNIEST > FINNY

FINNING > FIN

FINNMARK *n* Finnish monetary unit

FINNMARKS > FINNMARK

FINNOCHIO *variant of* > FINOCCHIO

FINNOCK *n* young sea trout on its first return to fresh water

FINNOCKS > FINNOCK

FINNSKO *variant of* > FINNESKO

FINNY *adj* relating to or containing many fishes

FINO *n* very dry sherry

FINOCCHIO *n* variety of fennel, *Foeniculum vulgare dulce*, with thickened stalks that resemble celery and are eaten as a vegetable, esp in S Europe

FINOCHIO *same as* > FINOCCHIO

FINOCHIOS > FINOCHIO

FINOS > FINO

FINS > FIN

FINSKO *variant of* > FINNESKO

FIORATURA *same as* > FIORITURA

FIORD *same as* > FJORD

FIORDS > FIORD

FIORIN *n* temperate perennial grass, *Agrostis stolonifera*

FIORINS > FIORIN

FIORITURA *n* embellishment, esp ornamentation added by the performer

FIORITURE > FIORITURA

FIPPENCE *n* fivepence

FIPPENCES > FIPPENCE

FIPPLE *n* wooden plug forming a flue in the end of a pipe, as the mouthpiece of a recorder

FIPPLES > FIPPLE

FIQUE *n* hemp

FIQUES > FIQUE

FIR *n* pyramid-shaped tree with needle-like leaves and erect cones

FIRE *n* state of combustion producing heat, flames, and smoke ▷ *vb* operate (a weapon) so that a bullet or missile is released

FIREABLE > FIRE

FIREARM *n* rifle, pistol, or shotgun

FIREARMED *adj* carrying firearm

FIREARMS > FIREARM

FIREBACK *n* ornamental iron slab against the back wall of a hearth

FIREBACKS > FIREBACK

FIREBALL *n* ball of fire at the centre of an explosion

FIREBALLS > FIREBALL

FIREBASE *n* artillery base from which heavy fire is directed at the enemy

FIREBASES > FIREBASE

FIREBIRD *n* any of various songbirds having a bright red plumage, esp the Baltimore oriole

FIREBIRDS > FIREBIRD

FIREBOARD *n* mantelpiece

FIREBOAT *n* motor vessel with fire-fighting apparatus

FIREBOATS > FIREBOAT

FIREBOMB *n* bomb that is designed to cause fires

FIREBOMBS > FIREBOMB

FIREBOX *n* furnace chamber of a boiler in a steam locomotive

FIREBOXES > FIREBOX

FIREBRAND *n* person who causes unrest

FIREBRAT *n* small primitive wingless insect, *Thermobia domestica*, that occurs in warm buildings, feeding on starchy food scraps, fabric, etc: order *Thysanura* (bristletails)

FIREBRATS > FIREBRAT

FIREBREAK *n* strip of cleared land to stop the advance of a fire

FIREBRICK *n* heat-resistant brick used for lining furnaces, fireplaces, etc

FIREBUG *n* person who deliberately sets fire to property

FIREBUGS > FIREBUG

FIREBUSH as in *Chilean firebush* South American shrub with scarlet flowers

FIRECLAY *n* heat-resistant clay used in the making of firebricks, furnace linings, etc

FIRECLAYS > FIRECLAY

FIRECREST *n* small European warbler, *Regulus ignicapillus*, having a crown striped with yellow, black, and white

FIRED > FIRE

FIREDAMP *n* explosive gas, composed mainly of methane, formed in mines

FIREDAMPS > FIREDAMP

FIREDOG *n* either of a pair of decorative metal stands used to support logs in an open fire

FIREDOGS > FIREDOG

FIREDRAKE *n* fire-breathing dragon

FIREFANG *vb* become overheated through decomposition

FIREFANGS > FIREFANG

FIREFIGHT *n* brief small-scale engagement between opposing military ground forces using short-range light weapons

FIREFLIES > FIREFLY

FIREFLOAT *n* boat used for firefighting

FIREFLOOD *n* method of extracting oil from a well by burning some of the oil to increase the rate of flow

FIREFLY *n* beetle that glows in the dark

FIREGUARD *same as* > FIREBREAK

FIREHALL *n* US and Canadian word for fire station

FIREHALLS > FIREHALL

FIREHOUSE *n* firestation

FIRELESS > FIRE

FIRELIGHT *n* light from a fire

FIRELIT *adj* lit by firelight

FIRELOCK *n* obsolete type of gunlock with a priming mechanism ignited by sparks

FIRELOCKS > FIRELOCK

FIREMAN *n* man whose job is to put out fires and rescue people endangered by them

FIREMANIC > FIREMAN

FIREMARK *n* plaque indicating that a building is insured

FIREMARKS > FIREMARK

FIREMEN > FIREMAN

FIREPAN *n* metal container for a fire in a room

FIREPANS > FIREPAN

FIREPINK *n* wildflower belonging to the pink family

FIREPINKS > FIREPINK

FIREPLACE *n* recess in a room for a fire

FIREPLUG *n* US and New Zealand name for a fire hydrant

FIREPLUGS > FIREPLUG

FIREPOT *n* Chinese fondue-like cooking pot

FIREPOTS > FIREPOT

FIREPOWER *n* amount of fire that may be delivered by a unit or weapon

FIREPROOF *adj* capable of resisting damage by fire ▷ *vb* make resistant to fire

FIRER > FIRE

FIREROOM *n* stokehold

FIREROOMS > FIREROOM

FIRERS > FIRE

FIRES > FIRE

FIRESHIP *n* vessel loaded with flammable materials, ignited, and directed among enemy warships to set them alight

FIRESHIPS > FIRESHIP

FIRESIDE *n* hearth

FIRESIDES > FIRESIDE

FIRESTONE *n* sandstone that withstands intense heat, esp one used for lining kilns, furnaces, etc

FIRESTORM *n* uncontrollable blaze sustained by violent winds

that are drawn into the column of rising hot air over the burning area: often the result of heavy bombing

FIRETHORN *n* any rosaceous evergreen spiny shrub of the genus *Pyracantha*, of SE Europe and Asia, having bright red or orange fruits: cultivated for ornament

FIRETRAP *n* building that would burn easily or one without fire escapes

FIRETRAPS > FIRETRAP

FIRETRUCK *n* fire engine

FIREWALL *n* appliance that prevents unauthorized access to a computer network from the internet

FIREWALLS > FIREWALL

FIREWATER *n* any alcoholic spirit

FIREWEED *n* any of various plants that appear as first vegetation in burnt-over areas, esp rosebay willowherb

FIREWEEDS > FIREWEED

FIREWOMAN *n* female firefighter

FIREWOMEN > FIREWOMAN

FIREWOOD *n* wood for burning

FIREWOODS > FIREWOOD

FIREWORK *n* device containing chemicals that is ignited to produce spectacular explosions and coloured sparks

FIREWORKS *pl n* show in which fireworks are let off

FIREWORM *n* cranberry worm

FIREWORMS > FIREWORM

FIRIE *n* in Australian English, informal word for a firefighter

FIRIES > FIRIE

FIRING *n* discharge of a firearm

FIRINGS > FIRING

FIRK *vb* beat

FIRKED > FIRK

FIRKIN *n* small wooden barrel or similar container

FIRKING > FIRK

FIRKINS > FIRKIN

FIRKS > FIRK

FIRLOT *n* unit of measurement for grain

FIRLOTS > FIRLOT

FIRM *adj* not soft or yielding ▷ *adv* in an unyielding manner ▷ *vb* make or become firm ▷ *n* business company

FIRMAMENT *n* sky or the heavens

FIRMAN *n* edict of an Oriental sovereign

FIRMANS > FIRMAN

FIRMED > FIRM

FIRMER > FIRM

FIRMERS > FIRM

FIRMEST > FIRM

FIRMING > FIRM

FIRMLESS *adj* unstable

FIRMLY > FIRM

FIRMNESS > FIRM

FIRMS > FIRM

FIRMWARE *n* fixed form of software programmed into a read-only memory

FIRMWARES > FIRMWARE

FIRN *another name for* > NEVE

FIRNS > FIRN

FIRRIER > FIRRY

FIRRIEST > FIRRY

FIRRING *n* wooden battens used in building construction

FIRRINGS > FIRRING

FIRRY *adj* of, relating to, or made from fir trees

FIRS > FIR

FIRST *adj* earliest in time or order ▷ *n* person or thing coming before all others ▷ *adv* before anything else

FIRSTBORN *adj* eldest of the children in a family ▷ *n* eldest child in a family

FIRSTHAND *adj* from the original source

FIRSTLING *n* first, esp the first offspring

FIRSTLY *adv* coming before other points, questions, etc

FIRSTNESS > FIRST

FIRSTS *pl n* saleable goods of the highest quality

FIRTH *n* narrow inlet of the sea, esp in Scotland

FIRTHS > FIRTH

FISC *n* state or royal treasury

FISCAL *adj* of government finances, esp taxes ▷ *n* (in some countries) a public prosecutor

FISCALIST > FISCAL

FISCALLY > FISCAL

FISCALS > FISCAL

FISCS > FISC

FISGIG *variant of* > FISHGIG

FISGIGS > FISGIG

FISH *n* cold-blooded vertebrate with gills, that lives in water ▷ *vb* try to catch fish

FISHABLE > FISH

FISHBALL *n* fried ball of flaked fish and mashed potato

FISHBALLS > FISHBALL

FISHBOLT *n* bolt used for fastening a fishplate to a rail

FISHBOLTS > FISHBOLT

FISHBONE *n* bone of a fish

FISHBONES > FISHBONE

FISHBOWL *n* goldfish bowl

FISHBOWLS > FISHBOWL

FISHCAKE *n* mixture of flaked fish and mashed potatoes formed into a flat circular shape

FISHCAKES > FISHCAKE

FISHED > FISH

FISHER *n* fisherman

FISHERIES > FISHERY

FISHERMAN *n* person who catches fish for a living or for pleasure

FISHERMEN > FISHERMAN

FISHERS > FISHER

FISHERY *n* area of the sea used for fishing

FISHES > FISH

FISHEYE *n* in photography, a lens of small focal length, having a highly curved protruding front element, that covers an angle of view of almost 180°

FISHEYES > FISHEYE

FISHFUL *adj* teeming with fish

FISHGIG *n* pole with barbed prongs for impaling fish

FISHGIGS > FISHGIG

FISHHOOK *n* sharp hook used in angling, esp one with a barb

FISHHOOKS > FISHHOOK

FISHIER > FISHY

FISHIEST > FISHY

FISHIFIED > FISHIFY

FISHIFIES > FISHIFY

FISHIFY *vb* change into fish

FISHILY > FISHY

FISHINESS > FISHY

FISHING *n* job or pastime of catching fish

FISHINGS > FISHING

FISHKILL *n* mass killing of fish by pollution

FISHKILLS > FISHKILL

FISHLESS > FISH

FISHLIKE > FISH

FISHLINE *n* line used on a fishing-rod

FISHLINES > FISHLINE

FISHMEAL *n* ground dried fish used as feed for farm animals or as a fertilizer

FISHMEALS > FISHMEAL

FISHNET *n* open mesh fabric resembling netting

FISHNETS > FISHNET

FISHPLATE *n* metal plate holding rails together

FISHPOLE *n* boom arm for a microphone

FISHPOLES > FISHPOLE

FISHPOND > FISH

FISHPONDS > FISH

FISHSKIN *n* skin of a fish

FISHSKINS > FISHSKIN

FISHTAIL *n* nozzle having a long narrow slot at the top, placed over a Bunsen burner to produce a thin fanlike flame ▷ *vb* slow an aeroplane by moving the tail from side to side

FISHTAILS > FISHTAIL

FISHWAY *n* fish ladder

FISHWAYS > FISHWAY

FISHWIFE *n* coarse scolding woman

FISHWIVES > FISHWIFE

FISHWORM *n* worm used as fishing bait

FISHWORMS > FISHWORM

FISHY *adj* of or like fish

FISHYBACK *n* goods supply chain involving container transfer from lorry to ship

FISK *vb* frisk

FISKED > FISK

FISKING > FISK

FISKS > FISK
FISNOMIE n physiognomy
FISNOMIES > FISNOMIE
FISSATE > FISSILE
FISSILE adj capable of undergoing nuclear fission
FISSILITY > FISSILE
FISSION n splitting
FISSIONAL > FISSION
FISSIONED adj split or broken into parts
FISSIONS > FISSION
FISSIPED adj having toes that are separated from one another, as dogs, cats, bears, and similar carnivores ▷ n fissiped animal
FISSIPEDE > FISSIPED
FISSIPEDS > FISSIPED
FISSIVE > FISSILE
FISSLE vb rustle
FISSLED > FISSLE
FISSLES > FISSLE
FISSLING > FISSLE
FISSURAL > FISSURE
FISSURE n long narrow cleft or crack ▷ vb crack or split apart
FISSURED > FISSURE
FISSURES > FISSURE
FISSURING > FISSURE
FIST n clenched hand ▷ vb hit with the fist
FISTED > FIST
FISTFIGHT n fight using bare fists
FISTFUL n quantity that can be held in a fist or hand
FISTFULS > FISTFUL
FISTIANA n world of boxing
FISTIC adj of or relating to fisticuffs or boxing
FISTICAL > FISTIC
FISTICUFF > FISTICUFFS
FISTIER > FIST
FISTIEST > FIST
FISTING > FIST
FISTMELE n measure of the width of a hand and the extended thumb, used to calculate the approximate height of the string of a braced bow
FISTMELES > FISTMELE
FISTNOTE n note in printed text preceded by the fist symbol
FISTNOTES > FISTNOTE
FISTS > FIST
FISTULA n long narrow ulcer
FISTULAE > FISTULA
FISTULAR same as > FISTULOUS
FISTULAS > FISTULA
FISTULATE same as > FISTULOUS
FISTULOSE variant of > FISTULOUS
FISTULOUS adj containing, relating to, or resembling a fistula
FISTY > FIST
FIT vb be appropriate or suitable for ▷ adj appropriate ▷ n way in which something fits

FITCH n fur of the polecat or ferret
FITCHE adj pointed
FITCHEE variant of > FITCHE
FITCHES > FITCH
FITCHET same as > FITCH
FITCHETS > FITCHET
FITCHEW archaic name for > POLECAT
FITCHEWS > FITCHEW
FITCHY variant of > FITCHE
FITFUL adj occurring in irregular spells
FITFULLY > FITFUL
FITLIER > FITLY
FITLIEST > FITLY
FITLY adv in a proper manner or place or at a proper time
FITMENT n accessory attached to a machine
FITMENTS > FITMENT
FITNA n state of trouble or chaos
FITNAS > FITNA
FITNESS n state of being fit
FITNESSES > FITNESS
FITS > FIT
FITT n song
FITTABLE > FIT
FITTE variant of > FITT
FITTED > FIT
FITTER > FIT
FITTERS > FIT
FITTES > FITTE
FITTEST > FIT
FITTING > FIT
FITTINGLY > FIT
FITTINGS > FIT
FITTS > FITT
FIVE n one more than four ▷ adj amounting to five ▷ determiner amounting to five
FIVEFOLD adj having five times as many or as much ▷ adv by five times as many or as much
FIVEPENCE n five-penny coin
FIVEPENNY adj (of a nail) one and three-quarters of an inch in length
FIVEPIN > FIVEPINS
FIVEPINS n bowling game played esp in Canada
FIVER n five-pound note
FIVERS > FIVER
FIVES n ball game resembling squash but played with bats or the hands
FIX vb make or become firm, stable, or secure ▷ n difficult situation
FIXABLE > FIX
FIXATE vb become or cause to become fixed
FIXATED > FIXATE
FIXATES > FIXATE
FIXATIF variant of > FIXATIVE
FIXATIFS > FIXATIF
FIXATING > FIXATE
FIXATION n obsessive interest in something
FIXATIONS > FIXATION
FIXATIVE n liquid used to

preserve or hold things in place ▷ adj serving or tending to fix
FIXATIVES > FIXATIVE
FIXATURE n something that holds an object in place
FIXATURES > FIXATURE
FIXED adj attached or placed so as to be immovable
FIXEDLY > FIXED
FIXEDNESS > FIXED
FIXER n solution used to make a photographic image permanent
FIXERS > FIXER
FIXES > FIX
FIXING n means of attaching one thing to another, as a pipe to a wall, slate to a roof, etc
FIXINGS pl n apparatus or equipment
FIXIT n solution to a complex problem
FIXITIES > FIXITY
FIXITY n state or quality of a person's gaze, attitude, or concentration not changing or weakening
FIXIVE > FIX
FIXT adj fixed
FIXTURE n permanently fitted piece of household equipment
FIXTURES > FIXTURE
FIXURE n firmness
FIXURES > FIXURE
FIZ variant of > FIZZ
FIZGIG vb inform on someone to the police
FIZGIGGED > FIZGIG
FIZGIGS > FIZGIG
FIZZ vb make a hissing or bubbling noise ▷ n hissing or bubbling noise
FIZZED > FIZZ
FIZZEN variant of > FOISON
FIZZENS > FIZZEN
FIZZER n anything that fizzes
FIZZERS > FIZZER
FIZZES > FIZZ
FIZZGIG variant of > FISHGIG
FIZZGIGS > FIZZGIG
FIZZIER > FIZZ
FIZZIEST > FIZZ
FIZZINESS > FIZZ
FIZZING > FIZZ
FIZZINGS > FIZZ
FIZZLE vb make a weak hissing or bubbling sound ▷ n hissing or bubbling sound
FIZZLED > FIZZLE
FIZZLES > FIZZLE
FIZZLING > FIZZLE
FIZZY > FIZZ
FJELD n high rocky plateau with little vegetation in Scandinavian countries
FJELDS > FJELD
FJORD n long narrow inlet of the sea between cliffs, esp in Norway
FJORDIC > FJORD

FJORDS > FJORD
FLAB n unsightly body fat
FLABBIER > FLABBY
FLABBIEST > FLABBY
FLABBILY > FLABBY
FLABBY adj having flabby flesh
FLABELLA > FLABELLUM
FLABELLUM n fan-shaped organ or part, such as the tip of the proboscis of a honeybee
FLABS > FLAB
FLACCID adj soft and limp
FLACCIDER > FLACCID
FLACCIDLY > FLACCID
FLACK vb flutter
FLACKED > FLACK
FLACKER vb flutter like a bird
FLACKERED > FLACKER
FLACKERS > FLACKER
FLACKERY > FLACK
FLACKET n flagon
FLACKETS > FLACKET
FLACKING > FLACK
FLACKS > FLACK
FLACON n small stoppered bottle or flask, such as one used for perfume
FLACONS > FLACON
FLAFF vb flap
FLAFFED > FLAFF
FLAFFER vb flutter
FLAFFERED > FLAFFER
FLAFFERS > FLAFFER
FLAFFING > FLAFF
FLAFFS > FLAFF
FLAG n piece of cloth attached to a pole as an emblem or signal ▷ vb mark with a flag or sticker
FLAGELLA > FLAGELLUM
FLAGELLAR > FLAGELLUM
FLAGELLIN n structural protein of bacterial flagella
FLAGELLUM n whiplike outgrowth from a cell that acts as an organ of movement
FLAGEOLET n small instrument like a recorder
FLAGGED > FLAG
FLAGGER > FLAG
FLAGGERS > FLAG
FLAGGIER > FLAGGY
FLAGGIEST > FLAGGY
FLAGGING > FLAG
FLAGGINGS > FLAG
FLAGGY adj drooping
FLAGITATE vb importune
FLAGLESS > FLAG
FLAGMAN n person who has charge of, carries, or signals with a flag, esp a railway employee
FLAGMEN > FLAGMAN
FLAGON n wide bottle for wine or cider
FLAGONS > FLAGON
FLAGPOLE n pole for a flag
FLAGPOLES > FLAGPOLE
FLAGRANCE > FLAGRANT
FLAGRANCY > FLAGRANT
FLAGRANT adj openly outrageous
FLAGS > FLAG
FLAGSHIP n admiral's ship

FLAGSHIPS > FLAGSHIP

FLAGSTAFF *same as* > FLAGPOLE

FLAGSTICK *n* in golf, pole used to indicate position of hole

FLAGSTONE *n* flat slab of hard stone for paving

FLAIL *vb* wave about wildly ▷ *n* tool formerly used for threshing grain by hand

FLAILED > FLAIL

FLAILING > FLAIL

FLAILS > FLAIL

FLAIR *n* natural ability

FLAIRS > FLAIR

FLAK *n* anti-aircraft fire

FLAKE *n* small thin piece, esp chipped off something ▷ *vb* peel off in flakes

FLAKED > FLAKE

FLAKER > FLAKE

FLAKERS > FLAKE

FLAKES > FLAKE

FLAKEY *same as* > FLAKY

FLAKIER > FLAKY

FLAKIES *n* dandruff

FLAKIEST > FLAKY

FLAKILY > FLAKY

FLAKINESS > FLAKY

FLAKING > FLAKE

FLAKS > FLAK

FLAKY *adj* like or made of flakes

FLAM *n* falsehood, deception, or sham ▷ *vb* cheat or deceive

FLAMBE *vb* cook or serve (food) in flaming brandy ▷ *adj* (of food, such as steak or pancakes) served in flaming brandy

FLAMBEAU *n* burning torch, as used in night processions

FLAMBEAUS > FLAMBEAU

FLAMBEAUX > FLAMBEAU

FLAMBEE *same as* > FLAMBE

FLAMBEED > FLAMBEE

FLAMBEES > FLAMBEE

FLAMBEING > FLAMBEE

FLAMBES > FLAMBE

FLAME *n* luminous burning gas coming from burning material ▷ *vb* burn brightly

FLAMED > FLAME

FLAMELESS > FLAME

FLAMELET > FLAME

FLAMELETS > FLAME

FLAMELIKE > FLAME

FLAMEN *n* (in ancient Rome) any of 15 priests who each served a particular deity

FLAMENCO *n* rhythmical Spanish dance accompanied by a guitar and vocalist

FLAMENCOS > FLAMENCO

FLAMENS > FLAMEN

FLAMEOUT *n* failure of an aircraft jet engine in flight due to extinction of the flame ▷ *vb* (of a jet engine) to fail in flight or to cause (a jet engine) to fail in flight

FLAMEOUTS > FLAMEOUT

FLAMER > FLAME

FLAMERS > FLAME

FLAMES > FLAME

FLAMFEW *n* fantastic trifle

FLAMFEWS > FLAMFEW

FLAMIER > FLAME

FLAMIEST > FLAME

FLAMINES > FLAMEN

FLAMING *adj* burning with flames ▷ *adv* extremely

FLAMINGLY > FLAMING

FLAMINGO *n* large pink wading bird with a long neck and legs

FLAMINGOS > FLAMINGO

FLAMM *variant of* > FLAM

FLAMMABLE *adj* easily set on fire

FLAMMED > FLAM

FLAMMING > FLAM

FLAMMS > FLAMM

FLAMMULE *n* small flame

FLAMMULES > FLAMMULE

FLAMS > FLAM

FLAMY > FLAME

FLAN *n* open sweet or savoury tart

FLANCARD *n* armour covering a horse's flank

FLANCARDS > FLANCARD

FLANCH *variant of* > FLAUNCH

FLANCHED > FLANCH

FLANCHES > FLANCH

FLANCHING > FLANCH

FLANERIE *n* aimless strolling or lounging

FLANERIES > FLANERIE

FLANES *n* arrows

FLANEUR *n* idler or loafer

FLANEURS > FLANEUR

FLANGE *n* projecting rim or collar ▷ *vb* attach or provide (a component) with a flange

FLANGED > FLANGE

FLANGER > FLANGE

FLANGERS > FLANGE

FLANGES > FLANGE

FLANGING > FLANGE

FLANK *n* part of the side between the hips and ribs ▷ *vb* be at or move along the side of

FLANKED > FLANK

FLANKEN *n* cut of beef

FLANKER *n* one of a detachment of soldiers detailed to guard the flanks, esp of a formation

FLANKERED > FLANKER

FLANKERS > FLANKER

FLANKING > FLANK

FLANKS > FLANK

FLANNEL *n* small piece of cloth for washing the face ▷ *vb* talk evasively

FLANNELED > FLANNEL

FLANNELET *n* cotton imitation of flannel

FLANNELLY > FLANNEL

FLANNELS > FLANNEL

FLANNEN *adj* made of flannel

FLANNENS > FLANNEN

FLANS > FLAN

FLAP *vb* move back and forwards or up and down ▷ *n* action or sound of flapping

FLAPERON *n* control flap on aircraft wing

FLAPERONS > FLAPERON

FLAPJACK *n* chewy biscuit made with oats

FLAPJACKS > FLAPJACK

FLAPLESS > FLAP

FLAPPABLE > FLAP

FLAPPED > FLAP

FLAPPER *n* (in the 1920s) a lively young woman who dressed and behaved unconventionally

FLAPPERS > FLAPPER

FLAPPIER > FLAPPY

FLAPPIEST > FLAPPY

FLAPPING > FLAP

FLAPPINGS > FLAP

FLAPPY *adj* loose

FLAPS > FLAP

FLAPTRACK *n* component in an aircraft wing

FLARE *vb* blaze with a sudden unsteady flame ▷ *n* sudden unsteady flame

FLAREBACK *n* flame in the breech of a gun when fired

FLARED > FLARE

FLARES *pl n* trousers with legs that widen below the knee

FLAREUP *n* outbreak of something

FLAREUPS > FLAREUP

FLARIER > FLARE

FLARIEST > FLARE

FLARING > FLARE

FLARINGLY > FLARE

FLARY > FLARE

FLASER *n* type of sedimentary structure in rock

FLASERS > FLASER

FLASH *n* sudden burst of light or flame ▷ *adj* vulgarly showy ▷ *vb* (cause to) burst into flame

FLASHBACK *n* scene in a book, play, or film, that shows earlier events ▷ *vb* return in a novel, film, etc, to a past event

FLASHBULB *n* small light bulb that produces a bright flash of light

FLASHCARD *n* card shown briefly as a memory test

FLASHCUBE *n* in photography, a cube with a bulb that is attached to a camera

FLASHED > FLASH

FLASHER *n* man who exposes himself indecently

FLASHERS > FLASHER

FLASHES > FLASH

FLASHEST > FLASH

FLASHGUN *n* type of electronic flash, attachable to or sometimes incorporated in a camera, that emits a very brief flash of light when the shutter is open

FLASHGUNS > FLASHGUN

FLASHIER > FLASHY

FLASHIEST > FLASHY

FLASHILY > FLASHY

FLASHING *n* watertight material used to cover joins in a roof

FLASHINGS > FLASHING

FLASHLAMP *n* electric lamp producing a flash of intense light

FLASHOVER *n* electric discharge over or around the surface of an insulator

FLASHTUBE *n* tube used in a flashlamp

FLASHY *adj* showy in a vulgar way

FLASK *n* flat bottle for carrying alcoholic drink in the pocket

FLASKET *n* long shallow basket

FLASKETS > FLASKET

FLASKS > FLASK

FLAT *adj* level and horizontal ▷ *adv* in or into a flat position ▷ *n* flat surface ▷ *vb* live in a flat

FLATBACK *n* flat-backed ornament, designed for viewing from front

FLATBACKS > FLATBACK

FLATBED *n* printing machine on which the type forme is carried on a flat bed under a revolving paper-bearing cylinder

FLATBEDS > FLATBED

FLATBOAT *n* flat-bottomed boat for transporting goods on a canal

FLATBOATS > FLATBOAT

FLATBREAD *n* type of thin unleavened bread

FLATCAP *n* Elizabethan man's hat with a narrow down-turned brim

FLATCAPS > FLATCAP

FLATCAR *n* flatbed

FLATCARS > FLATCAR

FLATETTE *n* very small flat

FLATETTES > FLATETTE

FLATFEET > FLATFOOT

FLATFISH *n* sea fish, such as the sole, which has a flat body

FLATFOOT *n* condition in which the entire sole of the foot is able to touch the ground because of flattening of the instep arch

FLATFOOTS > FLATFOOT

FLATHEAD *n* common Australian flatfish

FLATHEADS > FLATHEAD

FLATIRON *n* (formerly) an iron for pressing clothes that was heated by being placed on a stove

FLATIRONS > FLATIRON

FLATLAND *n* land notable for its levelness

FLATLANDS > FLATLAND

FLATLET *n* small flat

FLATLETS > FLATLET

FLATLINE *vb* die or be so near death that the display of one's vital signs on medical monitoring equipment shows a flat line rather than peaks and troughs

FLATLINED > FLATLINE

FLATLINER > FLATLINE

FLATLINES > FLATLINE

FLATLING adv in a flat or prostrate position ▷ adj with the flat side, as of a sword

FLATLINGS same as > FLATLING

FLATLONG adv prostrate

FLATLY > FLAT

FLATMATE n person with whom one shares a flat

FLATMATES > FLATMATE

FLATNESS > FLAT

FLATPACK n (of a piece of furniture, equipment, or other construction) supplied in pieces packed into a flat box for assembly by the buyer

FLATPACKS > FLATPACK

FLATS > FLAT

FLATSHARE n state of living in a flat where each occupant shares the facilities and expenses ▷ vb live in a flat with other people who are not relatives

FLATTED > FLAT

FLATTEN vb make or become flat or flatter

FLATTENED > FLATTEN

FLATTENER > FLATTEN

FLATTENS > FLATTEN

FLATTER vb praise insincerely

FLATTERED > FLATTER

FLATTERER > FLATTER

FLATTERS > FLATTER

FLATTERY n excessive or insincere praise

FLATTEST > FLAT

FLATTIE n flat tyre

FLATTIES > FLATTIE

FLATTING > FLAT

FLATTINGS > FLAT

FLATTISH adj somewhat flat

FLATTOP n informal name for an aircraft carrier

FLATTOPS > FLATTOP

FLATTY n flat shoe

FLATULENT adj suffering from or caused by too much gas in the intestines

FLATUOUS > FLATUS

FLATUS n gas generated in the alimentary canal

FLATUSES > FLATUS

FLATWARE n cutlery

FLATWARES > FLATWARE

FLATWASH n laundry that can be ironed mechanically

FLATWAYS adv with the flat or broad side down or in contact with another surface

FLATWISE same as > FLATWAYS

FLATWORK n laundry that can be ironed mechanically

FLATWORKS > FLATWORK

FLATWORM n worm, such as a tapeworm, with a

flattened body

FLATWORMS > FLATWORM

FLAUGHT vb flutter

FLAUGHTED > FLAUGHT

FLAUGHTER vb cut peat

FLAUGHTS > FLAUGHT

FLAUNCH n cement or mortar slope around a chimney top, manhole, etc, to throw off water ▷ vb cause to slope in this manner

FLAUNCHED > FLAUNCH

FLAUNCHES > FLAUNCH

FLAUNE variant of > FLAM

FLAUNES > FLAUNE

FLAUNT vb display (oneself or one's possessions) arrogantly ▷ n act of flaunting

FLAUNTED > FLAUNT

FLAUNTER > FLAUNT

FLAUNTERS > FLAUNT

FLAUNTIER > FLAUNTY

FLAUNTILY > FLAUNTY

FLAUNTING > FLAUNT

FLAUNTS > FLAUNT

FLAUNTY adj characterized by or inclined to ostentatious display or flaunting

FLAUTA n tortilla rolled around a filling

FLAUTAS > FLAUTA

FLAUTIST n flute player

FLAUTISTS > FLAUTIST

FLAVANOL n type of flavonoid

FLAVANOLS > FLAVANOL

FLAVANONE n flavone-derived compound

FLAVIN n heterocyclic ketone

FLAVINE same as > FLAVIN

FLAVINES > FLAVINE

FLAVINS > FLAVIN

FLAVONE n crystalline compound occurring in plants

FLAVONES > FLAVONE

FLAVONOID n any of a group of organic compounds that occur as pigments in fruit and flowers

FLAVONOL n flavonoid that occurs in red wine and is said to offer protection against heart disease

FLAVONOLS > FLAVONOL

FLAVOR same as > FLAVOUR

FLAVORED > FLAVOR

FLAVORER > FLAVOR

FLAVORERS > FLAVOR

FLAVORFUL same as > FLAVOURFUL

FLAVORING same as > FLAVORING

FLAVORIST n blender of ingredients, to create or enhance flavours

FLAVOROUS adj having flavour

FLAVORS > FLAVOR

FLAVORY adj flavoursome

FLAVOUR n distinctive taste ▷ vb give flavour to

FLAVOURED > FLAVOUR

FLAVOURER > FLAVOUR

FLAVOURS > FLAVOUR

FLAVOURY adj flavoursome

FLAW n imperfection or blemish ▷ vb make or become blemished, defective, or imperfect

FLAWED > FLAW

FLAWIER > FLAW

FLAWIEST > FLAW

FLAWING > FLAW

FLAWLESS > FLAW

FLAWN variant of > FLAM

FLAWNS > FLAWN

FLAWS > FLAW

FLAWY > FLAW

FLAX n plant grown for its stem fibres and seeds

FLAXEN adj (of hair) pale yellow

FLAXES > FLAX

FLAXIER > FLAXY

FLAXIEST > FLAXY

FLAXSEED n seed of the flax plant, which yields linseed oil

FLAXSEEDS > FLAXSEED

FLAXY same as > FLAXEN

FLAY same as > FLEY

FLAYED > FLAY

FLAYER > FLAY

FLAYERS > FLAY

FLAYING > FLAY

FLAYS > FLAY

FLAYSOME adj frightening

FLEA n small wingless jumping bloodsucking insect

FLEABAG n dirty or unkempt person, esp a woman

FLEABAGS > FLEABAG

FLEABANE as in Canadian fleabane

FLEABANES > FLEABANE

FLEABITE n bite of a flea

FLEABITES > FLEABITE

FLEAM n lancet used for letting blood

FLEAMS > FLEAM

FLEAPIT n shabby cinema or theatre

FLEAPITS > FLEAPIT

FLEAS > FLEA

FLEASOME > FLEA

FLEAWORT n any of various plants of the genus Senecio, esp S. integrifolius, a European species with yellow daisy-like flowers and rosettes of downy leaves: family Asteraceae (composites)

FLEAWORTS > FLEAWORT

FLECHE n slender spire, esp over the intersection of the nave and transept ridges of a church roof

FLECHES > FLECHE

FLECHETTE n steel dart or missile dropped from an aircraft, as in World War I

FLECK n small mark, streak, or speck ▷ vb speckle

FLECKED > FLECK

FLECKER same as > FLECK

FLECKERED > FLECKER

FLECKERS > FLECKER

FLECKING > FLECK

FLECKLESS > FLECK

FLECKS > FLECK

FLECKY > FLECK

FLECTION n act of bending or the state of being bent

FLECTIONS > FLECTION

FLED > FLEE

FLEDGE vb feed and care for (a young bird) until it is able to fly

FLEDGED > FLEDGE

FLEDGES > FLEDGE

FLEDGIER > FLEDGY

FLEDGIEST > FLEDGY

FLEDGING > FLEDGE

FLEDGLING n young bird ▷ adj new or inexperienced

FLEDGY adj feathery or feathered

FLEE vb run away (from)

FLEECE n sheep's coat of wool ▷ vb defraud or overcharge

FLEECED > FLEECE

FLEECER > FLEECE

FLEECERS > FLEECE

FLEECES > FLEECE

FLEECH vb flatter

FLEECHED > FLEECH

FLEECHES > FLEECH

FLEECHING > FLEECH

FLEECIE n person who collects fleeces after shearing and prepares them for baling

FLEECIER > FLEECY

FLEECIES > FLEECIE

FLEECIEST > FLEECY

FLEECILY > FLEECY

FLEECING > FLEECE

FLEECY adj made of or like fleece ▷ n person who collects fleeces after shearing and prepares them for baling

FLEEING > FLEE

FLEER vb grin or laugh at ▷ n derisory glance or grin

FLEERED > FLEER

FLEERER > FLEER

FLEERERS > FLEER

FLEERING > FLEER

FLEERINGS > FLEER

FLEERS > FLEER

FLEES > FLEE

FLEET n number of warships organized as a unit ▷ adj swift in movement ▷ vb move rapidly

FLEETED > FLEET

FLEETER > FLEET

FLEETEST > FLEET

FLEETING adj rapid and soon passing

FLEETLY > FLEET

FLEETNESS > FLEET

FLEETS > FLEET

FLEG vb scare

FLEGGED > FLEG

FLEGGING > FLEG

FLEGS > FLEG

FLEHMEN vb (of mammal) grimace

FLEHMENED > FLEHMEN

FLEHMENS > FLEHMEN

FLEISHIG same as > FLEISHIK

FLEISHIK adj (of food)

containing or derived from meat or meat products and therefore to be prepared and eaten separately from dairy foods

FLEME *vb* drive out

FLEMES > FLEME

FLEMING *n* native or inhabitant of Flanders or a Flemish-speaking Belgian

FLEMISH *vb* stow (a rope) in a Flemish coil

FLEMISHED > FLEMISH

FLEMISHES > FLEMISH

FLEMIT > FLEME

FLENCH *same as* > FLENSE

FLENCHED > FLENCH

FLENCHER > FLENCH

FLENCHERS > FLENCH

FLENCHES > FLENCH

FLENCHING > FLENCH

FLENSE *vb* strip (a whale, seal, etc) of (its blubber or skin)

FLENSED > FLENSE

FLENSER > FLENSE

FLENSERS > FLENSE

FLENSES > FLENSE

FLENSING > FLENSE

FLESH *n* soft part of a human or animal body

FLESHED > FLESH

FLESHER *n* person or machine that fleshes hides or skins

FLESHERS > FLESHER

FLESHES > FLESH

FLESHHOOD incarnation

FLESHIER > FLESHY

FLESHIEST > FLESHY

FLESHILY > FLESHY

FLESHING > FLESH

FLESHINGS *pl n* flesh-coloured tights

FLESHLESS > FLESH

FLESHLIER > FLESHLY

FLESHLING *n* voluptuary

FLESHLY *adj* carnal

FLESHMENT *n* act of fleshing

FLESHPOT *n* pot in which meat is cooked

FLESHPOTS *pl n* places, such as brothels and strip clubs, where sexual desires are catered to

FLESHWORM *n* flesh-eating worm

FLESHY *adj* plump

FLETCH *same as* > FLEDGE

FLETCHED > FLETCH

FLETCHER *n* person who makes arrows

FLETCHERS > FLETCHER

FLETCHES > FLETCH

FLETCHING > FLETCH

FLETTON *n* type of brick

FLETTONS > FLETTON

FLEURET *same as* > FLEURETTE

FLEURETS > FLEURET

FLEURETTE *n* ornament resembling a flower

FLEURON *n* decorative piece of pastry

FLEURONS > FLEURON

FLEURY *same as* > FLORY

FLEW > FLY

FLEWED *adj* having large flews

FLEWS *pl n* fleshy hanging upper lip of a bloodhound or similar dog

FLEX *n* flexible insulated electric cable ▷*vb* bend

FLEXAGON *n* hexagon made from a single pliable strip of triangles

FLEXAGONS > FLEXAGON

FLEXED > FLEX

FLEXES > FLEX

FLEXIBLE *adj* easily bent

FLEXIBLY > FLEXIBLE

FLEXILE *same as* > FLEXIBLE

FLEXING > FLEX

FLEXION *n* act of bending a joint or limb

FLEXIONAL > FLEXION

FLEXIONS > FLEXION

FLEXITIME *n* system permitting variation in starting and finishing times of work

FLEXO *n, adj, adv* flexography

FLEXOR *n* any muscle whose contraction serves to bend a joint or limb

FLEXORS > FLEXOR

FLEXOS > FLEXO

FLEXTIME *same as* > FLEXITIME

FLEXTIMER > FLEXTIME

FLEXTIMES > FLEXTIME

FLEXUOSE *same as* > FLEXUOUS

FLEXUOUS *adj* full of bends or curves

FLEXURAL > FLEXURE

FLEXURE *n* act of flexing or the state of being flexed

FLEXURES > FLEXURE

FLEY *vb* be afraid or cause to be afraid

FLEYED > FLEY

FLEYING > FLEY

FLEYS > FLEY

FLIBBERT *n* small piece or bit

FLIBBERTS > FLIBBERT

FLIC *n* French police officer

FLICHTER *vb* flutter

FLICHTERS > FLICHTER

FLICK *vb* touch or move with the finger or hand in a quick movement ▷*n* tap or quick stroke

FLICKABLE > FLICK

FLICKED > FLICK

FLICKER *vb* shine unsteadily or intermittently ▷*n* unsteady brief light

FLICKERED > FLICKER

FLICKERS > FLICKER

FLICKERY > FLICKER

FLICKING > FLICK

FLICKS > FLICK

FLICS > FLIC

FLIED > FLY

FLIER > FLY

FLIERS > FLY

FLIES > FLY

FLIEST > FLY

FLIGHT *n* journey by air ▷*vb* cause (a ball, dart, etc) to float slowly or deceptively towards its target

FLIGHTED > FLIGHT

FLIGHTIER > FLIGHTY

FLIGHTILY > FLIGHTY

FLIGHTING > FLIGHT

FLIGHTS > FLIGHT

FLIGHTY *adj* frivolous and fickle

FLIM *n* five-pound note

FLIMFLAM *n* nonsense ▷*vb* deceive

FLIMFLAMS > FLIMFLAM

FLIMP *vb* steal

FLIMPED > FLIMP

FLIMPING > FLIMP

FLIMPS > FLIMP

FLIMS > FLIM

FLIMSIER > FLIMSY

FLIMSIES > FLIMSY

FLIMSIEST > FLIMSY

FLIMSILY > FLIMSY

FLIMSY *adj* not strong or substantial ▷*n* thin paper used for making carbon copies of a letter, etc

FLINCH *same as* > FLENSE

FLINCHED > FLINCH

FLINCHER > FLINCH

FLINCHERS > FLINCH

FLINCHES > FLINCH

FLINCHING > FLINCH

FLINDER *n* fragment

FLINDERS > FLINDER

FLING *vb* throw, send, or move forcefully or hurriedly ▷*n* spell of self-indulgent enjoyment

FLINGER > FLING

FLINGERS > FLING

FLINGING > FLING

FLINGS > FLING

FLINKITE *n* anhydrous phosphate

FLINKITES > FLINKITE

FLINT *n* hard grey stone ▷*vb* fit or provide with a flint

FLINTED > FLINT

FLINTHEAD *n* American wading bird

FLINTIER > FLINTY

FLINTIEST > FLINTY

FLINTIFY *vb* turn to flint

FLINTILY > FLINTY

FLINTING > FLINT

FLINTLIKE > FLINT

FLINTLOCK *n* obsolete gun in which the powder was lit by a spark from a flint

FLINTS > FLINT

FLINTY *adj* cruel

FLIP *vb* throw (something small or light) carelessly ▷*n* snap or tap ▷*adj* flippant

FLIPBOOK *n* book of drawings made to seem animated by flipping pages

FLIPBOOKS > FLIPBOOK

FLIPFLOP *n* rubber sandal

FLIPFLOPS > FLIPFLOP

FLIPPANCY > FLIPPANT

FLIPPANT *adj* treating serious things lightly

FLIPPED > FLIP

FLIPPER *n* limb of a sea animal adapted for swimming

FLIPPERS > FLIPPER

FLIPPEST > FLIP

FLIPPING > FLIP

FLIPPY *adj* (of clothes) tending to move to and fro as the wearer walks

FLIPS > FLIP

FLIR *n* forward looking infrared radar

FLIRS > FLIR

FLIRT *vb* behave as if sexually attracted to someone ▷*n* person who flirts

FLIRTED > FLIRT

FLIRTER > FLIRT

FLIRTERS > FLIRT

FLIRTIER > FLIRT

FLIRTIEST > FLIRT

FLIRTING > FLIRT

FLIRTINGS > FLIRT

FLIRTISH > FLIRT

FLIRTS > FLIRT

FLIRTY > FLIRT

FLISK *vb* skip

FLISKED > FLISK

FLISKIER > FLISK

FLISKIEST > FLISK

FLISKING > FLISK

FLISKS > FLISK

FLISKY > FLISK

FLIT *vb* move lightly and rapidly ▷*n* act of flitting

FLITCH *n* side of pork salted and cured ▷*vb* cut (a tree trunk) into flitches

FLITCHED > FLITCH

FLITCHES > FLITCH

FLITCHING > FLITCH

FLITE *vb* scold or rail at ▷*n* dispute or scolding

FLITED > FLITE

FLITES > FLITE

FLITING > FLITE

FLITS > FLIT

FLITT *adj* fleet

FLITTED > FLIT

FLITTER > FLIT

FLITTERED > FLIT

FLITTERN *n* bark of young oak tree

FLITTERNS > FLITTERN

FLITTERS > FLIT

FLITTING > FLIT

FLITTINGS > FLIT

FLIVVER *n* old, cheap, or battered car

FLIVVERS > FLIVVER

FLIX *n* fur ▷*vb* have fur

FLIXED > FLIX

FLIXES > FLIX

FLIXING > FLIX

FLOAT *vb* rest on the surface of a liquid ▷*n* light object used to help someone or something float

FLOATABLE > FLOAT

FLOATAGE *same as* > FLOTAGE

FLOATAGES > FLOATAGE

FLOATANT *n* substance used in fly-fishing, to help dry flies to float

FLOATANTS > FLOATANT

FLOATCUT as in *floatcut file* file with rows of parallel teeth

f

FLOATED > FLOAT
FLOATEL *same as* > FLOTEL
FLOATELS > FLOATEL
FLOATER *n* person or thing that floats
FLOATERS > FLOATER
FLOATIER > FLOATY
FLOATIEST > FLOATY
FLOATING *adj* moving about, changing
FLOATINGS > FLOATING
FLOATS *pl n* footlights
FLOATY *adj* filmy and light
FLOC *same as* > FLOCK
FLOCCED > FLOC
FLOCCI > FLOCCUS
FLOCCING > FLOC
FLOCCOSE *adj* consisting of or covered with woolly tufts or hairs
FLOCCULAR > FLOCCUS
FLOCCULE *n* small aggregate of flocculent material
FLOCCULES > FLOCCULE
FLOCCULI > FLOCCULUS
FLOCCULUS *same as* > FLOCCULE
FLOCCUS *n* downy or woolly covering, as on the young of certain birds ▷ *adj* (of a cloud) having the appearance of woolly tufts at odd intervals in its structure
FLOCK *n* number of animals of one kind together ▷ *vb* gather in a crowd ▷ *adj* (of wallpaper) with a velvety raised pattern
FLOCKED > FLOCK
FLOCKIER > FLOCK
FLOCKIEST > FLOCK
FLOCKING > FLOCK
FLOCKINGS > FLOCK
FLOCKLESS > FLOCK
FLOCKS > FLOCK
FLOCKY > FLOCK
FLOCS > FLOC
FLOE *n* sheet of floating ice
FLOES > FLOE
FLOG *vb* beat with a whip or stick
FLOGGABLE > FLOG
FLOGGED > FLOG
FLOGGER > FLOG
FLOGGERS > FLOG
FLOGGING > FLOG
FLOGGINGS > FLOG
FLOGS > FLOG
FLOKATI *n* Greek hand-woven shaggy woollen rug
FLOKATIS > FLOKATI
FLONG *n* material, usually pulped paper or cardboard, used for making moulds in stereotyping
FLONGS > FLONG
FLOOD *n* overflow of water onto a normally dry area ▷ *vb* cover or become covered with water
FLOODABLE > FLOOD
FLOODED > FLOOD
FLOODER > FLOOD
FLOODERS > FLOOD
FLOODGATE *n* gate used to control the flow of water

FLOODING *n* submerging of land under water, esp due to heavy rain, a lake or river overflowing, etc
FLOODINGS > FLOODING
FLOODLESS > FLOOD
FLOODLIT *adj* illuminated with a floodlight
FLOODMARK *n* high-water mark
FLOODS > FLOOD
FLOODTIDE *n* rising tide
FLOODWALL *n* wall built as a defence against floods
FLOODWAY *n* conduit for floodwater
FLOODWAYS > FLOODWAY
FLOOEY *adj* awry
FLOOIE *same as* > FLOOEY
FLOOR *n* lower surface of a room ▷ *vb* knock down
FLOORAGE *n* area of floor
FLOORAGES > FLOORAGE
FLOORED > FLOOR
FLOORER *n* coup de grâce
FLOORERS > FLOORER
FLOORHEAD *n* upper side of a floor timber
FLOORING > FLOOR
FLOORINGS > FLOOR
FLOORLESS > FLOOR
FLOORS > FLOOR
FLOORSHOW *n* entertainment on floor of nightclub
FLOOSIE *same as* > FLOOZY
FLOOSIES > FLOOSIE
FLOOSY *variant of* > FLOOSIE
FLOOZIE *same as* > FLOOZY
FLOOZIES > FLOOZY
FLOOZY *n* disreputable woman
FLOP *vb* bend, fall, or collapse loosely or carelessly ▷ *n* failure
FLOPHOUSE *n* cheap lodging house, esp one used by tramps
FLOPOVER *n* TV visual effect of page being turned
FLOPOVERS > FLOPOVER
FLOPPED > FLOP
FLOPPER > FLOP
FLOPPERS > FLOP
FLOPPIER > FLOPPY
FLOPPIES > FLOPPY
FLOPPIEST > FLOPPY
FLOPPILY > FLOPPY
FLOPPING > FLOP
FLOPPY *adj* hanging downwards, loose ▷ *n* floppy disk
FLOPS > FLOP
FLOPTICAL *n* type of floppy disk
FLOR *n* yeast formed on the surface of sherry after fermentation
FLORA *n* plants of a given place or time
FLORAE > FLORA
FLORAL *adj* consisting of or decorated with flowers ▷ *n* class of perfume
FLORALLY > FLORAL
FLORALS > FLORAL
FLORAS > FLORA
FLOREANT > FLOREAT

FLOREAT *vb* may (a person, institution, etc) flourish
FLOREATED *same as* > FLORIATED
FLORENCE *n* type of fennel
FLORENCES > FLORENCE
FLORET *n* small flower forming part of a composite flower head
FLORETS > FLORET
FLORIATED *adj* having ornamentation based on flowers and leaves
FLORICANE *n* fruiting stem of plant
FLORID *adj* with a red or flushed complexion
FLORIDEAN *n* member of the red seaweed family
FLORIDER > FLORID
FLORIDEST > FLORID
FLORIDITY > FLORID
FLORIDLY > FLORID
FLORIER > FLORY
FLORIEST > FLORY
FLORIFORM *adj* flower-shaped
FLORIGEN *n* hypothetical plant hormone that induces flowering, thought to be synthesized in the leaves as a photoperiodic response and transmitted to the flower buds
FLORIGENS > FLORIGEN
FLORIN *n* former British and Australian coin
FLORINS > FLORIN
FLORIST *n* seller of flowers
FLORISTIC *adj* of or relating to flowers or a flora
FLORISTRY > FLORIST
FLORISTS > FLORIST
FLORS > FLOR
FLORUIT *vb* (he or she) flourished: used to indicate the period when a historical figure, whose birth and death dates are unknown, was most active
FLORUITS > FLORUIT
FLORULA *n* flora of a small single environment
FLORULAE > FLORULA
FLORULE *same as* > FLORULA
FLORULES > FLORULE
FLORY *adj* containing a fleur-de-lys
FLOSCULAR > FLOSCULE
FLOSCULE *n* floret
FLOSCULES > FLOSCULE
FLOSH *hopper-shaped box*
FLOSHES > FLOSH
FLOSS *n* fine silky fibres ▷ *vb* clean (between the teeth) with dental floss
FLOSSED > FLOSS
FLOSSER > FLOSS
FLOSSERS > FLOSS
FLOSSES > FLOSS
FLOSSIE *variant of* > FLOSSY
FLOSSIER > FLOSSY
FLOSSIES > FLOSSY
FLOSSIEST > FLOSSY
FLOSSILY > FLOSSY
FLOSSING > FLOSS
FLOSSINGS > FLOSS
FLOSSY *adj* consisting of or

resembling floss ▷ *n* floozy
FLOTA *n* formerly, Spanish commercial fleet
FLOTAGE *n* act or state of floating
FLOTAGES > FLOTAGE
FLOTANT *adj* in heraldry, flying in the air
FLOTAS > FLOTA
FLOTATION *n* launching or financing of a business enterprise
FLOTE *n* aquatic perennial grass
FLOTEL *n* (in the oil industry) an oil rig or boat used as accommodation for workers in off-shore oil fields
FLOTELS > FLOTEL
FLOTES > FLOTE
FLOTILLA *n* small fleet or fleet of small ships
FLOTILLAS > FLOTILLA
FLOTSAM *n* floating wreckage
FLOTSAMS > FLOTSAM
FLOUNCE *vb* go with emphatic movements ▷ *n* flouncing movement
FLOUNCED > FLOUNCE
FLOUNCES > FLOUNCE
FLOUNCIER > FLOUNCE
FLOUNCING *n* material, such as lace or embroidered fabric, used for making flounces
FLOUNCY > FLOUNCE
FLOUNDER *vb* move with difficulty, as in mud ▷ *n* edible flatfish
FLOUNDERS > FLOUNDER
FLOUR *n* powder made by grinding grain, esp wheat ▷ *vb* sprinkle with flour
FLOURED > FLOUR
FLOURIER > FLOUR
FLOURIEST > FLOUR
FLOURING > FLOUR
FLOURISH *vb* be active, successful, or widespread ▷ *n* dramatic waving motion
FLOURISHY > FLOURISH
FLOURLESS > FLOUR
FLOURS > FLOUR
FLOURY > FLOUR
FLOUSE *vb* splash
FLOUSED > FLOUSE
FLOUSES > FLOUSE
FLOUSH *variant of* > FLOUSE
FLOUSHED > FLOUSH
FLOUSHES > FLOUSH
FLOUSHING > FLOUSH
FLOUSING > FLOUSE
FLOUT *vb* deliberately disobey (a rule, law, etc)
FLOUTED > FLOUT
FLOUTER > FLOUT
FLOUTERS > FLOUT
FLOUTING > FLOUT
FLOUTS > FLOUT
FLOW *vb* (of liquid) move in a stream ▷ *n* act, rate, or manner of flowing
FLOWAGE *n* act of flowing or overflowing or the state of having overflowed

FLOWAGES > FLOWAGE

FLOWCHART n diagrammatic representation of the sequence of operations or equipment in an industrial process, computer program, etc

FLOWED > FLOW

FLOWER n part of a plant that produces seeds ▷ vb produce flowers, bloom

FLOWERAGE n mass of flowers

FLOWERBED n piece of ground for growing flowers

FLOWERED adj decorated with a floral design

FLOWERER n plant that flowers at a specified time or in a specified way

FLOWERERS > FLOWERER

FLOWERET another name for > FLORET

FLOWERETS > FLOWERET

FLOWERFUL adj having plentiful flowers

FLOWERIER > FLOWERY

FLOWERILY > FLOWERY

FLOWERING adj (of certain species of plants) capable of producing conspicuous flowers

FLOWERPOT n pot in which plants are grown

FLOWERS > FLOWER

FLOWERY adj decorated with a floral design

FLOWING > FLOW

FLOWINGLY > FLOW

FLOWMETER n instrument that measures the rate of flow of a liquid or gas within a pipe or tube

FLOWN > FLY

FLOWS > FLOW

FLOWSTONE n type of speleothem

FLU n any of various viral infections, esp a respiratory or intestinal infection

FLUATE n fluoride

FLUATES > FLUATE

FLUB vb bungle

FLUBBED > FLUB

FLUBBER > FLUB

FLUBBERS > FLUB

FLUBBING > FLUB

FLUBDUB n bunkum

FLUBDUBS > FLUBDUB

FLUBS > FLUB

FLUCTUANT adj inclined to vary or fluctuate

FLUCTUATE vb change frequently and erratically

FLUE n passage or pipe for smoke or hot air

FLUED adj having a flue

FLUELLEN n type of plant

FLUELLENS > FLUELLEN

FLUELLIN same as > FLUELLEN

FLUELLINS > FLUELLIN

FLUENCE > FLUENCY

FLUENCES > FLUENCY

FLUENCIES > FLUENCY

FLUENCY n quality of being fluent, esp facility in speech

or writing

FLUENT adj able to speak or write with ease ▷ n variable quantity in fluxions

FLUENTLY > FLUENT

FLUENTS > FLUENT

FLUERIC adj of or relating to fluidics

FLUERICS pl n fluidics

FLUES > FLUE

FLUEWORK n collectively, organ stops

FLUEWORKS > FLUEWORK

FLUEY adj involved in, caused by, or like influenza

FLUFF n soft fibres ▷ vb make or become soft and puffy

FLUFFED > FLUFF

FLUFFER n person employed on a pornographic film set to ensure that male actors are kept aroused

FLUFFERS n fluffer

FLUFFIER > FLUFFY

FLUFFIEST > FLUFFY

FLUFFILY > FLUFFY

FLUFFING > FLUFF

FLUFFS > FLUFF

FLUFFY adj of, resembling, or covered with fluff

FLUGEL n grand piano or harpsichord

FLUGELMAN variant of > FUGLEMAN

FLUGELMEN > FLUGELMAN

FLUGELS > FLUGEL

FLUID n substance able to flow and change its shape ▷ adj able to flow or change shape easily

FLUIDAL > FLUID

FLUIDALLY > FLUID

FLUIDIC > FLUIDICS

FLUIDICS n study and use of systems in which the flow of fluids in tubes simulates the flow of electricity in conductors. Such systems are used in place of electronics in certain applications, such as the control of apparatus

FLUIDIFY vb make fluid

FLUIDISE same as > FLUIDIZE

FLUIDISED > FLUIDISE

FLUIDISER > FLUIDISE

FLUIDISES > FLUIDISE

FLUIDITY n state of being fluid

FLUIDIZE vb make fluid, esp to make (solids) fluid by pulverizing them so that they can be transported in a stream of gas as if they were liquids

FLUIDIZED > FLUIDIZE

FLUIDIZER > FLUIDIZE

FLUIDIZES > FLUIDIZE

FLUIDLIKE > FLUID

FLUIDLY > FLUID

FLUIDNESS > FLUID

FLUIDRAM n British imperial measure

FLUIDRAMS > FLUIDRAM

FLUIDS > FLUID

FLUIER > FLUEY

FLUIEST > FLUEY

FLUISH > FLU

FLUKE n accidental stroke of luck ▷ vb gain, make, or hit by a fluke

FLUKED > FLUKE

FLUKES > FLUKE

FLUKEY same as > FLUKY

FLUKIER > FLUKY

FLUKIEST > FLUKY

FLUKILY > FLUKY

FLUKINESS > FLUKY

FLUKING > FLUKE

FLUKY adj done or gained by an accident, esp a lucky one

FLUME n narrow sloping channel for water ▷ vb transport (logs) in a flume

FLUMED > FLUME

FLUMES > FLUME

FLUMING > FLUME

FLUMMERY n silly or trivial talk

FLUMMOX vb puzzle or confuse

FLUMMOXED > FLUMMOX

FLUMMOXES > FLUMMOX

FLUMP vb move or fall heavily

FLUMPED > FLUMP

FLUMPING > FLUMP

FLUMPS > FLUMP

FLUNG > FLING

FLUNK vb fail ▷ n low grade below the pass standard

FLUNKED > FLUNK

FLUNKER > FLUNK

FLUNKERS > FLUNK

FLUNKEY same as > FLUNKY

FLUNKEYS > FLUNKEY

FLUNKIE same as > FLUNKY

FLUNKIES > FLUNKY

FLUNKING > FLUNK

FLUNKS > FLUNK

FLUNKY n servile person

FLUNKYISM > FLUNKY

FLUOR > FLUORSPAR

FLUORENE n white insoluble crystalline solid

FLUORENES > FLUORENE

FLUORESCE vb exhibit fluorescence

FLUORIC adj of, concerned with, or produced from fluorine or fluorspar

FLUORID same as > FLUORIDE

FLUORIDE n compound containing fluorine

FLUORIDES > FLUORIDE

FLUORIDS > FLUORID

FLUORIN same as > FLUORINE

FLUORINE n toxic yellow gas: most reactive of all the elements

FLUORINES > FLUORINE

FLUORINS > FLUORIN

FLUORITE same as > FLUORSPAR

FLUORITES > FLUORITE

FLUOROSES > FLUOROSIS

FLUOROSIS n fluoride poisoning, due to ingestion of too much fluoride in drinking water over a long

period or to ingestion of pesticides containing fluoride salts. Chronic fluorosis results in mottling of the teeth of children

FLUOROTIC > FLUOROSIS

FLUORS > FLUOR

FLUORSPAR n white or colourless mineral, consisting of calcium fluoride in crystalline form: the chief ore of fluorine

FLURR vb scatter

FLURRED > FLURR

FLURRIED > FLURRY

FLURRIES > FLURRY

FLURRING > FLURR

FLURRS > FLURR

FLURRY n sudden commotion ▷ vb confuse

FLURRYING > FLURRY

FLUS > FLU

FLUSH vb blush or cause to blush ▷ n blush ▷ adj level with the surrounding surface ▷ adv so as to be level

FLUSHABLE > FLUSH

FLUSHED > FLUSH

FLUSHER > FLUSH

FLUSHERS > FLUSH

FLUSHES > FLUSH

FLUSHEST > FLUSH

FLUSHIER > FLUSHY

FLUSHIEST > FLUSHY

FLUSHING n extra feeding given to ewes before mating to increase the lambing percentage

FLUSHINGS > FLUSHING

FLUSHNESS > FLUSH

FLUSHWORK n decorative treatment of the surface of an outside wall with flints split to show their smooth black surface, combined with dressed stone to form patterns such as tracery or initials

FLUSHY adj ruddy

FLUSTER vb make nervous or upset ▷ n nervous or upset state

FLUSTERED > FLUSTER

FLUSTERS > FLUSTER

FLUSTERY > FLUSTER

FLUSTRATE vb fluster

FLUTE n wind instrument consisting of a tube with sound holes and a mouth hole in the side ▷ vb utter in a high-pitched tone

FLUTED adj having decorative grooves

FLUTELIKE > FLUTE

FLUTER n craftsman who makes flutes or fluting

FLUTERS > FLUTER

FLUTES > FLUTE

FLUTEY > FLUTE

FLUTIER > FLUTE

FLUTIEST > FLUTE

FLUTINA n type of accordion

FLUTINAS > FLUTINA

FLUTING n design of decorative grooves

FLUTINGS > FLUTING

FLUTIST *same as* > FLAUTIST
FLUTISTS > FLUTIST
FLUTTER *vb* wave rapidly ▷ *n* flapping movement
FLUTTERED > FLUTTER
FLUTTERER > FLUTTER
FLUTTERS > FLUTTER
FLUTTERY *adj* flapping rapidly
FLUTY > FLUTE
FLUVIAL *adj* of rivers
FLUVIATIC > FLUVIAL
FLUX *n* constant change or instability ▷ *vb* make or become fluid
FLUXED > FLUX
FLUXES > FLUX
FLUXGATE *n* type of magnetometer
FLUXGATES > FLUXGATE
FLUXING > FLUX
FLUXION *n* rate of change of a function, especially the instantaneous velocity of a moving body
FLUXIONAL > FLUXION
FLUXIONS > FLUXION
FLUXIVE > FLUX
FLUXMETER *n* any instrument for measuring magnetic flux, usually by measuring the charge that flows through a coil when the flux changes
FLUYT *n* Dutch sailing ship
FLUYTS > FLUYT
FLY *vb* move through the air on wings or in an aircraft ▷ *n* fastening at the front of trousers ▷ *adj* sharp and cunning
FLYABLE > FLY
FLYAWAY *adj* (of hair) very fine and soft ▷ *n* person who is frivolous or flighty
FLYAWAYS > FLYAWAY
FLYBACK *n* fast return of the spot on a cathode-ray tube after completion of each trace
FLYBACKS > FLYBACK
FLYBANE *n* type of campion
FLYBANES > FLYBANE
FLYBELT *n* strip of tsetse-infested land
FLYBELTS > FLYBELT
FLYBLEW > FLYBLOW
FLYBLOW *vb* contaminate, esp with the eggs or larvae of the blowfly ▷ *n* egg or young larva of a blowfly, deposited on meat, paper, etc
FLYBLOWN *adj* covered with blowfly eggs
FLYBLOWS > FLYBLOW
FLYBOAT *n* any small swift boat
FLYBOATS > FLYBOAT
FLYBOOK *n* small case or wallet used by anglers for storing artificial flies
FLYBOOKS > FLYBOOK
FLYBOY *n* air force pilot
FLYBOYS > FLYBOY
FLYBRIDGE *n* highest navigational bridge on a ship

FLYBY *n* flight past a particular position or target, esp the close approach of a spacecraft to a planet or satellite for investigation of conditions
FLYBYS > FLYBY
FLYER > FLY
FLYERS > FLY
FLYEST > FLY
FLYHAND *n* device for transferring printed sheets from the press to a flat pile
FLYHANDS > FLYHAND
FLYING > FLY
FLYINGS > FLY
FLYLEAF *n* blank leaf at the beginning or end of a book
FLYLEAVES > FLYLEAF
FLYLESS > FLY
FLYMAKER *n* person who makes fishing flies
FLYMAKERS > FLYMAKER
FLYMAN *n* stagehand who operates the scenery, curtains, etc, in the flies
FLYMEN > FLYMAN
FLYOFF *n* total volume of water transferred from the earth to the atmosphere
FLYOFFS > FLYOFF
FLYOVER *n* road passing over another by a bridge
FLYOVERS > FLYOVER
FLYPAPER *n* paper with a sticky poisonous coating, used to kill flies
FLYPAPERS > FLYPAPER
FLYPAST *n* ceremonial flight of aircraft over a given area
FLYPASTS > FLYPAST
FLYPE *vb* fold back
FLYPED > FLYPE
FLYPES > FLYPE
FLYPING > FLYPE
FLYPITCH *n* area for unlicensed stalls at markets
FLYRODDER *n* angler using artificial fly
FLYSCH *n* marine sedimentary facies consisting of a sequence of sandstones, conglomerates, marls, shales, and clays that were formed by erosion during a period of mountain building and subsequently deformed as the mountain building continued
FLYSCHES > FLYSCH
FLYSCREEN *n* wire-mesh screen over a window to prevent flies from entering a room
FLYSHEET *n* part of tent
FLYSHEETS > FLYSHEET
FLYSPECK *n* small speck of the excrement of a fly ▷ *vb* mark with flyspecks
FLYSPECKS > FLYSPECK
FLYSTRIKE *n* infestation of wounded sheep by blowflies or maggots
FLYTE *same as* > FLITE
FLYTED > FLYTE

FLYTES > FLYTE
FLYTIER *n* person who makes his own fishing flies
FLYTIERS > FLYTIER
FLYTING > FLYTE
FLYTINGS > FLYTE
FLYTRAP *n* any of various insectivorous plants, esp Venus's flytrap
FLYTRAPS > FLYTRAP
FLYWAY *n* usual route used by birds when migrating
FLYWAYS > FLYWAY
FLYWEIGHT *n* boxer weighing up to 112lb (professional) or 51kg (amateur)
FLYWHEEL *n* heavy wheel regulating the speed of a machine
FLYWHEELS > FLYWHEEL
FOAL *n* young of a horse or related animal ▷ *vb* give birth to a foal
FOALED > FOAL
FOALFOOT *n* coltsfoot
FOALFOOTS > FOALFOOT
FOALING > FOAL
FOALS > FOAL
FOAM *n* mass of small bubbles on a liquid ▷ *vb* produce foam
FOAMABLE > FOAM
FOAMED > FOAM
FOAMER *n* (possibly obsessive) enthusiast
FOAMERS > FOAMER
FOAMIER > FOAMY
FOAMIEST > FOAMY
FOAMILY > FOAMY
FOAMINESS > FOAMY
FOAMING > FOAM
FOAMINGLY > FOAM
FOAMINGS > FOAM
FOAMLESS > FOAM
FOAMLIKE > FOAM
FOAMS > FOAM
FOAMY *adj* of, resembling, consisting of, or covered with foam
FOB *n* short watch chain ▷ *vb* cheat
FOBBED > FOB
FOBBING > FOB
FOBS > FOB
FOCACCIA *n* flat Italian bread made with olive oil and yeast
FOCACCIAS > FOCACCIA
FOCAL *adj* of or at a focus
FOCALISE > FOCUS
FOCALISED > FOCUS
FOCALISES > FOCUS
FOCALIZE *less common word for* > FOCUS
FOCALIZED > FOCALIZE
FOCALIZES > FOCALIZE
FOCALLY > FOCAL
FOCI > FOCUS
FOCIMETER *n* photographic focusing device
FOCOMETER *n* instrument for measuring the focal length of a lens
FOCUS *n* point at which light or sound waves converge ▷ *vb* bring or come into focus

FOCUSABLE > FOCUS
FOCUSED > FOCUS
FOCUSER > FOCUS
FOCUSERS > FOCUS
FOCUSES > FOCUS
FOCUSING > FOCUS
FOCUSINGS > FOCUS
FOCUSLESS > FOCUS
FOCUSSED > FOCUS
FOCUSSES > FOCUS
FOCUSSING > FOCUS
FODDER *n* feed for livestock ▷ *vb* supply (livestock) with fodder
FODDERED > FODDER
FODDERER > FODDER
FODDERERS > FODDER
FODDERING > FODDER
FODDERS > FODDER
FODGEL *adj* buxom
FOE *n* enemy, opponent
FOEDARIE *variant of* > FEDARIE
FOEDARIES > FOEDARIE
FOEDERATI > FOEDERATUS
FOEHN *same as* > FOHN
FOEHNS > FOEHN
FOEMAN *n* enemy in war
FOEMEN > FOEMAN
FOEN > FOE
FOES > FOE
FOETAL *same as* > FETAL
FOETATION *same as* > FETATION
FOETICIDE *same as* > FETICIDE
FOETID *same as* > FETID
FOETIDER > FOETID
FOETIDEST > FOETID
FOETIDLY > FOETID
FOETOR *same as* > FETOR
FOETORS > FOETOR
FOETUS *same as* > FETUS
FOETUSES > FOETUS
FOG *n* mass of condensed water vapour in the lower air, often greatly reducing visibility ▷ *vb* cover with steam
FOGASH *n* type of Hungarian pike perch
FOGASHES > FOGASH
FOGBOUND *adj* prevented from operating by fog
FOGBOW *n* faint arc of light sometimes seen in a fog bank
FOGBOWS > FOGBOW
FOGDOG *n* whitish spot sometimes seen in fog near the horizon
FOGDOGS > FOGDOG
FOGEY *n* old-fashioned person
FOGEYDOM > FOGEY
FOGEYDOMS > FOGEY
FOGEYISH > FOGEY
FOGEYISM > FOGEY
FOGEYISMS > FOGEY
FOGEYS > FOGEY
FOGFRUIT *n* wildflower of the verbena family
FOGFRUITS > FOGFRUIT
FOGGAGE *n* grass grown for winter grazing
FOGGAGES > FOGGAGE
FOGGED > FOG
FOGGER *n* device that

generates a fog

FOGGERS > FOGGER

FOGGIER > FOG

FOGGIEST > FOG

FOGGILY > FOG

FOGGINESS > FOG

FOGGING > FOG

FOGGY > FOG

FOGHORN n large horn sounded to warn ships in fog

FOGHORNS > FOGHORN

FOGIE variant of > FOGEY

FOGIES > FOGIE

FOGLE n silk handkerchief

FOGLES > FOGLE

FOGLESS > FOG

FOGMAN n person in charge of railway fog-signals

FOGMEN > FOGMAN

FOGRAM n fogey

FOGRAMITE > FOGRAM

FOGRAMITY > FOGRAM

FOGRAMS > FOGRAM

FOGS > FOG

FOGY same as > FOGEY

FOGYDOM > FOGY

FOGYDOMS > FOGY

FOGYISH > FOGY

FOGYISM > FOGY

FOGYISMS > FOGY

FOH interj expression of disgust

FOHN n warm dry wind blowing down the northern slopes of the Alps

FOHNS > FOHN

FOHS > FOH

FOIBLE n minor weakness or slight peculiarity

FOIBLES > FOIBLE

FOID same as > FELDSPATHOID

FOIDS > FOID

FOIL vb ruin (someone's plan) ▷ n metal in a thin sheet, esp for wrapping food

FOILABLE > FOIL

FOILBORNE adj moving by means of hydrofoils

FOILED > FOIL

FOILING > FOIL

FOILINGS > FOIL

FOILS > FOIL

FOILSMAN n person who uses or specializes in using a foil

FOILSMEN > FOILSMAN

FOIN n thrust or lunge with a weapon ▷ vb thrust with a weapon

FOINED > FOIN

FOINING > FOIN

FOININGLY > FOIN

FOINS > FOIN

FOISON n plentiful supply or yield

FOISONS > FOISON

FOIST vb force or impose on

FOISTED > FOIST

FOISTER > FOIST

FOISTERS > FOIST

FOISTING > FOIST

FOISTS > FOIST

FOLACIN n folic acid

FOLACINS > FOLACIN

FOLATE n folic acid

FOLATES > FOLIC

FOLD vb bend so that one part covers another ▷ n folded piece or part

FOLDABLE > FOLD

FOLDAWAY adj (of a bed) able to be folded and put away when not in use

FOLDAWAYS > FOLDAWAY

FOLDBACK n (in multitrack recording) a process for returning a signal to a performer instantly

FOLDBACKS > FOLDBACK

FOLDBOAT another name for > FALTBOAT

FOLDBOATS > FOLDBOAT

FOLDED > FOLD

FOLDER n piece of folded cardboard for holding loose papers

FOLDEROL same as > FALDERAL

FOLDEROLS > FOLDEROL

FOLDERS > FOLDER

FOLDING > FOLD

FOLDINGS > FOLDING

FOLDOUT another name for > GATEFOLD

FOLDOUTS > FOLDOUT

FOLDS > FOLD

FOLDUP n something that folds up

FOLDUPS > FOLDUP

FOLEY n footsteps editor

FOLEYS > FOLEY

FOLIA > FOLIUM

FOLIAGE n leaves

FOLIAGED adj having foliage

FOLIAGES > FOLIAGE

FOLIAR adj of or relating to a leaf or leaves

FOLIATE adj relating to, possessing, or resembling leaves ▷ vb ornament with foliage or with leaf forms such as foils

FOLIATED adj ornamented with or made up of foliage or foils

FOLIATES > FOLIATE

FOLIATING > FOLIATE

FOLIATION n process of producing leaves

FOLIATURE > FOLIATION

FOLIC as in folic acid, , any of a group of vitamins of the B complex, including pteroylglutamic acid and its derivatives: used in the treatment of megaloblastic anaemia

FOLIE n madness

FOLIES > FOLIE

FOLIO n sheet of paper folded in half to make two leaves of a book ▷ adj of or made in the largest book size, common esp in early centuries of European printing ▷ vb number the leaves of (a book) consecutively

FOLIOED > FOLIO

FOLIOING > FOLIO

FOLIOLATE adj possessing or relating to leaflets

FOLIOLE n part of a compound leaf

FOLIOLES > FOLIOLE

FOLIOLOSE > FOLIOLE

FOLIOS > FOLIO

FOLIOSE another word for > FOLIACEOUS

FOLIOUS adj foliose

FOLIUM n plane geometrical curve consisting of a loop whose two ends, intersecting at a node, are asymptotic to the same line. Standard equation: $x^3 + y^3 = 3a\,xy$ where $x = y + a$ is the equation of the line

FOLIUMS > FOLIUM

FOLK n people in general ▷ adj originating from or traditional to the common people of a country

FOLKIE n devotee of folk music ▷ adj of or relating to folk music

FOLKIER > FOLKIE

FOLKIES > FOLKIE

FOLKIEST > FOLKIE

FOLKISH > FOLK

FOLKLAND n former type of land tenure

FOLKLANDS > FOLKLAND

FOLKLIFE n traditional customs, arts, crafts, and other forms of cultural expression of a people

FOLKLIKE > FOLK

FOLKLIVES > FOLKLIFE

FOLKLORE n traditional beliefs and stories of a people

FOLKLORES > FOLKLORE

FOLKLORIC > FOLKLORE

FOLKMOOT n (in early medieval England) an assembly of the people of a district, town, or shire

FOLKMOOTS > FOLKMOOT

FOLKMOT same as > FOLKMOOT

FOLKMOTE same as > FOLKMOOT

FOLKMOTES > FOLKMOTE

FOLKMOTS > FOLKMOT

FOLKS > FOLK

FOLKSIER > FOLKSY

FOLKSIEST > FOLKSY

FOLKSILY > FOLKSY

FOLKSONG n traditional song

FOLKSONGS > FOLKSONG

FOLKSY adj simple and unpretentious

FOLKTALE n tale or legend originating among a people and typically becoming part of an oral tradition

FOLKTALES > FOLKTALE

FOLKWAY singular form of > FOLKWAYS

FOLKWAYS pl n traditional and customary ways of living

FOLKY same as > FOLKIE

FOLLES > FOLLIS

FOLLICLE n small cavity in the body, esp one from which a hair grows

FOLLICLES > FOLLICLE

FOLLIED > FOLLY

FOLLIES > FOLLY

FOLLIS n Roman coin

FOLLOW vb go or come after

FOLLOWED > FOLLOW

FOLLOWER n disciple or supporter

FOLLOWERS > FOLLOWER

FOLLOWING adj about to be mentioned ▷ n group of supporters ▷ prep as a result of

FOLLOWS > FOLLOW

FOLLOWUP n further action

FOLLOWUPS > FOLLOWUP

FOLLY n foolishness ▷ vb behave foolishly

FOLLYING > FOLLY

FOMENT vb encourage or stir up (trouble)

FOMENTED > FOMENT

FOMENTER > FOMENT

FOMENTERS > FOMENT

FOMENTING > FOMENT

FOMENTS > FOMENT

FOMES n any material, such as bedding or clothing, that may harbour pathogens and therefore convey disease

FOMITE > FOMES

FOMITES > FOMES

FON vb compel

FOND adj tender, loving ▷ n background of a design, as in lace ▷ vb dote

FONDA n Spanish hotel

FONDANT n (sweet made from) flavoured paste of sugar and water ▷ adj (of a colour) soft

FONDANTS > FONDANT

FONDAS > FONDA

FONDED > FOND

FONDER > FOND

FONDEST > FOND

FONDING > FOND

FONDLE vb caress

FONDLED > FONDLE

FONDLER > FONDLE

FONDLERS > FONDLE

FONDLES > FONDLE

FONDLING > FONDLE

FONDLINGS > FONDLE

FONDLY > FOND

FONDNESS > FOND

FONDS > FOND

FONDU n ballet movement, lowering the body by bending the leg(s)

FONDUE n Swiss dish of a hot melted cheese sauce into which pieces of bread are dipped ▷ vb cook and serve (food) as a fondue

FONDUED > FONDUE

FONDUEING > FONDUE

FONDUES > FONDUE

FONDUING > FONDUE

FONDUS > FONDU

FONE variant of > FOE

FONLY adv foolishly

FONNED > FON

FONNING > FON

FONS > FON

FONT n bowl in a church for baptismal water

FONTAL > FONT
FONTANEL same as > FONTANELLE
FONTANELS > FONTANEL
FONTANGE n type of tall headdress
FONTANGES > FONTANGE
FONTICULI > FONTICULUS
FONTINA n semihard, pale yellow, mild Italian cheese made from cow's milk
FONTINAS > FONTINA
FONTLET > FONT
FONTLETS > FONT
FONTS > FONT
FOOBAR same as > FUBAR
FOOD n what one eats; solid nourishment
FOODFUL adj supplying abundant food
FOODIE n gourmet
FOODIES > FOODIE
FOODISM n enthusiasm for and interest in the preparation and consumption of good food
FOODISMS > FOODISM
FOODLESS > FOOD
FOODS > FOOD
FOODSTUFF n substance used as food
FOODWAYS pl n customs and traditions relating to food and its preparation
FOODY same as > FOODIE
FOOFARAW n vulgar ornamentation
FOOFARAWS > FOOFARAW
FOOL n person lacking sense or judgment ▷ vb deceive (someone)
FOOLED > FOOL
FOOLERIES > FOOLERY
FOOLERY n foolish behaviour
FOOLFISH n orange filefish or winter flounder
FOOLHARDY adj recklessly adventurous
FOOLING > FOOL
FOOLINGS > FOOL
FOOLISH adj unwise, silly, or absurd
FOOLISHER > FOOLISH
FOOLISHLY > FOOLISH
FOOLPROOF adj unable to fail
FOOLS > FOOL
FOOLSCAP n size of paper, 34.3 x 43.2 centimetres
FOOLSCAPS > FOOLSCAP
FOOSBALL n US and Canadian name for table football
FOOSBALLS > FOOSBALL
FOOT n part of the leg below the ankle ▷ vb kick
FOOTAGE n amount of film used
FOOTAGES > FOOTAGE
FOOTBAG n sport of keeping small round object off the ground by kicking it
FOOTBAGS > FOOTBAG
FOOTBALL n game played by two teams of eleven players kicking a ball in an attempt to score goals

FOOTBALLS > FOOTBALL
FOOTBAR n any bar designed as a footrest or to be operated by the foot
FOOTBARS > FOOTBAR
FOOTBATH n vessel for bathing the feet
FOOTBATHS > FOOTBATH
FOOTBOARD n treadle or foot-operated lever on a machine
FOOTBOY n boy servant
FOOTBOYS > FOOTBOY
FOOTCLOTH obsolete word for > CAPARISON
FOOTED > FOOT
FOOTER n person who goes on foot ▷ vb potter
FOOTERED > FOOTER
FOOTERING > FOOTER
FOOTERS > FOOTER
FOOTFALL n sound of a footstep
FOOTFALLS > FOOTFALL
FOOTFAULT n fault that occurs when the server fails to keep both feet behind the baseline until he/she has served
FOOTGEAR another name for > FOOTWEAR
FOOTGEARS > FOOTGEAR
FOOTHILL n lower slope of a mountain or a relatively low hill at the foot of a mountain
FOOTHILLS > FOOTHILL
FOOTHOLD n secure position from which progress may be made
FOOTHOLDS > FOOTHOLD
FOOTIE same as > FOOTY
FOOTIER > FOOTY
FOOTIES > FOOTIE
FOOTIEST > FOOTY
FOOTING n basis or foundation
FOOTINGS > FOOTING
FOOTLE vb loiter aimlessly ▷ n foolishness
FOOTLED > FOOTLE
FOOTLER > FOOTLE
FOOTLERS > FOOTLE
FOOTLES > FOOTLE
FOOTLESS > FOOT
FOOTLIGHT n light illuminating the front of a stage
FOOTLIKE > FOOT
FOOTLING adj trivial ▷ n trifle
FOOTLINGS > FOOTLING
FOOTLOOSE adj free from ties
FOOTMAN n male servant in uniform
FOOTMARK n mark or trace of mud, wetness, etc, left by a person's foot on a surface
FOOTMARKS > FOOTMARK
FOOTMEN > FOOTMAN
FOOTMUFF n muff used to keep the feet warm
FOOTMUFFS > FOOTMUFF
FOOTNOTE n note printed at the foot of a page ▷ vb supply (a page, book, etc)

with footnotes
FOOTNOTED > FOOTNOTE
FOOTNOTES > FOOTNOTE
FOOTPACE n normal or walking pace
FOOTPACES > FOOTPACE
FOOTPAD n highwayman, on foot rather than horseback
FOOTPADS > FOOTPAD
FOOTPAGE n errand-boy
FOOTPAGES > FOOTPAGE
FOOTPATH n narrow path for walkers only
FOOTPATHS > FOOTPATH
FOOTPLATE n platform in the cab of a locomotive for the driver
FOOTPOST n post delivered on foot
FOOTPOSTS > FOOTPOST
FOOTPRINT n mark left by a foot
FOOTRA variant of > FOUTRA
FOOTRACE n race run on foot
FOOTRACES > FOOTRACE
FOOTRAS > FOOTRA
FOOTREST n something that provides a support for the feet, such as a low stool, rail, etc
FOOTRESTS > FOOTREST
FOOTROPE n part of a boltrope to which the foot of a sail is stitched
FOOTROPES > FOOTROPE
FOOTROT n contagious fungal disease of the feet of sheep
FOOTROTS > FOOTROT
FOOTRULE n rigid measure, one foot in length
FOOTRULES > FOOTRULE
FOOTS pl n sediment that accumulates at the bottom of a vessel containing any of certain liquids, such as vegetable oil or varnish
FOOTSIE n flirtation involving the touching together of feet
FOOTSIES > FOOTSIE
FOOTSLOG vb march
FOOTSLOGS > FOOTSLOG
FOOTSORE adj having sore or tired feet, esp from much walking
FOOTSTALK n small supporting stalk in animals and plants
FOOTSTALL n pedestal, plinth, or base of a column, pier, or statue
FOOTSTEP n step in walking
FOOTSTEPS > FOOTSTEP
FOOTSTOCK another name for > TAILSTOCK
FOOTSTONE n memorial stone at the foot of a grave
FOOTSTOOL n low stool used to rest the feet on while sitting
FOOTSY variant of > FOOTSIE
FOOTWALL n rocks on the lower side of an inclined fault plane or mineral vein
FOOTWALLS > FOOTWALL

FOOTWAY n way or path for pedestrians, such as a raised walk along the edge of a bridge
FOOTWAYS > FOOTWAY
FOOTWEAR n anything worn to cover the feet
FOOTWEARS > FOOTWEAR
FOOTWEARY adj tired from walking
FOOTWELL n part of a car in which the foot pedals are located
FOOTWELLS > FOOTWELL
FOOTWORK n skilful use of the feet, as in sport or dancing
FOOTWORKS > FOOTWORK
FOOTWORN adj footsore
FOOTY n football ▷ adj mean
FOOZLE vb bungle (a shot) ▷ n bungled shot
FOOZLED > FOOZLE
FOOZLER > FOOZLE
FOOZLERS > FOOZLE
FOOZLES > FOOZLE
FOOZLING > FOOZLE
FOOZLINGS > FOOZLE
FOP n man excessively concerned with fashion ▷ vb act like a fop
FOPLING n vain affected dandy
FOPLINGS > FOPLING
FOPPED > FOP
FOPPERIES > FOPPERY
FOPPERY n clothes, affectations, obsessions, etc, of or befitting a fop
FOPPING > FOP
FOPPISH > FOP
FOPPISHLY > FOP
FOPS > FOP
FOR prep indicating a person intended to benefit from or receive something, span of time or distance, person or thing represented by someone, etc
FORA > FORUM
FORAGE vb search about (for) ▷ n food for cattle or horses
FORAGED > FORAGE
FORAGER > FORAGE
FORAGERS > FORAGE
FORAGES > FORAGE
FORAGING > FORAGE
FORAM same as > FORAMINIFER
FORAMEN n natural hole, esp one in a bone through which nerves pass
FORAMENS > FORAMEN
FORAMINA > FORAMEN
FORAMINAL > FORAMEN
FORAMS > FORAM
FORANE as in vicar forane, , in the Roman Catholic church, vicar or priest appointed to act in a certain area of the diocese
FORASMUCH conj since
FORAY n brief raid or attack ▷ vb raid or ravage (a town, district, etc)
FORAYED > FORAY

FORAYER > FORAY
FORAYERS > FORAY
FORAYING > FORAY
FORAYS > FORAY
FORB n any herbaceous plant that is not a grass
FORBAD > FORBID
FORBADE > FORBID
FORBARE > FORBEAR
FORBEAR vb cease or refrain (from doing something)
FORBEARER > FORBEAR
FORBEARS > FORBEAR
FORBID vb prohibit, refuse to allow
FORBIDAL > FORBID
FORBIDALS > FORBIDAL
FORBIDDAL n prohibition
FORBIDDEN adj not permitted by order or law
FORBIDDER > FORBID
FORBIDS > FORBID
FORBODE vb obsolete word meaning forbid ▷ n obsolete word meaning forbidding
FORBODED > FORBODE
FORBODES > FORBODE
FORBODING > FORBODE
FORBORE past tense of > FORBEAR
FORBORNE > FORBEAR
FORBS > FORB
FORBY adv besides
FORBYE same as > FORBY
FORCAT n convict or galley slave
FORCATS > FORCAT
FORCE n strength or power ▷ vb compel, make (someone) do something
FORCEABLE > FORCE
FORCED adj compulsory
FORCEDLY > FORCED
FORCEFUL adj emphatic and confident
FORCELESS > FORCE
FORCEMEAT n mixture of chopped ingredients used for stuffing
FORCEPS pl n surgical pincers
FORCEPSES > FORCEPS
FORCER > FORCE
FORCERS > FORCE
FORCES > FORCE
FORCIBLE adj involving physical force or violence
FORCIBLY > FORCIBLE
FORCING > FORCE
FORCINGLY > FORCE
FORCIPATE > FORCEPS
FORCIPES > FORCEPS
FORD n shallow place where a river may be crossed ▷ vb cross (a river) at a ford
FORDABLE > FORD
FORDED > FORD
FORDID > FORDO
FORDING > FORD
FORDLESS > FORD
FORDO vb destroy
FORDOES > FORDO
FORDOING > FORDO
FORDONE > FORDO
FORDS > FORD
FORE adj in, at, or towards the front ▷ n front part

▷ interj golfer's shouted warning to a person in the path of a ball
FOREANENT prep opposite
FOREARM n arm from the wrist to the elbow ▷ vb prepare beforehand
FOREARMED > FOREARM
FOREARMS > FOREARM
FOREBAY n reservoir or canal
FOREBAYS > FOREBAY
FOREBEAR n ancestor
FOREBEARS > FOREBEAR
FOREBITT n post at a ship's foremast for securing cables
FOREBITTS > FOREBITT
FOREBODE vb warn of or indicate (an event, result, etc) in advance
FOREBODED > FOREBODE
FOREBODER > FOREBODE
FOREBODES > FOREBODE
FOREBODY n part of a ship forward of the foremast
FOREBOOM n boom of a foremast
FOREBOOMS > FOREBOOM
FOREBRAIN nontechnical name for > PROSENCEPHALON
FOREBY variant of > FORBY
FOREBYE variant of > FORBY
FORECABIN n forward cabin on a vessel
FORECAR n three-wheeled passenger vehicle attached to a motorcycle
FORECARS > FORECAR
FORECAST vb predict (weather, events, etc) ▷ n prediction
FORECASTS > FORECAST
FORECHECK vb in ice-hockey, to try to gain control of the puck while at opponents' end of rink
FORECLOSE vb take possession of (property bought with borrowed money which has not been repaid)
FORECLOTH n cloth hung over the front of something, especially an altar
FORECOURT n courtyard or open space in front of a building
FOREDATE vb antedate
FOREDATED > FOREDATE
FOREDATES > FOREDATE
FOREDECK n deck between the bridge and the forecastle
FOREDECKS > FOREDECK
FOREDID > FOREDO
FOREDO same as > FORDO
FOREDOES > FOREDO
FOREDOING > FOREDO
FOREDONE > FOREDO
FOREDOOM vb doom or condemn beforehand
FOREDOOMS > FOREDOOM
FOREFACE n muzzle of an animal
FOREFACES > FOREFACE

FOREFEEL vb have a premonition of
FOREFEELS > FOREFEEL
FOREFEET > FOREFOOT
FOREFELT > FOREFEEL
FOREFEND same as > FORFEND
FOREFENDS > FOREFEND
FOREFOOT n either of the front feet of an animal
FOREFRONT n most active or prominent position
FOREGLEAM n early or premonitory inkling or indication
FOREGO same as > FORGO
FOREGOER > FOREGO
FOREGOERS > FOREGO
FOREGOES > FOREGO
FOREGOING adj going before, preceding
FOREGONE adj gone or completed
FOREGUT n anterior part of the digestive tract of vertebrates, between the buccal cavity and the bile duct
FOREGUTS > FOREGUT
FOREHAND n stroke played with the palm of the hand facing forward ▷ adj (of a stroke) made so that the racket is held with the wrist facing the direction of play ▷ adv with a forehand stroke ▷ vb play (a shot) forehand
FOREHANDS > FOREHAND
FOREHEAD n part of the face above the eyebrows
FOREHEADS > FOREHEAD
FOREHENT vb seize in advance
FOREHENTS > FOREHENT
FOREHOCK n foreleg cut of bacon or pork
FOREHOCKS > FOREHOCK
FOREHOOF n front hoof
FOREHOOFS > FOREHOOF
FOREIGN adj not of, or in, one's own country
FOREIGNER n person from a foreign country
FOREIGNLY > FOREIGN
FOREJUDGE same as > FORJUDGE
FOREKING n previous king
FOREKINGS > FOREKING
FOREKNEW > FOREKNOW
FOREKNOW vb know in advance
FOREKNOWN > FOREKNOW
FOREKNOWS > FOREKNOW
FOREL n type of parchment
FORELADY n forewoman of a jury
FORELAID > FORELAY
FORELAIN > FORELIE
FORELAND n headland, cape, or coastal promontory
FORELANDS > FORELAND
FORELAY archaic word for > AMBUSH
FORELAYS > FORELAY
FORELEG n either of the front legs of an animal

FORELEGS > FORELEG
FORELEND vb give up
FORELENDS > FORELEND
FORELENT > FORELEND
FORELIE vb lie in front of
FORELIES > FORELIE
FORELIFT vb lift up in front
FORELIFTS > FORELIFT
FORELIMB n either of the front or anterior limbs of a four-limbed vertebrate: a foreleg, flipper, or wing
FORELIMBS > FORELIMB
FORELOCK n lock of hair over the forehead ▷ vb secure (a bolt) by means of a forelock
FORELOCKS > FORELOCK
FORELS > FOREL
FORELYING > FORELIE
FOREMAN n person in charge of a group of workers
FOREMAST n mast nearest the bow of a ship
FOREMASTS > FOREMAST
FOREMEAN vb intend in advance
FOREMEANS > FOREMEAN
FOREMEANT > FOREMEAN
FOREMEN > FOREMAN
FOREMILK n first milk drawn from a cow's udder prior to milking
FOREMILKS > FOREMILK
FOREMOST adv first in time, place, or importance ▷ adj first in time, place, or importance
FORENAME n first name
FORENAMED adj named or mentioned previously
FORENAMES > FORENAME
FORENIGHT n evening
FORENOON n morning
FORENOONS > FORENOON
FORENSIC adj used in or connected with courts of law
FORENSICS n art or study of formal debating
FOREPART n first or front part in place, order, or time
FOREPARTS > FOREPART
FOREPAST adj bygone
FOREPAW n either of the front feet of a land mammal that does not have hooves
FOREPAWS > FOREPAW
FOREPEAK n interior part of a vessel that is furthest forward
FOREPEAKS > FOREPEAK
FOREPLAN vb plan in advance
FOREPLANS > FOREPLAN
FOREPLAY n sexual stimulation before intercourse
FOREPLAYS > FOREPLAY
FOREPOINT vb predetermine or indicate in advance
FORERAN > FORERUN
FORERANK n first rank
FORERANKS > FORERANK
FOREREACH vb keep moving under momentum without

engine or sails

FOREREAD vb foretell

FOREREADS > FOREREAD

FORERUN vb serve as a herald for

FORERUNS > FORERUN

FORES > FORE

FORESAID less common word for > AFORESAID

FORESAIL n main sail on the foremast of a ship

FORESAILS > FORESAIL

FORESAW > FORESEE

FORESAY vb foretell

FORESAYS > FORESAY

FORESEE vb see or know beforehand

FORESEEN > FORESEE

FORESEER > FORESEE

FORESEERS > FORESEE

FORESEES > FORESEE

FORESHANK n top of the front leg of an animal

FORESHEET n sheet of a foresail

FORESHEW variant of > FORESHOW

FORESHEWN > FORESHEW

FORESHEWS > FORESHEW

FORESHIP n fore part of a ship

FORESHIPS > FORESHIP

FORESHOCK n relatively small earthquake heralding the arrival of a much larger one. Some large earthquakes are preceded by a series of foreshocks

FORESHORE n part of the shore between high- and low-tide marks

FORESHOW vb indicate in advance

FORESHOWN > FORESHOW

FORESHOWS > FORESHOW

FORESIDE n front or upper side or part

FORESIDES > FORESIDE

FORESIGHT n ability to anticipate and provide for future needs

FORESKIN n fold of skin covering the tip of the penis

FORESKINS > FORESKIN

FORESKIRT n front skirt of a garment (as opposed to the train)

FORESLACK variant of > FORSLACK

FORESLOW variant of > FORSLOW

FORESLOWS > FORESLOW

FORESPAKE > FORESPEAK

FORESPEAK vb predict

FORESPEND variant of > FORSPEND

FORESPENT > FORESPEND

FORESPOKE > FORESPEAK

FOREST n large area with a thick growth of trees ▷ vb create a forest (in)

FORESTAGE n part of a stage in front of the curtain

FORESTAIR n external stair

FORESTAL > FOREST

FORESTALL vb prevent or

guard against in advance

FORESTAY n adjustable stay leading from the truck of the foremast to the deck, stem, or bowsprit, for controlling the motion or bending of the mast

FORESTAYS > FORESTAY

FORESTEAL > FOREST

FORESTED > FOREST

FORESTER n person skilled in forestry

FORESTERS > FORESTER

FORESTIAL > FOREST

FORESTINE > FOREST

FORESTING > FOREST

FORESTRY n science of planting and caring for trees

FORESTS > FOREST

FORESWEAR vb forgo

FORESWORE > FORESWEAR

FORESWORN > FORESWEAR

FORETASTE n early limited experience of something to come ▷ vb have a foretaste of

FORETEACH vb teach beforehand

FORETEETH > FORETOOTH

FORETELL vb tell or indicate beforehand

FORETELLS > FORETELL

FORETHINK vb have prescience

FORETIME n time already gone

FORETIMES > FORETIME

FORETOKEN n sign of a future event ▷ vb foreshadow

FORETOLD > FORETELL

FORETOOTH another word for an > INCISOR

FORETOP n platform at the top of the foremast

FORETOPS > FORETOP

FOREVER adv without end

FOREVERS > FOREVER

FOREWARD n vanguard

FOREWARDS > FOREWARD

FOREWARN vb warn beforehand

FOREWARNS > FOREWARN

FOREWEIGH vb assess in advance

FOREWENT past tense of > FOREGO

FOREWIND n favourable wind

FOREWINDS > FOREWIND

FOREWING n either wing of the anterior pair of an insect's two pairs of wings

FOREWINGS > FOREWING

FOREWOMAN n woman in charge of a group of workers

FOREWOMEN > FOREWOMAN

FOREWORD n introduction to a book

FOREWORDS > FOREWORD

FOREWORN same as > FORWORN

FOREX n foreign exchange

FOREXES > FOREX

FOREYARD n yard for supporting the foresail of a

square-rigger

FOREYARDS > FOREYARD

FORFAIR vb perish

FORFAIRED > FORFAIR

FORFAIRN adj worn out

FORFAIRS > FORFAIR

FORFAITER > FORFAITING

FORFAULT variant of > FORFEIT

FORFAULTS > FORFAULT

FORFEIT n thing lost or given up as a penalty for a fault or mistake ▷ vb lose as a forfeit ▷ adj lost as a forfeit

FORFEITED > FORFEIT

FORFEITER > FORFEIT

FORFEITS > FORFEIT

FORFEND vb protect or secure

FORFENDED > FORFEND

FORFENDS > FORFEND

FORFEX n pair of pincers, esp the paired terminal appendages of an earwig

FORFEXES > FORFEX

FORFICATE adj (esp of the tails of certain birds) deeply forked

FORFOCHEN Scots word for > EXHAUSTED

FORGAT past tense of > FORGET

FORGATHER vb gather together

FORGAVE > FORGIVE

FORGE n place where metal is worked, smithy ▷ vb make a fraudulent imitation of (something)

FORGEABLE > FORGE

FORGED > FORGE

FORGEMAN > FORGE

FORGEMEN > FORGE

FORGER > FORGE

FORGERIES > FORGERY

FORGERS > FORGE

FORGERY n illegal copy of something

FORGES > FORGE

FORGET vb fail to remember

FORGETFUL adj tending to forget

FORGETIVE adj imaginative and inventive

FORGETS > FORGET

FORGETTER > FORGET

FORGING n process of producing a metal component by hammering

FORGINGS > FORGING

FORGIVE vb cease to blame or hold resentment against, pardon

FORGIVEN > FORGIVE

FORGIVER > FORGIVE

FORGIVERS > FORGIVE

FORGIVES > FORGIVE

FORGIVING adj willing to forgive

FORGO vb do without or give up

FORGOER > FORGO

FORGOERS > FORGO

FORGOES > FORGO

FORGOING > FORGO

FORGONE > FORGO

FORGOT past tense

of > FORGET

FORGOTTEN past participle of > FORGET

FORHAILE vb distress

FORHAILED > FORHAILE

FORHAILES > FORHAILE

FORHENT variant of > FOREHENT

FORHENTS > FORHENT

FORHOO vb forsake

FORHOOED > FORHOO

FORHOOIE variant of > FORHOO

FORHOOIED > FORHOOIE

FORHOOIES > FORHOOIE

FORHOOING > FORHOO

FORHOOS > FORHOO

FORHOW variant of > FORHOO

FORHOWED > FORHOW

FORHOWING > FORHOW

FORHOWS > FORHOW

FORINSEC adj foreign

FORINT n standard monetary unit of Hungary, divided into 100 fillér

FORINTS > FORINT

FORJASKIT adj exhausted

FORJESKIT variant of > FORJASKIT

FORJUDGE vb deprive of a right by the judgment of a court

FORJUDGED > FORJUDGE

FORJUDGES > FORJUDGE

FORK n tool for eating food, with prongs and a handle ▷ vb pick up, dig, etc with a fork

FORKBALL n method of pitching in baseball

FORKBALLS > FORKBALL

FORKED adj having a fork or forklike parts

FORKEDLY > FORKED

FORKER > FORK

FORKERS > FORK

FORKFUL > FORK

FORKFULS > FORK

FORKHEAD n forked head of a rod

FORKHEADS > FORKHEAD

FORKIER > FORKY

FORKIEST > FORKY

FORKINESS > FORKY

FORKING > FORK

FORKLESS > FORK

FORKLIFT n vehicle having two power-operated horizontal prongs that can be raised and lowered for loading, transporting, and unloading goods, esp goods that are stacked on wooden pallets

FORKLIFTS > FORKLIFT

FORKLIKE > FORK

FORKS > FORK

FORKSFUL > FORK

FORKTAIL n bird belonging to the flycatcher family

FORKTAILS > FORKTAIL

FORKY adj forked

FORLANA n Venetian dance

FORLANAS > FORLANA

FORLEND variant of > FORELEND

FORLENDS > FORLEND

FORLENT > FORLEND

FORLESE vb lose
FORLESES > FORLESE
FORLESING > FORLESE
FORLORE > FORLESE
FORLORN adj lonely and unhappy ▷ n forsaken person
FORLORNER > FORLORN
FORLORNLY > FORLORN
FORLORNS > FORLORN
FORM n shape or appearance ▷ vb give a (particular) shape to or take a (particular) shape
FORMABLE > FORM
FORMABLY > FORM
FORMAL adj of or characterized by established conventions of ceremony and behaviour
FORMALIN n solution of formaldehyde in water, used as a disinfectant or a preservative for biological specimens
FORMALINS > FORMALIN
FORMALISE same as > FORMALIZE
FORMALISM n concern with outward appearances and structure at the expense of content
FORMALIST > FORMALISM
FORMALITY n requirement of custom or etiquette
FORMALIZE vb make official or formal
FORMALLY > FORMAL
FORMALS > FORMAL
FORMAMIDE n amide derived from formic acid
FORMANT n any of several frequency ranges within which the partials of a sound, esp a vowel sound, are at their strongest, thus imparting to the sound its own special quality, tone colour, or timbre
FORMANTS > FORMANT
FORMAT n size and shape of a publication ▷ vb arrange in a format
FORMATE n any salt or ester of formic acid containing the ion HCOO⁻ or the group HCOO⁻
FORMATED > FORMAT
FORMATES > FORMATE
FORMATING > FORMAT
FORMATION n forming
FORMATIVE adj of or relating to development ▷ n inflectional or derivational affix
FORMATS > FORMAT
FORMATTED > FORMAT
FORMATTER > FORMAT
FORME n type matter, blocks, etc, assembled in a chase and ready for printing
FORMED > FORM
FORMEE n type of heraldic cross
FORMER adj of an earlier time, previous ▷ n person or thing that forms or

shapes
FORMERLY adv in the past
FORMERS > FORMER
FORMES > FORME
FORMFUL adj imaginative
FORMIATE variant of > FORMATE
FORMIATES > FORMIATE
FORMIC adj of, relating to, or derived from ants
FORMICA n tradename for any of various laminated plastic sheets, containing melamine, used esp for heat-resistant surfaces that can be easily cleaned
FORMICANT adj low-tension (of pulse)
FORMICARY n ant hill
FORMICAS > FORMICA
FORMICATE vb crawl around like ants
FORMING > FORM
FORMINGS > FORM
FORMLESS adj without a definite shape or form
FORMOL same as > FORMALIN
FORMOLS > FORMOL
FORMS > FORM
FORMULA n group of numbers, letters, or symbols expressing a scientific or mathematical rule
FORMULAE > FORMULA
FORMULAIC > FORMULA
FORMULAR adj of or relating to formulas
FORMULARY n book of prescribed formulas ▷ adj of, relating to, or of the nature of a formula
FORMULAS > FORMULA
FORMULATE vb plan or describe precisely and clearly
FORMULISE vb express in a formula
FORMULISM n adherence to or belief in formulas
FORMULIST > FORMULISM
FORMULIZE variant of > FORMULISE
FORMWORK n arrangement of wooden boards, bolts, etc, used to shape reinforced concrete while it is setting
FORMWORKS > FORMWORK
FORMYL n of, consisting of, or containing the monovalent group HCO-
FORMYLS > FORMYL
FORNENST prep situated against or facing towards
FORNENT variant of > FORNENST
FORNICAL > FORNIX
FORNICATE vb have sexual intercourse without being married ▷ adj arched or hoodlike in form
FORNICES > FORNIX
FORNIX n any archlike structure, esp the arched band of white fibres at the base of the brain
FORPET n quarter of a peck

(measure)
FORPETS > FORPET
FORPINE vb waste away
FORPINED > FORPINE
FORPINES > FORPINE
FORPINING > FORPINE
FORPIT variant of > FORPET
FORPITS > FORPIT
FORRAD adv forward
FORRADER > FORRAD
FORRARDER adv further forward
FORRAY archaic variant of > FORAY
FORRAYED > FORRAY
FORRAYING > FORRAY
FORRAYS > FORRAY
FORREN adj foreign
FORRIT adv forward(s)
FORSAID > FORSAY
FORSAKE vb withdraw support or friendship from
FORSAKEN adj completely deserted or helpless
FORSAKER > FORSAKE
FORSAKERS > FORSAKE
FORSAKES > FORSAKE
FORSAKING > FORSAKE
FORSAY vb renounce
FORSAYING > FORSAY
FORSAYS > FORSAY
FORSLACK vb be neglectful
FORSLACKS > FORSLACK
FORSLOE variant of > FORSLOW
FORSLOED > FORSLOE
FORSLOES > FORSLOE
FORSLOW vb hinder
FORSLOWED > FORSLOW
FORSLOWS > FORSLOW
FORSOOK past tense of > FORSAKE
FORSOOTH adv indeed
FORSPEAK vb bewitch
FORSPEAKS > FORSPEAK
FORSPEND vb exhaust
FORSPENDS > FORSPEND
FORSPENT > FORSPEND
FORSPOKE > FORSPEAK
FORSPOKEN > FORSPEAK
FORSWATT adj sweat-covered
FORSWEAR vb renounce or reject
FORSWEARS > FORSWEAR
FORSWINK vb exhaust through toil
FORSWINKS > FORSWINK
FORSWONCK variant of > FORSWUNK
FORSWORE > FORSWEAR
FORSWORN past participle of > FORSWEAR
FORSWUNK adj overworked
FORSYTHIA n shrub with yellow flowers in spring
FORT n fortified building or place ▷ vb fortify
FORTALICE n small fort or outwork of a fortification
FORTE n thing at which a person excels ▷ adv loudly
FORTED > FORT
FORTES > FORTIS
FORTH adv forwards, out, or away ▷ prep out of
FORTHCAME > FORTHCOME
FORTHCOME vb come forth

FORTHINK vb regret
FORTHINKS > FORTHINK
FORTHWITH adv at once
FORTHY adv therefore
FORTIES > FORTY
FORTIETH adj being the ordinal number of forty in numbering or counting order, position, time, etc Often written: 40th ▷ n one of 40 approximately equal parts of something
FORTIETHS > FORTIETH
FORTIFIED > FORTIFY
FORTIFIER > FORTIFY
FORTIFIES > FORTIFY
FORTIFY vb make (a place) defensible, as by building walls
FORTILAGE n small fort
FORTING > FORT
FORTIS adj (of a consonant) articulated with considerable muscular tension of the speech organs or with a great deal of breath pressure or plosion ▷ n consonant, such as English p or f, pronounced with considerable muscular force or breath pressure
FORTITUDE n courage in adversity or pain
FORTLET > FORT
FORTLETS > FORT
FORTNIGHT n two weeks
FORTRESS n large fort or fortified town ▷ vb protect with or as if with a fortress
FORTS > FORT
FORTUITY n chance or accidental occurrence
FORTUNATE adj having good luck
FORTUNE n luck, esp when favourable ▷ vb befall
FORTUNED > FORTUNE
FORTUNES > FORTUNE
FORTUNING > FORTUNE
FORTUNISE same as > FORTUNIZE
FORTUNIZE vb make happy
FORTY n four times ten ▷ adj amounting to forty ▷ determiner amounting to forty
FORTYISH > FORTY
FORUM n meeting or medium for open discussion or debate
FORUMS > FORUM
FORWANDER vb wander far
FORWARD same as > FORWARDS
FORWARDED > FORWARD
FORWARDER n person or thing that forwards
FORWARDLY > FORWARD
FORWARDS adv towards or at a place further ahead in space or time
FORWARN archaic word for > FORBID
FORWARNED > FORWARN
FORWARNS > FORWARN
FORWASTE vb lay waste
FORWASTED > FORWASTE

f

FORWASTES > FORWASTE
FORWEARY vb exhaust
FORWENT past tense
of > FORGO
FORWHY adv for what reason
FORWORN adj weary
FORZA n force
FORZANDI > FORZANDO
FORZANDO another word
for > SFORZANDO
FORZANDOS > FORZANDO
FORZATI > FORZATO
FORZATO variant
of > FORZANDO
FORZATOS > FORZATO
FORZE > FORZA
FOSCARNET n drug used to
treat AIDS
FOSS same as > FOSSE
FOSSA n anatomical
depression, trench, or
hollow area
FOSSAE > FOSSA
FOSSAS > FOSSA
FOSSATE adj having cavities
or depressions
FOSSE n ditch or moat, esp
one dug as a fortification
FOSSED adj having a ditch
or moat
FOSSES > FOSSE
FOSSETTE n small
depression or fossa, as in
a bone
FOSSETTES > FOSSETTE
FOSSICK vb search, esp for
gold or precious stones
FOSSICKED > FOSSICK
FOSSICKER > FOSSICK
FOSSICKS > FOSSICK
FOSSIL n hardened remains
of a prehistoric animal or
plant preserved in rock
▷ adj of, like, or being a
fossil
FOSSILISE same
as > FOSSILIZE
FOSSILIZE vb turn into a
fossil
FOSSILS > FOSSIL
FOSSOR n grave digger
FOSSORIAL adj (of the
forelimbs and skeleton
of burrowing animals)
adapted for digging
FOSSORS > FOSSOR
FOSSULA n small fossa
FOSSULAE > FOSSULA
FOSSULATE adj hollowed
FOSTER vb promote the
growth or development
of ▷ adj of or involved in
fostering a child
FOSTERAGE n act of caring
for or bringing up a foster
child
FOSTERED > FOSTER
FOSTERER > FOSTER
FOSTERERS > FOSTER
FOSTERING > FOSTER
FOSTERS > FOSTER
FOSTRESS n female fosterer
FOTHER vb stop a leak in a
ship's hull
FOTHERED > FOTHER
FOTHERING > FOTHER
FOTHERS > FOTHER
FOU adj full ▷ n bushel

FOUAT n succulent pink-
flowered plant
FOUATS > FOUAT
FOUD n sheriff in Orkney and
Shetland
FOUDRIE n foud's district
or office
FOUDRIES > FOUDRIE
FOUDS > FOUD
FOUER > FOU
FOUEST > FOU
FOUET n archaic word for
a whip
FOUETS > FOUET
FOUETTE n step in ballet in
which the dancer stands
on one foot and makes a
whiplike movement with
the other
FOUETTES > FOUETTE
FOUGADE n booby-trapped
pit or type of mine
FOUGADES > FOUGADE
FOUGASSE n type of bread
made with olive oil
FOUGASSES > FOUGASSE
FOUGHT > FIGHT
FOUGHTEN > FIGHT
FOUGHTIER > FOUGHTY
FOUGHTY adj musty
FOUL adj loathsome or
offensive ▷ n violation of
the rules ▷ vb make dirty
or polluted
FOULARD n soft light fabric
of plain-weave or twill-
weave silk or rayon, usually
with a printed design
FOULARDS > FOULARD
FOULBROOD n disease of
honeybees
FOULDER vb flash like
lightning
FOULDERED > FOULDER
FOULDERS > FOULDER
FOULE n type of woollen
cloth
FOULED > FOUL
FOULER > FOUL
FOULES > FOULE
FOULEST > FOUL
FOULIE n bad mood
FOULIES > FOULIE
FOULING > FOUL
FOULINGS > FOUL
FOULLY > FOUL
FOULMART n polecat
FOULMARTS > FOULMART
FOULNESS n state or quality
of being foul
FOULS > FOUL
FOUMART former name for
the > POLECAT
FOUMARTS > FOUMART
FOUND vb set up or establish
(an institution, etc)
FOUNDED > FOUND
FOUNDER vb break down
or fail ▷ n person who
establishes an institution,
company, society, etc
FOUNDERED > FOUNDER
FOUNDERS > FOUNDER
FOUNDING > FOUND
FOUNDINGS > FOUND
FOUNDLING n abandoned
baby
FOUNDRESS > FOUNDER

FOUNDRIES > FOUNDRY
FOUNDRY n place where
metal is melted and cast
FOUNDS > FOUND
FOUNT same as > FONT
FOUNTAIN n jet of water
FOUNTAINS > FOUNTAIN
FOUNTFUL adj full of springs
FOUNTS > FOUNT
FOUR n one more than three
▷ adj amounting to four
▷ determiner amounting
to four
FOURBALL n in golf, match
for two pairs in which each
player uses his own ball,
the better score of each
pair being counted at every
hole
FOURBALLS > FOURBALL
FOURCHEE n type of heraldic
cross
FOUREYED adj wearing
spectacles
FOURFOLD adj having four
times as many or as much
▷ adv by four times as
many or as much
FOURGON n long covered
wagon, used mainly for
carrying baggage, supplies,
etc
FOURGONS > FOURGON
FOURPENCE n former
English silver coin then
worth four pennies
FOURPENNY adj blow, esp
with the fist
FOURPLEX n building that
contains four separate
dwellings
FOURS > FOUR
FOURSCORE adj eighty
FOURSES n snack eaten at
four o'clock
FOURSOME n group of four
people
FOURSOMES > FOURSOME
FOURTEEN n four and
ten ▷ adj amounting to
fourteen ▷ determiner
amounting to fourteen
FOURTEENS > FOURTEEN
FOURTH n (of) number
four in a series ▷ adj of
or being number four in a
series ▷ adv after the third
person, position, event, etc
FOURTHLY > FOURTH
FOURTHS > FOURTH
FOUS > FOU
FOUSSA n Madagascan
civet-like animal
FOUSSAS > FOUSSA
FOUSTIER > FOUSTY
FOUSTIEST > FOUSTY
FOUSTY archaic variant
of > FUSTY
FOUTER same as > FOOTER
FOUTERED > FOUTER
FOUTERING > FOUTER
FOUTERS > FOUTER
FOUTH n abundance
FOUTHS > FOUTH
FOUTRA n fig; expression of
contempt
FOUTRAS > FOUTRA
FOUTRE vb footer

FOUTRED > FOUTRE
FOUTRES > FOUTRE
FOUTRING > FOUTRE
FOVEA n any small pit or
depression in the surface of
a bodily organ or part
FOVEAE > FOVEA
FOVEAL > FOVEA
FOVEAS > FOVEA
FOVEATE > FOVEA
FOVEATED > FOVEA
FOVEIFORM adj shaped like
small pit
FOVEOLA n small fovea
FOVEOLAE > FOVEOLA
FOVEOLAR > FOVEOLA
FOVEOLAS > FOVEOLA
FOVEOLATE > FOVEOLA
FOVEOLE same as > FOVEOLA
FOVEOLES > FOVEOLE
FOVEOLET same
as > FOVEOLA
FOVEOLETS > FOVEOLET
FOWL n domestic cock or
hen ▷ vb hunt or snare
wild birds
FOWLED > FOWL
FOWLER > FOWLING
FOWLERS > FOWLING
FOWLING n shooting or
trapping of birds for sport
or as a livelihood
FOWLINGS > FOWLING
FOWLPOX n viral infection of
poultry and other birds
FOWLPOXES > FOWLPOX
FOWLS > FOWL
FOWTH variant of > FOUTH
FOWTHS > FOWTH
FOX n reddish-brown bushy-
tailed animal of the dog
family ▷ vb perplex or
deceive
FOXBERRY n lingonberry
FOXED > FOX
FOXES > FOX
FOXFIRE n luminescent
glow emitted by certain
fungi on rotting wood
FOXFIRES > FOXFIRE
FOXFISH n type of shark
FOXFISHES > FOXFISH
FOXGLOVE n tall plant with
purple or white flowers
FOXGLOVES > FOXGLOVE
FOXHOLE n small pit dug for
protection
FOXHOLES > FOXHOLE
FOXHOUND n dog bred for
hunting foxes
FOXHOUNDS > FOXHOUND
FOXHUNT n hunting of foxes
with hounds ▷ vb hunt
foxes with hounds
FOXHUNTED > FOXHUNT
FOXHUNTER > FOXHUNT
FOXHUNTS > FOXHUNT
FOXIE n fox terrier
FOXIER > FOXY
FOXIES > FOXIE
FOXIEST > FOXY
FOXILY > FOXY
FOXINESS > FOXY
FOXING n piece of leather
used to reinforce or trim
part of the upper of a shoe
FOXINGS > FOXING
FOXLIKE > FOX

FOXSHARK n thresher shark
FOXSHARKS > FOXSHARK
FOXSHIP n cunning
FOXSHIPS > FOXSHIP
FOXSKIN adj made from the skin of a fox ▷ n skin of a fox
FOXSKINS > FOXSKIN
FOXTAIL n any grass of the genus *Alopecurus*, esp *A. pratensis*, of Europe, Asia, and South America, having soft cylindrical spikes of flowers: cultivated as a pasture grass
FOXTAILS > FOXTAIL
FOXTROT n ballroom dance with slow and quick steps ▷ vb perform this dance
FOXTROTS > FOXTROT
FOXY adj of or like a fox, esp in craftiness
FOY n loyalty
FOYBOAT n small rowing boat
FOYBOATS > FOYBOAT
FOYER n entrance hall in a theatre, cinema, or hotel
FOYERS > FOYER
FOYLE variant of > FOIL
FOYLED > FOYLE
FOYLES > FOYLE
FOYLING > FOYLE
FOYNE variant of > FOIN
FOYNED > FOYNE
FOYNES > FOYNE
FOYNING > FOYNE
FOYS > FOY
FOZIER > FOZY
FOZIEST > FOZY
FOZINESS > FOZY
FOZY adj spongy
FRA n brother: a title given to an Italian monk or friar
FRAB vb nag
FRABBED > FRAB
FRABBING > FRAB
FRABBIT adj peevish
FRABJOUS adj splendid
FRABS > FRAB
FRACAS n noisy quarrel
FRACASES > FRACAS
FRACK adj bold
FRACKING n method of releasing oil or gas from rock
FRACKINGS > FRACKING
FRACT vb break
FRACTAL n figure or surface generated by successive subdivisions of a simpler polygon or polyhedron, according to some iterative process ▷ adj of, relating to, or involving such a process
FRACTALS > FRACTAL
FRACTED > FRACT
FRACTI > FRACTUS
FRACTING > FRACT
FRACTION n numerical quantity that is not a whole number ▷ vb divide
FRACTIONS > FRACTION
FRACTIOUS adj easily upset and angered
FRACTS > FRACT
FRACTUR variant

of > FRAKTUR
FRACTURAL > FRACTURE
FRACTURE n breaking, esp of a bone ▷ vb break
FRACTURED > FRACTURE
FRACTURER > FRACTURE
FRACTURES > FRACTURE
FRACTURS > FRACTUR
FRACTUS n ragged-shaped cloud formation
FRAE Scot word for > FROM
FRAENA > FRAENUM
FRAENUM n fold of membrane or skin, such as the fold beneath the tongue, that supports an organ
FRAENUMS > FRAENUM
FRAG vb kill or wound (a fellow soldier or superior officer) deliberately with an explosive device
FRAGGED > FRAG
FRAGGING > FRAG
FRAGGINGS > FRAG
FRAGILE adj easily broken or damaged
FRAGILELY > FRAGILE
FRAGILER > FRAGILE
FRAGILEST > FRAGILE
FRAGILITY > FRAGILE
FRAGMENT n piece broken off ▷ vb break into pieces
FRAGMENTS > FRAGMENT
FRAGOR n sudden sound
FRAGORS > FRAGOR
FRAGRANCE n pleasant smell
FRAGRANCY same as > FRAGRANCE
FRAGRANT adj sweet-smelling
FRAGS > FRAG
FRAICHEUR n freshness
FRAIL adj physically weak ▷ n rush basket for figs or raisins
FRAILER > FRAIL
FRAILEST > FRAIL
FRAILISH > FRAIL
FRAILLY > FRAIL
FRAILNESS > FRAIL
FRAILS > FRAIL
FRAILTEE variant of > FRAILTY
FRAILTEES > FRAILTEE
FRAILTIES > FRAILTY
FRAILTY n physical or moral weakness
FRAIM n stranger
FRAIMS > FRAIM
FRAISE n neck ruff worn during the 16th century ▷ vb provide a rampart with a palisade
FRAISED > FRAISE
FRAISES > FRAISE
FRAISING > FRAISE
FRAKTUR n style of typeface, formerly used in German typesetting for many printed works
FRAKTURS > FRAKTUR
FRAMABLE > FRAME
FRAMBESIA same as > FRAMBOESIA
FRAMBOISE n brandy distilled from raspberries in

the Alsace-Lorraine region
FRAME n structure giving shape or support ▷ vb put together, construct
FRAMEABLE > FRAME
FRAMED > FRAME
FRAMELESS > FRAME
FRAMER > FRAME
FRAMERS > FRAME
FRAMES > FRAME
FRAMEWORK n supporting structure
FRAMING n frame, framework, or system of frames
FRAMINGS > FRAMING
FRAMPAL same as > FRAMPOLD
FRAMPLER n quarrelsome person
FRAMPLERS > FRAMPLER
FRAMPOLD adj peevish
FRANC n monetary unit of Switzerland, various African countries, and formerly of France and Belgium
FRANCHISE n right to vote ▷ vb grant (a person, firm, etc) a franchise
FRANCISE same as > FRANCIZE
FRANCISED > FRANCISE
FRANCISES > FRANCISE
FRANCIUM n radioactive metallic element
FRANCIUMS > FRANCIUM
FRANCIZE vb make French
FRANCIZED > FRANCIZE
FRANCIZES > FRANCIZE
FRANCO adj post-free
FRANCOLIN n any African or Asian partridge of the genus *Francolinus*
FRANCS > FRANC
FRANGER n condom
FRANGERS > FRANGER
FRANGIBLE adj breakable or fragile
FRANGLAIS n informal French containing a high proportion of words of English origin
FRANION n lover, paramour
FRANIONS > FRANION
FRANK adj honest and straightforward in speech or attitude ▷ n official mark on a letter permitting delivery ▷ vb put such a mark on (a letter)
FRANKABLE > FRANK
FRANKED > FRANK
FRANKER > FRANK
FRANKERS > FRANK
FRANKEST > FRANK
FRANKFORT same as > FRANKFURT
FRANKFURT n light brown smoked sausage
FRANKING > FRANK
FRANKLIN n (in 14th- and 15th-century England) a substantial landholder of free but not noble birth
FRANKLINS > FRANKLIN
FRANKLY adv in truth
FRANKNESS > FRANK

FRANKS > FRANK
FRANSERIA n American shrub
FRANTIC adj distracted with rage, grief, joy, etc
FRANTICLY > FRANTIC
FRANZIER > FRANZY
FRANZIEST > FRANZY
FRANZY adj irritable
FRAP vb lash down or together
FRAPE adj tightly bound
FRAPPANT adj striking, vivid
FRAPPE adj (of drinks) chilled ▷ n drink consisting of a liqueur, etc, poured over crushed ice
FRAPPED > FRAP
FRAPPEE > FRAPPE
FRAPPES > FRAPPE
FRAPPING > FRAP
FRAPS > FRAP
FRAS > FRA
FRASCATI n dry or semisweet white wine from the Lazio region of Italy
FRASCATIS > FRASCATI
FRASS n excrement or other refuse left by insects and insect larvae
FRASSES > FRASS
FRAT n member of a fraternity
FRATCH n quarrel ▷ vb quarrel
FRATCHES > FRATCH
FRATCHETY same as > FRATCHY
FRATCHIER > FRATCHY
FRATCHING > FRATCH
FRATCHY adj quarrelsome
FRATE n friar
FRATER n mendicant friar or a lay brother in a monastery or priory
FRATERIES > FRATER
FRATERNAL adj of a brother, brotherly
FRATERS > FRATER
FRATERY > FRATER
FRATI > FRATE
FRATRIES > FRATER
FRATRY > FRATER
FRATS > FRAT
FRAU n married German woman
FRAUD n (criminal) deception, swindle
FRAUDFUL > FRAUD
FRAUDS > FRAUD
FRAUDSMAN n practitioner of criminal fraud
FRAUDSMEN > FRAUDSMAN
FRAUDSTER n person who commits a fraud
FRAUGHAN Irish word for > WHORTLEBERRY
FRAUGHANS > FRAUGHAN
FRAUGHT adj tense or anxious ▷ vb archaic word for load ▷ n archaic word for freight
FRAUGHTED > FRAUGHT
FRAUGHTER > FRAUGHT
FRAUGHTS > FRAUGHT
FRAULEIN n unmarried German woman

FRAULEINS > FRAULEIN

FRAUS > FRAU

FRAUTAGE *variant of* > FRAUGHTAGE

FRAUTAGES > FRAUTAGE

FRAWZEY *n* celebration

FRAWZEYS > FRAWZEY

FRAY *n* noisy quarrel or conflict ▷ *vb* make or become ragged at the edge

FRAYED > FRAY

FRAYING > FRAY

FRAYINGS > FRAY

FRAYS > FRAY

FRAZIL *n* small pieces of ice that form in water moving turbulently enough to prevent the formation of a sheet of ice

FRAZILS > FRAZIL

FRAZZLE *n* exhausted state ▷ *vb* tire out

FRAZZLED > FRAZZLE

FRAZZLES > FRAZZLE

FRAZZLING > FRAZZLE

FREAK *n* abnormal person or thing ▷ *adj* abnormal ▷ *vb* streak with colour

FREAKED > FREAK

FREAKERY *as in control freakery* obsessive need to be in control of events

FREAKFUL *variant of* > FREAKISH

FREAKIER > FREAKY

FREAKIEST > FREAKY

FREAKILY > FREAKY

FREAKING > FREAK

FREAKISH *adj* of, related to, or characteristic of a freak

FREAKOUT *n* heightened emotional state

FREAKOUTS > FREAKOUT

FREAKS > FREAK

FREAKY *adj* weird, peculiar

FRECKLE *n* small brown spot on the skin ▷ *vb* mark or become marked with freckles

FRECKLED > FRECKLE

FRECKLES > FRECKLE

FRECKLIER > FRECKLE

FRECKLING > FRECKLE

FRECKLY > FRECKLE

FREDAINE *n* escapade

FREDAINES > FREDAINE

FREE *adj* able to act at will, not compelled or restrained ▷ *vb* release, liberate

FREEBASE *n* cocaine that has been refined by heating it in ether or some other solvent ▷ *vb* refine (cocaine) in this way

FREEBASED > FREEBASE

FREEBASER > FREEBASE

FREEBASES > FREEBASE

FREEBEE *variant of* > FREEBIE

FREEBEES > FREEBEE

FREEBIE *n* something provided without charge ▷ *adj* without charge

FREEBIES > FREEBIE

FREEBOARD *n* space or distance between the deck of a vessel and the water line

FREEBOOT *vb* act as a freebooter

FREEBOOTS > FREEBOOT

FREEBOOTY > FREEBOOT

FREEBORN *adj* not born in slavery

FREED > FREE

FREEDMAN *n* man freed from slavery

FREEDMEN > FREEDMAN

FREEDOM *n* being free

FREEDOMS > FREEDOM

FREEFORM *n* irregular flowing shape, often used in industrial or fabric design ▷ *adj* freely flowing, spontaneous

FREEGAN *n* person who avoids buying consumer goods, recycling discarded goods instead

FREEGANS > FREEGAN

FREEHAND *adj* drawn without guiding instruments

FREEHOLD *n* tenure of land for life without restrictions ▷ *adj* of or held by freehold

FREEHOLDS > FREEHOLD

FREEING > FREE

FREELANCE *n* (of) a self-employed person doing specific pieces of work for various employers ▷ *vb* work as a freelance ▷ *adv* of or as a freelance

FREELOAD *vb* act as a freeloader

FREELOADS > FREELOAD

FREELY > FREE

FREEMAN *n* person who has been given the freedom of a city

FREEMASON *n* member of a guild of itinerant skilled stonemasons, who had a system of secret signs and passwords with which they recognized each other

FREEMEN > FREEMAN

FREENESS > FREE

FREEPHONE *n* system of telephone use in which the cost of calls in response to an advertisement is borne by the advertiser

FREER *n* liberator

FREERS > FREER

FREES > FREE

FREESHEET *n* newspaper that is distributed free, paid for by its advertisers

FREESIA *n* plant with fragrant tubular flowers

FREESIAS > FREESIA

FREEST > FREE

FREESTONE *n* any fine-grained stone, esp sandstone or limestone, that can be cut and worked in any direction without breaking

FREESTYLE *n* competition, such as in swimming, in which each participant may use a style of his or her choice

FREET *n* omen or superstition

FREETIER > FREETY

FREETIEST > FREETY

FREETS > FREET

FREETY *adj* superstitious

FREEWARE *n* computer software that may be distributed and used without payment

FREEWARES > FREEWARE

FREEWAY *n* motorway

FREEWAYS > FREEWAY

FREEWHEEL *vb* travel downhill on a bicycle without pedalling ▷ *n* device in the rear hub of a bicycle wheel that permits it to rotate freely while the pedals are stationary

FREEWILL *n* apparent human ability to make choices that are not externally determined

FREEWOMAN *n* woman who is free or at liberty

FREEWOMEN > FREEWOMAN

FREEWRITE *vb* write freely without stopping or thinking

FREEWROTE > FREEWRITE

FREEZABLE > FREEZE

FREEZE *vb* change from a liquid to a solid by the reduction of temperature, as water to ice ▷ *n* period of very cold weather

FREEZER *n* insulated cabinet for cold-storage of perishable foods

FREEZERS > FREEZER

FREEZES > FREEZE

FREEZING > FREEZE

FREEZINGS > FREEZE

FREIGHT *n* commercial transport of goods ▷ *vb* send by freight

FREIGHTED > FREIGHT

FREIGHTER *n* ship or aircraft for transporting goods

FREIGHTS > FREIGHT

FREIT *variant of* > FREET

FREITIER > FREITY

FREITIEST > FREITY

FREITS > FREIT

FREITY *adj* superstitious

FREMD *adj* alien or strange

FREMDS > FREMD

FREMIT *same as* > FREMD

FREMITS > FREMIT

FREMITUS *n* vibration felt by the hand when placed on a part of the body, esp the chest, when the patient is speaking or coughing

FRENA > FRENUM

FRENCH *vb* (of food) cut into thin strips

FRENCHED > FRENCH

FRENCHES > FRENCH

FRENCHIFY *vb* make or become French in appearance, behaviour, etc

FRENCHING > FRENCH

FRENETIC *adj* uncontrolled, excited ▷ *n* madman

FRENETICS > FRENETIC

FRENNE *variant of* > FREMD

FRENULA > FRENULUM

FRENULAR > FRENULUM

FRENULUM *n* strong bristle or group of bristles on the hind wing of some moths and other insects, by which the forewing and hind wing are united during flight

FRENULUMS > FRENULUM

FRENUM *same as* > FRAENUM

FRENUMS > FRENUM

FRENZICAL > FRENZY

FRENZIED *adj* filled with or as if with frenzy

FRENZIES > FRENZY

FRENZILY > FRENZY

FRENZY *n* violent mental derangement ▷ *vb* make frantic

FRENZYING > FRENZY

FREON *n* trademark term meaning any of a group of chemically unreactive chlorofluorocarbons used as aerosol propellants, refrigerants, and solvents

FREONS > FREON

FREQUENCE *same as* > FREQUENCY

FREQUENCY *n* rate of occurrence

FREQUENT *adj* happening often ▷ *vb* visit habitually

FREQUENTS > FREQUENT

FRERE *n* friar

FRERES > FRERE

FRESCADE *n* shady place or cool walk

FRESCADES > FRESCADE

FRESCO *n* watercolour painting done on wet plaster on a wall ▷ *vb* paint a fresco

FRESCOED > FRESCO

FRESCOER > FRESCO

FRESCOERS > FRESCO

FRESCOES > FRESCO

FRESCOING > FRESCO

FRESCOIST > FRESCO

FRESCOS > FRESCO

FRESH *adj* newly made, acquired, etc ▷ *adv* recently ▷ *vb* freshen

FRESHED > FRESH

FRESHEN *vb* make or become fresh or fresher

FRESHENED > FRESHEN

FRESHENER > FRESHEN

FRESHENS > FRESHEN

FRESHER *n* first-year student

FRESHERS > FRESHER

FRESHES > FRESH

FRESHEST > FRESH

FRESHET *n* sudden overflowing of a river

FRESHETS > FRESHET

FRESHIE *n* in Indian English, new immigrant to the UK from the Asian subcontinent

FRESHIES > FRESHIE

FRESHING > FRESH

FRESHISH > FRESH

FRESHLY > FRESH

FRESHMAN *same as* > FRESHER

FRESHMEN > FRESHMAN
FRESHNESS > FRESH
FRESNEL n unit of frequency equivalent to 10 [12] hertz
FRESNELS > FRESNEL
FRET vb be worried ▷ n worried state
FRETBOARD n fingerboard with frets on a stringed musical instrument
FRETFUL adj irritable
FRETFULLY > FRETFUL
FRETLESS > FRET
FRETS > FRET
FRETSAW n fine saw with a narrow blade, used for fretwork
FRETSAWS > FRETSAW
FRETSOME adj vexing
FRETTED > FRET
FRETTER > FRET
FRETTERS > FRET
FRETTIER > FRETTY
FRETTIEST > FRETTY
FRETTING > FRET
FRETTINGS > FRET
FRETTY adj decorated with frets
FRETWORK n decorative carving in wood
FRETWORKS > FRETWORK
FRIABLE adj easily crumbled
FRIAND n small almond cake
FRIANDE variant of > FRIAND
FRIANDES > FRIANDE
FRIANDS > FRIAND
FRIAR n member of a male Roman Catholic religious order
FRIARBIRD n any of various Australian honeyeaters of the genus *Philemon*, having a naked head
FRIARIES > FRIARY
FRIARLY > FRIAR
FRIARS > FRIAR
FRIARY n house of friars
FRIB n short heavy-conditioned piece of wool removed from a fleece during classing
FRIBBLE vb fritter away ▷ n wasteful or frivolous person or action ▷ adj frivolous
FRIBBLED > FRIBBLE
FRIBBLER > FRIBBLE
FRIBBLERS > FRIBBLE
FRIBBLES > FRIBBLE
FRIBBLING > FRIBBLE
FRIBBLISH adj trifling
FRIBS > FRIB
FRICADEL variant of > FRIKKADEL
FRICADELS > FRICADEL
FRICANDO same as > FRICANDEAU
FRICASSEE n stewed meat served in a thick white sauce ▷ vb prepare (meat) as a fricassee
FRICATIVE n consonant produced by friction of the breath through a partially open mouth, such as (f) or (z) ▷ adj relating to or

being a fricative
FRICHT vb frighten
FRICHTED > FRICHT
FRICHTING > FRICHT
FRICHTS > FRICHT
FRICKING adj slang word for absolute
FRICTION n resistance met with by a body moving over another
FRICTIONS > FRICTION
FRIDGE n apparatus in which food and drinks are kept cool ▷ vb archaic word for chafe
FRIDGED > FRIDGE
FRIDGES > FRIDGE
FRIDGING > FRIDGE
FRIED > FRY
FRIEDCAKE n type of doughnut
FRIEND n person whom one knows well and likes ▷ vb befriend
FRIENDED > FRIEND
FRIENDING > FRIEND
FRIENDLY adj showing or expressing liking ▷ n match played for its own sake and not as part of a competition
FRIENDS > FRIEND
FRIER same as > FRYER
FRIERS > FRIER
FRIES > FRY
FRIEZE n ornamental band on a wall ▷ vb give a nap to (cloth)
FRIEZED > FRIEZE
FRIEZES > FRIEZE
FRIEZING > FRIEZE
FRIG vb taboo word meaning masturbate ▷ n fridge
FRIGATE n medium-sized fast warship
FRIGATES > FRIGATE
FRIGATOON n Venetian sailing ship
FRIGES > FRIG
FRIGGED > FRIG
FRIGGER > FRIG
FRIGGERS > FRIG
FRIGGING > FRIG
FRIGGINGS > FRIG
FRIGHT n sudden fear or alarm
FRIGHTED > FRIGHT
FRIGHTEN vb scare or terrify
FRIGHTENS > FRIGHTEN
FRIGHTFUL adj horrifying
FRIGHTING > FRIGHT
FRIGHTS > FRIGHT
FRIGID adj (of a woman) sexually unresponsive
FRIGIDER > FRIGID
FRIGIDEST > FRIGID
FRIGIDITY > FRIGID
FRIGIDLY > FRIGID
FRIGOT variant of > FRIGATE
FRIGOTS > FRIGOT
FRIGS > FRIG
FRIJOL n variety of bean, esp of the French bean, extensively cultivated for food in Mexico
FRIJOLE variant of > FRIJOL
FRIJOLES > FRIJOL

FRIKKADEL n South African meatball
FRILL n gathered strip of fabric attached at one edge ▷ vb adorn or fit with a frill or frills
FRILLED > FRILL
FRILLER > FRILL
FRILLERS > FRILL
FRILLIER > FRILLY
FRILLIES pl n flimsy women's underwear
FRILLIEST > FRILLY
FRILLING > FRILL
FRILLINGS > FRILL
FRILLS > FRILL
FRILLY adj with a frill or frills
FRINGE n hair cut short and hanging over the forehead ▷ vb decorate with a fringe ▷ adj (of theatre) unofficial or unconventional
FRINGED > FRINGE
FRINGES > FRINGE
FRINGIER > FRINGY
FRINGIEST > FRINGY
FRINGING > FRINGE
FRINGY adj having a fringe
FRIPON n rogue
FRIPONS > FRIPON
FRIPPER n dealer in old clothes
FRIPPERER same as > FRIPPER
FRIPPERS > FRIPPER
FRIPPERY n useless ornamentation
FRIPPET n frivolous or flamboyant young woman
FRIPPETS > FRIPPET
FRIS n frieze
FRISBEE n tradename of a light plastic disc, thrown with a spinning motion for recreation or in competition
FRISBEES > FRISBEE
FRISE n fabric with a long normally uncut nap used for upholstery and rugs
FRISEE n endive
FRISEES > FRISEE
FRISES > FRIS
FRISETTE n curly or frizzed fringe, often an artificial hairpiece, worn by women on the forehead
FRISETTES > FRISETTE
FRISEUR n hairdresser
FRISEURS > FRISEUR
FRISK vb move or leap playfully ▷ n playful movement
FRISKA n in Hungarian music, the fast movement of a piece
FRISKAS > FRISKA
FRISKED > FRISK
FRISKER > FRISK
FRISKERS > FRISK
FRISKET n light rectangular frame, attached to the tympan of a hand printing press, that carries a parchment sheet to protect the nonprinting areas

FRISKETS > FRISKET
FRISKFUL > FRISK
FRISKIER > FRISKY
FRISKIEST > FRISKY
FRISKILY > FRISKY
FRISKING > FRISK
FRISKINGS > FRISK
FRISKS > FRISK
FRISKY adj lively or high-spirited
FRISSON n shiver of fear or excitement
FRISSONS > FRISSON
FRIST archaic word for > POSTPONE
FRISTED > FRIST
FRISTING > FRIST
FRISTS > FRIST
FRISURE n styling the hair into curls
FRISURES > FRISURE
FRIT n basic materials, partially or wholly fused, for making glass, glazes for pottery, enamel, etc ▷ vb fuse (materials) in making frit
FRITES pl n chipped potatoes
FRITFLIES > FRITFLY
FRITFLY n small black dipterous fly, *Oscinella frit*, whose larvae are destructive to barley, wheat, rye, oats, etc
FRITH same as > FIRTH
FRITHBORH n type of pledge
FRITHS > FRITH
FRITS > FRIT
FRITT same as > FRIT
FRITTATA n Italian dish made with eggs and chopped vegetables or meat, resembling a flat thick omelette
FRITTATAS > FRITTATA
FRITTED > FRIT
FRITTER n piece of food fried in batter ▷ vb waste or squander
FRITTERED > FRITTER
FRITTERER > FRITTER
FRITTERS > FRITTER
FRITTING > FRIT
FRITTS > FRITTY
FRITURE archaic word for > FRITTER
FRITURES > FRITURE
FRITZ n derogatory term for a German soldier
FRITZES > FRITZ
FRIVOL vb behave frivolously
FRIVOLED > FRIVOL
FRIVOLER > FRIVOL
FRIVOLERS > FRIVOL
FRIVOLING > FRIVOL
FRIVOLITY > FRIVOLOUS
FRIVOLLED > FRIVOL
FRIVOLLER > FRIVOL
FRIVOLOUS adj not serious or sensible
FRIVOLS > FRIVOL
FRIZ variant of > FRIZZ
FRIZE n coarse woollen fabric ▷ vb freeze
FRIZED > FRIZE
FRIZER n person who gives

nap to cloth

FRIZERS > FRIZER

FRIZES > FRIZE

FRIZETTE same as > FRISETTE

FRIZETTES > FRIZETTE

FRIZING > FRIZE

FRIZZ vb form (hair) into stiff wiry curls ▷ n hair that has been frizzed

FRIZZANTE adj (of wine) slightly effervescent

FRIZZED > FRIZZ

FRIZZER > FRIZZ

FRIZZERS > FRIZZ

FRIZZES > FRIZZ

FRIZZIER > FRIZZY

FRIZZIES n condition of having frizzy hair

FRIZZIEST > FRIZZY

FRIZZILY > FRIZZY

FRIZZING > FRIZZ

FRIZZLE vb cook or heat until crisp and shrivelled ▷ n tight curl

FRIZZLED > FRIZZLE

FRIZZLER > FRIZZLE

FRIZZLERS > FRIZZLE

FRIZZLES > FRIZZLE

FRIZZLIER > FRIZZLE

FRIZZLING > FRIZZLE

FRIZZLY > FRIZZLE

FRIZZY adj (of the hair) in tight crisp wiry curls

FRO adv away ▷ n afro

FROCK n dress ▷ vb invest (a person) with the office or status of a cleric

FROCKED > FROCK

FROCKING n coarse material suitable for making frocks or work clothes

FROCKINGS > FROCKING

FROCKLESS > FROCK

FROCKS > FROCK

FROE n cutting tool with handle and blade at right angles, used for stripping young trees, etc

FROES > FROE

FROG n smooth-skinned tailless amphibian with long back legs used for jumping

FROGBIT n floating aquatic Eurasian plant

FROGBITS > FROGBIT

FROGEYE n plant disease

FROGEYED adj affected by frogeye

FROGEYES > FROGEYE

FROGFISH n any angler (fish) of the family Antennariidae, in which the body is covered with fleshy processes, including a fleshy lure on top of the head

FROGGED adj decorated with frogging

FROGGERY n place where frogs are kept

FROGGIER > FROGGY

FROGGIEST > FROGGY

FROGGING n decorative fastening of looped braid on a coat

FROGGINGS > FROGGING

FROGGY adj like a frog

FROGLET n young frog

FROGLETS > FROGLET

FROGLIKE > FROG

FROGLING n young frog

FROGLINGS > FROGLING

FROGMAN n swimmer with a rubber suit and breathing equipment for working underwater

FROGMARCH vb force (a resisting person) to move by holding his arms ▷ n method of carrying a resisting person in which each limb is held and the victim is face downwards

FROGMEN > FROGMAN

FROGMOUTH n any nocturnal insectivorous bird of the genera Podargus and Batrachostomus, of SE Asia and Australia, similar to the nightjars: family Podargidae, order Caprimulgiformes

FROGS > FROG

FROGSPAWN n jelly-like substance containing frog's eggs

FROIDEUR n coldness

FROIDEURS > FROIDEUR

FROING as in toing and froing going back and forth

FROINGS > FROING

FROISE n kind of pancake

FROISES > FROISE

FROLIC vb run and play in a lively way ▷ n lively and merry behaviour ▷ adj full of merriment or fun

FROLICKED > FROLIC

FROLICKER > FROLIC

FROLICKY same as > FROLICSOME

FROLICS > FROLIC

FROM prep indicating the point of departure, source, distance, cause, change of state, etc

FROMAGE as in fromage frais low-fat soft cheese

FROMAGES > FROMAGE

FROMENTY same as > FRUMENTY

FROND n long leaf or leaflike part of a fern, palm, or seaweed

FRONDAGE n fronds collectively

FRONDAGES > FRONDAGE

FRONDED adj having fronds

FRONDENT adj leafy

FRONDEUR 17th-century French rebel

FRONDEURS > FRONDEUR

FRONDLESS > FROND

FRONDOSE adj leafy or like a leaf

FRONDOUS adj leafy or like a leaf

FRONDS > FROND

FRONS n anterior cuticular plate on the head of some insects, in front of the clypeus

FRONT n fore part ▷ adj of or at the front ▷ vb face

(onto)

FRONTAGE n facade of a building

FRONTAGER n owner of a building or land on the front of a street

FRONTAGES > FRONTAGE

FRONTAL adj of, at, or in the front ▷ n decorative hanging for the front of an altar

FRONTALLY > FRONTAL

FRONTALS > FRONTAL

FRONTED > FRONT

FRONTENIS n racket used in Basque ball game

FRONTER > FRONT

FRONTES > FRONS

FRONTIER n area of a country bordering on another

FRONTIERS > FRONTIER

FRONTING > FRONT

FRONTLESS > FRONT

FRONTLET n small decorative loop worn on a woman's forehead, projecting from under her headdress, in the 15th century

FRONTLETS > FRONTLET

FRONTLINE adj of, relating to, or suitable for the front line of a military formation

FRONTLIST n list of books about to be published

FRONTMAN n nominal leader of an organization, etc, who lacks real power or authority, esp one who lends respectability to some nefarious activity

FRONTMEN > FRONTMAN

FRONTON n wall against which pelota or jai alai is played

FRONTONS > FRONTON

FRONTOON variant of > FRONTON

FRONTOONS > FRONTOON

FRONTPAGE adj on or suitable for the front page of a newspaper

FRONTS > FRONT

FRONTWARD same as > FRONTWARDS

FRONTWAYS adv with the front forward

FRONTWISE variant of > FRONTWAYS

FRORE adj very cold or frosty

FROREN variant of > FRORE

FRORN variant of > FRORE

FRORNE variant of > FRORE

FRORY adj frozen

FROS > FRO

FROSH n freshman

FROSHES > FROSH

FROST n white frozen dew or mist ▷ vb become covered with frost

FROSTBIT > FROSTBITE

FROSTBITE n destruction of tissue, esp of the fingers or ears, by cold ▷ vb affect with frostbite

FROSTED adj (of glass) having a rough surface to

make it opaque ▷ n type of ice cream dish

FROSTEDS > FROSTED

FROSTFISH n American fish appearing in frosty weather

FROSTIER > FROSTY

FROSTIEST > FROSTY

FROSTILY > FROSTY

FROSTING n sugar icing

FROSTINGS > FROSTING

FROSTLESS > FROST

FROSTLIKE > FROST

FROSTLINE n depth to which ground freezes in winter

FROSTNIP n milder form of frostbite

FROSTNIPS > FROSTNIP

FROSTS > FROST

FROSTWORK n patterns made by frost on glass, metal, etc

FROSTY adj characterized or covered by frost

FROTH n mass of small bubbles ▷ vb foam

FROTHED > FROTH

FROTHER > FROTH

FROTHERS > FROTH

FROTHERY n anything insubstantial, like froth

FROTHIER > FROTH

FROTHIEST > FROTH

FROTHILY > FROTH

FROTHING > FROTH

FROTHLESS > FROTH

FROTHS > FROTH

FROTHY > FROTH

FROTTAGE n act or process of taking a rubbing from a rough surface, such as wood, for a work of art

FROTTAGES > FROTTAGE

FROTTEUR n person who rubs against another person's body for a sexual thrill

FROTTEURS > FROTTEUR

FROUFROU n swishing sound, as made by a long silk dress

FROUFROUS > FROUFROU

FROUGHIER > FROUGHY

FROUGHY adj rancid

FROUNCE vb wrinkle

FROUNCED > FROUNCE

FROUNCES > FROUNCE

FROUNCING > FROUNCE

FROUZIER > FROUZY

FROUZIEST > FROUZY

FROUZY same as > FROWZY

FROW same as > FROE

FROWARD adj obstinate

FROWARDLY > FROWARD

FROWARDS > FROWARD

FROWIE variant of > FROUGHY

FROWIER > FROWIE

FROWIEST > FROWIE

FROWN vb wrinkle one's brows in worry, anger, or thought ▷ n frowning expression

FROWNED > FROWN

FROWNER > FROWN

FROWNERS > FROWN

FROWNING > FROWN

FROWNS > FROWN
FROWS > FROW
FROWSIER > FROWSY
FROWSIEST > FROWSY
FROWST n hot and stale atmosphere ▷ vb abandon oneself to such an atmosphere
FROWSTED > FROWST
FROWSTER > FROWST
FROWSTERS > FROWST
FROWSTIER > FROWSTY
FROWSTING > FROWST
FROWSTS > FROWST
FROWSTY adj stale or musty
FROWSY same as > FROWZY
FROWY variant of > FROUGHY
FROWZIER > FROWZY
FROWZIEST > FROWZY
FROWZILY > FROWZY
FROWZY adj dirty or unkempt
FROZE > FREEZE
FROZEN > FREEZE
FROZENLY > FREEZE
FRUCTAN n type of polymer of fructose, present in certain fruits
FRUCTANS > FRUCTAN
FRUCTED adj fruit-bearing
FRUCTIFY vb (cause to) bear fruit
FRUCTIVE adj fruitful
FRUCTOSE n crystalline sugar occurring in many fruits
FRUCTOSES > FRUCTOSE
FRUCTUARY n archaic word for a person who enjoys the fruits of something
FRUCTUATE vb bear fruit
FRUCTUOUS adj productive or fruitful
FRUG vb perform the frug, a 1960s dance
FRUGAL adj thrifty, sparing
FRUGALIST > FRUGAL
FRUGALITY > FRUGAL
FRUGALLY > FRUGAL
FRUGGED > FRUG
FRUGGING > FRUG
FRUGIVORE > FRUGIVOROUS
FRUGS > FRUG
FRUICT obsolete variant of > FRUIT
FRUICTS > FRUICT
FRUIT n part of a plant containing seeds, esp if edible ▷ vb bear fruit
FRUITAGE n process, state, or season of producing fruit
FRUITAGES > FRUITAGE
FRUITCAKE n cake containing dried fruit
FRUITED > FRUIT
FRUITER n fruit grower
FRUITERER n person who sells fruit
FRUITERS > FRUITER
FRUITERY n fruitage
FRUITFUL adj useful or productive
FRUITIER > FRUITY
FRUITIEST > FRUITY
FRUITILY > FRUITY
FRUITING > FRUIT
FRUITINGS > FRUIT
FRUITION n fulfilment of

something worked for or desired
FRUITIONS > FRUITION
FRUITIVE adj enjoying
FRUITLESS adj useless or unproductive
FRUITLET n small fruit
FRUITLETS > FRUITLET
FRUITLIKE > FRUIT
FRUITS > FRUIT
FRUITWOOD n wood of a fruit tree
FRUITY adj of or like fruit
FRUMENTY n kind of porridge made from hulled wheat boiled with milk, sweetened, and spiced
FRUMP n dowdy woman ▷ vb mock or taunt
FRUMPED > FRUMP
FRUMPIER > FRUMPY
FRUMPIEST > FRUMPY
FRUMPILY > FRUMPY
FRUMPING > FRUMP
FRUMPISH same as > FRUMPY
FRUMPLE vb wrinkle or crumple
FRUMPLED > FRUMPLE
FRUMPLES > FRUMPLE
FRUMPLING > FRUMPLE
FRUMPS > FRUMP
FRUMPY adj (of a woman, clothes, etc) dowdy, drab, or unattractive
FRUSEMIDE n diuretic used to relieve oedema, for example caused by heart or kidney disease
FRUSH vb break into pieces
FRUSHED > FRUSH
FRUSHES > FRUSH
FRUSHING > FRUSH
FRUST n fragment
FRUSTA > FRUSTUM
FRUSTRATE vb upset or anger ▷ adj frustrated or thwarted
FRUSTS > FRUST
FRUSTULE n hard siliceous cell wall of a diatom
FRUSTULES > FRUSTULE
FRUSTUM n part of a cone or pyramid contained between the base and a plane parallel to the base that intersects the solid
FRUSTUMS > FRUSTUM
FRUTEX n shrub
FRUTICES > FRUTEX
FRUTICOSE same as > FRUTESCENT
FRUTIFIED > FRUTIFY
FRUTIFIES > FRUTIFY
FRUTIFY vb malapropism for notify; used for comic effect by Shakespeare
FRY vb cook or be cooked in fat or oil ▷ n dish of fried food
FRYABLE > FRY
FRYBREAD n Native American fried bread
FRYBREADS > FRYBREAD
FRYER n person or thing that fries
FRYERS > FRYER
FRYING > FRY
FRYINGS > FRY

FRYPAN n long-handled shallow pan used for frying
FRYPANS > FRYPAN
FUB vb cheat
FUBAR adj irreparably damaged or bungled
FUBBED > FUB
FUBBERIES > FUBBERY
FUBBERY n cheating
FUBBIER > FUBBY
FUBBIEST > FUBBY
FUBBING > FUB
FUBBY adj chubby
FUBS > FUB
FUBSIER > FUBSY
FUBSIEST > FUBSY
FUBSY adj short and stout
FUCHSIA n ornamental shrub with hanging flowers
FUCHSIAS > FUCHSIA
FUCHSIN n greenish crystalline substance
FUCHSINE same as > FUCHSIN
FUCHSINES > FUCHSINE
FUCHSINS > FUCHSIN
FUCHSITE n form of mica
FUCHSITES > FUCHSITE
FUCI > FUCUS
FUCK vb taboo word meaning to have sexual intercourse (with) ▷ n taboo word for an act of sexual intercourse
FUCKED > FUCK
FUCKER n taboo word for a despicable or obnoxious person
FUCKERS > FUCKER
FUCKING > FUCK
FUCKINGS > FUCK
FUCKOFF n taboo word for an annoying or unpleasant person
FUCKOFFS > FUCKOFF
FUCKS > FUCK
FUCKUP vb taboo word meaning to damage or bungle ▷ n taboo word meaning an act or an instance of bungling
FUCKUPS > FUCKUP
FUCKWIT n taboo word for a fool or idiot
FUCKWITS > FUCKWIT
FUCOID adj of, relating to, or resembling seaweeds of the genus *Fucus* ▷ n any seaweed of the genus *Fucus*
FUCOIDAL adj of, relating to, or resembling seaweeds of the genus *Fucus* ▷ n any seaweed of the genus *Fucus*
FUCOIDS > FUCOID
FUCOSE n aldose
FUCOSES > FUCOSE
FUCOUS same as > FUCOIDAL
FUCUS n any seaweed of the genus *Fucus*, common in the intertidal regions of many shores and typically having greenish-brown slimy fronds
FUCUSED adj archaic word meaning made up with cosmetics
FUCUSES > FUCUS
FUD n rabbit's tail

FUDDIES > FUDDY
FUDDLE vb cause to be intoxicated or confused ▷ n confused state
FUDDLED > FUDDLE
FUDDLER > FUDDLE
FUDDLERS > FUDDLE
FUDDLES > FUDDLE
FUDDLING > FUDDLE
FUDDLINGS > FUDDLE
FUDDY n old-fashioned person
FUDGE n soft caramel-like sweet ▷ vb make (an issue) less clear deliberately ▷ interj mild exclamation of annoyance
FUDGED > FUDGE
FUDGES > FUDGE
FUDGING > FUDGE
FUDS > FUD
FUEHRER n leader: applied esp to Adolf Hitler
FUEHRERS > FUEHRER
FUEL n substance burned or treated to produce heat or power ▷ vb provide with fuel
FUELED > FUEL
FUELER > FUEL
FUELERS > FUEL
FUELING > FUEL
FUELLED > FUEL
FUELLER > FUEL
FUELLERS > FUEL
FUELLING > FUEL
FUELS > FUEL
FUELWOOD n any wood used as a fuel
FUELWOODS > FUELWOOD
FUERO n Spanish code of laws
FUEROS > FUERO
FUFF vb puff
FUFFED > FUFF
FUFFIER > FUFFY
FUFFIEST > FUFFY
FUFFING > FUFF
FUFFS > FUFF
FUFFY adj puffy
FUG n hot stale atmosphere ▷ vb sit in a fug
FUGACIOUS adj passing quickly away
FUGACITY n property of a gas that expresses its tendency to escape or expand
FUGAL adj of, relating to, or in the style of a fugue
FUGALLY > FUGAL
FUGATO adj in the manner or style of a fugue ▷ n movement, section, or piece in this style
FUGATOS > FUGATO
FUGGED > FUG
FUGGIER > FUG
FUGGIEST > FUG
FUGGILY > FUG
FUGGING > FUG
FUGGY > FUG
FUGHETTA n short fugue
FUGHETTAS > FUGHETTA
FUGIE n runaway
FUGIES > FUGIE
FUGIO n former US copper coin worth one dollar,

the first authorized by Congress (1787)
FUGIOS > FUGIO
FUGITIVE n person who flees, esp from arrest or pursuit ▷ adj fleeing
FUGITIVES > FUGITIVE
FUGLE vb act as a fugleman
FUGLED > FUGLE
FUGLEMAN n (formerly) a soldier used as an example for those learning drill
FUGLEMEN > FUGLEMAN
FUGLES > FUGLE
FUGLIER > FUGLY
FUGLIEST > FUGLY
FUGLING > FUGLE
FUGLY adj offensive word for very ugly
FUGS > FUG
FUGU n puffer fish
FUGUE n musical composition in which a theme is repeated in different parts ▷ vb be in a dreamlike, altered state of consciousness
FUGUED > FUGUE
FUGUELIKE > FUGUE
FUGUES > FUGUE
FUGUING > FUGUE
FUGUIST n composer of fugues
FUGUISTS > FUGUIST
FUGUS > FUGU
FUHRER same as > FUEHRER
FUHRERS > FUHRER
FUJI n type of African music
FUJIS > FUJI
FULCRA > FULCRUM
FULCRATE > FULCRUM
FULCRUM n pivot about which a lever turns
FULCRUMS > FULCRUM
FULFIL vb bring about the achievement of (a desire or promise)
FULFILL same as > FULFIL
FULFILLED > FULFILL
FULFILLER > FULFIL
FULFILLS > FULFILL
FULFILS > FULFIL
FULGENCY > FULGENT
FULGENT adj shining brilliantly
FULGENTLY > FULGENT
FULGID same as > FULGENT
FULGOR n brilliance
FULGOROUS > FULGOR
FULGORS > FULGOR
FULGOUR variant of > FULGOR
FULGOURS > FULGOUR
FULGURAL > FULGURATE
FULGURANT > FULGURATE
FULGURATE vb flash like lightning
FULGURITE n tube of glassy mineral matter found in sand and rock, formed by the action of lightning
FULGUROUS adj flashing like or resembling lightning
FULHAM n loaded die
FULHAMS > FULHAM
FULL adj containing as much or as many as possible ▷ adv completely

▷ vb clean, shrink, and press cloth
FULLAGE n price charged for fulling cloth
FULLAGES > FULLAGE
FULLAM variant of > FULHAM
FULLAMS > FULLAM
FULLAN variant of > FULHAM
FULLANS > FULLAN
FULLBACK n defensive player
FULLBACKS > FULLBACK
FULLBLOOD n person of unmixed race
FULLED > FULL
FULLER n person who fulls cloth for his living ▷ vb forge (a groove) or caulk (a riveted joint) with a fuller
FULLERED > FULLER
FULLERENE n any of various carbon molecules with a polyhedral structure similar to that of buckminsterfullerene, such as C_{70}, C_{76}, and C_{84}
FULLERIDE n compound of a fullerene in which atoms are trapped inside the cage of carbon atoms
FULLERIES > FULLERY
FULLERING > FULLER
FULLERITE n crystalline form of a fullerene
FULLERS > FULLER
FULLERY n place where fulling is carried out
FULLEST > FULL
FULLFACE n in printing, a letter that takes up full body size
FULLFACES > FULLFACE
FULLING > FULL
FULLISH > FULL
FULLNESS > FULL
FULLS > FULL
FULLY adv greatest degree or extent
FULMAR n Arctic sea bird
FULMARS > FULMAR
FULMINANT adj sudden and violent
FULMINATE vb criticize or denounce angrily ▷ n any salt or ester of fulminic acid, esp the mercury salt, which is used as a detonator
FULMINE vb fulminate
FULMINED > FULMINE
FULMINES > FULMINE
FULMINIC as in fulminic acid, , unstable volatile acid known only in solution and in the form of its salts and esters
FULMINING > FULMINE
FULMINOUS adj harshly critical
FULNESS > FULL
FULNESSES > FULL
FULSOME adj distastefully excessive or insincere
FULSOMELY > FULSOME
FULSOMER > FULSOME
FULSOMEST > FULSOME
FULVID variant of > FULVOUS
FULVOUS adj of a dull

brownish-yellow colour
FUM n phoenix, in Chinese mythology
FUMADO n salted, smoked fish
FUMADOES > FUMADO
FUMADOS > FUMADO
FUMAGE n hearth money
FUMAGES > FUMAGE
FUMARASE n enzyme
FUMARASES > FUMARASE
FUMARATE n salt of fumaric acid
FUMARATES > FUMARATE
FUMARIC as in fumaric acid, colourless crystalline acid with a fruity taste, found in some plants and manufactured from benzene
FUMAROLE n vent in or near a volcano from which hot gases, esp steam, are emitted
FUMAROLES > FUMAROLE
FUMAROLIC > FUMAROLE
FUMATORIA > FUMATORIUM
FUMATORY same as > FUMATORIUM
FUMBLE vb handle awkwardly ▷ n act of fumbling
FUMBLED > FUMBLE
FUMBLER > FUMBLE
FUMBLERS > FUMBLE
FUMBLES > FUMBLE
FUMBLING > FUMBLE
FUME vb be very angry ▷ pl n pungent smoke or vapour
FUMED adj (of wood, esp oak) having a dark colour and distinctive grain from exposure to ammonia fumes
FUMELESS > FUME
FUMELIKE > FUME
FUMER > FUME
FUMEROLE variant of > FUMAROLE
FUMEROLES > FUMEROLE
FUMERS > FUME
FUMES > FUME
FUMET n strong-flavoured liquor from cooking fish, meat, or game: used to flavour sauces
FUMETS > FUMET
FUMETTE variant of > FUMET
FUMETTES > FUMETTE
FUMETTI > FUMETTO
FUMETTO n speech balloon in a comic or cartoon
FUMIER > FUME
FUMIEST > FUME
FUMIGANT n substance used for fumigating
FUMIGANTS > FUMIGANT
FUMIGATE vb disinfect with fumes
FUMIGATED > FUMIGATE
FUMIGATES > FUMIGATE
FUMIGATOR > FUMIGATE
FUMING > FUME
FUMINGLY > FUME
FUMITORY n any plant of the chiefly European genus Fumaria, esp F. officinalis, having spurred flowers and

formerly used medicinally: family Fumariaceae
FUMOSITY > FUME
FUMOUS > FUME
FUMS > FUM
FUMULI > FUMULUS
FUMULUS n smokelike cloud
FUMY > FUME
FUN n enjoyment or amusement ▷ vb trick
FUNBOARD n type of surfboard
FUNBOARDS > FUNBOARD
FUNCTION n purpose something exists for ▷ vb operate or work
FUNCTIONS > FUNCTION
FUNCTOR n performer of a function
FUNCTORS > FUNCTOR
FUND n stock of money for a special purpose ▷ vb provide money to
FUNDABLE > FUND
FUNDAMENT n buttocks
FUNDED > FUND
FUNDER > FUND
FUNDERS > FUND
FUNDI n expert or boffin
FUNDIC > FUNDUS
FUNDIE n fundamentalist Christian
FUNDIES > FUNDIE
FUNDING > FUND
FUNDINGS > FUND
FUNDIS > FUNDI
FUNDLESS > FUND
FUNDRAISE vb raise money for a cause
FUNDS pl n money that is readily available
FUNDUS n base of an organ or the part farthest away from its opening
FUNDY n fundamentalist
FUNEBRAL variant of > FUNEBRIAL
FUNEBRE adj funereal or mournful
FUNEBRIAL same as > FUNEREAL
FUNERAL n ceremony of burying or cremating a dead person
FUNERALS > FUNERAL
FUNERARY adj of or for a funeral
FUNEREAL adj gloomy or sombre
FUNEST adj lamentable
FUNFAIR n entertainment with machines to ride on and stalls
FUNFAIRS > FUNFAIR
FUNFEST n enjoyable time
FUNFESTS > FUNFEST
FUNG same as > FUNK
FUNGAL adj of, derived from, or caused by a fungus or fungi ▷ n fungus or fungal infection
FUNGALS > FUNGAL
FUNGI > FUNGUS
FUNGIBLE n moveable perishable goods of a sort that may be estimated by number or weight, such as grain, wine, etc

▷ *adj* having the nature or quality of fungibles

FUNGIBLES > FUNGIBLE

FUNGIC > FUNGUS

FUNGICIDE *n* substance that destroys fungi

FUNGIFORM *adj* shaped like a mushroom or similar fungus

FUNGISTAT *n* substance that inhibits the growth of fungi

FUNGO *n* in baseball, act of tossing and hitting the ball ▷ *vb* toss and hit a ball

FUNGOES > FUNGO

FUNGOID *adj* resembling a fungus

FUNGOIDAL > FUNGOID

FUNGOIDS > FUNGOID

FUNGOSITY > FUNGOUS

FUNGOUS *adj* appearing suddenly and spreading quickly like a fungus

FUNGS > FUNG

FUNGUS *n* plant without leaves, flowers, or roots, such as a mushroom or mould

FUNGUSES > FUNGUS

FUNHOUSE *n* amusing place at fairground

FUNHOUSES > FUNHOUSE

FUNICLE *n* stalk that attaches an ovule or seed to the wall of the ovary

FUNICLES > FUNICLE

FUNICULAR *n* cable railway on a mountainside or cliff ▷ *adj* relating to or operated by a rope, cable, etc

FUNICULI > FUNICULUS

FUNICULUS *same as* > FUNICLE

FUNK *n* style of dance music with a strong beat ▷ *vb* avoid (doing something) through fear

FUNKED > FUNK

FUNKER > FUNK

FUNKERS > FUNK

FUNKHOLE *n* dugout

FUNKHOLES > FUNKHOLE

FUNKIA *n* hosta

FUNKIAS > FUNKIA

FUNKIER > FUNKY

FUNKIEST > FUNKY

FUNKILY > FUNKY

FUNKINESS > FUNKY

FUNKING > FUNK

FUNKS > FUNK

FUNKSTER *n* performer or fan of funk music

FUNKSTERS > FUNKSTER

FUNKY *adj* (of music) having a strong beat

FUNNED > FUN

FUNNEL *n* cone-shaped tube for pouring liquids into a narrow opening ▷ *vb* (cause to) move through or as if through a funnel

FUNNELED > FUNNEL

FUNNELING > FUNNEL

FUNNELLED > FUNNEL

FUNNELS > FUNNEL

FUNNER > FUN

FUNNEST > FUN

FUNNIER > FUNNY

FUNNIES *pl n* comic strips in a newspaper

FUNNIEST > FUNNY

FUNNILY > FUNNY

FUNNINESS > FUNNY

FUNNING > FUN

FUNNY *adj* comical, humorous ▷ *n* joke or witticism

FUNNYMAN *n* comedian

FUNNYMEN > FUNNYMAN

FUNPLEX *n* large amusement centre

FUNPLEXES > FUNPLEX

FUNS > FUN

FUNSTER *n* funnyman

FUNSTERS > FUNSTER

FUR *n* soft hair of a mammal ▷ *vb* cover or become covered with fur

FURACIOUS *adj* thievish

FURACITY > FURACIOUS

FURAL *n* furfural

FURALS > FURAL

FURAN *n* colourless flammable toxic liquid heterocyclic compound

FURANE *variant of* > FURAN

FURANES > FURANE

FURANOSE *n* simple sugar containing a furan ring

FURANOSES > FURANOSE

FURANS > FURAN

FURBEARER *n* mammal hunted for its pelt or fur

FURBELOW *n* flounce, ruffle, or other ornamental trim ▷ *vb* put a furbelow on (a garment)

FURBELOWS > FURBELOW

FURBISH *vb* smarten up

FURBISHED > FURBISH

FURBISHER > FURBISH

FURBISHES > FURBISH

FURCA *n* any forklike structure, esp in insects

FURCAE > FURCA

FURCAL > FURCA

FURCATE *vb* divide into two parts ▷ *adj* forked, branching

FURCATED > FURCATE

FURCATELY > FURCATE

FURCATES > FURCATE

FURCATING > FURCATE

FURCATION > FURCATE

FURCRAEA *n* plant belonging to the Agave family

FURCRAEAS > FURCRAEA

FURCULA *n* any forklike part or organ, esp the fused clavicles (wishbone) of birds

FURCULAE > FURCULA

FURCULAR > FURCULA

FURCULUM *same as* > FURCULA

FURDER *same as* > FURTHER

FUREUR *n* rage or anger

FUREURS > FUREUR

FURFAIR *variant of* > FURFUR

FURFAIRS > FURFAIR

FURFUR *n* scurf or scaling of the skin

FURFURAL *n* colourless liquid used as a solvent

FURFURALS > FURFURAL

FURFURAN *same as* > FURAN

FURFURANS > FURFURAN

FURFURES > FURFUR

FURFUROL *variant of* > FURFURAL

FURFUROLE *variant of* > FURFURAL

FURFUROLS > FURFUROL

FURFUROUS > FURFUR

FURFURS > FURFUR

FURIBUND *adj* furious

FURIES > FURY

FURIOSITY > FURIOUS

FURIOSO *adv* in a frantically rushing manner ▷ *n* passage or piece to be performed in this way

FURIOSOS > FURIOSO

FURIOUS *adj* very angry

FURIOUSLY > FURIOUS

FURKID *n* companion animal

FURKIDS > FURKID

FURL *vb* roll up and fasten (a sail, umbrella, or flag) ▷ *n* act or an instance of furling

FURLABLE > FURL

FURLANA *variant of* > FORLANA

FURLANAS > FURLANA

FURLED > FURL

FURLER > FURL

FURLERS > FURL

FURLESS > FUR

FURLING > FURL

FURLONG *n* unit of length equal to 220 yards (201.168 metres)

FURLONGS > FURLONG

FURLOUGH *n* leave of absence ▷ *vb* grant a furlough to

FURLOUGHS > FURLOUGH

FURLS > FURL

FURMENTY *same as* > FRUMENTY

FURMETIES > FURMETY

FURMETY *same as* > FRUMENTY

FURMITIES > FURMITY

FURMITY *same as* > FRUMENTY

FURNACE *n* enclosed chamber containing a very hot fire ▷ *vb* burn in a furnace

FURNACED > FURNACE

FURNACES > FURNACE

FURNACING > FURNACE

FURNIMENT *n* furniture

FURNISH *vb* provide (a house or room) with furniture

FURNISHED > FURNISH

FURNISHER > FURNISH

FURNISHES > FURNISH

FURNITURE *n* large movable articles such as chairs and wardrobes

FUROL *variant of* > FURFURAL

FUROLE *variant of* > FURFURAL

FUROLES > FUROLE

FUROLS > FUROL

FUROR *same as* > FURORE

FURORE *n* very excited or angry reaction

FURORES > FURORE

FURORS > FUROR

FURPHIES > FURPHY

FURPHY *n* rumour or fictitious story

FURR *vb* furrow

FURRED *same as* > FURRY

FURRIER *n* dealer in furs

FURRIERS > FURRIER

FURRIERY *n* occupation of a furrier

FURRIES > FURRY

FURRIEST > FURRY

FURRILY > FURRY

FURRINER *n* dialect rendering of foreigner

FURRINERS > FURRINER

FURRINESS > FURRY

FURRING > FUR

FURRINGS > FUR

FURROW *n* trench made by a plough ▷ *vb* make or become wrinkled

FURROWED > FURROW

FURROWER > FURROW

FURROWERS > FURROW

FURROWING > FURROW

FURROWS > FURROW

FURROWY > FURROW

FURRS > FURR

FURRY *adj* like or covered with fur or something furlike ▷ *n* child's fur-covered toy animal

FURS > FUR

FURTH *adv* out

FURTHER *adv* in addition ▷ *adj* more distant ▷ *vb* promote

FURTHERED > FURTHER

FURTHERER > FUTHER

FURTHERS > FURTHER

FURTHEST *adv* to the greatest degree ▷ *adj* most distant

FURTIVE *adj* sly and secretive

FURTIVELY > FURTIVE

FURUNCLE *technical name for* > BOIL

FURUNCLES > FURUNCLE

FURY *n* wild anger

FURZE *n* gorse

FURZES > FURZE

FURZIER > FURZE

FURZIEST > FURZE

FURZY > FURZE

FUSAIN *n* fine charcoal pencil or stick made from the spindle tree

FUSAINS > FUSAIN

FUSARIA > FUSARIUM

FUSARIUM *n* type of fungus

FUSAROL *variant of* > FUSAROLE

FUSAROLE *n* type of architectural moulding

FUSAROLES > FUSAROLE

FUSAROLS > FUSAROL

FUSC *adj* dark or dark-brown

FUSCOUS *adj* of a brownish-grey colour

FUSE *n* cord containing an explosive for detonating a bomb ▷ *vb* (cause to) fail as a result of a blown fuse

FUSED > FUSE

FUSEE n (in early clocks and watches) a spirally grooved spindle, functioning as an equalizing force on the unwinding of the mainspring

FUSEES > FUSEE

FUSEL n mixture of amyl alcohols, propanol, and butanol: a by-product in the distillation of fermented liquors used as a source of amyl alcohols

FUSELAGE n body of an aircraft

FUSELAGES > FUSELAGE

FUSELESS > FUSE

FUSELIKE > FUSE

FUSELS > FUSEL

FUSES > FUSE

FUSHION n spirit

FUSHIONS > FUSHION

FUSIBLE adj capable of being melted

FUSIBLY > FUSIBLE

FUSIFORM adj elongated and tapering at both ends

FUSIL n light flintlock musket

FUSILE adj easily melted

FUSILEER same as > FUSILIER

FUSILEERS > FUSILEER

FUSILIER n soldier of certain regiments

FUSILIERS > FUSILIER

FUSILLADE n continuous discharge of firearms ▷ vb attack with a fusillade

FUSILLI n spiral-shaped pasta

FUSILLIS > FUSILLI

FUSILS > FUSIL

FUSING > FUSE

FUSION n melting ▷ adj of a style of cooking that combines traditional Western techniques and ingredients with those used in Eastern cuisine

FUSIONAL > FUSION

FUSIONISM n favouring of coalitions among political groups

FUSIONIST > FUSIONISM

FUSIONS > FUSION

FUSS n needless activity or worry ▷ vb make a fuss

FUSSED > FUSS

FUSSER > FUSS

FUSSERS > FUSS

FUSSES > FUSS

FUSSIER > FUSSY

FUSSIEST > FUSSY

FUSSILY > FUSSY

FUSSINESS > FUSSY

FUSSING > FUSS

FUSSPOT n person who is difficult to please and complains often

FUSSPOTS > FUSSPOT

FUSSY adj inclined to fuss

FUST vb become mouldy

FUSTED > FUST

FUSTET n wood of the Venetian sumach shrub

FUSTETS > FUSTET

FUSTIAN n (formerly) a hard-wearing fabric of cotton mixed with flax or wool ▷ adj cheap

FUSTIANS > FUSTIAN

FUSTIC n large tropical American moraceous tree, *Chlorophora tinctoria*

FUSTICS > FUSTIC

FUSTIER > FUSTY

FUSTIEST > FUSTY

FUSTIGATE vb beat

FUSTILUGS n fat person

FUSTILY > FUSTY

FUSTINESS > FUSTY

FUSTING > FUST

FUSTOC variant of > FUSTIC

FUSTOCS > FUSTOC

FUSTS > FUST

FUSTY adj stale-smelling

FUSULINID n any of various extinct foraminifers

FUSUMA n Japanese sliding door

FUTCHEL n timber support in a carriage

FUTCHELS > FUTCHEL

FUTHARC same as > FUTHARK

FUTHARCS > FUTHARC

FUTHARK n phonetic alphabet consisting of runes

FUTHARKS > FUTHARK

FUTHORC same as > FUTHARK

FUTHORCS > FUTHORC

FUTHORK same as > FUTHARK

FUTHORKS > FUTHORK

FUTILE adj unsuccessful or useless

FUTILELY > FUTILE

FUTILER > FUTILE

FUTILEST > FUTILE

FUTILITY n lack of effectiveness or success

FUTON n Japanese-style bed

FUTONS > FUTON

FUTSAL n form of association football, played indoors with five players on each side

FUTSALS > FUTSAL

FUTTOCK n one of the ribs in the frame of a wooden vessel

FUTTOCKS > FUTTOCK

FUTURAL adj relating to the future

FUTURE n time to come ▷ adj yet to come or be

FUTURES pl n commodities bought or sold at an agreed price for delivery at a specified future date

FUTURISM n early 20th-century artistic movement making use of the characteristics of the machine age

FUTURISMS > FUTURISM

FUTURIST > FUTURISM

FUTURISTS > FUTURISM

FUTURITY n future

FUTZ vb fritter time away

FUTZED > FUTZ

FUTZES > FUTZ

FUTZING > FUTZ

FUZE same as > FUSE

FUZED > FUZE

FUZEE same as > FUSEE

FUZEES > FUZEE

FUZES > FUZE

FUZIL variant of > FUSIL

FUZILS > FUZIL

FUZING > FUZE

FUZZ n mass of fine or curly hairs or fibres ▷ vb make or become fuzzy

FUZZED > FUZZ

FUZZES > FUZZ

FUZZIER > FUZZY

FUZZIEST > FUZZY

FUZZILY > FUZZY

FUZZINESS > FUZZY

FUZZING > FUZZ

FUZZLE vb make drunk

FUZZLED > FUZZLE

FUZZLES > FUZZLE

FUZZLING > FUZZLE

FUZZTONE n device distorting electric guitar sound

FUZZTONES > FUZZTONE

FUZZY adj of, like, or covered with fuzz

FY variant of > FIE

FYCE variant of > FICE

FYCES > FYCE

FYKE n fish trap consisting of a net suspended over a series of hoops, laid horizontally in the water ▷ vb catch fish in this manner

FYKED > FYKE

FYKES > FYKE

FYKING > FYKE

FYLE variant of > FILE

FYLES > FYLE

FYLFOT rare word for > SWASTIKA

FYLFOTS > FYLFOT

FYNBOS n area of low-growing, evergreen vegetation

FYNBOSES > FYNBOS

FYRD n local militia of an Anglo-Saxon shire, in which all freemen had to serve

FYRDS > FYRD

FYTTE n song

FYTTES > FYTTE

Gg

GAB vb talk or chatter ▷ n hook or open notch in a rod or lever that drops over the spindle of a valve to form a temporary connection for operating the valve

GABARDINE n strong twill cloth used esp for raincoats

GABBARD same as > GABBART

GABBARDS > GABBARD

GABBART n Scottish sailing barge

GABBARTS > GABBART

GABBED > GAB

GABBER > GAB

GABBERS > GAB

GABBIER > GABBY

GABBIEST > GABBY

GABBINESS > GABBY

GABBING > GAB

GABBLE vb speak rapidly and indistinctly ▷ n rapid indistinct speech

GABBLED > GABBLE

GABBLER > GABBLE

GABBLERS > GABBLE

GABBLES > GABBLE

GABBLING > GABBLE

GABBLINGS > GABBLE

GABBRO n dark coarse-grained basic plutonic igneous rock consisting of plagioclase feldspar, pyroxene, and often olivine

GABBROIC > GABBRO

GABBROID adj gabbro-like

GABBROS > GABBRO

GABBY adj talkative

GABELLE n salt tax levied until 1790

GABELLED > GABELLE

GABELLER n person who collects the gabelle

GABELLERS > GABELLER

GABELLES > GABELLE

GABERDINE same as > GABARDINE

GABFEST n prolonged gossiping or conversation

GABFESTS > GABFEST

GABIES > GABY

GABION n cylindrical metal container filled with stones, used in the construction of underwater foundations

GABIONADE n row of gabions submerged in a waterway, stream, river, etc, to control the flow of water

GABIONAGE n structure composed of gabions

GABIONED > GABION

GABIONS > GABION

GABLE n triangular upper part of a wall between sloping roofs

GABLED > GABLE

GABLELIKE > GABLE

GABLES > GABLE

GABLET n small gable

GABLETS > GABLET

GABLING > GABLE

GABNASH n chatter

GABNASHES > GABNASH

GABOON n dark mahogany-like wood from a western and central African burseraceous tree, *Aucoumea klaineana*, used in plywood, for furniture, and as a veneer

GABOONS > GABOON

GABS > GAB

GABY n simpleton

GAD vb go about in search of pleasure ▷ n carefree adventure (esp in the phrase **on** or **upon the gad**)

GADABOUT n pleasure-seeker

GADABOUTS > GADABOUT

GADARENE adj headlong

GADDED > GAD

GADDER > GAD

GADDERS > GAD

GADDI n cushion on an Indian prince's throne

GADDING > GAD

GADDIS > GADDI

GADE same as > GAD

GADES > GADE

GADFLIES > GADFLY

GADFLY n fly that bites cattle

GADGE n man

GADGES > GADGE

GADGET n small mechanical device or appliance

GADGETEER n person who delights in gadgetry

GADGETRY n gadgets

GADGETS > GADGET

GADGETY > GADGET

GADGIE n fellow

GADGIES > GADGIE

GADI n Indian throne

GADID n any marine teleost fish of the family *Gadidae*, which includes the cod, haddock, whiting, and pollack ▷ adj of, relating to, or belonging to the *Gadidae*

GADIDS > GADID

GADIS > GADI

GADJE same as > GADGIE

GADJES > GADJE

GADJO variant of > GORGIO

GADLING n vagabond

GADLINGS > GADLING

GADOID adj of the cod family of marine fishes ▷ n gadoid fish

GADOIDS > GADOID

GADOLINIC adj relating to gadolinium, a silvery white metallic element

GADROON n moulding composed of a series of convex flutes and curves joined to form a decorative pattern, used esp as an edge to silver articles

GADROONED > GADROON

GADROONS > GADROON

GADS > GAD

GADSMAN n person who uses a gad when driving animals

GADSMEN > GADSMAN

GADSO n archaic expression of surprise

GADSOS > GADSO

GADWALL n duck, *Anas strepera*, related to the mallard

GADWALLS > GADWALL

GADZOOKS interj mild oath

GAE Scot word for > GO

GAED > GAE

GAEING > GAE

GAELICISE vb adapt to conform to Gaelic spelling and pronunciation

GAELICISM > GAELICISE

GAELICIZE same as > GAELICISE

GAEN > GAE

GAES > GAE

GAFF n stick with an iron hook for landing large fish ▷ vb hook or land (a fish) with a gaff

GAFFE n social blunder

GAFFED > GAFF

GAFFER n foreman or boss

GAFFERS > GAFFER

GAFFES > GAFFE

GAFFING > GAFF

GAFFINGS > GAFF

GAFFS > GAFF

GAFFSAIL n quadrilateral fore-and-aft sail on a sailing vessel

GAFFSAILS > GAFFSAIL

GAG vb choke or retch ▷ n cloth etc put into or tied across the mouth

GAGA adj senile

GAGAKU n type of traditional Japanese music

GAGAKUS > GAGAKU

GAGE vb gauge ▷ n (formerly) a glove or other object thrown down to indicate a challenge to fight

GAGEABLE > GAGE

GAGEABLY > GAGE

GAGED > GAGE

GAGER same as > GAUGER

GAGERS > GAGER

GAGES > GAGE

GAGGED > GAG

GAGGER n person or thing that gags

GAGGERIES > GAGGERY

GAGGERS > GAGGER

GAGGERY n practice of telling jokes

GAGGING > GAG

GAGGLE n disorderly crowd ▷ vb (of geese) to cackle

GAGGLED > GAGGLE

GAGGLES > GAGGLE

GAGGLING > GAGGLE

GAGGLINGS > GAGGLE

GAGING > GAGE

GAGMAN n person who writes gags for a comedian

GAGMEN > GAGMAN

GAGS > GAG

GAGSTER n standup comedian

GAGSTERS > GAGSTER

GAHNITE n dark green mineral of the spinel

group consisting of zinc aluminium oxide

GAHNITES > GAHNITE

GAID same as > GAD

GAIDS > GAID

GAIETIES > GAIETY

GAIETY n cheerfulness

GAIJIN n (in Japan) a foreigner

GAILLARD same as > GALLIARD

GAILLARDE same as > GAILLARD

GAILY adv merrily

GAIN vb acquire or obtain ▷ n profit or advantage ▷ adj straight or near

GAINABLE > GAIN

GAINED > GAIN

GAINER n person or thing that gains

GAINERS > GAINER

GAINEST > GAIN

GAINFUL adj useful or profitable

GAINFULLY > GAINFUL

GAINING > GAIN

GAININGS pl n profits or earnings

GAINLESS > GAIN

GAINLIER > GAINLY

GAINLIEST > GAINLY

GAINLY adj graceful or well-formed ▷ adv conveniently or suitably

GAINS pl n profits or winnings

GAINSAID > GAINSAY

GAINSAY vb deny or contradict

GAINSAYER > GAINSAY

GAINSAYS > GAINSAY

GAINST short for > AGAINST

GAIR n strip of green grass on a hillside

GAIRFOWL same as > GAREFOWL

GAIRFOWLS > GAIRFOWL

GAIRS > GAIR

GAIT n manner of walking ▷ vb teach (a horse) a particular gait

GAITED > GAIT

GAITER n cloth or leather covering for the lower leg

GAITERS > GAITER

GAITING > GAIT

GAITS > GAIT

GAITT Scots word for > GATE

GAITTS > GAITT

GAJO same as > GORGIO

GAJOS > GAJO

GAL n girl

GALA n festival

GALABEA same as > DJELLABA

GALABEAH same as > DJELLABA

GALABEAHS > GALABEAH

GALABEAS > GALABEA

GALABIA same as > DJELLABA

GALABIAH same as > DJELLABA

GALABIAHS > GALABIAH

GALABIAS > GALABIA

GALABIEH same as > DJELLABA

GALABIEHS > GALABIEH

GALABIYA same as > DJELLABA

GALABIYAH same as > DJELLABA

GALABIYAS > GALABIYA

GALACTIC adj of the Galaxy or other galaxies

GALACTOSE n white water-soluble monosaccharide found in lactose

GALAGE same as > GALOSH

GALAGES > GALAGE

GALAGO another name for > BUSHBABY

GALAGOS > GALAGO

GALAH n Australian cockatoo, Kakatoe roseicapilla, having grey wings, back, and crest and a pink body

GALAHS > GALAH

GALANGA same as > GALINGALE

GALANGAL same as > GALINGALE

GALANGALS > GALANGAL

GALANGAS > GALANGAL

GALANT n 18th-century style of music characterized by homophony and elaborate ornamentation

GALANTINE n cold dish of meat or poultry, which is boned, cooked, stuffed, then pressed into a neat shape and glazed

GALANTY as in galanty show pantomime shadow play, esp one in miniature using figures cut from paper

GALAPAGO n tortoise

GALAPAGOS > GALAPAGO

GALAS > GALA

GALATEA n strong twill-weave cotton fabric, striped or plain, for clothing

GALATEAS > GALATEA

GALAVANT same as > GALLIVANT

GALAVANTS > GALAVANT

GALAX n coltsfoot

GALAXES > GALAX

GALAXIES > GALAXY

GALAXY n system of stars

GALBANUM n bitter aromatic gum resin extracted from any of several Asian umbelliferous plants of the genus Ferula, esp F. galbaniflua, and used in incense and medicinally as a counterirritant

GALBANUMS > GALBANUM

GALDRAGON old Scots word for a > SORCERESS

GALE n strong wind

GALEA n part or organ shaped like a helmet or hood, such as the petals of certain flowers

GALEAE > GALEA

GALEAS > GALEA

GALEATE > GALEA

GALEATED > GALEA

GALEIFORM > GALEA

GALENA n soft bluish-grey

mineral consisting of lead sulphide: the chief source of lead

GALENAS > GALENA

GALENGALE same as > GALINGALE

GALENIC > GALENA

GALENICAL n any drug prepared from plant or animal tissue, esp vegetables, rather than being chemically synthesized ▷ adj denoting or belonging to this group of drugs

GALENITE same as > GALENA

GALENITES > GALENITE

GALENOID adj pertaining to galena

GALERE n group of people having a common interest, esp a coterie of undesirable people

GALERES > GALERE

GALES > GALE

GALETTE n type of savoury pancake

GALETTES > GALETTE

GALILEE n porch or chapel at the entrance to some medieval churches and cathedrals in England

GALILEES > GALILEE

GALINGALE n European cyperaceous plant, Cyperus longus, with rough-edged leaves, reddish spikelets of flowers, and aromatic roots

GALIONGEE n sailor

GALIOT n small swift galley formerly sailed on the Mediterranean

GALIOTS > GALIOT

GALIPOT n resin obtained from several species of pine

GALIPOTS > GALIPOT

GALIVANT same as > GALLIVANT

GALIVANTS > GALIVANT

GALL n impudence ▷ vb annoy

GALLABEA same as > DJELLABA

GALLABEAH same as > DJELLABA

GALLABEAS > GALLABEA

GALLABIA same as > DJELLABA

GALLABIAH same as > DJELLABA

GALLABIAS > GALLABIA

GALLABIEH same as > DJELLABA

GALLABIYA same as > DJELLABA

GALLAMINE n muscle relaxant used in anaesthesia

GALLANT adj brave and noble ▷ n young man who tried to impress women with his fashionable clothes or daring acts ▷ vb court or flirt (with)

GALLANTED > GALLANT

GALLANTER > GALLANT

GALLANTLY > GALLANT

GALLANTRY n showy, attentive treatment of women

GALLANTS > GALLANT

GALLATE n salt of gallic acid

GALLATES > GALLATE

GALLEASS n three-masted lateen-rigged galley used as a warship in the Mediterranean from the 15th to the 18th centuries

GALLED > GALL

GALLEIN n type of dyestuff

GALLEINS > GALLEIN

GALLEON n large three-masted sailing ship of the 15th–17th centuries

GALLEONS > GALLEON

GALLERIA n central court through several storeys of a shopping centre or department store onto which shops or departments open at each level

GALLERIAS > GALLERIA

GALLERIED adj having a gallery or galleries

GALLERIES > GALLERY

GALLERIST n person who owns or runs an art gallery

GALLERY n room or building for displaying works of art ▷ vb tunnel; form an underground gallery

GALLET vb (in roofing) use small pieces of slate mixed with mortar to support an upper slate

GALLETA n low-growing, coarse grass

GALLETAS > GALLETA

GALLETED > GALLET

GALLETING > GALLET

GALLETS > GALLET

GALLEY n kitchen of a ship or aircraft

GALLEYS > GALLEY

GALLFLIES > GALLFLY

GALLFLY n any of several small insects that produce galls in plant tissues, such as the gall wasp and gall midge

GALLIARD n spirited dance in triple time for two persons, popular in the 16th and 17th centuries ▷ adj lively

GALLIARDS > GALLIARD

GALLIASS same as > GALLEASS

GALLIC adj of or containing gallium in the trivalent state

GALLICA n variety of rose

GALLICAN adj of or relating to a movement favouring the restriction of papal control and greater autonomy for the French church

GALLICAS > GORGIO

GALLICISE same as > GALLICIZE

GALLICISM n word or idiom

g

borrowed from French

GALLICIZE *vb* make or become French in attitude, language, etc

GALLIED > GALLY

GALLIES > GALLY

GALLINAZO *n* black vulture

GALLING *adj* annoying or bitterly humiliating

GALLINGLY > GALLING

GALLINULE *n* moorhen

GALLIOT *same as* > GALIOT

GALLIOTS > GALLIOT

GALLIPOT *same as* > GALIPOT

GALLIPOTS > GALLIPOT

GALLISE *vb* add water and sugar to unfermented grape juice to increase the quantity of wine produced

GALLISED > GALLISE

GALLISES > GALLISE

GALLISING > GALLISE

GALLISISE *vb* gallise

GALLISIZE *same as* > GALLISE

GALLIUM *n* soft grey metallic element used in semiconductors

GALLIUMS > GALLIUM

GALLIVANT *vb* go about in search of pleasure

GALLIVAT *n* Oriental armed vessel

GALLIVATS > GALLIVAT

GALLIWASP *n* any lizard of the Central American genus *Diploglossus*, esp *D. monotropis* of the Caribbean: family *Anguidae*

GALLIZE *same as* > GALLISE

GALLIZED > GALLIZE

GALLIZES > GALLIZE

GALLIZING > GALLIZE

GALLNUT *n* type of plant gall that resembles a nut

GALLNUTS > GALLNUT

GALLOCK *adj* left-handed

GALLON *n* liquid measure of eight pints, equal to 4.55 litres

GALLONAGE *n* capacity measured in gallons

GALLONS > GALLON

GALLOON *n* narrow band of cord, embroidery, silver or gold braid, etc, used on clothes and furniture

GALLOONED > GALLOON

GALLOONS > GALLOON

GALLOOT *same as* > GALLOOT

GALLOOTS > GALOOT

GALLOP *n* horse's fastest pace ⊳ *vb* go or ride at a gallop

GALLOPADE *n* gallop ⊳ *vb* perform a gallopade

GALLOPED > GALLOP

GALLOPER > GALLOP

GALLOPERS > GALLOP

GALLOPING *adj* progressing at or as if at a gallop

GALLOPS > GALLOP

GALLOUS *adj* of or containing gallium in the divalent state

GALLOW *vb* frighten

GALLOWED > GALLOW

GALLOWING > GALLOW

GALLOWS *n* wooden structure used for hanging criminals

GALLOWSES > GALLOWS

GALLS > GALL

GALLSTONE *n* hard mass formed in the gall bladder or its ducts

GALLUMPH *same as* > GALUMPH

GALLUMPHS > GALLUMPH

GALLUS *adj* bold ⊳ *n* suspender for trousers

GALLUSED *adj* held up by galluses

GALLUSES > GALLUS

GALLY *vb* frighten

GALLYING > GALLY

GALOCHE *same as* > GALOSH.

GALOCHED > GALOCHE

GALOCHES > GALOCHE

GALOCHING > GALOCHE

GALOOT *n* clumsy or uncouth person

GALOOTS > GALOOT

GALOP *n* 19th-century dance in quick duple time ⊳ *vb* dance a galop

GALOPADE > GALOP

GALOPADES > GALOP

GALOPED > GALOP

GALOPIN *n* boy who ran errands for a cook

GALOPING > GALOP

GALOPINS > GALOPIN

GALOPPED > GALOP

GALOPPING > GALOP

GALOPS > GALOP

GALORE *adv* in abundance ⊳ *adj* in abundance ⊳ *n* abundance

GALORES > GALORE

GALOSH *n* waterproof overshoe ⊳ *vb* cover with galoshes

GALOSHE *same as* > GALOSH

GALOSHED > GALOSH

GALOSHES > GALOSH

GALOSHING > GALOSH

GALOWSES *Shakespearean plural for* > GALLOWS

GALRAVAGE *same as* > GILRAVAGE

GALS > GAL

GALTONIA *n* any plant of the bulbous genus *Galtonia*, esp *G. candicans*, with lanceolate leaves, drooping racemes of waxy white flowers, and a fragrant scent: family *Liliaceae*

GALTONIAS > GALTONIA

GALUMPH *vb* leap or move about clumsily

GALUMPHED > GALUMPH

GALUMPHER > GALUMPH

GALUMPHS > GALUMPH

GALUT *same as* > GALUTH

GALUTH *n* exile of Jews from Palestine

GALUTHS > GALUTH

GALUTS > GALUT

GALVANIC *adj* of or producing an electric current generated by chemical means

GALVANISE *same as* > GALVANIZE

GALVANISM *n* electricity, esp when produced by chemical means as in a cell or battery

GALVANIST > GALVANISM

GALVANIZE *vb* stimulate into action ⊳ *n* galvanized iron, usually in the form of corrugated sheets as used in roofing

GALVO *n* instrument for measuring electric current

GALVOS > GALVO

GALYAC *same as* > GALYAK

GALYACS > GALYAC

GALYAK *n* smooth glossy fur obtained from the skins of newborn or premature lambs and kids

GALYAKS > GALYAK

GAM *n* school of whales ⊳ *vb* (of whales) form a school

GAMA *n* tall perennial grass

GAMAHUCHE *derogatory term vb* practise cunnilingus or fellatio on ⊳ *n* cunnilingus or fellatio

GAMARUCHE *same as* > GAMAHUCHE

GAMAS > GAMA

GAMASH *n* type of gaiter

GAMASHES > GAMASH

GAMAY *n* red grape variety, or the wine made from it

GAMAYS > GAMAY

GAMB *n* in heraldry, the whole foreleg of a beast

GAMBA *n* second-largest member of the viol family

GAMBADE *same as* > GAMBADO

GAMBADES > GAMBADE

GAMBADO *n* leap or gambol; caper ⊳ *vb* perform a gambado

GAMBADOED > GAMBADO

GAMBADOES > GAMBADO

GAMBADOS > GAMBADO

GAMBAS > GAMBA

GAMBE *same as* > GAMB

GAMBES > GAMBE

GAMBESON *n* quilted and padded or stuffed leather or cloth garment worn under mail in the Middle Ages and later as a doublet by men and women

GAMBESONS > GAMBESON

GAMBET *n* tattler

GAMBETS > GAMBET

GAMBETTA *n* redshank

GAMBETTAS > GAMBETTA

GAMBIA *same as* > GAMBIER

GAMBIAS > GAMBIA

GAMBIER *n* astringent resinous substance obtained from a rubiaceous tropical Asian woody climbing plant, *Uncaria gambir* (or *U. gambier*)

GAMBIERS > GAMBIER

GAMBIR *same as* > GAMBIER

GAMBIRS > GAMBIR

GAMBIST *n* person who plays the (viola da) gamba

GAMBISTS > GAMBIST

GAMBIT *n* opening line or move intended to secure an advantage ⊳ *vb* sacrifice a chess piece, in opening, to gain a better position

GAMBITED > GAMBIT

GAMBITING > GAMBIT

GAMBITS > GAMBIT

GAMBLE *vb* play games of chance to win money ⊳ *n* risky undertaking

GAMBLED > GAMBLE

GAMBLER > GAMBLE

GAMBLERS > GAMBLE

GAMBLES > GAMBLE

GAMBLING > GAMBLE

GAMBLINGS > GAMBLE

GAMBO *n* farm cart

GAMBOGE *n* gum resin used as a yellow pigment and purgative

GAMBOGES > GAMBOGE

GAMBOGIAN > GAMBOGE

GAMBOGIC > GAMBOGE

GAMBOL *vb* jump about playfully, frolic ⊳ *n* frolic

GAMBOLED > GAMBOL

GAMBOLING > GAMBOL

GAMBOLLED > GAMBOL

GAMBOLS > GAMBOL

GAMBOS > GAMBO

GAMBREL *n* hock of a horse or similar animal

GAMBRELS > GAMBREL

GAMBROON *n* type of linen cloth

GAMBROONS > GAMBROON

GAMBS > GAMB

GAMBUSIA *n* small fish that feeds on mosquito larvae

GAMBUSIAS > GAMBUSIA

GAME *n* amusement or pastime ⊳ *vb* gamble ⊳ *adj* brave

GAMECOCK *n* cock bred and trained for fighting

GAMECOCKS > GAMECOCK

GAMED > GAME

GAMELAN *n* type of percussion orchestra common in the East Indies

GAMELANS > GAMELAN

GAMELIKE > GAME

GAMELY *adv* in a brave or sporting manner

GAMENESS *n* courage or bravery

GAMEPLAY *n* plot of a computer or video game or the way that it is played

GAMEPLAYS > GAMEPLAY

GAMER *n* person who plays computer games

GAMERS > GAMER

GAMES > GAME

GAMESIER > GAMESY

GAMESIEST > GAMESY

GAMESMAN *n* one who practises gamesmanship: the art of winning by cunning practices without actually cheating

GAMESMEN > GAMESMAN

GAMESOME *adj* full of merriment

GAMEST > GAME

g

GAMESTER n gambler
GAMESTERS > GAMESTER
GAMESY adj sporty
GAMETAL > GAMETE
GAMETE n reproductive cell
GAMETES > GAMETE
GAMETIC > GAMETE
GAMEY adj having the smell or flavour of game
GAMIC adj (esp of reproduction) requiring the fusion of gametes
GAMIER > GAMEY
GAMIEST > GAMEY
GAMILY > GAMEY
GAMIN n street urchin
GAMINE n slim boyish young woman
GAMINERIE n impish behaviour
GAMINES > GAMINE
GAMINESS > GAMEY
GAMING n gambling
GAMINGS > GAMING
GAMINS > GAMIN
GAMMA n third letter of the Greek alphabet
GAMMADIA > GAMMADION
GAMMADION n decorative figure composed of a number of Greek capital gammas, esp radiating from a centre, as in a swastika
GAMMAS > GAMMA
GAMMAT n derogatory term for a Cape Coloured person
GAMMATIA > GAMMATION
GAMMATION same as > GAMMADION
GAMMATS > GAMMAT
GAMME n musical scale
GAMMED > GAM
GAMMER n dialect word for an old woman: now chiefly humorous or contemptuous
GAMMERS > GAMMER
GAMMES > GAMME
GAMMIER > GAMMY
GAMMIEST > GAMMY
GAMMING > GAM
GAMMOCK vb clown around
GAMMOCKED > GAMMOCK
GAMMOCKS > GAMMOCK
GAMMON n cured or smoked ham ▷ vb score a double victory in backgammon over
GAMMONED > GAMMON
GAMMONER > GAMMON
GAMMONERS > GAMMON
GAMMONING > GAMMON
GAMMONS > GAMMON
GAMMY adj (of the leg) lame
GAMODEME n isolated breeding population
GAMODEMES > GAMODEME
GAMONE n any chemical substance secreted by a gamete that attracts another gamete during sexual reproduction
GAMONES > GAMONE
GAMP n umbrella
GAMPISH adj bulging
GAMPS > GAMP

GAMS > GAM
GAMUT n whole range or scale (of music, emotions, etc)
GAMUTS > GAMUT
GAMY same as > GAMEY
GAMYNESS > GAMY
GAN vb go
GANACHE n rich icing or filling made of chocolate and cream
GANACHES > GANACHE
GANCH vb impale
GANCHED > GANCH
GANCHES > GANCH
GANCHING > GANCH
GANDER n male goose ▷ vb look
GANDERED > GANDER
GANDERING > GANDER
GANDERISM > GANDER
GANDERS > GANDER
GANDY as in gandy dancer railway track maintenance worker
GANE > GANGUE
GANEF n unscrupulous opportunist who stoops to sharp practice
GANEFS > GANEF
GANEV same as > GANEF
GANEVS > GANEV
GANG n (criminal) group ▷ vb become or act as a gang
GANGBANG n sexual intercourse between one woman and several men one after the other, esp against her will ▷ vb force (a woman) to take part in a gangbang
GANGBANGS > GANGBANG
GANGBOARD n gangway
GANGED > GANG
GANGER n foreman of a gang of labourers
GANGERS > GANGER
GANGING > GANG
GANGINGS > GANG
GANGLAND n criminal underworld
GANGLANDS > GANGLAND
GANGLIA > GANGLION
GANGLIAL > GANGLION
GANGLIAR > GANGLION
GANGLIATE vb form a ganglion
GANGLIER > GANGLY
GANGLIEST > GANGLY
GANGLING adj lanky and awkward
GANGLION n group of nerve cells
GANGLIONS > GANGLION
GANGLY same as > GANGLING
GANGPLANK n portable bridge for boarding or leaving a ship
GANGPLOW n plough designed to produce parallel furrows
GANGPLOWS > GANGPLOW
GANGREL n wandering beggar
GANGRELS > GANGREL
GANGRENE n decay of body

tissue as a result of disease or injury ▷ vb become or cause to become affected with gangrene
GANGRENED > GANGRENE
GANGRENES > GANGRENE
GANGS > GANG
GANGSHAG vb participate in group sex with
GANGSHAGS > GANGSHAG
GANGSMAN n foreman
GANGSMEN > GANGSMAN
GANGSTA n member of a street gang
GANGSTAS > GANGSTA
GANGSTER n member of a criminal gang
GANGSTERS > GANGSTER
GANGUE n valueless material in an ore
GANGUES > GANGUE
GANGWAY same as > GANGPLANK
GANGWAYS > GANGWAY
GANISTER n highly refractory siliceous sedimentary rock occurring beneath coal seams: used for lining furnaces
GANISTERS > GANISTER
GANJA n highly potent form of cannabis, usually used for smoking
GANJAH same as > GANJA
GANJAHS > GANJAH
GANJAS > GANJA
GANNED > GAN
GANNET n large sea bird
GANNETRY n gannets' breeding-place
GANNETS > GANNET
GANNING > GAN
GANNISTER same as > GANISTER
GANOF same as > GANEF
GANOFS > GANOF
GANOID adj (of the scales of certain fishes) consisting of an inner bony layer covered with an enamel-like substance ▷ n ganoid fish
GANOIDS > GANOID
GANOIN n substance of which the outer layer of fish scales is composed
GANOINE same as > GANOIN
GANOINES > GANOINE
GANOINS > GANOIN
GANS > GAN
GANSEY n jersey or pullover
GANSEYS > GANSEY
GANT vb yawn
GANTED > GANT
GANTELOPE same as > GAUNTLET
GANTING > GANT
GANTLET n section of a railway where two tracks overlap ▷ vb make railway tracks form a gantlet
GANTLETED > GANTLET
GANTLETS > GANTLET
GANTLINE n line rove through a sheave for hoisting men or gear
GANTLINES > GANTLINE
GANTLOPE same

as > GAUNTLET
GANTLOPES > GANTLOPE
GANTRIES > GANTRY
GANTRY n structure supporting something such as a crane or rocket
GANTS > GANT
GANYMEDE n catamite
GANYMEDES > GANYMEDE
GAOL same as > JAIL
GAOLBIRD n person who is or has been confined to gaol, esp repeatedly
GAOLBIRDS > GAOLBIRD
GAOLBREAK n escape from gaol
GAOLED > GAOL
GAOLER > GAOL
GAOLERESS n female gaoler
GAOLERS > GAOL
GAOLING > GAOL
GAOLLESS > GAOL
GAOLS > GAOL
GAP n break or opening
GAPE vb stare in wonder ▷ n act of gaping
GAPED > GAPE
GAPER n person or thing that gapes
GAPERS > GAPER
GAPES n disease of young domestic fowl, characterized by gaping or gasping for breath and caused by gapeworms
GAPESEED n person who stares, mouth agape, at something
GAPESEEDS > GAPESEED
GAPEWORM n parasitic nematode worm, Syngamus trachea, that lives in the trachea of birds
GAPEWORMS > GAPEWORM
GAPIER > GAPES
GAPIEST > GAPES
GAPING adj wide open ▷ n state of having a gaping mouth
GAPINGLY > GAPING
GAPINGS > GAPING
GAPLESS > GAP
GAPO n forest near a river, regularly flooded in the rainy season
GAPOS > GAPO
GAPOSIS n gap between closed fastenings on a garment
GAPOSISES > GAPOSIS
GAPPED > GAP
GAPPER n in British English, person taking a year out between school and further education
GAPPERS > GAPPER
GAPPIER > GAP
GAPPIEST > GAP
GAPPING > GAP
GAPPY > GAP
GAPS > GAP
GAPY > GAPES
GAR same as > GARPIKE
GARAGE n building used to house cars ▷ vb put or keep a car in a garage
GARAGED > GARAGE

GARAGEMAN *n* car mechanic
GARAGEMEN > GARAGEMAN
GARAGES > GARAGE
GARAGING *n* accommodation for housing a motor vehicle
GARAGINGS > GARAGING
GARAGIST *n* person who runs a garage
GARAGISTE *n* small-scale wine-maker
GARAGISTS > GARAGIST
GARB *n* clothes ▷ *vb* clothe
GARBAGE *n* rubbish
GARBAGES > GARBAGE
GARBAGEY > GARBAGE
GARBAGY > GARBAGE
GARBANZO *another name for* > CHICKPEA
GARBANZOS > GARBANZO
GARBE *n* in heraldry, a wheat-sheaf
GARBED > GARB
GARBES > GARBE
GARBING > GARB
GARBLE *vb* jumble (a story, quotation, etc), esp unintentionally ▷ *n* act of garbling
GARBLED *adj* (of a story etc) jumbled and confused
GARBLER > GARBLE
GARBLERS > GARBLE
GARBLES > GARBLE
GARBLESS > GARB
GARBLING > GARBLE
GARBLINGS > GARBLE
GARBO *n* dustman
GARBOARD *n* bottommost plank of a vessel's hull
GARBOARDS > GARBOARD
GARBOIL *n* confusion or disturbance
GARBOILS > GARBOIL
GARBOLOGY *n* study of the contents of domestic dustbins to analyse the consumption patterns of households
GARBOS > GARBO
GARBS > GARB
GARBURE *n* thick soup from Bearn in France
GARBURES > GARBURE
GARCINIA *n* tropical tree
GARCINIAS > GARCINIA
GARCON *n* waiter
GARCONS > GARCON
GARDA *n* member of the police force of the Republic of Ireland
GARDAI > GARDA
GARDANT *same as* > GUARDANT
GARDANTS > GUARDANT
GARDEN *n* piece of land for growing flowers, fruit, or vegetables ▷ *vb* cultivate a garden
GARDENED > GARDEN
GARDENER *n* person who works in or takes care of a garden as an occupation or pastime
GARDENERS > GARDENER
GARDENFUL *n* quantity that will fill a garden

GARDENIA *n* large fragrant white waxy flower
GARDENIAS > GARDENIA
GARDENING *n* planning and cultivation of a garden
GARDENS > GARDEN
GARDEROBE *n* wardrobe or the contents of a wardrobe
GARDYLOO *n* act of throwing slops from a window
GARDYLOOS > GARDYLOO
GARE *n* filth
GAREFOWL *n* great auk
GAREFOWLS > GAREFOWL
GARFISH *same as* > GARPIKE
GARFISHES > GARFISH
GARGANEY *n* small Eurasian duck, closely related to the mallard
GARGANEYS > GARGANEY
GARGANTUA *n* monster in Japanese film
GARGARISE *vb* gargle
GARGARISM *n* gargle
GARGARIZE *same as* > GARGARISE
GARGET *n* inflammation of the mammary gland of domestic animals, esp cattle
GARGETS > GARGET
GARGETY > GARGET
GARGLE *vb* wash the throat with (a liquid) by breathing out slowly through the liquid ▷ *n* liquid used for gargling
GARGLED > GARGLE
GARGLER > GARGLE
GARGLERS > GARGLE
GARGLES > GARGLE
GARGLING > GARGLE
GARGOYLE *n* waterspout carved in the form of a grotesque face, esp on a church ▷ *vb* provide with gargoyles
GARGOYLED > GARGOYLE
GARGOYLES > GARGOYLE
GARI *n* thinly sliced pickled ginger, often served with sushi
GARIAL *same as* > GAVIAL
GARIALS > GARIAL
GARIBALDI *n* woman's loose blouse with long sleeves popular in the 1860s, copied from the red flannel shirt worn by Garibaldi's soldiers
GARIGUE *n* open shrubby vegetation of dry Mediterranean regions, consisting of spiny or aromatic dwarf shrubs interspersed with colourful ephemeral species
GARIGUES > GARIGUE
GARIS > GARI
GARISH *adj* crudely bright or colourful ▷ *vb* heal
GARISHED > GARISH
GARISHES > GARISH
GARISHING > GARISH
GARISHLY > GARISH
GARJAN *same as* > GURJUN
GARJANS > GARJAN

GARLAND *n* wreath of flowers worn or hung as a decoration ▷ *vb* decorate with garlands
GARLANDED > GARLAND
GARLANDRY *n* collective term for garlands
GARLANDS > GARLAND
GARLIC *n* pungent bulb of a plant of the onion family, used in cooking
GARLICKED *adj* flavoured with garlic
GARLICKY *adj* containing or resembling the taste or odour of garlic
GARLICS > GARLIC
GARMENT *n* article of clothing ▷ *vb* cover or clothe
GARMENTED > GARMENT
GARMENTS > GARMENT
GARNER *vb* collect or store ▷ *n* place for storage or safekeeping
GARNERED > GARNER
GARNERING > GARNER
GARNERS > GARNER
GARNET *n* red semiprecious stone
GARNETS > GARNET
GARNI *adj* garnished
GARNISH *vb* decorate (food) ▷ *n* decoration for food
GARNISHED > GARNISH
GARNISHEE *n* person upon whom a notice of warning has been served ▷ *vb* attach (a debt or other property) by a notice of warning
GARNISHER > GARNISH
GARNISHES > GARNISH
GARNISHRY *n* decoration
GARNITURE *n* decoration or embellishment
GAROTE *same as* > GARROTTE
GAROTED > GAROTE
GAROTES > GAROTE
GAROTING > GAROTE
GAROTTE *same as* > GARROTTE
GAROTTED > GAROTTE
GAROTTER > GAROTTE
GAROTTERS > GAROTTE
GAROTTES > GAROTTE
GAROTTING > GAROTTE
GAROUPA *in Chinese and SE Asian cookery, another name for* > GROPER
GAROUPAS > GAROUPA
GARPIKE *n* any primitive freshwater elongated bony fish of the genus *Lepisosteus*, of North and Central America, having very long toothed jaws and a body covering of thick scales
GARPIKES > GARPIKE
GARRAN *same as* > GARRON
GARRANS > GARRAN
GARRE *vb* compel
GARRED > GAR
GARRES > GARRE
GARRET *n* attic in a house
GARRETED *adj* living in a

garret
GARRETEER *n* person who lives in a garret
GARRETS > GARRET
GARRIGUE *same as* > GARIGUE
GARRIGUES > GARRIGUE
GARRING > GAR
GARRISON *n* troops stationed in a town or fort ▷ *vb* station troops in
GARRISONS > GARRISON
GARRON *n* small sturdy pony bred and used chiefly in Scotland and Ireland
GARRONS > GARRON
GARROT *n* goldeneye duck
GARROTE *same as* > GARROTTE
GARROTED > GARROTE
GARROTER > GARROTE
GARROTERS > GARROTE
GARROTES > GARROTE
GARROTING > GARROTE
GARROTS > GARROT
GARROTTE *n* Spanish method of execution by strangling ▷ *vb* kill by this method
GARROTTED > GARROTTE
GARROTTER > GARROTTE
GARROTTES > GARROTTE
GARRULITY > GARRULOUS
GARRULOUS *adj* talkative
GARRYA *n* any ornamental catkin-bearing evergreen shrub of the North American genus *Garrya*: family *Garryaceae*
GARRYAS > GARRYA
GARRYOWEN *n* (in rugby union) high kick forwards followed by a charge to the place where the ball lands
GARS > GAR
GART *vb* compel
GARTER *n* band worn round the leg to hold up a sock or stocking ▷ *vb* secure with a garter
GARTERED > GARTER
GARTERING > GARTER
GARTERS > GARTER
GARTH *n* courtyard surrounded by a cloister
GARTHS > GARTH
GARUDA *n* Hindu god
GARUDAS > GARUDA
GARUM *n* fermented fish sauce
GARUMS > GARUM
GARVEY *n* small flat-bottomed yacht
GARVEYS > GARVEY
GARVIE *n* sprat
GARVIES > GARVIE
GARVOCK *n* sprat
GARVOCKS > GARVOCK
GAS *n* airlike substance that is not liquid or solid ▷ *vb* poison or render unconscious with gas
GASAHOL *n* mixture of petrol and alcohol used as fuel
GASAHOLS > GASAHOL
GASALIER *same as* > GASOLIER

GASALIERS > GASALIER

GASBAG *n* person who talks too much ▷ *vb* talk in a voluble way, esp about unimportant matters

GASBAGGED > GASBAG

GASBAGS > GASBAG

GASCON *n* boaster

GASCONADE *n* boastful talk, bragging, or bluster ▷ *vb* boast, brag, or bluster

GASCONISM > GASCON

GASCONS > GASCON

GASEITIES > GASEITY

GASEITY *n* state of being gaseous

GASELIER *same as* > GASOLIER

GASELIERS > GASELIER

GASEOUS *adj* of or like gas

GASES > GAS

GASFIELD *n* area in which natural gas is found underground

GASFIELDS > GASFIELD

GASH *vb* make a long deep cut in ▷ *n* long deep cut ▷ *adj* surplus to requirements ▷ *adj* witty

GASHED > GASH

GASHER > GASH

GASHES > GASH

GASHEST > GASH

GASHFUL *adj* full of gashes

GASHING > GASH

GASHLY *adv* wittily

GASHOLDER *n* large tank for storing gas

GASHOUSE *n* gasworks

GASHOUSES > GASHOUSE

GASIFIED > GASIFY

GASIFIER > GASIFY

GASIFIERS > GASIFY

GASIFIES > GASIFY

GASIFORM *adj* in a gaseous form

GASIFY *vb* change into a gas

GASIFYING > GASIFY

GASKET *n* piece of rubber etc placed between the faces of a metal joint to act as a seal

GASKETS > GASKET

GASKIN *n* lower part of a horse's thigh, between the hock and the stifle

GASKING *same as* > GASKET

GASKINGS > GASKING

GASKINS > GASKIN

GASLESS > GAS

GASLIGHT *n* lamp in which light is produced by burning gas

GASLIGHTS > GASLIGHT

GASLIT *adj* lit by gas

GASMAN *n* man employed to read household gas meters and install or repair gas fittings, etc

GASMEN > GASMAN

GASOGENE *n* siphon bottle

GASOGENES > GASOGENE

GASOHOL *n* mixture of 80% or 90% petrol with 20% or 10% ethyl alcohol, for use as a fuel in internal-combustion engines

GASOHOLS > GASOHOL

GASOLENE *same as* > GASOLINE

GASOLENES > GASOLENE

GASOLIER *n* branched hanging fitting for gaslights

GASOLIERS > GASOLIER

GASOLINE *n* petrol

GASOLINES > GASOLINE

GASOLINIC > GASOLINE

GASOMETER *same as* > GASHOLDER

GASOMETRY *n* measurement of quantities of gases

GASP *vb* draw in breath sharply or with difficulty ▷ *n* convulsive intake of breath

GASPED > GASP

GASPER *n* person who gasps

GASPEREAU *another name for* > ALEWIFE

GASPERS > GASPER

GASPIER > GASP

GASPIEST > GASP

GASPINESS > GASP

GASPING > GASP

GASPINGLY > GASP

GASPINGS > GASP

GASPS > GASP

GASPY > GASP

GASSED > GAS

GASSER *n* drilling or well that yields natural gas

GASSERS > GASSER

GASSES > GAS

GASSIER > GASSY

GASSIEST > GASSY

GASSILY > GASSY

GASSINESS > GASSY

GASSING > GAS

GASSINGS > GAS

GASSY *adj* filled with gas

GAST *vb* frighten

GASTED > GAST

GASTER > GAST

GASTERS > GAST

GASTFULL *adj* dismal

GASTIGHT *adj* not allowing gas to enter or escape

GASTING > GAST

GASTNESS *n* dread

GASTNESSE *same as* > GASTNESS

GASTRAEA *n* hypothetical primeval form posited by Haeckel

GASTRAEAS > GASTRAEA

GASTRAEUM *n* underside of the body

GASTRAL *adj* relating to the stomach

GASTREA *same as* > GASTRAEA

GASTREAS > GASTREAS

GASTRIC *adj* of the stomach

GASTRIN *n* polypeptide hormone secreted by the stomach: stimulates secretion of gastric juice

GASTRINS > GASTRIN

GASTRITIC > GASTRITIS

GASTRITIS *n* inflammation of the stomach lining

GASTROPOD *n* mollusc, such as a snail, with a single flattened muscular foot ▷ *adj* of, relating to, or belonging to the *Gastropoda*

GASTRULA *n* saclike animal embryo consisting of three layers of cells (see ectoderm, mesoderm, and endoderm) surrounding a central cavity (archenteron) with a small opening (blastopore) to the exterior

GASTRULAE > GASTRULA

GASTRULAR > GASTRULA

GASTRULAS > GASTRULA

GASTS > GAST

GASWORKS *n* plant where coal gas is made

GAT *n* pistol or revolver

GATE *n* movable barrier, usu hinged, in a wall or fence ▷ *vb* provide with a gate or gates

GATEAU *n* rich elaborate cake

GATEAUS > GATEAU

GATEAUX > GATEAU

GATECRASH *vb* gain entry to (a party, concert, etc) without invitation or payment

GATED > GATE

GATEFOLD *n* oversize page in a book or magazine that is folded in

GATEFOLDS > GATEFOLD

GATEHOUSE *n* building at or above a gateway

GATELEG *adj* (of a table) with one or two drop leaves that are supported when in use by a hinged leg swung out from the frame

GATELESS > GATE

GATELIKE > GATE

GATEMAN *n* gatekeeper

GATEMEN > GATEMAN

GATEPOST *n* post on which a gate is hung

GATEPOSTS > GATEPOST

GATER *variant of* > GATOR

GATERS > GATER

GATES > GATE

GATEWAY *n* entrance with a gate

GATEWAYS > GATEWAY

GATH *n* (in Indian music) second section of a raga

GATHER *vb* assemble ▷ *n* act of gathering

GATHERED > GATHER

GATHERER > GATHER

GATHERERS > GATHER

GATHERING *n* assembly

GATHERS > GATHER

GATHS > GATH

GATING > GATE

GATINGS > GATE

GATOR *shortened form of* > ALLIGATOR

GATORS > GATOR

GATS > GAT

GATVOL *adj* in South African English, fed up

GAU *n* district set up by the Nazi Party during the Third Reich

GAUCHE *adj* socially awkward

GAUCHELY > GAUCHE

GAUCHER > GAUCHE

GAUCHERIE *n* quality of being gauche

GAUCHESCO *adj* relating to the folk traditions of the gauchos

GAUCHEST > GAUCHE

GAUCHO *n* S American cowboy

GAUCHOS > GAUCHO

GAUCIE *variant of* > GAUCY

GAUCIER > GAUCY

GAUCIEST > GAUCY

GAUCY *adj* plump or jolly

GAUD *n* article of cheap finery ▷ *vb* decorate gaudily

GAUDEAMUS *n* first word of a traditional graduation song, hence the song itself

GAUDED > GAUD

GAUDERIES > GAUDERY

GAUDERY *n* cheap finery or display

GAUDGIE *same as* > GADGIE

GAUDGIES > GADGIE

GAUDIER > GAUDY

GAUDIES > GAUDY

GAUDIEST > GAUDY

GAUDILY > GAUDY

GAUDINESS > GAUDY

GAUDING > GAUD

GAUDS > GAUD

GAUDY *adj* vulgarly bright or colourful ▷ *n* celebratory festival or feast held at some schools and colleges

GAUFER *n* wafer

GAUFERS > GAUFER

GAUFFER *same as* > GOFFER

GAUFFERED > GAUFFER

GAUFFERS > GAUFFER

GAUFRE *same as* > GAUFER

GAUFRES > GAUFRE

GAUGE *vb* estimate or judge ▷ *n* measuring instrument ▷ *adj* (of a pressure measurement) measured on a pressure gauge that registers zero at atmospheric pressure

GAUGEABLE > GAUGE

GAUGEABLY > GAUGE

GAUGED > GAUGE

GAUGER *n* person or thing that gauges

GAUGERS > GAUGER

GAUGES > GAUGE

GAUGING > GAUGE

GAUGINGS > GAUGE

GAUJE *same as* > GADGIE

GAUJES > GAUJE

GAULEITER *n* person in a position of authority who behaves in an overbearing authoritarian manner

GAULT *n* stiff compact clay or thick heavy clayey soil

GAULTER *n* person who digs gault

GAULTERS > GAULTER

GAULTS > GAULT

GAUM *vb* understand
GAUMED > GAUM
GAUMIER > GAUMY
GAUMIEST > GAUMY
GAUMING > GAUM
GAUMLESS *variant spelling of* > GORMLESS
GAUMS > GAUM
GAUMY *adj* clogged
GAUN > GO
GAUNCH *same as* > GANCH
GAUNCHED > GAUNCH
GAUNCHES > GAUNCH
GAUNCHING > GAUNCH
GAUNT *adj* lean and haggard ▷ *vb* yawn
GAUNTED > GAUNT
GAUNTER > GAUNT
GAUNTEST > GAUNT
GAUNTING > GAUNT
GAUNTLET *n* heavy glove with a long cuff ▷ *vb* run (or cause to run) the gauntlet
GAUNTLETS > GAUNTLET
GAUNTLY > GAUNT
GAUNTNESS > GAUNT
GAUNTREE *same as* > GANTRY
GAUNTREES > GAUNTREE
GAUNTRIES > GAUNTRY
GAUNTRY *same as* > GANTRY
GAUNTS > GAUNT
GAUP *same as* > GAWP
GAUPED > GAUP
GAUPER > GAUP
GAUPERS > GAUP
GAUPING > GAUP
GAUPS > GAUP
GAUPUS *same as* > GAWPUS
GAUPUSES > GAUPUS
GAUR *n* large wild member of the cattle tribe, *Bos gaurus*, inhabiting mountainous regions of S Asia
GAURS > GAUR
GAUS > GAU
GAUSS *n* cgs unit of magnetic flux density
GAUSSES > GAUSS
GAUSSIAN *adj* of or relating to the principles established by Karl Friedrich Gauss, the German mathematician
GAUZE *n* transparent loosely-woven fabric, often used for surgical dressings
GAUZELIKE > GAUZE
GAUZES > GAUZE
GAUZIER > GAUZY
GAUZIEST > GAUZY
GAUZILY > GAUZY
GAUZINESS > GAUZY
GAUZY *adj* resembling gauze
GAVAGE *n* forced feeding by means of a tube inserted into the stomach through the mouth
GAVAGES > GAVAGE
GAVE > GIVE
GAVEL *n* small hammer banged on a table by a judge, auctioneer, or chairman to call for attention ▷ *vb* use a gavel to restore order

GAVELED > GAVEL
GAVELING > GAVEL
GAVELKIND *n* former system of land tenure peculiar to Kent based on the payment of rent to the lord instead of the performance of services by the tenant
GAVELLED > GAVEL
GAVELLING > GAVEL
GAVELMAN *n* gavelkind tenant
GAVELMEN > GAVELMAN
GAVELOCK *n* iron crowbar
GAVELOCKS > GAVELOCK
GAVELS > GAVEL
GAVIAL *as in false gavial* small crocodile
GAVIALOID *adj* of or like gavials
GAVIALS > GAVIAL
GAVOT *same as* > GAVOTTE
GAVOTS > GAVOT
GAVOTTE *n* old formal dance ▷ *vb* dance a gavotte
GAVOTTED > GAVOTTE
GAVOTTES > GAVOTTE
GAVOTTING > GAVOTTE
GAWCIER > GAWCY
GAWCIEST > GAWCY
GAWCY *same as* > GAUCY
GAWD *same as* > GAUD
GAWDS > GAWD
GAWK *vb* stare stupidly ▷ *n* clumsy awkward person
GAWKED > GAWK
GAWKER > GAWK
GAWKERS > GAWK
GAWKIER > GAWKY
GAWKIES > GAWKY
GAWKIEST > GAWKY
GAWKIHOOD *n* state of being gawky
GAWKILY > GAWKY
GAWKINESS > GAWKY
GAWKING > GAWK
GAWKISH *same as* > GAWKY
GAWKISHLY > GAWKY
GAWKS > GAWK
GAWKY *adj* clumsy or awkward ▷ *n* simpleton
GAWP *vb* stare stupidly
GAWPED > GAWP
GAWPER > GAWP
GAWPERS > GAWP
GAWPING > GAWP
GAWPS > GAWP
GAWPUS *n* silly person
GAWPUSES > GAWPUS
GAWSIE *same as* > GAUCY
GAWSIER > GAWSIE
GAWSIEST > GAWSIE
GAWSY *same as* > GAUCY
GAY *adj* homosexual ▷ *n* homosexual
GAYAL *n* ox of India and Myanmar, *Bibos frontalis*, possibly a semidomesticated variety of gaur, black or brown with white stockings
GAYALS > GAYAL
GAYDAR *n* supposed ability of a homosexual person to determine whether or not another person is

homosexual
GAYDARS > GAYDAR
GAYER > GAY
GAYEST > GAY
GAYETIES > GAYETY
GAYETY *same as* > GAIETY
GAYLY > GAY
GAYNESS > GAY
GAYNESSES > GAY
GAYS > GAY
GAYSOME *adj* full of merriment
GAYWINGS *n* flowering wintergreen
GAZABO *n* fellow or companion
GAZABOES > GAZABO
GAZABOS > GAZABO
GAZAL *same as* > GHAZAL
GAZALS > GAZAL
GAZANIA *n* any plant of the S African genus *Gazania*, grown for their rayed flowers in variegated colours
GAZANIAS > GAZANIA
GAZAR *n* type of silk cloth
GAZARS > GAZAR
GAZE *vb* look fixedly ▷ *n* fixed look
GAZEBO *n* summerhouse with a good view
GAZEBOES > GAZEBO
GAZEBOS > GAZEBO
GAZED > GAZE
GAZEFUL *adj* gazing
GAZEHOUND *n* hound such as a greyhound that hunts by sight rather than by scent
GAZELLE *n* small graceful antelope
GAZELLES > GAZELLE
GAZEMENT *n* view
GAZEMENTS > GAZEMENT
GAZER > GAZE
GAZERS > GAZE
GAZES > GAZE
GAZETTE *n* official publication containing announcements ▷ *vb* announce or report (facts or an event) in a gazette
GAZETTED > GAZETTE
GAZETTEER *n* (part of) a book that lists and describes places ▷ *vb* list in a gazetteer
GAZETTES > GAZETTE
GAZETTING > GAZETTE
GAZIER > GAZY
GAZIEST > GAZY
GAZILLION *n* in informal English, an extremely large but unspecified number, quantity, or amount
GAZING > GAZE
GAZINGS > GAZE
GAZOGENE *same as* > GASOGENE
GAZOGENES > GAZOGENE
GAZON *n* sod used to cover a parapet in a fortification
GAZONS > GAZON
GAZOO *n* kazoo
GAZOOKA *same as* > GAZOO
GAZOOKAS > GAZOOKA
GAZOON *same as* > GAZON

GAZOONS > GAZOON
GAZOOS > GAZOO
GAZPACHO *n* Spanish soup made from tomatoes, peppers, etc, and served cold
GAZPACHOS > GAZPACHO
GAZUMP *vb* raise the price of a property after verbally agreeing it with (a prospective buyer) ▷ *n* act or an instance of gazumping
GAZUMPED > GAZUMP
GAZUMPER > GAZUMP
GAZUMPERS > GAZUMP
GAZUMPING > GAZUMP
GAZUMPS > GAZUMP
GAZUNDER *vb* reduce an offer on a property immediately before exchanging contracts having earlier agreed a higher price with the seller ▷ *n* act or instance of gazundering
GAZUNDERS > GAZUNDER
GAZY *adj* prone to gazing
GEAL *vb* congeal
GEALED > GEAL
GEALING > GEAL
GEALOUS *Spenserian spelling of* > JEALOUS
GEALOUSY *Spenserian spelling of* > JEALOUSY
GEALS > GEAL
GEAN *n* white-flowered rosaceous tree, *Prunus avium*, of Europe, W Asia, and N Africa, the ancestor of the cultivated sweet cherries
GEANS > GEAN
GEAR *n* set of toothed wheels connecting with another or with a rack to change the direction or speed of transmitted motion ▷ *vb* prepare or organize for something
GEARBOX *n* case enclosing a set of gears in a motor vehicle
GEARBOXES > GEARBOX
GEARCASE *n* protective casing for gears
GEARCASES > GEARCASE
GEARE *Spenserian spelling of* > JEER
GEARED > GEAR
GEARES > GEARE
GEARHEAD *n* part in engine gear system
GEARHEADS > GEARHEAD
GEARING *n* system of gears designed to transmit motion
GEARINGS > GEARING
GEARLESS > GEAR
GEARS > GEAR
GEARSHIFT *n* lever used to move gearwheels relative to each other, esp in a motor vehicle
GEARWHEEL *n* one of the toothed wheels in the gears of a motor vehicle

g

GEASON adj wonderful
GEAT n in casting, the channel through which molten metal runs into a mould
GEATS > GEAT
GEBUR n tenant farmer
GEBURS > GEBUR
GECK vb beguile
GECKED > GECK
GECKING > GECK
GECKO n small tropical lizard
GECKOES > GECKO
GECKOS > GECKO
GECKS > GECK
GED Scots word for > PIKE
GEDACT n flutelike stopped metal diapason organ pipe
GEDACTS > GEDACT
GEDDIT interj exclamation meaning do you understand it?
GEDECKT same as > GEDACT
GEDECKTS > GEDECKT
GEDS > GED
GEE interj mild exclamation of surprise, admiration, etc ▷ vb move (an animal, esp a horse) ahead
GEEBAG n in Irish slang, a disagreeable woman
GEEBAGS > GEEBAG
GEEBUNG n Australian tree or shrub with an edible but tasteless fruit
GEEBUNGS > GEEBUNG
GEECHEE n Black person from the southern states of the US
GEECHEES > GEECHEE
GEED > GEE
GEEGAW same as > GEWGAW
GEEGAWS > GEEGAW
GEEING > GEE
GEEK n boring, unattractive person
GEEKDOM > GEEK
GEEKDOMS > GEEK
GEEKED adj highly excited
GEEKIER > GEEK
GEEKIEST > GEEK
GEEKINESS > GEEK
GEEKS > GEEK
GEEKSPEAK n slang word for jargon used by geeks, esp computer enthusiasts
GEEKY > GEEK
GEELBEK n edible marine fish
GEELBEKS > GEELBEK
GEEP n cross between a goat and a sheep
GEEPOUND another name for > SLUG
GEEPOUNDS > SLUG
GEEPS > GEEP
GEES > GEE
GEESE > GOOSE
GEEST n area of sandy heathland in N Germany and adjacent areas
GEESTS > GEEST
GEEZ interj expression of surprise
GEEZAH variant spelling of > GEEZER
GEEZAHS > GEEZAH

GEEZER n man
GEEZERS > GEEZER
GEFILTE as in gefilte fish dish of fish stuffed with various ingredients
GEFUFFLE same as > KERFUFFLE
GEFUFFLED > GEFUFFLE
GEFUFFLES > GEFUFFLE
GEFULLTE as in gefullte fish dish of fish stuffed with various ingredients
GEGGIE Scottish, esp Glaswegian, slang word for the > MOUTH
GEGGIES > GEGGIE
GEHLENITE n green mineral consisting of calcium aluminium silicate in tetragonal crystalline form
GEISHA n (in Japan) professional female companion for men
GEISHAS > GEISHA
GEIST n spirit
GEISTS > GEIST
GEIT n border on clothing
GEITS > GEIT
GEL n jelly-like substance, esp one used to secure a hairstyle ▷ vb form a gel
GELABLE adj capable of forming a gel
GELADA n NE African baboon, Theropithecus gelada, with dark brown hair forming a mane over the shoulders, a bare red chest, and a ridge muzzle: family Cercopithecidae
GELADAS > GELADA
GELANDE as in gelande jump jump made in downhill skiing
GELANT same as > GELLANT
GELANTS > GELANT
GELASTIC adj relating to laughter
GELATE vb form a gel
GELATED > GELATE
GELATES > GELATE
GELATI n layered dessert of frozen custard and ice cream
GELATIN same as > GELATINE
GELATINE n substance made by boiling animal bones
GELATINES > GELATINE
GELATING > GELATE
GELATINS > GELATIN
GELATION n act or process of freezing a liquid
GELATIONS > GELATION
GELATIS > GELATI
GELATO n Italian frozen dessert, similar to ice cream
GELATOS > GELATO
GELCAP n dose of medicine enclosed in a soluble case of gelatine
GELCAPS > GELCAP
GELD vb castrate ▷ n tax on land levied in late Anglo-Saxon and Norman England

GELDED > GELD
GELDER > GELD
GELDERS > GELD
GELDING > GELD
GELDINGS > GELD
GELDS > GELD
GELEE n jelly
GELEES > GELEE
GELID adj very cold, icy, or frosty
GELIDER > GELID
GELIDEST > GELID
GELIDITY > GELID
GELIDLY > GELID
GELIDNESS > GELID
GELIGNITE n type of dynamite used for blasting
GELLANT n compound that forms a solid structure
GELLANTS > GELLANT
GELLED > GEL
GELLIES > GELLY
GELLING > GEL
GELLY same as > GELIGNITE
GELOSIES > GELOSY
GELOSY Spenserian spelling of > JEALOUSY
GELS > GEL
GELSEMIA > GELSEMIUM
GELSEMINE n alkaloid obtained from gelsemium
GELSEMIUM n any climbing shrub of the loganiaceous genus Gelsemium, of SE Asia and North America, esp the yellow jasmine, having fragrant yellow flowers
GELT > GELD
GELTS > GELD
GEM n precious stone or jewel ▷ vb set or ornament with gems
GEMATRIA n numerology of the Hebrew language and alphabet
GEMATRIAS > GEMATRIA
GEMCLIP n paperclip
GEMCLIPS > GEMCLIP
GEMEL n in heraldry, parallel bars
GEMELS > GEMEL
GEMFISH n Australian food fish with a delicate flavour
GEMFISHES > GEMFISH
GEMINAL adj occurring in pairs
GEMINALLY > GEMINAL
GEMINATE adj combined in pairs ▷ vb arrange or be arranged in pairs
GEMINATED > GEMINATE
GEMINATES > GEMINATE
GEMINI n expression of surprise
GEMINIES > GEMINY
GEMINOUS adj in pairs
GEMINY n pair
GEMLIKE > GEM
GEMMA n small asexual reproductive structure in liverworts, mosses, etc, that becomes detached from the parent and develops into a new individual
GEMMAE > GEMMA
GEMMAN dialect form

of > GENTLEMAN
GEMMATE adj (of some plants and animals) having or reproducing by gemmae ▷ vb produce or reproduce by gemmae
GEMMATED > GEMMATE
GEMMATES > GEMMATE
GEMMATING > GEMMATE
GEMMATION > GEMMATE
GEMMATIVE adj relating to gemmation
GEMMED > GEM
GEMMEN > GEMMAN
GEMMEOUS adj gem-like
GEMMERIES > GEMMERY
GEMMERY n gems collectively
GEMMIER > GEM
GEMMIEST > GEM
GEMMILY > GEM
GEMMINESS > GEM
GEMMING > GEM
GEMMOLOGY same as > GEMOLOGY
GEMMULE n cell or mass of cells produced asexually by sponges and developing into a new individual
GEMMULES > GEMMULE
GEMMY > GEM
GEMOLOGY n branch of mineralogy that is concerned with gems and gemstones
GEMONY same as > JIMINY
GEMOT n (in Anglo-Saxon England) a legal or administrative assembly of a community, such as a shire or hundred
GEMOTE same as > GEMOT
GEMOTES > GEMOTE
GEMOTS > GEMOT
GEMS > GEM
GEMSBOK same as > ORYX
GEMSBOKS > GEMSBOK
GEMSBUCK > ORYX
GEMSBUCKS > GEMSBUCK
GEMSHORN n type of medieval flute
GEMSHORNS > GEMSHORN
GEMSTONE n precious or semiprecious stone, esp one which has been cut and polished
GEMSTONES > GEMSTONE
GEMUTLICH adj having a feeling or atmosphere of warmth and friendliness
GEN n information ▷ vb gain information
GENA n cheek
GENAL > GENA
GENAPPE n smooth worsted yarn used for braid, etc
GENAPPES > GENAPPE
GENAS > GENA
GENDARME n member of the French police force
GENDARMES > GENDARME
GENDER n state of being male or female ▷ vb have sex
GENDERED > GENDER
GENDERING > GENDER
GENDERISE same

as > GENDERIZE
GENDERIZE *vb* make distinctions according to gender in or among
GENDERS > GENDER
GENE *n* part of a cell which determines inherited characteristics
GENEALOGY *n* (study of) the history and descent of a family or families
GENERA > GENUS
GENERABLE *adj* able to be generated
GENERAL *adj* common or widespread ▷*n* very senior army officer ▷*vb* act as a general
GENERALCY *n* rank of general
GENERALE *singular form of* > GENERALIA
GENERALIA *n* generalities
GENERALLY *adv* usually
GENERALS > GENERAL
GENERANT *n* something that generates
GENERANTS > GENERANT
GENERATE *vb* produce or bring into being
GENERATED > GENERATE
GENERATES > GENERATE
GENERATOR *n* machine for converting mechanical energy into electrical energy
GENERIC *adj* of a class, group, or genus ▷*n* drug, food product, etc that does not have a trademark
GENERICAL *same as* > GENERIC
GENERICS > GENERIC
GENEROUS *adj* free in giving
GENES > GENE
GENESES > GENESIS
GENESIS *n* beginning or origin
GENET *n* any agile catlike viverrine mammal of the genus *Genetta*, inhabiting wooded regions of Africa and S Europe, having an elongated head, thick spotted or blotched fur, and a very long tail
GENETIC *adj* of genes or genetics
GENETICAL *same as* > GENETIC
GENETICS *n* study of heredity and variation in organisms
GENETRIX *n* female progenitor
GENETS > GENET
GENETTE *same as* > GENET
GENETTES > GENETTE
GENEVA *n* gin
GENEVAS > GENEVA
GENIAL *adj* cheerful and friendly
GENIALISE *vb* make genial
GENIALITY > GENIAL
GENIALIZE *same as* > GENIALISE
GENIALLY > GENIAL

GENIC *adj* of or relating to a gene or genes
GENICALLY > GENIC
GENICULAR *adj* of or relating to the knee
GENIE *n* (in fairy tales) servant who appears by magic and grants wishes
GENIES > GENIE
GENII > GENIUS
GENIP *same as* > GENIPAP
GENIPAP *n* evergreen Caribbean rubiaceous tree, *Genipa americana*, with reddish-brown edible orange-like fruits
GENIPAPS > GENIPAP
GENIPS > GENIP
GENISTA *n* any member of the broom family
GENISTAS > GENISTA
GENISTEIN *n* substance found in plants, thought to fight cancer
GENITAL *adj* of the sexual organs or reproduction
GENITALIA *same as* > GENITALS
GENITALIC > GENITALIA
GENITALLY > GENITAL
GENITALS *pl n* external sexual organs
GENITIVAL > GENITIVE
GENITIVE *n* grammatical case indicating possession or association ▷*adj* denoting a case of nouns, pronouns, and adjectives in inflected languages used to indicate a relation of ownership or association, usually translated by English *of*
GENITIVES > GENITIVE
GENITOR *n* biological father as distinguished from the pater or legal father
GENITORS > GENITOR
GENITRIX *same as* > GENETRIX
GENITURE *n* birth
GENITURES > GENITURE
GENIUS *n* (person with) exceptional ability in a particular field
GENIUSES > GENIUS
GENIZAH *n* repository (usually in a synagogue) for books and other sacred objects which can no longer be used but which may not be destroyed
GENIZAHS > GENIZAH
GENIZOT > GENIZAH
GENIZOTH > GENIZAH
GENLOCK *n* generator locking device
GENLOCKS > GENLOCK
GENNAKER *n* type of sail for boats
GENNAKERS > GENNAKER
GENNED > GEN
GENNEL *same as* > GINNEL
GENNELS > GENNEL
GENNET *n* female donkey or ass
GENNETS > GENNET

GENNIES > GENNY
GENNING > GEN
GENNY *same as* > GENOA
GENOA *n* large triangular jib sail, often with a foot that extends as far aft as the clew of the mainsail
GENOAS > GENOA
GENOCIDAL > GENOCIDE
GENOCIDE *n* murder of a race of people
GENOCIDES > GENOCIDE
GENOGRAM *n* expanded family tree
GENOGRAMS > GENOGRAM
GENOISE *n* rich sponge cake
GENOISES > GENOISE
GENOM *same as* > GENOME
GENOME *n* full complement of genetic material within an organism
GENOMES > GENOME
GENOMIC > GENOME
GENOMICS *n* branch of molecular genetics concerned with the study of genomes
GENOMS > GENOM
GENOTYPE *n* genetic constitution of an organism
GENOTYPES > GENOTYPE
GENOTYPIC > GENOTYPE
GENRE *n* style of literary, musical, or artistic work
GENRES > GENRE
GENRO *n* group of highly respected elder statesmen in late 19th- and early 20th-century Japan
GENROS > GENRO
GENS *n* (in ancient Rome) any of a group of aristocratic families, having a common name and claiming descent from a common ancestor in the male line
GENSENG *same as* > GINSENG
GENSENGS > GENSENG
GENT *n* gentleman
GENTEEL *adj* affectedly proper and polite
GENTEELER > GENTEEL
GENTEELLY > GENTEEL
GENTES > GENS
GENTIAN *n* mountain plant with deep blue flowers
GENTIANS > GENTIAN
GENTIER > GENTY
GENTIEST > GENTY
GENTIL *adj* gentle
GENTILE *n* non-Jewish (person) ▷*adj* denoting an adjective or proper noun used to designate a place or the inhabitants of a place, as *Spanish* and *Spaniard*
GENTILES > GENTILE
GENTILIC *adj* tribal
GENTILISE *vb* live like a gentile
GENTILISH *adj* heathenish
GENTILISM *n* heathenism
GENTILITY *n* noble birth or ancestry
GENTILIZE *same*

as > GENTILISE
GENTLE *adj* mild or kindly ▷*vb* tame or subdue (a horse) ▷*n* maggot, esp when used as bait in fishing
GENTLED > GENTLE
GENTLEMAN *n* polite well-bred man
GENTLEMEN > GENTLEMAN
GENTLER > GENTLE
GENTLES > GENTLE
GENTLEST > GENTLE
GENTLING > GENTLE
GENTLY > GENTLE
GENTOO *n* grey-backed penguin
GENTOOS > GENTOO
GENTRICE *n* high birth
GENTRICES > GENTRICE
GENTRIES > GENTRY
GENTRIFY *vb* change the character of a neighbourhood by restoring property or introducing amenities that appeal to the middle classes
GENTRY *n* informal, often derogatory term for people just below the nobility in social rank
GENTS *n* men's public toilet
GENTY *adj* neat
GENU *n* any knee-like bend in a structure or part
GENUA > GENU
GENUFLECT *vb* bend the knee as a sign of reverence or deference
GENUINE *adj* not fake, authentic
GENUINELY > GENUINE
GENUS *n* group into which a family of animals or plants is divided
GENUSES > GENUS
GEO *n* (esp in Shetland) a small fjord or gully
GEOBOTANY *n* study of plants in relation to their geological habitat
GEOCARPIC > GEOCARPY
GEOCARPY *n* ripening of fruits below ground, as occurs in the peanut
GEOCORONA *n* outer layer of earth's atmosphere
GEODE *n* cavity, usually lined with crystals, within a rock mass or nodule
GEODES > GEODE
GEODESIC *adj* of the geometry of curved surfaces ▷*n* shortest line between two points on a curve
GEODESICS > GEODESIC
GEODESIES > GEODESY
GEODESIST > GEODESY
GEODESY *n* study of the shape and size of the earth
GEODETIC *same as* > GEODESIC
GEODETICS *same as* > GEODETIC
GEODIC > GEODE
GEODUCK *n* king clam

g

GEODUCKS > GEODUCK

GEOFACT n rock shaped by natural forces, as opposed to a manmade artefact

GEOFACTS > GEOFACT

GEOGENIES > GEOGENY

GEOGENY same as > GEOGONY

GEOGNOSES > GEOGNOSY

GEOGNOSIS same as > GEOGNOSY

GEOGNOST > GEOGNOSY

GEOGNOSTS > GEOGNOSY

GEOGNOSY n study of the origin and distribution of minerals and rocks in the earth's crust: superseded generally by the term 'geology'

GEOGONIC > GEOGONY

GEOGONIES > GEOGONY

GEOGONY n science of the earth's formation

GEOGRAPHY n study of the earth's physical features, climate, population, etc

GEOID n hypothetical surface that corresponds to mean sea level and extends at the same level under the continents

GEOIDAL > GEOID

GEOIDS > GEOID

GEOLATRY n worship of the earth

GEOLOGER > GEOLOGY

GEOLOGERS > GEOLOGY

GEOLOGIAN > GEOLOGY

GEOLOGIC > GEOLOGY

GEOLOGIES > GEOLOGY

GEOLOGISE same as > GEOLOGIZE

GEOLOGIST > GEOLOGY

GEOLOGIZE vb study the geological features of (an area)

GEOLOGY n study of the earth's origin, structure, and composition

GEOMANCER > GEOMANCY

GEOMANCY n prophecy from the pattern made when a handful of earth is cast down or dots are drawn at random and connected with lines

GEOMANT n geomancer

GEOMANTIC > GEOMANCY

GEOMANTS > GEOMANT

GEOMETER n person who is practised in or who studies geometry

GEOMETERS > GEOMETER

GEOMETRIC adj of geometry

GEOMETRID n any moth of the family Geometridae, the larvae of which are called measuring worms, inchworms, or loopers ▷ adj of, relating to, or belonging to the Geometridae

GEOMETRY n branch of mathematics dealing with points, lines, curves, and surfaces

GEOMYOID adj relating to burrowing rodents of the genus Geomys

GEOPHAGIA same as > GEOPHAGY

GEOPHAGY n practice of eating earth, clay, chalk, etc, found in some primitive tribes

GEOPHILIC adj soil-loving

GEOPHONE n device for recording seismic movement

GEOPHONES > GEOPHONE

GEOPHYTE n perennial plant that propagates by means of buds below the soil surface

GEOPHYTES > GEOPHYTE

GEOPHYTIC > GEOPHYTE

GEOPONIC adj of or relating to agriculture, esp as a science

GEOPONICS n science of agriculture

GEOPROBE n probing device used for sampling soil

GEOPROBES > GEOPROBE

GEORGETTE n fine silky fabric

GEORGIC adj agricultural ▷ n poem about rural or agricultural life

GEORGICAL same as > GEORGIC

GEORGICS > GEORGIC

GEOS > GEO

GEOSPHERE another name for > LITHOSPHERE

GEOSTATIC adj denoting or relating to the pressure exerted by a mass of rock or a similar substance

GEOTACTIC > GEOTAXIS

GEOTAXES > GEOTAXIS

GEOTAXIS n movement of an organism in response to the stimulus of gravity

GEOTHERM n line or surface within or on the earth connecting points of equal temperature

GEOTHERMS > GEOTHERM

GEOTROPIC adj of geotropism: the response of a plant to the stimulus of gravity

GERAH n ancient Hebrew unit of weight

GERAHS > GERAH

GERANIAL n cis- isomer of citral

GERANIALS > GERANIAL

GERANIOL n colourless or pale yellow terpine alcohol with an odour of roses, found in many essential oils: used in perfumery

GERANIOLS > GERANIOL

GERANIUM n cultivated plant with red, pink, or white flowers

GERANIUMS > GERANIUM

GERARDIA n any plant of the genus Gerardia

GERARDIAS > GERARDIA

GERBE same as > GARBE

GERBERA n any plant of the perennial genus Gerbera, esp the Barberton daisy from S. Africa, G. jamesonii, grown, usually as a greenhouse plant, for its large brightly coloured daisy-like flowers: family Asteraceae

GERBERAS > GERBERA

GERBES > GARBE

GERBIL n burrowing desert rodent of Asia and Africa

GERBILLE same as > GERBIL

GERBILLES > GERBILLE

GERBILS > GERBIL

GERE Spenserian spelling of > GEAR

GERENT n person who rules or manages

GERENTS > GERENT

GERENUK n slender E African antelope, Litocranius walleri, with a long thin neck and backward-curving horns

GERENUKS > GERENUK

GERES > GEAR

GERFALCON same as > GYRFALCON

GERIATRIC n derogatory term for old person ▷ adj of geriatrics or old people

GERLE Spenserian spelling of > GIRL

GERLES > GERLE

GERM n microbe, esp one causing disease ▷ vb sprout

GERMAIN same as > GERMEN

GERMAINE same as > GERMEN

GERMAINES > GERMAINE

GERMAINS > GERMAIN

GERMAN n dance consisting of complicated figures and changes of partners ▷ adj having the same parents as oneself

GERMANDER n any of several plants of the genus Teucrium

GERMANE adj relevant

GERMANELY > GERMANE

GERMANIC adj of or containing germanium in the tetravalent state

GERMANISE same as > GERMANIZE

GERMANITE n mineral consisting of a complex copper arsenic sulphide containing germanium, gallium, iron, zinc, and lead: an ore of germanium and gallium

GERMANIUM n brittle grey element that is a semiconductor

GERMANIZE vb adopt or cause to adopt German customs, speech, institutions, etc

GERMANOUS adj of or containing germanium in the divalent state

GERMANS > GERMAN

GERMED > GERM

GERMEN n mass of undifferentiated cells that gives rise to the germ cells

GERMENS > GERMEN

GERMFREE > GERM

GERMICIDE n substance that kills germs

GERMIER > GERMY

GERMIEST > GERMY

GERMIN same as > GERMEN

GERMINA > GERMEN

GERMINAL adj of or in the earliest stage of development

GERMINANT adj in the process of germinating

GERMINATE vb (cause to) sprout or begin to grow

GERMINESS > GERMY

GERMING > GERM

GERMINS > GERMIN

GERMLIKE > GERM

GERMPLASM n plant genetic material

GERMPROOF adj protected against the penetration of germs

GERMS > GERM

GERMY adj full of germs

GERNE vb grin

GERNED > GERNE

GERNES > GERNE

GERNING > GERNE

GERONIMO interj shout given by US paratroopers as they jump into battle

GERONTIC adj of or relating to the senescence of an organism

GEROPIGA n grape syrup used to sweeten inferior port wines

GEROPIGAS > GEROPIGA

GERT adv in dialect, great or very big

GERTCHA interj get out of here!

GERUND n noun formed from a verb

GERUNDIAL > GERUND

GERUNDIVE n (in Latin grammar) an adjective formed from a verb, expressing the desirability of the activity denoted by the verb ▷ adj of or relating to the gerund or gerundive

GERUNDS > GERUND

GESNERIA n any plant of the mostly tuberous-rooted S. American genus Gesneria, grown as a greenhouse plant for its large leaves and showy tubular flowers in a range of bright colours: family Gesneriaceae

GESNERIAD > GESNERIA

GESNERIAS > GESNERIA

GESSAMINE another word for > JASMINE

GESSE Spenserian spelling of > GUESS

GESSED > GESS

GESSES > GESS

GESSING > GESS

GESSO n plaster used for painting or in sculpture ▷ vb apply gesso to

GESSOED > GESSO

GESSOES > GESSO

GEST n notable deed or exploit

GESTALT n perceptual pattern or structure possessing qualities as a whole that cannot be described merely as a sum of its parts

GESTALTEN > GESTALT

GESTALTS > GESTALT

GESTANT adj laden

GESTAPO n any secret state police organization

GESTAPOS > GESTAPO

GESTATE vb carry (developing young) in the uterus during pregnancy

GESTATED > GESTATE

GESTATES > GESTATE

GESTATING > GESTATE

GESTATION n (period of) carrying of young in the womb between conception and birth

GESTATIVE > GESTATION

GESTATORY > GESTATION

GESTE same as > GEST

GESTES > GESTE

GESTIC adj consisting of gestures

GESTICAL > GESTIC

GESTS > GEST

GESTURAL > GESTURE

GESTURE n movement to convey meaning ▷ vb gesticulate

GESTURED > GESTURE

GESTURER > GESTURE

GESTURERS > GESTURE

GESTURES > GESTURE

GESTURING > GESTURE

GET vb obtain or receive

GETA n type of Japanese wooden sandal

GETABLE > GET

GETAS > GETA

GETATABLE adj accessible

GETAWAY n used in escape

GETAWAYS > GETAWAY

GETS > GET

GETTABLE > GET

GETTER n person or thing that gets ▷ vb remove (a gas) by the action of a getter

GETTERED > GETTER

GETTERING > GETTER

GETTERS > GETTER

GETTING > GET

GETTINGS > GET

GETUP n outfit

GETUPS > GETUP

GEUM n any herbaceous plant of the rosaceous genus Geum, having compound leaves and red, orange, or white flowers

GEUMS > GEUM

GEWGAW n showy but valueless trinket ▷ adj showy and valueless

GEWGAWED adj decorated gaudily

GEWGAWS > GEWGAW

GEY adv extremely ▷ adj gallant

GEYAN adv somewhat

GEYER > GEY

GEYEST > GEY

GEYSER n spring that discharges steam and hot water

GEYSERITE n mineral form of hydrated silica resembling opal, deposited from the waters of geysers and hot springs

GEYSERS > GEYSER

GHARIAL same as > GAVIAL

GHARIALS > GHARIAL

GHARRI same as > GHARRY

GHARRIES > GHARRY

GHARRIS > GHARRI

GHARRY n (in India) horse-drawn vehicle available for hire

GHAST vb terrify

GHASTED > GHAST

GHASTFUL adj dismal

GHASTING > GHAST

GHASTLIER > GHASTLY

GHASTLY adj unpleasant ▷ adv unhealthily

GHASTNESS n dread

GHASTS > GHAST

GHAT n (in India) steps leading down to a river

GHATS > GHAT

GHAUT n small cleft in a hill through which a rivulet runs down to the sea

GHAUTS > GHAUT

GHAZAL n Arabic love poem

GHAZALS > GHAZAL

GHAZEL same as > GHAZAL

GHAZELS > GHAZEL

GHAZI n Muslim fighter against infidels

GHAZIES > GHAZI

GHAZIS > GHAZI

GHEE n (in Indian cookery) clarified butter

GHEES > GHEE

GHERAO n form of industrial action in India in which workers imprison their employers on the premises until their demands are met ▷ vb trap an employer in his office, to indicate the workforce's discontent

GHERAOED > GHERAO

GHERAOES > GHERAO

GHERAOING > GHERAO

GHERAOS > GHERAO

GHERKIN n small pickled cucumber

GHERKINS > GHERKIN

GHESSE Spenserian spelling of > GUESS

GHESSED > GHESS

GHESSES > GHESS

GHESSING > GHESS

GHEST > GHESS

GHETTO n slum area inhabited by a deprived minority ▷ vb ghettoize

GHETTOED > GHETTO

GHETTOES > GHETTO

GHETTOING > GHETTO

GHETTOISE same as > GHETTOIZE

GHETTOIZE vb confine (someone or something) to a particular area or category

GHETTOS > GHETTO

GHI same as > GHEE

GHIBLI n fiercely hot wind of North Africa

GHIBLIS > GHIBLI

GHILGAI same as > GILGAI

GHILGAIS > GHILGAI

GHILLIE n type of tongueless shoe with lacing up the instep, originally worn by the Scots ▷ vb act as a g(h)illie

GHILLIED > GHILLIE

GHILLIES > GHILLIE

GHILLYING > GHILLIE

GHIS > GHI

GHOST n disembodied spirit of a dead person ▷ vb ghostwrite

GHOSTED > GHOST

GHOSTIER > GHOSTY

GHOSTIEST > GHOSTY

GHOSTING > GHOST

GHOSTINGS > GHOST

GHOSTLIER > GHOSTLY

GHOSTLIKE > GHOST

GHOSTLY adj frightening in appearance or effect

GHOSTS > GHOST

GHOSTY adj pertaining to ghosts

GHOUL n person with morbid interests

GHOULIE n goblin

GHOULIES > GHOULIE

GHOULISH adj of or relating to ghouls

GHOULS > GHOUL

GHYLL same as > GILL

GHYLLS > GHYLL

GI n loose-fitting white suit worn in judo, karate, and other martial arts

GIAMBEUX n jambeaux; leg armour

GIANT n mythical being of superhuman size ▷ adj huge

GIANTESS same as > GIANT

GIANTHOOD n condition of being a giant

GIANTISM same as > GIGANTISM

GIANTISMS > GIANTISM

GIANTLIER > GIANTLY

GIANTLIKE > GIANT

GIANTLY adj giantlike

GIANTRIES > GIANTRY

GIANTRY n collective term for giants

GIANTS > GIANT

GIANTSHIP n style of address for a giant

GIAOUR n derogatory term for a non-Muslim, esp a Christian, used esp by the Turks

GIAOURS > GIAOUR

GIARDIA n species of parasite

GIARDIAS > GIARDIA

GIB n metal wedge, pad, or thrust bearing, esp a brass plate let into a steam engine crosshead ▷ vb fasten or supply with a gib

GIBBED > GIB

GIBBER vb speak or utter rapidly and unintelligibly ▷ n boulder

GIBBERED > GIBBER

GIBBERING > GIBBER

GIBBERISH n rapid unintelligible talk

GIBBERS > GIBBER

GIBBET n gallows for displaying executed criminals ▷ vb put to death by hanging on a gibbet

GIBBETED > GIBBET

GIBBETING > GIBBET

GIBBETS > GIBBET

GIBBETTED > GIBBET

GIBBING > GIB

GIBBON n agile tree-dwelling ape of S Asia

GIBBONS > GIBBON

GIBBOSE same as > GIBBOUS

GIBBOSITY n state of being gibbous

GIBBOUS adj (of the moon) more than half but less than fully illuminated

GIBBOUSLY > GIBBOUS

GIBBSITE n mineral consisting of hydrated aluminium oxide

GIBBSITES > GIBBSITE

GIBE vb make jeering or scoffing remarks (at) ▷ n derisive or provoking remark

GIBED > GIBE

GIBEL n Prussian carp

GIBELS > GIBEL

GIBER > GIBE

GIBERS > GIBE

GIBES > GIBE

GIBING > GIBE

GIBINGLY > GIBE

GIBLET > GIBLETS

GIBLETS pl n gizzard, liver, heart, and neck of a fowl

GIBLI same as > GHIBLI

GIBLIS > GIBLI

GIBS > GIB

GIBSON n martini garnished with onion

GIBSONS > GIBSON

GIBUS n collapsible top hat operated by a spring

GIBUSES > GIBUS

GID n disease of sheep characterized by an unsteady gait and staggering, caused by infestation of the brain with tapeworms (Taenia caenuris)

GIDDAP interj exclamation used to make a horse go faster

GIDDAY interj expression of greeting

GIDDIED > GIDDY

GIDDIER > GIDDY

GIDDIES > GIDDY

GIDDIEST > GIDDY

GIDDILY > GIDDY

GIDDINESS > GIDDY

GIDDUP same as > GIDDYUP

GIDDY adj having or causing a feeling of dizziness ▷ vb make giddy

GIDDYAP same as > GIDDYUP

GIDDYING > GIDDY

GIDDYUP interj exclamation used to make a horse go faster

GIDGEE n small acacia tree, which at times emits an unpleasant smell

GIDGEES > GIDGEE

GIDJEE same as > GIDGEE

GIDJEES > GIDJEE

GIDS > GID

GIE Scot word for > GIVE

GIED > GIVE

GIEING > GIVE

GIEN > GIVE

GIES > GIVE

GIF obsolete word for > IF

GIFT n present ▷ vb make a present of

GIFTABLE adj suitable as gift ▷ n something suitable as gift

GIFTABLES > GIFTABLE

GIFTED adj talented

GIFTEDLY > GIFTED

GIFTEE n person given a gift

GIFTEES > GIFTEE

GIFTING > GIFT

GIFTLESS > GIFT

GIFTS > GIFT

GIFTSHOP n shop selling articles suitable for gifts

GIFTSHOPS > GIFTSHOP

GIFTWARE n anything that may be given as a present

GIFTWARES > GIFTWARE

GIFTWRAP vb wrap (a gift) in decorative wrapping paper

GIFTWRAPS > GIFTWRAP

GIG n single performance by pop or jazz musicians ▷ vb play a gig or gigs

GIGA same as > GIGUE

GIGABIT n unit of information in computing

GIGABITS > GIGABIT

GIGABYTE n one thousand and twenty-four megabytes

GIGABYTES > GIGABYTE

GIGACYCLE same as > GIGAHERTZ

GIGAFLOP n measure of processing speed, consisting of a thousand million floating-point operations a second

GIGAFLOPS > GIGAFLOP

GIGAHERTZ n unit of frequency equal to 10⁹ hertz.

GIGANTEAN adj gigantic

GIGANTIC adj enormous

GIGANTISM n excessive growth of the entire body, caused by overproduction of growth hormone by the pituitary gland during childhood or adolescence

GIGAS > GIGA

GIGATON n unit of explosive force

GIGATONS > GIGATON

GIGAWATT n unit of power equal to 1 billion watts

GIGAWATTS > GIGAWATT

GIGGED > GIG

GIGGING > GIG

GIGGIT vb move quickly

GIGGITED > GIGGIT

GIGGITING > GIGGIT

GIGGITS > GIGGIT

GIGGLE vb laugh nervously or foolishly ▷ n such a laugh

GIGGLED > GIGGLE

GIGGLER > GIGGLE

GIGGLERS > GIGGLE

GIGGLES > GIGGLE

GIGGLIER > GIGGLE

GIGGLIEST > GIGGLE

GIGGLING > GIGGLE

GIGGLINGS > GIGGLE

GIGGLY > GIGGLE

GIGHE > GIGA

GIGLET n flighty girl

GIGLETS > GIGLET

GIGLOT same as > GIGLET

GIGLOTS > GIGLOT

GIGMAN n one who places great importance on respectability

GIGMANITY > GIGMAN

GIGMEN > GIGMAN

GIGOLO n man paid by an older woman to be her escort or lover

GIGOLOS > GIGOLO

GIGOT n leg of lamb or mutton

GIGOTS > GIGOT

GIGS > GIG

GIGUE n piece of music, usually in six-eight time and often fugal, incorporated into the classical suite

GIGUES > GIGUE

GILA n large venomous brightly coloured lizard

GILAS > GILA

GILBERT n unit of magnetomotive force

GILBERTS > GILBERT

GILCUP same as > GILTCUP

GILCUPS > GILCUP

GILD vb put a thin layer of gold on

GILDED > GILD

GILDEN adj gilded

GILDER > GILD

GILDERS > GILD

GILDHALL same as > GUILDHALL

GILDHALLS > GILDHALL

GILDING > GILD

GILDINGS > GILD

GILDS > GILD

GILDSMAN > GILD

GILDSMEN > GILD

GILET n waist- or hip-length garment, usually sleeveless, fastening up the front

GILETS > GILET

GILGAI n natural water hole

GILGAIS > GILGAI

GILGIE n type of freshwater crayfish

GILGIES > GILGIE

GILL n radiating structure beneath the cap of a mushroom ▷ vb catch (fish) or (of fish) to be caught in a gill net

GILLAROO n type of brown trout

GILLAROOS > GILLAROO

GILLED > GILL

GILLER > GILL

GILLERS > GILL

GILLET n mare

GILLETS > GILLET

GILLFLIRT n flirtatious woman

GILLIE n (in Scotland) attendant for hunting or fishing ▷ vb act as a gillie

GILLIED > GILLIE

GILLIES > GILLY

GILLING > GILL

GILLION n (no longer in technical use) one thousand million

GILLIONS > GILLION

GILLNET n net designed to catch fish by the gills ▷ vb fish using a gillnet

GILLNETS > GILLNET

GILLS pl n breathing organs in fish and other water creatures

GILLY vb act as a gillie

GILLYING > GILLY

GILLYVOR n type of carnation

GILLYVORS > GILLYVOR

GILPEY n mischievous, frolicsome boy or girl

GILPEYS > GILPEY

GILPIES > GILPIE

GILPY same as > GILPEY

GILRAVAGE vb make merry, especially to excess

GILSONITE n very pure form of asphalt found in Utah and Colorado

GILT > GILD

GILTCUP n buttercup

GILTCUPS > GILTCUP

GILTHEAD n sparid fish, Sparus aurata, of Mediterranean and European Atlantic waters, having a gold-coloured band between the eyes

GILTHEADS > GILTHEAD

GILTS > GILD

GILTWOOD adj made of wood and gilded

GIMBAL vb support on gimbals

GIMBALED > GIMBAL

GIMBALING > GIMBAL

GIMBALLED > GIMBAL

GIMBALS pl n set of pivoted rings which allow nautical instruments to remain horizontal at sea

GIMCRACK adj showy but cheap ▷ n cheap showy trifle or gadget

GIMCRACKS > GIMCRACK

GIMEL n third letter of the Hebrew alphabet

GIMELS > GIMEL

GIMLET n small tool with a screwlike tip for boring holes in wood ▷ adj penetrating or piercing ▷ vb make holes in (wood) using a gimlet

GIMLETED > GIMLET

GIMLETING > GIMLET

GIMLETS > GIMLET

GIMMAL n ring composed of interlocking rings ▷ vb provide with gimmals

GIMMALLED > GIMMAL

GIMMALS > GIMMAL

GIMME interj give me! ▷ n short putt that one is excused by one's opponent from playing because it is considered too easy to miss

GIMMER n year-old ewe

GIMMERS > GIMMER

GIMMES > GIMME

GIMMICK n something designed to attract attention or publicity ▷ vb make gimmicky

GIMMICKED > GIMMICK

GIMMICKRY > GIMMICK

GIMMICKS > GIMMICK

GIMMICKY > GIMMICK

GIMMIE n in golf, an easy putt conceded to one's opponent

GIMMIES > GIMMIE

GIMMOR n mechanical device

GIMMORS > GIMMOR

GIMP n tapelike trimming of silk, wool, or cotton, often stiffened with wire ▷ vb derogatory term for limp

GIMPED > GIMP

GIMPIER > GIMPY

GIMPIEST > GIMPY

GIMPING > GIMP

GIMPS > GIMP

GIMPY same as > GAMMY

GIN n spirit flavoured with juniper berries ▷ vb free (cotton) of seeds with a gin; begin

GING n child's catapult

GINGAL n type of musket mounted on a swivel

GINGALL same as > GINGAL

GINGALLS > GINGALL

GINGALS > GINGAL

GINGE n person with ginger hair

GINGELEY same as > GINGILI

GINGELEYS > GINGELEY

GINGELI same as > GINGILI

GINGELIES > GINGELY

GINGELIS > GINGELI

GINGELLI same as > GINGILI

GINGELLIS > GINGILI

GINGELLY same as > GINGILI

GINGELY same as > GINGILI

GINGER n root of a tropical plant, used as a spice ▷ adj light reddish-brown ▷ vb add the spice ginger to (a dish)

GINGERADE n fizzy drink flavoured with ginger

GINGERED > GINGER

GINGERING > GINGER

GINGERLY adv cautiously ▷ adj cautious
GINGEROUS adj reddish
GINGERS > GINGER
GINGERY adj like or tasting of ginger
GINGES > GINGE
GINGHAM n cotton cloth, usu checked or striped
GINGHAMS > GINGHAM
GINGILI n oil obtained from sesame seeds
GINGILIS > GINGILI
GINGILLI same as > GINGILI
GINGILLIS > GINGILLI
GINGIVA same as > GUM
GINGIVAE > GINGIVA
GINGIVAL > GINGIVA
GINGKO same as > GINKGO
GINGKOES > GINGKO
GINGKOS > GINGKO
GINGLE same as > JINGLE
GINGLES > GINGLE
GINGLYMI > GINGLYMUS
GINGLYMUS n hinge joint
GINGS > GING
GINHOUSE n building where cotton is ginned
GINHOUSES > GINHOUSE
GINK n man or boy, esp one considered to be odd
GINKGO n ornamental Chinese tree
GINKGOES > GINKGO
GINKGOS > GINKGO
GINKS > GINK
GINN same as > JINN
GINNED > GIN
GINNEL n narrow passageway between buildings
GINNELS > GINNEL
GINNER > GIN
GINNERIES > GINHOUSE
GINNERS > GIN
GINNERY another word for > GINHOUSE
GINNIER > GINNY
GINNIEST > GINNY
GINNING > GIN
GINNINGS > GIN
GINNY adj relating to the spirit gin
GINORMOUS adj very large
GINS > GIN
GINSENG n (root of) a plant believed to have tonic and energy-giving properties
GINSENGS > GINSENG
GINSHOP n tavern
GINSHOPS > GINSHOP
GINZO n disparaging term for person of Italian descent
GINZOES > GINZO
GIO same as > GEO
GIOCOSO adv (of music) to be expressed joyfully or playfully
GIOS > GIO
GIP same as > GYP
GIPON another word for > JUPON
GIPONS > GIPON
GIPPED > GIP
GIPPER > GIP
GIPPERS > GIP

GIPPIES > GIPPY
GIPPING > GIP
GIPPO same as > GIPPY
GIPPOES > GIPPO
GIPPOS > GIPPO
GIPPY n starling
GIPS > GIP
GIPSEN obsolete word for > GYPSY
GIPSENS > GIPSEN
GIPSIED > GIPSY
GIPSIES > GIPSY
GIPSY n member of a nomadic people scattered throughout Europe and North America ▷ vb live like a gypsy
GIPSYDOM > GIPSY
GIPSYDOMS > GIPSY
GIPSYHOOD > GIPSY
GIPSYING > GIPSY
GIPSYISH > GIPSY
GIPSYWORT n hairy Eurasian plant, Lycopus europaeus, having two-lipped white flowers with purple dots on the lower lip: family Lamiaceae (labiates)
GIRAFFE n African ruminant mammal with a spotted yellow skin and long neck and legs
GIRAFFES > GIRAFFE
GIRAFFID adj giraffe-like
GIRAFFINE adj relating to a giraffe
GIRAFFISH > GIRAFFE
GIRAFFOID adj giraffe-like
GIRANDOLA same as > GIRANDOLE
GIRANDOLE n ornamental branched wall candleholder, usually incorporating a mirror
GIRASOL n type of opal that has a red or pink glow in bright light
GIRASOLE same as > GIRASOL
GIRASOLES > GIRASOLE
GIRASOLS > GIRASOL
GIRD vb put a belt round ▷ n blow or stroke
GIRDED > GIRD
GIRDER n large metal beam
GIRDERS > GIRDER
GIRDING > GIRD
GIRDINGLY > GIRD
GIRDINGS > GIRD
GIRDLE n woman's elastic corset ▷ vb surround or encircle
GIRDLED > GIRDLE
GIRDLER n person or thing that girdles
GIRDLERS > GIRDLER
GIRDLES > GIRDLE
GIRDLING > GIRDLE
GIRDS > GIRD
GIRKIN same as > GHERKIN
GIRKINS > GIRKIN
GIRL n female child
GIRLHOOD n state or time of being a girl
GIRLHOODS > GIRLHOOD
GIRLIE adj (of a magazine, calendar, etc) featuring pictures of naked or

scantily clad women ▷ n little girl
GIRLIER > GIRLY
GIRLIES > GIRLIE
GIRLIEST > GIRLY
GIRLISH adj of or like a girl in looks, behaviour, innocence, etc
GIRLISHLY > GIRLISH
GIRLOND obsolete word for > GARLAND
GIRLONDS > GIRLOND
GIRLS > GIRL
GIRLY same as > GIRLIE
GIRN vb snarl
GIRNED > GIRN
GIRNEL n large chest for storing meal
GIRNELS > GIRNEL
GIRNER > GIRN
GIRNERS > GIRN
GIRNEL adj peevish
GIRNIER > GIRNIE
GIRNIEST > GIRNIE
GIRNING > GIRN
GIRNS > GIRN
GIRO n (in some countries) system of transferring money within a post office or bank directly from one account to another
GIROLLE another word for > CHANTERELLE
GIROLLES > GIROLLE
GIRON n charge consisting of the lower half of a diagonally divided quarter, usually in the top left corner of the shield
GIRONIC > GIRON
GIRONNY adj divided into segments from the fesse point
GIRONS > GIRON
GIROS > GIRO
GIROSOL same as > GIRASOL
GIROSOLS > GIROSOL
GIRR same as > GIRD
GIRRS > GIRR
GIRSH n currency unit of Saudi Arabia
GIRSHES > GIRSH
GIRT vb gird; bind
GIRTED > GIRT
GIRTH n measurement round something ▷ vb fasten a girth on (a horse)
GIRTHED > GIRTH
GIRTHING > GIRTH
GIRTHLINE same as > GIRTLINE
GIRTHS > GIRTH
GIRTING > GIRT
GIRTLINE n gantline
GIRTLINES > GIRTLINE
GIRTS > GIRT
GIS > GI
GISARME n long-shafted battle-axe with a sharp point on the back of the axe head
GISARMES > GISARME
GISM n semen
GISMO same as > GIZMO
GISMOLOGY same as > GIZMOLOGY
GISMOS > GISMO

GISMS > GISM
GIST n substance or main point of a matter
GISTS > GIST
GIT n contemptible person ▷ vb dialect version of get
GITANA n female gypsy
GITANAS > GITANA
GITANO n male gypsy
GITANOS > GITANO
GITE n self-catering holiday cottage for let in France
GITES > GITE
GITS > GIT
GITTARONE n acoustic bass guitar
GITTED > GIT
GITTERN n obsolete medieval stringed instrument resembling the guitar ▷ vb play the gittern
GITTERNED > GITTERN
GITTERNS > GITTERN
GITTIN n Jewish divorce
GITTING > GIT
GIUST same as > JOUST
GIUSTED > GIUST
GIUSTING > GIUST
GIUSTO adv be observed strictly
GIUSTS > GIUST
GIVABLE > GIVE
GIVE vb present (something) to another person ▷ n resilience or elasticity
GIVEABLE > GIVE
GIVEAWAY n something that reveals hidden feelings or intentions ▷ adj very cheap or free
GIVEAWAYS > GIVEAWAY
GIVEBACK n reduction in wages in return for some other benefit, in time of recession
GIVEBACKS > GIVEBACK
GIVED same as > GYVED
GIVEN n assumed fact
GIVENNESS n condition of being given
GIVENS > GIVEN
GIVER > GIVE
GIVERS > GIVE
GIVES > GIVE
GIVING > GIVE
GIVINGS > GIVE
GIZMO n device
GIZMOLOGY n study of gadgets
GIZMOS > GIZMO
GIZZ n wig
GIZZARD n part of a bird's stomach
GIZZARDS > GIZZARD
GIZZEN vb (of wood) to warp
GIZZENED > GIZZEN
GIZZENING > GIZZEN
GIZZENS > GIZZEN
GIZZES > GIZZ
GJETOST n type of Norwegian cheese
GJETOSTS > GJETOST
GJU n type of violin used in Shetland
GJUS > GJU

g

GLABELLA *n* smooth elevation of the frontal bone just above the bridge of the nose: a reference point in physical anthropology or craniometry

GLABELLAE > GLABELLA

GLABELLAR > GLABELLA

GLABRATE *same as* > GLABROUS

GLABROUS *adj* without hair or a similar growth

GLACE *adj* preserved in a thick sugary syrup ▷ *vb* ice or candy (cakes, fruits, etc)

GLACEED > GLACE

GLACEING > GLACE

GLACES > GLACE

GLACIAL *adj* of ice or glaciers ▷ *n* ice age

GLACIALLY > GLACIAL

GLACIALS > GLACIAL

GLACIATE *vb* cover or become covered with glaciers or masses of ice

GLACIATED > GLACIATE

GLACIATES > GLACIATE

GLACIER *n* slow-moving mass of ice formed by accumulated snow

GLACIERED *adj* having a glacier or glaciers

GLACIERS > GLACIER

GLACIS *n* slight incline

GLACISES > GLACIS

GLAD *adj* pleased and happy ▷ *vb* become glad ▷ *n* gladiolus

GLADDED > GLAD

GLADDEN *vb* make glad

GLADDENED > GLADDEN

GLADDENER > GLADDEN

GLADDENS > GLADDEN

GLADDER > GLAD

GLADDEST > GLAD

GLADDIE *same as* > GLAD

GLADDIES > GLADDIE

GLADDING > GLAD

GLADDON *n* stinking iris

GLADDONS > GLADDON

GLADE *n* open space in a forest

GLADELIKE > GLADE

GLADES > GLADE

GLADFUL *adj* full of gladness

GLADIATE *adj* shaped like a sword

GLADIATOR *n* (in ancient Rome) man trained to fight in arenas to provide entertainment

GLADIER > GLADE

GLADIEST > GLADE

GLADIOLA *same as* > GLADIOLUS

GLADIOLAR > GLADIOLUS

GLADIOLAS > GLADIOLA

GLADIOLE *same as* > GLADIOLUS

GLADIOLES > GLADIOLE

GLADIOLI > GLADIOLUS

GLADIOLUS *n* garden plant with sword-shaped leaves

GLADIUS *n* short sword used by Roman legionaries

GLADIUSES > GLADIUS

GLADLIER > GLAD

GLADLIEST > GLAD

GLADLY > GLAD

GLADNESS > GLAD

GLADS > GLAD

GLADSOME *adj* joyous or cheerful

GLADSOMER > GLADSOME

GLADSTONE *n* light four-wheeled horse-drawn vehicle

GLADWRAP *n* in New Zealand English, thin film for wrapping food ▷ *vb* cover with gladwrap

GLADWRAPS > GLADWRAP

GLADY > GLADE

GLAIK *n* prank

GLAIKET *same as* > GLAIKIT

GLAIKIT *adj* foolish

GLAIKS > GLAIK

GLAIR *n* white of egg, esp when used as a size, glaze, or adhesive, usually in bookbinding ▷ *vb* apply glair to (something)

GLAIRE *same as* > GLAIR

GLAIRED > GLAIR

GLAIREOUS > GLAIR

GLAIRES > GLAIRE

GLAIRIER > GLAIR

GLAIRIEST > GLAIR

GLAIRIN *n* viscous deposit found in some mineral waters

GLAIRING > GLAIR

GLAIRINS > GLAIRIN

GLAIRS > GLAIR

GLAIRY > GLAIR

GLAIVE *archaic word for* > SWORD

GLAIVED *adj* armed with a sword

GLAIVES > GLAIVE

GLAM *n* magical illusion

GLAMOR *same as* > GLAMOUR

GLAMORED > GLAMOR

GLAMORING > GLAMOR

GLAMORISE *same as* > GLAMORIZE

GLAMORIZE *vb* cause to be or seem glamorous

GLAMOROUS *adj* alluring

GLAMORS > GLAMOR

GLAMOUR *n* alluring charm or fascination ▷ *vb* bewitch

GLAMOURED > GLAMOUR

GLAMOURS > GLAMOUR

GLAMS > GLAM

GLANCE *vb* look rapidly or briefly ▷ *n* brief look

GLANCED > GLANCE

GLANCER *n* log or pole used to protect standing trees from damage

GLANCERS > GLANCER

GLANCES > GLANCE

GLANCING > GLANCE

GLANCINGS > GLANCE

GLAND *n* organ that produces and secretes substances in the body

GLANDERED > GLANDERS

GLANDERS *n* highly infectious bacterial disease of horses, sometimes transmitted to man, caused by *Actinobacillus mallei* and characterized by inflammation and ulceration of the mucous membranes of the air passages, skin, and lymph glands

GLANDES > GLANS

GLANDLESS > GLAND

GLANDLIKE > GLAND

GLANDS > GLAND

GLANDULAR *adj* of or affecting a gland or glands

GLANDULE *n* small gland

GLANDULES > GLANDULE

GLANS *n* any small rounded body or glandlike mass, such as the head of the penis

GLARE *vb* stare angrily ▷ *n* angry stare ▷ *adj* smooth and glassy

GLAREAL *adj* (of a plant) growing in cultivated land

GLARED > GLARE

GLARELESS > GLARE

GLAREOUS *adj* resembling the white of an egg

GLARES > GLARE

GLARIER > GLARE

GLARIEST > GLARE

GLARINESS > GLARE

GLARING *adj* conspicuous

GLARINGLY > GLARING

GLARY > GLARE

GLASNOST *n* policy of openness and accountability, esp, formerly, in the USSR

GLASNOSTS > GLASNOST

GLASS *n* hard brittle, usu transparent substance consisting of metal silicates or similar compounds ▷ *vb* cover with, enclose in, or fit with glass

GLASSED > GLASS

GLASSEN *adj* glassy

GLASSES *pl n* pair of lenses for correcting faulty vision, in a frame that rests on the nose and hooks behind the ears

GLASSFUL *n* amount held by a full glass

GLASSFULS > GLASSFUL

GLASSIE *same as* > GLASSY

GLASSIER > GLASSY

GLASSIES > GLASSY

GLASSIEST > GLASSY

GLASSIFY *vb* turn into glass

GLASSILY > GLASSY

GLASSINE *n* glazed translucent paper used for book jackets

GLASSINES > GLASSINE

GLASSING > GLASS

GLASSLESS > GLASS

GLASSLIKE > GLASS

GLASSMAN *n* man whose work is making or selling glassware

GLASSMEN > GLASSMAN

GLASSWARE *n* articles made of glass

GLASSWORK *n* production of glassware

GLASSWORM *n* larva of gnat

GLASSWORT *n* any plant of the chenopodiaceous genus *Salicornia*, of salt marshes, having fleshy stems and scalelike leaves: formerly used as a source of soda for glass-making

GLASSY *adj* like glass ▷ *n* glass marble

GLAUCOMA *n* eye disease

GLAUCOMAS > GLAUCOMA

GLAUCOUS *adj* covered with a bluish waxy or powdery bloom

GLAUM *vb* snatch

GLAUMED > GLAUM

GLAUMING > GLAUM

GLAUMS > GLAUM

GLAUR *n* mud or mire

GLAURIER > GLAUR

GLAURIEST > GLAUR

GLAURS > GLAUR

GLAURY > GLAUR

GLAZE *vb* fit or cover with glass ▷ *n* transparent coating

GLAZED > GLAZE

GLAZEN *adj* glazed

GLAZER > GLAZE

GLAZERS > GLAZE

GLAZES > GLAZE

GLAZIER *n* person who fits windows with glass

GLAZIERS > GLAZIER

GLAZIERY > GLAZIER

GLAZIEST > GLAZE

GLAZILY > GLAZE

GLAZINESS > GLAZE

GLAZING *n* surface of a glazed object

GLAZINGS > GLAZING

GLAZY > GLAZE

GLEAM *n* small beam or glow of light ▷ *vb* emit a gleam

GLEAMED > GLEAM

GLEAMER *n* mirror used to cheat in card games

GLEAMERS > GLEAMER

GLEAMIER > GLEAM

GLEAMIEST > GLEAM

GLEAMING > GLEAM

GLEAMINGS > GLEAM

GLEAMS > GLEAM

GLEAMY > GLEAM

GLEAN *vb* gather (facts etc) bit by bit

GLEANABLE > GLEAN

GLEANED > GLEAN

GLEANER > GLEAN

GLEANERS > GLEAN

GLEANING > GLEAN

GLEANINGS *pl n* pieces of information that have been gleaned

GLEANS > GLEAN

GLEAVE *same as* > SWORD

GLEAVES > GLEAVE

GLEBA *n* mass of spores

GLEBAE > GLEBA

GLEBE *n* land granted to a member of the clergy as part of his or her benefice

GLEBELESS > GLEBE

GLEBES > GLEBE
GLEBOUS adj gleby
GLEBY adj relating to a glebe
GLED n kite
GLEDE same as > GLED
GLEDES > GLEDE
GLEDGE vb glance sideways
GLEDGED > GLEDGE
GLEDGES > GLEDGE
GLEDGING > GLEDGE
GLEDS > GLED
GLEE n triumph and delight ▷vb be full of glee
GLEED n burning ember or hot coal
GLEEDS > GLEED
GLEEFUL adj merry or joyful, esp over someone else's mistake or misfortune
GLEEFULLY > GLEEFUL
GLEEING > GLEE
GLEEK vb jeer
GLEEKED > GLEEK
GLEEKING > GLEEK
GLEEKS > GLEEK
GLEEMAN n minstrel
GLEEMEN > GLEEMAN
GLEENIE n guinea fowl
GLEENIES > GLEENIE
GLEES > GLEE
GLEESOME adj full of glee
GLEET n inflammation of the urethra with a slight discharge of thin pus and mucus: a stage of chronic gonorrhoea ▷vb discharge gleet
GLEETED > GLEET
GLEETIER > GLEET
GLEETIEST > GLEET
GLEETING > GLEET
GLEETS > GLEET
GLEETY > GLEET
GLEG adj quick
GLEGGER > GLEG
GLEGGEST > GLEG
GLEGLY > GLEG
GLEGNESS > GLEG
GLEI same as > GLEY
GLEIS > GLEI
GLEN n deep narrow valley, esp in Scotland
GLENGARRY n brimless Scottish cap with a crease down the crown
GLENLIKE > GLEN
GLENOID adj resembling or having a shallow cavity ▷n shallow cavity
GLENOIDAL > GLENOID
GLENOIDS > GLENOID
GLENS > GLEN
GLENT same as > GLINT
GLENTED > GLENT
GLENTING > GLENT
GLENTS > GLENT
GLEY n bluish-grey compact sticky soil occurring in certain humid regions ▷vb squint
GLEYED > GLEY
GLEYING > GLEY
GLEYINGS > GLEY
GLEYS > GLEY
GLIA n delicate web of connective tissue that surrounds and supports

nerve cells
GLIADIN n protein of cereals, esp wheat, with a high proline content: forms a sticky mass with water that binds flour into dough
GLIADINE same as > GLIADIN
GLIADINES > GLIADINE
GLIADINS > GLIADIN
GLIAL > GLIA
GLIAS > GLIA
GLIB adj fluent but insincere or superficial ▷vb castrate
GLIBBED > GLIB
GLIBBER > GLIB
GLIBBERY adj slippery
GLIBBEST > GLIB
GLIBBING > GLIB
GLIBLY > GLIB
GLIBNESS > GLIB
GLIBS > GLIB
GLID adj moving smoothly and easily
GLIDDER > GLID
GLIDDERY adj slippery
GLIDDEST > GLID
GLIDE vb move easily and smoothly ▷n smooth easy movement
GLIDED > GLIDE
GLIDEPATH n path followed by aircraft coming in to land
GLIDER n flying phalanger
GLIDERS > GLIDER
GLIDES > GLIDE
GLIDING n sport of flying gliders
GLIDINGLY > GLIDE
GLIDINGS > GLIDING
GLIFF vb slap
GLIFFING > GLIFF
GLIFFINGS > GLIFF
GLIFFS > GLIFF
GLIFT n moment
GLIFTS > GLIFT
GLIKE same as > GLEEK
GLIKES > GLIKE
GLIM n light or lamp
GLIME vb glance sideways
GLIMED > GLIME
GLIMES > GLIME
GLIMING > GLIME
GLIMMER vb shine faintly, flicker ▷n faint gleam
GLIMMERED > GLIMMER
GLIMMERS > GLIMMER
GLIMMERY > GLIMMER
GLIMPSE n brief or incomplete view ▷vb catch a glimpse of
GLIMPSED > GLIMPSE
GLIMPSER > GLIMPSE
GLIMPSERS > GLIMPSE
GLIMPSES > GLIMPSE
GLIMPSING > GLIMPSE
GLIMS > GLIM
GLINT vb gleam brightly ▷n bright gleam
GLINTED > GLINT
GLINTIER > GLINT
GLINTIEST > GLINT
GLINTING > GLINT
GLINTS > GLINT
GLINTY > GLINT
GLIOMA n tumour of the

brain and spinal cord, composed of neuroglia cells and fibres
GLIOMAS > GLIOMA
GLIOMATA > GLIOMA
GLIOSES > GLIOSIS
GLIOSIS n process leading to scarring in the central nervous system
GLISK n glimpse
GLISKS > GLISK
GLISSADE n gliding step in ballet ▷vb perform a glissade
GLISSADED > GLISSADE
GLISSADER > GLISSADE
GLISSADES > GLISSADE
GLISSANDI > GLISSANDO
GLISSANDO n slide between two notes in which all intermediate notes are played
GLISTEN vb gleam by reflecting light ▷n gleam or gloss
GLISTENED > GLISTEN
GLISTENS > GLISTEN
GLISTER archaic word for > GLITTER
GLISTERED > GLISTER
GLISTERS > GLISTER
GLIT n slimy matter
GLITCH n small problem that stops something from working properly
GLITCHES > GLITCH
GLITCHIER > GLITCH
GLITCHY > GLITCH
GLITS > GLIT
GLITTER vb shine with bright flashes ▷n sparkle or brilliance
GLITTERED > GLITTER
GLITTERS > GLITTER
GLITTERY > GLITTER
GLITZ n ostentatious showiness ▷vb make something more attractive
GLITZED > GLITZ
GLITZES > GLITZ
GLITZIER > GLITZY
GLITZIEST > GLITZY
GLITZILY > GLITZY
GLITZING > GLITZ
GLITZY adj showily attractive
GLOAM n dusk
GLOAMING n twilight
GLOAMINGS > GLOAMING
GLOAMS > GLOAM
GLOAT vb regard one's own good fortune or the misfortune of others with smug or malicious pleasure ▷n act of gloating
GLOATED > GLOAT
GLOATER > GLOAT
GLOATERS > GLOAT
GLOATING > GLOAT
GLOATS > GLOAT
GLOB n rounded mass of thick fluid
GLOBAL adj worldwide
GLOBALISE same as > GLOBALIZE
GLOBALISM n policy which is worldwide in scope

GLOBALIST > GLOBALISM
GLOBALIZE vb put (something) into effect worldwide
GLOBALLY > GLOBAL
GLOBATE adj shaped like a globe
GLOBATED same as > GLOBATE
GLOBBIER > GLOBBY
GLOBBIEST > GLOBBY
GLOBBY adj thick and lumpy
GLOBE n sphere with a map of the earth on it ▷vb form or cause to form into a globe
GLOBED > GLOBE
GLOBEFISH another name for > PUFFER
GLOBELIKE > GLOBE
GLOBES > GLOBE
GLOBESITY n informal word for obesity seen as a worldwide social problem
GLOBETROT vb regularly travel internationally
GLOBI > GLOBUS
GLOBIN n protein component of the pigments myoglobin and haemoglobin
GLOBING > GLOBE
GLOBINS > GLOBIN
GLOBOID adj shaped approximately like a globe ▷n globoid body, such as any of those occurring in certain plant granules
GLOBOIDS > GLOBOID
GLOBOSE adj spherical or approximately spherical ▷n globose object
GLOBOSELY > GLOBOSE
GLOBOSES > GLOBOSE
GLOBOSITY > GLOBOSE
GLOBOUS same as > GLOBOSE
GLOBS > GLOB
GLOBULAR adj shaped like a globe or globule ▷n globular star cluster
GLOBULARS > GLOBULAR
GLOBULE n small round drop
GLOBULES > GLOBULE
GLOBULET n small globule
GLOBULETS > GLOBULET
GLOBULIN n simple protein found in living tissue
GLOBULINS > GLOBULIN
GLOBULITE n spherical form of crystallite
GLOBULOUS same as > GLOBULAR
GLOBUS n any spherelike structure
GLOBY adj round
GLOCHID n barbed spine on a plant
GLOCHIDIA n, plural form of singular glochidium, a barbed hair on some plants
GLOCHIDS > GLOCHID
GLODE > GLIDE
GLOGG n hot alcoholic mixed drink, originally from Sweden, consisting of sweetened brandy, red wine, bitters or other

flavourings, and blanched almonds

GLOGGS > GLOGG

GLOIRE n glory

GLOIRES > GLOIRE

GLOM vb attach oneself to or associate oneself with

GLOMERA > GLOMUS

GLOMERATE adj gathered into a compact rounded mass ▷ vb wind into a ball

GLOMERULE n cymose inflorescence in the form of a ball-like cluster of flowers

GLOMERULI n, plural of singular glomerulus: a knot of blood vessels in the kidney

GLOMMED > GLOM

GLOMMING > GLOM

GLOMS > GLOM

GLOMUS n small anastomosis in an artery or vein

GLONOIN n nitroglycerin

GLONOINS > GLONOIN

GLOOM n melancholy or depression ▷ vb look sullen or depressed

GLOOMED > GLOOM

GLOOMFUL > GLOOM

GLOOMIER > GLOOMY

GLOOMIEST > GLOOMY

GLOOMILY > GLOOMY

GLOOMING > GLOOM

GLOOMINGS > GLOOM

GLOOMLESS > GLOOM

GLOOMS > GLOOM

GLOOMY adj despairing or sad

GLOOP vb cover with a viscous substance

GLOOPED > GLOOP

GLOOPIER > GLOOP

GLOOPIEST > GLOOP

GLOOPING > GLOOP

GLOOPS > GLOOP

GLOOPY > GLOOP

GLOP vb cover with a viscous substance

GLOPPED > GLOP

GLOPPIER > GLOP

GLOPPIEST > GLOP

GLOPPING > GLOP

GLOPPY > GLOP

GLOPS > GLOP

GLORIA n silk, wool, cotton, or nylon fabric used esp for umbrellas

GLORIAS > GLORIA

GLORIED > GLORY

GLORIES > GLORY

GLORIFIED > GLORIFY

GLORIFIER > GLORIFY

GLORIFIES > GLORIFY

GLORIFY vb make (something) seem more worthy than it is

GLORIOLE another name for a > HALO

GLORIOLES > GLORIOLE

GLORIOSA n bulbous African tropical plant

GLORIOSAS > GLORIOSA

GLORIOUS adj brilliantly beautiful

GLORY n praise or honour

▷ vb triumph or exalt

GLORYING > GLORY

GLOSS n surface shine or lustre ▷ vb make glossy

GLOSSA n paired tonguelike lobe in the labium of an insect

GLOSSAE > GLOSSA

GLOSSAL > GLOSSA

GLOSSARY n list of special or technical words with definitions

GLOSSAS > GLOSSA

GLOSSATOR n writer of glosses and commentaries, esp (in the Middle Ages) an interpreter of Roman and Canon Law

GLOSSED > GLOSS

GLOSSEME n smallest meaningful unit of a language, such as stress, form, etc

GLOSSEMES > GLOSSEME

GLOSSER > GLOSS

GLOSSERS > GLOSS

GLOSSES > GLOSS

GLOSSIER > GLOSSY

GLOSSIES > GLOSSY

GLOSSIEST > GLOSSY

GLOSSILY > GLOSSY

GLOSSINA n tsetse fly

GLOSSINAS > GLOSSINA

GLOSSING > GLOSS

GLOSSIST same as > GLOSSATOR

GLOSSISTS > GLOSSIST

GLOSSITIC > GLOSSITIS

GLOSSITIS n inflammation of the tongue

GLOSSLESS > GLOSS

GLOSSY adj smooth and shiny ▷ n expensively produced magazine

GLOST n lead glaze used for pottery

GLOSTS > GLOST

GLOTTAL adj of the glottis

GLOTTIC adj of or relating to the tongue or the glottis

GLOTTIDES > GLOTTIS

GLOTTIS n vocal cords and the space between them

GLOTTISES > GLOTTIS

GLOUT vb look sullen

GLOUTED > GLOUT

GLOUTING > GLOUT

GLOUTS > GLOUT

GLOVE n covering for the hand with individual sheaths for each finger and the thumb

GLOVED > GLOVE

GLOVELESS > GLOVE

GLOVER n person who makes or sells gloves

GLOVERS > GLOVER

GLOVES > GLOVE

GLOVING > GLOVE

GLOVINGS > GLOVE

GLOW vb emit light and heat without flames ▷ n glowing light

GLOWED > GLOW

GLOWER n scowl ▷ vb stare angrily

GLOWERED > GLOWER

GLOWERING > GLOWER

GLOWERS > GLOWER

GLOWFLIES > GLOWFLY

GLOWFLY n firefly

GLOWING adj full of praise

GLOWINGLY > GLOWING

GLOWLAMP n small light consisting of two or more electrodes in an inert gas

GLOWLAMPS > GLOWLAMP

GLOWS > GLOW

GLOWSTICK n plastic tube containing a luminescent material, waved or held aloft esp at gigs, raves, etc

GLOWWORM n European beetle, the females and larvae of which bear luminescent organs producing a greenish light

GLOWWORMS > GLOWWORM

GLOXINIA n tropical plant with large bell-shaped flowers

GLOXINIAS > GLOXINIA

GLOZE vb explain away ▷ n flattery or deceit

GLOZED > GLOZE

GLOZES > GLOZE

GLOZING > GLOZE

GLOZINGS > GLOZE

GLUCAGON n polypeptide hormone, produced in the pancreas by the islets of Langerhans, that stimulates the release of glucose into the blood

GLUCAGONS > GLUCAGON

GLUCAN n any polysaccharide consisting of a polymer of glucose, such as cellulose or starch

GLUCANS > GLUCAN

GLUCINA n oxide of glucinum

GLUCINAS > GLUCINA

GLUCINIC > GLUCINIUM

GLUCINIUM former name of > BERYLLIUM

GLUCINUM same as > GLUCINIUM

GLUCINUMS > GLUCINUM

GLUCONATE n compound formed when a mineral is bound to gluconic acid

GLUCOSE n kind of sugar found in fruit

GLUCOSES > GLUCOSE

GLUCOSIC > GLUCOSE

GLUCOSIDE n any of a large group of glycosides that yield glucose on hydrolysis

GLUE n natural or synthetic sticky substance used as an adhesive ▷ vb fasten with glue

GLUED > GLUE

GLUEING > GLUE

GLUELIKE > GLUE

GLUEPOT n container for holding glue

GLUEPOTS > GLUEPOT

GLUER > GLUE

GLUERS > GLUE

GLUES > GLUE

GLUEY > GLUE

GLUEYNESS > GLUE

GLUG n word representing a gurgling sound, as of liquid being poured from a bottle or swallowed ▷ vb drink noisily, taking big gulps

GLUGGABLE adj (of wine) easy and pleasant to drink

GLUGGED > GLUG

GLUGGING > GLUG

GLUGS > GLUG

GLUHWEIN n mulled wine

GLUHWEINS > GLUHWEIN

GLUIER > GLUE

GLUIEST > GLUE

GLUILY > GLUE

GLUINESS > GLUE

GLUING > GLUE

GLUISH > GLUE

GLUM adj sullen or gloomy

GLUME n one of a pair of dry membranous bracts at the base of the spikelet of grasses

GLUMELIKE > GLUME

GLUMELLA n palea

GLUMELLAS > GLUMELLA

GLUMES > GLUME

GLUMLY > GLUM

GLUMMER > GLUM

GLUMMEST > GLUM

GLUMNESS > GLUM

GLUMPIER > GLUMPY

GLUMPIEST > GLUMPY

GLUMPILY > GLUMPY

GLUMPISH > GLUMPY

GLUMPS n state of sulking

GLUMPY adj sullen

GLUMS n gloomy feelings

GLUNCH vb look sullen

GLUNCHED > GLUNCH

GLUNCHES > GLUNCH

GLUNCHING > GLUNCH

GLUON n hypothetical particle believed to be exchanged between quarks in order to bind them together to form particles

GLUONS > GLUON

GLURGE n stories, often sent by email, that are supposed to be true and uplifting, but which are often fabricated and sentimental

GLURGES > GLURGE

GLUT n excessive supply ▷ vb oversupply

GLUTAEAL > GLUTAEUS

GLUTAEI > GLUTAEUS

GLUTAEUS same as > GLUTEUS

GLUTAMATE n any salt of glutamic acid, esp its sodium salt

GLUTAMIC as in glutamic acid nonessential amino acid that plays a part in nitrogen metabolism

GLUTAMINE n nonessential amino acid occurring in proteins: plays an important role in protein metabolism

GLUTE n same as > GLUTEUS

GLUTEAL > GLUTEUS

GLUTEI > GLUTEUS

GLUTELIN n any of a group

of water-insoluble plant proteins found in cereals. They are precipitated by alcohol and are not coagulated by heat

GLUTELINS > GLUTELIN

GLUTEN n protein found in cereal grain

GLUTENIN n type of protein

GLUTENINS > GLUTENIN

GLUTENOUS > GLUTEN

GLUTENS > GLUTEN

GLUTES > GLUTE

GLUTEUS n any of the three muscles of the buttock

GLUTINOUS adj sticky or gluey

GLUTS > GLUT

GLUTTED > GLUT

GLUTTING > GLUT

GLUTTON n greedy person

GLUTTONS > GLUTTON

GLUTTONY n practice of eating too much

GLYCAEMIA n presence of glucose in blood

GLYCAEMIC > GLYCAEMIA

GLYCAN n polysaccharide

GLYCANS > GLYCAN

GLYCEMIA US spelling of > GLYCAEMIA

GLYCEMIAS > GLYCEMIA

GLYCEMIC > GLYCEMIA

GLYCERIA n manna grass

GLYCERIAS > GLYCERIA

GLYCERIC adj of, containing, or derived from glycerol

GLYCERIDE n any fatty-acid ester of glycerol

GLYCERIN same as > GLYCEROL

GLYCERINE same as > GLYCEROL

GLYCERINS > GLYCERIN

GLYCEROL n colourless odourless syrupy liquid obtained from animal and vegetable fats, used as a solvent, antifreeze, and sweetener, and in explosives

GLYCEROLS > GLYCEROL

GLYCERYL n (something) derived from glycerol by replacing or removing one or more of its hydroxyl groups

GLYCERYLS > GLYCERYL

GLYCIN same as > GLYCINE

GLYCINE n nonessential amino acid occurring in most proteins

GLYCINES > GLYCINE

GLYCINS > GLYCIN

GLYCOCOLL n glycine

GLYCOGEN n starchlike carbohydrate stored in the liver and muscles of humans and animals

GLYCOGENS > GLYCOGEN

GLYCOL n another name (not in technical usage) for or a diol

GLYCOLIC > GLYCOL

GLYCOLLIC > GLYCOL

GLYCOLS > GLYCOL

GLYCONIC n verse consisting of a spondee, choriamb and pyrrhic

GLYCONICS > GLYCONIC

GLYCOSE n any of various monosaccharides

GLYCOSES > GLYCOSE

GLYCOSIDE n any of a group of substances, such as digitoxin, derived from monosaccharides by replacing the hydroxyl group by another group

GLYCOSYL n glucose-derived radical

GLYCOSYLS > GLYCOSYL

GLYCYL n radical of glycine

GLYCYLS > GLYCYL

GLYPH n carved channel or groove, esp a vertical one as used on a Doric frieze

GLYPHIC > GLYPH

GLYPHS > GLYPH

GLYPTAL n alkyd resin obtained from polyhydric alcohols and polybasic organic acids or their anhydrides

GLYPTALS > GLYPTAL

GLYPTIC adj of or relating to engraving or carving, esp on precious stones

GLYPTICS n art of engraving precious stones

GMELINITE n zeolitic mineral

GNAMMA variant of > NAMMA

GNAR same as > GNARL

GNARL n any knotty protuberance or swelling on a tree ▷ vb knot or cause to knot

GNARLED adj rough, twisted, and knobbly

GNARLIER > GNARLY

GNARLIEST > GNARLY

GNARLING > GNARL

GNARLS > GNARL

GNARLY adj good

GNARR same as > GNARL

GNARRED > GNAR

GNARRING > GNAR

GNARRS > GNARR

GNARS > GNAR

GNASH vb grind (the teeth) together in anger or pain ▷ n act of gnashing the teeth

GNASHED > GNASH

GNASHER n tooth

GNASHERS pl n teeth, esp false ones

GNASHES > GNASH

GNASHING > GNASH

GNAT n small biting two-winged fly

GNATHAL same as > GNATHIC

GNATHIC adj of or relating to the jaw

GNATHION n lowest point of the midline of the lower jaw: a reference point in craniometry

GNATHIONS > GNATHION

GNATHITE n appendage of an arthropod that is specialized for grasping or

chewing

GNATHITES > GNATHITE

GNATHONIC adj deceitfully flattering

GNATLIKE > GNAT

GNATLING n small gnat

GNATLINGS > GNATLING

GNATS > GNAT

GNATTIER > GNATTY

GNATTIEST > GNATTY

GNATTY adj infested with gnats

GNAW vb bite or chew steadily ▷ n act or an instance of gnawing

GNAWABLE > GNAW

GNAWED > GNAW

GNAWER > GNAW

GNAWERS > GNAW

GNAWING > GNAW

GNAWINGLY > GNAW

GNAWINGS > GNAW

GNAWN > GNAW

GNAWS > GNAW

GNEISS n coarse-grained metamorphic rock

GNEISSES > GNEISS

GNEISSIC > GNEISS

GNEISSOID > GNEISS

GNEISSOSE > GNEISS

GNOCCHI n dumplings made of pieces of semolina pasta, or sometimes potato, used to garnish soup or served alone with sauce

GNOCCHIS > GNOCCHI

GNOMAE > GNOME

GNOME n imaginary creature like a little old man

GNOMELIKE > GNOME

GNOMES > GNOME

GNOMIC adj of pithy sayings

GNOMICAL same as > GNOMIC

GNOMISH > GNOME

GNOMIST n writer of pithy sayings

GNOMISTS > GNOMIST

GNOMON n stationary arm that projects the shadow on a sundial

GNOMONIC > GNOMON

GNOMONICS > GNOMON

GNOMONS > GNOMON

GNOSES > GNOSIS

GNOSIS n supposedly revealed knowledge of various spiritual truths, esp that said to have been possessed by ancient Gnostics

GNOSTIC adj of, relating to, or possessing knowledge, esp esoteric spiritual knowledge ▷ n one who knows

GNOSTICAL same as > GNOSTIC

GNOSTICS > GNOSTIC

GNOW n Australian wild bird

GNOWS > GNOW

GNU n ox-like S African antelope

GNUS > GNU

GO vb move to or from a place ▷ n attempt

GOA n gazelle, Procapra picticaudata, inhabiting

the plains of the Tibetan plateau, having a brownish-grey coat and backward-curving horns

GOAD vb provoke (someone) to take some kind of action, usu in anger ▷ n spur or provocation

GOADED > GOAD

GOADING > GOAD

GOADLIKE > GOAD

GOADS > GOAD

GOADSMAN n person who uses a goad

GOADSMEN > GOADSMAN

GOADSTER n goadsman

GOADSTERS > GOADSTER

GOAF n waste left in old mine workings

GOAFS > GOAF

GOAL n posts through which the ball or puck has to be propelled to score ▷ vb in rugby, to convert a try into a goal

GOALBALL n game played by two teams who compete to score goals by throwing a ball that emits audible sound when in motion. Players, who may be blind or sighted, are blindfolded during play

GOALBALLS > GOALBALL

GOALED > GOAL

GOALIE n goalkeeper

GOALIES > GOALIE

GOALING > GOAL

GOALLESS > GOAL

GOALMOUTH n area in front of the goal

GOALPOST n one of the two posts marking the limit of a goal

GOALPOSTS > GOALPOST

GOALS > GOAL

GOALWARD adv towards a goal

GOANNA n large Australian lizard

GOANNAS > GOANNA

GOARY variant spelling of > GORY

GOAS > GOA

GOAT n sure-footed ruminant animal with horns

GOATEE n pointed tuft-like beard

GOATEED > GOATEE

GOATEES > GOATEE

GOATFISH n red mullet

GOATHERD n person who looks after a herd of goats

GOATHERDS > GOATHERD

GOATIER > GOAT

GOATIEST > GOAT

GOATISH adj of, like, or relating to a goat

GOATISHLY > GOATISH

GOATLIKE > GOAT

GOATLING n young goat

GOATLINGS > GOATLING

GOATS > GOAT

GOATSKIN n leather made from the skin of a goat

GOATSKINS > GOATSKIN

g

g

GOATWEED *n* plant of the genus Capraria
GOATWEEDS > GOATWEED
GOATY > GOAT
GOB *n* lump of a soft substance ▷ *vb* spit
GOBAN *n* board on which go is played
GOBANG *n* Japanese board-game
GOBANGS > GOBANG
GOBANS > GOBAN
GOBBED > GOB
GOBBELINE *same as* > GOBLIN
GOBBET *n* lump, esp of food
GOBBETS > GOBBET
GOBBI > GOBBO
GOBBIER > GOBBY
GOBBIEST > GOBBY
GOBBING > GOB
GOBBLE *vb* eat hastily and greedily ▷ *n* rapid gurgling cry of the male turkey ▷ *interj* imitation of this sound
GOBBLED > GOBBLE
GOBBLER *n* turkey
GOBBLERS > GOBBLER
GOBBLES > GOBBLE
GOBBLING > GOBBLE
GOBBO *n* hunchback
GOBBY *adj* loudmouthed and offensive
GOBIES > GOBY
GOBIID *n* member of the genus Gobius
GOBIIDS > GOBIID
GOBIOID *adj* of or relating to the *Gobioidea*, a suborder of spiny-finned teleost fishes that includes gobies and mudskippers (family *Gobiidae*) and sleepers (family *Eleotridae*) ▷ *n any gobioid fish*
GOBIOIDS > GOBIOID
GOBLET *n* drinking cup without handles
GOBLETS > GOBLET
GOBLIN *n* (in folklore) small malevolent creature
GOBLINS > GOBLIN
GOBO *n* shield placed around a microphone to exclude unwanted sounds
GOBOES > GOBO
GOBONEE *same as* > GOBONY
GOBONY *adj* in heraldry, composed of a row of small, alternately-coloured, squares
GOBOS > GOBO
GOBS > GOB
GOBSHITE *n* stupid person
GOBSHITES > GOBSHITE
GOBURRA *n* kookaburra
GOBURRAS > GOBURRA
GOBY *n* small spiny-finned fish
GOD *n* spirit or being worshipped as having supernatural power ▷ *vb* deify
GODCHILD *n* child for whom a person stands as godparent

GODDAM *vb* damn
GODDAMMED > GODDAM
GODDAMN *interj* oath expressing anger, surprise, etc ▷ *adj* extremely ▷ *vb* damn
GODDAMNED > GODDAMN
GODDAMNS > GODDAMN
GODDAMS > GODDAM
GODDED > GOD
GODDEN *n* evening greeting
GODDENS > GODDEN
GODDESS *n* female divinity
GODDESSES > GODDESS
GODDING > GOD
GODET *n* triangular piece of material inserted into a garment, such as into a skirt to create a flare
GODETIA *n* plant with showy flowers
GODETIAS > GODETIA
GODETS > GODET
GODFATHER *n* male godparent ▷ *vb* be a godfather to
GODHEAD *n* essential nature and condition of being a god
GODHEADS > GODHEAD
GODHOOD *n* state of being divine
GODHOODS > GODHOOD
GODLESS *adj* wicked or unprincipled
GODLESSLY > GODLESS
GODLIER > GODLY
GODLIEST > GODLY
GODLIKE *adj* resembling or befitting a god or God
GODLILY > GODLY
GODLINESS > GODLY
GODLING *n* little god
GODLINGS > GODLING
GODLY *adj* devout or pious
GODMOTHER *n* female godparent
GODOWN *n* (in East Asia and India) warehouse
GODOWNS > GODOWN
GODPARENT *n* person who promises at a child's baptism to bring the child up as a Christian
GODROON *same as* > GADROON
GODROONED > GODROON
GODROONS > GODROON
GODS > GOD
GODSEND *n* something unexpected but welcome
GODSENDS > GODSEND
GODSHIP *n* divinity
GODSHIPS > GODSHIP
GODSLOT *n* time in a television or radio schedule traditionally reserved for religious broadcasts
GODSLOTS > GODSLOT
GODSO *same as* > GADSO
GODSON *n* male godchild
GODSONS > GODSON
GODSOS > GODSO
GODSPEED *n* expression of one's good wishes for a person's success and safety
GODSPEEDS > GODSPEED

GODSQUAD *n* informal, sometimes derogatory term for any group of evangelical Christians, members of which are regarded as intrusive and exuberantly pious
GODSQUADS > GODSQUAD
GODWARD *adv* towards God
GODWARDS *same as* > GODWARD
GODWIT *n* shore bird with long legs and an upturned bill
GODWITS > GODWIT
GOE *same as* > GO
GOEL *n* in Jewish law, blood-avenger
GOELS > GOEL
GOER *n* person who attends something regularly
GOERS > GOER
GOES > GO
GOETHITE *n* black, brown, or yellow mineral consisting of hydrated iron oxide in the form of orthorhombic crystals or fibrous masses
GOETHITES > GOETHITE
GOETIC > GOETY
GOETIES > GOETY
GOETY *n* witchcraft
GOEY *adj* go-ahead
GOFER *n* employee or assistant whose duties include menial tasks such as running errands
GOFERS > GOFER
GOFF *obsolete variant of* > GOLF
GOFFED > GOFF
GOFFER *vb* press pleats into (a frill) ▷ *n* ornamental frill made by pressing pleats
GOFFERED > GOFFER
GOFFERING > GOFFER
GOFFERS > GOFFER
GOFFING > GOFF
GOFFS > GOFF
GOGGA *n* any small insect
GOGGAS > GOGGA
GOGGLE *vb* (of the eyes) bulge ▷ *n* fixed or bulging stare
GOGGLEBOX *n* television set
GOGGLED > GOGGLE
GOGGLER *n* big-eyed scad
GOGGLERS > GOGGLER
GOGGLES > GOGGLE
GOGGLIER > GOGGLE
GOGGLIEST > GOGGLE
GOGGLING > GOGGLE
GOGGLINGS > GOGGLE
GOGGLY > GOGGLE
GOGLET *n* long-necked water-cooling vessel of porous earthenware, used esp in India
GOGLETS > GOGLET
GOGO *n* disco
GOGOS > GOGO
GOHONZON *n* (in Nichiren Buddhism) paper scroll to which devotional chanting is directed
GOHONZONS > GOHONZON

GOIER > GOEY
GOIEST > GOEY
GOING > GO
GOINGS > GO
GOITER *same as* > GOITRE
GOITERED > GOITER
GOITERS > GOITER
GOITRE *n* swelling of the thyroid gland in the neck
GOITRED > GOITRE
GOITRES > GOITRE
GOITROGEN *n* substance that induces the formation of a goitre
GOITROUS > GOITRE
GOLCONDA *n* source of wealth or riches, esp a mine
GOLCONDAS > GOLCONDA
GOLD *n* yellow precious metal ▷ *adj* made of gold
GOLDARN *euphemistic variant of* > GODDAMN
GOLDARNS > GODDAMN
GOLDBRICK *vb* swindle
GOLDBUG *n* American beetle with a bright metallic lustre
GOLDBUGS > GOLDBUG
GOLDCREST *n* small bird with a yellow crown
GOLDEN *adj* made of gold ▷ *vb* gild
GOLDENED > GOLDEN
GOLDENER > GOLDEN
GOLDENEST > GOLDEN
GOLDENEYE *n* either of two black-and-white diving ducks, *Bucephala clangula* or *B. islandica*, of northern regions
GOLDENING > GOLDEN
GOLDENLY > GOLDEN
GOLDENROD *n* tall plant with spikes of small yellow flowers
GOLDENS > GOLDEN
GOLDER > GOLD
GOLDEST > GOLD
GOLDEYE *n* North American clupeoid fish, *Hiodon alosoides*, with yellowish eyes, silvery sides, and a dark blue back: family *Hiodontidae* (mooneyes)
GOLDEYES > GOLDEYE
GOLDFIELD *n* area in which there are gold deposits
GOLDFINCH *n* kind of finch, the male of which has yellow-and-black wings
GOLDFINNY *same as* > GOLDSINNY
GOLDFISH *n* orange fish kept in ponds or aquariums
GOLDIER > GOLDY
GOLDIEST > GOLDY
GOLDISH > GOLD
GOLDLESS > GOLD
GOLDMINER *n* miner who works in a gold mine
GOLDS > GOLD
GOLDSINNY *n* any of various small European wrasses, esp the brightly coloured *Ctenolabrus rupestris*
GOLDSIZE *n* adhesive used

to fix gold leaf to a surface

GOLDSIZES > GOLDSIZE

GOLDSMITH n dealer in or maker of gold articles

GOLDSPINK n goldfinch

GOLDSTICK n colonel in the Life Guards who carries out ceremonial duties

GOLDSTONE another name for > AVENTURINE

GOLDTAIL as in goldtail moth European moth with white wings and a soft white furry body with a yellow tail tuft

GOLDTONE adj gold-coloured

GOLDURN variant of > GODDAMN

GOLDURNS > GOLDURN

GOLDY adj gold-like

GOLE obsolete spelling of > GOAL

GOLEM n (in Jewish legend) artificially created human being brought to life by supernatural means

GOLEMS > GOLEM

GOLES > GOLE

GOLF n outdoor game in which a ball is struck with clubs into a series of holes ▷vb play golf

GOLFED > GOLF

GOLFER n person who plays golf

GOLFERS > GOLFER

GOLFIANA n golfing collectibles

GOLFIANAS > GOLFIANA

GOLFING > GOLF

GOLFINGS > GOLF

GOLFS > GOLF

GOLGOTHA n place of burial

GOLGOTHAS > GOLGOTHA

GOLIARD n one of a number of wandering scholars in 12th- and 13th-century Europe famed for their riotous behaviour, intemperance, and composition of satirical and ribald Latin verse

GOLIARDIC > GOLIARD

GOLIARDS > GOLIARD

GOLIARDY > GOLIARD

GOLIAS vb behave outrageously

GOLIASED > GOLIAS

GOLIASES > GOLIAS

GOLIASING > GOLIAS

GOLIATH n giant

GOLIATHS > GOLIATH

GOLLAN n yellow flower

GOLLAND same as > GOLLAN

GOLLANDS > GOLLAND

GOLLANS > GOLLAN

GOLLAR same as > GOLLER

GOLLARED > GOLLAR

GOLLARING > GOLLAR

GOLLARS > GOLLAR

GOLLER vb roar

GOLLERED > GOLLER

GOLLERING > GOLLER

GOLLERS > GOLLER

GOLLIED > GOLLY

GOLLIES > GOLLY

GOLLIWOG n soft black-faced doll

GOLLIWOGG same as > GOLLIWOG

GOLLIWOGS > GOLLIWOG

GOLLOP vb eat or drink (something) quickly or greedily

GOLLOPED > GOLLOP

GOLLOPER > GOLLOP

GOLLOPERS > GOLLOP

GOLLOPING > GOLLOP

GOLLOPS > GOLLOP

GOLLY interj exclamation of mild surprise ▷n short for GOLLYWOG: used chiefly by children ▷vb spit

GOLLYING > GOLLY

GOLLYWOG same as > GOLLIWOG

GOLLYWOGS > GOLLYWOG

GOLOMYNKA n oily fish found only in Lake Baikal

GOLOSH same as > GALOSH

GOLOSHE same as > GALOSH

GOLOSHED > GOLOSH

GOLOSHES > GOLOSH

GOLOSHING > GOLOSH

GOLOSHOES > GOLOSH

GOLP same as > GOLPE

GOLPE n in heraldry, a purple circle

GOLPES > GOLPE

GOLPS > GOLP

GOMBEEN n usury

GOMBEENS > GOMBEEN

GOMBO same as > GUMBO

GOMBOS > GOMBO

GOMBRO same as > GUMBO

GOMBROON n Persian and Chinese pottery and porcelain wares

GOMBROONS > GOMBROON

GOMBROS > GOMBRO

GOMER n unwanted hospital patient

GOMERAL same as > GOMERIL

GOMERALS > GOMERAL

GOMEREL same as > GOMERIL

GOMERELS > GOMEREL

GOMERIL n slow-witted or stupid person

GOMERILS > GOMERIL

GOMERS > GOMER

GOMOKU another word for > GOBANG

GOMOKUS > GOMOKU

GOMPA n Tibetan monastery

GOMPAS > GOMPA

GOMPHOSES > GOMPHOSIS

GOMPHOSIS n form of immovable articulation in which a peglike part fits into a cavity, as in the setting of a tooth in its socket

GOMUTI n East Indian feather palm, Arenga pinnata, whose sweet sap is a source of sugar

GOMUTIS > GOMUTI

GOMUTO same as > GOMUTI

GOMUTOS > GOMUTO

GON n geometrical grade

GONAD n organ producing reproductive cells, such as a testicle or ovary

GONADAL > GONAD

GONADIAL > GONAD

GONADIC > GONAD

GONADS > GONAD

GONDELAY same as > GONDOLA

GONDELAYS > GONDELAY

GONDOLA n long narrow boat used in Venice

GONDOLAS > GONDOLA

GONDOLIER n person who propels a gondola

GONE > GO

GONEF same as > GANEF

GONEFS > GONEF

GONENESS n faintness from hunger

GONER n person or thing beyond help or recovery

GONERS > GONER

GONFALON n banner hanging from a crossbar, used esp by certain medieval Italian republics or in ecclesiastical processions

GONFALONS > GONFALON

GONFANON same as > GONFALON

GONFANONS > GONFANON

GONG n rimmed metal disc that produces a note when struck ▷vb sound a gong

GONGED > GONG

GONGING > GONG

GONGLIKE > GONG

GONGS > GONG

GONGSTER n person who strikes a gong

GONGSTERS > GONGSTER

GONGYO n (in Nichiren Buddhism) ceremony, performed twice a day, involving reciting parts of the Lotus Sutra and chanting the Daimoku to the Gohonzon

GONGYOS > GONGYO

GONIA > GONION

GONIATITE n any extinct cephalopod mollusc of the genus Goniatites and related genera, similar to ammonites

GONIDIA > GONIDIUM

GONIDIAL > GONIDIUM

GONIDIC > GONIDIUM

GONIDIUM n green algal cell in the thallus of a lichen

GONIF same as > GANEF

GONIFF same as > GANEF

GONIFFS > GONIFF

GONIFS > GANIF

GONION n point or apex of the angle of the lower jaw

GONIUM n immature reproductive cell

GONK n stuffed toy, often used as a mascot

GONKS > GONK

GONNA vb going to

GONOCOCCI n, plural of singular gonococcus: bacterium that causes gonorrhea

GONOCYTE n oocyte or spermatocyte

GONOCYTES > GONOCYTE

GONODUCT n duct leading from a gonad to the exterior, through which gametes pass

GONODUCTS > GONODUCT

GONOF same as > GANEF

GONOFS > GANOF

GONOPH same as > GANEF

GONOPHORE n polyp in certain coelenterates that bears gonads

GONOPHS > GONOPH

GONOPOD n either member of a pair of appendages that are the external reproductive organs of insects and some other arthropods

GONOPODS > GONOPOD

GONOPORE n external pore in insects, earthworms, etc, through which the gametes are extruded

GONOPORES > GONOPORE

GONORRHEA n infectious venereal disease

GONOSOME n individuals, collectively, in a colonial animal that are involved with reproduction

GONOSOMES > GONOSOME

GONS > GON

GONYS n lower outline of a bird's bill

GONYSES > GONYS

GONZO adj wild or crazy

GOO n sticky substance

GOOBER another name for > PEANUT

GOOBERS > GOOBER

GOOBIES > GOOBY

GOOBY n spittle

GOOD adj giving pleasure ▷n benefit

GOODBY same as > GOODBYE

GOODBYE n expression used on parting ▷interj expression used on parting ▷sentence substitute farewell: a conventional expression used at leave-taking or parting with people and at the loss or rejection of things or ideas

GOODBYES > GOODBYE

GOODBYS > GOODBY

GOODFACED adj with a handsome face

GOODIE same as > GOODY

GOODIER > GOODY

GOODIES > GOODY

GOODIEST > GOODY

GOODINESS > GOODY

GOODISH > GOOD

GOODLIER > GOODLY

GOODLIEST > GOODLY

GOODLY adj considerable

GOODMAN n husband

GOODMEN > GOODMAN

GOODNESS n quality of being good ▷interj exclamation of surprise

GOODNIGHT n conventional expression of farewell used in the evening or at night

GOODS > GOOD

g

GOODSIRE n grandfather
GOODSIRES > GOODSIRE
GOODTIME adj wildly seeking pleasure
GOODWIFE n mistress of a household
GOODWILL n kindly feeling
GOODWILLS > GOODWILL
GOODWIVES > GOODWIFE
GOODY n hero in a book or film ▷ interj child's exclamation of pleasure ▷ adj smug and sanctimonious
GOODYEAR n euphemistic term for the Devil
GOODYEARS > GOODYEAR
GOOEY adj sticky and soft
GOOEYNESS > GOOEY
GOOF n mistake ▷ vb make a mistake
GOOFBALL n barbiturate sleeping pill
GOOFBALLS > GOOFBALL
GOOFED > GOOF
GOOFIER > GOOFY
GOOFIEST > GOOFY
GOOFILY > GOOFY
GOOFINESS > GOOFY
GOOFING > GOOF
GOOFS > GOOF
GOOFY adj silly or ridiculous
GOOG n egg
GOOGLE vb search for (something) on the internet using a search engine
GOOGLED > GOOGLE
GOOGLES > GOOGLE
GOOGLIES > GOOGLY
GOOGLING > GOOGLE
GOOGLY n ball that spins unexpectedly from off to leg on the bounce
GOOGOL n number represented as one followed by 100 zeros (10^100)
GOOGOLS > GOOGOL
GOOGS > GOOG
GOOIER > GOOEY
GOOIEST > GOOEY
GOOILY > GOOEY
GOOK n derogatory word for a person from a Far Eastern country
GOOKS > GOOK
GOOKY adj sticky and messy
GOOL n corn marigold
GOOLD Scots word for > GOLD
GOOLDS > GOOLD
GOOLEY same as > GOOLIE
GOOLEYS > GOOLEY
GOOLIE n testicle
GOOLIES > GOOLIE
GOOLS > GOOL
GOOLY same as > GOOLIE
GOOMBAH n patron or mentor
GOOMBAHS > GOOMBAH
GOOMBAY n Bahamian soft drink
GOOMBAYS > GOOMBAY
GOON n stupid person
GOONDA n (in India) habitual criminal
GOONDAS > GOONDA

GOONEY n albatross
GOONEYS > GOONEY
GOONIE Scots word for a > GOWN
GOONIER > GOON
GOONIES > GOONIE
GOONIEST > GOON
GOONS > GOON
GOONY > GOON
GOOP n rude or ill-mannered person
GOOPIER > GOOP
GOOPIEST > GOOP
GOOPS > GOOP
GOOPY > GOOP
GOOR same as > GUR
GOORAL same as > GORAL
GOORALS > GOORAL
GOORIE See > KURI
GOORIES > GOORIE
GOOROO same as > GURU
GOOROOS > GOOROO
GOORS > GOOR
GOORY > GOOR
GOOS > GOO
GOOSANDER n type of duck
GOOSE n web-footed bird like a large duck ▷ vb prod (someone) playfully in the bottom
GOOSED > GOOSE
GOOSEFISH another name for > MONKFISH
GOOSEFOOT n any typically weedy chenopodiaceous plant of the genus Chenopodium, having small greenish flowers and leaves shaped like a goose's foot
GOOSEGOB > GOOSEBERRY
GOOSEGOBS > GOOSEBERRY
GOOSEGOG dialect or informal word for > GOOSEGOG
GOOSEGOGS > GOOSEBERRY
GOOSEHERD n person who herds geese
GOOSENECK n pivot between the forward end of a boom and a mast, to allow the boom to swing freely
GOOSERIES > GOOSERY
GOOSERY n place for keeping geese
GOOSES > GOOSE
GOOSEY same as > GOOSY
GOOSEYS > GOOSEY
GOOSIER > GOOSY
GOOSIES > GOOSY
GOOSIEST > GOOSY
GOOSINESS > GOOSY
GOOSING > GOOSE
GOOSY adj of or like a goose
GOPAK n spectacular high-leaping Russian peasant dance for men
GOPAKS > GOPAK
GOPHER n American burrowing rodent ▷ vb burrow
GOPHERED > GOPHER
GOPHERING > GOPHER
GOPHERS > GOPHER
GOPIK n money unit of Azerbaijan
GOPURA n gateway tower of an Indian temple

GOPURAM same as > GOPURA
GOPURAMS > GOPURA
GOPURAS > GOPURA
GOR interj God!
GORA n (in informal Indian English) White or fair-skinned male
GORAL n small goat antelope, Naemorhedus goral, inhabiting mountainous regions of S Asia. It has a yellowish-grey and black coat and small conical horns
GORALS > GORAL
GORAMIES > GORAMY
GORAMY same as > GOURAMI
GORAS > GORA
GORBELLY n large belly
GORBLIMEY interj exclamation of surprise or annoyance
GORBLIMY same as > GORBLIMEY
GORCOCK n male of the red grouse
GORCOCKS > GORCOCK
GORCROW n carrion crow
GORCROWS > GORCROW
GORDITA n small thick tortilla
GORDITAS > GORDITA
GORE n blood from a wound ▷ vb pierce with horns
GORED > GORE
GOREHOUND n enthusiast of gory horror films
GORES > GORE
GORGE n deep narrow valley ▷ vb eat greedily
GORGEABLE > GORGE
GORGED > GORGE
GORGEDLY > GORGE
GORGEOUS adj strikingly beautiful or attractive
GORGER > GORGE
GORGERIN another name for > NECKING
GORGERINS > GORGERIN
GORGERS > GORGE
GORGES > GORGE
GORGET n collar-like piece of armour worn to protect the throat
GORGETED > GORGET
GORGETS > GORGET
GORGIA n improvised sung passage
GORGIAS > GORGIA
GORGING > GORGE
GORGIO n word used by gypsies for a non-gypsy
GORGIOS > GORGIO
GORGON n terrifying or repulsive woman
GORGONEIA n plural of gorgoneion: representation of a Gorgon's head
GORGONIAN n any coral of the order Gorgonacea, having a horny or calcareous branching skeleton: includes the sea fans and red corals ▷ adj of, relating to, or belonging to the Gorgonacea

GORGONISE vb turn to stone
GORGONIZE same as > GORGONISE
GORGONS > GORGON
GORHEN n female red grouse
GORHENS > GORHEN
GORI n in informal Indian English, a White or fair-skinned female
GORIER > GORY
GORIEST > GORY
GORILLA n largest of the apes, found in Africa
GORILLAS > GORILLA
GORILLIAN > GORILLA
GORILLINE > GORILLA
GORILLOID > GORILLA
GORILY > GORY
GORINESS > GORY
GORING > GORE
GORINGS > GORE
GORIS > GORI
GORM n foolish person ▷ vb understand
GORMAND same as > GOURMAND
GORMANDS > GOURMAND
GORMED > GORM
GORMIER > GORMY
GORMIEST > GORMY
GORMING > GORM
GORMLESS adj stupid
GORMS > GORM
GORMY adj gormless
GORP same as > GAWP
GORPED > GAWP
GORPING > GAWP
GORPS > GAWP
GORSE n prickly yellow-flowered shrub
GORSEDD n meeting of bards and druids held daily before an eisteddfod
GORSEDDS > GORSEDD
GORSES > GORSE
GORSIER > GORSE
GORSIEST > GORSE
GORSOON n young boy
GORSOONS > GORSOON
GORSY > GORSE
GORY adj horrific or bloodthirsty
GOS > GO
GOSH interj exclamation of mild surprise or wonder
GOSHAWK n large hawk
GOSHAWKS > GOSHAWK
GOSHT n Indian meat dish
GOSHTS > GOSHT
GOSLARITE n hydrated zinc sulphate
GOSLET n pygmy goose
GOSLETS > GOSLET
GOSLING n young goose
GOSLINGS > GOSLING
GOSPEL n any of the first four books of the New Testament ▷ adj denoting a kind of religious music originating in the churches of the Black people in the Southern US ▷ vb teach the gospel
GOSPELER same as > GOSPELLER
GOSPELERS > GOSPELER
GOSPELISE vb evangelise

GOSPELIZE same as > GOSPELISE

GOSPELLED > GOSPEL

GOSPELLER n person who reads or chants the Gospel in a religious service

GOSPELLY > GOSPEL

GOSPELS > GOSPEL

GOSPODA > GOSPODIN

GOSPODAR n hospodar

GOSPODARS > GOSPODAR

GOSPODIN n Russian title of address, often indicating respect, equivalent to sir when used alone or to Mr when before a name

GOSPORT n aeroplane communication device

GOSPORTS > GOSPORT

GOSS vb spit

GOSSAMER n very fine fabric

GOSSAMERS > GOSSAMER

GOSSAMERY > GOSSAMER

GOSSAN n oxidised portion of a mineral vein in rock

GOSSANS > GOSSAN

GOSSE variant of > GORSE

GOSSED > GOSS

GOSSES > GOSSE

GOSSIB n gossip

GOSSIBS > GOSSIB

GOSSING > GOSS

GOSSIP n idle talk, esp about other people ▷ vb engage in gossip

GOSSIPED > GOSSIP

GOSSIPER > GOSSIP

GOSSIPERS > GOSSIP

GOSSIPING > GOSSIP

GOSSIPPED > GOSSIP

GOSSIPPER > GOSSIP

GOSSIPRY n idle talk

GOSSIPS > GOSSIP

GOSSIPY > GOSSIP

GOSSOON n boy, esp a servant boy

GOSSOONS > GOSSOON

GOSSYPINE adj cottony

GOSSYPOL n toxic crystalline pigment that is a constituent of cottonseed oil

GOSSYPOLS > GOSSYPOL

GOSTER vb laugh uncontrollably

GOSTERED > GOSTER

GOSTERING > GOSTER

GOSTERS > GOSTER

GOT > GET

GOTCHA as in gotcha lizard Australian name for a crocodile

GOTCHAS > GOTCHA

GOTH n aficionado of Goth music and fashion

GOTHIC adj of or relating to a literary style characterized by gloom, the grotesque, and the supernatural ▷ n family of heavy script typefaces

GOTHICISE same as > GOTHICIZE

GOTHICISM > GOTHIC

GOTHICIZE vb make gothic in style

GOTHICS > GOTHIC

GOTHITE same as > GOETHITE

GOTHITES > GOTHITE

GOTHS > GOTH

GOTTA vb got to

GOTTEN past participle of > GET

GOUACHE n (painting using) watercolours mixed with glue

GOUACHES > GOUACHE

GOUGE vb scoop or force out ▷ n hole or groove

GOUGED > GOUGE

GOUGER n person or tool that gouges

GOUGERE n choux pastry flavoured with cheese

GOUGERES > GOUGERE

GOUGERS > GOUGER

GOUGES > GOUGE

GOUGING > GOUGE

GOUJEERS same as > GOODYEAR

GOUJON n small strip of fish or chicken, coated in breadcrumbs and deep-fried

GOUJONS > GOUJON

GOUK same as > GOWK

GOUKS > GOUK

GOULASH n rich stew seasoned with paprika

GOULASHES > GOULASH

GOURA n large, crested ground pigeon found in New Guinea

GOURAMI n large SE Asian labyrinth fish, Osphronemus goramy, used for food and (when young) as an aquarium fish

GOURAMIES > GOURAMI

GOURAMIS > GOURAMI

GOURAS > GOURA

GOURD n fleshy fruit of a climbing plant

GOURDE n standard monetary unit of Haiti, divided into 100 centimes

GOURDES > GOURDE

GOURDIER > GOURDY

GOURDIEST > GOURDY

GOURDLIKE > GOURD

GOURDS > GOURD

GOURDY adj (of horses) swollen-legged

GOURMAND n person who is very keen on food and drink

GOURMANDS > GOURMAND

GOURMET n connoisseur of food and drink

GOURMETS > GOURMET

GOUSTIER > GOUSTY

GOUSTIEST > GOUSTY

GOUSTROUS adj stormy

GOUSTY adj dismal

GOUT n disease causing inflammation of the joints

GOUTFLIES > GOUTFLY

GOUTFLY n fly whose larvae infect crops

GOUTIER > GOUT

GOUTIEST > GOUT

GOUTILY > GOUT

GOUTINESS > GOUT

GOUTS > GOUT

GOUTTE n in heraldry, charge shaped like a drop of liquid

GOUTTES > GOUTTE

GOUTWEED n widely naturalized Eurasian umbelliferous plant, Aegopodium podagraria, with white flowers and creeping underground stems

GOUTWEEDS > GOUTWEED

GOUTWORT n bishop's weed

GOUTWORTS > GOUTWORT

GOUTY > GOUT

GOV n boss

GOVERN vb rule, direct, or control

GOVERNABLENESS

GOVERNALL n government

GOVERNED > GOVERN

GOVERNESS n woman teacher in a private household ▷ vb act as a governess

GOVERNING > GOVERN

GOVERNOR n official governing a province or state

GOVERNORS > GOVERNOR

GOVERNS > GOVERN

GOVS > GOV

GOWAN n any of various yellow or white flowers growing in fields, esp the common daisy

GOWANED > GOWAN

GOWANS > GOWAN

GOWANY > GOWAN

GOWD Scots word for > GOWD

GOWDER > GOWD

GOWDEST > GOWD

GOWDS > GOWD

GOWDSPINK n goldfinch

GOWF vb strike

GOWFED > GOWF

GOWFER > GOWF

GOWFERS > GOWF

GOWFING > GOWF

GOWFS > GOWF

GOWK n stupid person

GOWKS > GOWK

GOWL n substance often found in the corner of the eyes after sleep ▷ vb howl

GOWLAN same as > GOLLAN

GOWLAND same as > GOLLAN

GOWLANDS > GOWLAND

GOWLANS > GOWLAN

GOWLED > GOWL

GOWLING > GOWL

GOWLS > GOWL

GOWN n woman's long formal dress ▷ vb supply with or dress in a gown

GOWNBOY n foundationer schoolboy who wears a gown

GOWNBOYS > GOWNBOY

GOWNED > GOWN

GOWNING > GOWN

GOWNMAN n professional person, such as a lawyer, who wears a gown

GOWNMEN > GOWNMAN

GOWNS > GOWN

GOWNSMAN same as > GOWNMAN

GOWNSMEN > GOWNSMAN

GOWPEN n pair of cupped hands

GOWPENFUL n amount that can be contained in cupped hands

GOWPENS > GOWPEN

GOX n gaseous oxygen

GOXES > GOX

GOY n Jewish word for a non-Jew

GOYIM > GOY

GOYISCH > GOY

GOYISH > GOY

GOYS > GOY

GOZZAN same as > GOSSAN

GOZZANS > GOZZAN

GRAAL n holy grail

GRAALS > GRAAL

GRAB vb grasp suddenly, snatch ▷ n sudden snatch

GRABBABLE > GRAB

GRABBED > GRAB

GRABBER > GRAB

GRABBERS > GRAB

GRABBIER > GRABBY

GRABBIEST > GRABBY

GRABBING > GRAB

GRABBLE vb scratch or feel about with the hands

GRABBLED > GRABBLE

GRABBLER > GRABBLE

GRABBLERS > GRABBLE

GRABBLES > GRABBLE

GRABBLING > GRABBLE

GRABBY adj greedy or selfish

GRABEN n elongated trough of land produced by subsidence of the earth's crust between two faults

GRABENS > GRABEN

GRABS > GRAB

GRACE n beauty and elegance ▷ vb honour

GRACED > GRACE

GRACEFUL adj having beauty of movement, style, or form

GRACELESS adj lacking elegance

GRACES > GRACE

GRACILE adj gracefully thin or slender

GRACILES > GRACILIS

GRACILIS n thin muscle on the inner thigh

GRACILITY > GRACILE

GRACING > GRACE

GRACIOSO n clown in Spanish comedy

GRACIOSOS > GRACIOSO

GRACIOUS adj kind and courteous ▷ interj expression of mild surprise or wonder ▷ interj expression of surprise

GRACKLE n any American songbird of the genera Quiscalus and Cassidix, having a dark iridescent plumage: family Icteridae (American orioles)

GRACKLES > GRACKLE

GRAD n graduate

GRADABLE adj capable of being graded ▷ n word of

this kind

GRADABLES > GRADABLE

GRADATE *vb* change or cause to change imperceptibly, as from one colour, tone, or degree to another

GRADATED > GRADATE

GRADATES > GRADATE

GRADATIM *adv* step by step

GRADATING > GRADATE

GRADATION *n* (stage in) a series of degrees or steps

GRADATORY *adj* moving step by step

GRADDAN *vb* dress corn

GRADDANED > GRADDAN

GRADDANS > GRADDAN

GRADE *n* place on a scale of quality, rank, or size ▷ *vb* arrange in grades

GRADED > GRADE

GRADELESS > GRADE

GRADELIER > GRADELY

GRADELY *adj* fine

GRADER *n* person or thing that grades

GRADERS > GRADER

GRADES > GRADE

GRADIENT *n* (degree of) slope ▷ *adj* sloping uniformly

GRADIENTS > GRADIENT

GRADIN *n* ledge above or behind an altar on which candles, a cross, or other ornaments stand

GRADINE *same as* > GRADIN

GRADINES > GRADINE

GRADING > GRADE

GRADINI > GRADINO

GRADINO *n* step above an altar

GRADINS > GRADIN

GRADS > GRAD

GRADUAL *adj* occurring, developing, or moving in small stages ▷ *n* antiphon or group of several antiphons, usually from the Psalms, sung or recited immediately after the epistle at Mass

GRADUALLY > GRADUAL

GRADUALS > GRADUAL

GRADUAND *n* person who is about to graduate

GRADUANDS > GRADUAND

GRADUATE *vb* receive a degree or diploma ▷ *n* holder of a degree

GRADUATED > GRADUATE

GRADUATES > GRADUATE

GRADUATOR > GRADUATE

GRADUS *n* book of études or other musical exercises arranged in order of increasing difficulty

GRADUSES > GRADUS

GRAECISE *same as* > GRAECIZE

GRAECISED > GRAECISE

GRAECISES > GRAECISE

GRAECIZE *vb* make or become like the ancient Greeks

GRAECIZED > GRAECIZE

GRAECIZES > GRAECIZE

GRAFF *same as* > GRAFT

GRAFFED > GRAFF

GRAFFING > GRAFF

GRAFFITI *pl n* words or drawings scribbled or sprayed on walls etc

GRAFFITIS > GRAFFITI

GRAFFITO *n* instance of graffiti

GRAFFS > GRAFF

GRAFT *n* surgical transplant of skin or tissue ▷ *vb* transplant (living tissue) surgically

GRAFTAGE *n* in horticulture, the art of grafting

GRAFTAGES > GRAFTAGE

GRAFTED > GRAFT

GRAFTER > GRAFT

GRAFTERS > GRAFT

GRAFTING > GRAFT

GRAFTINGS > GRAFT

GRAFTS > GRAFT

GRAHAM *n* made of graham flour

GRAHAMS > GRAHAM

GRAIL *n* any desired ambition or goal

GRAILE *same as* > GRAIL

GRAILES > GRAILE

GRAILS > GRAIL

GRAIN *n* seedlike fruit of a cereal plant ▷ *vb* paint in imitation of the grain of wood or leather

GRAINAGE *n* duty paid on grain

GRAINAGES > GRAINAGE

GRAINE *n* eggs of the silkworm

GRAINED > GRAIN

GRAINER > GRAIN

GRAINERS > GRAIN

GRAINES > GRAINE

GRAINIER > GRAINY

GRAINIEST > GRAINY

GRAINING *n* pattern or texture of the grain of wood, leather, etc

GRAININGS > GRAINING

GRAINLESS > GRAIN

GRAINS > GRAIN

GRAINY *adj* resembling, full of, or composed of grain

GRAIP *n* long-handled gardening fork

GRAIPS > GRAIP

GRAITH *vb* clothe

GRAITHED > GRAITH

GRAITHING > GRAITH

GRAITHLY > GRAITH

GRAITHS > GRAITH

GRAKLE *same as* > GRACKLE

GRAKLES > GRAKLE

GRALLOCH *n* entrails of a deer ▷ *vb* disembowel (a deer killed in a hunt)

GRALLOCHS > GRALLOCH

GRAM *n* metric unit of mass equal to one thousandth of a kilogram

GRAMA *n* any of various grasses of the genus *Bouteloua*, of W North America and South America: often used as

pasture grasses

GRAMARIES > GRAMARY

GRAMARY *same as* > GRAMARYE

GRAMARYE *n* magic, necromancy, or occult learning

GRAMARYES > GRAMARYE

GRAMAS > GRAMA

GRAMASH *n* type of gaiter

GRAMASHES > GRAMASH

GRAME *n* sorrow

GRAMERCY *interj* many thanks

GRAMES > GRAME

GRAMMA *n* pasture grass of the South American plains

GRAMMAGE *n* weight of paper expressed as grams per square metre

GRAMMAGES > GRAMMAGE

GRAMMAR *n* branch of linguistics dealing with the form, function, and order of words

GRAMMARS > GRAMMAR

GRAMMAS > GRAMMA

GRAMMATIC *adj* of or relating to grammar

GRAMME *same as* > GRAME

GRAMMES > GRAM

GRAMOCHE *same as* > GRAMASH

GRAMOCHES > GRAMOCHE

GRAMP *n* grandfather

GRAMPA *variant of* > GRANDPA

GRAMPAS > GRAMPA

GRAMPS > GRAMP

GRAMPUS *n* dolphin-like mammal

GRAMPUSES > GRAMPUS

GRAMS > GRAM

GRAN *n* grandmother

GRANA > GRANUM

GRANARIES > GRANARY

GRANARY *n* storehouse for grain

GRAND *adj* large or impressive, imposing ▷ *n* thousand pounds or dollars

GRANDAD *n* grandfather

GRANDADDY *same as* > GRANDAD

GRANDADS > GRANDAD

GRANDAM *archaic word for* > GRANDMOTHER

GRANDAME *same as* > GRANDAM

GRANDAMES > GRANDAME

GRANDAMS > GRANDAM

GRANDAUNT *n* great-aunt

GRANDBABY *n* very young grandchild

GRANDDAD *same as* > GRANDDAD

GRANDDADS > GRANDAD

GRANDDAM *same as* > GRANDAM

GRANDDAMS > GRANDDAM

GRANDE *feminine form of* > GRAND

GRANDEE *n* Spanish nobleman of the highest rank

GRANDEES > GRANDEE

GRANDER > GRAND

GRANDEST > GRAND

GRANDEUR *n* magnificence

GRANDEURS > GRANDEUR

GRANDIOSE *adj* imposing

GRANDIOSO *adv* (to be played) in a grand manner

GRANDKID *n* grandchild

GRANDKIDS > GRANDKID

GRANDLY > GRAND

GRANDMA *n* grandmother

GRANDMAMA *same as* > GRANDMA

GRANDMAS > GRANDMA

GRANDNESS > GRAND

GRANDPA *n* grandfather

GRANDPAPA *same as* > GRANDPA

GRANDPAS > GRANDPA

GRANDS > GRAND

GRANDSIR *same as* > GRANDSIRE

GRANDSIRE *n* grandfather

GRANDSIRS > GRANDSIR

GRANDSON *n* male grandchild

GRANDSONS > GRANDSON

GRANFER *n* grandfather

GRANFERS > GRANFER

GRANGE *n* country house with farm buildings

GRANGER *n* keeper or member of a grange

GRANGERS > GRANGER

GRANGES > GRANGE

GRANITA *n* Italian iced drink

GRANITAS > GRANITA

GRANITE *n* very hard igneous rock often used in building

GRANITES > GRANITE

GRANITIC > GRANITE

GRANITISE *vb* form granite

GRANITITE *n* any granite with a high content of biotite

GRANITIZE *same as* > GRANITISE

GRANITOID > GRANITE

GRANIVORE *n* animal that feeds on seeds and grain

GRANNAM *n* old woman

GRANNAMS > GRANNAM

GRANNIE *vb* defeat (in a game or contest) so that one's opponent does not score a single point

GRANNIED > GRANNY

GRANNIES *pl n* Granny Smith apples

GRANNOM *n* widespread caddis fly, *Brachycentrus subnubilus*, the larvae of which attach their cases to vegetation under running water and are esteemed as a bait by anglers

GRANNOMS > GRANNOM

GRANNY *n* grandmother ▷ *vb* defeat (in a game or contest) so that one's opponent does not score a single point

GRANNYING > GRANNY

GRANNYISH *adj* typical of or suitable for an elderly woman

GRANOLA *n* muesli-like breakfast cereal

GRANOLAS > GRANOLA

GRANOLITH n paving material consisting of a mixture of cement and crushed granite or granite chippings

GRANS > GRAN

GRANT vb consent to fulfil (a request) ▷ n sum of money provided by a government for a specific purpose, such as education

GRANTABLE > GRANT

GRANTED > GRANT

GRANTEE n person to whom a grant is made

GRANTEES > GRANTEE

GRANTER > GRANT

GRANTERS > GRANT

GRANTING > GRANT

GRANTOR n person who makes a grant

GRANTORS > GRANTOR

GRANTS > GRANT

GRANTSMAN n student who specializes in obtaining grants

GRANTSMEN > GRANTSMAN

GRANULAR adj of or like grains

GRANULARY adj granular

GRANULATE vb make into grains

GRANULE n small grain

GRANULES > GRANULE

GRANULITE n granular foliated metamorphic rock in which the minerals form a mosaic of equal-sized granules

GRANULOMA n tumour composed of granulation tissue produced in response to chronic infection, inflammation, a foreign body, or to unknown causes

GRANULOSE less common word for > GRANULAR

GRANULOUS adj consisting of grains or granules

GRANUM n membrane layers in a chloroplast

GRAPE n small juicy green or purple berry, eaten raw or used to produce wine, raisins, currants, or sultanas ▷ vb grope

GRAPED > GRAPE

GRAPELESS > GRAPE

GRAPELIKE > GRAPE

GRAPERIES > GRAPERY

GRAPERY n building where grapes are grown

GRAPES n abnormal growth, resembling a bunch of grapes, on the fetlock of a horse

GRAPESEED n seed of the grape

GRAPESHOT n bullets which scatter when fired

GRAPETREE n sea grape, a shrubby plant resembling a grapevine

GRAPEVINE n grape-bearing vine

GRAPEY > GRAPE

GRAPH n drawing showing the relation of different numbers or quantities plotted against a set of axes ▷ vb draw or represent in a graph

GRAPHED > GRAPH

GRAPHEME n one of a set of orthographic symbols (letters or combinations of letters) in a given language that serve to distinguish one word from another and usually correspond to or represent phonemes, e.g. the f in fun, the ph in phantom, and the gh in laugh

GRAPHEMES > GRAPHEME

GRAPHEMIC > GRAPHEME

GRAPHIC adj vividly descriptive

GRAPHICAL same as > GRAPHIC

GRAPHICLY > GRAPHIC

GRAPHICS pl n diagrams, graphs, etc, esp as used on a television programme or computer screen

GRAPHING > GRAPH

GRAPHITE n soft black form of carbon, used in pencil leads

GRAPHITES > GRAPHITE

GRAPHITIC > GRAPHITE

GRAPHIUM n stylus (for writing)

GRAPHIUMS > GRAPHIUM

GRAPHS > GRAPH

GRAPIER > GRAPE

GRAPIEST > GRAPE

GRAPINESS > GRAPE

GRAPING > GRAPE

GRAPLE same as > GRAPPLE

GRAPLES > GRAPLE

GRAPLIN same as > GRAPNEL

GRAPLINE same as > GRAPNEL

GRAPLINES > GRAPLINE

GRAPLINS > GRAPLIN

GRAPNEL n device with several hooks, used to grasp or secure things

GRAPNELS > GRAPNEL

GRAPPA n spirit distilled from the fermented remains of grapes after pressing

GRAPPAS > GRAPPA

GRAPPLE vb try to cope with (something difficult) ▷ n grapnel

GRAPPLED > GRAPPLE

GRAPPLER > GRAPPLE

GRAPPLERS > GRAPPLE

GRAPPLES > GRAPPLE

GRAPPLING n act of gripping or seizing, as in wrestling

GRAPY > GRAPE

GRASP vb grip something firmly ▷ n grip or clasp

GRASPABLE > GRASP

GRASPED > GRASP

GRASPER > GRASP

GRASPERS > GRASP

GRASPING adj greedy or avaricious

GRASPLESS adj relaxed

GRASPS > GRASP

GRASS n common type of plant with jointed stems and long narrow leaves, including cereals and bamboo ▷ vb cover with grass

GRASSED > GRASS

GRASSER n police informant

GRASSERS > GRASSER

GRASSES > GRASS

GRASSHOOK another name for > SICKLE

GRASSIER > GRASSY

GRASSIEST > GRASSY

GRASSILY > GRASSY

GRASSING > GRASS

GRASSINGS > GRASS

GRASSLAND n land covered with grass

GRASSLESS > GRASS

GRASSLIKE > GRASS

GRASSPLOT n plot of ground overgrown with grass

GRASSQUIT n any tropical American finch of the genus Tiaris and related genera, such as T. olivacea (yellow-faced grassquit)

GRASSROOT adj relating to the ordinary people, especially as part of the electorate

GRASSUM n in Scots law, lump sum paid when taking up a lease

GRASSUMS > GRASSUM

GRASSY adj covered with, containing, or resembling grass

GRASTE archaic past participle of > GRACE

GRAT > GREET

GRATE vb rub into small bits on a rough surface ▷ n framework of metal bars for holding fuel in a fireplace

GRATED > GRATE

GRATEFUL adj feeling or showing gratitude

GRATELESS > GRATE

GRATER n tool with a sharp surface for grating food

GRATERS > GRATER

GRATES > GRATE

GRATICULE n grid of intersecting lines, esp of latitude and longitude on which a map is drawn

GRATIFIED > GRATIFY

GRATIFIER > GRATIFY

GRATIFIES > GRATIFY

GRATIFY vb satisfy or please ▷ adj giving one satisfaction or pleasure

GRATIN n crust of browned breadcrumbs

GRATINATE vb cook until the juice is absorbed and the surface crisps

GRATINE adj cooked au gratin

GRATINEE vb cook au gratin

GRATINEED > GRATINEE

GRATINEES > GRATINEE

GRATING adj harsh or rasping ▷ n framework of metal bars covering an opening

GRATINGLY > GRATING

GRATINGS > GRATING

GRATINS > GRATIN

GRATIS adj free, for nothing

GRATITUDE n feeling of being thankful for a favour or gift

GRATTOIR n scraper made of flint

GRATTOIRS > GRATTOIR

GRATUITY n money given for services rendered, tip

GRATULANT > GRATULATE

GRATULATE vb greet joyously

GRAUNCH vb crush or destroy

GRAUNCHED > GRAUNCH

GRAUNCHER > GRAUNCH

GRAUNCHES > GRAUNCH

GRAUPEL n soft hail or snow pellets

GRAUPELS > GRAUPEL

GRAV n unit of acceleration equal to the standard acceleration of free fall

GRAVADLAX same as > GRAVLAX

GRAVAMEN n that part of an accusation weighing most heavily against an accused

GRAVAMENS > GRAVAMEN

GRAVAMINA > GRAVAMEN

GRAVE n hole for burying a corpse ▷ adj causing concern ▷ vb cut, carve, sculpt, or engrave ▷ adv to be performed in a solemn manner

GRAVED > GRAVE

GRAVEL n mixture of small stones and coarse sand ▷ vb cover with gravel

GRAVELED > GRAVEL

GRAVELESS > GRAVE

GRAVELIKE > GRAVE

GRAVELING > GRAVEL

GRAVELISH > GRAVEL

GRAVELLED > GRAVEL

GRAVELLY adj covered with gravel

GRAVELS > GRAVEL

GRAVELY > GRAVE

GRAVEN > GRAVE

GRAVENESS > GRAVE

GRAVER n any of various engraving, chasing, or sculpting tools, such as a burin

GRAVERS > GRAVER

GRAVES > GRAVE

GRAVESIDE n area surrounding a grave

GRAVESITE n site of grave

GRAVEST > GRAVE

GRAVEWARD adj moving towards grave

GRAVEYARD n cemetery

GRAVID adj pregnant

GRAVIDA n pregnant woman

GRAVIDAE > GRAVIDA

g

GRAVIDAS > GRAVIDA
GRAVIDITY > GRAVID
GRAVIDLY > GRAVID
GRAVIES > GRAVY
GRAVING > GRAVE
GRAVINGS > GRAVE
> GRAVIPERCEPTION
GRAVIS as in *myasthenia gravis* chronic muscle-weakening disease
GRAVITAS *n* seriousness or solemnity
GRAVITATE *vb* be influenced or drawn towards
GRAVITIES > GRAVITY
GRAVITINO *n* hypothetical subatomic particle
GRAVITON *n* postulated quantum of gravitational energy
GRAVITONS > GRAVITON
GRAVITY *n* force of attraction of one object for another, esp of objects to the earth
GRAVLAKS *same as* > GRAVLAX
GRAVLAX *n* dry-cured salmon, marinated in salt, sugar, and spices, as served in Scandinavia
GRAVLAXES > GRAVLAX
GRAVS > GRAV
GRAVURE *n* method of intaglio printing using a plate with many small etched recesses
GRAVURES > GRAVURE
GRAVY *n* juices from meat in cooking
GRAY *same as* > GREY
GRAYBACK *same as* > GREYBACK
GRAYBACKS > GRAYBACK
GRAYBEARD *same as* > GREYBEARD
GRAYED > GRAY
GRAYER > GRAY
GRAYEST > GRAY
GRAYFISH *n* dogfish
GRAYFLIES > GRAYFLY
GRAYFLY *n* trumpet fly
GRAYHOUND *US spelling of* > GREYHOUND
GRAYING > GRAY
GRAYISH > GRAY
GRAYLAG *same as* > GREYLAG
GRAYLAGS > GRAYLAG
GRAYLE *n* holy grail
GRAYLES > GRAYLE
GRAYLING *n* fish of the salmon family
GRAYLINGS > GRAYLING
GRAYLY > GRAY
GRAYMAIL *n* tactic to avoid prosecution in espionage case by threatening to expose state secrets during trial
GRAYMAILS > GRAYMAIL
GRAYNESS > GREY
GRAYOUT *n* in aeronautics, impairment of vision due to lack of oxygen
GRAYOUTS > GRAYOUT
GRAYS > GRAY
GRAYSCALE *adj* in shades

of grey
GRAYWACKE *same as* > GREYWACKE
GRAYWATER *n* water that has been used
GRAZABLE > GRAZE
GRAZE *vb* feed on grass ▷ *n* slight scratch or scrape
GRAZEABLE > GRAZE
GRAZED > GRAZE
GRAZER > GRAZE
GRAZERS > GRAZE
GRAZES > GRAZE
GRAZIER *n* person who feeds cattle for market
GRAZIERS > GRAZIER
GRAZING *n* land on which grass for livestock is grown
GRAZINGLY > GRAZE
GRAZINGS > GRAZING
GRAZIOSO *adv* (of music) to be played gracefully
GREASE *n* soft melted animal fat ▷ *vb* apply grease to
GREASED > GREASE
GREASER *n* mechanic, esp of motor vehicles
GREASERS > GREASER
GREASES > GREASE
GREASIER > GREASY
GREASIES > GREASY
GREASIEST > GREASY
GREASILY > GREASY
GREASING > GREASE
GREASY *adj* covered with or containing grease ▷ *n* shearer
GREAT *adj* large in size or number ▷ *n* distinguished person
GREATCOAT *n* heavy overcoat
GREATEN *vb* make or become great
GREATENED > GREATEN
GREATENS > GREATEN
GREATER > GREAT
GREATEST *n* most outstanding individual in a given field
GREATESTS > GREATEST
GREATLY > GREAT
GREATNESS > GREAT
GREATS > GREAT
GREAVE *n* piece of armour for the shin ▷ *vb* grieve
GREAVED > GREAVE
GREAVES *pl n* residue left after the rendering of tallow
GREAVING > GREAVE
GREBE *n* diving water bird
GREBES > GREBE
GRECE *n* flight of steps
GRECES > GRECE
GRECIAN *same as* > GRECE
GRECIANS > GRECIAN
GRECISE *same as* > GRAECIZE
GRECISED > GRECISE
GRECISES > GRECISE
GRECISING > GRECISE
GRECIZE *same as* > GRAECIZE
GRECIZED > GRECIZE
GRECIZES > GRECIZE
GRECIZING > GRECIZE
GRECQUE *n* ornament of

Greek origin
GRECQUES > GRECQUE
GREE *n* superiority or victory ▷ *vb* come or cause to come to agreement or harmony
GREEBO *n* unkempt or dirty-looking young man
GREEBOES > GREEBO
GREECE *same as* > GRECE
GREECES > GREECE
GREED *n* excessive desire for food, wealth, etc
GREEDIER > GREEDY
GREEDIEST > GREEDY
GREEDILY > GREEDY
GREEDLESS > GREED
GREEDS > GREED
GREEDSOME *same as* > GREEDY
GREEDY *adj* having an excessive desire for something, such as food or money
GREEGREE *same as* > GRIGRI
GREEGREES > GREEGREE
GREEING > GREE
GREEK *vb* represent text as grey lines on a computer screen
GREEKED > GREEK
GREEKING > GREEK
GREEKINGS > GREEK
GREEN *adj* of a colour between blue and yellow ▷ *n* colour between blue and yellow ▷ *vb* make or become green
GREENBACK *n* inconvertible legal-tender US currency note originally issued during the Civil War in 1862
GREENBELT *n* zone of farmland, parks, and open country surrounding a town or city
GREENBONE *another name for* > BUTTERFISH
GREENBUG *n* common name for Schizaphis graminum
GREENBUGS > GREENBUG
GREENED > GREEN
GREENER *n* recent immigrant
GREENERS > GREENER
GREENERY *n* vegetation
GREENEST > GREEN
GREENFLY *n* green aphid, a common garden pest
GREENGAGE *n* sweet green plum
GREENHAND *n* greenhorn
GREENHEAD *n* male mallard
GREENHORN *n* novice
GREENIE *n* conservationist
GREENIER > GREEN
GREENIES > GREENIE
GREENIEST > GREEN
GREENING *n* process of making or becoming more aware of environmental considerations
GREENINGS > GREENING
GREENISH > GREEN
GREENLET *n* vireo, esp one of the genus Hylophilus
GREENLETS > GREENLET

GREENLING *n* any scorpaenoid food fish of the family *Hexagrammidae* of the North Pacific Ocean
GREENLIT *adj* given permission to proceed
GREENLY > GREEN
GREENMAIL *n* practice of a company buying sufficient shares in another company to threaten takeover and making a quick profit as a result of the threatened company buying back its shares at a higher price ▷ *vb* carry out the practice of greenmail
GREENNESS > GREEN
GREENROOM *n* backstage room in a theatre where performers rest or receive visitors
GREENS > GREEN
GREENSAND *n* olive-green sandstone consisting mainly of quartz and glauconite
GREENSICK *adj* suffering from greensickness: same as chlorosis
GREENSOME *n* match for two pairs in which each of the four players tees off and after selecting the better drive the partners of each pair play that ball alternately
GREENTH *n* greenness
GREENTHS > GREENTH
GREENWASH *n* superficial or insincere display of concern for the environment that is shown by an organization ▷ *vb* adopt a 'greenwash' policy
GREENWAY *n* linear open space, with pedestrian and cycle paths
GREENWAYS > GREENWAY
GREENWEED *n* woodwaxen
GREENWING *n* teal
GREENWOOD *n* forest or wood when the leaves are green
GREENY > GREEN
GREES > GREE
GREESE *same as* > GRECE
GREESES > GREESE
GREESING > GREESE
GREESINGS > GREESE
GREET *vb* meet with expressions of welcome ▷ *n* weeping
GREETE *same as* > GREET
GREETED > GREET
GREETER *n* person who greets people at the entrance of a shop, restaurant, casino, etc
GREETERS > GREETER
GREETES > GREETE
GREETING *n* act or words of welcoming on meeting
GREETINGS > GREETING
GREETS > GREET
GREFFIER *n* registrar
GREFFIERS > GREFFIER

GREGALE n northeasterly wind occurring in the Mediterranean
GREGALES > GREGALE
GREGARIAN adj gregarious
GREGARINE n any parasitic protozoan of the order Gregarinida, typically occurring in the digestive tract and body cavity of other invertebrates: phylum Apicomplexa (sporozoans) ▷ adj of, relating to, or belonging to the Gregarinida
GREGATIM adv in flocks or crowds
GREGE vb make heavy
GREGO n short, thick jacket
GREGOS > GREGO
GREIGE adj (of a fabric or material) not yet dyed ▷ n unbleached or undyed cloth or yarn
GREIGES > GREIGE
GREIN vb desire fervently
GREINED > GREIN
GREINING > GREIN
GREINS > GREIN
GREISEN n light-coloured metamorphic rock consisting mainly of quartz, white mica, and topaz formed by the pneumatolysis of granite
GREISENS > GREISEN
GREISLY same as > GRISLY
GREMIAL n cloth spread upon the lap of a bishop when seated during Mass
GREMIALS > GREMIAL
GREMLIN n imaginary being blamed for mechanical malfunctions
GREMLINS > GREMLIN
GREMMIE n young surfer
GREMMIES > GREMMIE
GREMMY same as > GREMMIE
GREMOLATA n garnish of finely chopped parsley, garlic and lemon
GREN same as > GRIN
GRENADE n small bomb thrown by hand or fired from a rifle
GRENADES > GRENADE
GRENADIER n soldier of a regiment formerly trained to throw grenades
GRENADINE n syrup made from pomegranates
GRENNED > GREN
GRENNING > GREN
GRENS > GREN
GRENZ as in grenz rays X-rays of long wavelength produced in a device when electrons are accelerated through 25 kilovolts or less
GRESE same as > GRECE
GRESES > GRESE
GRESSING same as > GRECE
GRESSINGS > GRESSING
GREVE same as > GREAVE
GREVES > GREVE
GREVILLEA n any of various Australian evergreen trees

and shrubs
GREW vb shudder
GREWED > GROW
GREWHOUND n greyhound
GREWING > GROW
GREWS > GROW
GREWSOME archaic or US spelling of > GRUESOME
GREWSOMER > GREWSOME
GREX n group of plants that has arisen from the same hybrid parent group
GREXES > GREX
GREY adj of a colour between black and white ▷ n grey colour ▷ vb become or make grey
GREYBACK n any of various animals having a grey back, such as the grey whale and the hooded crow
GREYBACKS > GREYBACK
GREYBEARD n old man, esp a sage
GREYED > GREY
GREYER > GREY
GREYEST > GREY
GREYHEN n female of the black grouse
GREYHENS > GREYHEN
GREYHOUND n swift slender dog used in racing
GREYING > GREY
GREYINGS > GREY
GREYISH > GREY
GREYLAG n large grey goose
GREYLAGS > GREYLAG
GREYLIST vb hold (someone) in suspicion, without actually excluding him or her from a particular activity
GREYLISTS > GREYLIST
GREYLY > GREY
GREYNESS > GREY
GREYS > GREY
GREYSTONE n type of grey rock
GREYWACKE n any dark sandstone or grit having a matrix of clay minerals
GRIBBLE n any small marine isopod crustacean of the genus Limnoria, which bores into and damages wharves and other submerged wooden structures
GRIBBLES > GRIBBLE
GRICE vb (of a railway enthusiast) to collect objects or visit places connected with trains and railways ▷ n object collected or place visited by a railway enthusiast
GRICED > GRICE
GRICER > GRICE
GRICERS > GRICE
GRICES > GRICE
GRICING > GRICE
GRICINGS > GRICE
GRID n network of horizontal and vertical lines, bars, etc
GRIDDED > GRID
GRIDDER n American

football player
GRIDDERS > GRIDDER
GRIDDLE n flat iron plate for cooking ▷ vb cook (food) on a griddle
GRIDDLED > GRIDDLE
GRIDDLES > GRIDDLE
GRIDDLING > GRIDDLE
GRIDE vb grate or scrape harshly ▷ n harsh or piercing sound
GRIDED > GRIDE
GRIDELIN n greyish violet colour
GRIDELINS > GRIDELIN
GRIDES > GRIDE
GRIDING > GRIDE
GRIDIRON n frame of metal bars for grilling food ▷ vb cover with parallel lines
GRIDIRONS > GRIDIRON
GRIDLOCK n situation where traffic is not moving ▷ vb (of traffic) to obstruct (an area)
GRIDLOCKS > GRIDLOCK
GRIDS > GRID
GRIECE same as > GRECE
GRIECED > GRIECE
GRIECES > GRIECE
GRIEF n deep sadness
GRIEFER n online game player who intentionally spoils the game for other players
GRIEFERS > GRIEFER
GRIEFFUL adj stricken with grief
GRIEFLESS > GRIEF
GRIEFS > GRIEF
GRIESIE same as > GRISY
GRIESLY same as > GRISY
GRIESY same as > GRISY
GRIEVANCE n real or imaginary cause for complaint
GRIEVANT n any person with a grievance
GRIEVANTS > GRIEVANT
GRIEVE vb (cause to) feel grief ▷ n farm manager or overseer
GRIEVED > GRIEVE
GRIEVER > GRIEVE
GRIEVERS > GRIEVE
GRIEVES > GRIEVE
GRIEVING > GRIEVE
GRIEVINGS > GRIEVE
GRIEVOUS adj very severe or painful
GRIFF n information
GRIFFE n carved ornament at the base of a column, often in the form of a claw
GRIFFES > GRIFFE
GRIFFIN n mythical monster with an eagle's head and wings and a lion's body
GRIFFINS > GRIFFIN
GRIFFON same as > GRIFFIN
GRIFFONS > GRIFFON
GRIFFS > GRIFF
GRIFT vb swindle
GRIFTED > GRIFT
GRIFTER > GRIFT
GRIFTERS > GRIFT

GRIFTING > GRIFT
GRIFTS > GRIFT
GRIG n lively person ▷ vb fish for grigs
GRIGGED > GRIG
GRIGGING > GRIG
GRIGRI n African talisman, amulet, or charm
GRIGRIS > GRIGRI
GRIGS > GRIG
GRIKE n solution fissure, a vertical crack about 0.5 m wide formed by the dissolving of limestone by water, that divides an exposed limestone surface into sections or clints
GRIKES > GRIKE
GRILL n device on a cooker that radiates heat downwards ▷ vb cook under a grill
GRILLADE n grilled food
GRILLADES > GRILLADE
GRILLAGE n arrangement of beams and crossbeams used as a foundation on soft ground
GRILLAGES > GRILLAGE
GRILLE n grating over an opening
GRILLED adj cooked on a grill or gridiron
GRILLER > GRILL
GRILLERS > GRILL
GRILLERY n place where food is grilled
GRILLES > GRILLE
GRILLING > GRILL
GRILLINGS > GRILL
GRILLION n extremely large but unspecified number, quantity, or amount ▷ determiner amounting to a grillion
GRILLIONS > GRILLION
GRILLROOM n restaurant serving grilled foods
GRILLS > GRILL
GRILLWORK same as > GRILL
GRILSE n salmon on its first return from the sea to fresh water
GRILSES > GRILSE
GRIM adj stern
GRIMACE n ugly or distorted facial expression of pain, disgust, etc ▷ vb make a grimace
GRIMACED > GRIMACE
GRIMACER > GRIMACE
GRIMACERS > GRIMACE
GRIMACES > GRIMACE
GRIMACING > GRIMACE
GRIMALKIN n old cat, esp an old female cat
GRIME n ingrained dirt ▷ vb make very dirty
GRIMED > GRIME
GRIMES > GRIME
GRIMIER > GRIME
GRIMIEST > GRIME
GRIMILY > GRIME
GRIMINESS > GRIME
GRIMING > GRIME
GRIMLY > GRIM
GRIMMER > GRIM

GRIMMEST > GRIM

GRIMNESS > GRIM

GRIMOIRE n textbook of sorcery and magic

GRIMOIRES > GRIMOIRE

GRIMY > GRIME

GRIN vb smile broadly, showing the teeth ▷ n broad smile

GRINCH n person whose lack of enthusiasm or bad temper has a depressing effect on others

GRINCHES > GRINCH

GRIND vb crush or rub to a powder ▷ n hard work

GRINDED obsolete past participle of > GRIND

GRINDELIA n any coarse plant of the American genus Grindelia, having yellow daisy-like flower heads: family Asteraceae (composites)

GRINDER n device for grinding substances

GRINDERS > GRINDER

GRINDERY n place in which tools and cutlery are sharpened

GRINDING > GRIND

GRINDINGS > GRIND

GRINDS > GRIND

GRINGA n female gringo

GRINGAS > GRINGA

GRINGO n person from an English-speaking country: used as a derogatory term by Latin Americans

GRINGOS > GRINGO

GRINNED > GRIN

GRINNER > GRIN

GRINNERS > GRIN

GRINNING > GRIN

GRINNINGS > GRIN

GRINS > GRIN

GRIOT n (in Western Africa) member of a caste responsible for maintaining an oral record of tribal history in the form of music, poetry, and storytelling

GRIOTS > GRIOT

GRIP n firm hold or grasp ▷ vb grasp or hold tightly

GRIPE vb complain persistently ▷ n complaint

GRIPED > GRIPE

GRIPER > GRIPE

GRIPERS > GRIPE

GRIPES > GRIPE

GRIPEY adj causing gripes

GRIPIER > GRIPEY

GRIPIEST > GRIPEY

GRIPING > GRIPE

GRIPINGLY > GRIPE

GRIPLE same as > GRIPPLE

GRIPMAN n cable-car operator

GRIPMEN > GRIPMAN

GRIPPE former name for > INFLUENZA

GRIPPED > GRIP

GRIPPER > GRIP

GRIPPERS > GRIP

GRIPPES > GRIPPE

GRIPPIER > GRIPPY

GRIPPIEST > GRIPPY

GRIPPING > GRIP

GRIPPLE adj greedy ▷ n hook

GRIPPLES > GRIPPLE

GRIPPY adj having grip

GRIPS > GRIP

GRIPSACK n travel bag

GRIPSACKS > GRIPSACK

GRIPT archaic variant of > GRIPPED

GRIPTAPE n rough tape for sticking to a surface to provide a greater grip

GRIPTAPES > GRIPTAPE

GRIPY same as > GRIPEY

GRIS same as > GRECE

GRISAILLE n technique of monochrome painting in shades of grey, as in an oil painting or a wall decoration, imitating the effect of relief

GRISE vb shudder

GRISED > GRISE

GRISELY same as > GRISLY

GRISEOUS adj streaked or mixed with grey

GRISES > GRISE

GRISETTE n (esp formerly) a French working-class girl, esp a pretty or flirtatious one

GRISETTES > GRISETTE

GRISGRIS same as > GRIGRI

GRISING > GRISE

GRISKIN n lean part of a loin of pork

GRISKINS > GRISKIN

GRISLED another word for > GRIZZLED

GRISLIER > GRISLY

GRISLIES > GRISLY

GRISLIEST > GRISLY

GRISLY adj horrifying or ghastly ▷ n large American bear

GRISON n either of two musteline mammals, Grison (or Galictis) cuja or G. vittata, of Central and South America, having a greyish back and black face and underparts

GRISONS > GRISON

GRISSINI pl n thin crisp breadsticks

GRIST n grain for grinding

GRISTER n device for grinding grain

GRISTERS > GRISTER

GRISTLE n tough stringy animal tissue found in meat

GRISTLES > GRISTLE

GRISTLIER > GRISTLE

GRISTLY > GRISTLE

GRISTMILL n mill, esp one equipped with large grinding stones for grinding grain

GRISTS > GRIST

GRISY adj grim

GRIT n rough particles of sand ▷ vb spread grit on (an icy road etc) ▷ adj great

GRITH n security, peace, or protection, guaranteed either in a certain place, such as a church, or for a period of time

GRITHS > GRITH

GRITLESS > GRIT

GRITS > GRIT

GRITSTONE same as > GRIT

GRITTED > GRIT

GRITTER n vehicle that spreads grit on the roads in icy weather

GRITTERS > GRITTER

GRITTEST > GRIT

GRITTIER > GRITTY

GRITTIEST > GRITTY

GRITTILY > GRITTY

GRITTING > GRIT

GRITTY adj courageous and tough

GRIVATION n (in navigation) grid variation

GRIVET n E African variety of a common guenon monkey, Cercopithecus aethiops, having long white tufts of hair on either side of the face

GRIVETS > GRIVET

GRIZE same as > GRECE

GRIZES > GRIZE

GRIZZLE vb whine or complain ▷ n grey colour

GRIZZLED adj grey-haired

GRIZZLER > GRIZZLE

GRIZZLERS > GRIZZLE

GRIZZLES > GRIZZLE

GRIZZLIER > GRIZZLY

GRIZZLIES > GRIZZLY

GRIZZLING > GRIZZLE

GRIZZLY n large American bear ▷ adj somewhat grey

GROAN n deep sound of grief or pain ▷ vb utter a groan

GROANED > GROAN

GROANER n person or thing that groans

GROANERS > GROANER

GROANFUL adj sad

GROANING > GROAN

GROANINGS > GROAN

GROANS > GROAN

GROAT n fourpenny piece

GROATS pl n hulled and crushed grain of various cereals

GROCER n shopkeeper selling foodstuffs

GROCERIES pl n food and other household supplies

GROCERS > GROCER

GROCERY n business or premises of a grocer

GROCKLE n tourist, esp one from the Midlands or the North of England

GROCKLES > GROCKLE

GRODIER > GRODY

GRODIEST > GRODY

GRODY adj unpleasant

GROG n spirit, usu rum, and water ▷ vb drink grog

GROGGED > GROG

GROGGERY n grogshop

GROGGIER > GROGGY

GROGGIEST > GROGGY

GROGGILY > GROGGY

GROGGING > GROG

GROGGY adj faint, shaky, or dizzy

GROGRAM n coarse fabric of silk, wool, or silk mixed with wool or mohair, often stiffened with gum, formerly used for clothing

GROGRAMS > GROGRAM

GROGS > GROG

GROGSHOP n drinking place, esp one of disreputable character

GROGSHOPS > GROGSHOP

GROIN n place where the legs join the abdomen ▷ vb provide or construct with groins

GROINED > GROIN

GROINING > GROIN

GROININGS > GROIN

GROINS > GROIN

GROK vb understand completely and intuitively

GROKKED > GROK

GROKKING > GROK

GROKS > GROK

GROMA n Roman surveying instrument

GROMAS > GROMA

GROMET same as > GROMMET

GROMETS > GROMET

GROMMET n ring or eyelet

GROMMETED adj having grommets

GROMMETS > GROMMET

GROMWELL n any of various hairy plants of the boraginaceous genus Lithospermum, esp L. officinale, having small greenish-white, yellow, or blue flowers, and smooth nutlike fruits

GROMWELLS > GROMWELL

GRONE obsolete word for > GROAN

GRONED > GRONE

GRONEFULL same as > GROANFUL

GRONES > GRONE

GRONING > GRONE

GROOF n face, or front of the body

GROOFS > GROOF

GROOLIER > GROOLY

GROOLIEST > GROOLY

GROOLY adj gruesome

GROOM n person who looks after horses ▷ vb make or keep one's clothes and appearance neat and tidy

GROOMED > GROOM

GROOMER > GROOM

GROOMERS > GROOM

GROOMING > GROOM

GROOMINGS > GROOM

GROOMS > GROOM

GROOMSMAN n man who attends the bridegroom at a wedding, usually the best man

GROOMSMEN > GROOMSMAN

GROOVE n long narrow channel in a surface

GROOVED > GROOVE

GROOVER n device that makes grooves

GROOVERS > GROOVER

GROOVES > GROOVE

GROOVIER > GROOVY

GROOVIEST > GROOVY

GROOVING > GROOVE

GROOVY adj attractive or exciting

GROPE vb feel about or search uncertainly ▷n instance of groping

GROPED > GROPE

GROPER n any large marine serranid fish of the genus Epinephelus and related genera, of warm and tropical seas

GROPERS > GROPER

GROPES > GROPE

GROPING > GROPE

GROPINGLY > GROPE

GROSBEAK n finch with a large powerful bill

GROSBEAKS > GROSBEAK

GROSCHEN n former Austrian monetary unit worth one hundredth of a schilling

GROSCHENS > GROSCHEN

GROSER n gooseberry

GROSERS > GROSER

GROSERT another word for > GROSER

GROSERTS > GROSERT

GROSET another word for > GROSER

GROSETS > GROSET

GROSGRAIN n heavy ribbed silk or rayon fabric

GROSS adj flagrant ▷n twelve dozen ▷vb make as total revenue before deductions ▷interj exclamation indicating disgust

GROSSART another word for > GROSER

GROSSARTS > GROSSART

GROSSED > GROSS

GROSSER > GROSS

GROSSERS > GROSS

GROSSES > GROSS

GROSSEST > GROSS

GROSSING > GROSS

GROSSLY > GROSS

GROSSNESS > GROSS

GROSSULAR n type of garnet

GROSZ n Polish monetary unit worth one hundredth of a zloty

GROSZE > GROSZ

GROSZY > GROSZ

GROT n rubbish

GROTESQUE adj strangely distorted ▷n grotesque person or thing

GROTS > GROT

GROTTIER > GROTTY

GROTTIEST > GROTTY

GROTTO n small picturesque cave

GROTTOED adj having grotto

GROTTOES > GROTTO

GROTTOS > GROTTO

GROTTY adj nasty or in bad condition

GROUCH vb grumble or complain ▷n person who is always complaining

GROUCHED > GROUCH

GROUCHES > GROUCH

GROUCHIER > GROUCHY

GROUCHILY > GROUCHY

GROUCHING > GROUCH

GROUCHY adj bad-tempered

GROUF same as > GROOF

GROUFS > GROUF

GROUGH n natural channel or fissure in a peat moor

GROUGHS > GROUGH

GROUND n surface of the earth ▷adj on or of the ground ▷vb base or establish

GROUNDAGE n fee levied on a vessel entering a port or anchored off a shore

GROUNDED adj sensible and down-to-earth

GROUNDEN obsolete variant of > GROUND

GROUNDER n (in baseball) ball that travels along the ground

GROUNDERS > GROUNDER

GROUNDHOG another name for > WOODCHUCK

GROUNDING n basic knowledge of a subject

GROUNDMAN n groundsman

GROUNDMEN > GROUNDMAN

GROUNDNUT n peanut

GROUNDOUT n (in baseball) being put out after hitting a grounder that is fielded and thrown to first base

GROUNDS > GROUND

GROUNDSEL n yellow-flowered weed

GROUP n number of people or things regarded as a unit ▷vb place or form into a group

GROUPABLE > GROUP

GROUPAGE n gathering people or objects into a group or groups

GROUPAGES > GROUPAGE

GROUPED > GROUP

GROUPER n large edible sea fish

GROUPERS > GROUPER

GROUPIE n ardent fan of a celebrity or of a sport or activity

GROUPIES > GROUPIE

GROUPING n set of people or organizations who act or work together to achieve a shared aim

GROUPINGS > GROUPING

GROUPIST n follower of a group

GROUPISTS > GROUPIST

GROUPLET n small group

GROUPLETS > GROUPLET

GROUPOID n magma

GROUPOIDS > GROUPOID

GROUPS > GROUP

GROUPWARE n software that enables computers within a group or organization to work together, allowing users to exchange electronic-mail messages, access shared files and databases, use video conferencing, etc

GROUPY same as > GROUPIE

GROUSE n stocky game bird ▷vb grumble or complain ▷adj fine or excellent ▷adj excellent

GROUSED > GROUSE

GROUSER > GROUSE

GROUSERS > GROUSE

GROUSES > GROUSE

GROUSEST > GROUSE

GROUSING > GROUSE

GROUT n thin mortar ▷vb fill up with grout

GROUTED > GROUT

GROUTER > GROUT

GROUTERS > GROUT

GROUTIER > GROUTY

GROUTIEST > GROUTY

GROUTING > GROUT

GROUTINGS > GROUT

GROUTS pl n sediment or grounds, as from making coffee

GROUTY adj sullen or surly

GROVE n small group of trees

GROVED > GROVE

GROVEL vb behave humbly in order to win a superior's favour

GROVELED > GROVEL

GROVELER > GROVEL

GROVELERS > GROVEL

GROVELESS > GROVE

GROVELING > GROVEL

GROVELLED > GROVEL

GROVELLER > GROVEL

GROVELS > GROVEL

GROVES > GROVE

GROVET n wrestling hold in which a wrestler in a kneeling position grips the head of his kneeling opponent with one arm and forces his shoulders down with the other

GROVETS > GROVET

GROW vb develop physically

GROWABLE adj able to be cultivated

GROWER n person who grows plants

GROWERS > GROWER

GROWING > GROW

GROWINGLY > GROW

GROWINGS > GROW

GROWL vb make a low rumbling sound ▷n growling sound

GROWLED > GROWL

GROWLER n person, animal, or thing that growls

GROWLERS > GROWLER

GROWLERY n place to retreat to, alone, when ill-humoured

GROWLIER > GROWL

GROWLIEST > GROWL

GROWLING > GROWL

GROWLINGS > GROWL

GROWLS > GROWL

GROWLY > GROWL

GROWN > GROW

GROWNUP n adult

GROWNUPS > GROWNUP

GROWS > GROW

GROWTH n growing ▷adj of or relating to growth

GROWTHIER > GROWTHY

GROWTHIST n advocate of the importance of economic growth

GROWTHS > GROWTH

GROWTHY adj rapid-growing

GROYNE n wall built out from the shore to control erosion

GROYNES > GROYNE

GROZING as in grozing iron iron for smoothing joints between lead pipes

GRUB n legless insect larva ▷vb search carefully for something by digging or by moving things about

GRUBBED > GRUB

GRUBBER n person who grubs

GRUBBERS > GRUBBER

GRUBBIER > GRUBBY

GRUBBIEST > GRUBBY

GRUBBILY > GRUBBY

GRUBBING > GRUB

GRUBBLE same as > GRABBLE

GRUBBLED > GRUBBLE

GRUBBLES > GRUBBLE

GRUBBLING > GRUBBLE

GRUBBY adj dirty

GRUBS > GRUB

GRUBSTAKE n supplies provided for a prospector on the condition that the donor has a stake in any finds ▷vb furnish with such supplies

GRUBWORM another word for > GRUB

GRUBWORMS > GRUBWORM

GRUDGE vb be unwilling to give or allow ▷n resentment ▷adj planned or carried out in order to settle a grudge

GRUDGED > GRUDGE

GRUDGEFUL adj envious

GRUDGER > GRUDGE

GRUDGERS > GRUDGE

GRUDGES > GRUDGE

GRUDGING > GRUDGE

GRUDGINGS > GRUDGE

GRUE n shiver or shudder ▷vb shiver or shudder

GRUED > GRUE

GRUEING > GRUE

GRUEL n thin porridge ▷vb subject to exhausting experiences

GRUELED > GRUEL

GRUELER > GRUEL

GRUELERS > GRUEL

GRUELING same as > GRUELLING

GRUELINGS > GRUELING

GRUELLED > GRUEL

GRUELLER > GRUEL

GRUELLERS > GRUEL

GRUELLING adj exhausting or severe ▷n severe

g

experience, esp
punishment
GRUELS > GRUEL
GRUES > GRUE
GRUESOME adj causing
horror and disgust
GRUESOMER > GRUESOME
GRUFE same as > GROOF
GRUFES > GRUFE
GRUFF adj rough or surly in
manner or voice ▷ vb talk
gruffly
GRUFFED > GRUFF
GRUFFER > GRUFF
GRUFFEST > GRUFF
GRUFFIER > GRUFFY
GRUFFIEST > GRUFFY
GRUFFILY > GRUFFY
GRUFFING > GRUFF
GRUFFISH > GRUFF
GRUFFLY > GRUFF
GRUFFNESS > GRUFF
GRUFFS > GRUFF
GRUFFY adj gruff
GRUFTED adj dirty
GRUGRU n any of several
tropical American palms,
esp Acrocomia sclerocarpa,
which has a spiny trunk
and leaves and edible nuts
GRUGRUS > GRUGRU
GRUIFORM adj relating to
an order of birds, including
cranes and bustards
GRUING > GRUE
GRUM adj surly
GRUMBLE vb complain ▷ n
complaint
GRUMBLED > GRUMBLE
GRUMBLER > GRUMBLE
GRUMBLERS > GRUMBLE
GRUMBLES > GRUMBLE
GRUMBLIER > GRUMBLE
GRUMBLING > GRUMBLE
GRUMBLY > GRUMBLE
GRUME n clot
GRUMES > GRUME
GRUMLY > GRUM
GRUMMER > GRUM
GRUMMEST > GRUM
GRUMMET same
as > GROMMET
GRUMMETED adj having
grummets
GRUMMETS > GRUMMET
GRUMNESS > GRUM
GRUMOSE same
as > GRUMOUS
GRUMOUS adj (esp of plant
parts) consisting of
granular tissue
GRUMP n surly or bad-
tempered person ▷ vb
complain or grumble
GRUMPED > GRUMP
GRUMPH vb grunt
GRUMPHED > GRUMPH
GRUMPHIE n pig
GRUMPHIES > GRUMPHIE
GRUMPHING > GRUMPH
GRUMPHS > GRUMPH
GRUMPHY same
as > GRUMPHIE
GRUMPIER > GRUMPY
GRUMPIEST > GRUMPY
GRUMPILY > GRUMPY
GRUMPING > GRUMP

GRUMPISH same as > GRUMPY
GRUMPS > GRUMP
GRUMPY adj bad-tempered
GRUNDIES pl n men's
underpants
GRUNGE n style of rock
music with a fuzzy guitar
sound
GRUNGER n fan of grunge
music
GRUNGERS > GRUNGER
GRUNGES > GRUNGE
GRUNGIER > GRUNGY
GRUNGIEST > GRUNGY
GRUNGY adj squalid or seedy
GRUNION n Californian
marine teleost fish,
Leuresthes tenuis, that
spawns on beaches: family
Atherinidae (silversides)
GRUNIONS > GRUNION
GRUNT vb make a low short
gruff sound, like a pig ▷ n
pig's sound
GRUNTED > GRUNT
GRUNTER n person or animal
that grunts, esp a pig
GRUNTERS > GRUNTER
GRUNTING > GRUNT
GRUNTINGS > GRUNT
GRUNTLE vb grunt or groan
GRUNTLED > GRUNTLE
GRUNTLES > GRUNTLE
GRUNTLING > GRUNTLE
GRUNTS > GRUNT
GRUPPETTI > GRUPPETTO
GRUPPETTO n turn
GRUSHIE adj healthy and
strong
GRUTCH vb grudge
GRUTCHED > GRUTCH
GRUTCHES > GRUTCH
GRUTCHING > GRUTCH
GRUTTEN > GREET
GRUYERE n hard flat whole-
milk cheese with holes
GRUYERES > GRUYERE
GRYCE same as > GRICE
GRYCES > GRYCE
GRYDE same as > GRYDE
GRYDED > GRYDE
GRYDES > GRYDE
GRYDING > GRYDE
GRYESY adj grey
GRYFON same as > GRIFFIN
GRYFONS > GRYFON
GRYKE same as > GRIKE
GRYKES > GRYKE
GRYPE same as > GRIPE
GRYPES > GRIPE
GRYPHON same as > GRIFFIN
GRYPHONS > GRYPHON
GRYPT archaic form
of > GRIPPED
GRYSBOK n either of two
small antelopes, Raphicerus
melanotis or R. sharpei,
of central and southern
Africa, having small
straight horns
GRYSBOKS > GRYSBOK
GRYSELY same as > GRISLY
GRYSIE same as > GRISY
GU same as > GJU
GUACAMOLE n spread of
mashed avocado, tomato
pulp, mayonnaise, and

seasoning
GUACHARO another name
for > OILBIRD
GUACHAROS > GUACHARO
GUACO n any of several
tropical American plants
whose leaves are used as
an antidote to snakebite
GUACOS > GUACO
GUAIAC same as > GUAIACUM
GUAIACOL n yellowish
oily creosote-like liquid
extracted from guaiacum
resin and hardwood tar,
used medicinally as an
expectorant
GUAIACOLS > GUAIACOL
GUAIACS > GUAIACUM
GUAIACUM n any tropical
American evergreen tree of
the zygophyllaceous genus
Guaiacum, such as the
lignum vitae
GUAIACUMS > GUAIACUM
GUAIOCUM same
as > GUAIACUM
GUAIOCUMS > GUAIOCUM
GUAN n any gallinaceous
bird of the genera Penelope,
Pipile, etc, of Central and
South America
GUANA another word
for > IGUANA
GUANABANA n tropical tree
or its fruit
GUANACO n S American
animal related to the llama
GUANACOS > GUANACO
GUANAS > GUANA
GUANASE n enzyme that
converts guanine to
xanthine by removal of an
amino group
GUANASES > GUANASE
GUANAY n type of cormorant
GUANAYS > GUANAY
GUANAZOLO n form of
guanine
GUANGO n rain tree
GUANGOS > GUANGO
GUANIDIN same
as > GUANIDINE
GUANIDINE n strongly
alkaline crystalline
substance, soluble in water
and found in plant and
animal tissues
GUANIDINS > GUANIDIN
GUANIN same as > GUANINE
GUANINE n white almost
insoluble compound:
one of the purine bases in
nucleic acids
GUANINES > GUANINE
GUANINS > GUANINE
GUANO n dried sea-bird
manure, used as fertilizer
GUANOS > GUANO
GUANOSINE n nucleoside
consisting of guanine and
ribose
GUANS > GUAN
GUANXI n Chinese social
concept based on the
exchange of favours
GUANXIS > GUANXI
GUANYLIC as in guanylic

acid nucleotide consisting
of guanine, ribose or
deoxyribose, and a
phosphate group
GUAR n leguminous
Indian plant, Cyamopsis
tetragonolobus, grown as
a fodder crop and for the
gum obtained from its
seeds
GUARANA n type of shrub
native to Venezuela
GUARANAS > GUARANA
GUARANI n standard
monetary unit of Paraguay,
divided into 100 céntimos
GUARANIES > GUARANI
GUARANIS > GUARANI
GUARANTEE n formal
assurance, esp in writing,
that a product will meet
certain standards ▷ vb
give a guarantee
GUARANTOR n person who
gives or is bound by a
guarantee
GUARANTY n pledge
of responsibility for
fulfilling another person's
obligations in case of
default
GUARD vb watch over to
protect or to prevent
escape ▷ n person or
group that guards
GUARDABLE > GUARD
GUARDAGE n state of being
in the care of a guardian
GUARDAGES > GUARDAGE
GUARDANT adj (of a beast)
shown full face ▷ n
guardian
GUARDANTS > GUARDANT
GUARDDOG n dog trained to
protect premises
GUARDDOGS > GUARDDOG
GUARDED adj cautious or
noncommittal
GUARDEDLY > GUARDED
GUARDEE n guardsman, esp
considered as representing
smartness and dash
GUARDEES > GUARDEE
GUARDER > GUARD
GUARDERS > GUARD
GUARDIAN n keeper or
protector ▷ adj protecting
or safeguarding
GUARDIANS > GUARDIAN
GUARDING > GUARD
GUARDLESS > GUARD
GUARDLIKE > GUARD
GUARDRAIL n railing at the
side of a staircase, road,
etc, as a safety barrier
GUARDROOM n room used by
guards
GUARDS > GUARD
GUARDSHIP n warship
responsible for the safety of
other ships in its company
GUARDSMAN n member of
the Guards
GUARDSMEN > GUARDSMAN
GUARISH vb heal
GUARISHED > GUARISH
GUARISHES > GUARISH

GUARS > GUAR

GUAVA n yellow-skinned tropical American fruit

GUAVAS > GUAVA

GUAYABERA n type of embroidered men's shirt

GUAYULE n bushy shrub, *Parthenium argentatum*, of the southwestern US: family *Asteraceae* (composites)

GUAYULES > GUAYULE

GUB n white man

GUBBAH *same as* > GUB

GUBBAHS > GUBBAH

GUBBINS n object of little or no value

GUBBINSES > GUBBINS

GUBERNIYA n territorial division of imperial Russia

GUBS > GUB

GUCK n slimy matter

GUCKIER > GUCKY

GUCKIEST > GUCKY

GUCKS > GUCK

GUCKY adj slimy and mucky

GUDDLE vb catch (fish) by groping with the hands under the banks or stones of a stream ▷n muddle

GUDDLED > GUDDLE

GUDDLES > GUDDLE

GUDDLING > GUDDLE

GUDE *Scots word for* > GOOD

GUDEMAN n male householder

GUDEMEN > GUDEMAN

GUDES n goods

GUDESIRE n grandfather

GUDESIRES > GUDESIRE

GUDEWIFE n female householder

GUDEWIVES > GUDEWIFE

GUDGEON n small freshwater fish ▷vb trick or cheat

GUDGEONED > GUDGEON

GUDGEONS > GUDGEON

GUE *same as* > GJU

GUENON n any slender agile Old World monkey of the genus *Cercopithecus*, inhabiting wooded regions of Africa and having long hind limbs and tail and long hair surrounding the face

GUENONS > GUENON

GUERDON n reward or payment ▷vb give a guerdon to

GUERDONED > GUERDON

GUERDONER > GUERDON

GUERDONS > GUERDON

GUEREZA n handsome colobus monkey of the mountain forests of Ethiopia

GUEREZAS > GUEREZA

GUERIDON n small ornately-carved table

GUERIDONS > GUERIDON

GUERILLA *same as* > GUERRILLA

GUERILLAS > GUERILLA

GUERITE n turret used by a sentry

GUERITES > GUERITE

GUERNSEY n seaman's knitted woolen sweater

GUERNSEYS > GUERNSEY

GUERRILLA n member of an unofficial armed force fighting regular forces

GUES > GUE

GUESS vb estimate or draw a conclusion without proper knowledge ▷n estimate or conclusion reached by guessing

GUESSABLE > GUESS

GUESSED > GUESS

GUESSER > GUESS

GUESSERS > GUESS

GUESSES > GUESS

GUESSING > GUESS

GUESSINGS > GUESS

GUESSWORK n process or results of guessing

GUEST n person entertained at another's house or at another's expense ▷vb appear as a visiting player or performer

GUESTED > GUEST

GUESTEN vb stay as a guest in someone's house

GUESTENED > GUESTEN

GUESTENS > GUESTEN

GUESTING > GUEST

GUESTS > GUEST

GUESTWISE adv as, or in the manner of, a guest

GUFF n nonsense

GUFFAW n crude noisy laugh ▷vb laugh in this way

GUFFAWED > GUFFAW

GUFFAWING > GUFFAW

GUFFAWS > GUFFAW

GUFFIE *Scots word for* > PIG

GUFFIES > GUFFIE

GUFFS > GUFF

GUGA n gannet chick

GUGAS > GUGA

GUGGLE vb drink making a gurgling sound

GUGGLED > GUGGLE

GUGGLES > GUGGLE

GUGGLING > GUGGLE

GUGLET *same as* > GOGLET

GUGLETS > GUGLET

GUICHET n grating, hatch, or small opening in a wall, esp a ticket-office window

GUICHETS > GUICHET

GUID *Scot word for* > GOOD

GUIDABLE > GUIDE

GUIDAGE n guidance

GUIDAGES > GUIDAGE

GUIDANCE n leadership, instruction, or advice

GUIDANCES > GUIDANCE

GUIDE n person who conducts tour expeditions ▷vb act as a guide for

GUIDEBOOK n handbook with information for visitors to a place

GUIDED > GUIDE

GUIDELESS > GUIDE

GUIDELINE n set principle for doing something

GUIDEPOST n sign on a post by a road indicating directions

GUIDER > GUIDE

GUIDERS > GUIDE

GUIDES > GUIDE

GUIDESHIP n supervision

GUIDEWAY n track controlling the motion of something

GUIDEWAYS > GUIDEWAY

GUIDEWORD n word at top of dictionary page indicating first entry on page

GUIDING > GUIDE

GUIDINGS > GUIDE

GUIDON n small pennant, used as a marker or standard, esp by cavalry regiments

GUIDONS > GUIDON

GUIDS n possessions

GUILD n organization or club

GUILDER n former monetary unit of the Netherlands

GUILDERS > GUILDER

GUILDHALL n hall where members of a guild meet

GUILDRIES > GUILDRY

GUILDRY n in Scotland, corporation of merchants in a burgh

GUILDS > GUILD

GUILDSHIP n condition of being a member of a guild

GUILDSMAN n man who is a member of a guild

GUILDSMEN > GUILDSMAN

GUILE n cunning or deceit ▷vb deceive

GUILED > GUILE

GUILEFUL > GUILE

GUILELESS adj free from guile

GUILER n deceiver

GUILERS > GUILER

GUILES > GUILE

GUILING > GUILE

GUILLEMET n (in printing) a duckfoot quote

GUILLEMOT n black-and-white diving sea bird of N hemisphere

GUILLOCHE n ornamental band or border with a repeating pattern of two or more interwoven wavy lines, as in architecture ▷vb decorate with guilloches

GUILT n fact or state of having done wrong

GUILTIER > GUILTY

GUILTIEST > GUILTY

GUILTILY > GUILTY

GUILTLESS adj innocent

GUILTS > GUILT

GUILTY adj responsible for an offence or misdeed

GUIMBARD n Jew's harp

GUIMBARDS > GUIMBARD

GUIMP *same as* > GUIMPE

GUIMPE n short blouse with sleeves worn under a pinafore dress ▷vb make with gimp

GUIMPED > GUIMPE

GUIMPES > GUIMPE

GUIMPING > GUIMPE

GUIMPS > GUIMP

GUINEA n former British monetary unit worth 21 shillings (1.05 pounds)

GUINEAS > GUINEA

GUIPURE n heavy lace that has its pattern connected by threads, rather than supported on a net mesh

GUIPURES > GUIPURE

GUIRO n percussion instrument made from a hollow gourd

GUIROS > GUIRO

GUISARD n guiser

GUISARDS > GUISARD

GUISE n false appearance ▷vb disguise or be disguised in fancy dress

GUISED > GUISE

GUISER n mummer, esp at Christmas or Halloween revels

GUISERS > GUISER

GUISES > GUISE

GUISING > GUISE

GUISINGS > GUISE

GUITAR n stringed instrument with a flat back and a long neck, played by plucking or strumming

GUITARIST > GUITAR

GUITARS > GUITAR

GUITGUIT n bird belonging to the family Coerebidae

GUITGUITS > GUITGUIT

GUIZER *same as* > GUISER

GUIZERS > GUIZER

GUL n design used in oriental carpets

GULA n gluttony

GULAG n forced-labour camp

GULAGS > GULAG

GULAR adj of, relating to, or situated in the throat or oesophagus

GULAS > GULA

GULCH n deep narrow valley ▷vb swallow fast

GULCHED > GULCH

GULCHES > GULCH

GULCHING > GULCH

GULDEN *same as* > GUILDER

GULDENS > GULDEN

GULE *Scots word for* > MARIGOLD

GULES n red in heraldry

GULF n large deep bay ▷vb swallow up

GULFED > GULF

GULFIER > GULF

GULFIEST > GULF

GULFING > GULF

GULFLIKE > GULF

GULFS > GULF

GULFWEED n any brown seaweed of the genus *Sargassum*

GULFWEEDS > GULFWEED

GULFY > GULF

GULL n long-winged sea bird ▷vb cheat or deceive

GULLABLE *same as* > GULLIBLE

GULLABLY > GULLABLE

GULLED > GULL

g

GULLER n deceiver

GULLERIES > GULLERY

GULLERS > GULLER

GULLERY n breeding-place for gulls

GULLET n muscular tube through which food passes from the mouth to the stomach

GULLETS > GULLET

GULLEY same as > GULLY

GULLEYED > GULLEY

GULLEYING > GULLEY

GULLEYS > GULLEY

GULLIBLE adj easily tricked

GULLIBLY > GULLIBLE

GULLIED > GULLY

GULLIES > GULLY

GULLING > GULL

GULLISH adj stupid

GULLS > GULL

GULLWING adj (of vehicle door) opening upwards

GULLY n channel cut by running water ▷ vb make (channels) in (the ground, sand, etc)

GULLYING > GULLY

GULOSITY n greed or gluttony

GULP vb swallow hastily ▷ n gulping

GULPED > GULP

GULPER > GULP

GULPERS > GULP

GULPH archaic word for > GULF

GULPHS > GULPH

GULPIER > GULP

GULPIEST > GULP

GULPING > GULP

GULPINGLY > GULP

GULPS > GULP

GULPY > GULP

GULS > GUL

GULY adj relating to gules

GUM n firm flesh in which the teeth are set ▷ vb stick with gum

GUMBALL n round piece of chewing gum

GUMBALLS > GUMBALL

GUMBO n mucilaginous pods of okra

GUMBOIL n abscess on the gum

GUMBOILS > GUMBOIL

GUMBOOT n rubber boot

GUMBOOTS pl n Wellington boots

GUMBOS > GUMBO

GUMBOTIL n sticky clay formed by the weathering of glacial drift

GUMBOTILS > GUMBOTIL

GUMDROP n hard jelly-like sweet

GUMDROPS > GUMDROP

GUMLANDS pl n infertile land from which the original kauri bush has been removed or burnt producing only kauri gum

GUMLESS > GUM

GUMLIKE > GUM

GUMLINE n line where gums meet teeth

GUMLINES > GUMLINE

GUMMA n rubbery tumour characteristic of advanced syphilis, occurring esp on the skin, liver, brain or heart

GUMMAS > GUMMA

GUMMATA > GUMMA

GUMMATOUS > GUMMA

GUMMED > GUM

GUMMER n punch-cutting tool

GUMMERS > GUMMER

GUMMIER > GUMMY

GUMMIES > GUMMY

GUMMIEST > GUMMY

GUMMILY > GUMMY

GUMMINESS > GUMMY

GUMMING > GUM

GUMMINGS > GUM

GUMMITE n orange or yellowish amorphous secondary mineral consisting of hydrated uranium oxides

GUMMITES > GUMMITE

GUMMOSE same as > GUMMOUS

GUMMOSES > GUMMOSE

GUMMOSIS n abnormal production of excessive gum in certain trees, esp fruit trees, as a result of wounding, infection, adverse weather conditions, severe pruning, etc

GUMMOSITY > GUMMOUS

GUMMOUS adj resembling or consisting of gum

GUMMY adj toothless ▷ n small crustacean-eating shark, Mustelus antarcticus, with bony ridges resembling gums in its mouth

GUMNUT n hardened seed container of the gumtree

GUMNUTS > GUMNUT

GUMP vb guddle

GUMPED > GUMP

GUMPHION n funeral banner

GUMPHIONS > GUMPHION

GUMPING > GUMP

GUMPS > GUMP

GUMPTION n resourcefulness

GUMPTIONS > GUMPTION

GUMPTIOUS > GUMPTION

GUMS > GUM

GUMSHIELD n plate or strip of soft waxy substance used by boxers to protect the teeth and gums

GUMSHOE n waterproof overshoe ▷ vb act stealthily

GUMSHOED > GUMSHOE

GUMSHOES > GUMSHOE

GUMSUCKER n native-born Australian

GUMTREE n any of various trees that yield gum, such as the eucalyptus, sweet gum, and sour gum

GUMTREES > GUMTREE

GUMWEED n any of several American yellow-flowered plants that have sticky flower heads

GUMWEEDS > GUMWEED

GUMWOOD same as > GUMTREE

GUMWOODS > GUMWOOD

GUN n weapon with a metal tube from which missiles are fired by explosion ▷ vb cause (an engine) to run at high speed

GUNBOAT n small warship

GUNBOATS > GUNBOAT

GUNCOTTON n form of cellulose nitrate used as an explosive

GUNDIES > GUNDY

GUNDOG n dog trained to work with a hunter or gamekeeper

GUNDOGS > GUNDOG

GUNDY n toffee

GUNFIGHT n fight between persons using firearms ▷ vb fight with guns

GUNFIGHTS > GUNFIGHT

GUNFIRE n repeated firing of guns

GUNFIRES > GUNFIRE

GUNFLINT n piece of flint in a flintlock's hammer used to strike the spark that ignites the charge

GUNFLINTS > GUNFLINT

GUNFOUGHT > GUNFIGHT

GUNG as in gung ho extremely or excessively enthusiastic about something

GUNGE n sticky unpleasant substance ▷ vb block or encrust with gunge

GUNGED > GUNGE

GUNGES > GUNGE

GUNGIER > GUNGE

GUNGIEST > GUNGE

GUNGING > GUNGE

GUNGY > GUNGE

GUNHOUSE n on a warship, an armoured rotatable enclosure for guns

GUNHOUSES > GUNHOUSE

GUNITE n cement-sand mortar that is sprayed onto formwork, walls, or rock by a compressed air ejector giving a very dense strong concrete layer: used to repair reinforced concrete, to line tunnel walls or mine airways, etc

GUNITES > GUNITE

GUNK n slimy or filthy substance

GUNKHOLE vb make a series of short boat excursions

GUNKHOLED > GUNKHOLE

GUNKHOLES > GUNKHOLE

GUNKIER > GUNK

GUNKIEST > GUNK

GUNKS > GUNK

GUNKY > GUNK

GUNLAYER n person who aims a ship's gun

GUNLAYERS > GUNLAYER

GUNLESS > GUN

GUNLOCK n mechanism in some firearms that causes the charge to be exploded

GUNLOCKS > GUNLOCK

GUNMAKER n person who makes guns

GUNMAKERS > GUNMAKER

GUNMAN n armed criminal

GUNMEN > GUNMAN

GUNMETAL n alloy of copper, tin, and zinc ▷ adj dark grey

GUNMETALS > GUNMETAL

GUNNAGE n number of guns carried by a warship

GUNNAGES > GUNNAGE

GUNNED > GUN

GUNNEL same as > GUNWALE

GUNNELS > GUNNEL

GUNNEN > GUN

GUNNER n artillery soldier

GUNNERA n any herbaceous perennial plant of the genus Gunnera, found throughout the S hemisphere and cultivated for its large leaves

GUNNERAS > GUNNERA

GUNNERIES > GUNNERY

GUNNERS > GUNNER

GUNNERY n use or science of large guns

GUNNIES > GUNNY

GUNNING > GUN

GUNNINGS > GUN

GUNNY n strong coarse fabric used for sacks

GUNNYBAG same as > GUNNYSACK

GUNNYBAGS > GUNNYBAG

GUNNYSACK n sack made from gunny

GUNPAPER n cellulose nitrate explosive made by treating paper with nitric acid

GUNPAPERS > GUNPAPER

GUNPLAY n use of firearms, as by criminals

GUNPLAYS > GUNPLAY

GUNPOINT n muzzle of a gun

GUNPOINTS > GUNPOINT

GUNPORT n porthole, or other, opening for a gun

GUNPORTS > GUNPORT

GUNPOWDER n explosive mixture of potassium nitrate, sulphur, and charcoal

GUNROOM n (esp in the Royal Navy) the mess allocated to subordinate or junior officers

GUNROOMS > GUNROOM

GUNRUNNER n person who smuggles guns and ammunition

GUNS > GUN

GUNSEL n catamite

GUNSELS > GUNSEL

GUNSHIP n ship or helicopter armed with heavy guns

GUNSHIPS > GUNSHIP

GUNSHOT n shot or range of a gun

GUNSHOTS > GUNSHOT

GUNSMITH n person who

manufactures or repairs firearms, esp portable guns
GUNSMITHS > GUNSMITH
GUNSTICK n ramrod
GUNSTICKS > GUNSTICK
GUNSTOCK n wooden handle to which the barrel of a rifle is attached
GUNSTOCKS > GUNSTOCK
GUNSTONE n cannonball
GUNSTONES > GUNSTONE
GUNTER n type of gaffing in which the gaff is hoisted parallel to the mast
GUNTERS > GUNTER
GUNWALE n top of a ship's side
GUNWALES > GUNWALE
GUNYAH n hut or shelter in the bush
GUNYAHS > GUNYAH
GUP n gossip
GUPPIES > GUPPY
GUPPY n small colourful aquarium fish
GUPS > GUP
GUR n unrefined cane sugar
GURAMI same as > GOURAMI
GURAMIS > GURAMI
GURDWARA n Sikh place of worship
GURDWARAS > GURDWARA
GURGE vb swallow up
GURGED > GURGE
GURGES > GURGE
GURGING > GURGE
GURGLE n bubbling noise ▷ vb (of water) to make low bubbling noises when flowing
GURGLED > GURGLE
GURGLES > GURGLE
GURGLING > GURGLE
GURGLET same as > GOGLET
GURGLETS > GURGLET
GURGLING > GURGLE
GURGOYLE same as > GARGOYLE
GURGOYLES > GURGOYLE
GURJUN n any of several S or SE Asian dipterocarpaceous trees of the genus *Dipterocarpus* that yield a resin
GURJUNS > GURJUN
GURL vb snarl
GURLED > GURL
GURLET n type of pickaxe
GURLETS > GURLET
GURLIER > GURLY
GURLIEST > GURLY
GURLING > GURL
GURLS > GURL
GURLY adj stormy
GURN variant spelling of > GIRN
GURNARD n spiny armour-headed sea fish
GURNARDS > GURNARD
GURNED > GURN
GURNET same as > GURNARD
GURNETS > GURNARD
GURNEY n wheeled stretcher for transporting hospital patients
GURNEYS > GURNEY
GURNING > GURN
GURNS > GURN

GURRAH n type of coarse muslin
GURRAHS > GURRAH
GURRIER n low-class tough ill-mannered person
GURRIERS > GURRIER
GURRIES > GURRY
GURRY n dog-fight
GURS > GUR
GURSH n unit of currency in Saudi Arabia
GURSHES > GURSH
GURU n Hindu or Sikh religious teacher or leader
GURUDOM n state of being a guru
GURUDOMS > GURUDOM
GURUISM > GURU
GURUISMS > GURU
GURUS > GURU
GURUSHIP > GURU
GURUSHIPS > GURU
GUS > GU
GUSH vb flow out suddenly and profusely ▷ n sudden copious flow
GUSHED > GUSH
GUSHER n spurting oil well
GUSHERS > GUSHER
GUSHES > GUSH
GUSHIER > GUSHY
GUSHIEST > GUSHY
GUSHILY > GUSHY
GUSHINESS > GUSHY
GUSHING > GUSH
GUSHINGLY > GUSH
GUSHY adj displaying excessive admiration or sentimentality
GUSLA n Balkan single-stringed musical instrument
GUSLAR n player of the gusla
GUSLARS > GUSLAR
GUSLAS > GUSLA
GUSLE same as > GUSLA
GUSLES > GUSLE
GUSLI n Russian harp-like musical instrument
GUSLIS > GUSLI
GUSSET n piece of material sewn into a garment to strengthen it ▷ vb put a gusset in (a garment)
GUSSETED > GUSSET
GUSSETING > GUSSET
GUSSETS > GUSSET
GUSSIE n young pig
GUSSIED > GUSSY
GUSSIES > GUSSY
GUSSY vb dress elaborately
GUSSYING > GUSSY
GUST n sudden blast of wind ▷ vb blow in gusts
GUSTABLE n anything that can be tasted
GUSTABLES > GUSTABLE
GUSTATION n act of tasting or the faculty of taste
GUSTATIVE > GUSTATION
GUSTATORY > GUSTATION
GUSTED > GUST
GUSTFUL adj tasty
GUSTIE adj tasty
GUSTIER > GUSTY
GUSTIEST > GUSTY
GUSTILY > GUSTY

GUSTINESS > GUSTY
GUSTING > GUST
GUSTLESS adj tasteless
GUSTO n enjoyment or zest
GUSTOES > GUSTO
GUSTOS > GUSTO
GUSTS > GUST
GUSTY adj blowing or occurring in gusts or characterized by blustery weather
GUT n intestine ▷ vb remove the guts from ▷ adj basic or instinctive
GUTBUCKET n highly emotional style of jazz playing
GUTCHER n grandfather
GUTCHERS > GUTCHER
GUTFUL n bellyful
GUTFULS > GUTFUL
GUTLESS adj cowardly
GUTLIKE > GUT
GUTROT n diarrhoea
GUTROTS > GUTROT
GUTS > GUT vb devour greedily
GUTSED > GUTS
GUTSER as in come a gutser fall heavily to the ground
GUTSERS > GUTSER
GUTSES > GUTS
GUTSFUL n bellyful
GUTSFULS > GUTSFUL
GUTSIER > GUTSY
GUTSIEST > GUTSY
GUTSILY > GUTSY
GUTSINESS > GUTSY
GUTSING > GUTS
GUTSY adj courageous
GUTTA n one of a set of small drop-like ornaments, esp as used on the architrave of a Doric entablature ▷ n rubber substance obtained from the coagulated latex of the guttapercha tree
GUTTAE > GUTTA
GUTTAS > GUTTA
GUTTATE adj (esp of plants) covered with small drops or drop-like markings, esp oil glands ▷ vb exude droplets of liquid
GUTTATED same as > GUTTATE
GUTTATES > GUTTATE
GUTTATING > GUTTATE
GUTTATION > GUTTATE
GUTTED > GUT
GUTTER n shallow channel for carrying away water from a roof or roadside ▷ vb (of a candle) burn unsteadily, with wax running down the sides
GUTTERED > GUTTER
GUTTERING n material for gutters
GUTTERS > GUTTER
GUTTERY > GUTTER
GUTTIER > GUTTY
GUTTIES > GUTTY
GUTTIEST > GUTTY
GUTTING > GUT
GUTTLE vb eat greedily
GUTTLED > GUTTLE

GUTTLER > GUTTLE
GUTTLERS > GUTTLE
GUTTLES > GUTTLE
GUTTLING > GUTTLE
GUTTURAL adj (of a sound) produced at the back of the throat ▷ n guttural consonant
> GUTTURALISATION
> GUTTURALIZATION
GUTTURALS > GUTTURAL
GUTTY n urchin or delinquent ▷ adj courageous
GUTZER n bad fall
GUTZERS > GUTZER
GUV informal name for > GOVERNOR
GUVS > GUV
GUY n man or boy ▷ vb make fun of
GUYED > GUY
GUYING > GUY
GUYLE same as > GUILE
GUYLED > GUYLE
GUYLER > GUYLE
GUYLERS > GUYLE
GUYLES > GUYLE
GUYLINE n guy rope
GUYLINES > GUYLINE
GUYLING > GUYLE
GUYOT n flat-topped submarine mountain, common in the Pacific Ocean, usually an extinct volcano whose summit did not reach above the sea surface
GUYOTS > GUYOT
GUYS > GUY
GUYSE same as > GUISE
GUYSES > GUYSE
GUZZLE vb eat or drink greedily
GUZZLED > GUZZLE
GUZZLER n person or thing that guzzles
GUZZLERS > GUZZLER
GUZZLES > GUZZLE
GUZZLING > GUZZLE
GWEDUC same as > GEODUCK
GWEDUCK same as > GEODUCK
GWEDUCKS > GWEDUCK
GWEDUCS > GWEDUCK
GWINE dialect form of > GOING
GWINIAD n powan
GWINIADS > GWINIAD
GWYNIAD n freshwater white fish, *Coregonus pennantii*, occurring in Lake Bala in Wales: related to the powan
GWYNIADS > GWYNIAD
GYAL same as > GAVAL
GYALS > GYAL
GYBE vb (of a fore-and-aft sail) swing suddenly from one side to the other ▷ n instance of gybing
GYBED > GYBE
GYBES > GYBE
GYBING > GYBE
GYELD n guild
GYELDS > GYELD
GYLDEN adj golden
GYM n gymnasium

9

GYMBAL *same as* > GIMBAL
GYMBALS > GYMBAL
GYMKHANA *n* horse-riding competition
GYMKHANAS > GYMKHANA
GYMMAL *same as* > GIMMAL
GYMMALS > GYMMAL
GYMNASIA > GYMNASIUM
GYMNASIAL > GYMNASIUM
GYMNASIC > GYMNASIUM
GYMNASIEN > GYMNASIUM
GYMNASIUM *n* large room with equipment for physical training
GYMNAST *n* expert in gymnastics
GYMNASTIC *adj* of, relating to, like, or involving gymnastics
GYMNASTS > GYMNAST
GYMNIC *adj* gymnastic
GYMNOSOPH *n* adherent of gymnosophy: belief that food and clothing are detrimental to purity of thought
GYMP *same as* > GIMP
GYMPED > GYMP
GYMPIE *n* tall tree with stinging hairs on its leaves
GYMPIES > GYMPIE
GYMPING > GYMP
GYMPS > GYMP
GYMS > GYM
GYMSLIP *n* tunic or pinafore formerly worn by schoolgirls
GYMSLIPS > GYMSLIP
GYNAE *adj* gynaecological ▷ *n* gynaecology
GYNAECEA > GYNAECIUM
GYNAECEUM *same as* > GYNAECIA
GYNAECIA > GYNAECIUM
GYNAECIUM *same as* > GYNOECIUM
GYNAECOID *adj* resembling, relating to, or like a woman
GYNAES > GYNAE
GYNANDRY *n* hermaphroditism
GYNARCHIC > GYNARCHY
GYNARCHY *n* government by women
GYNECIA > GYNECIUM
GYNECIC *adj* relating to the female sex

GYNECIUM *same as* > GYNOECIUM
GYNECOID *same as* > GYNAECOID
GYNIATRY *n* gynaecology: medicine concerned with diseases in women
GYNIE *n* gynaecology
GYNIES > GYNIE
GYNNEY *n* guinea hen
GYNNEYS > GYNNEY
GYNNIES > GYNNY
GYNNY *same as* > GYNNEY
GYNOCRACY *n* government by women
GYNOECIA > GYNOECIUM
GYNOECIUM *n* carpels of a flowering plant collectively
GYNOPHOBE *n* person who hates or fears women
GYNOPHORE *n* stalk in some plants that bears the gynoecium above the level of the other flower parts
GYNY *n* gynaecology
GYOZA *n* Japanese fried dumpling
GYOZAS > GYOZA
GYP *vb* swindle, cheat, or defraud ▷ *n* act of cheating
GYPLURE *n* synthetic version of the gypsy moth sex pheromone
GYPLURES > GYPLURE
GYPPED > GYP
GYPPER > GYP
GYPPERS > GYP
GYPPIE *same as* > GIPPY
GYPPIES > GYPPY
GYPPING > GYP
GYPPO *n* derogatory term for a gypsy
GYPPOS > GYPPO
GYPPY *same as* > GIPPY
GYPS > GYP
GYPSEIAN *adj* relating to gypsies
GYPSEOUS > GYPSUM
GYPSIED > GYPSY
GYPSIES > GYPSY
GYPSTER *n* swindler
GYPSTERS > GYPSTER
GYPSUM *n* chalklike mineral used to make plaster of Paris
GYPSUMS > GYPSUM

GYPSY *n* member of a nomadic people scattered throughout Europe and North America ▷ *vb* live like a gypsy
GYPSYDOM > GYPSY
GYPSYDOMS > GYPSYDOM
GYPSYHOOD > GYPSY
GYPSYING > GYPSY
GYPSYISH > GYPSY
GYPSYISM *n* state of being a gypsy
GYPSYISMS > GYPSYISM
GYPSYWORT *n* type of Eurasian herb with white flowers
GYRAL *adj* having a circular, spiral, or rotating motion
GYRALLY > GYRAL
GYRANT *adj* gyrating
GYRASE *n* topoisomerase enzyme
GYRASES > GYRASE
GYRATE *vb* rotate or spiral about a point or axis ▷ *adj* curved or coiled into a circle
GYRATED > GYRATE
GYRATES > GYRATE
GYRATING > GYRATE
GYRATION *n* act or process of gyrating
GYRATIONS > GYRATION
GYRATOR *n* electronic circuit that inverts the impedance
GYRATORS > GYRATOR
GYRATORY > GYRATE
GYRE *n* circular or spiral movement or path ▷ *vb* whirl
GYRED > GYRE
GYRENE *n* nickname for a member of the US Marine Corps
GYRENES > GYRENE
GYRES > GYRE
GYRFALCON *n* very large rare falcon of northern regions
GYRI > GYRUS
GYRING > GYRE
GYRO *n* gyrocompass: nonmagnetic compass that uses a motor-driven gyroscope to indicate true north
GYROCAR *n* two-wheeled car
GYROCARS > GYROCAR

GYRODYNE *n* aircraft that uses a powered rotor to take off and manoeuvre, but uses autorotation when cruising
GYRODYNES > GYRODYNE
GYROIDAL *adj* spiral
GYROLITE *n* silicate
GYROLITES > GYROLITE
GYROMANCY *n* divination by spinning in a circle, then falling on any of various letters that have been written on the ground
GYRON *same as* > GIRON
GYRONIC > GYRON
GYRONNY *same as* > GIRONNY
GYRONS > GYRON
GYROPILOT *n* type of automatic pilot
GYROPLANE *another name for* > AUTOGIRO
GYROS > GYRO
GYROSCOPE *n* disc rotating on an axis that can turn in any direction, so the disc maintains the same position regardless of the movement of the surrounding structure
GYROSE *adj* marked with sinuous lines
GYROSTAT *same as* > GYROSCOPE
GYROSTATS > GYROSTAT
GYROUS *adj* gyrose
GYROVAGUE *n* peripatetic monk
GYRUS *another name for* > CONVOLUTION
GYRUSES > GYRUS
GYTE *n* goat
GYTES > GYTE
GYTRASH *n* spirit that haunts lonely roads
GYTRASHES > GYTRASH
GYTTJA *n* sediment on lake bottom
GYTTJAS > GYTTJA
GYVE *vb* shackle or fetter ▷ *n* fetters
GYVED > GYVE
GYVES > GYVE
GYVING > GYVE

Hh

HA *interj* exclamation expressing triumph, surprise, or scorn

HAAF *n* deep-sea fishing ground off the Shetland and Orkney Islands

HAAFS > HAAF

HAANEPOOT *n* variety of grape

HAAR *n* cold sea mist or fog off the North Sea

HAARS > HAAR

HABANERA *n* slow Cuban dance in duple time

HABANERAS > HABANERA

HABANERO *n* variety of chilli pepper

HABANEROS > HABANERO

HABDABS *n* highly nervous state

HABDALAH *n* prayer at end of Jewish sabbath

HABDALAHS > HABDALAH

HABERDINE *n* dried cod

HABERGEON *n* light sleeveless coat of mail worn in the 14th century under the plated hauberk

HABILABLE *adj* able to wear clothes

HABILE *adj* skilful

HABIT *n* established way of behaving ▷ *vb* clothe

HABITABLE *adj* fit to be lived in

HABITABLY > HABITABLE

HABITAN *same as* > HABITANT

HABITANS > HABITAN

HABITANT *n* early French settler in Canada or Louisiana or a descendant of one, esp a farmer

HABITANTS > HABITANT

HABITAT *n* natural home of an animal or plant

HABITATS > HABITAT

HABITED *adj* dressed in a habit

HABITING > HABIT

HABITS > HABIT

HABITUAL *adj* done regularly and repeatedly ▷ *n* person with a habit

HABITUALS > HABITUAL

HABITUATE *vb* accustom

HABITUDE *n* habit or tendency

HABITUDES > HABITUDE

HABITUE *n* frequent visitor to a place

HABITUES > HABITUE

HABITUS *n* general physical state, esp with regard to susceptibility to disease

HABLE *old form of* > ABLE

HABOOB *n* sandstorm

HABOOBS > HABOOB

HABU *n* large venomous snake

HABUS > HABU

HACEK *n* pronunciation symbol in Slavonic language

HACEKS > HACEK

HACENDADO *n* owner of hacienda

HACHIS *n* hash

HACHURE *n* shading of short lines drawn on a map to indicate the degree of steepness of a hill ▷ *vb* mark or show by hachures

HACHURED > HACHURE

HACHURES > HACHURE

HACHURING > HACHURE

HACIENDA *n* ranch or large estate in Latin America

HACIENDAS > HACIENDA

HACK *vb* cut or chop violently ▷ *n* (inferior) writer or journalist ▷ *adj* unoriginal or of a low standard

HACKABLE > HACK

HACKAMORE *n* rope or rawhide halter used for unbroken foals

HACKBERRY *n* American tree or shrub with edible cherry-like fruits

HACKBOLT *n* shearwater

HACKBOLTS > HACKBOLT

HACKBUT *another word for* > ARQUEBUS

HACKBUTS > HACKBUT

HACKED > HACK

HACKEE *n* chipmunk

HACKEES > HACKEE

HACKER *n* computer enthusiast, esp one who breaks into the computer system of a company or government

HACKERIES > HACKERY

HACKERS > HACKER

HACKERY *n* journalism

HACKETTE *n* informal, derogatory term for female journalist

HACKETTES > HACKETTE

HACKIE *n* US word meaning cab driver

HACKIES > HACKIE

HACKING > HACK

HACKINGS > HACK

HACKLE *same as* > HECKLE

HACKLED > HACKLE

HACKLER > HACKLE

HACKLERS > HACKLE

HACKLES *pl n* hairs on the back of the neck and the back of a dog, cat, etc, which rise when the animal is angry or afraid

HACKLET *n* kittiwake

HACKLETS > HACKLET

HACKLIER > HACKLY

HACKLIEST > HACKLY

HACKLING > HACKLE

HACKLY *adj* rough or jagged

HACKMAN *n* taxi driver

HACKMEN > HACKMAN

HACKNEY *n* taxi ▷ *vb* make commonplace and banal by too frequent use

HACKNEYED *adj* (of a word or phrase) unoriginal and overused

HACKNEYS > HACKNEY

HACKS > HACK

HACKSAW *n* small saw for cutting metal ▷ *vb* cut with a hacksaw

HACKSAWED > HACKSAW

HACKSAWN > HACKSAW

HACKSAWS > HACKSAW

HACKWORK *n* dull repetitive work

HACKWORKS > HACKWORK

HACQUETON *n* padded jacket worn under chain mail

HAD *vb* Scots form of hold

HADAL *adj* of, relating to, or constituting very deep zones of the oceans

HADARIM > HEDER

HADAWAY *sentence substitute* exclamation urging the hearer to refrain from delay in the execution of a task

HACKERIES > HACKERY

HADDEN > HAVE

HADDEST *same as* > HADST

HADDIE *n* finnan haddock

HADDIES > HADDIE

HADDING > HAVE

HADDOCK *n* edible sea fish of N Atlantic

HADDOCKS > HADDOCK

HADE *n* angle made to the vertical by the plane of a fault or vein ▷ *vb* incline from the vertical

HADED > HADE

HADEDAH *n* large grey-green S African ibis

HADEDAHS > HADEDAH

HADES > HADE

HADING > HADE

HADITH *n* body of tradition and legend about Mohammed and his followers, used as a basis of Islamic law

HADITHS > HADITH

HADJ *same as* > HAJJ

HADJEE *same as* > HADJI

HADJEES > HADJEE

HADJES > HADJ

HADJI *same as* > HAJJI

HADJIS > HADJI

HADROME *n* part of xylem

HADROMES > HADROME

HADRON *n* any elementary particle capable of taking part in a strong nuclear interaction and therefore excluding leptons and photons

HADRONIC > HADRON

HADRONS > HADRON

HADROSAUR *n* any one of a large group of duck-billed partly aquatic bipedal dinosaurs

HADS > HAVE

HADST *singular form of the past tense (indicative mood) of* > HAVE

HAE *Scot variant of* > HAVE

HAECCEITY *n* property that uniquely identifies an object

HAED > HAE

HAEING > HAE

HAEM *n* complex red organic pigment containing ferrous iron, present in

h

h

haemoglobin

HAEMAL *adj* of the blood

HAEMATAL *same as* > HAEMAL

HAEMATEIN *n* dark purple water-insoluble crystalline substance obtained from logwood and used as an indicator and biological stain

HAEMATIC *n* agent that stimulates the production of red blood cells

HAEMATICS > HAEMATIC

HAEMATIN *n* dark bluish or brownish pigment containing iron in the ferric state, obtained by the oxidation of haem

HAEMATINS > HAEMATIN

HAEMATITE *same as* > HEMATITE

HAEMATOID *adj* resembling blood

HAEMATOMA *n* tumour of clotted or partially clotted blood

HAEMIC *same as* > HAEMATIC

HAEMIN *n* haematin chloride

HAEMINS > HAEMIN

HAEMOCOEL *n* body cavity of many invertebrates, including arthropods and molluscs, developed from part of the blood system

HAEMOCYTE *n* any blood cell, esp a red blood cell > HAEMOFLAGELLATE

HAEMOID *same as* > HAEMATOID

HAEMONIES > HAEMONY

HAEMONY *n* plant mentioned in Milton's poetry

HAEMOSTAT *n* surgical instrument that stops bleeding by compression of a blood vessel

HAEMS > HAEM

HAEN > HAE

HAEREDES > HAERES

HAEREMAI *interj* Māori expression of welcome

HAERES *same as* > HERES

HAES > HAE

HAET *n* whit

HAETS > HAET

HAFF *n* lagoon

HAFFET *n* side of head

HAFFETS > HAFFET

HAFFIT *same as* > HAFFET

HAFFITS > HAFFIT

HAFFLIN *same as* > HALFLING

HAFFLINS > HAFFLIN

HAFFS > HAFF

HAFIZ *n* title for a person who knows the Koran by heart

HAFIZES > HAFIZ

HAFNIUM *n* metallic element found in zirconium ores

HAFNIUMS > HAFNIUM

HAFT *n* handle of an axe, knife, or dagger ▷ *vb* provide with a haft

HAFTARA *same*

as > HAFTARAH

HAFTARAH *n* (in Judaism) short reading from the Prophets which follows the reading from the Torah on Sabbaths and festivals

HAFTARAHS > HAFTARAH

HAFTARAS > HAFTARA

HAFTAROT > HAFTARAH

HAFTAROTH > HAFTARAH

HAFTED > HAFT

HAFTER > HAFT

HAFTERS > HAFT

HAFTING > HAFT

HAFTORAH *same as* > HAFTARAH

HAFTORAHS > HAFTORAH

HAFTOROS > HAFTORAH

HAFTOROT > HAFTORAH

HAFTOROTH > HAFTORAH

HAFTS > HAFT

HAG *n* ugly old woman ▷ *vb* hack

HAGADIC > HAGGAD

HAGADIST *same as* > HAGGADIST

HAGADISTS > HAGADIST

HAGBERRY *same as* > HACKBERRY

HAGBOLT *same as* > HACKBOLT

HAGBOLTS > HAGBOLT

HAGBORN *adj* born of witch

HAGBUSH *same as* > ARQUEBUS

HAGBUSHES > HAGBUSH

HAGBUT > HAGBUT

HAGBUTEER > HAGBUT

HAGBUTS > HAGBUT

HAGBUTTER > HAGBUT

HAGDEN *same as* > HACKBOLT

HAGDENS > HAGDEN

HAGDON *same as* > HACKBOLT

HAGDONS > HAGDON

HAGDOWN *same as* > HACKBOLT

HAGDOWNS > HAGDOWN

HAGFISH *n* any of various primitive eel-like marine vertebrates

HAGFISHES > HAGFISH

HAGG *n* boggy place

HAGGADA *same as* > HAGGADAH

HAGGADAH *n* book containing the order of service of the traditional Jewish Passover meal

HAGGADAHS > HAGGADAH

HAGGADAS > HAGGADA

HAGGADIC > HAGGADAH

HAGGADIST *n* writer of Aggadoth

HAGGADOT > HAGGADAH

HAGGADOTH > HAGGADAH

HAGGARD *adj* looking tired and ill ▷ *n* hawk that has reached maturity before being caught

HAGGARDLY > HAGGARD

HAGGARDS > HAGGARD

HAGGED > HAG

HAGGING > HAG

HAGGIS *n* Scottish dish made from sheep's offal, oatmeal, suet, and seasonings, boiled in a bag

made from the sheep's stomach

HAGGISES > HAGGIS

HAGGISH > HAG

HAGGISHLY > HAG

HAGGLE *vb* bargain or wrangle over a price

HAGGLED > HAGGLE

HAGGLER > HAGGLE

HAGGLERS > HAGGLE

HAGGLES > HAGGLE

HAGGLING > HAGGLE

HAGGS > HAGG

HAGIARCHY *n* government by saints, holy men, or men in holy orders

HAGIOLOGY *n* literature about the lives and legends of saints

HAGLET *same as* > HACKLET

HAGLETS > HAGLET

HAGLIKE > HAG

HAGRIDDEN > HAGRIDE

HAGRIDE *vb* torment or obsess

HAGRIDER > HAGRIDE

HAGRIDERS > HAGRIDE

HAGRIDES > HAGRIDE

HAGRIDING > HAGRIDE

HAGRODE > HAGRIDE

HAGS > HAG

HAH *same as* > HA

HAHA *n* wall or other boundary marker that is set in a ditch so as not to interrupt the landscape

HAHAS > HAHA

HAHNIUM *n* transuranic element artificially produced from californium

HAHNIUMS > HAHNIUM

HAHS > HAH

HAICK *same as* > HAIK

HAICKS > HAICK

HAIDUK *n* rural brigand

HAIDUKS > HAIDUK

HAIK *n* Arab's outer garment of cotton, wool, or silk, for the head and body

HAIKA > HAIK

HAIKAI *same as* > HAIKU

HAIKS > HAIK

HAIKU *n* Japanese verse form in 17 syllables

HAIKUS > HAIKU

HAIL *n* (shower of) small pellets of ice ▷ *vb* fall as or like hail ▷ *sentence substitute* exclamation of greeting

HAILED > HAIL

HAILER > HAIL

HAILERS > HAIL

HAILIER > HAIL

HAILIEST > HAIL

HAILING > HAIL

HAILS > HAIL

HAILSHOT *n* small scattering shot

HAILSHOTS > HAILSHOT

HAILSTONE *n* pellet of hail

HAILSTORM *n* storm during which hail falls

HAILY > HAIL

HAIMISH *same as* > HEIMISH

HAIN *vb* Scots word

meaning save

HAINCH *Scots form of* > HAUNCH

HAINCHED > HAINCH

HAINCHES > HAINCH

HAINCHING > HAINCH

HAINED > HAIN

HAINING > HAIN

HAININGS > HAIN

HAINS > HAIN

HAINT *same as* > HAUNT

HAINTS > HAINT

HAIQUE *same as* > HAIK

HAIQUES > HAIK

HAIR *n* threadlike growth on the skin ▷ *vb* provide with hair

HAIRBALL *n* compact mass of hair that forms in the stomach of cats, calves, etc, as a result of licking and swallowing the fur, and causes vomiting, coughing, bloat, weight loss, and depression

HAIRBALLS > HAIRBALL

HAIRBAND *n* band worn around head to control hair

HAIRBANDS > HAIRBAND

HAIRBELL *same as* > HAREBELL

HAIRBELLS > HAIRBELL

HAIRBRUSH *n* brush for grooming the hair

HAIRCAP *n* type of moss

HAIRCAPS > HAIRCAP

HAIRCLOTH *n* cloth woven from horsehair, used in upholstery

HAIRCUT *n* act or an instance of cutting the hair

HAIRCUTS > HAIRCUT

HAIRDO *n* hairstyle

HAIRDOS > HAIRDO

HAIRDRIER *same as* > HAIRDRYER

HAIRDRYER *n* hand-held electric device that blows out hot air and is used to dry and, sometimes, assist in styling the hair, as in blow-drying

HAIRED *adj* with hair

HAIRGRIP *n* small bent clasp used to fasten the hair

HAIRGRIPS > HAIRGRIP

HAIRIER > HAIRY

HAIRIEST > HAIRY

HAIRIF *another name for* > CLEAVERS

HAIRIFS > HAIRIF

HAIRINESS > HAIRY

HAIRING > HAIR

HAIRLESS *adj* having little or no hair

HAIRLIKE > HAIR

HAIRLINE *n* edge of hair at the top of the forehead ▷ *adj* very fine or narrow

HAIRLINES > HAIRLINE

HAIRLOCK *n* lock of hair

HAIRLOCKS > HAIRLOCK

HAIRNET *n* any of several kinds of light netting worn over the hair to keep it in place

HAIRNETS > HAIRNET

HAIRPIECE n section of false hair added to a person's real hair

HAIRPIN n U-shaped wire used to hold the hair in place

HAIRPINS > HAIRPIN

HAIRS > HAIR

HAIRSPRAY n fixative solution sprayed onto the hair to keep a hairstyle in shape

HAIRST Scots form of > HARVEST

HAIRSTED > HAIRST

HAIRSTING > HAIRST

HAIRSTS > HAIRST

HAIRSTYLE n cut and arrangement of a person's hair

HAIRTAIL n any of various marine spiny-finned fish having a long whiplike scaleless body and long sharp teeth

HAIRTAILS > HAIRTAIL

HAIRWORK n thing made from hair

HAIRWORKS > HAIRWORK

HAIRWORM n any of various hairlike nematode worms

HAIRWORMS > HAIRWORM

HAIRY adj covered with hair

HAIRYBACK n offensive word for an Afrikaner

HAITH interj Scots oath

HAJ same as > HADJ

HAJES > HAJ

HAJI same as > HAJJI

HAJIS > HAJI

HAJJ n pilgrimage a Muslim makes to Mecca

HAJJAH n Muslim woman who has made a pilgrimage to Mecca

HAJJAHS > HAJJAH

HAJJES > HAJJ

HAJJI n Muslim who has made a pilgrimage to Mecca

HAJJIS > HAJJI

HAKA n ceremonial Māori dance with chanting

HAKAM n text written by a rabbi

HAKAMS > HAKAM

HAKARI n Māori ritual feast

HAKAS > HAKA

HAKE n edible sea fish of N hemisphere

HAKEA n Australian tree or shrub with hard woody fruit

HAKEAS > HAKEA

HAKEEM same as > HAKIM

HAKEEMS > HAKEEM

HAKES > HAKE

HAKIM n Muslim judge, ruler, or administrator

HAKIMS > HAKIM

HAKU in New Zealand English, same as > KINGFISH

HAKUS > HAKU

HALACHA n Jewish religious law

HALACHAS > HALACHA

HALACHIC > HALACHA

HALACHIST > HALACHA

HALACHOT > HALACHA

HALACHOTH > HALACHA

HALAKAH same as > HALACHA

HALAKAHS > HALAKAH

HALAKHA same as > HALACHA

HALAKHAH same as > HALACHA

HALAKHAHS > HALAKHAH

HALAKHAS > HALAKHA

HALAKHIC > HALAKHAH

HALAKHIST > HALAKHAH

HALAKHOT > HALAKHA

HALAKHOTH > HALAKHAH

HALAKIC > HALAKHA

HALAKIST > HALAKHA

HALAKISTS > HALAKHA

HALAKOTH > HALAKHA

HALAL n meat from animals slaughtered according to Muslim law ▷ adj of or relating to such meat ▷ vb kill (animals) in this way

HALALA n money unit in Saudi Arabia

HALALAH same as > HALALA

HALALAHS > HALALAH

HALALAS > HALALA

HALALLED > HALAL

HALALLING > HALAL

HALALS > HALAL

HALATION n fogging usually seen as a bright ring surrounding a source of light: caused by reflection from the back of the film

HALATIONS > HALATION

HALAVAH same as > HALVAH

HALAVAHS > HALAVAH

HALAZONE n type of disinfectant

HALAZONES > HALAZONE

HALBERD n spear with an axe blade

HALBERDS > HALBERD

HALBERT same as > HALBERD

HALBERTS > HALBERT

HALCYON adj peaceful and happy ▷ n (in Greek mythology) fabulous bird associated with the winter solstice

HALCYONIC adj peaceful and happy

HALCYONS > HALCYON

HALE adj healthy, robust ▷ vb pull or drag

HALED > HALE

HALENESS > HALE

HALER same as > HELLER

HALERS > HALER

HALERU > HALER

HALES > HALE

HALEST > HALE

HALF n either of two equal parts ▷ adj denoting one of two equal parts ▷ adv to the extent of half

HALFA n African grass

HALFAS > HALFA

HALFBACK n player positioned immediately behind the forwards

HALFBACKS > HALFBACK

HALFBEAK n type of fish with an elongated body, a short upper jaw, and a long protruding lower jaw

HALFBEAKS > HALFBEAK

HALFEN > HALF

HALFLIFE n time taken for half of the atoms in a radioactive material to undergo decay

HALFLIN same as > HALFLING

HALFLING n person only half-grown

HALFLINGS > HALFLING

HALFLINS > HALFLIN

HALFLIVES > HALFLIFE

HALFNESS > HALF

HALFPACE n landing on staircase

HALFPACES > HALFPACE

HALFPENCE > HALFPENNY

HALFPENNY n former British coin worth half an old penny

HALFPIPE n U-shaped object used in skateboarding stunts

HALFPIPES > HALFPIPE

HALFS > HALF

HALFTIME n rest period between the two halves of a game

HALFTIMES > HALFTIME

HALFTONE n illustration showing lights and shadows by means of very small dots ▷ adj relating to, used in, or made by halftone

HALFTONES > HALFTONE

HALFTRACK n vehicle with caterpillar tracks and wheels

HALFWAY adj at or to half the distance

HALFWIT n foolish or stupid person

HALFWITS > HALFWIT

HALIBUT n large edible flatfish of N Atlantic

HALIBUTS > HALIBUT

HALICORE n dugong

HALICORES > HALICORE

HALID same as > HALIDE

HALIDE n binary compound containing a halogen atom or ion in combination with a more electropositive element

HALIDES > HALIDE

HALIDOM n holy place or thing

HALIDOME same as > HALIDOM

HALIDOMES > HALIDOME

HALIDOMS > HALIDOM

HALIDS > HALID

HALIEUTIC adj of fishing

HALIMOT n court held by lord

HALIMOTE same as > HALIMOT

HALIMOTES > HALIMOTE

HALIMOTS > HALIMOT

HALING > HALE

HALIOTIS n type of shellfish

HALITE n colourless or white mineral sometimes tinted by impurities, found in beds as an evaporite

HALITES > HALITE

HALITOSES > HALITOSIS

HALITOSIS n unpleasant-smelling breath

HALITOTIC > HALITUS

HALITOUS > HALITUS

HALITUS n vapour

HALITUSES > HALITUS

HALL n entrance passage

HALLAH variant spelling of > CHALLAH

HALLAHS > HALLAH

HALLAL same as > HALAL

HALLALI n bugle call

HALLALIS > HALLALI

HALLALLED > HALLAL

HALLALOO same as > HALLOO

HALLALOOS > HALLALOO

HALLALS > HALLAL

HALLAN n partition in cottage

HALLANS > HALLAN

HALLEL n (in Judaism) section of the liturgy consisting of Psalms 113–18, read during the morning service on festivals, Chanukah, and Rosh Chodesh

HALLELS > HALLEL

HALLIAN same as > HALLION

HALLIANS > HALLIAN

HALLIARD same as > HALYARD

HALLIARDS > HALLIARD

HALLING n Norwegian country dance

HALLINGS > HALLING

HALLION n lout

HALLIONS > HALLION

HALLMARK n typical feature ▷ vb stamp with a hallmark

HALLMARKS > HALLMARK

HALLO same as > HALLOO

HALLOA same as > HALLOO

HALLOAED > HALLOA

HALLOAING > HALLOA

HALLOAS > HALLOA

HALLOED > HALLO

HALLOES > HALLO

HALLOING > HALLO

HALLOO interj shout used to call hounds at a hunt ▷ sentence substitute shout to attract attention, esp to call hounds at a hunt ▷ n shout of "halloo" ▷ vb shout (something) to (someone)

HALLOOED > HALLOO

HALLOOING > HALLOO

HALLOOS > HALLOO

HALLOS > HALLO

HALLOT > HALLAH

HALLOTH same as > CHALLAH

HALLOUMI n salty white sheep's cheese from Greece or Turkey, usually eaten grilled

HALLOUMIS > HALLOUMI

HALLOW vb consecrate or set apart as being holy

HALLOWED adj regarded as holy

HALLOWER > HALLOW

HALLOWERS > HALLOW
HALLOWING > HALLOW
HALLOWS > HALLOW
HALLS > HALL
HALLSTAND n piece of furniture on which are hung coats, hats, etc
HALLUCAL > HALLUX
HALLUCES > HALLUX
HALLUX n first digit on the hind foot of a mammal, bird, reptile, or amphibian
HALLWAY n entrance area
HALLWAYS > HALLWAY
HALLYON same as > HALLION
HALLYONS > HALLYON
HALM same as > HAULM
HALMA n board game in which players attempt to transfer their pieces from their own to their opponents' bases
HALMAS > HALMA
HALMS > HALM
HALO n ring of light round the head of a sacred figure ▷vb surround with a halo
HALOBIONT n plant or animal that lives in a salty environment such as the sea
HALOCLINE n gradient in salinity of sea
HALOED > HALO
HALOES > HALO
HALOGEN n any of a group of nonmetallic elements including chlorine and iodine
HALOGENS > HALOGEN
HALOGETON n herbaceous plant
HALOID adj resembling or derived from a halogen ▷n compound containing halogen atoms in its molecules
HALOIDS > HALOID
HALOING > HALO
HALOLIKE > HALO
HALON n any of a class of chemical compounds derived from hydrocarbons by replacing one or more hydrogen atoms by bromine atoms and other hydrogen atoms by other halogen atoms (chlorine, fluorine, or iodine). Halons are stable compounds that are used in fire extinguishers, although they may contribute to depletion of the ozone layer
HALONS > HALON
HALOPHILE n organism that thrives in an extremely salty environment, such as the Dead Sea
HALOPHILY n ability to live in salty environment
HALOPHOBE n plant unable to live in salty soil
HALOPHYTE n plant that grows in very salty soil, as in a salt marsh

HALOS > HALO
HALOSERE n plant community that originates and develops in conditions of high salinity
HALOSERES > HALOSERE
HALOTHANE n colourless volatile slightly soluble liquid with an odour resembling that of chloroform
HALOUMI same as > HALLOUMI
HALOUMIS > HALOUMI
HALSE vb embrace
HALSED > HALSE
HALSER > HALSE
HALSERS > HALSE
HALSES > HALSE
HALSING > HALSE
HALT vb come or bring to a stop ▷n temporary stop ▷adj lame
HALTED > HALT
HALTER n strap round a horse's head with a rope to lead it with ▷vb put a halter on (a horse)
HALTERE n one of a pair of short projections in dipterous insects that are modified hind wings, used for maintaining equilibrium during flight
HALTERED > HALTER
HALTERES > HALTERE
HALTERING > HALTER
HALTERS > HALTER
HALTING > HALT
HALTINGLY > HALT
HALTINGS > HALT
HALTLESS > HALT
HALTS > HALT
HALUTZ variant spelling of > CHALUTZ
HALUTZIM > HALUTZ
HALVA same as > HALVAH
HALVAH n Eastern Mediterranean, Middle Eastern, or Indian sweetmeat made of honey and containing sesame seeds, nuts, rose water, saffron, etc
HALVAHS > HALVAH
HALVAS > HALVA
HALVE vb divide in half
HALVED > HALVE
HALVER > HALVE
HALVERS > HALVE
HALVES > HALVE
HALVING > HALVE
HALYARD n rope for raising a ship's sail or flag
HALYARDS > HALYARD
HAM n smoked or salted meat from a pig's thigh ▷vb overact
HAMADA n rocky plateau in desert
HAMADAS > HAMADA
HAMADRYAD n one of a class of nymphs, each of which inhabits a tree and dies with it
HAMADRYAS n type of baboon

HAMAL n (in Middle Eastern countries) a porter, bearer, or servant
HAMALS > HAMAL
HAMAMELIS n any of several trees or shrubs native to E Asia and North America and cultivated as ornamentals
HAMARTIA n flaw in character which leads to the downfall of the protagonist in a tragedy
HAMARTIAS > HAMARTIA
HAMATE adj hook-shaped ▷n small bone in the wrist
HAMATES > HAMATE
HAMAUL same as > HAMAL
HAMAULS > HAMAUL
HAMBA interj usually offensive term for go away
HAMBLE vb mutilate
HAMBLED > HAMBLE
HAMBLES > HAMBLE
HAMBLING > HAMBLE
HAMBONE vb strike body to provide percussion
HAMBONED > HAMBONE
HAMBONES > HAMBONE
HAMBONING > HAMBONE
HAMBURG same as > HAMBURGER
HAMBURGER n minced beef shaped into a flat disc, cooked and usually served in a bread roll
HAMBURGS > HAMBURGER
HAME n either of the two curved bars holding the traces of the harness, attached to the collar of a draught animal
HAMED > HAME
HAMES > HAME
HAMEWITH adv Scots word meaning homewards
HAMFATTER n inferior actor or musician
HAMING > HAME
HAMLET n small village
HAMLETS > HAMLET
HAMMADA same as > HAMADA
HAMMADAS > HAMMADA
HAMMAL same as > HAMAL
HAMMALS > HAMMAL
HAMMAM n bathing establishment, such as a Turkish bath
HAMMAMS > HAMMAM
HAMMED > HAM
HAMMER n tool with a heavy metal head and a wooden handle, used to drive in nails etc ▷vb hit (as if) with a hammer
HAMMERED > HAMMER
HAMMERER > HAMMER
HAMMERERS > HAMMER
HAMMERING > HAMMER
HAMMERKOP n shark with hammer-shaped head
HAMMERMAN n person working with hammer
HAMMERMEN > HAMMERMAN
HAMMERS > HAMMER
HAMMERTOE n condition in which the toe is

permanently bent at the joint
HAMMIER > HAMMY
HAMMIEST > HAMMY
HAMMILY > HAMMY
HAMMINESS > HAMMY
HAMMING > HAM
HAMMOCK same as > HUMMOCK
HAMMOCKS > HAMMOCK
HAMMY adj (of an actor) overacting or tending to overact
HAMOSE adj shaped like hook
HAMOUS same as > HAMOSE
HAMPER vb make it difficult for (someone or something) to move or progress ▷n large basket with a lid
HAMPERED > HAMPER
HAMPERER > HAMPER
HAMPERERS > HAMPER
HAMPERING > HAMPER
HAMPERS > HAMPER
HAMPSTER same as > HAMSTER
HAMPSTERS > HAMPSTER
HAMS > HAM
HAMSTER n small rodent with a short tail and cheek pouches
HAMSTERS > HAMSTER
HAMSTRING n tendon at the back of the knee ▷vb make it difficult for (someone) to take any action
HAMSTRUNG > HAMSTRING
HAMULAR > HAMULUS
HAMULATE > HAMULUS
HAMULI > HAMULUS
HAMULOSE > HAMULUS
HAMULOUS > HAMULUS
HAMULUS n hook or hooklike process at the end of some bones or between the fore and hind wings of a bee or similar insect
HAMZA n sign used in Arabic to represent the glottal stop
HAMZAH same as > HAMZA
HAMZAHS > HAMZAH
HAMZAS > HAMZA
HAN archaic inflected form of > HAVE
HANAP n medieval drinking cup
HANAPER n small wickerwork basket, often used to hold official papers
HANAPERS > HANAPER
HANAPS > HANAP
HANCE same as > HAUNCH
HANCES > HANCE
HANCH vb try to bite
HANCHED > HANCH
HANCHES > HANCH
HANCHING > HANCH
HAND n part of the body at the end of the arm, consisting of a palm, four fingers, and a thumb ▷vb pass, give
HANDAX n small axe held in

one hand

HANDAXES > HANDAX

HANDBAG n woman's small bag for carrying personal articles in

HANDBAGS pl n incident in which people, esp sportsmen, fight or threaten to fight, but without real intent to inflict harm

HANDBALL n game in which two teams of seven players try to throw a ball into their opponent's goal ▷ vb pass (the ball) with a blow of the fist

HANDBALLS > HANDBALL

HANDBELL n bell rung by hand, esp one of a tuned set used in musical performance

HANDBELLS > HANDBELL

HANDBILL n small printed notice

HANDBILLS > HANDBILL

HANDBLOWN adj (of glass) made by hand

HANDBOOK n small reference or instruction book

HANDBOOKS > HANDBOOK

HANDBRAKE n brake in a motor vehicle operated by a hand lever

HANDCAR n small railway vehicle propelled by hand-pumped mechanism

HANDCARS > HANDCAR

HANDCART n simple cart pushed or pulled by hand, used for transporting goods

HANDCARTS > HANDCART

HANDCLAP n act of clapping hands

HANDCLAPS > HANDCLAP

HANDCLASP another word for > HANDSHAKE

HANDCRAFT same as > HANDICRAFT

HANDCUFF n one of a linked pair of metal rings designed to be locked round a prisoner's wrists by the police ▷ vb put handcuffs on

HANDCUFFS > HANDCUFF

HANDED > HAND

HANDER > HAND

HANDERS > HAND

HANDFAST n agreement, esp of marriage, confirmed by a handshake ▷ vb betroth or marry (two persons or another person) by joining the hands

HANDFASTS > HANDFAST

HANDFED > HANDFEED

HANDFEED vb feed (a person or an animal) by hand

HANDFEEDS > HANDFEED

HANDFUL n amount that can be held in the hand

HANDFULS > HANDFUL

HANDGRIP n covering, usually of towelling or rubber, that makes the

handle of a racket or club easier to hold

HANDGRIPS > HANDGRIP

HANDGUN n firearm that can be held, carried, and fired with one hand, such as a pistol

HANDGUNS > HANDGUN

HANDHELD adj held in position by the hand ▷ n computer that can be held in the hand

HANDHELDS > HANDHELD

HANDHOLD n object, crevice, etc, that can be used as a grip or support, as in climbing

HANDHOLDS > HANDHOLD

HANDICAP n physical or mental disability ▷ vb make it difficult for (someone) to do something

HANDICAPS > HANDICAP

HANDIER > HANDY

HANDIEST > HANDY

HANDILY adv in a handy way or manner

HANDINESS > HANDY

HANDING > HAND

HANDISM n discrimination against people on the grounds of whether they are left-handed or right-handed

HANDISMS > HANDISM

HANDIWORK n result of someone's work or activity

HANDJAR n Persian dagger

HANDJARS > HANDJAR

HANDLE n part of an object that is held so that it can be used ▷ vb hold, feel, or move with the hands

HANDLEBAR as in handlebar moustache: bushy extended moustache with curled ends that resembles the handlebars of a bicycle

HANDLED > HANDLE

HANDLER n person who controls an animal

HANDLERS > HANDLER

HANDLES > HANDLE

HANDLESS > HAND

HANDLIKE > HAND

HANDLING n act or an instance of picking up, turning over, or touching something

HANDLINGS > HANDLING

HANDLIST n rough list

HANDLISTS > HANDLIST

HANDLOOM n weaving device operated by hand

HANDLOOMS > HANDLOOM

HANDMADE adj made by hand, not by machine

HANDMAID n person or thing that serves as a useful but subordinate purpose

HANDMAIDS > HANDMAID

HANDOFF n (in rugby) act of warding off an opposing player with the open hand

HANDOFFS > HANDOFF

HANDOUT n clothing, food,

or money given to a needy person

HANDOUTS > HANDOUT

HANDOVER n transfer or surrender

HANDOVERS > HANDOVER

HANDPHONE n in SE Asian English, mobile phone

HANDPICK vb choose or select with great care, as for a special job or purpose

HANDPICKS > HANDPICK

HANDPLAY n fighting with fists

HANDPLAYS > HANDPLAY

HANDPRESS n printing press operated by hand

HANDPRINT n print of hand

HANDRAIL n rail alongside a stairway, to provide support

HANDRAILS > HANDRAIL

HANDROLL n large dried-seaweed cone filled with cold rice and other ingredients

HANDROLLS > HANDROLL

HANDS > HAND

HANDSAW n any saw for use in one hand only

HANDSAWS > HANDSAW

HANDSEL n gift for good luck at the beginning of a new year, new venture, etc ▷ vb give a handsel to (a person)

HANDSELED > HANDSEL

HANDSELS > HANDSEL

HANDSET n telephone mouthpiece and earpiece in a single unit

HANDSETS > HANDSET

HANDSEWN adj sewn by hand

HANDSFUL > HANDFUL

HANDSHAKE n act of grasping and shaking a person's hand, such as in greeting or when agreeing on a deal

HANDSOME adj (esp of a man) good-looking ▷ n term of endearment for a beloved person

HANDSOMER > HANDSOME

HANDSOMES > HANDSOME

HANDSPIKE n bar or length of pipe used as a lever

HANDSTAFF n staff held in hand

HANDSTAMP vb stamp by hand

HANDSTAND n act of supporting the body on the hands in an upside-down position

HANDSTURN n slightest amount of work

HANDTOWEL n towel for drying hands

HANDWHEEL n wheel operated by hand

HANDWORK n work done by hand rather than by machine

HANDWORKS > HANDWORK

HANDWOVEN adj woven by hand

HANDWRIT > HANDWRITE

HANDWRITE vb write by hand

HANDWROTE > HANDWRITE

HANDY adj convenient, useful

HANDYMAN n man who is good at making or repairing things

HANDYMEN > HANDYMAN

HANDYWORK same as > HANDIWORK

HANEPOOT n variety of muscat grape

HANEPOOTS > HANEPOOT

HANG vb attach or be attached at the top with the lower part free

HANGABLE adj suitable for hanging

HANGAR n large shed for storing aircraft ▷ vb put in a hangar

HANGARED > HANGAR

HANGARING > HANGAR

HANGARS > HANGAR

HANGBIRD n any bird, esp the Baltimore oriole, that builds a hanging nest

HANGBIRDS > HANGBIRD

HANGDOG adj guilty, ashamed ▷ n furtive or sneaky person

HANGDOGS > HANGDOG

HANGED > HANG

HANGER n curved piece of wood, wire, or plastic, with a hook, for hanging up clothes

HANGERS > HANGER

HANGFIRE n failure to fire

HANGFIRES > HANGFIRE

HANGI n Māori oven consisting of a hole in the ground filled with hot stones

HANGING > HANG

HANGINGS > HANG

HANGIS > HANGI

HANGMAN n man who executes people by hanging

HANGMEN > HANGMAN

HANGNAIL n piece of skin partly torn away from the base or side of a fingernail

HANGNAILS > HANGNAIL

HANGNEST same as > HANGBIRD

HANGNESTS > HANGNEST

HANGOUT n place where one lives or that one frequently visits

HANGOUTS > HANGOUT

HANGOVER n headache and nausea as a result of drinking too much alcohol

HANGOVERS > HANGOVER

HANGS > HANG

HANGTAG n attached label

HANGTAGS > HANGTAG

HANGUL n Korean language

HANGUP n emotional or psychological preoccupation or problem

HANGUPS > HANGUP

HANIWA n Japanese funeral offering

h

HANJAR same as > HANDJAR
HANJARS > HANJAR
HANK n coil, esp of yarn ▷ vb attach (a sail) to a stay by hanks
HANKED > HANK
HANKER vb desire intensely
HANKERED > HANKER
HANKERER > HANKER
HANKERERS > HANKER
HANKERING > HANKER
HANKERS > HANKER
HANKIE same as > HANKY
HANKIES > HANKY
HANKING > HANK
HANKS > HANK
HANKY n handkerchief
HANSA same as > HANSE
HANSAS > HANSA
HANSE n medieval guild of merchants
HANSEATIC > HANSA
HANSEL same as > HANDSEL
HANSELED > HANSEL
HANSELING > HANSEL
HANSELLED > HANSEL
HANSELS > HANSEL
HANSES > HANSE
HANSOM n formerly, a two-wheeled one-horse carriage with a fixed hood
HANSOMS > HANSOM
HANT same as > HAUNT
HANTED > HANT
HANTING > HANT
HANTLE n good deal
HANTLES > HANTLE
HANTS > HANT
HANUKIAH n candelabrum having nine branches that is lit during the festival of Hanukkah
HANUKIAHS > HANUKIAH
HANUMAN n type of monkey
HANUMANS > HANUMAN
HAO n monetary unit of Vietnam, worth one tenth of a dông
HAOLE n Hawaiian word for white person
HAOLES > HAOLE
HAOMA n type of ritual drink
HAOMAS > HAOMA
HAP n luck ▷ vb cover up
HAPAX n word that only appears in once in a work of literature, or in a body of work by a particular author
HAPAXES > HAPAX
HAPHAZARD adj not organized or planned ▷ n chance
HAPHTARA same as > HAFTARAH
HAPHTARAH same as > HAFTARAH
HAPHTARAS > HAPHTARA
HAPHTAROT > HAPHTARA
HAPKIDO n Korean martial art
HAPKIDOS > HAPKIDO
HAPLESS adj unlucky
HAPLESSLY > HAPLESS
HAPLITE variant of > APLITE
HAPLITES > HAPLITE
HAPLITIC > HAPLITE
HAPLOID adj denoting a cell

or organism with unpaired chromosomes ▷ n haploid cell or organism
HAPLOIDIC adj denoting a cell or organism with unpaired chromosomes
HAPLOIDS > HAPLOID
HAPLOIDY > HAPLOID
HAPLOLOGY n omission of a repeated occurrence of a sound or syllable in fluent speech
HAPLONT n organism, esp a plant, that has the haploid number of chromosomes in its somatic cells
HAPLONTIC > HAPLONT
HAPLONTS > HAPLONT
HAPLOPIA n normal single vision
HAPLOPIAS > HAPLOPIA
HAPLOSES > HAPLOSIS
HAPLOSIS n production of a haploid number of chromosomes during meiosis
HAPLOTYPE n collection of genetic markers usually inherited together
HAPLY archaic word for > PERHAPS
HAPPED > HAP
HAPPEN vb take place, occur
HAPPENED > HAPPEN
HAPPENING n event, occurrence ▷ adj fashionable and up-to-the-minute
HAPPENS > HAPPEN
HAPPIED > HAPPY
HAPPIER > HAPPY
HAPPIES > HAPPY
HAPPIEST > HAPPY
HAPPILY > HAPPY
HAPPINESS > HAPPY
HAPPING > HAP
HAPPY adj feeling or causing joy ▷ vb make happy
HAPPYING > HAPPY
HAPS > HAP
HAPTEN n incomplete antigen that can stimulate antibody production only when it is chemically combined with a particular protein
HAPTENE same as > HAPTEN
HAPTENES > HAPTENE
HAPTENIC > HAPTEN
HAPTENS > HAPTEN
HAPTERON n cell or group of cells that occurs in certain plants, esp seaweeds, and attaches the plant to its substratum
HAPTERONS > HAPTERON
HAPTIC adj relating to or based on the sense of touch
HAPTICAL same as > HAPTIC
HAPTICS n science of sense of touch
HAPU n subtribe
HAPUKA another name for > GROPER
HAPUKAS > HAPUKA
HAPUKU same as > HAPUKA
HAPUKUS same as > HAPUKU

HAPUS > HAPU
HAQUETON same as > HACQUETON
HAQUETONS > HAQUETON
HARAKEKE in New Zealand English, another name for > FLAX
HARAKEKES > HARAKEKE
HARAM n anything that is forbidden by Islamic law
HARAMBEE n work chant used on the E African coast ▷ interj cry of harambee
HARAMBEES > HARAMBEE
HARAMDA same as > HARAMZADA
HARAMDAS > HARAMDA
HARAMDI same as > HARAMZADI
HARAMDIS > HARAMDI
HARAMS > HARAM
HARAMZADA n in Indian English, slang word for an illegitimate male
HARAMZADI n in Indian English, slang word for an illegitimate female
HARANGUE vb address angrily or forcefully ▷ n angry or forceful speech
HARANGUED > HARANGUE
HARANGUER > HARANGUE
HARANGUES > HARANGUE
HARASS vb annoy or trouble constantly
HARASSED > HARASS
HARASSER > HARASS
HARASSERS > HARASS
HARASSES > HARASS
HARASSING > HARASS
HARBINGER n someone or something that announces the approach of something ▷ vb announce the approach or arrival of
HARBOR same as > HARBOUR
HARBORAGE same as > HARBOURAGE
HARBORED > HARBOR
HARBORER > HARBOR
HARBORERS > HARBOR
HARBORFUL n amount a harbour can hold
HARBORING > HARBOR
HARBOROUS adj hospitable
HARBORS > HARBOR
HARBOUR n sheltered port ▷ vb maintain secretly in the mind
HARBOURED > HARBOUR
HARBOURER > HARBOUR
HARBOURS > HARBOUR
HARD adj firm, solid, or rigid ▷ adv with great energy or effort
HARDASS n tough person
HARDASSES > HARDASS
HARDBACK n book with a stiff cover ▷ adj of or denoting a hardback
HARDBACKS > HARDBACK
HARDBAG n rigid container on motorcycle
HARDBAGS > HARDBAG
HARDBAKE n almond toffee
HARDBAKES > HARDBAKE
HARDBALL as in play

hardball act in a ruthless or uncompromising way
HARDBALLS > HARDBALL
HARDBEAM same as > HORNBEAM
HARDBEAMS > HARDBEAM
HARDBOARD n thin stiff board made of compressed sawdust and wood chips
HARDBOOT n type of skiing boot
HARDBOOTS > HARDBOOT
HARDBOUND same as > HARDBACK
HARDCASE n tough person
HARDCORE n style of rock music with short fast songs and little melody
HARDCORES > HARDCORE
HARDCOURT adj (of tennis) played on hard surface
HARDCOVER same as > HARDBACK
HARDEDGE n style of painting in which vividly coloured subjects are clearly delineated ▷ adj of, relating to, or denoting this style of painting
HARDEDGES > HARDEDGE
HARDEN vb make or become hard ▷ n rough fabric made from hards
HARDENED adj toughened by experience
HARDENER n person or thing that hardens
HARDENERS > HARDENER
HARDENING n act or process of becoming or making hard
HARDENS > HARDEN
HARDER > HARD
HARDEST > HARD
HARDFACE n uncompromising person
HARDFACES > HARDFACE
HARDGOODS same as > HARDWARE
HARDGRASS n coarse grass
HARDHACK n woody North American rosaceous plant with downy leaves and clusters of small pink or white flowers
HARDHACKS > HARDHACK
HARDHAT n hat made of a hard material for protection, worn esp by construction workers, equestrians, etc ▷ adj (in US English) characteristic of the presumed conservative attitudes and prejudices typified by construction workers
HARDHATS > HARDHAT
HARDHEAD same as > HARDHEADS
HARDHEADS n thistle-like plant
HARDIER > HARDY
HARDIES > HARDY
HARDIEST > HARDY
HARDIHEAD same as > HARDIHOOD
HARDIHOOD n courage or

daring

HARDILY *adv* in a hardy manner

HARDIMENT *same as* > HARDIHOOD

HARDINESS *n* condition or quality of being hardy, robust, or bold

HARDISH > HARD

HARDLINE *adj* uncompromising

HARDLINER > HARDLINE

HARDLY *adv* scarcely or not at all

HARDMAN *n* tough, ruthless, or violent man

HARDMEN > HARDMAN

HARDNESS *n* quality or condition of being hard

HARDNOSE *n* tough person

HARDNOSED *adj* tough, shrewd, and practical

HARDNOSES > HARDNOSE

HARDOKE *n* burdock

HARDOKES > HARDOKE

HARDPACK *n* rigid backpack

HARDPACKS > HARDPACK

HARDPAN *n* hard impervious layer of clay below the soil, resistant to drainage and root growth

HARDPANS > HARDPAN

HARDPARTS *n* skeleton

HARDROCK *adj* (of mining) concerned with extracting minerals other than coal, usually from solid rock ▷ *n* tough uncompromising man

HARDROCKS > HARDROCK

HARDS *pl n* coarse fibres and other refuse from flax and hemp

HARDSET *adj* in difficulties

HARDSHELL *adj* having a shell or carapace that is thick, heavy, or hard

HARDSHIP *n* suffering

HARDSHIPS > HARDSHIP

HARDSTAND *n* hard surface on which vehicles may be parked

HARDTACK *n* kind of hard saltless biscuit, formerly eaten by sailors

HARDTACKS > HARDTACK

HARDTOP *n* car equipped with a metal or plastic roof that is sometimes detachable

HARDTOPS > HARDTOP

HARDWARE *n* metal tools or implements

HARDWARES > HARDWARE

HARDWIRE *vb* instal permanently in computer

HARDWIRED *adj* (of a circuit or instruction) permanently wired into a computer, replacing separate software

HARDWIRES > HARDWIRE

HARDWOOD *n* wood of a broad-leaved tree such as oak or ash

HARDWOODS > HARDWOOD

HARDY *adj* able to stand

difficult conditions ▷ *n* any blacksmith's tool made with a square shank so that it can be lodged in a square hole in an anvil

HARE *n* animal like a large rabbit, with longer ears and legs ▷ *vb* run (away) quickly

HAREBELL *n* blue bell-shaped flower

HAREBELLS > HAREBELL

HARED > HARE

HAREEM *same as* > HAREM

HAREEMS > HAREEM

HARELD *n* long-tailed duck

HARELDS > HARELD

HARELIKE > HARE

HARELIP *n* slight split in the upper lip

HARELIPS > HARELIP

HAREM *n* (apartments of) a Muslim man's wives and concubines

HAREMS > HAREM

HARES > HARE

HARESTAIL *n* species of cotton grass

HAREWOOD *n* sycamore wood that has been stained for use in furniture making

HAREWOODS > HAREWOOD

HARIANA *n* Indian breed of cattle

HARIANAS > HARIANA

HARICOT *n* variety of French bean with light-coloured edible seeds, which can be dried and stored

HARICOTS > HARICOT

HARIGALDS *pl n* intestines

HARIGALS *same as* > HARIGALDS

HARIJAN *n* member of an Indian caste once considered untouchable

HARIJANS > HARIJAN

HARIM *same as* > HAREM

HARIMS > HARIM

HARING > HARE

HARIOLATE *vb* practise divination

HARIRA *n* Moroccan soup made from a variety of vegetables with lentils, chickpeas, and coriander

HARIRAS > HARIRA

HARISH *adj* like hare

HARISSA *n* hot paste made from chilli peppers, tomatoes, spices, and olive oil

HARISSAS > HARISSA

HARK *vb* listen

HARKED > HARK

HARKEN *same as* > HEARKEN

HARKENED > HARKEN

HARKENER > HARKEN

HARKENERS > HARKEN

HARKENING > HARKEN

HARKENS > HARKEN

HARKING > HARK

HARKS > HARK

HARL *same as* > HERL

HARLED > HARL

HARLEQUIN *n* stock comic

character with a diamond-patterned costume and mask ▷ *adj* in many colours

HARLING > HARL

HARLINGS > HARL

HARLOT *n* prostitute ▷ *adj* of or like a harlot

HARLOTRY > HARLOT

HARLOTS > HARLOT

HARLS > HARL

HARM *vb* injure physically, mentally, or morally ▷ *n* physical, mental, or moral injury

HARMALA *n* African plant

HARMALAS > HARMALA

HARMALIN *n* chemical derived from harmala

HARMALINE *same as* > HARMALIN

HARMALINS > HARMALIN

HARMAN *n* constable

HARMANS > HARMAN

HARMATTAN *n* dry dusty wind from the Sahara blowing towards the W African coast, esp from November to March

HARMDOING *n* doing of harm

HARMED > HARM

HARMEL *same as* > HARMALA

HARMELS > HARMEL

HARMER > HARM

HARMERS > HARM

HARMFUL *adj* causing or tending to cause harm, esp to a person's health

HARMFULLY > HARMFUL

HARMIN *same as* > HARMALIN

HARMINE *same as* > HARMALIN

HARMINES > HARMINE

HARMING > HARM

HARMINS > HARMIN

HARMLESS *adj* safe to use, touch, or be near

HARMONIC *adj* of harmony ▷ *n* overtone of a musical note produced when that note is played, but not usually heard as a separate note

HARMONICA *n* small wind instrument played by sucking and blowing

HARMONICS *n* science of musical sounds

HARMONIES > HARMONY

HARMONISE *same as* > HARMONIZE

HARMONIST *n* person skilled in the art and techniques of harmony

HARMONIUM *n* keyboard instrument like a small organ

HARMONIZE *vb* sing or play in harmony

HARMONY *n* peaceful agreement and cooperation

HARMOST *n* Spartan governor

HARMOSTS > HARMOST

HARMOSTY *n* office of a harmost

HARMOTOME *n* mineral of the zeolite group

HARMS > HARM

HARN *n* coarse linen

HARNESS *n* arrangement of straps for attaching a horse to a cart or plough ▷ *vb* put a harness on

HARNESSED > HARNESS

HARNESSER > HARNESS

HARNESSES > HARNESS

HARNS > HARN

HARO *interj* cry meaning alas

HAROS > HARO

HAROSET *n* Jewish dish eaten at Passover

HAROSETH *same as* > HAROSET

HAROSETHS > HAROSETH

HAROSETS > HAROSET

HARP *n* large triangular stringed instrument played with the fingers ▷ *vb* play the harp

HARPED > HARP

HARPER > HARP

HARPERS > HARP

HARPIES > HARPY

HARPIN *n* type of protein

HARPING > HARP

HARPINGS *pl n* wooden members used for strengthening the bow of a vessel

HARPINS *same as* > HARPINGS

HARPIST > HARP

HARPISTS > HARP

HARPOON *n* barbed spear attached to a rope used for hunting whales ▷ *vb* spear with a harpoon

HARPOONED > HARPOON

HARPOONER > HARPOON

HARPOONS > HARPOON

HARPS > HARP

HARPY *n* nasty or bad-tempered woman

HARPYLIKE > HARPY

HARQUEBUS *variant of* > ARQUEBUS

HARRIDAN *n* nagging or vicious woman

HARRIDANS > HARRIDAN

HARRIED > HARRY

HARRIER *n* cross-country runner

HARRIERS > HARRIER

HARRIES > HARRY

HARROW *n* implement used to break up lumps of soil ▷ *vb* draw a harrow over

HARROWED > HARROW

HARROWER > HARROW

HARROWERS > HARROW

HARROWING > HARROW

HARROWS > HARROW

HARRUMPH *vb* clear or make the noise of clearing the throat

HARRUMPHS > HARRUMPH

HARRY *vb* keep asking (someone) to do something, pester

HARRYING > HARRY

HARSH *adj* severe and difficult to cope with

h

HARSHEN *vb* make harsh
HARSHENED > HARSHEN
HARSHENS > HARSHEN
HARSHER > HARSH
HARSHEST > HARSH
HARSHLY > HARSH
HARSHNESS > HARSH
HARSLET *same as* > HASLET
HARSLETS > HARSLET
HART *n* adult male deer
HARTAL *n* (in India) the act of closing shops or suspending work, esp in political protest
HARTALS > HARTAL
HARTBEES *same as* > HARTBEEST
HARTBEEST *n* African antelope
HARTELY *archaic spelling of* > HEARTILY
HARTEN *same as* > HEARTEN
HARTENED > HARTEN
HARTENING > HARTEN
HARTENS > HARTEN
HARTLESSE *same as* > HEARTLESS
HARTS > HART
HARTSHORN *n* sal volatile
HARUMPH *same as* > HARRUMPH
HARUMPHED > HARUMPH
HARUMPHS > HARUMPH
HARUSPEX *n* (in ancient Rome) a priest who practised divination, esp by examining the entrails of animals
HARUSPICY > HARUSPEX
HARVEST *n* (season for) the gathering of crops ▷ *vb* gather (a ripened crop)
HARVESTED > HARVEST
HARVESTER *n* harvesting machine, esp a combine harvester
HARVESTS > HARVEST
HAS > HAVE
HASBIAN *n* former lesbian who has become heterosexual or bisexual
HASBIANS > HASBIAN
HASH *n* dish of diced cooked meat and vegetables reheated ▷ *vb* chop into small pieces
HASHED > HASH
HASHEESH *same as* > HASHISH
HASHES > HASH
HASHHEAD *n* regular marijuana user
HASHHEADS > HASHHEAD
HASHIER > HASH
HASHIEST > HASH
HASHING > HASH
HASHISH *n* drug made from the cannabis plant, smoked for its intoxicating effects
HASHISHES > HASHISH
HASHMARK *n* character (#)
HASHMARKS > HASHMARK
HASHY > HASH
HASK *n* archaic name for a basket for transporting fish
HASKS > HASK

HASLET *n* loaf of cooked minced pig's offal, eaten cold
HASLETS > HASLET
HASP *n* clasp that fits over a staple and is secured by a bolt or padlock, used as a fastening ▷ *vb* secure (a door, window, etc) with a hasp
HASPED > HASP
HASPING > HASP
HASPS > HASP
HASSAR *n* South American catfish
HASSARS > HASSAR
HASSEL *variant of* > HASSLE
HASSELS > HASSEL
HASSIUM *n* element synthetically produced in small quantities by high-energy ion bombardment
HASSIUMS > HASSIUM
HASSLE *n* trouble, bother ▷ *vb* bother or annoy
HASSLED > HASSLE
HASSLES > HASSLE
HASSLING > HASSLE
HASSOCK *n* cushion for kneeling on in church
HASSOCKS > HASSOCK
HASSOCKY > HASSOCK
HAST *singular form of the present tense (indicative mood) of* > HAVE
HASTA *Spanish for* > UNTIL
HASTATE *adj* (of a leaf) having a pointed tip and two outward-pointing lobes at the base
HASTATED *same as* > HASTATE
HASTATELY > HASTATE
HASTE *n* (excessive) quickness ▷ *vb* hasten
HASTED > HASTE
HASTEFUL > HASTE
HASTEN *vb* (cause to) hurry
HASTENED > HASTEN
HASTENER > HASTEN
HASTENERS > HASTEN
HASTENING > HASTEN
HASTENS > HASTEN
HASTES > HASTE
HASTIER > HASTY
HASTIEST > HASTY
HASTILY > HASTY
HASTINESS > HASTY
HASTING > HASTE
HASTINGS > HASTE
HASTY *adj* (too) quick
HAT *n* covering for the head, often with a brim ▷ *vb* supply (a person) with a hat or put a hat on (someone)
HATABLE > HATE
HATBAND *n* band or ribbon around the base of the crown of a hat
HATBANDS > HATBAND
HATBOX *n* box or case for a hat or hats
HATBOXES > HATBOX
HATBRUSH *n* brush for hats
HATCH *vb* (cause to) emerge from an egg ▷ *n* hinged door covering an opening

in a floor or wall
HATCHABLE > HATCH
HATCHBACK *n* car with a lifting door at the back
HATCHECK *n* cloakroom
HATCHECKS > HATCHECK
HATCHED > HATCH
HATCHEL *same as* > HECKLE
HATCHELED > HATCHEL
HATCHELS > HATCHEL
HATCHER > HATCH
HATCHERS > HATCH
HATCHERY *n* place where eggs are hatched under artificial conditions
HATCHES > HATCH
HATCHET *n* small axe
HATCHETS > HATCHET
HATCHETY *adj* like a hatchet
HATCHING > HATCH
HATCHINGS > HATCH
HATCHLING *n* young animal that has newly hatched from an egg
HATCHMENT *n* diamond-shaped tablet displaying the coat of arms of a dead person
HATCHWAY *n* opening in the deck of a ship
HATCHWAYS > HATCHWAY
HATE *vb* dislike intensely ▷ *n* intense dislike
HATEABLE > HATE
HATED > HATE
HATEFUL *adj* causing or deserving hate
HATEFULLY > HATEFUL
HATELESS > HATE
HATER > HATE
HATERENT *same as* > HATRED
HATERENTS > HATERENT
HATERS > HATE
HATES > HATE
HATFUL *n* amount a hat will hold
HATFULS > HATFUL
HATGUARD *n* string to keep a hat from blowing off
HATGUARDS > HATGUARD
HATH *form of the present tense (indicative mood) of* > HAVE
HATHA *as in* hatha yoga *form of yoga*
HATING > HATE
HATLESS > HAT
HATLIKE > HAT
HATMAKER *n* maker of hats
HATMAKERS > HATMAKER
HATPEG *n* peg to hang hat on
HATPEGS > HATPEG
HATPIN *n* sturdy pin used to secure a woman's hat to her hair, often having a decorative head
HATPINS > HATPIN
HATRACK *n* rack for hanging hats on
HATRACKS > HATRACK
HATRED *n* intense dislike
HATREDS > HATRED
HATS > HAT
HATSFUL > HATFUL
HATSTAND *n* frame or pole equipped with hooks or arms for hanging up hats,

coats, etc
HATSTANDS > HATSTAND
HATTED > HAT
HATTER *n* person who makes and sells hats ▷ *vb* annoy
HATTERED > HATTER
HATTERIA *n* species of reptile
HATTERIAS > HATTERIA
HATTERING > HATTER
HATTERS > HATTER
HATTING > HAT
HATTINGS > HAT
HATTOCK *n* small hat
HATTOCKS > HATTOCK
HAUBERK *n* long sleeveless coat of mail
HAUBERKS > HAUBERK
HAUBOIS *same as* > HAUTBOY
HAUD *Scot word for* > HOLD
HAUDING > HAUD
HAUDS > HAUD
HAUF *Scot word for* > HALF
HAUFS > HAUF
HAUGH *n* low-lying often alluvial riverside meadow
HAUGHS > HAUGH
HAUGHT *same as* > HAUGHTY
HAUGHTIER > HAUGHTY
HAUGHTILY > HAUGHTY
HAUGHTY *adj* proud, arrogant
HAUL *vb* pull or drag with effort ▷ *n* hauling
HAULAGE *n* (charge for) transporting goods
HAULAGES > HAULAGE
HAULD *Scots word for* > HOLD
HAULDS > HAULD
HAULED > HAUL
HAULER *same as* > HAULIER
HAULERS > HAULER
HAULIER *n* firm or person that transports goods by road
HAULIERS > HAULIER
HAULING > HAUL
HAULM *n* stalks of beans, peas, or potatoes collectively
HAULMIER > HAULMY
HAULMIEST > HAULMY
HAULMS > HAULM
HAULMY *adj* having haulms
HAULS > HAUL
HAULST *same as* > HALSE
HAULT *same as* > HAUGHTY
HAULYARD *same as* > HALYARD
HAULYARDS > HAULYARD
HAUNCH *n* human hip or fleshy hindquarter of an animal ▷ *vb* in archaic usage, cause (an animal) to come down on its haunches
HAUNCHED > HAUNCH
HAUNCHES > HAUNCH
HAUNCHING > HAUNCH
HAUNT *vb* visit in the form of a ghost ▷ *n* place visited frequently
HAUNTED *adj* frequented by ghosts
HAUNTER > HAUNT
HAUNTERS > HAUNT

HAUNTING adj memorably beautiful or sad

HAUNTINGS > HAUNT

HAUNTS > HAUNT

HAURIANT adj rising

HAURIENT same as > HAURIANT

HAUSE same as > HALSE

HAUSED > HAUSE

HAUSEN n variety of sturgeon

HAUSENS > HAUSEN

HAUSES > HAUSE

HAUSFRAU n German housewife

HAUSFRAUS > HAUSFRAU

HAUSING > HAUSE

HAUSTELLA n pl of haustellum: tip of the proboscis of an insect

HAUSTORIA n pl of haustorium: organ of a parasitic plant that absorbs food and water from host tissues

HAUT same as > HAUGHTY

HAUTBOIS same as > HAUTBOY

HAUTBOY n oboe

HAUTBOYS > HAUTBOY

HAUTE adj French word meaning high

HAUTEUR n haughtiness

HAUTEURS > HAUTEUR

HAUYNE n blue mineral containing calcium

HAUYNES > HAUYNE

HAVARTI n Danish cheese

HAVARTIS > HAVARTI

HAVDALAH n ceremony marking the end of the sabbath or of a festival, including the blessings over wine, candles, and spices

HAVDALAHS > HAVDALAH

HAVDOLOH same as > HAVDALAH

HAVDOLOHS > HAVDOLOH

HAVE vb possess, hold

HAVELOCK n light-coloured cover for a service cap with a flap extending over the back of the neck to protect the head and neck from the sun

HAVELOCKS > HAVELOCK

HAVEN n place of safety ▷ vb secure or shelter in or as if in a haven

HAVENED > HAVEN

HAVENING > HAVEN

HAVENLESS > HAVEN

HAVENS > HAVEN

HAVEOUR same as > HAVIOR

HAVEOURS > HAVEOUR

HAVER vb talk nonsense ▷ n nonsense

HAVERED > HAVER

HAVEREL n fool

HAVERELS > HAVEREL

HAVERING > HAVER

HAVERINGS > HAVER

HAVERS > HAVER

HAVERSACK n canvas bag carried on the back or shoulder

HAVERSINE n half the value of the versed sine

HAVES > HAVE

HAVILDAR n noncommissioned officer in the Indian army, equivalent in rank to sergeant

HAVILDARS > HAVILDAR

HAVING > HAVE

HAVINGS > HAVE

HAVIOR same as > HAVIOUR

HAVIORS > HAVIOR

HAVIOUR n possession

HAVIOURS > HAVIOUR

HAVOC n disorder and confusion ▷ vb lay waste

HAVOCKED > HAVOC

HAVOCKER > HAVOC

HAVOCKERS > HAVOC

HAVOCKING > HAVOC

HAVOCS > HAVOC

HAW n hawthorn berry ▷ vb make an inarticulate utterance

HAWALA n Middle Eastern system of money transfer

HAWALAS > HAWALA

HAWBUCK n bumpkin

HAWBUCKS > HAWBUCK

HAWED > HAW

HAWFINCH n European finch with a stout bill and brown plumage with black-and-white wings

HAWING > HAW

HAWK n bird of prey with a short hooked bill and very good eyesight ▷ vb offer (goods) for sale in the street or door-to-door

HAWKBELL n bell fitted to a hawk's leg

HAWKBELLS > HAWKBELL

HAWKBILL same as > HAWKSBILL

HAWKBILLS > HAWKBILL

HAWKBIT n any of three perennial plants with yellow dandelion-like flowers

HAWKBITS > HAWKBIT

HAWKED > HAWK

HAWKER n person who travels from place to place selling goods

HAWKERS > HAWKER

HAWKEY same as > HOCKEY

HAWKEYED adj having extremely keen sight

HAWKEYS > HAWKEY

HAWKIE n cow with white stripe on face

HAWKIES > HAWKIE

HAWKING another name for > FALCONRY

HAWKINGS > HAWKING

HAWKISH adj favouring the use or display of force rather than diplomacy to achieve foreign policy goals

HAWKISHLY > HAWKISH

HAWKIT adj having a white streak

HAWKLIKE > HAWK

HAWKMOTH n powerful narrow-winged moth with the ability to hover over flowers when feeding from the nectar

HAWKMOTHS > HAWKMOTH

HAWKNOSE n hooked nose

HAWKNOSES > HAWKNOSE

HAWKS > HAWK

HAWKSBILL n type of turtle

HAWKSHAW n private detective

HAWKSHAWS > HAWKSHAW

HAWKWEED n hairy plant with clusters of dandelion-like flowers

HAWKWEEDS > HAWKWEED

HAWM vb be idle and relaxed

HAWMED > HAWM

HAWMING > HAWM

HAWMS > HAWM

HAWS > HAW

HAWSE vb of boats, pitch violently when at anchor

HAWSED > HAWSE

HAWSEHOLE n one of the holes in the upper part of the bows of a vessel through which the anchor ropes pass

HAWSEPIPE n strong metal pipe through which an anchor rope passes

HAWSER n large rope used on a ship

HAWSERS > HAWSER

HAWSES > HAWSE

HAWSING > HAWSE

HAWTHORN n thorny shrub or tree

HAWTHORNS > HAWTHORN

HAWTHORNY > HAWTHORN

HAY n grass cut and dried as fodder ▷ vb cut, dry, and store (grass, clover, etc) as fodder

HAYBAND n rope made by twisting hay together

HAYBANDS > HAYBAND

HAYBOX n airtight box full of hay or other insulating material used to keep partially cooked food warm and allow cooking by retained heat

HAYBOXES > HAYBOX

HAYCOCK n small cone-shaped pile of hay left in the field until dry enough to carry to the rick or barn

HAYCOCKS > HAYCOCK

HAYED > HAY

HAYER n person who makes hay

HAYERS > HAYER

HAYEY > HAY

HAYFIELD n field of hay

HAYFIELDS > HAYFIELD

HAYFORK n long-handled fork with two long curved prongs, used for moving or turning hay

HAYFORKS > HAYFORK

HAYING > HAY

HAYINGS > HAY

HAYLAGE n type of hay for animal fodder

HAYLAGES > HAYLAGE

HAYLE n welfare

HAYLES > HAYLE

HAYLOFT n loft for storing hay

HAYLOFTS > HAYLOFT

HAYMAKER n person who helps to cut, turn, toss, spread, or carry hay

HAYMAKERS > HAYMAKER

HAYMAKING > HAYMAKER

HAYMOW n part of a barn where hay is stored

HAYMOWS > HAYMOW

HAYRACK n rack for holding hay for feeding to animals

HAYRACKS > HAYRACK

HAYRICK same as > HAYSTACK

HAYRICKS > HAYRICK

HAYRIDE n pleasure trip in hay wagon

HAYRIDES > HAYRIDE

HAYS > HAY

HAYSEED n seeds or fragments of grass or straw

HAYSEEDS > HAYSEED

HAYSEL n season for making hay

HAYSELS > HAYSEL

HAYSTACK n large pile of stored hay

HAYSTACKS > HAYSTACK

HAYWARD n parish officer in charge of enclosures and fences

HAYWARDS > HAYWARD

HAYWIRE adj (of things) not functioning properly ▷ n wire for binding hay

HAYWIRES > HAYWIRE

HAZAN same as > CANTOR

HAZANIM > HAZAN

HAZANS > HAZAN

HAZARD n something that could be dangerous ▷ vb put in danger

HAZARDED > HAZARD

HAZARDER > HAZARD

HAZARDERS > HAZARD

HAZARDING > HAZARD

HAZARDIZE same as > HAZARD

HAZARDOUS adj involving great risk

HAZARDRY n taking of risks

HAZARDS > HAZARD

HAZE n mist, often caused by heat ▷ vb make or become hazy

HAZED > HAZE

HAZEL n small tree producing edible nuts ▷ adj (of eyes) greenish-brown

HAZELHEN n type of grouse

HAZELHENS > HAZELHEN

HAZELLY > HAZEL

HAZELNUT n nut of a hazel shrub, which has a smooth shiny hard shell

HAZELNUTS > HAZELNUT

HAZELS > HAZEL

HAZER > HAZE

HAZERS > HAZE

HAZES > HAZE

HAZIER > HAZY

HAZIEST > HAZY

HAZILY > HAZY

HAZINESS > HAZY

HAZING > HAZE

HAZINGS > HAZE

HAZMAT n hazardous material

HAZMATS > HAZMAT

HAZY adj not clear, misty

HAZZAN same as > CANTOR

HAZZANIM > HAZZAN

HAZZANS > HAZZAN

HE pron male person or animal ▷ n male person or animal ▷ interj expression of amusement or derision

HEAD n upper or front part of the body, containing the sense organs and the brain ▷ adj chief, principal ▷ vb be at the top or front of

HEADACHE n continuous pain in the head

HEADACHES > HEADACHE

HEADACHEY same as > HEADACHY.

HEADACHY adj suffering from, caused by, or likely to cause a headache

HEADAGE n payment to farmer based on number of animals kept

HEADAGES > HEADAGE

HEADBAND n ribbon or band worn around the head

HEADBANDS > HEADBAND

HEADBANG vb nod one's head violently to the beat of loud rock music

HEADBANGS > HEADBANG

HEADBOARD n vertical board at the top end of a bed

HEADCASE n insane person

HEADCASES > HEADCASE

HEADCHAIR n chair with support for the head

HEADCLOTH n kerchief worn on the head

HEADCOUNT n count of number of people present

HEADDRESS n decorative head covering

HEADED adj having a head or heads

HEADEND n facility from which cable television is transmitted

HEADENDS > HEADEND

HEADER n striking a ball with the head

HEADERS > HEADER

HEADFAST n mooring rope at the bows of a ship

HEADFASTS > HEADFAST

HEADFIRST adv with the head foremost

HEADFISH same as > SUNFISH

HEADFRAME n structure supporting winding machinery at mine

HEADFUCK n taboo slang for experience that is wildly exciting or impressive

HEADFUCKS > HEADFUCK

HEADFUL n amount head will hold

HEADFULS > HEADFUL

HEADGATE n a gate that is used to control the flow of water at the upper end of a lock or conduit

HEADGATES > HEADGATE

HEADGEAR n hats collectively

HEADGEARS > HEADGEAR

HEADGUARD n padded helmet worn to protect the head in contact sports

HEADHUNT vb recruit employee from another company

HEADHUNTS > HEADHUNT

HEADIER > HEADY

HEADIEST > HEADY

HEADILY > HEADY

HEADINESS > HEADY

HEADING same as > HEAD

HEADINGS > HEADING

HEADLAMP same as > HEADLIGHT

HEADLAMPS > HEADLAMP

HEADLAND n area of land jutting out into the sea

HEADLANDS > HEADLAND

HEADLEASE n main lease often subdivided

HEADLESS adj without a head

HEADLIGHT n powerful light on the front of a vehicle

HEADLIKE > HEAD

HEADLINE n title at the top of a newspaper article, esp on the front page

HEADLINED > HEADLINE

HEADLINER n performer given prominent billing

HEADLINES > HEADLINE

HEADLOCK n wrestling hold in which a wrestler locks his opponent's head between the crook of his elbow and the side of his body

HEADLOCKS > HEADLOCK

HEADLONG adj with the head first ▷ adv with the head foremost

HEADMAN n chief or leader

HEADMARK n characteristic

HEADMARKS > HEADMARK

HEADMEN > HEADMAN

HEADMOST less common word for > FOREMOST

HEADNOTE n note at book chapter head

HEADNOTES > HEADNOTE

HEADPEACE archaic form of > HEADPIECE

HEADPHONE n small loudspeaker held against the ear

HEADPIECE n decorative band at the top of a page, chapter, etc

HEADPIN another word for > KINGPIN

HEADPINS > HEADPIN

HEADRACE n channel that carries water to a water wheel, turbine, etc

HEADRACES > HEADRACE

HEADRAIL n end of the table from which play is started, nearest the baulkline

HEADRAILS > HEADRAIL

HEADREACH n distance made to windward while tacking ▷ vb gain distance over (another boat) when tacking

HEADREST n support for the head, as on a dentist's chair or car seat

HEADRESTS > HEADREST

HEADRIG n edge of ploughed field

HEADRIGS > HEADRIG

HEADRING n African head decoration

HEADRINGS > HEADRING

HEADROOM n space below a roof or bridge which allows an object to pass or stay underneath it without touching it

HEADROOMS > HEADROOM

HEADROPE n rope round an animal's head

HEADROPES > HEADROPE

HEADS adv with the side of a coin which has a portrait of a head on it uppermost

HEADSAIL n any sail set forward of the foremast

HEADSAILS > HEADSAIL

HEADSCARF n scarf for the head, often worn tied under the chin

HEADSET n pair of headphones, esp with a microphone attached

HEADSETS > HEADSET

HEADSHAKE n gesture of shaking head

HEADSHIP n position or state of being a leader, esp the head teacher of a school

HEADSHIPS > HEADSHIP

HEADSHOT n photo of person's head

HEADSHOTS > HEADSHOT

HEADSMAN n (formerly) an executioner who beheaded condemned persons

HEADSMEN > HEADSMAN

HEADSPACE n space between bolt and cartridge in a rifle

HEADSTALL n part of a bridle that fits round a horse's head

HEADSTAND n act or an instance of balancing on the head, usually with the hands as support

HEADSTAY n rope from mast to bow on ship

HEADSTAYS > HEADSTAY

HEADSTICK n piece of wood formerly used in typesetting

HEADSTOCK n part of a machine that supports and transmits the drive to the chuck

HEADSTONE n memorial stone on a grave

HEADWARD same as > HEADWARDS

HEADWARDS adv backwards beyond the original source

HEADWATER n highest part of river

HEADWAY same as > HEADROOM

HEADWAYS > HEADWAY

HEADWIND n wind blowing against the course of an aircraft or ship

HEADWINDS > HEADWIND

HEADWORD n key word placed at the beginning of a line, paragraph, etc, as in a dictionary entry

HEADWORDS > HEADWORD

HEADWORK n mental work

HEADWORKS > HEADWORK

HEADY adj intoxicating or exciting

HEAL vb make or become well

HEALABLE > HEAL

HEALD same as > HEDDLE

HEALDED > HEALD

HEALDING > HEALD

HEALDS > HEALD

HEALED > HEAL

HEALEE n person who is being healed

HEALEES > HEALEE

HEALER > HEAL

HEALERS > HEAL

HEALING > HEAL

HEALINGLY > HEAL

HEALINGS > HEAL

HEALS > HEAL

HEALSOME Scots word for > WHOLESOME

HEALTH n normal (good) condition of someone's body ▷ interj exclamation wishing someone good health as part of a toast

HEALTHFUL same as > HEALTHY

HEALTHIER > HEALTHY

HEALTHILY > HEALTHY

HEALTHISM n lifestyle that prioritizes health and fitness over anything else

HEALTHS > HEALTH

HEALTHY adj having good health

HEAME old form of > HOME

HEAP n pile of things one on top of another ▷ vb gather into a pile

HEAPED > HEAP

HEAPER > HEAP

HEAPERS > HEAP

HEAPIER > HEAPY

HEAPIEST > HEAPY

HEAPING adj (of a spoonful) heaped

HEAPS > HEAP

HEAPSTEAD n buildings at mine

HEAPY adj having many heaps

HEAR vb perceive (a sound) by ear

HEARABLE > HEAR

HEARD same as > HERD

HEARDS > HERD

HEARE old form of > HAIR

HEARER > HEAR

HEARERS > HEAR

HEARES > HEARE

HEARIE *old form of* > HAIRY
HEARING > HEAR
HEARINGS > HEAR
HEARKEN *vb* listen
HEARKENED > HEARKEN
HEARKENER > HEARKEN
HEARKENS > HEARKEN
HEARS > HEAR
HEARSAY *n* gossip, rumour
HEARSAYS > HEARSAY
HEARSE *n* funeral car used to carry a coffin ▷*vb* put in hearse
HEARSED > HEARSE
HEARSES > HEARSE
HEARSIER > HEARSY
HEARSIEST > HEARSY
HEARSING > HEARSE
HEARSY *adj* like a hearse
HEART *n* organ that pumps blood round the body ▷*vb* (of vegetables) form a heart
HEARTACHE *n* intense anguish
HEARTBEAT *n* one complete pulsation of the heart
HEARTBURN *n* burning sensation in the chest caused by indigestion
HEARTED > HEART
HEARTEN *vb* encourage, make cheerful
HEARTENED > HEARTEN
HEARTENER > HEARTEN
HEARTENS > HEARTEN
HEARTFELT *adj* felt sincerely or strongly
HEARTFREE *adj* not in love
HEARTH *n* floor of a fireplace
HEARTHRUG *n* rug laid before fireplace
HEARTHS > HEARTH
HEARTIER > HEARTY
HEARTIES > HEARTY
HEARTIEST > HEARTY
HEARTIKIN *n* little heart
HEARTILY *adv* thoroughly or vigorously
HEARTING > HEART
HEARTLAND *n* central region of a country or continent
HEARTLESS *adj* cruel, unkind
HEARTLET *n* little heart
HEARTLETS > HEART
HEARTLING *n* little heart
HEARTLY *adv* vigorously
HEARTPEA *same as* > HEARTSEED
HEARTPEAS > HEARTPEA
HEARTS *n* card game in which players must avoid winning tricks containing hearts or the queen of spades
HEARTSEED *n* type of vine
HEARTSICK *adj* deeply dejected or despondent
HEARTSOME *adj* cheering or encouraging
HEARTSORE *adj* greatly distressed
HEARTWOOD *n* central core of dark hard wood in tree trunks
HEARTWORM *n* parasitic

nematode worm that lives in the heart and bloodstream of vertebrates
HEARTY *adj* substantial, nourishing ▷*n* comrade, esp a sailor
HEAST *same as* > HEST
HEASTE *same as* > HEST
HEASTES > HEASTE
HEASTS > HEAST
HEAT *vb* make or become hot ▷*n* state of being hot
HEATABLE > HEAT
HEATED *adj* angry and excited
HEATEDLY > HEATED
HEATER *n* device for supplying heat
HEATERS > HEATER
HEATH *n* area of open uncultivated land
HEATHBIRD *n* black grouse
HEATHCOCK *same as* > BLACKCOCK
HEATHEN *n* (of) a person who does not believe in an established religion ▷*adj* of or relating to heathen peoples
HEATHENRY > HEATHEN
HEATHENS > HEATHEN
HEATHER *n* low-growing plant with small purple, pinkish, or white flowers, growing on heaths and mountains ▷*adj* of a heather colour
HEATHERED > HEATHER
HEATHERS > HEATHER
HEATHERY > HEATHER
HEATHFOWL *Compare* > MOORFOWL
HEATHIER > HEATH
HEATHIEST > HEATH
HEATHLAND *n* area of heath
HEATHLESS > HEATH
HEATHLIKE > HEATH
HEATHS > HEATH
HEATHY > HEATH
HEATING *n* device or system for supplying heat, esp central heating, to a building
HEATINGS > HEATING
HEATLESS > HEAT
HEATPROOF > HEAT
HEATS > HEAT
HEATSPOT *n* spot on skin produced by heat
HEATSPOTS > HEATSPOT
HEAUME *n* (in the 12th and 13th centuries) a large helmet reaching and supported by the shoulders
HEAUMES > HEAUME
HEAVE *vb* lift with effort ▷*n* heaving
HEAVED > HEAVE
HEAVEN *n* place believed to be the home of God, where good people go when they die
HEAVENLY *adj* of or like heaven
HEAVENS > HEAVEN
HEAVER > HEAVE
HEAVERS > HEAVE

HEAVES > HEAVE
HEAVIER > HEAVY
HEAVIES > HEAVY
HEAVIEST > HEAVY
HEAVILY > HEAVY
HEAVINESS > HEAVY
HEAVING > HEAVE
HEAVINGS > HEAVE
HEAVY *adj* of great weight
HEAVYSET *adj* stockily built
HEBDOMAD *n* number seven or a group of seven
HEBDOMADS > HEBDOMAD
HEBE *n* any of various flowering shrubs
HEBEN *old form of* > EBONY
HEBENON *n* source of poison
HEBENONS > HEBENON
HEBENS > HEBEN
HEBES > HEBE
HEBETANT *adj* causing dullness
HEBETATE *adj* (of plant parts) having a blunt or soft point ▷*vb* make or become blunted
HEBETATED > HEBETATE
HEBETATES > HEBETATE
HEBETIC *adj* of or relating to puberty
HEBETUDE *n* mental dullness or lethargy
HEBETUDES > HEBETUDE
HEBONA *same as* > HEBENON
HEBONAS > HEBONA
HEBRAISE *same as* > HEBRAIZE
HEBRAISED > HEBRAISE
HEBRAISES > HEBRAISE
HEBRAIZE *vb* become or cause to become Hebrew or Hebraic
HEBRAIZED > HEBRAIZE
HEBRAIZES > HEBRAIZE
HECATOMB *n* (in ancient Greece or Rome) any great public sacrifice and feast, originally one in which 100 oxen were sacrificed
HECATOMBS > HECATOMB
HECH *interj* expression of surprise
HECHT *same as* > HIGHT
HECHTING > HECHT
HECHTS > HECHT
HECK *interj* mild exclamation of surprise, irritation, etc ▷*n* frame for obstructing the passage of fish in a river
HECKLE *vb* interrupt (a public speaker) with comments, questions, or taunts ▷*n* instrument for combing flax or hemp
HECKLED > HECKLE
HECKLER > HECKLE
HECKLERS > HECKLE
HECKLES > HECKLE
HECKLING > HECKLE
HECKLINGS > HECKLE
HECKS > HECK
HECOGENIN *n* plant chemical used in drugs
HECTARE *n* one hundred ares or 10 000 square metres (2.471 acres)

HECTARES > HECTARE
HECTIC *adj* rushed or busy ▷*n* hectic fever or flush
HECTICAL *same as* > HECTIC
HECTICLY > HECTIC
HECTICS > HECTIC
HECTOGRAM *n* one hundred grams. 1 hectogram is equivalent to 3.527 ounces.
HECTOR *vb* bully ▷*n* blustering bully
HECTORED > HECTOR
HECTORER > HECTOR
HECTORERS > HECTOR
HECTORING > HECTOR
HECTORISM > HECTOR
HECTORLY > HECTOR
HECTORS > HECTOR
HEDDLE *n* one of a set of frames of vertical wires on a loom, each wire having an eye through which a warp thread can be passed ▷*vb* pass thread through heddle
HEDDLED > HEDDLE
HEDDLES > HEDDLE
HEDDLING > HEDDLE
HEDER *variant spelling of* > CHEDER
HEDERA *See* > IVY
HEDERAL > HEDERA
HEDERAS > HEDERA
HEDERATED *adj* honoured with crown of ivy
HEDERS > HEDER
HEDGE *n* row of bushes forming a barrier or boundary ▷*vb* be evasive or noncommittal
HEDGEBILL *n* tool for pruning a hedge
HEDGED > HEDGE
HEDGEHOG *n* small mammal with a protective covering of spines
HEDGEHOGS > HEDGEHOG
HEDGEHOP *vb* (of an aircraft) to fly close to the ground, as in crop spraying
HEDGEHOPS > HEDGEHOP
HEDGEPIG *same as* > HEDGEHOG
HEDGEPIGS > HEDGEPIG
HEDGER > HEDGE
HEDGEROW *n* bushes forming a hedge
HEDGEROWS > HEDGEROW
HEDGERS > HEDGE
HEDGES > HEDGE
HEDGIER > HEDGE
HEDGIEST > HEDGE
HEDGING > HEDGE
HEDGINGLY > HEDGE
HEDGINGS > HEDGE
HEDGY > HEDGE
HEDONIC > HEDONISM
HEDONICS *n* branch of psychology concerned with the study of pleasant and unpleasant sensations
HEDONISM *n* doctrine that pleasure is the most important thing in life
HEDONISMS > HEDONISM
HEDONIST > HEDONISM
HEDONISTS > HEDONISM

h

HEDYPHANE *n* variety of lead ore

HEED *n* careful attention ▷ *vb* pay careful attention to

HEEDED > HEED

HEEDER > HEED

HEEDERS > HEED

HEEDFUL > HEED

HEEDFULLY > HEED

HEEDINESS > HEED

HEEDING > HEED

HEEDLESS *adj* taking no notice

HEEDS > HEED

HEEDY > HEED

HEEHAW *interj* representation of the braying sound of a donkey ▷ *vb* make braying sound

HEEHAWED > HEEHAW

HEEHAWING > HEEHAW

HEEHAWS > HEEHAW

HEEL *n* back part of the foot ▷ *vb* repair the heel of (a shoe)

HEELBALL *n* mixture of beeswax and lampblack used by shoemakers

HEELBALLS > HEELBALL

HEELED > HEEL

HEELER *n* dog that herds cattle by biting at their heels

HEELERS > HEELER

HEELING > HEEL

HEELINGS > HEEL

HEELLESS > HEEL

HEELPIECE *n* piece of a shoe, stocking, etc, designed to fit the heel

HEELPLATE *n* reinforcing piece of metal

HEELPOST *n* post for carrying the hinges of a door or gate

HEELPOSTS > HEELPOST

HEELS > HEEL

HEELTAP *n* layer of leather, etc, in the heel of a shoe

HEELTAPS > HEELTAP

HEEZE *Scots word for* > HOIST

HEEZED > HEEZE

HEEZES > HEEZE

HEEZIE *n* act of lifting

HEEZIES > HEEZIE

HEEZING > HEEZE

HEFT *vb* assess the weight of (something) by lifting ▷ *n* weight

HEFTE *same as* > HEAVE

HEFTED > HEFT

HEFTER > HEFT

HEFTERS > HEFT

HEFTIER > HEFTY

HEFTIEST > HEFTY

HEFTILY > HEFTY

HEFTINESS > HEFTY

HEFTING > HEFT

HEFTS > HEFT

HEFTY *adj* large, heavy, or strong

HEGARI *n* African sorghum

HEGARIS > HEGARI

HEGEMON *n* person in authority

HEGEMONIC > HEGEMONY

HEGEMONS > HEGEMON

HEGEMONY *n* political domination

HEGIRA *n* emigration escape or flight

HEGIRAS > HEGIRA

HEGUMEN *n* head of a monastery of the Eastern Church

HEGUMENE *n* head of Greek nunnery

HEGUMENES > HEGUMENE

HEGUMENOI > HEGUMENOS

HEGUMENOS *same as* > HEGUMEN

HEGUMENS > HEGUMEN

HEGUMENY *n* office of hegumen

HEH *interj* exclamation of surprise or inquiry

HEHS > HEH

HEID *Scot word for* > HEAD

HEIDS > HEID

HEIFER *n* young cow

HEIFERS > HEIFER

HEIGH *same as* > HEY

HEIGHT *n* distance from base to top

HEIGHTEN *vb* make or become higher or more intense

HEIGHTENS > HEIGHTEN

HEIGHTH *obsolete form of* > HEIGHT

HEIGHTHS > HEIGHTH

HEIGHTISM *n* discrimination based on people's heights

HEIGHTS > HEIGHT

HEIL *vb* give a German greeting

HEILED > HEIL

HEILING > HEIL

HEILS > HEIL

HEIMISH *adj* comfortable

HEINIE *n* buttocks

HEINIES > HEINIE

HEINOUS *adj* evil and shocking

HEINOUSLY > HEINOUS

HEIR *n* person entitled to inherit property or rank ▷ *vb* inherit

HEIRDOM *n* succession by right of blood

HEIRDOMS > HEIRDOM

HEIRED > HEIR

HEIRESS *n* woman who inherits or expects to inherit great wealth

HEIRESSES > HEIRESS

HEIRING > HEIR

HEIRLESS > HEIR

HEIRLOOM *n* object that has belonged to a family for generations

HEIRLOOMS > HEIRLOOM

HEIRS > HEIR

HEIRSHIP *n* state or condition of being an heir

HEIRSHIPS > HEIRSHIP

HEISHI *n* Native American shell jewellery

HEIST *n* robbery ▷ *vb* steal or burgle

HEISTED > HEIST

HEISTER > HEIST

HEISTERS > HEIST

HEISTING > HEIST

HEISTS > HEIST

HEITIKI *n* Māori neck ornament of greenstone

HEITIKIS > HEITIKI

HEJAB *same as* > HIJAB

HEJABS > HEJAB

HEJIRA *same as* > HEGIRA

HEJIRAS > HEJIRA

HEJRA *same as* > HEGIRA

HEJRAS > HEJRA

HEKETARA *n* small shrub that has flowers with white petals and yellow centres

HEKETARAS > HEKETARA

HEKTARE *same as* > HECTARE

HEKTARES > HEKTARE

HEKTOGRAM *same as* > HECTOGRAM

HELCOID *adj* having ulcers

HELD > HOLD

HELE as in *hele in* dialect expression meaning insert (cuttings, shoots, etc) into soil before planting to keep them moist

HELED > HELE

HELENIUM *n* plant with daisy-like yellow or variegated flowers

HELENIUMS > HELENIUM

HELES > HELE

HELIAC *same as* > HELIACAL

HELIACAL as in *heliacal rising* rising of a celestial object at approximately the same time as the rising of the sun

HELIAST *n* ancient Greek juror

HELIASTS > HELIAST

HELIBORNE *adj* carried in helicopter

HELIBUS *n* helicopter carrying passengers

HELIBUSES > HELIBUS

HELICAL *adj* spiral

HELICALLY > HELICAL

HELICES > HELIX

HELICITY *n* projection of the spin of an elementary particle on the direction of propagation

HELICLINE *n* spiral-shaped ramp

HELICOID *adj* shaped like a spiral ▷ *n* any surface resembling that of a screw thread

HELICOIDS > HELICOID

HELICON *n* bass tuba made to coil over the shoulder of a band musician

HELICONIA *n* tropical flowering plant

HELICONS > HELICON

HELICOPT *vb* transport using a helicopter

HELICOPTS > HELICOPT

HELICTITE *n* twisted stalactite

HELIDECK *n* landing deck for helicopters on ships, oil platforms, etc

HELIDECKS > HELIDECK

HELIDROME *n* small airport for helicopters

HELILIFT *vb* transport by helicopter

HELILIFTS > HELILIFT

HELIMAN *n* helicopter pilot

HELIMEN > HELIMAN

HELING > HELE

HELIO *n* instrument for sending messages in Morse code by reflecting the sun's rays

HELIODOR *n* clear yellow form of beryl used as a gemstone

HELIODORS > HELIODOR

HELIOGRAM *n* message sent by reflecting the sun's rays in a mirror

HELIOLOGY *n* study of sun

HELIOS > HELIO

HELIOSES > HELIOSIS

HELIOSIS *n* bad effect of overexposure to the sun

HELIOSTAT *n* astronomical instrument used to reflect the light of the sun in a constant direction

HELIOTYPE *n* printing process in which an impression is taken in ink from a gelatine surface that has been exposed under a negative and prepared for printing

HELIOTYPY *same as* > HELIOTYPE

HELIOZOAN *n* type of protozoan, typically having a siliceous shell and stiff radiating cytoplasmic projections

HELIOZOIC > HELIOZOAN

HELIPAD *n* place for helicopters to land and take off

HELIPADS > HELIPAD

HELIPILOT *n* helicopter pilot

HELIPORT *n* airport for helicopters

HELIPORTS > HELIPORT

HELISTOP *n* landing place for helicopter

HELISTOPS > HELISTOP

HELIUM *n* very light colourless odourless gas

HELIUMS > HELIUM

HELIX *n* spiral

HELIXES > HELIX

HELL *n* place believed to be where wicked people go when they die ▷ *vb* act wildly

HELLBENT *adj* intent

HELLBOX *n* (in printing) container for broken type

HELLBOXES > HELLBOX

HELLBROTH *n* evil concoction

HELLCAT *n* spiteful fierce-tempered woman

HELLCATS > HELLCAT

HELLDIVER *n* small greyish-brown North American grebe

HELLEBORE *n* plant with white flowers that bloom

in winter

HELLED > HELL

HELLENISE same as > HELLENIZE

HELLENIZE vb make or become like the ancient Greeks

HELLER n monetary unit of the Czech Republic and Slovakia

HELLERI n Central American fish

HELLERIES > HELLERY

HELLERIS > HELLERI

HELLERS > HELLER

HELLERY n wild or mischievous behaviour

HELLFIRE n torment of hell, imagined as eternal fire

HELLFIRES > HELLFIRE

HELLHOLE n unpleasant or evil place

HELLHOLES > HELLHOLE

HELLHOUND n hound of hell

HELLICAT n evil creature

HELLICATS > HELLICAT

HELLIER n slater

HELLIERS > HELLIER

HELLING > HELL

HELLION n rough or rowdy person, esp a child

HELLIONS > HELLION

HELLISH adj very unpleasant ▷ adv (intensifier)

HELLISHLY > HELLISH

HELLKITE n bird of prey from hell

HELLKITES > HELLKITE

HELLO interj expression of greeting or surprise ▷ n act of saying 'hello' ▷ sentence substitute expression of greeting used on meeting a person or at the start of a telephone call ▷ vb say hello

HELLOED > HELLO

HELLOES > HELLO

HELLOING > HELLO

HELLOS > HELLO

HELLOVA same as > HELLUVA

HELLS > HELL

HELLUVA adj (intensifier)

HELLWARD adj towards hell

HELLWARDS adv towards hell

HELM n tiller or wheel for steering a ship ▷ vb direct or steer

HELMED > HELM

HELMER n film director

HELMERS > HELMER

HELMET n hard hat worn for protection

HELMETED > HELMET

HELMETING n wearing or provision of a helmet

HELMETS > HELMET

HELMING > HELM

HELMINTH n any parasitic worm, esp a nematode or fluke

HELMINTHS > HELMINTH

HELMLESS > HELM

HELMS > HELM

HELMSMAN n person at the

helm who steers the ship

HELMSMEN > HELMSMAN

HELO n helicopter

HELOPHYTE n any perennial marsh plant that bears its overwintering buds in the mud below the surface

HELOS > HELO

HELOT n serf or slave

HELOTAGE same as > HELOTISM

HELOTAGES > HELOTAGE

HELOTISM n condition or quality of being a helot

HELOTISMS > HELOTISM

HELOTRIES > HELOTRY

HELOTRY n serfdom or slavery

HELOTS > HELOT

HELP vb make something easier, better, or quicker for (someone) ▷ n assistance or support

HELPABLE > HELP

HELPDESK n place where advice is given by telephone

HELPDESKS > HELPDESK

HELPED > HELP

HELPER > HELP

HELPERS > HELP

HELPFUL adj giving help

HELPFULLY > HELPFUL

HELPING n single portion of food

HELPINGS > HELPING

HELPLESS adj weak or incapable

HELPLINE n telephone line set aside for callers to contact an organization for help with a problem

HELPLINES > HELPLINE

HELPMATE n companion and helper, esp a husband or wife

HELPMATES > HELPMATE

HELPMEET less common word for > HELPMATE

HELPMEETS > HELPMEET

HELPS > HELP

HELVE n handle of a hand tool such as an axe or pick ▷ vb fit a helve to (a tool)

HELVED > HELVE

HELVES > HELVE

HELVETIUM same as > ASTATINE

HELVING > HELVE

HEM n bottom edge of a garment, folded under and stitched down ▷ vb provide with a hem

HEMAGOG same as > HEMAGOGUE

HEMAGOGS > HEMAGOGUE

HEMAGOGUE n haemagogue: drug that promotes the flow of blood

HEMAL same as > HAEMAL

HEMATAL same as > HEMAL

HEMATEIN same as > HAEMATEIN

HEMATEINS > HEMATEIN

HEMATIC same as > HAEMATIC

HEMATICS > HEMATIC

HEMATIN same as > HAEMATIN

HEMATINE n red dye

HEMATINES > HEMATINE

HEMATINIC same as > HAEMATIC

HEMATINS > HEMATIN

HEMATITE n red, grey, or black mineral

HEMATITES > HEMATITE

HEMATITIC > HEMATITE

HEMATOID same as > HAEMATOID

HEMATOMA same as > HAEMATOMA

HEMATOMAS > HEMATOMA

HEMATOSES > HEMATOSIS

HEMATOSIS n haematosis: oxygenation of venous blood in the lungs

HEMATOZOA n plural of > HEMATOZOON: protozoan that is parasitic in the blood

HEMATURIA same as > HAEMATURIA

HEMATURIC > HEMATURIA

HEME same as > HAEM

HEMELYTRA n plural of > HEMELYTRON: forewing of plant bugs

HEMES > HEME

HEMIALGIA n pain limited to one side of the body

HEMIC > HAEMATIC

HEMICYCLE n semicircular structure, room, arena, wall, etc

HEMIHEDRY n state of crystal having certain kind of symmetry

HEMIN same as > HAEMIN

HEMINA n old liquid measure

HEMINAS > HEMINA

HEMINS > HEMIN

HEMIOLA n rhythmic device involving the superimposition of, for example, two notes in the time of three

HEMIOLAS > HEMIOLA

HEMIOLIA same as > HEMIOLA

HEMIOLIAS > HEMIOLIA

HEMIOLIC > HEMIOLA

HEMIONE same as > HEMIONUS

HEMIONES > HEMIONE

HEMIONUS n Asian wild ass

HEMIOPIA n defective vision seeing only halves of things

HEMIOPIAS > HEMIOPIA

HEMIOPIC > HEMIOPIA

HEMIOPSIA same as > HEMIOPIA

HEMIPOD same as > HEMIPODE

HEMIPODE n button quail

HEMIPODES > HEMIPODE

HEMIPODS > HEMIPOD

HEMIPTER n insect with beaklike mouthparts

HEMIPTERS > HEMIPTER

HEMISPACE n area in brain

HEMISTICH n half line of verse

HEMITROPE another name for > TWIN

HEMITROPY n state of being a twin

HEMLINE n level to which the hem of a skirt hangs

HEMLINES > HEMLINE

HEMLOCK n poison made from a plant with spotted stems and small white flowers

HEMLOCKS > HEMLOCK

HEMMED > HEM

HEMMER n attachment on a sewing machine for hemming

HEMMERS > HEMMER

HEMMING > HEM

HEMOCOEL same as > HAEMOCOEL

HEMOCOELS > HEMOCOEL

HEMOCYTE same as > HAEMOCYTE

HEMOCYTES > HEMOCYTE

HEMOID same as > HAEMATOID

HEMOLYMPH n blood-like fluid in invertebrates

HEMOLYSE vb break down so that haemoglobulin is released

HEMOLYSED > HEMOLYSE

HEMOLYSES > HEMOLYSE

HEMOLYSIN n haemolysin: substance that breaks down red blood cells

HEMOLYSIS n haemolysis: disintegration of red blood cells

HEMOLYTIC > HEMOLYSIS

HEMOLYZE vb undergo or make undergo hemolysis

HEMOLYZED > HEMOLYZE

HEMOLYZES > HEMOLYZE

HEMOPHILE n haemophile: person with haemophilia

HEMOSTAT same as > HAEMOSTAT

HEMOSTATS > HEMOSTAT

HEMOTOXIC > HEMOTOXIN

HEMOTOXIN n substance that destroys red blood cells

HEMP n Asian plant with tough fibres

HEMPEN > HEMP

HEMPIE variant of > HEMPY

HEMPIER > HEMPY

HEMPIES > HEMPY

HEMPIEST > HEMPY

HEMPLIKE > HEMP

HEMPS > HEMP

HEMPSEED n seed of hemp

HEMPSEEDS > HEMPSEED

HEMPWEED n climbing weed

HEMPWEEDS > HEMPWEED

HEMPY adj of or like hemp ▷ n rogue

HEMS > HEM

HEMSTITCH n decorative edging stitch, usually for a hem, in which the cross threads are stitched in groups ▷ vb decorate (a hem, etc) with hemstitches

HEN n female domestic fowl ▷ vb lose one's courage

HENBANE *n* poisonous plant with sticky hairy leaves
HENBANES > HENBANE
HENBIT *n* European plant with small dark red flowers
HENBITS > HENBIT
HENCE *adv* from this time ▷ *interj* begone! away!
HENCHMAN *n* person employed by someone powerful to carry out orders ,
HENCHMEN > HENCHMAN
HENCOOP *n* cage for poultry
HENCOOPS > HENCOOP
HEND *vb* seize
HENDED > HEND
HENDIADYS *n* rhetorical device by which two nouns joined by a conjunction are used instead of a noun and modifier
HENDING > HEND
HENDS > HEND
HENEQUEN *n* agave plant native to Yucatán
HENEQUENS > HENEQUEN
HENEQUIN *same as* > HENEQUEN
HENEQUINS > HENEQUIN
HENGE *n* circular monument, often containing a circle of stones, dating from the Neolithic and Bronze Ages
HENGES > HENGE
HENHOUSE *n* coop for hens
HENHOUSES > HENHOUSE
HENIQUEN *same as* > HENEQUEN
HENIQUENS > HENIQUEN
HENIQUIN *same as* > HENIQUEN
HENIQUINS > HENIQUIN
HENLEY *n* type of sweater
HENLEYS > HENLEY
HENLIKE > HEN
HENNA *n* reddish dye made from a shrub or tree ▷ *vb* dye (the hair) with henna
HENNAED > HENNA
HENNAING > HENNA
HENNAS > HENNA
HENNED > HEN
HENNER *n* challenge
HENNERIES > HENNERY
HENNERS > HENNER
HENNERY *n* place or farm for keeping poultry
HENNIER > HENNY
HENNIES > HENNY
HENNIEST > HENNY
HENNIN *n* former women's hat
HENNING > HEN
HENNINS > HENNIN
HENNISH > HEN
HENNISHLY > HEN
HENNY *adj* like hen ▷ *n* cock that looks like hen
HENOTIC *adj* acting to reconcile
HENPECK *vb* (of a woman) to harass or torment (a man, esp her husband) by persistent nagging
HENPECKED *adj* (of a man)

dominated by his wife
HENPECKS > HENPECK
HENRIES > HENRY
HENRY *n* unit of electrical inductance
HENRYS > HENRY
HENS > HEN
HENT *vb* seize ▷ *n* anything that has been grasped, esp by the mind
HENTED > HENT
HENTING > HENT
HENTS > HENT
HEP *same as* > HIP
HEPAR *n* compound containing sulphur
HEPARIN *n* polysaccharide, containing sulphate groups, present in most body tissues: an anticoagulant used in the treatment of thrombosis
HEPARINS > HEPARIN
HEPARS > HEPAR
HEPATIC *adj* of the liver ▷ *n* any of various drugs for use in treating diseases of the liver
HEPATICA *n* woodland plant with white, mauve, or pink flowers
HEPATICAE > HEPATICA
HEPATICAL *same as* > HEPATIC
HEPATICAS > HEPATICA
HEPATICS > HEPATIC
HEPATISE *same as* > HEPATIZE
HEPATISED > HEPATISE
HEPATISES > HEPATISE
HEPATITE *n* mineral containing sulphur
HEPATITES > HEPATITE
HEPATITIS *n* inflammation of the liver
HEPATIZE *vb* turn into liver
HEPATIZED > HEPATIZE
HEPATIZES > HEPATIZE
HEPATOMA *n* cancer of liver
HEPATOMAS > HEPATOMA
HEPCAT *n* person who is hep, esp a player or admirer of jazz and swing in the 1940s
HEPCATS > HEPCAT
HEPPER > HEP
HEPPEST > HEP
HEPS > HEP
HEPSTER *same as* > HIPSTER
HEPSTERS > HEPSTER
HEPT *archaic spelling of* > HEAPED
HEPTAD *n* group or series of seven
HEPTADS > HEPTAD
HEPTAGLOT *n* book in seven languages
HEPTAGON *n* geometric figure with seven sides
HEPTAGONS > HEPTAGON
HEPTANE *n* alkane found in petroleum and used as an anaesthetic
HEPTANES > HEPTANE
HEPTAPODY *n* verse with seven beats in rhythm
HEPTARCH > HEPTARCHY

HEPTARCHS > HEPTARCHY
HEPTARCHY *n* government by seven rulers
HEPTOSE *n* any monosaccharide that has seven carbon atoms per molecule
HEPTOSES > HEPTOSE
HER *pron* refers to a female person or animal or anything personified as feminine when the object of a sentence or clause ▷ *adj* belonging to her ▷ *determiner* of, belonging to, or associated with her
HERALD *n* person who announces important news ▷ *vb* signal the approach of
HERALDED > HERALD
HERALDIC *adj* of or relating to heraldry
HERALDING > HERALD
HERALDIST > HERALDRY
HERALDRY *n* study of coats of arms and family trees
HERALDS > HERALD
HERB *n* plant used for flavouring in cookery, and in medicine
HERBAGE *n* herbaceous plants collectively, esp those on which animals graze
HERBAGED *adj* with grass growing on it
HERBAGES > HERBAGE
HERBAL *adj* of or relating to herbs, usually culinary or medicinal herbs ▷ *n* book describing and listing the properties of plants
HERBALISM *n* use of herbal medicine
HERBALIST *n* person who grows or specializes in the use of medicinal herbs
HERBALS > HERBAL
HERBAR *same as* > HERBARY
HERBARIA > HERBARIUM
HERBARIAL > HERBARIUM
HERBARIAN *same as* > HERBALIST
HERBARIES > HERBARY
HERBARIUM *n* collection of dried plants that are mounted and classified systematically
HERBARS > HERBAR
HERBARY *n* herb garden
HERBED *adj* flavoured with herbs
HERBELET *same as* > HERBLET
HERBELETS > HERBELET
HERBICIDE *n* chemical used to destroy plants, esp weeds
HERBIER > HERBY
HERBIEST > HERBY
HERBIST *same as* > HERBALIST
HERBISTS > HERBIST
HERBIVORA *n* animals that eat grass
HERBIVORE *n* animal that

eats only plants
HERBIVORY > HERBIVORE
HERBLESS > HERB
HERBLET *n* little herb
HERBLETS > HERBLET
HERBLIKE > HERB
HERBOLOGY *n* use or study of herbal medicine
HERBORISE *same as* > HERBORIZE
HERBORIST *same as* > HERBALIST
HERBORIZE *vb* collect herbs
HERBOSE *same as* > HERBOUS
HERBOUS *adj* with abundance of herbs
HERBS > HERB
HERBY *adj* abounding in herbs
HERCOGAMY *n* prevention of flower pollination
HERCULEAN *adj* requiring great strength or effort
HERCULES *as in hercules beetle* very large tropical American beetle
HERCYNITE *n* mineral containing iron
HERD *n* group of animals feeding and living together ▷ *vb* collect into a herd
HERDBOY *n* boy who looks after herd
HERDBOYS > HERDBOY
HERDED > HERD
HERDEN *n* type of coarse cloth
HERDENS > HERDEN
HERDER *same as* > HERDSMAN
HERDERS > HERDER
HERDESS *n* female herder
HERDESSES > HERDESS
HERDIC *n* small horse-drawn carriage with a rear entrance and side seats
HERDICS > HERDIC
HERDING > HERD
HERDLIKE > HERD
HERDMAN *same as* > HERDSMAN
HERDMEN > HERDMAN
HERDS > HERD
HERDSMAN *n* man who looks after a herd of animals
HERDSMEN > HERDSMAN
HERDWICK *n* hardy breed of sheep
HERDWICKS > HERDWICK
HERE *adv* in, at, or to this place or point
HEREABOUT *same as* > HEREABOUTS
HEREAFTER *adv* after this point or time ▷ *n* life after death
HEREAT *adv* because of this
HEREAWAY *same as* > HEREABOUT
HEREAWAYS *dialect form of* > HERE
HEREBY *adv* by means of or as a result of this
HEREDES > HERES
HEREDITY *n* passing on of characteristics from one

generation to another

HEREFROM adv from here

HEREIN adv in this place, matter, or document

HEREINTO adv into this place, circumstance, etc

HERENESS n state of being here

HEREOF adv of or concerning this

HEREON archaic word for > HEREUPON

HERES n heir

HERESIES > HERESY

HERESY n opinion contrary to accepted opinion or belief

HERETIC n person who holds unorthodox opinions

HERETICAL > HERETIC

HERETICS > HERETIC

HERETO adv this place, matter, or document

HERETRIX n in Scots law, female inheritor

HEREUNDER adv (in documents, etc) below this

HEREUNTO archaic word for > HERETO

HEREUPON adv following immediately after this

HEREWITH adv with this

HERIED > HERY

HERIES > HERY

HERIOT n (in medieval England) a death duty paid by villeins and free tenants to their lord, often consisting of the dead man's best beast or chattel

HERIOTS > HERIOT

HERISSE adj with bristles

HERISSON n spiked beam used as fortification

HERISSONS > HERISSON

HERITABLE adj capable of being inherited

HERITABLY > HERITABLE

HERITAGE n something inherited

HERITAGES > HERITAGE

HERITOR n person who inherits

HERITORS > HERITOR

HERITRESS > HERITOR

HERITRIX > HERITOR

HERKOGAMY same as > HERCOGAMY

HERL n barb or barbs of a feather, used to dress fishing flies

HERLING n Scots word for a type of fish

HERLINGS > HERL

HERLS > HERL

HERM n (in ancient Greece) a stone head of Hermes surmounting a square stone pillar

HERMA same as > HERM

HERMAE > HERMA

HERMAEAN adj type of statue

HERMAI > HERMA

HERMANDAD n organization of middle classes in Spain

HERMETIC adj sealed so as to be airtight

HERMETICS n alchemy

HERMETISM n belief in pagan mystical knowledge

HERMETIST > HERMETISM

HERMIT n person living in solitude, esp for religious reasons

HERMITAGE n home of a hermit

HERMITESS n female hermit

HERMITIC > HERMIT

HERMITISM n act of living as hermit

HERMITRY n life as hermit

HERMITS > HERMIT

HERMS > HERM

HERN archaic or dialect word for > HERON

HERNIA n protrusion of an organ or part through the lining of the surrounding body cavity

HERNIAE > HERNIA

HERNIAL > HERNIA

HERNIAS > HERNIA

HERNIATE n form hernia

HERNIATED > HERNIATE

HERNIATES > HERNIATE

HERNS > HERN

HERNSHAW same as > HERONSHAW

HERNSHAWS > HERNSHAW

HERO n principal character in a film, book, etc

HEROE variant of > HERO

HEROES > HERO

HEROIC adj courageous

HEROICAL same as > HEROIC

HEROICISE same as > HEROICIZE

HEROICIZE same as > HEROIZE

HEROICLY > HEROIC

HEROICS pl n extravagant behaviour

HEROIN n highly addictive drug derived from morphine

HEROINE n principal female character in a novel, play, etc

HEROINES > HEROINE

HEROINISM n addiction to heroin

HEROINS > HEROIN

HEROISE same as > HEROIZE

HEROISED > HEROISE

HEROISES > HEROISE

HEROISING > HEROISE

HEROISM n great courage and bravery

HEROISMS > HEROISM

HEROIZE vb make into hero

HEROIZED > HEROIZE

HEROIZES > HEROIZE

HEROIZING > HEROIZE

HERON n long-legged wading bird

HERONRIES > HERONRY

HERONRY n colony of breeding herons

HERONS > HERON

HERONSEW same as > HERONSHAW

HERONSEWS > HERONSEW

HERONSHAW n young heron

HEROON n temple or

monument dedicated to hero

HEROONS > HEROON

HEROS > HERO

HEROSHIP > HERO

HEROSHIPS > HERO

HERPES n any of several inflammatory skin diseases, including shingles and cold sores

HERPESES > HERPES

HERPETIC adj of or relating to any of the herpes diseases ▷ n person suffering from any of the herpes diseases

HERPETICS > HERPETIC

HERPETOID adj like reptile

HERPTILE adj denoting, relating to, or characterizing both reptiles and amphibians

HERRIED > HERRY

HERRIES > HERRY

HERRIMENT n act of plundering

HERRING n important food fish of northern seas

HERRINGER n person or boat catching herring

HERRINGS > HERRING

HERRY vb harry

HERRYING > HERRY

HERRYMENT same as > HERRIMENT

HERS pron something belonging to her

HERSALL n rehearsal

HERSALLS > HERSALL

HERSE n harrow

HERSED adj arranged like a harrow

HERSELF pron feminine singular reflexive form

HERSES > HERSE

HERSHIP n act of plundering

HERSHIPS > HERSHIP

HERSTORY n history from a female point of view or as it relates to women

HERTZ n unit of frequency

HERTZES > HERTZ

HERY vb praise

HERYE same as > HERY

HERYED > HERYE

HERYES > HERYE

HERYING > HERY

HES > HE

HESITANCE > HESITANT

HESITANCY > HESITANT

HESITANT adj undecided or wavering

HESITATE vb be slow or uncertain in doing something

HESITATED > HESITATE

HESITATER > HESITATE

HESITATES > HESITATE

HESITATOR > HESITATE

HESP same as > HASP

HESPED > HESP

HESPERID n species of butterfly

HESPERIDS > HESPERID

HESPING > HESP

HESPS > HESP

HESSIAN n coarse jute

fabric

HESSIANS > HESSIAN

HESSITE n black or grey metallic mineral consisting of silver telluride in cubic crystalline form

HESSITES > HESSITE

HESSONITE n orange-brown variety of grossularite garnet

HEST archaic word for > BEHEST

HESTERNAL adj belonging to yesterday

HESTS > HEST

HET n short for heterosexual ▷ past tense and past participle of heat ▷ adj Scot word for hot

HETAERA n (esp in ancient Greece) a female prostitute, esp an educated courtesan

HETAERAE > HETAERA

HETAERAS > HETAERA

HETAERIC > HETAERA

HETAERISM n state of being a concubine

HETAERIST > HETAERISM

HETAIRA same as > HETAERA

HETAIRAI > HETAIRA

HETAIRAS > HETAIRA

HETAIRIA n society

HETAIRIAS > HETAIRIA

HETAIRIC > HETAERA

HETAIRISM same as > HETAERISM

HETAIRIST > HETAERISM

HETE same as > HIGHT

HETERO short for > HETEROSEXUAL

HETERODOX adj differing from accepted doctrines or beliefs

HETERONYM n one of two or more words pronounced differently but spelt alike

HETEROPOD n marine invertebrate with a foot for swimming

HETEROS > HETERO

HETEROSES > HETEROSIS

HETEROSIS n increased size, strength, etc, of a hybrid as compared to either of its parents

HETEROTIC > HETEROSIS

HETES > HETE

HETH n eighth letter of the Hebrew alphabet

HETHER same as > HITHER

HETHS > HETH

HETING > HETE

HETMAN another word for > ATAMAN

HETMANATE > HETMAN

HETMANS > HETMAN

HETS > HET

HEUCH Scots word for > CRAG

HEUCHERA n N American plant with heart-shaped leaves and mostly red flowers

HEUCHERAS > HEUCHERA

HEUCHS > HEUCH

HEUGH same as > HEUCH

HEUGHS > HEUGH

h

HEUREKA *same as* > EUREKA
HEUREKAS > HEUREKA
HEURETIC *same as* > HEURISTIC
HEURETICS *n* use of logic
HEURISM *n* use of logic
HEURISMS > HEURISM
HEURISTIC *adj* involving learning by investigation ▷*n* science of heuristic procedure
HEVEA *n* rubber-producing South American tree
HEVEAS > HEVEA
HEW *vb* cut with an axe
HEWABLE > HEW
HEWED > HEW
HEWER > HEW
HEWERS > HEW
HEWGH *interj* sound made to imitate the flight of an arrow
HEWING > HEW
HEWINGS > HEW
HEWN > HEW
HEWS > HEW
HEX *adj* of or relating to hexadecimal notation ▷*n* evil spell ▷*vb* bewitch
HEXACHORD *n* (in medieval musical theory) any of three diatonic scales based upon C, F, and G, each consisting of six notes, from which solmization was developed
HEXACT *n* part of a sponge with six rays
HEXACTS > HEXACT
HEXAD *n* group or series of six
HEXADE *same as* > HEXAD
HEXADES > HEXADE
HEXADIC > HEXAD
HEXADS > HEXAD
HEXAFOIL *n* pattern with six lobes
HEXAFOILS > HEXAFOIL
HEXAGLOT *n* book in six languages
HEXAGON *n* geometrical figure with six sides
HEXAGONAL *adj* having six sides and six angles
HEXAGONS > HEXAGON
HEXAGRAM *n* star formed by extending the sides of a regular hexagon to meet at six points
HEXAGRAMS > HEXAGRAM
HEXAHEDRA *n* plural of hexahedron: solid figure with six plane faces
HEXAMERAL *adj* arranged in six groups
HEXAMETER *n* verse line consisting of six metrical feet
HEXAMINE *n* type of fuel produced in small solid blocks or tablets for use in miniature camping stoves
HEXAMINES > HEXAMINE
HEXANE *n* liquid alkane existing in five isomeric forms that are found in petroleum and used as

solvents
HEXANES > HEXANE
HEXANOIC *as in hexanoic acid* insoluble oily carboxylic acid found in coconut and palm oils and in milk
HEXAPLA *n* edition of the Old Testament compiled by Origen, containing six versions of the text
HEXAPLAR > HEXAPLA
HEXAPLAS > HEXAPLA
HEXAPLOID *adj* with six times the normal number of chromosomes
HEXAPOD *n* six-footed arthropod
HEXAPODIC > HEXAPODY
HEXAPODS > HEXAPOD
HEXAPODY *n* verse measure consisting of six metrical feet
HEXARCH *adj* (of plant) with six veins
HEXARCHY *n* alliance of six states
HEXASTICH *n* poem, stanza, or strophe that consists of six lines
HEXASTYLE *n* portico or façade with six columns ▷*adj* having six columns
HEXED > HEX
HEXENE *same as* > HEXYLENE
HEXENES > HEXENE
HEXER > HEX
HEXEREI *n* witchcraft
HEXEREIS > HEXEREI
HEXERS > HEX
HEXES > HEX
HEXING > HEX
HEXINGS > HEX
HEXONE *n* colourless insoluble liquid ketone used as a solvent for organic compounds
HEXONES > HEXONE
HEXOSAN *n* any of a group of polysaccharides that yield hexose on hydrolysis
HEXOSANS > HEXOSAN
HEXOSE *n* monosaccharide, such as glucose, that contains six carbon atoms per molecule
HEXOSES > HEXOSE
HEXYL *adj* of, consisting of, or containing the group of atoms C_6H_{13}, esp the isomeric form of this group, $CH_3(CH_2)_4CH_2$-
HEXYLENE *n* chemical compound similar to ethylene
HEXYLENES > HEXYLENE
HEXYLIC > HEXYL
HEXYLS > HEXYL
HEY *interj* expression of surprise or for catching attention ▷*vb* perform a country dance
HEYDAY *n* time of greatest success, prime
HEYDAYS > HEYDAY
HEYDEY *variant of* > HEYDAY
HEYDEYS > HEYDEY
HEYDUCK *same as* > HAIDUK

HEYDUCKS > HEYDUCK
HEYED > HEY
HEYING > HEY
HEYS > HEY
HI *interj* hello
HIANT *adj* gaping
HIATAL > HIATUS
HIATUS *n* pause or interruption in continuity
HIATUSES > HIATUS
HIBACHI *n* portable brazier for heating and cooking food
HIBACHIS > HIBACHI
HIBAKUSHA *n* survivor of either of the atomic-bomb attacks on Hiroshima and Nagasaki in 1945
HIBERNAL *adj* of or occurring in winter
HIBERNATE *vb* (of an animal) pass the winter as if in a deep sleep
HIBERNISE > HIBERNIZE
HIBERNIZE *vb* make Irish
HIBISCUS *n* tropical plant with large brightly coloured flowers
HIC *interj* representation of the sound of a hiccup
HICATEE *same as* > HICCATEE
HICATEES > HICATEE
HICCATEE *n* tortoise of West Indies
HICCATEES > HICCATEE
HICCOUGH *same as* > HICCUP
HICCOUGHS > HICCOUGH
HICCUP *n* spasm of the breathing organs with a sharp coughlike sound ▷*vb* make a hiccup
HICCUPED > HICCUP
HICCUPING > HICCUP
HICCUPPED > HICCUP
HICCUPS > HICCUP
HICCUPY > HICCUP
HICK *n* unsophisticated country person
HICKEY *n* object or gadget: used as a name when the correct name is forgotten, etc
HICKEYS > HICKEY
HICKIE *same as* > HICKEY
HICKIES > HICKIE
HICKISH > HICK
HICKORIES > HICKORY
HICKORY *n* N American nut-bearing tree
HICKS > HICK
HICKWALL *n* green woodpecker
HICKWALLS > HICKWALL
HICKYMAL *n* titmouse
HICKYMALS > HICKYMAL
HID > HIDE
HIDABLE > HIDE
HIDAGE *n* former tax on land
HIDAGES > HIDAGE
HIDALGA *n* Spanish noblewoman
HIDALGAS > HIDALGA
HIDALGO *n* member of the lower nobility in Spain
HIDALGOS > HIDALGO
HIDDEN > HIDE

HIDDENITE *n* green transparent variety of the mineral spodumene, used as a gemstone
HIDDENLY > HIDE
HIDDER *n* young ram
HIDDERS > HIDDER
HIDE *vb* put (oneself or an object) somewhere difficult to see or find ▷*n* place of concealment, esp for a bird-watcher
HIDEAWAY *n* private place
HIDEAWAYS > HIDEAWAY
HIDEBOUND *adj* unwilling to accept new ideas
HIDED > HIDE
HIDELESS > HIDE
HIDEOSITY > HIDEOUS
HIDEOUS *adj* ugly, revolting
HIDEOUSLY > HIDEOUS
HIDEOUT *n* hiding place, esp a remote place used by outlaws, etc; hideaway
HIDEOUTS > HIDEOUT
HIDER > HIDE
HIDERS > HIDE
HIDES > HIDE
HIDING > HIDE
HIDINGS > HIDE
HIDLING *n* hiding place
HIDLINGS *adv* in secret
HIDLINS *same as* > HIDLINGS
HIDROSES > HIDROSIS
HIDROSIS *n* any skin disease affecting the sweat glands
HIDROTIC > HIDROSIS
HIDROTICS > HIDROSIS
HIE *vb* hurry
HIED > HIE
HIEING > HIE
HIELAMAN *n* Australian Aboriginal shield
HIELAMANS > HIELAMAN
HIELAND *adj* characteristic of Highlanders, esp alluding to their supposed gullibility or foolishness in towns or cities
HIEMAL *less common word for* > HIBERNAL
HIEMS *n* winter
HIERACIUM *n* plant of hawkweed family
HIERARCH *n* person in a position of high-priestly authority
HIERARCHS > HIERARCH
HIERARCHY *n* system of people or things arranged in a graded order
HIERATIC *adj* of or relating to priests ▷*n* hieratic script of ancient Egypt
HIERATICA *n* type of papyrus
HIEROCRAT *n* person who believes in government by religious leaders
HIERODULE *n* (in ancient Greece) a temple slave, esp a sacral prostitute
HIEROGRAM *n* sacred symbol
HIEROLOGY *n* sacred literature

HIERURGY n performance of religious drama or music

HIES > HIE

HIFALUTIN adj pompous or pretentious

HIGGLE less common word for > HAGGLE

HIGGLED > HIGGLE

HIGGLER > HIGGLE

HIGGLERS > HIGGLE

HIGGLES > HIGGLE

HIGGLING > HIGGLE

HIGGLINGS > HIGGLE

HIGH adj being a relatively great distance from top to bottom; tall ▷ adv at or to a height ▷ n a high place or level ▷ vb hie

HIGHBALL n tall drink of whiskey with soda water or ginger ale and ice ▷ vb move at great speed

HIGHBALLS > HIGHBALL

HIGHBORN adj of noble or aristocratic birth

HIGHBOY n tall chest of drawers in two sections, the lower section being a lowboy

HIGHBOYS > HIGHBOY

HIGHBRED adj of noble breeding

HIGHBROW often disparaging n intellectual and serious person ▷ adj concerned with serious, intellectual subjects

HIGHBROWS > HIGHBROW

HIGHBUSH adj (of bush) growing tall

HIGHCHAIR n long-legged chair with a tray attached, used by a very young child at mealtimes

HIGHED > HIGH

HIGHER n advanced level of the Scottish Certificate of Education ▷ vb raise up

HIGHERED > HIGHER

HIGHERING > HIGHER

HIGHERS > HIGHER

HIGHEST > HIGH

HIGHFLIER same as > HIGHFLYER

HIGHFLYER n person who is extreme in aims, ambition, etc

HIGHING > HIGH

HIGHISH > HIGH

HIGHJACK same as > HIJACK

HIGHJACKS > HIGHJACK

HIGHLAND n relatively high ground

HIGHLANDS > HIGHLAND

HIGHLIFE n style of music combining West African elements with US jazz forms, found esp in the cities of West Africa

HIGHLIFES > HIGHLIFE

HIGHLIGHT n outstanding part or feature ▷ vb give emphasis to

HIGHLY adv extremely

HIGHMAN n dice weighted to make it fall in particular way

HIGHMEN > HIGHMAN

HIGHMOST adj highest

HIGHNESS n condition of being high or lofty

HIGHRISE n tall building

HIGHRISES > HIGHRISE

HIGHROAD n main road

HIGHROADS > HIGHROAD

HIGHS > HIGH

HIGHSPOT n highlight

HIGHSPOTS > HIGHSPOT

HIGHT vb archaic word for name or call

HIGHTAIL vb go or move in a great hurry

HIGHTAILS > HIGHTAIL

HIGHTED > HIGHT

HIGHTH old form of > HEIGHT

HIGHTHS > HIGHTH

HIGHTING n oath

HIGHTOP n top of ship's mast

HIGHTOPS > HIGHTOP

HIGHTS > HIGHT

HIGHVELD n high-altitude grassland region of E South Africa

HIGHVELDS > HIGHVELD

HIGHWAY n main road

HIGHWAYS > HIGHWAY

HIJAB n covering for the head and face, worn by Muslim women

HIJABS > HIJAB

HIJACK vb seize control of (an aircraft or other vehicle) while travelling ▷ n instance of hijacking

HIJACKED > HIJACK

HIJACKER > HIJACK

HIJACKERS > HIJACK

HIJACKING > HIJACK

HIJACKS > HIJACK

HIJINKS n lively enjoyment

HIJRA same as > HIJRAH

HIJRAH same as > HEGIRA

HIJRAHS > HIJRAH

HIJRAS > HIJRA

HIKE n long walk in the country, esp for pleasure ▷ vb go for a long walk

HIKED > HIKE

HIKER > HIKE

HIKERS > HIKE

HIKES > HIKE

HIKING > HIKE

HIKOI n walk or march, esp a Māori protest march ▷ vb take part in such a march

HIKOIED > HIKOI

HIKOIING > HIKOI

HIKOIS > HIKOI

HILA > HILUM

HILAR > HILUS

HILARIOUS adj very funny

HILARITY n mirth and merriment

HILCH vb hobble

HILCHED > HILCH

HILCHES > HILCH

HILCHING > HILCH

HILD same as > HOLD

HILDING n coward

HILDINGS > HILDING

HILI > HILUS

HILL n raised part of the earth's surface, less high than a mountain ▷ vb form into a hill or mound

HILLBILLY n usually disparaging term for an unsophisticated country person

HILLCREST n crest of hill

HILLED > HILL

HILLER > HILL

HILLERS > HILL

HILLFOLK n people living in the hills

HILLFORT n hilltop fortified with ramparts and ditches, dating from the second millennium BC

HILLFORTS > HILLFORT

HILLIER > HILL

HILLIEST > HILL

HILLINESS > HILL

HILLING > HILL

HILLMEN same as > HILLFOLK

HILLO same as > HELLO

HILLOA same as > HALLOA

HILLOAED > HILLOA

HILLOAING > HILLOA

HILLOAS > HILLOA

HILLOCK n small hill

HILLOCKED > HILLOCK

HILLOCKS > HILLOCK

HILLOCKY > HILLOCK

HILLOED > HILLO

HILLOES > HILLO

HILLOING > HILLO

HILLOS > HILLO

HILLS > HILL

HILLSIDE n side of a hill

HILLSIDES > HILLSIDE

HILLSLOPE same as > HILLSIDE

HILLTOP n top of hill

HILLTOPS > HILLTOP

HILLY > HILL

HILT n handle of a sword or knife ▷ vb supply with a hilt

HILTED > HILT

HILTING > HILT

HILTLESS > HILT

HILTS > HILT

HILUM n scar on a seed marking its point of attachment to the seed vessel

HILUS rare word for > HILUM

HIM pron refers to a male person or animal when the object of a sentence or clause ▷ n male person

HIMATIA > HIMATION

HIMATION n (in ancient Greece) a cloak draped around the body

HIMATIONS > HIMATION

HIMBO n slang, usually derogatory term for an attractive but empty-headed man

HIMBOS > HIMBO

HIMS > HIM

HIMSELF pron masculine singular reflexive form

HIN n Hebrew unit of capacity equal to about 12 pints or 3.5 litres

HINAHINA same as > MAHOE

HINAU n New Zealand tree

HIND adj situated at the back ▷ n female deer

HINDBERRY n raspberry

HINDBRAIN nontechnical name for > RHOMBENCEPHALON: part of the brain comprising the cerbellum, pons and medulla oblongata

HINDER vb get in the way of ▷ adj situated at the back

HINDERED > HINDER

HINDERER > HINDER

HINDERERS > HINDER

HINDERING > HINDER

HINDERS > HINDER

HINDFEET > HINDFOOT

HINDFOOT n back foot

HINDGUT n part of the vertebrate digestive tract comprising the colon and rectum

HINDGUTS > HINDGUT

HINDHEAD n back of head

HINDHEADS > HINDHEAD

HINDLEG n back leg

HINDLEGS > HINDLEG

HINDMOST > HIND

HINDRANCE n obstruction or snag

HINDS > HIND

HINDSHANK n meat from animal's hind leg

HINDSIGHT n ability to understand, after something has happened, what should have been done

HINDWARD adj at back

HINDWING n back wing

HINDWINGS > HINDWING

HING n asafoetida

HINGE n device for holding together two parts so that one can swing freely ▷ vb depend (on)

HINGED > HINGE

HINGELESS > HINGE

HINGELIKE > HINGE

HINGER n tool for making hinges

HINGERS > HINGER

HINGES > HINGE

HINGING > HINGE

HINGS > HING

HINKIER > HINKY

HINKIEST > HINKY

HINKY adj strange

HINNIED > HINNY

HINNIES > HINNY

HINNY n offspring of a male horse and a female donkey ▷ vb whinny

HINNYING > HINNY

HINS > HIN

HINT n indirect suggestion ▷ vb suggest indirectly

HINTED > HINT

HINTER > HINT

HINTERS > HINT

HINTING > HINT

HINTINGLY > HINT

HINTINGS > HINT

HINTS > HINT

HIOI n New Zealand plant

of the mint family

HIOIS > HIOI

HIP n either side of the body between the pelvis and the thigh ▷ adj aware of or following the latest trends ▷ interj exclamation used to introduce cheers

HIPBONE n either of the two bones that form the sides of the pelvis

HIPBONES > HIPBONE

HIPHUGGER adj (of trousers) having a low waist

HIPLESS > HIP

HIPLIKE > HIP

HIPLINE n widest part of a person's hips

HIPLINES > HIPLINE

HIPLY > HIP

HIPNESS > HIP

HIPNESSES > HIP

HIPPARCH n (in ancient Greece) a cavalry commander

HIPPARCHS > HIPPARCH

HIPPED adj having a hip or hips

HIPPEN n baby's nappy

HIPPENS > HIPPEN

HIPPER > HIP

HIPPEST > HIP

HIPPIATRY n treatment of disease in horses

HIPPIC adj of horses

HIPPIE same as > HIPPY

HIPPIEDOM > HIPPIE

HIPPIEISH > HIPPIE

HIPPIER > HIPPY

HIPPIES > HIPPY

HIPPIEST > HIPPY

HIPPIN same as > HIPPEN

HIPPINESS > HIPPY

HIPPING same as > HIPPEN

HIPPINGS > HIPPING

HIPPINS > HIPPIN

HIPPISH adj in low spirits

HIPPO n hippopotamus

HIPPOCRAS n old English drink of wine flavoured with spices

HIPPODAME n sea horse

HIPPOLOGY n study of horses

HIPPOS > HIPPO

HIPPURIC as in hippuric acid crystalline solid excreted in the urine of mammals

HIPPURITE n type of fossil

HIPPUS n spasm of eye

HIPPUSES > HIPPUS

HIPPY n (esp in the 1960s) person whose behaviour and dress imply a rejection of conventional values ▷ adj having large hips

HIPPYDOM > HIPPY

HIPPYDOMS > HIPPY

HIPS > HIP

HIPSHOT adj having a dislocated hip

HIPSTER n enthusiast of modern jazz

HIPSTERS pl n trousers cut so that the top encircles the hips

HIPT > HIP

HIRABLE > HIRE

HIRAGANA n one of the Japanese systems of syllabic writing based on Chinese cursive ideograms. The more widely used of the two current systems, it is employed in newspapers and general literature

HIRAGANAS > HIRAGANA

HIRAGE n fee for hiring

HIRAGES > HIRAGE

HIRCINE adj of or like a goat, esp in smell

HIRCOSITY n quality of being like a goat

HIRE vb pay to have temporary use of ▷ n hiring

HIREABLE > HIRE

HIREAGE same as > HIRAGE

HIREAGES > HIREAGE

HIRED > HIRE

HIREE n hired person

HIREES > HIREE

HIRELING n derogatory term for a person who works only for wages

HIRELINGS > HIRELING

HIRER > HIRE

HIRERS > HIRE

HIRES > HIRE

HIRING > HIRE

HIRINGS > HIRE

HIRLING n Scots word for a type of fish

HIRLINGS > HIRLING

HIRPLE vb limp ▷ n limping gait

HIRPLED > HIRPLE

HIRPLES > HIRPLE

HIRPLING > HIRPLE

HIRRIENT n trilled sound

HIRRIENTS > HIRRIENT

HIRSEL vb sort into groups

HIRSELED > HIRSEL

HIRSELING > HIRSEL

HIRSELLED > HIRSEL

HIRSELS > HIRSEL

HIRSLE vb wriggle or fidget

HIRSLED > HIRSLE

HIRSLES > HIRSLE

HIRSLING > HIRSLE

HIRSTIE adj dry

HIRSUTE adj hairy

HIRSUTISM > HIRSUTE

HIRUDIN n anticoagulant extracted from the mouth glands of leeches

HIRUDINS > HIRUDIN

HIRUNDINE adj of or resembling a swallow

HIS adj belonging to him

HISH same as > HISS

HISHED > HISH

HISHES > HISH

HISHING > HISH

HISN dialect form of > HIS

HISPANISM n Spanish turn of phrase

HISPID adj covered with stiff hairs or bristles

HISPIDITY > HISPID

HISS n sound like that of a long s (as an expression of contempt) ▷ vb utter a hiss ▷ interj exclamation of

derision or disapproval

HISSED > HISS

HISSELF dialect form of > HIMSELF

HISSER > HISS

HISSERS > HISS

HISSES > HISS

HISSIER > HISSY

HISSIES > HISSY

HISSIEST > HISSY

HISSING > HISS

HISSINGLY > HISS

HISSINGS > HISS

HISSY n temper tantrum ▷ adj sound similar to a hiss

HIST interj exclamation used to attract attention or as a warning to be silent ▷ vb make hist sound

HISTAMIN variant of > HISTAMINE

HISTAMINE n substance released by the body tissues in allergic reactions

HISTAMINS > HISTAMIN

HISTED > HIST

HISTIDIN variant of > HISTIDINE

HISTIDINE n nonessential amino acid that occurs in most proteins: a precursor of histamine

HISTIDINS > HISTIDIN

HISTIE same as > HIRSTIE

HISTING > HIST

HISTIOID same as > HISTOID

HISTOGEN n (formerly) any of three layers in an apical meristem that were thought to give rise to the different parts of the plant: the apical meristem is now regarded as comprising two layers

HISTOGENS > HISTOGEN

HISTOGENY > HISTOGEN

HISTOGRAM n statistical graph in which the frequency of values is represented by vertical bars of varying heights and widths

HISTOID adj (esp of a tumour)

HISTOLOGY n study of the tissues of an animal or plant

HISTONE n any of a group of basic proteins present in cell nuclei and implicated in the spatial organization of DNA

HISTONES > HISTONE

HISTORIAN n writer of history

HISTORIC adj famous or significant in history

HISTORIED adj recorded in history

HISTORIES > HISTORY

HISTORIFY vb make part of history

HISTORISM n idea that history influences present

HISTORY n (record or account of) past events and developments

HISTRIO n actor

HISTRION same as > HISTRIO

HISTRIONS > HISTRION

HISTRIOS > HISTRIO

HISTS > HIST

HIT vb strike, touch forcefully ▷ n hitting

HITCH n minor problem ▷ vb obtain (a lift) by hitchhiking

HITCHED > HITCH

HITCHER > HITCH

HITCHERS > HITCH

HITCHES > HITCH

HITCHHIKE vb travel by obtaining free lifts

HITCHIER > HITCH

HITCHIEST > HITCH

HITCHILY > HITCH

HITCHING > HITCH

HITCHY > HITCH

HITHE n small harbour

HITHER adv or towards this place ▷ vb come

HITHERED > HITHER

HITHERING > HITHER

HITHERS > HITHER

HITHERTO adv until this time

HITHES > HITHE

HITLESS > HIT

HITMAN n professional killer

HITMEN > HITMAN

HITS > HIT

HITTABLE > HIT

HITTER n boxer who has a hard punch rather than skill or finesse

HITTERS > HITTER

HITTING > HIT

HIVE n structure in which social bees live and rear their young ▷ vb cause (bees) to collect or (of bees) to collect inside a hive

HIVED > HIVE

HIVELESS > HIVE

HIVELIKE > HIVE

HIVER n person who keeps beehives

HIVERS > HIVER

HIVES n allergic reaction in which itchy red or whitish patches appear on the skin

HIVEWARD adj towards hive

HIVEWARDS adv towards hive

HIVING > HIVE

HIYA sentence substitute informal term of greeting

HIZEN n type of Japanese porcelain

HIZENS > HIZEN

HIZZ same as > HISS

HIZZED > HIZZ

HIZZES > HIZZ

HIZZING > HIZZ

HIZZONER n nickname for mayor

HIZZONERS > HIZZONER

HM interj sound made to express hesitation or doubt

HMM same as > HM

HO n derogatory term for a woman ▷ interj imitation or representation of the sound of a deep laugh ▷ vb halt

HOA *same as* > HO

HOACTZIN *same as* > HOATZIN

HOACTZINS > HOACTZIN

HOAED > HOA

HOAGIE *n* sandwich made with long bread roll

HOAGIES > HOAGIE

HOAGY *same as* > HOAGIE

HOAING > HOA

HOAR *adj* covered with hoarfrost ▷ *vb* make hoary

HOARD *n* store hidden away for future use ▷ *vb* save or store

HOARDED > HOARD

HOARDER > HOARD

HOARDERS > HOARD

HOARDING *n* large board for displaying advertisements

HOARDINGS > HOARDING

HOARDS > HOARD

HOARED > HOAR

HOARFROST *n* white ground frost

HOARHEAD *n* person with white hair

HOARHEADS > HOARHEAD

HOARHOUND *same as* > HOREHOUND

HOARIER > HOARY

HOARIEST > HOARY

HOARILY > HOARY

HOARINESS > HOARY

HOARING > HOAR

HOARS > HOAR

HOARSE *adj* (of a voice) rough and unclear

HOARSELY > HOARSE

HOARSEN *vb* make or become hoarse

HOARSENED > HOARSEN

HOARSENS > HOARSEN

HOARSER > HOARSE

HOARSEST > HOARSE

HOARY *adj* grey or white(-haired)

HOAS > HOA

HOAST *n* cough ▷ *vb* cough

HOASTED > HOAST

HOASTING > HOAST

HOASTMAN *n* shipper of coal

HOASTMEN > HOASTMAN

HOASTS > HOAST

HOATCHING *adj* infested

HOATZIN *n* South American bird with a brownish plumage and very small crested head

HOATZINES > HOATZIN

HOATZINS > HOATZIN

HOAX *n* deception or trick ▷ *vb* deceive or play a trick upon

HOAXED > HOAX

HOAXER > HOAX

HOAXERS > HOAX

HOAXES > HOAX

HOAXING > HOAX

HOB *n* flat top part of a cooker, or a separate flat surface, containing gas or electric rings for cooking on ▷ *vb* cut or form with a hob

HOBBED > HOB

HOBBER *n* machine used in making gears

HOBBERS > HOBBER

HOBBIES > HOBBY

HOBBING > HOB

HOBBISH *adj* like a clown

HOBBIT *n* one of an imaginary race of half-size people living in holes

HOBBITRY > HOBBIT

HOBBITS > HOBBIT

HOBBLE *vb* walk lamely ▷ *n* strap, rope, etc, used to hobble a horse

HOBBLED > HOBBLE

HOBBLER > HOBBLE

HOBBLERS > HOBBLE

HOBBLES > HOBBLE

HOBBLING > HOBBLE

HOBBLINGS > HOBBLE

HOBBY *n* activity pursued in one's spare time

HOBBYISM > HOBBY

HOBBYISMS > HOBBY

HOBBYIST > HOBBY

HOBBYISTS > HOBBY

HOBBYLESS > HOBBY

HOBDAY *vb* alleviate (a breathing problem in certain horses) by the surgical operation of removing soft tissue ventricles to pull back the vocal fold

HOBDAYED > HOBDAY

HOBDAYING > HOBDAY

HOBDAYS > HOBDAY

HOBGOBLIN *n* mischievous goblin

HOBJOB *vb* do odd jobs

HOBJOBBED > HOBJOB

HOBJOBBER > HOBJOB

HOBJOBS > HOBJOB

HOBLIKE > HOB

HOBNAIL *n* short nail with a large head for protecting the soles of heavy footwear ▷ *vb* provide with hobnails

HOBNAILED > HOBNAIL

HOBNAILS > HOBNAIL

HOBNOB *vb* be on friendly terms (with)

HOBNOBBED > HOBNOB

HOBNOBBER > HOBNOB

HOBNOBBY > HOBNOB

HOBNOBS > HOBNOB

HOBO *n* tramp or vagrant ▷ *vb* live as hobo

HOBODOM > HOBO

HOBODOMS > HOBO

HOBOED > HOBO

HOBOES > HOBO

HOBOING > HOBO

HOBOISM > HOBO

HOBOISMS > HOBO

HOBOS > HOBO

HOBS > HOB

HOC *adj* Latin for this

HOCK *n* joint in the back leg of an animal such as a horse that corresponds to the human ankle ▷ *vb* pawn

HOCKED > HOCK

HOCKER > HOCK

HOCKERS > HOCK

HOCKEY *n* team game played on a field with a ball and curved sticks

HOCKEYS > HOCKEY

HOCKING > HOCK

HOCKLE *vb* spit

HOCKLED > HOCKLE

HOCKLES > HOCKLE

HOCKLING > HOCKLE

HOCKS > HOCK

HOCKSHOP *n* pawnshop

HOCKSHOPS > HOCKSHOP

HOCUS *vb* take in

HOCUSED > HOCUS

HOCUSES > HOCUS

HOCUSING > HOCUS

HOCUSSED > HOCUS

HOCUSSES > HOCUS

HOCUSSING > HOCUS

HOD *n* open wooden box attached to a pole, for carrying bricks or mortar ▷ *vb* bob up and down

HODAD *n* person who pretends to be a surfer

HODADDIES > HODADDY

HODADDY *same as* > HODAD

HODADS > HODAD

HODDED > HOD

HODDEN *n* coarse homespun cloth produced in Scotland: hodden grey is made by mixing black and white wools

HODDENS > HODDEN

HODDIN *same as* > HODDEN

HODDING > HOD

HODDINS > HODDIN

HODDLE *vb* waddle

HODDLED > HODDLE

HODDLES > HODDLE

HODDLING > HODDLE

HODIERNAL *adj* of the present day

HODJA *n* respectful Turkish form of address

HODJAS > HODJA

HODMAN *n* hod carrier

HODMANDOD *n* snail

HODMEN > HODMAN

HODOGRAPH *n* curve of which the radius vector represents the velocity of a moving particle

HODOMETER *another name for* > ODOMETER

HODOMETRY > HODOMETER

HODOSCOPE *n* any device for tracing the path of a charged particle, esp a particle found in cosmic rays

HODS > HOD

HOE *n* long-handled tool used for loosening soil or weeding ▷ *vb* scrape or weed with a hoe

HOECAKE *n* maize cake

HOECAKES > HOECAKE

HOED > HOE

HOEDOWN *n* boisterous square dance

HOEDOWNS > HOEDOWN

HOEING > HOE

HOELIKE > HOE

HOER > HOE

HOERS > HOE

HOES > HOE

HOG *n* castrated male pig ▷ *vb* take more than one's share of

HOGAN *n* wooden dwelling covered with earth, typical of the Navaho Indians of N America

HOGANS > HOGAN

HOGBACK *n* narrow ridge that consists of steeply inclined rock strata

HOGBACKS > HOGBACK

HOGEN *n* strong alcoholic drink

HOGENS > HOGEN

HOGFISH *n* type of fish

HOGFISHES > HOGFISH

HOGG *same as* > HOG

HOGGED > HOG

HOGGER > HOG

HOGGEREL *n* year-old sheep

HOGGERELS > HOGGEREL

HOGGERIES > HOGGERY

HOGGERS > HOG

HOGGERY *n* hogs collectively

HOGGET *n* sheep up to the age of one year that has yet to be sheared

HOGGETS > HOGGET

HOGGIN *n* finely sifted gravel containing enough clay binder for it to be used in its natural form for making paths or roads

HOGGING *same as* > HOGGIN

HOGGINGS > HOGGING

HOGGINS > HOGGIN

HOGGISH *adj* selfish, gluttonous, or dirty

HOGGISHLY > HOGGISH

HOGGS > HOG

HOGH *n* ridge of land

HOGHOOD *n* condition of being hog

HOGHOODS > HOGHOOD

HOGHS > HOGH

HOGLIKE > HOG

HOGMANAY *n* New Year's Eve

HOGMANAYS > HOGMANAY

HOGMANE *n* short stiff mane

HOGMANES > HOGMANE

HOGMENAY *variant of* > HOGMANAY

HOGMENAYS > HOGMENAY

HOGNOSE *as in hognose snake* puff adder

HOGNOSED *as in hognosed skunk* any of several American skunks having a broad snoutlike nose

HOGNOSES > HOGNOSE

HOGNUT *another name for* > PIGNUT

HOGNUTS > HOGNUT

HOGS > HOG

HOGSHEAD *n* large cask

HOGSHEADS > HOGSHEAD

HOGTIE *vb* tie together the legs or the arms and legs of

HOGTIED > HOGTIE

HOGTIEING > HOGTIE

HOGTIES > HOGTIE

HOGTYING > HOGTIE

HOGWARD *n* person looking after hogs

HOGWARDS > HOGWARD

HOGWASH *n* nonsense

h

HOGWASHES > HOGWASH
HOGWEED n any of several coarse weedy umbelliferous plants, esp cow parsnip
HOGWEEDS > HOGWEED
HOH same as > HO
HOHA n nuisance
HOHED > HOH
HOHING > HOH
HOHS > HOH
HOI same as > HOY
HOICK vb raise abruptly and sharply
HOICKED > HOICK
HOICKING > HOICK
HOICKS interj cry used to encourage hounds to hunt ▷ vb shout hoicks
HOICKSED > HOICKS
HOICKSES > HOICKS
HOICKSING > HOICKS
HOIDEN same as > HOYDEN
HOIDENED > HOIDEN
HOIDENING > HOIDEN
HOIDENISH > HOIDEN
HOIDENS > HOIDEN
HOIK same as > HOICK
HOIKED > HOIK
HOIKING > HOIK
HOIKS > HOIK
HOING > HO
HOISE same as > HOIST
HOISED > HOISE
HOISES > HOISE
HOISIN n Chinese sweet spicy reddish-brown sauce made from soya beans, sugar, vinegar, and garlic
HOISING > HOISE
HOISINS > HOISIN
HOIST vb raise or lift up ▷ n device for lifting things
HOISTED > HOIST
HOISTER > HOIST
HOISTERS > HOIST
HOISTING > HOIST
HOISTINGS > HOIST
HOISTMAN n person operating a hoist
HOISTMEN > HOISTMAN
HOISTS > HOIST
HOISTWAY n shaft for a hoist
HOISTWAYS > HOISTWAY
HOKA n red cod
HOKE vb overplay (a part, etc)
HOKED > HOKE
HOKES > HOKE
HOKEY adj corny
HOKEYNESS > HOKEY
HOKI n fish of New Zealand waters
HOKIER > HOKEY
HOKIEST > HOKEY
HOKILY > HOKEY
HOKINESS > HOKEY
HOKING > HOKE
HOKIS > HOKI
HOKKU same as > HAIKU
HOKONUI n illicit whisky
HOKONUIS > HOKONUI
HOKUM n rubbish, nonsense
HOKUMS > HOKUM
HOKYPOKY n trickery
HOLANDRIC adj relating to Y-chromosomal genes

HOLARCHY n system composed of interacting holons
HOLARD n amount of water contained in soil
HOLARDS > HOLARD
HOLD vb keep or support in or with the hands or arms ▷ n act or way of holding
HOLDABLE > HOLD
HOLDALL n large strong travelling bag
HOLDALLS > HOLDALL
HOLDBACK n strap of the harness joining the breeching to the shaft, so that the horse can hold back the vehicle
HOLDBACKS > HOLDBACK
HOLDDOWN n control function in a computer
HOLDDOWNS > HOLDDOWN
HOLDEN past participle of > HOLD
HOLDER n person or thing that holds
HOLDERBAT n part of pipe used as fastening
HOLDERS > HOLDER
HOLDFAST n act of gripping strongly
HOLDFASTS > HOLDFAST
HOLDING > HOLD
HOLDINGS > HOLD
HOLDOUT n (in US English) person, country, organization, etc, that continues to resist or refuses to change
HOLDOUTS > HOLDOUT
HOLDOVER n (in US and Canadian English) elected official who continues in office after his term has expired
HOLDOVERS > HOLDOVER
HOLDS > HOLD
HOLDUP n robbery, esp an armed one
HOLDUPS > HOLDUP
HOLE n area hollowed out in a solid ▷ vb make holes in
HOLED > HOLE
HOLELESS > HOLE
HOLES > HOLE
HOLESOM same as > HOLESOME
HOLESOME same as > WHOLESOME
HOLEY adj full of holes
HOLEYER > HOLEY
HOLEYEST > HOLEY
HOLIBUT same as > HALIBUT
HOLIBUTS > HOLIBUT
HOLIDAY n time spent away from home for rest or recreation ▷ vb spend a holiday
HOLIDAYED > HOLIDAY
HOLIDAYER > HOLIDAY
HOLIDAYS > HOLIDAY
HOLIER > HOLY
HOLIES > HOLY
HOLIEST > HOLY
HOLILY adv in a holy, devout, or sacred manner
HOLINESS n state of being holy

HOLING > HOLE
HOLINGS > HOLE
HOLISM n view that a whole is greater than the sum of its parts
HOLISMS > HOLISM
HOLIST > HOLISM
HOLISTIC adj considering the complete person, physically and mentally, in the treatment of an illness
HOLISTS > HOLISM
HOLK vb dig
HOLKED > HOLK
HOLKING > HOLK
HOLKS > HOLK
HOLLA same as > HOLLO
HOLLAED > HOLLA
HOLLAING > HOLLA
HOLLAND n coarse linen cloth, used esp for furnishing
HOLLANDS > HOLLAND
HOLLAS > HOLLA
HOLLER n shout, yell ▷ vb shout or yell
HOLLERED > HOLLER
HOLLERING > HOLLER
HOLLERS > HOLLER
HOLLIDAM same as > HALIDOM
HOLLIDAMS > HOLLIDAM
HOLLIES > HOLLY
HOLLO interj cry for attention, or of encouragement ▷ vb shout
HOLLOA same as > HOLLO
HOLLOAED > HOLLOA
HOLLOAING > HOLLOA
HOLLOAS > HOLLOA
HOLLOED > HOLLO
HOLLOES > HOLLO
HOLLOING > HOLLO
HOLLOO same as > HALLOO
HOLLOOED > HOLLOO
HOLLOOING > HOLLOO
HOLLOOS > HOLLOO
HOLLOS > HOLLO
HOLLOW adj having a hole or space inside ▷ n cavity or space ▷ vb form a hollow in
HOLLOWARE n hollow utensils such as cups
HOLLOWED > HOLLOW
HOLLOWER > HOLLOW
HOLLOWEST > HOLLOW
HOLLOWING > HOLLOW
HOLLOWLY > HOLLOW
HOLLOWS > HOLLOW
HOLLY n evergreen tree with prickly leaves and red berries
HOLLYHOCK n tall garden plant with spikes of colourful flowers
HOLM n island in a river, lake, or estuary
HOLMIA n oxide of holmium
HOLMIAS > HOLMIA
HOLMIC adj of or containing holmium
HOLMIUM n silver-white metallic element, the compounds of which are

highly magnetic
HOLMIUMS > HOLMIUM
HOLMS > HOLM
HOLOCAUST n destruction or loss of life on a massive scale
HOLOCENE adj of, denoting, or formed in the second and most recent epoch of the Quaternary period, which began 10 000 years ago at the end of the Pleistocene
HOLOCRINE adj (of the secretion of glands) characterized by disintegration of the entire glandular cell in releasing its product, as in sebaceous glands
HOLOGAMY n condition of having gametes like ordinary cells
HOLOGRAM n three-dimensional photographic image
HOLOGRAMS > HOLOGRAM
HOLOGRAPH n document handwritten by the author
HOLOGYNIC adj passed down through females
HOLOGYNY n inheritance of genetic traits through females only
HOLOHEDRA n geometrical forms with particular symmetry
HOLON n autonomous self-reliant unit, esp in manufacturing
HOLONIC > HOLON
HOLONS > HOLON
HOLOPHOTE n device for directing light from lighthouse
HOLOPHYTE n plant capable of synthesizing food from inorganic molecules
HOLOPTIC adj with eyes meeting at the front
HOLOTYPE n original specimen from which a description of a new species is made
HOLOTYPES > HOLOTYPE
HOLOTYPIC > HOLOTYPE
HOLOZOIC adj (of animals) obtaining nourishment by feeding on plants or other animals
HOLP past tense of > HELP
HOLPEN past participle of > HELP
HOLS pl n holidays
HOLSTEIN n breed of cattle
HOLSTEINS > HOLSTEIN
HOLSTER n leather case for a pistol, hung from a belt ▷ vb return (a pistol) to its holster
HOLSTERED > HOLSTER
HOLSTERS > HOLSTER
HOLT n otter's lair
HOLTS > HOLT
HOLY adj of God or a god
HOLYDAM same as > HALIDOM
HOLYDAME same

Section 1: Words between 2 and 9 letters in length

as > HALIDOM
HOLYDAMES > HOLYDAME
HOLYDAMS > HOLYDAM
HOLYDAY *n* day on which a religious festival is observed
HOLYDAYS > HOLYDAY
HOLYSTONE *n* soft sandstone used for scrubbing the decks of a vessel ▷ *vb* scrub (a vessel's decks) with a holystone
HOLYTIDE *n* time for special religious observance
HOLYTIDES > HOLYTIDE
HOM *n* sacred plant of the Parsees and ancient Persians
HOMA *same as* > HOM
HOMAGE *n* show of respect or honour towards someone or something ▷ *vb* render homage to
HOMAGED > HOMAGE
HOMAGER > HOMAGE
HOMAGERS > HOMAGE
HOMAGES > HOMAGE
HOMAGING > HOMAGE
HOMALOID *n* geometrical plane
HOMALOIDS > HOMALOID
HOMAS > HOMA
HOMBRE *slang word for* > MAN
HOMBRES > HOMBRE
HOMBURG *n* man's soft felt hat with a dented crown and a stiff upturned brim
HOMBURGS > HOMBURG
HOME *n* place where one lives ▷ *adj* of one's home, birthplace, or native country ▷ *adv* to or at home ▷ *vb* direct towards (a point or target)
HOMEBIRTH *n* act of giving birth to a child in one's own home
HOMEBODY *n* person whose life and interests are centred on the home
HOMEBOUND *adj* heading for home
HOMEBOY *n* close friend
HOMEBOYS > HOMEBOY
HOMEBRED *adj* raised or bred at home ▷ *n* animal bred at home
HOMEBREDS > HOMEBRED
HOMEBREW *n* home-made beer
HOMEBREWS > HOMEBREW
HOMEBUILT *adj* built at home
HOMEBUYER *n* person buying a home
HOMECOMER *n* person coming home
HOMECRAFT *n* skills used in the home
HOMED > HOME
HOMEFELT *adj* felt personally
HOMEGIRL > HOMEBOY
HOMEGIRLS > HOMEBOY
HOMEGROWN *adj* (esp of fruit and vegetables) produced in one's own country,

district, estate, or garden
HOMELAND *n* country from which a person's ancestors came
HOMELANDS > HOMELAND
HOMELESS *adj* having nowhere to live ▷ *pl n* people who have nowhere to live
HOMELIER > HOMELY
HOMELIEST > HOMELY
HOMELIKE > HOME
HOMELILY > HOMELY
HOMELY *adj* simple, ordinary, and comfortable
HOMELYN *n* species of ray
HOMELYNS > HOMELYN
HOMEMADE *adj* (esp of cakes, jam, and other foods) made at home or on the premises, esp of high-quality ingredients
HOMEMAKER *n* person, esp a housewife, who manages a home
HOMEOBOX *adj* of genes that regulate cell development
HOMEOMERY *n* condition of being made up of similar parts
HOMEOPATH *n* person who treats disease by the use of small amounts of a drug that produces symptoms like those of the disease being treated
HOMEOSES > HOMEOSIS
HOMEOSIS *n* process of one part coming to resemble another
HOMEOTIC > HOMEOSIS
HOMEOWNER *n* person who owns the home in which he or she lives
HOMEPAGE *n* main page of website
HOMEPAGES > HOMEPAGE
HOMEPLACE *n* person's home
HOMEPORT *n* port where vessel is registered
HOMEPORTS > HOMEPORT
HOMER *n* homing pigeon ▷ *vb* score a home run in baseball
HOMERED > HOMER
HOMERIC *adj* grand or heroic
HOMERING > HOMER
HOMEROOM *n* common room at school
HOMEROOMS > HOMEROOM
HOMERS > HOMER
HOMES > HOME
HOMESICK *adj* sad because missing one's home and family
HOMESITE *n* site for building house
HOMESITES > HOMESITE
HOMESPUN *adj* (of philosophies or opinions) plain and unsophisticated ▷ *n* cloth made at home or made of yarn spun at home
HOMESPUNS > HOMESPUN
HOMESTALL *same as* > HOMESTEAD

HOMESTAND *n* series of games played at a team's home ground
HOMESTAY *n* period spent living as a guest in someone's home
HOMESTAYS > HOMESTAY
HOMESTEAD *n* farmhouse plus the adjoining land
HOMETOWN *n* town where one lives or was born
HOMETOWNS > HOMETOWN
HOMEWARD *adj* going home ▷ *adv* towards home
HOMEWARDS *adv* towards home
HOMEWARE *n* crockery, furniture, and furnishings with which a house, room, etc, is furnished
HOMEWARES > HOMEWARE
HOMEWORK *n* school work done at home
HOMEWORKS > HOMEWORK
HOMEY *same as* > HOMY
HOMEYNESS > HOMEY
HOMEYS > HOMEY
HOMICIDAL *adj* of, involving, or characterized by homicide
HOMICIDE *n* killing of a human being
HOMICIDES > HOMICIDE
HOMIE *short for* > HOMEBOY
HOMIER > HOMY
HOMIES > HOMIE
HOMIEST > HOMY
HOMILETIC *adj* of or relating to a homily or sermon
HOMILIES > HOMILY
HOMILIST > HOMILY
HOMILISTS > HOMILY
HOMILY *n* speech telling people how they should behave
HOMINES > HOMO
HOMINESS > HOMY
HOMING *adj* denoting the ability to return home after travelling great distances ▷ *n* relating to the ability to return home after travelling great distances
HOMINGS > HOMING
HOMINIAN *same as* > HOMINID
HOMINIANS > HOMINIAN
HOMINID *n* man or any extinct forerunner of man ▷ *adj* of or belonging to this family
HOMINIDS > HOMINID
HOMINIES > HOMINY
HOMININE *adj* characteristic of humans
HOMINISE *same as* > HOMINIZE
HOMINISED > HOMINISE
HOMINISES > HOMINISE
HOMINIZE *vb* make suitable for humans
HOMINIZED > HOMINIZE
HOMINIZES > HOMINIZE
HOMINOID *n* manlike animal ▷ *adj* of or like man
HOMINOIDS > HOMINOID

HOMINY *n* coarsely ground maize prepared as a food by boiling in milk or water
HOMME *French word for* > MAN
HOMMES > HOMME
HOMMOCK *same as* > HUMMOCK
HOMMOCKS > HOMMOCK
HOMMOS *same as* > HUMMUS
HOMMOSES > HOMMOS
HOMO *n* homogenized milk
HOMOCERCY *n* condition in fish of having a symmetrical tail
HOMODONT *adj* (of most nonmammalian vertebrates) having teeth that are all of the same type
HOMODYNE *adj* of strengthened radio waves
HOMOEOBOX *same as* > HOMEOBOX
HOMOEOSES > HOMOEOSIS
HOMOEOSIS *n* condition of controlling a system from within
HOMOEOTIC > HOMOEOSIS
HOMOGAMIC > HOMOGAMY
HOMOGAMY *n* condition in which all the flowers of an inflorescence are either of the same sex or hermaphrodite
HOMOGENY *n* similarity in structure of individuals or parts because of common ancestry
HOMOGONY *n* condition in a plant of having stamens and styles of the same length in all the flowers
HOMOGRAFT *n* tissue graft obtained from an organism of the same species as the recipient
HOMOGRAPH *n* word spelt the same as another, but with a different meaning
HOMOLOG *same as* > HOMOLOGUE
HOMOLOGIC *adj* having a related or similar position, structure, etc
HOMOLOGS > HOMOLOG
HOMOLOGUE *n* homologous part or organ
HOMOLOGY *n* condition of being homologous
HOMOLYSES > HOMOLYSIS
HOMOLYSIS *n* dissociation of a molecule into two neutral fragments
HOMOLYTIC > HOMOLYSIS
HOMOMORPH *n* thing same in form as something else
HOMONYM *n* word spelt or pronounced the same as another, but with a different meaning
HOMONYMIC > HOMONYM
HOMONYMS > HOMONYM
HOMONYMY > HOMONYMITY
HOMOPHILE *n* rare word for homosexual: person who is sexually attracted to members of the same sex
HOMOPHOBE *n* person who

has an intense hatred of homosexuality

HOMOPHONE *n* word pronounced the same as another, but with a different meaning or spelling

HOMOPHONY *n* linguistic phenomenon whereby words of different origins become identical in pronunciation

HOMOPHYLY *n* resemblance due to common ancestry

HOMOPLASY *n* state of being derived from an individual of the same species as the recipient

HOMOPOLAR *adj* of uniform charge

HOMOS > HOMO

HOMOSEX *n* sexual activity between homosexuals

HOMOSEXES > HOMOSEX

HOMOSPORY *n* state of producing spores of one kind only

HOMOSTYLY *n* (in flowers) existence of styles of only one length

HOMOTAXES > HOMOTAXIS

HOMOTAXIC > HOMOTAXIS

HOMOTAXIS *n* similarity of composition and arrangement in rock strata of different ages or in different regions

HOMOTONIC *adj* of same tone

HOMOTONY > HOMOTONIC

HOMOTYPAL *adj* of normal type

HOMOTYPE *n* something with same structure as something else

HOMOTYPES > HOMOTYPE

HOMOTYPIC *same as* > HOMOTYPAL

HOMOTYPY > HOMOTYPE

HOMOUSIAN *adj* believing God the Son and God the Father to be of the same essence

HOMS > HOM

HOMUNCLE *n* homunculus

HOMUNCLES > HOMUNCLE

HOMUNCULE *n* homunculus

HOMUNCULI *n* plural of homunculus: miniature man

HOMY *adj* like a home

HON *short for* > HONEY

HONAN *n* silk fabric of rough weave

HONANS > HONAN

HONCHO *n* person in charge ▷ *vb* supervise or be in charge of

HONCHOED > HONCHO

HONCHOING > HONCHO

HONCHOS > HONCHO

HOND *old form of* > HAND

HONDA *n* loop through which rope is threaded to make a lasso

HONDAS > HONDA

HONDLE *vb* negotiate on

price

HONDLED > HONDLE

HONDLES > HONDLE

HONDLING > HONDLE

HONDS > HOND

HONE *vb* sharpen ▷ *n* fine whetstone used for sharpening edged tools and knives

HONED > HONE

HONER > HONE

HONERS > HONE

HONES > HONE

HONEST *adj* truthful and moral

HONESTER > HONEST

HONESTEST > HONEST

HONESTIES > HONESTY

HONESTLY *adv* in an honest manner ▷ *interj* expression of disgust, surprise, etc

HONESTY *n* quality of being honest

HONEWORT *n* European plant that has clusters of small white flowers

HONEWORTS > HONEWORT

HONEY *n* sweet edible sticky substance made by bees from nectar; term of endearment ▷ *vb* sweeten with or as if with honey

HONEYBEE *n* bee widely domesticated as a source of honey and beeswax

HONEYBEES > HONEYBEE

HONEYBUN *n* term of endearment

HONEYBUNS > HONEYBUN

HONEYCOMB *n* waxy structure of six-sided cells in which honey is stored by bees in a beehive ▷ *vb* pierce or fill with holes, cavities, etc

HONEYDEW *n* sugary substance excreted by aphids and similar insects

HONEYDEWS > HONEYDEW

HONEYED > HONEY

HONEYEDLY > HONEY

HONEYFUL *adj* full of honey

HONEYING > HONEY

HONEYLESS > HONEY

HONEYMOON *n* holiday taken by a newly married couple ▷ *vb* take a honeymoon

HONEYPOT *n* container for honey

HONEYPOTS > HONEYPOT

HONEYS > HONEY

HONEYTRAP *n* scheme in which a victim is lured into a compromising sexual situation that provides the opportunity for blackmail

HONG *n* (in China) a factory, warehouse, etc ▷ *vb* archaic form of hang

HONGI *n* Māori greeting in which people touch noses ▷ *vb* touch noses

HONGIED > HONGI

HONGIES > HONGI

HONGIING > HONGI

HONGING > HONG

HONGIS > HONGI

HONGS > HONG

HONIED > HONEY

HONIEDLY > HONEY

HONING > HONE

HONK *n* sound made by a car horn ▷ *vb* (cause to) make this sound

HONKED > HONK

HONKER *n* person or thing that honks

HONKERS > HONKER

HONKEY *same as* > HONKY

HONKEYS > HONKEY

HONKIE *same as* > HONKY

HONKIES > HONKY

HONKING > HONK

HONKS > HONK

HONKY *n* derogatory slang for White man or White men collectively

HONOR *same as* > HONOUR

HONORABLE *adj* possessing high principles

HONORABLY > HONOURABLE

HONORAND *n* person being honoured

HONORANDS > HONORAND

HONORARIA *n* fee pain for a nominally free service

HONORARY *adj* held or given only as an honour

HONORED > HONOR

HONOREE *same as* > HONORAND

HONOREES > HONOREE

HONORER > HONOUR

HONORERS > HONOUR

HONORIFIC *adj* showing respect

HONORING > HONOR

HONORLESS > HONOUR

HONORS *same as* > HONOURS

HONOUR *n* sense of honesty and fairness ▷ *vb* give praise and attention to

HONOURED > HONOUR

HONOURER > HONOUR

HONOURERS > HONOUR

HONOURING > HONOUR

HONOURS > HONOUR

HONS > HON

HOO *pron* she

HOOCH *n* alcoholic drink, esp illicitly distilled spirits

HOOCHES > HOOCH

HOOCHIE *n* immoral woman

HOOCHIES > HOOCHIE

HOOD *n* head covering, often attached to a coat or jacket ▷ *vb* cover with or as if with a hood

HOODED *adj* (of a garment) having a hood

HOODIA *n* any of several southern African succulent plants whose sap has appetite-suppressing properties

HOODIAS > HOODIA

HOODIE *n* hooded sweatshirt

HOODIER > HOOD

HOODIES > HOODIE

HOODIEST > HOOD

HOODING > HOOD

HOODLESS > HOOD

HOODLIKE > HOOD

HOODLUM *n* violent criminal, gangster

HOODLUMS > HOODLUM

HOODMAN *n* blindfolded person in blindman's buff

HOODMEN > HOODMAN

HOODMOLD *n* moulding over door or window

HOODMOLDS > HOODMOLD

HOODOO *n* (cause of) bad luck ▷ *vb* bring bad luck to

HOODOOED > HOODOO

HOODOOING > HOODOO

HOODOOISM > HOODOO

HOODOOS > HOODOO

HOODS > HOOD

HOODWINK *vb* trick, deceive

HOODWINKS > HOODWINK

HOODY > HOOD

HOOEY *n* nonsense ▷ *interj* nonsense

HOOEYS > HOOEY

HOOF *n* horny covering of the foot of a horse, deer, etc ▷ *vb* kick or trample with the hooves

HOOFBEAT *n* sound made by hoof on the ground

HOOFBEATS > HOOFBEAT

HOOFBOUND *adj* (of a horse) having dry contracted hooves, with resultant pain and lameness

HOOFED *adj* having a hoof or hoofs

HOOFER *n* professional dancer

HOOFERS > HOOFER

HOOFING > HOOF

HOOFLESS > HOOF

HOOFLIKE > HOOF

HOOFPRINT *n* mark made by hoof on ground

HOOFROT *n* disease of hoof

HOOFROTS > HOOFROT

HOOFS > HOOF

HOOK *n* curved piece of metal, plastic, etc, used to hang, hold, or pull something ▷ *vb* fasten or catch (as if) with a hook

HOOKA *same as* > HOOKAH

HOOKAH *n* oriental pipe in which smoke is drawn through water and a long tube

HOOKAHS > HOOKAH

HOOKAS > HOOKA

HOOKCHECK *n* in ice hockey, act of hooking an opposing player

HOOKED *adj* bent like a hook

HOOKER *n* prostitute

HOOKERS > HOOKER

HOOKEY *same as* > HOOKY

HOOKEYS > HOOKEY

HOOKIER > HOOKY

HOOKIES > HOOKY

HOOKIEST > HOOKY

HOOKING > HOOK

HOOKLESS > HOOK

HOOKLET *n* little hook

HOOKLETS > HOOKLET

HOOKLIKE > HOOK

HOOKNOSE *n* nose with a pronounced outward and downward curve

HOOKNOSED > HOOKNOSE
HOOKNOSES > HOOKNOSE
HOOKS > HOOK
HOOKUP n contact of an aircraft in flight with the refuelling hose of a tanker aircraft
HOOKUPS > HOOKUP
HOOKWORM n blood-sucking worm with hooked mouthparts
HOOKWORMS > HOOKWORM
HOOKY n truancy, usually from school (esp in the phrase play hooky) ▷ adj hooklike
HOOLACHAN n Highland reel
HOOLEY n lively party
HOOLEYS > HOOLEY
HOOLICAN same as > HOOLACHAN
HOOLICANS > HOOLICAN
HOOLIE same as > HOOLEY
HOOLIER > HOOLY
HOOLIES > HOOLIE
HOOLIEST > HOOLY
HOOLIGAN n rowdy young person
HOOLIGANS > HOOLIGAN
HOOLOCK n Indian gibbon
HOOLOCKS > HOOLOCK
HOOLY adj careful or gentle
HOON n loutish youth who drives irresponsibly ▷ vb drive irresponsibly
HOONS > HOON
HOOP n rigid circular band, used esp as a child's toy or for animals to jump through in the circus ▷ vb surround with or as if with a hoop
HOOPED > HOOP
HOOPER rare word for > COOPER
HOOPERS > HOOPER
HOOPING > HOOP
HOOPLA n fairground game in which hoops are thrown over objects in an attempt to win them
HOOPLAS > HOOPLA
HOOPLESS > HOOP
HOOPLIKE > HOOP
HOOPOE n bird with a pinkish-brown plumage and a fanlike crest
HOOPOES > HOOPOE
HOOPOO same as > HOOPOE
HOOPOOS > HOOPOO
HOOPS > HOOP
HOOPSKIRT n skirt stiffened by hoops
HOOPSTER n basketball player
HOOPSTERS > HOOPSTER
HOORAH same as > HURRAH
HOORAHED > HOORAH
HOORAHING > HOORAH
HOORAHS > HOORAH
HOORAY same as > HURRAH
HOORAYED > HOORAY
HOORAYING > HOORAY
HOORAYS > HOORAY
HOORD same as > HOARD
HOORDS > HOORD
HOOROO same as > HURRAH

HOOSEGOW slang word for > JAIL
HOOSEGOWS > HOOSEGOW
HOOSGOW > JAIL
HOOSGOWS > JAIL
HOOSH vb shoo away
HOOSHED > HOOSH
HOOSHES > HOOSH
HOOSHING > HOOSH
HOOT n sound of a car horn ▷ vb sound (a car horn) ▷ interj exclamation of impatience or dissatisfaction: a supposed Scotticism
HOOTCH same as > HOOCH
HOOTCHES > HOOTCH
HOOTED > HOOT
HOOTER n device that hoots
HOOTERS > HOOTER
HOOTIER > HOOT
HOOTIEST > HOOT
HOOTING > HOOT
HOOTNANNY n informal performance by folk singers
HOOTS same as > HOOT
HOOTY > HOOT
HOOVE same as > HEAVE
HOOVED > HOOVE
HOOVEN > HOOVE
HOOVER vb vacuum-clean (a carpet, furniture, etc)
HOOVERED > HOOVER
HOOVERING > HOOVER
HOOVERS > HOOVER
HOOVES > HOOF
HOOVING > HOOVE
HOP vb jump on one foot ▷ n instance of hopping
HOPBIND n stalk of the hop
HOPBINDS > HOPBIND
HOPBINE same as > HOPBIND
HOPBINES > HOPBINE
HOPDOG n species of caterpillar
HOPDOGS > HOPDOG
HOPE vb want (something) to happen or be true ▷ n expectation of something desired
HOPED > HOPE
HOPEFUL adj having, expressing, or inspiring hope ▷ n person considered to be on the brink of success
HOPEFULLY adv in a hopeful manner
HOPEFULS > HOPEFUL
HOPELESS adj having or offering no hope
HOPER > HOPE
HOPERS > HOPE
HOPES > HOPE
HOPHEAD n heroin or opium addict
HOPHEADS > HOPHEAD
HOPING > HOPE
HOPINGLY > HOPE
HOPLITE n (in ancient Greece) a heavily armed infantryman
HOPLITES > HOPLITE
HOPLITIC > HOPLITE
HOPLOLOGY n study of weapons or armour

HOPPED > HOP
HOPPER n container for storing substances such as grain or sand
HOPPERCAR same as > HOPPER
HOPPERS > HOPPER
HOPPIER > HOPPY
HOPPIEST > HOPPY
HOPPING > HOP
HOPPINGS > HOP
HOPPLE same as > HOBBLE
HOPPLED > HOPPLE
HOPPLER > HOPPLE
HOPPLERS > HOPPLE
HOPPLES > HOPPLE
HOPPLING > HOPPLE
HOPPY adj tasting of hops
HOPS > HOP
HOPSACK n roughly woven fabric of wool, cotton, etc, used for clothing
HOPSACKS > HOPSACK
HOPSCOTCH n children's game of hopping in a pattern drawn on the ground
HOPTOAD n toad
HOPTOADS > HOPTOAD
HORA n traditional Israeli or Romanian circle dance
HORAH same as > HORA
HORAHS > HORAH
HORAL less common word for > HOURLY
HORARY adj relating to the hours
HORAS > HORA
HORDE n large crowd ▷ vb form, move in, or live in a horde
HORDED > HORDE
HORDEIN n simple protein, rich in proline, that occurs in barley
HORDEINS > HORDEIN
HORDEOLA > HORDEOLUM
HORDEOLUM n (in medicine) stye
HORDES > HORDE
HORDING > HORDE
HORDOCK same as > HARDOKE
HORDOCKS > HORDOCK
HORE same as > HOAR
HOREHOUND n plant that produces a bitter juice formerly used as a cough medicine
HORI n Māori ▷ adj of or relating to the Māori
HORIATIKI n traditional Greek salad consisting of tomatoes, cucumber, onion, olives, and feta cheese
HORIS > HORI
HORIZON n apparent line that divides the earth and the sky
HORIZONAL > HORIZON
HORIZONS > HORIZON
HORKEY same as > HOCKEY
HORKEYS > HORKEY
HORLICKS as in make a horlicks make a mistake or a mess

HORME n (in the psychology of C. G. Jung) fundamental vital energy
HORMES > HORME
HORMIC > HORME
HORMONAL > HORMONE
HORMONE n substance secreted by certain glands which stimulates certain organs of the body
HORMONES > HORMONE
HORMONIC > HORMONE
HORN n one of a pair of bony growths sticking out of the heads of cattle, sheep, etc ▷ vb provide with a horn or horns
HORNBAG n in Australian slang, a promiscuous woman
HORNBAGS > HORNBAG
HORNBEAK n garfish
HORNBEAKS > HORNBEAK
HORNBEAM n tree with smooth grey bark
HORNBEAMS > HORNBEAM
HORNBILL n bird with a bony growth on its large beak
HORNBILLS > HORNBILL
HORNBOOK n page bearing a religious text or the alphabet, held in a frame with a thin window of flattened cattle horn over it
HORNBOOKS > HORNBOOK
HORNBUG n stag beetle
HORNBUGS > HORNBUG
HORNED adj having a horn, horns, or hornlike parts
HORNER n dealer in horn
HORNERS > HORNER
HORNET n large wasp with a severe sting
HORNETS > HORNET
HORNFELS n hard compact fine-grained metamorphic rock formed by the action of heat from a magmatic intrusion on neighbouring sedimentary rocks
HORNFUL n amount a horn will hold
HORNFULS > HORNFUL
HORNGELD n feudal rent based on number of cattle
HORNGELDS > HORNGELD
HORNIER > HORNY
HORNIEST > HORNY
HORNILY > HORNY
HORNINESS > HORNY
HORNING > HORN
HORNINGS > HORN
HORNISH adj like horn
HORNIST n horn player
HORNISTS > HORNIST
HORNITO n small vent in volcano
HORNITOS > HORNITO
HORNLESS > HORN
HORNLET n small horn
HORNLETS > HORNLET
HORNLIKE > HORN
HORNPIPE n (music for) a solo dance, traditionally performed by sailors
HORNPIPES > HORNPIPE

HORNPOUT *n* catfish
HORNPOUTS > HORNPOUT
HORNS > HORN
HORNSTONE *same as* > HORNFELS
HORNTAIL *n* wasplike insect
HORNTAILS > HORNTAIL
HORNWORK *n* bastion in fortifications
HORNWORKS > HORNWORK
HORNWORM *n* caterpillar of hawk moth
HORNWORMS > HORNWORM
HORNWORT *n* aquatic plant
HORNWORTS > HORNWORT
HORNWRACK *n* yellowish bryozoan or sea mat sometimes found on beaches after a storm
HORNY *adj* of or like horn
HORNYHEAD *n* species of fish
HORNYWINK *n* lapwing
HOROEKA *n* New Zealand tree
HOROKAKA *n* low-growing New Zealand plant with fleshy leaves and pink or white flowers
HOROLOGE *rare word for* > TIMEPIECE
HOROLOGER *same as* > HOROLOGIST
HOROLOGES > HOROLOGE
HOROLOGIA *n* plural of horologium: clocktower
HOROLOGIC > HOROLOGY
HOROLOGY *n* art of making clocks and watches or of measuring time
HOROMETRY *n* measurement of time
HOROPITO *n* New Zealand plant
HOROPITOS > HOROPITO
HOROPTER *n* locus of all points in space that stimulate points on each eye that yield the same visual direction as each other
HOROPTERS > HOROPTER
HOROSCOPE *n* prediction of a person's future based on the positions of the planets, sun, and moon at his or her birth
HOROSCOPY *n* casting and interpretation of horoscopes
HORRENT *adj* bristling
HORRIBLE *adj* disagreeable, unpleasant ▷ *n* horrible thing
HORRIBLES > HORRIBLE
HORRIBLY *adv* in a horrible manner
HORRID *adj* disagreeable, unpleasant
HORRIDER > HORRID
HORRIDEST > HORRID
HORRIDLY > HORRID
HORRIFIC *adj* causing horror
HORRIFIED *adj* terrified
HORRIFIES > HORRIFY
HORRIFY *vb* cause to feel horror or shock

HORROR *n* (thing or person causing) terror or hatred ▷ *adj* having a frightening subject, usually concerned with the supernatural
HORRORS *pl n* fit of depression or anxiety ▷ *interj* expression of dismay, sometimes facetious
HORS *as in* hors d'oeuvre appetizer
HORSE *n* large animal with hooves, a mane, and a tail, used for riding and pulling carts etc ▷ *vb* provide with a horse
HORSEBACK *n* horse's back
HORSEBEAN *n* broad bean
HORSEBOX *n* trailer used for transporting horses
HORSECAR *n* streetcar drawn by horses
HORSECARS > HORSECAR
HORSED > HORSE
HORSEFLY *n* large bloodsucking fly
HORSEHAIR *n* hair from the tail or mane of a horse
HORSEHIDE *n* hide of a horse
HORSELESS > HORSE
HORSELIKE > HORSE
HORSEMAN *n* person skilled in riding
HORSEMEAT *n* flesh of the horse used as food
HORSEMEN > HORSEMAN
HORSEMINT *n* European mint plant
HORSEPLAY *n* rough or rowdy play
HORSEPOND *n* pond where horses drink
HORSEPOX *n* viral infection of horses
HORSERACE *n* race for horses
HORSES > HORSE
HORSESHIT *n* rubbish
HORSESHOD > HORSESHOE
HORSESHOE *n* protective U-shaped piece of iron nailed to a horse's hoof, regarded as a symbol of good luck ▷ *vb* fit with a horseshoe
HORSETAIL *n* plant with small dark toothlike leaves
HORSEWAY *n* road for horses
HORSEWAYS > HORSEWAY
HORSEWEED *n* US name for Canadian fleabane
HORSEWHIP *n* whip with a long thong, used for managing horses ▷ *vb* beat (a person or animal) with such a whip
HORSEY *adj* very keen on horses
HORSIER > HORSY
HORSIEST > HORSY
HORSILY > HORSEY
HORSINESS > HORSEY
HORSING > HORSE
HORSINGS > HORSE
HORSON *same as* > WHORESON

HORSONS > HORSON
HORST *n* ridge of land that has been forced upwards between two parallel faults
HORSTE *variant of* > HORST
HORSTES > HORSTE
HORSTS > HORST
HORSY *same as* > HORSEY
HORTATION > HORTATORY
HORTATIVE *same as* > HORTATORY
HORTATORY *adj* encouraging
HOS > HO
HOSANNA *interj* exclamation of praise to God ▷ *n* act of crying "hosanna" ▷ *vb* cry hosanna
HOSANNAED > HOSANNA
HOSANNAH *same as* > HOSANNA
HOSANNAHS > HOSANNAH
HOSANNAS > HOSANNA
HOSE *n* flexible pipe for conveying liquid ▷ *vb* water with a hose
HOSED > HOSE
HOSEL *n* socket in head of golf club
HOSELIKE > HOSE
HOSELS > HOSEL
HOSEMAN *n* fireman in charge of hose
HOSEMEN > HOSEMAN
HOSEN > HOSE
HOSEPIPE *n* hose
HOSEPIPES > HOSEPIPE
HOSER *n* person who swindles or deceives others
HOSERS > HOSER
HOSES > HOSE
HOSEY *vb* claim possession
HOSEYED > HOSEY
HOSEYING > HOSEY
HOSEYS > HOSEY
HOSIER *n* person who sells stockings, etc
HOSIERIES > HOSIERY
HOSIERS > HOSIER
HOSIERY *n* stockings, socks, and tights collectively
HOSING > HOSE
HOSPICE *n* nursing home for the terminally ill
HOSPICES > HOSPICE
HOSPITAGE *n* behaviour of guest
HOSPITAL *n* place where people who are ill are looked after and treated
HOSPITALE *n* lodging
HOSPITALS > HOSPITAL
HOSPITIA > HOSPITIUM
HOSPITIUM *same as* > HOSPICE
HOSPODAR *n* (formerly) the governor or prince of Moldavia or Wallachia under Ottoman rule
HOSPODARS > HOSPODAR
HOSS *n* horse
HOSSES > HOSS
HOST *n* person who entertains guests, esp in his own home ▷ *vb* be the host of
HOSTA *n* ornamental plant

HOSTAGE *n* person who is illegally held prisoner until certain demands are met by other people
HOSTAGES > HOSTAGE
HOSTAS > HOSTA
HOSTED > HOST
HOSTEL *n* building providing accommodation at a low cost for a specific group of people such as students, travellers, homeless people, etc ▷ *vb* stay in hostels
HOSTELED > HOSTEL
HOSTELER *same as* > HOSTELLER
HOSTELERS > HOSTELER
HOSTELING > HOSTEL
HOSTELLED > HOSTEL
HOSTELLER *n* person who stays at youth hostels
HOSTELRY *n* inn, pub
HOSTELS > HOSTEL
HOSTESS *n* woman who receives and entertains guests, esp in her own house ▷ *vb* act as hostess
HOSTESSED > HOSTESS
HOSTESSES > HOSTESS
HOSTIE *n* informal Australian word for an air hostess
HOSTIES > HOSTIE
HOSTILE *adj* unfriendly ▷ *n* hostile person
HOSTILELY > HOSTILE
HOSTILES > HOSTILE
HOSTILITY *n* unfriendly and aggressive feelings or behaviour
HOSTING > HOST
HOSTINGS > HOST
HOSTLER *another name (esp Brit) for* > OSTLER
HOSTLERS > HOSTLER
HOSTLESSE *adj* inhospitable
HOSTLY > HOST
HOSTRIES > HOSTRY
HOSTRY *n* lodging
HOSTS > HOST
HOT *adj* having a high temperature
HOTBED *n* any place encouraging a particular activity
HOTBEDS > HOTBED
HOTBLOOD *n* type of horse
HOTBLOODS > HOTBLOOD
HOTBOX *n* closed room where marijuana is smoked
HOTBOXES > HOTBOX
HOTCAKE *n* pancake
HOTCAKES > HOTCAKE
HOTCH *vb* jog
HOTCHED > HOTCH
HOTCHES > HOTCH
HOTCHING > HOTCH
HOTCHPOT *n* collecting of property so that it may be redistributed in equal shares, esp on the intestacy of a parent who has given property to his children in his lifetime
HOTCHPOTS > HOTCHPOT
HOTDOG *vb* perform a series

of manoeuvres in skiing, surfing, etc, esp in a showy manner

HOTDOGGED > HOTDOG

HOTDOGGER > HOTDOG

HOTDOGS > HOTDOG

HOTE > HIGHT

HOTEL *n* commercial establishment providing lodging and meals

HOTELDOM *n* hotel business

HOTELDOMS > HOTELDOM

HOTELIER *n* owner or manager of a hotel

HOTELIERS > HOTELIER

HOTELMAN *n* hotel owner

HOTELMEN > HOTELMAN

HOTELS > HOTEL

HOTEN > HIGHT

HOTFOOT *adv* quickly and eagerly ▷ *vb* move quickly

HOTFOOTED > HOTFOOT

HOTFOOTS > HOTFOOT

HOTHEAD *n* excitable or fiery person

HOTHEADED *adj* impetuous, rash, or hot-tempered

HOTHEADS > HOTHEAD

HOTHOUSE *n* greenhouse

HOTHOUSED *adj* taught intensively

HOTHOUSES > HOTHOUSE

HOTLINE *n* direct telephone link for emergency use

HOTLINES > HOTLINE

HOTLINK *n* area on website connecting to another site

HOTLINKS > HOTLINK

HOTLY > HOT

HOTNESS > HOT

HOTNESSES > HOT

HOTPLATE *n* heated metal surface on an electric cooker

HOTPLATES > HOTPLATE

HOTPOT *n* casserole of meat and vegetables, topped with potatoes

HOTPOTS > HOTPOT

HOTPRESS *vb* subject (paper, cloth, etc) to heat and pressure to give it a smooth surface or extract oil

HOTROD *n* car with an engine that has been radically modified to produce increased power

HOTRODS > HOTROD

HOTS as in *the hots* feeling of lust

HOTSHOT *n* important person or expert, esp when showy

HOTSHOTS > HOTSHOT

HOTSPOT *n* place where wireless broadband services are provided through a wireless local area network

HOTSPOTS > HOTSPOT

HOTSPUR *n* impetuous or fiery person

HOTSPURS > HOTSPUR

HOTTED > HOT

HOTTENTOT as in *hottentot fig* perennial plant with

fleshy leaves, showy yellow or purple flowers, and edible fruits

HOTTER *vb* simmer

HOTTERED > HOTTIER

HOTTERING > HOTTER

HOTTERS > HOTTER

HOTTEST > HOT

HOTTIE *n* sexually attractive person

HOTTIES > HOTTIE

HOTTING *n* practice of stealing fast cars and putting on a show of skilful but dangerous driving

HOTTINGS > HOTTING

HOTTISH *adj* fairly hot

HOTTY *same as* > HOTTIE

HOUDAH *same as* > HOWDAH

HOUDAHS > HOUDAH

HOUDAN *n* breed of light domestic fowl originally from France, with a distinctive full crest

HOUDANS > HOUDAN

HOUF *same as* > HOWF

HOUFED > HOUF

HOUFF *same as* > HOWF

HOUFFED > HOUFF

HOUFFING > HOUFF

HOUFFS > HOUFF

HOUFING > HOUF

HOUFS > HOUF

HOUGH *n* in Scotland, a cut of meat corresponding to shin ▷ *vb* hamstring (cattle, horses, etc)

HOUGHED > HOUGH

HOUGHING > HOUGH

HOUGHS > HOUGH

HOUHERE *n* small evergreen New Zealand tree

HOUMMOS *same as* > HUMMUS

HOUMMOSES > HOUMMOS

HOUMOUS > HUMMUS

HOUMOUSES > HOUMOUS

HOUMUS *same as* > HUMMUS

HOUMUSES > HOUMUS

HOUND *n* hunting dog ▷ *vb* pursue relentlessly

HOUNDED > HOUND

HOUNDER > HOUND

HOUNDERS > HOUND

HOUNDFISH *n* name given to various small sharks or dogfish

HOUNDING > HOUND

HOUNDS > HOUND

HOUNGAN *n* voodoo priest

HOUNGANS > HOUNGAN

HOUR *n* twenty-fourth part of a day, sixty minutes

HOURGLASS *n* device with two glass compartments, containing a quantity of sand that takes an hour to trickle from the top section to the bottom one

HOURI *n* any of the nymphs of paradise

HOURIS > HOURI

HOURLIES > HOURLY

HOURLONG *adj* lasting an hour

HOURLY *adv* (happening) every hour ▷ *adj* of, occurring, or done once

every hour ▷ *n* something that is done by the hour; someone who is paid by the hour

HOURPLATE *n* dial of clock

HOURS *pl n* indefinite time

HOUSE *n* building used as a home ▷ *vb* give accommodation to ▷ *adj* (of wine) sold in a restaurant at a lower price than wines on the wine list

HOUSEBOAT *n* stationary boat used as a home

HOUSEBOY *n* male domestic servant

HOUSEBOYS > HOUSEBOY

HOUSECARL *n* (in medieval Europe) a household warrior of Danish kings and noblemen

HOUSECOAT *n* woman's long loose coat-shaped garment for wearing at home

HOUSED > HOUSE

HOUSEFLY *n* common fly often found in houses

HOUSEFUL *n* full amount or number that can be accommodated in a particular house

HOUSEFULS > HOUSEFUL

HOUSEHOLD *n* all the people living in a house ▷ *adj* relating to the running of a household

HOUSEKEEP *vb* run household

HOUSEKEPT > HOUSEKEEP

HOUSEL *vb* give the Eucharist to (someone)

HOUSELED > HOUSEL

HOUSELEEK *n* plant that has a rosette of succulent leaves and pinkish flowers and grows on walls

HOUSELESS > HOUSE

HOUSELINE *n* tarred marline

HOUSELING > HOUSEL

HOUSELLED > HOUSEL

HOUSELS > HOUSEL

HOUSEMAID *n* female servant employed to do housework

HOUSEMAN *n* junior hospital doctor

HOUSEMATE *n* person who is not part of the same family, but with whom one shares a house

HOUSEMEN > HOUSEMAN

HOUSER > HOUSE

HOUSEROOM *n* room for storage or lodging

HOUSERS > HOUSE

HOUSES > HOUSE

HOUSESAT > HOUSESIT

HOUSESIT *vb* live in and look after a house during the absence of its owner or owners

HOUSESITS > HOUSESIT

HOUSETOP *n* rooftop

HOUSETOPS > HOUSETOP

HOUSEWIFE *n* woman who

runs her own household and does not have a job

HOUSEWORK *n* work of running a home, such as cleaning, cooking, and shopping

HOUSEY *adj* of or like house music

HOUSIER > HOUSEY

HOUSIEST > HOUSEY

HOUSING *n* (providing of) houses

HOUSINGS > HOUSING

HOUSLING *adj* of sacrament

HOUSTONIA *n* small North American plant with blue, white or purple flowers

HOUT *same as* > HOOT

HOUTED > HOUT

HOUTING *n* type of fish that lives in salt water but spawns in freshwater lakes and is valued for its edible flesh

HOUTINGS > HOUTING

HOUTS > HOUT

HOVE > HEAVE

HOVEA *n* Australian plant with purple flowers

HOVEAS > HOVEA

HOVED > HEAVE

HOVEL *n* small dirty house or hut ▷ *vb* shelter or be sheltered in a hovel

HOVELED > HOVEL

HOVELING > HOVEL

HOVELLED > HOVEL

HOVELLER *n* man working on boat

HOVELLERS > HOVELLER

HOVELLING > HOVEL

HOVELS > HOVEL

HOVEN > HEAVE

HOVER *vb* (of a bird etc) remain suspended in one place in the air ▷ *n* act of hovering

HOVERED > HOVER

HOVERER > HOVER

HOVERERS > HOVER

HOVERFLY *n* hovering wasp-like fly

HOVERING > HOVER

HOVERPORT *n* port for hovercraft

HOVERS > HOVER

HOVES > HEAVE

HOVING > HEAVE

HOW *adv* in what way, by what means ▷ *n* the way a thing is done ▷ *sentence substitute* greeting supposed to be or have been used by American Indians and often used humorously

HOWBE *same as* > HOWBEIT

HOWBEIT *adv* in archaic usage, however

HOWDAH *n* canopied seat on an elephant's back

HOWDAHS > HOWDAH

HOWDIE *n* midwife

HOWDIED > HOWDY

HOWDIES > HOWDY

HOWDY *vb* greet someone

HOWDYING > HOWDY

HOWE n depression in the earth's surface, such as a basin or valley

HOWES > HOWE

HOWEVER adv nevertheless

HOWF n haunt, esp a public house ▷ vb visit place frequently

HOWFED > HOWF

HOWFF vb visit place frequently

HOWFFED > HOWFF

HOWFFING > HOWFF

HOWFFS > HOWFF

HOWFING > HOWF

HOWFS > HOWF

HOWITZER n large gun firing shells at a steep angle

HOWITZERS > HOWITZER

HOWK vb dig (out or up)

HOWKED > HOWK

HOWKER > HOWK

HOWKERS > HOWK

HOWKING > HOWK

HOWKS > HOWK

HOWL n loud wailing cry ▷ vb utter a howl

HOWLBACK same as > HOWLROUND

HOWLBACKS > HOWLBACK

HOWLED > HOWL

HOWLER n stupid mistake

HOWLERS > HOWLER

HOWLET another word for > OWL

HOWLETS > HOWLET

HOWLING adj great

HOWLINGLY > HOWL

HOWLINGS > HOWL

HOWLROUND n condition, resulting in a howling noise, when sound from a loudspeaker is fed back into the microphone of a public-address or recording system

HOWLS > HOWL

HOWRE same as > HOUR

HOWRES > HOWRE

HOWS > HOW

HOWSO same as > HOWSOEVER

HOWSOEVER less common word for > HOWEVER

HOWTOWDIE n Scottish dish of boiled chicken with poached eggs and spinach

HOWZAT > HOW

HOWZIT informal word for > HELLO

HOX vb hamstring

HOXED > HOX

HOXES > HOX

HOXING > HOX

HOY interj cry used to attract someone's attention ▷ n freight barge ▷ vb drive animal with cry

HOYA n any of various E Asian or Australian plants

HOYAS > HOYA

HOYDEN n wild or boisterous girl ▷ vb behave like a hoyden

HOYDENED > HOYDEN

HOYDENING > HOYDEN

HOYDENISH > HOYDEN

HOYDENISM > HOYDEN

HOYDENS > HOYDEN

HOYED > HOY

HOYING > HOY

HOYLE n archer's mark used as a target

HOYLES > HOYLE

HOYS > HOY

HRYVNA n standard monetary unit of Ukraine, divided into 100 kopiykas

HRYVNAS > HRYVNA

HRYVNIA n money unit of Ukraine

HRYVNIAS > HRYVNIA

HRYVNYA same as > HRYVNA

HRYVNYAS > HRYVNYA

HUANACO same as > GUANACO

HUANACOS > HUANACO

HUAQUERO n Central American tomb robber

HUAQUEROS > HUAQUERO

HUARACHE n Mexican sandal

HUARACHES > HUARACHE

HUARACHO same as > HUARACHE

HUARACHOS > HUARACHO

HUB n centre of a wheel, through which the axle passes

HUBBIES > HUBBY

HUBBLY adj having an irregular surface

HUBBUB n confused noise of many voices

HUBBUBOO same as > HUBBUB

HUBBUBOOS > HUBBUBOO

HUBBUBS > HUBBUB

HUBBY n husband

HUBCAP n metal disc that fits on to and protects the hub of a wheel, esp on a car

HUBCAPS > HUBCAP

HUBRIS n pride, arrogance

HUBRISES > HUBRIS

HUBRISTIC > HUBRIS

HUBS > HUB

HUCK same as > HUCKABACK

HUCKABACK n coarse absorbent linen or cotton fabric used for towels and informal shirts, etc

HUCKERY adj ugly

HUCKLE n hip or haunch

HUCKLES > HUCKLE

HUCKS > HUCK

HUCKSTER n person using aggressive methods of selling ▷ vb peddle

HUCKSTERS > HUCKSTER

HUCKSTERY > HUCKSTER

HUDDEN > HAUD

HUDDLE vb hunch (oneself) through cold or fear ▷ n small group

HUDDLED > HUDDLE

HUDDLER > HUDDLE

HUDDLERS > HUDDLE

HUDDLES > HUDDLE

HUDDLING > HUDDLE

HUDDUP interj get up

HUDNA n truce or ceasefire for a fixed duration

HUDNAS > HUDNA

HUDUD n set of laws and punishments specified by Allah in the Koran

HUDUDS > HUDUD

HUE n colour, shade

HUED adj having a hue or colour as specified

HUELESS > HUE

HUER n pilchard fisherman

HUERS > HUER

HUES > HUE

HUFF n passing mood of anger or resentment ▷ vb blow or puff heavily

HUFFED > HUFF

HUFFER > HUFFING

HUFFERS > HUFFING

HUFFIER > HUFF

HUFFIEST > HUFF

HUFFILY > HUFF

HUFFINESS > HUFF

HUFFING n practice of inhaling toxic fumes from glue and other household products for their intoxicating effects

HUFFINGS > HUFFING

HUFFISH > HUFF

HUFFISHLY > HUFF

HUFFKIN n type of muffin

HUFFKINS > HUFFKIN

HUFFS > HUFF

HUFFY > HUFF

HUG vb clasp tightly in the arms, usu with affection ▷ n tight or fond embrace

HUGE adj very big

HUGELY adv very much

HUGENESS > HUGE

HUGEOUS same as > HUGE

HUGEOUSLY > HUGEOUS

HUGER > HUGE

HUGEST > HUGE

HUGGABLE > HUG

HUGGED > HUG

HUGGER > HUG

HUGGERS > HUG

HUGGIER > HUGGY

HUGGIEST > HUGGY

HUGGING > HUG

HUGGY adj sensitive and caring

HUGS > HUG

HUGY same as > HUGE

HUH interj exclamation of derision, bewilderment, or inquiry

HUHU n type of hairy New Zealand beetle

HUHUS > HUHU

HUI n meeting of Māori people

HUIA n extinct bird of New Zealand, prized by early Māoris for its distinctive tail feathers

HUIAS > HUIA

HUIC interj in hunting, a call to hounds

HUIPIL n Mayan woman's blouse

HUIPILES > HUIPIL

HUIPILS > HUIPIL

HUIS > HUI

HUISACHE n American tree

HUISACHES > HUISACHE

HUISSIER n doorkeeper

HUISSIERS > HUISSIER

HUITAIN n verse of eighteen lines

HUITAINS > HUITAIN

HULA n swaying Hawaiian dance

HULAS > HULA

HULE same as > ULE

HULES > HULE

HULK n body of an abandoned ship ▷ vb move clumsily

HULKED > HULK

HULKIER > HULKY

HULKIEST > HULKY

HULKING adj bulky, unwieldy

HULKS > HULK

HULKY same as > HULKING

HULL n main body of a boat ▷ vb remove the hulls from

HULLED > HULL

HULLER > HULL

HULLERS > HULL

HULLIER > HULLY

HULLIEST > HULLY

HULLING > HULL

HULLO same as > HELLO

HULLOA same as > HALLOA

HULLOAED > HULLOA

HULLOAING > HULLOA

HULLOAS > HULLOA

HULLOED > HULLO

HULLOES > HULLO

HULLOING > HULLO

HULLOO same as > HALLOO

HULLOOED > HULLOO

HULLOOING > HULLOO

HULLOOS > HULLOO

HULLOS > HULLO

HULLS > HULL

HULLY adj having husks

HUM vb make a low continuous vibrating sound ▷ n humming sound

HUMA n mythical bird

HUMAN adj of or typical of people ▷ n human being

HUMANE adj kind or merciful

HUMANELY > HUMANE

HUMANER > HUMANE

HUMANEST > HUMANE

HUMANHOOD n state of being human

HUMANISE same as > HUMANIZE

HUMANISED > HUMANISE

HUMANISER > HUMANISE

HUMANISES > HUMANISE

HUMANISM n belief in human effort rather than religion

HUMANISMS > HUMANISM

HUMANIST > HUMANISM

HUMANISTS > HUMANISM > HUMANITARIANIST

HUMANITY n human race

HUMANIZE vb make human or humane

HUMANIZED > HUMANIZE

HUMANIZER > HUMANIZE

HUMANIZES > HUMANIZE

HUMANKIND n human race

HUMANLIKE > HUMAN

HUMANLY adv by human powers or means

HUMANNESS > HUMAN

HUMANOID adj resembling a human being in

appearance ▷ n (in science fiction) a robot or creature resembling a human being
HUMANOIDS > HUMANOID
HUMANS > HUMAN
HUMAS > HUMA
HUMATE n decomposed plants used as fertilizer
HUMATES > HUMATE
HUMBLE adj conscious of one's failings ▷ vb cause to feel humble, humiliate
HUMBLEBEE another name for the > BUMBLEBEE
HUMBLED > HUMBLE
HUMBLER > HUMBLE
HUMBLERS > HUMBLE
HUMBLES > HUMBLE
HUMBLESSE n quality of being humble
HUMBLEST > HUMBLE
HUMBLING > HUMBLE
HUMBLINGS > HUMBLE
HUMBLY > HUMBLE
HUMBUCKER n twin-coil guitar pick-up
HUMBUG n hard striped peppermint sweet ▷ vb cheat or deceive (someone)
HUMBUGGED > HUMBUG
HUMBUGGER > HUMBUG
HUMBUGS > HUMBUG
HUMBUZZ n type of beetle
HUMBUZZES > HUMBUZZ
HUMDINGER n excellent person or thing
HUMDRUM adj ordinary, dull ▷ n monotonous routine, task, or person
HUMDRUMS > HUMDRUM
HUMECT vb make moist
HUMECTANT adj producing moisture ▷ n substance added to another substance to keep it moist
HUMECTATE vb produce moisture
HUMECTED > HUMECT
HUMECTING > HUMECT
HUMECTIVE > HUMECT
HUMECTS > HUMECT
HUMEFIED > HUMEFY
HUMEFIES > HUMEFY
HUMEFY same as > HUMIFY
HUMEFYING > HUMEFY
HUMERAL adj of or relating to the humerus ▷ n silk shawl worn by a priest at High Mass; humeral veil
HUMERALS > HUMERAL
HUMERI > HUMERUS
HUMERUS n bone from the shoulder to the elbow
HUMF same as > HUMPH
HUMFED > HUMF
HUMFING > HUMF
HUMFS > HUMF
HUMHUM n Indian cotton cloth
HUMHUMS > HUMHUM
HUMIC adj of, relating to, derived from, or resembling humus
HUMICOLE n any plant that thrives on humus
HUMICOLES > HUMICOLE
HUMID adj damp and hot

HUMIDER > HUMID
HUMIDEST > HUMID
HUMIDEX n system of measuring discomfort showing the combined effect of humidity and temperature
HUMIDEXES > HUMIDEX
HUMIDICES > HUMIDEX
HUMIDIFY vb make the air in (a room) more humid or damp
HUMIDITY n dampness
HUMIDLY > HUMID
HUMIDNESS > HUMID
HUMIDOR n humid place or container for storing cigars, tobacco, etc
HUMIDORS > HUMIDOR
HUMIFIED > HUMIFY
HUMIFIES > HUMIFY
HUMIFY vb convert or be converted into humus
HUMIFYING > HUMIFY
HUMILIANT adj humiliating
HUMILIATE vb lower the dignity or hurt the pride of
HUMILITY n quality of being humble
HUMINT n human intelligence
HUMINTS > HUMINT
HUMITE n mineral containing magnesium
HUMITES > HUMITE
HUMITURE n measure of both humidity and temperature
HUMITURES > HUMITURE
HUMLIE n hornless cow
HUMLIES > HUMLIE
HUMMABLE > HUM
HUMMAUM same as > HAMMAM
HUMMAUMS > HUMMAUM
HUMMED > HUM
HUMMEL adj (of cattle) hornless ▷ vb remove horns from
HUMMELLED > HUMMEL
HUMMELLER > HUMMEL
HUMMELS > HUMMEL
HUMMER > HUM
HUMMERS > HUM
HUMMING > HUM
HUMMINGS > HUM
HUMMOCK n very small hill ▷ vb form into a hummock or hummocks
HUMMOCKED > HUMMOCK
HUMMOCKS > HUMMOCK
HUMMOCKY > HUMMOCK
HUMMUM same as > HAMMAM
HUMMUMS > HUMMUM
HUMMUS n creamy dip originating in the Middle East, made from puréed chickpeas
HUMMUSES > HUMMUS
HUMOGEN n type of fertilizer
HUMOGENS > HUMOGEN
HUMONGOUS same as > HUMUNGOUS
HUMOR same as > HUMOUR
HUMORAL adj denoting or relating to a type of immunity caused by free

antibodies circulating in the blood
HUMORALLY > HUMORAL
HUMORED > HUMOR
HUMORESK n humorous musical composition
HUMORESKS > HUMORESK
HUMORFUL > HUMOR
HUMORING > HUMOR
HUMORIST n writer or entertainer who uses humour in his or her work
HUMORISTS > HUMORIST
HUMORLESS > HUMOR
HUMOROUS adj amusing, esp in a witty or clever way
HUMORS > HUMOR
HUMORSOME same as > HUMOURSOME
HUMOUR n ability to say or perceive things that are amusing ▷ vb be kind and indulgent to
HUMOURED > HUMOUR
HUMOURFUL > HUMOUR
HUMOURING > HUMOUR
HUMOURS > HUMOUR
HUMOUS same as > HUMUS
HUMP n raised piece of ground ▷ vb carry or heave
HUMPBACK same as > HUNCHBACK
HUMPBACKS > HUMPBACK
HUMPED > HUMP
HUMPEN n old German drinking glass
HUMPENS > HUMPEN
HUMPER > HUMP
HUMPERS > HUMP
HUMPH interj exclamation of annoyance or scepticism ▷ vb exclaim humph
HUMPHED > HUMPH
HUMPHING > HUMPH
HUMPHS > HUMPH
HUMPIER > HUMPY
HUMPIES > HUMPY
HUMPIEST > HUMPY
HUMPINESS > HUMPY
HUMPING > HUMP
HUMPLESS > HUMP
HUMPLIKE > HUMP
HUMPS > HUMP
HUMPTIES > HUMPTY
HUMPTY n low padded seat
HUMPY adj full of humps ▷ n primitive hut
HUMS > HUM
HUMSTRUM n medieval musical instrument
HUMSTRUMS > HUMSTRUM
HUMUNGOUS adj very large
HUMUS n decomposing vegetable and animal mould in the soil
HUMUSES > HUMUS
HUMUSY > HUMUS
HUMVEE n military vehicle
HUMVEES > HUMVEE
HUN n member of any of several Asiatic nomadic peoples speaking Mongoloid or Turkic languages
HUNCH n feeling or suspicion not based on facts ▷ vb draw (one's shoulders) up

or together
HUNCHBACK n person with an abnormal curvature of the spine
HUNCHED > HUNCH
HUNCHES > HUNCH
HUNCHING > HUNCH
HUNDRED n ten times ten ▷ adj amounting to a hundred
HUNDREDER n inhabitant of a hundred
HUNDREDOR same as > HUNDREDER
HUNDREDS > HUNDRED
HUNDREDTH adj being the ordinal number of 100 in numbering or counting order, position, time, etc ▷ n one of 100 approximately equal parts of something
HUNG > HANG
HUNGAN same as > HOUNGAN
HUNGANS > HUNGAN
HUNGER n discomfort or weakness from lack of food ▷ vb want very much
HUNGERED > HUNGER
HUNGERFUL adj hungry
HUNGERING > HUNGER
HUNGERLY adj hungry
HUNGERS > HUNGER
HUNGOVER adj suffering from hangover
HUNGRIER > HUNGRY
HUNGRIEST > HUNGRY
HUNGRILY > HUNGRY
HUNGRY adj desiring food
HUNH same as > HUH
HUNK n large piece
HUNKER vb squat
HUNKERED > HUNKER
HUNKERING > HUNKER
HUNKERS pl n haunches
HUNKEY n person of Hungarian descent
HUNKEYS > HUNKEY
HUNKIE same as > HUNKEY
HUNKIER > HUNKY
HUNKIES > HUNKY
HUNKIEST > HUNKY
HUNKS n crotchety old person
HUNKSES > HUNKS
HUNKY adj excellent
HUNNISH > HUN
HUNS > HUN
HUNT vb seek out and kill (wild animals) for food or sport ▷ n hunting
HUNTABLE > HUNT
HUNTAWAY n sheepdog trained to drive sheep by barking
HUNTAWAYS > HUNTAWAY
HUNTED adj harassed and worn
HUNTEDLY > HUNT
HUNTER n person or animal that hunts wild animals for food or sport
HUNTERS > HUNTER
HUNTING n pursuit and killing or capture of game and wild animals, regarded as a sport

h

HUNTINGS > HUNTING
HUNTRESS *same as* > HUNTER
HUNTS > HUNT
HUNTSMAN *n* man who hunts wild animals, esp foxes
HUNTSMEN > HUNTSMAN
HUP *vb* cry hup to get a horse to move
HUPIRO *in New Zealand English, same as* > STINKWOOD
HUPPAH *variant spelling of* > CHUPPAH
HUPPAHS > HUPPAH
HUPPED > HUP
HUPPING > HUP
HUPS > HUP
HURCHEON *same as* > URCHIN
HURCHEONS > HURCHEON
HURDEN *same as* > HARDEN
HURDENS > HURDEN
HURDIES *pl n* buttocks or haunches
HURDLE *n* light barrier for jumping over in some races ▷ *vb* jump over (something)
HURDLED > HURDLE
HURDLER > HURDLE
HURDLERS > HURDLE
HURDLES > HURDLE
HURDLING > HURDLE
HURDLINGS > HURDLE
HURDS *same as* > HARDS
HURL *vb* throw or utter forcefully ▷ *n* act or an instance of hurling
HURLBAT *same as* > WHIRLBAT
HURLBATS > HURLBAT
HURLED > HURL
HURLER > HURL
HURLERS > HURL
HURLEY *n* another word for the game of hurling
HURLEYS > HURLEY
HURLIES > HURLY
HURLING *n* Irish game like hockey
HURLINGS > HURLING
HURLS > HURL
HURLY *n* wheeled barrow
HURRA *same as* > HURRAH
HURRAED > HURRA
HURRAH *interj* exclamation of joy or applause ▷ *n* cheer of joy or victory ▷ *vb* shout "hurrah"
HURRAHED > HURRAH
HURRAHING > HURRAH
HURRAHS > HURRAH
HURRAING > HURRA
HURRAS > HURRA
HURRAY *same as* > HURRAH
HURRAYED > HURRAY
HURRAYING > HURRAY
HURRAYS > HURRAY
HURRICANE *n* very strong, often destructive, wind or storm
HURRICANO *same as* > HURRICANE
HURRIED *adj* done quickly or too quickly
HURRIEDLY > HURRIED
HURRIER > HURRY

HURRIERS > HURRY
HURRIES > HURRY
HURRY *vb* (cause to) move or act very quickly ▷ *n* doing something quickly or the need to do something quickly
HURRYING > HURRY
HURRYINGS > HURRY
HURST *n* wood
HURSTS > HURST
HURT *vb* cause physical or mental pain to ▷ *n* physical or mental pain ▷ *adj* injured or pained
HURTER > HURT
HURTERS > HURT
HURTFUL *adj* unkind
HURTFULLY > HURTFUL
HURTING > HURT
HURTLE *vb* move quickly or violently
HURTLED > HURTLE
HURTLES > HURTLE
HURTLESS *adj* uninjured
HURTLING > HURTLE
HURTS > HURT
HUSBAND *n* woman's partner in marriage ▷ *vb* use economically
HUSBANDED > HUSBAND
HUSBANDER > HUSBAND
HUSBANDLY > HUSBAND
HUSBANDRY *n* farming
HUSBANDS > HUSBAND
HUSH *vb* make or be silent ▷ *n* stillness or silence ▷ *interj* plea or demand for silence
HUSHABIED > HUSHABY
HUSHABIES > HUSHABY
HUSHABY *interj* used in quietening a baby or child to sleep ▷ *n* lullaby ▷ *vb* quieten to sleep
HUSHED > HUSH
HUSHEDLY > HUSH
HUSHER *same as* > USHER
HUSHERED > HUSHER
HUSHERING > HUSHER
HUSHERS > HUSHER
HUSHES > HUSH
HUSHFUL *adj* quiet
HUSHIER > HUSHY
HUSHIEST > HUSHY
HUSHING > HUSH
HUSHPUPPY *n* snack of deep-fried dough
HUSHY *adj* secret
HUSK *n* outer covering of certain seeds and fruits ▷ *vb* remove the husk from
HUSKED > HUSK
HUSKER > HUSK
HUSKERS > HUSK
HUSKIER > HUSKY
HUSKIES > HUSKY
HUSKIEST > HUSKY
HUSKILY > HUSKY
HUSKINESS > HUSKY
HUSKING > HUSK
HUSKINGS > HUSK
HUSKLIKE > HUSK
HUSKS > HUSK
HUSKY *adj* slightly hoarse ▷ *n* Arctic sledge dog with thick hair and a curled tail

HUSO *n* sturgeon
HUSOS > HUSO
HUSS *n* flesh of the European dogfish, when used as food
HUSSAR *n* lightly armed cavalry soldier
HUSSARS > HUSSAR
HUSSES > HUSS
HUSSIES > HUSSY
HUSSIF *n* sewing kit
HUSSIFS > HUSSIF
HUSSY *n* immodest or promiscuous woman
HUSTINGS *pl n* political campaigns and speeches before an election
HUSTLE *vb* push about, jostle ▷ *n* lively activity or bustle
HUSTLED > HUSTLE
HUSTLER > HUSTLE
HUSTLERS > HUSTLE
HUSTLES > HUSTLE
HUSTLING > HUSTLE
HUSTLINGS > HUSTLE
HUSWIFE *same as* > HOUSEWIFE
HUSWIFES > HUSWIFE
HUSWIVES > HUSWIFE
HUT *n* small house, shelter, or shed
HUTCH *n* cage for pet rabbits etc ▷ *vb* store or keep in or as if in a hutch
HUTCHED > HUTCH
HUTCHES > HUTCH
HUTCHIE *n* groundsheet draped over an upright stick, used as a temporary shelter
HUTCHIES > HUTCHIE
HUTCHING > HUTCH
HUTIA *n* rodent of West Indies
HUTIAS > HUTIA
HUTLIKE > HUT
HUTMENT *n* number or group of huts
HUTMENTS > HUTMENT
HUTS > HUT
HUTTED > HUT
HUTTING > HUT
HUTTINGS > HUT
HUTZPA *same as* > HUTZPAH
HUTZPAH *variant spelling of* > CHUTZPAH
HUTZPAHS > HUTZPAH
HUTZPAS > HUTZPA
HUZOOR *n* person of rank in India
HUZOORS > HUZOOR
HUZZA *same as* > HUZZAH
HUZZAED > HUZZA
HUZZAH *archaic word for* > HURRAH
HUZZAHED > HUZZAH
HUZZAHING > HUZZAH
HUZZAHS > HUZZAH
HUZZAING > HUZZA
HUZZAS > HUZZA
HUZZIES > HUZZY
HUZZY *same as* > HUSSY
HWAN *another name for* > WON
HWYL *n* emotional fervour, as in the recitation of poetry

HWYLS > HWYL
HYACINE *same as* > HYACINTH
HYACINES > HYACINE
HYACINTH *n* sweet-smelling spring flower that grows from a bulb
HYACINTHS > HYACINTH
HYAENA *same as* > HYENA
HYAENAS > HYAENA
HYAENIC > HYAENA
HYALIN *n* glassy translucent substance, such as occurs in certain degenerative skin conditions or in hyaline cartilage
HYALINE *adj* clear and translucent, with no fibres or granules ▷ *n* glassy transparent surface
HYALINES > HYALINE
HYALINISE *same as* > HYALINIZE
HYALINIZE *vb* give a glassy consistency to
HYALINS > HYALIN
HYALITE *n* clear and colourless variety of opal in globular form
HYALITES > HYALITE
HYALOGEN *n* insoluble substance in body structures
HYALOGENS > HYALOGEN
HYALOID *adj* clear and transparent ▷ *n* delicate transparent membrane enclosing the vitreous humour of the eye
HYALOIDS > HYALOID
HYALONEMA *n* species of sponge
HYBRID *n* offspring of two plants or animals of different species ▷ *adj* of mixed origin
HYBRIDISE *same as* > HYBRIDIZE
HYBRIDISM > HYBRID
HYBRIDIST > HYBRID
HYBRIDITY > HYBRID
HYBRIDIZE *vb* produce or cause (species) to produce hybrids
HYBRIDOMA *n* hybrid cell formed by the fusion of two different types of cell, esp one capable of producing antibodies, but of limited lifespan, fused with an immortal tumour cell
HYBRIDOUS > HYBRID
HYBRIDS > HYBRID
HYBRIS *same as* > HUBRIS
HYBRISES > HYBRIS
HYBRISTIC > HYBRIS
HYDANTOIN *n* colourless odourless crystalline compound present in beet molasses and used in the manufacture of pharmaceuticals and synthetic resins
HYDATHODE *n* pore in plants, esp on the leaves, specialized for excreting water

h

HYDATID *n* cyst containing tapeworm larvae

HYDATIDS > HYDATID

HYDATOID *adj* watery

HYDRA *n* mythical many-headed water serpent

HYDRACID *n* acid, such as hydrochloric acid, that does not contain oxygen

HYDRACIDS > HYDRACID

HYDRAE > HYDRA

HYDRAEMIA *n* wateriness of blood

HYDRAGOG *n* drug that removes water

HYDRAGOGS > HYDRAGOG

HYDRANGEA *n* ornamental shrub with clusters of pink, blue, or white flowers

HYDRANT *n* outlet from a water main with a nozzle for a hose

HYDRANTH *n* polyp in a colony of hydrozoan coelenterates that is specialized for feeding rather than reproduction

HYDRANTHS > HYDRANTH

HYDRANTS > HYDRANT

HYDRAS > HYDRA

HYDRASE *n* enzyme that removes water

HYDRASES > HYDRASE

HYDRASTIS *n* any of various Japanese and E North American plants, such as goldenseal, having showy foliage and ornamental red fruits

HYDRATE *n* chemical compound of water with another substance ▷ *vb* treat or impregnate with water

HYDRATED *adj* (of a compound) chemically bonded to water molecules

HYDRATES > HYDRATE

HYDRATING > HYDRATE

HYDRATION > HYDRATE

HYDRATOR > HYDRATE

HYDRATORS > HYDRATE

HYDRAULIC *adj* operated by pressure forced through a pipe by a liquid such as water or oil

HYDRAZIDE *n* any of a class of chemical compounds that result when hydrogen in hydrazine or any of its derivatives is replaced by an acid radical

HYDRAZINE *n* colourless basic liquid made from sodium hypochlorite and ammonia: a strong reducing agent, used chiefly as a rocket fuel

HYDRAZOIC as in *hydrazoic acid* colourless highly explosive liquid

HYDREMIA *same as* > HYDRAEMIA

HYDREMIAS > HYDREMIA

HYDRIA *n* (in ancient Greece and Rome) a large water jar

HYDRIAE > HYDRIA

HYDRIC *adj* of or containing hydrogen

HYDRID *same as* > HYDROID

HYDRIDE *n* compound of hydrogen with another element

HYDRIDES > HYDRIDE

HYDRIDS > HYDRID

HYDRILLA *n* aquatic plant used as an oxygenator in aquaria and pools

HYDRILLAS > HYDRILLA

HYDRIODIC as in *hydriodic acid* colourless or pale yellow aqueous solution of hydrogen iodide: a strong acid

HYDRO *n* hotel offering facilities for hydropathy ▷ *adj* electricity as supplied to a residence, business, etc

HYDROCAST *n* gathering of water samples for analysis

HYDROCELE *n* abnormal collection of fluid in any saclike space, esp around the testicles

HYDROFOIL *n* fast light boat with its hull raised out of the water on one or more pairs of fins

HYDROGEL *n* gel in which the liquid constituent is water

HYDROGELS > HYDROGEL

HYDROGEN *n* light flammable colourless gas that combines with oxygen to form water > HYDROGENISATION > HYDROGENIZATION

HYDROGENS > HYDROGEN

HYDROID *adj* of or relating to an order of colonial hydrozoan coelenterates that have the polyp phase dominant ▷ *n* hydroid colony or individual

HYDROIDS > HYDROID

HYDROLASE *n* enzyme, such as an esterase, that controls hydrolysis

HYDROLOGY *n* study of the distribution, conservation, and use of the water of the earth and its atmosphere

HYDROLYSE *vb* subject to or undergo hydrolysis

HYDROLYTE *n* substance subjected to hydrolysis

HYDROLYZE *same as* > HYDROLYSE

HYDROMA *same as* > HYGROMA

HYDROMAS > HYDROMA

HYDROMATA > HYDROMA

HYDROMEL *n* another word for 'mead' (the drink)

HYDROMELS > HYDROMEL

HYDRONAUT *n* person trained to operate deep submergence vessels

HYDRONIC *adj* using hot water in heating system

HYDRONIUM as in *hydronium ion* positive ion, formed by the attachment of a proton to a water molecule: occurs in solutions of acids and behaves like a hydrogen ion

HYDROPATH > HYDROPATHY

HYDROPIC > HYDROPSY

HYDROPS *n* anaemia in a fetus

HYDROPSES > HYDROPS

HYDROPSY *same as* > DROPSY

HYDROPTIC > HYDROPSY

HYDROPULT *n* type of water pump

HYDROS > HYDRO

HYDROSERE *n* sere that begins in an aquatic environment

HYDROSKI *n* hydrofoil used on some seaplanes to provide extra lift when taking off

HYDROSKIS > HYDROSKI

HYDROSOL *n* sol that has water as its liquid phase

HYDROSOLS > HYDROSOL

HYDROSOMA *same as* > HYDROSOME

HYDROSOME *n* body of a colonial hydrozoan

HYDROSTAT *n* device that detects the presence of water as a prevention against drying out, overflow, etc, esp one used as a warning in a steam boiler

HYDROUS *adj* containing water

HYDROVANE *n* vane on a seaplane conferring stability on water (a sponson) or facilitating take-off (a hydrofoil)

HYDROXIDE *n* compound containing a hydroxyl group or ion

HYDROXY *adj* (of a chemical compound) containing one or more hydroxyl groups

HYDROXYL *adj* of or containing the monovalent group –OH or the ion OH⁻ ▷ *n* of, consisting of, or containing the monovalent group -OH or the ion OH⁻

HYDROXYLS > HYDROXYL

HYDROZOA > HYDROZOON

HYDROZOAN *n* any colonial or solitary coelenterate of the class *Hydrozoa*, which includes the hydra, Portuguese man-of-war, and the sertularians ▷ *adj* of, relating to, or belonging to the *Hydrozoa*

HYDROZOON *same as* > HYDROZOAN

HYDYNE *n* type of rocket fuel

HYDYNES > HYDYNE

HYE *same as* > HIE

HYED > HYE

HYEING > HYE

HYEN *same as* > HYENA

HYENA *n* scavenging doglike mammal of Africa and S Asia

HYENAS > HYENA

HYENIC > HYENA

HYENINE *adj* of hyenas

HYENOID *adj* of or like hyenas

HYENS > HYEN

HYES > HYE

HYETAL *adj* of or relating to rain, rainfall, or rainy regions

HYETOLOGY *n* study of rainfall

HYGEIST *same as* > HYGIENIST

HYGEISTS > HYGEIST

HYGIEIST *same as* > HYGIENIST

HYGIEISTS > HYGIEIST

HYGIENE *n* principles and practice of health and cleanliness

HYGIENES > HYGIENE

HYGIENIC *adj* promoting health or cleanliness

HYGIENICS *same as* > HYGIENE

HYGIENIST *n* person skilled in the practice of hygiene

HYGRISTOR *n* electronic component the resistance of which varies with humidity

HYGRODEIK *n* type of thermometer

HYGROLOGY *n* study of humidity of air

HYGROMA *n* swelling in the soft tissue that occurs over a joint, usually caused by repeated injury

HYGROMAS > HYGROMA

HYGROMATA > HYGROMA

HYGROPHIL *adj* moisture-loving

HYGROSTAT *same as* > HUMIDISTAT

HYING > HIE

HYKE *same as* > HAIK

HYKES > HYKE

HYLA *n* type of tropical American tree frog

HYLAS > HYLA

HYLDING *same as* > HILDING

HYLDINGS > HYLDING

HYLE *n* wood

HYLEG *n* dominant planet when someone is born

HYLEGS > HYLEG

HYLES > HYLE

HYLIC *adj* solid

HYLICISM *n* materialism

HYLICISMS > HYLICISM

HYLICIST > HYLICISM

HYLICISTS > HYLICISM

HYLISM *same as* > HYLICISM

HYLISMS > HYLISM

HYLIST > HYLISM

HYLISTS > HYLISM

HYLOBATE *n* gibbon

HYLOBATES > HYLOBATE

HYLOIST *n* materialist

HYLOISTS > HYLOIST

HYLOPHYTE *n* plant that grows in woods

HYLOZOIC > HYLOZOISM

HYLOZOISM *n* philosophical doctrine that life is one of the properties of matter

HYLOZOIST > HYLOZOISM

h

HYMEN n membrane partly covering the opening of a girl's vagina, which breaks before puberty or at the first occurrence of sexual intercourse

HYMENAEAL same as > HYMENEAL

HYMENAEAN > HYMEN

HYMENAL > HYMEN

HYMENEAL adj of or relating to marriage ▷ n wedding song or poem

HYMENEALS > HYMENEAL

HYMENEAN > HYMEN

HYMENIA > HYMENIUM

HYMENIAL > HYMENIUM

HYMENIUM n (in basidiomycetous and ascomycetous fungi) a layer of cells some of which produce the spores

HYMENIUMS > HYMENIUM

HYMENS > HYMEN

HYMN n Christian song of praise sung to God or a saint ▷ vb express (praises, thanks, etc) by singing hymns

HYMNAL n book of hymns ▷ adj of, relating to, or characteristic of hymns

HYMNALS > HYMNAL

HYMNARIES > HYMNARY

HYMNARY same as > HYMNAL

HYMNBOOK n book containing the words and music of hymns

HYMNBOOKS > HYMNBOOK

HYMNED > HYMN

HYMNIC > HYMN

HYMNING > HYMN

HYMNIST n person who composes hymns

HYMNISTS > HYMNIST

HYMNLESS > HYMN

HYMNLIKE > HYMN

HYMNODIES > HYMNODY

HYMNODIST same as > HYMNIST

HYMNODY n composition or singing of hymns

HYMNOLOGY same as > HYMNODY

HYMNS > HYMN

HYNDE same as > HIND

HYNDES > HYNDE

HYOID adj of or relating to the hyoid bone ▷ n horseshoe-shaped bone that lies at the base of the tongue and above the thyroid cartilage

HYOIDAL adj of or relating to the hyoid bone

HYOIDEAN same as > HYOIDAL

HYOIDS > HYOID

HYOSCINE another name for > SCOPOLAMINE

HYOSCINES > HYOSCINE

HYP same as > HYPOTENUSE

HYPALGIA n reduced ability to feel pain

HYPALGIAS > HYPALGIA

HYPALLAGE n figure of speech in which the natural relations of two words in a statement are interchanged, as in *the fire spread the wind*

HYPANTHIA n plural of hypanthium: cup-shaped receptacle of perigynous or epigynous flowers

HYPATE n string of lyre

HYPATES > HYPATE

HYPE n intensive or exaggerated publicity or sales promotion ▷ vb promote (a product) using intensive or exaggerated publicity

HYPED > HYPE

HYPER > HYPE

HYPERACID adj having excess acidity

HYPERARID adj extremely dry

HYPERBOLA n curve produced when a cone is cut by a plane at a steeper angle to its base than its side

HYPERBOLE n deliberate exaggeration for effect

HYPERCUBE n figure in a space of four or more dimensions having all its sides equal and all its angles right angles

HYPEREMIA n excessive blood in an organ or part

HYPEREMIC > HYPEREMIA

HYPERFINE as in *hyperfine structure* splitting of a spectral line of an atom or molecule into two or more closely spaced components as a result of interaction of the electrons with the magnetic moments of the nuclei

HYPERGAMY n custom that forbids a woman to marry a man of lower social status

HYPERGOL n type of fuel

HYPERGOLS > HYPERGOL

HYPERICUM n herbaceous plant or shrub

HYPERLINK n link from a hypertext file that gives users instant access to related material in another file ▷ vb link (files) in this way

HYPERMART n very large supermarket

HYPERNOVA n exploding star that produces even more energy and light than a supernova

HYPERNYM n superordinate

HYPERNYMS > HYPERNYM

HYPERNYMY > HYPERNYM

HYPERON n any baryon that is not a nucleon

HYPERONS > HYPERON

HYPEROPE n person with hyperopia

HYPEROPES > HYPEROPE

HYPEROPIA n inability to see near objects clearly because the images received by the eye are focused behind the retina

HYPEROPIC > HYPEROPIA

HYPERPNEA n increase in breathing rate

HYPERPURE adj extremely pure

HYPERREAL adj involving or characterized by particularly realistic graphic representation ▷ n that which constitutes hyperreality

HYPERS > HYPE

HYPERTEXT n computer software and hardware that allows users to store and view text and move between related items easily

HYPES > HYPE

HYPESTER n person or organization that gives an idea or product intense publicity in order to promote it

HYPESTERS > HYPESTER

HYPETHRAL adj having no roof

HYPHA n any of the filaments that constitute the body (mycelium) of a fungus

HYPHAE > HYPHA

HYPHAL > HYPHA

HYPHEMIA n bleeding inside eye

HYPHEMIAS > HYPHEMIA

HYPHEN n punctuation mark (-) indicating that two words or syllables are connected ▷ vb hyphenate

HYPHENATE vb separate (words) with a hyphen

HYPHENED > HYPHEN

HYPHENIC > HYPHEN

HYPHENING > HYPHEN

HYPHENISE same as > HYPHENIZE

HYPHENISM > HYPHEN

HYPHENIZE same as > HYPHENATE

HYPHENS > HYPHEN

HYPING > HYPE

HYPINGS > HYPE

HYPINOSES > HYPINOSIS

HYPINOSIS n protein deficiency in blood

HYPNIC n sleeping drug

HYPNICS > HYPNIC

HYPNOGENY n hypnosis

HYPNOID adj of or relating to a state resembling sleep or hypnosis

HYPNOIDAL same as > HYPNOID

HYPNOLOGY n study of sleep and hypnosis

HYPNONE n sleeping drug

HYPNONES > HYPNONE

HYPNOSES > HYPNOSIS

HYPNOSIS n artificially induced state of relaxation in which the mind is more than usually receptive to suggestion

HYPNOTEE n person being hypnotized

HYPNOTEES > HYPNOTEE

HYPNOTIC adj of or (as if) producing hypnosis ▷ n drug that induces sleep

HYPNOTICS > HYPNOTIC

HYPNOTISE same as > HYPNOTIZE

HYPNOTISM n inducing hypnosis in someone

HYPNOTIST n person skilled in the theory and practice of hypnosis

HYPNOTIZE vb induce hypnosis in (a person)

HYPNOTOID adj like hypnosis

HYPNUM n species of moss

HYPNUMS > HYPNUM

HYPO vb inject with a hypodermic syringe

HYPOACID adj abnormally acidic

HYPOBARIC adj below normal pressure

HYPOBLAST n inner layer of an embryo at an early stage of development that becomes the endoderm at gastrulation

HYPOBOLE n act of anticipating objection

HYPOBOLES > HYPOBOLE

HYPOCAUST n ancient Roman heating system in which hot air circulated under the floor and between double walls

HYPOCIST n type of juice

HYPOCISTS > HYPOCIST

HYPOCOTYL n part of an embryo plant between the cotyledons and the radicle

HYPOCRISY n (instance of) pretence of having standards or beliefs that are contrary to one's real character or actual behaviour

HYPOCRITE n person who pretends to be what he or she is not

HYPODERM n layer of thick-walled tissue in some plants

HYPODERMA n layer of skin tissue

HYPODERMS > HYPODERM

HYPOED > HYPO

HYPOGAEA > HYPOGAEUM

HYPOGAEAL > HYPOGAEUM

HYPOGAEAN > HYPOGAEUM

HYPOGAEUM same as > HYPOGEUM

HYPOGEA > HYPOGEUM

HYPOGEAL adj occurring or living below the surface of the ground

HYPOGEAN > HYPOGEUM

HYPOGENE adj formed, taking place, or originating beneath the surface of the earth

HYPOGENIC > HYPOGENE

HYPOGEOUS same as > HYPOGEAL

HYPOGEUM n underground

vault, esp one used for burials

HYPOGYNY *adj* having the gynoecium above the other floral parts

HYPOID as in *hypoid gear* gear having a tooth form generated by a hypocycloidal curve; used extensively in motor vehicle transmissions to withstand a high surface loading

HYPOING > HYPO

HYPOMANIA *n* abnormal condition of extreme excitement, milder than mania but characterized by great optimism and overactivity and often by reckless spending of money

HYPOMANIC > HYPOMANIA

HYPOMORPH *n* mutant gene

HYPONASTY *n* increased growth of the lower surface of a plant part, resulting in an upward bending of the part

HYPONEA *same as* > HYPOPNEA

HYPONEAS > HYPONEA

HYPONOIA *n* underlying meaning

HYPONOIAS > HYPONOIA

HYPONYM *n* word whose meaning is included in that of another word

HYPONYMS > HYPONYM

HYPONYMY > HYPONYM

HYPOPHYGE *another name for* > APOPHYGE

HYPOPLOID *adj* having or designating a chromosome number that is less than a multiple of the haploid number

HYPOPNEA *same as* > HYPOPNOEA

HYPOPNEAS > HYPOPNEA

HYPOPNEIC > HYPOPNEA

HYPOPNOEA *n* abnormally shallow breathing, usually accompanied by a decrease in the breathing rate

HYPOPYON *n* pus in eye

HYPOPYONS > HYPOPYON

HYPOS > HYPO

HYPOSTOME *n* invertebrate body part

HYPOSTYLE *adj* having a roof supported by columns ▷ *n* building constructed in this way

HYPOTAXES > HYPOTAXIS

HYPOTAXIS *n* subordination of one clause to another by a conjunction

HYPOTHEC *n* charge on property in favour of a creditor

HYPOTHECA *n* inner and younger layer of the cell wall of a diatom

HYPOTHECS > HYPOTHEC

HYPOTONIA *n* state of being hypnotized

HYPOTONIC *adj* (of muscles) lacking normal tone or tension

HYPOXEMIA *n* lack of oxygen in blood

HYPOXEMIC > HYPOXEMIA

HYPOXIA *n* deficiency in the amount of oxygen delivered to the body tissues

HYPOXIAS > HYPOXIA

HYPOXIC > HYPOXIA

HYPPED > HYP

HYPPING > HYP

HYPS > HYP

HYPURAL *adj* below the tail

HYRACES > HYRAX

HYRACOID *adj* of, relating to, or belonging to the mammalian order *Hyracoidea*, which contains the hyraxes ▷ *n hyrax*

HYRACOIDS > HYRACOID

HYRAX *n* type of hoofed rodent-like animal of Africa and Asia

HYRAXES > HYRAX

HYSON *n* Chinese green tea

HYSONS > HYSON

HYSSOP *n* sweet-smelling herb used in folk medicine

HYSSOPS > HYSSOP

HYSTERIA *n* state of uncontrolled excitement, anger, or panic

HYSTERIAS > HYSTERIA

HYSTERIC *adj* of or suggesting hysteria

HYSTERICS *pl n* attack of hysteria

HYSTEROID *adj* resembling hysteria

HYTE *adj* insane

HYTHE *same as* > HITHE

HYTHES > HYTHE

h

Ii

IAMB n metrical foot of two syllables, a short one followed by a long one

IAMBI > IAMBUS

IAMBIC adj written in metrical units of one short and one long syllable ▷ n iambic foot, line, or stanza

IAMBICS > IAMBIC

IAMBIST n one who writes iambs

IAMBISTS > IAMBIST

IAMBS > IAMB

IAMBUS same as > IAMB

IAMBUSES > IAMBUS

IANTHINE adj violet

IATRIC adj relating to medicine or physicians

IATRICAL same as > IATRIC

IATROGENY n disease caused by medical intervention

IBERIS n plant with white or purple flowers

IBERISES > IBERIS

IBEX n wild goat with large backward-curving horns

IBEXES > IBEX

IBICES > IBEX

IBIDEM adv in the same place

IBIS n large wading bird with long legs

IBISES > IBIS

IBOGAINE n dopamine blocker

IBOGAINES > IBOGAINE

IBUPROFEN n drug that relieves pain and reduces inflammation

ICE n water in the solid state, formed by freezing liquid water ▷ vb form or cause to form ice

ICEBALL n ball of ice

ICEBALLS > ICEBALL

ICEBERG n large floating mass of ice

ICEBERGS > ICEBERG

ICEBLINK n yellowish-white reflected glare in the sky over an ice field

ICEBLINKS > ICEBLINK

ICEBOAT n boat that breaks up bodies of ice in water

ICEBOATER > ICEBOAT

ICEBOATS > ICEBOAT

ICEBOUND adj covered or made immobile by ice

ICEBOX n refrigerator

ICEBOXES > ICEBOX

ICECAP n mass of ice permanently covering an area

ICECAPPED adj having an icecap

ICECAPS > ICECAP

ICED adj covered with icing

ICEFALL n very steep part of a glacier that has deep crevasses and resembles a frozen waterfall

ICEFALLS > ICEFALL

ICEFIELD n very large flat expanse of ice floating in the sea; large ice floe

ICEFIELDS > ICEFIELD

ICEHOUSE n building for storing ice

ICEHOUSES > ICEHOUSE

ICEKHANA n motor race on a frozen lake

ICEKHANAS > ICEKHANA

ICELESS > ICE

ICELIKE > ICE

ICEMAKER n device for making ice

ICEMAKERS > ICEMAKER

ICEMAN n person who sells or delivers ice

ICEMEN > ICEMAN

ICEPACK n bag or folded cloth containing ice, applied to a part of the body, esp the head, to cool, reduce swelling, etc

ICEPACKS > ICEPACK

ICER n person who ices cakes

ICERS > ICER

ICES > ICE

ICESTONE n cryolite

ICESTONES > ICESTONE

ICEWINE n dessert wine made from grapes that have frozen before being harvested

ICEWINES > ICEWINE

ICH archaic form of > EKE

ICHABOD interj the glory has departed

ICHED > ICH

ICHES > ICH

ICHING > ICH

ICHNEUMON n greyish-brown mongoose

ICHNITE n trace fossil

ICHNITES > ICHNITE

ICHNOLITE same as > ICHNITE

ICHNOLOGY n study of trace fossils

ICHOR n fluid said to flow in the veins of the gods

ICHOROUS > ICHOR

ICHORS > ICHOR

ICHS > ICH

ICHTHIC same as > ICHTHYIC

ICHTHYIC adj of, relating to, or characteristic of fishes

ICHTHYOID adj resembling a fish ▷ n fishlike vertebrate

ICHTHYS n early Christian emblem

ICHTHYSES > ICHTHYS

ICICLE n tapering spike of ice hanging where water has dripped

ICICLED adj covered with icicles

ICICLES > ICICLE

ICIER > ICY

ICIEST > ICY

ICILY adv in an icy or reserved manner

ICINESS n condition of being icy or very cold

ICINESSES > ICINESS

ICING n mixture of sugar and water etc, used to cover and decorate cakes

ICINGS > ICING

ICK interj expression of disgust

ICKER n ear of corn

ICKERS > ICKER

ICKIER > ICKY

ICKIEST > ICKY

ICKILY > ICKY

ICKINESS > ICKY

ICKLE ironically childish word for > LITTLE

ICKLER > ICKLE

ICKLEST > ICKLE

ICKY adj sticky

ICON n picture of Christ or another religious figure, regarded as holy in the Orthodox Church

ICONES > ICON

ICONIC adj relating to, resembling, or having the character of an icon

ICONICAL same as > ICONIC

ICONICITY > ICONIC

ICONIFIED > ICONIFY

ICONIFIES > ICONIFY

ICONIFY vb render as an icon

ICONISE same as > ICONIZE

ICONISED > ICONISE

ICONISES > ICONISE

ICONISING > ICONISE

ICONIZE vb render as an icon

ICONIZED > ICONIZE

ICONIZES > ICONIZE

ICONIZING > ICONIZE

ICONOLOGY n study or field of art history concerning icons

ICONOSTAS same as > ICONOSTASIS

ICONS > ICON

ICTAL > ICTUS

ICTERIC > ICTERUS

ICTERICAL > ICTERUS

ICTERICS > ICTERUS

ICTERID n bird of the oriole family

ICTERIDS > ICTERID

ICTERINE > ICTERID

ICTERUS n yellowing of plant leaves, caused by excessive cold or moisture

ICTERUSES > ICTERUS

ICTIC > ICTUS

ICTUS n metrical or rhythmic stress in verse feet, as contrasted with the stress accent on words

ICTUSES > ICTUS

ICY adj very cold

ID n mind's instinctive unconscious energies

IDANT n chromosome

IDANTS > IDANT

IDE n silver orfe fish

IDEA n plan or thought formed in the mind ▷ vb have or form an idea

IDEAED > IDEA

IDEAL adj most suitable ▷ n conception of something that is perfect

IDEALESS > IDEA

IDEALISE same as > IDEALIZE

IDEALISED > IDEALISE

IDEALISER > IDEALISE

IDEALISES > IDEALISE

IDEALISM n tendency to seek perfection in everything

IDEALISMS > IDEALISM

IDEALIST > IDEALISM

IDEALISTS > IDEALISM

IDEALITY > IDEAL

IDEALIZE vb regard or portray as perfect or nearly perfect

IDEALIZED > IDEALIZE

IDEALIZER > IDEALIZE

IDEALIZES > IDEALIZE

IDEALLESS > IDEAL

IDEALLY > IDEAL

IDEALNESS > IDEAL

IDEALOGUE corruption of > IDEOLOGUE

IDEALOGY corruption of > IDEOLOGY

IDEALS > IDEAL

IDEAS > IDEA

IDEATA > IDEATUM

IDEATE vb form or have an idea of

IDEATED > IDEATE

IDEATES > IDEATE

IDEATING > IDEATE

IDEATION > IDEATE

IDEATIONS > IDEATE

IDEATIVE > IDEATE

IDEATUM n objective reality with which human ideas are supposed to correspond

IDEE n idea

IDEES > IDEE

IDEM adj same: used to refer to an article, chapter, or book already quoted

IDENT n short visual image employed between television programmes that works as a logo to locate the viewer to the channel

IDENTIC adj (esp of opinions expressed by two or more governments) having the same wording or intention regarding another power

IDENTICAL adj exactly the same

IDENTIFY vb prove or recognize as being a certain person or thing

IDENTIKIT n trademark name for a set of transparencies of various typical facial characteristics that can be superimposed on one another to build up a picture of a person sought by the police

IDENTITY n state of being a specified person or thing

IDENTS > IDENT

IDEOGRAM n character or symbol that directly represents a concept or

thing, rather than the sounds that form its name

IDEOGRAMS > IDEOGRAM

IDEOGRAPH same as > IDEOGRAM

IDEOLOGIC > IDEOLOGY

IDEOLOGUE same as > IDEOLOGIST

IDEOLOGY n body of ideas and beliefs of a group, nation, etc

IDEOMOTOR adj designating automatic muscular movements stimulated by ideas

IDEOPHONE n sound that represents a complete idea

IDES n (in the Ancient Roman calendar) the 15th of March, May, July, or October, or the 13th of other months

IDIOBLAST n plant cell that differs from those around it in the same tissue

IDIOCIES > IDIOCY

IDIOCY n utter stupidity

IDIOGRAM another name for > KARYOGRAM

IDIOGRAMS > IDIOGRAM

IDIOGRAPH n trademark

IDIOLECT n variety or form of a language used by an individual

IDIOLECTS > IDIOLECT

IDIOM n group of words which when used together have a different meaning from the words individually

IDIOMATIC > IDIOM

IDIOMS > IDIOM

IDIOPATHY n any disease of unknown cause

IDIOPHONE n percussion instrument, such as a cymbal or xylophone, made of naturally sonorous material

IDIOPLASM n germ plasm

IDIOT n foolish or stupid person

IDIOTCIES > IDIOTCY

IDIOTCY same as > IDIOCY

IDIOTIC adj of or resembling an idiot

IDIOTICAL same as > IDIOTIC

IDIOTICON n dictionary of dialect

IDIOTISH same as > IDIOTIC

IDIOTISM archaic word for > IDIOCY

IDIOTISMS > IDIOTISM

IDIOTS > IDIOT

IDIOTYPE n unique part of antibody

IDIOTYPES > IDIOTYPE

IDIOTYPIC > IDIOTYPE

IDLE adj not doing anything ▷ vb spend (time) doing very little

IDLED > IDLE

IDLEHOOD > IDLE

IDLEHOODS > IDLE

IDLENESS > IDLE

IDLER n person who idles

IDLERS > IDLER

IDLES > IDLE

IDLESSE > IDLE

IDLESSES > IDLE

IDLEST > IDLE

IDLING > IDLE

IDLY > IDLE

IDOCRASE n green, brown, or yellow mineral

IDOCRASES > IDOCRASE

IDOL n object of excessive devotion

IDOLA > IDOLUM

IDOLATER > IDOLATRY

IDOLATERS > IDOLATRY

IDOLATOR > IDOLATRY

IDOLATORS > IDOLATRY

IDOLATRY n worship of idols

IDOLISE same as > IDOLIZE

IDOLISED > IDOLISE

IDOLISER > IDOLISE

IDOLISERS > IDOLISE

IDOLISES > IDOLISE

IDOLISING > IDOLISE

IDOLISM > IDOLIZE

IDOLISMS > IDOL

IDOLIST > IDOLIZE

IDOLISTS > IDOLIZE

IDOLIZE vb love or admire excessively

IDOLIZED > IDOLIZE

IDOLIZER > IDOLIZE

IDOLIZERS > IDOLIZE

IDOLIZES > IDOLIZE

IDOLIZING > IDOLIZE

IDOLS > IDOL

IDOLUM n mental picture

IDONEITY > IDONEOUS

IDONEOUS adj appropriate

IDS > ID

IDYL same as > IDYLL

IDYLIST same as > IDYLLIST

IDYLISTS > IDYLIST

IDYLL n scene or time of great peace and happiness

IDYLLIAN same as > IDYLLIC

IDYLLIC adj of or relating to an idyll

IDYLLIST n writer of idylls

IDYLLISTS > IDYLLIST

IDYLLS > IDYLL

IDYLS > IDYL

IF n uncertainty or doubt

IFF n military system using radar transmissions to which equipment carried by friendly forces automatically responds with a precoded signal

IFFIER > IFFY

IFFIEST > IFFY

IFFINESS > IFFY

IFFY adj doubtful, uncertain

IFS > IF

IFTAR n meal eaten by Muslims to break their fast after sunset every day during Ramadan

IFTARS > IFTAR

IGAD same as > EGAD

IGAPO n flooded forest

IGAPOS > IGAPO

IGARAPE n canoe route

IGARAPES > IGARAPE

IGG vb antagonize

IGGED > IGG

IGGING > IGG

IGGS > IGG

IGLOO n dome-shaped Inuit house made of snow and ice

IGLOOS > IGLOO

IGLU same as > IGLOO

IGLUS > IGLU

IGNARO n ignoramus

IGNAROES > IGNARO

IGNAROS > IGNARO

IGNATIA n dried seed

IGNATIAS > IGNATIA

IGNEOUS adj (of rock) formed as molten rock cools and hardens

IGNESCENT adj giving off sparks when struck, as a flint ▷ n ignescent substance

IGNIFIED > IGNIFY

IGNIFIES > IGNIFY

IGNIFY vb turn into fire

IGNIFYING > IGNIFY

IGNITABLE > IGNITE

IGNITE vb catch fire or set fire to

IGNITED > IGNITE

IGNITER n person or thing that ignites

IGNITERS > IGNITER

IGNITES > IGNITE

IGNITIBLE > IGNITE

IGNITING > IGNITE

IGNITION n system that ignites the fuel-and-air mixture to start an engine

IGNITIONS > IGNITION

IGNITOR same as > IGNITER

IGNITORS > IGNITER

IGNITRON n mercury-arc rectifier controlled by a subsidiary electrode

IGNITRONS > IGNITRON

IGNOBLE adj dishonourable

IGNOBLER > IGNOBLE

IGNOBLEST > IGNOBLE

IGNOBLY > IGNOBLE

IGNOMIES > IGNOMY

IGNOMINY n humiliating disgrace

IGNOMY Shakespearean variant of > IGNOMINY

IGNORABLE > IGNORE

IGNORAMI > IGNORAMUS

IGNORAMUS n ignorant person

IGNORANCE n lack of knowledge or education

IGNORANT adj lacking knowledge ▷ n ignorant person

IGNORANTS > IGNORANT

IGNORE vb refuse to notice, disregard deliberately ▷ n disregard

IGNORED > IGNORE

IGNORER > IGNORE

IGNORERS > IGNORE

IGNORES > IGNORE

IGNORING > IGNORE

IGUANA n large tropical American lizard

IGUANAS > IGUANA

IGUANIAN > IGUANA

IGUANIANS > IGUANA

IGUANID same as > IGUANA

IGUANIDS > IGUANID

IGUANODON n massive herbivorous long-tailed bipedal dinosaur

IHRAM n customary white robes worn by Muslim pilgrims to Mecca, symbolizing a sacred or consecrated state

IHRAMS > IHRAM

IJTIHAD n effort of a Muslim scholar to derive a legal ruling from the Koran

IJTIHADS > IJTIHAD

IKAN n (in Malaysia) fish used esp in names of cooked dishes

IKANS > IKAN

IKAT n method of creating patterns in fabric by tie-dyeing the yarn before weaving

IKATS > IKAT

IKEBANA n Japanese art of flower arrangement

IKEBANAS > IKEBANA

IKON same as > ICON

IKONS > IKON

ILEA > ILEUM

ILEAC adj of or relating to the ileum

ILEAL same as > ILEAC

ILEITIDES > ILEITIS

ILEITIS n inflammation of the ileum

ILEITISES > ILEITIS

ILEOSTOMY n surgical formation of a permanent opening through the abdominal wall into the ileum

ILEUM n lowest part of the small intestine

ILEUS n obstruction of the intestine, esp the ileum, by mechanical occlusion or as the result of distension of the bowel following loss of muscular action

ILEUSES > ILEUS

ILEX n any of a genus of trees or shrubs that includes holly

ILEXES > ILEX

ILIA > ILIUM

ILIAC adj of or relating to the ilium

ILIACUS n iliac

ILIACUSES > ILIACUS

ILIAD n epic poem

ILIADS > ILIAD

ILIAL > ILIUM

ILICES > ILEX

ILIUM n uppermost and widest of the three sections of the hipbone

ILK n type ⊳ determiner each

ILKA same as > ILK

ILKADAY n every day

ILKADAYS > ILKADAY

ILKS > ILK

ILL adj not in good health ⊳n evil, harm ⊳adv badly

ILLAPSE vb slide in

ILLAPSED > ILLAPSE

ILLAPSES > ILLAPSE

ILLAPSING > ILLAPSE

ILLATION rare word for > INFERENCE

ILLATIONS > ILLATION

ILLATIVE adj of or relating to illation ⊳n illative case

ILLATIVES > ILLATIVE

ILLEGAL adj against the law ⊳n person who has entered or attempted to enter a country illegally

ILLEGALLY > ILLEGAL

ILLEGALS > ILLEGAL

ILLEGIBLE adj unable to be read or deciphered

ILLEGIBLY > ILLEGIBLE

ILLER > ILL

ILLEST > ILL

ILLIAD n wink

ILLIADS > ILLIAD

ILLIBERAL adj narrow-minded, intolerant

ILLICIT adj illegal

ILLICITLY > ILLICIT

ILLIMITED adj infinite

ILLINIUM n type of radioactive element

ILLINIUMS > ILLINIUM

ILLIPE n Asian tree

ILLIPES > ILLIPE

ILLIQUID adj (of an asset) not easily convertible into cash

ILLISION n act of striking against

ILLISIONS > ILLISION

ILLITE n clay mineral of the mica group, found in shales and mudstones

ILLITES > ILLITE

ILLITIC > ILLITE

ILLNESS n disease or indisposition

ILLNESSES > ILLNESS

ILLOGIC n reasoning characterized by lack of logic

ILLOGICAL adj unreasonable

ILLOGICS > ILLOGIC

ILLS > ILL

ILLTH n condition of poverty or misery

ILLTHS > ILLTH

ILLUDE vb trick or deceive

ILLUDED > ILLUDE

ILLUDES > ILLUDE

ILLUDING > ILLUDE

ILLUME vb illuminate

ILLUMED > ILLUME

ILLUMES > ILLUME

ILLUMINE vb throw light in or into

ILLUMINED > ILLUMINE

ILLUMINER n illuminator

ILLUMINES > ILLUMINE

ILLUMING > ILLUME

ILLUPI same as > ILLIPE

ILLUPIS > ILLUPI

ILLUSION n deceptive appearance or belief

ILLUSIONS > ILLUSION

ILLUSIVE same as > ILLUSORY

ILLUSORY adj seeming to be true, but actually false

ILLUVIA > ILLUVIUM

ILLUVIAL > ILLUVIUM

ILLUVIATE vb deposit illuvium

ILLUVIUM n material, which includes colloids and mineral salts, that is washed down from one layer of soil to a lower layer

ILLUVIUMS > ILLUVIUM

ILLY adv badly

ILMENITE n black mineral found in igneous rocks as layered deposits and in veins

ILMENITES > ILMENITE

IMAGE n mental picture of someone or something ⊳vb picture in the mind

IMAGEABLE > IMAGE

IMAGED > IMAGE

IMAGELESS > IMAGE

IMAGER n device that produces images

IMAGERIES > IMAGERY

IMAGERS > IMAGER

IMAGERY n images collectively, esp in the arts

IMAGES > IMAGE

IMAGINAL adj of, relating to, or resembling an imago

IMAGINARY adj existing only in the imagination

IMAGINE vb form a mental image of ⊳ sentence substitute exclamation of surprise

IMAGINED > IMAGINE

IMAGINER > IMAGINE

IMAGINERS > IMAGINE

IMAGINES > IMAGO

IMAGING > IMAGE

IMAGINGS > IMAGE

IMAGINING > IMAGINE

IMAGINIST n imaginative person

IMAGISM n poetic movement in England and America between 1912 and 1917

IMAGISMS > IMAGISM

IMAGIST > IMAGISM

IMAGISTIC > IMAGISM

IMAGISTS > IMAGISM

IMAGO n sexually mature adult insect

IMAGOES > IMAGO

IMAGOS > IMAGO

IMAM n leader of prayers in a mosque

IMAMATE n region or territory governed by an imam

IMAMATES > IMAMATE

IMAMS > IMAM

IMARET n (in Turkey) a hospice for pilgrims or travellers

IMARETS > IMARET

IMARI n Japanese porcelain

IMARIS > IMARI

IMAUM same as > IMAM

IMAUMS > IMAUM

IMBALANCE n lack of balance or proportion

IMBALM same as > EMBALM

IMBALMED > IMBALM

IMBALMER > IMBALM

IMBALMERS > IMBALM

IMBALMING > IMBALM

IMBALMS > IMBALM

IMBAR vb bar in

IMBARK vb cover in bark

IMBARKED > IMBARK

IMBARKING > IMBARK

IMBARKS > IMBARK

IMBARRED > IMBAR

IMBARRING > IMBAR

IMBARS > IMBAR

IMBASE vb degrade

IMBASED > IMBASE

IMBASES > IMBASE

IMBASING > IMBASE

IMBATHE vb bathe

IMBATHED > IMBATHE

IMBATHES > IMBATHE

IMBATHING > IMBATHE

IMBECILE n stupid person ⊳ adj stupid or senseless

IMBECILES > IMBECILE

IMBECILIC > IMBECILE

IMBED same as > EMBED

IMBEDDED > IMBED

IMBEDDING > IMBED

IMBEDS > IMBED

IMBIBE vb drink (alcoholic drinks)

IMBIBED > IMBIBE

IMBIBER > IMBIBE

IMBIBERS > IMBIBE

IMBIBES > IMBIBE

IMBIBING > IMBIBE

IMBITTER same as > EMBITTER

IMBITTERS > IMBITTER

IMBIZO n meeting, esp a gathering of the Zulu people called by the king or a traditional leader

IMBIZOS > IMBIZO

IMBLAZE vb depict heraldically

IMBLAZED > IMBLAZE

IMBLAZES > IMBLAZE

IMBLAZING > IMBLAZE

IMBODIED > IMBODY

IMBODIES > IMBODY

IMBODY same as > EMBODY

IMBODYING > IMBODY

IMBOLDEN same as > EMBOLDEN

IMBOLDENS > IMBOLDEN

IMBORDER vb enclose in a border

IMBORDERS > IMBORDER

IMBOSK vb conceal

IMBOSKED > IMBOSK

IMBOSKING > IMBOSK

IMBOSKS > IMBOSK

IMBOSOM vb hold in one's heart

IMBOSOMED > IMBOSOM

IMBOSOMS > IMBOSOM

IMBOSS same as > EMBOSS

IMBOSSED > IMBOSS

IMBOSSES > IMBOSS

IMBOSSING > IMBOSS

IMBOWER vb enclose in a bower

IMBOWERED > IMBOWER

IMBOWERS > IMBOWER

IMBRANGLE vb entangle

IMBRAST Spenserian past participle of > EMBRACE

IMBREX n curved tile

IMBRICATE *adj* having tiles or slates that overlap ▷ *vb* decorate with a repeating pattern resembling scales or overlapping tiles

IMBRICES > IMBREX

IMBROGLIO *n* confusing and complicated situation

IMBROWN *vb* make brown

IMBROWNED > IMBROWN

IMBROWNS > IMBROWN

IMBRUE *vb* stain, esp with blood

IMBRUED > IMBRUE

IMBRUES > IMBRUE

IMBRUING > IMBRUE

IMBRUTE *vb* reduce to a bestial state

IMBRUTED > IMBRUTE

IMBRUTES > IMBRUTE

IMBRUTING > IMBRUTE

IMBUE *vb* fill or inspire with (ideals or principles)

IMBUED > IMBUE

IMBUEMENT > IMBUE

IMBUES > IMBUE

IMBUING > IMBUE

IMBURSE *vb* pay

IMBURSED > IMBURSE

IMBURSES > IMBURSE

IMBURSING > IMBURSE

IMID *n* immunomodulatory drug

IMIDAZOLE *n* white crystalline basic heterocyclic compound

IMIDE *n* any of a class of organic compounds

IMIDES > IMIDE

IMIDIC > IMIDE

IMIDO > IMIDE

IMIDS > IMID

IMINAZOLE *same as* > IMIDAZOLE

IMINE *n* any of a class of organic compounds

IMINES > IMINE

IMINO > IMINE

IMINOUREA *another name for* > GUANIDINE

IMITABLE > IMITATE

IMITANCY *n* tendency to imitate

IMITANT *same as* > IMITATION

IMITANTS > IMITANT

IMITATE *vb* take as a model

IMITATED > IMITATE

IMITATES > IMITATE

IMITATING > IMITATE

IMITATION *n* copy of an original ▷ *adj* made to look like a material of superior quality

IMITATIVE *adj* imitating or tending to copy

IMITATOR > IMITATE

IMITATORS > IMITATE

IMMANACLE *vb* fetter

IMMANE *adj* monstrous

IMMANELY > IMMANE

IMMANENCE > IMMANENT

IMMANENCY > IMMANENT

IMMANENT *adj* present within and throughout something

IMMANITY > IMMANE

IMMANTLE *vb* cover with a mantle

IMMANTLED > IMMANTLE

IMMANTLES > IMMANTLE

IMMASK *vb* disguise

IMMASKED > IMMASK

IMMASKING > IMMASK

IMMASKS > IMMASK

IMMATURE *n* young animal ▷ *adj* not fully developed

IMMATURES > IMMATURE

IMMEDIACY > IMMEDIATE

IMMEDIATE *adj* occurring at once

IMMENSE *adj* extremely large

IMMENSELY > IMMENSE

IMMENSER > IMMENSE

IMMENSEST > IMMENSE

IMMENSITY *n* state or quality of being immense

IMMERGE *archaic word for* > IMMERSE

IMMERGED > IMMERGE

IMMERGES > IMMERGE

IMMERGING > IMMERGE

IMMERSE *vb* involve deeply, engross

IMMERSED *adj* sunk or submerged

IMMERSER > IMMERSE

IMMERSERS > IMMERSE

IMMERSES > IMMERSE

IMMERSING > IMMERSE

IMMERSION *n* form of baptism in which part or the whole of a person's body is submerged in the water

IMMERSIVE *adj* providing information or stimulation for a number of senses, not only sight and sound

IMMESH *variant of* > ENMESH

IMMESHED > IMMESH

IMMESHES > IMMESH

IMMESHING > IMMESH

IMMEW *vb* confine

IMMEWED > IMMEW

IMMEWING > IMMEW

IMMEWS > IMMEW

IMMIES > IMMY

IMMIGRANT *n* person who comes to a foreign country in order to settle there

IMMIGRATE *vb* come to a place or country of which one is not a native in order to settle there

IMMINENCE > IMMINENT

IMMINENCY > IMMINENT

IMMINENT *adj* about to happen

IMMINGLE *vb* blend or mix together

IMMINGLED > IMMINGLE

IMMINGLES > IMMINGLE

IMMINUTE *adj* reduced

IMMISSION *n* insertion

IMMIT *vb* insert

IMMITS > IMMIT

IMMITTED > IMMIT

IMMITTING > IMMIT

IMMIX *vb* mix in

IMMIXED > IMMIX

IMMIXES > IMMIX

IMMIXING > IMMIX

IMMIXTURE > IMMIX

IMMOBILE *adj* not moving

IMMODEST *adj* behaving in an indecent or improper manner

IMMODESTY > IMMODEST

IMMOLATE *vb* kill as a sacrifice

IMMOLATED > IMMOLATE

IMMOLATES > IMMOLATE

IMMOLATOR > IMMOLATE

IMMOMENT *adj* of no value

IMMORAL *adj* morally wrong, corrupt

IMMORALLY > IMMORAL

IMMORTAL *adj* living forever ▷ *n* person whose fame will last for all time

IMMORTALS > IMMORTAL

IMMOTILE *adj* (esp of living organisms or their parts) not capable of moving spontaneously and independently.

IMMOVABLE *adj* unable to be moved

IMMOVABLY > IMMOVABLE

IMMUNE *adj* protected against a specific disease ▷ *n* immune person or animal

IMMUNES > IMMUNE

IMMUNISE *same as* > IMMUNIZE

IMMUNISED > IMMUNISE

IMMUNISER > IMMUNISE

IMMUNISES > IMMUNISE

IMMUNITY *n* ability to resist disease

IMMUNIZE *vb* make immune to a disease

IMMUNIZED > IMMUNIZE

IMMUNIZER > IMMUNIZE

IMMUNIZES > IMMUNIZE

IMMUNOGEN *n* any substance that evokes an immune response

IMMURE *vb* imprison

IMMURED > IMMURE

IMMURES > IMMURE

IMMURING > IMMURE

IMMUTABLE *adj* unchangeable

IMMUTABLY > IMMUTABLE

IMMY *n* image-orthicon camera

IMP *n* (in folklore) mischievous small creature with magical powers ▷ *vb* insert (new feathers) into the stumps of broken feathers in order to repair the wing of a hawk or falcon

IMPACABLE *adj* incapable of being placated or pacified

IMPACT *n* strong effect ▷ *vb* have a strong effect on

IMPACTED > IMPACT

IMPACTER > IMPACT

IMPACTERS > IMPACT

IMPACTFUL > IMPACT

IMPACTING > IMPACT

IMPACTION > IMPACT

IMPACTITE *n* glassy rock formed in a meteor collision

IMPACTIVE *adj* of or relating to a physical impact

IMPACTOR > IMPACT

IMPACTORS > IMPACT

IMPACTS > IMPACT

IMPAINT *vb* paint

IMPAINTED > IMPAINT

IMPAINTS > IMPAINT

IMPAIR *vb* weaken or damage

IMPAIRED > IMPAIR

IMPAIRER > IMPAIR

IMPAIRERS > IMPAIR

IMPAIRING > IMPAIR

IMPAIRS > IMPAIR

IMPALA *n* southern African antelope

IMPALAS > IMPALA

IMPALE *vb* pierce with a sharp object

IMPALED > IMPALE

IMPALER > IMPALE

IMPALERS > IMPALE

IMPALES > IMPALE

IMPALING > IMPALE

IMPANATE *adj* embodied in bread

IMPANEL *variant spelling (esp US) of* > EMPANEL

IMPANELED > IMPANEL

IMPANELS > IMPANEL

IMPANNEL *same as* > IMPANEL

IMPANNELS > IMPANNEL

IMPARITY *less common word for* > DISPARITY

IMPARK *vb* make into a park

IMPARKED > IMPARK

IMPARKING > IMPARK

IMPARKS > IMPARK

IMPARL *vb* parley

IMPARLED > IMPARL

IMPARLING > IMPARL

IMPARLS > IMPARL

IMPART *vb* communicate (information)

IMPARTED > IMPART

IMPARTER > IMPART

IMPARTERS > IMPART

IMPARTIAL *adj* not favouring one side or the other

IMPARTING > IMPART

IMPARTS > IMPART

IMPASSE *n* situation in which progress is impossible

IMPASSES > IMPASSE

IMPASSION *vb* arouse the passions of

IMPASSIVE *adj* showing no emotion, calm

IMPASTE *vb* apply paint thickly to

IMPASTED > IMPASTE

IMPASTES > IMPASTE

IMPASTING > IMPASTE

IMPASTO *n* technique of applying paint thickly, so that brush marks are evident ▷ *vb* apply impasto

IMPASTOED > IMPASTO

IMPASTOS > IMPASTO

IMPATIENS *n* plant such as balsam, touch-me-

not, busy Lizzie, and policeman's helmet
IMPATIENT *adj* irritable at any delay or difficulty
IMPAVE *vb* set in a pavement
IMPAVED > IMPAVE
IMPAVES > IMPAVE
IMPAVID *adj* fearless
IMPAVIDLY > IMPAVID
IMPAVING > IMPAVE
IMPAWN *vb* pawn
IMPAWNED > IMPAWN
IMPAWNING > IMPAWN
IMPAWNS > IMPAWN
IMPEACH *vb* charge with a serious crime against the state
IMPEACHED > IMPEACH
IMPEACHER > IMPEACH
IMPEACHES > IMPEACH
IMPEARL *vb* adorn with pearls
IMPEARLED > IMPEARL
IMPEARLS > IMPEARL
IMPECCANT *adj* not sinning
IMPED > IMP
IMPEDANCE *n* measure of the opposition to the flow of an alternating current
IMPEDE *vb* hinder in action or progress
IMPEDED > IMPEDE
IMPEDER > IMPEDE
IMPEDERS > IMPEDE
IMPEDES > IMPEDE
IMPEDING > IMPEDE
IMPEDOR *n* component, such as an inductor or resistor, that offers impedance
IMPEDORS > IMPEDOR
IMPEL *vb* push or force (someone) to do something
IMPELLED > IMPEL
IMPELLENT > IMPEL
IMPELLER *n* vaned rotating disc of a centrifugal pump, compressor, etc
IMPELLERS > IMPELLER
IMPELLING > IMPEL
IMPELLOR *same as* > IMPELLER
IMPELLORS > IMPELLOR
IMPELS > IMPEL
IMPEND *vb* (esp of something threatening) to be about to happen
IMPENDED > IMPEND
IMPENDENT > IMPEND
IMPENDING > IMPEND
IMPENDS > IMPEND
IMPENNATE *adj* (of birds) lacking true functional wings or feathers
IMPERATOR *n* (in imperial Rome) a title of the emperor
IMPERFECT *adj* having faults or mistakes ▷ *n* imperfect tense
IMPERIA > IMPERIUM
IMPERIAL *adj* of or like an empire or emperor ▷ *n* wine bottle holding the equivalent of eight normal

bottles
IMPERIALS > IMPERIAL
IMPERIL *vb* put in danger
IMPERILED > IMPERIL
IMPERILS > IMPERIL
IMPERIOUS *adj* proud and domineering
IMPERIUM *n* (in ancient Rome) the supreme power, held esp by consuls and emperors, to command and administer in military, judicial, and civil affairs
IMPERIUMS > IMPERIUM
IMPETICOS *vb* put in a pocket
IMPETIGO *n* contagious skin disease
IMPETIGOS > IMPETIGO
IMPETRATE *vb* supplicate or entreat for, esp by prayer
IMPETUOUS *adj* done or acting without thought, rash
IMPETUS *n* incentive, impulse
IMPETUSES > IMPETUS
IMPHEE *n* African sugar cane
IMPHEES > IMPHEE
IMPI *n* group of Zulu warriors
IMPIES > IMPI
IMPIETIES > IMPIETY
IMPIETY *n* lack of respect or religious reverence
IMPING > IMP
IMPINGE *vb* affect or restrict
IMPINGED > IMPINGE
IMPINGENT > IMPINGE
IMPINGER > IMPINGE
IMPINGERS > IMPINGE
IMPINGES > IMPINGE
IMPINGING > IMPINGE
IMPINGS > IMP
IMPIOUS *adj* showing a lack of respect or reverence
IMPIOUSLY > IMPIOUS
IMPIS > IMPI
IMPISH *adj* mischievous
IMPISHLY > IMPISH
IMPLANT *n* something put into someone's body, usu by surgical operation ▷ *vb* put (something) into someone's body, usu by surgical operation
IMPLANTED > IMPLANT
IMPLANTER > IMPLANT
IMPLANTS > IMPLANT
IMPLATE *vb* sheathe
IMPLATED > IMPLATE
IMPLATES > IMPLATE
IMPLATING > IMPLATE
IMPLEACH *vb* intertwine
IMPLEAD *vb* sue or prosecute
IMPLEADED > IMPLEAD
IMPLEADER > IMPLEAD
IMPLEADS > IMPLEAD
IMPLED > IMPLEAD
IMPLEDGE *vb* pledge
IMPLEDGED > IMPLEDGE
IMPLEDGES > IMPLEDGE
IMPLEMENT *vb* carry out (instructions etc) ▷ *n* tool, instrument

IMPLETE *vb* fill
IMPLETED > IMPLETE
IMPLETES > IMPLETE
IMPLETING > IMPLETE
IMPLETION > IMPLETE
IMPLEX *n* part of an arthropod
IMPLEXES > IMPLEX
IMPLEXION *n* complication
IMPLICATE *vb* show to be involved, esp in a crime
IMPLICIT *adj* expressed indirectly
IMPLICITY > IMPLICIT
IMPLIED *adj* hinted at or suggested
IMPLIEDLY > IMPLIED
IMPLIES > IMPLY
IMPLODE *vb* collapse inwards
IMPLODED > IMPLODE
IMPLODENT *n* sound of an implosion
IMPLODES > IMPLODE
IMPLODING > IMPLODE
IMPLORE *vb* beg earnestly
IMPLORED > IMPLORE
IMPLORER > IMPLORE
IMPLORERS > IMPLORE
IMPLORES > IMPLORE
IMPLORING > IMPLORE
IMPLOSION *n* act or process of imploding
IMPLOSIVE *n* consonant pronounced in a particular way
IMPLUNGE *vb* submerge
IMPLUNGED > IMPLUNGE
IMPLUNGES > IMPLUNGE
IMPLUVIA > IMPLUVIUM
IMPLUVIUM *n* rain-filled water tank
IMPLY *vb* indicate by hinting, suggest
IMPLYING > IMPLY
IMPOCKET *vb* put in a pocket
IMPOCKETS > IMPOCKET
IMPOLDER *vb* make into a polder
IMPOLDERS > IMPOLDER
IMPOLICY *n* act or an instance of being unjudicious or impolitic
IMPOLITE *adj* showing bad manners
IMPOLITER > IMPOLITE
IMPOLITIC *adj* unwise or inadvisable
IMPONE *vb* impose
IMPONED > IMPONE
IMPONENT *n* person who imposes a duty, etc
IMPONENTS > IMPONENT
IMPONES > IMPONE
IMPONING > IMPONE
IMPOROUS *adj* not porous
IMPORT *vb* bring in (goods) from another country ▷ *n* something imported
IMPORTANT *adj* of great significance or value
IMPORTED > IMPORT
IMPORTER > IMPORT
IMPORTERS > IMPORT
IMPORTING > IMPORT
IMPORTS > IMPORT
IMPORTUNE *vb* harass with

persistent requests
IMPOSABLE > IMPOSE
IMPOSE *vb* force the acceptance of
IMPOSED > IMPOSE
IMPOSER > IMPOSE
IMPOSERS > IMPOSE
IMPOSES > IMPOSE
IMPOSING *adj* grand, impressive
IMPOST *n* tax, esp a customs duty ▷ *vb* classify (imported goods) according to the duty payable on them
IMPOSTED > IMPOST
IMPOSTER > IMPOST
IMPOSTERS > IMPOST
IMPOSTING > IMPOST
IMPOSTOR *n* person who cheats or swindles by pretending to be someone else
IMPOSTORS > IMPOSTOR
IMPOSTS > IMPOST
IMPOSTUME *archaic word for* > ABSCESS
IMPOSTURE *n* deception, esp by pretending to be someone else
IMPOT *n* slang term for the act of imposing
IMPOTENCE > IMPOTENT
IMPOTENCY > IMPOTENT
IMPOTENT *n* one who is impotent ▷ *adj* powerless
IMPOTENTS > IMPOTENT
IMPOTS > IMPOT
IMPOUND *vb* take legal possession of, confiscate
IMPOUNDED > IMPOUND
IMPOUNDER > IMPOUND
IMPOUNDS > IMPOUND
IMPOWER *less common spelling of* > EMPOWER
IMPOWERED > IMPOWER
IMPOWERS > IMPOWER
IMPRECATE *vb* swear, curse, or blaspheme
IMPRECISE *adj* inexact or inaccurate
IMPREGN *vb* impregnate
IMPREGNED > IMPREGN
IMPREGNS > IMPREGN
IMPRESA *n* heraldic device
IMPRESARI *n* impresarios
IMPRESAS > IMPRESA
IMPRESE *same as* > IMPRESA
IMPRESES > IMPRESE
IMPRESS *vb* affect strongly, usu favourably ▷ *n* impressing
IMPRESSE *n* heraldic device
IMPRESSED > IMPRESS
IMPRESSER > IMPRESS
IMPRESSES > IMPRESS
IMPREST *n* fund of cash from which a department or other unit pays incidental expenses, topped up periodically from central funds
IMPRESTS > IMPREST
IMPRIMIS *adv* in the first place
IMPRINT *n* mark made by printing or stamping

▷ *vb* produce (a mark) by printing or stamping
IMPRINTED > IMPRINT
IMPRINTER > IMPRINT
IMPRINTS > IMPRINT
IMPRISON *vb* put in prison
IMPRISONS > IMPRISON
IMPROBITY *n* dishonesty or wickedness
IMPROMPTU *adj* without planning or preparation ▷ *adv* in a spontaneous or improvised way ▷ *n* short piece of instrumental music resembling improvisation
IMPROPER *adj* indecent
IMPROV *n* improvisational comedy
IMPROVE *vb* make or become better
IMPROVED > IMPROVE
IMPROVER > IMPROVE
IMPROVERS > IMPROVE
IMPROVES > IMPROVE
IMPROVING > IMPROVE
IMPROVISE *vb* make use of whatever materials are available
IMPROVS > IMPROV
IMPRUDENT *adj* not sensible or wise
IMPS > IMP
IMPSONITE *n* asphaltite compound
IMPUDENCE *n* quality of being impudent
IMPUDENCY *same as* > IMPUDENCE
IMPUDENT *adj* cheeky, disrespectful
IMPUGN *vb* challenge the truth or validity of
IMPUGNED > IMPUGN
IMPUGNER > IMPUGN
IMPUGNERS > IMPUGN
IMPUGNING > IMPUGN
IMPUGNS > IMPUGN
IMPULSE *vb* give an impulse to ▷ *n* sudden urge to do something
IMPULSED > IMPULSE
IMPULSES > IMPULSE
IMPULSING > IMPULSE
IMPULSION *n* act of impelling or the state of being impelled
IMPULSIVE *adj* acting or done without careful consideration
IMPUNDULU *n* mythical bird associated with witchcraft, frequently manifested as the secretary bird
IMPUNITY *n* exemption or immunity from punishment or recrimination
IMPURE *adj* having dirty or unwanted substances mixed in
IMPURELY > IMPURE
IMPURER > IMPURE
IMPUREST > IMPURE
IMPURITY *n* impure element or thing
IMPURPLE *vb* colour purple

IMPURPLED > IMPURPLE
IMPURPLES > IMPURPLE
IMPUTABLE *adj* capable of being imputed
IMPUTABLY > IMPUTABLE
IMPUTE *vb* attribute responsibility to
IMPUTED > IMPUTE
IMPUTER > IMPUTE
IMPUTERS > IMPUTE
IMPUTES > IMPUTE
IMPUTING > IMPUTE
IMSHI *interj* go away!
IMSHY *same as* > IMSHI
IN *prep* indicating position inside, state or situation, etc ▷ *adv* indicating position inside, entry into, etc ▷ *adj* fashionable ▷ *n* way of approaching or befriending a person
INABILITY *n* lack of means or skill to do something
INACTION *n* act of doing nothing
INACTIONS > INACTION
INACTIVE *adj* idle
INAIDABLE *adj* beyond help
INAMORATA *n* woman with whom one is in love
INAMORATO *n* man with whom one is in love
INANE *adj* senseless, silly ▷ *n* something that is inane
INANELY > INANE
INANENESS > INANE
INANER > INANE
INANES > INANE
INANEST > INANE
INANGA *n* common type of New Zealand grass tree
INANGAS > INANGA
INANIMATE *adj* not living
INANITIES > INANITY
INANITION *n* exhaustion or weakness, as from lack of food
INANITY *n* lack of intelligence or imagination
INAPT *adj* not apt or fitting
INAPTLY > INAPT
INAPTNESS > INAPT
INARABLE *adj* not arable
INARCH *vb* graft (a plant) by uniting stock and scion while both are still growing independently
INARCHED > INARCH
INARCHES > INARCH
INARCHING > INARCH
INARM *vb* embrace
INARMED > INARM
INARMING > INARM
INARMS > INARM
INASMUCH as in *inasmuch as*, , in view of the fact that
INAUDIBLE *adj* not loud enough to be heard
INAUDIBLY > INAUDIBLE
INAUGURAL *adj* of or for an inauguration ▷ *n* speech made at an inauguration
INAURATE *adj* gilded
INBEING *n* existence in something else
INBEINGS > INBEING

INBENT *adj* bent inwards
INBOARD *adj* (of a boat's engine) inside the hull ▷ *adv* within the sides of or towards the centre of a vessel or aircraft
INBOARDS *same as* > INBOARD
INBORN *adj* existing from birth, natural
INBOUND *vb* pass into the playing area from outside it ▷ *adj* coming in
INBOUNDED > INBOUND
INBOUNDS > INBOUND
INBREAK *n* breaking in
INBREAKS > INBREAK
INBREATHE *vb* infuse or imbue
INBRED *n* inbred person or animal ▷ *adj* produced as a result of inbreeding
INBREDS > INBRED
INBREED *vb* breed from closely related individuals
INBREEDER > INBREED
INBREEDS > INBREED
INBRING *vb* bring in
INBRINGS > INBRING
INBROUGHT > INBRING
INBUILT *adj* present from the start
INBURNING *adj* burning within
INBURST *n* irruption
INBURSTS > INBURST
INBY *adv* into the house or an inner room ▷ *adj* located near or nearest to the house
INBYE *adv* near the house
INCAGE *vb* confine in or as in a cage
INCAGED > INCAGE
INCAGES > INCAGE
INCAGING > INCAGE
INCANT *vb* chant (a spell)
INCANTED > INCANT
INCANTING > INCANT
INCANTS > INCANT
INCAPABLE *adj* unable (to do something)
INCAPABLY > INCAPABLE
INCARNATE *adj* in human form ▷ *vb* give a bodily or concrete form to
INCASE *variant spelling of* > ENCASE
INCASED > INCASE
INCASES > INCASE
INCASING > INCASE
INCAUTION *n* act of not being cautious
INCAVE *vb* hide
INCAVED > INCAVE
INCAVES > INCAVE
INCAVI > INCAVO
INCAVING > INCAVE
INCAVO *n* incised part of a carving
INCEDE *vb* advance
INCEDED > INCEDE
INCEDES > INCEDE
INCEDING > INCEDE
INCENSE *vb* make very angry ▷ *n* substance that gives off a sweet perfume

when burned
INCENSED > INCENSE
INCENSER *n* incense burner
INCENSERS > INCENSER
INCENSES > INCENSE
INCENSING > INCENSE
INCENSOR *n* incense burner
INCENSORS > INCENSOR
INCENSORY *less common name for* > CENSER
INCENT *vb* provide incentive
INCENTED > INCENT
INCENTER *same as* > INCENTRE
INCENTERS > INCENTER
INCENTING > INCENT
INCENTIVE *n* something that encourages effort or action ▷ *adj* encouraging greater effort
INCENTRE *n* centre of an inscribed circle
INCENTRES > INCENTRE
INCENTS > INCENT
INCEPT *vb* (of organisms) to ingest (food) ▷ *n* rudimentary organ
INCEPTED > INCEPT
INCEPTING > INCEPT
INCEPTION *n* beginning
INCEPTIVE *adj* beginning ▷ *n* type of verb
INCEPTOR > INCEPT
INCEPTORS > INCEPT
INCEPTS > INCEPT
INCERTAIN *archaic form of* > UNCERTAIN
INCESSANT *adj* never stopping
INCEST *n* sexual intercourse between two people too closely related to marry
INCESTS > INCEST
INCH *n* unit of length equal to one twelfth of a foot or 2.54 centimetres ▷ *vb* move slowly and gradually
INCHASE *same as* > ENCHASE
INCHASED > INCHASE
INCHASES > INCHASE
INCHASING > INCHASE
INCHED > INCH
INCHER *n* something measuring given amount of inches
INCHERS > INCHER
INCHES > INCH
INCHING > INCH
INCHMEAL *adv* gradually
INCHOATE *adj* just begun and not yet properly developed ▷ *vb* begin
INCHOATED > INCHOATE
INCHOATES > INCHOATE
INCHPIN *n* cervine sweetbread
INCHPINS > INCHPIN
INCHWORM *n* larva of a type of moth
INCHWORMS > INCHWORM
INCIDENCE *n* extent or frequency of occurrence
INCIDENT *n* something that happens ▷ *adj* related (to) or dependent (on)
INCIDENTS > INCIDENT

i

INCIPIENT adj just starting to appear or happen

INCIPIT n Latin introductory phrase

INCIPITS > INCIPIT

INCISAL adj relating to the cutting edge of incisors and cuspids

INCISE vb cut into with a sharp tool

INCISED > INCISE

INCISES > INCISE

INCISING > INCISE

INCISION n cut, esp one made during a surgical operation

INCISIONS > INCISION

INCISIVE adj direct and forceful

INCISOR n front tooth, used for biting into food

INCISORS > INCISOR

INCISORY > INCISOR

INCISURAL > INCISURE

INCISURE n incision or notch in an organ or part

INCISURES > INCISURE

INCITABLE > INCITE

INCITANT n something that incites

INCITANTS > INCITANT

INCITE vb stir up, provoke

INCITED > INCITE

INCITER > INCITE

INCITERS > INCITE

INCITES > INCITE

INCITING > INCITE

INCIVIL archaic form of > UNCIVIL

INCIVISM n neglect of a citizen's duties

INCIVISMS > INCIVISM

INCLASP vb clasp

INCLASPED > INCLASP

INCLASPS > INCLASP

INCLE same as > INKLE

INCLEMENT adj (of weather) stormy or severe

INCLES > INCLE

INCLINE vb lean, slope ▷ n slope

INCLINED adj having a disposition

INCLINER > INCLINE

INCLINERS > INCLINE

INCLINES > INCLINE

INCLINING > INCLINE

INCLIP vb embrace

INCLIPPED > INCLIP

INCLIPS > INCLIP

INCLOSE less common spelling of > ENCLOSE

INCLOSED > INCLOSE

INCLOSER > INCLOSE

INCLOSERS > INCLOSE

INCLOSES > INCLOSE

INCLOSING > INCLOSE

INCLOSURE > INCLOSE

INCLUDE vb have as part of the whole

INCLUDED adj (of the stamens or pistils of a flower) not protruding beyond the corolla

INCLUDES > INCLUDE

INCLUDING > INCLUDE

INCLUSION n including or being included

INCLUSIVE adj including everything (specified)

INCOG n incognito

INCOGNITA n female who is in disguise or unknown

INCOGNITO adv having adopted a false identity ▷ n false identity ▷ adj under an assumed name or appearance

INCOGS > INCOG

INCOME n amount of money earned from work, investments, etc

INCOMER n person who comes to live in a place in which he or she was not born

INCOMERS > INCOMER

INCOMES > INCOME

INCOMING adj coming in ▷ n act of coming in

INCOMINGS > INCOMING

INCOMMODE vb cause inconvenience to

INCOMPACT adj not compact

INCONDITE adj poorly constructed or composed

INCONIE adj fine or delicate

INCONNU n whitefish of Arctic waters

INCONNUE n unknown woman

INCONNUES > INCONNUE

INCONNUS > INCONNU

INCONY adj fine or delicate

INCORPSE vb incorporate

INCORPSED > INCORPSE

INCORPSES > INCORPSE

INCORRECT adj wrong

INCORRUPT adj free from corruption

INCREASE vb make or become greater in size, number, etc ▷ n rise in number, size, etc

INCREASED > INCREASE

INCREASER > INCREASE

INCREASES > INCREASE

INCREATE adj (esp of gods) never having been created

INCREMATE vb cremate

INCREMENT n increase in money or value, esp a regular salary increase

INCRETION n direct secretion into the bloodstream, esp of a hormone from an endocrine gland

INCRETORY > INCRETION

INCROSS n plant or animal produced by continued inbreeding ▷ vb inbreed or produce by inbreeding

INCROSSED > INCROSS

INCROSSES > INCROSS

INCRUST same as > ENCRUST

INCRUSTED > INCRUST

INCRUSTS > INCRUST

INCUBATE vb (of a bird) hatch (eggs) by sitting on them

INCUBATED > INCUBATE

INCUBATES > INCUBATE

INCUBATOR n heated enclosed apparatus for rearing premature babies

INCUBI > INCUBUS

INCUBOUS adj (of a liverwort) having the leaves arranged so that the upper margin of each leaf lies above the lower margin of the next leaf along

INCUBUS n (in folklore) demon believed to have sex with sleeping women

INCUBUSES > INCUBUS

INCUDAL > INCUS

INCUDATE > INCUS

INCUDES > INCUS

INCULCATE vb fix in someone's mind by constant repetition

INCULPATE vb cause (someone) to be blamed for a crime

INCULT adj (of land) uncultivated

INCUMBENT n person who holds a particular office or position ▷ adj morally binding as a duty

INCUMBER less common spelling of > ENCUMBER

INCUMBERS > INCUMBER

INCUNABLE n early printed book

INCUR vb cause (something unpleasant) to happen

INCURABLE adj not able to be cured ▷ n person with an incurable disease

INCURABLY > INCURABLE

INCURIOUS adj showing no curiosity or interest

INCURRED > INCUR

INCURRENT adj (of anatomical ducts, tubes, channels, etc) having an inward flow

INCURRING > INCUR

INCURS > INCUR

INCURSION n sudden brief invasion

INCURSIVE > INCURSION

INCURVATE vb curve or cause to curve inwards ▷ adj curved inwards

INCURVE vb curve or cause to curve inwards

INCURVED > INCURVE

INCURVES > INCURVE

INCURVING > INCURVE

INCURVITY > INCURVE

INCUS n central of the three small bones in the middle ear of mammals

INCUSE n design stamped or hammered onto a coin ▷ vb impress (a design) in a coin or to impress (a coin) with a design by hammering or stamping ▷ adj stamped or hammered onto a coin

INCUSED > INCUSE

INCUSES > INCUSE

INCUSING > INCUSE

INCUT adj cut or etched in

INDABA n (among native peoples of southern Africa) a meeting to discuss a serious topic

INDABAS > INDABA

INDAGATE vb investigate

INDAGATED > INDAGATE

INDAGATES > INDAGATE

INDAGATOR > INDAGATE

INDAMIN same as > INDAMINE

INDAMINE n organic base used in the production of the dye safranine

INDAMINES > INDAMINE

INDAMINS > INDAMIN

INDART vb dart in

INDARTED > INDART

INDARTING > INDART

INDARTS > INDART

INDEBTED adj owing gratitude for help or favours

INDECENCY n state or quality of being indecent

INDECENT adj morally or sexually offensive

INDECORUM n indecorous behaviour or speech

INDEED adv really, certainly ▷ interj expression of indignation or surprise

INDELIBLE adj impossible to erase or remove

INDELIBLY > INDELIBLE

INDEMNIFY vb secure against loss, damage, or liability

INDEMNITY n insurance against loss or damage

INDENE n colourless liquid hydrocarbon extracted from petroleum and coal tar and used in making synthetic resins

INDENES > INDENE

INDENT vb make a dent in

INDENTED > INDENT

INDENTER > INDENT

INDENTERS > INDENT

INDENTING > INDENT

INDENTION n space between a margin and the start of the line of text

INDENTOR > INDENT

INDENTORS > INDENT

INDENTS > INDENT

INDENTURE n contract, esp one binding an apprentice to his or her employer ▷ vb bind (an apprentice) by indenture

INDEVOUT adj not devout

INDEW same as > INDUE

INDEWED > INDEW

INDEWING > INDEW

INDEWS > INDEW

INDEX n alphabetical list of names or subjects dealt with in a book ▷ vb provide (a book) with an index

INDEXABLE > INDEX

INDEXAL > INDEX

INDEXED > INDEX

INDEXER > INDEX

INDEXERS > INDEX

INDEXES > INDEX

INDEXICAL adj arranged as

or relating to an index or indexes ▷ n term whose reference depends on the context of utterance, such as I, you, here, now, or tomorrow
INDEXING > INDEX
INDEXINGS > INDEX
INDEXLESS > INDEX
INDICAN n compound secreted in the urine, usually in the form of its potassium salt
INDICANS > INDICAN
INDICANT n something that indicates
INDICANTS > INDICANT
INDICATE vb be a sign or symptom of
INDICATED > INDICATE
INDICATES > INDICATE
INDICATOR n something acting as a sign or indication
INDICES plural of > INDEX
INDICIA > INDICIUM
INDICIAL > INDICIUM
INDICIAS > INDICIUM
INDICIUM n notice
INDICIUMS > INDICIUM
INDICT vb formally charge with a crime
INDICTED > INDICT
INDICTEE > INDICT
INDICTEES > INDICT
INDICTER > INDICT
INDICTERS > INDICT
INDICTING > INDICT
INDICTION n recurring fiscal period of 15 years, often used as a unit for dating events
INDICTOR > INDICT
INDICTORS > INDICT
INDICTS > INDICT
INDIE adj (of rock music) released by an independent record company ▷ n independent record company
INDIES > INDIE
INDIGEN same as > INDIGENE
INDIGENCE > INDIGENT
INDIGENCY > INDIGENT
INDIGENE n indigenous person, animal, or thing
INDIGENES > INDIGENE
INDIGENS > INDIGEN
INDIGENT adj extremely poor ▷ n impoverished person
INDIGENTS > INDIGENT
INDIGEST n undigested mass
INDIGESTS > INDIGEST
INDIGN adj undeserving
INDIGNANT adj feeling or showing indignation
INDIGNIFY vb treat in a humiliating manner
INDIGNITY n embarrassing or humiliating treatment
INDIGNLY > INDIGN
INDIGO adj deep violet-blue ▷ n dye of this colour
INDIGOES > INDIGO
INDIGOID adj of, concerned

with, or resembling indigo or its blue colour ▷ n any of a number of synthetic dyes or pigments related in chemical structure to indigo
INDIGOIDS > INDIGOID
INDIGOS > INDIGO
INDIGOTIC > INDIGO
INDIGOTIN same as > INDIGO
INDINAVIR n drug used to treat AIDS
INDIRECT adj done or caused by someone or something else
INDIRUBIN n isomer of indigotin
INDISPOSE vb make unwilling or opposed
INDITE vb write
INDITED > INDITE
INDITER > INDITE
INDITERS > INDITE
INDITES > INDITE
INDITING > INDITE
INDIUM n soft silvery-white metallic element
INDIUMS > INDIUM
INDIVIDUA pl n indivisible entities
INDOCIBLE same as > INDOCILE
INDOCILE adj difficult to discipline or instruct
INDOL same as > INDOLE
INDOLE n white or yellowish crystalline heterocyclic compound extracted from coal tar and used in perfumery, medicine, and as a flavouring agent
INDOLENCE > INDOLENT
INDOLENCY > INDOLENT
INDOLENT adj lazy
INDOLES > INDOLE
INDOLS > INDOL
INDOOR adj inside a building
INDOORS adj inside or into a building
INDORSE variant spelling of > ENDORSE
INDORSED > INDORSE
INDORSEE > INDORSE
INDORSEES > INDORSE
INDORSER > INDORSE
INDORSERS > INDORSE
INDORSES > INDORSE
INDORSING > INDORSE
INDORSOR > INDORSE
INDORSORS > INDORSE
INDOW archaic variant of > INDOW
INDOWED > INDOW
INDOWING > INDOW
INDOWS > INDOW
INDOXYL n yellow water-soluble crystalline compound occurring in woad as its glucoside and in urine as its ester
INDOXYLS > INDOXYL
INDRAFT same as > INDRAUGHT
INDRAFTS > INDRAFT
INDRAUGHT n act of drawing or pulling in

INDRAWN adj drawn or pulled in
INDRENCH vb submerge
INDRI same as > INDRIS
INDRIS n large Madagascan arboreal lemuroid primate
INDRISES > INDRIS
INDUBIOUS adj certain
INDUCE vb persuade or influence
INDUCED > INDUCE
INDUCER > INDUCE
INDUCERS > INDUCE
INDUCES > INDUCE
INDUCIAE n time limit for a defendant to appear in court
INDUCIBLE > INDUCE
INDUCING > INDUCE
INDUCT vb formally install (someone, esp a clergyman) in office
INDUCTED > INDUCT
INDUCTEE n military conscript
INDUCTEES > INDUCTEE
INDUCTILE adj not ductile, pliant, or yielding
INDUCTING > INDUCT
INDUCTION > INDUCT
INDUCTIVE adj of or using induction
INDUCTOR n device designed to create inductance in an electrical circuit
INDUCTORS > INDUCTOR
INDUCTS > INDUCT
INDUE variant spelling of > ENDUE
INDUED > INDUE
INDUES > INDUE
INDUING > INDUE
INDULGE vb allow oneself pleasure
INDULGED > INDULGE
INDULGENT adj kind or lenient, often to excess
INDULGER > INDULGE
INDULGERS > INDULGE
INDULGES > INDULGE
INDULGING > INDULGE
INDULIN same as > INDULINE
INDULINE n any of a class of blue dyes obtained from aniline and aminoazobenzene
INDULINES > INDULINE
INDULINS > INDULIN
INDULT n faculty granted by the Holy See allowing a specific deviation from the Church's common law
INDULTS > INDULT
INDUMENTA pl n outer coverings of feather, fur, etc
INDUNA n (in South Africa) a Black African overseer in a factory, mine, etc
INDUNAS > INDUNA
INDURATE vb make or become hard or callous ▷ adj hardened, callous, or unfeeling
INDURATED > INDURATE

INDURATES > INDURATE
INDUSIA > INDUSIUM
INDUSIAL > INDUSIUM
INDUSIATE adj covered in indusia
INDUSIUM n membranous outgrowth on the undersurface of fern leaves that covers and protects the developing sporangia
INDUSTRY n manufacture of goods
INDUVIAE pl n withered leaves
INDUVIAL > INDUVIAE
INDUVIATE > INDUVIAE
INDWELL vb (of a spirit, principle, etc) to inhabit
INDWELLER > INDWELL
INDWELLS > INDWELL
INDWELT > INDWELL
INEARTH poetic word for > BURY
INEARTHED > INEARTH
INEARTHS > INEARTH
INEBRIANT adj causing intoxication, esp drunkenness ▷ n something that inebriates
INEBRIATE adj (person who is) habitually drunk ▷ n person who is habitually drunk ▷ vb make drunk
INEBRIETY > INEBRIATE
INEBRIOUS adj drunk
INEDIBLE adj not fit to be eaten
INEDIBLY > INEDIBLE
INEDITA pl n unpublished writings
INEDITED adj not edited
INEFFABLE adj too great for words
INEFFABLY > INEFFABLE
INELASTIC adj not elastic
INELEGANT adj lacking elegance or refinement
INEPT adj clumsy, lacking skill
INEPTER > INEPT
INEPTEST > INEPT
INEPTLY > INEPT
INEPTNESS > INEPT
INEQUABLE adj unfair
INEQUITY n injustice or unfairness
INERM adj without thorns
INERMOUS same as > INERM
INERRABLE adj not liable to error ▷ n person or thing that is incapable of error
INERRABLY > INERRABLE
INERRANCY > INERRABLE
INERRANT same as > INERRABLE
INERT n inert thing ▷ adj without the power of motion or resistance
INERTER > INERT
INERTEST > INERT
INERTIA n feeling of unwillingness to do anything
INERTIAE > INERTIA
INERTIAL > INERTIA
INERTIAS > INERTIA
INERTLY > INERT

INERTNESS > INERT
INERTS > INERT
INERUDITE adj not erudite
INESSIVE n grammatical case in Finnish
INESSIVES > INESSIVE
INEXACT adj not exact or accurate
INEXACTLY > INEXACT
INEXPERT n unskilled person ▷ adj lacking skill
INEXPERTS > INEXPERT
INFALL vb move towards a black hole, etc, under the influence of gravity
INFALLING > INFALL
INFALLS > INFALL
INFAME vb defame
INFAMED > INFAME
INFAMES > INFAME
INFAMIES > INFAMY
INFAMING > INFAME
INFAMISE same as > INFAMIZE
INFAMISED > INFAMISE
INFAMISES > INFAMISE
INFAMIZE vb make infamous
INFAMIZED > INFAMIZE
INFAMIZES > INFAMIZE
INFAMOUS adj well-known for something bad
INFAMY n state of being infamous
INFANCIES > INFANCY
INFANCY n early childhood
INFANT n very young child ▷ adj of, relating to, or designed for young children
INFANTA n (formerly) daughter of a king of Spain or Portugal
INFANTAS > INFANTA
INFANTE n (formerly) any son of a king of Spain or Portugal, except the heir to the throne
INFANTES > INFANTE
INFANTILE adj childish
INFANTINE adj infantile
INFANTRY n soldiers who fight on foot
INFANTS > INFANT
INFARCT n localized area of dead tissue (necrosis) resulting from obstruction of the blood supply to that part, esp by an embolus ▷ vb obstruct the blood supply to part of a body
INFARCTED > INFARCT
INFARCTS > INFARCT
INFARE vb enter
INFARES > INFARE
INFATUATE vb inspire or fill with an intense and unreasoning passion ▷ n person who is infatuated
INFAUNA n animals that live in ocean and river beds
INFAUNAE > INFAUNA
INFAUNAL > INFAUNA
INFAUNAS > INFAUNA
INFAUST adj unlucky
INFECT vb affect with a disease ▷ adj

contaminated or polluted with or as if with a disease
INFECTANT n something that infects
INFECTED > INFECT
INFECTER > INFECT
INFECTERS > INFECT
INFECTING > INFECT
INFECTION n infectious disease
INFECTIVE adj capable of causing infection
INFECTOR > INFECT
INFECTORS > INFECT
INFECTS > INFECT
INFECUND less common word for > INFERTILE
INFEFT vb give possession of heritable property
INFEFTED > INFEFT
INFEFTING > INFEFT
INFEFTS > INFEFT
INFELT adj heartfelt
INFEOFF same as > ENFEOFF
INFEOFFED > INFEOFF
INFEOFFS > INFEOFF
INFER vb work out from evidence
INFERABLE > INFER
INFERABLY > INFER
INFERE adv together
INFERENCE n act or process of reaching a conclusion by reasoning from evidence
INFERIAE pl n offerings made to the spirits of the dead
INFERIBLE > INFER
INFERIOR adj lower in quality, position, or status ▷ n person of lower position or status
INFERIORS > INFERIOR
INFERNAL adj of hell
INFERNO n intense raging fire
INFERNOS > INFERNO
INFERRED > INFER
INFERRER > INFER
INFERRERS > INFER
INFERRING > INFER
INFERS > INFER
INFERTILE adj unable to produce offspring
INFEST vb inhabit or overrun in unpleasantly large numbers
INFESTANT n parasite
INFESTED > INFEST
INFESTER > INFEST
INFESTERS > INFEST
INFESTING > INFEST
INFESTS > INFEST
INFICETE adj not witty
INFIDEL n person with no religion ▷ adj of unbelievers or unbelief
INFIDELIC > INFIDEL
INFIDELS > INFIDEL
INFIELD n area of the field near the pitch
INFIELDER n player positioned in the infield
INFIELDS > INFIELD
INFIGHT vb box at close quarters
INFIGHTER > INFIGHT

INFIGHTS > INFIGHT
INFILL vb fill in ▷ n act of filling or closing gaps, etc, in something, such as a row of buildings
INFILLED > INFILL
INFILLING > INFILL
INFILLS > INFILL
INFIMA > INFIMUM
INFIMUM n greatest lower bound
INFIMUMS > INFIMUM
INFINITE adj without any limit or end ▷ n something without any limit or end
INFINITES > INFINITE
INFINITY n endless space, time, or number
INFIRM vb make infirm ▷ adj physically or mentally weak
INFIRMARY n hospital
INFIRMED > INFIRM
INFIRMER > INFIRM
INFIRMEST > INFIRM
INFIRMING > INFIRM
INFIRMITY n state of being infirm
INFIRMLY > INFIRM
INFIRMS > INFIRM
INFIX vb fix firmly in ▷ n affix inserted into the middle of a word
INFIXED > INFIX
INFIXES > INFIX
INFIXING > INFIX
INFIXION > INFIX
INFIXIONS > INFIX
INFLAME vb make angry or excited
INFLAMED > INFLAME
INFLAMER > INFLAME
INFLAMERS > INFLAME
INFLAMES > INFLAME
INFLAMING > INFLAME
INFLATE vb expand by filling with air or gas
INFLATED > INFLATE
INFLATER > INFLATE
INFLATERS > INFLATE
INFLATES > INFLATE
INFLATING > INFLATE
INFLATION n inflating
INFLATIVE adj causing inflation
INFLATOR > INFLATE
INFLATORS > INFLATE
INFLATUS n act of breathing in
INFLECT vb change (the voice) in tone or pitch
INFLECTED > INFLECT
INFLECTOR > INFLECT
INFLECTS > INFLECT
INFLEXED adj curved or bent inwards and downwards towards the axis
INFLEXION n modulation of the voice
INFLEXURE same as > INFLEXION
INFLICT vb impose (something unpleasant) on
INFLICTED > INFLICT
INFLICTER > INFLICT
INFLICTOR > INFLICT

INFLICTS > INFLICT
INFLIGHT adj provided during flight in an aircraft
INFLOW n something, such as liquid or gas, that flows in ▷ vb flow in
INFLOWING same as > INFLOW
INFLOWS > INFLOW
INFLUENCE n effect of one person or thing on another ▷ vb have an effect on
INFLUENT adj flowing in ▷ n something flowing in, esp a tributary
INFLUENTS > INFLUENT
INFLUENZA n contagious viral disease causing headaches, muscle pains, and fever
INFLUX n arrival or entry of many people or things
INFLUXES > INFLUX
INFLUXION same as > INFLUX
INFO n information
INFOBAHN same as > INTERNET
INFOBAHNS > INFOBAHN
INFOLD variant spelling of > ENFOLD
INFOLDED > INFOLD
INFOLDER > INFOLD
INFOLDERS > INFOLD
INFOLDING > INFOLD
INFOLDS > INFOLD
INFOMANIA n obsessive devotion to gathering information
INFORCE same as > ENFORCE
INFORCED > INFORCE
INFORCES > INFORCE
INFORCING > INFORCE
INFORM vb tell ▷ adj without shape
INFORMAL adj relaxed and friendly
INFORMANT n person who gives information
INFORMED > INFORM
INFORMER n person who informs to the police
INFORMERS > INFORMER
INFORMING > INFORM
INFORMS > INFORM
INFORTUNE n misfortune
INFOS > INFO
INFOUGHT > INFIGHT
INFRA adv (esp in textual annotation) below
INFRACT vb violate or break (a law, an agreement, etc)
INFRACTED > INFRACT
INFRACTOR > INFRACT
INFRACTS > INFRACT
INFRARED adj of or using rays below the red end of the visible spectrum ▷ n infrared part of the spectrum
INFRAREDS > INFRARED
INFRINGE vb break (a law or agreement)
INFRINGED > INFRINGE
INFRINGER > INFRINGE
INFRINGES > INFRINGE
INFRUGAL adj wasteful

INFULA same as > INFULAE
INFULAE pl n two ribbons hanging from the back of a bishop's mitre
INFURIATE vb make very angry ▷ adj furious
INFUSCATE adj (esp of the wings of an insect) tinged with brown
INFUSE vb fill (with an emotion or quality)
INFUSED > INFUSE
INFUSER n any device used to make an infusion, esp a tea maker
INFUSERS > INFUSER
INFUSES > INFUSE
INFUSIBLE adj unable to be fused or melted
INFUSING > INFUSE
INFUSION n infusing
INFUSIONS > INFUSION
INFUSIVE > INFUSION
INFUSORIA pl n tiny water-dwelling animals
INFUSORY adj containing infusoria
INGAN Scots word for > ONION
INGANS > INGAN
INGATE n entrance
INGATES > INGATE
INGATHER vb gather together or in (a harvest)
INGATHERS > INGATHER
INGENER Shakespearean form of > ENGINEER
INGENERS > INGENER
INGENIOUS adj showing cleverness and originality
INGENIUM n genius
INGENIUMS > INGENIUM
INGENU n artless or inexperienced boy or young man
INGENUE n artless or inexperienced girl or young woman
INGENUES > INGENUE
INGENUITY n cleverness at inventing things
INGENUOUS adj unsophisticated and trusting
INGENUS > INGENU
INGEST vb take (food or liquid) into the body
INGESTA pl n nourishment taken into the body through the mouth
INGESTED > INGEST
INGESTING > INGEST
INGESTION > INGEST
INGESTIVE > INGEST
INGESTS > INGEST
INGINE n genius
INGINES > INGINE
INGLE n fire in a room or a fireplace
INGLENEUK same as > INGLENOOK
INGLENOOK n corner by a fireplace
INGLES > INGLE
INGLOBE vb shape as a sphere
INGLOBED > INGLOBE

INGLOBES > INGLOBE
INGLOBING > INGLOBE
INGLUVIAL > INGLUVIES
INGLUVIES n bird's craw
INGO vb reveal
INGOES > INGO
INGOING same as > INGO
INGOINGS > INGO
INGOT n oblong block of cast metal ▷ vb shape (metal) into ingots
INGOTED > INGOT
INGOTING > INGOT
INGOTS > INGOT
INGRAFT variant spelling of > ENGRAFT
INGRAFTED > INGRAFT
INGRAFTS > INGRAFT
INGRAIN vb impress deeply on the mind or nature ▷ adj (of carpets) made of dyed yarn or of fibre that is dyed before being spun into yarn ▷ n carpet made from ingrained yarn
INGRAINED > INGRAIN
INGRAINS > INGRAIN
INGRAM adj ignorant
INGRATE n ungrateful person ▷ adj ungrateful
INGRATELY > INGRATE
INGRATES > INGRATE
INGRESS n entrance
INGRESSES > INGRESS
INGROOVE vb cut a groove into
INGROOVED > INGROOVE
INGROOVES > INGROOVE
INGROSS archaic form of > ENGROSS
INGROSSED > INGROSS
INGROSSES > INGROSS
INGROUND adj sunk into ground
INGROUP n highly cohesive and relatively closed social group
INGROUPS > INGROUP
INGROWING adj (of a toenail) growing abnormally into the flesh
INGROWN adj (esp of a toenail) grown abnormally into the flesh
INGROWTH n act of growing inwards
INGROWTHS > INGROWTH
INGRUM adj ignorant
INGUINAL adj of or relating to the groin
INGULF variant spelling of > ENGULF
INGULFED > INGULF
INGULFING > INGULF
INGULFS > INGULF
INGULPH archaic form of > ENGULF
INGULPHED > INGULPH
INGULPHS > INGULPH
INHABIT vb live in
INHABITED > INHABIT
INHABITER n inhabitant
INHABITOR n inhabitant
INHABITS > INHABIT
INHALANT n medical preparation inhaled to help breathing problems ▷ adj

inhaled for its soothing or therapeutic effect
INHALANTS > INHALANT
INHALATOR n device for converting drugs into a fine spray for inhaling
INHALE vb breathe in (air, smoke, etc)
INHALED > INHALE
INHALER n container for an inhalant
INHALERS > INHALER
INHALES > INHALE
INHALING > INHALE
INHARMONY n discord
INHAUL n line for hauling in a sail
INHAULER same as > INHAUL
INHAULERS > INHAULER
INHAULS > INHAUL
INHAUST vb drink in
INHAUSTED > INHAUST
INHAUSTS > INHAUST
INHEARSE vb bury
INHEARSED > INHEARSE
INHEARSES > INHEARSE
INHERCE same as > INHEARSE
INHERCED > INHERCE
INHERCES > INHERCE
INHERCING > INHERCE
INHERE vb be an inseparable part (of)
INHERED > INHERE
INHERENCE n state or condition of being inherent
INHERENCY same as > INHERENCE
INHERENT adj existing as an inseparable part
INHERES > INHERE
INHERING > INHERE
INHERIT vb receive (money etc) from someone who has died
INHERITED > INHERIT
INHERITOR > INHERIT
INHERITS > INHERIT
INHESION less common word for > INHERENCE
INHESIONS > INHESION
INHIBIN n peptide hormone
INHIBINS > INHIBIN
INHIBIT vb restrain (an impulse or desire)
INHIBITED > INHIBIT
INHIBITER same as > INHIBITOR
INHIBITOR n person or thing that inhibits
INHIBITS > INHIBIT
INHOLDER n inhabitant
INHOLDERS > INHOLDER
INHOLDING n privately owned land inside a federal reserve
INHOOP vb confine
INHOOPED > INHOOP
INHOOPING > INHOOP
INHOOPS > INHOOP
INHUMAN adj cruel or brutal
INHUMANE same as > INHUMAN
INHUMANLY > INHUMAN
INHUMATE vb bury
INHUMATED > INHUMATE

INHUMATES > INHUMATE
INHUME vb inter
INHUMED > INHUME
INHUMER > INHUME
INHUMERS > INHUME
INHUMES > INHUME
INHUMING > INHUME
INIA > INION
INIMICAL adj unfavourable or hostile
INION n most prominent point at the back of the head, used as a point of measurement in craniometry
INIONS > INION
INIQUITY n injustice or wickedness
INISLE vb put on or make into an island
INISLED > INISLE
INISLES > INISLE
INISLING > INISLE
INITIAL adj first, at the beginning ▷ n first letter, esp of a person's name ▷ vb sign with one's initials
INITIALED > INITIAL
INITIALER > INITIAL
INITIALLY > INITIAL
INITIALS > INITIAL
INITIATE vb begin or set going ▷ n recently initiated person ▷ adj initiated
INITIATED > INITIATE
INITIATES > INITIATE
INITIATOR n person or thing that initiates
INJECT vb put (a fluid) into the body with a syringe
INJECTANT n injected substance
INJECTED > INJECT
INJECTING > INJECT
INJECTION n fluid injected into the body, esp for medicinal purposes
INJECTIVE > INJECTION
INJECTOR same as > INJECT
INJECTORS > INJECT
INJECTS > INJECT
INJELLIED > INJELLY
INJELLIES > INJELLY
INJELLY vb place in jelly
INJERA n white Ethiopian flatbread, similar to a crepe
INJERAS > INJERA
INJOINT vb join
INJOINTED > INJOINT
INJOINTS > INJOINT
INJUNCT vb issue a legal injunction against (a person)
INJUNCTED > INJUNCT
INJUNCTS > INJUNCT
INJURABLE > INJURE
INJURE vb hurt physically or mentally
INJURED > INJURE
INJURER > INJURE
INJURERS > INJURE
INJURES > INJURE
INJURIES > INJURY
INJURING > INJURE
INJURIOUS adj causing harm

INJURY *n* physical hurt

INJUSTICE *n* unfairness

INK *n* coloured liquid used for writing or printing ▷ *vb* mark in ink (something already marked in pencil)

INKBERRY *n* North American holly tree

INKBLOT *n* abstract patch of ink, one of ten commonly used in the Rorschach test

INKBLOTS > INKBLOT

INKED > INK

INKER > INK

INKERS > INK

INKHOLDER *same as* > INKHORN

INKHORN *n* (formerly) a small portable container for ink, usually made from horn

INKHORNS > INKHORN

INKIER > INKY

INKIEST > INKY

INKINESS > INKY

INKING > INK

INKJET *n* method of printing streams of electrically charged ink

INKLE *n* kind of linen tape used for trimmings

INKLED *adj* trimmed with inkle

INKLES > INKLE

INKLESS > INK

INKLIKE > INK

INKLING *n* slight idea or suspicion

INKLINGS > INKLING

INKPOT *n* ink-bottle

INKPOTS > INKPOT

INKS > INK

INKSPOT *n* ink stain

INKSPOTS > INKSPOT

INKSTAND *n* stand or tray for holding writing tools and containers for ink

INKSTANDS > INKSTAND

INKSTONE *n* stone used in making ink

INKSTONES > INKSTONE

INKWELL *n* small container for ink, often fitted into the surface of a desk

INKWELLS > INKWELL

INKWOOD *n* type of tree

INKWOODS > INKWOOD

INKY *adj* dark or black

INLACE *variant spelling of* > ENLACE

INLACED > INLACE

INLACES > INLACE

INLACING > INLACE

INLAID > INLAY

INLAND *adv* in or towards the interior of a country, away from the sea ▷ *adj* of or in the interior of a country or region, away from a sea or border ▷ *n* interior of a country or region

INLANDER > INLAND

INLANDERS > INLAND

INLANDS > INLAND

INLAY *n* inlaid substance or pattern ▷ *vb* decorate (an article, esp of furniture) by inserting pieces of wood, ivory, or metal so that the surfaces are smooth and flat

INLAYER > INLAY

INLAYERS > INLAY

INLAYING > INLAY

INLAYINGS > INLAY

INLAYS > INLAY

INLET *n* narrow strip of water extending from the sea into the land ▷ *vb* insert or inlay

INLETS > INLET

INLETTING > INLET

INLIER *n* outcrop of rocks that is entirely surrounded by younger rocks

INLIERS > INLIER

INLOCK *vb* lock up

INLOCKED > INLOCK

INLOCKING > INLOCK

INLOCKS > INLOCK

INLY *adv* inwardly

INLYING *adj* situated within or inside

INMATE *n* person living in an institution such as a prison

INMATES > INMATE

INMESH *variant spelling of* > ENMESH

INMESHED > INMESH

INMESHES > INMESH

INMESHING > INMESH

INMIGRANT *adj* coming in from another area of the same country ▷ *n* inmigrant person or animal

INMOST *adj* innermost

INN *n* pub or small hotel, esp in the country ▷ *vb* stay at an inn

INNAGE *n* measurement from bottom of container to surface of liquid

INNAGES > INNAGE

INNARDS *pl n* internal organs

INNATE *adj* being part of someone's nature, inborn

INNATELY > INNATE

INNATIVE *adj* native

INNED > INN

INNER *adj* happening or located inside ▷ *n* red innermost ring on a target

INNERLY > INNER

INNERMOST *adj* furthest inside

INNERNESS > INNER

INNERS > INNER

INNERSOLE *same as* > INSOLE

INNERVATE *vb* supply nerves to (a bodily organ or part)

INNERVE *vb* supply with nervous energy

INNERVED > INNERVE

INNERVES > INNERVE

INNERVING > INNERVE

INNERWEAR *n* underwear

INNING *n* division of the game consisting of a turn at batting and a turn in the field for each side

INNINGS > INNING

INNKEEPER *n* owner or manager of an inn

INNLESS *adj* without inns

INNOCENCE *n* quality or state of being innocent

INNOCENCY *same as* > INNOCENCE

INNOCENT *adj* not guilty of a crime ▷ *n* innocent person, esp a child

INNOCENTS > INNOCENT

INNOCUITY > INNOCUOUS

INNOCUOUS *adj* not harmful

INNOVATE *vb* introduce new ideas or methods

INNOVATED > INNOVATE

INNOVATES > INNOVATE

INNOVATOR > INNOVATE

INNOXIOUS *adj* not noxious

INNS > INN

INNUENDO *n* (remark making) an indirect reference to something rude or unpleasant

INNUENDOS > INNUENDO

INNYARD *n* courtyard of an inn

INNYARDS > INNYARD

INOCULA > INOCULUM

INOCULANT *same as* > INOCULUM

INOCULATE *vb* protect against disease by injecting with a vaccine

INOCULUM *n* substance used in giving an inoculation

INOCULUMS > INOCULUM

INODOROUS *adj* odourless

INOPINATE *adj* unexpected

INORB *vb* enclose in or as if in an orb

INORBED > INORB

INORBING > INORB

INORBS > INORB

INORGANIC *adj* not having the characteristics of living organisms

INORNATE *adj* simple

INOSINE *n* type of molecule making up cell

INOSINES > INOSINE

INOSITE *same as* > INOSITOL

INOSITES > INOSITE

INOSITOL *n* cyclic alcohol

INOSITOLS > INOSITOL

INOTROPIC *adj* affecting or controlling the contraction of muscles, esp those of the heart

INPATIENT *n* patient who stays in a hospital for treatment

INPAYMENT *n* money paid into a bank account

INPHASE *adj* in the same phase

INPOUR *vb* pour in

INPOURED > INPOUR

INPOURING > INPOUR

INPOURS > INPOUR

INPUT *n* resources put into a project etc ▷ *vb* enter (data) in a computer

INPUTS > INPUT

INPUTTED > INPUT

INPUTTER > INPUT

INPUTTERS > INPUT

INPUTTING > INPUT

INQILAB *n* (in India, Pakistan, etc) revolution

INQILABS > INQILAB

INQUERE *Spenserian form of* > INQUIRE

INQUERED > INQUERE

INQUERES > INQUERE

INQUERING > INQUERE

INQUEST *n* official inquiry into a sudden death

INQUESTS > INQUEST

INQUIET *vb* disturb

INQUIETED > INQUIET

INQUIETLY > INQUIET

INQUIETS > INQUIET

INQUILINE *n* animal that lives in close association with another animal without harming it ▷ *adj* of or living as an inquiline

INQUINATE *vb* corrupt

INQUIRE *vb* seek information or ask (about)

INQUIRED > INQUIRE

INQUIRER > INQUIRE

INQUIRERS > INQUIRE

INQUIRES > INQUIRE

INQUIRIES > INQUIRY

INQUIRING > INQUIRE

INQUIRY *n* question

INQUORATE *adj* without enough people present to make a quorum

INRO *n* Japanese seal-box

INROAD *n* invasion or hostile attack

INROADS > INROAD

INRUN *n* slope down which ski jumpers ski

INRUNS > INRUN

INRUSH *n* sudden and overwhelming inward flow ▷ *vb* flow or rush suddenly and overwhelmingly

INRUSHES > INRUSH

INRUSHING > INRUSH

INS > IN

INSANE *adj* mentally ill

INSANELY > INSANE

INSANER > INSANE

INSANEST > INSANE

INSANIE *n* insanity

INSANIES > INSANIE

INSANITY *n* state of being insane

INSATIATE *adj* not able to be satisfied

INSATIETY *n* insatiability

INSCAPE *n* essential inner nature of a person, an object, etc

INSCAPES > INSCAPE

INSCIENCE *n* ignorance

INSCIENT *adj* ignorant

INSCONCE *vb* fortify

INSCONCED > INSCONCE

INSCONCES > INSCONCE

INSCRIBE *vb* write or carve words on

INSCRIBED > INSCRIBE

INSCRIBER > INSCRIBE

INSCRIBES > INSCRIBE

INSCROLL *vb* write on a scroll

INSCROLLS > INSCROLL
INSCULP vb engrave
INSCULPED > INSCULP
INSCULPS > INSCULP
INSCULPT adj engraved
INSEAM vb contain
INSEAMED > INSEAM
INSEAMING > INSEAM
INSEAMS > INSEAM
INSECT n small animal with six legs and usu wings, such as an ant or fly
INSECTAN > INSECT
INSECTARY n place where insects are kept
INSECTEAN > INSECT
INSECTILE > INSECT
INSECTION n incision
INSECTS > INSECT
INSECURE adj anxious, not confident
INSEEM vb cover with grease
INSEEMED > INSEEM
INSEEMING > INSEEM
INSEEMS > INSEEM
INSELBERG n isolated rocky hill rising abruptly from a flat plain
INSENSATE adj without sensation, unconscious
INSERT vb put inside or include ▷ n something inserted
INSERTED adj (of a muscle) attached to the bone that it moves
INSERTER > INSERT
INSERTERS > INSERT
INSERTING > INSERT
INSERTION n act of inserting
INSERTS > INSERT
INSET n small picture inserted within a larger one ▷ vb place in or within ▷ adj decorated with something inserted
INSETS > INSET
INSETTED > INSET
INSETTER > INSET
INSETTERS > INSET
INSETTING > INSET
INSHALLAH sentence substitute if Allah wills it
INSHEATH vb sheathe
INSHEATHE vb sheathe
INSHEATHS > INSHEATH
INSHELL vb retreat, as into a shell
INSHELLED > INSHELL
INSHELLS > INSHELL
INSHELTER vb put in a shelter
INSHIP vb travel or send by ship
INSHIPPED > INSHIP
INSHIPS > INSHIP
INSHORE adj close to the shore ▷ adv towards the shore
INSHRINE variant spelling of > ENSHRINE
INSHRINED > INSHRINE
INSHRINES > INSHRINE
INSIDE prep in or to the interior of ▷ adj on or of

the inside ▷ adv on, in, or to the inside, indoors ▷ n inner side, surface, or part
INSIDER n member of a group who has privileged knowledge about it
INSIDERS > INSIDER
INSIDES > INSIDE
INSIDIOUS adj subtle or unseen but dangerous
INSIGHT n deep understanding
INSIGHTS > INSIGHT
INSIGNE same as > INSIGNIA
INSIGNIA n badge or emblem of honour or office
INSIGNIAS > INSIGNIA
INSINCERE adj showing false feelings, not genuine
INSINEW vb connect or strengthen, as with sinews
INSINEWED > INSINEW
INSINEWS > INSINEW
INSINUATE vb suggest indirectly
INSIPID adj lacking interest, spirit, or flavour
INSIPIDLY > INSIPID
INSIPIENT adj lacking wisdom
INSIST vb demand or state firmly
INSISTED > INSIST
INSISTENT adj making persistent demands
INSISTER > INSIST
INSISTERS > INSIST
INSISTING > INSIST
INSISTS > INSIST
INSNARE less common spelling of > ENSNARE
INSNARED > INSNARE
INSNARER > INSNARE
INSNARERS > INSNARE
INSNARES > INSNARE
INSNARING > INSNARE
INSOFAR adv to the extent
INSOLATE vb expose to sunlight, as for bleaching
INSOLATED > INSOLATE
INSOLATES > INSOLATE
INSOLE n inner sole of a shoe or boot
INSOLENCE > INSOLENT
INSOLENT n insolent person ▷ adj rude and disrespectful
INSOLENTS > INSOLENT
INSOLES > INSOLE
INSOLUBLE adj incapable of being solved
INSOLUBLY > INSOLUBLE
INSOLVENT adj unable to pay one's debts ▷ n person who is insolvent
INSOMNIA n inability to sleep
INSOMNIAC adj exhibiting or causing insomnia ▷ n person experiencing insomnia
INSOMNIAS > INSOMNIA
INSOMUCH adv such an extent
INSOOTH adv indeed
INSOUL variant of > ENSOUL
INSOULED > INSOUL

INSOULING > INSOUL
INSOULS > INSOUL
INSPAN vb harness (animals) to (a vehicle)
INSPANNED > INSPAN
INSPANS > INSPAN
INSPECT vb check closely or officially
INSPECTED > INSPECT
INSPECTOR n person who inspects
INSPECTS > INSPECT
INSPHERE variant spelling of > ENSPHERE
INSPHERED > INSPHERE
INSPHERES > INSPHERE
INSPIRE vb fill with enthusiasm, stimulate
INSPIRED adj brilliantly creative
INSPIRER > INSPIRE
INSPIRERS > INSPIRE
INSPIRES > INSPIRE
INSPIRING > INSPIRE
INSPIRIT vb fill with vigour
INSPIRITS > INSPIRIT
INSTABLE less common word for > UNSTABLE
INSTAL same as > INSTALL
INSTALL vb put in and prepare (equipment) for use
INSTALLED > INSTALL
INSTALLER > INSTALL
INSTALLS > INSTALL
INSTALS > INSTAL
INSTANCE n particular example ▷ vb mention as an example
INSTANCED > INSTANCE
INSTANCES > INSTANCE
INSTANCY n quality of being urgent or imminent
INSTANT n very brief time ▷ adj happening at once
INSTANTER adv without delay
INSTANTLY adv immediately
INSTANTS > INSTANT
INSTAR vb decorate with stars ▷ n stage in the development of an insect between any two moults
INSTARRED > INSTAR
INSTARS > INSTAR
INSTATE vb place in a position or office
INSTATED > INSTATE
INSTATES > INSTATE
INSTATING > INSTATE
INSTEAD adv as a replacement or substitute
INSTEP n part of the foot forming the arch between the ankle and toes
INSTEPS > INSTEP
INSTIGATE vb cause to happen
INSTIL vb introduce (an idea etc) gradually into someone's mind
INSTILL same as > INSTIL
INSTILLED > INSTIL
INSTILLER > INSTIL
INSTILLS > INSTIL
INSTILS > INSTIL

INSTINCT n inborn tendency to behave in a certain way ▷ adj animated or impelled (by)
INSTINCTS > INSTINCT
INSTITUTE n organization set up for a specific purpose, esp research or teaching ▷ vb start or establish
INSTRESS vb create or sustain
INSTROKE n inward stroke
INSTROKES > INSTROKE
INSTRUCT vb order to do something
INSTRUCTS > INSTRUCT
INSUCKEN adj of a sucken
INSULA n pyramid-shaped area of the brain within each cerebral hemisphere beneath parts of the frontal and temporal lobes
INSULAE > INSULA
INSULANT same as > INSULATION
INSULANTS > INSULANT
INSULAR adj not open to new ideas, narrow-minded ▷ n islander
INSULARLY > INSULAR
INSULARS > INSULAR
INSULAS > INSULA
INSULATE vb prevent or reduce the transfer of electricity, heat, or sound by surrounding or lining with a nonconducting material
INSULATED > INSULATE
INSULATES > INSULATE
INSULATOR n any material or device that insulates
INSULIN n hormone produced in the pancreas that controls the amount of sugar in the blood
INSULINS > INSULIN
INSULSE adj stupid
INSULSITY n stupidity
INSULT vb behave rudely to, offend ▷ n insulting remark or action
INSULTANT adj insulting
INSULTED > INSULT
INSULTER > INSULT
INSULTERS > INSULT
INSULTING > INSULT
INSULTS > INSULT
INSURABLE > INSURE
INSURANCE n agreement by which one makes regular payments to a company who pay an agreed sum if damage, loss, or death occurs
INSURANT n holder of an insurance policy
INSURANTS > INSURANT
INSURE vb protect by insurance
INSURED adj covered by insurance ▷ n person, persons, or organization covered by an insurance policy
INSUREDS > INSURED

INSURER n person or company that sells insurance
INSURERS > INSURER
INSURES > INSURE
INSURGENT adj in revolt against an established authority ▷ n person who takes part in a rebellion
INSURING > INSURE
INSWATHE vb bind or wrap
INSWATHED > INSWATHE
INSWATHES > INSWATHE
INSWEPT adj narrowed towards the front
INSWING n movement of a bowled ball from off to leg through the air
INSWINGER n ball bowled so as to move from off to leg through the air
INSWINGS > INSWING
INTACT adj not changed or damaged in any way
INTACTLY > INTACT
INTAGLI > INTAGLIO
INTAGLIO n (gem carved with) an engraved design
INTAGLIOS > INTAGLIO
INTAKE n amount or number taken in
INTAKES > INTAKE
INTARSIA n decorative or pictorial mosaic of inlaid wood or sometimes ivory of a style developed in the Italian Renaissance and used esp on wooden wall panels
INTARSIAS > INTARSIA
INTEGER n positive or negative whole number or zero
INTEGERS > INTEGER
INTEGRAL adj being an essential part of a whole ▷ n sum of a large number of very small quantities
INTEGRALS > INTEGRAL
INTEGRAND n mathematical function to be integrated
INTEGRANT adj part of a whole ▷ n integrant thing or part
INTEGRATE vb combine into a whole ▷ adj made up of parts
INTEGRITY n quality of having high moral principles
INTEL n US military intelligence
INTELLECT n power of thinking and reasoning
INTELS > INTEL
INTENABLE adj untenable
INTEND vb propose or plan (to do something)
INTENDANT n provincial or colonial official of France, Spain, or Portugal
INTENDED adj planned or future ▷ n person whom one is to marry
INTENDEDS > INTENDED
INTENDER > INTEND
INTENDERS > INTEND

INTENDING > INTEND
INTENDS > INTEND
INTENIBLE adj incapable of holding
INTENSATE vb intensify
INTENSE adj of great strength or degree
INTENSELY > INTENSE
INTENSER > INTENSE
INTENSEST > INTENSE
INTENSIFY vb make or become more intense
INTENSION n set of characteristics or properties by which the referent or referents of a given word are determined
INTENSITY n state or quality of being intense
INTENSIVE adj using or needing concentrated effort or resources ▷ n intensifier or intensive pronoun or grammatical construction
INTENT n intention ▷ adj paying close attention
INTENTION n something intended
INTENTIVE adj intent
INTENTLY > INTENT
INTENTS > INTENT
INTER vb bury (a corpse)
INTERACT vb act on or in close relation with each other
INTERACTS > INTERACT
INTERAGE adj between different ages
INTERARCH vb have intersecting arches
INTERBANK adj conducted between or involving two or more banks
INTERBED vb lie between strata of different minerals
INTERBEDS > INTERBED
INTERBRED adj having been bred within a single family or strain so as to produce particular characteristics
INTERCEDE vb try to end a dispute between two people or groups
INTERCELL adj occurring between cells
INTERCEPT vb seize or stop in transit ▷ n point at which two figures intersect
INTERCITY adj (in Britain) denoting a fast train or passenger rail service, esp between main towns
INTERCLAN adj occurring between clans
INTERCLUB adj of, relating to, or conducted between two or more clubs
INTERCOM n internal communication system with loudspeakers
INTERCOMS > INTERCOM
INTERCROP n crop grown between the rows of another crop ▷ vb grow (one crop) between the rows of (another)

INTERCUT another word for > CROSSCUT
INTERCUTS > INTERCUT
INTERDASH vb dash between
INTERDEAL vb intrigue or plot
INTERDICT n official prohibition or restraint ▷ vb prohibit or forbid
INTERDINE vb eat together
INTERESS vb interest
INTERESSE vb interest
INTEREST n desire to know or hear more about something ▷ vb arouse the interest of
INTERESTS > INTEREST
INTERFACE n area where two things interact or link ▷ vb connect or be connected with by interface
INTERFERE vb try to influence other people's affairs where one is not involved or wanted
INTERFILE vb place (one or more items) among other items in a file or arrangement
INTERFIRM adj occurring between companies
INTERFLOW vb flow together
INTERFOLD vb fold together
INTERFUSE vb mix or become mixed
INTERGANG adj occurring between gangs
INTERGREW > INTERGROW
INTERGROW vb grow among
INTERIM adj temporary, provisional, or intervening ▷ n intervening time ▷ adv meantime
INTERIMS > INTERIM
INTERIOR n inside ▷ adj inside, inner
INTERIORS > INTERIOR
INTERJECT vb make (a remark) suddenly or as an interruption
INTERJOIN vb join together
INTERKNIT vb knit together
INTERKNOT vb knot together
INTERLACE vb join together as if by weaving
INTERLAID > INTERLAY
INTERLAP less common word for > OVERLAP
INTERLAPS > INTERLAP
INTERLARD vb insert in or occur throughout
INTERLAY vb insert (layers) between ▷ n material, such as paper, placed between a printing plate and its base
INTERLAYS > INTERLAY
INTERLEAF n extra leaf which is inserted
INTERLEND vb lend between libraries
INTERLENT > INTERLEND
INTERLINE vb write or print

(matter) between the lines of (a text or book)
INTERLINK vb connect together
INTERLOAN n loan between one library and another
INTERLOCK vb join firmly together ▷ n device used to prevent a mechanism from operating independently or unsafely ▷ adj (of fabric) closely knitted
INTERLOOP vb loop together
INTERLOPE vb intrude
INTERLUDE n short rest or break in an activity or event
INTERMALE adj occurring between males
INTERMAT n patch of seabed devoid of vegetation
INTERMATS > INTERMAT
INTERMENT n burial
INTERMESH vb net together
INTERMIT vb suspend (activity) or (of activity) to be suspended temporarily or at intervals
INTERMITS > INTERMIT
INTERMIX vb mix together
INTERMONT adj located between mountains
INTERMURE vb wall in
INTERN vb imprison, esp during a war ▷ n trainee doctor in a hospital
INTERNAL adj of or on the inside ▷ n medical examination of the vagina, uterus, or rectum
INTERNALS > INTERNAL
INTERNE same as > INTERN
INTERNED > INTERN
INTERNEE n person who is interned
INTERNEES > INTERNEE
INTERNES > INTERNE
INTERNET n worldwide computer network
INTERNETS > INTERNET
INTERNING > INTERN
INTERNIST n physician who specializes in internal medicine
INTERNODE n part of a plant stem between two nodes
INTERNS > INTERN
INTERPAGE vb print (matter) on intervening pages
INTERPLAY n action and reaction of two things upon each other
INTERPLED adj having instituted a particular type of proceedings
INTERPONE vb interpose
INTERPOSE vb insert between or among things
INTERPRET vb explain the meaning of
INTERRACE adj between races
INTERRAIL vb travel on an international rail pass

INTERRED > INTER

INTERREX n person who governs during an interregnum

INTERRING > INTER

INTERROW adj occurring between rows

INTERRUPT vb break into (a conversation etc) ▷ n signal to initiate the stopping of the running of one computer program in order to run another

INTERS > INTER

INTERSECT vb (of roads) meet and cross

INTERSERT vb insert between

INTERSEX n condition of having characteristics intermediate between those of a male and a female

INTERTERM adj occurring between terms

INTERTEXT adj text seen as modifying another text in literary theory

INTERTIE n short roofing timber

INTERTIES > INTERTIE

INTERTILL vb cultivate between rows of crops

INTERUNIT adj occurring between units

INTERVAL n time between two particular moments or events

INTERVALE dialect form of > INTERVAL

INTERVALS > INTERVAL

INTERVEIN vb intersect

INTERVENE vb involve oneself in a situation, esp to prevent conflict

INTERVIEW n formal discussion, esp between a job-seeker and an employer ▷ vb conduct an interview with

INTERWAR adj of or happening in the period between World War I and World War II

INTERWIND vb wind together

INTERWORK same as > INTERWEAVE

INTERWOVE adj having been woven together

INTERZONE n area between two occupied zones

INTESTACY > INTESTATE

INTESTATE adj not having made a will ▷ n person who dies without having made a will

INTESTINE n lower part of the alimentary canal between the stomach and the anus

INTHRAL archaic form of > ENTHRAL

INTHRALL archaic form of > ENTHRAL

INTHRALLS > INTHRALL

INTHRALS > INTHRAL

INTHRONE archaic form of > ENTHRONE

INTHRONED > INTHRONE

INTHRONES > INTHRONE

INTI n former monetary unit of Peru

INTIFADA n Palestinian uprising against Israel in the West Bank and Gaza Strip

INTIFADAH same as > INTIFADA

INTIFADAS > INTIFADA

INTIFADEH same as > INTIFADA

INTIL Scot form of > INTO

INTIMA n innermost layer of an organ or part, esp of a blood vessel

INTIMACY n close or warm friendship

INTIMAE > INTIMA

INTIMAL > INTIMA

INTIMAS > INTIMA

INTIMATE adj having a close personal relationship ▷ n close friend ▷ vb hint at or suggest

INTIMATED > INTIMATE

INTIMATER > INTIMATE

INTIMATES > INTIMATE

INTIME adj intimate

INTIMISM n school of impressionist painting

INTIMISMS > INTIMISM

INTIMIST > INTIMISM

INTIMISTE > INTIMISM

INTIMISTS > INTIMISM

INTIMITY n intimacy

INTINE n inner wall of a pollen grain or a spore

INTINES > INTINE

INTIRE archaic form of > ENTIRE

INTIS > INTI

INTITLE archaic form of > ENTITLE

INTITLED > INTITLE

INTITLES > INTITLE

INTITLING > INTITLE

INTITULE vb (in Britain) to entitle (an act of parliament)

INTITULED > INTITULE

INTITULES > INTITULE

INTO prep indicating motion towards the centre, result of a change, division, etc

INTOED adj having inward-turning toes

INTOMB same as > ENTOMB

INTOMBED > INTOMB

INTOMBING > INTOMB

INTOMBS > INTOMB

INTONACO n wet plaster surface on which frescoes are painted

INTONACOS > INTONACO

INTONATE vb pronounce or articulate (continuous connected speech) with a characteristic rise and fall of the voice

INTONATED > INTONATE

INTONATES > INTONATE

INTONATOR > INTONATE

INTONE vb speak or recite in an unvarying tone of voice

INTONED > INTONE

INTONER > INTONE

INTONERS > INTONE

INTONES > INTONE

INTONING > INTONE

INTONINGS > INTONE

INTORSION n spiral twisting in plant stems or other parts

INTORT vb twist inward

INTORTED > INTORT

INTORTING > INTORT

INTORTION > INTORT

INTORTS > INTORT

INTOWN adj infield

INTRA prep within

INTRACITY same as > INTERCITY

INTRADA n prelude

INTRADAS > INTRADA

INTRADAY adj occurring within one day

INTRADOS n inner curve or surface of an arch or vault

INTRANET n internal network that makes use of Internet technology

INTRANETS > INTRANET

INTRANT n one who enters

INTRANTS > INTRANT

INTREAT archaic spelling of > ENTREAT

INTREATED > INTREAT

INTREATS > INTREAT

INTRENCH less common spelling of > ENTRENCH

INTREPID adj fearless, bold

INTRICACY > INTRICATE

INTRICATE adj involved or complicated

INTRIGANT n person who intrigues

INTRIGUE vb make interested or curious ▷ n secret plotting

INTRIGUED > INTRIGUE

INTRIGUER > INTRIGUE

INTRIGUES > INTRIGUE

INTRINCE adj intricate

INTRINSIC adj essential to the basic nature of something

INTRO n introduction

INTRODUCE vb present (someone) by name (to another person)

INTROFIED > INTROFY

INTROFIES > INTROFY

INTROFY vb increase the wetting properties

INTROIT n short prayer said or sung as the celebrant is entering the sanctuary to celebrate Mass

INTROITAL > INTROIT

INTROITS > INTROIT

INTROITUS n entrance to a body cavity

INTROJECT vb (esp of a child) to incorporate ideas of others, or (in fantasy) of objects

INTROLD variant of > ENTROLD

INTROMIT vb enter or insert or allow to enter or be inserted

INTROMITS > INTROMIT

INTRON n stretch of DNA that interrupts a gene and does not contribute to the specification of a protein

INTRONS > INTRON

INTRORSE adj turned inwards or towards the axis

INTROS > INTRO

INTROVERT n person concerned more with his or her thoughts and feelings than with the outside world ▷ adj shy and quiet ▷ vb turn (a hollow organ or part) inside out

INTRUDE vb come in or join in without being invited

INTRUDED > INTRUDE

INTRUDER n person who enters a place without permission

INTRUDERS > INTRUDER

INTRUDES > INTRUDE

INTRUDING > INTRUDE

INTRUSION n act of intruding

INTRUSIVE adj characterized by intrusion or tending to intrude

INTRUST same as > ENTRUST

INTRUSTED > INTRUST

INTRUSTS > INTRUST

INTUBATE vb insert a tube or cannula into (a hollow organ)

INTUBATED > INTUBATE

INTUBATES > INTUBATE

INTUIT vb know or discover by intuition

INTUITED > INTUIT

INTUITING > INTUIT

INTUITION n instinctive knowledge or insight without conscious reasoning

INTUITIVE adj of, possessing, or resulting from intuition

INTUITS > INTUIT

INTUMESCE vb swell or become swollen

INTURN n inward turn

INTURNED adj turned inward

INTURNS > INTURN

INTUSE n contusion

INTUSES > INTUSE

INTWINE less common spelling of > ENTWINE

INTWINED > INTWINE

INTWINES > INTWINE

INTWINING > INTWINE

INTWIST vb twist together

INTWISTED > INTWIST

INTWISTS > INTWIST

INUKSHUIT > INUKSHUK

INUKSHUK n stone used by Inuit people to mark a location

INUKSHUKS > INUKSHUK

INULA n plant of the elecampane genus

INULAS > INULA

INULASE n enzyme that hydrolyses inulin to

fructose

INULASES > INULASE

INULIN n fructose polysaccharide present in the tubers and rhizomes of some plants

INULINS > INULIN

INUMBRATE vb shade

INUNCTION n application of an ointment to the skin, esp by rubbing

INUNDANT > INUNDATE

INUNDATE vb flood

INUNDATED > INUNDATE

INUNDATES > INUNDATE

INUNDATOR > INUNDATE

INURBANE adj not urbane

INURE vb cause to accept or become hardened to

INURED > INURE

INUREMENT > INURE

INURES > INURE

INURING > INURE

INURN vb place (esp cremated ashes) in an urn

INURNED > INURN

INURNING > INURN

INURNMENT > INURN

INURNS > INURN

INUSITATE adj out of use

INUST adj burnt in

INUSTION > INUST

INUSTIONS > INUST

INUTILE adj useless

INUTILELY > INUTILE

INUTILITY > INUTILE

INVADABLE > INVADE

INVADE vb enter (a country) by military force

INVADED > INVADE

INVADER > INVADE

INVADERS > INVADE

INVADES > INVADE

INVADING > INVADE

INVALID n disabled or chronically ill person ▷ vb dismiss from active service because of illness or injury ▷ adj having no legal force

INVALIDED > INVALID

INVALIDLY > INVALID

INVALIDS > INVALID

INVAR n alloy made from iron and nickel

INVARIANT n entity, quantity, etc, that is unaltered by a particular transformation of coordinates

INVARS > INVAR

INVASION n invading

INVASIONS > INVASION

INVASIVE adj of or relating to an invasion, intrusion, etc

INVEAGLE archaic form of > INVEIGLE

INVEAGLED > INVEAGLE

INVEAGLES > INVEAGLE

INVECKED same as > INVECTED

INVECTED adj bordered with small convex curves

INVECTIVE n abusive speech or writing ▷ adj characterized by or using abusive language, bitter

sarcasm, etc

INVEIGH vb criticize strongly

INVEIGHED > INVEIGH

INVEIGHER > INVEIGH

INVEIGHS > INVEIGH

INVEIGLE vb coax by cunning or trickery

INVEIGLED > INVEIGLE

INVEIGLER > INVEIGLE

INVEIGLES > INVEIGLE

INVENIT (he or she) designed it: used formerly on objects such as pocket watches next to the designer's name

INVENT vb think up or create (something new)

INVENTED > INVENT

INVENTER same as > INVENTOR

INVENTERS > INVENTER

INVENTING > INVENT

INVENTION n something invented

INVENTIVE adj creative and resourceful

INVENTOR n person who invents, esp as a profession

INVENTORS > INVENTOR

INVENTORY n detailed list of goods or furnishings ▷ vb make a list of

INVENTS > INVENT

INVERITY n untruth

INVERNESS n type of cape

INVERSE vb make something opposite or contrary in effect ▷ adj reversed in effect, sequence, direction, etc ▷ n exact opposite

INVERSED > INVERSE

INVERSELY > INVERSE

INVERSES > INVERSE

INVERSING > INVERSE

INVERSION n act of inverting or state of being inverted

INVERSIVE > INVERSION

INVERT vb turn upside down or inside out ▷ n homosexual

INVERTASE n enzyme, occurring in the intestinal juice of animals and in yeasts

INVERTED > INVERT

INVERTER n any device for converting a direct current into an alternating current

INVERTERS > INVERTER

INVERTIN same as > INVERTASE

INVERTING > INVERT

INVERTINS > INVERTIN

INVERTOR same as > INVERTER

INVERTORS > INVERTOR

INVERTS > INVERT

INVEST vb spend (money, time, etc) on something with the expectation of profit

INVESTED > INVEST

INVESTING > INVEST

INVESTOR > INVEST

INVESTORS > INVEST

INVESTS > INVEST

INVEXED adj concave

INVIABLE adj not viable, esp financially

INVIABLY > INVIABLE

INVIDIOUS adj likely to cause resentment

INVIOLACY > INVIOLATE

INVIOLATE adj unharmed, unaffected

INVIOUS adj without paths or roads

INVIRILE adj unmanly

INVISCID adj not viscid

INVISIBLE adj not able to be seen ▷ n invisible item of trade

INVISIBLY > INVISIBLE

INVITAL adj not vital

INVITE vb request the company of ▷ n invitation

INVITED > INVITE

INVITEE n one who is invited

INVITEES > INVITEE

INVITER > INVITE

INVITERS > INVITE

INVITES > INVITE

INVITING adj tempting, attractive ▷ n old word for invitation

INVITINGS > INVITING

INVOCABLE > INVOKE

INVOCATE archaic word for > INVOKE

INVOCATED > INVOCATE

INVOCATES > INVOCATE

INVOCATOR > INVOCATE

INVOICE n (present with) a bill for goods or services supplied ▷ vb present (a customer) with an invoice

INVOICED > INVOICE

INVOICES > INVOICE

INVOICING > INVOICE

INVOKE vb put (a law or penalty) into operation

INVOKED > INVOKE

INVOKER > INVOKE

INVOKERS > INVOKE

INVOKES > INVOKE

INVOKING > INVOKE

INVOLUCEL n ring of bracts at the base of the florets of a compound umbel

INVOLUCRA n involucres

INVOLUCRE n ring of bracts at the base of an inflorescence in such plants as the composites

INVOLUTE adj complex, intricate, or involved ▷ n curve described by the free end of a thread as it is wound around another curve on the same plane ▷ vb become involute

INVOLUTED > INVOLUTE

INVOLUTES > INVOLUTE

INVOLVE vb include as a necessary part

INVOLVED > INVOLVE

INVOLVER > INVOLVE

INVOLVERS > INVOLVE

INVOLVES > INVOLVE

INVOLVING > INVOLVE

INWALL vb surround with a wall

INWALLED > INWALL

INWALLING > INWALL

INWALLS > INWALL

INWARD adj directed towards the middle ▷ adv towards the inside or middle ▷ n inward part

INWARDLY adv within the private thoughts or feelings

INWARDS adv towards the inside or middle of something

INWEAVE vb weave together into or as if into a design, fabric, etc

INWEAVED > INWEAVE

INWEAVES > INWEAVE

INWEAVING > INWEAVE

INWICK vb perform a curling stroke in which the stone bounces off another stone

INWICKED > INWICK

INWICKING > INWICK

INWICKS > INWICK

INWIND vb wind or coil around

INWINDING > INWIND

INWINDS > INWIND

INWIT n conscience

INWITH adv within

INWITS > INWIT

INWORK vb work in

INWORKED > INWORK

INWORKING > INWORK

INWORKS > INWORK

INWORN adj worn in

INWOUND > INWIND

INWOVE > INWEAVE

INWOVEN > INWEAVE

INWRAP less common spelling of > ENWRAP

INWRAPPED > INWRAP

INWRAPS > INWRAP

INWREATHE same as > ENWREATHE

INWROUGHT adj worked or woven into material, esp decoratively

INYALA n antelope

INYALAS > INYALA

IO n type of moth

IODATE same as > IODIZE

IODATED > IODATE

IODATES > IODATE

IODATING > IODATE

IODATION > IODATE

IODATIONS > IODATE

IODIC adj of or containing iodine

IODID same as > IODIDE

IODIDE n compound containing an iodine atom, such as methyl iodide

IODIDES > IODIDE

IODIDS > IODID

IODIN same as > IODINE

IODINATE vb cause to combine with iodine

IODINATED > IODINATE

IODINATES > IODINATE

IODINE n bluish-black element used in medicine and photography

IODINES > IODINE

IODINS > IODIN
IODISE same as > IODIZE
IODISED > IODISE
IODISER > IODISE
IODISERS > IODISE
IODISES > IODISE
IODISING > IODISE
IODISM n poisoning induced by ingestion of iodine or its compounds
IODISMS > IODISM
IODIZE vb treat with iodine
IODIZED > IODIZE
IODIZER > IODIZE
IODIZERS > IODIZE
IODIZES > IODIZE
IODIZING > IODIZE
IODOFORM n yellow crystalline insoluble volatile solid
IODOFORMS > IODOFORM
IODOMETRY n procedure used in volumetric analysis for determining the quantity of substance present that contains iodine
IODOPHILE adj taking an intense iodine stain
IODOPHOR n substance in which iodine is combined with an agent that renders it soluble
IODOPHORS > IODOPHOR
IODOPSIN n violet light-sensitive pigment in the cones of the retina of the eye that is responsible for colour vision
IODOPSINS > IODOPSIN
IODOUS adj of or containing iodine, esp in the trivalent state
IODURET n iodide
IODURETS > IODURET
IODYRITE n silver iodide
IODYRITES > IODYRITE
IOLITE n grey or violet-blue dichroic mineral
IOLITES > IOLITE
ION n electrically charged atom
IONIC adj of or in the form of ions
IONICITY n ionic character
IONICS pl n study of ions
IONISABLE > IONISE
IONISE same as > IONIZE
IONISED > IONISE
IONISER same as > IONIZER
IONISERS > IONISER
IONISES > IONISE
IONISING > IONISE
IONIUM n naturally occurring radioisotope of thorium
IONIUMS > IONIUM
IONIZABLE > IONIZE
IONIZE vb change into ions
IONIZED > IONIZE
IONIZER n person or thing that ionizes, esp an electrical device used within a room to refresh its atmosphere by restoring negative ions
IONIZERS > IONIZER

IONIZES > IONIZE
IONIZING > IONIZE
IONOGEN n compound that exists as ions when dissolved
IONOGENIC adj forming ions
IONOGENS > IONOGEN
IONOMER n thermoplastic with ionic bonding between polymer chains
IONOMERS > IONOMER
IONONE n yellowish liquid mixture of two isomers with an odour of violets
IONONES > IONONE
IONOPAUSE n transitional zone in the atmosphere between the ionosphere and the exosphere
IONOPHORE n chemical compound capable of forming a complex with an ion and transporting it through a biological membrane
IONOSONDE n instrument measuring ionization
IONOTROPY n reversible interconversion of a pair of organic isomers as a result of the migration of an ionic part of the molecule
IONS > ION
IOS > IO
IOTA n ninth letter in the Greek alphabet
IOTACISM n pronunciation tendency in Modern Greek
IOTACISMS > IOTACISM
IOTAS > IOTA
IPECAC n type of S American shrub
IPECACS > IPECAC
IPOMOEA n tropical or subtropical convolvulaceous plant
IPOMOEAS > IPOMOEA
IPPON n winning point awarded in a judo or karate competition
IPPONS > IPPON
IPRINDOLE n antidepressant
IRACUND adj easily angered
IRADE n written edict of a Muslim ruler
IRADES > IRADE
IRASCIBLE adj easily angered
IRASCIBLY > IRASCIBLE
IRATE adj very angry
IRATELY > IRATE
IRATENESS > IRATE
IRATER > IRATE
IRATEST > IRATE
IRE vb anger ▷ n anger
IRED > IRE
IREFUL > IRE
IREFULLY > IRE
IRELESS > IRE
IRENIC adj tending to conciliate or promote peace
IRENICAL same as > IRENIC
IRENICISM > IRENICS
IRENICON variant spelling of > EIRENICON

IRENICONS > IRENICON
IRENICS n that branch of theology that is concerned with unity between Christian sects and denominations
IRENOLOGY n study of peace
IRES > IRE
IRID n type of iris
IRIDAL > IRID
IRIDEAL > IRID
IRIDES > IRIS
IRIDIAL > IRID
IRIDIAN > IRID
IRIDIC adj of or containing iridium, esp in the tetravalent state
IRIDISE vb make iridescent
IRIDISED > IRIDISE
IRIDISES > IRIDISE
IRIDISING > IRIDISE
IRIDIUM n very hard corrosion-resistant metal
IRIDIUMS > IRIDIUM
IRIDIZE vb make iridescent
IRIDIZED > IRIDIZE
IRIDIZES > IRIDIZE
IRIDIZING > IRIDIZE
IRIDOCYTE n cell in the skin of fish that gives them iridescence
IRIDOLOGY n technique used in complementary medicine to diagnose illness by studying a patient's eyes
IRIDOTOMY n surgical incision into the iris, esp to create an artificial pupil
IRIDS > IRID
IRING > IRE
IRIS n coloured circular membrane of the eye containing the pupil ▷ vb display iridescence
IRISATE vb make iridescent
IRISATED > IRISATE
IRISATES > IRISATE
IRISATING > IRISATE
IRISATION > IRISATE
IRISCOPE n instrument that displays the prismatic colours
IRISCOPES > IRISCOPE
IRISED > IRIS
IRISES > IRIS
IRISING > IRIS
IRITIC > IRITIS
IRITIS n inflammation of the iris of the eye
IRITISES > IRITIS
IRK vb irritate, annoy
IRKED > IRK
IRKING > IRK
IRKS > IRK
IRKSOME adj irritating, annoying
IRKSOMELY > IRKSOME
IROKO n tropical African hardwood tree
IROKOS > IROKO
IRON n strong silvery-white metallic element, widely used for structural and engineering purposes ▷ adj made of iron ▷ vb smooth (clothes or fabric) with an

iron
IRONBARK n Australian eucalyptus with hard rough bark
IRONBARKS > IRONBARK
IRONBOUND adj bound with iron
IRONCLAD adj covered or protected with iron ▷ n large wooden 19th-century warship with armoured plating
IRONCLADS > IRONCLAD
IRONE n fragrant liquid
IRONED > IRON
IRONER > IRON
IRONERS > IRON
IRONES > IRONE
IRONIC adj using irony
IRONICAL same as > IRONIC
IRONIER > IRONY
IRONIES > IRONY
IRONIEST > IRONY
IRONING n clothes to be ironed
IRONINGS > IRONING
IRONISE same as > IRONIZE
IRONISED > IRONISE
IRONISES > IRONISE
IRONISING > IRONISE
IRONIST > IRONIZE
IRONISTS > IRONIZE
IRONIZE vb use or indulge in irony
IRONIZED > IRONIZE
IRONIZES > IRONIZE
IRONIZING > IRONIZE
IRONLESS > IRON
IRONLIKE > IRON
IRONMAN n very strong man
IRONMEN > IRONMAN
IRONNESS > IRON
IRONS > IRON
IRONSIDE n person with great stamina or resistance
IRONSIDES > IRONSIDE
IRONSMITH adj blacksmith
IRONSTONE n rock consisting mainly of iron ore
IRONWARE n domestic articles made of iron
IRONWARES > IRONWARE
IRONWEED n plant with purplish leaves
IRONWEEDS > IRONWEED
IRONWOMAN n very strong woman
IRONWOMEN > IRONWOMAN
IRONWOOD n any of various trees, such as hornbeam, with exceptionally hard wood
IRONWOODS > IRONWOOD
IRONWORK n work done in iron, esp decorative work
IRONWORKS n building in which iron is smelted, cast, or wrought
IRONY n mildly sarcastic use of words to imply the opposite of what is said ▷ adj of, resembling, or containing iron
IRRADIANT adj radiating light
IRRADIATE vb subject to or

treat with radiation

IRREAL *adj* unreal

IRREALITY *n* unreality

IRREDENTA > IRRIDENTA

IRREGULAR *adj* not regular or even ▷ *n* soldier not in a regular army

IRRELATED *adj* irrelevant

IRRIDENTA *n* region that is ethnically or historically tied to one country, but which is ruled by another

IRRIGABLE > IRRIGATE

IRRIGABLY > IRRIGATE

IRRIGATE *vb* supply (land) with water by artificial channels or pipes

IRRIGATED > IRRIGATE

IRRIGATES > IRRIGATE

IRRIGATOR > IRRIGATE

IRRIGUOUS *adj* well-watered

IRRISION *n* mockery

IRRISIONS > IRRISION

IRRISORY *adj* mocking

IRRITABLE *adj* easily annoyed

IRRITABLY > IRRITABLE

IRRITANCY > IRRITANT

IRRITANT *adj* causing irritation ▷ *n* something that annoys or irritates

IRRITANTS > IRRITANT

IRRITATE *vb* annoy, anger

IRRITATED > IRRITATE

IRRITATES > IRRITATE

IRRITATOR > IRRITATE

IRRUPT *vb* enter forcibly or suddenly

IRRUPTED > IRRUPT

IRRUPTING > IRRUPT

IRRUPTION > IRRUPT

IRRUPTIVE *adj* irrupting or tending to irrupt

IRRUPTS > IRRUPT

IS *third person singular present tense of* > BE

ISABEL *n* brown yellow colour

ISABELLA *same as* > ISABEL

ISABELLAS > ISABELLA

ISABELS > ISABEL

ISAGOGE *n* academic introduction to a specialized subject field or area of research

ISAGOGES > ISAGOGE

ISAGOGIC > ISAGOGICS

ISAGOGICS *n* introductory studies, esp in the history of the Bible

ISALLOBAR *n* line on a map connecting places with equal pressure changes

ISARITHM *n* line on a map connecting places with the same population density

ISARITHMS > ISARITHM

ISATIN *n* yellowish-red crystalline compound soluble in hot water, used for the preparation of vat dyes

ISATINE *same as* > ISATIN

ISATINES > ISATINE

ISATINIC > ISATIN

ISATINS > ISATIN

ISBA *n* log hut

ISBAS > ISBA

ISCHAEMIA *n* inadequate supply of blood to an organ or part, as from an obstructed blood flow

ISCHAEMIC > ISCHAEMIA

ISCHEMIA *same as* > ISCHAEMIA

ISCHEMIAS > ISCHEMIA

ISCHEMIC > ISCHAEMIA

ISCHIA > ISCHIUM

ISCHIADIC > ISCHIUM

ISCHIAL > ISCHIUM

ISCHIATIC > ISCHIUM

ISCHIUM *n* one of the three sections of the hipbone, situated below the ilium

ISCHURIA *n* retention of urine

ISCHURIAS > ISCHURIA

ISEIKONIA *n* seeing of same image in both eyes

ISEIKONIC > ISEIKONIA

ISENERGIC *adj* of equal energy

ISH *n* issue

ISHES > ISH

ISINGLASS *n* kind of gelatine obtained from some freshwater fish

ISIT *sentence substitute* expression used to seek confirmation of something or show one is listening

ISLAND *n* piece of land surrounded by water ▷ *vb* cause to become an island

ISLANDED > ISLAND

ISLANDER *n* person who lives on an island

ISLANDERS > ISLANDER

ISLANDING > ISLAND

ISLANDS > ISLAND

ISLE *vb* make an isle of ▷ *n* island

ISLED > ISLE

ISLELESS *adj* without islands

ISLEMAN *n* islander

ISLEMEN > ISLEMAN

ISLES > ISLE

ISLESMAN > ISLESMAN

ISLESMEN > ISLESMAN

ISLET *n* small island

ISLETED *adj* having islets

ISLETS > ISLET

ISLING > ISLE

ISLOMANIA *n* obsessional enthusiasm or partiality for islands

ISM *n* doctrine, system, or practice

ISMATIC *adj* following fashionable doctrines

ISMATICAL *same as* > ISMATIC

ISMS > ISM

ISNA *vb* is not

ISNAE *same as* > ISNA

ISO *n* short segment of film that can be replayed easily

ISOAMYL as in *isoamyl acetate*, , colourless volatile compound used as a solvent for cellulose lacquers and as a

flavouring

ISOAMYLS > ISOAMYL

ISOBAR *n* line on a map connecting places of equal atmospheric pressure

ISOBARE *same as* > ISOBAR

ISOBARES > ISOBARE

ISOBARIC *adj* having equal atmospheric pressure

ISOBARISM > ISOBAR

ISOBARS > ISOBAR

ISOBASE *n* line connecting points of equal land upheaval

ISOBASES > ISOBASE

ISOBATH *n* line on a map connecting points of equal underwater depth

ISOBATHIC > ISOBATH

ISOBATHS > ISOBATH

ISOBRONT *n* line connecting points of simultaneous storm development

ISOBRONTS > ISOBRONT

ISOBUTANE *n* form of butane

ISOBUTENE *n* isomer of butene

ISOBUTYL as in *methyl isobutyl ketone* colourless insoluble liquid ketone used as a solvent for organic compounds

ISOBUTYLS > ISOBUTYL

ISOCHASM *n* line connecting points of equal aurorae frequency

ISOCHASMS > ISOCHASM

ISOCHEIM *n* line on a map connecting places with the same mean winter temperature

ISOCHEIMS > ISOCHEIM

ISOCHIMAL > ISOCHIME

ISOCHIME *same as* > ISOCHEIM

ISOCHIMES > ISOCHIME

ISOCHOR *n* line on a graph showing the variation of the temperature of a fluid with its pressure, when the volume is kept constant

ISOCHORE *same as* > ISOCHOR

ISOCHORES > ISOCHORE

ISOCHORIC > ISOCHOR

ISOCHORS > ISOCHOR

ISOCHRON *n* line on an isotope ratio diagram denoting a suite of rock or mineral samples all formed at the same time

ISOCHRONE *n* line on a map or diagram connecting places from which it takes the same time to travel to a certain point

ISOCHRONS > ISOCHRON

ISOCLINAL *adj* sloping in the same direction and at the same angle ▷ *n* imaginary line connecting points on the earth's surface having equal angles of dip

ISOCLINE *same as* > ISOCLINAL

ISOCLINES > ISOCLINE

ISOCLINIC *same as* > ISOCLINAL

ISOCRACY *n* form of government in which all people have equal powers

ISOCRATIC > ISOCRACY

ISOCRYMAL *same as* > ISOCRYME

ISOCRYME *n* line connecting points of equal winter temperature

ISOCRYMES > ISOCRYME

ISOCYANIC as in *isocyanic acid*, , hypothetical acid known only in the form of its compounds

ISOCYCLIC *adj* containing a closed ring of atoms of the same kind, esp carbon atoms

ISODICA > ISODICON

ISODICON *n* short anthem

ISODOMA > ISODOMON

ISODOMON *n* masonry formed of uniform blocks, with courses are of equal height

ISODOMONS > ISODOMON

ISODOMOUS > ISODOMON

ISODOMUM *same as* > ISODOMON

ISODONT *n* animal in which the teeth are of similar size

ISODONTAL *same as* > ISONDONT

ISODONTS > ISODONT

ISODOSE *n* dose of radiation applied to a part of the body in radiotherapy that is equal to the dose applied to a different part

ISODOSES > ISODOSE

ISOENZYME *same as* > ISOZYME

ISOETES *n* quillwort

ISOFORM *n* protein similar in function but not form to another

ISOFORMS > ISOFORM

ISOGAMETE *n* gamete that is similar in size and form to the one with which it unites in fertilization

ISOGAMIC > ISOGAMY

ISOGAMIES > ISOGAMY

ISOGAMOUS > ISOGAMY

ISOGAMY *n* (in some algae and fungi) sexual fusion of gametes of similar size and form

ISOGENEIC *same as* > ISOGENIC

ISOGENIC *same as* > ISOGENOUS

ISOGENIES > ISOGENOUS

ISOGENOUS *adj* of similar origin, as parts derived from the same embryonic tissue

ISOGENY > ISOGENOUS

ISOGLOSS *n* line drawn on a map around the area in which a linguistic feature is to be found, such as a particular pronunciation of a given word

ISOGON *n* equiangular polygon
ISOGONAL *same as* > ISOGONIC
ISOGONALS > ISOGONAL
ISOGONE *same as* > ISOGONIC
ISOGONES > ISOGONE
ISOGONIC *adj* having, making, or involving equal angles ▷ *n* imaginary line connecting points on the earth's surface having equal magnetic declination
ISOGONICS > ISOGONIC
ISOGONIES > ISOGONY
ISOGONS > ISOGON
ISOGONY > ISOGONIC
ISOGRAFT *vb* grafting tissue from a donor genetically identical to the recipient
ISOGRAFTS > ISOGRAFT
ISOGRAM *same as* > ISOPLETH
ISOGRAMS > ISOGRAM
ISOGRAPH *n* line connecting points of the same linguistic usage
ISOGRAPHS > ISOGRAPH
ISOGRIV *n* line connecting points of equal angular difference between magnetic north and grid north
ISOGRIVS > ISOGRIV
ISOHEL *n* line on a map connecting places with an equal period of sunshine
ISOHELS > ISOHEL
ISOHYDRIC *adj* having the same acidity or hydrogen-ion concentration
ISOHYET *n* line on a map connecting places having equal rainfall
ISOHYETAL > ISOHYET
ISOHYETS > ISOHYET
ISOKONT *same as* > ISOKONTAN
ISOKONTAN *n* alga whose zoophores have equal cilia
ISOKONTS > ISOKONT
ISOLABLE > ISOLATE
ISOLATE *vb* place apart or alone ▷ *n* isolated person or group
ISOLATED > ISOLATE
ISOLATES > ISOLATE
ISOLATING > ISOLATE
ISOLATION > ISOLATE
ISOLATIVE *adj* concerned with isolation
ISOLATOR > ISOLATE
ISOLATORS > ISOLATE
ISOLEAD *n* line on a ballistic graph
ISOLEADS > ISOLEAD
ISOLEX *n* isogloss marking off the area in which a particular item of vocabulary is found
ISOLEXES > ISOLEX
ISOLINE *same as* > ISOPLETH
ISOLINES > ISOLINE
ISOLOG > ISOLOGOUS
ISOLOGOUS *adj* (of two or more organic compounds) having a similar structure but containing different

atoms of the same valency
ISOLOGS > ISOLOGOUS
ISOLOGUE > ISOLOGOUS
ISOLOGUES > ISOLOGOUS
ISOMER *n* substance whose molecules contain the same atoms as another but in a different arrangement
ISOMERASE *n* any enzyme that catalyses the conversion of one isomeric form of a compound to another
ISOMERE *same as* > ISOMER
ISOMERES > ISOMERE
ISOMERIC > ISOMER
ISOMERISE *same as* > ISOMERIZE
ISOMERISM *n* existence of two or more compounds having the same molecular formula but a different arrangement of atoms within the molecule
ISOMERIZE *vb* change or cause to change from one isomer to another
ISOMEROUS *adj* having an equal number of parts or markings
ISOMERS > ISOMER
ISOMETRIC *adj* relating to muscular contraction without shortening of the muscle ▷ *n* drawing made in this way
ISOMETRY *n* rigid motion of a plane or space such that the distance between any two points before and after this motion is unaltered
ISOMORPH *n* substance or organism that exhibits isomorphism
ISOMORPHS > ISOMORPH
ISONIAZID *n* soluble colourless crystalline compound used to treat tuberculosis
ISONOME *n* line on a chart connecting points of equal abundance values of a plant species sampled in different sections of an area
ISONOMES > ISONOME
ISONOMIC > ISONOMY
ISONOMIES > ISONOMY
ISONOMOUS > ISONOMY
ISONOMY *n* equality before the law of the citizens of a state
ISOOCTANE *n* colourless liquid alkane hydrocarbon produced from petroleum and used in standardizing petrol
ISOPACH *n* line on a map connecting points below which a particular rock stratum has the same thickness
ISOPACHS > ISOPACH
ISOPHONE *n* isogloss marking off an area in which a particular feature of pronunciation is found

ISOPHONES > ISOPHONE
ISOPHOTAL > ISOPHOTE
ISOPHOTE *n* line on a diagram or image of a galaxy, nebula, or other celestial object joining points of equal surface brightness
ISOPHOTES > ISOPHOTE
ISOPLETH *n* line on a map connecting places registering the same amount or ratio of some geographical or meteorological phenomenon or phenomena
ISOPLETHS > ISOPLETH
ISOPOD *n* type of crustacean including woodlice and pill bugs ▷ *adj* of this type of crustacean
ISOPODAN > ISOPOD
ISOPODANS > ISOPOD
ISOPODOUS > ISOPOD
ISOPODS > ISOPOD
ISOPOLITY *n* equality of political rights
ISOPRENE *n* colourless volatile liquid with a penetrating odour
ISOPRENES > ISOPRENE
ISOPROPYL *n* group of atoms
ISOPYCNAL *n* line on a map connecting points of equal atmospheric density
ISOPYCNIC *same as* > ISOPYCNAL
ISOS > ISO
ISOSCELES *adj* (of a triangle) having two sides of equal length
ISOSMOTIC *same as* > ISOTONIC
ISOSPIN *n* internal quantum number used in the classification of elementary particles
ISOSPINS > ISOSPIN
ISOSPORY *n* condition of having spores of only one kind
ISOSTACY *n* state of balance in earth's crust
ISOSTASY *n* state of balance, or equilibrium, which sections of the earth's lithosphere are thought ultimately to achieve when the vertical forces upon them remain unchanged
ISOSTATIC > ISOSTASY
ISOSTERIC *adj* (of two different molecules) having the same number of atoms and the same number and configuration of valency electrons
ISOTACH *n* line on a map connecting points of equal wind speed
ISOTACHS > ISOTACH
ISOTACTIC *adj* (of a stereospecific polymer)

having identical steric configurations of the groups on each asymmetric carbon atom on the chain
ISOTHERAL > ISOTHERE
ISOTHERE *n* line on a map linking places with the same mean summer temperature
ISOTHERES > ISOTHERE
ISOTHERM *n* line on a map connecting points of equal temperature
ISOTHERMS > ISOTHERM
ISOTONE *n* one of two or more atoms of different atomic number that contain the same number of neutrons
ISOTONES > ISOTONE
ISOTONIC *adj* (of two or more muscles) having equal tension
ISOTOPE *n* one of two or more atoms with the same number of protons in the nucleus but a different number of neutrons
ISOTOPES > ISOTOPE
ISOTOPIC > ISOTOPE
ISOTOPIES > ISOTOPE
ISOTOPY > ISOTOPE
ISOTRON *n* device for separating small quantities of isotopes by ionizing them and separating the ions by a mass spectrometer
ISOTRONS > ISOTRON
ISOTROPIC *adj* having uniform physical properties, such as elasticity or conduction in all directions
ISOTROPY > ISOTROPIC
ISOTYPE *n* presentation of statistical information in a row of diagrams
ISOTYPES > ISOTYPE
ISOTYPIC > ISOTYPE
ISOZYME *n* any of a set of structural variants of an enzyme occurring in different tissues in a single species
ISOZYMES > ISOZYME
ISOZYMIC > ISOZYME
ISPAGHULA *n* dietary fibre derived from seed husks and used as a thickener or stabilizer in the food industry
ISSEI *n* first-generation Japanese immigrant
ISSEIS > ISSEI
ISSUABLE *adj* capable of issuing or being issued
ISSUABLY > ISSUABLE
ISSUANCE *n* act of issuing
ISSUANCES > ISSUANCE
ISSUANT *adj* emerging or issuing
ISSUE *n* topic of interest or discussion ▷ *vb* make (a statement etc) publicly
ISSUED > ISSUE

i

ISSUELESS > ISSUE
ISSUER > ISSUE
ISSUERS > ISSUE
ISSUES > ISSUE
ISSUING > ISSUE
ISTANA *n* (in Malaysia) a royal palace
ISTANAS > ISTANA
ISTHMI > ISTHMUS
ISTHMIAN *n* inhabitant of an isthmus ▷ *adj* relating to or situated in an isthmus
ISTHMIANS > ISTHMIAN
ISTHMIC > ISTHMUS
ISTHMOID > ISTHMUS
ISTHMUS *n* narrow strip of land connecting two areas of land
ISTHMUSES > ISTHMUS
ISTLE *n* fibre obtained from various tropical American agave and yucca trees used in making carpets, cord, etc
ISTLES > ISTLE
IT *pron* refers to a nonhuman, animal, plant, or inanimate object ▷ *n* player whose turn it is to catch the others in children's games
ITA *n* type of palm
ITACISM *n* pronunciation of the Greek letter eta as in Modern Greek
ITACISMS > ITACISM
ITACONIC as in *itaconic acid*, , white colourless crystalline carboxylic acid
ITALIC *adj* (of printing type) sloping to the right ▷ *n* style of printing type

modelled on this, chiefly used to indicate emphasis, a foreign word, etc
ITALICISE *same as* > ITALICIZE
ITALICIZE *vb* put in italics
ITALICS > ITALIC
ITAS > ITA
ITCH *n* skin irritation causing a desire to scratch ▷ *vb* have an itch
ITCHED > ITCH
ITCHES > ITCH
ITCHIER > ITCH
ITCHIEST > ITCH
ITCHILY > ITCH
ITCHINESS > ITCH
ITCHING > ITCH
ITCHINGS > ITCH
ITCHWEED *n* white hellebore
ITCHWEEDS > ITCHWEED
ITCHY > ITCH
ITEM *n* single thing in a list or collection ▷ *adv* likewise ▷ *vb* itemize
ITEMED > ITEM
ITEMING > ITEM
ITEMISE *same as* > ITEMIZE
ITEMISED > ITEMISE
ITEMISER > ITEMISE
ITEMISERS > ITEMISE
ITEMISES > ITEMISE
ITEMISING > ITEMISE
ITEMIZE *vb* make a list of
ITEMIZED > ITEMIZE
ITEMIZER > ITEMIZE
ITEMIZERS > ITEMIZE
ITEMIZES > ITEMIZE
ITEMIZING > ITEMIZE
ITEMS > ITEM
ITERANCE > ITERATE

ITERANCES > ITERATE
ITERANT > ITERATE
ITERATE *vb* repeat
ITERATED > ITERATE
ITERATES > ITERATE
ITERATING > ITERATE
ITERATION > ITERATE
ITERATIVE *adj* repetitious or frequent
ITERUM *adv* again
ITHER *Scot word for* > OTHER
ITINERACY *same as* > ITINERANCY
ITINERANT *adj* travelling from place to place ▷ *n* itinerant worker or other person
ITINERARY *n* detailed plan of a journey ▷ *adj* of or relating to travel or routes of travel
ITINERATE *vb* travel from place to place
ITS *pron* belonging to it ▷ *adj* of or belonging to it
ITSELF *pron* reflexive form of *it*
IURE *adv* by law
IVIED *adj* covered with ivy
IVIES > IVY
IVORIED > IVORY
IVORIES *pl n* keys of a piano
IVORIST *n* worker in ivory
IVORISTS > IVORIST
IVORY *n* hard white bony substance forming the tusks of elephants ▷ *adj* yellowish-white
IVORYBILL *n* large American woodpecker
IVORYLIKE > IVORY

IVORYWOOD *n* yellowish-white wood of an Australian tree, used for engraving, inlaying, and turnery
IVRESSE *n* drunkenness
IVRESSES > IVRESSE
IVY *n* evergreen climbing plant
IVYLIKE > IVY
IWI *n* MÐori tribe
IWIS *archaic word for* > CERTAINLY
IXIA *n* southern African plant of the iris family with showy ornamental funnel-shaped flowers
IXIAS > IXIA
IXODIASES > IXODIASIS
IXODIASIS *n* disease transmitted by ticks
IXODID *n* hard-bodied tick
IXODIDS > IXODID
IXORA *n* flowering shrub
IXORAS > IXORA
IXTLE *same as* > ISTLE
IXTLES > IXTLE
IZAR *n* long garment worn by Muslim women
IZARD *n* type of goat-antelope
IZARDS > IZARD
IZARS > IZAR
IZVESTIA *n* news
IZVESTIAS > IZVESTIA
IZVESTIYA *same as* > IZVESTIA
IZZARD *n* letter Z
IZZARDS > IZZARD
IZZAT *n* honour or prestige
IZZATS > IZZAT

Jj

JA interj yes ▷ sentence substitute yes

JAAP n S African offensive word for a simpleton or country bumpkin

JAAPS > JAAP

JAB vb poke sharply ▷ n quick punch or poke

JABBED > JAB

JABBER vb talk rapidly or incoherently ▷ n rapid or incoherent talk

JABBERED > JABBER

JABBERER > JABBER

JABBERERS > JABBER

JABBERING > JABBER

JABBERS > JABBER

JABBING > JAB

JABBINGLY > JAB

JABBLE vb ripple

JABBLED > JABBLE

JABBLES > JABBLE

JABBLING > JABBLE

JABERS interj Irish exclamation

JABIRU n large white-and-black Australian stork

JABIRUS > JABIRU

JABORANDI n any of several tropical American rutaceous shrubs

JABOT n frill or ruffle on the front of a blouse or shirt

JABOTS > JABOT

JABS > JAB

JACAL n Mexican daub hut

JACALES > JACAL

JACALS > JACAL

JACAMAR n tropical American bird with an iridescent plumage

JACAMARS > JACAMAR

JACANA n long-legged long-toed bird of tropical and subtropical marshy regions

JACANAS > JACANA

JACARANDA n tropical tree with sweet-smelling wood

JACARE another name for > CAYMAN

JACARES > JACARE

JACCHUS n small monkey

JACCHUSES > JACCHUS

JACENT adj lying

JACINTH another name for > HYACINTH

JACINTHE n hyacinth

JACINTHES > JACINTHE

JACINTHS > JACINTH

JACK n device for raising a motor vehicle or other heavy object ▷ vb lift or push (an object) with a jack

JACKAL n doglike wild animal of Africa and Asia ▷ vb behave like a jackal

JACKALLED > JACKAL

JACKALS > JACKAL

JACKAROO same as > JACKEROO

JACKAROOS > JACKAROO

JACKASS n fool

JACKASSES > JACKASS

JACKBOOT n high military boot ▷ vb oppress

JACKBOOTS > JACKBOOT

JACKDAW n black-and-grey Eurasian bird of the crow family

JACKDAWS > JACKDAW

JACKED > JACK

JACKEEN n slick self-assertive lower-class Dubliner

JACKEENS > JACKEEN

JACKER n labourer

JACKEROO n young male management trainee on a sheep or cattle station ▷ vb work as a jackeroo

JACKEROOS > JACKEROO

JACKERS > JACKER

JACKET n short coat ▷ vb put a jacket on (someone or something)

JACKETED > JACKET

JACKETING > JACKET

JACKETS > JACKET

JACKFISH n small pike fish

JACKFRUIT n tropical Asian tree

JACKIES > JACKY

JACKING > JACK

JACKINGS > JACK

JACKKNIFE vb (of an articulated truck) go out of control so that the trailer swings round at a sharp angle to the cab ▷ n large clasp knife

JACKLEG n unskilled worker

JACKLEGS > JACKLEG

JACKLIGHT > JACK

JACKMAN n retainer

JACKMEN > JACKMAN

JACKPLANE n large woodworking plane

JACKPOT n largest prize that may be won in a game

JACKPOTS > JACKPOT

JACKROLL vb gang-rape

JACKROLLS > JACKROLL

JACKS n game in which metal, bone, or plastic pieces are thrown and then picked up between throws of a small ball

JACKSCREW n lifting device

JACKSHAFT n short length of shafting that transmits power from an engine or motor to a machine

JACKSIE n buttocks or anus

JACKSIES > JACKSIE

JACKSMELT n food fish of the North Pacific

JACKSMITH n smith who makes jacks

JACKSNIPE n small Eurasian short-billed snipe

JACKSTAY n metal rod, wire rope, or wooden batten to which an edge of a sail is fastened along a yard

JACKSTAYS > JACKSTAY

JACKSTONE n JACK

JACKSTRAW n straw mannequin

JACKSY same as > JACKSIE

JACKY n offensive word for a native Australian

JACOBIN n variety of fancy pigeon with a hood of feathers swept up over and around the head

JACOBINS > JACOBIN

JACOBUS n English gold coin minted in the reign of James I

JACOBUSES > JACOBUS

JACONET n light cotton fabric used for clothing, bandages, etc

JACONETS > JACONET

JACQUARD n fabric in which the design is incorporated into the weave instead of being printed or dyed on

JACQUARDS > JACQUARD

JACQUERIE n peasant rising or revolt

JACTATION n act of boasting

JACULATE vb hurl

JACULATED > JACULATE

JACULATES > JACULATE

JACULATOR > JACULATE

JACUZZI n bath or pool equipped with a system of underwater jets

JACUZZIS > JACUZZI

JADE n ornamental semiprecious stone, usu dark green ▷ adj bluish-green ▷ vb exhaust or make exhausted from work or use

JADED adj tired and unenthusiastic

JADEDLY > JADED

JADEDNESS > JADED

JADEITE n usually green or white mineral, found in igneous and metamorphic rocks

JADEITES > JADEITE

JADELIKE > JADE

JADERIES > JADERY

JADERY n shrewishness

JADES > JADE

JADING > JADE

JADISH > JADE

JADISHLY > JADE

JADITIC > JADE

JAEGER n marksman in certain units of the German or Austrian armies

JAEGERS > JAEGER

JAFA n offensive name for a person from Auckland

JAFAS > JAFA

JAG n period of uncontrolled indulgence in an activity ▷ vb cut unevenly

JAGA n guard ▷ vb guard or watch

JAGAED > JAGA

JAGAING > JAGA

JAGAS > JAGA

JAGER same as > JAEGER

JAGERS > JAGER

JAGG same as > JAG

JAGGARIES > JAGGARY

JAGGARY same as > JAGGERY

JAGGED > JAG

JAGGEDER > JAG

JAGGEDEST > JAG

JAGGEDLY > JAG

JAGGER n pedlar
JAGGERIES > JAGGERY
JAGGERS > JAGGER
JAGGERY n coarse brown sugar made in the East Indies from the sap of the date palm
JAGGHERY same as > JAGGERY
JAGGIER > JAGGY
JAGGIES > JAGGY
JAGGIEST > JAGGY
JAGGING > JAG
JAGGS > JAGG
JAGGY adj prickly ▷ n jagged computer image
JAGHIR n Indian regional governance
JAGHIRDAR n Indian regional governor
JAGHIRE n Indian regional governance
JAGHIRES > JAGHIRE
JAGHIRS > JAGHIR
JAGIR n Indian regional governance
JAGIRS > JAGIR
JAGLESS > JAG
JAGRA n Hindu festival
JAGRAS > JAGRA
JAGS > JAG
JAGUAR n large S American spotted cat
JAGUARS > JAGUAR
JAI interj victory (to)
JAIL n prison ▷ vb send to prison
JAILABLE > JAIL
JAILBAIT n young woman, or young women collectively, considered sexually attractive but below the age of consent
JAILBIRD n person who has often been in prison
JAILBIRDS > JAILBIRD
JAILBREAK n escape from jail
JAILED > JAIL
JAILER n person in charge of a jail
JAILERESS > JAILER
JAILERS > JAILER
JAILHOUSE n jail
JAILING > JAIL
JAILLESS > JAIL
JAILOR same as > JAILER
JAILORESS > JAILOR
JAILORS > JAILOR
JAILS > JAIL
JAK > JACK
JAKE adj slang word meaning all right
JAKES n human excrement
JAKESES > JAKES
JAKEY n derogatory Scots word for a homeless alcoholic
JAKEYS > JAKEY
JAKFRUIT same as > JACKFRUIT
JAKFRUITS > JAKFRUIT
JAKS > JACK
JALAP n Mexican convolvulaceous plant
JALAPENO n very hot type of green chilli pepper, used esp in Mexican cookery

JALAPENOS > JALAPENO
JALAPIC > JALAP
JALAPIN n purgative resin
JALAPINS > JALAPIN
JALAPS > JALAP
JALOP same as > JALAP
JALOPIES > JALOPY
JALOPPIES > JALOPPY
JALOPPY same as > JALOPY
JALOPS > JALOP
JALOPY n old car
JALOUSE vb suspect
JALOUSED > JALOUSE
JALOUSES > JALOUSE
JALOUSIE n window blind or shutter constructed from angled slats of wood, plastic, etc
JALOUSIED > JALOUSIE
JALOUSIES > JALOUSIE
JALOUSING > JALOUSE
JAM vb pack tightly into a place ▷ n fruit preserve or hold-up of traffic
JAMADAR n Indian army officer
JAMADARS > JAMADAR
JAMB n side post of a door or window frame ▷ vb climb up a crack in rock
JAMBALAYA n Creole dish made of shrimps, ham, rice, onions, etc
JAMBART same as > GREAVE
JAMBARTS > JAMBART
JAMBE same as > JAMB
JAMBEAU another word for > GREAVE
JAMBEAUX > JAMBEAU
JAMBED > JAMB
JAMBEE n light cane
JAMBEES > JAMBEE
JAMBER same as > GREAVE
JAMBERS > JAMBER
JAMBES > JAMBE
JAMBEUX > JAMBEAU
JAMBIER n greave
JAMBIERS > JAMBIER
JAMBING > JAMB
JAMBIYA n curved dagger
JAMBIYAH same as > JAMBIYA
JAMBIYAHS > JAMBIYAH
JAMBIYAS > JAMBIYA
JAMBO sentence substitute E African salutation
JAMBOK same as > SJAMBOK
JAMBOKKED > JAMBOK
JAMBOKS > JAMBOK
JAMBOLAN n Asian tree
JAMBOLANA same as > JAMBOLAN
JAMBOLANS > JAMBOLAN
JAMBONE n type of play in the card game euchre
JAMBONES > JAMBONE
JAMBOOL same as > JAMBOLAN
JAMBOOLS > JAMBOOL
JAMBOREE n large gathering or celebration
JAMBOREES > JAMBOREE
JAMBOS > JAMBO
JAMBS > JAMB
JAMBU same as > JAMBOLAN
JAMBUL same as > JAMBOLAN
JAMBULS > JAMBUL
JAMBUS > JAMBU

JAMDANI n patterned muslin
JAMDANIS > JAMDANI
JAMES n jemmy
JAMESES > JAMES
JAMJAR n container for preserves
JAMJARS > JAMJAR
JAMLIKE > JAM
JAMMABLE > JAM
JAMMED > JAM
JAMMER > JAM
JAMMERS > JAM
JAMMIER > JAMMY
JAMMIES informal word for > PYJAMAS
JAMMIEST > JAMMY
JAMMING > JAM
JAMMINGS > JAM
JAMMY adj lucky
JAMPACKED adj very crowded
JAMPAN n type of sedan chair used in India
JAMPANEE n jampan bearer
JAMPANEES > JAMPANEE
JAMPANI same as > JAMPANEE
JAMPANIS > JAMPANI
JAMPANS > JAMPAN
JAMPOT n container for preserves
JAMPOTS > JAMPOT
JAMS > JAM
JANDAL n sandal with a strap between the toes
JANDALS > JANDAL
JANE n girl or woman
JANES > JANE
JANGLE vb (cause to) make a harsh ringing noise ▷ n harsh ringing noise
JANGLED > JANGLE
JANGLER > JANGLE
JANGLERS > JANGLE
JANGLES > JANGLE
JANGLIER > JANGLY
JANGLIEST > JANGLY
JANGLING > JANGLE
JANGLINGS > JANGLE
JANGLY adj making a jangling sound
JANIFORM adj with two faces
JANISARY same as > JANISSARY
JANISSARY n infantryman in the Turkish army, originally a member of the sovereign's personal guard, from the 14th to the early 19th century
JANITOR n caretaker of a school or other building
JANITORS > JANITOR
JANITRESS > JANITOR
JANITRIX > JANITOR
JANIZAR same as > JANISSARY
JANIZARS > JANIZAR
JANIZARY same as > JANISSARY
JANKER n device for transporting logs
JANKERS > JANKER
JANN n lesser jinn
JANNIES > JANNY

JANNOCK same as > JONNOCK
JANNOCKS > JANNOCK
JANNS > JANN
JANNY n janitor
JANSKY n unit of flux density used predominantly in radio and infrared astronomy
JANSKYS > JANSKY
JANTEE archaic version of > JAUNTY
JANTIER > JANTY
JANTIES > JANTY
JANTIEST > JANTY
JANTY n petty officer ▷ adj (in archaic usage) jaunty
JAP vb splash
JAPAN n very hard varnish, usu black ▷ vb cover with this varnish ▷ adj relating to or varnished with japan
JAPANISE same as > JAPANIZE
JAPANISED > JAPANISE
JAPANISES > JAPANISE
JAPANIZE vb make Japanese
JAPANIZED > JAPANIZE
JAPANIZES > JAPANIZE
JAPANNED > JAPAN
JAPANNER > JAPAN
JAPANNERS > JAPAN
JAPANNING > JAPAN
JAPANS > JAPAN
JAPE n joke or prank ▷ vb joke or jest (about)
JAPED > JAPE
JAPER > JAPE
JAPERIES > JAPE
JAPERS > JAPE
JAPERY > JAPE
JAPES > JAPE
JAPING > JAPE
JAPINGLY > JAPE
JAPINGS > JAPE
JAPONICA n shrub with red flowers
JAPONICAS > JAPONICA
JAPPED > JAP
JAPPING > JAP
JAPS > JAP
JAR n wide-mouthed container, usu round and made of glass ▷ vb have a disturbing or unpleasant effect
JARARACA n South American snake
JARARACAS > JARARACA
JARARAKA same as > JARARACA
JARARAKAS > JARARAKA
JARFUL same as > JAR
JARFULS > JARFUL
JARGON n specialized technical language of a particular subject ▷ vb use or speak in jargon
JARGONED > JARGON
JARGONEER n user of jargon
JARGONEL n pear
JARGONELS > JARGONEL
JARGONING > JARGON
JARGONISE same as > JARGONIZE
JARGONISH > JARGON
JARGONIST > JARGON

JARGONIZE vb render into jargon
JARGONS > JARGON
JARGONY > JARGON
JARGOON same as > JARGON
JARGOONS > JARGOON
JARHEAD n US Marine
JARHEADS > JARHEAD
JARINA n South American palm tree
JARINAS > JARINA
JARK n seal or pass
JARKMAN n forger of passes or licences
JARKMEN > JARKMAN
JARKS > JARK
JARL n Scandinavian chieftain or noble
JARLDOM > JARL
JARLDOMS > JARL
JARLS > JARL
JARLSBERG n Norwegian cheese
JAROOL n Indian tree
JAROOLS > JAROOL
JAROSITE n yellow to brown mineral
JAROSITES > JAROSITE
JAROVISE same as > JAROVIZE
JAROVISED > JAROVISE
JAROVISES > JAROVISE
JAROVIZE vb vernalize
JAROVIZED > JAROVIZE
JAROVIZES > JAROVIZE
JARP vb strike or smash, esp to break the shell of (an egg) at Easter
JARPED > JARP
JARPING > JARP
JARPS > JARP
JARRAH n Australian eucalypt yielding valuable timber
JARRAHS > JARRAH
JARRED > JAR
JARRING > JAR
JARRINGLY > JAR
JARRINGS > JAR
JARS > JAR
JARSFUL > JARFUL
JARTA n heart
JARTAS > JARTA
JARUL variant of > JAROOL
JARULS > JARUL
JARVEY n hackney coachman
JARVEYS > JARVEY
JARVIE same as > JARVEY
JARVIES > JARVIE
JASEY n wig
JASEYS > JASEY
JASIES > JASEY
JASMIN same as > JASMINE
JASMINE n shrub with sweet-smelling yellow or white flowers
JASMINES > JASMINE
JASMINS > JASMIN
JASP another word for > JASPER
JASPE adj resembling jasper ▷ n subtly striped woven fabric
JASPER n red, yellow, dark green, or brown variety of quartz

JASPERISE same as > JASPERIZE
JASPERIZE vb turn into jasper
JASPEROUS > JASPER
JASPERS > JASPER
JASPERY > JASPER
JASPES > JASPE
JASPIDEAN > JASPER
JASPILITE n rock like jasper
JASPIS archaic word for > JASPER
JASPISES > JASPIS
JASPS > JASP
JASS obsolete variant of > JAZZ
JASSES > JASS
JASSID n leafhopper
JASSIDS > JASSID
JASY n wig
JATAKA n text describing the birth of Buddha
JATAKAS > JATAKA
JATO n jet-assisted takeoff
JATOS > JATO
JAUK vb dawdle
JAUKED > JAUK
JAUKING > JAUK
JAUKS > JAUK
JAUNCE vb prance
JAUNCED > JAUNCE
JAUNCES > JAUNCE
JAUNCING > JAUNCE
JAUNDICE n disease marked by yellowness of the skin ▷ vb distort (the judgment, etc) adversely
JAUNDICED > JAUNDICE
JAUNDICES > JAUNDICE
JAUNSE same as > JAUNCE
JAUNSED > JAUNSE
JAUNSES > JAUNSE
JAUNSING > JAUNSE
JAUNT n short journey for pleasure ▷ vb make such a journey
JAUNTED > JAUNT
JAUNTEE old spelling of > JAUNTY
JAUNTIE old spelling of > JAUNTY
JAUNTIER > JAUNTY
JAUNTIES > JAUNTY
JAUNTIEST > JAUNTY
JAUNTILY > JAUNTY
JAUNTING > JAUNT
JAUNTS > JAUNT
JAUNTY adj sprightly and cheerful ▷ n master-at-arms on a naval ship
JAUP same as > JARP
JAUPED > JAUP
JAUPING > JAUP
JAUPS > JAUP
JAVA n coffee or a variety of it
JAVAS > JAVA
JAVEL as in javel water aqueous solution containing sodium hypochlorite and some sodium chloride, used as a bleach and disinfectant
JAVELIN n light spear thrown in sports competitions ▷ vb spear

with a javelin
JAVELINA n collared peccary
JAVELINAS > JAVELINA
JAVELINED > JAVELIN
JAVELINS > JAVELIN
JAVELS > JAVEL
JAW n one of the bones in which the teeth are set ▷ vb talk lengthily
JAWAN n (in India) a soldier
JAWANS > JAWAN
JAWARI n variety of sorghum
JAWARIS > JAWARI
JAWBATION n scolding
JAWBONE n lower jaw of a person or animal ▷ vb try to persuade or bring pressure to bear (on) by virtue of one's high office or position, esp in urging compliance with official policy
JAWBONED > JAWBONE
JAWBONER > JAWBONE
JAWBONERS > JAWBONE
JAWBONES > JAWBONE
JAWBONING > JAWBONE
JAWBOX n metal sink
JAWBOXES > JAWBOX
JAWED > JAW
JAWFALL n depression
JAWFALLS > JAWFALL
JAWHOLE n cesspit
JAWHOLES > JAWHOLE
JAWING > JAW
JAWINGS > JAW
JAWLESS > JAW
JAWLIKE > JAW
JAWLINE n outline of the jaw
JAWLINES > JAWLINE
JAWS > JAW
JAXIE same as > JACKSIE
JAXIES > JAXIE
JAXY same as > JACKSIE
JAY n bird with a pinkish body and blue-and-black wings
JAYBIRD n jay
JAYBIRDS > JAYBIRD
JAYGEE n lieutenant junior grade in the US army
JAYGEES > JAYGEE
JAYHAWKER n Unionist guerrilla in US Civil War
JAYS > JAY
JAYVEE n junior varsity sports team
JAYVEES > JAYVEE
JAYWALK vb cross or walk in a street recklessly or illegally
JAYWALKED > JAYWALK
JAYWALKER > JAYWALK
JAYWALKS > JAYWALK
JAZERANT n coat of metal plates sewn onto cloth
JAZERANTS > JAZERANT
JAZIES > JAZY
JAZY n wig
JAZZ n kind of music with an exciting rhythm, usu involving improvisation ▷ vb play or dance to jazz music

JAZZBO n jazz musician or fan
JAZZBOS > JAZZBO
JAZZED > JAZZ
JAZZER > JAZZ
JAZZERS > JAZZ
JAZZES > JAZZ
JAZZIER > JAZZY
JAZZIEST > JAZZY
JAZZILY > JAZZY
JAZZINESS > JAZZY
JAZZING > JAZZ
JAZZLIKE > JAZZ
JAZZMAN > JAZZ
JAZZMEN > JAZZ
JAZZY adj flashy or showy
JEALOUS adj fearful of losing a partner or possession to a rival
JEALOUSE vb be jealous of
JEALOUSED > JEALOUSE
JEALOUSES > JEALOUSE
JEALOUSLY > JEALOUS
JEALOUSY n state of or an instance of feeling jealous
JEAN n tough twill-weave cotton fabric used for hard-wearing trousers, overalls, etc
JEANED adj wearing jeans
JEANETTE n light jean cloth
JEANETTES > JEANETTE
JEANS pl n casual denim trousers
JEAT n jet
JEATS > JEAT
JEBEL n hill or mountain in an Arab country
JEBELS > JEBEL
JEDI n person claiming to live according to a philosophy based on that of the fictional Jedi, from the StarWars films
JEDIS > JEDI
JEE variant of > GEE
JEED > JEE
JEEING > JEE
JEEL vb make into jelly
JEELED > JEEL
JEELIE same as > JEELY
JEELIED > JEELY
JEELIEING > JEELIE
JEELIES > JEELY
JEELING > JEEL
JEELS > JEEL
JEELY n jelly ▷ vb make into jelly
JEELYING > JEELY
JEEP n small military four-wheel drive road vehicle ▷ vb travel in a jeep
JEEPED > JEEP
JEEPERS interj mild exclamation of surprise
JEEPING > JEEP
JEEPNEY n Filipino bus converted from a jeep
JEEPNEYS > JEEPNEY
JEEPS > JEEP
JEER vb scoff or deride ▷ n cry of derision
JEERED > JEER
JEERER > JEER
JEERERS > JEER
JEERING > JEER
JEERINGLY > JEER

JEERINGS > JEER

JEERS > JEER

JEES > JEE

JEEZ *interj* expression of surprise or irritation

JEFE *n* (in Spanish-speaking countries) a military or political leader

JEFES > JEFE

JEFF *vb* downsize or close down (an organization)

JEFFED > JEFF

JEFFING > JEFF

JEFFS > JEFF

JEHAD *same as* > JIHAD

JEHADI *same as* > JIHADI

JEHADIS > JEHADI

JEHADISM *same as* > JIHADISM

JEHADISMS > JEHADISM

JEHADIST > JEHADISM

JEHADISTS > JEHADISM

JEHADS > JEHAD

JEHU *n* fast driver

JEHUS > JEHU

JEJUNA > JEJUNUM

JEJUNAL > JEJUNUM

JEJUNE *adj* simple or naive

JEJUNELY > JEJUNE

JEJUNITY > JEJUNE

JEJUNUM *n* part of the small intestine between the duodenum and the ileum

JELAB *same as* > JELLABA

JELABS > JELAB

JELL *vb* form into a jelly-like substance

JELLABA *n* loose robe with a hood, worn by some Arab men

JELLABAH *same as* > JELLABA

JELLABAHS > JELLABAH

JELLABAS > JELLABA

JELLED > JELL

JELLIED > JELLY

JELLIES > JELLY

JELLIFIED > JELLIFY

JELLIFIES > JELLIFY

JELLIFY *vb* make into or become jelly

JELLING > JELL

JELLO *n* (in US English) fruit-flavoured clear dessert set with gelatine

JELLOS > JELLO

JELLS > JELL

JELLY *n* fruit-flavoured clear dessert set with gelatine ▷ *vb* jellify

JELLYBEAN *n* bean-shaped sweet with a brightly coloured coating around a gelatinous filling

JELLYFISH *n* small jelly-like sea animal

JELLYING > JELLY

JELLYLIKE > JELLY

JELLYROLL *n* type of cake

JELUTONG *n* Malaysian tree

JELUTONGS > JELUTONG

JEMADAR *n* native junior officer belonging to a locally raised regiment serving as mercenaries in India, esp with the British Army (until 1947)

JEMADARS > JEMADAR

JEMBE *n* hoe

JEMBES > JEMBE

JEMIDAR *same as* > JEMADAR

JEMIDARS > JEMIDAR

JEMIMA *n* boot with elastic sides

JEMIMAS > JEMIMA

JEMMIED > JEMMY

JEMMIER > JEMMY

JEMMIES > JEMMY

JEMMIEST > JEMMY

JEMMINESS > JEMMY

JEMMY *n* short steel crowbar used by burglars ▷ *vb* prise (something) open with a jemmy ▷ *adj* neat

JEMMYING > JEMMY

JENNET *n* female donkey or ass

JENNETING *n* early-season apple

JENNETS > JENNET

JENNIES > JENNY

JENNY *same as* > JENNET

JEOFAIL *n* oversight in legal pleading

JEOFAILS > JEOFAIL

JEON *n* Korean pancake

JEOPARD *vb* put in jeopardy

JEOPARDED > JEOPARD

JEOPARDER > JEOPARD

JEOPARDS > JEOPARD

JEOPARDY *n* danger ▷ *vb* put in jeopardy

JEQUERITY *same as* > JEQUIRITY

JEQUIRITY *n* seed of the Indian liquorice

JERBIL *variant spelling of* > GERBIL

JERBILS > JERBIL

JERBOA *n* small mouselike rodent with long hind legs

JERBOAS > JERBOA

JEREED *same as* > JERID

JEREEDS > JEREED

JEREMIAD *n* long mournful complaint

JEREMIADS > JEREMIAD

JEREPIGO *n* sweet fortified wine similar to port

JEREPIGOS > JEREPIGO

JERFALCON *variant of* > GYRFALCON

JERID *n* wooden javelin used in Muslim countries in military displays on horseback

JERIDS > JERID

JERK *vb* move or throw abruptly ▷ *n* sharp or abruptly stopped movement

JERKED > JERK

JERKER > JERK

JERKERS > JERK

JERKIER > JERKY

JERKIES > JERKY

JERKIEST > JERKY

JERKILY > JERKY

JERKIN *n* sleeveless jacket

JERKINESS > JERKY

JERKING > JERK

JERKINGLY > JERK

JERKINGS > JERK

JERKINS > JERKIN

JERKS > JERK

JERKWATER *adj* inferior and insignificant

JERKY *adj* characterized by jerks ▷ *n* type of cured meat

JEROBOAM *n* wine bottle holding the equivalent of four normal bottles (approximately 104 ounces)

JEROBOAMS > JEROBOAM

JERQUE *vb* search for contraband

JERQUED > JERQUE

JERQUER > JERQUE

JERQUERS > JERQUE

JERQUES > JERQUE

JERQUING > JERQUE

JERQUINGS > JERQUE

JERREED *variant spelling of* > JERID

JERREEDS > JERREED

JERRICAN *n* five-gallon fuel can

JERRICANS > JERRICAN

JERRID *n* blunt javelin

JERRIDS > JERRID

JERRIES > JERRY

JERRY *short for* > JEROBOAM

JERRYCAN *n* flat-sided can used for storing or transporting liquids, esp motor fuel

JERRYCANS > JERRYCAN

JERSEY *n* knitted jumper

JERSEYED > JERSEY

JERSEYS > JERSEY

JESS *n* short leather strap, one end of which is permanently attached to the leg of a hawk or falcon while the other can be attached to a leash ▷ *vb* put jesses on (a hawk or falcon)

JESSAMIES > JESSAMY

JESSAMINE *same as* > JASMINE

JESSAMY *n* fop

JESSANT *adj* emerging

JESSE *same as* > JESS

JESSED > JESS

JESSERANT *n* coat of metal plates sewn onto cloth

JESSES > JESS

JESSIE *n* effeminate, weak, or cowardly boy or man

JESSIES > JESSIE

JESSING > JESS

JEST *vb* joke ▷ *n* something done or said for amusement

JESTBOOK *n* book of amusing stories

JESTBOOKS > JESTBOOK

JESTED > JEST

JESTEE *n* person about whom a joke is made

JESTEES > JESTEE

JESTER *n* professional clown at court

JESTERS > JESTER

JESTFUL > JEST

JESTING > JEST

JESTINGLY > JEST

JESTINGS > JEST

JESTS > JEST

JESUIT *n* offensive term for a person given to subtle and equivocating arguments

JESUITIC > JESUIT

JESUITISM > JESUIT

JESUITRY > JESUIT

JESUITS > JESUIT

JESUS *n* French paper size

JET *n* aircraft driven by jet propulsion ▷ *vb* fly by jet aircraft

JETBEAD *n* ornamental shrub

JETBEADS > JETBEAD

JETE *n* step in which the dancer springs from one leg and lands on the other

JETES > JETE

JETFOIL *n* type of hydrofoil that is propelled by water jets

JETFOILS > JETFOIL

JETLAG *n* tiredness caused by crossing timezones in jet flight

JETLAGS > JETLAG

JETLIKE > JET

JETLINER *n* commercial airliner powered by jet engines

JETLINERS > JETLINER

JETON *n* gambling chip

JETONS > JETON

JETPLANE *n* aircraft powered by one or more jet engines

JETPLANES > JETPLANE

JETPORT *n* airport for jet planes

JETPORTS > JETPORT

JETS > JET

JETSAM *n* goods thrown overboard to lighten a ship

JETSAMS > JETSAM

JETSOM *same as* > JETSAM

JETSOMS > JETSOM

JETSON *archaic form of* > JETSAM

JETSONS > JETSON

JETSTREAM *n* narrow belt of high-altitude winds moving east at high speeds)

JETTATURA *n* evil eye

JETTED > JET

JETTIED > JETTY

JETTIER > JETTY

JETTIES > JETTY

JETTIEST > JETTY

JETTINESS > JETTY

JETTING > JET

JETTISON *vb* abandon

JETTISONS > JETTISON

JETTON *n* counter or token, esp a chip used in such gambling games as roulette

JETTONS > JETTON

JETTY *n* small pier ▷ *adj* of or resembling jet, esp in colour or polish ▷ *vb* equip with a cantilevered floor

JETTYING > JETTY

JETWAY *n* tradename of a mobile elevated gangway connecting an aircraft to a departure gate, allowing passengers to board and disembark

JETWAYS > JETWAY

JEU n game

JEUNE adj young

JEUX > JEU

JEW vb obsolete offensive word for haggle ▷ n obsolete offensive word for a haggler

JEWED > JEW

JEWEL n precious or semiprecious stone ▷ vb fit or decorate with a jewel or jewels

JEWELED > JEWEL

JEWELER same as > JEWELLER

JEWELERS > JEWELER

JEWELFISH n beautifully coloured fish popular in aquaria

JEWELING > JEWEL

JEWELLED > JEWEL

JEWELLER n dealer in jewels

JEWELLERS > JEWELLER

JEWELLERY n objects decorated with precious stones

JEWELLIKE > JEWEL

JEWELLING > JEWEL

JEWELRIES > JEWELRY

JEWELRY same as > JEWELLERY

JEWELS > JEWEL

JEWELWEED n small bushy plant

JEWFISH n freshwater catfish

JEWFISHES > JEWFISH

JEWIE n jewfish

JEWIES > JEWIE

JEWING > JEW

JEWS > JEW

JEZAIL n Afghan musket

JEZAILS > JEZAIL

JEZEBEL n shameless or scheming woman

JEZEBELS > JEZEBEL

JHALA n Indian musical style

JHALAS > JHALA

JHATKA n slaughter of animals for food according to Sikh law

JHATKAS > JHATKA

JIAO n Chinese currency unit

JIAOS > JIAO

JIB same as > JIBE

JIBB same as > JIBE

JIBBAH same as > JUBBAH

JIBBAHS > JIBBAH

JIBBED > JIBB

JIBBER variant of > GIBBER

JIBBERED > JIBBER

JIBBERING > JIBBER

JIBBERS > JIBBER

JIBBING > JIBB

JIBBINGS > JIBB

JIBBONS pl n spring onions

JIBBOOM n spar forming an extension of the bowsprit

JIBBOOMS > JIBBOOM

JIBBS > JIBB

JIBE vb taunt or jeer ▷ n

insulting or taunting remark

JIBED > JIBE

JIBER > JIBE

JIBERS > JIBE

JIBES > JIBE

JIBING > JIBE

JIBINGLY > JIBE

JIBS > JIB

JICAMA n pale brown turnip with crisp sweet flesh, originating in Mexico

JICAMAS > JICAMA

JICKAJOG vb engage in sexual intercourse

JICKAJOGS > JICKAJOG

JIFF same as > JIFFY

JIFFIES > JIFFY

JIFFS > JIFF

JIFFY n very short period of time

JIG n type of lively dance ▷ vb dance a jig

JIGABOO n offensive term for a Black person

JIGABOOS > JIGABOO

JIGAJIG vb engage in sexual intercourse

JIGAJIGS > JIGAJIG

JIGAJOG variant of > JIGAJIG

JIGAJOGS > JIGAJOG

JIGAMAREE n thing

JIGGED > JIG

JIGGER n small whisky glass ▷ vb interfere or alter

JIGGERED > JIGGER

JIGGERING > JIGGER

JIGGERS > JIGGER

JIGGIER > JIGGY

JIGGIEST > JIGGY

JIGGING > JIG

JIGGINGS > JIG

JIGGISH > JIG

JIGGLE vb move up and down with short jerky movements ▷ n short jerky motion

JIGGLED > JIGGLE

JIGGLES > JIGGLE

JIGGLIER > JIGGLE

JIGGLIEST > JIGGLE

JIGGLING > JIGGLE

JIGGLY > JIGGLE

JIGGUMBOB n thing

JIGGY adj resembling a jig

JIGJIG variant of > JIGAJIG

JIGJIGGED > JIGJIG

JIGJIGS > JIGJIG

JIGLIKE > JIG

JIGOT same as > GIGOT

JIGOTS > JIGOT

JIGS > JIG

JIGSAW n picture cut into interlocking pieces, which the user tries to fit together again ▷ vb cut with a jigsaw

JIGSAWED > JIGSAW

JIGSAWING > JIGSAW

JIGSAWN > JIGSAW

JIGSAWS > JIGSAW

JIHAD n Islamic holy war against unbelievers

JIHADI n person who takes part in a jihad

JIHADIS > JIHADI

JIHADISM n Islamic

fundamentalist movement that favours the pursuit of jihads in defence of the Islamic faith

JIHADISMS > JIHADISM

JIHADIST > JIHADISM

JIHADISTS > JIHADISM

JIHADS > JIHAD

JILBAB n long robe worn by Muslim women

JILBABS > JILBAB

JILGIE n freshwater crayfish

JILGIES > JILGIE

JILL variant spelling of > GILL

JILLAROO n female jackeroo

JILLAROOS > JILLAROO

JILLET n wanton woman

JILLETS > JILLET

JILLFLIRT same as > JILLET

JILLION n extremely large number or amount

JILLIONS > JILLION

JILLIONTH > JILLION

JILLS > JILL

JILT vb leave or reject (one's lover) ▷ n woman who jilts a lover

JILTED > JILT

JILTER > JILT

JILTERS > JILT

JILTING > JILT

JILTS > JILT

JIMCRACK same as > GIMCRACK

JIMCRACKS > JIMCRACK

JIMINY interj expression of surprise

JIMJAM > JIMJAMS

JIMJAMS pl n state of nervous tension, excitement, or anxiety

JIMMIE same as > JIMMY

JIMMIED > JIMMY

JIMMIES > JIMMY

JIMMINY interj expression of surprise

JIMMY same as > JEMMY

JIMMYING > JIMMY

JIMP adj handsome

JIMPER > JIMP

JIMPEST > JIMP

JIMPIER > JIMPY

JIMPIEST > JIMPY

JIMPLY adv neatly

JIMPNESS > JIMP

JIMPY adj neat and tidy

JIMSON as in jimson weed type of poisonous plant with white flowers and shiny fruits

JIN n Chinese unit of weight

JINGAL n swivel-mounted gun

JINGALL same as > JINGAL

JINGALLS > JINGALL

JINGALS > JINGAL

JINGBANG n entirety of something

JINGBANGS > JINGBANG

JINGKO same as > GINGKO

JINGKOES > JINGKO

JINGLE n catchy verse or song used in a radio or

television advert ▷ vb (cause to) make a gentle ringing sound

JINGLED > JINGLE

JINGLER > JINGLE

JINGLERS > JINGLE

JINGLES > JINGLE

JINGLET n sleigh-bell clapper

JINGLETS > JINGLET

JINGLIER > JINGLE

JINGLIEST > JINGLE

JINGLING > JINGLE

JINGLY > JINGLE

JINGO n loud and bellicose patriot; chauvinism

JINGOES > JINGO

JINGOISH > JINGO

JINGOISM n aggressive nationalism

JINGOISMS > JINGOISM

JINGOIST > JINGOISM

JINGOISTS > JINGOISM

JINJILI n type of sesame

JINJILIS > JINJILI

JINK vb move quickly or jerkily in order to dodge someone ▷ n jinking movement

JINKED > JINK

JINKER n vehicle for transporting timber, consisting of a tractor and two sets of wheels for supporting the logs

JINKERS > JINKER

JINKING > JINK

JINKS > JINK

JINN > JINNI

JINNE interj South African exclamation expressing surprise, admiration, shock, etc

JINNEE same as > JINNI

JINNI n spirit in Muslim mythology

JINNIS > JINNI

JINNS > JINNI

JINRIKSHA same as > RICKSHAW

JINS > JIN

JINX n person or thing bringing bad luck ▷ vb be or put a jinx on

JINXED > JINX

JINXES > JINX

JINXING > JINX

JIPIJAPA n palmlike Central and South American plant whose fanlike leaves are bleached for making panama hats

JIPIJAPAS > JIPIJAPA

JIPYAPA same as > JIPIJAPA

JIPYAPAS > JIPYAPA

JIRBLE vb pour carelessly

JIRBLED > JIRBLE

JIRBLES > JIRBLE

JIRBLING > JIRBLE

JIRD n gerbil

JIRDS > JIRD

JIRGA n Afghan council

JIRGAS > JIRGA

JIRKINET n bodice

JIRKINETS > JIRKINET

JIRRE same as > JINNE

JISM slang word for > SEMEN

JISMS > JISM

JISSOM *slang word for* > SEMEN

JISSOMS > JISSOM

JITNEY *n* small bus that carries passengers for a low price, originally five cents

JITNEYS > JITNEY

JITTER *vb* be anxious or nervous

JITTERBUG *n* fast jerky American dance that was popular in the 1940s ▷ *vb* dance the jitterbug

JITTERED > JITTER

JITTERIER > JITTERY

JITTERING > JITTER

JITTERS > JITTER

JITTERY *adj* nervous

JIUJITSU *variant spelling of* > JUJITSU

JIUJITSUS > JIUJITSU

JIUJUTSU *same as* > JUJITSU

JIUJUTSUS > JIUJUTSU

JIVE *n* lively dance of the 1940s and '50s ▷ *vb* dance the jive

JIVEASS *adj* misleading or phoney

JIVED > JIVE

JIVER > JIVE

JIVERS > JIVE

JIVES > JIVE

JIVEY > JIVE

JIVIER > JIVE

JIVIEST > JIVE

JIVING > JIVE

JIVY > JIVE

JIZ *n* wig

JIZZ *n* term for the total combination of characteristics that serve to identify a particular species of bird or plant

JIZZES > JIZZ

JNANA *n* type of yoga

JNANAS > JNANA

JO *n* Scots word for sweetheart

JOANNA *n* piano

JOANNAS > JOANNA

JOANNES *same as* > JOHANNES

JOANNESES > JOANNES

JOB *n* occupation or paid employment ▷ *vb* work at casual jobs

JOBATION *n* scolding

JOBATIONS > JOBATION

JOBBED > JOB

JOBBER *n* person who jobs

JOBBERIES > JOBBERY

JOBBERS > JOBBER

JOBBERY *n* practice of making private profit out of a public office

JOBBIE *n* piece of excrement

JOBBIES > JOBBIE

JOBBING *adj* doing individual jobs for payment ▷ *n* act of seeking work

JOBBINGS > JOBBING

JOBCENTRE *n* office where unemployed people can find out about job vacancies

JOBE *vb* scold

JOBED > JOBE

JOBERNOWL *n* stupid person

JOBES > JOBE

JOBHOLDER *n* person who has a job

JOBING > JOBE

JOBLESS *pl n* unemployed people ▷ *adj* unemployed

JOBNAME *n* title of position

JOBNAMES > JOBNAME

JOBS > JOB

JOBSEEKER *n* person looking for employment

JOBSHARE *n* arrangement in which two or more people divide the duties and payment for one position between them, working at different times

JOBSHARES > JOBSHARE

JOBSWORTH *n* person in a position of minor authority who invokes the letter of the law in order to avoid any action requiring initiative, cooperation, etc

JOCK *n* athlete

JOCKETTE *n* female athlete

JOCKETTES > JOCKETTE

JOCKEY *n* person who rides horses in races, esp as a profession or for hire ▷ *vb* ride (a horse) in a race

JOCKEYED > JOCKEY

JOCKEYING > JOCKEY

JOCKEYISH > JOCKEY

JOCKEYISM *n* skills and practices of jockeys

JOCKEYS > JOCKEY

JOCKNEY *n* Scots dialect influenced by cockney speech patterns

JOCKNEYS > JOCKNEY

JOCKO *n* chimpanzee

JOCKOS > JOCKO

JOCKS > JOCK

JOCKSTRAP *n* belt with a pouch to support the genitals, worn by male athletes

JOCKTELEG *n* clasp knife

JOCO *adj* relaxed

JOCOSE *adj* playful or humorous

JOCOSELY > JOCOSE

JOCOSITY > JOCOSE

JOCULAR *adj* fond of joking

JOCULARLY > JOCULAR

JOCULATOR *n* joker

JOCUND *adj* merry or cheerful

JOCUNDITY > JOCUND

JOCUNDLY > JOCUND

JODEL *same as* > YODEL

JODELLED > JODEL

JODELLING > JODEL

JODELS > JODEL

JODHPUR *as in* jodphur boots ankle-length leather riding boots

JODHPURS *pl n* riding breeches, loose-fitting around the hips and tight-fitting from the thighs to the ankles

JOE *same as* > JO

JOES > JOE

JOEY *n* young kangaroo

JOEYS > JOEY

JOG *vb* run at a gentle pace, esp for exercise ▷ *n* slow run

JOGGED > JOG

JOGGER *n* person who runs at a jog trot over some distance for exercise, usually regularly

JOGGERS > JOGGER

JOGGING > JOG

JOGGINGS > JOG

JOGGLE *vb* shake or move jerkily ▷ *n* act of joggling

JOGGLED > JOGGLE

JOGGLER > JOGGLE

JOGGLERS > JOGGLE

JOGGLES > JOGGLE

JOGGLING > JOGGLE

JOGPANTS *pl n* trousers worn for jogging

JOGS > JOG

JOGTROT *n* easy bouncy gait, esp of a horse, midway between a walk and a trot

JOGTROTS > JOGTROT

JOHANNES *n* Portuguese gold coin minted in the early 18th century

JOHN *n* toilet

JOHNBOAT *n* small flat-bottomed boat

JOHNBOATS > JOHNBOAT

JOHNNIE *same as* > JOHNNY

JOHNNIES > JOHNNY

JOHNNY *n* chap

JOHNS > JOHN

JOHNSON *slang word for* > PENIS

JOHNSONS > JOHNSON

JOIN *vb* become a member (of) ▷ *n* place where two things are joined

JOINABLE > JOIN

JOINDER *n* act of joining, esp in legal contexts

JOINDERS > JOINDER

JOINED > JOIN

JOINER *n* maker of finished woodwork

JOINERIES > JOINERY

JOINERS > JOINER

JOINERY *n* joiner's work

JOINING > JOIN

JOININGS > JOIN

JOINS > JOIN

JOINT *adj* shared by two or more ▷ *n* place where bones meet but can move ▷ *vb* divide meat into joints

JOINTED *adj* having a joint or joints

JOINTEDLY > JOINTED

JOINTER *n* tool for pointing mortar joints, as in brickwork

JOINTERS > JOINTER

JOINTING > JOINT

JOINTLESS > JOINT

JOINTLY > JOINT

JOINTNESS > JOINT

JOINTRESS *n* woman entitled to a jointure

JOINTS > JOINT

JOINTURE *n* provision made by a husband for his wife by settling property upon her at marriage for her use after his death

JOINTURED > JOINTURE

JOINTURES > JOINTURE

JOINTWEED *n* American wild plant

JOINTWORM *n* larva of chalcid flies which form galls on the stems of cereal plants

JOIST *n* horizontal beam that helps support a floor or ceiling ▷ *vb* construct (a floor, roof, etc) with joists

JOISTED > JOIST

JOISTING > JOIST

JOISTS > JOIST

JOJOBA *n* shrub of SW North America whose seeds yield oil used in cosmetics

JOJOBAS > JOJOBA

JOKE *n* thing said or done to cause laughter ▷ *vb* make jokes

JOKED > JOKE

JOKER *n* person who jokes

JOKERS > JOKER

JOKES > JOKE

JOKESMITH *n* comedian

JOKESOME > JOKE

JOKESTER *n* person who makes jokes

JOKESTERS > JOKESTER

JOKEY *adj* intended as a joke

JOKIER > JOKEY

JOKIEST > JOKEY

JOKILY > JOKE

JOKINESS > JOKE

JOKING > JOKE

JOKINGLY > JOKE

JOKOL *Shetland word for* > YES

JOKY *same as* > JOKEY

JOL *n* party ▷ *vb* have a good time

JOLE *vb* knock

JOLED > JOLE

JOLES > JOLE

JOLING > JOLE

JOLL *variant of* > JOLE

JOLLED > JOL

JOLLEY *same as* > JOLLY

JOLLEYER > JOLLEY

JOLLEYERS > JOLLEY

JOLLEYING > JOLLEY

JOLLEYS > JOLLEY

JOLLIED > JOLLY

JOLLIER *n* joker

JOLLIERS > JOLLIER

JOLLIES > JOLLY

JOLLIEST > JOLLY

JOLLIFIED > JOLLIFY

JOLLIFIES > JOLLIFY

JOLLIFY *vb* be or cause to be jolly

JOLLILY > JOLLY

JOLLIMENT > JOLLY

JOLLINESS > JOLLY

JOLLING > JOL

JOLLITIES > JOLLITY

JOLLITY *n* condition of being jolly

JOLLOP *n* cream or unguent

JOLLOPS > JOLLOP

JOLLS > JOLL

JOLLY adj full of good humour ▷ adv extremely ▷ vb try to make or keep (someone) cheerful ▷ n festivity or celebration

JOLLYBOAT n small boat used as a utility tender for a vessel

JOLLYER > JOLLY

JOLLYERS > JOLLY

JOLLYHEAD same as > JOLLITY

JOLLYING > JOLLY

JOLLYINGS > JOLLY

JOLS > JOL

JOLT n unpleasant surprise or shock ▷ vb surprise or shock

JOLTED > JOLT

JOLTER > JOLT

JOLTERS > JOLT

JOLTHEAD n fool

JOLTHEADS > JOLTHEAD

JOLTIER > JOLT

JOLTIEST > JOLT

JOLTILY > JOLT

JOLTING > JOLT

JOLTINGLY > JOLT

JOLTS > JOLT

JOLTY > JOLT

JOMO same as > ZO

JOMON n particular era in Japanese history

JOMOS > JOMO

JONCANOE n Jamaican ceremony

JONCANOES > JONCANOE

JONES vb desire

JONESED > JONES

JONESES > JONES

JONESING > JONES

JONG n friend, often used in direct address

JONGLEUR n (in medieval France) an itinerant minstrel

JONGLEURS > JONGLEUR

JONGS > JONG

JONNOCK adj genuine ▷ adv honestly

JONNYCAKE n type of flat bread

JONQUIL n fragrant narcissus

JONQUILS > JONQUIL

JONTIES > JONTY

JONTY n petty officer

JOOK vb poke or puncture (the skin) ▷ n jab or the resulting wound

JOOKED > JOOK

JOOKERIES > JOOKERY

JOOKERY n mischief

JOOKING > JOOK

JOOKS > JOOK

JOR n movement in Indian music

JORAM same as > JORUM

JORAMS > JORAM

JORDAN n chamber pot

JORDANS > JORDAN

JORDELOO same as > GARDYLOO

JORDELOOS > JORDELOO

JORS > JOR

JORUM n large drinking bowl or vessel or its contents

JORUMS > JORUM

JOSEPH n woman's floor-length riding coat with a small cape, worn esp in the 18th century

JOSEPHS > JOSEPH

JOSH vb tease ▷ n teasing or bantering joke

JOSHED > JOSH

JOSHER > JOSH

JOSHERS > JOSH

JOSHES > JOSH

JOSHING > JOSH

JOSHINGLY > JOSH

JOSKIN n bumpkin

JOSKINS > JOSKIN

JOSS n Chinese deity worshipped in the form of an idol

JOSSER n simpleton

JOSSERS > JOSSER

JOSSES > JOSS

JOSTLE vb knock or push against ▷ n act of jostling

JOSTLED > JOSTLE

JOSTLER > JOSTLE

JOSTLERS > JOSTLE

JOSTLES > JOSTLE

JOSTLING > JOSTLE

JOSTLINGS > JOSTLE

JOT vb write briefly ▷ n very small amount

JOTA n Spanish dance with castanets in fast triple time, usually to a guitar and voice accompaniment

JOTAS > JOTA

JOTS > JOT

JOTTED > JOT

JOTTER n notebook

JOTTERS > JOTTER

JOTTING > JOT

JOTTINGS > JOT

JOTTY > JOT

JOTUN n giant

JOTUNN same as > JOTUN

JOTUNNS > JOTUNN

JOTUNS > JOTUN

JOUAL n nonstandard variety of Canadian French

JOUALS > JOUAL

JOUGS pl n iron ring, fastened by a chain to a wall, post, or tree, in which an offender was held by the neck

JOUISANCE n joy

JOUK vb duck or dodge ▷ n sudden evasive movement

JOUKED > JOUK

JOUKERIES > JOUKERY

JOUKERY same as > JOOKERY

JOUKING > JOUK

JOUKS > JOUK

JOULE n unit of work or energy ▷ vb knock

JOULED > JOULE

JOULES > JOULE

JOULING > JOULE

JOUNCE vb shake or jolt or cause to shake or jolt ▷ n jolting movement

JOUNCED > JOUNCE

JOUNCES > JOUNCE

JOUNCIER > JOUNCE

JOUNCIEST > JOUNCE

JOUNCING > JOUNCE

JOUNCY > JOUNCE

JOUR n day

JOURNAL n daily newspaper or magazine ▷ vb record in a journal

JOURNALED > JOURNAL

JOURNALS > JOURNAL

JOURNEY n act or process of travelling from one place to another ▷ vb travel

JOURNEYED > JOURNEY

JOURNEYER > JOURNEY

JOURNEYS > JOURNEY

JOURNO n journalist

JOURNOS > JOURNO

JOURS > JOUR

JOUST n combat with lances between two mounted knights ▷ vb fight on horseback using lances

JOUSTED > JOUST

JOUSTER > JOUST

JOUSTERS > JOUST

JOUSTING > JOUST

JOUSTS > JOUST

JOVIAL adj happy and cheerful

JOVIALITY > JOVIAL

JOVIALLY > JOVIAL

JOVIALTY same as > JOVIAL

JOW vb ring (a bell)

JOWAR n variety of sorghum

JOWARI same as > JOWAR

JOWARIS > JOWAR

JOWARS > JOWAR

JOWED > JOW

JOWING > JOW

JOWL n lower jaw ▷ vb knock

JOWLED > JOWL

JOWLER n dog with prominent jowls

JOWLERS > JOWLER

JOWLIER > JOWL

JOWLIEST > JOWL

JOWLINESS > JOWL

JOWLING > JOWL

JOWLS > JOWL

JOWLY > JOWL

JOWS > JOW

JOY n feeling of great delight or pleasure ▷ vb feel joy

JOYANCE n joyous feeling or festivity

JOYANCES > JOYANCE

JOYED > JOY

JOYFUL adj feeling or bringing great joy

JOYFULLER > JOYFUL

JOYFULLY > JOYFUL

JOYING > JOY

JOYLESS adj feeling or bringing no joy

JOYLESSLY > JOYLESS

JOYOUS adj extremely happy and enthusiastic

JOYOUSLY > JOYOUS

JOYPOP vb take addictive drugs occasionally without becoming addicted

JOYPOPPED > JOYPOP

JOYPOPPER > JOYPOP

JOYPOPS > JOYPOP

JOYRIDDEN > JOYRIDE

JOYRIDE n drive in a car one has stolen ▷ vb take such a ride

JOYRIDER > JOYRIDE

JOYRIDERS > JOYRIDE

JOYRIDES > JOYRIDE

JOYRIDING > JOYRIDE

JOYRODE > JOYRIDE

JOYS > JOY

JOYSTICK n control device for an aircraft or computer

JOYSTICKS > JOYSTICK

JUBA n lively African-American dance developed in the southern US

JUBAS > JUBA

JUBATE adj possessing a mane

JUBBAH n long loose outer garment with wide sleeves, worn by Muslim men and women, esp in India

JUBBAHS > JUBBAH

JUBE n gallery or loft over the rood screen in a church or cathedral

JUBES > JUBE

JUBHAH same as > JUBBAH

JUBHAHS > JUBHAH

JUBILANCE > JUBILANT

JUBILANCY > JUBILANT

JUBILANT adj feeling or expressing great joy

JUBILATE vb have or express great joy

JUBILATED > JUBILATE

JUBILATES > JUBILATE

JUBILE same as > JUBILEE

JUBILEE n special anniversary, esp 25th or 50th

JUBILEES > JUBILEE

JUBILES > JUBILE

JUCO n junior college in America

JUCOS > JUCO

JUD n large block of coal

JUDAS n peephole or a very small window in a door

JUDASES > JUDAS

JUDDER vb vibrate violently ▷ n violent vibration

JUDDERED > JUDDER

JUDDERING > JUDDER

JUDDERS > JUDDER

JUDGE n public official who tries cases and passes sentence in a court of law ▷ vb act as a judge

JUDGEABLE > JUDGE

JUDGED > JUDGE

JUDGELESS > JUDGE

JUDGELIKE > JUDGE

JUDGEMENT same as > JUDGMENT

JUDGER > JUDGE

JUDGERS > JUDGE

JUDGES > JUDGE

JUDGESHIP n position, office, or function of a judge

JUDGING > JUDGE

JUDGINGLY > JUDGE

JUDGMATIC adj judicious

JUDGMENT n opinion reached after careful

thought
JUDGMENTS > JUDGMENT
JUDICABLE adj capable of being judged, esp in a court of law
JUDICATOR n person who acts as a judge
JUDICIAL adj of or by a court or judge
JUDICIARY n system of courts and judges ▷ adj of or relating to courts of law, judgment, or judges
JUDICIOUS adj well-judged and sensible
JUDIES > JUDY
JUDO n sport in which two opponents try to throw each other to the ground
JUDOGI n white two-piece cotton costume worn during judo contests
JUDOGIS > JUDOGI
JUDOIST > JUDO
JUDOISTS > JUDO
JUDOKA n competitor or expert in judo
JUDOKAS > JUDOKA
JUDOS > JUDO
JUDS > JUD
JUDY n woman
JUG n container for liquids, with a handle and small spout ▷ vb stew or boil (meat, esp hare) in an earthenware container
JUGA > JUGUM
JUGAL adj of or relating to the zygomatic bone ▷ n cheekbone
JUGALS > JUGAL
JUGATE adj (esp of compound leaves) having parts arranged in pairs
JUGFUL same as > JUG
JUGFULS > JUGFUL
JUGGED > JUG
JUGGING > JUG
JUGGINGS > JUG
JUGGINS n silly person
JUGGINSES > JUGGINS
JUGGLE vb throw and catch (several objects) so that most are in the air at the same time ▷ n act of juggling
JUGGLED > JUGGLE
JUGGLER n person who juggles, esp a professional entertainer
JUGGLERS > JUGGLER
JUGGLERY > JUGGLE
JUGGLES > JUGGLE
JUGGLING > JUGGLE
JUGGLINGS > JUGGLE
JUGHEAD n clumsy person
JUGHEADS > JUGHEAD
JUGLET n small jug
JUGLETS > JUGLET
JUGS > JUG
JUGSFUL > JUGFUL
JUGULA > JUGULUM
JUGULAR n one of three large veins of the neck that return blood from the head to the heart
JUGULARS > JUGULAR

JUGULATE vb check (a disease) by extreme measures or remedies
JUGULATED > JUGULATE
JUGULATES > JUGULATE
JUGULUM n lower throat
JUGUM n small process at the base of each forewing in certain insects by which the forewings are united to the hindwings during flight
JUGUMS > JUGUM
JUICE n liquid part of vegetables, fruit, or meat ▷ vb extract juice from fruits and vegetables
JUICED > JUICE
JUICEHEAD n alcoholic
JUICELESS > JUICE
JUICER n kitchen appliance, usually operated by electricity, for extracting juice from fruits and vegetables
JUICERS > JUICER
JUICES > JUICE
JUICIER > JUICY
JUICIEST > JUICY
JUICILY > JUICY
JUICINESS > JUICY
JUICING > JUICE
JUICY adj full of juice
JUJITSU n Japanese art of wrestling and self-defence
JUJITSUS > JUJITSU
JUJU n W African magic charm or fetish
JUJUBE n chewy sweet made of flavoured gelatine
JUJUBES > JUJUBE
JUJUISM > JUJU
JUJUISMS > JUJU
JUJUIST > JUJU
JUJUISTS > JUJU
JUJUS > JUJU
JUJUTSU same as > JUJITSU
JUJUTSUS > JUJITSU
JUKE vb dance or play dance music
JUKEBOX n coin-operated machine on which records, CDs, or videos can be played
JUKEBOXES > JUKEBOX
JUKED > JUKE
JUKES > JUKE
JUKING > JUKE
JUKSKEI n game in which a peg is thrown over a fixed distance at a stake fixed into the ground
JUKSKEIS > JUKE
JUKU n Japanese martial art
JUKUS > JUKU
JULEP n sweet alcoholic drink
JULEPS > JULEP
JULIENNE adj (of vegetables or meat) cut into thin shreds ▷ n clear soup containing thinly shredded vegetables ▷ vb cut into thin pieces
JULIENNED > JULIENNE
JULIENNES > JULIENNE
JUMAR n clamp with a handle that can move

freely up a rope on which it is clipped but locks when downward pressure is applied ▷ vb climb (up a fixed rope) using jumars
JUMARED > JUMAR
JUMARING > JUMAR
JUMARRED > JUMAR
JUMARRING > JUMAR
JUMARS > JUMAR
JUMART n mythical offspring of a bull and a mare
JUMARTS > JUMART
JUMBAL same as > JUMBLE
JUMBALS > JUMBAL
JUMBIE n Caribbean ghost
JUMBIES > JUMBIE
JUMBLE n confused heap or state ▷ vb mix in a disordered way
JUMBLED > JUMBLE
JUMBLER > JUMBLE
JUMBLERS > JUMBLE
JUMBLES > JUMBLE
JUMBLIER > JUMBLE
JUMBLIEST > JUMBLE
JUMBLING > JUMBLE
JUMBLY > JUMBLE
JUMBO adj very large ▷ n large jet airliner
JUMBOISE same as > JUMBOIZE
JUMBOISED > JUMBOISE
JUMBOISES > JUMBOISE
JUMBOIZE vb extend (a ship, esp a tanker) by cutting out the middle part and inserting a new larger part between the original bow and stern
JUMBOIZED > JUMBOIZE
JUMBOIZES > JUMBOIZE
JUMBOS > JUMBO
JUMBUCK n sheep
JUMBUCKS > JUMBUCK
JUMBY n Caribbean ghost
JUMELLE n paired objects
JUMELLES > JUMELLE
JUMP vb leap or spring into the air using the leg muscles ▷ n act of jumping
JUMPABLE > JUMP
JUMPED > JUMP
JUMPER n sweater or pullover
JUMPERS > JUMPER
JUMPIER > JUMPY
JUMPIEST > JUMPY
JUMPILY > JUMPY
JUMPINESS > JUMPY
JUMPING > JUMP
JUMPINGLY > JUMP
JUMPINGS > JUMP
JUMPOFF n extra round in a showjumping contest when two or more horses are equal first, the fastest round deciding the winner
JUMPOFFS > JUMPOFF
JUMPS > JUMP
JUMPSUIT n one-piece garment of combined trousers and jacket or shirt
JUMPSUITS > JUMPSUIT
JUMPY adj nervous
JUN variant of > CHON

JUNCATE same as > JUNKET
JUNCATES > JUNCATE
JUNCO n North American bunting
JUNCOES > JUNCO
JUNCOS > JUNCO
JUNCTION n place where routes, railway lines, or roads meet
JUNCTIONS > JUNCTION
JUNCTURAL > JUNCTURE
JUNCTURE n point in time, esp a critical one
JUNCTURES > JUNCTURE
JUNCUS n type of rush
JUNCUSES > JUNCUS
JUNEATING n early-season apple
JUNGLE n tropical forest of dense tangled vegetation
JUNGLED adj covered with jungle
JUNGLEGYM n climbing frame for children
JUNGLES > JUNGLE
JUNGLI n uncultured person
JUNGLIER > JUNGLE
JUNGLIEST > JUNGLE
JUNGLIS > JUNGLI
JUNGLIST n jungle-music enthusiast
JUNGLISTS > JUNGLIST
JUNGLY > JUNGLE
JUNIOR adj of lower standing ▷ n junior person
JUNIORATE n preparatory course for candidates for religious orders
JUNIORITY n condition of being junior
JUNIORS > JUNIOR
JUNIPER n evergreen shrub with purple berries
JUNIPERS > JUNIPER
JUNK n discarded or useless objects ▷ vb discard as junk
JUNKANOO n Bahamian ceremony
JUNKANOOS > JUNKANOO
JUNKED > JUNK
JUNKER n (formerly) young German nobleman
JUNKERS > JUNKER
JUNKET n excursion by public officials paid for from public funds ▷ vb (of a public official, committee, etc) to go on a junket
JUNKETED > JUNKET
JUNKETEER > JUNKET
JUNKETER > JUNKET
JUNKETERS > JUNKET
JUNKETING > JUNKET
JUNKETS > JUNKET
JUNKETTED > JUNKET
JUNKETTER > JUNKET
JUNKIE n drug addict
JUNKIER > JUNKY
JUNKIES > JUNKY
JUNKIEST > JUNKY
JUNKINESS > JUNKY
JUNKING > JUNK
JUNKMAN n man who buys and sells discarded

clothing, furniture, etc

JUNKMEN > JUNKMAN

JUNKS > JUNK

JUNKY n drug addict ▷ adj of low quality

JUNKYARD n place where junk is stored or collected for sale

JUNKYARDS > JUNKYARD

JUNTA n group of military officers holding power in a country, esp after a coup

JUNTAS > JUNTA

JUNTO same as > JUNTA

JUNTOS > JUNTO

JUPATI n type of palm tree

JUPATIS > JUPATI

JUPE n sleeveless jacket

JUPES > JUPE

JUPON n short close-fitting sleeveless padded garment, used in the late 14th and early 15th centuries with armour

JUPONS > JUPON

JURA > JUS

JURAL adj of or relating to law or to the administration of justice

JURALLY > JURAL

JURANT n person taking oath

JURANTS > JURANT

JURASSIC adj of, denoting, or formed in the second period of the Mesozoic era, between the Triassic and Cretaceous periods, lasting

for 55 million years during which dinosaurs and ammonites flourished

JURAT n statement at the foot of an affidavit, naming the parties, stating when, where, and before whom it was sworn, etc

JURATORY adj of, relating to, or expressed in an oath

JURATS > JURAT

JURE adv by legal right

JUREL n edible fish found in warm American Atlantic waters

JURELS > JUREL

JURIDIC same as > JURIDICAL

JURIDICAL adj of law or the administration of justice

JURIED > JURY

JURIES > JURY

JURIST n expert in law

JURISTIC adj of or relating to jurists

JURISTS > JURIST

JUROR n member of a jury

JURORS > JUROR

JURY n group of people sworn to deliver a verdict in a court of law ▷ adj makeshift ▷ vb evaluate by jury

JURYING > JURY

JURYLESS > JURY

JURYMAN n member of a jury, esp a man

JURYMAST n replacement

mast

JURYMASTS > JURYMAST

JURYMEN > JURYMAN

JURYWOMAN n female member of a jury

JURYWOMEN > JURYWOMAN

JUS n right, power, or authority

JUSSIVE n mood of verbs used for giving orders; imperative

JUSSIVES > JUSSIVE

JUST adv very recently ▷ adj fair or impartial in action or judgment ▷ vb joust

JUSTED > JUST

JUSTER > JUST

JUSTERS > JUST

JUSTEST > JUST

JUSTICE n quality of being just

JUSTICER n magistrate

JUSTICERS > JUSTICER

JUSTICES > JUSTICE

JUSTICIAR n chief political and legal officer from the time of William I to that of Henry III, who deputized for the king in his absence and presided over the kings' courts

JUSTIFIED > JUSTIFY

JUSTIFIER > JUSTIFY

JUSTIFIES > JUSTIFY

JUSTIFY vb prove right or reasonable

JUSTING > JOUST

JUSTLE less common word

for > JOSTLE

JUSTLED > JUSTLE

JUSTLES > JUSTLE

JUSTLING > JUSTLE

JUSTLY > JUST

JUSTNESS > JUST

JUSTS same as > JOUST

JUT vb project or stick out ▷ n something that juts out

JUTE n plant fibre, used for rope, canvas, etc

JUTELIKE > JUTE

JUTES > JUTE

JUTS > JUT

JUTTED > JUT

JUTTIED > JUTTY

JUTTIES > JUTTY

JUTTING > JUT

JUTTINGLY > JUT

JUTTY vb project beyond

JUTTYING > JUTTY

JUVE same as > JUVENILE

JUVENAL variant spelling (esp US) of > JUVENILE

JUVENALS > JUVENAL

JUVENILE adj young ▷ n young person or child

JUVENILES > JUVENILE

JUVENILIA pl n works produced in an author's youth

JUVES > JUVE

JUXTAPOSE vb put side by side

JYMOLD adj having a hinge

JYNX n woodpecker

JYNXES > JYNX

Kk

KA *n* (in ancient Egypt) attendant spirit supposedly dwelling as a vital force in a man or statue ▷ *vb* (in archaic usage) help

KAAL *adj* naked

KAAMA *n* large African antelope with lyre-shaped horns

KAAMAS > KAAMA

KAAS *n* Dutch cabinet or wardrobe

KAB *variant spelling of* > CAB

KABAB *same as* > KEBAB

KABABBED > KABAB

KABABBING > KABAB

KABABS > KABAB

KABADDI *n* game in which players try to touch opposing players but avoid being captured by them

KABADDIS > KABADDI

KABAKA *n* any of the former rulers of the Baganda people of S Uganda

KABAKAS > KABAKA

KABALA *same as* > KABBALAH

KABALAS > KABALA

KABALISM > KABALA

KABALISMS > KABALA

KABALIST > KABALA

KABALISTS > KABALA

KABAR *archaic form of* > CABER

KABARS > KABAR

KABAYA *n* tunic

KABAYAS > KABAYA

KABBALA *same as* > KABBALAH

KABBALAH *n* ancient Jewish mystical tradition

KABBALAHS > KABBALAH

KABBALAS > KABBALA

KABBALISM > KABBALAH

KABBALIST > KABBALAH

KABELE *same as* > KEBELE

KABELES > KABELE

KABELJOU *n* large fish that is an important food fish of South African waters

KABELJOUS > KABELJOU

KABELJOUW *same as* > KABELJOU

KABIKI *n* fruit tree found in India

KABIKIS > KABIKI

KABOB *same as* > KEBAB

KABOBBED > KABOB

KABOBBING > KABOB

KABOBS > KABOB

KABS > KAB

KABUKI *n* form of Japanese drama based on popular legends and characterized by elaborate costumes, stylized acting, and the use of male actors for all roles

KABUKIS > KABUKI

KACCHA *n* trousers worn traditionally by Sikhs

KACCHAS > KACCHA

KACHA *adj* crude

KACHAHRI *n* Indian courthouse

KACHAHRIS > KACHAHRI

KACHCHA *same as* > KACHA

KACHERI *same as* > KACHAHRI

KACHERIS > KACHERI

KACHINA *n* any of the supernatural beings believed by the Hopi Indians to be the ancestors of living humans

KACHINAS > KACHINA

KADAITCHA *n* (in certain Central Australian Aboriginal tribes) man with the mission of avenging the death of a tribesman

KADDISH *n* ancient Jewish liturgical prayer

KADDISHES > KADDISH

KADDISHIM > KADDISH

KADE *same as* > KED

KADES > KADE

KADI *variant spelling of* > CADI

KADIS > KADI

KAE *n* dialect word for jackdaw or jay ▷ *vb* (in archaic usage) help

KAED > KAE

KAEING > KAE

KAES > KAE

KAF *n* letter of the Hebrew alphabet

KAFFIR *n* Southern African variety of sorghum, cultivated in dry regions for its grain and as fodder

KAFFIRS > KAFFIR

KAFFIYAH *same*

as > KAFFIYEH

KAFFIYAHS > KAFFIYAH

KAFFIYEH *same as* > KEFFIYEH

KAFFIYEHS > KAFFIYEH

KAFILA *n* caravan

KAFILAS > KAFILA

KAFIR *same as* > KAFFIR

KAFIRS > KAFIR

KAFS > KAF

KAFTAN *n* long loose Eastern garment

KAFTANS > KAFTAN

KAGO *n* Japanese sedan chair

KAGOOL *variant spelling of* > CAGOULE

KAGOOLS > KAGOOL

KAGOS > KAGO

KAGOUL *variant spelling of* > CAGOULE

KAGOULE *same as* > KAGOUL

KAGOULES > KAGOULE

KAGOULS > KAGOUL

KAGU *n* crested nocturnal bird of New Caledonia with a red bill and greyish plumage

KAGUS > KAGU

KAHAL *n* Jewish community

KAHALS > KAHAL

KAHAWAI *n* food and game fish of New Zealand

KAHAWAIS > KAHAWAI

KAHIKATEA *n* tall New Zealand coniferous tree

KAHIKATOA *n* tall New Zealand coniferous tree

KAHUNA *n* Hawaiian priest, shaman, or expert

KAHUNAS > KAHUNA

KAI *n* food

KAIAK *same as* > KAYAK

KAIAKED > KAIAK

KAIAKING > KAIAK

KAIAKS > KAIAK

KAID *n* North African chieftan or leader

KAIDS > KAID

KAIE *archaic form of* > KEY

KAIES > KAIE

KAIF *same as* > KIF

KAIFS > KAIF

KAIK *same as* > KAINGA

KAIKA *same as* > KAINGA

KAIKAI *n* food

KAIKAIS > KAIKAI

KAIKAS > KAIKA

KAIKAWAKA *n* small pyramid-shaped New Zealand conifer

KAIKOMAKO *n* small New Zealand tree with white flowers and black fruit

KAIKS > KAIK

KAIL *same as* > KALE

KAILS > KAIL

KAILYAIRD *same as* > KALEYARD

KAILYARD *same as* > KALEYARD

KAILYARDS > KAILYARD

KAIM *same as* > KAME

KAIMAKAM *n* Turkish governor

KAIMAKAMS > KAIMAKAM

KAIMS > KAIM

KAIN *variant spelling of* > CAIN

KAING > KA

KAINGA *n* (in New Zealand) a Māori village or small settlement

KAINGAS > KAINGA

KAINIT *same as* > KAINITE

KAINITE *n* white mineral consisting of potassium chloride and magnesium sulphate: a fertilizer and source of potassium salts

KAINITES > KAINITE

KAINITS > KAINIT

KAINS > KAIN

KAIROMONE *n* substance secreted by animal

KAIS > KAI

KAISER *n* German or Austro-Hungarian emperor

KAISERDOM > KAISER

KAISERIN *n* empress

KAISERINS > KAISERIN

KAISERISM > KAISER

KAISERS > KAISER

KAIZEN *n* philosophy of continuous improvement of working practices that underlies total quality management and just-in-time business techniques

KAIZENS > KAIZEN

KAJAWAH *n* type of seat or panier used on a camel

KAJAWAHS > KAJAWAH

KAJEPUT *n* variety of Australian melaleuca
KAJEPUTS > KAJEPUT
KAK *n* South African slang word for faeces
KAKA *n* parrot of New Zealand
KAKAPO *n* ground-living nocturnal New Zealand parrot that resembles an owl
KAKAPOS > KAKAPO
KAKARIKI *n* green-feathered New Zealand parrot
KAKAS > KAKA
KAKEMONO *n* Japanese paper or silk wall hanging, usually long and narrow, with a picture or inscription on it and a roller at the bottom
KAKEMONOS > KAKEMONO
KAKI *n* Asian persimmon tree
KAKIEMON *n* type of 17th century Japanese porcelain
KAKIEMONS > KAKIEMON
KAKIS > KAKI
KAKODYL *variant spelling of* > CACODYL
KAKODYLS > KAKODYL
KAKS > KAK
KALAM *n* discussion and debate, especially relating to Islamic theology
KALAMATA *as in* kalamata olive aubergine-coloured Greek olive
KALAMATAS > KALAMATA
KALAMDAN *n* Persian box in which to keep pens
KALAMDANS > KALAMDAN
KALAMKARI *n* Indian cloth printing and printed Indian cloth
KALAMS > KALAM
KALANCHOE *n* tropical succulent plant having small brightly coloured flowers and dark shiny leaves
KALE *n* cabbage with crinkled leaves
KALENDAR *variant form of* > CALENDAR
KALENDARS > KALENDAR
KALENDS *same as* > CALENDS
KALES > KALE
KALEWIFE *n* Scots word for a female vegetable or cabbage seller
KALEWIVES > KALEWIFE
KALEYARD *n* vegetable garden
KALEYARDS > KALEYARD
KALI *another name for* > SALTWORT
KALIAN *another name for* > HOOKAH
KALIANS > KALIAN
KALIF *variant spelling of* > CALIPH
KALIFATE *same as* > CALIPHATE
KALIFATES > KALIFATE
KALIFS > KALIF
KALIMBA *n* musical instrument

KALIMBAS > KALIMBA
KALINITE *n* alum
KALINITES > KALINITE
KALIPH *variant spelling of* > CALIPH
KALIPHATE *same as* > CALIPHATE
KALIPHS > KALIPH
KALIS > KALI
KALIUM *n* Latin for potassium
KALIUMS > KALIUM
KALLIDIN *n* type of peptide
KALLIDINS > KALLIDIN
KALLITYPE *n* old printing process
KALMIA *n* N American evergreen ericaceous shrub with showy clusters of white or pink flowers
KALMIAS > KALMIA
KALONG *n* fruit bat
KALONGS > KALONG
KALOTYPE *variant spelling of* > CALOTYPE
KALOTYPES > KALOTYPE
KALPA *n* (in Hindu cosmology) period in which the universe experiences a cycle of creation and destruction
KALPAC *same as* > CALPAC
KALPACS > KALPAC
KALPAK *variant spelling of* > CALPAC
KALPAKS > KALPAK
KALPAS > KALPA
KALPIS *n* Greek water jar
KALPISES > KALPIS
KALSOMINE *variant of* > CALCIMINE
KALUMPIT *n* type of Filipino fruit tree or its fruit
KALUMPITS > KALUMPIT
KALYPTRA *n* Greek veil
KALYPTRAS > KALYPTRA
KAM *Shakespearean word for* > CROOKED
KAMA *n* large African antelope with lyre-shaped horns
KAMAAINA *n* Hawaiian local
KAMAAINAS > KAMAAINA
KAMACITE *n* alloy of iron and nickel, occurring in meteorites
KAMACITES > KAMACITE
KAMAHI *n* tall New Zealand hardwood tree with pinkish flowers
KAMALA *n* East Indian tree
KAMALAS > KAMALA
KAMAS > KAMA
KAME *n* irregular mound or ridge of gravel, sand, etc, deposited by water derived from melting glaciers
KAMEES > KAMEEZ
KAMEESES > KAMEES
KAMEEZ *n* long tunic worn in the Indian subcontinent, often with shalwar
KAMEEZES > KAMEEZ
KAMELA *same as* > KAMALA
KAMELAS > KAMELA
KAMERAD *interj* shout of

surrender ▷ *vb* surrender
KAMERADED > KAMERAD
KAMERADS > KAMERAD
KAMES > KAME
KAMI *n* divine being or spiritual force in Shinto
KAMICHI *n* South American bird
KAMICHIS > KAMICHI
KAMIK *n* traditional Inuit boot made of caribou hide or sealskin
KAMIKAZE *n* (in World War II) Japanese pilot who performed a suicide mission ▷ *adj* (of an action) undertaken in the knowledge that it will kill or injure the person performing it
KAMIKAZES > KAMIKAZE
KAMIKS > KAMIK
KAMILA *same as* > KAMALA
KAMILAS > KAMILA
KAMIS *same as* > KAMEEZ
KAMISES > KAMIS
KAMME *same as* > KAM
KAMOKAMO *n* kind of marrow found in New Zealand
KAMPONG *n* (in Malaysia) village
KAMPONGS > KAMPONG
KAMSEEN *same as* > KHAMSIN
KAMSEENS > KAMSEEN
KAMSIN *same as* > KAMSEEN
KAMSINS > KAMSIN
KANA *n* Japanese syllabary, which consists of two written varieties
KANAE *n* grey mullet
KANAKA *n* Australian word for any native of the South Pacific islands, esp (formerly) one abducted to work in Australia
KANAKAS > KANAKA
KANAMYCIN *n* type of antibiotic
KANAS > KANA
KANBAN *n* just-in-time manufacturing process in which the movements of materials through a process are recorded on specially designed cards
KANBANS > KANBAN
KANDIES > KANDY
KANDY *same as* > CANDIE
KANE *n* Hawaiian man or boy
KANEH *n* 6-cubit Hebrew measure
KANEHS > KANEH
KANES > KANE
KANG *n* Chinese heatable platform used for sleeping and sitting on
KANGA *n* piece of gaily decorated thin cotton cloth used as a garment by women in E Africa
KANGAROO *n* Australian marsupial which moves by jumping with its powerful hind legs ▷ *vb* (of a car) move forward or to cause (a car) to move forward

with short sudden jerks, as a result of improper use of the clutch
KANGAROOS > KANGAROO
KANGAS > KANGA
KANGHA *n* comb traditionally worn by Sikhs as a symbol of their religious and cultural loyalty
KANGHAS > KANGHA
KANGS > KANG
KANJI *n* Japanese writing system using characters mainly derived from Chinese ideograms
KANJIS > KANJI
KANS *n* Indian wild sugar cane
KANSES > KANS
KANT *archaic spelling of* > CANT
KANTAR *n* unit of weight used in E Mediterranean countries, equivalent to 100 pounds or 45 kilograms but varying from place to place
KANTARS > KANTAR
KANTED > KANT
KANTELA *same as* > KANTELE
KANTELAS > KANTELA
KANTELE *n* Finnish stringed instrument
KANTELES > KANTELE
KANTEN *same as* > AGAR
KANTENS > KANTEN
KANTHA *n* Bengali embroidered quilt
KANTHAS > KANTHA
KANTIKOY *vb* dance ceremonially
KANTIKOYS > KANTIKOY
KANTING > KANT
KANTS > KANT
KANUKA *n* New Zealand myrtaceous tree
KANZU *n* long garment, usually white, with long sleeves, worn by E African men
KANZUS > KANZU
KAOLIANG *n* any of various E Asian varieties of sorghum
KAOLIANGS > KAOLIANG
KAOLIN *n* fine white clay used to make porcelain and in some medicines
KAOLINE *same as* > KAOLIN
KAOLINES > KAOLINE
KAOLINIC > KAOLIN
KAOLINISE *same as* > KAOLINIZE
KAOLINITE *n* white or grey clay mineral consisting of hydrated aluminium silicate in triclinic crystalline form, the main constituent of kaolin
KAOLINIZE *vb* change into kaolin
KAOLINS > KAOLIN
KAON *n* meson that has a positive or negative charge and a rest mass of about 966 electron masses, or no charge and a rest mass of

974 electron masses

KAONIC > KAON

KAONS > KAON

KAPA *n* Hawaiian cloth made from beaten mulberry bark

KAPAS > KAPA

KAPH *n* 11th letter of the Hebrew alphabet

KAPHS > KAPH

KAPOK *n* fluffy fibre from a tropical tree, used to stuff cushions etc

KAPOKS > KAPOK

KAPPA *n* tenth letter in the Greek alphabet

KAPPAS > KAPPA

KAPUKA *same as* > BROADLEAF

KAPUT *adj* ruined or broken

KAPUTT *same as* > KAPUT

KARA *n* steel bangle traditionally worn by Sikhs as a symbol of their religious and cultural loyalty

KARABINER *n* metal clip with a spring for attaching to a piton, belay, etc

KARAISM *n* beliefs and doctrines of a Jewish sect rejecting Rabbinism

KARAISMS > KARAISM

KARAIT *same as* > KRAIT

KARAITS > KRAIT

KARAKA *n* New Zealand tree

KARAKAS > KARAKA

KARAKIA *n* prayer

KARAKIAS > KARAKIA

KARAKUL *n* sheep of central Asia, the lambs of which have soft curled dark hair

KARAKULS > KARAKUL

KARAMU *n* small New Zealand tree with glossy leaves and orange fruit

KARAMUS > KARAMU

KARANGA *n* call or chant of welcome, sung by a female elder ▷ *vb* perform a karanga

KARANGAED > KARANGA

KARANGAS > KARANGA

KARAOKE *n* form of entertainment in which people sing over a prerecorded backing tape

KARAOKES > KARAOKE

KARAS > KARA

KARAT *n* measure of the proportion of gold in an alloy, expressed as the number of parts of gold in 24 parts of the alloy

KARATE *n* Japanese system of unarmed combat using blows with the feet, hands, elbows, and legs

KARATEIST *same as* > KARATEKA

KARATEKA *n* competitor or expert in karate

KARATEKAS > KARATEKA

KARATES > KARATE

KARATS > KARAT

KAREAREA *n* New Zealand falcon

KARENGO *n* edible type of Pacific seaweed

KARENGOS > KARENGO

KARITE *n* shea tree

KARITES > KARITE

KARK *variant spelling of* > CARK

KARKED > KARK

KARKING > KARK

KARKS > KARK

KARMA *n* person's actions affecting his or her fate in the next reincarnation

KARMAS > KARMA

KARMIC > KARMA

KARN *old word for* > CAIRN

KARNS > KARN

KARO *n* small New Zealand tree or shrub with sweet-smelling brown flowers

KAROO *n* high arid plateau

KAROOS > KAROO

KARORO *n* large seagull with black feathers on its back

KAROROS > KARORO

KAROSHI *n* (in Japan) death caused by overwork

KAROSHIS > KAROSHI

KAROSS *n* blanket made of animal skins sewn together

KAROSSES > KAROSS

KARRI *n* Australian eucalypt

KARRIS > KARRI

KARROO *same as* > KAROO

KARROOS > KARROO

KARSEY *variant spelling of* > KHAZI

KARSEYS > KARSEY

KARSIES > KARSY

KARST *n* denoting the characteristic scenery of a limestone region, including underground streams, gorges, etc

KARSTIC > KARST

KARSTIFY *vb* become karstic

KARSTS > KARST

KARSY *variant spelling of* > KHAZI

KART *n* light low-framed vehicle with small wheels and engine used for recreational racing

KARTER > KART

KARTERS > KART

KARTING > KART

KARTINGS > KART

KARTS > KART

KARYOGAMY *n* fusion of two gametic nuclei during fertilization

KARYOGRAM *n* diagram or photograph of the chromosomes of a cell, arranged in homologous pairs and in a numbered sequence

KARYOLOGY *n* study of cell nuclei, esp with reference to the number and shape of the chromosomes

KARYON *n* nucleus of a cell

KARYONS > KARYON

KARYOSOME *n* any of the dense aggregates of

chromatin in the nucleus of a cell

KARYOTIN *less common word for* > CHROMATIN

KARYOTINS > KARYOTIN

KARYOTYPE *n* appearance of the chromosomes in a somatic cell of an individual or species, with reference to their number, size, shape, etc ▷ *vb* determine the karyotype of (a cell)

KARZIES > KARZY

KARZY *variant spelling of* > KHAZI

KAS > KA

KASBAH *n* citadel of any of various North African cities

KASBAHS > KASBAH

KASHA *n* dish originating in Eastern Europe, consisting of boiled or baked buckwheat

KASHAS > KASHA

KASHER *vb* make fit for use

KASHERED > KASHER

KASHERING > KASHER

KASHERS > KASHER

KASHMIR *variant spelling of* > CASHMERE

KASHMIRS > KASHMIR

KASHRUS *same as* > KASHRUTH

KASHRUSES > KASHRUS

KASHRUT *same as* > KASHRUTH

KASHRUTH *n* condition of being fit for ritual use in general

KASHRUTHS > KASHRUTH

KASHRUTS > KASHRUT

KASME *interj* (in Indian English) I swear

KAT *same as* > KHAT

KATA *n* exercise consisting of a sequence of the specific movements of a martial art, used in training and designed to show skill in technique

KATABASES > KATABASIS

KATABASIS *n* retreat of the Greek mercenaries of Cyrus the Younger, after his death at Cunaxa, from the Euphrates to the Black Sea in 401–400 BC under the leadership of Xenophon

KATABATIC *adj* (of winds) blowing downhill through having become denser with cooling, esp at night when heat is lost from the earth's surface

KATABOLIC *same as* > CATABOLIC

KATAKANA *n* one of the two systems of syllabic writing employed for the representation of Japanese, based on Chinese ideograms. It is used mainly for foreign or foreign-derived words

KATAKANAS > KATAKANA

KATANA *n* Japanese samurai sword

KATANAS > KATANA

KATAS > KATA

KATCHINA *variant spelling of* > KACHINA

KATCHINAS > KATCHINA

KATCINA *variant spelling of* > KACHINA

KATCINAS > KATCINA

KATHAK *n* form of N Indian classical dancing that tells a story

KATHAKALI *n* form of dance drama of S India using mime and based on Hindu literature

KATHAKS > KATHAK

KATHARSES > KATHARSIS

KATHARSIS *variant spelling of* > CATHARSIS

KATHODAL > KATHODE

KATHODE *variant spelling of* > CATHODE

KATHODES > KATHODE

KATHODIC > KATHODE

KATI *variant spelling of* > CATTY

KATION *variant spelling of* > CATION

KATIONS > KATION

KATIPO *n* small poisonous New Zealand spider

KATIPOS > KATIPO

KATIS > KATI

KATORGA *n* labour camp in Imperial Russia or the Soviet Union

KATORGAS > KATORGA

KATS > KAT

KATSURA *n* Asian tree

KATSURAS > KATSURA

KATTI *variant spelling of* > CATTY

KATTIS > KATTI

KATYDID *n* large green grasshopper of N America

KATYDIDS > KATYDID

KAUGH *same as* > KIAUGH

KAUGHS > KAUGH

KAUMATUA *n* senior member of a tribe

KAUMATUAS > KAUMATUA

KAUPAPA *n* strategy, policy, or cause

KAUPAPAS > KAUPAPA

KAURI *n* large NZ conifer that yields valuable timber and resin

KAURIES > KAURY

KAURIS > KAURI

KAURU *n* edible stem of the cabbage tree

KAURY *variant spelling of* > KAURI

KAVA *n* Polynesian shrub

KAVAKAVA *same as* > KAVA

KAVAKAVAS > KAVAKAVA

KAVAS > KAVA

KAVASS *n* armed Turkish constable

KAVASSES > KAVASS

KAW *variant spelling of* > CAW

KAWA *n* protocol or etiquette, particularly in a Māori tribal meeting place

KAWAKAWA *n* aromatic shrub or small tree of New Zealand

KAWAKAWAS > KAWAKAWA

KAWAS > KAWA

KAWAU n New Zealand name for black shag

KAWED > KAW

KAWING > KAW

KAWS > KAW

KAY n name of the letter K

KAYAK n Inuit canoe made of sealskins stretched over a frame ▷ vb travel by kayak

KAYAKED > KAYAK

KAYAKER > KAYAK

KAYAKERS > KAYAK

KAYAKING > KAYAK

KAYAKINGS > KAYAK

KAYAKS > KAYAK

KAYLE n one of a set of ninepins

KAYLES pl n ninepins

KAYLIED adj (in British slang) intoxicated or drunk

KAYO another term for > KNOCKOUT

KAYOED > KAYO

KAYOES > KAYO

KAYOING > KAYO

KAYOINGS > KAYO

KAYOS > KAYO

KAYS > KAY

KAZACHKI same as > KAZACHOK

KAZACHOK n Russian folk dance in which the performer executes high kicks from a squatting position

KAZATSKI same as > KAZACHOK

KAZATSKY same as > KAZACHOK

KAZATZKA same as > KAZACHOK

KAZATZKAS > KAZACHOK

KAZI variant spelling of > KHAZI

KAZILLION same as > GAZILLION

KAZIS > KAZI

KAZOO n cigar-shaped metal musical instrument that produces a buzzing sound when the player hums into it

KAZOOS > KAZOO

KBAR n kilobar

KBARS > KBAR

KEA n large brownish-green parrot of NZ

KEAS > KEA

KEASAR archaic variant of > KAISER

KEASARS > KEASAR

KEAVIE n archaic or dialect word for a type of crab

KEAVIES > KEAVIE

KEB vb Scots word meaning miscarry or reject a lamb

KEBAB n dish of small pieces of meat grilled on skewers ▷ vb skewer

KEBABBED > KEBAB

KEBABBING > KEBAB

KEBABS > KEBAB

KEBAR n Scots word for beam or rafter

KEBARS > KEBAR

KEBBED > KEB

KEBBIE n Scots word for shepherd's crook

KEBBIES > KEBBIE

KEBBING > KEB

KEBBOCK n Scots word for a cheese

KEBBOCKS > KEBBOCK

KEBBUCK same as > KEBBOCK

KEBBUCKS > KEBBUCK

KEBELE n Ethiopian local council

KEBELES > KEBELE

KEBLAH same as > KIBLAH

KEBLAHS > KEBLAH

KEBOB same as > KEBAB

KEBOBBED > KEBOB

KEBOBBING > KEBOB

KEBOBS > KEBOB

KEBS > KEB

KECK vb retch or feel nausea

KECKED > KECK

KECKING > KECK

KECKLE Scots variant of > CACKLE

KECKLED > KECKLE

KECKLES > KECKLE

KECKLING > KECKLE

KECKLINGS > KECKLE

KECKS pl n trousers

KECKSES > KECKS

KECKSIES > KECKSY

KECKSY n dialect word meaning hollow plant stalk

KED as in sheep ked sheep tick

KEDDAH same as > KHEDA

KEDDAHS > KEDDAH

KEDGE vb move (a ship) along by hauling in on the cable of a light anchor ▷ n light anchor used for kedging

KEDGED > KEDGE

KEDGER n small anchor

KEDGEREE n dish of fish with rice and eggs

KEDGEREES > KEDGEREE

KEDGERS > KEDGER

KEDGES > KEDGE

KEDGIER > KEDGY

KEDGIEST > KEDGY

KEDGING > KEDGE

KEDGY adj dialect word for happy or lively

KEDS > KED

KEECH n old word for lump of fat

KEECHES > KEECH

KEEF same as > KIF

KEEFS > KEEF

KEEK Scot word for > PEEP

KEEKED > KEEK

KEEKER > KEEK

KEEKERS > KEEK

KEEKING > KEEK

KEEKS > KEEK

KEEL n main lengthways timber or steel support along the base of a ship ▷ vb mark with this stain

KEELAGE n fee charged by certain ports to allow a ship to dock

KEELAGES > KEELAGE

KEELBOAT n river boat with a shallow draught and a keel, used for freight and moved by towing, punting, or rowing

KEELBOATS > KEELBOAT

KEELED > KEEL

KEELER n bargeman

KEELERS > KEELER

KEELHALE same as > KEELHAUL

KEELHALED > KEELHALE

KEELHALES > KEELHALE

KEELHAUL vb reprimand (someone) harshly

KEELHAULS > KEELHAUL

KEELIE n kestrel

KEELIES > KEELIE

KEELING > KEEL

KEELINGS > KEEL

KEELIVINE Scots word for > PENCIL

KEELLESS > KEEL

KEELMAN n bargeman

KEELMEN > KEELMAN

KEELS > KEEL

KEELSON n lengthways beam fastened to the keel of a ship for strength

KEELSONS > KEELSON

KEELYVINE same as > KEELIVINE

KEEN adj eager or enthusiastic ▷ vb wail over the dead ▷ n lament for the dead

KEENED > KEEN

KEENER > KEEN

KEENERS > KEEN

KEENEST > KEEN

KEENING > KEEN

KEENINGS > KEEN

KEENLY > KEEN

KEENNESS > KEEN

KEENO same as > KENO

KEENOS > KEENO

KEENS > KEEN

KEEP vb have or retain possession of ▷ n cost of food and everyday expenses

KEEPABLE > KEEP

KEEPER n person who looks after animals in a zoo

KEEPERS > KEEPER

KEEPING > KEEP

KEEPINGS > KEEP

KEEPNET n cylindrical net strung on wire hoops and sealed at one end, suspended in water by anglers to keep alive the fish they have caught

KEEPNETS > KEEPNET

KEEPS > KEEP

KEEPSAKE n gift treasured for the sake of the giver

KEEPSAKES > KEEPSAKE

KEEPSAKY > KEEPSAKE

KEESHOND n breed of dog of the spitz type with a shaggy greyish coat and tightly curled tail, originating in Holland

KEESHONDS > KEESHOND

KEESTER same as > KEISTER

KEESTERS > KEESTER

KEET short for > PARAKEET

KEETS > KEET

KEEVE n tub or vat

KEEVES > KEEVE

KEF same as > KIF

KEFFEL dialect word for > HORSE

KEFFELS > KEFFEL

KEFFIYAH same as > KAFFIYEH

KEFFIYAHS > KEFFIYAH

KEFFIYEH n cotton headdress worn by Arabs

KEFFIYEHS > KEFFIYEH

KEFIR n effervescent drink of the Caucasus made from fermented milk

KEFIRS > KEFIR

KEFS > KEF

KEFTEDES n Greek dish of meatballs cooked with herbs and onions

KEFUFFLE same as > KERFUFFLE

KEFUFFLED > KEFUFFLE

KEFUFFLES > KEFUFFLE

KEG n small metal beer barrel ▷ vb put in kegs

KEGELER same as > KEGLER

KEGELERS > KEGELER

KEGGED > KEG

KEGGER > KEG

KEGGERS > KEG

KEGGING > KEG

KEGLER n participant in a game of tenpin bowling

KEGLERS > KEGLER

KEGLING n bowling

KEGLINGS > KEGLING

KEGS > KEG

KEHUA n ghost or spirit

KEHUAS > KEHUA

KEIGHT > KETCH

KEIR same as > KIER

KEIRETSU n group of Japanese businesses

KEIRETSUS > KEIRETSU

KEIRS > KEIR

KEISTER n rump

KEISTERS > KEISTER

KEITLOA n southern African black two-horned rhinoceros

KEITLOAS > KEITLOA

KEKENO n New Zealand fur seal

KEKERENGU n Māori bug

KEKS same as > KECKS

KEKSYE same as > KEX

KEKSYES > KEKSYE

KELEP n large ant found in Central and South America

KELEPS > KELEP

KELIM same as > KILIM

KELIMS > KELIM

KELL dialect word for > HAIRNET

KELLAUT same as > KHILAT

KELLAUTS > KELLAUT

KELLIES > KELLY

KELLS > KELL

KELLY n part of a drill system

KELOID n hard smooth pinkish raised growth of scar tissue at the site of an injury, tending to occur more frequently in dark-skinned races

KELOIDAL > KELOID

KELOIDS > KELOID

KELP *n* large brown seaweed ▷*vb* burn seaweed to make a type of ash used as a source for iodine and potash

KELPED > KELP

KELPER *n* Falkland Islander

KELPERS > KELPER

KELPIE *n* Australian sheepdog with a smooth coat and upright ears

KELPIES > KELPY

KELPING > KELP

KELPS > KELP

KELPY *same as* > KELPIE

KELSON *same as* > KEELSON

KELSONS > KELSON

KELT *n* salmon that has recently spawned

KELTER *same as* > KILTER

KELTERS > KELTER

KELTIE *variant spelling of* > KELTY

KELTIES > KELTY

KELTS > KELT

KELTY *n* old Scots word for an extra drink imposed on someone not thought to be drinking enough

KELVIN *n* SI unit of temperature

KELVINS > KELVIN

KEMB *old word for* > COMB

KEMBED > KEMB

KEMBING > KEMB

KEMBLA *n* small change

KEMBLAS > KEMBLA

KEMBO *same as* > KIMBO

KEMBOED > KEMBO

KEMBOING > KEMBO

KEMBOS > KEMBO

KEMBS > KEMB

KEMP *n* coarse hair or strand of hair, esp one in a fleece that resists dyeing ▷*vb* dialect word meaning to compete or try to come first

KEMPED > KEMP

KEMPER > KEMP

KEMPERS > KEMP

KEMPIER > KEMPY

KEMPIEST > KEMPY

KEMPING > KEMP

KEMPINGS > KEMP

KEMPLE *n* variable Scottish measure for hay or straw

KEMPLES > KEMPLE

KEMPS > KEMP

KEMPT *adj* (of hair) tidy

KEMPY > KEMP

KEN *vb* know ▷*n* range of knowledge or perception

KENAF *another name for* > AMBARY

KENAFS > KENAF

KENCH *n* bin for salting and preserving fish

KENCHES > KENCH

KENDO *n* Japanese sport of fencing using wooden staves

KENDOS > KENDO

KENNED > KEN

KENNEL *n* hutlike shelter for a dog ▷*vb* put or go into a kennel

KENNELED > KENNEL

KENNELING > KENNEL

KENNELLED > KENNEL

KENNELS > KENNEL

KENNER > KEN

KENNERS > KEN

KENNET *n* old word for a small hunting dog

KENNETS > KENNET

KENNETT *vb* spoil or destroy ruthlessly

KENNETTED > KENNETT

KENNETTS > KENNETT

KENNING > KEN

KENNINGS > KEN

KENO *n* game of chance similar to bingo

KENOS > KENO

KENOSES > KENOSIS

KENOSIS *n* Christ's voluntary renunciation of certain divine attributes, in order to identify himself with mankind

KENOSISES > KENOSIS

KENOTIC > KENOSIS

KENOTICS > KENOSIS

KENOTRON *n* signal-amplifying device

KENOTRONS > KENOTRON

KENS > KEN

KENSPECK *adj* Scots for easily seen or recognized

KENT *dialect word for* > PUNT

KENTE *n* brightly coloured handwoven cloth of Ghana, usually with some gold thread

KENTED > KENT

KENTES > KENTE

KENTIA *n* plant name formerly used to include palms now allotted to several different genera

KENTIAS > KENTIA

KENTING > KENT

KENTLEDGE *n* scrap metal used as ballast in a vessel

KENTS > KENT

KEP *vb* catch

KEPHALIC *variant spelling of* > CEPHALIC

KEPHALICS > KEPHALIC

KEPHALIN *same as* > CEPHALIN

KEPHALINS > KEPHALIN

KEPHIR *same as* > KEFIR

KEPHIRS > KEPHIR

KEPI *n* French military cap with a flat top and a horizontal peak

KEPIS > KEPI

KEPPED > KEP

KEPPEN > KEP

KEPPING > KEP

KEPPIT > KEP

KEPS > KEP

KEPT > KEEP

KERAMIC *rare variant of* > CERAMIC

KERAMICS *rare variant of* > CERAMICS

KERATIN *n* fibrous protein found in the hair and nails

KERATINS > KERATIN

KERATITIS *n* inflammation of the cornea

KERATOID *adj* resembling horn

KERATOMA *n* horny growth on the skin

KERATOMAS > KERATOMA

KERATOSE *adj* (esp of certain sponges) having a horny skeleton

KERATOSES > KERATOSIS

KERATOSIC > KERATOSE

KERATOSIS *n* any skin condition marked by a horny growth, such as a wart

KERATOTIC > KERATOSIS

KERB *n* edging to a footpath ▷*vb* provide with or enclose with a kerb

KERBAYA *n* blouse worn by Malay women

KERBAYAS > KERBAYA

KERBED > KERB

KERBING *n* material used for a kerb

KERBINGS > KERBING

KERBS > KERB

KERBSIDE *n* edge of a pavement where it drops to the level of the road

KERBSIDES > KERBSIDE

KERBSTONE *n* one of a series of stones that form a kerb

KERCHIEF *n* piece of cloth worn over the head or round the neck

KERCHIEFS > KERCHIEF

KERCHOO *interj* atishoo

KEREL *n* chap or fellow

KERELS > KEREL

KERERU *n* New Zealand pigeon

KERF *n* cut made by a saw, an axe, etc ▷*vb* cut

KERFED > KERF

KERFING > KERF

KERFLOOEY *adv* into state of destruction or malfunction

KERFS > KERF

KERFUFFLE *n* commotion or disorder ▷*vb* put into disorder or disarray

KERKIER > KERKY

KERKIEST > KERKY

KERKY *adj* stupid

KERMA *n* quotient of the sum of the initial kinetic energies of all the charged particles liberated by indirectly ionizing radiation in a volume element of a material divided by the mass of the volume element

KERMAS > KERMA

KERMES *n* dried bodies of female scale insects, used as a red dyestuff

KERMESITE *n* red antimony

KERMESS *same as* > KERMIS

KERMESSE *same as* > KERMIS

KERMESSES > KERMESSE

KERMIS *n* (formerly, esp in Holland and Northern Germany) annual country festival or carnival

KERMISES > KERMIS

KERN *n* part of the character on a piece of printer's type that projects beyond the body ▷*vb* furnish (a typeface) with a kern

KERNE *same as* > KERN

KERNED > KERNE

KERNEL *n* seed of a nut, cereal, or fruit stone ▷*vb* form kernels

KERNELED > KERNEL

KERNELING > KERNEL

KERNELLED > KERNEL

KERNELLY *adj* with or like kernels

KERNELS > KERNEL

KERNES > KERNE

KERNING *n* adjustment of space between the letters of words to improve the appearance of text matter

KERNINGS > KERNING

KERNISH *adj* of, belonging to, or resembling an armed foot soldier or peasant

KERNITE *n* light soft colourless or white mineral consisting of a hydrated sodium borate in monoclinic crystalline form: an important source of borax and other boron compounds

KERNITES > KERNITE

KERNS > KERN

KERO *short for* > KEROSENE

KEROGEN *n* solid organic material found in some rocks, such as oil shales, that produces hydrocarbons similar to petroleum when heated

KEROGENS > KEROGEN

KEROS > KERO

KEROSENE *n* liquid mixture distilled from petroleum and used as a fuel or solvent

KEROSENES > KEROSENE

KEROSINE *same as* > KEROSENE

KEROSINES > KEROSINE

KERPLUNK *vb* land noisily

KERPLUNKS > KERPLUNK

KERRIA *n* type of shrub with yellow flowers

KERRIAS > KERRIA

KERRIES > KERRY

KERRY *n* breed of dairy cattle

KERSEY *n* smooth woollen cloth used for overcoats, etc

KERSEYS > KERSEY

KERVE *dialect word for* > CARVE

KERVED > KERVE

KERVES > KERVE

KERVING > KERVE

KERYGMA *n* essential news of Jesus, as preached by the early Christians to elicit faith rather than to educate or instruct

KERYGMAS > KERYGMA

KERYGMATA > KERYGMA
KESAR old variant of > KAISER
KESARS > KESAR
KESH n beard and uncut hair, covered by the turban, traditionally worn by Sikhs as a symbol of their religious and cultural loyalty
KESHES > KESH
KEST old form of > CAST
KESTING > KEST
KESTREL n type of small falcon
KESTRELS > KESTREL
KESTS > KEST
KET n dialect word for carrion
KETA n type of salmon
KETAMINE n drug, chemically related to PCP, that is used in medicine as a general anaesthetic, being administered by injection
KETAMINES > KETAMINE
KETAS > KETA
KETCH n two-masted sailing vessel ▷ vb (in archaic usage) catch
KETCHES > KETCH
KETCHING > KETCH
KETCHUP n thick cold sauce, usu made of tomatoes
KETCHUPS > KETCHUP
KETE n basket woven from flax
KETENE n colourless irritating toxic gas used as an acetylating agent in organic synthesis
KETENES > KETENE
KETMIA as in bladder ketmia plant with pale yellow flowers and a bladder-like calyx
KETMIAS > KETMIA
KETO as in keto form form of tautomeric compounds when they are ketones rather than enol
KETOGENIC adj forming or able to stimulate the production of ketone bodies
KETOL n nitrogenous substance
KETOLS > KETOL
KETONE n type of organic solvent
KETONEMIA n excess of ketone bodies in the blood
KETONES > KETONE
KETONIC > KETONE
KETONURIA n presence of ketone bodies in the urine
KETOSE n any monosaccharide that contains a ketone group
KETOSES > KETOSIS
KETOSIS n high concentration of ketone bodies in the blood
KETOTIC > KETOSIS
KETOXIME n oxime formed by reaction between hydroxylamine and a

ketone
KETOXIMES > KETOXIME
KETS > KET
KETTLE n container with a spout and handle used for boiling water
KETTLEFUL > KETTLE
KETTLES > KETTLE
KETUBAH n contract that states the obligations within Jewish marriage
KETUBAHS > KETUBAH
KETUBOT > KETUBAH
KETUBOTH > KETUBAH
KEVEL n strong bitt or bollard for securing heavy hawsers
KEVELS > KEVEL
KEVIL old variant of > KEVEL
KEVILS > KEVIL
KEWL nonstandard variant spelling of > COOL
KEWLER > KEWL
KEWLEST > KEWL
KEWPIE n type of brightly coloured doll, commonly given as a prize at carnival
KEWPIES > KEWPIE
KEX n any of several large hollow-stemmed umbelliferous plants, such as cow parsnip and chervil
KEXES > KEX
KEY n device for operating a lock by moving a bolt ▷ adj of great importance ▷ vb enter (text) using a keyboard
KEYBOARD n set of keys on a piano, computer, etc ▷ vb enter (text) using a keyboard
KEYBOARDS > KEYBOARD
KEYBUGLE n bugle with keys
KEYBUGLES > KEYBUGLE
KEYBUTTON n on a keyboard, an object which, when pressed, causes the letter, number, or symbol shown on it to be printed in a document
KEYCARD n card with an electronic strip or code on it that allows it to open a corresponding keycard-operated door
KEYCARDS > KEYCARD
KEYED > KEY
KEYHOLE n opening for inserting a key into a lock
KEYHOLES > KEYHOLE
KEYING > KEY
KEYINGS > KEY
KEYLESS > KEY
KEYLINE n outline image of something on artwork or plans to show where it is to be placed
KEYLINES > KEYLINE
KEYLOGGER n device or software application used for covertly recording and monitoring keystrokes made on a remote computer
KEYNOTE adj central or dominating ▷ n dominant

idea of a speech etc ▷ vb deliver a keynote address to (a political convention, etc)
KEYNOTED > KEYNOTE
KEYNOTER n person delivering a keynote address
KEYNOTERS > KEYNOTER
KEYNOTES > KEYNOTE
KEYNOTING > KEYNOTE
KEYPAD n small panel with a set of buttons for operating a Teletext system, electronic calculator, etc
KEYPADS > KEYPAD
KEYPAL n person with whom one regularly exchanges emails for fun
KEYPALS > KEYPAL
KEYPUNCH n device having a keyboard that is operated manually to transfer data onto punched cards, paper tape, etc ▷ vb transfer (data) onto punched cards, paper tape, etc, by using a key punch
KEYRING n split ring designed for holding keys
KEYS interj children's cry for truce or respite from the rules of a game
KEYSET n set of computer keys used for a particular purpose
KEYSETS > KEYSET
KEYSTER same as > KEISTER
KEYSTERS > KEYSTER
KEYSTONE n most important part of a process, organization, etc ▷ vb project or provide with a distorted image
KEYSTONED > KEYSTONE
KEYSTONES > KEYSTONE
KEYSTROKE n single operation of the mechanism of a typewriter or keyboard-operated typesetting machine by the action of a key ▷ vb enter or cause to be recorded by pressing a key
KEYWAY n longitudinal slot cut into a component to accept a key that engages with a similar slot on a mating component to prevent relative motion of the two components
KEYWAYS > KEYWAY
KEYWORD n word or phrase that a computer will search for in order to locate the information or file that the computer user has requested
KEYWORDS > KEYWORD
KGOTLA n (in South African English) meeting place for village assemblies, court cases, and meetings of village leaders
KGOTLAS > KGOTLA
KHADDAR n cotton cloth of plain weave, produced in

India
KHADDARS > KHADDAR
KHADI same as > KHADDAR
KHADIS > KHADI
KHAF n letter of the Hebrew alphabet
KHAFS > KHAF
KHAKI adj dull yellowish-brown ▷ n hard-wearing fabric of this colour used for military uniforms
KHAKILIKE > KHAKI
KHAKIS > KHAKI
KHALAT same as > KHILAT
KHALATS > KHALAT
KHALIF variant spelling of > CALIPH
KHALIFA same as > CALIPH
KHALIFAH same as > CALIPH
KHALIFAHS > KHALIFAH
KHALIFAS > KHALIFA
KHALIFAT same as > CALIPHATE
KHALIFATE same as > CALIPHATE
KHALIFATS > KHALIFAT
KHALIFS > KHALIF
KHAMSEEN same as > KHAMSIN
KHAMSEENS > KHAMSEEN
KHAMSIN n hot southerly wind blowing from about March to May, esp in Egypt
KHAMSINS > KHAMSIN
KHAN n title of respect in Afghanistan and central Asia
KHANATE n territory ruled by a khan
KHANATES > KHANATE
KHANDA n double-edged sword that appears as the emblem on the Sikh flag and is used in the Amrit ceremony to stir the amrit
KHANDAS > KHANDA
KHANGA same as > KANGA
KHANGAS > KHANGA
KHANJAR n type of dagger
KHANJARS > KHANJAR
KHANS > KHAN
KHANSAMA same as > KHANSAMAH
KHANSAMAH n Indian cook or other male servant
KHANSAMAS > KHANSAMA
KHANUM feminine form of > KHAN
KHANUMS > KHANUM
KHAPH n letter of the Hebrew alphabet
KHAPHS > KHAPH
KHARIF n (in Pakistan, India, etc) crop that is harvested at the beginning of winter
KHARIFS > KHARIF
KHAT n white-flowered evergreen shrub of Africa and Arabia whose leaves have narcotic properties
KHATS > KHAT
KHAYA n type of African tree
KHAYAL n kind of Indian classical vocal music
KHAYALS > KHAYAL
KHAYAS > KHAYA

KHAZEN *same as* > CHAZAN
KHAZENIM > KHAZEN
KHAZENS > KHAZEN
KHAZI *n* lavatory
KHAZIS > KHAZI
KHEDA *n* (in India, Myanmar, etc) enclosure into which wild elephants are driven to be captured
KHEDAH *same as* > KHEDA
KHEDAHS > KHEDAH
KHEDAS > KHEDA
KHEDIVA *n* khedive's wife
KHEDIVAL > KHEDIVE
KHEDIVAS > KHEDIVA
KHEDIVATE > KHEDIVE
KHEDIVE *n* viceroy of Egypt under Ottoman suzerainty
KHEDIVES > KHEDIVE
KHEDIVIAL > KHEDIVE
KHET *n* Thai district
KHETH *same as* > HETH
KHETHS > KHETH
KHETS > KHET
KHI *n* letter of the Greek alphabet
KHILAFAT *same as* > CALIPHATE
KHILAFATS > KHILAFAT
KHILAT *n* (in the Middle East) robe or other gift given to someone by a superior as a mark of honour
KHILATS > KHILAT
KHILIM *same as* > KILIM
KHILIMS > KHILIM
KHIRKAH *n* dervish's woollen or cotton outer garment
KHIRKAHS > KHIRKAH
KHIS > KHI
KHODJA *same as* > KHOJA
KHODJAS > KHODJA
KHOJA *n* teacher in a Muslim school
KHOJAS > KHOJA
KHOR *n* watercourse
KHORS > KHOR
KHOTBAH *same as* > KHUTBAH
KHOTBAHS > KHOTBAH
KHOTBEH *same as* > KHUTBAH
KHOTBEHS > KHOTBEH
KHOUM *n* Mauritanian monetary unit
KHOUMS > KHOUM
KHUD *n* Indian ravine
KHUDS > KHUD
KHURTA *same as* > KURTA
KHURTAS > KHURTA
KHUSKHUS *n* aromatic perennial Indian grass whose roots are woven into mats, fans, and baskets
KHUTBAH *n* sermon in a Mosque, especially on a Friday
KHUTBAHS > KHUTBAH
KI *n* Japanese martial art
KIAAT *n* tropical African leguminous tree
KIAATS > KIAAT
KIANG *n* variety of wild ass that occurs in Tibet and surrounding regions
KIANGS > KIANG

KIAUGH *n* (in Scots) anxiety
KIAUGHS > KIAUGH
KIBBE *n* Middle Eastern dish made with minced meat and bulgur
KIBBEH *same as* > KIBBE
KIBBEHS > KIBBEH
KIBBES > KIBBE
KIBBI *same as* > KIBBE
KIBBIS > KIBBI
KIBBITZ *same as* > KIBITZ
KIBBITZED > KIBBITZ
KIBBITZER > KIBBITZ
KIBBITZES > KIBBITZ
KIBBLE *n* bucket used in wells or in mining for hoisting ▷ *vb* grind into small pieces
KIBBLED > KIBBLE
KIBBLES > KIBBLE
KIBBLING > KIBBLE
KIBBUTZ *n* communal farm or factory in Israel
KIBBUTZIM > KIBBUTZ
KIBE *n* chilblain, esp an ulcerated one on the heel
KIBEI *n* someone of Japanese ancestry born in the US and educated in Japan
KIBEIS > KIBEI
KIBES > KIBE
KIBITKA *n* (in Russia) covered sledge or wagon
KIBITKAS > KIBITKA
KIBITZ *vb* interfere or offer unwanted advice, esp as a spectator at a card game
KIBITZED > KIBITZ
KIBITZER > KIBITZ
KIBITZERS > KIBITZ
KIBITZES > KIBITZ
KIBITZING > KIBITZ
KIBLA *same as* > KIBLAH
KIBLAH *n* direction of Mecca, to which Muslims turn in prayer, indicated in mosques by a niche (mihrab) in the wall
KIBLAHS > KIBLAH
KIBLAS > KIBLA
KIBOSH *vb* put a stop to
KIBOSHED > KIBOSH
KIBOSHES > KIBOSH
KIBOSHING > KIBOSH
KICK *vb* drive, push, or strike with the foot ▷ *n* thrust or blow with the foot
KICKABLE > KICK
KICKABOUT *n* informal game of soccer
KICKBACK *n* money paid illegally for favours done ▷ *vb* have a strong reaction
KICKBACKS > KICKBACK
KICKBALL *n* children's ball game or the large ball used in it
KICKBALLS > KICKBALL
KICKBOARD *n* type of float held on to by a swimmer when practising leg strokes
KICKBOX *vb* box with hands and feet
KICKBOXED > KICKBOX
KICKBOXER *n* someone who

practises kickboxing, a martial art that resembles boxing but in which kicks are permitted
KICKBOXES > KICKBOX
KICKDOWN *n* method of changing gear in a car with automatic transmission, by fully depressing the accelerator
KICKDOWNS > KICKDOWN
KICKED > KICK
KICKER *n* person or thing that kicks
KICKERS > KICKER
KICKIER > KICKY
KICKIEST > KICKY
KICKING > KICK
KICKOFF *n* kick from the centre of the field that starts a game of football
KICKOFFS > KICKOFF
KICKS > KICK
KICKSHAW *n* valueless trinket
KICKSHAWS *same as* > KICKSHAW
KICKSTAND *n* short metal bar on a motorcycle, which when kicked into a vertical position holds the cycle upright when stationary
KICKSTART *vb* start by kicking pedal
KICKUP *n* fuss
KICKUPS > KICKUP
KICKY *adj* excitingly unusual and different
KID *n* child ▷ *vb* tease or deceive (someone) ▷ *adj* younger
KIDDED > KID
KIDDER > KID
KIDDERS > KID
KIDDIE *same as* > KIDDY
KIDDIED > KIDDY
KIDDIER *n* old word for a market trader
KIDDIERS > KIDDIER
KIDDIES > KIDDY
KIDDING > KID
KIDDINGLY > KID
KIDDISH > KID
KIDDLE *n* device, esp a barrier constructed of nets and stakes, for catching fish in a river or in the sea
KIDDLES > KIDDLE
KIDDO *n* very informal term of address for a young person
KIDDOES > KIDDO
KIDDOS > KIDDO
KIDDUSH *n* (in Judaism) special blessing said before a meal on sabbaths and festivals
KIDDUSHES > KIDDUSH
KIDDY *n* affectionate word for a child ▷ *vb* tease or deceive
KIDDYING > KIDDY
KIDDYWINK *n* humorous word for a child
KIDEL *same as* > KIDDLE
KIDELS > KIDEL
KIDGE *dialect word*

for > LIVELY
KIDGIE *adj* dialect word for friendly and welcoming
KIDGIER > KIDGIE
KIDGIEST > KIDGIE
KIDGLOVE *adj* overdelicate or overrefined
KIDLET *n* humorous word for small child
KIDLETS > KIDLET
KIDLIKE > KID
KIDLING *n* young kid
KIDLINGS > KIDLING
KIDNAP *vb* seize and hold (a person) to ransom
KIDNAPED > KIDNAP
KIDNAPEE > KIDNAP
KIDNAPEES > KIDNAP
KIDNAPER > KIDNAP
KIDNAPERS > KIDNAP
KIDNAPING > KIDNAP
KIDNAPPED > KIDNAP
KIDNAPPEE > KIDNAP
KIDNAPPER > KIDNAP
KIDNAPS > KIDNAP
KIDNEY *n* either of the pair of organs that filter waste products from the blood to produce urine
KIDNEYS > KIDNEY
KIDOLOGY *n* practice of bluffing or deception in order to gain a psychological advantage over someone
KIDS > KID
KIDSKIN *n* soft smooth leather made from the hide of a young goat
KIDSKINS > KIDSKIN
KIDSTAKES *pl n* pretence
KIDULT *n* adult who is interested in forms of entertainment such as computer games, television programmes, etc that are intended for children ▷ *adj* aimed at or suitable for kidults, or both children and adults
KIDULTS > KIDULT
KIDVID *n* informal word for children's video or television
KIDVIDS > KIDVID
KIEF *same as* > KIF
KIEFS > KIEF
KIEKIE *n* climbing bush plant of New Zealand
KIEKIES > KIEKIE
KIELBASA *n* Polish sausage
KIELBASAS > KIELBASA
KIELBASI *same as* > KIELBASA
KIELBASY *same as* > KIELBASA
KIER *n* vat in which cloth is bleached
KIERIE *n* South African cudgel
KIERIES > KIERIE
KIERS > KIER
KIESELGUR *n* type of mineral
KIESERITE *n* white mineral consisting of hydrated magnesium sulphate

KIESTER *same as* > KEISTER
KIESTERS > KIESTER
KIEVE *same as* > KEEVE
KIEVES > KIEVE
KIF *n* any drug or agent that when smoked is capable of producing a euphoric condition
KIFF *adj* South African slang for excellent
KIFS > KIF
KIGHT *n* archaic spelling of kite, the bird of prey
KIGHTS > KIGHT
KIKE *n* offensive word for a Jewish person
KIKES > KIKE
KIKOI *n* piece of cotton cloth with coloured bands, worn wrapped around the body
KIKOIS > KIKOI
KIKUMON *n* chrysanthemum emblem of the imperial family of Japan
KIKUMONS > KIKUMON
KIKUYU *n* type of grass
KIKUYUS > KIKUYU
KILD *old spelling of* > KILLED
KILDERKIN *n* obsolete unit of liquid capacity equal to 16 or 18 Imperial gallons or of dry capacity equal to 16 or 18 wine gallons
KILERG *n* 1000 ergs
KILERGS > KILERG
KILEY *same as* > KYLIE
KILEYS > KILEY
KILIM *n* pileless woven rug of intricate design made in the Middle East
KILIMS > KILIM
KILL *vb* cause the death of ▷ *n* act of killing
KILLABLE > KILL
KILLADAR *n* fort commander or governor
KILLADARS > KILLADAR
KILLAS *n* Cornish clay slate
KILLASES > KILLAS
KILLCOW *n* important person
KILLCOWS > KILLCOW
KILLCROP *n* ever-hungry baby, thought to be a fairy changeling
KILLCROPS > KILLCROP
KILLDEE *same as* > KILLDEER
KILLDEER *n* large brown-and-white North American plover with a noisy cry
KILLDEERS > KILLDEER
KILLDEES > KILLDEE
KILLED > KILL
KILLER *n* person or animal that kills, esp habitually
KILLERS > KILLER
KILLICK *n* small anchor, esp one made of a heavy stone
KILLICKS > KILLICK
KILLIE *same as* > KILLIFISH
KILLIES > KILLIE
KILLIFISH *n* any of various chiefly American minnow-like fishes
KILLING *adj* very tiring ▷ *n*

sudden financial success
KILLINGLY > KILLING
KILLINGS > KILLING
KILLJOY *n* person who spoils others' pleasure
KILLJOYS > KILLJOY
KILLOCK *same as* > KILLICK
KILLOCKS > KILLOCK
KILLOGIE *n* sheltered place in front of a kiln
KILLOGIES > KILLOGIE
KILLS > KILL
KILLUT *same as* > KHILAT
KILLUTS > KILLUT
KILN *n* oven for baking, drying, or processing pottery, bricks, etc ▷ *vb* fire or process in a kiln
KILNED > KILN
KILNING > KILN
KILNS > KILN
KILO *n* code word for the letter k
KILOBAR *n* 1000 bars
KILOBARS > KILOBAR
KILOBASE *n* unit of measurement for DNA and RNA equal to 1000 base pairs
KILOBASES > KILOBASE
KILOBAUD *n* 1000 baud
KILOBAUDS > KILOBAUD
KILOBIT *n* 1024 bits
KILOBITS > KILOBIT
KILOBYTE *n* 1024 units of information
KILOBYTES > KILOBYTE
KILOCURIE *n* unit of thousand curies
KILOCYCLE *n* short for kilocycle per second: a former unit of frequency equal to 1 kilohertz
KILOGAUSS *n* 1000 gauss
KILOGRAM *n* one thousand grams
KILOGRAMS > KILOGRAM
KILOGRAY *n* 1000 gray
KILOGRAYS > KILOGRAY
KILOHERTZ *n* one thousand hertz
KILOJOULE *n* 1000 joules
KILOLITER *US spelling of* > KILOLITRE
KILOLITRE *n* 1000 litres
KILOMETER *same as* > KILOMETRE
KILOMETRE *n* one thousand metres
KILOMOLE *n* 1000 moles
KILOMOLES > KILOMOLE
KILORAD *n* 1000 rads
KILORADS > KILORAD
KILOS > KILO
KILOTON *n* one thousand tons
KILOTONS > KILOTON
KILOVOLT *n* one thousand volts
KILOVOLTS > KILOVOLT
KILOWATT *n* one thousand watts
KILOWATTS > KILOWATT
KILP *dialect form of* > KELP
KILPS > KILP
KILT *n* knee-length pleated tartan skirt-like garment

worn orig. by Scottish Highlanders ▷ *vb* put pleats in (cloth)
KILTED > KILT
KILTER *n* working order or alignment
KILTERS > KILTER
KILTIE *n* someone wearing a kilt
KILTIES > KILTIE
KILTING > KILT
KILTINGS > KILT
KILTLIKE > KILT
KILTS > KILT
KILTY *same as* > KILTIE
KIMBO *vb* place akimbo
KIMBOED > KIMBO
KIMBOING > KIMBO
KIMBOS > KIMBO
KIMCHEE *same as* > KIMCHI
KIMCHEES > KIMCHEE
KIMCHI *n* Korean dish made from fermented cabbage or other vegetables, garlic, and chillies
KIMCHIS > KIMCHI
KIMMER *same as* > CUMMER
KIMMERS > KIMMER
KIMONO *n* loose wide-sleeved Japanese robe, fastened with a sash
KIMONOED > KIMONO
KIMONOS > KIMONO
KIN *n* person's relatives collectively ▷ *adj* related by blood
KINA *n* standard monetary unit of Papua New Guinea, divided into 100 toea
KINAKINA *same as* > QUININE
KINAKINAS > KINAKINA
KINARA *n* African candle holder
KINARAS > KINARA
KINAS > KINA
KINASE *n* any enzyme that can convert an inactive zymogen to the corresponding enzyme
KINASES > KINASE
KINCHIN *old slang word for* > CHILD
KINCHINS > KINCHIN
KINCOB *n* fine silk fabric embroidered with threads of gold or silver, of a kind made in India
KINCOBS > KINCOB
KIND *adj* considerate, friendly, and helpful ▷ *n* class or group with common characteristics ▷ *vb* old word for beget or father
KINDA *adv* very informal shortening of kind of
KINDED > KIND
KINDER *adj* more kind ▷ *n* kindergarten or nursery school
KINDERS > KIND
KINDEST > KIND
KINDIE *same as* > KINDY
KINDIES > KINDY
KINDING > KIND
KINDLE *vb* set (a fire) alight

KINDLED > KINDLE
KINDLER > KINDLE
KINDLERS > KINDLE
KINDLES > KINDLE
KINDLESS *adj* heartless
KINDLIER > KINDLY
KINDLIEST > KINDLY
KINDLILY > KINDLY
KINDLING *n* dry wood or straw for starting fires
KINDLINGS > KINDLING
KINDLY *adj* having a warm-hearted nature ▷ *adv* in a considerate way
KINDNESS *n* quality of being kind
KINDRED *adj* having similar qualities ▷ *n* blood relationship
KINDREDS > KINDRED
KINDS > KIND
KINDY *n* kindergarten
KINE *pl n* cows or cattle ▷ *n* Japanese pestle
KINEMA *same as* > CINEMA
KINEMAS > KINEMA
KINEMATIC *adj* of or relating to the study of the motion of bodies without reference to mass or force
KINES *n* > KINE
KINESCOPE *n* US name for a television tube ▷ *vb* record on film
KINESES > KINESIS
KINESIC *adj* of or relating to kinesics
KINESICS *n* study of the role of body movements, such as winking, shrugging, etc, in communication
KINESIS *n* nondirectional movement of an organism or cell in response to a stimulus, the rate of movement being dependent on the strength of the stimulus
KINETIC *adj* relating to or caused by motion
KINETICAL *same as* > KINETIC
KINETICS *n* branch of mechanics concerned with the study of bodies in motion
KINETIN *n* plant hormone
KINETINS > KINETIN
KINFOLK *another word for* > KINSFOLK
KINFOLKS > KINFOLK
KING *n* male ruler of a monarchy ▷ *vb* make king
KINGBIRD *n* any of several large American flycatchers
KINGBIRDS > KINGBIRD
KINGBOLT *n* pivot bolt that connects the body of a horse-drawn carriage to the front axle and provides the steering joint
KINGBOLTS > KINGBOLT
KINGCRAFT *n* art of ruling as a king, esp by diplomacy and cunning
KINGCUP *n* yellow-flowered

k

plant
KINGCUPS > KINGCUP
KINGDOM n state ruled by a king or queen
KINGDOMED adj old word for with a kingdom
KINGDOMS > KINGDOM
KINGED > KING
KINGFISH n food and game fish occurring in warm American Atlantic coastal waters
KINGHOOD > KING
KINGHOODS > KING
KINGING > KING
KINGKLIP n edible eel-like marine fish of S Africa
KINGKLIPS > KINGKLIP
KINGLE n Scots word for a type of hard rock
KINGLES > KINGLE
KINGLESS > KING
KINGLET n king of a small or insignificant territory
KINGLETS > KINGLET
KINGLIER > KINGLY
KINGLIEST > KINGLY
KINGLIKE > KING
KINGLING n minor king
KINGLINGS > KINGLING
KINGLY adj appropriate to a king ▷ adv in a manner appropriate to a king
KINGMAKER n person who has control over appointments to positions of authority
KINGPIN n most important person in an organization
KINGPINS > KINGPIN
KINGPOST n vertical post connecting the apex of a triangular roof truss to the tie beam
KINGPOSTS > KINGPOST
KINGS > KING
KINGSHIP n position or authority of a king
KINGSHIPS > KINGSHIP
KINGSIDE n (in chess) side of the board on which a particular king is at the start of a game as opposed to the side the queen is on
KINGSIDES > KINGSIDE
KINGSNAKE n North American snake
KINGWOOD n hard fine-grained violet-tinted wood of a Brazilian leguminous tree
KINGWOODS > KINGWOOD
KININ n any of a group of polypeptides in the blood that cause dilation of the blood vessels and make smooth muscles contract
KININS > KININ
KINK n twist or bend in rope, wire, hair, etc ▷ vb form or cause to form a kink
KINKAJOU n arboreal fruit-eating mammal of Central and South America, with a long prehensile tail
KINKAJOUS > KINKAJOU

KINKED > KINK
KINKIER > KINKY
KINKIEST > KINKY
KINKILY > KINKY
KINKINESS > KINKY
KINKING > KINK
KINKLE n little kink
KINKLES > KINKLE
KINKS > KINK
KINKY adj given to unusual sexual practices
KINLESS adj without any relatives
KINO same as > KENO
KINONE n benzoquinone, a yellow crystalline water-soluble ketone used in the production of dyestuffs
KINONES > KINONE
KINOS > KINO
KINRED old form of > KINDRED
KINREDS > KINRED
KINS > KIN
KINSFOLK pl n one's family or relatives
KINSFOLKS > KINSFOLK
KINSHIP n blood relationship
KINSHIPS > KINSHIP
KINSMAN n relative
KINSMEN > KINSMAN
KINSWOMAN > KINSMAN
KINSWOMEN > KINSMAN
KIORE n small brown rat native to New Zealand
KIOSK n small booth selling drinks, cigarettes, newspapers, etc
KIOSKS > KIOSK
KIP vb sleep ▷ n sleep or slumber
KIPE n dialect word for a basket for catching fish
KIPES > KIPE
KIPP uncommon variant of > KIP
KIPPA n skullcap worn by orthodox male Jews at all times and by others for prayer, esp a crocheted one worn by those with a specifically religious Zionist affiliation
KIPPAGE n Scots word for a state of anger or excitement
KIPPAGES > KIPPAGE
KIPPAS > KIPPA
KIPPED > KIP
KIPPEN > KEP
KIPPER n cleaned, salted, and smoked herring ▷ vb cure (a herring) by salting and smoking it
KIPPERED adj (of fish, esp herring) having been cleaned, salted, and smoked
KIPPERER > KIPPER
KIPPERERS > KIPPER
KIPPERING > KIPPER
KIPPERS > KIPPER
KIPPING > KIP
KIPPS > KIPP
KIPS > KIP
KIPSKIN same as > KIP

KIPSKINS > KIPSKIN
KIR n drink made from dry white wine and cassis
KIRBEH n leather bottle
KIRBEHS > KIRBEH
KIRBIGRIP n hairgrip
KIRBY as in kirby grip hairgrip consisting of a piece of wire bent back on itself and partly bent into ridges
KIRIGAMI n art, originally Japanese, of folding and cutting paper into decorative shapes
KIRIGAMIS > KIRIGAMI
KIRIMON n Japanese imperial crest
KIRIMONS > KIRIMON
KIRK Scot word for > CHURCH
KIRKED > KIRK
KIRKING > KIRK
KIRKINGS > KIRK
KIRKMAN n member or strong upholder of the Kirk
KIRKMEN > KIRKMAN
KIRKS > KIRK
KIRKTON n village or town with a parish church
KIRKTONS > KIRKTON
KIRKWARD adv towards the church
KIRKYAIRD same as > KIRKYARD
KIRKYARD n churchyard
KIRKYARDS > KIRKYARD
KIRMESS same as > KERMIS
KIRMESSES > KIRMESS
KIRN dialect word for > CHURN
KIRNED > KIRN
KIRNING > KIRN
KIRNS > KIRN
KIRPAN n short sword traditionally carried by Sikhs as a symbol of their religious and cultural loyalty
KIRPANS > KIRPAN
KIRRI n Hottentot stick
KIRRIS > KIRRI
KIRS > KIR
KIRSCH n cherry brandy
KIRSCHES > KIRSCH
KIRTAN n devotional singing, usually accompanied by musical instruments
KIRTANS > KIRTAN
KIRTLE n woman's skirt or dress ▷ vb dress with a kirtle
KIRTLED > KIRTLE
KIRTLES > KIRTLE
KIS > KI
KISAN n peasant or farmer
KISANS > KISAN
KISH n graphite formed on the surface of molten iron that contains a large amount of carbon
KISHES > KISH
KISHKA same as > KISHKE
KISHKAS > KISHKA
KISHKE n beef or fowl intestine or skin stuffed with flour, onion, etc, and

boiled and roasted
KISHKES > KISHKE
KISMAT same as > KISMET
KISMATS > KISMAT
KISMET n fate or destiny
KISMETIC > KISMET
KISMETS > KISMET
KISS vb touch with the lips in affection or greeting ▷ n touch with the lips
KISSABLE > KISS
KISSABLY > KISS
KISSAGRAM n greetings service in which a messenger kisses the person celebrating
KISSED > KISS
KISSEL n Russian dessert of sweetened fruit purée thickened with arrowroot
KISSELS > KISSEL
KISSER n mouth or face
KISSERS > KISSER
KISSES > KISS
KISSING > KISS
KISSOGRAM same as > KISSAGRAM
KISSY adj showing exaggerated affection, esp by frequent touching or kissing
KIST n large wooden chest ▷ vb place in a coffin
KISTED > KIST
KISTFUL > KIST
KISTFULS > KIST
KISTING > KIST
KISTS > KIST
KISTVAEN n stone tomb
KISTVAENS > KISTVAEN
KIT n outfit or equipment for a specific purpose ▷ vb fit or provide
KITBAG n bag for a soldier's or traveller's belongings
KITBAGS > KITBAG
KITCHEN n room used for cooking ▷ vb (in archaic usage) provide with food
KITCHENED > KITCHEN
KITCHENER n someone employed in kitchen work
KITCHENET n small kitchen or part of another room equipped for use as a kitchen
KITCHENS > KITCHEN
KITE n light frame covered with a thin material flown on a string in the wind ▷ vb soar and glide
KITED > KITE
KITELIKE > KITE
KITENGE n thick cotton cloth
KITENGES > KITENGE
KITER > KITE
KITERS > KITE
KITES > KITE
KITH n one's friends and acquaintances
KITHARA variant of > CITHARA
KITHARAS > KITHARA
KITHE same as > KYTHE
KITHED > KITHE
KITHES > KITHE

KITHING > KITHE
KITHS > KITH
KITING > KITE
KITINGS > KITE
KITLING *dialect word for* > KITTEN
KITLINGS > KITLING
KITS > KIT
KITSCH *n* art or literature with popular sentimental appeal ▷ *n* object or art that is tawdry, vulgarized, oversentimental or pretentious
KITSCHES > KITSCH
KITSCHIER > KITSCH
KITSCHIFY *vb* make kitsch
KITSCHILY > KITSCH
KITSCHY > KITSCH
KITSET *n* New Zealand word for a piece of furniture supplied in pieces for the purchaser to assemble
KITSETS > KITSET
KITTED > KIT
KITTEL *n* white garment worn for certain Jewish rituals or burial
KITTELS > KITTEL
KITTEN *n* young cat ▷ *vb* (of cats) give birth
KITTENED > KITTEN
KITTENING > KITTEN
KITTENISH *adj* lively and flirtatious
KITTENS > KITTEN
KITTENY > KITTEN
KITTIES > KITTY
KITTING > KIT
KITTIWAKE *n* type of seagull
KITTLE *adj* capricious and unpredictable ▷ *vb* be troublesome or puzzling to (someone)
KITTLED > KITTLE
KITTLER > KITTLE
KITTLES > KITTLE
KITTLEST > KITTLE
KITTLIER > KITTLY
KITTLIEST > KITTLY
KITTLING > KITTLE
KITTLY *Scots word for* > TICKLISH
KITTUL *n* type of palm from which jaggery sugar comes
KITTULS > KITTUL
KITTY *n* communal fund
KIVA *n* large underground or partly underground room in a Pueblo Indian village, used chiefly for religious ceremonies
KIVAS > KIVA
KIWI *n* New Zealand flightless bird with a long beak and no tail
KIWIFRUIT *n* edible oval fruit of the kiwi plant
KIWIS > KIWI
KLANG *n* (in music) kind of tone
KLANGS > KLANG
KLAP *vb* slap or spank
KLAPPED > KLAP
KLAPPING > KLAP
KLAPS > KLAP

KLATCH *n* gathering, especially over coffee
KLATCHES > KLATCH
KLATSCH *same as* > KLATCH
KLATSCHES > KLATSCH
KLAVERN *n* local Ku Klux Klan group
KLAVERNS > KLAVERN
KLAVIER *same as* > CLAVIER
KLAVIERS > KLAVIER
KLAXON *n* loud horn used on emergency vehicles as a warning signal ▷ *vb* hoot with a klaxon
KLAXONED > KLAXON
KLAXONING > KLAXON
KLAXONS > KLAXON
KLEAGLE *n* person with a particular rank in the Ku Klux Klan
KLEAGLES > KLEAGLE
KLEENEX *n* tradename for a kind of soft paper tissue, used esp as a handkerchief
KLEENEXES > KLEENEX
KLENDUSIC *adj* disease-resistant
KLEPHT *n* any of the Greeks who fled to the mountains after the 15th-century Turkish conquest of Greece and whose descendants survived as brigands into the 19th century
KLEPHTIC > KLEPHT
KLEPHTISM > KLEPHT
KLEPHTS > KLEPHT
KLEPTO *n* compulsive thief
KLEPTOS > KLEPTO
KLETT *n* lightweight climbing boot
KLETTS > KLETT
KLEZMER *n* Jewish folk musician, usually a member of a small band
KLEZMERS > KLEZMER
KLEZMORIM > KLEZMER
KLICK *n* kilometre
KLICKS > KLICK
KLIEG *as in* klieg light intense carbon-arc light used for illumination in producing films
KLIK *US military slang word for* > KILOMETRE
KLIKS > KLIK
KLINKER *n* type of brick used in paving
KLINKERS > KLINKER
KLINOSTAT *n* rotating and tilting plant holder for studying and experimenting with plant growth
KLIPDAS *n* rock hyrax
KLIPDASES > KLIPDAS
KLISTER *n* type of ski dressing for improving grip on snow
KLISTERS > KLISTER
KLONDIKE *n* rich source of something ▷ *vb* transfer (bulk loads of fish) to factory ships at sea for processing
KLONDIKED > KLONDIKE
KLONDIKER *same*

as > KLONDYKER
KLONDIKES > KLONDIKE
KLONDYKE *n* rich source of something ▷ *vb* transfer (bulk loads of fish) to factory ships at sea for processing
KLONDYKED > KLONDYKE
KLONDYKER *n* East European factory ship
KLONDYKES > KLONDYKE
KLONG *n* type of canal in Thailand
KLONGS > KLONG
KLOOCH *same as* > KLOOCHMAN
KLOOCHES > KLOOCH
KLOOCHMAN *n* North American Indian woman
KLOOCHMEN > KLOOCHMAN
KLOOF *n* mountain pass or gorge
KLOOFS > KLOOF
KLOOTCH *same as* > KLOOCHMAN
KLOOTCHES > KLOOTCH
KLUDGE *n* untidy solution involving a variety of cobbled-together elements ▷ *vb* cobble something together
KLUDGED > KLUDGE
KLUDGES > KLUDGE
KLUDGEY > KLUDGE
KLUDGIER > KLUDGE
KLUDGIEST > KLUDGE
KLUDGING > KLUDGE
KLUDGY > KLUDGE
KLUGE *same as* > KLUDGE
KLUGED > KLUGE
KLUGES > KLUGE
KLUGING > KLUGE
KLUTZ *n* clumsy or stupid person
KLUTZES > KLUTZ
KLUTZIER > KLUTZ
KLUTZIEST > KLUTZ
KLUTZY > KLUTZ
KLYSTRON *n* electron tube for the amplification or generation of microwaves by means of velocity modulation
KLYSTRONS > KLYSTRON
KNACK *n* skilful way of doing something ▷ *vb* dialect word for crack or snap
KNACKED *adj* broken or worn out
KNACKER *n* buyer of old horses for killing ▷ *vb* exhaust
KNACKERED *adj* extremely tired
KNACKERS > KNACKER
KNACKERY *n* slaughterhouse for horses
KNACKIER > KNACKY
KNACKIEST > KNACKY
KNACKING > KNACK
KNACKISH *adj* old word meaning cunning or artful
KNACKS > KNACK
KNACKY *adj* old or dialect word for cunning or artful
KNAG *n* knot in wood
KNAGGIER > KNAGGY

KNAGGIEST > KNAGGY
KNAGGY *adj* knotty
KNAGS > KNAG
KNAIDEL *same as* > KNEIDEL
KNAIDLACH > KNAIDEL
KNAP *n* crest of a hill ▷ *vb* hit, hammer, or chip
KNAPPED > KNAP
KNAPPER > KNAP
KNAPPERS > KNAP
KNAPPING > KNAP
KNAPPLE *old word for* > NIBBLE
KNAPPLED > KNAPPLE
KNAPPLES > KNAPPLE
KNAPPLING > KNAPPLE
KNAPS > KNAP
KNAPSACK *n* soldier's or traveller's bag worn strapped on the back
KNAPSACKS > KNAPSACK
KNAPWEED *n* plant with purplish thistle-like flowers
KNAPWEEDS > KNAPWEED
KNAR *old spelling of* > GNAR
KNARL *old spelling of* > GNARL
KNARLS > KNARL
KNARLY *same as* > GNARLY
KNARRED > KNAR
KNARRIER > KNAR
KNARRIEST > KNAR
KNARRING > KNAR
KNARRY > KNAR
KNARS > KNAR
KNAUR *variant form of* > KNUR
KNAURS > KNAUR
KNAVE *n* jack at cards
KNAVERIES > KNAVERY
KNAVERY *n* dishonest behaviour
KNAVES > KNAVE
KNAVESHIP *n* old Scottish legal term for the small proportion of milled grain due to the person doing the milling
KNAVISH > KNAVE
KNAVISHLY > KNAVE
KNAWE *same as* > KNAWEL
KNAWEL *n* any of several Old World caryophyllaceous plants of the genus *Scleranthus*, having heads of minute petal-less flowers
KNAWELS > KNAWEL
KNAWES > KNAWE
KNEAD *vb* work (dough) into a smooth mixture with the hands
KNEADABLE > KNEAD
KNEADED > KNEAD
KNEADER > KNEAD
KNEADERS > KNEAD
KNEADING > KNEAD
KNEADS > KNEAD
KNEE *n* joint between thigh and lower leg ▷ *vb* strike or push with the knee
KNEECAP *nontechnical name for* > PATELLA
KNEECAPS > KNEECAP
KNEED > KNEE
KNEEHOLE *n* space for the knees, esp under a desk
KNEEHOLES > KNEEHOLE
KNEEING > KNEE

k

KNEEJERK *adj* (of a reply or reaction) automatic and predictable

KNEEL *vb* fall or rest on one's knees ▷ *n* act or position of kneeling

KNEELED > KNEEL

KNEELER > KNEEL

KNEELERS > KNEEL

KNEELING > KNEEL

KNEELS > KNEEL

KNEEPAD *n* any of several types of protective covering for the knees

KNEEPADS > KNEEPAD

KNEEPAN *another word for* > PATELLA

KNEEPANS > KNEEPAN

KNEEPIECE *n* knee-shaped piece of timber in ship

KNEES > KNEE

KNEESIES *n* flirtatious touching of knees under table

KNEESOCK *n* type of sock that comes up to the knee

KNEESOCKS > KNEESOCK

KNEIDEL *n* (in Jewish cookery) small dumpling, usually served in chicken soup

KNEIDLACH > KNEIDEL

KNELL *n* sound of a bell, esp at a funeral or death ▷ *vb* ring a knell

KNELLED > KNELL

KNELLING > KNELL

KNELLS > KNELL

KNELT > KNEEL

KNESSET *n* parliament or assembly

KNESSETS > KNESSET

KNEVELL *vb* old Scots word meaning beat

KNEVELLED > KNEVELL

KNEVELLS > KNEVELL

KNEW > KNOW

KNICKER *n* woman's or girl's undergarment covering the lower trunk and having legs or legholes

KNICKERED > KNICKER

KNICKERS *pl n* woman's or girl's undergarment covering the lower trunk and having legs or legholes

KNICKS *pl n* knickers

KNIFE *n* cutting tool or weapon consisting of a sharp-edged blade with a handle ▷ *vb* cut or stab with a knife

KNIFED > KNIFE

KNIFELESS > KNIFE

KNIFELIKE > KNIFE

KNIFEMAN *n* man who is armed with a knife

KNIFEMEN > KNIFEMAN

KNIFER > KNIFE

KNIFEREST *n* support on which a carving knife or carving fork is placed at the table

KNIFERS > KNIFE

KNIFES > KNIFE

KNIFING > KNIFE

KNIFINGS > KNIFE

KNIGHT *n* man who has been given a knighthood ▷ *vb* award a knighthood to

KNIGHTAGE *n* group of knights or knights collectively

KNIGHTED > KNIGHT

KNIGHTING > KNIGHT

KNIGHTLY *adj* of, resembling, or appropriate for a knight

KNIGHTS > KNIGHT

KNIPHOFIA *n* any of several perennial southern African flowering plants

KNISH *n* piece of dough stuffed with potato, meat, or some other filling and baked or fried

KNISHES > KNISH

KNIT *vb* make (a garment) by interlocking a series of loops in wool or other yarn ▷ *n* fabric made by knitting

KNITCH *dialect word for* > BUNDLE

KNITCHES > KNITCH

KNITS > KNIT

KNITTABLE > KNIT

KNITTED > KNIT

KNITTER > KNIT

KNITTERS > KNIT

KNITTING > KNIT

KNITTINGS > KNIT

KNITTLE *n* old word for string or cord

KNITTLES > KNITTLE

KNITWEAR *n* knitted clothes, such as sweaters

KNITWEARS > KNITWEAR

KNIVE *rare variant of* > KNIFE

KNIVED > KNIVE

KNIVES > KNIFE

KNIVING > KNIVE

KNOB *n* rounded projection, such as a switch on a radio ▷ *vb* supply with knobs

KNOBBED > KNOB

KNOBBER *n* two-year-old male deer

KNOBBERS > KNOBBER

KNOBBIER > KNOB

KNOBBIEST > KNOB

KNOBBING > KNOB

KNOBBLE *n* small knob ▷ *vb* dialect word meaning strike

KNOBBLED *same as* > KNOBBLY

KNOBBLES > KNOBBLE

KNOBBLIER > KNOBBLY

KNOBBLING > KNOBBLE

KNOBBLY *adj* covered with small bumps

KNOBBY > KNOB

KNOBHEAD *n* stupid person

KNOBHEADS > KNOBHEAD

KNOBLIKE > KNOB

KNOBS > KNOB

KNOBSTICK *n* stick with a round knob at the end, used as a club or missile by South African tribesmen

KNOCK *vb* give a blow or push to ▷ *n* blow or rap

KNOCKDOWN *adj* (of a price) very low

KNOCKED > KNOCK

KNOCKER *n* metal fitting for knocking on a door

KNOCKERS > KNOCKER

KNOCKING > KNOCK

KNOCKINGS > KNOCK

KNOCKLESS > KNOCK

KNOCKOFF *n* informal word for a cheap, often illegal, copy of something

KNOCKOFFS > KNOCKOFF

KNOCKOUT *n* blow that renders an opponent unconscious ▷ *vb* render (someone) unconscious

KNOCKOUTS > KNOCKOUT

KNOCKS > KNOCK

KNOLL *n* small rounded hill ▷ *vb* (in archaic or dialect usage) knell

KNOLLED > KNOLL

KNOLLER > KNOLL

KNOLLERS > KNOLL

KNOLLIER > KNOLL

KNOLLIEST > KNOLL

KNOLLING > KNOLL

KNOLLS > KNOLL

KNOLLY > KNOLL

KNOP *n* knob, esp an ornamental one

KNOPPED > KNOP

KNOPS > KNOP

KNOSP *n* budlike architectural feature

KNOSPS > KNOSP

KNOT *n* fastening made by looping and pulling tight strands of string, cord, or rope ▷ *vb* tie with or into a knot

KNOTGRASS *n* polygonaceous weedy plant whose small green flowers produce numerous seeds

KNOTHOLE *n* hole in a piece of wood where a knot has been

KNOTHOLES > KNOTHOLE

KNOTLESS > KNOT

KNOTLIKE > KNOT

KNOTS > KNOT

KNOTTED > KNOT

KNOTTER > KNOT

KNOTTERS > KNOT

KNOTTIER > KNOTTY

KNOTTIEST > KNOTTY

KNOTTILY > KNOTTY

KNOTTING > KNOT

KNOTTINGS > KNOT

KNOTTY *adj* full of knots

KNOTWEED *n* any of several polygonaceous plants of the genus *Polygonum*, having small flowers and jointed stems

KNOTWEEDS > KNOTWEED

KNOTWORK *n* ornamentation consisting of a mass of intertwined and knotted cords

KNOTWORKS > KNOTWORK

KNOUT *n* stout whip used formerly in Russia as an instrument of punishment ▷ *vb* whip

KNOUTED > KNOUT

KNOUTING > KNOUT

KNOUTS > KNOUT

KNOW *vb* be or feel certain of the truth of (information etc)

KNOWABLE > KNOW

KNOWE *same as* > KNOLL

KNOWER > KNOW

KNOWERS > KNOW

KNOWES > KNOW

KNOWHOW *n* ingenuity, knack, or skill

KNOWHOWS > KNOWHOW

KNOWING > KNOW

KNOWINGER > KNOW

KNOWINGLY > KNOW

KNOWINGS > KNOW

KNOWLEDGE *n* facts, feelings or experiences known by a person or group of people ▷ *vb* (in archaic usage) acknowledge

KNOWN > KNOW

KNOWNS > KNOW

KNOWS > KNOW

KNUB *dialect word for* > KNOB

KNUBBIER > KNUB

KNUBBIEST > KNUB

KNUBBLE *vb* dialect word for beat or pound using one's fists

KNUBBLED > KNUBBLE

KNUBBLES > KNUBBLE

KNUBBLIER > KNUBBLY

KNUBBLING > KNUBBLE

KNUBBLY *adj* having small lumps or protuberances

KNUBBY *adj* knub

KNUBS > KNUB

KNUCKLE *n* bone at the finger joint

KNUCKLED > KNUCKLE

KNUCKLER *n* type of throw in baseball

KNUCKLERS > KNUCKLER

KNUCKLES > KNUCKLE

KNUCKLIER > KNUCKLE

KNUCKLING > KNUCKLE

KNUCKLY > KNUCKLE

KNUR *n* knot or protuberance in a tree trunk or in wood

KNURL *n* small ridge, often one of a series ▷ *vb* impress with a series of fine ridges or serrations

KNURLED > KNURL

KNURLIER > KNURLY

KNURLIEST > KNURLY

KNURLING > KNURL

KNURLINGS > KNURL

KNURLS > KNURL

KNURLY *rare word for* > GNARLED

KNURR *same as* > KNUR

KNURRS > KNURR

KNURS > KNUR

KNUT *n* dandy

KNUTS > KNUT

KO *n* (in New Zealand) traditional digging tool

KOA *n* Hawaiian leguminous tree

KOALA *n* tree-dwelling Australian marsupial with dense grey fur

KOALAS > KOALA

KOAN n (in Zen Buddhism) problem or riddle that admits no logical solution

KOANS > KOAN

KOAP n (in Papua New Guinean slang) sexual intercourse

KOAPS > KOAP

KOAS > KOA

KOB n any of several waterbuck-like species of African antelope

KOBAN n old oval-shaped Japanese gold coin

KOBANG same as > KOBAN

KOBANGS > KOBANG

KOBANS > KOBAN

KOBO n Nigerian monetary unit, worth one hundredth of a naira

KOBOLD n mischievous household sprite

KOBOLDS > KOBOLD

KOBOS > KOBO

KOBS > KOB

KOCHIA n any of several plants whose foliage turns dark red in late summer

KOCHIAS > KOCHIA

KOEKOEA n long-tailed cuckoo of New Zealand

KOEL n any of several parasitic cuckoos of S and SE Asia and Australia

KOELS > KOEL

KOFF n Dutch masted merchant vessel

KOFFS > KOFF

KOFTA n Indian dish of seasoned minced meat shaped into small balls and cooked

KOFTAS > KOFTA

KOFTGAR n (in India) person skilled in the art of inlaying steel with gold

KOFTGARI n ornamental Indian metalwork

KOFTGARIS > KOFTGARI

KOFTGARS > KOFTGAR

KOFTWORK same as > KOFTGARI

KOFTWORKS > KOFTWORK

KOHA n gift or donation, esp of cash

KOHAS > KOHA

KOHEKOHE n New Zealand tree with large glossy leaves and reddish wood

KOHL n cosmetic powder used to darken the edges of the eyelids

KOHLRABI n type of cabbage with an edible stem

KOHLRABIS > KOHLRABI

KOHLS > KOHL

KOI n any of various ornamental forms of the common carp

KOINE n common language among speakers of different languages

KOINES > KOINE

KOIS > KOI

KOJI n Japanese steamed rice

KOJIS > KOJI

KOKAKO n dark grey long-tailed wattled crow of New Zealand

KOKAKOS > KOKAKO

KOKANEE n freshwater salmon of lakes and rivers in W North America

KOKANEES > KOKANEE

KOKER n Guyanese sluice

KOKERS > KOKER

KOKIRI n rough-skinned New Zealand triggerfish, *Parika scaber*

KOKOBEH adj (of certain fruit) having a rough skin

KOKOPU n any of several small freshwater fish of New Zealand

KOKOWAI n type of clay used in decoration because of its red colour

KOKOWAIS > KOKOWAI

KOKRA n type of wood

KOKRAS > KOKRA

KOKUM n tropical tree

KOKUMS > KOKUM

KOLA as in *kola nut* caffeine-containing seed used in medicine and soft drinks

KOLACKY n sweet bun with a fruit, jam, or nut filling

KOLAS > KOLA

KOLBASI same as > KOLBASSI

KOLBASIS > KOLBASI

KOLBASSI n type of sausage

KOLBASSIS > KOLBASSI

KOLHOZ same as > KOLKHOZ

KOLHOZES > KOLHOZ

KOLHOZY same as > KOLKHOZ

KOLINSKI same as > KOLINSKY

KOLINSKY n Asian mink

KOLKHOS same as > KOLKHOZ

KOLKHOSES > KOLKHOS

KOLKHOSY > KOLKHOS

KOLKHOZ n (formerly) collective farm in the Soviet Union

KOLKHOZES > KOLKHOZ

KOLKHOZY > KOLKHOZ

KOLKOZ same as > KOLKHOZ

KOLKOZES > KOLKOZ

KOLKOZY > KOLKOZ

KOLO n Serbian folk dance in which a circle of people dance slowly around one or more dancers in the centre

KOLOS > KOLO

KOMATIK n sledge with wooden runners and crossbars bound with animal hides

KOMATIKS > KOMATIK

KOMBU n dark brown seaweed, the leaves of which are dried and used esp in Japanese cookery

KOMBUS > KOMBU

KOMISSAR same as > COMMISSAR

KOMISSARS > KOMISSAR

KOMITAJI n rebel or revolutionary

KOMITAJIS > KOMITAJI

KOMONDOR n large powerful dog of an ancient Hungarian breed, originally used for sheep herding

KOMONDORS > KOMONDOR

KON old word for > KNOW

KONAKI same as > KONEKE

KONBU same as > KOMBU

KONBUS > KONBU

KOND > KON

KONDO n (in Uganda) thief or armed robber

KONDOS > KONDO

KONEKE n farm vehicle with runners in front and wheels at the rear

KONFYT n South African fruit preserve

KONFYTS > KONFYT

KONGONI n E African hartbeest, *Alcelaphus buselaphus*

KONIMETER n device for measuring airborne dust concentration in which samples are obtained by sucking the air through a hole and allowing it to pass over a glass plate coated with grease on which the particles collect

KONINI n edible dark purple berry of the kotukutuku or tree fuchsia

KONIOLOGY n study of atmospheric dust and its effects

KONISCOPE n device for detecting and measuring dust in the air

KONK same as > CONK

KONKED > KONK

KONKING > KONK

KONKS > KONK

KONNING > KON

KONS > KON

KOODOO same as > KUDU

KOODOOS > KOODOO

KOOK n eccentric person ▷ vb dialect word for vanish

KOOKED > KOOK

KOOKIE same as > KOOKY

KOOKIER > KOOKY

KOOKIEST > KOOKY

KOOKINESS > KOOKY

KOOKING > KOOK

KOOKS > KOOK

KOOKY adj crazy, eccentric, or foolish

KOOLAH old form of > KOALA

KOOLAHS > KOOLAH

KOORI n Australian Aborigine

KOORIES > KOORI

KOORIS > KOORI

KOP n prominent isolated hill or mountain in southern Africa

KOPASETIC same as > COPACETIC

KOPECK n former Russian monetary unit, one hundredth of a rouble

KOPECKS > KOPECK

KOPEK same as > KOPECK

KOPEKS > KOPEK

KOPH n 19th letter in the Hebrew alphabet

KOPHS > KOPH

KOPIYKA n monetary unit of Ukraine, worth one hundredth of a hryvna

KOPIYKAS > KOPIYKA

KOPJE n small hill

KOPJES > KOPJE

KOPPA n consonantal letter in the Greek alphabet pronounced like kappa (K) with the point of articulation further back in the throat

KOPPAS > KOPPA

KOPPIE same as > KOPJE

KOPPIES > KOPPIE

KOPS > KOP

KOR n ancient Hebrew unit of capacity

KORA n West African instrument with twenty-one strings, combining features of the harp and the lute

KORAI > KORE

KORARI n native New Zealand flax plant, *Phormium tenax*

KORAS > KORA

KORAT as in *korat cat* rare blue-grey breed of cat with brilliant green eyes

KORATS > KORAT

KORE n ancient Greek statue of a young woman wearing clothes

KORERO n talk or discussion ▷ vb speak or converse

KOREROED > KORERO

KOREROING > KORERO

KOREROS > KORERO

KORES > KORE

KORFBALL n game similar to basketball, in which each team consists of six men and six women

KORFBALLS > KORFBALL

KORIMAKO another name for > BELLBIRD

KORKIR n variety of lichen used in dyeing

KORKIRS > KORKIR

KORMA n type of mild Indian dish consisting of meat or vegetables cooked in water, yoghurt, or cream

KORMAS > KORMA

KORO n elderly Māori man

KOROMIKO n flowering New Zealand shrub, *Hebe salicifolia*

KORORA n small New Zealand penguin

KORORAS > KORORA

KOROWAI n decorative woven cloak worn by a Māori chief

KORS > KOR

KORU n stylized curved pattern used esp in carving

KORUN > KORUNA

KORUNA n standard monetary unit of the Czech Republic and Slovakia, divided into 100 hellers

KORUNAS > KORUNA

KORUNY > KORUNA

KORUS > KORU

KOS *n* Indian unit of distance having different values in different localities

KOSES > KOS

KOSHER *adj* conforming to Jewish religious law, esp (of food) to Jewish dietary law ▷ *n* kosher food ▷ *vb* prepare in accordance with Jewish dietary rules

KOSHERED > KOSHER

KOSHERING > KOSHER

KOSHERS > KOSHER

KOSMOS *variant form of* > COSMOS

KOSMOSES > KOSMOS

KOSS *same as* > KOS

KOSSES > KOSS

KOTARE *n* small greenish-blue kingfisher found in New Zealand, Australia, and some Pacific islands to the north

KOTCH *vb* South African slang for vomit

KOTCHED > KOTCH

KOTCHES > KOTCH

KOTCHING > KOTCH

KOTO *n* Japanese stringed instrument, consisting of a rectangular wooden body over which are stretched silk strings, which are plucked with plectrums or a nail-like device

KOTOS > KOTO

KOTOW *same as* > KOWTOW

KOTOWED > KOTOW

KOTOWER > KOTOW

KOTOWERS > KOTOW

KOTOWING > KOTOW

KOTOWS > KOTOW

KOTTABOS > COTTABUS

KOTUKU *n* white heron with brilliant white plumage, black legs and yellow eyes and bill

KOTWAL *n* senior police officer or magistrate in an Indian town

KOTWALS > KOTWAL

KOULAN *same as* > KULAN

KOULANS > KOULAN

KOUMIS *same as* > KUMISS

KOUMISES > KOUMIS

KOUMISS *same as* > KUMISS

KOUMISSES > KOUMISS

KOUMYS *same as* > KUMISS

KOUMYSES > KOUMYS

KOUMYSS *same as* > KUMISS

KOUMYSSES > KOUMYSS

KOUPREY *n* large wild SE Asian ox

KOUPREYS > KOUPREY

KOURA *n* New Zealand freshwater crayfish

KOURBASH *same as* > KURBASH

KOUROI > KOUROS

KOUROS *n* ancient Greek statue of a young man

KOUSKOUS *same as* > COUSCOUS

KOUSSO *n* Abyssinian tree whose flowers have useful antiparasitic properties

KOUSSOS > KOUSSO

KOW *old variant of* > COW

KOWHAI *n* New Zealand tree with clusters of yellow flowers

KOWHAIS > KOWHAI

KOWS > KOW

KOWTOW *vb* be servile (towards) ▷ *n* act of kowtowing

KOWTOWED > KOWTOW

KOWTOWER > KOWTOW

KOWTOWERS > KOWTOW

KOWTOWING > KOWTOW

KOWTOWS > KOWTOW

KRAAL *n* S African village surrounded by a strong fence ▷ *adj* denoting or relating to the tribal aspects of the Black African way of life ▷ *vb* enclose (livestock) in a kraal

KRAALED > KRAAL

KRAALING > KRAAL

KRAALS > KRAAL

KRAB *same as* > KARABINER

KRABS > KRAB

KRAFT *n* strong wrapping paper, made from pulp processed with a sulphate solution

KRAFTS > KRAFT

KRAIT *n* any nonaggressive brightly coloured venomous elapid snake of the genus *Bungarus*, of S and SE Asia

KRAITS > KRAIT

KRAKEN *n* legendary sea monster

KRAKENS > KRAKEN

KRAKOWIAK *n* Polish dance

KRAMERIA *another name for* > RHATANY

KRAMERIAS > KRAMERIA

KRANG *n* dead whale from which the blubber has been removed

KRANGS > KRANG

KRANS *n* sheer rock face

KRANSES > KRANS

KRANTZ *same as* > KRANS

KRANTZES > KRANTZ

KRANZ *same as* > KRANS

KRANZES > KRANS

KRATER *same as* > CRATER

KRATERS > KRATER

KRAUT *n* sauerkraut

KRAUTS > KRAUT

KREASOTE *same as* > CREOSOTE

KREASOTED > KREASOTE

KREASOTES > KREASOTE

KREATINE *same as* > CREATINE

KREATINES > KREATINE

KREEP *n* lunar substance that is high in potassium, rare earth elements, and phosphorus

KREEPS > KREEP

KREESE *same as* > KRIS

KREESED > KREESE

KREESES > KREESE

KREESING > KREESE

KREMLIN *n* citadel of any Russian city

KREMLINS > KREMLIN

KRENG *same as* > KRANG

KRENGS > KRENG

KREOSOTE *same as* > CREOSOTE

KREOSOTED > KREOSOTE

KREOSOTES > KREOSOTE

KREPLACH *pl n* small filled dough casings usually served in soup

KREPLECH *same as* > KREPLACH

KREUTZER *n* any of various former copper and silver coins of Germany or Austria

KREUTZERS > KREUTZER

KREUZER *same as* > KREUTZER

KREUZERS > KREUZER

KREWE *n* club taking part in New Orleans carnival parade

KREWES > KREWE

KRILL *n* small shrimplike sea creature

KRILLS > KRILL

KRIMMER *n* tightly curled light grey fur obtained from the skins of lambs from the Crimean region

KRIMMERS > KRIMMER

KRIS *n* Malayan and Indonesian stabbing or slashing knife with a scalloped edge ▷ *vb* stab or slash with a kris

KRISED > KRIS

KRISES > KRIS

KRISING > KRIS

KROMESKY *n* croquette consisting of a piece of bacon wrapped round minced meat or fish

KRONA *n* standard monetary unit of Sweden

KRONE *n* standard monetary unit of Norway and Denmark

KRONEN > KRONE

KRONER > KRONE

KRONOR > KRONA

KRONUR > KRONA

KROON *n* standard monetary unit of Estonia, divided into 100 senti

KROONI > KROON

KROONS > KROON

KRUBI *n* aroid plant with an unpleasant smell

KRUBIS > KRUBI

KRUBUT *same as* > KRUBI

KRUBUTS > KRUBUT

KRULLER *variant spelling of* > CRULLER

KRULLERS > KRULLER

KRUMHORN *variant spelling of* > CRUMHORN

KRUMHORNS > KRUMHORN

KRUMKAKE *n* Scandinavian biscuit

KRUMKAKES > KRUMKAKE

KRUMMHOLZ *n* zone of stunted wind-blown trees growing at high altitudes

just above the timberline on tropical mountains

KRUMMHORN *variant spelling of* > CRUMHORN

KRYOLITE *variant spelling of* > CRYOLITE

KRYOLITES > KRYOLITE

KRYOLITH *same as* > CRYOLITE

KRYOLITHS > KRYOLITH

KRYOMETER *same as* > CRYOMETER

KRYPSES > KRYPSIS

KRYPSIS *n* idea that Christ made secret use of his divine attributes

KRYPTON *n* colourless gas present in the atmosphere and used in fluorescent lights

KRYPTONS > KRYPTON

KRYTRON *n* type of fast electronic gas-discharge switch, used as a trigger in nuclear weapons

KRYTRONS > KRYTRON

KSAR *old form of* > TSAR

KSARS > KSAR

KUCHCHA *same as* > KACHA

KUCHEN *n* breadlike cake containing apple, nuts, and sugar, originating from Germany

KUCHENS > KUCHEN

KUDLIK *n* Inuit soapstone seal-oil lamp

KUDLIKS > KUDLIK

KUDO *variant of* > KUDOS

KUDOS *n* fame or credit

KUDOSES > KUDOS

KUDU *n* African antelope with spiral horns

KUDUS > KUDU

KUDZU *n* hairy leguminous climbing plant of China and Japan, with trifoliate leaves and purple fragrant flowers

KUDZUS > KUDZU

KUE *n* name of the letter Q

KUEH *n* (in Malaysia) any cake of Malay, Chinese, or Indian origin

KUES > KUE

KUFI *n* cap for Muslim man

KUFIS > KUFI

KUFIYAH *same as* > KEFFIYEH

KUFIYAHS > KUFIYAH

KUGEL *n* baked pudding in traditional Jewish cooking

KUGELS > KUGEL

KUIA *n* Māori female elder or elderly woman

KUIAS > KUIA

KUKRI *n* heavy, curved knife used by Gurkhas

KUKRIS > KUKRI

KUKU *n* mussel

KUKUS > KUKU

KULA *n* ceremonial gift exchange practised among a group of islanders in the W Pacific, used to establish relations between islands

KULAK *n* (formerly) property-owning Russian peasant

KULAKI > KULAK

k

KULAKS > KULAK

KULAN *n* Asiatic wild ass of the Russian steppes, probably a variety of kiang or onager

KULANS > KULAN

KULAS > KULA

KULFI *n* Indian dessert made by freezing milk which has been concentrated by boiling away some of the water in it, and flavoured with nuts and cardamom seeds

KULFIS > KULFI

KULTUR *n* German civilization

KULTURS > KULTUR

KUMARA *n* tropical root vegetable with yellow flesh

KUMARAHOU *n* New Zealand shrub

KUMARAS > KUMARA

KUMARI *n* (in Indian English) maiden

KUMARIS > KUMARI

KUMBALOI *pl n* worry beads

KUMERA *same as* > KUMARA

KUMERAS > KUMERA

KUMIKUMI *same as* > KAMOKAMO

KUMISS *n* drink made from fermented mare's or other milk, drunk by certain Asian tribes, esp in Russia or used for dietetic and medicinal purposes

KUMISSES > KUMISS

KUMITE *n* freestyle sparring or fighting

KUMITES > KUMITE

KUMMEL *n* German liqueur flavoured with aniseed and cumin

KUMMELS > KUMMEL

KUMQUAT *n* citrus fruit resembling a tiny orange

KUMQUATS > KUMQUAT

KUMYS *same as* > KUMISS

KUMYSES > KUMYS

KUNA *n* standard monetary unit of Croatia, divided into 100 lipa

KUNDALINI *n* (in yoga) life force that resides at the base of the spine

KUNE > KUNA

KUNJOOS *adj* (in Indian English) mean or stingy

KUNKAR *n* type of limestone

KUNKARS > KUNKAR

KUNKUR *same as* > KUNKAR

KUNKURS > KUNKUR

KUNZITE *n* pink-coloured transparent variety of the mineral spodumene: a gemstone

KUNZITES > KUNZITE

KURBASH *vb* whip with a hide whip

KURBASHED > KURBASH

KURBASHES > KURBASH

KURFUFFLE *same as* > KERFUFFLE

KURGAN *n* Russian burial mound

KURGANS > KURGAN

KURI *n* mongrel dog

KURIS > KURI

KURRAJONG *n* Australian tree or shrub with tough fibrous bark

KURRE *old variant of* > CUR

KURRES > KURRE

KURSAAL *n* public room at a health resort

KURSAALS > KURSAAL

KURTA *n* long loose garment like a shirt without a collar worn in India

KURTAS > KURTA

KURTOSES > KURTOSIS

KURTOSIS *n* measure of the concentration of a distribution around its mean

KURU *n* degenerative disease of the nervous system, restricted to certain tribes in New Guinea, marked by loss of muscular control and thought to be caused by a slow virus

KURUS > KURU

KURVEY *vb* (in old South African English) transport goods by ox cart

KURVEYED > KURVEY

KURVEYING > KURVEY

KURVEYOR > KURVEY

KURVEYORS > KURVEY

KURVEYS > KURVEY

KUSSO *variant spelling of* > KOUSSO

KUSSOS > KUSSO

KUTA *n* (in Indian English) male dog

KUTAS > KUTA

KUTCH *same as* > CATECHU

KUTCHA *adj* makeshift or not solid

KUTCHES > KUTCH

KUTI *n* (in Indian English) female dog or bitch

KUTIS > KUTI

KUTU *n* body louse

KUTUS > KUTU

KUVASZ *n* breed of dog from Hungary

KUVASZOK > KUVASZ

KUZU *same as* > KUDZU

KUZUS > KUZU

KVAS *same as* > KVASS

KVASES > KVAS

KVASS *n* alcoholic drink of low strength made in Russia and E Europe from cereals and stale bread

KVASSES > KVASS

KVELL *vb* US word meaning be happy

KVELLED > KVELL

KVELLING > KVELL

KVELLS > KVELL

KVETCH *vb* complain or grumble

KVETCHED > KVETCH

KVETCHER > KVETCH

KVETCHERS > KVETCH

KVETCHES > KVETCH

KVETCHIER > KVETCHY

KVETCHILY > KVETCHY

KVETCHING > KVETCH

KVETCHY *adj* tending to grumble or complain

KWACHA *n* standard monetary unit of Zambia, divided into 100 ngwee

KWACHAS > KWACHA

KWAITO *n* type of South African pop music with lyrics spoken over an instrumental backing usually consisting of slowed-down house music layered with African percussion and melodies

KWAITOS > KWAITO

KWANZA *n* standard monetary unit of Angola, divided into 100 lwei

KWANZAS > KWANZA

KWELA *n* type of pop music popular among the Black communities of South Africa

KWELAS > KWELA

KY *pl n* Scots word for cows

KYACK *n* type of panier

KYACKS > KYACK

KYAK *same as* > KAYAK

KYAKS > KYAK

KYANG *same as* > KIANG

KYANGS > KYANG

KYANISE *same as* > KYANIZE

KYANISED > KYANISE

KYANISES > KYANISE

KYANISING > KYANISE

KYANITE *n* grey, green, or blue mineral consisting of aluminium silicate in triclinic crystalline form

KYANITES > KYANITE

KYANITIC > KYANITE

KYANIZE *vb* treat (timber) with corrosive sublimate to make it resistant to decay

KYANIZED > KYANIZE

KYANIZES > KYANIZE

KYANIZING > KYANIZE

KYAR *same as* > COIR

KYARS > KYAR

KYAT *n* standard monetary unit of Myanmar, divided into 100 pyas

KYATS > KYAT

KYBO *n* temporary lavatory constructed for use when camping

KYBOS > KYBO

KYBOSH *same as* > KIBOSH

KYBOSHED > KYBOSH

KYBOSHES > KYBOSH

KYBOSHING > KYBOSH

KYDST > KYTHE

KYE *n* Korean fundraising meeting

KYES > KYE

KYLE *n* narrow strait or channel

KYLES > KYLE

KYLICES > KYLIX

KYLIE *n* boomerang that is flat on one side and convex on the other

KYLIES > KYLIE

KYLIKES > KYLIX

KYLIN *n* (in Chinese art) mythical animal of composite form

KYLINS > KYLIN

KYLIX *n* shallow two-handled drinking vessel used in ancient Greece

KYLLOSES > KYLLOSIS

KYLLOSIS *n* club foot

KYLOE *n* breed of small long-horned long-haired beef cattle from NW Scotland

KYLOES > KYLOE

KYMOGRAM *n* image or other visual record created by a kymograph

KYMOGRAMS > KYMOGRAM

KYMOGRAPH *n* rotatable drum for holding paper on which a tracking stylus continuously records variations in blood pressure, respiratory movements, etc

KYND *old variant of* > KIND

KYNDE *old variant of* > KIND

KYNDED > KYND

KYNDES > KYNDE

KYNDING > KYND

KYNDS > KYND

KYNE *pl n* archaic word for cows

KYOGEN *n* type of Japanese drama

KYOGENS > KYOGEN

KYPE *n* hook on the lower jaw of a mature male salmon

KYPES > KYPE

KYPHOSES > KYPHOSIS

KYPHOSIS *n* backward curvature of the thoracic spine

KYPHOTIC > KYPHOSIS

KYRIE *n* type of prayer

KYRIELLE *n* verse form of French origin characterized by repeated lines or words

KYRIELLES > KYRIELLE

KYRIES > KYRIE

KYTE *n* belly

KYTES > KYTE

KYTHE *vb* appear

KYTHED > KYTHE

KYTHES > KYTHE

KYTHING > KYTHE

KYU *n* (in judo) one of the five student grades for inexperienced competitors

KYUS > KYU

k

L1

LA *n* exclamation of surprise or emphasis
LAAGER *n* (in Africa) a camp defended by a circular formation of wagons ▷ *vb* form (wagons) into a laager
LAAGERED > LAAGER
LAAGERING > LAAGER
LAAGERS > LAAGER
LAARI *same as* > LARI
LAARIS > LAARI
LAB *n* laboratory
LABARA > LABARUM
LABARUM *n* standard or banner carried in Christian religious processions
LABARUMS > LABARUM
LABDA *same as* > LAMBDA
LABDACISM *n* excessive use or idiosyncratic pronunciation of (l)
LABDANUM *n* dark resinous juice obtained from various rockroses
LABDANUMS > LABDANUM
LABDAS > LABDA
LABEL *n* piece of card or other material fixed to an object to show its ownership, destination, etc ▷ *vb* give a label to
LABELABLE > LABEL
LABELED > LABEL
LABELER > LABEL
LABELERS > LABEL
LABELING > LABEL
LABELLA > LABELLUM
LABELLATE > LABELLUM
LABELLED > LABEL
LABELLER > LABEL
LABELLERS > LABEL
LABELLING > LABEL
LABELLIST *n* person who wears only clothes with fashionable brand names
LABELLOID > LABELLUM
LABELLUM *n* lip-like part of certain plants
LABELS > LABEL
LABIA > LABIUM
LABIAL *adj* of the lips ▷ *n* speech sound that involves the lips
LABIALISE *same as* > LABIALIZE
LABIALISM > LABIALIZE

LABIALITY > LABIAL
LABIALIZE *vb* pronounce with articulation involving rounded lips
LABIALLY > LABIAL
LABIALS > LABIAL
LABIATE *n* any of a family of plants with square stems, aromatic leaves, and a two-lipped flower, such as mint or thyme ▷ *adj* of this family
LABIATED *adj* having a lip
LABIATES > LABIATE
LABILE *adj* (of a compound) prone to chemical change
LABILITY > LABILE
LABIS *n* cochlear
LABISES > LABIS
LABIUM *n* lip or liplike structure
LABLAB *n* twining leguminous plant
LABLABS > LABLAB
LABOR *same as* > LABOUR
LABORED *same as* > LABOURED
LABOREDLY > LABOURED
LABORER *same as* > LABOURER
LABORERS > LABORER
LABORING > LABOR
LABORIOUS *adj* involving great prolonged effort
LABORISM *same as* > LABOURISM
LABORISMS > LABORISM
LABORIST *same as* > LABOURIST
LABORISTS > LABORIST
LABORITE *n* adherent of the Labour party
LABORITES > LABORITE
LABORS > LABOR
LABOUR *n* physical work or exertion ▷ *vb* work hard
LABOURED *adj* uttered or done with difficulty
LABOURER *n* person who labours, esp someone doing manual work for wages
LABOURERS > LABOURER
LABOURING > LABOUR
LABOURISM *n* dominance of the working classes
LABOURIST *n* person who

supports workers' rights
LABOURS > LABOUR
LABRA > LABRUM
LABRADOR *n* large retriever dog with a usu gold or black coat
LABRADORS > LABRADOR
LABRET *n* piece of bone, shell, etc
LABRETS > LABRET
LABRID *same as* > LABROID
LABRIDS > LABRID
LABROID *n* type of fish ▷ *adj* of or relating to such fish
LABROIDS > LABROID
LABROSE *adj* thick-lipped
LABRUM *n* lip or liplike part
LABRUMS > LABRUM
LABRUSCA *n* grape variety
LABRYS *n* type of axe
LABRYSES > LABRYS
LABS > LAB
LABURNUM *n* ornamental tree with yellow hanging flowers
LABURNUMS > LABURNUM
LABYRINTH *n* complicated network of passages
LAC *same as* > LAKH
LACCOLITE *same as* > LACCOLITH
LACCOLITH *n* dome-shaped body of igneous rock between two layers of older sedimentary rock
LACE *n* delicate loosely woven decorative fabric ▷ *vb* fasten with shoelaces, cords, etc
LACEBARK *n* small evergreen tree
LACEBARKS > LACEBARK
LACED > LACE
LACELESS > LACE
LACELIKE > LACE
LACER > LACE
LACERABLE > LACERATE
LACERANT *adj* painfully distressing
LACERATE *vb* tear (flesh) ▷ *adj* having edges that are jagged or torn
LACERATED > LACERATE
LACERATES > LACERATE
LACERS > LACE
LACERTIAN *n* type of reptile
LACERTID *n* type of lizard

LACERTIDS > LACERTID
LACERTINE *adj* relating to lacertid
LACES > LACE
LACET *n* braidwork
LACETS > LACET
LACEWING *n* any of various neuropterous insects
LACEWINGS > LACEWING
LACEWOOD *n* wood of sycamore tree
LACEWOODS > LACEWOOD
LACEWORK *n* work made from lace
LACEWORKS > LACEWORK
LACEY *same as* > LACY
LACHES *n* negligence or unreasonable delay in pursuing a legal remedy
LACHESES > LACHES
LACHRYMAL *same as* > LACRIMAL
LACIER > LACY
LACIEST > LACY
LACILY > LACY
LACINESS > LACY
LACING > LACE
LACINGS > LACE
LACINIA *n* narrow fringe on petal
LACINIAE > LACINIA
LACINIATE *adj* jagged
LACK *n* shortage or absence of something needed or wanted ▷ *vb* need or be short of (something)
LACKADAY *another word for* > ALAS
LACKED > LACK
LACKER *variant spelling of* > LACQUER
LACKERED > LACKER
LACKERING > LACKER
LACKERS > LACKER
LACKEY *n* servile follower ▷ *vb* act as a lackey (to)
LACKEYED > LACKEY
LACKEYING > LACKEY
LACKEYS > LACKEY
LACKING > LACK
LACKLAND *n* fool
LACKLANDS > LACKLAND
LACKS > LACK
LACMUS *n* old form of litmus
LACMUSES > LACMUS
LACONIC *adj* using only a few words, terse

LACONICAL *same as* > LACONIC

LACONISM *n* economy of expression

LACONISMS > LACONISM

LACQUER *n* hard varnish for wood or metal ▷*vb* apply lacquer to

LACQUERED > LACQUER

LACQUERER > LACQUER

LACQUERS > LACQUER

LACQUEY *same as* > LACKEY

LACQUEYED > LACQUEY

LACQUEYS > LACQUEY

LACRIMAL *adj* of tears or the glands which produce them ▷*n* bone near tear gland

LACRIMALS > LACRIMAL

LACRIMOSO *adj* tearful

LACROSSE *n* sport in which teams catch and throw a ball using long sticks with a pouched net at the end, in an attempt to score goals

LACROSSES > LACROSSE

LACRYMAL *same as* > LACRIMAL

LACRYMALS > LACRYMAL

LACS > LAC

LACTAM *n* any of a group of inner amides

LACTAMS > LACTAM

LACTARIAN *n* vegetarian who eats dairy products

LACTARY *adj* relating to milk

LACTASE *n* any of a group of enzymes that hydrolyse lactose to glucose and galactose

LACTASES > LACTASE

LACTATE *vb* (of mammals) to secrete milk ▷*n* ester or salt of lactic acid

LACTATED > LACTATE

LACTATES > LACTATE

LACTATING > LACTATE

LACTATION *n* secretion of milk by female mammals to feed young

LACTEAL *adj* of or like milk ▷*n* any of the lymphatic vessels that convey chyle from the small intestine to the blood

LACTEALLY > LACTEAL

LACTEALS > LACTEAL

LACTEAN *another word for* > LACTEOUS

LACTEOUS *adj* milky

LACTIC *adj* of or derived from milk > LACTIFEROUS

LACTIFIC *adj* yielding milk

LACTONE *n* any of a class of organic compounds

LACTONES > LACTONE

LACTONIC > LACTONE

LACTOSE *n* white crystalline sugar found in milk

LACTOSES > LACTOSE

LACUNA *n* gap or missing part, esp in a document or series

LACUNAE > LACUNA

LACUNAL > LACUNA

LACUNAR *n* ceiling, soffit, or vault having coffers

▷*adj* of, relating to, or containing a lacuna or lacunas

LACUNARIA > LACUNAR

LACUNARS > LACUNAR

LACUNARY > LACUNA

LACUNAS > LACUNA

LACUNATE > LACUNA

LACUNE *n* hiatus

LACUNES > LACUNE

LACUNOSE > LACUNA

LACY *adj* fine, like lace

LAD *n* boy or young man

LADANUM *same as* > LABDANUM

LADANUMS > LADANUM

LADDER *n* frame of two poles connected by horizontal steps used for climbing ▷*vb* have or cause to have such a line of undone stitches

LADDERED > LADDER

LADDERING > LADDER

LADDERS > LADDER

LADDERY > LADDER

LADDIE *n* familiar term for a male, esp a young man

LADDIES > LADDIE

LADDISH *adj* informal word for behaving in a macho or immature manner

LADE *vb* put cargo on board (a ship) or (of a ship) to take on cargo ▷*n* watercourse, esp a millstream

LADED > LADE

LADEN *adj* loaded ▷*vb* load with cargo

LADENED > LADEN

LADENING > LADEN

LADENS > LADEN

LADER > LADE

LADERS > LADE

LADES > LADE

LADETTE *n* young woman whose social behaviour is similar to that of male adolescents or young men

LADETTES > LADETTE

LADHOOD > LAD

LADHOODS > LAD

LADIES *n* women's public toilet

LADIFIED > LADIFY

LADIFIES > LADIFY

LADIFY *same as* > LADYFY

LADIFYING > LADIFY

LADING > LADE

LADINGS > LADE

LADINO *n* Italian variety of white clover

LADINOS > LADINO

LADLE *n* spoon with a long handle and a large bowl, used for serving soup etc ▷*vb* serve out

LADLED > LADLE

LADLEFUL > LADLE

LADLEFULS > LADLE

LADLER *n* person who serves with a ladle

LADLERS > LADLER

LADLES > LADLE

LADLING > LADLE

LADRON *same as* > LADRONE

LADRONE *n* thief

LADRONES > LADRONE

LADRONS > LADRON

LADS > LAD

LADY *n* woman regarded as having characteristics of good breeding or high rank ▷*adj* female

LADYBIRD *n* small red beetle with black spots

LADYBIRDS > LADYBIRD

LADYBOY *n* transvestite or transsexual, esp one from the Far East

LADYBOYS > LADYBOY

LADYBUG *same as* > LADYBIRD

LADYBUGS > LADYBUG

LADYCOW *another word for* > LADYBIRD

LADYCOWS > LADYCOW

LADYFIED > LADYFY

LADYFIES > LADYFY

LADYFISH *n* type of game fish

LADYFLIES > LADYFLY

LADYFLY *another word for* > LADYBIRD

LADYFY *vb* make a lady of (someone)

LADYFYING > LADYFY

LADYHOOD > LADY

LADYHOODS > LADY

LADYISH > LADY

LADYISM > LADY

LADYISMS > LADY

LADYKIN *n* endearing form of lady

LADYKINS > LADYKIN

LADYLIKE *adj* polite and dignified

LADYLOVE *n* beloved woman

LADYLOVES > LADYLOVE

LADYPALM *n* small palm, grown indoors

LADYPALMS > LADYPALM

LADYSHIP *n* title of a peeress

LADYSHIPS > LADYSHIP

LAER *another word for* > LAAGER

LAERED > LAER

LAERING > LAER

LAERS > LAER

LAESIE *old form of* > LAZY

LAETARE *n* fourth Sunday of Lent

LAETARES > LAETARE

LAETRILE *n* drug used to treat cancer

LAETRILES > LAETRILE

LAEVIGATE *same as* > LEVIGATE

LAEVO *adj* on the left

LAEVULIN *n* polysaccharide occurring in the tubers of certain helianthus plants

LAEVULINS > LAEVULIN

LAEVULOSE *n* fructose

LAG *vb* go too slowly, fall behind ▷*n* delay between events

LAGAN *n* goods or wreckage on the sea bed, sometimes attached to a buoy to permit recovery

LAGANS > LAGAN

LAGENA *n* bottle with a

narrow neck

LAGENAS > LAGENA

LAGEND *same as* > LAGAN

LAGENDS > LAGEND

LAGER *n* light-bodied beer ▷*vb* ferment into lager

LAGERED > LAGER

LAGERING > LAGER

LAGERS > LAGER

LAGGARD *n* person who lags behind ▷*adj* sluggish, slow, or dawdling

LAGGARDLY > LAGGARD

LAGGARDS > LAGGARD

LAGGED > LAG

LAGGEN *n* spar of a barrel

LAGGENS > LAGGEN

LAGGER *n* person who lags pipes

LAGGERS > LAGGER

LAGGIN *same as* > LAGGEN

LAGGING > LAG

LAGGINGLY > LAG

LAGGINGS > LAG

LAGGINS > LAGGIN

LAGNAPPE *same as* > LAGNIAPPE

LAGNAPPES > LAGNAPPE

LAGNIAPPE *n* small gift, esp one given to a customer who makes a purchase

LAGOMORPH *n* any placental mammal of the order *Lagomorpha*

LAGOON *n* body of water cut off from the open sea by coral reefs or sand bars

LAGOONAL > LAGOON

LAGOONS > LAGOON

LAGRIMOSO *adj* mournful

LAGS > LAG

LAGUNA *n* lagoon

LAGUNAS > LAGUNA

LAGUNE *same as* > LAGOON

LAGUNES > LAGUNE

LAH *n* (in tonic sol-fa) sixth degree of any major scale

LAHAR *n* landslide of volcanic debris and water

LAHARS > LAHAR

LAHS > LAH

LAIC *adj* laical ▷*n* layman

LAICAL *adj* secular

LAICALLY > LAIC

LAICH *n* low-lying piece of land

LAICHS > LAICH

LAICISE *same as* > LAICIZE

LAICISED > LAICISE

LAICISES > LAICISE

LAICISING > LAICISE

LAICISM > LAIC

LAICISMS > LAIC

LAICITIES > LAICITY

LAICITY *n* state of being laical

LAICIZE *vb* withdraw clerical or ecclesiastical character or status from (an institution, building, etc)

LAICIZED > LAICIZE

LAICIZES > LAICIZE

LAICIZING > LAICIZE

LAICS > LAIC

LAID *Scots form of* > LOAD

LAIDED > LAID

LAIDING > LAID
LAIDLY adj very ugly
LAIDS > LAID
LAIGH adj low-lying ▷ n area of low-lying ground
LAIGHER > LAIGH
LAIGHEST > LAIGH
LAIGHS > LAIGH
LAIK vb play (a game, etc)
LAIKA n type of small dog
LAIKAS > LAIKA
LAIKED > LAIK
LAIKER > LAIK
LAIKERS > LAIK
LAIKING > LAIK
LAIKS > LAIK
LAIN > LIE
LAIPSE vb beat soundly
LAIPSED > LAIPSE
LAIPSES > LAIPSE
LAIPSING > LAIPSE
LAIR n resting place of an animal ▷ vb (esp of a wild animal) to retreat to or rest in a lair
LAIRAGE n accommodation for farm animals, esp at docks or markets
LAIRAGES > LAIRAGE
LAIRD n Scottish landowner
LAIRDLY adj pertaining to laird or lairds
LAIRDS > LAIRD
LAIRDSHIP n state of being laird
LAIRED > LAIR
LAIRIER > LAIRY
LAIRIEST > LAIRY
LAIRING > LAIR
LAIRISE same as > LAIRIZE
LAIRISED > LAIRISE
LAIRISES > LAIRISE
LAIRISING > LAIRISE
LAIRIZE vb show off
LAIRIZED > LAIRIZE
LAIRIZES > LAIRIZE
LAIRIZING > LAIRIZE
LAIRS > LAIR
LAIRY adj gaudy or flashy
LAISSE n type of rhyme scheme
LAISSES > LAISSE
LAITANCE n white film forming on drying concrete
LAITANCES > LAITANCE
LAITH Scots form of > LOATH
LAITHLY same as > LAIDLY
LAITIES > LAITY
LAITY n people who are not members of the clergy
LAKE n expanse of water entirely surrounded by land ▷ vb take time away from work
LAKEBED n bed of lake
LAKEBEDS > LAKEBED
LAKED > LAKE
LAKEFRONT n area at edge of lake
LAKELAND n countryside with a lot of lakes
LAKELANDS > LAKELAND
LAKELET n small lake
LAKELETS > LAKELET
LAKELIKE > LAKE
LAKEPORT n port on lake

LAKEPORTS > LAKEPORT
LAKER n cargo vessel used on lakes
LAKERS > LAKER
LAKES > LAKE
LAKESHORE n area at edge of lake
LAKESIDE n area at edge of lake
LAKESIDES > LAKESIDE
LAKH n (in India) 100 000, esp referring to this sum of rupees
LAKHS > LAKH
LAKIER > LAKY
LAKIEST > LAKY
LAKIN short form of > LADYKIN
LAKING > LAKE
LAKINGS > LAKE
LAKINS > LAKIN
LAKISH adj similar to poetry of Lake poets
LAKSA n (in Malaysia) a dish of Chinese origin consisting of rice noodles served in curry or hot soup
LAKSAS > LAKSA
LAKY adj of the reddish colour of the pigment lake
LALANG n coarse weedy Malaysian grass
LALANGS > LALANG
LALDIE n great gusto
LALDIES > LALDIE
LALDY same as > LALDIE
LALIQUE n type of ornamental glass
LALIQUES > LALIQUE
LALL vb make imperfect 'l' or 'r' sounds
LALLAN n literary version of the English spoken in Lowland Scotland
LALLAND same as > LALLAN
LALLANDS > LALLAND
LALLANS > LALLAN
LALLATION n defect of speech consisting of the pronunciation of 'r' as 'l'
LALLED > LALL
LALLING > LALL
LALLINGS > LALL
LALLS > LALL
LALLYGAG vb loiter aimlessly
LALLYGAGS > LALLYGAG
LAM vb attack vigorously
LAMA n Buddhist priest in Tibet or Mongolia
LAMAISTIC adj relating to the Mahayana form of Buddhism
LAMANTIN another word for > MANATEE
LAMANTINS > LAMANTIN
LAMAS > LAMA
LAMASERAI same as > LAMASERY
LAMASERY n monastery of lamas
LAMB n young sheep ▷ vb (of sheep) give birth to a lamb or lambs
LAMBADA n erotic Brazilian dance
LAMBADAS > LAMBADA

LAMBAST vb beat or thrash
LAMBASTE same as > LAMBAST
LAMBASTED > LAMBAST
LAMBASTES > LAMBASTE
LAMBASTS > LAMBAST
LAMBDA n 11th letter of the Greek alphabet
LAMBDAS > LAMBDA
LAMBDOID adj having the shape of the Greek letter lambda
LAMBED > LAMB
LAMBENCY > LAMBENT
LAMBENT adj (of a flame) flickering softly
LAMBENTLY > LAMBENT
LAMBER n person that attends to lambing ewes
LAMBERS > LAMBER
LAMBERT n cgs unit of illumination, equal to 1 lumen per square centimetre
LAMBERTS > LAMBERT
LAMBIE same as > LAMBKIN
LAMBIER > LAMBY
LAMBIES > LAMBIE
LAMBIEST > LAMBY
LAMBING n birth of lambs at the end of winter
LAMBINGS > LAMBING
LAMBITIVE n medicine taken by licking
LAMBKILL n N American dwarf shrub
LAMBKILLS > LAMBKILL
LAMBKIN n small or young lamb
LAMBKINS > LAMBKIN
LAMBLIKE > LAMB
LAMBLING n small lamb
LAMBLINGS > LAMBLING
LAMBOYS n skirt-like piece of armour made from metal strips
LAMBRUSCO n Italian sparkling wine
LAMBS > LAMB
LAMBSKIN n skin of a lamb, usually with the wool still on, used to make coats, slippers, etc
LAMBSKINS > LAMBSKIN
LAMBY adj lamb-like
LAME adj having an injured or disabled leg or foot ▷ vb make lame ▷ n fabric interwoven with gold or silver threads
LAMEBRAIN n stupid or slow-witted person
LAMED n 12th letter in the Hebrew alphabet
LAMEDH same as > LAMED
LAMEDHS > LAMEDH
LAMEDS > LAMED
LAMELLA n thin layer, plate, or membrane, esp any of the calcified layers of which bone is formed
LAMELLAE > LAMELLA
LAMELLAR > LAMELLA
LAMELLAS > LAMELLA
LAMELLATE > LAMELLA
LAMELLOID another word for > LAMELLA

LAMELLOSE > LAMELLA
LAMELY > LAME
LAMENESS > LAME
LAMENT vb feel or express sorrow (for) ▷ n passionate expression of grief
LAMENTED adj grieved for
LAMENTER > LAMENT
LAMENTERS > LAMENT
LAMENTING > LAMENT
LAMENTS > LAMENT
LAMER > LAME
LAMES > LAME
LAMEST > LAME
LAMETER Scots form of > LAMIGER
LAMETERS > LAMETER
LAMIA n one of a class of female monsters depicted with a snake's body and a woman's head and breasts
LAMIAE > LAMIA
LAMIAS > LAMIA
LAMIGER n disabled person
LAMIGERS > LAMIGER
LAMINA n thin plate, esp of bone or mineral
LAMINABLE > LAMINATE
LAMINAE > LAMINA
LAMINAL n consonant articulated with blade of tongue
LAMINALS > LAMINAL
LAMINAR > LAMINA
LAMINARIA n any brown seaweed of the genus Laminaria
LAMINARIN n carbohydrate, consisting of repeated glucose units, that is the main storage product of brown algae
LAMINARY > LAMINA
LAMINAS > LAMINA
LAMINATE vb make (a sheet of material) by sticking together thin sheets ▷ n laminated sheet ▷ adj composed of lamina
LAMINATED adj composed of many layers stuck together
LAMINATES > LAMINATE
LAMINATOR > LAMINATE
LAMING > LAME
LAMINGTON n sponge cake coated with a sweet coating
LAMININ n type of protein
LAMININS > LAMININ
LAMINITIS n (in animals with hooves) inflammation of the tissue to which the hoof is attached
LAMINOSE > LAMINA
LAMINOUS > LAMINA
LAMISH adj rather lame
LAMISTER n fugitive
LAMISTERS > LAMISTER
LAMITER same as > LAMETER
LAMITERS > LAMITER
LAMMED > LAM
LAMMER Scots word for > AMBER
LAMMERS > LAMMER
LAMMIE same as > LAMMY

LAMMIES > LAMMY

LAMMIGER same as > LAMIGER

LAMMIGERS > LAMIGER

LAMMING > LAM

LAMMINGS > LAM

LAMMY n thick woollen jumper

LAMP n device which produces light from electricity, oil, or gas ▷ vb go quickly with long steps

LAMPAD n candlestick

LAMPADARY n person who lights the lamps in an Orthodox Greek Church

LAMPADIST n prize-winner in race run by young men with torches

LAMPADS > LAMPAD

LAMPAS n swelling of the mucous membrane of the hard palate of horses

LAMPASES > LAMPAS

LAMPASSE same as > LAMPAS

LAMPASSES > LAMPASSE

LAMPBLACK n fine black soot used as a pigment in paint and ink

LAMPED > LAMP

LAMPER n lamprey

LAMPERN n migratory European lamprey

LAMPERNS > LAMPERN

LAMPERS > LAMPER

LAMPERSES > LAMPERS

LAMPHOLE n hole in ground for lowering lamp into sewer

LAMPHOLES > LAMPHOLE

LAMPING > LAMP

LAMPINGS > LAMP

LAMPION n oil-burning lamp

LAMPIONS > LAMPION

LAMPLIGHT n light produced by lamp

LAMPOON n humorous satire ridiculing someone ▷ vb satirize or ridicule

LAMPOONED > LAMPOON

LAMPOONER > LAMPOON

LAMPOONS > LAMPOON

LAMPPOST n post supporting a lamp in the street

LAMPPOSTS > LAMPPOST

LAMPREY n eel-like fish with a round sucking mouth

LAMPREYS > LAMPREY

LAMPS > LAMP

LAMPSHADE n shade used to reduce light shed by light bulb

LAMPSHELL n brachiopod

LAMPUKA same as > LAMPUKI

LAMPUKAS > LAMPUKA

LAMPUKI n type of fish

LAMPUKIS > LAMPUKI

LAMPYRID n firefly

LAMPYRIDS > LAMPYRID

LAMS > LAM

LAMSTER n fugitive

LAMSTERS > LAMSTER

LANA n wood from genipap tree

LANAI Hawaiian word for > VERANDA

LANAIS > LANAI

LANAS > LANA

LANATE adj having or consisting of a woolly covering of hairs

LANATED same as > LANATE

LANCE n long spear used by a mounted soldier ▷ vb pierce (a boil or abscess) with a lancet

LANCED > LANCE

LANCEGAY n kind of ancient spear

LANCEGAYS > LANCEGAY

LANCEJACK n lance corporal

LANCELET n any of several marine animals of the genus Branchiostoma

LANCELETS > LANCELET

LANCEOLAR adj narrow and tapering to a point at each end

LANCER n formerly, cavalry soldier armed with a lance

LANCERS n quadrille for eight or sixteen couples

LANCES > LANCE

LANCET n pointed two-edged surgical knife

LANCETED adj having one or more lancet arches or windows

LANCETS > LANCET

LANCEWOOD n New Zealand tree with slender leaves

LANCH obsolete form of > LAUNCH

LANCHED > LANCH

LANCHES > LANCH

LANCHING > LANCH

LANCIERS pl n type of dance

LANCIFORM adj in the form of a lance

LANCINATE adj (esp of pain) sharp or cutting

LANCING > LANCE

LAND n solid part of the earth's surface ▷ vb come or bring to earth after a flight, jump, or fall

LANDAMMAN n chairman of the governing council in some Swiss cantons

LANDAU n four-wheeled carriage with two folding hoods

LANDAULET n small landau

LANDAUS > LANDAU

LANDBOARD n narrow board, with wheels larger than those on a skateboard, usually ridden while standing

LANDDAMNE vb Shakespearian word for make (a person's life) unbearable

LANDDROS n sheriff

LANDDROST n South African magistrate

LANDE n type of moorland in SW France

LANDED adj possessing or consisting of lands

LANDER n spacecraft designed to land on a planet or other body

LANDERS > LANDER

LANDES > LANDE

LANDFALL n ship's first landing after a voyage

LANDFALLS > LANDFALL

LANDFILL n disposing of rubbish by covering it with earth

LANDFILLS > LANDFILL

LANDFORCE n body of people trained for land warfare

LANDFORM n any natural feature of the earth's surface, such as valleys and mountains

LANDFORMS > LANDFORM

LANDGRAB n sudden attempt to establish ownership of or copyright on something in advance of competitors

LANDGRABS > LANDGRAB

LANDGRAVE n (from the 13th century to 1806) a count who ruled over a specified territory

LANDING n floor area at the top of a flight of stairs

LANDINGS > LANDING

LANDLADY n woman who owns and leases property

LANDLER n Austrian country dance in which couples spin and clap

LANDLERS > LANDLER

LANDLESS > LAND

LANDLINE n telecommunications cable laid over land

LANDLINES > LANDLINE

LANDLOPER n vagabond or vagrant

LANDLORD n person who rents out land, houses, etc

LANDLORDS > LANDLORD

LANDMAN n person who lives and works on land

LANDMARK n prominent object in or feature of a landscape

LANDMARKS > LANDMARK

LANDMASS n large continuous area of land

LANDMEN > LANDMAN

LANDOWNER n person who owns land

LANDRACE n white very long-bodied lop-eared breed of pork pig

LANDRACES > LANDRACE

LANDRAIL n type of bird

LANDRAILS > LANDRAIL

LANDS pl n holdings in land

LANDSCAPE n extensive piece of inland scenery seen from one place ▷ vb improve natural features of (a piece of land) ▷ adj (of a publication or an illustration in a publication) of greater width than height

LANDSHARK n person who makes inordinate profits by buying and selling land

LANDSIDE n part of an airport farthest from the aircraft

LANDSIDES > LANDSIDE

LANDSKIP another word for > LANDSCAPE

LANDSKIPS > LANDSKIP

LANDSLEIT > LANDSMAN

LANDSLID > LANDSLIDE

LANDSLIDE vb cause land or rock to fall from hillside

LANDSLIP same as > LANDSLIDE

LANDSLIPS > LANDSLIP

LANDSMAN n person who works or lives on land, as distinguished from a seaman

LANDSMEN > LANDSMAN

LANDWARD same as > LANDWARDS

LANDWARDS adv towards land

LANDWIND n wind that comes from the land

LANDWINDS > LANDWIND

LANE n narrow road

LANELY Scots form of > LONELY

LANES > LANE

LANEWAY n lane

LANEWAYS > LANEWAY

LANG Scot word for > LONG

LANGAHA n type of Madagascan snake

LANGAHAS > LANGAHA

LANGAR n dining hall in a gurdwara

LANGARS > LANGAR

LANGER informal Irish word for > PENIS

LANGERED adj drunk

LANGERS > LANGER

LANGEST > LANG

LANGLAUF n cross-country skiing

LANGLAUFS > LANGLAUF

LANGLEY n unit of solar radiation

LANGLEYS > LANGLEY

LANGOUSTE n spiny lobster

LANGRAGE n shot consisting of scrap iron packed into a case, formerly used in naval warfare

LANGRAGES > LANGRAGE

LANGREL same as > LANGRAGE

LANGRELS > LANGREL

LANGRIDGE same as > LANGRAGE

LANGSHAN n breed of chicken

LANGSHANS > LANGSHAN

LANGSPEL n type of Scandinavian stringed instrument

LANGSPELS > LANGSPEL

LANGSPIEL same as > LANGSPEL

LANGSYNE adv long ago ▷ n times long past, esp those fondly remembered

LANGSYNES > LANGSYNE

LANGUAGE n system of sounds, symbols, etc for communicating thought ▷ vb express in language

Section 1: Words between 2 and 9 letters in length

LANGUAGED > LANGUAGE
LANGUAGES > LANGUAGE
LANGUE n language considered as an abstract system or a social institution
LANGUED adj having a tongue
LANGUES > LANGUE
LANGUET n anything resembling a tongue in shape or function
LANGUETS > LANGUET
LANGUETTE same as > LANGUET
LANGUID adj lacking energy or enthusiasm
LANGUIDLY > LANGUID
LANGUISH vb suffer neglect or hardship
LANGUOR n state of dreamy relaxation
LANGUORS > LANGUOR
LANGUR n any of various agile arboreal Old World monkeys of the genus Presbytis
LANGURS > LANGUR
LANIARD same as > LANYARD
LANIARDS > LANIARD
LANIARIES > LANIARY
LANIARY adj (esp of canine teeth) adapted for tearing ▷ n tooth adapted for tearing
LANITAL n fibre used in production of synthetic wool
LANITALS > LANITAL
LANK adj (of hair) straight and limp ▷ vb become or cause to become lank
LANKED > LANK
LANKER > LANK
LANKEST > LANK
LANKIER > LANKY
LANKIEST > LANKY
LANKILY > LANKY
LANKINESS > LANKY
LANKING > LANK
LANKLY > LANK
LANKNESS > LANK
LANKS > LANK
LANKY adj ungracefully tall and thin
LANNER n large falcon of Mediterranean regions, N Africa, and S Asia
LANNERET n male or tercel of the lanner falcon
LANNERETS > LANNERET
LANNERS > LANNER
LANOLATED > LANOLIN
LANOLIN n grease from sheep's wool used in ointments etc
LANOLINE same as > LANOLIN
LANOLINES > LANOLINE
LANOLINS > LANOLIN
LANOSE same as > LANATE
LANOSITY > LANOSE
LANT n stale urine
LANTANA n shrub with orange or yellow flowers, considered a weed in Australia

LANTANAS > LANTANA
LANTERLOO n old card game
LANTERN n light in a transparent protective case ▷ vb supply with lantern
LANTERNED > LANTERN
LANTERNS > LANTERN
LANTHANON n one of a group of chemical elements
LANTHANUM n silvery-white metallic element
LANTHORN archaic word for > LANTERN
LANTHORNS > LANTHORN
LANTS > LANT
LANTSKIP another word for > LANDSCAPE
LANTSKIPS > LANTSKIP > LANUGO
LANUGO n layer of fine hairs, esp the covering of the human fetus before birth
LANUGOS > LANUGO
LANX n dish; plate
LANYARD n cord worn round the neck to hold a knife or whistle
LANYARDS > LANYARD
LAODICEAN adj indifferent, esp in religious matters ▷ n person having a lukewarm attitude towards religious matters
LAOGAI n forced labour camp in China
LAOGAIS > LAOGAI
LAP n part between the waist and knees of a person when sitting ▷ vb overtake an opponent so as to be one or more circuits ahead
LAPBOARD n flat board that can be used on the lap as a makeshift table or desk
LAPBOARDS > LAPBOARD
LAPDOG n small pet dog
LAPDOGS > LAPDOG
LAPEL n part of the front of a coat or jacket folded back towards the shoulders
LAPELED > LAPEL
LAPELLED > LAPEL
LAPELS > LAPEL
LAPFUL same as > LAP
LAPFULS > LAPFUL
LAPHELD adj (esp of a personal computer) small enough to be used on one's lap
LAPIDARY adj of or relating to stones ▷ n person who cuts, polishes, sets, or deals in gemstones
LAPIDATE vb pelt with stones
LAPIDATED > LAPIDATE
LAPIDATES > LAPIDATE
LAPIDEOUS adj having appearance or texture of stone
LAPIDES > LAPIS
LAPIDIFIC adj transforming into stone
LAPIDIFY vb change into stone

LAPIDIST n cutter and engraver of precious stones
LAPIDISTS > LAPIDIST
LAPILLI > LAPILLUS
LAPILLUS n small piece of lava thrown from a volcano
LAPIN n castrated rabbit
LAPINS > LAPIN
LAPIS as in lapis lazuli brilliant blue mineral used as a gemstone
LAPISES > LAPIS
LAPJE same as > LAPPIE
LAPJES > LAPJE
LAPPED > LAP
LAPPEL same as > LAPEL
LAPPELS > LAPPEL
LAPPER n one that laps ▷ vb curdle
LAPPERED > LAPPER
LAPPERING > LAPPER
LAPPERS > LAPPER
LAPPET n small hanging flap or piece of lace
LAPPETED > LAPPET
LAPPETS > LAPPET
LAPPIE n rag
LAPPIES > LAPPIE
LAPPING > LAP
LAPPINGS > LAP
LAPS > LAP
LAPSABLE > LAPSE
LAPSANG n smoky-tasting Chinese tea
LAPSANGS > LAPSANG
LAPSE n temporary drop in a standard, esp through forgetfulness or carelessness ▷ vb drop in standard
LAPSED > LAPSE
LAPSER > LAPSE
LAPSERS > LAPSE
LAPSES > LAPSE
LAPSIBLE > LAPSE
LAPSING > LAPSE
LAPSTONE n device used by a cobbler on which leather is beaten
LAPSTONES > LAPSTONE
LAPSTRAKE n clinker-built boat
LAPSTREAK same as > LAPSTRAKE
LAPSUS n lapse or error
LAPTOP adj small enough to fit on a user's lap ▷ n computer small enough to fit on a user's lap
LAPTOPS > LAPTOP
LAPTRAY n tray with a cushioned underside, designed to rest in a person's lap while supporting reading material, etc
LAPTRAYS > LAPTRAY
LAPWING n plover with a tuft of feathers on the head
LAPWINGS > LAPWING
LAPWORK n work with lapping edges
LAPWORKS > LAPWORK
LAQUEARIA n ceiling made of panels
LAR n boy or young man
LARBOARD n port (side of

a ship)
LARBOARDS > LARBOARD
LARCENER > LARCENY
LARCENERS > LARCENY
LARCENIES > LARCENY
LARCENIST > LARCENY
LARCENOUS > LARCENY
LARCENY n theft
LARCH n deciduous coniferous tree
LARCHEN adj of larch
LARCHES > LARCH
LARD n soft white fat obtained from a pig ▷ vb insert strips of bacon in (meat) before cooking
LARDALITE n type of mineral
LARDED > LARD
LARDER n storeroom for food
LARDERER n person in charge of larder
LARDERERS > LARDERER
LARDERS > LARDER
LARDIER > LARDY
LARDIEST > LARDY
LARDING > LARD
LARDLIKE > LARD
LARDON n strip or cube of fat or bacon used in larding meat
LARDONS > LARDON
LARDOON same as > LARDON
LARDOONS > LARDOON
LARDS > LARD
LARDY adj fat
LARE another word for > LORE
LAREE n Asian fish-hook formerly used as currency
LAREES > LAREE
LARES > LARE
LARGANDO adv (music) growing slower and more marked
LARGE adj great in size, number, or extent ▷ n formerly, musical note of particular length
LARGELY adv principally
LARGEN another word for > ENLARGE
LARGENED > LARGEN
LARGENESS > LARGE
LARGENING > LARGEN
LARGENS > LARGEN
LARGER > LARGE
LARGES > LARGE
LARGESS same as > LARGESSE
LARGESSE n generous giving, esp of money
LARGESSES > LARGESSE
LARGEST > LARGE
LARGHETTO adv be performed moderately slowly ▷ n piece or passage to be performed in this way
LARGISH adj fairly large
LARGITION n act of being generous
LARGO adv in a slow and dignified manner ▷ n piece or passage to be performed in a slow and stately manner

LARGOS > LARGO

LARI n standard monetary unit of Georgia, divided into 100 tetri

LARIAT n lasso ▷ vb tether with lariat

LARIATED > LARIAT

LARIATING > LARIAT

LARIATS > LARIAT

LARINE adj of, relating to, or resembling a gull

LARIS > LARI

LARK n small brown songbird, skylark ▷ vb have a good time by frolicking

LARKED > LARK

LARKER > LARK

LARKERS > LARK

LARKIER > LARKY

LARKIEST > LARKY

LARKINESS > LARKY

LARKING > LARK

LARKISH > LARK

LARKS > LARK

LARKSOME adj mischievous

LARKSPUR n plant with spikes of blue, pink, or white flowers with spurs

LARKSPURS > LARKSPUR

LARKY adj frolicsome or mischievous

LARMIER n pouch under lower eyelid of deer

LARMIERS > LARMIER

LARN vb learn

LARNAKES > LARNAX

LARNAX n coffin made of terracotta

LARNED > LARN

LARNEY n white person ▷ adj (of clothes) smart

LARNEYS > LARNEY

LARNIER > LARNEY

LARNIEST > LARNEY

LARNING > LARN

LARNS > LARN

LAROID adj relating to Larus genus of gull family

LARRIGAN n knee-high oiled leather moccasin boot worn by trappers, etc

LARRIGANS > LARRIGAN

LARRIKIN n mischievous or unruly person

LARRIKINS > LARRIKIN

LARRUP vb beat or flog

LARRUPED > LARRUP

LARRUPER > LARRUP

LARRUPERS > LARRUP

LARRUPING > LARRUP

LARRUPS > LARRUP

LARS > LAR

LARUM archaic word for > ALARM

LARUMS > LARUM

LARVA n insect in an immature stage, often resembling a worm

LARVAE > LARVA

LARVAL > LARVA

LARVAS > LARVA

LARVATE adj masked; concealed

LARVATED same as > LARVATE

LARVICIDE n chemical used for killing larvae

LARVIFORM adj in the form of a larva

LARVIKITE n type of mineral

LARYNGAL adj laryngeal ▷ n sound articulated in the larynx

LARYNGALS > LARYNGAL

LARYNGEAL adj of or relating to the larynx

LARYNGES > LARYNX

LARYNX n part of the throat containing the vocal cords

LARYNXES > LARYNX

LAS > LA

LASAGNA same as > LASAGNE

LASAGNAS > LASAGNA

LASAGNE n pasta in wide flat sheets

LASAGNES > LASAGNE

LASCAR n East Indian seaman

LASCARS > LASCAR

LASE vb (of a substance, such as carbon dioxide or ruby) to be capable of acting as a laser

LASED > LASE

LASER n device that produces a very narrow intense beam of light, used for cutting very hard materials and in surgery etc

LASERDISC n disk similar in size to a long-playing record, on which data is stored in pits in a similar way to data storage on a compact disk

LASERDISK same as > LASERDISC

LASERS > LASER

LASERWORT n type of plant

LASES > LASE

LASH n eyelash ▷ vb hit with a whip

LASHED > LASH

LASHER > LASH

LASHERS > LASH

LASHES > LASH

LASHING > LASH

LASHINGLY > LASH

LASHINGS pl n great amount of

LASHINS variant of > LASHINGS

LASHKAR n troop of Indian men with weapons

LASHKARS > LASHKAR

LASING > LASE

LASINGS > LASE

LASKET n loop at the foot of a sail onto which an extra sail may be fastened

LASKETS > LASKET

LASQUE n flat-cut diamond

LASQUES > LASQUE

LASS n girl

LASSES > LASS

LASSI n cold drink made with yoghurt or buttermilk and flavoured with sugar, salt, or a mild spice

LASSIE n little lass

LASSIES > LASSIE

LASSIS > LASSI

LASSITUDE n physical or mental weariness

LASSLORN adj abandoned by a young girl

LASSO n rope with a noose for catching cattle and horses ▷ vb catch with a lasso

LASSOCK another word for > LASS

LASSOCKS > LASSOCK

LASSOED > LASSO

LASSOER > LASSO

LASSOERS > LASSO

LASSOES > LASSO

LASSOING > LASSO

LASSOS > LASSO

LASSU n slow part of csárdás folk dance

LASSUS > LASSU

LAST adv coming at the end or after all others ▷ adj only remaining ▷ n last person or thing ▷ vb continue

LASTAGE n space for storing goods in ship

LASTAGES > LASTAGE

LASTBORN n last child to be born

LASTBORNS > LASTBORN

LASTED > LAST

LASTER > LAST

LASTERS > LAST

LASTING adj existing or remaining effective for a long time ▷ n strong durable closely woven fabric used for shoe uppers, etc

LASTINGLY > LASTING

LASTINGS > LASTING

LASTLY adv at the end or at the last point

LASTS > LAST

LAT n former coin of Latvia

LATAH n psychological condition in which a traumatized individual becomes anxious and suggestible

LATAHS > LATAH

LATAKIA n type of Turkish tobacco

LATAKIAS > LATAKIA

LATCH n fastening for a door with a bar and lever ▷ vb fasten with a latch

LATCHED > LATCH

LATCHES > LATCH

LATCHET n shoe fastening, such as a thong or lace

LATCHETS > LATCHET

LATCHING > LATCH

LATCHKEY n key for an outside door or gate, esp one that lifts a latch

LATCHKEYS > LATCHKEY

LATE adj after the normal or expected time ▷ adv after the normal or expected time

LATECOMER n person or thing that comes late

LATED archaic word for > BELATED

LATEEN adj denoting a rig with a triangular sail bent to a yard hoisted to the head of a low mast

LATEENER n lateen-rigged ship

LATEENERS > LATEEN

LATEENS > LATEEN

LATELY adv in recent times

LATEN vb become or cause to become late

LATENCE > LATENT

LATENCES > LATENCE

LATENCIES > LATENT

LATENCY > LATENT

LATENED > LATEN

LATENESS > LATE

LATENING > LATEN

LATENS > LATEN

LATENT adj hidden and not yet developed ▷ n fingerprint that is not visible to the eye

LATENTLY > LATENT

LATENTS > LATENT

LATER adv afterwards

LATERAD adv towards the side

LATERAL adj of or relating to the side or sides ▷ n lateral object, part, passage, or movement ▷ vb pass laterally

LATERALED > LATERAL

LATERALLY > LATERAL

LATERALS > LATERAL

LATERBORN adj born later

LATERISE same as > LATERIZE

LATERISED > LATERISE

LATERISES > LATERISE

LATERITE n any of a group of deposits consisting of residual insoluble ferric and aluminium oxides

LATERITES > LATERITE

LATERITIC > LATERITE

LATERIZE vb develop into a laterite

LATERIZED > LATERIZE

LATERIZES > LATERIZE

LATESCENT n becoming latent

LATEST n the most recent news, fashion, etc

LATESTS > LATEST

LATEWAKE n vigil held over corpse

LATEWAKES > LATEWAKE

LATEWOOD n wood formed later in tree's growing season

LATEWOODS > LATEWOOD

LATEX n milky fluid found in some plants, esp the rubber tree, used in making rubber

LATEXES > LATEX

LATH n thin strip of wood used to support plaster, tiles, etc ▷ vb attach laths to (a ceiling, roof, floor, etc)

LATHE n machine for turning wood or metal while it is being shaped ▷ vb shape, bore, or cut a screw thread in or on (a workpiece) on a lathe

LATHED > LATHE
LATHEE *same as* > LATHI
LATHEES > LATHEE
LATHEN *adj* covered with laths
LATHER *n* froth of soap and water ▷ *vb* make frothy
LATHERED > LATHER
LATHERER > LATHER
LATHERERS > LATHER
LATHERIER > LATHER
LATHERING > LATHER
LATHERS > LATHER
LATHERY > LATHER
LATHES > LATHE
LATHI *n* long heavy wooden stick used as a weapon in India, esp by the police
LATHIER > LATHY
LATHIEST > LATHY
LATHING > LATHE
LATHINGS > LATHE
LATHIS > LATHI
LATHLIKE > LATH
LATHS > LATH
LATHWORK *n* work made of laths
LATHWORKS > LATHWORK
LATHY *adj* resembling a lath, esp in being tall and thin
LATHYRISM *n* neurological disease often resulting in weakness and paralysis of the legs
LATHYRUS *n* genus of climbing plant
LATI > LATUS
LATICES > LATEX
LATICIFER *n* cell or group of cells in a plant that contains latex
LATICLAVE *n* broad stripe on Roman senator's tunic
LATIFONDI *pl n* large agricultural estates in ancient Rome
LATIGO *n* strap on horse's saddle
LATIGOES > LATIGO
LATIGOS > LATIGO
LATILLA *n* stick making up part of ceiling
LATILLAS > LATILLA
LATIMERIA *n* any coelacanth fish of the genus *Latimeria*
LATINA *n* female inhabitant of the US who is of Latin American origin
LATINAS > LATINA
LATINISE *same as* > LATINIZE
LATINISED > LATINISE
LATINISES > LATINISE
LATINITY *n* facility in the use of Latin
LATINIZE *vb* translate into Latin
LATINIZED > LATINIZE
LATINIZES > LATINIZE
LATINO *n* male inhabitant of the US who is of Latin American origin
LATINOS > LATINO
LATISH *adv* rather late ▷ *adj* rather late

LATITANCY > LATITANT
LATITANT *adj* concealed
LATITAT *n* writ presuming that person accused was hiding
LATITATS > LATITAT
LATITUDE *n* angular distance measured in degrees N or S of the equator
LATITUDES > LATITUDE
LATKE *n* crispy Jewish pancake
LATKES > LATKE
LATOSOL *n* type of deep, well-drained soil
LATOSOLIC > LATOSOL
LATOSOLS > LATOSOL
LATRANT *adj* barking
LATRATION *n* instance of barking
LATRIA *n* adoration that may be offered to God alone
LATRIAS > LATRIA
LATRINE *n* toilet in a barracks or camp
LATRINES > LATRINE
LATROCINY *n* banditry
LATRON *n* bandit
LATRONS > LATRON
LATS > LAT
LATTE *n* coffee made with hot milk
LATTEN *n* metal or alloy, esp brass, made in thin sheets
LATTENS > LATTEN
LATTER *adj* second of two
LATTERLY *adv* recently
LATTES > LATTE
LATTICE *n* framework of intersecting strips of wood, metal, etc ▷ *vb* make, adorn, or supply with a lattice
LATTICED > LATTICE
LATTICES > LATTICE
LATTICING > LATTICE
LATTICINI > LATTICINO
LATTICINO *n* type of Italian glass
LATTIN *n* brass alloy beaten into a thin sheet
LATTINS > LATTIN
LATU *n* type of seaweed
LAUAN *n* type of wood used in furniture-making
LAUANS > LAUAN
LAUCH *Scots form of* > LAUGH
LAUCHING > LAUCH
LAUCHS > LAUCH
LAUD *vb* praise or glorify ▷ *n* praise or glorification
LAUDABLE *adj* praiseworthy
LAUDABLY > LAUDABLE
LAUDANUM *n* opium-based sedative
LAUDANUMS > LAUDANUM
LAUDATION *formal word for* > PRAISE
LAUDATIVE *same as* > LAUDATORY
LAUDATOR *n* one who praises highly
LAUDATORS > LAUDATOR
LAUDATORY *adj* praising or glorifying

LAUDED > LAUD
LAUDER > LAUD
LAUDERS > LAUD
LAUDING > LAUD
LAUDS *n* traditional morning prayer of the Western Church, constituting with matins the first of the seven canonical hours
LAUF *n* run in bobsleighing
LAUFS > LAUF
LAUGH *vb* make inarticulate sounds with the voice expressing amusement, merriment, or scorn ▷ *n* act or instance of laughing
LAUGHABLE *adj* ridiculously inadequate
LAUGHABLY > LAUGHABLE
LAUGHED > LAUGH
LAUGHER > LAUGH
LAUGHERS > LAUGH
LAUGHFUL > LAUGH
LAUGHIER > LAUGHY
LAUGHIEST > LAUGHY
LAUGHING > LAUGH
LAUGHINGS > LAUGH
LAUGHLINE *n* funny line in dialogue
LAUGHS > LAUGH
LAUGHSOME *adj* causing laughter
LAUGHTER *n* sound or action of laughing
LAUGHTERS > LAUGHTER
LAUGHY *adj* tending to laugh a lot
LAUNCE *old form of* > LANCE
LAUNCED > LAUNCE
LAUNCES > LAUNCE
LAUNCH *vb* put (a ship or boat) into the water, esp for the first time ▷ *n* launching
LAUNCHED > LAUNCH
LAUNCHER *n* any installation, vehicle, or other device for launching rockets, missiles, or other projectiles
LAUNCHERS > LAUNCHER
LAUNCHES > LAUNCH
LAUNCHING > LAUNCH
LAUNCHPAD *n* platform from which a spacecraft is launched
LAUNCING > LAUNCE
LAUND *n* open grassy space
LAUNDER *vb* wash and iron (clothes and linen) ▷ *n* water trough, esp one used for washing ore in mining
LAUNDERED > LAUNDER
LAUNDERER > LAUNDER
LAUNDERS > LAUNDER
LAUNDRESS *n* woman who launders clothes, sheets, etc, for a living
LAUNDRIES > LAUNDRY
LAUNDRY *n* clothes etc for washing or which have recently been washed
LAUNDS > LAUND
LAURA *n* group of monastic cells
LAURAE > LAURA

LAURAS > LAURA
LAUREATE *adj* crowned with laurel leaves as a sign of honour ▷ *n* person honoured with an award for art or science ▷ *vb* crown with laurel
LAUREATED > LAUREATE
LAUREATES > LAUREATE
LAUREL *n* glossy-leaved shrub, bay tree ▷ *vb* crown with laurel
LAURELED > LAUREL
LAURELING > LAUREL
LAURELLED > LAUREL
LAURELS > LAUREL
LAURIC *as in* *lauric acid* dodecanoic acid
LAURYL *as in* *lauryl alcohol* crystalline solid used to make detergents
LAURYLS > LAURYL
LAUWINE *n* avalanche
LAUWINES > LAUWINE
LAV *short for* > LAVATORY
LAVA *n* molten rock thrown out by volcanoes, which hardens as it cools
LAVABO *n* ritual washing of the celebrant's hands after the offertory at Mass
LAVABOES > LAVABO
LAVABOS > LAVABO
LAVAFORM *n* in form of lava
LAVAGE *n* washing out of a hollow organ by flushing with water
LAVAGES > LAVAGE
LAVALAVA *n* draped skirtlike garment worn by Polynesians
LAVALAVAS > LAVALAVA
LAVALIER *n* decorative pendant worn on chain
LAVALIERE *same as* > LAVALIER
LAVALIERS > LAVALIER
LAVALIKE > LAVA
LAVAS > LAVA
LAVASH *n* Armenian flat bread
LAVASHES > LAVASH
LAVATERA *n* any plant of the genus *Lavatera*, closely resembling mallow
LAVATERAS > LAVATERA
LAVATION *n* act or process of washing
LAVATIONS > LAVATION
LAVATORY *n* toilet
LAVE *archaic word for* > WASH
LAVED > LAVE
LAVEER *vb* (in sailing) tack
LAVEERED > LAVEER
LAVEERING > LAVEER
LAVEERS > LAVEER
LAVEMENT *n* washing with injections of water
LAVEMENTS > LAVEMENT
LAVENDER *n* shrub with fragrant flowers ▷ *adj* bluish-purple
LAVENDERS > LAVENDER
LAVER *n* large basin of water used by priests for ritual ablutions
LAVEROCK *Scot and northern*

English dialect word for > SKYLARK

LAVEROCKS > LAVEROCK

LAVERS > LAVER

LAVES > LAVE

LAVING > LAVE

LAVISH *adj* great in quantity or richness ▷ *vb* give or spend generously

LAVISHED > LAVISH

LAVISHER > LAVISH

LAVISHERS > LAVISH

LAVISHES > LAVISH

LAVISHEST > LAVISH

LAVISHING > LAVISH

LAVISHLY > LAVISH

LAVOLT *same as* > LAVOLTA

LAVOLTA *n* Italian dance of the 16th and 17th centuries ▷ *vb* dance the lavolta

LAVOLTAED > LAVOLTA

LAVOLTAS > LAVOLTA

LAVOLTED > LAVOLT

LAVOLTING > LAVOLT

LAVOLTS > LAVOLT

LAVRA *same as* > LAURA

LAVRAS > LAVRA

LAVROCK *same as* > LAVEROCK

LAVROCKS > LAVROCK

LAVS > LAV

LAW *n* rule binding on a community ▷ *vb* prosecute ▷ *adj* (in archaic usage) low

LAWBOOK *n* book on subject of law

LAWBOOKS > LAWBOOK

LAWED > LAW

LAWER > LAW

LAWEST > LAW

LAWFUL *adj* allowed by law

LAWFULLY > LAWFUL

LAWGIVER *n* giver of a code of laws

LAWGIVERS > LAWGIVER

LAWGIVING > LAWGIVER

LAWIN *n* bill or reckoning

LAWINE *n* avalanche

LAWINES > LAWINE

LAWING *same as* > LAWIN

LAWINGS > LAWING

LAWINS > LAWIN

LAWK *interj* used to show surprise

LAWKS *same as* > LAWK

LAWLAND *same as* > LOWLAND

LAWLANDS > LAWLAND

LAWLESS *adj* breaking the law, esp in a violent way

LAWLESSLY > LAWLESS

LAWLIKE > LAW

LAWMAKER *same as* > LAWGIVER

LAWMAKERS > LAWMAKER

LAWMAKING *n* process of legislating

LAWMAN *n* officer of the law, such as a policeman or sheriff

LAWMEN > LAWMAN

LAWMONGER *n* inferior lawyer

LAWN *n* area of tended and mown grass

LAWNIER > LAWN

LAWNIEST > LAWN

LAWNMOWER *n* machine for cutting grass on lawns

LAWNS > LAWN

LAWNY > LAWN

LAWS > LAW

LAWSUIT *n* court case brought by one person or group against another

LAWSUITS > LAWSUIT

LAWYER *n* professionally qualified legal expert ▷ *vb* act as lawyer

LAWYERED > LAWYER

LAWYERING > LAWYER

LAWYERLY > LAWYER

LAWYERS > LAWYER

LAX *adj* not strict ▷ *n* laxative

LAXATION *n* act of making lax or the state of being lax

LAXATIONS > LAXATION

LAXATIVE *adj* (medicine) inducing the emptying of the bowels ▷ *n* medicine that induces the emptying of the bowels

LAXATIVES > LAXATIVE

LAXATOR *n* muscle that loosens body part

LAXATORS > LAXATOR

LAXER > LAX

LAXES > LAX

LAXEST > LAX

LAXISM > LAXIST

LAXISMS > LAXIST

LAXIST *n* lenient or tolerant person

LAXISTS > LAXIST

LAXITIES > LAX

LAXITY > LAX

LAXLY > LAX

LAXNESS > LAX

LAXNESSES > LAX

LAY > LIE

LAYABOUT *n* lazy person ▷ *vb* hit out with violent and repeated blows in all directions

LAYABOUTS > LAYABOUT

LAYAWAY *n* merchandise reserved for future delivery

LAYAWAYS > LAYAWAY

LAYBACK *n* technique for climbing cracks by pulling on one side of the crack with the hands and pressing on the other with the feet ▷ *vb* in climbing, use layback technique

LAYBACKED > LAYBACK

LAYBACKS > LAYBACK

LAYDEEZ *pl n* jocular spelling of ladies, as pronounced in a mid-Atlantic accent

LAYED > LAY

LAYER *n* single thickness of some substance, as a cover or coating on a surface ▷ *vb* form a layer

LAYERAGE *n* covering stem or branch with soil to encourage new roots

LAYERAGES > LAYERAGE

LAYERED > LAYER

LAYERING *n* method of propagation that induces a shoot or branch to take root while it is still attached to the parent plant

LAYERINGS > LAYERING

LAYERS > LAYER

LAYETTE *n* clothes for a newborn baby

LAYETTES > LAYETTE

LAYIN *n* basketball score made by dropping ball into basket

LAYING > LAY

LAYINGS > LAY

LAYINS > LAYIN

LAYLOCK *old form of* > LILAC

LAYLOCKS > LAYLOCK

LAYMAN *n* person who is not a member of the clergy

LAYMEN > LAYMAN

LAYOFF *n* act of suspending employees

LAYOFFS > LAYOFF

LAYOUT *n* arrangement, esp of matter for printing or of a building

LAYOUTS > LAYOUT

LAYOVER *n* break in a journey

LAYOVERS > LAYOVER

LAYPEOPLE > LAYPERSON

LAYPERSON *n* person who is not a member of the clergy

LAYS > LIE

LAYSHAFT *n* auxiliary shaft in a gearbox

LAYSHAFTS > LAYSHAFT

LAYSTALL *n* place where waste is deposited

LAYSTALLS > LAYSTALL

LAYTIME *n* time allowed for loading cargo

LAYTIMES > LAYTIME

LAYUP *n* period of incapacity through illness

LAYUPS > LAYUP

LAYWOMAN *n* woman who is not a member of the clergy

LAYWOMEN > LAYWOMAN

LAZAR *archaic word for* > LEPER

LAZARET *same as* > LAZARETTO

LAZARETS > LAZARET

LAZARETTE *same as* > LAZARETTO

LAZARETTO *n* small locker at the stern of a boat or a storeroom between decks of a ship

LAZARS > LAZAR

LAZE *vb* be idle or lazy ▷ *n* time spent lazing

LAZED > LAZE

LAZES > LAZE

LAZIED > LAZY

LAZIER > LAZY

LAZIES > LAZY

LAZIEST > LAZY

LAZILY > LAZY

LAZINESS > LAZY

LAZING > LAZE

LAZO *another word for* > LASSO

LAZOED > LAZO

LAZOES > LAZO

LAZOING > LAZO

LAZOS > LAZO

LAZULI *n* lapis lazuli

LAZULIS > LAZULI

LAZULITE *n* blue mineral, consisting of hydrated magnesium iron phosphate, occurring in metamorphic rocks

LAZULITES > LAZULITE

LAZURITE *n* rare blue mineral consisting of a sodium–calcium–aluminium silicate

LAZURITES > LAZURITE

LAZY *vb* laze ▷ *adj* not inclined to work or exert oneself

LAZYBONES *n* lazy person

LAZYING > LAZY

LAZYISH > LAZY

LAZZARONE *n* Italian street beggar

LAZZARONI > LAZZARONE

LAZZI > LAZZO

LAZZO *n* comic routine in the commedia dell'arte

LEA *n* meadow

LEACH *vb* remove or be removed from a substance by a liquid passing through it ▷ *n* act or process of leaching

LEACHABLE > LEACH

LEACHATE *n* water that carries salts dissolved out of materials through which it has percolated

LEACHATES > LEACHATE

LEACHED > LEACH

LEACHER > LEACH

LEACHERS > LEACH

LEACHES > LEACH

LEACHIER > LEACHY

LEACHIEST > LEACHY

LEACHING > LEACH

LEACHINGS > LEACH

LEACHOUR *old form of* > LECHER

LEACHOURS > LEACHOUR

LEACHY *adj* porous

LEAD *vb* guide or conduct ▷ *n* first or most prominent place ▷ *adj* acting as a leader or lead

LEADED *adj* (of windows) made from many small panes of glass held together by lead strips

LEADEN *adj* heavy or sluggish ▷ *vb* become or cause to become leaden

LEADENED > LEADEN

LEADENING > LEADEN

LEADENLY > LEADEN

LEADENS > LEADEN

LEADER *n* person who leads

LEADERENE *n* strong female leader

LEADERS > LEADER

LEADIER > LEADY

LEADIEST > LEADY

LEADING > LEAD

LEADINGLY > LEAD

LEADINGS > LEAD

LEADLESS *adj* without lead

LEADMAN *n* man who leads

LEADMEN > LEADMAN

LEADOFF n initial move or action
LEADOFFS > LEADOFF
LEADPLANT n N American shrub
LEADS > LEAD
LEADSCREW n threaded rod in a lathe
LEADSMAN n sailor who takes soundings with a lead line
LEADSMEN > LEADSMAN
LEADWORK n maintenance work involving lead pipes, etc
LEADWORKS > LEADWORK
LEADWORT n any shrub of the plumbaginaceous genus *Plumbago*
LEADWORTS > LEADWORT
LEADY adj like lead
LEAF n flat usu green blade attached to the stem of a plant ▷ vb turn (pages) cursorily
LEAFAGE n leaves of plants
LEAFAGES > LEAFAGE
LEAFBUD n bud producing leaves rather than flowers
LEAFBUDS > LEAFBUD
LEAFED > LEAF
LEAFERIES > LEAFERY
LEAFERY n foliage
LEAFIER > LEAFY
LEAFIEST > LEAFY
LEAFINESS > LEAFY
LEAFING > LEAF
LEAFLESS > LEAF
LEAFLET n sheet of printed matter for distribution ▷ vb distribute leaflets (to)
LEAFLETED > LEAFLET
LEAFLETER > LEAFLET
LEAFLETS > LEAFLET
LEAFLIKE > LEAF
LEAFS > LEAF
LEAFSTALK n stalk attaching a leaf to a stem or branch
LEAFWORM n cotton plant pest
LEAFWORMS > LEAFWORM
LEAFY adj covered with leaves
LEAGUE n association promoting the interests of its members
LEAGUED > LEAGUE
LEAGUER vb harass; beset ▷ n encampment, esp of besiegers
LEAGUERED > LEAGUER
LEAGUERS > LEAGUER
LEAGUES > LEAGUE
LEAGUING > LEAGUE
LEAK n hole or defect that allows the escape or entrance of liquid, gas, radiation, etc ▷ vb let liquid etc in or out
LEAKAGE n act or instance of leaking
LEAKAGES > LEAKAGE
LEAKED > LEAK
LEAKER > LEAK
LEAKERS > LEAK
LEAKIER > LEAKY

LEAKIEST > LEAKY
LEAKILY > LEAKY
LEAKINESS > LEAKY
LEAKING > LEAK
LEAKLESS > LEAK
LEAKPROOF adj not likely to leak
LEAKS > LEAK
LEAKY adj leaking or tending to leak
LEAL adj loyal
LEALER > LEAL
LEALEST > LEAL
LEALLY > LEAL
LEALTIES > LEAL
LEALTY > LEAL
LEAM vb shine
LEAMED > LEAM
LEAMING > LEAM
LEAMS > LEAM
LEAN vb rest (against) ▷ adj thin but healthy-looking ▷ n lean part of meat
LEANED > LEAN
LEANER > LEAN
LEANERS > LEAN
LEANEST > LEAN
LEANING > LEAN
LEANINGS > LEAN
LEANLY > LEAN
LEANNESS > LEAN
LEANS > LEAN
LEANT > LEAN
LEANY old form of > LEAN
LEAP vb make a sudden powerful jump ▷ n sudden powerful jump
LEAPED > LEAP
LEAPER > LEAP
LEAPEROUS old form of > LEPROUS
LEAPERS > LEAP
LEAPFROG n game in which a player vaults over another bending down ▷ vb play leapfrog
LEAPFROGS > LEAPFROG
LEAPING > LEAP
LEAPOROUS old form of > LEPROUS
LEAPROUS old form of > LEPROUS
LEAPS > LEAP
LEAPT > LEAP
LEAR vb instruct
LEARE same as > LEAR
LEARED > LEAR
LEARES > LEARE
LEARIER > LEARY
LEARIEST > LEARY
LEARINESS > LEARY
LEARING > LEAR
LEARN vb gain skill or knowledge by study, practice, or teaching
LEARNABLE > LEARN
LEARNED > LEARN
LEARNEDLY > LEARN
LEARNER n someone who is learning something
LEARNERS > LEARNER
LEARNING > LEARN
LEARNINGS > LEARN
LEARNS > LEARN
LEARNT > LEARN
LEARS > LEAR
LEARY same as > LEERY

LEAS > LEA
LEASABLE > LEASE
LEASE n contract by which land or property is rented for a stated time by the owner to a tenant ▷ vb let or rent by lease
LEASEBACK n property transaction in which the buyer leases the property to the seller
LEASED > LEASE
LEASEHOLD adj (land or property) held on lease ▷ n land or property held under a lease
LEASER > LEASE
LEASERS > LEASE
LEASES > LEASE
LEASH n lead for a dog ▷ vb control by a leash
LEASHED > LEASH
LEASHES > LEASH
LEASHING > LEASH
LEASING > LEASE
LEASINGS > LEASE
LEASOW vb pasture
LEASOWE same as > LEASOW
LEASOWED > LEASOW
LEASOWES > LEASOWE
LEASOWING > LEASOW
LEASOWS > LEASOW
LEAST n smallest amount ▷ adj smallest ▷ n smallest one ▷ adv in the smallest degree
LEASTS > LEAST
LEASTWAYS adv at least
LEASTWISE same as > LEASTWAYS
LEASURE old form of > LEISURE
LEASURES > LEASURE
LEAT n trench or ditch that conveys water to a mill wheel
LEATHER n material made from specially treated animal skins ▷ adj made of leather ▷ vb beat or thrash
LEATHERED > LEATHER
LEATHERN adj made of or resembling leather
LEATHERS > LEATHER
LEATHERY adj like leather, tough
LEATS > LEAT
LEAVE vb go away from ▷ n permission to be absent from work or duty
LEAVED adj with leaves
LEAVEN n substance that causes dough to rise ▷ vb raise with leaven
LEAVENED > LEAVEN
LEAVENING > LEAVEN
LEAVENOUS adj containing leaven
LEAVENS > LEAVEN
LEAVER > LEAVE
LEAVERS > LEAVE
LEAVES > LEAF
LEAVIER > LEAVY
LEAVIEST > LEAVY
LEAVING > LEAVE
LEAVINGS pl n something remaining, such as refuse

LEAVY same as > LEAFY
LEAZE same as > LEASE
LEAZES > LEAZE
LEBBEK n type of timber tree
LEBBEKS > LEBBEK
LEBEN n semiliquid food made from curdled milk in N Africa and the Levant
LEBENS > LEBEN
LEBKUCHEN n biscuit, originating from Germany, usually containing honey, spices, etc
LECANORA n type of lichen
LECANORAS > LECANORA
LECCIES > LECCY
LECCY n electricity
LECH vb behave lecherously (towards) ▷ n lecherous act or indulgence
LECHAIM interj drinking toast ▷ n small drink with which to toast something or someone
LECHAIMS > LECHAIM
LECHAYIM same as > LECHAIM
LECHAYIMS > LECHAYIM
LECHED > LECH
LECHER n man who has or shows excessive sexual desire ▷ vb behave lecherously
LECHERED > LECHER
LECHERIES > LECHERY
LECHERING > LECHER
LECHEROUS adj (of a man) having or showing excessive sexual desire
LECHERS > LECHER
LECHERY n unrestrained and promiscuous sexuality
LECHES > LECH
LECHING > LECH
LECHWE n African antelope
LECHWES > LECHWE
LECITHIN n yellow-brown compound found in plant and animal tissues
LECITHINS > LECITHIN
LECTERN n sloping reading desk, esp in a church
LECTERNS > LECTERN
LECTIN n type of protein possessing high affinity for a specific sugar
LECTINS > LECTIN
LECTION n variant reading of a passage in a particular copy or edition of a text
LECTIONS > LECTION
LECTOR n lecturer or reader in certain universities
LECTORATE > LECTOR
LECTORS > LECTOR
LECTOTYPE n specimen designated by author after the publication of a species name
LECTRESS n female reader
LECTURE n informative talk to an audience on a subject ▷ vb give a talk
LECTURED > LECTURE
LECTURER n person who lectures, esp in a university

or college
LECTURERS > LECTURER
LECTURES > LECTURE
LECTURING > LECTURE
LECTURN old form
of > LECTERN
LECTURNS > LECTURN
LECYTHI > LECYTHUS
LECYTHIS n genus of very
tall trees
LECYTHUS n (in ancient
Greece) a vase with a
narrow neck
LED > LEAD
LEDDEN n language; speech
LEDDENS > LEDDEN
LEDGE n narrow shelf
sticking out from a wall
LEDGED > LEDGE
LEDGER n book of debit and
credit accounts of a firm
▷ vb fish using a wire trace
that allows the bait to float
freely while the weight
sinks
LEDGERED > LEDGER
LEDGERING > LEDGER
LEDGERS > LEDGER
LEDGES > LEDGE
LEDGIER > LEDGE
LEDGIEST > LEDGE
LEDGY > LEDGE
LEDUM n evergreen shrub
LEDUMS > LEDUM
LEE n sheltered side ▷ vb
(Scots) lie
LEEAR Scots form of > LIAR
LEEARS > LEEAR
LEEBOARD n one of two
paddle-like boards that can
be lowered along the lee
side of a vessel to reduce
sideways drift
LEEBOARDS > LEEBOARD
LEECH n species of
bloodsucking worm ▷ vb
use leeches to suck the
blood of
LEECHDOM n remedy
LEECHDOMS > LEECHDOM
LEECHED > LEECH
LEECHEE same as > LITCHI
LEECHEES > LEECHEE
LEECHES > LEECH
LEECHING > LEECH
LEECHLIKE > LEECH
LEED > LEE
LEEING > LEE
LEEK n vegetable of the
onion family with a long
bulb and thick stem
LEEKS > LEEK
LEEP vb boil; scald
LEEPED > LEEP
LEEPING > LEEP
LEEPS > LEEP
LEER vb look or grin at in
a sneering or suggestive
manner ▷ n sneering or
suggestive look or grin
LEERED > LEER
LEERIER > LEERY
LEERIEST > LEERY
LEERILY > LEERY
LEERINESS > LEERY
LEERING > LEER
LEERINGLY > LEER

LEERINGS > LEER
LEERS > LEER
LEERY adj suspicious or
wary (of)
LEES pl n sediment of wine
LEESE old form of > LOOSE
LEESES > LEESE
LEESING > LEESE
LEET n list of candidates for
an office
LEETLE form of > LITTLE
LEETS > LEET
LEEWARD n lee side ▷ adv
towards this side ▷ adj
of, in, or moving in the
direction towards which
the wind blows
LEEWARDLY > LEEWARD
LEEWARDS adv towards the
lee side
LEEWAY n room for free
movement within limits
LEEWAYS > LEEWAY
LEFT adj on the opposite
side from right ▷ n left side
LEFTE old past tense of > LIFT
LEFTER > LEFT
LEFTEST > LEFT
LEFTIE same as > LEFTY
LEFTIES > LEFTY
LEFTISH > LEFT
LEFTISM > LEFTIST
LEFTISMS > LEFTIST
LEFTIST adj (person) of the
political left ▷ n person
who supports the political
left
LEFTISTS > LEFTIST
LEFTMOST > LEFT
LEFTMOSTS > LEFT
LEFTOVER n unused portion
of food or material ▷ adj
left as an unused portion
LEFTOVERS > LEFTOVER
LEFTS > LEFT
LEFTWARD same
as > LEFTWARDS
LEFTWARDS adv towards or
on the left
LEFTWING adj of or relating
to the leftist faction of a
party, etc
LEFTY n left-winger
LEG n one of the limbs on
which a person or animal
walks, runs, or stands
LEGACIES > LEGACY
LEGACY n thing left in a will
LEGAL adj established or
permitted by law ▷ n legal
expert
LEGALESE n conventional
language in which legal
documents are written
LEGALESES > LEGALESE
LEGALISE same
as > LEGALIZE
LEGALISED > LEGALISE
LEGALISER > LEGALISE
LEGALISES > LEGALISE
LEGALISM n strict
adherence to the letter of
the law
LEGALISMS > LEGALISM
LEGALIST > LEGALISM
LEGALISTS > LEGALISM
LEGALITY n state or quality

of being legal or lawful
LEGALIZE vb make legal
LEGALIZED > LEGALIZE
LEGALIZER > LEGALIZE
LEGALIZES > LEGALIZE
LEGALLY > LEGAL
LEGALS > LEGAL
LEGATARY n legatee
LEGATE n messenger or
representative, esp from
the Pope ▷ vb leave as
legacy
LEGATED > LEGATE
LEGATEE n recipient of a
legacy
LEGATEES > LEGATEE
LEGATES > LEGATE
LEGATINE > LEGATE
LEGATING > LEGATE
LEGATION n diplomatic
minister and his staff
LEGATIONS > LEGATION
LEGATO adv (piece to be
played) smoothly ▷ n style
of playing with no gaps
between notes
LEGATOR n person who
gives a legacy or makes a
bequest
LEGATORS > LEGATOR
LEGATOS > LEGATO
LEGEND n traditional story
or myth
LEGENDARY adj famous
LEGENDISE same
as > LEGENDIZE
LEGENDIST n writer of
legends
LEGENDIZE vb make into
legend
LEGENDRY > LEGEND
LEGENDS > LEGEND
LEGER variant of > LEDGER
LEGERING > LEGER
LEGERINGS > LEGER
LEGERITY n agility
LEGERS > LEGER
LEGES > LEX
LEGGE vb lighten or lessen
LEGGED > LEG
LEGGER n man who moves
barge through tunnel using
legs
LEGGERS > LEGGER
LEGGES > LEGGE
LEGGIER > LEGGY
LEGGIERO adj light; delicate
LEGGIEST > LEGGY
LEGGIN same as > LEGGING
LEGGINESS > LEGGY
LEGGING n extra outer
covering for the lower leg
LEGGINGED > LEGGING
LEGGINGS > LEGGING
LEGGINS > LEGGIN
LEGGISM n blacklegging
LEGGISMS > LEGGISM
LEGGY adj having long legs
LEGHORN n type of Italian
wheat straw that is woven
into hats
LEGHORNS > LEGHORN
LEGIBLE adj easily read
LEGIBLY > LEGIBLE
LEGION n large military
force ▷ adj very large or
numerous

LEGIONARY adj of or
relating to a legion ▷ n
soldier belonging to a
legion
LEGIONED adj arranged in
legions
LEGIONS > LEGION
LEGISLATE vb make laws
LEGIST n person versed in
the law
LEGISTS > LEGIST
LEGIT n legitimate or
professionally respectable
drama ▷ adj legitimate
LEGITIM n amount of
inheritance due to children
from father
LEGITIMS > LEGITIM
LEGITS > LEGIT
LEGLAN same as > LEGLIN
LEGLANS > LEGLAN
LEGLEN same as > LEGLIN
LEGLENS > LEGLEN
LEGLESS adj without legs
LEGLET n jewellery worn
around the leg
LEGLETS > LEGLET
LEGLIKE > LEG
LEGLIN n milk-pail
LEGLINS > LEGLIN
LEGMAN n newsman who
reports on news stories
from the scene of action or
original source
LEGMEN > LEGMAN
LEGONG n Indonesian dance
LEGONGS > LEGONG
LEGROOM n space to move
one's legs comfortably, as
in a car
LEGROOMS > LEGROOM
LEGS > LEG
LEGUAAN n large S African
lizard
LEGUAANS > LEGUAAN
LEGUME n pod of a plant of
the pea or bean family
LEGUMES > LEGUME
LEGUMIN n protein obtained
mainly from the seeds of
leguminous plants
LEGUMINS > LEGUMIN
LEGWARMER n one of a pair
of garments resembling
stockings without feet
LEGWEAR n clothing worn
on the legs
LEGWEARS > LEGWEAR
LEGWORK n work that
involves travelling on foot
or as if on foot
LEGWORKS > LEGWORK
LEHAIM same as > LECHAIM
LEHAIMS > LEHAIM
LEHAYIM same as > LEHAIM
LEHAYIMS > LEHAYIM
LEHR n long tunnel-shaped
oven used for annealing
glass
LEHRJAHRE n
apprenticeship
LEHRS > LEHR
LEHUA n flower of Hawaii
LEHUAS > LEHUA
LEI > LEU
LEIDGER same as > LEDGER
LEIDGERS > LEIDGER

LEIGER same as > LEDGER
LEIGERS > LEIGER
LEIOMYOMA same as > FIBROID
LEIPOA n Australian bird
LEIPOAS > LEIPOA
LEIR same as > LEAR
LEIRED > LEIR
LEIRING > LEIR
LEIRS > LEIR
LEIS > LEU
LEISH adj agile
LEISHER > LEISH
LEISHEST > LEISH
LEISLER n small bat
LEISLERS > LEISLER
LEISTER n spear with three or more prongs for spearing fish, esp salmon ▷ vb spear (a fish) with a leister
LEISTERED > LEISTER
LEISTERS > LEISTER
LEISURE n time for relaxation or hobbies ▷ vb have leisure
LEISURED > LEISURE
LEISURELY adj deliberate, unhurried ▷ adv slowly
LEISURES > LEISURE
LEISURING > LEISURE
LEITMOTIF n recurring theme associated with a person, situation, or thought
LEITMOTIV same as > LEITMOTIF
LEK n area where birds gather for sexual display and courtship ▷ vb (of birds) gather at lek
LEKE old form of > LEAK
LEKGOTLA n meeting place for village assemblies, court cases, and meetings of village leaders
LEKGOTLAS > LEKGOTLA
LEKKED > LEK
LEKKER adj attractive or nice
LEKKING > LEK
LEKKINGS > LEK
LEKS > LEK
LEKU > LEK
LEKVAR n prune or apricot pie filling
LEKVARS > LEKVAR
LEKYTHI > LEKYTHOS
LEKYTHOI > LEKYTHOS
LEKYTHOS n Greek flask
LEKYTHUS same as > LEKYTHOS
LEMAN n beloved
LEMANS > LEMAN
LEME same as > LEAM
LEMED > LEME
LEMEL n metal filings
LEMELS > LEMEL
LEMES > LEME
LEMING > LEME
LEMMA n subsidiary proposition, proved for use in the proof of another proposition
LEMMAS > LEMMA
LEMMATA > LEMMA
LEMMATISE same as > LEMMATIZE
LEMMATIZE vb group together the inflected forms of (a word) for analysis as a single item
LEMMING n rodent of arctic regions, reputed to run into the sea and drown during mass migrations
LEMMINGS > LEMMING
LEMNISCAL adj relating to a type of closed plane curve
LEMNISCI > LEMNISCUS
LEMNISCUS technical name for > FILLET
LEMON n yellow oval fruit that grows on trees ▷ adj pale-yellow ▷ vb flavour with lemon
LEMONADE n lemon-flavoured soft drink, often fizzy
LEMONADES > LEMONADE
LEMONED > LEMON
LEMONFISH n type of game fish
LEMONIER > LEMONY
LEMONIEST > LEMONY
LEMONING > LEMON
LEMONISH > LEMON
LEMONLIKE > LEMON
LEMONS > LEMON
LEMONWOOD n small tree of New Zealand
LEMONY adj having or resembling the taste or colour of a lemon
LEMPIRA n standard monetary unit of Honduras, divided into 100 centavos
LEMPIRAS > LEMPIRA
LEMUR n nocturnal animal like a small monkey, found in Madagascar
LEMURES pl n spirits of the dead
LEMURIAN same as > LEMUROID
LEMURIANS > LEMURIAN
LEMURINE same as > LEMUROID
LEMURINES > LEMURINE
LEMURLIKE > LEMUR
LEMUROID adj of, relating to, or belonging to the superfamily which includes the lemurs and indrises ▷ n animal that resembles or is closely related to a lemur
LEMUROIDS > LEMUROID
LEMURS > LEMUR
LEND vb give the temporary use of
LENDABLE > LEND
LENDER > LEND
LENDERS > LEND
LENDING > LEND
LENDINGS > LEND
LENDS > LEND
LENES > LENIS
LENG vb linger ▷ adj long
LENGED > LENG
LENGER > LENG
LENGEST > LENG
LENGING > LENG
LENGS > LENG
LENGTH n extent or measurement from end to end
LENGTHEN vb make or become longer
LENGTHENS > LENGTHEN
LENGTHFUL > LENGTH
LENGTHIER > LENGTHY
LENGTHILY > LENGTHY
LENGTHMAN n person whose job it is to maintain a particular length of road or railway line
LENGTHMEN > LENGTHMAN
LENGTHS > LENGTH
LENGTHY adj very long or tiresome
LENIENCE > LENIENT
LENIENCES > LENIENT
LENIENCY > LENIENT
LENIENT adj tolerant, not strict or severe ▷ n lenient person
LENIENTLY > LENIENT
LENIENTS > LENIENT
LENIFIED > LENIFY
LENIFIES > LENIFY
LENIFY vb make lenient
LENIFYING > LENIFY
LENIS adj (of a consonant) pronounced with little muscular tension ▷ n consonant pronounced like this
LENITE vb undergo lenition
LENITED > LENITE
LENITES > LENITE
LENITIES > LENITY
LENITING > LENITE
LENITION n weakening of consonant sound
LENITIONS > LENITION
LENITIVE adj soothing or alleviating of pain or distress ▷ n lenitive drug
LENITIVES > LENITIVE
LENITY n mercy or clemency
LENO n (in textiles) a weave in which the warp yarns are twisted together in pairs between the weft or filling yarns
LENOS > LENO
LENS n piece of glass or similar material with one or both sides curved, used to bring together or spread light rays in cameras, spectacles, telescopes, etc
LENSE same as > LENS
LENSED adj incorporating a lens
LENSES > LENS
LENSING n materials which colour and diffuse light
LENSLESS > LENS
LENSMAN n camera operator
LENSMEN > LENSMAN
LENT > LEND
LENTANDO adv slowing down
LENTEN adj of or relating to Lent
LENTI > LENTO
LENTIC adj of, relating to, or inhabiting still water
LENTICEL n any of numerous pores in the stem of a woody plant
LENTICELS > LENTICEL
LENTICLE n lens-shaped layer of mineral or rock embedded in a matrix of different constitution
LENTICLES > LENTICLE
LENTICULE n small lentil
LENTIFORM adj shaped like a biconvex lens
LENTIGO technical name for a > FRECKLE
LENTIL n edible seed of a leguminous Asian plant
LENTILS > LENTIL
LENTISK n mastic tree
LENTISKS > LENTISK
LENTO adv slowly ▷ n movement or passage performed slowly
LENTOID adj lentiform ▷ n lentiform object
LENTOIDS > LENTOID
LENTOR n lethargy
LENTORS > LENTOR
LENTOS > LENTO
LENTOUS adj lethargic
LENVOY another word for > ENVOY
LENVOYS > LENVOY
LEONE n standard monetary unit of Sierra Leone, divided into 100 cents
LEONES > LEONE
LEONINE adj like a lion
LEOPARD n large spotted carnivorous animal of the cat family
LEOPARDS > LEOPARD
LEOTARD n tight-fitting garment covering the upper body, worn for dancing or exercise
LEOTARDED adj wearing a leotard
LEOTARDS > LEOTARD
LEP dialect word for > LEAP
LEPER n person suffering from leprosy
LEPERS > LEPER
LEPID adj amusing
LEPIDOTE adj covered with scales, scaly leaves, or spots ▷ n lepidote person, creature, or thing
LEPIDOTES > LEPIDOTE
LEPORID adj of, relating to, or belonging to the family of mammals that includes rabbits and hares ▷ n any animal belonging to this family
LEPORIDAE > LEPORID
LEPORIDS > LEPORID
LEPORINE adj of, relating to, or resembling a hare
LEPPED > LEP
LEPPING > LEP
LEPRA n leprosy
LEPRAS > LEPRA
LEPROSE adj having or denoting a whitish scurfy surface
LEPROSERY n hospital for leprosy sufferers

LEPROSIES > LEPROSY
LEPROSITY n state of being leprous
LEPROSY n disease attacking the nerves and skin, resulting in loss of feeling in the affected parts
LEPROTIC adj relating to leprosy
LEPROUS adj having leprosy
LEPROUSLY > LEPROUS
LEPS > LEP
LEPT > LEAP
LEPTA > LEPTON
LEPTIN n protein, produced by fat cells in the body, that acts on the brain to regulate the amount of additional fat laid down in the body
LEPTINS > LEPTIN
LEPTOME n tissue of plant conducting food
LEPTOMES > LEPTOME
LEPTON n any of a group of elementary particles with weak interactions
LEPTONIC > LEPTON
LEPTONS > LEPTON
LEPTOPHOS n type of pesticide
LEPTOSOME n person with a small bodily frame and a slender physique
LEPTOTENE n (in reproduction) early stage in cell division
LEQUEAR same as > LACUNAR
LEQUEARS > LEQUEAR
LERE same as > LEAR
LERED > LERE
LERES > LERE
LERING > LERE
LERNAEAN adj relating to Lerna
LERNEAN same as > LERNAEAN
LERP n crystallized honeydew
LERPS > LERP
LES short form of > LESBIAN
LESBIAN n homosexual woman ▷ adj of homosexual women
LESBIANS > LESBIAN
LESBIC adj relating to lesbians
LESBO n lesbian
LESBOS > LESBO
LESES > LES
LESION n structural change in an organ of the body caused by illness or injury ▷ vb cause lesions
LESIONED > LESION
LESIONING > LESION
LESIONS > LESION
LESPEDEZA n bush clover
LESS n smaller amount ▷ adj smaller in extent, degree, or duration ▷ pron smaller part or quantity ▷ adv smaller extent or degree ▷ prep after deducting, minus
LESSEE n person to whom a lease is granted

LESSEES > LESSEE
LESSEN vb make or become smaller or not as much
LESSENED > LESSEN
LESSENING > LESSEN
LESSENS > LESSEN
LESSER adj not as great in quantity, size, or worth
LESSES > LESS
LESSON n class or single period of instruction in a subject ▷ vb censure or punish
LESSONED > LESSON
LESSONING > LESSON
LESSONS > LESSON
LESSOR n person who grants a lease of property
LESSORS > LESSOR
LEST conj so as to prevent any possibility that ▷ vb listen
LESTED > LEST
LESTING > LEST
LESTS > LEST
LET n act of letting property ▷ vb obstruct
LETCH same as > LECH
LETCHED > LETCH
LETCHES > LETCH
LETCHING > LETCH
LETCHINGS > LETCH
LETDOWN n disappointment
LETDOWNS > LETDOWN
LETHAL adj deadly ▷ n weapon, etc capable of causing death
LETHALITY > LETHAL
LETHALLY > LETHAL
LETHALS > LETHAL
LETHARGIC > LETHARGY
LETHARGY n sluggishness or dullness
LETHE n forgetfulness
LETHEAN > LETHE
LETHEE n life-blood
LETHEES > LETHEE
LETHES > LETHE
LETHIED adj forgetful
LETS > LET
LETTABLE > LET
LETTED > LET
LETTER n written message, usu sent by post ▷ vb inscribe letters on
LETTERBOX n slot through which letters are delivered into a building
LETTERED adj learned
LETTERER > LETTER
LETTERERS > LETTER
LETTERING n act, art, or technique of inscribing letters on to something
LETTERMAN n successful college sportsman
LETTERMEN > LETTERMAN
LETTERN another word for > LECTERN
LETTERNS > LETTERN
LETTERS pl n literary knowledge or ability
LETTERSET n method of rotary printing in which ink is transferred from raised surfaces to paper via a rubber-covered cylinder

LETTING > LET
LETTINGS > LET
LETTRE n letter
LETTRES > LETTRE
LETTUCE n plant with large green leaves used in salads
LETTUCES > LETTUCE
LETUP n lessening or abatement
LETUPS > LETUP
LEU n standard monetary unit of Romania and Moldova, divided into 100 bani
LEUCAEMIA same as > LEUKAEMIA
LEUCAEMIC > LEUCAEMIA
LEUCEMIA same as > LEUKAEMIA
LEUCEMIAS > LEUCEMIA
LEUCEMIC > LEUCEMIA
LEUCH > LAUCH
LEUCHEN > LAUCH
LEUCIN same as > LEUCINE
LEUCINE n essential amino acid found in many proteins
LEUCINES > LEUCINE
LEUCINS > LEUCIN
LEUCITE n grey or white mineral consisting of potassium aluminium silicate
LEUCITES > LEUCITE
LEUCITIC > LEUCITE
LEUCO as in leuco base colourless compound formed by reducing a dye
LEUCOCYTE n white blood cell
LEUCOMA n white opaque scar of the cornea
LEUCOMAS > LEUCOMA
LEUCOSIN n albumin in cereal grains
LEUCOSINS > LEUCOSIN
LEUCOTOME n needle used in leucotomy
LEUCOTOMY n surgical operation of cutting some of the nerve fibres in the frontal lobes of the brain
LEUD Scots word for > BREADTH
LEUDES > LEUD
LEUDS > LEUD
LEUGH > LAUCH
LEUGHEN > LAUCH
LEUKAEMIA n disease caused by uncontrolled overproduction of white blood cells
LEUKEMIA same as > LEUKAEMIA
LEUKEMIAS > LEUKEMIA
LEUKEMIC > LEUKEMIA
LEUKEMICS > LEUKEMIA
LEUKEMOID adj resembling leukaemia
LEUKOCYTE same as > LEUCOCYTE
LEUKOMA same as > LEUCOMA
LEUKOMAS > LEUKOMA
LEUKON n white blood cell count
LEUKONS > LEUKON

LEUKOSES > LEUKOSIS
LEUKOSIS n abnormal growth of white blood cells
LEUKOTIC > LEUKOSIS
LEUKOTOMY n lobotomy
LEV n standard monetary unit of Bulgaria, divided into 100 stotinki
LEVA > LEV
LEVANT n type of leather made from the skins of goats, sheep, or seals ▷ vb bolt or abscond, esp to avoid paying debts
LEVANTED > LEVANT
LEVANTER n easterly wind in the W Mediterranean area, esp in the late summer
LEVANTERS > LEVANTER
LEVANTINE n cloth of twilled silk
LEVANTING > LEVANT
LEVANTS > LEVANT
LEVATOR n any of various muscles that raise a part of the body
LEVATORES > LEVATOR
LEVATORS > LEVATOR
LEVE adj darling ▷ adv gladly
LEVEE n natural or artificial river embankment ▷ vb go to the reception of
LEVEED > LEVEE
LEVEEING > LEVEE
LEVEES > LEVEE
LEVEL adj horizontal ▷ vb make even or horizontal ▷ n horizontal line or surface
LEVELED > LEVEL
LEVELER same as > LEVELLER
LEVELERS > LEVELER
LEVELING > LEVEL
LEVELLED > LEVEL
LEVELLER n person or thing that levels
LEVELLERS > LEVELLER
LEVELLEST > LEVEL
LEVELLING > LEVEL
LEVELLY > LEVEL
LEVELNESS > LEVEL
LEVELS > LEVEL
LEVER n handle used to operate machinery ▷ vb prise or move with a lever
LEVERAGE n action or power of a lever ▷ vb borrow capital required
LEVERAGED > LEVERAGE
LEVERAGES > LEVERAGE
LEVERED > LEVER
LEVERET n young hare
LEVERETS > LEVERET
LEVERING > LEVER
LEVERS > LEVER
LEVIABLE adj (of taxes, tariffs, etc) liable to be levied
LEVIATHAN n sea monster
LEVIED > LEVY
LEVIER > LEVY
LEVIERS > LEVY
LEVIES > LEVY
LEVIGABLE > LEVIGATE
LEVIGATE vb grind into a

fine powder or a smooth paste ▷ *adj* having a smooth polished surface
LEVIGATED > LEVIGATE
LEVIGATES > LEVIGATE
LEVIGATOR > LEVIGATE
LEVIN *archaic word for* > LIGHTNING
LEVINS > LEVIN
LEVIRATE *n* practice, required by Old Testament law, of marrying the widow of one's brother
LEVIRATES > LEVIRATE
LEVIRATIC > LEVIRATE
LEVIS *n* jeans
LEVITATE *vb* rise or cause to rise into the air
LEVITATED > LEVITATE
LEVITATES > LEVITATE
LEVITATOR > LEVITATE
LEVITE *n* Christian clergyman
LEVITES > LEVITE
LEVITIC > LEVITE
LEVITICAL > LEVITE
LEVITIES > LEVITY
LEVITY *n* inclination to make a joke of serious matters
LEVO *adj* anticlockwise
LEVODOPA *n* substance occurring naturally in the body and used to treat Parkinson's disease
LEVODOPAS > LEVODOPA
LEVOGYRE *n* counterclockwise spiral
LEVULIN *n* substance obtained from certain bulbs
LEVULINS > LEVULIN
LEVULOSE *n* fructose
LEVULOSES > LEVULOSE
LEVY *vb* impose and collect (a tax) ▷ *n* imposition or collection of taxes
LEVYING > LEVY
LEW *adj* tepid
LEWD *adj* lustful or indecent
LEWDER > LEWD
LEWDEST > LEWD
LEWDLY > LEWD
LEWDNESS > LEWD
LEWDSBIES > LEWDSBY
LEWDSBY *another word for* > LEWDSTER
LEWDSTER *n* lewd person
LEWDSTERS > LEWDSTER
LEWIS *n* lifting device for heavy stone or concrete blocks
LEWISES > LEWIS
LEWISIA *n* type of herb
LEWISIAS > LEWISIA
LEWISITE *n* colourless oily poisonous liquid
LEWISITES > LEWISITE
LEWISSON *same as* > LEWIS
LEWISSONS > LEWISSON
LEX *n* system or body of laws
LEXEME *n* minimal meaningful unit of language, the meaning of which cannot be understood from that of its

component morphemes
LEXEMES > LEXEME
LEXEMIC > LEXEME
LEXES > LEX
LEXICA > LEXICON
LEXICAL *adj* relating to the vocabulary of a language
LEXICALLY > LEXICAL
LEXICON *n* dictionary
LEXICONS > LEXICON
LEXIGRAM *n* figure or symbol that represents a word
LEXIGRAMS > LEXIGRAM
LEXIS *n* totality of vocabulary items in a language, including all forms having lexical meaning or grammatical function
LEXISES > LEXIS
LEY *n* land temporarily under grass
LEYLANDI *same as* > LEYLANDII
LEYLANDII *n* type of fast-growing cypress tree
LEYLANDIS > LEYLANDI
LEYS > LEY
LEZ *short form of* > LESBIAN
LEZES > LEZ
LEZZ *short form of* > LESBIAN
LEZZA *same as* > LEZZIE
LEZZAS > LEZZA
LEZZES > LEZZ
LEZZIE *n* lesbian
LEZZIES > LEZZIE
LEZZY *short form of* > LESBIAN
LI *n* Chinese measurement of distance
LIABILITY *n* hindrance or disadvantage
LIABLE *adj* legally obliged or responsible
LIAISE *vb* establish and maintain communication (with)
LIAISED > LIAISE
LIAISES > LIAISE
LIAISING > LIAISE
LIAISON *n* communication and contact between groups
LIAISONS > LIAISON
LIANA *n* climbing plant in tropical forests
LIANAS > LIANA
LIANE *same as* > LIANA
LIANES > LIANE
LIANG *n* Chinese unit of weight
LIANGS > LIANG
LIANOID > LIANA
LIAR *n* person who tells lies
LIARD *adj* grey ▷ *n* former small coin of various European countries
LIARDS > LIARD
LIARS > LIAR
LIART *Scots form of* > LIARD
LIAS *n* lowest series of rocks of the Jurassic system
LIASES > LIAS
LIATRIS *n* type of North American plant with small white flowers

LIATRISES > LIATRIS
LIB *n* informal, sometimes derogatory word for liberation ▷ *vb* geld
LIBANT *adj* touching lightly
LIBATE *vb* offer as gift to the gods
LIBATED > LIBATE
LIBATES > LIBATE
LIBATING > LIBATE
LIBATION *n* drink poured as an offering to the gods
LIBATIONS > LIBATION
LIBATORY > LIBATE
LIBBARD *another word for* > LEOPARD
LIBBARDS > LIBBARD
LIBBED > LIB
LIBBER *n* liberationist
LIBBERS > LIBBER
LIBBING > LIB
LIBECCHIO *same as* > LIBECCIO
LIBECCIO *n* strong westerly or southwesterly wind blowing onto the W coast of Corsica
LIBECCIOS > LIBECCIO
LIBEL *n* published statement falsely damaging a person's reputation ▷ *vb* falsely damage the reputation of (someone)
LIBELANT *same as* > LIBELLANT
LIBELANTS > LIBELANT
LIBELED > LIBEL
LIBELEE *same as* > LIBELLEE
LIBELEES > LIBELEE
LIBELER > LIBEL
LIBELERS > LIBEL
LIBELING > LIBEL
LIBELINGS > LIBEL
LIBELIST > LIBEL
LIBELISTS > LIBEL
LIBELLANT *n* party who brings an action in the ecclesiastical courts by presenting a libel
LIBELLED > LIBEL
LIBELLEE *n* person against whom a libel has been filed in an ecclesiastical court
LIBELLEES > LIBELLEE
LIBELLER > LIBEL
LIBELLERS > LIBEL
LIBELLING > LIBEL
LIBELLOUS > LIBEL
LIBELOUS > LIBEL
LIBELS > LIBEL
LIBER *n* tome or book
LIBERAL *adj* having social and political views that favour progress and reform ▷ *n* person who has liberal ideas or opinions
LIBERALLY > LIBERAL
LIBERALS > LIBERAL
LIBERATE *vb* set free
LIBERATED *adj* not bound by traditional sexual and social roles
LIBERATES > LIBERATE
LIBERATOR > LIBERATE
LIBERO *another name for* > SWEEPER

LIBEROS > LIBERO
LIBERS > LIBER
LIBERTIES > LIBERTY
LIBERTINE *n* morally dissolute person ▷ *adj* promiscuous and unscrupulous
LIBERTY *n* freedom
LIBIDINAL > LIBIDO
LIBIDO *n* psychic energy
LIBIDOS > LIBIDO
LIBKEN *n* lodging
LIBKENS > LIBKEN
LIBLAB *n* 19th century British liberal
LIBLABS > LIBLAB
LIBRA *n* ancient Roman unit of weight corresponding to 1 pound, but equal to about 12 ounces
LIBRAE > LIBRA
LIBRAIRE *n* bookseller
LIBRAIRES > LIBRAIRE
LIBRAIRIE *n* bookshop
LIBRARIAN *n* keeper of or worker in a library
LIBRARIES > LIBRARY
LIBRARY *n* room or building where books are kept
LIBRAS > LIBRA
LIBRATE *vb* oscillate or waver
LIBRATED > LIBRATE
LIBRATES > LIBRATE
LIBRATING > LIBRATE
LIBRATION *n* act or an instance of oscillating
LIBRATORY > LIBRATE
LIBRETTI > LIBRETTO
LIBRETTO *n* words of an opera
LIBRETTOS > LIBRETTO
LIBRI > LIBER
LIBRIFORM *adj* (of a fibre of woody tissue) elongated and having a pitted thickened cell wall
LIBS > LIB
LICE > LOUSE
LICENCE *n* document giving official permission to do something ▷ *vb* (in the US) give permission to
LICENCED > LICENCE
LICENCEE *same as* > LICENSEE
LICENCEES > LICENCEE
LICENCER > LICENCE
LICENCERS > LICENCE
LICENCES > LICENCE
LICENCING > LICENCE
LICENSE *vb* grant or give a licence for
LICENSED > LICENSE
LICENSEE *n* holder of a licence, esp to sell alcohol
LICENSEES > LICENSEE
LICENSER > LICENSE
LICENSERS > LICENSE
LICENSES > LICENSE
LICENSING > LICENSE
LICENSOR > LICENSE
LICENSORS > LICENSE
LICENSURE *n* act of conferring licence
LICENTE *adj* permitted;

allowed
LICH n dead body
LICHANOS n note played using forefinger
LICHEE *same as* > LITCHI
LICHEES > LICHEE
LICHEN n small flowerless plant forming a crust on rocks, trees, etc ▷ vb cover with lichen
LICHENED > LICHEN
LICHENIN n complex polysaccharide occurring in certain species of moss
LICHENING > LICHEN
LICHENINS > LICHENIN
LICHENISM n type of fungus
LICHENIST n person who studies lichens
LICHENOID > LICHEN
LICHENOSE > LICHEN
LICHENOUS > LICHEN
LICHENS > LICHEN
LICHES > LICH
LICHGATE n roofed gate to a churchyard
LICHGATES > LICHGATE
LICHI *same as* > LITCHI
LICHIS > LICHI
LICHT *Scot word for* > LIGHT
LICHTED > LICHT
LICHTER > LICHT
LICHTEST > LICHT
LICHTING > LICHT
LICHTLIED > LICHTLY
LICHTLIES > LICHTLY
LICHTLY vb treat discourteously
LICHTS > LICHT
LICHWAKE n night vigil over a dead body
LICHWAKES > LICHWAKE
LICHWAY n path used to carry coffin into church
LICHWAYS > LICHWAY
LICIT adj lawful, permitted
LICITLY > LICIT
LICITNESS > LICIT
LICK vb pass the tongue over ▷ n licking
LICKED > LICK
LICKER > LICK
LICKERISH adj lecherous or lustful
LICKERS > LICK
LICKING n beating
LICKINGS > LICKING
LICKPENNY n something that uses up large amounts of money
LICKS > LICK
LICKSPIT n flattering or servile person
LICKSPITS > LICKSPIT
LICORICE *same as* > LIQUORICE
LICORICES > LICORICE
LICTOR n one of a group of ancient Roman officials
LICTORIAN > LICTOR
LICTORS > LICTOR
LID n movable cover
LIDAR n radar-type instrument
LIDARS > LIDAR
LIDDED > LID
LIDDING n lids

LIDGER *variant form of* > LEDGER
LIDGERS > LEDGER
LIDLESS adj having no lid or top
LIDO n open-air centre for swimming and water sports
LIDOCAINE n powerful local anaesthetic administered by injection
LIDOS > LIDO
LIDS > LID
LIE vb make a deliberately false statement ▷ n deliberate falsehood
LIED n setting for solo voice and piano of a poem
LIEDER > LIED
LIEF adv gladly ▷ adj ready ▷ n beloved person
LIEFER > LIEF
LIEFEST > LIEF
LIEFLY > LIEF
LIEFS > LIEF
LIEGE adj bound to give or receive feudal service ▷ n lord
LIEGEDOM > LIEGE
LIEGEDOMS > LIEGE
LIEGELESS > LIEGE
LIEGEMAN n (formerly) the subject of a sovereign or feudal lord
LIEGEMEN > LIEGEMAN
LIEGER *same as* > LEDGER
LIEGERS > LIEGER
LIEGES > LIEGE
LIEN n right to hold another's property until a debt is paid
LIENABLE adj that can be subject of a lien
LIENAL adj of or relating to the spleen
LIENS > LIEN
LIENTERIC > LIENTERY
LIENTERY n passage of undigested food in the faeces
LIER n person who lies down
LIERNE n short secondary rib that connects the intersections of the primary ribs, esp as used in Gothic vaulting
LIERNES > LIERNE
LIERS > LIER
LIES > LIE
LIEU n stead
LIEUS > LIEU
LIEVE *same as* > LEVE
LIEVER > LIEVE
LIEVEST > LIEVE
LIFE n state of living beings, characterized by growth, reproduction, and response to stimuli
LIFEBELT n ring filled with air, used to keep a person afloat when in danger of drowning
LIFEBELTS > LIFEBELT
LIFEBLOOD n blood vital to life
LIFEBOAT n boat used for

rescuing people at sea
LIFEBOATS > LIFEBOAT
LIFEBUOY n any of various kinds of buoyant device for keeping people afloat
LIFEBUOYS > LIFEBUOY
LIFECARE n care of person's health and welfare
LIFECARES > LIFECARE
LIFEFUL adj full of life
LIFEGUARD n person who saves people from drowning ▷ vb work as lifeguard
LIFEHOLD adj (of land) held while one is alive
LIFELESS adj dead
LIFELIKE adj closely resembling or representing life
LIFELINE n means of contact or support
LIFELINES > LIFELINE
LIFELONG adj lasting all of a person's life
LIFER n prisoner sentenced to imprisonment for life
LIFERS > LIFER
LIFES *as in* still lifes paintings or drawings of inanimate objects
LIFESAVER n saver of a person's life
LIFESOME adj full of life
LIFESPAN n period of time during which a person or animal may be expected to live
LIFESPANS > LIFESPAN
LIFESTYLE n particular attitudes, habits, etc ▷ adj suggestive of a fashionable or desirable lifestyle
LIFETIME n length of time a person is alive
LIFETIMES > LIFETIME
LIFEWAY n way of life
LIFEWAYS > LIFEWAY
LIFEWORK n work to which a person has devoted their life
LIFEWORKS > LIFEWORK
LIFEWORLD n way individual experiences world
LIFT vb move upwards in position, status, volume, etc ▷ n cage raised and lowered in a vertical shaft to transport people or goods
LIFTABLE > LIFT
LIFTBACK n hatchback
LIFTBACKS > LIFTBACK
LIFTBOY n person who operates a lift, esp in large public or commercial buildings and hotels
LIFTBOYS > LIFTBOY
LIFTED > LIFT
LIFTER > LIFT
LIFTERS > LIFT
LIFTGATE n rear opening of hatchback
LIFTGATES > LIFTGATE
LIFTING > LIFT
LIFTMAN *same as* > LIFTBOY

LIFTMEN > LIFTMAN
LIFTOFF n moment a rocket leaves the ground ▷ vb (of a rocket) to leave its launch pad
LIFTOFFS > LIFTOFF
LIFTS > LIFT
LIFULL *obsolete form of* > LIFEFUL
LIG n (esp in the media) a function with free entertainment and refreshments ▷ vb attend such a function
LIGAMENT n band of tissue joining bones
LIGAMENTS > LIGAMENT
LIGAN *same as* > LAGAN
LIGAND n atom, molecule, radical, or ion forming a complex with a central atom
LIGANDS > LIGAND
LIGANS > LIGAN
LIGASE n any of a class of enzymes
LIGASES > LIGASE
LIGATE vb tie up or constrict (something) with a ligature
LIGATED > LIGATE
LIGATES > LIGATE
LIGATING > LIGATE
LIGATION > LIGATE
LIGATIONS > LIGATE
LIGATIVE > LIGATE
LIGATURE n link, bond, or tie ▷ vb bind with a ligature
LIGATURED > LIGATURE
LIGATURES > LIGATURE
LIGER n hybrid offspring of a female tiger and a male lion
LIGERS > LIGER
LIGGE *obsolete form of* > LIE
LIGGED > LIG
LIGGEN > LIG
LIGGER > LIG
LIGGERS > LIG
LIGGES > LIGGE
LIGGING > LIG
LIGGINGS > LIG
LIGHT n electromagnetic radiation by which things are visible ▷ adj bright ▷ vb ignite ▷ adv with little equipment or luggage
LIGHTBULB n glass bulb containing gas that emits light when a current is passed through it
LIGHTED > LIGHT
LIGHTEN vb make less dark
LIGHTENED > LIGHTEN
LIGHTENER > LIGHTEN
LIGHTENS > LIGHTEN
LIGHTER n device for lighting cigarettes etc ▷ vb convey in a type of flat-bottomed barge
LIGHTERED > LIGHTER
LIGHTERS > LIGHTER
LIGHTEST > LIGHT
LIGHTFACE n weight of type in printing
LIGHTFAST adj (of a dye)

unaffected by light
LIGHTFUL *adj* full of light
LIGHTING > LIGHT
LIGHTINGS > LIGHT
LIGHTISH > LIGHT
LIGHTLESS > LIGHT
LIGHTLIED > LIGHTLY
LIGHTLIES > LIGHTLY
LIGHTLY *adv* in a light way ▷ *vb* belittle
LIGHTNESS *n* quality of being light
LIGHTNING *n* visible discharge of electricity in the atmosphere ▷ *adj* fast and sudden
LIGHTS > LIGHT
LIGHTSHIP *n* moored ship used as a lighthouse
LIGHTSOME *adj* lighthearted
LIGHTWAVE *n* wave of light
LIGHTWOOD *n* Australian acacia
LIGNAGE *another word for* > LINEAGE
LIGNAGES > LIGNAGE
LIGNALOES *another name for* > EAGLEWOOD
LIGNAN *n* beneficial substance found in plants
LIGNANS > LIGNAN
LIGNE *n* unit of measurement
LIGNEOUS *adj* of or like wood
LIGNES > LIGNE
LIGNICOLE *adj* growing or living in wood
LIGNIFIED > LIGNIFY
LIGNIFIES > LIGNIFY
LIGNIFORM *adj* having the appearance of wood
LIGNIFY *vb* make or become woody as a result of the deposition of lignin in the cell walls
LIGNIN *n* complex polymer occurring in certain plant cell walls making the plant rigid
LIGNINS > LIGNIN
LIGNITE *n* woody textured rock used as fuel
LIGNITES > LIGNITE
LIGNITIC > LIGNITE
LIGNOSE *n* explosive compound
LIGNOSES > LIGNOSE
LIGNUM *n* wood
LIGNUMS > LIGNUM
LIGROIN *n* volatile fraction of petroleum that is used as a solvent
LIGROINE *same as* > LIGROIN
LIGROINES > LIGROINE
LIGROINS > LIGROIN
LIGS > LIG
LIGULA *same as* > LIGULE
LIGULAE > LIGULA
LIGULAR > LIGULA
LIGULAS > LIGULA
LIGULATE *adj* having the shape of a strap
LIGULATED *same as* > LIGULATE
LIGULE *n* membranous outgrowth at the junction

between the leaf blade and sheath in many grasses and sedges
LIGULES > LIGULE
LIGULOID > LIGULA
LIGURE *n* any of the 12 precious stones used in the breastplates of high priests
LIGURES > LIGURE
LIKABLE *adj* easy to like
LIKE *adj* similar ▷ *vb* find enjoyable ▷ *n* favourable feeling, desire, or preference
LIKEABLE *same as* > LIKABLE
LIKED > LIKE
LIKELIER > LIKELY
LIKELIEST > LIKELY
LIKELY *adj* tending or inclined ▷ *adv* probably
LIKEN *vb* compare
LIKENED > LIKEN
LIKENESS *n* resemblance
LIKENING > LIKEN
LIKENS > LIKEN
LIKER > LIKE
LIKERS > LIKE
LIKES > LIKE
LIKEST > LIKE
LIKEWAKE *same as* > LYKEWAKE
LIKEWAKES > LIKEWAKE
LIKEWALK *same as* > LYKEWAKE
LIKEWALKS > LIKEWALK
LIKEWISE *adv* similarly
LIKIN *n* historically, Chinese tax
LIKING *n* fondness
LIKINGS > LIKING
LIKINS > LIKIN
LIKUTA *n* (formerly) a coin used in Zaïre
LILAC *n* shrub with pale mauve or white flowers ▷ *adj* light-purple
LILACS > LILAC
LILANGENI *n* standard monetary unit of Swaziland, divided into 100 cents
LILIED *adj* decorated with lilies
LILIES > LILY
LILL *obsolete form of* > LOLL
LILLED > LILL
LILLING > LILL
LILLIPUT *adj* tiny ▷ *n* tiny person or being
LILLIPUTS > LILLIPUTIAN
LILLS > LILL
LILO *n* trademark for a type of inflatable plastic mattress
LILOS > LILO
LILT *n* pleasing musical quality in speaking ▷ *vb* speak with a lilt
LILTED > LILT
LILTING > LILT
LILTINGLY > LILT
LILTS > LILT
LILY *n* plant which grows from a bulb and has large, often white, flowers
LILYLIKE *adj* resembling a lily

LIMA *n* type of edible bean
LIMACEL *n* small shell inside some kinds of slug
LIMACELS > LIMACEL
LIMACEOUS *adj* relating to the slug
LIMACES > LIMAX
LIMACINE *adj* of, or relating to slugs, esp those of the genus *Limax*
LIMACON *n* heart-shaped curve
LIMACONS > LIMACON
LIMAIL *same as* > LEMEL
LIMAILS > LIMAIL
LIMAN *n* lagoon
LIMANS > LIMAN
LIMAS > LIMA
LIMATION *n* polishing
LIMATIONS > LIMATION
LIMAX *n* slug
LIMB *n* arm, leg, or wing ▷ *vb* dismember
LIMBA *n* type of African tree
LIMBAS > LIMBA
LIMBATE *adj* having an edge or border of a different colour from the rest
LIMBEC *obsolete form of* > ALEMBIC
LIMBECK *obsolete form of* > ALEMBIC
LIMBECKS > LIMBECK
LIMBECS > LIMBEC
LIMBED > LIMB
LIMBER *vb* loosen stiff muscles by exercising ▷ *adj* pliant or supple ▷ *n* part of a gun carriage, consisting of an axle, pole, and two wheels
LIMBERED > LIMBER
LIMBERER > LIMBER
LIMBEREST > LIMBER
LIMBERING > LIMBER
LIMBERLY > LIMBER
LIMBERS > LIMBER
LIMBI > LIMBUS
LIMBIC > LIMBUS
LIMBIER > LIMBY
LIMBIEST > LIMBY
LIMBING > LIMB
LIMBLESS > LIMB
LIMBMEAL *adv* piece by piece
LIMBO *n* supposed region intermediate between Heaven and Hell for the unbaptized
LIMBOS > LIMBO
LIMBOUS *adj* with overlapping edges
LIMBS > LIMB
LIMBUS *n* border
LIMBUSES > LIMBUS
LIMBY *adj* with long legs, stem, branches, etc
LIME *n* calcium compound used as a fertilizer or in making cement ▷ *vb* spread a calcium compound upon (land) ▷ *adj* having the flavour of lime fruit
LIMEADE *n* drink made from sweetened lime juice and plain or carbonated water

LIMEADES > LIMEADE
LIMED > LIME
LIMEKILN *n* kiln in which calcium carbonate is burned to produce quicklime
LIMEKILNS > LIMEKILN
LIMELESS > LIME
LIMELIGHT *n* glare of publicity ▷ *vb* illuminate with limelight
LIMELIT > LIMELIGHT
LIMEN *another term for* > THRESHOLD
LIMENS > LIMEN
LIMEPIT *n* pit containing lime in which hides are placed to remove the hair
LIMEPITS > LIMEPIT
LIMERICK *n* humorous verse of five lines
LIMERICKS > LIMERICK
LIMES *n* fortified boundary of the Roman Empire
LIMESCALE *n* flaky deposit left in containers such as kettles by the action of heat on water containing calcium salts
LIMESTONE *n* sedimentary rock used in building
LIMEWASH *n* mixture of lime and water used to whitewash walls, ceilings, etc
LIMEWATER *n* clear colourless solution of calcium hydroxide in water
LIMEY *n* British person ▷ *adj* British
LIMEYS > LIMEY
LIMIER > LIMY
LIMIEST > LIMY
LIMINA > LIMEN
LIMINAL *adj* relating to the point (or threshold) beyond which a sensation becomes too faint to be experienced
LIMINESS > LIMY
LIMING > LIME
LIMINGS > LIME
LIMIT *n* ultimate extent, degree, or amount of something ▷ *vb* restrict or confine
LIMITABLE > LIMIT
LIMITARY *adj* of, involving, or serving as a limit
LIMITED *adj* having a limit ▷ *n* limited train, bus, etc
LIMITEDLY > LIMITED
LIMITEDS > LIMITED
LIMITER *n* electronic circuit that produces an output signal whose positive or negative amplitude, or both, is limited to some predetermined value above which the peaks become flattened
LIMITERS > LIMITER
LIMITES > LIMES
LIMITING > LIMIT
LIMITINGS > LIMIT
LIMITLESS > LIMIT
LIMITS > LIMIT
LIMMA *n* semitone

LIMMAS > LIMMA
LIMMER n scoundrel
LIMMERS > LIMMER
LIMN vb represent in drawing or painting
LIMNAEID n type of snail
LIMNAEIDS > LIMNAEID
LIMNED > LIMN
LIMNER > LIMN
LIMNERS > LIMN
LIMNETIC adj of, relating to, or inhabiting the open water of lakes down to the depth of light penetration
LIMNIC adj relating to lakes
LIMNING > LIMN
LIMNOLOGY n study of bodies of fresh water with reference to their plant and animal life, physical properties, geographical features, etc
LIMNS > LIMN
LIMO short for > LIMOUSINE
LIMONENE n liquid optically active terpene with a lemon-like odour
LIMONENES > LIMONENE
LIMONITE n common brown, black, or yellow amorphous secondary mineral
LIMONITES > LIMONITE
LIMONITIC > LIMONITE
LIMOS > LIMO
LIMOSES > LIMOSIS
LIMOSIS n excessive hunger
LIMOUS adj muddy
LIMOUSINE n large luxurious car
LIMP vb walk with an uneven step ▷ n limping walk ▷ adj without firmness or stiffness
LIMPA n type of rye bread
LIMPAS > LIMPA
LIMPED > LIMP
LIMPER > LIMP
LIMPERS > LIMP
LIMPEST > LIMP
LIMPET n shellfish which sticks tightly to rocks ▷ adj denoting certain weapons that are magnetically attached to their targets and resist removal
LIMPETS > LIMPET
LIMPID adj clear or transparent
LIMPIDITY > LIMPID
LIMPIDLY > LIMPID
LIMPING > LIMP
LIMPINGLY > LIMP
LIMPINGS > LIMP
LIMPKIN n rail-like wading bird
LIMPKINS > LIMPKIN
LIMPLY > LIMP
LIMPNESS > LIMP
LIMPS > LIMP
LIMPSEY same as > LIMPSY
LIMPSIER > LIMPSY
LIMPSIEST > LIMPSY
LIMPSY adj limp
LIMULI > LIMULUS
LIMULOID n type of crab

LIMULOIDS > LIMULOID
LIMULUS n any horseshoe crab of the genus Limulus
LIMULUSES > LIMULUS
LIMY adj of, like, or smeared with birdlime
LIN vb cease
LINABLE > LINE
LINAC n linear accelerator
LINACS > LINAC
LINAGE n number of lines in written or printed matter
LINAGES > LINAGE
LINALOL same as > LINALOOL
LINALOLS > LINALOL
LINALOOL n optically active colourless fragrant liquid
LINALOOLS > LINALOOL
LINCH n ledge
LINCHES > LINCH
LINCHET another word for > LINCH
LINCHETS > LINCHET
LINCHPIN n pin to hold a wheel on its axle
LINCHPINS > LINCHPIN
LINCRUSTA n type of wallpaper having a hard embossed surface
LINCTURE n medicine taken by licking
LINCTURES > LINCTURE
LINCTUS n syrupy cough medicine
LINCTUSES > LINCTUS
LIND variant of > LINDEN
LINDANE n white poisonous crystalline powder
LINDANES > LINDANE
LINDEN n large tree with heart-shaped leaves and fragrant yellowish flowers
LINDENS > LINDEN
LINDIES > LINDY
LINDS > LIND
LINDWORM n wingless serpent-like dragon
LINDWORMS > LINDWORM
LINDY n lively dance
LINE n long narrow mark ▷ vb mark with lines
LINEABLE > LINE
LINEAGE n descent from an ancestor
LINEAGES > LINEAGE
LINEAL adj in direct line of descent
LINEALITY > LINEAL
LINEALLY > LINEAL
LINEAMENT n facial feature
LINEAR adj of or in lines
LINEARISE same as > LINEARIZE
LINEARITY > LINEAR
LINEARIZE vb make linear
LINEARLY > LINEAR
LINEATE adj marked with lines
LINEATED same as > LINEATE
LINEATION n act of marking with lines
LINEBRED adj having an ancestor that is common to sire and dam
LINECUT n method of relief printing
LINECUTS > LINECUT

LINED > LINE
LINELESS > LINE
LINELIKE > LINE
LINEMAN same as > LINESMAN
LINEMEN > LINEMAN
LINEN n cloth or thread made from flax
LINENS > LINEN
LINENY > LINEN
LINEOLATE adj marked with very fine parallel lines
LINER n large passenger ship or aircraft
LINERLESS > LINER
LINERS > LINER
LINES > LINE
LINESMAN n (in some sports) an official who helps the referee or umpire
LINESMEN > LINESMAN
LINEUP n row or arrangement of people or things
LINEUPS > LINEUP
LINEY > LINE
LING n slender food fish
LINGA same as > LINGAM
LINGAM n (in Sanskrit grammar) the masculine gender
LINGAMS > LINGAM
LINGAS > LINGA
LINGBERRY same as > COWBERRY
LINGCOD n any scorpaenoid food fish of the family Ophiodontidae
LINGCODS > LINGCOD
LINGEL n strong shoemaker's thread
LINGELS > LINGEL
LINGER vb delay or prolong departure
LINGERED > LINGER
LINGERER > LINGER
LINGERERS > LINGER
LINGERIE n women's underwear or nightwear
LINGERIES > LINGERIE
LINGERING > LINGER
LINGERS > LINGER
LINGIER > LINGY
LINGIEST > LINGY
LINGLE same as > LINGEL
LINGLES > LINGLE
LINGO n foreign or unfamiliar language or jargon
LINGOES > LINGO
LINGOT n ingot
LINGOTS > LINGOT
LINGS > LING
LINGSTER n person able to communicate with aliens
LINGSTERS > LINGSTER
LINGUA n any tongue-like structure
LINGUAE > LINGUA
LINGUAL adj of the tongue ▷ n lingual consonant, such as Scots (r)
LINGUALLY > LINGUAL
LINGUALS > LINGUAL
LINGUAS > LINGUA
LINGUICA n Portuguese sausage

LINGUICAS > LINGUICA
LINGUINE n kind of pasta in the shape of thin flat strands
LINGUINES > LINGUINE
LINGUINI same as > LINGUINE
LINGUINIS > LINGUINI
LINGUISA same as > LINGUICA
LINGUISAS > LINGUISA
LINGUIST n person skilled in foreign languages
LINGUISTS > LINGUIST
LINGULA n small tongue
LINGULAE > LINGULA
LINGULAR > LINGULA
LINGULAS > LINGULA
LINGULATE adj shaped like a tongue
LINGY adj heather-covered
LINHAY n farm building with an open front
LINHAYS > LINHAY
LINIER > LINE
LINIEST > LINE
LINIMENT n medicated liquid rubbed on the skin to relieve pain or stiffness
LINIMENTS > LINIMENT
LININ n network of viscous material in the nucleus of a cell that connects the chromatin granules
LINING n layer of cloth attached to the inside of a garment etc
LININGS > LINING
LININS > LININ
LINISH vb polish metal
LINISHED > LINISH
LINISHER > LINISH
LINISHERS > LINISH
LINISHES > LINISH
LINISHING > LINISH
LINK n any of the rings forming a chain ▷ vb connect with or as if with links
LINKABLE > LINK
LINKAGE n act of linking or the state of being linked
LINKAGES > LINKAGE
LINKBOY n (formerly) a boy who carried a torch for pedestrians in dark streets
LINKBOYS > LINKBOY
LINKED > LINK
LINKER n person or thing that links
LINKERS > LINKER
LINKING > LINK
LINKMAN same as > LINKBOY
LINKMEN > LINKMAN
LINKS > LINK
LINKSLAND n land near sea used for golf
LINKSMAN same as > LINKBOY
LINKSMEN > LINKSMAN
LINKSTER n interpreter
LINKSTERS > LINKSTER
LINKUP n establishing of a connection or union between objects, groups, organizations, etc
LINKUPS > LINKUP

LINKWORK n something made up of links
LINKWORKS > LINKWORK
LINKY adj (of countryside) consisting of links
LINN n waterfall or a pool at the foot of it
LINNED > LIN
LINNET n songbird of the finch family
LINNETS > LINNET
LINNEY same as > LINHAY
LINNEYS > LINNEY
LINNIES > LINNY
LINNING > LIN
LINNS > LINN
LINNY same as > LINHAY
LINO same as > LINOLEUM
LINOCUT n design cut in relief in linoleum mounted on a block of wood
LINOCUTS > LINOCUT
LINOLEATE n ester or salt of linoleic acid
LINOLEIC as in linoleic acid colourless oily essential fatty acid found in linseed
LINOLENIC as in linolenic acid colourless unsaturated essential fatty acid
LINOLEUM n type of floor covering
LINOLEUMS > LINOLEUM
LINOS > LINO
LINOTYPE n line of metal type produced by machine ▷ vb set as line of type
LINOTYPED > LINOTYPE
LINOTYPER > LINOTYPE
LINOTYPES > LINOTYPE
LINS > LIN
LINSANG n any of several forest-dwelling viverrine mammals
LINSANGS > LINSANG
LINSEED n seed of the flax plant
LINSEEDS > LINSEED
LINSEY n type of cloth
LINSEYS > LINSEY
LINSTOCK n long staff holding a lighted match, formerly used to fire a cannon
LINSTOCKS > LINSTOCK
LINT n soft material for dressing a wound
LINTED adj having lint
LINTEL n horizontal beam at the top of a door or window
LINTELLED adj having a lintel
LINTELS > LINTEL
LINTER n machine for stripping the short fibres of ginned cotton seeds
LINTERS > LINTER
LINTIE Scot word for > LINNET
LINTIER > LINT
LINTIES > LINTIE
LINTIEST > LINT
LINTING n process of making lint
LINTLESS > LINT

LINTOL same as > LINTEL
LINTOLS > LINTEL
LINTS > LINT
LINTSEED same as > LINSEED
LINTSEEDS > LINTSEED
LINTSTOCK same as > LINSTOCK
LINTWHITE n linnet
LINTY > LINT
LINUM n any plant of the annual or perennial genus Linum
LINUMS > LINUM
LINURON n type of herbicide
LINURONS > LINURON
LINUX n nonproprietary computer operating system suitable for use on personal computers
LINUXES > LINUX
LINY > LINE
LION n large animal of the cat family, the male of which has a shaggy mane
LIONCEL n (heraldry) small lion
LIONCELLE same as > LIONCEL
LIONCELS > LIONCEL
LIONEL same as > LIONCEL
LIONELS > LIONEL
LIONESS n female lion
LIONESSES > LIONESS
LIONET n young lion
LIONETS > LIONET
LIONFISH n any of various scorpion fishes of the Pacific
> LIONHEARTEDNESS
LIONISE same as > LIONIZE
LIONISED > LIONISE
LIONISER > LIONISE
LIONISERS > LIONISE
LIONISES > LIONISE
LIONISING > LIONISE
LIONISM n lion-like appearance of leprosy
LIONISMS > LIONISM
LIONIZE vb treat as a celebrity
LIONIZED > LIONIZE
LIONIZER > LIONIZE
LIONIZERS > LIONIZE
LIONIZES > LIONIZE
LIONIZING > LIONIZE
LIONLIKE > LION
LIONLY > LION
LIONS > LION
LIP n either of the fleshy edges of the mouth ▷ vb touch with the lips
LIPA n monetary unit of Croatia worth one hundredth of a kuna
LIPAEMIA n abnormally large amount of fat in the blood
LIPAEMIAS > LIPAEMIA
LIPARITE n type of igneous rock
LIPARITES > LIPARITE
LIPASE n any of a group of enzymes that digest fat
LIPASES > LIPASE
LIPE n lurch
LIPECTOMY n surgical

operation to remove fat
LIPEMIA same as > LIPAEMIA
LIPEMIAS > LIPEMIA
LIPID n any of a group of organic compounds including fats, oils, waxes, and sterols
LIPIDE same as > LIPID
LIPIDES > LIPIDE
LIPIDIC > LIPID
LIPIDS > LIPID
LIPIN n family of nuclear proteins
LIPINS > LIPIN
LIPLESS > LIP
LIPLIKE > LIP
LIPO n liposuction
LIPOCYTE n fat-storing cell
LIPOCYTES > LIPOCYTE
LIPOGRAM n piece of writing in which all words containing a particular letter have been deliberately omitted
LIPOGRAMS > LIPOGRAM
LIPOIC as in lipoic acid sulphur-containing fatty acid
LIPOID n fatlike substance, such as wax
LIPOIDAL > LIPOID
LIPOIDS > LIPOID
LIPOLITIC same as > LIPOLYTIC
LIPOLYSES > LIPOLYSIS
LIPOLYSIS n hydrolysis of fats resulting in the production of carboxylic acids and glycerol
LIPOLYTIC adj fat-burning
LIPOMA n benign tumour composed of fatty tissue
LIPOMAS > LIPOMA
LIPOMATA > LIPOMA
LIPOPLAST n small particle in plant cytoplasm, esp that of seeds, in which fat is stored
LIPOS > LIPO
LIPOSOMAL > LIPOSOME
LIPOSOME n particle formed by lipids
LIPOSOMES > LIPOSOME
LIPOSUCK vb subject to liposuction
LIPOSUCKS > LIPOSUCK
LIPOTROPY n breaking down of fat in body
LIPPED > LIP
LIPPEN vb trust
LIPPENED > LIPPEN
LIPPENING > LIPPEN
LIPPENS > LIPPEN
LIPPER Scots word for > RIPPLE
LIPPERED > LIPPER
LIPPERING > LIPPER
LIPPERS > LIPPER
LIPPIE variant of > LIPPY
LIPPIER > LIPPY
LIPPIES > LIPPIE
LIPPIEST > LIPPY
LIPPINESS > LIPPY
LIPPING > LIP
LIPPINGS > LIP
LIPPITUDE n state of having bleary eyes

LIPPY adj insolent or cheeky ▷ n lipstick
LIPREAD vb follow what someone says by watching their lips
LIPREADER > LIPREAD
LIPREADS > LIPREAD
LIPS > LIP
LIPSTICK n cosmetic in stick form, for colouring the lips ▷ vb put lipstick on
LIPSTICKS > LIPSTICK
LIPURIA n presence of fat in the urine
LIPURIAS > LIPURIA
LIQUABLE adj that can be melted
LIQUATE vb separate one component of (an alloy, impure metal, or ore) by heating so that the more fusible part melts
LIQUATED > LIQUATE
LIQUATES > LIQUATE
LIQUATING > LIQUATE
LIQUATION > LIQUATE
LIQUEFIED > LIQUEFY
LIQUEFIER > LIQUEFY
LIQUEFIES > LIQUEFY
LIQUEFY vb make or become liquid
LIQUESCE vb become liquid
LIQUESCED > LIQUESCE
LIQUESCES > LIQUESCE
LIQUEUR n flavoured and sweetened alcoholic spirit ▷ vb flavour with liqueur
LIQUEURED > LIQUEUR
LIQUEURS > LIQUEUR
LIQUID n substance in a physical state which can change shape but not size ▷ adj of or being a liquid
LIQUIDATE vb pay (a debt)
LIQUIDISE same as > LIQUIDIZE
LIQUIDITY n state of being able to meet financial obligations
LIQUIDIZE vb make or become liquid
LIQUIDLY > LIQUID
LIQUIDS > LIQUID
LIQUIDUS n line on graph above which a substance is in liquid form
LIQUIFIED > LIQUIFY
LIQUIFIES > LIQUIFY
LIQUIFY same as > LIQUEFY
LIQUOR n alcoholic drink, esp spirits ▷ vb steep (malt) in warm water to form wort in brewing
LIQUORED > LIQUOR
LIQUORICE n black substance used in medicine and as a sweet
LIQUORING > LIQUOR
LIQUORISH same as > LICKERISH
LIQUORS > LIQUOR
LIRA n monetary unit of Turkey, Malta, and formerly of Italy
LIRAS > LIRA
LIRE > LIRA
LIRI > LIRA

LIRIOPE *n* grasslike plant
LIRIOPES > LIRIOPE
LIRIPIPE *n* tip of a graduate's hood
LIRIPIPES > LIRIPIPE
LIRIPOOP *same as* > LIRIPIPE
LIRIPOOPS > LIRIPOOP
LIRK *vb* wrinkle
LIRKED > LIRK
LIRKING > LIRK
LIRKS > LIRK
LIROT > LIRA
LIROTH > LIRA
LIS *n* fleur-de-lis
LISENTE > SENTE
LISK *Yorkshire dialect for* > GROIN
LISKS > LISK
LISLE *n* strong fine cotton thread or fabric
LISLES > LISLE
LISP *n* speech defect in which *s* and *z* are pronounced *th* ▷ *vb* speak or utter with a lisp
LISPED > LISP
LISPER > LISP
LISPERS > LISP
LISPING > LISP
LISPINGLY > LISP
LISPINGS > LISP
LISPOUND *n* unit of weight
LISPOUNDS > LISPOUND
LISPS > LISP
LISPUND *same as* > LISPOUND
LISPUNDS > LISPUND
LISSES > LIS
LISSOM *adj* supple, agile
LISSOME *same as* > LISSOM
LISSOMELY > LISSOM
LISSOMLY > LISSOM
LIST *n* item-by-item record of names or things, usu written one below another ▷ *vb* make a list of
LISTABLE > LIST
LISTED > LIST
LISTEE *n* person on list
LISTEES > LISTEE
LISTEL *another name for* > FILLET
LISTELS > LISTEL
LISTEN *vb* concentrate on hearing something
LISTENED > LISTEN
LISTENER > LISTEN
LISTENERS > LISTEN
LISTENING > LISTEN
LISTENS > LISTEN
LISTER *n* plough with a double mouldboard designed to throw soil to either side of a central furrow
LISTERIA *n* any rodlike Gram-positive bacterium of the genus *Listeria*
LISTERIAL > LISTERIA
LISTERIAS > LISTERIA
LISTERS > LISTER
LISTETH > LIST
LISTFUL *adj* paying attention
LISTING *n* list or an entry in a list
LISTINGS > LISTING

LISTLESS *adj* lacking interest or energy
LISTS *pl n* field of combat in a tournament
LISTSERV *n* service on the internet that provides an electronic mailing to subscribers with similar interests
LISTSERVS > LISTSERV
LIT *n* archaic word for dye or colouring
LITAI > LITAS
LITANIES > LITANY
LITANY *n* prayer with responses from the congregation
LITAS *n* standard monetary unit of Lithuania, divided into 100 centai
LITCHI *n* Chinese sapindaceous tree cultivated for its round edible fruits
LITCHIS > LITCHI
LITE *same as* > LIGHT
LITED > LIGHT
LITENESS > LITE
LITER *same as* > LITRE
LITERACY *n* ability to read and write
LITERAL *adj* according to the explicit meaning of a word or text, not figurative ▷ *n* misprint or misspelling in a text
LITERALLY *adv* in a literal manner
LITERALS > LITERAL
LITERARY *adj* of or knowledgeable about literature
LITERATE *adj* able to read and write ▷ *n* literate person
LITERATES > LITERATE
LITERATI *pl n* literary people
LITERATIM *adv* letter for letter
LITERATO > LITERATI
LITERATOR *n* professional writer
LITERATUS > LITERATI
LITEROSE *adj* affectedly literary
LITERS > LITER
LITES > LITE
LITH *n* limb or joint
LITHARGE *n* lead monoxide
LITHARGES > LITHARGE
LITHATE *n* salt of uric acid
LITHATES > LITHATE
LITHE *adj* flexible or supple, pliant ▷ *vb* listen
LITHED > LITHE
LITHELY > LITHE
LITHEMIA *n* gout
LITHEMIAS > LITHEMIA
LITHEMIC > LITHEMIA
LITHENESS > LITHE
LITHER > LITHE
LITHERLY *adj* crafty; cunning
LITHES > LITHE
LITHESOME *less common word for* > LISSOM

LITHEST > LITHE
LITHIA *n* lithium present in mineral waters as lithium salts
LITHIAS > LITHIA
LITHIASES > LITHIASIS
LITHIASIS *n* formation of a calculus
LITHIC *adj* of, relating to, or composed of stone
LITHIFIED > LITHIFY
LITHIFIES > LITHIFY
LITHIFY *vb* turn into rock
LITHING > LITHE
LITHISTID *n* type of sponge
LITHITE *n* part of cell with sensory element
LITHITES > LITHITE
LITHIUM *n* chemical element, the lightest known metal
LITHIUMS > LITHIUM
LITHO *n* lithography ▷ *vb* print using lithography
LITHOCYST *n* sac containing otoliths
LITHOED > LITHO
LITHOID *adj* resembling stone or rock
LITHOIDAL *same as* > LITHOID
LITHOING > LITHO
LITHOLOGY *n* physical characteristics of a rock
LITHOPONE *n* white pigment consisting of a mixture of zinc sulphide, zinc oxide, and barium sulphate
LITHOPS *n* fleshy-leaved plant
LITHOS > LITHO
LITHOSOL *n* type of azonal soil consisting chiefly of unweathered or partly weathered rock fragments
LITHOSOLS > LITHOSOL
LITHOTOME *n* instrument used in lithotomy operation
LITHOTOMY *n* surgical removal of a calculus, esp one in the urinary bladder
LITHS > LITH
LITIGABLE *adj* that may be the subject of litigation
LITIGANT *n* person involved in a lawsuit ▷ *adj* engaged in litigation
LITIGANTS > LITIGANT
LITIGATE *vb* bring or contest a law suit
LITIGATED > LITIGATE
LITIGATES > LITIGATE
LITIGATOR > LITIGATE
LITIGIOUS *adj* frequently going to law
LITING > LITE
LITMUS *n* blue dye turned red by acids and restored to blue by alkalis
LITMUSES > LITMUS
LITORAL *same as* > LITTORAL
LITOTES *n* ironical understatement used for effect

LITOTIC > LITOTES
LITRE *n* unit of liquid measure equal to 1000 cubic centimetres or 1.76 pints
LITRES > LITRE
LITS > LIT
LITTEN *adj* lighted
LITTER *n* untidy rubbish dropped in public places ▷ *vb* strew with litter
LITTERBAG *n* bag for putting rubbish in
LITTERBUG *n* person who tends to drop rubbish in public places
LITTERED > LITTER
LITTERER *n* one who litters
LITTERERS > LITTERER
LITTERING > LITTER
LITTERS > LITTER
LITTERY *adj* covered in litter
LITTLE *adj* small or smaller than average ▷ *adv* not a lot ▷ *n* small amount, extent, or duration
LITTLER > LITTLE
LITTLES > LITTLE
LITTLEST > LITTLE
LITTLIE *n* young child
LITTLIES > LITTLIE
LITTLIN *same as* > LITTLING
LITTLING *n* child
LITTLINGS > LITTLING
LITTLINS > LITTLIN
LITTLISH *adj* rather small
LITTORAL *adj* of or by the seashore ▷ *n* coastal district
LITTORALS > LITTORAL
LITU > LITAS
LITURGIC > LITURGY
LITURGICS *n* study of liturgies
LITURGIES > LITURGY
LITURGISM > LITURGIST
LITURGIST *n* student or composer of liturgical forms
LITURGY *n* prescribed form of public worship
LITUUS *n* type of curved trumpet
LITUUSES > LITUUS
LIVABLE *adj* tolerable or pleasant to live (with)
LIVE *vb* be alive ▷ *adj* living, alive ▷ *adv* in the form of a live performance
LIVEABLE *same as* > LIVABLE
LIVED > LIVE
LIVEDO *n* reddish discoloured patch on the skin
LIVEDOS > LIVEDO
LIVELIER > LIVELY
LIVELIEST > LIVELY
LIVELILY > LIVELY
LIVELOD *n* livelihood
LIVELODS > LIVELOD
LIVELONG *adj* long or seemingly long
LIVELONGS > LIVELONG
LIVELOOD *n* livelihood
LIVELOODS > LIVELOOD
LIVELY *adj* full of life or

vigour

LIVEN vb make or become lively

LIVENED > LIVEN

LIVENER > LIVEN

LIVENERS > LIVEN

LIVENESS n state of being alive

LIVENING > LIVEN

LIVENS > LIVEN

LIVER n person who lives in a specified way

LIVERED adj having liver

LIVERIED adj wearing livery

LIVERIES > LIVERY

LIVERING n process of liquid becoming lumpy

LIVERISH adj having a disorder of the liver

LIVERLEAF n woodland plant

LIVERLESS > LIVER

LIVERS > LIVER

LIVERWORT n plant resembling seaweed or leafy moss

LIVERY n distinctive dress, esp of a servant or servants ▷ adj of or resembling liver

LIVERYMAN n member of a livery company

LIVERYMEN > LIVERYMAN

LIVES > LIFE

LIVEST > LIVE

LIVESTOCK n farm animals

LIVETRAP n box constructed to trap an animal without injuring it

LIVETRAPS > LIVETRAP

LIVEWARE n programmers, systems analysts, operating staff, and other personnel working in a computer system

LIVEWARES > LIVEWARE

LIVEYER n (in Newfoundland) a full-time resident

LIVEYERE same as > LIVEYER

LIVEYERES > LIVEYERE

LIVEYERS > LIVEYER

LIVID adj angry or furious

LIVIDER > LIVID

LIVIDEST > LIVID

LIVIDITY n state of being livid

LIVIDLY > LIVID

LIVIDNESS > LIVID

LIVIER same as > LIVEYER

LIVIERS > LIVIER

LIVING adj possessing life, not dead or inanimate ▷ n condition of being alive

LIVINGLY > LIVING

LIVINGS > LIVING

LIVOR another word for > LIVIDITY

LIVORS > LIVOR

LIVRAISON n one of the numbers of a book published in parts

LIVRE n former French unit of money of account, equal to 1 pound of silver

LIVRES > LIVRE

LIVYER same as > LIVEYER

LIVYERS > LIVYER

LIXIVIA > LIXIVIUM

LIXIVIAL > LIXIVIATE

LIXIVIATE less common word for > LEACH

LIXIVIOUS > LIXIVIUM

LIXIVIUM n alkaline solution obtained by leaching wood ash with water

LIXIVIUMS > LIXIVIUM

LIZARD n four-footed reptile with a long body and tail

LIZARDS > LIZARD

LIZZIE as in busy lizzie plant with pink, white, or red flowers

LIZZIES > LIZZIE

LLAMA n woolly animal of the camel family used as a beast of burden in S America

LLAMAS > LLAMA

LLANERO n native of llanos

LLANEROS > LLANERO

LLANO n extensive grassy treeless plain, esp in South America

LLANOS > LLANO

LO interj look!

LOACH n carplike freshwater fish

LOACHES > LOACH

LOAD n burden or weight ▷ vb put a load on or into

LOADED adj (of a question) containing a hidden trap or implication

LOADEN vb load

LOADENED > LOADEN

LOADENING > LOADEN

LOADENS > LOADEN

LOADER n person who loads a gun or other firearm

LOADERS > LOADER

LOADING n load or burden

LOADINGS > LOADING

LOADS pl n lots or a lot

LOADSPACE n area in a motor vehicle where a load can be carried

LOADSTAR same as > LODESTAR

LOADSTARS > LOADSTAR

LOADSTONE same as > LODESTONE

LOAF n shaped mass of baked bread ▷ vb idle, loiter

LOAFED > LOAF

LOAFER n person who avoids work

LOAFERISH > LOAFER

LOAFERS > LOAFER

LOAFING > LOAF

LOAFINGS > LOAF

LOAFS > LOAF

LOAM n fertile soil ▷ vb cover, treat, or fill with loam

LOAMED > LOAM

LOAMIER > LOAM

LOAMIEST > LOAM

LOAMINESS > LOAM

LOAMING > LOAM

LOAMLESS > LOAM

LOAMS > LOAM

LOAMY > LOAM

LOAN n money lent at interest ▷ vb lend

LOANABLE > LOAN

LOANBACK n facility by which an individual can borrow from his or her pension fund ▷ vb make use of this facility

LOANBACKS > LOANBACK

LOANED > LOAN

LOANER > LOAN

LOANERS > LOAN

LOANING > LOAN

LOANINGS > LOANING

LOANS > LOAN

LOANSHIFT n adaptation of word from one language by another

LOANWORD n word adopted from one language into another

LOANWORDS > LOANWORD

LOAST > LOOSE

LOATH adj unwilling or reluctant (to)

LOATHE vb hate, be disgusted by

LOATHED > LOATHE

LOATHER > LOATHE

LOATHERS > LOATHE

LOATHES > LOATHE

LOATHEST > LOATH

LOATHFUL adj causing loathing

LOATHING n strong disgust

LOATHINGS > LOATHING

LOATHLY adv with reluctance

LOATHNESS > LOATH

LOATHSOME adj causing loathing

LOATHY obsolete form of > LOATHSOME

LOAVE vb make into the form of a loaf

LOAVED > LOAVE

LOAVES > LOAF

LOAVING > LOAVE

LOB n ball struck or thrown in a high arc ▷ vb strike or throw (a ball) in a high arc

LOBAR adj of or affecting a lobe

LOBATE adj with or like lobes

LOBATED same as > LOBATE

LOBATELY > LOBATE

LOBATION n division into lobes

LOBATIONS > LOBATION

LOBBED > LOB

LOBBER n one who lobs

LOBBERS > LOBBER

LOBBIED > LOBBY

LOBBIES > LOBBY

LOBBING > LOB

LOBBY n corridor into which rooms open ▷ vb try to influence (legislators) in the formulation of policy

LOBBYER > LOBBY

LOBBYERS > LOBBY

LOBBYGOW n errand boy

LOBBYGOWS > LOBBYGOW

LOBBYING > LOBBY

LOBBYINGS > LOBBY

LOBBYISM > LOBBYIST

LOBBYISMS > LOBBYIST

LOBBYIST n person who lobbies on behalf of a particular interest

LOBBYISTS > LOBBYIST

LOBE n rounded projection

LOBECTOMY n surgical removal of a lobe from any organ or gland in the body

LOBED > LOBE

LOBEFIN n type of fish

LOBEFINS > LOBEFIN

LOBELET n small lobe

LOBELETS > LOBELET

LOBELIA n garden plant with blue, red, or white flowers

LOBELIAS > LOBELIA

LOBELINE n crystalline alkaloid extracted from the seeds of the Indian tobacco plant

LOBELINES > LOBELINE

LOBES > LOBE

LOBI > LOBUS

LOBING n formation of lobes

LOBINGS > LOBING

LOBIPED adj with lobed toes

LOBLOLLY n southern US pine tree

LOBO n timber wolf

LOBOLA n (in African custom) price paid by a bridegroom's family to his bride's family

LOBOLAS > LOBOLA

LOBOLO same as > LOBOLA

LOBOLOS > LOBOLO

LOBOS > LOBO

LOBOSE another word for > LOBATE

LOBOTOMY n surgical incision into a lobe of the brain to treat mental disorders

LOBS > LOB

LOBSCOUSE n sailor's stew of meat, vegetables, and hardtack

LOBSTER n shellfish with a long tail and claws, which turns red when boiled ▷ vb fish for lobsters

LOBSTERED > LOBSTER

LOBSTERER n person who catches lobsters

LOBSTERS > LOBSTER

LOBSTICK n tree used as landmark

LOBSTICKS > LOBSTICK

LOBULAR > LOBULE

LOBULARLY > LOBULE

LOBULATE > LOBULE

LOBULATED > LOBULE

LOBULE n small lobe or a subdivision of a lobe

LOBULES > LOBULE

LOBULI > LOBULUS

LOBULOSE > LOBULUS

LOBULUS n small lobe

LOBUS n lobe

LOBWORM same as > LUGWORM

LOBWORMS > LOBWORM
LOCA > LOCUS
LOCAL *adj* of or existing in a particular place ▷ *n* person belonging to a particular district
LOCALE *n* scene of an event
LOCALES > LOCALE
LOCALISE *same as* > LOCALIZE
LOCALISED > LOCALISE
LOCALISER > LOCALISE
LOCALISES > LOCALISE
LOCALISM *n* pronunciation, phrase, etc, peculiar to a particular locality
LOCALISMS > LOCALISM
LOCALIST > LOCALISM
LOCALISTS > LOCALISM
LOCALITE *n* resident of an area
LOCALITES > LOCALITE
LOCALITY *n* neighbourhood or area
LOCALIZE *vb* restrict to a particular place
LOCALIZED > LOCALIZE
LOCALIZER > LOCALIZE
LOCALIZES > LOCALIZE
LOCALLY *adv* within a particular area or place
LOCALNESS > LOCAL
LOCALS > LOCAL
LOCATABLE > LOCATE
LOCATE *vb* discover the whereabouts of
LOCATED > LOCATE
LOCATER > LOCATE
LOCATERS > LOCATE
LOCATES > LOCATE
LOCATING > LOCATE
LOCATION *n* site or position
LOCATIONS > LOCATION
LOCATIVE *adj* (of a word or phrase) indicating place or direction ▷ *n* locative case
LOCATIVES > LOCATIVE
LOCATOR *n* part of index that indicates where to look for information
LOCATORS > LOCATOR
LOCELLATE *adj* split into secondary cells
LOCH *n* lake
LOCHAN *n* small inland loch
LOCHANS > LOCHAN
LOCHIA *n* vaginal discharge of cellular debris, mucus, and blood following childbirth
LOCHIAL > LOCHIA
LOCHS > LOCH
LOCI > LOCUS
LOCK *n* appliance for fastening a door, case, etc ▷ *vb* fasten or become fastened securely
LOCKABLE > LOCK
LOCKAGE *n* system of locks in a canal
LOCKAGES > LOCKAGE
LOCKAWAY *n* investment intended to be held for a relatively long time
LOCKAWAYS > LOCKAWAY
LOCKBOX *n* system of collecting funds from

companies by banks
LOCKBOXES > LOCKBOX
LOCKDOWN *n* device used to secure equipment, etc
LOCKDOWNS > LOCKDOWN
LOCKED > LOCK
LOCKER *n* small cupboard with a lock
LOCKERS > LOCKER
LOCKET *n* small hinged pendant for a portrait etc
LOCKETS > LOCKET
LOCKFAST *adj* securely fastened with a lock
LOCKFUL *n* sufficient to fill a canal lock
LOCKFULS > LOCKFUL
LOCKHOUSE *n* house of lock-keeper
LOCKING > LOCK
LOCKINGS > LOCK
LOCKJAW *n* tetanus
LOCKJAWS > LOCKJAW
LOCKMAKER *n* maker of locks
LOCKMAN *n* lock-keeper
LOCKMEN > LOCKMAN
LOCKNUT *n* supplementary nut screwed down upon a primary nut to prevent it from shaking loose
LOCKNUTS > LOCKNUT
LOCKOUT *n* closing of a workplace by an employer to force workers to accept terms
LOCKOUTS > LOCKOUT
LOCKPICK *another word for* > PICKLOCK
LOCKPICKS > LOCKPICK
LOCKRAM *n* type of linen cloth
LOCKRAMS > LOCKRAM
LOCKS > LOCK
LOCKSET *n* hardware used to lock door
LOCKSETS > LOCKSET
LOCKSMAN *same as* > LOCKMAN
LOCKSMEN > LOCKSMAN
LOCKSMITH *n* person who makes and mends locks
LOCKSTEP *n* method of marching in step as closely as possible
LOCKSTEPS > LOCKSTEP
LOCKUP *n* prison
LOCKUPS > LOCKUP
LOCO *n* locomotive ▷ *adj* insane ▷ *vb* poison with locoweed
LOCOED > LOCO
LOCOES > LOCO
LOCOFOCO *n* match
LOCOFOCOS > LOCOFOCO
LOCOING > LOCO
LOCOISM *n* disease of cattle, sheep, and horses caused by eating locoweed
LOCOISMS > LOCOISM
LOCOMAN *n* railwayman, esp an engine-driver
LOCOMEN > LOCOMAN
LOCOMOTE *vb* move from one place to another
LOCOMOTED > LOCOMOTE
LOCOMOTES > LOCOMOTE

LOCOMOTOR *adj* of or relating to locomotion
LOCOPLANT *another word for* > LOCOWEED
LOCOS > LOCO
LOCOWEED *n* any of several perennial leguminous plants
LOCOWEEDS > LOCOWEED
LOCULAR *adj* divided into compartments by septa
LOCULATE *same as* > LOCULAR
LOCULATED *same as* > LOCULATE
LOCULE *n* any of the chambers of an ovary or anther
LOCULED *adj* having locules
LOCULES > LOCULE
LOCULI > LOCULUS
LOCULUS *same as* > LOCULE
LOCUM *n* temporary stand-in for a doctor or clergyman
LOCUMS > LOCUM
LOCUPLETE *adj* well-stored
LOCUS *n* area or place where something happens
LOCUST *n* destructive insect that flies in swarms and eats crops ▷ *vb* ravage, as locusts
LOCUSTA *n* flower cluster unit in grasses
LOCUSTAE > LOCUSTA
LOCUSTAL > LOCUSTA
LOCUSTED > LOCUST
LOCUSTING > LOCUST
LOCUSTS > LOCUST
LOCUTION *n* manner or style of speech
LOCUTIONS > LOCUTION
LOCUTORY *adj* room intended for conversation
LOD *n* type of logarithm
LODE *n* vein of ore
LODEN *n* thick heavy waterproof woollen cloth with a short pile, used to make garments, esp coats
LODENS > LODEN
LODES > LODE
LODESMAN *n* pilot
LODESMEN > LODESMAN
LODESTAR *n* star used in navigation or astronomy as a point of reference
LODESTARS > LODESTAR
LODESTONE *n* magnetic iron ore
LODGE *n* gatekeeper's house ▷ *vb* live in another's house at a fixed charge
LODGEABLE > LODGE
LODGED > LODGE
LODGEMENT *same as* > LODGMENT
LODGEPOLE *n* type of pine tree
LODGER *n* person who pays rent in return for accommodation in someone else's home
LODGERS > LODGER
LODGES > LODGE
LODGING *n* temporary residence

LODGINGS *pl n* rented room or rooms in which to live, esp in another person's house
LODGMENT *n* act of lodging or the state of being lodged
LODGMENTS > LODGMENT
LODICULA *n* delicate scale in grass
LODICULAE > LODICULA
LODICULE *n* any of two or three minute scales at the base of the ovary in grass flowers that represent the corolla
LODICULES > LODICULE
LODS > LOD
LOERIE *same as* > LOURIE
LOERIES > LOERIE
LOESS *n* fine-grained soil, found mainly in river valleys, originally deposited by the wind
LOESSAL > LOESS
LOESSES > LOESS
LOESSIAL > LOESS
LOFT *n* space between the top storey and roof of a building ▷ *vb* strike, throw, or kick (a ball) high into the air
LOFTED > LOFT
LOFTER *n* type of golf club
LOFTERS > LOFTER
LOFTIER > LOFTY
LOFTIEST > LOFTY
LOFTILY > LOFTY
LOFTINESS > LOFTY
LOFTING > LOFT
LOFTLESS > LOFT
LOFTLIKE > LOFT
LOFTS > LOFT
LOFTSMAN *n* person who reproduces in actual size a draughtsman's design for a ship or an aircraft
LOFTSMEN > LOFTSMAN
LOFTY *adj* of great height
LOG *n* portion of a felled tree stripped of branches ▷ *vb* saw logs from a tree
LOGAN *another name for* > BOGAN
LOGANIA *n* type of Australian plant
LOGANIAS > LOGANIA
LOGANS > LOGAN
LOGAOEDIC *adj* of or relating to verse in which mixed metres are combined within a single line to give the effect of prose ▷ *n* line or verse of this kind
LOGARITHM *n* one of a series of arithmetical functions used to make certain calculations easier
LOGBOARD *n* board used for logging a ship's records
LOGBOARDS > LOGBOARD
LOGBOOK *n* book recording the details about a car or a ship's journeys
LOGBOOKS > LOGBOOK
LOGE *n* small enclosure or box in a theatre or opera

house
LOGES > LOGE
LOGGAT n small piece of wood
LOGGATS > LOGGAT
LOGGED > LOG
LOGGER n tractor or crane for handling logs
LOGGERS > LOGGER
LOGGETS n old-fashioned game played with sticks
LOGGIA n covered gallery at the side of a building
LOGGIAS > LOGGIA
LOGGIE > LOGGIA
LOGGIER > LOGGY
LOGGIEST > LOGGY
LOGGING > LOG
LOGGINGS > LOG
LOGGISH > LOG
LOGGY adj slow, sluggish, or listless
LOGIA > LOGION
LOGIC n philosophy of reasoning
LOGICAL adj of logic
LOGICALLY > LOGICAL
LOGICIAN n person who specializes in or is skilled at logic
LOGICIANS > LOGICIAN
LOGICISE same as > LOGICIZE
LOGICISED > LOGICISE
LOGICISES > LOGICISE
LOGICISM n philosophical theory that all of mathematics can be deduced from logic
LOGICISMS > LOGICISM
LOGICIST > LOGICISM
LOGICISTS > LOGICISM
LOGICIZE vb present reasons for or against
LOGICIZED > LOGICIZE
LOGICIZES > LOGICIZE
LOGICLESS > LOGIC
LOGICS > LOGIC
LOGIE n fire-place of a kiln
LOGIER > LOGY
LOGIES > LOGIE
LOGIEST > LOGY
LOGILY > LOGY
LOGIN n process by which a computer user logs on
LOGINESS > LOGY
LOGINS > LOGIN
LOGION n saying of Christ regarded as authentic
LOGIONS > LOGION
LOGISTIC n uninterpreted calculus or system of symbolic logic ▷ adj (of a curve) having a particular form of equation
LOGISTICS n detailed planning and organization of a large, esp military, operation
LOGJAM n blockage caused by the crowding together of a number of logs floating in a river ▷ vb cause a logjam
LOGJAMMED > LOGJAM
LOGJAMS > LOGJAM
LOGJUICE n poor quality

port wine
LOGJUICES > LOGJUICE
LOGLINE n synopsis of screenplay
LOGLINES > LOGLINE
LOGLOG n logarithm of a logarithm (in equations, etc)
LOGLOGS > LOGLOG
LOGNORMAL adj (maths) having a natural logarithm with normal distribution
LOGO same as > LOGOTYPE
LOGOFF n process by which a computer user logs out
LOGOFFS > LOGOFF
LOGOGRAM n single symbol representing an entire morpheme, word, or phrase
LOGOGRAMS > LOGOGRAM
LOGOGRAPH same as > LOGOGRAM
LOGOGRIPH n word puzzle, esp one based on recombination of the letters of a word
LOGOI > LOGOS
LOGOMACH n one who argues over words
LOGOMACHS > LOGOMACH
LOGOMACHY n argument about words or the meaning of words
LOGON variant of > LOGIN
LOGONS > LOGON
LOGOPEDIC adj of or relating to speech therapy
LOGOPHILE n one who loves words
LOGORRHEA n excessive or uncontrollable talkativeness
LOGOS n reason or the rational principle expressed in words and things, argument, or justification
LOGOTHETE n officer of Byzantine empire
LOGOTYPE n piece of type with several uncombined characters cast on it
LOGOTYPES > LOGOTYPE
LOGOTYPY > LOGOTYPE
LOGOUT variant of > LOGOFF
LOGOUTS > LOGOUT
LOGROLL vb use logrolling in order to procure the passage of (legislation)
LOGROLLED > LOGROLL
LOGROLLER > LOGROLL
LOGROLLS > LOGROLL
LOGS > LOG
LOGWAY another name for > GANGWAY
LOGWAYS > LOGWAY
LOGWOOD n leguminous tree of the Caribbean and Central America
LOGWOODS > LOGWOOD
LOGY adj dull or listless
LOHAN another word for > ARHAT
LOHANS > LOHAN
LOID vb open (a lock) using a celluloid strip
LOIDED > LOID

LOIDING > LOID
LOIDS > LOID
LOIN n part of the body between the ribs and the hips
LOINCLOTH n piece of cloth covering the loins only
LOINS pl n hips and the inner surface of the legs where they join the body
LOIPE n cross-country skiing track
LOIPEN > LOIPE
LOIR n large dormouse
LOIRS > LOIR
LOITER vb stand or wait aimlessly or idly
LOITERED > LOITER
LOITERER > LOITER
LOITERERS > LOITER
LOITERING > LOITER
LOITERS > LOITER
LOKE n track
LOKES > LOKE
LOKSHEN pl n noodles
LOLIGO n type of squid
LOLIGOS > LOLIGO
LOLIUM n type of grass
LOLIUMS > LOLIUM
LOLL vb lounge lazily ▷ n act or instance of lolling
LOLLED > LOLL
LOLLER > LOLL
LOLLERS > LOLL
LOLLIES > LOLLY
LOLLING > LOLL
LOLLINGLY > LOLL
LOLLIPOP n boiled sweet on a small wooden stick
LOLLIPOPS > LOLLIPOP
LOLLOP vb move clumsily
LOLLOPED > LOLLOP
LOLLOPING > LOLLOP
LOLLOPS > LOLLOP
LOLLOPY > LOLLOP
LOLLS > LOLL
LOLLY n lollipop or ice lolly
LOLLYGAG same as > LALLYGAG
LOLLYGAGS > LOLLYGAG
LOLLYPOP same as > LOLLIPOP
LOLLYPOPS > LOLLYPOP
LOLOG same as > LOGLOG
LOLOGS > LOLOG
LOMA n lobe
LOMAS > LOMA
LOMATA > LOMA
LOME vb cover with lome
LOMED > LOME
LOMEIN n Chinese dish
LOMEINS > LOMEIN
LOMENT n pod of certain leguminous plants
LOMENTA > LOMENTUM
LOMENTS > LOMENT
LOMENTUM same as > LOMENT
LOMENTUMS > LOMENTUM
LOMES > LOME
LOMING > LOME
LOMPISH another word for > LUMPISH
LONE adj solitary
LONELIER > LONELY
LONELIEST > LONELY
LONELILY > LONELY

LONELY adj sad because alone
LONENESS > LONE
LONER n person who prefers to be alone
LONERS > LONER
LONESOME adj lonely ▷ n own
LONESOMES > LONESOME
LONG adj having length, esp great length, in space or time ▷ adv for a certain time ▷ vb have a strong desire (for)
LONGA n long note
LONGAEVAL adj long-lived
LONGAN n sapindaceous tree of tropical and subtropical Asia
LONGANS > LONGAN
LONGAS > LONGA
LONGBOARD n type of surfboard
LONGBOAT n largest boat carried on a ship
LONGBOATS > LONGBOAT
LONGBOW n large powerful bow
LONGBOWS > LONGBOW
LONGCASE as in longcase clock grandfather clock
LONGCLOTH n fine plain-weave cotton cloth made in long strips
LONGE n rope used in training a horse ▷ vb train using a longe
LONGED > LONG
LONGEING > LONGE
LONGER n line of barrels on a ship
LONGERON n main longitudinal structural member of an aircraft
LONGERONS > LONGERON
LONGERS > LONGER
LONGES > LONGE
LONGEST > LONG
LONGEVAL another word for > LONGAEVAL
LONGEVITY n long life
LONGEVOUS > LONGEVITY
LONGHAIR n cat with long hair
LONGHAIRS > LONGHAIR
LONGHAND n ordinary writing, not shorthand or typing
LONGHANDS > LONGHAND
LONGHEAD n person with long head
LONGHEADS > LONGHEAD
LONGHORN n British breed of beef cattle with long curved horns
LONGHORNS > LONGHORN
LONGHOUSE n long communal dwelling of Native American peoples
LONGICORN n any beetle of the family Cerambycidae ▷ adj having or designating long antennae
LONGIES n long johns
LONGING n yearning ▷ adj having or showing desire
LONGINGLY > LONGING

LONGINGS > LONGING

LONGISH *adj* rather long

LONGITUDE *n* distance east or west from a standard meridian

LONGJUMP *n* jumping contest decided by length

LONGJUMPS > LONGJUMP

LONGLEAF *n* North American pine tree

LONGLINE *n* (tennis) straight stroke played down court

LONGLINES > LONGLINE

LONGLY > LONG

LONGNECK *n* US, Canadian and Australian word for a 330-ml beer bottle with a long narrow neck

LONGNECKS > LONGNECK

LONGNESS > LONG

LONGS *pl n* full-length trousers

LONGSHIP *n* narrow open boat with oars and a square sail, used by the Vikings

LONGSHIPS > LONGSHIP

LONGSHORE *adj* situated on, relating to, or along the shore

LONGSOME *adj* slow; boring

LONGSPUR *n* any of various Arctic and North American buntings

LONGSPURS > LONGSPUR

LONGTIME *adj* of long standing

LONGUEUR *n* period of boredom or dullness

LONGUEURS > LONGUEUR

LONGWALL *n* long face in coal mine

LONGWALLS > LONGWALL

LONGWAYS *adv* lengthways

LONGWISE *same as* > LONGWAYS

LONICERA *n* honeysuckle

LONICERAS > LONICERA

LOO *n* informal word meaning lavatory ▷ *vb* Scots word meaning love

LOOBIER > LOOBY

LOOBIES > LOOBY

LOOBIEST > LOOBY

LOOBILY > LOOBY

LOOBY *adj* foolish ▷ *n* foolish or stupid person

LOOED > LOO

LOOEY *n* lieutenant

LOOEYS > LOOEY

LOOF *n* part of ship's side

LOOFA *same as* > LOOFAH

LOOFAH *n* sponge made from the dried pod of a gourd

LOOFAHS > LOOFAH

LOOFAS > LOOFA

LOOFFUL *n* handful

LOOFFULS > LOOFFUL

LOOFS > LOOF

LOOIE *same as* > LOOEY

LOOIES > LOOIE

LOOING > LOO

LOOK *vb* direct the eyes or attention (towards) ▷ *n* instance of looking

LOOKALIKE *n* person who is the double of another

LOOKDOWN *n* way paper appears when looked at under reflected light

LOOKDOWNS > LOOKDOWN

LOOKED > LOOK

LOOKER *n* person who looks

LOOKERS > LOOKER

LOOKING > LOOK

LOOKISM *n* discrimination against a person on the grounds of physical appearance

LOOKISMS > LOOKISM

LOOKIST > LOOKISM

LOOKISTS > LOOKISM

LOOKOUT *n* act of watching for danger or for an opportunity ▷ *vb* be careful

LOOKOUTS > LOOKOUT

LOOKOVER *n* inspection, esp a brief one

LOOKOVERS > LOOKOVER

LOOKS > LOOK

LOOKSISM *same as* > LOOKISM

LOOKSISMS > LOOKSISM

LOOKUP *n* act of looking up information, esp on the internet

LOOKUPS > LOOKUP

LOOM *n* machine for weaving cloth ▷ *vb* appear dimly

LOOMED > LOOM

LOOMING > LOOM

LOOMS > LOOM

LOON *n* diving bird

LOONEY *same as* > LOONY

LOONEYS > LOONY

LOONIE *n* Canadian dollar coin with a loon bird on one of its faces

LOONIER > LOONY

LOONIES > LOONY

LOONIEST > LOONY

LOONILY > LOONY

LOONINESS > LOONY

LOONING *n* cry of the loon

LOONINGS > LOONING

LOONS > LOON

LOONY *adj* foolish or insane ▷ *n* foolish or insane person

LOOP *n* rounded shape made by a curved line or rope crossing itself ▷ *vb* form or fasten with a loop

LOOPED > LOOP

LOOPER *n* person or thing that loops or makes loops

LOOPERS > LOOPER

LOOPHOLE *n* means of evading a rule without breaking it ▷ *vb* provide with loopholes

LOOPHOLED > LOOPHOLE

LOOPHOLES > LOOPHOLE

LOOPIER > LOOPY

LOOPIEST > LOOPY

LOOPILY > LOOPY

LOOPINESS > LOOPY

LOOPING > LOOP

LOOPINGS > LOOP

LOOPS > LOOP

LOOPY *adj* slightly mad or crazy

LOOR > LIEF

LOORD *obsolete word for* > LOUT

LOORDS > LOORD

LOOS > LOO

LOOSE *adj* not tight, fastened, fixed, or tense ▷ *adv* in a loose manner ▷ *vb* free

LOOSEBOX *n* enclosed stall with a door in which an animal can be kept

LOOSED > LOOSE

LOOSELY > LOOSE

LOOSEN *vb* make loose

LOOSENED > LOOSEN

LOOSENER > LOOSEN

LOOSENERS > LOOSEN

LOOSENESS > LOOSE

LOOSENING > LOOSEN

LOOSENS > LOOSEN

LOOSER > LOOSE

LOOSES > LOOSE

LOOSEST > LOOSE

LOOSIE *n* informal word for loose forward

LOOSIES *pl n* cigarettes sold individually

LOOSING *n* celebration of one's 21st birthday

LOOSINGS > LOOSING

LOOT *vb* pillage ▷ *n* goods stolen during pillaging

LOOTED > LOOT

LOOTEN *Scots past form of* > LET

LOOTER > LOOT

LOOTERS > LOOT

LOOTING > LOOT

LOOTINGS > LOOT

LOOTS > LOOT

LOOVES > LOOF

LOP *vb* cut away (twigs and branches) ▷ *n* part or parts lopped off, as from a tree

LOPE *vb* run with long easy strides ▷ *n* loping stride

LOPED > LOPE

LOPER > LOPE

LOPERS > LOPE

LOPES > LOPE

LOPGRASS *n* smooth-bladed grass

LOPHODONT *adj* (of teeth) having elongated ridges

LOPING > LOPE

LOPOLITH *n* saucer- or lens-shaped body of intrusive igneous rock

LOPOLITHS > LOPOLITH

LOPPED > LOP

LOPPER *n* tool for lopping ▷ *vb* curdle

LOPPERED > LOPPER

LOPPERING > LOPPER

LOPPERS > LOPPER

LOPPIER > LOPPY

LOPPIES > LOPPY

LOPPIEST > LOPPY

LOPPING > LOP

LOPPINGS > LOP

LOPPY *adj* floppy ▷ *n* man employed to do maintenance tasks on a ranch

LOPS > LOP

LOPSIDED *adj* greater in height, weight, or size on one side

LOPSTICK *variant of* > LOBSTICK

LOPSTICKS > LOPSTICK

LOQUACITY *n* tendency to talk a great deal

LOQUAT *n* ornamental evergreen rosaceous tree

LOQUATS > LOQUAT

LOQUITUR *n* stage direction meaning *he or she speaks*

LOR *interj* exclamation of surprise or dismay

LORAL *adj* of part of side of bird's head

LORAN *n* radio navigation system operating over long distances

LORANS > LORAN

LORATE *adj* like a strap

LORAZEPAM *n* type of tranquillizer

LORCHA *n* junk-rigged vessel

LORCHAS > LORCHA

LORD *n* person with power over others, such as a monarch or master ▷ *vb* act in a superior manner

LORDED > LORD

LORDING *n* gentleman

LORDINGS > LORDING

LORDKIN *n* little lord

LORDKINS > LORDKIN

LORDLESS > LORD

LORDLIER > LORDLY

LORDLIEST > LORDLY

LORDLIKE > LORD

LORDLING *n* young lord

LORDLINGS > LORDLING

LORDLY *adj* imperious, proud ▷ *adv* in the manner of a lord

LORDOMA *same as* > LORDOSIS

LORDOMAS > LORDOMA

LORDOSES > LORDOSIS

LORDOSIS *n* forward curvature of the lumbar spine

LORDOTIC > LORDOSIS

LORDS > LORD

LORDSHIP *n* position or authority of a lord

LORDSHIPS > LORDSHIP

LORDY *interj* exclamation of surprise or dismay

LORE *n* body of traditions on a subject

LOREAL *adj* concerning or relating to lore

LOREL *another word for* > LOSEL

LORELS > LOREL

LORES > LORE

LORETTE *n* concubine

LORETTES > LORETTE

LORGNETTE *n* pair of spectacles mounted on a long handle

LORGNON *n* monocle or pair of spectacles

LORGNONS > LORGNON

LORIC > LORICA

LORICA *n* hard outer

covering of rotifers, ciliate protozoans, and similar organisms

LORICAE > LORICA

LORICATE > LORICA

LORICATED > LORICA

LORICATES > LORICA

LORICS > LORICA

LORIES > LORY

LORIKEET n small brightly coloured Australian parrot

LORIKEETS > LORIKEET

LORIMER n (formerly) a person who made bits, spurs, and other small metal objects

LORIMERS > LORIMER

LORINER same as > LORIMER

LORINERS > LORINER

LORING n teaching

LORINGS > LORING

LORIOT n golden oriole (bird)

LORIOTS > LORIOT

LORIS n any of several omnivorous nocturnal slow-moving prosimian primates

LORISES > LORIS

LORN adj forsaken or wretched

LORNNESS > LORN

LORRELL obsolete word for > LOSEL

LORRELLS > LORRELL

LORRIES > LORRY

LORRY n large vehicle for transporting loads by road

LORY n any of various small brightly coloured parrots of Australia and Indonesia

LOS n approval

LOSABLE > LOOSE

LOSE vb part with or come to be without

LOSED > LOSE

LOSEL n worthless person ▷ adj (of a person) worthless, useless, or wasteful

LOSELS > LOSEL

LOSEN > LOOSE

LOSER n person or thing that loses

LOSERS > LOSER

LOSES > LOOSE

LOSH interj lord

LOSING > LOSE

LOSINGLY > LOSE

LOSINGS pl n losses, esp money lost in gambling

LOSLYF n South African slang for a promiscuous female

LOSLYFS > LOSLYF

LOSS n losing

LOSSES > LOSS

LOSSIER > LOSSY

LOSSIEST > LOSSY

LOSSLESS > LOSS

LOSSMAKER n organization, industry, or enterprise that consistently fails to make a profit

LOSSY adj (of a dielectric material, transmission line, etc) designed to have a

high attenuation

LOST adj missing

LOSTNESS > LOST

LOT pron great number ▷ n collection of people or things ▷ vb draw lots for

LOTA n globular water container, usually of brass, used in India, Myanmar, etc

LOTAH same as > LOTA

LOTAHS > LOTAH

LOTAS > LOTA

LOTE another word for > LOTUS

LOTES > LOTE

LOTH same as > LOATH

LOTHARIO n rake, libertine, or seducer

LOTHARIOS > LOTHARIO

LOTHEFULL obsolete form of > LOATHFUL

LOTHER > LOTH

LOTHEST > LOTH

LOTHFULL obsolete form of > LOATHFUL

LOTHNESS > LOTH

LOTHSOME same as > LOATHSOME

LOTI n standard monetary unit of Lesotho, divided into 100 lisente

LOTIC adj of, relating to, or designating natural communities living in rapidly flowing water

LOTION n medical or cosmetic liquid for use on the skin

LOTIONS > LOTION

LOTO same as > LOTTO

LOTOS same as > LOTUS

LOTOSES > LOTOS

LOTS > LOT

LOTTE n type of fish

LOTTED > LOT

LOTTER n someone who works an allotment

LOTTERIES > LOTTERY

LOTTERS > LOTTER

LOTTERY n method of raising money by selling tickets that win prizes by chance

LOTTES > LOTTE

LOTTING > LOT

LOTTO n game of chance like bingo

LOTTOS > LOTTO

LOTUS n legendary plant whose fruit induces forgetfulness

LOTUSES > LOTUS

LOTUSLAND n idyllic place of contentment

LOU Scot word for > LOVE

LOUCHE adj shifty or disreputable

LOUCHELY > LOUCHE

LOUD adj relatively great in volume

LOUDEN vb make or become louder

LOUDENED > LOUDEN

LOUDENING > LOUDEN

LOUDENS > LOUDEN

LOUDER > LOUD

LOUDEST > LOUD

LOUDISH adj fairly loud

LOUDLIER > LOUD

LOUDLIEST > LOUD

LOUDLY > LOUD

LOUDMOUTH n person who talks too much, esp in a boastful or indiscreet way

LOUDNESS > LOUD

LOUED > LOU

LOUGH n loch

LOUGHS > LOUGH

LOUIE same as > LOOEY

LOUIES > LOUIE

LOUING > LOU

LOUIS n former French gold coin

LOUMA n weekly market in rural areas of developing countries

LOUMAS > LOUMA

LOUN same as > LOWN

LOUND same as > LOUN

LOUNDED > LOUND

LOUNDER vb beat severely

LOUNDERED > LOUNDER

LOUNDERS > LOUNDER

LOUNDING > LOUND

LOUNDS > LOUND

LOUNED > LOUN

LOUNGE n living room in a private house ▷ vb sit, lie, or stand in a relaxed manner

LOUNGED > LOUNGE

LOUNGER n comfortable sometimes adjustable couch or extending chair designed for someone to relax on

LOUNGERS > LOUNGER

LOUNGES > LOUNGE

LOUNGING > LOUNGE

LOUNGINGS > LOUNGE

LOUNGY adj casual; relaxed

LOUNING > LOUN

LOUNS > LOUN

LOUP Scot word for > LEAP

LOUPE n magnifying glass used by jewellers, horologists, etc

LOUPED > LOUP

LOUPEN > LOUP

LOUPES > LOUPE

LOUPING > LOUP

LOUPIT > LOUP

LOUPS > LOUP

LOUR vb (esp of the sky, weather, etc) to be overcast, dark, and menacing ▷ n menacing scowl or appearance

LOURE n slow, former French dance

LOURED > LOUR

LOURES > LOURE

LOURIE n type of African bird with either crimson or grey plumage

LOURIER > LOURY

LOURIES > LOURIE

LOURIEST > LOURY

LOURING > LOUR

LOURINGLY > LOUR

LOURINGS > LOUR

LOURS > LOUR

LOURY adj sombre

LOUS > LOU

LOUSE n wingless parasitic insect ▷ vb ruin or spoil

LOUSED > LOUSE

LOUSER n mean nasty person

LOUSERS > LOUSER

LOUSES > LOUSE

LOUSEWORT n any of various N temperate scrophulariaceous plants

LOUSIER > LOUSY

LOUSIEST > LOUSY

LOUSILY > LOUSY

LOUSINESS > LOUSY

LOUSING > LOUSE

LOUSY adj mean or unpleasant

LOUT n crude, oafish, or aggressive person ▷ vb bow or stoop

LOUTED > LOUT

LOUTING > LOUT

LOUTISH adj characteristic of a lout

LOUTISHLY > LOUTISH

LOUTS > LOUT

LOUVAR n large silvery whalelike scombroid fish

LOUVARS > LOUVAR

LOUVER same as > LOUVRE

LOUVERED same as > LOUVRED

LOUVERS > LOUVER

LOUVRE n one of a set of parallel slats slanted to admit air but not rain

LOUVRED adj (of a window, door, etc) having louvres

LOUVRES > LOUVRE

LOVABLE adj attracting or deserving affection

LOVABLY > LOVABLE

LOVAGE n European plant used for flavouring food

LOVAGES > LOVAGE

LOVAT n yellowish-green or bluish-green mixture, esp in tweeds or woollens

LOVATS > LOVAT

LOVE vb have a great affection for ▷ n great affection

LOVEABLE same as > LOVABLE

LOVEABLY > LOEVABLE

LOVEBIRD n small parrot

LOVEBIRDS > LOVEBIRD

LOVEBITE n temporary red mark left on a person's skin by someone biting or sucking it

LOVEBITES > LOVEBITE

LOVEBUG n small US flying insect

LOVEBUGS > LOVEBUG

LOVED > LOVE

LOVEFEST n event when people talk about loving one another

LOVEFESTS > LOVEFEST

LOVELESS adj without love

LOVELIER > LOVELY

LOVELIES > LOVELY

LOVELIEST > LOVELY

LOVELIGHT n brightness of eyes of one in love

LOVELILY > LOVELY

LOVELOCK n long lock of hair worn on the forehead

LOVELOCKS > LOVELOCK

LOVELORN adj miserable because of unhappiness in love

LOVELY adj very attractive ▷ n attractive woman

LOVEMAKER n one involved in lovemaking

LOVER n person having a sexual relationship outside marriage

LOVERED adj having a lover

LOVERLESS > LOVER

LOVERLY adj loverlike

LOVERS > LOVER

LOVES > LOVE

LOVESEAT n armchair for two people

LOVESEATS > LOVESEAT

LOVESICK adj pining or languishing because of love

LOVESOME adj full of love

LOVEVINE n leafless parasitic vine

LOVEVINES > LOVEVINE

LOVEY another word for > LOVE

LOVEYS > LOVEY

LOVING adj affectionate, tender

LOVINGLY > LOVING

LOVINGS > LOVING

LOW adj not tall, high, or elevated ▷ adv in or to a low position, level, or degree ▷ n low position, level, or degree ▷ vb moo

LOWAN n type of Australian bird

LOWANS > LOWAN

LOWBALL vb deliberately under-charge

LOWBALLED > LOWBALL

LOWBALLS > LOWBALL

LOWBORN adj of ignoble or common parentage

LOWBOY n table fitted with drawers

LOWBOYS > LOWBOY

LOWBRED same as > LOWBORN

LOWBROW adj with nonintellectual tastes and interests ▷ n person with uncultivated or nonintellectual tastes

LOWBROWED > LOWBROW

LOWBROWS > LOWBROW

LOWDOWN n inside information

LOWDOWNS > LOWDOWN

LOWE variant of > LOW

LOWED > LOW

LOWER adj below one or more other things ▷ vb cause or allow to move down

LOWERABLE > LOWER

LOWERCASE n small letters ▷ adj non-capitalized

LOWERED > LOWER

LOWERIER > LOWERY

LOWERIEST > LOWERY

LOWERING > LOWER

LOWERINGS > LOWER

LOWERMOST adj lowest

LOWERS > LOWER

LOWERY adj sombre

LOWES > LOWE

LOWEST > LOW

LOWING > LOW

LOWINGS > LOW

LOWISH > LOW

LOWLAND n low-lying country ▷ adj of a lowland or lowlands

LOWLANDER > LOWLAND

LOWLANDS > LOWLAND

LOWLIER > LOWLY

LOWLIEST > LOWLY

LOWLIFE n member or members of the underworld

LOWLIFER > LOWLIFE

LOWLIFERS > LOWLIFE

LOWLIFES > LOWLIFE

LOWLIGHT n unenjoyable or unpleasant part of an event

LOWLIGHTS > LOWLIGHT

LOWLIHEAD n state of being humble

LOWLILY > LOWLY

LOWLINESS > LOWLY

LOWLIVES > LOWLIFE

LOWLY adj modest, humble ▷ adv in a low or lowly manner

LOWN vb calm

LOWND same as > LOWN

LOWNDED > LOWND

LOWNDING > LOWND

LOWNDS > LOWND

LOWNE same as > LOON

LOWNED > LOWN

LOWNES > LOWNE

LOWNESS > LOW

LOWNESSES > LOW

LOWNING > LOWN

LOWNS > LOWN

LOWP same as > LOUP

LOWPED > LOWP

LOWPING > LOWP

LOWPS > LOWP

LOWRIDER n car with body close to ground

LOWRIDERS > LOWRIDER

LOWRIE another name for same as > LORY

LOWRIES > LOWRY

LOWRY another name for > LORY

LOWS > LOW

LOWSE vb release or loose ▷ adj loose

LOWSED > LOWSE

LOWSENING same as > LOOSING

LOWSER > LOWSE

LOWSES > LOWSE

LOWSEST > LOWSE

LOWSING > LOWSE

LOWSIT > LOWSE

LOWT same as > LOUT

LOWTED > LOWT

LOWTING > LOWT

LOWTS > LOWT

LOWVELD n low ground in S Africa

LOWVELDS > LOWVELD

LOX vb load fuel tanks of spacecraft with liquid oxygen ▷ n kind of smoked salmon

LOXED > LOX

LOXES > LOX

LOXING > LOX

LOXODROME n line on globe crossing all meridians at same angle

LOXODROMY n technique of navigating using rhumb lines

LOXYGEN n liquid oxygen

LOXYGENS > LOXYGEN

LOY n narrow spade with a single footrest

LOYAL adj faithful to one's friends, country, or government

LOYALER > LOYAL

LOYALEST > LOYAL

LOYALISM > LOYALIST

LOYALISMS > LOYALIST

LOYALIST n patriotic supporter of the sovereign or government

LOYALISTS > LOYALIST

LOYALLER > LOYAL

LOYALLEST > LOYAL

LOYALLY > LOYAL

LOYALNESS > LOYAL

LOYALTIES > LOYALTY

LOYALTY n quality of being loyal

LOYS > LOY

LOZELL obsolete form of > LOSEL

LOZELLS > LOZELL

LOZEN n window pane

LOZENGE n medicated tablet held in the mouth until it dissolves

LOZENGED adj decorated with lozenges

LOZENGES > LOZENGE

LOZENGY adj divided by diagonal lines to form a lattice

LOZENS > LOZEN

LUACH n calendar that shows the dates of festivals and, usually, the times of start and finish of the Sabbath

LUAU n feast of Hawaiian food

LUAUS > LUAU

LUBBARD same as > LUBBER

LUBBARDS > LUBBARD

LUBBER n big, awkward, or stupid person

LUBBERLY > LUBBER

LUBBERS > LUBBER

LUBE n lubricating oil ▷ vb lubricate with oil

LUBED > LUBE

LUBES > LUBE

LUBFISH n type of fish

LUBFISHES > LUBFISH

LUBING > LUBE

LUBRA n Aboriginal woman

LUBRAS > LUBRA

LUBRIC adj slippery

LUBRICAL same as > LUBRIC

LUBRICANT n lubricating substance, such as oil ▷ adj serving to lubricate

LUBRICATE vb oil or grease to lessen friction

LUBRICITY n lewdness or salaciousness

LUBRICOUS adj lewd or lascivious

LUCARNE n type of dormer window

LUCARNES > LUCARNE

LUCE another name for > PIKE

LUCENCE > LUCENT

LUCENCES > LUCENT

LUCENCIES > LUCENT

LUCENCY > LUCENT

LUCENT adj brilliant, shining, or translucent

LUCENTLY > LUCENT

LUCERN same as > LUCERNE

LUCERNE n alfalfa

LUCERNES > LUCERNE

LUCERNS > LUCERN

LUCES > LUCE

LUCHOT pl n engraved tablets of stone

LUCHOTH same as > LUCHOT

LUCID adj clear and easily understood

LUCIDER > LUCID

LUCIDEST > LUCID

LUCIDITY > LUCID

LUCIDLY > LUCID

LUCIDNESS > LUCID

LUCIFER n friction match

LUCIFERIN n substance occurring in bioluminescent organisms, such as glow-worms and fireflies

LUCIFERS > LUCIFER

LUCIGEN n lamp burning oil mixed with hot air

LUCIGENS > LUCIGEN

LUCITE n brand name of a type of transparent acrylic-based plastic

LUCITES > LUCITE

LUCK n fortune, good or bad ▷ vb have good fortune

LUCKED > LUCK

LUCKEN adj shut

LUCKIE same as > LUCKY

LUCKIER > LUCKY

LUCKIES > LUCKIE

LUCKIEST > LUCKY

LUCKILY > LUCKY

LUCKINESS > LUCKY

LUCKING > LUCK

LUCKLESS adj having bad luck

LUCKPENNY n coin kept for luck

LUCKS > LUCK

LUCKY adj having or bringing good luck ▷ n old woman

LUCRATIVE adj very profitable

LUCRE n money or wealth

LUCRES > LUCRE

LUCTATION n effort; struggle

LUCUBRATE vb write or study, esp at night

LUCULENT adj easily understood

LUCUMA n type of S American tree

LUCUMAS > LUCUMA

LUCUMO *n* Etruscan king

LUCUMONES > LUCUMO

LUCUMOS > LUCUMO

LUD *n* lord ▷ *interj* exclamation of dismay or surprise

LUDE *n* slang word for drug for relieving anxiety

LUDERICK *n* Australian fish, usu black or dark brown in colour

LUDERICKS > LUDERICK

LUDES > LUDE

LUDIC *adj* playful

LUDICALLY > LUDIC

LUDICROUS *adj* absurd or ridiculous

LUDO *n* game played with dice and counters on a board

LUDOS > LUDO

LUDS > LUD

LUDSHIP > LUD

LUDSHIPS > LUD

LUES *n* any venereal disease

LUETIC > LUES

LUETICS > LUES

LUFF *vb* sail (a ship) towards the wind ▷ *n* leading edge of a fore-and-aft sail

LUFFA *same as* > LOOFAH

LUFFAS > LUFFA

LUFFED > LUFF

LUFFING > LUFF

LUFFS > LUFF

LUG *vb* carry or drag with great effort ▷ *n* projection serving as a handle

LUGE *n* racing toboggan on which riders lie on their backs, descending feet first ▷ *vb* ride on a luge

LUGED > LUGE

LUGEING > LUGE

LUGEINGS > LUGE

LUGER *n* tradename for a type of German automatic pistol

LUGERS > LUGER

LUGES > LUGE

LUGGABLE *n* unwieldy portable computer

LUGGABLES > LUGGABLE

LUGGAGE *n* suitcases, bags, etc

LUGGAGES > LUGGAGE

LUGGED > LUG

LUGGER *n* small working boat with an oblong sail

LUGGERS > LUGGER

LUGGIE *n* wooden bowl with handles

LUGGIES > LUGGIE

LUGGING > LUG

LUGHOLE *informal word for* > EAR

LUGHOLES > LUGHOLE

LUGING > LUGE

LUGINGS > LUGE

LUGS > LUG

LUGSAIL *n* four-sided sail bent and hoisted on a yard

LUGSAILS > LUGSAIL

LUGWORM *n* large worm used as bait

LUGWORMS > LUGWORM

LUIT *Scots past form of* > LET

LUITEN > LET

LUKE *variant of* > LUKEWARM

LUKEWARM *adj* moderately warm, tepid

LULIBUB *obsolete form of* > LOLLIPOP

LULIBUBS > LULIBUB

LULL *vb* soothe (someone) by soft sounds or motions ▷ *n* brief time of quiet in a storm etc

LULLABIED > LULLABY

LULLABIES > LULLABY

LULLABY *n* quiet song to send a child to sleep ▷ *vb* quiet or soothe with or as if with a lullaby

LULLED > LULL

LULLER > LULL

LULLERS > LULL

LULLING > LULL

LULLS > LULL

LULU *n* person or thing considered to be outstanding in size, appearance, etc

LULUS > LULU

LUM *n* chimney

LUMA *n* black and white element of TV signal

LUMAS > LUMA

LUMBAGO *n* pain in the lower back

LUMBAGOS > LUMBAGO

LUMBANG *n* type of tree

LUMBANGS > LUMBANG

LUMBAR *adj* of the part of the body between the lowest ribs and the hipbones ▷ *n* old-fashioned kind of ship

LUMBARS > LUMBAR

LUMBER *n* unwanted disused household articles ▷ *vb* burden with something unpleasant

LUMBERED > LUMBER

LUMBERER > LUMBER

LUMBERERS > LUMBER

LUMBERING *n* business or trade of cutting, transporting, preparing, or selling timber ▷ *adj* awkward in movement

LUMBERLY *adj* heavy; clumsy

LUMBERMAN *n* person whose work involves felling trees

LUMBERMEN > LUMBERMAN

LUMBERS > LUMBER

LUMBRICAL *adj* relating to any of the the four wormlike muscles in the hand or foot

LUMBRICI > LUMBRICUS

LUMBRICUS *n* type of worm

LUMEN *n* derived SI unit of luminous flux

LUMENAL > LUMEN

LUMENS > LUMEN

LUMINA > LUMEN

LUMINAIRE *n* light fixture

LUMINAL > LUMEN

LUMINANCE *n* state or quality of radiating or reflecting light

LUMINANT *n* something used to give light

LUMINANTS > LUMINANT

LUMINARIA *n* type of candle

LUMINARY *n* famous person ▷ *adj* of, involving, or characterized by light or enlightenment

LUMINE *vb* illuminate

LUMINED > LUMINE

LUMINES > LUMINE

LUMINESCE *vb* exhibit luminescence

LUMINING > LUMINE

LUMINISM *n* US artistic movement

LUMINISMS > LUMINISM

LUMINIST > LUMINISM

LUMINISTS > LUMINISM

LUMINOUS *adj* reflecting or giving off light

LUMME *interj* exclamation of surprise or dismay

LUMMIER > LUMMY

LUMMIEST > LUMMY

LUMMOX *n* clumsy or stupid person

LUMMOXES > LUMMOX

LUMMY *interj* exclamation of surprise ▷ *adj* excellent

LUMP *n* shapeless piece or mass ▷ *vb* consider as a single group

LUMPED > LUMP

LUMPEN *adj* stupid or unthinking ▷ *n* member of underclass

LUMPENLY > LUMPEN

LUMPENS > LUMPEN

LUMPER *n* stevedore

LUMPERS > LUMPER

LUMPFISH *n* North Atlantic scorpaenoid fish

LUMPIER > LUMPY

LUMPIEST > LUMPY

LUMPILY > LUMPY

LUMPINESS > LUMPY

LUMPING > LUMP

LUMPINGLY > LUMP

LUMPISH *adj* stupid or clumsy

LUMPISHLY > LUMPISH

LUMPKIN *n* lout

LUMPKINS > LUMPKIN

LUMPS > LUMP

LUMPY *adj* full of or having lumps

LUMS > LUM

LUNA *n* type of large American moth

LUNACIES > LUNACY

LUNACY *n* foolishness

LUNANAUT *same as* > LUNARNAUT

LUNANAUTS > LUNANAUT

LUNAR *adj* relating to the moon ▷ *n* lunar distance

LUNARIAN *n* inhabitant of the moon

LUNARIANS > LUNARIAN

LUNARIES > LUNARY

LUNARIST *n* one believing the moon influences weather

LUNARISTS > LUNARIST

LUNARNAUT *n* astronaut who travels to moon

LUNARS > LUNAR

LUNARY *n* moonwort herb

LUNAS > LUNA

LUNATE *adj* shaped like a crescent ▷ *n* crescent-shaped bone forming part of the wrist

LUNATED *variant of* > LUNATE

LUNATELY > LUNATE

LUNATES > LUNATE

LUNATIC *adj* foolish and irresponsible ▷ *n* foolish or annoying person

LUNATICAL *variant of* > LUNATIC

LUNATICS > LUNATIC

LUNATION *See* > MONTH

LUNATIONS > LUNATION

LUNCH *n* meal taken in the middle of the day ▷ *vb* eat lunch

LUNCHBOX *n* container for carrying a packed lunch

LUNCHED > LUNCH

LUNCHEON *n* formal lunch

LUNCHEONS > LUNCHEON

LUNCHER > LUNCH

LUNCHERS > LUNCH

LUNCHES > LUNCH

LUNCHING > LUNCH

LUNCHMEAT *n* mixture of meat and cereal

LUNCHROOM *n* room where lunch is served or people may eat lunches they bring

LUNCHTIME *n* time at which lunch is usually eaten

LUNE *same as* > LUNETTE

LUNES > LUNE

LUNET *n* small moon or satellite

LUNETS > LUNET

LUNETTE *n* anything that is shaped like a crescent

LUNETTES > LUNETTE

LUNG *n* organ that allows an animal or bird to breathe air

LUNGAN *same as* > LONGAN

LUNGANS > LUNGAN

LUNGE *n* sudden forward motion ▷ *vb* move with or make a lunge

LUNGED > LUNGE

LUNGEE *same as* > LUNGI

LUNGEES > LUNGEE

LUNGEING > LUNGE

LUNGER > LUNGE

LUNGERS > LUNGE

LUNGES > LUNGE

LUNGFISH *n* freshwater bony fish with an air-breathing lung

LUNGFUL > LUNG

LUNGFULS > LUNG

LUNGI *n* long piece of cotton cloth worn as a loincloth, sash, or turban by Indian men or as a skirt

LUNGIE *n* guillemot

LUNGIES > LUNGIE

LUNGING > LUNGE

LUNGIS > LUNGI

LUNGS > LUNG

LUNGWORM *n* any parasitic nematode worm of the family *Metastrongylidae*

LUNGWORMS > LUNGWORM

LUNGWORT *n* any of several

Eurasian plants of the boraginaceous genus *Pulmonaria*

LUNGWORTS > LUNGWORT

LUNGYI *same as* > LUNGI

LUNGYIS > LUNGYI

LUNIER > LUNY

LUNIES > LUNY

LUNIEST > LUNY

LUNINESS > LUNY

LUNISOLAR *adj* resulting from or based on the combined gravitational attraction of the sun and moon

LUNITIDAL *adj* of or relating to tidal phenomena as produced by the moon

LUNK *n* awkward, heavy, or stupid person

LUNKER *n* very large fish, esp bass

LUNKERS > LUNKER

LUNKHEAD *n* stupid person

LUNKHEADS > LUNKHEAD

LUNKS > LUNK

LUNT *vb* produce smoke

LUNTED > LUNT

LUNTING > LUNT

LUNTS > LUNT

LUNULA *n* white crescent-shaped area at the base of the human fingernail

LUNULAE > LUNULA

LUNULAR *same as* > LUNULATE

LUNULATE *adj* having markings shaped like crescents

LUNULATED *same as* > LUNULATE

LUNULE *same as* > LUNULA

LUNULES > LUNULE

LUNY *same as* > LOONY

LUNYIE *same as* > LUNGIE

LUNYIES > LUNYIE

LUPANAR *n* brothel

LUPANARS > LUPANAR

LUPIN *n* garden plant with tall spikes of flowers

LUPINE *adj* like a wolf ▷ *n* lupin

LUPINES > LUPINE

LUPINS > LUPIN

LUPOUS *adj* relating to lupus

LUPPEN > SCOTS PAST FORM OF > LEAP

LUPULIN *n* resinous powder extracted from the female flowers of the hop plant

LUPULINE *adj* relating to lupulin

LUPULINIC *same as* > LUPULINE

LUPULINS > LUPULIN

LUPUS *n* ulcerous skin disease

LUPUSES > LUPUS

LUR *n* large bronze musical horn found in Danish peat bogs

LURCH *vb* tilt or lean suddenly to one side ▷ *n* lurching movement

LURCHED > LURCH

LURCHER *n* crossbred dog trained to hunt silently

LURCHERS > LURCHER

LURCHES > LURCH

LURCHING > LURCH

LURDAN *n* stupid or dull person ▷ *adj* dull or stupid

LURDANE *same as* > LURDAN

LURDANES > LURDANE

LURDANS > LURDAN

LURDEN *same as* > LURDAN

LURDENS > LURDEN

LURE *vb* tempt or attract by the promise of reward ▷ *n* person or thing that lures

LURED > LURE

LURER > LURE

LURERS > LURE

LURES > LURE

LUREX *n* thin glittery thread

LUREXES > LUREX

LURGI *same as* > LURGY

LURGIES > LURGY

LURGIS > LURGI

LURGY *n* any undetermined illness

LURID *adj* vivid in shocking detail, sensational

LURIDER > LURID

LURIDEST > LURID

LURIDLY > LURID

LURIDNESS > LURID

LURING > LURE

LURINGLY > LURE

LURK *vb* lie hidden or move stealthily, esp for sinister purposes

LURKED > LURK

LURKER > LURK

LURKERS > LURK

LURKING *adj* lingering but almost unacknowledged

LURKINGLY > LURKING

LURKINGS > LURKING

LURKS > LURK

LURRIES > LURRY

LURRY *n* confused jumble

LURS > LUR

LURVE *n* love

LURVES > LURVE

LUSCIOUS *adj* extremely pleasurable to taste or smell

LUSER *n* user of a computer system, as considered by a systems administator or other member of a technical support team

LUSERS > LUSER

LUSH *adj* (of grass etc) growing thickly and healthily ▷ *n* alcoholic ▷ *vb* drink (alcohol) to excess

LUSHED > LUSH

LUSHER *adj* more lush ▷ *n* drunkard

LUSHERS > LUSHER

LUSHES > LUSH

LUSHEST > LUSH

LUSHIER > LUSHY

LUSHIEST > LUSHY

LUSHING > LUSH

LUSHLY > LUSH

LUSHNESS > LUSH

LUSHY *adj* slightly intoxicated

LUSK *vb* lounge around

LUSKED > LUSK

LUSKING > LUSK

LUSKISH *adj* lazy

LUSKS > LUSK

LUST *n* strong sexual desire ▷ *vb* have passionate desire (for)

LUSTED > LUST

LUSTER *same as* > LUSTRE

LUSTERED > LUSTER

LUSTERING > LUSTER

LUSTERS > LUSTER

LUSTFUL *adj* driven by lust

LUSTFULLY > LUSTFUL

LUSTICK *obsolete word for* > LUSTY

LUSTIER > LUSTY

LUSTIEST > LUSTY

LUSTIHEAD *n* vigour

LUSTIHOOD *n* vigour

LUSTILY > LUSTY

LUSTINESS > LUSTY

LUSTING > LUST

LUSTIQUE *obsolete word for* > LUSTY

LUSTLESS > LUST

LUSTRA > LUSTRUM

LUSTRAL *adj* of or relating to a ceremony of purification

LUSTRATE *vb* purify by means of religious rituals or ceremonies

LUSTRATED > LUSTRATE

LUSTRATES > LUSTRATE

LUSTRE *n* gloss, sheen ▷ *vb* make, be, or become lustrous

LUSTRED > LUSTRE

LUSTRES > LUSTRE

LUSTRINE *same as* > LUSTRING

LUSTRINES > LUSTRINE

LUSTRING *n* glossy silk cloth, formerly used for clothing, upholstery, etc

LUSTRINGS > LUSTRING

LUSTROUS > LUSTRE

LUSTRUM *n* period of five years

LUSTRUMS > LUSTRUM

LUSTS > LUST

LUSTY *adj* vigorous, healthy

LUSUS *n* freak, mutant, or monster

LUSUSES > LUSUS

LUTANIST *same as* > LUTENIST

LUTANISTS > LUTANIST

LUTE *n* ancient guitar-like musical instrument with a body shaped like a half pear ▷ *vb* seal (a joint or surface) with a mixture of cement and clay

LUTEA *adj* yellow

LUTEAL *adj* relating to or characterized by the development of the corpus luteum

LUTECIUM *same as* > LUTETIUM

LUTECIUMS > LUTECIUM

LUTED > LUTE

LUTEFISK *n* Scandinavian fish dish

LUTEFISKS > LUTEFISK

LUTEIN *n* xanthophyll pigment that has a light-absorbing function in photosynthesis

LUTEINISE *same as* > LUTEINIZE

LUTEINIZE *vb* develop into part of corpus luteum

LUTEINS > LUTEIN

LUTENIST *n* person who plays the lute

LUTENISTS > LUTENIST

LUTEOLIN *n* yellow crystalline compound found in many plants

LUTEOLINS > LUTEOLIN

LUTEOLOUS > LUTEOLIN

LUTEOUS *adj* of a light to moderate greenish-yellow colour

LUTER *n* lute player

LUTERS > LUTER

LUTES > LUTE

LUTESCENT *adj* yellowish in colour

LUTETIUM *n* silvery-white metallic element

LUTETIUMS > LUTETIUM

LUTEUM *adj* yellow

LUTFISK *same as* > LUTEFISK

LUTFISKS > LUTFISK

LUTHERN *another name for* > DORMER

LUTHERNS > LUTHERN

LUTHIER *n* lute-maker

LUTHIERS > LUTHIER

LUTING *n* mixture of cement and clay

LUTINGS > LUTING

LUTIST *same as* > LUTENIST

LUTISTS > LUTIST

LUTITE *another name for* > PELITE

LUTITES > LUTITE

LUTTEN > LOOT

LUTZ *n* jump in which the skater takes off from the back outside edge of one skate, makes one, two, or three turns in the air, and lands on the back outside edge of the other skate

LUTZES > LUTZ

LUV *n* love

LUVS > LOVE

LUVVIE *n* person who is involved in acting or the theatre

LUVVIES > LUVVY

LUVVY *same as* > LUVVIE

LUX *n* unit of illumination

LUXATE *vb* put (a shoulder, knee, etc) out of joint

LUXATED > LUXATE

LUXATES > LUXATE

LUXATING > LUXATE

LUXATION > LUXATE

LUXATIONS > LUXATE

LUXE *as in* de luxe rich, elegant, or sumptuous

LUXES > LUXE

LUXMETER *n* device for measuring light

LUXMETERS > LUXMETER

LUXURIANT *adj* rich and abundant

LUXURIATE *vb* take self-indulgent pleasure (in)

LUXURIES > LUXURY

LUXURIOUS *adj* full of luxury, sumptuous
LUXURIST *n* lover of luxury
LUXURISTS > LUXURIST
LUXURY *n* enjoyment of rich, very comfortable living ▷ *adj* of or providing luxury
LUZ *n* supposedly indestructible bone of the human body
LUZERN *n* alfalfa
LUZERNS > LUZERN
LUZZES > LUZ
LWEI *n* Angolan monetary unit
LWEIS > LWEI
LYAM *n* leash
LYAMS > LYAM
LYARD *same as* > LIARD
LYART *same as* > LIARD
LYASE *n* any enzyme that catalyses the separation of two parts of a molecule
LYASES > LYASE
LYCEA > LYCEUM
LYCEE *n* secondary school
LYCEES > LYCEE
LYCEUM *n* public building for events such as concerts and lectures
LYCEUMS > LYCEUM
LYCH *same as* > LICH
LYCHEE *same as* > LITCHI
LYCHEES > LYCHEE
LYCHES > LYCH
LYCHGATE *same as* > LICHGATE
LYCHGATES > LYCHGATE
LYCHNIS *n* any caryophyllaceous plant of the genus *Lychnis*
LYCHNISES > LYCHNIS
LYCOPENE *n* red pigment
LYCOPENES > LYCOPENE
LYCOPOD *n* type of moss
LYCOPODS > LYCOPOD
LYCRA *n* tradename for a type of synthetic elastic fabric and fibre used for tight-fitting garments, such as swimming costumes
LYCRAS > LYCRA
LYDDITE *n* explosive consisting chiefly of fused picric acid
LYDDITES > LYDDITE
LYE *n* caustic solution obtained by leaching wood ash
LYES > LYE
LYFULL *obsolete form of* > LIFEFUL
LYING > LIE
LYINGLY > LIE
LYINGS > LIE

LYKEWAKE *n* watch held over a dead person, often with festivities
LYKEWAKES > LYKEWAKE
LYKEWALK *variant of* > LYKEWAKE
LYKEWALKS > LYKEWALK
LYM *obsolete form of* > LYAM
LYME as in *lyme grass* type of perennial dune grass
LYMES > LYME
LYMITER *same as* > LIMITER
LYMITERS > LIMITER
LYMPH *n* colourless bodily fluid consisting mainly of white blood cells
LYMPHAD *n* ancient rowing boat
LYMPHADS > LYMPHAD
LYMPHATIC *adj* of, relating to, or containing lymph ▷ *n* lymphatic vessel
LYMPHOID *adj* of or resembling lymph, or relating to the lymphatic system
LYMPHOMA *n* any form of cancer of the lymph nodes
LYMPHOMAS > LYMPHOMA
LYMPHS *n* lymph
LYMS > LYM
LYNAGE *obsolete form of* > LINEAGE
LYNAGES > LYNAGE
LYNCEAN *adj* of or resembling a lynx
LYNCH *vb* put to death without a trial
LYNCHED > LYNCH
LYNCHER > LYNCH
LYNCHERS > LYNCH
LYNCHES > LYNCH
LYNCHET *n* terrace or ridge formed in prehistoric or medieval times by ploughing a hillside
LYNCHETS > LYNCHET
LYNCHING > LYNCH
LYNCHINGS > LYNCH
LYNCHPIN *same as* > LINCHPIN
LYNCHPINS > LYNCHPIN
LYNE *n* flax
LYNES > LYNE
LYNX *n* animal of the cat family with tufted ears and a short tail
LYNXES > LYNX
LYNXLIKE > LYNX
LYOLYSES > LYOLYSIS
LYOLYSIS *n* formation of an acid and a base from the interaction of a salt with a solvent
LYOMEROUS *adj* relating to Lyomeri fish

LYONNAISE *adj* (of food) cooked or garnished with onions, usually fried
LYOPHIL *same as* > LYOPHILIC
LYOPHILE *same as* > LYOPHILIC
LYOPHILED *adj* lyophiliized
LYOPHILIC *adj* (of a colloid) having a dispersed phase with a high affinity for the continuous phase
LYOPHOBE *same as* > LYOPHOBIC
LYOPHOBIC *adj* (of a colloid) having a dispersed phase with little or no affinity for the continuous phase
LYRA as in *lyra viol* lutelike musical instrument of the 16th and 17th centuries
LYRATE *adj* shaped like a lyre
LYRATED *same as* > LYRATE
LYRATELY > LYRATE
LYRE *n* ancient musical instrument like a U-shaped harp
LYREBIRD *n* Australian bird, the male of which spreads its tail into the shape of a lyre
LYREBIRDS > LYREBIRD
LYRES > LYRE
LYRIC *adj* (of poetry) expressing personal emotion in songlike style ▷ *n* short poem in a songlike style
LYRICAL *same as* > LYRIC
LYRICALLY > LYRIC
LYRICISE *same as* > LYRICIZE
LYRICISED > LYRICISE
LYRICISES > LYRICISE
LYRICISM *n* quality or style of lyric poetry
LYRICISMS > LYRICISM
LYRICIST *n* person who writes the words of songs or musicals
LYRICISTS > LYRICIST
LYRICIZE *vb* write lyrics
LYRICIZED > LYRICIZE
LYRICIZES > LYRICIZE
LYRICON *n* wind synthesizer
LYRICONS > LYRICON
LYRICS > LYRIC
LYRIFORM *adj* lyre-shaped
LYRISM *n* art or technique of playing the lyre
LYRISMS > LYRISM
LYRIST *same as* > LYRICIST
LYRISTS > LYRIST
LYSATE *n* material formed by lysis

LYSATES > LYSATE
LYSE *vb* undergo or cause to undergo lysis
LYSED > LYSE
LYSERGIC as in *lysergic acid* crystalline compound used in medical research
LYSERGIDE *n* LSD
LYSES > LYSIS
LYSIGENIC *adj* caused by breaking down of cells
LYSIMETER *n* instrument for determining solubility, esp the amount of water-soluble matter in soil
LYSIN *n* any of a group of antibodies that cause dissolution of cells against which they are directed
LYSINE *n* essential amino acid that occurs in proteins
LYSINES > LYSINE
LYSING > LYSE
LYSINS > LYSIN
LYSIS *n* destruction or dissolution of cells by the action of a particular lysin
LYSOGEN *n* lysis-inducing agent
LYSOGENIC > LYSOGEN
LYSOGENS > LYSOGEN
LYSOGENY > LYSOGEN
LYSOL *n* tradename for a solution used as an antiseptic and disinfectant
LYSOLS > LYSOL
LYSOSOMAL > LYSOSOME
LYSOSOME *n* any of numerous small particles that are present in the cytoplasm of most cells
LYSOSOMES > LYSOSOME
LYSOZYME *n* enzyme occurring in tears, certain body tissues, and egg white
LYSOZYMES > LYSOZYME
LYSSA *less common word for* > RABIES
LYSSAS > LYSSA
LYTE *vb* dismount
LYTED > LYTE
LYTES > LYTE
LYTHE *n* type of fish
LYTHES > LYTHE
LYTIC *adj* relating to, causing, or resulting from lysis
LYTICALLY > LYTIC
LYTING > LYTE
LYTTA *n* rodlike mass of cartilage beneath the tongue in the dog and other carnivores
LYTTAE > LYTTA
LYTTAS > LYTTA

Mm

MA *n* mother

MAA *vb* (of goats) bleat

MAAED > MAA

MAAING > MAA

MAAR *n* coneless volcanic crater that has been formed by a single explosion

MAARE > MAAR

MAARS > MAAR

MAAS *n* thick soured milk

MAASES > MAAS

MAATJES *n* pickled herring

MABE *n* type of pearl

MABELA *n* ground kaffir corn used for making porridge

MABELAS > MABELA

MABES > MABE

MAC *n* macintosh

MACABER *same as* > MACABRE

MACABRE *adj* strange and horrible, gruesome

MACABRELY > MACABRE

MACACO *n* any of various lemurs, esp *Lemur macaco*, the males of which are usually black and the females brown

MACACOS > MACACO

MACADAM *n* road surface of pressed layers of small broken stones

MACADAMIA *n* Australian tree with edible nuts

MACADAMS > MACADAM

MACAHUBA *n* South American palm tree

MACAHUBAS > MACAHUBA

MACALLUM *n* ice cream with raspberry sauce

MACALLUMS > MACALLUM

MACAQUE *n* monkey of Asia and Africa with cheek pouches and either a short tail or no tail

MACAQUES > MACAQUE

MACARISE *vb* congratulate

MACARISED > MACARISE

MACARISES > MACARISE

MACARISM *n* blessing

MACARISMS > MACARISM

MACARIZE *same as* > MACARISE

MACARIZED > MACARIZE

MACARIZES > MACARIZE

MACARONI *n* pasta in short tube shapes

MACARONIC *adj* (of verse) characterized by a mixture of vernacular words jumbled together with Latin words or Latinized words or with words from one or more other foreign languages ▷ *n* macaronic verse

MACARONIS > MACARONI

MACAROON *n* small biscuit or cake made with ground almonds

MACAROONS > MACAROON

MACASSAR *n* oily preparation formerly put on the hair to make it smooth and shiny

MACASSARS > MACASSAR

MACAW *n* large tropical American parrot

MACAWS > MACAW

MACCABAW *same as* > MACCABOY

MACCABAWS > MACCABAW

MACCABOY *n* dark rose-scented snuff

MACCABOYS > MACCABOY

MACCARONI *same as* > MACARONI

MACCHIA *n* thicket in Italy

MACCHIATO *n* espresso coffee served with a dash of hot or cold milk

MACCHIE > MACCHIA

MACCOBOY *same as* > MACCABOY

MACCOBOYS > MACCOBOY

MACE *n* club, usually having a spiked metal head, used esp in the Middle Ages ▷ *vb* use a mace

MACED > MACE

MACEDOINE *n* hot or cold mixture of diced vegetables

MACER *n* macebearer, esp (in Scotland) an official who acts as usher in a court of law

MACERAL *n* any of the organic units that constitute coal: equivalent to any of the mineral constituents of a rock

MACERALS > MACERAL

MACERATE *vb* soften by soaking

MACERATED > MACERATE

MACERATER > MACERATE

MACERATES > MACERATE

MACERATOR > MACERATE

MACERS > MACER

MACES > MACE

MACH *n* ratio of the speed of a body in a particular medium to the speed of sound in that medium

MACHAIR *n* (in the western Highlands of Scotland) a strip of sandy, grassy, often lime-rich land just above the high-water mark at a sandy shore: used as grazing or arable land

MACHAIRS > MACHAIR

MACHAN *n* (in India) a raised platform used in tiger hunting

MACHANS > MACHAN

MACHE *n* papier-mâché

MACHER *n* important or influential person: often used ironically

MACHERS > MACHER

MACHES > MACHE

MACHETE *n* broad heavy knife used for cutting or as a weapon

MACHETES > MACHETE

MACHI as in *machi chips* in Indian English, fish and chips

MACHINATE *vb* contrive, plan, or devise (schemes, plots, etc)

MACHINE *n* apparatus, usu powered by electricity, designed to perform a particular task ▷ *vb* make or produce by machine

MACHINED > MACHINE

MACHINERY *n* machines or machine parts collectively

MACHINES > MACHINE

MACHINING > MACHINE

MACHINIST *n* person who operates a machine

MACHISMO *n* exaggerated or strong masculinity

MACHISMOS > MACHISMO

MACHMETER *n* instrument for measuring the Mach number of an aircraft in flight

MACHO *adj* strongly or exaggeratedly masculine ▷ *n* strong or exaggerated masculinity

MACHOISM > MACHO

MACHOISMS > MACHO

MACHOS > MACHO

MACHREE *n* Irish form of address meaning my dear

MACHREES > MACHREE

MACHS > MACH

MACHZOR *n* Jewish prayer book containing prescribed holiday rituals

MACHZORIM > MACHZOR

MACHZORS > MACHZOR

MACING > MACE

MACINTOSH *n* waterproof raincoat

MACK *same as* > MAC

MACKEREL *n* edible sea fish

MACKERELS > MACKEREL

MACKINAW *n* thick short double-breasted plaid coat

MACKINAWS > MACKINAW

MACKLE *n* double or blurred impression caused by shifting paper or type ▷ *vb* mend hurriedly or in a makeshift way

MACKLED > MACKLE

MACKLES > MACKLE

MACKLING > MACKLE

MACKS > MACK

MACLE *n* crystal consisting of two parts

MACLED > MACLE

MACLES > MACLE

MACON *n* red or white wine from the Mâcon area, heavier than the other burgundies

MACONS > MACON

MACOYA *n* South American tree

MACOYAS > MACOYA

MACRAME *n* ornamental work of knotted cord

MACRAMES > MACRAME

MACRAMI *same as* > MACRAME

MACRAMIS > MACRAMI

MACRO *n* close-up lens

MACROBIAN *adj* long-lived

MACROCODE *n* computer instruction that triggers many other instructions

m

MACROCOPY n enlargement of printed material for easier reading

MACROCOSM n universe

MACROCYST n unusually large cyst

MACROCYTE n abnormally large red blood cell

MACRODOME n dome shape in crystal structure

MACRODONT adj having large teeth

MACROGLIA n one of the two types of non-nervous tissue (glia) found in the central nervous system: includes astrocytes

MACROLOGY n verbose but meaningless talk

MACROMERE n any of the large yolk-filled cells formed by unequal cleavage of a fertilized ovum

MACROMOLE n large chemistry mole

MACRON n mark placed over a letter to represent a long vowel

MACRONS > MACRON

MACROPOD n member of kangaroo family

MACROPODS > MACROPOD

MACROPSIA n condition of seeing everything in the field of view as larger than it really is, which can occur in diseases of the retina or in some brain disorders

MACROS > MACRO

MACROTOUS adj having large ears

MACRURAL > MACRURAN

MACRURAN n any decapod crustacean of the group (formerly suborder) Macrura, which includes the lobsters, prawns, and crayfish ▷ adj of, relating to, or belonging to the Macrura

MACRURANS > MACRURAN

MACRUROID > MACRURAN

MACRUROUS > MACRURAN

MACS > MAC

MACTATION n sacrificial killing

MACULA n small spot or area of distinct colour, such as a freckle

MACULAE > MACULA

MACULAR > MACULA

MACULAS > MACULA

MACULATE vb spot, stain, or pollute ▷ adj spotted or polluted

MACULATED > MACULATE

MACULATES > MACULATE

MACULE same as > MACKLE

MACULED > MACULE

MACULES > MACULE

MACULING > MACULE

MACULOSE adj having spots

MACUMBA n religious cult in Brazil that combines Christian and voodoo elements

MACUMBAS > MACUMBA

MAD adj mentally deranged, insane ▷ vb make mad

MADAFU n coconut milk

MADAFUS > MADAFU

MADAM n polite term of address for a woman ▷ vb call someone madam

MADAME n French title equivalent to Mrs

MADAMED > MADAM

MADAMES > MADAME

MADAMING > MADAM

MADAMS > MADAM

MADAROSES > MADAROSIS

MADAROSIS n abnormal loss of eyebrows or eyelashes

MADBRAIN adj insane

MADCAP adj foolish or reckless ▷ n impulsive or reckless person

MADCAPS > MADCAP

MADDED > MAD

MADDEN vb infuriate or irritate

MADDENED > MADDEN

MADDENING adj serving to send mad

MADDENS > MADDEN

MADDER n type of rose

MADDERS > MADAM

MADDEST > MAD

MADDING > MAD

MADDINGLY > MAD

MADDISH > MAD

MADDOCK same as > MATTOCK

MADDOCKS > MADDOCK

MADE > MAKE

MADEFIED > MADEFY

MADEFIES > MADEFY

MADEFY vb make moist

MADEFYING > MADEFY

MADEIRA n kind of rich sponge cake

MADEIRAS > MADEIRA

MADELEINE n small fancy sponge cake

MADERISE vb become reddish

MADERISED > MADERISE

MADERISES > MADERISE

MADERIZE same as > MADERISE

MADERIZED > MADERIZE

MADERIZES > MADERIZE

MADGE n type of hammer

MADGES > MADGE

MADHOUSE n place filled with uproar or confusion

MADHOUSES > MADHOUSE

MADID adj wet

MADISON n type of cycle relay race

MADISONS > MADISON

MADLING n insane person

MADLINGS > MADLING

MADLY adv with great speed and energy

MADMAN n person who is insane

MADMEN > MADMAN

MADNESS n insanity

MADNESSES > MADNESS

MADONNA n picture or statue of the Virgin Mary

MADONNAS > MADONNA

MADOQUA n Ethiopian antelope

MADOQUAS > MADOQUA

MADRAS n medium-hot curry

MADRASA same as > MADRASAH

MADRASAH n educational institution, particularly for Islamic religious instruction

MADRASAHS > MADRASAH

MADRASAS > MADRASA

MADRASES > MADRAS

MADRASSA same as > MADRASAH

MADRASSAH same as > MADRASAH

MADRASSAS > MADRASSA

MADRE Spanish word for > MOTHER

MADREPORE n any coral of the genus Madrepora, many of which occur in tropical seas and form large coral reefs: order Zoantharia

MADRES > MADRE

MADRIGAL n 16th–17th-century part song for unaccompanied voices

MADRIGALS > MADRIGAL

MADRILENE n cold consommé flavoured with tomato juice

MADRONA n ericaceous North American evergreen tree or shrub, Arbutus menziesii, with white flowers and red berry-like fruits

MADRONAS > MADRONA

MADRONE same as > MADRONA

MADRONES > MADRONE

MADRONO same as > MADRONA

MADRONOS > MADRONO

MADS > MAD

MADTOM n species of catfish

MADTOMS > MADTOM

MADURO adj (of cigars) dark and strong ▷ n cigar of this type

MADUROS > MADURO

MADWOMAN n woman who is insane, esp one who behaves violently

MADWOMEN > MADWOMAN

MADWORT n low-growing Eurasian boraginaceous plant, Asperugo procumbens, with small blue flowers

MADWORTS > MADWORT

MADZOON same as > MATZOON

MADZOONS > MADZOON

MAE as in mae west inflatable life jacket, esp as issued to the US armed forces for emergency use

MAELID n mythical spirit of apple

MAELIDS > MAELID

MAELSTROM n great whirlpool

MAENAD n female disciple of Dionysus, the Greek god of wine

MAENADES > MAENAD

MAENADIC > MAENAD

MAENADISM > MAENAD

MAENADS > MAENAD

MAES > MAE

MAESTOSO adv be performed majestically ▷ n piece or passage directed to be played in this way

MAESTOSOS > MAESTOSO

MAESTRI > MAESTRO

MAESTRO n outstanding musician or conductor

MAESTROS > MAESTRO

MAFFIA same as > MAFIA

MAFFIAS > MAFFIA

MAFFICK vb celebrate extravagantly and publicly

MAFFICKED > MAFFICK

MAFFICKER > MAFFICK

MAFFICKS > MAFFICK

MAFFLED adj baffled

MAFFLIN n half-witted person

MAFFLING same as > MAFFLIN

MAFFLINGS > MAFFLING

MAFFLINS > MAFFLIN

MAFIA n international secret organization founded in Sicily, probably in opposition to tyranny. It developed into a criminal organization and in the late 19th century was carried to the US by Italian immigrants

MAFIAS > MAFIA

MAFIC n collective term for minerals present in igneous rock

MAFICS > MAFIC

MAFIOSI > MAFIOSO

MAFIOSO n member of the Mafia

MAFIOSOS > MAFIOSO

MAFTED adj suffering under oppressive heat

MAFTIR n final section of the weekly Torah reading

MAFTIRS > MAFTIR

MAG vb talk ▷ n talk

MAGAININ n any of a series of related substances with antibacterial properties, derived from the skins of frogs

MAGAININS > MAGAININ

MAGALOG same as > MAGALOGUE

MAGALOGS > MAGALOG

MAGALOGUE n combination of a magazine and a catalogue

MAGAZINE n periodical publication with articles by different writers

MAGAZINES > MAGAZINE

MAGDALEN n reformed prostitute

MAGDALENE same as > MAGDALEN

MAGDALENS > MAGDALEN

MAGE archaic word for > MAGICIAN

MAGENTA adj deep purplish-red ▷ n deep purplish red

that is the complementary colour of green and, with yellow and cyan, forms a set of primary colours

MAGENTAS > MAGENTA

MAGES > MAGE

MAGESHIP > MAGE

MAGESHIPS > MAGE

MAGG *same as* > MAG

MAGGED > MAG

MAGGIE *n* magpie

MAGGIES > MAGGIE

MAGGING > MAG

MAGGOT *n* larva of an insect

MAGGOTIER > MAGGOTY

MAGGOTS > MAGGOT

MAGGOTY *adj* relating to, resembling, or ridden with maggots

MAGGS > MAGG

MAGI > MAGUS

MAGIAN > MAGUS

MAGIANISM > MAGUS

MAGIANS > MAGUS

MAGIC *n* supposed art of invoking supernatural powers to influence events ▷ *vb* to transform or produce by or as if by magic ▷ *adj* of, using, or like magic

MAGICAL > MAGIC

MAGICALLY > MAGIC

MAGICIAN *n* conjuror

MAGICIANS > MAGICIAN

MAGICKED > MAGIC

MAGICKING > MAGIC

MAGICS > MAGIC

MAGILP *same as* > MEGILP

MAGILPS > MAGILP

MAGISM > MAGUS

MAGISMS > MAGUS

MAGISTER *n* person entitled to teach in medieval university

MAGISTERS > MAGISTER

MAGISTERY *n* agency or substance, such as the philosopher's stone, believed to transmute other substances

MAGISTRAL *adj* of, relating to, or characteristic of a master ▷ *n* fortification in a determining position

MAGLEV *n* type of high-speed train that runs on magnets supported by a magnetic field generated around the track

MAGLEVS > MAGLEV

MAGMA *n* molten rock inside the earth's crust

MAGMAS > MAGMA

MAGMATA > MAGMA

MAGMATIC > MAGMA

MAGMATISM > MAGMA

MAGNALIUM *n* alloy of magnesium and aluminium

MAGNATE *n* influential or wealthy person, esp in industry

MAGNATES > MAGNATE

MAGNES *n* magnetic iron ore

MAGNESES > MAGNES

MAGNESIA *n* white tasteless substance used as an antacid and a laxative

MAGNESIAL > MAGNESIA

MAGNESIAN > MAGNESIA

MAGNESIAS > MAGNESIA

MAGNESIC > MAGNESIA

MAGNESITE *n* white, colourless, or lightly tinted mineral

MAGNESIUM *n* silvery-white metallic element

MAGNET *n* piece of iron or steel capable of attracting iron and pointing north when suspended

MAGNETAR *n* type of neutron star that has a very intense magnetic field, over 1000 times greater than that of a pulsar

MAGNETARS > MAGNETAR

MAGNETIC *adj* having the properties of a magnet

MAGNETICS *n* branch of physics concerned with magnetism

MAGNETISE *same as* > MAGNETIZE

MAGNETISM *n* magnetic property

MAGNETIST > MAGNETISM

MAGNETITE *n* black magnetizable mineral that is an important source of iron

MAGNETIZE *vb* make into a magnet

MAGNETO *n* apparatus for ignition in an internal-combustion engine

MAGNETON *n* unit of magnetic moment

MAGNETONS > MAGNETON

MAGNETOS > MAGNETO

MAGNETRON *n* electronic valve used with a magnetic field to generate microwave oscillations, used. esp in radar

MAGNETS > MAGNET

MAGNIFIC *adj* magnificent, grandiose, or pompous

MAGNIFICO *n* magnate

MAGNIFIED > MAGNIFY

MAGNIFIER > MAGNIFY

MAGNIFIES > MAGNIFY

MAGNIFY *vb* increase in apparent size, as with a lens

MAGNITUDE *n* relative importance or size

MAGNOLIA *n* shrub or tree with showy white or pink flowers

MAGNOLIAS > MAGNOLIA

MAGNON *n* short for Cro-Magnon

MAGNONS > MAGNON

MAGNOX *n* alloy composed mainly of magnesium, used in fuel elements of some nuclear reactors

MAGNOXES > MAGNOX

MAGNUM *n* large wine bottle holding about 1.5 litres

MAGNUMS > MAGNUM

MAGNUS *as in magnus hitch*

knot similar to a clove hitch but having one more turn

MAGOT *n* Chinese or Japanese figurine in a crouching position, usually grotesque

MAGOTS > MAGOT

MAGPIE *n* black-and-white bird

MAGPIES > MAGPIE

MAGS > MAG

MAGSMAN *n* raconteur

MAGSMEN > MAGSMAN

MAGUEY *n* any of various tropical American agave plants of the genera *Agave* or *Furcraea*, esp one that yields a fibre or is used in making an alcoholic beverage

MAGUEYS > MAGUEY

MAGUS *n* Zoroastrian priest of the ancient Medes and Persians

MAGYAR *adj* of or relating to a style of sleeve cut in one piece with the bodice

MAHARAJA *same as* > MAHARAJAH

MAHARAJAH *n* former title of some Indian princes

MAHARAJAS > MAHARAJA

MAHARANEE *same as* > MAHARANI

MAHARANI *n* wife of a maharaja

MAHARANIS > MAHARANI

MAHARISHI *n* Hindu religious teacher or mystic

MAHATMA *n* person revered for holiness and wisdom

MAHATMAS > MAHATMA

MAHEWU *n* (in South Africa) fermented liquid mealie-meal porridge, used as a stimulant, esp by Black Africans

MAHEWUS > MAHEWU

MAHIMAHI *n* Pacific fish

MAHIMAHIS > MAHIMAHI

MAHJONG *n* game of Chinese origin, usually played by four people, in which tiles bearing various designs are (drawn and discarded until one player has an entire hand of winning combinations

MAHJONGG *same as* > MAHJONG

MAHJONGGS > MAHJONGG

MAHJONGS > MAHJONG

MAHLSTICK *same as* > MAULSTICK

MAHMAL *n* litter used in Muslim ceremony

MAHMALS > MAHMAL

MAHOE *n* New Zealand tree

MAHOES > MAHOE

MAHOGANY *n* hard reddish-brown wood of several tropical trees ▷ *adj* reddish-brown

MAHONIA *n* any evergreen berberidaceous shrub of the Asian and American genus *Mahonia*, esp *M.*

aquifolium: cultivated for their ornamental spiny divided leaves and clusters of small yellow flowers

MAHONIAS > MAHONIA

MAHOUT *n* (in India and the East Indies) elephant driver or keeper

MAHOUTS > MAHOUT

MAHSEER *n* any of various large freshwater Indian cyprinid fishes, such as *Barbus tor*

MAHSEERS > MAHSEER

MAHSIR *same as* > MAHSEER

MAHSIRS > MAHSIR

MAHUA *n* Indian tree

MAHUANG *n* herbal medicine from shrub

MAHUANGS > MAHUANG

MAHUAS > MAHUA

MAHWA *same as* > MAHUA

MAHWAS > MAHWA

MAHZOR *same as* > MACHZOR

MAHZORIM > MAHZOR

MAHZORS > MAHZOR

MAIASAUR *same as* > MAIASAURA

MAIASAURA *n* species of dinosaur

MAIASAURS > MAIASAUR

MAID *n* female servant ▷ *vb* work as maid

MAIDAN *n* (in Pakistan, India, etc) an open space used for meetings, sports, etc

MAIDANS > MAIDAN

MAIDED > MAID

MAIDEN *n* young unmarried woman ▷ *adj* unmarried

MAIDENISH > MAIDEN

MAIDENLY *adj* modest

MAIDENS > MAIDEN

MAIDHOOD > MAID

MAIDHOODS > MAID

MAIDING > MAID

MAIDISH > MAID

MAIDISM *n* pellagra

MAIDISMS > MAIDISM

MAIDLESS > MAID

MAIDS > MAID

MAIEUTIC *adj* of or relating to the Socratic method of eliciting knowledge by a series of questions and answers

MAIEUTICS *n* Socratic method

MAIGRE *adj* not containing flesh, and so permissible as food on days of religious abstinence ▷ *n* species of fish

MAIGRES > MAIGRE

MAIHEM *same as* > MAYHEM

MAIHEMS > MAIHEM

MAIK *n* old halfpenny

MAIKO *n* apprentice geisha

MAIKOS > MAIKO

MAIKS > MAIK

MAIL *n* letters and packages transported and delivered by the post office ▷ *vb* send by mail

MAILABLE > MAIL

MAILBAG *n* large bag for

transporting or delivering mail

MAILBAGS > MAILBAG

MAILBOX n box into which letters and parcels are delivered

MAILBOXES > MAILBOX

MAILCAR same as > MAILCOACH

MAILCARS > MAILCAR

MAILCOACH n railway coach specially constructed for the transportation of mail

MAILE n halfpenny

MAILED > MAIL

MAILER n person who addresses or mails letters, etc

MAILERS > MAILER

MAILES > MAILE

MAILGRAM n telegram

MAILGRAMS > MAILGRAM

MAILING > MAIL

MAILINGS > MAILING

MAILL n Scots word meaning rent

MAILLESS > MAIL

MAILLOT n tights worn for ballet, gymnastics, etc

MAILLOTS > MAILLOT

MAILLS > MAILL

MAILMAN n postman

MAILMEN > MAILMAN

MAILMERGE n computer program for sending mass mailings

MAILPOUCH same as > MAILBAG

MAILROOM n room where mail to and from building is dealt with

MAILROOMS > MAILROOM

MAILS > MAIL

MAILSACK same as > MAILBAG

MAILSACKS > MAILSACK

MAILSHOT n posting of advertising material to many selected people at once

MAILSHOTS > MAILSHOT

MAILVAN n vehicle used to transport post

MAILVANS > MAILVAN

MAIM vb cripple or mutilate ▷ n injury or defect

MAIMED > MAIM

MAIMER > MAIM

MAIMERS > MAIM

MAIMING > MAIM

MAIMINGS > MAIM

MAIMS > MAIM

MAIN adj chief or principal ▷ n principal pipe or line carrying water, gas, or electricity ▷ vb lower sails

MAINBOOM spar for mainsail

MAINBOOMS > MAINBOOM

MAINBRACE n brace attached to the mainyard

MAINDOOR n door from street into house

MAINDOORS > MAINDOOR

MAINED > MAIN

MAINER > MAIN

MAINEST > MAIN

MAINFRAME adj denoting

a high-speed general-purpose computer ▷ n high-speed general-purpose computer, with a large store capacity

MAINING > MAIN

MAINLAND n stretch of land which forms the main part of a country

MAINLANDS > MAINLAND

MAINLINE n the trunk route between two points, usually fed by branch lines ▷ vb to inject a drug into a vein ▷ adj having an important position, esp having responsibility for the main areas of activity

MAINLINED > MAINLINE

MAINLINER > MAINLINE

MAINLINES > MAINLINE

MAINLY adv for the most part, chiefly

MAINMAST n chief mast of a ship

MAINMASTS > MAINMAST

MAINOR n act of doing something

MAINORS > MAINOR

MAINOUR same as > MAINOR

MAINOURS > MAINOUR

MAINPRISE n former legal surety

MAINS > MAIN

MAINSAIL n largest sail on a mainmast

MAINSAILS > MAINSAIL

MAINSHEET n line used to control the angle of the mainsail to the wind

MAINSTAY n chief support

MAINSTAYS > MAINSTAY

MAINTAIN vb continue or keep in existence

MAINTAINS > MAINTAIN

MAINTOP n top or platform at the head of the mainmast

MAINTOPS > MAINTOP

MAINYARD n yard for a square mainsail

MAINYARDS > MAINYARD

MAIOLICA same as > MAJOLICA

MAIOLICAS > MAIOLICA

MAIR Scots form of > MORE

MAIRE n New Zealand tree

MAIREHAU n small aromatic shrub of New Zealand

MAIREHAUS > MAIREHAU

MAIRES > MAIRE

MAIRS > MAIR

MAISE n measure of herring

MAISES > MAISE

MAIST Scot word for > MOST

MAISTER Scots word for > MASTER

MAISTERED > MAISTER

MAISTERS > MAISTER

MAISTRIES > MAISTER

MAISTRING > MAISTER

MAISTRY > MAISTER

MAISTS > MAIST

MAIZE n type of corn with spikes of yellow grains

MAIZES > MAIZE

MAJAGUA same as > MAHOE

MAJAGUAS > MAJAGUA

MAJESTIC adj beautiful, dignified, and impressive

MAJESTIES > MAJESTY

MAJESTY n stateliness or grandeur

MAJLIS n (in various N African and Middle Eastern countries) an assembly; council

MAJLISES > MAJLIS

MAJOLICA n type of ornamented Italian pottery

MAJOLICAS > MAJOLICA

MAJOR adj greater in number, quality, or extent ▷ n middle-ranking army officer ▷ vb do one's principal study in (a particular subject)

MAJORAT n estate, the right to which is that of the first born child of a family

MAJORATS > MAJORAT

MAJORDOMO n chief steward or butler of a great household

MAJORED > MAJOR

MAJORETTE n one of a group of girls who practise formation marching and baton twirling

MAJORING > MAJOR

MAJORITY n greater number

MAJORLY adv very

MAJORS > MAJOR

MAJORSHIP > MAJOR

MAJUSCULE n large letter, either capital or uncial, used in printing or writing ▷ adj relating to, printed, or written in such letters

MAK Scot word for > MAKE

MAKABLE > MAKE

MAKAR same as > MAKER

MAKARS > MAKAR

MAKE vb create, construct, or establish ▷ n brand, type, or style

MAKEABLE > MAKE

MAKEBATE n troublemaker

MAKEBATES > MAKEBATE

MAKEFAST n strong support to which a vessel is secured

MAKEFASTS > MAKEFAST

MAKELESS > MAKE

MAKEOVER vb to transfer the title or possession of (property, etc) ▷ n a series of alterations, including beauty treatments and new clothes, intended to make a noticeable improvement in a person's appearance

MAKEOVERS > MAKEOVER

MAKER n person or company that makes something

MAKEREADY n process of preparing the forme and the cylinder or platen packing to achieve the correct impression all over the forme

MAKERS > MAKER

MAKES > MAKE

MAKESHIFT adj serving as a temporary substitute ▷ n something serving in this capacity

MAKEUP n cosmetics, such as powder, lipstick, etc, applied to the face to improve its appearance ▷ vb devise, construct, or compose, sometimes with the intent to deceive

MAKEUPS > MAKEUP

MAKI n in Japanese cuisine, rice and other ingredients wrapped in a short seaweed roll

MAKIMONO n Japanese scroll

MAKIMONOS > MAKIMONO

MAKING > MAKE

MAKINGS pl n potentials, qualities, or materials

MAKIS > MAKI

MAKO n powerful shark of the Atlantic and Pacific Oceans

MAKOS > MAKO

MAKS > MAK

MAKUTA plural of > LIKUTA

MAKUTU n Polynesian witchcraft ▷ vb cast a spell on

MAKUTUED > MAKUTU

MAKUTUING > MAKUTU

MAKUTUS > MAKUTU

MAL n illness

MALA n string of beads or knots, used in praying and meditating

MALACCA n stem of the rattan palm

MALACCAS > MALACCA

MALACHITE n green mineral

MALACIA n pathological softening of an organ or tissue, such as bone

MALACIAS > MALACIA

MALADIES > MALADY

MALADROIT adj clumsy or awkward

MALADY n disease or illness

MALAGUENA n Spanish dance similar to the fandango

MALAISE n something wrong which affects a section of society or area of activity

MALAISES > MALAISE

MALAM same as > MALLAM

MALAMS > MALAM

MALAMUTE n Alaskan sled dog of the spitz type, having a dense usually greyish coat

MALAMUTES > MALAMUTE

MALANDER same as > MALANDERS

MALANDERS pl n disease of horses characterized by an eczematous inflammation behind the knee

MALANGA same as > COCOYAM

MALANGAS > MALANGA

MALAPERT adj saucy or impudent ▷ n saucy or impudent person

MALAPERTS > MALAPERT
MALAPROP n a word unintentionally confused with one of similar sound, esp when creating a ridiculous effect, as in *I am not under the affluence of alcohol*
MALAPROPS > MALAPROP
MALAR n cheekbone ▷ *adj* of or relating to the cheek or cheekbone
MALARIA n infectious disease caused by the bite of some mosquitoes
MALARIAL > MALARIA
MALARIAN > MALARIA
MALARIAS > MALARIA
MALARIOUS > MALARIA
MALARKEY n nonsense or rubbish
MALARKEYS > MALARKEY
MALARKIES > MALARKY
MALARKY *same as* > MALARKEY
MALAROMA n bad smell
MALAROMAS > MALAROMA
MALARS > MALAR
MALAS > MALA
MALATE n any salt or ester of malic acid
MALATES > MALATE
MALATHION n yellow organophosphorus insecticide used as a dust or mist for the control of house flies and garden pests
MALAX *vb* soften
MALAXAGE > MALAX
MALAXAGES > MALAX
MALAXATE *same as* > MALAX
MALAXATED > MALAXATE
MALAXATES > MALAXATE
MALAXATOR n machine for kneading or grinding
MALAXED > MALAX
MALAXES > MALAX
MALAXING > MALAX
MALE *adj* of the sex which can fertilize female reproductive cells ▷ *n* male person or animal
MALEATE n any salt or ester of maleic acid
MALEATES > MALEATE
MALEDICT *vb* utter a curse against ▷ *adj* cursed or detestable
MALEDICTS > MALEDICT
MALEFFECT n bad effect
MALEFIC *adj* causing evil
MALEFICE n wicked deed
MALEFICES > MALEFICE
MALEIC *as in* maleic acid colourless soluble crystalline substance used to synthesize other compounds
MALEMIUT *same as* > MALAMUTE
MALEMIUTS > MALEMIUT
MALEMUTE *same as* > MALAMUTE
MALEMUTES > MALEMUTE
MALENESS > MALE
MALENGINE n wicked plan

MALES > MALE
MALFED *adj* having malfunctioned
MALFORMED *adj* deformed
MALGRADO *prep* in spite of
MALGRE *same as* > MAUGRE
MALGRED > MALGRE
MALGRES > MALGRE
MALGRING > MALGRE
MALI n member of an Indian caste
MALIBU *as in* malibu board lightweight surfboard
MALIC *as in* malic acid colourless crystalline compound occurring in apples and other fruit
MALICE n desire to cause harm to others ▷ *vb* wish harm to
MALICED > MALICE
MALICES > MALICE
MALICHO n mischief
MALICHOS > MALICHO
MALICING > MALICE
MALICIOUS *adj* characterized by malice
MALIGN *vb* slander or defame ▷ *adj* evil in influence or effect
MALIGNANT *adj* seeking to harm others
MALIGNED > MALIGN
MALIGNER > MALIGN
MALIGNERS > MALIGN
MALIGNING > MALIGN
MALIGNITY n evil disposition
MALIGNLY > MALIGN
MALIGNS > MALIGN
MALIHINI n (in Hawaii) a foreigner or stranger
MALIHINIS > MALIHINI
MALIK n person of authority in India
MALIKS > MALIK
MALINE n stiff net
MALINES > MALINE
MALINGER *vb* feign illness to avoid work
MALINGERS > MALINGER
MALINGERY > MALINGER
MALIS > MALI
MALISM n belief that evil dominates world
MALISMS > MALISM
MALISON *archaic or poetic word for* > CURSE
MALISONS > MALISON
MALIST > MALISM
MALKIN *archaic or dialect name for a* > CAT
MALKINS > MALKIN
MALL n street or shopping area closed to vehicles ▷ *vb* maul
MALLAM n (in Islamic W Africa) a man learned in Koranic studies
MALLAMS > MALLAM
MALLANDER *same as* > MALANDERS
MALLARD n wild duck
MALLARDS > MALLARD
MALLEABLE *adj* capable of being hammered or pressed into shape

MALLEABLY > MALLEABLE
MALLEATE *vb* hammer
MALLEATED > MALLEATE
MALLEATES > MALLEATE
MALLECHO *same as* > MALICHO
MALLECHOS > MALLECHO
MALLED > MALL
MALLEE n low-growing eucalypt in dry regions
MALLEES > MALLEE
MALLEI > MALLEUS
MALLEMUCK n any of various sea birds, such as the albatross, fulmar, or shearwater
MALLENDER *same as* > MALANDERS
MALLEOLAR > MALLEOLUS
MALLEOLI > MALLEOLUS
MALLEOLUS n either of two rounded bony projections of the tibia and fibula on the sides of each ankle joint
MALLET n (wooden) hammer
MALLETS > MALLET
MALLEUS n outermost and largest of the three small bones in the middle ear of mammals
MALLEUSES > MALLEUS
MALLING > MALL
MALLINGS > MALL
MALLOW n plant with pink or purple flowers
MALLOWS > MALLOW
MALLS > MALL
MALM n soft greyish limestone that crumbles easily
MALMAG n Asian monkey
MALMAGS > MALMAG
MALMIER > MALMY
MALMIEST > MALMY
MALMS > MALM
MALMSEY n sweet Madeira wine
MALMSEYS > MALMSEY
MALMSTONE *same as* > MALM
MALMY *adj* looking like malm
MALODOR *same as* > MALODOUR
MALODORS > MALODOR
MALODOUR n unpleasant smell
MALODOURS > MALODOUR
MALONATE n salt of malonic acid
MALONATES > MALONATE
MALONIC *as in* malonic acid colourless crystalline compound occurring in sugar beet
MALOTI *plural of* > LOTI
MALPIGHIA n tropical shrub
MALPOSED *adj* in abnormal position
MALS > MAL
MALSTICK *same as* > MAULSTICK
MALSTICKS > MALSTICK
MALT n grain, such as barley, prepared for use in making beer or whisky ▷ *vb* make into or make with malt
MALTALENT n evil intention

MALTASE n enzyme that hydrolyses maltose and similar glucosides to glucose
MALTASES > MALTASE
MALTED > MALT
MALTEDS > MALT
MALTHA n any of various naturally occurring mixtures of hydrocarbons, such as ozocerite
MALTHAS > MALTHA
MALTIER > MALTY
MALTIEST > MALTY
MALTINESS > MALTY
MALTING n building in which malt is made or stored
MALTINGS > MALTING
MALTMAN *same as* > MALTSTER
MALTMEN > MALTMAN
MALTOL n food additive
MALTOLS > MALTOL
MALTOSE n sugar formed by the action of enzymes on starch
MALTOSES > MALTOSE
MALTREAT *vb* treat badly
MALTREATS > MALTREAT
MALTS > MALT
MALTSTER n person who makes or deals in malt
MALTSTERS > MALTSTER
MALTWORM n heavy drinker
MALTWORMS > MALTWORM
MALTY *adj* of, like, or containing malt
MALVA n mallow plant
MALVAS > MALVA
MALVASIA n type of grape used to make malmsey
MALVASIAN > MALVASIA
MALVASIAS > MALVASIA
MALVESIE *same as* > MALMSEY
MALVESIES > MALVESIE
MALVOISIE n amber dessert wine made in France, similar to malmsey
MALWA n Ugandan drink brewed from millet
MALWARE n computer program designed to cause damage or disruption to a system
MALWARES > MALWARE
MALWAS > MALWA
MAM *same as* > MOTHER
MAMA n mother
MAMAGUY *vb* deceive or tease, either in jest or by deceitful flattery ▷ *n* instance of such deception or flattery
MAMAGUYED > MAMAGUY
MAMAGUYS > MAMAGUY
MAMAKAU *same as* > MAMAKU
MAMAKO *same as* > MAMAKU
MAMAKU n tall edible New Zealand tree fern
MAMALIGA *same as* > POLENTA
MAMALIGAS > MAMALIGA
MAMAS > MAMA
MAMBA n deadly S African snake

MAMBAS > MAMBA
MAMBO n Latin American dance resembling the rumba ▷ vb perform this dance
MAMBOED > MAMBO
MAMBOES > MAMBO
MAMBOING > MAMBO
MAMBOS > MAMBO
MAMEE same as > MAMEY
MAMEES > MAMEE
MAMELON n small rounded hillock
MAMELONS > MAMELON
MAMELUCO n Brazilian of mixed European and South American descent
MAMELUCOS > MAMELUCO
MAMELUKE n member of a military class, originally of Turkish slaves, ruling in Egypt from about 1250 to 1517 and remaining powerful until crushed in 1811
MAMELUKES > MAMELUKE
MAMEY n tropical tree
MAMEYES > MAMEY
MAMEYS > MAMEY
MAMIE n tropical tree
MAMIES > MAMIE
MAMILLA n nipple or teat
MAMILLAE > MAMILLA
MAMILLAR adj of breast
MAMILLARY > MAMILLA
MAMILLATE adj having nipples or nipple-like protuberances
MAMLUK same as > MAMELUKE
MAMLUKS > MAMLUK
MAMMA n buxom and voluptuous woman
MAMMAE > MAMMA
MAMMAL n animal of the type that suckles its young
MAMMALIAN > MAMMAL
MAMMALITY > MAMMAL
MAMMALOGY n branch of zoology concerned with the study of mammals
MAMMALS > MAMMAL
MAMMARY adj of the breasts or milk-producing glands
MAMMAS > MAMMA
MAMMATE adj having breasts
MAMMATI > MAMMATUS
MAMMATUS n breast-shaped cloud
MAMMEE same as > MAMEY
MAMMEES > MAMMEE
MAMMER vb hesitate
MAMMERED > MAMMER
MAMMERING > MAMMER
MAMMERS > MAMMER
MAMMET same as > MAUMET
MAMMETRY n worship of idols
MAMMETS > MAMMET
MAMMEY same as > MAMEY
MAMMEYS > MAMMEY
MAMMIE same as > MAMMY
MAMMIES > MAMMY
MAMMIFER same as > MAMMAL
MAMMIFERS > MAMMIFER
MAMMIFORM adj in form of

breast
MAMMILLA same as > MAMILLA
MAMMILLAE > MAMMILLA
MAMMITIS same as > MASTITIS
MAMMOCK n fragment ▷ vb tear or shred
MAMMOCKED > MAMMOCK
MAMMOCKS > MAMMOCK
MAMMOGRAM n xray to examine the breasts in early detection of cancer
MAMMON n wealth regarded as a source of evil
MAMMONISH > MAMMON
MAMMONISM > MAMMON
MAMMONIST > MAMMON
MAMMONITE > MAMMON
MAMMONS > MAMMON
MAMMOTH n extinct elephant-like mammal ▷ adj colossal
MAMMOTHS > MAMMOTH
MAMMY n Black woman employed as a nurse or servant to a White family
MAMPARA n foolish person, idiot
MAMPARAS > MAMPARA
MAMPOER n home-distilled brandy made from peaches, prickly pears, etc
MAMPOERS > MAMPOER
MAMS > MAM
MAMSELLE n mademoiselle
MAMSELLES > MAMSELLE
MAMZER n child of an incestuous or adulterous union
MAMZERIM > MAMZER
MAMZERS > MAMZER
MAN n adult male ▷ vb supply with sufficient people for operation or defence
MANA n authority, influence
MANACLE vb handcuff or fetter ▷ n metal ring or chain put round the wrists or ankles, used to restrict the movements of a prisoner or convict
MANACLED > MANACLE
MANACLES > MANACLE
MANACLING > MANACLE
MANAGE vb succeed in doing
MANAGED > MANAGE
MANAGER n person in charge of a business, institution, actor, sports team, etc
MANAGERS > MANAGER
MANAGES > MANAGE
MANAGING adj having administrative control or authority
MANAIA n common figure in Māori carving consisting of a human body and a bird-like head
MANAKIN same as > MANIKIN
MANAKINS > MANAKIN
MANANA n tomorrow ▷ adv tomorrow
MANANAS > MANANA
MANAS > MANA
MANAT n standard monetary

unit of Azerbaijan, divided into 100 gopik
MANATEE n large tropical plant-eating aquatic mammal
MANATEES > MANATEE
MANATI same as > MANATEE
MANATIS > MANATI
MANATOID > MANATEE
MANATS > MANAT
MANATU n large flowering deciduous New Zealand tree
MANAWA in New Zealand, same as > MANGROVE
MANAWAS > MANAWA
MANCALA n African and Asian board game
MANCALAS > MANCALA
MANCANDO adv musical direction meaning fading away
MANCHE n long sleeve
MANCHES > MANCHE
MANCHET n type of bread
MANCHETS > MANCHET
MANCIPATE vb make legal transfer in ancient Rome
MANCIPLE n steward who buys provisions, esp in a college, Inn of Court, or monastery
MANCIPLES > MANCIPLE
MANCUS n former English coin
MANCUSES > MANCUS
MAND > MAN
MANDALA n circular design symbolizing the universe
MANDALAS > MANDALA
MANDALIC > MANDALA
MANDAMUS n formerly a writ from, now an order of, a superior court commanding an inferior tribunal, public official, corporation, etc, to carry out a public duty
MANDARIN n high-ranking government official
MANDARINE same as > MANDARIN
MANDARINS > MANDARIN
MANDATARY same as > MANDATORY
MANDATE n official or authoritative command ▷ vb give authority to
MANDATED > MANDATE
MANDATES > MANDATE
MANDATING > MANDATE
MANDATOR > MANDATE
MANDATORS > MANDATE
MANDATORY adj compulsory ▷ n person or state holding a mandate
MANDI n (in India) a big market
MANDIBLE n lower jawbone or jawlike part
MANDIBLES > MANDIBLE
MANDILION same as > MANDYLION
MANDIOC same as > MANIOC
MANDIOCA same as > MANIOC
MANDIOCAS > MANDIOCA
MANDIOCCA same

as > MANIOC
MANDIOCS > MANDIOC
MANDIR n Hindu or Jain temple
MANDIRA same as > MANDIR
MANDIRAS > MANDIRA
MANDIRS > MANDIR
MANDIS > MANDI
MANDOLA n early type of mandolin
MANDOLAS > MANDOLA
MANDOLIN n musical instrument with four pairs of strings
MANDOLINE same as > MANDOLIN
MANDOLINS > MANDOLIN
MANDOM n mankind
MANDOMS > MANDOM
MANDORA n ancestor of mandolin
MANDORAS > MANDORA
MANDORLA n (in painting, sculpture, etc) an almond-shaped area of light, usually surrounding the resurrected Christ or the Virgin at the Assumption
MANDORLAS > MANDORLA
MANDRAKE n plant with a forked root, formerly used as a narcotic
MANDRAKES > MANDRAKE
MANDREL n shaft on which work is held in a lathe
MANDRELS > MANDREL
MANDRIL same as > MANDREL
MANDRILL n large blue-faced baboon
MANDRILLS > MANDRILL
MANDRILS > MANDRIL
MANDUCATE vb eat or chew
MANDYLION n loose garment formerly worn over armour
MANE n long hair on the neck of a horse, lion, etc
MANED > MANE
MANEGE n art of training horses and riders ▷ vb train horse
MANEGED > MANEGE
MANEGES > MANEGE
MANEGING > MANEGE
MANEH same as > MINA
MANEHS > MANEH
MANELESS > MANE
MANENT > MANET
MANES pl n spirits of the dead, often revered as minor deities
MANET vb theatre direction, remain on stage
MANEUVER same as > MANOEUVRE
MANEUVERS > MANEUVER
MANFUL adj determined and brave
MANFULLY > MANFUL
MANG vb speak
MANGA n type of Japanese comic book with an adult theme
MANGABEY n any of several large agile arboreal Old World monkeys of the

genus *Cercocebus*, of central Africa, having long limbs and tail and white upper eyelids

MANGABEYS > MANGABEY

MANGABIES > MANGABY

MANGABY *same as* > MANGABEY

MANGAL *n* Turkish brazier

MANGALS > MANGAL

MANGANATE *n* salt of manganic acid

MANGANESE *n* brittle greyish-white metallic element

MANGANIC *adj* of or containing manganese in the trivalent state

MANGANIN *n* copper-based alloy

MANGANINS > MANGANIN

MANGANITE *n* blackish mineral

MANGANOUS *adj* of or containing manganese in the divalent state

MANGAS > MANGA

MANGE *n* skin disease of domestic animals

MANGEAO *n* small New Zealand tree with glossy leaves

MANGED *adj* having mange

MANGEL *n* Eurasian variety of the beet plant, *Beta vulgaris*, cultivated as a cattle food, having a large yellowish root

MANGELS > MANGEL

MANGER *n* eating trough in a stable or barn

MANGERS > MANGER

MANGES > MANGE

MANGETOUT *n* variety of pea with an edible pod

MANGEY *same as* > MANGY

MANGIER > MANGY

MANGIEST > MANGY

MANGILY > MANGY

MANGINESS > MANGY

MANGING > MANG

MANGLE *vb* destroy by crushing and twisting ▷ *n* machine with rollers for squeezing water from washed clothes

MANGLED > MANGLE

MANGLER > MANGLE

MANGLERS > MANGLE

MANGLES > MANGLE

MANGLING > MANGLE

MANGO *n* tropical fruit with sweet juicy yellow flesh

MANGOES > MANGO

MANGOLD *n* type of root vegetable

MANGOLDS > MANGOLD

MANGONEL *n* war engine for hurling stones

MANGONELS > MANGONEL

MANGOS > MANGO

MANGOSTAN *n* East Indian tree with thick leathery leaves and edible fruit

MANGOUSTE *same as* > MONGOOSE

MANGROVE *n* tropical tree with exposed roots, which grows beside water

MANGROVES > MANGROVE

MANGS > MANG

MANGULATE *vb* bend or twist out of shape

MANGY *adj* having mange

MANHANDLE *vb* treat roughly

MANHATTAN *n* mixed drink consisting of four parts whisky, one part vermouth, and a dash of bitters

MANHOLE *n* hole with a cover, through which a person can enter a drain or sewer

MANHOLES > MANHOLE

MANHOOD *n* state or quality of being a man or being manly

MANHOODS > MANHOOD

MANHUNT *n* organized search, usu by police, for a wanted man or a fugitive

MANHUNTER > MANHUNT

MANHUNTS > MANHUNT

MANI *n* place to pray

MANIA *n* extreme enthusiasm

MANIAC *n* mad person

MANIACAL *adj* affected with or characteristic of mania

MANIACS > MANIAC

MANIAS > MANIA

MANIC *adj* extremely excited or energetic ▷ *n* person afflicted with mania

MANICALLY > MANIC

MANICOTTI *pl n* large tubular noodles, usually stuffed with ricotta cheese and baked in a tomato sauce

MANICS > MANIC

MANICURE *n* cosmetic care of the fingernails and hands ▷ *vb* care for (the fingernails and hands) in this way

MANICURED > MANICURE

MANICURES > MANICURE

MANIES > MANY

MANIFEST *adj* easily noticed, obvious ▷ *vb* show plainly ▷ *n* list of cargo or passengers for customs

MANIFESTO *n* declaration of policy as issued by a political party ▷ *vb* issued manifesto

MANIFESTS > MANIFEST

MANIFOLD *adj* numerous and varied ▷ *n* pipe with several outlets, esp in an internal-combustion engine ▷ *vb* duplicate (a page, book, etc)

MANIFOLDS > MANIFOLD

MANIFORM *adj* like hand

MANIHOC *variation of* > MANIOC

MANIHOCS > MANIHOC

MANIHOT *n* tropical American plant

MANIHOTS > MANIHOT

MANIKIN *n* little man or dwarf

MANIKINS > MANIKIN

MANILA *n* strong brown paper used for envelopes

MANILAS > MANILA

MANILLA *n* early currency in W Africa in the form of a small bracelet

MANILLAS > MANILLA

MANILLE *n* (in ombre and quadrille) the second best trump

MANILLES > MANILLE

MANIOC *same as* > CASSAVA

MANIOCA *same as* > MANIOC

MANIOCAS > MANIOCA

MANIOCS > MANIOC

MANIPLE *n* (in ancient Rome) a unit of 120 to 200 foot soldiers

MANIPLES > MANIPLE

MANIPLIES *same as* > MANYPLIES

MANIPULAR *adj* of or relating to an ancient Roman maniple

MANIS *n* pangolin

MANITO *same as* > MANITOU

MANITOS > MANITO

MANITOU *n* (among the Algonquian Indians) a deified spirit or force

MANITOUS > MANITOU

MANITU *same as* > MANITOU

MANITUS > MANITU

MANJACK *n* single individual

MANJACKS > MANJACK

MANKIER > MANKY

MANKIEST > MANKY

MANKIND *n* human beings collectively

MANKINDS > MANKIND

MANKY *adj* worthless, rotten, or in bad taste

MANLESS > MAN

MANLIER > MANLY

MANLIEST > MANLY

MANLIKE *adj* resembling or befitting a man

MANLIKELY > MANLIKE

MANLILY > MANLY

MANLINESS > MANLY

MANLY *adj* (possessing qualities) appropriate to a man

MANMADE *adj* made or produced by man

MANNA *n* miraculous food which sustained the Israelites in the wilderness

MANNAN *n* drug derived from mannose

MANNANS > MANNAN

MANNAS > MANNA

MANNED > MAN

MANNEQUIN *n* woman who models clothes at a fashion show

MANNER *n* way a thing happens or is done

MANNERED *adj* affected

MANNERISM *n* person's distinctive habit or trait

MANNERIST > MANNERISM

MANNERLY *adj* having good manners, polite ▷ *adv* with good manners

MANNERS *pl n* person's social conduct viewed in the light of whether it is regarded as polite or acceptable or not

MANNIKIN *same as* > MANIKIN

MANNIKINS > MANNIKIN

MANNING > MAN

MANNISH *adj* (of a woman) like a man

MANNISHLY > MANNISH

MANNITE *same as* > MANNITOL

MANNITES > MANNITE

MANNITIC > MANNITOL

MANNITOL *n* white crystalline water-soluble sweet-tasting alcohol

MANNITOLS > MANNITOL

MANNOSE *n* hexose sugar

MANNOSES > MANNOSE

MANO *n* stone for grinding grain

MANOAO *n* New Zealand shrub

MANOAOS > MANOAO

MANOEUVRE *n* skilful movement ▷ *vb* manipulate or contrive skilfully or cunningly

MANOMETER *n* instrument for comparing pressures

MANOMETRY > MANOMETER

MANOR *n* large country house and its lands

MANORIAL > MANOR

MANORS > MANOR

MANOS > MANO

MANOSCOPY *n* measurement of the densities of gases

MANPACK *n* load carried by one person

MANPACKS > MANPACK

MANPOWER *n* available number of workers

MANPOWERS > MANPOWER

MANQUE *adj* would-be

MANRED *n* homage

MANREDS > MANRED

MANRENT *same as* > MANRED

MANRENTS > MANRENT

MANRIDER *n* train carrying miners in coal mine

MANRIDERS > MANRIDER

MANRIDING *adj* carrying people rather than goods

MANROPE *n* rope railing

MANROPES > MANROPE

MANS > MAN

MANSARD *n* roof with two slopes on both sides and both ends, the lower slopes being steeper than the upper

MANSARDED *adj* having mansard roof

MANSARDS > MANSARD

MANSE *n* house provided for a minister in some religious denominations

MANSES > MANSE

MANSHIFT *n* work done by one person in one shift

MANSHIFTS > MANSHIFT

MANSION *n* large house

MANSIONS > MANSION

MANSLAYER n person who kills man
MANSONRY n mansions collectively
MANSUETE adj gentle
MANSWORN adj perjured
MANTA n any large ray (fish) of the family *Mobulidae*, having very wide winglike pectoral fins and feeding on plankton
MANTAS > MANTA
MANTEAU n cloak or mantle
MANTEAUS > MANTEAU
MANTEAUX > MANTEAU
MANTEEL n cloak
MANTEELS > MANTEEL
MANTEL n structure round a fireplace ▷ vb construct a mantel
MANTELET n woman's short mantle, often lace-trimmed, worn in the mid-19th century
MANTELETS > MANTELET
MANTELS > MANTEL
MANTES > MANTIS
MANTIC adj of or relating to divination and prophecy
MANTICORA same as > MANTICORE
MANTICORE n mythical monster with body of lion and human head
MANTID same as > MANTIS
MANTIDS > MANTID
MANTIES > MANTY
MANTILLA n (in Spain) a lace scarf covering a woman's head and shoulders
MANTILLAS > MANTILLA
MANTIS n carnivorous insect like a grasshopper
MANTISES > MANTIS
MANTISSA n part of a common logarithm consisting of the decimal point and the figures following it
MANTISSAS > MANTISSA
MANTLE same as > MANTEL
MANTLED > MANTLE
MANTLES > MANTLE
MANTLET same as > MANTELET
MANTLETS > MANTLET
MANTLING n drapery or scrollwork around a shield
MANTLINGS > MANTLING
MANTO same as > MANTEAU
MANTOES > MANTO
MANTOS > MANTO
MANTRA n any sacred word or syllable used as an object of concentration
MANTRAM same as > MANTRA
MANTRAMS > MANTRAM
MANTRAP n snare for catching people, esp trespassers
MANTRAPS > MANTRAP
MANTRAS > MANTRA
MANTRIC > MANTRA
MANTUA n loose gown of the 17th and 18th centuries, worn open in front to show the underskirt

MANTUAS > MANTUA
MANTY Scots variant of > MANTUA
MANUAL adj of or done with the hands ▷ n handbook
MANUALLY > MANUAL
MANUALS > MANUAL
MANUARY same as > MANUAL
MANUBRIA > MANUBRIUM
MANUBRIAL > MANUBRIUM
MANUBRIUM n any handle-shaped part, esp the upper part of the sternum
MANUHIRI n visitor to a Māori marae
MANUHIRIS > MANUHIRI
MANUKA n New Zealand tree with strong elastic wood and aromatic leaves
MANUKAS > MANUKA
MANUL n Asian wildcat
MANULS > MANUL
MANUMEA n pigeon of Samoa
MANUMEAS > MANUMEA
MANUMIT vb free from slavery
MANUMITS > MANUMIT
MANURANCE n cultivation of land
MANURE n animal excrement used as a fertilizer ▷ vb fertilize (land) with this
MANURED > MANURE
MANURER > MANURE
MANURERS > MANURE
MANURES > MANURE
MANURIAL > MANURE
MANURING > MANURE
MANURINGS > MANURE
MANUS n wrist and hand
MANWARD adv towards humankind
MANWARDS same as > MANWARD
MANWISE adv in human way
MANY adj numerous ▷ n large number
MANYATA same as > MANYATTA
MANYATAS > MANYATA
MANYATTA n settlement of Masai people
MANYATTAS > MANYATTA
MANYFOLD adj many in number
MANYPLIES n third component of the stomach of ruminants
MANZANITA n Californian plant
MANZELLO n instrument like saxophone
MANZELLOS > MANZELLO
MAOMAO n fish of New Zealand seas
MAORMOR same as > MORMAOR
MAORMORS > MAORMOR
MAP n representation of the earth's surface or some part of it, showing geographical features ▷ vb make a map of
MAPAU n small New Zealand tree with reddish bark, aromatic leaves, and dark berries

MAPLE n tree with broad leaves, a variety of which yields sugar
MAPLELIKE > MAPLE
MAPLES > MAPLE
MAPLESS > MAP
MAPLIKE > MAP
MAPMAKER n person who draws maps
MAPMAKERS > MAPMAKER
MAPMAKING > MAPMAKER
MAPPABLE > MAP
MAPPED > MAP
MAPPEMOND n map of world
MAPPER > MAP
MAPPERIES > MAPPERY
MAPPERS > MAP
MAPPERY n making of maps
MAPPING > MAP
MAPPINGS > MAP
MAPPIST > MAP
MAPPISTS > MAP
MAPS > MAP
MAPSTICK same as > MOPSTICK
MAPSTICKS > MAPSTICK
MAPWISE adv like map
MAQUETTE n sculptor's small preliminary model or sketch
MAQUETTES > MAQUETTE
MAQUI n Chilean shrub
MAQUILA n US-owned factory in Mexico
MAQUILAS > MAQUILA
MAQUIS n French underground movement that fought against the German occupying forces in World War II
MAQUISARD n member of French maquis
MAR vb spoil or impair ▷ n disfiguring mark
MARA n harelike South American rodent, *Dolichotis patagonum*, inhabiting the pampas of Argentina: family *Caviidae* (cavies)
MARABI n kind of music popular in S African townships in the 1930s
MARABIS > MARABI
MARABOU n large black-and-white African stork
MARABOUS > MARABOU
MARABOUT n Muslim holy man or hermit of North Africa
MARABOUTS > MARABOUT
MARABUNTA n any of several social wasps
MARACA n shaken percussion instrument made from a gourd containing dried seeds etc
MARACAS > MARACA
MARAE n enclosed space in front of a Māori meeting house
MARAES > MARAE
MARAGING as in *maraging steel* strong low-carbon steel containing nickel and small amounts of titanium, aluminium, and niobium, produced by transforming

to a martensitic structure and heating at 500°C
MARAGINGS > MARAGING
MARAH n bitterness
MARAHS > MARAH
MARANATHA n member of Christian sect
MARANTA n any plant of the tropical American rhizomatous genus *Maranta*, some species of which are grown as pot plants for their showy leaves in variegated shades of green: family *Marantaceae*
MARANTAS > MARANTA
MARARI n eel-like blennoid food fish
MARARIS > MARARI
MARAS > MARA
MARASCA n European cherry tree, *Prunus cerasus marasca*, with red acid-tasting fruit from which maraschino is made
MARASCAS > MARASCA
MARASMIC > MARASMUS
MARASMOID > MARASMUS
MARASMUS n general emaciation and wasting, esp of infants, thought to be associated with severe malnutrition or impaired utilization of nutrients
MARATHON n long-distance race of 26 miles 385 yards (42.195 kilometres) ▷ adj of or relating to a race on foot of 26 miles 385 yards (42.195 kilometres)
MARATHONS > MARATHON
MARAUD vb wander or raid in search of plunder
MARAUDED > MARAUD
MARAUDER > MARAUD
MARAUDERS > MARAUD
MARAUDING adj wandering or raiding in search of plunder
MARAUDS > MARAUD
MARAVEDI n any of various Spanish coins of copper or gold
MARAVEDIS > MARAVEDI
MARBELISE same as > MARBLEIZE
MARBELIZE same as > MARBLEIZE
MARBLE n kind of limestone with a mottled appearance, which can be highly polished ▷ vb mottle with variegated streaks in imitation of marble
MARBLED > MARBLE
MARBLEISE same as > MARBLEIZE
MARBLEIZE vb give a marble-like appearance to
MARBLER > MARBLE
MARBLERS > MARBLE
MARBLES n game in which marble balls are rolled at one another
MARBLIER > MARBLE

MARBLIEST > MARBLE

MARBLING n mottled effect or pattern resembling marble

MARBLINGS > MARBLING

MARBLY > MARBLE

MARC n remains of grapes or other fruit that have been pressed for wine-making

MARCASITE n crystals of iron pyrites, used in jewellery

MARCATO adj (of notes) heavily accented ▷ adv with each note heavily accented

MARCATOS > MARCATO

MARCEL n hairstyle characterized by repeated regular waves, popular in the 1920s ▷ vb make such waves in (the hair) with special hot irons

MARCELLA n type of fabric

MARCELLAS > MARCELLA

MARCELLED > MARCEL

MARCELLER > MARCEL

MARCELS > MARCEL

MARCH vb walk with a military step ▷ n action of marching

MARCHED > MARCH

MARCHEN n German story

MARCHER n person who marches

MARCHERS > MARCHER

MARCHES > MARCH

MARCHESA n (in Italy) the wife or widow of a marchese

MARCHESAS > MARCHESA

MARCHESE n (in Italy) a nobleman ranking below a prince and above a count

MARCHESES > MARCHESE

MARCHESI > MARCHESE

MARCHING > MARCH

MARCHLAND n border land

MARCHLIKE adj like march in rhythm

MARCHMAN n person living on border

MARCHMEN > MARCHMAN

MARCHPANE same as > MARZIPAN

MARCONI vb communicate by wireless

MARCONIED > MARCONI

MARCONIS > MARCONI

MARCS > MARC

MARD > MAR

MARDIED > MARDY

MARDIER > MARDY

MARDIES > MARDY

MARDIEST > MARDY

MARDY adj (of a child) spoilt ▷ vb behave in mardy way

MARDYING > MARDY

MARE n female horse or zebra

MAREMMA n marshy unhealthy region near the shore, esp in Italy

MAREMMAS > MAREMMA

MAREMME > MAREMMA

MARENGO adj browned in oil and cooked with tomatoes, mushrooms, garlic, wine, etc

MARES > MARE

MARESCHAL same as > MARSHAL

MARG short for > MARGARINE

MARGARIC adj of or resembling pearl

MARGARIN n ester of margaric acid

MARGARINE n butter substitute made from animal or vegetable fats

MARGARINS > MARGARIN

MARGARITA n mixed drink consisting of tequila and lemon juice

MARGARITE n pink pearly micaceous mineral

MARGAY n feline mammal, Felis wiedi, of Central and South America, having a dark-striped coat

MARGAYS > MARGAY

MARGE n margarine

MARGENT same as > MARGIN

MARGENTED > MARGENT

MARGENTS > MARGENT

MARGES > MARGE

MARGIN n edge or border ▷ vb provide with a margin

MARGINAL adj insignificant, unimportant ▷ n marginal constituency

MARGINALS > MARGINAL

MARGINATE vb provide with a margin or margins ▷ adj having a margin of a distinct colour or form

MARGINED > MARGIN

MARGINING > MARGIN

MARGINS > MARGIN

MARGOSA n Indian tree

MARGOSAS > MARGOSA

MARGRAVE n (formerly) a German nobleman ranking above a count

MARGRAVES > MARGRAVE

MARGS > MARG

MARIA > MARE

MARIACHI n small ensemble of street musicians in Mexico

MARIACHIS > MARIACHI

MARIALITE n silicate mineral

MARID n spirit in Muslim mythology

MARIDS > MARID

MARIES > MARY

MARIGOLD n plant with yellow or orange flowers

MARIGOLDS > MARIGOLD

MARIGRAM n graphic record of the tide levels at a particular coastal station

MARIGRAMS > MARIGRAM

MARIGRAPH n gauge for recording the levels of the tides

MARIHUANA same as > MARIJUANA

MARIJUANA n dried flowers and leaves of the cannabis plant, used as a drug, esp in cigarettes

MARIMBA n Latin American percussion instrument resembling a xylophone

MARIMBAS > MARIMBA

MARIMBIST > MARIMBA

MARINA n harbour for yachts and other pleasure boats

MARINADE n seasoned liquid in which fish or meat is soaked before cooking

MARINADED > MARINADE

MARINADES > MARINADE

MARINARA n Italian pasta sauce

MARINARAS > MARINARA

MARINAS > MARINA

MARINATE vb soak in marinade

MARINATED > MARINATE

MARINATES > MARINATE

MARINE adj of the sea or shipping ▷ n (esp in Britain and the US) soldier trained for land and sea combat

MARINER n sailor

MARINERA n folk dance of Peru

MARINERAS > MARINERA

MARINERS > MARINER

MARINES > MARINE

MARINIERE adj served in white wine and onion sauce

MARIPOSA n any of several liliaceous plants of the genus Calochortus, of the southwestern US and Mexico, having brightly coloured tulip-like flowers

MARIPOSAS > MARIPOSA

MARISCHAL Scots variant of > MARSHAL

MARISH n marsh

MARISHES > MARISH

MARITAGE n right of a lord to choose the spouses of his wards

MARITAGES > MARITAGE

MARITAL adj relating to marriage

MARITALLY > MARITAL

MARITIME adj relating to shipping

MARJORAM n aromatic herb used for seasoning food and in salads

MARJORAMS > MARJORAM

MARK n line, dot, scar, etc visible on a surface ▷ vb make a mark on

MARKA n unit of currency introduced as an interim currency in Bosnia-Herzegovina

MARKAS > MARKA

MARKDOWN n price reduction ▷ vb reduce in price

MARKDOWNS > MARKDOWN

MARKED adj noticeable

MARKEDLY > MARKED

MARKER n object used to show the position of something

MARKERS > MARKER

MARKET n assembly or place for buying and selling ▷ vb offer or produce for sale

MARKETED > MARKET

MARKETEER n supporter of the European Union and of Britain's membership of it

MARKETER > MARKET

MARKETERS > MARKET

MARKETING n part of a business that controls the way that goods or services are sold

MARKETS > MARKET

MARKHOOR same as > MARKHOR

MARKHOORS > MARKHOOR

MARKHOR n large wild Himalayan goat, Capra falconeri, with a reddish-brown coat and large spiralled horns

MARKHORS > MARKHOR

MARKING n arrangement of colours on an animal or plant

MARKINGS > MARKING

MARKKA n former standard monetary unit of Finland, divided into 100 penniä

MARKKAA > MARKKA

MARKKAS > MARKKA

MARKMAN n person owning land

MARKMEN > MARKMAN

MARKS > MARK

MARKSMAN n person skilled at shooting

MARKSMEN > MARKSMAN

MARKUP n percentage or amount added to the cost of a commodity to provide the seller with a profit and to cover overheads, costs, etc ▷ vb increase the price of

MARKUPS > MARKUP

MARL n soil formed of clay and lime, used as fertilizer ▷ vb fertilize (land) with marl

MARLE same as > MARVEL

MARLED > MARL

MARLES > MARLE

MARLIER > MARLY

MARLIEST > MARLY

MARLIN same as > MARLINE

MARLINE n light rope, usually tarred, made of two strands laid left-handed

MARLINES > MARLINE

MARLING same as > MARLINE

MARLINGS > MARLING

MARLINS > MARLIN

MARLITE n type of marl that contains clay and calcium carbonate and is resistant to the decomposing action of air

MARLITES > MARLITE

MARLITIC > MARLITE

MARLS > MARL

MARLSTONE same as > MARLITE

MARLY adj marl-like

MARM same as > MADAM

MARMALADE n jam made from citrus fruits ▷ adj (of cats) streaked orange or yellow and brown

MARMALISE *vb* beat soundly or defeat utterly

MARMALIZE *same as* > MARMALISE

MARMARISE *same as* > MARMARIZE

MARMARIZE *vb* turn to marble

MARMELISE *same as* > MARMELIZE

MARMELIZE *vb* beat soundly

MARMITE *n* large cooking pot

MARMITES > MARMITE

MARMOREAL *adj* of or like marble

MARMOREAN *same as* > MARMOREAL

MARMOSE *n* South American opossum

MARMOSES > MARMOSE

MARMOSET *n* small bushy-tailed monkey

MARMOSETS > MARMOSET

MARMOT *n* burrowing rodent

MARMOTS > MARMOT

MARMS > MARM

MAROCAIN *n* fabric of ribbed crepe

MAROCAINS > MAROCAIN

MARON *n* freshwater crustacean

MARONS > MARON

MAROON *adj* reddish-purple ▷ *vb* abandon ashore, esp on an island ▷ *n* exploding firework or flare used as a warning signal

MAROONED > MAROON

MAROONER > MAROON

MAROONERS > MAROON

MAROONING > MAROON

MAROONS > MAROON

MAROQUIN *n* morocco leather

MAROQUINS > MAROQUIN

MAROR *n* Jewish ceremonial dish of bitter herbs

MARORS > MAROR

MARPLOT *n* person interfering with plot

MARPLOTS > MARPLOT

MARQUE *n* brand of product, esp of a car

MARQUEE *n* large tent used for a party or exhibition

MARQUEES > MARQUEE

MARQUES > MARQUE

MARQUESS *n* nobleman of the rank below a duke

MARQUETRY *n* ornamental inlaid work of wood

MARQUIS *n* (in some European countries) nobleman of the rank above a count

MARQUISE *same as* > MARQUEE

MARQUISES > MARQUISE

MARRAM as in *marram grass* any of several grasses of the genus that grow on sandy shores and can withstand drying

MARRAMS > MARRAM

MARRANO *n* Spanish or Portuguese Jew of the late Middle Ages who was converted to Christianity, esp one forcibly converted but secretly adhering to Judaism

MARRANOS > MARRANO

MARRED > MAR

MARRELS *same as* > MERILS

MARRER > MAR

MARRERS > MAR

MARRI *n* species of eucalyptus, *Eucalyptus calophylla*, of Western Australia, widely cultivated for its coloured flowers

MARRIAGE *n* state of being married

MARRIAGES > MARRIAGE

MARRIED > MARRY

MARRIEDS *pl n* married people

MARRIER > MARRY

MARRIERS > MARRY

MARRIES > MARRY

MARRING > MAR

MARRIS > MARRI

MARRON *n* large edible sweet chestnut

MARRONS > MARRON

MARROW *n* fatty substance inside bones ▷ *vb* be mate to

MARROWED > MARROW

MARROWFAT *n* variety of large pea

MARROWING > MARROW

MARROWISH > MARROW

MARROWS > MARROW

MARROWSKY *n* spoonerism

MARROWY > MARROW

MARRUM *same as* > MARRAM

MARRUMS > MARRUM

MARRY *vb* take as a husband or wife ▷ *interj* exclamation of surprise or anger

MARRYING > MARRY

MARRYINGS > MARRY

MARS > MAR

MARSALA *n* dark sweet dessert wine made in Sicily

MARSALAS > MARSALA

MARSE *same as* > MASTER

MARSEILLE *n* strong cotton fabric with a raised pattern, used for bedspreads, etc

MARSES > MARSE

MARSH *n* low-lying wet land

MARSHAL *n* officer of the highest rank ▷ *vb* arrange in order

MARSHALCY > MARSHAL

MARSHALED > MARSHAL

MARSHALER > MARSHAL

MARSHALL *n* shortened form of Marshall Plan, programme of US economic aid for the reconstruction of post-World War II Europe (1948–52)

MARSHALLS > MARSHALL

MARSHALS > MARSHAL

MARSHBUCK *n* antelope of the central African swamplands, *Strepsiceros spekei*, with spreading hoofs adapted to boggy ground

MARSHES > MARSH

MARSHIER > MARSHY

MARSHIEST > MARSHY

MARSHLAND *n* land consisting of marshes

MARSHLIKE > MARSH

MARSHWORT *n* prostrate creeping aquatic perennial umbelliferous plant of the genus *Apium*, esp *A. inundatum*, having small white flowers: related to wild celery

MARSHY *adj* of, involving, or like a marsh

MARSPORT *n* spoilsport

MARSPORTS > MARSPORT

MARSQUAKE *n* Martian equivalent of earthquake

MARSUPIA > MARSUPIUM

MARSUPIAL *n* animal that carries its young in a pouch, such as a kangaroo ▷ *adj* of or like a marsupial

MARSUPIAN > MARSUPIAL

MARSUPIUM *n* external pouch in most female marsupials within which the newly born offspring are suckled and complete their development

MART *n* market ▷ *vb* sell or trade

MARTAGON *n* Eurasian lily plant, *Lilium martagon*, cultivated for its mottled purplish-red flowers with reflexed petals

MARTAGONS > MARTAGON

MARTED > MART

MARTEL *n* hammer-shaped weapon ▷ *vb* use such a weapon

MARTELLED > MARTEL

MARTELLO *n* small circular tower for coastal defence, formerly much used in Europe

MARTELLOS > MARTELLO

MARTELS > MARTEL

MARTEN *n* weasel-like animal

MARTENS > MARTEN

MARTEXT *n* preacher who makes many mistakes

MARTEXTS > MARTEXT

MARTIAL *adj* of war, warlike

MARTIALLY > MARTIAL

MARTIALS as in *court martials* military courts that try people subject to military law

MARTIAN *n* inhabitant of Mars

MARTIANS > MARTIAN

MARTIN *n* bird with a slightly forked tail

MARTINET *n* person who maintains strict discipline

MARTINETS > MARTINET

MARTING > MART

MARTINGAL *n* strap of a horse's harness

MARTINI *n* cocktail of vermouth and gin

MARTINIS > MARTINI

MARTINS > MARTIN

MARTLET *n* footless bird often found in coats of arms, standing for either a martin or a swallow

MARTLETS > MARTLET

MARTS > MART

MARTYR *n* person who dies or suffers for his or her beliefs ▷ *vb* make a martyr of

MARTYRDOM *n* sufferings or death of a martyr

MARTYRED > MARTYR

MARTYRIA > MARTYRIUM

MARTYRIES > MARTYRY

MARTYRING > MARTYR

MARTYRISE > MARTYR

MARTYRIUM *same as* > MARTYRY

MARTYRIZE > MARTYR

MARTYRLY > MARTYR

MARTYRS > MARTYR

MARTYRY *n* shrine or chapel erected in honour of a martyr

MARVEL *vb* be filled with wonder ▷ *n* wonderful thing

MARVELED > MARVEL

MARVELING > MARVEL

MARVELLED > MARVEL

MARVELOUS *adj* causing great wonder

MARVELS > MARVEL

MARVER *vb* roll molten glass on slab

MARVERED > MARVER

MARVERING > MARVER

MARVERS > MARVER

MARVY *shortened form of* > MARVELOUS

MARXISANT *adj* sympathetic to Marxism

MARY *shortened form of* > MARYJANE

MARYBUD *n* bud of marigold

MARYBUDS > MARYBUD

MARYJANE *n* slang for marijuana

MARYJANES > MARYJANE

MARZIPAN *n* paste of ground almonds, sugar, and egg whites ▷ *modifier* of or relating to the stratum of middle managers in a financial institution or other business

MARZIPANS > MARZIPAN

MAS > MA

MASA *n* Mexican maize dough

MASALA *n* mixture of spices ground into a paste ▷ *adj* spicy

MASALAS > MASALA

MASAS > MASA

MASCARA *n* cosmetic for darkening the eyelashes

MASCARAED *adj* wearing mascara

MASCARAS > MASCARA

MASCARON *n* in architecture, a face carved in stone or metal

MASCARONS *n* grotesque face used as decoration

MASCLE *n* charge consisting of a lozenge with a lozenge-shaped hole in the middle

MASCLED > MASCLE

MASCLES > MASCLE

MASCON *n* any of several lunar regions of high gravity

MASCONS > MASCON

MASCOT *n* person, animal, or thing supposed to bring good luck

MASCOTS > MASCOT

MASCULINE *adj* relating to males

MASCULIST *n* advocate of rights of men)

MASCULY > MASCLE

MASE *vb* function as maser

MASED > MASE

MASER *n* device for amplifying microwaves

MASERS > MASER

MASES > MASE

MASH *n* soft pulpy mass ▷ *vb* crush into a soft mass

MASHALLAH *interj* what Allah wishes

MASHED > MASH

MASHER > MASH

MASHERS > MASH

MASHES > MASH

MASHGIACH *n* person who ensures adherence to kosher rules

MASHGIAH *same as* > MASHGIACH

MASHGIHIM > MASHGIACH

MASHIACH *n* messiah

MASHIACHS > MASHIACH

MASHIE *n* (formerly) a club, corresponding to the modern No. 5 or No. 6 iron, used for approach shots

MASHIER > MASHY

MASHIES > MASHIE

MASHIEST > MASHY

MASHING > MASH

MASHINGS > MASH

MASHLAM *same as* > MASLIN

MASHLAMS > MASHLAM

MASHLIM *same as* > MASLIN

MASHLIMS > MASHLIM

MASHLIN *same as* > MASLIN

MASHLINS > MASHLIN

MASHLOCH *same as* > MASLIN

MASHLOCHS > MASHLOCH

MASHLUM *same as* > MASLIN

MASHLUMS > MASHLUM

MASHMAN *n* brewery worker

MASHMEN > MASHMAN

MASHUA *n* South American plant

MASHUAS > MASHUA

MASHUP *n* piece of recorded or live music in which a producer or DJ blends together two or more tracks, often of contrasting genres

MASHUPS > MASHUP

MASHY *adj* like mash

MASING > MASE

MASJID *same as* > MOSQUE

MASJIDS > MASJID

MASK *n* covering for the face, as a disguise or protection ▷ *vb* cover with a mask

MASKABLE > MASK

MASKED *adj* disguised or covered by or as if by a mask

MASKEG *n* North American bog

MASKEGS > MASKEG

MASKER *n* person who wears a mask or takes part in a masque

MASKERS > MASKER

MASKING *n* act or practice of masking

MASKINGS > MASKING

MASKLIKE > MASK

MASKS > MASK

MASLIN *n* mixture of wheat, rye or other grain

MASLINS > MASLIN

MASOCHISM *n* condition in which (sexual) pleasure is obtained from feeling pain or from being humiliated

MASOCHIST > MASOCHISM

MASON *n* person who works with stone ▷ *vb* construct or strengthen with masonry

MASONED > MASON

MASONIC *adj* of, characteristic of, or relating to Freemasons or Freemasonry

MASONING ≥ MASON

MASONITE *n* tradename for a kind of dark brown hardboard used for partitions, lining, etc

MASONITES > MASONITE

MASONRIED *adj* built of masonry

MASONRIES > MASONRY

MASONRY *n* stonework

MASONS > MASON

MASOOLAH *n* Indian boat used in surf

MASOOLAHS > MASOOLAH

MASQUE *n* 16th–17th-century form of dramatic entertainment

MASQUER *same as* > MASKER

MASQUERS > MASQUER

MASQUES > MASQUE

MASS *n* coherent body of matter ▷ *adj* large-scale ▷ *vb* form into a mass

MASSA *old fashioned variant of* > MASTER

MASSACRE *n* indiscriminate killing of large numbers of people ▷ *vb* kill in large numbers

MASSACRED > MASSACRE

MASSACRER > MASSACRE

MASSACRES > MASSACRE

MASSAGE *n* rubbing and kneading of parts of the body to reduce pain or stiffness ▷ *vb* give a massage to

MASSAGED > MASSAGE

MASSAGER > MASSAGE

MASSAGERS > MASSAGE

MASSAGES > MASSAGE

MASSAGING > MASSAGE

MASSAGIST > MASSAGE

MASSAS > MASSA

MASSCULT *n* culture of masses

MASSCULTS > MASSCULT

MASSE *n* stroke made by hitting the cue ball off centre with the cue held nearly vertically, esp so as to make the ball move in a curve around another ball before hitting the object ball

MASSED > MASS

MASSEDLY > MASS

MASSES *pl n* body of common people

MASSETER *n* muscle of the cheek used in moving the jaw, esp in chewing

MASSETERS > MASSETER

MASSEUR *n* person who gives massages

MASSEURS > MASSEUR

MASSEUSE *n* woman who gives massages, esp as a profession

MASSEUSES > MASSEUSE

MASSICOT *n* yellow earthy secondary mineral

MASSICOTS > MASSICOT

MASSIER > MASSY

MASSIEST > MASSY

MASSIF *n* connected group of mountains

MASSIFS > MASSIF

MASSINESS > MASSY

MASSING > MASS

MASSIVE *adj* large and heavy ▷ *n* group of friends or associates

MASSIVELY > MASSIVE

MASSIVES > MASSIVE

MASSLESS > MASS

MASSOOLA *same as* > MASOOLAH

MASSOOLAS > MASSOOLA

MASSY *literary word for* > MASSIVE

MASSYMORE *n* underground prison

MAST *n* tall pole for supporting something, esp a ship's sails

MASTABA *n* mud-brick superstructure above tombs in ancient Egypt

MASTABAH *same as* > MASTABA

MASTABAHS > MASTABAH

MASTABAS > MASTABA

MASTED > MAST

MASTER *n* person in control, such as an employer or an owner of slaves or animals ▷ *adj* overall or controlling ▷ *vb* acquire knowledge of or skill in ▷ *modifier* overall or controlling

MASTERATE *n* status of master

MASTERDOM > MASTER

MASTERED > MASTER

MASTERFUL *adj* domineering

MASTERIES > MASTERY

MASTERING > MASTER

MASTERLY *adj* showing great skill

MASTERS > MASTER

MASTERY *n* expertise

MASTFUL > MAST

MASTHEAD *n* head of a mast ▷ *vb* send (a sailor) to the masthead as a punishment

MASTHEADS > MASTHEAD

MASTHOUSE *n* place for storing masts

MASTIC *n* gum obtained from certain trees

MASTICATE *vb* chew

MASTICH *same as* > MASTIC

MASTICHE *same as* > MASTIC

MASTICHES > MASTICHE

MASTICHS > MASTICH

MASTICOT *same as* > MASSICOT

MASTICOTS > MASTICOT

MASTICS > MASTIC

MASTIER > MAST

MASTIEST > MAST

MASTIFF *n* large dog

MASTIFFS > MASTIFF

MASTING > MAST

MASTITIC > MASTITIS

MASTITIS *n* inflammation of a breast or udder

MASTIX *n* type of gum

MASTIXES > MASTIX

MASTLESS > MAST

MASTLIKE > MAST

MASTODON *n* extinct elephant-like mammal

MASTODONS > MASTODON

MASTODONT > MASTODON

MASTOID *n* projection of the bone behind the ear ▷ *adj* shaped like a nipple or breast

MASTOIDAL > MASTOID

MASTOIDS > MASTOID

MASTOPEXY *n* cosmetic surgery of breasts

MASTS > MAST

MASTY > MAST

MASU *n* Japanese salmon

MASULA *same as* > MASOOLAH

MASULAS > MASULA

MASURIUM *n* silver-grey metallic element

MASURIUMS > MASURIUM

MASUS > MASU

MAT *n* piece of fabric used as a floor covering or to protect a surface ▷ *vb* tangle or become tangled into a dense mass ▷ *adj* having a dull, lustreless, or roughened surface

MATACHIN *n* dancer with sword

MATACHINA *n* feamale matachin

MATACHINI > MATACHIN

MATADOR *n* man who kills the bull in bullfights

MATADORA *n* female matador

MATADORAS > MATADORA

MATADORE *n* form of dominoes game

MATADORES > MATADORE
MATADORS > MATADOR
MATAGOURI n thorny bush of New Zealand, *Discaria toumatou*, that forms thickets in open country
MATAI n New Zealand tree, the wood of which is used for timber for building
MATAIS > MATAI
MATAMATA (in Malaysia) a former name for > POLICE
MATAMATAS > MATAMATA
MATAMBALA > TAMBALA
MATATA same as > FERNBIRD
MATCH n contest in a game or sport ▷ vb be exactly like, equal to, or in harmony with
MATCHABLE > MATCH
MATCHBOOK n number of carboard matches attached in folder
MATCHBOX n small box for holding matches
MATCHED > MATCH
MATCHER > MATCH
MATCHERS > MATCH
MATCHES > MATCH
MATCHET same as > MACHETE
MATCHETS > MATCHET
MATCHING > MATCH
MATCHLESS adj unequalled
MATCHLOCK n obsolete type of gunlock igniting the powder by means of a slow match
MATCHMADE > MATCHMAKE
MATCHMAKE vb bring suitable people together for marriage
MATCHMARK n mark made on mating components of an engine, machine, etc, to ensure that the components are assembled in the correct relative positions ▷ vb stamp (an object) with matchmarks
MATCHPLAY adj of a golf scoring system relating to holes won and lost
MATCHUP n sports match
MATCHUPS > MATCHUP
MATCHWOOD n small splinters
MATE n friend ▷ vb pair (animals) or (of animals) be paired for reproduction
MATED > MATE
MATELASSE adj (in textiles) having a raised design, as quilting
MATELESS > MATE
MATELOT n sailor
MATELOTE n fish served with a sauce of wine, onions, seasonings, and fish stock
MATELOTES > MATELOTE
MATELOTS > MATELOT
MATELOTTE same as > MATELOTE
MATER n mother: often used facetiously
MATERIAL n substance of which a thing is made ▷ adj of matter or substance

MATERIALS pl n equipment necessary for a particular activity
MATERIEL n materials and equipment of an organization, esp of a military force
MATERIELS > MATERIEL
MATERNAL adj of a mother
MATERNITY n motherhood ▷ adj of or for pregnant women
MATERS > MATER
MATES > MATE
MATESHIP n comradeship of friends, usually male, viewed as an institution
MATESHIPS > MATESHIP
MATEY adj friendly or intimate ▷ n friend or fellow: usually used in direct address
MATEYNESS > MATEY
MATEYS > MATEY
MATFELON n knapweed
MATFELONS > MATFELON
MATGRASS n widespread perennial European grass with dense tufts of bristly leaves, characteristic of peaty moors
MATH same as > MATHS
MATHESES > MATHESIS
MATHESIS n learning or wisdom
MATHS n the study of numbers, measurements, and shapes
MATICO n Peruvian shrub
MATICOS > MATICO
MATIER > MATY
MATIES > MATY
MATIEST > MATY
MATILDA n bushman's swag
MATILDAS > MATILDA
MATILY > MATY
MATIN adj of or relating to matins
MATINAL same as > MATIN
MATINEE n afternoon performance in a theatre or cinema
MATINEES > MATINEE
MATINESS > MATY
MATING > MATE
MATINGS > MATE
MATINS pl n early morning service in various Christian Churches
MATIPO n New Zealand shrub
MATIPOS > MATIPO
MATJES same as > MAATJES
MATLESS > MAT
MATLO same as > MATELOT
MATLOS > MATLO
MATLOW same as > MATELOT
MATLOWS > MATLOW
MATOKE n (in Uganda) the flesh of bananas, boiled and mashed as a food
MATOKES > MATOKE
MATOOKE same as > MATOKE
MATOOKES > MATOOKE
MATRASS n long-necked glass flask, used for distilling, dissolving

substances, etc
MATRASSES > MATRASS
MATRES > MATER
MATRIARCH n female head of a tribe or family
MATRIC n matriculation
MATRICE same as > MATRIX
MATRICES > MATRIX
MATRICIDE n crime of killing one's mother
MATRICS > MATRIC
MATRICULA n register
MATRILINY n attention to descent of kinship through the female line
MATRIMONY n marriage
MATRIX n substance or situation in which something originates, takes form, or is enclosed
MATRIXES > MATRIX
MATRON n staid or dignified married woman
MATRONAGE n state of being a matron
MATRONAL > MATRON
MATRONISE same as > MATRONIZE
MATRONIZE vb make matronly
MATRONLY adj (of a woman) middle-aged and plump
MATRONS > MATRON
MATROSS n gunner's assitant
MATROSSES > MATROSS
MATS > MAT
MATSAH same as > MATZO
MATSAHS > MATSAH
MATSURI n Japanese religious ceremony
MATSURIS > MATSURI
MATSUTAKE n Japanese mushroom
MATT adj dull, not shiny
MATTAMORE n subterranean storehouse or dwelling
MATTE same as > MATT
MATTED > MAT
MATTEDLY > MAT
MATTER n substance of which something is made ▷ vb be of importance
MATTERED > MATTER
MATTERFUL > MATTER
MATTERING > MATTER
MATTERS > MATTER
MATTERY adj discharging pus
MATTES > MATTE
MATTIE n young herring
MATTIES > MATTIE
MATTIFIED > MATTIFY
MATTIFIES > MATTIFY
MATTIFY vb make (the skin of the face) less oily or shiny using cosmetics
MATTIN same as > MATIN
MATTING > MAT
MATTINGS > MAT
MATTINS same as > MATINS
MATTOCK n large pick with one of its blade ends flattened for loosening soil
MATTOCKS > MATTOCK
MATTOID n person displaying eccentric

behaviour and mental characteristics that approach the psychotic
MATTOIDS > MATTOID
MATTRASS same as > MATRASS
MATTRESS n large stuffed flat case, often with springs, used on or as a bed
MATTS > MATT
MATURABLE > MATURE
MATURATE vb mature or bring to maturity
MATURATED > MATURATE
MATURATES > MATURATE
MATURE adj fully developed or grown-up ▷ vb make or become mature
MATURED > MATURE
MATURELY > MATURE
MATURER > MATURE
MATURERS > MATURE
MATURES > MATURE
MATUREST > MATURE
MATURING > MATURE
MATURITY n state of being mature
MATUTINAL adj of, occurring in, or during the morning
MATUTINE same as > MATUTINAL
MATWEED n grass found on moors
MATWEEDS > MATWEED
MATY same as > MATEY
MATZA same as > MATZO
MATZAH same as > MATZO
MATZAHS > MATZAH
MATZAS > MATZA
MATZO n large very thin biscuit of unleavened bread, traditionally eaten by Jews during Passover
MATZOH same as > MATZO
MATZOHS > MATZOH
MATZOON n fermented milk product similar to yogurt
MATZOONS > MATZOON
MATZOS > MATZO
MATZOT > MATZO
MATZOTH > MATZO
MAUBIES > MAUBY
MAUBY n (in the E Caribbean) a bittersweet drink made from the bark of a rhamnaceous tree
MAUD n shawl or rug of grey wool plaid formerly worn in Scotland
MAUDLIN adj foolishly or tearfully sentimental
MAUDLINLY > MAUDLIN
MAUDS > MAUD
MAUGER same as > MAUGRE
MAUGRE prep in spite of ▷ vb behave spitefully towards
MAUGRED > MAUGRE
MAUGRES > MAUGRE
MAUGRING > MAUGRE
MAUL vb handle roughly ▷ n loose scrum
MAULED > MAUL
MAULER > MAUL
MAULERS pl n hands
MAULGRE same as > MAUGRE
MAULGRED > MAULGRE
MAULGRES > MAULGRE

MAULGRING > MAULGRE
MAULING > MAUL
MAULS > MAUL
MAULSTICK *n* long stick used by artists to steady the hand holding the brush
MAULVI *n* expert in Islamic law
MAULVIS > MAULVI
MAUMET *n* false god
MAUMETRY > MAUMET
MAUMETS > MAUMET
MAUN *dialect word for* > MUST
MAUND *n* unit of weight used in Asia, esp India, having different values in different localities. A common value in India is 82 pounds or 37 kilograms ▷ *vb* beg
MAUNDED > MAUND
MAUNDER *vb* talk or act aimlessly or idly
MAUNDERED > MAUNDER
MAUNDERER > MAUNDER
MAUNDERS > MAUNDER
MAUNDIES > MAUNDY
MAUNDING > MAUND
MAUNDS > MAUND
MAUNDY *n* ceremonial washing of the feet of poor persons in commemoration of Jesus' washing of his disciples' feet (John 13:4–34) re-enacted in some churches on Maundy Thursday
MAUNGIER > MAUNGY
MAUNGIEST > MAUNGY
MAUNGY *adj* (esp of a child) sulky, bad-tempered, or peevish
MAUNNA *vb* Scots term meaning must not
MAURI *n* soul
MAURIS > MAURI
MAUSOLEA > MAUSOLEUM
MAUSOLEAN > MAUSOLEUM
MAUSOLEUM *n* stately tomb
MAUT *same as* > MAHOUT
MAUTHER *n* girl
MAUTHERS > MAUTHER
MAUTS > MAUT
MAUVAIS *adj* bad
MAUVAISE *feminine form of* > MAUVAIS
MAUVE *adj* pale purple ▷ *n* any of various pale to moderate pinkish-purple or bluish-purple colours
MAUVEIN *same as* > MAUVEINE
MAUVEINE *same as* > MAUVE
MAUVEINES > MAUVEINE
MAUVEINS > MAUVEIN
MAUVER > MAUVE
MAUVES > MAUVE
MAUVEST > MAUVE
MAUVIN *same as* > MAUVEINE
MAUVINE *same as* > MAUVEINE
MAUVINES > MAUVINE
MAUVINS > MAUVIN
MAVEN *n* expert or connoisseur
MAVENS > MAVEN
MAVERICK *adj* independent

and unorthodox (person) ▷ *n* person of independent or unorthodox views ▷ *vb* take illegally
MAVERICKS > MAVERICK
MAVIE *n* type of thrush
MAVIES > MAVIE
MAVIN *same as* > MAVEN
MAVINS > MAVIN
MAVIS *n* song thrush
MAVISES > MAVIS
MAVOURNIN *n* Irish form of address meaning my darling
MAW *n* animal's mouth, throat, or stomach ▷ *vb* eat or bite
MAWBOUND *adj* (of cattle) constipated
MAWED > MAW
MAWGER *adj* (of persons or animals) thin or lean
MAWING > MAW
MAWK *n* maggot
MAWKIER > MAWK
MAWKIEST > MAWK
MAWKIN *n* slovenly woman
MAWKINS > MAWKIN
MAWKISH *adj* foolishly sentimental
MAWKISHLY > MAWKISH
MAWKS > MAWK
MAWKY > MAWK
MAWMET *same as* > MAUMET
MAWMETRY > MAWMET
MAWMETS > MAWMET
MAWN *n* dialect word for a quantity
MAWPUS *same as* > MOPUS
MAWPUSES > MAWPUS
MAWR *same as* > MAUTHER
MAWRS > MAWR
MAWS > MAW
MAWSEED *n* poppy seed
MAWSEEDS > MAWSEED
MAWTHER *same as* > MAUTHER
MAWTHERS > MAWTHER
MAX *vb* reach the full extent
MAXED > MAX
MAXES > MAX
MAXI *adj* (of a garment) very long ▷ *n* type of large racing yacht
MAXICOAT *n* long coat
MAXICOATS > MAXICOAT
MAXILLA *n* upper jawbone of a vertebrate
MAXILLAE > MAXILLA
MAXILLAR > MAXILLA
MAXILLARY > MAXILLA
MAXILLAS > MAXILLA
MAXILLULA *n* jaw in crustacean
MAXIM *n* general truth or principle
MAXIMA > MAXIMUM
MAXIMAL *adj* maximum ▷ *n* maximum
MAXIMALLY > MAXIMAL
MAXIMALS > MAXIMAL
MAXIMIN *n* highest of a set of minimum values
MAXIMINS > MAXIMIN
MAXIMISE *same as* > MAXIMIZE
MAXIMISED > MAXIMISE

MAXIMISER > MAXIMIZE
MAXIMISES > MAXIMISE
MAXIMIST > MAXIM
MAXIMISTS > MAXIM
MAXIMITE *n* type of explosive
MAXIMITES > MAXIMITE
MAXIMIZE *vb* increase to a maximum
MAXIMIZED > MAXIMIZE
MAXIMIZER > MAXIMIZE
MAXIMIZES > MAXIMIZE
MAXIMS > MAXIM
MAXIMUM *n* greatest possible (amount or number) ▷ *adj* of, being, or showing a maximum or maximums
MAXIMUMLY > MAXIMUM
MAXIMUMS > MAXIMUM
MAXIMUS *n* method rung on twelve bells
MAXIMUSES > MAXIMUS
MAXING > MAX
MAXIS > MAXI
MAXIXE *n* Brazilian dance in duple time, a precursor of the tango
MAXIXES > MAXIXE
MAXWELL *n* cgs unit of magnetic flux
MAXWELLS > MAXWELL
MAY *vb* used as an auxiliary to express possibility, permission, opportunity, etc ▷ *vb* gather may
MAYA *n* illusion, esp the material world of the senses regarded as illusory
MAYAN > MAYA
MAYAPPLE *n* American plant
MAYAPPLES > MAYAPPLE
MAYAS > MAYA
MAYBE *adv* perhaps, possibly ▷ *sentence substitute* possibly
MAYBES > MAYBE
MAYBIRD *n* American songbird
MAYBIRDS > MAYBIRD
MAYBUSH *n* flowering shrub
MAYBUSHES > MAYBUSH
MAYDAY *n* international radiotelephone distress signal
MAYDAYS > MAYDAY
MAYED > MAY
MAYEST *same as* > MAYST
MAYFLIES > MAYFLY
MAYFLOWER *n* any of various plants that bloom in May
MAYFLY *n* short-lived aquatic insect
MAYHAP *archaic word for* > PERHAPS
MAYHAPPEN *same as* > MAYHAP
MAYHEM *n* violent destruction or confusion
MAYHEMS > MAYHEM
MAYING > MAY
MAYINGS > MAYING
MAYO *n* mayonnaise
MAYOR *n* head of a municipality
MAYORAL > MAYOR
MAYORALTY *n* (term of)

office of a mayor
MAYORESS *n* mayor's wife
MAYORS > MAYOR
MAYORSHIP > MAYOR
MAYOS > MAYO
MAYPOLE *n* pole set up for dancing round on the first day of May to celebrate spring
MAYPOLES > MAYPOLE
MAYPOP *n* American wild flower
MAYPOPS > MAYPOP
MAYS > MAY
MAYST *singular form of the present tense of* > MAY
MAYSTER *same as* > MASTER
MAYSTERS > MAYSTER
MAYVIN *same as* > MAVEN
MAYVINS > MAYVIN
MAYWEED *n* widespread Eurasian weedy plant, having evil-smelling leaves and daisy-like flower heads
MAYWEEDS > MAYWEED
MAZAEDIA > MAZAEDIUM
MAZAEDIUM *n* part of lichen
MAZARD *same as* > MAZER
MAZARDS > MAZARD
MAZARINE *n* blue colour
MAZARINES > MAZARINE
MAZE *n* complex network of paths or lines designed to puzzle
MAZED > MAZE
MAZEDLY *adv* in bewildered way
MAZEDNESS *n* bewilderment
MAZEFUL > MAZE
MAZELIKE > MAZE
MAZELTOV *interj* congratulations
MAZEMENT > MAZE
MAZEMENTS > MAZE
MAZER *n* large hardwood drinking bowl
MAZERS > MAZER
MAZES > MAZE
MAZEY *adj* dizzy
MAZHBI *n* low-caste Sikh
MAZHBIS > MAZHBI
MAZIER > MAZY
MAZIEST > MAZY
MAZILY > MAZY
MAZINESS > MAZY
MAZING > MAZE
MAZOURKA *same as* > MAZURKA
MAZOURKAS > MAZOURKA
MAZOUT *same as* > MAZUT
MAZOUTS > MAZOUT
MAZUMA *n* money
MAZUMAS > MAZUMA
MAZURKA *n* lively Polish dance
MAZURKAS > MAZURKA
MAZUT *n* residue left after distillation of petrol
MAZUTS > MAZUT
MAZY *adj* of or like a maze
MAZZARD *same as* > MAZARD
MAZZARDS > MAZZARD
MBAQANGA *n* style of Black popular music of urban South Africa
MBAQANGAS > MBAQANGA
MBIRA *n* African musical

instrument consisting of tuned metal strips attached to a resonating box, which are plucked with the thumbs

MBIRAS > MBIRA

ME n (in tonic sol-fa) third degree of any major scale ▷ pron refers to the speaker or writer

MEACOCK n timid person

MEACOCKS > MEACOCK

MEAD n alcoholic drink made from honey

MEADOW n piece of grassland

MEADOWS > MEADOW

MEADOWY > MEADOW

MEADS > MEAD

MEAGER same as > MEAGRE

MEAGERLY > MEAGRE

MEAGRE adj scanty or insufficient ▷ n Mediterranean fish

MEAGRELY > MEAGRE

MEAGRER > MEAGRE

MEAGRES > MEAGRE

MEAGREST > MEAGRE

MEAL n occasion when food is served and eaten ▷ vb cover with meal

MEALED > MEAL

MEALER n person eating but not lodging at boarding house

MEALERS > MEALER

MEALIE n maize

MEALIER > MEALY

MEALIES South African word for > MAIZE

MEALIEST > MEALY

MEALINESS > MEALY

MEALING > MEAL

MEALLESS > MEAL

MEALS > MEAL

MEALTIME n time for meal

MEALTIMES > MEALTIME

MEALWORM n larva of various beetles of the genus Tenebrio, esp T. molitor, feeding on meal, flour, and similar stored foods: family Tenebrionidae

MEALWORMS > MEALWORM

MEALY adj resembling meal

MEALYBUG n plant-eating homopterous insect

MEALYBUGS > MEALYBUG

MEAN vb intend to convey or express ▷ adj miserly, ungenerous, or petty ▷ n middle point between two extremes

MEANDER vb follow a winding course ▷ n winding course

MEANDERED > MEANDER

MEANDERER > MEANDER

MEANDERS > MEANDER

MEANDRIAN > MEANDER

MEANDROUS > MEANDER

MEANE vb moan

MEANED > MEANE

MEANER > MEAN

MEANERS > MEAN

MEANES > MEANE

MEANEST > MEAN

MEANIE n unkind or miserly

person

MEANIES > MEANY

MEANING n what something means

MEANINGLY > MEAN

MEANINGS > MEANING

MEANLY > MEAN

MEANNESS > MEAN

MEANS > MEAN

MEANT > MEAN

MEANTIME n intervening period ▷ adv meanwhile

MEANTIMES > MEANTIME

MEANWHILE adv during the intervening period

MEANY same as > MEANIE

MEARE same as > MERE

MEARES > MEARE

MEARING adj forming boundary

MEASE vb assuage

MEASED > MEASE

MEASES > MEASE

MEASING > MEASE

MEASLE vb infect with measles

MEASLED adj (of cattle, sheep, or pigs) infested with tapeworm larvae

MEASLES n infectious disease producing red spots

MEASLIER > MEASLY

MEASLIEST > MEASLY

MEASLING > MEASLE

MEASLY adj meagre

MEASURE n size or quantity ▷ vb determine the size or quantity of

MEASURED adj slow and steady

MEASURER > MEASURE

MEASURERS > MEASURE

MEASURES pl n rock strata that contain a particular type of deposit

MEASURING adj used to measure quantities, esp in cooking

MEAT n animal flesh as food

MEATAL > MEATUS

MEATAXE n meat cleaver

MEATAXES > MEATAXE

MEATBALL n minced beef, shaped into a ball before cooking

MEATBALLS > MEATBALL

MEATED adj fattened

MEATH same as > MEAD

MEATHE same as > MEAD

MEATHEAD n stupid person

MEATHEADS > MEATHEAD

MEATHES > MEATHE

MEATHS > MEATH

MEATIER > MEATY

MEATIEST > MEATY

MEATILY > MEATY

MEATINESS > MEATY

MEATLESS > MEAT

MEATLOAF n chopped meat served in loaf-shaped mass

MEATMAN n meat seller

MEATMEN > MEATMAN

MEATS > MEAT

MEATSPACE n real physical world, as contrasted with the world of cyberspace

MEATUS n natural opening or channel, such as the canal leading from the outer ear to the eardrum

MEATUSES > MEATUS

MEATY adj (tasting) of or like meat

MEAWES same as > MEWS

MEAZEL same as > MESEL

MEAZELS > MEAZEL

MEBOS n South African dried apricots

MEBOSES > MEBOS

MECCA n place that attracts many visitors

MECCAS > MECCA

MECHANIC n person skilled in repairing or operating machinery

MECHANICS n scientific study of motion and force

MECHANISE same as > MECHANIZE

MECHANISM n way a machine works

MECHANIST same as > MECHANIC

MECHANIZE vb equip with machinery

MECHITZA n screen in synagogue separating men and women

MECHITZAS > MECHITZA

MECHITZOT > MECHITZA

MECK same as > MAIK

MECKS > MECK

MECLIZINE n drug used to treat motion sickness

MECONATE n salt of meconic acid

MECONATES > MECONATE

MECONIC adj derived from poppies

MECONIN n substance found in opium

MECONINS > MECONIN

MECONIUM n dark green mucoid material that forms the first faeces of a newborn infant

MECONIUMS > MECONIUM

MED n doctor

MEDACCA n Japanese freshwater fish

MEDACCAS > MEDACCA

MEDAILLON n small round thin piece of food

MEDAKA same as > MEDACCA

MEDAKAS > MEDAKA

MEDAL n piece of metal with an inscription etc, given as a reward or memento ▷ vb honour with a medal

MEDALED > MEDAL

MEDALET n small medal

MEDALETS > MEDALET

MEDALING > MEDAL

MEDALIST same as > MEDALLIST

MEDALISTS > MEDALIST

MEDALLED > MEDAL

MEDALLIC > MEDAL

MEDALLING > MEDAL

MEDALLION n disc-shaped ornament worn on a chain round the neck

MEDALLIST n winner of a

medal

MEDALS > MEDAL

MEDCINAL same as > MEDICINAL

MEDDLE vb interfere annoyingly

MEDDLED > MEDDLE

MEDDLER > MEDDLE

MEDDLERS > MEDDLE

MEDDLES > MEDDLE

MEDDLING > MEDDLE

MEDDLINGS > MEDDLE

MEDEVAC n evacuation of casualties from forward areas to the nearest hospital or base ▷ vb transport (a wounded or sick person) to hospital by medevac

MEDEVACED > MEDEVAC

MEDEVACS > MEDEVAC

MEDFLIES > MEDFLY

MEDFLY n Mediterranean fruit fly

MEDIA > MEDIUM

MEDIACIES > MEDIACY

MEDIACY n quality or state of being mediate

MEDIAD adj situated near the median line or plane of an organism

MEDIAE > MEDIUM

MEDIAEVAL adj of, relating to, or in the style of the Middle Ages ▷ n person living in medieval times

MEDIAL adj of or in the middle ▷ n speech sound between being fortis and lenis

MEDIALLY > MEDIAL

MEDIALS > MEDIAL

MEDIAN n middle (point or line) ▷ adj of, relating to, situated in, or directed towards the middle

MEDIANLY > MEDIAN

MEDIANS > MEDIAN

MEDIANT n third degree of a major or minor scale

MEDIANTS > MEDIANT

MEDIAS > MEDIUM

MEDIATE vb intervene in a dispute to bring about agreement ▷ adj occurring as a result of or dependent upon mediation

MEDIATED > MEDIATE

MEDIATELY > MEDIATE

MEDIATES > MEDIATE

MEDIATING > MEDIATE

MEDIATION n act of mediating

MEDIATISE same as > MEDIATIZE

MEDIATIVE > MEDIATE

MEDIATIZE vb annex (a state) to another state, allowing the former ruler to retain his title and some authority

MEDIATOR > MEDIATE

MEDIATORS > MEDIATE

MEDIATORY > MEDIATE

MEDIATRIX n female mediator

MEDIC n doctor or medical

student
MEDICABLE *adj* potentially able to be treated or cured medically
MEDICABLY > MEDICABLE
MEDICAID *n* health assistance programme financed by federal, state, and local taxes to help pay hospital and medical costs for persons of low income
MEDICAIDS > MEDICAID
MEDICAL *adj* of the science of medicine ▷ *n* medical examination
MEDICALLY > MEDICAL
MEDICALS > MEDICAL
MEDICANT *n* medicinal substance
MEDICANTS > MEDICANT
MEDICARE *n* (in the US) a federally sponsored health insurance programme for persons of 65 or older
MEDICARES > MEDICARE
MEDICATE *vb* treat with a medicinal substance
MEDICATED *adj* (of a patient) having been treated with a medicine or drug
MEDICATES > MEDICATE
MEDICIDE *n* suicide assisted by doctor
MEDICIDES > MEDICIDE
MEDICINAL *adj* having therapeutic properties ▷ *n* medicinal substance
MEDICINE *n* substance used to treat disease ▷ *vb* treat with medicine
MEDICINED > MEDICINE
MEDICINER *n* physician
MEDICINES > MEDICINE
MEDICK *n* any small leguminous plant of the genus *Medicago*, such as black medick or sickle medick, having yellow or purple flowers and trifoliate leaves
MEDICKS > MEDICK
MEDICO *n* doctor or medical student
MEDICOS > MEDICO
MEDICS > MEDIC
MEDIEVAL *adj* of the Middle Ages ▷ *n* person living in medieval times
MEDIEVALS > MEDIEVAL
MEDIGAP *n* private health insurance
MEDIGAPS > MEDIGAP
MEDII > MEDIUS
MEDINA *n* ancient quarter of any of various North African cities
MEDINAS > MEDINA
MEDIOCRE *adj* average in quality
MEDITATE *vb* reflect deeply, esp on spiritual matters
MEDITATED > MEDITATE
MEDITATES > MEDITATE
MEDITATOR > MEDITATE
MEDIUM *adj* midway between extremes,

average ▷ *n* middle state, degree, or condition
MEDIUMS *pl n* medium-dated gilt-edged securities
MEDIUS *n* middle finger
MEDIUSES > MEDIUS
MEDIVAC *variant spelling of* > MEDEVAC
MEDIVACED > MEDIVAC
MEDIVACS > MEDIVAC
MEDLAR *n* apple-like fruit of a small tree, eaten when it begins to decay
MEDLARS > MEDLAR
MEDLE *same as* > MEDDLE
MEDLED > MEDLE
MEDLES > MEDLE
MEDLEY *n* miscellaneous mixture ▷ *adj* of, being, or relating to a mixture or variety
MEDLEYS > MEDLEY
MEDLING > MEDLE
MEDRESE *same as* > MADRASAH
MEDRESES > MEDRESE
MEDRESSEH *same as* > MADRASAH
MEDS > MED
MEDULLA *n* marrow, pith, or inner tissue
MEDULLAE > MEDULLA
MEDULLAR > MEDULLA
MEDULLARY > MEDULLA
MEDULLAS > MEDULLA
MEDULLATE *adj* having medulla
MEDUSA *n* jellyfish
MEDUSAE > MEDUSA
MEDUSAL > MEDUSA
MEDUSAN > MEDUSA
MEDUSANS > MEDUSA
MEDUSAS > MEDUSA
MEDUSOID *same as* > MEDUSA
MEDUSOIDS > MEDUSOID
MEE *n* Malaysian noodle dish
MEED *n* recompense
MEEDS > MEED
MEEK *adj* submissive or humble
MEEKEN *vb* make meek
MEEKENED > MEEKEN
MEEKENING > MEEKEN
MEEKENS > MEEKEN
MEEKER > MEEK
MEEKEST > MEEK
MEEKLY > MEEK
MEEKNESS > MEEK
MEEMIE *n* hysterical person
MEEMIES > MEEMIE
MEER *same as* > MERE
MEERCAT *same as* > MEERKAT
MEERCATS > MEERCAT
MEERED > MEER
MEERING > MEER
MEERKAT *n* S African mongoose
MEERKATS > MEERKAT
MEERS > MEER
MEES > MEE
MEET *vb* come together (with) ▷ *n* meeting, esp a sports meeting ▷ *adj* fit or suitable
MEETER > MEET

MEETERS > MEET
MEETEST > MEET
MEETING > MEET
MEETINGS > MEET
MEETLY > MEET
MEETNESS *n* properness
MEETS > MEET
MEFF *dialect word for* > TRAMP
MEFFS > MEFF
MEG *short for* > MEGABYTE
MEGA *adj* extremely good, great, or successful
MEGABAR *n* unit of million bars
MEGABARS > MEGABAR
MEGABIT *n* one million bits
MEGABITS > MEGABIT
MEGABUCK *n* million dollars
MEGABUCKS > MEGABUCK
MEGABYTE *n* 2S2SO or 1 048 576 bytes
MEGABYTES > MEGABYTE
MEGACITY *n* city with over 10 million inhabitants
MEGACURIE *n* unit of million curies
MEGACYCLE *same as* > MEGAHERTZ
MEGADEAL *n* very good deal
MEGADEALS > MEGADEAL
MEGADEATH *n* death of a million people, esp in a nuclear war or attack
MEGADOSE *n* very large dose, as of a medicine, vitamin, etc
MEGADOSES > MEGADOSE
MEGADYNE *n* unit of million dynes
MEGADYNES > MEGADYNE
MEGAFARAD *n* unit of million farads
MEGAFAUNA *n* component of the fauna of a region or period that comprises the larger terrestrial animals
MEGAFLOP *n* measure of processing speed, consisting of a million floating-point operations a second
MEGAFLOPS > MEGAFLOP
MEGAFLORA *n* plants large enough to be seen by naked eye
MEGAFOG *n* amplified fog signal
MEGAFOGS > MEGAFOG
MEGAGAUSS *n* unit of million gauss
MEGAHERTZ *n* one million hertz
MEGAHIT *n* great success
MEGAHITS > MEGAHIT
MEGAJOULE *n* unit of million joules
MEGALITH *n* great stone, esp as part of a prehistoric monument
MEGALITHS > MEGALITH
MEGALITRE *n* one million litres
MEGALOPIC *adj* having large eyes
MEGALOPS *n* crab in larval stage

MEGAPHONE *n* cone-shaped instrument used to amplify the voice ▷ *vb* speak through megaphone
MEGAPHYLL *n* relatively large type of leaf produced by ferns and seed plants
MEGAPIXEL *n* one million pixels
MEGAPLEX *n* cinema complex containing a large number of separate screens, and usually a restaurant or bar
MEGAPOD *same as* > MEGAPODE
MEGAPODE *n* bird of Australia, New Guinea, and adjacent islands
MEGAPODES > MEGAPODE
MEGAPODS > MEGAPOD
MEGARA > MEGARON
MEGARAD *n* unit of million rads
MEGARADS > MEGARAD
MEGARON *n* tripartite rectangular room containing a central hearth surrounded by four pillars, found in Bronze Age Greece and Asia Minor
MEGARONS > MEGARON
MEGASCOPE *n* type of image projector
MEGASPORE *n* larger of the two types of spore produced by some spore-bearing plants, which develops into the female gametophyte
MEGASS *another name for* > BAGASSE
MEGASSE *same as* > MEGASS
MEGASSES > MEGASS
MEGASTAR *n* very well-known personality in the entertainment business
MEGASTARS > MEGASTAR
MEGASTORE *n* very large store
MEGATHERE *n* any of various gigantic extinct American sloths of the genus *Megatherium* and related genera, common in late Cenozoic times
MEGATON *n* explosive power equal to that of one million tons of TNT
MEGATONIC > MEGATON
MEGATONS > MEGATON
MEGAVOLT *n* one million volts
MEGAVOLTS > MEGAVOLT
MEGAWATT *n* one million watts
MEGAWATTS > MEGAWATT
MEGILLA *same as* > MEGILLAH
MEGILLAH *n* scroll of the Book of Esther, read on the festival of Purim
MEGILLAHS > MEGILLAH
MEGILLAS > MEGILLA
MEGILLOTH > MEGILLAH
MEGILP *n* oil-painting medium of linseed oil

m

mixed with mastic varnish or turpentine

MEGILPH *same as* > MEGILP

MEGILPHS > MEGILPH

MEGILPS > MEGILP

MEGOHM *n* one million ohms.

MEGOHMS > MEGOHM

MEGRIM *n* caprice

MEGRIMS *n* fit of depression

MEGS > MEG

MEHNDI *n* (esp in India) the practice of painting designs on the hands, feet, etc using henna

MEHNDIS > MEHNDI

MEIBOMIAN as in *meibomian gland* any of the small sebaceous glands in the eyelid, beneath the conjunctiva

MEIKLE *adj* Scots word meaning large

MEIN *Scots word for* > MOAN

MEINED > MEIN

MEINEY *same as* > MEINY

MEINEYS > MEINEY

MEINIE *same as* > MEINY

MEINIES > MEINY

MEINING > MEIN

MEINS > MEIN

MEINT *same as* > MING

MEINY *n* retinue or household

MEIOCYTE *n* cell that divides by meiosis to produce four haploid spores

MEIOCYTES > MEIOCYTE

MEIOFAUNA *n* component of the fauna of a sea or lake bed comprising small (but not microscopic) animals, such as tiny worms and crustaceans

MEIONITE *n* mineral containing silica

MEIONITES > MEIONITE

MEIOSES > MEIOSIS

MEIOSIS *n* type of cell division in which reproductive cells are produced, each containing half the chromosome number of the parent nucleus

MEIOSPORE *n* haploid spore

MEIOTIC > MEIOSIS

MEISHI *n* business card in Japan

MEISHIS > MEISHI

MEISTER *n* person who excels at a particular activity

MEISTERS > MEISTER

MEITH *n* landmark

MEITHS > MEITH

MEJLIS *same as* > MAJLIS

MEJLISES > MEJLIS

MEKKA *same as* > MECCA

MEKKAS > MEKKA

MEKOMETER *n* device for measuring distance

MEL *n* pure form of honey formerly used in pharmaceutical products

MELA *n* Asian cultural or religious fair or festival

MELALEUCA *n* Australian shrub or tree with a white trunk and black branches

MELAMDIM > MELAMED

MELAMED *n* Hebrew teacher

MELAMINE *n* colourless crystalline compound used in making synthetic resins

MELAMINES > MELAMINE

MELAMPODE *n* poisonous plant

MELANGE *n* mixture

MELANGES > MELANGE

MELANIAN *n* freshwater mollusc

MELANIC *adj* relating to melanism or melanosis ▷ *n* darker form of creature

MELANICS > MELANIC

MELANIN *n* dark pigment found in the hair, skin, and eyes of humans and animals

MELANINS > MELANIN

MELANISE *same as* > MELANIZE

MELANISED > MELANISE

MELANISES > MELANISE

MELANISM *same as* > MELANOSIS

MELANISMS > MELANISM

MELANIST > MELANISM

MELANISTS > MELANISM

MELANITE *n* black variety of andradite garnet

MELANITES > MELANITE

MELANITIC > MELANITE

MELANIZE *vb* turn into melanin

MELANIZED > MELANIZE

MELANIZES > MELANIZE

MELANO *n* person with abnormally dark skin

MELANOID *adj* resembling melanin ▷ *n* dark substance formed in skin

MELANOIDS > MELANOID

MELANOMA *n* tumour composed of dark-coloured cells, occurring in some skin cancers

MELANOMAS > MELANOMA

MELANOS > MELANO

MELANOSES > MELANOSIS

MELANOSIS *n* skin condition characterized by excessive deposits of melanin

MELANOTIC > MELANOSIS

MELANOUS *adj* having a dark complexion and black hair

MELANURIA *n* presence of melanin in urine

MELANURIC > MELANURIA

MELAPHYRE *n* type of weathered amygdaloidal basalt or andesite

MELAS > MELA

MELASTOME *n* tropical flowering plant

MELATONIN *n* hormone-like secretion of the pineal gland, causing skin colour changes in some animals and thought to be involved in reproductive function

MELD *vb* merge or blend ▷ *n* act of melding

MELDED > MELD

MELDERS > MELD

MELDING > MELD

MELDS > MELD

MELEE *n* noisy confused fight or crowd

MELEES > MELEE

MELENA *n* excrement or vomit stained by blood

MELENAS > MELENA

MELIC *adj* (of poetry, esp ancient Greek lyric poems) intended to be sung ▷ *n* tpye of grass

MELICK *n* either of two pale green perennial grasses

MELICKS > MELICK

MELICS > MELIC

MELIK *same as* > MALIK

MELIKS > MELIK

MELILITE *n* mineral containing calcium

MELILITES > MELILITE

MELILOT *n* any leguminous plant of the Old World genus *Melilotus*, having narrow clusters of small white or yellow fragrant flowers

MELILOTS > MELILOT

MELINITE *n* high explosive made from picric acid

MELINITES > MELINITE

MELIORATE *vb* improve

MELIORISM *n* notion that the world can be improved by human effort

MELIORIST > MELIORISM

MELIORITY *n* improved state

MELISMA *n* expressive vocal phrase or passage consisting of several notes sung to one syllable

MELISMAS > MELISMA

MELISMATA > MELISMA

MELL *vb* mix

MELLAY *same as* > MELEE

MELLAYS > MELLAY

MELLED > MELL

MELLIFIC *adj* forming or producing honey

MELLING > MELL

MELLITE *n* soft yellow mineral

MELLITES > MELLITE

MELLITIC > MELLITE

MELLOTRON *n* musical synthesizer

MELLOW *adj* soft, not harsh ▷ *vb* make or become mellow

MELLOWED > MELLOW

MELLOWER > MELLOW

MELLOWEST > MELLOW

MELLOWING > MELLOW

MELLOWLY > MELLOW

MELLOWS > MELLOW

MELLOWY *same as* > MELLOW

MELLS > MELL

MELOCOTON *n* variety of peach

MELODEON *n* small accordion

MELODEONS > MELODEON

MELODIA *same as* > MELODICA

MELODIAS > MELODIA

MELODIC *adj* of melody

MELODICA *n* type of flute

MELODICAS > MELODICA

MELODICS *n* study of melody

MELODIES > MELODY

MELODION *same as* > MELODEON

MELODIONS > MELODION

MELODIOUS *adj* pleasing to the ear

MELODISE *same as* > MELODIZE

MELODISED > MELODISE

MELODISER > MELODISE

MELODISES > MELODISE

MELODIST *n* composer of melodies

MELODISTS > MELODIST

MELODIZE *vb* provide with a melody

MELODIZED > MELODIZE

MELODIZER > MELODIZE

MELODIZES > MELODIZE

MELODRAMA *n* play full of extravagant action and emotion

MELODRAME *same as* > MELODRAMA

MELODY *n* series of musical notes which make a tune

MELOID *n* any long-legged beetle of the family *Meloidae*, which includes the blister beetles and oil beetles ▷ *adj* of, relating to, or belonging to the *Meloidae*

MELOIDS > MELOID

MELOMANIA *n* great enthusiasm for music

MELOMANIC > MELOMANIA

MELON *n* large round juicy fruit with a hard rind

MELONGENE *n* aubergine

MELONS > MELON

MELPHALAN *n* drug used to treat leukaemia

MELS > MEL

MELT *vb* (cause to) become liquid by heat ▷ *n* act or process of melting

MELTABLE > MELT

MELTAGE *n* process or result of melting or the amount melted

MELTAGES > MELTAGE

MELTDOWN *n* (in a nuclear reactor) melting of the fuel rods, with the possible release of radiation

MELTDOWNS > MELTDOWN

MELTED > MELT

MELTEMI *n* northerly wind in the northeast Mediterranean

MELTEMIS > MELTEMI

MELTER > MELT

MELTERS > MELT

MELTIER > MELTY

MELTIEST > MELTY

MELTING > MELT

MELTINGLY > MELT

MELTINGS > MELT

MELTITH *n* meal

MELTITHS > MELTITH

m

MELTON *n* heavy smooth woollen fabric with a short nap, used esp for overcoats
MELTONS > MELTON
MELTS > MELT
MELTWATER *n* melted snow or ice
MELTY *adj* tending to melt
MELUNGEON *n* any of a dark-skinned group of people of the Appalachians in E Tennessee, of mixed Indian, White, and Black ancestry
MEM *n* 13th letter in the Hebrew alphabet, transliterated as *m*
MEMBER *n* individual making up a body or society ▷ *adj* (of a (country or group) belonging to an organization or alliance
MEMBERED *adj* having members
MEMBERS > MEMBER
MEMBRAL *adj* of limbs
MEMBRANAL > MEMBRANE
MEMBRANE *n* thin flexible tissue in a plant or animal body
MEMBRANED *adj* having membrane
MEMBRANES > MEMBRANE
MEME *n* idea or element of social behaviour (passed on through generations in a culture, esp by imitation
MEMENTO *n* thing serving to remind, souvenir
MEMENTOES > MEMENTO
MEMENTOS > MEMENTO
MEMES > MEME
MEMETICS *n* study of gentic transmission of culture
MEMO *n* memorandum
MEMOIR *n* biography or historical account based on personal knowledge
MEMOIRISM *n* writing of memoirs
MEMOIRIST > MEMOIRISM
MEMOIRS *pl n* collection of reminiscences about a period or series of events, written from personal experience
MEMORABLE *adj* worth remembering, noteworthy
MEMORABLY > MEMORABLE
MEMORANDA *n* plural of memorandum: written statement of communications
MEMORIAL *n* something serving to commemorate a person or thing ▷ *adj* serving as a memorial
MEMORIALS > MEMORIAL
MEMORIES > MEMORY
MEMORISE *same as* > MEMORIZE
MEMORISED > MEMORISE
MEMORISER > MEMORIZE
MEMORISES > MEMORISE
MEMORITER *adv* from memory
MEMORIZE *vb* commit to memory

MEMORIZED > MEMORIZE
MEMORIZER > MEMORIZE
MEMORIZES > MEMORIZE
MEMORY *n* ability to remember
MEMOS > MEMO
MEMS > MEM
MEMSAHIB *n* (formerly, in India) term of respect used for a European married woman
MEMSAHIBS > MEMSAHIB
MEN > MAN
MENACE *n* threat ▷ *vb* threaten, endanger
MENACED > MENACE
MENACER > MENACE
MENACERS > MENACE
MENACES > MENACE
MENACING > MENACE
MENAD *same as* > MAENAD
MENADIONE *n* yellow crystalline compound
MENADS > MENAD
MENAGE *old form of* > MANAGE
MENAGED > MENAGE
MENAGERIE *n* collection of wild animals for exhibition
MENAGES > MENAGE
MENAGING > MENAGE
MENARCHE *n* first occurrence of menstruation in a woman's life
MENARCHES > MENARCHE
MENAZON *n* type of insecticide
MENAZONS > MENAZON
MEND *vb* repair or patch ▷ *n* mended area
MENDABLE > MEND
MENDACITY *n* (tendency to) untruthfulness
MENDED > MEND
MENDER > MEND
MENDERS > MEND
MENDICANT *adj* begging ▷ *n* beggar
MENDICITY > MENDICANT
MENDIGO *n* Spanish beggar or vagrant
MENDIGOS > MENDIGO
MENDING *n* something to be mended, esp clothes
MENDINGS > MENDING
MENDS > MEND
MENE *Scots form of* > MOAN
MENED > MENE
MENEER *n* South African title of address equivalent to *sir* when used alone or *Mr* when placed before a name
MENEERS > MENEER
MENES > MENE
MENFOLK *pl n* men collectively, esp the men of a particular family
MENFOLKS *same as* > MENFOLK
MENG *vb* mix
MENGE *same as* > MENG
MENGED > MENG
MENGES > MENGE
MENGING > MENG
MENGS > MENG
MENHADEN *n* marine North

American fish, *Brevoortia tyrannus*: source of fishmeal, fertilizer, and oil: family *Clupeidae* (herrings, etc)
MENHADENS > MENHADEN
MENHIR *n* single upright prehistoric stone
MENHIRS > MENHIR
MENIAL *adj* involving boring work of low status ▷ *n* person with a menial job
MENIALLY > MENIAL
MENIALS > MENIAL
MENILITE *n* liver opal
MENILITES > MENILITE
MENING > MENE
MENINGEAL > MENINX
MENINGES > MENINX
MENINX *n* one of three membranes that envelop the brain and spinal cord
MENISCAL > MENISCUS
MENISCATE > MENISCUS
MENISCI > MENISCUS
MENISCOID > MENISCUS
MENISCUS *n* curved surface of a liquid
MENO *adv* (esp preceding a dynamic or tempo marking) to be played less quickly, less softly, etc
MENOLOGY *n* ecclesiastical calendar of the months
MENOMINEE *n* whitefish, found in N America and Siberia
MENOMINI *same as* > MENOMINEE
MENOMINIS > MENOMINI
MENOPAUSE *n* time when a woman's menstrual cycle ceases
MENOPOLIS *n* informal word for an area with a high proportion of single men
MENOPOME *n* American salamander
MENOPOMES > MENOPOME
MENORAH *n* seven-branched candelabrum used as an emblem of Judaism
MENORAHS > MENORAH
MENORRHEA *n* normal bleeding in menstruation
MENSA *n* faint constellation in the S hemisphere lying between Hydrus and Volans and containing part of the Large Magellanic Cloud
MENSAE *n* star of the mensa constellation
MENSAL *adj* monthly
MENSAS > MENSA
MENSCH *n* decent person
MENSCHEN > MENSCH
MENSCHES > MENSCH
MENSCHY > MENSCH
MENSE *vb* grace
MENSED > MENSE
MENSEFUL *adj* gracious
MENSELESS *adj* graceless
MENSES *n* menstruation
MENSH *vb* mention
MENSHED > MENSH
MENSHEN *n* Chinese door

god
MENSHES > MENSH
MENSHING > MENSH
MENSING > MENSE
MENSTRUA > MENSTRUUM
MENSTRUAL *adj* of or relating to menstruation
MENSTRUUM *n* solvent, esp one used in the preparation of a drug
MENSUAL *same as* > MENSAL
MENSURAL *adj* of or involving measure
MENSWEAR *n* clothing for men
MENSWEARS > MENSWEAR
MENT *same as* > MING
MENTA > MENTUM
MENTAL *adj* of, in, or done by the mind
MENTALESE *n* picturing of concepts in mind without words
MENTALISM *n* doctrine that mind is the fundamental reality and that objects of knowledge exist only as aspects of the subject's consciousness
MENTALIST > MENTALISM
MENTALITY *n* way of thinking
MENTALLY > MENTAL
MENTATION *n* process or result of mental activity
MENTEE *n* person trained by mentor
MENTEES > MENTEE
MENTHENE *n* liquid obtained from menthol
MENTHENES > MENTHENE
MENTHOL *n* organic compound found in peppermint, used medicinally
MENTHOLS > MENTHOL
MENTICIDE *n* destruction of person's mental independence
MENTION *vb* refer to briefly ▷ *n* brief reference to a person or thing
MENTIONED > MENTION
MENTIONER > MENTION
MENTIONS > MENTION
MENTO *n* Jamaican song
MENTOR *n* adviser or guide ▷ *vb* act as a mentor to (someone) ▷ *vb* act as mentor for
MENTORED > MENTOR
MENTORIAL > MENTOR
MENTORING *n* (in business) the practice of assigning a junior member of staff to the care of a more experienced person who assists him in his career
MENTORS > MENTOR
MENTOS > MENTO
MENTUM *n* chin
MENU *n* list of dishes to be served, or from which to order
MENUDO *n* Mexican soup
MENUDOS > MENUDO
MENUISIER *n* joiner**

MENUS > MENU

MENYIE *same as* > MEINIE

MENYIES > MENYIE

MEOU *same as* > MEOW

MEOUED > MEOU

MEOUING > MEOU

MEOUS > MEOU

MEOW *vb* (of a cat) to make a characteristic crying sound ▷ *interj* imitation of this sound

MEOWED > MEOW

MEOWING > MEOW

MEOWS > MEOW

MEPACRINE *n* drug formerly widely used to treat malaria

MEPHITIC *adj* poisonous

MEPHITIS *n* foul-smelling discharge

MEPHITISM *n* poisoning

MERANTI *n* wood from any of several Malaysian trees of the dipterocarpaceous genus *Shorea*

MERANTIS > MERANTI

MERBROMIN *n* green iridescent crystalline compound

MERC *n* mercenary

MERCAPTAN *another name* (*not in technical usage*) *for* > THIOL

MERCAPTO *adj* of a particular chemical group

MERCAT *Scots word for* > MARKET

MERCATS > MERCAT

MERCENARY *adj* influenced by greed ▷ *n* hired soldier

MERCER *n* dealer in textile fabrics and fine cloth

MERCERIES > MERCER

MERCERISE *same as* > MERCERIZE

MERCERIZE *vb* treat (cotton yarn) with an alkali to increase its strength and reception to dye and impart a lustrous silky appearance

MERCERS > MERCER

MERCERY > MERCER

MERCES > MERC

MERCH *n* merchandise

MERCHANT *n* person engaged in trade, wholesale trader ▷ *adj* of ships involved in commercial trade or their crews ▷ *vb* conduct trade in

MERCHANTS > MERCHANT

MERCHES > MERCH

MERCHET *n* (in feudal England) a fine paid by a tenant, esp a villein, to his lord for allowing the marriage of his daughter

MERCHETS > MERCHET

MERCHILD *n* mythical creature with upper body of child and lower body of fish

MERCIABLE *adj* merciful

MERCIES > MERCY

MERCIFIDE > MERCIFY

MERCIFIED > MERCIFY

MERCIFIES > MERCIFY

MERCIFUL *adj* compassionate

MERCIFY *vb* show mercy to

MERCILESS *adj* without mercy

MERCS > MERC

MERCURATE *vb* treat or mix with mercury

MERCURIAL *adj* lively, changeable ▷ *n* any salt of mercury for use as a medicine

MERCURIC *adj* of or containing mercury in the divalent state

MERCURIES > MERCURY

MERCURISE *same as* > MERCURATE

MERCURIZE *same as* > MERCURISE

MERCUROUS *adj* of or containing mercury in the monovalent state

MERCURY *n* silvery liquid metal

MERCY *n* compassionate treatment of an offender or enemy who is in one's power

MERDE *French word for* > EXCREMENT

MERDES > MERDE

MERE *adj* nothing more than ▷ *n* lake ▷ *vb* old form of survey

MERED *adj* forming a boundary

MEREL *same as* > MERIL

MERELL *same as* > MERIL

MERELLS *same as* > MERILS

MERELS > MERILS

MERELY *adv* only

MERENGUE *n* type of lively dance music originating in the Dominican Republic, which combines African and Spanish elements

MERENGUES > MERENGUE

MEREOLOGY *n* formal study of the logical properties of the relation of part and whole

MERER > MERE

MERES > MERE

MERESMAN *n* man who decides on boundaries

MERESMEN > MERESMAN

MEREST > MERE

MERESTONE *n* stone marking boundary

MERFOLK *n* mermaids and mermen

MERFOLKS > MERFOLK

MERGANSER *n* large crested diving duck

MERGE *vb* combine or blend

MERGED > MERGE

MERGEE *n* business taken over by merger

MERGEES > MERGEE

MERGENCE > MERGE

MERGENCES > MERGE

MERGER *n* combination of business firms into one

MERGERS > MERGER

MERGES > MERGE

MERGING > MERGE

MERGINGS > MERGE

MERI *n* Māori war club

MERICARP *n* part of plant fruit

MERICARPS > MERICARP

MERIDIAN *n* imaginary circle of the earth passing through both poles ▷ *adj* along or relating to a meridian

MERIDIANS > MERIDIAN

MERIL *n* counter used in merils

MERILS *n* old board game

MERIMAKE *n* merrymaking

MERIMAKES > MERIMAKE

MERING > MERE

MERINGS > MERING

MERINGUE *n* baked mixture of egg whites and sugar

MERINGUES > MERINGUE

MERINO *n* breed of sheep with fine soft wool

MERINOS > MERINO

MERIS > MERI

MERISES > MERISIS

MERISIS *n* growth by division of cells

MERISM *n* duplication of biological parts

MERISMS > MERISM

MERISTEM *n* plant tissue responsible for growth, whose cells divide and differentiate to form the tissues and organs of the plant

MERISTEMS > MERISTEM

MERISTIC *adj* of or relating to the number of organs or parts in an animal or plant body

MERIT *n* excellence or worth ▷ *vb* deserve

MERITED > MERIT

MERITING > MERIT

MERITLESS > MERIT

MERITS > MERIT

MERK *n* old Scots coin

MERKIN *n* artificial hairpiece for the pudendum

MERKINS > MERKIN

MERKS > MERK

MERL *same as* > MERLE

MERLE *adj* (of a dog, esp a collie) having a bluish-grey coat with speckles or streaks of black

MERLES > MERLE

MERLIN *n* small falcon

MERLING *n* whiting

MERLINGS > MERLING

MERLINS > MERLIN

MERLON *n* solid upright section in a crenellated battlement

MERLONS > MERLON

MERLOT *n* black grape grown in France and now throughout the wine-producing world, used, often in a blend, for making wine

MERLOTS > MERLOT

MERLS > MERL

MERMAID *n* imaginary sea creature with the upper part of a woman and the lower part of a fish

MERMAIDEN *same as* > MERMAID

MERMAIDS > MERMAID

MERMAN *n* male counterpart of the mermaid

MERMEN > MERMAN

MEROCRINE *adj* (of the secretion of glands) characterized by formation of the product without undergoing disintegration

MEROGONY *n* development of embryo from part of ovum

MEROISTIC *adj* producing yolk and ova

MEROME *same as* > MEROSOME

MEROMES > MEROME

MERONYM *n* part of something used to refer to the whole, such as *faces* meaning *people*, as in *they've seen a lot of faces come and go*

MERONYMS > MERONYM

MERONYMY > MERONYM

MEROPIA *n* partial blindness

MEROPIAS > MEROPIA

MEROPIC > MEROPIA

MEROPIDAN *n* bird of bee-eater family

MEROSOME *n* segment in body of worm

MEROSOMES > MEROSOME

MEROZOITE *n* any of the cells formed by fission of a schizont during the life cycle of sporozoan protozoans, such as the malaria parasite

MERPEOPLE *same as* > MERFOLK

MERRIER > MERRY

MERRIES > MERRY

MERRIEST > MERRY

MERRILY > MERRY

MERRIMENT *n* gaiety, fun, or mirth

MERRINESS > MERRY

MERRY *adj* cheerful or jolly ▷ *n* gean

MERRYMAN *n* jester

MERRYMEN > MERRYMAN

MERSALYL *n* salt of sodium

MERSALYLS > MERSALYL

MERSE *n* low level ground by a river or shore, often alluvial and fertile

MERSES > MERSE

MERSION *n* dipping in water

MERSIONS > MERSION

MERYCISM *n* rumination

MERYCISMS > MERYCISM

MES > ME

MESA *n* flat-topped hill found in arid regions

MESAIL *n* visor

MESAILS > MESAIL

MESAL *same as* > MESIAL

MESALLY > MESAL

MESARAIC *adj* of mesentery

MESARCH *adj* (of a xylem

strand) having the first-formed xylem surrounded by that formed later, as in fern stems
MESAS *same as* > MESA
MESCAL *n* spineless globe-shaped cactus of Mexico and the SW of the USA
MESCALIN *same as* > MESCALINE
MESCALINE *n* hallucinogenic drug obtained from the tops of mescals
MESCALINS > MESCALIN
MESCALISM *n* addiction to mescal
MESCALS > MESCAL
MESCLUM *same as* > MESCLUN
MESCLUMS > MESCLUM
MESCLUN *n* type of green salad
MESCLUNS > MESCLUN
MESDAMES > MADAM
MESE *n* middle string on lyre
MESEEMED > MESEEMS
MESEEMETH *same as* > MESEEMS
MESEEMS *vb* it seems to me
MESEL *n* leper
MESELED *adj* afflicted by leprosy
MESELS > MESEL
MESENTERA > MESENTERON
MESENTERY *n* double layer of peritoneum that is attached to the back wall of the abdominal cavity and supports most of the small intestine
MESES > MESE
MESETA *n* plateau in Spain
MESETAS > MESETA
MESH *n* network or net ▷ *vb* (of gear teeth) engage ▷ *adj* made from mesh
MESHED > MESH
MESHES > MESH
MESHIER > MESH
MESHIEST > MESH
MESHING > MESH
MESHINGS > MESH
MESHUGA *adj* crazy
MESHUGAAS *n* madness
MESHUGAH *same as* > MESHUGA
MESHUGAS *adj* crazy
MESHUGGA *same as* > MESHUGA
MESHUGGAH *same as* > MESHUGA
MESHUGGE *same as* > MESHUGA
MESHWORK *n* network
MESHWORKS > MESHWORK
MESHY > MESH
MESIAD *adj* relating to or situated at the middle or centre
MESIAL *another word for* > MEDIAL
MESIALLY > MESIAL
MESIAN *same as* > MESIAL
MESIC > MESON
MESICALLY > MESON
MESMERIC *adj* holding (someone) as if spellbound

MESMERISE *same as* > MESMERIZE
MESMERISM *n* hypnotic state induced by the operator's imposition of his will on that of the patient
MESMERIST > MESMERISM
MESMERIZE *vb* hold spellbound
MESNALTY *n* lands of a mesne lord
MESNE *adj* in Law, intermediate or intervening: used esp of any assignment of property before the last
MESNES > MESNE
MESOBLAST *another name for* > MESODERM
MESOCARP *n* middle layer of the pericarp of a fruit, such as the flesh of a peach
MESOCARPS > MESOCARP
MESOCRANY *n* medium skull breadth
MESODERM *n* middle germ layer of an animal embryo, giving rise to muscle, blood, bone, connective tissue, etc
MESODERMS > MESODERM
MESOGLEA *n* gelatinous material between the outer and inner cellular layers of jellyfish and other coelenterates
MESOGLEAL > MESOGLEA
MESOGLEAS > MESOGLEA
MESOGLOEA *same as* > MESOGLEA
MESOLITE *n* type of mineral
MESOLITES > MESOLITE
MESOMERE *n* cell in fertilized ovum
MESOMERES > MESOMERE
MESOMORPH *n* person with a muscular body build: said to be correlated with somatotonia
MESON *n* elementary atomic particle
MESONIC > MESON
MESONS > MESON
MESOPAUSE *n* zone of minimum temperature between the mesosphere and the thermosphere
MESOPHILE *n* ideal growth temperature of 20-45 degrees
MESOPHYL *same as* > MESOPHYLL
MESOPHYLL *n* soft chlorophyll-containing tissue of a leaf between the upper and lower layers of epidermis: involved in photosynthesis
MESOPHYLS > MESOPHYLL
MESOPHYTE *n* any plant that grows in surroundings receiving an average supply of water
MESOSCALE *adj* of weather phenomena of medium duration
MESOSOME *n* part of

bacterial cell
MESOSOMES > MESOSOME
MESOTRON *same as* > MESON
MESOTRONS > MESOTRON
MESOZOAN *n* type of parasite
MESOZOANS > MESOZOAN
MESOZOIC *adj* of, denoting, or relating to an era of geological time
MESPRISE *same as* > MISPRISE
MESPRISES > MESPRISE
MESPRIZE *same as* > MISPRISE
MESPRIZES > MESPRIZE
MESQUIN *adj* mean
MESQUINE *same as* > MESQUIN
MESQUIT *same as* > MESQUITE
MESQUITE *n* small tree whose sugary pods are used as animal fodder
MESQUITES > MESQUITE
MESQUITS > MESQUIT
MESS *n* untidy or dirty confusion ▷ *vb* muddle or dirty
MESSAGE *n* communication sent ▷ *vb* send as a message
MESSAGED > MESSAGE
MESSAGES > MESSAGE
MESSAGING *n* sending and receiving of messages
MESSALINE *n* light lustrous twilled-silk fabric
MESSAN *Scots word for* > DOG
MESSANS > MESSAN
MESSED > MESS
MESSENGER *n* bearer of a message ▷ *vb* send by messenger
MESSES > MESS
MESSIAH *n* exceptional or hoped for liberator of a country or people
MESSIAHS > MESSIAH
MESSIANIC *adj* of or relating to the Messiah, his awaited deliverance of the Jews, or the new age of peace expected to follow this
MESSIAS *same as* > MESSIAH
MESSIASES > MESSIAS
MESSIER > MESSY
MESSIEST > MESSY
MESSIEURS > MONSIEUR
MESSILY > MESSY
MESSINESS > MESSY
MESSING > MESS
MESSMAN *n* sailor working in ship's mess
MESSMATE *n* person with whom one shares meals in a mess, esp in the army
MESSMATES > MESSMATE
MESSMEN > MESSMAN
MESSUAGE *n* dwelling house together with its outbuildings, curtilage, and the adjacent land appropriated to its use
MESSUAGES > MESSUAGE
MESSY *adj* dirty, confused, or untidy

MESTEE *same as* > MUSTEE
MESTEES > MESTEE
MESTER *n* master: used as a term of address for a man who is the head of a house
MESTERS > MESTER
MESTESO *n* Spanish music genre
MESTESOES > MESTESO
MESTESOS > MESTESO
MESTINO *n* person of mixed race
MESTINOES > MESTINO
MESTINOS > MESTINO
MESTIZA > MESTIZO
MESTIZAS > MESTIZO
MESTIZO *n* person of mixed parentage, esp the offspring of a Spanish American and an American Indian
MESTIZOES > MESTIZO
MESTIZOS > MESTIZO
MESTO *adj* sad
MESTOM *same as* > MESTOME
MESTOME *n* conducting tissue associated with parenchyma
MESTOMES > MESTOME
MESTOMS > MESTOM
MESTRANOL *n* synthetic oestrogen
MET *n* measuring stick
META *n* indicating change, alteration, or alternation
METABASES > METABASIS
METABASIS *n* change
METABATIC > METABASIS
METABOLIC *adj* of or related to the sum total of the chemical processes that occurs in living organisms, resulting in growth, production of energy, elimination of waste material, etc
METABOLY *n* ability of some cells, esp protozoans, to alter their shape
METACARPI *n* skeleton of the hand between the wrist and the fingers
METAGE *n* official measuring of weight or contents
METAGENIC *adj* of or relating to the production within the life cycle of an organism of alternating asexual and sexual reproductive forms
METAGES > METAGE
METAIRIE *n* area of land on which farmer pays rent in kind
METAIRIES > METAIRIE
METAL *n* chemical element, such as iron or copper, that is malleable and capable of conducting heat and electricity ▷ *adj* made of metal ▷ *vb* fit or cover with metal
METALED > METAL
METALHEAD *n* fan of heavy metal music
METALING > METAL
METALISE *same*

m

as > METALLIZE
METALISED > METALISE
METALISES > METALISE
METALIST *same*

as > METALLIST
METALISTS > METALIST
METALIZE *same*

as > METALLIZE
METALIZED > METALIZE
METALIZES > METALIZE
METALLED > METAL
METALLIC *adj* of or consisting of metal ▷ *n* something metallic
METALLICS > METALLIC
METALLIKE > METAL
METALLINE *adj* of, resembling, or relating to metals
METALLING > METAL
METALLISE *same*

as > METALLIZE
METALLIST *n* person who works with metals
METALLIZE *vb* make metallic or to coat or treat with metal
METALLOID *n* nonmetallic element, such as arsenic or silicon, that has some of the properties of a metal ▷ *adj* of or being a metalloid
METALLY *adj* like metal
METALMARK *n* variety of butterfly
METALS > METAL
METALWARE *n* items made of metal
METALWORK *n* craft of making objects from metal
METAMALE *n* sterile male organism, esp a fruit fly (*Drosophila*) that has one X chromosome and three sets of autosomes
METAMALES > METAMALE
METAMER *n* any of two or more isomeric compounds exhibiting metamerism
METAMERAL > METAMERE
METAMERE *n* one of the similar body segments into which earthworms, crayfish, and similar animals are divided longitudinally
METAMERES > METAMERE
METAMERIC *adj* divided into or consisting of metameres
METAMERS > METAMER
METAMICT *adj* of or denoting the amorphous state of a substance that has lost its crystalline structure as a result of the radioactivity of uranium or thorium within it
METANOIA *n* repentance
METANOIAS > METANOIA
METAPELET *n* foster mother
METAPHASE *n* second stage of mitosis during which the condensed chromosomes attach to the centre of the spindle
METAPHOR *n* figure of speech

in which a term is applied to something it does not literally denote in order to imply a resemblance
METAPHORS > METAPHOR
METAPLASM *n* nonliving constituents, such as starch and pigment granules, of the cytoplasm of a cell
METAPLOT > METAPELET
METARCHON *n* nontoxic substance, such as a chemical to mask pheromones, that reduces the persistence of a pest
METASOMA *n* posterior part of an arachnid's abdomen (opisthosoma) that never carries appendages
METASOMAS > METASOMA
METATAG *n* element of HTML describing the contents of a web page and used by search engines to index pages by subject
METATAGS > METATAG
METATARSI *pl n* skeleton of human foot between toes and tarsus
METATE *n* stone for grinding grain on
METATES > METATE
METAXYLEM *n* xylem tissue that consists of rigid thick-walled cells and occurs in parts of the plant that have finished growing
METAYAGE *n* farming in which rent is paid in kind
METAYAGES > METAYAGE
METAYER *n* farmer who pays rent in kind
METAYERS > METAYER
METAZOA > METAZOAN
METAZOAL > METAZOAN
METAZOAN *n* any animal having a body composed of many cells: includes all animals except sponges and protozoans ▷ *adj* of the metazoans
METAZOANS > METAZOAN
METAZOIC *adj* of, relating to, or belonging to the *Metazoa*
METAZOON *same*

as > METAZOAN
METCAST *n* weather forecast
METCASTS > METCAST
METE *vb* deal out as punishment ▷ *n* (to) measure
METED > METE
METEOR *n* small fast-moving heavenly body, visible as a streak of incandescence if it enters the earth's atmosphere
METEORIC *adj* of a meteor
METEORISM *another name* *for* > TYMPANITES
METEORIST *n* person who studies meteors
METEORITE *n* meteor that has fallen to earth

METEOROID *n* any of the small celestial bodies that are thought to orbit the sun. When they enter the earth's atmosphere, they become visible as meteors
METEOROUS > METEOR
METEORS > METEOR
METEPA *n* type of pesticide
METEPAS > METEPA
METER *same as* > METRE
METERAGE *n* act of measuring
METERAGES > METERAGE
METERED > METER
METERING > METER
METERS > METER
METES > METE
METESTICK *n* measuring rod
METESTRUS *n* period in the oestrous cycle following oestrus, characterized by lack of sexual activity
METEWAND *same*

as > METESTICK
METEWANDS > METEWAND
METEYARD *same*

as > METESTICK
METEYARDS > METEYARD
METFORMIN *n* drug used to treat diabetes
METH *n* variety of amphetamine
METHADON *same*

as > METHADONE
METHADONE *n* drug similar to morphine, sometimes prescribed as a heroin substitute
METHADONS > METHADON
METHANAL *n* colourless poisonous irritating gas with a pungent characteristic odour, made by the oxidation of methanol and used as formalin and in the manufacture of synthetic resins
METHANALS > METHANAL
METHANE *n* colourless inflammable gas
METHANES > METHANE
METHANOIC *as in* *methanoic acid* systematic name for formic acid
METHANOL *n* colourless poisonous liquid used as a solvent and fuel
METHANOLS > METHANOL
METHEGLIN *n* (esp formerly) spiced or medicated mead
METHINK *same*

as > METHINKS
METHINKS *vb* it seems to me
METHO *n* methylated spirits
METHOD *n* way or manner
METHODIC *same*

as > METHOD
METHODISE *same*

as > METHODIZE
METHODISM *n* system and practices of the Methodist Church, developed by the English preacher John Wesley (1703–91) and his

followers
METHODIST > METHODISM
METHODIZE *vb* organize according to a method
METHODS > METHOD
METHOS > METHO
METHOUGHT > METHINKS
METHOXIDE *n* saltlike compound in which the hydrogen atom in the hydroxyl group of methanol has been replaced by a metal atom, usually an alkali metal atom as in sodium methoxide, $NaOCH_3$
METHOXY *n* steroid drug
METHOXYL *n* chemical compound of methyl and hydroxyl
METHS *n* methylated spirits
METHYL *n* compound containing a saturated hydrocarbon group of atoms
METHYLAL *n* colourless volatile flammable liquid
METHYLALS > METHYLAL
METHYLASE *n* enzyme
METHYLATE *vb* mix with methanol
METHYLENE *adj* of, consisting of, or containing the divalent group of atoms $=CH_2$
METHYLIC > METHYL
METHYLS > METHYL
METHYSES > METHYSIS
METHYSIS *n* drunkenness
METHYSTIC *adj* intoxicating
METIC *n* (in ancient Greece) an alien having some rights of citizenship in the city in which he lives
METICALS > METICAL
METICAL *n* money unit in Mozambique
METICALS > METICAL
METICS > METIC
METIER *n* profession or trade
METIERS > METIER
METIF *n* person of mixed race
METIFS > METIF
METING > METE
METIS *n* person of mixed parentage
METISSE > METIS
METISSES > METIS
METOL *n* colourless soluble organic substance used, (in the form of its sulphate, as a photographic developer
METOLS > METOL
METONYM *n* word used in a metonymy. For example *the bottle* is a metonym for *alcoholic drink*
METONYMIC > METONYMY
METONYMS > METONYM
METONYMY *n* figure of speech in which one thing is replaced by another associated with it, such (as 'the Crown' for 'the queen'
METOPAE > METOPE

METOPE n square space between two triglyphs in a Doric frieze

METOPES > METOPE

METOPIC adj of or relating to the forehead

METOPISM n congenital disfigurement of forehead

METOPISMS > METOPISM

METOPON n painkilling drug

METOPONS > METOPON

METOPRYL n type of anaesthetic

METOPRYLS > METOPRYL

METRALGIA n pain in the uterus

METRAZOL n drug used to improve blood circulation

METRAZOLS > METRAZOL

METRE n basic unit of length equal to about 1.094 yards (100 centimetres) ▷ vb express in poetry

METRED > METRE

METRES > METRE

METRIC adj of the decimal system of weights and measures based on the metre

METRICAL adj of measurement

METRICATE vb convert a measuring system or instrument to metric units

METRICIAN n writer of metrical verse

METRICISE vb study metre of poetry

METRICISM > METRICISE

METRICIST same as > METRICIAN

METRICIZE same as > METRICISE

METRICS n art of using poetic metre

METRIFIED > METRIFY

METRIFIER > METRIFY

METRIFIES > METRIFY

METRIFY vb render into poetic metre

METRING > METRE

METRIST n person skilled in the use of poetic metre

METRISTS > METRIST

METRITIS n inflammation of the uterus

METRO n underground railway system, esp in Paris

METROLOGY n science of weights and measures

METRONOME n instrument which marks musical time by means of a ticking pendulum

METROPLEX n large urban area

METROS > METRO

METS > MET

METTLE n courage or spirit

METTLED adj spirited, courageous, or valiant

METTLES > METTLE

METUMP n band for carrying a load or burden

METUMPS > METUMP

MEU another name for > SPIGNEL

MEUNIERE adj (of fish) dredged with flour, fried in butter, and served with butter, lemon juice, and parsley

MEUS > MEU

MEUSE n gap (in fence, wall etc) through which an animal passed ▷ vb go through this gap

MEUSED > MEUSE

MEUSES > MEUSE

MEUSING > MEUSE

MEVE same as > MOVE

MEVED > MEVE

MEVES > MEVE

MEVING > MEVE

MEVROU n South African title of address equivalent to *Mrs* when placed before a surname or *madam* when used alone

MEVROUS > MEVROU

MEW n cry of a cat ▷ vb utter this cry

MEWED > MEW

MEWING > MEW

MEWL vb (esp of a baby) to cry weakly ▷ n weak or whimpering cry

MEWLED > MEWL

MEWLER > MEWL

MEWLERS > MEWL

MEWLING > MEWL

MEWLS > MEWL

MEWS same as > MEUSE

MEWSED > MEWS

MEWSES > MEWS

MEWSING > MEWS

MEYNT > MING

MEZAIL same as > MESAIL

MEZAILS > MEZAIL

MEZCAL variant spelling of > MESCAL

MEZCALINE variant spelling of > MESCALINE

MEZCALS > MEZCAL

MEZE n type of hors d'oeuvre eaten esp with an apéritif or other drink in Greece and the Near (East

MEZEREON same as > MEZEREUM

MEZEREONS > MEZEREON

MEZEREUM n dried bark of certain shrubs of the genus *Daphne*, esp mezereon, formerly used as a vesicant and to treat arthritis

MEZEREUMS > MEZEREUM

MEZES > MEZE

MEZQUIT same as > MESQUITE

MEZQUITE same as > MESQUITE

MEZQUITES > MEZQUITE

MEZQUITS > MEZQUIT

MEZUZA same as > MEZUZAH

MEZUZAH n piece of parchment inscribed with biblical passages and fixed to the doorpost of the rooms of a Jewish house

MEZUZAHS > MEZUZAH

MEZUZAS > MEZUZA

MEZUZOT > MEZUZAH

MEZUZOTH > MEZUZAH

MEZZ same as > MEZZANINE

MEZZALUNA n half-moon shaped kitchen chopper

MEZZANINE n intermediate storey, esp between the ground and first floor ▷ adj of or relating to an intermediate stage in a financial process

MEZZE same as > MEZE

MEZZES > MEZZE

MEZZO adv moderately

MEZZOS > MEZZO

MEZZOTINT n method of engraving by scraping the roughened surface of a metal plate ▷ vb engrave (a copper plate) in this fashion

MGANGA n witch doctor

MGANGAS > MGANGA

MHO former name for > SIEMENS

MHORR n African gazelle

MHORRS > MHORR

MHOS > MHO

MI n (in tonic sol-fa) the third degree of any major scale

MIAOU same as > MEOW

MIAOUED > MIAOU

MIAOUING > MIAOU

MIAOUS > MIAOU

MIAOW same as > MEOW

MIAOWED > MIAOW

MIAOWING > MIAOW

MIAOWS > MIAOW

MIASM same as > MIASMA

MIASMA n unwholesome or foreboding atmosphere

MIASMAL > MIASMA

MIASMAS > MIASMA

MIASMATA > MIASMA

MIASMATIC > MIASMA

MIASMIC > MIASMA

MIASMOUS > MIASMA

MIASMS > MIASM

MIAUL same as > MEOW

MIAULED > MIAUL

MIAULING > MIAUL

MIAULS > MIAUL

MIB n marble used in games

MIBS > MIB

MIC n microphone

MICA n glasslike mineral used as an electrical insulator

MICACEOUS > MICA

MICAS > MICA

MICATE vb add mica to

MICATED > MICATE

MICATES > MICATE

MICATING > MICATE

MICAWBER n person who idles and trusts to fortune

MICAWBERS > MICAWBER

MICE > MOUSE

MICELL same as > MICELLE

MICELLA same as > MICELLE

MICELLAE > MICELLA

MICELLAR > MICELLE

MICELLAS > MICELLA

MICELLE n charged aggregate of molecules of colloidal size in a solution

MICELLES > MICELLE

MICELLS > MICELL

MICH same as > MITCH

MICHE same as > MICH

MICHED > MICH

MICHER > MICH

MICHERS > MICH

MICHES > MICH

MICHIGAN US name for > NEWMARKET

MICHIGANS > MICHIGAN

MICHING > MICH

MICHINGS > MICH

MICHT n Scots word for might

MICHTS > MICHT

MICK n derogatory term for an Irish person

MICKEY n young bull, esp one that is wild and unbranded ▷ vb drug person's drink

MICKEYED > MICKEY

MICKEYING > MICKEY

MICKEYS > MICKEY

MICKIES > MICKY

MICKLE adj large or abundant ▷ adv much ▷ n great amount

MICKLER > MICKLE

MICKLES > MICKLE

MICKLEST > MICKLE

MICKS > MICK

MICKY same as > MICKEY

MICO n marmoset

MICOS > MICO

MICRA > MICRON

MICRIFIED > MICRIFY

MICRIFIES > MICRIFY

MICRIFY vb make very small

MICRO n small computer

MICROBAR n millionth of bar of pressure

MICROBARS > MICROBAR

MICROBE n minute organism, esp one causing disease

MICROBEAM n X-ray machine with narrow focussed beam

MICROBES > MICROBE

MICROBIAL > MICROBE

MICROBIAN > MICROBE

MICROBIC > MICROBE

MICROBREW n beer made in small brewery

MICROBUS n small bus

MICROCAP adj (of investments) involving very small amount of capital

MICROCAR n small car

MICROCARD n card containing microprint

MICROCARS > MICROCAR

MICROCHIP n small wafer of silicon containing electronic circuits ▷ vb implant (an animal) with a microchip tag for purposes of identification

MICROCODE n set of computer instructions

MICROCOPY n greatly reduced photographic copy of a printed page, drawing, etc, on microfilm or microfiche

m

MICROCOSM *n* miniature representation of something

MICROCYTE *n* unusually small red blood cell

MICRODONT *adj* having unusually small teeth

MICRODOT *n* photographic copy of a document reduced to pinhead size

MICRODOTS > MICRODOT

MICROFILM *n* miniaturized recording of books or documents on a roll of film ▷ *vb* photograph a page or document on microfilm

MICROFORM *n* method of storing symbolic information by using photographic reduction techniques, such as microfilm, microfiche, etc

MICROGLIA *n* one of the two types of non-nervous tissue (glia) found in the central nervous system, having macrophage activity

MICROGRAM *n* photograph or drawing of an object as viewed through a microscope

MICROHM *n* millionth of ohm

MICROHMS > MICROHM

MICROINCH *n* millionth of inch

MICROJET *n* light jet-propelled aircraft

MICROJETS > MICROJET

MICROLITE *n* small private aircraft carrying no more than two people, with an empty weight of not more than 150 kg and a wing area not less than 10 square metres: used in pleasure flying and racing

MICROLITH *n* small Mesolithic flint tool which was made from a blade and formed part of hafted tools

MICROLOAN *n* very small loan

MICROLOGY *n* study of microscopic things

MICROLUX *n* millionth of a lux

MICROMERE *n* any of the small cells formed by unequal cleavage of a fertilized ovum

MICROMESH *n* very fine mesh

MICROMHO *n* millionth of mho

MICROMHOS > MICROMHO

MICROMINI *n* very short skirt

MICROMOLE *n* millionth of mole

MICRON *n* unit of length equal to 10^{-6} metre

MICRONISE *same as* > MICRONIZE

MICRONIZE *vb* break down to very small particles

MICRONS > MICRON

MICROPORE *n* very small pore

MICROPSIA *n* defect of vision in which objects appear to be smaller than they appear to a person with normal vision

MICROPUMP *n* small pump inserted in skin to automatically deliver medicine

MICROPYLE *n* small opening in the integuments of a plant ovule through which the male gametes pass

MICROS > MICRO

MICROSITE *n* website that is intended for a specific limited purpose and is often temporary

MICROSOME *n* any of the small particles consisting of ribosomes and fragments of attached endoplasmic reticulum that can be isolated from cells by centrifugal action

MICROTOME *n* instrument used for cutting thin sections, esp of biological material, for microscopical examination

MICROTOMY *n* cutting of sections with a microtome

MICROTONE *n* any musical interval smaller than a semitone

MICROVOLT *n* millionth of volt

MICROWATT *n* millionth of watt

MICROWAVE *n* electromagnetic wave with a wavelength of a few centimetres, used in radar and cooking ▷ *vb* cook in a microwave oven

MICROWIRE *n* very fine wire

MICRURGY *n* manipulation and examination of single cells under a microscope

MICS > MIC

MICTION *n* urination

MICTIONS > MICTION

MICTURATE *vb* urinate

MID *adj* intermediate, middle ▷ *n* middle ▷ *prep* amid

MIDAIR *n* some point above ground level, in the air

MIDAIRS > MIDAIR

MIDBRAIN *n* part of the brain that develops from the middle portion of the embryonic neural tube

MIDBRAINS > MIDBRAIN

MIDCAP *adj* (of investments) involving very small amount

MIDCOURSE *adj* in middle of course

MIDCULT *n* middlebrow culture

MIDCULTS > MIDCULT

MIDDAY *n* noon

MIDDAYS > MIDDAY

MIDDEN *n* dunghill or rubbish heap

MIDDENS > MIDDEN

MIDDEST *adj* in middle

MIDDIE *n* glass or bottle containing 285ml of beer

MIDDIES > MIDDY

MIDDLE *adj* equidistant from two extremes ▷ *n* middle point or part ▷ *vb* place in the middle

MIDDLED > MIDDLE

MIDDLEMAN *n* trader who buys from the producer and sells to the consumer

MIDDLEMEN > MIDDLEMAN

MIDDLER *n* pupil in middle years at school

MIDDLERS > MIDDLER

MIDDLES > MIDDLE

MIDDLING *adj* mediocre ▷ *adv* moderately

MIDDLINGS *pl n* poorer or coarser part of flour or other products

MIDDORSAL *adj* in middle or back

MIDDY *n* middle-sized glass of beer

MIDFIELD *n* area between the two opposing defences

MIDFIELDS > MIDFIELD

MIDGE *n* small mosquito-like insect

MIDGES > MIDGE

MIDGET *n* very small person or thing ▷ *adj* much smaller than normal

MIDGETS > MIDGET

MIDGIE *n* informal word for a small winged biting insect such as the midge or sandfly

MIDGIER > MIDGE

MIDGIES > MIDGIE

MIDGIEST > MIDGE

MIDGUT *n* middle part of the digestive tract of vertebrates, including the small intestine

MIDGUTS > MIDGUT

MIDGY > MIDGE

MIDI *adj* (of a skirt, coat, etc) reaching to below the knee or midcalf

MIDINETTE *n* Parisian seamstress or salesgirl in a clothes shop

MIDIRON *n* club, usually a No. 5, 6, or 7 iron, used for medium-length approach shots

MIDIRONS > MIDIRON

MIDIS > MIDI

MIDISKIRT *n* skirt of medium length

MIDLAND *n* middle part of a country

MIDLANDS > MIDLAND

MIDLEG *n* middle of leg

MIDLEGS > MIDLEG

MIDLIFE as in *midlife crisis* crisis that may be experienced in middle age involving frustration, panic, and feelings of pointlessness, sometimes resulting in radical and often ill-advised changes of lifestyle

MIDLIFER *n* middle-aged person

MIDLIFERS > MIDLIFER

MIDLINE *n* line at middle of something

MIDLINES > MIDLINE

MIDLIST *n* books in publisher's range that sell reasonably well

MIDLISTS > MIDLIST

MIDLIVES > MIDLIFE

MIDMONTH *n* middle of month

MIDMONTHS > MIDMONTH

MIDMOST *adv* in the middle or midst

MIDMOSTS > MIDMOST

MIDNIGHT *n* twelve o'clock at night

MIDNIGHTS > MIDNIGHT

MIDNOON *n* noon

MIDNOONS > MIDNOON

MIDPOINT *n* point on a line equally distant from either end

MIDPOINTS > MIDPOINT

MIDRANGE *n* part of loudspeaker

MIDRANGES > MIDRANGE

MIDRASH *n* homily on a scriptural passage derived by traditional Jewish exegetical methods and consisting usually of embellishment of the scriptural narrative

MIDRASHIC > MIDRASH

MIDRASHIM > MIDRASH

MIDRASHOT > MIDRASH

MIDRIB *n* main vein of a leaf, running down the centre of the blade

MIDRIBS > MIDRIB

MIDRIFF *n* middle part of the body

MIDRIFFS > MIDRIFF

MIDS > MID

MIDSHIP *adj* in, of, or relating to the middle of a vessel ▷ *n* middle of a vessel

MIDSHIPS *See* > AMIDSHIPS

MIDSIZE *adj* medium-sized

MIDSIZED *same as* > MIDSIZE

MIDSOLE *n* layer between the inner and the outer sole of a shoe, contoured for absorbing shock

MIDSOLES > MIDSOLE

MIDSPACE *n* area in middle of space

MIDSPACES > MIDSPACE

MIDST *See* > AMID

MIDSTORY *n* level of forest trees between smallest and tallest

MIDSTREAM *n* middle of a stream or river ▷ *adj* in or towards the middle of a stream or river

MIDSTS > MIDST

MIDSUMMER *n* middle of summer

MIDTERM *n* middle of a term in a school, university, etc

MIDTERMS > MIDTERM
MIDTOWN *n* centre of a town
MIDTOWNS > MIDTOWN
MIDWATCH *n* naval watch period beginning at midnight
MIDWAY *adv* halfway ▷ *adj* in or at the middle of the distance ▷ *n* place in a fair, carnival, etc, where sideshows are located
MIDWAYS > MIDWAY
MIDWEEK *n* middle of the week
MIDWEEKLY > MIDWEEK
MIDWEEKS > MIDWEEK
MIDWIFE *n* trained person who assists at childbirth ▷ *vb* act as midwife
MIDWIFED > MIDWIFE
MIDWIFERY *n* art or practice of a midwife
MIDWIFES > MIDWIFE
MIDWIFING > MIDWIFE
MIDWINTER *n* middle or depth of winter
MIDWIVE *vb* act as midwife
MIDWIVED > MIDWIVE
MIDWIVES > MIDWIVE
MIDWIVING > MIDWIVE
MIDYEAR *n* middle of the year
MIDYEARS > MIDYEAR
MIELIE *same as* > MEALIE
MIELIES > MIELIE
MIEN *n* person's bearing, demeanour, or appearance
MIENS > MIEN
MIEVE *same as* > MOVE
MIEVED > MIEVE
MIEVES > MIEVE
MIEVING > MIEVE
MIFF *vb* take offence or offend ▷ *n* petulant mood
MIFFED > MIFF
MIFFIER > MIFFY
MIFFIEST > MIFFY
MIFFILY > MIFFY
MIFFINESS > MIFFY
MIFFING > MIFF
MIFFS > MIFF
MIFFY *adj* easily upset
MIFTY *same as* > MIFFY
MIG *n* marble used in games
MIGG *same as* > MIG
MIGGLE *n* US word for playing marble
MIGGLES > MIGGLE
MIGGS > MIGG
MIGHT > MAY
MIGHTEST > MAY
MIGHTFUL *same as* > MIGHTY
MIGHTIER > MIGHTY
MIGHTIEST > MIGHTY
MIGHTILY *adv* great extent, amount, or degree
MIGHTS > MAY
MIGHTST > MAY
MIGHTY *adj* powerful ▷ *adv* very
MIGMATITE *n* composite rock body containing two types of rock (esp igneous and metamorphic rock) that have interacted with each other but are nevertheless still

distinguishable
MIGNON *adj* small and pretty ▷ *n* tender boneless cut of meat
MIGNONNE > MIGNON
MIGNONNES > MIGNON
MIGNONS > MIGNON
MIGRAINE *n* severe headache, often with nausea and visual disturbances
MIGRAINES > MIGRAINE
MIGRANT *n* person or animal that moves from one place to another ▷ *adj* moving from one place to another
MIGRANTS > MIGRANT
MIGRATE *vb* move from one place to settle in another
MIGRATED > MIGRATE
MIGRATES > MIGRATE
MIGRATING > MIGRATE
MIGRATION *n* act or an instance of migrating
MIGRATOR > MIGRATE
MIGRATORS > MIGRATE
MIGRATORY *adj* (of an animal) migrating every year
MIGS > MIG
MIHA *n* young fern frond which has not yet opened
MIHI *n* Māori ceremonial greeting ▷ *vb* greet
MIHIED > MIHI
MIHIING > MIHI
MIHIS > MIHI
MIHRAB *n* niche in a mosque showing the direction of Mecca
MIHRABS > MIHRAB
MIJNHEER *same as* > MYNHEER
MIJNHEERS > MIJNHEER
MIKADO *n* Japanese emperor
MIKADOS > MIKADO
MIKE *n* microphone
MIKED > MIKE
MIKES > MIKE
MIKING > MIKE
MIKRA > MIKRON
MIKRON *same as* > MICRON
MIKRONS > MIKRON
MIKVAH *n* pool used esp by women for ritual purification after their monthly period
MIKVAHS > MIKVAH
MIKVEH *same as* > MIKVAH
MIKVEHS > MIKVEH
MIKVOS > MIKVEH
MIKVOT > MIKVEH
MIKVOTH > MIKVAH
MIL *n* unit of length equal to one thousandth of an inch
MILADI *same as* > MILADY
MILADIES > MILADY
MILADIS > MILADI
MILADY *n* (formerly) a continental title for an English gentlewoman
MILAGE *same as* > MILEAGE
MILAGES > MILAGE
MILCH *adj* (of a cow) giving milk
MILCHIG *same as* > MILCHIK
MILCHIK *adj* containing or

used in the preparation of milk products and so not to be used with meat products
MILD *adj* not strongly flavoured ▷ *n* dark beer flavoured with fewer hops than bitter ▷ *vb* become gentle
MILDED > MILD
MILDEN *vb* make or become mild or milder
MILDENED > MILDEN
MILDENING > MILDEN
MILDENS > MILDEN
MILDER > MILD
MILDEST > MILD
MILDEW *same as* > MOULD
MILDEWED > MILDEW
MILDEWING > MILDEW
MILDEWS > MILDEW
MILDEWY > MILDEW
MILDING > MILD
MILDLY > MILD
MILDNESS > MILD
MILDS > MILD
MILE *n* unit of length equal to 1760 yards or 1.609 kilometres
MILEAGE *n* distance travelled in miles
MILEAGES > MILEAGE
MILEPOST *n* signpost that shows the distance in miles to or from a place
MILEPOSTS > MILEPOST
MILER *n* athlete, horse, etc, that specializes in races of one mile
MILERS > MILER
MILES > MILE
MILESIAN *adj* Irish
MILESIMO *n* Spanish word meaning thousandth
MILESIMOS > MILESIMO
MILESTONE *same as* > MILEPOST
MILFOIL *same as* > YARROW
MILFOILS > MILFOIL
MILIA > MILIUM
MILIARIA *n* acute itching eruption of the skin, caused by blockage of the sweat glands
MILIARIAL > MILIARIA
MILIARIAS > MILIARIA
MILIARY *adj* resembling or relating to millet seeds
MILIEU *n* environment or surroundings
MILIEUS > MILIEU
MILIEUX > MILIEU
MILITANCE > MILITANT
MILITANCY > MILITANT
MILITANT *adj* aggressive or vigorous in support of a cause ▷ *n* militant person
MILITANTS > MILITANT
MILITAR *same as* > MILITARY
MILITARIA *pl n* items of military interest, such as weapons, uniforms, medals, etc, esp from the past
MILITARY *adj* of or for soldiers, armies, or war ▷ *n* armed services

MILITATE *vb* have a strong influence or effect
MILITATED > MILITATE
MILITATES > MILITATE
MILITIA *n* military force of trained citizens for use in emergency only
MILITIAS > MILITIA
MILIUM *n* pimple
MILK *n* white fluid produced by female mammals to feed their young ▷ *vb* draw milk from
MILKED > MILK
MILKEN *adj* of or like milk
MILKER *n* cow, goat, etc, that yields milk, esp of a specified quality or amount
MILKERS > MILKER
MILKFISH *n* large silvery tropical clupeoid food and game fish, *Chanos chanos*: family *Chanidae*
MILKIER > MILKY
MILKIEST > MILKY
MILKILY > MILKY
MILKINESS > MILKY
MILKING > MILK
MILKINGS > MILKING
MILKLESS > MILK
MILKLIKE > MILK
MILKMAID *n* (esp in former times) woman who milks cows
MILKMAIDS > MILKMAID
MILKMAN *n* man who delivers milk to people's houses
MILKMEN > MILKMAN
MILKO *informal name for* > MILKMAN
MILKOS > MILKO
MILKS > MILK
MILKSHAKE *n* drink of flavoured milk
MILKSHED *n* area where milk is produced
MILKSHEDS > MILKSHED
MILKSOP *n* feeble man
MILKSOPPY > MILKSOP
MILKSOPS > MILKSOP
MILKTOAST *n* meek, submissive, or timid person
MILKWEED *same as* > MONARCH
MILKWEEDS > MILKWEED
MILKWOOD *n* tree producing latex
MILKWOODS > MILKWOOD
MILKWORT *n* any of several plants of the genus *Polygala*, having small blue, pink, or white flowers with two petal-like sepals: family *Polygalaceae*. They were formerly believed to increase milk production in cows
MILKWORTS > MILKWORT
MILKY *adj* of or like milk
MILL *n* factory ▷ *vb* grind, press, or process in or as if in a mill
MILLABLE > MILL
MILLAGE *adj* American tax rate calculated in thousandths per dollar

MILLAGES > MILLAGE
MILLBOARD n strong pasteboard, used esp in book covers
MILLCAKE n food for livestock
MILLCAKES > MILLCAKE
MILLDAM n dam built in a stream to raise the water level sufficiently for it to turn a millwheel
MILLDAMS > MILLDAM
MILLE French word for > THOUSAND
MILLED adj crushed or ground in a mill
MILLENARY adj of or relating to a thousand or to a thousand years ▷ n adherent of millenarianism
MILLENNIA n plural of millennium: period or cycle of one thousand years
MILLEPED same as > MILLEPEDE
MILLEPEDE same as > MILLIPEDE
MILLEPEDS > MILLEPED
MILLEPORE n any tropical colonial coral-like medusoid hydrozoan of the order Milleporina, esp of the genus Millepora, having a calcareous skeleton
MILLER n person who works in a mill
MILLERITE n yellow mineral consisting of nickel sulphide
MILLERS > MILLER
MILLES > MILLE
MILLET n type of cereal grass
MILLETS > MILLET
MILLHOUSE n house attached to mill
MILLIARD n one thousand millions
MILLIARDS > MILLIARD
MILLIARE n ancient Roman unit of distance
MILLIARES > MILLIARE
MILLIARY adj relating to or marking a distance equal to an ancient Roman mile of a thousand paces
MILLIBAR n unit of atmospheric pressure
MILLIBARS > MILLIBAR
MILLIE n derogatory name for a young working-class woman
MILLIEME n Tunisian monetary unit worth one thousandth of a dinar
MILLIEMES > MILLIEME
MILLIER n metric weight of million grams
MILLIERS > MILLIER
MILLIES > MILLIE
MILLIGAL n unit of gravity
MILLIGALS > MILLIGAL
MILLIGRAM n thousandth part of a gram
MILLILUX n thousandth of lux
MILLIME same

as > MILLIEME
MILLIMES > MILLIME
MILLIMHO n thousandth of mho
MILLIMHOS > MILLIMHO
MILLIMOLE n thousandth of mole
MILLINE n measurement of advertising space
MILLINER n maker or seller of women's hats
MILLINERS > MILLINER
MILLINERY n hats, trimmings, etc, sold by a milliner
MILLINES > MILLINE
MILLING n act or process of grinding, cutting, pressing, or crushing in a mill
MILLINGS > MILLING
MILLIOHM n thousandth of ohm
MILLIOHMS > MILLIOHM
MILLION n one thousand thousands
MILLIONS > MILLION
MILLIONTH n one of 1 000 000 approximately equal parts of something ▷ adj being the ordinal number of 1 000 000 in numbering or counting order, etc
MILLIPED same as > MILLIPEDE
MILLIPEDE n small animal with a jointed body and many pairs of legs
MILLIPEDS > MILLIPED
MILLIREM n unit of radiation
MILLIREMS > MILLIREM
MILLIVOLT n thousandth of volt
MILLIWATT n thousandth of watt
MILLOCRAT n member of a government of millowners
MILLPOND n pool which provides water to turn a millwheel
MILLPONDS > MILLPOND
MILLRACE n current of water that turns a millwheel
MILLRACES > MILLRACE
MILLRIND n iron support fitted across an upper millstone
MILLRINDS > MILLRIND
MILLRUN same as > MILLRACE
MILLRUNS > MILLRUN
MILLS > MILL
MILLSCALE n scale on metal being heated
MILLSTONE n flat circular stone for grinding corn
MILLTAIL n channel carrying water away from mill
MILLTAILS > MILLTAIL
MILLWHEEL n waterwheel that drives a mill
MILLWORK n work done in a mill
MILLWORKS > MILLWORK

MILNEB n type of pesticide
MILNEBS > MILNEB
MILO n any of various early-growing cultivated varieties of sorghum with heads of yellow or pinkish seeds resembling millet
MILOMETER n device that records the number of miles that a bicycle or motor vehicle has travelled
MILOR same as > MILORD
MILORD n (formerly) a continental title used for an English gentleman
MILORDS > MILORD
MILORS > MILOR
MILOS > MILO
MILPA n form of subsistence agriculture in Mexico
MILPAS > MILPA
MILREIS n former monetary unit of Portugal and Brazil, divided into 1000 reis
MILS > MIL
MILSEY n milk strainer
MILSEYS > MILSEY
MILT n sperm of fish ▷ vb fertilize (the roe of a female fish) with milt, esp artificially
MILTED > MILT
MILTER n male fish that is mature and ready to breed
MILTERS > MILTER
MILTIER > MILTY
MILTIEST > MILTY
MILTING > MILT
MILTONIA n tropical American orchid
MILTONIAS > MILTONIA
MILTS > MILT
MILTY adj full of milt
MILTZ same as > MILT
MILTZES > MILTZ
MILVINE adj of kites and related birds
MIM adj prim, modest, or demure
MIMBAR n pulpit in mosque
MIMBARS > MIMBAR
MIME n acting without the use of words ▷ vb act in mime
MIMED > MIME
MIMEO vb mimeograph
MIMEOED > MIMEO
MIMEOING > MIMEO
MIMEOS > MIMEO
MIMER > MIME
MIMERS > MIME
MIMES > MIME
MIMESES > MIMESIS
MIMESIS n imitative representation of nature or human behaviour
MIMESISES > MIMESIS
MIMESTER > MIME
MIMESTERS > MIME
MIMETIC adj imitating or representing something
MIMETICAL > MIMETIC
MIMETITE n rare secondary mineral
MIMETITES > MIMETITE
MIMIC vb imitate (a person

or manner), esp for satirical effect ▷ n person or animal that is good at mimicking ▷ adj of, relating to, or using mimicry
MIMICAL > MIMIC
MIMICKED > MIMIC
MIMICKER > MIMIC
MIMICKERS > MIMIC
MIMICKING > MIMIC
MIMICRIES > MIMICRY
MIMICRY n act or art of copying or imitating closely
MIMICS > MIMIC
MIMING > MIME
MIMMER > MIM
MIMMEST > MIM
MIMMICK same as > MINNICK
MIMMICKED > MIMMICK
MIMMICKS > MIMMICK
MIMOSA n shrub with fluffy yellow flowers and sensitive leaves
MIMOSAS > MIMOSA
MIMSEY same as > MIMSY
MIMSIER > MIMSY
MIMSIEST > MIMSY
MIMSY adj prim, underwhelming, and ineffectual
MIMULUS n plants cultivated for their yellow or red flowers
MIMULUSES > MIMULUS
MINA n ancient unit of weight and money, used in Asia Minor, equal to one sixtieth of a talent
MINABLE > MINE
MINACIOUS adj threatening
MINACITY > MINACIOUS
MINAE > MINA
MINAR n tower
MINARET n tall slender tower of a mosque
MINARETED > MINARET
MINARETS > MINARET
MINARS > MINAR
MINAS > MINA
MINATORY adj threatening or menacing
MINBAR same as > MIMBAR
MINBARS > MINBAR
MINCE vb cut or grind into very small pieces ▷ n minced meat
MINCED > MINCE
MINCEMEAT n sweet mixture of dried fruit and spices
MINCER n machine for mincing meat
MINCERS > MINCER
MINCES > MINCE
MINCEUR adj (of food) low-fat
MINCIER > MINCY
MINCIEST > MINCY
MINCING adj affected in manner
MINCINGLY > MINCING
MINCINGS > MINCING
MINCY adj effeminate
MIND n thinking faculties ▷ vb take offence at
MINDED adj having an inclination as specified

MINDER *n* aide or bodyguard
MINDERS > MINDER
MINDFUCK *n* taboo term for deliberate infliction of psychological damage
MINDFUCKS > MINDFUCK
MINDFUL *adj* heedful
MINDFULLY > MINDFUL
MINDING > MIND
MINDINGS > MIND
MINDLESS *adj* stupid
MINDS > MIND
MINDSET *n* ideas and attitudes with which a person approaches a situation, esp when these are seen as being difficult to alter
MINDSETS > MINDSET
MINDSHARE *n* level of awareness in the minds of consumers that a particular product commands
MINE *pron* belonging to me ▷ *n* deep hole for digging out coal, ores, etc ▷ *vb* dig for minerals
MINEABLE > MINE
MINED > MINE
MINEFIELD *n* area of land or water containing mines
MINELAYER *n* warship or aircraft for carrying and laying mines
MINEOLA *same as* > MINNEOLA
MINEOLAS > MINEOLA
MINER *n* person who works in a mine
MINERAL *n* naturally occurring inorganic substance, such as metal ▷ *adj* of, containing, or like minerals
MINERALS > MINERAL
MINERS > MINER
MINES > MINE
MINESHAFT *n* vertical entrance into mine
MINESTONE *n* ore
MINETTE *n* type of rock
MINETTES > MINETTE
MINEVER *same as* > MINIVER
MINEVERS > MINEVER
MING *vb* mix
MINGE *n* taboo word fore female genitals
MINGED > MING
MINGER *n* unattractive person
MINGERS > MINGER
MINGES > MINGE
MINGIER > MINGY
MINGIEST > MINGY
MINGIN *same as* > MINGING
MINGINESS > MINGY
MINGING *adj* unattractive or unpleasant
MINGLE *vb* mix or blend
MINGLED > MINGLE
MINGLER > MINGLE
MINGLERS > MINGLE
MINGLES > MINGLE
MINGLING > MINGLE
MINGLINGS > MINGLE
MINGS > MING

MINGY *adj* miserly
MINI *same as* > MINIDRESS
MINIATE *vb* paint with minium
MINIATED > MINIATE
MINIATES > MINIATE
MINIATING > MINIATE
MINIATION > MINIATE
MINIATURE *n* small portrait, model, or copy ▷ *adj* small-scale ▷ *vb* reproduce in miniature
MINIBAR *n* selection of drinks and confectionery provided in a hotel room
MINIBARS > MINIBAR
MINIBIKE *n* light motorcycle
MINIBIKER > MINIBIKE
MINIBIKES > MINIBIKE
MINIBREAK *n* short holiday
MINIBUS *n* small bus
MINIBUSES > MINIBUS
MINICAB *n* ordinary car used as a taxi
MINICABS > MINICAB
MINICAM *n* portable television camera
MINICAMP *n* period spent together in isolation by sports team
MINICAMPS > MINICAMP
MINICAMS > MINICAM
MINICAR *n* small car
MINICARS > MINICAR
MINICOM *n* device used by deaf and hard-of-hearing people, allowing typed telephone messages to be sent and received
MINICOMS > MINICOM
MINIDISC *n* small recordable compact disc
MINIDISCS > MINIDISC
MINIDISH *n* small parabolic aerial for reception or transmission to a communications satellite
MINIDISK *same as* > MINIDISC
MINIDISKS > MINIDISK
MINIDRESS *n* very short dress, at least four inches above the knee
MINIER > MINY
MINIEST > MINY
MINIFIED > MINIFY
MINIFIES > MINIFY
MINIFY *vb* minimize or lessen the size or importance of (something)
MINIFYING > MINIFY
MINIKIN *n* small, dainty, or affected person or thing ▷ *adj* dainty, prim, or affected
MINIKINS > MINIKIN
MINILAB *n* equipment for processing photographic film
MINILABS > MINILAB
MINIM *n* note half the length of a semibreve ▷ *adj* very small
MINIMA > MINIMUM
MINIMAL *adj* minimum ▷ *n* small surfboard

MINIMALLY > MINIMAL
MINIMALS > MINIMAL
MINIMAX *n* lowest of a set of maximum values ▷ *vb* make maximum as low as possible
MINIMAXED > MINIMAX
MINIMAXES > MINIMAX
MINIMENT *same as* > MUNIMENT
MINIMENTS > MINIMENT
MINIMILL *n* small mill
MINIMILLS > MINIMILL
MINIMISE *same as* > MINIMIZE
MINIMISED > MINIMISE
MINIMISER > MINIMIZE
MINIMISES > MINIMISE
MINIMISM *n* desire to reduce to minimum
MINIMISMS > MINIMISM
MINIMIST > MINIMISM
MINIMISTS > MINIMISM
MINIMIZE *vb* reduce to a minimum
MINIMIZED > MINIMIZE
MINIMIZER > MINIMIZE
MINIMIZES > MINIMIZE
MINIMOTO *n* reduced-size replica motorcycle used for racing
MINIMOTOS > MINIMOTO
MINIMS > MINIM
MINIMUM *n* least possible (amount or number) ▷ *adj* of, being, or showing a minimum or minimums
MINIMUMS > MINIMUM
MINIMUS *adj* youngest: sometimes used after the surname of a schoolboy having elder brothers at the same school
MINIMUSES > MINIMUS
MINING *n* act, process, or industry of extracting coal or ores from the earth
MININGS > MINING
MINION *n* servile assistant ▷ *adj* dainty, pretty, or elegant
MINIONS > MINION
MINIPARK *n* small park
MINIPARKS > MINIPARK
MINIPILL *n* low-dose oral contraceptive containing a progestogen only
MINIPILLS > MINIPILL
MINIRUGBY *n* version of rugby with fewer players
MINIS > MINI
MINISCULE *same as* > MINUSCULE
MINISH *vb* diminish
MINISHED > MINISH
MINISHES > MINISH
MINISHING > MINISH
MINISKI *n* short ski
MINISKIRT *n* very short skirt
MINISKIS > MINISKI
MINISTATE *n* small independent state
MINISTER *n* head of a government department ▷ *vb* attend to the needs of
MINISTERS > MINISTER

MINISTRY *n* profession or duties of a clergyman
MINITOWER *n* computer in small vertical cabinet
MINITRACK *n* satellite tracking system
MINIUM *n* bright red poisonous insoluble oxide of lead usually obtained as a powder by heating litharge in air
MINIUMS > MINIUM
MINIVAN *n* small van, esp one with seats in the back for carrying passengers
MINIVANS > MINIVAN
MINIVER *n* white fur, used in ceremonial costumes
MINIVERS > MINIVER
MINIVET *n* any brightly coloured tropical Asian cuckoo shrike of the genus *Pericrocotus*
MINIVETS > MINIVET
MINK *n* stoatlike animal
MINKE *as in* *minke whale* type of small whalebone whale or rorqual
MINKES > MINKE
MINKS > MINK
MINNEOLA *n* juicy citrus fruit that is a cross between a tangerine and a grapefruit
MINNEOLAS > MINNEOLA
MINNICK *vb* behave in fussy way
MINNICKED > MINNICK
MINNICKS > MINNICK
MINNIE *n* mother
MINNIES > MINNIE
MINNOCK *same as* > MINNICK
MINNOCKED > MINNOCK
MINNOCKS > MINNOCK
MINNOW *n* small freshwater fish
MINNOWS > MINNOW
MINNY *same as* > MINNIE
MINO *same as* > MYNAH
MINOR *adj* lesser ▷ *n* person regarded legally as a child ▷ *vb* take a minor
MINORCA *n* breed of light domestic fowl with glossy white, black, or blue plumage
MINORCAS > MINORCA
MINORED > MINOR
MINORING > MINOR
MINORITY *n* lesser number
MINORS > MINOR
MINORSHIP > MINOR
MINOS > MINO
MINOXIDIL *n* drug used to counter baldness
MINSHUKU *n* guesthouse in Japan
MINSHUKUS > MINSHUKU
MINSTER *n* cathedral or large church
MINSTERS > MINSTER
MINSTREL *n* medieval singer or musician
MINSTRELS > MINSTREL
MINT *n* plant with aromatic leaves used for seasoning and flavouring ▷ *vb* make (coins)

MINTAGE n process of minting
MINTAGES > MINTAGE
MINTED > MINT
MINTER > MINT
MINTERS > MINT
MINTIER > MINT
MINTIEST > MINT
MINTING > MINT
MINTS > MINT
MINTY > MINT
MINUEND n number from which another number is to be subtracted
MINUENDS > MINUEND
MINUET n stately dance
MINUETS > MINUET
MINUS adj indicating subtraction ▷ n sign (-) denoting subtraction or a number less than zero ▷ prep reduced by the subtraction of
MINUSCULE adj very small ▷ n lower-case letter
MINUSES > MINUS
MINUTE n 60th part of an hour or degree ▷ vb record in the minutes ▷ adj very small
MINUTED > MINUTE
MINUTELY adv in great detail ▷ adj occurring every minute
MINUTEMAN n (in the War of American Independence) colonial militiaman who promised to be ready to fight at one minute's notice
MINUTEMEN > MINUTEMAN
MINUTER > MINUTE
MINUTES pl n official record of the proceedings of a meeting or conference
MINUTEST > MINUTE
MINUTIA singular noun of > MINUTIAE
MINUTIAE pl n trifling or precise details
MINUTIAL > MINUTIAE
MINUTING > MINUTE
MINUTIOSE > MINUTIAE
MINX n bold or flirtatious girl
MINXES > MINX
MINXISH > MINX
MINY adj of or like mines
MINYAN n number of persons required by Jewish law to be present for a religious service, namely, at least ten males over thirteen years of age
MINYANIM > MINYAN
MINYANS > MINYAN
MIOCENE adj of, denoting, or formed in the fourth epoch of the Tertiary period, between the Oligocene and Pliocene epochs, which lasted for 19 million years
MIOMBO n (in E Africa) a dry wooded area with sparse deciduous growth
MIOMBOS > MIOMBO
MIOSES > MIOSIS

MIOSIS n excessive contraction of the pupil of the eye, as in response to drugs
MIOTIC > MIOSIS
MIOTICS > MIOSIS
MIPS n million instructions per second: a unit used to express the speed of a computer's central processing unit
MIQUELET n type of lock on old firearm
MIQUELETS > MIQUELET
MIR n peasant commune in prerevolutionary Russia
MIRABELLE n small sweet yellow-orange fruit that is a variety of greengage
MIRABILIA n wonders
MIRABILIS n tropical American plant
MIRABLE adj wonderful
MIRACIDIA n plural form of singular miracidium: flat ciliated larva of flukes that hatches from the egg and gives rise asexually to other larval forms
MIRACLE n wonderful supernatural event
MIRACLES > MIRACLE
MIRADOR n window, balcony, or turret
MIRADORS > MIRADOR
MIRAGE n optical illusion, esp one caused by hot air
MIRAGES > MIRAGE
MIRANDISE same as > MIRANDIZE
MIRANDIZE vb (in USA) inform arrested person of rights
MIRBANE n substance used in perfumes
MIRBANES > MIRBANE
MIRCHI Indian English word for > HOT
MIRE n swampy ground ▷ vb sink or be stuck in a mire
MIRED > MIRE
MIREPOIX n mixture of sautéed root vegetables used as a base for braising meat or for various sauces
MIRES > MIRE
MIREX n type of insecticide
MIREXES > MIREX
MIRI > MIR
MIRIER > MIRE
MIRIEST > MIRE
MIRIFIC adj achieving wonderful things
MIRIFICAL same as > MIRIFIC
MIRIN n Japanese rice wine
MIRINESS > MIRE
MIRING > MIRE
MIRINS > MIRIN
MIRITI n South American palm
MIRITIS > MIRITI
MIRK same as > MURK
MIRKER > MIRK
MIRKEST > MIRK
MIRKIER > MIRK

MIRKIEST > MURKY
MIRKILY > MIRK
MIRKINESS > MIRK
MIRKS > MIRK
MIRKY > MIRK
MIRLIER > MIRLY
MIRLIEST > MIRLY
MIRLIGOES n dizzy feeling
MIRLITON another name (chiefly US) for > CHAYOTE
MIRLITONS > MIRLITON
MIRLY same as > MARLY
MIRO n tall New Zealand tree
MIROMIRO n small New Zealand bird
MIRROR n coated glass surface for reflecting images ▷ vb reflect in or as if in a mirror
MIRRORED > MIRROR
MIRRORING > MIRROR
MIRRORS > MIRROR
MIRS > MIR
MIRTH n laughter, merriment, or gaiety
MIRTHFUL > MIRTH
MIRTHLESS > MIRTH
MIRTHS > MIRTH
MIRV n missile that has several warheads, each one being directed to different enemy targets ▷ vb arm with mirvs
MIRVED > MIRV
MIRVING > MIRV
MIRVS > MIRV
MIRY > MIRE
MIRZA n title of respect placed before the surname of an official, scholar, or other distinguished man
MIRZAS > MIRZA
MIS > MI
MISACT vb act wrongly
MISACTED > MISACT
MISACTING > MISACT
MISACTS > MISACT
MISADAPT vb adapt badly
MISADAPTS > MISADAPT
MISADD vb add badly
MISADDED > MISADD
MISADDING > MISADD
MISADDS > MISADD
MISADJUST vb adjust wrongly
MISADVICE n bad advice
MISADVISE vb give bad advice to
MISAGENT n bad agent
MISAGENTS > MISAGENT
MISAIM vb aim badly
MISAIMED > MISAIM
MISAIMING > MISAIM
MISAIMS > MISAIM
MISALIGN vb align badly
MISALIGNS > MISALIGN
MISALLEGE vb allege wrongly
MISALLIED > MISALLY
MISALLIES > MISALLY
MISALLOT vb allot wrongly
MISALLOTS > MISALLOT
MISALLY vb form unsuitable alliance
MISALTER vb alter wrongly
MISALTERS > MISALTER

MISANDRY n hatred of men
MISAPPLY vb use something for a purpose for which it is not intended or is not suited
MISARRAY n disarray
MISARRAYS > MISARRAY
MISASSAY vb assay wrongly
MISASSAYS > MISASSAY
MISASSIGN vb assign wrongly
MISATE > MISEAT
MISATONE vb atone wrongly
MISATONED > MISATONE
MISATONES > MISATONE
MISAUNTER n misadventure
MISAVER vb claim wrongly
MISAVERS > MISAVER
MISAVISED adj badly advised
MISAWARD vb award wrongly
MISAWARDS > MISAWARD
MISBECAME > MISBECOME
MISBECOME vb be unbecoming to or unsuitable for
MISBEGAN > MISBEGIN
MISBEGIN vb begin badly
MISBEGINS > MISBEGIN
MISBEGOT adj illegitimate
MISBEGUN > MISBEGIN
MISBEHAVE vb behave badly
MISBELIEF n false or unorthodox belief
MISBESEEM vb be unsuitable for
MISBESTOW vb bestow wrongly
MISBIAS vb prejudice wrongly
MISBIASED > MISBIAS
MISBIASES > MISBIAS
MISBILL vb present inaccurate bill
MISBILLED > MISBILL
MISBILLS > MISBILL
MISBIND vb bind wrongly
MISBINDS > MISBIND
MISBIRTH n abortion
MISBIRTHS > MISBIRTH
MISBORN adj abortive
MISBOUND > MISBIND
MISBRAND vb put misleading label on
MISBRANDS > MISBRAND
MISBUILD vb build badly
MISBUILDS > MISBUILD
MISBUILT > MISBUILD
MISBUTTON vb button wrongly
MISCALL vb call by the wrong name
MISCALLED > MISCALL
MISCALLER > MISCALL
MISCALLS > MISCALL
MISCARRY vb have a miscarriage
MISCAST vb cast (a role or actor) in (a play or film) inappropriately
MISCASTS > MISCAST
MISCEGEN n person of mixed race
MISCEGENE same as > MISCEGEN
MISCEGENS > MISCEGEN

m

MISCEGINE *same as* > MISCEGEN

MISCH *as in* misch metal alloy of cerium and other rare earth metals, used esp as a flint in cigarette lighters

MISCHANCE *n* unlucky event

MISCHANCY *adj* unlucky

MISCHARGE *vb* charge wrongly

MISCHIEF *n* annoying but not malicious behaviour

MISCHIEFS > MISCHIEF

MISCHOICE *n* bad choice

MISCHOOSE *vb* make bad choice

MISCHOSE > MISCHOOSE

MISCHOSEN > MISCHOOSE

MISCIBLE *adj* able to be mixed

MISCITE *vb* cite wrongly

MISCITED > MISCITE

MISCITES > MISCITE

MISCITING > MISCITE

MISCLAIM *vb* claim wrongly

MISCLAIMS > MISCLAIM

MISCLASS *adj* class badly

MISCODE *vb* code wrongly

MISCODED > MISCODE

MISCODES > MISCODE

MISCODING > MISCODE

MISCOIN *vb* coin wrongly

MISCOINED > MISCOIN

MISCOINS > MISCOIN

MISCOLOR *same as* > MISCOLOUR

MISCOLORS > MISCOLOR

MISCOLOUR *vb* give wrong colour to

MISCOOK *vb* cook badly

MISCOOKED > MISCOOK

MISCOOKS > MISCOOK

MISCOPIED > MISCOPY

MISCOPIES > MISCOPY

MISCOPY *vb* copy badly

MISCOUNT *vb* count or calculate incorrectly ▷ *n* false count or calculation

MISCOUNTS > MISCOUNT

MISCREANT *n* wrongdoer ▷ *adj* evil or villainous

MISCREATE *vb* create (something) badly or incorrectly ▷ *adj* badly or unnaturally formed or made

MISCREDIT *vb* disbelieve

MISCREED *n* false creed

MISCREEDS > MISCREED

MISCUE *n* faulty stroke in which the cue tip slips off the cue ball or misses it altogether ▷ *vb* make a miscue

MISCUED > MISCUE

MISCUEING > MISCUE

MISCUES > MISCUE

MISCUING > MISCUE

MISCUT *n* cut wrongly

MISCUTS > MISCUT

MISDATE *vb* date (a letter, event, etc) wrongly

MISDATED > MISDATE

MISDATES > MISDATE

MISDATING > MISDATE

MISDEAL *vb* deal out cards incorrectly ▷ *n* faulty deal

MISDEALER > MISDEAL

MISDEALS > MISDEAL

MISDEALT > MISDEAL

MISDEED *n* wrongful act

MISDEEDS > MISDEED

MISDEEM *vb* form bad opinion of

MISDEEMED > MISDEEM

MISDEEMS > MISDEEM

MISDEFINE *vb* define badly

MISDEMEAN *rare word for* > MISBEHAVE

MISDEMPT > MISDEEM

MISDESERT *n* quality of being undeserving

MISDIAL *vb* dial telephone number incorrectly

MISDIALED > MISDIAL

MISDIALS > MISDIAL

MISDID > MISDO

MISDIET *n* wrong diet

MISDIETS > MISDIET

MISDIGHT *adj* done badly

MISDIRECT *vb* give (someone) wrong directions or instructions

MISDIVIDE *vb* divide wrongly

MISDO *vb* do badly or wrongly

MISDOER > MISDO

MISDOERS > MISDO

MISDOES > MISDO

MISDOING > MISDO

MISDOINGS > MISDO

MISDONE *adj* done badly

MISDONNE *same as* > MISDONE

MISDOUBT *archaic word for* > DOUBT

MISDOUBTS > MISDOUBT

MISDRAW *vb* draw poorly

MISDRAWN > MISDRAW

MISDRAWS > MISDRAW

MISDREAD *n* fear of approaching evil

MISDREADS > MISDREAD

MISDREW > MISDRAW

MISDRIVE *vb* drive badly

MISDRIVEN > MISDRIVE

MISDRIVES > MISDRIVE

MISDROVE > MISDRIVE

MISE *n* issue in the obsolete writ of right

MISEASE *n* unease

MISEASES > MISEASE

MISEAT *vb* eat unhealthy food

MISEATEN > MISEAT

MISEATING > MISEAT

MISEATS > MISEAT

MISEDIT *vb* edit badly

MISEDITED > MISEDIT

MISEDITS > MISEDIT

MISEMPLOY *vb* employ badly

MISENROL *vb* enrol wrongly

MISENROLL *same as* > MISENROL

MISENROLS > MISENROL

MISENTER *vb* enter wrongly

MISENTERS > MISENTER

MISENTRY *n* wrong or mistaken entry

MISER *n* person who hoards money and hates spending it

MISERABLE *adj* very unhappy, wretched ▷ *n* wretched person

MISERABLY > MISERABLE

MISERE *n* call in solo whist and other card games declaring a hand that will win no tricks

MISERERE *n* type of psalm

MISERERES > MISERERE

MISERES > MISERE

MISERIES > MISERY

MISERLIER > MISERLY

MISERLY *adj* of or resembling a miser

MISERS > MISER

MISERY *n* great unhappiness

MISES > MISE

MISESTEEM *n* lack of respect

MISEVENT *n* mishap

MISEVENTS > MISEVENT

MISFAITH *n* distrust

MISFAITHS > MISFAITH

MISFALL *vb* happen as piece of bad luck

MISFALLEN > MISFALL

MISFALLS > MISFALL

MISFALNE > MISFALL

MISFARE *vb* get on badly

MISFARED > MISFARE

MISFARES > MISFARE

MISFARING > MISFARE

MISFEASOR *n* someone who carries out the improper performance of an act that is lawful in itself

MISFED > MISFEED

MISFEED *vb* feed wrongly

MISFEEDS > MISFEED

MISFEIGN *vb* feign with evil motive

MISFEIGNS > MISFEIGN

MISFELL > MISFALL

MISFIELD *vb* fail to field properly

MISFIELDS > MISFIELD

MISFILE *vb* file (papers, records, etc) wrongly

MISFILED > MISFILE

MISFILES > MISFILE

MISFILING > MISFILE

MISFIRE *vb* (of a firearm or engine) fail to fire correctly ▷ *n* act or an instance of misfiring

MISFIRED > MISFIRE

MISFIRES > MISFIRE

MISFIRING > MISFIRE

MISFIT *n* person not suited to his or her social environment ▷ *vb* fail to fit or be fitted

MISFITS > MISFIT

MISFITTED > MISFIT

MISFOCUS *n* wrong or poor focus

MISFORM *vb* form badly

MISFORMED > MISFORM

MISFORMS > MISFORM

MISFRAME *vb* frame wrongly

MISFRAMED > MISFRAME

MISFRAMES > MISFRAME

MISGAUGE *vb* gauge badly

MISGAUGED > MISGAUGE

MISGAUGES > MISGAUGE

MISGAVE > MISGIVE

MISGIVE *vb* make or be apprehensive or suspicious

MISGIVEN > MISGIVE

MISGIVES > MISGIVE

MISGIVING *n* feeling of fear or doubt

MISGO *vb* go wrong way

MISGOES > MISGO

MISGOING > MISGO

MISGONE > MISGO

MISGOTTEN *adj* obtained dishonestly

MISGOVERN *vb* govern badly

MISGRADE *vb* grade wrongly

MISGRADED > MISGRADE

MISGRADES > MISGRADE

MISGRAFF *adj* badly done

MISGRAFT *vb* graft wrongly

MISGRAFTS > MISGRAFT

MISGREW > MISGROW

MISGROW *vb* grow in unsuitable way

MISGROWN > MISGROW

MISGROWS > MISGROW

MISGROWTH > MISGROW

MISGUESS *vb* guess wrongly

MISGUGGLE *vb* handle incompetently

MISGUIDE *vb* guide or direct wrongly or badly

MISGUIDED *adj* mistaken or unwise

MISGUIDER > MISGUIDE

MISGUIDES > MISGUIDE

MISHANDLE *vb* handle badly or inefficiently

MISHANTER *n* misfortune

MISHAP *n* minor accident ▷ *vb* happen as bad luck

MISHAPPED > MISHAP

MISHAPPEN *vb* happen as bad luck

MISHAPS > MISHAP

MISHAPT *same as* > MISSHAPEN

MISHEAR *vb* hear (what someone says) wrongly

MISHEARD > MISHEAR

MISHEARS > MISHEAR

MISHEGAAS *same as* > MESHUGAAS

MISHEGOSS *same as* > MESHUGAAS

MISHIT *n* faulty shot, kick, or stroke ▷ *vb* hit or kick a ball with a faulty stroke

MISHITS > MISHIT

MISHMASH *n* confused collection or mixture

MISHMEE *n* root of Asian plant

MISHMEES > MISHMEE

MISHMI *n* evergreen perennial plant

MISHMIS > MISHMI

MISHMOSH *same as* > MISHMASH

MISINFER *vb* infer wrongly

MISINFERS > MISINFER

MISINFORM *vb* give incorrect information to

MISINTEND *vb* intend to harm

MISINTER *vb* bury wrongly

MISINTERS > MISINTER

MISJOIN *vb* join badly

MISJOINED > MISJOIN

m

MISJOINS > MISJOIN
MISJUDGE vb judge wrongly or unfairly
MISJUDGED > MISJUDGE
MISJUDGER > MISJUDGE
MISJUDGES > MISJUDGE
MISKAL n unit of weight in Iran
MISKALS > MISKAL
MISKEEP vb keep wrongly
MISKEEPS > MISKEEP
MISKEN vb be unaware of
MISKENNED > MISKEN
MISKENS > MISKEN
MISKENT > MISKEN
MISKEPT > MISKEEP
MISKEY vb key wrongly
MISKEYED > MISKEY
MISKEYING > MISKEY
MISKEYS > MISKEY
MISKICK vb fail to kick properly
MISKICKED > MISKICK
MISKICKS > MISKICK
MISKNEW vb > MISKNOW
MISKNOW have wrong idea about
MISKNOWN > MISKNOW
MISKNOWS > MISKNOW
MISLABEL vb label badly
MISLABELS > MISLABEL
MISLABOR vb labour wrongly
MISLABORS > MISLABOR
MISLAID > MISLAY
MISLAIN > MISLAY
MISLAY vb lose (something) temporarily
MISLAYER > MISLAY
MISLAYERS > MISLAY
MISLAYING > MISLAY
MISLAYS > MISLAY
MISLEAD vb give false or confusing information to
MISLEADER > MISLEAD
MISLEADS > MISLEAD
MISLEARED adj badly brought up
MISLEARN vb learn wrongly
MISLEARNS > MISLEARN
MISLEARNT > MISLEARN
MISLED > MISLEAD
MISLEEKE same as > MISLIKE
MISLEEKED > MISLEEKE
MISLEEKES > MISLEEKE
MISLETOE same as > MISTLETOE
MISLETOES > MISLETOE
MISLIE vb lie wrongly
MISLIES > MISLIE
MISLIGHT vb use light to lead astray
MISLIGHTS > MISLIGHT
MISLIKE vb dislike ▷ n dislike or aversion
MISLIKED > MISLIKE
MISLIKER > MISLIKE
MISLIKERS > MISLIKE
MISLIKES > MISLIKE
MISLIKING > MISLIKE
MISLIPPEN vb distrust
MISLIT > MISLIGHT
MISLIVE vb live wickedly
MISLIVED > MISLIVE
MISLIVES > MISLIVE
MISLIVING > MISLIVE
MISLOCATE vb put in wrong place

MISLODGE vb lodge wrongly
MISLODGED > MISLODGE
MISLODGES > MISLODGE
MISLUCK vb have bad luck
MISLUCKED > MISLUCK
MISLUCKS > MISLUCK
MISLYING > MISLIE
MISMADE > MISMAKE
MISMAKE vb make badly
MISMAKES > MISMAKE
MISMAKING > MISMAKE
MISMANAGE vb organize or run (something) badly
MISMARK vb mark wrongly
MISMARKED > MISMARK
MISMARKS > MISMARK
MISMARRY vb make unsuitable marriage
MISMATCH vb form an unsuitable partner, opponent, or set ▷ n unsuitable match
MISMATE vb mate wrongly
MISMATED > MISMATE
MISMATES > MISMATE
MISMATING > MISMATE
MISMEET vb fail to meet
MISMEETS > MISMEET
MISMET > MISMEET
MISMETRE vb fail to follow metre of poem
MISMETRED > MISMETRE
MISMETRES > MISMETRE
MISMOVE vb move badly
MISMOVED > MISMOVE
MISMOVES > MISMOVE
MISMOVING > MISMOVE
MISNAME vb name badly
MISNAMED > MISNAME
MISNAMES > MISNAME
MISNAMING > MISNAME
MISNOMER n incorrect or unsuitable name ▷ vb apply misnomer to
MISNOMERS > MISNOMER
MISNUMBER vb number wrongly
MISO n thick brown salty paste made from soya beans, used to flavour savoury dishes, esp soups
MISOCLERE adj hostile to clergy
MISOGAMIC > MISOGAMY
MISOGAMY n hatred of marriage
MISOGYNIC > MISOGYNY
MISOGYNY n hatred of women
MISOLOGY n hatred of reasoning or reasoned argument
MISONEISM n hatred of anything new
MISONEIST > MISONEISM
MISORDER vb order badly
MISORDERS > MISORDER
MISORIENT vb orient incorrectly
MISOS > MISO
MISPAGE vb page wrongly
MISPAGED > MISPAGE
MISPAGES > MISPAGE
MISPAGING > MISPAGE
MISPAINT vb paint badly or wrongly

MISPAINTS > MISPAINT
MISPARSE vb parse wrongly
MISPARSED > MISPARSE
MISPARSES > MISPARSE
MISPART vb part wrongly
MISPARTED > MISPART
MISPARTS > MISPART
MISPATCH vb patch wrongly
MISPEN vb write wrongly
MISPENNED > MISPEN
MISPENS > MISPEN
MISPHRASE vb phrase badly
MISPICKEL n white or grey metallic mineral consisting of a sulphide of iron and arsenic that forms monoclinic crystals with an orthorhombic shape: an ore of arsenic
MISPLACE vb mislay
MISPLACED adj (of an emotion or action) directed towards a person or thing that does not deserve it
MISPLACES > MISPLACE
MISPLAN vb plan badly or wrongly
MISPLANS > MISPLAN
MISPLANT vb plant badly or wrongly
MISPLANTS > MISPLANT
MISPLAY vb play badly or wrongly in games or sports ▷ n wrong or unskilful play
MISPLAYED > MISPLAY
MISPLAYS > MISPLAY
MISPLEAD vb plead incorrectly
MISPLEADS > MISPLEAD
MISPLEASE vb displease
MISPLED > MISPLEAD
MISPOINT vb punctuate badly
MISPOINTS > MISPOINT
MISPOISE n lack of poise ▷ vb lack poise
MISPOISED > MISPOISE
MISPOISES > MISPOISE
MISPRAISE vb fail to praise properly
MISPRICE vb give wrong price to
MISPRICED > MISPRICE
MISPRICES > MISPRICE
MISPRINT n printing error ▷ vb print a letter incorrectly
MISPRINTS > MISPRINT
MISPRISE same as > MISPRIZE
MISPRISED > MISPRISE
MISPRISES > MISPRISE
MISPRIZE vb fail to appreciate the value of
MISPRIZED > MISPRIZE
MISPRIZER > MISPRIZE
MISPRIZES > MISPRIZE
MISPROUD adj undeservedly proud
MISQUOTE vb quote inaccurately
MISQUOTED > MISQUOTE
MISQUOTER > MISQUOTE
MISQUOTES > MISQUOTE
MISRAISE vb raise wrongly or excessively
MISRAISED > MISRAISE

MISRAISES > MISRAISE
MISRATE vb rate wrongly
MISRATED > MISRATE
MISRATES > MISRATE
MISRATING > MISRATE
MISREAD vb misinterpret (a situation etc)
MISREADS > MISREAD
MISRECKON vb reckon wrongly
MISRECORD vb record wrongly
MISREFER vb refer wrongly
MISREFERS > MISREFER
MISREGARD n lack of attention
MISRELATE vb relate badly
MISRELIED > MISRELY
MISRELIES > MISRELY
MISRELY vb rely wrongly
MISRENDER vb render wrongly
MISREPORT vb report falsely or inaccurately ▷ n inaccurate or false report
MISRHYMED adj badly rhymed
MISROUTE vb send wrong way
MISROUTED > MISROUTE
MISROUTES > MISROUTE
MISRULE vb govern inefficiently or unjustly ▷ n inefficient or unjust government
MISRULED > MISRULE
MISRULES > MISRULE
MISRULING > MISRULE
MISS vb fail to notice, hear, hit, reach, find, or catch ▷ n fact or instance of missing
MISSA n Roman Catholic mass
MISSABLE > MISS
MISSAE > MISSA
MISSAID > MISSAY
MISSAL n book containing the prayers and rites of the Mass
MISSALS > MISSAL
MISSAW > MISSEE
MISSAY vb say wrongly
MISSAYING > MISSAY
MISSAYS > MISSAY
MISSEAT vb seat wrongly
MISSEATED > MISSEAT
MISSEATS > MISSEAT
MISSED > MISS
MISSEE vb see wrongly
MISSEEING > MISSEE
MISSEEM vb be unsuitable for
MISSEEMED > MISSEEM
MISSEEMS > MISSEEM
MISSEEN > MISSEE
MISSEES > MISSEE
MISSEL as in missel thrush large European thrush with a brown back and spotted breast, noted for feeding on mistletoe berries
MISSELS > MISSEL
MISSEND vb send wrongly
MISSENDS > MISSEND
MISSENSE n type of genetic mutation
MISSENSES > MISSENSE

MISSENT > MISSEND
MISSES > MISS
MISSET *vb* set wrongly
MISSETS > MISSET
MISSHAPE *vb* shape badly ▷ *n* something that is badly shaped
MISSHAPED > MISSHAPE
MISSHAPEN *adj* badly shaped, deformed
MISSHAPER > MISSHAPE
MISSHAPES > MISSHAPE
MISSHOD *adj* badly shod
MISSHOOD *n* state of being unmarried woman
MISSHOODS > MISSHOOD
MISSIER > MISSY
MISSIES > MISSY
MISSIEST > MISSY
MISSILE *n* rocket with an exploding warhead, used as a weapon
MISSILEER *n* serviceman or servicewoman who is responsible for firing missiles
MISSILERY *n* missiles collectively
MISSILES > MISSILE
MISSILRY *same as* > MISSILERY
MISSING *adj* lost or absent
MISSINGLY > MISSING
MISSION *n* specific task or duty ▷ *vb* direct a mission to or establish a mission in (a given region)
MISSIONAL *adj* emphasizing preaching of gospel
MISSIONED > MISSION
MISSIONER *n* person heading a parochial mission in a Christian country
MISSIONS > MISSION
MISSIS *same as* > MISSUS
MISSISES > MISSIS
MISSISH *adj* like schoolgirl
MISSIVE *n* letter ▷ *adj* sent or intended to be sent
MISSIVES > MISSIVE
MISSORT *vb* sort wrongly
MISSORTED > MISSORT
MISSORTS > MISSORT
MISSOUND *vb* sound wrongly
MISSOUNDS > MISSOUND
MISSOUT *n* someone who has been overlooked
MISSOUTS > MISSOUT
MISSPACE *vb* space out wrongly
MISSPACED > MISSPACE
MISSPACES > MISSPACE
MISSPEAK *vb* speak wrongly
MISSPEAKS > MISSPEAK
MISSPELL *vb* spell (a word) wrongly
MISSPELLS > MISSPELL
MISSPELT > MISSPELL
MISSPEND *vb* waste or spend unwisely
MISSPENDS > MISSPEND
MISSPENT > MISSPEND
MISSPOKE > MISSPEAK
MISSPOKEN > MISSPEAK

MISSTAMP *vb* stamp badly
MISSTAMPS > MISSTAMP
MISSTART *vb* start wrongly
MISSTARTS > MISSTART
MISSTATE *vb* state incorrectly
MISSTATED > MISSTATE
MISSTATES > MISSTATE
MISSTEER *vb* steer badly
MISSTEERS > MISSTEER
MISSTEP *n* false step ▷ *vb* take false step
MISSTEPS > MISSTEP
MISSTOP *vb* stop wrongly
MISSTOPS > MISSTOP
MISSTRIKE *vb* fail to strike properly
MISSTRUCK > MISSTRIKE
MISSTYLE *vb* call by wrong name
MISSTYLED > MISSTYLE
MISSTYLES > MISSTYLE
MISSUIT *vb* be unsuitable for
MISSUITED > MISSUIT
MISSUITS > MISSUIT
MISSUS *n* one's wife or the wife of the person addressed or referred to
MISSUSES > MISSUS
MISSY *n* affectionate or disparaging form of address to a girl ▷ *adj* missish
MIST *n* thin fog ▷ *vb* cover or be covered with mist
MISTAKE *n* error or blunder ▷ *vb* misunderstand
MISTAKEN *adj* wrong in judgment or opinion
MISTAKER > MISTAKE
MISTAKERS > MISTAKE
MISTAKES > MISTAKE
MISTAKING > MISTAKE
MISTAL *n* cow shed
MISTALS > MISTAL
MISTAUGHT > MISTEACH
MISTBOW *same as* > FOGBOW
MISTBOWS > MISTBOW
MISTEACH *vb* teach badly
MISTED > MIST
MISTELL *vb* tell wrongly
MISTELLS > MISTELL
MISTEMPER *vb* make disordered
MISTEND *vb* tend wrongly
MISTENDED > MISTEND
MISTENDS > MISTEND
MISTER *n* informal form of address for a man ▷ *vb* call (someone) mister
MISTERED > MISTER
MISTERIES > MISTERY
MISTERING > MISTER
MISTERM *vb* term badly
MISTERMED > MISTERM
MISTERMS > MISTERM
MISTERS > MISTER
MISTERY *same as* > MYSTERY
MISTEUK *Scots variant of* > MISTOOK
MISTFUL > MIST
MISTHINK *vb* have poor opinion of
MISTHINKS > MISTHINK
MISTHREW > MISTHROW
MISTHROW *vb* fail to throw

properly
MISTHROWN > MISTHROW
MISTHROWS > MISTHROW
MISTICO *n* small Mediterranean sailing ship
MISTICOS > MISTICO
MISTIER > MISTY
MISTIEST > MISTY
MISTIGRIS *n* joker or a blank card used as a wild card in a variety of draw poker
MISTILY > MISTY
MISTIME *vb* do (something) at the wrong time
MISTIMED > MISTIME
MISTIMES > MISTIME
MISTIMING > MISTIME
MISTINESS > MISTY
MISTING *n* application of a fake suntan by spray
MISTINGS > MISTING
MISTITLE *vb* name badly
MISTITLED > MISTITLE
MISTITLES > MISTITLE
MISTLE *same as* > MIZZLE
MISTLED > MISTLE
MISTLES > MISTLE
MISTLETOE *n* evergreen plant with white berries growing as a parasite on trees
MISTLING > MISTLE
MISTOLD > MISTELL
MISTOOK *past tense of* > MISTAKE
MISTOUCH *vb* fail to touch properly
MISTRACE *vb* trace wrongly
MISTRACED > MISTRACE
MISTRACES > MISTRACE
MISTRAIN *vb* train wrongly
MISTRAINS > MISTRAIN
MISTRAL *n* strong dry northerly wind of S France
MISTRALS > MISTRAL
MISTREAT *vb* treat (a person or animal) badly
MISTREATS > MISTREAT
MISTRESS *n* woman who has a continuing sexual relationship with a married man ▷ *vb* make into mistress
MISTRIAL *n* trial made void because of some error
MISTRIALS > MISTRIAL
MISTRUST *vb* have doubts or suspicions about ▷ *n* lack of trust
MISTRUSTS > MISTRUST
MISTRUTH *n* something untrue
MISTRUTHS > MISTRUTH
MISTRYST *vb* fail to keep appointment with
MISTRYSTS > MISTRYST
MISTS > MIST
MISTUNE *vb* fail to tune properly
MISTUNED > MISTUNE
MISTUNES > MISTUNE
MISTUNING > MISTUNE
MISTUTOR *vb* instruct badly
MISTUTORS > MISTUTOR
MISTY *adj* full of mist
MISTYPE *vb* type badly

MISTYPED > MISTYPE
MISTYPES > MISTYPE
MISTYPING > MISTYPE
MISUNION *n* wrong or bad union
MISUNIONS > MISUNION
MISUSAGE > MISUSE
MISUSAGES > MISUSE
MISUSE *n* incorrect, improper, or careless use ▷ *vb* use wrongly
MISUSED > MISUSE
MISUSER *n* abuse of some right, privilege, office, etc, such as one that may lead to its forfeiture
MISUSERS > MISUSER
MISUSES > MISUSE
MISUSING > MISUSE
MISUST > MISUSE
MISVALUE *vb* value badly
MISVALUED > MISVALUE
MISVALUES > MISVALUE
MISWEEN *vb* assess wrongly
MISWEENED > MISWEEN
MISWEENS > MISWEEN
MISWEND *vb* become lost
MISWENDS > MISWEND
MISWENT > MISWEND
MISWORD *vb* word badly
MISWORDED > MISWORD
MISWORDS > MISWORD
MISWRIT > MISWRITE
MISWRITE *vb* write badly
MISWRITES > MISWRITE
MISWROTE > MISWRITE
MISYOKE *vb* join wrongly
MISYOKED > MISYOKE
MISYOKES > MISYOKE
MISYOKING > MISYOKE
MITCH *vb* play truant from school
MITCHED > MITCH
MITCHES > MITCH
MITCHING > MITCH
MITE *n* very small spider-like animal
MITER *same as* > MITRE
MITERED > MITER
MITERER > MITER
MITERERS > MITER
MITERING > MITER
MITERS > MITER
MITERWORT *same as* > MITREWORT
MITES > MITE
MITHER *vb* fuss over or moan about something
MITHERED > MITHER
MITHERING > MITHER
MITHERS > MITHER
MITICIDAL > MITICIDE
MITICIDE *n* any drug or agent that destroys mites
MITICIDES > MITICIDE
MITIER > MITY
MITIEST > MITY
MITIGABLE > MITIGATE
MITIGANT *adj* acting to mitigate
MITIGATE *vb* make less severe
MITIGATED > MITIGATE
MITIGATES > MITIGATE
MITIGATOR > MITIGATE
MITIS *n* malleable iron, fluid enough for casting,

m

made by adding a small amount of aluminium to wrought iron

MITISES > MITIS

MITOGEN n any agent that induces mitosis

MITOGENIC > MITOGEN

MITOGENS > MITOGEN

MITOMYCIN n

MITOSES > MITOSIS

MITOSIS n type of cell division in which the nucleus divides into two nuclei which each contain the same number of chromosomes as the original nucleus

MITOTIC > MITOSIS

MITRAILLE n hail of bullets

MITRAL adj of or like a mitre

MITRE n bishop's pointed headdress ▷vb join with a mitre joint

MITRED > MITRE

MITRES > MITRE

MITREWORT n any of several Asian and North American saxifragaceous plants of the genus *Mitella*, having clusters of small white flowers and capsules resembling a bishop's mitre

MITRIFORM adj shaped like mitre

MITRING > MITRE

MITSVAH same as > MITZVAH

MITSVAHS > MITSVAH

MITSVOTH > MITSVAH

MITT same as > MITTEN

MITTEN n glove with one section for the thumb and one for the four fingers together

MITTENED adj wearing mittens

MITTENS > MITTEN

MITTIMUS n warrant of commitment to prison or a command to a jailer directing him to hold someone in prison

MITTS > MITT

MITUMBA n used clothes imported for sale in African countries

MITUMBAS > MITUMBA

MITY adj having mites

MITZVAH n commandment or precept, esp one found in the Bible

MITZVAHS > MITZVAH

MITZVOTH > MITZVAH

MIURUS n type of rhythm in poetry

MIURUSES > MIURUS

MIX vb combine or blend into one mass ▷n mixture

MIXABLE > MIX

MIXDOWN n (in sound recording) the transfer of a multitrack master mix to two-track stereo tape

MIXDOWNS > MIXDOWN

MIXED adj formed or blended together by mixing

MIXEDLY > MIXED

MIXEDNESS > MIXED

MIXEN n dunghill

MIXENS > MIXEN

MIXER n kitchen appliance used for mixing foods

MIXERS > MIXER

MIXES > MIX

MIXIBLE > MIX

MIXIER > MIX

MIXIEST > MIX

MIXING > MIX

MIXMASTER n disc jockey

MIXOLOGY n art of mixing cocktails

MIXT > MIX

MIXTE adj of or denoting a type of bicycle frame, usually for women, in which angled twin lateral tubes run back to the rear axle

MIXTION n amber-based mixture used in making gold leaf

MIXTIONS > MIXTION

MIXTURE n something mixed

MIXTURES > MIXTURE

MIXUP vb confuse or confound ▷n something that is mixed up

MIXUPS > MIXUP

MIXY adj mixed

MIZ shortened form of > MISERY

MIZEN same as > MIZZEN

MIZENMAST n (on a yawl, ketch, or dandy) the after mast

MIZENS > MIZEN

MIZMAZE n maze

MIZMAZES > MIZMAZE

MIZUNA n Japanese variety of lettuce having crisp green leaves

MIZUNAS > MIZUNA

MIZZ same as > MIZ

MIZZEN n sail set on a mizzenmast ▷adj of or relating to any kind of gear used with a mizzenmast

MIZZENS > MIZZEN

MIZZES > MIZ

MIZZLE vb decamp

MIZZLED > MIZZLE

MIZZLES > MIZZLE

MIZZLIER > MIZZLE

MIZZLIEST > MIZZLE

MIZZLING > MIZZLE

MIZZLINGS > MIZZLE

MIZZLY > MIZZLE

MIZZONITE n mineral containing sodium

MIZZY as in *mizzy maze* dialect expression meaning state of confusion

MM interj expression of enjoyment of taste or smell

MNA same as > MINA

MNAS > MNA

MNEME n ability to retain memory

MNEMES > MNEME

MNEMIC > MNEME

MNEMON n unit of memory

MNEMONIC adj intended to help the memory ▷n something, for instance a verse, intended to help the memory

MNEMONICS n art or practice of improving or of aiding the memory

MNEMONIST > MNEMONICS

MNEMONS > MNEMON

MO n moment

MOA n large extinct flightless New Zealand bird

MOAI n any of the gigantic carved stone figures found on Easter Island (Rapa Nui)

MOAN n low cry of pain ▷vb make or utter with a moan

MOANED > MOAN

MOANER > MOAN

MOANERS > MOAN

MOANFUL > MOAN

MOANFULLY > MOAN

MOANING > MOAN

MOANINGLY > MOAN

MOANINGS > MOAN

MOANS > MOAN

MOAS > MOA

MOAT n deep wide ditch, esp round a castle ▷vb surround with or as if with a moat

MOATED > MOAT

MOATING > MOAT

MOATLIKE > MOAT

MOATS > MOAT

MOB n disorderly crowd ▷vb surround in a mob to acclaim or attack

MOBBED > MOB

MOBBER > MOB

MOBBERS > MOB

MOBBIE same as > MOBBY

MOBBIES > MOBBY

MOBBING > MOB

MOBBINGS > MOB

MOBBISH > MOB

MOBBISHLY > MOB

MOBBISM n behaviour as mob

MOBBISMS > MOBBISM

MOBBLE same as > MOBLE

MOBBLED > MOBBLE

MOBBLES > MOBBLE

MOBBLING > MOBBLE

MOBBY n West Indian drink

MOBCAP n woman's 18th-century cotton cap with a pouched crown

MOBCAPS > MOBCAP

MOBE n mobile phone

MOBES > MOBE

MOBIE n mobile phone

MOBIES > MOBY

MOBILE adj able to move ▷n hanging structure designed to move in air currents

MOBILES > MOBILE

MOBILISE same as > MOBILIZE

MOBILISED > MOBILISE

MOBILISER > MOBILISE

MOBILISES > MOBILISE

MOBILITY n ability to move physically

MOBILIZE vb (of the armed services) prepare for active service

MOBILIZED > MOBILIZE

MOBILIZER > MOBILIZE

MOBILIZES > MOBILIZE

MOBLE vb muffle

MOBLED > MOBLE

MOBLES > MOBLE

MOBLING > MOBLE

MOBLOG n chronicle, which may be shared with others, of someone's thoughts and experiences recorded in the form of mobile phone calls, text messages, and photographs

MOBLOGGER > MOBLOG

MOBLOGS > MOBLOG

MOBOCRACY n rule or domination by a mob

MOBOCRAT > MOBOCRACY

MOBOCRATS > MOBOCRACY

MOBS > MOB

MOBSMAN n person in mob

MOBSMEN > MOBSMAN

MOBSTER n member of a criminal organization

MOBSTERS > MOBSTER

MOBY n mobile phone

MOC shortening of > MOCCASIN

MOCCASIN same as > MOCCASIN

MOCCASINS > MOCCASIN

MOCCASIN n soft leather shoe

MOCCASINS > MOCCASIN

MOCCIES pl n informal Australian word for moccasins

MOCH n spell of humid weather

MOCHA n kind of strong dark coffee

MOCHAS > MOCHA

MOCHELL same as > MUCH

MOCHELLS > MOCHELL

MOCHIE adj damp or humid

MOCHIER > MOCHIE

MOCHIEST > MOCHIE

MOCHILA n South American shoulder bag

MOCHILAS > MOCHILA

MOCHINESS > MOCHIE

MOCHS > MOCH

MOCHY same as > MOCHIE

MOCK vb make fun of ▷adj sham or imitation ▷n act of mocking

MOCKABLE > MOCK

MOCKADO n imitation velvet

MOCKADOES > MOCKADO

MOCKAGE same as > MOCKERY

MOCKAGES > MOCKAGE

MOCKED > MOCK

MOCKER vb dress up

MOCKERED > MOCKER

MOCKERIES > MOCKERY

MOCKERING > MOCKER

MOCKERNUT n species of smooth-barked hickory, *Carya tomentosa*, with fragrant foliage that turns bright yellow in autumn

MOCKERS > MOCKER

MOCKERY n derision

MOCKING > MOCK

MOCKINGLY > MOCK

MOCKINGS > MOCK

MOCKNEY *n* person who affects a cockney accent ▷ *adj* denoting an affected cockney accent or a person who has one

MOCKNEYS > MOCKNEY

MOCKS > MOCK

MOCKTAIL *n* cocktail without alcohol

MOCKTAILS > MOCKTAIL

MOCKUP *n* working full-scale model of a machine, apparatus, etc, for testing, research, etc

MOCKUPS > MOCKUP

MOCOCK *n* Native American birchbark container

MOCOCKS > MOCOCK

MOCS > MOC

MOCUCK *same as* > MOCOCK

MOCUCKS > MOCUCK

MOCUDDUM *same as* > MUQADDAM

MOCUDDUMS > MOCUDDUM

MOD *n* member of a group of young people, orig. in the mid-1960s, who were very clothes-conscious and rode motor scooters

MODAL *adj* of or relating to mode or manner ▷ *n* modal word

MODALISM *n* type of Christian doctrine

MODALISMS > MODALISM

MODALIST > MODALISM

MODALISTS > MODALISM

MODALITY *n* condition of being modal

MODALLY > MODAL

MODALS > MODAL

MODE *n* method or manner

MODEL *n* (miniature) representation ▷ *adj* excellent or perfect ▷ *vb* make a model of

MODELED > MODEL

MODELER > MODEL

MODELERS > MODEL

MODELING *same as* > MODELLING

MODELINGS > MODELING

MODELIST *n* person who constructs models

MODELISTS > MODELIST

MODELLED > MODEL

MODELLER > MODEL

MODELLERS > MODEL

MODELLI > MODELLO

MODELLING *n* act or an instance of making a model

MODELLO *n* artist's preliminary sketch or model

MODELLOS > MODELLO

MODELS > MODEL

MODEM *n* device for connecting two computers by a telephone line ▷ *vb* send or receive by modem

MODEMED > MODEM

MODEMING > MODEM

MODEMS > MODEM

MODENA *n* popular variety of domestic fancy pigeon originating in Modena

MODENAS > MODENA

MODER *n* intermediate layer in humus

MODERATE *adj* not extreme ▷ *n* person of moderate views ▷ *vb* make or become less violent or extreme

MODERATED > MODERATE

MODERATES > MODERATE

MODERATO *adv* at a moderate speed ▷ *n* moderato piece

MODERATOR *n* (Presbyterian Church) minister appointed to preside over a Church court, general assembly, etc

MODERATOS > MODERATO

MODERN *adj* of present or recent times ▷ *n* contemporary person

MODERNE *adj* of or relating to the style of architecture and design, prevalent in Europe and the US in the late 1920s and 1930s, typified by the use of straight lines, tubular chromed steel frames, contrasting inlaid woods, etc

MODERNER > MODERN

MODERNES *n* being modern

MODERNEST > MODERN

MODERNISE *same as* > MODERNIZE

MODERNISM *n* (support of) modern tendencies, thoughts, or styles

MODERNIST > MODERNISM

MODERNITY *n* quality or state of being modern

MODERNIZE *vb* bring up to date

MODERNLY > MODERN

MODERNS > MODERN

MODERS > MODER

MODES > MODE

MODEST *adj* not vain or boastful

MODESTER > MODEST

MODESTEST > MODEST

MODESTIES > MODESTY

MODESTLY > MODEST

MODESTY *n* quality or condition of being modest

MODGE *vb* do shoddily

MODGED > MODGE

MODGES > MODGE

MODGING > MODGE

MODI > MODUS

MODICA > MODICUM

MODICUM *n* small quantity

MODICUMS > MODICUM

MODIFIED > MODIFY

MODIFIER *n* word that qualifies the sense of another

MODIFIERS > MODIFIER

MODIFIES > MODIFY

MODIFY *vb* change slightly

MODIFYING > MODIFY

MODII > MODIUS

MODILLION *n* one of a set of ornamental brackets under a cornice, esp as used in the Corinthian order

MODIOLAR > MODIOLUS

MODIOLI > MODIOLUS

MODIOLUS *n* central bony pillar of the cochlea

MODISH *adj* in fashion

MODISHLY > MODISH

MODIST *n* follower of fashion

MODISTE *n* fashionable dressmaker or milliner

MODISTES > MODISTE

MODISTS > MODIST

MODIUS *n* ancient Roman quantity measure

MODIWORT *Scots variant of* > MOULDWARP

MODIWORTS > MODIWORT

MODS > MOD

MODULAR *adj* of, consisting of, or resembling a module or modulus ▷ *n* thing comprised of modules

MODULARLY > MODULAR

MODULARS > MODULAR

MODULATE *vb* vary in tone

MODULATED > MODULATE

MODULATES > MODULATE

MODULATOR > MODULATE

MODULE *n* self-contained unit, section, or component with a specific function

MODULES > MODULE

MODULI > MODULUS

MODULO *adv* with reference to modulus

MODULUS *n* coefficient expressing a specified property, for instance elasticity, of a specified substance

MODUS *n* way of doing something

MOE *same as* > MORE

MOELLON *n* rubble

MOELLONS > MOELLON

MOER *n* in South Africa, slang word for the womb ▷ *vb* in South Africa, attack (someone or something) violently

MOERED > MOER

MOERING > MOER

MOERS > MOER

MOES > MOE

MOFETTE *n* opening in a region of nearly extinct volcanic activity, through which carbon dioxide, nitrogen, and other gases pass

MOFETTES > MOFETTE

MOFFETTE *same as* > MOFETTE

MOFFETTES > MOFFETTE

MOFFIE *n* homosexual ▷ *adj* homosexual

MOFFIES > MOFFIE

MOFO *n* offensive term, a shortened form of motherfucker

MOFOS > MOFO

MOFUSSIL *n* provincial area in India

MOFUSSILS > MOFUSSIL

MOG *vb* go away

MOGGAN *n* stocking without foot

MOGGANS > MOGGAN

MOGGED > MOG

MOGGIE *same as* > MOGGY

MOGGIES > MOGGY

MOGGING > MOG

MOGGY *n* cat

MOGHUL *same as* > MOGUL

MOGHULS > MOGHUL

MOGS > MOG

MOGUL *n* important or powerful person

MOGULED *adj* having moguls

MOGULS > MOGUL

MOHAIR *n* fine hair of the Angora goat

MOHAIRS > MOHAIR

MOHALIM *same as* > MOHELIM

MOHAWK *n* half turn from either edge of either skate to the corresponding edge of the other skate

MOHAWKS > MOHAWK

MOHEL *n* man qualified to conduct circumcisions

MOHELIM > MOHEL

MOHELS > MOHEL

MOHICAN *n* punk hairstyle

MOHICANS > MOHICAN

MOHR *same as* > MHORR

MOHRS > MOHR

MOHUA *n* small New Zealand bird with a yellow head and breast

MOHUR *n* former Indian gold coin worth 15 rupees

MOHURS > MOHUR

MOI > ME

MOIDER *same as* > MOITHER

MOIDERED > MOIDER

MOIDERING > MOIDER

MOIDERS > MOIDER

MOIDORE *n* former Portuguese gold coin

MOIDORES > MOIDORE

MOIETIES > MOIETY

MOIETY *n* half

MOIL *vb* moisten or soil or become moist, soiled, etc ▷ *n* toil

MOILED > MOIL

MOILER > MOIL

MOILERS > MOIL

MOILING > MOIL

MOILINGLY > MOIL

MOILS > MOIL

MOINEAU *n* small fortification

MOINEAUS > MOINEAU

MOIRA *n* fate

MOIRAI > MOIRA

MOIRE *adj* having a watered or wavelike pattern ▷ *n* any fabric that has such a pattern

MOIRES > MOIRE

MOISER *n* informer

MOISERS > MOISER

MOIST *adj* slightly wet ▷ *vb* moisten

MOISTED > MOIST

MOISTEN *vb* make or become moist

MOISTENED > MOISTEN

MOISTENER > MOISTEN

MOISTENS > MOISTEN

MOISTER > MOIST
MOISTEST > MOIST
MOISTFUL *adj* full of moisture
MOISTIFY *vb* moisten
MOISTING > MOIST
MOISTLY > MOIST
MOISTNESS > MOIST
MOISTS > MOIST
MOISTURE *n* liquid diffused as vapour or condensed in drops
MOISTURES > MOISTURE
MOIT *same as* > MOTE
MOITHER *vb* bother or bewilder
MOITHERED > MOITHER
MOITHERS > MOITHER
MOITS > MOIT
MOJARRA *n* tropical American sea fish
MOJARRAS > MOJARRA
MOJO *n* charm or magic spell
MOJOES > MOJO
MOJOS > MOJO
MOKADDAM *same as* > MUQADDAM
MOKADDAMS > MOKADDAM
MOKE *n* donkey
MOKES > MOKE
MOKI *n* either of two edible sea fish of New Zealand, the blue cod (*Percis colias*) or the bastard trumpeter (*Latridopsis ciliaris*)
MOKIHI *n* Māori raft
MOKIS > MOKI
MOKO *n* Māori tattoo or tattoo pattern
MOKOMOKO *n* type of skink found in New Zealand
MOKOPUNA *n* grandchild or young person
MOKOPUNAS > MOKOPUNA
MOKORO *n* (in Botswana) the traditional dugout canoe of the people of the Okavango Delta
MOKOROS > MOKORO
MOKOS > MOKO
MOKSHA *n* freedom from the endless cycle of transmigration into a state of bliss
MOKSHAS > MOKSHA
MOL *same as* > MOLE
MOLA *another name for* > SUNFISH
MOLAL *adj* of or consisting of a solution containing one mole of solute per thousand grams of solvent
MOLALITY *n* (not in technical usage) a measure of concentration equal to the number of moles of solute in a thousand grams of solvent
MOLAR *n* large back tooth used for grinding ▷ *adj* of any of these teeth
MOLARITY *n* concentration
MOLARS > MOLAR
MOLAS > MOLA
MOLASSE *n* soft sediment produced by the erosion of mountain ranges after the final phase of mountain building
MOLASSES *n* dark syrup, a by-product of sugar refining
MOLD *same as* > MOULD
MOLDABLE > MOLD
MOLDAVITE *n* green tektite found in the Czech Republic, thought to be the product of an ancient meteorite impact in Germany
MOLDBOARD *n* curved blade of a plough
MOLDED > MOLD
MOLDER *same as* > MOULDER
MOLDERED > MOLDER
MOLDERING > MOLDER
MOLDERS > MOLDER
MOLDIER > MOLDY
MOLDIEST > MOLDY
MOLDINESS > MOLDY
MOLDING *same as* > MOULDING
MOLDINGS > MOLDING
MOLDS > MOLD
MOLDWARP *same as* > MOULDWARP
MOLDWARPS > MOLDWARP
MOLDY *same as* > MOULDY
MOLE *n* small dark raised spot on the skin
MOLECAST *n* molehill
MOLECASTS > MOLECAST
MOLECULAR *adj* of or relating to molecules
MOLECULE *n* simplest freely existing chemical unit, composed of two or more atoms
MOLECULES > MOLECULE
MOLEHILL *n* small mound of earth thrown up by a burrowing mole
MOLEHILLS > MOLEHILL
MOLEHUNT *n* hunt for moles
MOLEHUNTS > MOLEHUNT
MOLERAT *n* any burrowing molelike African rodent of the famil
MOLERATS > MOLERAT
MOLES > MOLE
MOLESKIN *n* dark grey dense velvety pelt of a mole, used as a fur
MOLESKINS *pl n* clothing of moleskin
MOLEST *vb* interfere with sexually
MOLESTED > MOLEST
MOLESTER > MOLEST
MOLESTERS > MOLEST
MOLESTFUL *adj* molesting
MOLESTING > MOLEST
MOLESTS > MOLEST
MOLIES > MOLY
MOLIMEN *n* effort needed to perform bodily function
MOLIMENS > MOLIMEN
MOLINE *adj* (of a cross) having arms of equal length, forked and curved back at the ends ▷ *n* moline cross
MOLINES > MOLINE
MOLINET *n* stick for whipping chocolate
MOLINETS > MOLINET
MOLL *n* gangster's female accomplice
MOLLA *same as* > MOLLAH
MOLLAH *same as* > MULLAH
MOLLAHS > MOLLAH
MOLLAS > MOLLA
MOLLIE *same as* > MOLLY
MOLLIES > MOLLY
MOLLIFIED > MOLLIFY
MOLLIFIER > MOLLIFY
MOLLIFIES > MOLLIFY
MOLLIFY *vb* pacify or soothe
MOLLITIES *n* softness
MOLLS > MOLL
MOLLUSC *n* soft-bodied, usu hard-shelled, animal, such as a snail or oyster
MOLLUSCA *n* molluscs collectively
MOLLUSCAN > MOLLUSC
MOLLUSCS > MOLLUSC
MOLLUSCUM *n* viral skin infection
MOLLUSK *same as* > MOLLUSC
MOLLUSKAN > MOLLUSK
MOLLUSKS > MOLLUSK
MOLLY *n* any brightly coloured tropical or subtropical American freshwater cyprinodont fish of the genus *Mollienisia*
MOLLYHAWK *n* juvenile of the southern black-backed gull (*Larus dominicanus*)
MOLLYMAWK *informal name for* > MALLEMUCK
MOLOCH *n* spiny Australian desert-living lizard, *Moloch horridus*, that feeds on ants: family *Agamidae* (agamas)
MOLOCHISE *vb* sacrifice to deity
MOLOCHIZE *same as* > MOLOCHISE
MOLOCHS > MOLOCH
MOLOSSI > MOLOSSUS
MOLOSSUS *n* division of metre in poetry
MOLS > MOL
MOLT *same as* > MOULT
MOLTED > MOLT
MOLTEN > MELT
MOLTENLY > MELT
MOLTER > MOLT
MOLTERS > MOLT
MOLTING > MOLT
MOLTO *adv* very
MOLTS > MOLT
MOLY *n* magic herb given by Hermes to Odysseus to nullify the spells of Circe
MOLYBDATE *n* salt or ester of a molybdic acid
MOLYBDIC *adj* of or containing molybdenum in the trivalent or hexavalent state
MOLYBDOUS *adj* of or containing molybdenum, esp in a low valence state
MOM *same as* > MOTHER
MOME *n* fool
MOMENT *n* short space of time
MOMENTA > MOMENTUM
MOMENTANY *same as* > MOMENTARY
MOMENTARY *adj* lasting only a moment
MOMENTLY *same as* > MOMENT
MOMENTO *same as* > MEMENTO
MOMENTOES > MOMENTO
MOMENTOS > MOMENTO
MOMENTOUS *adj* of great significance
MOMENTS > MOMENT
MOMENTUM *n* impetus to go forward, develop, or get stronger
MOMENTUMS > MOMENTUM
MOMES > MOME
MOMI *same as* > MOM
MOMISM *n* excessive domination of a child by his or her mother
MOMISMS > MOMISM
MOMMA *same as* > MAMMA
MOMMAS > MOMMA
MOMMET *same as* > MAMMET
MOMMETS > MOMMET
MOMMIES > MOMMY
MOMMY *same as* > MOM
MOMS > MOM
MOMSER *same as* > MOMZER
MOMSERS > MOMSER
MOMUS *n* person who ridicules
MOMUSES > MOMUS
MOMZER *same as* > MAMZER
MOMZERIM > MOMZER
MOMZERS > MOMZER
MON *dialect variant of* > MAN
MONA *n* W African guenon monkey, *Cercopithecus mona*, with dark fur on the back and white or yellow underparts
MONACHAL *less common word for* > MONASTIC
MONACHISM > MONACHAL
MONACHIST > MONACHAL
MONACID *same as* > MONACIDIC
MONACIDIC *same as* > MONACID
MONACIDS > MONACID
MONACT *adj* (of sponge) with single-spiked structures in skeleton
MONACTINE > MONACT
MONAD *n* any fundamental singular metaphysical entity
MONADAL > MONAD
MONADES > MONAS
MONADIC *adj* being or relating to a monad
MONADICAL > MONAD
MONADISM *n* (esp in the writings of Gottfried Leibnitz, the German rationalist philosopher and mathematician (1646–1716)) the philosophical doctrine that monads are the ultimate units of reality
MONADISMS > MONADISM
MONADNOCK *n* residual hill that consists of hard rock in

an otherwise eroded area

MONADS > MONAD

MONAL *n* any of several S Asian pheasants of the genus *Lophophorus*, the males of which have a brilliantly coloured plumage

MONALS > MONAL

MONANDRY *n* preference of only one male sexual partner over a period of time

MONARCH *n* sovereign ruler of a state

MONARCHAL > MONARCH

MONARCHIC > MONARCH

MONARCHS > MONARCH

MONARCHY *n* government by or a state ruled by a sovereign

MONARDA *n* any mintlike North American plant of the genus *Monarda*: family *Lamiaceae* (labiates)

MONARDAS > MONARDA

MONAS *same as* > MONAD

MONASES > MONAS

MONASTERY *n* residence of a community of monks

MONASTIC *adj* of monks, nuns, or monasteries ▷*n* person who is committed to this way of life, esp a monk

MONASTICS > MONASTIC

MONATOMIC *adj* consisting of single atoms

MONAUL *same as* > MONAL

MONAULS > MONAUL

MONAURAL *adj* relating to, having, or hearing with only one ear

MONAXIAL *another word for* > UNIAXIAL

MONAXON *n* type of sponge

MONAXONIC > MONAXON

MONAXONS > MONAXON

MONAZITE *n* yellow to reddish-brown mineral consisting of a phosphate of thorium, cerium, and lanthanum in monoclinic crystalline form

MONAZITES > MONAZITE

MONDAIN *n* man who moves in fashionable society ▷*adj* characteristic of fashionable society

MONDAINE *n* woman who moves in fashionable society ▷*adj* characteristic of fashionable society

MONDAINES > MONDAINE

MONDAINS > MONDAIN

MONDE *n* French word meaning world or society

MONDES > MONDE

MONDIAL *adj* of or involving the whole world

MONDO *n* Buddhist questioning technique

MONDOS > MONDO

MONECIAN *same as* > MONECIOUS

MONECIOUS *adj* (of some flowering plants) having

the male and female reproductive organs in separate flowers on the same plant

MONELLIN *n* sweet protein

MONELLINS > MONELLIN

MONEME *less common word for* > MORPHEME

MONEMES > MONEME

MONER *n* hypothetical simple organism

MONERA > MONER

MONERAN *n* type of bacterium

MONERANS > MONERAN

MONERGISM *n* Christian doctrine on spiritual regeneration

MONERON *same as* > MONER

MONETARY *adj* of money or currency

MONETH *same as* > MONTH

MONETHS > MONETH

MONETISE *same as* > MONETIZE

MONETISED > MONETISE

MONETISES > MONETISE

MONETIZE *vb* establish as the legal tender of a country

MONETIZED > MONETIZE

MONETIZES > MONETIZE

MONEY *n* medium of exchange, coins or banknotes

MONEYBAG *n* bag for money

MONEYBAGS *n* very rich person

MONEYED *adj* rich

MONEYER *n* person who coins money

MONEYERS > MONEYER

MONEYLESS > MONEY

MONEYMAN *n* person supplying money

MONEYMEN > MONEY

MONEYS > MONEY

MONEYWORT *n* European and North American creeping primulaceous plant, *Lysimachia nummularia*, with round leaves and yellow flowers

MONG *n* stupid or foolish person

MONGCORN *same as* > MASLIN

MONGCORNS > MONGCORN

MONGED *adj* under the influence of drugs

MONGEESE > MONGOOSE

MONGER *n* trader or dealer ▷*vb* deal in

MONGERED > MONGER

MONGERIES > MONGER

MONGERING > MONGER

MONGERS > MONGER

MONGERY > MONGER

MONGO *same as* > MUNGO

MONGOE *same as* > MONGO

MONGOES > MONGOE

MONGOL *adj* offensive word for a person affected by Down's syndrome

MONGOLIAN *adj* offensive term meaning affected by Down's syndrome

MONGOLISM > MONGOL

MONGOLOID *adj* offensive term meaning characterized by Down's syndrome ▷*n* offensive word for a person affected by Down's syndrome

MONGOLS > MONGOL

MONGOOSE *n* stoatlike mammal of Asia and Africa that kills snakes

MONGOOSES > MONGOOSE

MONGOS > MONGO

MONGREL *n* animal, esp a dog, of mixed breed ▷*adj* of mixed breed or origin

MONGRELLY > MONGREL

MONGRELS > MONGREL

MONGS > MONG

MONGST *short for* > AMONGST

MONIAL *n* mullion

MONIALS > MONIAL

MONICKER *same as* > MONIKER

MONICKERS > MONICKER

MONIE *Scots word for* > MANY

MONIED *same as* > MONEYED

MONIES > MONEY

MONIKER *n* person's name or nickname

MONIKERS > MONIKER

MONILIA *n* type of fungus

MONILIAL *adj* denoting a thrush infection, caused by the fungus *Candida* (formerly *Monilia*) *albicans*

MONILIAS > MONILIA

MONIMENT *same as* > MONUMENT

MONIMENTS > MONIMENT

MONIPLIES *same as* > MANYPLIES

MONISH *same as* > ADMONISH

MONISHED > MONISH

MONISHES > MONISH

MONISHING > MONISH

MONISM *n* doctrine that reality consists of only one basic substance or element, such as mind or matter

MONISMS > MONISM

MONIST > MONISM

MONISTIC > MONISM

MONISTS > MONISM

MONITION *n* warning or caution

MONITIONS > MONITION

MONITIVE *adj* reproving

MONITOR *n* person or device that checks, controls, warns, or keeps a record of something ▷*vb* watch and check on

MONITORED > MONITOR

MONITORS > MONITOR

MONITORY *adj* acting as or giving a warning ▷*n* letter containing a monition

MONITRESS > MONITOR

MONK *n* member of an all-male religious community bound by vows

MONKERIES > MONKERY

MONKERY *n* derogatory word for monastic life or practices

MONKEY *n* long-tailed primate ▷*vb* meddle or fool

MONKEYED > MONKEY

MONKEYING > MONKEY

MONKEYISH > MONKEY

MONKEYISM *n* practice of behaving like monkey

MONKEYPOD *n* Central American tree

MONKEYPOT *n* any of various tropical trees of the genus *Lecythis*: family *Lecythidaceae*

MONKEYS > MONKEY

MONKFISH *n* any of various fish of the genus *Lophius*

MONKHOOD *n* condition of being a monk

MONKHOODS > MONKHOOD

MONKISH *adj* of, relating to, or resembling a monk or monks

MONKISHLY > MONKISH

MONKS > MONK

MONKSHOOD *n* poisonous plant with hooded flowers

MONO *n* monophonic sound

MONOACID *adj* a base which is capable of reacting with only one molecule of a monobasic acid

MONOACIDS > MONOACID

MONOAMINE *n* substance, such as adrenaline, noradrenaline, or serotonin, that contains a single amine group

MONOAO *n* New Zealand plant with rigid leaves

MONOBASIC *adj* (of an acid, such as hydrogen chloride) having only one replaceable hydrogen atom per molecule

MONOBROW *n* appearance of a single eyebrow as a result of the eyebrows joining above a person's nose

MONOBROWS > MONOBROW

MONOCARP *n* plant that is monocarpic

MONOCARPS > MONOCARP

MONOCEROS *n* faint constellation on the celestial equator crossed by the Milky Way and lying close to Orion and Canis Major

MONOCHORD *n* instrument employed in acoustic analysis or investigation, consisting usually of one string stretched over a resonator of wood

MONOCLE *n* eyeglass for one eye only

MONOCLED > MONOCLE

MONOCLES > MONOCLE

MONOCLINE *n* fold in stratified rocks in which the strata are inclined in the same direction from the horizontal

MONOCOQUE *n* vehicle body moulded from a single piece of material with no separate load-bearing parts ▷ *adj* of or relating to the design characteristic of a monocoque

MONOCOT *n* any flowering plant of the class *Monocotyledonae*, having a single embryonic seed leaf, leaves with parallel veins, and flowers with parts in threes: includes grasses, lilies, palms, and orchids

MONOCOTS > MONOCOT

MONOCOTYL *same as* > MONOCOT

MONOCRACY *n* government by one person

MONOCRAT > MONOCRACY

MONOCRATS > MONOCRACY

MONOCULAR *adj* having or for one eye only ▷ *n* device for use with one eye, such as a field glass

MONOCYCLE *another name for* > UNICYCLE

MONOCYTE *n* large phagocytic leucocyte with a spherical nucleus and clear cytoplasm

MONOCYTES > MONOCYTE

MONOCYTIC > MONOCYTE

MONODIC > MONODY

MONODICAL > MONODY

MONODIES > MONODY

MONODIST > MONODY

MONODISTS > MONODY

MONODONT *adj* (of certain animals, esp the male narwhal) having a single tooth throughout life

MONODRAMA *n* play or other dramatic piece for a single performer

MONODY *n* (in Greek tragedy) an ode sung by a single actor

MONOECIES > MONOECY

MONOECISM *n* being both male and female

MONOECY *same as* > MONOECISM

MONOESTER *n* type of ester

MONOFIL *n* synthetic thread or yarn composed of a single strand rather than twisted fibres

MONOFILS > MONOFIL

MONOFUEL *n* single type of fuel

MONOFUELS > MONOFUEL

MONOGAMIC > MONOGAMY

MONOGAMY *n* custom of being married to one person at a time

MONOGENIC *adj* of or relating to an inherited character difference that is controlled by a single gene

MONOGENY *n* the hypothetical descent of all organisms from a single cell or organism

MONOGERM *adj* containing single seed

MONOGLOT *n* person speaking only one language

MONOGLOTS > MONOGLOT

MONOGONY *n* asexual reproduction

MONOGRAM *n* design of combined letters, esp a person's initials ▷ *vb* decorate (clothing, stationery, etc) with a monogram

MONOGRAMS > MONOGRAM

MONOGRAPH *n* book or paper on a single subject ▷ *vb* write a monograph on

MONOGYNY *n* custom of having only one female sexual partner over a period of time

MONOHULL *n* sailing vessel with a single hull

MONOHULLS > MONOHULL

MONOICOUS *adj* (of some flowering plants) having the male and female reproductive organs in separate flowers on the same plant

MONOKINE *n* type of protein

MONOKINES > MONOKINE

MONOKINI *n* bottom half of bikini

MONOKINIS > MONOKINI

MONOLATER > MONOLATRY

MONOLATRY *n* exclusive worship of one god without excluding the existence of others

MONOLAYER *n* single layer of atoms or molecules adsorbed on a surface

MONOLITH *n* large upright block of stone

MONOLITHS > MONOLITH

MONOLOG *same as* > MONOLOGUE

MONOLOGIC > MONOLOGUE

MONOLOGS > MONOLOG

MONOLOGUE *n* long speech by one person

MONOLOGY > MONOLOGUE

MONOMACHY *n* combat between two individuals

MONOMANIA *n* obsession with one thing

MONOMARK *n* series of letters or figures to identify goods, personal articles, etc

MONOMARKS > MONOMARK

MONOMER *n* compound whose molecules can join together to form a polymer

MONOMERIC > MONOMER

MONOMERS > MONOMER

MONOMETER *n* line of verse consisting of one metrical foot

MONOMIAL *n* expression consisting of a single term, such as 5*ax* ▷ *adj* consisting of a single algebraic term

MONOMIALS > MONOMIAL

MONOMODE *adj* denoting or relating to a type of optical fibre with a core less than 10 micrometres in diameter

MONONYM *n* person who is famous enough to be known only by one name,

usually the first name

MONONYMS > MONONYM

MONOPHAGY *n* feeding on only one type of food

MONOPHASE *adj* having single alternating electric current

MONOPHONY > MONO

MONOPHYLY *n* group of ancestor and all descendants

MONOPITCH *adj* (of roof) having only one slope

MONOPLANE *n* aeroplane with one pair of wings

MONOPLOID *less common word for* > HAPLOID

MONOPOD *same as* > MONOPODE

MONOPODE *n* member of a legendary one-legged race of Africa

MONOPODES > MONOPODE

MONOPODIA *n* plural of monopodium: the main axis of growth in the pine tree and similar plants: the main stem, which elongates from the tip and gives rise to lateral branches

MONOPODS > MONOPOD

MONOPODY *n* single-foot measure in poetry

MONOPOLE *n* magnetic pole considered in isolation

MONOPOLES > MONOPOLE

MONOPOLY *n* exclusive possession of or right to do something

MONOPSONY *n* situation in which the entire market demand for a product or service consists of only one buyer

MONOPTERA *n* plural of monopteron: circular classical building, esp a temple, that has a single ring of columns surrounding it

MONOPTOTE *n* word with only one form

MONOPULSE *n* radar transmitting single pulse only

MONORAIL *n* single-rail railway

MONORAILS > MONORAIL

MONORCHID *adj* having only one testicle ▷ *n* animal or person with only one testicle

MONORHINE *adj* having single nostril

MONORHYME *n* poem in which all lines rhyme

MONOS > MONO

MONOSEMY *n* fact of having only a single meaning

MONOSES > MONOSIS

MONOSIES > MONOSY

MONOSIS *n* abnormal separation

MONOSKI *n* wide ski on which the skier stands with both feet

MONOSKIER > MONOSKI

MONOSKIS > MONOSKI

MONOSOME *n* unpaired chromosome, esp an X-chromosome in an otherwise diploid cell

MONOSOMES > MONOSOME

MONOSOMIC > MONOSOME

MONOSOMY *n* condition with missing pair of chromosomes

MONOSTELE *n* type of plant tissue

MONOSTELY > MONOSTELE

MONOSTICH *n* poem of a single line

MONOSTOME *adj* having only one mouth, pore, or similar opening

MONOSTYLE *adj* having single shaft

MONOSY *same as* > MONOSIS

MONOTINT *n* black-and-white photograph or transparency

MONOTINTS > MONOTINT

MONOTONE *n* unvaried pitch in speech or sound ▷ *adj* unvarying ▷ *vb* speak in monotone

MONOTONED > MONOTONE

MONOTONES > MONOTONE

MONOTONIC *same as* > MONOTONE

MONOTONY *n* wearisome routine, dullness

MONOTREME *n* any mammal of the primitive order *Monotremata*, of Australia and New Guinea: egg-laying toothless animals with a single opening (cloaca) for the passage of eggs or sperm, faeces, and urine. The group contains only the echidnas and the platypus

MONOTROCH *n* wheelbarrow

MONOTYPE *n* single print made from a metal or glass plate on which a picture has been painted

MONOTYPES > MONOTYPE

MONOTYPIC *adj* (of a genus or species) consisting of only one type of animal or plant

MONOVULAR *adj* of single ovum

MONOXIDE *n* oxide that contains one oxygen atom per molecule

MONOXIDES > MONOXIDE

MONOXYLON *n* canoe made from one log

MONS > MON

MONSIEUR *n* French title of address equivalent to *sir* or *Mr*

MONSIGNOR *n* ecclesiastical title attached to certain offices or distinctions usually bestowed by the Pope

MONSOON *n* seasonal wind of SE Asia

MONSOONAL > MONSOON

MONSOONS > MONSOON

MONSTER n imaginary, usu frightening, beast ▷ adj huge ▷ vb criticize (a person or group) severely

MONSTERA n any plant of the tropical climbing genus *Monstera*, some species of which are grown as greenhouse or pot plants for their unusual leathery perforated leaves: family *Araceae. M. deliciosa* is the Swiss cheese plant

MONSTERAS > MONSTERA

MONSTERED > MONSTER

MONSTERS > MONSTER

MONSTROUS adj unnatural or ugly

MONTADALE n breed of sheep

MONTAGE n (making of) a picture composed from pieces of others ▷ vb make as montage

MONTAGED > MONTAGE

MONTAGES > MONTAGE

MONTAGING > MONTAGE

MONTAN as in *montan wax* hard wax obtained from lignite and peat used in polishes and candles

MONTANE n area of mountain dominated by vegetation ▷ adj of or inhabiting mountainous regions

MONTANES > MONTANE

MONTANT n vertical part in woodwork

MONTANTO n rising blow

MONTANTOS > MONTANTO

MONTANTS > MONTANT

MONTARIA n Brazilian canoe

MONTARIAS > MONTARIA

MONTE n gambling card game of Spanish origin

MONTEITH n large ornamental bowl, usually of silver, for cooling wineglasses, which are suspended from the notched rim

MONTEITHS > MONTEITH

MONTEM n former money-raising practice at Eton school

MONTEMS > MONTEM

MONTERO n round cap with a flap at the back worn by hunters, esp in Spain in the 17th and 18th centuries

MONTEROS > MONTERO

MONTES > MONTE

MONTH n one of the twelve divisions of the calendar year

MONTHLIES > MONTHLY

MONTHLING n month-old child

MONTHLONG adj lasting all month

MONTHLY adj happening or payable once a month ▷ adv once a month ▷ n monthly magazine

MONTHS > MONTH

MONTICLE same as > MONTICULE

MONTICLES > MONTICLE

MONTICULE n small hill or mound, such as a secondary volcanic cone

MONTIES > MONTY

MONTRE n pipes of organ

MONTRES > MONTRE

MONTURE n mount or frame

MONTURES > MONTURE

MONTY n complete form of something

MONUMENT n something, esp a building or statue, that commemorates something

MONUMENTS > MONUMENT

MONURON n type of weedkiller

MONURONS > MONURON

MONY *Scot word for* > MANY

MONYPLIES same as > MANYPLIES

MONZONITE n coarse-grained plutonic igneous rock consisting of equal amounts of plagioclase and orthoclase feldspar, with ferromagnesian minerals

MOO n long deep cry of a cow ▷ vb make this noise ▷ interj instance or imitation of this sound

MOOCH vb loiter about aimlessly

MOOCHED > MOOCH

MOOCHER > MOOCH

MOOCHERS > MOOCH

MOOCHES > MOOCH

MOOCHING > MOOCH

MOOD n temporary (gloomy) state of mind

MOODIED > MOODY

MOODIER > MOODY

MOODIES > MOODY

MOODIEST > MOODY

MOODILY > MOODY

MOODINESS > MOODY

MOODS > MOOD

MOODY adj sullen or gloomy ▷ vb flatter

MOODYING > MOODY

MOOED > MOO

MOOI adj pleasing or nice

MOOING > MOO

MOOK n person regarded with contempt, esp a stupid person

MOOKS > MOOK

MOOKTAR same as > MUKHTAR

MOOKTARS > MOOKTAR

MOOL same as > MOULD

MOOLA same as > MOOLAH

MOOLAH slang word for > MONEY

MOOLAHS > MOOLAH

MOOLAS > MOOLA

MOOLED > MOOL

MOOLEY same as > MOOLY

MOOLEYS > MOOLEY

MOOLI n type of large white radish

MOOLIES > MOOLY

MOOLING > MOOL

MOOLIS > MOOLI

MOOLOO n person from the Waikato

MOOLOOS > MOOLOO

MOOLS > MOOL

MOOLVI same as > MOOLVIE

MOOLVIE n (esp in India) a Muslim doctor of the law, teacher, or learned man also used as a title of respect

MOOLVIES > MOOLVIE

MOOLVIS > MOOLVI

MOOLY same as > MULEY

MOON n natural satellite of the earth ▷ vb be idle in a listless or dreamy way

MOONBEAM n ray of moonlight

MOONBEAMS > MOONBEAM

MOONBLIND adj (in horses), having a disorder which causes inflammation of the eyes and sometimes blindness

MOONBOW n rainbow made by moonlight

MOONBOWS > MOONBOW

MOONCALF n born fool

MOONCHILD n someone who is born under the Cancer star sign

MOONDUST n dust on surface of moon

MOONDUSTS > MOONDUST

MOONED adj decorated with a moon

MOONER > MOON

MOONERS > MOON

MOONEYE n any of several North American large-eyed freshwater clupeoid fishes of the family *Hiodontidae*, esp *Hiodon tergisus*

MOONEYES > MOONEYE

MOONFACE n big round face ▷ vb have a moon face

MOONFACED > MOONFACE

MOONFACES > MOONFACE

MOONFISH n any of several deep-bodied silvery carangid fishes, occurring in warm and tropical American coastal waters

MOONIER > MOONY

MOONIES > MOONY

MOONIEST > MOONY

MOONILY > MOONY

MOONINESS > MOONY

MOONING > MOON

MOONISH > MOON

MOONISHLY > MOON

MOONLESS > MOON

MOONLET n small moon

MOONLETS > MOONLET

MOONLIGHT n light from the moon ▷ adj illuminated by the moon ▷ vb work at a secondary job, esp illegally

MOONLIKE > MOON

MOONLIT adj illuminated by the moon

MOONPHASE n phase of moon

MOONPORT n place from which flights leave for moon

MOONPORTS > MOONPORT

MOONQUAKE n light tremor of the moon, detected on the moon's surface

MOONRAKER n small square sail set above a skysail

MOONRISE n moment when the moon appears above the horizon

MOONRISES > MOONRISE

MOONROCK n rock from moon

MOONROCKS > MOONROCK

MOONROOF same as > SUNROOF

MOONROOFS > MOONROOF

MOONS > MOON

MOONSAIL n small sail high on mast

MOONSAILS > MOONSAIL

MOONSCAPE n surface of the moon or a picture or model of it

MOONSEED n any menispermaceous climbing plant of the genus *Menispermum* and related genera, having red or black fruits with crescent-shaped or ring-shaped seeds

MOONSEEDS > MOONSEED

MOONSET n moment when the moon disappears below the horizon

MOONSETS > MOONSET

MOONSHEE same as > MUNSHI

MOONSHEES > MOONSHEE

MOONSHINE same as > MOONLIGHT

MOONSHINY > MOONSHINE

MOONSHOT n launching of a spacecraft to the moon

MOONSHOTS > MOONSHOT

MOONSTONE n translucent semiprecious stone

MOONWALK n instance of walking on moon

MOONWALKS > MOONWALK

MOONWARD adj towards moon

MOONWARDS adv towards moon

MOONWORT n any of various ferns of the genus *Botrychium*, esp *B. lunaria*, which has crescent-shaped leaflets

MOONWORTS > MOONWORT

MOONY adj dreamy or listless ▷ n crazy or foolish person

MOOP same as > MOUP

MOOPED > MOOP

MOOPING > MOOP

MOOPS > MOOP

MOOR n tract of open uncultivated ground covered with grass and heather ▷ vb secure (a ship) with ropes etc

MOORAGE n place for mooring a vessel

MOORAGES > MOORAGE

MOORBURN n practice of burning off old growth on a heather moor to encourage new growth for grazing

MOORBURNS > MOORBURN

MOORCOCK *n* male of the red grouse

MOORCOCKS > MOORCOCK

MOORED > MOOR

MOORFOWL *n* red grouse

MOORFOWLS > MOORFOWL

MOORHEN *n* small black water bird

MOORHENS > MOORHEN

MOORIER > MOOR

MOORIEST > MOOR

MOORILL *n* disease of cattle on moors

MOORILLS > MOORILL

MOORING *n* place for mooring a ship

MOORINGS *pl n* ropes and anchors used in mooring a vessel

MOORISH *adj* of or relating to the Moor people of North Africa

MOORLAND *n* area of moor

MOORLANDS > MOORLAND

MOORLOG *n* rotted wood below surface of moor

MOORLOGS > MOOR

MOORMAN *n* person living on moor

MOORMEN > MOORMAN

MOORS > MOOR

MOORVA *same as* > MURVA

MOORVAS > MOORVA

MOORWORT *n* low-growing pink-flowered shrub that grows in peaty bogs

MOORWORTS > MOORWORT

MOORY > MOOR

MOOS > MOO

MOOSE *n* large N American deer

MOOSEBIRD *n* North American jay

MOOSEWOOD *n* North American tree

MOOSEYARD *n* place where moose spend winter

MOOT *adj* debatable ▷ *vb* bring up for discussion ▷ *n* (in Anglo-Saxon England) a local administrative assembly

MOOTABLE > MOOT

MOOTED > MOOT

MOOTER > MOOT

MOOTERS > MOOT

MOOTEST > MOOT

MOOTING > MOOT

MOOTINGS > MOOT

MOOTMAN *n* person taking part in moot

MOOTMEN > MOOTMAN

MOOTNESS > MOOT

MOOTS > MOOT

MOOVE *same as* > MOVE

MOOVED > MOOVE

MOOVES > MOOVE

MOOVING > MOOVE

MOP *n* long stick with twists of cotton or a sponge on the end, used for cleaning ▷ *vb* clean or soak up with or as if with a mop

MOPANE *same as* > MOPANI

MOPANES > MOPANE

MOPANI *n* leguminous tree, *Colophospermum* (or *Copaifera*) *mopane*, native to southern Africa, that is highly resistant to drought and produces very hard wood

MOPANIS > MOPANI

MOPBOARD *n* wooden border fixed round the base of an interior wall

MOPBOARDS > MOPBOARD

MOPE *vb* be gloomy and apathetic ▷ *n* gloomy person

MOPED *n* light motorized cycle

MOPEDS > MOPED

MOPEHAWK *same as* > MOPOKE

MOPEHAWKS > MOPEHAWK

MOPER > MOPE

MOPERIES > MOPERY

MOPERS > MOPE

MOPERY *n* gloominess

MOPES > MOPE

MOPEY > MOPE

MOPHEAD *n* person with shaggy hair

MOPHEADS > MOPHEAD

MOPIER > MOPE

MOPIEST > MOPE

MOPINESS > MOPE

MOPING > MOPE

MOPINGLY > MOPE

MOPISH > MOPE

MOPISHLY > MOPE

MOPOKE *n* species of owl

MOPOKES > MOPOKE

MOPPED > MOP

MOPPER > MOP

MOPPERS > MOP

MOPPET *same as* > POPPET

MOPPETS > MOPPET

MOPPIER > MOPPY

MOPPIEST > MOPPY

MOPPING > MOP

MOPPY *adj* drunk

MOPS > MOP

MOPSIES > MOPSY

MOPSTICK *n* mop handle

MOPSTICKS > MOPSTICK

MOPSY *n* untidy or dowdy person

MOPUS *n* person who mopes

MOPUSES > MOPUS

MOPY > MOPE

MOQUETTE *n* thick velvety fabric used for carpets and upholstery

MOQUETTES > MOQUETTE

MOR *n* layer of acidic humus formed in cool moist areas where decomposition is slow

MORA *n* quantity of a short syllable in verse

MORACEOUS *adj* of, relating to, or belonging to the *Moraceae*, mostly tropical and subtropical family of trees and shrubs, including fig, mulberry, breadfruit, and hop, many of which have latex in the stems and heads enclosed in a fleshy receptacle

MORAE > MORA

MORAINAL > MORAINE

MORAINE *n* accumulated mass of debris deposited by a glacier

MORAINES > MORAINE

MORAINIC > MORAINE

MORAL *adj* concerned with right and wrong conduct ▷ *n* lesson to be obtained from a story or event ▷ *vb* moralize

MORALE *n* degree of confidence or hope of a person or group

MORALES > MORALE

MORALISE *same as* > MORALIZE

MORALISED > MORALISE

MORALISER > MORALIZE

MORALISES > MORALISE

MORALISM *n* habit or practice of moralizing

MORALISMS > MORALISM

MORALIST *n* person with a strong sense of right and wrong

MORALISTS > MORALIST

MORALITY *n* good moral conduct

MORALIZE *vb* make moral pronouncements

MORALIZED > MORALIZE

MORALIZER > MORALIZE

MORALIZES > MORALIZE

MORALL *same as* > MURAL

MORALLED > MORALL

MORALLER > MORAL

MORALLERS > MORAL

MORALLING > MORALL

MORALLS > MORALL

MORALLY > MORAL

MORALS > MORAL

MORAS > MORA

MORASS *n* marsh

MORASSES > MORASS

MORASSY > MORASS

MORAT *n* drink containing mulberry juice

MORATORIA *n* plural form of singular moratorium: legally authorized postponement of the fulfilment of an obligation

MORATORY > MORATORIA

MORATS > MORAT

MORAY *n* large voracious eel

MORAYS > MORAY

MORBID *adj* unduly interested in death or unpleasant events

MORBIDER > MORBID

MORBIDEST > MORBID

MORBIDITY *n* state of being morbid

MORBIDLY > MORBID

MORBIFIC *adj* causing disease

MORBILLI *same as* > MEASLES

MORBUS *n* disease

MORBUSES > MORBUS

MORCEAU *n* fragment or morsel

MORCEAUX > MORCEAU

MORCHA *n* (in India) a hostile demonstration against the government

MORCHAS > MORCHA

MORDACITY *n* quality of sarcasm

MORDANCY > MORDANT

MORDANT *adj* sarcastic or scathing ▷ *n* substance used to fix dyes ▷ *vb* treat (a fabric, yarn, etc) with a mordant

MORDANTED > MORDANT

MORDANTLY > MORDANT

MORDANTS > MORDANT

MORDENT *n* melodic ornament consisting of the rapid alternation of a note with a note one degree lower than it

MORDENTS > MORDENT

MORE *adj* greater in amount or degree ▷ *adv* greater extent ▷ *pron* greater or additional amount or number

MOREEN *n* heavy, usually watered, fabric of wool or wool and cotton, used esp in furnishing

MOREENS > MOREEN

MOREISH *adj* (of food) causing a desire for more

MOREL *n* edible mushroom with a pitted cap

MORELLE *n* nightshade

MORELLES > MORELLE

MORELLO *n* variety of small very dark sour cherry

MORELLOS > MORELLO

MORELS > MOREL

MORENDO *adv* (in music) dying away

MORENESS > MORE

MOREOVER *adv* in addition to what has already been said

MOREPORK *same as* > MOPOKE

MOREPORKS > MOREPORK

MORES *pl n* customs and conventions embodying the fundamental values of a community

MORESQUE *adj* (esp of decoration and architecture) of Moorish style ▷ *n* Moorish design or decoration

MORESQUES > MORESQUE

MORGAN *n* American breed of small compact saddle horse

MORGANITE *n* pink variety of beryl, used as a gemstone

MORGANS > MORGAN

MORGAY *n* small dogfish

MORGAYS > MORGAY

MORGEN *n* South African unit of area, equal to about two acres or 0.8 hectare

MORGENS > MORGEN

MORGUE *same as* > MORTUARY

MORGUES > MORGUE

MORIA *n* folly

MORIAS > MORIA

MORIBUND *adj* without force or vitality

MORICHE *same as* > MIRITI

MORICHES > MORICHE

MORION *n* 16th-century

helmet with a brim and wide comb

MORIONS > MORION

MORISCO *n* a morris dance

MORISCOES > MORISCO

MORISCOS > MORISCO

MORISH *same as* > MOREISH

MORKIN *n* animal dying in accident

MORKINS > MORKIN

MORLING *n* sheep killed by disease

MORLINGS > MORLING

MORMAOR *n* former high-ranking Scottish nobleman

MORMAORS > MORMAOR

MORN *n* morning

MORNAY *adj* served with a cheese sauce

MORNAYS > MORNAY

MORNE *same as* > MOURN

MORNED > MORNE

MORNES > MORNE

MORNING *n* part of the day before noon

MORNINGS > MORNING

MORNS > MORN

MOROCCO *n* goatskin leather

MOROCCOS > MOROCCO

MORON *n* foolish or stupid person

MORONIC > MORON

MORONISM > MORON

MORONISMS > MORON

MORONITY > MORON

MORONS > MORON

MOROSE *adj* sullen or moody

MOROSELY > MOROSE

MOROSER > MOROSE

MOROSEST > MOROSE

MOROSITY > MOROSE

MORPH *n* phonological representation of a morpheme ▷*vb* undergo or cause to undergo morphing

MORPHEAN *adj* of or relating to Morpheus, the god of sleep and dreams

MORPHED > MORPH

MORPHEME *n* speech element having a meaning or grammatical function that cannot be subdivided into further such elements

MORPHEMES > MORPHEME

MORPHEMIC > MORPHEME

MORPHETIC *same as* > MORPHEAN

MORPHEW *n* blemish on skin

MORPHEWS > MORPHEW

MORPHIA *same as* > MORPHINE

MORPHIAS > MORPHIA

MORPHIC *as in morphic resonance* idea that, through a telepathic effect or sympathetic vibration, an event or act can lead to similar events or acts in the future or an idea conceived in one mind can then arise in another

MORPHIN *variant form of* > MORPHINE

MORPHINE *n* drug extracted from opium, used as an anaesthetic and sedative

MORPHINES > MORPHINE

MORPHING *n* computer technique used for graphics and in films, in which one image is gradually transformed into another image without individual changes being noticeable in the process

MORPHINGS > MORPHING

MORPHINIC > MORPHINE

MORPHINS > MORPHINE

MORPHO *n* type of butterfly

MORPHOGEN *n* chemical in body that influences growth

MORPHOS > MORPHO

MORPHOSES > MORPHOSIS

MORPHOSIS *n* development in an organism or its parts characterized by structural change

MORPHOTIC > MORPHOSIS

MORPHS > MORPH

MORRA *same as* > MORA

MORRAS > MORRA

MORRELL *n* tall eucalyptus, *Eucalyptus longicornis*, of SW Australia, having pointed buds

MORRELLS > MORRELL

MORRHUA *n* cod

MORRHUAS > MORRHUA

MORRICE *same as* > MORRIS

MORRICES > MORRICE

MORRION *same as* > MORION

MORRIONS > MORRION

MORRIS *vb* perform morris dance

MORRISED > MORRIS

MORRISES > MORRIS

MORRISING > MORRIS

MORRO *n* rounded hill or promontory

MORROS > MORRO

MORROW *n* next day

MORROWS > MORROW

MORS > MOR

MORSAL > MORSURE

MORSE *n* clasp or fastening on a cope

MORSEL *n* small piece, esp of food ▷*vb* divide into morsels

MORSELED > MORSEL

MORSELING > MORSEL

MORSELLED > MORSEL

MORSELS > MORSEL

MORSES > MORSE

MORSURE *n* bite

MORSURES > MORSURE

MORT *n* call blown on a hunting horn to signify the death of the animal hunted

MORTAL *adj* subject to death ▷*n* human being

MORTALISE *same as* > MORTALIZE

MORTALITY *n* state of being mortal

MORTALIZE *vb* make mortal

MORTALLY > MORTAL

MORTALS > MORTAL

MORTAR *n* small cannon with a short range ▷*vb* fire on with mortars

MORTARED > MORTAR

MORTARING > MORTAR

MORTARMAN *n* person firing mortar

MORTARMEN > MORTAR

MORTARS > MORTAR

MORTARY *adj* of or like mortar

MORTBELL *n* bell rung for funeral

MORTBELLS > MORTBELL

MORTCLOTH *n* cloth spread over coffin

MORTGAGE *n* conditional pledging of property, esp a house, as security for the repayment of a loan ▷*vb* pledge (property) as security thus ▷*adj* of or relating to a mortgage

MORTGAGED > MORTGAGE

MORTGAGEE *n* creditor in a mortgage

MORTGAGER *same as* > MORTGAGOR

MORTGAGES > MORTGAGE

MORTGAGOR *n* debtor in a mortgage

MORTICE *same as* > MORTISE

MORTICED > MORTICE

MORTICER > MORTICE

MORTICERS > MORTICE

MORTICES > MORTICE

MORTICIAN *n* undertaker

MORTICING > MORTICE

MORTIFIC *adj* causing death

MORTIFIED > MORTIFY

MORTIFIER > MORTIFY

MORTIFIES > MORTIFY

MORTIFY *vb* humiliate

MORTISE *n* slot or recess, usually rectangular, cut into a piece of wood, stone, etc, to receive a matching projection (tenon) of another piece, or a mortise lock ▷*vb* cut a slot or recess in (a piece of wood, stone, etc)

MORTISED > MORTISE

MORTISER > MORTISE

MORTISERS > MORTISE

MORTISES > MORTISE

MORTISING > MORTISE

MORTLING *n* corpse

MORTLINGS > MORTLING

MORTMAIN *n* state or condition of lands, buildings, etc, held inalienably, as by an ecclesiastical or other corporation

MORTMAINS > MORTMAIN

MORTS > MORT

MORTSAFE *n* heavy iron cage or grille placed over the grave of a newly deceased person during the 19th century in order to deter body snatchers

MORTSAFES > MORTSAFE

MORTUARY *n* building where corpses are kept before burial or cremation ▷*adj* of or relating to death or burial

MORULA *n* solid ball of cells resulting from cleavage of a fertilized ovum

MORULAE > MORULA

MORULAR > MORULA

MORULAS > MORULA

MORWONG *n* food fish of Australasian coastal waters belonging to the *Cheilodactylidae* family

MORWONGS > MORWONG

MORYAH *interj* exclamation of annoyance, disbelief, etc

MOS > MO

MOSAIC *n* design or decoration using small pieces of coloured stone or glass

MOSAICISM *n* occurrence of different types of tissue side by side

MOSAICIST > MOSAIC

MOSAICKED *adj* arranged in mosaic form

MOSAICS > MOSAIC

MOSASAUR *n* any of various extinct Cretaceous giant marine lizards of the genus *Mosasaurus* and related genera, typically having paddle-like limbs

MOSASAURI > MOSASAUR

MOSASAURS > MOSASAUR

MOSCHATE *n* odour like musk

MOSCHATEL *n* small N temperate plant, *Adoxa moschatellina*, with greenish-white musk-scented flowers on top of the stem, arranged as four pointing sideways at right angles to each other and one facing upwards: family *Adoxaceae*

MOSE *vb* have glanders

MOSED > MOSE

MOSELLE *n* German white wine from the Moselle valley

MOSELLES > MOSELLE

MOSES > MOSE

MOSEY *vb* walk in a leisurely manner

MOSEYED > MOSEY

MOSEYING > MOSEY

MOSEYS > MOSEY

MOSH *n* type of dance, performed to loud rock music, in which people throw themselves about in a frantic and violent manner ▷*vb* dance in this manner

MOSHAV *n* cooperative settlement in Israel, consisting of a number of small farms

MOSHAVIM > MOSHAV

MOSHED > MOSH

MOSHER > MOSH

MOSHERS > MOSH

MOSHES > MOSH

MOSHING > MOSH

MOSHINGS > MOSH

MOSING > MOSE

MOSK *same as* > MOSQUE

MOSKONFYT n South African grape syrup
MOSKS > MOSK
MOSLINGS n shavings from animal skin being prepared
MOSQUE n Muslim temple
MOSQUES > MOSQUE
MOSQUITO n blood-sucking flying insect
MOSQUITOS > MOSQUITO
MOSS n small flowerless plant growing in masses on moist surfaces ▷vb gather moss
MOSSBACK n old turtle, shellfish, etc, that has a growth of algae on its back
MOSSBACKS > MOSSBACK
MOSSED > MOSS
MOSSER > MOSS
MOSSERS > MOSS
MOSSES > MOSS
MOSSGROWN adj covered in moss
MOSSIE n common sparrow
MOSSIER > MOSS
MOSSIES > MOSSIE
MOSSIEST > MOSS
MOSSINESS > MOSS
MOSSING > MOSS
MOSSLAND n land covered in peat
MOSSLANDS > MOSSLAND
MOSSLIKE > MOSS
MOSSO adv to be performed with rapidity
MOSSPLANT n individual plant in moss
MOSSY > MOSS
MOST n greatest number or degree ▷adj greatest in number or degree ▷adv in the greatest degree
MOSTE > MOTE
MOSTEST > MOST
MOSTESTS > MOST
MOSTLY adv for the most part, generally
MOSTS > MOST
MOSTWHAT adv mostly
MOT n girl or young woman, esp one's girlfriend
MOTE n tiny speck ▷vb may or might
MOTED adj containing motes
MOTEL n roadside hotel for motorists
MOTELIER n person running motel
MOTELIERS > MOTELIER
MOTELS > MOTEL
MOTEN > MOTE
MOTES > MOTE
MOTET n short sacred choral song
MOTETS > MOTET
MOTETT same as > MOTET
MOTETTIST > MOTET
MOTETTS > MOTET
MOTEY adj containing motes
MOTH n nocturnal insect like a butterfly
MOTHBALL n small ball of camphor or naphthalene used to repel moths from stored clothes ▷vb store (something operational)

for future use
MOTHBALLS > MOTHBALL
MOTHED adj damaged by moths
MOTHER n female parent ▷adj native or inborn ▷vb look after as a mother
MOTHERED > MOTHER
MOTHERESE n simplified and repetitive type of speech, with exaggerated intonation and rhythm, often used by adults when speaking to babies
MOTHERING > MOTHER
MOTHERLY adj of or resembling a mother, esp in warmth, or protectiveness
MOTHERS > MOTHER
MOTHERY > MOTHER
MOTHIER > MOTHY
MOTHIEST > MOTHY
MOTHLIKE > MOTH
MOTHPROOF adj (esp of clothes) chemically treated so as to repel clothes moths ▷vb make mothproof
MOTHS > MOTH
MOTHY adj ragged
MOTI n derogatory Indian English word for a fat woman or girl
MOTIER > MOTEY
MOTIEST > MOTEY
MOTIF n (recurring) theme or design
MOTIFIC adj causing motion
MOTIFS > MOTIF
MOTILE adj capable of independent movement ▷n person whose mental imagery strongly reflects movement, esp his own
MOTILES > MOTILE
MOTILITY > MOTILE
MOTION n process, action, or way of moving ▷vb direct (someone) by gesture
MOTIONAL > MOTION
MOTIONED > MOTION
MOTIONER > MOTION
MOTIONERS > MOTION
MOTIONING > MOTION
MOTIONIST n person proposing many motions
MOTIONS > MOTION
MOTIS > MOTI
MOTIVATE vb give incentive to
MOTIVATED > MOTIVATE
MOTIVATES > MOTIVATE
MOTIVATOR > MOTIVATE
MOTIVE n reason for a course of action ▷adj causing motion ▷vb motivate
MOTIVED > MOTIVE
MOTIVES > MOTIVE
MOTIVIC adj of musical motif
MOTIVING > MOTIVE
MOTIVITY n power of moving or of initiating motion
MOTLEY adj miscellaneous ▷n costume of a jester

MOTLEYER > MOTLEY
MOTLEYEST > MOTLEY
MOTLEYS > MOTLEY
MOTLIER > MOTLEY
MOTLIEST > MOTLEY
MOTMOT n any tropical American bird of the family Momotidae, having a long tail and blue and brownish-green plumage: order Coraciiformes (kingfishers, etc)
MOTMOTS > MOTMOT
MOTOCROSS n motorcycle race over a rough course
MOTOR n engine, esp of a vehicle ▷vb travel by car ▷adj of or relating to cars and other vehicles powered by petrol or diesel engines
MOTORABLE adj (of a road) suitable for use by motor vehicles
MOTORAIL n transport of cars by train
MOTORAILS > MOTORAIL
MOTORBIKE n motorcycle
MOTORBOAT n any boat powered by a motor
MOTORBUS n bus driven by an internal-combustion engine
MOTORCADE n procession of cars carrying important people
MOTORCAR n self-propelled electric railway car
MOTORCARS > MOTORCAR
MOTORDOM n world of motor cars
MOTORDOMS > MOTORDOM
MOTORED > MOTOR
MOTORHOME n large motor vehicle with living quarters behind the driver's compartment
MOTORIAL > MOTOR
MOTORIC > MOTOR
MOTORING > MOTOR
MOTORINGS > MOTOR
MOTORISE same as > MOTORIZE
MOTORISED > MOTORISE
MOTORISES > MOTORISE
MOTORIST n driver of a car
MOTORISTS > MOTORIST
MOTORIUM n area of nervous system involved in movement
MOTORIUMS > MOTORIUM
MOTORIZE vb equip with a motor
MOTORIZED > MOTORIZE
MOTORIZES > MOTORIZE
MOTORLESS > MOTOR
MOTORMAN n driver of an electric train
MOTORMEN > MOTORMAN
MOTORS > MOTOR
MOTORSHIP n ship with motor
MOTORWAY n main road for fast-moving traffic
MOTORWAYS > MOTORWAY
MOTORY > MOTOR
MOTOSCAFI > MOTOSCAFO
MOTOSCAFO n motorboat

MOTS > MOT
MOTSER n large sum of money, esp a gambling win
MOTSERS > MOTSER
MOTT n clump of trees
MOTTE n mound on which a castle was built
MOTTES > MOTTE
MOTTIER > MOTTY
MOTTIES > MOTTY
MOTTIEST > MOTTY
MOTTLE vb colour with streaks or blotches of different shades ▷n mottled appearance, as of the surface of marble
MOTTLED > MOTTLE
MOTTLER n paintbrush for mottled effects
MOTTLERS > MOTTLER
MOTTLES > MOTTLE
MOTTLING > MOTTLE
MOTTLINGS > MOTTLE
MOTTO n saying expressing an ideal or rule of conduct
MOTTOED adj having motto
MOTTOES > MOTTO
MOTTOS > MOTTO
MOTTS > MOTT
MOTTY n target at which coins are aimed in pitch-and-toss ▷adj containing motes
MOTU n derogatory Indian English word for a fat man or boy
MOTUCA n Brazilian fly
MOTUCAS > MOTUCA
MOTUS > MOTU
MOTZA same as > MOTSER
MOTZAS > MOTZA
MOU Scots word for > MOUTH
MOUCH same as > MOOCH
MOUCHARD n police informer
MOUCHARDS > MOUCHARD
MOUCHED > MOUCH
MOUCHER > MOUCH
MOUCHERS > MOUCH
MOUCHES > MOUCH
MOUCHING > MOUCH
MOUCHOIR n handkerchief
MOUCHOIRS > MOUCHOIR
MOUDIWART same as > MOULDWARP
MOUDIWORT same as > MOULDWARP
MOUE n disdainful or pouting look
MOUES > MOUE
MOUFFLON same as > MOUFLON
MOUFFLONS > MOUFFLON
MOUFLON n wild short-fleeced mountain sheep, Ovis musimon, of Corsica and Sardinia
MOUFLONS > MOUFLON
MOUGHT > MOTE
MOUILLE adj palatalized, as in the sounds represented by Spanish ll or ñ
MOUJIK same as > MUZHIK
MOUJIKS > MOUJIK
MOULAGE n mould making
MOULAGES > MOULAGE
MOULD n hollow container in which metal etc is cast

▷ *vb* shape
MOULDABLE > MOULD
MOULDED > MOULD
MOULDER *vb* decay into dust ▷ *n* person who moulds or makes moulds
MOULDERED > MOULDER
MOULDERS > MOULDER
MOULDIER > MOULDY
MOULDIEST > MOULDY
MOULDING *n* moulded ornamental edging
MOULDINGS > MOULDING
MOULDS > MOULD
MOULDWARP *archaic or dialect name for a* > MOLE
MOULDY *adj* stale or musty
MOULIN *n* vertical shaft in a glacier, maintained by a constant descending stream of water and debris
MOULINET *n* device for bending crossbow
MOULINETS > MOULINET
MOULINS > MOULIN
MOULS *Scots word for* > MOULD
MOULT *vb* shed feathers, hair, or skin to make way for new growth ▷ *n* process of moulting
MOULTED > MOULT
MOULTEN *adj* having moulted
MOULTER > MOULT
MOULTERS > MOULT
MOULTING > MOULT
MOULTINGS > MOULT
MOULTS > MOULT
MOUND *n* heap, esp of earth or stones ▷ *vb* gather into a mound
MOUNDBIRD *n* Australian bird laying eggs in mounds
MOUNDED > MOUND
MOUNDING > MOUND
MOUNDS > MOUND
MOUNSEER *same as* > MONSIEUR
MOUNSEERS > MOUNSEER
MOUNT *vb* climb or ascend ▷ *n* backing or support on which something is fixed
MOUNTABLE > MOUNT
MOUNTAIN *n* hill of great size ▷ *adj* of, found on, or for use on a mountain or mountains
MOUNTAINS > MOUNTAIN
MOUNTAINY > MOUNTAIN
MOUNTANT *n* adhesive for mounting pictures
MOUNTANTS > MOUNTANT
MOUNTED *adj* riding horses
MOUNTER > MOUNT
MOUNTERS > MOUNT
MOUNTING *same as* > MOUNT
MOUNTINGS > MOUNTING
MOUNTS > MOUNT
MOUP *n* nibble
MOUPED > MOUP
MOUPING > MOUP
MOUPS > MOUP
MOURN *vb* feel or express sorrow for (a dead person or lost thing)
MOURNED > MOURN

MOURNER *n* person attending a funeral
MOURNERS > MOURNER
MOURNFUL *adj* sad or dismal
MOURNING *n* grieving ▷ *adj* of or relating to mourning
MOURNINGS > MOURNING
MOURNIVAL *n* card game
MOURNS > MOURN
MOUS > MOU
MOUSAKA *same as* > MOUSSAKA
MOUSAKAS > MOUSAKA
MOUSE *n* small long-tailed rodent ▷ *vb* stalk and catch mice
MOUSEBIRD *another name for* > COLY
MOUSED > MOUSE
MOUSEKIN *n* little mouse
MOUSEKINS > MOUSEKIN
MOUSELIKE > MOUSE
MOUSEMAT *n* piece of material on which a computer mouse is moved
MOUSEMATS > MOUSEMAT
MOUSEOVER *n* on a web page, any item that changes or pops up when the pointer of a mouse moves over it
MOUSEPAD *n* pad for computer mouse
MOUSEPADS > MOUSEPAD
MOUSER *n* cat used to catch mice
MOUSERIES > MOUSERY
MOUSERS > MOUSER
MOUSERY *n* place infested with mice
MOUSES > MOUSE
MOUSETAIL *n* any of various N temperate ranunculaceous plants of the genus *Myosurus*, esp *M. minimus*, with tail-like flower spikes
MOUSETRAP *n* spring-loaded trap for killing mice
MOUSEY *same as* > MOUSY
MOUSIE *n* little mouse
MOUSIER > MOUSY
MOUSIES > MOUSIE
MOUSIEST > MOUSY
MOUSILY > MOUSY
MOUSINESS > MOUSY
MOUSING *n* lashing, shackle, etc, for closing off a hook to prevent a load from slipping off
MOUSINGS > MOUSING
MOUSLE *vb* handle roughly
MOUSLED > MOUSLE
MOUSLES > MOUSLE
MOUSLING > MOUSLE
MOUSME *n* Japanese girl
MOUSMEE *same as* > MOUSME
MOUSMEES > MOUSMEE
MOUSMES > MOUSME
MOUSSAKA *n* dish made with meat, aubergines, and tomatoes, topped with cheese sauce
MOUSSAKAS > MOUSSAKA
MOUSSE *n* dish of flavoured cream whipped and set ▷ *vb* apply mousse to

MOUSSED > MOUSSE
MOUSSES > MOUSSE
MOUSSING > MOUSSE
MOUST *same as* > MUST
MOUSTACHE *n* hair on the upper lip
MOUSTED > MOUST
MOUSTING > MOUST
MOUSTS > MOUST
MOUSY *adj* like a mouse, esp in hair colour
MOUTAN *n* variety of peony
MOUTANS > MOUTAN
MOUTER *same as* > MULTURE
MOUTERED > MOUTER
MOUTERER > MOUTER
MOUTERERS > MOUTER
MOUTERING > MOUTER
MOUTERS > MOUTER
MOUTH *n* opening in the head for eating and issuing sounds ▷ *vb* form (words) with the lips without speaking
MOUTHABLE *adj* able to be recited
MOUTHED > MOUTH
MOUTHER > MOUTH
MOUTHERS > MOUTH
MOUTHFEEL *n* texture of a substance as it is perceived in the mouth
MOUTHFUL *n* amount of food or drink put into the mouth at any one time when eating or drinking
MOUTHFULS > MOUTHFUL
MOUTHIER > MOUTHY
MOUTHIEST > MOUTHY
MOUTHILY > MOUTHY
MOUTHING > MOUTH
MOUTHLESS > MOUTH
MOUTHLIKE > MOUTH
MOUTHPART *n* any of the paired appendages in arthropods that surround the mouth and are specialized for feeding
MOUTHS > MOUTH
MOUTHWASH *n* medicated liquid for gargling and cleansing the mouth
MOUTHY *adj* bombastic
MOUTON *n* sheepskin processed to resemble the fur of another animal, esp beaver or seal
MOUTONNEE *n* rounded by action of glacier
MOUTONS > MOUTON
MOVABLE *adj* able to be moved or rearranged ▷ *n* movable article, esp a piece of furniture
MOVABLES > MOVABLE
MOVABLY > MOVABLE
MOVE *vb* change in place or position ▷ *n* moving
MOVEABLE *same as* > MOVABLE
MOVEABLES > MOVEABLE
MOVEABLY > MOVEABLE
MOVED > MOVE
MOVELESS *adj* immobile
MOVEMENT *n* action or process of moving
MOVEMENTS > MOVEMENT

MOVER *n* person or animal that moves in a particular way
MOVERS > MOVER
MOVES > MOVE
MOVIE *n* cinema film
MOVIEDOM *n* world of cinema
MOVIEDOMS > MOVIEDOM
MOVIEGOER *n* person who goes to cinema
MOVIELAND *same as* > MOVIEDOM
MOVIEOKE *n* entertainment in which people act out well-known scenes from movies that are silently playing in the background
MOVIEOKES > MOVIEOKE
MOVIEOLA *same as* > MOVIOLA
MOVIEOLAS > MOVIEOLA
MOVIES > MOVIE
MOVING *adj* arousing or touching the emotions
MOVINGLY > MOVING
MOVIOLA *n* viewing machine used in cutting and editing film
MOVIOLAS > MOVIOLA
MOW *vb* cut (grass or crops) ▷ *n* part of a barn where hay, straw, etc, is stored
MOWA *same as* > MAHUA
MOWAS > MOWA
MOWBURN *vb* heat up in mow
MOWBURNED > MOWBURN
MOWBURNS > MOWBURN
MOWBURNT *adj* (of hay, straw, etc) damaged by overheating in a mow
MOWDIE *Scot words for* > MOLE
MOWDIES > MOWDIE
MOWED > MOW
MOWER > MOW
MOWERS > MOW
MOWING > MOW
MOWINGS > MOW
MOWN > MOW
MOWRA *same as* > MAHUA
MOWRAS > MOWRA
MOWS > MOW
MOXA *n* downy material obtained from various plants and used in Oriental medicine by being burned on the skin as a cauterizing agent or counterirritant for the skin
MOXAS > MOXA
MOXIE *n* courage, nerve, or vigour
MOXIES > MOXIE
MOY *n* coin
MOYA *n* mud emitted from a volcano
MOYAS > MOYA
MOYGASHEL *n* type of linen
MOYITIES > MOIETY
MOYITY *same as* > MOIETY
MOYL *same as* > MOYLE
MOYLE *vb* toil
MOYLED > MOYLE
MOYLES > MOYLE
MOYLING > MOYLE
MOYLS > MOYL

m

MOYS > MOY
MOZ n hex ▷ vb jinx someone or something
MOZE vb give nap to
MOZED > MOZE
MOZES > MOZ
MOZETTA same as > MOZZETTA
MOZETTAS > MOZETTA
MOZETTE > MOZETTA
MOZING > MOZE
MOZO n porter in southwest USA
MOZOS > MOZO
MOZZ same as > MOZ
MOZZES > MOZZ
MOZZETTA n short hooded cape worn by the pope, cardinals, etc
MOZZETTAS > MOZZETTA
MOZZETTE > MOZZETTA
MOZZIE same as > MOSSIE
MOZZIES > MOZZIE
MOZZLE n luck
MOZZLES > MOZZLE
MPRET n former Albanian ruler
MPRETS > MPRET
MRIDAMGAM same as > MRIDANG
MRIDANG n drum used in Indian music
MRIDANGA same as > MRIDANG
MRIDANGAM same as > MRIDANG
MRIDANGAS > MRIDANGA
MRIDANGS > MRIDANG
MU n 12th letter in the Greek alphabet, a consonant, transliterated as m
MUCATE n salt of mucic acid
MUCATES > MUCATE
MUCH adj large amount or degree of ▷ n large amount or degree ▷ adv great degree
MUCHACHO n young man
MUCHACHOS > MUCHACHO
MUCHEL same as > MUCH
MUCHELL same as > MUCH
MUCHELLS > MUCHELL
MUCHELS > MUCHEL
MUCHES > MUCH
MUCHLY > MUCH
MUCHNESS n magnitude
MUCHO adv Spanish for very
MUCIC as in mucic acid colourless crystalline solid carboxylic acid found in milk sugar and used in the manufacture of pyrrole
MUCID adj mouldy, musty, or slimy
MUCIDITY > MUCID
MUCIDNESS > MUCID
MUCIGEN n substance present in mucous cells that is converted into mucin
MUCIGENS > MUCIGEN
MUCILAGE n gum or glue
MUCILAGES > MUCILAGE
MUCIN n any of a group of nitrogenous mucoproteins occurring in saliva, skin, tendon, etc, that produce

a very viscous solution in water
MUCINOGEN n substance forming mucin
MUCINOID adj of or like mucin
MUCINOUS > MUCIN
MUCINS > MUCIN
MUCK n dirt, filth
MUCKAMUCK n food ▷ vb consume food
MUCKED > MUCK
MUCKENDER n handkerchief
MUCKER n person who shifts broken rock or waste ▷ vb hoard
MUCKERED > MUCKER
MUCKERING > MUCKER
MUCKERISH > MUCKER
MUCKERS > MUCKER
MUCKHEAP n dunghill
MUCKHEAPS > MUCKHEAP
MUCKIER > MUCKY
MUCKIEST > MUCKY
MUCKILY > MUCKY
MUCKINESS > MUCKY
MUCKING > MUCK
MUCKLE same as > MICKLE
MUCKLES > MUCKLE
MUCKLUCK same as > MUKLUK
MUCKLUCKS > MUCKLUCK
MUCKRAKE n agricultural rake for spreading manure ▷ vb seek out and expose scandal, esp concerning public figures
MUCKRAKED > MUCKRAKE
MUCKRAKER > MUCKRAKE
MUCKRAKES > MUCKRAKE
MUCKS > MUCK
MUCKSWEAT n profuse sweat
MUCKWORM n any larva or worm that lives in mud
MUCKWORMS > MUCKWORM
MUCKY adj dirty or muddy
MUCLUC same as > MUKLUK
MUCLUCS > MUCLUC
MUCOID adj of the nature of or resembling mucin ▷ n substance like mucin
MUCOIDAL same as > MUCOID
MUCOIDS > MUCOID
MUCOLYTIC adj breaking down mucus
MUCOR n any fungus belonging to the genus Mucor, which comprises many common moulds
MUCORS > MUCOR
MUCOSA n mucous membrane: mucus-secreting membrane that lines body cavities or passages that are open to the external environment
MUCOSAE > MUCOSA
MUCOSAL > MUCOSA
MUCOSAS > MUCOSA
MUCOSE same as > MUCOUS
MUCOSITY > MUCOUS
MUCOUS adj of, resembling, or secreting mucus
MUCRO n short pointed projection from certain parts or organs, as from the tip of a leaf

MUCRONATE adj terminating in a sharp point
MUCRONES > MUCRO
MUCROS > MUCRO
MUCULENT adj like mucus
MUCUS n slimy secretion of the mucous membranes
MUCUSES > MUCUS
MUD n wet soft earth ▷ vb cover in mud
MUDBATH n medicinal bath in heated mud
MUDBATHS > MUDBATH
MUDBUG n crayfish
MUDBUGS > MUDBUG
MUDCAP vb use explosive charge in blasting
MUDCAPPED > MUDCAP
MUDCAPS > MUDCAP
MUDCAT n any of several large North American catfish living in muddy rivers, esp in the Mississippi valley
MUDCATS > MUDCAT
MUDDED > MUD
MUDDER n horse that runs well in mud
MUDDERS > MUDDER
MUDDIED > MUDDY
MUDDIER > MUDDY
MUDDIES > MUDDY
MUDDIEST > MUDDY
MUDDILY > MUDDY
MUDDINESS > MUDDY
MUDDING > MUD
MUDDLE vb confuse ▷ n state of confusion
MUDDLED > MUDDLE
MUDDLER n person who muddles or muddles through
MUDDLERS > MUDDLER
MUDDLES > MUDDLE
MUDDLIER > MUDDLE
MUDDLIEST > MUDDLE
MUDDLING > MUDDLE
MUDDLINGS > MUDDLE
MUDDLY > MUDDLE
MUDDY adj covered or filled with mud ▷ vb make muddy
MUDDYING > MUDDY
MUDEJAR n Spanish Moor, esp one permitted to stay in Spain after the Christian reconquest ▷ adj of or relating to a style of architecture orginated by Mudéjares
MUDEJARES > MUDEJAR
MUDEYE n larva of the dragonfly, commonly used as a fishing bait
MUDEYES > MUDEYE
MUDFISH n any of various fishes, such as the bowfin and cichlids, that live at or frequent the muddy bottoms of rivers, lakes, etc
MUDFISHES > MUDFISH
MUDFLAP n flap above wheel to deflect mud
MUDFLAPS > MUDFLAP
MUDFLAT n tract of low muddy land, esp near an estuary, that is covered at

high tide and exposed at low tide
MUDFLATS > MUDFLAT
MUDFLOW n flow of soil or fine-grained sediment mixed with water down a steep unstable slope
MUDFLOWS > MUDFLOW
MUDGE vb speak vaguely
MUDGED > MUDGE
MUDGER > MUDGE
MUDGERS > MUDGE
MUDGES > MUDGE
MUDGING > MUDGE
MUDGUARD n cover over a wheel to prevent mud or water being thrown up by it
MUDGUARDS > MUDGUARD
MUDHEN n water bird living in muddy place
MUDHENS > MUDHEN
MUDHOLE n hole with mud at bottom
MUDHOLES > MUDHOLE
MUDHOOK n anchor
MUDHOOKS > MUDHOOK
MUDIR n local governor
MUDIRIA n province of mudir
MUDIRIAS > MUDIRIA
MUDIRIEH same as > MUDIRIA
MUDIRIEHS > MUDIRIEH
MUDIRS > MUDIR
MUDLARK n street urchin ▷ vb play in mud
MUDLARKED > MUDLARK
MUDLARKS > MUDLARK
MUDLOGGER n person checking mud for traces of oil
MUDPACK n cosmetic paste applied to the face to improve the complexion
MUDPACKS > MUDPACK
MUDPUPPY n aquatic North American salamander of the genus with red feathery external gills and other persistent larval features
MUDRA n any of various ritual hand movements in Hindu religious dancing
MUDRAS > MUDRA
MUDROCK n type of sedimentary rock
MUDROCKS > MUDROCK
MUDROOM n room where muddy shoes may be left
MUDROOMS > MUDROOM
MUDS > MUD
MUDSCOW n boat for travelling over mudflats
MUDSCOWS > MUDSCOW
MUDSILL n support for building at or below ground
MUDSILLS > MUDSILL
MUDSLIDE n landslide of mud
MUDSLIDES > MUDSLIDE
MUDSTONE n dark grey clay rock similar to shale but with the lamination less well developed
MUDSTONES > MUDSTONE

MUDWORT n plant growing in mud

MUDWORTS > MUDWORT

MUEDDIN same as > MUEZZIN

MUEDDINS > MUEDDIN

MUENSTER n whitish-yellow semihard whole milk cheese, often flavoured with caraway or aniseed

MUENSTERS > MUENSTER

MUESLI n mixture of grain, nuts, and dried fruit, eaten with milk

MUESLIS > MUESLI

MUEZZIN n official who summons Muslims to prayer

MUEZZINS > MUEZZIN

MUFF n tube-shaped covering to keep the hands warm ▷ vb bungle (an action)

MUFFED > MUFF

MUFFIN n light round flat yeast cake

MUFFINEER n muffin dish

MUFFING > MUFF

MUFFINS > MUFFIN

MUFFISH > MUFF

MUFFLE vb wrap up for warmth or to deaden sound ▷ n something that muffles

MUFFLED > MUFFLE

MUFFLER n scarf

MUFFLERED adj with muffler

MUFFLERS > MUFFLER

MUFFLES > MUFFLE

MUFFLING > MUFFLE

MUFFS > MUFF

MUFLON same as > MOUFFLON

MUFLONS > MUFLON

MUFTI n civilian clothes worn by a person who usually wears a uniform

MUFTIS > MUFTI

MUG n large drinking cup ▷ vb attack in order to rob

MUGEARITE n crystalline rock

MUGFUL same as > MUG

MUGFULS > MUGFUL

MUGG same as > MUG

MUGGA n Australian eucalyptus tree with dark bark and pink flowers, Eucalyptus sideroxylon

MUGGAR same as > MUGGER

MUGGARS > MUGGAR

MUGGAS > MUGGA

MUGGED > MUG

MUGGEE n mugged person

MUGGEES > MUGGEE

MUGGER n person who commits robbery with violence, esp in the street

MUGGERS > MUGGER

MUGGIER > MUGGY

MUGGIEST > MUGGY

MUGGILY > MUGGY

MUGGINESS > MUGGY

MUGGING > MUG

MUGGINGS > MUG

MUGGINS n stupid or gullible person

MUGGINSES > MUGGINS

MUGGISH same as > MUGGY

MUGGS > MUG

MUGGUR same as > MUGGER

MUGGURS > MUGGUR

MUGGY adj (of weather) damp and stifling

MUGHAL same as > MOGUL

MUGHALS > MUGHAL

MUGS > MUG

MUGSHOT n police photograph of person's face

MUGSHOTS > MUGSHOT

MUGWORT n N temperate perennial herbaceous plant, Artemisia vulgaris, with aromatic leaves and clusters of small greenish-white flowers: family Asteraceae (composites)

MUGWORTS > MUGWORT

MUGWUMP n neutral or independent person, esp in politics

MUGWUMPS > MUGWUMP

MUHLIES > MUHLY

MUHLY n American grass

MUID n former French measure of capacity

MUIDS > MUID

MUIL same as > MULE

MUILS > MUIL

MUIR same as > MOOR

MUIRBURN same as > MOORBURN

MUIRBURNS > MUIRBURN

MUIRS > MUIR

MUIST same as > MUST

MUISTED > MUIST

MUISTING > MUIST

MUISTS > MUIST

MUJAHEDIN n Muslim guerrilla

MUJAHIDIN same as > MUJAHEDIN

MUJIK same as > MUZHIK

MUJIKS > MUJIK

MUKHTAR n lawyer in India

MUKHTARS > MUKHTAR

MUKLUK n soft boot, usually of sealskin, worn in the American Arctic

MUKLUKS > MUKLUK

MUKTUK n thin outer skin of the beluga, used as food

MUKTUKS > MUKTUK

MULATTA n female mulatto

MULATTAS > MULATTA

MULATTO n child of one Black and one White parent ▷ adj of a light brown colour

MULATTOES > MULATTO

MULATTOS > MULATTO

MULBERRY n tree whose leaves are used to feed silkworms ▷ adj dark purple

MULCH n mixture of wet straw, leaves, etc, used to protect the roots of plants ▷ vb cover (land) with mulch

MULCHED > MULCH

MULCHES > MULCH

MULCHING > MULCH

MULCT vb cheat or defraud ▷ n fine or penalty

MULCTED > MULCT

MULCTING > MULCT

MULCTS > MULCT

MULE n offspring of a horse and a donkey ▷ vb strike coin with different die on each side

MULED > MULE

MULES vb surgically remove folds of skin from a sheep

MULESED > MULES

MULESES > MULES

MULESING > MULES

MULETA n small cape attached to a stick used by the matador during the final stages of a bullfight

MULETAS > MULETA

MULETEER n mule driver

MULETEERS > MULETEER

MULEY adj (of cattle) having no horns ▷ n any hornless cow

MULEYS > MULEY

MULGA n Australian acacia shrub growing in desert regions

MULGAS > MULGA

MULING > MULE

MULISH adj obstinate

MULISHLY > MULISH

MULL vb think (over) or ponder ▷ n promontory or headland

MULLA same as > MULLAH

MULLAH n Muslim scholar, teacher, or religious leader

MULLAHISM n rule by mullahs

MULLAHS > MULLAH

MULLARKY same as > MALARKEY

MULLAS > MULLA

MULLED > MULL

MULLEIN n type of European plant

MULLEINS > MULLEIN

MULLEN same as > MULLEIN

MULLENS > MULLEN

MULLER n flat heavy implement of stone or iron used to grind material against a slab of stone

MULLERED adj drunk

MULLERS > MULLER

MULLET n edible sea fish

MULLETS > MULLET

MULLEY same as > MULEY

MULLEYS > MULLEY

MULLIGAN n stew made from odds and ends of food

MULLIGANS > MULLIGAN

MULLING > MULL

MULLION n vertical dividing bar in a window ▷ vb furnish (a window, screen, etc) with mullions

MULLIONED > MULLION

MULLIONS > MULLION

MULLITE n colourless mineral

MULLITES > MULLITE

MULLOCK n waste material from a mine

MULLOCKS > MULLOCK

MULLOCKY > MULLOCK

MULLOWAY n large Australian sea fish, valued for sport and food

MULLOWAYS > MULLOWAY

MULLS > MULL

MULMUL n muslin

MULMULL same as > MULMUL

MULMULLS > MULMULL

MULMULS > MULMUL

MULSE n drink containing honey

MULSES > MULSE

MULSH same as > MULCH

MULSHED > MULSH

MULSHES > MULSH

MULSHING > MULSH

MULTEITY n manifoldness

MULTIAGE adj involving different age groups

MULTIATOM adj involving many atoms

MULTIBAND adj involving more than one waveband

MULTIBANK adj involving more than one bank

MULTICAR adj involving several cars

MULTICAST n broadcast from one source simultaneously to several receivers on a network

MULTICELL adj involving many cells

MULTICIDE n mass murder

MULTICITY adj involving more than one city

MULTICOPY adj involving many copies

MULTIDAY adj involving more than one day

MULTIDISC adj involving more than one disc

MULTIDRUG adj involving more than one drug

MULTIFID adj having or divided into many lobes or similar segments

MULTIFIL n fibre made up of many filaments

MULTIFILS > MULTIFIL

MULTIFOIL n ornamental design having a large number of foils

MULTIFOLD adj many times doubled

MULTIFORM adj having many shapes or forms

MULTIGERM adj (of plants) having the ability to multiply germinate

MULTIGRID adj involving several grids

MULTIGYM n exercise apparatus incorporating a variety of weights, used for toning the muscles

MULTIGYMS > MULTIGYM

MULTIHUED adj having many colours

MULTIHULL n sailing vessel with two or more hulls

MULTIJET adj involving more than one jet

MULTILANE adj having several lanes

MULTILINE adj involving several lines

m

MULTILOBE adj having more than one lobe

MULTIMODE adj involving several modes

MULTIPACK n form of packaging of foodstuffs, etc, that contains several units and is offered at a price below that of the equivalent number of units

MULTIPAGE adj involving many pages

MULTIPARA n woman who has given birth to more than one viable fetus or living child

MULTIPART adj involving many parts

MULTIPATH adj relating to television or radio signals that travel by more than one route from a transmitter and arrive at slightly different times, causing ghost images or audio distortion

MULTIPED adj having many feet ▷ n insect or animal having many feet

MULTIPEDE same as > MULTIPED

MULTIPEDS > MULTIPED

MULTIPION adj involving many pions

MULTIPLE adj having many parts ▷ n quantity which contains another an exact number of times

MULTIPLES > MULTIPLE

MULTIPLET n set of closely spaced lines in a spectrum, resulting from small differences between the energy levels of atoms or molecules

MULTIPLEX n purpose-built complex containing several cinemas and usu restaurants and bars ▷ adj having many elements, complex ▷ vb send (messages or signals) or (of messages or signals) be sent by multiplex

MULTIPLY vb increase in number or degree

MULTIPOLE adj involving more than one pole

MULTIPORT adj involving more than one port

MULTIROLE adj having a number of roles, functions, etc

MULTIROOM adj having many rooms

MULTISITE adj involving more than one site

MULTISIZE adj involving more than size

MULTISTEP adj involving several steps

MULTITASK vb work at several different tasks simultaneously

MULTITON adj weighing several tons

MULTITONE adj involving more than one tone

MULTITUDE n great number

MULTIUNIT adj involving more than one unit

MULTIUSE adj suitable for more than one use

MULTIUSER > MULTIUSE

MULTIWALL adj involving several layers

MULTIYEAR adj involving more than one year

MULTUM n substance used in brewing

MULTUMS > MULTUM

MULTURE n fee formerly paid to a miller for grinding grain ▷ vb take multure

MULTURED > MULTURE

MULTURER > MULTURE

MULTURERS > MULTURE

MULTURES > MULTURE

MULTURING > MULTURE

MUM n mother ▷ vb act in a mummer's play

MUMBLE vb speak indistinctly, mutter ▷ n indistinct utterance

MUMBLED > MUMBLE

MUMBLER > MUMBLE

MUMBLERS > MUMBLE

MUMBLES > MUMBLE

MUMBLING > MUMBLE

MUMBLINGS > MUMBLE

MUMBLY > MUMBLE

MUMCHANCE adj silent

MUMM same as > MUM

MUMMED > MUM

MUMMER n actor in a traditional English folk play or mime

MUMMERIES > MUMMERY

MUMMERS > MUMMER

MUMMERY n performance by mummers

MUMMIA n mummified flesh used as medicine

MUMMIAS > MUMMIA

MUMMICHOG n small American fish

MUMMIED > MUMMY

MUMMIES > MUMMY

MUMMIFIED > MUMMIFY

MUMMIFIES > MUMMIFY

MUMMIFORM adj like mummy

MUMMIFY vb preserve the body of (a human or animal) as a mummy

MUMMING > MUM

MUMMINGS > MUM

MUMMOCK same as > MAMMOCK

MUMMOCKS > MUMMOCK

MUMMS > MUMM

MUMMY n body embalmed and wrapped for burial in ancient Egypt ▷ vb mummify

MUMMYING > MUMMY

MUMP vb be silent

MUMPED > MUMP

MUMPER > MUMP

MUMPERS > MUMP

MUMPING > MUMP

MUMPISH > MUMPS

MUMPISHLY > MUMPS

MUMPS n infectious disease with swelling in the glands

of the neck

MUMPSIMUS n opinion held obstinately

MUMS > MUM

MUMSIER > MUMSY

MUMSIEST > MUMSY

MUMSY adj out of fashion

MUMU n oven in Papua New Guinea

MUMUS > MUMU

MUN same as > MAUN

MUNCH vb chew noisily and steadily

MUNCHABLE > MUNCH

MUNCHED > MUNCH

MUNCHER > MUNCH

MUNCHERS > MUNCH

MUNCHES > MUNCH

MUNCHIES pl n craving for food, induced by alcohol or drugs

MUNCHING > MUNCH

MUNCHKIN n undersized person or a child, esp an appealing one

MUNCHKINS > MUNCHKIN

MUNDANE adj everyday

MUNDANELY > MUNDANE

MUNDANER > MUNDANE

MUNDANEST > MUNDANE

MUNDANITY > MUNDANE

MUNDIC n iron pyrites

MUNDICS > MUNDIC

MUNDIFIED > MUNDIFY

MUNDIFIES > MUNDIFY

MUNDIFY vb cleanse

MUNDUNGO n tripe in Spain

MUNDUNGOS > MUNDUNGO

MUNDUNGUS n smelly tobacco

MUNG vb process (computer data)

MUNGA n army canteen

MUNGAS > MUNGA

MUNGCORN n maslin

MUNGCORNS > MUNGCORN

MUNGED > MUNG

MUNGING > MUNG

MUNGO n cheap felted fabric made from waste wool

MUNGOES > MUNGO

MUNGOOSE same as > MONGOOSE

MUNGOOSES > MUNGOOSE

MUNGOS > MUNGO

MUNGS > MUNG

MUNI n municipal radio broadcast

MUNICIPAL adj relating to a city or town

MUNIFIED > MUNIFY

MUNIFIES > MUNIFY

MUNIFY vb fortify

MUNIFYING > MUNIFY

MUNIMENT n means of defence

MUNIMENTS pl n title deeds or similar documents

MUNIS > MUNI

MUNITE vb strengthen

MUNITED > MUNITE

MUNITES > MUNITE

MUNITING > MUNITE

MUNITION vb supply with munitions

MUNITIONS pl n military stores

MUNNION archaic word for > MULLION

MUNNIONS > MUNNION

MUNS > MUN

MUNSHI n secretary in India

MUNSHIS > MUNSHI

MUNSTER variant of > MUENSTER

MUNSTERS > MUNSTER

MUNT n derogatory word for a Black African

MUNTER n unattractive person

MUNTERS > MUNTER

MUNTIN n supporting or strengthening bar for a glass window, door, etc

MUNTING same as > MUNTIN

MUNTINGS > MUNTING

MUNTINS > MUNTIN

MUNTJAC n any small Asian deer of the genus Muntiacus, typically having a chestnut-brown coat, small antlers, and a barklike cry

MUNTJACS > MUNTJAC

MUNTJAK same as > MUNTJAC

MUNTJAKS > MUNTJAK

MUNTRIE n Australian shrub with green-red edible berries

MUNTRIES > MUNTRIE

MUNTS > MUNT

MUNTU same as > MUNT

MUNTUS > MUNTU

MUON n positive or negative elementary particle with a mass 207 times that of an electron

MUONIC > MUON

MUONIUM n form of hydrogen

MUONIUMS > MUONIUM

MUONS > MUON

MUPPET n stupid person

MUPPETS > MUPPET

MUQADDAM n person of authority in India

MUQADDAMS > MUQADDAM

MURA n group of people living together in Japanese countryside

MURAENA n moray eel

MURAENAS > MURAENA

MURAENID n eel of moray family

MURAENIDS > MURAENID

MURAGE n tax levied for the construction or maintenance of town walls

MURAGES > MURAGE

MURAL n painting on a wall ▷ adj of or relating to a wall

MURALED same as > MURALLED

MURALIST > MURAL

MURALISTS > MURAL

MURALLED adj decorated with mural

MURALS > MURAL

MURAS > MURA

MURDABAD interj down with

MURDER n unlawful intentional killing of a human being ▷ vb kill in this way

MURDERED > MURDER

MURDEREE n murder victim

MURDEREES > MURDEREE

MURDERER > MURDER

MURDERERS > MURDER

MURDERESS > MURDER

MURDERING > MURDER

MURDEROUS adj intending, capable of, or guilty of murder

MURDERS > MURDER

MURE archaic or literary word for > IMMURE

MURED > MURE

MUREIN n polymer found in cells

MUREINS > MUREIN

MURENA same as > MURAENA

MURENAS > MURENA

MURES > MURE

MUREX n any of various spiny-shelled marine gastropods of the genus Murex and related genera: formerly used as a source of the dye Tyrian purple

MUREXES > MUREX

MURGEON vb grimace at

MURGEONED > MURGEON

MURGEONS > MURGEON

MURIATE obsolete name for a > CHLORIDE

MURIATED > MURIATE

MURIATES > MURIATE

MURIATIC as in muriatic acid former name for a strong acid used in many industrial processes

MURICATE adj having a surface roughened by numerous short points

MURICATED same as > MURICATE

MURICES > MUREX

MURID n animal of mouse family

MURIDS > MURID

MURIFORM adj like mouse

MURINE adj of, relating to, or belonging to the Muridae, an Old World family of rodents, typically having long hairless tails: includes rats and mice ▷ n any animal belonging to the Muridae

MURINES > MURINE

MURING > MURE

MURK n thick darkness ▷ adj dark or gloomy

MURKER > MURK

MURKEST > MURK

MURKIER > MURKY

MURKIEST > MURKY

MURKILY > MURKY

MURKINESS > MURKY

MURKISH > MURK

MURKLY > MURK

MURKS > MURK

MURKSOME > MURK

MURKY adj dark or gloomy

MURL vb crumble

MURLAIN n type of basket

MURLAINS > MURLAIN

MURLAN same as > MURLAIN

MURLANS > MURLAN

MURLED > MURL

MURLIER > MURL

MURLIEST > MURL

MURLIN same as > MURLAIN

MURLING > MURL

MURLINS > MURLIN

MURLS > MURL

MURLY > MURL

MURMUR vb speak or say in a quiet indistinct way ▷ n continuous low indistinct sound

MURMURED > MURMUR

MURMURER > MURMUR

MURMURERS > MURMUR

MURMURING > MURMUR

MURMUROUS > MURMUR

MURMURS > MURMUR

MURPHIES > MURPHY

MURPHY dialect or informal word for > POTATO

MURR n former name for a cold

MURRA same as > MURRHINE

MURRAGH n type of large caddis fly

MURRAGHS > MURRAGH

MURRAIN n cattle plague

MURRAINED > MURRAIN

MURRAINS > MURRAIN

MURRAM n type of gravel

MURRAMS > MURRAM

MURRAS > MURRA

MURRAY n large Australian freshwater fish

MURRAYS > MURRAY

MURRE n any guillemot of the genus Uria

MURREE n native Australian

MURREES > MURREE

MURRELET n any of several small diving birds of the genus Brachyramphus and related genera, similar and related to the auks: family Alcidae, order Charadriiformes

MURRELETS > MURRELET

MURREN same as > MURRAIN

MURRENS > MURREN

MURRES > MURRE

MURREY adj mulberry colour

MURREYS > MURREY

MURRHA same as > MURRA

MURRHAS > MURRHA

MURRHINE adj of or relating to an unknown substance used in ancient Rome to make vases, cups, etc ▷ n substance so used

MURRI same as > MURREE

MURRIES > MURRY

MURRIN same as > MURRAIN

MURRINE same as > MURRHINE

MURRINS > MURRIN

MURRION same as > MURRAIN

MURRIONS > MURRION

MURRIS > MURRI

MURRS > MURR

MURRY same as > MORAY

MURTHER same as > MURDER

MURTHERED > MURTHER

MURTHERER > MURTHER

MURTHERS > MURTHER

MURTI n image of a deity, which itself is considered divine once consecrated

MURTIS > MURTI

MURVA n type of hemp

MURVAS > MURVA

MUS > MU

MUSACEOUS adj of, relating to, a family of tropical flowering plants with large leaves and clusters of elongated berry fruits: includes the banana, edible plantain, and Manila hemp

MUSANG n catlike aninal of Malaysia

MUSANGS > MUSANG

MUSAR n rabbinic literature concerned with ethics, right conduct, etc

MUSARS > MUSAR

MUSCA n small constellation in the S hemisphere lying between the Southern Cross and Chamaeleon

MUSCADEL same as > MUSCATEL

MUSCADELS > MUSCADEL

MUSCADET n white grape, grown esp in the Loire valley, used for making wine

MUSCADETS > MUSCADET

MUSCADIN n Parisian dandy

MUSCADINE n woody climbing vitaceous plant, Vitis rotundifolia, of the southeastern US

MUSCADINS > MUSCADIN

MUSCAE > MUSCA

MUSCARINE n poisonous alkaloid occurring in certain mushrooms

MUSCAT same as > MUSCATEL

MUSCATEL n rich sweet wine made from muscat grapes

MUSCATELS > MUSCATEL

MUSCATS > MUSCAT

MUSCAVADO same as > MUSCOVADO

MUSCID n any fly of the dipterous family Muscidae, including the housefly and tsetse fly ▷ adj of, relating to, or belonging to the Muscidae

MUSCIDS > MUSCID

MUSCLE n tissue in the body which produces movement by contracting ▷ vb force one's way (in)

MUSCLED > MUSCLE

MUSCLEMAN n man with highly developed muscles

MUSCLEMEN > MUSCLEMAN

MUSCLES > MUSCLE

MUSCLIER > MUSCLE

MUSCLIEST > MUSCLE

MUSCLING > MUSCLE

MUSCLINGS > MUSCLE

MUSCLY > MUSCLE

MUSCOID adj of family of plants

MUSCOLOGY n branch of botany

MUSCONE same as > MUSKONE

MUSCONES > MUSCONE

MUSCOSE adj like moss

MUSCOVADO n raw sugar

obtained from the juice of sugar cane by evaporating the molasses

MUSCOVITE n pale brown, or green, or colourless mineral of the mica group

MUSCULAR adj with well-developed muscles

MUSCULOUS adj muscular

MUSE vb ponder quietly ▷ n state of abstraction

MUSED > MUSE

MUSEFUL > MUSE

MUSEFULLY > MUSE

MUSEOLOGY n science of museum organization

MUSER > MUSE

MUSERS > MUSE

MUSES > MUSE

MUSET same as > MUSIT

MUSETS > MUSET

MUSETTE n type of bagpipe with a bellows popular in France during the 17th and 18th centuries

MUSETTES > MUSETTE

MUSEUM n building where natural, artistic, historical, or scientific objects are exhibited and preserved

MUSEUMS > MUSEUM

MUSH n soft pulpy mass ▷ interj order to dogs in a sled team to start up or go faster ▷ vb travel by or drive a dogsled

MUSHA interj Irish exclamation of surprise

MUSHED > MUSH

MUSHER > MUSH

MUSHERS > MUSH

MUSHES > MUSH

MUSHIER > MUSHY

MUSHIEST > MUSHY

MUSHILY > MUSHY

MUSHINESS > MUSHY

MUSHING > MUSH

MUSHMOUTH n person speaking indistinctly

MUSHROOM n edible fungus with a stem and cap ▷ vb grow rapidly

MUSHROOMS > MUSHROOM

MUSHY adj soft and pulpy

MUSIC n art form using a melodious and harmonious combination of notes ▷ vb play music

MUSICAL adj of or like music ▷ n play or film with songs and dancing

MUSICALE n party or social evening with a musical programme

MUSICALES > MUSICALE

MUSICALLY > MUSICAL

MUSICALS > MUSICAL

MUSICIAN n person who plays or composes music, esp as a profession

MUSICIANS > MUSICIAN

MUSICK same as > MUSIC

MUSICKED > MUSIC

MUSICKER > MUSIC

MUSICKERS > MUSIC

MUSICKING > MUSIC

MUSICKS > MUSICK

m

MUSICLESS > MUSIC
MUSICS > MUSIC
MUSIMON same
　as > MOUFFLON
MUSIMONS > MUSIMON
MUSING > MUSE
MUSINGLY > MUSE
MUSINGS > MUSE
MUSIT n gap in fence
MUSITS > MUSIT
MUSIVE adj mosaic
MUSJID same as > MASJID
MUSJIDS > MUSJID
MUSK n scent obtained from
　a gland of the musk deer
　or produced synthetically
　▷ vb perfume with musk
MUSKED > MUSK
MUSKEG n area of undrained
　boggy land
MUSKEGS > MUSKEG
MUSKET n long-barrelled
　gun
MUSKETEER n (formerly)
　a soldier armed with a
　musket
MUSKETOON n small musket
MUSKETRY n (use of)
　muskets
MUSKETS > MUSKET
MUSKIE n large North
　American freshwater game
　fish,
MUSKIER > MUSKIE
MUSKIES > MUSKIE
MUSKIEST > MUSKIE
MUSKILY > MUSKY
MUSKINESS > MUSKY
MUSKING > MUSK
MUSKIT same as > MESQUITE
MUSKITS > MUSKIT
MUSKLE same as > MUSSEL
MUSKLES > MUSKLE
MUSKMELON n any of several
　varieties of melon, such
　as the cantaloupe and
　honeydew
MUSKONE n substance in
　musk
MUSKONES > MUSKONE
MUSKOX n large Canadian
　mammal
MUSKOXEN > MUSKOX
MUSKRAT n N American
　beaver-like rodent
MUSKRATS > MUSKRAT
MUSKROOT same
　as > MOSCHATEL
MUSKROOTS > MUSKROOT
MUSKS > MUSK
MUSKY same as > MUSKIE
MUSLIN n fine cotton fabric
MUSLINED adj wearing
　muslin
MUSLINET n coarse muslin
MUSLINETS > MUSLINET
MUSLINS > MUSLIN
MUSMON same as > MUSIMON
MUSMONS > MUSMON
MUSO n musician, esp a
　pop musician, regarded
　as being overconcerned
　with technique rather
　than musical content or
　expression
MUSOS > MUSO
MUSPIKE n Canadian

freshwater fish
MUSPIKES > MUSPIKE
MUSQUASH same
　as > MUSKRAT
MUSROL n part of bridle
MUSROLS > MUSROL
MUSS vb make untidy ▷ n
　state of disorder
MUSSE same as > MUSS
MUSSED > MUSS
MUSSEL n edible shellfish
　with a dark hinged shell
MUSSELLED adj poisoned
　through eating bad
　mussels
MUSSELS > MUSSEL
MUSSES > MUSS
MUSSIER > MUSSY
MUSSIEST > MUSSY
MUSSILY > MUSSY
MUSSINESS > MUSSY
MUSSING > MUSS
MUSSITATE vb mutter
MUSSY adj untidy or
　disordered
MUST vb used as an auxiliary
　to express obligation,
　certainty, or resolution
　▷ n essential or necessary
　thing ▷ vb powder
MUSTACHE same
　as > MOUSTACHE
MUSTACHED > MUSTACHE
MUSTACHES > MUSTACHE
MUSTACHIO n moustache,
　esp a bushy or elaborate
　one
MUSTANG n wild horse of
　SW USA
MUSTANGS > MUSTANG
MUSTARD n paste made from
　the powdered seeds of a
　plant, used as a condiment
　▷ adj brownish-yellow
MUSTARDS > MUSTARD
MUSTARDY > MUSTARD
MUSTED > MUST
MUSTEE n offspring of a
　White and a quadroon
MUSTEES > MUSTEE
MUSTELID n member of
　weasel family
MUSTELIDS > MUSTELID
MUSTELINE adj of, relating
　to, or belonging to
　the Mustelidae, family
　of typically predatory
　mammals including
　weasels, ferrets, minks,
　polecats, badgers, skunks,
　and otters: order Carnivora
　(carnivores) ▷ n any
　musteline animal
MUSTER vb summon up
　(strength, energy, or
　support) ▷ n assembly of
　military personnel
MUSTERED > MUSTER
MUSTERER > MUSTER
MUSTERERS > MUSTER
MUSTERING > MUSTER
MUSTERS > MUSTER
MUSTH n state of frenzied
　sexual excitement in the
　males of certain large
　mammals, esp elephants,
　associated with discharge

from a gland between the
　ear and eye
MUSTHS > MUSTH
MUSTIER > MUSTY
MUSTIEST > MUSTY
MUSTILY > MUSTY
MUSTINESS > MUSTY
MUSTING > MUST
MUSTS > MUST
MUSTY adj smelling mouldy
　and stale
MUT another word for > EM
MUTABLE adj liable to
　change
MUTABLY > MUTABLE
MUTAGEN n any substance
　that can induce genetic
　mutation
MUTAGENIC > MUTAGEN
MUTAGENS > MUTAGEN
MUTANDA > MUTANDUM
MUTANDUM n something to
　be changed
MUTANT n mutated animal,
　plant, etc ▷ adj of or
　resulting from mutation
MUTANTS > MUTANT
MUTASE n type of enzyme
MUTASES > MUTASE
MUTATE vb (cause to)
　undergo mutation
MUTATED > MUTATE
MUTATES > MUTATE
MUTATING > MUTATE
MUTATION same
　as > MUTANT
MUTATIONS > MUTATION
MUTATIVE > MUTATE
MUTATORY adj subject to
　change
MUTCH n close-fitting linen
　cap formerly worn by
　women and children in
　Scotland ▷ vb cadge
MUTCHED > MUTCH
MUTCHES > MUTCH
MUTCHING > MUTCH
MUTCHKIN n Scottish unit
　of liquid measure equal to
　slightly less than one pint
MUTCHKINS > MUTCHKIN
MUTE adj silent ▷ n person
　who is unable to speak
　▷ vb reduce the volume or
　soften the tone of a musical
　instrument by means of a
　mute or soft pedal
MUTED adj (of sound or
　colour) softened
MUTEDLY > MUTED
MUTELY > MUTE
MUTENESS > MUTE
MUTER > MUTE
MUTES > MUTE
MUTEST > MUTE
MUTHA n taboo slang word
　derived from motherfucker
MUTHAS > MUTHA
MUTI n medicine, esp herbal
　medicine
MUTICATE same
　as > MUTICOUS
MUTICOUS adj lacking an
　awn, spine, or point
MUTILATE vb deprive of a
　limb or other part
MUTILATED > MUTILATE

MUTILATES > MUTILATE
MUTILATOR > MUTILATE
MUTINE vb mutiny
MUTINED > MUTINE
MUTINEER n person who
　mutinies
MUTINEERS > MUTINEER
MUTINES > MUTINE
MUTING > MUTE
MUTINIED > MUTINY
MUTINIES > MUTINY
MUTINING > MUTINE
MUTINOUS adj openly
　rebellious
MUTINY n rebellion against
　authority, esp by soldiers
　or sailors ▷ vb commit
　mutiny
MUTINYING > MUTINY
MUTIS > MUTI
MUTISM n state of being
　mute
MUTISMS > MUTISM
MUTON n part of gene
MUTONS > MUTON
MUTOSCOPE n early form of
　cine camera
MUTS > MUT
MUTT n mongrel dog
MUTTER vb utter or speak
　indistinctly ▷ n muttered
　sound or grumble
MUTTERED > MUTTER
MUTTERER > MUTTER
MUTTERERS > MUTTER
MUTTERING > MUTTER
MUTTERS > MUTTER
MUTTON n flesh of sheep,
　used as food
MUTTONS > MUTTON
MUTTONY > MUTTON
MUTTS > MUTT
MUTUAL adj felt or expressed
　by each of two people
　about the other ▷ n
　mutual company
MUTUALISE same
　as > MUTUALIZE
MUTUALISM another name
　for > SYMBIOSIS
MUTUALIST > MUTUALISM
MUTUALITY > MUTUAL
MUTUALIZE vb make or
　become mutual
MUTUALLY > MUTUAL
MUTUALS > MUTUAL
MUTUCA same as > MOTUCA
MUTUCAS > MUTUCA
MUTUEL n system of betting
　in which those who have
　bet on the winners of a race
　share in the total amount
　wagered less a percentage
　for the management
MUTUELS > MUTUEL
MUTULAR > MUTULE
MUTULE n one of a set of flat
　blocks below the corona of
　a Doric cornice
MUTULES > MUTULE
MUTUUM n contract for loan
　of goods
MUTUUMS > MUTUUM
MUUMUU n loose brightly-
　coloured dress worn by
　women in Hawaii
MUUMUUS > MUUMUU

MUX *vb* spoil
MUXED > MUX
MUXES > MUX
MUXING > MUX
MUZAKY *adj* having a bland sound
MUZHIK *n* Russian peasant, esp under the tsars
MUZHIKS > MUZHIK
MUZJIK *same as* > MUZHIK
MUZJIKS > MUZJIK
MUZZ *vb* make (something) muzzy
MUZZED > MUZZ
MUZZES > MUZZ
MUZZIER > MUZZY
MUZZIEST > MUZZY
MUZZILY > MUZZY
MUZZINESS > MUZZY
MUZZING > MUZZ
MUZZLE *n* animal's mouth and nose ▷ *vb* prevent from being heard or noticed
MUZZLED > MUZZLE
MUZZLER > MUZZLE
MUZZLERS > MUZZLE
MUZZLES > MUZZLE
MUZZLING > MUZZLE
MUZZY *adj* confused or muddled
MVULE *n* tropical African tree
MVULES > MVULE
MWALIMU *n* teacher
MWALIMUS > MWALIMU
MY *adj* belonging to me ▷ *interj* exclamation of surprise or awe ▷ *determiner* of, belonging to, or associated with the speaker or writer (me)
MYAL > MYALISM
MYALGIA *n* pain in a muscle or a group of muscles
MYALGIAS > MYALGIA
MYALGIC > MYALGIA
MYALISM *n* kind of witchcraft, similar to obi, practised esp in the Caribbean
MYALISMS > MYALISM
MYALIST > MYALISM
MYALISTS > MYALISM
MYALL *n* Australian acacia with hard scented wood
MYALLS > MYALL
MYASES > MYASIS
MYASIS *same as* > MYIASIS
MYC *n* oncogene that aids the growth of tumorous cells
MYCELE *n* microscopic spike-like structure in mucus
MYCELES > MYCELE
MYCELIA > MYCELIUM
MYCELIAL > MYCELIUM
MYCELIAN > MYCELIUM
MYCELIUM *n* mass forming the body of a fungus
MYCELLA *n* blue-veined Danish cream cheese, less strongly flavoured than Danish blue
MYCELLAS > MYCELLA
MYCELOID > MYCELIUM

MYCETES *n* fungus
MYCETOMA *n* chronic fungal infection, esp of the foot, characterized by swelling, usually resulting from a wound
MYCETOMAS > MYCETOMA
MYCOBIONT *n* fungal constituent of a lichen
MYCOFLORA *n* all fungus growing in particular place
MYCOLOGIC > MYCOLOGY
MYCOLOGY *n* study of fungi
MYCOPHAGY *n* eating of mushrooms
MYCOPHILE *n* person who likes eating mushrooms
MYCORHIZA *n* association of a fungus and a plant in which the fungus lives within or on the outside of the plant's roots forming a symbiotic or parasitic relationship
MYCOSES > MYCOSIS
MYCOSIS *n* any infection or disease caused by fungus
MYCOTIC > MYCOSIS
MYCOTOXIN *n* any of various toxic substances produced by fungi some of which may affect food and others of which are alleged to have been used in warfare
MYCOVIRUS *n* virus attacking fungi
MYCS > MYC
MYDRIASES > MYDRIASIS
MYDRIASIS *n* abnormal dilation of the pupil of the eye, produced by drugs, coma, etc
MYDRIATIC *adj* relating to or causing mydriasis ▷ *n* mydriatic drug
MYELIN *n* white tissue forming an insulating sheath around certain nerve fibres
MYELINE *same as* > MYELIN
MYELINES > MYELINE
MYELINIC > MYELIN
MYELINS > MYELIN
MYELITIS *n* inflammation of the spinal cord or of the bone marrow
MYELOCYTE *n* immature granulocyte, normally occurring in the bone marrow but detected in the blood in certain diseases
MYELOGRAM *n* X-ray of the spinal cord, after injection with a radio-opaque medium
MYELOID *adj* of or relating to the spinal cord or the bone marrow
MYELOMA *n* tumour of the bone marrow
MYELOMAS > MYELOMA
MYELOMATA > MYELOMA
MYELON *n* spinal cord
MYELONS > MYELON
MYGALE *n* large American spider
MYGALES > MYGALE

MYIASES > MYIASIS
MYIASIS *n* infestation of the body by the larvae of flies
MYIOPHILY *same as* > MYOPHILY
MYLAR *n* tradename for a kind of strong polyester film
MYLARS > MYLAR
MYLODON *n* prehistoric giant sloth
MYLODONS > MYLODON
MYLODONT *same as* > MYLODON
MYLODONTS > MYLODONT
MYLOHYOID *n* muscle in neck
MYLONITE *n* fine-grained metamorphic rock, often showing banding and micaceous fracture, formed by the crushing, grinding, or rolling of the original structure
MYLONITES > MYLONITE
MYLONITIC > MYLONITE
MYNA *same as* > MYNAH
MYNAH *n* tropical Asian starling which can mimic human speech
MYNAHS > MYNAH
MYNAS > MYNA
MYNHEER *n* Dutch title of address
MYNHEERS > MYNHEER
MYOBLAST *n* cell from which muscle develops
MYOBLASTS > MYOBLAST
MYOCARDIA *pl n* muscular tissues of the heart
MYOCLONIC > MYOCLONUS
MYOCLONUS *n* sudden involuntary muscle contraction
MYOFIBRIL *n* type of cell in muscle
MYOGEN *n* albumin found in muscle
MYOGENIC *adj* originating in or forming muscle tissue
MYOGENS > MYOGEN
MYOGLOBIN *n* protein that is the main oxygen-carrier of muscle
MYOGRAM *n* tracings of muscular contractions
MYOGRAMS > MYOGRAM
MYOGRAPH *n* instrument for recording tracings of muscular contractions
MYOGRAPHS > MYOGRAPH
MYOGRAPHY > MYOGRAPH
MYOID *adj* like muscle
MYOLOGIC > MYOLOGY
MYOLOGIES > MYOLOGY
MYOLOGIST > MYOLOGY
MYOLOGY *n* branch of medical science concerned with the structure and diseases of muscles
MYOMA *n* benign tumour composed of muscle tissue
MYOMANCY *n* divination through observing mice
MYOMANTIC > MYOMANCY
MYOMAS > MYOMA

MYOMATA > MYOMA
MYOMATOUS > MYOMA
MYONEURAL *adj* involving muscle and nerve
MYOPATHIC > MYOPATHY
MYOPATHY *n* any disease affecting muscles or muscle tissue
MYOPE *n* any person afflicted with myopia
MYOPES > MYOPE
MYOPHILY *n* pollination of plants by flies
MYOPIA *n* short-sightedness
MYOPIAS > MYOPIA
MYOPIC *n* shortsighted person
MYOPICS > MYOPIC
MYOPIES > MYOPY
MYOPS *same as* > MYOPE
MYOPSES > MYOPS
MYOPY *same as* > MYOPIA
MYOSCOPE *n* electrical instrument for stimulating muscles
MYOSCOPES > MYOSCOPE
MYOSES > MYOSIS
MYOSIN *n* chief protein of muscle that interacts with actin to form actomyosin during muscle contraction
MYOSINS > MYOSIN
MYOSIS *same as* > MIOSIS
MYOSITIS *n* inflammation of muscle
MYOSOTE *same as* > MYOSOTIS
MYOSOTES > MYOSOTE
MYOSOTIS *n* any plant of the boraginaceous genus *Myosotis*
MYOTIC > MIOSIS
MYOTICS > MIOSIS
MYOTOME *n* any segment of embryonic mesoderm that develops into skeletal muscle in the adult
MYOTOMES > MYOTOME
MYOTONIA *n* lack of muscle tone, frequently including muscle spasm or rigidity
MYOTONIAS > MYOTONIA
MYOTONIC > MYOTONIA
MYOTUBE *n* cylindrical cell in muscle
MYOTUBES > MYOTUBE
MYRBANE *same as* > MIRBANE
MYRBANES > MYRBANE
MYRIAD *adj* innumerable ▷ *n* large indefinite number
MYRIADS > MYRIAD
MYRIADTH > MYRIAD
MYRIADTHS > MYRIAD
MYRIAPOD *n* invertebrate with a long segmented body and many legs, such as a centipede ▷ *adj* of, relating to, or belonging to the *Myriapoda*
MYRIAPODS > MYRIAPOD
MYRICA *n* dried root bark of the wax myrtle, used as a tonic and to treat diarrhoea
MYRICAS > MYRICA
MYRINGA *n* eardrum

MYRINGAS > MYRINGA
MYRIOPOD *same as* > MYRIAPOD
MYRIOPODS > MYRIOPOD
MYRIORAMA *n* picture made up of different parts
MYRISTIC *adj* of nutmeg plant family
MYRMECOID *adj* like ant
MYRMIDON *n* follower or henchman
MYRMIDONS > MYRMIDON
MYROBALAN *n* dried plumlike fruit of various tropical trees of the genus *Terminalia*, used in dyeing, tanning, ink, and medicine
MYRRH *n* aromatic gum used in perfume, incense, and medicine
MYRRHIC > MYRRH
MYRRHINE > MURRA
MYRRHOL *n* oil of myrrh
MYRRHOLS > MYRRHOL
MYRRHS > MYRRH
MYRTLE *n* flowering evergreen shrub
MYRTLES > MYRTLE
MYSELF *pron* reflexive form of *I* or *me*
MYSID *n* small shrimplike crustacean
MYSIDS > MYSID
MYSOST *n* Norwegian cheese
MYSOSTS > MYSOST
MYSTAGOG *n* person instructing others in religious mysteries
MYSTAGOGS > MYSTAGOG
MYSTAGOGY *n* instruction of those who are preparing for initiation into the mysteries
MYSTERIES > MYSTERY
MYSTERY *n* strange or inexplicable event or phenomenon
MYSTIC *n* person who seeks spiritual knowledge ▷ *adj* mystical
MYSTICAL *adj* having a spiritual or religious significance beyond human understanding
MYSTICETE *n* species of whale
MYSTICISM *n* belief in or experience of a reality beyond normal human understanding or experience
MYSTICLY > MYSTIC
MYSTICS > MYSTIC
MYSTIFIED > MYSTIFY
MYSTIFIER > MYSTIFY
MYSTIFIES > MYSTIFY
MYSTIFY *vb* bewilder or puzzle
MYSTIQUE *n* aura of mystery or power
MYSTIQUES > MYSTIQUE
MYTH *n* tale with supernatural characters, usu of how the world and mankind began
MYTHI > MYTHUS
MYTHIC *same as* > MYTHICAL
MYTHICAL *adj* of or relating to myth
MYTHICISE *same as* > MYTHICIZE
MYTHICISM *n* theory that explains miracles as myths
MYTHICIST > MYTHICIZE
MYTHICIZE *vb* make into or treat as a myth
MYTHIER > MYTHY
MYTHIEST > MYTHY
MYTHISE *same as* > MYTHIZE
MYTHISED > MYTHISE
MYTHISES > MYTHISE
MYTHISING > MYTHISE
MYTHISM *same as* > MYTHICISM
MYTHISMS > MYTHISM
MYTHIST > MYTHISM
MYTHISTS > MYTHISM
MYTHIZE *same as* > MYTHICIZE
MYTHIZED > MYTHIZE
MYTHIZES > MYTHIZE
MYTHIZING > MYTHIZE
MYTHMAKER *n* person who creates myth
MYTHOI > MYTHOS
MYTHOLOGY *n* myths collectively
MYTHOMANE *n* obsession with lying, exaggerating, or relating incredible imaginary adventures as if they had really happened
MYTHOPEIC *adj* of myths
MYTHOPOET *n* poet writing on mythical theme
MYTHOS *n* complex of beliefs, values, attitudes, etc, characteristic of a specific group or society
MYTHS > MYTH
MYTHUS *same as* > MYTHOS
MYTHY *adj* of or like myth
MYTILOID *adj* like mussel
MYXAMEBA *same as* > MYXAMOEBA
MYXAMEBAE > MYXAMEBA
MYXAMEBAS > MYXAMEBA
MYXAMOEBA *n* cell produced by spore
MYXEDEMA *same as* > MYXOEDEMA
MYXEDEMAS > MYXEDEMA
MYXEDEMIC > MYXOEDEMA
MYXO *n* infectious and usually fatal viral disease of rabbits characterized by swelling of the mucous membranes and formation of skin tumours
MYXOCYTE *n* cell in mucous tissue
MYXOCYTES > MYXOCYTE
MYXOEDEMA *n* disease caused by an underactive thyroid gland, characterized by puffy eyes, face, and hands, and mental sluggishness
MYXOID *adj* containing mucus
MYXOMA *n* tumour composed of mucous connective tissue, usually situated in subcutaneous tissue
MYXOMAS > MYXOMA
MYXOMATA > MYXOMA
MYXOS > MYXO
MYXOVIRAL > MYXOVIRUS
MYXOVIRUS *n* any of a group of viruses that cause influenza, mumps, and certain other diseases
MZEE *n* old person ▷ *adj* advanced in years
MZEES > MZEE
MZUNGU *n* White person
MZUNGUS > MZUNGU

Nn

NA *same as* > NAE

NAAM *same as* > NAM

NAAMS > NAAM

NAAN *n* slightly leavened flat Indian bread

NAANS > NAAN

NAARTJE *same as* > NAARTJIE

NAARTJES > NAARTJE

NAARTJIE *n* tangerine

NAARTJIES > NAARTJIE

NAB *vb* arrest (someone)

NABBED > NAB

NABBER *n* thief

NABBERS > NABBER

NABBING > NAB

NABE *n* Japanese hotpot

NABES > NABE

NABIS *n* Parisian art movement

NABK *n* edible berry

NABKS > NABK

NABLA *another name* for > DEL

NABLAS > NABLA

NABOB *same as* > NAWAB

NABOBERY > NABOB

NABOBESS *n* rich, powerful, or important woman

NABOBISH > NABOB

NABOBISM > NABOB

NABOBISMS > NABOB

NABOBS > NABOB

NABS > NAB

NACARAT *n* red-orange colour

NACARATS > NACARAT

NACELLE *n* streamlined enclosure on an aircraft, esp one housing an engine

NACELLES > NACELLE

NACH *n* Indian dance

NACHAS *n* pleasure

NACHE *n* rump

NACHES *same as* > NACHAS

NACHO *n* snack of a piece of tortilla topped with cheese, peppers, etc

NACHOS > NACHO

NACHTMAAL *same as* > NAGMAAL

NACKET *n* light lunch, snack

NACKETS > NACKET

NACRE *n* mother of pearl

NACRED > NACRE

NACREOUS *adj* relating to or consisting of mother-of-pearl

NACRES > NACRE

NACRITE *n* mineral

NACRITES > NACRITE

NACROUS > NACRE

NADA *n* nothing

NADAS > NADA

NADIR *n* point in the sky opposite the zenith

NADIRAL > NADIR

NADIRS > NADIR

NADORS *n* thirst brought on by excessive consumption of alcohol

NADS *pl n* testicles

NAE *Scot word for* > NO

NAEBODIES > NAEBODY

NAEBODY *Scots variant of* > NOBODY

NAETHING *Scots variant of* > NOTHING

NAETHINGS > NAETHING

NAEVE *n* birthmark

NAEVES > NAEVUS

NAEVI > NAEVUS

NAEVOID > NAEVUS

NAEVUS *n* birthmark or mole

NAFF *adj* lacking quality or taste ▷ *vb* go away

NAFFED > NAFF

NAFFER > NAFF

NAFFEST > NAFF

NAFFING > NAFF

NAFFLY > NAFF

NAFFNESS > NAFF

NAFFS > NAFF

NAG *vb* scold or find fault constantly ▷ *n* person who nags

NAGA *n* cobra

NAGANA *n* disease of all domesticated animals of central and southern Africa

NAGANAS > NAGANA

NAGAPIE *n* bushbaby

NAGAPIES > NAGAPIE

NAGARI *n* set of scripts used as the writing systems for several languages of India

NAGARIS > NAGARI

NAGAS > NAGA

NAGGED > NAG

NAGGER > NAG

NAGGERS > NAG

NAGGIER > NAG

NAGGIEST > NAG

NAGGING > NAG

NAGGINGLY > NAG

NAGGY > NAG

NAGMAAL *n* Communion

NAGMAALS > NAGMAAL

NAGOR *another name* for > REEDBUCK

NAGORS > NAGOR

NAGS > NAG

NAH *same as* > NO

NAHAL *n* agricultural settlement run by an Israeli military youth organization

NAHALS > NAHAL

NAIAD *n* nymph living in a lake or river

NAIADES > NAIAD

NAIADS > NAIAD

NAIANT *adj* swimming

NAIF *less common word* for > NAIVE

NAIFER > NAIF

NAIFEST > NAIF

NAIFLY > NAIVE

NAIFNESS > NAIVE

NAIFS > NAIF

NAIK *n* chief

NAIKS > NAIK

NAIL *n* pointed piece of metal with a head, hit with a hammer to join two objects together ▷ *vb* attach (something) with nails

NAILBITER *n* person who bites his or her nails

NAILBRUSH *n* small stiff-bristled brush for cleaning the fingernails

NAILED > NAIL

NAILER > NAIL

NAILERIES > NAILERY

NAILERS > NAIL

NAILERY *n* nail factory

NAILFILE *n* small metal file used to shape and smooth the nails

NAILFILES > NAILFILE

NAILFOLD *n* skin at base of fingernail

NAILFOLDS > NAILFOLD

NAILHEAD *n* decorative device, as on tooled leather, resembling the round head of a nail

NAILHEADS > NAILHEAD

NAILING > NAIL

NAILINGS > NAIL

NAILLESS > NAIL

NAILS > NAIL

NAILSET *n* punch for driving the head of a nail below the surrounding surface

NAILSETS > NAILSET

NAIN *adj* own

NAINSELL *n* own self

NAINSELLS > NAINSELL

NAINSOOK *n* light soft plain-weave cotton fabric, used esp for babies' wear

NAINSOOKS > NAINSOOK

NAIRA *n* standard monetary unit of Nigeria, divided into 100 kobo

NAIRAS > NAIRA

NAIRU *n* Non-Accelerating Inflation Rate of Unemployment

NAIRUS > NAIRU

NAISSANCE *French* for > BIRTH

NAISSANT *adj* (of a beast) having only the forepart shown above a horizontal division of a shield

NAIVE *adj* innocent and gullible ▷ *n* person who is naive, esp in artistic style

NAIVELY > NAIVE

NAIVENESS > NAIVE

NAIVER > NAIVE

NAIVES > NAIVE

NAIVEST > NAIVE

NAIVETE *variant of* > NAIVETY

NAIVETES > NAIVETE

NAIVETIES > NAIVETY

NAIVETY *n* state or quality of being naive

NAIVIST > NAIVE

NAKED *adj* without clothes

NAKEDER > NAKED

NAKEDEST > NAKED

NAKEDLY > NAKED

NAKEDNESS > NAKED

NAKER *n* one of a pair of small kettledrums used in medieval music

NAKERS > NAKER

NAKFA *n* standard currency unit of Eritrea

NAKFAS > NAKFA

NALA *n* ravine

NALAS > NALA

NALED n type of insecticide
NALEDS > NALED
NALLA n ravine
NALLAH same as > NALLA
NALLAHS > NALLAH
NALLAS > NALLA
NALOXONE n chemical substance that counteracts the effects of opiates by binding to opiate receptors on cells
NALOXONES > NALOXONE
NAM n distraint
NAMABLE > NAME
NAMASKAR n salutation used in India
NAMASKARS > NAMASKAR
NAMASTE n Indian greeting
NAMASTES > NAMASTE
NAMAYCUSH n North American freshwater fish
NAME n word by which a person or thing is known ▷ vb give a name to
NAMEABLE > NAME
NAMECHECK vb mention (someone) by name ▷ n mention of someone's name, for example on a radio programme
NAMED > NAME
NAMELESS adj without a name
NAMELY adv that is to say
NAMEPLATE n small sign on or by a door giving the occupant's name and, sometimes, profession
NAMER > NAME
NAMERS > NAME
NAMES > NAME
NAMESAKE n person with the same name as another
NAMESAKES > NAMESAKE
NAMETAG n identification badge
NAMETAGS > NAMETAG
NAMETAPE n narrow cloth tape bearing the owner's name and attached to an article
NAMETAPES > NAMETAPE
NAMING > NAME
NAMINGS > NAME
NAMMA as in namma hole Australian word for a natural well in rock
NAMS > NAM
NAMU n black New Zealand sandfly
NAN n grandmother
NANA same as > NAN
NANAS > NANA
NANCE n homosexual man
NANCES > NANCE
NANCIES > NANCY
NANCIFIED adj effeminate
NANCY n effeminate or homosexual boy or man
NANDIN n type of shrub
NANDINA n type of shrub
NANDINAS > NANDINA
NANDINE n African palm civet
NANDINES > NANDINE
NANDINS > NANDIN
NANDOO > NANDU

NANDOOS > NANDOO
NANDU n type of ostrich
NANDUS > NANDU
NANE Scot word for > NONE
NANISM n dwarfism
NANISMS > NANISM
NANKEEN n hard-wearing buff-coloured cotton fabric
NANKEENS > NANKEEN
NANKIN same as > NANKEEN
NANKINS > NANKIN
NANNA same as > NAN
NANNAS > NANNA
NANNIE same as > NANNY
NANNIED > NANNY
NANNIES > NANNY
NANNY n woman whose job is looking after young children ▷ vb be too protective towards
NANNYGAI n edible sea fish of Australia which is red in colour and has large prominent eyes
NANNYGAIS > NANNYGAI
NANNYING > NANNY
NANNYISH > NANNY
NANOBE n microbe that is smaller than the smallest known bacterium
NANOBES > NANOBE
NANODOT n microscopic cluster of several hundred nickel atoms used to store large amounts of data in a computer chip
NANODOTS > NANODOT
NANOGRAM n unit of measurement
NANOGRAMS > NANOGRAM
NANOMETER same as > NANOMETRE
NANOMETRE n one thousand-millionth of a metre
NANOOK n polar bear
NANOOKS > NANOOK
NANOSCALE adj on very small scale
NANOTECH n technology of very small objects
NANOTECHS > NANOTECH
NANOTESLA n unit of measurement
NANOTUBE n cylindrical molecule of carbon
NANOTUBES > NANOTUBE
NANOWATT n unit of measurement
NANOWATTS > NANOWATT
NANOWORLD n world at a microscopic level, as dealt with by nanotechnology
NANS > NAN
NANUA same as > MOKI
NAOI > NAOS
NAOS n ancient classical temple
NAOSES > NAOS
NAP n short sleep ▷ vb have a short sleep
NAPA n type of leather
NAPALM n highly inflammable jellied petrol, used in bombs ▷ vb attack (people or places) with napalm

NAPALMED > NAPALM
NAPALMING > NAPALM
NAPALMS > NAPALM
NAPAS > NAPA
NAPE n back of the neck ▷ vb attack with napalm)
NAPED > NAPE
NAPERIES > NAPERY
NAPERY n household linen, esp table linen
NAPES > NAPE
NAPHTHA n liquid mixture distilled from coal tar or petroleum, used as a solvent and in petrol
NAPHTHAS > NAPHTHA
NAPHTHENE n any of a class of cycloalkanes found in petroleum
NAPHTHOL n white crystalline solid used in dyes
NAPHTHOLS > NAPHTHOL
NAPHTHOUS > NAPHTHA
NAPHTHYL n of, consisting of, or containing either of two forms of the monovalent group $C_{10}H_7-$
NAPHTHYLS > NAPHTHYL
NAPHTOL same as > NAPHTHOL
NAPHTOLS > NAPHTOL
NAPIFORM adj shaped like a turnip)
NAPING > NAPE
NAPKIN same as > NAPPY
NAPKINS > NAPKIN
NAPLESS adj threadbare
NAPOLEON n former French gold coin worth 20 francs
NAPOLEONS > NAPOLEON
NAPOO vb kill
NAPOOED > NAPOO
NAPOOING > NAPOO
NAPOOS > NAPOO
NAPPA n soft leather, used in gloves and clothes, made from sheepskin, lambskin, or kid
NAPPAS > NAPPA
NAPPE n large sheet or mass of rock that has been thrust from its original position by earth movements
NAPPED > NAP
NAPPER n person or thing that raises the nap on cloth
NAPPERS > NAPPER
NAPPES > NAPPE
NAPPIE same as > NAPPY
NAPPIER > NAPPY
NAPPIES > NAPPY
NAPPIEST > NAPPY
NAPPINESS > NAPPY
NAPPING > NAP
NAPPY n piece of absorbent material fastened round a baby's lower torso to absorb urine and faeces ▷ adj having a nap
NAPRON same as > APRON
NAPRONS > NAPRON
NAPROXEN n pain-killing drug
NAPROXENS > NAPROXEN
NAPS > NAP
NARAS same as > NARRAS

NARASES > NARAS
NARC n narcotics agent
NARCEEN same as > NARCEINE
NARCEENS > NARCEEN
NARCEIN same as > NARCEINE
NARCEINE n narcotic alkaloid that occurs in opium
NARCEINES > NARCEINE
NARCEINS > NARCEIN
NARCISM n exceptional admiration for oneself
NARCISMS > NARCISM
NARCISSI > NARCISSUS
NARCISSUS n yellow, orange, or white flower related to the daffodil
NARCIST same as > NARCISSIST
NARCISTIC adj excessively admiring of oneself
NARCISTS > NARCIST
NARCO n officer working in the area of anti-drug operations
NARCOMA n coma caused by intake of narcotic drugs
NARCOMAS > NARCOMA
NARCOMATA > NARCOMA
NARCOS n drug smugglers
NARCOSE same as > NARCOSIS
NARCOSES > NARCOSIS
NARCOSIS n effect of a narcotic
NARCOTIC adj of a drug, such as morphine or opium, which produces numbness and drowsiness, used medicinally but addictive ▷ n such a drug
NARCOTICS > NARCOTIC
NARCOTINE n type of drug
NARCOTISE same as > NARCOTIZE
NARCOTISM n stupor or addiction induced by narcotic drugs
NARCOTIST n person affected by narcotics
NARCOTIZE vb place under the influence of a narcotic drug
NARCS > NARC
NARD n any of several plants whose aromatic roots were formerly used in medicine ▷ vb anoint with nard oil
NARDED > NARD
NARDINE > NARD
NARDING > NARD
NARDOO n any of certain cloverlike ferns which grow in swampy areas
NARDOOS > NARDOO
NARDS > NARD
NARE n nostril
NARES pl n nostrils
NARGHILE another name for > HOOKAH
NARGHILES > NARGHILE
NARGHILLY same as > NARGHILE
NARGHILY same as > NARGHILE
NARGILE same

as > NARGHILE

NARGILEH *same*
as > NARGHILE

NARGILEHS > NARGILEH

NARGILES > NARGILE

NARGILIES > NARGILE

NARGILY *same*
as > NARGHILE

NARIAL *adj* of or relating to
the nares

NARIC > NARE

NARICORN *n* bird's nostril

NARICORNS > NARICORN

NARINE *same as* > NARIAL

NARIS > NARES

NARK *vb* annoy ▷ *n*
informer or spy

NARKED > NARK

NARKIER > NARKY

NARKIEST > NARKY

NARKING > NARK

NARKS > NARK

NARKY *adj* irritable or
complaining

NARQUOIS *adj* malicious

NARRAS *n* type of shrub

NARRASES > NARRAS

NARRATE *vb* tell (a story)

NARRATED > NARRATE

NARRATER *same*
as > NARRATOR

NARRATERS > NARRATER

NARRATES > NARRATE

NARRATING > NARRATE

NARRATION *n* narrating

NARRATIVE *n* account,
story ▷ *adj* telling a story

NARRATOR *n* person who
tells a story or gives an
account of something

NARRATORS > NARRATOR

NARRATORY > NARRATIVE

NARRE *adj* nearer

NARROW *adj* small in breadth
in comparison to length
▷ *vb* make or become
narrow

NARROWED > NARROW

NARROWER > NARROW

NARROWEST > NARROW

NARROWING > NARROW

NARROWISH > NARROW

NARROWLY > NARROW

NARROWS *pl n* narrow part of
a strait, river, or current

NARTHEX *n* portico at the
west end of a basilica or
church

NARTHEXES > NARTHEX

NARTJIE *same as* > NAARTJIE

NARTJIES > NARTJIE

NARWAL *same as* > NARWHAL

NARWALS > NARWAL

NARWHAL *n* arctic whale
with a long spiral tusk

NARWHALE *same*
as > NARWHAL

NARWHALES > NARWHALE

NARWHALS > NARWHAL

NARY *adv* not

NAS *obsolete contraction of*
has not

NASAL *adj* of the nose ▷ *n*
nasal speech sound, such
as English *m*, *n*, or *ng*

NASALISE *same*
as > NASALIZE

NASALISED > NASALISE

NASALISES > NASALISE

NASALISM *n* nasal
pronunciation

NASALISMS > NASALISM

NASALITY > NASAL

NASALIZE *vb* pronounce
nasally

NASALIZED > NASALIZE

NASALIZES > NASALIZE

NASALLY > NASAL

NASALS > NASAL

NASARD *n* organ stop

NASARDS > NASARD

NASCENCE > NASCENT

NASCENCES > NASCENT

NASCENCY > NASCENT

NASCENT *adj* starting to
grow or develop

NASEBERRY *another name*
for > SAPODILLA

NASHGAB *n* chatter

NASHGABS > NASHGAB

NASHI *n* fruit of the
Japanese pear

NASHIS > NASHI

NASIAL > NASION

NASION *n* craniometric
point where the top of the
nose meets the ridge of the
forehead

NASIONS > NASION

NASSELLA *as in nassella*
tussock type of tussock
grass

NASTALIK *n* type of script

NASTALIKS > NASTALIK

NASTIC *adj* (of movement of
plants) independent of the
direction of the external
stimulus

NASTIER > NASTY

NASTIES > NASTY

NASTIEST > NASTY

NASTILY > NASTY

NASTINESS > NASTY

NASTY *adj* unpleasant ▷ *n*
something unpleasant

NASUTE *n* type of termite

NASUTES > NASUTE

NAT *n* supporter of
nationalism

NATAL *adj* of or relating to
birth

NATALITY *n* birth rate in a
given place

NATANT *adj* (of aquatic
plants) floating on the
water

NATANTLY *adv* in a floating
manner

NATATION *n* swimming

NATATIONS > NATATION

NATATORIA *pl n* indoor
swimming pools

NATATORY *adj* of or relating
to swimming

NATCH *sentence substitute*
naturally ▷ *n* notch

NATCHES > NATCH

NATES *pl n* buttocks

NATHELESS *prep*
notwithstanding

NATHEMO *same*
as > NATHEMORE

NATHEMORE *adv* nevermore

NATHLESS *same*

as > NATHELESS

NATIFORM *adj* resembling
buttocks

NATION *n* people of one
or more cultures or races
organized as a single state

NATIONAL *adj* of or serving
a nation as a whole ▷ *n*
citizen of a nation

NATIONALS > NATIONAL

NATIONS > NATION

NATIS > NATES

NATIVE *adj* relating to a
place where a person was
born ▷ *n* person born in a
specified place

NATIVELY > NATIVE

NATIVES > NATIVE

NATIVISM *n* policy of
favouring the natives
of a country over the
immigrants

NATIVISMS > NATIVISM

NATIVIST > NATIVISM

NATIVISTS > NATIVISM

NATIVITY *n* birth or origin

NATRIUM *obsolete name*
for > SODIUM

NATRIUMS > NATRIUM

NATROLITE *n* colourless,
white, or yellow zeolite
mineral

NATRON *n* whitish or yellow
mineral

NATRONS > NATRON

NATS > NAT

NATTER *vb* talk idly or
chatter ▷ *n* long idle chat

NATTERED > NATTER

NATTERER > NATTER

NATTERERS > NATTER

NATTERING > NATTER

NATTERS > NATTER

NATTERY *adj* irritable

NATTIER > NATTY

NATTIEST > NATTY

NATTILY > NATTY

NATTINESS > NATTY

NATTY *adj* smart and spruce

NATURA *n* nature

NATURAE > NATURA

NATURAL *adj* normal or to be
expected ▷ *n* person with
an inborn talent or skill

NATURALLY > NATURAL

NATURALS > NATURAL

NATURE *n* whole system
of the existence, forces,
and events of the physical
world that are not
controlled by human
beings

NATURED *adj* having a
certain disposition

NATURES > NATURE

NATURING *adj* creative

NATURISM *n* nudism

NATURISMS > NATURISM

NATURIST > NATURISM

NATURISTS > NATURISM

NAUCH *same as* > NAUTCH

NAUCHES > NAUCH

NAUGAHYDE *n* type of vinyl-
coated fabric

NAUGHT *n* nothing ▷ *adv*
not at all

NAUGHTIER > NAUGHTY

NAUGHTIES > NAUGHTY

NAUGHTILY > NAUGHTY

NAUGHTS > NAUGHT

NAUGHTY *adj* disobedient
or mischievous ▷ *n* act of
sexual intercourse

NAUMACHIA *n* mock sea
fight performed as an
entertainment

NAUMACHY *same*
as > NAUMACHIA

NAUNT *n* aunt

NAUNTS > NAUNT

NAUPLIAL > NAUPLIUS

NAUPLII > NAUPLIUS

NAUPLIOID > NAUPLIUS

NAUPLIUS *n* larva of many
crustaceans

NAUSEA *n* feeling of being
about to vomit

NAUSEANT *n* substance
inducing nausea

NAUSEANTS > NAUSEANT

NAUSEAS > NAUSEA

NAUSEATE *vb* make
(someone) feel sick

NAUSEATED > NAUSEATE

NAUSEATES > NAUSEATE

NAUSEOUS *adj* as if about to
vomit

NAUTCH *n* intricate
traditional Indian dance
performed by professional
dancing girls

NAUTCHES > NAUTCH

NAUTIC *same as* > NAUTICAL

NAUTICAL *adj* of the sea or
ships

NAUTICS > NAUTIC

NAUTILI > NAUTILUS

NAUTILOID *n* type of
mollusc ▷ *adj* of this type
of mollusc

NAUTILUS *n* shellfish with
many tentacles

NAVAID *n* navigational aid

NAVAIDS > NAVAID

NAVAL *adj* of or relating to a
navy or ships

NAVALISM *n* domination of
naval interests

NAVALISMS > NAVALISM

NAVALLY > NAVAL

NAVAR *n* system of air
navigation

NAVARCH *n* admiral

NAVARCHS > NAVARCH

NAVARCHY *n* navarch's term
of office

NAVARHO *n* aircraft
navigation system

NAVARHOS > NAVARHO

NAVARIN *n* stew of
mutton or lamb with root
vegetables

NAVARINS > NAVARIN

NAVARS > NAVAR

NAVE *n* long central part of
a church

NAVEL *n* hollow in the
middle of the abdomen
where the umbilical cord
was attached

NAVELS > NAVEL

NAVELWORT *another name*
for > PENNYWORT

NAVES > NAVE

Section 1: Words between 2 and 9 letters in length

NAVETTE n gem cut

NAVETTES > NAVETTE

NAVEW another name for > TURNIP

NAVEWS > NAVEW

NAVICERT n certificate specifying the contents of a neutral ship's cargo

NAVICERTS > NAVICERT

NAVICULA n incense holder

NAVICULAR adj shaped like a boat ▷ n small boat-shaped bone of the wrist or foot

NAVICULAS > NAVICULA

NAVIES > NAVY

NAVIGABLE adj wide, deep, or safe enough to be sailed through

NAVIGABLY > NAVIGABLE

NAVIGATE vb direct or plot the path or position of a ship, aircraft, or car

NAVIGATED > NAVIGATE

NAVIGATES > NAVIGATE

NAVIGATOR n person who is skilled in or performs navigation, esp on a ship or aircraft

NAVVIED > NAVVY

NAVVIES > NAVVY

NAVVY n labourer employed on a road or a building site ▷ vb work as a navvy

NAVVYING > NAVVY

NAVY n branch of a country's armed services comprising warships with their crews and organization ▷ adj navy-blue

NAW same as > NO

NAWAB n (formerly) a Muslim ruler or powerful landowner in India

NAWABS > NAWAB

NAY interj no ▷ n person who votes against a motion ▷ adv used for emphasis ▷ sentence substitute no

NAYS > NAY

NAYSAID > NAYSAY

NAYSAY vb say no

NAYSAYER n refuser

NAYSAYERS > NAYSAYER

NAYSAYING > NAYSAY

NAYSAYS > NAYSAY

NAYTHLES same as > NATHELESS

NAYWARD n towards denial

NAYWARDS same as > NAYWARD

NAYWORD n proverb

NAYWORDS > NAYWORD

NAZE n flat marshy headland

NAZES > NAZE

NAZI n person who thinks or acts in a brutal or dictatorial way

NAZIFIED > NAZIFY

NAZIFIES > NAZIFY

NAZIFY vb make nazi in character

NAZIFYING > NAZIFY

NAZIR n Muslim official

NAZIRS > NAZIR

NAZIS > NAZI

NE conj nor

NEAFE same as > NIEVE

NEAFES > NEAFE

NEAFFE same as > NIEVE

NEAFFES > NEAFFE

NEAL same as > ANNEAL

NEALED > NEAL

NEALING > NEAL

NEALS > NEAL

NEANIC adj of or relating to the early stages in the life cycle of an organism

NEAP adj of, relating to, or constituting a neap tide ▷ vb be grounded by a neap tide

NEAPED > NEAP

NEAPING > NEAP

NEAPS > NEAP

NEAR adj indicating a place or time not far away ▷ vb draw close (to) ▷ prep at or to a place or time not far away from ▷ adv at or to a place or time not far away ▷ n left side of a horse or vehicle

NEARBY adj not far away ▷ adv close at hand

NEARED > NEAR

NEARER > NEAR

NEAREST > NEAR

NEARING > NEAR

NEARLIER > NEARLY

NEARLIEST > NEARLY

NEARLY adv almost

NEARNESS > NEAR

NEARS > NEAR

NEARSHORE n area of coastline water

NEARSIDE n side of a vehicle that is nearer the kerb

NEARSIDES > NEARSIDE

NEAT adj tidy and clean ▷ n domestic bovine animal

NEATEN vb make neat

NEATENED > NEATEN

NEATENING > NEATEN

NEATENS > NEATEN

NEATER > NEAT

NEATEST > NEAT

NEATH short for > BENEATH

NEATHERD n cowherd

NEATHERDS > NEATHERD

NEATLY > NEAT

NEATNESS > NEAT

NEATNIK n very neat and tidy person

NEATNIKS > NEATNIK

NEATS > NEAT

NEB n beak of a bird or the nose of an animal ▷ vb look around nosily

NEBBED > NEB

NEBBICH same as > NEBBISH

NEBBICHS > NEBBICH

NEBBING > NEB

NEBBISH n unfortunate simpleton

NEBBISHE same as > NEBBISH

NEBBISHER same as > NEBBISH

NEBBISHES > NEBBISH

NEBBISHY > NEBBISH

NEBBUK n type of shrub

NEBBUKS > NEBBUK

NEBECK same as > NEBBUK

NEBECKS > NEBECK

NEBEK same as > NEBBUK

NEBEKS > NEBEK

NEBEL n Hebrew musical instrument

NEBELS > NEBEL

NEBENKERN n component of insect sperm

NEBISH same as > NEBBISH

NEBISHES > NEBISH

NEBRIS n fawn-skin

NEBRISES > NEBRIS

NEBS > NEB

NEBULA n hazy cloud of particles and gases

NEBULAE > NEBULA

NEBULAR > NEBULA

NEBULAS > NEBULA

NEBULE n cloud

NEBULES > NEBULE

NEBULISE same as > NEBULIZE

NEBULISED > NEBULISE

NEBULISER same as > NEBULIZER

NEBULISES > NEBULISE

NEBULIUM n element

NEBULIUMS > NEBULIUM

NEBULIZE vb turn (a liquid) into a fine spray

NEBULIZED > NEBULIZE

NEBULIZER n device which turns a drug from a liquid into a fine spray which can be inhaled

NEBULIZES > NEBULIZE

NEBULOSE same as > NEBULOUS

NEBULOUS adj vague and unclear

NEBULY adj wavy

NECESSARY adj needed to obtain the desired result

NECESSITY n circumstances that inevitably require a certain result

NECK n part of the body joining the head to the shoulders ▷ vb kiss and cuddle

NECKATEE n piece of ornamental cloth worn around the neck

NECKATEES > NECKATEE

NECKBAND n band around the neck of a garment

NECKBANDS > NECKBAND

NECKBEEF n cheap cattle flesh

NECKBEEFS > NECKBEEF

NECKCLOTH n large ornamental usually white cravat worn formerly by men

NECKED > NECK

NECKER > NECK

NECKERS > NECK

NECKGEAR n any neck covering

NECKGEARS > NECKGEAR

NECKING n activity of kissing and embracing passionately

NECKINGS > NECKING

NECKLACE n decorative piece of jewellery worn around the neck ▷ vb kill (someone) by placing a burning tyre round his or her neck

NECKLACED > NECKLACE

NECKLACES > NECKLACE

NECKLESS > NECK

NECKLET n ornament worn round the neck

NECKLETS > NECKLET

NECKLIKE > NECK

NECKLINE n shape or position of the upper edge of a dress or top

NECKLINES > NECKLINE

NECKPIECE n piece of fur, cloth, etc, worn around the neck or neckline

NECKS > NECK

NECKTIE same as > TIE

NECKTIES > NECKTIE

NECKVERSE n verse read to prove clergy membership

NECKWEAR n articles of clothing, such as ties, scarves, etc, worn around the neck

NECKWEARS > NECKWEAR

NECKWEED n type of plant

NECKWEEDS > NECKWEED

NECROLOGY n list of people recently dead

NECROPHIL n person who is sexually attracted to dead bodies

NECROPOLI pl n burial sites or cemeteries

NECROPSY n postmortem examination ▷ vb carry out a necropsy

NECROSE vb cause or undergo necrosis

NECROSED > NECROSE

NECROSES > NECROSE

NECROSING > NECROSE

NECROSIS n death of cells in the body

NECROTIC > NECROSIS

NECROTISE same as > NECROTIZE

NECROTIZE vb undergo necrosis

NECROTOMY n dissection of a dead body

NECTAR n sweet liquid collected from flowers by bees

NECTAREAL > NECTAR

NECTAREAN > NECTAR

NECTARED adj filled with nectar

NECTARIAL > NECTARY

NECTARIED adj having nectaries

NECTARIES > NECTARY

NECTARINE n smooth-skinned peach

NECTAROUS > NECTAR

NECTARS > NECTAR

NECTARY n any of various glandular structures secreting nectar in a plant

NED n derogatory name for an adolescent hooligan

NEDDIER > NEDDY

NEDDIES > NEDDY
NEDDIEST > NEDDY
NEDDISH > NEDDY
NEDDY n donkey ▷ adj of or relating to neds
NEDETTE n derogatory name for a female adolescent hooligan
NEDETTES > NEDETTE
NEDS > NED
NEE prep indicating the maiden name of a married woman ▷ adj indicating the maiden name of a married woman
NEED vb require or be in want of ▷ n condition of lacking something
NEEDED > NEED
NEEDER > NEED
NEEDERS > NEED
NEEDFIRE n beacon
NEEDFIRES > NEEDFIRE
NEEDFUL adj necessary or required
NEEDFULLY > NEEDFUL
NEEDFULS n must-haves
NEEDIER > NEEDY
NEEDIEST > NEEDY
NEEDILY > NEEDY
NEEDINESS n state of being needy
NEEDING > NEED
NEEDLE n thin pointed piece of metal with an eye through which thread is passed for sewing ▷ vb goad or provoke
NEEDLED > NEEDLE
NEEDLEFUL n length of thread cut for use in a needle
NEEDLER n needle maker
NEEDLERS > NEEDLER
NEEDLES > NEEDLE
NEEDLESS adj unnecessary
NEEDLIER > NEEDLE
NEEDLIEST > NEEDLE
NEEDLING > NEEDLE
NEEDLINGS > NEEDLE
NEEDLY > NEEDLE
NEEDMENT > NEED
NEEDMENTS > NEED
NEEDS adv necessarily ▷ pl n what is required
NEEDY adj poor, in need of financial support
NEELD same as > NEEDLE
NEELDS > NEELD
NEELE same as > NEEDLE
NEELES > NEELE
NEEM n type of large Indian tree
NEEMB same as > NEEM
NEEMBS > NEEMB
NEEMS > NEEM
NEEP dialect name for > TURNIP
NEEPS > NEEP
NEESBERRY same as > NASEBERRY
NEESE same as > NEEZE
NEESED > NEESE
NEESES > NEESE
NEESING > NEESE
NEEZE vb sneeze
NEEZED > NEEZE

NEEZES > NEEZE
NEEZING > NEEZE
NEF n church nave
NEFANDOUS adj unmentionable
NEFARIOUS adj wicked
NEFAST adj wicked
NEFS > NEF
NEG n photographic negative
NEGATE vb invalidate
NEGATED > NEGATE
NEGATER > NEGATE
NEGATERS > NEGATE
NEGATES > NEGATE
NEGATING > NEGATE
NEGATION n opposite or absence of something
NEGATIONS > NEGATION
NEGATIVE adj expressing a denial or refusal ▷ n negative word or statement
NEGATIVED > NEGATIVE
NEGATIVES > NEGATIVE
NEGATON same as > NEGATRON
NEGATONS > NEGATON
NEGATOR > NEGATE
NEGATORS > NEGATE
NEGATORY > NEGATION
NEGATRON obsolete word for > ELECTRON
NEGATRONS > NEGATRON
NEGLECT vb take no care of ▷ n neglecting or being neglected
NEGLECTED > NEGLECT
NEGLECTER > NEGLECT
NEGLECTOR > NEGLECT
NEGLECTS > NEGLECT
NEGLIGE variant of > NEGLIGEE
NEGLIGEE n woman's lightweight usu lace-trimmed dressing gown
NEGLIGEES > NEGLIGEE
NEGLIGENT adj habitually neglecting duties, responsibilities, etc
NEGLIGES > NEGLIGE
NEGOCIANT n wine merchant
NEGOTIANT n person, nation, organization, etc, involved in a negotiation
NEGOTIATE vb discuss in order to reach (an agreement)
NEGRESS n old-fashioned offensive name for a Black woman
NEGRESSES > NEGRESS
NEGRITUDE n fact of being a Negro
NEGRO n old-fashioned offensive name for a Black man
NEGROES > NEGRO
NEGROHEAD n type of rubber
NEGROID n member of one of the major racial groups of mankind, which is characterized by brown-black skin and tightly-curled hair
NEGROIDAL > NEGROID

NEGROIDS > NEGROID
NEGROISM > NEGRO
NEGROISMS > NEGRO
NEGRONI n type of cocktail
NEGRONIS > NEGRONI
NEGROPHIL n person who admires Black people and their culture
NEGS > NEG
NEGUS n hot drink of port and lemon juice, usually spiced and sweetened
NEGUSES > NEGUS
NEIF same as > NIEVE
NEIFS > NEIF
NEIGH n loud high-pitched sound made by a horse ▷ vb make this sound
NEIGHBOR same as > NEIGHBOUR
NEIGHBORS > NEIGHBOR
NEIGHBOUR n person who lives or is situated near another ▷ vb be or live close (to a person or thing)
NEIGHED > NEIGH
NEIGHING > NEIGH
NEIGHS > NEIGH
NEINEI n type of plant
NEINEIS > NEINEI
NEIST Scots variant of > NEXT
NEITHER pron not one nor the other ▷ adj not one nor the other (of two)
NEIVE same as > NIEVE
NEIVES > NEIVE
NEK n mountain pass
NEKS > NEK
NEKTON n population of free-swimming animals that inhabits the middle depths of a sea or lake
NEKTONIC > NEKTON
NEKTONS > NEKTON
NELIES same as > NELIS
NELIS n type of pear
NELLIE n effeminate man
NELLIES > NELLIE
NELLY as in not on your nelly not under any circumstances
NELSON n type of wrestling hold
NELSONS > NELSON
NELUMBIUM same as > NELUMBO
NELUMBO n type of aquatic plant
NELUMBOS > NELUMBO
NEMA n filament
NEMAS > NEMA
NEMATIC adj (of a substance) existing in or having a mesomorphic state in which a linear orientation of the molecules causes anisotropic properties
NEMATODE n slender cylindrical unsegmented worm
NEMATODES > NEMATODE
NEMATOID > NEMATODE
NEMERTEAN n type of ribbon-like marine worm ▷ adj of this worm

NEMERTIAN same as > NEMERTEAN
NEMERTINE same as > NEMERTEAN
NEMESES > NEMESIS
NEMESIA n type of southern African plant
NEMESIAS > NEMESIA
NEMESIS n retribution or vengeance
NEMN vb name
NEMNED > NEMN
NEMNING > NEMN
NEMNS > NEMN
NEMOPHILA n any of a genus of low-growing hairy annual plants
NEMORAL adj of a wood
NEMOROUS adj woody
NEMPT adj named
NENE n rare black-and-grey short-winged Hawaiian goose
NENES > NENE
NENNIGAI same as > NANNYGAI
NENNIGAIS > NENNIGAI
NENUPHAR n type of water lily
NENUPHARS > NENUPHAR
NEOBLAST n worm cell
NEOBLASTS > NEOBLAST
NEOCON n supporter of conservative politics
NEOCONS > NEOCON
NEOCORTEX n part of the brain
NEODYMIUM n silvery-white metallic element of lanthanide series
NEOGENE adj of, denoting, or formed during the Miocene and Pliocene epochs
NEOGOTHIC n style of architecture popular in Britain in the 18th and 19th centuries
NEOLITH n Neolithic stone implement
NEOLITHIC adj relating to the Neolithic period
NEOLITHS > NEOLITH
NEOLOGIAN > NEOLOGY
NEOLOGIC > NEOLOGISM
NEOLOGIES > NEOLOGY
NEOLOGISE same as > NEOLOGIZE
NEOLOGISM n newly-coined word or an established word used in a new sense
NEOLOGIST > NEOLOGISM
NEOLOGIZE vb invent or use neologisms
NEOLOGY same as > NEOLOGISM
NEOMORPH n genetic component
NEOMORPHS > NEOMORPH
NEOMYCIN n type of antibiotic obtained from a bacterium
NEOMYCINS > NEOMYCIN
NEON n colourless odourless gaseous element used in illuminated signs and lights ▷ adj of or illuminated by neon

NEONATAL *adj* relating to the first few weeks of a baby's life

NEONATE *n* newborn child, esp in the first week of life and up to four weeks old

NEONATES > NEONATE

NEONED *adj* lit with neon

NEONOMIAN *n* Christian religious belief

NEONS > NEON

NEOPAGAN *n* advocate of the revival of paganism

NEOPAGANS > NEOPAGAN

NEOPHILE *n* person who welcomes new things

NEOPHILES > NEOPHILE

NEOPHILIA *n* tendency to like anything new

NEOPHOBE > NEOPHOBIA

NEOPHOBES > NEOPHOBIA

NEOPHOBIA *n* tendency to dislike anything new

NEOPHOBIC > NEOPHOBIA

NEOPHYTE *n* beginner or novice

NEOPHYTES > NEOPHYTE

NEOPHYTIC > NEOPHYTE

NEOPILINA *n* type of mollusc

NEOPLASIA *n* abnormal growth of tissue

NEOPLASM *n* any abnormal new growth of tissue

NEOPLASMS > NEOPLASM

NEOPLASTY *n* surgical formation of new tissue structures or repair of damaged structures

NEOPRENE *n* synthetic rubber used in waterproof products

NEOPRENES > NEOPRENE

NEOTEINIA *n* state of prolonged immaturity

NEOTENIC > NEOTENY

NEOTENIES > NEOTENY

NEOTENOUS > NEOTENY

NEOTENY *n* persistence of larval or fetal features in the adult form of an animal

NEOTERIC *adj* belonging to a new fashion or trend ▷ *n* new writer or philosopher

NEOTERICS > NEOTERIC

NEOTERISE *same as* > NEOTERIZE

NEOTERISM > NEOTERIC

NEOTERIST > NEOTERIC

NEOTERIZE *vb* introduce new things

NEOTOXIN *n* harmful agent

NEOTOXINS > NEOTOXIN

NEOTROPIC *adj* of tropical America

NEOTYPE *n* specimen selected to replace a type specimen that has been lost or destroyed

NEOTYPES > NEOTYPE

NEP *n* catmint

NEPENTHE *n* drug that ancient writers referred to as a means of forgetting grief or trouble

NEPENTHES > NEPENTHE

NEPER *n* unit expressing the ratio of two quantities

NEPERS > NEPER

NEPETA *same as* > CATMINT

NEPETAS > NEPETA

NEPHALISM *n* teetotalism

NEPHALIST > NEPHALISM

NEPHELINE *n* whitish mineral

NEPHELITE *same as* > NEPHELINE

NEPHEW *n* son of one's sister or brother

NEPHEWS > NEPHEW

NEPHOGRAM *n* photograph of a cloud

NEPHOLOGY *n* study of clouds

NEPHRALGY *n* pain in a kidney

NEPHRIC *adj* renal

NEPHRIDIA *pl n* simple excretory organs of many invertebrates

NEPHRISM *n* chronic kidney disease

NEPHRISMS > NEPHRISM

NEPHRITE *n* tough fibrous amphibole mineral

NEPHRITES > NEPHRITE

NEPHRITIC *adj* of or relating to the kidneys

NEPHRITIS *n* inflammation of a kidney

NEPHROID *adj* kidney-shaped

NEPHRON *n* minute urine-secreting tubule in the kidney

NEPHRONS > NEPHRON

NEPHROSES > NEPHROSIS

NEPHROSIS *n* any noninflammatory degenerative kidney disease

NEPHROTIC > NEPHROSIS

NEPIONIC *adj* of or relating to the juvenile period in the life cycle of an organism

NEPIT *same as* > NIT

NEPITS > NEPIT

NEPOTIC > NEPOTISM

NEPOTISM *n* favouritism in business shown to relatives and friends

NEPOTISMS > NEPOTISM

NEPOTIST > NEPOTISM

NEPOTISTS > NEPOTISM

NEPS > NEP

NEPTUNIUM *n* synthetic radioactive metallic element

NERAL *n* isomer of citral

NERALS > NERAL

NERD *n* boring person obsessed with a particular subject

NERDIER > NERD

NERDIEST > NERD

NERDINESS > NERD

NERDISH > NERD

NERDS > NERD

NERDY > NERD

NEREID *n* sea nymph in Greek mythology

NEREIDES > NEREID

NEREIDS > NEREID

NEREIS *n* any polychaete worm of the genus *Nereis*

NERINE *n* type of S African plant related to the amaryllis

NERINES > NERINE

NERITE *n* type of sea snail

NERITES > NERITE

NERITIC *adj* of or formed in the region of shallow seas near a coastline

NERK *n* fool

NERKA *n* type of salmon

NERKAS > NERKA

NERKS > NERK

NEROL *n* scented liquid

NEROLI *n* brown oil used in perfumery

NEROLIS > NEROLI

NEROLS > NEROL

NERTS *interj* nuts

NERTZ *same as* > NERTS

NERVAL > NERVE

NERVATE *adj* (of leaves) with veins

NERVATION *less common word for* > VENATION

NERVATURE *same as* > NERVATION

NERVE *n* cordlike bundle of fibres that conducts impulses between the brain and other parts of the body ▷ *vb* give courage to oneself

NERVED > NERVE

NERVELESS *adj* numb, without feeling

NERVELET *n* small nerve

NERVELETS > NERVELET

NERVER > NERVE

NERVERS > NERVE

NERVES > NERVE

NERVIER > NERVY

NERVIEST > NERVY

NERVILY > NERVY

NERVINE *adj* having a soothing or calming effect upon the nerves ▷ *n* nervine drug or agent

NERVINES > NERVINE

NERVINESS > NERVY

NERVING > NERVE

NERVINGS > NERVE

NERVOSITY *n* nervousness

NERVOUS *adj* apprehensive or worried

NERVOUSLY > NERVOUS

NERVULAR > NERVULE

NERVULE *n* small vein

NERVULES > NERVULE

NERVURE *n* any of the stiff rods that form the supporting framework of an insect's wing

NERVURES > NERVURE

NERVY *adj* excitable or nervous

NESCIENCE *formal or literary word for* > IGNORANCE

NESCIENT > NESCIENCE

NESCIENTS > NESCIENCE

NESH *adj* sensitive to the cold

NESHER > NESH

NESHEST > NESH

NESHNESS > NESH

NESS *n* headland, cape

NESSES > NESS

NEST *n* place or structure in which birds or certain animals lay eggs or give birth to young ▷ *vb* make or inhabit a nest

NESTABLE > NEST

NESTED > NEST

NESTER > NEST

NESTERS > NEST

NESTFUL > NEST

NESTFULS > NEST

NESTING > NEST

NESTINGS > NEST

NESTLE *vb* snuggle

NESTLED > NESTLE

NESTLER > NESTLE

NESTLERS > NESTLE

NESTLES > NESTLE

NESTLIKE > NEST

NESTLING *n* bird too young to leave the nest

NESTLINGS > NESTLING

NESTOR *n* wise old man

NESTORS > NESTOR

NESTS > NEST

NET *n* fabric of meshes of string, thread, or wire with many openings ▷ *vb* catch (a fish or animal) in a net ▷ *adj* left after all deductions

NETBALL *n* team game in which a ball has to be thrown through a net hanging from a ring at the top of a pole

NETBALLER > NETBALL

NETBALLS > NETBALL

NETE *n* lyre string

NETES > NETE

NETFUL > NET

NETFULS > NET

NETHEAD *n* person who is enthusiastic about or an expert on the internet

NETHEADS > NETHEAD

NETHELESS *same as* > NATHELESS

NETHER *adj* lower

NETIZEN *n* person who regularly uses the internet

NETIZENS > NETIZEN

NETLESS > NET

NETLIKE > NET

NETMINDER *n* goalkeeper

NETOP *n* friend

NETOPS > NETOP

NETS > NET

NETSPEAK *n* jargon, abbreviations, and emoticons typically used by frequent internet users

NETSPEAKS > NETSPEAK

NETSUKE *n* (in Japan) a carved toggle worn dangling from the waist

NETSUKES > NETSUKE

NETT *same as* > NET

NETTABLE > NETT

NETTED > NET

NETTER *n* person that makes nets

NETTERS > NETTER

NETTIE *n* habitual and enthusiastic user of the internet

NETTIER > NET
NETTIES > NETTY
NETTIEST > NET
NETTING > NET
NETTINGS > NET
NETTLE *n* plant with stinging hairs on the leaves ▷ *vb* bother or irritate
NETTLED > NETTLE
NETTLER > NETTLE
NETTLERS > NETTLE
NETTLES > NETTLE
NETTLIER > NETTLE
NETTLIEST > NETTLE
NETTLING > NETTLE
NETTLY > NETTLE
NETTS > NETT
NETTY *n* lavatory, originally an earth closet
NETWORK *n* system of intersecting lines, roads, etc ▷ *vb* broadcast (a programme) over a network
NETWORKED > NETWORK
NETWORKER *n* person who forms business contacts through informal social meetings
NETWORKS > NETWORK
NEUK *Scot word for* > NOOK
NEUKS > NEUK
NEUM *same as* > NEUME
NEUMATIC > NEUME
NEUME *n* one of a series of notational symbols used before the 14th century
NEUMES > NEUME
NEUMIC > NEUME
NEUMS > NEUM
NEURAL *adj* of a nerve or the nervous system
NEURALGIA *n* severe pain along a nerve
NEURALGIC > NEURALGIA
NEURALLY > NEURAL
NEURATION *n* arrangement of veins
NEURAXON *n* biological cell component
NEURAXONS > NEURAXON
NEURILITY *n* properties of the nerves
NEURINE *n* poisonous alkaloid
NEURINES > NEURINE
NEURISM *n* nerve force
NEURISMS > NEURISM
NEURITE *n* biological cell component
NEURITES > NEURITE
NEURITIC > NEURITIS
NEURITICS > NEURITIS
NEURITIS *n* inflammation of a nerve or nerves
NEUROCHIP *n* semiconductor chip designed for use in an electronic neural network
NEUROCOEL *n* cavity in brain
NEUROGLIA *another name for* > GLIA
NEUROGRAM *same as* > ENGRAM
NEUROID *adj* nervelike
NEUROLOGY *n* scientific study of the nervous system

NEUROMA *n* any tumour composed of nerve tissue
NEUROMAS > NEUROMA
NEUROMAST *n* sensory cell in fish
NEUROMATA > NEUROMA
NEURON *same as* > NEURONE
NEURONAL > NEURONE
NEURONE *n* cell specialized to conduct nerve impulses
NEURONES > NEURONE
NEURONIC > NEURONE
NEURONS > NEURON
NEUROPATH *n* person suffering from or predisposed to a disorder of the nervous system
NEUROPIL *n* dense network of neurons and glia in the central nervous system
NEUROPILS > NEUROPIL
NEUROSAL > NEUROSIS
NEUROSES > NEUROSIS
NEUROSIS *n* mental disorder producing hysteria, anxiety, depression, or obsessive behaviour
NEUROTIC *adj* emotionally unstable ▷ *n* neurotic person
NEUROTICS > NEUROTIC
NEUROTOMY *n* surgical cutting of a nerve, esp to relieve intractable pain
NEURULA *n* stage of embryonic development
NEURULAE > NEURULA
NEURULAR > NEURULA
NEURULAS > NEURULA
NEUSTIC > NEUSTON
NEUSTON *n* organisms, similar to plankton, that float on the surface film of open water
NEUSTONIC > NEUSTON
NEUSTONS > NEUSTON
NEUTER *adj* belonging to a particular class of grammatical inflections in some languages ▷ *vb* castrate (an animal) ▷ *n* neuter gender
NEUTERED > NEUTER
NEUTERING > NEUTER
NEUTERS > NEUTER
NEUTRAL *adj* taking neither side in a war or dispute ▷ *n* neutral person or nation
NEUTRALLY > NEUTRAL
NEUTRALS > NEUTRAL
NEUTRETTO *n* neutrino associated with the muon
NEUTRINO *n* elementary particle with no mass or electrical charge
NEUTRINOS > NEUTRINO
NEUTRON *n* electrically neutral elementary particle of about the same mass as a proton
NEUTRONIC > NEUTRON
NEUTRONS > NEUTRON
NEVE *n* mass of porous ice, formed from snow, that has not yet become frozen

into glacier ice
NEVEL *vb* beat with the fists
NEVELLED > NEVEL
NEVELLING > NEVEL
NEVELS > NEVEL
NEVER *adv* at no time ▷ *sentence substitute* at no time ▷ *interj* surely not!
NEVERMIND *n* difference
NEVERMORE *adv* never again
NEVES > NEVE
NEVI > NEVUS
NEVOID > NAEVUS
NEVUS *same as* > NAEVUS
NEW *adj* not existing before ▷ *adv* recently ▷ *vb* make new
NEWBIE *n* person new to a job, club, etc
NEWBIES > NEWBIE
NEWBORN *adj* recently or just born ▷ *n* newborn baby
NEWBORNS > NEWBORN
NEWCOME > NEWCOMER
NEWCOMER *n* recent arrival or participant
NEWCOMERS > NEWCOMER
NEWED > NEW
NEWEL *n* post at the top or bottom of a flight of stairs that supports the handrail
NEWELL *n* new thing
NEWELLED > NEWEL
NEWELLS > NEWELL
NEWELS > NEWEL
NEWER > NEW
NEWEST > NEW
NEWFANGLE *adj* newly come into existence or fashion
NEWFOUND *adj* newly or recently discovered
NEWIE *n* fresh idea or thing
NEWIES > NEWIE
NEWING > NEW
NEWISH *adj* fairly new
NEWISHLY > NEWISH
NEWLY *adv* recently
NEWLYWED *n* recently married person
NEWLYWEDS > NEWLYWED
NEWMARKET *n* double-breasted waisted coat with a full skirt
NEWMOWN *adj* freshly cut
NEWNESS > NEW
NEWNESSES > NEW
NEWS *n* important or interesting new happenings ▷ *vb* report
NEWSAGENT *n* shopkeeper who sells newspapers and magazines
NEWSBEAT *n* particular area of news reporting
NEWSBEATS > NEWSBEAT
NEWSBOY *n* boy who sells or delivers newspapers
NEWSBOYS > NEWSBOY
NEWSBREAK *n* newsflash
NEWSCAST *n* radio or television broadcast of the news
NEWSCASTS > NEWSCAST
NEWSDESK *n* news gathering and reporting department
NEWSDESKS > NEWSDESK

NEWSED > NEWS
NEWSES > NEWS
NEWSFLASH *n* brief important news item, which interrupts a radio or television programme
NEWSGIRL *n* female newsreader or reporter
NEWSGIRLS > NEWSGIRL
NEWSGROUP *n* forum where subscribers exchange information about a specific subject by e-mail
NEWSHAWK *n* newspaper reporter
NEWSHAWKS > NEWSHAWK
NEWSHOUND *same as* > NEWSHAWK
NEWSIE *same as* > NEWSY
NEWSIER > NEWSY
NEWSIES > NEWSIE
NEWSIEST > NEWSY
NEWSINESS > NEWSY
NEWSING > NEWS
NEWSLESS > NEWS
NEWSMAKER *n* person whose activities are reported in news
NEWSMAN *n* male newsreader or reporter
NEWSMEN > NEWSMAN
NEWSPAPER *n* weekly or daily publication containing news ▷ *vb* do newspaper related work
NEWSPEAK *n* language of politicians and officials regarded as deliberately ambiguous and misleading
NEWSPEAKS > NEWSPEAK
NEWSPRINT *n* inexpensive paper used for newspapers
NEWSREEL *n* short film giving news
NEWSREELS > NEWSREEL
NEWSROOM *n* room where news is received and prepared for publication or broadcasting
NEWSROOMS > NEWSROOM
NEWSSTAND *n* portable stand from which newspapers are sold
NEWSTRADE *n* newspaper retail
NEWSWIRE *n* electronic means of delivering up-to-the-minute news
NEWSWIRES > NEWSWIRE
NEWSWOMAN *n* female newsreader or reporter
NEWSWOMEN > NEWSWOMAN
NEWSY *adj* full of news ▷ *n* newsagent
NEWT *n* small amphibious creature with a long slender body and tail
NEWTON *n* unit of force
NEWTONS > NEWTON
NEWTS > NEWT
NEWWAVER *n* member of new wave
NEWWAVERS > NEWWAVER
NEXT *adv* immediately following ▷ *n* next person or thing
NEXTDOOR *adj* in or at the

adjacent house or building
NEXTLY > NEXT
NEXTNESS > NEXT
NEXTS > NEXT
NEXUS n connection or link
NEXUSES > NEXUS
NGAIO n small New Zealand tree
NGAIOS > NGAIO
NGANA same as > NAGANA
NGANAS > NGANA
NGARARA n lizard found in New Zealand
NGATI n (occurring as part of the tribe name) a tribe or clan
NGATIS > NGATI
NGOMA n type of drum
NGOMAS > NGOMA
NGULTRUM n standard monetary unit of Bhutan, divided into 100 chetrum
NGULTRUMS > NGULTRUM
NGWEE n Zambian monetary unit worth one hundredth of a kwacha
NHANDU n type of spider
NHANDUS > NHANDU
NIACIN n vitamin of the B complex that occurs in milk, liver, and yeast
NIACINS > NIACIN
NIAISERIE n simplicity
NIALAMIDE n type of drug
NIB n writing point of a pen ▷ vb provide with a nib
NIBBED > NIB
NIBBING > NIB
NIBBLE vb take little bites (of) ▷ n little bite
NIBBLED > NIBBLE
NIBBLER n person, animal, or thing that nibbles
NIBBLERS > NIBBLER
NIBBLES > NIBBLE
NIBBLING > NIBBLE
NIBBLINGS > NIBBLE
NIBLICK n (formerly) a club, a No. 9 iron, giving a great deal of lift
NIBLICKS > NIBLICK
NIBLIKE > NIB
NIBS > NIB
NICAD n rechargeable dry-cell battery
NICADS > NICAD
NICCOLITE n copper-coloured mineral
NICE adj pleasant
NICEISH > NICE
NICELY > NICE
NICENESS > NICE
NICER > NICE
NICEST > NICE
NICETIES > NICETY
NICETY n subtle point
NICHE n hollow area in a wall ▷ adj of or aimed at a specialist group or market ▷ vb place (a statue) in a niche
NICHED > NICHE
NICHER vb snigger
NICHERED > NICHER
NICHERING > NICHER
NICHERS > NICHER
NICHES > NICHE

NICHING > NICHE
NICHT Scot word for > NIGHT
NICHTS > NICHT
NICISH > NICE
NICK vb make a small cut in ▷ n small cut
NICKAR n hard seed
NICKARS > NICKAR
NICKED > NICK
NICKEL n silvery-white metal often used in alloys ▷ vb plate with nickel
NICKELED > NICKEL
NICKELIC adj of or containing metallic nickel
NICKELINE another name for > NICCOLITE
NICKELING > NICKEL
NICKELISE same as > NICKELIZE
NICKELIZE vb treat with nickel
NICKELLED > NICKEL
NICKELOUS adj of or containing nickel, esp in the divalent state
NICKELS > NICKEL
NICKER n pound sterling ▷ vb (of a horse) to neigh softly
NICKERED > NICKER
NICKERING > NICKER
NICKERS > NICKER
NICKING > NICK
NICKLE same as > NICKEL
NICKLED > NICKLE
NICKLES > NICKLE
NICKLING > NICKLE
NICKNACK n cheap ornament or trinket
NICKNACKS > NICKNACK
NICKNAME n familiar name given to a person or place ▷ vb call by a nickname
NICKNAMED > NICKNAME
NICKNAMER > NICKNAME
NICKNAMES > NICKNAME
NICKPOINT n break in the slope of a river caused by renewed erosion
NICKS > NICK
NICKSTICK n tally
NICKUM n mischievous person
NICKUMS > NICKUM
NICKY as in nicky nicky nine doors Canadian game
NICOISE adj prepared with tomatoes, black olives, garlic and anchovies
NICOL n device for producing plane-polarized light
NICOLS > NICOL
NICOMPOOP n stupid person
NICOTIAN n tobacco user
NICOTIANA n any plant of the American and Australian genus Nicotiana, such as tobacco
NICOTIANS > NICOTIAN
NICOTIN same as > NICOTINE
NICOTINE n poisonous substance found in tobacco
NICOTINED > NICOTINE
NICOTINES > NICOTINE
NICOTINIC > NICOTINE

NICOTINS same as > NICOTIN
NICTATE same as > NICTITATE
NICTATED > NICTATE
NICTATES > NICTATE
NICTATING > NICTATE
NICTATION n act of blinking
NICTITANT adj blinking
NICTITATE vb blink
NID same as > NIDE
NIDAL > NIDUS
NIDAMENTA pl n egg capsules
NIDATE vb undergo nidation
NIDATED > NIDATE
NIDATES > NIDATE
NIDATING > NIDATE
NIDATION n implantation
NIDATIONS > NIDATION
NIDDERING n coward ▷ adj cowardly
NIDDICK n nape of the neck
NIDDICKS > NIDDICK
NIDE vb nest
NIDED > NIDE
NIDERING same as > NIDDERING
NIDERINGS > NIDERING
NIDERLING same as > NIDDERING
NIDES > NIDE
NIDGET n fool
NIDGETS > NIDGET
NIDI > NIDUS
NIDIFIED > NIDIFY
NIDIFIES > NIDIFY
NIDIFY vb (of a bird) to make or build a nest
NIDIFYING > NIDIFY
NIDING n coward
NIDINGS > NIDING
NIDOR n cooking smell
NIDOROUS > NIDOR
NIDORS > NIDOR
NIDS > NID
NIDUS n nest in which insects or spiders deposit their eggs
NIDUSES > NIDUS
NIE archaic spelling of > NIGH
NIECE n daughter of one's sister or brother
NIECES > NIECE
NIED > NIE
NIEF same as > NIEVE
NIEFS > NIEF
NIELLATED > NIELLO
NIELLI > NIELLO
NIELLIST > NIELLO
NIELLISTS > NIELLO
NIELLO n black compound of sulphur and silver, lead, or copper ▷ vb decorate or treat with niello
NIELLOED > NIELLO
NIELLOING > NIELLO
NIELLOS > NIELLO
NIES > NIE
NIEVE n closed hand
NIEVEFUL > NIEVE
NIEVEFULS > NIEVE
NIEVES > NIEVE
NIFE n earth's core, thought to be composed of nickel and iron
NIFES > NIFE

NIFF n stink ▷ vb stink
NIFFED > NIFF
NIFFER vb barter
NIFFERED > NIFFER
NIFFERING > NIFFER
NIFFERS > NIFFER
NIFFIER > NIFF
NIFFIEST > NIFF
NIFFING > NIFF
NIFFNAFF vb trifle
NIFFNAFFS > NIFFNAFF
NIFFS > NIFF
NIFFY > NIFF
NIFTIER > NIFTY
NIFTIES > NIFTY
NIFTIEST > NIFTY
NIFTILY > NIFTY
NIFTINESS > NIFTY
NIFTY adj neat or smart ▷ n nifty thing
NIGELLA n type of plant the Mediterranean and W Asia
NIGELLAS > NIGELLA
NIGER n obsolete offensive term for a Black person
NIGERS > NIGER
NIGGARD n stingy person ▷ adj miserly ▷ vb act in a niggardly way
NIGGARDED > NIGGARD
NIGGARDLY adj stingy ▷ adv stingily
NIGGARDS > NIGGARD
NIGGER n offensive name for a Black person ▷ vb burn
NIGGERDOM > NIGGER
NIGGERED > NIGGER
NIGGERING > NIGGER
NIGGERISH > NIGGER
NIGGERISM n offensive name for an idiom supposedly characteristic of Black people
NIGGERS > NIGGER
NIGGERY > NIGGER
NIGGLE vb worry slightly ▷ n small worry or doubt
NIGGLED > NIGGLE
NIGGLER > NIGGLE
NIGGLERS > NIGGLE
NIGGLES > NIGGLE
NIGGLIER > NIGGLE
NIGGLIEST > NIGGLE
NIGGLING adj petty ▷ n act or instance of niggling
NIGGLINGS > NIGGLING
NIGGLY > NIGGLE
NIGH prep near ▷ adv nearly ▷ adj near ▷ vb approach
NIGHED > NIGH
NIGHER > NIGH
NIGHEST > NIGH
NIGHING > NIGH
NIGHLY > NIGH
NIGHNESS > NIGH
NIGHS > NIGH
NIGHT n time of darkness between sunset and sunrise ▷ adj of, occurring, or working at night
NIGHTBIRD same as > NIGHTHAWK
NIGHTCAP n drink taken just before bedtime
NIGHTCAPS > NIGHTCAP
NIGHTCLUB n

establishment for dancing, music, etc, open late at night ▷ *vb* go to nightclubs
NIGHTED *adj* darkened
NIGHTFALL *n* approach of darkness
NIGHTFIRE *n* fire burned at night
NIGHTGEAR *n* nightclothes
NIGHTGLOW *n* faint light from the upper atmosphere in the night sky, esp in low latitudes
NIGHTGOWN *n* loose dress worn in bed by women
NIGHTHAWK *n* type of American nightjar
NIGHTIE *same as* > NIGHTGOWN
NIGHTIES > NIGHTY
NIGHTJAR *n* nocturnal bird with a harsh cry
NIGHTJARS > NIGHTJAR
NIGHTLESS > NIGHT
NIGHTLIFE *n* entertainment and social activities available at night in a town or city
NIGHTLIKE > NIGHT
NIGHTLONG *adv* throughout the night
NIGHTLY *adv* (happening) each night ▷ *adj* happening each night
NIGHTMARE *n* very bad dream
NIGHTMARY > NIGHTMARE
NIGHTS *adv* at night or on most nights
NIGHTSIDE *n* dark side
NIGHTSPOT *n* nightclub
NIGHTTIDE *same as* > NIGHTTIME
NIGHTTIME *n* time from sunset to sunrise
NIGHTWARD > NIGHT
NIGHTWEAR *n* apparel worn in bed or before retiring to bed
NIGHTY *same as* > NIGHTIE
NIGIRI *n* small oval block of cold rice, wasabi and fish, sometimes held together by a seaweed band
NIGIRIS > NIGIRI
NIGRICANT *adj* black
NIGRIFIED > NIGRIFY
NIGRIFIES > NIGRIFY
NIGRIFY *vb* blacken
NIGRITUDE *n* blackness
NIGROSIN *same as* > NIGROSINE
NIGROSINE *n* type of black pigment and dye used in inks and shoe polishes
NIGROSINS > NIGROSIN
NIHIL *n* nil
NIHILISM *n* rejection of all established authority and institutions
NIHILISMS > NIHILISM
NIHILIST > NIHILISM
NIHILISTS > NIHILISM
NIHILITY *n* state or condition of being nothing
NIHILS > NIHIL
NIHONGA *n* Japanese form of

painting
NIHONGAS > NIHONGA
NIKAU *n* palm tree native to New Zealand
NIKAUS > NIKAU
NIL *n* nothing, zero
NILGAI *n* large Indian antelope
NILGAIS > NILGAI
NILGAU *same as* > NILGHAU
NILGAUS > NILGAU
NILGHAI *same as* > NILGAI
NILGHAIS > NILGHAI
NILGHAU *same as* > NILGAI
NILGHAUS > NILGHAU
NILL *vb* be unwilling
NILLED > NILL
NILLING > NILL
NILLS > NILL
NILPOTENT *n* mathematical term
NILS > NIL
NIM *n* game in which two players alternately remove one or more small items from one of several rows or piles ▷ *vb* steal
NIMB *n* halo
NIMBED > NIMB
NIMBI > NIMBUS
NIMBLE *adj* agile and quick
NIMBLER > NIMBLE
NIMBLESSE > NIMBLE
NIMBLEST > NIMBLE
NIMBLEWIT *n* alert, bright, and clever person
NIMBLY > NIMBLE
NIMBS > NIMB
NIMBUS *n* dark grey rain cloud
NIMBUSED > NIMBUS
NIMBUSES > NIMBUS
NIMBYISM *n* practice of objecting to something that will affect one or take place in one's locality
NIMBYISMS > NIMBYISM
NIMBYNESS *same as* > NIMBYISM
NIMIETIES > NIMIETY
NIMIETY *rare word for* > EXCESS
NIMIOUS > NIMIETY
NIMMED > NIM
NIMMER > NIM
NIMMERS > NIM
NIMMING > NIM
NIMONIC as in *nimonic alloy* type of nickel-based alloy used at high temperature
NIMPS *adj* easy
NIMROD *n* hunter
NIMRODS > NIMROD
NIMS > NIM
NINCOM *same as* > NICOMPOOP
NINCOMS > NINCOM
NINCUM *same as* > NICOMPOOP
NINCUMS > NINCUM
NINE *n* one more than eight
NINEBARK *n* North American shrub
NINEBARKS > NINEBARK
NINEFOLD *adj* having nine times as many or as much ▷ *adv* by nine times as

much or as many
NINEHOLES *n* type of game
NINEPENCE *n* coin worth nine pennies
NINEPENNY *same as* > NINEPENCE
NINEPIN *n* skittle used in ninepins
NINEPINS *n* game of skittles
NINES > NINE
NINESCORE *n* product of nine times twenty
NINETEEN *n* ten and nine
NINETEENS > NINETEEN
NINETIES > NINETY
NINETIETH *adj* being the ordinal number of *ninety* in numbering order ▷ *n* one of 90 approximately equal parts of something
NINETY *n* ten times nine ▷ *determiner* amounting to ninety
NINHYDRIN *n* chemical reagent used for the detection and analysis of primary amines
NINJA *n* person skilled in ninjutsu
NINJAS > NINJA
NINJITSU *same as* > NINJUTSU
NINJITSUS > NINJITSU
NINJUTSU *n* Japanese martial art
NINJUTSUS > NINJUTSU
NINNIES > NINNY
NINNY *n* stupid person
NINNYISH > NINNY
NINON *n* fine strong silky fabric
NINONS > NINON
NINTH *n* (of) number nine in a series ▷ *adj* coming after the eighth in counting order, position, time, etc ▷ *adv* after the eighth person, position, event, etc
NINTHLY *same as* > NINTH
NINTHS > NINTH
NIOBATE *n* type of salt crystal
NIOBATES > NIOBATE
NIOBIC *adj* of or containing niobium in the pentavalent state
NIOBITE *another name for* > COLUMBITE
NIOBITES > NIOBITE
NIOBIUM *n* white superconductive metallic element
NIOBIUMS > NIOBIUM
NIOBOUS *adj* of or containing niobium in the trivalent state
NIP *vb* hurry ▷ *n* pinch or light bite
NIPA *n* palm tree of S and SE Asia
NIPAS > NIPA
NIPCHEESE *n* ship's purser
NIPPED > NIP
NIPPER *n* small child ▷ *vb* secure with rope
NIPPERED > NIPPER

NIPPERING > NIPPER
NIPPERKIN *n* small quantity of alcohol
NIPPERS *pl n* instrument or tool for snipping, pinching, or squeezing
NIPPIER > NIPPY
NIPPIEST > NIPPY
NIPPILY > NIPPY
NIPPINESS > NIPPY
NIPPING > NIP
NIPPINGLY > NIP
NIPPLE *n* projection in the centre of a breast ▷ *vb* provide with a nipple
NIPPLED > NIPPLE
NIPPLES > NIPPLE
NIPPLING > NIPPLE
NIPPY *adj* frosty or chilly
NIPS > NIP
NIPTER *n* type of religious ceremony
NIPTERS > NIPTER
NIQAB *n* type of veil worn by some Muslim women
NIQABS > NIQAB
NIRAMIAI *n* sumo wrestling procedure
NIRAMIAIS > NIRAMIAI
NIRL *vb* shrivel
NIRLED > NIRL
NIRLIE *variant of* > NIRLY
NIRLIER > NIRLY
NIRLIEST > NIRLY
NIRLING > NIRL
NIRLIT > NIRL
NIRLS > NIRL
NIRLY *adj* shrivelled
NIRVANA *n* absolute spiritual enlightenment and bliss
NIRVANAS > NIRVANA
NIRVANIC > NIRVANA
NIS *n* friendly goblin
NISBERRY *same as* > NASEBERRY
NISEI *n* native-born citizen of the US or Canada whose parents were Japanese immigrants
NISEIS > NISEI
NISGUL *n* smallest and weakest bird in a brood of chickens
NISGULS > NISGUL
NISH *n* nothing
NISHES > NISH
NISI *adj* (of a court order) coming into effect on a specified date
NISSE *same as* > NIS
NISSES > NISSE
NISUS *n* impulse towards or striving after a goal
NIT *n* egg or larva of a louse
NITCHIE *n* offensive term for a Native American person
NITCHIES > NITCHIE
NITE *variant of* > NIGHT
NITER *same as* > NITRE
NITERIE *n* nightclub
NITERIES > NITERIE
NITERS > NITER
NITERY > NITER
NITES > NITE
NITHER *vb* shiver

NITHERED > NITHER
NITHERING > NITHER
NITHERS > NITHER
NITHING n coward
NITHINGS > NITHING
NITID adj bright
NITINOL n metal alloy
NITINOLS > NITINOL
NITON less common name for > RADON
NITONS > NITON
NITPICK vb criticize unnecessarily
NITPICKED > NITPICK
NITPICKER > NITPICK
NITPICKS > NITPICK
NITPICKY > NITPICK
NITRAMINE another name for > TETRYL
NITRATE n compound of nitric acid, used as a fertilizer ▷ vb treat with nitric acid or a nitrate
NITRATED > NITRATE
NITRATES > NITRATE
NITRATINE n type of mineral
NITRATING > NITRATE
NITRATION > NITRATE
NITRATOR > NITRATE
NITRATORS > NITRATE
NITRE n potassium nitrate
NITRES > NITRE
NITRIC adj of or containing nitrogen
NITRID same as > NITRIDE
NITRIDE n compound of nitrogen with a more electropositive element ▷ vb make into a nitride
NITRIDED > NITRIDE
NITRIDES > NITRIDE
NITRIDING > NITRIDE
NITRIDS > NITRID
NITRIFIED > NITRIFY
NITRIFIER > NITRIFY
NITRIFIES > NITRIFY
NITRIFY vb treat (a substance) or cause (a substance) to react with nitrogen
NITRIL same as > NITRILE
NITRILE n any one of a particular class of organic compounds
NITRILES > NITRILE
NITRILS > NITRIL
NITRITE n salt or ester of nitrous acid
NITRITES > NITRITE
NITRO n nitrogylcerine
NITROGEN n colourless odourless gas that forms four fifths of the air
NITROGENS > NITROGEN
NITROLIC adj pertaining to a group of acids
NITROS > NITRO
NITROSO adj of a particular monovalent group
NITROSYL another word for > NITROSO
NITROSYLS > NITROSYL
NITROUS adj derived from or containing nitrogen in a low valency state
NITROXYL n type of

chemical
NITROXYLS > NITROXYL
NITRY adj nitrous
NITRYL n chemical compound
NITRYLS > NITRYL
NITS > NIT
NITTIER > NITTY
NITTIEST > NITTY
NITTY adj infested with nits
NITWIT n stupid person
NITWITS > NITWIT
NITWITTED > NITWIT
NIVAL adj of or growing in or under snow
NIVATION n weathering of rock around a patch of snow by alternate freezing and thawing
NIVATIONS > NIVATION
NIVEOUS adj resembling snow, esp in colour
NIX sentence substitute be careful! watch out! ▷ n rejection or refusal ▷ vb veto, deny, reject, or forbid (plans, suggestions, etc)
NIXE n water sprite
NIXED > NIX
NIXER n spare-time job
NIXERS > NIXER
NIXES > NIX
NIXIE n female water sprite, usually unfriendly to humans
NIXIES > NIXIE
NIXING > NIX
NIXY same as > NIXIE
NIZAM n (formerly) a Turkish regular soldier
NIZAMATE n territory of the nizam
NIZAMATES > NIZAMATE
NIZAMS > NIZAM
NKOSI n term of address to a superior
NKOSIS > NKOSI
NO interj expresses denial, disagreement, or refusal ▷ adj not any, not a ▷ adv not at all ▷ n answer or vote of 'no'
NOAH n shark
NOAHS > NOAH
NOB n person of wealth or social distinction
NOBBIER > NOB
NOBBIEST > NOB
NOBBILY > NOB
NOBBINESS > NOB
NOBBLE vb attract the attention of (someone) in order to talk to him or her
NOBBLED > NOBBLE
NOBBLER > NOBBLE
NOBBLERS > NOBBLE
NOBBLES > NOBBLE
NOBBLING > NOBBLE
NOBBUT adv nothing but
NOBBY > NOB
NOBELIUM n artificially-produced radioactive element
NOBELIUMS > NOBELIUM
NOBILESSE same as > NOBLESSE
NOBILIARY adj of or

relating to the nobility
NOBILITY n quality of being noble
NOBLE adj showing or having high moral qualities ▷ n member of the nobility
NOBLEMAN n person of noble rank
NOBLEMEN > NOBLEMAN
NOBLENESS > NOBLE
NOBLER > NOBLE
NOBLES > NOBLE
NOBLESSE n noble birth or condition
NOBLESSES > NOBLESSE
NOBLEST > NOBLE
NOBLY > NOBLE
NOBODIES > NOBODY
NOBODY pron no person ▷ n person of no importance
NOBS > NOB
NOCAKE n Indian meal made from dried corn
NOCAKES > NOCAKE
NOCENT n guilty person
NOCENTLY > NOCENT
NOCENTS > NOCENT
NOCHEL vb refuse to pay someone else's debt
NOCHELLED > NOCHEL
NOCHELS > NOCHEL
NOCK n notch on an arrow or a bow for the bowstring ▷ vb fit (an arrow) on a bowstring
NOCKED > NOCK
NOCKET same as > NACKET
NOCKETS > NOCKET
NOCKING > NOCK
NOCKS > NOCK
NOCTILIO n type of bat
NOCTILIOS > NOCTILIO
NOCTILUCA n any bioluminescent marine dinoflagellate of the genus Noctiluca
NOCTUA n type of moth
NOCTUARY n nightly journal
NOCTUAS > NOCTUA
NOCTUID n type of nocturnal moth ▷ adj of or relating to this type of moth
NOCTUIDS > NOCTUID
NOCTULE n any of several large Old World insectivorous bats
NOCTULES > NOCTULE
NOCTUOID > NOCTUA
NOCTURIA n excessive urination during the night
NOCTURIAS > NOCTURIA
NOCTURN n any of the main sections of the office of matins
NOCTURNAL adj of the night ▷ n something active at night
NOCTURNE n short dreamy piece of music
NOCTURNES > NOCTURNE
NOCTURNS > NOCTURN
NOCUOUS adj harmful
NOCUOUSLY > NOCUOUS
NOD vb lower and raise (one's head) briefly in agreement or greeting ▷ n

act of nodding
NODAL adj of or like a node
NODALISE same as > NODALIZE
NODALISED same as > NODALISE
NODALISES same as > NODALISE
NODALITY > NODAL
NODALIZE vb make something nodal
NODALIZED > NODALIZE
NODALIZES > NODALIZE
NODALLY > NODAL
NODATED adj knotted
NODATION n knottiness
NODATIONS > NODATION
NODDED > NOD
NODDER > NOD
NODDERS > NOD
NODDIER > NODDY
NODDIES > NODDY
NODDIEST > NODDY
NODDING > NOD
NODDINGLY > NOD
NODDINGS > NOD
NODDLE n head ▷ vb nod (the head), as through drowsiness
NODDLED > NODDLE
NODDLES > NODDLE
NODDLING > NODDLE
NODDY n tropical tern with a dark plumage ▷ adj very easy to use or understand
NODE n point on a plant stem from which leaves grow
NODES > NODE
NODI > NODUS
NODICAL adj of or relating to the nodes of a celestial body, esp of the moon
NODOSE adj having nodes or knotlike swellings
NODOSITY > NODOSE
NODOUS same as > NODOSE
NODS > NOD
NODULAR > NODULE
NODULATED > NODULE
NODULE n small knot or lump
NODULED > NODULE
NODULES > NODULE
NODULOSE > NODULE
NODULOUS > NODULE
NODUS n problematic idea, situation, etc
NOEL n Christmas
NOELS > NOEL
NOES > NO
NOESES > NOESIS
NOESIS n exercise of reason, esp in the apprehension of universal forms
NOESISES > NOESIS
NOETIC adj of or relating to the mind, esp to its rational and intellectual faculties
NOG same as > NOGGING
NOGAKU n Japanese style of drama
NOGG same as > NOG
NOGGED adj built with timber and brick
NOGGIN n head

NOGGING *n* short horizontal timber member used between the studs of a framed partition
NOGGINGS > NOGGING
NOGGINS > NOGGIN
NOGGS > NOGG
NOGS > NOG
NOH *n* stylized classic drama of Japan
NOHOW *adv* under any conditions
NOHOWISH > NOHOW
NOIL *n* short or knotted fibres that are separated from the long fibres by combing
NOILS > NOIL
NOILY > NOIL
NOINT *vb* anoint
NOINTED > NOINT
NOINTER *n* mischievous child
NOINTERS > NOINTER
NOINTING > NOINT
NOINTS > NOINT
NOIR *adj* (of a film) showing characteristics of a *film noir*, in plot or style ▷ *n* film noir
NOIRISH > NOIR
NOIRS > NOIR
NOISE *n* sound, usu a loud or disturbing one
NOISED > NOISE
NOISEFUL > NOISE
NOISELESS *adj* making little or no sound
NOISENIK *n* rock musician who performs loud harsh music
NOISENIKS > NOISENIK
NOISES > NOISE
NOISETTE *n* hazelnut chocolate ▷ *adj* flavoured or made with hazelnuts
NOISETTES > NOISETTE
NOISIER > NOISY
NOISIEST > NOISY
NOISILY > NOISY
NOISINESS > NOISY
NOISING > NOISE
NOISOME *adj* (of smells) offensive
NOISOMELY > NOISOME
NOISY *adj* making a lot of noise
NOLE *same as* > NOLL
NOLES > NOLE
NOLITION *n* unwillingness
NOLITIONS > NOLITION
NOLL *n* head
NOLLS > NOLL
NOLO as in *nolo contendere* plea indicating that the defendant does not wish to contest the case
NOLOS > NOLO
NOM *n* name
NOMA *n* gangrenous inflammation of the mouth, esp one affecting malnourished children
NOMAD *n* member of a tribe with no fixed dwelling place, wanderer
NOMADE *same as* > NOMAD
NOMADES > NOMADE

NOMADIC *adj* relating to or characteristic of nomads or their way of life
NOMADIES > NOMADY
NOMADISE *same as* > NOMADIZE
NOMADISED > NOMADISE
NOMADISES > NOMADISE
NOMADISM > NOMAD
NOMADISMS > NOMAD
NOMADIZE *vb* live as nomads
NOMADIZED > NOMADIZE
NOMADIZES > NOMADIZE
NOMADS > NOMAD
NOMADY *n* practice of living like nomads
NOMARCH *n* head of an ancient Egyptian nome
NOMARCHS > NOMARCH
NOMARCHY *n* any of the provinces of modern Greece
NOMAS > NOMA
NOMBLES *variant spelling of* > NUMBLES
NOMBRIL *n* point on a shield between the fesse point and the lowest point
NOMBRILS > NOMBRIL
NOME *n* any of the former provinces of modern Greece
NOMEN *n* ancient Roman's second name, designating his gens or clan
NOMES > NOME
NOMIC *adj* normal or habitual
NOMINA > NOMEN
NOMINABLE > NOMINATE
NOMINAL *adj* in name only ▷ *n* nominal element
NOMINALLY > NOMINAL
NOMINALS > NOMINAL
NOMINATE *vb* suggest as a candidate ▷ *adj* having a particular name
NOMINATED > NOMINATE
NOMINATES > NOMINATE
NOMINATOR > NOMINATE
NOMINEE *n* candidate
NOMINEES > NOMINEE
NOMISM *n* adherence to a law or laws as a primary exercise of religion
NOMISMS > NOMISM
NOMISTIC > NOMISM
NOMOCRACY *n* government based on the rule of law rather than arbitrary will, terror, etc
NOMOGENY *n* law of life originating as a natural process
NOMOGRAM *n* arrangement of two linear or logarithmic scales
NOMOGRAMS > NOMOGRAM
NOMOGRAPH *same as* > NOMOGRAM
NOMOI > NOMOS
NOMOLOGIC > NOMOLOGY
NOMOLOGY *n* science of law and law-making
NOMOS *n* convention
NOMOTHETE *n* legislator
NOMS > NOM

NON *adv* not
NONA *n* sleeping sickness
NONACID *adj* not acid ▷ *n* nonacid substance
NONACIDIC *adj* not acidic
NONACIDS > NONACID
NONACTING *adj* not acting
NONACTION *n* not action
NONACTIVE *adj* not active
NONACTOR *n* person who is not an actor
NONACTORS > NONACTOR
NONADDICT *n* person who is not an addict
NONADULT *n* person who is not an adult
NONADULTS > NONADULT
NONAGE *n* state of being under full legal age for various actions
NONAGED > NONAGE
NONAGES > NONAGE
NONAGON *n* geometric figure with nine sides
NONAGONAL > NONAGON
NONAGONS > NONAGON
NONANE *n* type of chemical compound
NONANES > NONANE
NONANIMAL *adj* not animal
NONANOIC as in *nonanoic acid* colourless oily fatty acid with a rancid odour
NONANSWER *n* unsatisfactory reply
NONARABLE *adj* not arable
NONART *n* something that does not constitute art
NONARTIST *n* person who is not an artist
NONARTS > NONART
NONARY *adj* based on the number nine
NONAS > NONES
NONATOMIC *adj* not atomic
NONAUTHOR *n* person who is not the author
NONBANK *n* business or institution that is not a bank but provides similar services
NONBANKS > NONBANK
NONBASIC *adj* not basic
NONBEING *n* philosophical problem relating to the question of existence
NONBEINGS > NONBEING
NONBELIEF *n* state of not believing
NONBINARY *adj* not binary
NONBITING *adj* not biting
NONBLACK *n* person or thing that is not black
NONBLACKS > NONBLACK
NONBODIES > NONBODY
NONBODY *n* nonphysical nature of a person
NONBONDED *adj* not bonded
NONBOOK *n* book with little substance
NONBOOKS > NONBOOK
NONBRAND *adj* not produced by a well-known company
NONBUYING *adj* not buying
NONCAKING *adj* not liable to cake
NONCAMPUS *adj* not on

campus
NONCAREER *adj* not career-related
NONCASH *adj* other than cash
NONCASUAL *adj* not casual
NONCAUSAL *adj* not causal
NONCE *n* present time or occasion
NONCEREAL *adj* not cereal
NONCES > NONCE
NONCHURCH *adj* not related to the church
NONCLASS *n* lack of class
NONCLING *adj* not liable to stick
NONCODING *adj* (of DNA) not containing instructions for making protein
NONCOITAL *adj* not involving sexual intercourse
NONCOKING *adj* not liable to coke
NONCOLA *n* soft drink other than cola
NONCOLAS > NONCOLA
NONCOLOR *n* achromatic colour such as black or white
NONCOLORS > NONCOLOR
NONCOM *n* person not involved in combat
NONCOMBAT *adj* not involved in combat
NONCOMS > NONCOM
NONCONCUR *vb* disagree
NONCORE *adj* not central or essential
NONCOUNTY *adj* not controlled or run by a county
NONCREDIT *adj* relating to an educational course not providing a credit towards a degree
NONCRIME *n* incident that is not a crime
NONCRIMES > NONCRIME
NONCRISES > NONCRISIS
NONCRISIS *n* situation that is not a crisis
NONCYCLIC *adj* not cyclic
NONDAIRY *adj* not containing dairy products
NONDANCE *n* series of movements that do not constitute a dance
NONDANCER *n* person who is not a dancer
NONDANCES > NONDANCE
NONDEGREE *adj* not leading to a degree
NONDEMAND *adj* not involving demand
NONDESERT *adj* not belonging to the desert
NONDOCTOR *n* person who is not a doctor
NONDOLLAR *adj* not involving the dollar
NONDRIP *adj* (of paint) specially formulated to minimize dripping during application
NONDRIVER *n* person who does not drive

NONDRUG adj not involving the use of drugs

NONDRYING adj not drying

NONE pron not any

NONEDIBLE adj not edible

NONEGO n everything that is outside one's conscious self, such as one's environment

NONEGOS > NONEGO

NONELECT n person not chosen

NONELITE adj not elite

NONEMPTY adj mathematical term

NONENDING adj not ending

NONENERGY adj without energy

NONENTITY n insignificant person or thing

NONENTRY n failure to enter

NONEQUAL adj not equal ▷ n person who is not the equal of another person

NONEQUALS > NONEQUAL

NONEROTIC adj not erotic

NONES n (in the Roman calendar) the ninth day before the ides of each month

NONESUCH n matchless person or thing

NONET n piece of music composed for a group of nine instruments

NONETHNIC n not ethnic

NONETS > NONET

NONETTE same as > NONET

NONETTES > NONETTE

NONETTI same as > NONET

NONETTO same as > NONET

NONETTOS > NONETTO

NONEVENT n disappointing or insignificant occurrence

NONEVENTS > NONEVENT

NONEXEMPT adj not exempt

NONEXOTIC adj not exotic

NONEXPERT n person who is not an expert

NONEXTANT adj no longer in existence

NONFACT n event or thing not provable

NONFACTOR n something that is not a factor

NONFACTS > NONFACT

NONFADING adj colourfast

NONFAMILY n household that does not consist of a family

NONFAN n person who is not a fan

NONFANS > NONFAN

NONFARM adj not connected with a farm

NONFARMER n person who is not a farmer

NONFAT adj fat free

NONFATAL adj not resulting in or capable of causing death

NONFATTY adj not fatty

NONFEUDAL adj not feudal

NONFILIAL adj not involving parent-child relationship

NONFINAL adj not final

NONFINITE adj not finite

NONFISCAL adj not involving government funds

NONFLUID adj not fluid ▷ n something that is not a fluid

NONFLUIDS > NONFLUID

NONFLYING adj not capable of flying

NONFOCAL adj not focal

NONFOOD n item that is not food

NONFORMAL adj not formal

NONFOSSIL adj not consisting of fossils

NONFROZEN adj not frozen

NONFUEL adj not relating to fuel

NONFUNDED adj not receiving funding

NONG n stupid or incompetent person

NONGAME adj not pursued for competitive sport purposes

NONGAY n person who is not gay

NONGAYS > NONGAY

NONGHETTO adj not belonging to the ghetto

NONGLARE adj not causing glare ▷ n any of various nonglare materials

NONGLARES > NONGLARE

NONGLAZED adj not glazed

NONGLOSSY adj not glossy

NONGOLFER n person who is not a golfer

NONGRADED adj not graded

NONGREASY adj not greasy

NONGREEN adj not green

NONGROWTH n failure to grow

NONGS > NONG

NONGUEST n person who is not a guest

NONGUESTS > NONGUEST

NONGUILT n state of being innocent

NONGUILTS > NONGUILT

NONHARDY adj fragile

NONHEME adj of dietary iron, obtained from vegetable foods

NONHERO n person who is not a hero

NONHEROES > NONHERO

NONHEROIC adj not heroic

NONHOME adj not of the home

NONHUMAN n something not human

NONHUMANS > NONHUMAN

NONHUNTER n person or thing that does not hunt

NONI n type of tree of SE Asia and the Pacific islands whose fruit provides a possibly health-promoting juice

NONIDEAL adj not ideal

NONILLION n (in Britain, France, and Germany) the number represented as one followed by 54 zeros

NONIMAGE n person who is

not a celebrity

NONIMAGES > NONIMAGE

NONIMMUNE adj not immune

NONIMPACT adj not involving impact

NONINERT adj not inert

NONINJURY adj not involving injury

NONINSECT n animal that is not an insect

NONIONIC adj not ionic

NONIRON adj not requiring ironing

NONIS > NONI

NONISSUE n matter of little importance

NONISSUES > NONISSUE

NONJOINER n person who does not join (an organisation, etc)

NONJURIES > NONJURY

NONJURING adj refusing the oath of allegiance

NONJUROR n person who refuses to take an oath, as of allegiance

NONJURORS > NONJUROR

NONJURY n trial without a jury

NONKOSHER adj not kosher

NONLABOR adj not concerned with labour

NONLAWYER n person who is not a lawyer

NONLEADED adj not leaded

NONLEAFY adj not leafy

NONLEAGUE adj not belonging to a league

NONLEGAL adj not legal

NONLEGUME n not a pod of the pea or bean family

NONLETHAL adj not resulting in or capable of causing death

NONLEVEL adj not level

NONLIABLE adj not liable

NONLIFE n matter which is not living

NONLINEAL same as > NONLINEAR

NONLINEAR adj not of, in, along, or relating to a line

NONLIQUID n substance which is not liquid

NONLIVES > NONLIFE

NONLIVING adj not living

NONLOCAL adj not of, affecting, or confined to a limited area or part ▷ n person who is not local to an area

NONLOCALS > NONLOCAL

NONLOVING adj not loving

NONLOYAL adj not loyal

NONLYRIC adj without lyrics

NONMAJOR n student who is not majoring in a specified subject

NONMAJORS > NONMAJOR

NONMAN n being that is not a man

NONMANUAL adj not manual

NONMARKET adj not relating to markets

NONMATURE adj not mature

NONMEAT n not containing meat

NONMEMBER n person who is not a member of a particular club or organization

NONMEN > NONMAN

NONMENTAL adj not mental

NONMETAL n chemical element that forms acidic oxides and is a poor conductor of heat and electricity

NONMETALS > NONMETAL

NONMETRIC adj not metric

NONMETRO adj not metropolitan

NONMOBILE adj not mobile

NONMODAL adj not modal

NONMODERN adj not modern

NONMONEY adj not involving money

NONMORAL adj not involving morality

NONMORTAL adj not fatal

NONMOTILE adj not capable of movement

NONMOVING adj not moving

NONMUSIC n (unpleasant) noise

NONMUSICS > NONMUSIC

NONMUTANT n person or thing that is not mutated

NONMUTUAL adj not mutual

NONNASAL adj not nasal

NONNATIVE adj not native ▷ n person who is not native to a place

NONNAVAL adj not belonging to the navy

NONNEURAL adj not neural

NONNEWS adj not concerned with news

NONNIES > NONNY

NONNOBLE adj not noble

NONNORMAL adj not normal

NONNOVEL n literary work that is not a novel

NONNOVELS > NONNOVEL

NONNY n meaningless word

NONOBESE adj not obese

NONOHMIC adj not having electrical resistance

NONOILY adj not oily

NONORAL adj not oral

NONORALLY > NONORAL

NONOWNER n person who is not an owner

NONOWNERS > NONOWNER

NONPAGAN n person who is not a pagan

NONPAGANS > NONPAGAN

NONPAID adj without payment

NONPAPAL adj not of the pope

NONPAPIST adj not papist

NONPAR adj nonparticipating

NONPAREIL n person or thing that is unsurpassed ▷ adj having no match or equal

NONPARENT n person who is not a parent

NONPARITY n state of not being equal

NONPAROUS adj never having given birth

NONPARTY adj not connected with a political party

NONPAST n grammatical term

NONPASTS > NONPAST

NONPAYING adj (of guests, customers, etc) not expected or requested to pay

NONPEAK n period of low demand

NONPERSON n person regarded as nonexistent or unimportant

NONPLANAR adj not planar

NONPLAY n social behaviour that is not classed as play

NONPLAYER n person not playing

NONPLAYS > NONPLAY

NONPLIANT adj not pliant

NONPLUS vb put at a loss ▷ n state of utter perplexity prohibiting action or speech

NONPLUSED > NONPLUS

NONPLUSES > NONPLUS

NONPOETIC adj not poetic

NONPOINT adj without a specific site

NONPOLAR adj not polar

NONPOLICE adj not related to the police

NONPOOR adj not poor

NONPOROUS adj not permeable to water, air, or other fluids

NONPOSTAL adj not postal

NONPRINT adj published in a format other than print on paper

NONPROFIT n organization that is not intended to make a profit

NONPROS vb enter a judgment of non prosequitur against a plaintiff

NONPROVEN adj not tried and tested

NONPUBLIC adj not public

NONQUOTA adj not included in a quota

NONRACIAL adj not related to racial factors or discrimination

NONRANDOM adj not random

NONRATED adj not rated

NONREADER n person who does not or cannot read

NONRETURN adj denoting a mechanism that permits flow in a pipe in one direction only

NONRHOTIC adj denoting or speaking a dialect of English in which preconsonantal r s are not pronounced

NONRIGID adj not rigid

NONRIOTER n person who does not participate in a riot

NONRIVAL n person or thing not competing for success

NONRIVALS > NONRIVAL

NONROYAL adj not royal

NONRUBBER adj not containing rubber

NONRULING adj not ruling

NONRURAL adj not rural

NONSACRED adj not sacred

NONSALINE adj not containing salt

NONSCHOOL adj not relating to school

NONSECRET adj not sacred

NONSECURE adj not secure

NONSELF n foreign molecule in the body

NONSELVES > NONSELF

NONSENSE n something that has or makes no sense ▷ interj exclamation of disagreement

NONSENSES > NONSENSE

NONSERIAL adj not serial

NONSEXIST adj not discriminating on the basis of sex, esp not against women

NONSEXUAL adj not of, relating to, or characterized by sex or sexuality

NONSHRINK adj not likely to shrink

NONSIGNER n person who cannot use sign language

NONSKATER n person who does not skate

NONSKED n non-scheduled aeroplane

NONSKEDS > NONSKED

NONSKID adj designed to reduce skidding

NONSKIER n person who does not ski

NONSKIERS > NONSKIER

NONSLIP adj designed to prevent slipping

NONSMOKER n person who does not smoke

NONSOCIAL adj not social

NONSOLAR adj not related to the sun

NONSOLID n substance that is not a solid

NONSOLIDS > NONSOLID

NONSPEECH adj not involving speech

NONSTAPLE adj not staple

NONSTATIC adj not static

NONSTEADY adj not steady

NONSTICK adj coated with a substance that food will not stick to when cooked

NONSTICKY adj not sticky

NONSTOP adv without a stop ▷ adj without a stop ▷ n nonstop flight

NONSTOPS > NONSTOP

NONSTORY n story of little substance or importance

NONSTYLE n style that cannot be identified

NONSTYLES > NONSTYLE

NONSUCH same as > NONESUCH

NONSUCHES > NONSUCH

NONSUGAR n substance that is not a sugar

NONSUGARS > NONSUGAR

NONSUIT n order of a judge dismissing a suit when the plaintiff fails to show a good cause of action or to produce any evidence ▷ vb order the dismissal of the suit of (a person)

NONSUITED > NONSUIT

NONSUITS > NONSUIT

NONSYSTEM adj having no system

NONTALKER n person who does not talk

NONTARGET adj not being a target

NONTARIFF adj without tariff

NONTAX n tax that has little real effect

NONTAXES > NONTAX

NONTHEIST n person who believes the existence or non-existence of God is irrelevant

NONTIDAL adj not having a tide

NONTITLE adj without title

NONTONAL adj not written in a key

NONTONIC adj not tonic

NONTOXIC adj not poisonous

NONTRAGIC adj not tragic

NONTRIBAL adj not tribal

NONTRUMP adj not of the trump suit

NONTRUTH same as > UNTRUTH

NONTRUTHS > NONTRUTH

NONUNION adj (of a company) not employing trade union members ▷ n failure of broken bones or bone fragments to heal

NONUNIONS > NONUNION

NONUNIQUE adj not unique

NONUPLE adj ninefold ▷ n ninefold number

NONUPLES > NONUPLE

NONUPLET n child born in a multiple birth of nine siblings

NONUPLETS > NONUPLET

NONURBAN adj rural

NONURGENT adj not urgent

NONUSABLE adj not usable

NONUSE n failure to use

NONUSER > NONUSE

NONUSERS > NONUSE

NONUSES > NONUSE

NONUSING > NONUSE

NONVACANT adj not vacant

NONVALID adj not valid

NONVECTOR n quantity without size and direction

NONVENOUS adj not venous

NONVERBAL adj not involving the use of language

NONVESTED adj not vested

NONVIABLE adj not viable

NONVIEWER n person who does not watch (television)

NONVIRAL adj not caused by a virus

NONVIRGIN n person who is not a virgin

NONVIRILE adj not virile

NONVISUAL adj not visual

NONVITAL adj not vital

NONVOCAL n music track without singing

NONVOCALS > NONVOCAL

NONVOTER n person who does not vote

NONVOTERS > NONVOTER

NONVOTING adj (of shares in a company) not entitling the owner to vote at company meetings

NONWAGE adj not part of wages

NONWAR n state of nonviolence

NONWARS > NONWAR

NONWHITE n person who is not white

NONWHITES > NONWHITE

NONWINGED adj without wings

NONWOODY adj not woody

NONWOOL adj not wool

NONWORD n series of letters not recognised as a word

NONWORDS > NONWORD

NONWORK adj not involving work

NONWORKER n person who does not work

NONWOVEN n material made by a method other than weaving

NONWOVENS > NONWOVEN

NONWRITER n person who is not a writer

NONYL n type of chemical

NONYLS > NONYL

NONZERO adj not equal to zero

NOO n type of Japanese musical drama

NOODGE vb annoy persistently

NOODGED > NOODGE

NOODGES > NOODGE

NOODGING > NOODGE

NOODLE n simpleton ▷ vb improvise aimlessly on a musical instrument

NOODLED > NOODLE

NOODLEDOM n state of being a simpleton

NOODLES > NOODLE

NOODLING n aimless musical improvisation

NOODLINGS > NOODLING

NOOGIE n act of inflicting pain by rubbing someone's head hard

NOOGIES > NOOGIE

NOOIT interj South African exclamation of pleased or shocked surprise

NOOK n corner or recess

NOOKIE same as > NOOKY

NOOKIER > NOOKY

NOOKIES > NOOKIE

NOOKIEST > NOOKY

NOOKLIKE > NOOK

NOOKS > NOOK

NOOKY n sexual intercourse ▷ adj resembling a nook

NOOLOGIES > NOOLOGY

NOOLOGY n study of

intuition

NOOMETRY *n* mind measurement

NOON *n* twelve o'clock midday ▷ *vb* take a rest at noon

NOONDAY *adj* happening at noon ▷ *n* middle of the day

NOONDAYS > NOONDAY

NOONED > NOON

NOONER *n* sexual encounter during a lunch hour

NOONERS > NOONER

NOONING *n* midday break for rest or food

NOONINGS > NOONING

NOONS > NOON

NOONTIDE same as > NOONTIME

NOONTIDES > NOONTIDE

NOONTIME *n* middle of the day

NOONTIMES > NOONTIME

NOOP *n* point of the elbow

NOOPS > NOOP

NOOSE *n* loop in the end of a rope, tied with a slipknot

NOOSED > NOOSE

NOOSER *n* person who uses a noose

NOOSERS > NOOSER

NOOSES > NOOSE

NOOSING > NOOSE

NOOSPHERE *n* sphere of human thought

NOOTROPIC *adj* acting on mind

NOPAL *n* type of cactus

NOPALES > NOPAL

NOPALITO *n* small cactus

NOPALITOS > NOPALITO

NOPALS > NOPAL

NOPE *interj* no

NOPLACE same as > NOWHERE

NOR *prep* and not

NORDIC *adj* of competitions in cross-country racing and ski-jumping

NORI *n* edible seaweed often used in Japanese cookery, esp for wrapping sushi or rice balls

NORIA *n* water wheel with buckets attached to its rim for raising water from a stream into irrigation canals

NORIAS > NORIA

NORIMON *n* Japanese passenger vehicle

NORIMONS > NORIMON

NORIS > NORI

NORITE *n* variety of gabbro composed mainly of hypersthene and labradorite feldspar

NORITES > NORITE

NORITIC > NORITE

NORK *n* female breast

NORKS > NORK

NORLAND *n* north part of a country or the earth

NORLANDS > NORLAND

NORM *n* standard that is regarded as normal

NORMA *n* norm or standard

NORMAL *adj* usual, regular, or typical ▷ *n* usual or regular state, degree or form

NORMALCY > NORMAL

NORMALISE same as > NORMALIZE

NORMALITY > NORMAL

NORMALIZE *vb* make or become normal

NORMALLY *adv* as a rule

NORMALS > NORMAL

NORMAN *n* post used for winding on a ship

NORMANDE *n* type of cattle

NORMANS > NORMAN

NORMAS > NORMA

NORMATIVE *adj* of or setting a norm or standard

NORMED *n* mathematical term

NORMLESS *adj* without a norm

NORMS > NORM

NORSEL *vb* fit with short lines for fastening hooks

NORSELLED > NORSEL

NORSELLER > NORSEL

NORSELS > NORSEL

NORTENA same as > NORTENO

NORTENAS > NORTENA

NORTENO *n* type of Mexican music

NORTENOS > NORTENO

NORTH *n* direction towards the North Pole, opposite south ▷ *adj* or in the north ▷ *adv* in, to, or towards the north ▷ *vb* move north

NORTHEAST *adv* (in or to) direction between north and east ▷ *n* point of the compass or direction midway between north and east ▷ *adj* of or denoting the northeastern part of a specified country, area, etc

NORTHED > NORTH

NORTHER *n* wind or storm from the north ▷ *vb* move north

NORTHERED > NORTHER

NORTHERLY *adj* of or in the north ▷ *adv* towards the north ▷ *n* wind from the north

NORTHERN *adj* situated in or towards the north ▷ *n* person from the north

NORTHERNS > NORTHERN

NORTHERS > NORTHER

NORTHING *n* movement or distance covered in a northerly direction

NORTHINGS > NORTHING

NORTHLAND *n* lands that are far to the north

NORTHMOST *adj* situated furthest north

NORTHS > NORTH

NORTHWARD *adv* towards the north

NORTHWEST *adv* (in or to) direction between north and west ▷ *n* point of the compass or direction midway between north and west ▷ *adj* of or denoting the northwestern part of a specified country, area, etc

NORWARD same as > NORTHWARD

NORWARDS same as > NORWARD

NOS > NO

NOSE *n* organ of smell, used also in breathing ▷ *vb* move forward slowly and carefully

NOSEAN *n* type of mineral

NOSEANS > NOSEAN

NOSEBAG *n* bag containing feed fastened round a horse's head

NOSEBAGS > NOSEBAG

NOSEBAND *n* part of a horse's bridle that goes around the nose

NOSEBANDS > NOSEBAND

NOSEBLEED *n* bleeding from the nose

NOSED > NOSE

NOSEDIVE *vb* (of an aircraft) plunge suddenly with the nose pointing downwards

NOSEDIVED > NOSEDIVE

NOSEDIVES > NOSEDIVE

NOSEDOVE > NOSEDIVE

NOSEGAY *n* small bunch of flowers

NOSEGAYS > NOSEGAY

NOSEGUARD *n* position in American football

NOSELESS > NOSE

NOSELIKE > NOSE

NOSELITE same as > NOSEAN

NOSELITES > NOSELITE

NOSEPIECE same as > NOSEBAND

NOSER *n* strong headwind

NOSERS > NOSER

NOSES > NOSE

NOSEWHEEL *n* wheel fitted under the nose of an aircraft

NOSEY *adj* prying or inquisitive ▷ *n* nosey person

NOSEYS > NOSEY

NOSH *n* food ▷ *vb* eat

NOSHED > NOSH

NOSHER > NOSH

NOSHERIE same as > NOSHERY

NOSHERIES > NOSHERIE

NOSHERS > NOSH

NOSHERY *n* restaurant or other place where food is served

NOSHES > NOSH

NOSHING > NOSH

NOSIER > NOSY

NOSIES > NOSY

NOSIEST > NOSY

NOSILY > NOSY

NOSINESS > NOSY

NOSING *n* edge of a step or stair tread that projects beyond the riser

NOSINGS > NOSING

NOSODE *n* homeopathic remedy

NOSODES > NOSODE

NOSOLOGIC > NOSOLOGY

NOSOLOGY *n* branch of medicine concerned with the classification of diseases

NOSTALGIA *n* sentimental longing for the past

NOSTALGIC *adj* of or characterized by nostalgia ▷ *n* person who indulges in nostalgia

NOSTOC *n* type of bacterium occurring in moist places

NOSTOCS > NOSTOC

NOSTOI > NOSTOS

NOSTOLOGY *n* scientific study of ageing

NOSTOS *n* story of a return home

NOSTRIL *n* one of the two openings at the end of the nose

NOSTRILS > NOSTRIL

NOSTRO as in *nostro account* bank account conducted by a British bank with a foreign bank

NOSTRUM *n* quack medicine

NOSTRUMS > NOSTRUM

NOSY *adj* prying or inquisitive

NOT *adv* expressing negation, refusal, or denial

NOTA > NOTUM

NOTABILIA *n* things worthy of notice

NOTABLE *adj* worthy of being noted, remarkable ▷ *n* person of distinction

NOTABLES > NOTABLE

NOTABLY *adv* particularly or especially

NOTAEUM *n* back of a bird's body

NOTAEUMS > NOTAEUM

NOTAL > NOTUM

NOTANDA > NOTANDUM

NOTANDUM *n* notable fact

NOTAPHILY *n* study of paper money

NOTARIAL > NOTARY

NOTARIES > NOTARY

NOTARISE same as > NOTARIZE

NOTARISED > NOTARISE

NOTARISES > NOTARISE

NOTARIZE *vb* attest to or authenticate (a document, contract, etc), as a notary

NOTARIZED > NOTARIZE

NOTARIZES > NOTARIZE

NOTARY *n* person authorized to witness the signing of legal documents

NOTATE *vb* write (esp music) in notation

NOTATED > NOTATE

NOTATES > NOTATE

NOTATING > NOTATE

NOTATION *n* representation of numbers or quantities in a system by a series of symbols

NOTATIONS > NOTATION

NOTCH *n* V-shaped cut ▷ *vb*

make a notch in
NOTCHBACK *n* type of car
NOTCHED > NOTCH
NOTCHEL *vb* refuse to pay another person's debts
NOTCHELS > NOTCHEL
NOTCHER *n* person who cuts notches
NOTCHERS > NOTCHER
NOTCHES > NOTCH
NOTCHIER > NOTCHY
NOTCHIEST > NOTCHY
NOTCHING > NOTCH
NOTCHINGS > NOTCH
NOTCHY *adj* (of a motor vehicle gear mechanism) requiring careful gear-changing
NOTE *n* short letter ▷*vb* notice, pay attention to
NOTEBOOK *n* book for writing in
NOTEBOOKS > NOTEBOOK
NOTECARD *n* greetings card with space to write note
NOTECARDS > NOTECARD
NOTECASE *same as* > WALLET
NOTECASES > NOTECASE
NOTED *adj* well-known
NOTEDLY > NOTED
NOTEDNESS > NOTED
NOTELESS > NOTE
NOTELET *n* small folded card with a design on the front, used for writing informal letters
NOTELETS > NOTELET
NOTEPAD *n* number of sheets of paper fastened together along one edge
NOTEPADS > NOTEPAD
NOTEPAPER *n* paper used for writing letters
NOTER *n* person who takes notes
NOTERS > NOTER
NOTES *pl n* short descriptive or summarized jottings taken down for future reference
NOTHER *same as* > OTHER
NOTHING *pron* not anything ▷*adv* not at all ▷*n* person or thing of no importance
NOTHINGS > NOTHING
NOTICE *n* observation or attention ▷*vb* observe, become aware of
NOTICED > NOTICE
NOTICER *n* person who takes notice
NOTICERS > NOTICER
NOTICES > NOTICE
NOTICING > NOTICE
NOTIFIED > NOTIFY
NOTIFIER > NOTIFY
NOTIFIERS > NOTIFY
NOTIFIES > NOTIFY
NOTIFY *vb* inform
NOTIFYING > NOTIFY
NOTING > NOTE
NOTION *n* idea or opinion
NOTIONAL *adj* speculative, imaginary, or unreal
NOTIONIST *n* person whose opinions are merely notions

NOTIONS *pl n* pins, cotton, ribbon, and similar wares used for sewing
NOTITIA *n* register or list, esp of ecclesiastical districts
NOTITIAE > NOTITIA
NOTITIAS > NOTITIA
NOTOCHORD *n* fibrous longitudinal rod in all embryo and some adult chordate animals
NOTORIETY > NOTORIOUS
NOTORIOUS *adj* well known for something bad
NOTORNIS *n* rare flightless rail of New Zealand
NOTOUR *adj* notorious
NOTT *same as* > NOT
NOTTURNI > NOTTURNO
NOTTURNO *n* piece of music
NOTUM *n* cuticular plate covering the dorsal surface of a thoracic segment of an insect
NOUGAT *n* chewy sweet containing nuts and fruit
NOUGATS > NOUGAT
NOUGHT *n* figure o
NOUGHTIES *pl n* decade from 2000 to 2009
NOUGHTS > NOUGHT
NOUL *same as* > NOLL
NOULD *vb* would not
NOULDE *same as* > NOULD
NOULE *same as* > NOLL
NOULES > NOULE
NOULS > NOUL
NOUMENA > NOUMENON
NOUMENAL > NOUMENON
NOUMENON *n* (in the philosophy of Kant) a thing as it is in itself, incapable of being known, but only inferred from the nature of experience
NOUN *n* word that refers to a person, place, or thing
NOUNAL > NOUN
NOUNALLY > NOUN
NOUNIER > NOUNY
NOUNIEST > NOUNY
NOUNLESS > NOUN
NOUNS > NOUN
NOUNY *adj* nounlike
NOUP *n* steep headland
NOUPS > NOUP
NOURICE *n* nurse
NOURICES > NOURICE
NOURISH *vb* feed
NOURISHED > NOURISH
NOURISHER > NOURISH
NOURISHES > NOURISH
NOURITURE *n* nourishment
NOURSLE *vb* nurse
NOURSLED > NOURSLE
NOURSLES > NOURSLE
NOURSLING > NOURSLE
NOUS *n* common sense
NOUSELL *vb* foster
NOUSELLED > NOUSELL
NOUSELLS > NOUSELL
NOUSES > NOUS
NOUSLE *vb* nuzzle
NOUSLED > NOUSLE
NOUSLES > NOUSLE
NOUSLING > NOUSLE

NOUT *same as* > NOUGHT
NOUVEAU *adj* having recently become the thing specified
NOUVEAUX *same as* > NOUVEAU
NOUVELLE *n* long short story
NOUVELLES > NOUVELLE
NOVA *n* star that suddenly becomes brighter and then gradually decreases to its original brightness
NOVAE > NOVA
NOVALIA *n* newly reclaimed land
NOVALIKE *adj* resembling a nova
NOVAS > NOVA
NOVATED as in *novated lease* Australian system of employer-aided car purchase
NOVATION *n* substitution of a new obligation for an old one by mutual agreement between the parties
NOVATIONS > NOVATION
NOVEL *n* long fictitious story in book form ▷*adj* fresh, new, or original
NOVELDOM *n* realm of fiction
NOVELDOMS > NOVELDOM
NOVELESE *n* style of writing characteristic of poor novels
NOVELESES > NOVELESE
NOVELETTE *n* short novel, esp one regarded as trivial or sentimental
NOVELISE *same as* > NOVELIZE
NOVELISED > NOVELISE
NOVELISER *n* person who novelizes
NOVELISES > NOVELISE
NOVELISH *adj* resembling a novel
NOVELISM *n* innovation
NOVELISMS > NOVELISM
NOVELIST *n* writer of novels
NOVELISTS > NOVELIST
NOVELIZE *vb* convert (a true story, film, etc) into a novel
NOVELIZED > NOVELIZE
NOVELIZER *n* person who novelizes
NOVELIZES > NOVELIZE
NOVELLA *n* short novel
NOVELLAE > NOVELLA
NOVELLAS > NOVELLA
NOVELLE > NOVELLA
NOVELLY > NOVEL
NOVELS > NOVEL
NOVELTIES > NOVELTY
NOVELTY *n* newness
NOVENA *n* set of prayers or services on nine consecutive days
NOVENAE > NOVENA
NOVENARY *n* set of nine
NOVENAS > NOVENA
NOVENNIAL *adj* recurring every ninth year
NOVERCAL *adj* stepmotherly
NOVERINT *n* writ

NOVERINTS > NOVERINT
NOVICE *n* beginner
NOVICES > NOVICE
NOVICIATE *same as* > NOVITIATE
NOVITIATE *n* period of being a novice
NOVITIES > NOVITY
NOVITY *n* novelty
NOVOCAINE *n* tradename of a painkilling substance used as a local anaesthetic
NOVODAMUS *n* type of charter
NOVUM *n* game played with dice
NOVUMS > NOVUM
NOW *adv* at or for the present time
NOWADAYS *adv* in these times
NOWAY *adv* in no manner ▷*sentence substitute* used to make an emphatic refusal, denial etc
NOWAYS *same as* > NOWAY
NOWED *adj* knotted
NOWHENCE *adv* from no place
NOWHERE *adv* not anywhere ▷*n* nonexistent or insignicant place
NOWHERES > NOWHERE
NOWHITHER *adv* no place
NOWISE *another word for* > NOWAY
NOWL *n* crown of the head
NOWLS > NOWL
NOWN *same as* > OWN
NOWNESS > NOWN
NOWNESSES > NOWN
NOWS > NOW
NOWT *n* nothing
NOWTIER > NOWTY
NOWTIEST > NOWTY
NOWTS > NOWT
NOWTY *adj* bad-tempered
NOWY *adj* having a small projection at the centre (of a cross)
NOX *n* nitrogen oxide
NOXAL *adj* relating to damage done by something belonging to another
NOXES > NOX
NOXIOUS *adj* poisonous or harmful
NOXIOUSLY > NOXIOUS
NOY *vb* harrass
NOYADE *n* execution by drowning
NOYADES > NOYADE
NOYANCE *n* nuisance
NOYANCES > NOYANCE
NOYAU *n* liqueur made from brandy flavoured with nut kernels
NOYAUS > NOYAU
NOYED > NOY
NOYES *archaic form of* > NOISE
NOYESES > NOYES
NOYING > NOY
NOYOUS > NOY
NOYS > NOY
NOYSOME > NOY
NOZZER *n* new recruit (in

the Navy)

NOZZERS > NOZZER

NOZZLE n projecting spout through which fluid is discharged

NOZZLES > NOZZLE

NTH adj of an unspecified number

NU n 13th letter in the Greek alphabet

NUANCE n subtle difference in colour, meaning, or tone ▷ vb give subtle differences to

NUANCED > NUANCE

NUANCES > NUANCE

NUANCING > NUANCE

NUB n point or gist (of a story etc) ▷ vb hang from the gallows

NUBBED > NUB

NUBBIER > NUBBY

NUBBIEST > NUBBY

NUBBIN n something small or undeveloped, esp a fruit or ear of corn

NUBBINESS > NUBBY

NUBBING > NUB

NUBBINS > NUBBIN

NUBBLE n small lump

NUBBLED > NUBBLE

NUBBLES > NUBBLE

NUBBLIER > NUBBLE

NUBBLIEST > NUBBLE

NUBBLING > NUBBLE

NUBBLY > NUBBLE

NUBBY adj having small lumps or protuberances

NUBECULA n small irregular galaxy near the S celestial pole

NUBECULAE > NUBECULA

NUBIA n fleecy scarf for the head, worn by women

NUBIAS > NUBIA

NUBIFORM adj cloudlike

NUBILE adj sexually attractive

NUBILITY > NUBILE

NUBILOSE same as > NUBILOUS

NUBILOUS adj cloudy

NUBS > NUB

NUBUCK n type of leather with a velvety finish

NUBUCKS > NUBUCK

NUCELLAR > NUCELLUS

NUCELLI > NUCELLUS

NUCELLUS n central part of a plant ovule containing the embryo sac

NUCHA n back or nape of the neck

NUCHAE > NUCHA

NUCHAL n scale on a reptile's neck

NUCHALS > NUCHAL

NUCLEAL > NUCLEUS

NUCLEAR adj of nuclear weapons or energy

NUCLEASE n any of a group of enzymes that hydrolyse nucleic acids to simple nucleotides

NUCLEASES > NUCLEASE

NUCLEATE adj having a nucleus ▷ vb form a

nucleus

NUCLEATED > NUCLEATE

NUCLEATES > NUCLEATE

NUCLEATOR > NUCLEATE

NUCLEI > NUCLEUS

NUCLEIC as in nucleic acid type of complex compound that is a vital constituent of living cells

NUCLEIDE same as > NUCLIDE

NUCLEIDES > NUCLEIDE

NUCLEIN n any of a group of proteins that occur in the nuclei of living cells

NUCLEINIC > NUCLEIN

NUCLEINS > NUCLEIN

NUCLEOID n component of a bacterium

NUCLEOIDS > NUCLEOID

NUCLEOLAR > NUCLEOLUS

NUCLEOLE variant of > NUCLEOLUS

NUCLEOLES > NUCLEOLE

NUCLEOLI > NUCLEOLUS

NUCLEOLUS n small rounded body within a resting nucleus that contains RNA and proteins

NUCLEON n proton or neutron

NUCLEONIC adj relating to the branch of physics concerned with the applications of nuclear energy

NUCLEONS > NUCLEON

NUCLEUS n centre, esp of an atom or cell

NUCLEUSES > NUCLEUS

NUCLIDE n species of atom characterized by its atomic number and its mass number

NUCLIDES > NUCLIDE

NUCLIDIC > NUCLIDE

NUCULE n small seed

NUCULES > NUCULE

NUDATION n act of stripping

NUDATIONS > NUDATION

NUDDIES > NUDDY

NUDDY as in in the nuddy in the nude

NUDE adj naked ▷ n naked figure in painting, sculpture, or photography

NUDELY > NUDE

NUDENESS > NUDE

NUDER > NUDE

NUDES > NUDE

NUDEST > NUDE

NUDGE vb push gently, esp with the elbow ▷ n gentle push or touch

NUDGED > NUDGE

NUDGER > NUDGE

NUDGERS > NUDGE

NUDGES > NUDGE

NUDGING > NUDGE

NUDICAUL adj (of plants) having stems without leaves

NUDIE n film, show, or magazine depicting nudity

NUDIES > NUDIE

NUDISM n practice of not wearing clothes

NUDISMS > NUDISM

NUDIST > NUDISM

NUDISTS > NUDISM

NUDITIES > NUDITY

NUDITY n state or fact of being nude

NUDNICK same as > NUDNIK

NUDNICKS > NUDNICK

NUDNIK n boring person

NUDNIKS > NUDNIK

NUDZH same as > NUDGE

NUDZHED > NUDZH

NUDZHES > NUDZH

NUDZHING > NUDZH

NUFF slang form of > ENOUGH

NUFFIN slang form of > NOTHING

NUFFINS > NUFFIN

NUFFS > NUFF

NUGAE n jests

NUGATORY adj of little value

NUGGAR n sailing boat used to carry cargo on the Nile

NUGGARS > NUGGAR

NUGGET n small lump of gold in its natural state ▷ vb polish footwear

NUGGETED > NUGGET

NUGGETING > NUGGET

NUGGETS > NUGGET

NUGGETTED > NUGGET

NUGGETY adj of or resembling a nugget

NUISANCE n something or someone that causes annoyance or bother ▷ adj causing annoyance or bother

NUISANCER n person or thing causing a nuisance

NUISANCES > NUISANCE

NUKE vb attack with nuclear weapons ▷ n nuclear weapon

NUKED > NUKE

NUKES > NUKE

NUKING > NUKE

NULL adj without legal force ▷ vb make negative

NULLA same as > NULLAH

NULLAH n stream or drain

NULLAHS > NULLAH

NULLAS > NULLA

NULLED > NULL

NULLIFIED > NULLIFY

NULLIFIER > NULLIFY

NULLIFIES > NULLIFY

NULLIFY vb make ineffective

NULLING n knurling

NULLINGS > NULLING

NULLIPARA n woman who has never borne a child

NULLIPORE n any of several red seaweeds

NULLITIES > NULLITY

NULLITY n state of being null

NULLNESS > NULL

NULLS > NULL

NUMB adj without feeling, as through cold, shock, or fear ▷ vb make numb

NUMBAT n small Australian marsupial with a long snout and tongue

NUMBATS > NUMBAT

NUMBED > NUMB

NUMBER n sum or quantity ▷ vb count

NUMBERED > NUMBER

NUMBERER n person who numbers

NUMBERERS > NUMBERER

NUMBERING > NUMBER

NUMBERS > NUMBER

NUMBEST > NUMB

NUMBFISH n any of several electric ray fish

NUMBING > NUMB

NUMBINGLY > NUMB

NUMBLES pl n heart, lungs, liver, etc, of a deer or other animal, cooked for food

NUMBLY > NUMB

NUMBNESS > NUMB

NUMBS > NUMB

NUMBSKULL n stupid person

NUMCHUCK same as > NUNCHAKU

NUMCHUCKS > NUMCHUCK

NUMDAH n coarse felt made esp in India

NUMDAHS > NUMDAH

NUMEN n (esp in ancient Roman religion) a deity or spirit presiding over a thing or place

NUMERABLE adj able to be numbered or counted

NUMERABLY > NUMERABLE

NUMERACY n ability to use numbers, esp in arithmetical operations

NUMERAIRE n unit in which prices are measured

NUMERAL n word or symbol used to express a sum or quantity ▷ adj of, consisting of, or denoting a number

NUMERALLY > NUMERAL

NUMERALS > NUMERAL

NUMERARY adj of or relating to numbers

NUMERATE adj able to do basic arithmetic ▷ vb read (a numerical expression)

NUMERATED > NUMERATE

NUMERATES > NUMERATE

NUMERATOR n number above the line in a fraction

NUMERIC n number or numeral

NUMERICAL adj measured or expressed in numbers

NUMERICS > NUMERIC

NUMEROUS adj existing or happening in large numbers

NUMINA plural of > NUMEN

NUMINOUS adj arousing religious or spiritual emotions ▷ n something that arouses religious or spiritual emotions

NUMMARY adj of or relating to coins

NUMMULAR adj shaped like a coin

NUMMULARY > NUMMULAR

NUMMULINE > NUMMULAR

NUMMULITE n type of large fossil protozoan

n

NUMNAH *same as* > NUMDAH
NUMNAHS > NUMNAH
NUMPTIES > NUMPTY
NUMPTY *n* stupid person
NUMSKULL *same as* > NUMBSKULL
NUMSKULLS > NUMSKULL
NUN *n* female member of a religious order
NUNATAK *n* isolated mountain peak projecting through the surface of surrounding glacial ice
NUNATAKER > NUNATAK
NUNATAKS > NUNATAK
NUNCHAKU *n* rice flail used as a weapon
NUNCHAKUS > NUNCHAKU
NUNCHEON *n* light snack
NUNCHEONS > NUNCHEON
NUNCIO *n* pope's ambassador
NUNCIOS > NUNCIO
NUNCLE *archaic or dialect word for* > UNCLE
NUNCLES > NUNCLE
NUNCUPATE *vb* declare publicly
NUNDINAL > NUNDINE
NUNDINE *n* market day
NUNDINES > NUNDINE
NUNHOOD *n* condition, practice, or character of a nun
NUNHOODS > NUNHOOD
NUNLIKE > NUN
NUNNATION *n* pronunciation of n at the end of words
NUNNERIES > NUNNERY
NUNNERY *n* convent
NUNNISH > NUN
NUNNY *as in* *nunny bag* small sealskin haversack used in Canada
NUNS > NUN
NUNSHIP > NUN
NUNSHIPS > NUN
NUPTIAL *adj* relating to marriage
NUPTIALLY > NUPTIAL
NUPTIALS *pl n* wedding
NUR *n* wooden ball
NURAGHE *n* Sardinian round tower
NURAGHI > NURAGHE
NURAGHIC > NURAGHE
NURD *same as* > NERD
NURDIER > NERD
NURDIEST > NERD
NURDISH > NERD
NURDLE *vb* score runs in cricket by deflecting the ball rather than striking it hard
NURDLED > NURDLE
NURDLES > NURDLE
NURDLING > NURDLE
NURDS > NURD
NURDY > NURD
NURHAG *n* Sardinian round tower
NURHAGS > NURHAG
NURL *variant of* > KNURL
NURLED > NURL
NURLING > NURL
NURLS > NURL
NURR *n* wooden ball

NURRS > NURR
NURS > NUR
NURSE *n* person employed to look after sick people, usu in a hospital ▷ *vb* look after (a sick person)
NURSED > NURSE
NURSELIKE > NURSE
NURSELING *same as* > NURSLING
NURSEMAID *n* woman employed to look after children
NURSER *n* person who treats something carefully
NURSERIES > NURSERY
NURSERS > NURSER
NURSERY *n* room where children sleep or play
NURSES > NURSE
NURSING *n* practice or profession of caring for the sick and injured
NURSINGS > NURSING
NURSLE *vb* nuzzle
NURSLED > NURSLE
NURSLES > NURSLE
NURSLING *n* child or young animal that is being suckled, nursed, or fostered
NURSLINGS > NURSLING
NURTURAL > NURTURE
NURTURANT > NURTURE
NURTURE *n* act or process of promoting the development of a child or young plant ▷ *vb* promote or encourage the development of
NURTURED > NURTURE
NURTURER > NURTURE
NURTURERS > NURTURE
NURTURES > NURTURE
NURTURING > NURTURE
NUS > NU
NUT *n* fruit consisting of a hard shell and a kernel ▷ *vb* to gather nuts
NUTANT *adj* having the apex hanging down
NUTARIAN *n* person whose diet is based around nuts
NUTARIANS > NUTARIAN
NUTATE *vb* nod
NUTATED > NUTATE
NUTATES > NUTATE
NUTATING > NUTATE
NUTATION *n* periodic variation in the precession of the earth's axis
NUTATIONS > NUTATION
NUTBROWN *adj* of a brownish colour, esp a reddish-brown
NUTBUTTER *n* ground nuts blended with butter
NUTCASE *n* insane person
NUTCASES > NUTCASE
NUTGALL *n* nut-shaped gall caused by gall wasps on the oak and other trees
NUTGALLS > NUTGALL
NUTGRASS *n* type of plant
NUTHATCH *n* small songbird
NUTHOUSE *n* mental hospital or asylum
NUTHOUSES > NUTHOUSE

NUTJOBBER *n* nuthatch
NUTLET *n* any of the one-seeded portions of a fruit that fragments when mature
NUTLETS > NUTLET
NUTLIKE > NUT
NUTMEAL *n* type of grain
NUTMEALS > NUTMEAL
NUTMEAT *n* kernel of a nut
NUTMEATS > NUTMEAT
NUTMEG *n* spice made from the seed of a tropical tree ▷ *vb* kick or hit the ball between the legs of (an opposing player)
NUTMEGGED > NUTMEG
NUTMEGGY > NUTMEG
NUTMEGS > NUTMEG
NUTPECKER *n* nuthatch
NUTPICK *n* tool used to dig the meat from nuts
NUTPICKS > NUTPICK
NUTRIA *n* fur of the coypu
NUTRIAS > NUTRIA
NUTRIENT *n* substance that provides nourishment ▷ *adj* providing nourishment
NUTRIENTS > NUTRIENT
NUTRIMENT *n* food or nourishment required by all living things to grow and stay healthy
NUTRITION *n* process of taking in and absorbing nutrients
NUTRITIVE *adj* of nutrition ▷ *n* nutritious food
NUTS > NUT
NUTSEDGE *same as* > NUTGRASS
NUTSEDGES > NUTSEDGE
NUTSHELL *n* shell around the kernel of a nut
NUTSHELLS > NUTSHELL
NUTSIER > NUTSY
NUTSIEST > NUTSY
NUTSO *adj* insane
NUTSY *adj* lunatic
NUTTED > NUT
NUTTER *n* insane person
NUTTERIES > NUTTERY
NUTTERS > NUTTER
NUTTERY *n* place where nut trees grow
NUTTIER > NUTTY
NUTTIEST > NUTTY
NUTTILY > NUTTY
NUTTINESS > NUTTY
NUTTING *n* act of gathering nuts
NUTTINGS > NUTTING
NUTTY *adj* containing or resembling nuts
NUTWOOD *n* any of various nut-bearing trees, such as walnut
NUTWOODS > NUTWOOD
NUZZER *n* present given to a superior in India
NUZZERS > NUZZER
NUZZLE *vb* push or rub gently with the nose or snout
NUZZLED > NUZZLE
NUZZLER *n* person or thing

that nuzzles
NUZZLERS > NUZZLER
NUZZLES > NUZZLE
NUZZLING > NUZZLE
NY *same as* > NIGH
NYAFF *n* small or contemptible person ▷ *vb* yelp like a small dog
NYAFFED > NYAFF
NYAFFING > NYAFF
NYAFFS > NYAFF
NYALA *n* spiral-horned southern African antelope
NYALAS > NYALA
NYANZA *n* (in E Africa) a lake
NYANZAS > NYANZA
NYAS *n* young hawk
NYASES > NYAS
NYBBLE *n* small byte
NYBBLES > NYBBLE
NYCTALOPS *n* person or thing with night-vision
NYE *n* flock of pheasants ▷ *vb* near
NYED > NYE
NYES > NYE
NYING > NYE
NYLGHAI *same as* > NILGAI
NYLGHAIS > NYLGHAI
NYLGHAU *same as* > NILGAI
NYLGHAUS > NYLGHAU
NYLON *n* synthetic material used for clothing etc
NYLONS *pl n* stockings made of nylon
NYMPH *n* mythical spirit of nature, represented as a beautiful young woman
NYMPHA *n* either one of the labia minora
NYMPHAE > NYMPHA
NYMPHAEA *n* water lily
NYMPHAEUM *n* shrine of the nymphs
NYMPHAL > NYMPH
NYMPHALID *n* butterfly of the family that includes the fritillaries and red admirals ▷ *adj* of this family of butterflies
NYMPHEAN > NYMPH
NYMPHET *n* sexually precocious young girl
NYMPHETIC > NYMPHET
NYMPHETS > NYMPHET
NYMPHETTE *same as* > NYMPHET
NYMPHIC > NYMPH
NYMPHICAL > NYMPH
NYMPHISH > NYMPH
NYMPHLIKE > NYMPH
NYMPHLY > NYMPH
NYMPHO *n* nymphomaniac
NYMPHOS > NYMPHO
NYMPHS > NYMPH
NYS > NY
NYSSA *n* type of tree
NYSSAS > NYSSA
NYSTAGMIC > NYSTAGMUS
NYSTAGMUS *n* involuntary movement of the eye comprising a smooth drift followed by a flick back
NYSTATIN *n* type of antibiotic obtained from a bacterium
NYSTATINS > NYSTATIN

n

Oo

OAF *n* stupid or clumsy person
OAFISH > OAF
OAFISHLY > OAF
OAFS > OAF
OAK *n* deciduous forest tree
OAKED *adj* relating to wine that is stored for a time in oak barrels prior to bottling
OAKEN *adj* made of the wood of the oak
OAKENSHAW *n* small forest of oaks
OAKER *same as* > OCHRE
OAKERS > OAKER
OAKIER > OAKY
OAKIES > OAKY
OAKIEST > OAKY
OAKLEAF *n* leaf on oak tree
OAKLEAVES > OAKLEAF
OAKLIKE > OAK
OAKLING *n* young oak
OAKLINGS > OAKLING
OAKMOSS *n* type of lichen
OAKMOSSES > OAKMOSS
OAKS > OAK
OAKUM *n* fibre obtained by unravelling old rope
OAKUMS > OAKUM
OAKY *adj* hard like the wood of an oak ▷ *n* ice cream
OANSHAGH *n* foolish girl or woman
OANSHAGHS > OANSHAGH
OAR *n* pole with a broad blade, used for rowing a boat ▷ *vb* propel with oars
OARAGE *n* use or number of oars
OARAGES > OARAGE
OARED *adj* equipped with oars
OARFISH *n* very long ribbonfish with long slender ventral fins
OARFISHES > OARFISH
OARIER > OARY
OARIEST > OARY
OARING > OAR
OARLESS > OAR
OARLIKE > OAR
OARLOCK *n* swivelling device attached to the gunwale of a boat that holds an oar in place
OARLOCKS > OARLOCK
OARS > OAR

OARSMAN *n* person who rows
OARSMEN > OARSMAN
OARSWOMAN *n* female oarsman
OARSWOMEN > OARSWOMAN
OARWEED *n* type of brown seaweed
OARWEEDS > OARWEED
OARY *adj* of or like an oar
OASES > OASIS
OASIS *n* fertile area in a desert
OAST *n* oven for drying hops
OASTHOUSE *n* building with kilns for drying hops
OASTS > OAST
OAT *n* hard cereal grown as food
OATCAKE *n* thin flat biscuit of oatmeal
OATCAKES > OATCAKE
OATEN *adj* made of oats or oat straw
OATER *n* film about the American Wild West
OATERS > OATER
OATH *n* solemn promise, esp to be truthful in court
OATHABLE *adj* able to take an oath
OATHS > OATH
OATLIKE > OAT
OATMEAL *n* coarse flour made from oats ▷ *adj* pale brownish-cream
OATMEALS > OATMEAL
OATS > OAT
OAVES > OAF
OB *n* expression of opposition
OBA *n* (in W Africa) a Yoruba chief or ruler
OBANG *n* former Japanese coin
OBANGS > OBANG
OBAS > OBA
OBBLIGATI > OBBLIGATO
OBBLIGATO *n* essential part or accompaniment ▷ *adj* not to be omitted in performance
OBCONIC *adj* (of a fruit or similar part) shaped like a cone and attached at the pointed end
OBCONICAL *same*

as > OBCONIC
OBCORDATE *adj* heart-shaped and attached at the pointed end
OBDURACY > OBDURATE
OBDURATE *adj* hardhearted or stubborn ▷ *vb* make obdurate
OBDURATED > OBDURATE
OBDURATES > OBDURATE
OBDURE *vb* make obdurate
OBDURED > OBDURE
OBDURES > OBDURE
OBDURING > OBDURE
OBE *n* ancient Laconian village
OBEAH *vb* cast spell on
OBEAHED > OBEAH
OBEAHING > OBEAH
OBEAHISM > OBEAH
OBEAHISMS > OBEAH
OBEAHS > OBEAH
OBECHE *n* African tree
OBECHES > OBECHE
OBEDIENCE *n* condition or quality of being obedient
OBEDIENT *adj* obeying or willing to obey
OBEISANCE *n* attitude of respect
OBEISANT > OBEISANCE
OBEISM *n* belief in obeah
OBEISMS > OBEISM
OBELI > OBELUS
OBELIA *n* type of jellyfish
OBELIAS > OBELIA
OBELION *n* area of skull
OBELISCAL > OBELISK
OBELISE *same as* > OBELIZE
OBELISED > OBELISE
OBELISES > OBELISE
OBELISING > OBELISE
OBELISK *n* four-sided stone column tapering to a pyramid at the top
OBELISKS > OBELISK
OBELISM *n* practice of marking passages in text
OBELISMS > OBELISM
OBELIZE *vb* mark (a word or passage) with an obelus
OBELIZED > OBELIZE
OBELIZES > OBELIZE
OBELIZING > OBELIZE
OBELUS *n* mark used in editions of ancient documents to indicate

spurious words or passages
OBENTO *n* Japanese lunch box
OBENTOS > OBENTO
OBES > OBE
OBESE *adj* very fat
OBESELY > OBESE
OBESENESS > OBESE
OBESER > OBESE
OBESEST > OBESE
OBESITIES > OBESE
OBESITY > OBESE
OBEY *vb* carry out instructions or orders
OBEYABLE > OBEY
OBEYED > OBEY
OBEYER > OBEY
OBEYERS > OBEY
OBEYING > OBEY
OBEYS > OBEY
OBFUSCATE *vb* make (something) confusing
OBI *n* broad sash tied in a large flat bow at the back, worn by Japanese women and children ▷ *vb* bewitch
OBIA *same as* > OBEAH
OBIAS > OBIA
OBIED > OBI
OBIING > OBI
OBIISM > OBI
OBIISMS > OBI
OBIIT *vb* died
OBIS > OBI
OBIT *n* memorial service
OBITAL *adj* of obits
OBITER *adv* by the way
OBITS > OBIT
OBITUAL *adj* of obits
OBITUARY *n* announcement of someone's death, esp in a newspaper
OBJECT *n* physical thing ▷ *vb* express disapproval
OBJECTED > OBJECT
OBJECTIFY *vb* represent concretely
OBJECTING > OBJECT
OBJECTION *n* expression or feeling of opposition or disapproval
OBJECTIVE *n* aim or purpose ▷ *adj* not biased
OBJECTOR > OBJECT
OBJECTORS > OBJECT
OBJECTS > OBJECT
OBJET *n* object

OBJETS > OBJET
OBJURE vb put on oath
OBJURED > OBJURE
OBJURES > OBJURE
OBJURGATE vb scold or reprimand
OBJURING > OBJURE
OBLAST n administrative division of the constituent republics of Russia
OBLASTI > OBLAST
OBLASTS > OBLAST
OBLATE adj (of a sphere) flattened at the poles ▷ n person dedicated to a monastic or religious life
OBLATELY > OBLATE
OBLATES > OBLATE
OBLATION n religious offering
OBLATIONS > OBLATION
OBLATORY > OBLATION
OBLIGABLE > OBLIGATE
OBLIGANT n person promising to pay a sum
OBLIGANTS > OBLIGANT
OBLIGATE vb compel, constrain, or oblige morally or legally ▷ adj compelled, bound, or restricted
OBLIGATED > OBLIGATE
OBLIGATES > OBLIGATE
OBLIGATI > OBLIGATO
OBLIGATO same as > OBBLIGATO
OBLIGATOR > OBLIGATE
OBLIGATOS > OBLIGATO
OBLIGE vb compel (someone) morally or by law to do something
OBLIGED > OBLIGE
OBLIGEE n person in whose favour an obligation, contract, or bond is created
OBLIGEES > OBLIGEE
OBLIGER > OBLIGE
OBLIGERS > OBLIGE
OBLIGES > OBLIGE
OBLIGING adj ready to help other people
OBLIGOR n person who binds himself by contract to perform some obligation
OBLIGORS > OBLIGOR
OBLIQUE adj slanting ▷ n symbol (/) ▷ vb take or have an oblique direction
OBLIQUED > OBLIQUE
OBLIQUELY > OBLIQUE
OBLIQUER > OBLIQUE
OBLIQUES > OBLIQUE
OBLIQUEST > OBLIQUE
OBLIQUID adj oblique
OBLIQUING > OBLIQUE
OBLIQUITY n state or condition of being oblique
OBLIVION n state of being forgotten
OBLIVIONS > OBLIVION
OBLIVIOUS adj unaware
OBLONG adj having two long sides, two short sides, and four right angles ▷ n oblong figure
OBLONGLY > OBLONG
OBLONGS > OBLONG
OBLOQUIAL > OBLOQUY

OBLOQUIES > OBLOQUY
OBLOQUY n verbal abuse
OBNOXIOUS adj offensive
OBO n ship carrying oil and ore
OBOE n double-reeded woodwind instrument
OBOES > OBOE
OBOIST > OBOE
OBOISTS > OBOE
OBOL same as > OBOLUS
OBOLARY adj very poor
OBOLE n former weight unit in pharmacy
OBOLES > OBOLE
OBOLI > OBOLUS
OBOLS > OBOL
OBOLUS n modern Greek unit of weight equal to one tenth of a gram
OBOS > OBO
OBOVATE adj (of a leaf) shaped like the longitudinal section of an egg with the narrower end at the base
OBOVATELY > OBOVATE
OBOVOID adj (of a fruit) egg-shaped with the narrower end at the base
OBREPTION n obtaining of something by giving false information
OBS > OB
OBSCENE adj portraying sex offensively
OBSCENELY > OBSCENE
OBSCENER > OBSCENE
OBSCENEST > OBSCENE
OBSCENITY n state or quality of being obscene
OBSCURANT n opposer of reform and enlightenment ▷ adj of or relating to an obscurant
OBSCURE adj not well known ▷ vb make (something) obscure
OBSCURED > OBSCURE
OBSCURELY > OBSCURE
OBSCURER > OBSCURE
OBSCURERS > OBSCURE
OBSCURES > OBSCURE
OBSCUREST > OBSCURE
OBSCURING > OBSCURE
OBSCURITY n state or quality of being obscure
OBSECRATE rare word for > BESEECH
OBSEQUENT adj (of a river) flowing into a subsequent stream in the opposite direction to the original slope of the land
OBSEQUIAL > OBSEQUIES
OBSEQUIE same as > OBSEQUY
OBSEQUIES pl n funeral rites
OBSEQUY singular of > OBSEQUIES
OBSERVANT adj quick to notice things
OBSERVE vb see or notice
OBSERVED > OBSERVE
OBSERVER n person who observes, esp one who watches someone or

something carefully
OBSERVERS > OBSERVER
OBSERVES > OBSERVE
OBSERVING > OBSERVE
OBSESS vb preoccupy (someone) compulsively
OBSESSED > OBSESS
OBSESSES > OBSESS
OBSESSING > OBSESS
OBSESSION n something that preoccupies a person to the exclusion of other things
OBSESSIVE adj motivated by a persistent overriding idea or impulse ▷ n person subject to obsession
OBSESSOR > OBSESS
OBSESSORS > OBSESS
OBSIDIAN n dark glassy volcanic rock
OBSIDIANS > OBSIDIAN
OBSIGN vb confirm
OBSIGNATE same as > OBSIGN
OBSIGNED > OBSIGN
OBSIGNING > OBSIGN
OBSIGNS > OBSIGN
OBSOLESCE vb become obsolete
OBSOLETE adj no longer in use ▷ vb make obsolete
OBSOLETED > OBSOLETE
OBSOLETES > OBSOLETE
OBSTACLE n something that makes progress difficult
OBSTACLES > OBSTACLE
OBSTETRIC adj of or relating to childbirth
OBSTINACY n state or quality of being obstinate
OBSTINATE adj stubborn
OBSTRUCT vb block with an obstacle
OBSTRUCTS > OBSTRUCT
OBSTRUENT adj causing obstruction, esp of the intestinal tract ▷ n anything that causes obstruction
OBTAIN vb acquire intentionally
OBTAINED > OBTAIN
OBTAINER > OBTAIN
OBTAINERS > OBTAIN
OBTAINING > OBTAIN
OBTAINS > OBTAIN
OBTECT adj (of a pupa) encased in a hardened secretion
OBTECTED same as > OBTECT
OBTEMPER vb comply (with)
OBTEMPERS > OBTEMPER
OBTEND vb put forward
OBTENDED > OBTEND
OBTENDING > OBTEND
OBTENDS > OBTEND
OBTENTION n act of obtaining
OBTEST vb beg (someone) earnestly
OBTESTED > OBTEST
OBTESTING > OBTEST
OBTESTS > OBTEST
OBTRUDE vb push oneself or one's ideas on others

OBTRUDED > OBTRUDE
OBTRUDER > OBTRUDE
OBTRUDERS > OBTRUDE
OBTRUDES > OBTRUDE
OBTRUDING > OBTRUDE
OBTRUSION > OBTRUDE
OBTRUSIVE adj unpleasantly noticeable
OBTUND vb deaden or dull
OBTUNDED > OBTUND
OBTUNDENT > OBTUND
OBTUNDING > OBTUND
OBTUNDITY n semi-conscious state
OBTUNDS > OBTUND
OBTURATE vb stop up (an opening, esp the breech of a gun)
OBTURATED > OBTURATE
OBTURATES > OBTURATE
OBTURATOR > OBTURATE
OBTUSE adj mentally slow
OBTUSELY > OBTUSE
OBTUSER > OBTUSE
OBTUSEST > OBTUSE
OBTUSITY > OBTUSE
OBUMBRATE vb overshadow
OBVENTION n incidental expense
OBVERSE n opposite way of looking at an idea ▷ adj facing or turned towards the observer
OBVERSELY > OBVERSE
OBVERSES > OBVERSE
OBVERSION > OBVERT
OBVERT vb deduce the obverse of (a proposition)
OBVERTED > OBVERT
OBVERTING > OBVERT
OBVERTS > OBVERT
OBVIABLE > OBVIATE
OBVIATE vb make unnecessary
OBVIATED > OBVIATE
OBVIATES > OBVIATE
OBVIATING > OBVIATE
OBVIATION > OBVIATE
OBVIATOR > OBVIATE
OBVIATORS > OBVIATE
OBVIOUS adj easy to see or understand, evident
OBVIOUSLY adv in a way that is easy to see or understand
OBVOLUTE adj (of leaves or petals in the bud) folded so that the margins overlap each other
OBVOLUTED same as > OBVOLUTE
OBVOLVENT adj curving around something
OCA n any of various South American herbaceous plants
OCARINA n small oval wind instrument
OCARINAS > OCARINA
OCAS > OCA
OCCAM n computer programming language
OCCAMIES > OCCAMY
OCCAMS > OCCAM
OCCAMY n type of alloy
OCCASION n time at which a particular thing happens

O

▷ *vb* cause

OCCASIONS *pl n* needs

OCCIDENT *literary or formal word for* > WEST

OCCIDENTS > OCCIDENT

OCCIES > OCCY

OCCIPITA > OCCIPUT

OCCIPITAL *adj* of or relating to the back of the head or skull

OCCIPUT *n* back of the head

OCCIPUTS > OCCIPUT

OCCLUDE *vb* obstruct

OCCLUDED > OCCLUDE

OCCLUDENT > OCCLUDE

OCCLUDER > OCCLUDE

OCCLUDERS > OCCLUDE

OCCLUDES > OCCLUDE

OCCLUDING > OCCLUDE

OCCLUSAL > OCCLUSION

OCCLUSION *n* act or process of occluding or the state of being occluded

OCCLUSIVE *adj* of or relating to the act of occlusion ▷ *n* occlusive speech sound

OCCLUSOR *n* muscle for closing opening

OCCLUSORS > OCCLUSOR

OCCULT *adj* relating to the supernatural ▷ *vb* (of a celestial body) to hide (another celestial body) from view

OCCULTED > OCCULT

OCCULTER *n* something that obscures

OCCULTERS > OCCULTER

OCCULTING > OCCULT

OCCULTISM *n* belief in and the study and practice of magic, astrology, etc

OCCULTIST > OCCULTISM

OCCULTLY > OCCULT

OCCULTS > OCCULT

OCCUPANCE *same as* > OCCUPANCY

OCCUPANCY *n* (length of) a person's stay in a specified place

OCCUPANT *n* person occupying a specified place

OCCUPANTS > OCCUPANT

OCCUPATE *same as* > OCCUPY

OCCUPATED > OCCUPATE

OCCUPATES > OCCUPATE

OCCUPIED > OCCUPY

OCCUPIER *n* person who lives in a particular house, whether as owner or tenant

OCCUPIERS > OCCUPIER

OCCUPIES > OCCUPY

OCCUPY *vb* live or work in (a building)

OCCUPYING > OCCUPY

OCCUR *vb* happen

OCCURRED > OCCUR

OCCURRENT *adj* (of a property) relating to some observable feature of its bearer

OCCURRING > OCCUR

OCCURS > OCCUR

OCCY as in *all over the occy* dialect expression meaning in every direction

OCEAN *n* vast area of sea between continents

OCEANARIA *pl n* large saltwater aquaria for marine life

OCEANAUT *n* undersea explorer

OCEANAUTS > OCEANAUT

OCEANIC *adj* of or relating to the ocean

OCEANID *n* ocean nymph in Greek mythology

OCEANIDES > OCEANID

OCEANIDS > OCEANID

OCEANS > OCEAN

OCELLAR > OCELLUS

OCELLATE > OCELLUS

OCELLATED > OCELLUS

OCELLI > OCELLUS

OCELLUS *n* simple eye of insects and some other invertebrates

OCELOID *adj* of or like an ocelot

OCELOT *n* American wild cat with a spotted coat

OCELOTS > OCELOT

OCH *interj* expression of surprise, annoyance, or disagreement

OCHE *n* (in darts) mark on the floor behind which a player must stand

OCHER *same as* > OCHRE

OCHERED > OCHER

OCHERING > OCHER

OCHEROUS > OCHER

OCHERS > OCHER

OCHERY > OCHER

OCHES > OCHE

OCHIDORE *n* type of crab

OCHIDORES > OCHIDORE

OCHLOCRAT *n* supporter of rule by the mob

OCHONE *interj* expression of sorrow or regret

OCHRE *n* brownish-yellow earth ▷ *adj* moderate yellow-orange to orange ▷ *vb* colour with ochre

OCHREA *n* cup-shaped structure that sheathes the stems of certain plants

OCHREAE > OCHREA

OCHREATE *same as* > OCREATE

OCHRED > OCHRE

OCHREOUS > OCHRE

OCHRES > OCHRE

OCHREY > OCHRE

OCHRING > OCHRE

OCHROID > OCHRE

OCHROUS > OCHRE

OCHRY > OCHRE

OCICAT *n* breed of large short-haired cat with a spotted coat

OCICATS > OCICAT

OCKER *n* uncultivated or boorish Australian

OCKERISM *n* Australian boorishness

OCKERISMS > OCKERISM

OCKERS > OCKER

OCKODOLS *pl n* one's feet when wearing boots

OCOTILLO *n* cactus-like tree

OCOTILLOS > OCOTILLO

OCREA *same as* > OCHREA

OCREAE > OCREA

OCREATE *adj* possessing an ocrea

OCTA *same as* > OKTA

OCTACHORD *n* eight-stringed musical instrument

OCTAD *n* group or series of eight

OCTADIC > OCTAD

OCTADS > OCTAD

OCTAGON *n* geometric figure with eight sides

OCTAGONAL *adj* having eight sides and eight angles

OCTAGONS > OCTAGON

OCTAHEDRA *pl n* solid eight-sided figures; octahedrons

OCTAL *n* number system with a base 8

OCTALS > OCTAL

OCTAMETER *n* verse line consisting of eight metrical feet

OCTAN *n* illness that occurs weekly

OCTANE *n* hydrocarbon found in petrol

OCTANES > OCTANE

OCTANGLE *same as* > OCTAGON

OCTANGLES > OCTANGLE

OCTANOL *n* alcohol containing eight carbon atoms

OCTANOLS > OCTANOL

OCTANS > OCTAN

OCTANT *n* any of the eight parts into which the three planes containing the Cartesian coordinate axes divide space

OCTANTAL > OCTANT

OCTANTS > OCTANT

OCTAPLA *n* book with eight texts

OCTAPLAS > OCTAPLA

OCTAPLOID *adj* having eight parts

OCTAPODIC > OCTAPODY

OCTAPODY *n* line of verse with eight metrical feet

OCTARCHY *n* government by eight rulers

OCTAROON *same as* > OCTOROON

OCTAROONS > OCTAROON

OCTAS > OCTA

OCTASTICH *n* verse of eight lines

OCTASTYLE *adj* (of building) having eight columns

OCTAVAL > OCTAVE

OCTAVE *n* (interval between the first and) eighth note of a scale ▷ *adj* consisting of eight parts

OCTAVES > OCTAVE

OCTAVO *n* book size in which the sheets are folded into eight leaves

OCTAVOS > OCTAVO

OCTENNIAL *adj* occurring every eight years

OCTET *n* group of eight performers

OCTETS > OCTET

OCTETT *same as* > OCTET

OCTETTE *same as* > OCTET

OCTETTES > OCTETTE

OCTETTS > OCTETT

OCTILLION *n* (in Britain and Germany) the number represented as one followed by 48 zeros

OCTOFID *adj* divided into eight

OCTOHEDRA *same as* > OCTAHEDRA

OCTONARII *pl n* lines with eight feet

OCTONARY *adj* relating to or based on the number eight ▷ *n* stanza of eight lines

OCTOPI > OCTOPUS

OCTOPLOID *same as* > OCTAPLOID

OCTOPOD *n* type of mollusc ▷ *adj* of these molluscs

OCTOPODAN > OCTOPOD

OCTOPODES > OCTOPOD

OCTOPODS > OCTOPOD

OCTOPUS *n* sea creature with a soft body and eight tentacles

OCTOPUSES > OCTOPUS

OCTOPUSH *n* hockey-like game played underwater

OCTOROON *n* person having one quadroon and one White parent

OCTOROONS > OCTOROON

OCTOSTYLE *same as* > OCTASTYLE

OCTOTHORP *n* type of symbol used in printing

OCTROI *n* duty on various goods brought into certain European towns

OCTROIS > OCTROI

OCTUOR *n* octet

OCTUORS > OCTUOR

OCTUPLE *n* quantity or number eight times as great as another ▷ *adj* eight times as much or as many ▷ *vb* multiply by eight

OCTUPLED > OCTUPLE

OCTUPLES > OCTUPLE

OCTUPLET *n* one of eight offspring from one birth

OCTUPLETS > OCTUPLET

OCTUPLEX *n* something made up of eight parts

OCTUPLING > OCTUPLE

OCTUPLY *adv* by eight times

OCTYL *n* group of atoms

OCTYLS > OCTYL

OCULAR *adj* relating to the eyes or sight ▷ *n* lens in an optical instrument

OCULARIST *n* person who makes artificial eyes

OCULARLY > OCULAR

OCULARS > OCULAR

OCULATE *adj* possessing eyes

OCULATED *same as* > OCULATE

OCULI > OCULUS

OCULIST n ophthalmologist
OCULISTS > OCULIST
OCULUS n round window
OD n hypothetical force formerly thought to be responsible for many natural phenomena
ODA n room in a harem
ODAH same as > ODA
ODAHS > ODAH
ODAL same as > UDAL
ODALIQUE same as > ODALISQUE
ODALIQUES > ODALIQUE
ODALISK same as > ODALISQUE
ODALISKS > ODALISK
ODALISQUE n female slave in a harem
ODALLER > ODAL
ODALLERS > ODAL
ODALS > ODAL
ODAS > ODA
ODD adj unusual
ODDBALL n eccentric person ▷ adj strange or peculiar
ODDBALLS > ODDBALL
ODDER > ODD
ODDEST > ODD
ODDISH > ODD
ODDITIES > ODDITY
ODDITY n odd person or thing
ODDLY > ODD
ODDMENT n odd piece or thing
ODDMENTS > ODDMENT
ODDNESS > ODD
ODDNESSES > ODD
ODDS pl n (ratio showing) the probability of something happening
ODDSMAKER n person setting odds in betting
ODDSMAN n umpire
ODDSMEN > ODDSMAN
ODE n lyric poem, usu addressed to a particular subject
ODEA > ODEUM
ODEON same as > ODEUM
ODEONS > ODEON
ODES > ODE
ODEUM n (esp in ancient Greece and Rome) a building for musical performances
ODEUMS > ODEUM
ODIC > OD
ODIFEROUS adj having odour
ODIOUS adj offensive
ODIOUSLY > ODIOUS
ODISM > OD
ODISMS > OD
ODIST > OD
ODISTS > OD
ODIUM n widespread dislike
ODIUMS > ODIUM
ODOGRAPH same as > ODOMETER
ODOGRAPHS > ODOGRAPH
ODOMETER n device that records the number of miles that a bicycle or motor vehicle has travelled
ODOMETERS > ODOMETER

ODOMETRY > ODOMETER
ODONATE n dragonfly or related insect
ODONATES > ODONATE
ODONATIST n dragonfly expert
ODONTALGY n toothache
ODONTIC adj of teeth
ODONTIST n dentist
ODONTISTS > ODONTIST
ODONTOID adj toothlike ▷ n bone in the spine
ODONTOIDS > ODONTOID
ODONTOMA n tumour near teeth
ODONTOMAS > ODONTOMA
ODOR same as > ODOUR
ODORANT n something with a strong smell
ODORANTS > ODORANT
ODORATE adj having a strong smell
ODORED same as > ODOURED
ODORFUL same as > ODOURFUL
ODORISE same as > ODORIZE
ODORISED > ODORISE
ODORISES > ODORISE
ODORISING > ODORISE
ODORIZE vb give an odour to
ODORIZED > ODORIZE
ODORIZES > ODORIZE
ODORIZING > ODORIZE
ODORLESS > ODOR
ODOROUS adj having or emitting a characteristic smell or odour
ODOROUSLY > ODOROUS
ODORS > ODOR
ODOUR n particular smell
ODOURED adj having odour
ODOURFUL adj full of odour
ODOURLESS > ODOUR
ODOURS > ODOUR
ODS > OD
ODSO n cry of suprise
ODSOS > ODSO
ODYL same as > OD
ODYLE same as > OD
ODYLES > ODYLE
ODYLISM > ODYL
ODYLISMS > ODYL
ODYLS > ODYL
ODYSSEY n long eventful journey
ODYSSEYS > ODYSSEY
ODZOOKS interj cry of surprise
OE n grandchild
OECIST n colony founder
OECISTS > OECIST
OECOLOGY less common spelling of > ECOLOGY
OECUMENIC variant of > ECUMENIC
OEDEMA n abnormal swelling
OEDEMAS > OEDEMA
OEDEMATA > OEDEMA
OEDIPAL adj relating to an Oedipus complex, whereby a male child wants to replace his father
OEDIPALLY > OEDIPAL
OEDIPEAN same as > OEDIPAL

OEDOMETER n instrument for measuring the consolidation of a soil specimen under pressure
OEILLADE n amorous or suggestive glance
OEILLADES > OEILLADE
OENANTHIC adj smelling of or like wine
OENOLOGY n study of wine
OENOMANCY n divination by studying the colour of wine
OENOMANIA n craving for wine
OENOMEL n drink made of wine and honey
OENOMELS > OENOMEL
OENOMETER n device for measuring the strength of wine
OENOPHIL same as > OENOPHILE
OENOPHILE n lover or connoisseur of wines
OENOPHILS > OENOPHIL
OENOPHILY n love of wine
OENOTHERA n type of American plant with yellow flowers that open in the evening
OERLIKON n type of cannon
OERLIKONS > OERLIKON
OERSTED n cgs unit of magnetic field strength
OERSTEDS > OERSTED
OES > OE
OESOPHAGI pl n gullets
OESTRAL > OESTRUS
OESTRIN obsolete term for > OESTROGEN
OESTRINS > OESTRIN
OESTRIOL n weak oestrogenic hormone secreted by the mammalian ovary
OESTRIOLS > OESTRIOL
OESTROGEN n female hormone that controls the reproductive cycle
OESTRONE n weak oestrogenic hormone secreted by the mammalian ovary
OESTRONES > OESTRONE
OESTROUS > OESTRUS
OESTRUM same as > OESTRUS
OESTRUMS > OESTRUM
OESTRUS n regularly occurring period of fertility and sexual receptivity in most female mammals
OESTRUSES > OESTRUS
OEUVRE n work of art, literature, music, etc
OEUVRES > OEUVRE
OF prep belonging to
OFAY n derogatory term for a White person
OFAYS > OFAY
OFF prep away from ▷ adv away ▷ adj not operating ▷ n side of the field to which the batsman's feet point ▷ vb kill
OFFAL n edible organs of an animal, such as liver or kidneys

OFFALS > OFFAL
OFFBEAT adj unusual or eccentric ▷ n any of the normally unaccented beats in a bar
OFFBEATS > OFFBEAT
OFFCAST n cast-off
OFFCASTS > OFFCAST
OFFCUT n piece remaining after the required parts have been cut out
OFFCUTS > OFFCUT
OFFED > OFF
OFFENCE n (cause of) hurt feelings or annoyance
OFFENCES > OFFENCE
OFFEND vb hurt the feelings of, insult
OFFENDED > OFFEND
OFFENDER > OFFEND
OFFENDERS > OFFEND
OFFENDING > OFFEND
OFFENDS > OFFEND
OFFENSE same as > OFFENCE
OFFENSES > OFFENSE
OFFENSIVE adj disagreeable ▷ n position or action of attack
OFFER vb present (something) for acceptance or rejection ▷ n something offered
OFFERABLE > OFFER
OFFERED > OFFER
OFFEREE n person to whom an offer is made
OFFEREES > OFFEREE
OFFERER > OFFER
OFFERERS > OFFER
OFFERING n thing offered
OFFERINGS > OFFERING
OFFEROR > OFFER
OFFERORS > OFFER
OFFERS > OFFER
OFFERTORY n offering of the bread and wine for Communion
OFFHAND adj casual, curt ▷ adv without preparation
OFFHANDED adj without care oe consideration
OFFICE n room or building where people work at desks
OFFICER n person in authority in the armed services ▷ vb furnish with officers
OFFICERED > OFFICER
OFFICERS > OFFICER
OFFICES > OFFICE
OFFICIAL adj of a position of authority ▷ n person who holds a position of authority
OFFICIALS > OFFICIAL
OFFICIANT n person who presides and officiates at a religious ceremony
OFFICIARY n body of officials ▷ adj of, relating to, or derived from office
OFFICIATE vb act in an official role
OFFICINAL adj (of pharmaceutical products) available without

prescription ▷ *n* official preparation or plant

OFFICIOUS *adj* interfering unnecessarily

OFFING *n* area of the sea visible from the shore

OFFINGS > OFFING

OFFISH *adj* aloof or distant in manner

OFFISHLY > OFFISH

OFFKEY *adj* out of tune

OFFLINE *adj* disconnected from a computer or the internet

OFFLOAD *vb* pass responsibilty for (something unpleasant) to someone else

OFFLOADED > OFFLOAD

OFFLOADS > OFFLOAD

OFFPEAK *adj* relating to times outside periods of intensive use

OFFPRINT *n* separate reprint of an article that originally appeared in a larger publication ▷ *vb* reprint (an article taken from a larger publication) separately

OFFPRINTS > OFFPRINT

OFFPUT *n* act of putting off

OFFPUTS > OFFPUT

OFFRAMP *n* road allowing traffic to leave a motorway

OFFRAMPS > OFFRAMP

OFFS > OFF

OFFSADDLE *vb* unsaddle

OFFSCREEN *adj* unseen by film viewers

OFFSCUM *n* scum

OFFSCUMS > OFFSCUM

OFFSEASON *n* period of little trade in a business

OFFSET *vb* cancel out, compensate for ▷ *n* printing method in which the impression is made onto a surface which transfers it to the paper

OFFSETS > OFFSET

OFFSHOOT *n* something developed from something else

OFFSHOOTS > OFFSHOOT

OFFSHORE *adv* away from or at some distance from the shore ▷ *adj* sited or conducted at sea ▷ *n* company operating abroad where the tax system is more advantageous than at home

OFFSHORES > OFFSHORE

OFFSIDE *adv* (positioned) illegally ahead of the ball ▷ *n* side of a vehicle nearest the centre of the road

OFFSIDER *n* partner or assistant

OFFSIDERS > OFFSIDER

OFFSIDES > OFFSIDE

OFFSPRING *n* child

OFFSTAGE *adv* out of the view of the audience ▷ *n* something that happens offstage

OFFSTAGES > OFFSTAGE

OFFTAKE *n* act of taking off

OFFTAKES > OFFTAKE

OFFTRACK *adj* not at a racetrack

OFLAG *n* German prisoner-of-war camp for officers in World War II

OFLAGS > OFLAG

OFT *adv* often

OFTEN *adv* frequently, much of the time

OFTENER > OFTEN

OFTENEST > OFTEN

OFTENNESS > OFTEN

OFTER > OFT

OFTEST > OFT

OFTTIMES *same as* > OFTEN

OGAM *same as* > OGHAM

OGAMIC > OGAM

OGAMS > OGAM

OGDOAD *n* group of eight

OGDOADS > OGDOAD

OGEE *n* moulding having a cross section in the form of a letter S

OGEES > OGEE

OGGIN *n* sea

OGGINS > OGGIN

OGHAM *n* ancient alphabetical writing system used by the Celts in Britain and Ireland

OGHAMIC > OGHAM

OGHAMIST > OGHAM

OGHAMISTS > OGHAM

OGHAMS > OGHAM

OGIVAL > OGIVE

OGIVE *n* diagonal rib or groin of a Gothic vault

OGIVES > OGIVE

OGLE *vb* stare at (someone) lustfully ▷ *n* flirtatious or lewd look

OGLED > OGLE

OGLER > OGLE

OGLERS > OGLE

OGLES > OGLE

OGLING > OGLE

OGLINGS > OGLE

OGMIC > OGAM

OGRE *n* giant that eats human flesh

OGREISH > OGRE

OGREISHLY > OGRE

OGREISM > OGRE

OGREISMS > OGRE

OGRES > OGRE

OGRESS > OGRE

OGRESSES > OGRE

OGRISH > OGRE

OGRISHLY > OGRE

OGRISM > OGRE

OGRISMS > OGRE

OH *interj* exclamation of surprise, pain, etc ▷ *vb* say oh

OHED > OH

OHIA *n* Hawaiian plant

OHIAS > OHIA

OHING > OH

OHM *n* unit of electrical resistance

OHMAGE *n* electrical resistance in ohms

OHMAGES > OHMAGE

OHMIC *adj* of or relating to a circuit element

OHMICALLY > OHMIC

OHMMETER *n* instrument for measuring electrical resistance

OHMMETERS > OHMMETER

OHMS > OHM

OHO *n* exclamation expressing surprise, exultation, or derision

OHONE *same as* > OCHONE

OHOS > OHO

OHS > OH

OI *interj* shout to attract attention

OIDIA > OIDIUM

OIDIOID > OIDIUM

OIDIUM *n* type of fungal spore

OIK *n* person regarded as inferior because ignorant or lower-class

OIKIST *same as* > OECIST

OIKISTS > OIKIST

OIKS > OIK

OIL *n* viscous liquid, insoluble in water and usu flammable ▷ *vb* lubricate (a machine) with oil

OILBIRD *n* type of nocturnal gregarious cave-dwelling bird

OILBIRDS > OILBIRD

OILCAMP *n* camp for oilworkers

OILCAMPS > OILCAMP

OILCAN *n* container with a long nozzle for applying oil to machinery

OILCANS > OILCAN

OILCLOTH *n* waterproof material

OILCLOTHS > OILCLOTH

OILCUP *n* cup-shaped oil reservoir in a machine providing continuous lubrication for a bearing

OILCUPS > OILCUP

OILED > OIL

OILER *n* person, device, etc, that lubricates or supplies oil

OILERIES > OILERY

OILERS > OILER

OILERY *n* oil business

OILFIELD *n* area containing oil reserves

OILFIELDS > OILFIELD

OILFIRED *adj* using oil as fuel

OILGAS *n* gaseous mixture of hydrocarbons used as a fuel

OILGASES > OILGAS

OILHOLE *n* hole for oil

OILHOLES > OILHOLE

OILIER > OILY

OILIEST > OILY

OILILY > OILY

OILINESS > OILY

OILING > OIL

OILLET *same as* > EYELET

OILLETS > OILLET

OILMAN *n* person who owns or operates oil wells

OILMEN > OILMAN

OILNUT *n* nut from which oil is extracted

OILNUTS > OILNUT

OILPAPER *n* oiled paper

OILPAPERS > OILPAPER

OILPROOF *adj* resistant to oil

OILS > OIL

OILSEED *n* seed from which oil is extracted

OILSEEDS > OILSEED

OILSKIN *n* (garment made from) waterproof material

OILSKINS > OILSKIN

OILSTONE *n* stone with a fine grain lubricated with oil and used for sharpening cutting tools

OILSTONES > OILSTONE

OILTIGHT *adj* not allowing oil through

OILWAY *n* channel for oil

OILWAYS > OILWAY

OILY *adj* soaked or covered with oil

OINK *n* grunt of a pig or an imitation of this ▷ *interj* imitation or representation of the grunt of a pig ▷ *vb* make noise of pig

OINKED > OINK

OINKING > OINK

OINKS > OINK

OINOLOGY *same as* > OENOLOGY

OINOMEL *same as* > OENOMEL

OINOMELS > OINOMEL

OINT *vb* anoint

OINTED > OINT

OINTING > OINT

OINTMENT *n* greasy substance used for healing skin or as a cosmetic

OINTMENTS > OINTMENT

OINTS > OINT

OITICICA *n* South American tree

OITICICAS > OITICICA

OJIME *n* Japanese bead used to secure cords

OJIMES > OJIME

OKA *n* unit of weight used in Turkey

OKAPI *n* African animal related to the giraffe but with a shorter neck

OKAPIS > OKAPI

OKAS > OKA

OKAY *adj* satisfactory ▷ *vb* approve or endorse ▷ *n* approval or agreement ▷ *interj* expression of approval

OKAYED > OKAY

OKAYING > OKAY

OKAYS > OKAY

OKE *same as* > OKA

OKEH *variant of* > OKAY

OKEHS > OKEH

OKES > OKE

OKEYDOKE *variant of* > OKAY

OKEYDOKEY *variant of* > OKAY

OKIMONO *n* Japanese ornamental item

OKIMONOS > OKIMONO

OKRA *n* tropical plant with edible green pods

OKRAS > OKRA

OKTA *n* unit used in meteorology to measure cloud cover

OKTAS > OKTA

OLD *adj* having lived or existed for a long time ▷ *n* earlier or past time

OLDEN *adj* old ▷ *vb* grow old

OLDENED > OLDEN

OLDENING > OLDEN

OLDENS > OLDEN

OLDER *adj* having lived or existed longer

OLDEST > OLD

OLDIE *n* old but popular song or film

OLDIES > OLDIE

OLDISH > OLD

OLDNESS > OLD

OLDNESSES > OLD

OLDS > OLD

OLDSQUAW *n* type of long-tailed sea duck

OLDSQUAWS > OLDSQUAW

OLDSTER *n* older person

OLDSTERS > OLDSTER

OLDSTYLE *n* printing type style

OLDSTYLES > OLDSTYLE

OLDWIFE *n* any of various fishes, esp the menhaden or the alewife

OLDWIVES > OLDWIFE

OLDY *same as* > OLDIE

OLE *interj* exclamation of approval or encouragement customary at bullfights ▷ *n* cry of olé

OLEA > OLEUM

OLEACEOUS *adj* relating to a family of trees and shrubs, including the ash, jasmine, and olive

OLEANDER *n* Mediterranean flowering evergreen shrub

OLEANDERS > OLEANDER

OLEARIA *n* daisy bush

OLEARIAS > OLEARIA

OLEASTER *n* type of shrub with silver-white twigs and yellow flowers

OLEASTERS > OLEASTER

OLEATE *n* any salt or ester of oleic acid

OLEATES > OLEATE

OLECRANAL > OLECRANON

OLECRANON *n* bony projection of the ulna behind the elbow joint

OLEFIANT *adj* forming oil

OLEFIN *same as* > OLEFINE

OLEFINE *another name for* > ALKENE

OLEFINES > OLEFINE

OLEFINIC > OLEFINE

OLEFINS > OLEFIN

OLEIC *as in oleic acid* colourless oily liquid used in making soap

OLEIN *another name for* > TRIOLEIN

OLEINE *same as* > OLEIN

OLEINES > OLEINE

OLEINS > OLEIN

OLENT *adj* having smell

OLEO *as in oleo oil* oil

extracted from beef fat

OLEOGRAPH *n* chromolithograph printed in oil colours to imitate the appearance of an oil painting

OLEORESIN *n* semisolid mixture of a resin and essential oil

OLEOS > OLEO

OLES > OLE

OLESTRA *n* trademark term for an artificial fat

OLESTRAS > OLESTRA

OLEUM *n* type of sulphuric acid

OLEUMS > OLEUM

OLFACT *vb* smell something

OLFACTED > OLFACT

OLFACTING > OLFACT

OLFACTION *n* sense of smell

OLFACTIVE *adj* of sense of smell

OLFACTORY *adj* relating to the sense of smell ▷ *n* organ or nerve concerned with the sense of smell

OLFACTS > OLFACT

OLIBANUM *n* frankincense

OLIBANUMS > OLIBANUM

OLICOOK *n* doughnut

OLICOOKS > OLICOOK

OLID *adj* foul-smelling

OLIGAEMIA *n* reduction in the volume of the blood, as occurs after haemorrhage

OLIGAEMIC > OLIGAEMIA

OLIGARCH *n* member of an oligarchy

OLIGARCHS > OLIGARCH

OLIGARCHY *n* government by a small group of people

OLIGEMIA *same as* > OLIGAEMIA

OLIGEMIAS > OLIGEMIA

OLIGEMIC > OLIGAEMIA

OLIGIST *n* type of iron ore

OLIGISTS > OLIGIST

OLIGOCENE *adj* belonging to geological time period

OLIGOGENE *n* type of gene

OLIGOMER *n* compound of relatively low molecular weight containing up to five monomer units

OLIGOMERS > OLIGOMER

OLIGOPOLY *n* market situation in which control over the supply of a commodity is held by a small number of producers

OLIGURIA *n* excretion of an abnormally small volume of urine

OLIGURIAS > OLIGURIA

OLINGO *n* South American mammal

OLINGOS > OLINGO

OLIO *n* dish of many different ingredients

OLIOS > OLIO

OLIPHANT *archaic variant of* > ELEPHANT

OLIPHANTS > OLIPHANT

OLITORIES > OLITORY

OLITORY *n* kitchen garden

OLIVARY *adj* shaped like

an olive

OLIVE *n* small green or black fruit used as food or pressed for its oil ▷ *adj* greyish-green

OLIVENITE *n* green to black rare secondary mineral

OLIVER *as in Bath oliver* type of unsweetened biscuit

OLIVERS > OLIVER

OLIVES > OLIVE

OLIVET *n* button shaped like olive

OLIVETS > OLIVET

OLIVINE *n* olive-green mineral of the olivine group

OLIVINES > OLIVINE

OLIVINIC *adj* containing olivine

OLLA *n* cooking pot

OLLAMH *n* old Irish term for a wise man

OLLAMHS > OLLAMH

OLLAS > OLLA

OLLAV *same as* > OLLAMH

OLLAVS > OLLAV

OLLER *n* waste ground

OLLERS > OLLER

OLLIE *n* (in skateboarding and snowboarding) a jump into the air executed by stamping on the tail of the board

OLLIES > OLLIE

OLM *n* pale blind eel-like salamander

OLMS > OLM

OLOGIES > OLOGY

OLOGIST *n* scientist

OLOGISTS > OLOGIST

OLOGOAN *vb* complain loudly without reason

OLOGOANED > OLOGOAN

OLOGOANS > OLOGOAN

OLOGY *n* science or other branch of knowledge

OLOLIUQUI *n* medicinal plant used by the Aztecs

OLOROSO *n* golden-coloured sweet sherry

OLOROSOS > OLOROSO

OLPAE > OLPE

OLPE *n* ancient Greek jug

OLPES > OLPE

OLYCOOK *same as* > OLYKOEK

OLYCOOKS > OLYCOOK

OLYKOEK *n* American type of doughnut

OLYKOEKS > OLYKOEK

OLYMPIAD *n* staging of the modern Olympic Games

OLYMPIADS > OLYMPIAD

OLYMPICS *pl n* modern revival of the ancient Greek games, featuring sporting contests

OM *n* sacred syllable in Hinduism

OMADHAUN *n* foolish man or boy

OMADHAUNS > OMADHAUN

OMASA > OMASUM

OMASAL > OMASUM

OMASUM *n* compartment in the stomach of a ruminant animal

OMBER *same as* > OMBRE

OMBERS > OMBER

OMBRE *n* 18th-century card game

OMBRELLA *old form of* > UMBRELLA

OMBRELLAS > OMBRELLA

OMBRES > OMBRE

OMBROPHIL *n* plant flourishing in rainy conditions

OMBU *n* South American tree

OMBUDSMAN *n* official who investigates complaints against government organizations

OMBUDSMEN > OMBUDSMAN

OMBUS > OMBU

OMEGA *n* last letter in the Greek alphabet

OMEGAS > OMEGA

OMELET *same as* > OMELETTE

OMELETS > OMELET

OMELETTE *n* dish of eggs beaten and fried

OMELETTES > OMELETTE

OMEN *n* happening or object thought to foretell success or misfortune ▷ *vb* portend

OMENED > OMEN

OMENING > OMEN

OMENS > OMEN

OMENTA > OMENTUM

OMENTAL > OMENTUM

OMENTUM *n* double fold of the peritoneum connecting the stomach with other abdominal organs

OMENTUMS > OMENTUM

OMER *n* ancient Hebrew unit of dry measure equal to one tenth of an ephah

OMERS > OMER

OMERTA *n* conspiracy of silence

OMERTAS > OMERTA

OMICRON *n* 15th letter in the Greek alphabet

OMICRONS > OMICRON

OMIGOD *interj* exclamation of surprise, pleasure, dismay, etc

OMIKRON *same as* > OMICRON

OMIKRONS > OMIKRON

OMINOUS *adj* worrying, seeming to foretell misfortune

OMINOUSLY > OMINOUS

OMISSIBLE > OMIT

OMISSION *n* something that has been left out or passed over

OMISSIONS > OMISSION

OMISSIVE > OMISSION

OMIT *vb* leave out

OMITS > OMIT

OMITTANCE *n* omission

OMITTED > OMIT

OMITTER > OMIT

OMITTERS > OMIT

OMITTING > OMIT

OMLAH *n* staff team in India

OMLAHS > OMLAH

OMMATEA > OMMATEUM

o

OMMATEUM *n* insect eye

OMMATIDIA *pl n* cone-shaped parts of the eyes of some arthropods

OMNEITIES > OMNEITY

OMNEITY *n* state of being all

OMNIANA *n* miscellaneous collection

OMNIARCH *n* ruler of everything

OMNIARCHS > OMNIARCH

OMNIBUS *n* several books or TV or radio programmes made into one ▷ *adj* consisting of or dealing with several different things at once

OMNIBUSES > OMNIBUS

OMNIETIES > OMNIETY

OMNIETY *same as* > OMNEITY

OMNIFIC *adj* creating all things

OMNIFIED > OMNIFY

OMNIFIES > OMNIFY

OMNIFORM *adj* of all forms

OMNIFY *vb* make something universal

OMNIFYING > OMNIFY

OMNIMODE *adj* of all functions

OMNIRANGE *n* very-high-frequency ground radio navigational system

OMNIUM *n* total value

OMNIUMS > OMNIUM

OMNIVORA *n* group of omnivorous mammals

OMNIVORE *n* omnivorous animal

OMNIVORES > OMNIVORE

OMNIVORY *n* state of being omnivorous

OMOHYOID *n* muscle in shoulder

OMOHYOIDS > OMOHYOID

OMOPHAGIA *n* eating of raw food, esp meat

OMOPHAGIC > OMOPHAGIA

OMOPHAGY *same as* > OMOPHAGIA

OMOPHORIA *pl n* stole-like bands worn by some bishops

OMOPLATE *n* shoulder blade

OMOPLATES > OMOPLATE

OMOV *n* one member one vote: a voting system in which each voter has one vote to cast

OMOVS > OMOV

OMPHACITE *n* type of mineral

OMPHALI > OMPHALOS

OMPHALIC > OMPHALOS

OMPHALOID *adj* like navel

OMPHALOS *n* (in the ancient world) a sacred conical object, esp a stone

OMRAH *n* Muslim noble

OMRAHS > OMRAH

OMS > OM

ON *prep* indicating position above, attachment, closeness, etc ▷ *adv* in operation ▷ *adj* operating ▷ *n* side of the field on which the batsman stands

▷ *vb* go on

ONAGER *n* wild ass of Persia

ONAGERS > ONAGER

ONAGRI > ONAGER

ONANISM *n* withdrawal in sexual intercourse before ejaculation

ONANISMS > ONANISM

ONANIST > ONANISM

ONANISTIC > ONANISM

ONANISTS > ONANISM

ONBEAT *n* first and third beats in a bar of four-four time

ONBEATS > ONBEAT

ONBOARD *adj* on a ship or other craft

ONCE *adv* on one occasion ▷ *n* one occasion

ONCER *n* (formerly) a one-pound note

ONCERS > ONCER

ONCES > ONCE

ONCET *dialect form of* > ONCE

ONCIDIUM *n* American orchid

ONCIDIUMS > ONCIDIUM

ONCOGEN *n* substance causing tumours to form

ONCOGENE *n* gene that can cause cancer when abnormally activated

ONCOGENES > ONCOGENE

ONCOGENIC *adj* causing the formation of a tumour

ONCOGENS > ONCOGEN

ONCOLOGIC > ONCOLOGY

ONCOLOGY *n* branch of medicine concerned with the study, classification, and treatment of tumours

ONCOLYSES > ONCOLYSIS

ONCOLYSIS *n* destruction of tumours

ONCOLYTIC *adj* destroying tumours

ONCOME *n* act of coming on

ONCOMES > ONCOME

ONCOMETER *n* instrument for measuring body organs

ONCOMICE > ONCOMOUSE

ONCOMING *adj* approaching from the front ▷ *n* approach or onset

ONCOMINGS > ONCOMING

ONCOMOUSE *n* mouse bred for cancer treatment research

ONCOST *same as* > OVERHEADS

ONCOSTMAN *n* miner paid daily

ONCOSTMEN > ONCOSTMAN

ONCOSTS > ONCOST

ONCOTOMY *n* surgical cutting of a tumour

ONCOVIRUS *n* virus causing cancer

ONCUS *same as* > ONKUS

ONDATRA *same as* > MUSQUASH

ONDATRAS > ONDATRA

ONDINE *same as* > UNDINE

ONDINES > ONDINE

ONDING *Scots word for* > ONSET

ONDINGS > ONDING

ONDOGRAM *n* record made by ondograph

ONDOGRAMS > ONDOGRAM

ONDOGRAPH *n* instrument for producing a graphical recording of an alternating current

ONE *adj* single, lone ▷ *n* number or figure 1 ▷ *pron* any person

ONEFOLD *adj* simple

ONEIRIC *adj* of or relating to dreams

ONELY *same as* > ONLY

ONENESS *n* unity

ONENESSES > ONENESS

ONER *n* single continuous action

ONERIER > ONERY

ONERIEST > ONERY

ONEROUS *adj* (of a task) difficult to carry out

ONEROUSLY > ONEROUS

ONERS > ONER

ONERY *same as* > ORNERY

ONES > ONE

ONESELF *pron* reflexive form of *one*

ONETIME *adj* at some time in the past

ONEYER *old form of* > ONE

ONEYERS > ONEYER

ONEYRE *same as* > ONEYER

ONEYRES > ONEYRE

ONFALL *n* attack or onset

ONFALLS > ONFALL

ONFLOW *n* flowing on

ONFLOWS > ONFLOW

ONGAONGA *n* New Zealand nettle with a severe or fatal sting

ONGAONGAS > ONGAONGA

ONGOING *adj* in progress, continuing

ONGOINGS *pl n* things that are happening

ONIE *variant spelling of* > ONY

ONION *n* strongly flavoured edible bulb ▷ *vb* add onion to

ONIONED > ONION

ONIONIER > ONION

ONIONIEST > ONION

ONIONING > ONION

ONIONS > ONION

ONIONSKIN *n* glazed translucent paper

ONIONY > ONION

ONIRIC *same as* > ONEIRIC

ONISCOID *adj* of or like woodlice

ONIUM *as in onium compound* type of chemical salt

ONIUMS > ONIUM

ONKUS *adj* bad

ONLAY *n* artificial veneer for a tooth

ONLAYS > ONLAY

ONLIEST *same as* > ONLY

ONLINE *adj* connected to a computer or the internet

ONLINER *n* person who uses the internet regularly

ONLINERS > ONLINER

ONLOAD *vb* load files on to a computer

ONLOADED > ONLOAD

ONLOADING > ONLOAD

ONLOADS > ONLOAD

ONLOOKER *n* person who watches without taking part

ONLOOKERS > ONLOOKER

ONLOOKING > ONLOOKER

ONLY *adj* alone of its kind ▷ *adv* exclusively

ONNED > ON

ONNING > ON

ONO *n* Hawaiian fish

ONOMASTIC *adj* of or relating to proper names

ONOS > ONO

ONRUSH *n* forceful forward rush or flow

ONRUSHES > ONRUSH

ONRUSHING *adj* approaching quickly

ONS > ON

ONSCREEN *adj* appearing on screen

ONSET *n* beginning

ONSETS > ONSET

ONSETTER *n* attacker

ONSETTERS > ONSET

ONSETTING *n* attack

ONSHORE *adv* towards the land

ONSHORING *n* practice of employing white-collar workers from abroad

ONSIDE *adv* (of a player in various sports) in a legal position ▷ *adj* taking one's part or side ▷ *n* part of cricket field where a batsman stands

ONSIDES > ONSIDE

ONSLAUGHT *n* violent attack

ONST *same as* > ONCE

ONSTAGE *adj* visible by audience

ONSTEAD *Scots word for* > FARMSTEAD

ONSTEADS > ONSTEAD

ONSTREAM *adj* in operation

ONTIC *adj* having real existence

ONTICALLY > ONTIC

ONTO *prep* a position on

ONTOGENIC > ONTOGENY

ONTOGENY *n* entire sequence of events involved in the development of an individual organism

ONTOLOGIC > ONTOLOGY

ONTOLOGY *n* branch of philosophy concerned with existence

ONUS *n* responsibility or burden

ONUSES > ONUS

ONWARD *same as* > ONWARDS

ONWARDLY > ONWARD

ONWARDS *adv* at or towards a point or position ahead, in advance, etc

ONY *Scots word for* > ANY

ONYCHA *n* part of mollusc

ONYCHAS > ONYCHA

ONYCHIA *n* inflammation of the nails or claws of animals

ONYCHIAS > ONYCHIA
ONYCHITE *n* type of stone
ONYCHITES > ONYCHITE
ONYCHITIS *n* inflammation of nails
ONYCHIUM *n* part of insect foot
ONYCHIUMS > ONYCHIUM
ONYMOUS *adj* (of a book) bearing its author's name
ONYX *n* type of quartz with coloured layers
ONYXES > ONYX
OO *Scots word for* > WOOL
OOBIT *n* hairy caterpillar
OOBITS > OOBIT
OOCYST *n* type of zygote
OOCYSTS > OOCYST
OOCYTE *n* immature female germ cell that gives rise to an ovum
OOCYTES > OOCYTE
OODLES *pl n* great quantities
OODLINS *same as* > OODLES
OOF *n* money
OOFIER > OOF
OOFIEST > OOF
OOFS > OOF
OOFTISH *n* money
OOFTISHES > OOFTISH
OOFY > OOF
OOGAMETE *n* female gamete
OOGAMETES > OOGAMETE
OOGAMIES > OOGAMY
OOGAMOUS > OOGAMY
OOGAMY *n* sexual reproduction involving a small motile male gamete and a large much less motile female gamete
OOGENESES > OOGENESIS
OOGENESIS *n* formation and maturation of ova from undifferentiated cells in the ovary
OOGENETIC > OOGENESIS
OOGENIES > OOGENY
OOGENY *same as* > OOGENESIS
OOGONIA > OOGONIUM
OOGONIAL > OOGONIUM
OOGONIUM *n* immature female germ cell forming oocytes by repeated divisions
OOGONIUMS > OOGONIUM
OOH *interj* exclamation of surprise, pleasure, pain, etc ▷ *vb* say ooh
OOHED > OOH
OOHING > OOH
OOHS > OOH
OOIDAL *adj* shaped like egg
OOLACHAN *same as* > EULACHON
OOLACHANS > OOLACHAN
OOLAKAN *same as* > EULACHON
OOLAKANS > OOLAKAN
OOLITE *n* limestone made up of tiny grains of calcium carbonate
OOLITES > OOLITE
OOLITH *n* any of the tiny spherical grains of sedimentary rock of which oolite is composed

OOLITHS > OOLITH
OOLITIC > OOLITE
OOLOGIC > OOLOGY
OOLOGICAL > OOLOGY
OOLOGIES > OOLOGY
OOLOGIST > OOLOGY
OOLOGISTS > OOLOGY
OOLOGY *n* branch of ornithology concerned with the study of birds' eggs
OOLONG *n* kind of dark tea that is partly fermented before being dried
OOLONGS > OOLONG
OOM *n* title of respect used to refer to an elderly man
OOMIAC *same as* > UMIAK
OOMIACK *same as* > UMIAK
OOMIACKS > OOMIACK
OOMIACS > OOMIAC
OOMIAK *same as* > UMIAK
OOMIAKS > OOMIAK
OOMPAH *n* representation of the sound made by a deep brass instrument ▷ *vb* make the noise of a brass instrument
OOMPAHED > OOMPAH
OOMPAHING > OOMPAH
OOMPAHS > OOMPAH
OOMPH *n* enthusiasm, vigour, or energy
OOMPHS > OOMPH
OOMS > OOM
OOMYCETE *n* organism formerly classified as fungi
OOMYCETES > OOMYCETE
OON *Scots word for* > OVEN
OONS > OON
OONT *n* camel
OONTS > OONT
OOP *vb* Scots word meaning to bind
OOPED > OOP
OOPHORON *n* ovary
OOPHORONS > OOPHORON
OOPHYTE *n* gametophyte in mosses, liverworts, and ferns
OOPHYTES > OOPHYTE
OOPHYTIC > OOPHYTE
OOPING > OOP
OOPS *interj* exclamation of surprise or apology
OOR *Scots form of* > OUR
OORALI *n* member of Indian people
OORALIS > OORALI
OORIAL *n* Himalayan sheep
OORIALS > OORIAL
OORIE *adj* Scots word meaning shabby
OORIER > OORIE
OORIEST > OORIE
OOS > OO
OOSE *n* dust
OOSES > OOSE
OOSIER > OOSE
OOSIEST > OOSE
OOSPERM *n* fertilized ovum
OOSPERMS > OOSPERM
OOSPHERE *n* large female gamete produced in the oogonia of algae and fungi
OOSPHERES > OOSPHERE
OOSPORE *n* thick-walled

sexual spore that develops from a fertilized oosphere
OOSPORES > OOSPORE
OOSPORIC > OOSPORE
OOSPOROUS > OOSPORE
OOSY > OOSE
OOT *Scots word for* > OUT
OOTHECA *n* capsule containing eggs that is produced by some insects and molluscs
OOTHECAE > OOTHECA
OOTHECAL > OOTHECA
OOTID *n* immature female gamete that develops into an ovum
OOTIDS > OOTID
OOTS > OOT
OOZE *vb* flow slowly ▷ *n* sluggish flow
OOZED > OOZE
OOZES > OOZE
OOZIER > OOZY
OOZIEST > OOZY
OOZILY > OOZY
OOZINESS > OOZY
OOZING > OOZE
OOZY *adj* moist or dripping
OP *n* operation
OPACIFIED > OPACIFY
OPACIFIER > OPACIFY
OPACIFIES > OPACIFY
OPACIFY *vb* become or make opaque
OPACITIES > OPACITY
OPACITY *n* state or quality of being opaque
OPACOUS *same as* > OPAQUE
OPAH *n* large soft-finned deep-sea fish
OPAHS > OPAH
OPAL *n* iridescent precious stone
OPALED *adj* made like opal
OPALESCE *vb* exhibit a milky iridescence
OPALESCED > OPALESCE
OPALESCES > OPALESCE
OPALINE *adj* opalescent ▷ *n* opaque or semiopaque whitish glass
OPALINES > OPALINE
OPALISED *same as* > OPALIZED
OPALIZED *adj* made into opal
OPALS > OPAL
OPAQUE *adj* not able to be seen through, not transparent ▷ *n* opaque pigment used to block out particular areas on a negative ▷ *vb* make opaque
OPAQUED > OPAQUE
OPAQUELY > OPAQUE
OPAQUER > OPAQUE
OPAQUES > OPAQUE
OPAQUEST > OPAQUE
OPAQUING > OPAQUE
OPCODE *n* computer code containing operating instructions
OPCODES > OPCODE
OPE *archaic or poetic word for* > OPEN
OPED > OPE

OPEN *adj* not closed ▷ *vb* (cause to) become open ▷ *n* competition which all may enter
OPENABLE > OPEN
OPENCAST *as in opencast mining* mining by excavating from the surface
OPENED > OPEN
OPENER *n* tool for opening cans and bottles
OPENERS > OPENER
OPENEST > OPEN
OPENING *n* beginning ▷ *adj* first
OPENINGS > OPENING
OPENLY > OPEN
OPENNESS > OPEN
OPENS > OPEN
OPENSIDE *n* in rugby, flanker who plays on the open side of the scrum
OPENSIDES > OPENSIDE
OPENWORK *n* ornamental work, as of metal or embroidery, having a pattern of openings or holes
OPENWORKS > OPENWORK
OPEPE *n* African tree
OPEPES > OPEPE
OPERA *n* drama in which the text is sung to an orchestral accompaniment
OPERABLE *adj* capable of being treated by a surgical operation
OPERABLY > OPERABLE
OPERAGOER *n* person who goes to operas
OPERAND *n* quantity, variable, or function upon which an operation is performed
OPERANDS > OPERAND
OPERANT *adj* producing effects ▷ *n* person or thing that operates
OPERANTLY > OPERANT
OPERANTS > OPERANT
OPERAS > OPERA
OPERATE *vb* (cause to) work
OPERATED > OPERATE
OPERATES > OPERATE
OPERATIC *adj* of or relating to opera
OPERATICS *n* performance of operas
OPERATING > OPERATE
OPERATION *n* method or procedure of working
OPERATISE *same as* > OPERATIZE
OPERATIVE *adj* working ▷ *n* worker with a special skill
OPERATIZE *vb* turn (a play, novel, etc) into an opera
OPERATOR *n* person who operates a machine or instrument
OPERATORS > OPERATOR
OPERCELE *same as* > OPERCULE
OPERCELES > OPERCELE
OPERCULA > OPERCULUM
OPERCULAR > OPERCULUM

OPERCULE n gill cover

OPERCULES > OPERCULE

OPERCULUM n covering flap or lidlike structure in animals or plants

OPERETTA n light-hearted comic opera

OPERETTAS > OPERETTA

OPERON n group of adjacent genes in bacteria functioning as a unit

OPERONS > OPERON

OPEROSE adj laborious

OPEROSELY > OPEROSE

OPEROSITY > OPEROSE

OPES > OPE

OPGEFOK adj South African taboo slang for damaged or bungled

OPHIDIAN adj snakelike ▷ n any reptile of the suborder Ophidia; a snake

OPHIDIANS > OPHIDIAN

OPHIOLITE n type of mineral

OPHIOLOGY n branch of zoology that is concerned with the study of snakes

OPHITE n any of several greenish mottled rocks

OPHITES > OPHITE

OPHITIC adj having small elongated feldspar crystals enclosed

OPHIURA n sea creature like a starfish

OPHIURAN same as > OPHIURA

OPHIURANS > OPHIURAN

OPHIURAS > OPHIURA

OPHIURID same as > OPHIURA

OPHIURIDS > OPHIURID

OPHIUROID adj of or like ophiura

OPIATE n narcotic drug containing opium ▷ adj containing or consisting of opium ▷ vb treat with an opiate

OPIATED > OPIATE

OPIATES > OPIATE

OPIATING > OPIATE

OPIFICER n craftsman

OPIFICERS > OPIFICER

OPINABLE adj thinkable

OPINE vb express an opinion

OPINED > OPINE

OPINES > OPINE

OPING > OPE

OPINICUS n mythical monster

OPINING > OPINE

OPINION n personal belief or judgment

OPINIONED adj having strong opinions

OPINIONS > OPINION

OPIOID n substance that resembles morphine in its physiological or pharmacological effect

OPIOIDS > OPIOID

OPIUM n addictive narcotic drug made from poppy seeds

OPIUMISM n addiction to opium

OPIUMISMS > OPIUMISM

OPIUMS > OPIUM

OPOBALSAM n soothing ointment

OPODELDOC n medical ointment

OPOPANAX n medical resin from plant

OPORICE n former medicine made from fruit

OPORICES > OPORICE

OPOSSUM n small marsupial of America or Australasia

OPOSSUMS > OPOSSUM

OPPIDAN adj of a town ▷ n person living in a town

OPPIDANS > OPPIDAN

OPPILANT > OPPILATE

OPPILATE vb block (the pores, bowels, etc)

OPPILATED > OPPILATE

OPPILATES > OPPILATE

OPPO n counterpart in another organization

OPPONENCY > OPPONENT

OPPONENT n person one is working against in a contest, battle, or argument ▷ adj opposite, as in position

OPPONENTS > OPPONENT

OPPORTUNE adj happening at a suitable time

OPPOS > OPPO

OPPOSABLE adj (of the thumb) capable of touching the tip of all the other fingers

OPPOSABLY > OPPOSABLE

OPPOSE vb work against

OPPOSED > OPPOSE

OPPOSER > OPPOSE

OPPOSERS > OPPOSE

OPPOSES > OPPOSE

OPPOSING > OPPOSE

OPPOSITE adj situated on the other side ▷ n person or thing that is opposite ▷ prep facing ▷ adv on the other side

OPPOSITES > OPPOSITE

OPPRESS vb control by cruelty or force

OPPRESSED > OPPRESS

OPPRESSES > OPPRESS

OPPRESSOR > OPPRESS

OPPUGN vb call into question

OPPUGNANT adj combative, antagonistic, or contrary

OPPUGNED > OPPUGN

OPPUGNER > OPPUGN

OPPUGNERS > OPPUGN

OPPUGNING > OPPUGN

OPPUGNS > OPPUGN

OPS > OP

OPSIMATH n person who learns late in life

OPSIMATHS > OPSIMATH

OPSIMATHY > OPSIMATH

OPSIN n type of protein

OPSINS > OPSIN

OPSOMANIA n extreme enthusiasm for a particular food

OPSONIC > OPSONIN

OPSONIFY same as > OPSONIZE

OPSONIN n constituent of blood serum

OPSONISE same as > OPSONIZE

OPSONISED > OPSONISE

OPSONISES > OPSONISE

OPSONIUM n relish eaten with bread

OPSONIUMS > OPSONIUM

OPSONIZE vb subject (bacteria) to the action of opsonins

OPSONIZED > OPSONIZE

OPSONIZES > OPSONIZE

OPT vb show a preference, choose

OPTANT n person who opts

OPTANTS > OPTANT

OPTATIVE adj indicating or expressing choice, preference, or wish ▷ n optative mood

OPTATIVES > OPTATIVE

OPTED > OPT

OPTER > OPT

OPTERS > OPT

OPTIC adj relating to the eyes or sight

OPTICAL adj of or involving light or optics

OPTICALLY > OPTICAL

OPTICIAN n person qualified to prescribe glasses

OPTICIANS > OPTICIAN

OPTICIST n optics expert

OPTICISTS > OPTICIST

OPTICS n science of sight and light

OPTIMA > OPTIMUM

OPTIMAL adj best or most favourable

OPTIMALLY > OPTIMAL

OPTIMATE n Roman aristocrat

OPTIMATES > OPTIMATE

OPTIME n mathematics student at Cambridge University

OPTIMES > OPTIME

OPTIMISE same as > OPTIMIZE

OPTIMISED > OPTIMISE

OPTIMISER > OPTIMISE

OPTIMISES > OPTIMISE

OPTIMISM n tendency to take the most hopeful view

OPTIMISMS > OPTIMISM

OPTIMIST > OPTIMISM

OPTIMISTS > OPTIMISM

OPTIMIZE vb make the most of

OPTIMIZED > OPTIMIZE

OPTIMIZER > OPTIMIZE

OPTIMIZES > OPTIMIZE

OPTIMUM n best possible conditions ▷ adj most favourable

OPTIMUMS > OPTIMUM

OPTING > OPT

OPTION n choice ▷ vb obtain an option on

OPTIONAL adj possible but not compulsory ▷ n optional thing

OPTIONALS > OPTIONAL

OPTIONED > OPTION

OPTIONEE n holder of a financial option

OPTIONEES > OPTIONEE

OPTIONING > OPTION

OPTIONS > OPTION

OPTOLOGY n science of sight

OPTOMETER n any of various instruments for measuring the refractive power of the eye

OPTOMETRY n science or practice of testing visual acuity and prescribing corrective lenses

OPTOPHONE n device for blind people that converts printed words into sounds

OPTRONICS n science of electronic and light signals

OPTS > OPT

OPULENCE > OPULENT

OPULENCES > OPULENT

OPULENCY > OPULENT

OPULENT adj having or indicating wealth

OPULENTLY > OPULENT

OPULUS n flowering shrub

OPULUSES > OPULUS

OPUNTIA n type of cactus

OPUNTIAS > OPUNTIA

OPUS n artistic creation, esp a musical work

OPUSCLE same as > OPUSCULE

OPUSCLES > OPUSCLE

OPUSCULA > OPUSCULUM

OPUSCULAR > OPUSCULE

OPUSCULE n small or insignificant artistic work

OPUSCULES > OPUSCULE

OPUSCULUM same as > OPUSCULE

OPUSES > OPUS

OQUASSA n American trout

OQUASSAS > OQUASSA

OR prep before ▷ adj of the metal gold ▷ n gold

ORA > OS

ORACH same as > ORACHE

ORACHE n type of plant

ORACHES > ORACHE

ORACIES > ORACY

ORACLE n shrine of an ancient god ▷ vb utter as an oracle

ORACLED > ORACLE

ORACLES > ORACLE

ORACLING > ORACLE

ORACULAR adj of or like an oracle

ORACULOUS adj of an oracle

ORACY n capacity to express oneself in and understand speech

ORAD adv towards the mouth

ORAGIOUS adj stormy

ORAL adj spoken ▷ n spoken examination

ORALISM n oral method of communicating with deaf people

ORALISMS > ORALISM

ORALIST > ORALISM

ORALISTS > ORALISM

ORALITIES > ORALITY
ORALITY n state of being oral
ORALLY > ORAL
ORALS > ORAL
ORANG n orangutan
ORANGE n reddish-yellow citrus fruit ▷ adj reddish-yellow
ORANGEADE n orange-flavoured, usu fizzy drink
ORANGER > ORANGE
ORANGERIE archaic variant of > ORANGERY
ORANGERY n greenhouse for growing orange trees
ORANGES > ORANGE
ORANGEST > ORANGE
ORANGEY > ORANGE
ORANGIER > ORANGE
ORANGIEST > ORANGE
ORANGISH > ORANGE
ORANGS > ORANG
ORANGUTAN n large ape with shaggy reddish-brown hair
ORANGY > ORANGE
ORANT n artistic representation of worshipper
ORANTS > ORANT
ORARIA > ORARIUM
ORARIAN n person who lives on the coast
ORARIANS > ORARIAN
ORARION n garment worn by Greek clergyman
ORARIONS > ORARION
ORARIUM n handkerchief
ORARIUMS > ORARIUM
ORATE vb make or give an oration
ORATED > ORATE
ORATES > ORATE
ORATING > ORATE
ORATION n formal speech
ORATIONS > ORATION
ORATOR n skilful public speaker
ORATORIAL adj of oratory
ORATORIAN n clergyman of a particular type of church
ORATORIES > ORATORY
ORATORIO n musical composition for choir and orchestra
ORATORIOS > ORATORIO
ORATORS > ORATOR
ORATORY n art of making speeches
ORATRESS n female orator
ORATRICES > ORATRIX
ORATRIX n female orator
ORATRIXES > ORATRIX
ORB n ceremonial decorated sphere with a cross on top, carried by a monarch ▷ vb make or become circular or spherical
ORBED > ORB
ORBICULAR adj circular or spherical
ORBIER > ORBY
ORBIEST > ORBY
ORBING > ORB
ORBIT n curved path of a planet, satellite, or spacecraft around another

body ▷ vb move in an orbit around
ORBITA same as > ORBIT
ORBITAL adj of or denoting an orbit ▷ n region surrounding an atomic nucleus
ORBITALLY > ORBITAL
ORBITALS > ORBITAL
ORBITAS > ORBITA
ORBITED > ORBIT
ORBITER n spacecraft or satellite designed to orbit a planet without landing on it
ORBITERS > ORBITER
ORBITIES > ORBITY
ORBITING > ORBIT
ORBITS > ORBIT
ORBITY n bereavement
ORBLESS > ORB
ORBS > ORB
ORBY adj orb-shaped
ORC n any of various whales, such as the killer and grampus
ORCA n killer whale
ORCAS > ORCA
ORCEIN n brown crystalline material
ORCEINS > ORCEIN
ORCHARD n area where fruit trees are grown
ORCHARDS > ORCHARD
ORCHAT same as > ORCHARD
ORCHATS > ORCHAT
ORCHEL same as > ORCHIL
ORCHELLA same as > ORCHIL
ORCHELLAS > ORCHELLA
ORCHELS > ORCHEL
ORCHESES > ORCHESIS
ORCHESIS n art of dance
ORCHESTIC adj of dance
ORCHESTRA n large group of musicians, esp playing a variety of instruments
ORCHID n plant with flowers that have unusual lip-shaped petals
ORCHIDIST n orchid grower
ORCHIDS > ORCHID
ORCHIL n any of various lichens
ORCHILLA same as > ORCHIL
ORCHILLAS > ORCHILLA
ORCHILS > ORCHIL
ORCHIS n type of orchid
ORCHISES > ORCHIS
ORCHITIC > ORCHITIS
ORCHITIS n inflammation of one or both testicles
ORCIN same as > ORCINOL
ORCINE same as > ORCINOL
ORCINES > ORCINE
ORCINOL n colourless crystalline water-soluble solid
ORCINOLS > ORCINOL
ORCINS > ORCIN
ORCS > ORC
ORD n pointed weapon
ORDAIN vb make (someone) a member of the clergy
ORDAINED > ORDAIN
ORDAINER > ORDAIN
ORDAINERS > ORDAIN
ORDAINING > ORDAIN

ORDAINS > ORDAIN
ORDALIAN adj of an ordeal
ORDALIUM same as > ORDEAL
ORDALIUMS > ORDALIUM
ORDEAL n painful or difficult experience
ORDEALS > ORDEAL
ORDER n instruction to be carried out ▷ vb give an instruction to
ORDERABLE > ORDER
ORDERED > ORDER
ORDERER > ORDER
ORDERERS > ORDER
ORDERING > ORDER
ORDERINGS > ORDER
ORDERLESS > ORDER
ORDERLIES > ORDERLY
ORDERLY adj well-organized ▷ n hospital attendant ▷ adv according to custom or rule
ORDERS > ORDER
ORDINAIRE adj ordinary
ORDINAL adj denoting a certain position in a sequence of numbers ▷ n book containing the forms of services for the ordination of ministers
ORDINALLY > ORDINAL
ORDINALS > ORDINAL
ORDINANCE n official rule or order
ORDINAND n candidate for ordination
ORDINANDS > ORDINAND
ORDINANT n person who ordains
ORDINANTS > ORDINANT
ORDINAR Scots word for > ORDINARY
ORDINARS > ORDINAR
ORDINARY adj usual or normal
ORDINATE n vertical coordinate of a point in a two-dimensional system of coordinates ▷ vb ordain
ORDINATED > ORDINATE
ORDINATES > ORDINATE
ORDINEE n person being ordained
ORDINEES > ORDINEE
ORDINES > ORDO
ORDNANCE n weapons and military supplies
ORDNANCES > ORDNANCE
ORDO n religious order
ORDOS > ORDO
ORDS > ORD
ORDURE n excrement
ORDURES > ORDURE
ORDUROUS > ORDURE
ORE n (rock containing) a mineral which yields metal
OREAD n mountain nymph
OREADES > OREAD
OREADS > OREAD
ORECTIC adj of or relating to the desires
ORECTIVE > OREXIS
OREGANO n sweet-smelling herb used in cooking
OREGANOS > OREGANO
OREIDE same as > OROIDE
OREIDES > OREIDE

OREODONT n extinct prehistoric mammal
OREODONTS > OREODONT
OREOLOGY same as > OROLOGY
OREPEARCH same as > OVERPERCH
ORES > ORE
ORESTUNCK > OVERSTINK
OREWEED n seaweed
OREWEEDS > OREWEED
OREXIS n appetite
OREXISES > OREXIS
ORF n infectious disease of sheep and sometimes goats and cattle
ORFE n small slender European fish
ORFES > ORFE
ORFRAY same as > ORPHREY
ORFRAYS > ORFRAY
ORFS > ORF
ORGAN n part of an animal or plant that has a particular function
ORGANA > ORGANON
ORGANDIE n fine cotton fabric
ORGANDIES > ORGANDY
ORGANDY same as > ORGANDIE
ORGANELLE n structural and functional unit in a cell
ORGANIC adj of or produced from animals or plants ▷ n substance that is derived from animal or vegetable matter
ORGANICAL same as > ORGANIC
ORGANICS > ORGANIC
ORGANISE same as > ORGANIZE
ORGANISED same as > ORGANIZED
ORGANISER same as > ORGANIZER
ORGANISES > ORGANISE
ORGANISM n any living animal or plant
ORGANISMS > ORGANISM
ORGANIST n organ player
ORGANISTS > ORGANIST
ORGANITY same as > ORGANISM
ORGANIZE vb make arrangements for
ORGANIZED > ORGANIZE
ORGANIZER n person who organizes or is capable of organizing
ORGANIZES > ORGANIZE
ORGANON n system of logical or scientific rules, esp that of Aristotle
ORGANONS > ORGANON
ORGANOSOL n resin-based coating
ORGANOTIN adj of an organic compound used as a pesticide
ORGANS > ORGAN
ORGANUM same as > ORGANON
ORGANUMS > ORGANUM
ORGANZA n thin stiff fabric of silk, cotton, or synthetic

fibre

ORGANZAS > ORGANZA

ORGANZINE n strong thread made of twisted strands of raw silk

ORGASM n most intense point of sexual pleasure ▷ vb experience orgasm

ORGASMED > ORGASM

ORGASMIC > ORGASM

ORGASMING > ORGASM

ORGASMS > ORGASM

ORGASTIC > ORGASM

ORGEAT n drink made from barley or almonds, and orange flower water

ORGEATS > ORGEAT

ORGIA same as > ORGY

ORGIAC > ORGY

ORGIAS > ORGIA

ORGIAST n participant in orgy

ORGIASTIC > ORGY

ORGIASTS > ORGIAST

ORGIC > ORGY

ORGIES > ORGY

ORGILLOUS same as > ORGULOUS

ORGONE n substance claimed to be needed in people for sexual activity and mental health

ORGONES > ORGONE

ORGUE n number of stakes lashed together

ORGUES > ORGUE

ORGULOUS adj proud

ORGY n party involving promiscuous sexual activity

ORIBATID n type of mite

ORIBATIDS > ORIBATID

ORIBI n small African antelope

ORIBIS > ORIBI

ORICALCHE same as > ORICHALC

ORICHALC n type of alloy

ORICHALCS > ORICHALC

ORIEL n type of bay window

ORIELLED adj having an oriel

ORIELS > ORIEL

ORIENCIES > ORIENCY

ORIENCY n state of being orient

ORIENT vb position (oneself) according to one's surroundings ▷ n eastern sky or the dawn ▷ adj eastern

ORIENTAL adj eastern ▷ n native of the orient

ORIENTALS > ORIENTAL

ORIENTATE vb position (oneself) according to one's surroundings

ORIENTED > ORIENT

ORIENTEER vb take part in orienteering ▷ n person who takes part in orienteering

ORIENTER > ORIENT

ORIENTERS > ORIENT

ORIENTING > ORIENT

ORIENTS > ORIENT

ORIFEX same as > ORIFICE

ORIFEXES > ORIFEX

ORIFICE n opening or hole

ORIFICES > ORIFICE

ORIFICIAL > ORIFICE

ORIFLAMME n scarlet flag adopted as the national banner of France in the Middle Ages

ORIGAMI n Japanese decorative art of paper folding

ORIGAMIS > ORIGAMI

ORIGAN another name for > MARJORAM

ORIGANE same as > ORIGAN

ORIGANES > ORIGANE

ORIGANS > ORIGAN

ORIGANUM n type of aromatic plant

ORIGANUMS > ORIGANUM

ORIGIN n point from which something develops

ORIGINAL adj first or earliest ▷ n first version, from which others are copied

ORIGINALS > ORIGINAL

ORIGINATE vb come or bring into existence

ORIGINS > ORIGIN

ORIHOU n small New Zealand tree

ORILLION n part of bastion

ORILLIONS > ORILLION

ORINASAL adj pronounced with simultaneous oral and nasal articulation ▷ n orinasal speech sound

ORINASALS > ORINASAL

ORIOLE n tropical or American songbird

ORIOLES > ORIOLE

ORISHA n any of the minor gods or spirits of traditional Yoruba religion

ORISHAS > ORISHA

ORISON another word for > PRAYER

ORISONS > ORISON

ORIXA same as > ORISHA

ORIXAS > ORIXA

ORLE n border around a shield

ORLEANS n type of fabric

ORLEANSES > ORLEANS

ORLES > ORLE

ORLON n tradename for a crease-resistant acrylic fibre or fabric used for clothing, furnishings, etc

ORLONS > ORLON

ORLOP n (in a vessel with four or more decks) the lowest deck

ORLOPS > ORLOP

ORMER n edible marine mollusc

ORMERS > ORMER

ORMOLU n gold-coloured alloy used for decoration

ORMOLUS > ORMOLU

ORNAMENT n decorative object ▷ vb decorate

ORNAMENTS > ORNAMENT

ORNATE adj highly decorated, elaborate

ORNATELY > ORNATE

ORNATER > ORNATE

ORNATEST > ORNATE

ORNERIER > ORNERY

ORNERIEST > ORNERY

ORNERY adj stubborn or vile-tempered

ORNIS less common word for > AVIFAUNA

ORNISES > ORNIS

ORNITHES n birds in Greek myth

ORNITHIC adj of or relating to birds or a bird fauna

ORNITHINE n type of amino acid

ORNITHOID adj like bird

OROGEN n part of earth subject to orogeny

OROGENIC > OROGENY

OROGENIES > OROGENY

OROGENS > OROGEN

OROGENY n formation of mountain ranges by intense upward displacement of the earth's crust

OROGRAPHY n study or mapping of relief, esp of mountains

OROIDE n alloy containing copper, tin, and other metals, used as imitation gold

OROIDES > OROIDE

OROLOGIES > OROLOGY

OROLOGIST > OROLOGY

OROLOGY same as > OROGRAPHY

OROMETER n aneroid barometer with an altitude scale

OROMETERS > OROMETER

ORONASAL adj of or relating to the mouth and nose

OROPESA n float used in minesweeping

OROPESAS > OROPESA

OROTUND adj (of the voice) resonant and booming

ORPHAN n child whose parents are dead ▷ vb deprive of parents

ORPHANAGE n children's home for orphans

ORPHANED > ORPHAN

ORPHANING > ORPHAN

ORPHANISM n state of being an orphan

ORPHANS > ORPHAN

ORPHARION n large lute in use during the 16th and 17th centuries

ORPHIC adj mystical or occult

ORPHICAL same as > ORPHIC

ORPHISM n style of abstract art

ORPHISMS > ORPHISM

ORPHREY n richly embroidered band or border

ORPHREYED adj emroidered with gold

ORPHREYS > ORPHREY

ORPIMENT n yellow mineral

ORPIMENTS > ORPIMENT

ORPIN same as > ORPINE

ORPINE n type of plant

ORPINES > ORPINE

ORPINS > ORPIN

ORRA adj odd or unmatched

ORRAMAN n man who does odd jobs

ORRAMEN > ORRAMAN

ORRERIES > ORRERY

ORRERY n mechanical model of the solar system

ORRICE same as > ORRIS

ORRICES > ORRICE

ORRIS n kind of iris

ORRISES > ORRIS

ORRISROOT n rhizome of a type of iris, used as perfume

ORS > OR

ORSEILLE same as > ORCHIL

ORSEILLES > ORSEILLE

ORSELLIC > ORSEILLE

ORT n fragment

ORTANIQUE n hybrid between an orange and a tangerine

ORTHIAN adj having high pitch

ORTHICON n type of television camera tube

ORTHICONS > ORTHICON

ORTHO n type of photographic plate

ORTHOAXES > ORTHOAXIS

ORTHOAXIS n axis in a crystal

ORTHODOX adj conforming to established views

ORTHODOXY n orthodox belief or practice

ORTHOEPIC > ORTHOEPY

ORTHOEPY n study of correct or standard pronunciation

ORTHOPEDY n treatment of deformity

ORTHOPOD n surgeon

ORTHOPODS > ORTHOPOD

ORTHOPTER n type of aircraft propelled by flapping wings

ORTHOPTIC adj relating to normal binocular vision

ORTHOS > ORTHO

ORTHOSES > ORTHOSIS

ORTHOSIS n artificial or mechanical aid to support a weak part of the body

ORTHOTIC > ORTHOTICS

ORTHOTICS n use of artificial or mechanical aids to assist movement of weak joints or muscles

ORTHOTIST n person who is qualified to practise orthotics

ORTHOTONE adj (of a word) having an independent accent ▷ n independently accented word

ORTHROS n canonical hour in the Greek Church

ORTHROSES > ORTHROS

ORTOLAN n small European songbird eaten as a delicacy

ORTOLANS > ORTOLAN

ORTS pl n scraps or leavings

ORVAL n plant of sage family

ORVALS > ORVAL
ORYX n large African antelope
ORYXES > ORYX
ORZO n pasta in small grain shapes
ORZOS > ORZO
OS n mouth or mouthlike part or opening
OSAR > OS
OSCAR n cash
OSCARS > OSCAR
OSCHEAL adj of scrotum
OSCILLATE vb swing back and forth
OSCINE n songbird ▷ adj of songbirds
OSCINES > OSCINE
OSCININE > OSCINE
OSCITANCE same as > OSCITANCY
OSCITANCY n state of being drowsy, lazy, or inattentive
OSCITANT > OSCITANCY
OSCITATE vb yawn
OSCITATED > OSCITATE
OSCITATES > OSCITATE
OSCULA > OSCULUM
OSCULANT adj possessing some of the characteristics of two different taxonomic groups
OSCULAR adj of or relating to an osculum
OSCULATE vb kiss
OSCULATED > OSCULATE
OSCULATES > OSCULATE
OSCULE n small mouth or opening
OSCULES > OSCULE
OSCULUM n mouthlike aperture
OSE same as > ESKER
OSES > OSE
OSETRA n type of caviar
OSETRAS > OSETRA
OSHAC n plant smelling of ammonia
OSHACS > OSHAC
OSIER n willow tree
OSIERED adj covered with osiers
OSIERIES > OSIERY
OSIERS > OSIER
OSIERY n work done with osiers
OSMATE n salt of osmic acid
OSMATES > OSMATE
OSMATIC adj relying on sense of smell
OSMETERIA pl n glands in some caterpillars that secrete foul-smelling substances to deter predators
OSMIATE same as > OSMATE
OSMIATES > OSMIATE
OSMIC adj of or containing osmium in a high valence state
OSMICALLY > OSMIC
OSMICS n science of smell
OSMIOUS same as > OSMOUS
OSMIUM n heaviest known metallic element
OSMIUMS > OSMIUM
OSMOL same as > OSMOLE

OSMOLAL > OSMOLE
OSMOLAR adj containing one osmole per litre
OSMOLE n unit of osmotic pressure
OSMOLES > OSMOLE
OSMOLS > OSMOL
OSMOMETER n instrument for measuring osmotic pressure
OSMOMETRY > OSMOMETER
OSMOSE vb undergo or cause to undergo osmosis
OSMOSED > OSMOSE
OSMOSES > OSMOSE
OSMOSING > OSMOSE
OSMOSIS n movement of a liquid through a membrane from a lower to a higher concentration
OSMOTIC > OSMOSIS
OSMOUS adj of or containing osmium in a low valence state
OSMUND same as > OSMUNDA
OSMUNDA n type of fern
OSMUNDAS > OSMUNDA
OSMUNDINE n type of compost
OSMUNDS > OSMUND
OSNABURG n coarse plain-woven cotton used for sacks, furnishings, etc
OSNABURGS > OSNABURG
OSPREY n large fish-eating bird of prey
OSPREYS > OSPREY
OSSA > OS
OSSARIUM same as > OSSUARY
OSSARIUMS > OSSARIUM
OSSATURE n skeleton
OSSATURES > OSSATURE
OSSEIN n protein that forms the organic matrix of bone
OSSEINS > OSSEIN
OSSELET n growth on knee of horse
OSSELETS > OSSELET
OSSEOUS adj consisting of or like bone
OSSEOUSLY > OSSEOUS
OSSETER n sturgeon
OSSETERS > OSSETER
OSSETRA same as > OSETRA
OSSETRAS > OSSETRA
OSSIA conj (in music) or
OSSICLE n small bone, esp one of those in the middle ear
OSSICLES > OSSICLE
OSSICULAR > OSSICLE
OSSIFIC adj making something turn to bone
OSSIFIED adj converted into bone
OSSIFIER > OSSIFY
OSSIFIERS > OSSIFY
OSSIFIES > OSSIFY
OSSIFRAGA n large sea bird
OSSIFRAGE n osprey
OSSIFY vb (cause to) become bone, harden
OSSIFYING > OSSIFY
OSSUARIES > OSSUARY
OSSUARY n any container

for the burial of human bones, such as an urn or vault
OSTEAL adj of or relating to bone or to the skeleton
OSTEITIC > OSTEITIS
OSTEITIS n inflammation of a bone
OSTENSIVE adj directly showing or pointing out
OSTENSORY n (in the RC Church) receptacle for displaying the consecrated Host
OSTENT n appearance
OSTENTS > OSTENT
OSTEOCYTE n bone cell
OSTEODERM n bony area in skin
OSTEOGEN n material from which bone forms
OSTEOGENS > OSTEOGEN
OSTEOGENY n forming of bone
OSTEOID adj of or resembling bone ▷ n bony deposit
OSTEOIDS > OSTEOID
OSTEOLOGY n study of the structure and function of bones
OSTEOMA n benign tumour composed of bone or bonelike tissue
OSTEOMAS > OSTEOMA
OSTEOMATA > OSTEOMA
OSTEOPATH n person who practises osteopathy
OSTEOSES > OSTEOSIS
OSTEOSIS n forming of bony tissue
OSTEOTOME n surgical instrument for cutting bone, usually a special chisel
OSTEOTOMY n surgical cutting or dividing of bone
OSTIA > OSTIUM
OSTIAL > OSTIUM
OSTIARIES > OSTIARY
OSTIARY another word for > PORTER
OSTIATE adj having ostium
OSTINATI > OSTINATO
OSTINATO n persistently repeated phrase or rhythm
OSTINATOS > OSTINATO
OSTIOLAR > OSTIOLE
OSTIOLATE > OSTIOLE
OSTIOLE n pore in the reproductive bodies of certain algae and fungi through which spores pass
OSTIOLES > OSTIOLE
OSTIUM n any of the pores in sponges through which water enters the body
OSTLER n stableman at an inn
OSTLERESS n female ostler
OSTLERS > OSTLER
OSTMARK n currency of the former East Germany
OSTMARKS > OSTMARK
OSTOMATE n person with an ostomy
OSTOMATES > OSTOMATE

OSTOMIES > OSTOMY
OSTOMY n surgically made opening connecting organ to surface of body
OSTOSES > OSTOSIS
OSTOSIS n formation of bone
OSTOSISES > OSTOSIS
OSTRACA > OSTRACON
OSTRACEAN adj of oysters
OSTRACISE same as > OSTRACIZE
OSTRACISM > OSTRACIZE
OSTRACIZE vb exclude (a person) from a group
OSTRACOD n type of minute crustacean
OSTRACODE adj of ostracods
OSTRACODS > OSTRACOD
OSTRACON n (in ancient Greece) a potsherd used for ostracizing
OSTRAKA > OSTRAKON
OSTRAKON same as > OSTRACON
OSTREGER n keeper of hawks
OSTREGERS > OSTREGER
OSTRICH n large African bird that runs fast but cannot fly
OSTRICHES > OSTRICH
OTAKU n Japanese computer geeks
OTALGIA technical name for > EARACHE
OTALGIAS > OTALGIA
OTALGIC > OTALGIA
OTALGIES > OTALGY
OTALGY same as > OTALGIA
OTARIES > OTARY
OTARINE > OTARY
OTARY n seal with ears
OTHER adj remaining in a group of which one or some have been specified ▷ n other person or thing
OTHERNESS n quality of being different or distinct in appearance, character, etc
OTHERS > OTHER
OTHERWISE adv differently, in another way ▷ adj of an unexpected nature ▷ pron something different in outcome
OTIC adj of or relating to the ear
OTIOSE adj not useful
OTIOSELY > OTIOSE
OTIOSITY > OTIOSE
OTITIC > OTITIS
OTITIDES > OTITIS
OTITIS n inflammation of the ear
OTITISES > OTITIS
OTOCYST n embryonic structure in vertebrates that develops into the inner ear in the adult
OTOCYSTIC > OTOCYST
OTOCYSTS > OTOCYST
OTOLITH n granule of calcium carbonate in the inner ear of vertebrates
OTOLITHIC > OTOLITH

OTOLITHS > OTOLITH
OTOLOGIES > OTOLOGY
OTOLOGIST > OTOLOGY
OTOLOGY n branch of medicine concerned with the ear
OTOPLASTY n cosmetic surgery on ears
OTORRHOEA n discharge from the ears
OTOSCOPE another name for > AURISCOPE
OTOSCOPES > OTOSCOPE
OTOSCOPIC > OTOSCOPY
OTOSCOPY n examination of ear using otoscope
OTOTOXIC adj toxic to the ear
OTTAR variant of > ATTAR
OTTARS > OTTAR
OTTAVA n interval of an octave
OTTAVAS > OTTAVA
OTTAVINO n piccolo
OTTAVINOS > OTTAVINO
OTTER n small brown freshwater mammal that eats fish ▷ vb fish using an otter board
OTTERED > OTTER
OTTERING > OTTER
OTTERS > OTTER
OTTO another name for > ATTAR
OTTOMAN n storage chest with a padded lid for use as a seat
OTTOMANS > OTTOMAN
OTTOS > OTTO
OTTRELITE n type of mineral
OU n man, bloke, or chap
OUABAIN n poisonous white crystalline glycoside
OUABAINS > OUABAIN
OUAKARI n South American monkey
OUAKARIS > OUAKARI
OUBAAS n man in authority
OUBAASES > OUBAAS
OUBIT n hairy caterpillar
OUBITS > OUBIT
OUBLIETTE n dungeon entered only by a trapdoor
OUCH interj exclamation of sudden pain ▷ n brooch or clasp set with gems ▷ vb say ouch
OUCHED > OUCH
OUCHES > OUCH
OUCHING > OUCH
OUCHT Scots word for > ANYTHING
OUCHTS > OUCHT
OUD n Arabic stringed musical instrument resembling a lute or mandolin
OUDS > OUD
OUGHLIED > OUGHLY
OUGHLIES > OUGHLY
OUGHLY variant of > UGLY
OUGHLYING > OUGHLIE
OUGHT vb have an obligation ▷ n zero
OUGHTED > OUGHT
OUGHTING > OUGHT

OUGHTNESS n state of being right
OUGHTS > OUGHT
OUGLIE variant of > UGLY
OUGLIED > OUGLIE
OUGLIEING > OUGLIE
OUGLIES > OUGLIE
OUGUIYA n standard monetary unit of Mauritania
OUGUIYAS > OUGUIYA
OUIJA n tradename for a board through which spirits supposedly answer questions
OUIJAS > OUIJA
OUISTITI n marmoset
OUISTITIS > OUISTITI
OUK Scots word for > WEEK
OUKS > OUK
OULACHON same as > EULACHON
OULACHONS > OULACHON
OULAKAN same as > EULACHON
OULAKANS > OULAKAN
OULD Scots or Irish form of > OLD
OULDER > OULD
OULDEST > OULD
OULK Scots form of > WEEK
OULKS > OULK
OULONG same as > OOLONG
OULONGS > OULONG
OUMA n grandmother, often as a title with a surname
OUMAS > OUMA
OUNCE n unit of weight equal to one sixteenth of a pound
OUNCES > OUNCE
OUNDY adj wavy
OUP same as > OOP
OUPA n grandfather, often as a title with a surname
OUPAS > OUPA
OUPED > OUP
OUPH same as > OAF
OUPHE same as > OAF
OUPHES > OUPHE
OUPHS > OUPH
OUPING > OUP
OUPS > OUP
OUR adj belonging to us ▷ determiner of, belonging to, or associated in some way with us
OURALI n plant from which curare comes
OURALIS > OURALI
OURANG same as > ORANG
OURANGS > OURANG
OURARI same as > OURALI
OURARIS > OURARI
OUREBI same as > ORIBI
OUREBIS > OUREBI
OURIE same as > OORIE
OURIER > OURIE
OURIEST > OURIE
OURN dialect form of > OUR
OUROBOROS n mythical serpent
OUROLOGY same as > UROLOGY
OUROSCOPY same as > UROSCOPY
OURS pron thing(s)

belonging to us
OURSELF pron formal word for myself used by monarchs
OURSELVES pron reflexive form of we or us
OUS > OU
OUSEL same as > OUZEL
OUSELS > OUSEL
OUST vb force (someone) out, expel
OUSTED > OUST
OUSTER n act or instance of forcing someone out of a position
OUSTERS > OUSTER
OUSTING > OUST
OUSTITI n device for opening locked door
OUSTITIS > OUSTITI
OUSTS > OUST
OUT adj denoting movement or distance away from ▷ vb name (a public figure) as being homosexual
OUTACT vb surpass in acting
OUTACTED > OUTACT
OUTACTING > OUTACT
OUTACTS > OUTACT
OUTADD vb beat or surpass at adding
OUTADDED > OUTADD
OUTADDING > OUTADD
OUTADDS > OUTADD
OUTAGE n period of power failure
OUTAGES > OUTAGE
OUTARGUE vb defeat in argument
OUTARGUED > OUTARGUE
OUTARGUES > OUTARGUE
OUTASIGHT adj excellent or wonderful
OUTASK vb declare wedding banns
OUTASKED > OUTASK
OUTASKING > OUTASK
OUTASKS > OUTASK
OUTATE > OUTEAT
OUTBACK n remote bush country of Australia
OUTBACKER > OUTBACK
OUTBACKS > OUTBACK
OUTBAKE vb bake more or better than
OUTBAKED > OUTBAKE
OUTBAKES > OUTBAKE
OUTBAKING > OUTBAKE
OUTBAR vb keep out
OUTBARK vb bark more or louder than
OUTBARKED > OUTBARK
OUTBARKS > OUTBARK
OUTBARRED > OUTBAR
OUTBARS > OUTBAR
OUTBAWL vb bawl more or louder than
OUTBAWLED > OUTBAWL
OUTBAWLS > OUTBAWL
OUTBEAM vb beam more or brighter than
OUTBEAMED > OUTBEAM
OUTBEAMS > OUTBEAM
OUTBEG vb beg more or better than
OUTBEGGED > OUTBEG

OUTBEGS > OUTBEG
OUTBID vb offer a higher price than
OUTBIDDEN > OUTBID
OUTBIDDER > OUTBID
OUTBIDS > OUTBID
OUTBITCH vb bitch more or better than
OUTBLAZE vb blaze more or hotter than
OUTBLAZED > OUTBLAZE
OUTBLAZES > OUTBLAZE
OUTBLEAT vb bleat more or louder than
OUTBLEATS > OUTBLEAT
OUTBLESS vb bless more than
OUTBLOOM vb bloom more or better than
OUTBLOOMS > OUTBLOOM
OUTBLUFF vb surpass in bluffing
OUTBLUFFS > OUTBLUFF
OUTBLUSH vb blush more than
OUTBOARD adj (of a boat's engine) portable, with its own propeller ▷ adv away from the centre line of a vessel or aircraft ▷ n outboard motor
OUTBOARDS > OUTBOARD
OUTBOAST vb surpass in boasting
OUTBOASTS > OUTBOAST
OUTBOUGHT > OUTBUY
OUTBOUND adj going out
OUTBOUNDS n boundaries
OUTBOX vb surpass in boxing
OUTBOXED > OUTBOX
OUTBOXES > OUTBOX
OUTBOXING > OUTBOX
OUTBRAG vb brag more or better than
OUTBRAGS > OUTBRAG
OUTBRAVE vb surpass in bravery
OUTBRAVED > OUTBRAVE
OUTBRAVES > OUTBRAVE
OUTBRAWL vb defeat in a brawl
OUTBRAWLS > OUTBRAWL
OUTBRAZEN vb be more brazen than
OUTBREAK n sudden occurrence (of something unpleasant) ▷ vb break out
OUTBREAKS > OUTBREAK
OUTBRED > OUTBREED
OUTBREED vb produce offspring through sexual relations outside a particular family or tribe
OUTBREEDS > OUTBREED
OUTBRIBE vb bribe more than
OUTBRIBED > OUTBRIBE
OUTBRIBES > OUTBRIBE
OUTBROKE > OUTBREAK
OUTBROKEN > OUTBREAK
OUTBUILD vb exceed in building
OUTBUILDS > OUTBUILD
OUTBUILT > OUTBUILD
OUTBULGE vb bulge outwards

OUTBULGED > OUTBULGE
OUTBULGES > OUTBULGE
OUTBULK *vb* exceed in bulk
OUTBULKED > OUTBULK
OUTBULKS > OUTBULK
OUTBULLY *vb* exceed in bullying
OUTBURN *vb* burn longer or brighter than
OUTBURNED > OUTBURN
OUTBURNS > OUTBURN
OUTBURNT > OUTBURN
OUTBURST *n* sudden expression of emotion ▷ *vb* burst out
OUTBURSTS > OUTBURST
OUTBUY *vb* buy more than
OUTBUYING > OUTBUY
OUTBUYS > OUTBUY
OUTBY *adv* outside
OUTBYE *same as* > OUTBY
OUTCALL *n* visit to customer's home by professional
OUTCALLS > OUTCALL
OUTCAPER *vb* exceed in capering
OUTCAPERS > OUTCAPER
OUTCAST *n* person rejected by a particular group ▷ *adj* rejected, abandoned, or discarded
OUTCASTE *n* person who has been expelled from a caste ▷ *vb* cause (someone) to lose his caste
OUTCASTED > OUTCASTE
OUTCASTES > OUTCASTE
OUTCASTS > OUTCAST
OUTCATCH *vb* catch more than
OUTCAUGHT > OUTCATCH
OUTCAVIL *vb* exceed in cavilling
OUTCAVILS > OUTCAVIL
OUTCHARGE *vb* charge more than
OUTCHARM *vb* exceed in charming
OUTCHARMS > OUTCHARM
OUTCHEAT *vb* exceed in cheating
OUTCHEATS > OUTCHEAT
OUTCHID > OUTCHIDE
OUTCHIDE *vb* exceed in chiding
OUTCHIDED > OUTCHIDE
OUTCHIDES > OUTCHIDE
OUTCITIES > OUTCITY
OUTCITY *n* anywhere outside a city's confines
OUTCLASS *vb* surpass in quality
OUTCLIMB *vb* exceed in climbing
OUTCLIMBS > OUTCLIMB
OUTCLOMB > OUTCLIMB
OUTCOACH *vb* exceed in coaching
OUTCOME *n* result
OUTCOMES > OUTCOME
OUTCOOK *vb* cook more or better than
OUTCOOKED > OUTCOOK
OUTCOOKS > OUTCOOK
OUTCOUNT *vb* exceed in counting

OUTCOUNTS > OUTCOUNT
OUTCRAFTY *vb* be craftier than
OUTCRAWL *vb* crawl further or faster than
OUTCRAWLS > OUTCRAWL
OUTCRIED > OUTCRY
OUTCRIES > OUTCRY
OUTCROP *n* part of a rock formation that sticks out of the earth ▷ *vb* (of rock strata) to protrude through the surface of the earth
OUTCROPS > OUTCROP
OUTCROSS *vb* breed (animals or plants of the same breed but different strains) ▷ *n* animal or plant produced as a result of outcrossing
OUTCROW *vb* exceed in crowing
OUTCROWD *vb* have more crowd than
OUTCROWDS > OUTCROWD
OUTCROWED > OUTCROW
OUTCROWS > OUTCROW
OUTCRY *n* vehement or widespread protest ▷ *vb* cry louder or make more noise than (someone or something)
OUTCRYING > OUTCRY
OUTCURSE *vb* exceed in cursing
OUTCURSED > OUTCURSE
OUTCURSES > OUTCURSE
OUTCURVE *n* baseball thrown to curve away from batter
OUTCURVES > OUTCURVE
OUTDANCE *vb* surpass in dancing
OUTDANCED > OUTDANCE
OUTDANCES > OUTDANCE
OUTDARE *vb* be more brave than
OUTDARED > OUTDARE
OUTDARES > OUTDARE
OUTDARING > OUTDARE
OUTDATE *vb* make or become old-fashioned or obsolete
OUTDATED *adj* old-fashioned
OUTDATES > OUTDATE
OUTDATING > OUTDATE
OUTDAZZLE *vb* exceed in dazzling
OUTDEBATE *vb* exceed in debate
OUTDESIGN *vb* exceed in designing
OUTDID > OUTDO
OUTDO *vb* surpass in performance
OUTDODGE *vb* surpass in doding
OUTDODGED > OUTDODGE
OUTDODGES > OUTDODGE
OUTDOER > OUTDO
OUTDOERS > OUTDO
OUTDOES > OUTDO
OUTDOING > OUTDO
OUTDONE > OUTDO
OUTDOOR *adj* taking place, existing, or intended for use in the open air

OUTDOORS *adv* in(to) the open air ▷ *n* open air
OUTDOORSY *adj* taking part in activities relating to the outdoors
OUTDRAG *vb* beat in drag race
OUTDRAGS > OUTDRAG
OUTDRANK > OUTDRINK
OUTDRAW *vb* draw (a gun) faster than
OUTDRAWN > OUTDRAW
OUTDRAWS > OUTDRAW
OUTDREAM *vb* exceed in dreaming
OUTDREAMS > OUTDREAM
OUTDREAMT > OUTDREAM
OUTDRESS *vb* dress better than
OUTDREW > OUTDRAW
OUTDRINK *vb* drink more than
OUTDRINKS > OUTDRINK
OUTDRIVE *vb* exceed in driving
OUTDRIVEN > OUTDRIVE
OUTDRIVES > OUTDRIVE
OUTDROP *same as* > OUTCROP
OUTDROPS > OUTDROP
OUTDROVE > OUTDRIVE
OUTDRUNK > OUTDRINK
OUTDUEL *vb* defeat in duel
OUTDUELED > OUTDUEL
OUTDUELS > OUTDUEL
OUTDURE *vb* last longer than
OUTDURED > OUTDURE
OUTDURES > OUTDURE
OUTDURING > OUTDURE
OUTDWELL *vb* live outside something
OUTDWELLS > OUTDWELL
OUTDWELT > OUTDWELL
OUTEARN *vb* earn more than
OUTEARNED > OUTEARN
OUTEARNS > OUTEARN
OUTEAT *vb* eat more than
OUTEATEN > OUTEAT
OUTEATING > OUTEAT
OUTEATS > OUTEAT
OUTECHO *vb* echo more than
OUTECHOED > OUTECHO
OUTECHOES > OUTECHO
OUTED > OUT
OUTEDGE *n* furthest limit
OUTEDGES > OUTEDGE
OUTER *adj* on the outside ▷ *n* white outermost ring on a target
OUTERCOAT *same as* > OVERCOAT
OUTERMOST *adj* furthest out
OUTERS > OUTER
OUTERWEAR *n* clothes worn on top of other clothes
OUTFABLE *vb* exceed in creating fables
OUTFABLED > OUTFABLE
OUTFABLES > OUTFABLE
OUTFACE *vb* subdue or disconcert (someone) by staring
OUTFACED > OUTFACE
OUTFACES > OUTFACE
OUTFACING > OUTFACE
OUTFALL *n* mouth of a river or drain
OUTFALLS > OUTFALL

OUTFAST *vb* fast longer than
OUTFASTED > OUTFAST
OUTFASTS > OUTFAST
OUTFAWN *vb* exceed in fawning
OUTFAWNED > OUTFAWN
OUTFAWNS > OUTFAWN
OUTFEAST *vb* exceed in feasting
OUTFEASTS > OUTFEAST
OUTFEEL *vb* exceed in feeling
OUTFEELS > OUTFEEL
OUTFELT > OUTFEEL
OUTFENCE *vb* surpass at fencing
OUTFENCED > OUTFENCE
OUTFENCES > OUTFENCE
OUTFIELD *n* area far from the pitch
OUTFIELDS > OUTFIELD
OUTFIGHT *vb* surpass in fighting
OUTFIGHTS > OUTFIGHT
OUTFIGURE *same as* > OUTTHINK
OUTFIND *vb* exceed in finding
OUTFINDS > OUTFIND
OUTFIRE *vb* exceed in firing
OUTFIRED > OUTFIRE
OUTFIRES > OUTFIRE
OUTFIRING > OUTFIRE
OUTFISH *vb* catch more fish than
OUTFISHED > OUTFISH
OUTFISHES > OUTFISH
OUTFIT *n* matching set of clothes ▷ *vb* furnish or be furnished with an outfit, equipment, etc
OUTFITS > OUTFIT
OUTFITTED > OUTFIT
OUTFITTER *n* supplier of men's clothes
OUTFLANK *vb* get round the side of (an enemy army)
OUTFLANKS > OUTFLANK
OUTFLASH *vb* be flashier than
OUTFLEW > OUTFLY
OUTFLIES > OUTFLY
OUTFLING *n* cutting remark
OUTFLINGS > OUTFLING
OUTFLOAT *vb* surpass at floating
OUTFLOATS > OUTFLOAT
OUTFLOW *n* anything that flows out, such as liquid or money ▷ *vb* flow faster than
OUTFLOWED > OUTFLOW
OUTFLOWN > OUTFLY
OUTFLOWS > OUTFLOW
OUTFLUSH *n* burst of light
OUTFLY *vb* fly better or faster than
OUTFLYING > OUTFLY
OUTFOOL *vb* be more foolish than
OUTFOOLED > OUTFOOL
OUTFOOLS > OUTFOOL
OUTFOOT *vb* (of a boat) to go faster than (another boat)
OUTFOOTED > OUTFOOT
OUTFOOTS > OUTFOOT
OUTFOUGHT > OUTFIGHT

OUTFOUND > OUTFIND
OUTFOX *vb* defeat or foil (someone) by being more cunning
OUTFOXED > OUTFOX
OUTFOXES > OUTFOX
OUTFOXING > OUTFOX
OUTFROWN *vb* dominate by frowning more than
OUTFROWNS > OUTFROWN
OUTFUMBLE *vb* exceed in fumbling
OUTGAIN *vb* gain more than
OUTGAINED > OUTGAIN
OUTGAINS > OUTGAIN
OUTGALLOP *vb* gallop faster than
OUTGAMBLE *vb* defeat at gambling
OUTGAS *vb* undergo the removal of adsorbed or absorbed gas from solids
OUTGASES > OUTGAS
OUTGASSED > OUTGAS
OUTGASSES > OUTGAS
OUTGATE *n* way out
OUTGATES > OUTGATE
OUTGAVE > OUTGIVE
OUTGAZE *vb* gaze beyond
OUTGAZED > OUTGAZE
OUTGAZES > OUTGAZE
OUTGAZING > OUTGAZE
OUTGIVE *vb* exceed in giving
OUTGIVEN > OUTGIVE
OUTGIVES > OUTGIVE
OUTGIVING > OUTGIVE
OUTGLARE *vb* exceed in glaring
OUTGLARED > OUTGLARE
OUTGLARES > OUTGLARE
OUTGLEAM *vb* gleam more than
OUTGLEAMS > OUTGLEAM
OUTGLOW *vb* glow more than
OUTGLOWED > OUTGLOW
OUTGLOWS > OUTGLOW
OUTGNAW *vb* exceed in gnawing
OUTGNAWED > OUTGNAW
OUTGNAWN > OUTGNAW
OUTGNAWS > OUTGNAW
OUTGO *vb* exceed or outstrip ▷ *n* cost
OUTGOER > OUTGO
OUTGOERS > OUTGO
OUTGOES > OUTGO
OUTGOING *adj* leaving ▷ *n* act of going out
OUTGOINGS *pl n* expenses
OUTGONE > OUTGO
OUTGREW > OUTGROW
OUTGRIN *vb* exceed in grinning
OUTGRINS > OUTGRIN
OUTGROSS *vb* earn more than
OUTGROUP *n* group of people outside one's own group of people
OUTGROUPS > OUTGROUP
OUTGROW *vb* become too large or too old for
OUTGROWN > OUTGROW
OUTGROWS > OUTGROW
OUTGROWTH *n* natural development
OUTGUARD *n* guard furthest

away from main party
OUTGUARDS > OUTGUARD
OUTGUESS *vb* surpass in guessing
OUTGUIDE *n* folder in filing system ▷ *vb* beat or surpass at guiding
OUTGUIDED > OUTGUIDE
OUTGUIDES > OUTGUIDE
OUTGUN *vb* surpass in fire power
OUTGUNNED > OUTGUN
OUTGUNS > OUTGUN
OUTGUSH *vb* gush out
OUTGUSHED > OUTGUSH
OUTGUSHES > OUTGUSH
OUTHANDLE *vb* handle better than
OUTHAUL *n* line or cable for tightening the foot of a sail
OUTHAULER *same as* > OUTHAUL
OUTHAULS > OUTHAUL
OUTHEAR *vb* exceed in hearing
OUTHEARD > OUTHEAR
OUTHEARS > OUTHEAR
OUTHER *same as* > OTHER
OUTHIRE *vb* hire out
OUTHIRED > OUTHIRE
OUTHIRES > OUTHIRE
OUTHIRING > OUTHIRE
OUTHIT *vb* hit something further than (someone else)
OUTHITS > OUTHIT
OUTHOMER *vb* score more home runs than
OUTHOMERS > OUTHOMER
OUTHOUSE *n* building near a main building
OUTHOUSES > OUTHOUSE
OUTHOWL *vb* exceed in howling
OUTHOWLED > OUTHOWL
OUTHOWLS > OUTHOWL
OUTHUMOR *vb* exceed in humouring
OUTHUMORS > OUTHUMOR
OUTHUNT *vb* exceed in hunting
OUTHUNTED > OUTHUNT
OUTHUNTS > OUTHUNT
OUTHUSTLE *vb* be more competitive than
OUTHYRE *same as* > OUTHIRE
OUTHYRED > OUTHYRE
OUTHYRES > OUTHYRE
OUTHYRING > OUTHYRE
OUTING *n* leisure trip
OUTINGS > OUTING
OUTJEST *vb* exceed in jesting
OUTJESTED > OUTJEST
OUTJESTS > OUTJEST
OUTJET *n* projecting part
OUTJETS > OUTJET
OUTJINX *vb* exceed in jinxing
OUTJINXED > OUTJINX
OUTJINXES > OUTJINX
OUTJOCKEY *vb* outwit by deception
OUTJUGGLE *vb* surpass at juggling
OUTJUMP *vb* jump higher or farther than

OUTJUMPED > OUTJUMP
OUTJUMPS > OUTJUMP
OUTJUT *vb* jut out ▷ *n* projecting part
OUTJUTS > OUTJUT
OUTJUTTED > OUTJUT
OUTKEEP *vb* beat or surpass at keeping
OUTKEEPS > OUTKEEP
OUTKEPT > OUTKEEP
OUTKICK *vb* exceed in kicking
OUTKICKED > OUTKICK
OUTKICKS > OUTKICK
OUTKILL *vb* exceed in killing
OUTKILLED > OUTKILL
OUTKILLS > OUTKILL
OUTKISS *vb* exceed in kissing
OUTKISSED > OUTKISS
OUTKISSES > OUTKISS
OUTLAID > OUTLAY
OUTLAIN > OUTLAY
OUTLAND *adj* outlying or distant ▷ *n* outlying areas of a country or region
OUTLANDER *n* foreigner or stranger
OUTLANDS > OUTLAND
OUTLASH *n* sudden attack
OUTLASHES > OUTLASH
OUTLAST *vb* last longer than
OUTLASTED > OUTLAST
OUTLASTS > OUTLAST
OUTLAUGH *vb* laugh longer or louder than
OUTLAUGHS > OUTLAUGH
OUTLAUNCE *same as* > OUTLAUNCH
OUTLAUNCH *vb* send out
OUTLAW *n* criminal deprived of legal protection, bandit ▷ *vb* make illegal
OUTLAWED > OUTLAW
OUTLAWING > OUTLAW
OUTLAWRY *n* act of outlawing or the state of being outlawed
OUTLAWS > OUTLAW
OUTLAY *n* expenditure ▷ *vb* spend (money)
OUTLAYING > OUTLAY
OUTLAYS > OUTLAY
OUTLEAD *vb* be better leader than
OUTLEADS > OUTLEAD
OUTLEAP *vb* leap higher or farther than
OUTLEAPED > OUTLEAP
OUTLEAPS > OUTLEAP
OUTLEAPT > OUTLEAP
OUTLEARN *vb* exceed in learning
OUTLEARNS > OUTLEARN
OUTLEARNT > OUTLEARN
OUTLED > OUTLEAD
OUTLER *n* farm animal kept out of doors
OUTLERS > OUTLER
OUTLET *n* means of expressing emotion
OUTLETS > OUTLET
OUTLIE *vb* lie outside a particular place
OUTLIED > OUTLIE
OUTLIER *n* outcrop of rocks that is entirely surrounded

by older rocks
OUTLIERS > OUTLIER
OUTLIES > OUTLIE
OUTLINE *n* short general explanation ▷ *vb* summarize
OUTLINEAR > OUTLINE
OUTLINED > OUTLINE
OUTLINER > OUTLINE
OUTLINERS > OUTLINE
OUTLINES > OUTLINE
OUTLINING > OUTLINE
OUTLIVE *vb* live longer than
OUTLIVED > OUTLIVE
OUTLIVER > OUTLIVE
OUTLIVERS > OUTLIVE
OUTLIVES > OUTLIVE
OUTLIVING > OUTLIVE
OUTLOOK *n* attitude ▷ *vb* look out
OUTLOOKED > OUTLOOK
OUTLOOKS > OUTLOOK
OUTLOVE *vb* exceed in loving
OUTLOVED > OUTLOVE
OUTLOVES > OUTLOVE
OUTLOVING > OUTLOVE
OUTLUSTRE *vb* outshine
OUTLYING *adj* distant from the main area
OUTMAN *vb* surpass in manpower
OUTMANNED > OUTMAN
OUTMANS > OUTMAN
OUTMANTLE *vb* be better dressed than
OUTMARCH *vb* exceed in marching
OUTMASTER *vb* surpass
OUTMATCH *vb* surpass or outdo (someone)
OUTMODE *vb* make unfashionable
OUTMODED *adj* no longer fashionable or accepted
OUTMODES > OUTMODE
OUTMODING > OUTMODE
OUTMOST *another word for* > OUTERMOST
OUTMOVE *vb* move faster or better than
OUTMOVED > OUTMOVE
OUTMOVES > OUTMOVE
OUTMOVING > OUTMOVE
OUTMUSCLE *vb* dominate by physical strength
OUTNAME *vb* be more notorious than
OUTNAMED > OUTNAME
OUTNAMES > OUTNAME
OUTNAMING > OUTNAME
OUTNESS *n* state or quality of being external
OUTNESSES > OUTNESS
OUTNIGHT *vb* refer to night more often than
OUTNIGHTS > OUTNIGHT
OUTNUMBER *vb* exceed in number
OUTOFFICE *n* outbuilding
OUTPACE *vb* go faster than (someone)
OUTPACED > OUTPACE
OUTPACES > OUTPACE
OUTPACING > OUTPACE
OUTPAINT *vb* exceed in painting
OUTPAINTS > OUTPAINT

OUTPART n remote region

OUTPARTS > OUTPART

OUTPASS vb exceed in passing

OUTPASSED > OUTPASS

OUTPASSES > OUTPASS

OUTPEEP vb peep out

OUTPEEPED > OUTPEEP

OUTPEEPS > OUTPEEP

OUTPEER vb surpass

OUTPEERED > OUTPEER

OUTPEERS > OUTPEER

OUTPEOPLE vb rid a country of its people

OUTPITCH vb exceed in pitching

OUTPITIED > OUTPITY

OUTPITIES > OUTPITY

OUTPITY vb exceed in pitying

OUTPLACE vb find job for ex-employee

OUTPLACED > OUTPLACE

OUTPLACER > OUTPLACE

OUTPLACES > OUTPLACE

OUTPLAN vb exceed in planning

OUTPLANS > OUTPLAN

OUTPLAY vb perform better than one's opponent in a sport or game

OUTPLAYED > OUTPLAY

OUTPLAYS > OUTPLAY

OUTPLOD vb exceed in plotting

OUTPLODS > OUTPLOD

OUTPLOT vb exceed in plotting

OUTPLOTS > OUTPLOT

OUTPOINT vb score more points than

OUTPOINTS > OUTPOINT

OUTPOLL vb win more votes than

OUTPOLLED > OUTPOLL

OUTPOLLS > OUTPOLL

OUTPORT n isolated fishing village, esp in Newfoundland

OUTPORTER n inhabitant or native of a Newfoundland outport

OUTPORTS > OUTPORT

OUTPOST n outlying settlement

OUTPOSTS > OUTPOST

OUTPOUR n act of flowing or pouring out ▷ vb pour or cause to pour out freely or rapidly

OUTPOURED > OUTPOUR

OUTPOURER > OUTPOUR

OUTPOURS > OUTPOUR

OUTPOWER vb have more power than

OUTPOWERS > OUTPOWER

OUTPRAY vb exceed in praying

OUTPRAYED > OUTPRAY

OUTPRAYS > OUTPRAY

OUTPREACH vb outdo in preaching

OUTPREEN vb exceed in preening

OUTPREENS > OUTPREEN

OUTPRESS vb exceed in pressing

OUTPRICE vb sell at better price than

OUTPRICED > OUTPRICE

OUTPRICES > OUTPRICE

OUTPRIZE vb prize more highly than

OUTPRIZED > OUTPRIZE

OUTPRIZES > OUTPRIZE

OUTPULL vb exceed in pulling

OUTPULLED > OUTPULL

OUTPULLS > OUTPULL

OUTPUNCH vb punch better than

OUTPUPIL n student sent to a different school to the one he or she would normally attend

OUTPUPILS > OUTPUPIL

OUTPURSUE vb pursue farther than

OUTPUSH vb exceed in pushing

OUTPUSHED > OUTPUSH

OUTPUSHES > OUTPUSH

OUTPUT n amount produced ▷ vb produce (data) at the end of a process

OUTPUTS > OUTPUT

OUTPUTTED > OUTPUT

OUTQUOTE vb exceed in quoting

OUTQUOTED > OUTQUOTE

OUTQUOTES > OUTQUOTE

OUTRACE vb surpass in racing

OUTRACED > OUTRACE

OUTRACES > OUTRACE

OUTRACING > OUTRACE

OUTRAGE n great moral indignation ▷ vb offend morally

OUTRAGED > OUTRAGE

OUTRAGES > OUTRAGE

OUTRAGING > OUTRAGE

OUTRAISE vb raise more money than

OUTRAISED > OUTRAISE

OUTRAISES > OUTRAISE

OUTRAN > OUTRUN

OUTRANCE n furthest extreme

OUTRANCES > OUTRANCE

OUTRANG > OUTRING

OUTRANGE vb have a greater range than

OUTRANGED > OUTRANGE

OUTRANGES > OUTRANGE

OUTRANK vb be of higher rank than (someone)

OUTRANKED > OUTRANK

OUTRANKS > OUTRANK

OUTRATE vb offer better rate than

OUTRATED > OUTRATE

OUTRATES > OUTRATE

OUTRATING > OUTRATE

OUTRAVE vb outdo in raving

OUTRAVED > OUTRAVE

OUTRAVES > OUTRAVE

OUTRAVING > OUTRAVE

OUTRE adj shockingly eccentric

OUTREACH vb surpass in reach ▷ n act or process of reaching out

OUTREAD vb outdo in reading

OUTREADS > OUTREAD

OUTREASON vb surpass in reasoning

OUTRECKON vb surpass in reckoning

OUTRED vb be redder than

OUTREDDED > OUTRED

OUTREDDEN same as > OUTRED

OUTREDS > OUTRED

OUTREIGN vb reign for longer than

OUTREIGNS > OUTREIGN

OUTRELIEF n aid given outdoors

OUTREMER n land overseas

OUTREMERS > OUTREMER

OUTRIDDEN > OUTRIDE

OUTRIDE vb outdo by riding faster, farther, or better than ▷ n extra unstressed syllable within a metrical foot

OUTRIDER n motorcyclist acting as an escort

OUTRIDERS > OUTRIDER

OUTRIDES > OUTRIDE

OUTRIDING > OUTRIDE

OUTRIG vb supply with outfit

OUTRIGGED > OUTRIG

OUTRIGGER n stabilizing frame projecting from a boat

OUTRIGHT adv absolute(ly) ▷ adj complete

OUTRIGS > OUTRIG

OUTRING vb exceed in ringing

OUTRINGS > OUTRING

OUTRIVAL vb surpass

OUTRIVALS > OUTRIVAL

OUTRO n instrumental passage that concludes a piece of music

OUTROAR vb roar louder than

OUTROARED > OUTROAR

OUTROARS > OUTROAR

OUTROCK vb outdo in rocking

OUTROCKED > OUTROCK

OUTROCKS > OUTROCK

OUTRODE > OUTRIDE

OUTROLL vb exceed in rolling

OUTROLLED > OUTROLL

OUTROLLS > OUTROLL

OUTROOP n auction

OUTROOPER > OUTROOP

OUTROOPS > OUTROOP

OUTROOT vb root out

OUTROOTED > OUTROOT

OUTROOTS > OUTROOT

OUTROPE same as > OUTROOP

OUTROPER > OUTROPE

OUTROPERS > OUTROPE

OUTROPES > OUTROPE

OUTROS > OUTRO

OUTROW vb outdo in rowing

OUTROWED > OUTROW

OUTROWING > OUTROW

OUTROWS > OUTROW

OUTRUN vb run faster than

OUTRUNG > OUTRING

OUTRUNNER n attendant who runs in front of a carriage, etc

OUTRUNS > OUTRUN

OUTRUSH n flowing or rushing out ▷ vb rush out

OUTRUSHED > OUTRUSH

OUTRUSHES > OUTRUSH

OUTS > OUT

OUTSAID > OUTSAY

OUTSAIL vb sail better than

OUTSAILED > OUTSAIL

OUTSAILS > OUTSAIL

OUTSANG > OUTSING

OUTSAT > OUTSIT

OUTSAVOR vb exceed in savouring

OUTSAVORS > OUTSAVOR

OUTSAW > OUTSEE

OUTSAY vb say something out loud

OUTSAYING > OUTSAY

OUTSAYS > OUTSAY

OUTSCHEME vb outdo in scheming

OUTSCOLD vb outdo in scolding

OUTSCOLDS > OUTSCOLD

OUTSCOOP vb outdo in achieving scoops

OUTSCOOPS > OUTSCOOP

OUTSCORE vb score more than

OUTSCORED > OUTSCORE

OUTSCORES > OUTSCORE

OUTSCORN vb defy with scorn

OUTSCORNS > OUTSCORN

OUTSCREAM vb scream louder than

OUTSEE vb exceed in seeing

OUTSEEING > OUTSEE

OUTSEEN > OUTSEE

OUTSEES > OUTSEE

OUTSELL vb be sold in greater quantities than

OUTSELLS > OUTSELL

OUTSERT another word for > WRAPROUND

OUTSERTS > OUTSERT

OUTSERVE vb serve better at tennis than

OUTSERVED > OUTSERVE

OUTSERVES > OUTSERVE

OUTSET n beginning

OUTSETS > OUTSET

OUTSHAME vb greatly shame

OUTSHAMED > OUTSHAME

OUTSHAMES > OUTSHAME

OUTSHINE vb surpass (someone) in excellence

OUTSHINED > OUTSHINE

OUTSHINES > OUTSHINE

OUTSHONE > OUTSHINE

OUTSHOOT vb surpass or excel in shooting ▷ n thing that projects or shoots out

OUTSHOOTS > OUTSHOOT

OUTSHOT > OUTSHOOT n projecting part

OUTSHOTS > OUTSHOT

OUTSHOUT vb shout louder than

OUTSHOUTS > OUTSHOUT

OUTSIDE adv indicating movement to or position on the exterior ▷ adj unlikely ▷ n external area or surface

OUTSIDER n person outside a specific group

OUTSIDERS > OUTSIDER

OUTSIDES > OUTSIDE

OUTSIGHT n power of seeing

OUTSIGHTS > OUTSIGHT

OUTSIN vb sin more than

OUTSING vb sing better or louder than

OUTSINGS > OUTSING

OUTSINNED > OUTSIN

OUTSINS > OUTSIN

OUTSIT vb sit longer than

OUTSITS > OUTSIT

OUTSIZE adj larger than normal ▷ n outsize garment

OUTSIZED same as > OUTSIZE

OUTSIZES > OUTSIZE

OUTSKATE vb skate better than

OUTSKATED > OUTSKATE

OUTSKATES > OUTSKATE

OUTSKIRT singular of > OUTSKIRTS

OUTSKIRTS pl n outer areas, esp of a town

OUTSLEEP vb sleep longer than

OUTSLEEPS > OUTSLEEP

OUTSLEPT > OUTSLEEP

OUTSLICK vb outsmart

OUTSLICKS > OUTSLICK

OUTSMART vb outwit

OUTSMARTS > OUTSMART

OUTSMELL vb surpass in smelling

OUTSMELLS > OUTSMELL

OUTSMELT > OUTSMELL

OUTSMILE vb outdo in smiling

OUTSMILED > OUTSMILE

OUTSMILES > OUTSMILE

OUTSMOKE vb smoke more than

OUTSMOKED > OUTSMOKE

OUTSMOKES > OUTSMOKE

OUTSNORE vb outdo in snoring

OUTSNORED > OUTSNORE

OUTSNORES > OUTSNORE

OUTSOAR vb fly higher than

OUTSOARED > OUTSOAR

OUTSOARS > OUTSOAR

OUTSOLD > OUTSELL

OUTSOLE n outermost sole of a shoe

OUTSOLES > OUTSOLE

OUTSOURCE vb subcontract (work) to another company

OUTSPAN vb relax

OUTSPANS > OUTSPAN

OUTSPEAK vb speak better or louder than

OUTSPEAKS > OUTSPEAK

OUTSPED > OUTSPEED

OUTSPEED vb go faster than

OUTSPEEDS > OUTSPEED

OUTSPELL vb exceed at spelling

OUTSPELLS > OUTSPELL

OUTSPELT > OUTSPELL

OUTSPEND vb spend more

than

OUTSPENDS > OUTSPEND

OUTSPENT > OUTSPEND

OUTSPOKE > OUTSPEAK

OUTSPOKEN adj tending to say what one thinks

OUTSPORT vb sport in excess of

OUTSPORTS > OUTSPORT

OUTSPRANG > OUTSPRING

OUTSPREAD adj spread or stretched out as far as possible ▷ vb spread out or cause to spread out ▷ n spreading out

OUTSPRING vb spring out

OUTSPRINT vb run faster than (someone)

OUTSPRUNG > OUTSPRING

OUTSTAND vb be outstanding or excel

OUTSTANDS > OUTSTAND

OUTSTARE vb stare longer than

OUTSTARED > OUTSTARE

OUTSTARES > OUTSTARE

OUTSTART vb jump out ▷ n outset

OUTSTARTS > OUTSTART

OUTSTATE vb surpass in stating

OUTSTATED > OUTSTATE

OUTSTATES > OUTSTATE

OUTSTAY vb overstay

OUTSTAYED > OUTSTAY

OUTSTAYS > OUTSTAY

OUTSTEER vb steer better than

OUTSTEERS > OUTSTEER

OUTSTEP vb step farther than

OUTSTEPS > OUTSTEP

OUTSTOOD > OUTSTAND

OUTSTRAIN vb strain too much

OUTSTRIDE vb surpass in striding

OUTSTRIKE vb exceed in striking

OUTSTRIP vb surpass

OUTSTRIPS > OUTSTRIP

OUTSTRIVE vb strive harder than

OUTSTRODE > OUTSTRIDE

OUTSTROKE n outward stroke

OUTSTROVE > OUTSTRIVE

OUTSTRUCK > OUTSTRIKE

OUTSTUDY vb outdo in studying

OUTSTUNT vb outdo in performing stunts

OUTSTUNTS > OUTSTUNT

OUTSULK vb outdo in sulking

OUTSULKED > OUTSULK

OUTSULKS > OUTSULK

OUTSUM vb add up to more than

OUTSUMMED > OUTSUM

OUTSUMS > OUTSUM

OUTSUNG > OUTSING

OUTSWAM > OUTSWIM

OUTSWARE > OUTSWEAR

OUTSWEAR vb swear more than

OUTSWEARS > OUTSWEAR

OUTSWEEP n outward movement of arms in swimming breaststroke

OUTSWEEPS > OUTSWEEP

OUTSWELL vb exceed in swelling

OUTSWELLS > OUTSWELL

OUTSWEPT adj curving outwards

OUTSWIM vb outdo in swimming

OUTSWIMS > OUTSWIM

OUTSWING n (in cricket) movement of a ball from leg to off through the air

OUTSWINGS > OUTSWING

OUTSWORE > OUTSWEAR

OUTSWORN > OUTSWEAR

OUTSWUM > OUTSWIM

OUTSWUNG adj made to curve outwards

OUTTAKE n unreleased take from a recording session, film, or TV programme ▷ vb take out

OUTTAKEN > OUTTAKE

OUTTAKES > OUTTAKE

OUTTAKING > OUTTAKE

OUTTALK vb talk more, longer, or louder than (someone)

OUTTALKED > OUTTALK

OUTTALKS > OUTTALK

OUTTASK vb assign task to staff outside organization

OUTTASKED > OUTTASK

OUTTASKS > OUTTASK

OUTTELL vb make known

OUTTELLS > OUTTELL

OUTTHANK vb outdo in thanking

OUTTHANKS > OUTTHANK

OUTTHIEVE vb surpass in stealing

OUTTHINK vb outdo in thinking

OUTTHINKS > OUTTHINK

OUTTHREW > OUTTHROW

OUTTHROB vb outdo in throbbing

OUTTHROBS > OUTTHROB

OUTTHROW vb throw better than

OUTTHROWN > OUTTHROW

OUTTHROWS > OUTTHROW

OUTTHRUST vb extend outwards

OUTTOLD > OUTTELL

OUTTONGUE vb speak louder than

OUTTOOK > OUTTAKE

OUTTOP vb rise higher than

OUTTOPPED > OUTTOP

OUTTOPS > OUTTOP

OUTTOWER vb tower over

OUTTOWERS > OUTTOWER

OUTTRADE vb surpass in trading

OUTTRADED > OUTTRADE

OUTTRADES > OUTTRADE

OUTTRAVEL vb oudo in travelling

OUTTRICK vb outdo in trickery

OUTTRICKS > OUTTRICK

OUTTROT vb exceed at trotting

OUTTROTS > OUTTROT

OUTTRUMP vb count for more than

OUTTRUMPS > OUTTRUMP

OUTTURN same as > OUTPUT

OUTTURNS > OUTTURN

OUTVALUE vb surpass in value

OUTVALUED > OUTVALUE

OUTVALUES > OUTVALUE

OUTVAUNT vb outdo in boasting

OUTVAUNTS > OUTVAUNT

OUTVENOM vb surpass in venomousness

OUTVENOMS > OUTVENOM

OUTVIE vb outdo in competition

OUTVIED > OUTVIE

OUTVIES > OUTVIE

OUTVOICE vb surpass in noise

OUTVOICED > OUTVOICE

OUTVOICES > OUTVOICE

OUTVOTE vb defeat by getting more votes than

OUTVOTED > OUTVOTE

OUTVOTER > OUTVOTE

OUTVOTERS > OUTVOTE

OUTVOTES > OUTVOTE

OUTVOTING > OUTVOTE

OUTVYING > OUTVIE

OUTWAIT vb wait longer than

OUTWAITED > OUTWAIT

OUTWAITS > OUTWAIT

OUTWALK vb walk farther or longer than

OUTWALKED > OUTWALK

OUTWALKS > OUTWALK

OUTWAR vb surpass or exceed in warfare

OUTWARD same as > OUTWARDS

OUTWARDLY adv in outward appearance

OUTWARDS adv towards the outside

OUTWARRED > OUTWAR

OUTWARS > OUTWAR

OUTWASH n mass of gravel carried and deposited by the water derived from melting glaciers

OUTWASHES > OUTWASH

OUTWASTE vb outdo in wasting

OUTWASTED > OUTWASTE

OUTWASTES > OUTWASTE

OUTWATCH vb surpass in watching

OUTWEAR vb use up or destroy by wearing

OUTWEARS > OUTWEAR

OUTWEARY vb exhaust

OUTWEED vb root out

OUTWEEDED > OUTWEED

OUTWEEDS > OUTWEED

OUTWEEP vb outdo in weeping

OUTWEEPS > OUTWEEP

OUTWEIGH vb be more important, significant, or influential than

OUTWEIGHS > OUTWEIGH

OUTWELL vb pour out

OUTWELLED > OUTWELL

OUTWELLS > OUTWELL

OUTWENT > OUTGO

OUTWEPT > OUTWEEP

OUTWHIRL vb surpass at whirling

OUTWHIRLS > OUTWHIRL

OUTWICK vb move one curling stone by striking with another

OUTWICKED > OUTWICK

OUTWICKS > OUTWICK

OUTWILE vb surpass in cunning

OUTWILED > OUTWILE

OUTWILES > OUTWILE

OUTWILING > OUTWILE

OUTWILL vb demonstrate stronger will than

OUTWILLED > OUTWILL

OUTWILLS > OUTWILL

OUTWIN vb get out of

OUTWIND vb unwind

OUTWINDED > OUTWIND

OUTWINDS > OUTWIND

OUTWING vb surpass in flying

OUTWINGED > OUTWING

OUTWINGS > OUTWING

OUTWINS > OUTWIN

OUTWISH vb surpass in wishing

OUTWISHED > OUTWISH

OUTWISHES > OUTWISH

OUTWIT vb get the better of (someone) by cunning

OUTWITH prep outside

OUTWITS > OUTWIT

OUTWITTED > OUTWIT

OUTWON > OUTWIN

OUTWORE > OUTWEAR

OUTWORK n defences which lie outside main defensive works ▷vb work better, harder, etc, than

OUTWORKED > OUTWORK

OUTWORKER > OUTWORK

OUTWORKS > OUTWORK

OUTWORN adj no longer in use

OUTWORTH vb be more valuable than

OUTWORTHS > OUTWORTH

OUTWOUND > OUTWIND

OUTWREST vb extort

OUTWRESTS > OUTWREST

OUTWRIT > OUTWRITE

OUTWRITE vb outdo in writing

OUTWRITES > OUTWRITE

OUTWROTE > OUTWRITE

OUTYELL vb outdo in yelling

OUTYELLED > OUTYELL

OUTYELLS > OUTYELL

OUTYELP vb outdo in yelping

OUTYELPED > OUTYELP

OUTYELPS > OUTYELP

OUTYIELD vb yield more than

OUTYIELDS > OUTYIELD

OUVERT adj open

OUVERTE feminine form of > OUVERT

OUVRAGE n work

OUVRAGES > OUVRAGE

OUVRIER n worker

OUVRIERE feminine form of > OUVRIER

OUVRIERES > OUVRIERE

OUVRIERS > OUVRIER

OUZEL n type of bird

OUZELS > OUZEL

OUZO n strong aniseed-flavoured spirit from Greece

OUZOS > OUZO

OVA > OVUM

OVAL adj egg-shaped ▷n anything that is oval in shape

OVALBUMIN n albumin in egg whites

OVALITIES > OVAL

OVALITY > OVAL

OVALLY > OVAL

OVALNESS > OVAL

OVALS > OVAL

OVARIAL > OVARY

OVARIAN > OVARY

OVARIES > OVARY

OVARIOLE n tube in insect ovary

OVARIOLES > OVARIOLE

OVARIOUS adj of eggs

OVARITIS n inflammation of an ovary

OVARY n female egg-producing organ

OVATE adj shaped like an egg ▷vb give ovation

OVATED > OVATE

OVATELY > OVATE

OVATES > OVATE

OVATING > OVATE

OVATION n enthusiastic round of applause

OVATIONAL > OVATION

OVATIONS > OVATION

OVATOR > OVATE

OVATORS > OVATE

OVEL n mourner, esp during the first seven days after a death

OVELS > OVEL

OVEN n heated compartment or container for cooking or for drying or firing ceramics ▷vb cook in an oven

OVENABLE adj (of food) suitable for cooking in an oven

OVENBIRD n type of small brownish South American bird

OVENBIRDS > OVENBIRD

OVENED > OVEN

OVENING > OVEN

OVENLIKE > OVEN

OVENPROOF adj able to be used in an oven

OVENS > OVEN

OVENWARE n heat-resistant dishes in which food can be both cooked and served

OVENWARES > OVENWARE

OVENWOOD n pieces of wood for burning in an oven

OVENWOODS > OVENWOOD

OVER adv indicating position on the top of, amount greater than, etc ▷adj finished ▷n (in cricket) series of six balls bowled from one end ▷vb jump over

OVERABLE adj too able

OVERACT vb act in an exaggerated way

OVERACTED > OVERACT

OVERACTS > OVERACT

OVERACUTE adj too acute

OVERAGE adj beyond a specified age ▷n amount beyond given limit

OVERAGED adj very old

OVERAGES > OVERAGE

OVERALERT adj abnormally alert

OVERALL adv in total ▷n coat-shaped protective garment ▷adj from one end to the other

OVERALLED adj wearing overalls

OVERALLS > OVERALL

OVERAPT adj tending excessively

OVERARCH vb form an arch over

OVERARM adv with the arm above the shoulder ▷adj bowled, thrown, or performed with the arm raised above the shoulder ▷vb throw (a ball) overarm

OVERARMED > OVERARM

OVERARMS > OVERARM

OVERATE > OVEREAT

OVERAWE vb affect (someone) with an overpowering sense of awe

OVERAWED > OVERAWE

OVERAWES > OVERAWE

OVERAWING > OVERAWE

OVERBAKE vb bake too long

OVERBAKED > OVERBAKE

OVERBAKES > OVERBAKE

OVERBEAR vb dominate or overcome

OVERBEARS > OVERBEAR

OVERBEAT vb beat too much

OVERBEATS > OVERBEAT

OVERBED adj fitting over bed

OVERBET vb bet too much

OVERBETS > OVERBET

OVERBID vb bid for more tricks than one can expect to win ▷n bid higher than someone else's bid

OVERBIDS > OVERBID

OVERBIG adj too big

OVERBILL vb charge too much money

OVERBILLS > OVERBILL

OVERBITE n extension of the upper front teeth over the lower front teeth when the mouth is closed

OVERBITES > OVERBITE

OVERBLEW > OVERBLOW

OVERBLOW vb blow into (a wind instrument) with greater force than normal

OVERBLOWN adj excessive

OVERBLOWS > OVERBLOW

OVERBOARD adv from a boat into the water

OVERBOIL vb boil too much

OVERBOILS > OVERBOIL

OVERBOLD adj too bold

OVERBOOK vb accept too many bookings

OVERBOOKS > OVERBOOK

OVERBOOT n protective boot worn over an ordinary boot or shoe

OVERBOOTS > OVERBOOT

OVERBORE > OVERBEAR

OVERBORN > OVERBEAR

OVERBORNE > OVERBEAR

OVERBOUND vb jump over

OVERBRAKE vb brake too much

OVERBRED adj produced by too much selective breeding

OVERBREED vb produce by too much selective breeding

OVERBRIEF adj too brief

OVERBRIM vb overflow

OVERBRIMS > OVERBRIM

OVERBROAD adj not specific enough

OVERBROW vb hang over

OVERBROWS > OVERBROW

OVERBUILD vb build over or on top of

OVERBUILT > OVERBUILD

OVERBULK vb loom large over

OVERBULKS > OVERBULK

OVERBURN vb copy information onto CD

OVERBURNS > OVERBURN

OVERBURNT > OVERBURN

OVERBUSY adj too busy ▷vb make too busy

OVERBUY vb buy too much or too many

OVERBUYS > OVERBUY

OVERBY adv Scots expression meaning over the road or across the way

OVERCALL n bid higher than the preceding one ▷vb bid higher than (an opponent)

OVERCALLS > OVERCALL

OVERCAME > OVERCOME

OVERCARRY vb carry too far or too many

OVERCAST adj (of the sky) covered by clouds ▷vb make or become overclouded or gloomy ▷n covering, as of clouds or mist

OVERCASTS > OVERCAST

OVERCATCH vb overtake

OVERCHEAP adj too cheap

OVERCHECK n thin leather strap attached to a horse's bit to keep its head up

OVERCHILL vb make too cold

OVERCIVIL adj too civil

OVERCLAD adj wearing too many clothes

OVERCLAIM vb claim too much

OVERCLASS n dominant group in society

OVERCLEAN adj too clean

OVERCLEAR adj too clear

OVERCLOSE adj too close

OVERCLOUD vb make or become covered with clouds

OVERCLOY vb weary with excess
OVERCLOYS > OVERCLOY
OVERCOACH vb coach too much
OVERCOAT n heavy coat
OVERCOATS > OVERCOAT
OVERCOLD adj too cold
OVERCOLOR vb colour too highly
OVERCOME vb gain control over after an effort
OVERCOMER > OVERCOME
OVERCOMES > OVERCOME
OVERCOOK vb spoil food by cooking it for too long
OVERCOOKS > OVERCOOK
OVERCOOL vb cool too much
OVERCOOLS > OVERCOOL
OVERCOUNT vb outnumber
OVERCOVER vb cover up
OVERCOY adj too modest
OVERCRAM vb fill too full
OVERCRAMS > OVERCRAM
OVERCRAW same as > OVERCROW
OVERCRAWS > OVERCRAW
OVERCROP vb exhaust (land) by excessive cultivation
OVERCROPS > OVERCROP
OVERCROW vb crow over
OVERCROWD vb fill with more people or things than is desirable
OVERCROWS > OVERCROW
OVERCURE vb take curing process too far
OVERCURED > OVERCURE
OVERCURES > OVERCURE
OVERCUT vb cut too much
OVERCUTS > OVERCUT
OVERDARE vb dare too much
OVERDARED > OVERDARE
OVERDARES > OVERDARE
OVERDATED adj outdated
OVERDEAR adj too dear
OVERDECK n upper deck
OVERDECKS > OVERDECK
OVERDID > OVERDO
OVERDIGHT adj covered up
OVERDO vb do to excess
OVERDOER > OVERDO
OVERDOERS > OVERDO
OVERDOES > OVERDO
OVERDOG n person or side in an advantageous position
OVERDOGS > OVERDOG
OVERDOING > OVERDO
OVERDONE > OVERDO
OVERDOSE n excessive dose of a drug ▷ vb take an overdose
OVERDOSED > OVERDOSE
OVERDOSES > OVERDOSE
OVERDRAFT n overdrawing
OVERDRANK > OVERDRINK
OVERDRAW vb withdraw more money than is in (one's bank account)
OVERDRAWN > OVERDRAW
OVERDRAWS > OVERDRAW
OVERDRESS vb dress (oneself or another) too elaborately or finely ▷ n dress that may be worn over a jumper, blouse, etc
OVERDREW > OVERDRAW

OVERDRIED > OVERDRY
OVERDRIES > OVERDRY
OVERDRINK vb drink too much alcohol
OVERDRIVE n very high gear in a motor vehicle
OVERDROVE > OVERDRIVE
OVERDRUNK > OVERDRINK
OVERDRY vb dry too much
OVERDUB vb add (new sounds) to a tape so that the old and the new sounds can be heard ▷ n sound or series of sounds added by this method
OVERDUBS > OVERDUB
OVERDUE adj still due after the time allowed
OVERDUST vb dust too much
OVERDUSTS > OVERDUST
OVERDYE vb dye (a fabric, yarn, etc) excessively
OVERDYED > OVERDYE
OVERDYER > OVERDYE
OVERDYERS > OVERDYE
OVERDYES > OVERDYE
OVEREAGER adj excessively eager or keen
OVEREASY adj too easy
OVEREAT vb eat more than is necessary or healthy
OVEREATEN > OVEREAT
OVEREATER > OVEREAT
OVEREATS > OVEREAT
OVERED > OVER
OVEREDIT vb edit too much
OVEREDITS > OVEREDIT
OVEREGG vb exaggerate absurdly
OVEREGGED > OVEREGG
OVEREGGS > OVEREGG
OVEREMOTE vb emote too much
OVEREXERT vb exhaust or injure (oneself) by doing too much
OVEREYE vb survey
OVEREYED > OVEREYE
OVEREYES > OVEREYE
OVEREYING > OVEREYE
OVERFALL n turbulent stretch of water caused by marine currents over an underwater ridge
OVERFALLS > OVERFALL
OVERFAR adv too far
OVERFAST adj too fast
OVERFAT adj too fat
OVERFAVOR vb favour too much
OVERFEAR vb fear too much
OVERFEARS > OVERFEAR
OVERFED > OVERFEED
OVERFEED vb give (a person, plant, or animal) more food than is necessary or healthy
OVERFEEDS > OVERFEED
OVERFELL > OVERFALL
OVERFILL vb put more into (something) than there is room for
OVERFILLS > OVERFILL
OVERFINE adj too fine
OVERFISH vb fish too much
OVERFIT adj too fit
OVERFLEW > OVERFLY

OVERFLIES > OVERFLY
OVERFLOOD vb flood excessively
OVERFLOW vb flow over ▷ n something that overflows
OVERFLOWN > OVERFLY
OVERFLOWS > OVERFLOW
OVERFLUSH adj too flush
OVERFLY vb fly over (a territory) or past (a point)
OVERFOCUS vb focus too much
OVERFOLD n fold in which one or both limbs have been inclined more than 90° from their original orientation
OVERFOLDS > OVERFOLD
OVERFOND adj excessively keen (on)
OVERFOUL adj too foul
OVERFRANK adj too frank
OVERFREE adj too forward
OVERFULL adj excessively full
OVERFUND vb supply with too much money
OVERFUNDS > OVERFUND
OVERFUSSY adj too fussy
OVERGALL vb make sore all over
OVERGALLS > OVERGALL
OVERGANG vb dominate
OVERGANGS > OVERGANG
OVERGAVE > OVERGIVE
OVERGEAR vb cause (a company) to have too high a proportion of loan stock
OVERGEARS > OVERGEAR
OVERGET vb overtake
OVERGETS > OVERGET
OVERGILD vb gild too much
OVERGILDS > OVERGILD
OVERGILT > OVERGILD
OVERGIRD vb gird too tightly
OVERGIRDS > OVERGIRD
OVERGIRT > OVERGIRD
OVERGIVE vb give up
OVERGIVEN > OVERGIVE
OVERGIVES > OVERGIVE
OVERGLAD adj too glad
OVERGLAZE adj (of decoration or colours) applied to porcelain above the glaze
OVERGLOOM vb make gloomy
OVERGO vb go beyond
OVERGOAD vb goad too much
OVERGOADS > OVERGOAD
OVERGOES > OVERGO
OVERGOING > OVERGO
OVERGONE > OVERGO
OVERGORGE vb overeat
OVERGOT > OVERGET
OVERGRADE vb grade too highly
OVERGRAIN vb apply grainy texture to
OVERGRASS vb grow grass on top of
OVERGRAZE vb graze (land) too intensively
OVERGREAT adj too great
OVERGREEN vb cover with

vegetation
OVERGREW > OVERGROW
OVERGROW vb grow over or across (an area, path, lawn, etc)
OVERGROWN > OVERGROW
OVERGROWS > OVERGROW
OVERHAILE vb pull over
OVERHAIR n outer coat of animal
OVERHAIRS > OVERHAIR
OVERHALE same as > OVERHAILE
OVERHALED > OVERHALE
OVERHALES > OVERHALE
OVERHAND adj thrown or performed with the hand raised above the shoulder ▷ adv with the hand above the shoulder ▷ vb sew with the thread passing over two edges in one direction
OVERHANDS > OVERHAND
OVERHANG vb project beyond something ▷ n overhanging part
OVERHANGS > OVERHANG
OVERHAPPY adj too happy
OVERHARD adj too hard
OVERHASTE n excessive haste
OVERHASTY > OVERHASTE
OVERHATE vb hate too much
OVERHATED > OVERHATE
OVERHATES > OVERHATE
OVERHAUL vb examine and repair ▷ n examination and repair
OVERHAULS > OVERHAUL
OVERHEAD adj above one's head ▷ adv over or above head height ▷ n stroke in racket games played from above head height
OVERHEADS pl n general cost of maintaining a business
OVERHEAP vb supply too much
OVERHEAPS > OVERHEAP
OVERHEAR vb hear (a speaker or remark) unintentionally
OVERHEARD > OVERHEAR
OVERHEARS > OVERHEAR
OVERHEAT vb make or become excessively hot ▷ n condition of being overheated
OVERHEATS > OVERHEAT
OVERHELD > OVERHOLD
OVERHENT vb overtake
OVERHENTS > OVERHENT
OVERHIGH adj too high
OVERHIT vb hit too strongly
OVERHITS > OVERHIT
OVERHOLD vb value too highly
OVERHOLDS > OVERHOLD
OVERHOLY adj too holy
OVERHONOR vb honour too highly
OVERHOPE vb hope too much
OVERHOPED > OVERHOPE
OVERHOPES > OVERHOPE
OVERHOT adj too hot

OVERHUNG > OVERHANG
OVERHUNT vb hunt too much
OVERHUNTS > OVERHUNT
OVERHYPE vb hype too much
OVERHYPED > OVERHYPE
OVERHYPES > OVERHYPE
OVERIDLE adj too idle
OVERING > OVER
OVERINKED adj printed using too much ink
OVERISSUE vb issue (shares, banknotes, etc) in excess of demand or ability to pay ▷ n shares, banknotes, etc, thus issued
OVERJOY vb give great delight to
OVERJOYED adj extremely pleased
OVERJOYS > OVERJOY
OVERJUMP vb jump too far
OVERJUMPS > OVERJUMP
OVERJUST adj too just
OVERKEEN adj too keen
OVERKEEP vb keep too long
OVERKEEPS > OVERKEEP
OVERKEPT > OVERKEEP
OVERKEST same as > OVERCAST
OVERKILL n treatment that is greater than required
OVERKILLS > OVERKILL
OVERKIND adj too kind
OVERKING n supreme king
OVERKINGS > OVERKING
OVERKNEE adj reaching to above knee
OVERLABOR vb spend too much work on
OVERLADE vb overburden
OVERLADED > OVERLADE
OVERLADEN > OVERLADE
OVERLADES > OVERLADE
OVERLAID > OVERLAY
OVERLAIN > OVERLIE
OVERLAND adv by land ▷ vb drive (cattle or sheep) overland
OVERLANDS > OVERLAND
OVERLAP vb share part of the same space or period of time (as) ▷ n area overlapping
OVERLAPS > OVERLAP
OVERLARD vb cover with lard
OVERLARDS > OVERLARD
OVERLARGE adj excessively large
OVERLATE adj too late
OVERLAX adj too lax
OVERLAY vb cover with a thin layer ▷ n something that is laid over something else
OVERLAYS > OVERLAY
OVERLEAF adv on the back of the current page
OVERLEAP vb leap too far
OVERLEAPS > OVERLEAP
OVERLEAPT > OVERLEAP
OVERLEARN vb study too intensely
OVERLEND vb lend too much
OVERLENDS > OVERLEND

OVERLENT > OVERLEND
OVERLET vb let to too many
OVERLETS > OVERLET
OVERLEWD adj too lewd
OVERLIE vb lie on or cover (something or someone)
OVERLIER > OVERLIE
OVERLIERS > OVERLIE
OVERLIES > OVERLIE
OVERLIGHT vb illuminate too brightly
OVERLIT > OVERLIGHT
OVERLIVE vb live longer than (another person)
OVERLIVED > OVERLIVE
OVERLIVES > OVERLIVE
OVERLOAD vb put too large a load on or in ▷ n excessive load
OVERLOADS > OVERLOAD
OVERLOCK vb sew fabric with interlocking stitch
OVERLOCKS > OVERLOCK
OVERLONG adj too or excessively long
OVERLOOK vb fail to notice ▷ n high place affording a view
OVERLOOKS > OVERLOOK
OVERLORD n supreme lord or master
OVERLORDS > OVERLORD
OVERLOUD adj too loud
OVERLOVE vb love too much
OVERLOVED > OVERLOVE
OVERLOVES > OVERLOVE
OVERLUSH adj too lush
OVERLUSTY adj too lusty
OVERLY adv excessively
OVERLYING > OVERLIE
OVERMAN vb provide with too many staff ▷ n man who oversees others
OVERMANS > OVERMAN
OVERMANY adj too many
OVERMAST vb provide mast that is too big
OVERMASTS > OVERMAST
OVERMATCH vb be more than a match for ▷ n person superior in ability
OVERMEEK adj too meek
OVERMELT vb melt too much
OVERMELTS > OVERMELT
OVERMEN > OVERMAN
OVERMERRY adj very merry
OVERMILD adj too mild
OVERMILK vb milk too much
OVERMILKS > OVERMILK
OVERMINE vb mine too much
OVERMINED > OVERMINE
OVERMINES > OVERMINE
OVERMIX vb mix too much
OVERMIXED > OVERMIX
OVERMIXES > OVERMIX
OVERMOUNT vb surmount
OVERMUCH adj too much ▷ n excessive amount
OVERNAME vb repeat (someone's) name
OVERNAMED > OVERNAME
OVERNAMES > OVERNAME
OVERNEAR adj too near
OVERNEAT adj too neat
OVERNET vb cover with net

OVERNETS > OVERNET
OVERNEW adj too new
OVERNICE adj too fastidious, precise, etc
OVERNIGHT adv (taking place) during one night ▷ adj done in, occurring in, or lasting the night ▷ vb stay the night
OVERPACK vb pack too much
OVERPACKS > OVERPACK
OVERPAGE same as > OVERLEAF
OVERPAID > OVERPAY
OVERPAINT vb apply too much paint
OVERPART vb give an actor too difficult a role
OVERPARTS > OVERPART
OVERPASS vb pass over, through, or across
OVERPAST > OVERPASS
OVERPAY vb pay (someone) at too high a rate
OVERPAYS > OVERPAY
OVERPEDAL vb use piano pedal too much
OVERPEER vb look down over
OVERPEERS > OVERPEER
OVERPERCH vb fly up to perch on
OVERPERT adj too insolent
OVERPITCH vb bowl (a cricket ball) so that it pitches too close to the stumps
OVERPLAID n plaid in double layer
OVERPLAN vb plan excessively
OVERPLANS > OVERPLAN
OVERPLANT vb plant more than is necessary
OVERPLAST adj put above
OVERPLAY same as > OVERACT
OVERPLAYS > OVERPLAY
OVERPLIED > OVERPLY
OVERPLIES > OVERPLY
OVERPLOT vb plot onto existing graph or map
OVERPLOTS > OVERPLOT
OVERPLUS n surplus or excess quantity
OVERPLY vb ply too much
OVERPOISE vb weigh more than
OVERPOST vb hurry over
OVERPOSTS > OVERPOST
OVERPOWER vb subdue or overcome (someone)
OVERPRESS vb oppress
OVERPRICE vb put too high a price on
OVERPRINT vb print (additional matter) onto (something already printed) ▷ n additional matter printed onto something already printed
OVERPRIZE vb prize too highly
OVERPROOF adj containing more alcohol than standard spirit

OVERPROUD adj too proud
OVERPUMP vb pump too much
OVERPUMPS > OVERPUMP
OVERQUICK adj too quick
OVERRACK vb strain too much
OVERRACKS > OVERRACK
OVERRAKE vb rake over
OVERRAKED > OVERRAKE
OVERRAKES > OVERRAKE
OVERRAN > OVERRUN
OVERRANK adj too rank
OVERRASH adj too rash
OVERRATE vb have too high an opinion of
OVERRATED > OVERRATE
OVERRATES > OVERRATE
OVERREACH vb defeat or thwart (oneself) by attempting to do or gain too much
OVERREACT vb react more strongly than is necessary
OVERREAD vb read over
OVERREADS > OVERREAD
OVERRED vb paint over in red
OVERREDS > OVERRED
OVERREN same as > OVERRUN
OVERRENS > OVERREN
OVERRICH adj (of food) excessively flavoursome or fatty
OVERRIDE vb overrule ▷ n device or system that can override an automatic control
OVERRIDER > OVERRIDE
OVERRIDES > OVERRIDE
OVERRIFE adj too rife
OVERRIGID adj too rigid
OVERRIPE adj (of a fruit or vegetable) so ripe that it has started to decay
OVERRIPEN vb become overripe
OVERROAST vb roast too long
OVERRODE > OVERRIDE
OVERRUDE adj very rude
OVERRUFF vb defeat trump card by playing higher trump
OVERRUFFS > OVERRUFF
OVERRULE vb reverse the decision of (a person with less power)
OVERRULED > OVERRULE
OVERRULER > OVERRULE
OVERRULES > OVERRULE
OVERRUN vb conquer rapidly ▷ n act or an instance of overrunning
OVERRUNS > OVERRUN
OVERS > OVER
OVERSAD adj too sad
OVERSAIL vb project beyond
OVERSAILS > OVERSAIL
OVERSALE n selling of more than is available
OVERSALES > OVERSALE
OVERSALT vb put too much salt in
OVERSALTS > OVERSALT

OVERSAUCE *vb* put too much sauce on

OVERSAVE *vb* put too much money in savings

OVERSAVED > OVERSAVE

OVERSAVES > OVERSAVE

OVERSAW > OVERSEE

OVERSCALE *adj* at higher scale than standard

OVERSCORE *vb* cancel by drawing a line or lines over or through

OVERSEA *same as* > OVERSEAS

OVERSEAS *adj* to, of, or from a distant country ▷ *adv* across the sea ▷ *n* foreign country or foreign countries collectively

OVERSEE *vb* watch over from a position of authority

OVERSEED *vb* plant too much seed in

OVERSEEDS > OVERSEED

OVERSEEN > OVERSEE

OVERSEER *n* person who oversees others, esp workmen

OVERSEERS > OVERSEER

OVERSEES > OVERSEE

OVERSELL *vb* exaggerate the merits or abilities of

OVERSELLS > OVERSELL

OVERSET *vb* disturb or upset

OVERSETS > OVERSET

OVERSEW *vb* sew (two edges) with stitches that pass over them both

OVERSEWED > OVERSEW

OVERSEWN > OVERSEW

OVERSEWS > OVERSEW

OVERSEXED *adj* more interested in sex than is thought decent

OVERSHADE *vb* appear more important than

OVERSHARP *adj* too sharp

OVERSHINE *vb* shine down on

OVERSHIRT *n* shirt worn over lighter clothes

OVERSHOE *n* protective shoe worn over an ordinary shoe

OVERSHOES > OVERSHOE

OVERSHONE > OVERSHINE

OVERSHOOT *vb* go beyond (a mark or target) ▷ *n* act or instance of overshooting

OVERSHOT *adj* (of a water wheel) driven by a flow of water that passes over the wheel ▷ *n* type of fishing rod

OVERSHOTS > OVERSHOT

OVERSICK *adj* too sick

OVERSIDE *adv* over the side (of a ship) ▷ *n* top side

OVERSIDES > OVERSIDE

OVERSIGHT *n* mistake caused by not noticing something

OVERSIZE *adj* larger than the usual size ▷ *n* size larger than the usual or proper size

OVERSIZED *same as* > OVERSIZE

OVERSIZES > OVERSIZE

OVERSKIP *vb* skip over

OVERSKIPS > OVERSKIP

OVERSKIRT *n* outer skirt, esp one that reveals a decorative underskirt

OVERSLEEP *vb* sleep beyond the intended time

OVERSLEPT > OVERSLEEP

OVERSLIP *vb* slip past

OVERSLIPS > OVERSLIP

OVERSLIPT > OVERSLIP

OVERSLOW *adj* too slow

OVERSMAN *n* overseer

OVERSMEN > OVERSMAN

OVERSMOKE *vb* smoke something too much

OVERSOAK *vb* soak too much

OVERSOAKS > OVERSOAK

OVERSOFT *adj* too soft

OVERSOLD > OVERSELL

OVERSOON *adv* too soon

OVERSOUL *n* universal divine essence

OVERSOULS > OVERSOUL

OVERSOW *vb* sow again after first sowing

OVERSOWED > OVERSOW

OVERSOWN > OVERSOW

OVERSOWS > OVERSOW

OVERSPEND *vb* spend more than one can afford ▷ *n* amount by which someone or something is overspent

OVERSPENT > OVERSPEND

OVERSPICE *vb* add too much spice to

OVERSPILL *n* rehousing of people from crowded cities in smaller towns ▷ *vb* overflow

OVERSPILT > OVERSPILL

OVERSPIN *n* forward spinning motion

OVERSPINS > OVERSPIN

OVERSTAFF *vb* provide an excessive number of staff for (a factory, hotel, etc)

OVERSTAIN *vb* stain too much

OVERSTAND *vb* remain longer than

OVERSTANK > OVERSTINK

OVERSTARE *vb* outstare

OVERSTATE *vb* state too strongly

OVERSTAY *vb* stay beyond the limit or duration of

OVERSTAYS > OVERSTAY

OVERSTEER *vb* (of a vehicle) to turn more sharply than is desirable or anticipated

OVERSTEP *vb* go beyond (a certain limit)

OVERSTEPS > OVERSTEP

OVERSTINK *vb* exceed in stinking

OVERSTIR *vb* stir too much

OVERSTIRS > OVERSTIR

OVERSTOCK *vb* hold or supply (a commodity) in excess of requirements

OVERSTOOD > OVERSTAND

OVERSTORY *n* highest level of trees in a rainforest

OVERSTREW *vb* scatter over

OVERSTUDY *vb* study too much

OVERSTUFF *vb* force too much into

OVERSTUNK > OVERSTINK

OVERSUDS *vb* produce too much lather

OVERSUP *vb* sup too much

OVERSUPS > OVERSUP

OVERSURE *adj* too sure

OVERSWAM > OVERSWIM

OVERSWAY *vb* overrule

OVERSWAYS > OVERSWAY

OVERSWEAR *vb* swear again

OVERSWEET *adj* too sweet

OVERSWELL *vb* overflow

OVERSWIM *vb* swim across

OVERSWIMS > OVERSWIM

OVERSWING *vb* swing too much or too far

OVERSWORE > OVERSWEAR

OVERSWORN > OVERSWEAR

OVERSWUM > OVERSWIM

OVERSWUNG > OVERSWING

OVERT *adj* open, not hidden

OVERTAKE *vb* move past (a vehicle or person) travelling in the same direction

OVERTAKEN > OVERTAKE

OVERTAKES > OVERTAKE

OVERTALK *vb* talk over

OVERTALKS > OVERTALK

OVERTAME *adj* too tame

OVERTART *adj* too bitter

OVERTASK *vb* impose too heavy a task upon

OVERTASKS > OVERTASK

OVERTAX *vb* put too great a strain on

OVERTAXED > OVERTAX

OVERTAXES > OVERTAX

OVERTEACH *vb* teach too much

OVERTEEM *vb* be too full of something

OVERTEEMS > OVERTEEM

OVERTHICK *adj* too thick

OVERTHIN *adj* too thin

OVERTHINK *vb* give too much thought to

OVERTHREW > OVERTHROW

OVERTHROW *vb* defeat and replace ▷ *n* downfall, destruction

OVERTIGHT *adj* too tight

OVERTIME *adv* in addition to one's normal working hours ▷ *n* work at a regular job done in addition to regular working hours ▷ *vb* exceed the required time for (a photographic exposure)

OVERTIMED > OVERTIME

OVERTIMER > OVERTIME

OVERTIMES > OVERTIME

OVERTIMID *adj* too timid

OVERTIP *vb* give too much money as a tip

OVERTIPS > OVERTIP

OVERTIRE *vb* make too tired

OVERTIRED > OVERTIRE

OVERTIRES > OVERTIRE

OVERTLY > OVERT

OVERTNESS > OVERT

OVERTOIL *vb* work too hard

OVERTOILS > OVERTOIL

OVERTONE *n* additional meaning

OVERTONES > OVERTONE

OVERTOOK > OVERTAKE

OVERTOP *vb* exceed in height

OVERTOPS > OVERTOP

OVERTOWER *vb* tower above

OVERTRADE *vb* (of an enterprise) to trade in excess of working capital

OVERTRAIN *vb* train too much

OVERTREAT *vb* give too much medical treatment to

OVERTRICK *n* trick by which a player exceeds his contract

OVERTRIM *vb* trim too much

OVERTRIMS > OVERTRIM

OVERTRIP *vb* tread lightly over

OVERTRIPS > OVERTRIP

OVERTRUMP *vb* (in cards) play a trump higher than (one previously played to the trick)

OVERTRUST *vb* trust too much

OVERTURE *n* orchestral introduction ▷ *vb* make or present an overture to

OVERTURED > OVERTURE

OVERTURES > OVERTURE

OVERTURN *vb* turn upside down ▷ *n* act of overturning or the state of being overturned

OVERTURNS > OVERTURN

OVERTYPE *vb* type over existing text

OVERTYPED > OVERTYPE

OVERTYPES > OVERTYPE

OVERURGE *vb* urge too strongly

OVERURGED > OVERURGE

OVERURGES > OVERURGE

OVERUSE *vb* use excessively ▷ *n* excessive use

OVERUSED > OVERUSE

OVERUSES > OVERUSE

OVERUSING > OVERUSE

OVERVALUE *vb* regard (someone or something) as much more important than is the case

OVERVEIL *vb* cover over

OVERVEILS > OVERVEIL

OVERVIEW *n* general survey

OVERVIEWS > OVERVIEW

OVERVIVID *adj* too vivid

OVERVOTE *vb* vote more times than is allowed

OVERVOTED > OVERVOTE

OVERVOTES > OVERVOTE

OVERWARM *vb* make too warm

OVERWARMS > OVERWARM

OVERWARY *adj* excessively wary

OVERWASH *n* act of washing over something

OVERWATCH *vb* watch over

OVERWATER *vb* give too much water to

OVERWEAK *adj* too weak

OVERWEAR *vb* wear out
OVERWEARS > OVERWEAR
OVERWEARY *vb* make too tired
OVERWEEN *vb* think too highly of
OVERWEENS > OVERWEEN
OVERWEIGH *vb* exceed in weight
OVERWENT > OVERGO
OVERWET *vb* make too wet
OVERWETS > OVERWET
OVERWHELM *vb* overpower, esp emotionally
OVERWIDE *adj* too wide
OVERWILY *adj* too crafty
OVERWIND *vb* wind (a watch) beyond the proper limit
OVERWINDS > OVERWIND
OVERWING *vb* fly above
OVERWINGS > OVERWING
OVERWISE *adj* too wise
OVERWORD *n* repeated word or phrase
OVERWORDS > OVERWORD
OVERWORE > OVERWEAR
OVERWORK *vb* work too much ▷ *n* excessive work
OVERWORKS > OVERWORK
OVERWORN > OVERWEAR
OVERWOUND > OVERWIND
OVERWREST *vb* strain too much
OVERWRITE *vb* write (something) in an excessively ornate or prolix style
OVERWROTE > OVERWRITE
OVERYEAR *vb* keep for later year
OVERYEARS > OVERYEAR
OVERZEAL *n* excess of zeal
OVERZEALS > OVERZEAL
OVIBOS *n* type of ox
OVIBOSES > OVIBOS
OVIBOVINE > OVIBOS
OVICIDAL > OVICIDE
OVICIDE *n* killing of sheep
OVICIDES > OVICIDE
OVIDUCAL > OVIDUCT
OVIDUCT *n* tube through which eggs are conveyed from the ovary
OVIDUCTAL > OVIDUCT
OVIDUCTS > OVIDUCT
OVIFEROUS *adj* carrying or producing eggs or ova
OVIFORM *adj* shaped like an egg
OVIGEROUS *same as* > OVIFEROUS
OVINE *adj* of or like a sheep ▷ *n* member of sheep family
OVINES > OVINE
OVIPARA *n* all oviparous animals
OVIPARITY > OVIPAROUS
OVIPAROUS *adj* producing eggs that hatch outside the body of the mother
OVIPOSIT *vb* (of insects and fishes) to deposit eggs through an ovipositor
OVIPOSITS > OVIPOSIT
OVIRAPTOR *n* egg-eating dinosaur
OVISAC *n* capsule or sac, such as an ootheca, in which egg cells are produced
OVISACS > OVISAC
OVIST *n* person believing ovum contains all subsequent generations
OVISTS > OVIST
OVOID *adj* egg-shaped ▷ *n* something that is ovoid
OVOIDAL *adj* ovoid ▷ *n* something that is ovoid
OVOIDALS > OVOIDAL
OVOIDS > OVOID
OVOLI > OVOLO
OVOLO *n* convex moulding having a cross section in the form of a quarter of a circle or ellipse
OVOLOS > OVOLO
OVONIC *adj* using particular electronic storage batteries
OVONICS *n* science of ovonic equipment
OVOTESTES > OVOTESTIS
OVOTESTIS *n* reproductive organ of snails
OVULAR > OVULE
OVULARY > OVULE
OVULATE *vb* produce or release an egg cell from an ovary
OVULATED > OVULATE
OVULATES > OVULATE
OVULATING > OVULATE
OVULATION > OVULATE
OVULATORY > OVULATE
OVULE *n* plant part that contains the egg cell and becomes the seed after fertilization
OVULES > OVULE
OVUM *n* unfertilized egg cell
OW *interj* exclamation of pain
OWCHE *same as* > OUCH
OWCHES > OWCHE
OWE *vb* be obliged to pay (a sum of money) to (a person)
OWED > OWE
OWELTIES > OWELTY
OWELTY *n* equality, esp in financial transactions
OWER *Scots word for* > OVER
OWERBY *adv* over there
OWERLOUP *n* Scots word meaning encroachment
OWERLOUPS > OWERLOUP
OWES > OWE
OWING > OWE
OWL *n* night bird of prey ▷ *vb* act like an owl
OWLED > OWL
OWLER *vb* smuggler
OWLERIES > OWLERY
OWLERS > OWLER
OWLERY *n* place where owls live
OWLET *n* young or nestling owl
OWLETS > OWLET
OWLIER > OWLY
OWLIEST > OWLY
OWLING > OWL

OWLISH *adj* like an owl
OWLISHLY > OWLISH
OWLLIKE > OWL
OWLS > OWL
OWLY *same as* > OWLISH
OWN *adj* used to emphasize possession ▷ *pron* thing(s) belonging to a particular person ▷ *vb* possess
OWNABLE *adj* able to be owned
OWNED > OWN
OWNER *n* person who owns
OWNERLESS > OWNER
OWNERS > OWNER
OWNERSHIP *n* state or fact of being an owner
OWNING > OWN
OWNS > OWN
OWRE *same as* > OWER
OWRECOME *n* chorus of song
OWRECOMES > OWRECOME
OWRELAY *Scots form of* > OVERLAY
OWRELAYS > OWRELAY
OWRES > OWRE
OWREWORD *variant of* > OVERWORD
OWREWORDS > OWREWORD
OWRIE *same as* > OORIE
OWRIER > OWRIE
OWRIEST > OWRIE
OWSE *Scots form of* > OX
OWSEN *pl n Scots word for* > OXEN
OWT *dialect word for* > ANYTHING
OWTS > OWT
OX *n* castrated bull
OXACILLIN *n* antibiotic drug
OXALATE *n* salt or ester of oxalic acid ▷ *vb* treat with oxalate
OXALATED > OXALATE
OXALATES > OXALATE
OXALATING > OXALATE
OXALIC *as in* *oxalic acid* poisonous acid found in many plants
OXALIS *n* type of plant
OXALISES > OXALIS
OXAZEPAM *n* drug used to relieve anxiety
OXAZEPAMS > OXAZEPAM
OXAZINE *n* type of chemical compound
OXAZINES > OXAZINE
OXBLOOD *n* dark reddish-brown colour ▷ *adj* of this colour
OXBLOODS > OXBLOOD
OXBOW *n* U-shaped piece of wood fitted around the neck of a harnessed ox and attached to the yoke
OXBOWS > OXBOW
OXCART *n* cart pulled by ox
OXCARTS > OXCART
OXEN > OX
OXER *n* high fence
OXERS > OXER
OXES > OX
OXEYE *n* daisy-like flower
OXEYES > OXEYE
OXFORD *n* type of stout laced shoe with a low heel

OXFORDS > OXFORD
OXGANG *n* old measure of farmland
OXGANGS > OXGANG
OXGATE *same as* > OXGANG
OXGATES > OXGATE
OXHEAD *n* head of an ox
OXHEADS > OXHEAD
OXHEART *n* heart-shaped cherry
OXHEARTS > OXHEART
OXHIDE *n* leather made from the hide of an ox
OXHIDES > OXHIDE
OXID *same as* > OXIDE
OXIDABLE *adj* able to undergo oxidation
OXIDANT *n* substance that acts or is used as an oxidizing agent
OXIDANTS > OXIDANT
OXIDASE *n* any of a group of enzymes that bring about biological oxidation
OXIDASES > OXIDASE
OXIDASIC > OXIDASE
OXIDATE *another word for* > OXIDIZE
OXIDATED > OXIDATE
OXIDATES > OXIDATE
OXIDATING > OXIDATE
OXIDATION *n* oxidizing
OXIDATIVE > OXIDATION
OXIDE *n* compound of oxygen and one other element
OXIDES > OXIDE
OXIDIC > OXIDE
OXIDISE *same as* > OXIDIZE
OXIDISED > OXIDISE
OXIDISER *same as* > OXIDIZER
OXIDISERS > OXIDISER
OXIDISES > OXIDISE
OXIDISING > OXIDISE
OXIDIZE *vb* combine chemically with oxygen, as in burning or rusting
OXIDIZED > OXIDIZE
OXIDIZER *same as* > OXIDANT
OXIDIZERS > OXIDIZER
OXIDIZES > OXIDIZE
OXIDIZING > OXIDIZE
OXIDS > OXID
OXIM *same as* > OXIME
OXIME *n* type of chemical compound
OXIMES > OXIME
OXIMETER *n* instrument for measuring oxygen in blood
OXIMETERS > OXIMETER
OXIMETRY > OXIMETER
OXIMS > OXIM
OXLAND *same as* > OXGANG
OXLANDS > OXLAND
OXLIKE > OX
OXLIP *n* type of woodland plant with small drooping pale yellow flowers
OXLIPS > OXLIP
OXO *as in* *oxo acid* acid that contains oxygen
OXONIUM *as in* *oxonium compound* type of salt derived from an organic ether

OXONIUMS > OXONIUM
OXPECKER n type of African starling
OXPECKERS > OXPECKER
OXSLIP same as > OXLIP
OXSLIPS > OXSLIP
OXTAIL n tail of an ox, used in soups and stews
OXTAILS > OXTAIL
OXTER n armpit ▷ vb grip under arm
OXTERED > OXTER
OXTERING > OXTER
OXTERS > OXTER
OXTONGUE n type of plant
OXTONGUES > OXTONGUE
OXY > OX
OXYACID n any acid that contains oxygen
OXYACIDS > OXYACID
OXYCODONE as in oxycodone hydrochloride opiate drug used as a painkiller
OXYGEN n gaseous element essential to life and combustion
OXYGENASE n enzyme
OXYGENATE vb add oxygen to
OXYGENIC > OXYGEN
OXYGENISE variant of > OXYGENIZE
OXYGENIZE vb add oxygen to
OXYGENOUS > OXYGEN
OXYGENS > OXYGEN
OXYMEL n mixture of vinegar

and honey
OXYMELS > OXYMEL
OXYMORA > OXYMORON
OXYMORON n figure of speech that combines two apparently contradictory ideas
OXYMORONS > OXYMORON
OXYNTIC adj of or denoting stomach cells that secrete acid
OXYPHIL n type of cell found in glands
OXYPHILE same as > OXYPHIL
OXYPHILES > OXYPHILE
OXYPHILIC > OXYPHIL
OXYPHILS > OXYPHIL
OXYSALT n any salt of an oxyacid
OXYSALTS > OXYSALT
OXYSOME n group of molecules
OXYSOMES > OXYSOME
OXYTOCIC adj accelerating childbirth by stimulating uterine contractions ▷ n oxytocic drug or agent
OXYTOCICS > OXYTOCIC
OXYTOCIN n hormone that stimulates the ejection of milk in mammals
OXYTOCINS > OXYTOCIN
OXYTONE adj having an accent on the final syllable ▷ n oxytone word
OXYTONES > OXYTONE

OY n grandchild
OYE same as > OY
OYER n (in the 13th century) an assize
OYERS > OYER
OYES same as > OYEZ
OYESES > OYES
OYESSES > OYES
OYEZ interj shouted three times by a public crier calling for attention before a proclamation ▷ n such a cry
OYEZES > OYEZ
OYS > OY
OYSTER n edible shellfish ▷ vb dredge for, gather, or raise oysters
OYSTERED > OYSTER
OYSTERER n person fishing for oysters
OYSTERERS > OYSTERER
OYSTERING > OYSTER
OYSTERMAN n person who gathers, cultivates, or sells oysters
OYSTERMEN > OYSTERMAN
OYSTERS > OYSTER
OYSTRIGE archaic variant of > OSTRICH
OYSTRIGES > OYSTRIGE
OZAENA n inflammation of nasal mucous membrane
OZAENAS > OZAENA
OZALID n method of duplicating writing or illustrations

OZALIDS > OZALID
OZEKI n sumo wrestling champion
OZEKIS > OZEKI
OZOCERITE n brown or greyish wax
OZOKERITE same as > OZOCERITE
OZONATE vb add ozone to
OZONATED > OZONATE
OZONATES > OZONATE
OZONATING > OZONATE
OZONATION > OZONATE
OZONE n strong-smelling form of oxygen
OZONES > OZONE
OZONIC > OZONE
OZONIDE n type of unstable explosive compound
OZONIDES > OZONIDE
OZONISE same as > OZONIZE
OZONISED > OZONISE
OZONISER > OZONISE
OZONISERS > OZONISE
OZONISES > OZONISE
OZONISING > OZONISE
OZONIZE vb convert (oxygen) into ozone
OZONIZED > OZONIZE
OZONIZER > OZONIZE
OZONIZERS > OZONIZE
OZONIZES > OZONIZE
OZONIZING > OZONIZE
OZONOUS > OZONE
OZZIE n hospital
OZZIES > OZZIE

Pp

PA n (formerly) fortified Māori settlement

PAAL n stake driven into the ground

PAALS > PAAL

PABLUM same as > PABULUM

PABLUMS > PABLUM

PABOUCHE n soft shoe

PABOUCHES > PABOUCHE

PABULAR > PABULUM

PABULOUS > PABULUM

PABULUM n food

PABULUMS > PABULUM

PAC n soft shoe

PACA n large burrowing hystricomorph rodent of Central and South America

PACABLE adj easily appeased

PACAS > PACA

PACATION n act of making peace

PACATIONS > PACATION

PACE n single step in walking ▷ vb walk up and down, esp in anxiety ▷ prep with due respect to: used to express polite disagreement

PACED > PACE

PACEMAKER n electronic device surgically implanted in a person with heart disease to regulate the heartbeat

PACER n horse trained to move at a special gait, esp for racing

PACERS > PACER

PACES > PACE

PACEWAY n racecourse for trotting and pacing

PACEWAYS > PACEWAY

PACEY adj fast-moving, quick, lively

PACHA same as > PASHA

PACHADOM n rank of pacha

PACHADOMS > PACHADOM

PACHAK n fragrant roots of Asian plant

PACHAKS > PACHAK

PACHALIC n jurisdiction of pasha

PACHALICS > PACHALIC

PACHAS > PACHA

PACHINKO n Japanese game similar to pinball

PACHINKOS > PACHINKO

PACHISI n Indian game somewhat resembling backgammon, played on a cruciform board using six cowries as dice

PACHISIS > PACHISI

PACHOULI same as > PATCHOULI

PACHOULIS > PACHOULI

PACHUCO n young Mexican living in the US, esp one of low social status who belongs to a street gang

PACHUCOS > PACHUCO

PACHYDERM n thick-skinned animal such as an elephant

PACHYTENE n third stage of the prophase of meiosis during which the chromosomes become shorter and thicker and divide into chromatids

PACIER > PACY

PACIEST > PACY

PACIFIC adj tending to bring peace

PACIFICAL > PACIFIC

PACIFIED > PACIFY

PACIFIER n baby's dummy

PACIFIERS > PACIFIER

PACIFIES > PACIFY

PACIFISM n belief that violence of any kind is unjustifiable and that one should not participate in war

PACIFISMS > PACIFISM

PACIFIST n person who refuses on principle to take part in war ▷ adj advocating, relating to, or characterized by pacifism

PACIFISTS > PACIFIST

PACIFY vb soothe, calm

PACIFYING > PACIFY

PACING > PACE

PACK vb put (clothes etc) together in a suitcase or bag ▷ n bag carried on a person's or animal's back

PACKABLE > PACK

PACKAGE same as > PACKET

PACKAGED > PACKAGE

PACKAGER n independent firm specializing in design and production, as of illustrated books or television programmes which are sold to publishers or television companies as finished products

PACKAGERS > PACKAGER

PACKAGES > PACKAGE

PACKAGING n box or wrapping in which a product is offered for sale

PACKBOARD n frame for carrying goods

PACKED adj completely filled

PACKER n person or company whose business is to pack goods, esp food

PACKERS > PACKER

PACKET n small container (and contents) ▷ vb wrap up in a packet or as a packet

PACKETED > PACKET

PACKETING > PACKET

PACKETS > PACKET

PACKFONG n Chinese alloy

PACKFONGS > PACKFONG

PACKFRAME n light metal frame with shoulder straps, used for carrying heavy or awkward loads

PACKHORSE n horse used for carrying goods

PACKING n material, such as paper or plastic, used to protect packed goods

PACKINGS > PACKING

PACKLY > PACK

PACKMAN n person carrying pack

PACKMEN > PACKMAN

PACKNESS > PACK

PACKS > PACK

PACKSACK n bag carried strapped on the back or shoulder

PACKSACKS > PACKSACK

PACKSHEET n cover for pack

PACKSTAFF n staff for supporting pack

PACKWAX n neck ligament

PACKWAXES > PACKWAX

PACKWAY n path for pack animals

PACKWAYS > PACKWAY

PACO n S American mammal

PACOS > PACO

PACS > PAC

PACT n formal agreement

PACTA > PACTUM

PACTION vb concur with

PACTIONAL > PACTION

PACTIONED > PACTION

PACTIONS > PACTION

PACTS > PACT

PACTUM n pact

PACY same as > PACEY

PAD n piece of soft material used for protection, support, absorption of liquid, etc ▷ vb protect or fill with soft material

PADANG n (in Malaysia) playing field

PADANGS > PADANG

PADAUK n tropical African or Asian leguminous tree with reddish wood

PADAUKS > PADAUK

PADDED > PAD

PADDER n highwayman who robs on foot

PADDERS > PADDER

PADDIES > PADDY

PADDING > PAD

PADDINGS > PAD

PADDLE n short oar with a broad blade at one or each end ▷ vb move (a canoe etc) with a paddle

PADDLED > PADDLE

PADDLER > PADDLE

PADDLERS > PADDLE

PADDLES > PADDLE

PADDLING > PADDLE

PADDLINGS > PADDLE

PADDOCK n small field or enclosure for horses ▷ vb place (a horse) in a paddock

PADDOCKED > PADDOCK

PADDOCKS > PADDOCK

PADDY n fit of temper

PADDYWACK vb spank or smack

PADELLA n type of candle

PADELLAS > PADELLA

PADEMELON n small Australian wallaby

PADERERO same as > PATERERO

PADEREROS > PADERERO

PADI same as > PADDY

PADIS > PADI

PADISHAH n Iranian ruler

PADISHAHS > PADISHAH
PADKOS n snacks and provisions for a journey
PADLE another name for > LUMPFISH
PADLES > PADLE
PADLOCK n detachable lock with a hinged hoop fastened over a ring on the object to be secured ▷ vb fasten (something) with a padlock
PADLOCKED > PADLOCK
PADLOCKS > PADLOCK
PADMA n type of lotus
PADMAS > PADMA
PADNAG n ambling horse
PADNAGS > PADNAG
PADOUK same as > PADAUK
PADOUKS > PADOUK
PADRE n chaplain to the armed forces
PADRES > PADRE
PADRI > PADRE
PADRONE n owner or proprietor of an inn, esp in Italy
PADRONES > PADRONE
PADRONI > PADRONE
PADRONISM n system of work controlled by a padrone
PADS > PAD
PADSAW n small narrow saw used for cutting curves
PADSAWS > PADSAW
PADSHAH same as > PADISHAH
PADSHAHS > PADSHAH
PADUASOY n rich strong silk fabric used for hangings, vestments, etc
PADUASOYS > PADUASOY
PADYMELON same as > PADEMELON
PAEAN n song of triumph or thanksgiving
PAEANISM > PAEAN
PAEANISMS > PAEAN
PAEANS > PAEAN
PAEDERAST same as > PEDERAST
PAEDEUTIC adj of or relating to the study of teaching
PAEDIATRY n branch of medical science concerned with children and their diseases
PAEDOLOGY n study of the character, growth, and development of children
PAELLA n Spanish dish of rice, chicken, shellfish, and vegetables
PAELLAS > PAELLA
PAENULA n ancient Roman cloak
PAENULAE > PAENULA
PAENULAS > PAENULA
PAEON n metrical foot of four syllables, with one long one and three short ones in any order
PAEONIC > PAEON
PAEONICS > PAEON
PAEONIES > PAEONY

PAEONS > PAEON
PAEONY same as > PEONY
PAESAN n fellow countryman
PAESANI > PAESANO
PAESANO n Italian-American man
PAESANOS > PAESANO
PAESANS > PAESAN
PAGAN adj not belonging to one of the world's main religions ▷ n pagan person
PAGANDOM > PAGAN
PAGANDOMS > PAGAN
PAGANISE same as > PAGANIZE
PAGANISED > PAGANISE
PAGANISER > PAGANISE
PAGANISES > PAGANISE
PAGANISH > PAGAN
PAGANISM > PAGAN
PAGANISMS > PAGAN
PAGANIST > PAGAN
PAGANISTS > PAGAN
PAGANIZE vb become pagan, render pagan, or convert to paganism
PAGANIZED > PAGANIZE
PAGANIZER > PAGANIZE
PAGANIZES > PAGANIZE
PAGANS > PAGAN
PAGE n (one side of) sheet of paper forming a book etc ▷ vb summon (someone) by bleeper or loudspeaker, in order to pass on a message
PAGEANT n parade or display of people in costume, usu illustrating a scene from history
PAGEANTRY n spectacular display or ceremony
PAGEANTS > PAGEANT
PAGEBOY n hairstyle in which the hair is smooth and the same medium length with the ends curled under
PAGEBOYS > PAGEBOY
PAGED > PAGE
PAGEFUL n amount (of text, etc) that a page will hold
PAGEFULS > PAGEFUL
PAGEHOOD n state of being a page
PAGEHOODS > PAGEHOOD
PAGER n small electronic device, capable of receiving short messages
PAGERS > PAGER
PAGES > PAGE
PAGEVIEW n electronic page of information displayed at the request of a user
PAGEVIEWS > PAGEVIEW
PAGINAL adj page-for-page
PAGINATE vb number the pages of (a book, manuscript, etc) in sequence
PAGINATED > PAGINATE
PAGINATES > PAGINATE
PAGING > PAGE
PAGINGS > PAGE
PAGLE same as > PAIGLE
PAGLES > PAGLE

PAGOD n oriental idol
PAGODA n pyramid-shaped Asian temple or tower
PAGODAS > PAGODA
PAGODS > PAGOD
PAGRI n type of turban
PAGRIS > PAGRI
PAGURIAN n any decapod crustacean of the family Paguridae, which includes the hermit crabs ▷ adj of, relating to, or belonging to the Paguridae
PAGURIANS > PAGURIAN
PAGURID same as > PAGURIAN
PAGURIDS > PAGURID
PAH same as > PA
PAHAUTEA same as > KAIKAWAKA
PAHLAVI n Iranian coin
PAHLAVIS > PAHLAVI
PAHOEHOE n hardened lava
PAHOEHOES > PAHOEHOE
PAHS > PAH
PAID > PAY
PAIDEUTIC same as > PAEDEUTIC
PAIDLE Scots variant of > PADDLE
PAIDLES > PAIDLE
PAIGLE n cowslip
PAIGLES > PAIGLE
PAIK vb thump or whack
PAIKED > PAIK
PAIKING > PAIK
PAIKS > PAIK
PAIL n bucket
PAILFUL same as > PAIL
PAILFULS > PAILFUL
PAILLARD n thin slice of meat
PAILLARDS > PAILLARD
PAILLASSE same as > PALLIASSE
PAILLETTE n sequin or spangle sewn onto a costume
PAILLON n thin leaf of metal
PAILLONS > PAILLON
PAILS > PAIL
PAILSFUL > PAILFUL
PAIN n physical or mental suffering ▷ vb cause (someone) mental or physical suffering
PAINCH Scots variant of > PAUNCH
PAINCHES > PAINCH
PAINED adj having or suggesting pain or distress
PAINFUL adj causing pain or distress
PAINFULLY > PAINFUL
PAINIM n heathen or pagan
PAINIMS > PAINIM
PAINING > PAIN
PAINLESS adj not causing pain or distress
PAINS pl n care or trouble
PAINT n coloured substance, spread on a surface with a brush or roller ▷ vb colour or coat with paint
PAINTABLE > PAINT
PAINTBALL n game in

which teams of players simulate a military skirmish, shooting each other with paint pellets
PAINTBOX n box containing a tray of dry watercolour paints
PAINTED > PAINT
PAINTER n rope at the front of a boat, for tying it up
PAINTERLY adj having qualities peculiar to painting, esp the depiction of shapes by means of solid masses of colour, rather than by lines
PAINTERS > PAINTER
PAINTIER > PAINT
PAINTIEST > PAINT
PAINTING n picture produced by using paint
PAINTINGS > PAINTING
PAINTRESS n female painter
PAINTS > PAINT
PAINTURE n art of painting
PAINTURES > PAINTURE
PAINTWORK n covering of paint on parts of a vehicle, building, etc
PAINTY > PAINT
PAIOCK obsolete word for > PEACOCK
PAIOCKE obsolete word for > PEACOCK
PAIOCKES > PAIOCKE
PAIOCKS > PAIOCK
PAIR n set of two things matched for use together ▷ vb group or be grouped in twos
PAIRE obsolete spelling of > PAIR
PAIRED > PAIR
PAIRER > PAIR
PAIRES > PAIRE
PAIREST > PAIR
PAIRIAL variant of > PRIAL
PAIRIALS > PAIRIAL
PAIRING > PAIR
PAIRINGS > PAIR
PAIRS > PAIR
PAIRWISE adv in pairs
PAIS n country
PAISA n monetary unit of Bangladesh, Bhutan, India, Nepal, and Pakistan worth one hundredth of a rupee
PAISAN n fellow countryman
PAISANA n female peasant
PAISANAS > PAISANA
PAISANO n friend
PAISANOS > PAISANO
PAISANS > PAISAN
PAISAS > PAISA
PAISE > PAISA
PAISLEY n pattern of small curving shapes with intricate detailing, usually printed in bright colours
PAISLEYS > PAISLEY
PAITRICK Scots word for > PARTRIDGE
PAITRICKS > PAITRICK
PAJAMA same as > PYJAMA
PAJAMAED adj wearing

pajamas

PAJAMAS > PAJAMA

PAJOCK *obsolete word for* > PEACOCK

PAJOCKE *obsolete word for* > PEACOCK

PAJOCKES > PAJOCKE

PAJOCKS > PAJOCK

PAKAHI *n* acid land that is unsuitable for cultivation

PAKAHIS > PAKAHI

PAKAPOO *n* Chinese lottery with betting slips marked with Chinese characters

PAKAPOOS > PAKAPOO

PAKEHA *n* person of European descent, as distinct from a Māori

PAKEHAS > PAKEHA

PAKFONG *same as* > PACKFONG

PAKFONGS > PAKFONG

PAKIHI *n* area of swampy infertile land

PAKIHIS > PAKIHI

PAKKA *variant of* > PUKKA

PAKOKO *n* small freshwater fish

PAKOKOS > PAKOKO

PAKORA *n* Indian dish consisting of pieces of vegetable, chicken, etc, dipped in a spiced batter and deep-fried

PAKORAS > PAKORA

PAKTHONG *n* white alloy containing copper, zinc, and nickel

PAKTHONGS > PAKTHONG

PAKTONG *same as* > PAKTHONG

PAKTONGS > PAKTONG

PAL *n* friend ▷ *vb* associate as friends

PALABRA *n* word

PALABRAS > PALABRA

PALACE *n* residence of a king, bishop, etc

PALACED *adj* having palaces

PALACES > PALACE

PALADIN *n* knight who did battle for a monarch

PALADINS > PALADIN

PALAESTRA *n* (in ancient Greece or Rome) public place devoted to the training of athletes

PALAFITTE *n* prehistoric dwelling

PALAGI *n* (in Samoa) European

PALAGIS > PALAGI

PALAIS *n* dance hall

PALAMA *n* webbing on bird's feet

PALAMAE > PALAMA

PALAMATE > PALAMA

PALAMINO *same as* > PALOMINO

PALAMINOS > PALAMINO

PALAMPORE *same as* > PALEMPORE

PALANKEEN *same as* > PALANQUIN

PALANQUIN *n* (formerly, in the Orient) covered bed in which someone could be

carried on the shoulders of four men

PALAPA *n* open-sided tropical building

PALAPAS > PALAPA

PALAS *n* East Indian tree

PALASES > PALAS

PALATABLE *adj* pleasant to taste

PALATABLY > PALATABLE

PALATAL *adj* of or relating to the palate ▷ *n* bony plate that forms the palate

PALATALLY > PALATAL

PALATALS > PALATAL

PALATE *n* roof of the mouth ▷ *vb* perceive by taste

PALATED > PALATE

PALATES > PALATE

PALATIAL *adj* like a palace, magnificent

PALATINE *same as* > PALATAL

PALATINES > PALATINE

PALATING > PALATE

PALAVER *n* time-wasting fuss ▷ *vb* (often used humorously) have a conference

PALAVERED > PALAVER

PALAVERER > PALAVER

PALAVERS > PALAVER

PALAY *n* type of rubber

PALAYS > PALAY

PALAZZI > PALAZZO

PALAZZO *n* Italian palace

PALAZZOS > PALAZZO

PALE *adj* light, whitish ▷ *vb* become pale ▷ *n* wooden or metal post used in fences

PALEA *n* inner of two bracts surrounding each floret in a grass spikelet

PALEAE > PALEA

PALEAL > PALEA

PALEATE *adj* having scales

PALEBUCK *n* small African antelope

PALEBUCKS > PALEBUCK

PALED > PALE

PALEFACE *n* offensive term for a White person, said to have been used by Native Americans of N America

PALEFACES > PALEFACE

PALELY > PALE

PALEMPORE *n* bed covering

PALENESS > PALE

PALEOCENE *adj* belonging to geological time period

PALEOGENE *adj* early geological time period

PALEOLITH *n* Stone Age artefact

PALEOLOGY *n* study of prehistory

PALEOSOL *n* ancient soil horizon

PALEOSOLS > PALEOSOL

PALEOZOIC *adj* belonging to geological time period

PALER > PALE

PALES > PALE

PALEST > PALE

PALESTRA *same as* > PALAESTRA

PALESTRAE > PALESTRA

PALESTRAL > PALESTRA

PALESTRAS > PALESTRA

PALET *n* perpendicular band on escutcheon

PALETOT *n* loose outer garment

PALETOTS > PALETOT

PALETS > PALET

PALETTE *n* artist's flat board for mixing colours on

PALETTES > PALETTE

PALEWAYS *same as* > PALEWISE

PALEWISE *adv* by perpendicular lines

PALFREY *n* light saddle horse, esp ridden by women

PALFREYED > PALFREY

PALFREYS > PALFREY

PALIER > PALY

PALIEST > PALY

PALIFORM *adj* resembling coral

PALIKAR *n* Greek soldier in the war of independence against Turkey

PALIKARS > PALIKAR

PALILALIA *n* speech disorder in which a word or phrase is rapidly repeated

PALILLOGY *n* repetition of word or phrase

PALIMONY *n* alimony awarded to a nonmarried partner after the break-up of a long-term relationship

PALING *n* wooden or metal post used in fences

PALINGS > PALING

PALINKA *n* type of apricot brandy, originating in Central and Eastern Europe

PALINKAS > PALINKA

PALINODE *n* poem in which the poet recants something he has said in a former poem

PALINODES > PALINODE

PALINODY > PALINODE

PALINOPIA *n* visual disorder in which the patient perceives a prolonged afterimage

PALISADE *n* fence made of wooden posts driven into the ground ▷ *vb* enclose with a palisade

PALISADED > PALISADE

PALISADES > PALISADE

PALISADO *same as* > PALISADE

PALISH *adj* rather pale

PALKEE *n* covered Oriental litter

PALKEES > PALKEE

PALKI *same as* > PALKEE

PALKIS > PALKI

PALL *n* cloth spread over a coffin ▷ *vb* become boring

PALLA *n* ancient Roman cloak

PALLADIA > PALLADIUM

PALLADIC *adj* of or containing palladium in the trivalent or tetravalent state

PALLADIUM *n* silvery-white element of the platinum metal group

PALLADOUS *adj* of or containing palladium in the divalent state

PALLAE > PALLA

PALLAH *n* S African antelope

PALLAHS > PALLAH

PALLED > PALL

PALLET *same as* > PALETTE

PALLETED > PALLET

PALLETING > PALLET

PALLETISE *same as* > PALLETIZE

PALLETIZE *vb* stack or transport on a pallet or pallets

PALLETS > PALLET

PALLETTE *n* armpit plate of a suit of armour

PALLETTES > PALLETTE

PALLIA > PALLIUM

PALLIAL *adj* relating to cerebral cortex

PALLIARD *n* person who begs

PALLIARDS > PALLIARD

PALLIASSE *n* straw-filled mattress

PALLIATE *vb* lessen the severity of (something) without curing it

PALLIATED > PALLIATE

PALLIATES > PALLIATE

PALLIATOR > PALLIATE

PALLID *adj* pale, esp because ill or weak

PALLIDER > PALLID

PALLIDEST > PALLID

PALLIDITY > PALLID

PALLIDLY > PALLID

PALLIER > PALLY

PALLIEST > PALLY

PALLING > PALL

PALLIUM *n* garment worn by men in ancient Greece or Rome, made by draping a large rectangular cloth about the body

PALLIUMS > PALLIUM

PALLONE *n* Italian ball game

PALLONES > PALLONE

PALLOR *n* paleness of complexion, usually because of illness, shock, or fear

PALLORS > PALLOR

PALLS > PALL

PALLY *adj* on friendly terms

PALM *n* inner surface of the hand ▷ *vb* conceal in or about the hand, as in sleight-of-hand tricks

PALMAR *adj* of or relating to the palm of the hand

PALMARIAN *adj* pre-eminent

PALMARY *adj* worthy of praise

PALMATE *adj* shaped like an open hand

PALMATED *same as* > PALMATE

PALMATELY > PALMATE

PALMATION *n* state of being palmate

PALMED > PALM

PALMER n (in Medieval Europe) pilgrim bearing a palm branch as a sign of his visit to the Holy Land
PALMERS > PALMER
PALMETTE n ornament or design resembling the palm leaf
PALMETTES > PALMETTE
PALMETTO n small palm tree with fan-shaped leaves
PALMETTOS > PALMETTO
PALMFUL n amount that can be held in the palm of a hand
PALMFULS > PALMFUL
PALMHOUSE n greenhouse for palms, etc
PALMIE n palmtop computer
PALMIER > PALMY
PALMIES > PALMIE
PALMIEST > PALMY
PALMIET n South African rush
PALMIETS > PALMIET
PALMING > PALM
PALMIPED n web-footed bird
PALMIPEDE same as > PALMIPED
PALMIPEDS > PALMIPED
PALMIST > PALMISTRY
PALMISTER n person telling fortunes by reading palms
PALMISTRY n fortune-telling from lines on the palm of the hand
PALMISTS > PALMISTRY
PALMITATE n any salt or ester of palmitic acid
PALMITIC as in *palmitic acid* white crystalline solid that is a saturated fatty acid
PALMITIN n colourless glyceride of palmitic acid
PALMITINS > PALMITIN
PALMLIKE > PALM
PALMS > PALM
PALMTOP adj small enough to be held in the hand ▷ n computer small enough to be held in the hand
PALMTOPS > PALMTOP
PALMY adj successful, prosperous and happy
PALMYRA n tall tropical Asian palm
PALMYRAS > PALMYRA
PALOLO n polychaete worm of the S Pacific Ocean
PALOLOS > PALOLO
PALOMINO n gold-coloured horse with a white mane and tail
PALOMINOS > PALOMINO
PALOOKA n stupid or clumsy boxer or other person
PALOOKAS > PALOOKA
PALOVERDE n thorny American shrub
PALP n either of a pair of sensory appendages that arise from the mouthparts of crustaceans and insects ▷ vb feel
PALPABLE adj obvious

PALPABLY > PALPABLE
PALPAL > PALP
PALPATE vb examine (an area of the body) by touching ▷ adj of, relating to, or possessing a palp or palps
PALPATED > PALPATE
PALPATES > PALPATE
PALPATING > PALPATE
PALPATION > PALPATE
PALPATOR n type of beetle
PALPATORS > PALPATOR
PALPATORY > PALPATE
PALPEBRA n eyelid
PALPEBRAE > PALPEBRA
PALPEBRAL adj of or relating to the eyelid
PALPEBRAS > PALPEBRA
PALPED > PALP
PALPI > PALPUS
PALPING > PALP
PALPITANT > PALPITATE
PALPITATE vb (of the heart) beat rapidly
PALPS > PALP
PALPUS same as > PALP
PALS > PAL
PALSGRAVE n German count palatine
PALSHIP n state of being pals
PALSHIPS > PALSHIP
PALSIED > PALSY
PALSIER > PALSY
PALSIES > PALSY
PALSIEST > PALSY
PALSTAFF variant of > PALSTAVE
PALSTAFFS > PALSTAFF
PALSTAVE n kind of celt, usually of bronze, made to fit into a split wooden handle rather than having a socket for the handle
PALSTAVES > PALSTAVE
PALSY n paralysis ▷ vb paralyse ▷ adj friendly
PALSYING > PALSY
PALSYLIKE > PALSY
PALTER vb act or talk insincerely
PALTERED > PALTER
PALTERER > PALTER
PALTERERS > PALTER
PALTERING > PALTER
PALTERS > PALTER
PALTRIER > PALTRY
PALTRIEST > PALTRY
PALTRILY > PALTRY
PALTRY adj insignificant
PALUDAL adj of, relating to, or produced by marshes
PALUDIC adj of malaria
PALUDINAL adj inhabiting swamps
PALUDINE adj relating to marsh
PALUDISM rare word for > MALARIA
PALUDISMS > PALUDISM
PALUDOSE adj growing or living in marshes
PALUDOUS adj marshy
PALUSTRAL adj marshy
PALY adj vertically striped
PAM n knave of clubs

PAMPA n grassland area
PAMPAS pl n vast grassy plains in S America
PAMPASES > PAMPAS
PAMPEAN > PAMPAS
PAMPEANS > PAMPAS
PAMPER vb treat (someone) with great indulgence, spoil
PAMPERED > PAMPER
PAMPERER > PAMPER
PAMPERERS > PAMPER
PAMPERING > PAMPER
PAMPERO n dry cold wind in South America blowing across the pampas from the south or southwest
PAMPEROS > PAMPERO
PAMPERS > PAMPER
PAMPHLET n thin paper-covered booklet
PAMPHLETS > PAMPHLET
PAMPHREY n cabbage
PAMPHREYS > PAMPHREY
PAMPOEN n pumpkin
PAMPOENS > PAMPOEN
PAMPOOTIE n rawhide slipper worn by men in the Aran Islands
PAMS > PAM
PAN n wide long-handled metal container used in cooking ▷ vb sift gravel from (a river) in a pan to search for gold
PANACEA n remedy for all diseases or problems
PANACEAN > PANACEA
PANACEAS > PANACEA
PANACHAEA variant of > PANACEA
PANACHE n confident elegant style
PANACHES > PANACHE
PANADA n mixture of flour, water, etc, or of breadcrumbs soaked in milk, used as a thickening
PANADAS > PANADA
PANAMA n hat made of the plaited leaves of the jipijapa plant
PANAMAS > PANAMA
PANARIES > PANARY
PANARY n storehouse for bread
PANATELA same as > PANATELLA
PANATELAS > PANATELA
PANATELLA n long slender cigar
PANAX n genus of perennial herbs
PANAXES > PANAX
PANBROIL vb broil in a pan
PANBROILS > PANBROIL
PANCAKE n thin flat circle of fried batter ▷ vb cause (an aircraft) to make a pancake landing or (of an aircraft) to make a pancake landing
PANCAKED > PANCAKE
PANCAKES > PANCAKE
PANCAKING > PANCAKE
PANCE n pansy
PANCES > PANCE
PANCETTA n lightly spiced

cured bacon from Italy
PANCETTAS > PANCETTA
PANCHAX n brightly coloured tropical Asian cyprinodont fish
PANCHAXES > PANCHAX
PANCHAYAT n village council in India
PANCHEON n shallow bowl
PANCHEONS > PANCHEON
PANCHION same as > PANCHEON
PANCHIONS > PANCHION
PANCOSMIC adj of every cosmos
PANCRATIA n wrestling and boxing contests
PANCRATIC > PANCRATIA
PANCREAS n large gland behind the stomach that produces insulin and helps digestion
PAND n valance
PANDA n large black-and-white bearlike mammal from China
PANDANI n tropical tree
PANDANUS n Old World tropical palmlike plant
PANDAR vb act as a pimp
PANDARED > PANDAR
PANDARING > PANDAR
PANDARS > PANDAR
PANDAS > PANDA
PANDATION n warping
PANDECT n treatise covering all aspects of a particular subject
PANDECTS > PANDECT
PANDEMIA n epidemic affecting everyone
PANDEMIAN adj sensual
PANDEMIAS > PANDEMIA
PANDEMIC adj (of a disease) occurring over a wide area ▷ n pandemic disease
PANDEMICS > PANDEMIC
PANDER vb indulge (a person his or her desires) ▷ n person who procures a sexual partner for someone
PANDERED > PANDER
PANDERER n person who procures a sexual partner for someone
PANDERERS > PANDERER
PANDERESS n female panderer
PANDERING > PANDER
PANDERISM > PANDER
PANDERLY > PANDER
PANDEROUS > PANDER
PANDERS > PANDER
PANDIED > PANDY
PANDIES > PANDY
PANDIT same as > PUNDIT
PANDITS > PANDIT
PANDOOR same as > PANDOUR
PANDOORS > PANDOOR
PANDORA n handsome red sea bream
PANDORAS > PANDORA
PANDORE another word for > BANDORE
PANDORES > PANDORE
PANDOUR n one of an 18th-century force of

Croatian soldiers in the Austrian service, notorious for their brutality

PANDOURS > PANDOUR

PANDOWDY n deep-dish pie made from fruit, esp apples, with a cake topping

PANDS > PAND

PANDURA n ancient stringed instrument

PANDURAS > PANDURA

PANDURATE adj (of plant leaves) shaped like the body of a fiddle

PANDY n (in schools) stroke on the hand with a strap as a punishment ▷vb punish with such strokes

PANDYING > PANDY

PANE n sheet of glass in a window or door ▷adj (of fish, meat, etc) dipped or rolled in breadcrumbs before cooking

PANED > PANE

PANEER n soft white cheese, used in Indian cookery

PANEERS > PANEER

PANEGOISM n form of scepticism

PANEGYRIC n formal speech or piece of writing in praise of someone or something

PANEGYRY n panegyric

PANEITIES > PANEITY

PANEITY n state of being bread

PANEL n flat distinct section of a larger surface, for example in a door ▷vb cover or decorate with panels ▷adj of a group acting as a panel

PANELED > PANEL

PANELESS > PANE

PANELING same as > PANELLING

PANELINGS > PANELING

PANELISED same as > PANELIZED

PANELIST same as > PANELLIST

PANELISTS > PANELIST

PANELIZED adj made in sections for quick assembly

PANELLED > PANEL

PANELLING n panels collectively, esp on a wall

PANELLIST n member of a panel

PANELS > PANEL

PANES > PANE

PANETELA same as > PANATELA

PANETELAS > PANETELA

PANETELLA n long thin cigar

PANETTONE n kind of Italian spiced brioche containing sultanas

PANETTONI > PANETTONE

PANFISH n small food fish

PANFISHES > PANFISH

PANFRIED > PANFRY

PANFRIES > PANFRY

PANFRY vb fry in a pan

PANFRYING > PANFRY

PANFUL > PAN

PANFULS > PAN

PANG n sudden sharp feeling of pain or sadness ▷vb cause pain

PANGA n broad heavy knife of E Africa, used as a tool or weapon

PANGAMIC > PANGAMY

PANGAMIES > PANGAMY

PANGAMY n unrestricted mating

PANGAS > PANGA

PANGED > PANG

PANGEN same as > PANGENE

PANGENE n hypothetical particle of protoplasm

PANGENES > PANGENE

PANGENS > PANGEN

PANGING > PANG

PANGLESS adj without pangs

PANGOLIN n animal of tropical countries with a scaly body and a long snout for eating ants and termites

PANGOLINS > PANGOLIN

PANGRAM n sentence incorporating all the letters of the alphabet

PANGRAMS > PANGRAM

PANGS > PANG

PANHANDLE n (in the US) narrow strip of land that projects from one state into another ▷vb accost and beg from (passers-by), esp on the street

PANHUMAN adj relating to all humanity

PANIC n sudden overwhelming fear, often affecting a whole group of people ▷vb feel or cause to feel panic ▷adj of or resulting from such terror

PANICALLY > PANIC

PANICK old word for > PANIC

PANICKED > PANIC

PANICKIER > PANIC

PANICKING > PANIC

PANICKS > PANICK

PANICKY > PANIC

PANICLE n loose, irregularly branched cluster of flowers

PANICLED > PANICLE

PANICLES > PANICLE

PANICS > PANIC

PANICUM n type of grass

PANICUMS > PANICUM

PANIER same as > PANNIER

PANIERS > PANIER

PANIM n heathen or pagan

PANIMS > PANIM

PANING > PANE

PANINI > PANINO

PANINO n Italian sandwich

PANISC n faun; attendant of Pan

PANISCS > PANISC

PANISK same as > PANISC

PANISKS > PANISK

PANISLAM n all of Islam

PANISLAMS > PANISLAM

PANJANDRA n pompous self-important officials of

people of rank

PANLOGISM n metaphysics of Leibniz

PANMICTIC > PANMIXIA

PANMIXES > PANMIXIA

PANMIXIA n (in population genetics) random mating within an interbreeding population

PANMIXIAS > PANMIXIA

PANMIXIS same as > PANMIXIA

PANNAGE n pasturage for pigs, esp in a forest

PANNAGES > PANNAGE

PANNE n lightweight velvet fabric

PANNED > PAN

PANNELLED adj divided into panels

PANNER > PAN

PANNERS > PAN

PANNES > PANNE

PANNICK old spelling of the noun > PANIC

PANNICKS > PANNICK

PANNICLE n thin layer of body tissue

PANNICLES > PANNICLE

PANNIER n bag fixed on the back of a cycle

PANNIERED > PANNIER

PANNIERS > PANNIER

PANNIKEL n skull

PANNIKELL same as > PANNIKEL

PANNIKELS > PANNIKEL

PANNIKIN n small metal cup or pan

PANNIKINS > PANNIKIN

PANNING > PAN

PANNINGS > PAN

PANNOSE adj like felt

PANNUS n inflammatory fleshy lesion on the surface of the eye

PANNUSES > PANNUS

PANOCHA n coarse grade of sugar made in Mexico

PANOCHAS > PANOCHA

PANOCHE n type of dark sugar

PANOCHES > PANOCHE

PANOISTIC adj producing ova

PANOPLIED > PANOPLY

PANOPLIES > PANOPLY

PANOPLY n magnificent array

PANOPTIC adj taking in all parts, aspects, etc, in a single view

PANORAMA n wide unbroken view of a scene

PANORAMAS > PANORAMA

PANORAMIC > PANORAMA

PANPIPE n wind instrument

PANPIPES > PANPIPE

PANS > PAN

PANSEXUAL n person open to any sexual activity

PANSIED adj covered with pansies

PANSIES > PANSY

PANSOPHIC > PANSOPHY

PANSOPHY n universal knowledge

PANSPERMY n 19th-century evolutionary theory

PANSY n small garden flower with velvety purple, yellow, or white petals

PANT vb breathe quickly and noisily during or after exertion ▷n act of panting

PANTABLE n soft shoe

PANTABLES > PANTABLE

PANTAGAMY n marriage to everyone

PANTALEON n percussion instrument

PANTALET same as > PANTALETS

PANTALETS pl n long drawers, usually trimmed with ruffles, extending below the skirts

PANTALON n keyboard instrument

PANTALONE n Italian comic character

PANTALONS > PANTALON

PANTALOON n (in pantomime) absurd old man, the butt of the clown's tricks

PANTDRESS n dress with divided skirt

PANTED > PANT

PANTER n person who pants

PANTERS > PANTER

PANTHEISM n belief that God is present in everything

PANTHEIST > PANTHEISM

PANTHENOL n pantothenyl alcohol

PANTHEON n (in ancient Greece and Rome) temple built to honour all the gods

PANTHEONS > PANTHEON

PANTHER n leopard, esp a black one

PANTHERS > PANTHER

PANTIE same as > PANTY

PANTIES pl n women's underpants

PANTIHOSE same as > PANTYHOSE

PANTILE n roofing tile with an S-shaped cross section ▷vb tile roof with pantiles

PANTILED > PANTILE

PANTILES > PANTILE

PANTILING > PANTILE

PANTINE n pasteboard puppet

PANTINES > PANTINE

PANTING > PANT

PANTINGLY > PANT

PANTINGS > PANT

PANTLER n pantry servant

PANTLERS > PANTLER

PANTO same as > PANTOMIME

PANTOFFLE same as > PANTOFLE

PANTOFLE n kind of slipper

PANTOFLES > PANTOFLE

PANTOMIME n play based on a fairy tale, performed at Christmas time

PANTON n type of horseshoe

PANTONS > PANTON

PANTOS > PANTO

PANTOUFLE *same as* > PANTOFLE
PANTOUM *n* verse form
PANTOUMS > PANTOUM
PANTRIES > PANTRY
PANTROPIC *adj* found throughout tropics
PANTRY *n* small room or cupboard for storing food
PANTRYMAN *n* pantry servant
PANTRYMEN > PANTRYMAN
PANTS *pl n* undergarment for the lower part of the body
PANTSUIT *n* woman's suit of a jacket or top and trousers
PANTSUITS > PANTSUIT
PANTUN *n* Malayan poetry
PANTUNS > PANTUN
PANTY *n* woman's undergarment
PANTYHOSE *pl n* women's tights
PANZER *n* German tank
PANZERS > PANZER
PANZOOTIC *n* disease that affects all the animals in a geographical area
PAOLI > PAOLO
PAOLO *n* Italian silver coin
PAP *n* soft food for babies or invalids ▷ *vb* (of the paparazzi) to follow and photograph (a famous person) ▷ *vb* feed with pap
PAPA *n* father
PAPABLE *adj* suitable for papacy
PAPACIES > PAPACY
PAPACY *n* position or term of office of a pope
PAPADAM *variant of* > POPPADOM
PAPADAMS > PAPADAM
PAPADOM *variant of* > POPPADOM
PAPADOMS > PAPADOM
PAPADUM *variant of* > POPPADOM
PAPADUMS > PAPADUM
PAPAIN *n* proteolytic enzyme occurring in the unripe fruit of the papaya tree
PAPAINS > PAPAIN
PAPAL *adj* of the pope
PAPALISE *same as* > PAPALIZE
PAPALISED > PAPALISE
PAPALISES > PAPALISE
PAPALISM *n* papal system
PAPALISMS > PAPALISM
PAPALIST *n* supporter of a pope
PAPALISTS > PAPALIST
PAPALIZE *vb* make papal
PAPALIZED > PAPALIZE
PAPALIZES > PAPALIZE
PAPALLY > PAPAL
PAPARAZZI > PAPARAZZO
PAPARAZZO *n* photographer specializing in candid photographs of famous people
PAPAS > PAPA
PAPAUMA *n* New Zealand

word for broadleaf
PAPAW *same as* > PAPAYA
PAPAWS > PAPAW
PAPAYA *n* large sweet West Indian fruit
PAPAYAN > PAPAYA
PAPAYAS > PAPAYA
PAPE *n* spiritual father
PAPER *n* material made in sheets from wood pulp or other fibres ▷ *vb* cover (walls) with wallpaper
PAPERBACK *n* book with covers made of flexible card ▷ *adj* of a paperback or publication of paperbacks ▷ *vb* publish in paperback
PAPERBARK *n* Australian tree of swampy regions, with spear-shaped leaves and papery bark
PAPERBOY *n* boy employed to deliver newspapers to people's homes
PAPERBOYS > PAPERBOY
PAPERCLIP *n* bent wire clip for holding sheets of paper together
PAPERED > PAPER
PAPERER > PAPER
PAPERERS > PAPER
PAPERGIRL *n* girl employed to deliver newspapers to people's homes
PAPERIER > PAPERY
PAPERIEST > PAPERY
PAPERING > PAPER
PAPERINGS > PAPER
PAPERLESS *adj* of, relating to, or denoting a means of communication, record keeping, etc, esp electronic, that does not use paper
PAPERS > PAPER
PAPERWARE *n* printed matter
PAPERWORK *n* clerical work, such as writing reports and letters
PAPERY *adj* like paper, esp in thinness, flimsiness, or dryness
PAPES > PAPE
PAPETERIE *n* box or case for papers and other writing materials
PAPHIAN *n* prostitute
PAPHIANS > PAPHIAN
PAPILIO *n* butterfly
PAPILIOS > PAPILIO
PAPILLA *n* small projection of tissue at the base of a hair, tooth, or feather
PAPILLAE > PAPILLA
PAPILLAR > PAPILLA
PAPILLARY > PAPILLA
PAPILLATE > PAPILLA
PAPILLOMA *n* benign tumour derived from epithelial tissue and forming a rounded or lobulated mass
PAPILLON *n* breed of toy spaniel with large ears
PAPILLONS > PAPILLON
PAPILLOSE > PAPILLA

PAPILLOTE *n* paper frill around cutlets, etc
PAPILLOUS > PAPILLA
PAPILLULE *n* tubercle
PAPISH *n* Catholic
PAPISHER *n* derogatory term for a Roman Catholic
PAPISHERS > PAPISHER
PAPISHES > PAPISH
PAPISM *n* derogatory term for Roman Catholicism
PAPISMS > PAPISM
PAPIST *n* derogatory term for a Roman Catholic
PAPISTIC > PAPIST
PAPISTRY > PAPIST
PAPISTS > PAPIST
PAPOOSE *n* Native American child
PAPOOSES > PAPOOSE
PAPPADAM *same as* > POPPADOM
PAPPADAMS > PAPPADAM
PAPPADOM *same as* > POPPADOM
PAPPADOMS > PAPPADOM
PAPPED > PAP
PAPPI > PAPPUS
PAPPIER > PAPPY
PAPPIES > PAPPY
PAPPIEST > PAPPY
PAPPING > PAP
PAPPOOSE *same as* > PAPOOSE
PAPPOOSES > PAPPOOSE
PAPPOSE > PAPPUS
PAPPOUS > PAPPUS
PAPPUS *n* ring of fine feathery hairs surrounding the fruit in composite plants, such as the thistle
PAPPUSES > PAPPUS
PAPPY *adj* resembling pap
PAPRICA *same as* > PAPRIKA
PAPRICAS > PAPRICA
PAPRIKA *n* mild powdered seasoning made from red peppers
PAPRIKAS > PAPRIKA
PAPS > PAP
PAPULA *same as* > PAPULE
PAPULAE > PAPULA
PAPULAR > PAPULE
PAPULE *n* small solid usually round elevation of the skin
PAPULES > PAPULE
PAPULOSE > PAPULE
PAPULOUS > PAPULE
PAPYRAL > PAPYRUS
PAPYRI > PAPYRUS
PAPYRIAN > PAPYRUS
PAPYRINE > PAPYRUS
PAPYRUS *n* tall water plant
PAPYRUSES > PAPYRUS
PAR *n* usual or average condition ▷ *vb* play (a golf hole) in par
PARA *n* paratrooper
PARABASES > PARABASIS
PARABASIS *n* (in classical Greek comedy) address from the chorus to the audience
PARABEMA *n* architectural feature
PARABLAST *n* yolk of an egg, such as a hen's egg, that

undergoes meroblastic cleavage
PARABLE *n* story that illustrates a religious teaching ▷ *vb* write parable
PARABLED > PARABLE
PARABLES > PARABLE
PARABLING > PARABLE
PARABOLA *n* regular curve resembling the course of an object thrown forward and up
PARABOLAS > PARABOLA
PARABOLE *n* similitude
PARABOLES > PARABOLE
PARABOLIC *adj* of, relating to, or shaped like a parabola
PARABRAKE *n* parachute attached to the rear of a vehicle and opened to assist braking
PARACHOR *n* quantity constant over range of temperatures
PARACHORS > PARACHOR
PARACHUTE *n* large fabric canopy that slows the descent of a person or object from an aircraft ▷ *vb* land or drop by parachute
PARACLETE *n* mediator or advocate
PARACME *n* phase where fever lessens
PARACMES > PARACME
PARACRINE *adj* of signalling between biological cells
PARACUSES > PARACUSIS
PARACUSIS *n* hearing disorder
PARADE *n* procession or march ▷ *vb* display or flaunt
PARADED > PARADE
PARADER > PARADE
PARADERS > PARADE
PARADES > PARADE
PARADIGM *n* example or model
PARADIGMS > PARADIGM
PARADING > PARADE
PARADISAL *adj* of, relating to, or resembling paradise
PARADISE *n* heaven
PARADISES > PARADISE
PARADISIC > PARADISE
PARADOR *n* state-run hotel in Spain
PARADORES > PARADOR
PARADORS > PARADOR
PARADOS *n* bank behind a trench or other fortification, giving protection from being fired on from the rear
PARADOSES > PARADOS
PARADOX *n* person or thing made up of contradictory elements
PARADOXAL *adj* paradoxical
PARADOXER *n* proposer of paradox
PARADOXES > PARADOX
PARADOXY *n* state of being paradoxical

PARADROP *n* delivery of personnel or equipment from an aircraft by parachute

PARADROPS > PARADROP

PARAE *n* type of fish

PARAFFIN *n* liquid mixture distilled from petroleum and used as a fuel or solvent ▷ *vb* treat with paraffin or paraffin wax

PARAFFINE *same as* > PARAFFIN

PARAFFINS > PARAFFIN

PARAFFINY *adj* like paraffin

PARAFFLE *n* extravagant display

PARAFFLES > PARAFFLE

PARAFLE *same as* > PARAFFLE

PARAFLES > PARAFLE

PARAFOIL *n* airfoil used on a paraglider

PARAFOILS > PARAFOIL

PARAFORM *n* paraformaldehyde

PARAFORMS > PARAFORM

PARAGE *n* type of feudal land tenure

PARAGES > PARAGE

PARAGLIDE *vb* glide through the air on a special parachute

PARAGOGE *n* addition of a sound or a syllable to the end of a word, such as *st* in *amongst*

PARAGOGES > PARAGOGE

PARAGOGIC > PARAGOGE

PARAGOGUE *same as* > PARAGOGE

PARAGON *n* model of perfection ▷ *vb* equal or surpass

PARAGONED > PARAGON

PARAGONS > PARAGON

PARAGRAM *n* pun

PARAGRAMS > PARAGRAM

PARAGRAPH *n* section of a piece of writing starting on a new line ▷ *vb* put (a piece of writing) into paragraphs

PARAKEET *n* small long-tailed parrot

PARAKEETS > PARAKEET

PARAKELIA *n* succulent herb of the genus *Calandrinia*, with purple flowers, that thrives in inland Australia

PARAKITE *n* series of linked kites

PARAKITES > PARAKITE

PARALALIA *n* any of various speech disorders, esp the production of a sound different from that intended

PARALEGAL *n* person trained to assist lawyers but not qualified to practise law ▷ *adj* of or designating such a person

PARALEXIA *n* disorder of the ability to read in which words and syllables are meaninglessly transposed

PARALEXIC > PARALEXIA

PARALLAX *n* apparent change in an object's position due to a change in the observer's position

PARALLEL *adj* separated by an equal distance at every point ▷ *n* line separated from another by an equal distance at every point ▷ *vb* correspond to

PARALLELS > PARALLEL

PARALOGIA *n* self-deception

PARALOGY *n* anatomical similarity

PARALYSE *vb* affect with paralysis

PARALYSED > PARALYSE

PARALYSER > PARALYSE

PARALYSES > PARALYSIS

PARALYSIS *n* inability to move or feel, because of damage to the nervous system

PARALYTIC *adj* affected with paralysis ▷ *n* person who is paralysed

PARALYZE *same as* > PARALYSE

PARALYZED > PARALYZE

PARALYZER > PARALYZE

PARALYZES > PARALYZE

PARAMATTA *n* lightweight twill-weave fabric of wool with silk or cotton

PARAMECIA *n* freshwater protozoans

PARAMEDIC *n* person working in support of the medical profession ▷ *adj* of or designating such a person

PARAMENT *n* ecclesiastical vestment or decorative hanging

PARAMENTA > PARAMENT

PARAMENTS > PARAMENT

PARAMESE *n* note in ancient Greek music

PARAMESES > PARAMESE

PARAMETER *n* limiting factor, boundary

PARAMO *n* high plateau in the Andes between the tree line and the permanent snow line

PARAMORPH *n* mineral that has undergone paramorphism

PARAMOS > PARAMO

PARAMOUNT *adj* of the greatest importance ▷ *n* supreme ruler

PARAMOUR *n* lover, esp of a person married to someone else

PARAMOURS > PARAMOUR

PARAMYLUM *n* starch-like substance

PARANETE *n* note in ancient Greek music

PARANETES > PARANETE

PARANG *n* short stout straight-edged knife used by the Dyaks of Borneo

PARANGS > PARANG

PARANOEA *same*

as > PARANOIA

PARANOEAS > PARANOEA

PARANOEIC *same as* > PARANOIAC

PARANOIA *n* mental illness causing delusions of grandeur or persecution

PARANOIAC > PARANOIA

PARANOIAS > PARANOIA

PARANOIC > PARANOIA

PARANOICS > PARANOIA

PARANOID *adj* of, characterized by, or resembling paranoia ▷ *n* person who shows the behaviour patterns associated with paranoia

PARANOIDS > PARANOID

PARANYM *n* euphemism

PARANYMPH *n* bridesmaid or best man

PARANYMS > PARANYM

PARAPARA *n* small carnivorous New Zealand tree

PARAPENTE *n* sport of jumping off high mountains wearing skis and a light parachute

PARAPET *n* low wall or railing along the edge of a balcony or roof ▷ *vb* provide with a parapet

PARAPETED > PARAPET

PARAPETS > PARAPET

PARAPH *n* flourish after a signature, originally to prevent forgery ▷ *vb* embellish signature

PARAPHED > PARAPH

PARAPHING > PARAPH

PARAPHS > PARAPH

PARAPODIA *n* paired unjointed lateral appendages of polychaete worms

PARAQUAT *n* yellow extremely poisonous soluble solid used in solution as a weedkiller

PARAQUATS > PARAQUAT

PARAQUET *n* long-tailed parrot

PARAQUETS > PARAQUET

PARAQUITO *n* parakeet

PARARHYME *n* type of rhyme

PARAS > PARA

PARASAIL *vb* glide through air on parachute towed by boat

PARASAILS > PARASAIL

PARASANG *n* Persian unit of distance equal to about 5.5 km or 3.4 miles

PARASANGS > PARASANG

PARASCEVE *n* preparation

PARASHAH *n* section of the Torah read in the synagogue

PARASHAHS > PARASHAH

PARASHOT > PARASHAH

PARASHOTH > PARASHAH

PARASITE *n* animal or plant living in or on another

PARASITES > PARASITE

PARASITIC > PARASITE

PARASOL *n* umbrella-like sunshade

PARASOLED *adj* having a parasol

PARASOLS > PARASOL

PARATAXES > PARATAXIS

PARATAXIS *n* juxtaposition of clauses in a sentence without the use of a conjunction

PARATHA *n* (in Indian cookery) flat unleavened bread, resembling a small nan bread, that is fried on a griddle

PARATHAS > PARATHA

PARATHION *n* slightly water-soluble toxic oil, odourless and colourless when pure, used as an insecticide

PARATONIC *adj* (of a plant movement) occurring in response to an external stimulus

PARATROOP *n* paratrooper

PARAVAIL *adj* lowest

PARAVANE *n* torpedo-shaped device towed from the bow of a vessel so that the cables will cut the anchors of any moored mines

PARAVANES > PARAVANE

PARAVANT *adv* in front

PARAVAUNT *same*

as > PARAVANT

PARAWING *n* paraglider

PARAWINGS > PARAWING

PARAXIAL *adj* (of a light ray) parallel to the axis of an optical system

PARAZOA > PARAZOAN

PARAZOAN *n* sea sponge

PARAZOANS > PARAZOAN

PARAZOON *n* parasitic animal

PARBAKE *vb* partially bake

PARBAKED > PARBAKE

PARBAKES > PARBAKE

PARBAKING > PARBAKE

PARBOIL *vb* boil until partly cooked

PARBOILED > PARBOIL

PARBOILS > PARBOIL

PARBREAK *vb* vomit

PARBREAKS > PARBREAK

PARBUCKLE *n* rope sling for lifting or lowering a heavy cylindrical object, such as a cask or tree trunk ▷ *vb* raise or lower (an object) with such a sling

PARCEL *n* something wrapped up, package ▷ *vb* wrap up

PARCELED > PARCEL

PARCELING > PARCEL

PARCELLED > PARCEL

PARCELS > PARCEL

PARCENARY *n* joint heirship

PARCENER *n* person who takes an equal share with another or others

PARCENERS > PARCENER

PARCH *vb* make very hot and dry

PARCHED > PARCH

P

PARCHEDLY > PARCH

PARCHEESI n modern board game derived from the ancient game of pachisi

PARCHES > PARCH

PARCHESI same as > PARCHEESI

PARCHESIS > PARCHESI

PARCHING > PARCH

PARCHISI same as > PARCHEESI

PARCHISIS > PARCHISI

PARCHMENT n thick smooth writing material made from animal skin

PARCIMONY obsolete variant of > PARSIMONY

PARCLOSE n screen or railing in a church separating off an altar, chapel, etc

PARCLOSES > PARCLOSE

PARD n leopard or panther

PARDAH same as > PURDAH

PARDAHS > PARDAH

PARDAL variant spelling of > PARDALE

PARDALE n leopard

PARDALES > PARDALE

PARDALIS n leopard

PARDALOTE n small Australian songbird

PARDALS > PARDAL

PARDED adj having spots

PARDEE adv certainly

PARDI same as > PARDEE

PARDIE same as > PARDEE

PARDINE adj spotted

PARDNER n friend or partner: used as a term of address

PARDNERS > PARDNER

PARDON vb forgive, excuse ▷ n forgiveness ▷ interj sorry ▷ sentence substitute sorry

PARDONED > PARDON

PARDONER n (before the Reformation) person licensed to sell ecclesiastical indulgences

PARDONERS > PARDONER

PARDONING > PARDON

PARDONS > PARDON

PARDS > PARD

PARDY same as > PARDEE

PARE vb cut off the skin or top layer of

PARECIOUS adj having the male and female reproductive organs at different levels on the same stem

PARECISM n state of having male and female organs close together

PARECISMS > PARECISM

PARED > PARE

PAREGORIC n medicine containing opium, benzoic acid, camphor or ammonia, and anise oil

PAREIRA n root of a South American menispermaceous climbing plant

PAREIRAS > PAREIRA

PARELLA n type of lichen

PARELLAS > PARELLA

PARELLE same as > PARELLA

PARELLES > PARELLE

PARENESES > PARENESIS

PARENESIS n exhortation

PARENT n father or mother ▷ vb raise offspring

PARENTAGE n ancestry or family

PARENTAL adj of or relating to a parent or parenthood

PARENTED > PARENT

PARENTING n activity of bringing up children

PARENTS > PARENT

PAREO same as > PAREU

PAREOS > PAREU

PARER > PARE

PARERA n New Zealand duck with grey-edged brown feathers

PARERGA > PARERGON

PARERGON n work that is not one's main employment

PARERS > PARE

PARES > PARE

PARESES > PARESIS

PARESIS n incomplete or slight paralysis of motor functions

PARETIC > PARESIS

PARETICS > PARESIS

PAREU n rectangle of fabric worn by Polynesians as a skirt or loincloth

PAREUS > PAREU

PAREV adj containing neither meat nor milk products and so fit for use with either meat or milk dishes

PAREVE same as > PAREV

PARFAIT n dessert consisting of layers of ice cream, fruit, and sauce, topped with whipped cream, and served in a tall glass

PARFAITS > PARFAIT

PARFLECHE n sheet of rawhide that has been dried after soaking in lye and water to remove the hair

PARFLESH same as > PARFLECHE

PARFOCAL adj with focal points in the same plane

PARGANA n Indian sub-district

PARGANAS > PARGANA

PARGASITE n dark green mineral

PARGE vb coat with plaster

PARGED > PARGE

PARGES > PARGE

PARGET n plaster, mortar, etc, used to line chimney flues or cover walls ▷ vb cover or decorate with parget

PARGETED > PARGET

PARGETER > PARGET

PARGETERS > PARGET

PARGETING same

as > PARGET

PARGETS > PARGET

PARGETTED > PARGET

PARGING > PARGE

PARGINGS > PARGE

PARGO n sea bream

PARGOS > PARGO

PARGYLINE n monoamine oxidase inhibitor

PARHELIA > PARHELION

PARHELIC > PARHELION

PARHELION n one of several bright spots on the parhelic circle or solar halo

PARHYPATE n note in ancient Greek music

PARIAH n social outcast

PARIAHS > PARIAH

PARIAL n pair royal of playing cards

PARIALS > PARIAL

PARIAN n type of marble or porcelain

PARIANS > PARIAN

PARIES n wall of an organ or bodily cavity

PARIETAL adj of the walls of a body cavity such as the skull ▷ n parietal bone

PARIETALS > PARIETAL

PARIETES > PARIES

PARING n piece pared off

PARINGS > PARING

PARIS n type of herb

PARISCHAN variant of > PAROCHIN

PARISES > PARIS

PARISH n area that has its own church and a priest or pastor

PARISHAD n Indian assembly

PARISHADS > PARISHAD

PARISHEN n member of parish

PARISHENS > PARISHEN

PARISHES > PARISH

PARISON n unshaped mass of glass before it is moulded into its final form

PARISONS > PARISON

PARITIES > PARITY

PARITOR n official who summons witnesses

PARITORS > PARITOR

PARITY n equality or equivalence

PARK n area of open land for recreational use by the public ▷ vb stop and leave (a vehicle) temporarily

PARKA n large waterproof jacket with a hood

PARKADE n building used as a car park

PARKADES > PARKADE

PARKAS > PARKA

PARKED > PARK

PARKEE n Eskimo outer garment

PARKEES > PARKEE

PARKER > PARK

PARKERS > PARK

PARKETTE n small public car park

PARKETTES > PARKETTE

PARKI variant of > PARKA

PARKIE n park keeper

PARKIER > PARKY

PARKIES > PARKIE

PARKIEST > PARKY

PARKIN n moist spicy ginger cake usually containing oatmeal

PARKING > PARK

PARKINGS > PARK

PARKINS > PARKIN

PARKIS > PARKI

PARKISH adj like a park

PARKLAND n grassland with scattered trees

PARKLANDS > PARKLAND

PARKLIKE > PARK

PARKLY adj having many parks or resembling a park

PARKOUR n sport of running in urban areas performing gymnastics on manmade obstacles

PARKOURS > PARKOUR

PARKS > PARK

PARKWARD adv towards a park

PARKWARDS adv towards a park

PARKWAY n (in the US and Canada) wide road planted with trees, turf, etc

PARKWAYS > PARKWAY

PARKY adj (of the weather) chilly

PARLANCE n particular way of speaking, idiom

PARLANCES > PARLANCE

PARLANDO adv to be performed as though speaking

PARLANTE same as > PARLANDO

PARLAY vb stake (winnings from one bet) on a subsequent wager ▷ n bet in which winnings from one wager are staked on another, or a series of such bets

PARLAYED > PARLAY

PARLAYING > PARLAY

PARLAYS > PARLAY

PARLE vb speak

PARLED > PARLE

PARLEMENT n parliament

PARLES > PARLE

PARLEY n meeting between leaders or representatives of opposing forces to discuss terms ▷ vb have a parley

PARLEYED > PARLEY

PARLEYER > PARLEY

PARLEYERS > PARLEY

PARLEYING > PARLEY

PARLEYS > PARLEY

PARLEYVOO vb speak French ▷ n French language

PARLIES pl n small Scottish biscuits

PARLING > PARLE

PARLOR same as > PARLOUR

PARLORS > PARLOR

PARLOUR n living room for receiving visitors

PARLOURS > PARLOUR

PARLOUS adj dire ▷ adv

extremely

PARLOUSLY > PARLOUS

PARLY n short form of parliament

PARMESAN n Italian hard cheese

PARMESANS > PARMESAN

PAROCHIAL adj narrow in outlook

PAROCHIN n old Scottish parish

PAROCHINE same as > PAROCHIN

PAROCHINS > PAROCHIN

PARODIC > PARODY

PARODICAL > PARODY

PARODIED > PARODY

PARODIES > PARODY

PARODIST > PARODY

PARODISTS > PARODY

PARODOI n path leading to Greek theatre

PARODOS n ode sung by Greek chorus

PARODY n exaggerated and amusing imitation of someone else's style ▷ vb make a parody of

PARODYING > PARODY

PAROEMIA n proverb

PAROEMIAC adj of proverbs

PAROEMIAL adj of proverbs

PAROEMIAS > PAROEMIA

PAROICOUS same as > PARECIOUS

PAROL n (formerly) pleadings in an action when presented by word of mouth ▷ adj (of a contract, lease, etc) made orally or in writing but not under seal

PAROLABLE > PAROLE

PAROLE n early freeing of a prisoner on condition that he or she behaves well ▷ vb put on parole

PAROLED > PAROLE

PAROLEE > PAROLE

PAROLEES > PAROLE

PAROLES > PAROLE

PAROLING > PAROLE

PAROLS > PAROL

PARONYM n cognate word

PARONYMIC > PARONYM

PARONYMS > PARONYM

PARONYMY > PARONYM

PAROQUET n small long-tailed parrot

PAROQUETS > PARROQUET

PARORE n type of fish found around Australia and New Zealand

PAROSMIA n any disorder of the sense of smell

PAROSMIAS > PAROSMIA

PAROTIC adj situated near the ear

PAROTID adj relating to or situated near the parotid gland ▷ n parotid gland

PAROTIDS > PAROTID

PAROTIS n parotid gland

PAROTISES > PAROTIS

PAROTITIC > PAROTITIS

PAROTITIS n inflammation of the parotid gland

PAROTOID n any of various warty poison glands on the head and back of certain toads and salamanders ▷ adj resembling a parotid gland

PAROTOIDS > PAROTOID

PAROUS adj having given birth

PAROUSIA n Second Coming

PAROUSIAS > PAROUSIA

PAROXYSM n uncontrollable outburst of rage, delight, etc

PAROXYSMS > PAROXYSM

PARP vb make a honking sound

PARPANE n parapet on bridge

PARPANES > PARPANE

PARPED > PARP

PARPEN same as > PARPEND

PARPEND same as > PERPEND

PARPENDS > PARPEND

PARPENS > PARPEN

PARPENT n parapet on bridge

PARPENTS > PARPENT

PARPING > PARP

PARPOINT n parapet on bridge

PARPOINTS > PARPOINT

PARPS > PARP

PARQUET n floor covering made of wooden blocks arranged in a geometric pattern ▷ vb cover with parquet

PARQUETED > PARQUET

PARQUETRY n pieces of wood arranged in a geometric pattern, used to cover floors

PARQUETS > PARQUET

PARR n salmon up to two years of age

PARRA n tourist or non-resident on a beach

PARRAKEET same as > PARAKEET

PARRAL same as > PARREL

PARRALS > PARRAL

PARRAS > PARRA

PARRED > PAR

PARREL n ring that holds the jaws of a boom to the mast but lets it slide up and down

PARRELS > PARREL

PARRHESIA n boldness of speech

PARRICIDE n crime of killing either of one's parents

PARRIDGE Scottish variant of > PORRIDGE

PARRIDGES > PARRIDGE

PARRIED > PARRY

PARRIER > PARRY

PARRIERS > PARRY

PARRIES > PARRY

PARRING > PAR

PARRITCH Scottish variant of > PORRIDGE

PARROCK vb put (an animal) in a small field

PARROCKED > PARROCK

PARROCKS > PARROCK

PARROKET n small long-tailed parrot

PARROKETS > PARROKET

PARROQUET n small long-tailed parrot

PARROT n tropical bird with a short hooked beak and an ability to imitate human speech ▷ vb repeat (someone else's words) without thinking

PARROTED > PARROT

PARROTER n person who repeats what is said

PARROTERS > PARROTER

PARROTING > PARROT

PARROTRY > PARROT

PARROTS > PARROT

PARROTY adj like a parrot; chattering

PARRS > PARR

PARRY vb ward off (an attack) ▷ n parrying

PARRYING > PARRY

PARS > PAR

PARSABLE > PARSE

PARSE vb analyse (a sentence) in terms of grammar

PARSEC n unit of astronomical distance

PARSECS > PARSEC

PARSED > PARSE

PARSER n program or part of a program that interprets input to a computer by recognizing key words or analysing sentence structure

PARSERS > PARSER

PARSES > PARSE

PARSIMONY n extreme caution in spending money

PARSING > PARSE

PARSINGS > PARSE

PARSLEY n herb used for seasoning and decorating food ▷ vb garnish with parsley

PARSLEYED > PARSLEY

PARSLEYS > PARSLEY

PARSLIED > PARSLEY

PARSNEP same as > PARSNIP

PARSNEPS > PARSNEP

PARSNIP n long tapering cream-coloured root vegetable

PARSNIPS > PARSNIP

PARSON n Anglican parish priest

PARSONAGE n parson's house

PARSONIC > PARSON

PARSONISH adj like a parson

PARSONS > PARSON

PART n one of the pieces that make up a whole ▷ vb divide or separate

PARTAKE vb take (food or drink)

PARTAKEN > PARTAKE

PARTAKER > PARTAKE

PARTAKERS > PARTAKE

PARTAKES > PARTAKE

PARTAKING > PARTAKE

PARTAN Scottish word for > CRAB

PARTANS > PARTAN

PARTED adj divided almost to the base

PARTER n thing that parts

PARTERRE n formally patterned flower garden

PARTERRES > PARTERRE

PARTERS > PARTER

PARTI n concept of architectural design

PARTIAL adj not complete ▷ n any of the component tones of a single musical sound, including both those that belong to the harmonic series of the sound and those that do not

PARTIALLY > PARTIAL

PARTIALS > PARTIAL

PARTIBLE adj (esp of property or an inheritance) divisible

PARTICLE n extremely small piece or amount

PARTICLES > PARTICLE

PARTIED > PARTY

PARTIER n person who parties

PARTIERS > PARTIER

PARTIES > PARTY

PARTIM adv in part

PARTING same as > PART

PARTINGS > PARTING

PARTIS > PARTI

PARTISAN n strong supporter of a party or group ▷ adj prejudiced or one-sided

PARTISANS > PARTISAN

PARTITA n type of suite

PARTITAS > PARTITA

PARTITE adj composed of or divided into a specified number of parts

PARTITION n screen or thin wall that divides a room ▷ vb divide with a partition

PARTITIVE adj (of a noun) referring to part of something ▷ n partitive word, such as some or any

PARTITURA n music score for several parts

PARTIZAN same as > PARTISAN

PARTIZANS > PARTIZAN

PARTLET n woman's garment covering the neck and shoulders

PARTLETS > PARTLET

PARTLY adv not completely

PARTNER n either member of a couple in a relationship or activity ▷ vb be the partner of

PARTNERED > PARTNER

PARTNERS > PARTNER

PARTON n hypothetical elementary particle postulated as a constituent of neutrons and protons

PARTONS > PARTON

PARTOOK > PARTAKE

PARTRIDGE n game bird of the grouse family

PARTS *pl n* abilities or talents

PARTURE *n* departure

PARTURES > PARTURE

PARTWAY *adv* some of the way

PARTWORK *n* series of magazines issued at weekly or monthly intervals, which are designed to be bound together to form a complete course or book

PARTWORKS > PARTWORK

PARTY *n* social gathering for pleasure ▷ *vb* celebrate, have fun ▷ *adj* (of a shield) divided vertically into two colours, metals, or furs

PARTYER *n* person who parties

PARTYERS > PARTYER

PARTYGOER *n* person who goes to party

PARTYING > PARTY

PARTYISM *n* devotion to political party

PARTYISMS > PARTYISM

PARULIDES > PARULIS

PARULIS *another name for* > GUMBOIL

PARULISES > PARULIS

PARURA *same as* > PARURE

PARURAS > PARURA

PARURE *n* set of jewels or other ornaments

PARURES > PARURE

PARVE *same as* > PAREV

PARVENU *n* person newly risen to a position of power or wealth ▷ *adj* of or characteristic of a parvenu

PARVENUE *n* woman who, having risen socially or economically, is considered to be an upstart or to lack the appropriate refinement for her new position ▷ *adj* of or characteristic of a parvenue

PARVENUES > PARVENUE

PARVENUS > PARVENU

PARVIS *n* court or portico in front of a building, esp a church

PARVISE *same as* > PARVIS

PARVISES > PARVISE

PARVO *n* disease of cattle and dogs

PARVOLIN *n* substance resulting from the putrefaction of flesh

PARVOLINE *n* liquid derived from coal tar

PARVOLINS > PARVOLIN

PARVOS > PARVO

PAS *n* dance step or movement, esp in ballet

PASCAL *n* unit of pressure

PASCALS > PASCAL

PASCHAL *adj* of the Passover or Easter ▷ *n* Passover or Easter

PASCHALS > PASCHAL

PASCUAL *adj* relating to pasture

PASE *n* movement of

the cape or muleta by a matador to attract the bull's attention and guide its attack

PASEAR *vb* go for a rambling walk

PASEARED > PASEAR

PASEARING > PASEAR

PASEARS > PASEAR

PASELA *same as* > BONSELA

PASELAS > PASELA

PASEO *n* bullfighters' procession

PASEOS > PASEO

PASES > PASE

PASH *n* infatuation ▷ *vb* throw or be thrown and break or be broken to bits

PASHA *n* high official of the Ottoman Empire

PASHADOM *n* territory of a pasha

PASHADOMS > PASHADOM

PASHALIC *same as* > PASHALIK

PASHALICS > PASHALIC

PASHALIK *n* province or jurisdiction of a pasha

PASHALIKS > PASHALIK

PASHAS > PASHA

PASHED > PASH

PASHES > PASH

PASHIM *same as* > PASHM

PASHIMS > PASHM

PASHING > PASH

PASHKA *n* rich Russian dessert made of cottage cheese, cream, almonds, currants, etc

PASHKAS > PASHKA

PASHM *n* underfur of various Tibetan animals, esp goats, used for cashmere shawls

PASHMINA *n* type of cashmere scarf or shawl made from the underfur of Tibetan goats

PASHMINAS > PASHMINA

PASHMS > PASHM

PASODOBLE *n* fast modern ballroom dance

PASPALUM *n* type of grass with wide leaves

PASPALUMS > PASPALUM

PASPIES > PASPY

PASPY *n* piece of music in triple time

PASQUIL *n* abusive lampoon or satire ▷ *vb* ridicule with pasquil

PASQUILER *n* person who lampoons

PASQUILS > PASQUIL

PASS *vb* go by, past, or through ▷ *n* successful result in a test or examination

PASSABLE *adj* (just) acceptable

PASSABLY *adv* fairly

PASSADE *n* act of moving back and forth in the same place

PASSADES > PASSADE

PASSADO *n* forward thrust with sword

PASSADOES > PASSADO

PASSADOS > PASSADO

PASSAGE *n* channel or opening providing a way through ▷ *vb* move or cause to move at a passage

PASSAGED > PASSAGE

PASSAGER *as in passager hawk* young hawk or falcon caught while on migration

PASSAGES > PASSAGE

PASSAGING > PASSAGE

PASSALONG *adj* (of plants) easily propagated and given to others

PASSAMENT *vb* sew border on garment

PASSANT *adj* (of a beast) walking, with the right foreleg raised

PASSATA *n* sauce made from sieved tomatoes, often used in Italian cookery

PASSATAS > PASSATA

PASSBAND *n* band of frequencies that is transmitted with maximum efficiency through a circuit, filter, etc

PASSBANDS > PASSBAND

PASSBOOK *n* book issued by a bank or building society for keeping a record of deposits and withdrawals

PASSBOOKS > PASSBOOK

PASSE *adj* out-of-date

PASSED > PASS

PASSEE *adj* out of fashion

PASSEL *n* group or quantity of no fixed number

PASSELS > PASSEL

PASSEMENT *vb* sew border on garment

PASSENGER *n* person travelling in a vehicle driven by someone else

PASSEPIED *n* lively minuet of Breton origin

PASSER *n* person or thing that passes

PASSERBY *n* person that is passing or going by, esp on foot

PASSERINE *adj* belonging to the order of perching birds ▷ *n* any bird of this order

PASSERS > PASSER

PASSERSBY > PASSERBY

PASSES > PASS

PASSIBLE *adj* susceptible to emotion or suffering

PASSIBLY > PASSIBLE

PASSIM *adv* everywhere, throughout

PASSING *adj* brief or transitory ▷ *n* death

PASSINGLY > PASSING

PASSINGS > PASSING

PASSION *n* intense sexual love ▷ *vb* give passionate character to

PASSIONAL *adj* of, relating to, or due to passion or the passions ▷ *n* book recounting the sufferings of Christian martyrs or

saints

PASSIONED > PASSION

PASSIONS > PASSION

PASSIVATE *vb* render (a metal) less susceptible to corrosion by coating the surface with a substance, such as an oxide

PASSIVE *adj* not playing an active part ▷ *n* passive form of a verb

PASSIVELY > PASSIVE

PASSIVES > PASSIVE

PASSIVISM *n* theory, belief, or practice of passive resistance

PASSIVIST > PASSIVISM

PASSIVITY > PASSIVE

PASSKEY *n* private key

PASSKEYS > PASSKEY

PASSLESS *adj* having no pass

PASSMAN *n* student who passes without honours

PASSMEN > PASSMAN

PASSMENT *same as* > PASSEMENT

PASSMENTS > PASSMENT

PASSOUT *n* (in ice hockey) pass by an attacking player from behind the opposition goal line

PASSOUTS > PASSOUT

PASSOVER *n* lamb eaten during Passover

PASSOVERS > PASSOVER

PASSPORT *n* official document of nationality granting permission to travel abroad

PASSPORTS > PASSPORT

PASSUS *n* (esp in medieval literature) division or section of a poem, story, etc

PASSUSES > PASSUS

PASSWORD *n* secret word or phrase that ensures admission

PASSWORDS > PASSWORD

PAST *adj* of the time before the present ▷ *n* period of time before the present ▷ *adv* ago ▷ *prep* beyond

PASTA *n* type of food, such as spaghetti, that is made in different shapes from flour and water

PASTALIKE > PASTA

PASTANCE *n* activity that passes time

PASTANCES > PASTANCE

PASTAS > PASTA

PASTE *n* moist soft mixture, such as toothpaste ▷ *vb* fasten with paste

PASTED > PASTE

PASTEDOWN *n* portion of endpaper pasted to cover of book

PASTEL *n* coloured chalk crayon for drawing ▷ *adj* pale and delicate in colour

PASTELIST > PASTEL

PASTELS > PASTEL

PASTER *n* person or thing that pastes

PASTERN n part of a horse's foot between the fetlock and the hoof

PASTERNS > PASTERN

PASTERS > PASTER

PASTES > PASTE

PASTEUP n assembly of typeset matter, illustrations, etc, pasted on a sheet of paper or board

PASTEUPS > PASTEUP

PASTICCI > PASTICCIO

PASTICCIO n art work borrowing various styles

PASTICHE n work of art that mixes styles or copies the style of another artist

PASTICHES > PASTICHE

PASTIE n decorative cover for nipple

PASTIER > PASTY

PASTIES > PASTY

PASTIEST > PASTY

PASTIL same as > PASTILLE

PASTILLE n small fruit-flavoured and sometimes medicated sweet

PASTILLES > PASTILLE

PASTILS > PASTIL

PASTILY > PASTY

PASTIME n activity that makes time pass pleasantly

PASTIMES > PASTIME

PASTINA n small pieces of pasta

PASTINAS > PASTINA

PASTINESS > PASTY

PASTING n heavy defeat

PASTINGS > PASTING

PASTIS n anise-flavoured alcoholic drink

PASTISES > PASTIS

PASTITSIO n Greek dish consisting of minced meat and macaroni topped with bechamel sauce

PASTITSO n Greek dish of baked pasta

PASTITSOS > PASTITSO

PASTLESS adj having no past

PASTNESS n quality of being past

PASTOR n member of the clergy in charge of a congregation ▷ vb act as a pastor

PASTORAL adj of or depicting country life ▷ n poem or picture portraying country life

PASTORALE n musical composition that suggests country life

PASTORALI > PASTORALE

PASTORALS > PASTORAL

PASTORATE n office or term of office of a pastor

PASTORED > PASTOR

PASTORING > PASTOR

PASTORIUM n residence of pastor

PASTORLY > PASTOR

PASTORS > PASTOR

PASTRAMI n highly seasoned smoked beef

PASTRAMIS > PASTRAMI

PASTRIES > PASTRY

PASTROMI same as > PASTRAMI

PASTROMIS > PASTROMI

PASTRY n baking dough made of flour, fat, and water

PASTS > PAST

PASTURAGE n business of grazing cattle

PASTURAL adj of pasture

PASTURE n grassy land for farm animals to graze on ▷ vb cause (livestock) to graze or (of livestock) to graze (a pasture)

PASTURED > PASTURE

PASTURER n person who tends cattle

PASTURERS > PASTURER

PASTURES > PASTURE

PASTURING > PASTURE

PASTY adj (of a complexion) pale and unhealthy ▷ n round of pastry folded over a savoury filling

PAT vb tap lightly ▷ n gentle tap or stroke ▷ adj quick, ready, or glib

PATACA n monetary unit of Macao

PATACAS > PATACA

PATAGIA > PATAGIUM

PATAGIAL > PATAGIUM

PATAGIUM n web of skin between the neck, limbs, and tail in bats and gliding mammals that functions as a wing

PATAKA n building on stilts, used for storing provisions

PATAMAR n type of boat

PATAMARS > PATAMAR

PATBALL n game like squash but using hands instead of rackets

PATBALLS > PATBALL

PATCH n piece of material sewn on a garment ▷ vb mend with a patch

PATCHABLE > PATCH

PATCHED > PATCH

PATCHER > PATCH

PATCHERS > PATCH

PATCHERY n bungling work

PATCHES > PATCH

PATCHIER > PATCHY

PATCHIEST > PATCHY

PATCHILY > PATCHY

PATCHING > PATCH

PATCHINGS > PATCH

PATCHOCKE Spenserian word for > CLOWN

PATCHOULI n Asiatic tree, the leaves of which yield a heavy fragrant oil

PATCHOULY same as > PATCHOULI

PATCHWORK n needlework made of pieces of different materials sewn together

PATCHY adj of uneven quality or intensity

PATE n head

PATED > PATE

PATELLA n kneecap

PATELLAE > PATELLA

PATELLAR > PATELLA

PATELLAS > PATELLA

PATELLATE adj having the shape of a patella

PATEN n plate, usually made of silver or gold, used for the bread at Communion

PATENCIES > PATENCY

PATENCY n condition of being obvious

PATENS > PATEN

PATENT n document giving the exclusive right to make or sell an invention ▷ adj open to public inspection ▷ vb obtain a patent for

PATENTED > PATENT

PATENTEE n person, group, company, etc, that has been granted a patent

PATENTEES > PATENTEE

PATENTING > PATENT

PATENTLY adv obviously

PATENTOR n person who or official body that grants a patent or patents

PATENTORS > PATENTOR

PATENTS > PATENT

PATER n father

PATERA n shallow ancient Roman bowl

PATERAE > PATERA

PATERCOVE n fraudulent priest

PATERERO n type of cannon

PATEREROS > PATERERO

PATERNAL adj fatherly

PATERNITY n fact or state of being a father

PATERS > PATER

PATES > PATE

PATH n surfaced walk or track ▷ vb make a path

PATHED > PATH

PATHETIC adj causing feelings of pity or sadness ▷ pl n pathetic sentiments ▷ n pathetic person

PATHETICS > PATHETIC

PATHIC n catamite ▷ adj of or relating to a catamite

PATHICS > PATHIC

PATHING > PATH

PATHLESS > PATH

PATHNAME n name of a file or directory together with its position in relation to other directories traced back in a line to the root

PATHNAMES > PATHNAME

PATHOGEN n thing that causes disease

PATHOGENE same as > PATHOGEN

PATHOGENS > PATHOGEN

PATHOGENY n origin, development, and resultant effects of a disease

PATHOLOGY n scientific study of diseases

PATHOS n power of arousing pity or sadness

PATHOSES > PATHOS

PATHS > PATH

PATHWAY n path

PATHWAYS > PATHWAY

PATIBLE adj endurable

PATIENCE n quality of being patient

PATIENCES > PATIENCE

PATIENT adj enduring difficulties or delays calmly ▷ n person receiving medical treatment ▷ vb make calm

PATIENTED > PATIENT

PATIENTER > PATIENT

PATIENTLY > PATIENT

PATIENTS > PATIENT

PATIKI n New Zealand sand flounder or dab

PATIN same as > PATEN

PATINA n fine layer on a surface

PATINAE > PATINA

PATINAED adj having a patina

PATINAS > PATINA

PATINATE vb coat with patina

PATINATED > PATINATE

PATINATES > PATINATE

PATINE vb cover with patina

PATINED > PATINE

PATINES > PATINE

PATINING > PATINE

PATINISE same as > PATINIZE

PATINISED > PATINISE

PATINISES > PATINISE

PATINIZE vb coat with patina

PATINIZED > PATINIZE

PATINIZES > PATINIZE

PATINS > PATIN

PATIO n paved area adjoining a house

PATIOS > PATIO

PATISSIER n pastry chef

PATLY adv fitly

PATNESS n appropriateness

PATNESSES > PATNESS

PATOIS n regional dialect, esp of French

PATONCE adj (of cross) with limbs which broaden from centre

PATOOTIE n person's bottom

PATOOTIES > PATOOTIE

PATRIAL n (in Britain, formerly) person with a right by statute to live in the United Kingdom, and so not subject to immigration control

PATRIALS > PATRIAL

PATRIARCH n male head of a family or tribe

PATRIATE vb bring under the authority of an autonomous country

PATRIATED > PATRIATE

PATRIATES > PATRIATE

PATRICIAN n member of the nobility ▷ adj of noble birth

PATRICIDE n crime of killing one's father

PATRICK n former Irish coin

PATRICKS > PATRICK

PATRICO n fraudulent priest

p

PATRICOES > PATRICO
PATRILINY n tracing of family descent through males
PATRIMONY n property inherited from ancestors
PATRIOT n person who loves his or her country and supports its interests
PATRIOTIC > PATRIOT
PATRIOTS > PATRIOT
PATRISTIC adj of or relating to the Fathers of the Church, their writings, or the study of these
PATROL n regular circuit by a guard ▷ vb go round on guard, or reconnoitring
PATROLLED > PATROL
PATROLLER > PATROL
PATROLMAN n man, esp a policeman, who patrols a certain area
PATROLMEN > PATROLMAN
PATROLOGY n study of the writings of the Fathers of the Church
PATROLS > PATROL
PATRON n person who gives financial support to charities, artists, etc
PATRONAGE n support given by a patron
PATRONAL > PATRONESS
PATRONESS n woman who sponsors or aids artists, charities, etc
PATRONISE same as > PATRONIZE
PATRONIZE vb treat in a condescending way
PATRONLY > PATRONESS
PATRONNE n woman who owns or manages a hotel, restaurant, or bar
PATRONNES > PATRONNE
PATRONS > PATRON
PATROON n Dutch land-holder in New Netherland and New York with manorial rights in the colonial era
PATROONS > PATROON
PATS > PAT
PATSIES > PATSY
PATSY n person who is easily cheated, victimized, etc
PATTAMAR n Indian courier
PATTAMARS > PATTAMAR
PATTE n band keeping belt in place
PATTED > PAT
PATTEE adj (of a cross) having triangular arms widening outwards
PATTEN n wooden clog or sandal on a raised wooden platform or metal ring ▷ vb wear pattens
PATTENED > PATTEN
PATTENING > PATTEN
PATTENS > PATTEN
PATTER vb make repeated soft tapping sounds ▷ n quick succession of taps
PATTERED > PATTER

PATTERER > PATTER
PATTERERS > PATTER
PATTERING > PATTER
PATTERN n arrangement of repeated parts or decorative designs ▷ vb model
PATTERNED > PATTERN
PATTERNS > PATTERN
PATTERS > PATTER
PATTES > PATTE
PATTIE same as > PATTY
PATTIES > PATTY
PATTING > PAT
PATTLE dialect for > PADDLE
PATTLES > PATTLE
PATTY n small flattened cake of minced food
PATTYPAN n small round flattish squash
PATTYPANS > PATTYPAN
PATU n short Māori club, now used ceremonially
PATULENT adj spreading widely
PATULIN n toxic antibiotic
PATULINS > PATULIN
PATULOUS adj spreading widely or expanded
PATUS > PATU
PATUTUKI n blue cod
PATUTUKIS > PATUTUKI
PATY adj (of cross) having arms of equal length
PATZER n novice chess player
PATZERS > PATZER
PAUA n edible shellfish of New Zealand, which has a pearly shell used for jewellery
PAUAS > PAUA
PAUCAL n grammatical number occurring in some languages for words in contexts where a few of their referents are described or referred to ▷ adj relating to or inflected for this number
PAUCALS > PAUCAL
PAUCITIES > PAUCITY
PAUCITY n scarcity
PAUGHTIER > PAUGHTY
PAUGHTY Scots word for > HAUGHTY
PAUL same as > PAWL
PAULDRON n either of two metal plates worn with armour to protect the shoulders
PAULDRONS > PAULDRON
PAULIN n tarpaulin
PAULINS > PAULIN
PAULOWNIA n Japanese tree with large heart-shaped leaves and clusters of purplish or white flowers
PAULS > PAUL
PAUNCE n pansy
PAUNCES > PAUNCE
PAUNCH n protruding belly ▷ vb stab in the stomach
PAUNCHED > PAUNCH
PAUNCHES > PAUNCH
PAUNCHIER > PAUNCHY
PAUNCHING > PAUNCH

PAUNCHY adj having a protruding belly or abdomen
PAUPER n very poor person ▷ vb reduce to beggary
PAUPERED > PAUPER
PAUPERESS n female pauper
PAUPERING > PAUPER
PAUPERISE same as > PAUPERIZE
PAUPERISM > PAUPER
PAUPERIZE vb make a pauper of
PAUPERS > PAUPER
PAUPIETTE n rolled stuffed fish or meat
PAUROPOD n minute myriapod
PAUROPODS > PAUROPOD
PAUSAL > PAUSE
PAUSE vb stop for a time ▷ n stop or rest in speech or action
PAUSED > PAUSE
PAUSEFUL adj taking pauses
PAUSELESS adj without pauses
PAUSER > PAUSE
PAUSERS > PAUSE
PAUSES > PAUSE
PAUSING > PAUSE
PAUSINGLY adv with pauses
PAUSINGS > PAUSE
PAV short for > PAVLOVA
PAVAGE n tax towards paving streets, or the right to levy such a tax
PAVAGES > PAVAGE
PAVAN same as > PAVANE
PAVANE n slow and stately dance of the 16th and 17th centuries
PAVANES > PAVANE
PAVANS > PAVAN
PAVE vb form (a surface) with stone or brick ▷ n paved surface, esp an uneven one
PAVED > PAVE
PAVEED adj (of jewels) set close together
PAVEMENT n paved path for pedestrians ▷ vb provide with pavement
PAVEMENTS > PAVEMENT
PAVEN same as > PAVANE
PAVENS > PAVEN
PAVER > PAVE
PAVERS > PAVE
PAVES > PAVE
PAVID adj fearful
PAVILION n building on a playing field etc ▷ vb place or set in or as if in a pavilion
PAVILIONS > PAVILION
PAVILLON n bell of wind instrument
PAVILLONS > PAVILLON
PAVIN same as > PAVANE
PAVING n paved surface ▷ adj of or for a paved surface or pavement
PAVINGS > PAVING
PAVINS > PAVIN
PAVIOR same as > PAVIOUR
PAVIORS > PAVIOR

PAVIOUR n person who lays paving
PAVIOURS > PAVIOUR
PAVIS n large square shield, developed in the 15th century, at first portable but later heavy and set up in a permanent position
PAVISE same as > PAVIS
PAVISER n soldier holding pavise
PAVISERS > PAVISER
PAVISES > PAVISE
PAVISSE same as > PAVIS
PAVISSES > PAVISSE
PAVLOVA n meringue cake topped with whipped cream and fruit
PAVLOVAS > PAVLOVA
PAVONAZZO n white Italian marble
PAVONE n peacock
PAVONES > PAVONE
PAVONIAN same as > PAVONINE
PAVONINE adj of or resembling a peacock or the colours, design, or iridescence of a peacock's tail
PAVS > PAV
PAW n animal's foot with claws and pads ▷ vb scrape with the paw or hoof
PAWA old word for > PEACOCK
PAWAS > PAWA
PAWAW vb recite N American incantation
PAWAWED > PAWAW
PAWAWING > PAWAW
PAWAWS > PAWAW
PAWED > PAW
PAWER n person or animal that paws
PAWERS > PAWER
PAWING > PAW
PAWK Scots word for > TRICK
PAWKIER > PAWKY
PAWKIEST > PAWKY
PAWKILY > PAWKY
PAWKINESS > PAWKY
PAWKS > PAWK
PAWKY adj having or characterized by a dry wit
PAWL n pivoted lever shaped to engage with a ratchet to prevent motion in a particular direction
PAWLS > PAWL
PAWN vb deposit (an article) as security for money borrowed ▷ n chessman of the lowest value
PAWNABLE > PAWN
PAWNAGE > PAWN
PAWNAGES > PAWN
PAWNCE old word for > PANSY
PAWNCES > PAWNCE
PAWNED > PAWN
PAWNEE n one who accepts goods in pawn
PAWNEES > PAWNEE
PAWNER n one who pawns his or her possessions
PAWNERS > PAWNER
PAWNING > PAWN

PAWNOR *same as* > PAWNER
PAWNORS > PAWNOR
PAWNS > PAWN
PAWNSHOP *n* premises of a pawnbroker
PAWNSHOPS > PAWNSHOP
PAWPAW *same as* > PAPAW
PAWPAWS > PAWPAW
PAWS > PAW
PAX *n* kiss of peace ▷ *interj* call signalling a desire to end hostilities
PAXES > PAX
PAXIUBA *n* tropical tree
PAXIUBAS > PAXIUBA
PAWWAX *n* strong ligament in the neck of many mammals, which supports the head
PAXWAXES > PAXWAX
PAY *vb* give money etc in return for goods or services ▷ *n* wages or salary
PAYABLE *adj* due to be paid
PAYABLES *n* debts to be paid
PAYABLY > PAYABLE
PAYBACK *n* return on an investment
PAYBACKS > PAYBACK
PAYCHECK *n* payment for work done
PAYCHECKS > PAYCHECK
PAYDAY *n* day on which wages or salaries are paid
PAYDAYS > PAYDAY
PAYED > PAY
PAYEE *n* person to whom money is paid or due
PAYEES > PAYEE
PAYER *n* person who pays
PAYERS > PAYER
PAYFONE *US spelling of* > PAYPHONE
PAYFONES > PAYFONE
PAYGRADE *n* military rank
PAYGRADES > PAYGRADE
PAYING > PAY
PAYINGS > PAY
PAYLOAD *n* passengers or cargo of an aircraft
PAYLOADS > PAYLOAD
PAYMASTER *n* official responsible for the payment of wages and salaries
PAYMENT *n* act of paying
PAYMENTS > PAYMENT
PAYNIM *n* heathen or pagan
PAYNIMRY *n* state of being heathen
PAYNIMS > PAYNIM
PAYOFF *n* final settlement, esp in retribution
PAYOFFS > PAYOFF
PAYOLA *n* bribe to get special treatment, esp to promote a commercial product
PAYOLAS > PAYOLA
PAYOR *same as* > PAYER
PAYORS > PAYOR
PAYOUT *n* sum of money paid out
PAYOUTS > PAYOUT
PAYPHONE *n* coin-operated telephone

PAYPHONES > PAYPHONE
PAYROLL *n* list of employees who receive regular pay
PAYROLLS > PAYROLL
PAYS > PAY
PAYSAGE *n* landscape
PAYSAGES > PAYSAGE
PAYSAGIST *n* painter of landscapes
PAYSD *Spenserian form of* > POISED
PAYSLIP *n* note of payment given to employee
PAYSLIPS > PAYSLIP
PAZAZZ *same as* > PIZZAZZ
PAZAZZES > PAZAZZ
PAZZAZZ *same as* > PIZZAZZ
PAZZAZZES > PAZZAZZ
PE *n* 17th letter in the Hebrew alphabet
PEA *n* climbing plant with seeds growing in pods
PEABERRY *n* coffee berry containing one seed
PEACE *n* calm, quietness
PEACEABLE *adj* inclined towards peace
PEACEABLY > PEACEABLE
PEACED > PEACE
PEACEFUL *adj* not in a state of war or disagreement
PEACELESS *adj* without peace
PEACENIK *n* activist who opposes war
PEACENIKS > PEACENIK
PEACES > PEACE
PEACETIME *n* period without war
PEACH *n* soft juicy fruit with a stone and a downy skin ▷ *adj* pinkish-orange ▷ *vb* inform against an accomplice
PEACHBLOW *n* type of glaze on porcelain
PEACHED > PEACH
PEACHER > PEACH
PEACHERS > PEACH
PEACHES > PEACH
PEACHIER > PEACHY
PEACHIEST > PEACHY
PEACHILY > PEACHY
PEACHING > PEACH
PEACHY *adj* of or like a peach, esp in colour or texture
PEACING > PEACE
PEACOAT *n* woollen jacket
PEACOATS > PEACOAT
PEACOCK *n* large male bird with a brilliantly coloured fanlike tail ▷ *vb* display (oneself) proudly
PEACOCKED > PEACOCK
PEACOCKS > PEACOCK
PEACOCKY > PEACOCK
PEACOD *same as* > PEACOD
PEACODS > PEACOD
PEAFOWL *n* peacock or peahen
PEAFOWLS > PEAFOWL
PEAG *n* (formerly) money used by North American Indians, made of cylindrical shells strung or woven together

PEAGE *same as* > PEAG
PEAGES > PEAGE
PEAGS > PEAG
PEAHEN > PEACOCK
PEAHENS > PEACOCK
PEAK *n* pointed top, esp of a mountain ▷ *vb* form or reach a peak ▷ *adj* of or at the point of greatest demand
PEAKED *adj* having a peak
PEAKIER > PEAK
PEAKIEST > PEAK
PEAKING > PEAK
PEAKISH *adj* sickly
PEAKLESS > PEAK
PEAKLIKE > PEAK
PEAKS > PEAK
PEAKY > PEAK
PEAL *n* long loud echoing sound, esp of bells or thunder ▷ *vb* sound with a peal or peals
PEALED > PEAL
PEALIKE > PEA
PEALING > PEAL
PEALS > PEAL
PEAN *n* paean ▷ *vb* deliver a pean
PEANED > PEAN
PEANING > PEAN
PEANS > PEAN
PEANUT *n* pea-shaped nut that ripens underground
PEANUTS > PEANUT
PEAPOD *n* pod of the pea plant
PEAPODS > PEAPOD
PEAR *n* sweet juicy fruit with a narrow top and rounded base
PEARCE *old spelling of* > PIERCE
PEARCED > PEARCE
PEARCES > PEARCE
PEARCING > PEARCE
PEARE *obsolete spelling of* > PEAR
PEARES > PEARE
PEARL *same as* > PURL
PEARLASH *n* granular crystalline form of potassium carbonate
PEARLED > PEARL
PEARLER *n* person who dives for or trades in pearls ▷ *adj* excellent
PEARLERS > PEARLER
PEARLIER > PEARLY
PEARLIES > PEARLY
PEARLIEST > PEARLY
PEARLIN *n* type of lace used to trim clothes
PEARLING > PEARL
PEARLINGS > PEARL
PEARLINS *n* type of lace
PEARLISED *same as* > PEARLIZED
PEARLITE *same as* > PERLITE
PEARLITES > PEARLITE
PEARLITIC > PEARLITE
PEARLIZED *adj* having or given a pearly lustre
PEARLS > PEARL
PEARLWORT *n* plant with small white flowers that are spherical in bud

PEARLY *adj* resembling a pearl, esp in lustre ▷ *n* London costermonger who wears on ceremonial occasions a traditional dress of dark clothes covered with pearl buttons
PEARMAIN *n* any of several varieties of apple having a red skin
PEARMAINS > PEARMAIN
PEARS > PEAR
PEARST *archaic variant of* > PIERCED
PEART *adj* lively
PEARTER > PEART
PEARTEST > PEART
PEARTLY > PEART
PEARTNESS > PEART
PEARWOOD *n* wood from pear tree
PEARWOODS > PEARWOOD
PEAS > PEA
PEASANT *n* person working on the land, esp in poorer countries or in the past
PEASANTRY *n* peasants collectively
PEASANTS > PEASANT
PEASANTY *adj* having qualities ascribed to traditional country life or people
PEASCOD *same as* > COD
PEASCODS > PEASCOD
PEASE *n* archaic or dialect word for pea ▷ *vb* appease
PEASECOD *n* pod of a pea plant
PEASECODS > PEASECOD
PEASED > PEASE
PEASEN *obsolete plural of* > PEASE
PEASES > PEASE
PEASING > PEASE
PEASON *obsolete plural of* > PEASE
PEASOUPER *n* thick fog
PEAT *n* decayed vegetable material found in bogs, used as fertilizer or fuel
PEATARIES > PEATARY
PEATARY *n* area covered with peat
PEATERIES > PEATERY
PEATERY *same as* > PEATARY
PEATIER > PEAT
PEATIEST > PEAT
PEATLAND *n* area of land consisting of peat bogs, usually containing many species of flora and fauna
PEATLANDS > PEATLAND
PEATMAN *n* person who collects peat
PEATMEN > PEATMAN
PEATS > PEAT
PEATSHIP *n* ship carrying peat
PEATSHIPS > PEATSHIP
PEATY > PEAT
PEAVEY *n* wooden lever with a metal pointed end and a hinged hook, used for handling logs
PEAVEYS > PEAVEY
PEAVIES > PEAVY

PEAVY *same as* > PEAVEY

PEAZE *same as* > PEASE

PEAZED > PEAZE

PEAZES > PEAZE

PEAZING > PEAZE

PEBA *n* type of armadillo

PEBAS > PEBA

PEBBLE *n* small roundish stone ▷ *vb* cover with pebbles

PEBBLED > PEBBLE

PEBBLES > PEBBLE

PEBBLIER > PEBBLE

PEBBLIEST > PEBBLE

PEBBLING *n* act of spraying the rink with drops of hot water to slow down the stone

PEBBLINGS > PEBBLING

PEBBLY > PEBBLE

PEBRINE *n* disease of silkworms

PEBRINES > PEBRINE

PEC *n* pectoral muscle

PECAN *n* edible nut of a N American tree

PECANS > PECAN

PECCABLE *adj* liable to sin

PECCANCY > PECCANT

PECCANT *adj* guilty of an offence

PECCANTLY > PECCANT

PECCARIES > PECCARY

PECCARY *n* piglike animal of American forests

PECCAVI *n* confession of guilt

PECCAVIS > PECCAVI

PECH *Scottish word for* > PANT

PECHAN *Scots word for* > STOMACH

PECHANS > PECHAN

PECHED > PECH

PECHING > PECH

PECHS > PECH

PECK *vb* strike or pick up with the beak ▷ *n* pecking movement

PECKE *n* quarter of bushel

PECKED > PECK

PECKER *n* slang word for penis

PECKERS > PECKER

PECKES > PECKE

PECKIER > PECKY

PECKIEST > PECKY

PECKING peck

PECKINGS > PECK

PECKISH *adj* slightly hungry

PECKISHLY > PECKISH

PECKS > PECK

PECKY *adj* discoloured

PECORINI > PECORINO

PECORINO *n* Italian cheese made from ewes' milk

PECORINOS > PECORINO

PECS *pl n* pectoral muscles

PECTASE *n* enzyme occurring in certain ripening fruits

PECTASES > PECTASE

PECTATE *n* salt or ester of pectic acid

PECTATES > PECTATE

PECTEN *n* comblike structure in the eye of birds and reptiles

PECTENS > PECTEN

PECTIC > PECTIN

PECTIN *n* substance in fruit that makes jam set

PECTINAL *adj* resembling a comb

PECTINATE *adj* shaped like a comb

PECTINEAL *adj* relating to pubic bone

PECTINES > PECTEN

PECTINOUS > PECTIN

PECTINS > PECTIN

PECTISE *same as* > PECTIZE

PECTISED > PECTISE

PECTISES > PECTISE

PECTISING > PECTISE

PECTIZE *vb* change into a jelly

PECTIZED > PECTIZE

PECTIZES > PECTIZE

PECTIZING > PECTIZE

PECTOLITE *n* silicate of lime and soda

PECTORAL *adj* of the chest or thorax ▷ *n* pectoral muscle or fin

PECTORALS > PECTORAL

PECTOSE *n* insoluble carbohydrate found in the cell walls of unripe fruit that is converted to pectin by enzymic processes

PECTOSES > PECTOSE

PECULATE *vb* embezzle (public money)

PECULATED > PECULATE

PECULATES > PECULATE

PECULATOR > PECULATE

PECULIA > PECULIUM

PECULIAR *adj* strange ▷ *n* special sort, esp an accented letter

PECULIARS > PECULIAR

PECULIUM *n* property that a father or master allowed his child or slave to hold as his own

PECUNIARY *adj* relating to, or consisting of, money

PECUNIOUS *adj* having lots of money

PED *n* pannier

PEDAGOG *same as* > PEDAGOGUE

PEDAGOGIC > PEDAGOGUE

PEDAGOGS > PEDAGOG

PEDAGOGUE *n* schoolteacher, esp a pedantic one

PEDAGOGY *n* principles, practice, or profession of teaching

PEDAL *n* foot-operated lever used to control a vehicle or machine, or to modify the tone of a musical instrument ▷ *vb* propel (a bicycle) by using its pedals ▷ *adj* of or relating to the foot or the feet

PEDALED > PEDAL

PEDALER > PEDAL

PEDALERS > PEDAL

PEDALFER *n* type of zonal soil deficient in lime but containing deposits of aluminium and iron

PEDALFERS > PEDALFER

PEDALIER *n* pedal piano

PEDALIERS > PEDALIER

PEDALING > PEDAL

PEDALLED > PEDAL

PEDALLER *n* person who pedals

PEDALLERS > PEDALLER

PEDALLING > PEDAL

PEDALO *n* pleasure craft driven by pedal-operated paddle wheels

PEDALOES > PEDALO

PEDALOS > PEDALO

PEDALS > PEDAL

PEDANT *n* person who is excessively concerned with details and rules, esp in academic work

PEDANTIC *adj* of, relating to, or characterized by pedantry

PEDANTISE *same as* > PEDANTIZE

PEDANTISM > PEDANT

PEDANTIZE *vb* make pedantic comments

PEDANTRY *n* practice of being a pedant, esp in the minute observance of petty rules or details

PEDANTS > PEDANT

PEDATE *adj* (of a plant leaf) divided into several lobes arising at a common point, the lobes often being stalked and the lateral lobes sometimes divided into smaller lobes

PEDATELY > PEDATE

PEDATIFID *adj* (of a plant leaf) pedately divided, with the divisions less deep than in a pedate leaf

PEDDER *old form of* > PEDLAR

PEDDERS > PEDDER

PEDDLE *vb* sell (goods) from door to door

PEDDLED > PEDDLE

PEDDLER *same as* > PEDLAR

PEDDLERS > PEDDLER

PEDDLERY *n* business of peddler

PEDDLES > PEDDLE

PEDDLING > PEDDLE

PEDDLINGS > PEDDLE

PEDERAST *n* man who has homosexual relations with boys

PEDERASTS > PEDERAST

PEDERASTY *n* homosexual relations between men and boys

PEDERERO *n* type of cannon

PEDEREROS > PEDERERO

PEDES > PES

PEDESES > PEDESIS

PEDESIS *n* random motion of small particles

PEDESTAL *n* base supporting a column, statue, etc

PEDESTALS > PEDESTAL

PEDETIC *adj* of feet

PEDIATRIC *adj* of or relating to the medical science of children and their diseases

PEDICAB *n* pedal-operated tricycle, available for hire, with an attached seat for one or two passengers

PEDICABS > PEDICAB

PEDICEL *n* stalk bearing a single flower of an inflorescence

PEDICELS > PEDICEL

PEDICLE *n* any small stalk

PEDICLED > PEDICLE

PEDICLES > PEDICLE

PEDICULAR *adj* relating to, infested with, or caused by lice

PEDICULI > PEDICULUS

PEDICULUS *n* wingless parasite

PEDICURE *n* medical or cosmetic treatment of the feet ▷ *vb* give a pedicure

PEDICURED > PEDICURE

PEDICURES > PEDICURE

PEDIFORM *adj* shaped like a foot

PEDIGREE *n* register of ancestors, esp of a purebred animal

PEDIGREED > PEDIGREE

PEDIGREES > PEDIGREE

PEDIMENT *n* triangular part over a door etc

PEDIMENTS > PEDIMENT

PEDIPALP *n* either member of the second pair of head appendages of arachnids

PEDIPALPI > PEDIPALP

PEDIPALPS > PEDIPALP

PEDLAR *n* person who sells goods from door to door

PEDLARIES > PEDLARY

PEDLARS > PEDLAR

PEDLARY *same as* > PEDLERY

PEDLER *same as* > PEDLAR

PEDLERIES > PEDLERY

PEDLERS > PEDLER

PEDLERY *n* business of pedler

PEDOCAL *n* type of zonal soil that is rich in lime and characteristic of relatively dry areas

PEDOCALIC > PEDOCAL

PEDOCALS > PEDOCAL

PEDOGENIC *adj* relating to soil

PEDOLOGIC > PEDOLOGY

PEDOLOGY *same as* > PAEDOLOGY

PEDOMETER *n* instrument which measures the distance walked

PEDOPHILE *n* person who is sexually attracted to children

PEDORTHIC *adj* (of footwear) designed to alleviate foot problems

PEDRAIL *n* device replacing wheel on rough surfaces

PEDRAILS > PEDRAIL

PEDRERO *n* type of cannon

PEDREROES > PEDRERO

PEDREROS > PEDRERO

PEDRO *n* card game

PEDROS > PEDRO

PEDS > PED

PEDUNCLE same as > PEDICEL

PEDUNCLED > PEDUNCLE

PEDUNCLES > PEDUNCLE

PEE vb urinate ▷ n urine

PEEBEEN n type of large evergreen

PEEBEENS > PEEBEEN

PEECE obsolete variant of > PIECE

PEECES > PEECE

PEED > PEE

PEEING > PEE

PEEK n peep or glance ▷ vb glance quickly or secretly

PEEKABO same as > PEEKABOO

PEEKABOO n game for young children, in which one person hides his face and suddenly reveals it and cries 'peekaboo' ▷ adj (of a garment) made of fabric that is almost transparent or patterned with small holes

PEEKABOOS > PEEKABOO

PEEKABOS > PEEKABO

PEEKAPOO n dog which is cross between Pekingese and poodle

PEEKAPOOS > PEEKAPOO

PEEKED > PEEK

PEEKING > PEEK

PEEKS > PEEK

PEEL vb remove the skin or rind of (a vegetable or fruit) ▷ n rind or skin

PEELABLE > PEEL

PEELED > PEEL

PEELER n special knife or mechanical device for peeling vegetables, fruit, etc

PEELERS > PEELER

PEELING n strip of skin, rind, bark, etc, that has been peeled off

PEELINGS > PEELING

PEELS > PEEL

PEEN n end of a hammer head opposite the striking face, often rounded or wedge-shaped ▷ vb strike with the peen of a hammer or with a stream of metal shot in order to bend or shape (a sheet of metal)

PEENED > PEEN

PEENGE vb complain

PEENGED > PEENGE

PEENGEING > PEENGE

PEENGES > PEENGE

PEENGING > PEENGE

PEENING > PEEN

PEENS > PEEN

PEEOY n homemade firework

PEEOYS > PEEOY

PEEP vb look slyly or quickly ▷ n peeping look

PEEPE old spelling of > PIP

PEEPED > PEEP

PEEPER n person who peeps

PEEPERS > PEEPER

PEEPES archaic spelling

of > PEEPS

PEEPHOLE n small aperture, such as one in the door of a flat for observing callers before opening

PEEPHOLES > PEEPHOLE

PEEPING > PEEP

PEEPS > PEEP

PEEPSHOW n box containing a series of pictures that can be seen through a small hole

PEEPSHOWS > PEEPSHOW

PEEPUL n Indian moraceous tree

PEEPULS > PEEPUL

PEER n (in Britain) member of the nobility ▷ vb look closely and intently

PEERAGE n whole body of peers

PEERAGES > PEERAGE

PEERED > PEER

PEERESS n (in Britain) woman holding the rank of a peer

PEERESSES > PEERESS

PEERIE n spinning top ▷ adj small

PEERIER > PEERIE

PEERIES > PEERIE

PEERIEST > PEERIE

PEERING > PEER

PEERLESS adj unequalled, unsurpassed

PEERS > PEER

PEERY n child's spinning top

PEES > PEE

PEESWEEP n early spring storm

PEESWEEPS > PEESWEEP

PEETWEET n spotted sandpiper

PEETWEETS > PEETWEET

PEEVE vb irritate or annoy ▷ n something that irritates

PEEVED > PEEVE

PEEVER n hopscotch

PEEVERS > PEEVER

PEEVES > PEEVE

PEEVING > PEEVE

PEEVISH adj fretful or irritable

PEEVISHLY > PEEVISH

PEEWEE same as > PEWEE

PEEWEES > PEEWEE

PEEWIT same as > LAPWING

PEEWITS > PEEWIT

PEG n pin or clip for joining, fastening, marking, etc ▷ vb fasten with pegs

PEGASUS n winged horse

PEGASUSES > PEGASUS

PEGBOARD n board with a pattern of holes into which small pegs can be fitted, used for playing certain games or keeping a score

PEGBOARDS > PEGBOARD

PEGBOX n part of stringed instrument that holds tuning pegs

PEGBOXES > PEGBOX

PEGGED > PEG

PEGGIES > PEGGY

PEGGING > PEG

PEGGINGS > PEG

PEGGY n ship's steward

PEGH variant of > PECH

PEGHED > PEGH

PEGHING > PEGH

PEGHS > PEGH

PEGLEGGED adj having wooden leg

PEGLESS > PEG

PEGLIKE > PEG

PEGMATITE n exceptionally coarse-grained intrusive igneous rock

PEGS > PEG

PEH n letter in the Hebrew alphabet

PEHS > PEH

PEIGNOIR n woman's light dressing gown

PEIGNOIRS > PEIGNOIR

PEIN same as > PEEN

PEINCT vb paint

PEINCTED > PEINCT

PEINCTING > PEINCT

PEINCTS > PEINCT

PEINED > PEIN

PEINING > PEIN

PEINS > PEIN

PEIRASTIC adj experimental

PEISE same as > PEIZE

PEISED > PEISE

PEISES > PEISE

PEISHWA n Indian leader

PEISHWAH same as > PEISHWA

PEISHWAHS > PEISHWAH

PEISHWAS > PEISHWA

PEISING > PEISE

PEIZE vb weight or poise

PEIZED > PEIZE

PEIZES > PEIZE

PEIZING > PEIZE

PEJORATE vb change for the worse

PEJORATED > PEJORATE

PEJORATES > PEJORATE

PEKAN n large North American marten

PEKANS > PEKAN

PEKE n Pekingese dog

PEKEPOO same as > PEEKAPOO

PEKEPOOS > PEKEPOO

PEKES > PEKE

PEKIN n silk fabric

PEKINS > PEKIN

PEKOE n high-quality tea made from the downy tips of the young buds of the tea plant

PEKOES > PEKOE

PELA n insect living on wax

PELAGE n coat of a mammal, consisting of hair, wool, fur, etc

PELAGES > PELAGE

PELAGIAL adj of the open sea

PELAGIAN adj of or inhabiting the open sea ▷ n pelagic creature

PELAGIANS > PELAGIAN

PELAGIC adj of or relating to the open sea ▷ n any pelagic creature

PELAGICS > PELAGIC

PELAS > PELA

PELE Spenserian variant of > PEAL

PELECYPOD another word for > BIVALVE

PELERINE n woman's narrow cape with long pointed ends in front

PELERINES > PELERINE

PELES > PELE

PELF n money or wealth

PELFS > PELF

PELHAM n horse's bit for a double bridle, less severe than a curb but more severe than a snaffle

PELHAMS > PELHAM

PELICAN n large water bird with a pouch beneath its bill for storing fish

PELICANS > PELICAN

PELISSE n cloak or loose coat which is usually fur-trimmed

PELISSES > PELISSE

PELITE n any argillaceous rock such as shale

PELITES > PELITE

PELITIC > PELITE

PELL n hide of an animal

PELLACH same as > PELLACK

PELLACHS > PELLACK

PELLACK n porpoise

PELLACKS > PELLACK

PELLAGRA n disease caused by lack of vitamin B

PELLAGRAS > PELLAGRA

PELLAGRIN n person who suffers from pellagra

PELLET n small ball of something ▷ vb strike with pellets

PELLETAL > PELLET

PELLETED > PELLET

PELLETIFY vb shape into pellets

PELLETING > PELLET

PELLETISE vb shape into pellets

PELLETIZE vb shape into pellets

PELLETS > PELLET

PELLICLE n thin skin or film

PELLICLES > PELLICLE

PELLITORY n urticaceous plant

PELLMELL n disorder

PELLMELLS > PELLMELL

PELLOCK n porpoise

PELLOCKS > PELLOCK

PELLS > PELL

PELLUCID adj very clear

PELLUM n dust

PELLUMS > PELLUM

PELMA n sole of the foot

PELMANISM n memory card game

PELMAS > PELMA

PELMATIC > PELMA

PELMET n ornamental drapery or board, concealing a curtain rail

PELMETS > PELMET

PELOID n mud used therapeutically

PELOIDS > PELOID

PELOLOGY n study of

P

therapeutic uses of mud

PELON *adj* hairless

PELORIA *n* abnormal production of actinomorphic flowers in a plant of a species that usually produces zygomorphic flowers

PELORIAN > PELORIA

PELORIAS > PELORIA

PELORIC > PELORIA

PELORIES > PELORY

PELORISED *adj* affected by peloria

PELORISM *n* floral mutation

PELORISMS > PELORISM

PELORIZED *same as* > PELORISED

PELORUS *n* sighting device used in conjunction with a magnetic compass or a gyrocompass for measuring the relative bearings of observed points

PELORUSES > PELORUS

PELORY *n* floral mutation

PELOTA *n* game played by two players who use a basket strapped to their wrists or a wooden racket to propel a ball against a specially marked wall

PELOTAS > PELOTA

PELOTON *n* main field of riders in a road race

PELOTONS > PELOTON

PELT *vb* throw missiles at ▷ *n* skin of a fur-bearing animal

PELTA *n* small ancient shield

PELTAE > PELTA

PELTAS > PELTA

PELTAST *n* (in ancient Greece) lightly armed foot soldier

PELTASTS > PELTAST

PELTATE *adj* (of leaves) having the stalk attached to the centre of the lower surface

PELTATELY > PELTATE

PELTATION > PELTATE

PELTED > PELT

PELTER > PELT *vb* rain heavily

PELTERED > PELT

PELTERING > PELT

PELTERS > PELT

PELTING > PELT

PELTINGLY > PELT

PELTINGS > PELT

PELTLESS > PELT

PELTRIES > PELTRY

PELTRY *n* pelts of animals collectively

PELTS > PELT

PELVES > PELVIS

PELVIC *adj* of, near, or relating to the pelvis ▷ *n* pelvic bone

PELVICS > PELVIC

PELVIFORM *adj* shaped like pelvis

PELVIS *n* framework of bones at the base of the

spine, to which the hips are attached

PELVISES > PELVIS

PEMBINA *n* type of cranberry

PEMBINAS > PEMBINA

PEMBROKE *n* small table

PEMBROKES > PEMBROKE

PEMICAN *same as* > PEMMICAN

PEMICANS > PEMICAN

PEMMICAN *n* small pressed cake of shredded dried meat, pounded into paste with fat and berries or dried fruits

PEMMICANS > PEMMICAN

PEMOLINE *n* mild stimulant

PEMOLINES > PEMOLINE

PEMPHIGUS *n* any of a group of blistering skin diseases

PEMPHIX *n* type of crustacean

PEMPHIXES > PEMPHIX

PEN *n* instrument for writing in ink ▷ *vb* write or compose

PENAL *adj* of or used in punishment

PENALISE *same as* > PENALIZE

PENALISED > PENALISE

PENALISES > PENALISE

PENALITY > PENAL

PENALIZE *vb* impose a penalty on

PENALIZED > PENALIZE

PENALIZES > PENALIZE

PENALLY > PENAL

PENALTIES > PENALTY

PENALTY *n* punishment for a crime or offence

PENANCE *n* voluntary self-punishment to make amends for wrongdoing ▷ *vb* (of ecclesiastical authorities) impose a penance upon (a sinner)

PENANCED > PENANCE

PENANCES > PENANCE

PENANCING > PENANCE

PENANG *variant of* > PINANG

PENANGS > PENANG

PENATES *pl n* household gods

PENCE > PENNY

PENCEL *n* small pennon, originally one carried by a knight's squire

PENCELS > PENCEL

PENCES > PENNY

PENCHANT *n* inclination or liking

PENCHANTS > PENCHANT

PENCIL *n* thin cylindrical instrument containing graphite, for writing or drawing ▷ *vb* draw, write, or mark with a pencil

PENCILED > PENCIL

PENCILER > PENCIL

PENCILERS > PENCIL

PENCILING > PENCIL

PENCILLED > PENCIL

PENCILLER > PENCIL

PENCILS > PENCIL

PENCRAFT *n* skill in writing

PENCRAFTS > PENCRAFT

PEND *vb* await judgment or settlement ▷ *n* archway or vaulted passage

PENDANT *n* ornament worn on a chain round the neck

PENDANTLY > PENDANT

PENDANTS > PENDANT

PENDED > PEND

PENDENCY > PENDENT

PENDENT *adj* hanging ▷ *n* pendant

PENDENTLY > PENDENT

PENDENTS > PENDENT

PENDICLE *n* something dependent on another

PENDICLER *n* person who rents a croft

PENDICLES > PENDICLE

PENDING *prep* while waiting for ▷ *adj* not yet decided or settled

PENDRAGON *n* supreme war chief or leader of the ancient Britons

PENDS > PEND

PENDU *adj* in informal Indian English, culturally backward

PENDULAR *adj* pendulous

PENDULATE *vb* swing as pendulum

PENDULE *n* manoeuvre by which a climber on a rope from above swings in a pendulum-like series of movements to reach another line of ascent

PENDULES > PENDULE

PENDULINE *adj* building nests that hang down

PENDULOUS *adj* hanging, swinging

PENDULUM *same as* > PENDULE

PENDULUMS > PENDULUM

PENE *variant of* > PEEN

PENED > PENE

PENEPLAIN *n* relatively flat land surface produced by a long period of erosion

PENEPLANE *same as* > PENEPLAIN

PENES > PENIS

PENETRANT *adj* sharp ▷ *n* substance that lowers the surface tension of a liquid and thus causes it to penetrate or be absorbed more easily

PENETRATE *vb* find or force a way into or through

PENFOLD *same as* > PINFOLD

PENFOLDS > PENFOLD

PENFUL *n* contents of pen

PENFULS > PENFUL

PENGO *n* standard monetary unit of Hungary, replaced by the forint in 1946

PENGOS > PENGO

PENGUIN *n* flightless black-and-white sea bird of the southern hemisphere

PENGUINRY *n* breeding place of penguins

PENGUINS > PENGUIN

PENHOLDER *n* container for

pens

PENI *old spelling of* > PENNY

PENIAL > PENIS

PENICIL *n* small pad for wounds

PENICILS > PENICIL

PENIE *old spelling of* > PENNY

PENIES > PENIE

PENILE *adj* of or relating to the penis

PENILL > PENILLION

PENILLION *pl n* Welsh art or practice of singing poetry in counterpoint to a traditional melody played on the harp

PENING > PENE

PENINSULA *n* strip of land nearly surrounded by water

PENIS *n* organ of copulation and urination in male mammals

PENISES > PENIS

PENISTONE *n* coarse woollen cloth

PENITENCE > PENITENT

PENITENCY > PENITENT

PENITENT *adj* feeling sorry for having done wrong ▷ *n* someone who is penitent

PENITENTS > PENITENT

PENK *n* small fish

PENKNIFE *n* small knife with blade(s) that fold into the handle

PENKNIVES > PENKNIFE

PENKS > PENK

PENLIGHT *n* small thin flashlight

PENLIGHTS > PENLIGHT

PENLITE *same as* > PENLIGHT

PENLITES > PENLITE

PENMAN *n* person skilled in handwriting

PENMEN > PENMAN

PENNA *n* any large feather that has a vane and forms part of the main plumage of a bird

PENNAE > PENNA

PENNAL *n* first-year student of Protestant university

PENNALISM *n* menial choring at college

PENNALS > PENNAL

PENNAME *n* author's pseudonym

PENNAMES > PENNAME

PENNANT *same as* > PENDANT

PENNANTS > PENNANT

PENNATE *adj* having feathers, wings, or winglike structures

PENNATED *same as* > PENNATE

PENNATULA *n* sea pen

PENNE *n* pasta in the form of short tubes

PENNED > PEN

PENNEECH *n* card game

PENNEECHS > PENNEECH

PENNEECK *same as* > PENNEECH

PENNEECKS > PENNEECK

PENNER *n* person who

writes
PENNERS > PENNER
PENNES > PENNE
PENNI n former Finnish monetary unit worth one hundredth of a markka
PENNIA > PENNI
PENNIED adj having money
PENNIES > PENNY
PENNIFORM adj shaped like a feather
PENNILESS adj very poor
PENNILL n stanza in a Welsh poem
PENNINE n mineral found in the Pennine Alps
PENNINES > PENNINE
PENNING > PEN
PENNINITE n bluish-green variety of chlorite occurring in the form of thick crystals
PENNIS > PENNI
PENNON n triangular or tapering flag
PENNONCEL n small narrow flag
PENNONED adj equipped with a pennon
PENNONS > PENNON
PENNY n British bronze coin worth one hundredth of a pound
PENNYBOY n employee whose duties include menial tasks, such as running errands
PENNYBOYS > PENNYBOY
PENNYFEE n small payment
PENNYFEES > PENNYFEE
PENNYLAND n old Scottish division of land
PENNYWISE adj careful with small amounts of money
PENNYWORT n Eurasian rock plant with whitish-green tubular flowers and rounded leaves
PENOCHE n type of fudge
PENOCHES > PENOCHE
PENOLOGY n study of punishment and prison management
PENONCEL n small narrow flag
PENONCELS > PENONCEL
PENPOINT n tip of pen
PENPOINTS > PENPOINT
PENPUSHER n person whose work involves a lot of boring paperwork
PENS > PEN
PENSEE n thought put down on paper
PENSEES > PENSEE
PENSEL same as > PENCEL
PENSELS > PENSEL
PENSIL same as > PENCEL
PENSILE adj designating or building a hanging nest
PENSILITY > PENSILE
PENSILS > PENSIL
PENSION n regular payment to people above a certain age, retired employees, widows, etc ▷ vb grant a pension to

PENSIONE n Italian boarding house
PENSIONED > PENSION
PENSIONER n person receiving a pension
PENSIONES > PENSIONE
PENSIONS > PENSION
PENSIVE adj deeply thoughtful, often with a tinge of sadness
PENSIVELY > PENSIVE
PENSTEMON n North American flowering plant with five stamens
PENSTER n writer
PENSTERS > PENSTER
PENSTOCK n conduit that supplies water to a hydroelectric power plant
PENSTOCKS > PENSTOCK
PENSUM n school exercise
PENSUMS > PENSUM
PENT n penthouse
PENTACLE same as > PENTAGRAM
PENTACLES > PENTACLE
PENTACT n sponge spicule with five rays
PENTACTS > PENTACT
PENTAD n group or series of five
PENTADIC > PENTAD
PENTADS > PENTAD
PENTAGON n geometric figure with five sides
PENTAGONS > PENTAGON
PENTAGRAM n five-pointed star
PENTALOGY n combination of five closely related symptoms
PENTALPHA n five-pointed star
PENTAMERY n state of consisting of five parts
PENTANE n alkane hydrocarbon with three isomers
PENTANES > PENTANE
PENTANGLE same as > PENTAGRAM
PENTANOIC as in pentanoic acid colourless liquid carboxylic acid
PENTANOL n colourless oily liquid
PENTANOLS > PENTANOL
PENTAPODY n series or measure of five feet
PENTARCH n member of pentarchy
PENTARCHS > PENTARCH
PENTARCHY n government by five rulers
PENTATHLA n pentathlons
PENTEL n ballpoint pen with free-flowing ink
PENTELS > PENTEL
PENTENE n colourless flammable liquid alkene with several straight-chained isomeric forms
PENTENES > PENTENE
PENTHIA n child born fifth
PENTHIAS > PENTHIA
PENTHOUSE n flat built on the roof or top floor of a

building
PENTICE vb accommodate in a penthouse
PENTICED > PENTICE
PENTICES > PENTICE
PENTICING > PENTICE
PENTISE same as > PENTICE
PENTISED > PENTISE
PENTISES > PENTISE
PENTISING > PENTISE
PENTITI > PENTITO
PENTITO n person involved in organized crime who offers information to the police in return for immunity from prosecution
PENTODE n electronic valve having five electrodes: a cathode, anode, and three grids
PENTODES > PENTODE
PENTOMIC adj denoting or relating to the subdivision of an army division into five battle groups, esp for nuclear warfare
PENTOSAN n polysaccharide occuring in plants, humus, etc
PENTOSANE same as > PENTOSAN
PENTOSANS > PENTOSAN
PENTOSE n monosaccharide containing five atoms of carbon per molecule
PENTOSES > PENTOSE
PENTOSIDE n compound containing sugar
PENTOXIDE n oxide of an element with five atoms of oxygen per molecule
PENTROOF n lean-to
PENTROOFS > PENTROOF
PENTS > PENT
PENTYL n one of a particular chemical group
PENTYLENE n type of chemical
PENTYLS > PENTYL
PENUCHE same as > PANOCHA
PENUCHES > PENUCHE
PENUCHI same as > PANOCHA
PENUCHIS > PENUCHI
PENUCHLE same as > PINOCHLE
PENUCHLES > PENUCHLE
PENUCKLE same as > PENUCHLE
PENUCKLES > PENUCKLE
PENULT n last syllable but one in a word
PENULTIMA same as > PENULT
PENULTS > PENULT
PENUMBRA n (in an eclipse) partially shadowed region which surrounds the full shadow
PENUMBRAE > PENUMBRA
PENUMBRAL > PENUMBRA
PENUMBRAS > PENUMBRA
PENURIES > PENURY
PENURIOUS adj niggardly with money
PENURY n extreme poverty
PENWOMAN n female writer

PENWOMEN > PENWOMAN
PEON n Spanish-American farm labourer or unskilled worker
PEONAGE n state of being a peon
PEONAGES > PEONAGE
PEONES > PEON
PEONIES > PEONY
PEONISM same as > PEONAGE
PEONISMS > PEONISM
PEONS > PEON
PEONY n garden plant with showy red, pink, or white flowers
PEOPLE pl n persons generally ▷ vb provide with inhabitants
PEOPLED > PEOPLE
PEOPLER n settler
PEOPLERS > PEOPLER
PEOPLES > PEOPLE
PEOPLING > PEOPLE
PEP n high spirits, energy, or enthusiasm ▷ vb liven by imbuing with new vigour
PEPERINO n type of volcanic rock
PEPERINOS > PEPERINO
PEPEROMIA n plant from tropical and subtropical America with slightly fleshy ornamental leaves
PEPERONI same as > PEPPERONI
PEPERONIS > PEPPERONI
PEPFUL adj full of vitality
PEPINO n purple-striped yellow fruit
PEPINOS > PEPINO
PEPLA > PEPLUM
PEPLOS n (in ancient Greece) top part of a woman's attire, caught at the shoulders and hanging in folds to the waist
PEPLOSES > PEPLOS
PEPLUM same as > PEPLOS
PEPLUMED > PEPLUM
PEPLUMS > PEPLUM
PEPLUS same as > PEPLOS
PEPLUSES > PEPLUS
PEPO n fruit such as the melon, squash, cucumber, or pumpkin
PEPONIDA variant of > PEPO
PEPONIDAS > PEPO
PEPONIUM variant of > PEPO
PEPONIUMS > PEPONIUM
PEPOS > PEPO
PEPPED > PEP
PEPPER n sharp hot condiment made from the fruit of an East Indian climbing plant ▷ vb season with pepper
PEPPERBOX n container for pepper
PEPPERED > PEPPER
PEPPERER > PEPPER
PEPPERERS > PEPPER
PEPPERIER > PEPPERY
PEPPERING > PEPPER
PEPPERONI n dry sausage of pork and beef spiced with pepper
PEPPERS > PEPPER

PEPPERY *adj* tasting of pepper

PEPPIER > PEPPY

PEPPIEST > PEPPY

PEPPILY > PEPPY

PEPPINESS > PEPPY

PEPPING > PEP

PEPPY *adj* full of vitality

PEPS > PEP

PEPSIN *n* enzyme produced in the stomach, which, when activated by acid, breaks down proteins

PEPSINATE *vb* treat (a patient) with pepsin

PEPSINE *same as* > PEPSIN

PEPSINES > PEPSINE

PEPSINS > PEPSIN

PEPTALK *n* talk meant to inspire ▷ *vb* give a peptalk to

PEPTALKED > PEPTALK

PEPTALKS > PEPTALK

PEPTIC *adj* relating to digestion or the digestive juices ▷ *n* substance that aids digestion

PEPTICITY > PEPTIC

PEPTICS > PEPTIC

PEPTID *variant of* > PEPTIDE

PEPTIDASE *n* any of a group of proteolytic enzymes that hydrolyse peptides to amino acids

PEPTIDE *n* compound consisting of two or more amino acids linked by chemical bonding between the amino group of one and the carboxyl group of another

PEPTIDES > PEPTIDE

PEPTIDIC *adj* of peptides

PEPTIDS > PEPTID

PEPTISE *same as* > PEPTIZE

PEPTISED > PEPTISE

PEPTISER > PEPTISE

PEPTISERS > PEPTISE

PEPTISES > PEPTISE

PEPTISING > PEPTISE

PEPTIZE *vb* disperse (a substance) into a colloidal state, usually to form a sol

PEPTIZED > PEPTIZE

PEPTIZER > PEPTIZE

PEPTIZERS > PEPTIZE

PEPTIZES > PEPTIZE

PEPTIZING > PEPTIZE

PEPTONE *n* any of a group of compounds that form an intermediary group in the digestion of proteins to amino acids

PEPTONES > PEPTONE

PEPTONIC > PEPTONE

PEPTONISE *same as* > PEPTONIZE

PEPTONIZE *vb* hydrolyse (a protein) to peptones by enzymic action, esp by pepsin or pancreatic extract

PEQUISTE *n* in Canada, member or supporter of the Parti Québécois

PEQUISTES > PEQUISTE

PER *prep* for each

PERACID *n* acid, such as perchloric acid, in which the element forming the acid radical exhibits its highest valency

PERACIDS > PERACID

PERACUTE *adj* very acute

PERAEA > PERAEON

PERAEON *same as* > PEREION

PERAEONS > PERAEON

PERAEOPOD *same as* > PEREIOPOD

PERAI *another name for* > PIRANHA

PERAIS > PERAI

PERBORATE *n* salt derived, or apparently derived, from perboric acid

PERCALE *n* close-textured woven cotton fabric, plain or printed, used esp for sheets

PERCALES > PERCALE

PERCALINE *n* fine light cotton fabric, used esp for linings

PERCASE *adv* perchance

PERCE *obsolete word for* > PIERCE

PERCEABLE *adj* pierceable

PERCEANT *adj* piercing

PERCED > PERCE

PERCEIVE *vb* become aware of (something) through the senses

PERCEIVED > PERCEIVE

PERCEIVER > PERCEIVE

PERCEIVES > PERCEIVE

PERCEN > PERCE

PERCENT *n* percentage or proportion

PERCENTAL > PERCENT

PERCENTS > PERCENT

PERCEPT *n* concept that depends on recognition by the senses, such as sight, of some external object or phenomenon

PERCEPTS > PERCEPT

PERCES > PERCE

PERCH *n* resting place for a bird ▷ *vb* alight, rest, or place on or as if on a perch

PERCHANCE *adv* perhaps

PERCHED > PERCH

PERCHER > PERCH

PERCHERON *n* compact heavy breed of carthorse

PERCHERS > PERCH

PERCHERY *n* barn in which hens are allowed to move without restriction

PERCHES > PERCH

PERCHING > PERCH

PERCHINGS > PERCH

PERCIFORM *adj* of perch-like fishes

PERCINE *adj* of perches

PERCING > PERCE

PERCOCT *adj* well-cooked

PERCOID *adj* of, relating to, or belonging to the *Percoidea*, a suborder of spiny-finned teleost fishes ▷ *n* any fish belonging to the suborder *Percoidea*

PERCOIDS > PERCOID

PERCOLATE *vb* pass or filter through small holes ▷ *n* product of percolation

PERCOLIN *n* pain-relieving drug

PERCOLINS > PERCOLIN

PERCUSS *vb* strike sharply, rapidly, or suddenly

PERCUSSED > PERCUSS

PERCUSSES > PERCUSS

PERCUSSOR > PERCUSS

PERDENDO *adj* (of music) getting gradually quieter and slower

PERDIE *adv* certainly

PERDITION *n* spiritual ruin

PERDU *adj* (of a soldier) placed on hazardous sentry duty ▷ *n* soldier placed on hazardous sentry duty

PERDUE *same as* > PERDU

PERDUES > PERDUE

PERDURE *vb* last for long time

PERDURED > PERDURE

PERDURES > PERDURE

PERDURING > PERDURE

PERDUS > PERDU

PERDY *adv* certainly

PERE *n* addition to a French surname to specify the father rather than the son of the same name

PEREA > PEREON

PEREGAL *adj* equal ▷ *n* equal

PEREGALS > PEREGAL

PEREGRIN *variant spelling of* > PEREGRINE

PEREGRINE *adj* coming from abroad

PEREGRINS > PEREGRIN

PEREIA > PEREION

PEREION *n* thorax of some crustaceans

PEREIONS > PEREION

PEREIOPOD *n* appendage of the pereion

PEREIRA *n* bark of a South American apocynaceous tree

PEREIRAS > PEREIRA

PERENNATE *vb* (of plants) live from one growing season to another

PERENNIAL *adj* lasting through many years ▷ *n* plant lasting more than two years

PERENNITY *n* state of being perennial

PERENTIE *n* large dark-coloured Australian monitor lizard

PERENTIES > PERENTY

PERENTY *same as* > PERENTIE

PEREON *same as* > PEREION

PEREONS > PEREON

PEREOPOD *same as* > PEREIOPOD

PEREOPODS > PEREOPOD

PERES > PERE

PERFAY *interj* by my faith

PERFECT *adj* having all the essential elements ▷ *n* perfect tense ▷ *vb* improve

PERFECTA *n* bet on the order of the first and second in a race

PERFECTAS > PERFECTA

PERFECTED > PERFECT

PERFECTER *same as* > PERFECTOR

PERFECTI *n* ascetic group of elite Cathars

PERFECTLY *adv* completely, utterly, or absolutely

PERFECTO *n* large cigar that is tapered from both ends

PERFECTOR *n* person who completes or makes something perfect

PERFECTOS > PERFECTO

PERFECTS > PERFECT

PERFERVID *adj* extremely ardent, enthusiastic, or zealous

PERFERVOR *n* zealous person

PERFET *obsolete variant of* > PERFECT

PERFIDIES > PERFIDY

PERFIDY *n* perfidious act

PERFIN *former name for* > SPIF

PERFING *n* practice of taking early retirement, with financial compensation, from the police force

PERFINGS > PERFING

PERFINS > PERFIN

PERFORANS *adj* perforating or penetrating

PERFORANT *adj* perforating

PERFORATE *vb* make holes in ▷ *adj* pierced by small holes

PERFORCE *adv* of necessity

PERFORM *vb* carry out (an action)

PERFORMED > PERFORM

PERFORMER > PERFORM

PERFORMS > PERFORM

PERFUME *n* liquid cosmetic worn for its pleasant smell ▷ *vb* give a pleasant smell to

PERFUMED > PERFUME

PERFUMER *n* person who makes or sells perfume

PERFUMERS > PERFUMER

PERFUMERY *n* perfumes in general

PERFUMES > PERFUME

PERFUMIER *same as* > PERFUMER

PERFUMING > PERFUME

PERFUMY *adj* like perfume

PERFUSATE *n* fluid flowing through tissue or organ

PERFUSE *vb* permeate (a liquid, colour, etc) through or over (something)

PERFUSED > PERFUSE

PERFUSES > PERFUSE

PERFUSING > PERFUSE

PERFUSION > PERFUSE

PERFUSIVE > PERFUSE

PERGOLA *n* arch or framework of trellis supporting climbing plants

PERGOLAS > PERGOLA

PERGUNNAH *same*

as > PARGANA

PERHAPS *adv* possibly, maybe ▷ *sentence substitute* it may happen, be so, etc ▷ *n* something that might have happened

PERHAPSES > PERHAPS

PERI *n* (in Persian folklore) one of a race of beautiful supernatural beings

PERIAGUA *n* dugout canoe

PERIAGUAS > PERIAGUA

PERIAKTOI > PERIAKTOS

PERIAKTOS *n* ancient device for changing theatre scenery

PERIANTH *n* outer part of a flower

PERIANTHS > PERIANTH

PERIAPSES > PERIAPSIS

PERIAPSIS *n* closest point to a central body reached by a body in orbit

PERIAPT *n* charm or amulet

PERIAPTS > PERIAPT

PERIBLAST *n* tissue surrounding blastoderm in meroblastic eggs

PERIBLEM *n* layer of meristematic tissue in stems and roots that gives rise to the cortex

PERIBLEMS > PERIBLEM

PERIBOLI > PERIBOLOS

PERIBOLOI > PERIBOLOS

PERIBOLOS *n* enclosed court surrounding ancient temple

PERIBOLUS *same as* > PERIBOLOS

PERICARP *n* part of a fruit enclosing the seed that develops from the wall of the ovary

PERICARPS > PERICARP

PERICLASE *n* mineral consisting of magnesium oxide in the form of isometric crystals or grains

PERICLINE *n* white translucent variety of albite in the form of elongated crystals

PERICON *n* Argentinian dance

PERICONES > PERICON

PERICOPAE > PERICOPE

PERICOPAL > PERICOPE

PERICOPE *n* selection from a book, esp a passage from the Bible read at religious services

PERICOPES > PERICOPE

PERICOPIC > PERICOPE

PERICYCLE *n* layer of plant tissue beneath the endodermis

PERIDERM *n* outer corky protective layer of woody stems and roots

PERIDERMS > PERIDERM

PERIDIA > PERIDIUM

PERIDIAL > PERIDIUM

PERIDINIA *n* genus of flagellate organisms

PERIDIUM *n* distinct outer layer of the spore-bearing organ in many fungi

PERIDIUMS > PERIDIUM

PERIDOT *n* pale green transparent gemstone

PERIDOTE *same as* > PERIDOT

PERIDOTES > PERIDOTE

PERIDOTIC > PERIDOT

PERIDOTS > PERIDOT

PERIDROME *n* space between the columns and inner room of a classical temple

PERIGEAL > PERIGEE

PERIGEAN > PERIGEE

PERIGEE *n* point in the orbit of the moon or a satellite that is nearest the earth

PERIGEES > PERIGEE

PERIGON *n* angle of 360°

PERIGONE *n* part enclosing the essential organs of a flower

PERIGONES > PERIGONE

PERIGONIA *n* perigones

PERIGONS > PERIGON

PERIGYNY *n* (of a flower) condition of having a concave or flat receptacle with the gynoecium and other floral parts at the same level

PERIHELIA *n* points in the orbits of planets at which they are nearest the sun

PERIKARYA *n* parts of nerve cells that contain the nuclei

PERIL *n* great danger ▷ *vb* expose to danger

PERILED > PERIL

PERILING > PERIL

PERILLA *n* type of mint

PERILLAS > PERILLA

PERILLED > PERIL

PERILLING > PERIL

PERILOUS *adj* very hazardous or dangerous

PERILS > PERIL

PERILUNE *n* point in a lunar orbit when a spacecraft launched from the moon is nearest the moon

PERILUNES > PERILUNE

PERILYMPH *n* fluid filling the space between the membranous and bony labyrinths of the internal ear

PERIMETER *n* outer edge of an area

PERIMETRY > PERIMETER

PERIMORPH *n* mineral that encloses another mineral of a different type

PERIMYSIA *n* sheaths of fibrous connective tissue surrounding the primary bundles of muscle fibres

PERINAEUM *same as* > PERINEUM

PERINATAL *adj* of or in the weeks shortly before or after birth

PERINEA > PERINEUM

PERINEAL > PERINEUM

PERINEUM *n* region of the body between the anus and the genitals

PERINEUMS > PERINEUM

PERIOD *n* particular portion of time ▷ *adj* (of furniture, dress, a play, etc) dating from or in the style of an earlier time ▷ *vb* divide into periods

PERIODATE *n* any salt or ester of a periodic acid

PERIODED > PERIOD

PERIODIC *adj* recurring at intervals

PERIODID *n* kind of iodide

PERIODIDE *variant of* > PERIODID

PERIODIDS > PERIODID

PERIODING > PERIOD

PERIODS > PERIOD

PERIOST *n* thick fibrous two-layered membrane covering the surface of bones

PERIOSTEA > PERIOSTS

PERIOSTS > PERIOST

PERIOTIC *adj* of or relating to the structures situated around the internal ear ▷ *n* periotic bone

PERIOTICS > PERIOTIC

PERIPATUS *n* wormlike arthropod with a segmented body and short unjointed limbs

PERIPETIA *n* abrupt turn of events or reversal of circumstances

PERIPETY *same as* > PERIPETEIA

PERIPHERY *n* boundary or edge

PERIPLASM *n* region inside wall of biological cell

PERIPLAST *n* nutritive and supporting tissue in animal organ

PERIPLUS *n* circumnavigation

PERIPROCT *n* tough membrane surrounding anus in echinoderms

PERIPTER *n* type of ancient temple

PERIPTERS > PERIPTER

PERIPTERY *n* region surrounding moving body

PERIQUE *n* strong highly-flavoured tobacco cured in its own juices and grown in Louisiana

PERIQUES > PERIQUE

PERIS > PERI

PERISARC *n* outer chitinous layer secreted by colonial hydrozoan coelenterates

PERISARCS > PERISARC

PERISCIAN *adj* person whose shadow moves round every point of compass during day

PERISCOPE *n* instrument used, esp in submarines, to give a view of objects on a different level

PERISH *vb* be destroyed or die

PERISHED *adj* (of a person, part of the body, etc) extremely cold

PERISHER *n* mischievous person

PERISHERS > PERISHER

PERISHES > PERISH

PERISHING *adj* very cold

PERISPERM *n* nutritive tissue surrounding the embryo in certain seeds, and developing from the nucellus of the ovule

PERISTOME *n* fringe of pointed teeth surrounding the opening of a moss capsule

PERISTYLE *n* colonnade that surrounds a court or building

PERITI > PERITUS

PERITONEA *n* thin translucent serous sacs that line the walls of abdominal cavities and cover the viscera

PERITRACK *another name for* > TAXIWAY

PERITRICH *n* ciliate protozoan in which the cilia are restricted to a spiral around the mouth

PERITUS *n* Catholic theology consultant

PERIWIG *same as* > PERUKE

PERIWIGS > PERIWIG

PERJINK *adj* prim or finicky

PERJURE *vb* render (oneself) guilty of perjury

PERJURED *adj* having sworn falsely

PERJURER > PERJURE

PERJURERS > PERJURE

PERJURES > PERJURE

PERJURIES > PERJURY

PERJURING > PERJURE

PERJUROUS > PERJURY

PERJURY *n* act or crime of lying while under oath in a court

PERK *n* incidental benefit gained from a job, such as a company car ▷ *adj* pert ▷ *vb* (of coffee) percolate

PERKED > PERK

PERKIER > PERKY

PERKIEST > PERKY

PERKILY > PERKY

PERKIN *same as* > PARKIN

PERKINESS > PERKY

PERKING > PERK

PERKINS > PERKIN

PERKISH *adj* perky

PERKS > PERK

PERKY *adj* lively or cheerful

PERLEMOEN *n* edible sea creature with a shell lined with mother of pearl

PERLITE *n* variety of obsidian consisting of masses of small pearly globules

PERLITES > PERLITE

PERLITIC > PERLITE

PERLOUS *same as* > PERILOUS

PERM *n* long-lasting curly hairstyle produced by treating the hair with chemicals ▷ *vb* give (hair) a perm

PERMALLOY *n* any of various alloys containing iron and nickel

PERMANENT *adj* lasting forever

PERMEABLE *adj* able to be permeated, esp by liquid

PERMEABLY > PERMEABLE

PERMEANCE *n* act of permeating

PERMEANT > PERMEANCE

PERMEANTS > PERMEANCE

PERMEASE *n* carrier protein

PERMEASES > PERMEASE

PERMEATE *vb* pervade or pass through the whole of (something)

PERMEATED > PERMEATE

PERMEATES > PERMEATE

PERMEATOR > PERMEATE

PERMED > PERM

PERMIAN *adj* of, denoting, or formed in the last period of the Palaeozoic era

PERMIE *n* person, esp an office worker, employed by a firm on a permanent basis

PERMIES > PERMIE

PERMING > PERM

PERMIT *vb* give permission, allow ▷ *n* document giving permission to do something

PERMITS > PERMIT

PERMITTED > PERMIT

PERMITTEE *n* person given a permit

PERMITTER > PERMIT

PERMS > PERM

PERMUTATE *vb* alter the sequence or arrangement (of)

PERMUTE *vb* change the sequence of

PERMUTED > PERMUTE

PERMUTES > PERMUTE

PERMUTING > PERMUTE

PERN *n* type of buzzard

PERNANCY *n* receiving of rents

PERNIO *n* chilblain

PERNIONES > PERNIO

PERNOD *n* aniseed-flavoured aperitif from France

PERNODS > PERNOD

PERNS > PERN

PERONE *n* fibula

PERONEAL *adj* of or relating to the fibula or the outer side of the leg

PERONES > PERONE

PERONEUS *n* lateral muscle of the leg

PERORAL *adj* administered through mouth

PERORALLY > PERORAL

PERORATE *vb* speak at length, esp in a formal manner

PERORATED > PERORATE

PERORATES > PERORATE

PERORATOR > PERORATE

PEROVSKIA *n* Russian sage

PEROXID *variant*

of > PEROXIDE

PEROXIDE *n* hydrogen peroxide used as a hair bleach ▷ *adj* bleached with or resembling peroxide ▷ *vb* bleach (the hair) with peroxide

PEROXIDED > PEROXIDE

PEROXIDES > PEROXIDE

PEROXIDIC > PEROXIDE

PEROXIDS > PEROXID

PEROXO *n* type of acid

PEROXY *adj* containing the peroxide group

PERP *n* informal US and Canadian word for someone who has committed a crime

PERPEND *n* large stone that passes through a wall from one side to the other ▷ *vb* ponder

PERPENDED > PERPEND

PERPENDS > PERPEND

PERPENT *same as* > PERPEND

PERPENTS > PERPENT

PERPETUAL *adj* lasting forever ▷ *n* (of a crop plant) continually producing edible parts

PERPLEX *vb* puzzle, bewilder

PERPLEXED > PERPLEX

PERPLEXER > PERPLEX

PERPLEXES > PERPLEX

PERPS > PERP

PERRADIAL *adj* situated around radii of radiate

PERRADII > PERRADIUS

PERRADIUS *n* primary tentacle of a polyp

PERRIER *n* short mortar

PERRIERS > PERRIER

PERRIES > PERRY

PERRON *n* external flight of steps, esp one at the front entrance of a building

PERRONS > PERRON

PERRUQUE *old spelling of* > PERUKE

PERRUQUES > PERRUQUE

PERRY *n* alcoholic drink made from fermented pears

PERSALT *n* any salt of a peracid

PERSALTS > PERSALT

PERSANT *adj* piercing

PERSAUNT *adj* piercing

PERSE *old variant of* > PIERCE

PERSECUTE *vb* treat cruelly because of race, religion, etc

PERSEITY *n* quality of having substance independently of real objects

PERSELINE *same as* > PURSLANE

PERSES > PERSE

PERSEVERE *vb* keep making an effort despite difficulties

PERSICO *same as* > PERSICOT

PERSICOS > PERSICO

PERSICOT *n* cordial made from apricots

PERSICOTS > PERSICOT

PERSIENNE *n* printed calico

PERSIMMON *n* sweet red tropical fruit

PERSING > PERSE

PERSIST *vb* continue to be or happen, last

PERSISTED > PERSIST

PERSISTER > PERSIST

PERSISTS > PERSIST

PERSON *n* human being

PERSONA *n* someone's personality as presented to others

PERSONAE > PERSONA

PERSONAGE *n* important person

PERSONAL *adj* individual or private ▷ *n* item of movable property

PERSONALS > PERSONAL

PERSONAS > PERSONA

PERSONATE *vb* assume the identity of (another person) with intent to deceive ▷ *adj* (of the corollas of certain flowers) having two lips in the form of a face

PERSONIFY *vb* give human characteristics to

PERSONISE *same as* > PERSONIZE

PERSONIZE *vb* personify

PERSONNED *adj* manned

PERSONNEL *n* people employed in an organization

PERSONS > PERSON

PERSPEX *n* tradename for any of various clear acrylic resins, used chiefly as a substitute for glass

PERSPEXES > PERSPEX

PERSPIRE *vb* sweat

PERSPIRED > PERSPIRE

PERSPIRES > PERSPIRE

PERSPIRY *adj* perspiring

PERST *adj* perished

PERSUADE *vb* make (someone) do something by argument, charm, etc

PERSUADED > PERSUADE

PERSUADER > PERSUADE

PERSUADES > PERSUADE

PERSUE *obsolete form of* > PURSUE

PERSUED > PERSUE

PERSUES > PERSUE

PERSUING > PERSUE

PERSWADE *obsolete form of* > PERSUADE

PERSWADED > PERSWADE

PERSWADES > PERSWADE

PERT *adj* saucy and cheeky ▷ *n* pert person

PERTAIN *vb* belong or be relevant (to)

PERTAINED > PERTAIN

PERTAINS > PERTAIN

PERTAKE *obsolete form of* > PARTAKE

PERTAKEN > PERTAKE

PERTAKES > PERTAKE

PERTAKING > PERTAKE

PERTER > PERT

PERTEST > PERT

PERTHITE *n* type of feldspar

PERTHITES > PERTHITE

PERTHITIC > PERTHITE

PERTINENT *adj* relevant

PERTLY > PERT

PERTNESS > PERT

PERTOOK > PERTAKE

PERTS > PERT

PERTURB *vb* disturb greatly

PERTURBED > PERTURB

PERTURBER > PERTURB

PERTURBS > PERTURB

PERTUSATE *adj* pierced at apex

PERTUSE *adj* having holes

PERTUSED *adj* having holes

PERTUSION *n* punched hole

PERTUSSAL > PERTUSSIS

PERTUSSES > PERTUSSIS

PERTUSSIS *n* whooping cough

PERUKE *n* wig for men worn in the 17th and 18th centuries

PERUKED *adj* wearing wig

PERUKES > PERUKE

PERUSABLE > PERUSE

PERUSAL > PERUSE

PERUSALS > PERUSE

PERUSE *vb* read in a careful or leisurely manner

PERUSED > PERUSE

PERUSER > PERUSE

PERUSERS > PERUSE

PERUSES > PERUSE

PERUSING > PERUSE

PERV *n* pervert ▷ *vb* give a person an erotic look

PERVADE *vb* spread right through (something)

PERVADED > PERVADE

PERVADER > PERVADE

PERVADERS > PERVADE

PERVADES > PERVADE

PERVADING > PERVADE

PERVASION > PERVADE

PERVASIVE *adj* pervading or tending to pervade

PERVE *same as* > PERV

PERVED > PERV

PERVERSE *adj* deliberately doing something different from what is thought normal or proper

PERVERSER > PERVERSE

PERVERT *vb* use or alter for a wrong purpose ▷ *n* person who practises sexual perversion

PERVERTED *adj* deviating greatly from what is regarded as normal or right

PERVERTER > PERVERT

PERVERTS > PERVERT

PERVES > PERV

PERVIATE *vb* perforate or burrow

PERVIATED > PERVIATE

PERVIATES > PERVIATE

PERVICACY *n* obstinacy

PERVING > PERV

PERVIOUS *adj* able to be penetrated, permeable

PERVS > PERV

PES *n* animal part corresponding to the human foot

PESADE *n* position in which

the horse stands on the hind legs with the forelegs in the air

PESADES > PESADE

PESANT *obsolete spelling of* > PEASANT

PESANTE *adv* to be performed clumsily

PESANTS > PESANT

PESAUNT *obsolete spelling of* > PEASANT

PESAUNTS > PESAUNT

PESETA *n* former monetary unit of Spain

PESETAS > PESETA

PESEWA *n* Ghanaian monetary unit worth one hundredth of a cedi

PESEWAS > PESEWA

PESHWA *same as* > PEISHWA

PESHWAS > PESHWA

PESKIER > PESKY

PESKIEST > PESKY

PESKILY > PESKY

PESKINESS > PESKY

PESKY *adj* troublesome

PESO *n* monetary unit of Argentina, Mexico, etc

PESOS > PESO

PESSARIES > PESSARY

PESSARY *n* appliance worn in the vagina, either to prevent conception or to support the womb

PESSIMA *n* lowest point

PESSIMAL *adj* (of animal's environment) least favourable for survival

PESSIMISM *n* tendency to expect the worst in all things

PESSIMIST > PESSIMISM

PESSIMUM *same as* > PESSIMAL

PEST *n* annoying person

PESTER *vb* annoy or nag continually

PESTERED > PESTER

PESTERER > PESTER

PESTERERS > PESTER

PESTERING > PESTER

PESTEROUS *adj* inclined to annoy

PESTERS > PESTER

PESTFUL *adj* causing annoyance

PESTHOLE *n* breeding ground for disease

PESTHOLES > PESTHOLE

PESTHOUSE *n* hospital for treating persons with infectious diseases

PESTICIDE *n* chemical for killing insect pests

PESTIER > PESTY

PESTIEST > PESTY

PESTILENT *adj* annoying, troublesome

PESTLE *n* club-shaped implement for grinding things to powder in a mortar ▷ *vb* pound (a substance or object) with or as if with a pestle

PESTLED > PESTLE

PESTLES > PESTLE

PESTLING > PESTLE

PESTO *n* sauce for pasta, consisting of basil leaves, pine nuts, garlic, oil, and Parmesan cheese, all crushed together

PESTOLOGY *n* study of pests

PESTOS > PESTO

PESTS > PEST

PESTY *adj* persistently annoying

PET *n* animal kept for pleasure and companionship ▷ *adj* kept as a pet ▷ *vb* treat as a pet

PETABYTE *n* in computing, 10^{15} or 2^{50} bytes

PETABYTES > PETABYTE

PETAHERTZ *n* very large unit of electrical frequency

PETAL *n* one of the brightly coloured outer parts of a flower

PETALED > PETAL

PETALINE > PETAL

PETALISM *n* ostracism in ancient Syracuse

PETALISMS > PETALISM

PETALLED > PETAL

PETALLIKE > PETAL

PETALODIC > PETALODY

PETALODY *n* condition in certain plants in which stamens or other parts of the flower assume the form and function of petals

PETALOID *adj* resembling a petal, esp in shape

PETALOUS *adj* bearing or having petals

PETALS > PETAL

PETANQUE *n* game, popular in France, in which metal bowls are thrown to land as near as possible to a target ball

PETANQUES > PETANQUE

PETAR *obsolete variant of* > PETARD

PETARA *n* clothes basket

PETARAS > PETARA

PETARD *n* device containing explosives used to breach a wall, doors, etc

PETARDS > PETARD

PETARIES > PETARY

PETARS > PETAR

PETARY *n* weapon for hurling stones

PETASOS *same as* > PETASUS

PETASOSES > PETASOS

PETASUS *n* broad-brimmed hat worn by the ancient Greeks

PETASUSES > PETASUS

PETAURINE *adj* similar to a flying phalanger

PETAURIST *n* flying phalanger

PETCHARY *n* type of kingbird

PETCOCK *n* small valve for checking the water level in a steam boiler or draining condensed steam from the cylinder of a steam engine

PETCOCKS > PETCOCK

PETECHIA *n* minute discoloured spot on

the surface of the skin or mucous membrane, caused by an underlying ruptured blood vessel

PETECHIAE > PETECHIA

PETECHIAL > PETECHIA

PETER *vb* fall (off) in volume, intensity, etc, and finally cease ▷ *n* act of petering

PETERED > PETER

PETERING > PETER

PETERMAN *n* burglar skilled in safe-breaking

PETERMEN > PETERMAN

PETERS > PETER

PETERSHAM *n* thick corded ribbon used to stiffen belts, button bands, etc

PETHER *old variant of* > PEDLAR

PETHERS > PETHER

PETHIDINE *n* white crystalline water-soluble drug used to relieve pain

PETILLANT *adj* (of wine) slightly effervescent

PETIOLAR > PETIOLE

PETIOLATE *adj* (of a plant or leaf) having a leafstalk

PETIOLE *n* stalk which attaches a leaf to a plant

PETIOLED > PETIOLE

PETIOLES > PETIOLE

PETIOLULE *n* stalk of any of the leaflets making up a compound leaf

PETIT *adj* of little or lesser importance

PETITE *adj* (of a woman) small and dainty ▷ *n* clothing size for small women

PETITES > PETITE

PETITION *n* formal request, esp one signed by many people and presented to parliament ▷ *vb* present a petition to

PETITIONS > PETITION

PETITORY *adj* soliciting

PETNAP *vb* steal pet

PETNAPER > PETNAP

PETNAPERS > PETNAP

PETNAPING > PETNAP

PETNAPPED > PETNAP

PETNAPPER > PETNAP

PETNAPS > PETNAP

PETRALE *n* type of sole

PETRALES > PETRALE

PETRARIES > PETRARY

PETRARY *n* weapon for hurling stones

PETRE *same as* > SALTPETRE

PETREL *n* sea bird with a hooked bill and tubular nostrils

PETRELS > PETREL

PETRES > PETRE

PETRIFIC *adj* petrifying

PETRIFIED > PETRIFY

PETRIFIER > PETRIFY

PETRIFIES > PETRIFY

PETRIFY *vb* frighten severely

PETROGENY *n* origin of rocks

PETROGRAM *n* prehistoric

rock painting

PETROL *n* flammable liquid obtained from petroleum, used as fuel in internal-combustion engines ▷ *vb* supply with petrol

PETROLAGE *n* addition of petrol (to a body of water) to get rid of mosquitoes

PETROLEUM *n* thick dark oil found underground

PETROLEUR *n* person using petrol to cause explosions

PETROLIC *adj* of, relating to, containing, or obtained from petroleum

PETROLLED > PETROL

PETROLOGY *n* study of the composition, origin, structure, and formation of rocks

PETROLS > PETROL

PETRONEL *n* firearm of large calibre used in the 16th and early 17th centuries, esp by cavalry soldiers

PETRONELS > PETRONEL

PETROSAL *adj* of, relating to, or situated near the dense part of the temporal bone that surrounds the inner ear ▷ *n* petrosal bone

PETROSALS > PETROSAL

PETROUS *adj* denoting the dense part of the temporal bone that surrounds the inner ear

PETS > PET

PETSAI *n* Chinese cabbage

PETSAIS > PETSAI

PETTABLE > PET

PETTED > PET

PETTEDLY > PET

PETTER > PET

PETTERS > PET

PETTI *n* petticoat

PETTICOAT *n* woman's skirt-shaped undergarment

PETTIER > PETTY

PETTIES > PETTI

PETTIEST > PETTY

PETTIFOG *vb* quibble or fuss over details

PETTIFOGS > PETTIFOG

PETTILY > PETTY

PETTINESS > PETTY

PETTING > PET

PETTINGS > PET

PETTISH *adj* peevish or fretful

PETTISHLY > PETTISH

PETTITOES *pl n* pig's trotters, esp when used as food

PETTLE *vb* pat animal

PETTLED > PETTLE

PETTLES > PETTLE

PETTLING > PETTLE

PETTO *n* breast of animal

PETTY *adj* unimportant, trivial

PETULANCE > PETULANT

PETULANCY > PETULANT

PETULANT *adj* childishly irritable or peevish

PETUNIA *n* garden plant

with funnel-shaped flowers

PETUNIAS > PETUNIA

PETUNTSE n fusible feldspathic mineral used in hard-paste porcelain

PETUNTSES > PETUNTSE

PETUNTZE same as > PETUNTSE

PETUNTZES > PETUNTZE

PEW n fixed benchlike seat in a church

PEWEE n any of several small North American flycatchers of the genus *Contopus*, having a greenish-brown plumage

PEWEES > PEWEE

PEWHOLDER n renter of pew

PEWIT another name for > LAPWING

PEWITS > PEWIT

PEWS > PEW

PEWTER n greyish metal made of tin and lead

PEWTERER > PEWTER

PEWTERERS > PEWTER

PEWTERS > PEWTER

PEYOTE another name for > MESCAL

PEYOTES > PEYOTE

PEYOTISM n ritual use of peyote

PEYOTISMS > PEYOTISM

PEYOTIST n person who uses peyote

PEYOTISTS > PEYOTIST

PEYOTL same as > PEYOTE

PEYOTLS > PEYOTL

PEYSE vb weight or poise

PEYSED > PEYSE

PEYSES > PEYSE

PEYSING > PEYSE

PEYTRAL same as > PEYTREL

PEYTRALS > PEYTRAL

PEYTREL n breastplate of horse's armour

PEYTRELS > PEYTREL

PEZANT obsolete spelling of > PEASANT

PEZANTS > PEZANT

PEZIZOID adj having cup-like form

PFENNIG n former German monetary unit worth one hundredth of a mark

PFENNIGE > PFENNIG

PFENNIGS > PFENNIG

PFENNING old variant of > PFENNIG

PFENNINGS > PFENNING

PFFT interj sound indicating sudden disappearance of something

PFUI interj phooey

PHACELIA n plant grown for its large, deep blue bell flowers

PHACELIAS > PHACELIA

PHACOID adj lentil- or lens-shaped

PHACOIDAL same as > PHACOID

PHACOLITE n colourless variety of chabazite

PHACOLITH n lens-shaped igneous rock structure

PHAEIC adj (of animals) having dusky coloration

PHAEISM > PHAEIC

PHAEISMS > PHAEIC

PHAENOGAM n seed-bearing plant

PHAETON n light four-wheeled horse-drawn carriage with or without a top

PHAETONS > PHAETON

PHAGE n virus that is parasitic in a bacterium and multiplies within its host, which is destroyed when the new viruses are released

PHAGEDENA n rapidly spreading ulcer that destroys tissues as it increases in size

PHAGES > PHAGE

PHAGOCYTE n cell or protozoan that engulfs particles, such as microorganisms

PHAGOSOME n part of biological cell

PHALANGAL > PHALANGE

PHALANGE another name for > PHALANX

PHALANGER same as > POSSUM

PHALANGES > PHALANX

PHALANGID n type of arachnid

PHALANX n closely grouped mass of people

PHALANXES > PHALANX

PHALAROPE n aquatic shore bird of northern oceans and lakes

PHALLI > PHALLUS

PHALLIC adj of or resembling a phallus

PHALLIN n poisonous substance from mushroom

PHALLINS > PHALLIN

PHALLISM n worship or veneration of the phallus

PHALLISMS > PHALLISM

PHALLIST > PHALLICISM

PHALLISTS > PHALLICISM

PHALLOID adj resembling penis

PHALLUS n penis, esp as a symbol of reproductive power in primitive rites

PHALLUSES > PHALLUS

PHANG old variant spelling of > FANG

PHANGED > PHANG

PHANGING > PHANG

PHANGS > PHANG

PHANSIGAR n Indian assassin

PHANTASIM same as > PHANTASM

PHANTASM n unreal vision, illusion

PHANTASMA same as > PHANTASM

PHANTASMS > PHANTASM

PHANTAST same as > FANTAST

PHANTASTS > PHANTAST

PHANTASY same

as > FANTASY

PHANTOM n ghost ▷ adj deceptive or unreal

PHANTOMS > PHANTOM

PHANTOMY adj of phantoms

PHANTOSME old spelling of > PHANTASM

PHARAOH n ancient Egyptian king

PHARAOHS > PHARAOH

PHARAONIC > PHARAOH

PHARE n beacon tower

PHARES > PHARE

PHARISAIC n righteously hypocritical

PHARISEE n self-righteous or hypocritical person

PHARISEES > PHARISEE

PHARMA n pharmaceutical companies considered together as an industry

PHARMACY n preparation and dispensing of drugs and medicines

PHARMAS > PHARMA

PHARMING n practice of rearing or growing genetically-modified animals or plants in order to develop pharmaceutical products

PHARMINGS > PHARMING

PHAROS n lighthouse

PHAROSES > PHAROS

PHARYNGAL adj of, relating to, or situated in or near the pharynx

PHARYNGES > PHARYNX

PHARYNX n cavity forming the back part of the mouth

PHARYNXES > PHARYNX

PHASE n any distinct or characteristic stage in a development or chain of events ▷ vb arrange or carry out in stages or to coincide with something else

PHASEAL > PHASE

PHASED > PHASE

PHASEDOWN n gradual reduction

PHASELESS > PHASE

PHASEOLIN n anti-fungal substance from kidney bean

PHASEOUT n gradual reduction

PHASEOUTS > PHASEOUT

PHASES > PHASE

PHASIC > PHASE

PHASING n tonal sweep achieved by varying the phase relationship of two similar audio signals by mechanical or electronic means

PHASINGS > PHASING

PHASIS another word for > PHASE

PHASMID n stick insect or leaf insect

PHASMIDS > PHASMID

PHASOR n rotating vector representing a quantity, such as an alternating current or voltage, that

varies sinusoidally

PHASORS > PHASOR

PHAT adj terrific

PHATIC adj (of speech, esp of conversational phrases) used to establish social contact and to express sociability rather than specific meaning

PHATTER > PHAT

PHATTEST > PHAT

PHEASANT n game bird with bright plumage

PHEASANTS > PHEASANT

PHEAZAR old variant of > VIZIER

PHEAZARS > PHEAZAR

PHEER same as > FERE

PHEERE same as > FERE

PHEERES > PHEERE

PHEERS > PHEER

PHEESE vb worry

PHEESED > PHEESE

PHEESES > PHEESE

PHEESING > PHEESE

PHEEZE same as > PHEESE

PHEEZED > PHEEZE

PHEEZES > PHEEZE

PHEEZING > PHEEZE

PHELLEM technical name for > CORK

PHELLEMS > PHELLEM

PHELLOGEN n cork cambium

PHELLOID adj like cork

PHELONIA > PHELONION

PHELONION n vestment for an Orthodox priest

PHENACITE n colourless or white glassy mineral

PHENAKISM n deception

PHENAKITE same as > PHENACITE

PHENATE n ester or salt of phenol

PHENATES > PHENATE

PHENAZIN same as > PHENAZINE

PHENAZINE n yellow crystalline tricyclic compound

PHENAZINS > PHENAZIN

PHENE n genetically determined characteristic of organism

PHENES > PHENE

PHENETIC > PHENETICS

PHENETICS n system of classification based on similarities between organisms without regard to their evolutionary relationships

PHENETOL same as > PHENETOLE

PHENETOLE n colourless oily compound

PHENETOLS > PHENETOL

PHENGITE n type of alabaster

PHENGITES > PHENGITE

PHENIC adj of phenol

PHENIX same as > PHOENIX

PHENIXES > PHENIX

PHENOCOPY n noninheritable change in an organism that is caused by environmental influence during development but resembles the effects of a genetic mutation

PHENOGAM same as > PHAENOGAM

PHENOGAMS > PHENOGAM

PHENOL n chemical used in disinfectants and antiseptics

PHENOLATE vb treat or disinfect with phenol

PHENOLIC adj of, containing, or derived from phenol ▷ n derivative of phenol

PHENOLICS > PHENOLIC

PHENOLOGY n study of recurring phenomena, such as animal migration, esp as influenced by climatic conditions

PHENOLS > PHENOL

PHENOM n person or thing of outstanding abilities or qualities

PHENOMENA n phenomenons

PHENOMS > PHENOM

PHENOTYPE n physical form of an organism as determined by the interaction of its genetic make-up and its environment

PHENOXIDE n any of a class of salts of phenol

PHENOXY as in phenoxy resin any of a class of resins dervied from polyhydroxy ethers

PHENYL n chemical substance

PHENYLENE n compound derived from benzene

PHENYLIC > PHENYL

PHENYLS > PHENYL

PHENYTOIN n anticonvulsant drug

PHEON n barbed iron head of dart

PHEONS > PHEON

PHERESES > PHERESIS

PHERESIS n specialized form of blood donation

PHEROMONE n chemical substance, secreted externally by certain animals, such as insects, affecting the behaviour or physiology of other animals of the same species

PHESE same as > PHEESE

PHESED > PHESE

PHESES > PHESE

PHESING > PHESE

PHEW interj exclamation of relief, surprise, etc

PHI n 21st letter in the Greek alphabet

PHIAL n small bottle for medicine etc ▷ vb put in phial

PHIALLED > PHIAL

PHIALLING > PHIAL

PHIALS > PHIAL

PHILABEG same as > FILIBEG

PHILABEGS > PHILABEG

PHILAMOT variant of > FILEMOT

PHILAMOTS > PHILAMOT

PHILANDER vb (of a man) flirt or have many casual love affairs with women

PHILATELY n stamp collecting

PHILHORSE n last horse in a team

PHILIBEG variant spelling of > FILIBEG

PHILIBEGS > PHILIBEG

PHILIPPIC n bitter or impassioned speech of denunciation, invective

PHILISTIA n domain of cultural philistine

PHILLABEG same as > FILIBEG

PHILLIBEG same as > FILIBEG

PHILOGYNY n fondness for women

PHILOLOGY n science of the structure and development of languages

PHILOMATH n lover of learning

PHILOMEL n nightingale

PHILOMELA same as > PHILOMEL

PHILOMELS > PHILOMEL

PHILOMOT n colour of dead leaf

PHILOMOTS > PHILOMOT

PHILOPENA n gift made as forfeit in game

PHILTER vb drink supposed to arouse love, desire, etc ▷ vb arouse sexual or romantic feelings by means of a philter

PHILTERED > PHILTER

PHILTERS > PHILTER

PHILTRA > PHILTRUM

PHILTRE n magic drink supposed to arouse love in the person who drinks it ▷ vb mix with love potion

PHILTRED > PHILTRE

PHILTRES > PHILTRE

PHILTRING > PHILTRE

PHILTRUM n indentation above the upper lip

PHIMOSES > PHIMOSIS

PHIMOSIS n abnormal tightness of the foreskin, preventing its being retracted over the tip of the penis

PHIMOTIC > PHIMOSIS

PHINNOCK variant spelling of > FINNOCK

PHINNOCKS > PHINNOCK

PHIS > PHI

PHISHING n use of fraudulent e-mails and lookalike websites to extract personal and financial details for criminal purposes

PHISHINGS > PHISHING

PHISNOMY n physiognomy

PHIZ n face or a facial expression

PHIZES > PHIZ

PHIZOG same as > PHIZ

PHIZOGS > PHIZOG

PHIZZES > PHIZ

PHLEBITIC > PHLEBITIS

PHLEBITIS n inflammation of a vein

PHLEGM n thick yellowish substance formed in the nose and throat during a cold

PHLEGMIER > PHLEGM

PHLEGMON n inflammatory mass that may progress to abscess

PHLEGMONS > PHLEGMON

PHLEGMS > PHLEGM

PHLEGMY > PHLEGM

PHLOEM n plant tissue that acts as a path for the distribution of food substances to all parts of the plant

PHLOEMS > PHLOEM

PHLOMIS n plant of Phlomis genus

PHLOMISES > PHLOMIS

PHLORIZIN n chemical found in root bark of fruit trees

PHLOX n flowering garden plant

PHLOXES > PHLOX

PHLYCTENA n small blister, vesicle, or pustule

PHO n Vietnamese noodle soup

PHOBIA n intense and unreasoning fear or dislike

PHOBIAS > PHOBIA

PHOBIC adj of, relating to, or arising from a phobia ▷ n person suffering from a phobia

PHOBICS > PHOBIC

PHOBISM n phobia

PHOBISMS > PHOBISM

PHOBIST > PHOBISM

PHOBISTS > PHOBISM

PHOCA n genus of seals

PHOCAE > PHOCA

PHOCAS > PHOCA

PHOCINE adj of, relating to, or resembling a seal

PHOCOMELY n congenital deformity resulting from prenatal interference with the development of the fetal limbs, characterized esp by short stubby hands or feet attached close to the body

PHOEBE n greyish-brown North American flycatcher

PHOEBES > PHOEBE

PHOEBUS n sun

PHOEBUSES > PHOEBUS

PHOENIX n legendary bird said to set fire to itself and rise anew from its ashes

PHOENIXES > PHOENIX

PHOH variant of > FOH

PHOHS > PHOH

PHOLADES > PHOLAS

PHOLAS n type of bivalve mollusc

PHON n unit of loudness

PHONAL adj relating to voice

PHONATE vb articulate speech sounds, esp to cause the vocal cords to vibrate in the execution of a voiced speech sound

PHONATED > PHONATE

PHONATES > PHONATE

PHONATHON n telephone-based fund-raising campaign

PHONATING > PHONATE

PHONATION > PHONATE

PHONATORY > PHONATE

PHONE vb telephone ▷ n single uncomplicated speech sound

PHONECAM n digital camera incorporated in a mobile phone

PHONECAMS > PHONECAM

PHONECARD n card used to operate certain public telephones

PHONED > PHONE

PHONEME n one of the set of speech sounds in any given language that serve to distinguish one word from another

PHONEMES > PHONEME

PHONEMIC adj of or relating to the phoneme

PHONEMICS n classification and analysis of the phonemes of a language

PHONER n person making a telephone call

PHONERS > PHONER

PHONES > PHONE

PHONETIC adj of speech sounds

PHONETICS n science of speech sounds

PHONETISE same as > PHONETIZE

PHONETISM n phonetic writing

PHONETIST n person who advocates or uses a system of phonetic spelling

PHONETIZE vb represent by phonetic signs

PHONEY adj not genuine ▷ n phoney person or thing ▷ vb fake

PHONEYED > PHONEY

PHONEYING > PHONEY

PHONEYS > PHONEY

PHONIC > PHONICS

PHONICS n method of teaching people to read by training them to associate letters with their phonetic values

PHONIED > PHONY

PHONIER > PHONY

PHONIES > PHONY

PHONIEST > PHONY

PHONILY > PHONY

PHONINESS > PHONY

PHONING > PHONE

PHONMETER n instrument measuring sound levels

PHONO n phonograph

PHONOGRAM n any written symbol standing for

a sound, syllable, morpheme, or word

PHONOLITE n fine-grained volcanic igneous rock consisting of alkaline feldspars and nepheline

PHONOLOGY n study of the speech sounds in a language

PHONON n quantum of vibrational energy in the acoustic vibrations of a crystal lattice

PHONONS > PHONON

PHONOPORE n device for conveying sound

PHONOS > PHONO

PHONOTYPE n letter or symbol representing a sound

PHONOTYPY n transcription of speech into phonetic symbols

PHONS > PHON

PHONY vb fake

PHONYING > PHONY

PHOOEY interj exclamation of scorn or contempt

PHORATE n type of insecticide

PHORATES > PHORATE

PHORESIES > PHORESY

PHORESY n association in which one animal clings to another to ensure movement from place to place, as some mites use some insects

PHORMINX n ancient Greek stringed instrument

PHORMIUM n New Zealand plant with leathery evergreen leaves and red or yellow flowers in panicles

PHORMIUMS > PHORMIUM

PHORONID n small wormlike marine animal

PHORONIDS > PHORONID

PHOS > PHO

PHOSGENE n poisonous gas used in warfare

PHOSGENES > PHOSGENE

PHOSPHATE n compound of phosphorus

PHOSPHENE n sensation of light caused by pressure on the eyelid of a closed eye or by other mechanical or electrical interference with the visual system

PHOSPHID same as > PHOSPHIDE

PHOSPHIDE n any compound of phosphorus with another element, esp a more electropositive element

PHOSPHIDS > PHOSPHID

PHOSPHIN same as > PHOSPHINE

PHOSPHINE n colourless flammable gas that is slightly soluble in water and has a strong fishy odour

PHOSPHINS > PHOSPHIN

PHOSPHITE n any salt or

ester of phosphorous acid

PHOSPHOR n substance capable of emitting light when irradiated with particles of electromagnetic radiation

PHOSPHORE same as > PHOSPHOR

PHOSPHORI n plural of phosphorus

PHOSPHORS > PHOSPHOR

PHOSSY as in phossy jaw gangrenous condition of the lower jawbone caused by prolonged exposure to phosphorus fumes

PHOT n unit of illumination equal to one lumen per square centimetre

PHOTIC adj of or concerned with light

PHOTICS n science of light

PHOTINIA n genus of garden plants

PHOTINIAS > PHOTINIA

PHOTISM n sensation of light or colour caused by stimulus of another sense

PHOTISMS > PHOTISM

PHOTO n photograph ▷ vb take a photograph of

PHOTOCELL n cell which produces a current or voltage when exposed to light or other electromagnetic radiation

PHOTOCOPY n photographic reproduction ▷ vb make a photocopy of

PHOTOED > PHOTO

PHOTOFIT n method of combining photographs of facial features, hair, etc, into a composite picture of a face

PHOTOFITS > PHOTOFIT

PHOTOG n photograph

PHOTOGEN same as > PHOTOGENE

PHOTOGENE n afterimage

PHOTOGENS > PHOTOGEN

PHOTOGENY n photography

PHOTOGRAM n picture, usually abstract, produced on a photographic material without the use of a camera, as by placing an object on the material and exposing to light

PHOTOGS > PHOTOG

PHOTOING > PHOTO

PHOTOLYSE vb cause to undergo photolysis

PHOTOLYZE same as > PHOTOLYZE

PHOTOMAP n map constructed by adding grid lines, place names, etc, to one or more aerial photographs ▷ vb map (an area) using aerial photography

PHOTOMAPS > PHOTOMAP

PHOTOMASK n material on which etching pattern for integrated circuit is drawn

PHOTON n quantum of

electromagnetic radiation energy, such as light, having both particle and wave behaviour

PHOTONIC > PHOTON

PHOTONICS n study and design of devices and systems, such as optical fibres, that depend on the transmission, modulation, or amplification of streams of photons

PHOTONS > PHOTON

PHOTOPHIL n light-seeking organism

PHOTOPIA n normal adaptation of the eye to light

PHOTOPIAS > PHOTOPIA

PHOTOPIC > PHOTOPIA

PHOTOPLAY n play filmed as movie

PHOTOPSIA n appearance of flashes due to retinal irritation

PHOTOPSY same as > PHOTOPSIA

PHOTOS > PHOTO

PHOTOSCAN n photographic scan

PHOTOSET vb set (type matter) by photosetting

PHOTOSETS > PHOTOSET

PHOTOSTAT n copy made by photocopying machine ▷ vb make a photostat copy (of)

PHOTOTAXY n movement of an entire organism in response to light

PHOTOTUBE n type of photocell in which radiation falling on a photocathode causes electrons to flow to an anode and thus produce an electric current

PHOTOTYPE n printing plate produced by photography ▷ vb reproduce (an illustration) using a phototype

PHOTOTYPY n process of producing phototypes

PHOTS > PHOT

PHPHT interj expressing irritation or reluctance

PHRASAL adj of, relating to, or composed of phrases

PHRASALLY > PHRASAL

PHRASE n group of words forming a unit of meaning, esp within a sentence ▷ vb express in words

PHRASED > PHRASE

PHRASEMAN n coiner of phrases

PHRASEMEN > PHRASEMAN

PHRASER > PHRASE

PHRASERS > PHRASE

PHRASES > PHRASE

PHRASIER > PHRASY

PHRASIEST > PHRASY

PHRASING n exact words used to say or write something

PHRASINGS > PHRASING

PHRASY adj containing phrases

PHRATRAL > PHRATRY

PHRATRIC > PHRATRY

PHRATRIES > PHRATRY

PHRATRY n group of people within a tribe who have a common ancestor

PHREAK vb hack into a telecommunications system

PHREAKED > PHREAK

PHREAKER > PHREAK

PHREAKERS > PHREAK

PHREAKING > PHREAK

PHREAKS > PHREAK

PHREATIC adj of or relating to ground water occurring below the water table

PHRENESES > PHRENESIS

PHRENESIS n mental confusion

PHRENETIC obsolete spelling of > FRENETIC

PHRENIC adj of or relating to the diaphragm

PHRENISM n belief in non-physical life force

PHRENISMS > PHRENISM

PHRENITIC > PHRENITIS

PHRENITIS n state of frenzy

PHRENSIED > PHRENSY

PHRENSIES > PHRENSY

PHRENSY obsolete spelling of > FRENZY

PHRENTICK obsolete spelling of > PHRENETIC

PHRYGANA another name for > GARIGUE

PHRYGANAS > PHRYGANA

PHT same as > PHPHT

PHTHALATE n salt or ester of phthalic acid

PHTHALEIN n any of a class of organic compounds obtained by the reaction of phthalic anhydride with a phenol and used in dyes

PHTHALIC as in phthalic anhydride white crystalline substance used mainly in producing dyestuffs

PHTHALIN n colourless compound formed by reduction of phthalein

PHTHALINS > PHTHALIN

PHTHISES > PHTHISIS

PHTHISIC adj relating to or affected with phthisis ▷ n person suffering from phthisis

PHTHISICS > PHTHISIC

PHTHISIS n any disease that causes wasting of the body, esp pulmonary tuberculosis

PHUT vb make muffled explosive sound

PHUTS > PHUT

PHUTTED > PHUT

PHUTTING > PHUT

PHYCOCYAN n type of protein found in some algae

PHYCOLOGY n study of algae

PHYLA > PHYLUM

PHYLAE > PHYLE**

PHYLAR > PHYLUM

PHYLARCH n chief of tribe

PHYLARCHS > PHYLARCH

PHYLARCHY > PHYLARCH

PHYLAXIS n protection against infection

PHYLE n tribe or clan of an ancient Greek people such as the Ionians

PHYLESES > PHYLESIS

PHYLESIS n evolutionary events that modify taxon without causing speciation

PHYLETIC adj of or relating to the evolution of a species or group of organisms

PHYLETICS n study of the evolution of species

PHYLIC > PHYLE

PHYLLARY n bract subtending flower head of composite plant

PHYLLID n leaf of a liverwort or moss

PHYLLIDS > PHYLLID

PHYLLITE n compact lustrous metamorphic rock, rich in mica, derived from a shale or other clay-rich rock

PHYLLITES > PHYLLITE

PHYLLITIC > PHYLLITE

PHYLLO variant of > FILO

PHYLLODE n flattened leafstalk that resembles and functions as a leaf

PHYLLODES > PHYLLODE

PHYLLODIA > PHYLLODE

PHYLLODY n abnormal development of leaves from parts of flower

PHYLLOID adj resembling a leaf ▷ n leaf-like organ

PHYLLOIDS > PHYLLOID

PHYLLOME n leaf or a leaflike organ

PHYLLOMES > PHYLLOME

PHYLLOMIC > PHYLLOME

PHYLLOPOD n crustacean with leaf-like appendages

PHYLLOS > PHYLLO

PHYLOGENY n sequence of events involved in the evolution of a species, genus, etc

PHYLON n tribe

PHYLUM n major taxonomic division of animals and plants that contains one or more classes

PHYSALIA n Portuguese man-of-war

PHYSALIAS > PHYSALIA

PHYSALIS n strawberry tomato

PHYSED n physical education

PHYSEDS > PHYSED

PHYSES > PHYSIS

PHYSETER n creature such as the sperm whale

PHYSETERS > PHYSETER

PHYSIATRY n treatment of injury by physical means

PHYSIC n medicine or drug, esp a cathartic or purge

▷ vb treat (a patient) with medicine

PHYSICAL adj of the body, as contrasted with the mind or spirit

PHYSICALS pl n commodities that can be purchased and used, as opposed to those bought and sold in a futures market

PHYSICIAN n doctor of medicine

PHYSICISM n belief in the physical as opposed to the spiritual

PHYSICIST n person skilled in or studying physics

PHYSICKED > PHYSIC

PHYSICKY > PHYSIC

PHYSICS n science of the properties of matter and energy

PHYSIO n physiotherapy

PHYSIOS > PHYSIO

PHYSIQUE n person's bodily build and muscular development

PHYSIQUED adj having particular physique

PHYSIQUES > PHYSIQUE

PHYSIS n part of bone responsible for lengthening

PHYTANE n hydrocarbon found in some fossilised plant remains

PHYTANES > PHYTANE

PHYTIN n substance from plants used as an energy supplement

PHYTINS > PHYTIN

PHYTOGENY n branch of botany that is concerned with the detailed description of plants

PHYTOID adj resembling plant

PHYTOL n alcohol used to synthesize some vitamins

PHYTOLITH n microscopic particle in plants

PHYTOLOGY rare name for > BOTANY

PHYTOLS > PHYTOL

PHYTON n unit of plant structure, usually considered as the smallest part of the plant that is capable of growth when detached from the parent plant

PHYTONIC > PHYTON

PHYTONS > PHYTON

PHYTOSES > PHYTOSIS

PHYTOSIS n disease caused by vegetable parasite

PHYTOTOMY n dissection of plants

PHYTOTRON n building in which plants can be grown on a large scale, under controlled conditions

PI n sixteenth letter in the Greek alphabet ▷ vb spill and mix (set type) indiscriminately

PIA n innermost of the

three membranes that cover the brain and the spinal cord

PIACEVOLE adv to be performed in playful manner

PIACULAR adj making expiation for a sacrilege

PIAFFE n passage done on the spot ▷ vb strut on the spot

PIAFFED > PIAFFE

PIAFFER > PIAFFE

PIAFFERS > PIAFFE

PIAFFES > PIAFFE

PIAFFING > PIAFFE

PIAL adj relating to pia mater

PIAN n contagious tropical skin disease

PIANETTE n small piano

PIANETTES > PIANETTE

PIANIC adj of piano

PIANINO n small upright piano

PIANINOS > PIANINO

PIANISM n technique, skill, or artistry in playing the piano

PIANISMS > PIANISM

PIANIST n person who plays the piano

PIANISTE variant of > PIANIST

PIANISTES > PIANISTE

PIANISTIC > PIANISM

PIANISTS > PIANIST

PIANO n musical instrument with strings which are struck by hammers worked by a keyboard ▷ adv quietly

PIANOLIST n person who plays the Pianola

PIANOS > PIANO

PIANS > PIAN

PIARIST n member of a Roman religious order

PIARISTS > PIARIST

PIAS > PIA

PIASABA same as > PIASSAVA

PIASABAS > PIASABA

PIASAVA same as > PIASSAVA

PIASAVAS > PIASAVA

PIASSABA same as > PIASSAVA

PIASSABAS > PIASSABA

PIASSAVA n South American palm tree

PIASSAVAS > PIASSAVA

PIASTER same as > PIASTRE

PIASTERS > PIASTER

PIASTRE n standard monetary unit of South Vietnam, divided into 100 cents

PIASTRES > PIASTRE

PIAZZA n square or marketplace, esp in Italy

PIAZZAS > PIAZZA

PIAZZE > PIAZZA

PIAZZIAN > PIAZZA

PIBAL n method of measuring wind

PIBALS > PIBAL

PIBROCH n form of bagpipe music

PIBROCHS > PIBROCH

PIC n photograph or illustration

PICA n abnormal craving to ingest substances such as clay, dirt, and hair

PICACHO n pointed solitary mountain

PICACHOS > PICACHO

PICADILLO n Mexican dish

PICADOR n mounted bullfighter with a lance

PICADORES > PICADOR

PICADORS > PICADOR

PICAL adj relating to pica

PICAMAR n hydrocarbon extract of beechwood tar

PICAMARS > PICAMAR

PICANINNY n offensive term for a small Black or Aboriginal child

PICANTE adj spicy

PICARA n female adventurer

PICARAS > PICARA

PICARIAN n tree-haunting bird

PICARIANS > PICARIAN

PICARO n roguish adventurer

PICAROON n adventurer or rogue

PICAROONS > PICAROON

PICAROS > PICARO

PICAS > PICA

PICAYUNE adj of small value or importance ▷ n any coin of little value, such as a five-cent piece

PICAYUNES > PICAYUNE

PICCADILL n high stiff collar

PICCANIN n offensive word for a Black African child

PICCANINS > PICCANIN

PICCATA n Italian sauce

PICCIES > PICCY

PICCOLO n small flute

PICCOLOS > PICCOLO

PICCY n picture or photograph

PICE n former Indian coin worth one sixty-fourth of a rupee

PICENE n type of hydrocarbon

PICENES > PICENE

PICEOUS adj of, relating to, or resembling pitch

PICHOLINE n variety of olive

PICHURIM n S American laurel tree

PICHURIMS > PICHURIM

PICIFORM adj relating to certain tree-haunting birds

PICINE adj relating to woodpeckers

PICK vb choose ▷ n choice

PICKABACK same as > PIGGYBACK

PICKABLE > PICK

PICKADIL same as > PICCADILL

PICKADILL same as > PICCADILL

PICKADILS > PICKADIL

P

PICKAPACK same as > PICKABACK

PICKAROON same as > PICAROON

PICKAX same as > PICKAXE

PICKAXE n large pick ▷ vb use a pickaxe on (earth, rocks, etc)

PICKAXED > PICKAXE

PICKAXES > PICKAXE

PICKAXING > PICKAXE

PICKBACK same as > PICKABACK

PICKBACKS > PICKBACK

PICKED > PICK

PICKEER vb make raid for booty

PICKEERED > PICKEER

PICKEERER > PICKEER

PICKEERS > PICKEER

PICKER n person or thing that picks, esp that gathers fruit, crops, etc

PICKEREL n North American freshwater game fish

PICKERELS > PICKEREL

PICKERIES > PICKERY

PICKERS > PICKER

PICKERY n petty theft

PICKET n person or group standing outside a workplace to deter would-be workers during a strike ▷ vb form a picket outside (a workplace)

PICKETED > PICKET

PICKETER > PICKET

PICKETERS > PICKET

PICKETING > PICKET

PICKETS > PICKET

PICKIER > PICKY

PICKIEST > PICKY

PICKILY > PICKY

PICKIN n small child

PICKINESS > PICKY

PICKING > PICK

PICKINGS pl n money easily acquired

PICKINS > PICKIN

PICKLE n food preserved in vinegar or salt water ▷ vb preserve in vinegar or salt water

PICKLED adj (of food) preserved

PICKLER > PICKLE

PICKLERS > PICKLE

PICKLES > PICKLE

PICKLING > PICKLE

PICKLOCK n person who picks locks, esp one who gains unlawful access to premises by this means

PICKLOCKS > PICKLOCK

PICKMAW n type of gull

PICKMAWS > PICKMAW

PICKOFF n baseball play

PICKOFFS > PICKOFF

PICKPROOF adj (of a lock) unable to be picked

PICKS > PICK

PICKTHANK n flatterer

PICKUP n small truck with an open body and low sides

PICKUPS > PICKUP

PICKWICK n tool for raising

the short wick of an oil lamp

PICKWICKS > PICKWICK

PICKY adj fussy

PICLORAM n type of herbicide

PICLORAMS > PICLORAM

PICNIC n informal meal out of doors ▷ vb have a picnic

PICNICKED > PICNIC

PICNICKER > PICNIC

PICNICKY > PICNIC

PICNICS > PICNIC

PICOCURIE n unit of radioactivity

PICOFARAD n unit of capacitance

PICOGRAM n trillionth of gram

PICOGRAMS > PICOGRAM

PICOLIN variant of > PICOLINE

PICOLINE n liquid derivative of pyridine found in bone oil and coal tar

PICOLINES > PICOLINE

PICOLINIC > PICOLINE

PICOLINS > PICOLIN

PICOMETER same as > PICOMETRE

PICOMETRE n trillionth fraction of metre

PICOMOLE n trillionth of a mole

PICOMOLES > PICOMOLE

PICONG n any teasing or satirical banter, originally a verbal duel in song

PICONGS > PICONG

PICOT n any of pattern of small loops, as on lace ▷ vb decorate material with small loops

PICOTE adj (of material) picoted

PICOTED > PICOT

PICOTEE n type of carnation having pale petals edged with a darker colour, usually red

PICOTEES > PICOTEE

PICOTING > PICOT

PICOTITE n dark-brown mineral

PICOTITES > PICOTITE

PICOTS > PICOT

PICOWAVE vb treat food with gamma waves

PICOWAVED > PICOWAVE

PICOWAVES > PICOWAVE

PICQUET vb provide early warning of attack

PICQUETED > PICQUET

PICQUETS > PICQUET

PICRA n powder of aloes and canella

PICRAS > PICRA

PICRATE n any salt or ester of picric acid, such as sodium picrate

PICRATED adj containing picrate

PICRATES > PICRATE

PICRIC as in picric acid toxic sparingly soluble crystalline yellow acid

PICRITE n coarse-grained

ultrabasic igneous rock consisting of olivine and augite with small amounts of plagioclase feldspar

PICRITES > PICRITE

PICRITIC > PICRITE

PICS > PIC

PICTARNIE Scots word for > TERN

PICTOGRAM n picture or symbol standing for a word or group of words, as in written Chinese

PICTORIAL adj of or in painting or pictures ▷ n newspaper etc with many pictures

PICTURAL n picture

PICTURALS > PICTURAL

PICTURE n drawing or painting ▷ vb visualize, imagine

PICTURED > PICTURE

PICTURES > PICTURE

PICTURING > PICTURE

PICTURISE same as > PICTURIZE

PICTURIZE vb adorn with pictures

PICUL n unit of weight, used in China, Japan, and SE Asia

PICULS > PICUL

PIDDLE vb urinate

PIDDLED > PIDDLE

PIDDLER > PIDDLE

PIDDLERS > PIDDLE

PIDDLES > PIDDLE

PIDDLING adj small or unimportant

PIDDLY adj trivial

PIDDOCK n marine bivalve that bores into rock, clay, or wood

PIDDOCKS > PIDDOCK

PIDGEON variant of > PIDGIN

PIDGEONS > PIDGEON

PIDGIN n language, not a mother tongue, made up of elements of two or more other languages

PIDGINISE same as > PIDGINIZE

PIDGINIZE vb create pidgin language

PIDGINS > PIDGIN

PIE n dish of meat, fruit, etc baked in pastry

PIEBALD adj (horse) with irregular black-and-white markings ▷ n black-and-white horse

PIEBALDS > PIEBALD

PIECE n separate bit or part

PIECED > PIECE

PIECELESS > PIECE

PIECEMEAL adv bit by bit ▷ adj fragmentary or unsystematic

PIECEN vb join broken threads

PIECENED > PIECEN

PIECENER > PIECEN

PIECENERS > PIECEN

PIECENING > PIECEN

PIECENS > PIECEN

PIECER n person who

mends, repairs, or joins something, esp broken threads on a loom

PIECERS > PIECER

PIECES > PIECE

PIECEWISE adv with respect to number of discrete pieces

PIECEWORK n work paid for according to the quantity produced

PIECING > PIECE

PIECINGS > PIECE

PIECRUST n pastry used for making pies

PIECRUSTS > PIECRUST

PIED > PI

PIEDFORT n coin thicker than normal

PIEDFORTS > PIEDFORT

PIEDISH n container for baking pies

PIEDISHES > PIEDISH

PIEDMONT adj (of glaciers, plains, etc) formed or situated at the foot of a mountain or mountain range ▷ n gentle slope leading from mountains to flat land

PIEDMONTS > PIEDMONT

PIEDNESS n state of being pied

PIEFORT same as > PIEDFORT

PIEFORTS > PIEFORT

PIEHOLE n person's mouth

PIEHOLES > PIEHOLE

PIEING > PIE

PIEMAN n seller of pies

PIEMEN > PIEMAN

PIEND same as > PEEN

PIENDS > PIEND

PIEPLANT n rhubarb

PIEPLANTS > PIEPLANT

PIEPOWDER n former court for dealing with certain disputes

PIER n platform on stilts sticking out into the sea

PIERAGE n accommodation for ships at piers

PIERAGES > PIERAGE

PIERCE vb make a hole in or through with a sharp instrument

PIERCED > PIERCE

PIERCER > PIERCE

PIERCERS > PIERCE

PIERCES > PIERCE

PIERCING adj (of a sound) shrill and high-pitched ▷ n art or practice of piercing body parts for the insertion of jewellery

PIERCINGS > PIERCING

PIERID n type of butterfly

PIERIDINE adj > PIERID

PIERIDS > PIERID

PIERIS n American or Asiatic shrub

PIERISES > PIERIS

PIEROGI n Polish dumpling

PIEROGIES > PIEROGI

PIERRETTE n female pierrot

PIERROT n clown or masquerader with a whitened face, white

costume, and pointed hat
PIERROTS > PIERROT
PIERS > PIER
PIERST *archaic spelling of* > PIERCED
PIERT *n* small plant with small greenish flowers
PIERTS > PIERT
PIES > PIE
PIET *n* magpie
PIETA *n* sculpture, painting, or drawing of the dead Christ, supported by the Virgin Mary
PIETAS > PIETA
PIETIES > PIETY
PIETISM *n* exaggerated piety
PIETISMS > PIETISM
PIETIST > PIETISM
PIETISTIC > PIETISM
PIETISTS > PIETISM
PIETS > PIET
PIETY *n* deep devotion to God and religion
PIEZO *adj* piezoelectric
PIFFERARI > PIFFERARO
PIFFERARO *n* player of piffero
PIFFERO *n* small rustic flute
PIFFEROS > PIFFERO
PIFFLE *n* nonsense ▷ *vb* talk or behave feebly
PIFFLED > PIFFLE
PIFFLER *n* talker of nonsense
PIFFLERS > PIFFLER
PIFFLES > PIFFLE
PIFFLING *adj* worthless
PIG *n* animal kept and killed for pork, ham, and bacon ▷ *vb* eat greedily
PIGBOAT *n* submarine
PIGBOATS > PIGBOAT
PIGEON *n* bird with a heavy body and short legs, sometimes trained to carry messages ▷ *vb* pigeonhole
PIGEONED > PIGEON
PIGEONING > PIGEON
PIGEONITE *n* brownish mineral
PIGEONRY *n* loft for keeping pigeons
PIGEONS > PIGEON
PIGFACE *n* creeping succulent plant with bright-coloured flowers and red fruits
PIGFACES > PIGFACE
PIGFEED *n* food for pigs
PIGFEEDS > PIGFEED
PIGFISH *n* grunting fish of the North American Atlantic coast
PIGFISHES > PIGFISH
PIGGED > PIG
PIGGERIES > PIGGERY
PIGGERY *n* place for keeping and breeding pigs
PIGGIE *same as* > PIGGY
PIGGIER > PIGGY
PIGGIES > PIGGY
PIGGIEST > PIGGY
PIGGIN *n* small wooden bucket or tub
PIGGINESS > PIGGY

PIGGING > PIG
PIGGINGS > PIG
PIGGINS > PIGGIN
PIGGISH *adj* like a pig, esp in appetite or manners
PIGGISHLY > PIGGISH
PIGGY *n* child's word for a pig, esp a piglet ▷ *adj* like a pig, esp in appetite
PIGGYBACK *n* ride on someone's shoulders ▷ *adv* carried on someone's shoulders ▷ *adj* on the back and shoulders of another person ▷ *vb* give (a person) a piggyback on one's back and shoulders
PIGHEADED *adj* stupidly stubborn
PIGHT *vb* pierce
PIGHTED > PIGHT
PIGHTING > PIGHT
PIGHTLE *n* small enclosure
PIGHTLES > PIGHTLE
PIGHTS > PIGHT
PIGLET *n* young pig
PIGLETS > PIGLET
PIGLIKE > PIG
PIGLING *n* young pig
PIGLINGS > PIGLING
PIGMAEAN *same as* > PYGMAEAN
PIGMEAN *same as* > PYGMAEAN
PIGMEAT *less common name for* > PORK
PIGMEATS > PIGMEAT
PIGMENT *n* colouring matter, paint or dye ▷ *vb* colour with pigment
PIGMENTAL > PIGMENT
PIGMENTED > PIGMENT
PIGMENTS > PIGMENT
PIGMIES > PIGMY
PIGMOID *adj* of pygmies
PIGMY *same as* > PYGMY
PIGNERATE *vb* pledge or pawn
PIGNOLI *same as* > PIGNOLIA
PIGNOLIA *n* edible seed of nut pine
PIGNOLIAS > PIGNOLIA
PIGNOLIS > PIGNOLI
PIGNORA > PIGNUS
PIGNORATE *same as* > PIGNERATE
PIGNUS *n* pawn or pledge
PIGNUT *n* bitter nut of any of several North American hickory trees
PIGNUTS > PIGNUT
PIGOUT *n* binge
PIGOUTS > PIGOUT
PIGPEN *same as* > PIGSTY
PIGPENS > PIGPEN
PIGS > PIG
PIGSCONCE *n* foolish person
PIGSKIN *n* skin of the domestic pig ▷ *adj* made of pigskin
PIGSKINS > PIGSKIN
PIGSNEY *same as* > PIGSNY
PIGSNEYS > PIGSNEY
PIGSNIE *same as* > PIGSNY
PIGSNIES > PIGSNIE
PIGSNY *n* former pet name for girl

PIGSTICK *vb* (esp in India) hunt and spear wild boar, esp from horseback
PIGSTICKS > PIGSTICK
PIGSTIES > PIGSTY
PIGSTUCK > PIGSTICK
PIGSTY *same as* > PIGPEN
PIGSWILL *n* waste food or other edible matter fed to pigs
PIGSWILLS > PIGSWILL
PIGTAIL *n* plait of hair hanging from the back or either side of the head
PIGTAILED > PIGTAIL
PIGTAILS > PIGTAIL
PIGWASH *n* wet feed for pigs
PIGWASHES > PIGWASH
PIGWEED *n* coarse North American amaranthaceous weed
PIGWEEDS > PIGWEED
PIHOIHOI *n* variety of New Zealand pipit
PIING > PI
PIKA *n* burrowing lagomorph mammal of mountainous regions of North America and Asia
PIKAKE *n* type of Asian vine
PIKAKES > PIKAKE
PIKAS > PIKA
PIKAU *n* pack, knapsack, or rucksack
PIKAUS > PIKAU
PIKE *n* large predatory freshwater fish ▷ *vb* stab or pierce using a pike ▷ *adj* (of the body position of a diver) bent at the hips but with the legs straight
PIKED > PIKE
PIKELET *n* small thick pancake
PIKELETS > PIKELET
PIKEMAN *n* (formerly) soldier armed with a pike
PIKEMEN > PIKEMAN
PIKEPERCH *n* pikelike freshwater teleost fish
PIKER *n* shirker
PIKERS > PIKER
PIKES > PIKE
PIKESTAFF *n* wooden handle of a pike
PIKEY *n* in British English, derogatory word for gypsy or vagrant
PIKEYS > PIKEY
PIKI *n* bread made from blue cornmeal
PIKING > PIKE
PIKINGS > PIKE
PIKIS > PIKI
PIKUL *same as* > PICUL
PIKULS > PIKUL
PILA *n* pillar-like anatomical structure
PILAF *same as* > PILAU
PILAFF *same as* > PILAU
PILAFFS > PILAFF
PILAFS > PILAF
PILAO *same as* > PILAU
PILAOS > PILAO
PILAR *adj* relating to hair
PILASTER *n* square column, usu set in a wall

PILASTERS > PILASTER
PILAU *n* Middle Eastern dish of meat, fish, or poultry boiled with rice, spices, etc
PILAUS > PILAU
PILAW *same as* > PILAU
PILAWS > PILAW
PILCH *n* outer garment, originally one made of skin
PILCHARD *n* small edible sea fish of the herring family
PILCHARDS > PILCHARD
PILCHER *n* scabbard for sword
PILCHERS > PILCHER
PILCHES > PILCH
PILCORN *n* type if oat
PILCORNS > PILCORN
PILCROW *n* paragraph mark
PILCROWS > PILCROW
PILE *n* number of things lying on top of each other ▷ *vb* collect into a pile
PILEA *n* artillery or gunpowder plant, which releases a cloud of pollen when shaken
PILEAS > PILEA
PILEATE *adj* (of birds) having a crest
PILEATED *same as* > PILEATE
PILED > PILE
PILEI > PILEUS
PILELESS > PILE
PILEOUS *adj* hairy
PILER *n* placer of things on pile
PILERS > PILER
PILES *pl n* swollen veins in the rectum, haemorrhoids
PILEUM *n* top of a bird's head from the base of the bill to the occiput
PILEUP *n* multiple collision of vehicles
PILEUPS > PILEUP
PILEUS *n* upper cap-shaped part of a mushroom or similar spore-producing body
PILEWORK *n* construction built from heavy stakes or cylinders
PILEWORKS > PILEWORK
PILEWORT *n* any of several plants, such as lesser celandine, thought to be effective in treating piles
PILEWORTS > PILEWORT
PILFER *vb* steal in small quantities
PILFERAGE *n* act or practice of stealing small quantities or articles
PILFERED > PILFER
PILFERER > PILFER
PILFERERS > PILFER
PILFERIES > PILFERY
PILFERING > PILFER
PILFERS > PILFER
PILFERY *n* theft
PILGARLIC *n* bald head or a man with a bald head
PILGRIM *n* person who journeys to a holy place
PILGRIMER *n* one who

undertakes a pilgrimage

PILGRIMS > PILGRIM

PILI n Philippine tree with edible seeds resembling almonds

PILIFORM adj resembling a long hair

PILING n act of driving piles

PILINGS > PILING

PILIS > PILI

PILL n small ball of medicine swallowed whole ▷ vb peel or skin (something)

PILLAGE vb steal property by violence in war ▷ n violent seizure of goods, esp in war

PILLAGED > PILLAGE

PILLAGER > PILLAGE

PILLAGERS > PILLAGE

PILLAGES > PILLAGE

PILLAGING > PILLAGE

PILLAR n upright post, usu supporting a roof ▷ vb provide or support with pillars

PILLARED > PILLAR

PILLARING > PILLAR

PILLARIST n recluse who sat on high pillar

PILLARS > PILLAR

PILLAU same as > PILAU

PILLAUS > PILLAU

PILLBOX n small box for pills

PILLBOXES > PILLBOX

PILLED > PILL

PILLHEAD n person addicted to pills

PILLHEADS > PILLHEAD

PILLICOCK n penis

PILLIE n pilchard

PILLIES > PILLIE

PILLING > PILL

PILLINGS > PILL

PILLION n seat for a passenger behind the rider of a motorcycle ▷ adv on a pillion ▷ vb ride pillion

PILLIONED > PILLION

PILLIONS > PILLION

PILLOCK n stupid or annoying person

PILLOCKS > PILLOCK

PILLORIED > PILLORY

PILLORIES > PILLORY

PILLORISE same as > PILLORIZE

PILLORIZE vb put in pillory

PILLORY n frame with holes for the head and hands in which an offender was locked and exposed to public abuse ▷ vb ridicule publicly

PILLOW n stuffed cloth bag for supporting the head in bed ▷ vb rest as if on a pillow

PILLOWED > PILLOW

PILLOWING > PILLOW

PILLOWS > PILLOW

PILLOWY > PILLOW

PILLS > PILL

PILLWORM n worm that rolls up spirally

PILLWORMS > PILLWORM

PILLWORT n small Eurasian water fern

PILLWORTS > PILLWORT

PILOMOTOR adj causing movement of hairs

PILONIDAL adj of crease above buttocks

PILOSE adj covered with fine soft hairs

PILOSITY > PILOSE

PILOT n person qualified to fly an aircraft or spacecraft ▷ adj experimental and preliminary ▷ vb act as the pilot of

PILOTAGE n act of piloting an aircraft or ship

PILOTAGES > PILOTAGE

PILOTED > PILOT

PILOTFISH n fish that accompanies sharks

PILOTING n navigational handling of a ship near land using buoys, soundings, landmarks, etc, or the finding of a ship's position by such means

PILOTINGS > PILOTING

PILOTIS pl n posts raising a building up from the ground

PILOTLESS > PILOT

PILOTMAN n railway worker who directs trains through hazardous stretches of track

PILOTMEN > PILOTMAN

PILOTS > PILOT

PILOUS same as > PILOSE

PILOW same as > PILAU

PILOWS > PILOW

PILSENER same as > PILSNER

PILSENERS > PILSENER

PILSNER n type of pale beer with a strong flavour of hops

PILSNERS > PILSNER

PILULA n pill

PILULAE > PILULA

PILULAR > PILULE

PILULAS > PILULA

PILULE n small pill

PILULES > PILULE

PILUM n ancient Roman javelin

PILUS > PILI

PILY adj like wool or pile

PIMA n type of cotton

PIMAS > PIMA

PIMENT n wine flavoured with spices

PIMENTO same as > PIMIENTO

PIMENTON n smoked chilli powder

PIMENTONS > PIMENTON

PIMENTOS > PIMENTO

PIMENTS > PIMENT

PIMIENTO n Spanish pepper with a red fruit used as a vegetable

PIMIENTOS > PIMIENTO

PIMP n man who gets customers for a prostitute in return for a share of his or her earnings ▷ vb act as a pimp

PIMPED > PIMP

PIMPERNEL n wild plant with small star-shaped flowers

PIMPING > PIMP

PIMPLE n small pus-filled spot on the skin

PIMPLED > PIMPLE

PIMPLES > PIMPLE

PIMPLIER > PIMPLE

PIMPLIEST > PIMPLE

PIMPLY > PIMPLE

PIMPS > PIMP

PIN n short thin piece of stiff wire with a point and head, for fastening things ▷ vb fasten with a pin

PINA n cone of silver amalgam

PINACEOUS adj of, relating to, or belonging to the Pinaceae, a family of conifers with needle-like leaves: includes pine, spruce, fir, larch, and cedar

PINACOID n pair of opposite parallel faces of crystal

PINACOIDS > PINACOID

PINAFORE n apron

PINAFORED > PINAFORE

PINAFORES > PINAFORE

PINAKOID same as > PINACOID

PINAKOIDS > PINAKOID

PINANG n areca tree

PINANGS > PINANG

PINAS > PINA

PINASTER n Mediterranean pine tree

PINASTERS > PINASTER

PINATA n papier-mâché party decoration filled with sweets, hung up during parties, and struck with a stick until it breaks open

PINATAS > PINATA

PINBALL vb ricochet

PINBALLED > PINBALL

PINBALLS > PINBALL

PINBONE n part of sirloin

PINBONES > PINBONE

PINCASE n case for holding pins

PINCASES > PINCASE

PINCER vb grip with pincers

PINCERED > PINCER

PINCERING > PINCER

PINCERS pl n tool consisting of two hinged arms, for gripping

PINCH vb squeeze between finger and thumb ▷ n act of pinching

PINCHBECK n alloy of zinc and copper, used as imitation gold ▷ adj sham or cheap

PINCHBUG n type of crab

PINCHBUGS > PINCHBUG

PINCHCOCK n clamp used to compress a flexible tube to control the flow of fluid through it

PINCHECK n small check woven into fabric

PINCHECKS > PINCHECK

PINCHED > PINCH

PINCHER > PINCH

PINCHERS > PINCH

PINCHES > PINCH

PINCHFIST n mean person

PINCHGUT n miserly person

PINCHGUTS > PINCHGUT

PINCHING > PINCH

PINCHINGS > PINCH

PINDAN n desert region of Western Australia

PINDANS > PINDAN

PINDAREE same as > PINDARI

PINDAREES > PINDAREE

PINDARI n former irregular Indian horseman

PINDARIS > PINDARI

PINDER n person who impounds

PINDERS > PINDER

PINDLING adj peevish or fractious

PINDOWN n wrestling manoeuvre

PINDOWNS > PINDOWN

PINE n evergreen coniferous tree ▷ vb feel great longing (for)

PINEAL adj resembling a pine cone ▷ n pineal gland

PINEALS > PINEAL

PINEAPPLE n large tropical fruit with juicy yellow flesh and a hard skin

PINECONE n seed-producing structure of a pine tree

PINECONES > PINECONE

PINED > PINE

PINEDROPS n parasitic herb of pine trees

PINELAND n area covered with pine forest

PINELANDS > PINELAND

PINELIKE > PINE

PINENE n isomeric terpene found in many essential oils

PINENES > PINENE

PINERIES > PINERY

PINERY n place, esp a hothouse, where pineapples are grown

PINES > PINE

PINESAP n red herb of N America

PINESAPS > PINESAP

PINETA > PINETUM

PINETUM n area of land where pine trees and other conifers are grown

PINEWOOD n wood of pine trees

PINEWOODS > PINEWOOD

PINEY > PINE

PINFALL another name for > FALL

PINFALLS > PINFALL

PINFISH n small porgy of the SE North American coast of the Atlantic

PINFISHES > PINFISH

PINFOLD n pound for stray cattle ▷ vb gather or confine in or as if in a pinfold

PINFOLDED > PINFOLD

PINFOLDS > PINFOLD

PING n short high-pitched sound ▷ vb make such a noise

PINGED > PING

PINGER n device, esp a timer, that makes a pinging sound

PINGERS > PINGER

PINGING > PING

PINGLE vb enclose small area of ground

PINGLED > PINGLE

PINGLER > PINGLE

PINGLERS > PINGLE

PINGLES > PINGLE

PINGLING > PINGLE

PINGO n mound of earth or gravel formed through pressure from a layer of water trapped between newly frozen ice and underlying permafrost in Arctic regions

PINGOES > PINGO

PINGOS > PINGO

PINGPONG n table tennis

PINGPONGS > PINGPONG

PINGRASS n weed with fernlike leaves

PINGS > PING

PINGUEFY vb become greasy or fat

PINGUID adj fatty, oily, or greasy

PINGUIN same as > PENGUIN

PINGUINS > PINGUIN

PINHEAD n head of a pin

PINHEADED adj stupid or silly

PINHEADS > PINHEAD

PINHOLE n small hole made with or as if with a pin

PINHOLES > PINHOLE

PINHOOKER n trader of young thoroughbred horses

PINIER > PINY

PINIES > PINY

PINIEST > PINY

PINING > PINE

PINION n bird's wing ▷ vb immobilize (someone) by tying or holding his or her arms

PINIONED > PINION

PINIONING > PINION

PINIONS > PINION

PINITE n greyish-green or brown mineral containing amorphous aluminium and potassium sulphates

PINITES > PINITE

PINITOL n compound found in pinewood

PINITOLS > PINITOL

PINK n pale reddish colour ▷ adj of the colour pink ▷ vb (of an engine) make a metallic noise because not working properly, knock

PINKED > PINK

PINKEN vb turn pink

PINKENED > PINKEN

PINKENING > PINKEN

PINKENS > PINKEN

PINKER n something that

pinks

PINKERS > PINKER

PINKERTON n private detective

PINKEST > PINK

PINKEY variant of > PINKY

PINKEYE n acute contagious inflammation of the conjunctiva of the eye

PINKEYES > PINKEYE

PINKEYS > PINKEY

PINKIE n little finger

PINKIER > PINKY

PINKIES > PINKIE

PINKIEST > PINKY

PINKINESS n quality of being pink

PINKING > PINK

PINKINGS > PINK

PINKISH > PINK

PINKLY > PINK

PINKNESS > PINK

PINKO n person regarded as mildly left-wing

PINKOES > PINKO

PINKOS > PINKO

PINKROOT n plant with red-and-yellow flowers and pink roots

PINKROOTS > PINKROOT

PINKS > PINK

PINKY adj of a pink colour

PINNA n external part of the ear

PINNACE n ship's boat

PINNACES > PINNACE

PINNACLE n highest point of fame or success ▷ vb set on or as if on a pinnacle

PINNACLED > PINNACLE

PINNACLES > PINNACLE

PINNAE > PINNA

PINNAL > PINNA

PINNAS > PINNA

PINNATE adj (of compound leaves) having leaflets growing opposite each other in pairs

PINNATED same as > PINNATE

PINNATELY > PINNATE

PINNATION > PINNATE

PINNED > PIN

PINNER n person or thing that pins

PINNERS > PINNER

PINNET n pinnacle

PINNETS > PINNET

PINNIE same as > PINNY

PINNIES > PINNIE

PINNING > PIN

PINNINGS > PIN

PINNIPED n aquatic placental mammal such as the seal, sea lion, walrus, etc

PINNIPEDE same as > PINNIPED

PINNIPEDS > PINNIPED

PINNOCK n small bird

PINNOCKS > PINNOCK

PINNOED adj held or bound by the arms

PINNULA same as > PINNULE

PINNULAE > PINNULA

PINNULAR > PINNULE

PINNULAS > PINNULA

PINNULATE > PINNULE

PINNULE n any of the lobes of a leaflet of a pinnate compound leaf, which is itself pinnately divided

PINNULES > PINNULE

PINNY informal or child's name for > PINAFORE

PINOCHLE n card game for two to four players similar to bezique

PINOCHLES > PINOCHLE

PINOCLE same as > PINOCHLE

PINOCLES > PINOCLE

PINOCYTIC adj of process of pinocytosis

PINOLE n (in the southwestern United States) flour made of parched ground corn, mesquite beans, sugar, etc

PINOLES > PINOLE

PINON n low-growing pine

PINONES > PINON

PINONS > PINON

PINOT n any of several grape varieties

PINOTS > PINOT

PINPOINT vb locate or identify exactly ▷ adj exact ▷ n insignificant or trifling thing

PINPOINTS > PINPOINT

PINPRICK n small irritation or annoyance ▷ vb puncture with or as if with a pin

PINPRICKS > PINPRICK

PINS > PIN

PINSCHER n breed of dog

PINSCHERS > PINSCHER

PINSETTER n device that sets pins in bowling alley

PINSTRIPE n very narrow stripe in fabric

PINSWELL n small boil

PINSWELLS > PINSWELL

PINT n liquid measure, 1/8 gallon (.568 litre)

PINTA n pint of milk

PINTABLE n pinball machine

PINTABLES > PINTABLE

PINTADA same as > PINTADO

PINTADAS > PINTADA

PINTADERA n decorative stamp, usually made of clay, found in the Neolithic of the E Mediterranean and in many American cultures

PINTADO n species of seagoing petrel

PINTADOES > PINTADO

PINTADOS > PINTADO

PINTAIL n greyish-brown duck with a pointed tail

PINTAILED adj having tapered tail

PINTAILS > PINTAIL

PINTANO n tropical reef fish

PINTANOS > PINTANO

PINTAS > PINTA

PINTLE n pin or bolt forming the pivot of a hinge

PINTLES > PINTLE

PINTO adj marked with patches of white ▷ n pinto horse

PINTOES > PINTO

PINTOS > PINTO

PINTS > PINT

PINTSIZE same as > PINTSIZED

PINTSIZED adj very small

PINUP n picture of a sexually attractive person, esp when partially or totally undressed

PINUPS > PINUP

PINWALE n fabric with narrow ridges

PINWALES > PINWALE

PINWEED n herb with tiny flowers

PINWEEDS > PINWEED

PINWHEEL n cogwheel whose teeth are formed by small pins projecting either axially or radially from the rim of the wheel

PINWHEELS > PINWHEEL

PINWORK n (in needlepoint lace) fine raised stitches

PINWORKS > PINWORK

PINWORM n parasitic nematode worm

PINWORMS > PINWORM

PINWRENCH n wrench with a projection to fit a hole

PINXIT vb (he or she) painted (it): used formerly on paintings next to the artist's name

PINY variant of > PEONY

PINYIN n system of romanized spelling for the Chinese language

PINYON n low-growing pine

PINYONS > PINYON

PIOLET n type of ice axe

PIOLETS > PIOLET

PION n any of three subatomic particles which are classified as mesons

PIONED adj abounding in marsh marigolds

PIONEER n explorer or early settler of a new country ▷ vb be the pioneer or leader of

PIONEERED > PIONEER

PIONEERS > PIONEER

PIONER obsolete spelling of > PIONEER

PIONERS > PIONER

PIONEY same as > PEONY

PIONEYS > PIONEY

PIONIC > PION

PIONIES > PIONY

PIONING n work of pioneers

PIONINGS > PIONING

PIONS > PION

PIONY same as > PEONY

PIOPIO n New Zealand thrush, thought to be extinct

PIOSITIES > PIOSITY

PIOSITY n grandiose display of piety

PIOTED adj pied

PIOUS adj deeply religious, devout

PIOUSLY > PIOUS
PIOUSNESS > PIOUS
PIOY variant of > PEEOY
PIOYE variant of > PEEOY
PIOYES > PIOYE
PIOYS > PIOY
PIP n small seed in a fruit ▷ vb chirp
PIPA n tongueless South American toad, *Pipa pipa*, that carries its young in pits in the skin of its back
PIPAGE n pipes collectively
PIPAGES > PIPAGE
PIPAL same as > PEEPUL
PIPALS > PIPAL
PIPAS > PIPA
PIPE n tube for conveying liquid or gas ▷ vb play on a pipe
PIPEAGE same as > PIPAGE
PIPEAGES > PIPEAGE
PIPECLAY n fine white pure clay, used in tobacco pipes and pottery and to whiten leather and similar materials ▷ vb whiten with pipeclay
PIPECLAYS > PIPECLAY
PIPED > PIPE
PIPEFISH n teleost fish with a long tubelike snout and an elongated body covered with bony plates
PIPEFUL > PIPE
PIPEFULS > PIPE
PIPELESS > PIPE
PIPELIKE > PIPE
PIPELINE n long pipe for transporting oil, water, etc
PIPELINED > PIPELINE
PIPELINES > PIPELINE
PIPER n player on a pipe or bagpipes
PIPERIC > PIPERINE
PIPERINE n crystalline insoluble alkaloid that is the active ingredient of pepper
PIPERINES > PIPERINE
PIPERONAL n white fragrant aldehyde used in flavourings, perfumery, and suntan lotions
PIPERS > PIPER
PIPES > PIPE
PIPESTEM n hollow stem of pipe
PIPESTEMS > PIPESTEM
PIPESTONE n variety of consolidated red clay used by American Indians to make tobacco pipes
PIPET same as > PIPETTE
PIPETS > PIPET
PIPETTE n slender glass tube used to transfer or measure fluids ▷ vb transfer or measure out (a liquid) using a pipette
PIPETTED > PIPETTE
PIPETTES > PIPETTE
PIPETTING > PIPETTE
PIPEWORK n stops and flues on pipe organ
PIPEWORKS > PIPEWORK
PIPEWORT n perennial plant

with a twisted flower stalk and a greenish-grey scaly flower head
PIPEWORTS > PIPEWORT
PIPI n edible mollusc often used as bait
PIPIER > PIPE
PIPIEST > PIPE
PIPINESS n material's suitability for use as pipe
PIPING n system of pipes
PIPINGLY > PIPING
PIPINGS > PIPING
PIPIS > PIPI
PIPISTREL n species of bat
PIPIT n small brownish songbird
PIPITS > PIPIT
PIPKIN same as > PIGGIN
PIPKINS > PIPKIN
PIPLESS > PIP
PIPPED > PIP
PIPPIER > PIPPY
PIPPIEST > PIPPY
PIPPIN n type of eating apple
PIPPING > PIP
PIPPINS > PIPPIN
PIPPY adj containing many pips
PIPS > PIP
PIPSQUEAK n insignificant or contemptible person
PIPUL n Indian fig tree
PIPULS > PIPUL
PIPY > PIPE
PIQUANCE same as > PIQUANT
PIQUANCES > PIQUANT
PIQUANCY > PIQUANT
PIQUANT adj having a pleasant spicy taste
PIQUANTLY > PIQUANT
PIQUE n feeling of hurt pride, baffled curiosity, or resentment ▷ vb hurt the pride of
PIQUED > PIQUE
PIQUES > PIQUE
PIQUET n card game for two ▷ vb play game of piquet
PIQUETED > PIQUET
PIQUETING > PIQUET
PIQUETS > PIQUET
PIQUILLO n variety of sweet red pepper
PIQUILLOS > PIQUILLO
PIQUING > PIQUE
PIR n Sufi master
PIRACETAM n drug used to treat muscle spasm
PIRACIES > PIRACY
PIRACY n robbery on the seas
PIRAGUA same as > PIROGUE
PIRAGUAS > PIRAGUA
PIRAI n large S American fish
PIRAIS > PIRAI
PIRANA same as > PIRANHA
PIRANAS > PIRANA
PIRANHA n small fierce freshwater fish of tropical America
PIRANHAS > PIRANHA
PIRARUCU n large S American food fish

PIRARUCUS > PIRARUCU
PIRATE n sea robber ▷ vb sell or reproduce (artistic work etc) illegally
PIRATED > PIRATE
PIRATES > PIRATE
PIRATIC > PIRATE
PIRATICAL > PIRATE
PIRATING > PIRATE
PIRAYA same as > PIRAI
PIRAYAS > PIRAYA
PIRIFORM adj shaped like pear
PIRL n ripple in water
PIRLICUE same as > PURLICUE
PIRLICUED > PIRLICUE
PIRLICUES > PIRLICUE
PIRLS > PIRL
PIRN n reel or bobbin
PIRNIE n stripy nightcap
PIRNIES > PIRNIE
PIRNIT adj striped
PIRNS > PIRN
PIROG n large pie filled with meat, vegetables, etc
PIROGEN n turnovers made from kneaded dough
PIROGHI > PIROG
PIROGI > PIROG
PIROGIES > PIROG
PIROGUE n any of various kinds of dugout canoes
PIROGUES > PIROGUE
PIROJKI same as > PIROSHKI
PIROPLASM n parasite of red blood cells
PIROQUE same as > PIROGUE
PIROQUES > PIROQUE
PIROSHKI same as > PIROZHKI
PIROUETTE n spinning turn balanced on the toes of one foot ▷ vb perform a pirouette
PIROZHKI > PIROZHOK
PIROZHOK n small triangular pastry filled with meat, vegetables, etc
PIRS > PIR
PIS > PI
PISCARIES > PISCARY
PISCARY n place where fishing takes place
PISCATOR n fisherman
PISCATORS > PISCATOR
PISCATORY adj of or relating to fish, fishing, or fishermen
PISCATRIX n female angler
PISCIFORM adj having form of fish
PISCINA n stone basin, with a drain, in a church or sacristy where water used at Mass is poured away
PISCINAE > PISCINA
PISCINAL > PISCINA
PISCINAS > PISCINA
PISCINE n pond or pool
PISCINES > PISCINE
PISCIVORE n eater of fish
PISCO n S American brandy
PISCOS > PISCO
PISE n rammed earth or clay used to make floors or walls

PISES > PISE
PISH interj exclamation of impatience or contempt ▷ vb make this exclamation at (someone or something)
PISHED > PISH
PISHER n Yiddish term for small boy
PISHERS > PISHER
PISHES > PISH
PISHING > PISH
PISHOGE same as > PISHOGUE
PISHOGES > PISHOGE
PISHOGUE n sorcery
PISHOGUES > PISHOGUE
PISIFORM adj resembling a pea ▷ n small pealike bone on the ulnar side of the carpus
PISIFORMS > PISIFORM
PISKIES > PISKY
PISKY n Cornish fairy
PISMIRE archaic or dialect word for > ANT
PISMIRES > PISMIRE
PISO n peso of the Philippines
PISOLITE n sedimentary rock
PISOLITES > PISOLITE
PISOLITH same as > PISOLITE
PISOLITHS > PISOLITH
PISOLITIC > PISOLITE
PISOS > PISO
PISS vb urinate ▷ n act of urinating
PISSANT n insignificant person
PISSANTS > PISSANT
PISSED adj drunk
PISSER n someone or something that pisses
PISSERS > PISSER
PISSES > PISS
PISSHEAD n drunkard
PISSHEADS > PISSHEAD
PISSING > PISS
PISSOIR n public urinal, usu enclosed by a wall or screen
PISSOIRS > PISSOIR
PISTACHE n tree yielding pistachio nut
PISTACHES > PISTACHE
PISTACHIO n edible nut of a Mediterranean tree ▷ adj of a yellowish-green colour
PISTAREEN n Spanish coin, used in the US and the West Indies until the 18th century
PISTE n ski slope
PISTES > PISTE
PISTIL n seed-bearing part of a flower
PISTILS > PISTIL
PISTOL n short-barrelled handgun ▷ vb shoot with a pistol
PISTOLE n any of various gold coins of varying value, formerly used in Europe
PISTOLED > PISTOL
PISTOLEER n person, esp a

soldier, who is armed with or fires a pistol

PISTOLERO *n* shooter of pistols

PISTOLES > PISTOLE

PISTOLET *n* small pistol

PISTOLETS > PISTOLET

PISTOLIER *n* shooter of pistols

PISTOLING > PISTOL

PISTOLLED > PISTOL

PISTOLS > PISTOL

PISTON *n* cylindrical part in an engine that slides to and fro in a cylinder

PISTONS > PISTON

PISTOU *n* French sauce

PISTOUS > PISTOU

PIT *n* deep hole in the ground ▷ *vb* mark with small dents or scars

PITA *n* any of several agave plants yielding a strong fibre

PITAHAYA *n* any giant cactus of Central America and the SW United States

PITAHAYAS > PITAHAYA

PITAPAT *adv* with quick light taps ▷ *n* such taps ▷ *vb* make quick light taps or beats

PITAPATS > PITAPAT

PITARA *variant of* > PETARA

PITARAH *variant of* > PETARA

PITARAHS > PITARAH

PITARAS > PITARA

PITAS > PITA

PITAYA *same as* > PITAHAYA

PITAYAS > PITAYA

PITCH *vb* throw, hurl ▷ *n* area marked out for playing sport

PITCHBEND *n* electronic device that enables a player to bend the pitch of a note being sounded on a synthesizer, usually with a pitch wheel, strip, or lever

PITCHED > PITCH

PITCHER *n* large jug with a narrow neck

PITCHERS > PITCHER

PITCHES > PITCH

PITCHFORK *n* large long-handled fork for lifting hay ▷ *vb* thrust abruptly or violently

PITCHIER > PITCHY

PITCHIEST > PITCHY

PITCHILY > PITCHY

PITCHING > PITCH

PITCHINGS > PITCH

PITCHMAN *n* itinerant pedlar of small merchandise who operates from a stand at a fair, etc

PITCHMEN > PITCHMAN

PITCHOUT *n* type of baseball pitch

PITCHOUTS > PITCHOUT

PITCHPINE *n* large N American pine tree

PITCHPIPE *n* small one-note pipe used for tuning instruments

PITCHPOLE *vb* turn end

over end

PITCHY *adj* full of or covered with pitch

PITEOUS *adj* arousing pity

PITEOUSLY > PITEOUS

PITFALL *n* hidden difficulty or danger

PITFALLS > PITFALL

PITH *n* soft white lining of the rind of oranges etc ▷ *vb* destroy the brain and spinal cord of (a laboratory animal) by piercing or severing

PITHBALL *n* type of conductor

PITHBALLS > PITHBALL

PITHEAD *n* top of a mine shaft and the buildings and hoisting gear around it

PITHEADS > PITHEAD

PITHECOID *adj* relating to apes

PITHED > PITH

PITHFUL > PITH

PITHIER > PITHY

PITHIEST > PITHY

PITHILY > PITHY

PITHINESS > PITHY

PITHING > PITH

PITHLESS > PITH

PITHLIKE > PITH

PITHOI > PITHOS

PITHOS *n* large ceramic container for oil or grain

PITHS > PITH

PITHY *adj* short and full of meaning

PITIABLE *adj* arousing or deserving pity or contempt

PITIABLY > PITIABLE

PITIED > PITY

PITIER > PITY

PITIERS > PITY

PITIES > PITY

PITIFUL *adj* arousing pity

PITIFULLY > PITIFUL

PITILESS *adj* feeling no pity or mercy

PITMAN *n* connecting rod (in a machine)

PITMANS > PITMAN

PITMEN > PITMAN

PITON *n* metal spike used in climbing to secure a rope

PITONS > PITON

PITPROP *n* support beam in mine shaft

PITPROPS > PITPROP

PITS > PIT

PITSAW *n* large saw formerly used for cutting logs into planks, operated by two men, one standing on top of the log and the other in a pit underneath it

PITSAWS > PITSAW

PITTA *n* small brightly coloured ground-dwelling tropical bird

PITTANCE *n* very small amount of money

PITTANCES > PITTANCE

PITTAS > PITTA

PITTED > PIT

PITTEN *adj* having been put

PITTER *vb* make pattering

sound

PITTERED > PITTER

PITTERING > PITTER

PITTERS > PITTER

PITTING > PIT

PITTINGS > PIT

PITTITE *n* occupant of a theatre pit

PITTITES > PITTITE

PITUITA *n* thick nasal secretion

PITUITARY *n* gland at the base of the brain, that helps to control growth ▷ *adj* of or relating to the pituitary gland

PITUITAS > PITUITA

PITUITE *n* mucus

PITUITES > PITUITE

PITUITRIN *n* extract from pituitary gland

PITURI *n* Australian solanaceous shrub

PITURIS > PITURI

PITY *n* sympathy or sorrow for others' suffering ▷ *vb* feel pity for

PITYING > PITY

PITYINGLY > PITY

PITYROID *adj* resembling bran

PIU *adv* more (quickly, softly, etc)

PIUM *n* stinging insect

PIUMS > PIUM

PIUPIU *n* skirt made from the leaves of the New Zealand flax, worn by Māoris on ceremonial occasions

PIUPIUS > PIUPIU

PIVOT *n* central shaft on which something turns ▷ *vb* provide with or turn on a pivot

PIVOTABLE > PIVOT

PIVOTAL *adj* of crucial importance

PIVOTALLY > PIVOTAL

PIVOTED > PIVOT

PIVOTER > PIVOT

PIVOTERS > PIVOT

PIVOTING > PIVOT

PIVOTINGS > PIVOT

PIVOTMAN *n* person in rank around whom others wheel

PIVOTMEN > PIVOTMAN

PIVOTS > PIVOT

PIX *less common spelling of* > PYX

PIXEL *n* any of a number of very small picture elements that make up a picture, as on a visual display unit

PIXELS > PIXEL

PIXES > PIX

PIXIE *n* (in folklore) fairy

PIXIEISH > PIXIE

PIXIES > PIXY

PIXILATED *adj* eccentric or whimsical

PIXINESS > PIXIE

PIXY *same as* > PIXIE

PIXYISH > PIXY

PIZAZZ *same as* > PIZZAZZ

PIZAZZES > PIZAZZ

PIZAZZY > PIZAZZ

PIZE *vb* strike (someone a blow)

PIZED > PIZE

PIZES > PIZE

PIZING > PIZE

PIZZA *n* flat disc of dough covered with a wide variety of savoury toppings and baked

PIZZAIOLA *adj* having a type of tomato sauce

PIZZALIKE > PIZZA

PIZZAS > PIZZA

PIZZAZ *same as* > PZAZZ

PIZZAZES > PIZZAZ

PIZZAZZ *n* attractive combination of energy and style

PIZZAZZES > PIZZAZZ

PIZZAZZY > PIZZAZZ

PIZZELLE *n* Italian sweet wafer

PIZZELLES > PIZZELLE

PIZZERIA *n* place where pizzas are made, sold, or eaten

PIZZERIAS > PIZZERIA

PIZZICATI > PIZZICATO

PIZZICATO *adj* played by plucking the string of a violin etc with the finger ▷ *adv* (in music for the violin family) to be plucked with the finger ▷ *n* style or technique of playing a normally bowed stringed instrument in this manner

PIZZLE *n* penis of an animal, esp a bull

PIZZLES > PIZZLE

PLAAS *n* farm

PLAASES > PLAAS

PLACABLE *adj* easily placated or appeased

PLACABLY > PLACABLE

PLACARD *n* notice that is carried or displayed in public ▷ *vb* attach placards to

PLACARDED > PLACARD

PLACARDS > PLACARD

PLACATE *vb* make (someone) stop feeling angry or upset

PLACATED > PLACATE

PLACATER > PLACATE

PLACATERS > PLACATE

PLACATES > PLACATE

PLACATING > PLACATE

PLACATION > PLACATE

PLACATIVE *same as* > PLACATORY

PLACATORY *adj* placating or intended to placate

PLACCAT *variant of* > PLACKET

PLACCATE *variant of* > PLACKET

PLACCATES > PLACCATE

PLACCATS > PLACCAT

PLACE *n* particular part of an area or space ▷ *vb* put in a particular place

PLACEABLE > PLACE

PLACEBO *n* sugar pill etc given to an unsuspecting

patient instead of an active drug

PLACEBOES > PLACEBO

PLACEBOS > PLACEBO

PLACED > PLACE

PLACEKICK n (in football) kick in which the ball is placed in position before it is kicked ▷ vb take a placekick

PLACELESS adj not rooted in a specific place or community

PLACEMAN n person who holds a public office, esp for private profit and as a reward for political support

PLACEMEN > PLACEMAN

PLACEMENT n arrangement

PLACENTA n organ formed in the womb during pregnancy, providing nutrients for the fetus

PLACENTAE > PLACENTA

PLACENTAL adj (esp of animals) having a placenta

PLACENTAS > PLACENTA

PLACER n surface sediment containing particles of gold or some other valuable mineral

PLACERS > PLACER

PLACES > PLACE

PLACET n vote or expression of assent by saying the word placet

PLACETS > PLACET

PLACID adj not easily excited or upset, calm

PLACIDER > PLACID

PLACIDEST > PLACID

PLACIDITY > PLACID

PLACIDLY > PLACID

PLACING n method of issuing securities to the public using an intermediary, such as a stockbroking firm

PLACINGS > PLACING

PLACIT n decree or dictum

PLACITA > PLACITUM

PLACITORY > PLACIT

PLACITS > PLACIT

PLACITUM n court or assembly in Middle Ages

PLACK n small former Scottish coin

PLACKET n opening at the waist of a dress or skirt for buttons or zips or for access to a pocket

PLACKETS > PLACKET

PLACKLESS adj lacking money

PLACKS > PLACK

PLACODERM n extinct bony-plated fishlike vertebrate

PLACOID adj platelike or flattened ▷ n fish with placoid scales

PLACOIDS > PLACOID

PLAFOND n ceiling, esp one having ornamentation

PLAFONDS > PLAFOND

PLAGAL adj (of a cadence) progressing from the subdominant to the tonic

chord, as in the Amen of a hymn

PLAGE n bright patch in the sun's chromosphere

PLAGES > PLAGE

PLAGIARY n person who plagiarizes or a piece of plagiarism

PLAGIUM n crime of kidnapping

PLAGIUMS > PLAGIUM

PLAGUE n fast-spreading fatal disease ▷ vb trouble or annoy continually

PLAGUED > PLAGUE

PLAGUER > PLAGUE

PLAGUERS > PLAGUE

PLAGUES > PLAGUE

PLAGUEY same as > PLAGUY

PLAGUIER > PLAGUEY

PLAGUIEST > PLAGUEY

PLAGUILY > PLAGUY

PLAGUING > PLAGUE

PLAGUY adj disagreeable or vexing ▷ adv disagreeably or annoyingly

PLAICE n edible European flatfish

PLAICES > PLAICE

PLAID n long piece of tartan cloth worn as part of Highland dress ▷ vb weave cloth into plaid

PLAIDED > PLAID

PLAIDING > PLAID

PLAIDINGS > PLAID

PLAIDMAN n wearer of plaid

PLAIDMEN > PLAIDMAN

PLAIDS > PLAID

PLAIN adj easy to see or understand ▷ n large stretch of level country ▷ adv clearly or simply ▷ vb complain

PLAINANT n plaintiff

PLAINANTS > PLAINANT

PLAINED > PLAIN

PLAINER > PLAIN

PLAINEST > PLAIN

PLAINFUL adj apt to complain

PLAINING > PLAIN

PLAININGS > PLAIN

PLAINISH > PLAIN

PLAINLY > PLAIN

PLAINNESS > PLAIN

PLAINS pl n extensive tracts of level or almost level treeless countryside

PLAINSMAN n person who lives in a plains region, esp in the Great Plains of North America

PLAINSMEN > PLAINSMAN

PLAINSONG n unaccompanied singing, esp in a medieval church

PLAINT n complaint or lamentation

PLAINTEXT n (in telecommunications) message set in a directly readable form rather than in coded groups

PLAINTFUL adj complaining

PLAINTIFF n person who sues in a court of law

PLAINTIVE adj sad, mournful

PLAINTS > PLAINT

PLAINWORK n weaving

PLAISTER n plaster

PLAISTERS > PLAISTER

PLAIT n intertwined length of hair ▷ vb intertwine separate strands in a pattern

PLAITED > PLAIT

PLAITER > PLAIT

PLAITERS > PLAIT

PLAITING > PLAIT

PLAITINGS > PLAIT

PLAITS > PLAIT

PLAN n way thought out to do or achieve something ▷ vb arrange beforehand

PLANAR adj of or relating to a plane

PLANARIA n type of flatworm

PLANARIAN n type of flatworm

PLANARIAS > PLANARIA

PLANARITY > PLANAR

PLANATE adj having been flattened

PLANATION n erosion of a land surface until it is basically flat

PLANCH vb cover with planks

PLANCHE same as > PLANCH

PLANCHED > PLANCH

PLANCHES > PLANCH

PLANCHET n piece of metal ready to be stamped as a coin, medal, etc

PLANCHETS > PLANCHET

PLANCHING > PLANCH

PLANE n aeroplane ▷ adj perfectly flat or level ▷ vb glide or skim

PLANED > PLANE

PLANELOAD n amount or number carried by plane

PLANENESS > PLANE

PLANER n machine with a cutting tool that makes repeated horizontal strokes across the surface of a workpiece

PLANERS > PLANER

PLANES > PLANE

PLANESIDE n area next to aeroplane

PLANET n large body in space that revolves round the sun or another star

PLANETARY adj of or relating to a planet ▷ n train of planetary gears

PLANETIC > PLANET

PLANETOID See > ASTEROID

PLANETS > PLANET

PLANFORM n outline or silhouette of an object, esp an aircraft, as seen from above

PLANFORMS > PLANFORM

PLANGENCY > PLANGENT

PLANGENT adj (of sounds) mournful and resounding

PLANING > PLANE

PLANISH vb give a final

finish to (metal) by hammering or rolling to produce a smooth surface

PLANISHED > PLANISH

PLANISHER > PLANISH

PLANISHES > PLANISH

PLANK n long flat piece of sawn timber ▷ vb cover or provide (an area) with planks

PLANKED > PLANK

PLANKING n number of planks

PLANKINGS > PLANKING

PLANKS > PLANK

PLANKTER n organism in plankton

PLANKTERS > PLANKTER

PLANKTON n minute animals and plants floating in the surface water of a sea or lake

PLANKTONS > PLANKTON

PLANLESS adj having no plan

PLANNED > PLAN

PLANNER n person who makes plans, esp for the development of a town, building, etc

PLANNERS > PLANNER

PLANNING > PLAN

PLANNINGS > PLAN

PLANOSOL n type of intrazonal soil of humid or subhumid uplands having a strongly leached upper layer overlying a clay hardpan

PLANOSOLS > PLANOSOL

PLANS > PLAN

PLANT n living organism that grows in the ground and has no power to move ▷ vb put in the ground to grow

PLANTA n sole of foot

PLANTABLE > PLANT

PLANTAE > PLANTA

PLANTAGE n plants

PLANTAGES > PLANTAGE

PLANTAIN n low-growing wild plant with broad leaves

PLANTAINS > PLANTAIN

PLANTAR adj of, relating to, or occurring on the sole of the foot or a corresponding part

PLANTAS > PLANTA

PLANTED > PLANT

PLANTER n owner of a plantation

PLANTERS > PLANTER

PLANTING > PLANT

PLANTINGS > PLANT

PLANTLESS > PLANT

PLANTLET n small plant

PLANTLETS > PLANTLET

PLANTLIKE > PLANT

PLANTLING n young plant

PLANTS > PLANT

PLANTSMAN n experienced gardener who specializes in collecting rare or interesting plants

PLANTSMEN > PLANTSMAN

PLANTULE n embryo in act of germination
PLANTULES > PLANTULE
PLANULA n ciliated free-swimming larva of hydrozoan coelenterates such as the hydra
PLANULAE > PLANULA
PLANULAR > PLANULA
PLANULATE adj flat
PLANULOID adj of planula
PLANURIA n expulsion of urine from abnormal opening
PLANURIAS > PLANURIA
PLANURIES > PLANURY
PLANURY another name for > PLANURY
PLANXTIES > PLANXTY
PLANXTY n Celtic melody for harp
PLAP same as > PLOP
PLAPPED > PLAP
PLAPPING > PLAP
PLAPS > PLAP
PLAQUE n inscribed commemorative stone or metal plate
PLAQUES > PLAQUE
PLAQUETTE n small plaque
PLASH same as > PLEACH
PLASHED > PLASH
PLASHER n type of farm tool
PLASHERS > PLASHER
PLASHES > PLASH
PLASHET n small pond
PLASHETS > PLASHET
PLASHIER > PLASHY
PLASHIEST > PLASHY
PLASHING > PLASH
PLASHINGS > PLASH
PLASHY adj wet or marshy
PLASM same as > PLASMA
PLASMA n clear liquid part of blood
PLASMAGEL another name for > ECTOPLASM
PLASMAS > PLASMA
PLASMASOL another name for > ENDOPLASM
PLASMATIC > PLASMA
PLASMIC > PLASMA
PLASMID n small circle of bacterial DNA that is independent of the main bacterial chromosome
PLASMIDS > PLASMID
PLASMIN n proteolytic enzyme that causes fibrinolysis in blood clots
PLASMINS > PLASMIN
PLASMODIA n amoeboid masses of protoplasm, each containing many nuclei
PLASMOID n section of a plasma having a characteristic shape
PLASMOIDS > PLASMOID
PLASMON n sum total of plasmagenes in a cell
PLASMONS > PLASMON
PLASMS > PLASM
PLAST archaic past participle of > PLACE
PLASTE archaic past participle of > PLACE

PLASTER n mixture of lime, sand, etc for coating walls ▷ vb cover with plaster
PLASTERED adj drunk
PLASTERER > PLASTER
PLASTERS > PLASTER
PLASTERY > PLASTER
PLASTIC n synthetic material that can be moulded when soft but sets in a hard long-lasting shape ▷ adj made of plastic
PLASTICKY adj made of or resembling plastic
PLASTICLY > PLASTIC
PLASTICS > PLASTIC
PLASTID n any of various small particles in the cytoplasm of the cells of plants and some animals
PLASTIDS > PLASTID
PLASTIQUE n easily-moulded plastic explosive
PLASTISOL n suspension of resin particles convertible into solid plastic
PLASTRAL > PLASTRON
PLASTRON n bony plate forming the ventral part of the shell of a tortoise or turtle
PLASTRONS > PLASTRON
PLASTRUM variant of > PLASTRON
PLASTRUMS > PLASTRUM
PLAT n small area of ground
PLATAN n plane tree
PLATANE same as > PLATAN
PLATANES > PLATANE
PLATANNA n S African frog
PLATANNAS > PLATANNA
PLATANS > PLATAN
PLATBAND n border of flowers in garden
PLATBANDS > PLATBAND
PLATE n shallow dish for holding food ▷ vb cover with a thin coating of gold, silver, or other metal
PLATEASM n talking with mouth open too wide
PLATEASMS > PLATEASM
PLATEAU n area of level high land ▷ vb remain stable for a long period
PLATEAUED > PLATEAU
PLATEAUS > PLATEAU
PLATEAUX > PLATEAU
PLATED adj coated with a layer of metal
PLATEFUL same as > PLATE
PLATEFULS > PLATEFUL
PLATELET n minute particle occurring in blood of vertebrates and involved in clotting of blood
PLATELETS > PLATELET
PLATELIKE > PLATE
PLATEMAN n one of crew of steam train
PLATEMARK another name for > HALLMARK
PLATEMEN > PLATEMAN
PLATEN n roller of a typewriter, against which the paper is held

PLATENS > PLATEN
PLATER n person or thing that plates
PLATERS > PLATER
PLATES > PLATE
PLATESFUL > PLATEFUL
PLATFORM n raised floor
PLATFORMS > PLATFORM
PLATIER > PLATY
PLATIES > PLATY
PLATIEST > PLATY
PLATINA n alloy of platinum and several other metals, including palladium, osmium, and iridium
PLATINAS > PLATINA
PLATING n coating of metal
PLATINGS > PLATING
PLATINIC adj of or containing platinum, esp in the tetravalent state
PLATINISE same as > PLATINIZE
PLATINIZE vb coat with platinum
PLATINOID adj containing or resembling platinum
PLATINOUS adj of or containing platinum, esp in the divalent state
PLATINUM n valuable silvery-white metal
PLATINUMS > PLATINUM
PLATITUDE n remark that is true but not interesting or original
PLATONIC adj (of a relationship) friendly or affectionate but not sexual ▷ n platonic friend
PLATONICS > PLATONIC
PLATONISM n philosophy of Plato
PLATOON n smaller unit within a company of soldiers ▷ vb organise into platoons
PLATOONED > PLATOON
PLATOONS > PLATOON
PLATS > PLAT
PLATTED > PLAT
PLATTER n large dish
PLATTERS > PLATTER
PLATTING > PLAT
PLATTINGS > PLAT
PLATY adj of, relating to, or designating rocks the constituents of which occur in flaky layers ▷ n small brightly coloured freshwater cyprinodont fish
PLATYFISH same as > PLATY
PLATYPI > PLATYPUS
PLATYPUS n Australian egg-laying amphibious mammal, with dense fur, webbed feet, and a ducklike bill
PLATYS > PLATY
PLATYSMA n muscle located on side of neck
PLATYSMAS > PLATYSMA
PLAUDIT n expression of enthusiastic approval
PLAUDITE interj give a round of applause!

PLAUDITS > PLAUDIT
PLAUSIBLE adj apparently true or reasonable
PLAUSIBLY > PLAUSIBLE
PLAUSIVE adj expressing praise or approval
PLAUSTRAL adj relating to wagons
PLAY vb occupy oneself in (a game or recreation) ▷ n story performed on stage or broadcast
PLAYA n (in the US) temporary lake, or its dry often salty bed, in a desert basin
PLAYABLE > PLAY
PLAYACT vb pretend or make believe
PLAYACTED > PLAYACT
PLAYACTOR > PLAYACT
PLAYACTS > PLAYACT
PLAYAS > PLAYA
PLAYBACK n playing of a recording on magnetic tape ▷ vb listen to or watch (something recorded)
PLAYBACKS > PLAYBACK
PLAYBILL n poster or bill advertising a play
PLAYBILLS > PLAYBILL
PLAYBOOK n book containing a range of possible set plays
PLAYBOOKS > PLAYBOOK
PLAYBOY n rich man who lives only for pleasure
PLAYBOYS > PLAYBOY
PLAYBUS n mobile playground
PLAYBUSES > PLAYBUS
PLAYDATE n gathering of children at house for play
PLAYDATES > PLAYDATE
PLAYDAY n day given to play
PLAYDAYS > PLAYDAY
PLAYDOWN same as > PLAYOFF
PLAYDOWNS > PLAYDOWN
PLAYED > PLAY
PLAYER n person who plays a game or sport
PLAYERS > PLAYER
PLAYFIELD n field for sports
PLAYFUL adj lively
PLAYFULLY > PLAYFUL
PLAYGIRL n rich woman devoted to pleasure
PLAYGIRLS > PLAYGIRL
PLAYGOER n person who goes often to the theatre
PLAYGOERS > PLAYGOER
PLAYGOING > PLAYGOER
PLAYGROUP same as > PLAYSCHOOL
PLAYHOUSE n theatre
PLAYING
PLAYLAND US variant of > PLAYGROUND
PLAYLANDS > PLAYLAND
PLAYLESS > PLAY
PLAYLET n short play
PLAYLETS > PLAYLET
PLAYLIKE > PLAY
PLAYLIST n list of records chosen for playing, such

as on a radio station ▷ vb put (a song or record) on a playlist
PLAYLISTS > PLAYLIST
PLAYMAKER n player who creates scoring opportunities for his or her team-mates
PLAYMATE n companion in play
PLAYMATES > PLAYMATE
PLAYOFF n extra contest to decide the winner when two or more competitors are tied
PLAYOFFS > PLAYOFF
PLAYPEN n small portable enclosure in which a young child can safely be left to play
PLAYPENS > PLAYPEN
PLAYROOM n recreation room, esp for children
PLAYROOMS > PLAYROOM
PLAYS > PLAY
PLAYSOME adj playful
PLAYSUIT n woman's or child's outfit, usually comprising shorts and a top
PLAYSUITS > PLAYSUIT
PLAYTHING n toy
PLAYTIME n time for play or recreation, such as a school break
PLAYTIMES > PLAYTIME
PLAYWEAR n clothes suitable for playing in
PLAZA n open space or square
PLAZAS > PLAZA
PLEA n serious or urgent request, entreaty
PLEACH vb interlace the stems or boughs of (a tree or hedge)
PLEACHED > PLEACH
PLEACHES > PLEACH
PLEACHING > PLEACH
PLEAD vb ask urgently or with deep feeling
PLEADABLE > PLEAD
PLEADED > PLEAD
PLEADER > PLEAD
PLEADERS > PLEAD
PLEADING > PLEAD
PLEADINGS > PLEAD
PLEADS > PLEAD
PLEAED > PLEA
PLEAING > PLEA
PLEAS > PLEA
PLEASABLE > PLEASE
PLEASANCE n secluded part of a garden laid out with trees, walks, etc
PLEASANT adj pleasing, enjoyable
PLEASE vb give pleasure or satisfaction to ▷ adv polite word of request
PLEASED > PLEASE
PLEASEDLY > PLEASE
PLEASEMAN n person who courts favour
PLEASEMEN > PLEASEMAN
PLEASER > PLEASE
PLEASERS > PLEASE

PLEASES > PLEASE
PLEASETH obsolete inflection of > PLEASE
PLEASING adj giving pleasure or satisfaction ▷ n act of giving pleasure
PLEASINGS > PLEASING
PLEASURE n feeling of happiness and satisfaction ▷ vb give pleasure to or take pleasure (in)
PLEASURED > PLEASURE
PLEASURER > PLEASURE
PLEASURES > PLEASURE
PLEAT n fold made by doubling material back on itself ▷ vb arrange (material) in pleats
PLEATED > PLEAT
PLEATER n attachment on a sewing machine that makes pleats
PLEATERS > PLEATER
PLEATHER n synthetic leather
PLEATHERS > PLEATHER
PLEATING > PLEAT
PLEATLESS > PLEAT
PLEATS > PLEAT
PLEB n common vulgar person
PLEBBIER > PLEBBY
PLEBBIEST > PLEBBY
PLEBBY adj common or vulgar
PLEBE n member of the lowest class at the US Naval Academy or Military Academy
PLEBEAN old variant of > PLEBEIAN
PLEBEIAN adj of the lower social classes ▷ n member of the lower social classes
PLEBEIANS > PLEBEIAN
PLEBES > PLEBE
PLEBIFIED > PLEBIFY
PLEBIFIES > PLEBIFY
PLEBIFY vb make plebeian
PLEBS n common people
PLECTRA > PLECTRUM
PLECTRE variant of > PLECTRUM
PLECTRES > PLECTRE
PLECTRON same as > PLECTRUM
PLECTRONS > PLECTRON
PLECTRUM n small implement for plucking the strings of a guitar etc
PLECTRUMS > PLECTRUM
PLED > PLEAD
PLEDGABLE > PLEDGE
PLEDGE n solemn promise ▷ vb promise solemnly
PLEDGED > PLEDGE
PLEDGEE n person to whom a pledge is given
PLEDGEES > PLEDGEE
PLEDGEOR same as > PLEDGOR
PLEDGEORS > PLEDGEOR
PLEDGER same as > PLEDGOR
PLEDGERS > PLEDGER
PLEDGES > PLEDGE
PLEDGET n small flattened pad of wool, cotton, etc,

esp for use as a pressure bandage to be applied to wounds or sores
PLEDGETS > PLEDGET
PLEDGING > PLEDGE
PLEDGOR n person who gives or makes a pledge
PLEDGORS > PLEDGOR
PLEIAD n brilliant or talented group, esp one with seven members
PLEIADES > PLEIAD
PLEIADS > PLEIAD
PLEIOCENE variant spelling of > PLIOCENE
PLEIOMERY n state of having more than normal number
PLEIOTAXY n increase in whorls in flower
PLENA > PLENUM
PLENARIES > PLENARY
PLENARILY > PLENARY
PLENARTY n state of endowed church office when occupied
PLENARY adj (of a meeting) attended by all members ▷ n book of the gospels or epistles and homilies read at the Eucharist
PLENCH n tool combining wrench and pliers
PLENCHES > PLENCH
PLENILUNE n full moon
PLENIPO n plenipotentiary diplomat
PLENIPOES > PLENIPO
PLENIPOS > PLENIPO
PLENISH vb fill, stock, or resupply
PLENISHED > PLENISH
PLENISHER > PLENISH
PLENISHES > PLENISH
PLENISM n philosophical theory
PLENISMS > PLENISM
PLENIST > PLENISM
PLENISTS > PLENISM
PLENITUDE n completeness, abundance
PLENTEOUS adj plentiful
PLENTIES > PLENTY
PLENTIFUL adj existing in large amounts or numbers
PLENTY n large amount or number ▷ adj very many ▷ adv more than adequately
PLENUM n enclosure containing gas at a higher pressure than the surrounding environment
PLENUMS > PLENUM
PLEON n abdomen of crustacean
PLEONAL adj of abdomen or crustacean
PLEONASM n use of more words than necessary
PLEONASMS > PLEONASM
PLEONAST n person using more words than necessary
PLEONASTE n type of black mineral
PLEONASTS > PLEONAST

PLEONEXIA n greed
PLEONIC > PLEON
PLEONS > PLEON
PLEOPOD another name for > SWIMMERET
PLEOPODS > PLEOPOD
PLERION n filled-centre supernova remnant in which radiation is emitted by the centre as well as the shell
PLERIONS > PLERION
PLEROMA n abundance
PLEROMAS > PLEROMA
PLEROME n central column in growing stem or root
PLEROMES > PLEROME
PLESH n small pool
PLESHES > PLESH
PLESSOR same as > PLEXOR
PLESSORS > PLESSOR
PLETHORA n excess
PLETHORAS > PLETHORA
PLETHORIC > PLETHORA
PLEUCH same as > PLEUGH
PLEUCHED > PLEUCH
PLEUCHING > PLEUCH
PLEUCHS > PLEUCH
PLEUGH Scottish word for > PLOUGH
PLEUGHED > PLEUGH
PLEUGHING > PLEUGH
PLEUGHS > PLEUGH
PLEURA > PLEURON
PLEURAE > PLEURON
PLEURAL > PLEURON
PLEURAS > PLEURON
PLEURISY n inflammation of the membrane covering the lungs
PLEURITIC > PLEURISY
PLEURITIS n pleurisy
PLEURON n part of the cuticle of arthropods that covers the lateral surface of a body segment
PLEUSTON n mass of small organisms, esp algae, floating at the surface of shallow pools
PLEUSTONS > PLEUSTON
PLEW n (formerly in Canada) beaver skin used as a standard unit of value in the fur trade
PLEWS > PLEW
PLEX n shortening of multiplex
PLEXAL > PLEXUS
PLEXES > PLEX
PLEXIFORM adj like or having the form of a network or plexus
PLEXOR n small hammer with a rubber head for use in percussion of the chest and testing reflexes
PLEXORS > PLEXOR
PLEXURE n act of weaving together
PLEXURES > PLEXURE
PLEXUS n complex network of nerves or blood vessels
PLEXUSES > PLEXUS
PLIABLE adj easily bent
PLIABLY > PLIABLE
PLIANCIES > PLIANT

PLIANCY > PLIANT
PLIANT adj pliable
PLIANTLY > PLIANT
PLICA n folding over of parts, such as a fold of skin, muscle, peritoneum, etc
PLICAE > PLICA
PLICAL > PLICA
PLICATE adj having or arranged in parallel folds or ridges ▷vb arrange into parallel folds
PLICATED > PLICATE
PLICATELY > PLICATE
PLICATES > PLICATE
PLICATING > PLICATE
PLICATION n act of folding or the condition of being folded or plicate
PLICATURE same as > PLICATION
PLIE n classic ballet practice posture with back erect and knees bent
PLIED > PLY
PLIER n person who plies a trade
PLIERS pl n tool with hinged arms and jaws for gripping
PLIES > PLY
PLIGHT n difficult or dangerous situation
PLIGHTED > PLIGHT
PLIGHTER > PLIGHT
PLIGHTERS > PLIGHT
PLIGHTFUL > PLIGHT
PLIGHTING > PLIGHT
PLIGHTS > PLIGHT
PLIM vb swell with water
PLIMMED > PLIM
PLIMMING > PLIM
PLIMS > PLIM
PLIMSOL same as > PLIMSOLE
PLIMSOLE same as > PLIMSOLL
PLIMSOLES > PLIMSOLE
PLIMSOLL n light rubber-soled canvas shoe worn for various sports
PLIMSOLLS > PLIMSOLL
PLIMSOLS > PLIMSOL
PLING n (in computer jargon) an exclamation mark
PLINGS > PLING
PLINK n short sharp often metallic sound as of a string on a musical instrument being plucked or a bullet striking metal ▷vb make such a noise
PLINKED > PLINK
PLINKER > PLINK
PLINKERS > PLINK
PLINKING > PLINK
PLINKINGS > PLINK
PLINKS > PLINK
PLINTH n slab forming the base of a statue, column, etc
PLINTHS > PLINTH
PLIOCENE adj of the Pliocene geological time period
PLIOFILM n transparent

plastic material
PLIOFILMS > PLIOFILM
PLIOSAUR n type of dinosaur
PLIOSAURS > PLIOSAUR
PLIOTRON n type of vacuum tube
PLIOTRONS > PLIOTRON
PLISKIE n practical joke
PLISKIES > PLISKIE
PLISKY same as > PLISKIE
PLISSE n fabric with a wrinkled finish, achieved by treatment involving caustic soda
PLISSES > PLISSE
PLOAT vb thrash
PLOATED > PLOAT
PLOATING > PLOAT
PLOATS > PLOAT
PLOD vb walk with slow heavy steps ▷n act of plodding
PLODDED > PLOD
PLODDER n person who plods, esp one who works in a slow and persevering but uninspired manner
PLODDERS > PLODDER
PLODDING > PLOD
PLODDINGS > PLOD
PLODGE vb wade in water, esp the sea ▷n act of wading
PLODGED > PLODGE
PLODGES > PLODGE
PLODGING > PLODGE
PLODS > PLOD
PLOIDIES > PLOIDY
PLOIDY n number of copies of set of chromosomes in cell
PLONG obsolete variant of > PLUNGE
PLONGD > PLONG
PLONGE vb clean drains by action of tide
PLONGED > PLONGE
PLONGES > PLONGE
PLONGING > PLONGE
PLONGS > PLONG
PLONK vb put (something) down heavily and carelessly ▷n cheap inferior wine ▷interj exclamation imitative of this sound
PLONKED > PLONK
PLONKER n stupid person
PLONKERS > PLONKER
PLONKIER > PLONK
PLONKIEST > PLONK
PLONKING > PLONK
PLONKINGS > PLONK
PLONKO n alcoholic, esp one who drinks wine
PLONKOS > PLONKO
PLONKS > PLONK
PLONKY > PLONK
PLOOK same as > PLOUK
PLOOKIE same as > PLOUKY
PLOOKIER > PLOUK
PLOOKIEST > PLOUK
PLOOKS > PLOOK
PLOOKY same as > PLOUKY
PLOP n sound of an object falling into water without

a splash ▷vb make this sound ▷interj exclamation imitative of this sound
PLOPPED > PLOP
PLOPPING > PLOP
PLOPS > PLOP
PLOSION n sound of an abrupt break or closure, esp the audible release of a stop
PLOSIONS > PLOSION
PLOSIVE adj pronounced with a sudden release of breath ▷n plosive consonant
PLOSIVES > PLOSIVE
PLOT n secret plan to do something illegal or wrong ▷vb plan secretly, conspire
PLOTFUL > PLOT
PLOTLESS > PLOT
PLOTLINE n literary or dramatic plot
PLOTLINES > PLOTLINE
PLOTS > PLOT
PLOTTAGE n land that makes up plot
PLOTTAGES > PLOTTAGE
PLOTTED > PLOT
PLOTTER same as > PLOUTER
PLOTTERED > PLOTTER
PLOTTERS > PLOTTER
PLOTTIE n hot spiced drink
PLOTTIER > PLOTTY
PLOTTIES > PLOTTIE
PLOTTIEST > PLOTTY
PLOTTING > PLOT
PLOTTINGS > PLOT
PLOTTY adj intricately plotted
PLOTZ vb faint or collapse
PLOTZED > PLOTZ
PLOTZES > PLOTZ
PLOTZING > PLOTZ
PLOUGH n agricultural tool for turning over soil ▷vb turn over (earth) with a plough
PLOUGHBOY n boy who guides the animals drawing a plough
PLOUGHED > PLOUGH
PLOUGHER > PLOUGH
PLOUGHERS > PLOUGH
PLOUGHING > PLOUGH
PLOUGHMAN n man who ploughs
PLOUGHMEN > PLOUGHMAN
PLOUGHS > PLOUGH
PLOUK n pimple
PLOUKIE > PLOUK
PLOUKIER > PLOUK
PLOUKIEST > PLOUK
PLOUKS > PLOUK
PLOUKY > PLOUK
PLOUTER same as > PLOWTER
PLOUTERED > PLOUTER
PLOUTERS > PLOUTER
PLOVER n shore bird with a straight bill and long pointed wings
PLOVERS > PLOVER
PLOVERY > PLOVER
PLOW same as > PLOUGH
PLOWABLE > PLOW
PLOWBACK n reinvestment of profits

PLOWBACKS > PLOWBACK
PLOWBOY same as > PLOUGHBOY
PLOWBOYS > PLOWBOY
PLOWED > PLOW
PLOWER > PLOW
PLOWERS > PLOW
PLOWHEAD n draught iron of plow
PLOWHEADS > PLOWHEAD
PLOWING > PLOW
PLOWLAND n land plowed
PLOWLANDS > PLOWLAND
PLOWMAN same as > PLOUGHMAN
PLOWMEN > PLOWMAN
PLOWS > PLOW
PLOWSHARE n horizontal pointed cutting blade of a mouldboard plow
PLOWSTAFF n one of the handles of a plow
PLOWTER vb work or play in water or mud ▷n act of plowtering
PLOWTERED > PLOWTER
PLOWTERS > PLOWTER
PLOY n manoeuvre designed to gain an advantage ▷vb form a column from a line of troops
PLOYED > PLOY
PLOYING > PLOY
PLOYS > PLOY
PLU same as > PLEW
PLUCK vb pull or pick off ▷n courage
PLUCKED > PLUCK
PLUCKER > PLUCK
PLUCKERS > PLUCK
PLUCKIER > PLUCKY
PLUCKIEST > PLUCKY
PLUCKILY > PLUCKY
PLUCKING > PLUCK
PLUCKS > PLUCK
PLUCKY adj brave
PLUE same as > PLEW
PLUES > PLUE
PLUFF vb expel in puffs
PLUFFED > PLUFF
PLUFFIER > PLUFF
PLUFFIEST > PLUFF
PLUFFING > PLUFF
PLUFFS > PLUFF
PLUFFY > PLUFF
PLUG n thing fitting into and filling a hole ▷vb block or seal (a hole or gap) with a plug
PLUGBOARD n device with a large number of sockets in which electrical plugs can be inserted to form many different temporary circuits
PLUGGED > PLUG
PLUGGER > PLUG
PLUGGERS > PLUG
PLUGGING > PLUG
PLUGGINGS > PLUG
PLUGHOLE n hole, esp in a bath, basin, or sink, through which waste water drains and which can be closed with a plug
PLUGHOLES > PLUGHOLE

P

PLUGLESS > PLUG

PLUGOLA n plugging of products on television

PLUGOLAS > PLUGOLA

PLUGS > PLUG

PLUGUGLY n city tough; ruffian

PLUM n oval usu dark red fruit with a stone in the middle ▷ adj dark purplish-red

PLUMAGE n bird's feathers

PLUMAGED > PLUMAGE

PLUMAGES > PLUMAGE

PLUMATE adj of, relating to, or possessing one or more feathers or plumes

PLUMB vb understand (something obscure) ▷ adv exactly ▷ n weight, usually of lead, suspended at the end of a line and used to determine water depth or verticality

PLUMBABLE > PLUMB

PLUMBAGO n plant of warm regions with clusters of blue, white, or red flowers

PLUMBAGOS > PLUMBAGO

PLUMBATE n compound formed from lead oxide

PLUMBATES > PLUMBATE

PLUMBED > PLUMB

PLUMBEOUS adj made of or relating to lead or resembling lead in colour

PLUMBER n person who fits and repairs pipes and fixtures for water and drainage systems

PLUMBERS > PLUMBER

PLUMBERY same as > PLUMBING

PLUMBIC adj of or containing lead in the tetravalent state

PLUMBING n pipes and fixtures used in water and drainage systems

PLUMBINGS > PLUMBING

PLUMBISM n chronic lead poisoning

PLUMBISMS > PLUMBISM

PLUMBITE n substance containing lead oxide

PLUMBITES > PLUMBITE

PLUMBLESS adj incapable of being sounded

PLUMBNESS > PLUMB

PLUMBOUS adj of or containing lead in the divalent state

PLUMBS > PLUMB

PLUMBUM n obsolete name for lead (the metal)

PLUMBUMS > PLUMBUM

PLUMCOT n hybrid of apricot and plum

PLUMCOTS > PLUMCOT

PLUMDAMAS n prune

PLUME n feather, esp one worn as an ornament ▷ vb adorn or decorate with feathers or plumes

PLUMED > PLUME

PLUMELESS > PLUME

PLUMELET n small plume

PLUMELETS > PLUMELET

PLUMELIKE > PLUME

PLUMERIA n tropical tree with candelabra-like branches

PLUMERIAS > PLUMERIA

PLUMERIES > PLUMERY

PLUMERY n plumes collectively

PLUMES > PLUME

PLUMIER > PLUMY

PLUMIEST > PLUMY

PLUMING > PLUME

PLUMIPED n bird with feathered feet

PLUMIPEDS > PLUMIPED

PLUMIST n person who makes plumes

PLUMISTS > PLUMIST

PLUMLIKE > PLUM

PLUMMER > PLUM

PLUMMEST > PLUM

PLUMMET vb plunge downward ▷ n weight on a plumb line or fishing line

PLUMMETED > PLUMMET

PLUMMETS > PLUMMET

PLUMMIER > PLUMMY

PLUMMIEST > PLUMMY

PLUMMY adj of, full of, or like plums

PLUMOSE same as > PLUMATE

PLUMOSELY > PLUMOSE

PLUMOSITY > PLUMOSE

PLUMOUS adj having plumes or feathers

PLUMP adj moderately or attractively fat ▷ vb sit or fall heavily and suddenly ▷ n heavy abrupt fall or the sound of this ▷ adv suddenly or heavily

PLUMPED > PLUMP

PLUMPEN vb make or become plump

PLUMPENED > PLUMPEN

PLUMPENS > PLUMPEN

PLUMPER n pad carried in the mouth by actors to round out the cheeks

PLUMPERS > PLUMPER

PLUMPEST > PLUMP

PLUMPIE same as > PLUMPY

PLUMPIER > PLUMPY

PLUMPIEST > PLUMPY

PLUMPING > PLUMP

PLUMPISH adj on the plump side

PLUMPLY > PLUMP

PLUMPNESS > PLUMP

PLUMPS > PLUMP

PLUMPY adj plump

PLUMS > PLUM

PLUMULA n down feather

PLUMULAE > PLUMULA

PLUMULAR > PLUMULE

PLUMULATE adj covered with soft fine feathers

PLUMULE n embryonic shoot of seed-bearing plants

PLUMULES > PLUMULE

PLUMULOSE adj having hairs branching out like feathers

PLUMY adj like a feather

PLUNDER vb take by force, esp in time of war ▷ n

things plundered, spoils

PLUNDERED > PLUNDER

PLUNDERER > PLUNDER

PLUNDERS > PLUNDER

PLUNGE vb put or throw forcibly or suddenly (into) ▷ n plunging dive

PLUNGED > PLUNGE

PLUNGER n rubber suction cup used to clear blocked pipes

PLUNGERS > PLUNGER

PLUNGES > PLUNGE

PLUNGING > PLUNGE

PLUNGINGS > PLUNGE

PLUNK vb pluck the strings of (a banjo etc) to produce a twanging sound ▷ n act or sound of plunking ▷ interj exclamation imitative of the sound of something plunking ▷ adv exactly

PLUNKED > PLUNK

PLUNKER > PLUNK

PLUNKERS > PLUNK

PLUNKIER > PLUNKY

PLUNKIEST > PLUNKY

PLUNKING > PLUNK

PLUNKS > PLUNK

PLUNKY adj sounding like plucked banjo string

PLURAL adj of or consisting of more than one ▷ n word indicating more than one

PLURALISE same as > PLURALIZE

PLURALISM n existence and toleration of a variety of peoples, opinions, etc in a society

PLURALIST > PLURALISM

PLURALITY n state of being plural

PLURALIZE vb make or become plural

PLURALLY > PLURAL

PLURALS > PLURAL

PLURIPARA n woman who has borne more than one child

PLURISIE same as > PLEURISY

PLURISIES > PLURISIE

PLURRY euphemism for > BLOODY

PLUS vb make or become greater in value

PLUSAGE same as > PLUSSAGE

PLUSAGES > PLUSAGE

PLUSED > PLUS

PLUSES > PLUS

PLUSH n fabric with long velvety pile ▷ adj luxurious

PLUSHER > PLUSH

PLUSHES > PLUSH

PLUSHEST > PLUSH

PLUSHIER > PLUSHY

PLUSHIEST > PLUSHY

PLUSHILY > PLUSHY

PLUSHLY > PLUSH

PLUSHNESS > PLUSH

PLUSHY same as > PLUSH

PLUSING > PLUS

PLUSSAGE n amount over and above another amount

PLUSSAGES > PLUSSAGE

PLUSSED > PLUS

PLUSSES > PLUS

PLUSSING > PLUS

PLUTEAL > PLUTEUS

PLUTEI > PLUTEUS

PLUTEUS n larva of sea urchin

PLUTEUSES > PLUTEUS

PLUTOCRAT n person who is powerful because of being very rich

PLUTOLOGY n study of wealth

PLUTON n any mass of igneous rock that has solidified below the surface of the earth

PLUTONIAN adj of or relating to the underworld

PLUTONIC adj (of igneous rocks) formed from molten rock that has cooled and solidified below the earth's surface

PLUTONISM n theory that the earth's crust was formed by volcanoes

PLUTONIUM n radioactive metallic element used esp in nuclear reactors and weapons

PLUTONOMY n economics

PLUTONS > PLUTON

PLUVIAL adj of or caused by the action of rain ▷ n of or relating to rainfall or precipitation

PLUVIALS > PLUVIAL

PLUVIAN n crocodile bird

PLUVIOSE same as > PLUVIOUS

PLUVIOUS adj of or relating to rain

PLY vb work at (a job or trade) ▷ n thickness of wool, fabric, etc

PLYER n person who plies trade

PLYERS > PLYER

PLYING > PLY

PLYINGLY > PLY

PLYWOOD n board made of thin layers of wood glued together

PLYWOODS > PLYWOOD

PNEUMA n person's vital spirit, soul, or creative energy

PNEUMAS > PNEUMA

PNEUMATIC adj worked by or inflated with wind or air

PNEUMONIA n inflammation of the lungs

PNEUMONIC adj of, relating to, or affecting the lungs

PO n chamber pot

POA n type of grass

POACEOUS adj of, relating to, or belonging to the plant family *Poaceae* (grasses)

POACH vb catch (animals) illegally on someone else's land

POACHABLE > POACH

POACHED > POACH

POACHER n person who

catches animals illegally on someone else's land

POACHERS > POACHER

POACHES > POACH

POACHIER > POACHY

POACHIEST > POACHY

POACHING > POACH

POACHINGS > POACH

POACHY adj (of land) wet and soft

POAKA n type of stilt (bird) native to New Zealand

POAKAS > POAKA

POAKE n waste matter from tanning of hides

POAKES > POAKE

POAS > POA

POBLANO n variety of chilli pepper

POBLANOS > POBLANO

POBOY n New Orleans sandwich

POBOYS > POBOY

POCHARD n European diving duck

POCHARDS > POCHARD

POCHAY n post chaise: a closed horse-drawn four-wheeled coach

POCHAYS > POCHAY

POCHETTE n envelope-shaped handbag used by women and men

POCHETTES > POCHETTE

POCHOIR n print made from stencils

POCHOIRS > POCHOIR

POCK n pus-filled blister resulting from smallpox ▷ vb mark with scars

POCKARD variant of > POCHARD

POCKARDS > POCKARD

POCKED > POCK

POCKET n small bag sewn into clothing for carrying things ▷ vb put into one's pocket ▷ adj small

POCKETED > POCKET

POCKETER > POCKET

POCKETERS > POCKET

POCKETFUL n as much as a pocket will hold

POCKETING > POCKET

POCKETS > POCKET

POCKIER > POCK

POCKIES pl n woollen mittens

POCKIEST > POCK

POCKILY > POCK

POCKING > POCK

POCKMANKY n portmanteau

POCKMARK n pitted scar left on the skin after the healing of a smallpox or similar pustule ▷ vb scar or pit (a surface) with pockmarks

POCKMARKS > POCKMARK

POCKPIT n mark left on skin after a pock has gone

POCKPITS > POCKPIT

POCKS > POCK

POCKY > POCK

POCO adv little

POCOSEN same as > POCOSIN

POCOSENS > POCOSEN

POCOSIN n swamp in US upland coastal region

POCOSINS > POCOSIN

POCOSON same as > POCOSIN

POCOSONS > POCOSON

POD n long narrow seed case of peas, beans, etc ▷ vb remove the pod from

PODAGRA n gout of the foot or big toe

PODAGRAL > PODAGRA

PODAGRAS > PODAGRA

PODAGRIC > PODAGRA

PODAGROUS > PODAGRA

PODAL adj relating to feet

PODALIC adj relating to feet

PODARGUS n bird of SE Asia and Australia

PODCAST n audio file similar to a radio broadcast, which can be downloaded and listened to on a computer or MP3 player ▷ vb make available in this format

PODCASTED > PODCAST

PODCASTER > PODCAST

PODCASTS > PODCAST

PODDED > POD

PODDIE n user of or enthusiast for the iPod, a portable digital music player

PODDIER > PODDY

PODDIES > PODDY

PODDIEST > PODDY

PODDING > POD

PODDLE vb move or travel in a leisurely manner

PODDLED > PODDLE

PODDLES > PODDLE

PODDLING > PODDLE

PODDY n handfed calf or lamb ▷ adj fat

PODESTA n (in modern Italy) subordinate magistrate in some towns

PODESTAS > PODESTA

PODEX n posterior

PODEXES > PODEX

PODGE n short chubby person

PODGES > PODGE

PODGIER > PODGY

PODGIEST > PODGY

PODGILY > PODGY

PODGINESS > PODGY

PODGY adj short and fat

PODIA > PODIUM

PODIAL > PODIUM

PODIATRIC > PODIATRY

PODIATRY another word for > CHIROPODY

PODITE n crustacean leg

PODITES > PODITE

PODITIC adj similar to the limb segment of an arthropod

PODIUM n small raised platform for a conductor or speaker

PODIUMS > PODIUM

PODLEY n young coalfish

PODLEYS > PODLEY

PODLIKE > POD

PODOCARP n stem supporting fruit

PODOCARPS > PODOCARP

PODOLOGY n study of feet

PODOMERE n segment of limb of arthropod

PODOMERES > PODOMERE

PODS > POD

PODSOL same as > PODZOL

PODSOLIC > PODZOL

PODSOLISE same as > PODZOLIZE

PODSOLIZE same as > PODZOLIZE

PODSOLS > PODSOL

PODZOL n type of soil characteristic of coniferous forest regions having a greyish-white colour in its upper leached layers

PODZOLIC > PODZOL

PODZOLISE same as > PODZOLIZE

PODZOLIZE vb make into or form a podzol

PODZOLS > PODZOL

POECHORE n dry region

POECHORES > POECHORE

POEM n imaginative piece of writing in rhythmic lines

POEMATIC adj of poetry

POEMS > POEM

POENOLOGY same as > PENOLOGY

POEP n emission of gas from the anus

POEPOL n South African slang for anus

POEPOLS > POEPOL

POEPS > POEP

POESIED > POESY

POESIES > POESY

POESY n poetry ▷ vb write poems

POESYING > POESY

POET n writer of poems

POETASTER n writer of inferior verse

POETASTRY > POETASTER

POETESS n female poet

POETESSES > POETESS

POETIC adj of or like poetry

POETICAL n poet

POETICALS > POETICAL

POETICISE same as > POETICIZE

POETICISM > POETICISE

POETICIZE vb put into poetry or make poetic

POETICS n principles and forms of poetry or the study of these, esp as a form of literary criticism

POETICULE n inferior poet

POETISE same as > POETICIZE

POETISED > POETISE

POETISER > POETISE

POETISERS > POETISE

POETISES > POETISE

POETISING > POETISE

POETIZE same as > POETICIZE

POETIZED > POETIZE

POETIZER > POETIZE

POETIZERS > POETIZE

POETIZES > POETIZE

POETIZING > POETIZE

POETLESS > POET

POETLIKE > POET

POETRESSE old variant of > POETESS

POETRIES > POETRY

POETRY n poems

POETS > POET

POETSHIP n state of being poet

POETSHIPS > POETSHIP

POFFLE n small piece of land

POFFLES > POFFLE

POGEY n financial or other relief given to the unemployed by the government

POGEYS > POGEY

POGGE n European marine scorpaenoid fish

POGGES > POGGE

POGIES > POGY

POGO vb jump up and down in one spot, as in a punk dance of the 1970s

POGOED > POGO

POGOER > POGO

POGOERS > POGO

POGOING > POGO

POGONIA n orchid with pink or white fragrant flowers

POGONIAS > POGONIA

POGONIP n icy winter fog

POGONIPS > POGONIP

POGOS > POGO

POGROM n organized persecution and massacre ▷ vb carry out a pogrom

POGROMED > POGROM

POGROMING > POGROM

POGROMIST > POGROM

POGROMS > POGROM

POGY same as > POGEY

POH interj exclamation expressing contempt or disgust

POHIRI variant spelling of > POWHIRI

POHIRIS > POHIRI

POI n ball of woven flax swung rhythmically by Māori women during poi dances

POIGNADO old variant of > PONIARD

POIGNANCE > POIGNANT

POIGNANCY > POIGNANT

POIGNANT adj sharply painful to the feelings

POILU n infantryman in the French Army, esp one in the front lines in World War I

POILUS > POILU

POINADO old variant of > PONIARD

POINADOES > POINADO

POINCIANA n tropical leguminous tree with large orange or red flowers

POIND vb take (property of a debtor) in execution or by way of distress

POINDED > POIND

POINDER > POIND

POINDERS > POIND

POINDING > POIND

POINDINGS > POIND

POINDS > POIND

POINT n main idea in a discussion, argument, etc

▷ *vb* show the direction or position of something or draw attention to it by extending a finger or other pointed object towards it

POINTABLE > POINT

POINTE *n* tip of the toe

POINTED *adj* having a sharp end

POINTEDLY > POINTED

POINTEL *n* engraver's tool

POINTELLE *n* fabric design in form of chevrons

POINTELS > POINTEL

POINTER *n* helpful hint

POINTERS > POINTER

POINTES > POINTE

POINTIER > POINTY

POINTIEST > POINTY

POINTILLE *n* dotted lines and curves impressed on cover of book

POINTING *n* insertion of mortar between the joints in brickwork

POINTINGS > POINTING

POINTLESS *adj* meaningless, irrelevant

POINTMAN *n* soldier who walks at the front of an infantry patrol in combat

POINTMEN > POINTMAN

POINTS > POINT

POINTSMAN *n* person who operates railway points

POINTSMEN > POINTSMAN

POINTY *adj* having a sharp point or points

POIS > POI

POISE *n* calm dignified manner ▷ *vb* be balanced or suspended

POISED *adj* absolutely ready

POISER *n* balancing organ of some insects

POISERS > POISER

POISES > POISE

POISHA *n* monetary unit of Bangladesh

POISING > POISE

POISON *n* substance that kills or injures when swallowed or absorbed ▷ *vb* give poison to

POISONED > POISON

POISONER > POISON

POISONERS > POISON

POISONING > POISON

POISONOUS *adj* of or like a poison

POISONS > POISON

POISSON *n* fish

POISSONS > POISSON

POITIN *variant spelling of* > POTEEN

POITINS > POITIN

POITREL *n* breastplate of horse's armour

POITRELS > POITREL

POITRINE *n* woman's bosom

POITRINES > POITRINE

POKABLE > POKE

POKAL *n* tall drinking cup

POKALS > POKAL

POKE *vb* jab or prod with one's finger, a stick, etc ▷ *n*

poking

POKEBERRY *same as* > POKEWEED

POKED > POKE

POKEFUL *n* contents of small bag

POKEFULS > POKEFUL

POKELOGAN *another name for* > BOGAN

POKER *n* metal rod for stirring a fire

POKERISH *adj* stiff like poker

POKEROOT *same as* > POKEWEED

POKEROOTS > POKEROOT

POKERS > POKER

POKERWORK *n* art of producing pictures or designs on wood by burning it with a heated metal point

POKES > POKE

POKEWEED *n* tall North American plant that has small white flowers, juicy purple berries, and a poisonous purple root used medicinally

POKEWEEDS > POKEWEED

POKEY *same as* > POKIE

POKEYS > POKEY

POKIE *n* poker machine

POKIER > POKY

POKIES > POKY

POKIEST > POKY

POKILY > POKY

POKINESS > POKY

POKING > POKE

POKY *adj* small and cramped

POL *n* political campaigner

POLACCA *same as* > POLACRE

POLACCAS > POLACCA

POLACRE *n* three-masted sailing vessel used in the Mediterranean

POLACRES > POLACRE

POLAR *adj* of or near either of the earth's poles ▷ *n* type of line in geometry

POLARISE *same as* > POLARIZE

POLARISED > POLARISE

POLARISER *same as* > POLARIZER

POLARISES > POLARISE

POLARITY *n* state of having two directly opposite tendencies or opinions

POLARIZE *vb* form or cause to form into groups with directly opposite views

POLARIZED > POLARIZE

POLARIZER *n* person or a device that causes polarization

POLARIZES > POLARIZE

POLARON *n* kind of electron

POLARONS > POLARON

POLARS > POLAR

POLDER *n* land reclaimed from the sea, esp in the Netherlands ▷ *vb* reclaim land from the sea

POLDERED > POLDER

POLDERING > POLDER

POLDERS > POLDER

POLE *n* long rounded piece

of wood etc ▷ *vb* strike or push with a pole

POLEAX *same as* > POLEAXE

POLEAXE *vb* hit or stun with a heavy blow ▷ *n* axe formerly used in battle or used by a butcher

POLEAXED > POLEAXE

POLEAXES > POLEAXE

POLEAXING > POLEAXE

POLECAT *n* small animal of the weasel family

POLECATS > POLECAT

POLED > POLE

POLEIS > POLIS

POLELESS > POLE

POLEMARCH *n* (in ancient Greece) civilian official, originally a supreme general

POLEMIC *n* fierce attack on or defence of a particular opinion, belief, etc ▷ *adj* of or involving dispute or controversy

POLEMICAL > POLEMIC

POLEMICS *n* art of dispute

POLEMISE *same as* > POLEMIZE

POLEMISED > POLEMISE

POLEMISES > POLEMISE

POLEMIST > POLEMIC

POLEMISTS > POLEMIC

POLEMIZE *vb* engage in controversy

POLEMIZED > POLEMIZE

POLEMIZES > POLEMIZE

POLENTA *n* thick porridge made in Italy, usually from maize

POLENTAS > POLENTA

POLER *n* person or thing that poles, esp a punter

POLERS > POLER

POLES > POLE

POLESTAR *n* guiding principle, rule, standard, etc

POLESTARS > POLESTAR

POLEWARD *adv* towards a pole

POLEY *adj* (of cattle) hornless or polled ▷ *n* animal with horns removed

POLEYN *n* piece of armour for protecting the knee

POLEYNS > POLEYN

POLEYS > POLEY

POLIANITE *n* manganese dioxide occurring as hard crystals

POLICE *n* organized force in a state which keeps law and order ▷ *vb* control or watch over with police or a similar body

POLICED > POLICE

POLICEMAN *n* member of a police force

POLICEMEN > POLICEMAN

POLICER *n* computer device controlling use

POLICERS > POLICER

POLICES > POLICE

POLICIES > POLICY

POLICING > POLICE

POLICINGS > POLICE

POLICY *n* plan of action adopted by a person, group, or state

POLIES > POLY

POLING > POLE

POLINGS > POLE

POLIO *n* acute viral disease

POLIOS > POLIO

POLIS *n* ancient Greek city-state

POLISH *vb* make smooth and shiny by rubbing ▷ *n* substance used for polishing

POLISHED *adj* accomplished

POLISHER > POLISH

POLISHERS > POLISH

POLISHES > POLISH

POLISHING > POLISH

POLITBURO *n* supreme policy-making authority in most communist countries

POLITE *adj* showing consideration for others in one's manners, speech, etc

POLITELY > POLITE

POLITER > POLITE

POLITESSE *n* formal or genteel politeness

POLITEST > POLITE

POLITIC *adj* wise and likely to prove advantageous

POLITICAL *adj* of the state, government, or public administration

POLITICK *vb* engage in politics

POLITICKS > POLITICK

POLITICLY > POLITIC

POLITICO *n* politician

POLITICOS > POLITICO

POLITICS *n* winning and using of power to govern society

POLITIES > POLITY

POLITIQUE *n* 16th-century French moderate

POLITY *n* politically organized state, church, or society

POLJE *n* large elliptical depression in karst regions, sometimes containing a marsh or small lake

POLJES > POLJE

POLK *vb* dance a polka

POLKA *n* lively 19th-century dance ▷ *vb* dance a polka

POLKAED > POLKA

POLKAING > POLKA

POLKAS > POLKA

POLKED > POLK

POLKING > POLK

POLKS > POLK

POLL *n* questioning of a random sample of people to find out general opinion ▷ *vb* receive (votes)

POLLACK *n* food fish related to the cod, found in northern seas

POLLACKS > POLLACK

POLLAN *n* whitefish that occurs in lakes in Northern Ireland

POLLANS > POLLAN

p

POLLARD *n* animal that has shed its horns or has had them removed ▷ *vb* cut off the top of (a tree) to make it grow bushy

POLLARDED > POLLARD

POLLARDS > POLLARD

POLLED *adj* (of animals, esp cattle) having the horns cut off or being naturally hornless

POLLEE > POLL

POLLEES > POLL

POLLEN *n* fine dust produced by flowers to fertilize other flowers ▷ *vb* collect pollen

POLLENATE *same as* > POLLINATE

POLLENED > POLLEN

POLLENING > POLLEN

POLLENS > POLLEN

POLLENT *adj* strong

POLLER > POLL

POLLERS > POLL

POLLEX *n* first digit of the forelimb of amphibians, reptiles, birds, and mammals, such as the thumb of man and other primates

POLLICAL > POLLEX

POLLICES > POLLEX

POLLICIE *obsolete spelling of* > POLICY

POLLICIES > POLLICIE

POLLICY *obsolete spelling of* > POLICY

POLLIES > POLLY

POLLINATE *vb* fertilize with pollen

POLLING *n* casting or registering of votes at an election

POLLINGS > POLLING

POLLINIA > POLLINIUM

POLLINIC > POLLEN

POLLINISE *same as* > POLLINIZE

POLLINIUM *n* mass of cohering pollen grains, produced by plants such as orchids and transported as a whole during pollination

POLLINIZE *same as* > POLLINATE

POLLIST *n* one advocating the use of polls

POLLISTS > POLLIST

POLLIWIG *same as* > POLLIWOG

POLLIWIGS > POLLIWOG

POLLIWOG *n* sailor who has not crossed the equator

POLLIWOGS > POLLIWOG

POLLMAN *n* one passing a degree without honours

POLLMEN > POLLMAN

POLLOCK *same as* > POLLACK

POLLOCKS > POLLOCK

POLLS > POLL

POLLSTER *n* person who conducts opinion polls

POLLSTERS > POLLSTER

POLLTAKER *n* person conducting poll

POLLUCITE *n* colourless

rare mineral consisting of a hydrated caesium aluminium silicate

POLLUSION *n* comic Shakespearian character's version of "allusion"

POLLUTANT *n* something that pollutes

POLLUTE *vb* contaminate with something poisonous or harmful

POLLUTED *adj* made unclean or impure

POLLUTER > POLLUTE

POLLUTERS > POLLUTE

POLLUTES > POLLUTE

POLLUTING > POLLUTE

POLLUTION *n* act of polluting or the state of being polluted

POLLUTIVE *adj* causing pollution

POLLY *n* politician

POLLYANNA *n* person who is constantly or excessively optimistic

POLLYWIG *same as* > POLLIWOG

POLLYWIGS > POLLYWIG

POLLYWOG *same as* > POLLIWOG

POLLYWOGS > POLLYWOG

POLO *n* game like hockey played by teams of players on horseback

POLOIDAL *adj* relating to a type of magnetic field

POLOIST *n* devotee of polo

POLOISTS > POLOIST

POLONAISE *n* old stately dance

POLONIE *same as* > POLONY

POLONIES > POLONY

POLONISE *same as* > POLONIZE

POLONISED > POLONISE

POLONISES > POLONISE

POLONISM > POLONISE

POLONISMS > POLONISE

POLONIUM *n* radioactive element that occurs in trace amounts in uranium ores

POLONIUMS > POLONIUM

POLONIZE *vb* make Polish

POLONIZED > POLONIZE

POLONIZES > POLONIZE

POLONY *n* bologna sausage

POLOS > POLO

POLS > POL

POLT *n* thump or blow ▷ *vb* strike

POLTED > POLT

POLTFEET > POLTFOOT

POLTFOOT *adj* having a club foot ▷ *n* club foot

POLTING > POLT

POLTROON *n* utter coward

POLTROONS > POLTROON

POLTS > POLT

POLVERINE *n* glassmakers' potash

POLY *n* polytechnic

POLYACID *adj* having two or more hydroxyl groups

POLYACT *adj* (of a sea creature) having many

tentacles or limb-like protrusions

POLYADIC *adj* (of a relation, operation, etc) having several argument places

POLYAMIDE *n* synthetic polymeric material

POLYAMINE *n* compound containing two or more amine groups

POLYANDRY *n* practice of having more than one husband at the same time

POLYANTHA *n* type of flower

POLYANTHI *n* hybrid garden primroses

POLYARCH *n* member of polyarchy

POLYARCHY *n* political system in which power is dispersed

POLYAXIAL *n* joint in which movement occurs in more than one axis

POLYAXON *n* nerve cell with multiple branches

POLYAXONS > POLYAXON

POLYBASIC *adj* (of an acid) having two or more replaceable hydrogen atoms per molecule

POLYBRID *n* hybrid plant with more than two parental groups

POLYBRIDS > POLYBRID

POLYCARPY *n* condition of being able to produce flowers and fruit several times in successive years or seasons

POLYCHETE *n* variety of worm

POLYCONIC *as in* *polyconic projection* type of projection used in making maps of large areas

POLYCOT *n* plant that has or appears to have more than two cotyledons

POLYCOTS > POLYCOT

POLYDEMIC *adj* growing in or inhabiting more than two regions

POLYENE *n* chemical compound containing a chain of alternating single and double carbon-carbon bonds

POLYENES > POLYENE

POLYENIC > POLYENE

POLYESTER *n* synthetic material used to make plastics and textile fibres

POLYGALA *n* herbaceous plant or small shrub

POLYGALAS > POLYGALA

POLYGAM *n* plant of the Polygamia class

POLYGAMIC > POLYGAMY

POLYGAMS > POLYGAM

POLYGAMY *n* practice of having more than one husband or wife at the same time

POLYGENE *n* any of a group of genes that each produce a small quantitative

effect on a particular characteristic of the phenotype, such as height

POLYGENES > POLYGENE

POLYGENIC *adj* of, relating to, or controlled by polygenes

POLYGENY > POLYGENIC

POLYGLOT *adj* (person) able to speak or write several languages ▷ *n* person who can speak many languages

POLYGLOTS > POLYGLOT

POLYGLOTT *variant of* > POLYGLOT

POLYGON *n* geometrical figure with three or more angles and sides

POLYGONAL > POLYGON

POLYGONS > POLYGON

POLYGONUM *n* plant with stems with knotlike joints and spikes of small white, green, or pink flowers

POLYGONY > POLYGON

POLYGRAPH *n* instrument for recording pulse rate and perspiration, used esp as a lie detector

POLYGYNY *n* practice of having more than one wife at the same time

POLYHEDRA *n* solid figures, each consisting of four or more plane faces

POLYIMIDE *n* type of polymer

POLYLEMMA *n* debate forcing choice between contradictory positions

POLYMASTY *n* condition in which more than two breasts are present

POLYMATH *n* person of great and varied learning

POLYMATHS > POLYMATH

POLYMATHY > POLYMATH

POLYMER *n* chemical compound with large molecules made of simple molecules of the same kind

POLYMERIC *adj* of or being a polymer

POLYMERS > POLYMER

POLYMERY > POLYMER

POLYMORPH *n* species of animal or plant that exhibits polymorphism

POLYMYXIN *n* polypeptide antibiotic

POLYNIA *same as* > POLYNYA

POLYNIAS > POLYNIA

POLYNYA *n* stretch of open water surrounded by ice, esp near the mouths of large rivers, in arctic seas

POLYNYAS > POLYNYA

POLYNYI > POLYNYA

POLYOL *n* type of alcohol

POLYOLS > POLYOL

POLYOMA *n* type of tumour caused by virus

POLYOMAS > POLYOMA

POLYOMINO *n* polygon made from joining identical squares at their edges

POLYONYM *n* object with

many names
POLYONYMS > POLYONYM
POLYONYMY > POLYONYM
POLYP n small simple sea creature with a hollow cylindrical body
POLYPARIA n polyparies
POLYPARY n common base and connecting tissue of a colony of coelenterate polyps, esp coral
POLYPE variant of > POLYP
POLYPED same as > POLYPOD
POLYPEDS > POLYPED
POLYPES > POLYPE
POLYPHAGY n insatiable appetite
POLYPHASE adj (of an electrical system, circuit, or device) having, generating, or using two or more alternating voltages of the same frequency, the phases of which are cyclically displaced by fractions of a period
POLYPHON n musical instrument resembling a lute
POLYPHONE n letter or character with more than one phonetic value
POLYPHONS > POLYPHON
POLYPHONY n polyphonic style of composition or a piece of music using it
POLYPI > POLYPUS
POLYPIDE n polyp forming part of a colonial animal
POLYPIDES > POLYPIDE
POLYPIDOM same as > POLYPARY
POLYPILL n proposed combined medication intended to reduce the likelihood of heart attacks and strokes
POLYPILLS > POLYPILL
POLYPINE adj of or relating to polyps
POLYPITE same as > POLYPIDE
POLYPITES > POLYPITE
POLYPLOID adj (of cells, organisms, etc) having more than twice the basic (haploid) number of chromosomes ▷n individual or cell of this type
POLYPNEA n rapid breathing
POLYPNEAS > POLYPNEA
POLYPNEIC > POLYPNEA
POLYPOD adj (esp of insect larvae) having many legs or similar appendages ▷n animal of this type
POLYPODS > POLYPOD
POLYPODY n fern with deeply divided leaves and round naked sori
POLYPOID > POLYP
POLYPORE n type of fungi
POLYPORES > POLYPORE
POLYPOSES > POLYPOSIS
POLYPOSIS n formation of many polyps

POLYPOUS > POLYP
POLYPS > POLYP
POLYPTYCH n altarpiece consisting of more than three panels, set with paintings or carvings, and usually hinged for folding
POLYPUS same as > POLYP
POLYPUSES > POLYPUS
POLYS > POLY
POLYSEME n word with many meanings
POLYSEMES > POLYSEME
POLYSEMIC > POLYSEME
POLYSEMY n existence of several meanings in a single word
POLYSOME n assemblage of ribosomes associated with a messenger RNA molecule
POLYSOMES > POLYSOME
POLYSOMIC adj of, relating to, or designating a basically diploid chromosome complement, in which some but not all the chromosomes are represented more than twice
POLYSOMY > POLYSOME
POLYSTYLE adj with many columns
POLYTENE adj denoting a type of giant-size chromosome consisting of many replicated genes in parallel, found esp in Drosophila larvae
POLYTENY > POLYTENE
POLYTHENE n light plastic used for bags etc
POLYTONAL adj using more than two different tones or keys simultaneously
POLYTYPE n crystal occurring in more than one form
POLYTYPES > POLYTYPE
POLYTYPIC adj existing in, consisting of, or incorporating several different types or forms
POLYURIA n state or condition of discharging abnormally large quantities of urine, often accompanied by a need to urinate frequently
POLYURIAS > POLYURIA
POLYURIC > POLYURIA
POLYVINYL n designating a plastic or resin formed by polymerization of a vinyl derivative
POLYWATER n liquid formerly supposed to be polymeric form of water
POLYZOA n small mosslike aquatic creatures
POLYZOAN another word for > BRYOZOAN
POLYZOANS > POLYZOAN
POLYZOARY n colony of bryozoan animals
POLYZOIC adj (of certain colonial animals) having many zooids or similar

polyps
POLYZONAL adj having many zones
POLYZOOID adj resembling a polyzoon
POLYZOON n individual zooid within polyzoan
POM same as > POMMY
POMACE n apple pulp left after pressing for juice
POMACEOUS adj of, relating to, or bearing pomes, such as the apple, pear, and quince trees
POMACES > POMACE
POMADE n perfumed oil put on the hair to make it smooth and shiny ▷vb put pomade on
POMADED > POMADE
POMADES > POMADE
POMADING > POMADE
POMANDER n mixture of sweet-smelling petals, herbs, etc
POMANDERS > POMANDER
POMATO n hybrid of tomato and potato
POMATOES > POMATO
POMATUM same as > POMADE
POMATUMS > POMATUM
POMBE n any alcoholic drink
POMBES > POMBE
POME n fleshy fruit of the apple and related plants, consisting of an enlarged receptacle enclosing the ovary and seeds
POMELO n edible yellow fruit, like a grapefruit, of a tropical tree
POMELOS > POMELO
POMEROY n bullet used to down airships
POMEROYS > POMEROY
POMES > POME
POMFRET n small black rounded liquorice sweet
POMFRETS > POMFRET
POMMEE adj (of cross) having end of each arm ending in disk
POMMEL same as > PUMMEL
POMMELE adj having a pommel
POMMELED > POMMEL
POMMELING > POMMEL
POMMELLED > POMMEL
POMMELS > POMMEL
POMMETTY adj having a pommel
POMMIE same as > POMMY
POMMIES > POMMY
POMMY n word used by Australians and New Zealanders for a British person
POMO n postmodernism
POMOERIUM n space around town within city walls
POMOLOGY n branch of horticulture that is concerned with the study and cultivation of fruit
POMOS > POMO
POMP n stately display or ceremony

POMPADOUR n early 18th-century hairstyle for women, having the front hair arranged over a pad to give it greater height and bulk
POMPANO n deep-bodied carangid food fish
POMPANOS > POMPANO
POMPELO n large Asian citrus fruit
POMPELOS > POMPELO
POMPEY vb mollycoddle
POMPEYED > POMPEY
POMPEYING > POMPEY
POMPEYS > POMPEY
POMPHOLYX n type of eczema
POMPIER adj slavishly conventional
POMPILID n spider-hunting wasp
POMPILIDS > POMPILID
POMPION n pumpkin
POMPIONS > POMPION
POMPOM n decorative ball of tufted wool, silk, etc
POMPOMS > POMPOM
POMPON same as > POMPOM
POMPONS > POMPON
POMPOON variant of > POMPOM
POMPOONS > POMPOON
POMPOSITY n vain or ostentatious display of dignity or importance
POMPOUS adj foolishly serious and grand, self-important
POMPOUSLY > POMPOUS
POMPS > POMP
POMROY variant of > POMEROY
POMROYS > POMROY
POMS > POM
POMWATER n kind of apple
POMWATERS > POMWATER
PONCE n derogatory word for an effeminate man ▷vb act stupidly or waste time
PONCEAU n scarlet red
PONCEAUS > PONCEAU
PONCEAUX > PONCEAU
PONCED > PONCE
PONCES > PONCE
PONCEY adj ostentatious, pretentious, or effeminate
PONCHO n loose circular cloak with a hole for the head
PONCHOED adj wearing poncho
PONCHOS > PONCHO
PONCIER > PONCEY
PONCIEST > PONCEY
PONCING > PONCE
PONCY same as > PONCEY
POND n small area of still water ▷vb hold back (flowing water)
PONDAGE n water held in reservoir
PONDAGES > PONDAGE
PONDED > POND
PONDER vb think thoroughly or deeply (about)
PONDERAL adj relating to

weight

PONDERATE *vb* consider

PONDERED > PONDER

PONDERER > PONDER

PONDERERS > PONDER

PONDERING > PONDER

PONDEROSA *n* N American pine tree

PONDEROUS *adj* serious and dull

PONDERS > PONDER

PONDING > POND

PONDOK *n* (in southern Africa) crudely made house or shack

PONDOKKIE *same as* > PONDOK

PONDOKS > PONDOK

PONDS > POND

PONDWEED *n* plant that grows in ponds

PONDWEEDS > PONDWEED

PONE *n* bread made of maize

PONENT *n* west wind

PONES > PONE

PONEY *same as* > PONY

PONEYS > PONEY

PONG *n* strong unpleasant smell ▷ *vb* give off a strong unpleasant smell

PONGA *n* tall New Zealand tree fern with large leathery leaves

PONGAS > PONGA

PONGED > PONG

PONGEE *n* thin plain-weave silk fabric from China or India, left in its natural colour

PONGEES > PONGEE

PONGID *n* any primate of the family *Pongidae*, which includes the gibbons and the great apes ▷ *adj* of, relating to, or belonging to the family *Pongidae*

PONGIDS > PONGID

PONGIER > PONG

PONGIEST > PONG

PONGING > PONG

PONGO *n* anthropoid ape, esp an orang-utan or (formerly) a gorilla

PONGOES > PONGO

PONGOS > PONGO

PONGS > PONG

PONGY > PONG

PONIARD *n* small slender dagger ▷ *vb* stab with a poniard

PONIARDED > PONIARD

PONIARDS > PONIARD

PONIED > PONY

PONIES > PONY

PONK *n* evil spirit ▷ *vb* stink

PONKED > PONK

PONKING > PONK

PONKS > PONK

PONS *n* bridge of connecting tissue

PONT *n* (in South Africa) river ferry, esp one that is guided by a cable from one bank to the other

PONTAGE *n* tax paid for repairing bridge

PONTAGES > PONTAGE

PONTAL *adj* of or relating to the pons

PONTES > PONS

PONTIANAC *same as* > PONTIANAK

PONTIANAK *n* (in Malay folklore) female vampire

PONTIC *adj* of or relating to the pons

PONTIE *same as* > PONTY

PONTIES > PONTY

PONTIFEX *n* (in ancient Rome) any of the senior members of the Pontifical College

PONTIFF *n* Pope

PONTIFFS > PONTIFF

PONTIFIC > PONTIFF

PONTIFICE *n* structure of bridge

PONTIFIED > PONTIFY

PONTIFIES > PONTIFY

PONTIFY *vb* speak or behave in a pompous or dogmatic manner

PONTIL *same as* > PUNTY

PONTILE *adj* relating to pons ▷ *n* metal bar used in glass-making

PONTILES > PONTILE

PONTILS > PONTIL

PONTINE *adj* of or relating to bridges

PONTLEVIS *n* horse rearing repeatedly

PONTON *variant of* > PONTOON

PONTONEER *same as* > PONTONIER

PONTONIER *n* person in charge of or involved in building a pontoon bridge

PONTONS > PONTON

PONTOON *n* floating platform supporting a temporary bridge ▷ *vb* cross a river using pontoons

PONTOONED > PONTOON

PONTOONER > PONTOON

PONTOONS > PONTOON

PONTS > PONT

PONTY *n* rod used for shaping molten glass

PONY *n* small horse ▷ *vb* settle bill or debt

PONYING > PONY

PONYSKIN *n* leather from pony hide

PONYSKINS > PONYSKIN

PONYTAIL *n* long hair tied in one bunch at the back of the head

PONYTAILS > PONYTAIL

PONZU *n* type of Japanese dipping sauce made from orange juice, sake, sugar, soy sauce, and red pepper

PONZUS > PONZU

POO *vb* defecate

POOCH *n* slang word for dog ▷ *vb* bulge or protrude

POOCHED > POOCH

POOCHES > POOCH

POOCHING > POOCH

POOD *n* unit of weight, used in Russia, equal to 36.1

pounds or 16.39 kilograms

POODLE *n* dog with curly hair often clipped fancifully

POODLES > POODLE

POODS > POOD

POOED > POO

POOF *n* derogatory word for a homosexual man

POOFIER > POOF

POOFIEST > POOF

POOFS > POOF

POOFTAH *same as* > POOFTER

POOFTAHS > POOFTAH

POOFTER *n* derogatory word for a man who is considered effeminate or homosexual

POOFTERS > POOFTER

POOFY > POOF

POOGYE *n* Hindu nose-flute

POOGYES > POOGYE

POOH *interj* exclamation of disdain, contempt, or disgust ▷ *vb* make such an exclamation

POOHED > POOH

POOHING > POOH

POOHS > POOH

POOING > POO

POOJA *variant of* > PUJA

POOJAH *variant of* > PUJA

POOJAHS > POOJAH

POOJAS > POOJA

POOK *vb* pluck

POOKA *n* malevolent Irish spirit

POOKAS > POOKA

POOKING > POOK

POOKIT > POOK

POOKS > POOK

POOL *n* small body of still water ▷ *vb* put in a common fund

POOLED > POOL

POOLER *n* person taking part in pool

POOLERS > POOLER

POOLHALL *n* room containing pool tables

POOLHALLS > POOLHALL

POOLING > POOL

POOLROOM *n* hall or establishment where pool, billiards, etc, are played

POOLROOMS > POOLROOM

POOLS *pl n* organized nationwide principally postal gambling pool betting on the result of football matches

POOLSIDE *n* area surrounding swimming pool

POOLSIDES > POOLSIDE

POON *n* SE Asian tree with lightweight hard wood and shiny leathery leaves

POONAC *n* coconut residue

POONACS > POONAC

POONCE *n* derogatory word for a homosexual man ▷ *vb* behave effeminately

POONCED > POONCE

POONCES > POONCE

POONCING > POONCE

POONS > POON

POONTANG *n* taboo word for

the female pudenda

POONTANGS > POONTANG

POOP *n* raised part at the back of a sailing ship ▷ *vb* (of a wave or sea) break over the stern of (a vessel)

POOPED > POOP

POOPER as in *party pooper* person whose behaviour or personality spoils other people's enjoyment

POOPERS > POOPER

POOPING > POOP

POOPS > POOP

POOR *adj* having little money and few possessions

POORER > POOR

POOREST > POOR

POORHOUSE *n* (formerly) publicly maintained institution offering accommodation to the poor

POORI *n* unleavened Indian bread

POORIS > POORI

POORISH > POOR

POORLIER > POORLY

POORLIEST > POORLY

POORLY *adv* in a poor manner ▷ *adj* not in good health

POORMOUTH *vb* complain about being poor

POORNESS > POOR

POORT *n* (in South Africa) steep narrow mountain pass, usually following a river or stream

POORTITH *same as* > PUIRTITH

POORTITHS > POORTITH

POORTS > POORT

POORWILL *n* bird of N America

POORWILLS > POORWILL

POOS > POO

POOT *vb* break wind

POOTED > POOT

POOTER > POOT

POOTERS > POOT

POOTING > POOT

POOTLE *vb* travel or go in a relaxed or leisurely manner

POOTLED > POOTLE

POOTLES > POOTLE

POOTLING > POOTLE

POOTS > POOT

POOVE *same as* > POOF

POOVERIES > POOVERY

POOVERY *n* derogatory word for homosexuality

POOVES > POOVE

POOVIER > POOVE

POOVIEST > POOVE

POOVY > POOVE

POP *vb* make or cause to make a small explosive sound ▷ *n* small explosive sound ▷ *adj* popular

POPADUM *same as* > POPPADOM

POPADUMS > POPADUM

POPCORN *n* grains of maize heated until they puff up and burst

POPCORNS > POPCORN

P

POPE n bishop of Rome as head of the Roman Catholic Church
POPEDOM n office or dignity of a pope
POPEDOMS > POPEDOM
POPEHOOD > POPE
POPEHOODS > POPE
POPELESS > POPE
POPELIKE > POPE
POPELING n deputy or supporter of pope
POPELINGS > POPELING
POPERA n music drawing on opera or classical music and aiming for popular appeal
POPERAS > POPERA
POPERIES > POPERY
POPERIN n kind of pear
POPERINS > POPERIN
POPERY n derogatory word for Roman Catholicism
POPES > POPE
POPESEYE adj denoting a cut of steak
POPESHIP > POPE
POPESHIPS > POPE
POPETTE n young female fan or performer of pop music
POPETTES > POPETTE
POPEYED adj staring in astonishment
POPGUN n toy gun that fires a pellet or cork by means of compressed air
POPGUNS > POPGUN
POPINJAY n conceited, foppish, or overly talkative person
POPINJAYS > POPINJAY
POPISH adj derogatory word for Roman Catholic
POPISHLY > POPISH
POPJOY vb amuse oneself
POPJOYED > POPJOY
POPJOYING > POPJOY
POPJOYS > POPJOY
POPLAR n tall slender tree
POPLARS > POPLAR
POPLIN n ribbed cotton material
POPLINS > POPLIN
POPLITEAL adj of, relating to, or near the part of the leg behind the knee
POPLITEI > POPLITEUS
POPLITEUS n muscle in leg
POPLITIC same as > POPLITEAL
POPOVER n individual Yorkshire pudding, often served with roast beef
POPOVERS > POPOVER
POPPA same as > PAPA
POPPADOM n thin round crisp Indian bread
POPPADOMS > POPPADOM
POPPADUM same as > POPPADOM
POPPADUMS > POPPADUM
POPPAS > POPPA
POPPED > POP
POPPER n press stud
POPPERING n method of fishing

POPPERS > POPPER
POPPET n term of affection for a small child or sweetheart
POPPETS > POPPET
POPPIED adj covered with poppies
POPPIER > POPPY
POPPIES > POPPY
POPPIEST > POPPY
POPPING > POP
POPPISH adj like pop music
POPPIT n bead used to form necklace
POPPITS > POPPIT
POPPLE vb (of boiling water or a choppy sea) to heave or toss
POPPLED > POPPLE
POPPLES > POPPLE
POPPLIER > POPPLY
POPPLIEST > POPPLY
POPPLING > POPPLE
POPPLY adj covered in small bumps
POPPY n plant with a large red flower ▷ adj reddish-orange
POPPYCOCK n nonsense
POPPYHEAD n hard dry seed-containing capsule of a poppy
POPRIN same as > POPERIN
POPRINS > POPRIN
POPS > POP
POPSICLE n tradename for a kind of ice lolly
POPSICLES > POPSICLE
POPSIE same as > POPSY
POPSIES > POPSY
POPSTER n pop star
POPSTERS > POPSTER
POPSY n attractive young woman
POPULACE n ordinary people
POPULACES > POPULACE
POPULAR adj widely liked and admired ▷ n cheap newspapers with mass circulation
POPULARLY adv by the public as a whole
POPULARS > POPULAR
POPULATE vb live in, inhabit
POPULATED > POPULATE
POPULATES > POPULATE
POPULISM n political strategy based on a calculated appeal to the interests or prejudices of ordinary people
POPULISMS > POPULISM
POPULIST adj (person) appealing to the interests or prejudices of ordinary people ▷ n person, esp a politician, who appeals to the interests or prejudices of ordinary people
POPULISTS > POPULIST
POPULOUS adj densely populated
PORAE n large edible sea fish of New Zealand waters
PORAL adj relating to pores
PORANGI adj crazy

PORBEAGLE n kind of shark
PORCELAIN n fine china
PORCH n covered approach to the entrance of a building
PORCHES > PORCH
PORCINE adj of or like a pig
PORCINI > PORCINO
PORCINIS > PORCINO
PORCINO n edible woodland fungus
PORCUPINE n animal covered with long pointed quills
PORCUPINY > PORCUPINE
PORE n tiny opening in the skin or in the surface of a plant ▷ vb make a close intent examination or study (of a book, map, etc)
PORED > PORE
PORER n person who pores
PORERS > PORE
PORES > PORE
PORGE vb cleanse (slaughtered animal) ceremonially
PORGED > PORGE
PORGES > PORGE
PORGIE same as > PORGY
PORGIES > PORGY
PORGING > PORGE
PORGY n any of various sparid fishes, many of which occur in American Atlantic waters
PORIER > PORY
PORIEST > PORY
PORIFER n type of invertebrate
PORIFERAL > PORIFERAN
PORIFERAN n sponge ▷ adj of, relating to, or belonging to the phylum Porifera
PORIFERS > PORIFER
PORINA n larva of a moth which causes damage to grassland
PORINAS > PORINA
PORINESS > PORY
PORING > PORE
PORISM n type of mathematical proposition, the meaning of which is now obscure
PORISMS > PORISM
PORISTIC > PORISM
PORK vb (of eg a raven) make a croaking sound
PORKED > PORK
PORKER n pig raised for food
PORKERS > PORKER
PORKIER > PORKY
PORKIES > PORKY
PORKIEST > PORKY
PORKINESS > PORKY
PORKING > PORK
PORKLING n pig
PORKLINGS > PORKLING
PORKPIE n hat with a round flat crown and a brim that can be turned up or down
PORKPIES > PORKPIE
PORKS > PORK
PORKWOOD n wood of small American tree
PORKWOODS > PORKWOOD

PORKY adj of or like pork ▷ n lie
PORN n pornography
PORNIER > PORNY
PORNIEST > PORNY
PORNO same as > PORN
PORNOMAG n pornographic magazine
PORNOMAGS > PORNOMAG
PORNOS > PORNO
PORNS > PORN
PORNY adj pornographic
POROGAMIC > POROGAMY
POROGAMY n fertilization of seed plants
POROMERIC adj (of a plastic) permeable to water vapour ▷ n substance having this characteristic, esp one based on polyurethane and used in place of leather in making shoe uppers
POROSCOPE n instrument for assessing porosity
POROSCOPY > POROSCOPE
POROSE adj pierced with small pores
POROSES > POROSIS
POROSIS n porous condition of bones
POROSITY n state or condition of being porous
POROUS adj allowing liquid to pass through gradually
POROUSLY > POROUS
PORPESS n type of fish
PORPESSE same as > PORPOISE
PORPESSES > PORPESS
PORPHYRIA n hereditary disease of body metabolism, producing abdominal pain, mental confusion, etc
PORPHYRIC > PORPHYRIA
PORPHYRIN n any of a group of pigments occurring widely in animal and plant tissues and having a heterocyclic structure formed from four pyrrole rings linked by four methylene groups
PORPHYRIO n aquatic bird
PORPHYRY n reddish rock with large crystals in it
PORPOISE n fishlike sea mammal ▷ vb (of an aeroplane) nose-dive during landing
PORPOISED > PORPOISE
PORPOISES > PORPOISE
PORPORATE adj wearing purple
PORRECT adj extended forwards ▷ vb stretch forward
PORRECTED > PORRECT
PORRECTS > PORRECT
PORRENGER same as > PORRINGER
PORRIDGE n breakfast food made of oatmeal cooked in water or milk
PORRIDGES > PORRIDGE
PORRIDGY > PORRIDGE
PORRIGO n disease of the

scalp

PORRIGOS > PORRIGO

PORRINGER *n* small dish, often with a handle, used esp formerly for soup or porridge

PORT *same as* > PORTHOLE

PORTA *n* aperture in an organ, such as the liver, esp one providing an opening for blood vessels

PORTABLE *adj* easily carried ▷ *n* article designed to be easily carried, such as a television or typewriter

PORTABLES > PORTABLE

PORTABLY > PORTABLE

PORTAGE *n* (route for) transporting boats and supplies overland between navigable waterways ▷ *vb* transport (boats and supplies) in this way

PORTAGED > PORTAGE

PORTAGES > PORTAGE

PORTAGING > PORTAGE

PORTAGUE *n* Portuguese gold coin

PORTAGUES > PORTAGUE

PORTAL *n* large imposing doorway or gate

PORTALED > PORTAL

PORTALS > PORTAL

PORTANCE *n* person's bearing

PORTANCES > PORTANCE

PORTAPACK *n* combined videotape recorder and camera

PORTAPAK *same as* > PORTAPACK

PORTAPAKS > PORTAPAK

PORTAS > PORTA

PORTASES *variant of* > PORTESSE

PORTATE *adj* diagonally athwart escutcheon

PORTATILE *adj* portable

PORTATIVE *adj* concerned with the act of carrying

PORTED > PORT

PORTEND *vb* be a sign of

PORTENDED > PORTEND

PORTENDS > PORTEND

PORTENT *n* sign of a future event

PORTENTS > PORTENT

PORTEOUS *variant of* > PORTESSE

PORTER *n* man who carries luggage ▷ *vb* carry luggage

PORTERAGE *n* work of carrying supplies, goods, etc, done by porters

PORTERED > PORTER

PORTERESS *n* female porter

PORTERING > PORTER

PORTERLY > PORTER

PORTERS > PORTER

PORTESS *variant of* > PORTESSE

PORTESSE *n* prayer book

PORTESSES > PORTESSE

PORTFIRE *n* (formerly) slow-burning fuse used for firing rockets and fireworks and, in mining, for igniting explosives

PORTFIRES > PORTFIRE

PORTFOLIO *n* (flat case for carrying) examples of an artist's work

PORTHOLE *n* small round window in a ship or aircraft

PORTHOLES > PORTHOLE

PORTHORS *same as* > PORTESSE

PORTHOS *same as* > PORTESSE

PORTHOSES > PORTHOS

PORTHOUSE *n* company producing port

PORTICO *n* porch or covered walkway with columns supporting the roof

PORTICOED > PORTICO

PORTICOES > PORTICO

PORTICOS > PORTICO

PORTIER > PORT

PORTIERE *n* curtain hung in a doorway

PORTIERED > PORTIERE

PORTIERES > PORTIERE

PORTIEST > PORT

PORTIGUE *same as* > PORTAGUE

PORTIGUES > PORTIGUE

PORTING > PORT

PORTION *n* part or share ▷ *vb* divide (something) into shares

PORTIONED > PORTION

PORTIONER > PORTION

PORTIONS > PORTION

PORTLAND *n* type of rose

PORTLANDS > PORTLAND

PORTLAST *n* gunwale of ship

PORTLASTS > PORTLAST

PORTLESS > PORT

PORTLIER > PORTLY

PORTLIEST > PORTLY

PORTLY *adj* rather fat

PORTMAN *n* inhabitant of port

PORTMEN > PORTMAN

PORTOISE *same as* > PORTLAST

PORTOISES > PORTOISE

PORTOLAN *n* book of sailing charts

PORTOLANI > PORTOLANO

PORTOLANO *variant of* > PORTOLAN

PORTOLANS > PORTOLAN

PORTOUS *variant of* > PORTESSE

PORTOUSES > PORTOUS

PORTRAIT *n* picture of a person ▷ *adj* (of a publication or an illustration in a publication) of greater height than width

PORTRAITS > PORTRAIT

PORTRAY *vb* describe or represent by artistic means, as in writing or film

PORTRAYAL > PORTRAY

PORTRAYED > PORTRAY

PORTRAYER > PORTRAY

PORTRAYS > PORTRAY

PORTREEVE *n* Saxon magistrate

PORTRESS *n* female porter, esp a doorkeeper

PORTS > PORT

PORTSIDE *adj* beside port

PORTULACA *n* tropical American plant with yellow, pink, or purple showy flowers

PORTULAN *same as* > PORTOLAN

PORTULANS > PORTULAN

PORTY *adj* like port

PORWIGGLE *n* tadpole

PORY *adj* containing pores

POS > PO

POSABLE > POSE

POSADA *n* inn in a Spanish-speaking country

POSADAS > POSADA

POSAUNE *n* organ chorus reed

POSAUNES > POSAUNE

POSE *vb* place in or take up a particular position to be photographed or drawn ▷ *n* position while posing

POSEABLE *adj* able to be manipulated into poses

POSED > POSE

POSER *n* puzzling question

POSERISH *same as* > POSEY

POSERS > POSER

POSES > POSE

POSEUR *n* person who behaves in an affected way to impress others

POSEURS > POSEUR

POSEUSE *n* female poseur

POSEUSES > POSEUSE

POSEY *adj* (of a place) for, characteristic of, or full of posers

POSH *adj* smart, luxurious ▷ *adv* in a manner associated with the upper class ▷ *vb* make posh

POSHED > POSH

POSHER > POSH

POSHES > POSH

POSHEST > POSH

POSHING > POSH

POSHLY > POSH

POSHNESS > POSH

POSHO *n* corn meal

POSHOS > POSHO

POSHTEEN *same as* > POSTEEN

POSHTEENS > POSHTEEN

POSIER > POSY

POSIES > POSY

POSIEST > POSY

POSIGRADE *adj* producing positive thrust

POSING > POSE

POSINGLY > POSE

POSINGS > POSE

POSIT *vb* lay down as a basis for argument ▷ *n* fact, idea, etc, that is posited

POSITED > POSIT

POSITIF *n* (on older organs) manual controlling soft stops

POSITIFS > POSITIF

POSITING > POSIT

POSITION *n* place ▷ *vb* place

POSITIONS > POSITION

POSITIVE *same as* > PLUS

POSITIVER > POSITIVE

POSITIVES > POSITIVE

POSITON *n* part of chromosome

POSITONS > POSITON

POSITRON *n* particle with same mass as electron but positive charge

POSITRONS > POSITRON

POSITS > POSIT

POSNET *n* small basin or dish

POSNETS > POSNET

POSOLE *n* hominy

POSOLES > POSOLE

POSOLOGIC > POSOLOGY

POSOLOGY *n* branch of medicine concerned with the determination of appropriate doses of drugs or agents

POSS *vb* wash (clothes) by agitating them with a long rod, pole, etc

POSSE *n* group of men organized to maintain law and order

POSSED > POSS

POSSER *n* short stick used for stirring clothes in a washtub

POSSERS > POSSER

POSSES > POSSE

POSSESS *vb* have as one's property

POSSESSED *adj* owning or having

POSSESSES > POSSESS

POSSESSOR > POSSESS

POSSET *n* drink of hot milk curdled with ale, beer, etc, flavoured with spices, formerly used as a remedy for colds ▷ *vb* treat with a posset

POSSETED > POSSET

POSSETING > POSSET

POSSETS > POSSET

POSSIBLE *adj* able to exist, happen, or be done ▷ *n* person or thing that might be suitable or chosen

POSSIBLER > POSSIBLE

POSSIBLES > POSSIBLE

POSSIBLY *adv* perhaps, not necessarily

POSSIE *n* place

POSSIES > POSSIE

POSSING > POSS

POSSUM *vb* pretend to be dead, asleep, ignorant, etc, to deceive an opponent

POSSUMED > POSSUM

POSSUMING > POSSUM

POSSUMS > POSSUM

POST *n* official system of delivering letters and parcels ▷ *vb* send by post

POSTAGE *n* charge for sending a letter or parcel by post

POSTAGES > POSTAGE

POSTAL *adj* of a Post Office

or the mail-delivery service ▷ *n* postcard

POSTALLY > POSTAL

POSTALS > POSTAL

POSTANAL *adj* behind the anus

POSTAXIAL *adj* situated or occurring behind the axis of the body

POSTBAG *n* postman's bag

POSTBAGS > POSTBAG

POSTBASE *adv* (in linguistics) coming immediately after a base word

POSTBOX *n* box into which mail is put for collection by the postal service

POSTBOXES > POSTBOX

POSTBOY *n* man or boy who brings the post round to offices

POSTBOYS > POSTBOY

POSTBURN *adj* after injury from burns

POSTBUS *n* (in Britain, esp in rural districts) vehicle carrying the mail that also carries passengers

POSTBUSES > POSTBUS

POSTCARD *n* card for sending a message by post without an envelope

POSTCARDS > POSTCARD

POSTCAVA *n* inferior vena cava

POSTCAVAE > POSTCAVA

POSTCAVAL > POSTCAVA

POSTCAVAS > POSTCAVA

POSTCODE *n* system of letters and numbers used to aid the sorting of mail ▷ *vb* put a postcode on a letter

POSTCODED > POSTCODE

POSTCODES > POSTCODE

POSTCOUP *adj* after coup

POSTCRASH *adj* after a crash

POSTDATE *vb* write a date on (a cheque) that is later than the actual date

POSTDATED > POSTDATE

POSTDATES > POSTDATE

POSTDIVE *adj* following a dive

POSTDOC *n* postdoctoral degree

POSTDOCS > POSTDOC

POSTDRUG *adj* of time after drug has been taken

POSTED > POST

POSTEEN *n* Afghan leather jacket

POSTEENS > POSTEEN

POSTER *n* large picture or notice stuck on a wall ▷ *vb* cover with posters

POSTERED > POSTER

POSTERING > POSTER

POSTERIOR *n* buttocks ▷ *adj* behind, at the back of

POSTERITY *n* future generations, descendants

POSTERN *n* small back door or gate ▷ *adj* situated at the rear or the side

POSTERNS > POSTERN

POSTERS > POSTER

POSTFACE *n* note added to the end of a text

POSTFACES > POSTFACE

POSTFAULT *adj* after a fault

POSTFIRE *adj* of the period after a fire

POSTFIX *vb* add or append at the end of something

POSTFIXAL > POSTFIX

POSTFIXED > POSTFIX

POSTFIXES > POSTFIX

POSTFORM *vb* mould or shape (plastic) while it hot from reheating

POSTFORMS > POSTFORM

POSTGAME *adj* of period after sports match

POSTGRAD *n* graduate taking further degree

POSTGRADS > POSTGRAD

POSTHASTE *adv* with great speed ▷ *n* great haste

POSTHEAT *n* industrial heating process

POSTHEATS > POSTHEAT

POSTHOLE *n* hole dug in ground to hold fence post

POSTHOLES > POSTHOLE

POSTHORSE *n* horse kept at an inn or posthouse for use by postriders or for hire to travellers

POSTHOUSE *n* house or inn where horses were kept for postriders or for hire to travellers

POSTICAL *adj* (of the position of plant parts) behind another part

POSTICHE *adj* (of architectural ornament) inappropriately applied ▷ *n* imitation, counterfeit, or substitute

POSTICHES > POSTICHE

POSTICOUS *same as* > POSTICAL

POSTIE *n* postman

POSTIES > POSTIE

POSTIL *n* commentary or marginal note, as in a Bible ▷ *vb* annotate (a biblical passage)

POSTILED > POSTIL

POSTILING > POSTIL

POSTILION *n* person riding one of a pair of horses drawing a carriage

POSTILLED > POSTIL

POSTILLER > POSTIL

POSTILS > POSTIL

POSTIN *variant of* > POSTEEN

POSTING *n* job to which someone is assigned by his or her employer which involves moving to a particular town or country

POSTINGS > POSTING

POSTINS > POSTIN

POSTIQUE *variant of* > POSTICHE

POSTIQUES > POSTIQUE

POSTLUDE *n* final or concluding piece or movement

POSTLUDES > POSTLUDE

POSTMAN *n* person who collects and delivers post

POSTMARK *n* official mark stamped on letters showing place and date of posting ▷ *vb* put such a mark on (mail)

POSTMARKS > POSTMARK

POSTMEN > POSTMAN

POSTNASAL *adj* situated at the back of the nose

POSTNATAL *adj* occurring after childbirth

POSTNATI *n* those born in Scotland after its union with England

POSTOP *n* person recovering from surgery

POSTOPS > POSTOP

POSTORAL *adj* situated at the back of the mouth

POSTPAID *adj* with the postage prepaid

POSTPONE *vb* put off to a later time

POSTPONED > POSTPONE

POSTPONER > POSTPONE

POSTPONES > POSTPONE

POSTPOSE *vb* place (word or phrase) after other constituents in sentence

POSTPOSED > POSTPOSE

POSTPOSES > POSTPOSE

POSTPUNK *adj* (of pop music) belonging to a style that followed punk rock

POSTRACE *adj* of the period after a race

POSTRIDER *n* (formerly) person who delivered post on horseback

POSTRIOT *adj* of the period after a riot

POSTS > POST

POSTSHOW *adj* of the period after a show

POSTSYNC *vb* add a sound recording to (and synchronize with) an existing video or film recording

POSTSYNCS > POSTSYNC

POSTTAX *adj* of the period after tax is paid

POSTTEEN *n* young adult

POSTTEENS > POSTTEEN

POSTTEST *n* test taken after a lesson

POSTTESTS > POSTTEST

POSTTRIAL *adj* of the period after a trial

POSTULANT *n* candidate for admission to a religious order

POSTULATA *n* things postulated

POSTULATE *vb* assume to be true as the basis of an argument or theory ▷ *n* something postulated

POSTURAL > POSTURE

POSTURE *n* position or way in which someone stands, walks, etc ▷ *vb* behave in an exaggerated way to get attention

POSTURED > POSTURE

POSTURER > POSTURE

POSTURERS > POSTURE

POSTURES > POSTURE

POSTURING > POSTURE

POSTURISE *same as* > POSTURIZE

POSTURIST > POSTURE

POSTURIZE *less common word for* > POSTURE

POSTVIRAL as in *postviral syndrome* debilitating condition occurring as a sequel to viral illness

POSTWAR *adj* occurring or existing after a war

POSTWOMAN *n* woman who carries and delivers mail as a profession

POSTWOMEN > POSTWOMAN

POSY *n* small bunch of flowers

POT *n* round deep container ▷ *vb* plant in a pot

POTABLE *adj* drinkable ▷ *n* something fit to drink

POTABLES > POTABLE

POTAE *n* hat

POTAES > POTAE

POTAGE *n* thick soup

POTAGER *n* small kitchen garden

POTAGERS > POTAGER

POTAGES > POTAGE

POTAMIC *adj* of or relating to rivers

POTASH *n* white powdery substance obtained from ashes and used as fertilizer ▷ *vb* treat with potash

POTASHED > POTASH

POTASHES > POTASH

POTASHING > POTASH

POTASS *abbreviated form of* > POTASSIUM

POTASSA *n* potassium oxide

POTASSAS > POTASSA

POTASSES > POTASS

POTASSIC > POTASSIUM

POTASSIUM *n* silvery metallic element

POTATION *n* act of drinking

POTATIONS > POTATION

POTATO *n* roundish starchy vegetable that grows underground

POTATOBUG *n* Colorado beetle

POTATOES > POTATO

POTATORY *adj* of, relating to, or given to drinking

POTBELLY *n* bulging belly

POTBOIL *vb* boil in a pot

POTBOILED > POTBOIL

POTBOILER *n* inferior work of art produced quickly to make money

POTBOILS > POTBOIL

POTBOUND *adj* (of plant) unable to grow because pot is too small

POTBOY *n* (esp formerly) youth or man employed at a public house to serve beer, etc

POTBOYS > POTBOY

POTCH *n* inferior quality opal used in jewellery for

mounting precious opals

POTCHE *vb* stab

POTCHED > POTCHE

POTCHER > POTCHE

POTCHERS > POTCHE

POTCHES > POTCH

POTCHING > POTCHE

POTE *vb* push

POTED > POTE

POTEEN *n* (in Ireland) illegally made alcoholic drink

POTEENS > POTEEN

POTENCE *same as* > POTENCY

POTENCES > POTENCE

POTENCIES > POTENCY

POTENCY *n* state or quality of being potent

POTENT *adj* having great power or influence ▷ *n* potentate or ruler

POTENTATE *n* ruler or monarch

POTENTIAL *adj* possible but not yet actual ▷ *n* ability or talent not yet fully used

POTENTISE *same as* > POTENTIZE

POTENTIZE *vb* make more potent

POTENTLY > POTENT

POTENTS > POTENT

POTES > POTE

POTFUL *n* amount held by a pot

POTFULS > POTFUL

POTGUN *n* pot-shaped mortar

POTGUNS > POTGUN

POTHEAD *n* habitual user of cannabis

POTHEADS > POTHEAD

POTHECARY *n* pharmacist

POTHEEN *rare variant of* > POTEEN

POTHEENS > POTHEEN

POTHER *n* fuss or commotion ▷ *vb* make or be troubled or upset

POTHERB *n* plant whose leaves, flowers, or stems are used in cooking

POTHERBS > POTHERB

POTHERED > POTHER

POTHERING > POTHER

POTHERS > POTHER

POTHERY *adj* stuffy

POTHOLDER *n* piece of material used to protect hands while lifting pot from oven

POTHOLE *n* hole in the surface of a road

POTHOLED > POTHOLE

POTHOLER > POTHOLING

POTHOLERS > POTHOLING

POTHOLES > POTHOLE

POTHOLING *n* sport of exploring underground caves

POTHOOK *n* S-shaped hook for suspending a pot over a fire

POTHOOKS > POTHOOK

POTHOS *n* climbing plant

POTHOUSE *n* (formerly) small tavern or pub

POTHOUSES > POTHOUSE

POTHUNTER *n* person who hunts for food or for profit without regard to the rules of sport

POTICARY *obsolete spelling of* > POTHECARY

POTICHE *n* tall vase or jar, as of porcelain, with a round or polygonal body that narrows towards the neck and a detached lid or cover

POTICHES > POTICHE

POTIN *n* bronze alloy with high tin content

POTING > POTE

POTINS > POTIN

POTION *n* dose of medicine or poison

POTIONS > POTION

POTLACH *same as* > POTLATCH

POTLACHE *same as* > POTLATCH

POTLACHES > POTLACHE

POTLATCH *n* competitive ceremonial activity among certain North American Indians

POTLIKE > POT

POTLINE *n* row of electrolytic cells for reducing metals

POTLINES > POTLINE

POTLUCK *n* whatever food happens to be available without special preparation

POTLUCKS > POTLUCK

POTMAN *same as* > POTBOY

POTMEN > POTMAN

POTOMETER *n* apparatus that measures the rate of water uptake by a plant or plant part

POTOO *n* nocturnal tropical bird

POTOOS > POTOO

POTOROO *n* Australian leaping rodent

POTOROOS > POTOROO

POTPIE *n* meat and vegetable stew with a pie crust on top

POTPIES > POTPIE

POTPOURRI *n* fragrant mixture of dried flower petals

POTS > POT

POTSHARD *same as* > POTSHERD

POTSHARDS > POTSHARD

POTSHARE *same as* > POTSHERD

POTSHARES > POTSHARE

POTSHERD *n* broken fragment of pottery

POTSHERDS > POTSHERD

POTSHOP *n* public house

POTSHOPS > POTSHOP

POTSHOT *n* chance shot taken casually, hastily, or without careful aim

POTSHOTS > POTSHOT

POTSIE *same as* > POTSY

POTSIES > POTSY

POTSTONE *n* impure

massive variety of soapstone, formerly used for making cooking vessels

POTSTONES > POTSTONE

POTSY *n* hopscotch

POTT *old variant of* > POT

POTTAGE *n* thick soup or stew

POTTAGES > POTTAGE

POTTED > POT

POTTEEN *same as* > POTEEN

POTTEENS > POTTEEN

POTTER *same as* > PUTTER

POTTERED > POTTER

POTTERER > POTTER

POTTERERS > POTTER

POTTERIES > POTTERY

POTTERING > POTTER

POTTERS > POTTER

POTTERY *n* articles made from baked clay

POTTIER > POTTY

POTTIES > POTTY

POTTIEST > POTTY

POTTINESS > POTTY

POTTING > POT

POTTINGAR *same as* > POTTINGER

POTTINGER *n* apothecary

POTTLE *n* liquid measure equal to half a gallon

POTTLES > POTTLE

POTTO *n* short-tailed prosimian primate

POTTOS > POTTO

POTTS > POTT

POTTY *adj* crazy or silly ▷ *n* bowl used by a small child as a toilet

POTWALLER *n* man entitled to the franchise before 1832 by virtue of possession of his own fireplace

POTZER *same as* > PATZER

POTZERS > POTZER

POUCH *n* small bag ▷ *vb* place in or as if in a pouch

POUCHED > POUCH

POUCHES > POUCH

POUCHFUL *n* amount a pouch will hold

POUCHFULS > POUCHFUL

POUCHIER > POUCH

POUCHIEST > POUCH

POUCHING > POUCH

POUCHY > POUCH

POUDER *obsolete spelling of* > POWDER

POUDERS > POUDER

POUDRE *old spelling of* > POWDER

POUDRES > POUDRE

POUF *n* large solid cushion used as a seat ▷ *vb* pile up hair into rolled puffs

POUFED > POUF

POUFF *same as* > POUF

POUFFE *same as* > POUF

POUFFED > POUFFE

POUFFES > POUFFE

POUFFING > POUFFE

POUFFS > POUFF

POUFFY *same as* > POOFY

POUFING > POUF

POUFS > POUF

POUFTAH *same as* > POOFTER

POUFTAHS > POUFTAH

POUFTER *same as* > POOFTER

POUFTERS > POUFTER

POUK *Scots variant of* > POKE

POUKE *n* mischievous spirit

POUKES > POUKE

POUKING > POUK

POUKIT > POUK

POUKS > POUK

POULAINE *n* tapering toe of shoe

POULAINES > POULAINE

POULARD *n* hen that has been spayed for fattening

POULARDE *same as* > POULARD

POULARDES > POULARDE

POULARDS > POULARD

POULDER *obsolete spelling of* > POWDER

POULDERS > POULDER

POULDRE *archaic spelling of* > POWDER

POULDRES > POULDRE

POULDRON *same as* > PAULDRON

POULDRONS > POULDRON

POULE *n* fowl suitable for slow stewing

POULES > POULE

POULP *n* octopus

POULPE *variant of* > POULP

POULPES > POULPE

POULPS > POULP

POULT *n* young of a gallinaceous bird, esp of domestic fowl

POULTER *n* poultry dealer

POULTERER *same as* > POULTER

POULTERS > POULTER

POULTICE *n* moist dressing, often heated, applied to inflamed skin ▷ *vb* apply poultice to

POULTICED > POULTICE

POULTICES > POULTICE

POULTRIES > POULTRY

POULTRY *n* domestic fowls

POULTS > POULT

POUNCE *vb* spring upon suddenly to attack or capture ▷ *n* pouncing

POUNCED > POUNCE

POUNCER > POUNCE

POUNCERS > POUNCE

POUNCES > POUNCE

POUNCET *n* box with a perforated top used for perfume

POUNCETS > POUNCET

POUNCHING *old variant of* > PUNCHING

POUNCING > POUNCE

POUND *n* monetary unit of Britain and some other countries ▷ *vb* hit heavily and repeatedly

POUNDAGE *n* charge of so much per pound of weight or sterling

POUNDAGES > POUNDAGE

POUNDAL *n* fps unit of force

POUNDALS > POUNDAL

POUNDCAKE *n* cake containing a pound of each ingredient

POUNDED > POUND

P

POUNDER > POUND
POUNDERS > POUND
POUNDING > POUND
POUNDS > POUND
POUPE *vb* make sudden blowing sound
POUPED > POUPE
POUPES > POUPE
POUPING > POUPE
POUPT > POUPE
POUR *vb* flow or cause to flow out in a stream
POURABLE > POUR
POURBOIRE *n* tip or gratuity
POURED > POUR
POURER > POUR
POURERS > POUR
POURIE *n* jug
POURIES > POURIE
POURING > POUR
POURINGLY > POUR
POURINGS > POUR
POURPOINT *n* man's stuffed quilted doublet of a kind worn between the Middle Ages and the 17th century
POURS > POUR
POURSEW *obsolete spelling of* > PURSUE
POURSEWED > POURSEW
POURSEWS > POURSEW
POURSUE *obsolete spelling of* > PURSUE
POURSUED > PURSUE
POURSUES > POURSUE
POURSUING > POURSUE
POURSUIT *same as* > PURSUIT
POURSUITS > POURSUIT
POURTRAY *obsolete spelling of* > PORTRAY
POURTRAYD > POURTRAY
POURTRAYS > POURTRAY
POUSOWDIE *n* Scottish stew made from sheep's head
POUSSE *same as* > PEASE
POUSSES > POUSSE
POUSSETTE *n* figure in country dancing in which couples hold hands and move up or down the set to change positions ▷ *vb* perform such a figure
POUSSIE *old variant of* > PUSSY
POUSSIES > POUSSIE
POUSSIN *n* young chicken reared for eating
POUSSINS > POUSSIN
POUT *vb* thrust out one's lips, look sulky ▷ *n* pouting look
POUTED > POUT
POUTER *n* pigeon that can puff out its crop
POUTERS > POUTER
POUTFUL *adj* tending to pout
POUTHER *Scots variant of* > POWDER
POUTHERED > POUTHER
POUTHERS > POUTHER
POUTIER > POUT
POUTIEST > POUT
POUTINE *n* dish of chipped potatoes topped with curd cheese and a tomato-based sauce
POUTINES > POUTINE
POUTING > POUT
POUTINGLY > POUT
POUTINGS > POUT
POUTS > POUT
POUTY > POUT
POVERTIES > POVERTY
POVERTY *n* state of being without enough food or money
POW *interj* exclamation to indicate that a collision or explosion has taken place ▷ *n* head or a head of hair
POWAN *n* freshwater whitefish, *Coregonus clupeoides*, occurring in some Scottish lakes
POWANS > POWAN
POWDER *n* substance in the form of tiny loose particles ▷ *vb* apply powder to
POWDERED > POWDER
POWDERER > POWDER
POWDERERS > POWDER
POWDERIER > POWDER
POWDERING > POWDER
POWDERS > POWDER
POWDERY > POWDER
POWELLISE > POWELLIZE
POWELLITE *n* type of mineral
POWELLIZE *vb* treat wood with a sugar solution
POWER *n* ability to do or act ▷ *vb* give or provide power to
POWERBOAT *n* fast powerful motorboat
POWERED > POWER
POWERFUL *adj* having great power or influence ▷ *adv* extremely
POWERING > POWER
POWERLESS *adj* without power or authority
POWERPLAY *n* behaviour intended to maximise person's power
POWERS > POWER
POWFAGGED *adj* exhausted
POWHIRI *n* Māori ceremony of welcome, esp to a marae
POWHIRIS > POWHIRI
POWIN *n* peacock
POWINS > POWIN
POWN *variant of* > POWIN
POWND *obsolete spelling of* > POUND
POWNDED > POWND
POWNDING > POWND
POWNDS > POWND
POWNEY *old Scots spelling of* > PONY
POWNEYS > POWNEY
POWNIE *old Scots spelling of* > PONY
POWNIES > POWNIE
POWNS > POWN
POWNY *old Scots spelling of* > PONY
POWRE *obsolete spelling of* > POWER
POWRED > POWRE
POWRES > POWRE
POWRING > POWRE
POWS > POW
POWSOWDY *same as* > POUSOWDIE
POWTER *vb* scrabble about
POWTERED > POWTER
POWTERING > POWTER
POWTERS > POWTER
POWWAW *interj* expression of disbelief or contempt
POWWOW *n* talk or conference ▷ *vb* hold a powwow
POWWOWED > POWWOW
POWWOWING > POWWOW
POWWOWS > POWWOW
POX *n* disease in which skin pustules form ▷ *vb* infect with pox
POXED > POX
POXES > POX
POXIER > POXY
POXIEST > POXY
POXING > POX
POXVIRUS *n* virus such as smallpox
POXY *adj* having or having had syphilis
POYNANT *old variant of* > POIGNANT
POYNT *obsolete spelling of* > POINT
POYNTED > POYNT
POYNTING > POYNT
POYNTS > POYNT
POYOU *n* type of armadillo
POYOUS > POYOU
POYSE *obsolete variant of* > POISE
POYSED > POYSE
POYSES > POYSE
POYSING > POYSE
POYSON *obsolete spelling of* > POISON
POYSONED > POYSON
POYSONING > POYSON
POYSONS > POYSON
POZ *adj* positive
POZOLE *same as* > POSOLE
POZOLES > POZOLE
POZZ *adj* positive
POZZIES > POZZY
POZZOLAN *same as* > POZZOLANA
POZZOLANA *n* type of porous volcanic ash
POZZOLANS > POZZOLAN
POZZY *same as* > POSSIE
PRAAM *same as* > PRAM
PRAAMS > PRAAM
PRABBLE *variant of* > BRABBLE
PRABBLES > PRABBLE
PRACHARAK *n* (in India) person appointed to propagate a cause through personal contact, meetings, public lectures, etc
PRACTIC *adj* practical ▷ *n* practice
PRACTICAL *adj* involving experience or actual use rather than theory ▷ *n* examination in which something has to be done or made
PRACTICE *same as* > PRACTISE
PRACTICED > PRACTICE
PRACTICER > PRACTICE
PRACTICES > PRACTICE
PRACTICK *obsolete word for* > PRACTICE
PRACTICKS > PRACTICK
PRACTICS > PRACTIC
PRACTICUM *n* course in which theory is put into practice
PRACTIQUE *variant of* > PRACTIC
PRACTISE *vb* do repeatedly so as to gain skill
PRACTISED > PRACTISE
PRACTISER > PRACTISE
PRACTISES > PRACTISE
PRACTIVE *obsolete word for* > ACTIVE
PRACTOLOL *n* type of drug
PRAD *n* horse
PRADS > PRAD
PRAEAMBLE *same as* > PREAMBLE
PRAECIPE *n* written request addressed to court
PRAECIPES > PRAECIPE
PRAECOCES *n* division of birds whose young are able to run when first hatched
PRAEDIAL *adj* of or relating to land, farming, etc ▷ *n* slave attached to a farm
PRAEDIALS > PRAEDIAL
PRAEFECT *same as* > PREFECT
PRAEFECTS > PRAEFECT
PRAELECT *same as* > PRAELECT
PRAELECTS > PRAELECT
PRAELUDIA *n* musical preludes
PRAENOMEN *n* ancient Roman's first or given name
PRAESES *n* Roman governor
PRAESIDIA *n* presidiums
PRAETOR *n* (in ancient Rome) senior magistrate ranking just below the consuls
PRAETORS > PRAETOR
PRAGMATIC *adj* concerned with practical consequences rather than theory
PRAHU *same as* > PROA
PRAHUS > PRAHU
PRAIRIE *n* large treeless area of grassland, esp in N America and Canada
PRAIRIED > PRAIRIE
PRAIRIES > PRAIRIE
PRAISE *vb* express approval or admiration of (someone or something) ▷ *n* something said or written to show approval or admiration
PRAISEACH *n* type of porridge
PRAISED > PRAISE
PRAISEFUL > PRAISE
PRAISER > PRAISE
PRAISERS > PRAISE
PRAISES > PRAISE

PRAISING > PRAISE
PRAISINGS > PRAISE
PRAJNA n wisdom or understanding considered as the goal of Buddhist contemplation
PRAJNAS > PRAJNA
PRALINE n sweet made of nuts and caramelized sugar
PRALINES > PRALINE
PRAM n four-wheeled carriage for a baby, pushed by hand
PRAMS > PRAM
PRANA n (in Oriental medicine, martial arts, etc) cosmic energy believed to come from the sun and connecting the elements of the universe
PRANAS > PRANA
PRANAYAMA n breath control in yoga
PRANCE vb walk with exaggerated bouncing steps ▷ n act of prancing
PRANCED > PRANCE
PRANCER > PRANCE
PRANCERS > PRANCE
PRANCES > PRANCE
PRANCING > PRANCE
PRANCINGS > PRANCE
PRANCK obsolete variant of > PRANK
PRANCKE obsolete variant of > PRANK
PRANCKED > PRANCK
PRANCKES > PRANCKE
PRANCKING > PRANCK
PRANCKS > PRANCK
PRANDIAL adj of or relating to a meal
PRANG n crash in a car or aircraft ▷ vb crash or damage (an aircraft or car)
PRANGED > PRANG
PRANGING > PRANG
PRANGS > PRANG
PRANK n mischievous trick ▷ vb dress or decorate showily or gaudily
PRANKED > PRANK
PRANKFUL > PRANK
PRANKIER > PRANK
PRANKIEST > PRANK
PRANKING > PRANK
PRANKINGS > PRANK
PRANKISH > PRANK
PRANKLE obsolete variant of > PRANCE
PRANKLED > PRANKLE
PRANKLES > PRANKLE
PRANKLING > PRANKLE
PRANKS > PRANK
PRANKSOME > PRANK
PRANKSTER n practical joker
PRANKY > PRANK
PRAO same as > PROA
PRAOS > PRAO
PRASE n light green translucent variety of chalcedony
PRASES > PRASE
PRAT n stupid person
PRATE vb talk idly and at length ▷ n chatter

PRATED > PRATE
PRATER > PRATE
PRATERS > PRATE
PRATES > PRATE
PRATFALL vb fall upon one's buttocks
PRATFALLS > PRATFALL
PRATFELL > PRATFALL
PRATIE n potato
PRATIES > PRATIE
PRATING > PRATE
PRATINGLY > PRATE
PRATINGS > PRATE
PRATIQUE n formal permission given to a vessel to use a foreign port upon satisfying the requirements of local health authorities
PRATIQUES > PRATIQUE
PRATS > PRAT
PRATT n buttocks ▷ vb hit on the buttocks
PRATTED > PRATT
PRATTING > PRATT
PRATTLE vb chatter in a childish or foolish way ▷ n childish or foolish talk
PRATTLED > PRATTLE
PRATTLER > PRATTLE
PRATTLERS > PRATTLE
PRATTLES > PRATTLE
PRATTLING > PRATTLE
PRATTS > PRATT
PRATY obsolete variant of > PRETTY
PRAU same as > PROA
PRAUNCE obsolete variant of > PRANCE
PRAUNCED > PRAUNCE
PRAUNCES > PRAUNCE
PRAUNCING > PRAUNCE
PRAUS > PRAU
PRAVITIES > PRAVITY
PRAVITY n moral degeneracy
PRAWLE n Shakespearian phonetic spelling of "brawl" meant to indicate that the speaker is Welsh
PRAWLES > PRAWLE
PRAWLIN variant of > PRALINE
PRAWLINS > PRAWLIN
PRAWN n edible shellfish like a large shrimp ▷ vb catch prawns
PRAWNED > PRAWN
PRAWNER > PRAWN
PRAWNERS > PRAWN
PRAWNING > PRAWN
PRAWNS > PRAWN
PRAXES > PRAXIS
PRAXIS n practice as opposed to theory
PRAXISES > PRAXIS
PRAY vb say prayers ▷ adv I beg you ▷ interj I beg you
PRAYED > PRAY
PRAYER n thanks or appeal addressed to one's God
PRAYERFUL adj inclined to or characterized by prayer
PRAYERS > PRAYER
PRAYING > PRAY
PRAYINGLY > PRAY
PRAYINGS > PRAY

PRAYS > PRAY
PRE prep before
PREABSORB vb absorb beforehand
PREACCUSE vb accuse beforehand
PREACE obsolete variant of > PRESS
PREACED > PREACE
PREACES > PREACE
PREACH vb give a talk on a religious theme as part of a church service
PREACHED > PREACH
PREACHER n person who preaches, esp in church
PREACHERS > PREACHER
PREACHES > PREACH
PREACHIER > PREACHY
PREACHIFY vb preach or moralize in a tedious manner
PREACHILY > PREACHY
PREACHING > PREACH
PREACHY adj inclined to or marked by preaching
PREACING > PREACE
PREACT vb act beforehand
PREACTED > PREACT
PREACTING > PREACT
PREACTS > PREACT
PREADAMIC adj of or relating to the belief that there were people on earth before Adam
PREADAPT vb adapt beforehand
PREADAPTS > PREADAPT
PREADJUST vb adjust beforehand
PREADMIT vb prepare patient prior to treatment
PREADMITS > PREADMIT
PREADOPT vb adopt in advance
PREADOPTS > PREADOPT
PREADULT n animal or person who has not reached adulthood
PREADULTS > PREADULT
PREAGED adj treated to appear older
PREALLOT vb allot beforehand
PREALLOTS > PREALLOT
PREALTER vb alter beforehand
PREALTERS > PREALTER
PREAMBLE n introductory part to something said or written ▷ vb write a preamble
PREAMBLED > PREAMBLE
PREAMBLES > PREAMBLE
PREAMP n electronic amplifier used to improve the signal-to-noise ratio of an electronic device
PREAMPS > PREAMP
PREANAL adj situated in front of anus
PREAPPLY vb apply beforehand
PREARM vb arm beforehand
PREARMED > PREARM
PREARMING > PREARM
PREARMS > PREARM

PREASE vb crowd or press
PREASED > PREASE
PREASES > PREASE
PREASING > PREASE
PREASSE obsolete spelling of > PRESS
PREASSED > PREASSE
PREASSES > PREASSE
PREASSIGN vb assign beforehand
PREASSING > PREASSE
PREASSURE vb assure beforehand
PREATOMIC adj before the atomic age
PREATTUNE vb attune beforehand
PREAUDIT n examination of contracts before a transaction
PREAUDITS > PREAUDIT
PREAVER vb aver in advance
PREAVERS > PREAVER
PREAXIAL adj situated or occurring in front of the axis of the body
PREBADE > PREBID
PREBAKE vb bake before further cooking
PREBAKED > PREBAKE
PREBAKES > PREBAKE
PREBAKING > PREBAKE
PREBASAL adj in front of a base
PREBATTLE adj of the period before a battle
PREBEND n allowance paid by a cathedral or collegiate church to a canon or member of the chapter
PREBENDAL > PREBEND
PREBENDS > PREBEND
PREBID vb bid beforehand
PREBIDDEN > PREBID
PREBIDS > PREBID
PREBILL vb issue an invoice before the service has been provided
PREBILLED > PREBILL
PREBILLS > PREBILL
PREBIND vb bind a book in a hard-wearing binding
PREBINDS > PREBIND
PREBIOTIC adj of the period before the existence of life on earth
PREBIRTH n period of life before birth
PREBIRTHS > PREBIRTH
PREBLESS vb bless a couple before they marry
PREBOARD vb board an aircraft before other passengers
PREBOARDS > PREBOARD
PREBOIL vb boil beforehand
PREBOILED > PREBOIL
PREBOILS > PREBOIL
PREBOOK vb book well in advance
PREBOOKED > PREBOOK
PREBOOKS > PREBOOK
PREBOOM adj of the period before an economic boom
PREBORN adj unborn
PREBOUGHT > PREBUY
PREBOUND > PREBIND

PREBUDGET adj before budget

PREBUILD vb build beforehand

PREBUILDS > PREBUILD

PREBUILT > PREBUILD

PREBUTTAL n prepared response to an anticipated criticism

PREBUY vb buy in advance

PREBUYING > PREBUY

PREBUYS > PREBUY

PRECANCEL vb cancel (postage stamps) before placing them on mail ▷ n precancelled stamp

PRECANCER n condition that may develop into cancer

PRECAST adj (esp of concrete when employed as a structural element in building) cast in a particular form before being used ▷ vb cast (concrete) in a particular form before use

PRECASTS > PRECAST

PRECATIVE same as > PRECATORY

PRECATORY adj of, involving, or expressing entreaty

PRECAUDAL adj in front of the caudal fin

PRECAVA n superior vena cava

PRECAVAE > PRECAVA

PRECAVAL > PRECAVA

PRECEDE vb go or be before

PRECEDED > PRECEDE

PRECEDENT n previous case or occurrence regarded as an example to be followed ▷ adj preceding

PRECEDES > PRECEDE

PRECEDING adj going or coming before

PRECEESE Scots variant of > PRECISE

PRECENSOR vb censor (a film, play, book, etc) before its publication

PRECENT vb issue a command or law

PRECENTED > PRECENT

PRECENTOR n person who leads the singing in a church

PRECENTS > PRECENT

PRECEPIT old word for > PRECIPICE

PRECEPITS > PRECEPIT

PRECEPT n rule of behaviour

PRECEPTOR n instructor

PRECEPTS > PRECEPT

PRECESS vb undergo or cause to undergo precession

PRECESSED > PRECESS

PRECESSES > PRECESS

PRECHARGE vb charge beforehand

PRECHECK vb check beforehand

PRECHECKS > PRECHECK

PRECHILL vb chill

beforehand

PRECHILLS > PRECHILL

PRECHOOSE vb choose in advance

PRECHOSE > PRECHOOSE

PRECHOSEN > PRECHOOSE

PRECIEUSE n pretentious female

PRECIEUX n pretentious male

PRECINCT n area in a town closed to traffic

PRECINCTS pl n surrounding region

PRECIOUS adj of great value and importance ▷ adv very

PRECIPE n type of legal document

PRECIPES > PRECIPE

PRECIPICE n very steep face of a cliff

PRECIS n short written summary of a longer piece ▷ vb make a precis of

PRECISE adj exact, accurate in every detail

PRECISED > PRECIS

PRECISELY adv in a precise manner

PRECISER > PRECISE

PRECISES > PRECIS

PRECISEST > PRECISE

PRECISIAN n punctilious observer of rules or forms, esp in the field of religion

PRECISING > PRECIS

PRECISION n quality of being precise ▷ adj accurate

PRECISIVE adj limiting by cutting off all that is unnecessary

PRECITED adj cited previously

PRECLEAN vb clean beforehand

PRECLEANS > PRECLEAN

PRECLEAR vb approve in advance

PRECLEARS > PRECLEAR

PRECLUDE vb make impossible to happen

PRECLUDED > PRECLUDE

PRECLUDES > PRECLUDE

PRECOCIAL adj (of the young of some species of birds after hatching) covered with down, having open eyes, and capable of leaving the nest within a few days of hatching ▷ n precocial bird

PRECOCITY n early maturing or development

PRECODE vb code beforehand

PRECODED > PRECODE

PRECODES > PRECODE

PRECODING > PRECODE

PRECOITAL adj before sex

PRECONISE same as > PRECONIZE

PRECONIZE vb announce or commend publicly

PRECOOK vb cook (food) beforehand

PRECOOKED > PRECOOK

PRECOOKER n device for preparing food before cooking

PRECOOKS > PRECOOK

PRECOOL vb cool in advance

PRECOOLED > PRECOOL

PRECOOLS > PRECOOL

PRECOUP adj of the period before a coup

PRECRASH adj of the period before a crash

PRECREASE vb provide with a crease in advance

PRECRISIS adj occurring before a crisis

PRECURE vb cure in advance

PRECURED > PRECURE

PRECURES > PRECURE

PRECURING > PRECURE

PRECURRER > PRECURE

PRECURSE n forerunning

PRECURSES > PRECURSE

PRECURSOR n something that precedes and is a signal of something else, forerunner

PRECUT vb cut in advance

PRECUTS > PRECUT

PREDACITY n predatory nature

PREDATE vb occur at an earlier date than

PREDATED > PREDATE

PREDATES > PREDATE

PREDATING > PREDATE

PREDATION n relationship between two species of animal in a community, in which one (the predator) hunts, kills, and eats the other (the prey)

PREDATISM n state of preying on other animals

PREDATIVE > PREDATE

PREDATOR n predatory animal

PREDATORS > PREDATOR

PREDATORY adj habitually hunting and killing other animals for food

PREDAWN n period before dawn

PREDAWNS > PREDAWN

PREDEATH n period immediately before death

PREDEATHS > PREDEATH

PREDEBATE adj before a debate

PREDEDUCT vb deduct beforehand

PREDEFINE vb define in advance

PREDELLA n painting or sculpture or a series of small paintings or sculptures in a long narrow strip forming the lower edge of an altarpiece or the face of an altar step or platform

PREDELLAS > PREDELLA

PREDELLE > PREDELLA

PREDESIGN vb design beforehand

PREDEVOTE adj preordained

PREDIAL same as > PRAEDIAL

PREDIALS > PREDIAL

PREDICANT same as > PREDIKANT

PREDICATE n part of a sentence in which something is said about the subject ▷ vb declare or assert ▷ adj of or relating to something that has been predicated

PREDICT vb tell about in advance, prophesy

PREDICTED > PREDICT

PREDICTER > PREDICT

PREDICTOR n person or thing that predicts

PREDICTS > PREDICT

PREDIED > PREDY

PREDIES > PREDY

PREDIGEST vb treat (food) artificially to aid subsequent digestion in the body

PREDIKANT n minister in the Dutch Reformed Church in South Africa

PREDILECT adj chosen or preferred

PREDINNER adj of the period before dinner

PREDIVE adj happening before a dive

PREDOOM vb pronounce (someone or something's) doom beforehand

PREDOOMED > PREDOOM

PREDOOMS > PREDOOM

PREDRAFT adj before a draft

PREDRIED > PREDRY

PREDRIES > PREDRY

PREDRILL vb drill in advance

PREDRILLS > PREDRILL

PREDRY vb dry beforehand

PREDRYING > PREDRY

PREDUSK n period before dawn

PREDUSKS > PREDUSK

PREDY vb prepare for action

PREDYING > PREDY

PREE vb try or taste

PREED > PREE

PREEDIT vb edit beforehand

PREEDITED > PREEDIT

PREEDITS > PREEDIT

PREEING > PREE

PREELECT vb elect beforehand

PREELECTS > PREELECT

PREEMIE n premature infant

PREEMIES > PREEMIE

PREEMPT vb acquire in advance of or to the exclusion of others

PREEMPTED > PREEMPT

PREEMPTOR > PREEMPT

PREEMPTS > PREEMPT

PREEN vb (of a bird) clean or trim (feathers) with the beak ▷ n pin, esp a decorative one

PREENACT vb enact beforehand

PREENACTS > PREENACT

PREENED > PREEN

PREENER > PREEN

PREENERS > PREEN

PREENING > PREEN
PREENS > PREEN
PREERECT vb erect beforehand
PREERECTS > PREERECT
PREES > PREE
PREEVE old form of > PROVE
PREEVED > PREEVE
PREEVES > PREEVE
PREEVING > PREEVE
PREEXCITE vb stimulate in preparation
PREEXEMPT vb exempt beforehand
PREEXILIC adj prior to the Babylonian exile of the Jews
PREEXIST vb exist beforehand
PREEXISTS > PREEXIST
PREEXPOSE vb expose beforehand
PREFAB n prefabricated house ▷ vb manufacture sections of (building) in factory
PREFABBED > PREFAB
PREFABS > PREFAB
PREFACE n introduction to a book ▷ vb serve as an introduction to (a book, speech, etc)
PREFACED > PREFACE
PREFACER > PREFACE
PREFACERS > PREFACE
PREFACES > PREFACE
PREFACIAL adj anterior to face
PREFACING > PREFACE
PREFADE vb fade beforehand
PREFADED > PREFADE
PREFADES > PREFADE
PREFADING > PREFADE
PREFARD vb old form of preferred
PREFATORY adj concerning a preface
PREFECT n senior pupil in a school, with limited power over others
PREFECTS > PREFECT
PREFER vb like better
PREFERRED > PREFER
PREFERRER > PREFER
PREFERS > PREFER
PREFEUDAL adj of the period before the feudal era
PREFIGHT adj of the period before a boxing match
PREFIGURE vb represent or suggest in advance
PREFILE vb file beforehand
PREFILED > PREFILE
PREFILES > PREFILE
PREFILING > PREFILE
PREFILLED adj having been filled beforehand
PREFIRE vb fire beforehand
PREFIRED > PREFIRE
PREFIRES > PREFIRE
PREFIRING > PREFIRE
PREFIX n letter or group of letters put at the beginning of a word to make a new word, such as un- in unhappy ▷ vb put as an

introduction or prefix (to)
PREFIXAL > PREFIX
PREFIXED > PREFIX
PREFIXES > PREFIX
PREFIXING > PREFIX
PREFIXION > PREFIX
PREFLAME adj of the period before combustion
PREFLIGHT adj of or relating to the period just prior to a plane taking off
PREFOCUS vb focus in advance
PREFORM vb form beforehand
PREFORMAT vb format in advance
PREFORMED > PREFORM
PREFORMS > PREFORM
PREFRANK vb frank in advance
PREFRANKS > PREFRANK
PREFREEZE vb freeze beforehand
PREFROZE > PREFREEZE
PREFROZEN > PREFREEZE
PREFUND vb pay for in advance
PREFUNDED > PREFUND
PREFUNDS > PREFUND
PREGAME adj of the period before a sports match ▷ n such a period
PREGAMES > PREGAME
PREGGERS informal word for > PREGNANT
PREGGIER > PREGGY
PREGGIEST > PREGGY
PREGGY informal word for > PREGNANT
PREGNABLE adj capable of being assailed or captured
PREGNANCE obsolete word for > PREGNANCY
PREGNANCY n state or condition of being pregnant
PREGNANT adj carrying a fetus in the womb
PREGROWTH n period before something begins to grow
PREGUIDE vb give guidance in advance
PREGUIDED > PREGUIDE
PREGUIDES > PREGUIDE
PREHALLUX n extra first toe
PREHANDLE vb handle beforehand
PREHARDEN vb harden beforehand
PREHEAT vb heat (an oven, grill, pan, etc) beforehand
PREHEATED > PREHEAT
PREHEATER > PREHEAT
PREHEATS > PREHEAT
PREHEND vb take hold of
PREHENDED > PREHEND
PREHENDS > PREHEND
PREHENSOR n part that grasps
PREHIRING adj relating to early hiring
PREHNITE n green mineral
PREHNITES > PREHNITE
PREHUMAN n hominid that predates man
PREHUMANS > PREHUMAN

PREIF old form of > PROOF
PREIFE old form of > PROOF
PREIFES > PREIFE
PREIFS > PREIF
PREIMPOSE vb impose beforehand
PREINFORM vb inform beforehand
PREINSERT vb insert beforehand
PREINVITE vb invite before others
PREJINK variant of > PERJINK
PREJUDGE vb judge beforehand without sufficient evidence
PREJUDGED > PREJUDGE
PREJUDGER > PREJUDGE
PREJUDGES > PREJUDGE
PREJUDICE n unreasonable or unfair dislike or preference ▷ vb cause (someone) to have a prejudice
PREJUDIZE old form of > PREJUDICE
PRELACIES > PRELACY
PRELACY n office or status of a prelate
PRELATE n bishop or other churchman of high rank
PRELATES > PRELATE
PRELATESS n female prelate
PRELATIAL > PRELATE
PRELATIC > PRELATE
PRELATIES > PRELATY
PRELATION n setting of one above another
PRELATISE same as > PRELATIZE
PRELATISH > PRELATE
PRELATISM same as > PRELACY
PRELATIST > PRELATISM
PRELATIZE vb exercise prelatical power
PRELATURE same as > PRELACY
PRELATY n prelacy
PRELAUNCH adj of the period before a launch
PRELAW adj before taking up study of law
PRELECT vb lecture or discourse in public
PRELECTED > PRELECT
PRELECTOR > PRELECT
PRELECTS > PRELECT
PRELEGAL adj of the period before the start of a law course
PRELIFE n life lived before one's life on earth
PRELIM n event which precedes another
PRELIMIT vb limit beforehand
PRELIMITS > PRELIMIT
PRELIMS pl n pages of a book, such as the title page and contents, which come before the main text
PRELIVES > PRELIFE
PRELOAD vb load beforehand

PRELOADED > PRELOAD
PRELOADS > PRELOAD
PRELOCATE vb locate beforehand
PRELOVED adj previously owned or used
PRELUDE n introductory movement in music ▷ vb act as a prelude to (something)
PRELUDED > PRELUDE
PRELUDER > PRELUDE
PRELUDERS > PRELUDE
PRELUDES > PRELUDE
PRELUDI > PRELUDIO
PRELUDIAL > PRELUDE
PRELUDING > PRELUDE
PRELUDIO n musical prelude
PRELUNCH adj of the period before lunch
PRELUSION > PRELUDE
PRELUSIVE > PRELUDE
PRELUSORY > PRELUDE
PREM n informal word for a premature infant
PREMADE adj made in advance
PREMAN n Indonesian gangster
PREMARKET adj of the period before a product is available
PREMATURE adj happening or done before the normal or expected time
PREMEAL adj of the period before a meal
PREMED n premedical student
PREMEDIC same as > PREMED
PREMEDICS > PREMEDIC
PREMEDS > PREMED
PREMEET adj happening before a meet
PREMEN > PREMAN
PREMERGER adj of the period prior to a merger
PREMIA > PREMIUM
PREMIE same as > PREEMIE
PREMIER n prime minister ▷ adj chief, leading
PREMIERE n first performance of a play, film, etc ▷ vb give, or (of a film, play, or opera) be, a premiere
PREMIERED > PREMIERE
PREMIERES > PREMIERE
PREMIERS > PREMIER
PREMIES > PREMIE
PREMISE n statement assumed to be true and used as the basis of reasoning ▷ vb state or assume (a proposition) as a premise in an argument, theory, etc
PREMISED > PREMISE
PREMISES > PREMISE
PREMISING > PREMISE
PREMISS same as > PREMISE
PREMISSES > PREMISS
PREMIUM n additional sum of money, as on a wage or charge

P

PREMIUMS > PREMIUM

PREMIX vb mix beforehand

PREMIXED > PREMIX

PREMIXES > PREMIX

PREMIXING > PREMIX

PREMIXT > PREMIX

PREMODERN adj of the period before a modern era

PREMODIFY vb modify in advance

PREMOLAR n tooth between the canine and first molar in adult humans ▷ adj situated before a molar tooth

PREMOLARS > PREMOLAR

PREMOLD vb mold in advance

PREMOLDED > PREMOLD

PREMOLDS > PREMOLD

PREMOLT adj happening in the period before an animal molts

PREMONISH vb admonish beforehand

PREMORAL adj not governed by sense of right and wrong

PREMORSE adj appearing as though the end had been bitten off

PREMOSAIC adj of the period before Moses

PREMOTION n previous motion

PREMOVE vb prompt to action

PREMOVED > PREMOVE

PREMOVES > PREMOVE

PREMOVING > PREMOVE

PREMS > PREM

PREMUNE adj having immunity to a disease as a result of latent infection

PREMY variant of > PREEMIE

PRENAME n forename

PRENAMES > PRENAME

PRENASAL n bone in the front of the nose

PRENASALS > PRENASAL

PRENATAL adj before birth, during pregnancy ▷ n prenatal examination

PRENATALS > PRENATAL

PRENOMEN less common spelling of > PRAENOMEN

PRENOMENS > PRENOMEN

PRENOMINA > PRENOMEN

PRENOON adj of the period before noon

PRENOTIFY vb notify in advance

PRENOTION n preconception

PRENT Scots variant of > PRINT

PRENTED > PRENT

PRENTICE vb bind as an apprentice

PRENTICED > PRENTICE

PRENTICES > PRENTICE

PRENTING > PRENT

PRENTS > PRENT

PRENUBILE adj of the period from birth to puberty

PRENUMBER vb number in advance

PRENUP n prenuptial agreement

PRENUPS > PRENUP

PRENZIE adj Shakespearian word, possibly a mistake, supposed by some to mean "princely"

PREOBTAIN vb obtain in advance

PREOCCUPY vb fill the thoughts or attention of (someone) to the exclusion of other things

PREOCULAR adj relating to the scale in front of the eye of a reptile or fish

PREOP n patient being prepared for surgery

PREOPS > PREOP

PREOPTION n right of first choice

PREORAL adj situated in front of mouth

PREORDAIN vb ordain, decree, or appoint beforehand

PREORDER vb order in advance

PREORDERS > PREORDER

PREOWNED adj second-hand

PREP vb prepare

PREPACK vb pack in advance of sale

PREPACKED adj sold already wrapped

PREPACKS > PREPACK

PREPAID > PREPAY

PREPARE vb make or get ready

PREPARED > PREPARE

PREPARER > PREPARE

PREPARERS > PREPARE

PREPARES > PREPARE

PREPARING > PREPARE

PREPASTE vb paste in advance

PREPASTED > PREPASTE

PREPASTES > PREPASTE

PREPAVE vb pave beforehand

PREPAVED > PREPAVE

PREPAVES > PREPAVE

PREPAVING > PREPAVE

PREPAY vb pay for in advance

PREPAYING > PREPAY

PREPAYS > PREPAY

PREPENSE adj (usually in legal contexts) arranged in advance ▷ vb consider beforehand

PREPENSED > PREPENSE

PREPENSES > PREPENSE

PREPILL adj of the period before the contraceptive pill became available

PREPLACE vb place in advance

PREPLACED > PREPLACE

PREPLACES > PREPLACE

PREPLAN vb plan beforehand

PREPLANS > PREPLAN

PREPLANT adj planted in advance

PREPOLLEX n additional digit on thumb of some animals

PREPONE vb bring forward to an earlier time

PREPONED > PREPONE

PREPONES > PREPONE

PREPONING > PREPONE

PREPOSE vb place before

PREPOSED > PREPOSE

PREPOSES > PREPOSE

PREPOSING > PREPOSE

PREPOSTOR n prefect in certain public shcools

PREPOTENT adj greater in power, force, or influence

PREPPED > PREP

PREPPIE same as > PREPPY

PREPPIER > PREPPY

PREPPIES > PREPPY

PREPPIEST > PREPPY

PREPPILY > PREPPY

PREPPING > PREP

PREPPY adj characteristic of or denoting a fashion style of neat, understated, and often expensive clothes ▷ n person exhibiting such style

PREPREG n material already impregnated with synthetic resin

PREPREGS > PREPREG

PREPRESS adj before printing

PREPRICE vb price in advance

PREPRICED > PREPRICE

PREPRICES > PREPRICE

PREPRINT vb print in advance

PREPRINTS > PREPRINT

PREPS > PREP

PREPUBES > PREPUBIS

PREPUBIS n animal hip bone

PREPUCE n foreskin

PREPUCES > PREPUCE

PREPUEBLO adj belonging to the period before the Pueblo Indians

PREPUNCH vb pierce with holes in advance

PREPUPA n insect in stage of life before pupa

PREPUPAE > PREPUPA

PREPUPAL adj of the period between the larval and pupal stages

PREPUPAS > PREPUPA

PREPUTIAL > PREPUCE

PREQUEL n film or book about an earlier stage of a story or a character's life, released because the later part of it has already been successful

PREQUELS > PREQUEL

PRERACE adj of the period before a race

PRERADIO adj before the invention of radio

PRERECORD vb record (music or a programme) in advance so that it can be played or broadcast later

PRERECTAL adj in front of the rectum

PREREFORM adj before reform

PRERENAL adj anterior to kidney

PRERETURN adj of the period before return

PREREVIEW adj of the period before review

PRERINSE vb treat before rinsing

PRERINSED > PRERINSE

PRERINSES > PRERINSE

PRERIOT adj of the period before a riot

PREROCK adj of the era before rock music

PRERUPT adj abrupt

PRESA n sign or symbol used in a canon, round, etc, to indicate the entry of each part.

PRESAGE vb be a sign or warning of ▷ n omen

PRESAGED > PRESAGE

PRESAGER > PRESAGE

PRESAGERS > PRESAGE

PRESAGES > PRESAGE

PRESAGING > PRESAGE

PRESALE n practice of arranging the sale of a product before it is available

PRESALES > PRESALE

PRESBYOPE n person with presbyopy

PRESBYOPY n diminishing ability of the eye to focus

PRESBYTE n person with presbyopy

PRESBYTER n (in some episcopal Churches) official with administrative and priestly duties

PRESBYTES > PRESBYTE

PRESBYTIC > PRESBYTE

PRESCHOOL adj of or for children below the age of five

PRESCIENT adj having knowledge of events before they take place

PRESCIND vb withdraw attention (from something)

PRESCINDS > PRESCIND

PRESCIOUS adj prescient

PRESCORE vb record (the score of a film) before shooting

PRESCORED > PRESCORE

PRESCORES > PRESCORE

PRESCREEN vb screen in advance

PRESCRIBE vb recommend the use of (a medicine)

PRESCRIPT n something laid down or prescribed ▷ adj prescribed as a rule

PRESCUTA > PRESCUTUM

PRESCUTUM n part of an insect's thorax

PRESE > PRESA

PRESEASON n period before the start of a sport season

PRESELECT vb select beforehand

PRESELL vb promote (a product, entertainment, etc) with publicity in advance of its appearance

PRESELLS > PRESELL

PRESENCE *n* fact of being in a specified place

PRESENCES > PRESENCE

PRESENILE *adj* occurring before the onset of old age

PRESENT *adj* being in a specified place ▷ *n* present time or tense ▷ *vb* introduce formally or publicly

PRESENTED > PRESENT

PRESENTEE *n* person who is presented, as at court

PRESENTER *n* person introducing a TV or radio show

PRESENTLY *adv* soon

PRESENTS *pl n* used in a deed or document to refer to itself

PRESERVE *vb* keep from being damaged, changed, or ended ▷ *n* area of interest restricted to a particular person or group

PRESERVED > PRESERVE

PRESERVER > PRESERVE

PRESERVES > PRESERVE

PRESES *variant of* > PRAESES

PRESET *vb* set the timer on a piece of equipment so that it starts to work at a specific time ▷ *adj* (of equipment) with the controls set in advance ▷ *n* control, such as a variable resistor, that is not as accessible as the main controls and is used to set initial conditions

PRESETS > PRESET

PRESETTLE *vb* settle beforehand

PRESHAPE *vb* shape beforehand

PRESHAPED > PRESHAPE

PRESHAPES > PRESHAPE

PRESHIP *vb* ship in advance

PRESHIPS > PRESHIP

PRESHOW *vb* show in advance

PRESHOWED > PRESHOW

PRESHOWN > PRESHOW

PRESHOWS > PRESHOW

PRESHRANK > PRESHRINK

PRESHRINK *vb* subject to a shrinking process so that further shrinkage will not occur

PRESHRUNK > PRESHRINK

PRESIDE *vb* be in charge, esp of a meeting

PRESIDED > PRESIDE

PRESIDENT *n* head of state in many countries

PRESIDER > PRESIDE

PRESIDERS > PRESIDE

PRESIDES > PRESIDE

PRESIDIA > PRESIDIUM

PRESIDIAL *adj* presidential

PRESIDING > PRESIDE

PRESIDIO *n* military post or establishment, esp in countries under Spanish control

PRESIDIOS > PRESIDIO

PRESIDIUM *n* (in Communist countries) permanent administrative committee

PRESIFT *vb* sift beforehand

PRESIFTED > PRESIFT

PRESIFTS > PRESIFT

PRESIGNAL *vb* signal in advance

PRESLEEP *adj* of the period before sleep

PRESLICE *vb* slice in advance

PRESLICED > PRESLICE

PRESLICES > PRESLICE

PRESOAK *vb* soak beforehand

PRESOAKED > PRESOAK

PRESOAKS > PRESOAK

PRESOLD > PRESELL

PRESOLVE *vb* solve beforehand

PRESOLVED > PRESOLVE

PRESOLVES > PRESOLVE

PRESONG *adj* of the period before a song is sung

PRESORT *vb* sort in advance

PRESORTED > PRESORT

PRESORTS > PRESORT

PRESPLIT *adj* of the period prior to a split

PRESS *vb* apply force or weight to ▷ *n* printing machine

PRESSED > PRESS

PRESSER > PRESS

PRESSERS > PRESS

PRESSES > PRESS

PRESSFAT *n* wine vat

PRESSFATS > PRESSFAT

PRESSFUL > PRESS

PRESSFULS > PRESS

PRESSGANG *n* squad of sailors forcing others into navy

PRESSIE *informal word for* > PRESENT

PRESSIES > PRESSIE

PRESSING *adj* urgent ▷ *n* large number of gramophone records produced at one time

PRESSINGS > PRESSING

PRESSION *n* act of pressing

PRESSIONS > PRESSION

PRESSMAN *n* person who works for the press

PRESSMARK *n* location mark on a book indicating a specific bookcase

PRESSMEN > PRESSMAN

PRESSOR *n* something that produces an increase in blood pressure

PRESSORS > PRESSOR

PRESSROOM *n* room in a printing establishment that houses the printing presses

PRESSRUN *n* number of books printed at one time

PRESSRUNS > PRESSRUN

PRESSURE *n* force produced by pressing ▷ *vb* persuade forcefully

PRESSURED > PRESSURE

PRESSURES > PRESSURE

PRESSWORK *n* operation of a printing press

PREST *adj* prepared for action or use ▷ *n* loan of money ▷ *vb* give as a loan

PRESTAMP *vb* stamp in advance

PRESTAMPS > PRESTAMP

PRESTED > PREST

PRESTER > PREST

PRESTERNA *adj* anterior to sternum

PRESTERS > PREST

PRESTIGE *n* high status or respect resulting from success or achievements

PRESTIGES > PRESTIGE

PRESTING > PREST

PRESTO *adv* very quickly ▷ *n* passage to be played very quickly

PRESTORE *vb* store in advance

PRESTORED > PRESTORE

PRESTORES > PRESTORE

PRESTOS > PRESTO

PRESTRESS *vb* apply tensile stress to (the steel cables, wires, etc, of a precast concrete part) before the load is applied

PRESTRIKE *adj* of the period before a strike

PRESTS > PREST

PRESUME *vb* suppose to be the case

PRESUMED > PRESUME

PRESUMER > PRESUME

PRESUMERS > PRESUME

PRESUMES > PRESUME

PRESUMING > PRESUME

PRESUMMIT *n* meeting held prior to a summit

PRESURVEY *vb* survey in advance

PRETAPE *vb* tape in advance

PRETAPED > PRETAPE

PRETAPES > PRETAPE

PRETAPING > PRETAPE

PRETASTE *vb* taste in advance

PRETASTED > PRETASTE

PRETASTES > PRETASTE

PRETAX *adj* before tax

PRETEEN *n* boy or girl approaching his or her teens

PRETEENS > PRETEEN

PRETELL *vb* predict

PRETELLS > PRETELL

PRETENCE *n* behaviour intended to deceive, pretending

PRETENCES > PRETENCE

PRETEND *vb* claim or give the appearance of (something untrue) to deceive or in play ▷ *adj* fanciful

PRETENDED > PRETEND

PRETENDER *n* person who makes a false or disputed claim to a position of power

PRETENDS > PRETEND

PRETENSE *same*

as > PRETENCE

PRETENSES > PRETENSE

PRETERIST *n* person interested in past

PRETERIT *same*

as > PRETERITE

PRETERITE *n* past tense of verbs, such as *jumped*, *swam* ▷ *adj* expressing such a past tense

PRETERITS > PRETERIT

PRETERM *n* premature baby

PRETERMIT *vb* overlook intentionally

PRETERMS > PRETERM

PRETEST *vb* test (something) before presenting it to its intended public or client ▷ *n* act or instance of pretesting

PRETESTED > PRETEST

PRETESTS > PRETEST

PRETEXT *n* false reason given to hide the real one ▷ *vb* get personal information under false pretences

PRETEXTED > PRETEXT

PRETEXTS > PRETEXT

PRETOLD > PRETELL

PRETONIC *adj* denoting or relating to the syllable before the one bearing the primary stress in a word

PRETOR *same as* > PRAETOR

PRETORIAL > PRETOR

PRETORIAN *n* person with the rank of praetor

PRETORS > PRETOR

PRETRAIN *vb* train in advance

PRETRAINS > PRETRAIN

PRETRAVEL *adj* of the period before travel

PRETREAT *vb* treat in advance

PRETREATS > PRETREAT

PRETRIAL *n* hearing prior to a trial

PRETRIALS > PRETRIAL

PRETRIM *vb* trim in advance

PRETRIMS > PRETRIM

PRETTIED > PRETTY

PRETTIER > PRETTY

PRETTIES > PRETTY

PRETTIEST > PRETTY

PRETTIFY *vb* make pretty

PRETTILY > PRETTY

PRETTY *adj* pleasing to look at ▷ *adv* fairly, moderately ▷ *vb* pretty

PRETTYING > PRETTY

PRETTYISH *adj* quite pretty

PRETTYISM *n* affectedly pretty style

PRETYPE *vb* type in advance

PRETYPED > PRETYPE

PRETYPES > PRETYPE

PRETYPING > PRETYPE

PRETZEL *n* brittle salted biscuit

PRETZELS > PRETZEL

PREUNION *n* early form of trade union

PREUNIONS > PREUNION

PREUNITE *vb* unite in

advance
PREUNITED > PREUNITE
PREUNITES > PREUNITE
PREVAIL vb gain mastery
PREVAILED > PREVAIL
PREVAILER > PREVAIL
PREVAILS > PREVAIL
PREVALENT adj widespread, common
PREVALUE vb value beforehand
PREVALUED > PREVALUE
PREVALUES > PREVALUE
PREVE vb prove
PREVED > PREVE
PREVENE vb come before
PREVENED > PREVENE
PREVENES > PREVENE
PREVENING > PREVENE
PREVENT vb keep from happening or doing
PREVENTED > PREVENT
PREVENTER n person or thing that prevents
PREVENTS > PREVENT
PREVERB n particle preceding root of verb
PREVERBAL > PREVERB
PREVERBS > PREVERB
PREVES > PREVE
PREVIABLE adj not yet viable
PREVIEW n advance showing of a film or exhibition before it is shown to the public ▷ vb view in advance
PREVIEWED > PREVIEW
PREVIEWER > PREVIEW
PREVIEWS > PREVIEW
PREVING > PREVE
PREVIOUS adj coming or happening before
PREVISE vb predict or foresee
PREVISED > PREVISE
PREVISES > PREVISE
PREVISING > PREVISE
PREVISION n act or power of foreseeing
PREVISIT vb visit beforehand
PREVISITS > PREVISIT
PREVISOR > PREVISE
PREVISORS > PREVISE
PREVUE same as > PREVIEW
PREVUED > PREVUE
PREVUES > PREVUE
PREVUING > PREVUE
PREWAR adj relating to the period before a war, esp before World War I or II
PREWARM vb warm beforehand
PREWARMED > PREWARM
PREWARMS > PREWARM
PREWARN vb warn in advance
PREWARNED > PREWARN
PREWARNS > PREWARN
PREWASH vb give a preliminary wash to (clothes), esp in a washing machine ▷ n preliminary wash, esp in a washing machine
PREWASHED > PREWASH

PREWASHES > PREWASH
PREWEIGH vb weigh beforehand
PREWEIGHS > PREWEIGH
PREWIRE vb wire beforehand
PREWIRED > PREWIRE
PREWIRES > PREWIRE
PREWIRING > PREWIRE
PREWORK vb work in advance
PREWORKED > PREWORK
PREWORKS > PREWORK
PREWORN adj (of clothes) second-hand
PREWRAP vb wrap in advance
PREWRAPS > PREWRAP
PREWYN obsolete spelling of > PRUNE
PREWYNS > PREWYN
PREX same as > PREXY
PREXES > PREX
PREXIES > PREXY
PREXY n US college president
PREY n animal hunted and killed for food by another animal ▷ vb hunt or seize food by killing other animals
PREYED > PREY
PREYER > PREY
PREYERS > PREY
PREYFUL adj rich in prey
PREYING > PREY
PREYS > PREY
PREZ n president
PREZES > PREZ
PREZZIE same as > PRESSIE
PREZZIES > PREZZIE
PRIAL n pair royal of cards
PRIALS > PRIAL
PRIAPEAN same as > PRIAPIC
PRIAPI > PRIAPUS
PRIAPIC adj phallic
PRIAPISM n prolonged painful erection of the penis, caused by neurological disorders, obstruction of the penile blood vessels, etc
PRIAPISMS > PRIAPISM
PRIAPUS n representation of the penis
PRIAPUSES > PRIAPUS
PRIBBLE variant of > PRABBLE
PRIBBLES > PRIBBLE
PRICE n amount of money for which a thing is bought or sold ▷ vb fix or ask the price of
PRICEABLE > PRICE
PRICED > PRICE
PRICELESS adj very valuable
PRICER > PRICE
PRICERS > PRICE
PRICES > PRICE
PRICEY adj expensive
PRICIER > PRICY
PRICIEST > PRICY
PRICILY > PRICEY
PRICINESS > PRICEY
PRICING > PRICE
PRICINGS > PRICE

PRICK vb pierce lightly with a sharp point ▷ n sudden sharp pain caused by pricking
PRICKED > PRICK
PRICKER n person or thing that pricks
PRICKERS > PRICKER
PRICKET n male deer in the second year of life having unbranched antlers
PRICKETS > PRICKET
PRICKIER > PRICKY
PRICKIEST > PRICKY
PRICKING > PRICK
PRICKINGS > PRICK
PRICKLE n thorn or spike on a plant ▷ vb have a tingling or pricking sensation
PRICKLED > PRICKLE
PRICKLES > PRICKLE
PRICKLIER > PRICKLY
PRICKLING > PRICKLE
PRICKLY adj having prickles
PRICKS > PRICK
PRICKWOOD n shrub with wood used for skewers
PRICKY adj covered with pricks
PRICY same as > PRICEY
PRIDE n feeling of pleasure and satisfaction when one has done well
PRIDED > PRIDE
PRIDEFUL > PRIDE
PRIDELESS > PRIDE
PRIDES > PRIDE
PRIDIAN adj relating to yesterday
PRIDING > PRIDE
PRIED > PRY
PRIEDIEU n piece of furniture consisting of a low surface for kneeling upon and a narrow front surmounted by a rest for the elbows or for books, for use when praying
PRIEDIEUS > PRIEDIEU
PRIEDIEUX > PRIEDIEU
PRIEF obsolete variant of > PROOF
PRIEFE obsolete variant of > PROOF
PRIEFES > PRIEFE
PRIEFS > PRIEF
PRIER n person who pries
PRIERS > PRIER
PRIES > PRY
PRIEST n (in the Christian church) person who can administer the sacraments and preach ▷ vb make a priest
PRIESTED > PRIEST
PRIESTESS n female official who offers sacrifice on behalf of the people and peforms various other religious ceremonies
PRIESTING > PRIEST
PRIESTLY adj of, relating to, characteristic of, or befitting a priest
PRIESTS > PRIEST
PRIEVE obsolete variant of > PROOF

PRIEVED > PRIEVE
PRIEVES > PRIEVE
PRIEVING > PRIEVE
PRIG n self-righteous person who acts as if superior to others
PRIGGED > PRIG
PRIGGER n thief
PRIGGERS > PRIGGER
PRIGGERY > PRIG
PRIGGING > PRIG
PRIGGINGS > PRIG
PRIGGISH > PRIG
PRIGGISM > PRIG
PRIGGISMS > PRIG
PRIGS > PRIG
PRILL vb convert (a material) into a granular free-flowing form ▷ n prilled material
PRILLED > PRILL
PRILLING > PRILL
PRILLS > PRILL
PRIM adj formal, proper, and rather prudish ▷ vb make prim
PRIMA same as > PRIMO
PRIMACIES > PRIMACY
PRIMACY n state of being first in rank, grade, etc
PRIMAEVAL same as > PRIMEVAL
PRIMAGE n tax added to customs duty
PRIMAGES > PRIMAGE
PRIMAL adj of basic causes or origins
PRIMALITY n state of being prime
PRIMALLY > PRIMAL
PRIMARIES > PRIMARY
PRIMARILY adv chiefly or mainly
PRIMARY adj chief, most important ▷ n person or thing that is first in position, time, or importance
PRIMAS > PRIMA
PRIMATAL n primate
PRIMATALS > PRIMATAL
PRIMATE n member of an order of mammals including monkeys and humans ▷ adj of, relating to, or belonging to the order Primates
PRIMATES > PRIMATE
PRIMATIAL > PRIMATE
PRIMATIC > PRIMATE
PRIMAVERA n springtime
PRIME adj main, most important ▷ n time when someone is at his or her best or most vigorous ▷ vb give (someone) information in advance to prepare them for something
PRIMED > PRIME
PRIMELY > PRIME
PRIMENESS > PRIME
PRIMER n special paint applied to bare wood etc before the main paint
PRIMERO n 16th- and 17th-century card game

PRIMEROS > PRIMERO
PRIMERS > PRIMER
PRIMES > PRIME
PRIMETIME adj occurring during or designed for prime time
PRIMEUR n anything (esp fruit) produced early
PRIMEURS > PRIMEUR
PRIMEVAL adj of the earliest age of the world
PRIMI > PRIMO
PRIMINE n integument surrounding an ovule or the outer of two such integuments
PRIMINES > PRIMINE
PRIMING same as > PRIMER
PRIMINGS > PRIMING
PRIMIPARA n woman who has borne only one child
PRIMITIAE pl n first fruits of the season
PRIMITIAL > PRIMITIAE
PRIMITIAS > PRIMITIAE
PRIMITIVE adj of an early simple stage of development ▷ n primitive person or thing
PRIMLY > PRIM
PRIMMED > PRIM
PRIMMER > PRIM
PRIMMERS > PRIM
PRIMMEST > PRIM
PRIMMING > PRIM
PRIMNESS > PRIM
PRIMO n upper or right-hand part in a piano duet
PRIMORDIA n organs or parts in the earliest stage of development
PRIMOS > PRIMO
PRIMP vb tidy (one's hair or clothes) fussily
PRIMPED > PRIMP
PRIMPING > PRIMP
PRIMPS > PRIMP
PRIMROSE n pale yellow spring flower ▷ adj pale yellow
PRIMROSED > PRIMROSE
PRIMROSES > PRIMROSE
PRIMROSY > PRIMROSE
PRIMS > PRIM
PRIMSIE Scots variant of > PRIM
PRIMSIER > PRIMSIE
PRIMSIEST > PRIMSIE
PRIMULA n type of primrose with brightly coloured flowers
PRIMULAS > PRIMULA
PRIMULINE n type of dye
PRIMUS n presiding bishop in the Synod
PRIMUSES > PRIMUS
PRIMY adj prime
PRINCE vb act the prince
PRINCED > PRINCE
PRINCEDOM n dignity, rank, or position of a prince
PRINCEKIN n young prince
PRINCELET n petty or minor prince
PRINCELY adj of or like a prince ▷ adv in a princely manner

PRINCES > PRINCE
PRINCESS n female member of a royal family, esp the daughter of the king or queen
PRINCESSE same as > PRINCESS
PRINCING > PRINCE
PRINCIPAL adj main, most important ▷ n head of a school or college
PRINCIPE n prince
PRINCIPI > PRINCIPE
PRINCIPIA n principles
PRINCIPLE n moral rule guiding behaviour
PRINCOCK same as > PRINCOX
PRINCOCKS > PRINCOCK
PRINCOX n pert youth
PRINCOXES > PRINCOX
PRINK vb dress (oneself) finely
PRINKED > PRINK
PRINKER > PRINK
PRINKERS > PRINK
PRINKING > PRINK
PRINKS > PRINK
PRINT vb reproduce (a newspaper, book, etc) in large quantities by mechanical or electronic means ▷ n printed words etc
PRINTABLE adj capable of being printed or of producing a print
PRINTED > PRINT
PRINTER n person or company engaged in printing
PRINTERS > PRINTER
PRINTERY n establishment in which printing is carried out
PRINTHEAD n component in a printer that forms a printed character
PRINTING n process of producing printed matter
PRINTINGS > PRINTING
PRINTLESS > PRINT
PRINTOUT n printed information produced by a computer output device
PRINTOUTS > PRINTOUT
PRINTS > PRINT
PRION n dovelike petrel with a serrated bill
PRIONS > PRION
PRIOR adj earlier ▷ n head monk in a priory
PRIORATE n office, status, or term of office of a prior
PRIORATES > PRIORATE
PRIORESS n deputy head nun in a convent
PRIORIES > PRIORY
PRIORITY n most important thing that must be dealt with first
PRIORLY > PRIOR
PRIORS > PRIOR
PRIORSHIP n office of prior
PRIORY n place where certain orders of monks or nuns live

PRISAGE n customs duty levied until 1809 upon wine imported into England
PRISAGES > PRISAGE
PRISE same as > PRY
PRISED > PRISE
PRISER > PRISE
PRISERE n primary sere or succession from bare ground to the community climax
PRISERES > PRISERE
PRISERS > PRISE
PRISES > PRISE
PRISING > PRISE
PRISM n transparent block usu with triangular ends and rectangular sides, used to disperse light into a spectrum or refract it in optical instruments
PRISMATIC adj of or shaped like a prism
PRISMOID n prismatoid having an equal number of vertices in each of the two parallel planes and whose sides are trapeziums or parallelograms
PRISMOIDS > PRISMOID
PRISMS > PRISM
PRISMY > PRISM
PRISON n building where criminals and accused people are held ▷ vb imprison
PRISONED > PRISON
PRISONER n person held captive
PRISONERS > PRISONER
PRISONING > PRISON
PRISONOUS > PRISON
PRISONS > PRISON
PRISS n prissy person ▷ vb act prissily
PRISSED > PRISS
PRISSES > PRISS
PRISSIER > PRISSY
PRISSIES > PRISSY
PRISSIEST > PRISSY
PRISSILY > PRISSY
PRISSING > PRISS
PRISSY adj prim, correct, and easily shocked ▷ n prissy person
PRISTANE n colourless combustible liquid
PRISTANES > PRISTANE
PRISTINE adj clean, new, and unused
PRITHEE interj pray thee
PRIVACIES > PRIVACY
PRIVACY n condition of being private
PRIVADO n close friend
PRIVADOES > PRIVADO
PRIVADOS > PRIVADO
PRIVATE adj for the use of one person or group only ▷ n soldier of the lowest rank
PRIVATEER n privately owned armed vessel authorized by the government to take part in a war ▷ vb competitor, esp in motor racing, who

is privately financed rather than sponsored by a manufacturer
PRIVATELY > PRIVATE
PRIVATER > PRIVATE
PRIVATES > PRIVATE
PRIVATEST > PRIVATE
PRIVATION n loss or lack of the necessities of life
PRIVATISE same as > PRIVATIZE
PRIVATISM n lack of concern for public life
PRIVATIST > PRIVATISM
PRIVATIVE adj causing privation
PRIVATIZE vb sell (a publicly owned company) to individuals or a private company
PRIVET n bushy evergreen shrub used for hedges
PRIVETS > PRIVET
PRIVIER > PRIVY
PRIVIES > PRIVY
PRIVIEST > PRIVY
PRIVILEGE n advantage or favour that only some people have ▷ vb bestow a privilege or privileges upon
PRIVILY adv in a secret way
PRIVITIES > PRIVITY
PRIVITY n legally recognized relationship existing between two parties, such as that between lessor and lessee and between the parties to a contract
PRIVY adj sharing knowledge of something secret ▷ n toilet, esp an outside one
PRIZABLE adj of worth
PRIZE n reward given for success in a competition etc ▷ adj winning or likely to win a prize ▷ vb value highly
PRIZED > PRIZE
PRIZEMAN n winner of prize
PRIZEMEN > PRIZEMAN
PRIZER n contender for prize
PRIZERS > PRIZER
PRIZES > PRIZE
PRIZING > PRIZE
PRO prep in favour of ▷ n professional ▷ adv in favour of a motion etc
PROA n any of several kinds of canoe-like boats used in the South Pacific, esp one equipped with an outrigger and sails
PROACTION n action that initiates change as opposed to reaction to events
PROACTIVE adj tending to initiate change rather than reacting to events
PROAS > PROA
PROB n problem
PROBABLE adj likely to happen or be true ▷ n person who is likely to be

P

chosen for a team, event, etc

PROBABLES > PROBABLE

PROBABLY *adv* in all likelihood ▷ *sentence substitute* I believe such a thing or situation may be the case

PROBALL *adj* believable

PROBAND *n* first patient to be investigated in a family study, to whom all relationships are referred

PROBANDS > PROBAND

PROBANG *n* long flexible rod, often with a small sponge at one end, for inserting into the oesophagus, as to apply medication

PROBANGS > PROBANG

PROBATE *n* process of proving the validity of a will ▷ *vb* establish officially the authenticity and validity of (a will)

PROBATED > PROBATE

PROBATES > PROBATE

PROBATING > PROBATE

PROBATION *n* system of dealing with law-breakers, esp juvenile ones, by placing them under supervision

PROBATIVE *adj* serving to test or designed for testing

PROBATORY *same as* > PROBATIVE

PROBE *vb* search into or examine closely ▷ *n* surgical instrument used to examine a wound, cavity, etc

PROBEABLE > PROBE

PROBED > PROBE

PROBER > PROBE

PROBERS > PROBE

PROBES > PROBE

PROBING > PROBE

PROBINGLY > PROBE

PROBIOTIC *n* bacterium that protects the body from harmful bacteria

PROBIT *n* statistical measurement

PROBITIES > PROBITY

PROBITS > PROBIT

PROBITY *n* honesty, integrity

PROBLEM *n* something difficult to deal with or solve ▷ *adj* of a literary work that deals with difficult moral questions

PROBLEMS > PROBLEM

PROBOSCIS *n* long trunk or snout

PROBS > PROB

PROCACITY *n* insolence

PROCAINE *n* colourless or white crystalline water-soluble substance

PROCAINES > PROCAINE

PROCAMBIA *n* plant part in stem and root

PROCARP *n* female reproductive organ in red algae

PROCARPS > PROCARP

PROCARYON *same as* > PROKARYON

PROCEDURE *n* way of doing something, esp the correct or usual one

PROCEED *vb* start or continue doing

PROCEEDED > PROCEED

PROCEEDER > PROCEED

PROCEEDS *pl n* money obtained from an event or activity

PROCERITY *n* tallness

PROCESS *n* series of actions or changes ▷ *vb* handle or prepare by a special method of manufacture

PROCESSED > PROCESS

PROCESSER *same as* > PROCESSOR

PROCESSES > PROCESS

PROCESSOR *n* person or thing that carries out a process

PROCHAIN *variant of* > PROCHEIN

PROCHEIN *adj* next or nearest

PROCHOICE *adj* in favour of women's right to abortion

PROCHURCH *adj* favourable to church

PROCIDENT *adj* relating to prolapsus

PROCINCT *n* state of preparedness

PROCINCTS > PROCINCT

PROCLAIM *vb* declare publicly

PROCLAIMS > PROCLAIM

PROCLISES > PROCLITIC

PROCLISIS > PROCLITIC

PROCLITIC *adj* relating to or denoting a monosyllabic word or form having no stress or accent and pronounced as a prefix of the following word, as in English 't for it in 'twas ▷ *n* proclitic word or form

PROCLIVE *adj* prone

PROCONSUL *n* administrator or governor of a colony, occupied territory, or other dependency

PROCREANT > PROCREATE

PROCREATE *vb* produce offspring

PROCTAL *adj* relating to the rectum

PROCTITIS *n* inflammation of the rectum

PROCTODEA *pl n* parts of the anus

PROCTOR *n* member of the staff of certain universities having duties including the enforcement of discipline ▷ *vb* invigilate (an examination)

PROCTORED > PROCTOR

PROCTORS > PROCTOR

PROCURACY *n* office of a procurator

PROCURAL > PROCURE

PROCURALS > PROCURE

PROCURE *vb* get, provide

PROCURED > PROCURE

PROCURER *n* person who obtains people to act as prostitutes

PROCURERS > PROCURER

PROCURES > PROCURE

PROCURESS *same as* > PROCURER

PROCUREUR *n* law officer in Guernsey

PROCURING > PROCURE

PROD *vb* poke with something pointed ▷ *n* prodding

PRODDED > PROD

PRODDER > PROD

PRODDERS > PROD

PRODDING > PROD

PRODIGAL *adj* recklessly extravagant, wasteful ▷ *n* person who spends lavishly or squanders money

PRODIGALS > PRODIGAL

PRODIGIES > PRODIGY

PRODIGY *n* person with some marvellous talent

PRODITOR *n* traitor

PRODITORS > PRODITOR

PRODITORY > PRODITOR

PRODNOSE *vb* make uninvited inquiries (about someone else's business, for example)

PRODNOSED > PRODNOSE

PRODNOSES > PRODNOSE

PRODROMAL > PRODROME

PRODROME *n* any symptom that signals the impending onset of a disease

PRODROMES > PRODROME

PRODROMI > PRODROME

PRODROMIC > PRODROME

PRODROMUS *same as* > PRODROME

PRODRUG *n* compound that is itself biologically inactive but is metabolized in the body to produce an active therapeutic drug

PRODRUGS > PRODRUG

PRODS > PROD

PRODUCE *vb* bring into existence ▷ *n* food grown for sale

PRODUCED > PRODUCE

PRODUCER *n* person with control over the making of a film, record, etc

PRODUCERS > PRODUCER

PRODUCES > PRODUCE

PRODUCING > PRODUCE

PRODUCT *n* something produced

PRODUCTS > PRODUCT

PROEM *n* introduction or preface

PROEMBRYO *n* stage prior to embryo in plants

PROEMIAL > PROEM

PROEMS > PROEM

PROENZYME *n* inactive form of an enzyme

PROESTRUS *n* period in the estrous cycle that immediately precedes estrus

PROETTE *n* female golfing professional

PROETTES > PROETTE

PROF *short for* > PROFESSOR

PROFACE *interj* much good may it do you

PROFAMILY *adj* in favour of family

PROFANE *adj* showing disrespect for religion or holy things ▷ *vb* treat (something sacred) irreverently, desecrate

PROFANED > PROFANE

PROFANELY > PROFANE

PROFANER > PROFANE

PROFANERS > PROFANE

PROFANES > PROFANE

PROFANING > PROFANE

PROFANITY *n* profane talk or behaviour, blasphemy

PROFESS *vb* state or claim (something as true), sometimes falsely

PROFESSED *adj* supposed

PROFESSES > PROFESS

PROFESSOR *n* teacher of the highest rank in a university

PROFFER *vb* offer ▷ *n* act of proffering

PROFFERED > PROFFER

PROFFERER > PROFFER

PROFFERS > PROFFER

PROFILE *n* outline, esp of the face, as seen from the side ▷ *vb* draw, write, or make a profile of

PROFILED > PROFILE

PROFILER *n* person or device that creates a profile, esp someone with psychological training who assists police investigations by identifying the likely characteristics of the perpetrator of a particular crime

PROFILERS > PROFILER

PROFILES > PROFILE

PROFILING > PROFILE

PROFILIST > PROFILE

PROFIT *n* money gained ▷ *vb* gain or benefit

PROFITED > PROFIT

PROFITEER *n* person who makes excessive profits at the expense of the public ▷ *vb* make excessive profits

PROFITER > PROFIT

PROFITERS > PROFIT

PROFITING > PROFIT

PROFITS > PROFIT

PROFLUENT *adj* flowing smoothly or abundantly

PROFORMA *n* invoice issued before an order is placed or before the goods are delivered giving all the details and the cost of the goods

PROFORMAS > PROFORMA

PROFOUND *adj* showing or needing great knowledge ▷ *n* great depth

PROFOUNDS > PROFOUND

PROFS > PROF

PROFUSE *adj* plentiful
PROFUSELY > PROFUSE
PROFUSER > PROFUSE
PROFUSERS > PROFUSE
PROFUSION > PROFUSE
PROFUSIVE *same as* > PROFUSE
PROG *vb* prowl about for or as if for food or plunder ▷ *n* food obtained by begging
PROGENIES > PROGENY
PROGENY *n* children
PROGERIA *n* premature old age, a rare condition occurring in children and characterized by small stature, absent or greying hair, wrinkled skin, and other signs of old age
PROGERIAS > PROGERIA
PROGESTIN *n* type of steroid hormone
PROGGED > PROG
PROGGER *n* fan of progressive rock
PROGGERS > PROGGER
PROGGING > PROG
PROGGINS *n* proctor
PROGNOSE *vb* predict course of disease
PROGNOSED > PROGNOSE
PROGNOSES > PROGNOSIS
PROGNOSIS *n* doctor's forecast about the progress of an illness
PROGRADE *vb* (of beach) advance towards sea
PROGRADED > PROGRADE
PROGRADES > PROGRADE
PROGRAM *same as* > PROGRAMME
PROGRAMED > PROGRAM
PROGRAMER *n* US spelling of programmer
PROGRAMME *same as* > PROGRAM
PROGRAMS > PROGRAM
PROGRESS *n* improvement, development ▷ *vb* become more advanced or skilful
PROGS > PROG
PROGUN *adj* in favour of public owning firearms
PROHIBIT *vb* forbid or prevent from happening
PROHIBITS > PROHIBIT
PROIGN *same as* > PROIN
PROIGNED > PROIGN
PROIGNING > PROIGN
PROIGNS > PROIGN
PROIN *vb* trim or prune
PROINE *same as* > PROIN
PROINED > PROIN
PROINES > PROINE
PROINING > PROIN
PROINS > PROIN
PROJECT *n* planned scheme to do or examine something over a period ▷ *vb* make a forecast based on known data
PROJECTED > PROJECT
PROJECTOR *n* apparatus for projecting photographic images, films, or slides on a screen
PROJECTS > PROJECT

PROJET *n* draft of a proposed treaty
PROJETS > PROJET
PROKARYON *n* nucleus of a prokaryote
PROKARYOT *n* any organism having cells in each of which the genetic material is in a single DNA chain, not enclosed in a nucleus
PROKE *vb* thrust or poke
PROKED > PROKE
PROKER > PROKE
PROKERS > PROKE
PROKES > PROKE
PROKING > PROKE
PROLABOR *adj* favouring the Labor party
PROLACTIN *n* gonadotrophic hormone secreted by the anterior lobe of the pituitary gland
PROLAMIN *same as* > PROLAMINE
PROLAMINE *n* any of a group of simple plant proteins, including gliadin, hordein, and zein
PROLAMINS > PROLAMIN
PROLAN *n* constituent of human pregnancy urine
PROLANS > PROLAN
PROLAPSE *n* slipping down of an internal organ of the body from its normal position ▷ *vb* (of an internal organ) slip from its normal position
PROLAPSED > PROLAPSE
PROLAPSES > PROLAPSE
PROLAPSUS *same as* > PROLAPSE
PROLATE *adj* having a polar diameter which is longer than the equatorial diameter ▷ *vb* pronounce or utter
PROLATED > PROLATE
PROLATELY > PROLATE
PROLATES > PROLATE
PROLATING > PROLATE
PROLATION > PROLATE
PROLATIVE > PROLATE
PROLE *old form of* > PROWL
PROLED > PROLE
PROLEG *n* any of the short paired unjointed appendages on each abdominal segment of a caterpillar and any of certain other insect larvae
PROLEGS > PROLEG
PROLEPSES > PROLEPSIS
PROLEPSIS *n* rhetorical device by which objections are anticipated and answered in advance
PROLEPTIC > PROLEPSIS
PROLER *n* prowler
PROLERS > PROLER
PROLES > PROLE
PROLETARY *n* member of the proletariat
PROLICIDE *n* killing of one's child
PROLIFIC *adj* very productive

PROLINE *n* nonessential amino acid that occurs in protein
PROLINES > PROLINE
PROLING > PROLE
PROLIX *adj* (of speech or a piece of writing) overlong and boring
PROLIXITY > PROLIX
PROLIXLY > PROLIX
PROLL *vb* prowl or search
PROLLED > PROLL
PROLLER > PROLL
PROLLERS > PROLL
PROLLING > PROLL
PROLLS > PROLL
PROLOG *same as* > PROLOGUE
PROLOGED > PROLOG
PROLOGING > PROLOG
PROLOGISE *same as* > PROLOGIZE
PROLOGIST *n* prologue writer
PROLOGIZE *vb* write a prologue
PROLOGS > PROLOG
PROLOGUE *n* introduction to a play or book ▷ *vb* introduce or preface with or as if with a prologue
PROLOGUED > PROLOGUE
PROLOGUES > PROLOGUE
PROLONG *vb* make (something) last longer
PROLONGE *n* (formerly) specially fitted rope used as part of the towing equipment of a gun carriage
PROLONGED > PROLONG
PROLONGER > PROLONG
PROLONGES > PROLONGE
PROLONGS > PROLONG
PROLUSION *n* preliminary written exercise
PROLUSORY > PROLUSION
PROM *n* formal dance held at a high school or college
PROMACHOS *n* defender or champion
PROMENADE *n* paved walkway along the seafront at a holiday resort ▷ *vb* take a leisurely walk
PROMETAL *n* type of cast iron
PROMETALS > PROMETAL
PROMETRIC *adj* in favour of the metric system
PROMINE *n* substance promoting cell growth
PROMINENT *adj* very noticeable
PROMINES > PROMINE
PROMISE *vb* say that one will definitely do or not do something ▷ *n* undertaking to do or not to do something
PROMISED > PROMISE
PROMISEE *n* person to whom a promise is made
PROMISEES > PROMISEE
PROMISER > PROMISE
PROMISERS > PROMISE
PROMISES > PROMISE
PROMISING *adj* likely to

succeed or turn out well
PROMISOR *n* person who makes a promise
PROMISORS > PROMISOR
PROMISSOR *n* (in law) person who makes a promise
PROMMER *n* spectator at promenade concert
PROMMERS > PROMMER
PROMO *vb* promote (something) using a promo
PROMODERN *adj* in favour of the modern
PROMOED > PROMO
PROMOING > PROMO
PROMOS > PROMO
PROMOTE *vb* help to make (something) happen or increase
PROMOTED > PROMOTE
PROMOTER *n* person who organizes or finances an event etc
PROMOTERS > PROMOTER
PROMOTES > PROMOTE
PROMOTING > PROMOTE
PROMOTION > PROMOTE
PROMOTIVE *adj* tending to promote
PROMOTOR *variant of* > PROMOTER
PROMOTORS > PROMOTOR
PROMPT *vb* cause (an action) ▷ *adj* done without delay ▷ *adv* exactly ▷ *n* anything that serves to remind
PROMPTED > PROMPT
PROMPTER *n* person offstage who prompts actors
PROMPTERS > PROMPTER
PROMPTEST > PROMPT
PROMPTING > PROMPT
PROMPTLY > PROMPT
PROMPTS > PROMPT
PROMPTURE *n* prompting
PROMS > PROM
PROMULGE *vb* bring to public knowledge
PROMULGED > PROMULGE
PROMULGES > PROMULGE
PROMUSCES > PROMUSCIS
PROMUSCIS *n* proboscis of certain insects
PRONAOI > PRONAOS
PRONAOS *n* inner area of the portico of a classical temple
PRONATE *vb* turn (a limb, hand, or foot) so that the palm or sole is directed downwards
PRONATED > PRONATE
PRONATES > PRONATE
PRONATING > PRONATE
PRONATION > PRONATE
PRONATOR *n* any muscle whose contractions produce or affect pronation
PRONATORS > PRONATOR
PRONE *n* sermon
PRONELY > PRONE
PRONENESS > PRONE
PRONEPHRA *n* parts of the kidneys of lower vertebrates
PRONER > PRONE

PRONES > PRONE

PRONEST > PRONE

PRONEUR n flatterer

PRONEURS > PRONEUR

PRONG n one spike of a fork or similar instrument ▷ vb prick or spear with or as if with a prong

PRONGBUCK n horned N American ruminant

PRONGED > PRONG

PRONGHORN n ruminant mammal inhabiting rocky deserts of North America and having small branched horns

PRONGING > PRONG

PRONGS > PRONG

PRONK vb jump straight up

PRONKED > PRONK

PRONKING > PRONK

PRONKS > PRONK

PRONOTA > PRONOTUM

PRONOTAL > PRONOTUM

PRONOTUM n notum of the prothorax of an insect

PRONOUN n word, such as she or it, used to replace a noun

PRONOUNCE vb form the sounds of (words or letters), esp clearly or in a particular way

PRONOUNS > PRONOUN

PRONTO adv at once

PRONUCLEI n nuclei of mature ova or spermatozoa before fertilization

PRONUNCIO n papal ambassador

PROO interj (to a horse) stop!

PROOEMION n preface

PROOEMIUM n preface

PROOF n evidence that shows that something is true or has happened ▷ adj able to withstand ▷ vb take a proof from (type matter)

PROOFED > PROOF

PROOFER n reader of proofs

PROOFERS > PROOFER

PROOFING > PROOF

PROOFINGS > PROOF

PROOFLESS > PROOF

PROOFREAD vb read and correct (printer's proofs)

PROOFROOM n room for proofreading

PROOFS > PROOF

PROOTIC n bone in front of ear

PROOTICS > PROOTIC

PROP vb support (something) so that it stays upright or in place ▷ n pole, beam, etc used as a support

PROPAGATE vb spread (information and ideas)

PROPAGE vb propagate

PROPAGED > PROPAGE

PROPAGES > PROPAGE

PROPAGING > PROPAGE

PROPAGULA > PROPAGULE

PROPAGULE n plant part,

such as a bud, that becomes detached from the rest of the plant and grows into a new plant

PROPALE vb publish (something)

PROPALED > PROPALE

PROPALES > PROPALE

PROPALING > PROPALE

PROPANE n flammable gas found in petroleum and used as a fuel

PROPANES > PROPANE

PROPANOIC as in propanoic acid colourless liquid carboxylic acid

PROPANOL n colourless alcohol

PROPANOLS > PROPANOL

PROPANONE n systematic name of acetone

PROPEL vb cause to move forward

PROPELLED > PROPEL

PROPELLER n revolving shaft with blades for driving a ship or aircraft

PROPELLOR same as > PROPELLER

PROPELS > PROPEL

PROPEND vb be inclined or disposed

PROPENDED > PROPEND

PROPENDS > PROPEND

PROPENE n colourless gaseous alkene obtained by cracking petroleum

PROPENES > PROPENE

PROPENOIC as in propenoic acid systematic name of acrylic acid

PROPENOL n liquid used to make allylic alcohol

PROPENOLS > PROPENOL

PROPENSE adj inclining forward

PROPENYL n three-carbon radical

PROPER adj real or genuine ▷ n service or psalm regarded as appropriate to a specific day, season, etc

PROPERDIN n protein present in blood serum that, acting with complement, is involved in the destruction of alien cells, such as bacteria

PROPERER > PROPER

PROPEREST > PROPER

PROPERLY > PROPER

PROPERS > PROPER

PROPERTY same as > PROPRIUM

PROPHAGE n virus that exists in a bacterial cell and undergoes division with its host without destroying it

PROPHAGES > PROPHAGE

PROPHASE n first stage of mitosis, during which the nuclear membrane disappears and the nuclear material resolves itself into chromosomes

PROPHASES > PROPHASE

PROPHASIC > PROPHASE

PROPHECY n prediction

PROPHESY vb foretell

PROPHET n person supposedly chosen by God to spread His word

PROPHETIC adj foretelling what will happen

PROPHETS > PROPHET

PROPHYLL n leaf-shaped plant structure

PROPHYLLS > PROPHYLL

PROPINE vb to drink a toast to

PROPINED > PROPINE

PROPINES > PROPINE

PROPINING > PROPINE

PROPIONIC as in propionic acid former name for propanoic acid

PROPJET another name for > TURBOPROP

PROPJETS > PROPJET

PROPMAN n member of the stage crew in charge of the stage props

PROPMEN > PROPMAN

PROPODEON n part of an insect's thorax

PROPODEUM variant of > PROPODEON

PROPOLIS n greenish-brown resinous aromatic substance collected by bees from the buds of trees for use in the construction of hives

PROPONE vb propose or put forward, esp before a court

PROPONED > PROPONE

PROPONENT n person who argues in favour of something

PROPONES > PROPONE

PROPONING > PROPONE

PROPOSAL n act of proposing

PROPOSALS > PROPOSAL

PROPOSE vb put forward for consideration

PROPOSED > PROPOSE

PROPOSER > PROPOSE

PROPOSERS > PROPOSE

PROPOSES > PROPOSE

PROPOSING > PROPOSE

PROPOSITA n woman from whom a line of descent is traced

PROPOSITI n people from whom lines of descent are traced

PROPOUND vb put forward for consideration

PROPOUNDS > PROPOUND

PROPPANT n material used in the oil extraction process

PROPPANTS > PROPPANT

PROPPED > PROP

PROPPING > PROP

PROPRETOR n (in ancient Rome) citizen, esp an ex-praetor, granted a praetor's imperium, to be exercised outside Rome

PROPRIA > PROPRIUM

PROPRIETY n quality of being appropriate or fitting

PROPRIUM n attribute

that is not essential to a species but is common and peculiar to it

PROPS > PROP

PROPTOSES > PROPTOSIS

PROPTOSIS n forward displacement of an organ or part, such as the eyeball

PROPULSOR n propeller

PROPYL n of, consisting of, or containing the monovalent group of atoms C_3H_7-

PROPYLA > PROPYLON

PROPYLAEA n porticos, esp those that form the entrances to temples

PROPYLENE n gas found in petroleum and used to produce many organic compounds

PROPYLIC > PROPYL

PROPYLITE n altered andesite or similar rock containing calcite, chlorite, etc, produced by the action of hot water

PROPYLON n portico, esp one that forms the entrance to a temple

PROPYLONS > PROPYLON

PROPYLS > PROPYL

PRORATE vb divide, assess, or distribute (something) proportionately

PRORATED > PRORATE

PRORATES > PRORATE

PRORATING > PRORATE

PRORATION > PRORATE

PRORE n forward part of ship

PRORECTOR n official in German academia

PROREFORM adj in favour of or supporting reform, esp within politics

PRORES > PRORE

PROROGATE vb discontinue legislative meetings

PROROGUE vb suspend (parliament) without dissolving it

PROROGUED > PROROGUE

PROROGUES > PROROGUE

PROS > PRO

PROSAIC adj lacking imagination, dull

PROSAICAL same as > PROSAIC

PROSAISM n prosaic quality or style

PROSAISMS > PROSAISM

PROSAIST > PROSAISM

PROSAISTS > PROSAISM

PROSATEUR n writer of prose

PROSCENIA n arches or openings separating stages from auditoria together with the areas immediately in front of the arches

PROSCRIBE vb prohibit, outlaw

PROSCRIPT n proscription or prohibition

PROSE n ordinary speech

or writing in contrast to poetry ▷ *vb* speak or write in a tedious style

PROSECT *vb* dissect a cadaver for a public demonstration

PROSECTED > PROSECT

PROSECTOR *n* person who prepares or dissects anatomical subjects for demonstration

PROSECTS > PROSECT

PROSECUTE *vb* bring a criminal charge against

PROSED > PROSE

PROSELIKE > PROSE

PROSELYTE *n* recent convert

PROSEMAN *n* writer of prose

PROSEMEN > PROSEMAN

PROSER *n* writer of prose

PROSERS > PROSER

PROSES > PROSE

PROSEUCHA *n* place of prayer

PROSEUCHE *n* prayer

PROSIER > PROSY

PROSIEST > PROSY

PROSIFIED > PROSIFY

PROSIFIES > PROSIFY

PROSIFY *vb* write prose

PROSILY > PROSY

PROSIMIAN *n* any primate of the primitive suborder *Prosimii*, including lemurs, lorises, and tarsiers ▷ *adj* of, relating to, or belonging to the *Prosimii*

PROSINESS > PROSY

PROSING > PROSE

PROSINGS > PROSE

PROSIT *interj* good health! cheers!

PROSO *n* millet

PROSODIAL *adj* of prosody

PROSODIAN *n* writer of prose

PROSODIC > PROSODY

PROSODIES > PROSODY

PROSODIST > PROSODY

PROSODY *n* study of poetic metre and techniques

PROSOMA *n* head and thorax of an arachnid

PROSOMAL > PROSOMA

PROSOMAS > PROSOMA

PROSOMATA > PROSOMA

PROSOPON *n* (in Christianity) manifestation of any of the persons of the Trinity

PROSOPONS > PROSOPON

PROSOS > PROSO

PROSPECT *n* something anticipated ▷ *vb* explore, esp for gold

PROSPECTS > PROSPECT

PROSPER *vb* be successful

PROSPERED > PROSPER

PROSPERS > PROSPER

PROSS *n* prostitute

PROSSES > PROSS

PROSSIE *n* prostitute

PROSSIES > PROSSIE

PROST *same as* > PROSIT

PROSTATE *n* gland in male mammals that surrounds the neck of the bladder

▷ *adj* of or relating to the prostate gland

PROSTATES > PROSTATE

PROSTATIC *same as* > PROSTATE

PROSTERNA *n* sternums or thoraces of insects

PROSTIE *n* prostitute

PROSTIES > PROSTIE

PROSTOMIA *n* lobes at the head ends of earthworms and other annelids

PROSTRATE *adj* lying face downwards ▷ *vb* lie face downwards

PROSTYLE *adj* (of a building) having a row of columns in front, esp as in the portico of a Greek temple ▷ *n* prostyle building, portico, etc

PROSTYLES > PROSTYLE

PROSUMER *n* amateur user of electronic equipment suitable for professionals

PROSUMERS > PROSUMER

PROSY *adj* dull and long-winded

PROTAMIN *same as* > PROTAMINE

PROTAMINE *n* any of a group of basic simple proteins that occur, in association with nucleic acids, in the sperm of some fish

PROTAMINS > PROTAMIN

PROTANDRY *n* condition (in hermaphrodite plants) of maturing the anthers before the stigma

PROTANOPE *n* person with type of colour blindness

PROTASES > PROTASIS

PROTASIS *n* antecedent of a conditional statement

PROTATIC > PROTASIS

PROTEA *n* African shrub with showy flowers

PROTEAN *adj* constantly changing ▷ *n* creature that can change shape

PROTEANS > PROTEAN

PROTEAS > PROTEA

PROTEASE *n* any enzyme involved in proteolysis

PROTEASES > PROTEASE

PROTECT *vb* defend from trouble, harm, or loss

PROTECTED > PROTECT

PROTECTER *same as* > PROTECTOR

PROTECTOR *n* person or thing that protects

PROTECTS > PROTECT

PROTEGE *n* person who is protected and helped by another

PROTEGEE *n* woman or girl who is protected and helped by another

PROTEGEES > PROTEGEE

PROTEGES > PROTEGE

PROTEI > PROTEUS

PROTEID *n* protein

PROTEIDE *variant of* > PROTEID

PROTEIDES > PROTEIDE

PROTEIDS > PROTEID

PROTEIN *n* any of a group of complex organic compounds that are essential for life

PROTEINIC > PROTEIN

PROTEINS > PROTEIN

PROTEND *vb* hold out or stretch

PROTENDED > PROTEND

PROTENDS > PROTEND

PROTENSE *n* extension

PROTENSES > PROTENSE

PROTEOME *n* full complement of proteins that occur within a cell, tissue, or organism

PROTEOMES > PROTEOME

PROTEOMIC > PROTEOME

PROTEOSE *n* compounds formed during proteolysis that is less complex than metaproteins but more so than peptones

PROTEOSES > PROTEOSE

PROTEST *n* declaration or demonstration of objection ▷ *vb* object, disagree

PROTESTED > PROTEST

PROTESTER > PROTEST

PROTESTOR > PROTEST

PROTESTS > PROTEST

PROTEUS *n* aerobic bacterium

PROTEUSES > PROTEUS

PROTHALLI *n* small flat free-living gametophtyes in ferns, club mosses etc

PROTHESES > PROTHESIS

PROTHESIS *n* process in the development of a language by which a phoneme or syllable is prefixed to a word to facilitate pronunciation

PROTHETIC > PROTHESIS

PROTHORAX *n* first segment of the thorax of an insect, which bears the first pair of walking legs

PROTHYL *variant of* > PROTYLE

PROTHYLS > PROTHYL

PROTIST *n* (in some classification systems) any organism belonging to the kingdom *Protista*

PROTISTAN > PROTIST

PROTISTIC > PROTIST

PROTISTS > PROTIST

PROTIUM *n* most common isotope of hydrogen

PROTIUMS > PROTIUM

PROTOAVIS *n* bird-like fossil

PROTOCOL *n* rules of behaviour for formal occasions

PROTOCOLS > PROTOCOL

PROTODERM *n* outer primary meristem of a plant

PROTOGINE *n* type of granite

PROTOGYNY *n* (in hermaphrodite plants and animals) condition of producing female gametes

before male ones

PROTON *n* positively charged particle in the nucleus of an atom

PROTONATE *vb* provide atom with proton

PROTONEMA *n* branched threadlike structure that grows from a moss spore and eventually develops into the moss plant

PROTONIC *adj* (of a solvent, such as water) able to donate hydrogen ions to solute molecules

PROTONS > PROTON

PROTOPOD *n* part of crustacean's leg

PROTOPODS > PROTOPOD

PROTORE *n* primary mineral deposit

PROTORES > PROTORE

PROTOSTAR *n* cloud of interstellar gas and dust that gradually collapses, forming a hot dense core, and evolves into a star once nuclear fusion can occur in the core

PROTOTYPE *n* original or model to be copied or developed

PROTOXID *variant of* > PROTOXIDE

PROTOXIDE *n* oxide of an element that contains the smallest amount of oxygen of any of its oxides

PROTOXIDS > PROTOXID

PROTOZOA > PROTOZOAN

PROTOZOAL > PROTOZOAN

PROTOZOAN *n* microscopic one-celled creature ▷ *adj* of or relating to protozoans

PROTOZOIC > PROTOZOAN

PROTOZOON *same as* > PROTOZOAN

PROTRACT *vb* lengthen or extend (a situation etc)

PROTRACTS > PROTRACT

PROTRADE *adj* in favour of trade

PROTRUDE *vb* stick out, project

PROTRUDED > PROTRUDE

PROTRUDES > PROTRUDE

PROTYL *same as* > PROTYLE

PROTYLE *n* hypothetical primitive substance from which the chemical elements were supposed to have been formed

PROTYLES > PROTYLE

PROTYLS > PROTYL

PROUD *adj* feeling pleasure and satisfaction

PROUDER > PROUD

PROUDEST > PROUD

PROUDFUL *adj* full of pride

PROUDISH *adj* rather proud

PROUDLY > PROUD

PROUDNESS > PROUD

PROUL *variant of* > PROWL

PROULED > PROWL

PROULER *Scots variant of* > PROWLER

PROULERS > PROULER

PROULING > PROUL
PROULS > PROUL
PROUNION adj in favour of or supporting the constitutional union between two or more countries
PROUSTITE n red mineral consisting of silver arsenic sulphide in hexagonal crystalline form
PROVABLE > PROVE
PROVABLY > PROVE
PROVAND n food
PROVANDS > PROVAND
PROVANT adj supplied with provisions
PROVE vb establish the validity of
PROVEABLE > PROVE
PROVEABLY > PROVEABLE
PROVED > PROVE
PROVEDOR variant of > PROVEDORE
PROVEDORE n purveyor
PROVEDORS > PROVEDOR
PROVEN > PROVE
PROVEND same as > PROVAND
PROVENDER n fodder
PROVENDS > PROVEND
PROVENLY > PROVE
PROVER > PROVE
PROVERB n short saying that expresses a truth or gives a warning ▷ vb utter or describe (something) in the form of a proverb
PROVERBED > PROVERB
PROVERBS > PROVERB
PROVERS > PROVE
PROVES > PROVE
PROVIANT variant of > PROVAND
PROVIANTS > PROVIANT
PROVIDE vb make available
PROVIDED > PROVIDE
PROVIDENT adj thrifty
PROVIDER > PROVIDE
PROVIDERS > PROVIDE
PROVIDES > PROVIDE
PROVIDING > PROVIDE
PROVIDOR variant of > PROVEDORE
PROVIDORS > PROVIDOR
PROVINCE n area governed as a unit of a country or empire
PROVINCES > PROVINCE
PROVINE vb plant branch of vine in ground for propagation
PROVINED > PROVINE
PROVINES > PROVINE
PROVING > PROVE
PROVINGS > PROVE
PROVINING > PROVINE
PROVIRAL > PROVIRUS
PROVIRUS n inactive form of a virus in a host cell
PROVISION n act of supplying something ▷ vb supply with food
PROVISO n condition, stipulation
PROVISOES > PROVISO
PROVISOR n person who receives provision

PROVISORS > PROVISOR
PROVISORY adj containing a proviso
PROVISOS > PROVISO
PROVOCANT n provocateur; one who deliberately behaves controversially to provoke argument or other strong reactions
PROVOKE vb deliberately anger
PROVOKED > PROVOKE
PROVOKER > PROVOKE
PROVOKERS > PROVOKE
PROVOKES > PROVOKE
PROVOKING > PROVOKE
PROVOLONE n mellow, pale yellow, soft, and sometimes smoked cheese, made of cow's milk: usually moulded in the shape of a pear
PROVOST n head of certain university colleges in Britain
PROVOSTRY n office of provost
PROVOSTS > PROVOST
PROW n bow of a vessel ▷ adj gallant
PROWAR adj in favour of or supporting war
PROWER > PROW
PROWESS n superior skill or ability
PROWESSED adj brave or skilful
PROWESSES > PROWESS
PROWEST > PROW
PROWL vb move stealthily around a place as if in search of prey or plunder ▷ n prowling
PROWLED > PROWL
PROWLER > PROWL
PROWLERS > PROWL
PROWLING > PROWL
PROWLINGS > PROWL
PROWLS > PROWL
PROWS > PROW
PROXEMIC > PROXEMICS
PROXEMICS n study of spatial interrelationships in humans or in populations of animals of the same species
PROXIES > PROXY
PROXIMAL same as > PROXIMATE
PROXIMATE adj next or nearest in space or time
PROXIMITY n nearness in space or time
PROXIMO adv in or during the next or coming month
PROXY n person authorized to act on behalf of someone else
PROYN obsolete spelling of > PRUNE
PROYNE obsolete spelling of > PRUNE
PROYNED > PROYN
PROYNES > PROYNE
PROYNING > PROYN
PROYNS > PROYN
PROZYMITE n Christian

using leavened bread for the Eucharist
PRUDE n person who is excessively modest, prim, or proper
PRUDENCE n caution in practical affairs
PRUDENCES > PRUDENCE
PRUDENT adj cautious, discreet, and sensible
PRUDENTLY > PRUDENT
PRUDERIES > PRUDE
PRUDERY > PRUDE
PRUDES > PRUDE
PRUDISH > PRUDE
PRUDISHLY > PRUDE
PRUH variant of > PROO
PRUINA n woolly white covering on some lichens
PRUINAS > PRUINA
PRUINE obsolete spelling of > PRUNE
PRUINES > PRUINE
PRUINOSE adj coated with a powdery or waxy bloom
PRUNABLE > PRUNE
PRUNE n dried plum ▷ vb cut off dead parts or excessive branches from (a tree or plant)
PRUNED > PRUNE
PRUNELLA n strong fabric, esp a twill-weave worsted, used for gowns and the uppers of some shoes
PRUNELLAS > PRUNELLA
PRUNELLE same as > PRUNELLA
PRUNELLES > PRUNELLE
PRUNELLO same as > PRUNELLA
PRUNELLOS > PRUNELLO
PRUNER > PRUNE
PRUNERS > PRUNE
PRUNES > PRUNE
PRUNING > PRUNE
PRUNINGS > PRUNE
PRUNT n glass ornamentation
PRUNTED > PRUNT
PRUNTS > PRUNT
PRUNUS n type of ornamental tree or shrub
PRUNUSES > PRUNUS
PRURIENCE > PRURIENT
PRURIENCY n sexual desire
PRURIENT adj excessively interested in sexual matters
PRURIGO n chronic inflammatory disease of the skin characterized by the formation of papules and intense itching
PRURIGOS > PRURIGO
PRURITIC > PRURITUS
PRURITUS n any intense sensation of itching
PRUSIK n sliding knot that locks under pressure and can be used to form a loop in which a climber can place his or her foot in order to stand or ascend a rope ▷ vb climb (up a standing rope) using prusiks
PRUSIKED > PRUSIK

PRUSIKING > PRUSIK
PRUSIKS > PRUSIK
PRUSSIATE n any cyanide, ferrocyanide, or ferricyanide
PRUSSIC as in prussic acid weakly acidic extremely poisonous aqueous solution of hydrogen cyanide
PRUTA same as > PRUTAH
PRUTAH n former Israeli coin
PRUTOT > PRUTAH
PRUTOTH > PRUTAH
PRY vb make an impertinent or uninvited inquiry into a private matter ▷ n act of prying
PRYER same as > PRIER
PRYERS > PRYER
PRYING > PRY
PRYINGLY > PRY
PRYINGS > PRY
PRYS old variant of > PRICE
PRYSE old variant of > PRICE
PRYSED > PRYSE
PRYSES > PRYSE
PRYSING > PRYSE
PRYTANEA > PRYTANEUM
PRYTANEUM n public hall of a city in ancient Greece
PRYTHEE same as > PRITHEE
PSALM n sacred song ▷ vb sing a psalm
PSALMBOOK n book of psalms
PSALMED > PSALM
PSALMIC > PSALM
PSALMING > PSALM
PSALMIST n writer of psalms
PSALMISTS > PSALMIST
PSALMODIC > PSALMODY
PSALMODY n singing of sacred music
PSALMS > PSALM
PSALTER n devotional or liturgical book containing a version of Psalms
PSALTERIA n omasums
PSALTERS > PSALTER
PSALTERY n ancient instrument played by plucking strings
PSALTRESS n woman who sings psalms
PSALTRIES > PSALTRY
PSALTRY same as > PSALTERY
PSAMMITE rare name for > SANDSTONE
PSAMMITES > PSAMMITE
PSAMMITIC > PSAMMITE
PSAMMON n community of microscopic life forms living between grains of sand on shores
PSAMMONS > PSAMMON
PSCHENT n ancient Egyptian crown
PSCHENTS > PSCHENT
PSELLISM n stammering
PSELLISMS > PSELLISM
PSEPHISM n proposition adopted by a majority vote
PSEPHISMS > PSEPHISM
PSEPHITE n any rock, such as a breccia, that

consists of large fragments embedded in a finer matrix

PSEPHITES > PSEPHITE

PSEPHITIC > PSEPHITE

PSEUD n pretentious person

PSEUDAXES > PSEUDAXIS

PSEUDAXIS another name for > SYMPODIUM

PSEUDERY n pretentious talk

PSEUDISH > PSEUD

PSEUDO n pretentious person

PSEUDONYM n fictitious name adopted esp by an author

PSEUDOPOD n temporary projection from the body of a single-celled animal

PSEUDOS > PSEUDO

PSEUDS > PSEUD

PSHAW n exclamation of disgust, impatience, disbelief, etc ▷ vb make this exclamation

PSHAWED > PSHAW

PSHAWING > PSHAW

PSHAWS > PSHAW

PSI n 23rd letter of the Greek alphabet

PSILOCIN n hallucinogenic substance

PSILOCINS > PSILOCIN

PSILOSES > PSILOSIS

PSILOSIS n disease of the small intestine

PSILOTIC > PSILOSIS

PSION n type of elementary particle

PSIONIC > PSIONICS

PSIONICS n study of the practical use of psychic powers

PSIONS > PSION

PSIS > PSI

PSOAE > PSOAS

PSOAI > PSOAS

PSOAS n either of two muscles of the loins that aid in flexing and rotating the thigh

PSOASES > PSOAS

PSOATIC > PSOAS

PSOCID n tiny wingless insect

PSOCIDS > PSOCID

PSORA n itching skin complaint

PSORALEA n any plant of the tropical and subtropical leguminous genus Psoralea, having curly leaves, white or purple flowers, and short one-seeded pods

PSORALEAS > PSORALEA

PSORALEN n treatment for some skin diseases

PSORALENS > PSORALEN

PSORAS > PSORA

PSORIASES > PSORIASIS

PSORIASIS n skin disease with reddish spots and patches covered with silvery scales

PSORIATIC > PSORIASIS

PSORIC > PSORA

PSST interj sound made

to attract someone's attention, esp without others noticing

PST interj sound made to attract someone's attention

PSYCH vb psychoanalyse

PSYCHE same as > PSYCH

PSYCHED > PSYCH

PSYCHES > PSYCH

PSYCHIC adj having mental powers which cannot be explained by natural laws ▷ n person with psychic powers

PSYCHICAL > PSYCHIC

PSYCHICS > PSYCHIC

PSYCHING > PSYCH

PSYCHISM n belief in a universal soul

PSYCHISMS > PSYCHISM

PSYCHIST > PSYCHISM

PSYCHISTS > PSYCHISM

PSYCHO n psychopath

PSYCHOGAS n gas with a mind-altering effect

PSYCHOID n name for an animal's innate impetus to perform actions

PSYCHOIDS > PSYCHOID

PSYCHOS > PSYCHO

PSYCHOSES > PSYCHOSIS

PSYCHOSIS n severe mental disorder in which the sufferer's contact with reality becomes distorted

PSYCHOTIC adj of, relating to, or characterized by psychosis ▷ n person suffering from psychosis

PSYCHS > PSYCH

PSYLLA same as > PSYLLID

PSYLLAS > PSYLLA

PSYLLID n any homopterous insect of the family Psyllidae, which comprises the jumping plant lice

PSYLLIDS > PSYLLID

PSYLLIUM n grain, the husks of which are used medicinally as a laxative and to reduce blood cholesterol levels

PSYLLIUMS > PSYLLIUM

PSYOP n psychological operation

PSYOPS > PSYOP

PSYWAR n psychological warfare

PSYWARS > PSYWAR

PTARMIC n material that causes sneezing

PTARMICS > PTARMIC

PTARMIGAN n bird of the grouse family which turns white in winter

PTERIA > PTERION

PTERIDINE n yellow crystalline base

PTERIN n compound such as folic acid

PTERINS > PTERIN

PTERION n point on the side of the skull where a number of bones meet

PTEROPOD n small marine

gastropod mollusc in which the foot is expanded into two winglike lobes for swimming and the shell is absent or thin-walled

PTEROPODS > PTEROPOD

PTEROSAUR n extinct flying reptile

PTERYGIA > PTERYGIUM

PTERYGIAL adj of or relating to a fin or wing

PTERYGIUM n abnormal tissue over corner of eye

PTERYGOID n either of two long bony plates extending downwards from each side of the sphenoid bone within the skull

PTERYLA n any of the tracts of skin that bear contour feathers, arranged in lines along the body of a bird

PTERYLAE > PTERYLA

PTILOSES > PTILOSIS

PTILOSIS n falling out of eye lashes

PTISAN n grape juice drained off without pressure

PTISANS > PTISAN

PTOMAIN same as > PTOMAINE

PTOMAINE n any of a group of poisonous alkaloids found in decaying matter

PTOMAINES > PTOMAINE

PTOMAINIC > PTOMAINE

PTOMAINS > PTOMAIN

PTOOEY interj imitation of the sound of spitting

PTOSES > PTOSIS

PTOSIS n prolapse or drooping of a part, esp the eyelid

PTOTIC > PTOSIS

PTUI same as > PTOOEY

PTYALIN n amylase secreted in the saliva of man and other animals

PTYALINS > PTYALIN

PTYALISE same as > PTYALIZE

PTYALISED > PTYALISE

PTYALISES > PTYALISE

PTYALISM n excessive secretion of saliva

PTYALISMS > PTYALISM

PTYALIZE vb expel saliva from the mouth

PTYALIZED > PTYALIZE

PTYALIZES > PTYALIZE

PTYXES > PTYXIS

PTYXIS n folding of a leaf in a bud

PTYXISES > PTYXIS

PUB n building with a bar licensed to sell alcoholic drinks ▷ vb visit a pub or pubs

PUBBED > PUB

PUBBING > PUB

PUBE n pubic hair

PUBERAL adj relating to puberty

PUBERTAL > PUBERTY

PUBERTIES > PUBERTY

PUBERTY n beginning of

sexual maturity

PUBES > PUBE

PUBESCENT adj reaching or having reached puberty

PUBIC adj of the lower abdomen

PUBIS n one of the three sections of the hipbone that forms part of the pelvis

PUBISES > PUBIS

PUBLIC adj of or concerning the people as a whole ▷ n community, people in general

PUBLICAN n person who owns or runs a pub

PUBLICANS > PUBLICAN

PUBLICISE same as > PUBLICIZE

PUBLICIST n person, esp a press agent or journalist, who publicizes something

PUBLICITY n process or information used to arouse public attention

PUBLICIZE vb bring to public attention

PUBLICLY adv in a public manner

PUBLICS > PUBLIC

PUBLISH vb produce and issue (printed matter) for sale

PUBLISHED > PUBLISH

PUBLISHER n company or person that publishes books, periodicals, music, etc

PUBLISHES > PUBLISH

PUBS > PUB

PUCAN n traditional Connemara open sailing boat

PUCANS > PUCAN

PUCCOON n any of several North American boraginaceous plants of the genus Lithospermum, esp L. canescens, that yield a red dye

PUCCOONS > PUCCOON

PUCE adj purplish-brown ▷ n colour varying from deep red to dark purplish-brown

PUCELAGE n virginity

PUCELAGES > PUCELAGE

PUCELLE n maid or virgin

PUCELLES > PUCELLE

PUCER > PUCE

PUCES > PUCE

PUCEST > PUCE

PUCK n mischievous or evil spirit ▷ vb strike (the ball) in hurling

PUCKA same as > PUKKA

PUCKED > PUCK

PUCKER vb gather into wrinkles ▷ n wrinkle or crease

PUCKERED > PUCKER

PUCKERER > PUCKER

PUCKERERS > PUCKER

PUCKERIER > PUCKERY

PUCKERING > PUCKER

PUCKEROOD adj ruined

p

PUCKERS > PUCKER

PUCKERY adj (of wine) high in tannins

PUCKFIST n puffball

PUCKFISTS > PUCKFIST

PUCKING > PUCK

PUCKISH > PUCK

PUCKISHLY > PUCK

PUCKLE n early type of machine gun

PUCKLES > PUCKLE

PUCKS > PUCK

PUD short for > PUDDING

PUDDEN dialect spelling of > PUDDING

PUDDENING n rope fender on boat

PUDDENS > PUDDEN

PUDDER vb make bother or fuss

PUDDERED > PUDDER

PUDDERING > PUDDER

PUDDERS > PUDDER

PUDDIES > PUDDY

PUDDING n dessert, esp a cooked one served hot

PUDDINGS > PUDDING

PUDDINGY > PUDDING

PUDDLE n small pool of water, esp of rain ▷ vb make (clay etc) into puddle

PUDDLED > PUDDLE

PUDDLER > PUDDLE

PUDDLERS > PUDDLE

PUDDLES > PUDDLE

PUDDLIER > PUDDLE

PUDDLIEST > PUDDLE

PUDDLING n process for converting pig iron into wrought iron by heating it with ferric oxide in a furnace to oxidize the carbon

PUDDLINGS > PUDDLING

PUDDLY > PUDDLE

PUDDOCK same as > PADDOCK

PUDDOCKS > PUDDOCK

PUDDY n paw

PUDENCIES > PUDENCY

PUDENCY n modesty, shame, or prudishness

PUDENDA > PUDENDUM

PUDENDAL > PUDENDUM

PUDENDOUS adj shameful

PUDENDUM n human external genital organs collectively, esp of a female

PUDENT adj lacking in ostentation; humble

PUDGE same as > PODGE

PUDGES > PUDGE

PUDGIER > PUDGY

PUDGIEST > PUDGY

PUDGILY > PUDGY

PUDGINESS > PUDGY

PUDGY adj podgy

PUDIBUND adj prudish

PUDIC > PUDENDUM

PUDICITY n modesty

PUDOR n sense of shame

PUDORS > PUDOR

PUDS > PUD

PUDSEY variant of > PUDSY

PUDSIER > PUDSY

PUDSIEST > PUDSY

PUDSY adj plump

PUDU n diminutive Andean antelope with short straight horns and reddish-brown spotted coat

PUDUS > PUDU

PUEBLO n communal village, built by certain Indians of the southwestern US and parts of Latin America, consisting of one or more flat-roofed stone or adobe houses

PUEBLOS > PUEBLO

PUER vb steep hides in an alkaline substance from the dung of dogs

PUERED > PUER

PUERILE adj silly and childish

PUERILELY > PUERILE

PUERILISM n immature or childish behaviour by an adult

PUERILITY > PUERILE

PUERING > PUER

PUERPERA n woman who has recently given birth

PUERPERAE > PUERPERA

PUERPERAL adj concerning the period following childbirth

PUERPERIA n periods of around six weeks following childbirths when uteruses return to their normal size and shape

PUERS > PUER

PUFF n (sound of) short blast of breath, wind, etc ▷ vb blow or breathe in short quick draughts

PUFFBALL n ball-shaped fungus

PUFFBALLS > PUFFBALL

PUFFBIRD n brownish tropical American bird with a large head

PUFFBIRDS > PUFFBIRD

PUFFED > PUFF

PUFFER n person or thing that puffs

PUFFERIES > PUFFERY

PUFFERS > PUFFER

PUFFERY n exaggerated praise, esp in publicity or advertising

PUFFIER > PUFFY

PUFFIEST > PUFFY

PUFFILY > PUFFY

PUFFIN n black-and-white sea bird with a brightly-coloured beak

PUFFINESS > PUFFY

PUFFING > PUFF

PUFFINGLY > PUFF

PUFFINGS > PUFF

PUFFINS > PUFFIN

PUFFS > PUFF

PUFFY adj short of breath

PUFTALOON n Australian fried scone

PUG n small snub-nosed dog ▷ vb mix or knead (clay) with water to form a malleable mass or paste

PUGAREE same as > PUGGREE

PUGAREES > PUGAREE

PUGGAREE same as > PUGGREE

PUGGAREES > PUGGAREE

PUGGED > PUG

PUGGERIES > PUGGERY

PUGGERY same as > PUGGREE

PUGGIE n Scottish word for fruit machine

PUGGIER > PUGGY

PUGGIES > PUGGIE

PUGGIEST > PUGGY

PUGGINESS > PUGGY

PUGGING > PUG

PUGGINGS > PUG

PUGGISH > PUG

PUGGLE vb stir up by poking

PUGGLED > PUGGLE

PUGGLES > PUGGLE

PUGGLING > PUGGLE

PUGGREE n scarf, usually pleated, around the crown of some hats, esp sun helmets

PUGGREES > PUGGREE

PUGGRIES > PUGGRY

PUGGRY same as > PUGGREE

PUGGY adj sticky, claylike ▷ n term of endearment

PUGH interj exclamation of disgust

PUGIL n pinch or small handful

PUGILISM n art, practice, or profession of fighting with the fists

PUGILISMS > PUGILISM

PUGILIST > PUGILISM

PUGILISTS > PUGILISM

PUGILS > PUGIL

PUGMARK n trail of an animal

PUGMARKS > PUGMARK

PUGNACITY n readiness to fight

PUGREE same as > PUGGREE

PUGREES > PUGREE

PUGS > PUG

PUH interj exclamation expressing contempt or disgust

PUHA n sow thistle

PUHAS > PUHA

PUIR Scottish word for > POOR

PUIRER > PUIR

PUIREST > PUIR

PUIRTITH n poverty

PUIRTITHS > PUIRTITH

PUISNE adj (esp of a subordinate judge) of lower rank ▷ n judge of lower rank

PUISNES > PUISNE

PUISNY adj younger or inferior

PUISSANCE n showjumping competition that tests a horse's ability to jump large obstacles

PUISSANT adj powerful

PUISSAUNT same as > PUISSANT

PUJA n ritual in honour of the gods, performed either at home or in the mandir (temple)

PUJAH same as > PUJA

PUJAHS > PUJAH

PUJAS > PUJA

PUKA in New Zealand English, same as > BROADLEAF

PUKATEA n aromatic New Zealand tree, valued for its high-quality timber

PUKATEAS > PUKATEA

PUKE vb vomit ▷ n act of vomiting

PUKED > PUKE

PUKEKO n brightly coloured New Zealand wading bird

PUKEKOS > PUKEKO

PUKER n person who vomits

PUKERS > PUKER

PUKES > PUKE

PUKING > PUKE

PUKKA adj properly done, constructed, etc

PUKU n belly or stomach

PUKUS > PUKU

PUL n Afghan monetary unit worth one hundredth of an afghani

PULA n standard monetary unit of Botswana, divided into 100 thebe

PULAO same as > PILAU

PULAOS > PULAO

PULAS > PULA

PULDRON same as > PAULDRON

PULDRONS > PULDRON

PULE vb whine or whimper

PULED > PULE

PULER > PULE

PULERS > PULE

PULES > PULE

PULI > PUL

PULICENE adj flea-ridden

PULICIDE n flea-killing substance

PULICIDES > PULICIDE

PULIER > PULY

PULIEST > PULY

PULIK > PUL

PULING > PULE

PULINGLY > PULE

PULINGS > PULE

PULIS > PUL

PULK same as > PULKA

PULKA n reindeer-drawn sleigh

PULKAS > PULKA

PULKHA same as > PULKA

PULKHAS > PULKHA

PULKS > PULK

PULL vb exert force on (an object) to move it towards the source of the force ▷ n act of pulling

PULLBACK n act of pulling back

PULLBACKS > PULLBACK

PULLED > PULL

PULLER > PULL

PULLERS > PULL

PULLET n young hen

PULLETS > PULLET

PULLEY n wheel with a grooved rim in which a belt, chain, or piece of rope runs in order to lift weights by a downward pull

PULLEYS > PULLEY

PULLI > PULLUS

PULLING > PULL

PULLMAN *n* luxurious railway coach, esp a sleeping car
PULLMANS > PULLMAN
PULLORUM as in *pullorum disease* acute serious bacterial disease of very young birds
PULLOUT *n* removable section of a magazine, etc
PULLOUTS > PULLOUT
PULLOVER *n* sweater that is pulled on over the head
PULLOVERS > PULLOVER
PULLS > PULL
PULLULATE *vb* (of animals, etc) breed rapidly or abundantly
PULLUP *n* exercise in which the body is raised up by the arms pulling on a horizontal bar fixed above the head
PULLUPS > PULLUP
PULLUS *n* technical term for a chick or young bird
PULMO *n* lung
PULMONARY *adj* of the lungs
PULMONATE *adj* having lungs or lung-like organs ▷ *n* any pulmonate mollusc
PULMONES > PULMO
PULMONIC *adj* of or relating to the lungs ▷ *n* person with lung disease
PULMONICS > PULMONIC
PULMOTOR *n* apparatus for pumping oxygen into the lungs during artificial respiration
PULMOTORS > PULMOTOR
PULP *n* soft wet substance made from crushed or beaten matter ▷ *vb* reduce to pulp
PULPAL > PULP
PULPALLY > PULP
PULPBOARD *n* board made from wood pulp
PULPED > PULP
PULPER > PULP
PULPERS > PULP
PULPIER > PULPY
PULPIEST > PULPY
PULPIFIED > PULPIFY
PULPIFIES > PULPIFY
PULPIFY *vb* reduce to pulp
PULPILY > PULPY
PULPINESS > PULPY
PULPING > PULP
PULPIT *n* raised platform for a preacher
PULPITAL > PULPIT
PULPITED > PULPIT
PULPITEER *n* deliverer of sermon
PULPITER *n* preacher
PULPITERS > PULPITER
PULPITRY *n* art of delivering sermons
PULPITS > PULPIT
PULPITUM *n* stone screen dividing nave and choir
PULPITUMS > PULPITUM
PULPLESS > PULP
PULPMILL *n* mill making raw material for paper

PULPMILLS > PULPMILL
PULPOUS *n* soft and yielding
PULPS > PULP
PULPSTONE *n* calcified mass in a tooth cavity
PULPWOOD *n* pine, spruce, or any other soft wood used to make paper
PULPWOODS > PULPWOOD
PULPY *adj* having a soft or soggy consistency
PULQUE *n* light alcoholic drink from Mexico made from the juice of various agave plants, esp the maguey
PULQUES > PULQUE
PULS > PUL
PULSANT *adj* vibrant
PULSAR *n* small dense star which emits regular bursts of radio waves
PULSARS > PULSAR
PULSATE *vb* throb, quiver
PULSATED > PULSATE
PULSATES > PULSATE
PULSATILE *adj* beating rhythmically
PULSATING > PULSATE
PULSATION *n* act of pulsating
PULSATIVE > PULSATE
PULSATOR *n* device that stimulates rhythmic motion of a body
PULSATORS > PULSATOR
PULSATORY *adj* of or relating to pulsation
PULSE *n* regular beating of blood through the arteries at each heartbeat ▷ *vb* beat, throb, or vibrate
PULSED > PULSE
PULSEJET *n* type of ramjet engine
PULSEJETS > PULSEJET
PULSELESS > PULSE
PULSER *n* thing that pulses
PULSERS > PULSER
PULSES > PULSE
PULSIDGE *archaic word for* > PULSE
PULSIDGES > PULSIDGE
PULSIFIC *adj* causing the pulse to increase
PULSING > PULSE
PULSION *n* act of driving forward
PULSIONS > PULSION
PULSOJET *same as* > PULSEJET
PULSOJETS > PULSOJET
PULTAN *n* native Indian regiment
PULTANS > PULTAN
PULTON *same as* > PULTAN
PULTONS > PULTON
PULTOON *same as* > PULTAN
PULTOONS > PULTOON
PULTUN *same as* > PULTAN
PULTUNS > PULTUN
PULTURE *n* food and drink claimed by foresters as their right from anyone within the limits of a given forest
PULTURES > PULTURE

PULU *n* substance from Hawaiian ferns, used for stuffing cushions, etc
PULUS > PULU
PULVER *vb* make into powder
PULVERED > PULVER
PULVERINE *n* ashes of the barilla plant
PULVERING > PULVER
PULVERISE *same as* > PULVERIZE
PULVERIZE *vb* reduce to fine pieces
PULVEROUS *adj* consisting of tiny particles
PULVERS > PULVER
PULVIL *vb* apply perfumed powder
PULVILIO *n* perfumed powder
PULVILIOS > PULVILIO
PULVILLAR *adj* like cushion
PULVILLE *same as* > PULVIL
PULVILLED > PULVIL
PULVILLES > PULVILLE
PULVILLI > PULVILLUS
PULVILLIO *same as* > PULVILIO
PULVILLUS *n* small pad between the claws at the end of an insect's leg
PULVILS > PULVIL
PULVINAR *n* part of the thalamus
PULVINARS > PULVINAR
PULVINATE *adj* (of a frieze) curved convexly
PULVINI > PULVINUS
PULVINULE *n* part of a leaf
PULVINUS *n* swelling at the base of a leafstalk
PULWAR *n* light Indian river boat
PULWARS > PULWAR
PULY *adj* whiny
PUMA *n* large American wild cat with a greyish-brown coat
PUMAS > PUMA
PUMELO *same as* > POMELO
PUMELOS > PUMELO
PUMICATE *vb* pound fruit with pumice to make juice
PUMICATED > PUMICATE
PUMICATES > PUMICATE
PUMICE *n* light porous stone used for scouring ▷ *vb* rub or polish with pumice
PUMICED > PUMICE
PUMICEOUS > PUMICE
PUMICER > PUMICE
PUMICERS > PUMICE
PUMICES > PUMICE
PUMICING > PUMICE
PUMICITE *n* fine-grained variety of pumice
PUMICITES > PUMICITE
PUMIE *n* small stone
PUMIES > PUMIE
PUMMEL *vb* strike repeatedly with or as if with the fists
PUMMELED > PUMMEL
PUMMELING > PUMMEL
PUMMELLED > PUMMEL
PUMMELO *same as* > POMELO
PUMMELOS > PUMMELO

PUMMELS > PUMMEL
PUMP *n* machine used to force a liquid or gas to move in a particular direction ▷ *vb* raise or drive with a pump
PUMPED > PUMP
PUMPER > PUMP
PUMPERS > PUMP
PUMPHOOD *n* cover for the upper wheel of a chain pump
PUMPHOODS > PUMPHOOD
PUMPING > PUMP
PUMPION *archaic word for* > PUMPKIN
PUMPIONS > PUMPION
PUMPKIN *n* large round fruit with an orange rind, soft flesh, and many seeds
PUMPKING *n* person involved in a web-based project who has temporary but exclusive authority to make changes to the master source code
PUMPKINGS > PUMPKING
PUMPKINS > PUMPKIN
PUMPLESS > PUMP
PUMPLIKE > PUMP
PUMPS > PUMP
PUMY *adj* large and round
PUN *n* use of words to exploit double meanings for humorous effect ▷ *vb* make puns
PUNA *n* high cold dry plateau, esp in the Andes
PUNALUA *n* marriage between the sisters of one family to the brothers of another
PUNALUAN > PUNALUA
PUNALUAS > PUNALUA
PUNAS > PUNA
PUNCE *n* kick ▷ *vb* kick
PUNCED > PUNCE
PUNCES > PUNCE
PUNCH *vb* strike at with a clenched fist ▷ *n* blow with a clenched fist
PUNCHBAG *n* stuffed or inflated bag suspended by a flexible rod, that is punched for exercise, esp boxing training
PUNCHBAGS > PUNCHBAG
PUNCHBALL *n* stuffed or inflated ball supported by a flexible rod, that is punched for exercise, esp boxing training
PUNCHBOWL *n* large bowl for serving punch
PUNCHED > PUNCH
PUNCHEON *n* large cask of variable capacity, usually between 70 and 120 gallons
PUNCHEONS > PUNCHEON
PUNCHER > PUNCH
PUNCHERS > PUNCH
PUNCHES > PUNCH
PUNCHIER > PUNCHY
PUNCHIEST > PUNCHY
PUNCHILY > PUNCHY
PUNCHING > PUNCH
PUNCHLESS > PUNCH

PUNCHY adj forceful
PUNCING > PUNCE
PUNCTA > PUNCTUM
PUNCTATE adj having or marked with minute spots, holes, or depressions
PUNCTATED same as > PUNCTATE
PUNCTATOR n marker of points
PUNCTILIO n strict attention to minute points of etiquette
PUNCTO n tip of a fencing sword
PUNCTOS > PUNCTO
PUNCTUAL adj arriving or taking place at the correct time
PUNCTUATE vb put punctuation marks in
PUNCTULE n very small opening
PUNCTULES > PUNCTULE
PUNCTUM n tip or small point
PUNCTURE n small hole made by a sharp object, esp in a tyre ▷vb pierce a hole in
PUNCTURED > PUNCTURE
PUNCTURER > PUNCTURE
PUNCTURES > PUNCTURE
PUNDIT n expert who speaks publicly on a subject
PUNDITIC adj of or relating to pundits
PUNDITRY n expressing of expert opinions
PUNDITS > PUNDIT
PUNDONOR n point of honour
PUNG n horse-drawn sleigh with a boxlike body on runners
PUNGA variant spelling of > PONGA
PUNGAS > PUNGA
PUNGENCE n pungency
PUNGENCES > PUNGENCE
PUNGENCY > PUNGENT
PUNGENT adj having a strong sharp bitter flavour
PUNGENTLY > PUNGENT
PUNGLE vb make payment
PUNGLED > PUNGLE
PUNGLES > PUNGLE
PUNGLING > PUNGLE
PUNGS > PUNG
PUNIER > PUNY
PUNIEST > PUNY
PUNILY > PUNY
PUNINESS > PUNY
PUNISH vb cause (someone) to suffer or undergo a penalty for some wrongdoing
PUNISHED > PUNISH
PUNISHER > PUNISH
PUNISHERS > PUNISH
PUNISHES > PUNISH
PUNISHING > PUNISH
PUNITION n punishment
PUNITIONS > PUNITION
PUNITIVE adj relating to punishment
PUNITORY same as > PUNITIVE
PUNJI n sharpened bamboo stick
PUNJIS > PUNJI
PUNK n anti-Establishment youth movement and style of rock music of the late 1970s ▷adj relating to the punk youth movement of the late 1970s
PUNKA n fan made of a palm leaf or leaves
PUNKAH same as > PUNKA
PUNKAHS > PUNKAH
PUNKAS > PUNKA
PUNKER > PUNK
PUNKERS > PUNK
PUNKEST > PUNK
PUNKEY n small winged insect
PUNKEYS > PUNKEY
PUNKIE same as > PUNKEY
PUNKIER > PUNKY
PUNKIES > PUNKIE
PUNKIEST > PUNKY
PUNKIN same as > PUMPKIN
PUNKINESS > PUNKY
PUNKINS > PUNKIN
PUNKISH > PUNK
PUNKS > PUNK
PUNKY adj of punk music
PUNNED > PUN
PUNNER > PUN
PUNNERS > PUN
PUNNET n small basket for fruit
PUNNETS > PUNNET
PUNNIER > PUNNY
PUNNIEST > PUNNY
PUNNING > PUN
PUNNINGLY > PUN
PUNNINGS > PUN
PUNNY adj of puns
PUNS > PUN
PUNSTER n person who is fond of making puns
PUNSTERS > PUNSTER
PUNT n open flat-bottomed boat propelled by a pole ▷vb travel in a punt
PUNTED > PUNT
PUNTEE same as > PUNTY
PUNTEES > PUNTEE
PUNTER n person who bets
PUNTERS > PUNTER
PUNTIES > PUNTY
PUNTING > PUNT
PUNTO n hit in fencing
PUNTOS > PUNTO
PUNTS > PUNT
PUNTSMAN n man in charge of a river punt
PUNTSMEN > PUNTSMAN
PUNTY n long iron rod used in the finishing process of glass-blowing
PUNY adj small and feeble
PUP n young of certain animals, such as dogs and seals ▷vb (of dogs, seals, etc) to give birth to pups
PUPA n insect at the stage of development between a larva and an adult
PUPAE > PUPA
PUPAL > PUPA
PUPARIA > PUPARIUM
PUPARIAL > PUPARIUM
PUPARIUM n hard barrel-shaped case enclosing the pupae of the housefly and other dipterous insects
PUPAS > PUPA
PUPATE vb (of an insect larva) to develop into a pupa
PUPATED > PUPATE
PUPATES > PUPATE
PUPATING > PUPATE
PUPATION > PUPATE
PUPATIONS > PUPATE
PUPFISH n type of small fish
PUPFISHES > PUPFISH
PUPIL n person who is taught by a teacher
PUPILAGE same as > PUPILLAGE
PUPILAGES > PUPILAGE
PUPILAR > PUPIL
PUPILARY same as > PUPILLARY
PUPILLAGE n condition of being a pupil or duration for which one is a pupil
PUPILLAR > PUPIL
PUPILLARY adj of or relating to a pupil or a legal ward
PUPILLATE adj with a spot of a different colour in the middle
PUPILS > PUPIL
PUPILSHIP n state of being a pupil
PUPPED > PUP
PUPPET n small doll or figure moved by strings or by the operator's hand
PUPPETEER n person who operates puppets
PUPPETRY n art of making and manipulating puppets and presenting puppet shows
PUPPETS > PUPPET
PUPPIED > PUPPY
PUPPIES > PUPPY
PUPPING > PUP
PUPPODUM same as > POPPADOM
PUPPODUMS > PUPPODUM
PUPPY n young dog ▷vb have puppies
PUPPYDOM n state of being a puppy
PUPPYDOMS > PUPPYDOM
PUPPYHOOD > PUPPY
PUPPYING > PUPPY
PUPPYISH > PUPPY
PUPPYISM n impudence
PUPPYISMS > PUPPYISM
PUPPYLIKE > PUPPY
PUPS > PUP
PUPU n Hawaiian dish
PUPUNHA n fruit of a type of palm tree
PUPUNHAS > PUPUNHA
PUPUS > PUPU
PUR same as > PURR
PURANA n any of a class of Sanskrit writings not included in the Vedas, characteristically recounting the birth and deeds of Hindu gods and the creation, destruction, or recreation of the universe
PURANAS > PURANA
PURANIC > PURANA
PURBLIND adj partly or nearly blind
PURCHASE vb obtain by payment ▷n thing that is bought
PURCHASED > PURCHASE
PURCHASER > PURCHASE
PURCHASES > PURCHASE
PURDA same as > PURDAH
PURDAH n Muslim and Hindu custom of keeping women in seclusion, with clothing that conceals them completely when they go out
PURDAHED > PURDAH
PURDAHS > PURDAH
PURDAS > PURDA
PURDONIUM n type of coal scuttle having a slanted cover that is raised to open it, and an inner removable metal container for the coal
PURE adj unmixed, untainted ▷vb make pure
PUREBLOOD n purebred animal
PUREBRED adj denoting a pure strain obtained through many generations of controlled breeding ▷n purebred animal
PUREBREDS > PUREBRED
PURED > PURE
PUREE n smooth thick pulp of cooked and sieved fruit, vegetables, meat, or fish ▷vb make (cooked foods) into a puree
PUREED > PUREE
PUREEING > PUREE
PUREES > PUREE
PURELY adv in a pure manner
PURENESS > PURE
PURER > PURE
PURES > PURE
PUREST > PURE
PURFLE n ruffled or curved ornamental band, as on clothing, furniture, etc ▷vb decorate with such a band or bands
PURFLED > PURFLE
PURFLER > PURFLE
PURFLERS > PURFLE
PURFLES > PURFLE
PURFLING same as > PURFLE
PURFLINGS > PURFLING
PURFLY > PURFLE
PURGATION n act of purging or state of being purged
PURGATIVE adj (medicine) designed to cause defecation ▷n medicine for emptying the bowels
PURGATORY n place or state of temporary suffering
PURGE vb rid (a thing or place) of (unwanted things or people) ▷n purging
PURGEABLE > PURGE

PURGED > PURGE
PURGER > PURGE
PURGERS > PURGE
PURGES > PURGE
PURGING > PURGE
PURGINGS > PURGE
PURI *n* unleavened flaky Indian bread, that is deep-fried in ghee and served hot
PURIFIED > PURIFY
PURIFIER *n* device or substance that frees something of extraneous, contaminating, or debasing matter
PURIFIERS > PURIFIER
PURIFIES > PURIFY
PURIFY *vb* make or become pure
PURIFYING > PURIFY
PURIM *n* Jewish holiday
PURIMS > PURIM
PURIN *same as* > PURINE
PURINE *n* colourless crystalline solid that can be prepared from uric acid
PURINES > PURINE
PURING > PURE
PURINS > PURIN
PURIRI *n* forest tree of New Zealand
PURIRIS > PURIRI
PURIS > PURI
PURISM *n* strict insistence on the correct usage or style, such as in grammar or art
PURISMS > PURISM
PURIST > PURISM
PURISTIC > PURISM
PURISTS > PURISM
PURITAN *n* person who follows strict moral or religious principles *▷adj* of or like a puritan
PURITANIC > PURITAN
PURITANS > PURITAN
PURITIES > PURITY
PURITY *n* state or quality of being pure
PURL *n* stitch made by knitting a plain stitch backwards *▷vb* knit in purl
PURLED > PURL
PURLER *n* headlong or spectacular fall
PURLERS > PURLER
PURLICUE *vb* finish a pen stroke with a flourish
PURLICUED > PURLICUE
PURLICUES > PURLICUE
PURLIEU *n* land on the edge of a royal forest
PURLIEUS > PURLIEU
PURLIN *n* horizontal beam that supports the rafters of a roof
PURLINE *same as* > PURLIN
PURLINES > PURLINE
PURLING > PURL
PURLINGS > PURL
PURLINS > PURLIN
PURLOIN *vb* steal
PURLOINED > PURLOIN
PURLOINER > PURLOIN
PURLOINS > PURLOIN

PURLS > PURL
PUROMYCIN *n* type of antibiotic
PURPIE *old Scots word for* > PURSLANE
PURPIES > PURPIE
PURPLE *n* colour between red and blue *▷adj* of a colour between red and blue *▷vb* make purple
PURPLED > PURPLE
PURPLER > PURPLE
PURPLES > PURPLE
PURPLEST > PURPLE
PURPLIER > PURPLE
PURPLIEST > PURPLE
PURPLING > PURPLE
PURPLISH > PURPLE
PURPLY > PURPLE
PURPORT *vb* claim (to be or do something) *▷n* apparent meaning, significance
PURPORTED *adj* alleged
PURPORTS > PURPORT
PURPOSE *n* reason for which something is done or exists
PURPOSED > PURPOSE
PURPOSELY *adv* intentionally
PURPOSES > PURPOSE
PURPOSING > PURPOSE
PURPOSIVE *adj* having or showing a definite intention
PURPURA *n* any of several blood diseases causing purplish spots or patches on the skin due to subcutaneous bleeding
PURPURAS > PURPURA
PURPURE *n* purple
PURPUREAL *adj* having a purple colour
PURPURES > PURPURE
PURPURIC > PURPURA
PURPURIN *n* red crystalline compound used as a stain for biological specimens
PURPURINS > PURPURIN
PURPY *variant of* > PURPIE
PURR *vb* (of cats) make low vibrant sound, usu when pleased *▷n* this sound
PURRED > PURR
PURRING > PURR
PURRINGLY > PURR
PURRINGS > PURR
PURRS > PURR
PURS > PUR
PURSE *n* small bag for money *▷vb* draw (one's lips) together into a small round shape
PURSED > PURSE
PURSEFUL *n* that which can be contained in purse
PURSEFULS > PURSEFUL
PURSELIKE > PURSE
PURSER *n* ship's officer who keeps the accounts
PURSERS > PURSER
PURSES > PURSE
PURSEW *archaic spelling of* > PURSUE
PURSEWED > PURSEW
PURSEWING > PURSEW

PURSEWS > PURSEW
PURSIER > PURSY
PURSIEST > PURSY
PURSILY > PURSY
PURSINESS > PURSY
PURSING > PURSE
PURSLAIN *same as* > PURSLANE
PURSLAINS > PURSLAIN
PURSLANE *n* weedy portulacaceous plant, *Portulaca oleracea*, with small yellow flowers and fleshy leaves, which are used in salads and as a potherb
PURSLANES > PURSLANE
PURSUABLE > PURSUE
PURSUAL *n* act of pursuit
PURSUALS > PURSUAL
PURSUANCE *n* carrying out of an action or plan
PURSUANT *adj* in agreement or conformity
PURSUE *vb* chase
PURSUED > PURSUE
PURSUER > PURSUE
PURSUERS > PURSUE
PURSUES > PURSUE
PURSUING > PURSUE
PURSUINGS > PURSUE
PURSUIT *n* pursuing
PURSUITS > PURSUIT
PURSY *adj* short-winded
PURTIER > PURTY
PURTIEST > PURTY
PURTRAID > PURTRAYD
PURTRAYD *adj* archaic spelling of portayed
PURTY *adj* pretty
PURULENCE > PURULENT
PURULENCY > PURULENT
PURULENT *adj* of or containing pus
PURVEY *vb* supply (provisions) *▷n* food and drink laid on at a wedding reception, etc
PURVEYED > PURVEY
PURVEYING > PURVEY
PURVEYOR *n* person, organization, etc, that supplies food and provisions
PURVEYORS > PURVEYOR
PURVEYS > PURVEY
PURVIEW *n* scope or range of activity or outlook
PURVIEWS > PURVIEW
PUS *n* yellowish matter produced by infected tissue
PUSES > PUS
PUSH *vb* move or try to move by steady force *▷n* act of pushing
PUSHBALL *n* game in which two teams try to push a heavy ball towards opposite goals
PUSHBALLS > PUSHBALL
PUSHCART *n* handcart, typically having two wheels and a canvas roof, used esp by street vendors
PUSHCARTS > PUSHCART
PUSHCHAIR *n* folding chair on wheels for a baby

PUSHDOWN *n* list in which the last item added is at the top
PUSHDOWNS > PUSHDOWN
PUSHED *adj* short of
PUSHER *n* person who sells illegal drugs
PUSHERS > PUSHER
PUSHES > PUSH
PUSHFUL > PUSH
PUSHFULLY > PUSH
PUSHIER > PUSHY
PUSHIEST > PUSHY
PUSHILY > PUSHY
PUSHINESS > PUSHY
PUSHING *prep* almost or nearly (a certain age, speed, etc) *▷adj* aggressively ambitious *▷adv* almost or nearly (a certain age, speed, etc)
PUSHINGLY > PUSHING
PUSHOVER *n* something easily achieved
PUSHOVERS > PUSHOVER
PUSHPIN *n* pin with a small ball-shaped head
PUSHPINS > PUSHPIN
PUSHROD *n* metal rod transmitting the reciprocating motion that operates the valves of an internal-combustion engine having the camshaft in the crankcase
PUSHRODS > PUSHROD
PUSHUP *n* exercise in which the body is alternately raised from and lowered to the floor by the arms only, the trunk being kept straight with the toes and hands resting on the floor
PUSHUPS > PUSHUP
PUSHY *adj* too assertive or ambitious
PUSLE *old spelling of* > PUZZLE
PUSLED > PUSLE
PUSLES > PUSLE
PUSLEY *same as* > PURSLANE
PUSLEYS > PUSLEY
PUSLIKE > PUS
PUSLING > PUSLE
PUSS *same as* > PUSSY
PUSSEL *n* slatternly woman
PUSSELS > PUSSEL
PUSSER *n* naval purser
PUSSERS > PUSSER
PUSSES > PUSS
PUSSIER > PUSSY
PUSSIES > PUSSY
PUSSIEST > PUSSY
PUSSLEY *n* weedy trailing herb
PUSSLEYS > PUSSLEY
PUSSLIES > PUSSLY
PUSSLIKE > PUSS
PUSSLY *variant of* > PUSSLEY
PUSSY *n* cat *▷adj* containing or full of pus
PUSSYCAT *same as* > PUSSY
PUSSYCATS > PUSSYCAT
PUSSYFOOT *vb* behave too cautiously *▷n* person who pussyfoots
PUSSYTOES *n* type of low-

P

growing plant

PUSTULANT *adj* causing the formation of pustules ▷ *n* agent causing such formation

PUSTULAR > PUSTULE

PUSTULATE *vb* form into pustules ▷ *adj* covered with pustules

PUSTULE *n* pimple containing pus

PUSTULED > PUSTULE

PUSTULES > PUSTULE

PUSTULOUS > PUSTULE

PUT *vb* cause to be (in a position, state, or place) ▷ *n* throw in putting the shot

PUTAMEN *n* hard endocarp or stone of fruits such as the peach, plum, and cherry

PUTAMINA > PUTAMEN

PUTATIVE *adj* reputed, supposed

PUTCHEON *n* trap for catching salmon

PUTCHEONS > PUTCHEON

PUTCHER *n* trap for catching salmon

PUTCHERS > PUTCHER

PUTCHOCK *same as* > PACHAK

PUTCHOCKS > PUTCHOCK

PUTCHUK *same as* > PACHAK

PUTCHUKS > PUTCHUK

PUTDOWN *n* snub or insult

PUTDOWNS > PUTDOWN

PUTEAL *n* enclosure around a well

PUTEALS > PUTEAL

PUTELI *same as* > PATELA

PUTELIS > PUTELI

PUTID *adj* having an unpleasant odour

PUTLOCK *same as* > PUTLOG

PUTLOCKS > PUTLOCK

PUTLOG *n* short horizontal beam that with others supports the floor planks of a scaffold

PUTLOGS > PUTLOG

PUTOFF *n* pretext or delay

PUTOFFS > PUTOFF

PUTOIS *n* brush to paint pottery

PUTON *n* hoax or piece of mockery

PUTONGHUA *n* Chinese language

PUTONS > PUTON

PUTOUT *n* baseball play in which the batter or runner is put out

PUTOUTS > PUTOUT

PUTREFIED > PUTREFY

PUTREFIER > PUTREFY

PUTREFIES > PUTREFY

PUTREFY *vb* rot and produce an offensive smell

PUTRID *adj* rotten and foul-smelling

PUTRIDER > PUTRID

PUTRIDEST > PUTRID

PUTRIDITY > PUTRID

PUTRIDLY > PUTRID

PUTS > PUT

PUTSCH *n* sudden violent

attempt to remove a government from power

PUTSCHES > PUTSCH

PUTSCHIST *n* person taking part in putsch

PUTT *n* stroke on the putting green to roll the ball into or near the hole ▷ *vb* strike (the ball) in this way

PUTTED > PUTT

PUTTEE *n* (esp as part of a military uniform) strip of cloth worn wound around the leg from the ankle to the knee

PUTTEES > PUTTEE

PUTTEN *old Scots past participle of* > PUT

PUTTER *n* golf club for putting ▷ *vb* busy oneself in a desultory though agreeable manner

PUTTERED > PUTTER

PUTTERER > PUTTER

PUTTERERS > PUTTER

PUTTERING > PUTTER

PUTTERS > PUTTER

PUTTI > PUTTO

PUTTIE *same as* > PUTTEE

PUTTIED > PUTTY

PUTTIER *n* glazier

PUTTIERS > PUTTIER

PUTTIES > PUTTY

PUTTING > PUT

PUTTINGS > PUT

PUTTO *n* representation of a small boy, a cherub or cupid, esp in baroque painting or sculpture

PUTTOCK *n* type of bird of prey

PUTTOCKS > PUTTOCK

PUTTS > PUTT

PUTTY *n* stiff paste of whiting and linseed oil ▷ *vb* fill, fix, or coat with putty

PUTTYING > PUTTY

PUTTYLESS > PUTTY

PUTTYLIKE > PUTTY

PUTTYROOT *n* North American orchid

PUTURE *n* claim of foresters for food for men, horses, hawks, and hounds, within the bounds of the forest

PUTURES > PUTURE

PUTZ *n* despicable or stupid person ▷ *vb* waste time

PUTZED > PUTZ

PUTZES > PUTZ

PUTZING > PUTZ

PUY *n* small volcanic cone

PUYS > PUY

PUZEL *same as* > PUCELLE

PUZELS > PUZEL

PUZZEL *n* prostitute

PUZZELS > PUZZEL

PUZZLE *vb* perplex and confuse or be perplexed or confused ▷ *n* problem that cannot be easily solved

PUZZLED > PUZZLE

PUZZLEDLY > PUZZLE

PUZZLEDOM > PUZZLE

PUZZLER *n* person or thing that puzzles

PUZZLERS > PUZZLER

PUZZLES > PUZZLE

PUZZLING > PUZZLE

PUZZOLANA *same as* > POZZOLANA

PYA *n* monetary unit of Myanmar worth one hundredth of a kyat

PYAEMIA *n* blood poisoning with pus-forming microorganisms in the blood

PYAEMIAS > PYAEMIA

PYAEMIC > PYAEMIA

PYAS > PYA

PYAT *n* magpie ▷ *adj* pied

PYATS > PYAT

PYCNIC *same as* > PYKNIC

PYCNIDIA > PYCNIDIUM

PYCNIDIAL > PYCNIDIUM

PYCNIDIUM *n* small flask-shaped structure containing spores that occurs in ascomycetes and certain other fungi

PYCNITE *n* variety of topaz

PYCNITES > PYCNITE

PYCNON *old word for* > SEMITONE

PYCNONS > PYCNON

PYCNOSES > PYCNOSIS

PYCNOSIS *n* process of shrinking in a cell nucleus

PYCNOTIC > PYCNOSIS

PYE *same as* > PIE

PYEBALD *same as* > PIEBALD

PYEBALDS > PYEBALD

PYEING > PYE

PYELITIC > PYELITIS

PYELITIS *n* inflammation of the pelvis of the kidney

PYELOGRAM *n* film produced by pyelography

PYEMIA *same as* > PYAEMIA

PYEMIAS > PYEMIA

PYEMIC > PYAEMIA

PYENGADU *variant of* > PYINKADO

PYENGADUS > PYENGADU

PYES > PYE

PYET *same as* > PYAT

PYETS > PYET

PYGAL *n* rear part

PYGALS > PYGAL

PYGARG *n* type of horned mammal

PYGARGS > PYGARG

PYGIDIA > PYGIDIUM

PYGIDIAL > PYGIDIUM

PYGIDIUM *n* terminal segment, division, or other structure in certain annelids, arthropods, and other invertebrates

PYGIDIUMS > PYGIDIUM

PYGMAEAN > PYGMY

PYGMEAN > PYGMY

PYGMIES > PYGMY

PYGMOID *adj* of or like pygmies

PYGMY *n* something that is a very small example of its type ▷ *adj* very small

PYGMYISH > PYGMY

PYGMYISM > PYGMY

PYGMYISMS > PYGMY

PYGOSTYLE *n* vertebral

bone in birds

PYIC *adj* relating to pus

PYIN *n* constituent of pus

PYINKADO *n* leguminous tree native to India and Myanmar

PYINKADOS > PYINKADO

PYINS > PYIN

PYJAMA *same as* > PYJAMAS

PYJAMAED > PYJAMAS

PYJAMAS *pl n* loose-fitting trousers and top worn in bed

PYKNIC *adj* (of a physical type) characterized by a broad squat fleshy physique with a large chest and abdomen ▷ *n* person with this physical type

PYKNICS > PYKNIC

PYKNOSES > PYKNOSIS

PYKNOSIS *n* thickening of a cell

PYKNOSOME *n* stocky body type

PYKNOTIC > PYKNOSIS

PYLON *n* steel tower-like structure supporting electrical cables

PYLONS > PYLON

PYLORI > PYLORUS

PYLORIC > PYLORUS

PYLORUS *n* small circular opening at the base of the stomach through which partially digested food (chyme) passes to the duodenum

PYLORUSES > PYLORUS

PYNE *archaic variant of* > PINE

PYNED > PYNE

PYNES > PYNE

PYNING > PYNE

PYODERMA *n* any skin eruption characterized by pustules or the formation of pus

PYODERMAS > PYODERMA

PYODERMIC > PYODERMA

PYOGENIC *adj* of or relating to the formation of pus

PYOID *adj* resembling pus

PYONER *old variant of* > PIONEER

PYONERS > PYONER

PYONINGS *n* old term for the work of pioneers

PYORRHEA *same as* > PYORRHOEA

PYORRHEAL > PYORRHOEA

PYORRHEAS > PYORRHEA

PYORRHEIC > PYORRHOEA

PYORRHOEA *n* disease of the gums and tooth sockets which causes bleeding of the gums and the formation of pus

PYOSES > PYOSIS

PYOSIS *n* formation of pus

PYOT *same as* > PYAT

PYOTS > PYOT

PYRACANTH *n* type of thorny shrub

PYRAL > PYRE

PYRALID *n* tropical moth

PYRALIDID *same*

as > PYRALID

PYRALIDS > PYRALID

PYRALIS *same as* > PYRALID

PYRALISES > PYRALIS

PYRAMID *n* solid figure with a flat base and triangular sides sloping upwards to a point ▷ *vb* build up or be arranged in the form of a pyramid

PYRAMIDAL > PYRAMID

PYRAMIDED > PYRAMID

PYRAMIDES > PYRAMIS

PYRAMIDIA *n* pyramidal apices of obelisks

PYRAMIDIC > PYRAMID

PYRAMIDON *n* type of pipe for an organ

PYRAMIDS > PYRAMID

PYRAMIS *n* pyramid-shaped structure

PYRAMISES > PYRAMIS

PYRAN *n* unsaturated heterocyclic compound having a ring containing five carbon atoms and one oxygen atom and two double bonds

PYRANOID > PYRAN

PYRANOSE *n* structure in many sugars

PYRANOSES > PYRANOSE

PYRANS > PYRAN

PYRAZOLE *n* crystalline soluble basic heterocyclic compound

PYRAZOLES > PYRAZOLE

PYRE *n* pile of wood for burning a corpse on

PYRENE *n* solid polynuclear aromatic hydrocarbon extracted from coal tar

PYRENEITE *n* dark mineral found in the Pyrenees

PYRENES > PYRENE

PYRENOID *n* any of various small protein granules that occur in certain algae, mosses, and protozoans and are involved in the synthesis of starch

PYRENOIDS > PYRENOID

PYRES > PYRE

PYRETHRIN *n* oily water-insoluble compound used as an insecticide

PYRETHRUM *n* Eurasian chrysanthemum with white, pink, red, or purple flowers

PYRETIC *adj* of, relating to, or characterized by fever

PYREX *n* tradename for any of a variety of borosilicate glasses that have low coefficients of expansion,

making them suitable for heat-resistant glassware used in cookery and chemical apparatus

PYREXES > PYREX

PYREXIA *technical name for* > FEVER

PYREXIAL > PYREXIA

PYREXIAS > PYREXIA

PYREXIC > PYREXIA

PYRIC *adj* of or relating to burning

PYRIDIC > PYRIDINE

PYRIDINE *n* colourless hygroscopic liquid with a characteristic odour

PYRIDINES > PYRIDINE

PYRIDOXAL *n* naturally occurring derivative of pyridoxine that is a precursor of a coenzyme involved in several enzymic reactions

PYRIDOXIN *n* derivative of pyridine

PYRIFORM *adj* (esp of organs of the body) pear-shaped

PYRITE *n* yellow mineral consisting of iron sulphide in cubic crystalline form

PYRITES *same as* > PYRITE

PYRITIC > PYRITE

PYRITICAL > PYRITE

PYRITISE *same as* > PYRITIZE

PYRITISED > PYRITISE

PYRITISES > PYRITISE

PYRITIZE *vb* convert into pyrites

PYRITIZED > PYRITIZE

PYRITIZES > PYRITIZE

PYRITOUS > PYRITE

PYRO *n* pyromaniac

PYROCERAM *n* transparent ceramic material

PYROCLAST *n* piece of lava ejected from a volcano

PYROGEN *n* any of a group of substances that cause a rise in temperature in an animal body

PYROGENIC *adj* produced by or producing heat

PYROGENS > PYROGEN

PYROLA *n* evergreen perennial

PYROLAS > PYROLA

PYROLATER *n* worshipper of fire

PYROLATRY > PYROLATER

PYROLISE *same as* > PYROLIZE

PYROLISED > PYROLISE

PYROLISES > PYROLISE

PYROLIZE *vb* subject to pyrolysis

PYROLIZED > PYROLIZE

PYROLIZES > PYROLIZE

PYROLOGY *n* study of heat

PYROLYSE *vb* subject to pyrolysis

PYROLYSED > PYROLYSE

PYROLYSER > PYROLYSE

PYROLYSES > PYROLYSE

PYROLYSIS *n* application of heat to chemical compounds in order to cause decomposition

PYROLYTIC > PYROLYSIS

PYROLYZE *same as* > PYROLYSE

PYROLYZED > PYROLYSE

PYROLYZER > PYROLYSE

PYROLYZES > PYROLYSE

PYROMANCY *n* divination by fire or flames

PYROMANIA *n* uncontrollable urge to set things on fire

PYROMETER *n* instrument for measuring high temperatures

PYROMETRY > PYROMETER

PYRONE *n* type of heterocyclic compound

PYRONES > PYRONE

PYRONINE *n* red dye used as biological stain

PYRONINES > PYRONINE

PYROPE *n* deep yellowish-red garnet that consists of magnesium aluminium silicate and is used as a gemstone

PYROPES > PYROPE

PYROPHONE *n* musical instrument using hydrogen flames

PYROPUS *variant of* > PYROPE

PYROPUSES > PYROPUS

PYROS > PYRO

PYROSCOPE *n* instrument for measuring intensity of heat

PYROSES > PYROSIS

PYROSIS *technical name for* > HEARTBURN

PYROSISES > PYROSIS

PYROSOME *n* tube-shaped glowing marine creature

PYROSOMES > PYROSOME

PYROSTAT *n* device that activates an alarm or extinguisher in the event of a fire

PYROSTATS > PYROSTAT

PYROXENE *n* silicate mineral

PYROXENES > PYROXENE

PYROXENIC > PYROXENE

PYROXYLE *same as* > PYROXYLIN

PYROXYLES > PYROXYLE

PYROXYLIC > PYROXYLIN

PYROXYLIN *n* yellow substance obtained by nitrating cellulose with a mixture of nitric and sulphuric acids

PYRRHIC *n* metrical foot of two short or unstressed syllables ▷ *adj* of or relating to such a metrical foot

PYRRHICS > PYRRHIC

PYRRHOUS *adj* ruddy or reddish

PYRROL *same as* > PYRROLE

PYRROLE *n* colourless insoluble toxic liquid with a five-membered ring containing one nitrogen atom

PYRROLES > PYRROLE

PYRROLIC > PYRROLE

PYRROLS > PYRROL

PYRUVATE *n* ester or salt of pyruvic acid

PYRUVATES > PYRUVATE

PYRUVIC *as in pyruvic acid* colourless pleasant-smelling liquid

PYTHIUM *n* type of fungi

PYTHIUMS > PYTHIUM

PYTHON *n* large nonpoisonous snake that crushes its prey

PYTHONESS *n* woman, such as Apollo's priestess at Delphi, believed to be possessed by an oracular spirit

PYTHONIC > PYTHON

PYTHONS > PYTHON

PYURIA *n* any condition characterized by the presence of pus in the urine

PYURIAS > PYURIA

PYX *n* any receptacle for the Eucharistic Host ▷ *vb* put (something) in a pyx

PYXED > PYX

PYXES > PYX

PYXIDES > PYXIS

PYXIDIA > PYXIDIUM

PYXIDIUM *n* dry fruit of such plants as the plantain

PYXIE *n* creeping evergreen shrub of the eastern US with small white or pink star-shaped flowers

PYXIES > PYXIE

PYXING > PYX

PYXIS *same as* > PYXIDIUM

PZAZZ *same as* > PIZZAZZ

PZAZZES > PZAZZ

Qq

QABALA *same as* > KABBALAH

QABALAH *same as* > KABBALAH

QABALAHS > QABALAH

QABALAS > QABALA

QABALISM > QABALAH

QABALISMS > QABALAH

QABALIST > QABALAH

QABALISTS > QABALAH

QADI *variant spelling of* > CADI

QADIS > QADI

QAID *n* chief

QAIDS > QAID

QAIMAQAM *n* Turkish officer or official

QAIMAQAMS > QAIMAQAM

QALAMDAN *n* writing case

QALAMDANS > QALAMDAN

QANAT *n* underground irrigation channel

QANATS > QANAT

QASIDA *n* Arabic verse form

QASIDAS > QASIDA

QAT *variant spelling of* > KHAT

QATS > QAT

QAWWAL *n* qawwali singer

QAWWALI *n* Islamic religious song, esp in Asia

QAWWALIS > QAWWALI

QAWWALS > QAWWAL

QI *variant of* > CHI

QIBLA *variant of* > KIBLAH

QIBLAS > QIBLA

QIGONG *n* system of breathing and exercise designed to benefit both physical and mental health

QIGONGS > QIGONG

QINDAR *n* Albanian monetary unit worth one hundredth of a lek

QINDARKA > QINDAR

QINDARS > QINDAR

QINGHAOSU *n* Chinese herb

QINTAR *same as* > QINDAR

QINTARS > QINTAR

QIS > QI

QIVIUT *n* soft muskox wool

QIVIUTS > QIVIUT

QOPH *variant of* > KOPH

QOPHS > QOPH

QORMA *variant spelling of* > KORMA

QORMAS > QORMA

QUA *prep* in the capacity of

QUAALUDE *n* methaqualone

QUAALUDES > QUAALUDE

QUACK *vb* (of a duck) utter a harsh guttural sound ▷ *n* an unqualified person who claims medical knowledge

QUACKED > QUACK

QUACKER > QUACK

QUACKERS > QUACK

QUACKERY *n* activities or methods of a quack

QUACKIER > QUACK

QUACKIEST > QUACK

QUACKING > QUACK

QUACKISH > QUACK

QUACKISM *same as* > QUACKERY

QUACKISMS > QUACKISM

QUACKLE *same as* > QUACK

QUACKLED > QUACKLE

QUACKLES > QUACKLE

QUACKLING > QUACKLE

QUACKS > QUACK

QUACKY > QUACK

QUAD *n* quadrangle

QUADDED *adj* formed of multiple quads

QUADDING *n* birdwatching in a specified area

QUADPLEX *n* apartment on four floors

QUADRANS *n* Roman coin

QUADRANT *n* quarter of a circle

QUADRANTS > QUADRANT

QUADRAT *n* area of vegetation, often one square metre, marked out for study of the plants in the surrounding area

QUADRATE *n* cube or square, or a square or cubelike object ▷ *vb* make square or rectangular ▷ *adj* of or relating to this bone

QUADRATED > QUADRATE

QUADRATES > QUADRATE

QUADRATIC *n* equation in which the variable is raised to the power of two, but nowhere raised to a higher power ▷ *adj* of the second power

QUADRATS > QUADRAT

QUADRATUS *n* type of muscle

QUADRELLA *n* four nominated horseraces in which the punter bets on selecting the four winners

QUADRIC *adj* having or characterized by an equation of the second degree, usually in two or three variables ▷ *n* quadric curve, surface, or function

QUADRICEP *n* muscle in thigh

QUADRICS > QUADRIC

QUADRIFID *adj* divided into four lobes or other parts

QUADRIGA *n* (in the classical world) a two-wheeled chariot drawn by four horses abreast

QUADRIGAE > QUADRIGA

QUADRIGAS > QUADRIGA

QUADRILLE *n* square dance for four couples

QUADRIVIA *n* higher divisions of the seven liberal arts

QUADROON *n* an offensive term for the offspring of a mulatto and a white person

QUADROONS > QUADROON

QUADRUMAN *n* nonhuman primate

QUADRUPED *n* any animal with four legs ▷ *adj* having four feet

QUADRUPLE *vb* multiply by four ▷ *adj* four times as much or as many ▷ *n* quantity or number four times as great as another

QUADRUPLY > QUADRUPLE

QUADS > QUAD

QUAERE *n* query or question ▷ *interj* ask or inquire: used esp to introduce a question ▷ *vb* ask

QUAERED > QUAERE

QUAEREING > QUAERE

QUAERES > QUAERE

QUAERITUR *sentence substitute* question is asked

QUAESITUM *n* object sought

QUAESTOR *n* any of several magistrates of ancient Rome, usually a financial administrator

QUAESTORS > QUAESTOR

QUAFF *vb* drink heartily or in one draught

QUAFFABLE > QUAFF

QUAFFED > QUAFF

QUAFFER > QUAFF

QUAFFERS > QUAFF

QUAFFING > QUAFF

QUAFFS > QUAFF

QUAG *another word for* > QUAGMIRE

QUAGGA *n* recently extinct zebra, striped only on the head and shoulders

QUAGGAS > QUAGGA

QUAGGIER > QUAGGY

QUAGGIEST > QUAGGY

QUAGGY *adj* resembling a marsh or quagmire

QUAGMIRE *n* soft wet area of land ▷ *vb* bog down

QUAGMIRED > QUAGMIRE

QUAGMIRES > QUAGMIRE

QUAGMIRY > QUAGMIRE

QUAGS > QUAG

QUAHAUG *same as* > QUAHOG

QUAHAUGS > QUAHAUG

QUAHOG *n* edible clam

QUAHOGS > QUAHOG

QUAI *same as* > QUAY

QUAICH *n* small shallow drinking cup, usually with two handles

QUAICHES > QUAICH

QUAICHS > QUAICH

QUAIGH *same as* > QUAICH

QUAIGHS > QUAIGH

QUAIL *n* small game bird of the partridge family ▷ *vb* shrink back with fear

QUAILED > QUAIL

QUAILING > QUAIL

QUAILINGS > QUAIL

QUAILS > QUAIL

QUAINT *adj* attractively unusual, esp in an old-fashioned style

QUAINTER > QUAINT

QUAINTEST > QUAINT

QUAINTLY > QUAINT

QUAIR *n* book

QUAIRS > QUAIR

QUAIS > QUAI

QUAKE *vb* shake or tremble with or as if with fear ▷ *n* earthquake

QUAKED > QUAKE

QUAKER > QUAKE

QUAKERS > QUAKE

QUAKES > QUAKE
QUAKIER > QUAKY
QUAKIEST > QUAKY
QUAKILY > QUAKY
QUAKINESS > QUAKY
QUAKING > QUAKE
QUAKINGLY > QUAKE
QUAKINGS > QUAKE
QUAKY *adj* inclined to quake
QUALE *n* essential property or quality
QUALIA > QUALE
QUALIFIED > QUALIFY
QUALIFIER *n* person or thing that qualifies, esp a contestant in a competition who wins a preliminary heat or contest and so earns the right to take part in the next round
QUALIFIES > QUALIFY
QUALIFY *vb* provide or be provided with the abilities necessary for a task, office, or duty
QUALITIED *adj* possessing qualities
QUALITIES > QUALITY
QUALITY *n* degree or standard of excellence ▷ *adj* excellent or superior
QUALM *n* pang of conscience
QUALMIER > QUALM
QUALMIEST > QUALM
QUALMING *adj* having a qualm
QUALMISH > QUALM
QUALMLESS > QUALM
QUALMS > QUALM
QUALMY > QUALM
QUAMASH *another name for* > CAMASS
QUAMASHES > QUAMASH
QUANDANG *same as* > QUANDONG
QUANDANGS > QUANDANG
QUANDARY *n* difficult situation or dilemma
QUANDONG *n* small Australian tree with edible fruit and nuts used in preserves
QUANDONGS > QUANDONG
QUANGO *n* quasi-autonomous nongovernmental organization: any partly independent official body set up by a government
QUANGOS > QUANGO
QUANNET *n* flat file with handle at one end
QUANNETS > QUANNET
QUANT *n* long pole for propelling a boat, esp a punt, by pushing on the bottom of a river or lake ▷ *vb* propel (a boat) with a quant
QUANTA > QUANTUM
QUANTAL *adj* of or relating to a quantum or an entity that is quantized
QUANTALLY > QUANTAL
QUANTED > QUANT
QUANTIC *n* mathematical function

QUANTICAL > QUANTIC
QUANTICS > QUANTIC
QUANTIFY *vb* discover or express the quantity of
QUANTILE *n* element of a division
QUANTILES > QUANTILE
QUANTING > QUANT
QUANTISE *same as* > QUANTIZE
QUANTISED > QUANTISE
QUANTISER > QUANTISE
QUANTISES > QUANTISE
QUANTITY *n* specified or definite amount or number
QUANTIZE *vb* restrict (a physical quantity) to one of a set of values characterized by quantum numbers
QUANTIZED > QUANTIZE
QUANTIZER > QUANTIZE
QUANTIZES > QUANTIZE
QUANTONG *same as* > QUANDONG
QUANTONGS > QUANTONG
QUANTS > QUANT
QUANTUM *n* desired or required amount, esp a very small one ▷ *adj* of or designating a major breakthrough or sudden advance
QUARE *adj* remarkable or strange
QUARENDEN *n* dark-red apple
QUARENDER *same as* > QUARENDEN
QUARER > QUARE
QUAREST > QUARE
QUARK *n* subatomic particle thought to be the fundamental unit of matter
QUARKS > QUARK
QUARREL *n* angry disagreement ▷ *vb* have a disagreement or dispute
QUARRELED > QUARREL
QUARRELER > QUARREL
QUARRELS > QUARREL
QUARRIAN *n* cockatiel of scrub and woodland regions of inland Australia
QUARRIANS > QUARRIAN
QUARRIED > QUARRY
QUARRIER *another word for* > QUARRYMAN
QUARRIERS > QUARRIER
QUARRIES > QUARRY
QUARRION *same as* > QUARRIAN
QUARRIONS > QUARRION
QUARRY *n* place where stone is dug from the surface of the earth ▷ *vb* extract (stone) from a quarry
QUARRYING > QUARRY
QUARRYMAN *n* man who works in or manages a quarry
QUARRYMEN > QUARRYMAN
QUART *n* unit of liquid measure equal to two pints (1.136 litres)
QUARTAN *adj* (esp of a

malarial fever) occurring every third day ▷ *n* quartan malaria
QUARTANS > QUARTAN
QUARTE *n* fourth of eight basic positions from which a parry or attack can be made in fencing
QUARTER *n* one of four equal parts of something ▷ *vb* divide into four equal parts ▷ *adj* being or consisting of one of four equal parts
QUARTERED *adj* (of a shield) divided into four sections, each having contrasting arms or having two sets of arms, each repeated in diagonally opposite corners
QUARTERER > QUARTER
QUARTERLY *adj* occurring, due, or issued at intervals of three months ▷ *n* magazine issued every three months ▷ *adv* once every three months
QUARTERN *n* fourth part of certain weights or measures, such as a peck or a pound
QUARTERNS > QUARTERN
QUARTERS *pl n* accommodation, esp as provided for military personnel
QUARTES > QUARTE
QUARTET *n* group of four performers
QUARTETS > QUARTET
QUARTETT *same as* > QUARTET
QUARTETTE *same as* > QUARTET
QUARTETTI > QUARTETTO
QUARTETTO *same as* > QUARTET
QUARTETTS > QUARTETT
QUARTIC *n* biquadratic equation
QUARTICS > QUARTIC
QUARTIER *n* city district
QUARTIERS > QUARTIER
QUARTILE *n* one of three values of a variable dividing its distribution into four groups with equal frequencies ▷ *adj* of a quartile
QUARTILES > QUARTILE
QUARTO *n* book size in which the sheets are folded into four leaves
QUARTOS > QUARTO
QUARTS > QUART
QUARTZ *n* hard glossy mineral
QUARTZES > QUARTZ
QUARTZIER > QUARTZ
QUARTZITE *n* very hard metamorphic rock consisting of a mosaic of intergrown quartz crystals
QUARTZOSE > QUARTZ
QUARTZOUS > QUARTZ
QUARTZY > QUARTZ
QUASAR *n* extremely distant

starlike object that emits powerful radio waves
QUASARS > QUASAR
QUASH *vb* annul or make void
QUASHED > QUASH
QUASHEE *same as* > QUASHIE
QUASHEES > QUASHEE
QUASHER > QUASH
QUASHERS > QUASH
QUASHES > QUASH
QUASHIE *n* in the Carribbean, an unsophisticated or gullible male Black peasant
QUASHIES > QUASHIE
QUASHING > QUASH
QUASI *adv* as if
QUASS *variant of* > KVASS
QUASSES > QUASS
QUASSIA *n* tropical American tree, the wood of which yields a substance used in insecticides
QUASSIAS > QUASSIA
QUASSIN *n* bitter crystalline substance
QUASSINS > QUASSIN
QUAT *n* spot
QUATCH *vb* move
QUATCHED > QUATCH
QUATCHES > QUATCH
QUATCHING > QUATCH
QUATE *n* fortune
QUATORZE *n* cards worth 14 points in piquet
QUATORZES > QUATORZE
QUATRAIN *n* stanza or poem of four lines
QUATRAINS > QUATRAIN
QUATRE *n* playing card with four pips
QUATRES > QUATRE
QUATS > QUAT
QUAVER *vb* (of a voice) quiver or tremble ▷ *n* note half the length of a crotchet
QUAVERED > QUAVER
QUAVERER > QUAVER
QUAVERERS > QUAVER
QUAVERIER > QUAVER
QUAVERING > QUAVER
QUAVERS > QUAVER
QUAVERY > QUAVER
QUAY *n* wharf built parallel to the shore
QUAYAGE *n* system of quays
QUAYAGES > QUAYAGE
QUAYD *archaic past participle of* > QUAIL
QUAYLIKE > QUAY
QUAYS > QUAY
QUAYSIDE *n* edge of a quay along the water
QUAYSIDES > QUAYSIDE
QUAZZIER > QUAZZY
QUAZZIEST > QUAZZY
QUAZZY *adj* unwell
QUBIT *n* quantum bit
QUBITS > QUBIT
QUBYTE *n* unit of eight qubits
QUBYTES > QUBYTE
QUEACH *n* thicket
QUEACHES > QUEACH
QUEACHIER > QUEACHY
QUEACHY *adj* unwell

QUEAN n boisterous, impudent, or disreputable woman
QUEANS > QUEAN
QUEASIER > QUEASY
QUEASIEST > QUEASY
QUEASILY > QUEASY
QUEASY adj having the feeling that one is about to vomit
QUEAZIER > QUEAZY
QUEAZIEST > QUEAZY
QUEAZY same as > QUEASY
QUEBRACHO n anacardiaceous South American tree
QUEECHIER > QUEECHY
QUEECHY same as > QUEACHY
QUEEN n female sovereign who is the official ruler or head of state ▷ vb flaunt one's homosexuality
QUEENCAKE n small light cake containing currants
QUEENDOM n territory, state, people, or community ruled over by a queen
QUEENDOMS > QUEENDOM
QUEENED > QUEEN
QUEENHOOD > QUEEN
QUEENIE n scallop
QUEENIER > QUEENY
QUEENIES > QUEENIE
QUEENIEST > QUEENY
QUEENING > QUEEN
QUEENINGS > QUEEN
QUEENITE n supporter of a queen
QUEENITES > QUEENITE
QUEENLESS > QUEEN
QUEENLET n queen of a small realm
QUEENLETS > QUEENLET
QUEENLIER > QUEENLY
QUEENLY adj resembling or appropriate to a queen ▷ adv in a manner appropriate to a queen
QUEENS > QUEEN
QUEENSHIP > QUEEN
QUEENSIDE n half of a chessboard in which the queen starts
QUEENY adj effeminate
QUEER adj not normal or usual ▷ n derogatory name for a homosexual person ▷ vb spoil or thwart
QUEERCORE n gay-oriented punk music
QUEERDOM n gay culture
QUEERDOMS > QUEERDOM
QUEERED > QUEER
QUEERER > QUEER
QUEEREST > QUEER
QUEERING > QUEER
QUEERISH > QUEER
QUEERITY > QUEER
QUEERLY > QUEER
QUEERNESS > QUEER
QUEERS > QUEER
QUEEST n wood pigeon
QUEESTS > QUEEST
QUEINT same as > QUAINT
QUELCH same as > SQUELCH
QUELCHED > QUELCH

QUELCHES > QUELCH
QUELCHING > QUELCH
QUELEA n East African weaver bird
QUELEAS > QUELEA
QUELL vb suppress
QUELLABLE > QUELL
QUELLED > QUELL
QUELLER > QUELL
QUELLERS > QUELL
QUELLING > QUELL
QUELLS > QUELL
QUEME vb please
QUEMED > QUEME
QUEMES > QUEME
QUEMING > QUEME
QUENA n Andean flute
QUENAS > QUENA
QUENCH vb satisfy (one's thirst)
QUENCHED > QUENCH
QUENCHER > QUENCH
QUENCHERS > QUENCH
QUENCHES > QUENCH
QUENCHING > QUENCH
QUENELLE n finely sieved mixture of cooked meat or fish, shaped into various forms and cooked in stock or fried as croquettes
QUENELLES > QUENELLE
QUEP interj expression of derision
QUERCETIC > QUERCETIN
QUERCETIN n yellow crystalline pigment found naturally in the rind and bark of many plants
QUERCETUM n group of oak trees
QUERCINE adj of or relating to oak trees
QUERCITIN same as > QUERCETIN
QUERIDA n sweetheart
QUERIDAS > QUERIDA
QUERIED > QUERY
QUERIER > QUERY
QUERIERS > QUERY
QUERIES > QUERY
QUERIMONY n complaint
QUERIST n person who makes inquiries or queries
QUERISTS > QUERIST
QUERN n stone hand mill for grinding corn
QUERNS > QUERN
QUERULOUS adj complaining or whining
QUERY n question, esp one raising doubt ▷ vb express uncertainty, doubt, or an objection concerning (something)
QUERYING > QUERY
QUERYINGS > QUERY
QUEST n long and difficult search ▷ vb go in search of
QUESTANT n one who quests
QUESTANTS > QUEST
QUESTED > QUEST
QUESTER > QUEST
QUESTERS > QUEST
QUESTING > QUEST
QUESTINGS > QUEST
QUESTION n form of words

addressed to a person in order to obtain an answer ▷ vb put a question or questions to (a person)
QUESTIONS > QUESTION
QUESTOR same as > QUAESTOR
QUESTORS > QUESTOR
QUESTRIST n one who quests
QUESTS > QUEST
QUETCH vb move
QUETCHED > QUETCH
QUETCHES > QUETCH
QUETCHING > QUETCH
QUETHE vb say
QUETHES > QUETHE
QUETHING > QUETHE
QUETSCH n plum brandy
QUETSCHES > QUETSCH
QUETZAL n crested bird of Central and N South America
QUETZALES > QUETZAL
QUETZALS > QUETZAL
QUEUE n line of people or vehicles waiting for something ▷ vb form or remain in a line while waiting
QUEUED > QUEUE
QUEUEING > QUEUE
QUEUEINGS > QUEUE
QUEUER > QUEUE
QUEUERS > QUEUE
QUEUES > QUEUE
QUEUING > QUEUE
QUEUINGS > QUEUE
QUEY n young cow
QUEYN n girl
QUEYNIE same as > QUEYN
QUEYNIES > QUEYNIE
QUEYNS > QUEYN
QUEYS > QUEY
QUEZAL same as > QUETZAL
QUEZALES > QUEZAL
QUEZALS > QUEZAL
QUIBBLE vb make trivial objections ▷ n trivial objection
QUIBBLED > QUIBBLE
QUIBBLER > QUIBBLE
QUIBBLERS > QUIBBLE
QUIBBLES > QUIBBLE
QUIBBLING > QUIBBLE
QUIBLIN same as > QUIBBLE
QUIBLINS > QUIBLIN
QUICH vb move
QUICHE n savoury flan with an egg custard filling to which vegetables etc are added
QUICHED > QUICH
QUICHES > QUICHE
QUICHING > QUICH
QUICK adj speedy, fast ▷ n area of sensitive flesh under a nail ▷ adv in a rapid manner
QUICKBEAM n rowan tree
QUICKEN vb make or become faster ▷ n rowan tree
QUICKENED > QUICKEN
QUICKENER > QUICKEN
QUICKENS > QUICKEN
QUICKER > QUICK

QUICKEST > QUICK
QUICKIE n anything done or made hurriedly ▷ adj made or done rapidly
QUICKIES > QUICKIE
QUICKLIME n white solid used in the manufacture of glass and steel
QUICKLY > QUICK
QUICKNESS > QUICK
QUICKS > QUICK
QUICKSAND n deep mass of loose wet sand that sucks anything on top of it into it
QUICKSET adj (of plants or cuttings) planted so as to form a hedge ▷ n hedge composed of such plants
QUICKSETS > QUICKSET
QUICKSTEP n fast modern ballroom dance ▷ vb perform this dance
QUID n pound (sterling)
QUIDAM n specified person
QUIDAMS > QUIDAM
QUIDDANY n quince jelly
QUIDDIT same as > QUIDDITY
QUIDDITCH n imaginary game in which players fly on broomsticks
QUIDDITS > QUIDDIT
QUIDDITY n essential nature of something
QUIDDLE vb waste time
QUIDDLED > QUIDDLE
QUIDDLER > QUIDDLE
QUIDDLERS > QUIDDLE
QUIDDLES > QUIDDLE
QUIDDLING > QUIDDLE
QUIDNUNC n person eager to learn news and scandal
QUIDNUNCS > QUIDNUNC
QUIDS > QUID
QUIESCE vb quieten
QUIESCED > QUIETEN
QUIESCENT adj quiet, inactive, or dormant
QUIESCES > QUIESCE
QUIESCING > QUIESCE
QUIET adj with little noise ▷ n quietness ▷ vb make or become quiet
QUIETED > QUIET
QUIETEN vb make or become quiet
QUIETENED > QUIETEN
QUIETENER > QUIETEN
QUIETENS > QUIETEN
QUIETER > QUIET
QUIETERS > QUIET
QUIETEST > QUIET
QUIETING > QUIET
QUIETINGS > QUIET
QUIETISM n passivity and calmness of mind towards external events
QUIETISMS > QUIETISM
QUIETIST > QUIETISM
QUIETISTS > QUIETISM
QUIETIVE n sedative drug
QUIETIVES > QUIETIVE
QUIETLY > QUIET
QUIETNESS > QUIET
QUIETS > QUIET
QUIETSOME > QUIET
QUIETUDE n quietness,

peace, or tranquillity

QUIETUDES > QUIETUDE

QUIETUS *n* release from life

QUIETUSES > QUIETUS

QUIFF *n* tuft of hair brushed up above the forehead

QUIFFS > QUIFF

QUIGHT *vb* quit

QUIGHTED > QUIGHT

QUIGHTING > QUIGHT

QUIGHTS > QUIGHT

QUILL *n* pen made from the feather of a bird's wing or tail ▷ *vb* wind (thread, yarn, etc) onto a spool or bobbin

QUILLAI *another name for* > SOAPBARK

QUILLAIA *same as* > QUILLAI

QUILLAIAS > QUILLAIA

QUILLAIS > QUILLAI

QUILLAJA *same as* > QUILLAI

QUILLAJAS > QUILLAJA

QUILLBACK *n* freshwater fish

QUILLED > QUILL

QUILLET *n* quibble or subtlety

QUILLETS > QUILLET

QUILLING *n* decorative craftwork in which material such as glass, fabric or paper is formed into small bands or rolls that form the basis of a design

QUILLINGS > QUILLING

QUILLMAN *n* clerk

QUILLMEN > QUILLMAN

QUILLON *n* either half of the extended crosspiece of a sword or dagger

QUILLONS > QUILLON

QUILLS > QUILL

QUILLWORK *n* embroidery using porcupine quills

QUILLWORT *n* aquatic tracheophyte plant with quill-like leaves

QUILT *n* padded covering for a bed ▷ *vb* stitch together two layers of (fabric) with padding between them

QUILTED > QUILT

QUILTER > QUILT

QUILTERS > QUILT

QUILTING *n* material used for making a quilt

QUILTINGS > QUILTING

QUILTS > QUILT

QUIM *n* taboo word for the female genitals

QUIMS > QUIM

QUIN *same as* > QUINT

QUINA *n* quinine

QUINARIES > QUINARY

QUINARY *adj* consisting of fives or by fives ▷ *n* set of five

QUINAS > QUINA

QUINATE *adj* arranged in or composed of five parts

QUINCE *n* acid-tasting pear-shaped fruit

QUINCES > QUINCE

QUINCHE *vb* move

QUINCHED > QUINCHE

QUINCHES > QUINCHE

QUINCHING > QUINCHE

QUINCUNX *n* group of five objects arranged in the shape of a rectangle with one at each corner and the fifth in the centre

QUINE *variant of* > QUEAN

QUINELA *same as* > QUINELLA

QUINELAS > QUINELA

QUINELLA *n* form of betting on a horse race in which the punter bets on selecting the first and second place-winners in any order

QUINELLAS > QUINELLA

QUINES > QUINE

QUINIC *as in* *quinic acid* white crystalline soluble optically active carboxylic acid

QUINIDINE *n* crystalline alkaloid drug

QUINIE *n* girl

QUINIELA *same as* > QUINELLA

QUINIELAS > QUINIELA

QUINIES > QUINIE

QUININ *same as* > QUININE

QUININA *same as* > QUININE

QUININAS > QUININA

QUININE *n* bitter drug used as a tonic and formerly to treat malaria

QUININES > QUININE

QUININS > QUININ

QUINNAT *n* Pacific salmon

QUINNATS > QUINNAT

QUINO *same as* > KENO

QUINOA *n* type of grain high in nutrients

QUINOAS > QUINOA

QUINOID *same as* > QUINONOID

QUINOIDAL > QUINOID

QUINOIDS > QUINOID

QUINOL *n* white crystalline soluble phenol used as a photographic developer

QUINOLIN *same as* > QUINOLINE

QUINOLINE *n* oily colourless insoluble basic heterocyclic compound

QUINOLINS > QUINOLIN

QUINOLONE *n* any of a group of synthetic antibiotics

QUINOLS > QUINOL

QUINONE *n* yellow crystalline water-soluble unsaturated ketone

QUINONES > QUINONE

QUINONOID *adj* of, resembling, or derived from quinone

QUINOS > QUINO

QUINQUINA *same as* > QUININE

QUINS > QUIN

QUINSIED > QUINSY

QUINSIES > QUINSY

QUINSY *n* inflammation of the throat or tonsils

QUINT *same as* > QUIN

QUINTA *n* Portuguese vineyard where grapes for wine or port are grown

QUINTAIN *n* post or target set up for tilting exercises for mounted knights or foot soldiers

QUINTAINS > QUINTAIN

QUINTAL *n* unit of weight equal to (esp in Britain) 112 pounds (50.85 kg) or (esp in US) 100 pounds (45.36 kg)

QUINTALS > QUINTAL

QUINTAN *adj* (of a fever) occurring every fourth day ▷ *n* quintan fever

QUINTANS > QUINTAN

QUINTAR *n* Albanian unit of currency

QUINTARS > QUINTAR

QUINTAS > QUINTA

QUINTE *n* fifth of eight basic positions from which a parry or attack can be made in fencing

QUINTES > QUINTE

QUINTET *n* group of five performers

QUINTETS > QUINTET

QUINTETT *same as* > QUINTET

QUINTETTE *same as* > QUINTET

QUINTETTI > QUINTETTO

QUINTETTO *same as* > QUINTET

QUINTETTS > QUINTETT

QUINTIC *adj* of or relating to the fifth degree ▷ *n* mathematical function

QUINTICS > QUINTIC

QUINTILE *n* aspect of 72° between two heavenly bodies

QUINTILES > QUINTILE

QUINTIN *same as* > QUINTAIN

QUINTINS > QUINTIN

QUINTROON *n* person with one Black great-great-grandparent

QUINTS > QUINT

QUINTUPLE *vb* multiply by five ▷ *adj* five times as much or as many ▷ *n* quantity or number five times as great as another

QUINTUPLY > QUINTUPLE

QUINZE *n* card game with rules similar to those of vingt-et-un, except that the score aimed at is 15 rather than 21

QUINZES > QUINZE

QUIP *n* witty saying ▷ *vb* make a quip

QUIPO *same as* > QUIPU

QUIPOS > QUIPO

QUIPPED > QUIP

QUIPPER > QUIP

QUIPPERS > QUIP

QUIPPIER > QUIP

QUIPPIEST > QUIP

QUIPPING > QUIP

QUIPPISH > QUIP

QUIPPU *same as* > QUIPU

QUIPPUS > QUIPPU

QUIPPY > QUIP

QUIPS > QUIP

QUIPSTER *n* person inclined to make sarcastic or witty remarks

QUIPSTERS > QUIPSTER

QUIPU *n* device of the Incas of Peru used to record information, consisting of an arrangement of variously coloured and knotted cords attached to a base cord

QUIPUS > QUIPU

QUIRE *n* set of 24 or 25 sheets of paper ▷ *vb* arrange in quires

QUIRED > QUIRE

QUIRES > QUIRE

QUIRING > QUIRE

QUIRISTER *same as* > CHORISTER

QUIRK *n* peculiarity of character ▷ *vb* quip

QUIRKED > QUIRK

QUIRKIER > QUIRK

QUIRKIEST > QUIRK

QUIRKILY > QUIRK

QUIRKING > QUIRK

QUIRKISH > QUIRK

QUIRKS > QUIRK

QUIRKY > QUIRK

QUIRT *n* whip with a leather thong at one end ▷ *vb* strike with a quirt

QUIRTED > QUIRT

QUIRTING > QUIRT

QUIRTS > QUIRT

QUISLING *n* traitor who aids an occupying enemy force

QUISLINGS > QUISLING

QUIST *n* wood pigeon

QUISTS > QUIST

QUIT *vb* stop (doing something) ▷ *adj* free (from)

QUITCH *vb* move

QUITCHED > QUITCH

QUITCHES > QUITCH

QUITCHING > QUITCH

QUITCLAIM *n* formal renunciation of any claim against a person or of a right to land ▷ *vb* renounce (a claim) formally

QUITE *archaic form of* > QUIT

QUITED > QUITE

QUITES > QUITE

QUITING > QUITE

QUITRENT *n* (formerly) a rent payable by a freeholder or copyholder to his lord that released him from liability to perform services

QUITRENTS > QUITRENT

QUITS > QUIT

QUITTAL *n* repayment of an action with a similar action

QUITTALS > QUITTAL

QUITTANCE *n* release from debt or other obligation

QUITTED > QUIT

QUITTER *n* person who lacks perseverance

QUITTERS > QUITTER

QUITTING > QUIT

QUITTOR *n* infection of the cartilages on the side of a horse's foot, characterized by inflammation and the formation of pus

QUITTORS > QUITTOR

QUIVER *vb* shake with a tremulous movement ▷ *n* shaking or trembling

QUIVERED > QUIVER

QUIVERER > QUIVER

QUIVERERS > QUIVER

QUIVERFUL *n* amount that a quiver can hold

QUIVERIER > QUIVER

QUIVERING > QUIVER

QUIVERISH > QUIVER

QUIVERS > QUIVER

QUIVERY > QUIVER

QUIXOTE *n* impractical idealist

QUIXOTES > QUIXOTE

QUIXOTIC *adj* romantic and unrealistic

QUIXOTISM > QUIXOTIC

QUIXOTRY > QUIXOTE

QUIZ *n* entertainment in which the knowledge of the players is tested by a series of questions ▷ *vb* investigate by close questioning

QUIZZED > QUIZ

QUIZZER > QUIZ

QUIZZERS > QUIZ

QUIZZERY > QUIZ

QUIZZES > QUIZ

QUIZZICAL *adj* questioning and mocking

QUIZZIFY > QUIZ

QUIZZING > QUIZ

QUIZZINGS > QUIZ

QUOAD *adv* as far as

QUOD *n* jail ▷ *vb* say

QUODDED > QUOD

QUODDING > QUOD

QUODLIBET *n* light piece of music based on two or more popular tunes

QUODLIN *n* cooking apple

QUODLINS > QUODLIN

QUODS > QUOD

QUOHOG *n* edible clam

QUOHOGS > QUOHOG

QUOIF *vb* arrange (the hair)

QUOIFED > QUOIF

QUOIFING > QUOIF

QUOIFS > QUOIF

QUOIN *n* external corner of a building ▷ *vb* wedge

QUOINED > QUOIN

QUOINING > QUOIN

QUOINS > QUOIN

QUOIST *n* wood pigeon

QUOISTS > QUOIST

QUOIT *n* large ring used in the game of quoits ▷ *vb* throw as a quoit

QUOITED > QUOIT

QUOITER > QUOIT

QUOITERS > QUOIT

QUOITING > QUOIT

QUOITS *n* game in which quoits are tossed at a stake in the ground in attempts to encircle it

QUOKKA *n* small Australian wallaby

QUOKKAS > QUOKKA

QUOLL *n* Australian catlike carnivorous marsupial

QUOLLS > QUOLL

QUOMODO *n* manner

QUOMODOS > QUOMODO

QUONDAM *adj* of an earlier time

QUONK *vb* make an accidental noise while broadcasting

QUONKED > QUONK

QUONKING > QUONK

QUONKS > QUONK

QUOOKE *archaic past participle of* > QUAKE

QUOP *vb* pulsate or throb

QUOPPED > QUOP

QUOPPING > QUOP

QUOPS > QUOP

QUORATE *adj* having or being a quorum

QUORUM *n* minimum number of people required to be present at a meeting before any transactions can take place

QUORUMS > QUORUM

QUOTA *n* share that is due from, due to, or allocated to a group or person

QUOTABLE *adj* apt or suitable for quotation

QUOTABLY > QUOTABLE

QUOTAS > QUOTA

QUOTATION *n* written or spoken passage repeated exactly in a later work, speech, or conversation

QUOTATIVE *n* word indicating quotation

QUOTE *vb* repeat (words) exactly from (an earlier work, speech, or conversation) ▷ *n* quotation ▷ *interj* expression used parenthetically to indicate that the words that follow it form a quotation

QUOTED > QUOTE

QUOTER > QUOTE

QUOTERS > QUOTE

QUOTES > QUOTE

QUOTH *vb* said

QUOTHA *interj* expression of mild sarcasm, used in picking up a word or phrase used by someone else

QUOTIDIAN *adj* daily ▷ *n* malarial fever characterized by attacks that recur daily

QUOTIENT *n* result of the division of one number or quantity by another

QUOTIENTS > QUOTIENT

QUOTING > QUOTE

QUOTITION *n* division by repeated subtraction

QUOTUM *same as* > QUOTA

QUOTUMS > QUOTUM

QURSH *same as* > QURUSH

QURSHES > QURUSH

QURUSH *n* Saudi Arabian currency unit

QURUSHES > QURUSH

QUYTE *same as* > QUIT

QUYTED > QUYTE

QUYTES > QUYTE

QUYTING > QUYTE

QWERTIES > QWERTY

QWERTY *n* standard English-language typewriter or computer keyboard

QWERTYS > QWERTY

q

Rr

RABANNA *n* Madagascan woven raffia

RABANNAS > RABANNA

RABAT *vb* rotate so that the plane rotated coincides with another

RABATINE *n* type of collar

RABATINES > RABATINE

RABATMENT > RABAT

RABATO *n* wired or starched collar, often of intricate lace, that stood up at the back and sides: worn in the 17th century

RABATOES > RABATO

RABATOS > RABATO

RABATS > RABAT

RABATTE *same as* > RABAT

RABATTED > RABAT

RABATTES > RABATTE

RABATTING > RABAT

RABBET *n* recess, groove, or step, usually of rectangular section, cut into a surface or along the edge of a piece of timber to receive a mating piece ▷ *vb* cut or form a rabbet in (timber)

RABBETED > RABBET

RABBETING > RABBET

RABBETS > RABBET

RABBI *n* Jewish spiritual leader

RABBIES > RABBI

RABBIN *same as* > RABBI

RABBINATE *n* position, function, or tenure of office of a rabbi

RABBINIC *adj* of or relating to the rabbis, their teachings, writings, views, language, etc

RABBINICS *n* study of rabbinic literature of the post-Talmudic period

RABBINISM *n* teachings and traditions of the rabbis of the Talmudic period

RABBINIST > RABBINISM

RABBINITE > RABBINISM

RABBINS > RABBIN

RABBIS > RABBI

RABBIT *n* small burrowing mammal with long ears ▷ *vb* talk too much

RABBITED > RABBIT

RABBITER *n* person who traps and sells rabbits

RABBITERS > RABBITER

RABBITING *n* activity of hunting rabbits

RABBITO *same as* > RABBITOH

RABBITOH *n* (formerly) an itinerant seller of rabbits for eating

RABBITOHS > RABBITOH

RABBITOS > RABBITO

RABBITRY *n* place where tame rabbits are kept and bred

RABBITS > RABBIT

RABBITY *adj* rabbitlike

RABBLE *n* disorderly crowd of noisy people ▷ *vb* stir, mix, or skim (the molten charge) in a roasting furnace

RABBLED > RABBLE

RABBLER *n* iron tool or device for stirring, mixing, or skimming a molten charge in a roasting furnace

RABBLERS > RABBLER

RABBLES > RABBLE

RABBLING > RABBLE

RABBLINGS > RABBLE

RABBONI *n* very respectful Jewish title or form of address meaning my great master

RABBONIS > RABBONI

RABI *n* (in Pakistan, India, etc) a crop that is harvested at the end of winter

RABIC > RABIES

RABID *adj* fanatical

RABIDER > RABID

RABIDEST > RABID

RABIDITY > RABID

RABIDLY > RABID

RABIDNESS > RABID

RABIES *n* usu fatal viral disease transmitted by dogs and certain other animals

RABIETIC > RABIES

RABIS > RABI

RACA *adj* biblical word meaning worthless or empty-headed

RACAHOUT *n* acorn flour or drink made from it

RACAHOUTS > RACAHOUT

RACCAHOUT *same as* > RACAHOUT

RACCOON *n* small N American mammal with a long striped tail

RACCOONS > RACCOON

RACE *n* contest of speed ▷ *vb* compete with in a race

RACECARD *n* card or booklet at a race meeting with the times of the races, names of the runners, etc, printed on it

RACECARDS > RACECARD

RACED > RACE

RACEGOER *n* one who attends a race meeting, esp a habitual frequenter of race meetings

RACEGOERS > RACEGOER

RACEGOING > RACEGOER

RACEHORSE *n* horse specially bred for racing

RACEMATE *n* racemic compound

RACEMATES > RACEMATE

RACEME *n* cluster of flowers along a central stem, as in the foxglove

RACEMED *adj* with or in racemes

RACEMES > RACEME

RACEMIC *adj* of, concerned with, or being a mixture of equal amounts of enantiomers and consequently having no optical activity

RACEMISE *same as* > RACEMIZE

RACEMISED > RACEMISE

RACEMISES > RACEMISE

RACEMISM > RACEMIC

RACEMISMS > RACEMIC

RACEMIZE *vb* change or cause to change into a racemic mixture

RACEMIZED > RACEMIZE

RACEMIZES > RACEMIZE

RACEMOID *adj* resembling a raceme

RACEMOSE *adj* being or resembling a raceme

RACEMOUS *same as* > RACEMOSE

RACEPATH *same*

RACAHOUTS > RACAHOUT

RACAHOUT *same as* > RACAHOUT

as > RACETRACK

RACEPATHS > RACEPATH

RACER *n* person, animal, or machine that races

RACERS > RACER

RACES > RACE

RACETRACK *n* track for racing

RACEWALK *vb* race by walking fast rather than running

RACEWALKS > RACEWALK

RACEWAY *n* racetrack, esp one for banger racing

RACEWAYS > RACEWAY

RACH *n* scent hound

RACHE *same as* > RACH

RACHES > RACH

RACHET *same as* > RATCHET

RACHETED > RACHET

RACHETING > RACHET

RACHETS > RACHET

RACHIAL > RACHIS

RACHIDES > RACHIS

RACHIDIAL > RACHIS

RACHIDIAN > RACHIS

RACHILLA *n* (in grasses) the short stem of a spikelet that bears the florets

RACHILLAE > RACHILLA

RACHILLAS > RACHILLA

RACHIS *n* main axis or stem of an inflorescence or compound leaf

RACHISES > RACHIS

RACHITIC > RACHITIS

RACHITIS *another name for* > RICKETS

RACIAL *adj* relating to the division of the human species into races

RACIALISE *same as* > RACIALIZE

RACIALISM *same as* > RACISM

RACIALIST > RACIALISM

RACIALIZE *vb* render racial in tone or content

RACIALLY > RACIAL

RACIATION *n* evolutionary development of races

RACIER > RACY

RACIEST > RACY

RACILY > RACY

RACINESS > RACY

RACING *adj* denoting or associated with horse

races ▷ n practice of engaging horses (or sometimes greyhounds) in contests of speed

RACINGS > RACING

RACISM n hostile attitude or behaviour to members of other races, based on a belief in the innate superiority of one's own race

RACISMS > RACISM

RACIST > RACISM

RACISTS > RACISM

RACK n framework for holding particular articles, such as coats or luggage ▷ vb cause great suffering to

RACKED > RACK

RACKER > RACK

RACKERS > RACK

RACKET n noisy disturbance ▷ vb make a commotion

RACKETED > RACKET

RACKETEER n person making illegal profits ▷ vb operate a racket

RACKETER n someone making a racket

RACKETERS > RACKETER

RACKETIER > RACKETY

RACKETING > RACKET

RACKETRY n noise and commotion

RACKETS n ball game played in a paved walled court

RACKETT n early double-reeded wind instrument

RACKETTS > RACKETT

RACKETY adj involving noise, commotion and excitement

RACKFUL > RACK

RACKFULS > RACK

RACKING > RACK

RACKINGLY > RACK

RACKINGS > RACK

RACKLE adj dialect word meaning rash

RACKS > RACK

RACKWORK n mechanism with a rack and pinion

RACKWORKS > RACKWORK

RACLETTE n Swiss dish of melted cheese served on boiled potatoes

RACLETTES > RACLETTE

RACLOIR n scraper

RACLOIRS > RACLOIR

RACON n radar beacon

RACONS > RACON

RACONTEUR n skilled storyteller

RACOON same as > RACCOON

RACOONS > RACOON

RACQUET same as > RACKET

RACQUETED > RACQUET

RACQUETS > RACQUET

RACY adj slightly shocking

RAD n former unit of absorbed ionizing radiation dose equivalent to an energy absorption per unit mass of 0.01 joule per kilogram of irradiated material. 1 rad is equivalent

to 0.01 gray ▷ vb fear ▷ adj slang term for great

RADAR n device for tracking distant objects by bouncing high-frequency radio pulses off them

RADARS > RADAR

RADDED > RAD

RADDER > RAD

RADDEST > RAD

RADDING > RAD

RADDLE same as > RUDDLE

RADDLED adj (of a person) unkempt or run-down in appearance

RADDLEMAN same as > RUDDLEMAN

RADDLEMEN > RADDLEMAN

RADDLES > RADDLE

RADDLING > RADDLE

RADDOCKE same as > RUDDOCK

RADDOCKES > RADDOCKE

RADE (in Scots dialect) past tense of > RIDE

RADGE adj angry or uncontrollable ▷ n person acting in such a way

RADGER > RADGE

RADGES > RADGE

RADGEST > RADGE

RADIABLE adj able to be x-rayed

RADIAL adj spreading out from a common central point ▷ n radial-ply tyre

RADIALE n bone in the wrist

RADIALIA > RADIALE

RADIALISE same as > RADIALIZE

RADIALITY > RADIAL

RADIALIZE vb arrange in a pattern of radii

RADIALLY > RADIAL

RADIALS > RADIAL

RADIAN n unit for measuring angles, equal to 57.296°

RADIANCE n quality or state of being radiant

RADIANCES > RADIANCE

RADIANCY same as > RADIANCE

RADIANS > RADIAN

RADIANT adj looking happy ▷ n point or object that emits radiation, esp the part of a heater that gives out heat

RADIANTLY > RADIANT

RADIANTS > RADIANT

RADIATA as in radiata pine type of pine tree

RADIATAS > RADIATA

RADIATE vb spread out from a centre ▷ adj having rays or a radial structure

RADIATED > RADIATE

RADIATELY > RADIATE

RADIATES > RADIATE

RADIATING > RADIATE

RADIATION n transmission of energy from one body to another

RADIATIVE adj emitting or causing the emission of radiation

RADIATOR n arrangement of pipes containing hot water or steam to heat a room

RADIATORS > RADIATOR

RADIATORY same as > RADIATIVE

RADICAL adj fundamental ▷ n person advocating fundamental (political) change

RADICALLY adv thoroughly

RADICALS > RADICAL

RADICAND n number or quantity from which a root is to be extracted, usually preceded by a radical sign

RADICANDS > RADICAND

RADICANT adj forming roots from the stem

RADICATE vb root or cause to take root

RADICATED > RADICATE

RADICATES > RADICATE

RADICCHIO n Italian variety of chicory, with purple leaves streaked with white that are eaten raw in salads

RADICEL n very small root

RADICELS > RADICEL

RADICES > RADIX

RADICLE n small or developing root

RADICLES > RADICLE

RADICULAR adj root-related

RADICULE same as > RADICLE

RADICULES > RADICULE

RADII > RADIUS

RADIO n use of electromagnetic waves for broadcasting, communication, etc ▷ vb transmit (a message) by radio ▷ adj of, relating to, or using radio

RADIOED > RADIO

RADIOGOLD n radioactive isotope of gold

RADIOGRAM n image produced on a specially sensitized photographic film or plate by radiation, usually by X-rays or gamma rays

RADIOING > RADIO

RADIOLOGY n science of using x-rays in medicine

RADIOMAN n radio operator

RADIOMEN > RADIOMAN

RADIONICS n dowsing technique using a pendulum to detect the energy fields that are emitted by all forms of matter

RADIOS > RADIO

RADIOTHON n lengthy radio programme to raise charity funds, etc

RADISH n small hot-flavoured root vegetable eaten raw in salads

RADISHES > RADISH

RADIUM n radioactive metallic element

RADIUMS > RADIUM

RADIUS n (length of) a straight line from the centre to the circumference of a circle

RADIUSES > RADIUS

RADIX n any number that is the base of a number system or of a system of logarithms

RADIXES > RADIX

RADOME n protective housing for a radar antenna made from a material that is transparent to radio waves

RADOMES > RADOME

RADON n radioactive gaseous element

RADONS > RADON

RADS > RAD

RADULA n horny tooth-bearing strip on the tongue of molluscs that is used for rasping food

RADULAE > RADULA

RADULAR > RADULA

RADULAS > RADULA

RADULATE > RADULA

RADWASTE n radioactive wast

RADWASTES > RADWASTE

RAFALE n burst of artillery fire

RAFALES > RAFALE

RAFF n rubbish

RAFFIA n prepared palm fibre for weaving mats etc

RAFFIAS > RAFFIA

RAFFINATE n liquid left after a solute has been extracted by solvent extraction

RAFFINOSE n trisaccharide of fructose, glucose, and galactose that occurs in sugar beet, cotton seed, certain cereals, etc

RAFFISH adj slightly disreputable

RAFFISHLY > RAFFISH

RAFFLE n lottery with goods as prizes ▷ vb offer as a prize in a raffle

RAFFLED > RAFFLE

RAFFLER > RAFFLE

RAFFLERS > RAFFLE

RAFFLES > RAFFLE

RAFFLESIA n any of various tropical Asian parasitic leafless plants whose flowers smell of putrid meat and are pollinated by carrion flies

RAFFLING > RAFFLE

RAFFS > RAFF

RAFT n floating platform of logs, planks, etc ▷ vb convey on or travel by raft, or make a raft from

RAFTED > RAFT

RAFTER n one of the main beams of a roof ▷ vb to fit with rafters

RAFTERED > RAFTER

RAFTERING > RAFTER

RAFTERS > RAFTER

RAFTING > RAFT

RAFTINGS > RAFT

RAFTMAN *same as* > RAFTSMAN

RAFTMEN > RAFTMAN

RAFTS > RAFT

RAFTSMAN *n* someone who does rafting

RAFTSMEN > RAFTSMAN

RAG *n* fragment of cloth ▷ *vb* tease ▷ *adj* (in British universities and colleges) of various events organized to raise money for charity

RAGA *n* any of several conventional patterns of melody and rhythm that form the basis for freely interpreted compositions. Each pattern is associated with different aspects of religious devotion

RAGAS > RAGA

RAGBAG *n* confused assortment, jumble

RAGBAGS > RAGBAG

RAGBOLT *n* bolt that has angled projections on it to prevent it working loose once it has been driven home

RAGBOLTS > RAGBOLT

RAGDE *archaic past form of* > RAGE

RAGE *n* violent anger or passion ▷ *vb* speak or act with fury

RAGED > RAGE

RAGEE *same as* > RAGI

RAGEES > RAGEE

RAGEFUL > RAGE

RAGER > RAGE

RAGERS > RAGE

RAGES > RAGE

RAGG *same as* > RAGSTONE

RAGGA *n* dance-oriented style of reggae

RAGGAS > RAGGA

RAGGED > RAG

RAGGEDER > RAG

RAGGEDEST > RAG

RAGGEDIER > RAGGEDY

RAGGEDLY > RAG

RAGGEDY *adj* somewhat ragged

RAGGEE *same as* > RAGI

RAGGEES > RAGGEE

RAGGERIES > RAGGERY

RAGGERY *n* rags

RAGGIER > RAGGY

RAGGIES > RAGGY

RAGGIEST > RAGGY

RAGGING > RAG

RAGGINGS > RAG

RAGGLE *n* thin groove cut in stone or brickwork, esp to hold the edge of a roof ▷ *vb* cut a raggle in

RAGGLED > RAGGLE

RAGGLES > RAGGLE

RAGGLING > RAGGLE

RAGGS > RAGG

RAGGY *adj* raglike ▷ *n* cereal grass cultivated in Africa and Asia for its edible grain

RAGHEAD *n* offensive term for an Arab person

RAGHEADS > RAGHEAD

RAGI *n* cereal grass cultivated in Africa and Asia for its edible grain

RAGING > RAGE

RAGINGLY > RAGE

RAGINGS > RAGE

RAGINI *n* Indian musical form related to a raga

RAGINIS > RAGINI

RAGIS > RAGI

RAGLAN *adj* (of a sleeve) joined to a garment by diagonal seams from the neck to the underarm ▷ *n* coat with sleeves that continue to the collar instead of having armhole seams

RAGLANS > RAGLAN

RAGMAN *n* rag-and-bone man

RAGMANS > RAGMAN

RAGMEN > RAGMAN

RAGMENT *n* statute, roll, or list

RAGMENTS > RAGMENT

RAGOUT *n* richly seasoned stew of meat and vegetables ▷ *vb* make into a ragout

RAGOUTED > RAGOUT

RAGOUTING > RAGOUT

RAGOUTS > RAGOUT

RAGPICKER *n* rag-and-bone man

RAGS > RAG

RAGSTONE *n* hard sandstone or limestone, esp when used for building

RAGSTONES > RAGSTONE

RAGTAG *n* disparaging term for common people

RAGTAGS > RAGTAG

RAGTIME *n* style of jazz piano music

RAGTIMER > RAGTIME

RAGTIMERS > RAGTIME

RAGTIMES > RAGTIME

RAGTOP *n* informal word for a car with a folding or removable roof

RAGTOPS > RAGTOP

RAGULED *same as* > RAGULY

RAGULY *adj* (in heraldry) having toothlike or stublike projections

RAGWEED *n* any of several plants regarded as weeds, some of which produce a large amount of hay-fever-causing pollen

RAGWEEDS > RAGWEED

RAGWHEEL *n* toothed wheel

RAGWHEELS > RAGWHEEL

RAGWORK *n* weaving or needlework using rags

RAGWORKS > RAGWORK

RAGWORM *n* type of worm that lives chiefly in burrows in sand or mud

RAGWORMS > RAGWORM

RAGWORT *n* plant with ragged leaves and yellow flowers

RAGWORTS > RAGWORT

RAH *informal US word for* > CHEER

RAHED > RAH

RAHING > RAH

RAHS > RAH

RAHUI *n* Māori prohibition

RAHUIS > RAHUI

RAI *n* type of Algerian popular music based on traditional Algerian music influenced by modern Western pop

RAIA *same as* > RAYAH

RAIAS > RAIA

RAID *n* sudden surprise attack or search ▷ *vb* make a raid on

RAIDED > RAID

RAIDER > RAID

RAIDERS > RAID

RAIDING > RAID

RAIDINGS > RAID

RAIDS > RAID

RAIK *n* wander ▷ *vb* wander

RAIKED > RAIK

RAIKING > RAIK

RAIKS > RAIK

RAIL *n* horizontal bar, esp as part of a fence or track ▷ *vb* complain bitterly or loudly

RAILBED *n* ballast layer supporting the sleepers of a railway track

RAILBEDS > RAILBED

RAILBIRD *n* racing aficionado

RAILBIRDS > RAILBIRD

RAILBUS *n* buslike vehicle for use on railway lines

RAILBUSES > RAILBUS

RAILCAR *n* passenger-carrying railway vehicle consisting of a single coach with its own power unit

RAILCARD *n* card which pensioners, young people, etc can buy, entitling them to cheaper rail travel

RAILCARDS > RAILCARD

RAILCARS > RAILCAR

RAILE *archaic spelling of* > RAIL

RAILED > RAIL

RAILER > RAIL

RAILERS > RAIL

RAILES > RAILE

RAILHEAD *n* terminal of a railway

RAILHEADS > RAILHEAD

RAILING *n* fence made of rails supported by posts

RAILINGLY > RAIL

RAILINGS > RAILING

RAILLERY *n* teasing or joking

RAILLESS > RAIL

RAILLIES > RAILLY

RAILLY *old word for* > MOCK

RAILMAN *n* railway employee

RAILMEN > RAILMAN

RAILROAD *same as* > RAILWAY

RAILROADS > RAILROAD

RAILS > RAIL

RAILWAY *n* track of iron rails on which trains run

RAILWAYS > RAILWAY

RAILWOMAN *n* female railway employee

RAILWOMEN > RAILWOMAN

RAIMENT *n* clothing

RAIMENTS > RAIMENT

RAIN *n* water falling in drops from the clouds ▷ *vb* fall or pour down as rain

RAINBAND *n* dark band in the solar spectrum caused by water in the atmosphere

RAINBANDS > RAINBAND

RAINBIRD *n* a bird whose call is believed to be a sign of impending rain

RAINBIRDS > RAINBIRD

RAINBOW *n* arch of colours in the sky

RAINBOWED *adj* resembling or involving a rainbow

RAINBOWS > RAINBOW

RAINBOWY > RAINBOW

RAINCHECK *n* ticket stub allowing readmission to a game on a later date should bad weather prevent play

RAINCOAT *n* water-resistant overcoat

RAINCOATS > RAINCOAT

RAINDATE *n* US term for an alternative date in case of rain

RAINDATES > RAINDATE

RAINDROP *n* water droplet that falls from the sky when it is raining

RAINDROPS > RAINDROP

RAINE *archaic spelling of* > REIGN

RAINED > RAIN

RAINES > RAINE

RAINFALL *n* amount of rain

RAINFALLS > RAINFALL

RAINIER > RAINY

RAINIEST > RAINY

RAINILY > RAINY

RAININESS > RAINY

RAINING > RAIN

RAINLESS > RAIN

RAINMAKER *n* (among American Indians) a professional practitioner of ritual incantations or other actions intended to cause rain to fall

RAINOUT *n* radioactive fallout or atmospheric pollution carried to the earth by rain

RAINOUTS > RAINOUT

RAINPROOF *adj* (of garments, materials, buildings, etc) impermeable to rainwater ▷ *vb* make rainproof

RAINS > RAIN

RAINSPOUT *n* waterspout

RAINSTORM *n* storm with heavy rain

RAINTIGHT *same as* > RAINPROOF

RAINWASH *n* action of rain ▷ *vb* erode or wet as a result of rain

RAINWATER *n* water from

rain
RAINWEAR *n* protective garments intended for use in wet weather
RAINWEARS > RAINWEAR
RAINY *adj* characterized by a large rainfall
RAIRD *same as* > REIRD
RAIRDS > RAIRD
RAIS > RAI
RAISABLE > RAISE
RAISE *vb* lift up ▷ *n* increase in pay
RAISEABLE > RAISE
RAISED > RAISE
RAISER > RAISE
RAISERS > RAISE
RAISES > RAISE
RAISIN *n* dried grape
RAISING *n* rule that moves a constituent from an embedded clause into the main clause
RAISINGS > RAISING
RAISINS > RAISIN
RAISINY > RAISIN
RAISONNE *adj* carefully thought out
RAIT *same as* > RET
RAITA *n* Indian dish of chopped cucumber, mint, etc, in yogurt, served with curries
RAITAS > RAITA
RAITED > RAIT
RAITING > RAIT
RAITS > RAIT
RAIYAT *same as* > RYOT
RAIYATS > RAIYAT
RAJ *n* (in India) government
RAJA *same as* > RAJAH
RAJAH *n* (in India, formerly) a ruler or landlord: sometimes used as a form of address or as a title preceding a name
RAJAHS > RAJAH
RAJAHSHIP > RAJAH
RAJAS > RAJA
RAJASHIP > RAJA
RAJASHIPS > RAJA
RAJES > RAJ
RAKE *n* tool with a long handle and a crosspiece with teeth, used for smoothing earth or gathering leaves, hay, etc ▷ *vb* gather or smooth with a rake
RAKED > RAKE
RAKEE *same as* > RAKI
RAKEES > RAKEE
RAKEHELL *n* dissolute man ▷ *adj* profligate
RAKEHELLS > RAKEHELL
RAKEHELLY *adj* profligate
RAKEOFF *n* share of profits, esp one that is illegal or given as a bribe
RAKEOFFS > RAKEOFF
RAKER *n* person who rakes
RAKERIES > RAKERY
RAKERS > RAKER
RAKERY *n* rakish behaviour
RAKES > RAKE
RAKESHAME *n* old word for someone shamefully

dissolute
RAKI *n* strong spirit distilled in Turkey, the former Yugoslavia, etc, from grain, usually flavoured with aniseed or other aromatics
RAKING *n* offence committed when a player deliberately scrapes an opponent's leg, arm, etc with the studs of his or her boots
RAKINGS > RAKING
RAKIS > RAKI
RAKISH *adj* dashing or jaunty
RAKISHLY > RAKISH
RAKSHAS *same as* > RAKSHASA
RAKSHASA *n* Hindu demon
RAKSHASAS > RAKSHASA
RAKSHASES > RAKSHAS
RAKU *n* type of Japanese pottery
RAKUS > RAKU
RALE *n* abnormal coarse crackling sound heard on auscultation of the chest, usually caused by the accumulation of fluid in the lungs
RALES > RALE
RALLIED > RALLY
RALLIER > RALLY
RALLIERS > RALLY
RALLIES > RALLY
RALLIFORM *adj* of rail family of birds
RALLINE *adj* of, relating to, or belonging to the *Rallidae*, a family of birds that includes the rails, crakes, and coots
RALLY *n* large gathering of people for a meeting ▷ *vb* bring or come together after dispersal or for a common cause
RALLYE *US variant of* > RALLY
RALLYES > RALLYE
RALLYING > RALLY
RALLYINGS > RALLY
RALLYIST > RALLY
RALLYISTS > RALLY
RALPH *vb* slang word meaning vomit
RALPHED > RALPH
RALPHING > RALPH
RALPHS > RALPH
RAM *n* male sheep ▷ *vb* strike against with force
RAMADA *n* outdoor eating area with roof but open sides
RAMADAS > RAMADA
RAMAKIN *same as* > RAMEKIN
RAMAKINS > RAMAKIN
RAMAL *adj* relating to a branch or branches
RAMATE *adj* with branches
RAMBLA *n* dried-up (riverbed
RAMBLAS > RAMBLA
RAMBLE *vb* walk without a definite route ▷ *n* walk, esp in the country
RAMBLED > RAMBLE
RAMBLER *n* person who

rambles
RAMBLERS > RAMBLER
RAMBLES > RAMBLE
RAMBLING *adj* large and irregularly shaped ▷ *n* activity of going for long walks in the country
RAMBLINGS > RAMBLING
RAMBUTAN *n* SE Asian tree that has bright red edible fruit
RAMBUTANS > RAMBUTAN
RAMCAT *n* dialect word for a male cat
RAMCATS > RAMCAT
RAMEAL *same as* > RAMAL
RAMEE *same as* > RAMIE
RAMEES > RAMEE
RAMEKIN *n* small ovenproof dish for a single serving of food
RAMEKINS > RAMEKIN
RAMEN *n* Japanese dish consisting of a clear broth containing thin white noodles and sometimes vegetables, meat, etc
RAMENS > RAMEN
RAMENTA > RAMENTUM
RAMENTUM *n* any of the thin brown scales that cover the stems and leaves of young ferns
RAMEOUS *same as* > RAMAL
RAMEQUIN *same as* > RAMEKIN
RAMEQUINS > RAMEQUIN
RAMET *n* any of the individuals in a group of clones
RAMETS > RAMET
RAMI *same as* > RAMIE
RAMIE *n* woody Asian shrub with broad leaves and a stem that yields a flaxlike fibre
RAMIES > RAMIE
RAMIFIED > RAMIFY
RAMIFIES > RAMIFY
RAMIFORM *adj* having a branchlike shape
RAMIFY *vb* become complex
RAMIFYING > RAMIFY
RAMILIE *same as* > RAMILLIE
RAMILIES > RAMILIE
RAMILLIE *n* wig with a plait at the back fashionable in the 18th century
RAMILLIES > RAMILLIE
RAMIN *n* swamp-growing tree found in Malaysia and Indonesia
RAMINS > RAMIN
RAMIS > RAMI
RAMJET *n* type of jet engine in which fuel is burned in a duct using air compressed by the forward speed of the aircraft
RAMJETS > RAMJET
RAMMED > RAM
RAMMEL *n* discarded or waste matter
RAMMELS > RAMMEL
RAMMER > RAM
RAMMERS > RAM
RAMMIER > RAMMISH

RAMMIES > RAMMISH
RAMMIEST > RAMMISH
RAMMING > RAM
RAMMISH *adj* like a ram, esp in being lustful or foul-smelling
RAMMISHLY > RAMMISH
RAMMLE *n* collection of items saved in case they become useful
RAMMLES > RAMMLE
RAMMY *n* noisy disturbance or free-for-all ▷ *vb* make a rammy
RAMONA *same as* > SAGEBRUSH
RAMONAS > RAMONA
RAMOSE *adj* having branches
RAMOSELY > RAMOSE
RAMOSITY > RAMOSE
RAMOUS *same as* > RAMOSE
RAMOUSLY > RAMOSE
RAMP *n* slope joining two level surfaces ▷ *vb* (esp of animals) to rush around in a wild excited manner
RAMPAGE *vb* dash about violently
RAMPAGED > RAMPAGE
RAMPAGER > RAMPAGE
RAMPAGERS > RAMPAGE
RAMPAGES > RAMPAGE
RAMPAGING > RAMPAGE
RAMPANCY > RAMPANT
RAMPANT *adj* growing or spreading uncontrollably
RAMPANTLY > RAMPANT
RAMPART *n* mound or wall for defence ▷ *vb* provide with a rampart
RAMPARTED > RAMPART
RAMPARTS > RAMPART
RAMPAUGE *Scots variant of* > RAMPAGE
RAMPAUGED > RAMPAUGE
RAMPAUGES > RAMPAUGE
RAMPED > RAMP
RAMPER > RAMP
RAMPERS > RAMP
RAMPICK *same as* > RAMPIKE
RAMPICKED > RAMPICK
RAMPICKS > RAMPICK
RAMPIKE *n* US or dialect word for a dead tree
RAMPIKES > RAMPIKE
RAMPING > RAMP
RAMPINGS > RAMP
RAMPION *n* European and Asian plant that has clusters of bluish flowers and an edible white tuberous root used in salads
RAMPIONS > RAMPION
RAMPIRE *archaic variant of* > RAMPART
RAMPIRED > RAMPIRE
RAMPIRES > RAMPIRE
RAMPOLE *same as* > RAMPIKE
RAMPOLES > RAMPOLE
RAMPS > RAMP
RAMPSMAN *n* mugger
RAMPSMEN > RAMPSMAN
RAMROD *n* long thin rod used for cleaning the barrel of a gun or forcing gunpowder into an old-fashioned

gun ▷ *adj* (of someone's posture) very straight and upright ▷ *vb* drive

RAMRODDED > RAMROD

RAMRODS > RAMROD

RAMS > RAM

RAMSHORN as in *ramshorn snail* any of various freshwater snails

RAMSHORNS > RAMSHORN

RAMSON *n* type of garlic

RAMSONS > RAMSON

RAMSTAM *adv* headlong ▷ *adj* headlong

RAMTIL *n* African plant grown in India esp for its oil

RAMTILLA *same as* > RAMTIL

RAMTILLAS > RAMTILLA

RAMTILS > RAMTIL

RAMULAR *adj* relating to a branch or branches

RAMULI > RAMULUS

RAMULOSE *adj* (of the parts or organs of animals and plants) having many small branches

RAMULOUS *same as* > RAMULOSE

RAMULUS *n* small branch

RAMUS *n* barb of a bird's feather

RAN > RUN

RANA *n* genus of frogs

RANARIAN *adj* of or relating to frogs

RANARIUM *n* place for keeping frogs

RANARIUMS > RANARIUM

RANAS > RANA

RANCE *Scots word for* > PROP

RANCED > RANCE

RANCEL *vb* (in Shetland and Orkney) carry out a search

RANCELS > RANCEL

RANCES > RANCE

RANCH *n* large cattle farm in the American West ▷ *vb* run a ranch

RANCHED > RANCH

RANCHER *n* person who owns, manages, or works on a ranch

RANCHERIA *n* native American settlement or home of a rancher

RANCHERIE *n* (in British Columbia, Canada) a settlement of North American Indians, esp on a reserve

RANCHERO *another word for* > RANCHER

RANCHEROS > RANCHERO

RANCHERS > RANCHER

RANCHES > RANCH

RANCHING > RANCH

RANCHINGS > RANCH

RANCHLESS > RANCH

RANCHLIKE > RANCH

RANCHMAN *n* man who owns, manages, or works on a ranch

RANCHMEN > RANCHMAN

RANCHO *n* hut or group of huts for housing ranch workers

RANCHOS > RANCHO

RANCID *adj* (of butter, bacon, etc) stale and having an offensive smell

RANCIDER > RANCID

RANCIDEST > RANCID

RANCIDITY > RANCID

RANCIDLY > RANCID

RANCING > RANCE

RANCOR *same as* > RANCOUR

RANCORED > RANCOR

RANCOROUS > RANCOUR

RANCORS > RANCOR

RANCOUR *n* deep bitter hate

RANCOURED > RANCOUR

RANCOURS > RANCOUR

RAND *n* monetary unit of South Africa; leather strip on the heel of a shoe ▷ *vb* cut into rands

RANDAN *n* boat rowed by three people, in which the person in the middle uses two oars and the people fore and aft use one oar each

RANDANS > RANDAN

RANDED > RAND

RANDEM *adv* with three horses harnessed together as a team ▷ *n* carriage or team of horses so driven

RANDEMS > RANDEM

RANDIE *same as* > RANDY

RANDIER > RANDY

RANDIES > RANDY

RANDIEST > RANDY

RANDILY > RANDY

RANDINESS > RANDY

RANDING > RAND

RANDLORD *n* mining magnate during the 19th-century gold boom in Johannesburg

RANDLORDS > RANDLORD

RANDOM *adj* made or done by chance or without plan ▷ *n* (in mining) the course of a vein of ore

RANDOMISE *same as* > RANDOMIZE

RANDOMIZE *vb* set up (a selection process, sample, etc) in a deliberately random way in order to enhance the statistical validity of any results obtained

RANDOMLY > RANDOM

RANDOMS > RANDOM

RANDON *old variant of* > RANDOM

RANDONS > RANDON

RANDS > RAND

RANDY *adj* sexually aroused ▷ *n* rude or reckless person

RANEE *same as* > RANI

RANEES > RANEE

RANG > RING

RANGATIRA *n* Māori chief of either sex

RANGE *n* limits of effectiveness or variation ▷ *vb* vary between one point and another

RANGED > RANGE

RANGELAND *n* land that naturally produces forage

plants suitable for grazing but where rainfall is too low or erratic for growing crops

RANGER *n* official in charge of a nature reserve etc

RANGERS > RANGER

RANGES > RANGE

RANGI *n* sky

RANGIER > RANGY

RANGIEST > RANGY

RANGILY > RANGY

RANGINESS > RANGY

RANGING > RANGE

RANGINGS > RANGE

RANGIORA *n* evergreen New Zealand shrub or small tree with large ovate leaves and small greenish-white flowers

RANGIORAS > RANGIORA

RANGIS > RANGI

RANGOLI *n* traditional Indian ground decoration using coloured sand or chalks

RANGOLIS > RANGOLI

RANGY *adj* having long slender limbs

RANI *n* wife or widow of a rajah

RANID *n* frog

RANIDS > RANID

RANIFORM *n* froglike

RANINE *adj* relating to frogs

RANIS > RANI

RANK *n* relative place or position ▷ *vb* have a specific rank or position ▷ *adj* complete or absolute

RANKE *archaic variant of* > RANK

RANKED > RANK

RANKER *n* soldier in the ranks

RANKERS > RANKER

RANKES > RANKE

RANKEST > RANK

RANKING *adj* prominent ▷ *n* position on a scale

RANKINGS > RANKING

RANKISH *adj* old word meaning rather rank

RANKISM *n* discrimination against people on the grounds of rank

RANKISMS > RANKISM

RANKLE *vb* continue to cause resentment or bitterness

RANKLED > RANKLE

RANKLES > RANKLE

RANKLESS > RANK

RANKLING > RANKLE

RANKLY > RANK

RANKNESS > RANK

RANKS > RANK

RANKSHIFT *n* phenomenon in which a unit at one rank in the grammar has the function of a unit at a lower rank, as for example in the phrase *the house on the corner*, where the words *on the corner* shift down from the rank of group to the rank of word ▷ *vb*

shift or be shifted from one linguistic rank to another

RANPIKE *same as* > RAMPIKE

RANPIKES > RANPIKE

RANSACK *vb* search thoroughly

RANSACKED > RANSACK

RANSACKER > RANSACK

RANSACKS > RANSACK

RANSEL *same as* > RANCEL

RANSELS > RANSEL

RANSHAKLE *Scots word for* > RANSACK

RANSOM *n* money demanded in return for the release of someone who has been kidnapped ▷ *vb* pay money to obtain the release of a captive

RANSOMED > RANSOM

RANSOMER > RANSOM

RANSOMERS > RANSOM

RANSOMING > RANSOM

RANSOMS > RANSOM

RANT *vb* talk in a loud and excited way ▷ *n* loud excited speech

RANTED > RANT

RANTER > RANT

RANTERISM > RANT

RANTERS > RANT

RANTING > RANT

RANTINGLY > RANT

RANTINGS > RANT

RANTIPOLE *n* reckless person ▷ *vb* behave like a rantipole

RANTS > RANT

RANULA *n* saliva-filled cyst that develops under the tongue

RANULAR *n* cyst of lower surface of tongue

RANULAS > RANULA

RANUNCULI *pl n* plants of the genus that includes the buttercup, crowfoot, spearwort, and lesser celandine

RANZEL *same as* > RANCEL

RANZELMAN *n* (in Shetland and Orkney) type of constable

RANZELMEN > RANZELMAN

RANZELS > RANZEL

RAOULIA *n* flowering plant of New Zealand

RAOULIAS > RAOULIA

RAP *vb* hit with a sharp quick blow ▷ *n* quick sharp blow

RAPACIOUS *adj* greedy or grasping

RAPACITY > RAPACIOUS

RAPE *vb* force to submit to sexual intercourse ▷ *n* act of raping

RAPED > RAPE

RAPER > RAPE

RAPERS > RAPE

RAPES > RAPE

RAPESEED *n* seed of the oilseed rape plant

RAPESEEDS > RAPESEED

RAPHAE > RAPHE

RAPHANIA *n* type of ergotism possibly resulting

from consumption of radish seeds

RAPHANIAS > RAPHANIA

RAPHE n elongated ridge of conducting tissue along the side of certain seeds

RAPHES > RAPHE

RAPHIA same as > RAFFIA

RAPHIAS > RAPHIA

RAPHIDE n any of numerous needle-shaped crystals, usually of calcium oxalate, that occur in many plant cells as a metabolic product

RAPHIDES > RAPHIDE

RAPHIS same as > RAPHIDE

RAPID adj quick, swift

RAPIDER > RAPID

RAPIDEST > RAPID

RAPIDITY > RAPID

RAPIDLY > RAPID

RAPIDNESS > RAPID

RAPIDS pl n part of a river with a fast turbulent current

RAPIER n fine-bladed sword

RAPIERED adj carrying a rapier

RAPIERS > RAPIER

RAPINE n pillage or plundering

RAPINES > RAPINE

RAPING > RAPE

RAPINI pl n type of leafy vegetable

RAPIST n person who commits rape

RAPISTS > RAPIST

RAPLOCH n Scots word for homespun woollen material ▷ adj Scots word meaning coarse or homemade

RAPLOCHS > RAPLOCH

RAPPAREE n Irish irregular soldier of the late 17th century

RAPPAREES > RAPPAREE

RAPPE n Arcadian dish of grated potatoes and pork or chicken

RAPPED > RAP

RAPPEE n moist English snuff of the 18th and 19th centuries

RAPPEES > RAPPEE

RAPPEL n (formerly) a drumbeat to call soldiers to arms ▷ vb abseil

RAPPELED > RAPPEL

RAPPELING > RAPPEL

RAPPELLED > RAPPEL

RAPPELS > RAPPEL

RAPPEN n Swiss coin equal to one hundredth of a franc

RAPPER n something used for rapping, such as a knocker on a door

RAPPERS > RAPPER

RAPPES > RAPPE

RAPPING > RAP

RAPPINGS > RAP

RAPPINI same as > RAPINI

RAPPORT n harmony or agreement

RAPPORTS > RAPPORT

RAPS > RAP

RAPT adj engrossed or spellbound

RAPTLY > RAPT

RAPTNESS > RAPT

RAPTOR n any bird of prey

RAPTORIAL adj (of the feet of birds) adapted for seizing prey

RAPTORS > RAPTOR

RAPTURE n ecstasy ▷ vb entrance

RAPTURED > RAPTURE

RAPTURES > RAPTURE

RAPTURING > RAPTURE

RAPTURISE same as > RAPTURIZE

RAPTURIST > RAPTURE

RAPTURIZE vb go into ecstasies

RAPTUROUS adj experiencing or manifesting ecstatic joy or delight

RARE adj uncommon archaic spelling of > REAR

RAREBIT as in Welsh rarebit dish made from melted cheese and sometimes milk and seasonings and served on toast

RAREBITS > RAREBIT

RARED > RARE

RAREE as in raree show street show or carnival

RAREFIED adj highly specialized, exalted

RAREFIER > RAREFY

RAREFIERS > RAREFY

RAREFIES > RAREFY

RAREFY vb make or become rarer or less dense

RAREFYING > RAREFY

RARELY adv seldom

RARENESS > RARE

RARER > RARE

RARERIPE adj ripening early ▷ n fruit or vegetable that ripens early

RARERIPES > RARERIPE

RARES > RARE

RAREST > RARE

RARIFIED same as > RAREFIED

RARIFIES > RARIFY

RARIFY same as > RAREFY

RARIFYING > RARIFY

RARING adj ready

RARITIES > RARITY

RARITY n something that is valuable because it is unusual

RARK as in rark up informal New Zealand expression meaning reprimand severely

RARKED > RARK

RARKING > RARK

RARKS > RARK

RAS n headland

RASBORA n often brightly coloured tropical fish

RASBORAS > RASBORA

RASCAILLE n rabble

RASCAL n rogue ▷ adj belonging to the mob or rabble

RASCALDOM > RASCAL

RASCALISM > RASCAL

RASCALITY n mischievous, disreputable, or dishonest character, behaviour, or action

RASCALLY adj dishonest or mean ▷ adv in a dishonest or mean fashion

RASCALS > RASCAL

RASCASSE n any of various fishes with venomous spines on the dorsal and anal fins

RASCASSES > RASCASSE

RASCHEL n type of loosely knitted fabric

RASCHELS > RASCHEL

RASE same as > RAZE

RASED > RASE

RASER > RASE

RASERS > RASE

RASES > RASE

RASH adj hasty, reckless, or incautious ▷ n eruption of spots or patches on the skin ▷ vb (in old usage) cut

RASHED > RASH

RASHER n thin slice of bacon

RASHERS > RASHER

RASHES > RASH

RASHEST > RASH

RASHIE n Australian word for a shirt worn by surfers as protection against sunburn, heat rash, etc

RASHIES > RASHIE

RASHING > RASH

RASHLIKE > RASH

RASHLY > RASH

RASHNESS > RASH

RASING > RASE

RASMALAI n Indian dessert made from cheese, milk, and almonds

RASMALAIS > RASMALAI

RASORIAL adj (of birds such as domestic poultry) adapted for scratching the ground for food

RASP n harsh grating noise ▷ vb speak in a grating voice

RASPATORY n surgical instrument for abrading

RASPBERRY n red juicy edible berry

RASPED > RASP

RASPER > RASP

RASPERS > RASP

RASPIER > RASPY

RASPIEST > RASPY

RASPINESS > RASPY

RASPING adj (esp of a noise) harsh or grating

RASPINGLY > RASPING

RASPINGS pl n browned breadcrumbs for coating fish and other foods before frying, baking, etc

RASPISH > RASP

RASPS > RASP

RASPY same as > RASPING

RASSE n small S Asian civet

RASSES > RASSE

RASSLE dialect variant of > WRESTLE

RASSLED > RASSLE

RASSLES > RASSLE

RASSLING > RASSLE

RAST archaic past form of > RACE

RASTA n member of a particular Black religious movement

RASTAFARI n Black religious movement

RASTER n image consisting of rows of pixel information, such as a JPEG, GIF etc ▷ vb use web-based technology to turn a digital image into a large picture composed of a grid of black and white dots

RASTERED > RASTER

RASTERING > RASTER

RASTERISE same as > RASTERIZE

RASTERIZE vb (in computing) convert into pixels for screen output

RASTERS > RASTER

RASTRUM n pen for drawing the five lines of a musical stave simultaneously

RASTRUMS > RASTRUM

RASURE n scraping

RASURES > RASURE

RAT n small rodent ▷ vb inform (on)

RATA n New Zealand hard-wood forest tree with crimson flowers

RATABLE adj able to be rated or evaluated

RATABLES pl n property that is liable to rates

RATABLY > RATABLE

RATAFEE same as > RATAFIA

RATAFEES > RATAFEE

RATAFIA n liqueur made from fruit

RATAFIAS > RATAFIA

RATAL n amount on which rates are assessed ▷ adj of or relating to rates (local taxation)

RATALS > RATAL

RATAN same as > RATTAN

RATANIES > RATANY

RATANS > RATAN

RATANY n flowering desert shrub

RATAPLAN n drumming sound ▷ vb drum

RATAPLANS > RATAPLAN

RATAS > RATA

RATATAT n sound of knocking on a door

RATATATS > RATATAT

RATBAG n eccentric, stupid, or unreliable person

RATBAGS > RATBAG

RATBITE as in ratbite fever acute infectious disease that can be caught from the bite of an infected rat

RATCH same as > RATCHET

RATCHED > RATCH

RATCHES > RATCH

RATCHET n set of teeth on a bar or wheel allowing motion in one direction only ▷ vb move using or as if using a ratchet system

RATCHETED > RATCHET

RATCHETS > RATCHET

RATCHING > RATCH

RATE n degree of speed or progress ▷ vb consider or value

RATEABLE same as > RATABLE

RATEABLY > RATEABLE

RATED > RATE

RATEEN same as > RATINE

RATEENS > RATEEN

RATEL n large African and S Asian musteline mammal

RATELS > RATEL

RATEMETER n device for counting and averaging the number of events in a given time

RATEPAYER n person who pays local rates on a building

RATER > RATE

RATERS > RATE

RATES pl n (in some countries) a tax on property levied by a local authority

RATFINK n contemptible or undesirable person

RATFINKS > RATFINK

RATFISH n deep-sea fish with a whiplike tail

RATFISHES > RATFISH

RATH same as > RATHE

RATHA n (in India) a four-wheeled carriage drawn by horses or bullocks

RATHAS > RATHA

RATHE adj blossoming or ripening early in the season

RATHER adv some extent ▷ interj expression of strong affirmation ▷ sentence substitute expression of strong affirmation, often in answer to a question

RATHEREST adv archaic word equivalent to soonest

RATHERIPE same as > RATHRIPE

RATHERISH adv (in informal English) quite or fairly

RATHEST adv dialect or archaic word meaning soonest

RATHOLE n rat's hiding place or burrow

RATHOLES > RATHOLE

RATHOUSE n psychiatric hospital or asylum

RATHOUSES > RATHOUSE

RATHRIPE adj dialect word meaning mature or ripe ahead of time ▷ n variety of apple or other fruit that is quick to ripen

RATHRIPES > RATHRIPE

RATHS > RATH

RATICIDE n rat poison

RATICIDES > RATICIDE

RATIFIED > RATIFY

RATIFIER > RATIFY

RATIFIERS > RATIFY

RATIFIES > RATIFY

RATIFY vb give formal approval to

RATIFYING > RATIFY

RATINE n coarse loosely woven cloth

RATINES > RATINE

RATING n valuation or assessment

RATINGS > RATING

RATIO n relationship between two numbers or amounts expressed as a proportion

RATION n fixed allowance of food etc ▷ vb limit to a certain amount per person

RATIONAL adj reasonable, sensible ▷ n rational number

RATIONALE n reason for an action or decision

RATIONALS > RATIONAL

RATIONED > RATION

RATIONING > RATION

RATIONS pl n fixed daily allowance of food, esp to military personnel or when supplies are limited

RATIOS > RATIO

RATITE adj (of flightless birds) having a breastbone that lacks a keel for the attachment of flight muscles ▷ n bird, such as an ostrich, kiwi, or rhea, that belongs to this group

RATITES > RATITE

RATLIKE > RAT

RATLIN same as > RATLINE

RATLINE n any of a series of light lines tied across the shrouds of a sailing vessel for climbing aloft

RATLINES > RATLINE

RATLING n young rat

RATLINGS > RATLING

RATLINS > RATLIN

RATO n rocket-assisted take-off

RATOO same as > RATU

RATOON n new shoot that grows from near the root or crown of crop plants, esp the sugar cane, after the old growth has been cut back ▷ vb propagate or cause to propagate by such a growth

RATOONED > RATOON

RATOONER n plant that spreads by ratooning

RATOONERS > RATOONER

RATOONING > RATOON

RATOONS > RATOON

RATOOS > RATOO

RATOS > RATO

RATPACK n members of the press who pursue celebrities and give wide coverage of their private lives

RATPACKS > RATPACK

RATPROOF adj impenetrable by rats

RATS > RAT

RATSBANE n rat poison, esp arsenic oxide

RATSBANES > RATSBANE

RATTAIL n type of fish

RATTAILED adj having tail like rat

RATTAILS > RATTAIL

RATTAN n climbing palm with jointed stems used for canes

RATTANS > RATTAN

RATTED > RAT

RATTEEN same as > RATINE

RATTEENS > RATTEEN

RATTEN vb sabotage or steal tools in order to disrupt the work of

RATTENED > RATTEN

RATTENER > RATTEN

RATTENERS > RATTEN

RATTENING > RATTEN

RATTENS > RATTEN

RATTER n dog or cat that catches and kills rats

RATTERIES > RATTERY

RATTERS > RATTER

RATTERY n rats' dwelling area

RATTIER > RATTY

RATTIEST > RATTY

RATTILY > RATTY

RATTINESS > RATTY

RATTING > RAT

RATTINGS > RAT

RATTISH adj of, resembling, or infested with rats

RATTLE vb give out a succession of short sharp sounds ▷ n short sharp sound

RATTLEBAG n rattle made out of a bag containing a variety of different things

RATTLEBOX n any of various tropical and subtropical leguminous plants that have inflated pods within which the seeds rattle

RATTLED > RATTLE

RATTLER n something that rattles

RATTLERS > RATTLER

RATTLES > RATTLE

RATTLIER > RATTLY

RATTLIEST > RATTLY

RATTLIN same as > RATLINE

RATTLINE same as > RATLINE

RATTLINES > RATTLINE

RATTLING adv exceptionally, very ▷ n succession of short sharp sounds

RATTLINGS > RATTLING

RATTLINS > RATTLIN

RATTLY adj having a rattle

RATTON n dialect word for a little rat

RATTONS > RATTON

RATTOON same as > RATOON

RATTOONED > RATTOON

RATTOONS > RATTOON

RATTRAP n device for catching rats

RATTRAPS > RATTRAP

RATTY adj bad-tempered, irritable

RATU n title used by Fijian chiefs or nobles

RATUS > RATU

RAUCID adj raucous

RAUCITIES > RAUCOUS

RAUCITY > RAUCOUS

RAUCLE adj Scots word for rough or tough

RAUCLER > RAUCLE

RAUCLEST > RAUCLE

RAUCOUS adj hoarse or harsh

RAUCOUSLY > RAUCOUS

RAUGHT archaic past form of > REACH

RAUN n fish roe or spawn

RAUNCH n lack of polish or refinement ▷ vb behave in a raunchy manner

RAUNCHED > RAUNCH

RAUNCHES > RAUNCH

RAUNCHIER > RAUNCHY

RAUNCHILY > RAUNCHY

RAUNCHING > RAUNCH

RAUNCHY adj earthy, sexy

RAUNGE archaic word for > RANGE

RAUNGED > RAUNGE

RAUNGES > RAUNGE

RAUNGING > RAUNGE

RAUNS > RAUN

RAUPATU n confiscation or seizure of land

RAUPATUS > RAUPATU

RAUPO n New Zealand bulrush

RAURIKI n sow thistle, any of various plants with prickly leaves, milky juice and yellow heads

RAURIKIS > RAURIKI

RAUWOLFIA n tropical tree or shrub

RAVAGE vb cause extensive damage to ▷ n destructive action

RAVAGED > RAVAGE

RAVAGER > RAVAGE

RAVAGERS > RAVAGE

RAVAGES > RAVAGE

RAVAGING > RAVAGE

RAVE vb talk wildly or with enthusiasm ▷ n enthusiastically good review

RAVED > RAVE

RAVEL vb tangle or become entangled ▷ n tangle or complication

RAVELED > RAVEL

RAVELER > RAVEL

RAVELERS > RAVEL

RAVELIN n outwork having two embankments at a salient angle

RAVELING > RAVEL

RAVELINGS > RAVEL

RAVELINS > RAVELIN

RAVELLED > RAVEL

RAVELLER > RAVEL

RAVELLERS > RAVEL

RAVELLING > RAVEL

RAVELLY > RAVEL

RAVELMENT n ravel or tangle

RAVELS > RAVEL

RAVEN n black bird like a large crow ▷ adj (of hair) shiny black ▷ vb seize or seek (plunder, prey, etc)

RAVENED > RAVEN
RAVENER > RAVEN
RAVENERS > RAVEN
RAVENING adj (of animals) hungrily searching for prey
RAVENINGS pl n rapacious behaviour and activities
RAVENLIKE > RAVEN
RAVENOUS adj very hungry
RAVENS > RAVEN
RAVER n person who leads a wild or uninhibited social life
RAVERS > RAVER
RAVES > RAVE
RAVIGOTE n rich white sauce with herbs and shallots
RAVIGOTES > RAVIGOTE
RAVIGOTTE n French salad sauce
RAVIN archaic spelling of > RAVEN
RAVINE n narrow steep-sided valley worn by a stream
RAVINED > RAVIN
RAVINES > RAVINE
RAVING adj delirious ▷ n frenzied, irrational, or wildly extravagant talk or utterances
RAVINGLY > RAVING
RAVINGS > RAVING
RAVINING > RAVIN
RAVINS > RAVIN
RAVIOLI n small squares of pasta with a savoury filling
RAVIOLIS > RAVIOLI
RAVISH vb enrapture
RAVISHED > RAVISH
RAVISHER > RAVISH
RAVISHERS > RAVISH
RAVISHES > RAVISH
RAVISHING adj lovely or entrancing
RAW adj uncooked as in in the raw without clothes
RAWARU n New Zealand name for blue cod
RAWBONE archaic variant of > RAWBONED
RAWBONED adj having a lean bony physique
RAWER > RAW
RAWEST > RAW
RAWHEAD n bogeyman
RAWHEADS > RAWHEAD
RAWHIDE n untanned hide ▷ vb whip
RAWHIDED > RAWHIDE
RAWHIDES > RAWHIDE
RAWHIDING > RAWHIDE
RAWIN n monitoring of winds in the upper atmosphere using radar and a balloon
RAWING (in dialect) same as > ROWEN
RAWINGS > RAWING
RAWINS > RAWIN
RAWISH > RAW
RAWLY > RAW
RAWMAISH n Irish word for foolish or exaggerated talk
RAWN (in dialect) same as > ROWEN

RAWNESS > RAW
RAWNESSES > RAW
RAWNS > RAWN
RAWS > RAW
RAX vb stretch or extend ▷ n act of stretching or straining
RAXED > RAX
RAXES > RAX
RAXING > RAX
RAY n single line or narrow beam of light ▷ vb (of an object) to emit (light) in rays or (of light) to issue in the form of rays
RAYA same as > RAYAH
RAYAH n (formerly) a non-Muslim subject of the Ottoman Empire
RAYAHS > RAYAH
RAYAS > RAYA
RAYED > RAY
RAYGRASS same as > RYEGRASS
RAYING > RAY
RAYLE archaic spelling of > RAIL
RAYLED > RAYLE
RAYLES > RAYLE
RAYLESS adj dark
RAYLESSLY > RAYLESS
RAYLET n small ray
RAYLETS > RAYLET
RAYLIKE adj resembling a ray
RAYLING > RAYLE
RAYNE archaic spelling of > REIGN
RAYNES > RAYNE
RAYON n (fabric made of) a synthetic fibre
RAYONS > RAYON
RAYS > RAY
RAZE vb destroy (buildings or a town) completely
RAZED > RAZE
RAZEE n sailing ship that has had its upper deck or decks removed ▷ vb remove the upper deck or decks of (a sailing ship)
RAZEED > RAZEE
RAZEEING > RAZEE
RAZEES > RAZEE
RAZER > RAZE
RAZERS > RAZE
RAZES > RAZE
RAZING > RAZE
RAZMATAZ n noisy or showy fuss or activity
RAZOO n imaginary coin
RAZOOS > RAZOO
RAZOR n sharp instrument for shaving ▷ vb cut or shave with a razor
RAZORABLE adj able to be shaved
RAZORBACK n another name for the common rorqual
RAZORBILL n sea bird of the North Atlantic with a stout sideways flattened bill
RAZORED > RAZOR
RAZORING > RAZOR
RAZORS > RAZOR
RAZURE same as > RASURE
RAZURES > RAZURE

RAZZ vb make fun of
RAZZBERRY US variant of > RASPBERRY
RAZZED > RAZZ
RAZZES > RAZZ
RAZZIA n raid for plunder or slaves, esp one carried out by Moors in North Africa
RAZZIAS > RAZZIA
RAZZING > RAZZ
RAZZLE as in on the razzle celebration
RAZZLES > RAZZLE
RE prep concerning
REABSORB vb absorb again
REABSORBS > REABSORB
REACCEDE vb accede again
REACCEDED > REACCEDE
REACCEDES > REACCEDE
REACCENT vb accent again
REACCENTS > REACCENT
REACCEPT vb accept again
REACCEPTS > REACCEPT
REACCLAIM vb acclaim again
REACCUSE vb accuse again
REACCUSED > REACCUSE
REACCUSES > REACCUSE
REACH vb arrive at ▷ n distance that one can reach
REACHABLE > REACH
REACHED > REACH
REACHER > REACH
REACHERS > REACH
REACHES > REACH
REACHING > REACH
REACHLESS adj unreachable or unattainable
REACQUIRE vb get or gain (something) again which one has owned
REACT vb act in response (to)
REACTANCE n resistance to the flow of an alternating current caused by the inductance or capacitance of the circuit
REACTANT n substance that participates in a chemical reaction
REACTANTS > REACTANT
REACTED > REACT
REACTING > REACT
REACTION n physical or emotional response to a stimulus
REACTIONS > REACTION
REACTIVE adj chemically active
REACTOR n apparatus in which a nuclear reaction is maintained and controlled to produce nuclear energy
REACTORS > REACTOR
REACTS > REACT
REACTUATE vb activate again
READ vb look at and understand or take in (written or printed matter) ▷ n matter suitable for reading
READABLE adj enjoyable to read
READABLY > READABLE
READAPT vb adapt again

READAPTED > READAPT
READAPTS > READAPT
READD vb add again
READDED > READD
READDICT vb cause to become addicted again
READDICTS > READDICT
READDING > READD
READDRESS vb look at or discuss (an issue, situation, etc) from a new or different point of view
READDS > READD
READER n person who reads
READERLY adj pertaining to or suitable for a reader
READERS > READER
READIED > READY
READIER > READY
READIES pl n ready money
READIEST > READY
READILY adv promptly
READINESS n state of being ready or prepared
READING > READ
READINGS > READ
READJUST vb adapt to a new situation
READJUSTS > READJUST
READMIT vb let (a person, country, etc) back in to a place or organization
READMITS > READMIT
READOPT vb adopt again
READOPTED > READOPT
READOPTS > READOPT
READORN vb adorn again
READORNED > READORN
READORNS > READORN
READOUT n act of retrieving information from a computer memory or storage device
READOUTS > READOUT
READS > READ
READVANCE vb advance again
READVISE vb advise again
READVISED > READVISE
READVISES > READVISE
READY adj prepared for use or action ▷ vb prepare
READYING > READY
READYMADE adj made for purchase and immediate use by any customer
REAEDIFY vb rebuild
REAEDIFYE same as > REAEDIFY
REAFFIRM vb state again, confirm
REAFFIRMS > REAFFIRM
REAFFIX vb affix again
REAFFIXED > REAFFIX
REAFFIXES > REAFFIX
REAGENCY > REAGENT
REAGENT n chemical substance that reacts with another, used to detect the presence of the other
REAGENTS > REAGENT
REAGIN n type of antibody that is formed against an allergen and is attached to the cells of a tissue. The antigen–antibody reaction that occurs on subsequent

contact with the allergen causes tissue damage, leading to the release of histamine and other substances responsible for an allergic reaction
REAGINIC > REAGIN
REAGINS > REAGIN
REAK *same as* > RECK
REAKED > REAK
REAKING > REAK
REAKS > REAK
REAL *adj* existing in fact ▷*n* name of a former small Spanish or Spanish-American silver coin as well as of the standard monetary unit of Brazil
REALER > REAL
REALES > REAL
REALEST > REAL
REALGAR *n* rare orange-red soft mineral consisting of arsenic sulphide in monoclinic crystalline form
REALGARS > REALGAR
REALIA *pl n* real-life facts and material used in teaching
REALIGN *vb* change or put back to a new or former place or position
REALIGNED > REALIGN
REALIGNS > REALIGN
REALISE *same as* > REALIZE
REALISED > REALISE
REALISER > REALISE
REALISERS > REALISE
REALISES > REALISE
REALISING > REALISE
REALISM *n* awareness or acceptance of things as they are
REALISMS > REALISM
REALIST *n* person who is aware of and accepts the physical universe, events, etc, as they are
REALISTIC *adj* seeing and accepting things as they really are, practical
REALISTS > REALIST
REALITIES > REALITY
REALITY *n* state of things as they are
REALIZE *vb* become aware or grasp the significance of
REALIZED > REALIZE
REALIZER > REALIZE
REALIZERS > REALIZE
REALIZES > REALIZE
REALIZING > REALIZE
REALLIE *old or dialect variant of* > REALLY
REALLIED > REALLY
REALLIES > REALLY
REALLOT *vb* allot again
REALLOTS > REALLOT
REALLY *adv* very ▷*interj* exclamation of dismay, doubt, or surprise ▷*vb* (in archaic usage) rally
REALLYING > REALLY
REALM *n* kingdom
REALMLESS > REALM
REALMS > REALM
REALNESS > REAL

REALO *n* member of the German Green party with moderate views
REALOS > REALO
REALS > REAL
REALTER *vb* alter again
REALTERED > REALTER
REALTERS > REALTER
REALTIE *n* archaic word meaning sincerity
REALTIES > REALTY
REALTIME *adj* (of a data-processing system) constantly updating to reflect the latest changes in data
REALTOR *n* estate agent
REALTORS > REALTOR
REALTY *n* immovable property
REAM *n* twenty quires of paper, generally 500 sheets ▷*vb* enlarge (a hole) by use of a reamer
REAME *archaic variant of* > REALM
REAMED > REAM
REAMEND *vb* amend again
REAMENDED > REAMEND
REAMENDS > REAMEND
REAMER *n* steel tool with a cylindrical or tapered shank around which longitudinal teeth are ground, used for smoothing the bores of holes accurately to size
REAMERS > REAMER
REAMES > REAME
REAMIER > REAMY
REAMIEST > REAMY
REAMING > REAM
REAMS > REAM
REAMY *Scots for* > CREAMY
REAN *same as* > REEN
REANALYSE *vb* analyse again
REANALYZE *US spelling of* > REANALYSE
REANIMATE *vb* refresh or enliven (something) again
REANNEX *vb* annex again
REANNEXED > REANNEX
REANNEXES > REANNEX
REANOINT *vb* anoint again
REANOINTS > REANOINT
REANS > REAN
REANSWER *vb* answer again
REANSWERS > REANSWER
REAP *vb* cut and gather (a harvest)
REAPABLE > REAP
REAPED > REAP
REAPER *n* person who reaps or machine for reaping
REAPERS > REAPER
REAPHOOK *n* sickle
REAPHOOKS > REAPHOOK
REAPING > REAP
REAPPAREL *vb* clothe again
REAPPEAR *vb* appear again
REAPPEARS > REAPPEAR
REAPPLIED > REAPPLY
REAPPLIES > REAPPLY
REAPPLY *vb* put or spread (something) on again
REAPPOINT *vb* assign (a person, committee, etc) to

a post or role again
REAPPROVE *vb* approve again
REAPS > REAP
REAR *n* back part ▷*vb* care for and educate (children)
REARED > REAR
REARER > REAR
REARERS > REAR
REARGUARD *n* troops protecting the rear of an army
REARGUE *vb* argue again
REARGUED > REARGUE
REARGUES > REARGUE
REARGUING > REARGUE
REARHORSE *n* mantis
REARING > REAR
REARISE *vb* arise again
REARISEN > REARISE
REARISES > REARISE
REARISING > REARISE
REARLY *old word for* > EARLY
REARM *vb* arm again
REARMED > REARM
REARMICE > REARMOUSE
REARMING > REARM
REARMOST *adj* nearest the back
REARMOUSE *same as* > REREMOUSE
REARMS > REARM
REAROSE > REARISE
REAROUSAL > REAROUSE
REAROUSE *vb* arouse again
REAROUSED > REAROUSE
REAROUSES > REAROUSE
REARRANGE *vb* organize differently, alter
REARREST *vb* arrest again
REARRESTS > REARREST
REARS > REAR
REARWARD *adj* in the rear ▷*adv* towards the rear ▷*n* position in the rear, esp the rear division of a military formation
REARWARDS *same as* > REARWARD
REASCEND *vb* ascend again
REASCENDS > REASCEND
REASCENT *n* new ascent
REASCENTS > REASCENT
REASON *n* cause or motive ▷*vb* think logically in forming conclusions
REASONED *adj* well thought out or well presented
REASONER > REASON
REASONERS > REASON
REASONING *n* process of drawing conclusions from facts or evidence
REASONS > REASON
REASSAIL *vb* assail again
REASSAILS > REASSAIL
REASSERT *vb* assert (rights, claims, etc) again
REASSERTS > REASSERT
REASSESS *vb* reconsider the value or importance of
REASSIGN *vb* move (personnel, resources, etc) to a new post, department, location, etc
REASSIGNS > REASSIGN
REASSORT *vb* assort again

REASSORTS > REASSORT
REASSUME *vb* assume again
REASSUMED > REASSUME
REASSUMES > REASSUME
REASSURE *vb* restore confidence to
REASSURED > REASSURE
REASSURER > REASSURE
REASSURES > REASSURE
REAST *same as* > REEST
REASTED > REAST
REASTIER > REASTY
REASTIEST > REASTY
REASTING > REAST
REASTS > REAST
REASTY *adj* (in dialect) rancid
REATA *n* lasso
REATAS > REATA
REATE *n* type of crowfoot
REATES > REATE
REATTACH *vb* attach again
REATTACK *vb* attack again
REATTACKS > REATTACK
REATTAIN *vb* attain again
REATTAINS > REATTAIN
REATTEMPT *vb* attempt again
REAVAIL *vb* avail again
REAVAILED > REAVAIL
REAVAILS > REAVAIL
REAVE *vb* carry off (property, prisoners, etc) by force
REAVED > REAVE
REAVER > REAVE
REAVERS > REAVE
REAVES > REAVE
REAVING > REAVE
REAVOW *vb* avow again
REAVOWED > REAVOW
REAVOWING > REAVOW
REAVOWS > REAVOW
REAWAKE *vb* awake again
REAWAKED > REAWAKE
REAWAKEN *vb* emerge or rouse from sleep
REAWAKENS > REAWAKEN
REAWAKES > REAWAKE
REAWAKING > REAWAKE
REAWOKE > REAWAKE
REAWOKEN > REAWAKE
REB *n* Confederate soldier in the American Civil War (1861–65)
REBACK *vb* provide with a new back, backing, or lining
REBACKED > REBACK
REBACKING > REBACK
REBACKS > REBACK
REBADGE *vb* relaunch (a product) under a new name, brand, or logo
REBADGED > REBADGE
REBADGES > REBADGE
REBADGING > REBADGE
REBAIT *vb* bait again
REBAITED > REBAIT
REBAITING > REBAIT
REBAITS > REBAIT
REBALANCE *vb* balance again
REBAPTISE *same as* > REBAPTIZE
REBAPTISM *n* new baptism
REBAPTIZE *vb* baptize

r

again

REBAR n rod providing reinforcement in concrete structures

REBARS > REBAR

REBATABLE > REBATE

REBATE n discount or refund ▷ vb cut a rabbet in

REBATED > REBATE

REBATER > REBATE

REBATERS > REBATE

REBATES > REBATE

REBATING > REBATE

REBATO same as > RABATO

REBATOES > REBATO

REBATOS > REBATO

REBBE n individual's chosen spiritual mentor

REBBES > REBBE

REBBETZIN n wife of a rabbi

REBEC n medieval stringed instrument resembling the violin but having a lute-shaped body

REBECK same as > REBEC

REBECKS > REBECK

REBECS > REBEC

REBEGAN > REBEGIN

REBEGIN vb begin again

REBEGINS > REBEGIN

REBEGUN > REBEGIN

REBEL vb revolt against the ruling power ▷ n person who rebels ▷ adj rebelling

REBELDOM > REBEL

REBELDOMS > REBEL

REBELLED > REBEL

REBELLER > REBEL

REBELLERS > REBEL

REBELLING > REBEL

REBELLION n organized open resistance to authority

REBELLOW vb re-echo loudly

REBELLOWS > REBELLOW

REBELS > REBEL

REBID vb bid again

REBIDDEN > REBID

REBIDDING > REBID

REBIDS > REBID

REBILL vb bill again

REBILLED > REBILL

REBILLING > REBILL

REBILLS > REBILL

REBIND vb bind again

REBINDING > REBIND

REBINDS > REBIND

REBIRTH n revival or renaissance

REBIRTHS > REBIRTH

REBIT > REBITE

REBITE vb (in printing) to give another application of acid in order to cause further cutting of a plate

REBITES > REBITE

REBITING > REBITE

REBITTEN > REBITE

REBLEND vb blend again

REBLENDED > REBLEND

REBLENDS > REBLEND

REBLENT same as > REBLEND

REBLOOM vb bloom again

REBLOOMED > REBLOOM

REBLOOMS > REBLOOM

REBLOSSOM vb blossom again

REBOANT adj resounding or reverberating

REBOARD vb board again

REBOARDED > REBOARD

REBOARDS > REBOARD

REBOATION n repeated bellow

REBODIED > REBODY

REBODIES > REBODY

REBODY vb give a new body to

REBODYING > REBODY

REBOIL vb boil again

REBOILED > REBOIL

REBOILING > REBOIL

REBOILS > REBOIL

REBOOK vb book again

REBOOKED > REBOOK

REBOOKING > REBOOK

REBOOKS > REBOOK

REBOOT vb shut down and then restart (a computer system)

REBOOTED > REBOOT

REBOOTING > REBOOT

REBOOTS > REBOOT

REBOP same as > BEBOP

REBOPS > REBOP

REBORE n boring of a cylinder to restore its true shape ▷ vb carry out this process

REBORED > REBORE

REBORES > REBORE

REBORING > REBORE

REBORN adj active again after a period of inactivity

REBORROW vb borrow again

REBORROWS > REBORROW

REBOTTLE vb bottle again

REBOTTLED > REBOTTLE

REBOTTLES > REBOTTLE

REBOUGHT > REBUY

REBOUND vb spring back ▷ n act of rebounding

REBOUNDED > REBOUND

REBOUNDER > REBOUND

REBOUNDS > REBOUND

REBOZO n long wool or linen scarf covering the shoulders and head, worn by Latin American women

REBOZOS > REBOZO

REBRACE vb brace again

REBRACED > REBRACE

REBRACES > REBRACE

REBRACING > REBRACE

REBRANCH vb branch again

REBRAND vb change or update the image of (an organization or product)

REBRANDED > REBRAND

REBRANDS > REBRAND

REBRED > REBREED

REBREED vb breed again

REBREEDS > REBREED

REBS > REB

REBUFF vb reject or snub ▷ n blunt refusal, snub

REBUFFED > REBUFF

REBUFFING > REBUFF

REBUFFS > REBUFF

REBUILD vb build (a building or town) again, after severe damage

REBUILDED archaic past form of > REBUILD

REBUILDS > REBUILD

REBUILT > REBUILD

REBUKABLE > REBUKE

REBUKE vb scold sternly ▷ n stern scolding

REBUKED > REBUKE

REBUKEFUL > REBUKE

REBUKER > REBUKE

REBUKERS > REBUKE

REBUKES > REBUKE

REBUKING > REBUKE

REBURIAL > REBURY

REBURIALS > REBURY

REBURIED > REBURY

REBURIES > REBURY

REBURY vb bury again

REBURYING > REBURY

REBUS n puzzle consisting of pictures and symbols representing words or syllables

REBUSES > REBUS

REBUT vb prove that (a claim) is untrue

REBUTMENT > REBUT

REBUTS > REBUT

REBUTTAL > REBUT

REBUTTALS > REBUT

REBUTTED > REBUT

REBUTTER n defendant's pleading in reply to a claimant's surrejoinder

REBUTTERS > REBUTTER

REBUTTING > REBUT

REBUTTON vb button again

REBUTTONS > REBUTTON

REBUY vb buy again

REBUYING > REBUY

REBUYS > REBUY

REC n short for recreation

RECAL same as > RECALL

RECALESCE vb glow again

RECALL vb recollect or remember ▷ n ability to remember

RECALLED > RECALL

RECALLER > RECALL

RECALLERS > RECALL

RECALLING > RECALL

RECALLS > RECALL

RECALMENT > RECAL

RECALS > RECALL

RECAMIER n shade of pink

RECAMIERS > RECAMIER

RECANE vb cane again

RECANED > RECANE

RECANES > RECANE

RECANING > RECANE

RECANT vb withdraw (a statement or belief) publicly

RECANTED > RECANT

RECANTER > RECANT

RECANTERS > RECANT

RECANTING > RECANT

RECANTS > RECANT

RECAP vb recapitulate ▷ n recapitulation

RECAPPED > RECAP

RECAPPING > RECAP

RECAPS > RECAP

RECAPTION n process of taking back one's own wife, child, property, etc, without causing a breach of the peace

RECAPTOR > RECAPTURE

RECAPTORS > RECAPTURE

RECAPTURE vb experience again ▷ n act of recapturing

RECARPET vb replace one carpet with another

RECARPETS > RECARPET

RECARRIED > RECARRY

RECARRIES > RECARRY

RECARRY vb carry again

RECAST vb organize or set out in a different way

RECASTING > RECAST

RECASTS > RECAST

RECATALOG vb catalogue again

RECATCH vb catch again

RECATCHES > RECATCH

RECAUGHT > RECATCH

RECAUTION vb caution again

RECCE vb reconnoitre ▷ n reconnaissance

RECCED > RECCE

RECCEED > RECCE

RECCEING > RECCE

RECCES > RECCE

RECCIED > RECCY

RECCIES > RECCY

RECCO same as > RECCE

RECCOS > RECCO

RECCY same as > RECCE

RECCYING > RECCY

RECEDE vb move to a more distant place

RECEDED > RECEDE

RECEDES > RECEDE

RECEDING > RECEDE

RECEIPT n written acknowledgment of money or goods received ▷ vb acknowledge payment of (a bill), as by marking it

RECEIPTED > RECEIPT

RECEIPTOR n person who receipts

RECEIPTS > RECEIPT

RECEIVAL n act of receiving or state of being received

RECEIVALS > RECEIVAL

RECEIVE vb take, accept, or get

RECEIVED adj generally accepted

RECEIVER n part of telephone that is held to the ear

RECEIVERS > RECEIVER

RECEIVES > RECEIVE

RECEIVING > RECEIVE

RECEMENT vb cement again

RECEMENTS > RECEMENT

RECENCIES > RECENT

RECENCY > RECENT

RECENSE vb revise

RECENSED > RECENSE

RECENSES > RECENSE

RECENSING > RECENSE

RECENSION n critical revision of a literary work

RECENSOR vb censor again

RECENSORS > RECENSOR

RECENT adj having happened lately

RECENTER > RECENT

RECENTEST > RECENT

RECENTLY > RECENT

RECENTRE *vb* centre again

RECENTRED > RECENTRE

RECENTRES > RECENTRE

RECEPT *n* idea or image formed in the mind by repeated experience of a particular pattern of sensory stimulation

RECEPTION *n* area for receiving guests, clients, etc

RECEPTIVE *adj* willing to accept new ideas, suggestions, etc

RECEPTOR *n* sensory nerve ending that changes specific stimuli into nerve impulses

RECEPTORS > RECEPTOR

RECEPTS > RECEPT

RECERTIFY *vb* certify again

RECESS *n* niche or alcove ▷ *vb* place or set (something) in a recess

RECESSED > RECESS

RECESSES > RECESS

RECESSING > RECESS

RECESSION *n* period of economic difficulty when little is being bought or sold

RECESSIVE *adj* receding ▷ *n* recessive gene or character

RECHANGE *vb* change again

RECHANGED > RECHANGE

RECHANGES > RECHANGE

RECHANNEL *vb* channel again

RECHARGE *vb* cause (a battery) to take in and store electricity again

RECHARGED > RECHARGE

RECHARGER > RECHARGE

RECHARGES > RECHARGE

RECHART *vb* chart again

RECHARTED > RECHART

RECHARTER *vb* charter again

RECHARTS > RECHART

RECHATE *same as* > RECHEAT

RECHATES > RECHATE

RECHAUFFE *n* warmed-up leftover food

RECHEAT *n* (in a hunt) sounding of the horn to call back the hounds ▷ *vb* sound the horn to call back the hounds

RECHEATED > RECHEAT

RECHEATS > RECHEAT

RECHECK *vb* check again

RECHECKED > RECHECK

RECHECKS > RECHECK

RECHERCHE *adj* refined or elegant

RECHEW *vb* chew again

RECHEWED > RECHEW

RECHEWING > RECHEW

RECHEWS > RECHEW

RECHIE *adj* smoky

RECHLESSE *archaic form of* > RECKLESS

RECHOOSE *vb* choose again

RECHOOSES > RECHOOSE

RECHOSE > RECHOOSE

RECHOSEN > RECHOOSE

RECIPE *n* directions for cooking a dish

RECIPES > RECIPE

RECIPIENT *n* person who receives something

RECIRCLE *vb* circle again

RECIRCLED > RECIRCLE

RECIRCLES > RECIRCLE

RECISION *n* act of cancelling or rescinding

RECISIONS > RECISION

RECIT *n* narrative

RECITABLE > RECITE

RECITAL *n* musical performance by a soloist or soloists

RECITALS > RECITAL

RECITE *vb* repeat (a poem, story, etc) aloud to an audience

RECITED > RECITE

RECITER > RECITE

RECITERS > RECITE

RECITES > RECITE

RECITING > RECITE

RECITS > RECIT

RECK *vb* mind or care about (something)

RECKAN *adj* strained, tormented, or twisted

RECKED > RECK

RECKING > RECK

RECKLESS *adj* heedless of danger

RECKLING *dialect word for* > RUNT

RECKLINGS > RECKLING

RECKON *vb* consider or think

RECKONED > RECKON

RECKONER *n* any of various devices or tables used to facilitate reckoning, esp a ready reckoner

RECKONERS > RECKONER

RECKONING *n* counting or calculating

RECKONS > RECKON

RECKS > RECK

RECLAD *vb* cover in a different substance

RECLADDED > RECLAD

RECLADS > RECLAD

RECLAIM *vb* regain possession of ▷ *n* act of reclaiming or state of being reclaimed

RECLAIMED > RECLAIM

RECLAIMER > RECLAIM

RECLAIMS > RECLAIM

RECLAME *n* public acclaim or attention

RECLAMES > RECLAME

RECLASP *vb* clasp again

RECLASPED > RECLASP

RECLASPS > RECLASP

RECLEAN *vb* clean again

RECLEANED > RECLEAN

RECLEANS > RECLEAN

RECLIMB *vb* climb again

RECLIMBED > RECLIMB

RECLIMBS > RECLIMB

RECLINATE *adj* (esp of a leaf or stem) naturally curved or bent backwards so that the upper part rests on the ground

RECLINE *vb* rest in a leaning position

RECLINED > RECLINE

RECLINER *n* type of armchair having a back that can be adjusted to slope at various angles and, usually, a leg rest

RECLINERS > RECLINER

RECLINES > RECLINE

RECLINING > RECLINE

RECLOSE *vb* close again

RECLOSED > RECLOSE

RECLOSES > RECLOSE

RECLOSING > RECLOSE

RECLOTHE *vb* clothe again

RECLOTHED > RECLOTHE

RECLOTHES > RECLOTHE

RECLUSE *n* person who avoids other people ▷ *adj* solitary

RECLUSELY > RECLUSE

RECLUSES > RECLUSE

RECLUSION > RECLUSE

RECLUSIVE > RECLUSE

RECLUSORY *n* recluse's dwelling or cell

RECOAL *vb* supply or be supplied with fresh coal

RECOALED > RECOAL

RECOALING > RECOAL

RECOALS > RECOAL

RECOAT *vb* coat again

RECOATED > RECOAT

RECOATING > RECOAT

RECOATS > RECOAT

RECOCK *vb* cock again

RECOCKED > RECOCK

RECOCKING > RECOCK

RECOCKS > RECOCK

RECODE *vb* put into a new code

RECODED > RECODE

RECODES > RECODE

RECODIFY *vb* codify again

RECODING > RECODE

RECOGNISE *same as* > RECOGNIZE

RECOGNIZE *vb* identify as (a person or thing) already known

RECOIL *vb* jerk or spring back ▷ *n* backward jerk

RECOILED > RECOIL

RECOILER > RECOIL

RECOILERS > RECOIL

RECOILING > RECOIL

RECOILS > RECOIL

RECOIN *vb* coin again

RECOINAGE *n* new coinage

RECOINED > RECOIN

RECOINING > RECOIN

RECOINS > RECOIN

RECOLLECT *vb* call back to mind, remember

RECOLLET *n* member of a particular Franciscan order

RECOLLETS > RECOLLET

RECOLOR *vb* give a new colour to

RECOLORED > RECOLOR

RECOLORS > RECOLOR

RECOMB *vb* comb again

RECOMBED > RECOMB

RECOMBINE *vb* join together again

RECOMBING > RECOMB

RECOMBS > RECOMB

RECOMFORT *archaic word for* > COMFORT

RECOMMEND *vb* advise or counsel

RECOMMIT *vb* send (a bill) back to a committee for further consideration

RECOMMITS > RECOMMIT

RECOMPACT *vb* compact again

RECOMPILE *vb* compile again

RECOMPOSE *vb* restore to composure or calmness

RECOMPUTE *vb* compute again

RECON *n* smallest genetic unit capable of recombining

RECONCILE *vb* harmonize (conflicting beliefs etc)

RECONDITE *adj* difficult to understand

RECONDUCT *vb* conduct again

RECONFER *vb* confer again

RECONFERS > RECONFER

RECONFINE *vb* confine again

RECONFIRM *vb* confirm (an arrangement, agreement, etc) again

RECONNECT *vb* link or be linked together again

RECONNED > RECON

RECONNING > RECON

RECONQUER *vb* conquer again

RECONS > RECON

RECONSIGN *vb* consign again

RECONSOLE *vb* console again

RECONSULT *vb* consult again

RECONTACT *vb* contact again

RECONTOUR *vb* contour again

RECONVENE *vb* gather together again after an interval

RECONVERT *vb* change (something) back to a previous state or form

RECONVEY *vb* convey again

RECONVEYS > RECONVEY

RECONVICT *vb* convict again

RECOOK *vb* cook again

RECOOKED > RECOOK

RECOOKING > RECOOK

RECOOKS > RECOOK

RECOPIED > RECOPY

RECOPIES > RECOPY

RECOPY *vb* copy again

RECOPYING > RECOPY

RECORD *n* document or other thing that preserves information ▷ *vb* put in writing

RECORDED > RECORD

RECORDER *n* person or machine that records, esp a video, cassette, or tape recorder

RECORDERS > RECORDER

RECORDING *n* something,

esp music, that has been recorded

RECORDIST *n* person that records

RECORDS > RECORD

RECORK *vb* cork again

RECORKED > RECORK

RECORKING > RECORK

RECORKS > RECORK

RECOUNT *vb* tell in detail

RECOUNTAL > RECOUNT

RECOUNTED > RECOUNT

RECOUNTER *n* narrator of a story

RECOUNTS > RECOUNT

RECOUP *vb* regain or make good (a loss)

RECOUPE *vb* (in law) keep back or withhold

RECOUPED > RECOUP

RECOUPING > RECOUP

RECOUPLE *vb* couple again

RECOUPLED > RECOUPLE

RECOUPLES > RECOUPLE

RECOUPS > RECOUP

RECOURE *archaic variant of* > RECOVER

RECOURED > RECOURE

RECOURES > RECOURE

RECOURING > RECOURE

RECOURSE *archaic word for* > RETURN

RECOURSED > RECOURSE

RECOURSES > RECOURSE

RECOVER *vb* become healthy again

RECOVERED > RECOVER

RECOVEREE *n* (in law) person found against in a recovery case

RECOVERER > RECOVER

RECOVEROR *n* (in law) person successfully demanding a right in a recovery case

RECOVERS > RECOVER

RECOVERY *n* act of recovering from sickness, a shock, or a setback

RECOWER *archaic variant of* > RECOVER

RECOWERED > RECOWER

RECOWERS > RECOWER

RECOYLE *archaic spelling of* > RECOIL

RECOYLED > RECOYLE

RECOYLES > RECOYLE

RECOYLING > RECOYLE

RECRATE *vb* crate again

RECRATED > RECRATE

RECRATES > RECRATE

RECRATING > RECRATE

RECREANCE > RECREANT

RECREANCY > RECREANT

RECREANT *n* disloyal or cowardly person ▷ *adj* cowardly

RECREANTS > RECREANT

RECREATE *vb* amuse (oneself or someone else)

RECREATED > RECREATE

RECREATES > RECREATE

RECREATOR > RECREATE

RECREMENT *n* any substance, such as bile, that is secreted from a part of the body and later

reabsorbed instead of being excreted

RECROSS *vb* move or go across (something) again

RECROSSED > RECROSS

RECROSSES > RECROSS

RECROWN *vb* crown again

RECROWNED > RECROWN

RECROWNS > RECROWN

RECRUIT *vb* enlist (new soldiers, members, etc) ▷ *n* newly enlisted soldier

RECRUITAL *n* act of recruiting

RECRUITED > RECRUIT

RECRUITER > RECRUIT

RECRUITS > RECRUIT

RECS > REC

RECTA > RECTUM

RECTAL *adj* of the rectum

RECTALLY > RECTAL

RECTANGLE *n* oblong four-sided figure with four right angles

RECTI > RECTUS

RECTIFIED > RECTIFY

RECTIFIER *n* electronic device, such as a semiconductor diode or valve, that converts an alternating current to a direct current by suppression or inversion of alternate half cycles

RECTIFIES > RECTIFY

RECTIFY *vb* put right, correct

RECTION *n* (in grammar) the determination of the form of one word by another word

RECTIONS > RECTION

RECTITIC > RECTITIS

RECTITIS *n* inflammation of the rectum

RECTITUDE *n* moral correctness

RECTO *n* right-hand page of a book

RECTOCELE *n* protrusion or herniation of the rectum into the vagina

RECTOR *n* clergyman in charge of a parish

RECTORAL *adj* of or relating to God's rule or to a rector

RECTORATE > RECTOR

RECTORESS *n* female rector or the wife or widow of a rector

RECTORIAL *adj* of or relating to a rector ▷ *n* election of a rector

RECTORIES > RECTORY

RECTORS > RECTOR

RECTORY *n* rector's house

RECTOS > RECTO

RECTRESS *same as* > RECTORESS

RECTRICES > RECTRIX

RECTRIX *n* any of the large stiff feathers of a bird's tail, used in controlling the direction of flight

RECTUM *n* final section of the large intestine

RECTUMS > RECTUM

RECTUS *n* straight muscle, esp either of two muscles of the anterior abdominal wall

RECUILE *archaic variant of* > RECOIL

RECUILED > RECUILE

RECUILES > RECUILE

RECUILING > RECUILE

RECULE *archaic variant of* > RECOIL

RECULED > RECULE

RECULES > RECULE

RECULING > RECULE

RECUMBENT *adj* lying down

RECUR *vb* happen again

RECURE *vb* archaic word for cure or recover

RECURED > RECURE

RECURES > RECURE

RECURING > RECURE

RECURRED > RECUR

RECURRENT *adj* happening or tending to happen again or repeatedly

RECURRING > RECUR

RECURS > RECUR

RECURSION *n* act or process of returning or running back

RECURSIVE > RECURSION

RECURVATE *adj* bent back

RECURVE *vb* curve or bend (something) back or down or (of something) to be so curved or bent

RECURVED > RECURVE

RECURVES > RECURVE

RECURVING > RECURVE

RECUSAL *n* withdrawal of a judge from a case

RECUSALS > RECUSAL

RECUSANCE > RECUSANT

RECUSANCY > RECUSANT

RECUSANT *n* Roman Catholic who did not attend the services of the Church of England ▷ *adj* (formerly, of Catholics) refusing to attend services of the Church of England

RECUSANTS > RECUSANT

RECUSE *vb* (in law) object to or withdraw (a judge)

RECUSED > RECUSE

RECUSES > RECUSE

RECUSING > RECUSE

RECUT *vb* cut again

RECUTS > RECUT

RECUTTING > RECUT

RECYCLATE *n* recyclable material

RECYCLE *vb* reprocess (used materials) for further use ▷ *n* repetition of a fixed sequence of events

RECYCLED > RECYCLE

RECYCLER > RECYCLE

RECYCLERS > RECYCLE

RECYCLES > RECYCLE

RECYCLING > RECYCLE

RECYCLIST > RECYCLE

RED *adj* of a colour varying from crimson to orange and seen in blood, fire, etc ▷ *n* red colour

REDACT *vb* compose or draft

(an edict, proclamation, etc)

REDACTED > REDACT

REDACTING > REDACT

REDACTION > REDACT

REDACTOR > REDACT

REDACTORS > REDACT

REDACTS > REDACT

REDAMAGE *vb* damage again

REDAMAGED > REDAMAGE

REDAMAGES > REDAMAGE

REDAN *n* fortification of two parapets at a salient angle

REDANS > REDAN

REDARGUE *vb* archaic word for disprove or refute

REDARGUED > REDARGUE

REDARGUES > REDARGUE

REDATE *vb* change date of

REDATED > REDATE

REDATES > REDATE

REDATING > REDATE

REDBACK *n* small venomous Australian spider

REDBACKS > REDBACK

REDBAIT *vb* harass those with leftwing leanings

REDBAITED > REDBAIT

REDBAITER *n* person who deliberately antagonizes communists

REDBAITS > REDBAIT

REDBAY *n* type of tree

REDBAYS > REDBAY

REDBELLY *n* any of various animals having red underparts, especially the char or the redbelly turtle

REDBIRD *n* type of bird, the male of which is distinguished by its bright red plumage and black wings

REDBIRDS > REDBIRD

REDBONE *n* type of American dog

REDBONES > REDBONE

REDBREAST *n* robin

REDBRICK *adj* (of a university in Britain) founded in the late 19th or early 20th century ▷ *n* denoting, relating to, or characteristic of a provincial British university of relatively recent foundation, esp as distinguished from Oxford and Cambridge

REDBRICKS > REDBRICK

REDBUD *n* American leguminous tree with heart-shaped leaves and small budlike pink flowers

REDBUDS > REDBUD

REDBUG *another name for* > CHIGGER

REDBUGS > REDBUG

REDCAP *n* military policeman

REDCAPS > REDCAP

REDCOAT *n* British soldier

REDCOATS > REDCOAT

REDD *vb* bring order to ▷ *n* act or an instance of redding

REDDED > REDD

REDDEN *vb* make or become red

REDDENDA > REDDENDUM

REDDENDO *n* (in Scotland) legal clause specifying what payment or duties are required in exchange for something

REDDENDOS > REDDENDO

REDDENDUM *n* legal clause specifying what shall be given in return for the granting of a lease

REDDENED > REDDEN

REDDENING > REDDEN

REDDENS > REDDEN

REDDER > REDD

REDDERS > REDD

REDDEST > RED

REDDIER > REDDY

REDDIEST > REDDY

REDDING > REDD

REDDINGS > REDD

REDDISH *adj* somewhat red

REDDISHLY > REDDISH

REDDLE *same as* > RUDDLE

REDDLED > REDDLE

REDDLEMAN *same as* > RUDDLEMAN

REDDLEMEN > REDDLEMAN

REDDLES > REDDLE

REDDLING > REDDLE

REDDS > REDD

REDDY *adj* reddish

REDE *n* advice or counsel ▷ *vb* advise

REDEAL *vb* deal again

REDEALING > REDEAL

REDEALS > REDEAL

REDEALT > REDEAL

REDEAR *n* variety of sunfish with a red flash above the gills

REDEARS > REDEAR

REDECIDE *vb* decide again

REDECIDED > REDECIDE

REDECIDES > REDECIDE

REDECRAFT *n* logic

REDED > REDE

REDEEM *vb* make up for

REDEEMED > REDEEM

REDEEMER > REDEEM

REDEEMERS > REDEEM

REDEEMING *adj* making up for faults or deficiencies

REDEEMS > REDEEM

REDEFEAT *vb* defeat again

REDEFEATS > REDEFEAT

REDEFECT *vb* defect back or again

REDEFECTS > REDEFECT

REDEFIED > REDEFY

REDEFIES > REDEFY

REDEFINE *vb* define (something) again or differently

REDEFINED > REDEFINE

REDEFINES > REDEFINE

REDEFY *vb* defy again

REDEFYING > REDEFY

REDELESS > REDE

REDELIVER *vb* deliver again

REDEMAND *vb* demand again

REDEMANDS > REDEMAND

REDENIED > REDENY

REDENIES > REDENY

REDENY *vb* deny again

REDENYING > REDENY

REDEPLOY *vb* assign to a new position or task

REDEPLOYS > REDEPLOY

REDEPOSIT *vb* deposit again

REDES > REDE

REDESCEND *vb* descend again

REDESIGN *vb* change the design of (something) ▷ *n* something that has been redesigned

REDESIGNS > REDESIGN

REDEVELOP *vb* rebuild or renovate (an area or building)

REDEYE *n* inferior whiskey

REDEYES > REDEYE

REDFIN *n* any of various small fishes with reddish fins that are popular aquarium fishes

REDFINS > REDFIN

REDFISH *n* male salmon that has recently spawned

REDFISHES > REDFISH

REDFOOT *n* fatal disease of newborn lambs of unknown cause in which the horny layers of the feet become separated, exposing the red laminae below

REDFOOTS > REDFOOT

REDHANDED *adj* in the act of doing something criminal, wrong, or shameful

REDHEAD *n* person with reddish hair

REDHEADED > REDHEAD

REDHEADS > REDHEAD

REDHORSE *n* type of fish

REDHORSES > REDHORSE

REDIA *n* parasitic larva of flukes that has simple locomotory organs, pharynx, and intestine and gives rise either to other rediae or to a different larva (the cercaria)

REDIAE > REDIA

REDIAL *vb* dial (a telephone number) again

REDIALED > REDIAL

REDIALING > REDIAL

REDIALLED > REDIAL

REDIALS > REDIAL

REDIAS > REDIA

REDICTATE *vb* dictate again

REDID > REDO

REDIGEST *vb* digest again

REDIGESTS > REDIGEST

REDIGRESS *vb* digress again

REDING > REDE

REDINGOTE *n* woman's coat with a close-fitting top and a full skirt

REDIP *vb* dip again

REDIPPED > REDIP

REDIPPING > REDIP

REDIPS > REDIP

REDIPT *archaic past form of* > REDIP

REDIRECT *vb* send in a new direction or course

REDIRECTS > REDIRECT

REDISCUSS *vb* discuss again

REDISPLAY *vb* display again

REDISPOSE *vb* dispose again

REDISTIL *vb* distil again

REDISTILL *US spelling of* > REDISTIL

REDISTILS > REDISTIL

REDIVIDE *vb* divide again

REDIVIDED > REDIVIDE

REDIVIDES > REDIVIDE

REDIVIVUS *adj* returned to life

REDIVORCE *vb* divorce again

REDLEG *n* derogatory term for poor White

REDLEGS > REDLEG

REDLINE *vb* (esp of a bank or group of banks) to refuse a loan to (a person or country) because of the presumed risks involved

REDLINED > REDLINE

REDLINER > REDLINE

REDLINERS > REDLINE

REDLINES > REDLINE

REDLINING > REDLINE

REDLY > RED

REDNECK *n* (in the southwestern US) derogatory term for a poor uneducated White farm worker ▷ *adj* reactionary and bigoted

REDNECKED *adj* with a red neck

REDNECKS > REDNECK

REDNESS > RED

REDNESSES > RED

REDO *vb* do over again in order to improve ▷ *n* instance of redoing something

REDOCK *vb* dock again

REDOCKED > REDOCK

REDOCKING > REDOCK

REDOCKS > REDOCK

REDOES > REDO

REDOING > REDO

REDOLENCE > REDOLENT

REDOLENCY > REDOLENT

REDOLENT *adj* reminiscent (of)

REDON *vb* don again

REDONE > REDO

REDONNED > REDON

REDONNING > REDON

REDONS > REDON

REDOS > REDO

REDOUBLE *vb* increase, multiply, or intensify ▷ *n* act of redoubling

REDOUBLED > REDOUBLE

REDOUBLER > REDOUBLE

REDOUBLES > REDOUBLE

REDOUBT *n* small fort defending a hilltop or pass ▷ *vb* fear

REDOUBTED > REDOUBT

REDOUBTS > REDOUBT

REDOUND *vb* cause advantage or disadvantage (to)

REDOUNDED > REDOUND

REDOUNDS > REDOUND

REDOUT *n* reddened vision and other symptoms caused by a rush of blood to the head in response to negative gravitational stresses

REDOUTS > REDOUT

REDOWA *n* Bohemian folk dance similar to the waltz

REDOWAS > REDOWA

REDOX *n* chemical reaction in which one substance is reduced and the other is oxidized

REDOXES > REDOX

REDPOLL *n* mostly grey-brown finch with a red crown and pink breast

REDPOLLS > REDPOLL

REDRAFT *vb* write a second copy of (a letter, proposal, essay, etc) ▷ *n* second draft

REDRAFTED > REDRAFT

REDRAFTS > REDRAFT

REDRAW *vb* draw or draw up (something) again or differently

REDRAWER > REDRAW

REDRAWERS > REDRAW

REDRAWING > REDRAW

REDRAWN > REDRAW

REDRAWS > REDRAW

REDREAM *vb* dream again

REDREAMED > REDREAM

REDREAMS > REDREAM

REDREAMT > REDREAM

REDRESS *vb* make amends for ▷ *n* compensation or amends

REDRESSED > REDRESS

REDRESSER > REDRESS

REDRESSES > REDRESS

REDRESSOR > REDRESS

REDREW > REDRAW

REDRIED > REDRY

REDRIES > REDRY

REDRILL *vb* drill again

REDRILLED > REDRILL

REDRILLS > REDRILL

REDRIVE *vb* drive again

REDRIVEN > REDRIVE

REDRIVES > REDRIVE

REDRIVING > REDRIVE

REDROOT *n* yellow-flowered bog plant of E North America whose roots yield a red dye

REDROOTS > REDROOT

REDROVE > REDRIVE

REDRY *vb* dry again

REDRYING > REDRY

REDS > RED

REDSEAR *same as* > REDSHORT

REDSHANK *n* large Eurasian sandpiper with red legs

REDSHANKS > REDSHANK

REDSHARE *n* red algae

REDSHIFT *n* shift in the lines of the spectrum of an astronomical object

REDSHIFTS > REDSHIFT

REDSHIRE *same as* > REDSHARE

REDSHIRT *vb* take a year out of a sports team

REDSHIRTS > REDSHIRT

REDSHORT *vb* become brittle

at red-hot temperatures

REDSKIN *n* offensive term for Native American

REDSKINS > REDSKIN

REDSTART *n* European bird of the thrush family, the male of which has an orange-brown tail and breast

REDSTARTS > REDSTART

REDSTREAK *n* variety of apple

REDTAIL *n* variety of bird with red colouring on its tail

REDTAILS > REDTAIL

REDTOP *n* sensationalist tabloid newspaper

REDTOPS > REDTOP

REDUB *vb* fix or repair

REDUBBED > REDUB

REDUBBING > REDUB

REDUBS > REDUB

REDUCE *vb* bring down, lower

REDUCED > REDUCE

REDUCER *n* chemical solution used to lessen the density of a negative or print by oxidizing some of the blackened silver to soluble silver compounds

REDUCERS > REDUCER

REDUCES > REDUCE

REDUCIBLE > REDUCE

REDUCIBLY > REDUCE

REDUCING > REDUCE

REDUCTANT *n* reducing agent

REDUCTASE *n* any enzyme that catalyses a biochemical reduction reaction

REDUCTION *n* act of reducing

REDUCTIVE > REDUCTION

REDUCTOR *n* apparatus in which substances can be reduced

REDUCTORS > REDUCTOR

REDUIT *n* fortified part from which a garrison may fight on once an enemy has taken outworks

REDUITS > REDUIT

REDUNDANT *adj* (of a worker) no longer needed

REDUVIID *n* any hemipterous bug of the family *Reduviidae*, which includes the assassin bugs and the wheel bug ▷ *adj* of, relating to, or belonging to the family *Reduviidae*

REDUVIIDS > REDUVIID

REDUX *adj* brought back or returned

REDWARE *another name for* > KELP

REDWARES > REDWARE

REDWATER *n* tick-borne disease of cattle

REDWATERS > REDWATER

REDWING *n* small European thrush

REDWINGS > REDWING

REDWOOD *n* giant Californian

conifer with reddish bark

REDWOODS > REDWOOD

REDYE *vb* dye again

REDYED > REDYE

REDYEING > REDYE

REDYES > REDYE

REE *n* Scots word for walled enclosure

REEARN *vb* earn again

REEARNED > REEARN

REEARNING > REEARN

REEARNS > REEARN

REEBOK *same as* > RHEBOK

REEBOKS > REEBOK

REECH *vb* (in dialect) smoke

REECHED > REECH

REECHES > REECH

REECHIE *same as* > REECHY

REECHIER > REECHY

REECHIEST > REECHY

REECHING > REECH

REECHO *vb* echo again

REECHOED > REECHO

REECHOES > REECHO

REECHOING > REECHO

REECHY *adj* (in dialect) smoky

REED *n* tall grass that grows in swamps and shallow water

REEDBED *n* area of wetland with reeds growing in it

REEDBEDS > REEDBED

REEDBIRD *n* any of several birds that frequent reed beds, esp (in the US and Canada) the bobolink

REEDBIRDS > REEDBIRD

REEDBUCK *n* buff-coloured African antelope with inward-curving horns

REEDBUCKS > REEDBUCK

REEDE *obsolete variant of* > RED

REEDED > REED

REEDEN *adj* of or consisting of reeds

REEDER *n* thatcher

REEDERS > REEDER

REEDES > REEDE

REEDIER > REEDY

REEDIEST > REEDY

REEDIFIED > REEDIFY

REEDIFIES > REEDIFY

REEDIFY *vb* edify again or rebuild

REEDILY > REEDY

REEDINESS > REEDY

REEDING *n* set of small semicircular architectural mouldings

REEDINGS > REEDING

REEDIT *vb* edit again

REEDITED > REEDIT

REEDITING > REEDIT

REEDITION *n* new edition

REEDITS > REEDIT

REEDLIKE *adj* resembling a reed

REEDLING *n* tawny titlike Eurasian songbird common in reed beds

REEDLINGS > REEDLING

REEDMACE *n* tall reedlike marsh plant

REEDMACES > REEDMACE

REEDMAN *n* musician who

plays a wind instrument that has a reed

REEDMEN > REEDMAN

REEDS > REED

REEDSTOP *n* organ stop controlling a rank of reed pipes

REEDSTOPS > REEDSTOP

REEDUCATE *vb* educate again

REEDY *adj* harsh and thin in tone

REEF *n* ridge of rock or coral near the surface of the sea ▷ *vb* roll up part of a sail

REEFABLE > REEF

REEFED > REEF

REEFER *n* short thick jacket worn esp by sailors

REEFERS > REEFER

REEFIER > REEFY

REEFIEST > REEFY

REEFING > REEF

REEFINGS > REEF

REEFS > REEF

REEFY *adj* with reefs

REEJECT *vb* eject again

REEJECTED > REEJECT

REEJECTS > REEJECT

REEK *vb* smell strongly ▷ *n* strong unpleasant smell

REEKED > REEK

REEKER > REEK

REEKERS > REEK

REEKIE *same as* > REEKY

REEKIER > REEK

REEKIEST > REEK

REEKING > REEK

REEKINGLY > REEK

REEKS > REEK

REEKY *adj* steamy or smoky

REEL *n* cylindrical object on which film, tape, thread, or wire is wound ▷ *vb* stagger, sway, or whirl

REELABLE > REEL

REELECT *vb* elect again

REELECTED > REELECT

REELECTS > REELECT

REELED > REEL

REELER > REEL

REELERS > REEL

REELEVATE *vb* elevate again

REELING > REEL

REELINGLY > REEL

REELINGS > REEL

REELMAN *n* (formerly) member of a beach life-saving team operating a winch

REELMEN > REELMAN

REELS > REEL

REEMBARK *vb* embark again

REEMBARKS > REEMBARK

REEMBODY *vb* embody again

REEMBRACE *vb* embrace again

REEMERGE *vb* emerge again

REEMERGED > REEMERGE

REEMERGES > REEMERGE

REEMIT *vb* emit again

REEMITS > REEMIT

REEMITTED > REEMIT

REEMPLOY *vb* employ again

REEMPLOYS > REEMPLOY

REEN *n* ditch, esp a drainage channel

REENACT *vb* enact again

REENACTED > REENACT

REENACTOR > REENACT

REENACTS > REENACT

REENDOW *vb* endow again

REENDOWED > REENDOW

REENDOWS > REENDOW

REENFORCE *vb* enforce again

REENGAGE *vb* engage again

REENGAGED > REENGAGE

REENGAGES > REENGAGE

REENGRAVE *vb* engrave again

REENJOY *vb* enjoy again

REENJOYED > REENJOY

REENJOYS > REENJOY

REENLARGE *vb* enlarge again

REENLIST *vb* enlist again

REENLISTS > REENLIST

REENROLL *vb* enrol again

REENROLLS > REENROLL

REENS > REEN

REENSLAVE *vb* enslave again

REENTER *vb* enter again

REENTERED > REENTER

REENTERS > REENTER

REENTRANT *n* reentering angle ▷ *adj* (of an angle) pointing inwards

REENTRIES > REENTRY

REENTRY *n* return of a spacecraft into the earth's atmosphere

REEQUIP *vb* equip again

REEQUIPS > REEQUIP

REERECT *vb* erect again

REERECTED > REERECT

REERECTS > REERECT

REES > REE

REEST *vb* (esp of horses) to be noisily uncooperative

REESTED > REEST

REESTIER > REESTY

REESTIEST > REESTY

REESTING > REEST

REESTS > REEST

REESTY *same as* > REASTY

REEVE *n* local representative of the king in a shire until the early 11th century ▷ *vb* pass (a rope or cable) through an eye or other narrow opening

REEVED > REEVE

REEVES > REEVE

REEVING > REEVE

REEVOKE *vb* evoke again

REEVOKED > REEVOKE

REEVOKES > REEVOKE

REEVOKING > REEVOKE

REEXAMINE *vb* examine again

REEXECUTE *vb* execute again

REEXHIBIT *vb* exhibit again

REEXPEL *vb* expel again

REEXPELS > REEXPEL

REEXPLAIN *vb* explain again

REEXPLORE *vb* explore again

REEXPORT *vb* export again

REEXPORTS > REEXPORT

REEXPOSE *vb* expose again

REEXPOSED > REEXPOSE

REEXPOSES > REEXPOSE
REEXPRESS *vb* express again
REF *n* referee in sport ▷ *vb* referee
REFACE *vb* repair or renew the facing of (a wall)
REFACED > REFACE
REFACES > REFACE
REFACING > REFACE
REFALL *vb* fall again
REFALLEN > REFALL
REFALLING > REFALL
REFALLS > REFALL
REFASHION *vb* give a new form to (something)
REFASTEN *vb* fasten again
REFASTENS > REFASTEN
REFECT *vb* archaic word for restore or refresh with food and drink
REFECTED > REFECT
REFECTING > REFECT
REFECTION *n* refreshment with food and drink
REFECTIVE > REFECT
REFECTORY *n* room for meals in a college etc
REFECTS > REFECT
REFED > REFEED
REFEED *vb* feed again
REFEEDING > REFEED
REFEEDS > REFEED
REFEEL *vb* feel again
REFEELING > REFEEL
REFEELS > REFEEL
REFEL *vb* refute
REFELL > REFALL
REFELLED > REFEL
REFELLING > REFEL
REFELS > REFEL
REFELT > REFEEL
REFENCE *vb* fence again
REFENCED > REFENCE
REFENCES > REFENCE
REFENCING > REFENCE
REFER *vb* allude (to)
REFERABLE > REFER
REFEREE *n* umpire in sports, esp soccer or boxing ▷ *vb* act as referee of
REFEREED > REFEREE
REFEREES > REFEREE
REFERENCE *n* act of referring
REFERENDA *pl n* polls to determine the view of the electorate on something; referendums
REFERENT *n* object or idea to which a word or phrase refers
REFERENTS > REFERENT
REFERRAL > REFER
REFERRALS > REFER
REFERRED > REFER
REFERRER > REFER
REFERRERS > REFER
REFERRING > REFER
REFERS > REFER
REFFED > REF
REFFING > REF
REFFO *n* offensive name for a European refugee after World War II
REFFOS > REFFO
REFIGHT *vb* fight again ▷ *n*

second or new fight
REFIGHTS > REFIGHT
REFIGURE *vb* figure again
REFIGURED > REFIGURE
REFIGURES > REFIGURE
REFILE *vb* file again
REFILED > REFILE
REFILES > REFILE
REFILING > REFILE
REFILL *vb* fill again ▷ *n* second or subsequent filling
REFILLED > REFILL
REFILLING > REFILL
REFILLS > REFILL
REFILM *vb* film again
REFILMED > REFILM
REFILMING > REFILM
REFILMS > REFILM
REFILTER *vb* filter again
REFILTERS > REFILTER
REFINABLE > REFINE
REFINANCE *vb* finance again
REFIND *vb* find again
REFINDING > REFIND
REFINDS > REFIND
REFINE *vb* purify
REFINED *adj* cultured or polite
REFINEDLY > REFINED
REFINER *n* person, device, or substance that removes impurities, sediment, or other unwanted matter from something
REFINERS > REFINER
REFINERY *n* place where sugar, oil, etc is refined
REFINES > REFINE
REFINING > REFINE
REFININGS > REFINE
REFINISH *vb* finish again
REFIRE *vb* fire again
REFIRED > REFIRE
REFIRES > REFIRE
REFIRING > REFIRE
REFIT *vb* make ready for use again by repairing or re-equipping ▷ *n* repair or re-equipping for further use
REFITMENT > REFIT
REFITS > REFIT
REFITTED > REFIT
REFITTING > REFIT
REFIX *vb* fix again
REFIXED > REFIX
REFIXES > REFIX
REFIXING > REFIX
REFLAG *vb* flag again
REFLAGGED > REFLAG
REFLAGS > REFLAG
REFLATE *vb* inflate or be inflated again
REFLATED > REFLATE
REFLATES > REFLATE
REFLATING > REFLATE
REFLATION *n* increase in the supply of money and credit designed to encourage economic activity
REFLECT *vb* throw back, esp rays of light, heat, etc
REFLECTED > REFLECT
REFLECTER *n* archaic word for a critic

REFLECTOR *n* polished surface for reflecting light etc
REFLECTS > REFLECT
REFLET *n* iridescent glow or lustre, as on ceramic ware
REFLETS > REFLET
REFLEW > REFLY
REFLEX *n* involuntary response to a stimulus or situation ▷ *adj* (of a muscular action) involuntary ▷ *vb* bend, turn, or reflect backwards
REFLEXED > REFLEX
REFLEXES > REFLEX
REFLEXING > REFLEX
REFLEXION *n* act of reflecting or the state of being reflected
REFLEXIVE *adj* denoting a pronoun that refers back to the subject of a sentence or clause ▷ *n* reflexive pronoun or verb
REFLEXLY > REFLEX
REFLIES > REFLY
REFLOAT *vb* float again
REFLOATED > REFLOAT
REFLOATS > REFLOAT
REFLOOD *vb* flood again
REFLOODED > REFLOOD
REFLOODS > REFLOOD
REFLOW *vb* flow again
REFLOWED > REFLOW
REFLOWER *vb* flower again
REFLOWERS > REFLOWER
REFLOWING > REFLOW
REFLOWN > REFLY
REFLOWS > REFLOW
REFLUENCE > REFLUENT
REFLUENT *adj* flowing back
REFLUX *vb* boil or be boiled in a vessel attached to a condenser, so that the vapour condenses and flows back into the vessel ▷ *n* act of refluxing
REFLUXED > REFLUX
REFLUXES > REFLUX
REFLUXING > REFLUX
REFLY *vb* fly again
REFLYING > REFLY
REFOCUS *vb* focus again or anew
REFOCUSED > REFOCUS
REFOCUSES > REFOCUS
REFOLD *vb* fold again
REFOLDED > REFOLD
REFOLDING > REFOLD
REFOLDS > REFOLD
REFOOT *vb* foot again
REFOOTED > REFOOT
REFOOTING > REFOOT
REFOOTS > REFOOT
REFOREST *vb* replant (an area that was formerly forested) with trees
REFORESTS > REFOREST
REFORGE *vb* forge again
REFORGED > REFORGE
REFORGES > REFORGE
REFORGING > REFORGE
REFORM *n* improvement ▷ *vb* improve
REFORMADE *archaic variant of* > REFORMADO

REFORMADO *n* formerly, an officer whose men have been disbanded
REFORMAT *vb* format again
REFORMATE *n* gas formed in certain processes
REFORMATS > REFORMAT
REFORMED > REFORM
REFORMER > REFORM
REFORMERS > REFORM
REFORMING > REFORM
REFORMISM *n* doctrine or movement advocating reform, esp political or religious reform, rather than abolition
REFORMIST > REFORMISM
REFORMS > REFORM
REFORTIFY *vb* fortify again or further
REFOUGHT > REFIGHT
REFOUND *vb* found again
REFOUNDED > REFOUND
REFOUNDER > REFOUND
REFOUNDS > REFOUND
REFRACT *vb* change the course of (light etc) passing from one medium to another
REFRACTED > REFRACT
REFRACTOR *n* object or material that refracts
REFRACTS > REFRACT
REFRAIN *n* frequently repeated part of a song ▷ *vb* abstain (from action)
REFRAINED > REFRAIN
REFRAINER > REFRAIN
REFRAINS > REFRAIN
REFRAME *vb* support or enclose (a picture, photograph, etc) in a new or different frame
REFRAMED > REFRAME
REFRAMES > REFRAME
REFRAMING > REFRAME
REFREEZE *vb* freeze or be frozen again after having defrosted
REFREEZES > REFREEZE
REFRESH *vb* revive or reinvigorate, as through food, drink, or rest
REFRESHED > REFRESH
REFRESHEN *vb* freshen again
REFRESHER *n* something that refreshes, such as a cold drink
REFRESHES > REFRESH
REFRIED > REFRY
REFRIES > REFRY
REFRINGE *formerly used to mean* > REFRACT
REFRINGED > REFRINGE
REFRINGES > REFRINGE
REFRONT *vb* put a new front on
REFRONTED > REFRONT
REFRONTS > REFRONT
REFROZE > REFREEZE
REFROZEN > REFREEZE
REFRY *vb* fry again
REFRYING > REFRY
REFS > REF
REFT > REAVE
REFUEL *vb* supply or be

supplied with fresh fuel

REFUELED > REFUEL

REFUELING > REFUEL

REFUELLED > REFUEL

REFUELS > REFUEL

REFUGE n (source of) shelter or protection ▷ vb take refuge or give refuge to

REFUGED > REFUGE

REFUGEE n person who seeks refuge, esp in a foreign country

REFUGEES > REFUGEE

REFUGES > REFUGE

REFUGIA > REFUGIUM

REFUGING > REFUGE

REFUGIUM n geographical region that has remained unaltered by a climatic change affecting surrounding regions and that therefore forms a haven for relict fauna and flora

REFULGENT adj shining, radiant

REFUND vb pay back ▷ n return of money

REFUNDED > REFUND

REFUNDER > REFUND

REFUNDERS > REFUND

REFUNDING > REFUND

REFUNDS > REFUND

REFURBISH vb renovate and brighten up

REFURNISH vb furnish again

REFUSABLE > REFUSE

REFUSAL n denial of anything demanded or offered

REFUSALS > REFUSAL

REFUSE vb decline, deny, or reject ▷ n rubbish or useless matter

REFUSED > REFUSE

REFUSENIK n person who refuses to obey a law or cooperate with the government because of strong beliefs

REFUSER > REFUSE

REFUSERS > REFUSE

REFUSES > REFUSE

REFUSING > REFUSE

REFUSION n new or further fusion

REFUSIONS > REFUSION

REFUSNIK same as > REFUSENIK

REFUSNIKS > REFUSNIK

REFUTABLE > REFUTE

REFUTABLY > REFUTE

REFUTAL n act or process of refuting

REFUTALS > REFUTAL

REFUTE vb disprove

REFUTED > REFUTE

REFUTER > REFUTE

REFUTERS > REFUTE

REFUTES > REFUTE

REFUTING > REFUTE

REG n large expanse of stony desert terrain

REGAIN vb get back or recover ▷ n process of getting something back, esp lost weight

REGAINED > REGAIN

REGAINER > REGAIN

REGAINERS > REGAIN

REGAINING > REGAIN

REGAINS > REGAIN

REGAL adj of or like a king or queen ▷ n portable organ equipped only with small reed pipes, popular from the 15th century and recently revived for modern performance

REGALE vb entertain (someone) with stories etc ▷ n feast

REGALED > REGALE

REGALER > REGALE

REGALERS > REGALE

REGALES > REGALE

REGALIA pl n ceremonial emblems of royalty or high office

REGALIAN adj royal

REGALIAS > REGALIA

REGALING > REGALE

REGALISM n principle that the sovereign has supremacy in church affairs

REGALISMS > REGALISM

REGALIST > REGALISM

REGALISTS > REGALISM

REGALITY n state or condition of being royal

REGALLY > REGAL

REGALNESS > REGAL

REGALS > REGAL

REGAR same as > REGUR

REGARD vb consider ▷ n respect or esteem

REGARDANT adj (of a beast) shown looking backwards over its shoulder

REGARDED > REGARD

REGARDER > REGARD

REGARDERS > REGARD

REGARDFUL adj showing regard (for)

REGARDING prep on the subject of

REGARDS > REGARD

REGARS > REGAR

REGATHER vb gather again

REGATHERS > REGATHER

REGATTA n meeting for yacht or boat races

REGATTAS > REGATTA

REGAUGE vb gauge again

REGAUGED > REGAUGE

REGAUGES > REGAUGE

REGAUGING > REGAUGE

REGAVE > REGIVE

REGEAR vb readjust

REGEARED > REGEAR

REGEARING > REGEAR

REGEARS > REGEAR

REGELATE vb undergo or cause to undergo regelation

REGELATED > REGELATE

REGELATES > REGELATE

REGENCE old variant of > REGENCY

REGENCES > REGENCE

REGENCIES > REGENCY

REGENCY n status or period of office of a regent

REGENT n ruler of a kingdom during the absence, childhood, or illness of its monarch ▷ adj ruling as a regent

REGENTAL > REGENT

REGENTS > REGENT

REGES > REX

REGEST n archaic word for register

REGESTS > REGEST

REGGAE n style of Jamaican popular music with a strong beat

REGGAES > REGGAE

REGGO same as > REGO

REGGOS > REGGO

REGICIDAL > REGICIDE

REGICIDE n killing of a king

REGICIDES > REGICIDE

REGIE n government-directed management or government monopoly

REGIES > REGIE

REGILD vb gild again

REGILDED > REGILD

REGILDING > REGILD

REGILDS > REGILD

REGILT archaic past form of > REGILD

REGIME n system of government

REGIMEN n prescribed system of diet etc

REGIMENS > REGIMEN

REGIMENT n organized body of troops as a unit of the army ▷ vb force discipline or order on, esp in a domineering manner

REGIMENTS > REGIMENT

REGIMES > REGIME

REGIMINAL adj regimen-related

REGINA n queen

REGINAE > REGINA

REGINAL adj queenly

REGINAS > REGINA

REGION n administrative division of a country

REGIONAL adj of, characteristic of, or limited to a region ▷ n regional heat of a competition

REGIONALS > REGIONAL

REGIONARY same as > REGIONAL

REGIONS > REGION

REGISSEUR n official in a dance company with varying duties, usually including directing productions

REGISTER n (book containing) an official list or record of things ▷ vb enter in a register or set down in writing

REGISTERS > REGISTER

REGISTRAR n keeper of official records

REGISTRY n place where official records are kept

REGIUS as in regius professor Crown-appointed holder of a university chair

REGIVE vb give again or back

REGIVEN > REGIVE

REGIVES > REGIVE

REGIVING > REGIVE

REGLAZE vb glaze again

REGLAZED > REGLAZE

REGLAZES > REGLAZE

REGLAZING > REGLAZE

REGLET n flat narrow architectural moulding

REGLETS > REGLET

REGLORIFY vb glorify again

REGLOSS vb gloss again or give a new gloss to

REGLOSSED > REGLOSS

REGLOSSES > REGLOSS

REGLOW vb glow again

REGLOWED > REGLOW

REGLOWING > REGLOW

REGLOWS > REGLOW

REGLUE vb glue again

REGLUED > REGLUE

REGLUES > REGLUE

REGLUING > REGLUE

REGMA n type of fruit with cells that break open and break away when ripe

REGMAKER n drink taken to relieve the symptoms of a hangover

REGMAKERS > REGMAKER

REGMATA > REGMA

REGNA > REGNUM

REGNAL adj of a sovereign, reign, or kingdom

REGNANCY > REGNANT

REGNANT adj reigning

REGNUM n reign or rule

REGO n registration of a motor vehicle

REGOLITH n layer of loose material covering the bedrock of the earth and moon, etc, comprising soil, sand, rock fragments, volcanic ash, glacial drift, etc

REGOLITHS > REGOLITH

REGORGE vb vomit up

REGORGED > REGORGE

REGORGES > REGORGE

REGORGING > REGORGE

REGOS > REGO

REGOSOL n type of azonal soil consisting of unconsolidated material derived from freshly deposited alluvium or sands

REGOSOLS > REGOSOL

REGRADE vb grade again

REGRADED > REGRADE

REGRADES > REGRADE

REGRADING > REGRADE

REGRAFT vb graft again

REGRAFTED > REGRAFT

REGRAFTS > REGRAFT

REGRANT vb grant again

REGRANTED > REGRANT

REGRANTS > REGRANT

REGRATE vb buy up (commodities) in advance so as to raise their price for profitable resale

REGRATED > REGRATE

REGRATER > REGRATE

REGRATERS > REGRATE

REGRATES > REGRATE

REGRATING > REGRATE
REGRATOR > REGRATE
REGRATORS > REGRATE
REGREDE vb go back
REGREDED > REGREDE
REGREDES > REGREDE
REGREDING > REGREDE
REGREEN vb green again
REGREENED > REGREEN
REGREENS > REGREEN
REGREET vb greet again or return greetings of
REGREETED > REGREET
REGREETS > REGREET
REGRESS vb revert to a former worse condition ▷ n return to a former and worse condition
REGRESSED > REGRESS
REGRESSES > REGRESS
REGRESSOR > REGRESS
REGRET vb feel sorry about ▷ n feeling of repentance, guilt, or sorrow
REGRETFUL > REGRET
REGRETS > REGRET
REGRETTED > REGRET
REGRETTER > REGRET
REGREW > REGROW
REGRIND vb grind again
REGRINDS > REGRIND
REGROOM vb groom again
REGROOMED > REGROOM
REGROOMS > REGROOM
REGROOVE vb groove again
REGROOVED > REGROOVE
REGROOVES > REGROOVE
REGROUND > REGRIND
REGROUP vb reorganize (military forces) after an attack or a defeat
REGROUPED > REGROUP
REGROUPS > REGROUP
REGROW vb grow or be grown again after having been cut or having died or withered
REGROWING > REGROW
REGROWN > REGROW
REGROWS > REGROW
REGROWTH n growing back of hair, plants, etc
REGROWTHS > REGROWTH
REGS > REG
REGUERDON vb reward
REGULA n rule
REGULABLE adj able to be regulated
REGULAE > REGULA
REGULAR adj normal, customary, or usual ▷ n regular soldier
REGULARLY > REGULAR
REGULARS > REGULAR
REGULATE vb control, esp by rules
REGULATED > REGULATE
REGULATES > REGULATE
REGULATOR n device that automatically controls pressure, temperature, etc
REGULI > REGULUS
REGULINE > REGULUS
REGULISE variant spelling of > REGULIZE
REGULISED > REGULISE
REGULISES > REGULISE

REGULIZE vb turn into regulus
REGULIZED > REGULIZE
REGULIZES > REGULIZE
REGULO n any of a number of temperatures to which a gas oven may be set
REGULOS > REGULO
REGULUS n impure metal forming beneath the slag during the smelting of ores
REGULUSES > REGULUS
REGUR n black loamy Indian soil
REGURS > REGUR
REH n (in India) salty surface crust on the soil
REHAB vb help (addict, disabled person, prisoner, etc) to readapt to society or a new job ▷ n treatment or help given to an addict, disabled person, or prisoner, etc
REHABBED > REHAB
REHABBER > REHAB
REHABBERS > REHAB
REHABBING > REHAB
REHABS > REHAB
REHAMMER vb hammer again
REHAMMERS > REHAMMER
REHANDLE vb handle again
REHANDLED > REHANDLE
REHANDLES > REHANDLE
REHANG vb hang again
REHANGED > REHANG
REHANGING > REHANG
REHANGS > REHANG
REHARDEN vb harden again
REHARDENS > REHARDEN
REHASH vb rework or reuse ▷ n old ideas presented in a new form
REHASHED > REHASH
REHASHES > REHASH
REHASHING > REHASH
REHEAR vb hear again
REHEARD > REHEAR
REHEARING > REHEAR
REHEARS > REHEAR
REHEARSAL n preparatory practice session
REHEARSE vb practise (a play, concert, etc)
REHEARSED > REHEARSE
REHEARSER > REHEARSE
REHEARSES > REHEARSE
REHEAT vb heat or be heated again
REHEATED > REHEAT
REHEATER > REHEAT
REHEATERS > REHEAT
REHEATING > REHEAT
REHEATS > REHEAT
REHEEL vb put a new heel or new heels on
REHEELED > REHEEL
REHEELING > REHEEL
REHEELS > REHEEL
REHEM vb hem again
REHEMMED > REHEM
REHEMMING > REHEM
REHEMS > REHEM
REHINGE vb put a new hing or new hinges on
REHINGED > REHINGE

REHINGES > REHINGE
REHINGING > REHINGE
REHIRE vb hire again
REHIRED > REHIRE
REHIRES > REHIRE
REHIRING > REHIRE
REHOBOAM n wine bottle holding the equivalent of six normal bottles (approximately 156 ounces)
REHOBOAMS > REHOBOAM
REHOUSE vb provide with a new (and better) home
REHOUSED > REHOUSE
REHOUSES > REHOUSE
REHOUSING > REHOUSE
REHS > REH
REHUNG > REHANG
REHYDRATE vb hydrate again
REI n name for a former Portuguese coin, more properly called a real
REIF n Scots word meaning robbery or plunder
REIFIED > REIFY
REIFIER > REIFY
REIFIERS > REIFY
REIFIES > REIFY
REIFS > REIF
REIFY vb consider or make (an abstract idea or concept) real or concrete
REIFYING > REIFY
REIGN n period of a sovereign's rule ▷ vb rule (a country)
REIGNED > REIGN
REIGNING > REIGN
REIGNITE vb catch fire or cause to catch fire again
REIGNITED > REIGNITE
REIGNITES > REIGNITE
REIGNS > REIGN
REIK Scots word for > SMOKE
REIKI n form of therapy in which the practitioner is believed to channel energy into the patient in order to encourage healing or restore wellbeing
REIKIS > REIKI
REIKS > REIK
REILLUME vb relight
REILLUMED > REILLUME
REILLUMES > REILLUME
REIMAGE vb image again
REIMAGED > REIMAGE
REIMAGES > REIMAGE
REIMAGINE vb imagine again
REIMAGING > REIMAGE
REIMBURSE vb refund, pay back
REIMMERSE vb immerse again
REIMPLANT vb implant again
REIMPORT vb import (goods manufactured from exported raw materials) ▷ n act of reimporting
REIMPORTS > REIMPORT
REIMPOSE vb establish previously imposed laws, controls, etc, again
REIMPOSED > REIMPOSE

REIMPOSES > REIMPOSE
REIN vb check or manage with reins
REINCITE vb incite again
REINCITED > REINCITE
REINCITES > REINCITE
REINCUR vb incur again
REINCURS > REINCUR
REINDEER n deer of arctic regions with large branched antlers
REINDEERS > REINDEER
REINDEX vb index again
REINDEXED > REINDEX
REINDEXES > REINDEX
REINDICT vb indict again
REINDICTS > REINDICT
REINDUCE vb induce again
REINDUCED > REINDUCE
REINDUCES > REINDUCE
REINDUCT vb induct again
REINDUCTS > REINDUCT
REINED > REIN
REINETTE n variety of apple
REINETTES > REINETTE
REINFECT vb infect or contaminate again
REINFECTS > REINFECT
REINFLAME vb inflame again
REINFLATE vb inflate again
REINFORCE vb give added emphasis to
REINFORM vb inform again
REINFORMS > REINFORM
REINFUND vb archaic word for pour in again
REINFUNDS > REINFUND
REINFUSE vb infuse again
REINFUSED > REINFUSE
REINFUSES > REINFUSE
REINHABIT vb inhabit again
REINING > REIN
REINJECT vb inject again
REINJECTS > REINJECT
REINJURE vb injure again
REINJURED > REINJURE
REINJURES > REINJURE
REINJURY n further injury
REINK vb ink again
REINKED > REINK
REINKING > REINK
REINKS > REINK
REINLESS > REIN
REINS pl n narrow straps attached to a bit to guide a horse
REINSERT vb insert again
REINSERTS > REINSERT
REINSMAN n driver in a trotting race
REINSMEN > REINSMAN
REINSPECT vb inspect again
REINSPIRE vb inspire again
REINSTAL same as > REINSTALL
REINSTALL vb put in place and connect (machinery, equipment, etc) again
REINSTALS > REINSTAL
REINSTATE vb restore to a former position
REINSURE vb insure again
REINSURED > REINSURE
REINSURER > REINSURE
REINSURES > REINSURE
REINTER vb inter again

REINTERS > REINTER
REINVADE vb invade again
REINVADED > REINVADE
REINVADES > REINVADE
REINVENT vb replace (a product, etc) with an entirely new version
REINVENTS > REINVENT
REINVEST vb put back profits from a previous investment into the same enterprise
REINVESTS > REINVEST
REINVITE vb invite again
REINVITED > REINVITE
REINVITES > REINVITE
REINVOKE vb invoke again
REINVOKED > REINVOKE
REINVOKES > REINVOKE
REINVOLVE vb involve again
REIRD Scots word for > DIN
REIRDS > REIRD
REIS > REI
REISES > REI
REISSUE n book, record, etc, that is published or released again after being unavailable for a time ▷ vb publish or release (a book, record, etc) again after a period of unavailability
REISSUED > REISSUE
REISSUER > REISSUE
REISSUERS > REISSUE
REISSUES > REISSUE
REISSUING > REISSUE
REIST same as > REEST
REISTAFEL same as > RIJSTAFEL
REISTED > REIST
REISTING > REIST
REISTS > REIST
REITBOK same as > REEDBUCK
REITBOKS > REITBOK
REITER n soldier in the German cavalry
REITERANT > REITERATE
REITERATE vb repeat again and again
REITERS > REITER
REIVE vb go on a plundering raid
REIVED > REIVE
REIVER > REIVE
REIVERS > REIVE
REIVES > REIVE
REIVING > REIVE
REJACKET n put a new jacket on
REJACKETS > REJACKET
REJECT vb refuse to accept or believe ▷ n person or thing rejected as not up to standard
REJECTED > REJECT
REJECTEE n someone who has been rejected
REJECTEES > REJECTEE
REJECTER > REJECT
REJECTERS > REJECT
REJECTING > REJECT
REJECTION > REJECT
REJECTIVE > REJECT
REJECTOR > REJECT
REJECTORS > REJECT
REJECTS > REJECT

REJIG vb re-equip (a factory or plant) ▷ n act or process of rejigging
REJIGGED > REJIG
REJIGGER > REJIG
REJIGGERS > REJIG
REJIGGING > REJIG
REJIGS > REJIG
REJOICE vb feel or express great happiness
REJOICED > REJOICE
REJOICER > REJOICE
REJOICERS > REJOICE
REJOICES > REJOICE
REJOICING > REJOICE
REJOIN vb join again
REJOINDER n answer, retort
REJOINED > REJOIN
REJOINING > REJOIN
REJOINS > REJOIN
REJON n bullfighting lance
REJONEO n bullfighting activity in which a mounted bullfighter spears the bull with lances
REJONEOS > REJONEO
REJONES > REJON
REJOURN vb archaic word meaning postpone or adjourn
REJOURNED > REJOURN
REJOURNS > REJOURN
REJUDGE vb judge again
REJUDGED > REJUDGE
REJUDGES > REJUDGE
REJUDGING > REJUDGE
REJUGGLE vb juggle again
REJUGGLED > REJUGGLE
REJUGGLES > REJUGGLE
REJUSTIFY vb justify again
REKE same as > RECK
REKED > REKE
REKES > REKE
REKEY vb key again
REKEYED > REKEY
REKEYING > REKEY
REKEYS > REKEY
REKINDLE vb arouse former emotions or interests
REKINDLED > REKINDLE
REKINDLES > REKINDLE
REKING > REKE
REKNIT vb knit again
REKNITS > REKNIT
REKNITTED > REKNIT
REKNOT vb knot again
REKNOTS > REKNOT
REKNOTTED > REKNOT
RELABEL vb label again
RELABELED > RELABEL
RELABELS > RELABEL
RELACE vb lace again
RELACED > RELACE
RELACES > RELACE
RELACHE n break
RELACHES > RELACHE
RELACING > RELACE
RELACQUER vb apply a new coat of lacquer to
RELAID > RELAY
RELAND vb land again
RELANDED > RELAND
RELANDING > RELAND
RELANDS > RELAND
RELAPSE vb fall back into bad habits, illness, etc ▷ n return of bad habits,

illness, etc
RELAPSED > RELAPSE
RELAPSER > RELAPSE
RELAPSERS > RELAPSE
RELAPSES > RELAPSE
RELAPSING > RELAPSE
RELATA > RELATUM
RELATABLE > RELATE
RELATE vb establish a relation between
RELATED adj linked by kinship or marriage
RELATEDLY > RELATED
RELATER > RELATE
RELATERS > RELATE
RELATES > RELATE
RELATING > RELATE
RELATION n connection between things
RELATIONS pl n social or political dealings between individuals or groups
RELATIVAL adj of or relating to a relative
RELATIVE adj true to a certain degree or extent ▷ n person connected by blood or marriage
RELATIVES > RELATIVE
RELATOR n person who relates a story
RELATORS > RELATOR
RELATUM n one of the objects between which a relation is said to hold
RELAUNCH vb launch again ▷ n another launching, or something that is relaunched
RELAUNDER vb launder again
RELAX vb make or become looser, less tense, or less rigid
RELAXABLE > RELAX
RELAXANT n drug or agent that relaxes, esp one that relaxes tense muscles ▷ adj of, relating to, or tending to produce relaxation
RELAXANTS > RELAXANT
RELAXED > RELAX
RELAXEDLY > RELAX
RELAXER n person or thing that relaxes, esp a substance used to straighten curly hair
RELAXERS > RELAXER
RELAXES > RELAX
RELAXIN n mammalian polypeptide hormone secreted by the corpus luteum during pregnancy, which relaxes the pelvic ligaments
RELAXING > RELAX
RELAXINS > RELAXIN
RELAY n fresh set of people or animals relieving others ▷ vb pass on (a message)
RELAYED > RELAY
RELAYING > RELAY
RELAYS > RELAY
RELEARN vb learn (something previously known) again
RELEARNED > RELEARN

RELEARNS > RELEARN
RELEARNT > RELEARN
RELEASE vb set free ▷ n setting free
RELEASED > RELEASE
RELEASEE n someone to whom an estate is released or someone released from captivity
RELEASEES > RELEASEE
RELEASER > RELEASE
RELEASERS > RELEASE
RELEASES > RELEASE
RELEASING > RELEASE
RELEASOR n someone releasing an estate to someone else
RELEASORS > RELEASOR
RELEGABLE adj able to be relegated
RELEGATE vb put in a less important position
RELEGATED > RELEGATE
RELEGATES > RELEGATE
RELEND vb lend again
RELENDING > RELEND
RELENDS > RELEND
RELENT vb give up a harsh intention, become less severe
RELENTED > RELENT
RELENTING > RELENT
RELENTS > RELENT
RELET vb let again
RELETS > RELET
RELETTER vb redo lettering of
RELETTERS > RELETTER
RELETTING > RELET
RELEVANCE > RELEVANT
RELEVANCY > RELEVANT
RELEVANT adj do with the matter in hand
RELEVE n dance move in which heels are off the ground
RELEVES > RELEVE
RELIABLE adj able to be trusted, dependable ▷ n something or someone believed to be reliable
RELIABLES > RELIABLE
RELIABLY > RELIABLE
RELIANCE n dependence, confidence, or trust
RELIANCES > RELIANCE
RELIANT > RELIANCE
RELIANTLY > RELIANCE
RELIC n something that has survived from the past
RELICENSE vb license again
RELICS > RELIC
RELICT n relic
RELICTION n process by which sea water or fresh water recedes over time, changing the waterline and leaving land exposed
RELICTS > RELICT
RELIDE archaic past form of > RELY
RELIE archaic spelling of > RELY
RELIED > RELY
RELIEF n gladness at the end or removal of pain, distress, etc

RELIEFS > RELIEF
RELIER > RELY
RELIERS > RELY
RELIES > RELY
RELIEVE vb bring relief to
RELIEVED adj experiencing relief, esp from worry or anxiety
RELIEVER n person or thing that relieves
RELIEVERS > RELIEVER
RELIEVES > RELIEVE
RELIEVING > RELIEVE
RELIEVO same as > RELIEF
RELIEVOS > RELIEVO
RELIGHT vb ignite or cause to ignite again
RELIGHTED > RELIGHT
RELIGHTS > RELIGHT
RELIGIEUX n member of a monastic order or clerical body
RELIGION n system of belief in and worship of a supernatural power or god
RELIGIONS > RELIGION
RELIGIOSE adj affectedly or extremely pious
RELIGIOSO adj religious ▷ adv in a religious manner
RELIGIOUS adj of religion ▷ n monk or nun
RELINE vb line again or anew
RELINED > RELINE
RELINES > RELINE
RELINING > RELINE
RELINK vb link again
RELINKED > RELINK
RELINKING > RELINK
RELINKS > RELINK
RELIQUARY n case or shrine for holy relics
RELIQUE archaic spelling of > RELIC
RELIQUEFY vb liquefy again
RELIQUES > RELIQUE
RELIQUIAE pl n fossil remains of animals or plants
RELISH vb enjoy, like very much ▷ n liking or enjoyment
RELISHED > RELISH
RELISHES > RELISH
RELISHING > RELISH
RELIST vb list again
RELISTED > RELIST
RELISTING > RELIST
RELISTS > RELIST
RELIT > RELIGHT
RELIVABLE > RELIVE
RELIVE vb experience (a sensation etc) again, esp in the imagination
RELIVED > RELIVE
RELIVER vb deliver up again
RELIVERED > RELIVER
RELIVERS > RELIVER
RELIVES > RELIVE
RELIVING > RELIVE
RELLENO n Mexican dish of stuffed vegetable
RELLENOS > RELLENO
RELLIES pl n relatives or relations
RELLISH (in music) variant

of > RELISH
RELLISHED > RELLISH
RELLISHES > RELLISH
RELOAD vb put fresh ammunition into (a firearm)
RELOADED > RELOAD
RELOADER > RELOAD
RELOADERS > RELOAD
RELOADING > RELOAD
RELOADS > RELOAD
RELOAN vb loan again
RELOANED > RELOAN
RELOANING > RELOAN
RELOANS > RELOAN
RELOCATE vb move to a new place to live or work
RELOCATED > RELOCATE
RELOCATEE n someone who is relocated
RELOCATES > RELOCATE
RELOCATOR n program designed to transfer files from one computer to another
RELOCK vb lock again
RELOCKED > RELOCK
RELOCKING > RELOCK
RELOCKS > RELOCK
RELOOK vb look again
RELOOKED > RELOOK
RELOOKING > RELOOK
RELOOKS > RELOOK
RELUCENT adj bright
RELUCT vb struggle or rebel
RELUCTANT adj unwilling or disinclined
RELUCTATE vb be or appear reluctant
RELUCTED > RELUCT
RELUCTING > RELUCT
RELUCTS > RELUCT
RELUME vb light or brighten again
RELUMED > RELUME
RELUMES > RELUME
RELUMINE same as > RELUME
RELUMINED > RELUMINE
RELUMINES > RELUMINE
RELUMING > RELUME
RELY vb depend (on)
RELYING > RELY
REM n dose of ionizing radiation that produces the same effect in man as one roentgen of x- or gamma-radiation
REMADE n object that has been reconstructed from original materials
REMADES > REMADE
REMAIL vb mail again
REMAILED > REMAIL
REMAILING > REMAIL
REMAILS > REMAIL
REMAIN vb continue
REMAINDER n part which is left ▷ vb offer (copies of a poorly selling book) at reduced prices
REMAINED > REMAIN
REMAINING > REMAIN
REMAINS pl n relics, esp of ancient buildings
REMAKE vb make again in a different way ▷ n new version of an old film

REMAKER > REMAKE
REMAKERS > REMAKE
REMAKES > REMAKE
REMAKING > REMAKE
REMAN vb man again or afresh
REMAND vb send back into custody or put on bail before trial
REMANDED > REMAND
REMANDING > REMAND
REMANDS > REMAND
REMANENCE n ability of a material to retain magnetization, equal to the magnetic flux density of the material after the removal of the magnetizing field
REMANENCY archaic variant of > REMANENCE
REMANENT adj remaining or left over ▷ n archaic word meaning remainder
REMANENTS > REMANENT
REMANET n something left over
REMANETS > REMANET
REMANIE n fragments and fossils of older origin found in a more recent deposit
REMANIES > REMANIE
REMANNED > REMAN
REMANNING > REMAN
REMANS > REMAN
REMAP vb map again
REMAPPED > REMAP
REMAPPING > REMAP
REMAPS > REMAP
REMARK vb make a casual comment (on) ▷ n observation or comment
REMARKED > REMARK
REMARKER > REMARK
REMARKERS > REMARK
REMARKET vb market again
REMARKETS > REMARKET
REMARKING > REMARK
REMARKS > REMARK
REMARQUE n printing mark in the margin of a plate
REMARQUED adj having had a remarque put on
REMARQUES > REMARQUE
REMARRIED > REMARRY
REMARRIES > REMARRY
REMARRY vb marry again following a divorce or the death of one's previous husband or wife
REMASTER vb make a new master audio recording, now usually digital, from (an earlier recording), to produce compact discs or stereo records with improved sound reproduction
REMASTERS > REMASTER
REMATCH n second or return game or contest between two players ▷ vb match (two contestants) again
REMATCHED > REMATCH
REMATCHES > REMATCH
REMATE vb mate again ▷ n finishing pass in

bullfighting
REMATED > REMATE
REMATES > REMATE
REMATING > REMATE
REMBLAI n earth used for an embankment or rampart
REMBLAIS > REMBLAI
REMBLE dialect word for > REMOVE
REMBLED > REMBLE
REMBLES > REMBLE
REMBLING > REMBLE
REMEAD archaic or dialect word for > REMEDY
REMEADED > REMEAD
REMEADING > REMEAD
REMEADS > REMEAD
REMEASURE vb measure again
REMEDE archaic or dialect word for > REMEDY
REMEDED > REMEDE
REMEDES > REMEDE
REMEDIAL adj intended to correct a specific disability, handicap, etc
REMEDIAT archaic word for > REMEDIAL
REMEDIATE archaic word for > REMEDIAL
REMEDIED > REMEDY
REMEDIES > REMEDY
REMEDING > REMEDE
REMEDY n means of curing pain or disease ▷ vb put right
REMEDYING > REMEDY
REMEET vb meet again
REMEETING > REMEET
REMEETS > REMEET
REMEID archaic or dialect word for > REMEDY
REMEIDED > REMEID
REMEIDING > REMEID
REMEIDS > REMEID
REMELT vb melt again
REMELTED > REMELT
REMELTING > REMELT
REMELTS > REMELT
REMEMBER vb retain in or recall to one's memory
REMEMBERS > REMEMBER
REMEN n ancient Egyptian measurement unit
REMEND vb mend again
REMENDED > REMEND
REMENDING > REMEND
REMENDS > REMEND
REMENS > REMEN
REMERCIED > REMERCY
REMERCIES > REMERCY
REMERCY vb archaic word for thank
REMERGE vb merge again
REMERGED > REMERGE
REMERGES > REMERGE
REMERGING > REMERGE
REMET > REMEET
REMEX n any of the large flight feathers of a bird's wing
REMIGATE vb row
REMIGATED > REMIGATE
REMIGATES > REMIGATE
REMIGES > REMEX
REMIGIAL > REMEX
REMIGRATE vb migrate

Section 1: Words between 2 and 9 letters in length

again

REMIND *vb* cause to remember

REMINDED > REMIND

REMINDER *n* something that recalls the past

REMINDERS > REMINDER

REMINDFUL *adj* serving to remind

REMINDING > REMIND

REMINDS > REMIND

REMINISCE *vb* talk or write of past times, experiences, etc

REMINT *vb* mint again

REMINTED > REMINT

REMINTING > REMINT

REMINTS > REMINT

REMISE *vb* give up or relinquish (a right, claim, etc) ▷ *n* second thrust made on the same lunge after the first has missed

REMISED > REMISE

REMISES > REMISE

REMISING > REMISE

REMISS *adj* negligent or careless

REMISSION *n* reduction in the length of a prison term

REMISSIVE > REMISSION

REMISSLY > REMISS

REMISSORY *adj* liable to or intended to gain remission

REMIT *vb* send (money) for goods, services, etc, esp by post ▷ *n* area of competence or authority

REMITMENT *n* archaic word for remittance or remission

REMITS > REMIT

REMITTAL > REMIT

REMITTALS > REMIT

REMITTED > REMIT

REMITTEE *n* recipient of a remittance

REMITTEES > REMITTEE

REMITTENT *adj* (of a disease) periodically less severe

REMITTER *n* person who remits

REMITTERS > REMITTER

REMITTING > REMIT

REMITTOR *same as* > REMITTER

REMITTORS > REMITTOR

REMIX *vb* change the relative prominence of each performer's part of (a recording) ▷ *n* remixed version of a recording

REMIXED > REMIX

REMIXES > REMIX

REMIXING > REMIX

REMIXT *informal past form of* > REMIX

REMIXTURE > REMIX

REMNANT *n* small piece, esp of fabric, left over ▷ *adj* remaining

REMNANTAL *adj* existing as remnant

REMNANTS > REMNANT

REMODEL *vb* give a different shape or form to ▷ *n* something that has been

remodelled

REMODELED > REMODEL

REMODELER > REMODEL

REMODELS > REMODEL

REMODIFY *vb* modify again

REMOISTEN *vb* moisten again

REMOLADE *same as* > REMOULADE

REMOLADES > REMOLADE

REMOLD *US spelling of* > REMOULD

REMOLDED > REMOLD

REMOLDING > REMOLD

REMOLDS > REMOLD

REMONTANT *adj* (esp of cultivated roses) flowering more than once in a single season ▷ *n* rose having such a growth

REMONTOIR *n* any of various devices used in watches, clocks, etc, to compensate for errors arising from the changes in the force driving the escapement

REMORA *n* spiny-finned fish

REMORAS > REMORA

REMORID > REMORA

REMORSE *n* feeling of sorrow and regret for something one did

REMORSES > REMORSE

REMOTE *adj* far away, distant ▷ *n* (in informal usage) remote control

REMOTELY > REMOTE

REMOTER > REMOTE

REMOTES > REMOTE

REMOTEST > REMOTE

REMOTION *n* removal

REMOTIONS > REMOTION

REMOUD *Spenserian variant of* > REMOVED

REMOULADE *n* mayonnaise sauce flavoured with herbs, mustard, and capers, served with salads, cold meat, etc

REMOULD *vb* change completely ▷ *n* renovated tyre

REMOULDED > REMOULD

REMOULDS > REMOULD

REMOUNT *vb* get on (a horse, bicycle, etc) again ▷ *n* fresh horse, esp (formerly) to replace one killed or injured in battle

REMOUNTED > REMOUNT

REMOUNTS > REMOUNT

REMOVABLE > REMOVE

REMOVABLY > REMOVE

REMOVAL *n* removing, esp changing residence

REMOVALS > REMOVAL

REMOVE *vb* take away or off ▷ *n* degree of difference

REMOVED *adj* very different or distant

REMOVEDLY *adv* at a distance

REMOVER > REMOVE

REMOVERS > REMOVE

REMOVES > REMOVE

REMOVING > REMOVE

REMS > REM

REMUAGE *n* (in the making of sparkling wine) process of turning the bottles to let the sediment out

REMUAGES > REMUAGE

REMUDA *n* stock of horses enabling riders to change mounts

REMUDAS > REMUDA

REMUEUR *n* (in the making of sparkling wine) person carrying out remuage, or the turning of bottles

REMUEURS > REMUEUR

REMURMUR *vb* murmur again or murmur in reply

REMURMURS > REMURMUR

REN *archaic variant of* > RUN

RENAGUE *same as* > RENEGE

RENAGUED > RENAGUE

RENAGUES > RENAGUE

RENAGUING > RENAGUE

RENAIL *vb* nail again

RENAILED > RENAIL

RENAILING > RENAIL

RENAILS > RENAIL

RENAL *adj* of the kidneys

RENAME *vb* change the name of (someone or something)

RENAMED > RENAME

RENAMES > RENAME

RENAMING > RENAME

RENASCENT *adj* becoming active or vigorous again

RENATURE *vb* return to natural state

RENATURED > RENATURE

RENATURES > RENATURE

RENAY *vb* archaic word meaning renounce

RENAYED > RENAY

RENAYING > RENAY

RENAYS > RENAY

RENCONTRE *n* unexpected meeting

REND *vb* tear or wrench apart

RENDED > REND

RENDER *vb* cause to become ▷ *n* first thin coat of plaster applied to a surface

RENDERED > RENDER

RENDERER > RENDER

RENDERERS > RENDER

RENDERING *n* act or an instance of performing a play, piece of music, etc

RENDERS > RENDER

RENDIBLE > REND

RENDING > REND

RENDITION *n* performance

RENDS > REND

RENDZINA *n* dark interzonal type of soil found in grassy or formerly grassy areas of moderate rainfall, esp on chalklands

RENDZINAS > RENDZINA

RENEGADE *n* person who deserts a cause ▷ *vb* become a renegade

RENEGADED > RENEGADE

RENEGADES > RENEGADE

RENEGADO *archaic word for* > RENEGADE

RENEGADOS > RENEGADO

RENEGATE *old variant of* > RENEGADE

RENEGATES > RENEGATE

RENEGE *vb* go back (on a promise etc)

RENEGED > RENEGE

RENEGER > RENEGE

RENEGERS > RENEGE

RENEGES > RENEGE

RENEGING > RENEGE

RENEGUE *same as* > RENEGE

RENEGUED > RENEGUE

RENEGUER > RENEGUE

RENEGUERS > RENEGE

RENEGUES > RENEGUE

RENEGUING > RENEGUE

RENEST *vb* nest again or form a new nest

RENESTED > RENEST

RENESTING > RENEST

RENESTS > RENEST

RENEW *vb* begin again

RENEWABLE > RENEW

RENEWABLY > RENEW

RENEWAL *n* act of renewing or state of being renewed

RENEWALS > RENEWAL

RENEWED > RENEW

RENEWEDLY > RENEW

RENEWER > RENEW

RENEWERS > RENEW

RENEWING > RENEW

RENEWINGS > RENEW

RENEWS > RENEW

RENEY *same as* > RENAY

RENEYED > RENEY

RENEYING > RENEY

RENEYS > RENEY

RENFIERST *adj* archaic word for turned fierce

RENFORCE *vb* archaic word for reinforce

RENFORCED > RENFORCE

RENFORCES > RENFORCE

RENFORST > RENFORCE

RENGA *n* type of collaborative poetry found in Japan

RENGAS > RENGA

RENIED > RENY

RENIES > RENY

RENIFORM *adj* having the shape or profile of a kidney

RENIG *same as* > RENEGE

RENIGGED > RENIG

RENIGGING > RENIG

RENIGS > RENIG

RENIN *n* proteolytic enzyme secreted by the kidneys, which plays an important part in the maintenance of blood pressure

RENINS > RENIN

RENITENCE > RENITENT

RENITENCY > RENITENT

RENITENT *adj* reluctant

RENK *adj* unpleasant

RENKER > RENK

RENKEST > RENK

RENMINBI *same as* > YUAN

RENMINBIS > RENMINBI

RENNASE *same as* > RENNIN

RENNASES > RENNASE

RENNE *archaic variant of* > RUN

RENNED > REN

RENNES > RENNE

RENNET *n* substance for curdling milk to make cheese

RENNETS > RENNET

RENNIN *n* enzyme that occurs in gastric juice and is a constituent of rennet. It coagulates milk by converting caseinogen to casein

RENNING > REN

RENNINGS > REN

RENNINS > RENNIN

RENOGRAM *n* X-ray kidney image

RENOGRAMS > RENOGRAM

RENOTIFY *vb* notify again

RENOUNCE *vb* give up (a belief, habit, etc) voluntarily ▷ *n* failure to follow suit in a card game

RENOUNCED > RENOUNCE

RENOUNCER > RENOUNCE

RENOUNCES > RENOUNCE

RENOVATE *vb* restore to good condition

RENOVATED > RENOVATE

RENOVATES > RENOVATE

RENOVATOR > RENOVATE

RENOWN *n* widespread good reputation ▷ *vb* make famous

RENOWNED *adj* famous

RENOWNER *n* renown giver

RENOWNERS > RENOWNER

RENOWNING > RENOWN

RENOWNS > RENOWN

RENS > REN

RENT *n* payment made by a tenant to a landlord or owner of a property ▷ *vb* grant the right to use one's property for payment

RENTABLE > REND

RENTAL *n* sum payable as rent ▷ *adj* of or relating to rent

RENTALLER *n* (in Scots law) tenant with very favourable terms

RENTALS > RENTAL

RENTE *n* annual income from capital investment

RENTED > RENT

RENTER *n* person who lets his property in return for rent, esp a landlord

RENTERS > RENTER

RENTES > RENTE

RENTIER *n* person who lives off unearned income such as rents or interest

RENTIERS > RENTIER

RENTING > RENT

RENTINGS > RENT

RENTS > RENT

RENUMBER *vb* number again or afresh

RENUMBERS > RENUMBER

RENVERSE *vb* archaic word meaning overturn

RENVERSED > RENVERSE

RENVERSES > RENVERSE

RENVERST > RENVERSE

RENVOI *n* referring of a dispute or other legal question to a jurisdiction other than that in which it arose

RENVOIS > RENVOI

RENVOY old variant of > RENVOI

RENVOYS > RENVOY

RENY same as > RENAY

RENYING > RENY

REO *n* language

REOBJECT *vb* object again

REOBJECTS > REOBJECT

REOBSERVE *vb* observe again

REOBTAIN *vb* obtain again

REOBTAINS > REOBTAIN

REOCCUPY *vb* occupy (a building, area, etc) again

REOCCUR *vb* happen, take place, or come about again

REOCCURS > REOCCUR

REOFFEND *vb* commit another offence

REOFFENDS > REOFFEND

REOFFER *vb* offer again

REOFFERED > REOFFER

REOFFERS > REOFFER

REOIL *vb* oil again

REOILED > REOIL

REOILING > REOIL

REOILS > REOIL

REOPEN *vb* open again after a period of being closed or suspended

REOPENED > REOPEN

REOPENER *n* clause in a legal document allowing for an issue to be revisited at a subsequent date

REOPENERS > REOPENER

REOPENING > REOPEN

REOPENS > REOPEN

REOPERATE *vb* operate again

REOPPOSE *vb* oppose again

REOPPOSED > REOPPOSE

REOPPOSES > REOPPOSE

REORDAIN *vb* ordain again

REORDAINS > REORDAIN

REORDER *vb* change the order of

REORDERED > REORDER

REORDERS > REORDER

REORIENT *vb* adjust or align (something) in a new or different way

REORIENTS > REORIENT

REOS > REO

REOUTFIT *vb* outfit again

REOUTFITS > REOUTFIT

REOVIRUS *n* type of virus

REOXIDISE same as > REOXIDIZE

REOXIDIZE *vb* oxidize again

REP *n* sales representative ▷ *vb* work as a representative

REPACIFY *vb* pacify again

REPACK *vb* place or arrange (articles) in (a container) again or in a different way

REPACKAGE *vb* wrap or put (something) in a package again

REPACKED > REPACK

REPACKING > REPACK

REPACKS > REPACK

REPAID > REPAY

REPAINT *vb* apply a new or fresh coat of paint

REPAINTED > REPAINT

REPAINTS > REPAINT

REPAIR *vb* restore to good condition, mend ▷ *n* act of repairing

REPAIRED > REPAIR

REPAIRER > REPAIR

REPAIRERS > REPAIR

REPAIRING > REPAIR

REPAIRMAN *n* man whose job it is to repair machines, appliances, etc

REPAIRMEN > REPAIRMAN

REPAIRS > REPAIR

REPAND *adj* having a wavy margin

REPANDLY > REPAND

REPANEL *vb* panel again or anew

REPANELED > REPANEL

REPANELS > REPANEL

REPAPER *vb* paper again or afresh

REPAPERED > REPAPER

REPAPERS > REPAPER

REPARABLE *adj* able to be repaired or remedied

REPARABLY > REPARABLE

REPARK *vb* park again

REPARKED > REPARK

REPARKING > REPARK

REPARKS > REPARK

REPARTEE *n* interchange of witty retorts ▷ *vb* retort

REPARTEED > REPARTEE

REPARTEES > REPARTEE

REPASS *vb* pass again

REPASSAGE *n* passage back or return

REPASSED > REPASS

REPASSES > REPASS

REPASSING > REPASS

REPAST *n* meal ▷ *vb* feed (on)

REPASTED > REPAST

REPASTING > REPAST

REPASTS > REPAST

REPASTURE old word for > FOOD

REPATCH *vb* patch again

REPATCHED > REPATCH

REPATCHES > REPATCH

REPATTERN *vb* pattern again

REPAVE *vb* pave again

REPAVED > REPAVE

REPAVES > REPAVE

REPAVING > REPAVE

REPAY *vb* pay back, refund

REPAYABLE > REPAY

REPAYING > REPAY

REPAYMENT > REPAY

REPAYS > REPAY

REPEAL *vb* cancel (a law) officially ▷ *n* act of repealing

REPEALED > REPEAL

REPEALER > REPEAL

REPEALERS > REPEAL

REPEALING > REPEAL

REPEALS > REPEAL

REPEAT *vb* say or do again ▷ *n* act or instance of repeating

REPEATED *adj* done, made, or said again and again

REPEATER *n* firearm that may be discharged many times without reloading

REPEATERS > REPEATER

REPEATING > REPEAT

REPEATS > REPEAT

REPECHAGE *n* extra heat or test providing second chance to previous losers or failing candidates

REPEG *vb* peg again

REPEGGED > REPEG

REPEGGING > REPEG

REPEGS > REPEG

REPEL *vb* be disgusting to

REPELLANT same as > REPELLENT

REPELLED > REPEL

REPELLENT *adj* distasteful ▷ *n* something that repels, esp a chemical to repel insects

REPELLER > REPEL

REPELLERS > REPEL

REPELLING > REPEL

REPELS > REPEL

REPENT *vb* feel regret for (a deed or omission) ▷ *adj* lying or creeping along the ground

REPENTANT *adj* reproaching oneself for one's past actions or sins

REPENTED > REPENT

REPENTER > REPENT

REPENTERS > REPENT

REPENTING > REPENT

REPENTS > REPENT

REPEOPLE *vb* people again

REPEOPLED > REPEOPLE

REPEOPLES > REPEOPLE

REPERCUSS *vb* have repercussions

REPEREPE *n* New Zealand word for the elephant fish, a large fish of the southwest Pacific with a trunk-like snout

REPERK *vb* perk again

REPERKED > REPERK

REPERKING > REPERK

REPERKS > REPERK

REPERTORY *n* repertoire

REPERUSAL *n* fresh perusal

REPERUSE *vb* peruse again

REPERUSED > REPERUSE

REPERUSES > REPERUSE

REPETEND *n* digit or series of digits in a recurring decimal that repeats itself

REPETENDS > REPETEND

REPHRASE *vb* express in different words

REPHRASED > REPHRASE

REPHRASES > REPHRASE

REPIGMENT *vb* pigment again

REPIN *vb* pin again

REPINE *vb* fret or complain

REPINED > REPINE

REPINER > REPINE

REPINERS > REPINE

REPINES > REPINE

REPINING > REPINE

REPININGS > REPINE

REPINNED > REPIN

REPINNING > REPIN
REPINS > REPIN
REPIQUE n score of 30 points made from the cards held by a player before play begins ▷ vb score a repique against (someone)
REPIQUED > REPIQUE
REPIQUES > REPIQUE
REPIQUING > REPIQUE
REPLA > REPLUM
REPLACE vb substitute for
REPLACED > REPLACE
REPLACER > REPLACE
REPLACERS > REPLACE
REPLACES > REPLACE
REPLACING > REPLACE
REPLAN vb plan again
REPLANNED > REPLAN
REPLANS > REPLAN
REPLANT vb plant again
REPLANTED > REPLANT
REPLANTS > REPLANT
REPLASTER vb plaster again
REPLATE vb plate again
REPLATED > REPLATE
REPLATES > REPLATE
REPLATING > REPLATE
REPLAY n immediate reshowing on TV of an incident in sport, esp in slow motion ▷ vb play (a match, recording, etc) again
REPLAYED > REPLAY
REPLAYING > REPLAY
REPLAYS > REPLAY
REPLEAD vb plead again
REPLEADED > REPLEAD
REPLEADER n right to plead again
REPLEADS > REPLEAD
REPLED > REPLEAD
REPLEDGE vb pledge again
REPLEDGED > REPLEDGE
REPLEDGES > REPLEDGE
REPLENISH vb fill up again, resupply
REPLETE adj filled or gorged ▷ vb fill again
REPLETED > REPLETE
REPLETELY > REPLETE
REPLETES > REPLETE
REPLETING > REPLETE
REPLETION n state or condition of being replete
REPLEVIED > REPLEVY
REPLEVIES > REPLEVY
REPLEVIN n recovery of goods unlawfully taken, made subject to establishing the validity of the recovery in a legal action and returning the goods if the decision is adverse
REPLEVINS > REPLEVIN
REPLEVY vb recover possession of (goods) by replevin
REPLICA n exact copy
REPLICAS > REPLICA
REPLICASE n type of enzyme
REPLICATE vb make or be a copy of ▷ adj folded back on itself

REPLICON n region of a DNA molecule that is replicated from a single origin
REPLICONS > REPLICON
REPLIED > REPLY
REPLIER > REPLY
REPLIERS > REPLY
REPLIES > REPLY
REPLOT vb plot again
REPLOTS > REPLOT
REPLOTTED > REPLOT
REPLOW vb plow again
REPLOWED > REPLOW
REPLOWING > REPLOW
REPLOWS > REPLOW
REPLUM n internal separating wall in some fruits
REPLUMB vb plumb again
REPLUMBED > REPLUMB
REPLUMBS > REPLUMB
REPLUNGE vb plunge again
REPLUNGED > REPLUNGE
REPLUNGES > REPLUNGE
REPLY vb answer or respond ▷ n answer or response
REPLYING > REPLY
REPO n act of repossessing
REPOINT vb repair the joints of (brickwork, masonry, etc) with mortar or cement
REPOINTED > REPOINT
REPOINTS > REPOINT
REPOLISH vb polish again
REPOLL vb poll again
REPOLLED > REPOLL
REPOLLING > REPOLL
REPOLLS > REPOLL
REPOMAN n informal word for a man employed to repossess goods in cases of non-payment
REPOMEN > REPOMAN
REPONE vb restore (someone) to his former status, office, etc
REPONED > REPONE
REPONES > REPONE
REPONING > REPONE
REPORT vb give an account of ▷ n account or statement
REPORTAGE n act or process of reporting news or other events of general interest
REPORTED > REPORT
REPORTER n person who gathers news for a newspaper, TV, etc
REPORTERS > REPORTER
REPORTING > REPORT
REPORTS > REPORT
REPOS > REPO
REPOSAL n repose
REPOSALL archaic spelling of > REPOSAL
REPOSALLS > REPOSALL
REPOSALS > REPOSE
REPOSE n peace ▷ vb lie or lay at rest
REPOSED > REPOSE
REPOSEDLY > REPOSE
REPOSEFUL > REPOSE
REPOSER > REPOSE
REPOSERS > REPOSE
REPOSES > REPOSE
REPOSING > REPOSE

REPOSIT vb put away, deposit, or store up
REPOSITED > REPOSIT
REPOSITOR n any instrument used for correcting the position of displaced organs or bones
REPOSITS > REPOSIT
REPOSSESS vb (of a lender) take back property from a customer who is behind with payments
REPOST vb post again
REPOSTED > REPOST
REPOSTING > REPOST
REPOSTS > REPOST
REPOSURE old word for > REPOSE
REPOSURES > REPOSURE
REPOT vb put (a house plant) into a new usually larger pot
REPOTS > REPOT
REPOTTED > REPOT
REPOTTING > REPOT
REPOUR vb pour back or again
REPOURED > REPOUR
REPOURING > REPOUR
REPOURS > REPOUR
REPOUSSE adj raised in relief, as a design on a thin piece of metal hammered through from the underside ▷ n design or surface made in this way
REPOUSSES > REPOUSSE
REPOWER vb put new engine in
REPOWERED > REPOWER
REPOWERS > REPOWER
REPP same as > REP
REPPED > REP
REPPING > REP
REPPINGS > REP
REPPS > REPP
REPREEVE archaic spelling of > REPRIEVE
REPREEVED > REPREEVE
REPREEVES > REPREEVE
REPREHEND vb find fault with
REPRESENT vb act as a delegate or substitute for
REPRESS vb keep (feelings) in check
REPRESSED adj (of a person) repressing feelings, instincts, desires, etc
REPRESSER > REPRESS
REPRESSES > REPRESS
REPRESSOR n protein synthesized under the control of a repressor gene, which has the capacity to bind to the operator gene and thereby shut off the expression of the structural genes of an operon
REPRICE vb price again
REPRICED > REPRICE
REPRICES > REPRICE
REPRICING > REPRICE
REPRIEFE n (in archaic usage) reproof
REPRIEFES > REPRIEFE
REPRIEVAL old word

for > REPRIEVE
REPRIEVE vb postpone the execution of (a condemned person) ▷ n (document granting) postponement or cancellation of a punishment
REPRIEVED > REPRIEVE
REPRIEVER > REPRIEVE
REPRIEVES > REPRIEVE
REPRIMAND vb blame (someone) officially for a fault ▷ n official blame
REPRIME vb prime again
REPRIMED > REPRIME
REPRIMES > REPRIME
REPRIMING > REPRIME
REPRINT vb print further copies of (a book) ▷ n reprinted copy
REPRINTED > REPRINT
REPRINTER > REPRINT
REPRINTS > REPRINT
REPRISAL n retaliation
REPRISALS > REPRISAL
REPRISE n repeating of an earlier theme ▷ vb repeat an earlier theme
REPRISED > REPRISE
REPRISES > REPRISE
REPRISING > REPRISE
REPRIVE archaic spelling of > REPRIEVE
REPRIVED > REPRIVE
REPRIVES > REPRIVE
REPRIVING > REPRIVE
REPRIZE archaic spelling of > REPRISE
REPRIZED > REPRIZE
REPRIZES > REPRIZE
REPRIZING > REPRIZE
REPRO n imitation or facsimile of a work of art; reproduction
REPROACH vb blame, rebuke
REPROBACY > REPROBATE
REPROBATE n depraved or disreputable (person) ▷ adj morally unprincipled ▷ vb disapprove of
REPROBE vb probe again
REPROBED > REPROBE
REPROBES > REPROBE
REPROBING > REPROBE
REPROCESS vb treat or prepare (something) by a special method again
REPRODUCE vb produce a copy of
REPROGRAM vb program again
REPROOF n severe blaming of someone for a fault ▷ vb treat (a coat, jacket, etc) so as to renew its texture, waterproof qualities, etc
REPROOFED > REPROOF
REPROOFS > REPROOF
REPROS > REPRO
REPROVAL same as > REPROOF
REPROVALS > REPROVAL
REPROVE vb speak severely to (someone) about a fault
REPROVED > REPROVE
REPROVER > REPROVE
REPROVERS > REPROVE

REPROVES > REPROVE
REPROVING > REPROVE
REPRYVE *archaic spelling of* > REPRIEVE
REPRYVED > REPRYVE
REPRYVES > REPRYVE
REPRYVING > REPRYVE
REPS > REP
REPTANT *adj* creeping, crawling, or lying along the ground
REPTATION *n* creeping action
REPTILE *n* cold-blooded egg-laying vertebrate with horny scales or plates, such as a snake or tortoise ▷ *adj* creeping, crawling, or squirming
REPTILES > REPTILE
REPTILIA > REPTILIUM
REPTILIAN *adj* of, relating to, resembling, or characteristic of reptiles
REPTILIUM *n* place where live reptiles are kept for show
REPTILOID *adj* resembling a reptile
REPUBLIC *n* form of government in which the people or their elected representatives possess the supreme power
REPUBLICS > REPUBLIC
REPUBLISH *vb* publish again
REPUDIATE *vb* reject the authority or validity of
REPUGN *vb* oppose or conflict (with)
REPUGNANT *adj* offensive or distasteful
REPUGNED > REPUGN
REPUGNING > REPUGN
REPUGNS > REPUGN
REPULP *vb* pulp again
REPULPED > REPULP
REPULPING > REPULP
REPULPS > REPULP
REPULSE *vb* be disgusting to ▷ *n* driving back
REPULSED > REPULSE
REPULSER > REPULSE
REPULSERS > REPULSE
REPULSES > REPULSE
REPULSING > REPULSE
REPULSION *n* distaste or aversion
REPULSIVE *adj* loathsome, disgusting
REPUMP *vb* pump again
REPUMPED > REPUMP
REPUMPING > REPUMP
REPUMPS > REPUMP
REPUNIT *n* any number that consists entirely of the same repeated digits, such as 111 or 55,555
REPUNITS > REPUNIT
REPURE *vb* archaic word meaning make pure again
REPURED > REPURE
REPURES > REPURE
REPURIFY *vb* purify again
REPURING > REPURE
REPURPOSE *vb* find new

purpose for
REPURSUE *vb* pursue again
REPURSUED > REPURSUE
REPURSUES > REPURSUE
REPUTABLE *adj* of good reputation, respectable
REPUTABLY > REPUTABLE
REPUTE *n* reputation ▷ *vb* consider (a person or thing) to be as specified
REPUTED *adj* supposed
REPUTEDLY *adv* according to general belief or supposition
REPUTES > REPUTE
REPUTING > REPUTE
REPUTINGS > REPUTE
REQUALIFY *vb* qualify again
REQUERE *archaic variant of* > REQUIRE
REQUERED > REQUERE
REQUERES > REQUERE
REQUERING > REQUERE
REQUEST *vb* ask ▷ *n* asking
REQUESTED > REQUEST
REQUESTER > REQUEST
REQUESTOR > REQUEST
REQUESTS > REQUEST
REQUICKEN *vb* quicken again
REQUIEM *n* Mass celebrated for the dead
REQUIEMS > REQUIEM
REQUIGHT *archaic spelling of* > REQUITE
REQUIGHTS > REQUIGHT
REQUIN *vb* type of shark
REQUINS > REQUIN
REQUIRE *vb* want or need
REQUIRED > REQUIRE
REQUIRER > REQUIRE
REQUIRERS > REQUIRE
REQUIRES > REQUIRE
REQUIRING > REQUIRE
REQUISITE *adj* necessary, essential ▷ *n* essential thing
REQUIT *vb* quit again
REQUITAL *n* act or an instance of requiting
REQUITALS > REQUITAL
REQUITE *vb* return to someone (the same treatment or feeling as received)
REQUITED > REQUITE
REQUITER > REQUITE
REQUITERS > REQUITE
REQUITES > REQUITE
REQUITING > REQUITE
REQUITS > REQUIT
REQUITTED > REQUIT
REQUOTE *vb* quote again
REQUOTED > REQUOTE
REQUOTES > REQUOTE
REQUOTING > REQUOTE
REQUOYLE *archaic spelling of* > RECOIL
REQUOYLED > REQUOYLE
REQUOYLES > REQUOYLE
RERACK *vb* rack again
RERACKED > RERACK
RERACKING > RERACK
RERACKS > RERACK
RERADIATE *vb* radiate again
RERAIL *vb* put back on a railway line

RERAILED > RERAIL
RERAILING *n* replacement of existing rails on a railway line
RERAILS > RERAIL
RERAISE *vb* raise again
RERAISED > RERAISE
RERAISES > RERAISE
RERAISING > RERAISE
RERAN > RERUN
REREAD *vb* read (something) again
REREADING > REREAD
REREADS > REREAD
REREBRACE *n* armour worn on the upper arm
RERECORD *vb* record again
RERECORDS > RERECORD
REREDOS *n* ornamental screen behind an altar
REREDOSES > REREDOS
REREDOSSE *same as* > REREDOS
RERELEASE *vb* release again
REREMAI *n* New Zealand word for the basking shark
REREMICE > REREMOUSE
REREMIND *vb* remind again
REREMINDS > REREMIND
REREMOUSE *n* archaic or dialect word for 'bat' (the animal)
RERENT *vb* rent again
RERENTED > RERENT
RERENTING > RERENT
RERENTS > RERENT
REREPEAT *vb* repeat again
REREPEATS > REREPEAT
REREVIEW *vb* review again
REREVIEWS > REREVIEW
REREVISE *vb* revise again
REREVISED > REREVISE
REREVISES > REREVISE
REREWARD *archaic spelling of* > REARWARD
REREWARDS *archaic spelling of* > REARWARDS
RERIG *vb* rig again
RERIGGED > RERIG
RERIGGING > RERIG
RERIGS > RERIG
RERISE *vb* rise again
RERISEN > RERISE
RERISES > RERISE
RERISING > RERISE
REROLL *vb* roll again
REROLLED > REROLL
REROLLER > REROLL
REROLLERS > REROLL
REROLLING > REROLL
REROLLS > REROLL
REROOF *vb* put a new roof or roofs on
REROOFED > REROOF
REROOFING > REROOF
REROOFS > REROOF
REROSE > RERISE
REROUTE *vb* send or direct by a different route
REROUTED > REROUTE
REROUTES > REROUTE
REROUTING > REROUTE
RERUN *n* film or programme that is broadcast again, repeat ▷ *vb* put on (a film or programme) again
RERUNNING > RERUN

RERUNS > RERUN
RES *informal word for* > RESIDENCE
RESADDLE *vb* saddle again
RESADDLED > RESADDLE
RESADDLES > RESADDLE
RESAID > RESAY
RESAIL *vb* sail again
RESAILED > RESAIL
RESAILING > RESAIL
RESAILS > RESAIL
RESALABLE > RESALE
RESALE *n* selling of something purchased earlier
RESALES > RESALE
RESALGAR *archaic variant of* > REALGAR
RESALGARS > RESALGAR
RESALUTE *vb* salute back or again
RESALUTED > RESALUTE
RESALUTES > RESALUTE
RESAMPLE *vb* (in graphics or digital photography) change the size or resolution of
RESAMPLED > RESAMPLE
RESAMPLES > RESAMPLE
RESAT > RESIT
RESAW *vb* saw again
RESAWED > RESAW
RESAWING > RESAW
RESAWN > RESAW
RESAWS > RESAW
RESAY *vb* say again or in response
RESAYING > RESAY
RESAYS > RESAY
RESCALE *vb* resize
RESCALED > RESCALE
RESCALES > RESCALE
RESCALING > RESCALE
RESCHOOL *vb* retrain
RESCHOOLS > RESCHOOL
RESCIND *vb* annul or repeal
RESCINDED > RESCIND
RESCINDER > RESCIND
RESCINDS > RESCIND
RESCORE *vb* score afresh
RESCORED > RESCORE
RESCORES > RESCORE
RESCORING > RESCORE
RESCREEN *vb* screen again
RESCREENS > RESCREEN
RESCRIPT *n* (in ancient Rome) an ordinance taking the form of a reply by the emperor to a question on a point of law
RESCRIPTS > RESCRIPT
RESCUABLE > RESCUE
RESCUE *vb* deliver from danger or trouble, save ▷ *n* rescuing
RESCUED > RESCUE
RESCUER > RESCUE
RESCUERS > RESCUE
RESCUES > RESCUE
RESCUING > RESCUE
RESCULPT *vb* sculpt again
RESCULPTS > RESCULPT
RESEAL *vb* close or secure tightly again
RESEALED > RESEAL
RESEALING > RESEAL
RESEALS > RESEAL

r

r

RESEARCH n systematic investigation to discover facts or collect information ▷vb carry out investigations
RESEASON vb season again
RESEASONS > RESEASON
RESEAT vb show (a person) to a new seat
RESEATED > RESEAT
RESEATING > RESEAT
RESEATS > RESEAT
RESEAU n mesh background to a lace or other pattern
RESEAUS > RESEAU
RESEAUX > RESEAU
RESECT vb cut out part of (a bone, an organ, or other structure or part)
RESECTED > RESECT
RESECTING > RESECT
RESECTION n excision of part of a bone, organ, or other part
RESECTS > RESECT
RESECURE vb secure again
RESECURED > RESECURE
RESECURES > RESECURE
RESEDA n plant that has small spikes of grey-green flowers ▷adj of a greyish-green colour
RESEDAS > RESEDA
RESEE vb see again
RESEED vb form seed and reproduce naturally, forming a constant plant population
RESEEDED > RESEED
RESEEDING > RESEED
RESEEDS > RESEED
RESEEING > RESEE
RESEEK vb seek again
RESEEKING > RESEEK
RESEEKS > RESEEK
RESEEN > RESEE
RESEES > RESEE
RESEIZE vb seize again
RESEIZED > RESEIZE
RESEIZES > RESEIZE
RESEIZING > RESEIZE
RESEIZURE > RESEIZE
RESELECT vb choose (someone or something) again, esp to choose an existing office-holder as candidate for re-election
RESELECTS > RESELECT
RESELL vb sell (something) one has previously bought
RESELLER > RESELL
RESELLERS > RESELL
RESELLING > RESELL
RESELLS > RESELL
RESEMBLE vb be or look like
RESEMBLED > RESEMBLE
RESEMBLER > RESEMBLE
RESEMBLES > RESEMBLE
RESEND vb send again
RESENDING > RESEND
RESENDS > RESEND
RESENT vb feel bitter about
RESENTED > RESENT
RESENTER > RESENT
RESENTERS > RESENT
RESENTFUL adj feeling or characterized by

resentment
RESENTING > RESENT
RESENTIVE archaic word for > RESENTFUL
RESENTS > RESENT
RESERPINE n insoluble alkaloid, extracted from the roots of the plant *Rauwolfia serpentina*, used medicinally to lower blood pressure and as a sedative
RESERVE vb set aside, keep for future use ▷n something, esp money or troops, kept for emergencies
RESERVED adj not showing one's feelings, lacking friendliness
RESERVER > RESERVE
RESERVERS > RESERVE
RESERVES > RESERVE
RESERVICE vb service again
RESERVING > RESERVE
RESERVIST n member of a military reserve
RESERVOIR n natural or artificial lake storing water for community supplies
RESES > RES
RESET vb set again (a broken bone, matter in type, a gemstone, etc) ▷n act or an instance of setting again
RESETS > RESET
RESETTED same as > RESET
RESETTER > RESET
RESETTERS > RESET
RESETTING > RESET
RESETTLE vb settle to live in a different place
RESETTLED > RESETTLE
RESETTLES > RESETTLE
RESEW vb sew again
RESEWED > RESEW
RESEWING > RESEW
RESEWN > RESEW
RESEWS > RESEW
RESH n 20th letter of the Hebrew alphabet
RESHAPE vb shape (something) again or differently
RESHAPED > RESHAPE
RESHAPER > RESHAPE
RESHAPERS > RESHAPE
RESHAPES > RESHAPE
RESHAPING > RESHAPE
RESHARPEN vb sharpen again
RESHAVE vb shave again
RESHAVED > RESHAVE
RESHAVEN > RESHAVE
RESHAVES > RESHAVE
RESHAVING > RESHAVE
RESHES > RESH
RESHINE vb shine again
RESHINED > RESHINE
RESHINES > RESHINE
RESHINGLE vb put new shingles on
RESHINING > RESHINE
RESHIP vb ship again
RESHIPPED > RESHIP
RESHIPPER > RESHIP
RESHIPS > RESHIP

RESHOD > RESHOE
RESHOE vb put a new sho or shoes on
RESHOED > RESHOE
RESHOEING > RESHOE
RESHOES > RESHOE
RESHONE > RESHINE
RESHOOT vb shoot again
RESHOOTS > RESHOOT
RESHOT > RESHOOT
RESHOW vb show again
RESHOWED > RESHOW
RESHOWER vb have another shower
RESHOWERS > RESHOWER
RESHOWING > RESHOW
RESHOWN > RESHOW
RESHOWS > RESHOW
RESHUFFLE n reorganization ▷vb reorganize
RESIANCE archaic word for > RESIDENCE
RESIANCES > RESIANCE
RESIANT archaic word for > RESIDENT
RESIANTS > RESIANT
RESID n residual oil left over from the petroleum distillation process
RESIDE vb dwell permanently
RESIDED > RESIDE
RESIDENCE n home or house
RESIDENCY n regular series of concerts by a band or singer at one venue
RESIDENT n person who lives in a place ▷adj living in a place
RESIDENTS > RESIDENT
RESIDER > RESIDE
RESIDERS > RESIDE
RESIDES > RESIDE
RESIDING > RESIDE
RESIDS > RESID
RESIDUA > RESIDUUM
RESIDUAL adj of or being a remainder ▷n something left over as a residue
RESIDUALS > RESIDUAL
RESIDUARY adj of, relating to, or constituting a residue
RESIDUE n what is left, remainder
RESIDUES > RESIDUE
RESIDUOUS adj residual
RESIDUUM n residue
RESIDUUMS > RESIDUUM
RESIFT vb sift again
RESIFTED > RESIFT
RESIFTING > RESIFT
RESIFTS > RESIFT
RESIGHT vb sight again
RESIGHTED > RESIGHT
RESIGHTS > RESIGHT
RESIGN vb give up office, a job, etc
RESIGNED adj content to endure
RESIGNER > RESIGN
RESIGNERS > RESIGN
RESIGNING > RESIGN
RESIGNS > RESIGN
RESILE vb spring or shrink

back
RESILED > RESILE
RESILES > RESILE
RESILIENT adj (of a person) recovering quickly from a shock etc
RESILIN n substance found in insect bodies
RESILING > RESILE
RESILINS > RESILIN
RESILVER vb silver again
RESILVERS > RESILVER
RESIN n sticky substance from plants, esp pines ▷vb treat or coat with resin
RESINATA n type of wine
RESINATAS > RESINATA
RESINATE vb impregnate with resin
RESINATED > RESINATE
RESINATES > RESINATE
RESINED > RESIN
RESINER n applier or collector of resin
RESINERS > RESINER
RESINIFY vb become or cause to be resinous
RESINING > RESIN
RESINISE variant spelling of > RESINIZE
RESINISED > RESINISE
RESINISES > RESINISE
RESINIZE vb apply resin to
RESINIZED > RESINIZE
RESINIZES > RESINIZE
RESINLIKE > RESIN
RESINOID adj resembling, characteristic of, or containing resin ▷n any resinoid substance, esp a synthetic compound
RESINOIDS > RESINOID
RESINOSES > RESINOSIS
RESINOSIS n excessive resin loss in diseased or damaged conifers
RESINOUS > RESIN
RESINS > RESIN
RESINY adj resembling, containing or covered with resin
RESIST vb withstand or oppose ▷n substance used to protect something, esp a coating that prevents corrosion
RESISTANT adj characterized by or showing resistance ▷n person or thing that resists
RESISTED > RESIST
RESISTENT same as > RESISTANT
RESISTER > RESIST
RESISTERS > RESIST
RESISTING > RESIST
RESISTIVE adj exhibiting electrical resistance
RESISTOR n component of an electrical circuit producing resistance
RESISTORS > RESISTOR
RESISTS > RESIST
RESIT vb take (an exam) again ▷n exam that has to be taken again
RESITE vb move to a

different site
RESITED > RESITE
RESITES > RESITE
RESITING > RESITE
RESITS > RESIT
RESITTING > RESIT
RESITUATE *vb* situate elsewhere
RESIZE *vb* change size of
RESIZED > RESIZE
RESIZES > RESIZE
RESIZING > RESIZE
RESKETCH *vb* sketch again
RESKEW *archaic spelling of* > RESCUE
RESKEWED > RESKEW
RESKEWING > RESKEW
RESKEWS > RESKEW
RESKILL *vb* train (workers) to acquire new skills
RESKILLED > RESKILL
RESKILLS > RESKILL
RESKUE *archaic spelling of* > RESCUE
RESKUED > RESKUE
RESKUES > RESKUE
RESKUING > RESKUE
RESLATE *vb* slate again
RESLATED > RESLATE
RESLATES > RESLATE
RESLATING > RESLATE
RESMELT *vb* smelt again
RESMELTED > RESMELT
RESMELTS > RESMELT
RESMOOTH *vb* smooth again
RESMOOTHS > RESMOOTH
RESNATRON *n* tetrode used to generate high power at high frequencies
RESOAK *vb* soak again
RESOAKED > RESOAK
RESOAKING > RESOAK
RESOAKS > RESOAK
RESOD *vb* returf
RESODDED > RESOD
RESODDING > RESOD
RESODS > RESOD
RESOFTEN *vb* soften again
RESOFTENS > RESOFTEN
RESOJET *n* type of jet engine
RESOJETS > RESOJET
RESOLD > RESELL
RESOLDER *vb* solder again
RESOLDERS > RESOLDER
RESOLE *vb* put a new sole or new soles on
RESOLED > RESOLE
RESOLES > RESOLE
RESOLING > RESOLE
RESOLUBLE *adj* able to be resolved
RESOLUTE *adj* firm in purpose ▷ *n* someone resolute
RESOLUTER > RESOLUTE
RESOLUTES > RESOLUTE
RESOLVE *vb* decide with an effort of will ▷ *n* absolute determination
RESOLVED *adj* determined
RESOLVENT *adj* serving to dissolve or separate something into its elements ▷ *n* something that resolves
RESOLVER > RESOLVE

RESOLVERS > RESOLVE
RESOLVES > RESOLVE
RESOLVING > RESOLVE
RESONANCE *n* echoing, esp with a deep sound
RESONANT *adj* resounding or re-echoing ▷ *n* type of unobstructed speech sound
RESONANTS > RESONANT
RESONATE *vb* resound or cause to resound
RESONATED > RESONATE
RESONATES > RESONATE
RESONATOR *n* any body or system that displays resonance, esp a tuned electrical circuit or a conducting cavity in which microwaves are generated by a resonant current
RESORB *vb* absorb again
RESORBED > RESORB
RESORBENT > RESORB
RESORBING > RESORB
RESORBS > RESORB
RESORCIN *n* substance used principally in dyeing
RESORCINS > RESORCIN
RESORT *vb* have recourse (to) for help etc ▷ *n* place for holidays
RESORTED > RESORT
RESORTER > RESORT
RESORTERS > RESORT
RESORTING > RESORT
RESORTS > RESORT
RESOUGHT > RESEEK
RESOUND *vb* echo or ring with sound
RESOUNDED > RESOUND
RESOUNDS > RESOUND
RESOURCE *n* thing resorted to for support ▷ *vb* provide funding or other resources for
RESOURCED > RESOURCE
RESOURCES > RESOURCE
RESOW *vb* sow again
RESOWED > RESOW
RESOWING > RESOW
RESOWN > RESOW
RESOWS > RESOW
RESPACE *vb* change the spacing of
RESPACED > RESPACE
RESPACES > RESPACE
RESPACING > RESPACE
RESPADE *vb* dig over
RESPADED > RESPADE
RESPADES > RESPADE
RESPADING > RESPADE
RESPEAK *vb* speak further
RESPEAKS > RESPEAK
RESPECIFY *vb* specify again
RESPECT *n* consideration ▷ *vb* treat with esteem
RESPECTED > RESPECT
RESPECTER *n* person who respects someone or something
RESPECTS > RESPECT
RESPELL *vb* spell again
RESPELLED > RESPELL
RESPELLS > RESPELL
RESPELT > RESPELL
RESPIRE *vb* breathe

RESPIRED > RESPIRE
RESPIRES > RESPIRE
RESPIRING > RESPIRE
RESPITE *n* pause, interval of rest ▷ *vb* grant a respite to
RESPITED > RESPITE
RESPITES > RESPITE
RESPITING > RESPITE
RESPLEND *vb* be resplendent
RESPLENDS > RESPLEND
RESPLICE *vb* splice again
RESPLICED > RESPLICE
RESPLICES > RESPLICE
RESPLIT *vb* split again
RESPLITS > RESPLIT
RESPOKE > RESPEAK
RESPOKEN > RESPEAK
RESPOND *vb* answer ▷ *n* pilaster or an engaged column that supports an arch or a lintel
RESPONDED > RESPOND
RESPONDER > RESPOND
RESPONDS > RESPOND
RESPONSA *n* that part of rabbinic literature concerned with written rulings in answer to questions
RESPONSE *n* answer
RESPONSER *n* radio or radar receiver used in conjunction with an interrogator to receive and display signals from a transponder
RESPONSES > RESPONSE
RESPONSOR *same as* > RESPONSER
RESPONSUM *n* written answer from a rabbinic authority to a question submitted
RESPOOL *vb* rewind onto spool
RESPOOLED > RESPOOL
RESPOOLS > RESPOOL
RESPOT *vb* (in billiards) replace on one of the spots
RESPOTS > RESPOT
RESPOTTED > RESPOT
RESPRANG > RESPRING
RESPRAY *n* new coat of paint applied to a car, van, etc ▷ *vb* spray (a car, wheels, etc) with a new coat of paint
RESPRAYED > RESPRAY
RESPRAYS > RESPRAY
RESPREAD *vb* spread again
RESPREADS > RESPREAD
RESPRING *vb* put new springs in
RESPRINGS > RESPRING
RESPROUT *vb* sprout again
RESPROUTS > RESPROUT
RESPRUNG > RESPRING
RESSALDAR *n* native cavalry commander in mixed Anglo-Indian army
REST *n* freedom from exertion etc ▷ *vb* take a rest
RESTABLE *vb* put in stable again or elsewhere

RESTABLED > RESTABLE
RESTABLES > RESTABLE
RESTACK *vb* stack again
RESTACKED > RESTACK
RESTACKS > RESTACK
RESTAFF *vb* staff again
RESTAFFED > RESTAFF
RESTAFFS > RESTAFF
RESTAGE *vb* produce or perform a new production of (a play)
RESTAGED > RESTAGE
RESTAGES > RESTAGE
RESTAGING > RESTAGE
RESTAMP *vb* stamp again
RESTAMPED > RESTAMP
RESTAMPS > RESTAMP
RESTART *vb* commence (something) or set (something) in motion again ▷ *n* act or an instance of starting again
RESTARTED > RESTART
RESTARTER > RESTART
RESTARTS > RESTART
RESTATE *vb* state or affirm (something) again or in a different way
RESTATED > RESTATE
RESTATES > RESTATE
RESTATING > RESTATE
RESTATION *vb* station elsewhere
RESTED > REST
RESTEM *vb* stem again
RESTEMMED > RESTEM
RESTEMS > RESTEM
RESTER > REST
RESTERS > REST
RESTFUL *adj* relaxing or soothing
RESTFULLY > RESTFUL
RESTIER > RESTY
RESTIEST > RESTY
RESTIFF *same as* > RESTIVE
RESTIFORM *adj* (esp of bundles of nerve fibres) shaped like a cord or rope
RESTING > REST
RESTINGS > REST
RESTITCH *vb* stitch again
RESTITUTE *vb* restore
RESTIVE *adj* restless or impatient
RESTIVELY > RESTIVE
RESTLESS *adj* bored or dissatisfied
RESTO *n* restored antique, vintage car, etc
RESTOCK *vb* replenish stores or supplies
RESTOCKED > RESTOCK
RESTOCKS > RESTOCK
RESTOKE *vb* stoke again
RESTOKED > RESTOKE
RESTOKES > RESTOKE
RESTOKING > RESTOKE
RESTORAL *n* restoration
RESTORALS > RESTORAL
RESTORE *vb* return (a building, painting, etc) to its original condition
RESTORED > RESTORE
RESTORER > RESTORE
RESTORERS > RESTORE
RESTORES > RESTORE
RESTORING > RESTORE

r

RESTOS > RESTO
RESTRAIN vb hold (someone) back from action
RESTRAINS > RESTRAIN
RESTRAINT n something that restrains
RESTRESS vb stress again or differently
RESTRETCH vb stretch again
RESTRICT vb confine to certain limits
RESTRICTS > RESTRICT
RESTRIKE vb strike again
RESTRIKES > RESTRIKE
RESTRING vb string again or anew
RESTRINGE vb restrict
RESTRINGS > RESTRING
RESTRIVE vb strive again
RESTRIVEN > RESTRIVE
RESTRIVES > RESTRIVE
RESTROOM n room in a public building having lavatories, washing facilities, and sometimes couches
RESTROOMS > RESTROOM
RESTROVE > RESTRIVE
RESTRUCK > RESTRIKE
RESTRUNG > RESTRING
RESTS > REST
RESTUDIED > RESTUDY
RESTUDIES > RESTUDY
RESTUDY vb study again
RESTUFF vb put new stuffing in
RESTUFFED > RESTUFF
RESTUFFS > RESTUFF
RESTUMP vb Australian building term for provide with new stumps
RESTUMPED > RESTUMP
RESTUMPS > RESTUMP
RESTY adj restive
RESTYLE vb style again
RESTYLED > RESTYLE
RESTYLES > RESTYLE
RESTYLING > RESTYLE
RESUBJECT vb subject again
RESUBMIT vb submit again
RESUBMITS > RESUBMIT
RESULT n outcome or consequence ▷ vb be the outcome or consequence (of)
RESULTANT adj arising as a result ▷ n sum of two or more vectors, such as the force resulting from two or more forces acting on a single point
RESULTED > RESULT
RESULTFUL > RESULT
RESULTING > RESULT
RESULTS > RESULT
RESUMABLE > RESUME
RESUME vb begin again ▷ n summary
RESUMED > RESUME
RESUMER > RESUME
RESUMERS > RESUME
RESUMES > RESUME
RESUMING > RESUME
RESUMMON vb summon again
RESUMMONS > RESUMMON

RESUPINE adj lying on the back
RESUPPLY vb provide (with something) again
RESURFACE vb arise or occur again
RESURGE vb rise again from or as if from the dead
RESURGED > RESURGE
RESURGENT adj rising again, as to new life, vigour, etc
RESURGES > RESURGE
RESURGING > RESURGE
RESURRECT vb restore to life
RESURVEY vb survey again
RESURVEYS > RESURVEY
RESUSPEND vb put back into suspension
RESWALLOW vb swallow again
RET vb moisten or soak (flax, hemp, jute, etc) to promote bacterial action in order to facilitate separation of the fibres from the woody tissue by beating
RETABLE n ornamental screenlike structure above and behind an altar, esp one used as a setting for a religious picture or carving
RETABLES > RETABLE
RETACK vb tack again
RETACKED > RETACK
RETACKING > RETACK
RETACKLE vb tackle again
RETACKLED > RETACKLE
RETACKLES > RETACKLE
RETACKS > RETACK
RETAG vb tag again
RETAGGED > RETAG
RETAGGING > RETAG
RETAGS > RETAG
RETAIL n selling of goods individually or in small amounts to the public ▷ adj of or engaged in such selling ▷ adv by retail ▷ vb sell or be sold retail
RETAILED > RETAIL
RETAILER > RETAIL
RETAILERS > RETAIL
RETAILING > RETAIL
RETAILOR vb tailor afresh
RETAILORS > RETAILOR
RETAILS > RETAIL
RETAIN vb keep in one's possession
RETAINED > RETAIN
RETAINER n fee to retain someone's services
RETAINERS > RETAINER
RETAINING > RETAIN
RETAINS > RETAIN
RETAKE vb recapture ▷ n act of rephotographing a scene
RETAKEN > RETAKE
RETAKER > RETAKE
RETAKERS > RETAKE
RETAKES > RETAKE
RETAKING > RETAKE
RETAKINGS > RETAKE
RETALIATE vb repay an injury or wrong in kind
RETALLIED > RETALLY

RETALLIES > RETALLY
RETALLY vb count up again
RETAMA n type of shrub
RETAMAS > RETAMA
RETAPE vb tape again
RETAPED > RETAPE
RETAPES > RETAPE
RETAPING > RETAPE
RETARD vb delay or slow (progress or development) ▷ n offensive term for a retarded person
RETARDANT n substance that reduces the rate of a chemical reaction ▷ adj having a slowing effect
RETARDATE n person who is retarded
RETARDED adj underdeveloped, esp mentally
RETARDER n person or thing that retards
RETARDERS > RETARDER
RETARDING > RETARD
RETARDS > RETARD
RETARGET vb target afresh or differently
RETARGETS > RETARGET
RETASTE vb taste again
RETASTED > RETASTE
RETASTES > RETASTE
RETASTING > RETASTE
RETAUGHT > RETEACH
RETAX vb tax again
RETAXED > RETAX
RETAXES > RETAX
RETAXING > RETAX
RETCH vb try to vomit ▷ n involuntary spasm of the stomach
RETCHED > RETCH
RETCHES > RETCH
RETCHING > RETCH
RETCHLESS archaic variant of > RECKLESS
RETE n any network of nerves or blood vessels
RETEACH vb teach again
RETEACHES > RETEACH
RETEAM vb team up again
RETEAMED > RETEAM
RETEAMING > RETEAM
RETEAMS > RETEAM
RETEAR vb tear again
RETEARING > RETEAR
RETEARS > RETEAR
RETELL vb relate (a story, etc) again or differently
RETELLER > RETELL
RETELLERS > RETELL
RETELLING > RETELL
RETELLS > RETELL
RETEM n type of shrub
RETEMPER vb temper again
RETEMPERS > RETEMPER
RETEMS > RETEM
RETENE n yellow crystalline hydrocarbon found in tar oils from pine wood and in certain fossil resins
RETENES > RETENE
RETENTION n retaining
RETENTIVE adj capable of retaining or remembering
RETES > RETE
RETEST vb test (something)

again or differently
RETESTED > RETEST
RETESTIFY vb testify again
RETESTING > RETEST
RETESTS > RETEST
RETEXTURE vb restore natural texture to
RETHINK vb consider again, esp with a view to changing one's tactics ▷ n act or an instance of thinking again
RETHINKER > RETHINK
RETHINKS > RETHINK
RETHOUGHT > RETHINK
RETHREAD vb thread again
RETHREADS > RETHREAD
RETIA > RETE
RETIAL > RETE
RETIARII > RETIARIUS
RETIARIUS n (in ancient Rome) a gladiator armed with a net and trident
RETIARY adj of, relating to, or resembling a net or web
RETICELLA n form of lace
RETICENCE > RETICENT
RETICENCY > RETICENT
RETICENT adj uncommunicative, reserved
RETICLE n network of fine lines, wires, etc, placed in the focal plane of an optical instrument to assist measurement of the size or position of objects under observation
RETICLES > RETICLE
RETICULA > RETICULUM
RETICULAR adj in the form of a network or having a network of parts
RETICULE same as > RETICLE
RETICULES > RETICULE
RETICULUM n any fine network, esp one in the body composed of cells, fibres, etc
RETIE vb tie again
RETIED > RETIE
RETIEING > RETIE
RETIES > RETIE
RETIFORM adj netlike
RETIGHTEN vb tighten again
RETILE vb put new tiles in or on
RETILED > RETILE
RETILES > RETILE
RETILING > RETILE
RETIME vb time again or alter time of
RETIMED > RETIME
RETIMES > RETIME
RETIMING > RETIME
RETINA n light-sensitive membrane at the back of the eye
RETINAE > RETINA
RETINAL adj of or relating to the retina ▷ n aldehyde form of the polyene retinol (vitamin A) that associates with the protein opsin to form the visual purple pigment rhodopsin

RETINALS > RETINAL
RETINAS > RETINA
RETINE *n* chemical found in body cells that slows cell growth and division
RETINENE *n* aldehyde form of the polyene retinol (vitamin A) that associates with the protein opsin to form the visual purple pigment rhodopsin
RETINENES > RETINENE
RETINES > RETINE
RETINITE *n* any of various resins of fossil origin, esp one derived from lignite
RETINITES > RETINITE
RETINITIS *n* inflammation of the retina
RETINOID *adj* resinlike ▷ *n* derivative of vitamin A
RETINOIDS > RETINOID
RETINOL *n* another name for vitamin A and rosin oil
RETINOLS > RETINOL
RETINT *vb* tint again or change tint of
RETINTED > RETINT
RETINTING > RETINT
RETINTS > RETINT
RETINUE *n* band of attendants
RETINUED > RETINUE
RETINUES > RETINUE
RETINULA *n* part of the compound eye in certain arthropods
RETINULAE > RETINULA
RETINULAR > RETINULA
RETINULAS > RETINULA
RETIRACY *n* (in US English) retirement
RETIRAL *n* act of retiring from office, one's work, etc
RETIRALS > RETIRAL
RETIRANT *n* (in US English) retired person
RETIRANTS > RETIRANT
RETIRE *vb* (cause to) give up office or work, esp through age
RETIRED *adj* having retired from work etc
RETIREDLY > RETIRED
RETIREE *n* person who has retired from work
RETIREES > RETIREE
RETIRER > RETIRE
RETIRERS > RETIRE
RETIRES > RETIRE
RETIRING *adj* shy
RETITLE *vb* give a new title to
RETITLED > RETITLE
RETITLES > RETITLE
RETITLING > RETITLE
RETOLD > RETELL
RETOOK > RETAKE
RETOOL *vb* replace, re-equip, or rearrange the tools in (a factory, etc)
RETOOLED > RETOOL
RETOOLING > RETOOL
RETOOLS > RETOOL
RETORE > RETEAR
RETORN > RETEAR
RETORSION *n* retaliatory

action taken by a state whose citizens have been mistreated by a foreign power by treating the subjects of that power similarly
RETORT *vb* reply quickly, wittily, or angrily ▷ *n* quick, witty, or angry reply
RETORTED > RETORT
RETORTER > RETORT
RETORTERS > RETORT
RETORTING > RETORT
RETORTION *n* act of retorting
RETORTIVE > RETORT
RETORTS > RETORT
RETOTAL *vb* add up again
RETOTALED > RETOTAL
RETOTALS > RETOTAL
RETOUCH *vb* restore or improve by new touches, esp of paint ▷ *n* art or practice of retouching
RETOUCHED > RETOUCH
RETOUCHER > RETOUCH
RETOUCHES > RETOUCH
RETOUR *vb* (in Scottish law) to return as heir
RETOURED > RETOUR
RETOURING > RETOUR
RETOURS > RETOUR
RETRACE *vb* go back over (a route etc) again
RETRACED > RETRACE
RETRACER > RETRACE
RETRACERS > RETRACE
RETRACES > RETRACE
RETRACING > RETRACE
RETRACK *vb* track again
RETRACKED > RETRACK
RETRACKS > RETRACK
RETRACT *vb* withdraw (a statement etc)
RETRACTED > RETRACT
RETRACTOR *n* any of various muscles that retract an organ or part
RETRACTS > RETRACT
RETRAICT *archaic form of* > RETREAT
RETRAICTS > RETRAICT
RETRAIN *vb* train to do a new or different job
RETRAINED > RETRAIN
RETRAINEE > RETRAIN
RETRAINS > RETRAIN
RETRAIT *archaic form of* > RETREAT
RETRAITE *archaic form of* > RETREAT
RETRAITES > RETRAITE
RETRAITS > RETRAIT
RETRAITT *n* archaic word meaning portrait
RETRAITTS > RETRAITT
RETRAL *adj* at, near, or towards the back
RETRALLY > RETRAL
RETRATE *archaic form of* > RETREAT
RETRATED > RETRATE
RETRATES > RETRATE
RETRATING > RETRATE
RETREAD *n* remould ▷ *vb* remould tread again
RETREADED > RETREAD

RETREADS > RETREAD
RETREAT *vb* move back from a position, withdraw ▷ *n* act of or military signal for retiring or withdrawal
RETREATED > RETREAT
RETREATER > RETREAT
RETREATS > RETREAT
RETREE *n* imperfectly made paper
RETREES > RETREE
RETRENCH *vb* reduce expenditure, cut back
RETRIAL *n* second trial of a case or defendant in a court of law
RETRIALS > RETRIAL
RETRIBUTE *vb* give back
RETRIED > RETRY
RETRIES > RETRY
RETRIEVAL *n* act or process of retrieving
RETRIEVE *vb* fetch back again ▷ *n* chance of being retrieved
RETRIEVED > RETRIEVE
RETRIEVER *n* dog trained to retrieve shot game
RETRIEVES > RETRIEVE
RETRIM *vb* trim again
RETRIMMED > RETRIM
RETRIMS > RETRIM
RETRO *adj* associated with or revived from the past
RETROACT *vb* act in opposition
RETROACTS > RETROACT
RETROCEDE *vb* give back
RETROD > RETREAD
RETRODDEN > RETREAD
RETRODICT *vb* make surmises about the past using information from the present
RETROFIRE *n* act of firing a retrorocket
RETROFIT *vb* equip (a vehicle, piece of equipment, etc) with new parts, safety devices, etc, after manufacture
RETROFITS > RETROFIT
RETROFLEX *adj* bent or curved backwards
RETROJECT *vb* throw backwards (opposed to *project*)
RETRONYM *n* word coined for existing thing to distinguish it from new thing
RETRONYMS > RETRONYM
RETROPACK *n* system of retrorockets on a spacecraft
RETRORSE *adj* (esp of plant parts) pointing backwards or in a direction opposite to normal
RETROS > RETRO
RETROUSSE *adj* (of a nose) turned upwards
RETROVERT *vb* turn back
RETRY *vb* try again (a case already determined)
RETRYING > RETRY
RETS > RET

RETSINA *n* Greek wine flavoured with resin
RETSINAS > RETSINA
RETTED > RET
RETTERIES > RETTERY
RETTERY *n* flax-retting place
RETTING > RET
RETUND *vb* weaken or blunt
RETUNDED > RETUND
RETUNDING > RETUND
RETUNDS > RETUND
RETUNE *vb* tune (a musical instrument) differently or again
RETUNED > RETUNE
RETUNES > RETUNE
RETUNING > RETUNE
RETURF *vb* turf again
RETURFED > RETURF
RETURFING > RETURF
RETURFS > RETURF
RETURN *vb* go or come back ▷ *n* returning ▷ *adj* of or being a return
RETURNED > RETURN
RETURNEE *n* person who returns to his native country, esp after war service
RETURNEES > RETURNEE
RETURNER *n* person or thing that returns
RETURNERS > RETURNER
RETURNIK *n* someone returning or intending to return to their native land, especially when this is in the former Soviet Union
RETURNIKS > RETURNIK
RETURNING > RETURN
RETURNS > RETURN
RETUSE *adj* having a rounded apex and a central depression
RETWIST *vb* twist again
RETWISTED > RETWIST
RETWISTS > RETWIST
RETYING > RETIE
RETYPE *vb* type again
RETYPED > RETYPE
RETYPES > RETYPE
RETYPING > RETYPE
REUNIFIED > REUNIFY
REUNIFIES > REUNIFY
REUNIFY *vb* bring together again something previously divided
REUNION *n* meeting of people who have been apart
REUNIONS > REUNION
REUNITE *vb* bring or come together again after a separation
REUNITED > REUNITE
REUNITER > REUNITE
REUNITERS > REUNITE
REUNITES > REUNITE
REUNITING > REUNITE
REUPTAKE *vb* absorb again
REUPTAKES > REUPTAKE
REURGE *vb* urge again
REURGED > REURGE
REURGES > REURGE
REURGING > REURGE
REUSABLE *adj* able to be

r

used more than once

REUSABLES pl n products which can be used more than once

REUSE vb use again ▷ n act of using something again

REUSED > REUSE

REUSES > REUSE

REUSING > REUSE

REUTILISE same as > REUTILIZE

REUTILIZE vb utilize again

REUTTER vb utter again

REUTTERED > REUTTER

REUTTERS > REUTTER

REV n revolution (of an engine) ▷ vb increase the speed of revolution of (an engine)

REVALENTA n lentil flour

REVALUATE same as > REVALUE

REVALUE vb adjust the exchange value of (a currency) upwards

REVALUED > REVALUE

REVALUES > REVALUE

REVALUING > REVALUE

REVAMP vb renovate or restore ▷ n something that has been renovated or revamped

REVAMPED > REVAMP

REVAMPER > REVAMP

REVAMPERS > REVAMP

REVAMPING > REVAMP

REVAMPS > REVAMP

REVANCHE n revenge

REVANCHES > REVANCHE

REVARNISH vb varnish again

REVEAL vb make known ▷ n vertical side of an opening in a wall, esp the side of a window or door between the frame and the front of the wall

REVEALED > REVEAL

REVEALER > REVEAL

REVEALERS > REVEAL

REVEALING adj disclosing information that one did not know

REVEALS > REVEAL

REVEHENT adj (in anatomy) carrying back

REVEILLE n morning bugle call to waken soldiers

REVEILLES > REVEILLE

REVEL vb take pleasure (in) ▷ n occasion of noisy merrymaking

REVELATOR n revealer

REVELED > REVEL

REVELER > REVEL

REVELERS > REVEL

REVELING > REVEL

REVELLED > REVEL

REVELLER > REVEL

REVELLERS > REVEL

REVELLING > REVEL

REVELMENT > REVEL

REVELRIES > REVELRY

REVELROUS > REVELRY

REVELRY n festivity

REVELS > REVEL

REVENANT n something, esp

a ghost, that returns

REVENANTS > REVENANT

REVENGE n retaliation for wrong done ▷ vb make retaliation for

REVENGED > REVENGE

REVENGER > REVENGE

REVENGERS > REVENGE

REVENGES > REVENGE

REVENGING > REVENGE

REVENGIVE > REVENGE

REVENUAL > REVENUE

REVENUE n income, esp of a state

REVENUED > REVENUE

REVENUER n revenue officer or cutter

REVENUERS > REVENUER

REVENUES > REVENUE

REVERABLE > REVERE

REVERB n electronic device that creates artificial acoustics ▷ vb reverberate

REVERBED > REVERB

REVERBING > REVERB

REVERBS > REVERB

REVERE vb be in awe of and respect greatly

REVERED > REVERE

REVERENCE n awe mingled with respect and esteem

REVEREND adj worthy of reverence ▷ n clergyman

REVERENDS > REVEREND

REVERENT adj showing reverence

REVERER > REVERE

REVERERS > REVERE

REVERES > REVERE

REVERIE n absent-minded daydream

REVERIES > REVERIE

REVERIFY vb verify again

REVERING > REVERE

REVERIST n someone given to reveries

REVERISTS > REVERIST

REVERS n turned back part of a garment, such as the lapel

REVERSAL n act or an instance of reversing

REVERSALS > REVERSAL

REVERSE vb turn upside down or the other way round ▷ n opposite ▷ adj opposite or contrary

REVERSED > REVERSE

REVERSELY > REVERSE

REVERSER > REVERSE

REVERSERS > REVERSE

REVERSES > REVERSE

REVERSI n game played on a draughtboard with 64 pieces, black on one side and white on the other. When pieces are captured they are turned over to join the capturing player's forces

REVERSING > REVERSE

REVERSION n return to a former state, practice, or belief

REVERSIS n type of card game

REVERSO another name

for > VERSO

REVERSOS > REVERSO

REVERT vb return to a former state

REVERTANT n mutant that has reverted to an earlier form ▷ adj having mutated to an earlier form

REVERTED > REVERT

REVERTER > REVERT

REVERTERS > REVERT

REVERTING > REVERT

REVERTIVE > REVERT

REVERTS > REVERT

REVERY same as > REVERIE

REVEST vb restore (former power, authority, status, etc, to a person) or (of power, authority, etc) to be restored

REVESTED > REVEST

REVESTING > REVEST

REVESTRY same as > VESTRY

REVESTS > REVEST

REVET vb face (a wall or embankment) with stones

REVETMENT n facing of stones, sandbags, etc, to protect a wall, embankment, or earthworks

REVETS > REVET

REVETTED > REVET

REVETTING > REVET

REVEUR n daydreamer

REVEURS > REVEUR

REVEUSE n female daydreamer

REVEUSES > REVEUSE

REVIBRATE vb vibrate again

REVICTUAL vb victual again

REVIE vb archaic cards term meaning challenge by placing a larger stake

REVIED > REVIE

REVIES > REVIE

REVIEW n critical assessment of a book, concert, etc ▷ vb hold or write a review of

REVIEWAL same as > REVIEW

REVIEWALS > REVIEWAL

REVIEWED > REVIEW

REVIEWER > REVIEW

REVIEWERS > REVIEW

REVIEWING > REVIEW

REVIEWS > REVIEW

REVILE vb be abusively scornful of

REVILED > REVILE

REVILER > REVILE

REVILERS > REVILE

REVILES > REVILE

REVILING > REVILE

REVILINGS > REVILE

REVIOLATE vb violate again

REVISABLE > REVISE

REVISAL > REVISE

REVISALS > REVISE

REVISE vb change or alter ▷ n act, process, or result of revising

REVISED > REVISE

REVISER > REVISE

REVISERS > REVISE

REVISES > REVISE

REVISING > REVISE

REVISION n act of revising

REVISIONS > REVISION

REVISIT vb visit again

REVISITED > REVISIT

REVISITS > REVISIT

REVISOR > REVISE

REVISORS > REVISE

REVISORY adj of or having the power of revision

REVIVABLE > REVIVE

REVIVABLY > REVIVE

REVIVAL n reviving or renewal

REVIVALS > REVIVAL

REVIVE vb bring or come back to life, vigour, use, etc

REVIVED > REVIVE

REVIVER > REVIVE

REVIVERS > REVIVE

REVIVES > REVIVE

REVIVIFY vb give new life to

REVIVING > REVIVE

REVIVINGS > REVIVE

REVIVOR n means of reviving a lawsuit that has been suspended owing to the death or marriage of one of the parties

REVIVORS > REVIVOR

REVOCABLE adj capable of being revoked

REVOCABLY > REVOCABLE

REVOICE vb utter again

REVOICED > REVOICE

REVOICES > REVOICE

REVOICING > REVOICE

REVOKABLE same as > REVOCABLE

REVOKABLY > REVOCABLE

REVOKE vb cancel (a will, agreement, etc) ▷ n act of revoking

REVOKED > REVOKE

REVOKER > REVOKE

REVOKERS > REVOKE

REVOKES > REVOKE

REVOKING > REVOKE

REVOLT n uprising against authority ▷ vb rise in rebellion

REVOLTED > REVOLT

REVOLTER > REVOLT

REVOLTERS > REVOLT

REVOLTING adj disgusting, horrible

REVOLTS > REVOLT

REVOLUTE adj (esp of the margins of a leaf) rolled backwards and downwards

REVOLVE vb turn round, rotate ▷ n circular section of a stage that can be rotated by electric power to provide a scene change

REVOLVED > REVOLVE

REVOLVER n repeating pistol

REVOLVERS > REVOLVER

REVOLVES > REVOLVE

REVOLVING adj denoting or relating to an engine, such as a radial aero engine, in which the cylinders revolve about a fixed shaft

REVOTE vb decide or grant

again by a new vote
REVOTED > REVOTE
REVOTES > REVOTE
REVOTING > REVOTE
REVS > REV
REVUE n theatrical entertainment with topical sketches and songs
REVUES > REVUE
REVUIST > REVUE
REVUISTS > REVUE
REVULSED adj filled with disgust
REVULSION n strong disgust
REVULSIVE adj of or causing revulsion ▷ n counterirritant
REVVED > REV
REVVING > REV
REVYING > REVIE
REW archaic spelling of > RUE
REWAKE vb awaken again
REWAKED > REWAKE
REWAKEN vb awaken again
REWAKENED > REWAKEN
REWAKENS > REWAKEN
REWAKES > REWAKE
REWAKING > REWAKE
REWAN archaic past form of > REWIN
REWARD n something given in return for a service ▷ vb pay or give something to (someone) for a service, information, etc
REWARDED > REWARD
REWARDER > REWARD
REWARDERS > REWARD
REWARDFUL > REWARD
REWARDING adj giving personal satisfaction, worthwhile
REWARDS > REWARD
REWAREWA n New Zealand tree
REWAREWAS > REWAREWA
REWARM vb warm again
REWARMED > REWARM
REWARMING > REWARM
REWARMS > REWARM
REWASH vb wash again
REWASHED > REWASH
REWASHES > REWASH
REWASHING > REWASH
REWAX vb wax again
REWAXED > REWAX
REWAXES > REWAX
REWAXING > REWAX
REWEAR vb wear again
REWEARING > REWEAR
REWEARS > REWEAR
REWEAVE vb weave again
REWEAVED > REWEAVE
REWEAVES > REWEAVE
REWEAVING > REWEAVE
REWED vb wed again
REWEDDED > REWED
REWEDDING > REWED
REWEDS > REWED
REWEIGH vb weigh again
REWEIGHED > REWEIGH
REWEIGHS > REWEIGH
REWELD vb weld again
REWELDED > REWELD
REWELDING > REWELD
REWELDS > REWELD

REWET vb wet again
REWETS > REWET
REWETTED > REWET
REWETTING > REWET
REWIDEN vb widen again
REWIDENED > REWIDEN
REWIDENS > REWIDEN
REWIN vb win again
REWIND vb wind again
REWINDED > REWIND
REWINDER > REWIND
REWINDERS > REWIND
REWINDING > REWIND
REWINDS > REWIND
REWINNING > REWIN
REWINS > REWIN
REWIRABLE > REWIRE
REWIRE vb provide (a house, engine, etc) with new wiring
REWIRED > REWIRE
REWIRES > REWIRE
REWIRING > REWIRE
REWOKE > REWAKE
REWOKEN > REWAKE
REWON > REWIN
REWORD vb alter the wording of
REWORDED > REWORD
REWORDING > REWORD
REWORDS > REWORD
REWORE > REWEAR
REWORK vb improve or bring up to date
REWORKED > REWORK
REWORKING > REWORK
REWORKS > REWORK
REWORN > REWEAR
REWOUND > REWIND
REWOVE > REWEAVE
REWOVEN > REWEAVE
REWRAP vb wrap again
REWRAPPED > REWRAP
REWRAPS > REWRAP
REWRAPT > REWRAP
REWRITE vb write again in a different way ▷ n something rewritten
REWRITER > REWRITE
REWRITERS > REWRITE
REWRITES > REWRITE
REWRITING > REWRITE
REWRITTEN > REWRITE
REWROTE > REWRITE
REWROUGHT > REWORK
REWS > REW
REWTH archaic variant of > RUTH
REWTHS > REWTH
REX n king
REXES > REX
REXINE n tradename for a form of artificial leather
REXINES > REXINE
REYNARD n fox
REYNARDS > REYNARD
REZ n informal word for an instance of reserving; reservation
REZERO vb reset to zero
REZEROED > REZERO
REZEROES > REZERO
REZEROING > REZERO
REZEROS > REZERO
REZONE vb zone again
REZONED > REZONE
REZONES > REZONE

REZONING > REZONE
REZZES > REZ
RHABDOID adj rod-shaped ▷ n rod-shaped structure found in cells of some plants and animals
RHABDOIDS > RHABDOID
RHABDOM n (in insect anatomy) any of many similar rodlike structures found in the eye
RHABDOMAL > RHABDOM
RHABDOME same as > RHABDOM
RHABDOMES > RHABDOME
RHABDOMS > RHABDOM
RHABDUS n sponge spicule
RHABDUSES > RHABDUS
RHACHIAL > RACHIS
RHACHIDES > RHACHIS
RHACHILLA same as > RACHILLA
RHACHIS same as > RACHIS
RHACHISES > RHACHIS
RHACHITIS same as > RACHITIS
RHAGADES pl n cracks found in the skin
RHAMNOSE n type of plant sugar
RHAMNOSES > RHAMNOSE
RHAMNUS n buckthorn
RHAMNUSES > RHAMNUS
RHAMPHOID adj beaklike
RHANJA n Indian English word for a male lover
RHANJAS > RHANJA
RHAPHAE > RHAPHE
RHAPHE same as > RAPHE
RHAPHES > RHAPHE
RHAPHIDE same as > RAPHIDE
RHAPHIDES > RHAPHIDE
RHAPHIS same as > RAPHIDE
RHAPONTIC n rhubarb
RHAPSODE n (in ancient Greece) professional reciter of poetry
RHAPSODES > RHAPSODE
RHAPSODIC adj of or like a rhapsody
RHAPSODY n freely structured emotional piece of music
RHATANIES > RHATANY
RHATANY n South American leguminous shrub
RHEA n S American three-toed ostrich
RHEAS > RHEA
RHEBOK n woolly brownish-grey southern African antelope
RHEBOKS > RHEBOK
RHEMATIC adj of or relating to word formation
RHEME n constituent of a sentence that adds most new information, in addition to what has already been said in the discourse. The rheme is usually, but not always, associated with the subject
RHEMES > RHEME
RHENIUM n silvery-white metallic element with a

high melting point
RHENIUMS > RHENIUM
RHEOBASE n minimum nerve impulse required to elicit a response from a tissue
RHEOBASES > RHEOBASE
RHEOBASIC > RHEOBASE
RHEOCHORD n wire inserted into an electrical circuit to vary or regulate the current
RHEOCORD same as > RHEOCHORD
RHEOCORDS > RHEOCORD
RHEOLOGIC > RHEOLOGY
RHEOLOGY n branch of physics concerned with the flow and change of shape of matter
RHEOMETER n instrument for measuring the velocity of the blood flow
RHEOMETRY > RHEOMETER
RHEOPHIL adj liking flowing water
RHEOPHILE n something that likes flowing water
RHEOSTAT n instrument for varying the resistance of an electrical circuit
RHEOSTATS > RHEOSTAT
RHEOTAXES > RHEOTAXIS
RHEOTAXIS n movement of an organism towards or away from a current of water
RHEOTOME n interrupter
RHEOTOMES > RHEOTOME
RHEOTROPE n electric-current-reversing device
RHESUS n macaque monkey
RHESUSES > RHESUS
RHETOR n teacher of rhetoric
RHETORIC n art of effective speaking or writing
RHETORICS > RHETORIC
RHETORISE same as > RHETORIZE
RHETORIZE vb make use of rhetoric
RHETORS > RHETOR
RHEUM n watery discharge from the eyes or nose
RHEUMATIC adj (person) affected by rheumatism ▷ n person suffering from rheumatism
RHEUMATIZ n dialect word meaning rheumatism, any painful disorder of joints, muscles, or connective tissue
RHEUMED adj rheumy
RHEUMIC adj of or relating to rheum
RHEUMIER > RHEUMY
RHEUMIEST > RHEUMY
RHEUMS > RHEUM
RHEUMY adj of the nature of rheum
RHEXES > RHEXIS
RHEXIS n rupture
RHEXISES > RHEXIS
RHIES > RHY
RHIGOLENE n volatile liquid obtained from petroleum

r

and used as a local anaesthetic

RHIME *old spelling of* > RHYME

RHIMES > RHIME

RHINAL *adj* of or relating to the nose

RHINE *n* dialect word for a ditch

RHINES > RHINE

RHINITIC > RHINITIS

RHINITIS *n* inflammation of the mucous membrane that lines the nose

RHINO *n* rhinoceros

RHINOCERI *n* rhinoceroses

RHINOLITH *n* calculus formed in the nose

RHINOLOGY *n* branch of medical science concerned with the nose and its diseases

RHINOS > RHINO

RHIPIDATE *adj* shaped like a fan

RHIPIDION *n* fan found in Greek Orthodox churches

RHIPIDIUM *n* on a plant, a fan-shaped arrangement of flowers

RHIZIC *adj* of or relating to the root of an equation

RHIZINE *same as* > RHIZOID

RHIZINES > RHIZINE

RHIZOBIA > RHIZOBIUM

RHIZOBIAL > RHIZOBIUM

RHIZOBIUM *n* any rod-shaped bacterium of the genus *Rhizobium*, typically occurring in the root nodules of leguminous plants

RHIZOCARP *n* plant that fruits underground or whose root remains intact while the leaves die off annually

RHIZOCAUL *n* rootlike stem

RHIZOID *n* any of various slender hairlike structures that function as roots in the gametophyte generation of mosses, ferns, and related plants

RHIZOIDAL > RHIZOID

RHIZOIDS > RHIZOID

RHIZOMA *same as* > RHIZOME

RHIZOMATA > RHIZOMA

RHIZOME *n* thick underground stem producing new plants

RHIZOMES > RHIZOME

RHIZOMIC > RHIZOME

RHIZOPI > RHIZOPUS

RHIZOPOD *n* any protozoan of the phylum *Rhizopoda*, characterized by naked protoplasmic processes (pseudopodia). The group includes the amoebas ▷ *adj* of, relating to, or belonging to the *Rhizopoda*

RHIZOPODS > RHIZOPOD

RHIZOPUS *n* any zygomycetous fungus of the genus *Rhizopus*, esp *R. nigricans*, a bread mould

RHIZOTOMY *n* surgical incision into the roots of spinal nerves, esp for the relief of pain

RHO *n* 17th letter in the Greek alphabet, a consonant transliterated as r or rh

RHODAMIN *same as* > RHODAMINE

RHODAMINE *n* any one of a group of synthetic red or pink basic dyestuffs used for wool and silk. They are made from phthalic anhydride and aminophenols

RHODAMINS > RHODAMIN

RHODANATE *n* sulphocyanate

RHODANIC *adj* of or relating to sulphocyanic acid

RHODANISE *same as* > RHODANIZE

RHODANIZE *vb* plate with rhodium

RHODIC *adj* of or containing rhodium, esp in the tetravalent state

RHODIE *same as* > RHODY

RHODIES > RHODY

RHODINAL *n* substance with a lemon-like smell found esp in citronella and certain eucalyptus oils

RHODINALS > RHODINAL

RHODIUM *n* hard metallic element

RHODIUMS > RHODIUM

RHODOLITE *n* pale violet or red variety of garnet, used as a gemstone

RHODONITE *n* brownish translucent mineral

RHODOPSIN *n* red pigment in the rods of the retina in vertebrates. It is dissociated by light into retinene, the light energy being converted into nerve signals, and is re-formed in the dark

RHODORA *n* type of shrub

RHODORAS > RHODORA

RHODOUS *adj* of or containing rhodium (but proportionally more than a rhodic compound)

RHODY *n* rhododendron

RHOEADINE *n* alkaloid found in the poppy

RHOMB *same as* > RHOMBUS

RHOMBI > RHOMBUS

RHOMBIC *adj* relating to or having the shape of a rhombus

RHOMBICAL *same as* > RHOMBIC

RHOMBOI > RHOMBOS

RHOMBOID *n* parallelogram with adjacent sides of unequal length ▷ *adj* having such a shape

RHOMBOIDS > RHOMBOID

RHOMBOS *n* wooden slat attached to a thong that makes a roaring sound when the thong is whirled

RHOMBS > RHOMB

RHOMBUS *n* parallelogram with sides of equal length but no right angles, diamond-shaped figure

RHOMBUSES > RHOMBUS

RHONCHAL > RHONCHUS

RHONCHI > RHONCHUS

RHONCHIAL > RHONCHUS

RHONCHUS *n* rattling or whistling respiratory sound resembling snoring, caused by secretions in the trachea or bronchi

RHONE *same as* > RONE

RHONES > RHONE

RHOPALIC *adj* describes verse in which each successive word has one more syllable than the word before

RHOPALISM > RHOPALIC

RHOS > RHO

RHOTACISE *same as* > RHOTACIZE

RHOTACISM *n* excessive use or idiosyncratic pronunciation of r

RHOTACIST > RHOTACISM

RHOTACIZE *vb* pronounce r excessively or idiosyncratically

RHOTIC *adj* denoting or speaking a dialect of English in which postvocalic r s are pronounced

RHOTICITY > RHOTIC

RHUBARB *n* garden plant of which the fleshy stalks are cooked as fruit ▷ *interj* noise made by actors to simulate conversation, esp by repeating the word *rhubarb* ▷ *vb* simulate conversation in this way

RHUBARBED > RHUBARB

RHUBARBS > RHUBARB

RHUBARBY > RHUBARB

RHUMB *as in* *rhumb line* imaginary line on the surface of a sphere, such as the earth, that intersects all meridians at the same angle

RHUMBA *same as* > RUMBA

RHUMBAED > RHUMBA

RHUMBAING > RHUMBA

RHUMBAS > RHUMBA

RHUMBS > RHUMB

RHUS *n* genus of shrubs and small trees, several species of which are cultivated as ornamentals for their colourful autumn foliage

RHUSES > RHUS

RHY *archaic spelling of* > RYE

RHYME *n* sameness of the final sounds at the ends of lines of verse, or in words ▷ *vb* make a rhyme

RHYMED > RHYME

RHYMELESS > RHYME

RHYMER *same as* > RHYMESTER

RHYMERS > RHYMER

RHYMES > RHYME

RHYMESTER *n* mediocre poet

RHYMING > RHYME

RHYMIST > RHYME

RHYMISTS > RHYME

RHYNE *same as* > RHINE

RHYNES > RHYNE

RHYOLITE *n* fine-grained igneous rock consisting of quartz, feldspars, and mica or amphibole. It is the volcanic equivalent of granite

RHYOLITES > RHYOLITE

RHYOLITIC > RHYOLITE

RHYTA > RHYTON

RHYTHM *n* any regular movement or beat

RHYTHMAL *adj* rhythmic

RHYTHMED > RHYTHM

RHYTHMI > RHYTHMUS

RHYTHMIC *adj* of, relating to, or characterized by rhythm, as in movement or sound

RHYTHMICS *n* study of rhythmic movement

RHYTHMISE *same as* > RHYTHMIZE

RHYTHMIST *n* person who has a good sense of rhythm

RHYTHMIZE *vb* make rhythmic

RHYTHMS > RHYTHM

RHYTHMUS *n* rhythm

RHYTIDOME *n* bark

RHYTINA *n* type of sea cow

RHYTINAS > RHYTINA

RHYTON *n* (in ancient Greece) a horn-shaped drinking vessel with a hole in the pointed end through which to drink

RHYTONS > RHYTON

RIA *n* long narrow inlet of the seacoast, being a former valley that was submerged by a rise in the level of the sea. Rias are found esp on the coasts of SW Ireland and NW Spain

RIAL *n* standard monetary unit of Iran

RIALS > RIAL

RIALTO *n* market or exchange

RIALTOS > RIALTO

RIANCIES > RIANT

RIANCY > RIANT

RIANT *adj* laughing

RIANTLY > RIANT

RIAS > RIA

RIATA *same as* > REATA

RIATAS > RIATA

RIB *n* one of the curved bones forming the framework of the upper part of the body ▷ *vb* provide or mark with ribs

RIBA *n* (in Islam) interest or usury, as forbidden by the Koran

RIBALD *adj* humorously or mockingly rude or obscene ▷ *n* ribald person

RIBALDLY > RIBALD

RIBALDRY *n* ribald language

or behaviour

RIBALDS > RIBALD

RIBAND *n* ribbon awarded for some achievement

RIBANDS > RIBAND

RIBAS > RIBA

RIBATTUTA *n* (in music) type of trill

RIBAUD *archaic variant of* > RIBALD

RIBAUDRED *archaic variant of* > RIBALD

RIBAUDRY *archaic variant of* > RIBALDRY

RIBAUDS > RIBAUD

RIBAVIRIN *n* type of antiviral drug

RIBBAND *same as* > RIBAND

RIBBANDS > RIBBAND

RIBBED > RIB

RIBBER *n* someone who ribs

RIBBERS > RIBBER

RIBBIER > RIBBY

RIBBIEST > RIBBY

RIBBING > RIB

RIBBINGS > RIB

RIBBON *n* narrow band of fabric used for trimming, tying, etc ▷ *vb* adorn with a ribbon or ribbons

RIBBONED > RIBBON

RIBBONING > RIBBON

RIBBONRY *n* ribbons or ribbon work

RIBBONS > RIBBON

RIBBONY > RIBBON

RIBBY *adj* with noticeable ribs

RIBCAGE *n* bony structure of ribs enclosing the lungs

RIBCAGES > RIBCAGE

RIBES *n* genus of shrubs that includes currants

RIBGRASS *same as* > RIBWORT

RIBIBE *n* rebeck

RIBIBES > RIBIBE

RIBIBLE *same as* > RIBIBE

RIBIBLES > RIBIBLE

RIBIER *n* variety of grape

RIBIERS > RIBIER

RIBLESS > RIB

RIBLET *n* small rib

RIBLETS > RIBLET

RIBLIKE > RIB

RIBOSE *n* pentose sugar that is an isomeric form of arabinose and that occurs in RNA and riboflavin

RIBOSES > RIBOSE

RIBOSOMAL > RIBOSOME

RIBOSOME *n* any of numerous minute particles in the cytoplasm of cells, either free or attached to the endoplasmic reticulum, that contain RNA and protein and are the site of protein synthesis

RIBOSOMES > RIBOSOME

RIBOZYMAL > RIBOZYME

RIBOZYME *n* RNA molecule capable of catalysing a chemical reaction, usually the cleavage of another RNA molecule

RIBOZYMES > RIBOZYME

RIBS > RIB

RIBSTON *n* variety of apple

RIBSTONE *same as* > RIBSTON

RIBSTONES > RIBSTONE

RIBSTONS > RIBSTON

RIBWORK *n* work or structure involving ribs

RIBWORKS > RIBWORK

RIBWORT *n* Eurasian plant with lancelike ribbed leaves and a dense spike of small white flowers

RIBWORTS > RIBWORT

RICE *n* cereal plant grown on wet ground in warm countries ▷ *vb* sieve (potatoes or other vegetables) to a coarse mashed consistency

RICEBIRD *n* any of various birds frequenting rice fields, esp the Java sparrow

RICEBIRDS > RICEBIRD

RICED > RICE

RICER *n* kitchen utensil with small holes through which cooked potatoes and similar soft foods are pressed to form a coarse mash

RICERCAR *same as* > RICERCARE

RICERCARE *n* elaborate polyphonic composition making extensive use of contrapuntal imitation and usually very slow in tempo

RICERCARI > RICERCARE

RICERCARS > RICERCAR

RICERCATA *same as* > RICERCARE

RICERS > RICER

RICES > RICE

RICEY *adj* resembling or containing rice

RICH *adj* owning a lot of money or property, wealthy ▷ *vb* (in archaic usage) enrich

RICHED > RICH

RICHEN *vb* enrich

RICHENED > RICHEN

RICHENING > RICHEN

RICHENS > RICHEN

RICHER > RICH

RICHES *pl n* wealth

RICHESSE *n* wealth or richness

RICHESSES > RICHESSE

RICHEST > RICH

RICHING > RICH

RICHLY *adv* elaborately

RICHNESS *n* state or quality of being rich

RICHT *adj, adv, n, vb* right

RICHTED > RICHT

RICHTER > RICHT

RICHTEST > RICHT

RICHTING > RICHT

RICHTS > RICHT

RICHWEED *n* type of plant

RICHWEEDS > RICHWEED

RICIER > RICY

RICIEST > RICY

RICIN *n* highly toxic

protein, a lectin, derived from castor-oil seeds: used in experimental cancer therapy

RICING > RICE

RICINS > RICIN

RICINUS *n* genus of plants

RICINUSES > RICINUS

RICK *n* stack of hay etc ▷ *vb* wrench or sprain (a joint)

RICKED > RICK

RICKER *n* young kauri tree of New Zealand

RICKERS > RICKER

RICKETIER > RICKETY

RICKETILY > RICKETY

RICKETS *n* disease of children marked by softening of the bones, bow legs, etc, caused by vitamin D deficiency

RICKETTY *same as* > RICKETY

RICKETY *adj* shaky or unstable

RICKEY *n* cocktail consisting of gin or vodka, lime juice, and soda water, served iced

RICKEYS > RICKEY

RICKING > RICK

RICKLE *n* unsteady or shaky structure, esp a dilapidated building

RICKLES > RICKLE

RICKLY *adj* archaic word for run-down or rickety

RICKRACK *n* zigzag braid used for trimming

RICKRACKS > RICKRACK

RICKS > RICK

RICKSHA *same as* > RICKSHAW

RICKSHAS > RICKSHA

RICKSHAW *n* light two-wheeled man-drawn Asian vehicle

RICKSHAWS > RICKSHAW

RICKSTAND *n* platform on which to put a rick

RICKSTICK *n* tool used when making hayricks

RICKYARD *n* place where hayricks are put

RICKYARDS > RICKYARD

RICOCHET *vb* (of a bullet) rebound from a solid surface ▷ *n* such a rebound

RICOCHETS > RICOCHET

RICOTTA *n* soft white unsalted Italian cheese made from sheep's milk

RICOTTAS > RICOTTA

RICRAC *same as* > RICKRACK

RICRACS > RICRAC

RICTAL > RICTUS

RICTUS *n* gape or cleft of an open mouth or beak

RICTUSES > RICTUS

RICY *same as* > RICEY

RID *vb* clear or relieve (of)

RIDABLE > RIDE

RIDDANCE *n* act of getting rid of something undesirable or unpleasant

RIDDANCES > RIDDANCE

RIDDED > RID

RIDDEN > RIDE

RIDDER > RID

RIDDERS > RID

RIDDING > RID

RIDDLE *n* question made puzzling to test one's ingenuity ▷ *vb* speak in riddles

RIDDLED > RIDDLE

RIDDLER > RIDDLE

RIDDLERS > RIDDLE

RIDDLES > RIDDLE

RIDDLING > RIDDLE

RIDDLINGS > RIDDLE

RIDE *vb* sit on and control or propel (a horse, bicycle, etc) ▷ *n* journey on a horse etc, or in a vehicle

RIDEABLE > RIDE

RIDENT *adj* laughing, smiling, or gay

RIDER *n* person who rides

RIDERED > RIDER

RIDERLESS > RIDER

RIDERS > RIDER

RIDERSHIP > RIDER

RIDES > RIDE

RIDGE *n* long narrow hill ▷ *vb* form into a ridge or ridges

RIDGEBACK as in *Rhodesian ridgeback* large short-haired breed of dog characterized by a ridge of hair growing along the back in the opposite direction to the rest of the coat

RIDGED > RIDGE

RIDGEL *same as* > RIDGELING

RIDGELIKE > RIDGE

RIDGELINE *n* ridge

RIDGELING *n* domestic male animal with one or both testicles undescended, esp a horse

RIDGELS > RIDGEL

RIDGEPOLE *n* timber along the ridge of a roof, to which the rafters are attached

RIDGER *n* plough used to form furrows and ridges

RIDGERS > RIDGER

RIDGES > RIDGE

RIDGETOP *n* summit of ridge

RIDGETOPS > RIDGETOP

RIDGETREE *another name for* > RIDGEPOLE

RIDGEWAY *n* road or track along a ridge, esp one of great antiquity

RIDGEWAYS > RIDGEWAY

RIDGIER > RIDGE

RIDGIEST > RIDGE

RIDGIL *same as* > RIDGELING

RIDGILS > RIDGIL

RIDGING > RIDGE

RIDGINGS > RIDGE

RIDGLING *same as* > RIDGELING

RIDGLINGS > RIDGLING

RIDGY > RIDGE

RIDICULE *n* treatment of a person or thing as ridiculous ▷ *vb* laugh at, make fun of

RIDICULED > RIDICULE

r

RIDICULER > RIDICULE
RIDICULES > RIDICULE
RIDING > RIDE
RIDINGS > RIDE
RIDLEY n marine turtle
RIDLEYS > RIDLEY
RIDOTTO n entertainment with music and dancing, often in masquerade: popular in 18th-century England
RIDOTTOS > RIDOTTO
RIDS > RID
RIEL n standard monetary unit of Cambodia, divided into 100 sen
RIELS > RIEL
RIEM n strip of hide
RIEMPIE n leather thong or lace used mainly to make chair seats
RIEMPIES > RIEMPIE
RIEMS > RIEM
RIESLING n type of white wine
RIESLINGS > RIESLING
RIEVE n archaic word for rob or plunder
RIEVER n archaic word for robber or plunderer
RIEVERS > RIEVER
RIEVES > RIEVE
RIEVING > RIEVE
RIF vb lay off
RIFAMPIN n drug used in the treatment of tuberculosis, meningitis, and leprosy
RIFAMPINS > RIFAMPIN
RIFAMYCIN n antibiotic
RIFE adj widespread or common
RIFELY > RIFE
RIFENESS > RIFE
RIFER > RIFE
RIFEST > RIFE
RIFF n short repeated melodic figure ▷ vb play or perform riffs in jazz or rock music
RIFFAGE n (in jazz or rock music) act or an instance of playing a short series of chords
RIFFAGES > RIFFAGE
RIFFED > RIFF
RIFFING > RIFF
RIFFLE vb flick through (pages etc) quickly ▷ n rapid in a stream
RIFFLED > RIFFLE
RIFFLER n file with a curved face for filing concave surfaces
RIFFLERS > RIFFLER
RIFFLES > RIFFLE
RIFFLING > RIFFLE
RIFFOLA n use of an abundance of dominant riffs
RIFFOLAS > RIFFOLA
RIFFRAFF n rabble, disreputable people
RIFFRAFFS > RIFFRAFF
RIFFS > RIFF
RIFLE n firearm with a long barrel ▷ vb cut spiral

grooves inside the barrel of a gun
RIFLEBIRD n any of various birds of paradise
RIFLED > RIFLE
RIFLEMAN n person skilled in the use of a rifle, esp a soldier
RIFLEMEN > RIFLEMAN
RIFLER > RIFLE
RIFLERIES > RIFLERY
RIFLERS > RIFLE
RIFLERY n rifle shots
RIFLES > RIFLE
RIFLING n cutting of spiral grooves on the inside of a firearm's barrel
RIFLINGS > RIFLING
RIFLIP n genetic difference between two individuals
RIFLIPS > RIFLIP
RIFS > RIF
RIFT n break in friendly relations ▷ vb burst or cause to burst open
RIFTE archaic word for > RIFT
RIFTED > RIFT
RIFTIER > RIFT
RIFTIEST > RIFT
RIFTING > RIFT
RIFTLESS > RIFT
RIFTS > RIFT
RIFTY > RIFT
RIG vb arrange in a dishonest way ▷ n apparatus for drilling for oil and gas
RIGADOON n old Provençal couple dance, light and graceful, in lively duple time
RIGADOONS > RIGADOON
RIGATONI n macaroni in the form of short ridged often slightly curved pieces
RIGATONIS > RIGATONI
RIGAUDON same as > RIGADOON
RIGAUDONS > RIGAUDON
RIGG n type of fish
RIGGALD same as > RIDGELING
RIGGALDS > RIGGALD
RIGGED > RIG
RIGGER n workman who rigs vessels, etc
RIGGERS > RIGGER
RIGGING > RIG
RIGGINGS > RIG
RIGGISH adj dialect word meaning wanton
RIGGS > RIGG
RIGHT adj just ▷ adv correctly ▷ n claim, title, etc allowed or due ▷ vb bring or come back to a normal or correct state
RIGHTABLE adj capable of being righted
RIGHTABLY > RIGHTABLE
RIGHTED > RIGHT
RIGHTEN vb set right
RIGHTENED > RIGHTEN
RIGHTENS > RIGHTEN
RIGHTEOUS adj upright, godly, or virtuous
RIGHTER > RIGHT

RIGHTERS > RIGHT
RIGHTEST > RIGHT
RIGHTFUL adj in accordance with what is right
RIGHTIES > RIGHTY
RIGHTING > RIGHT
RIGHTINGS > RIGHT
RIGHTISH adj somewhat right, esp politically
RIGHTISM > RIGHTIST
RIGHTISMS > RIGHTIST
RIGHTIST adj (person) on the political right ▷ n supporter of the political right
RIGHTISTS > RIGHTIST
RIGHTLESS > RIGHT
RIGHTLY adv in accordance with the true facts or justice
RIGHTMOST > RIGHT
RIGHTNESS n state or quality of being right
RIGHTO n expression of agreement or compliance
RIGHTOS > RIGHTO
RIGHTS > RIGHT
RIGHTSIZE vb restructure (an organization) to cut costs and improve effectiveness without ruthlessly downsizing
RIGHTWARD adj situated on or directed towards the right ▷ adv towards or on the right
RIGHTY n informal word for a right-winger
RIGID adj inflexible or strict ▷ adv completely or excessively ▷ n strict and unbending person
RIGIDER > RIGID
RIGIDEST > RIGID
RIGIDIFY vb make or become rigid
RIGIDISE same as > RIGIDIZE
RIGIDISED > RIGIDISE
RIGIDISES > RIGIDISE
RIGIDITY > RIGID
RIGIDIZE vb make or become rigid
RIGIDIZED > RIGIDIZE
RIGIDIZES > RIGIDIZE
RIGIDLY > RIGID
RIGIDNESS > RIGID
RIGIDS > RIGID
RIGLIN same as > RIDGELING
RIGLING same as > RIDGELING
RIGLINGS > RIGLING
RIGLINS > RIGLIN
RIGMAROLE n long complicated procedure
RIGOL n (in dialect) ditch or gutter
RIGOLL same as > RIGOL
RIGOLLS > RIGOLL
RIGOLS > RIGOL
RIGOR same as > RIGOUR
RIGORISM n strictness in judgment or conduct
RIGORISMS > RIGORISM
RIGORIST > RIGORISM
RIGORISTS > RIGORISM
RIGOROUS adj harsh, severe,

or stern
RIGORS > RIGOR
RIGOUR n harshness, severity, or strictness
RIGOURS > RIGOUR
RIGOUT n person's clothing
RIGOUTS > RIGOUT
RIGS > RIG
RIGSDALER n any of various former Scandinavian or Dutch small silver coins
RIGWIDDIE n part of the carthorse's harness to which the shafts of the cart attach
RIGWOODIE same as > RIGWIDDIE
RIJSTAFEL n assortment of Indonesian rice dishes
RIKISHA same as > RICKSHAW
RIKISHAS > RIKISHA
RIKISHI n sumo wrestler
RIKSHAW same as > RICKSHAW
RIKSHAWS > RICKSHAW
RILE vb anger or annoy
RILED > RILE
RILES > RILE
RILEY adj cross or irritable
RILIER > RILEY
RILIEST > RILEY
RILIEVI > RILIEVO
RILIEVO same as > RELIEF
RILING > RILE
RILL n small stream ▷ vb trickle
RILLE same as > RILL
RILLED > RILL
RILLES > RILLE
RILLET n little rill
RILLETS > RILLET
RILLETTES pl n potted meat
RILLING > RILL
RILLMARK n mark left by the trickle of a rill
RILLMARKS > RILLMARK
RILLS > RILL
RIM n edge or border ▷ vb put a rim on (a pot, cup, wheel, etc)
RIMA n long narrow opening
RIMAE > RIMA
RIMAYE n crevasse at the head of a glacier
RIMAYES > RIMAYE
RIME same as > RHYME
RIMED > RIME
RIMELESS > RHYME
RIMER same as > RHYMESTER
RIMERS > RIMER
RIMES > RIME
RIMESTER same as > RHYMESTER
RIMESTERS > RIMESTER
RIMFIRE adj (of a cartridge) having the primer in the rim of the base ▷ n cartridge of this type
RIMFIRES > RIMFIRE
RIMIER > RIMY
RIMIEST > RIMY
RIMINESS > RIMY
RIMING > RIME
RIMLAND n area situated on

the outer edges of a region

RIMLANDS > RIMLAND

RIMLESS > RIM

RIMMED > RIM

RIMMER n tool for shaping the edge of something

RIMMERS > RIMMER

RIMMING > RIM

RIMMINGS > RIM

RIMOSE adj (esp of plant parts) having the surface marked by a network of intersecting cracks

RIMOSELY > RIMOSE

RIMOSITY > RIMOSE

RIMOUS same as > RIMOSE

RIMPLE vb crease or wrinkle

RIMPLED > RIMPLE

RIMPLES > RIMPLE

RIMPLING > RIMPLE

RIMROCK n rock forming the boundaries of a sandy or gravelly alluvial deposit

RIMROCKS > RIMROCK

RIMS > RIM

RIMSHOT n deliberate simultaneous striking of skin and rim of drum

RIMSHOTS > RIMSHOT

RIMU n New Zealand tree whose wood is used for building and furniture

RIMUS > RIMU

RIMY adj coated with rime

RIN Scots variant of > RUN

RIND n tough outer coating of fruits, cheese, or bacon ▷ vb take the bark off

RINDED > RIND

RINDIER > RINDY

RINDIEST > RINDY

RINDING > RIND

RINDLESS > RIND

RINDS > RIND

RINDY adj with a rind or rindlike skin

RINE archaic variant of > RIND

RINES > RINE

RING vb give out a clear resonant sound, as a bell ▷ n ringing

RINGBARK same as > RING

RINGBARKS > RINGBARK

RINGBIT n type of bit worn by a horse

RINGBITS > RINGBIT

RINGBOLT n bolt with a ring fitted through an eye attached to the bolt head

RINGBOLTS > RINGBOLT

RINGBONE n abnormal bony growth affecting the pastern of a horse, often causing lameness

RINGBONES > RINGBONE

RINGDOVE n large Eurasian pigeon with white patches on the wings and neck

RINGDOVES > RINGDOVE

RINGED > RING

RINGENT adj (of the corolla of plants such as the snapdragon) consisting of two distinct gaping lips

RINGER n person or thing apparently identical to

another

RINGERS > RINGER

RINGGIT n standard monetary unit of Malaysia, divided into 100 sen

RINGGITS > RINGGIT

RINGHALS n variety of cobra

RINGING > RING

RINGINGLY > RING

RINGINGS > RING

RINGLESS > RING

RINGLET n curly lock of hair

RINGLETED > RINGLET

RINGLETS > RINGLET

RINGLIKE > RING

RINGMAN n (in dialect) ring finger

RINGMEN > RINGMAN

RINGNECK n any bird that has ringlike markings round its neck

RINGNECKS > RINGNECK

RINGS > RING

RINGSIDE n row of seats nearest a boxing or circus ring ▷ adj providing a close uninterrupted view

RINGSIDER n someone with a ringside seat or position

RINGSIDES > RINGSIDE

RINGSTAND n stand for laboratory equipment

RINGSTER n member of a ring controlling a market in antiques, art treasures, etc

RINGSTERS > RINGSTER

RINGTAIL n possum with a curling tail used to grip branches while climbing

RINGTAILS > RINGTAIL

RINGTAW n game of marbles in which the aim is to knock other players' marbles out of a ring

RINGTAWS > RINGTAW

RINGTONE n musical tune played by a mobile phone when a call is received

RINGTONES > RINGTONE

RINGTOSS n game in which participants try to throw hoops onto an upright stick

RINGWAY n bypass

RINGWAYS > RINGWAY

RINGWISE adj used to being in the ring and able to respond appropriately

RINGWOMB n complication at lambing resulting from failure of the cervix to open

RINGWOMBS > RINGWOMB

RINGWORK n circular earthwork

RINGWORKS > RINGWORK

RINGWORM n fungal skin disease in circular patches

RINGWORMS > RINGWORM

RINK n sheet of ice for skating or curling ▷ vb skate on a rink

RINKED > RINK

RINKHALS n S African cobra that can spit venom

RINKING > RINK

RINKS > RINK

RINNING > RIN

RINS > RIN

RINSABLE > RINSE

RINSE vb remove soap from (washed clothes, hair, etc) by applying clean water ▷ n rinsing

RINSEABLE > RINSE

RINSED > RINSE

RINSER > RINSE

RINSERS > RINSE

RINSES > RINSE

RINSIBLE > RINSE

RINSING > RINSE

RINSINGS > RINSE

RIOJA n red or white Spanish wine with a vanilla bouquet and flavour

RIOJAS > RIOJA

RIOT n disorderly unruly disturbance ▷ vb take part in a riot

RIOTED > RIOT

RIOTER > RIOT

RIOTERS > RIOT

RIOTING > RIOT

RIOTINGS > RIOT

RIOTISE n archaic word for riotous behaviour and excess

RIOTISES > RIOTISE

RIOTIZE same as > RIOTISE

RIOTIZES > RIOTIZE

RIOTOUS adj unrestrained

RIOTOUSLY > RIOTOUS

RIOTRIES > RIOTRY

RIOTRY n riotous behaviour

RIOTS > RIOT

RIP vb tear violently ▷ n split or tear

RIPARIAL adj riparian

RIPARIAN adj of or on the banks of a river ▷ n person who owns land on a river bank

RIPARIANS > RIPARIAN

RIPCORD n cord pulled to open a parachute

RIPCORDS > RIPCORD

RIPE adj ready to be reaped, eaten, etc ▷ vb ripen

RIPECK same as > RYEPECK

RIPECKS > RIPECK

RIPED > RIPE

RIPELY > RIPE

RIPEN vb grow ripe

RIPENED > RIPEN

RIPENER > RIPEN

RIPENERS > RIPEN

RIPENESS > RIPE

RIPENING > RIPEN

RIPENS > RIPEN

RIPER adj more ripe ▷ n old Scots word meaning plunderer

RIPERS > RIPER

RIPES > RIPE

RIPEST > RIPE

RIPIENI > RIPIENO

RIPIENIST n orchestral member who is there to swell the sound rather than play solo

RIPIENO n (in baroque concertos and concerti grossi) the full orchestra, as opposed to the instrumental soloists

RIPIENOS > RIPIENO

RIPING > RIPE

RIPOFF n grossly overpriced article

RIPOFFS > RIPOFF

RIPOST same as > RIPOSTE

RIPOSTE n verbal retort ▷ vb make a riposte

RIPOSTED > RIPOSTE

RIPOSTES > RIPOSTE

RIPOSTING > RIPOSTE

RIPOSTS > RIPOST

RIPP n old Scots word for a handful of grain

RIPPABLE > RIP

RIPPED > RIP

RIPPER n person who rips

RIPPERS > RIPPER

RIPPIER n archaic word for fish seller

RIPPIERS > RIPPIER

RIPPING > RIP

RIPPINGLY > RIP

RIPPLE n slight wave or ruffling of a surface ▷ vb flow or form into little waves (on)

RIPPLED > RIPPLE

RIPPLER > RIPPLE

RIPPLERS > RIPPLE

RIPPLES > RIPPLE

RIPPLET n tiny ripple

RIPPLETS > RIPPLET

RIPPLIER > RIPPLE

RIPPLIEST > RIPPLE

RIPPLING > RIPPLE

RIPPLINGS > RIPPLE

RIPPLY > RIPPLE

RIPPS > RIPP

RIPRAP vb deposit broken stones in or on

RIPRAPPED > RIPRAP

RIPRAPS > RIPRAP

RIPS > RIP

RIPSAW n handsaw for cutting along the grain of timber ▷ vb saw with a ripsaw

RIPSAWED > RIPSAW

RIPSAWING > RIPSAW

RIPSAWN > RIPSAW

RIPSAWS > RIPSAW

RIPSTOP n tear-resistant cloth

RIPSTOPS > RIPSTOP

RIPT archaic past form of > RIP

RIPTIDE n stretch of turbulent water in the sea, caused by the meeting of currents or abrupt changes in depth

RIPTIDES > RIPTIDE

RIRORIRO n small NZ bush bird that hatches the eggs of the shining cuckoo

RIRORIROS > RIRORIRO

RISALDAR n Indian cavalry officer

RISALDARS > RISALDAR

RISE vb get up from a lying, sitting, or kneeling position ▷ n rising

RISEN > RISE

RISER n person who rises, esp from bed

RISERS > RISER

RISES > RISE
RISHI n Indian seer or sage
RISHIS > RISHI
RISIBLE adj causing laughter, ridiculous
RISIBLES pl n sense of humour
RISIBLY > RISIBLE
RISING > RISE
RISINGS > RISE
RISK n chance of disaster or loss ▷ vb act in spite of the possibility of (injury or loss)
RISKED > RISK
RISKER > RISK
RISKERS > RISK
RISKFUL > RISK
RISKIER > RISKY
RISKIEST > RISKY
RISKILY > RISKY
RISKINESS > RISKY
RISKING > RISK
RISKLESS > RISK
RISKS > RISK
RISKY adj full of risk, dangerous
RISOLUTO adj musical term meaning firm and decisive ▷ adv firmly and decisively
RISOTTO n dish of rice cooked in stock with vegetables, meat, etc
RISOTTOS > RISOTTO
RISP vb Scots word meaning rasp
RISPED > RISP
RISPETTI > RISPETTO
RISPETTO n kind of folk song
RISPING > RISP
RISPINGS > RISP
RISPS > RISP
RISQUE n risk
RISQUES > RISQUE
RISSOLE n cake of minced meat, coated with breadcrumbs and fried
RISSOLES > RISSOLE
RISTRA n string of dried chilli peppers
RISTRAS > RISTRA
RISUS n involuntary grinning expression
RISUSES > RISUS
RIT vb Scots word for cut or slit
RITARD n (in music) a slowing down
RITARDS > RITARD
RITE n formal practice or custom, esp religious
RITELESS > RITE
RITENUTO adv held back momentarily ▷ n (in music) a slowing down
RITENUTOS > RITENUTO
RITES > RITE
RITONAVIR n drug used to treat HIV
RITORNEL n (in music) orchestral passage
RITORNELL same as > RITORNEL
RITORNELS > RITORNEL
RITS > RIT
RITT same as > RIT
RITTED > RIT

RITTER n knight or horseman
RITTERS > RITTER
RITTING > RIT
RITTS > RITT
RITUAL n prescribed order of rites ▷ adj concerning rites
RITUALISE same as > RITUALIZE
RITUALISM n exaggerated emphasis on the importance of rites and ceremonies
RITUALIST > RITUALISM
RITUALIZE vb engage in ritualism or devise rituals
RITUALLY > RITUAL
RITUALS > RITUAL
RITZ as in put on the ritz assume a superior air or make an ostentatious display
RITZES > RITZ
RITZIER > RITZY
RITZIEST > RITZY
RITZILY > RITZY
RITZINESS > RITZY
RITZY adj luxurious or elegant
RIVA n rock cleft
RIVAGE n bank, shore, or coast
RIVAGES > RIVAGE
RIVAL n person or thing that competes with or equals another for favour, success, etc ▷ adj in the position of a rival ▷ vb (try to) equal
RIVALED > RIVAL
RIVALESS n female rival
RIVALING > RIVAL
RIVALISE same as > RIVALIZE
RIVALISED > RIVALISE
RIVALISES > RIVALISE
RIVALITY > RIVAL
RIVALIZE vb become a rival
RIVALIZED > RIVALIZE
RIVALIZES > RIVALIZE
RIVALLED > RIVAL
RIVALLESS > RIVAL
RIVALLING > RIVAL
RIVALRIES > RIVALRY
RIVALROUS > RIVALRY
RIVALRY n keen competition
RIVALS > RIVAL
RIVALSHIP > RIVAL
RIVAS > RIVA
RIVE vb split asunder
RIVED > RIVE
RIVEL vb archaic word meaning wrinkle
RIVELLED > RIVEL
RIVELLING > RIVEL
RIVELS > RIVEL
RIVEN > RIVE
RIVER n large natural stream of water
RIVERAIN same as > RIPARIAN
RIVERAINS > RIVERAIN
RIVERBANK n bank of a river
RIVERBED n bed of a river
RIVERBEDS > RIVERBOAT

RIVERBOAT n boat, especially a barge, designed for use on rivers
RIVERED adj with a river or rivers
RIVERET n archaic word for rivulet or stream
RIVERETS > RIVERET
RIVERHEAD n source of river
RIVERINE same as > RIPARIAN
RIVERLESS > RIVER
RIVERLIKE adj resembling a river
RIVERMAN n boatman or man earning his living working on a river
RIVERMEN > RIVERMAN
RIVERS > RIVER
RIVERSIDE n area beside a river
RIVERWARD adj towards the river ▷ adv towards the river
RIVERWAY n river serving as a waterway
RIVERWAYS > RIVERWAY
RIVERWEED n type of plant found growing near rivers
RIVERY adj riverlike
RIVES > RIVE
RIVET n bolt for fastening metal plates, the end being put through holes and then beaten flat ▷ vb fasten with rivets
RIVETED > RIVET
RIVETER > RIVET
RIVETERS > RIVET
RIVETING > RIVET
RIVETINGS > RIVET
RIVETS > RIVET
RIVETTED > RIVET
RIVETTING > RIVET
RIVIERA n coastline resembling the Mediterranean Riviera
RIVIERAS > RIVIERA
RIVIERE n necklace the diamonds or other precious stones of which gradually increase in size up to a large centre stone
RIVIERES > RIVIERE
RIVING > RIVE
RIVLIN n Scots word for rawhide shoe
RIVLINS > RIVLIN
RIVO interj (in the past) an informal toast
RIVOS > RIVO
RIVULET n small stream
RIVULETS > RIVULET
RIVULOSE adj having meandering lines
RIYAL n standard monetary unit of Qatar, divided into 100 dirhams
RIYALS > RIYAL
RIZ (in some dialects) past form of > RISE
RIZA n partial icon cover made from precious metal
RIZARD n redcurrant
RIZARDS > RIZARD
RIZAS > RIZA
RIZZAR n Scots word for red

currant ▷ vb Scots word for sun-dry
RIZZARED > RIZZAR
RIZZARING > RIZZAR
RIZZARS > RIZZAR
RIZZART n Scots word for red currant
RIZZARTS > RIZZART
RIZZER same as > RIZZAR
RIZZERED > RIZZER
RIZZERING > RIZZER
RIZZERS > RIZZER
RIZZOR vb dry
RIZZORED > RIZZOR
RIZZORING > RIZZOR
RIZZORS > RIZZOR
ROACH n Eurasian freshwater fish ▷ vb clip (mane) short so that it stands upright
ROACHED adj arched convexly, as the back of certain breeds of dog, such as the whippet
ROACHES > ROACH
ROACHING > ROACH
ROAD n way prepared for passengers, vehicles, etc
ROADBED n material used to make a road
ROADBEDS > ROADBED
ROADBLOCK n barricade across a road to stop traffic for inspection etc
ROADCRAFT n skills and knowledge of a road user
ROADEO n competition in which drivers or other road users put their skills on the road to the test
ROADEOS > ROADEO
ROADHOUSE n pub or restaurant on a country road
ROADIE n person who transports and sets up equipment for a band
ROADIES > ROADIE
ROADING n road building
ROADINGS > ROADING
ROADKILL n remains of an animal or animals killed on the road by motor vehicles
ROADKILLS > ROADKILL
ROADLESS > ROAD
ROADMAN n someone involved in road repair or construction
ROADMEN > ROADMAN
ROADS > ROAD
ROADSHOW n radio show broadcast live from one of a number of places being visited by a touring disc jockey
ROADSHOWS > ROADSHOW
ROADSIDE n side of a road ▷ adj situated beside a road
ROADSIDES > ROADSIDE
ROADSMAN same as > ROADMAN
ROADSMEN > ROADSMAN
ROADSTEAD same as > ROAD
ROADSTER n open car with only two seats
ROADSTERS > ROADSTER
ROADWAY n part of a road

used by vehicles

ROADWAYS > ROADWAY

ROADWORK n sports training by running along roads

ROADWORKS pl n repairs to a road, esp blocking part of the road

ROAM vb wander about ▷ n act of roaming

ROAMED > ROAM

ROAMER > ROAM

ROAMERS > ROAM

ROAMING > ROAM

ROAMINGS > ROAM

ROAMS > ROAM

ROAN adj (of a horse) having a brown or black coat sprinkled with white hairs ▷ n roan horse

ROANS > ROAN

ROAR vb make or utter a loud deep hoarse sound like that of a lion ▷ n such a sound

ROARED > ROAR

ROARER > ROAR

ROARERS > ROAR

ROARIE Scots word for > NOISY

ROARIER > ROARY

ROARIEST > ROARY

ROARING > ROAR

ROARINGLY > ROARING

ROARINGS > ROAR

ROARMING adj severe

ROARS > ROAR

ROARY adj roarlike or tending to roar

ROAST vb cook by dry heat, as in an oven ▷ n roasted joint of meat ▷ adj roasted

ROASTED > ROAST

ROASTER n person or thing that roasts

ROASTERS > ROASTER

ROASTING adj extremely hot ▷ n severe criticism or scolding

ROASTINGS > ROASTING

ROASTS > ROAST

ROATE archaic form of > ROTE

ROATED > ROATE

ROATES > ROATE

ROATING > ROATE

ROB vb steal from

ROBALO n tropical fish

ROBALOS > ROBALO

ROBAND n piece of marline used for fastening a sail to a spar

ROBANDS > ROBAND

ROBBED > ROB

ROBBER > ROB

ROBBERIES > ROBBERY

ROBBERS > ROB

ROBBERY n stealing of property from a person by using or threatening to use force

ROBBIN same as > ROBAND

ROBBING > ROB

ROBBINS > ROBBIN

ROBE n long loose outer garment ▷ vb put a robe on

ROBED > ROBE

ROBES > ROBE

ROBIN n small brown bird with a red breast

ROBING > ROBE

ROBINGS > ROBE

ROBINIA n type of leguminous tree

ROBINIAS > ROBINIA

ROBINS > ROBIN

ROBLE n oak tree

ROBLES > ROBLE

ROBORANT adj tending to fortify or increase strength ▷ n drug or agent that increases strength

ROBORANTS > ROBORANT

ROBOT n automated machine, esp one performing functions in a human manner

ROBOTIC > ROBOT

ROBOTICS n science of designing and using robots

ROBOTISE same as > ROBOTIZE

ROBOTISED > ROBOTISE

ROBOTISES > ROBOTISE

ROBOTISM > ROBOT

ROBOTISMS > ROBOT

ROBOTIZE vb automate

ROBOTIZED > ROBOTIZE

ROBOTIZES > ROBOTIZE

ROBOTRIES > ROBOT

ROBOTRY > ROBOT

ROBOTS > ROBOT

ROBS > ROB

ROBURITE n flameless explosive

ROBURITES > ROBURITE

ROBUST adj very strong and healthy

ROBUSTA n species of coffee tree

ROBUSTAS > ROBUSTA

ROBUSTER > ROBUST

ROBUSTEST > ROBUST

ROBUSTLY > ROBUST

ROC n monstrous bird of Arabian mythology

ROCAILLE n decorative rock or shell work, esp as ornamentation in a rococo fountain, grotto, or interior

ROCAILLES > ROCAILLE

ROCAMBOLE n variety of sand leek whose garlic-like bulb is used for seasoning

ROCH same as > ROTCH

ROCHES > ROTCH

ROCHET n white surplice with tight sleeves, worn by bishops, abbots, and certain other Church dignitaries

ROCHETS > ROCHET

ROCK n hard mineral substance that makes up part of the earth's crust, stone ▷ vb (cause to) sway to and fro ▷ adj of or relating to rock music

ROCKABIES > ROCKABY

ROCKABLE > ROCK

ROCKABY same as > ROCKABYE

ROCKABYE n lullaby or rocking motion used with a baby during lullabies

ROCKABYES > ROCKABYE

ROCKAWAY n four-wheeled horse-drawn carriage, usually with two seats and a hard top

ROCKAWAYS > ROCKAWAY

ROCKBOUND adj hemmed in or encircled by rocks

ROCKCRESS n low-growing plant with white flowers

ROCKED > ROCK

ROCKER n rocking chair

ROCKERIES > ROCKERY

ROCKERS > ROCKER

ROCKERY n mound of stones in a garden for rock plants

ROCKET n self-propelling device powered by the burning of explosive contents (used as a firework, weapon, etc) ▷ vb move fast, esp upwards, like a rocket

ROCKETED > ROCKET

ROCKETEER n engineer or scientist concerned with the design, operation, or launching of rockets

ROCKETER n bird that launches itself into the air like a rocket when flushed

ROCKETERS > ROCKETER

ROCKETING > ROCKET

ROCKETRY n science and technology of the design and operation of rockets

ROCKETS > ROCKET

ROCKFALL n instance of rocks breaking away and falling from an outcrop

ROCKFALLS > ROCKFALL

ROCKFISH n any of various fishes that live among rocks

ROCKHOUND n person interested in rocks and minerals

ROCKIER > ROCKY n archaic or dialect word for rock pigeon

ROCKIERS > ROCKY

ROCKIEST > ROCKY

ROCKILY > ROCKY

ROCKINESS > ROCKY

ROCKING > ROCK

ROCKINGLY > ROCKING

ROCKINGS > ROCK

ROCKLAY same as > ROKELAY

ROCKLAYS > ROCKLAY

ROCKLESS > ROCK

ROCKLIKE > ROCK

ROCKLING n any of various small sea fishes having an elongated body and barbels around the mouth

ROCKLINGS > ROCKLING

ROCKOON n rocket carrying scientific equipment for studying the upper atmosphere, fired from a balloon at high altitude

ROCKOONS > ROCKOON

ROCKROSE n any of various shrubs or herbaceous plants cultivated for their roselike flowers

ROCKROSES > ROCKROSE

ROCKS > ROCK

ROCKSHAFT n shaft that rotates backwards and forwards rather than continuously, esp one used in the valve gear of a steam engine

ROCKSLIDE n fall of rocks down hillside

ROCKWATER n water that comes out of rock

ROCKWEED n any of various seaweeds that grow on rocks exposed at low tide

ROCKWEEDS > ROCKWEED

ROCKWORK n structure made of rock

ROCKWORKS > ROCKWORK

ROCKY adj having many rocks

ROCOCO adj (of furniture, architecture, etc) having much elaborate decoration in an early 18th-century style ▷ n style of architecture and decoration that originated in France in the early 18th century, characterized by elaborate but graceful, light, ornamentation, often containing asymmetrical motifs

ROCOCOS > ROCOCO

ROCQUET n another name for the salad plant rocket

ROCQUETS > ROCQUET

ROCS > ROC

ROD n slender straight bar, stick ▷ vb clear with a rod

RODDED > ROD

RODDING > ROD

RODDINGS > ROD

RODE vb (of the male woodcock) to perform a display flight at dusk during the breeding season

RODED > RODE

RODENT n animal with teeth specialized for gnawing, such as a rat, mouse, or squirrel

RODENTS > RODENT

RODEO n display of skill by cowboys, such as bareback riding ▷ vb take part in a rodeo

RODEOED > RODEO

RODEOING > RODEO

RODEOS > RODEO

RODES > RODE

RODEWAY archaic spelling of > ROADWAY

RODEWAYS > RODEWAY

RODFISHER n angler

RODGERSIA n flowering plant

RODING > RODE

RODINGS > RODE

RODLESS > ROD

RODLIKE > ROD

RODMAN n someone who uses or fishes with a rod

RODMEN > RODMAN

RODS > ROD

RODSMAN same as > RODMAN

RODSMEN > RODSMAN

RODSTER n angler

RODSTERS > RODSTER

ROE n mass of eggs in a fish, sometimes eaten as food

ROEBUCK n male of the roe deer

ROEBUCKS > ROEBUCK

ROED adj with roe inside

ROEMER n drinking glass, typically having an ovoid bowl on a short stem

ROEMERS > ROEMER

ROENTGEN n unit measuring a radiation dose

ROENTGENS > ROENTGEN

ROES > ROE

ROESTONE same as > OOLITE

ROESTONES > ROESTONE

ROGALLO n flexible fabric delta wing, originally designed as a possible satellite retrieval vehicle but actually developed in the 1960s as the first successful hang-glider

ROGALLOS > ROGALLO

ROGATION n solemn supplication, esp in a form of ceremony prescribed by the Church

ROGATIONS > ROGATION

ROGATORY adj (esp in legal contexts) seeking or authorized to seek information

ROGER interj (used in signalling) message received ▷ vb (of a man) to copulate (with)

ROGERED > ROGER

ROGERING > ROGER

ROGERINGS > ROGER

ROGERS > ROGER

ROGNON n isolated rock outcrop on a glacier

ROGNONS > ROGNON

ROGUE n dishonest or unprincipled person ▷ adj (of a wild beast) having a savage temper and living apart from the herd ▷ vb rid (a field or crop) of plants that are inferior, diseased, or of an unwanted variety

ROGUED > ROGUE

ROGUEING > ROGUE

ROGUERIES > ROGUERY

ROGUERY n dishonest or immoral behaviour

ROGUES > ROGUE

ROGUESHIP n being a rogue

ROGUING > ROGUE

ROGUISH adj dishonest or unprincipled

ROGUISHLY > ROGUISH

ROGUY same as > ROGUISH

ROIL vb make (a liquid) cloudy or turbid by stirring up dregs or sediment

ROILED > ROIL

ROILIER > ROILY

ROILIEST > ROILY

ROILING > ROIL

ROILS > ROIL

ROILY adj cloudy or muddy

ROIN same as > ROYNE

ROINED > ROIN

ROINING > ROIN

ROINISH same as > ROYNISH

ROINS > ROIN

ROIST archaic variant of > ROISTER

ROISTED > ROIST

ROISTER vb make merry noisily or boisterously

ROISTERED > ROISTER

ROISTERER > ROISTER

ROISTERS > ROISTER

ROISTING > ROIST

ROISTS > ROIST

ROJAK n (in Malaysia) a salad dish served in chilli sauce

ROJAKS > ROJAK

ROJI n Japanese tea garden or its path of stones

ROJIS > ROJI

ROK same as > ROC

ROKE vb (in dialect) steam or smoke

ROKED > ROKE

ROKELAY n type of cloak

ROKELAYS > ROKELAY

ROKER n variety of ray

ROKERS > ROKER

ROKES > ROKE

ROKIER > ROKY

ROKIEST > ROKY

ROKING > ROKE

ROKKAKU n hexagonal Japanese kite

ROKS > ROK

ROKY adj (in dialect) steamy or smoky

ROLAG n roll of carded wool ready for spinning

ROLAGS > ROLAG

ROLAMITE n type of bearing using two rollers and a moving flexible band

ROLAMITES > ROLAMITE

ROLE n task or function

ROLES > ROLE

ROLF vb massage following a particular technique

ROLFED > ROLF

ROLFER > ROLF

ROLFERS > ROLF

ROLFING > ROLF

ROLFINGS > ROLF

ROLFS > ROLF

ROLL vb move by turning over and over ▷ n act of rolling over or from side to side

ROLLABLE > ROLL

ROLLAWAY n mounted on rollers so as to be easily moved, esp to be stored away after use

ROLLAWAYS > ROLLAWAY

ROLLBACK n reduction to a previous price

ROLLBACKS > ROLLBACK

ROLLBAR n bar that reinforces the frame of a car, esp one used for racing, rallying, etc, to protect the driver if the car should turn over

ROLLBARS > ROLLBAR

ROLLED > ROLL

ROLLER n rotating cylinder used for smoothing or supporting a thing to be moved, spreading paint, etc

ROLLERS > ROLLER

ROLLICK vb behave in a carefree, frolicsome, or boisterous manner ▷ n boisterous or carefree escapade or event

ROLLICKED > ROLLICK

ROLLICKS > ROLLICK

ROLLICKY adj rollicking

ROLLING > ROLL

ROLLINGS > ROLL

ROLLMOP n herring fillet rolled round onion slices and pickled

ROLLMOPS > ROLLMOP

ROLLNECK adj (of a garment) having a high neck that is worn rolled over ▷ n rollneck sweater or other garment

ROLLNECKS > ROLLNECK

ROLLOCK same as > ROWLOCK

ROLLOCKS > ROLLOCK

ROLLOUT n presentation to the public of a new aircraft, product, etc; launch

ROLLOUTS > ROLLOUT

ROLLOVER n instance of a prize continuing in force for an additional period

ROLLOVERS > ROLLOVER

ROLLS > ROLL

ROLLTOP as in rolltop desk desk having a slatted wooden panel that can be pulled down over the writing surface when not in use

ROLLWAY n incline down which logs are rolled

ROLLWAYS > ROLLWAY

ROM n male gypsy

ROMA n gypsy

ROMAGE archaic variant of > RUMMAGE

ROMAGES > ROMAGE

ROMAIKA n Greek dance

ROMAIKAS > ROMAIKA

ROMAINE n usual US and Canadian name for 'cos' (lettuce)

ROMAINES > ROMAINE

ROMAJI n Roman alphabet as used to write Japanese

ROMAJIS > ROMAJI

ROMAL same as > RUMAL

ROMALS > ROMAL

ROMAN adj in or relating to the vertical style of printing type used for most printed matter ▷ n roman type

ROMANCE n love affair ▷ vb exaggerate or fantasize

ROMANCED > ROMANCE

ROMANCER > ROMANCE

ROMANCERS > ROMANCE

ROMANCES > ROMANCE

ROMANCING > ROMANCE

ROMANISE same as > ROMANIZE

ROMANISED > ROMANISE

ROMANISES > ROMANISE

ROMANIZE vb impart a Roman Catholic character to (a ceremony, practice, etc)

ROMANIZED > ROMANIZE

ROMANIZES > ROMANIZE

ROMANO n hard light-coloured sharp-tasting cheese

ROMANOS > ROMANO

ROMANS > ROMAN

ROMANTIC adj of or dealing with love ▷ n romantic person or artist

ROMANTICS > ROMANTIC

ROMANZA n short instrumental piece of song-like character

ROMANZAS > ROMANZA

ROMAS > ROMA

ROMAUNT n verse romance

ROMAUNTS > ROMAUNT

ROMCOM n film or television comedy based around the romantic relationships of the characters

ROMCOMS > ROMCOM

ROMELDALE n type of sheep

ROMEO n ardent male lover

ROMEOS > ROMEO

ROMNEYA n bushy type of poppy

ROMNEYAS > ROMNEYA

ROMP vb play wildly and joyfully ▷ n boisterous activity

ROMPED > ROMP

ROMPER n playful or boisterous child

ROMPERS pl n child's overalls

ROMPING > ROMP

ROMPINGLY > ROMP

ROMPISH > ROMP

ROMPISHLY > ROMP

ROMPS > ROMP

ROMS > ROM

RONCADOR n any of several types of fish

RONCADORS > RONCADOR

RONDACHE n round shield

RONDACHES > RONDACHE

RONDAVEL n circular building, often thatched

RONDAVELS > RONDAVEL

RONDE n round dance

RONDEAU n poem consisting of 13 or 10 lines with the opening words of the first line used as a refrain

RONDEAUX > RONDEAU

RONDEL n rondeau consisting of three stanzas of 13 or 14 lines with a two-line refrain appearing twice or three times

RONDELET n brief rondeau, having five or seven lines and a refrain taken from the first line

RONDELETS > RONDELET

RONDELLE n type of bead

RONDELLES > RONDELLE

RONDELS > RONDEL

RONDES > RONDE

RONDINO n short rondo

RONDINOS > RONDINO

RONDO n piece of music with a leading theme

continually returned to

RONDOS > RONDO

RONDURE *n* circle or curve

RONDURES > RONDURE

RONE *n* drainpipe or gutter for carrying rainwater from a roof

RONEO *vb* duplicate (a document) from a stencil ▷ *n* document reproduced by this process

RONEOED > RONEO

RONEOING > RONEO

RONEOS > RONEO

RONEPIPE *same as* > RONE

RONEPIPES > RONEPIPE

RONES > RONE

RONG *archaic past participle of* > RING

RONGGENG *n* Malay traditional dance

RONGGENGS > RONGGENG

RONIN *n* lordless samurai, esp one whose feudal lord had been deprived of his territory

RONINS > RONIN

RONION *same as* > RUNNION

RONIONS > RONION

RONNE *archaic form of* > RUN

RONNEL *n* type of pesticide

RONNELS > RONNEL

RONNIE *n* Dublin slang word for moustache

RONNIES > RONNIE

RONNING > RONNE

RONT *archaic variant of* > RUNT

RONTE *archaic variant of* > RUNT

RONTES > RONTE

RONTGEN *variant spelling of* > ROENTGEN

RONTGENS > RONTGEN

RONTS > RONT

RONYON *same as* > RUNNION

RONYONS > RUNNION

RONZER *n* New Zealand word for a New Zealander not from Auckland

RONZERS > RONZER

ROO *n* kangaroo

ROOD *n* Cross

ROODS > ROOD

ROOF *n* outside upper covering of a building, car, etc ▷ *vb* put a roof on

ROOFED > ROOF

ROOFER > ROOF

ROOFERS > ROOF

ROOFIE *n* tablet of sedative drug

ROOFIER > ROOFY

ROOFIES > ROOFIE

ROOFIEST > ROOFY

ROOFING *n* material used to build a roof

ROOFINGS > ROOFING

ROOFLESS > ROOF

ROOFLIKE > ROOF

ROOFLINE *n* uppermost edge of a roof

ROOFLINES > ROOFLINE

ROOFS > ROOF

ROOFSCAPE *n* view of the rooftops of a town, city, etc

ROOFTOP *n* outside part of

the roof of a building

ROOFTOPS > ROOFTOP

ROOFTREE *same as* > RIDGEPOLE

ROOFTREES > ROOFTREE

ROOFY *adj* with roofs

ROOIBOS *n* tea prepared from the dried leaves of an African plant

ROOIKAT *n* South African lynx

ROOIKATS > ROOIKAT

ROOINEK *n* contemptuous name for an Englishman

ROOINEKS > ROOINEK

ROOK *n* Eurasian bird of the crow family ▷ *vb* swindle

ROOKED > ROOK

ROOKERIES > ROOKERY

ROOKERY *n* colony of rooks, penguins, or seals

ROOKIE *n* new recruit

ROOKIER > ROOKY

ROOKIES > ROOKIE

ROOKIEST > ROOKY

ROOKING > ROOK

ROOKISH > ROOK

ROOKS > ROOK

ROOKY *adj* abounding in rooks

ROOM *n* enclosed area in a building ▷ *vb* occupy or share a room

ROOMED > ROOM

ROOMER > ROOM

ROOMERS > ROOM

ROOMETTE *n* self-contained compartment in a railway sleeping car

ROOMETTES > ROOMETTE

ROOMFUL *n* number or quantity sufficient to fill a room

ROOMFULS > ROOMFUL

ROOMIE *n* roommate

ROOMIER > ROOMY

ROOMIES > ROOMIE

ROOMIEST > ROOMY

ROOMILY > ROOMY

ROOMINESS > ROOMY

ROOMING > ROOM

ROOMMATE *n* person with whom one shares a room or apartment

ROOMMATES > ROOMMATE

ROOMS > ROOM

ROOMSOME *adj* archaic word meaning roomy

ROOMY *adj* spacious

ROON *n* Scots word for shred or strip

ROONS > ROON

ROOP *same as* > ROUP

ROOPED > ROOP

ROOPIER > ROOPY

ROOPIEST > ROOPY

ROOPING > ROOP

ROOPIT *same as* > ROOPY

ROOPS > ROOP

ROOPY *adj* (in dialect) hoarse

ROORBACH *same as* > ROORBACK

ROORBACHS > ROORBACH

ROORBACK *n* false or distorted report or account, used to obtain political advantage

ROORBACKS > ROORBACK

ROOS > ROO

ROOSA *n* type of grass

ROOSAS > ROOSA

ROOSE *vb* flatter

ROOSED > ROOSE

ROOSER > ROOSE

ROOSERS > ROOSE

ROOSES > ROOSE

ROOSING > ROOSE

ROOST *n* perch for fowls ▷ *vb* perch

ROOSTED > ROOST

ROOSTER *n* domestic cock

ROOSTERS > ROOSTER

ROOSTING > ROOST

ROOSTS > ROOST

ROOT *n* part of a plant that grows down into the earth obtaining nourishment ▷ *vb* establish a root and start to grow

ROOTAGE *n* root system

ROOTAGES > ROOTAGE

ROOTCAP *n* layer of cells at root tip

ROOTCAPS > ROOTCAP

ROOTED > ROOT

ROOTEDLY > ROOT

ROOTER > ROOT

ROOTERS > ROOT

ROOTHOLD > ROOT

ROOTHOLDS > ROOT

ROOTIER > ROOT

ROOTIES > ROOTY

ROOTIEST > ROOT

ROOTINESS > ROOT

ROOTING > ROOT

ROOTINGS > ROOT

ROOTLE *same as* > ROOT

ROOTLED > ROOTLE

ROOTLES > ROOTLE

ROOTLESS *adj* having no sense of belonging

ROOTLET *n* small root or branch of a root

ROOTLETS > ROOTLET

ROOTLIKE > ROOT

ROOTLING > ROOTLE

ROOTS *adj* (of popular music) going back to the origins of a style, esp in being unpretentious

ROOTSIER > ROOTS

ROOTSIEST > ROOTS

ROOTSTALK *same as* > RHIZOME

ROOTSTOCK *same as* > RHIZOME

ROOTSY > ROOTS

ROOTWORM *n* beetle larvae feeding on roots

ROOTWORMS > ROOTWORM

ROOTY *adj* rootlike ▷ *n* (in military slang) bread

ROPABLE *adj* capable of being roped

ROPE *n* thick cord

ROPEABLE *same as* > ROPABLE

ROPED > ROPE

ROPELIKE > ROPE

ROPER *n* someone who makes ropes

ROPERIES > ROPERY

ROPERS > ROPER

ROPERY *n* place where ropes

are made

ROPES > ROPE

ROPEWALK *n* long narrow usually covered path or shed where ropes are made

ROPEWALKS > ROPEWALK

ROPEWAY *n* type of aerial lift

ROPEWAYS > ROPEWAY

ROPEWORK *n* making, mending, or tying ropes

ROPEWORKS > ROPEWORK

ROPEY *adj* inferior or inadequate

ROPIER > ROPY

ROPIEST > ROPY

ROPILY > ROPEY

ROPINESS > ROPEY

ROPING > ROPE

ROPINGS > ROPE

ROPY *same as* > ROPEY

ROQUE *n* game developed from croquet, played on a hard surface with a resilient surrounding border from which the ball can rebound

ROQUES > ROQUE

ROQUET *vb* drive one's ball against (another person's ball) in order to be allowed to croquet ▷ *n* act of roqueting

ROQUETED > ROQUET

ROQUETING > ROQUET

ROQUETS > ROQUET

ROQUETTE *n* another name for the salad plant rocket

ROQUETTES > ROQUETTE

RORAL *archaic word for* > DEWY

RORE *archaic spelling of* > ROAR

RORES > RORE

RORIC *same as* > RORAL

RORID *same as* > RORAL

RORIE *same as* > ROARY

RORIER > RORY

RORIEST > RORY

RORQUAL *n* toothless whale with a dorsal fin

RORQUALS > RORQUAL

RORT *n* dishonest scheme ▷ *vb* take unfair advantage of something

RORTED > RORT

RORTER *n* small-scale confidence trickster

RORTERS > RORTER

RORTIER > RORT

RORTIEST > RORT

RORTING > RORT

RORTS > RORT

RORTY > RORT

RORY *adj* dewy

ROSACE *another name for* > ROSETTE

ROSACEA *n* chronic inflammatory disease causing the skin of the face to become abnormally flushed and sometimes pustular

ROSACEAS > ROSACEA

ROSACEOUS *adj* of or belonging to a family of plants typically having five-petalled flowers,

r

which includes the rose, strawberry, and many fruit trees

ROSACES > ROSACE

ROSAKER *archaic word for* > REALGAR

ROSAKERS > ROSAKER

ROSALIA *n* melody which is repeated but at a higher pitch each time

ROSALIAS > ROSALIA

ROSANILIN *n* reddish-brown crystalline insoluble derivative of aniline used as a red dye

ROSARIA > ROSARIUM

ROSARIAN *n* person who cultivates roses, esp professionally

ROSARIANS > ROSARIAN

ROSARIES > ROSARY

ROSARIUM *n* rose garden

ROSARIUMS > ROSARIUM

ROSARY *n* series of prayers

ROSBIF *n* term used in France for an English person

ROSBIFS > ROSBIF

ROSCID *adj* dewy

ROSCOE *slang word for* > GUN

ROSCOES > ROSCOE

ROSE > RISE

ROSEAL *adj* rosy or roselike

ROSEATE *adj* rose-coloured

ROSEATELY > ROSEATE

ROSEBAY *as in rosebay willowherb* perennial plant with spikes of deep pink flowers

ROSEBAYS > ROSEBAY

ROSEBOWL *n* bowl for displaying roses or other flowers

ROSEBOWLS > ROSEBOWL

ROSEBUD *n* rose which has not yet fully opened

ROSEBUDS > ROSEBUD

ROSEBUSH *n* flowering shrub

ROSED > RISE

ROSEFINCH *n* any of various finches with pink patches

ROSEFISH *n* red food fish of North Atlantic coastal waters

ROSEHIP *n* berry-like fruit of a rose plant

ROSEHIPS > ROSEHIP

ROSELESS > RISE

ROSELIKE > RISE

ROSELLA *n* type of Australian parrot

ROSELLAS > ROSELLA

ROSELLE *n* Indian flowering plant

ROSELLES > ROSELLE

ROSEMARY *n* fragrant flowering shrub

ROSEOLA *n* feverish condition of young children that lasts for some five days during the last two of which the patient has a rose-coloured rash. It is caused by the human herpes virus

ROSEOLAR > ROSEOLA

ROSEOLAS > ROSEOLA

ROSERIES > ROSERY

ROSEROOT *n* Eurasian mountain plant

ROSEROOTS > ROSEROOT

ROSERY *n* bed or garden of roses

ROSES > RISE

ROSESLUG *n* one of various types of pest that feed on roses

ROSESLUGS > ROSESLUG

ROSET *n* Scots word meaning rosin ▷ *vb* rub rosin on

ROSETED > ROSET

ROSETING > ROSET

ROSETS > ROSET

ROSETTE *n* rose-shaped ornament, esp a circular bunch of ribbons

ROSETTED > ROSET

ROSETTES > ROSETTE

ROSETTY > ROSET

ROSETY > ROSET

ROSEWATER *n* scented water used as a perfume and in cooking, made by the distillation of rose petals or by impregnation with oil of roses

ROSEWOOD *n* fragrant wood used to make furniture

ROSEWOODS > ROSEWOOD

ROSHI *n* teacher of Zen Buddhism

ROSHIS > ROSHI

ROSIED > ROSY

ROSIER *archaic word for* > ROSEBUSH

ROSIERE *archaic word for* > ROSEBUSH

ROSIERES > ROSIERE

ROSIERS > ROSIER

ROSIES > ROSY

ROSIEST > ROSY

ROSILY > ROSY

ROSIN *n* resin used for treating the bows of violins etc ▷ *vb* apply rosin to

ROSINATE *n* chemical compound

ROSINATES > ROSINATE

ROSINED > ROSIN

ROSINER *n* strong alcoholic drink

ROSINERS > ROSINER

ROSINESS > ROSY

ROSING > RISE

ROSINING > ROSIN

ROSINOL *n* yellowish fluorescent oily liquid obtained from certain resins, used in the manufacture of carbon black, varnishes, and lacquers

ROSINOLS > ROSINOL

ROSINOUS *adj* rosiny

ROSINS > ROSIN

ROSINWEED *n* any of several North American plants of the genus *Silphium* and related genera, having resinous juice, sticky foliage, and a strong smell

ROSINY > ROSIN

ROSIT *same as* > ROSET

ROSITED > ROSIT

ROSITING > ROSIT

ROSITS > ROSIT

ROSMARINE *archaic form of* > ROSEMARY

ROSOGLIO *same as* > ROSOLIO

ROSOGLIOS > ROSOGLIO

ROSOLIO *n* type of cordial

ROSOLIOS > ROSOLIO

ROSSER *n* bark-removing machine

ROSSERS > ROSSER

ROST *archaic spelling of* > ROAST

ROSTED > ROST

ROSTELLA > ROSTELLUM

ROSTELLAR > ROSTELLUM

ROSTELLUM *n* small beaklike process, such as the hooked projection from the top of the head in tapeworms or the outgrowth from the stigma of an orchid

ROSTER *n* list of people and their turns of duty ▷ *vb* place on a roster

ROSTERED > ROSTER

ROSTERING > ROSTER

ROSTERS > ROSTER

ROSTI *n* cheese-topped fried Swiss dish consisting of grated potato and, optionally, onion

ROSTING > ROST

ROSTIS > ROSTI

ROSTRA > ROSTRUM

ROSTRAL *adj* of or like a beak or snout

ROSTRALLY > ROSTRAL

ROSTRATE *adj* having a beak or beaklike process

ROSTRATED *same as* > ROSTRATE

ROSTRUM *n* platform or stage

ROSTRUMS > ROSTRUM

ROSTS > ROST

ROSULA *n* rosette

ROSULAS > ROSULA

ROSULATE *adj* in the form of a rose

ROSY *adj* pink-coloured ▷ *vb* redden or make pink

ROSYING > ROSY

ROT *vb* decompose or decay ▷ *n* decay

ROTA *n* list of people who take it in turn to do a particular task

ROTACHUTE *n* device serving the same purpose as a parachute, in which the canopy is replaced by freely revolving rotor blades, used for the delivery of stores or recovery of missiles

ROTAL *adj* of or relating to wheels or rotation

ROTAMETER *n* device for measuring the flow of a liquid

ROTAN *another name for* > RATTAN

ROTANS > ROTAN

ROTAPLANE *n* aircraft that derives its lift from freely revolving rotor blades

ROTARIES > ROTARY

ROTARY *adj* revolving ▷ *n* traffic roundabout

ROTAS > ROTA

ROTATABLE > ROTATE

ROTATE *vb* (cause to) move round a centre or on a pivot ▷ *adj* designating a corolla the united petals of which radiate from a central point like the spokes of a wheel

ROTATED > ROTATE

ROTATES > ROTATE

ROTATING *adj* revolving around a central axis, line, or point

ROTATION *n* act of rotating

ROTATIONS > ROTATION

ROTATIVE *same as* > ROTATORY

ROTATOR *n* person, device, or part that rotates or causes rotation

ROTATORES > ROTATOR

ROTATORS > ROTATOR

ROTATORY *adj* of, relating to, possessing, or causing rotation

ROTAVATE *same as* > ROTOVATE

ROTAVATED > ROTAVATE

ROTAVATES > ROTAVATE

ROTAVATOR *n* type of machine with rotating blades that will break up soil

ROTAVIRUS *n* any member of a genus of viruses that cause worldwide endemic infections. They occur in birds and mammals, cause diarrhoea in children, and are usually transmitted in food prepared with unwashed hands

ROTCH *n* little auk

ROTCHE *same as* > ROTCH

ROTCHES > ROTCH

ROTCHIE *same as* > ROTCH

ROTCHIES > ROTCHIE

ROTE *n* mechanical repetition ▷ *vb* learn by rote

ROTED > ROTE

ROTENONE *n* white odourless crystalline substance extracted from the roots of derris: a powerful insecticide

ROTENONES > ROTENONE

ROTES > ROTE

ROTGRASS *n* type of grass blamed for sheeprot

ROTGUT *n* alcoholic drink of inferior quality

ROTGUTS > ROTGUT

ROTHER *dialect word for* > OX

ROTHERS > ROTHER

ROTI *n* (in India and the Caribbean) a type of unleavened bread

ROTIFER *n* minute aquatic multicellular invertebrate

ROTIFERAL > ROTIFER
ROTIFERAN > ROTIFER
ROTIFERS > ROTIFER
ROTIFORM *adj* in the shape of a wheel
ROTING > ROTE
ROTIS > ROTI
ROTL *n* unit of weight used in Muslim countries, varying in value between about one and five pounds
ROTLS > ROTL
ROTO *n* printing process using a cylinder etched with many small recesses, from which ink is transferred to a moving web of paper, plastic, etc, in a rotary press
ROTOGRAPH *n* photograph made using a particular method ▷ *vb* photograph using this method
ROTOLO *n* (in Italian cuisine) a roll
ROTOLOS > ROTOLO
ROTON *n* quantum of vortex motion
ROTONS > ROTON
ROTOR *n* revolving portion of a dynamo, motor, or turbine
ROTORS > ROTOR
ROTOS > ROTO
ROTOTILL *vb* break up the soil using a rototiller
ROTOTILLS > ROTOTILL
ROTOVATE *vb* break up (the surface of the earth, or an area of ground) using a rotavator
ROTOVATED > ROTOVATE
ROTOVATES > ROTOVATE
ROTOVATOR *same as* > ROTAVATOR
ROTS > ROT
ROTTAN *n* (in dialect) a rat
ROTTANS > ROTTAN
ROTTE *n* ancient stringed instrument
ROTTED > ROT
ROTTEN *adj* decaying ▷ *adv* extremely ▷ *n* (in dialect) a rat
ROTTENER > ROTTEN
ROTTENEST > ROTTEN
ROTTENLY > ROTTEN
ROTTENS > ROTTEN
ROTTER *n* despicable person
ROTTERS > ROTTER
ROTTES > ROTTE
ROTTING > ROT
ROTULA *n* kneecap
ROTULAE > ROTULA
ROTULAS > ROTULA
ROTUND *adj* round and plump ▷ *vb* make round
ROTUNDA *n* circular building or room, esp with a dome
ROTUNDAS > ROTUNDA
ROTUNDATE *adj* rounded
ROTUNDED > ROTUND
ROTUNDER > ROTUND
ROTUNDEST > ROTUND
ROTUNDING > ROTUND
ROTUNDITY > ROTUND
ROTUNDLY > ROTUND

ROTUNDS > ROTUND
ROTURIER *n* freeholder or ordinary person
ROTURIERS > ROTURIER
ROUBLE *n* monetary unit of Russia, Belarus, and Tajikistan
ROUBLES > ROUBLE
ROUCHE *same as* > RUCHE
ROUCHES > ROUCHE
ROUCOU *another name for* > ANNATTO
ROUCOUS > ROUCOU
ROUE *n* man given to immoral living
ROUEN *n* breed of duck
ROUENS > ROUEN
ROUES > ROUE
ROUGE *n* red cosmetic used to colour the cheeks ▷ *vb* apply rouge to
ROUGED > ROUGE
ROUGES > ROUGE
ROUGH *adj* uneven or irregular ▷ *vb* make rough ▷ *n* rough state or area
ROUGHAGE *n* indigestible constituents of food which aid digestion
ROUGHAGES > ROUGHAGE
ROUGHBACK *n* rough-skinned flatfish
ROUGHCAST *n* mixture of plaster and small stones for outside walls ▷ *vb* coat with this ▷ *adj* covered with or denoting roughcast
ROUGHDRY *vb* dry (clothes or linen) without smoothing
ROUGHED > ROUGH
ROUGHEN *vb* make or become rough
ROUGHENED > ROUGHEN
ROUGHENS > ROUGHEN
ROUGHER *n* person that does the rough preparatory work on something ▷ *adj* more rough
ROUGHERS > ROUGHER
ROUGHEST > ROUGH
ROUGHHEW *vb* cut or hew (timber, stone, etc) roughly without finishing the surfac
ROUGHHEWN > ROUGHHEW
ROUGHHEWS > ROUGHHEW
ROUGHIE *n* small food fish found in southern and western Australian waters
ROUGHIES > ROUGHIE
ROUGHING > ROUGH
ROUGHISH *adj* somewhat rough
ROUGHLEG *n* any of several kinds of large hawk with feathered legs
ROUGHLEGS > ROUGHLEG
ROUGHLY *adv* without being exact or fully authenticated
ROUGHNECK *n* violent person
ROUGHNESS > ROUGH
ROUGHS > ROUGH
ROUGHSHOD *adj* (of a horse) shod with rough-bottomed shoes to prevent slidi
ROUGHT *archaic past form of* > REACH

ROUGHY *spelling variant of* > ROUGHIE
ROUGING > ROUGE
ROUILLE *n* kind of sauce
ROUILLES > ROUILLE
ROUL *archaic form of* > ROLL
ROULADE *n* slice of meat rolled, esp around a stuffing, and cooked
ROULADES > ROULADE
ROULE *archaic form of* > ROLL
ROULEAU *n* roll of paper containing coins
ROULEAUS > ROULEAU
ROULEAUX > ROULEAU
ROULES > ROULE
ROULETTE *n* gambling game played with a revolving wheel and a ball ▷ *vb* use a toothed wheel on (something), as in engraving, making stationery, etc
ROULETTED > ROULETTE
ROULETTES > ROULETTE
ROULS > ROUL
ROUM *archaic spelling of* > ROOM
ROUMING *n* pasture given for an animal
ROUMINGS > ROUMING
ROUMS > ROUM
ROUNCE *n* handle that is turned to move paper and plates on a printing press
ROUNCES > ROUNCE
ROUNCEVAL *n* giant or monster
ROUNCIES > ROUNCY
ROUNCY *archaic word for* > HORSE
ROUND *adj* spherical, cylindrical, circular, or curved ▷ *prep* indicating an encircling movement, presence on all sides, etc ▷ *vb* move round ▷ *n* round shape
ROUNDARCH *adj* with rounded arches
ROUNDBALL *n* form of basketball
ROUNDED *adj* round or curved
ROUNDEDLY > ROUNDED
ROUNDEL *same as* > ROUNDELAY
ROUNDELAY *n* simple song with a refrain
ROUNDELS > ROUNDEL
ROUNDER *n* run round all four bases after one hit in rounders
ROUNDERS *n* bat-and-ball team game
ROUNDEST > ROUND
ROUNDHAND *n* style of handwriting with large rounded curves
ROUNDHEEL *n* immoral woman
ROUNDING *n* process in which a number is approximated as the closest number that can be expressed using the number of bits or digits

available
ROUNDINGS > ROUNDING
ROUNDISH *adj* somewhat round
ROUNDLE *same as* > ROUNDEL
ROUNDLES > ROUNDLE
ROUNDLET *n* small circle
ROUNDLETS > ROUNDLET
ROUNDLY *adv* thoroughly
ROUNDNESS > ROUND
ROUNDS > ROUND
ROUNDSMAN *n* person who makes rounds, as for inspection or to deliver goods
ROUNDSMEN > ROUNDSMAN
ROUNDTRIP *n* US term for return trip
ROUNDUP *n* act of gathering together livestock, people, facts, etc
ROUNDUPS > ROUNDUP
ROUNDURE *n* archaic word meaning roundness
ROUNDURES > ROUNDURE
ROUNDWOOD *n* small pieces of timber (about 5–15 cm, or 2–6 in.) in diameter
ROUNDWORM *n* worm that is a common intestinal parasite of man
ROUP *n* any of various chronic respiratory diseases of birds, esp poultry ▷ *vb* sell by auction
ROUPED > ROUP
ROUPET *adj* Scots word meaning hoarse or croaky
ROUPIER > ROUP
ROUPIEST > ROUP
ROUPILY > ROUP
ROUPING > ROUP
ROUPIT *same as* > ROUPET
ROUPS > ROUP
ROUPY > ROUP
ROUSANT *adj* (in heraldry) rising
ROUSE *same as* > REVEILLE
ROUSED > ROUSE
ROUSEMENT *n* stirring up
ROUSER *n* person or thing that rouses people, such as a stirring speech or compelling rock song
ROUSERS > ROUSER
ROUSES > ROUSE
ROUSING *adj* lively, vigorous
ROUSINGLY > ROUSING
ROUSSEAU *n* pemmican fried in its own fat
ROUSSEAUS > ROUSSEAU
ROUSSETTE *n* dogfish
ROUST *vb* rout or stir, as out of bed
ROUSTED > ROUST
ROUSTER *n* unskilled labourer on an oil rig
ROUSTERS > ROUSTER
ROUSTING > ROUST
ROUSTS > ROUST
ROUT *n* overwhelming defeat ▷ *vb* defeat and put to flight
ROUTE *n* roads taken to reach a destination ▷ *vb* send by a particular route

r

ROUTED > ROUTE

ROUTEING > ROUTE

ROUTEMAN n (in US English) delivery man or salesman doing a particular round

ROUTEMEN > ROUTEMAN

ROUTER n device that allows data to be moved efficiently between two points on a network

ROUTERS > ROUTER

ROUTES > ROUTE

ROUTEWAY n track, road, or waterway, etc, used as a route to somewhere

ROUTEWAYS > ROUTEWAY

ROUTH n abundance ▷ adj abundant

ROUTHIE adj abundant, plentiful, or well filled

ROUTHIER > ROUTHIE

ROUTHIEST > ROUTHIE

ROUTHS > ROUTH

ROUTINE n usual or regular method of procedure ▷ adj ordinary or regular

ROUTINEER n someone who believes in routine

ROUTINELY > ROUTINE

ROUTINES > ROUTINE

ROUTING > ROUT

ROUTINGS > ROUT

ROUTINISE same as > ROUTINIZE

ROUTINISM > ROUTINE

ROUTINIST > ROUTINE

ROUTINIZE vb make routine

ROUTOUS > ROUT

ROUTOUSLY > ROUT

ROUTS > ROUT

ROUX n fat and flour cooked together as a basis for sauces

ROVE > REEVE

ROVED > REEVE

ROVEN > REEVE

ROVER n wanderer, traveller

ROVERS > ROVER

ROVES > REEVE

ROVING > ROVE

ROVINGLY > ROVING

ROVINGS > ROVE

ROW n straight line of people or things ▷ vb propel (a boat) by oars

ROWABLE > ROW

ROWAN n tree producing bright red berries, mountain ash

ROWANS > ROWAN

ROWBOAT n small boat propelled by one or more pairs of oars

ROWBOATS > ROWBOAT

ROWDEDOW same as > ROWDYDOW

ROWDEDOWS > ROWDEDOW

ROWDIER > ROWDY

ROWDIES > ROWDY

ROWDIEST > ROWDY

ROWDILY > ROWDY

ROWDINESS > ROWDY

ROWDY adj disorderly, noisy, and rough ▷ n person like this

ROWDYDOW n hullabaloo

ROWDYDOWS > ROWDYDOW

ROWDYISH > ROWDY

ROWDYISM n rowdy behaviour or tendencies or a habitual pattern of rowdy behaviour

ROWDYISMS > ROWDYISM

ROWED > ROW

ROWEL n small spiked wheel on a spur ▷ vb goad (a horse) using a rowel

ROWELED > ROWEL

ROWELING > ROWEL

ROWELLED > ROWEL

ROWELLING > ROWEL

ROWELS > ROWEL

ROWEN another word for > AFTERMATH

ROWENS > ROWEN

ROWER > ROW

ROWERS > ROW

ROWING > ROW

ROWINGS > ROW

ROWLOCK n device on a boat that holds an oar in place

ROWLOCKS > ROWLOCK

ROWME archaic variant of > ROOM

ROWMES > ROWME

ROWND archaic variant of > ROUND

ROWNDED > ROWND

ROWNDELL archaic variant of > ROUNDEL

ROWNDELLS > ROWNDELL

ROWNDING > ROWND

ROWNDS > ROWND

ROWOVER n act of winning a rowing race unopposed, by rowing the course

ROWOVERS > ROWOVER

ROWS > ROW

ROWT archaic variant of > ROUT

ROWTED > ROWT

ROWTH same as > ROUTH

ROWTHS > ROWTH

ROWTING > ROWT

ROWTS > ROWT

ROYAL adj of, befitting, or supported by a king or queen ▷ n member of a royal family

ROYALET n minor king

ROYALETS > ROYALET

ROYALISE same as > ROYALIZE

ROYALISED > ROYALISE

ROYALISES > ROYALISE

ROYALISM > ROYALIST

ROYALISMS > ROYALIST

ROYALIST n supporter of monarchy ▷ adj of or relating to royalists

ROYALISTS > ROYALIST

ROYALIZE vb make royal

ROYALIZED > ROYALIZE

ROYALIZES > ROYALIZE

ROYALLER > ROYAL

ROYALLEST > ROYAL

ROYALLY > ROYAL

ROYALMAST n highest part of mast

ROYALS > ROYAL

ROYALTIES > ROYALTY

ROYALTY n royal people

ROYNE archaic word for > GNAW

ROYNED > ROYNE

ROYNES > ROYNE

ROYNING > ROYNE

ROYNISH archaic word for > MANGY

ROYST same as > ROIST

ROYSTED > ROYST

ROYSTER same as > ROISTER

ROYSTERED > ROYSTER

ROYSTERER > ROYSTER

ROYSTERS > ROISTER

ROYSTING > ROYST

ROYSTS > ROYST

ROZELLE same as > ROSELLE

ROZELLES > ROZELLE

ROZET same as > ROSET

ROZETED > ROZET

ROZETING > ROZET

ROZETS > ROZET

ROZIT same as > ROSET

ROZITED > ROZIT

ROZITING > ROZIT

ROZITS > ROZIT

ROZZER n policeman

ROZZERS > ROZZER

RUANA n woollen wrap resembling a poncho

RUANAS > RUANA

RUB vb apply pressure and friction to (something) with a circular or backwards-and-forwards movement ▷ n act of rubbing

RUBABOO n soup or stew made by boiling pemmican with, if available, flour and vegetables

RUBABOOS > RUBABOO

RUBACE same as > RUBASSE

RUBACES > RUBACE

RUBAI n verse form of Persian origin consisting of four-line stanzas

RUBAIYAT n (in Persian poetry) a verse form consisting of four-line stanzas

RUBASSE n type of quartz containing red haematite

RUBASSES > RUBASSE

RUBATI > RUBATO

RUBATO n (with) expressive flexibility of tempo ▷ adv be played with a flexible tempo

RUBATOS > RUBATO

RUBBABOO same as > RUBABOO

RUBBABOOS > RUBABOO

RUBBED > RUB

RUBBER n strong waterproof elastic material, orig. made from the dried sap of a tropical tree, now usu synthetic ▷ adj made of or producing rubber ▷ vb provide with rubber coating

RUBBERED > RUBBER

RUBBERIER > RUBBERY

RUBBERING > RUBBER

RUBBERISE same as > RUBBERIZE

RUBBERIZE vb coat or treat with rubber

RUBBERS > RUBBER

RUBBERY adj having the texture of or resembling rubber, esp in flexibility or toughness

RUBBET old Scots past form of > ROB

RUBBIDIES > RUBBIDY

RUBBIDY same as > RUBBITY

RUBBIES > RUBBY

RUBBING > RUB

RUBBINGS > RUB

RUBBISH n waste matter ▷ vb criticize

RUBBISHED > RUBBISH

RUBBISHES > RUBBISH

RUBBISHLY variant of > RUBBISHY

RUBBISHY adj worthless, of poor quality, or useless

RUBBIT old Scots past form of > ROB

RUBBITIES > RUBBITY

RUBBITY n pub

RUBBLE n fragments of broken stone, brick, etc ▷ vb turn into rubble

RUBBLED > RUBBLE

RUBBLES > RUBBLE

RUBBLIER > RUBBLE

RUBBLIEST > RUBBLE

RUBBLING > RUBBLE

RUBBLY > RUBBLE

RUBBOARD n board for scrubbing clothes on

RUBBOARDS > RUBBOARD

RUBBY n rubbing alcohol, esp when mixed with cheap wine for drinking

RUBDOWN n act of drying or cleaning vigorously

RUBDOWNS > RUBDOWN

RUBE n unsophisticated countryman

RUBEFIED > RUBEFY

RUBEFIES > RUBEFY

RUBEFY vb make red, esp (of a counterirritant) to make the skin go red

RUBEFYING > RUBEFY

RUBEL n currency unit of Belarus

RUBELLA n mild contagious viral disease characterized by cough, sore throat, and skin rash

RUBELLAN n red-coloured mineral

RUBELLANS > RUBELLAN

RUBELLAS > RUBELLA

RUBELLITE n red transparent variety of tourmaline, used as a gemstone

RUBELS > RUBEL

RUBEOLA technical name for > MEASLES

RUBEOLAR > RUBEOLA

RUBEOLAS > RUBEOLA

RUBES > RUBE

RUBESCENT adj reddening

RUBICELLE n variety of spinel that is orange or yellow in colour

RUBICON n point of no return ▷ vb (in bezique) to beat before the loser has managed to gain as many as 1000 points

RUBICONED > RUBICON

RUBICONS > RUBICON

RUBICUND *adj* ruddy

RUBIDIC > RUBIDIUM

RUBIDIUM *n* soft highly reactive radioactive element

RUBIDIUMS > RUBIDIUM

RUBIED > RUBY

RUBIER > RUBY

RUBIES > RUBY

RUBIEST > RUBY

RUBIFIED > RUBIFY

RUBIFIES > RUBIFY

RUBIFY *same as* > RUBEFY

RUBIFYING > RUBIFY

RUBIGO *old Scots word for* > PENIS

RUBIGOS > RUBIGO

RUBIN *archaic word for* > RUBY

RUBINE *archaic word for* > RUBY

RUBINEOUS *same as* > RUBIOUS

RUBINES > RUBINE

RUBINS > RUBIN

RUBIOUS *adj* of the colour ruby

RUBLE *same as* > ROUBLE

RUBLES > RUBLE

RUBOFF *n* resulting effect on something else; consequences

RUBOFFS > RUBOFF

RUBOUT *n* killing or elimination

RUBOUTS > RUBOUT

RUBRIC *n* set of rules for behaviour ▷ *adj* written, printed, or marked in red

RUBRICAL > RUBRIC

RUBRICATE *vb* print (a book or manuscript) with red titles, headings, etc

RUBRICIAN *n* authority on liturgical rubrics

RUBRICS > RUBRIC

RUBS > RUB

RUBSTONE *n* stone used for sharpening or smoothing, esp a whetstone

RUBSTONES > RUBSTONE

RUBUS *n* fruit-bearing genus of shrubs

RUBY *n* red precious gemstone ▷ *adj* deep red ▷ *vb* redden

RUBYING > RUBY

RUBYLIKE > RUBY

RUC *same as* > ROC

RUCHE *n* pleat or frill of lace etc as a decoration ▷ *vb* put a ruche on

RUCHED > RUCHE

RUCHES > RUCHE

RUCHING *n* material used for a ruche

RUCHINGS > RUCHING

RUCK *n* rough crowd of common people ▷ *vb* wrinkle or crease

RUCKED > RUCK

RUCKING > RUCK

RUCKLE *another word*

for > RUCK

RUCKLED > RUCKLE

RUCKLES > RUCKLE

RUCKLING > RUCKLE

RUCKMAN *n* person who plays in the ruck

RUCKMEN > RUCKMAN

RUCKS > RUCK

RUCKSACK *n* large pack carried on the back

RUCKSACKS > RUCKSACK

RUCKSEAT *n* seat fixed to or forming part of a rucksack

RUCKSEATS > RUCKSEAT

RUCKUS *n* uproar

RUCKUSES > RUCKUS

RUCOLA *n* another name for the salad plant rocket

RUCOLAS > RUCOLA

RUCS > RUC

RUCTATION *n* archaic word meaning eructation or belch

RUCTION *n* uproar

RUCTIONS > RUCTION

RUCTIOUS *adj* tending or likely to cause ructions

RUD *n* red or redness ▷ *vb* redden

RUDACEOUS *adj* (of conglomerate, breccia, and similar rocks) composed of coarse-grained material

RUDAS *n* Scots word for a coarse, rude old woman

RUDASES > RUDAS

RUDBECKIA *n* any plant of the North American genus *Rudbeckia*, cultivated for their showy flowers

RUDD *n* European freshwater fish

RUDDED > RUD

RUDDER *n* vertical hinged piece at the stern of a boat or at the rear of an aircraft, for steering

RUDDERS > RUDDER

RUDDIED > RUDDY

RUDDIER > RUDDY

RUDDIES > RUDDY

RUDDIEST > RUDDY

RUDDILY > RUDDY

RUDDINESS > RUDDY

RUDDING > RUD

RUDDLE *n* red ochre, used esp to mark sheep ▷ *vb* mark (sheep) with ruddle

RUDDLED > RUDDLE

RUDDLEMAN *n* ruddle dealer

RUDDLEMEN > RUDDLEMAN

RUDDLES > RUDDLE

RUDDLING > RUDDLE

RUDDOCK *dialect name for the* > ROBIN

RUDDOCKS > RUDDOCK

RUDDS > RUDD

RUDDY *adj* of a fresh healthy red colour ▷ *adv* bloody ▷ *vb* redden

RUDDYING > RUDDY

RUDE *archaic spelling of* > ROOD

RUDELY > RUDE

RUDENESS > RUDE

RUDER > RUDE

RUDERAL *n* plant that grows

on waste ground ▷ *adj* growing in waste places

RUDERALS > RUDERAL

RUDERIES > RUDE

RUDERY > RUDE

RUDES > RUDE

RUDESBIES > RUDESBY

RUDESBY *n* archaic word for rude person

RUDEST > RUDE

RUDIE *n* member of a youth movement originating in the 1960s

RUDIES > RUDIE

RUDIMENT *n* first principles or elementary stages of a subject

RUDIMENTS > RUDIMENT

RUDISH *adj* somewhat rude

RUDS > RUD

RUE *vb* feel regret for ▷ *n* plant with evergreen bitter leaves

RUED > RUE

RUEFUL *adj* regretful or sorry

RUEFULLY > RUEFUL

RUEING > RUE

RUEINGS > RUE

RUELLE *n* area between bed and wall, at one time used by French ladies of standing for receiving visitors

RUELLES > RUELLE

RUELLIA *n* genus of plants

RUELLIAS > RUELLIA

RUER > RUE

RUERS > RUE

RUES > RUE

RUFESCENT *adj* tinged with red or becoming red

RUFF *n* circular pleated, gathered, or fluted collar of lawn, muslin, etc, often starched or wired, worn by both men and women in the 16th and 17th centuries ▷ *vb* trump

RUFFE *n* European freshwater fish

RUFFED > RUFF

RUFFES > RUFFE

RUFFIAN *n* violent lawless person ▷ *vb* act like a ruffian

RUFFIANED > RUFFIAN

RUFFIANLY > RUFFIAN

RUFFIANS > RUFFIAN

RUFFIN *archaic name for* > RUFFE

RUFFING > RUFF

RUFFINS > RUFFIN

RUFFLE *vb* disturb the calm of ▷ *n* frill or pleat

RUFFLED > RUFFLE

RUFFLER *n* person or thing that ruffles

RUFFLERS > RUFFLER

RUFFLES > RUFFLE

RUFFLIER > RUFFLY

RUFFLIEST > RUFFLY

RUFFLIKE > RUFF

RUFFLING > RUFFLE

RUFFLINGS > RUFFLE

RUFFLY *adj* ruffled

RUFFS > RUFF

RUFIYAA *n* standard monetary unit of the Maldives, divided into 100 laari

RUFIYAAS > RUFIYAA

RUFOUS *adj* reddish-brown

RUG *n* small carpet ▷ *vb* (in dialect) tug

RUGA *n* fold, wrinkle, or crease

RUGAE > RUGA

RUGAL *adj* (in anatomy) with ridges or folds

RUGALACH *same as* > RUGELACH

RUGATE *same as* > RUGOSE

RUGBIES > RUGBY

RUGBY *n* form of football played with an oval ball which may be handled by the players

RUGELACH *n* fruit and nut pastry shaped like a croissant

RUGGED *adj* rocky or steep

RUGGEDER > RUGGED

RUGGEDEST > RUGGED

RUGGEDISE *same as* > RUGGEDIZE

RUGGEDIZE *vb* make durable, as for military use

RUGGEDLY > RUGGED

RUGGELACH *same as* > RUGELACH

RUGGER *same as* > RUGBY

RUGGERS > RUGGER

RUGGIER > RUGGY

RUGGIEST > RUGGY

RUGGING > RUG

RUGGINGS > RUG

RUGGY *adj* (in dialect) rough or rugged

RUGLIKE > RUG

RUGOLA *n* another name for the salad plant rocket

RUGOLAS > RUGOLA

RUGOSA *n* any of various shrubs descended from a particular type of wild rose

RUGOSAS > RUGOSA

RUGOSE *adj* wrinkled

RUGOSELY > RUGOSE

RUGOSITY > RUGOSE

RUGOUS *same as* > RUGOSE

RUGS > RUG

RUGULOSE *adj* with little wrinkles

RUIN *vb* destroy or spoil completely ▷ *n* destruction or decay

RUINABLE > RUIN

RUINATE *vb* archaic word for bring or come to ruin

RUINATED > RUINATE

RUINATES > RUINATE

RUINATING > RUINATE

RUINATION *n* act of ruining

RUINED > RUIN

RUINER > RUIN

RUINERS > RUIN

RUING > RUE

RUINGS > RUE

RUINING > RUIN

RUININGS > RUIN

RUINOUS *adj* causing ruin

RUINOUSLY > RUINOUS

RUINS > RUIN

r

RUKH *same as* > ROC
RUKHS > RUKH
RULABLE > RULE
RULE *n* statement of what is allowed, for example in a game or procedure ▷ *vb* govern
RULED > RULE
RULELESS > RULE
RULER *n* person who governs ▷ *vb* punish by hitting with a ruler
RULERED > RULER
RULERING > RULER
RULERS > RULER
RULERSHIP > RULER
RULES > RULE
RULESSE *adj* archaic word meaning ruleless or without rules
RULIER > RULY
RULIEST > RULY
RULING *n* formal decision ▷ *adj* controlling or exercising authority
RULINGS > RULING
RULLION *n* Scots word for rawhide shoe
RULLIONS > RULLION
RULLOCK *same as* > ROWLOCK
RULLOCKS > RULLOCK
RULY *adj* orderly
RUM *n* alcoholic drink distilled from sugar cane ▷ *adj* odd, strange
RUMAKI *n* savoury of chicken liver and sliced water chestnut wrapped in bacon
RUMAKIS > RUMAKI
RUMAL *n* handkerchief or type of cloth
RUMALS > RUMAL
RUMBA *n* lively ballroom dance of Cuban origin ▷ *vb* dance the rumba
RUMBAED > RUMBA
RUMBAING > RUMBA
RUMBAS > RUMBA
RUMBELOW *n* nonsense word used in the refrain of certain sea shanties
RUMBELOWS > RUMBELOW
RUMBLE *vb* make a low continuous noise ▷ *n* deep resonant sound
RUMBLED > RUMBLE
RUMBLER > RUMBLE
RUMBLERS > RUMBLE
RUMBLES > RUMBLE
RUMBLIER > RUMBLY
RUMBLIEST > RUMBLY
RUMBLING > RUMBLE
RUMBLINGS > RUMBLE
RUMBLY *adj* rumbling or liable to rumble
RUMBO *n* rum-based cocktail
RUMBOS > RUMBO
RUME *archaic form of* > RHEUM
RUMEN *n* first compartment of the stomach of ruminants, behind the reticulum, in which food is partly digested before being regurgitated as cud

RUMENS > RUMEN
RUMES > RUME
RUMINA > RUMEN
RUMINAL > RUMEN
RUMINANT *n* cud-chewing (animal, such as a cow, sheep, or deer) ▷ *adj* of ruminants
RUMINANTS > RUMINANT
RUMINATE *vb* chew the cud
RUMINATED > RUMINATE
RUMINATES > RUMINATE
RUMINATOR > RUMINATE
RUMKIN *n* archaic term for a drinking vessel
RUMKINS > RUMKIN
RUMLY > RUM
RUMMAGE *vb* search untidily and at length ▷ *n* untidy search through a collection of things
RUMMAGED > RUMMAGE
RUMMAGER > RUMMAGE
RUMMAGERS > RUMMAGE
RUMMAGES > RUMMAGE
RUMMAGING > RUMMAGE
RUMMER > RUM
RUMMERS > RUM
RUMMEST > RUM
RUMMIER > RUMMY
RUMMIES > RUMMY
RUMMIEST > RUMMY
RUMMILY > RUMMY
RUMMINESS > RUMMY
RUMMISH *adj* rather strange, peculiar or odd
RUMMY *n* card game in which players try to collect sets or sequences ▷ *adj* of or like rum in taste or smell
RUMNESS > RUM
RUMNESSES > RUM
RUMOR *same as* > RUMOUR
RUMORED > RUMOR
RUMORING > RUMOR
RUMOROUS *adj* involving or containing rumours
RUMORS > RUMOR
RUMOUR *n* unproved statement ▷ *vb* pass around or circulate in the form of a rumour
RUMOURED > RUMOUR
RUMOURER *n* someone given to spreading rumours
RUMOURERS > RUMOURER
RUMOURING > RUMOUR
RUMOURS > RUMOUR
RUMP *n* buttocks ▷ *vb* turn back on
RUMPED > RUMP
RUMPIES > RUMPY
RUMPING > RUMP
RUMPLE *vb* make untidy, crumpled, or dishevelled ▷ *n* wrinkle, fold, or crease
RUMPLED > RUMPLE
RUMPLES > RUMPLE
RUMPLESS > RUMP
RUMPLIER > RUMPLE
RUMPLIEST > RUMPLE
RUMPLING > RUMPLE
RUMPLY > RUMPLE
RUMPO *n* slang word for sexual intercourse
RUMPOS > RUMPO
RUMPS > RUMP

RUMPUS *n* noisy commotion
RUMPUSES > RUMPUS
RUMPY *n* tailless Manx cat ▷ *adj* with a large or noticeable rump
RUMRUNNER *n* alcohol smuggler
RUMS > RUM
RUN *vb* move with a more rapid gait than walking ▷ *n* act or spell of running
RUNABOUT *n* small car used for short journeys ▷ *vb* move busily from place to place
RUNABOUTS > RUNABOUT
RUNAGATE *n* vagabond, fugitive, or renegade
RUNAGATES > RUNAGATE
RUNANGA *n* Māori assembly or council
RUNAROUND *n* deceitful or evasive treatment of a person
RUNAWAY *n* person or animal that runs away
RUNAWAYS > RUNAWAY
RUNBACK *n* (in tennis) the areas behind the baselines of the court
RUNBACKS > RUNBACK
RUNCH *n* another name for white charlock
RUNCHES > RUNCH
RUNCIBLE *as in runcible spoon* forklike utensil with two prongs and one sharp curved prong
RUNCINATE *adj* (of a leaf) having a saw-toothed margin with the teeth or lobes pointing backwards
RUND *same as* > ROON
RUNDALE *n* (formerly) the name given, esp in Ireland and earlier in Scotland, to the system of land tenure in which each land-holder had several strips of land that were not contiguous
RUNDALES > RUNDALE
RUNDLE *n* rung of a ladder
RUNDLED *adj* rounded
RUNDLES > RUNDLE
RUNDLET *n* liquid measure, generally about 15 gallons
RUNDLETS > RUNDLET
RUNDOWN *adj* tired; exhausted ▷ *n* brief review, résumé, or summary
RUNDOWNS > RUNDOWN
RUNDS > RUND
RUNE *n* any character of the earliest Germanic alphabet
RUNECRAFT *n* understanding of and skill working with runes
RUNED *n* with runes on
RUNELIKE *adj* resembling a rune or runes
RUNES > RUNE
RUNFLAT *adj* having a safety feature that prevents tyres becoming dangerous or liable to damage when flat
RUNG > RING

RUNGLESS > RING
RUNGS > RING
RUNIC > RUNE
RUNKLE *vb* (in dialect) crease or wrinkle
RUNKLED > RUNKLE
RUNKLES > RUNKLE
RUNKLING > RUNKLE
RUNLESS > RUN
RUNLET *n* cask for wine, beer, etc
RUNLETS > RUNLET
RUNNABLE > RUN
RUNNEL *n* small brook
RUNNELS > RUNNEL
RUNNER *n* competitor in a race
RUNNERS > RUNNER
RUNNET *dialect word for* > RENNET
RUNNETS > RUNNET
RUNNIER > RUNNY
RUNNIEST > RUNNY
RUNNINESS > RUNNY
RUNNING > RUN
RUNNINGLY > RUN
RUNNINGS > RUN
RUNNION *n* archaic pejorative term for a woman
RUNNIONS > RUNNION
RUNNY *adj* tending to flow
RUNOFF *n* extra race to decide the winner after a tie
RUNOFFS > RUNOFF
RUNOUT *n* dismissal of a batsman by running him out
RUNOUTS > RUNOUT
RUNOVER *n* incident in which someone is run over by a vehicle
RUNOVERS > RUNOVER
RUNRIG *same as* > RUNDALE
RUNRIGS > RUNRIG
RUNROUND *same as* > RUNAROUND
RUNROUNDS > RUNROUND
RUNS > RUN
RUNT *n* smallest animal in a litter
RUNTED *adj* stunted
RUNTIER > RUNT
RUNTIEST > RUNT
RUNTINESS > RUNT
RUNTISH > RUNT
RUNTISHLY > RUNT
RUNTS > RUNT
RUNTY > RUNT
RUNWAY *n* hard level roadway where aircraft take off and land
RUNWAYS > RUNWAY
RUPEE *n* monetary unit of India and Pakistan
RUPEES > RUPEE
RUPIA *n* type of skin eruption
RUPIAH *n* standard monetary unit of Indonesia, divided into 100 sen
RUPIAHS > RUPIAH
RUPIAS > RUPIA
RUPTURE *n* breaking, breach ▷ *vb* break, burst, or sever

RUPTURED > RUPTURE

RUPTURES > RUPTURE

RUPTURING > RUPTURE

RURAL *adj* in or of the countryside ▷*n* country dweller

RURALISE *same as* > RURALIZE

RURALISED > RURALISE

RURALISES > RURALISE

RURALISM > RURAL

RURALISMS > RURAL

RURALIST > RURAL

RURALISTS > RURAL

RURALITE > RURAL

RURALITES > RURAL

RURALITY > RURAL

RURALIZE *vb* make rural in character, appearance, etc

RURALIZED > RURALIZE

RURALIZES > RURALIZE

RURALLY > RURAL

RURALNESS > RURAL

RURALS > RURAL

RURBAN *adj* part country, part urban

RURP *n* very small piton

RURPS > RURP

RURU *another name for* > MOPOKE

RURUS > RURU

RUSA *n* type of deer with a mane

RUSALKA *n* water nymph or spirit

RUSALKAS > RUSALKA

RUSAS > RUSA

RUSCUS *n* type of shrub

RUSCUSES > RUSCUS

RUSE *n* stratagem or trick

RUSES > RUSE

RUSH *vb* move or do very quickly ▷*n* sudden quick or violent movement ▷*adj* done with speed, hasty

RUSHED > RUSH

RUSHEE *n* someone interested in gaining fraternity or sorority membership

RUSHEES > RUSHEE

RUSHEN *adj* made of rushes

RUSHER > RUSH

RUSHERS > RUSH

RUSHES *pl n* (in film-making) the initial prints of a scene or scenes before editing, usually prepared daily

RUSHIER > RUSHY

RUSHIEST > RUSHY

RUSHINESS > RUSHY

RUSHING > RUSH

RUSHINGS > RUSH

RUSHLIGHT *n* narrow candle, formerly in use, made of the pith of various types of rush dipped in tallow

RUSHLIKE > RUSH

RUSHY *adj* full of rushes

RUSINE *adj* of or relating to

rusa deer

RUSK *n* hard brown crisp biscuit, used esp for feeding babies

RUSKS > RUSK

RUSMA *n* Turkish depilatory

RUSMAS > RUSMA

RUSSE *as in charlotte russe* cold dessert made from whipped cream, custard, etc, surrounded by sponge fingers

RUSSEL *n* type of woollen fabric

RUSSELS > RUSSEL

RUSSET *adj* reddish-brown ▷*n* apple with rough reddish-brown skin ▷*vb* become russet-coloured

RUSSETED > RUSSET

RUSSETING > RUSSET

RUSSETS > RUSSET

RUSSETY > RUSSET

RUSSIA *n* Russia leather

RUSSIAS > RUSSIA

RUSSIFIED > RUSSIFY

RUSSIFIES > RUSSIFY

RUSSIFY *vb* cause to become Russian in character

RUSSULA *n* any fungus of the large basidiomycetous genus *Russula*, of typical toadstool shape and often brightly coloured

RUSSULAE > RUSSULA

RUSSULAS > RUSSULA

RUST *n* reddish-brown coating formed on iron etc that has been exposed to moisture ▷*adj* reddish-brown ▷*vb* become coated with rust

RUSTABLE *adj* liable to rust

RUSTED > RUST

RUSTIC *adj* of or resembling country people ▷*n* person from the country

RUSTICAL *n* rustic

RUSTICALS > RUSTICAL

RUSTICANA *pl n* objects, such as agricultural implements, garden furniture, etc, relating to the countryside or made in imitation of rustic styles

RUSTICATE *vb* banish temporarily from university as a punishment

RUSTICIAL *made-up variant of* > RUSTIC

RUSTICISE *same as* > RUSTICIZE

RUSTICISM > RUSTIC

RUSTICITY > RUSTIC

RUSTICIZE *vb* make rustic

RUSTICLY > RUSTIC

RUSTICS > RUSTIC

RUSTIER > RUSTY

RUSTIEST > RUSTY

RUSTILY > RUSTY

RUSTINESS > RUSTY

RUSTING > RUST

RUSTINGS > RUST

RUSTLE *n* (make) a low whispering sound ▷*vb* steal (cattle)

RUSTLED > RUSTLE

RUSTLER *n* cattle thief

RUSTLERS > RUSTLER

RUSTLES > RUSTLE

RUSTLESS > RUST

RUSTLING > RUSTLE

RUSTLINGS > RUSTLE

RUSTPROOF *adj* treated against rusting

RUSTRE *n* (in heraldry) lozenge with a round hole in the middle showing the background colour

RUSTRED > RUSTRE

RUSTRES > RUSTRE

RUSTS > RUST

RUSTY *adj* coated with rust

RUT *n* furrow made by wheels ▷*vb* be in a period of sexual excitability

RUTABAGA *n* Eurasian plant with a bulbous edible root which is used as a vegetable and as cattle fodder

RUTABAGAS > RUTABAGA

RUTACEOUS *adj* of, relating to, or belonging to the *Rutaceae*, a family of tropical and temperate flowering plants many of which have aromatic leaves. The family includes rue and citrus trees

RUTH *n* pity

RUTHENIC *adj* of or containing ruthenium, esp in a high valency state

RUTHENIUM *n* rare hard brittle white element

RUTHFUL *adj* full of or causing sorrow or pity

RUTHFULLY > RUTHFUL

RUTHLESS *adj* pitiless, merciless

RUTHS > RUTH

RUTILANT *adj* of a reddish colour or glow

RUTILATED *adj* (of minerals, esp quartz) containing needles of rutile

RUTILE *n* black, yellowish, or reddish-brown mineral

RUTILES > RUTILE

RUTIN *n* bioflavonoid found in various plants including rue

RUTINS > RUTIN

RUTS > RUT

RUTTED > RUT

RUTTER *n* (in history) type of cavalry soldier

RUTTERS > RUTTER

RUTTIER > RUTTY

RUTTIEST > RUTTY

RUTTILY > RUTTY

RUTTINESS > RUTTY

RUTTING > RUT

RUTTINGS > RUT

RUTTISH *adj* (of an animal) in a condition of rut

RUTTISHLY > RUTTISH

RUTTY *adj* full of ruts or holes

RYA *n* type of rug originating in Scandinavia

RYAL *n* one of several old coins

RYALS > RYAL

RYAS > RYA

RYBAT *n* polished stone piece forming the side of a window or door

RYBATS > RYBAT

RYBAUDRYE *archaic variant of* > RIBALDRY

RYE *n* kind of grain used for fodder and bread

RYEBREAD *n* any of various breads made entirely or partly from rye flour, often with caraway seeds

RYEBREADS > RYEBREAD

RYEFLOUR *n* flour made from rye

RYEFLOURS > RYEFLOUR

RYEGRASS *n* any of various grasses of the genus *Lolium* native to Europe, N Africa, and Asia and widely cultivated as forage crops

RYEPECK *n* punt-mooring pole

RYEPECKS > RYEPECK

RYES > RYE

RYFE *archaic variant of* > RIFE

RYKE *Scots variant of* > REACH

RYKED > RYKE

RYKES > RYKE

RYKING > RYKE

RYMME *same as* > RIM

RYMMED > RYMME

RYMMES > RYMME

RYMMING > RYMME

RYND *n* (in milling) crossbar piece forming part of the support structure of the upper millstone

RYNDS > RYND

RYOKAN *n* traditional Japanese inn

RYOKANS > RYOKAN

RYOT *n* (in India) a peasant or tenant farmer

RYOTS > RYOT

RYOTWARI *n* (in India) system of land tenure in which land taxes are paid to the state

RYOTWARIS > RYOTWARI

RYPE *n* ptarmigan

RYPECK *same as* > RYEPECK

RYPECKS > RYEPECK

RYPER > RYPE

r

Ss

SAB *n* person engaged in direct action to prevent a targeted activity taking place ▷ *vb* take part in such action

SABADILLA *n* tropical American liliaceous plant

SABAL *n* variety of palm tree

SABALS > SABAL

SABATON *n* foot covering in suit of armour

SABATONS > SABATON

SABAYON *n* dessert or sweet sauce made with egg yolks, sugar, and wine beaten together over heat till thick

SABAYONS > SABAYON

SABBAT *n* midnight meeting of witches

SABBATH *n* period of rest

SABBATHS > SABBATH

SABBATIC *n* period of leave granted to university staff

SABBATICS > SABBATIC

SABBATINE *adj* of Saturday

SABBATISE same as > SABBATIZE

SABBATISM *n* sabbath observance

SABBATIZE *vb* observe as sabbath

SABBATS > SABBAT

SABBED > SAB

SABBING > SAB

SABE *n* very informal word meaning sense or savvy ▷ *vb* very informal word meaning know or savvy

SABED > SABE

SABEING > SABE

SABELLA *n* marine worm

SABELLAS > SABELLA

SABER same as > SABRE

SABERED > SABER

SABERING > SABER

SABERLIKE > SABER

SABERS > SABER

SABES > SABE

SABIN *n* unit of acoustic absorption equal to the absorption resulting from one square foot of a perfectly absorbing surface

SABINE variant of > SAVIN

SABINES > SABINE

SABINS > SABIN

SABIR *n* member of ancient

Turkic people

SABIRS > SABIR

SABKHA *n* flat coastal plain with a salt crust, common in Arabia

SABKHAH *n* sabkha

SABKHAHS > SABKHAH

SABKHAS > SABKHA

SABKHAT *n* sabkha

SABKHATS > SABKHAT

SABLE *n* dark fur from a small weasel-like Arctic animal ▷ *adj* black

SABLED > SABLE

SABLEFISH *n* North American fish

SABLES > SABLE

SABLING > SABLE

SABOT *n* wooden shoe traditionally worn by peasants in France

SABOTAGE *n* intentional damage done to machinery, systems, etc ▷ *vb* damage intentionally

SABOTAGED > SABOTAGE

SABOTAGES > SABOTAGE

SABOTEUR *n* person who commits sabotage

SABOTEURS > SABOTEUR

SABOTIER *n* wearer of wooden clogs

SABOTIERS > SABOTIER

SABOTS > SABOT

SABRA *n* native-born Israeli Jew

SABRAS > SABRA

SABRE *n* curved cavalry sword ▷ *vb* injure or kill with a sabre

SABRED > SABRE

SABRES > SABRE

SABREUR *n* person wielding sabre

SABREURS > SABREUR

SABRING > SABRE

SABS > SAB

SABULINE same as > SABULOUS

SABULOSE same as > SABULOUS

SABULOUS *adj* like sand in texture

SABURRA *n* granular deposit

SABURRAL > SABURRA

SABURRAS > SABURRA

SAC *n* pouchlike structure in

an animal or plant

SACATON *n* coarse grass of the southwestern US and Mexico, grown for hay and pasture

SACATONS > SACATON

SACBUT *n* medieval trombone

SACBUTS > SACBUT

SACCADE *n* movement of the eye when it makes a sudden change of fixation, as in reading

SACCADES > SACCADE

SACCADIC > SACCADE

SACCATE *adj* in the form of a sac

SACCHARIC as in saccharic acid white soluble solid acid

SACCHARIN *n* artificial sweetener

SACCHARUM *n* cane sugar

SACCIFORM *adj* like a sac

SACCOI > SACCOS

SACCOS *n* bishop's garment in the Orthodox Church

SACCOSES > SACCOS

SACCULAR *adj* of or resembling a sac

SACCULATE *adj* of, relating to, or possessing a saccule, saccules, or a sacculus

SACCULE *n* small sac

SACCULES > SACCULE

SACCULI > SACCULUS

SACCULUS same as > SACCULE

SACELLA > SACELLUM

SACELLUM *n* tomb within a church

SACHEM same as > SAGAMORE

SACHEMDOM > SACHEM

SACHEMIC > SACHEM

SACHEMS > SACHEM

SACHET *n* small envelope or bag containing a single portion

SACHETED *adj* contained in a sachet

SACHETS > SACHET

SACK *n* large bag made of coarse material ▷ *vb* dismiss

SACKABLE *adj* of or denoting an offence, infraction of rules, etc, that

is sufficiently serious to warrant dismissal from an employment

SACKAGE *n* act of sacking a place

SACKAGES > SACKAGE

SACKBUT *n* medieval form of trombone

SACKBUTS > SACKBUT

SACKCLOTH *n* coarse fabric used for sacks, formerly worn as a penance

SACKED > SACK

SACKER > SACK

SACKERS > SACK

SACKFUL > SACK

SACKFULS > SACKFUL

SACKING *n* rough woven material used for sacks

SACKINGS > SACKING

SACKLESS *adj* old word meaning innocent

SACKLIKE > SACK

SACKS > SACK

SACKSFUL > SACKFUL

SACLESS *adj* old word meaning unchallengeable

SACLIKE > SAC

SACQUE same as > SACK

SACQUES > SACQUE

SACRA > SACRUM

SACRAL *adj* of or associated with sacred rites ▷ *n* sacral vertebra

SACRALGIA *n* pain in sacrum

SACRALISE same as > SACRALIZE

SACRALIZE *vb* make sacred

SACRALS > SACRAL

SACRAMENT *n* ceremony of the Christian Church, esp Communion

SACRARIA > SACRARIUM

SACRARIAL > SACRARIUM

SACRARIUM *n* sanctuary of a church

SACRED *adj* holy

SACREDLY > SACRED

SACRIFICE *n* giving something up ▷ *vb* offer as a sacrifice

SACRIFIDE *vb* old form of sacrifice

SACRIFIED > SACRIFY

SACRIFIES > SACRIFY

SACRIFY *vb* old form of

sacrifice

SACRILEGE n misuse or desecration of something sacred

SACRING n act or ritual of consecration, esp of the Eucharist or of a bishop

SACRINGS > SACRING

SACRIST same as > SACRISTAN

SACRISTAN n person in charge of the contents of a church

SACRISTS > SACRIST

SACRISTY n room in a church where sacred objects are kept

SACRUM n wedge-shaped bone at the base of the spine

SACRUMS > SACRUM

SACS > SAC

SAD adj sorrowful, unhappy ▷ vb New Zealand word meaning express sadness or displeasure strongly

SADDED > SAD

SADDEN vb make (someone) sad

SADDENED > SADDEN

SADDENING > SADDEN

SADDENS > SADDEN

SADDER > SAD

SADDEST > SAD

SADDHU same as > SADHU

SADDHUS > SADDHU

SADDING > SAD

SADDISH > SAD

SADDLE n rider's seat on a horse or bicycle ▷ vb put a saddle on (a horse)

SADDLEBAG n pouch or small bag attached to the saddle of a horse, bicycle, or motorcycle

SADDLEBOW n pommel of a saddle

SADDLED > SADDLE

SADDLER n maker or seller of saddles

SADDLERS > SADDLER

SADDLERY n saddles and harness for horses collectively

SADDLES > SADDLE

SADDLING > SADDLE

SADDO vb make sad ▷ n socially inadequate or pathetic person

SADDOES > SADDO

SADDOS > SADDO

SADE same as > SADHE

SADES > SADE

SADHANA n one of a number of spiritual practices or disciplines which lead to perfection, these being contemplation, asceticism, worship of a god, and correct living

SADHANAS > SADHANA

SADHE n 18th letter in the Hebrew alphabet

SADHES > SADHE

SADHU n Hindu wandering holy man

SADHUS > SADHU

SADI variant of > SADHE

SADIRON n heavy iron pointed at both ends, for pressing clothes

SADIRONS > SADIRON

SADIS > SADI

SADISM n gaining of (sexual) pleasure from inflicting pain

SADISMS > SADISM

SADIST > SADISM

SADISTIC > SADISM

SADISTS > SADISM

SADLY > SAD

SADNESS > SAD

SADNESSES > SAD

SADO variant of > CHADO

SADOS > SADO

SADS > SAD

SADZA n southern African porridge

SADZAS > SADZA

SAE Scot word for > SO

SAECULUM n age in astronomy

SAECULUMS > SAECULUM

SAETER n upland pasture in Norway

SAETERS > SAETER

SAFARI n expedition to hunt or observe wild animals, esp in Africa ▷ vb go on safari

SAFARIED > SAFARI

SAFARIING > SAFARI

SAFARIS > SAFARI

SAFARIST n person on safari

SAFARISTS > SAFARIST

SAFE adj secure, protected ▷ n strong lockable container ▷ vb make safe

SAFED > SAFE

SAFEGUARD vb protect ▷ n protection

SAFELIGHT n light that can be used in a room in which photographic material is handled, transmitting only those colours to which a particular type of film, plate, or paper is relatively insensitive

SAFELY > SAFE

SAFENESS > SAFE

SAFER > SAFE

SAFES > SAFE

SAFEST > SAFE

SAFETIED > SAFETY

SAFETIES > SAFETY

SAFETY n state of being safe ▷ vb make safe

SAFETYING > SAFETY

SAFETYMAN n defensive player in American football

SAFETYMEN > SAFETYMAN

SAFFIAN n leather tanned with sumach and usually dyed a bright colour

SAFFIANS > SAFFIAN

SAFFLOWER n thistle-like plant with flowers used for dye and oil

SAFFRON n orange-coloured flavouring obtained from a crocus ▷ adj orange

SAFFRONED adj containing

saffron

SAFFRONS > SAFFRON

SAFFRONY adj like saffron

SAFING > SAFE

SAFRANIN same as > SAFRANINE

SAFRANINE n any of a class of azine dyes, used for textiles and biological stains

SAFRANINS > SAFRANIN

SAFROL n oily liquid obtained from sassafras

SAFROLE n colourless or yellowish oily water-insoluble liquid

SAFROLES > SAFROLE

SAFROLS > SAFROL

SAFRONAL n oily liquid derived from saffron

SAFRONALS > SAFRONAL

SAFT Scot word for > SOFT

SAFTER > SAFT

SAFTEST > SAFT

SAG vb sink in the middle ▷ n droop

SAGA n legend of Norse heroes

SAGACIOUS adj wise

SAGACITY n foresight, discernment, or keen perception

SAGAMAN n person reciting Norse sagas

SAGAMEN > SAGAMAN

SAGAMORE n (among some Native Americans) a chief or eminent man

SAGAMORES > SAGAMORE

SAGANASH n Algonquian term for an Englishman

SAGAPENUM n resin formerly used as drug

SAGAS > SAGA

SAGATHIES > SAGATHY

SAGATHY n type of light fabric

SAGBUT n medieval trombone

SAGBUTS > SAGBUT

SAGE n very wise man ▷ adj wise

SAGEBRUSH n aromatic plant of West N America

SAGELY > SAGE

SAGENE n fishing net

SAGENES > SAGENE

SAGENESS > SAGE

SAGENITE n mineral found in crystal form

SAGENITES > SAGENITE

SAGENITIC > SAGENITE

SAGER > SAGE

SAGES > SAGE

SAGEST > SAGE

SAGGAR n clay box in which fragile ceramic wares are placed for protection during firing ▷ vb put in a saggar

SAGGARD n saggar

SAGGARDS > SAGGARD

SAGGARED > SAGGAR

SAGGARING > SAGGAR

SAGGARS > SAGGAR

SAGGED > SAG

SAGGER same as > SAGGAR

SAGGERED > SAGGER

SAGGERING > SAGGER

SAGGERS > SAGGER

SAGGIER > SAGGY

SAGGIEST > SAGGY

SAGGING > SAG

SAGGINGS > SAG

SAGGY adj tending to sag

SAGIER > SAGY

SAGIEST > SAGY

SAGINATE vb fatten livestock

SAGINATED > SAGINATE

SAGINATES > SAGINATE

SAGITTA n sine of an arc

SAGITTAL adj resembling an arrow

SAGITTARY n centaur

SAGITTAS > SAGITTA

SAGITTATE adj (esp of leaves) shaped like the head of an arrow

SAGO n starchy cereal from the powdered pith of the sago palm tree

SAGOIN n South American monkey

SAGOINS > SAGOIN

SAGOS > SAGO

SAGOUIN n South American monkey

SAGOUINS > SAGOUIN

SAGRADA as in cascara sagrada dried bark of the cascara buckthorn, used as a stimulant and laxative

SAGS > SAG

SAGUARO n giant cactus of desert regions of Arizona, S California, and Mexico

SAGUAROS > SAGUARO

SAGUIN n South American monkey

SAGUINS > SAGUIN

SAGUM n Roman soldier's cloak

SAGY adj like or containing sage

SAHEB same as > SAHIB

SAHEBS > SAHEB

SAHIB n Indian term of address placed after a man's name as a mark of respect

SAHIBA n respectful Indian term of address for woman

SAHIBAH n sahiba

SAHIBAHS > SAHIBAH

SAHIBAS > SAHIBA

SAHIBS > SAHIB

SAHIWAL n breed of cattle in India

SAHIWALS > SAHIWAL

SAHUARO same as > SAGUARO

SAHUAROS > SAHUARO

SAI n South American monkey

SAIBLING n freshwater fish

SAIBLINGS > SAIBLING

SAIC n boat of eastern Mediterranean

SAICE same as > SYCE

SAICES > SAICE

SAICK n boat of eastern Mediterranean

SAICKS > SAICK

SAICS > SAIC

Section 1: Words between 2 and 9 letters in length

SAID *same as* > SAYYID
SAIDEST > SAY
SAIDS > SAID
SAIDST > SAY
SAIGA *n* either of two antelopes of the plains of central Asia
SAIGAS > SAIGA
SAIKEI *n* Japanese ornamental miniature landscape
SAIKEIS > SAIKEI
SAIKLESS *old Scots word for* > INNOCENT
SAIL *n* sheet of fabric stretched to catch the wind for propelling a sailing boat ▷ *vb* travel by water
SAILABLE > SAIL
SAILBOARD *n* board with a mast and single sail, used for windsurfing
SAILBOAT *n* boat propelled chiefly by sail
SAILBOATS > SAILBOAT
SAILCLOTH *n* fabric for making sails
SAILED > SAIL
SAILER *n* vessel, esp one equipped with sails, with specified sailing characteristics
SAILERS > SAILER
SAILFISH *n* large tropical game fish, with a long sail-like fin on its back
SAILING *n* practice, art, or technique of sailing a vessel
SAILINGS > SAILING
SAILLESS > SAIL
SAILMAKER *n* person who makes sails
SAILOR *n* member of a ship's crew
SAILORING *n* activity of working as sailor
SAILORLY > SAILOR
SAILORS > SAILOR
SAILPLANE *n* high-performance glider
SAILROOM *n* space on ship for storing sails
SAILROOMS > SAILROOM
SAILS > SAIL
SAIM *Scots word for* > LARD
SAIMIN *n* Hawaiian dish of noodles
SAIMINS > SAIMIN
SAIMIRI *n* South American monkey
SAIMIRIS > SAIMIRI
SAIMS > SAIM
SAIN *vb* make the sign of the cross over so as to bless or protect from evil or sin
SAINE *vb* old form of say
SAINED > SAIN
SAINFOIN *n* Eurasian plant with pink flowers, widely grown as feed for grazing farm animals
SAINFOINS > SAINFOIN
SAINING > SAIN
SAINS > SAIN
SAINT *n* person venerated after death as specially holy

▷ *vb* canonize
SAINTDOM > SAINT
SAINTDOMS > SAINT
SAINTED *adj* formally recognized by a Christian Church as a saint
SAINTESS *n* female saint
SAINTFOIN *n* sainfoin
SAINTHOOD *n* state or character of being a saint
SAINTING > SAINT
SAINTISH > SAINT
SAINTISM *n* quality of being saint
SAINTISMS > SAINTISM
SAINTLESS > SAINT
SAINTLIER > SAINTLY
SAINTLIKE > SAINT
SAINTLILY > SAINTLY
SAINTLING *n* little saint
SAINTLY *adj* behaving in a very good, patient, or holy way
SAINTS > SAINT
SAINTSHIP > SAINT
SAIQUE *n* boat in eastern Mediterranean
SAIQUES > SAIQUE
SAIR *Scot word for* > SORE
SAIRED > SAIR
SAIRER > SAIR
SAIREST > SAIR
SAIRING > SAIR
SAIRS > SAIR
SAIS > SAI
SAIST > SAY
SAITH *form of the present tense (indicative mood) of* > SAY
SAITHE *n* dark-coloured food fish found in northern seas
SAITHES > SAITHE
SAITHS > SAITH
SAIVID *n* Muslim descended from Mohammed's grandson
SAIYIDS > SAIVID
SAJOU *n* South American monkey
SAJOUS > SAJOU
SAKAI *n* Malaysian aborigine
SAKAIS > SAKAI
SAKE *n* benefit
SAKER *n* large falcon of E Europe and central Asia
SAKERET *n* male saker
SAKERETS > SAKERET
SAKERS > SAKER
SAKES > SAKE
SAKI *same as* > SAKE
SAKIA *n* water wheel in Middle East
SAKIAS > SAKIA
SAKIEH *n* water wheel in Middle East
SAKIEHS > SAKIEH
SAKIS > SAKI
SAKIYEH *n* water wheel in Middle East
SAKIYEHS > SAKIYEH
SAKKOI > SAKKOS
SAKKOS *n* bishop's garment in Orthodox Church
SAKKOSES > SAKKOS
SAKSAUL *n* Asian tree

SAKSAULS > SAKSAUL
SAL *pharmacological term for* > SALT
SALAAM *n* low bow of greeting among Muslims ▷ *vb* make a salaam
SALAAMED > SALAAM
SALAAMING > SALAAM
SALAAMS > SALAAM
SALABLE *same as* > SALEABLE
SALABLY > SALEABLY
SALACIOUS *adj* excessively concerned with sex
SALACITY *n* excessive interest in sex
SALAD *n* dish of raw vegetables, eaten as a meal or part of a meal
SALADANG *n* variety of ox
SALADANGS > SALADANG
SALADE *same as* > SALLET
SALADES > SALADE
SALADING *n* ingredients for salad
SALADINGS > SALADING
SALADS > SALAD
SALAL *n* North American shrub
SALALS > SALAL
SALAMI *n* highly spiced sausage
SALAMIS > SALAMI
SALAMON *n* word used in old oaths
SALAMONS > SALAMON
SALANGANE *n* Asian swift
SALARIAT *n* salary-earning class
SALARIATS > SALARIAT
SALARIED *adj* earning or providing a salary
SALARIES > SALARY
SALARY *n* fixed regular payment, usu monthly, to an employee ▷ *vb* pay a salary to
SALARYING > SALARY
SALARYMAN *n* (in Japan) an office worker
SALARYMEN > SALARYMAN
SALBAND *n* coating of mineral
SALBANDS > SALBAND
SALCHOW *n* type of figure-skating jump
SALCHOWS > SALCHOW
SALE *n* exchange of goods for money
SALEABLE *adj* fit or likely to be sold
SALEABLY > SALEABLE
SALEP *n* dried ground starchy tubers of various orchids, used for food and formerly as drugs
SALEPS > SALEP
SALERATUS *n* sodium bicarbonate when used in baking powder
SALERING *n* enclosed area for livestock at market
SALERINGS > SALERING
SALEROOM *n* place where goods are sold by auction
SALEROOMS > SALEROOM
SALES > SALE
SALESGIRL *n* person who

sells goods
SALESLADY *n* person who sells goods
SALESMAN *n* person who sells goods
SALESMEN > SALESMAN
SALESROOM *n* room in which merchandise on sale is displayed
SALET *same as* > SALLET
SALETS > SALET
SALEWD > SALUE
SALEYARD *n* area with pens for holding animals before auction
SALEYARDS > SALEYARD
SALFERN *n* plant of borage family
SALFERNS > SALFERN
SALIAUNCE *n* old word meaning onslaught
SALIC *adj* (of rocks and minerals) having a high content of silica and alumina
SALICES > SALIX
SALICET *n* soft-toned organ stop
SALICETA > SALICETUM
SALICETS > SALICET
SALICETUM *n* plantation of willows
SALICIN *n* colourless or white crystalline water-soluble glucoside
SALICINE *same as* > SALICIN
SALICINES > SALICINE
SALICINS > SALICIN
SALICYLIC *as in salicylic acid* white crystalline substance with a sweet taste and a bitter aftertaste
SALIENCE > SALIENT
SALIENCES > SALIENT
SALIENCY *n* quality of being prominent
SALIENT *adj* prominent, noticeable ▷ *n* projecting part of a front line
SALIENTLY > SALIENT
SALIENTS > SALIENT
SALIFIED > SALIFY
SALIFIES > SALIFY
SALIFY *vb* treat, mix with, or cause to combine with a salt
SALIFYING > SALIFY
SALIGOT *n* water chestnut
SALIGOTS > SALIGOT
SALIMETER *n* hydrometer for measuring salt in a solution
SALIMETRY > SALIMETER
SALINA *n* salt marsh, lake, or spring
SALINAS > SALINA
SALINE *adj* containing salt ▷ *n* solution of sodium chloride and water
SALINES > SALINE
SALINISE *same as* > SALINIZE
SALINISED > SALINISE
SALINISES > SALINISE
SALINITY > SALINE
SALINIZE *vb* treat with salt

SALINIZED > SALINIZE
SALINIZES > SALINIZE
SALIVA n liquid that forms in the mouth, spittle
SALIVAL > SALIVA
SALIVARY > SALIVA
SALIVAS > SALIVA
SALIVATE vb produce saliva
SALIVATED > SALIVATE
SALIVATES > SALIVATE
SALIVATOR > SALIVATE
SALIX n plant or tree of willow family
SALL archaic form of > SHALL
SALLAD old spelling of > SALAD
SALLADS > SALLAD
SALLAL n North American shrub
SALLALS > SALLAL
SALLE n hall
SALLEE n SE Australian eucalyptus with a pale grey bark
SALLEES > SALLEE
SALLES > SALLE
SALLET n light round helmet extending over the back of the neck
SALLETS > SALLET
SALLIED > SALLY
SALLIER > SALLY
SALLIERS > SALLY
SALLIES > SALLY
SALLOW adj of an unhealthy pale or yellowish colour ▷ vb make sallow ▷ n any of several small willow trees
SALLOWED > SALLOW
SALLOWER > SALLOW
SALLOWEST > SALLOW
SALLOWING > SALLOW
SALLOWISH > SALLOW
SALLOWLY > SALLOW
SALLOWS > SALLOW
SALLOWY > SALLOW
SALLY n violent excursion ▷ vb set or rush out
SALLYING > SALLY
SALLYPORT n opening in a fortified place from which troops may make a sally
SALMI n ragout of game stewed in a rich brown sauce
SALMIS same as > SALMI
SALMON n large fish with orange-pink flesh valued as food ▷ adj orange-pink
SALMONET n young salmon
SALMONETS > SALMONET
SALMONID n any fish of the family Salmonidiae
SALMONIDS > SALMONID
SALMONOID adj belonging to the order of soft-finned teleost fishes that includes the salmon, whitefish, grayling, and char ▷ n any of these fish
SALMONS > SALMON
SALOL n white sparingly soluble crystalline compound with a slight aromatic odour, used as a preservative and to absorb

light in sun-tan lotions, plastics, etc
SALOLS > SALOL
SALOMETER n instrument for measuring salt in solution
SALON n commercial premises of a hairdresser, beautician, etc
SALONS > SALON
SALOON n closed car with four or more seats
SALOONS > SALOON
SALOOP n infusion of aromatic herbs or other plant parts formerly used as a tonic or cure
SALOOPS > SALOOP
SALOP variant of > SALOOP
SALOPIAN > SALOOP
SALOPS > SALOP
SALP n minute animal floating in sea
SALPA n any of various minute floating animals of warm oceans
SALPAE > SALPA
SALPAS > SALPA
SALPIAN n minute animal floating in sea
SALPIANS > SALPIAN
SALPICON n mixture of chopped fish, meat, or vegetables in a sauce
SALPICONS > SALPICON
SALPID n minute animal floating in sea
SALPIDS > SALPID
SALPIFORM > SALPA
SALPINGES > SALPINX
SALPINX n Fallopian tube or Eustachian tube
SALPINXES > SALPINX
SALPS > SALP
SALS > SAL
SALSA n lively Puerto Rican dance ▷ vb dance the salsa
SALSAED > SALSA
SALSAING > SALSA
SALSAS > SALSA
SALSE n volcano expelling mud
SALSES > SALSE
SALSIFIES > SALSIFY
SALSIFY n Mediterranean plant with a long white edible root
SALSILLA n tropical American vine
SALSILLAS > SALSILLA
SALT n white crystalline substance used to season food ▷ vb season or preserve with salt
SALTANDO n staccato piece of violin playing
SALTANT adj (of an organism) differing from others of its species because of a saltation ▷ n saltant organism
SALTANTS > SALTANT
SALTATE vb go through saltation
SALTATED > SALTATE
SALTATES > SALTATE
SALTATING > SALTATE

SALTATION n abrupt variation in the appearance of an organism, usu caused by genetic mutation
SALTATO n saltando
SALTATORY adj specialized for jumping
SALTBOX n box for salt with a sloping lid
SALTBOXES > SALTBOX
SALTBUSH n shrub that grows in alkaline desert regions
SALTCAT n salty medicine for pigeons
SALTCATS > SALTCAT
SALTCHUCK n any body of salt water
SALTED adj seasoned, preserved, or treated with salt
SALTER n person who deals in or manufactures salt
SALTERN n place where salt is obtained from pools of evaporated sea water
SALTERNS > SALTERN
SALTERS > SALTER
SALTEST > SALT
SALTFISH n salted cod
SALTIE n saltwater crocodile
SALTIER > SALTIRE
SALTIERS > SALTIER
SALTIES > SALTIE
SALTIEST > SALTY
SALTILY > SALTY
SALTINE n salty biscuit
SALTINES > SALTINE
SALTINESS > SALTY
SALTING n area of low ground regularly inundated with salt water
SALTINGS > SALTING
SALTIRE n diagonal cross on a shield
SALTIRES > SALTIRE
SALTISH > SALT
SALTISHLY > SALT
SALTLESS > SALT
SALTLIKE > SALT
SALTLY > SALT
SALTNESS > SALT
SALTO n daring jump ▷ vb perform a daring jump
SALTOED > SALTO
SALTOING > SALTO
SALTOS > SALTO
SALTPAN n shallow basin containing salt, gypsum, etc, that was deposited from an evaporated salt lake
SALTPANS > SALTPAN
SALTPETER same as > SALTPETRE
SALTPETRE n compound used in gunpowder and as a preservative
SALTS > SALT
SALTUS n break in the continuity of a sequence, esp the omission of a necessary step in a logical argument
SALTUSES > SALTUS
SALTWATER adj living in

the sea
SALTWORK n place where salt is refined
SALTWORKS n place, building, or factory where salt is produced
SALTWORT n any of several chenopodiaceous plants with prickly leaves, striped stems, and small green flowers
SALTWORTS > SALTWORT
SALTY adj of, tasting of, or containing salt
SALUBRITY n quality of being favourable to health or wholesome
SALUE vb old word meaning salute
SALUED > SALUE
SALUES > SALUE
SALUING > SALUE
SALUKI n type of tall hound with a smooth coat
SALUKIS > SALUKI
SALURETIC n drug that increases secretion of salt in urine
SALUTARY adj producing a beneficial result
SALUTE n motion of the arm as a formal military sign of respect ▷ vb greet with a salute
SALUTED > SALUTE
SALUTER > SALUTE
SALUTERS > SALUTE
SALUTES > SALUTE
SALUTING > SALUTE
SALVABLE adj capable of or suitable for being saved or salvaged
SALVABLY > SALVABLE
SALVAGE n saving of a ship or other property from destruction ▷ vb save from destruction or waste
SALVAGED > SALVAGE
SALVAGEE n rope on sailing ship
SALVAGEES > SALVAGEE
SALVAGER > SALVAGE
SALVAGERS > SALVAGE
SALVAGES > SALVAGE
SALVAGING > SALVAGE
SALVARSAN n old medicine containing arsenic
SALVATION n fact or state of being saved from harm or the consequences of sin
SALVATORY n place for storing something safely
SALVE n healing or soothing ointment ▷ vb soothe or appease
SALVED > SALVE
SALVER same as > SALVOR
SALVERS > SALVER
SALVES > SALVE
SALVETE n Latin greeting
SALVETES > SALVETE
SALVIA n plant with blue or red flowers
SALVIAS > SALVIA
SALVIFIC adj acting to salve
SALVING > SALVE

SALVINGS > SALVE

SALVO n simultaneous discharge of guns etc ▷ vb attack with a salvo

SALVOED > SALVO

SALVOES > SALVO

SALVOING > SALVO

SALVOR n person instrumental in salvaging a vessel or its cargo

SALVORS > SALVOR

SALVOS > SALVO

SALWAR as in salwar kameez long tunic worn over a pair of baggy trousers, usually worn by women, esp in Pakistan

SAM vb collect

SAMA n Japanese title of respect

SAMAAN n South American tree

SAMAANS > SAMAAN

SAMADHI n state of deep meditative contemplation which leads to higher consciousness

SAMADHIS > SAMADHI

SAMAN n South American tree

SAMANS > SAMAN

SAMARA n dry indehiscent one-seeded fruit with a winglike extension to aid dispersal

SAMARAS > SAMARA

SAMARITAN n kindly person who helps another in distress

SAMARIUM n silvery metallic element

SAMARIUMS > SAMARIUM

SAMAS > SAMA

SAMBA n lively Brazilian dance ▷ vb perform such a dance

SAMBAED > SAMBA

SAMBAING > SAMBA

SAMBAL n Malaysian dish

SAMBALS > SAMBAL

SAMBAR n S Asian deer with three-tined antlers

SAMBARS > SAMBAR

SAMBAS > SAMBA

SAMBHAR n Indian dish

SAMBHARS > SAMBHAR

SAMBHUR n Asian deer

SAMBHURS > SAMBHUR

SAMBO n offensive word for a Black person

SAMBOS > SAMBO

SAMBUCA n Italian liqueur

SAMBUCAS > SAMBUCA

SAMBUKE n ancient Greek stringed instrument

SAMBUKES > SAMBUKE

SAMBUR same as > SAMBAR

SAMBURS > SAMBUR

SAME adj identical, not different, unchanged ▷ n something identical

SAMECH n letter in Hebrew alphabet

SAMECHS > SAMECH

SAMEK variant of > SAMEKH

SAMEKH n 15th letter in the Hebrew alphabet

transliterated as s

SAMEKHS > SAMEKH

SAMEKS > SAMEK

SAMEL adj of brick, not sufficiently fired

SAMELY adj the same

SAMEN old Scots form of > SAME

SAMENESS n state or quality of being the same

SAMES > SAME

SAMEY adj monotonous

SAMFOO n style of casual dress worn by Chinese women, consisting of a waisted blouse and trousers

SAMFOOS > SAMFOO

SAMFU n Chinese female outfit

SAMFUS > SAMFU

SAMIEL same as > SIMOOM

SAMIELS > SAMIEL

SAMIER > SAMEY

SAMIEST > SAMEY

SAMISEN n Japanese plucked stringed instrument with a long neck, an unfretted fingerboard, and a rectangular soundbox

SAMISENS > SAMISEN

SAMITE n heavy fabric of silk, often woven with gold or silver threads, used in the Middle Ages for clothing

SAMITES > SAMITE

SAMITHI same as > SAMITI

SAMITHIS > SAMITHI

SAMITI n (in India) an association, esp one formed to organize political activity

SAMITIS > SAMITI

SAMIZDAT n (in the former Soviet Union) a system of secret printing and distribution of banned literature

SAMIZDATS > SAMIZDAT

SAMLET n young salmon

SAMLETS > SAMLET

SAMLOR n motor vehicle in Thailand

SAMLORS > SAMLOR

SAMMED > SAM

SAMMIES > SAMMY

SAMMING > SAM

SAMMY n (in South Africa) an Indian fruit and vegetable vendor who goes from house to house

SAMNITIS n poisonous plant mentioned by Spenser

SAMOSA n (in Indian cookery) a small fried triangular spiced meat or vegetable pasty

SAMOSAS > SAMOSA

SAMOVAR n Russian tea urn

SAMOVARS > SAMOVAR

SAMOYED n Siberian breed of dog of the spitz type, having a dense white or cream coat with a distinct

ruff, and a tightly curled tail

SAMOYEDS > SAMOYED

SAMP n crushed maize used for porridge

SAMPAN n small boat with oars used in China

SAMPANS > SAMPAN

SAMPHIRE n plant found on rocks by the seashore

SAMPHIRES > SAMPHIRE

SAMPI n old Greek number character

SAMPIRE n samphire

SAMPIRES > SAMPIRE

SAMPIS > SAMPI

SAMPLE n part taken as representative of a whole ▷ vb take and test a sample of

SAMPLED > SAMPLE

SAMPLER n piece of embroidery showing the embroiderer's skill

SAMPLERS > SAMPLER

SAMPLERY n making of samplers

SAMPLES > SAMPLE

SAMPLING n process of selecting a random sample

SAMPLINGS > SAMPLING

SAMPS > SAMP

SAMS > SAM

SAMSARA n endless cycle of birth, death, and rebirth

SAMSARAS > SAMSARA

SAMSHOO n Chinese alcoholic drink

SAMSHOOS > SAMSHOO

SAMSHU n alcoholic drink from China that is made from fermented rice and resembles sake

SAMSHUS > SAMSHU

SAMURAI n member of an ancient Japanese warrior caste

SAMURAIS > SAMURAI

SAN n sanatorium

SANATIVE less common word for > CURATIVE

SANATORIA pl n institutions for the care of chronically ill people

SANATORY adj healing

SANBENITO n yellow garment bearing a red cross, worn by penitent heretics in the Inquisition

SANCAI n glaze in Chinese pottery

SANCAIS > SANCAI

SANCHO n African stringed instrument

SANCHOS > SANCHO

SANCTA > SANCTUM

SANCTIFY vb make holy

SANCTION n permission, authorization ▷ vb allow, authorize

SANCTIONS > SANCTION

SANCTITY n sacredness, inviolability

SANCTUARY n holy place

SANCTUM n sacred place

SANCTUMS > SANCTUM

SAND n substance consisting of small grains

of rock, esp on a beach or in a desert ▷ vb smooth with sandpaper

SANDABLE > SAND

SANDAL n light shoe consisting of a sole attached by straps ▷ vb put sandals on

SANDALED > SANDAL

SANDALING > SANDAL

SANDALLED > SANDAL

SANDALS > SANDAL

SANDARAC n either of two coniferous trees having hard fragrant dark wood

SANDARACH same as > SANDARAC

SANDARACS > SANDARAC

SANDBAG n bag filled with sand, used as protection against gunfire or flood water ▷ vb protect with sandbags

SANDBAGS > SANDBAG

SANDBANK n bank of sand below the surface of a river or sea

SANDBANKS > SANDBANK

SANDBAR n ridge of sand in a river or sea, often exposed at low tide

SANDBARS > SANDBAR

SANDBLAST n (clean with) a jet of sand blown from a nozzle under pressure ▷ vb clean or decorate (a surface) with a sandblast

SANDBOX n container on a railway locomotive from which sand is released onto the rails to assist the traction

SANDBOXES > SANDBOX

SANDBOY as in happy as a sandboy very happy or high-spirited

SANDBOYS > SANDBOY

SANDBUR n variety of wild grass

SANDBURR n variety of wild grass

SANDBURRS > SANDBURR

SANDBURS > SANDBUR

SANDCRACK n crack in horse's hoof

SANDDAB n type of small Pacific flatfish

SANDDABS > SANDDAB

SANDED > SAND

SANDEK n man who holds a baby being circumcised

SANDEKS > SANDEK

SANDER n power tool for smoothing surfaces

SANDERS > SANDER

SANDERSES > SANDER

SANDFISH n burrowing Pacific fish

SANDFLIES > SANDFLY

SANDFLY n any of various small mothlike dipterous flies: the bloodsucking females transmit diseases including leishmaniasis

SANDGLASS less common word for > HOURGLASS

SANDHEAP n heap of sand

SANDHEAPS > SANDHEAP
SANDHI n modification of the form or sound of a word under the influence of an adjacent word
SANDHILL n hill of sand
SANDHILLS > SANDHILL
SANDHIS > SANDHI
SANDHOG n person who works in underground or underwater construction projects
SANDHOGS > SANDHOG
SANDIER > SANDY
SANDIEST > SANDY
SANDINESS > SANDY
SANDING > SAND
SANDINGS > SAND
SANDIVER n scum forming on molten glass
SANDIVERS > SANDIVER
SANDLESS > SAND
SANDLIKE > SAND
SANDLING n sand eel
SANDLINGS > SANDLING
SANDLOT n area of vacant ground used by children for playing baseball and other games
SANDLOTS > SANDLOT
SANDMAN n (in folklore) a magical person supposed to put children to sleep by sprinkling sand in their eyes
SANDMEN > SANDMAN
SANDPAPER n paper coated with sand for smoothing a surface ▷ vb smooth with sandpaper
SANDPEEP n small sandpiper
SANDPEEPS > SANDPEEP
SANDPILE n pile of sand
SANDPILES > SANDPILE
SANDPIPER n shore bird with a long bill and slender legs
SANDPIT n shallow pit or container holding sand for children to play in
SANDPITS > SANDPIT
SANDPUMP n pump for wet sand
SANDPUMPS > SANDPUMP
SANDS > SAND
SANDSHOE n light canvas shoe with a rubber sole
SANDSHOES > SANDSHOE
SANDSOAP n gritty general-purpose soap
SANDSOAPS > SANDSOAP
SANDSPOUT n sand sucked into air by whirlwind
SANDSPUR n American wild grass
SANDSPURS > SANDSPUR
SANDSTONE n rock composed of sand
SANDSTORM n desert wind that whips up clouds of sand
SANDWICH n two slices of bread with a layer of food between ▷ vb insert between two other things
SANDWORM n any of various

polychaete worms that live in burrows on sandy shores, esp the lugworm
SANDWORMS > SANDWORM
SANDWORT n any of numerous caryophyllaceous plants which grow in dense tufts on sandy soil and have white or pink solitary flowers
SANDWORTS > SANDWORT
SANDY adj covered with sand
SANE adj of sound mind ▷ vb heal
SANED > SANE
SANELY > SANE
SANENESS > SANE
SANER > SANE
SANES > SANE
SANEST > SANE
SANG Scots word for > SONG
SANGA n Ethiopian ox
SANGAR n breastwork of stone or sods
SANGAREE n spiced drink similar to sangria
SANGAREES > SANGAREE
SANGARS > SANGAR
SANGAS > SANGA
SANGER n sandwich
SANGERS > SANGER
SANGFROID n composure or self-possession
SANGH n Indian union or association
SANGHAT n fellowship or assembly, esp a local Sikh community or congregation
SANGHATS > SANGHAT
SANGHS > SANGH
SANGLIER n wild boar
SANGLIERS > SANGLIER
SANGO same as > SANGER
SANGOMA n witch doctor or herbalist
SANGOMAS > SANGOMA
SANGOS > SANGO
SANGRIA n Spanish drink of red wine and fruit
SANGRIAS > SANGRIA
SANGS > SANG
SANGUIFY vb turn into blood
SANGUINE adj cheerful, optimistic ▷ n red pencil containing ferric oxide, used in drawing
SANGUINED > SANGUINE
SANGUINES > SANGUINE
SANICLE n type of plant with clusters of small white flowers and oval fruits with hooked bristles
SANICLES > SANICLE
SANIDINE n alkali feldspar that is found in lavas
SANIDINES > SANIDINE
SANIES n thin greenish foul-smelling discharge from a wound, etc, containing pus and blood
SANIFIED > SANIFY
SANIFIES > SANIFY
SANIFY vb make healthy

SANIFYING > SANIFY
SANING > SANE
SANIOUS > SANIES
SANITARIA variant of > SANATORIA
SANITARY adj promoting health by getting rid of dirt and germs
SANITATE vb make sanitary
SANITATED > SANITATE
SANITATES > SANITATE
SANITIES > SANITY
SANITISE same as > SANITIZE
SANITISED > SANITISE
SANITISER > SANITISE
SANITISES > SANITISE
SANITIZE vb omit unpleasant details to make (news) more acceptable
SANITIZED > SANITIZE
SANITIZER > SANITIZE
SANITIZES > SANITIZE
SANITORIA variant of > SANATORIA
SANITY n state of having a normal healthy mind
SANJAK n (in the Turkish Empire) a subdivision of a vilayet
SANJAKS > SANJAK
SANK > SINK
SANKO n African stringed instrument
SANKOS > SANKO
SANNIE Scots word for > SANDSHOE
SANNIES > SANNIE
SANNOP n Native American married man
SANNOPS > SANNOP
SANNUP n Native American married man
SANNUPS > SANNUP
SANNYASI n Brahman who having attained the fourth and last stage of life as a beggar will not be reborn, but will instead be absorbed into the Universal Soul
SANNYASIN same as > SANNYASI
SANNYASIS > SANNYASI
SANPAN n sampan
SANPANS > SANPAN
SANPRO n sanitary-protection products, collectively
SANPROS > SANPRO
SANS archaic word for > WITHOUT
SANSA n African musical instrument
SANSAR n name of a wind that blows in Iran
SANSARS > SANSAR
SANSAS > SANSA
SANSEI n American whose parents were Japanese immigrants
SANSEIS > SANSEI
SANSERIF n style of printer's typeface
SANSERIFS > SANSERIF
SANT n devout person in India

SANTAL n sandalwood
SANTALIC adj of sandalwood
SANTALIN n substance giving sandalwood its colour
SANTALINS > SANTALIN
SANTALOL n liquid from sandalwood used in perfume
SANTALOLS > SANTALOL
SANTALS > SANTAL
SANTERA n priestess of santeria
SANTERAS > SANTERA
SANTERIA n Caribbean religious cult
SANTERIAS > SANTERIA
SANTERO n priest of santeria
SANTEROS > SANTERO
SANTIMI > SANTIMS
SANTIMS n money unit in Latvia
SANTIMU same as > SANTIMS
SANTIR n Middle Eastern stringed instrument
SANTIRS > SANTIR
SANTO n saint or representation of one
SANTOL n fruit from Southeast Asia
SANTOLINA n any plant of an evergreen Mediterranean genus grown for its silvery-grey felted foliage
SANTOLS > SANTOL
SANTON n French figurine
SANTONICA n oriental wormwood plant
SANTONIN n white crystalline soluble substance extracted from the dried flower heads of santonica
SANTONINS > SANTONIN
SANTONS > SANTON
SANTOOR same as > SANTIR
SANTOORS > SANTOOR
SANTOS > SANTO
SANTOUR n Middle Eastern stringed instrument
SANTOURS > SANTOUR
SANTS > SANT
SANTUR n Middle Eastern stringed instrument
SANTURS > SANTUR
SANYASI same as > SANNYASI
SANYASIS > SANNYASI
SAOUARI n tropical American tree
SAOUARIS > SAOUARI
SAP n moisture that circulates in plants ▷ vb undermine
SAPAJOU n capuchin monkey
SAPAJOUS > SAPAJOU
SAPAN n tropical tree
SAPANS > SAPAN
SAPANWOOD n small S Asian tree
SAPEGO n skin disease
SAPEGOES > SAPEGO
SAPELE n type of W African tree
SAPELES > SAPELE

SAPFUL *adj* full of sap
SAPHEAD *n* simpleton, idiot, or fool
SAPHEADED > SAPHEAD
SAPHEADS > SAPHEAD
SAPHENA *n* either of two large superficial veins of the legs
SAPHENAE > SAPHENA
SAPHENAS > SAPHENA
SAPHENOUS > SAPHENA
SAPID *adj* having a pleasant taste
SAPIDITY > SAPID
SAPIDLESS *adj* lacking flavour
SAPIDNESS > SAPID
SAPIENCE > SAPIENT
SAPIENCES > SAPIENT
SAPIENCY > SAPIENT
SAPIENS *adj* relating to or like modern human beings
SAPIENT *adj* wise, shrewd ▷ *n* wise person
SAPIENTLY > SAPIENT
SAPIENTS > SAPIENT
SAPLESS > SAP
SAPLING *n* young tree
SAPLINGS > SAPLING
SAPODILLA *n* large tropical American evergreen tree
SAPOGENIN *n* substance derived from saponin
SAPONARIA *See* > SOAPWORT
SAPONATED *adj* treated or combined with soap
SAPONIFY *vb* convert (a fat) into a soap by treatment with alkali
SAPONIN *n* any of a group of plant glycosides
SAPONINE *n* saponin
SAPONINES > SAPONINE
SAPONINS > SAPONIN
SAPONITE *n* type of clay mineral
SAPONITES > SAPONITE
SAPOR *n* quality in a substance that is perceived by the sense of taste
SAPORIFIC > SAPOR
SAPOROUS > SAPOR
SAPORS > SAPOR
SAPOTA *same as* > SAPODILLA
SAPOTAS > SAPOTA
SAPOTE *n* Central American tree
SAPOTES > SAPOTE
SAPOUR *variant of* > SAPOR
SAPOURS > SAPOUR
SAPPAN *n* tropical tree
SAPPANS > SAPPAN
SAPPED > SAP
SAPPER *n* soldier in an engineering unit
SAPPERS > SAPPER
SAPPHIC *adj* lesbian ▷ *n* verse written in a particular form
SAPPHICS > SAPPHIC
SAPPHIRE *n* blue precious stone ▷ *adj* deep blue
SAPPHIRED *adj* blue-coloured
SAPPHIRES > SAPPHIRE
SAPPHISM *n* lesbianism
SAPPHISMS > SAPPHISM

SAPPHIST *n* lesbian
SAPPHISTS > SAPPHIST
SAPPIER > SAPPY
SAPPIEST > SAPPY
SAPPILY > SAPPY
SAPPINESS > SAPPY
SAPPING > SAP
SAPPLE *vb* Scots word meaning wash in water
SAPPLED > SAPPLE
SAPPLES > SAPPLE
SAPPLING > SAPPLE
SAPPY *adj* (of plants) full of sap
SAPRAEMIA *n* blood poisoning caused by toxins of putrefactive bacteria
SAPRAEMIC > SAPRAEMIA
SAPREMIA *American spelling of* > SAPRAEMIA
SAPREMIAS > SAPREMIA
SAPREMIC > SAPREMIA
SAPROBE *n* organism that lives on decaying organisms
SAPROBES > SAPROBE
SAPROBIAL > SAPROBE
SAPROBIC > SAPROBE
SAPROLITE *n* deposit of earth, etc, formed by decomposition of rocks that has remained in its original site
SAPROPEL *n* unconsolidated sludge consisting of the decomposed remains of aquatic organisms at the bottoms of lakes and oceans
SAPROPELS > SAPROPEL
SAPROZOIC *adj* (of animals or plants) feeding on dead organic matter
SAPS > SAP
SAPSAGO *n* hard greenish Swiss cheese made with sour skimmed milk and coloured and flavoured with clover
SAPSAGOS > SAPSAGO
SAPSUCKER *n* either of two North American woodpeckers
SAPUCAIA *n* Brazilian tree
SAPUCAIAS > SAPUCAIA
SAPWOOD *n* soft wood, just beneath the bark in tree trunks, that consists of living tissue
SAPWOODS > SAPWOOD
SAR *n* marine fish ▷ *vb* Scots word meaning savour
SARABAND *same as* > SARABANDE
SARABANDE *n* slow stately Spanish dance
SARABANDS > SARABAND
SARAFAN *n* Russian woman's cloak
SARAFANS > SARAFAN
SARAN *n* any one of a class of thermoplastic resins
SARANGI *n* stringed instrument of India played with a bow
SARANGIS > SARANGI

SARANS > SARAN
SARAPE *n* serape
SARAPES > SARAPE
SARBACANE *n* type of blowpipe
SARCASM *n* (use of) bitter or wounding ironic language
SARCASMS > SARCASM
SARCASTIC *adj* full of or showing sarcasm
SARCENET *n* fine soft silk fabric formerly from Italy and used for clothing, ribbons, etc
SARCENETS > SARCENET
SARCINA *n* type of bacterium
SARCINAE > SARCINA
SARCINAS > SARCINA
SARCOCARP *n* fleshy mesocarp of such fruits as the peach or plum
SARCODE *n* material making up living cell
SARCODES > SARCODE
SARCODIC > SARCODE
SARCOID *adj* of, relating to, or resembling flesh ▷ *n* tumour resembling a sarcoma
SARCOIDS > SARCOID
SARCOLOGY *n* study of flesh
SARCOMA *n* malignant tumour beginning in connective tissue
SARCOMAS > SARCOMA
SARCOMATA > SARCOMA
SARCOMERE *n* any of the units that together comprise skeletal muscle
SARCONET *n* type of silk
SARCONETS > SARCONET
SARCOPTIC *adj* relating to mange
SARCOSOME *n* energy-producing tissue in muscle
SARCOUS *adj* (of tissue) muscular or fleshy
SARD *n* orange, red, or brown variety of chalcedony, used as a gemstone
SARDANA *n* Catalan dance
SARDANAS > SARDANA
SARDAR *n* title used before the name of Sikh men
SARDARS > SARDAR
SARDEL *n* small fish
SARDELLE *n* small fish
SARDELLES > SARDELLE
SARDELS > SARDEL
SARDINE *n* small fish of the herring family, usu preserved tightly packed in tins ▷ *vb* cram together
SARDINED > SARDINE
SARDINES > SARDINE
SARDINING > SARDINE
SARDIUS *same as* > SARD
SARDIUSES > SARDIUS
SARDONIAN *adj* sardonic
SARDONIC *adj* mocking or scornful
SARDONYX *n* brown-and-white gemstone
SARDS > SARD
SARED > SAR

SAREE *same as* > SARI
SAREES > SAREE
SARGASSO *same as* > SARGASSUM
SARGASSOS > SARGASSO
SARGASSUM *n* type of floating seaweed
SARGE *n* sergeant
SARGES > SARGE
SARGO *same as* > SARGUS
SARGOS *variant of* > SARGUS
SARGOSES > SARGOS
SARGUS *n* species of sea fish
SARGUSES > SARGUS
SARI *n* long piece of cloth draped around the body and over one shoulder, worn by Hindu women
SARIN *n* chemical used in warfare as a lethal nerve gas producing asphyxia
SARING > SAR
SARINS > SARIN
SARIS > SARI
SARK *n* shirt or (formerly) chemise
SARKIER > SARKY
SARKIEST > SARKY
SARKING *n* flat planking supporting the roof cladding of a building
SARKINGS > SARKING
SARKS > SARK
SARKY *adj* sarcastic
SARMENT *n* thin twig
SARMENTA > SARMENTUM
SARMENTS > SARMENT
SARMENTUM *n* runner on plant
SARMIE *n* sandwich
SARMIES > SARMIE
SARNEY *n* sandwich
SARNEYS > SARNEY
SARNIE *n* sandwich
SARNIES > SARNIE
SAROD *n* Indian stringed musical instrument that may be played with a bow or plucked
SARODE *n* Indian stringed instrument
SARODES > SARODE
SARODIST *n* sarod player
SARODISTS > SARODIST
SARODS > SAROD
SARONG *n* long piece of cloth tucked around the waist or under the armpits, worn esp in Malaysia
SARONGS > SARONG
SARONIC > SAROS
SAROS *n* cycle of about 18 years 11 days in which eclipses of the sun and moon occur in the same sequence
SAROSES > SAROS
SARPANCH *n* head of a panchayat
SARRASIN *n* buckwheat
SARRASINS > SARRASIN
SARRAZIN *n* buckwheat
SARRAZINS > SARRAZIN
SARS > SAR
SARSAR *same as* > SANSAR
SARSARS > SARSAR
SARSDEN *n* sarsen

SARSDENS > SARSDEN

SARSEN *n* boulder of silicified sandstone found in large numbers in S England

SARSENET *same as* > SARCENET

SARSENETS > SARSENET

SARSENS > SARSEN

SARSNET *n* type of silk

SARSNETS > SARSNET

SARTOR *humorous or literary word for* > TAILOR

SARTORIAL *adj* of men's clothes or tailoring

SARTORIAN *adj* of tailoring

SARTORII > SARTORIUS

SARTORIUS *n* long ribbon-shaped muscle that aids in flexing the knee

SARTORS > SARTOR

SARUS *n* Indian bird of crane family

SARUSES > SARUS

SASARARA *n* scolding

SASARARAS > SASARARA

SASER *n* device for amplifying ultrasound, working on a similar principle to a laser

SASERS > SASER

SASH *n* decorative strip of cloth worn round the waist or over one shoulder ▷ *vb* furnish with a sash, sashes, or sash windows

SASHAY *vb* move or walk in a casual or a showy manner

SASHAYED > SASHAY

SASHAYING > SASHAY

SASHAYS > SASHAY

SASHED > SASH

SASHES > SASH

SASHIMI *n* Japanese dish of thin fillets of raw fish

SASHIMIS > SASHIMI

SASHING > SASH

SASHLESS > SASH

SASIN *another name for* > BLACKBUCK

SASINE *n* granting of legal possession of feudal property

SASINES > SASINE

SASINS > SASIN

SASKATOON *n* species of serviceberry of W Canada

SASQUATCH *n* (in Canadian folklore) hairy beast or manlike monster said to leave huge footprints

SASS *n* insolent or impudent talk or behaviour ▷ *vb* talk or answer back in such a way

SASSABIES > SASSABY

SASSABY *n* African antelope of grasslands and semideserts

SASSAFRAS *n* American tree with aromatic bark used medicinally

SASSARARA *n* scolding

SASSE *n* old word meaning canal lock

SASSED > SASS

SASSES > SASS

SASSIER > SASSY

SASSIES > SASSY

SASSIEST > SASSY

SASSILY > SASSY

SASSINESS > SASSY

SASSING > SASS

SASSOLIN *n* boric acid

SASSOLINS > SASSOLIN

SASSOLITE *n* boric acid

SASSWOOD *same as* > SASSY

SASSWOODS > SASSWOOD

SASSY *adj* insolent, impertinent ▷ *n* W African leguminous tree with poisonous bark

SASSYWOOD *n* trial by ordeal in Liberia

SASTRA *same as* > SHASTRA

SASTRAS > SASTRA

SASTRUGA *n* one of a series of ridges on snow-covered plains, caused by the action of wind laden with ice particles

SASTRUGI > SASTRUGA

SAT > SIT

SATAI *same as* > SATAY

SATAIS > SATAL

SATANG *n* monetary unit of Thailand worth one hundredth of a baht

SATANGS > SATANG

SATANIC *adj* of Satan

SATANICAL *same as* > SATANIC

SATANISM *n* worship of the devil

SATANISMS > SATANISM

SATANIST > SATANISM

SATANISTS > SATANISM

SATANITY *n* quality of being satanic

SATARA *n* type of cloth

SATARAS > SATARA

SATAY *n* Indonesian and Malaysian dish consisting of pieces of chicken, pork, etc, grilled on skewers and served with peanut sauce

SATAYS > SATAY

SATCHEL *n* bag, usu with a shoulder strap, for carrying books

SATCHELED *adj* carrying a satchel

SATCHELS > SATCHEL

SATE *vb* satisfy (a desire or appetite) fully

SATED > SATE

SATEDNESS > SATE

SATEEN *n* glossy linen or cotton fabric, woven in such a way that it resembles satin

SATEENS > SATEEN

SATELESS *adj* old word meaning insatiable

SATELLES *n* species of bacteria

SATELLITE *n* man-made device orbiting in space ▷ *adj* of or used in the transmission of television signals from a satellite to the home ▷ *vb* transmit by communications satellite

SATEM *adj* denoting or belonging to a particular group of Indo-European languages

SATES > SATE

SATI *n* Indian widow suicide

SATIABLE *adj* capable of being satiated

SATIABLY > SATIABLE

SATIATE *vb* provide with more than enough, so as to disgust

SATIATED > SATIATE

SATIATES > SATIATE

SATIATING > SATIATE

SATIATION > SATIATE

SATIETIES > SATIETY

SATIETY *n* feeling of having had too much

SATIN *n* silky fabric with a glossy surface on one side ▷ *adj* like satin in texture ▷ *vb* cover with satin

SATINED > SATIN

SATINET *n* thin or imitation satin

SATINETS > SATINET

SATINETTA *n* thin satin

SATINETTE *same as* > SATINET

SATING > SATE

SATINING > SATIN

SATINPOD *n* honesty (the plant)

SATINPODS > SATINPOD

SATINS > SATIN

SATINWOOD *n* tropical tree yielding hard wood

SATINY > SATIN

SATIRE *n* use of ridicule to expose vice or folly

SATIRES > SATIRE

SATIRIC *same as* > SATIRICAL

SATIRICAL *adj* of, relating to, or containing satire

SATIRISE *same as* > SATIRIZE

SATIRISED > SATIRISE

SATIRISER > SATIRIZE

SATIRISES > SATIRISE

SATIRIST *n* writer of satire

SATIRISTS > SATIRIST

SATIRIZE *vb* ridicule by means of satire

SATIRIZED > SATIRIZE

SATIRIZER > SATIRIZE

SATIRIZES > SATIRIZE

SATIS > SATI

SATISFICE *vb* act in such a way as to satisfy the minimum requirements for achieving a particular result

SATISFIED > SATISFY

SATISFIER > SATISFY

SATISFIES > SATISFY

SATISFY *vb* please, content

SATIVE *adj* old word meaning cultivated

SATORI *n* state of sudden indescribable intuitive enlightenment

SATORIS > SATORI

SATRAP *n* (in ancient Persia) a provincial governor or subordinate ruler

SATRAPAL > SATRAP

SATRAPIES > SATRAPY

SATRAPS > SATRAP

SATRAPY *n* province, office, or period of rule of a satrap

SATSUMA *n* kind of small orange

SATSUMAS > SATSUMA

SATURABLE *adj* capable of being saturated

SATURANT *n* substance that causes a solution, etc, to be saturated ▷ *adj* (of a substance) causing saturation

SATURANTS > SATURANT

SATURATE *vb* soak thoroughly

SATURATED *adj* (of a solution or solvent) containing the maximum amount of solute that can normally be dissolved at a given temperature and pressure

SATURATER > SATURATE

SATURATES > SATURATE

SATURATOR > SATURATE

SATURNIC *adj* poisoned by lead

SATURNIID *n* any moth of the mainly tropical family *Saturniidae*, typically having large brightly coloured wings ▷ *adj* of, relating to, or belonging to the *Saturniidae*

SATURNINE *adj* gloomy in temperament or appearance

SATURNISM *n* lead poisoning

SATURNIST *n* old word meaning glum person

SATYR *n* woodland god, part man, part goat

SATYRA *n* female satyr

SATYRAL *n* mythical beast in heraldry

SATYRALS > SATYRAL

SATYRAS > SATYRA

SATYRESS *n* female satyr

SATYRIC > SATYR

SATYRICAL > SATYR

SATYRID *n* butterfly with typically brown or dark wings with paler markings

SATYRIDS > SATYRID

SATYRISK *n* small satyr

SATYRISKS > SATYRISK

SATYRLIKE > SATYR

SATYRS > SATYR

SAU *archaic past tense of* > SEE

SAUBA *n* South American ant

SAUBAS > SAUBA

SAUCE *n* liquid added to food to enhance flavour ▷ *vb* prepare (food) with sauce

SAUCEBOAT *n* gravy boat

SAUCEBOX *n* saucy person

SAUCED > SAUCE

SAUCELESS > SAUCE

SAUCEPAN *n* cooking pot with a long handle

SAUCEPANS > SAUCEPAN

SAUCEPOT n cooking pot with lid
SAUCEPOTS > SAUCEPOT
SAUCER n small round dish put under a cup
SAUCERFUL > SAUCER
SAUCERS > SAUCER
SAUCES > SAUCE
SAUCH n sallow or willow
SAUCHS > SAUCH
SAUCIER n chef who makes sauces
SAUCIERS > SAUCIER
SAUCIEST > SAUCY
SAUCILY > SAUCY
SAUCINESS > SAUCY
SAUCING > SAUCE
SAUCISSE n type of explosive fuse
SAUCISSES > SAUCISSE
SAUCISSON n type of explosive fuse
SAUCY adj impudent
SAUFGARD old form of > SAFEGUARD
SAUFGARDS > SAUFGARD
SAUGER n small North American pikeperch
SAUGERS > SAUGER
SAUGH same as > SAUCH
SAUGHS > SAUGH
SAUGHY adj Scots word meaning made of willow
SAUL Scots word for > SOUL
SAULGE n old word for sage plant
SAULGES > SAULGE
SAULIE n Scots word meaning professional mourner
SAULIES > SAULIE
SAULS > SAUL
SAULT n waterfall in Canada
SAULTS > SAULT
SAUNA n Finnish-style steam bath ▷ vb have a sauna
SAUNAED > SAUNA
SAUNAING > SAUNA
SAUNAS > SAUNA
SAUNT Scots form of > SAINT
SAUNTED > SAUNT
SAUNTER vb walk in a leisurely manner, stroll ▷ n leisurely walk
SAUNTERED > SAUNTER
SAUNTERER > SAUNTER
SAUNTERS > SAUNTER
SAUNTING > SAUNT
SAUNTS > SAUNT
SAUREL n type of mackerel
SAURELS > SAUREL
SAURIAN adj of or like a lizard ▷ n former name for > LIZARD
SAURIANS > SAURIAN
SAURIES > SAURY
SAUROID adj like a lizard
SAUROPOD n type of herbivorous dinosaur including the brontosaurus and the diplodocus
SAUROPODS > SAUROPOD
SAURY n type of fish of tropical and temperate seas, having an elongated body and long toothed

jaws
SAUSAGE n minced meat in an edible tube-shaped skin
SAUSAGES > SAUSAGE
SAUT Scot word for > SALT
SAUTE vb fry quickly in a little fat ▷ n dish of sautéed food ▷ adj sautéed until lightly brown
SAUTED > SAUT
SAUTEED > SAUTE
SAUTEEING > SAUTE
SAUTEES > SAUTE
SAUTEING > SAUTE
SAUTERNE n sauternes
SAUTERNES n sweet white French wine
SAUTES > SAUTE
SAUTING > SAUT
SAUTOIR n long necklace or pendant
SAUTOIRE variant of > SAUTOIR
SAUTOIRES > SAUTOIRE
SAUTOIRS > SAUTOIR
SAUTS > SAUT
SAV short for > SAVELOY
SAVABLE > SAVE
SAVAGE adj wild, untamed ▷ n uncivilized person ▷ vb attack ferociously
SAVAGED > SAVAGE
SAVAGEDOM > SAVAGE
SAVAGELY > SAVAGE
SAVAGER > SAVAGE
SAVAGERY n viciousness and cruelty
SAVAGES > SAVAGE
SAVAGEST > SAVAGE
SAVAGING > SAVAGE
SAVAGISM > SAVAGE
SAVAGISMS > SAVAGE
SAVANNA n open grasslands, usually with scattered bushes or trees, characteristic of much of tropical Africa
SAVANNAH same as > SAVANNA
SAVANNAHS > SAVANNAH
SAVANNAS > SAVANNA
SAVANT n learned person
SAVANTE > SAVANT
SAVANTES > SAVANT
SAVANTS > SAVANT
SAVARIN n type of cake
SAVARINS > SAVARIN
SAVATE n form of boxing in which blows may be delivered with the feet as well as the hands
SAVATES > SAVATE
SAVE vb rescue or preserve from harm, protect ▷ n act of preventing a goal ▷ prep except
SAVEABLE > SAVE
SAVED > SAVE
SAVEGARD vb old word meaning protect
SAVEGARDS > SAVEGARD
SAVELOY n spicy smoked sausage
SAVELOYS > SAVELOY
SAVER > SAVE
SAVERS > SAVE
SAVES > SAVE

SAVEY vb understand
SAVEYED > SAVEY
SAVEYING > SAVEY
SAVEYS > SAVEY
SAVIN n small spreading juniper bush of Europe, N Asia, and North America
SAVINE same as > SAVIN
SAVINES > SAVINE
SAVING n economy ▷ prep except ▷ adj tending to save or preserve
SAVINGLY > SAVING
SAVINGS > SAVING
SAVINS > SAVIN
SAVIOR same as > SAVIOUR
SAVIORS > SAVIOR
SAVIOUR n person who rescues another
SAVIOURS > SAVIOUR
SAVOR same as > SAVOUR
SAVORED > SAVOR
SAVORER > SAVOR
SAVORERS > SAVOR
SAVORIER > SAVORY
SAVORIES > SAVORY
SAVORIEST > SAVORY
SAVORILY > SAVOUR
SAVORING > SAVOR
SAVORLESS > SAVOUR
SAVOROUS > SAVOUR
SAVORS > SAVOR
SAVORY same as > SAVOURY
SAVOUR vb enjoy, relish ▷ n characteristic taste or odour
SAVOURED > SAVOUR
SAVOURER > SAVOUR
SAVOURERS > SAVOUR
SAVOURIER > SAVOURY
SAVOURIES > SAVOURY
SAVOURILY > SAVOURY
SAVOURING > SAVOUR
SAVOURLY adv old word meaning refeshingly
SAVOURS > SAVOUR
SAVOURY adj salty or spicy ▷ n savoury dish served before or after a meal
SAVOY n variety of cabbage
SAVOYARD n person keenly interested in the operettas of Gilbert and Sullivan
SAVOYARDS > SAVOYARD
SAVOYS > SAVOY
SAVS > SAV
SAVVEY vb understand
SAVVEYED > SAVVEY
SAVVEYING > SAVVEY
SAVVEYS > SAVVEY
SAVVIED > SAVVY
SAVVIER > SAVVY
SAVVIES > SAVVY
SAVVIEST > SAVVY
SAVVILY > SAVVY
SAVVINESS > SAVVY
SAVVY vb understand ▷ n understanding, intelligence ▷ adj shrewd
SAVVYING > SAVVY
SAW n hand tool for cutting wood and metal ▷ vb cut with a saw
SAWAH n paddyfield
SAWAHS > SAWAH
SAWBILL n any of various hummingbirds of the

genus *Ramphodon*
SAWBILLS > SAWBILL
SAWBLADE n blade of a saw
SAWBLADES > SAWBLADE
SAWBONES n surgeon or doctor
SAWBUCK n sawhorse, esp one having an X-shaped supporting structure
SAWBUCKS > SAWBUCK
SAWDER n flattery ▷ vb flatter
SAWDERED > SAWDER
SAWDERING > SAWDER
SAWDERS > SAWDER
SAWDUST n fine wood fragments made in sawing ▷ vb cover with sawdust
SAWDUSTED > SAWDUST
SAWDUSTS > SAWDUST
SAWDUSTY > SAWDUST
SAWED > SAW
SAWER > SAW
SAWERS > SAW
SAWFISH n fish with a long toothed snout
SAWFISHES > SAWFISH
SAWFLIES > SAWFLY
SAWFLY n any of various hymenopterous insects
SAWHORSE n structure for supporting wood that is being sawn
SAWHORSES > SAWHORSE
SAWING > SAW
SAWINGS > SAW
SAWLIKE > SAW
SAWLOG n log suitable for sawing
SAWLOGS > SAWLOG
SAWMILL n mill where timber is sawn into planks
SAWMILLS > SAWMILL
SAWN past participle of > SAW
SAWNEY n derogatory word for a fool
SAWNEYS > SAWNEY
SAWPIT n pit above which a log is sawn into planks
SAWPITS > SAWPIT
SAWS > SAW
SAWSHARK n shark with long sawlike snout
SAWSHARKS > SAWSHARK
SAWTEETH > SAWTOOTH
SAWTIMBER n wood for sawing
SAWTOOTH adj (of a waveform) having an amplitude that varies linearly with time between two values
SAWYER n person who saws timber for a living
SAWYERS > SAWYER
SAX same as > SAXOPHONE
SAXATILE adj living among rocks
SAXAUL n Asian tree
SAXAULS > SAXAUL
SAXE as in *saxe blue* light greyish-blue colour
SAXES > SAX
SAXHORN n valved brass instrument used chiefly in brass and military bands
SAXHORNS > SAXHORN

SAXICOLE *variant of* > SAXATILE

SAXIFRAGE *n* alpine rock plant with small flowers

SAXITOXIN *n* poison extracted from mollusc

SAXONIES > SAXONY

SAXONITE *n* igneous rock

SAXONITES > SAXONITE

SAXONY *n* fine 3-ply yarn used for knitting and weaving

SAXOPHONE *n* brass wind instrument with keys and a curved body

SAXTUBA *n* bass saxhorn

SAXTUBAS > SAXTUBA

SAY *vb* speak or utter ▷ *n* right or chance to speak

SAYABLE > SAY

SAYED *same as* > SAYYID

SAYEDS > SAYED

SAYER > SAY

SAYERS > SAY

SAYEST > SAY

SAYID *same as* > SAYYID

SAYIDS > SAYID

SAYING > SAY

SAYINGS > SAY

SAYNE > SAY

SAYON *n* type of tunic

SAYONARA *n* Japanese farewell

SAYONARAS > SAYONARA

SAYONS > SAYON

SAYS > SAY

SAYST > SAY

SAYYID *n* Muslim claiming descent from Mohammed's grandson Husain

SAYYIDS > SAYYID

SAZ *n* Middle Eastern stringed instrument

SAZERAC *n* mixed drink of whisky, Pernod, syrup, bitters, and lemon

SAZERACS > SAZERAC

SAZES > SAZ

SAZHEN *n* Russian measure of length

SAZHENS > SAZHEN

SAZZES > SAZ

SBIRRI > SBIRRO

SBIRRO *n* Italian police officer

SCAB *n* crust formed over a wound ▷ *vb* become covered with a scab

SCABBARD *n* sheath for a sword or dagger

SCABBARDS > SCABBARD

SCABBED > SCAB

SCABBIER > SCABBY

SCABBIEST > SCABBY

SCABBILY > SCABBY

SCABBING > SCAB

SCABBLE *vb* shape (stone) roughly

SCABBLED > SCABBLE

SCABBLES > SCABBLE

SCABBLING > SCABBLE

SCABBY *adj* covered with scabs

SCABIES *n* itchy skin disease

SCABIETIC > SCABIES

SCABIOSA *n* flowering plant

SCABIOSAS > SCABIOSA

SCABIOUS *n* plant with showy blue, red, or whitish dome-shaped flower heads ▷ *adj* having or covered with scabs

SCABLAND *n* barren rocky land

SCABLANDS *pl n* type of terrain consisting of bare rock surfaces, with little or no soil cover and scanty vegetation

SCABLIKE > SCAB

SCABRID *adj* having a rough or scaly surface

SCABROUS *adj* rough and scaly

SCABS > SCAB

SCAD *n* any of various carangid fishes

SCADS *pl n* large amount or number

SCAFF *n* Scots word meaning food

SCAFFIE *n* Scots word meaning street cleaner

SCAFFIES > SCAFFIE

SCAFFOLD *n* temporary platform for workmen ▷ *vb* provide with a scaffold

SCAFFOLDS > SCAFFOLD

SCAFFS > SCAFF

SCAG *n* tear in a garment or piece of cloth ▷ *vb* make a tear in (cloth)

SCAGGED > SCAG

SCAGGING > SCAG

SCAGLIA *n* type of limestone

SCAGLIAS > SCAGLIA

SCAGLIOLA *n* type of imitation marble made of glued gypsum

SCAGS > SCAG

SCAIL *vb* Scots word meaning disperse

SCAILED > SCAIL

SCAILING > SCAIL

SCAILS > SCAIL

SCAITH *vb* old word meaning injure

SCAITHED > SCAITH

SCAITHING > SCAITH

SCAITHS > SCAITH

SCALA *n* passage inside the cochlea

SCALABLE *adj* capable of being scaled or climbed

SCALABLY > SCALABLE

SCALADE *short for* > ESCALADE

SCALADES > SCALADE

SCALADO *same as* > SCALADE

SCALADOS > SCALADO

SCALAE > SCALA

SCALAGE *n* percentage deducted from the price of goods liable to shrink or leak

SCALAGES > SCALAGE

SCALAR *adj* (variable quantity) having magnitude but no direction ▷ *n* quantity, such as time or temperature, that has magnitude but not direction

SCALARE *another name for* > ANGELFISH

SCALARES > SCALARE

SCALARS > SCALAR

SCALATION *n* way scales are arranged

SCALAWAG *same as* > SCALLYWAG

SCALAWAGS > SCALAWAG

SCALD *same as* > SKALD

SCALDED > SCALD

SCALDER > SCALD

SCALDERS > SCALD

SCALDFISH *n* small European flatfish

SCALDHEAD *n* diseased scalp

SCALDIC > SKALD

SCALDING > SCALD

SCALDINGS > SCALD

SCALDINI > SCALDINO

SCALDINO *n* Italian brazier

SCALDS > SCALD

SCALDSHIP *n* position of being Scandinavian poet

SCALE *n* one of the thin overlapping plates covering fishes and reptiles ▷ *vb* remove scales from

SCALED > SCALE

SCALELESS > SCALE

SCALELIKE > SCALE

SCALENE *adj* (of a triangle) with three unequal sides

SCALENI > SCALENUS

SCALENUS *n* any one of the three muscles situated on each side of the neck

SCALEPAN *n* part of scales holding weighed object

SCALEPANS > SCALEPAN

SCALER *n* person or thing that scales

SCALERS > SCALER

SCALES > SCALE

SCALETAIL *n* type of squirrel

SCALEUP *n* increase

SCALEUPS > SCALEUP

SCALEWORK *n* artistic representation of scales

SCALIER > SCALY

SCALIEST > SCALY

SCALINESS > SCALY

SCALING > SCALING

SCALINGS > SCALE

SCALL *n* disease of the scalp characterized by itching and scab formation

SCALLAWAG *same as* > SCALLYWAG

SCALLED > SCALL

SCALLIES > SCALLY

SCALLION *same as* > SHALLOT

SCALLIONS > SCALLION

SCALLOP *n* edible shellfish with two fan-shaped shells ▷ *vb* decorate (an edge) with scallops

SCALLOPED > SCALLOP

SCALLOPER > SCALLOP

SCALLOPS > SCALLOP

SCALLS > SCALL

SCALLY *n* rascal

SCALLYWAG *n* scamp, rascal

SCALOGRAM *n* scale for measuring opinion

SCALP *n* skin and hair on top of the head ▷ *vb* cut off the scalp of

SCALPED > SCALP

SCALPEL *n* small surgical knife

SCALPELS > SCALPEL

SCALPER > SCALP

SCALPERS > SCALP

SCALPING *n* process in which the top portion of a metal ingot is machined away before use

SCALPINGS > SCALPING

SCALPINS *n* small stones

SCALPLESS > SCALP

SCALPRUM *n* large scalpel

SCALPRUMS > SCALPRUM

SCALPS > SCALP

SCALY *adj* resembling or covered in scales

SCAM *n* dishonest scheme ▷ *vb* swindle (someone) by means of a trick

SCAMBLE *vb* scramble

SCAMBLED > SCAMBLE

SCAMBLER > SCAMBLE

SCAMBLERS > SCAMBLE

SCAMBLES > SCAMBLE

SCAMBLING > SCAMBLE

SCAMEL *n* Shakespearian word of uncertain meaning

SCAMELS > SCAMEL

SCAMMED > SCAM

SCAMMER *n* person who perpetrates a scam

SCAMMERS > SCAMMER

SCAMMING > SCAM

SCAMMONY *n* twining Asian convolvulus plant

SCAMP *n* mischievous child ▷ *vb* perform without care

SCAMPED > SCAMP

SCAMPER *vb* run about hurriedly or in play ▷ *n* scampering

SCAMPERED > SCAMP

SCAMPERER > SCAMPER

SCAMPERS > SCAMP

SCAMPI *pl n* large prawns

SCAMPIES > SCAMPI

SCAMPING > SCAMP

SCAMPINGS > SCAMP

SCAMPIS > SCAMPI

SCAMPISH > SCAMP

SCAMPS > SCAMP

SCAMS > SCAM

SCAMSTER *same as* > SCAMMER

SCAMSTERS > SCAMSTER

SCAMTO *n* argot of urban South African Blacks

SCAMTOS > SCAMTO

SCAN *vb* scrutinize carefully ▷ *n* scanning

SCAND > SCAN

SCANDAL *n* disgraceful action or event ▷ *vb* disgrace

SCANDALED > SCANDAL

SCANDALS > SCANDAL

SCANDENT *adj* (of plants) having a climbing habit

SCANDIA *n* scandium oxide

SCANDIAS > SCANDIA

SCANDIC *adj* of or

S

containing scandium

SCANDIUM *n* rare silvery-white metallic element

SCANDIUMS > SCANDIUM

SCANNABLE > SCAN

SCANNED > SCAN

SCANNER *n* electronic device used for scanning

SCANNERS > SCANNER

SCANNING > SCAN

SCANNINGS > SCAN

SCANS > SCAN

SCANSION *n* metrical scanning of verse

SCANSIONS > SCANSION

SCANT *adj* barely sufficient, meagre ▷ *vb* limit in size or quantity ▷ *adv* scarcely

SCANTED > SCANT

SCANTER > SCANT

SCANTEST > SCANT

SCANTIER > SCANTY

SCANTIES *n* women's underwear

SCANTIEST > SCANTY

SCANTILY > SCANTY

SCANTING > SCANT

SCANTITY *n* quality of being scant

SCANTLE *vb* stint

SCANTLED > SCANTLE

SCANTLES > SCANTLE

SCANTLING *n* piece of sawn timber, such as a rafter, that has a small cross section

SCANTLY > SCANT

SCANTNESS > SCANT

SCANTS > SCANT

SCANTY *adj* barely sufficient or not sufficient

SCAPA *variant of* > SCARPER

SCAPAED > SCAPA

SCAPAING > SCAPA

SCAPAS > SCAPA

SCAPE *n* leafless stalk in plants that arises from a rosette of leaves and bears one or more flowers ▷ *vb* archaic word for escape

SCAPED > SCAPE

SCAPEGOAT *n* person made to bear the blame for others ▷ *vb* make a scapegoat of

SCAPELESS *adj* allowing no escape

SCAPEMENT *n* escapement

SCAPES > SCAPE

SCAPHOID *obsolete word for* > NAVICULAR

SCAPHOIDS > SCAPHOID

SCAPHOPOD *n* any marine mollusc of the class *Scaphopoda*

SCAPI > SCAPUS

SCAPING > SCAPE

SCAPOLITE *n* any of a group of colourless, white, grey, or violet fluorescent minerals

SCAPOSE > SCAPE

SCAPPLE *vb* shape roughly

SCAPPLED > SCAPPLE

SCAPPLES > SCAPPLE

SCAPPLING > SCAPPLE

SCAPULA *n* shoulder blade

SCAPULAE > SCAPULA

SCAPULAR *adj* of the scapula ▷ *n* loose sleeveless garment worn by monks over their habits

SCAPULARS > SCAPULAR

SCAPULARY *same as* > SCAPULAR

SCAPULAS > SCAPULA

SCAPUS *n* flower stalk

SCAR *n* mark left by a healed wound ▷ *vb* mark or become marked with a scar

SCARAB *n* sacred beetle of ancient Egypt

SCARABAEI *pl n* scarabs

SCARABEE *n* old word for scarab beetle

SCARABEES > SCARABEE

SCARABOID *adj* resembling a scarab beetle ▷ *n* beetle that resembles a scarab

SCARABS > SCARAB

SCARCE *adj* insufficient to meet demand

SCARCELY *adv* hardly at all

SCARCER > SCARCE

SCARCEST > SCARCE

SCARCITY *n* inadequate supply

SCARE *vb* frighten or be frightened ▷ *n* fright, sudden panic ▷ *adj* causing (needless) fear or alarm

SCARECROW *n* figure dressed in old clothes, set up to scare birds away from crops

SCARED > SCARE

SCAREDER > SCARE

SCAREDEST > SCARE

SCAREHEAD *n* newspaper headline intended to shock

SCARER > SCARE

SCARERS > SCARE

SCARES > SCARE

SCAREY *adj* frightening

SCARF *n* piece of material worn round the neck, head, or shoulders ▷ *vb* join in this way

SCARFED > SCARF

SCARFER > SCARF

SCARFERS > SCARF

SCARFING > SCARF

SCARFINGS > SCARF

SCARFISH *n* type of fish

SCARFPIN *n* decorative pin securing scarf

SCARFPINS > SCARFPIN

SCARFS > SCARF

SCARFSKIN *n* outermost layer of the skin

SCARFWISE *adv* like scarf

SCARIER > SCARY

SCARIEST > SCARY

SCARIFIED > SCARIFY

SCARIFIER > SCARIFY

SCARIFIES > SCARIFY

SCARIFY *vb* scratch or cut slightly all over

SCARILY > SCARY

SCARINESS > SCARY

SCARING > SCARE

SCARIOSE *same as* > SCARIOUS

SCARIOUS *adj* (of plant

parts) membranous, dry, and brownish in colour

SCARLESS > SCAR

SCARLET *n* brilliant red ▷ *adj* bright red ▷ *vb* make scarlet

SCARLETED > SCARLET

SCARLETS > SCARLET

SCARMOGE *n* old form of skirmish

SCARMOGES > SCARMOGE

SCARP *n* steep slope ▷ *vb* wear or cut so as to form a steep slope

SCARPA *vb* run away

SCARPAED > SCARPA

SCARPAING > SCARPA

SCARPAS > SCARPA

SCARPED > SCARP

SCARPER *vb* run away ▷ *n* hasty departure

SCARPERED > SCARPER

SCARPERS > SCARPER

SCARPETTI > SCARPETTO

SCARPETTO *n* type of shoe

SCARPH *vb* join with scarf joint

SCARPHED > SCARPH

SCARPHING > SCARPH

SCARPHS > SCARPH

SCARPINES *n* device for torturing feet

SCARPING > SCARP

SCARPINGS > SCARP

SCARPS > SCARP

SCARRE *n* Shakespearian word of unknown meaning

SCARRED > SCAR

SCARRES > SCARRE

SCARRIER > SCAR

SCARRIEST > SCAR

SCARRING > SCAR

SCARRINGS > SCAR

SCARRY > SCAR

SCARS > SCAR

SCART *vb* scratch or scrape ▷ *n* scratch or scrape

SCARTED > SCART

SCARTH *Scots word for* > CORMORANT

SCARTHS > SCARTH

SCARTING > SCART

SCARTS > SCART

SCARVES > SCARF

SCARY *adj* frightening

SCAT *vb* go away ▷ *n* jazz singing using improvised vocal sounds instead of words

SCATBACK *n* American football player

SCATBACKS > SCATBACK

SCATCH *same as* > STILT

SCATCHES > SCATCH

SCATH *vb* old word meaning injure

SCATHE *vb* attack with severe criticism ▷ *n* harm

SCATHED > SCATHE

SCATHEFUL *adj* old word meaning harmful

SCATHES > SCATHE

SCATHING *adj* harshly critical

SCATHS > SCATH

SCATOLE *n* substance found in coal

SCATOLES > SCATOLE

SCATOLOGY *n* preoccupation with obscenity, esp with references to excrement

SCATS > SCAT

SCATT *n* old word meaning tax ▷ *vb* tax

SCATTED > SCAT

SCATTER *vb* throw about in various directions ▷ *n* scattering

SCATTERED > SCATTER

SCATTERER > SCATTER

SCATTERS > SCATTER

SCATTERY *adj* dispersed

SCATTIER > SCATTY

SCATTIEST > SCATTY

SCATTILY > SCATTY

SCATTING > SCAT

SCATTINGS > SCAT

SCATTS > SCATT

SCATTY *adj* empty-headed

SCAUD *Scot word for* > SCALD

SCAUDED > SCAUD

SCAUDING > SCAUD

SCAUDS > SCAUD

SCAUP *variant of* > SCALP

SCAUPED > SCAUP

SCAUPER *same as* > SCORPER

SCAUPERS > SCAUPER

SCAUPING > SCAUP

SCAUPS > SCAUP

SCAUR *same as* > SCAR

SCAURED > SCAUR

SCAURIES > SCAURY

SCAURING > SCAUR

SCAURS > SCAUR

SCAURY *n* young seagull

SCAVAGE *n* old word meaning toll

SCAVAGER > SCAVAGE

SCAVAGERS > SCAVAGE

SCAVAGES > SCAVAGE

SCAVENGE *vb* search for (anything usable) among discarded material

SCAVENGED > SCAVENGE

SCAVENGER *n* person who scavenges

SCAVENGES > SCAVENGE

SCAW *n* headland

SCAWS > SCAW

SCAWTITE *n* mineral containing calcium

SCAWTITES > SCAWTITE

SCAZON *n* metre in poetry

SCAZONS > SCAZON

SCAZONTES > SCAZON

SCAZONTIC > SCAZON

SCEAT *n* Anglo-Saxon coin

SCEATT *n* Anglo-Saxon coin

SCEATTAS > SCEAT

SCEDULE *old spelling of* > SCHEDULE

SCEDULED > SCEDULE

SCEDULES > SCEDULE

SCEDULING > SCEDULE

SCELERAT *n* villain

SCELERATE *n* villain

SCELERATS > SCELERAT

SCENA *n* scene in an opera, usually longer than a single aria

SCENARIES > SCENARY

SCENARIO *n* summary of the plot of a play or film

SCENARIOS > SCENARIO
SCENARISE same
  as > SCENARIZE
SCENARIST > SCENARIO
SCENARIZE vb create
  scenario
SCENARY n scenery
SCENAS > SCENA
SCEND vb (of a vessel) to
  surge upwards in a heavy
  sea ▷ n upward heaving of
  a vessel pitching
SCENDED > SCEND
SCENDING > SCEND
SCENDS > SCEND
SCENE n place of action of
  a real or imaginary event
  ▷ vb set in a scene
SCENED > SCENE
SCENEMAN n person shifting
  stage scenery
SCENEMEN > SCENEMAN
SCENERIES > SCENERY
SCENERY n natural features
  of a landscape
SCENES > SCENE
SCENIC adj picturesque ▷ n
  something scenic
SCENICAL > SCENE
SCENICS > SCENIC
SCENING > SCENE
SCENT n pleasant smell ▷ vb
  detect by smell
SCENTED > SCENT
SCENTFUL adj old word
  meaning having scent
SCENTING > SCENT
SCENTINGS > SCENT
SCENTLESS > SCENT
SCENTS > SCENT
SCEPSIS n doubt
SCEPSISES > SCEPSIS
SCEPTER same as > SCEPTRE
SCEPTERED > SCEPTER
SCEPTERS > SCEPTER
SCEPTIC n person who
  habitually doubts generally
  accepted beliefs ▷ adj of or
  relating to sceptics
SCEPTICAL adj not
  convinced that something
  is true
SCEPTICS > SCEPTIC
SCEPTRAL adj royal
SCEPTRE n ornamental rod
  symbolizing royal power
  ▷ vb invest with authority
SCEPTRED > SCEPTRE
SCEPTRES > SCEPTRE
SCEPTRING > SCEPTRE
SCEPTRY adj having sceptre
SCERNE vb old word
  meaning discern
SCERNED > SCERNE
SCERNES > SCERNE
SCERNING > SCERNE
SCHANSE n stones heaped
  to shelter soldier in battle
SCHANSES > SCHANSE
SCHANTZE n stones heaped
  to shelter soldier in battle
SCHANTZES > SCHANTZE
SCHANZE n stones heaped
  to shelter soldier in battle
SCHANZES > SCHANZE
SCHAPPE n yarn or fabric
  made from waste silk

SCHAPPED > SCHAPPE
SCHAPPES > SCHAPPE
SCHAPSKA n cap worn by
  lancer
SCHAPSKAS > SCHAPSKA
SCHATCHEN same
  as > SHADCHAN
SCHAV n Polish soup
SCHAVS > SCHAV
SCHECHITA n slaughter
  of animals according to
  Jewish law
SCHEDULAR > SCHEDULE
SCHEDULE n plan of
  procedure for a project ▷ vb
  plan to occur at a certain
  time
SCHEDULED adj arranged
  or planned according to a
  programme, timetable, etc
SCHEDULER > SCHEDULE
SCHEDULES > SCHEDULE
SCHEELITE n white,
  brownish, or greenish
  mineral
SCHELLUM n Scots word
  meaning rascal
SCHELLUMS > SCHELLUM
SCHELM n South African
  word meaning rascal
SCHELMS > SCHELM
SCHEMA n overall plan or
  diagram
SCHEMAS > SCHEMA
SCHEMATA > SCHEMA
SCHEMATIC adj presented
  as a plan or diagram ▷ n
  schematic diagram, esp of
  an electrical circuit
SCHEME n systematic plan
  ▷ vb plan in an underhand
  manner
SCHEMED > SCHEME
SCHEMER > SCHEME
SCHEMERS > SCHEME
SCHEMES > SCHEME
SCHEMIE n Scots
  derogatory word for a
  resident of a housing
  scheme
SCHEMIES > SCHEMIE
SCHEMING adj given to
  making plots ▷ n intrigues
SCHEMINGS > SCHEMING
SCHERZI > SCHERZO
SCHERZO n brisk lively piece
  of music
SCHERZOS > SCHERZO
SCHIAVONE n type of sword
SCHIEDAM n type of
  gin produced in the
  Netherlands
SCHIEDAMS > SCHIEDAM
SCHILLER n unusual
  iridescent or metallic lustre
  in some minerals
SCHILLERS > SCHILLER
SCHILLING n former
  monetary unit of Austria
SCHIMMEL n roan horse
SCHIMMELS > SCHIMMEL
SCHISM n (group resulting
  from) division in an
  organization
SCHISMA n musical term
SCHISMAS > SCHISMA
SCHISMS > SCHISM

SCHIST n crystalline rock
  which splits into layers
SCHISTOSE > SCHIST
SCHISTOUS > SCHIST
SCHISTS > SCHIST
SCHIZIER > SCHIZY
SCHIZIEST > SCHIZY
SCHIZO n derogatory
  term for a schizophrenic
  (person) ▷ adj
  schizophrenic
SCHIZOID adj abnormally
  introverted ▷ n schizoid
  person
SCHIZOIDS > SCHIZOID
SCHIZONT n cell formed
  from a trophozoite during
  the asexual stage of the
  life cycle of sporozoan
  protozoans
SCHIZONTS > SCHIZONT
SCHIZOPOD n any of various
  shrimplike crustaceans
SCHIZOS > SCHIZO
SCHIZY adj slang term
  meaning schizophrenic
SCHIZZIER > SCHIZZY
SCHIZZY adj slang term
  meaning schizophrenic
SCHLAGER n German
  duelling sword
SCHLAGERS > SCHLAGER
SCHLEMIEL n awkward
  or unlucky person whose
  endeavours usually fail
SCHLEMIHL same
  as > SCHLEMIEL
SCHLEP vb drag or lug
  (oneself or an object) with
  difficulty ▷ n stupid or
  clumsy person
SCHLEPP vb schlep
SCHLEPPED > SCHLEP
SCHLEPPER n incompetent
  person
SCHLEPPS > SCHLEPP
SCHLEPPY > SCHLEPP
SCHLEPS > SCHLEP
SCHLICH n finely crushed
  ore
SCHLICHS > SCHLICH
SCHLIERE n (in physics or
  geology) streak of different
  density or composition
  from surroundings
SCHLIEREN > SCHLIERE
SCHLIERIC > SCHLIERE
SCHLOCK n goods or
  produce of cheap or inferior
  quality ▷ adj cheap,
  inferior, or trashy
SCHLOCKER n thing of poor
  quality
SCHLOCKS > SCHLOCK
SCHLOCKY adj of poor
  quality
SCHLONG slang word
  for > PENIS
SCHLONGS > SCHLONG
SCHLOSS n castle
SCHLOSSES > SCHLOSS
SCHLUB n coarse or
  contemptible person
SCHLUBS > SCHLUB
SCHLUMP vb move in lazy
  way
SCHLUMPED > SCHLUMP

SCHLUMPS > SCHLUMP
SCHLUMPY > SCHLUMP
SCHMALTZ n excessive
  sentimentality
SCHMALTZY adj excessively
  sentimental
SCHMALZ same
  as > SCHMALTZ
SCHMALZES > SCHMALZ
SCHMALZY adj schmaltzy
SCHMATTE same
  as > SCHMUTTER
SCHMATTES > SCHMATTE
SCHMEAR n situation,
  matter, or affair ▷ vb
  spread or smear
SCHMEARED > SCHMEAR
SCHMEARS > SCHMEAR
SCHMECK n taste
SCHMECKS > SCHMECK
SCHMEER same as > SCHMEAR
SCHMEERED > SCHMEER
SCHMEERS > SCHMEER
SCHMELZ n ornamental
  glass
SCHMELZE variant
  of > SCHMELZ
SCHMELZES > SCHMELZ
SCHMICK n informal
  Australian word for
  excellent, elegant, or
  stylish
SCHMO n dull, stupid, or
  boring person
SCHMOCK n stupid person
SCHMOCKS > SCHMOCK
SCHMOE n stupid person
SCHMOES > SCHMO
SCHMOOS variant
  of > SCHMOOSE
SCHMOOSE vb chat
SCHMOOSED > SCHMOOSE
SCHMOOSES > SCHMOOSE
SCHMOOZ n chat
SCHMOOZE vb chat or gossip
  ▷ n trivial conversation
SCHMOOZED > SCHMOOZE
SCHMOOZER > SCHMOOZE
SCHMOOZES > SCHMOOZE
SCHMOOZY > SCHMOOZE
SCHMOS > SCHMO
SCHMUCK n stupid or
  contemptible person
SCHMUCKS > SCHMUCK
SCHMUTTER n cloth or
  clothing
SCHNAPPER same
  as > SNAPPER
SCHNAPPS n strong
  alcoholic spirit
SCHNAPS same
  as > SCHNAPPS
SCHNAPSES > SCHNAPS
SCHNAUZER n wire-haired
  breed of dog of the terrier
  type, originally from
  Germany
SCHNECKE > SCHNECKEN
SCHNECKEN pl n sweet
  spiral-shaped bread roll
  flavoured with cinnamon
  and nuts
SCHNELL adj German word
  meaning quick
SCHNITZEL n thin slice of
  meat, esp veal
SCHNOOK n stupid or gullible

person
SCHNOOKS > SCHNOOK
SCHNORKEL *less common variant of* > SNORKEL
SCHNORR *vb* beg
SCHNORRED > SCHNORR
SCHNORRER *n* person who lives off the charity of others
SCHNORRS > SCHNORR
SCHNOZ *n* nose
SCHNOZES > SCHNOZ
SCHNOZZ *n* nose
SCHNOZZES > SCHNOZZ
SCHNOZZLE *slang word for* > NOSE
SCHOLAR *n* learned person
SCHOLARCH *n* head of school
SCHOLARLY > SCHOLAR
SCHOLARS > SCHOLAR
SCHOLIA > SCHOLIUM
SCHOLIAST *n* medieval annotator, esp of classical texts
SCHOLION *n* scholarly annotation
SCHOLIUM *n* commentary or annotation, esp on a classical text
SCHOLIUMS > SCHOLIUM
SCHOOL *n* place where children are taught or instruction is given in a subject ▷*vb* educate or train
SCHOOLBAG *n* school pupil's bag
SCHOOLBOY *n* child attending school
SCHOOLDAY *n* day for going to school
SCHOOLE *n* old form of shoal
SCHOOLED > SCHOOL
SCHOOLERY *n* old word meaning something taught
SCHOOLES > SCHOOLE
SCHOOLIE *n* schoolteacher or a high-school student
SCHOOLIES > SCHOOLIE
SCHOOLING *n* education
SCHOOLKID *n* child who goes to school
SCHOOLMAN *n* scholar versed in the learning of the Schoolmen
SCHOOLMEN > SCHOOLMAN
SCHOOLS > SCHOOL
SCHOONER *n* sailing ship rigged fore-and-aft
SCHOONERS > SCHOONER
SCHORL *n* type of black tourmaline
SCHORLS > SCHORL
SCHOUT *n* council officer in Netherlands
SCHOUTS > SCHOUT
SCHRIK *variant of* > SKRIK
SCHRIKS > SCHRIK
SCHROD *n* young cod
SCHRODS > SCHROD
SCHTICK *same as* > SHTICK
SCHTICKS > SCHTICK
SCHTIK *n* schtick
SCHTIKS > SCHTIK
SCHTOOK *n* trouble
SCHTOOKS > SCHTOOK

SCHTOOM *adj* silent
SCHTUCK *n* trouble
SCHTUCKS > SCHTUCK
SCHUIT *n* Dutch boat with flat bottom
SCHUITS > SCHUIT
SCHUL *same as* > SHUL
SCHULN > SCHUL
SCHULS > SCHUL
SCHUSS *n* straight high-speed downhill run ▷*vb* perform a schuss
SCHUSSED > SCHUSS
SCHUSSER > SCHUSS
SCHUSSERS > SCHUSS
SCHUSSES > SCHUSS
SCHUSSING > SCHUSS
SCHUYT *n* Dutch boat with flat bottom
SCHUYTS > SCHUYT
SCHVARTZE *n* Yiddish word for black person
SCHWA *n* central vowel representing the sound that occurs in unstressed syllables in English
SCHWARTZE *same as* > SCHVARTZE
SCHWAS > SCHWA
SCIAENID *adj* of or relating to a family of mainly tropical and subtropical marine percoid fishes ▷*n* any of these fish
SCIAENIDS > SCIAENID
SCIAENOID *same as* > SCIAENID
SCIAMACHY *n* fight with an imaginary enemy
SCIARID *n* small fly
SCIARIDS > SCIARID
SCIATIC *adj* of the hip ▷*n* sciatic part of the body
SCIATICA *n* severe pain in the large nerve in the back of the leg
SCIATICAL > SCIATICA
SCIATICAS > SCIATICA
SCIATICS > SCIATIC
SCIENCE *n* systematic study and knowledge of natural or physical phenomena
SCIENCED *adj* old word meaning learned
SCIENCES > SCIENCE
SCIENT *adj* old word meaning scientific
SCIENTER *adv* knowingly
SCIENTIAL *adj* of or relating to science
SCIENTISE *same as* > SCIENTIZE
SCIENTISM *n* application of, or belief in, the scientific method
SCIENTIST *n* person who studies or practises a science
SCIENTIZE *vb* treat scientifically
SCILICET *adv* namely
SCILLA *n* a plant with small bell-shaped flowers
SCILLAS > SCILLA
SCIMETAR *n* scimitar
SCIMETARS > SCIMETAR

SCIMITAR *n* curved oriental sword
SCIMITARS > SCIMITAR
SCIMITER *n* scimitar
SCIMITERS > SCIMITER
SCINCOID *adj* of, relating to, or resembling a skink ▷*n* any animal, esp a lizard, resembling a skink
SCINCOIDS > SCINCOID
SCINTILLA *n* very small amount
SCIOLISM *n* practice of opinionating on subjects of which one has only superficial knowledge
SCIOLISMS > SCIOLISM
SCIOLIST > SCIOLISM
SCIOLISTS > SCIOLISM
SCIOLOUS > SCIOLISM
SCIOLTO *adv* musical direction meaning freely
SCIOMACHY *same as* > SCIAMACHY
SCIOMANCY *n* divination with the help of ghosts
SCION *n* descendant or heir
SCIONS > SCION
SCIOPHYTE *n* any plant that grows best in the shade
SCIOSOPHY *n* unscientific system of knowledge
SCIROC *n* hot Mediterranean wind
SCIROCCO *n* hot Mediterranean wind
SCIROCCOS > SCIROCCO
SCIROCS > SCIROC
SCIRRHI > SCIRRHUS
SCIRRHOID > SCIRRHUS
SCIRRHOUS *adj* of or resembling a scirrhus
SCIRRHUS *n* hard cancerous growth composed of fibrous tissues
SCISSEL *n* waste metal left over from sheet metal after discs have been punched out of it
SCISSELS > SCISSEL
SCISSIL *n* scissel
SCISSILE *adj* capable of being cut or divided
SCISSILS > SCISSIL
SCISSION *n* act or an instance of cutting, splitting, or dividing
SCISSIONS > SCISSION
SCISSOR *vb* cut (an object) with scissors
SCISSORED > SCISSOR
SCISSORER > SCISSOR
SCISSORS *pl n* cutting instrument with two crossed pivoted blades
SCISSURE *n* longitudinal cleft
SCISSURES > SCISSURE
SCIURID *n* squirrel or related rodent
SCIURIDS > SCIURID
SCIURINE *adj* relating to a family of rodents that includes squirrels, marmots, and chipmunks ▷*n* any sciurine animal
SCIURINES > SCIURINE

SCIUROID *adj* (of an animal) resembling a squirrel
SCLAFF *vb* cause (the club) to hit (the ground behind the ball) when making a stroke ▷*n* sclaffing stroke or shot
SCLAFFED > SCLAFF
SCLAFFER > SCLAFF
SCLAFFERS > SCLAFF
SCLAFFING > SCLAFF
SCLAFFS > SCLAFF
SCLATE *vb* Scots word meaning slate
SCLATED > SCLATE
SCLATES > SCLATE
SCLATING > SCLATE
SCLAUNDER *n* old form of slander
SCLAVE *n* old form of slave
SCLAVES > SCLAVE
SCLERA *n* tough white substance that forms the outer covering of the eyeball
SCLERAE > SCLERA
SCLERAL > SCLERA
SCLERAS > SCLERA
SCLERE *n* supporting anatomical structure, esp a sponge spicule
SCLEREID *n* type of biological cell
SCLEREIDE *n* type of biological cell
SCLEREIDS > SCLEREID
SCLEREMA *n* condition in which body tissues harden
SCLEREMAS > SCLEREMA
SCLERES > SCLERE
SCLERITE *n* any of the hard chitinous plates that make up the exoskeleton of an arthropod
SCLERITES > SCLERITE
SCLERITIC > SCLERITE
SCLERITIS *n* inflammation of the sclera
SCLEROID *adj* (of organisms and their parts) hard or hardened
SCLEROMA *n* any small area of abnormally hard tissue, esp in a mucous membrane
SCLEROMAS > SCLEROMA
SCLEROSAL > SCLEROSIS
SCLEROSE *vb* affect with sclerosis
SCLEROSED *adj* hardened
SCLEROSES > SCLEROSIS
SCLEROSIS *n* abnormal hardening of body tissues
SCLEROTAL *n* bony area in sclerotic
SCLEROTIA *pl n* masses of hyphae formed in certain fungi
SCLEROTIC *same as* > SCLERA
SCLEROTIN *n* protein in the cuticle of insects that becomes hard and dark
SCLEROUS *adj* hard
SCLIFF *n* Scots word for small piece
SCLIFFS > SCLIFF
SCLIM *vb* Scots word

Section 1: Words between 2 and 9 letters in length

meaning climb
SCLIMMED > SCLIM
SCLIMMING > SCLIM
SCLIMS > SCLIM
SCODIER > SCODY
SCODIEST > SCODY
SCODY *adj* unkempt
SCOFF *vb* express derision
▷ *n* mocking expression
SCOFFED > SCOFF
SCOFFER > SCOFF
SCOFFERS > SCOFF
SCOFFING > SCOFF
SCOFFINGS > SCOFF
SCOFFLAW *n* person who
habitually flouts or violates
the law
SCOFFLAWS > SCOFFLAW
SCOFFS > SCOFF
SCOG *vb* shelter
SCOGGED > SCOG
SCOGGING > SCOG
SCOGS > SCOG
SCOINSON *n* part of door or
window frame
SCOINSONS > SCOINSON
SCOLD *vb* find fault with,
reprimand ▷ *n* person who
scolds
SCOLDABLE > SCOLD
SCOLDED > SCOLD
SCOLDER > SCOLD
SCOLDERS > SCOLD
SCOLDING > SCOLD
SCOLDINGS > SCOLD
SCOLDS > SCOLD
SCOLECES > SCOLEX
SCOLECID *n* variety of
worm
SCOLECIDS > SCOLECID
SCOLECITE *n* white zeolite
mineral
SCOLECOID *adj* like scolex
SCOLEX *n* headlike part of a
tapeworm
SCOLIA > SCOLION
SCOLICES > SCOLEX
SCOLIOMA *n* condition with
abnormal curvature of
spine
SCOLIOMAS > SCOLIOMA
SCOLION *n* ancient Greek
drinking song
SCOLIOSES > SCOLIOSIS
SCOLIOSIS *n* abnormal
lateral curvature of the
spine
SCOLIOTIC > SCOLIOSIS
SCOLLOP *variant*
of > SCALLOP
SCOLLOPED > SCOLLOP
SCOLLOPS > SCOLLOP
SCOLYTID *n* type of beetle
SCOLYTIDS > SCOLYTID
SCOLYTOID *n* type of beetle
SCOMBRID *n* fish of mackerel
family
SCOMBRIDS > SCOMBRID
SCOMBROID *adj* relating to a
suborder of marine spiny-
finned fishes ▷ *n* any fish
belonging to this suborder
SCOMFISH *vb* Scots word
meaning stifle
SCONCE *n* bracket on a wall
for holding candles or lights
▷ *vb* challenge (a fellow

student) on the grounds
of a social misdemeanour
to drink a large quantity of
beer without stopping
SCONCED > SCONCE
SCONCES > SCONCE
SCONCHEON *n* part of door or
window frame
SCONCING > SCONCE
SCONE *n* small plain cake
baked in an oven or on a
griddle
SCONES > SCONE
SCONTION *n* part of door or
window frame
SCONTIONS > SCONTION
SCOOBIES > SCOOBY
SCOOBY *n* clue; notion
SCOOCH *vb* compress one's
body into smaller space
SCOOCHED > SCOOCH
SCOOCHES > SCOOCH
SCOOCHING > SCOOCH
SCOOG *vb* shelter
SCOOGED > SCOOG
SCOOGING > SCOOG
SCOOGS > SCOOG
SCOOP *n* shovel-like tool for
ladling or hollowing out
▷ *vb* take up or hollow out
with or as if with a scoop
SCOOPABLE > SCOOP
SCOOPED > SCOOP
SCOOPER > SCOOP
SCOOPERS > SCOOP
SCOOPFUL > SCOOP
SCOOPFULS > SCOOP
SCOOPING > SCOOP
SCOOPINGS > SCOOP
SCOOPS > SCOOP
SCOOPSFUL > SCOOP
SCOOSH *vb* squirt ▷ *n* squirt
or rush of liquid
SCOOSHED > SCOOSH
SCOOSHES > SCOOSH
SCOOSHING > SCOOSH
SCOOT *vb* leave or move
quickly ▷ *n* act of scooting
SCOOTCH *same as* > SCOOCH
SCOOTCHED > SCOOTCH
SCOOTCHES > SCOOTCH
SCOOTED > SCOOT
SCOOTER *n* child's vehicle
propelled by pushing on
the ground with one foot
SCOOTERS > SCOOTER
SCOOTING > SCOOT
SCOOTS > SCOOT
SCOP *n* (in Anglo-Saxon
England) a bard or minstrel
SCOPA *n* tuft of hairs on the
abdomen or hind legs of
bees, used for collecting
pollen
SCOPAE > SCOPA
SCOPAS > SCOPA
SCOPATE *adj* having tuft
SCOPE *n* opportunity for
using abilities ▷ *vb* look at
or examine carefully
SCOPED > SCOPE
SCOPELID *n* deep-sea fish
SCOPELIDS > SCOPELID
SCOPELOID *n* deep-sea fish
SCOPES > SCOPE
SCOPING > SCOPE
SCOPOLINE *n* soluble

crystalline alkaloid
SCOPS > SCOP
SCOPULA *n* small tuft of
dense hairs on the legs and
chelicerae of some spiders
SCOPULAE > SCOPULA
SCOPULAS > SCOPULA
SCOPULATE > SCOPULA
SCORBUTIC *adj* of or having
scurvy
SCORCH *vb* burn on the
surface ▷ *n* slight burn
SCORCHED > SCORCH
SCORCHER *n* very hot day
SCORCHERS > SCORCHER
SCORCHES > SCORCH
SCORCHING > SCORCH
SCORDATO *adj* musical term
meaning out of tune
SCORE *n* points gained in a
game or competition ▷ *vb*
gain (points) in a game
SCORECARD *n* card on which
scores are recorded in
games such as golf
SCORED > SCORE
SCORELESS *adj* without
anyone scoring
SCORELINE *n* final score in
game
SCOREPAD *n* pad for
recording score in game
SCOREPADS > SCOREPAD
SCORER > SCORE
SCORERS > SCORE
SCORES > SCORE
SCORIA *n* mass of solidified
lava containing many
cavities
SCORIAC > SCORIA
SCORIAE > SCORIA
SCORIFIED > SCORIFY
SCORIFIER > SCORIFY
SCORIFIES > SCORIFY
SCORIFY *vb* remove
(impurities) from metals by
forming scoria
SCORING *n* act or practice of
scoring
SCORINGS > SCORING
SCORIOUS > SCORIA
SCORN *n* open contempt
▷ *vb* despise
SCORNED > SCORN
SCORNER > SCORN
SCORNERS > SCORN
SCORNFUL > SCORN
SCORNING > SCORN
SCORNINGS > SCORN
SCORNS > SCORN
SCORODITE *n* mineral
containing iron and
aluminium
SCORPER *n* kind of fine
chisel with a square or
curved tip
SCORPERS > SCORPER
SCORPIOID *adj* of, relating
to, or resembling scorpions
SCORPION *n* small lobster-
shaped animal with a sting
at the end of a jointed tail
SCORPIONS > SCORPION
SCORRENDO *adj* musical
term meaning gliding
SCORSE *vb* exchange
SCORSED > SCORSE

SCORSER > SCORSE
SCORSERS > SCORSE
SCORSES > SCORSE
SCORSING > SCORSE
SCOT *n* payment or tax
SCOTCH *vb* put an end to
▷ *n* gash
SCOTCHED > SCOTCH
SCOTCHES > SCOTCH
SCOTCHING > SCOTCH
SCOTER *n* type of sea duck
SCOTERS > SCOTER
SCOTIA *n* deep concave
moulding
SCOTIAS > SCOTIA
SCOTOMA *n* blind spot
SCOTOMAS > SCOTOMA
SCOTOMATA > SCOTOMA
SCOTOMIA *n* dizziness
SCOTOMIAS > SCOTOMIA
SCOTOMIES > SCOTOMY
SCOTOMY *n* dizziness
SCOTOPHIL *adj* liking
darkness
SCOTOPIA *n* ability of the
eye to adjust for night
vision
SCOTOPIAS > SCOTOPIA
SCOTOPIC > SCOTOPIA
SCOTS > SCOT
SCOTTIE *n* type of small
sturdy terrier
SCOTTIES > SCOTTIE
SCOUG *vb* shelter
SCOUGED > SCOUG
SCOUGING > SCOUG
SCOUGS > SCOUG
SCOUNDREL *n* cheat or
deceiver
SCOUP *vb* Scots word
meaning jump
SCOUPED > SCOUP
SCOUPING > SCOUP
SCOUPS > SCOUP
SCOUR *vb* clean or polish by
rubbing with something
rough ▷ *n* scouring
SCOURED > SCOUR
SCOURER > SCOUR
SCOURERS > SCOUR
SCOURGE *n* person or thing
causing severe suffering
▷ *vb* cause severe suffering
to
SCOURGED > SCOURGE
SCOURGER > SCOURGE
SCOURGERS > SCOURGE
SCOURGES > SCOURGE
SCOURGING > SCOURGE
SCOURIE *n* young seagull
SCOURIES > SCOURIE
SCOURING > SCOUR
SCOURINGS *pl n* residue left
after cleaning grain
SCOURS > SCOUR
SCOURSE *vb* exchange
SCOURSED > SCOURSE
SCOURSES > SCOURSE
SCOURSING > SCOURSE
SCOUSE *n* stew made from
left-over meat
SCOUSER *n* inhabitant of
Liverpool
SCOUSERS > SCOUSER
SCOUSES > SCOUSE
SCOUT *n* person sent out to
reconnoitre ▷ *vb* act as a

scout
SCOUTED > SCOUT
SCOUTER > SCOUT
SCOUTERS > SCOUT
SCOUTH n Scots word meaning plenty of scope
SCOUTHER vb Scots word meaning scorch
SCOUTHERS > SCOUTHER
SCOUTHERY > SCOUTHER
SCOUTHS > SCOUTH
SCOUTING > SCOUT
SCOUTINGS > SCOUT
SCOUTS > SCOUT
SCOW n unpowered barge used for carrying freight ▷ vb transport by scow
SCOWDER vb Scots word meaning scorch
SCOWDERED > SCOWDER
SCOWDERS > SCOWDER
SCOWED > SCOW
SCOWING > SCOW
SCOWL n (have) an angry or sullen expression ▷ vb have an angry or bad-tempered facial expression
SCOWLED > SCOWL
SCOWLER n person who scowls
SCOWLERS > SCOWLER
SCOWLING > SCOWL
SCOWLS > SCOWL
SCOWP vb Scots word meaning jump
SCOWPED > SCOWP
SCOWPING > SCOWP
SCOWPS > SCOWP
SCOWRER n old word meaning hooligan
SCOWRERS > SCOWRER
SCOWRIE n young seagull
SCOWRIES > SCOWRIE
SCOWS > SCOW
SCOWTH n Scots word meaning plenty of scope
SCOWTHER vb Scots word meaning scorch
SCOWTHERS > SCOWTHER
SCOWTHS > SCOWTH
SCOZZA n rowdy person, esp one who drinks a lot of alcohol
SCOZZAS > SCOZZA
SCRAB vb scratch
SCRABBED > SCRAB
SCRABBING > SCRAB
SCRABBLE vb scrape at with the hands, feet, or claws ▷ n board game in which words are formed by letter tiles
SCRABBLED > SCRABBLE
SCRABBLER > SCRABBLE
SCRABBLES > SCRABBLE
SCRABBLY adj covered with stunted trees
SCRABS > SCRAB
SCRAE Scots word for > SCREE
SCRAES > SCRAE
SCRAG n thin end of a neck of mutton ▷ vb wring the neck of
SCRAGGED > SCRAG
SCRAGGIER > SCRAGGY
SCRAGGILY > SCRAGGY
SCRAGGING > SCRAG

SCRAGGLY adj untidy or irregular
SCRAGGY adj thin, bony
SCRAGS > SCRAG
SCRAICH vb Scots word meaning scream
SCRAICHED > SCRAICH
SCRAICHS > SCRAICH
SCRAIGH vb Scots word meaning scream
SCRAIGHED > SCRAIGH
SCRAIGHS > SCRAIGH
SCRAM vb go away quickly ▷ n emergency shutdown of a nuclear reactor
SCRAMB vb scratch with nails or claws
SCRAMBED > SCRAMB
SCRAMBING > SCRAMB
SCRAMBLE vb climb or crawl hastily or awkwardly ▷ n scrambling
SCRAMBLED > SCRAMBLE
SCRAMBLER n electronic device that makes transmitted speech unintelligible
SCRAMBLES > SCRAMBLE
SCRAMBS > SCRAMB
SCRAMJET n type of jet engine
SCRAMJETS > SCRAMJET
SCRAMMED > SCRAM
SCRAMMING > SCRAM
SCRAMS > SCRAM
SCRAN n food
SCRANCH vb crunch
SCRANCHED > SCRANCH
SCRANCHES > SCRANCH
SCRANNEL adj thin ▷ n thin person or thing
SCRANNELS > SCRANNEL
SCRANNIER > SCRANNY
SCRANNY adj scrawny
SCRANS > SCRAN
SCRAP n small piece ▷ vb discard as useless
SCRAPABLE > SCRAPE
SCRAPBOOK n book with blank pages in which newspaper cuttings or pictures are stuck
SCRAPE vb rub with something rough or sharp ▷ n act or sound of scraping
SCRAPED > SCRAPE
SCRAPEGUT n old word for fiddle player
SCRAPER > SCRAPE
SCRAPERS > SCRAPE
SCRAPES > SCRAPE
SCRAPHEAP n pile of discarded material
SCRAPIE n disease of sheep and goats
SCRAPIES > SCRAPIE
SCRAPING n act of scraping
SCRAPINGS > SCRAPING
SCRAPPAGE n act of scrapping
SCRAPPED > SCRAP
SCRAPPER n person who scraps
SCRAPPERS > SCRAPPER
SCRAPPIER > SCRAPPY
SCRAPPILY > SCRAPPY

SCRAPPING > SCRAP
SCRAPPLE n scraps of pork cooked with cornmeal and formed into a loaf
SCRAPPLES > SCRAPPLE
SCRAPPY adj fragmentary, disjointed
SCRAPS > SCRAP
SCRAPYARD n place for scrap metal
SCRAT vb scratch
SCRATCH vb mark or cut with claws, nails, or anything rough or sharp ▷ n wound, mark, or sound made by scratching ▷ adj put together at short notice
SCRATCHED > SCRATCH
SCRATCHER n person, animal, or thing that scratches
SCRATCHES n disease of horses characterized by dermatitis in the region of the fetlock
SCRATCHIE n scratchcard
SCRATCHY > SCRATCH
SCRATS > SCRAT
SCRATTED > SCRAT
SCRATTING > SCRAT
SCRATTLE vb dialect word meaning scratch
SCRATTLED > SCRATTLE
SCRATTLES > SCRATTLE
SCRAUCH vb squawk
SCRAUCHED > SCRAUCH
SCRAUCHS > SCRAUCH
SCRAUGH vb squawk
SCRAUGHED > SCRAUGH
SCRAUGHS > SCRAUGH
SCRAW n sod from the surface of a peat bog or from a field
SCRAWL vb write carelessly or hastily ▷ n scribbled writing
SCRAWLED > SCRAWL
SCRAWLER > SCRAWL
SCRAWLERS > SCRAWL
SCRAWLIER > SCRAWL
SCRAWLING > SCRAWL
SCRAWLS > SCRAWL
SCRAWLY > SCRAWL
SCRAWM vb dialect word meaning scratch
SCRAWMED > SCRAWM
SCRAWMING > SCRAWM
SCRAWMS > SCRAWM
SCRAWNIER > SCRAWNY
SCRAWNILY > SCRAWNY
SCRAWNY adj thin and bony
SCRAWP vb scratch (the skin) to relieve itching
SCRAWPED > SCRAWP
SCRAWPING > SCRAWP
SCRAWPS > SCRAWP
SCRAWS > SCRAW
SCRAY n tern
SCRAYE n tern
SCRAYES > SCRAYE
SCRAYS > SCRAY
SCREAK vb screech or creak ▷ n screech or creak
SCREAKED > SCREAK
SCREAKIER > SCREAK
SCREAKING > SCREAK

SCREAKS > SCREAK
SCREAKY > SCREAK
SCREAM vb utter a piercing cry, esp of fear or pain ▷ n shrill piercing cry
SCREAMED > SCREAM
SCREAMER n person or thing that screams
SCREAMERS > SCREAMER
SCREAMING > SCREAM
SCREAMS > SCREAM
SCREE n slope of loose shifting stones
SCREECH n (utter) a shrill cry ▷ vb utter a shrill cry
SCREECHED > SCREECH
SCREECHER > SCREECH
SCREECHES > SCREECH
SCREECHY adj loud and shrill
SCREED n long tedious piece of writing ▷ vb rip
SCREEDED > SCREED
SCREEDER > SCREED
SCREEDERS > SCREED
SCREEDING > SCREED
SCREEDS > SCREED
SCREEN n surface of a television set, VDU, etc, on which an image is formed ▷ vb shelter or conceal with or as if with a screen
SCREENED > SCREEN
SCREENER > SCREEN
SCREENERS > SCREEN
SCREENFUL > SCREEN
SCREENIE n informal Australian word for screensaver
SCREENIES > SCREENIE
SCREENING > SCREEN
SCREENS > SCREEN
SCREES > SCREE
SCREET vb shed tears ▷ n act or sound of crying
SCREETED > SCREET
SCREETING > SCREET
SCREETS > SCREET
SCREEVE vb write
SCREEVED > SCREEVE
SCREEVER > SCREEVE
SCREEVERS > SCREEVE
SCREEVES > SCREEVE
SCREEVING > SCREEVE
SCREICH same as > SCREIGH
SCREICHED > SCREICH
SCREICHS > SCREICH
SCREIGH Scot word for > SCREECH
SCREIGHED > SCREIGH
SCREIGHS > SCREIGH
SCREW n metal pin with a spiral ridge along its length, twisted into materials to fasten them together ▷ vb turn (a screw)
SCREWABLE > SCREW
SCREWBALL n odd or eccentric person ▷ adj crazy or eccentric
SCREWBEAN n variety of mesquite
SCREWED adj fastened by a screw or screws
SCREWER > SCREW
SCREWERS > SCREW
SCREWIER > SCREWY

SCREWIEST > SCREWY
SCREWING > SCREW
SCREWINGS > SCREW
SCREWLIKE > SCREW
SCREWS > SCREW
SCREWTOP *n* lid with a threaded rim that is turned to close it securely
SCREWTOPS > SCREWTOP
SCREWUP *n* something done badly
SCREWUPS > SCREWUP
SCREWWORM *n* larva of a fly that develops beneath the skin of living mammals often causing illness or death
SCREWY *adj* crazy or eccentric
SCRIBABLE > SCRIBE
SCRIBAL > SCRIBE
SCRIBBLE *vb* write hastily or illegibly ▷ *n* something scribbled
SCRIBBLED > SCRIBBLE
SCRIBBLER *n* often derogatory term for a writer of poetry, novels, journalism, etc
SCRIBBLES > SCRIBBLE
SCRIBBLY > SCRIBBLE
SCRIBE *n* person who copies documents ▷ *vb* to score a line with a pointed instrument
SCRIBED > SCRIBE
SCRIBER *n* pointed steel tool used to score materials as a guide to cutting, etc
SCRIBERS > SCRIBER
SCRIBES > SCRIBE
SCRIBING > SCRIBE
SCRIBINGS > SCRIBE
SCRIBISM > SCRIBE
SCRIBISMS > SCRIBE
SCRIECH *vb* Scots word meaning screech
SCRIECHED > SCRIECH
SCRIECHS > SCRIECH
SCRIED > SCRY
SCRIENE *n* old form of screen
SCRIENES > SCRIENE
SCRIES > SCRY
SCRIEVE *vb* Scots word meaning write
SCRIEVED > SCRIEVE
SCRIEVES > SCRIEVE
SCRIEVING > SCRIEVE
SCRIGGLE *vb* wriggle
SCRIGGLED > SCRIGGLE
SCRIGGLES > SCRIGGLE
SCRIGGLY > SCRIGGLE
SCRIKE *vb* old word meaning shriek
SCRIKED > SCRIKE
SCRIKES > SCRIKE
SCRIKING > SCRIKE
SCRIM *n* open-weave muslin or hessian fabric, used in upholstery, lining, building
SCRIMMAGE *n* rough or disorderly struggle ▷ *vb* engage in a scrimmage
SCRIMP *vb* be very economical

SCRIMPED > SCRIMP
SCRIMPER > SCRIMP
SCRIMPERS > SCRIMP
SCRIMPIER > SCRIMP
SCRIMPILY > SCRIMP
SCRIMPING > SCRIMP
SCRIMPIT *adj* Scots word meaning ungenerous
SCRIMPLY *adv* sparingly
SCRIMPS > SCRIMP
SCRIMPY > SCRIMP
SCRIMS > SCRIM
SCRIMSHAW *n* art of decorating or carving shells, etc, done by sailors as a leisure activity ▷ *vb* produce scrimshaw (from)
SCRIMURE *old word for* > FENCER
SCRIMURES > SCRIMURE
SCRINE *n* old form of shrine
SCRINES > SCRINE
SCRIP *n* certificate representing a claim to stocks or shares
SCRIPPAGE *n* contents of scrip
SCRIPS > SCRIP
SCRIPT *n* text of a film, play, or TV programme ▷ *vb* write a script for
SCRIPTED > SCRIPT
SCRIPTER *n* person who writes scripts for films, play, or television dramas
SCRIPTERS > SCRIPTER
SCRIPTING > SCRIPT
SCRIPTORY *adj* of writing
SCRIPTS > SCRIPT
SCRIPTURE *n* sacred writings of a religion
SCRITCH *vb* screech
SCRITCHED > SCRITCH
SCRITCHES > SCRITCH
SCRIVE *Scots word for* > WRITE
SCRIVED > SCRIVE
SCRIVENER *n* person who writes out deeds, letters, etc
SCRIVES > SCRIVE
SCRIVING > SCRIVE
SCROBE *n* groove
SCROBES > SCROBE
SCROD *n* young cod or haddock, esp one split and prepared for cooking
SCRODDLED *adj* made of scraps of pottery
SCRODS > SCROD
SCROFULA *n* tuberculosis of the lymphatic glands
SCROFULAS > SCROFULA
SCROG *n* Scots word meaning small tree
SCROGGIE *adj* having scrogs upon it
SCROGGIER > SCROGGIE
SCROGGIN *n* mixture of nuts and dried fruits
SCROGGINS > SCROGGIN
SCROGGY *variant of* > SCROGGIE
SCROGS > SCROG
SCROLL *n* roll of parchment or paper ▷ *vb* move (text) up or down on a VDU

screen
SCROLLED > SCROLL
SCROLLING > SCROLL
SCROLLS > SCROLL
SCROME *vb* crawl or climb, esp using the hands to aid movement
SCROMED > SCROME
SCROMES > SCROME
SCROMING > SCROME
SCROOCH *vb* scratch (the skin) to relieve itching
SCROOCHED > SCROOCH
SCROOCHES > SCROOCH
SCROOGE *variant of* > SCROUGE
SCROOGED > SCROOGE
SCROOGES > SCROOGE
SCROOGING > SCROOGE
SCROOP *vb* emit a grating or creaking sound ▷ *n* such a sound
SCROOPED > SCROOP
SCROOPING > SCROOP
SCROOPS > SCROOP
SCROOTCH *vb* hunch up
SCRORP *n* deep scratch or weal
SCRORPS > SCRORP
SCROTA > SCROTUM
SCROTAL > SCROTUM
SCROTE *n* slang derogatory word meaning a worthless fellow
SCROTES > SCROTE
SCROTUM *n* pouch of skin containing the testicles
SCROTUMS > SCROTUM
SCROUGE *vb* crowd or press
SCROUGED > SCROUGE
SCROUGER *n* American word meaning whopper
SCROUGERS > SCROUGER
SCROUGES > SCROUGE
SCROUGING > SCROUGE
SCROUNGE *vb* get by cadging or begging
SCROUNGED > SCROUNGE
SCROUNGER > SCROUNGE
SCROUNGES > SCROUNGE
SCROUNGY *adj* shabby
SCROW *n* scroll
SCROWDGE *vb* squeeze
SCROWDGED > SCROWDGE
SCROWDGES > SCROWDGE
SCROWL *vb* old form of scroll
SCROWLE *vb* old form of scroll
SCROWLED > SCROWL
SCROWLES > SCROWLE
SCROWLING > SCROWL
SCROWLS > SCROWL
SCROWS > SCROW
SCROYLE *n* old word meaning wretch
SCROYLES > SCROYLE
SCRUB *vb* clean by rubbing, often with a hard brush and water ▷ *n* scrubbing ▷ *adj* stunted or inferior
SCRUBBED > SCRUB
SCRUBBER *n* woman who has many sexual partners
SCRUBBERS > SCRUBBER
SCRUBBIER > SCRUBBY
SCRUBBILY > SCRUBBY
SCRUBBING > SCRUB

SCRUBBY *adj* covered with scrub
SCRUBLAND *n* area of scrub vegetation
SCRUBS > SCRUB
SCRUFF *same as* > SCUM
SCRUFFIER > SCRUFFY
SCRUFFILY > SCRUFFY
SCRUFFS > SCRUFF
SCRUFFY *adj* unkempt or shabby
SCRUM *n* restarting of play in which opposing packs of forwards push against each other to gain possession of the ball ▷ *vb* form a scrum
SCRUMDOWN *n* forming of scrum in rugby
SCRUMMAGE *same as* > SCRUM
SCRUMMED > SCRUM
SCRUMMIE *n* informal word for a scrum half
SCRUMMIER > SCRUMMY
SCRUMMIES > SCRUMMIE
SCRUMMING > SCRUM
SCRUMMY *adj* delicious
SCRUMP *vb* steal (apples) from an orchard or garden
SCRUMPED > SCRUMP
SCRUMPIES > SCRUMPY
SCRUMPING > SCRUMP
SCRUMPLE *vb* crumple or crush
SCRUMPLED > SCRUMPLE
SCRUMPLES > SCRUMPLE
SCRUMPOX *n* skin infection spread among players in scrum
SCRUMPS > SCRUMP
SCRUMPY *n* rough dry cider
SCRUMS > SCRUM
SCRUNCH *vb* crumple or crunch or be crumpled or crunched ▷ *n* act or sound of scrunching
SCRUNCHED > SCRUNCH
SCRUNCHES > SCRUNCH
SCRUNCHIE *n* loop of elastic covered loosely with fabric, used to hold the hair in a ponytail
SCRUNCHY *adj* crunchy
SCRUNT *n* Scots word meaning stunted thing
SCRUNTIER > SCRUNT
SCRUNTS > SCRUNT
SCRUNTY > SCRUNT
SCRUPLE *n* doubt produced by one's conscience or morals ▷ *vb* have doubts on moral grounds
SCRUPLED > SCRUPLE
SCRUPLER > SCRUPLE
SCRUPLERS > SCRUPLE
SCRUPLES > SCRUPLE
SCRUPLING > SCRUPLE
SCRUTABLE *adj* open to or able to be understood by scrutiny
SCRUTATOR *n* person who examines or scrutinizes
SCRUTINY *n* close examination
SCRUTO *n* trapdoor on stage
SCRUTOIRE *n* writing desk

S

SCRUTOS > SCRUTO
SCRUZE vb old word meaning squeeze
SCRUZED > SCRUZE
SCRUZES > SCRUZE
SCRUZING > SCRUZE
SCRY vb divine, esp by crystal gazing
SCRYDE > SCRY
SCRYER > SCRY
SCRYERS > SCRY
SCRYING > SCRY
SCRYINGS > SCRY
SCRYNE n old form of shrine
SCRYNES > SCRYNE
SCUBA n apparatus used in skin diving, consisting of cylinders containing compressed air attached to a breathing apparatus ▷vb dive using scuba equipment
SCUBAED > SCUBA
SCUBAING > SCUBA
SCUBAS > SCUBA
SCUCHIN n old form of scutcheon
SCUCHINS > SCUCHIN
SCUD vb move along swiftly ▷n act of scudding
SCUDDALER n Scots word meaning leader of festivities
SCUDDED > SCUD
SCUDDER > SCUD
SCUDDERS > SCUD
SCUDDING > SCUD
SCUDDLE vb scuttle
SCUDDLED > SCUDDLE
SCUDDLES > SCUDDLE
SCUDDLING > SCUDDLE
SCUDI > SCUDO
SCUDLER n Scots word meaning leader of festivities
SCUDLERS > SCUDLER
SCUDO n any of several former Italian coins
SCUDS > SCUD
SCUFF vb drag (the feet) while walking ▷n mark caused by scuffing
SCUFFED > SCUFF
SCUFFER n type of sandal
SCUFFERS > SCUFFER
SCUFFING > SCUFF
SCUFFLE vb fight in a disorderly manner ▷n disorderly struggle
SCUFFLED > SCUFFLE
SCUFFLER > SCUFFLE
SCUFFLERS > SCUFFLE
SCUFFLES > SCUFFLE
SCUFFLING > SCUFFLE
SCUFFS > SCUFF
SCUFT n dialect word meaning nape of neck
SCUFTS > SCUFT
SCUG vb shelter
SCUGGED > SCUG
SCUGGING > SCUG
SCUGS > SCUG
SCUL n old form of school
SCULCH n rubbish
SCULCHES > SCULCH
SCULK vb old form of skulk
SCULKED > SCULK

SCULKER > SCULK
SCULKERS > SCULK
SCULKING > SCULK
SCULKS > SCULK
SCULL n small oar ▷vb row (a boat) using sculls
SCULLE n old form of school
SCULLED > SCULL
SCULLER > SCULL
SCULLERS > SCULL
SCULLERY n small room where washing-up and other kitchen work is done
SCULLES > SCULLE
SCULLING > SCULL
SCULLINGS > SCULL
SCULLION n servant employed to do the hard work in a kitchen
SCULLIONS > SCULLION
SCULLS > SCULL
SCULP variant of > SCULPTURE
SCULPED > SCULP
SCULPIN n any of various fishes of the family Cottidae
SCULPING > SCULP
SCULPINS > SCULPIN
SCULPS > SCULP
SCULPSIT (he or she) sculptured it: used formerly on sculptures next to a sculptor's name
SCULPT same as > SCULPTURE
SCULPTED > SCULPT
SCULPTING > SCULPT
SCULPTOR n person who makes sculptures
SCULPTORS > SCULPTOR
SCULPTS > SCULPT
SCULPTURE n art of making figures or designs in wood, stone, etc ▷vb represent in sculpture
SCULS > SCUL
SCULTCH same as > SCULCH
SCULTCHES > SCULTCH
SCUM n impure or waste matter on the surface of a liquid ▷vb remove scum from
SCUMBAG n offensive or despicable person
SCUMBAGS > SCUMBAG
SCUMBER vb old word meaning defecate
SCUMBERED > SCUMBER
SCUMBERS > SCUMBER
SCUMBLE vb soften or blend (an outline or colour) with a thin upper coat of opaque colour ▷n upper layer of colour applied in this way
SCUMBLED > SCUMBLE
SCUMBLES > SCUMBLE
SCUMBLING > SCUMBLE
SCUMFISH vb Scots word meaning disgust
SCUMLESS > SCUM
SCUMLIKE > SCUM
SCUMMED > SCUM
SCUMMER > SCUM
SCUMMERS > SCUM
SCUMMIER > SCUMMY
SCUMMIEST > SCUMMY
SCUMMILY > SCUMMY

SCUMMING > SCUM
SCUMMINGS > SCUM
SCUMMY adj of, resembling, consisting of, or covered with scum
SCUMS > SCUM
SCUNCHEON n inner part of a door jamb or window frame
SCUNDERED adj Irish dialect word for embarrassed
SCUNGE vb borrow ▷n dirty or worthless person
SCUNGED > SCUNGE
SCUNGES > SCUNGE
SCUNGIER > SCUNGY
SCUNGIEST > SCUNGY
SCUNGILLI n seafood dish of conch
SCUNGING > SCUNGE
SCUNGY adj sordid or dirty
SCUNNER vb feel aversion ▷n strong aversion
SCUNNERED adj annoyed, discontented, or bored
SCUNNERS > SCUNNER
SCUP n common sparid fish of American coastal regions of the Atlantic
SCUPPAUG n sea fish
SCUPPAUGS > SCUPPAUG
SCUPPER vb defeat or ruin ▷n drain in the side of a ship
SCUPPERED > SCUPPER
SCUPPERS > SCUPPER
SCUPS > SCUP
SCUR n small unattached growth of horn at the site of a normal horn in cattle
SCURF n flaky skin on the scalp
SCURFIER > SCURF
SCURFIEST > SCURF
SCURFS > SCURF
SCURFY > SCURF
SCURRED > SCUR
SCURRIED > SCURRY
SCURRIER n old word meaning scout
SCURRIERS > SCURRIER
SCURRIES > SCURRY
SCURRIL adj old word meaning vulgar
SCURRILE adj old word meaning vulgar
SCURRING > SCUR
SCURRIOUR n old word meaning scout
SCURRY vb move hastily ▷n act or sound of scurrying
SCURRYING > SCURRY
SCURS > SCUR
SCURVIER > SCURVY
SCURVIES > SCURVY
SCURVIEST > SCURVY
SCURVILY > SCURVY
SCURVY n disease caused by lack of vitamin C ▷adj mean and despicable
SCUSE shortened form of > EXCUSE
SCUSED > SCUSE
SCUSES > SCUSE
SCUSING > SCUSE
SCUT n short tail of the hare, rabbit, or deer

SCUTA > SCUTUM
SCUTAGE n payment sometimes exacted by a lord from his vassal in lieu of military service
SCUTAGES > SCUTAGE
SCUTAL > SCUTE
SCUTATE adj (of animals) having or covered with large bony or horny plates
SCUTATION > SCUTATE
SCUTCH vb separate the fibres from the woody part of (flax) by pounding ▷n tool used for this
SCUTCHED > SCUTCH
SCUTCHEON same as > SHIELD
SCUTCHER same as > SCUTCH
SCUTCHERS > SCUTCHER
SCUTCHES > SCUTCH
SCUTCHING > SCUTCH
SCUTE n horny or chitinous plate that makes up part of the exoskeleton in armadillos, etc
SCUTELLA > SCUTELLUM
SCUTELLAR > SCUTELLUM
SCUTELLUM n last of three plates into which the notum of an insect's thorax is divided
SCUTES > SCUTE
SCUTIFORM adj (esp of plant parts) shaped like a shield
SCUTIGER n species of centipede
SCUTIGERS > SCUTIGER
SCUTS > SCUT
SCUTTER informal word for > SCURRY
SCUTTERED > SCUTTER
SCUTTERS > SCUTTER
SCUTTLE n fireside container for coal ▷vb run with short quick steps
SCUTTLED > SCUTTLE
SCUTTLER > SCUTTLE
SCUTTLERS > SCUTTLE
SCUTTLES > SCUTTLE
SCUTTLING > SCUTTLE
SCUTUM n middle of three plates into which the notum of an insect's thorax is divided
SCUTWORK n menial or dull work
SCUTWORKS > SCUTWORK
SCUZZ n dirt
SCUZZBALL n despicable person
SCUZZES > SCUZZ
SCUZZIER > SCUZZY
SCUZZIEST > SCUZZY
SCUZZY adj unkempt, dirty, or squalid
SCYBALA > SCYBALUM
SCYBALOUS > SCYBALUM
SCYBALUM n hard faeces in stomach
SCYE n Scots word meaning sleeve-hole
SCYES > SCYE
SCYPHATE adj shaped like cup
SCYPHI > SCYPHUS
SCYPHUS n ancient Greek

two-handled drinking cup without a footed base

SCYTALE *n* coded message in ancient Sparta

SCYTALES > SCYTALE

SCYTHE *n* long-handled tool with a curved blade for cutting grass ▷ *vb* cut with a scythe

SCYTHED > SCYTHE

SCYTHEMAN *n* scythe user

SCYTHEMEN > SCYTHEMAN

SCYTHER > SCYTHE

SCYTHERS > SCYTHE

SCYTHES > SCYTHE

SCYTHING > SCYTHE

SDAINE *vb* old form of disdain

SDAINED > SDAINE

SDAINES > SDAINE

SDAINING > SDAINE

SDAYN *vb* old form of disdain

SDAYNED > SDAYN

SDAYNING > SDAYN

SDAYNS > SDAYN

SDEIGN *vb* old form of disdain

SDEIGNE *vb* old form of disdain

SDEIGNED > SDEIGN

SDEIGNES > SDEIGNE

SDEIGNING > SDEIGN

SDEIGNS > SDEIGN

SDEIN *vb* old form of disdain

SDEINED > SDEIN

SDEINING > SDEIN

SDEINS > SDEIN

SEA *n* mass of salt water covering three quarters of the earth's surface

SEABAG *n* canvas bag for holding a sailor's belongings

SEABAGS > SEABAG

SEABANK *n* sea shore

SEABANKS > SEABANK

SEABEACH *n* beach at seaside

SEABED *n* bottom of sea

SEABEDS > SEABED

SEABIRD *n* bird that lives on the sea

SEABIRDS > SEABIRD

SEABLITE *n* prostrate annual plant of the goosefoot family

SEABLITES > SEABLITE

SEABOARD *n* coast

SEABOARDS > SEABOARD

SEABOOT *n* sailor's waterproof boot

SEABOOTS > SEABOOT

SEABORNE *adj* carried on or by the sea

SEABOTTLE *n* type of seaweed

SEACOAST *n* land bordering on the sea

SEACOASTS > SEACOAST

SEACOCK *n* valve in the hull of a vessel below the water line for admitting sea water or for pumping out bilge water

SEACOCKS > SEACOCK

SEACRAFT *n* skill as sailor

SEACRAFTS > SEACRAFT

SEACUNNY *n* quartermaster on Indian ship

SEADOG *another word for* > FOGBOW

SEADOGS > SEADOG

SEADROME *n* aerodrome floating on sea

SEADROMES > SEADROME

SEAFARER *n* traveller who goes by sea

SEAFARERS > SEAFARER

SEAFARING *adj* working or travelling by sea ▷ *n* act of travelling by sea

SEAFLOOR *n* bottom of the sea

SEAFLOORS > SEAFLOOR

SEAFOLK *n* people who sail sea

SEAFOLKS > SEAFOLK

SEAFOOD *n* edible saltwater fish or shellfish

SEAFOODS > SEAFOOD

SEAFOWL *n* seabird

SEAFOWLS > SEAFOWL

SEAFRONT *n* built-up area facing the sea

SEAFRONTS > SEAFRONT

SEAGIRT *adj* surrounded by the sea

SEAGOING *adj* built for travelling on the sea

SEAGULL *n* gull

SEAGULLS > SEAGULL

SEAHAWK *n* skua

SEAHAWKS > SEAHAWK

SEAHOG *n* porpoise

SEAHOGS > SEAHOG

SEAHORSE *n* marine fish with a horselike head that swims upright

SEAHORSES > SEAHORSE

SEAHOUND *n* dogfish

SEAHOUNDS > SEAHOUND

SEAKALE *n* European coastal plant

SEAKALES > SEAKALE

SEAL *n* piece of wax, lead, etc with a special design impressed upon it, attached to a letter or document as a mark of authentication ▷ *vb* close with or as if with a seal

SEALABLE > SEAL

SEALANT *n* any substance used for sealing

SEALANTS > SEALANT

SEALCH *Scots word for* > SEAL

SEALCHS > SEALCH

SEALED *adj* (of a road) having a hard surface

SEALER *n* person or thing that seals

SEALERIES > SEALERY

SEALERS > SEALER

SEALERY *n* occupation of hunting seals

SEALGH *Scots word for* > SEAL

SEALGHS > SEALGH

SEALIFT *vb* transport by ship

SEALIFTED > SEALIFT

SEALIFTS > SEALIFT

SEALINE *n* company running regular sailings

SEALINES > SEALINE

SEALING > SEAL

SEALINGS > SEAL

SEALLIKE *adj* resembling a seal

SEALPOINT *n* popular variety of Siamese cat

SEALS > SEAL

SEALSKIN *n* skin or prepared fur of a seal, used to make coats

SEALSKINS > SEALSKIN

SEALWAX *n* sealing wax

SEALWAXES > SEALWAX

SEALYHAM *n* type of short-legged terrier

SEALYHAMS > SEALYHAM

SEAM *n* line where two edges are joined, as by stitching ▷ *vb* mark with furrows or wrinkles

SEAMAID *n* mermaid

SEAMAIDS > SEAMAID

SEAMAN *n* sailor

SEAMANLY > SEAMAN

SEAMARK *n* aid to navigation, such as a conspicuous object on a shore used as a guide

SEAMARKS > SEAMARK

SEAME *n* old word meaning grease

SEAMED > SEAM

SEAMEN > SEAMAN

SEAMER *n* fast bowler who makes the ball bounce on its seam so that it will change direction

SEAMERS > SEAMER

SEAMES > SEAME

SEAMIER > SEAMY

SEAMIEST > SEAMY

SEAMINESS > SEAMY

SEAMING > SEAM

SEAMLESS *adj* (of a garment) without seams

SEAMLIKE > SEAM

SEAMOUNT *n* submarine mountain rising more than 1000 metres above the surrounding ocean floor

SEAMOUNTS > SEAMOUNT

SEAMS > SEAM

SEAMSET *n* tool for flattening seams in metal

SEAMSETS > SEAMSET

SEAMSTER *n* person who sews

SEAMSTERS > SEAMSTER

SEAMY *adj* sordid

SEAN *vb* fish with seine net

SEANCE *n* meeting at which spiritualists attempt to communicate with the dead

SEANCES > SEANCE

SEANED > SEAN

SEANING > SEAN

SEANS > SEAN

SEAPIECE *n* artwork depicting sea

SEAPIECES > SEAPIECE

SEAPLANE *n* aircraft designed to take off from and land on water

SEAPLANES > SEAPLANE

SEAPORT *n* town or city with a harbour for boats

and ships

SEAPORTS > SEAPORT

SEAQUAKE *n* agitation and disturbance of the sea caused by an earthquake at the sea bed

SEAQUAKES > SEAQUAKE

SEAQUARIA *pl n* areas of salt water where sea animals are kept

SEAR *vb* scorch, burn the surface of ▷ *n* mark caused by searing ▷ *adj* dried up

SEARAT *n* pirate

SEARATS > SEARAT

SEARCE *vb* sift

SEARCED > SEARCE

SEARCES > SEARCE

SEARCH *vb* examine closely in order to find something ▷ *n* searching

SEARCHED > SEARCH

SEARCHER > SEARCH

SEARCHERS > SEARCH

SEARCHES > SEARCH

SEARCHING *adj* keen or thorough

SEARCING > SEARCE

SEARE *adj* old word meaning dry and withered

SEARED > SEAR

SEARER > SEAR

SEAREST > SEAR

SEARING > SEAR

SEARINGLY > SEAR

SEARINGS > SEAR

SEARNESS > SEAR

SEAROBIN *n* type of American gurnard

SEAROBINS > SEAROBIN

SEARS > SEAR

SEAS > SEA

SEASCAPE *n* picture of a scene at sea

SEASCAPES > SEASCAPE

SEASCOUT *n* member of seagoing scouts

SEASCOUTS > SEASCOUT

SEASE *vb* old form of seize

SEASED > SEASE

SEASES > SEASE

SEASHELL *n* empty shell of a mollusc

SEASHELLS > SEASHELL

SEASHORE *n* land bordering on the sea

SEASHORES > SEASHORE

SEASICK *adj* suffering from nausea caused by the motion of a ship

SEASICKER > SEASICK

SEASIDE *n* area, esp a holiday resort, on the coast

SEASIDES > SEASIDE

SEASING > SEASE

SEASON *n* one of four divisions of the year, each of which has characteristic weather conditions ▷ *vb* flavour with salt, herbs, etc

SEASONAL *adj* depending on or varying with the seasons ▷ *n* seasonal thing

SEASONALS > SEASONAL

SEASONED > SEASON

SEASONER > SEASON

SEASONERS > SEASON

SEASONING n salt, herbs, etc added to food to enhance flavour
SEASONS > SEASON
SEASPEAK n language used by sailors
SEASPEAKS > SEASPEAK
SEASTRAND n seashore
SEASURE n old form of seizure
SEASURES > SEASURE
SEAT n thing designed or used for sitting on ▷ vb cause to sit
SEATBACK n back of seat
SEATBACKS > SEATBACK
SEATBELT n safety belt in vehicle
SEATBELTS > SEATBELT
SEATED > SEAT
SEATER n person or thing that seats
SEATERS > SEATER
SEATING n supply or arrangement of seats ▷ adj of or relating to the provision of places to sit
SEATINGS > SEATING
SEATLESS > SEAT
SEATMATE n person sitting in next seat
SEATMATES > SEATMATE
SEATRAIN n ship that can carry train
SEATRAINS > SEATRAIN
SEATROUT n trout living in the sea
SEATROUTS > SEATROUT
SEATS > SEAT
SEATWORK n school work done at pupils' desks
SEATWORKS > SEATWORK
SEAWALL n wall built to prevent encroachment or erosion by the sea
SEAWALLS > SEAWALL
SEAWAN n shell beads, usually unstrung, used by certain North American Indians as money
SEAWANS > SEAWAN
SEAWANT n Native American name for silver coins
SEAWANTS > SEAWANT
SEAWARD same as > SEAWARDS
SEAWARDLY > SEAWARD
SEAWARDS adv towards the sea
SEAWARE n any of numerous large coarse seaweeds
SEAWARES > SEAWARE
SEAWATER n water from sea
SEAWATERS > SEAWATER
SEAWAY n waterway giving access to an inland port, navigable by ocean-going ships
SEAWAYS > SEAWAY
SEAWEED n plant growing in the sea
SEAWEEDS > SEAWEED
SEAWIFE n variety of sea fish
SEAWIVES > SEAWIFE
SEAWOMAN n mermaid
SEAWOMEN > SEAWOMAN

SEAWORM n marine worm
SEAWORMS > SEAWORM
SEAWORTHY adj (of a ship) in fit condition for a sea voyage
SEAZE vb old form of seize
SEAZED > SEAZE
SEAZES > SEAZE
SEAZING > SEAZE
SEBACEOUS adj of, like, or secreting fat or oil
SEBACIC adj derived from sebacic acid, a white crystalline acid
SEBASIC same as > SEBACIC
SEBATE n salt of sebacic acid
SEBATES > SEBATE
SEBESTEN n Asian tree
SEBESTENS > SEBESTEN
SEBIFIC adj producing fat
SEBORRHEA n skin disease in which excessive oil is secreted
SEBUM n oily substance secreted by the sebaceous glands
SEBUMS > SEBUM
SEBUNDIES > SEBUNDY
SEBUNDY n irregular soldier in India
SEC same as > SECANT
SECALOSE n type of sugar
SECALOSES > SECALOSE
SECANT n (in trigonometry) the ratio of the length of the hypotenuse to the length of the adjacent side in a right-angled triangle
SECANTLY > SECANT
SECANTS > SECANT
SECATEUR n secateurs
SECATEURS pl n small pruning shears
SECCO n wall painting done on dried plaster with tempera or pigments ground in limewater
SECCOS > SECCO
SECEDE vb withdraw formally from a political alliance or federation
SECEDED > SECEDE
SECEDER > SECEDE
SECEDERS > SECEDE
SECEDES > SECEDE
SECEDING > SECEDE
SECERN vb (of a gland or follicle) to secrete
SECERNED > SECERN
SECERNENT > SECERN
SECERNING > SECERN
SECERNS > SECERN
SECESH n secessionist in US Civil War
SECESHER n secessionist in US Civil War
SECESHERS > SECESHER
SECESHES > SECESH
SECESSION n act of seceding
SECH n hyperbolic secant
SECHS > SECH
SECKEL variant of > SECKLE
SECKELS > SECKEL
SECKLE n type of pear
SECKLES > SECKLE

SECLUDE vb keep (a person) from contact with others
SECLUDED adj private, sheltered
SECLUDES > SECLUDE
SECLUDING > SECLUDE
SECLUSION n state of being secluded
SECLUSIVE adj tending to seclude
SECO adj (of wine) dry
SECODONT n animal with cutting back teeth
SECODONTS > SECODONT
SECONAL n tradename for secobarbitol
SECONALS > SECONAL
SECOND adj coming directly after the first ▷ n person or thing coming second ▷ vb express formal support for (a motion proposed in a meeting)
SECONDARY adj of less importance ▷ n person or thing that is secondary
SECONDE n second of eight positions from which a parry or attack can be made in fencing
SECONDED > SECOND
SECONDEE n person who is seconded
SECONDEES > SECONDEE
SECONDER > SECOND
SECONDERS > SECOND
SECONDES > SECONDE
SECONDI > SECONDO
SECONDING > SECOND
SECONDLY same as > SECOND
SECONDO n left-hand part in a piano duet
SECONDS > SECOND
SECPAR n distance unit in astronomy
SECPARS > SECPAR
SECRECIES > SECRECY
SECRECY n state of being secret
SECRET adj kept from the knowledge of others ▷ n something kept secret
SECRETA n secretions
SECRETAGE n use of mercury in treating furs
SECRETARY n person who deals with correspondence and general clerical work
SECRETE vb (of an organ, gland, etc) produce and release (a substance)
SECRETED > SECRETE
SECRETER > SECRET
SECRETES > SECRETE
SECRETEST > SECRET
SECRETIN n peptic hormone secreted by the mucosae of the duodenum and jejunum
SECRETING > SECRETE
SECRETINS > SECRETIN
SECRETION n substance that is released from a cell, organ, or gland
SECRETIVE adj inclined to keep things secret
SECRETLY > SECRET

SECRETOR > SECRETE
SECRETORS > SECRETE
SECRETORY adj of, relating to, or producing a secretion
SECRETS > SECRET
SECS > SEC
SECT n often disparaging term for a subdivision of a religious or political group, esp one with extreme beliefs
SECTARIAL > SECT
SECTARIAN adj of a sect ▷ n member of a sect
SECTARIES > SECTARY
SECTARY n member of a sect
SECTATOR n member of sect
SECTATORS > SECTATOR
SECTILE adj able to be cut smoothly
SECTILITY > SECTILE
SECTION n part cut off ▷ vb cut or divide into sections
SECTIONAL adj concerned with a particular area or group within a country or community
SECTIONED > SECTION
SECTIONS > SECTION
SECTOR n part or subdivision ▷ vb divide into sectors
SECTORAL > SECTOR
SECTORED > SECTOR
SECTORIAL adj of or relating to a sector
SECTORING > SECTOR
SECTORISE same as > SECTORIZE
SECTORIZE vb split into sectors
SECTORS > SECTOR
SECTS > SECT
SECULAR adj worldly, as opposed to sacred ▷ n member of the secular clergy
SECULARLY > SECULAR
SECULARS > SECULAR
SECULUM n age in astronomy
SECULUMS > SECULUM
SECUND adj having or designating parts arranged on or turned to one side of the axis
SECUNDINE n one of the two integuments surrounding the ovule of a plant
SECUNDLY > SECUND
SECUNDUM adj according to
SECURABLE > SECURE
SECURANCE > SECURE
SECURE adj free from danger ▷ vb obtain
SECURED > SECURE
SECURELY > SECURE
SECURER > SECURE
SECURERS > SECURE
SECURES > SECURE
SECUREST > SECURE
SECURING > SECURE
SECURITAN n person believing they are secure
SECURITY n precautions against theft, espionage,

or other danger

SED *old spelling of* > SAID

SEDAN *same as* > SALOON

SEDANS > SEDAN

SEDARIM > SEDER

SEDATE *adj* calm and dignified ▷ *vb* give a sedative drug to

SEDATED > SEDATE

SEDATELY > SEDATE

SEDATER > SEDATE

SEDATES > SEDATE

SEDATEST > SEDATE

SEDATING > SEDATE

SEDATION *n* state of calm, esp when brought about by sedatives

SEDATIONS > SEDATION

SEDATIVE *adj* having a soothing or calming effect ▷ *n* sedative drug

SEDATIVES > SEDATIVE

SEDENT *adj* seated

SEDENTARY *adj* done sitting down, involving little exercise

SEDER *n* Jewish ceremonial meal held on the first night or first two nights of Passover

SEDERS > SEDER

SEDERUNT *n* sitting of an ecclesiastical assembly, court, etc

SEDERUNTS > SEDERUNT

SEDES *Latin word for* > SEAT

SEDGE *n* coarse grasslike plant growing on wet ground

SEDGED *adj* having sedge

SEDGELAND *n* land covered with sedge

SEDGES > SEDGE

SEDGIER > SEDGE

SEDGIEST > SEDGE

SEDGY > SEDGE

SEDILE *n* seat for clergy in church

SEDILIA *n* group of three seats where the celebrant and ministers sit at certain points during High Mass

SEDILIUM *n* seat for clergy in church

SEDIMENT *n* matter which settles to the bottom of a liquid

SEDIMENTS > SEDIMENT

SEDITION *n* speech or action encouraging rebellion against the government

SEDITIONS > SEDITION

SEDITIOUS *adj* of, like, or causing sedition

SEDUCE *vb* persuade into sexual intercourse

SEDUCED > SEDUCE

SEDUCER *n* person who entices, allures, or seduces

SEDUCERS > SEDUCER

SEDUCES > SEDUCE

SEDUCIBLE > SEDUCE

SEDUCING > SEDUCE

SEDUCINGS > SEDUCE

SEDUCIVE *adj* seductive

SEDUCTION *n* act of

seducing or the state of being seduced

SEDUCTIVE *adj* (of a woman) sexually attractive

SEDUCTOR *n* person who seduces

SEDUCTORS > SEDUCTOR

SEDULITY > SEDULOUS

SEDULOUS *adj* diligent or persevering

SEDUM *n* rock plant

SEDUMS > SEDUM

SEE *vb* perceive with the eyes or mind ▷ *n* diocese of a bishop

SEEABLE > SEE

SEECATCH *n* male seal in Aleutians

SEED *n* mature fertilized grain of a plant ▷ *vb* sow with seed

SEEDBED *n* area of soil prepared for the growing of seedlings before they are transplanted

SEEDBEDS > SEEDBED

SEEDBOX *n* part of plant that contains seeds

SEEDBOXES > SEEDBED

SEEDCAKE *n* sweet cake flavoured with caraway seeds and lemon rind or essence

SEEDCAKES > SEEDCAKE

SEEDCASE *n* part of a fruit enclosing the seeds

SEEDCASES > SEEDCASE

SEEDEATER *n* bird feeding on seeds

SEEDED > SEED

SEEDER *n* person or thing that seeds

SEEDERS > SEEDER

SEEDIER > SEEDY

SEEDIEST > SEEDY

SEEDILY > SEEDY

SEEDINESS > SEEDY

SEEDING > SEED

SEEDINGS > SEED

SEEDLESS > SEED

SEEDLIKE > SEED

SEEDLING *n* young plant raised from a seed

SEEDLINGS > SEEDLING

SEEDLIP *n* basket holding seeds to be sown

SEEDLIPS > SEEDLIP

SEEDMAN *n* seller of seeds

SEEDMEN > SEEDMAN

SEEDNESS *n* old word meaning sowing of seeds

SEEDPOD *n* carpel enclosing the seeds of a flowering plant

SEEDPODS > SEEDPOD

SEEDS > SEED

SEEDSMAN *n* seller of seeds

SEEDSMEN > SEEDSMAN

SEEDSTOCK *n* livestock used for breeding

SEEDTIME *n* season when seeds are sown

SEEDTIMES > SEEDTIME

SEEDY *adj* shabby

SEEING > SEE

SEEINGS > SEE

SEEK *vb* try to find or obtain

SEEKER > SEEK

SEEKERS > SEEK

SEEKING > SEEK

SEEKS > SEEK

SEEL *vb* sew up the eyelids of (a hawk or falcon) so as to render it quiet and tame

SEELD *adj* old word meaning rare

SEELED > SEEL

SEELIE *pl n* good benevolent fairies

SEELIER > SEELY

SEELIEST > SEELY

SEELING > SEEL

SEELINGS > SEEL

SEELS > SEEL

SEELY *adj* old word meaning happy

SEEM *vb* appear to be

SEEMED > SEEM

SEEMER > SEEM

SEEMERS > SEEM

SEEMING *adj* apparent but not real ▷ *n* outward or false appearance

SEEMINGLY *adv* in appearance but not necessarily in actuality

SEEMINGS > SEEMING

SEEMLESS *adj* old word meaning unseemly

SEEMLIER > SEEMLY

SEEMLIEST > SEEMLY

SEEMLIHED *n* old word meaning seemliness

SEEMLY *adj* proper or fitting ▷ *adv* properly or decorously

SEEMLYHED *n* old word meaning seemliness

SEEMS > SEEM

SEEN > SEE

SEEP *vb* trickle through slowly, ooze ▷ *n* small spring or place where water, oil, etc, has oozed through the ground

SEEPAGE *n* act or process of seeping

SEEPAGES > SEEPAGE

SEEPED > SEEP

SEEPIER > SEEPY

SEEPIEST > SEEPY

SEEPING > SEEP

SEEPS > SEEP

SEEPY *adj* tending to seep

SEER *n* person who sees

SEERESS > SEER

SEERESSES > SEER

SEERS > SEER

SEES > SEE

SEESAW *n* plank balanced in the middle so that two people seated on either end ride up and down alternately ▷ *vb* move up and down

SEESAWED > SEESAW

SEESAWING > SEESAW

SEESAWS > SEESAW

SEETHE *vb* be very agitated ▷ *n* act or state of seething

SEETHED > SEETHE

SEETHER > SEETHE

SEETHERS > SEETHE

SEETHES > SEETHE

SEETHING *adj* boiling or foaming as if boiling

SEETHINGS > SEETHING

SEEWING *n* suing

SEFER *n* scrolls of the Law

SEG *n* metal stud on shoe sole

SEGAR *n* cigar

SEGARS > SEGAR

SEGETAL *adj* (of weeds) growing amongst crops

SEGGAR *n* box in which pottery is baked

SEGGARS > SEGGAR

SEGHOL *n* pronunciation mark in Hebrew

SEGHOLATE *n* vowel sound in Hebrew

SEGHOLS > SEGHOL

SEGMENT *n* one of several sections into which something may be divided ▷ *vb* divide into segments

SEGMENTAL *adj* of, like, or having the form of a segment

SEGMENTED > SEGMENT

SEGMENTS > SEGMENT

SEGNI > SEGNO

SEGNO *n* sign at the beginning or end of a section directed to be repeated

SEGNOS > SEGNO

SEGO *n* American variety of lily

SEGOL *variant of* > SEGHOL

SEGOLATE *variant of* > SEGHOLATE

SEGOLATES > SEGOLATE

SEGOLS > SEGOL

SEGOS > SEGO

SEGREANT *adj* having raised wings in heraldry

SEGREGANT *n* organism different because of segregation

SEGREGATE *vb* set apart

SEGS > SEG

SEGUE *vb* proceed from one section or piece of music to another without a break ▷ *n* practice or an instance of playing music in this way

SEGUED > SEGUE

SEGUEING > SEGUE

SEGUES > SEGUE

SEI *n* type of rorqual

SEICENTO *n* 17th century with reference to Italian art and literature

SEICENTOS > SEICENTO

SEICHE *n* periodic oscillation of the surface of an enclosed or semienclosed body of water

SEICHES > SEICHE

SEIDEL *n* vessel for drinking beer

SEIDELS > SEIDEL

SEIF *n* long ridge of blown sand in a desert

SEIFS > SEIF

SEIGNEUR *n* feudal lord

SEIGNEURS > SEIGNEUR

SEIGNEURY *n* estate of a

seigneur

SEIGNIOR *n* (in England) the lord of a seigniory

SEIGNIORS > SEIGNIOR

SEIGNIORY *n* (in England) the fee or manor of a seignior

SEIGNORAL *adj* relating to the quality of being a lord

SEIGNORY *n* lordship

SEIK *Scot word for* > SICK

SEIKER > SEIK

SEIKEST > SEIK

SEIL *vb* dialect word meaning strain

SEILED > SEIL

SEILING > SEIL

SEILS > SEIL

SEINE *n* large fishing net that hangs vertically from floats ▷ *vb* catch (fish) using this net

SEINED > SEINE

SEINER > SEINE

SEINERS > SEINE

SEINES > SEINE

SEINING > SEINE

SEININGS > SEINE

SEIR *n* fish of Indian seas

SEIRS > SEIR

SEIS > SEI

SEISABLE > SEISE

SEISE *vb* put into legal possession of (property, etc)

SEISED > SEISE

SEISER > SEISE

SEISERS > SEISE

SEISES > SEISE

SEISIN *n* feudal possession of an estate in land

SEISING > SEISE

SEISINGS > SEISE

SEISINS > SEISIN

SEISM *n* earthquake

SEISMAL *adj* of earthquakes

SEISMIC *adj* relating to earthquakes

SEISMICAL *same as* > SEISMIC

SEISMISM *n* occurrence of earthquakes

SEISMISMS > SEISMISM

SEISMS > SEISM

SEISOR *n* person who takes seisin

SEISORS > SEISOR

SEISURE *n* act of seisin

SEISURES > SEISURE

SEITAN *same as* > SEITEN

SEITANS > SEITAN

SEITEN *n* gluten from wheat

SEITENS > SEITEN

SEITIES > SEITY

SEITY *n* selfhood

SEIZABLE > SEIZE

SEIZE *vb* take hold of forcibly or quickly

SEIZED > SEIZE

SEIZER > SEIZE

SEIZERS > SEIZE

SEIZES > SEIZE

SEIZIN *same as* > SEISIN

SEIZING *n* binding used for holding together two ropes, two spars, etc, esp

by lashing with a separate rope

SEIZINGS > SEIZING

SEIZINS > SEIZIN

SEIZOR *n* person who takes seisin

SEIZORS > SEIZOR

SEIZURE *n* sudden violent attack of an illness

SEIZURES > SEIZURE

SEJANT *adj* (of a beast) shown seated

SEJEANT *same as* > SEJANT

SEKOS *n* holy place

SEKOSES > SEKOS

SEKT *n* German sparkling wine

SEKTS > SEKT

SEL *Scot word for* > SELF

SELACHIAN *adj* relating to a large subclass of cartilaginous fishes including the sharks, rays, dogfish, and skates ▷ *n* any fish belonging to this subclass

SELADANG *n* Malaysian tapir

SELADANGS > SELADANG

SELAH *n* Hebrew word of unknown meaning occurring in the Old Testament psalms, and thought to be a musical direction

SELAHS > SELAH

SELAMLIK *n* men's quarters in Turkish house

SELAMLIKS > SELAMLIK

SELCOUTH *adj* old word meaning strange

SELD *adj* old word meaning rare

SELDOM *adv* not often, rarely

SELDOMLY > SELDOM

SELDSEEN *adj* old word meaning seldom seen

SELDSHOWN *adj* old word meaning seldom shown

SELE *n* old word meaning happiness

SELECT *vb* pick out or choose ▷ *adj* chosen in preference to others

SELECTA *n* disc jockey

SELECTAS > SELECTA

SELECTED > SELECT

SELECTEE *n* person who is selected, esp for military service

SELECTEES > SELECTEE

SELECTING > SELECT

SELECTION *n* selecting

SELECTIVE *adj* chosen or choosing carefully

SELECTLY > SELECT

SELECTMAN *n* any of the members of the local boards of most New England towns

SELECTMEN > SELECTMAN

SELECTOR *n* person or thing that selects

SELECTORS > SELECTOR

SELECTS > SELECT

SELENATE *n* any salt or ester formed by replacing one or both of the hydrogens of

selenic acid with metal ions or organic groups

SELENATES > SELENATE

SELENIAN *adj* of the moon

SELENIC *adj* of or containing selenium, esp in the hexavalent state

SELENIDE *n* compound containing selenium

SELENIDES > SELENIDE

SELENIOUS *adj* of or containing selenium in the divalent or tetravalent state

SELENITE *n* colourless glassy variety of gypsum

SELENITES > SELENITE

SELENITIC > SELENITE

SELENIUM *n* nonmetallic element with photoelectric properties

SELENIUMS > SELENIUM

SELENOSES > SELENOSIS

SELENOSIS *n* poisoned condition caused by selenium

SELENOUS *same as* > SELENIOUS

SELES > SELE

SELF *n* distinct individuality or identity of a person or thing ▷ *pron* myself, yourself, himself, or herself ▷ *vb* reproduce by oneself

SELFDOM *n* selfhood

SELFDOMS > SELFDOM

SELFED > SELF

SELFHEAL *n* low-growing European herbaceous plant

SELFHEALS > SELFHEAL

SELFHOOD *n* state of having a distinct identity

SELFHOODS > SELFHOOD

SELFING > SELF

SELFINGS > SELF

SELFISH *adj* caring too much about oneself and not enough about others

SELFISHLY > SELFISH

SELFISM *n* emphasis on self

SELFISMS > SELFISM

SELFIST > SELFISM

SELFISTS > SELFISM

SELFLESS *adj* unselfish

SELFNESS *n* egotism

SELFS > SELF

SELFSAME *adj* very same

SELFWARD *adj* toward self

SELFWARDS *adv* towards self

SELICTAR *n* Turkish sword-bearer

SELICTARS > SELICTAR

SELKIE *same as* > SILKIE

SELKIES > SELKIE

SELL *vb* exchange (something) for money ▷ *n* manner of selling

SELLA *n* area of bone in body

SELLABLE > SELL

SELLAE > SELLA

SELLAS > SELLA

SELLE *n* old word meaning seat

SELLER *n* person who sells

SELLERS > SELLER

SELLES > SELLE

SELLING > SELL

SELLOFF *n* act of selling cheaply

SELLOFFS > SELLOFF

SELLOTAPE *n* tradename for a type of transparent adhesive tape

SELLOUT *n* performance of a show etc for which all the tickets are sold

SELLOUTS > SELLOUT

SELLS > SELL

SELS > SEL

SELSYN *same as* > SYNCHRO

SELSYNS > SELSYN

SELTZER *n* natural effervescent water containing minerals

SELTZERS > SELTZER

SELVA *n* dense equatorial forest characterized by tall broad-leaved evergreen trees, lianas, etc

SELVAGE *n* edge of cloth, woven so as to prevent unravelling ▷ *vb* edge or border

SELVAGED > SELVAGE

SELVAGEE *n* rope used as strap

SELVAGEES > SELVAGEE

SELVAGES > SELVAGE

SELVAGING > SELVAGE

SELVAS > SELVA

SELVEDGE *same as* > SELVAGE

SELVEDGED > SELVEDGE

SELVEDGES > SELVEDGE

SELVES > SELF

SEMAINIER *n* chest of drawers

SEMANTEME *same as* > SEMEME

SEMANTIC *adj* relating to the meaning of words

SEMANTICS *n* study of linguistic meaning

SEMANTIDE *n* type of molecule

SEMANTRA > SEMANTRON

SEMANTRON *n* bar struck instead of bell in Orthodox church

SEMAPHORE *n* system of signalling by holding two flags in different positions to represent letters of the alphabet ▷ *vb* signal (information) by semaphore

SEMATIC *adj* (of the conspicuous coloration of certain animals) acting as a warning, esp to potential predators

SEMBLABLE *adj* resembling or similar ▷ *n* something that resembles another thing

SEMBLABLY > SEMBLABLE

SEMBLANCE *n* outward or superficial appearance

SEMBLANT *n* semblance

SEMBLANTS > SEMBLANT

SEMBLE *vb* seem

SEMBLED > SEMBLE

S

SEMBLES > SEMBLE
SEMBLING > SEMBLE
SEME *adj* dotted (with)
SEMEE *variant of* > SEME
SEMEED *adj* seme
SEMEIA > SEMEION
SEMEION *n* unit of metre in ancient poetry
SEMEIOTIC *same as* > SEMIOTIC
SEMEME *n* meaning of a morpheme
SEMEMES > SEMEME
SEMEMIC > SEMEME
SEMEN *n* sperm-carrying fluid produced by male animals
SEMENS > SEMEN
SEMES > SEME
SEMESTER *n* either of two divisions of the academic year
SEMESTERS > SEMESTER
SEMESTRAL > SEMESTER
SEMI *n* semidetached house
SEMIANGLE *n* half angle
SEMIARID *adj* denoting land that lies on the edges of a desert but has a slightly higher rainfall
SEMIBALD *adj* partly bald
SEMIBOLD *adj* denoting a weight of typeface between medium and bold face ▷*n* semibold type
SEMIBOLDS > SEMIBOLD
SEMIBREVE *n* musical note four beats long
SEMIBULL *n* papal bull issued before coronation
SEMIBULLS > SEMIBULL
SEMICOLON *n* punctuation mark (;)
SEMICOMA *n* condition similar to a coma
SEMICOMAS > SEMICOMA
SEMICURED *adj* partly cured
SEMIDEAF *adj* partly deaf
SEMIDEIFY *vb* treat almost as god
SEMIDOME *n* half-dome, esp one used to cover a semicircular apse
SEMIDOMED *adj* having semidome
SEMIDOMES > SEMIDOME
SEMIDRY *adj* partly dry
SEMIDWARF *adj* smaller than standard variety
SEMIE *n* historical name for a student in second year at a Scottish university
SEMIERECT *adj* partly erect
SEMIES > SEMIE
SEMIFINAL *n* match or round before the final
SEMIFIT *adj* not fully fit
SEMIFLUID *adj* having properties between those of a liquid and those of a solid ▷*n* substance that has such properties because of high viscosity
SEMIGALA *adj* characterized by quite a lot of celebration and fun
SEMIGLOSS *adj* (of paint)

giving finish between matt and gloss
SEMIGROUP *n* type of set in mathematics
SEMIHARD *adj* partly hard
SEMIHIGH *adj* moderately high
SEMIHOBO *n* person looking almost like hobo
SEMIHOBOS > SEMIHOBO
SEMILLON *n* grape used to make wine
SEMILLONS > SEMILLON
SEMILOG *adj* semilogarithmic
SEMILUNAR *adj* shaped like a crescent or half-moon
SEMILUNE *n* half-moon shape
SEMILUNES > SEMILUNE
SEMIMAT *adj* semimatt
SEMIMATT *adj* with surface midway between matt and gloss
SEMIMATTE *adj* semimatt
SEMIMETAL *n* metal not fully malleable
SEMIMICRO *adj* using microwaves
SEMIMILD *adj* somewhat mild
SEMIMOIST *adj* slightly wet
SEMIMUTE *adj* having speech impairment through hearing loss
SEMINA > SEMEN
SEMINAL *adj* original and influential
SEMINALLY > SEMINAL
SEMINAR *n* meeting of a group of students for discussion
SEMINARS > SEMINAR
SEMINARY *n* college for priests
SEMINATE *vb* sow
SEMINATED > SEMINATE
SEMINATES > SEMINATE
SEMINOMA *n* malignant tumour of the testicle
SEMINOMAD *n* person living partly nomadic life
SEMINOMAS > SEMINOMA
SEMINUDE *adj* partly nude
SEMIOLOGY *same as* > SEMIOTICS
SEMIOPEN *adj* half-open
SEMIOSES > SEMIOSIS
SEMIOSIS *n* action involving establishing relationship between signs
SEMIOTIC *adj* relating to signs and symbols, esp spoken or written signs
SEMIOTICS *n* study of human communications, esp signs and symbols
SEMIOVAL *adj* shaped like half of oval
SEMIPED *n* measure in poetic metre
SEMIPEDS > SEMIPED
SEMIPIOUS *adj* quite pious
SEMIPLUME *n* type of bird feather
SEMIPOLAR *as in* *semipolar bond* type of chemical bond

SEMIPRO *n* semiprofessional
SEMIPROS > SEMIPRO
SEMIRAW *adj* not fully cooked or processed
SEMIRIGID *adj* (of an airship) maintaining shape by means of a main supporting keel and internal gas pressure
SEMIROUND *adj* with one flat side and one round side ▷*n* something semiround
SEMIRURAL *adj* partly rural
SEMIS > SEMI
SEMISES > SEMI
SEMISOFT *adj* partly soft
SEMISOLID *adj* having a viscosity and rigidity intermediate between that of a solid and a liquid ▷*n* substance in this state
SEMISOLUS *n* advertisement that appears on the same page as another advertisement but not adjacent to it
SEMISTIFF *adj* partly stiff
SEMISWEET *adj* partly sweet
SEMITAR *old spelling of* > SCIMITAR
SEMITARS > SEMITAR
SEMITAUR *old spelling of* > SCIMITAR
SEMITAURS > SEMITAR
SEMITIST *n* student of Semitic languages and culture
SEMITISTS > SEMITIST
SEMITONAL > SEMITONE
SEMITONE *n* smallest interval between two notes in Western music
SEMITONES > SEMITONE
SEMITONIC > SEMITONE
SEMITRUCK *n* articulated lorry
SEMIURBAN *adj* suburban
SEMIVOCAL *adj* of or relating to a semivowel
SEMIVOWEL *n* vowel-like sound that acts like a consonant, such as the sound *w* in *well*
SEMIWILD *adj* not fully domesticated
SEMIWORKS *adj* equipped to manufacture but not in great numbers
SEMMIT *n* vest
SEMMITS > SEMMIT
SEMOLINA *n* hard grains of wheat left after the milling of flour, used to make puddings and pasta
SEMOLINAS > SEMOLINA
SEMPER *adv* Latin word meaning always
SEMPLE *adj* Scots word meaning simple
SEMPLER > SEMPLE
SEMPLEST > SEMPLE
SEMPLICE *adv* be performed in a simple manner
SEMPRE *adv* (preceding a tempo or dynamic marking) always

SEMPSTER *n* person who sews
SEMPSTERS > SEMPSTER
SEMSEM *n* sesame
SEMSEMS > SEMSEM
SEMUNCIA *n* ancient Roman coin
SEMUNCIAE > SEMUNCIA
SEMUNCIAL > SEMUNCIA
SEMUNCIAS > SEMUNCIA
SEN *n* monetary unit of Brunei, Cambodia, Indonesia, Malaysia, and formerly of Japan
SENA *n* (in India) the army: used in the names of certain paramilitary political organizations
SENARIES > SENARY
SENARII > SENARIUS
SENARIUS *n* type of poem
SENARY *adj* of or relating to the number six
SENAS > SENA
SENATE *n* main governing body at some universities
SENATES > SENATE
SENATOR *n* member of a senate
SENATORS > SENATOR
SEND *vb* cause (a person or thing) to go to or be taken or transmitted to a place
SENDABLE > SEND
SENDAL *n* fine silk fabric used, esp in the Middle Ages, for ceremonial clothing, etc
SENDALS > SENDAL
SENDED *vb* old word meaning sent
SENDER > SEND
SENDERS > SEND
SENDING > SEND
SENDINGS > SEND
SENDOFF *n* demonstration of good wishes at a person's departure ▷*vb* dispatch (something, such as a letter)
SENDOFFS > SENDOFF
SENDS > SEND
SENDUP *n* parody or imitation
SENDUPS > SENDUP
SENE *n* money unit in Samoa
SENECA *variant of* > SENEGA
SENECAS > SENECA
SENECIO *n* any plant of the genus *Senecio*
SENECIOS > SENECIO
SENEGA *n* milkwort plant of the eastern US, with small white flowers
SENEGAS > SENEGA
SENESCENT *adj* growing old
SENESCHAL *n* steward of the household of a medieval prince or nobleman
SENGI *n* African shrew
SENGREEN *n* house leek
SENGREENS > SENGREEN
SENHOR *n* Portuguese term of address for man
SENHORA *n* Portuguese term of address for woman

SENHORAS > SENHORA
SENHORES > SENHOR
SENHORITA n Portuguese term of address for girl
SENHORS > SENHOR
SENILE adj mentally or physically weak because of old age ▷ n senile person
SENILELY > SENILE
SENILES > SENILE
SENILITY > SENILE
SENIOR adj superior in rank or standing ▷ n senior person
SENIORITY n state of being senior
SENIORS > SENIOR
SENITI n money unit in Tonga
SENNA n tropical plant
SENNACHIE n Gaelic storyteller
SENNAS > SENNA
SENNET n fanfare: used as a stage direction in Elizabethan drama
SENNETS > SENNET
SENNIGHT archaic word for > WEEK
SENNIGHTS > SENNIGHT
SENNIT n flat braided cordage used on ships
SENNITS > SENNIT
SENOPIA n short-sightedness in old age
SENOPIAS > SENOPIA
SENOR n Spanish term of address equivalent to sir or Mr
SENORA n Spanish term of address equivalent to madam or Mrs
SENORAS > SENORA
SENORES > SENOR
SENORITA n Spanish term of address equivalent to madam or Miss
SENORITAS > SENORITA
SENORS > SENOR
SENRYU n Japanese short poem
SENS > SEN
SENSA > SENSUM
SENSATE adj perceived by the senses ▷ vb make sensate
SENSATED > SENSATE
SENSATELY > SENSATE
SENSATES > SENSATE
SENSATING > SENSATE
SENSATION n ability to feel things physically
SENSE n any of the faculties of perception or feeling ▷ vb perceive
SENSED > SENSE
SENSEFUL adj full of sense
SENSEI n martial arts teacher
SENSEIS > SENSEI
SENSELESS adj foolish
SENSES > SENSE
SENSI same as > SENSEI
SENSIBLE adj having or showing good sense ▷ n sensible thing or person
SENSIBLER > SENSIBLE

SENSIBLES > SENSIBLE
SENSIBLY > SENSIBLE
SENSILE adj capable of feeling
SENSILLA > SENSILLUM
SENSILLAE > SENSILLUM
SENSILLUM n sense organ in insects
SENSING > SENSE
SENSINGS > SENSE
SENSIS > SENSI
SENSISM n theory that ideas spring from senses
SENSISMS > SENSISM
SENSIST > SENSISM
SENSISTS > SENSISM
SENSITISE same as > SENSITIZE
SENSITIVE adj easily hurt or offended
SENSITIZE vb make sensitive
SENSOR n device that detects or measures the presence of something, such as radiation
SENSORIA > SENSORIUM
SENSORIAL same as > SENSORY
SENSORILY > SENSORY
SENSORIUM n area of the brain considered responsible for receiving and integrating sensations from the outside world
SENSORS > SENSOR
SENSORY adj of the senses or sensation
SENSUAL adj giving pleasure to the body and senses rather than the mind
SENSUALLY > SENSUAL
SENSUM n sensation detached from the information it conveys and also from its source in the external world
SENSUOUS adj pleasing to the senses
SENT n former monetary unit of Estonia
SENTE n money unit in Lesotho
SENTED > SEND
SENTENCE n sequence of words capable of standing alone as a statement, question, or command ▷ vb pass sentence on (a convicted person)
SENTENCED > SENTENCE
SENTENCER > SENTENCE
SENTENCES > SENTENCE
SENTENTIA n opinion
SENTI > SENT
SENTIENCE n state or quality of being sentient
SENTIENCY same as > SENTIENCE
SENTIENT adj capable of feeling ▷ n sentient person or thing
SENTIENTS > SENTIENT
SENTIMENT n thought, opinion, or attitude
SENTIMO n money unit in Philippines

SENTIMOS > SENTIMO
SENTINEL n sentry ▷ vb guard as a sentinel
SENTINELS > SENTINEL
SENTING > SEND
SENTRIES > SENTRY
SENTRY n soldier on watch
SENTS > SENT
SENVIES > SENVY
SENVY n mustard
SENZA prep without
SEPAD vb suppose
SEPADDED > SEPAD
SEPADDING > SEPAD
SEPADS > SEPAD
SEPAL n leaflike division of the calyx of a flower
SEPALED > SEPAL
SEPALINE same as > SEPALOID
SEPALLED > SEPAL
SEPALODY n changing of flower part into sepal
SEPALOID adj (esp of petals) resembling a sepal in structure and function
SEPALOUS adj with sepals
SEPALS > SEPAL
SEPARABLE adj able to be separated
SEPARABLY > SEPARABLE
SEPARATA > SEPARATUM
SEPARATE vb act as a barrier between ▷ adj not the same, different ▷ n item of clothing that only covers half the body
SEPARATED > SEPARATE
SEPARATES > SEPARATE
SEPARATOR n person or thing that separates
SEPARATUM n separate printing of article from magazine
SEPHEN n stingray
SEPHENS > SEPHEN
SEPIA n reddish-brown pigment ▷ adj dark reddish-brown, like the colour of very old photographs
SEPIAS > SEPIA
SEPIC adj of sepia
SEPIMENT n hedge
SEPIMENTS > SEPIMENT
SEPIOLITE n meerschaum
SEPIOST n cuttlefish bone
SEPIOSTS > SEPIOST
SEPIUM n cuttlefish bone
SEPIUMS > SEPIUM
SEPMAG adj designating a film or television programme for which the sound is recorded on separate magnetic material and run in synchronism with the picture
SEPOY n (formerly) Indian soldier in the service of the British
SEPOYS > SEPOY
SEPPUKU n Japanese ritual suicide
SEPPUKUS > SEPPUKU
SEPS n species of lizard
SEPSES > SEPSIS

SEPSIS n poisoning caused by pus-forming bacteria
SEPT n clan, esp in Ireland or Scotland
SEPTA > SEPTUM
SEPTAGE n waste removed from septic tank
SEPTAGES > SEPTAGE
SEPTAL adj of or relating to a septum
SEPTARIA > SEPTARIUM
SEPTARIAN > SEPTARIUM
SEPTARIUM n mass of mineral substance having cracks filled with another mineral
SEPTATE adj divided by septa
SEPTATION n division by partitions
SEPTEMFID adj divided into seven
SEPTEMVIR n member of government of seven men
SEPTENARY adj of or relating to the number seven ▷ n number seven
SEPTENNIA pl n cycles of seven years
SEPTET n group of seven performers
SEPTETS > SEPTET
SEPTETTE same as > SEPTET
SEPTETTES > SEPTETTE
SEPTIC adj (of a wound) infected ▷ n infected wound
SEPTICAL > SEPTIC
SEPTICITY > SEPTIC
SEPTICS > SEPTIC
SEPTIFORM adj acting as partition
SEPTIMAL adj of number seven
SEPTIME n seventh of eight basic positions from which a parry can be made in fencing
SEPTIMES > SEPTIME
SEPTIMOLE n group of seven musical notes
SEPTLEVA n gambling term from old card game
SEPTLEVAS > SEPTLEVA
SEPTS > SEPT
SEPTUM n dividing partition between two cavities in the body
SEPTUMS > SEPTUM
SEPTUOR n group of seven musicians
SEPTUORS > SEPTUOR
SEPTUPLE vb multiply by seven ▷ adj seven times as much or as many ▷ n quantity or number seven times as great as another
SEPTUPLED > SEPTUPLE
SEPTUPLES > SEPTUPLE
SEPTUPLET n group of seven notes played in a time value of six, eight, etc
SEPULCHER same as > SEPULCHRE
SEPULCHRE n tomb or burial vault ▷ vb bury in a sepulchre

SEPULTURE *n* act of placing in a sepulchre

SEQUACITY quality of being pliant or controllable

SEQUEL *n* novel, play, or film that continues the story of an earlier one

SEQUELA *n* any abnormal bodily condition or disease related to or arising from a pre-existing disease

SEQUELAE > SEQUELA

SEQUELISE *same as* > SEQUELIZE

SEQUELIZE *vb* create sequel to

SEQUELS > SEQUEL

SEQUENCE *n* arrangement of two or more things in successive order ▷ *vb* arrange in a sequence

SEQUENCED > SEQUENCE

SEQUENCER *n* electronic device that determines the order in which a number of operations occur

SEQUENCES > SEQUENCE

SEQUENCY *n* number of changes in mathematical list

SEQUENT *adj* following in order or succession ▷ *n* something that follows

SEQUENTLY > SEQUENT

SEQUENTS > SEQUENT

SEQUESTER *vb* seclude

SEQUESTRA *pl n* detached pieces of necrotic bone that often migrate to wounds

SEQUIN *n* small ornamental metal disc on a garment ▷ *vb* apply sequins

SEQUINED > SEQUIN

SEQUINING > SEQUIN

SEQUINNED > SEQUIN

SEQUINS > SEQUIN

SEQUITUR *n* conclusion that follows from the premises

SEQUITURS > SEQUITUR

SEQUOIA *n* giant Californian coniferous tree

SEQUOIAS > SEQUOIA

SER *n* unit of weight used in India, usually taken as one fortieth of a maund

SERA > SERUM

SERAC *n* pinnacle of ice among crevasses on a glacier, usually on a steep slope

SERACS > SERAC

SERAFILE *n* line of soldiers

SERAFILES > SERAFILE

SERAFIN *n* old silver coin of Goa

SERAFINS > SERAFIN

SERAGLIO *n* harem of a Muslim palace

SERAGLIOS > SERAGLIO

SERAI *n* (in the East) a caravanserai or inn

SERAIL *same as* > SERAGLIO

SERAILS > SERAIL

SERAIS > SERAI

SERAL > SERE

SERANG *n* native captain of a crew of sailors in the East

Indies

SERANGS > SERANG

SERAPE *n* blanket-like shawl often of brightly-coloured wool worn by men in Latin America

SERAPES > SERAPE

SERAPH *n* member of the highest order of angels

SERAPHIC *adj* of or resembling a seraph

SERAPHIM > SERAPH

SERAPHIMS > SERAPH

SERAPHIN *n* angel

SERAPHINE *n* old keyboard instrument

SERAPHINS > SERAPHIN

SERAPHS > SERAPH

SERASKIER *n* Turkish military leader

SERDAB *n* secret chamber in an ancient Egyptian tomb

SERDABS > SERDAB

SERE *adj* dried up or withered ▷ *n* series of changes occurring in the ecological succession of a particular community ▷ *vb* sear

SERED > SERE

SEREIN *n* fine rain falling from a clear sky after sunset, esp in the tropics

SEREINS > SEREIN

SERENADE *n* music played or sung to a woman by a lover ▷ *vb* sing or play a serenade to (someone)

SERENADED > SERENADE

SERENADER > SERENADE

SERENADES > SERENADE

SERENATA *n* 18th-century cantata, often dramatic in form

SERENATAS > SERENATA

SERENATE *n* old form of serenade

SERENATES > SERENATE

SERENE *adj* calm, peaceful ▷ *vb* make serene

SERENED > SERENE

SERENELY > SERENE

SERENER > SERENE

SERENES > SERENE

SERENEST > SERENE

SERENING > SERENE

SERENITY *n* state or quality of being serene

SERER > SERE

SERES > SERE

SEREST > SERE

SERF *n* medieval farm labourer who could not leave the land he worked on

SERFAGE > SERF

SERFAGES > SERF

SERFDOM > SERF

SERFDOMS > SERF

SERFHOOD > SERF

SERFHOODS > SERF

SERFISH > SERF

SERFLIKE > SERF

SERFS > SERF

SERFSHIP > SERF

SERFSHIPS > SERF

SERGE *n* strong woollen

fabric

SERGEANCY > SERGEANT

SERGEANT *n* noncommissioned officer in the army

SERGEANTS > SERGEANT

SERGEANTY *n* form of feudal tenure

SERGED *adj* with sewn seam

SERGER *n* sewing machine attachment for finishing seams

SERGERS > SERGER

SERGES > SERGE

SERGING *n* type of sewing

SERGINGS > SERGING

SERIAL *n* story or play produced in successive instalments ▷ *adj* of or forming a series

SERIALISE *same as* > SERIALIZE

SERIALISM *n* musical technique using a sequence of notes in a definite order

SERIALIST *n* writer of serials

SERIALITY > SERIAL

SERIALIZE *vb* publish or present as a serial

SERIALLY > SERIAL

SERIALS > SERIAL

SERIATE *adj* forming a series ▷ *vb* form into a series

SERIATED > SERIATE

SERIATELY > SERIATE

SERIATES > SERIATE

SERIATIM *adv* in a series

SERIATING > SERIATE

SERIATION > SERIATE

SERIC *adj* of silk

SERICEOUS *adj* covered with a layer of small silky hairs

SERICIN *n* gelatinous protein found on the fibres of raw silk

SERICINS > SERICIN

SERICITE *n* type of mica

SERICITES > SERICITE

SERICITIC > SERICITE

SERICON *n* solution used in alchemy

SERICONS > SERICON

SERIEMA *n* either of two cranelike South American birds

SERIEMAS > SERIEMA

SERIES *n* group or succession of related things, usu arranged in order

SERIF *n* small line at the extremities of a main stroke in a type character

SERIFED *adj* having serifs

SERIFFED *adj* having serifs

SERIFS > SERIF

SERIGRAPH *n* colour print made by an adaptation of the silk-screen process

SERIN *n* any of various small yellow-and-brown finches

SERINE *n* sweet-tasting

amino acid

SERINES > SERINE

SERINETTE *n* barrel organ

SERING > SERE

SERINGA *n* any of several trees that yield rubber

SERINGAS > SERINGA

SERINS > SERIN

SERIOUS *adj* giving cause for concern

SERIOUSLY *adv* in a serious manner or to a serious degree

SERIPH *same as* > SERIF

SERIPHS > SERIPH

SERJEANCY *n* rank of sergeant

SERJEANT *same as* > SERGEANT

SERJEANTS > SERJEANT

SERJEANTY *n* type of feudal tenure

SERK *Scots word for* > SHIRT

SERKALI *n* government in Africa

SERKALIS > SERKALI

SERKS > SERK

SERMON *n* speech on a religious or moral subject by a clergyman in a church service ▷ *vb* deliver a sermon

SERMONED > SERMON

SERMONEER *n* preacher

SERMONER *variant of* > SERMONEER

SERMONERS > SERMONER

SERMONET *n* short sermon

SERMONETS > SERMONET

SERMONIC > SERMON

SERMONING > SERMON

SERMONISE *same as* > SERMONIZE

SERMONIZE *vb* make a long moralizing speech

SERMONS > SERMON

SEROLOGIC > SEROLOGY

SEROLOGY *n* science concerned with serums

SERON *n* crate

SERONS > SERON

SEROON *n* crate

SEROONS > SEROON

SEROPUS *n* liquid consisting of serum and pus

SEROPUSES > SEROPUS

SEROSA *n* one of the thin membranes surrounding the embryo in an insect's egg

SEROSAE > SEROSA

SEROSAL > SEROSA

SEROSAS > SEROSA

SEROSITY > SEROUS

SEROTINAL *same as* > SEROTINE

SEROTINE *adj* produced, flowering, or developing late in the season ▷ *n* either of two insectivorous bats

SEROTINES > SEROTINE

SEROTINY *n* state of being serotinous

SEROTONIN *n* compound that occurs in the brain, intestines, and blood

S

platelets and acts as a neurotransmitter

SEROTYPE *n* category into which material, usually a bacterium, is placed based on its serological activity ▷ *vb* class according to serotype

SEROTYPED > SEROTYPE

SEROTYPES > SEROTYPE

SEROUS *adj* of, containing, or like serum

SEROVAR *n* subdivision of species

SEROVARS > SEROVAR

SEROW *n* either of two antelopes of mountainous regions of S and SE Asia

SEROWS > SEROW

SERPENT *n* snake

SERPENTRY *n* serpents

SERPENTS > SERPENT

SERPIGO *n* any progressive skin eruption, such as ringworm or herpes

SERPIGOES > SERPIGO

SERPIGOS > SERPIGO

SERPULA *n* marine worm

SERPULAE > SERPULA

SERPULID *n* marine polychaete worm

SERPULIDS > SERPULID

SERPULITE *n* variety of fossil

SERR *vb* press close together

SERRA *n* sawlike part or organ

SERRAE > SERRA

SERRAN *n* species of fish

SERRANID *n* any of numerous marine fishes including the sea basses, and sea perches ▷ *adj* of or belonging to the family *Serranidae*

SERRANIDS > SERRANID

SERRANO *n* type of Spanish ham

SERRANOID *same as* > SERRANID

SERRANOS > SERRANO

SERRANS > SERRAN

SERRAS > SERRA

SERRATE *adj* (of leaves) having a margin of forward pointing teeth ▷ *vb* make serrate

SERRATED *adj* having a notched or sawlike edge

SERRATES > SERRATE

SERRATI > SERRATUS

SERRATING > SERRATE

SERRATION *n* state or condition of being serrated

SERRATURE *same as* > SERRATION

SERRATUS *n* muscle in thorax

SERRE *vb* press close together

SERRED > SERRE

SERREFILE *n* file of soldiers

SERRES > SERRE

SERRICORN *n* with serrate antennae

SERRIED *adj* in close formation

SERRIEDLY > SERRIED

SERRIES > SERRY

SERRIFORM *adj* resembling a notched or sawlike edge

SERRING > SERRE

SERRS > SERR

SERRULATE *adj* (esp of leaves) minutely serrate

SERRY *vb* close together

SERRYING > SERRY

SERS > SER

SERUEWE *vb* old word meaning survey

SERUEWED > SERUEWE

SERUEWES > SERUEWE

SERUEWING > SERUEWE

SERUM *n* watery fluid left after blood has clotted

SERUMAL > SERUM

SERUMS > SERUM

SERVABLE > SERVE

SERVAL *n* feline African mammal

SERVALS > SERVAL

SERVANT *n* person employed to do household work for another ▷ *vb* work as a servant

SERVANTED > SERVANT

SERVANTRY *n* servants

SERVANTS > SERVANT

SERVE *vb* work for (a person, community, or cause) ▷ *n* act of serving the ball

SERVEABLE > SERVE

SERVED > SERVE

SERVER *n* player who serves in racket games

SERVERIES > SERVERY

SERVERS > SERVER

SERVERY *n* room from which food is served

SERVES > SERVE

SERVEWE *vb* old word meaning survey

SERVEWED > SERVEWE

SERVEWES > SERVEWE

SERVEWING > SERVEWE

SERVICE *n* serving ▷ *adj* serving the public rather than producing goods ▷ *vb* provide a service or services to

SERVICED > SERVICE

SERVICER > SERVICE

SERVICERS > SERVICE

SERVICES > SERVICE

SERVICING > SERVICE

SERVIENT *adj* subordinate

SERVIETTE *n* table napkin

SERVILE *adj* too eager to obey people, fawning ▷ *n* servile person

SERVILELY > SERVILE

SERVILES > SERVILE

SERVILISM *n* condition of being servile

SERVILITY > SERVILE

SERVING *n* portion of food

SERVINGS > SERVING

SERVITOR *n* servant or attendant

SERVITORS > SERVITOR

SERVITUDE *n* bondage or slavery

SERVLET *n* small program that runs on a web server often accessing databases in response to client input

SERVLETS > SERVLET

SERVO *n* servomechanism ▷ *adj* of a servomechanism

SERVOS > SERVO

SERVQUAL *n* provision of high-quality products by an organization backed by a high level of service for consumers

SERVQUALS > SERVQUAL

SESAME *n* plant cultivated for its seeds and oil, which are used in cooking

SESAMES > SESAME

SESAMOID *adj* of or relating to various small bones formed in tendons ▷ *n* sesamoid bone

SESAMOIDS > SESAMOID

SESE *interj* exclamation found in Shakespeare

SESELI *n* garden plant

SESELIS > SESELI

SESEY *interj* exclamation found in Shakespeare

SESH *short for* > SESSION

SESHES > SESH

SESS *n* old word meaning tax

SESSA *interj* exclamation found in Shakespeare

SESSES > SESS

SESSILE *adj* (of flowers or leaves) having no stalk

SESSILITY > SESSILE

SESSION *n* period spent in an activity

SESSIONAL > SESSION

SESSIONS *pl n* sittings or a sitting of justice in court

SESSPOOL *n* cesspool

SESSPOOLS > SESSPOOL

SESTERCE *n* silver or, later, bronze coin of ancient Rome worth a quarter of a denarius

SESTERCES > SESTERCE

SESTERTIA *pl n* ancient Roman money accounts

SESTERTII *pl n* sesterces

SESTET *n* last six lines of a sonnet

SESTETS > SESTET

SESTETT *n* group of six

SESTETTE *n* group of six

SESTETTES > SESTETTE

SESTETTO *n* composition for six musicians

SESTETTOS > SESTETTO

SESTETTS > SESTETT

SESTINA *n* elaborate verse form of Italian origin

SESTINAS > SESTINA

SESTINE *n* poem of six lines

SESTINES > SESTINE

SESTON *n* type of plankton

SESTONS > SESTON

SET *vb* put in a specified position or state ▷ *n* setting or being set ▷ *adj* fixed or established beforehand

SETA *n* (in invertebrates and some plants) any bristle or bristle-like appendage

SETACEOUS > SETA

SETAE > SETA

SETAL > SETA

SETBACK *n* anything that delays progress

SETBACKS > SETBACK

SETENANT *n* pair of postage stamps of different values joined together

SETENANTS > SETENANT

SETIFORM *adj* shaped like a seta

SETLINE *n* any of various types of fishing line

SETLINES > SETLINE

SETNESS > SET

SETNESSES > SET

SETOFF *n* counterbalance

SETOFFS > SETOFF

SETON *n* surgical thread inserted below the skin

SETONS > SETON

SETOSE *adj* covered with setae

SETOUS > SETA

SETOUT *n* beginning or outset

SETOUTS > SETOUT

SETS > SET

SETSCREW *n* screw that fits into the boss or hub of a wheel, and prevents motion of the part relative to the shaft on which it is mounted

SETSCREWS > SETSCREW

SETT *n* badger's burrow

SETTEE *n* couch

SETTEES > SETTEE

SETTER *n* long-haired gun dog ▷ *vb* treat with a piece of setterwort

SETTERED > SETTER

SETTERING > SETTER

SETTERS > SETTER

SETTING > SET

SETTINGS > SET

SETTLE *vb* arrange or put in order ▷ *n* long wooden bench with high back and arms

SETTLED > SETTLE

SETTLER *n* colonist

SETTLERS > SETTLER

SETTLES > SETTLE

SETTLING > SETTLE

SETTLINGS *pl n* any matter or substance that has settled at the bottom of a liquid

SETTLOR *n* person who settles property on someone

SETTLORS > SETTLOR

SETTS > SETT

SETUALE *n* valerian

SETUALES > SETUALE

SETULE *n* small bristle

SETULES > SETULE

SETULOSE > SETULE

SETULOUS > SETULE

SETUP *n* way in which anything is organized or arranged

SETUPS > SETUP

SETWALL *n* valerian

SETWALLS > SETWALL

SEVEN *n* one more than six ▷ *adj* amounting to seven ▷ *determiner* amounting to seven

SEVENFOLD *adj* having seven times as many or as much ▷ *adv* by seven times as many or as much

SEVENS *n* Rugby Union match or series of matches played with seven players on each side

SEVENTEEN *n* ten and seven ▷ *adj* amounting to seventeen ▷ *determiner* amounting to seventeen

SEVENTH *n* (of) number seven in a series ▷ *adj* coming after the sixth and before the eighth ▷ *adv* after the sixth person, position, event, etc

SEVENTHLY *same as* > SEVENTH

SEVENTHS > SEVENTH

SEVENTIES > SEVENTY

SEVENTY *n* ten times seven ▷ *adj* amounting to seventy ▷ *determiner* amounting to seventy

SEVER *vb* cut through or off

SEVERABLE *adj* able to be severed

SEVERAL *adj* some, a few ▷ *n* individual person

SEVERALLY *adv* separately

SEVERALS > SEVERAL

SEVERALTY *n* state of being several or separate

SEVERANCE *n* act of severing or state of being severed

SEVERE *adj* strict or harsh

SEVERED > SEVER

SEVERELY > SEVERE

SEVERER > SEVERE

SEVEREST > SEVERE

SEVERIES > SEVERY

SEVERING > SEVER

SEVERITY > SEVERE

SEVERS > SEVER

SEVERY *n* part of vaulted ceiling

SEVICHE *n* Mexican fish dish

SEVICHES > SEVICHE

SEVRUGA *n* species of sturgeon

SEVRUGAS > SEVRUGA

SEW *vb* join with thread repeatedly passed through with a needle

SEWABLE > SEW

SEWAGE *n* waste matter or excrement carried away in sewers

SEWAGES > SEWAGE

SEWAN *same as* > SEAWAN

SEWANS > SEWAN

SEWAR *n* Asian dagger

SEWARS > SEWAR

SEWED > SEW

SEWEL *n* scarecrow

SEWELLEL *n* mountain beaver

SEWELLELS > SEWELLEL

SEWELS > SEWEL

SEWEN *same as* > SEWIN

SEWENS > SEWEN

SEWER *n* drain to remove waste water and sewage ▷ *vb* provide with sewers

SEWERAGE *n* system of sewers

SEWERAGES > SEWERAGE

SEWERED > SEWER

SEWERING > SEWER

SEWERINGS > SEWER

SEWERLESS > SEWER

SEWERLIKE > SEWER

SEWERS > SEWER

SEWIN *n* sea trout

SEWING > SEW

SEWINGS > SEW

SEWINS > SEWIN

SEWN > SEW

SEWS > SEW

SEX *n* state of being male or female ▷ *vb* find out the sex of ▷ *adj* of sexual matters

SEXAHOLIC *n* person who is addicted to sex

SEXED *adj* having a specified degree of sexuality

SEXENNIAL *adj* occurring once every six years or over a period of six years ▷ *n* sixth anniversary

SEXER *n* person checking sex of chickens

SEXERCISE *n* sexual activity, regarded as a way of keeping fit

SEXERS > SEXER

SEXES > SEX

SEXFID *adj* split into six

SEXFOIL *n* flower with six petals or leaves

SEXFOILS > SEXFOIL

SEXIER > SEXY

SEXIEST > SEXY

SEXILY > SEXY

SEXINESS > SEXY

SEXING > SEX

SEXISM *n* discrimination on the basis of a person's sex

SEXISMS > SEXISM

SEXIST > SEXISM

SEXISTS > SEXISM

SEXLESS *adj* neither male nor female

SEXLESSLY > SEXLESS

SEXLINKED *adj* (of a gene) found on a sex chromosome

SEXOLOGIC > SEXOLOGY

SEXOLOGY *n* study of sexual behaviour in human beings

SEXPERT *n* person who professes a knowledge of sexual matters

SEXPERTS > SEXPERT

SEXPOT *n* person, esp a young woman, considered as being sexually very attractive

SEXPOTS > SEXPOT

SEXT *n* fourth of the seven canonical hours of the divine office or the prayers prescribed for it: originally the sixth hour of the day (noon)

SEXTAIN *same as* > SESTINA

SEXTAINS > SEXTAIN

SEXTAN *adj* (of a fever) marked by paroxysms that recur after an interval of five days

SEXTANS *n* Roman coin

SEXTANSES > SEXTANS

SEXTANT *n* navigator's instrument for measuring angles to calculate one's position

SEXTANTAL > SEXTANT

SEXTANTS > SEXTANT

SEXTARII > SEXTARIUS

SEXTARIUS *n* ancient Roman quantity measure

SEXTET *n* group of six performers

SEXTETS > SEXTET

SEXTETT *n* sextet

SEXTETTE *same as* > SEXTET

SEXTETTES > SEXTETTE

SEXTETTS > SEXTETT

SEXTILE *n* one of five values of a variable dividing its distribution into six groups with equal frequencies

SEXTILES > SEXTILE

SEXTO *same as* > SIXMO

SEXTOLET *n* group of six musical notes

SEXTOLETS > SEXTOLET

SEXTON *n* official in charge of a church and churchyard

SEXTONESS *n* female sexton

SEXTONS > SEXTON

SEXTOS > SEXTO

SEXTS > SEXT

SEXTUOR *n* sextet

SEXTUORS > SEXTUOR

SEXTUPLE *vb* multiply by six ▷ *adj* six times as much or as many ▷ *n* quantity or number six times as great as another

SEXTUPLED > SEXTUPLE

SEXTUPLES > SEXTUPLE

SEXTUPLET *n* one of six children born at one birth

SEXTUPLY > SEXTUPLE

SEXUAL *adj* of or characterized by sex

SEXUALISE *same as* > SEXUALIZE

SEXUALISM *n* emphasising of sexuality

SEXUALIST > SEXUALISM

SEXUALITY *n* state or quality of being sexual

SEXUALIZE *vb* make or become sexual or sexually aware

SEXUALLY > SEXUAL

SEXVALENT *adj* with valency of six

SEXY *adj* sexually exciting or attractive

SEY *n* Scots word meaning part of cow carcase

SEYEN *n* old form of scion

SEYENS > SEYEN

SEYS > SEY

SEYSURE *n* old form of seizure

SEYSURES > SEYSURE

SEZ *vb* informal spelling of 'says'

SFERICS *same as* > SPHERICS

SFORZANDI > SFORZANDO

SFORZANDO *adv* be played with strong initial attack ▷ *n* symbol written above a note, indicating this

SFORZATI > SFORZATO

SFORZATO *same as* > SFORZANDO

SFORZATOS > SFORZATO

SFUMATO *n* gradual transition between areas of different colour in painting

SFUMATOS > SFUMATO

SGRAFFITI > SGRAFFITO

SGRAFFITO *n* technique in mural or ceramic decoration in which the top layer of glaze is incised with a design to reveal parts of the ground

SH *same as* > SHILLING

SHA *interj* be quiet

SHABASH *interj* (in Indian English) bravo or well done

SHABBATOT *pl n* Jewish sabbaths

SHABBIER > SHABBY

SHABBIEST > SHABBY

SHABBILY > SHABBY

SHABBLE *n* Scots word meaning old sword

SHABBLES > SHABBLE

SHABBY *adj* worn or dilapidated in appearance

SHABRACK *n* cavalryman's saddle cloth

SHABRACKS > SHABRACK

SHACK *n* rough hut ▷ *vb* evade (work or responsibility)

SHACKED > SHACK

SHACKING > SHACK

SHACKLE *n* metal ring for securing a person's wrists or ankles ▷ *vb* fasten with shackles

SHACKLED > SHACKLE

SHACKLER > SHACKLE

SHACKLERS > SHACKLE

SHACKLES > SHACKLE

SHACKLING > SHACKLE

SHACKO *same as* > SHAKO

SHACKOES > SHACKO

SHACKOS > SHACKO

SHACKS > SHACK

SHAD *n* herring-like fish

SHADBERRY *n* edible purplish berry of the shadbush

SHADBLOW *n* type of shrub

SHADBLOWS > SHADBLOW

SHADBUSH *n* type of N American tree or shrub

SHADCHAN *n* Jewish marriage broker

SHADCHANS > SHADCHAN

SHADDOCK *another name for* > POMELO

SHADDOCKS > SHADDOCK

SHADE *n* relative darkness ▷ *vb* screen from light

SHADED > SHADE

SHADELESS > SHADE

SHADER > SHADE
SHADERS > SHADE
SHADES *pl n* gathering darkness at nightfall
SHADFLIES > SHADFLY
SHADFLY *American name for* > MAYFLY
SHADIER > SHADY
SHADIEST > SHADY
SHADILY > SHADY
SHADINESS > SHADY
SHADING *n* graded areas of tone indicating light and dark in a painting or drawing
SHADINGS > SHADING
SHADKHAN *same as* > SHADCHAN
SHADKHANS > SHADKHAN
SHADOOF *n* mechanism for raising water, esp as used in Egypt and the Near East
SHADOOFS > SHADOOF
SHADOW *n* dark shape cast on a surface when something stands between a light and the surface ▷ *vb* cast a shadow over
SHADOWBOX *vb* practise boxing against an imaginary opponent
SHADOWED > SHADOW
SHADOWER > SHADOW
SHADOWERS > SHADOW
SHADOWIER > SHADOWY
SHADOWILY > SHADOWY
SHADOWING > SHADOW
SHADOWS > SHADOW
SHADOWY *adj* (of a place) full of shadows
SHADRACH *n* lump of iron that has not been melted in the furnace
SHADRACHS > SHADRACH
SHADS > SHAD
SHADUF *same as* > SHADOOF
SHADUFS > SHADUF
SHADY *adj* situated in or giving shade
SHAFT *n* long narrow straight handle of a tool or weapon ▷ *vb* treat badly
SHAFTED > SHAFT
SHAFTER > SHAFT
SHAFTERS > SHAFT
SHAFTING *n* assembly of rotating shafts for transmitting power
SHAFTINGS > SHAFTING
SHAFTLESS > SHAFT
SHAFTS > SHAFT
SHAG *n* coarse shredded tobacco ▷ *adj* (of a carpet) having a long pile ▷ *vb* have sexual intercourse with (a person)
SHAGBARK *n* North American hickory tree
SHAGBARKS > SHAGBARK
SHAGGABLE *adj* sexually attractive
SHAGGED > SHAG
SHAGGIER > SHAGGY
SHAGGIEST > SHAGGY
SHAGGILY > SHAGGY
SHAGGING > SHAG
SHAGGY *adj* covered with rough hair or wool
SHAGPILE *adj* (of carpet) having long fibres
SHAGREEN *n* sharkskin
SHAGREENS > SHAGREEN
SHAGROON *n* nineteenth-century Australian settler in Canterbury
SHAGROONS > SHAGROON
SHAGS > SHAG
SHAH *n* formerly, ruler of Iran
SHAHADA *n* Islamic declaration of faith, repeated daily by Muslims
SHAHADAS > SHAHADA
SHAHDOM > SHAH
SHAHDOMS > SHAH
SHAHS > SHAH
SHAHTOOSH *n* soft wool that comes from the protected Tibetan antelope
SHAIKH *n* sheikh
SHAIKHS > SHAIKH
SHAIRD *n* Scots word meaning shred
SHAIRDS > SHAIRD
SHAIRN *Scots word for* > DUNG
SHAIRNS > SHAIRN
SHAITAN *n* (in Muslim countries) an evil spirit
SHAITANS > SHAITAN
SHAKABLE > SHAKE
SHAKE *vb* move quickly up and down or back and forth ▷ *n* shaking
SHAKEABLE > SHAKE
SHAKED *vb* old form of shook
SHAKEDOWN *n* act of extortion
SHAKEN > SHAKE
SHAKEOUT *n* process of reducing the number of people in a workforce
SHAKEOUTS > SHAKEOUT
SHAKER *n* container in which drinks are mixed or from which powder is shaken
SHAKERS > SHAKER
SHAKES > SHAKE
SHAKEUP *n* radical reorganization
SHAKEUPS > SHAKEUP
SHAKIER > SHAKY
SHAKIEST > SHAKY
SHAKILY > SHAKY
SHAKINESS > SHAKY
SHAKING > SHAKE
SHAKINGS > SHAKE
SHAKO *n* tall cylindrical peaked military hat with a plume
SHAKOES > SHAKO
SHAKOS > SHAKO
SHAKT *vb* old form of shook
SHAKUDO *n* Japanese alloy of copper and gold
SHAKUDOS > SHAKUDO
SHAKY *adj* unsteady
SHALE *n* flaky sedimentary rock
SHALED > SHALE
SHALELIKE > SHALE
SHALES > SHALE
SHALEY > SHALE
SHALIER > SHALE
SHALIEST > SHALE
SHALING > SHALE
SHALL *vb* used as an auxiliary to make the future tense
SHALLI *n* type of fabric
SHALLIS > SHALLI
SHALLON *n* American shrub
SHALLONS > SHALLON
SHALLOON *n* light twill-weave woollen fabric used chiefly for coat linings, etc
SHALLOONS > SHALLOON
SHALLOP *n* light boat used for rowing in shallow water
SHALLOPS > SHALLOP
SHALLOT *n* kind of small onion
SHALLOTS > SHALLOT
SHALLOW *adj* not deep ▷ *n* shallow place in a body of water ▷ *vb* make or become shallow
SHALLOWED > SHALLOW
SHALLOWER > SHALLOW
SHALLOWLY > SHALLOW
SHALLOWS > SHALLOW
SHALM *n* old woodwind instrument
SHALMS > SHALM
SHALOM *n* Jewish greeting meaning 'peace be with you'
SHALOMS > SHALOM
SHALOT *n* shallot
SHALOTS > SHALOT
SHALT *singular form of the present tense (indicative mood) of* > SHALL
SHALWAR *n* pair of loose-fitting trousers tapering to a narrow fit around the ankles, worn in the Indian subcontinent, often with a kameez
SHALWARS > SHALWAR
SHALY > SHALE
SHAM *n* thing or person that is not genuine ▷ *adj* not genuine ▷ *vb* fake, feign
SHAMA *n* Indian songbird
SHAMABLE > SHAME
SHAMABLY > SHAME
SHAMAN *n* priest of shamanism
SHAMANIC > SHAMAN
SHAMANISM *n* religion of northern Asia, based on a belief in good and evil spirits
SHAMANIST > SHAMANISM
SHAMANS > SHAMAN
SHAMAS > SHAMA
SHAMATEUR *n* sportsperson who is officially an amateur but accepts payment
SHAMBA *n* (in E Africa) any field used for growing crops
SHAMBAS > SHAMBA
SHAMBLE *vb* walk in a shuffling awkward way ▷ *n* awkward or shuffling walk
SHAMBLED > SHAMBLE
SHAMBLES *n* disorderly event or place
SHAMBLIER > SHAMBLE
SHAMBLING > SHAMBLE
SHAMBLY > SHAMBLE
SHAMBOLIC *adj* completely disorganized
SHAME *n* painful emotion caused by awareness of having done something dishonourable or foolish ▷ *vb* cause to feel shame
SHAMEABLE > SHAME
SHAMEABLY > SHAME
SHAMED > SHAME
SHAMEFAST *adj* old form of shamefaced
SHAMEFUL *adj* causing or deserving shame
SHAMELESS *adj* with no sense of shame
SHAMER *n* cause of shame
SHAMERS > SHAME
SHAMES > SHAME
SHAMIANA *n* tent in India
SHAMIANAH *n* tent in India
SHAMIANAS > SHAMIANA
SHAMINA *n* wool blend of pashm and shahtoosh
SHAMINAS > SHAMINA
SHAMING > SHAME
SHAMISEN *n* Japanese stringed instrument
SHAMISENS > SHAMISEN
SHAMMAS *same as* > SHAMMES
SHAMMASH *same as* > SHAMMES
SHAMMASIM > SHAMMES
SHAMMED > SHAM
SHAMMER > SHAM
SHAMMERS > SHAM
SHAMMES *n* official acting as the beadle, sexton, and caretaker of a synagogue
SHAMMIED > SHAMMY
SHAMMIES > SHAMMY
SHAMMING > SHAM
SHAMMOS *same as* > SHAMMES
SHAMMOSIM > SHAMMES
SHAMMY *n* piece of chamois leather ▷ *vb* rub with a shammy
SHAMMYING > SHAMMY
SHAMOIS *n* chamois
SHAMOS *same as* > SHAMMES
SHAMOSIM > SHAMMES
SHAMOY *n* chamois ▷ *vb* rub with a shamoy
SHAMOYED > SHAMOY
SHAMOYING > SHAMOY
SHAMOYS > SHAMOY
SHAMPOO *n* liquid soap for washing hair, carpets, or upholstery ▷ *vb* wash with shampoo
SHAMPOOED > SHAMPOO
SHAMPOOER > SHAMPOO
SHAMPOOS > SHAMPOO
SHAMROCK *n* clover leaf, esp as the Irish emblem
SHAMROCKS > SHAMROCK
SHAMS > SHAM
SHAMUS *n* police or private detective
SHAMUSES > SHAMUS
SHAN *variant of* > SHAND
SHANACHIE *n* Gaelic

storyteller

SHAND n old word meaning fake coin

SHANDIES > SHANDY

SHANDRIES > SHANDRY

SHANDRY n light horse-drawn cart

SHANDS > SHAND

SHANDY n drink made of beer and lemonade

SHANGHAI vb force or trick (someone) into doing something ▷ n catapult

SHANGHAIS > SHANGHAI

SHANK n lower leg ▷ vb (of fruits, roots, etc) to show disease symptoms, esp discoloration

SHANKBONE n bone in lower leg

SHANKED > SHANK

SHANKING > SHANK

SHANKS > SHANK

SHANNIES > SHANNY

SHANNY n European blenny of rocky coastal waters

SHANS > SHAN

SHANTEY same as > SHANTY

SHANTEYS > SHANTEY

SHANTI n peace

SHANTIES > SHANTY

SHANTIH same as > SHANTI

SHANTIHS > SHANTIH

SHANTIS > SHANTI

SHANTUNG n soft Chinese silk with a knobbly surface

SHANTUNGS > SHANTUNG

SHANTY n shack or crude dwelling

SHANTYMAN n man living in shanty

SHANTYMEN > SHANTYMAN

SHAPABLE > SHAPE

SHAPE n outward form of an object ▷ vb form or mould

SHAPEABLE > SHAPE

SHAPED > SHAPE

SHAPELESS adj (of a person or object) lacking a pleasing shape

SHAPELIER > SHAPELY

SHAPELY adj having an attractive shape

SHAPEN vb old form of shaped

SHAPER > SHAPE

SHAPERS > SHAPE

SHAPES > SHAPE

SHAPEUP n system of hiring dockers for a day's work

SHAPEUPS > SHAPEUP

SHAPEWEAR n underwear that shapes body

SHAPING > SHAPE

SHAPINGS > SHAPE

SHAPS n leather over-trousers worn by cowboys

SHARABLE > SHARE

SHARD n broken piece of pottery or glass

SHARDED adj old word meaning hidden under dung

SHARDS > SHARD

SHARE n part of something that belongs to or is contributed by a person

▷ vb give or take a share of (something)

SHAREABLE > SHARE

SHARECROP vb cultivate (farmland) as a sharecropper

SHARED > SHARE

SHAREMAN n member of fishing-boat crew who shares profits

SHAREMEN > SHAREMAN

SHARER > SHARE

SHARERS > SHARE

SHARES > SHARE

SHARESMAN n member of fishing-boat crew who shares profits

SHARESMEN > SHARESMAN

SHAREWARE n software available to all users without the need for a licence

SHARIA n body of doctrines that regulate the lives of Muslims

SHARIAH same as > SHARIA

SHARIAHS > SHARIAH

SHARIAS > SHARIA

SHARIAT n Islamic religious law

SHARIATS > SHARIAT

SHARIF same as > SHERIF

SHARIFIAN > SHARIF

SHARIFS > SHARIF

SHARING > SHARE

SHARINGS > SHARE

SHARK n large usu predatory sea fish ▷ vb obtain (something) by cheating or deception

SHARKED > SHARK

SHARKER n shark hunter

SHARKERS > SHARKER

SHARKING > SHARK

SHARKINGS > SHARK

SHARKLIKE > SHARK

SHARKS > SHARK

SHARKSKIN n stiff glossy fabric

SHARN Scots word for > DUNG

SHARNIER > SHARN

SHARNIEST > SHARN

SHARNS > SHARN

SHARNY > SHARN

SHARON as in sharon fruit persimmon

SHARP adj having a keen cutting edge or fine point ▷ adv promptly ▷ n symbol raising a note one semitone above natural pitch ▷ vb make sharp

SHARPED > SHARP

SHARPEN vb make or become sharp or sharper

SHARPENED > SHARPEN

SHARPENER > SHARPEN

SHARPENS > SHARPEN

SHARPER n person who cheats

SHARPERS > SHARPER

SHARPEST > SHARP

SHARPIE n member of a teenage group having short hair and distinctive clothes

SHARPIES > SHARPIE

SHARPING > SHARP

SHARPINGS > SHARP

SHARPISH adj fairly sharp ▷ adv promptly

SHARPLY > SHARP

SHARPNESS > SHARP

SHARPS > SHARP

SHARPY n swindler

SHASH vb old form of sash

SHASHED > SHASH

SHASHES > SHASH

SHASHING > SHASH

SHASHLICK same as > SHASHLIK

SHASHLIK n type of kebab

SHASHLIKS > SHASHLIK

SHASLIK n type of kebab

SHASLIKS > SHASLIK

SHASTER same as > SHASTRA

SHASTERS > SHASTER

SHASTRA n any of the sacred writings of Hinduism

SHASTRAS > SHASTRA

SHAT past tense and past participle of > SHIT

SHATTER vb break into pieces ▷ n fragment

SHATTERED adj completely exhausted

SHATTERER > SHATTER

SHATTERS > SHATTER

SHATTERY adj liable to shatter

SHAUCHLE vb Scots word meaning shuffle

SHAUCHLED > SHAUCHLE

SHAUCHLES > SHAUCHLE

SHAUCHLY > SHAUCHLE

SHAUGH n old word meaning small wood

SHAUGHS > SHAUGH

SHAUL vb old form of shawl

SHAULED > SHAUL

SHAULING > SHAUL

SHAULS > SHAUL

SHAVABLE > SHAVE

SHAVE vb remove (hair) from (the face, head, or body) with a razor or shaver ▷ n shaving

SHAVEABLE > SHAVE

SHAVED > SHAVE

SHAVELING n derogatory term for a priest or clergyman with a shaven head

SHAVEN adj closely shaved or tonsured

SHAVER n electric razor

SHAVERS > SHAVER

SHAVES > SHAUL

SHAVETAIL n American slang for second lieutenant

SHAVIE n Scots word meaning trick

SHAVIES > SHAVIE

SHAVING > SHAVE

SHAVINGS > SHAVE

SHAW n small wood ▷ vb show

SHAWED > SHAW

SHAWING > SHAW

SHAWL n piece of cloth worn over a woman's shoulders or wrapped around a baby ▷ vb cover with a shawl

SHAWLED > SHAWL

SHAWLEY n Irish word for woman wearing shawl

SHAWLEYS > SHAWLEY

SHAWLIE n disparaging term for a working-class woman who wears a shawl

SHAWLIES > SHAWLIE

SHAWLING > SHAWL

SHAWLINGS > SHAWL

SHAWLLESS > SHAWL

SHAWLS > SHAWL

SHAWM n medieval form of the oboe with a conical bore and flaring bell

SHAWMS > SHAWM

SHAWN variant of > SHAWM

SHAWS > SHAW

SHAY dialect word for > CHAISE

SHAYA n Indian plant

SHAYAS > SHAYA

SHAYS > SHAY

SHAZAM interj magic slogan

SHCHI n Russian cabbage soup

SHCHIS > SHCHI

SHE pron female person or animal previously mentioned ▷ n female person or animal

SHEA n tropical African tree

SHEADING n any of the six subdivisions of the Isle of Man

SHEADINGS > SHEADING

SHEAF n bundle of papers ▷ vb tie into a sheaf

SHEAFED > SHEAF

SHEAFIER > SHEAF

SHEAFIEST > SHEAF

SHEAFING > SHEAF

SHEAFLIKE > SHEAF

SHEAFS > SHEAF

SHEAFY > SHEAF

SHEAL vb old word meaning shell

SHEALED > SHEAL

SHEALING > SHEAL

SHEALINGS > SHEAL

SHEALS > SHEAL

SHEAR vb clip hair or wool from ▷ n breakage caused through strain or twisting

SHEARED > SHEAR

SHEARER > SHEAR

SHEARERS > SHEAR

SHEARING > SHEAR

SHEARINGS > SHEAR

SHEARLEG n one spar of shearlegs

SHEARLEGS same as > SHEERLEGS

SHEARLING n young sheep after its first shearing

SHEARMAN n person who trims cloth

SHEARMEN > SHEARMAN

SHEARS > SHEAR

SHEAS > SHEA

SHEATFISH n European catfish

SHEATH n close-fitting cover, esp for a knife or sword

SHEATHE vb put into a sheath

SHEATHED > SHEATHE

SHEATHER > SHEATHE
SHEATHERS > SHEATHE
SHEATHES > SHEATHE
SHEATHIER > SHEATHE
SHEATHING n any material used as an outer layer
SHEATHS > SHEATH
SHEATHY > SHEATHE
SHEAVE vb gather or bind into sheaves ▷ n wheel with a grooved rim, esp one used as a pulley
SHEAVED > SHEAVE
SHEAVES > SHEAF
SHEAVING > SHEAVE
SHEBANG n situation, matter, or affair
SHEBANGS > SHEBANG
SHEBEAN same as > SHEBEEN
SHEBEANS > SHEBEAN
SHEBEEN n place where alcohol is sold illegally ▷ vb run a shebeen
SHEBEENED > SHEBEEN
SHEBEENER > SHEBEEN
SHEBEENS > SHEBEEN
SHECHITA n Jewish method of killing animals for food
SHECHITAH same as > SHECHITA
SHECHITAS > SHECHITA
SHED n building used for storage or shelter or as a workshop ▷ vb get rid of
SHEDABLE > SHED
SHEDDABLE > SHED
SHEDDED > SHED
SHEDDER n person or thing that sheds
SHEDDERS > SHEDDER
SHEDDING > SHED
SHEDDINGS > SHED
SHEDFUL n quantity or amount contained in a shed
SHEDFULS > SHEDFUL
SHEDLIKE > SHED
SHEDLOAD n very large amount or number
SHEDLOADS > SHEDLOAD
SHEDS > SHED
SHEEL vb old word meaning shell
SHEELED > SHEEL
SHEELING > SHEEL
SHEELS > SHEEL
SHEEN n glistening brightness on the surface of something ▷ adj shining and beautiful ▷ vb give a sheen to
SHEENED > SHEEN
SHEENEY n offensive word for Jew
SHEENEYS > SHEENEY
SHEENFUL > SHEEN
SHEENIE n offensive word for Jew
SHEENIER > SHEEN
SHEENIES > SHEENIE
SHEENIEST > SHEEN
SHEENING > SHEEN
SHEENS > SHEEN
SHEENY > SHEEN
SHEEP n ruminant animal bred for wool and meat
SHEEPCOT n sheepcote

SHEEPCOTE another word for > SHEEPFOLD
SHEEPCOTS > SHEEPCOT
SHEEPDOG n dog used for herding sheep
SHEEPDOGS > SHEEPDOG
SHEEPFOLD n pen or enclosure for sheep
SHEEPHEAD n species of fish
SHEEPIER > SHEEP
SHEEPIEST > SHEEP
SHEEPISH adj embarrassed because of feeling foolish
SHEEPLE pl n informal derogatory word for people who follow the majority in matters of opinion, taste, etc
SHEEPLIKE > SHEEP
SHEEPMAN n person who keeps sheep
SHEEPMEN > SHEEPMAN
SHEEPO n person employed to bring sheep to the catching pen in a shearing shed
SHEEPOS > SHEEPO
SHEEPSKIN n skin of a sheep with the fleece still on, used for clothing or rugs
SHEEPWALK n tract of land for grazing sheep
SHEEPY > SHEEP
SHEER adj absolute, complete ▷ adv steeply ▷ vb change course suddenly ▷ n any transparent fabric used for making garments
SHEERED > SHEER
SHEERER > SHEER
SHEEREST > SHEER
SHEERING > SHEER
SHEERLEG n one spar of sheerlegs
SHEERLEGS n device for lifting heavy weights
SHEERLY > SHEER
SHEERNESS > SHEER
SHEERS > SHEER
SHEESH interj exclamation of surprise or annoyance
SHEET n large piece of cloth used as an inner bed cover ▷ vb provide with, cover, or wrap in a sheet
SHEETED > SHEET
SHEETER > SHEET
SHEETERS > SHEET
SHEETFED adj printing on separate sheets of paper
SHEETIER > SHEET
SHEETIEST > SHEET
SHEETING n material from which sheets are made
SHEETINGS > SHEETING
SHEETLESS > SHEET
SHEETLIKE > SHEET
SHEETROCK n brand name for plasterboard
SHEETS > SHEET
SHEETY > SHEET
SHEEVE n part of mine winding gear
SHEEVES > SHEEVE
SHEGETZ n offensive word

for non-Jew
SHEHITA n slaughter of animal according to Jewish religious law
SHEHITAH n slaughter of animal according to Jewish religious law
SHEHITAHS > SHEHITAH
SHEHITAS > SHEHITA
SHEIK same as > SHEIKH
SHEIKDOM same as > SHEIKHDOM
SHEIKDOMS > SHEIKDOM
SHEIKH n Arab chief
SHEIKHA n chief wife of sheikh
SHEIKHAS > SHEIKHA
SHEIKHDOM n territory ruled by a sheikh
SHEIKHS > SHEIKH
SHEIKS > SHEIK
SHEILA n girl or woman
SHEILAS > SHEILA
SHEILING n hut used by shepherds
SHEILINGS > SHEILING
SHEITAN n Muslim demon
SHEITANS > SHEITAN
SHEKALIM > SHEKEL
SHEKEL n monetary unit of Israel
SHEKELIM > SHEKEL
SHEKELS > SHEKEL
SHELDDUCK n species of large duck
SHELDRAKE same as > SHELDUCK
SHELDUCK n large brightly coloured wild duck of Europe and Asia
SHELDUCKS > SHELDUCK
SHELF n board fixed horizontally for holding things ▷ vb put on a shelf
SHELFED > SHELF
SHELFFUL > SHELF
SHELFFULS > SHELF
SHELFIER > SHELF
SHELFIEST > SHELF
SHELFING > SHELF
SHELFLIKE > SHELF
SHELFROOM n space on shelf
SHELFS > SHELF
SHELFY > SHELF
SHELL n hard outer covering of an egg, nut, or certain animals ▷ vb take the shell from
SHELLAC n resin used in varnishes ▷ vb coat with shellac
SHELLACK vb shellac
SHELLACKS > SHELLAC
SHELLACS > SHELLAC
SHELLBACK n sailor who has crossed the equator
SHELLBARK same as > SHAGBARK
SHELLDUCK n shelduck
SHELLED > SHELL
SHELLER > SHELL
SHELLERS > SHELL
SHELLFIRE n firing of artillery shells
SHELLFISH n sea-living animal, esp one that can be eaten, with a shell

SHELLFUL > SHELL
SHELLFULS > SHELL
SHELLIER > SHELL
SHELLIEST > SHELL
SHELLING > SHELL
SHELLINGS > SHELL
SHELLS > SHELL
SHELLWORK n decoration with shells
SHELLY > SHELL
SHELTA n secret language used by some traveling people in Britain and Ireland
SHELTAS > SHELTA
SHELTER n structure providing protection from danger or the weather ▷ vb give shelter to
SHELTERED adj protected from wind and rain
SHELTERER > SHELTER
SHELTERS > SHELTER
SHELTERY > SHELTER
SHELTIE n small dog similar to a collie
SHELTIES > SHELTY
SHELTY same as > SHELTIE
SHELVE vb put aside or postpone
SHELVED > SHELVE
SHELVER > SHELVE
SHELVERS > SHELVE
SHELVES > SHELF
SHELVIER > SHELVY
SHELVIEST > SHELVY
SHELVING n (material for) shelves
SHELVINGS > SHELVING
SHELVY adj having shelves
SHEMOZZLE n noisy confusion or dispute
SHEND vb put to shame
SHENDING > SHEND
SHENDS > SHEND
SHENT > SHEND
SHEOL n hell
SHEOLS > SHEOL
SHEPHERD n person who tends sheep ▷ vb guide or watch over (people)
SHEPHERDS > SHEPHERD
SHEQALIM n plural of sheqel
SHEQEL same as > SHEKEL
SHEQELS > SHEQEL
SHERANG n person in charge
SHERANGS > SHERANG
SHERBERT same as > SHERBET
SHERBERTS > SHERBET
SHERBET n fruit-flavoured fizzy powder
SHERBETS > SHERBET
SHERD same as > SHARD
SHERDS > SHERD
SHERE old spelling of > SHEER
SHEREEF same as > SHERIF
SHEREEFS > SHEREEF
SHERIA same as > SHARIA
SHERIAS > SHERIA
SHERIAT n Muslim religious law
SHERIATS > SHERIAT
SHERIF n descendant of Mohammed through his daughter Fatima
SHERIFF n (in the US) chief

law enforcement officer of a county

SHERIFFS > SHERIFF

SHERIFIAN > SHERIF

SHERIFS > SHERIF

SHERLOCK n detective

SHERLOCKS > SHERLOCK

SHEROOT n cheroot

SHEROOTS > SHEROOT

SHERPA n official who assists at a summit meeting

SHERPAS > SHERPA

SHERRIES > SHERRY

SHERRIS n old form of sherry

SHERRISES > SHERRIS

SHERRY n pale or dark brown fortified wine

SHERWANI n long coat closed up to the neck, worn by men in India

SHERWANIS > SHERWANI

SHES > SHE

SHET vb old form of shut

SHETLAND n type of wool spun in the Shetland islands

SHETLANDS > SHETLAND

SHETS > SHET

SHETTING > SHET

SHEUCH n ditch or trough ▷ vb dig

SHEUCHED > SHEUCH

SHEUCHING > SHEUCH

SHEUCHS > SHEUCH

SHEUGH same as > SHEUCH

SHEUGHED > SHEUGH

SHEUGHING > SHEUGH

SHEUGHS > SHEUGH

SHEVA n mark in Hebrew writing

SHEVAS > SHEVA

SHEW archaic spelling of > SHOW

SHEWBREAD n loaves of bread placed every Sabbath on the table beside the altar of incense in the tabernacle of ancient Israel

SHEWED > SHEW

SHEWEL n old word meaning scarecrow

SHEWELS > SHEWEL

SHEWER > SHEW

SHEWERS > SHEW

SHEWING > SHEW

SHEWN > SHEW

SHEWS > SHEW

SHH interj sound made to ask for silence

SHIAI n judo contest

SHIAIS > SHIAI

SHIATSU n massage in which pressure is applied to the same points of the body as in acupuncture

SHIATSUS > SHIATSU

SHIATZU n shiatzu

SHIATZUS > SHIATZU

SHIBAH n Jewish period of mourning

SHIBAHS > SHIBAH

SHIBUICHI n Japanese alloy of copper and silver

SHICKER n alcoholic drink

SHICKERED adj drunk

SHICKERS > SHICKER

SHICKSA n non-Jewish girl

SHICKSAS > SHICKSA

SHIDDER n old word meaning female animal

SHIDDERS > SHIDDER

SHIDDUCH n arranged marriage

SHIED > SHY

SHIEL vb sheal

SHIELD n piece of armour carried on the arm to protect the body from blows or missiles ▷ vb protect

SHIELDED > SHIELD

SHIELDER > SHIELD

SHIELDERS > SHIELD

SHIELDING > SHIELD

SHIELDS > SHIELD

SHIELED > SHIEL

SHIELING n rough hut or shelter used by people tending cattle on high or remote ground

SHIELINGS > SHIELING

SHIELS > SHIEL

SHIER n horse that shies habitually

SHIERS > SHIER

SHIES > SHY

SHIEST > SHY

SHIFT vb move ▷ n shifting

SHIFTABLE > SHIFT

SHIFTED > SHIFT

SHIFTER > SHIFT

SHIFTERS > SHIFT

SHIFTIER > SHIFTY

SHIFTIEST > SHIFTY

SHIFTILY > SHIFTY

SHIFTING > SHIFT

SHIFTINGS > SHIFT

SHIFTLESS adj lacking in ambition or initiative

SHIFTS > SHIFT

SHIFTWORK n system of employment where an individual's normal hours of work are outside the period of normal day working

SHIFTY adj evasive or untrustworthy

SHIGELLA n any rod-shaped Gram-negative bacterium of the genus Shigella

SHIGELLAE > SHIGELLA

SHIGELLAS > SHIGELLA

SHIITAKE n kind of mushroom widely used in Oriental cookery

SHIITAKES > SHIITAKE

SHIKAR n hunting, esp big-game hunting ▷ vb hunt (game, esp big game)

SHIKAREE same as > SHIKARI

SHIKAREES > SHIKAREE

SHIKARI n (in India) a hunter

SHIKARIS > SHIKARI

SHIKARRED > SHIKAR

SHIKARS > SHIKAR

SHIKKER n Yiddish term for drunk person

SHIKKERS > SHIKKER

SHIKSA n often derogatory term for a non-Jewish girl

SHIKSAS > SHIKSA

SHIKSE n non-Jewish girl

SHIKSEH same as > SHIKSE

SHIKSEHS > SHIKSEH

SHIKSES > SHIKSE

SHILINGI n money unit in Tanzania

SHILL n confidence trickster's assistant ▷ vb act as a shill

SHILLABER n keen customer

SHILLALA n short Irish club or cudgel

SHILLALAH same as > SHILLALA

SHILLALAS > SHILLALA

SHILLED > SHILL

SHILLELAH same as > SHILLALA

SHILLING n former British coin

SHILLINGS > SHILLING

SHILLS > SHILL

SHILPIT adj puny

SHILY > SHY

SHIM n thin strip of material placed between two close surfaces to fill a gap ▷ vb fit or fill up with a shim

SHIMAAL n hot Middle Eastern wind

SHIMAALS > SHIMAAL

SHIMMED > SHIM

SHIMMER n (shine with) a faint unsteady light ▷ vb shine with a faint unsteady light

SHIMMERED > SHIMMER

SHIMMERS > SHIMMER

SHIMMERY adj shining with a glistening or tremulous light

SHIMMEY n chemise

SHIMMEYS > SHIMMEY

SHIMMIED > SHIMMY

SHIMMIES > SHIMMY

SHIMMING > SHIM

SHIMMY n American ragtime dance with much shaking of the hips and shoulders ▷ vb dance the shimmy

SHIMMYING > SHIMMY

SHIMOZZLE n predicament

SHIMS > SHIM

SHIN n front of the lower leg ▷ vb climb by using the hands or arms and legs

SHINBONE n tibia

SHINBONES > SHINBONE

SHINDIES > SHINDY

SHINDIG n noisy party

SHINDIGS > SHINDIG

SHINDY n quarrel or commotion

SHINDYS > SHINDY

SHINE vb give out or reflect light; cause to gleam ▷ n brightness or lustre

SHINED > SHINE

SHINELESS > SHINE

SHINER n black eye

SHINERS > SHINER

SHINES > SHINE

SHINESS > SHY

SHINESSES > SHY

SHINGLE n wooden roof tile ▷ vb cover (a roof) with shingles

SHINGLED > SHINGLE

SHINGLER > SHINGLE

SHINGLERS > SHINGLE

SHINGLES n disease causing a rash of small blisters along a nerve

SHINGLIER > SHINGLE

SHINGLING > SHINGLE

SHINGLY > SHINGLE

SHINGUARD n rigid piece of plastic to protect footballer's shin

SHINIER > SHINY

SHINIES > SHINY

SHINIEST > SHINY

SHINILY > SHINY

SHININESS > SHINY

SHINING > SHINE

SHININGLY > SHINE

SHINJU n (formerly, in Japan) a ritual double suicide of lovers

SHINJUS > SHINJU

SHINKIN n worthless person

SHINKINS > SHINKIN

SHINLEAF n wintergreen

SHINLEAFS > SHINLEAF

SHINNE n old form of chin

SHINNED > SHIN

SHINNERY n American oak tree

SHINNES > SHINNE

SHINNEY vb climb with hands and legs

SHINNEYED > SHINNEY

SHINNEYS > SHINNEY

SHINNIED > SHINNY

SHINNIES > SHINNY

SHINNING > SHIN

SHINNY same as > SHINTY

SHINNYING > SHINNY

SHINS > SHIN

SHINTIED > SHINTY

SHINTIES > SHINTY

SHINTY n game like hockey ▷ vb play shinty

SHINTYING > SHINTY

SHINY adj bright and polished

SHIP n large seagoing vessel ▷ vb send or transport by carrier, esp a ship

SHIPBOARD adj taking place or used aboard a ship

SHIPBORNE adj carried on ship

SHIPFUL n amount carried by ship

SHIPFULS > SHIPFUL

SHIPLAP n method of constructing ship hull

SHIPLAPS > SHIPLAP

SHIPLESS > SHIP

SHIPLOAD n quantity carried by a ship

SHIPLOADS > SHIPLOAD

SHIPMAN n master or captain of a ship

SHIPMATE n sailor serving on the same ship as another

SHIPMATES > SHIPMATE

SHIPMEN > SHIPMAN

SHIPMENT n act of shipping cargo

SHIPMENTS > SHIPMENT

SHIPOWNER n person who owns or has shares in a ship or ships

SHIPPABLE > SHIP

SHIPPED > SHIP

SHIPPEN n dialect word for cattle shed

SHIPPENS > SHIPPEN

SHIPPER n person or company that ships

SHIPPERS > SHIPPER

SHIPPIE n prostitute who solicits at a port

SHIPPIES > SHIPPIE

SHIPPING > SHIP

SHIPPINGS > SHIP

SHIPPO n Japanese enamel work

SHIPPON n dialect word for cattle shed

SHIPPONS > SHIPPON

SHIPPOS > SHIPPO

SHIPPOUND n Baltic weight measure

SHIPS > SHIP

SHIPSHAPE adj orderly or neat ▷ adv in a neat and orderly manner

SHIPSIDE n part of wharf next to ship

SHIPSIDES > SHIPSIDE

SHIPWAY n structure on which a vessel is built, then launched

SHIPWAYS > SHIPWAY

SHIPWORM n any wormlike marine bivalve mollusc of the genus Teredo

SHIPWORMS > SHIPWORM

SHIPWRECK n destruction of a ship through storm or collision ▷ vb cause to undergo shipwreck

SHIPYARD n place where ships are built

SHIPYARDS > SHIPYARD

SHIR n gathering in material

SHIRALEE n swag

SHIRALEES > SHIRALEE

SHIRE n county ▷ vb refresh or rest

SHIRED > SHIRE

SHIREMAN n sheriff

SHIREMEN > SHIREMAN

SHIRES > SHIRE

SHIRING > SHIRE

SHIRK vb avoid (duty or work) ▷ n person who shirks

SHIRKED > SHIRK

SHIRKER > SHIRK

SHIRKERS > SHIRK

SHIRKING > SHIRK

SHIRKS > SHIRK

SHIRR vb gather (fabric) into two or more parallel rows to decorate a dress, etc ▷ n series of gathered rows decorating a dress, blouse, etc

SHIRRA old Scots word for > SHERIFF

SHIRRALEE n swagman's bundle of possessions

SHIRRAS > SHIRRA

SHIRRED > SHIRR

SHIRRING > SHIRR

SHIRRINGS > SHIRR

SHIRRS > SHIRR

SHIRS > SHIR

SHIRT n garment for the upper part of the body ▷ vb put a shirt on

SHIRTBAND n neckband on shirt

SHIRTED > SHIRT

SHIRTIER > SHIRTY

SHIRTIEST > SHIRTY

SHIRTILY > SHIRTY

SHIRTING n fabric used in making men's shirts

SHIRTINGS > SHIRTING

SHIRTLESS > SHIRT

SHIRTS > SHIRT

SHIRTTAIL n part of a shirt that extends below the waist

SHIRTY adj bad-tempered or annoyed

SHISH as in shish kebab dish of meat and vegetables threaded onto skewers and grilled

SHISHA same as > HOOKAH

SHISHAS > SHISHA

SHISO n Asian plant with aromatic leaves that are used in cooking

SHISOS > SHISO

SHIST n schist

SHISTS > SHIST

SHIT taboo vb defecate ▷ n excrement ▷ interj exclamation of anger or disgust

SHITAKE same as > SHIITAKE

SHITAKES > SHITAKE

SHITE same as > SHIT

SHITED > SHITE

SHITES > SHITE

SHITFACED adj drunk

SHITHEAD n taboo slang fool

SHITHEADS > SHITHEAD

SHITHOLE n dirty place

SHITHOLES > SHITHOLE

SHITING > SHITE

SHITLESS adj very frightened

SHITLIST n list of hated things

SHITLISTS > SHITLIST

SHITLOAD n taboo slang for a lot

SHITLOADS > SHITLOAD

SHITS > SHIT

SHITTAH n tree mentioned in the Old Testament

SHITTAHS > SHITTAH

SHITTED > SHIT

SHITTIER > SHIT

SHITTIEST > SHIT

SHITTILY > SHIT

SHITTIM > SHITTAH

SHITTIMS > SHITTAH

SHITTING > SHIT

SHITTY > SHIT

SHIUR n lesson in which a passage of the Talmud is studied together by a group of people

SHIURIM > SHIUR

SHIV variant spelling of > CHIV

SHIVA variant of > SHIVAH

SHIVAH n Jewish period of formal mourning

SHIVAHS > SHIVAH

SHIVAREE n discordant mock serenade to newlyweds, made with pans, kettles, etc

SHIVAREED > SHIVAREE

SHIVAREES > SHIVAREE

SHIVAS > SHIVA

SHIVE n flat cork or bung for wide-mouthed bottles

SHIVER vb tremble, as from cold or fear ▷ n shivering

SHIVERED > SHIVER

SHIVERER > SHIVER

SHIVERERS > SHIVER

SHIVERIER > SHIVERY

SHIVERING > SHIVER

SHIVERS > SHIVER

SHIVERY adj inclined to shiver or tremble

SHIVES > SHIVE

SHIVITI n Jewish decorative plaque with religious message

SHIVITIS > SHIVITI

SHIVOO n Australian word meaning rowdy party

SHIVOOS > SHIVOO

SHIVS > SHIV

SHIVVED > SHIV

SHIVVING > SHIV

SHKOTZIM n plural of shegetz

SHLEMIEHL Yiddish word for > FOOL

SHLEMIEL same as > SCHLEMIEL

SHLEMIELS > SHLEMIEL

SHLEP vb schlep

SHLEPP vb schlep

SHLEPPED > SHLEP

SHLEPPER > SHLEP

SHLEPPERS > SHLEP

SHLEPPING > SHLEP

SHLEPPS > SHLEPP

SHLEPS > SHLEP

SHLIMAZEL n unlucky person

SHLOCK n something of poor quality

SHLOCKIER > SHLOCK

SHLOCKS > SHLOCK

SHLOCKY > SHLOCK

SHLOSHIM n period of thirty days' deep mourning following a death

SHLOSHIMS > SHLOSHIM

SHLUB same as > SCHLUB

SHLUBS > SHLUB

SHLUMP vb move in lazy way

SHLUMPED > SHLUMP

SHLUMPING > SHLUMP

SHLUMPS > SHLUMP

SHLUMPY > SHLUMP

SHMALTZ n schmaltz

SHMALTZES > SHMALTZ

SHMALTZY > SHMALTZ

SHMATTE n rag

SHMATTES > SHMATTE

SHMEAR n set of things

SHMEARS > SHMEAR

SHMEK n smell

SHMEKS > SHMEK

SHMO same as > SCHMO

SHMOCK n despicable person

SHMOCKS > SHMOCK

SHMOES > SHMO

SHMOOSE variant of > SCHMOOZE

SHMOOSED > SHMOOSE

SHMOOSES > SHMOOSE

SHMOOSING > SHMOOSE

SHMOOZE variant of > SCHMOOZE

SHMOOZED > SHMOOZE

SHMOOZES > SHMOOZE

SHMOOZING > SHMOOZE

SHMUCK n despicable person

SHMUCKS > SCHMUCK

SHNAPPS same as > SCHNAPPS

SHNAPS n schnaps

SHNOOK n stupid person

SHNOOKS > SHNOOK

SHNORRER same as > SCHNORRER

SHNORRERS > SHNORRER

SHOAL n large number of fish swimming together ▷ vb make or become shallow ▷ adj (of the draught of a vessel) drawing little water

SHOALED > SHOAL

SHOALER > SHOAL

SHOALEST > SHOAL

SHOALIER > SHOALY

SHOALIEST > SHOALY

SHOALING > SHOAL

SHOALINGS > SHOAL

SHOALNESS > SHOAL

SHOALS > SHOAL

SHOALWISE adv in a large group or in large groups

SHOALY adj shallow

SHOAT n piglet that has recently been weaned

SHOATS > SHOAT

SHOCHET n (in Judaism) a person who has been specially trained and licensed to slaughter animals and birds in accordance with the laws of shechita

SHOCHETIM > SHOCHET

SHOCHETS > SHOCHET

SHOCK vb horrify, disgust, or astonish ▷ n sudden violent emotional disturbance ▷ adj bushy

SHOCKABLE > SHOCK

SHOCKED > SHOCK

SHOCKER n person or thing that shocks or horrifies

SHOCKERS > SHOCK

SHOCKING adj causing horror, disgust, or astonishment

SHOCKS > SHOCK

SHOD > SHOE

SHODDEN vb old form of shod

SHODDIER > SHODDY

SHODDIES > SHODDY

SHODDIEST > SHODDY

SHODDILY > SHODDY

SHODDY adj made or done

badly ▷ *n* yarn or fabric made from wool waste or clippings

SHODER *n* skins used in making gold leaf

SHODERS > SHODER

SHOE *n* outer covering for the foot, ending below the ankle ▷ *vb* fit with a shoe or shoes

SHOEBILL *n* large wading bird of tropical E African swamps

SHOEBILLS > SHOEBILL

SHOEBLACK *n* (esp formerly) a person who shines boots and shoes

SHOEBOX *n* cardboard box for shoes

SHOEBOXES > SHOEBOX

SHOED > SHOE

SHOEHORN *n* smooth curved implement inserted at the heel of a shoe to ease the foot into it ▷ *vb* cram (people or things) into a very small space

SHOEHORNS > SHOEHORN

SHOEING > SHOE

SHOEINGS > SHOE

SHOELACE *n* cord for fastening shoes

SHOELACES > SHOELACE

SHOELESS > SHOE

SHOEMAKER *n* person who makes or repairs shoes or boots

SHOEPAC *n* waterproof boot

SHOEPACK *n* waterproof boot

SHOEPACKS > SHOEPACK

SHOEPACS > SHOEPAC

SHOER *n* person who shoes horses

SHOERS > SHOER

SHOES > SHOE

SHOESHINE *n* act or an instance of polishing a pair of shoes

SHOETREE *n* piece of metal, wood, or plastic inserted in a shoe to keep its shape

SHOETREES > SHOETREE

SHOFAR *n* ram's horn sounded in the synagogue daily during the month of Elul and repeatedly on Rosh Hashanah

SHOFARS > SHOFAR

SHOFROTH > SHOFAR

SHOG *vb* shake

SHOGGED > SHOG

SHOGGING > SHOG

SHOGGLE *vb* shake

SHOGGLED > SHOGGLE

SHOGGLES > SHOGGLE

SHOGGLIER > SHOGGLE

SHOGGLING > SHOGGLE

SHOGGLY > SHOGGLE

SHOGI *n* Japanese chess

SHOGIS > SHOGI

SHOGS > SHOG

SHOGUN *n* Japanese chief military commander

SHOGUNAL > SHOGUN

SHOGUNATE *n* office or rule of a shogun

SHOGUNS > SHOGUN

SHOJI *n* Japanese rice-paper screen in a sliding wooden frame

SHOJIS > SHOJI

SHOLA *n* Indian plant

SHOLAS > SHOLA

SHOLOM *n* Hebrew greeting

SHOLOMS > SHOLOM

SHONE > SHINE

SHONEEN *n* Irishman who imitates English ways

SHONEENS > SHONEEN

SHONKIER > SHONKY

SHONKIEST > SHONKY

SHONKY *adj* unreliable or unsound

SHOO *interj* go away! ▷ *vb* drive away as by saying 'shoo'

SHOOED > SHOO

SHOOFLIES > SHOOFLY

SHOOFLY as in *shoofly pie* US dessert similar to treacle tart

SHOOGIE *vb* Scots word meaning swing

SHOOGIED > SHOOGIE

SHOOGIES > SHOOGIE

SHOOGLE *vb* shake, sway, or rock back and forth ▷ *n* rocking motion

SHOOGLED > SHOOGLE

SHOOGLES > SHOOGLE

SHOOGLIER > SHOOGLE

SHOOGLING > SHOOGLE

SHOOGLY > SHOOGLE

SHOOING > SHOO

SHOOK *n* set of parts ready for assembly

SHOOKS > SHOOK

SHOOL *dialect word for* > SHOVEL

SHOOLE *dialect word for* > SHOVEL

SHOOLED > SHOOL

SHOOLES > SHOOLE

SHOOLING > SHOOL

SHOOLS > SHOOL

SHOON *plural of* > SHOE

SHOORA *same as* > SHURA

SHOORAS > SHOORA

SHOOS > SHOO

SHOOT *vb* hit, wound, or kill with a missile fired from a weapon ▷ *n* new branch or sprout of a plant

SHOOTABLE > SHOOT

SHOOTDOWN *n* act of shooting down aircraft

SHOOTER *n* person or thing that shoots

SHOOTERS > SHOOTER

SHOOTING > SHOOT

SHOOTINGS > SHOOT

SHOOTIST *n* person who shoots

SHOOTISTS > SHOOTIST

SHOOTOUT *n* conclusive gunfight

SHOOTOUTS > SHOOTOUT

SHOOTS > SHOOT

SHOP *n* place for sale of goods and services ▷ *vb* visit a shop or shops to buy goods

SHOPBOARD *n* shop counter

SHOPBOY *n* boy working in shop

SHOPBOYS > SHOPBOY

SHOPE *n* old form of shape

SHOPFRONT *n* area of shop facing street

SHOPFUL *n* amount stored in shop

SHOPFULS > SHOPFUL

SHOPGIRL *n* girl working in shop

SHOPGIRLS > SHOPGIRL

SHOPHAR *same as* > SHOFAR

SHOPHARS > SHOPHAR

SHOPHROTH > SHOPHAR

SHOPLIFT *vb* steal from shop

SHOPLIFTS > SHOPLIFT

SHOPMAN *n* man working in shop

SHOPMEN > SHOPMAN

SHOPPE *old-fashioned spelling of* > SHOP

SHOPPED > SHOP

SHOPPER *n* person who buys goods in a shop

SHOPPERS > SHOPPER

SHOPPES > SHOPPE

SHOPPIER > SHOPPY

SHOPPIEST > SHOPPY

SHOPPING > SHOP

SHOPPINGS > SHOP

SHOPPY *adj* of a shop

SHOPS > SHOP

SHOPTALK *n* conversation about one's work, carried on outside working hours

SHOPTALKS > SHOPTALK

SHOPWORN *adj* worn or faded from being displayed in a shop

SHORAN *n* short-range radar system

SHORANS > SHORAN

SHORE *n* edge of a sea or lake ▷ *vb* prop or support

SHOREBIRD *n* bird that lives close to the water

SHORED > SHORE

SHORELESS *adj* without a shore suitable for landing

SHORELINE *n* edge of a sea, lake, or wide river

SHOREMAN *n* person who lives on shore

SHOREMEN > SHOREMAN

SHORER > SHORE

SHORERS > SHORE

SHORES > SHORE

SHORESIDE *n* area at shore

SHORESMAN *n* fishing industry worker on shore

SHORESMEN > SHORESMAN

SHOREWARD *adj* near or facing the shore ▷ *adv* towards the shore

SHOREWEED *n* tufty aquatic perennial plant

SHORING > SHORE

SHORINGS > SHORE

SHORL *n* black mineral

SHORLS > SHORL

SHORN *past participle of* > SHEAR

SHORT *adj* not long ▷ *adv* abruptly ▷ *n* drink of spirits ▷ *vb* short-circuit

SHORTAGE *n* deficiency

SHORTAGES > SHORTAGE

SHORTARM *adj* (of a punch) with the arm bent

SHORTCAKE *n* shortbread

SHORTCUT *n* route that is shorter than the usual one

SHORTCUTS > SHORTCUT

SHORTED > SHORT

SHORTEN *vb* make or become shorter

SHORTENED > SHORTEN

SHORTENER > SHORTEN

SHORTENS > SHORTEN

SHORTER > SHORT

SHORTEST > SHORT

SHORTFALL *n* deficit

SHORTGOWN *n* old Scots word meaning woman's jacket

SHORTHAIR *n* cat with short fur

SHORTHAND *n* system of rapid writing using symbols to represent words

SHORTHEAD *n* species of fish

SHORTHOLD as in *shorthold tenancy* letting of a dwelling for between one and five years at a fair rent

SHORTHORN *n* member of a breed of cattle with short horns

SHORTIA *n* American flowering plant

SHORTIAS > SHORTIA

SHORTIE *n* person or thing that is extremely short

SHORTIES > SHORTY

SHORTING > SHORT

SHORTISH > SHORT

SHORTLIST *n* list of suitable applicants for a job, etc

SHORTLY *adv* soon

SHORTNESS > SHORT

SHORTS *pl n* trousers reaching the top of the thigh or partway to the knee

SHORTSTOP *n* fielding position to the left of second base viewed from home plate

SHORTWAVE *n* radio wave with a wavelength in the range 10–100 metres

SHORTY *same as* > SHORTIE

SHOT *vb* load with shot

SHOTE *same as* > SHOAT

SHOTES > SHOTE

SHOTFIRER *n* person detonating blasting charge

SHOTGUN *n* gun for firing a charge of shot at short range ▷ *adj* involving coercion or duress ▷ *vb* shoot or threaten with or as if with a shotgun

SHOTGUNS > SHOTGUN

SHOTHOLE *n* drilled hole in to which explosive is put for blasting

SHOTHOLES > SHOTHOLE

SHOTMAKER *n* sport player making good shots

SHOTPROOF *adj* able to

withstand shot
SHOTPUT *n* athletic event in which a heavy metal ball is thrown
SHOTPUTS > SHOTPUT
SHOTS > SHOT
SHOTT *n* shallow temporary salt lake or marsh in the North African desert
SHOTTE *n* old form of shoat
SHOTTED > SHOT
SHOTTEN *adj* (of fish, esp herring) having recently spawned
SHOTTES > SHOTTE
SHOTTING > SHOT
SHOTTLE *n* small drawer
SHOTTLES > SHOTTLE
SHOTTS > SHOTT
SHOUGH *n* old word meaning lapdog
SHOUGHS > SHOUGH
SHOULD > SHALL
SHOULDER *n* part of the body to which an arm, foreleg, or wing is attached ▷ *vb* bear (a burden or responsibility)
SHOULDERS > SHOULDER
SHOULDEST *same as* > SHOULDST
SHOULDST *form of the past tense of* > SHALL
SHOUSE *n* toilet ▷ *adj* unwell or in poor spirits
SHOUSES > SHOUSE
SHOUT *n* loud cry ▷ *vb* cry out loudly
SHOUTED > SHOUT
SHOUTER > SHOUT
SHOUTERS > SHOUT
SHOUTHER *Scots form of* > SHOULDER
SHOUTHERS > SHOUTHER
SHOUTIER > SHOUTY
SHOUTIEST > SHOUTY
SHOUTING > SHOUT
SHOUTINGS > SHOUT
SHOUTLINE *n* line in advertisement made prominent to catch attention
SHOUTS > SHOUT
SHOUTY *adj* characterized by or involving shouting
SHOVE *vb* push roughly ▷ *n* rough push
SHOVED > SHOVE
SHOVEL *n* tool for lifting or moving loose material ▷ *vb* lift or move as with a shovel
SHOVELED > SHOVEL
SHOVELER *n* type of duck
SHOVELERS > SHOVELER
SHOVELFUL > SHOVEL
SHOVELING > SHOVEL
SHOVELLED > SHOVEL
SHOVELLER > SHOVEL
SHOVELS > SHOVEL
SHOVER > SHOVE
SHOVERS > SHOVE
SHOVES > SHOVE
SHOVING *n* act of pushing hard
SHOVINGS > SHOVING
SHOW *vb* make, be, or become noticeable

or visible ▷ *n* public exhibition
SHOWABLE > SHOW
SHOWBIZ *n* entertainment industry including theatre, films, and TV
SHOWBIZZY > SHOWBIZ
SHOWBOAT *n* paddle-wheel river steamer with a theatre and a repertory company ▷ *vb* perform or behave in a showy and flamboyant way
SHOWBOATS > SHOWBOAT
SHOWBOX *n* box containing showman's material
SHOWBOXES > SHOWBOX
SHOWBREAD *same as* > SHEWBREAD
SHOWCASE *n* situation in which something is displayed to best advantage ▷ *vb* exhibit or display ▷ *adj* displayed or meriting display as in a showcase
SHOWCASED > SHOWCASE
SHOWCASES > SHOWCASE
SHOWD *vb* rock or sway to and fro ▷ *n* rocking motion
SHOWDED > SHOWD
SHOWDING > SHOWD
SHOWDOWN *n* confrontation that settles a dispute
SHOWDOWNS > SHOWDOWN
SHOWDS > SHOWD
SHOWED > SHOW
SHOWER *n* kind of bath in which a person stands while being sprayed with water ▷ *vb* wash in a shower
SHOWERED > SHOWER
SHOWERER > SHOWER
SHOWERERS > SHOWER
SHOWERFUL > SHOWER
SHOWERIER > SHOWER
SHOWERING > SHOWER
SHOWERS > SHOWER
SHOWERY > SHOWER
SHOWGHE *n* old word meaning lapdog
SHOWGHES > SHOWGHE
SHOWGIRL *n* girl who appears in shows, etc, esp as a singer or dancer
SHOWGIRLS > SHOWGIRL
SHOWIER > SHOWY
SHOWIEST > SHOWY
SHOWILY > SHOWY
SHOWINESS > SHOWY
SHOWING > SHOW
SHOWINGS > SHOW
SHOWMAN *n* man skilled at presenting anything spectacularly
SHOWMANLY > SHOWMAN
SHOWMEN > SHOWMAN
SHOWN > SHOW
SHOWOFF *n* person who makes a vain display of himself or herself
SHOWOFFS > SHOWOFF
SHOWPIECE *n* excellent specimen shown for display or as an example
SHOWPLACE *n* place visited

for its beauty or interest
SHOWRING *n* area where animals are displayed for sale or competition
SHOWRINGS > SHOWRING
SHOWROOM *n* room in which goods for sale are on display
SHOWROOMS > SHOWROOM
SHOWS > SHOW
SHOWTIME *n* time when show begins
SHOWTIMES > SHOWTIME
SHOWY *adj* gaudy
SHOWYARD *n* yard where cattle are displayed
SHOWYARDS > SHOWYARD
SHOYU *n* Japanese variety of soy sauce
SHOYUS > SHOYU
SHRADDHA *n* Hindu offering to an ancestor
SHRADDHAS > SHRADDHA
SHRANK > SHRINK
SHRAPNEL *n* artillery shell filled with pellets which scatter on explosion
SHRAPNELS > SHRAPNEL
SHRED *n* long narrow strip torn from something ▷ *vb* tear to shreds
SHREDDED > SHRED
SHREDDER > SHRED
SHREDDERS > SHRED
SHREDDIER > SHRED
SHREDDING > SHRED
SHREDDY > SHRED
SHREDLESS > SHRED
SHREDS > SHRED
SHREEK *old spelling of* > SHRIEK
SHREEKED > SHREEK
SHREEKING > SHREEK
SHREEKS > SHREEK
SHREIK *old spelling of* > SHRIEK
SHREIKED > SHREIK
SHREIKING > SHREIK
SHREIKS > SHREIK
SHREW *n* small mouselike animal ▷ *vb* curse or damn
SHREWD *adj* clever and perceptive
SHREWDER > SHREWD
SHREWDEST > SHREWD
SHREWDIE *n* shrewd person
SHREWDIES > SHREWDIE
SHREWDLY > SHREWD
SHREWED > SHREW
SHREWING > SHREW
SHREWISH *adj* (esp of a woman) bad-tempered and nagging
SHREWLIKE > SHREW
SHREWMICE *pl n* shrews
SHREWS > SHREW
SHRI *n* Indian title of respect
SHRIECH *old spelling of* > SHRIEK
SHRIECHED > SHRIECH
SHRIECHES > SHRIECH
SHRIEK *n* shrill cry ▷ *vb* utter (with) a shriek
SHRIEKED > SHRIEK
SHRIEKER > SHRIEK
SHRIEKERS > SHRIEK

SHRIEKIER > SHRIEK
SHRIEKING > SHRIEK
SHRIEKS > SHRIEK
SHRIEKY > SHRIEK
SHRIEVAL *adj* of or relating to a sheriff
SHRIEVE *archaic word for* > SHERIFF
SHRIEVED > SHRIEVE
SHRIEVES > SHRIEVE
SHRIEVING > SHRIEVE
SHRIFT *n* act or an instance of shriving or being shriven
SHRIFTS > SHRIFT
SHRIGHT *n* old word meaning shriek
SHRIGHTS > SHRIGHT
SHRIKE *n* songbird with a heavy hooked bill ▷ *vb* archaic word for shriek
SHRIKED > SHRIKE
SHRIKES > SHRIKE
SHRIKING > SHRIKE
SHRILL *adj* (of a sound) sharp and high-pitched ▷ *vb* utter shrilly
SHRILLED > SHRILL
SHRILLER > SHRILL
SHRILLEST > SHRILL
SHRILLIER > SHRILL
SHRILLING > SHRILL
SHRILLS > SHRILL
SHRILLY > SHRILL
SHRIMP *n* small edible shellfish ▷ *vb* fish for shrimps
SHRIMPED > SHRIMP
SHRIMPER > SHRIMP
SHRIMPERS > SHRIMP
SHRIMPIER > SHRIMP
SHRIMPING > SHRIMP
SHRIMPS > SHRIMP
SHRIMPY > SHRIMP
SHRINAL > SHRINE
SHRINE *n* place of worship associated with a sacred person or object ▷ *vb* enshrine
SHRINED > SHRINE
SHRINES > SHRINE
SHRINING > SHRINE
SHRINK *vb* become or make smaller ▷ *n* psychiatrist
SHRINKAGE *n* decrease in size, value, or weight
SHRINKER > SHRINK
SHRINKERS > SHRINK
SHRINKING > SHRINK
SHRINKS > SHRINK
SHRIS > SHRI
SHRITCH *vb* old word meaning shriek
SHRITCHED > SHRITCH
SHRITCHES > SHRITCH
SHRIVE *vb* hear the confession of (a penitent)
SHRIVED > SHRIVE
SHRIVEL *vb* shrink and wither
SHRIVELED > SHRIVEL
SHRIVELS > SHRIVEL
SHRIVEN > SHRIVE
SHRIVER > SHRIVE
SHRIVERS > SHRIVE
SHRIVES > SHRIVE
SHRIVING > SHRIVE
SHRIVINGS > SHRIVE

SHROFF n (in China and Japan) expert employed to separate counterfeit money from the genuine ▷ vb test (money) and separate out the counterfeit and base
SHROFFAGE > SHROFF
SHROFFED > SHROFF
SHROFFING > SHROFF
SHROFFS > SHROFF
SHROOM n slang for magic mushroom ▷ vb take magic mushrooms
SHROOMED > SHROOM
SHROOMER > SHROOM
SHROOMERS > SHROOM
SHROOMING > SHROOM
SHROOMS > SHROOM
SHROUD n piece of cloth used to wrap a dead body ▷ vb conceal
SHROUDED > SHROUD
SHROUDIER > SHROUD
SHROUDING > SHROUD
SHROUDS > SHROUD
SHROUDY > SHROUD
SHROVE vb dialect word meaning to observe Shrove-tide
SHROVED > SHROVE
SHROVES > SHROVE
SHROVING > SHROVE
SHROW vb old form of shrew
SHROWD adj old form of shrewd
SHROWED > SHROW
SHROWING > SHROW
SHROWS > SHROW
SHRUB n woody plant smaller than a tree ▷ vb plant shrubs
SHRUBBED > SHRUB
SHRUBBERY n area planted with shrubs
SHRUBBIER > SHRUBBY
SHRUBBING > SHRUB
SHRUBBY adj consisting of, planted with, or abounding in shrubs
SHRUBLAND n land covered by shrubs
SHRUBLESS > SHRUB
SHRUBLIKE > SHRUB
SHRUBS > SHRUB
SHRUG vb raise and then drop (the shoulders) as a sign of indifference or doubt ▷ n shrugging
SHRUGGED > SHRUG
SHRUGGING > SHRUG
SHRUGS > SHRUG
SHRUNK > SHRINK
SHRUNKEN adj reduced in size
SHTCHI n Russian cabbage soup
SHTCHIS > SHTCHI
SHTETEL n Jewish community in Eastern Europe
SHTETELS > SHTETEL
SHTETL n (formerly) a small Jewish community in Eastern Europe
SHTETLACH > SHTETL
SHTETLS > SHTETL

SHTICK n comedian's routine
SHTICKIER > SHTICK
SHTICKS > SHTICK
SHTICKY > SHTICK
SHTIK n shtick
SHTIKS > SHTIK
SHTOOK n trouble
SHTOOKS > SHTOOK
SHTOOM adj silent
SHTUCK n trouble
SHTUCKS > SHTUCK
SHTUM adj silent
SHTUMM adj silent
SHTUP vb have sex (with)
SHTUPPED > SHTUP
SHTUPPING > SHTUP
SHTUPS > SHTUP
SHUBUNKIN n type of goldfish
SHUCK n outer covering of something ▷ vb remove the shucks from
SHUCKED > SHUCK
SHUCKER > SHUCK
SHUCKERS > SHUCK
SHUCKING > SHUCK
SHUCKINGS > SHUCK
SHUCKS pl n something of little value ▷ interj exclamation of disappointment, annoyance, etc
SHUDDER vb shake or tremble violently, esp with horror ▷ n shaking or trembling
SHUDDERED > SHUDDER
SHUDDERS > SHUDDER
SHUDDERY > SHUDDER
SHUFFLE vb walk without lifting the feet ▷ n shuffling
SHUFFLED > SHUFFLE
SHUFFLER > SHUFFLE
SHUFFLERS > SHUFFLE
SHUFFLES > SHUFFLE
SHUFFLING > SHUFFLE
SHUFTI same as > SHUFTY
SHUFTIES > SHUFTY
SHUFTIS > SHUFTI
SHUFTY n look
SHUGGIES > SHUGGY
SHUGGY n swing, as at a fairground
SHUL Yiddish word for > SYNAGOGUE
SHULE vb saunter
SHULED > SHULE
SHULES > SHULE
SHULING > SHULE
SHULN > SHUL
SHULS > SHUL
SHUN vb avoid
SHUNLESS adj old word meaning not to be shunned
SHUNNABLE > SHUN
SHUNNED > SHUN
SHUNNER > SHUN
SHUNNERS > SHUN
SHUNNING > SHUN
SHUNPIKE vb take side road to avoid toll at turnpike
SHUNPIKED > SHUNPIKE
SHUNPIKER > SHUNPIKE
SHUNPIKES > SHUNPIKE
SHUNS > SHUN

SHUNT vb move (objects or people) to a different position ▷ n shunting
SHUNTED > SHUNT
SHUNTER n small railway locomotive used for manoeuvring coaches
SHUNTERS > SHUNTER
SHUNTING > SHUNT
SHUNTINGS > SHUNT
SHUNTS > SHUNT
SHURA n consultative council or assembly
SHURAS > SHURA
SHUSH interj be quiet! ▷ vb quiet by saying 'shush'
SHUSHED > SHUSH
SHUSHER > SHUSH
SHUSHERS > SHUSH
SHUSHES > SHUSH
SHUSHING > SHUSH
SHUT vb bring together or fold, close
SHUTDOWN n closing of a factory, shop, or other business ▷ vb discontinue operations permanently
SHUTDOWNS > SHUTDOWN
SHUTE variant of > CHUTE
SHUTED > SHUTE
SHUTES > SHUTE
SHUTEYE n sleep
SHUTEYES > SHUTEYE
SHUTING > SHUTE
SHUTOFF n device that shuts something off, esp a machine control
SHUTOFFS > SHUTOFF
SHUTOUT n game in which the opposing team does not score ▷ vb keep out or exclude
SHUTOUTS > SHUTOUT
SHUTS > SHUT
SHUTTER n hinged doorlike cover for closing off a window ▷ vb close or equip with a shutter
SHUTTERED > SHUTTER
SHUTTERS > SHUTTER
SHUTTING > SHUT
SHUTTLE n bobbin-like device used in weaving ▷ vb move by or as if by a shuttle
SHUTTLED > SHUTTLE
SHUTTLER > SHUTTLE
SHUTTLERS > SHUTTLE
SHUTTLES > SHUTTLE
SHUTTLING > SHUTTLE
SHVARTZE same as > SCHVARTZE
SHVARTZES > SHVARTZE
SHWA same as > SCHWA
SHWANPAN same as > SWANPAN
SHWANPANS > SHWANPAN
SHWAS > SHWA
SHWESHWE n African cotton print fabric
SHWESHWES > SHWESHWE
SHY adj not at ease in company ▷ vb start back in fear ▷ n throw
SHYER > SHY
SHYERS > SHY
SHYEST > SHY

SHYING > SHY
SHYISH > SHY
SHYLOCK vb lend money at an exorbitant rate of interest
SHYLOCKED > SHYLOCK
SHYLOCKS > SHYLOCK
SHYLY > SHY
SHYNESS > SHY
SHYNESSES > SHY
SHYPOO n liquor of poor quality
SHYPOOS > SHYPOO
SHYSTER n person, esp a lawyer or politician, who uses discreditable or unethical methods
SHYSTERS > SHYSTER
SI same as > TE
SIAL n silicon-rich and aluminium-rich rocks of the earth's continental upper crust
SIALIC > SIAL
SIALID n species of fly
SIALIDAN > SIALID
SIALIDANS > SIALID
SIALIDS > SIALID
SIALOGRAM n X-ray of salivary gland
SIALOID adj resembling saliva
SIALOLITH n hard deposit formed in salivary gland
SIALON n type of ceramic
SIALONS > SIALON
SIALS > SIAL
SIAMANG n large black gibbon
SIAMANGS > SIAMANG
SIAMESE variant of > SIAMEZE
SIAMESED > SIAMESE
SIAMESES > SIAMESE
SIAMESING > SIAMESE
SIAMEZE vb join together
SIAMEZED > SIAMEZE
SIAMEZES > SIAMEZE
SIAMEZING > SIAMEZE
SIB n blood relative
SIBB n sib
SIBBS > SIBB
SIBILANCE > SIBILANT
SIBILANCY > SIBILANT
SIBILANT adj hissing ▷ n consonant pronounced with a hissing sound
SIBILANTS > SIBILANT
SIBILATE vb pronounce or utter (words or speech) with a hissing sound
SIBILATED > SIBILATE
SIBILATES > SIBILATE
SIBILATOR > SIBILATE
SIBILOUS > SIBILANT
SIBLING n brother or sister
SIBLINGS > SIBLING
SIBS > SIB
SIBSHIP n group of children of the same parents
SIBSHIPS > SIBSHIP
SIBYL n (in ancient Greece and Rome) prophetess
SIBYLIC > SIBYL
SIBYLLIC > SIBYL
SIBYLLINE > SIBYL
SIBYLS > SIBYL

S

SIC *adv* thus ▷ *vb* attack
SICCAN *adj* Scots word meaning such
SICCAR *adj* sure
SICCATIVE *n* substance added to a liquid to promote drying
SICCED > SIC
SICCING > SIC
SICCITIES > SICCITY
SICCITY *n* dryness
SICE *same as* > SYCE
SICES > SICE
SICH *adj* old form of such
SICHT *Scot word for* > SIGHT
SICHTED > SICHT
SICHTING > SICHT
SICHTS > SICHT
SICILIANA *n* Sicilian dance
SICILIANE > SICILIANA
SICILIANO *n* old dance in six-beat or twelve-beat time
SICK *adj* vomiting or likely to vomit ▷ *n* vomit ▷ *vb* vomit
SICKBAY *n* room for the treatment of sick people, for example on a ship
SICKBAYS > SICKBAY
SICKBED *n* bed where sick person lies
SICKBEDS > SICKBED
SICKED > SICK
SICKEE *n* person off work through illness
SICKEES > SICKEE
SICKEN *vb* make nauseated or disgusted
SICKENED > SICKEN
SICKENER *n* something that induces sickness or nausea
SICKENERS > SICKENER
SICKENING *adj* causing horror or disgust
SICKENS > SICKEN
SICKER > SICK
SICKERLY *adv* Scots word meaning surely
SICKEST > SICK
SICKIE *n* day of sick leave from work
SICKIES > SICKIE
SICKING > SICK
SICKISH > SICK
SICKISHLY > SICK
SICKLE *n* tool with a curved blade for cutting grass or grain ▷ *vb* cut with a sickle
SICKLED > SICKLE
SICKLEMAN *n* person reaping with sickle
SICKLEMEN > SICKLEMAN
SICKLEMIA *n* form of anaemia
SICKLEMIC > SICKLEMIA
SICKLES > SICKLE
SICKLIED > SICKLY
SICKLIER > SICKLY
SICKLIES > SICKLY
SICKLIEST > SICKLY
SICKLILY > SICKLY
SICKLING > SICKLE
SICKLY *adj* unhealthy, weak ▷ *adv* suggesting sickness ▷ *vb* make sickly

SICKLYING > SICKLY
SICKNESS *n* particular illness or disease
SICKNURSE *n* person nursing sick person
SICKO *n* person who is mentally disturbed or perverted ▷ *adj* perverted or in bad taste
SICKOS > SICKO
SICKOUT *n* form of industrial action in which all workers in a workplace report sick simultaneously
SICKOUTS > SICKOUT
SICKROOM *n* room to which a person who is ill is confined
SICKROOMS > SICKROOM
SICKS > SICK
SICLIKE *adj* Scots word meaning suchlike
SICS > SIC
SIDA *n* Australian hemp plant
SIDALCEA *n* type of perennial N American plant
SIDALCEAS > SIDALCEA
SIDAS > SIDA
SIDDHA *n* (in Hinduism) person who has achieved perfection
SIDDHAS > SIDDHA
SIDDHI *n* (in Hinduism) power attained with perfection
SIDDHIS > SIDDHI
SIDDHUISM *n* (in Indian English) any contrived metaphor or simile
SIDDUR *n* Jewish prayer book
SIDDURIM > SIDDUR
SIDDURS > SIDDUR
SIDE *n* line or surface that borders anything ▷ *adj* at or on the side
SIDEARM *n* weapon worn on belt
SIDEARMS > SIDEARM
SIDEBAND *n* frequency band either above or below the carrier frequency
SIDEBANDS > SIDEBAND
SIDEBAR *n* small newspaper article beside larger one
SIDEBARS > SIDEBAR
SIDEBOARD *n* piece of furniture for holding plates, cutlery, etc in a dining room
SIDEBONES *n* part of horse's hoof
SIDEBURNS *pl n* man's side whiskers
SIDECAR *n* small passenger car on the side of a motorcycle
SIDECARS > SIDECAR
SIDECHECK *n* part of horse's harness
SIDED > SIDE
SIDEDNESS > SIDE
SIDEDRESS *vb* place fertilizer in the soil near the roots of a plant

SIDEHILL *n* side of hill
SIDEHILLS > SIDEHILL
SIDEKICK *n* close friend or associate
SIDEKICKS > SIDEKICK
SIDELIGHT *n* either of two small lights on the front of a vehicle
SIDELINE *n* subsidiary interest or source of income ▷ *vb* prevent (a player) from taking part in a game
SIDELINED > SIDELINE
SIDELINER > SIDELINE
SIDELINES *pl n* area immediately outside the playing area, where substitute players sit
SIDELING *adj* to one side
SIDELOCK *n* long lock of hair on side of head
SIDELOCKS > SIDELOCK
SIDELONG *adj* sideways ▷ *adv* obliquely
SIDEMAN *n* member of a dance band or a jazz group other than the leader
SIDEMEN > SIDEMAN
SIDENOTE *n* note written in margin
SIDENOTES > SIDENOTE
SIDEPATH *n* minor path
SIDEPATHS > SIDEPATH
SIDEPIECE *n* part forming side of something
SIDER *n* one who sides with another
SIDERAL *adj* from the stars
SIDERATE *vb* strike violently
SIDERATED > SIDERATE
SIDERATES > SIDERATE
SIDEREAL *adj* of or determined with reference to the stars
SIDERITE *n* pale yellow to brownish-black mineral
SIDERITES > SIDERITE
SIDERITIC > SIDERITE
SIDEROAD *n* (esp in Ontario) a road going at right angles to concession roads
SIDEROADS > SIDEROAD
SIDEROSES > SIDEROSIS
SIDEROSIS *n* lung disease caused by breathing in fine particles of iron or other metallic dust
SIDEROTIC > SIDEROSIS
SIDERS > SIDER
SIDES > SIDE
SIDESHOOT *n* minor shoot growing on plant
SIDESHOW *n* entertainment offered along with the main show
SIDESHOWS > SIDESHOW
SIDESLIP *same as* > SLIP
SIDESLIPS > SIDESLIP
SIDESMAN *n* man elected to help the parish church warden
SIDESMEN > SIDESMAN
SIDESPIN *n* horizontal spin put on ball
SIDESPINS > SIDESPIN

SIDESTEP *vb* dodge (an issue) ▷ *n* movement to one side, such as in dancing or boxing
SIDESTEPS > SIDESTEP
SIDESWIPE *n* unexpected criticism of someone or something while discussing another subject ▷ *vb* make a sideswipe
SIDETRACK *vb* divert from the main topic ▷ *n* railway siding
SIDEWALK *n* paved path for pedestrians, at the side of a road
SIDEWALKS > SIDEWALK
SIDEWALL *n* either of the sides of a pneumatic tyre between the tread and the rim
SIDEWALLS > SIDEWALL
SIDEWARD *adj* directed or moving towards one side ▷ *adv* towards one side
SIDEWARDS *adv* towards one side
SIDEWAY *variant of* > SIDEWAYS
SIDEWAYS *adv* or from the side ▷ *adj* moving or directed to or from one side
SIDEWHEEL *n* one of the paddle wheels of a sidewheeler
SIDEWISE *adv* sideways
SIDH *pl n* fairy people
SIDHA *n* (in Hinduism) person who has achieved perfection
SIDHAS > SIDHA
SIDHE *pl n* inhabitants of fairyland
SIDING *n* short stretch of railway track on which trains are shunted from the main line
SIDINGS > SIDING
SIDLE *vb* walk in a furtive manner ▷ *n* sideways movement
SIDLED > SIDLE
SIDLER > SIDLE
SIDLERS > SIDLE
SIDLES > SIDLE
SIDLING > SIDLE
SIDLINGLY > SIDLE
SIECLE *n* century, period, or era
SIECLES > SIECLE
SIEGE *n* surrounding and blockading of a place ▷ *vb* lay siege to
SIEGED > SIEGE
SIEGER *n* person who besieges
SIEGERS > SIEGER
SIEGES > SIEGE
SIEGING > SIEGE
SIELD *vb* old word meaning given a ceiling
SIEMENS *n* SI unit of electrical conductance
SIEN *n* old word meaning scion
SIENITE *n* type of igneous rock

SIENITES > SIENITE

SIENNA n reddish- or yellowish-brown pigment made from natural earth

SIENNAS > SIENNA

SIENS > SIEN

SIENT n old word meaning scion

SIENTS > SIENT

SIEROZEM n type of soil

SIEROZEMS > SIEROZEM

SIERRA n range of mountains in Spain or America with jagged peaks

SIERRAN > SIERRA

SIERRAS > SIERRA

SIES same as > SIS

SIESTA n afternoon nap, taken in hot countries

SIESTAS > SIESTA

SIETH n old form of scythe

SIETHS > SIETH

SIEUR n French word meaning lord

SIEURS > SIEUR

SIEVE n utensil with mesh through which a substance is sifted or strained ▷ vb sift or strain through a sieve

SIEVED > SIEVE

SIEVELIKE > SIEVE

SIEVERT n derived SI unit of dose equivalent, equal to 1 joule per kilogram

SIEVERTS > SIEVERT

SIEVES > SIEVE

SIEVING > SIEVE

SIF adj South African slang for disgusting

SIFAKA n either of two large rare arboreal lemuroid primates

SIFAKAS > SIFAKA

SIFFLE vb whistle

SIFFLED > SIFFLE

SIFFLES > SIFFLE

SIFFLEUR n male professional whistler

SIFFLEURS > SIFFLEUR

SIFFLEUSE n female professional whistler

SIFFLING > SIFFLE

SIFREI > SEFER

SIFT vb remove the coarser particles from a substance with a sieve

SIFTED > SIFT

SIFTER > SIFT

SIFTERS > SIFT

SIFTING > SIFT

SIFTINGLY > SIFT

SIFTINGS pl n material or particles separated out by or as if by a sieve

SIFTS > SIFT

SIGANID n tropical fish

SIGANIDS > SIGANID

SIGH n long audible breath expressing sadness, tiredness, relief, or longing ▷ vb utter a sigh

SIGHED > SIGH

SIGHER > SIGH

SIGHERS > SIGH

SIGHFUL > SIGH

SIGHING > SIGH

SIGHINGLY > SIGH

SIGHLESS > SIGH

SIGHLIKE > SIGH

SIGHS > SIGH

SIGHT n ability to see ▷ vb catch sight of

SIGHTABLE > SIGHT

SIGHTED adj not blind

SIGHTER n any of six practice shots allowed to each competitor in a tournament

SIGHTERS > SIGHTER

SIGHTING > SIGHT

SIGHTINGS > SIGHT

SIGHTLESS adj blind

SIGHTLIER > SIGHTLY

SIGHTLINE n uninterrupted line of vision

SIGHTLY adj pleasing or attractive to see

SIGHTS > SIGHT

SIGHTSAW > SIGHTSEE

SIGHTSEE vb visit the famous or interesting sights of (a place)

SIGHTSEEN > SIGHTSEE

SIGHTSEER > SIGHTSEE

SIGHTSEES > SIGHTSEE

SIGHTSMAN n tourist guide

SIGHTSMEN > SIGHTSMAN

SIGIL n seal or signet

SIGILLARY > SIGIL

SIGILLATE adj closed with seal

SIGILS > SIGIL

SIGISBEI > SIGISBEO

SIGISBEO n male escort for a married woman

SIGLA n list of symbols used in a book

SIGLAS > SIGLA

SIGLOI > SIGLOS

SIGLOS n silver coin of ancient Persia worth one twentieth of a daric

SIGLUM n symbol used in book

SIGMA n 18th letter in the Greek alphabet

SIGMAS > SIGMA

SIGMATE adj shaped like the Greek letter sigma or the Roman S ▷ n sigmate thing ▷ vb add a sigma

SIGMATED > SIGMATE

SIGMATES > SIGMATE

SIGMATIC > SIGMATE

SIGMATING > SIGMATE

SIGMATION > SIGMATE

SIGMATISM n repetition of letter s

SIGMATRON n machine for generating X-rays

SIGMOID adj shaped like the letter S ▷ n S-shaped bend in the final portion of the large intestine

SIGMOIDAL variant of > SIGMOID

SIGMOIDS > SIGMOID

SIGN n indication of something not immediately or outwardly observable ▷ vb write (one's name) on (a document or letter) to show its authenticity or one's agreement

SIGNA pl n symbols

SIGNABLE > SIGN

SIGNAGE n signs collectively, esp street signs or signs giving directions

SIGNAGES > SIGNAGE

SIGNAL n sign or gesture to convey information ▷ adj very important ▷ vb convey (information) by signal

SIGNALED > SIGNAL

SIGNALER > SIGNAL

SIGNALERS > SIGNAL

SIGNALING > SIGNAL

SIGNALISE same as > SIGNALIZE

SIGNALIZE vb make noteworthy or conspicuous

SIGNALLED > SIGNAL

SIGNALLER > SIGNAL

SIGNALLY adv conspicuously or especially

SIGNALMAN n railwayman in charge of signals and points

SIGNALMEN > SIGNALMAN

SIGNALS > SIGNAL

SIGNARIES > SIGNARY

SIGNARY n set of symbols

SIGNATORY n one of the parties who sign a document ▷ adj having signed a document or treaty

SIGNATURE n person's name written by himself or herself in signing something

SIGNBOARD n board carrying a sign or notice, often to advertise a business or product

SIGNED > SIGN

SIGNEE n person signing document

SIGNEES > SIGNEE

SIGNER n person who signs something

SIGNERS > SIGNER

SIGNET n small seal used to authenticate documents ▷ vb stamp or authenticate with a signet

SIGNETED > SIGNET

SIGNETING > SIGNET

SIGNETS > SIGNET

SIGNEUR old spelling of > SENIOR

SIGNEURIE n old word meaning seniority

SIGNIEUR n old word meaning lord

SIGNIEURS > SIGNIEUR

SIGNIFICS n study of meaning

SIGNIFIED > SIGNIFY

SIGNIFIER > SIGNIFY

SIGNIFIES > SIGNIFY

SIGNIFY vb indicate or suggest

SIGNING n system of communication using hand and arm movements, such as one used by deaf people

SIGNINGS > SIGNING

SIGNIOR same as > SIGNOR

SIGNIORI > SIGNIOR

SIGNIORS > SIGNIOR

SIGNIORY n old word meaning lordship

SIGNLESS > SIGN

SIGNOR n Italian term of address equivalent to sir or Mr

SIGNORA n Italian term of address equivalent to madam or Mrs

SIGNORAS > SIGNORA

SIGNORE n Italian man: a title of respect equivalent to sir

SIGNORES > SIGNORE

SIGNORI > SIGNORE

SIGNORIA n government of Italian city

SIGNORIAL > SIGNORIA

SIGNORIAS > SIGNORIA

SIGNORIES > SIGNORY

SIGNORINA n Italian term of address equivalent to madam or Miss

SIGNORINE > SIGNORINA

SIGNORINI > SIGNORINO

SIGNORINO n young gentleman

SIGNORS > SIGNOR

SIGNORY same as > SEIGNIORY

SIGNPOST n post bearing a sign that shows the way ▷ vb mark with signposts

SIGNPOSTS > SIGNPOST

SIGNS > SIGN

SIJO n Korean poem

SIJOS > SIJO

SIK adj excellent

SIKA n Japanese forest-dwelling deer

SIKAS > SIKA

SIKE n small stream

SIKER adj old spelling of sicker

SIKES > SIKE

SIKORSKY n type of helicopter

SILAGE n fodder crop harvested while green and partially fermented in a silo ▷ vb make silage

SILAGED > SILAGE

SILAGEING > SILAGE

SILAGES > SILAGE

SILAGING > SILAGE

SILANE n gas containing silicon

SILANES > SILANE

SILASTIC n tradename for a type of flexible silicone rubber

SILASTICS > SILASTIC

SILD n any of various small young herrings, esp when prepared and canned in Norway

SILDS > SILD

SILE vb pour with rain

SILED > SILE

SILEN n god of woodland

SILENCE n absence of noise

or speech ▷ vb make silent

SILENCED adj (of a clergyman) forbidden to preach or perform his clerical functions

SILENCER n device to reduce the noise of an engine exhaust or gun

SILENCERS > SILENCER

SILENCES > SILENCE

SILENCING > SILENCE

SILENE n any plant of the large perennial genus Silene

SILENES > SILENE

SILENI > SILENUS

SILENS > SILEN

SILENT adj tending to speak very little ▷ n silent film

SILENTER > SILENT

SILENTEST > SILENT

SILENTLY > SILENT

SILENTS > SILENT

SILENUS n woodland deity

SILER n strainer

SILERS > SILER

SILES > SILE

SILESIA n twill-weave fabric of cotton or other fibre

SILESIAS > SILESIA

SILEX n type of heat-resistant glass made from fused quartz

SILEXES > SILEX

SILICA n hard glossy mineral found as quartz and in sandstone

SILICAS > SILICA

SILICATE n compound of silicon, oxygen, and a metal

SILICATED > SILICATE

SILICATES > SILICATE

SILICEOUS adj of, relating to, or containing abundant silica

SILICIC adj of, concerned with, or containing silicon or an acid obtained from silicon

SILICIDE n any one of a class of binary compounds formed between silicon and certain metals

SILICIDES > SILICIDE

SILICIFY vb convert or be converted into silica

SILICIOUS same as > SILICEOUS

SILICIUM rare name for > SILICON

SILICIUMS > SILICIUM

SILICLE same as > SILICULA

SILICLES > SILICLE

SILICON n brittle nonmetallic element widely used in chemistry and industry ▷ adj denoting an area of a country that contains much high-technology industry

SILICONE n tough synthetic substance made from silicon and used in lubricants

SILICONES > SILICONE

SILICONS > SILICON

SILICOSES > SILICOSIS

SILICOSIS n lung disease caused by inhaling silica dust

SILICOTIC n person suffering from silicosis

SILICULA n short broad siliqua, occurring in such cruciferous plants as honesty and shepherd's-purse

SILICULAE > SILICULA

SILICULAS > SILICULA

SILICULE same as > SILICULA

SILICULES > SILICULE

SILING > SILE

SILIQUA n long dry dehiscent fruit of cruciferous plants such as the wallflower

SILIQUAE > SILIQUA

SILIQUAS > SILIQUA

SILIQUE same as > SILIQUA

SILIQUES > SILIQUE

SILIQUOSE > SILIQUA

SILIQUOUS > SILIQUA

SILK n fibre made by the larva of a certain moth ▷ vb (of maize) develop long hairlike styles

SILKALENE same as > SILKALINE

SILKALINE n fine smooth cotton fabric used for linings, etc

SILKED > SILK

SILKEN adj made of silk ▷ vb make like silk

SILKENED > SILKEN

SILKENING > SILKEN

SILKENS > SILKEN

SILKIE n Scots word for a seal

SILKIER > SILKY

SILKIES > SILKIE

SILKIEST > SILKY

SILKILY > SILKY

SILKINESS > SILKY

SILKING > SILK

SILKLIKE > SILK

SILKOLINE n material like silk

SILKS > SILK

SILKTAIL n waxwing

SILKTAILS > SILKTAIL

SILKWEED another name for > MILKWEED

SILKWEEDS > SILKWEED

SILKWORM n caterpillar that spins a cocoon of silk

SILKWORMS > SILKWORM

SILKY adj of or like silk

SILL n ledge at the bottom of a window or door

SILLABUB same as > SYLLABUB

SILLABUBS > SILLABUB

SILLADAR n Indian irregular cavalryman

SILLADARS > SILLADAR

SILLER n silver ▷ adj silver

SILLERS > SILLER

SILLIBUB n syllabub

SILLIBUBS > SILLIBUB

SILLIER > SILLY

SILLIES > SILLY

SILLIEST > SILLY

SILLILY > SILLY

SILLINESS > SILLY

SILLOCK n young coalfish

SILLOCKS > SILLOCK

SILLS > SILL

SILLY adj foolish ▷ n foolish person

SILO n pit or airtight tower for storing silage or grains ▷ vb put in a silo

SILOED > SILO

SILOING > SILO

SILOS > SILO

SILOXANE n any of a class of compounds containing alternate silicon and oxygen atoms

SILOXANES > SILOXANE

SILPHIA > SILPHIUM

SILPHIUM n American flowering wild plant

SILPHIUMS > SILPHIUM

SILT n mud deposited by moving water ▷ vb fill or be choked with silt

SILTATION > SILT

SILTED > SILT

SILTIER > SILT

SILTIEST > SILT

SILTING > SILT

SILTS > SILT

SILTSTONE n variety of fine sandstone formed from consolidated silt

SILTY > SILT

SILURIAN n formed in the third period of the Palaeozoic

SILURID n any freshwater fish of the family Siluridae including catfish ▷ adj of, relating to, or belonging to the family Siluridae

SILURIDS > SILURID

SILURIST n member of ancient Silurian tribe

SILURISTS > SILURIST

SILUROID n freshwater fish

SILUROIDS > SILUROID

SILVA same as > SYLVA

SILVAE > SILVA

SILVAN same as > SYLVAN

SILVANS > SILVAN

SILVAS > SILVA

SILVATIC adj wild, not domestic

SILVER n white precious metal ▷ adj made of or of the colour of silver ▷ vb coat with silver

SILVERED > SILVER

SILVERER > SILVER

SILVERERS > SILVER

SILVEREYE n greenish-coloured songbird of Africa, Australia, New Zealand, and Asia

SILVERIER > SILVERY

SILVERING > SILVER

SILVERISE same as > SILVERIZE

SILVERIZE vb coat with silver

SILVERLY adv like silver

SILVERN adj silver

SILVERS > SILVER

SILVERY adj like silver

SILVEX n type of weedkiller

SILVEXES > SILVEX

SILVICAL adj of trees

SILVICS n study of trees

SIM n computer game that simulates an activity such as flying or playing a sport

SIMA n silicon-rich and magnesium-rich rocks of the earth's oceanic crust

SIMAR variant spelling of > CYMAR

SIMAROUBA n any tropical American tree of the genus Simarouba

SIMARRE n woman's loose gown

SIMARRES > SIMARRE

SIMARS > SIMAR

SIMARUBA same as > SIMAROUBA

SIMARUBAS > SIMARUBA

SIMAS > SIMA

SIMATIC > SIMA

SIMAZINE n organic weedkiller

SIMAZINES > SIMAZINE

SIMBA E African word for > LION

SIMBAS > SIMBA

SIMI n East African sword

SIMIAL adj of apes

SIMIAN n a monkey or ape ▷ adj of or resembling a monkey or ape

SIMIANS > SIMIAN

SIMILAR adj alike but not identical

SIMILARLY > SIMILAR

SIMILE n figure of speech comparing one thing to another, using 'as' or 'like'

SIMILES > SIMILE

SIMILISE same as > SIMILIZE

SIMILISED > SIMILISE

SIMILISES > SIMILISE

SIMILIZE vb use similes

SIMILIZED > SIMILIZE

SIMILIZES > SIMILIZE

SIMILOR n alloy used in cheap jewellery

SIMILORS > SIMILOR

SIMIOID adj of apes

SIMIOUS adj of apes

SIMIS > SIMI

SIMITAR same as > SCIMITAR

SIMITARS > SIMITAR

SIMKIN word used in India for > CHAMPAGNE

SIMKINS > SIMKIN

SIMLIN n American variety of squash plant

SIMLINS > SIMLIN

SIMMER vb cook gently at just below boiling point ▷ n state of simmering

SIMMERED > SIMMER

SIMMERING > SIMMER

SIMMERS > SIMMER

SIMNEL as in simnel cake fruit cake with marzipan eaten at Easter

SIMNELS > SIMNEL

SIMOLEON n American slang

Section 1: Words between 2 and 9 letters in length

for dollar

SIMOLEONS > SIMOLEON

SIMONIAC n person who is guilty of practising simony

SIMONIACS > SIMONIAC

SIMONIES > SIMONY

SIMONIOUS > SIMONY

SIMONISE same as > SIMONIZE

SIMONISED > SIMONISE

SIMONISES > SIMONISE

SIMONIST > SIMONY

SIMONISTS > SIMONY

SIMONIZE vb polish with wax

SIMONIZED > SIMONIZE

SIMONIZES > SIMONIZE

SIMONY n practice of buying or selling Church benefits such as pardons

SIMOOM n hot suffocating sand-laden desert wind

SIMOOMS > SIMOOM

SIMOON same as > SIMOOM

SIMOONS > SIMOON

SIMORG n bird in Persian myth

SIMORGS > SIMORG

SIMP short for > SIMPLETON

SIMPAI n Indonesian monkey

SIMPAIS > SIMPAI

SIMPATICO adj pleasant or congenial

SIMPER vb smile in a silly or affected way ▷ n simpering smile

SIMPERED > SIMPER

SIMPERER > SIMPER

SIMPERERS > SIMPER

SIMPERING > SIMPER

SIMPERS > SIMPER

SIMPKIN word used in India for > CHAMPAGNE

SIMPKINS > SIMPKIN

SIMPLE adj easy to understand or do ▷ n simpleton ▷ vb archaic word meaning to look for medicinal herbs

SIMPLED > SIMPLE

SIMPLER > SIMPLE

SIMPLERS > SIMPLE

SIMPLES > SIMPLE

SIMPLESSE n old word meaning simplicity

SIMPLEST > SIMPLE

SIMPLETON n foolish or half-witted person

SIMPLEX adj permitting the transmission of signals in only one direction in a radio circuit ▷ n simple not a compound word

SIMPLEXES > SIMPLEX

SIMPLICES > SIMPLEX

SIMPLICIA n species of moth

SIMPLIFY vb make less complicated

SIMPLING > SIMPLE

SIMPLINGS > SIMPLE

SIMPLISM n quality of being extremely naive

SIMPLISMS > SIMPLISM

SIMPLIST n old word meaning expert in herbal

medicine

SIMPLISTE adj simplistic

SIMPLISTS > SIMPLIST

SIMPLY adv in a simple manner

SIMPS > SIMP

SIMS > SIM

SIMUL adj simultaneous ▷ n simultaneous broadcast

SIMULACRA pl n representations of things

SIMULACRE n resemblance

SIMULANT adj simulating ▷ n simulant thing

SIMULANTS > SIMULANT

SIMULAR n person or thing that simulates or imitates ▷ adj fake

SIMULARS > SIMULAR

SIMULATE vb make a pretence of ▷ adj assumed or simulated

SIMULATED adj being an imitation of the genuine article, usually made from cheaper material

SIMULATES > SIMULATE

SIMULATOR n device that simulates specific conditions for the purposes of research or training

SIMULCAST vb broadcast (a programme) simultaneously on radio and television ▷ n programme broadcast in this way

SIMULIUM n tropical fly

SIMULIUMS > SIMULIUM

SIMULS > SIMUL

SIMURG n bird in Persian myth

SIMURGH n bird in Persian myth

SIMURGHS > SIMURGH

SIMURGS > SIMURG

SIN n offence or transgression ▷ vb commit a sin

SINAPISM n mixture of black mustard seeds and an adhesive, applied to the skin

SINAPISMS > SINAPISM

SINCE prep during the period of time after ▷ adv from that time

SINCERE adj without pretence or deceit

SINCERELY > SINCERE

SINCERER > SINCERE

SINCEREST > SINCERE

SINCERITY > SINCERE

SINCIPITA > SINCIPUT

SINCIPUT n forward upper part of the skull

SINCIPUTS > SINCIPUT

SIND variant of > SYNE

SINDED > SIND

SINDING > SIND

SINDINGS > SIND

SINDON n type of cloth

SINDONS > SINDON

SINDS > SIND

SINE n ratio of the length of the opposite side to that of the hypotenuse in a right-

angled triangle ▷ vb variant of > SYNE

SINECURE n paid job with minimal duties

SINECURES > SINECURE

SINED > SINE

SINES > SINE

SINEW n tough fibrous tissue joining muscle to bone ▷ vb make strong

SINEWED adj having sinews

SINEWIER > SINEWY

SINEWIEST > SINEWY

SINEWING > SINEW

SINEWLESS > SINEW

SINEWS > SINEW

SINEWY adj lean and muscular

SINFONIA n symphony orchestra

SINFONIAS > SINFONIA

SINFONIE > SINFONIA

SINFUL adj guilty of sin

SINFULLY > SINFUL

SING vb make musical sounds with the voice ▷ n act or performance of singing

SINGABLE > SING

SINGALONG n act of singing along with a performer

SINGE vb burn the surface of ▷ n superficial burn

SINGED > SINGE

SINGEING > SINGE

SINGER n person who sings, esp professionally

SINGERS > SINGER

SINGES > SINGE

SINGING > SING

SINGINGLY > SING

SINGINGS > SING

SINGLE adj one only ▷ n single thing ▷ vb pick out from others

SINGLED > SINGLE

SINGLEDOM n state of being unmarried or not involved in a long-term relationship

SINGLES pl n match played with one person on each side

SINGLET n sleeveless vest

SINGLETON n only card of a particular suit held by a player

SINGLETS > SINGLET

SINGLING > SINGLE

SINGLINGS > SINGLE

SINGLY adv one at a time

SINGS > SING

SINGSONG n informal singing session ▷ adj (of the voice) repeatedly rising and falling in pitch

SINGSONGS > SINGSONG

SINGSONGY > SINGSONG

SINGSPIEL n type of German comic opera with spoken dialogue

SINGULAR adj (of a word or form) denoting one person or thing ▷ n singular form of a word

SINGULARS > SINGULAR

SINGULARY adj (of an operator) monadic

SINGULT n old word meaning sob

SINGULTS > SINGULT

SINGULTUS technical name for > HICCUP

SINH n hyperbolic sine

SINHS > SINH

SINICAL > SINE

SINICISE same as > SINICIZE

SINICISED > SINICISE

SINICISES > SINICISE

SINICIZE vb make Chinese

SINICIZED > SINICIZE

SINICIZES > SINICIZE

SINING > SINE

SINISTER adj threatening or suggesting evil or harm

SINISTRAL adj of, relating to, or located on the left side, esp the left side of the body

SINK vb submerge (in liquid) ▷ n fixed basin with a water supply and drainage pipe

SINKABLE > SINK

SINKAGE n act of sinking or degree to which something sinks or has sunk

SINKAGES > SINKAGE

SINKER n weight for a fishing line

SINKERS > SINKER

SINKHOLE n depression in the ground surface, esp in limestone, where a surface stream disappears underground

SINKHOLES > SINKHOLE

SINKIER > SINKY

SINKIEST > SINKY

SINKING > SINK

SINKINGS > SINK

SINKS > SINK

SINKY adj giving underfoot

SINLESS adj free from sin or guilt

SINLESSLY > SINLESS

SINNED > SIN

SINNER n person that sins ▷ vb behave like a sinner

SINNERED > SINNER

SINNERING > SINNER

SINNERS > SIN

SINNET n braided rope

SINNETS > SINNET

SINNING > SIN

SINNINGIA n tropical flowering plant

SINOLOGUE > SINOLOGY

SINOLOGY n study of Chinese culture, etc

SINOPIA n pigment made from iron ore

SINOPIAS > SINOPIA

SINOPIE > SINOPIA

SINOPIS n pigment made from iron ore

SINOPISES > SINOPIS

SINOPITE n iron ore

SINOPITES > SINOPITE

SINS > SIN

SINSYNE adv Scots word meaning since

SINTER n whitish porous incrustation that is

S

deposited from hot springs ▷ *vb* form large particles from (metal powders or powdery ores) by heating or pressure

SINTERED > SINTER

SINTERING > SINTER

SINTERS > SINTER

SINTERY > SINTER

SINUATE *vb* wind

SINUATED *same as* > SINUATE

SINUATELY > SINUATE

SINUATES > SINUATE

SINUATING > SINUATE

SINUATION *same as* > SINUOSITY

SINUITIS *variant of* > SINUSITIS

SINUOSE *adj* sinuous

SINUOSITY *n* quality of being sinuous

SINUOUS *adj* full of turns or curves

SINUOUSLY > SINUOUS

SINUS *n* hollow space in a bone, esp an air passage opening into the nose

SINUSES > SINUS

SINUSITIS *n* inflammation of a sinus membrane

SINUSLIKE > SINUS

SINUSOID *n* any of the irregular terminal blood vessels that replace capillaries in certain organs ▷ *adj* resembling a sinus

SINUSOIDS > SINUSOID

SIP *vb* drink in small mouthfuls ▷ *n* amount sipped

SIPE *vb* soak

SIPED > SIPE

SIPES > SIPE

SIPHON *n* bent tube which uses air pressure to draw liquid from a container ▷ *vb* draw off thus

SIPHONAGE > SIPHON

SIPHONAL > SIPHON

SIPHONATE *adj* having a syphon

SIPHONED > SIPHON

SIPHONET *n* sucking tube on an aphid

SIPHONETS > SIPHONET

SIPHONIC > SIPHON

SIPHONING > SIPHON

SIPHONS > SIPHON

SIPHUNCLE *n* tube inside shellfish

SIPING > SIPE

SIPPED > SIP

SIPPER > SIP

SIPPERS > SIP

SIPPET *n* small piece of toast eaten with soup or gravy

SIPPETS > SIPPET

SIPPING > SIP

SIPPLE *vb* sip

SIPPLED > SIPPLE

SIPPLES > SIPPLE

SIPPLING > SIPPLE

SIPPY as in *sippy cup* infant's drinking cup with a tight-fitting lid and

perforated spout

SIPS > SIP

SIR *n* polite term of address for a man ▷ *vb* call someone 'sir'

SIRCAR *n* government in India

SIRCARS > SIRCAR

SIRDAR *same as* > SARDAR

SIRDARS > SIRDAR

SIRE *n* male parent of a horse or other domestic animal ▷ *vb* father

SIRED > SIRE

SIREE *emphasized form of* > SIR

SIREES > SIREE

SIREN *n* device making a loud wailing noise as a warning

SIRENIAN *adj* belonging to the *Sirenia*, an order of aquatic herbivorous placental mammals that contains the dugong and manatee ▷ *n* any animal belonging to the order *Sirenia*

SIRENIANS > SIRENIAN

SIRENIC > SIREN

SIRENISE *variant of* > SIRENIZE

SIRENISED > SIRENISE

SIRENISES > SIRENISE

SIRENIZE *vb* bewitch

SIRENIZED > SIRENIZE

SIRENIZES > SIRENIZE

SIRENS > SIREN

SIRES > SIRE

SIRGANG *n* Asian bird

SIRGANGS > SIRGANG

SIRI *n* betel

SIRIASES > SIRIASIS

SIRIASIS *n* sunstroke

SIRIH *n* betel

SIRIHS > SIRIH

SIRING > SIRE

SIRIS > SIRI

SIRKAR *n* government in India

SIRKARS > SIRKAR

SIRLOIN *n* prime cut of loin of beef

SIRLOINS > SIRLOIN

SIRNAME *vb* old form of surname

SIRNAMED > SIRNAME

SIRNAMES > SIRNAME

SIRNAMING > SIRNAME

SIROC *n* sirocco

SIROCCO *n* hot wind blowing from N Africa into S Europe

SIROCCOS > SIROCCO

SIROCS > SIROC

SIRONISE *same as* > SIRONIZE

SIRONISED > SIRONISE

SIRONISES > SIRONISE

SIRONIZE *vb* treat (a woollen fabric) chemically to prevent it wrinkling after being washed

SIRONIZED > SIRONIZE

SIRONIZES > SIRONIZE

SIROSET *adj* of the chemical treatment of

woollen fabrics to give a permanent-press effect

SIRRA *disrespectful form of* > SIR

SIRRAH *n* contemptuous term used in addressing a man or boy

SIRRAHS > SIRRAH

SIRRAS > SIRRA

SIRRED > SIR

SIRREE *n* form of 'sir' used for emphasis

SIRREES > SIRREE

SIRRING > SIR

SIRS > SIR

SIRUP *same as* > SYRUP

SIRUPED > SIRUP

SIRUPIER > SIRUP

SIRUPIEST > SIRUP

SIRUPING > SIRUP

SIRUPS > SIRUP

SIRUPY > SIRUP

SIRVENTE *n* verse form employed by the troubadours of Provence to satirize political themes

SIRVENTES > SIRVENTE

SIS *n* sister

SISAL *n* (fibre of) plant used in making ropes

SISALS > SISAL

SISERARY *n* scolding

SISES > SIS

SISKIN *n* yellow-and-black finch

SISKINS > SISKIN

SISS *shortening of* > SISTER

SISSES > SISS

SISSIER > SISSY

SISSIES > SISSY

SISSIEST > SISSY

SISSIFIED > SISSY

SISSINESS > SISSY

SISSOO *n* Indian tree

SISSOOS > SISSOO

SISSY *n* weak or cowardly (person) ▷ *adj* effeminate, weak, or cowardly

SISSYISH > SISSY

SISSYNESS > SISSY

SIST *vb* Scottish law term meaning stop

SISTED > SIST

SISTER *n* girl or woman with the same parents as another person ▷ *adj* closely related, similar ▷ *vb* be or be like a sister

SISTERED > SISTER

SISTERING > SISTER

SISTERLY *adj* of or like a sister

SISTERS > SISTER

SISTING > SIST

SISTRA > SISTRUM

SISTROID *adj* contained between the convex sides of two intersecting curves

SISTRUM *n* musical instrument of ancient Egypt consisting of a metal rattle

SISTRUMS > SISTRUM

SISTS > SIST

SIT *vb* rest one's body upright on the buttocks

SITAR *n* Indian stringed

musical instrument

SITARIST > SITAR

SITARISTS > SITAR

SITARS > SITAR

SITATUNGA *another name for* > MARSHBUCK

SITCOM *n* situation comedy

SITCOMS > SITCOM

SITE *n* place where something is, was, or is intended to be located ▷ *vb* provide with a site

SITED > SITE

SITELLA *n* type of small generally black-and-white bird

SITELLAS > SITELLA

SITES > SITE

SITFAST *n* sore on a horse's back caused by rubbing of the saddle

SITFASTS > SITFAST

SITH *archaic word for* > SINCE

SITHE *vb* old form of scythe

SITHED > SITHE

SITHEE *interj* look here! listen!

SITHEN *adv* old word meaning since

SITHENCE *adv* old word meaning since

SITHENS *adv* old word meaning since

SITHES > SITHE

SITHING > SITHE

SITING > SITE

SITIOLOGY *n* study of diet and nutrition

SITKA as in *sitka spruce* tall North American spruce tree

SITKAMER *n* sitting room

SITKAMERS > SITKAMER

SITOLOGY *n* scientific study of food, diet, and nutrition

SITREP *n* military situation report

SITREPS > SITREP

SITS > SIT

SITTAR *n* sitar

SITTARS > SITTAR

SITTELLA *variant spelling of* > SITELLA

SITTELLAS > SITTELLA

SITTEN *adj* dialect word for in the saddle

SITTER *n* baby-sitter

SITTERS > SITTER

SITTINE *adj* of nuthatch bird family

SITTING > SIT

SITTINGS > SIT

SITUATE *vb* place ▷ *adj* (now used esp in legal contexts) situated

SITUATED > SITUATE

SITUATES > SITUATE

SITUATING > SITUATE

SITUATION *n* state of affairs

SITULA *n* bucket-shaped container, usually of metal or pottery and often richly decorated

SITULAE > SITULA

SITUP *n* exercise in which the body is brought into a sitting position from one

lying on the back
SITUPS > SITUP
SITUS *n* position or location, esp the usual or right position of an organ or part of the body
SITUSES > SITUS
SITUTUNGA *n* African antelope
SITZ as in *sitz bath* bath in which the buttocks and hips are immersed in hot water
SITZKRIEG *n* period during a war in which both sides change positions very slowly or not at all
SITZMARK *n* depression in the snow where a skier has fallen
SITZMARKS > SITZMARK
SIVER *same as* > SYVER
SIVERS > SIVER
SIWASH *vb* (in the Pacific Northwest) to camp out with only natural shelter
SIWASHED > SIWASH
SIWASHES > SIWASH
SIWASHING > SIWASH
SIX *n* one more than five
SIXAIN *n* stanza or poem of six lines
SIXAINE *n* six-line stanza of poetry
SIXAINES > SIXAINE
SIXAINS > SIXAIN
SIXER *same as* > SIX
SIXERS > SIXER
SIXES > SIX
SIXFOLD *adj* having six times as many or as much ▷ *adv* by six times as many or as much
SIXMO *n* book size resulting from folding a sheet of paper into six leaves or twelve pages, each one sixth the size of the sheet
SIXMOS > SIXMO
SIXPENCE *n* former British and Australian coin worth six pennies
SIXPENCES > SIXPENCE
SIXPENNY *adj* (of a nail) two inches in length
SIXSCORE *n* hundred and twenty
SIXSCORES > SIXSCORE
SIXTE *n* sixth of eight basic positions from which a parry or attack can be made in fencing
SIXTEEN *n* six and ten ▷ *adj* amounting to sixteen ▷ *determiner* amounting to sixteen
SIXTEENER *n* poem verse with sixteen syllables
SIXTEENMO *n* book size resulting from folding a sheet of paper into 16 leaves or 32 pages
SIXTEENS > SIXTEEN
SIXTEENTH *adj* coming after the fifteenth in numbering order ▷ *n* one of 16 equal or nearly equal

parts of something
SIXTES > SIXTE
SIXTH *n* (of) number six in a series ▷ *adj* coming after the fifth and before the seventh in numbering order ▷ *adv* after the fifth person, position, etc
SIXTHLY *same as* > SIXTH
SIXTHS > SIXTH
SIXTIES > SIXTY
SIXTIETH *adj* being the ordinal number of *sixty* in numbering order ▷ *n* one of 60 approximately equal parts of something
SIXTIETHS > SIXTIETH
SIXTY *n* six times ten ▷ *adj* amounting to sixty
SIXTYISH > SIXTY
SIZABLE *adj* quite large
SIZABLY > SIZABLE
SIZAR *n* (at certain universities) an undergraduate receiving a maintenance grant from the college
SIZARS > SIZAR
SIZARSHIP > SIZAR
SIZE *n* dimensions, bigness ▷ *vb* arrange according to size
SIZEABLE *same as* > SIZABLE
SIZEABLY > SIZABLE
SIZED *adj* of a specified size
SIZEISM *n* discrimination on the basis of a person's size, esp against people considered to be overweight
SIZEISMS > SIZEISM
SIZEIST > SIZEISM
SIZEISTS > SIZEISM
SIZEL *n* scrap metal clippings
SIZELS > SIZEL
SIZER > SIZE
SIZERS > SIZE
SIZES > SIZE
SIZIER > SIZE
SIZIEST > SIZE
SIZINESS > SIZE
SIZING > SIZE
SIZINGS > SIZE
SIZISM *n* discrimination against people because of weight
SIZISMS > SIZISM
SIZIST > SIZISM
SIZISTS > SIZISM
SIZY > SIZE
SIZZLE *vb* make a hissing sound like frying fat ▷ *n* hissing sound
SIZZLED > SIZZLE
SIZZLER *n* something that sizzles
SIZZLERS > SIZZLER
SIZZLES > SIZZLE
SIZZLING *adj* extremely hot
SIZZLINGS > SIZZLING
SJAMBOK *n* whip or riding crop made of hide ▷ *vb* beat with a sjambok
SJAMBOKED > SJAMBOK
SJAMBOKS > SJAMBOK
SJOE *interj* South African

exclamation of surprise, admiration, exhaustion, etc
SKA *n* type of West Indian pop music of the 1960s
SKAG *same as* > SCAG
SKAGS > SKAG
SKAIL *vb* Scots word meaning disperse
SKAILED > SKAIL
SKAILING > SKAIL
SKAILS > SKAIL
SKAITH *vb* Scots word meaning injure
SKAITHED > SKAITH
SKAITHING > SKAITH
SKAITHS > SKAITH
SKALD *n* (in ancient Scandinavia) a bard or minstrel
SKALDIC > SKALD
SKALDS > SKALD
SKALDSHIP > SKALD
SKANGER *n* Irish derogatory slang for a young working-class person who wears casual sports clothes
SKANGERS > SKANGER
SKANK *n* fast dance to reggae music ▷ *vb* perform this dance
SKANKED > SKANK
SKANKER > SKANK
SKANKERS > SKANK
SKANKIER > SKANKY
SKANKIEST > SKANKY
SKANKING > SKANK
SKANKINGS > SKANK
SKANKS > SKANK
SKANKY *adj* dirty or unattractive
SKART *Scots word for* > CORMORANT
SKARTH *Scots word for* > CORMORANT
SKARTHS > SKARTH
SKARTS > SKART
SKAS > SKA
SKAT *n* three-handed card game using 32 cards, popular in German-speaking communities
SKATE *n* boot with a steel blade or sets of wheels attached to the sole for gliding over ice or a hard surface ▷ *vb* glide on or as if on skates
SKATED > SKATE
SKATEPARK *n* place for skateboarding
SKATER *n* person who skates
SKATERS > SKATER
SKATES > SKATE
SKATING > SKATE
SKATINGS > SKATE
SKATOL *n* skatole
SKATOLE *n* white or brownish crystalline solid
SKATOLES > SKATOLE
SKATOLS > SKATOL
SKATS > SKAT
SKATT *n* dialect word meaning throw
SKATTS > SKATT
SKAW *variant of* > SCAW

SKAWS > SKAW
SKEAN *n* kind of double-edged dagger formerly used in Ireland and Scotland
SKEANE *same as* > SKEIN
SKEANES > SKEANE
SKEANS > SKEAN
SKEAR *dialect form of* > SCARE
SKEARED > SKEAR
SKEARIER > SKEARY
SKEARIEST > SKEARY
SKEARING > SKEAR
SKEARS > SKEAR
SKEARY *dialect form of* > SCARY
SKEDADDLE *vb* run off ▷ *n* hasty retreat
SKEE *variant spelling of* > SKI
SKEECHAN *n* old Scots type of beer
SKEECHANS > SKEECHAN
SKEED > SKEE
SKEEF *adj, adv* South African slang for at an oblique angle
SKEEING > SKEE
SKEELIER > SKEELY
SKEELIEST > SKEELY
SKEELY *adj* Scots word meaning skilful
SKEEN *n* type of ibex
SKEENS > SKEEN
SKEER *dialect form of* > SCARE
SKEERED > SKEER
SKEERIER > SKEERY
SKEERIEST > SKEERY
SKEERING > SKEER
SKEERS > SKEER
SKEERY *dialect form of* > SCARY
SKEES > SKEE
SKEESICKS *American word meaning* > ROGUE
SKEET *n* form of clay-pigeon shooting
SKEETER *informal word for* > MOSQUITO
SKEETERS > SKEETER
SKEETS > SKEET
SKEG *n* reinforcing brace between the after end of a keel and the rudderpost
SKEGG *n* skeg
SKEGGER *n* young salmon
SKEGGERS > SKEGGER
SKEGGS > SKEGG
SKEGS > SKEG
SKEIGH *adj* Scots word meaning shy
SKEIGHER > SKEIGH
SKEIGHEST > SKEIGH
SKEIN *n* yarn wound in a loose coil ▷ *vb* wind into a skein
SKEINED > SKEIN
SKEINING > SKEIN
SKEINS > SKEIN
SKELDER *vb* beg
SKELDERED > SKELDER
SKELDERS > SKELDER
SKELETAL > SKELETON
SKELETON *n* framework of bones inside a person's or animal's body ▷ *adj* reduced to a minimum
SKELETONS > SKELETON

S

SKELF *n* splinter of wood, esp when embedded accidentally in the skin
SKELFS > SKELF
SKELL *n* homeless person
SKELLIE *adj* skelly
SKELLIED > SKELLY
SKELLIER > SKELLY
SKELLIES > SKELLY
SKELLIEST > SKELLY
SKELLOCH *n* Scots word meaning scream
SKELLOCHS > SKELLOCH
SKELLS > SKELL
SKELLUM *n* rogue
SKELLUMS > SKELLUM
SKELLY *n* whitefish of certain lakes in the Lake District ▷ *vb* look sideways or squint ▷ *adj* cross-eyed
SKELLYING > SKELLY
SKELM *n* villain or crook
SKELMS > SKELM
SKELP *vb* slap ▷ *n* slap
SKELPED > SKELP
SKELPING > SKELP
SKELPINGS > SKELP
SKELPIT *vb* Scots word meaning skelped
SKELPS > SKELP
SKELTER *vb* scurry
SKELTERED > SKELTER
SKELTERS > SKELTER
SKELUM *n* Scots word meaning rascal
SKELUMS > SKELUM
SKEN *vb* squint or stare
SKENE *n* Scots word meaning dagger
SKENES > SKENE
SKENNED > SKEN
SKENNING > SKEN
SKENS > SKEN
SKEO *n* Scots dialect word meaning hut
SKEOS > SKEO
SKEP *n* beehive, esp one constructed of straw ▷ *vb* gather into a hive
SKEPFUL *n* amount skep will hold
SKEPFULS > SKEP
SKEPPED > SKEP
SKEPPING > SKEP
SKEPS > SKEP
SKEPSIS *n* doubt
SKEPSISES > SKEPSIS
SKEPTIC *same as* > SCEPTIC
SKEPTICAL > SKEPTIC
SKEPTICS > SKEPTIC
SKER *vb* scour
SKERRED > SKER
SKERRICK *n* small fragment or amount
SKERRICKS > SKERRICK
SKERRIES > SKERRY
SKERRING > SKER
SKERRY *n* rocky island or reef
SKERS > SKER
SKET *vb* splash (water)
SKETCH *n* rough drawing ▷ *vb* make a sketch (of)
SKETCHED > SKETCH
SKETCHER > SKETCH
SKETCHERS > SKETCH
SKETCHES > SKETCH

SKETCHIER > SKETCHY
SKETCHILY > SKETCHY
SKETCHING > SKETCH
SKETCHPAD *n* pad of paper for sketching
SKETCHY *adj* incomplete or inadequate
SKETS > SKET
SKETTED > SKET
SKETTING > SKET
SKEW *vb* make slanting or crooked ▷ *adj* slanting or crooked ▷ *n* slanting position
SKEWBACK *n* sloping surface on both sides of a segmental arch that takes the thrust
SKEWBACKS > SKEWBACK
SKEWBALD *adj* (horse) marked with patches of white and another colour ▷ *n* horse with this marking
SKEWBALDS > SKEWBALD
SKEWED > SKEW
SKEWER *n* pin to hold meat together during cooking ▷ *vb* fasten with a skewer
SKEWERED > SKEWER
SKEWERING > SKEWER
SKEWERS > SKEWER
SKEWEST > SKEW
SKEWING > SKEW
SKEWNESS *n* quality or condition of being skew
SKEWS > SKEW
SKEWWHIFF *adj* crooked or slanting
SKI *n* one of a pair of long runners fastened to boots for gliding over snow or water ▷ *vb* travel on skis
SKIABLE > SKI
SKIAGRAM *n* picture made from shadows
SKIAGRAMS > SKIAGRAM
SKIAGRAPH *n* skiagram
SKIAMACHY *same as* > SCIAMACHY
SKIASCOPE *n* medical instrument for examining the eye to detect errors of refraction
SKIASCOPY *n* retinoscopy
SKIATRON *n* type of cathode ray tube
SKIATRONS > SKIATRON
SKIBOB *n* vehicle made of two short skis for gliding down snow slopes
SKIBOBBED > SKIBOB
SKIBOBBER > SKIBOB
SKIBOBS > SKIBOB
SKID *vb* (of a moving vehicle) slide sideways uncontrollably ▷ *n* skidding
SKIDDED > SKID
SKIDDER > SKID
SKIDDERS > SKID
SKIDDIER > SKID
SKIDDIEST > SKID
SKIDDING > SKID
SKIDDOO *vb* go away quickly
SKIDDOOED > SKIDDOO
SKIDDOOS > SKIDDOO

SKIDDY > SKID
SKIDLID *n* crash helmet
SKIDLIDS > SKIDLID
SKIDOO *n* snowmobile ▷ *vb* travel on a skidoo
SKIDOOED > SKIDOO
SKIDOOING > SKIDOO
SKIDOOS > SKIDOO
SKIDPAN *n* area made slippery so that vehicle drivers can practise controlling skids
SKIDPANS > SKIDPAN
SKIDPROOF *adj* (of a road surface, tyre, etc) preventing or resistant to skidding
SKIDS > SKID
SKIDWAY *n* platform on which logs ready for sawing are piled
SKIDWAYS > SKIDWAY
SKIED > SKY
SKIER > SKI
SKIERS > SKI
SKIES > SKY
SKIEY *adj* of the sky
SKIEYER > SKIEY
SKIEYEST > SKIEY
SKIFF *n* small boat ▷ *vb* travel in a skiff
SKIFFED > SKIFF
SKIFFING > SKIFF
SKIFFLE *n* style of popular music of the 1950s, played chiefly on guitars and improvised percussion instruments ▷ *vb* play this style of music
SKIFFLED > SKIFFLE
SKIFFLES > SKIFFLE
SKIFFLESS > SKIFF
SKIFFLING > SKIFFLE
SKIFFS > SKIFF
SKIING > SKI
SKIINGS > SKI
SKIJORER > SKIJORING
SKIJORERS > SKIJORING
SKIJORING *n* sport in which a skier is pulled over snow or ice, usually by a horse
SKILFUL *adj* having or showing skill
SKILFULLY > SKILFUL
SKILL *n* special ability or expertise
SKILLED *adj* possessing or demonstrating accomplishment, skill, or special training
SKILLESS > SKILL
SKILLET *n* small frying pan or shallow cooking pot
SKILLETS > SKILLET
SKILLFUL *same as* > SKILFUL
SKILLIER > SKILLY
SKILLIES > SKILLY
SKILLIEST > SKILLY
SKILLING *n* former Scandinavian coin of low denomination
SKILLINGS > SKILLING
SKILLION *n* part of a building having a lower, esp sloping, roof
SKILLIONS > SKILLION
SKILLS > SKILL

SKILLY *n* thin soup or gruel ▷ *adj* skilled
SKIM *vb* remove floating matter from the surface of (a liquid) ▷ *n* act or process of skimming
SKIMBOARD *n* type of surfboard, shorter than standard and rounded at both ends ▷ *vb* surf on a skimboard
SKIMMED > SKIM
SKIMMER *n* person or thing that skims
SKIMMERS > SKIMMER
SKIMMIA *n* shrub of S and SE Asia grown for its ornamental red berries and evergreen foliage
SKIMMIAS > SKIMMIA
SKIMMING > SKIM
SKIMMINGS *pl n* material that is skimmed off a liquid
SKIMO *n* informal and offensive word for an Inuit
SKIMOBILE *n* motor vehicle with skis for travelling on snow
SKIMOS > SKIMO
SKIMP *vb* not invest enough time, money, material, etc
SKIMPED > SKIMP
SKIMPIER > SKIMPY
SKIMPIEST > SKIMPY
SKIMPILY > SKIMPY
SKIMPING > SKIMP
SKIMPS > SKIMP
SKIMPY *adj* scanty or insufficient
SKIMS > SKIM
SKIN *n* outer covering of the body ▷ *vb* remove the skin of
SKINCARE *n* use of cosmetics in taking care of skin
SKINCARES > SKINCARE
SKINFLICK *n* film containing much nudity and sex
SKINFLINT *n* miser
SKINFOOD *n* cosmetic cream for the skin
SKINFOODS > SKINFOOD
SKINFUL *n* sufficient alcoholic drink to make one drunk
SKINFULS > SKINFUL
SKINHEAD *n* youth with very short hair
SKINHEADS > SKINHEAD
SKINK *n* any lizard of the family *Scincidae* ▷ *vb* serve a drink
SKINKED > SKINK
SKINKER > SKINK
SKINKERS > SKINK
SKINKING > SKINK
SKINKS > SKINK
SKINLESS > SKIN
SKINLIKE > SKIN
SKINNED > SKIN
SKINNER *n* person who prepares or deals in animal skins
SKINNERS > SKINNER
SKINNIER > SKINNY

SKINNIEST > SKINNY
SKINNING > SKIN
SKINNY adj thin
SKINS > SKIN
SKINT adj having no money
SKINTER > SKINT
SKINTEST > SKINT
SKINTIGHT adj fitting tightly over the body
SKIO n Scots dialect word meaning hut
SKIORING n sport of being towed on skis by horse
SKIORINGS > SKIORING
SKIOS > SKIO
SKIP vb leap lightly from one foot to the other ▷ n skipping
SKIPJACK n important food fish of tropical seas
SKIPJACKS > SKIPJACK
SKIPLANE n aircraft fitted with skis to enable it to land on and take off from snow
SKIPLANES > SKIPLANE
SKIPPABLE > SKIP
SKIPPED > SKIP
SKIPPER vb captain ▷ n captain of a ship or aircraft
SKIPPERED > SKIPPER
SKIPPERS > SKIPPER
SKIPPET n small round box for preserving a document or seal
SKIPPETS > SKIPPET
SKIPPIER > SKIPPY
SKIPPIEST > SKIPPY
SKIPPING > SKIP
SKIPPINGS > SKIP
SKIPPY adj in high spirits
SKIPS > SKIP
SKIRL n sound of bagpipes ▷ vb (of bagpipes) to give out a shrill sound
SKIRLED > SKIRL
SKIRLING > SKIRL
SKIRLINGS > SKIRL
SKIRLS > SKIRL
SKIRMISH n brief or minor fight or argument ▷ vb take part in a skirmish
SKIRR vb move, run, or fly rapidly ▷ n whirring or grating sound, as of the wings of birds in flight
SKIRRED > SKIRR
SKIRRET n umbelliferous Old World plant
SKIRRETS > SKIRRET
SKIRRING > SKIRR
SKIRRS > SKIRR
SKIRT n woman's garment hanging from the waist ▷ vb border
SKIRTED > SKIRT
SKIRTER n man who skirts fleeces
SKIRTERS > SKIRTER
SKIRTING n border fixed round the base of an interior wall to protect it from kicks, dirt, etc
SKIRTINGS pl n ragged edges trimmed from the fleece of a sheep
SKIRTLESS > SKIRT

SKIRTLIKE > SKIRT
SKIRTS > SKIRT
SKIS > SKI
SKIT n brief satirical sketch
SKITCH vb (of a dog) to attack
SKITCHED > SKITCH
SKITCHES > SKITCH
SKITCHING > SKITCH
SKITE n boast ▷ vb boast
SKITED > SKITE
SKITES > SKITE
SKITING > SKITE
SKITS > SKIT
SKITTER vb move or run rapidly or lightly
SKITTERED > SKITTER
SKITTERS > SKITTER
SKITTERY adj moving lightly and rapidly
SKITTISH adj playful or lively
SKITTLE n bottle-shaped object used as a target in some games ▷ vb play skittles
SKITTLED > SKITTLE
SKITTLES > SKITTLE
SKITTLING > SKITTLE
SKIVE vb evade work or responsibility
SKIVED > SKIVE
SKIVER n tanned outer layer split from a skin ▷ vb cut leather
SKIVERED > SKIVER
SKIVERING > SKIVER
SKIVERS > SKIVER
SKIVES > SKIVE
SKIVIE adj old Scots word meaning disarranged
SKIVIER > SKIVIE
SKIVIEST > SKIVIE
SKIVING > SKIVE
SKIVINGS > SKIVE
SKIVVIED > SKIVVY
SKIVVIES > SKIVVY
SKIVVY n female servant who does menial work ▷ vb work as a skivvy
SKIVVYING > SKIVVY
SKIVY > SKIVE
SKIWEAR n clothes for skiing in
SKLATE Scots word for > SLATE
SKLATED > SKLATE
SKLATES > SKLATE
SKLATING > SKLATE
SKLENT Scots word for > SLANT
SKLENTED > SKLENT
SKLENTING > SKLENT
SKLENTS > SKLENT
SKLIFF n Scots word meaning little piece
SKLIFFS > SKLIFF
SKLIM vb Scots word meaning climb
SKLIMMED > SKLIM
SKLIMMING > SKLIM
SKLIMS > SKLIM
SKOAL same as > SKOL
SKOALED > SKOAL
SKOALING > SKOAL
SKOALS > SKOAL
SKOFF vb eat greedily

SKOFFED > SKOFF
SKOFFING > SKOFF
SKOFFS > SKOFF
SKOKIAAN n (in South Africa) a potent alcoholic beverage
SKOKIAANS > SKOKIAAN
SKOL sentence substitute good health! (a drinking toast) ▷ vb down (an alcoholic drink) in one go
SKOLIA > SKOLION
SKOLION n ancient Greek drinking song
SKOLLED > SKOL
SKOLLIE same as > SKOLLY
SKOLLIES > SKOLLY
SKOLLING > SKOL
SKOLLY n hooligan, usually one of a gang
SKOLS > SKOL
SKOOKUM adj strong or brave
SKOOL ironically illiterate or childish spelling of > SCHOOL
SKOOLS > SKOOL
SKOOSH vb Scots word meaning squirt
SKOOSHED > SKOOSH
SKOOSHES > SKOOSH
SKOOSHING > SKOOSH
SKORT n pair of shorts with a front panel which gives the appearance of a skirt
SKORTS > SKORT
SKOSH n little bit
SKOSHES > SKOSH
SKRAN n food
SKRANS > SKRAN
SKREEGH vb Scots word meaning screech
SKREEGHED > SKREEGH
SKREEGHS > SKREEGH
SKREEN n screen
SKREENS > SKREEN
SKREIGH vb Scots word meaning screech
SKREIGHED > SKREIGH
SKREIGHS > SKREIGH
SKRIECH vb Scots word meaning screech
SKRIECHED > SKRIECH
SKRIECHS > SKRIECH
SKRIED > SKRY
SKRIEGH vb Scots word meaning screech
SKRIEGHED > SKRIEGH
SKRIEGHS > SKRIEGH
SKRIES > SKRY
SKRIK n South African word meaning fright
SKRIKE vb cry
SKRIKED > SKRIKE
SKRIKES > SKRIKE
SKRIKING > SKRIKE
SKRIKS > SKRIK
SKRIMMAGE vb scrimmage
SKRIMP vb steal apples
SKRIMPED > SKRIMP
SKRIMPING > SKRIMP
SKRIMPS > SKRIMP
SKRUMP vb steal apples
SKRUMPED > SKRUMP
SKRUMPING > SKRUMP
SKRUMPS > SKRUMP
SKRY vb try to tell future
SKRYER > SKRY
SKRYERS > SKRY

SKRYING > SKRY
SKUA n large predatory gull
SKUAS > SKUA
SKUDLER n Scots word meaning leader of festivities
SKUDLERS > SKUDLER
SKUG vb shelter
SKUGGED > SKUG
SKUGGING > SKUG
SKUGS > SKUG
SKULK vb move stealthily ▷ n person who skulks
SKULKED > SKULK
SKULKER > SKULK
SKULKERS > SKULK
SKULKING > SKULK
SKULKINGS > SKULK
SKULKS > SKULK
SKULL n bony framework of the head ▷ vb strike on the head
SKULLCAP n close-fitting brimless cap
SKULLCAPS > SKULLCAP
SKULLED > SKULL
SKULLING > SKULL
SKULLS > SKULL
SKULPIN n North American fish
SKULPINS > SKULPIN
SKUMMER vb defecate
SKUMMERED > SKUMMER
SKUMMERS > SKUMMER
SKUNK n small black-and-white N American mammal which emits a foul-smelling fluid when attacked ▷ vb defeat overwhelmingly in a game
SKUNKBIRD n North American songbird
SKUNKED > SKUNK
SKUNKIER > SKUNK
SKUNKIEST > SKUNK
SKUNKING > SKUNK
SKUNKS > SKUNK
SKUNKWEED n low-growing fetid swamp plant of N America
SKUNKY > SKUNK
SKURRIED > SKURRY
SKURRIES > SKURRY
SKURRY vb scurry
SKURRYING > SKURRY
SKUTTLE vb scuttle
SKUTTLED > SKUTTLE
SKUTTLES > SKUTTLE
SKUTTLING > SKUTTLE
SKY n upper atmosphere as seen from the earth ▷ vb hit high in the air
SKYBOARD n small board used for skysurfing
SKYBOARDS > SKYBOARD
SKYBORN adj born in heaven
SKYBORNE adj flying through sky
SKYBOX n luxurious suite high up in the stand of a sports stadium
SKYBOXES > SKYBOX
SKYBRIDGE n covered, elevated bridge connecting two buildings
SKYCAP n luggage porter at American airport

SKYCAPS > SKYCAP
SKYCLAD *adj* naked
SKYDIVE *vb* take part in skydiving
SKYDIVED > SKYDIVE
SKYDIVER > SKYDIVE
SKYDIVERS > SKYDIVE
SKYDIVES > SKYDIVE
SKYDIVING *n* sport of jumping from an aircraft and performing manoeuvres before opening one's parachute
SKYDOVE > SKYDIVE
SKYED > SKY
SKYER *n* cricket ball hit up into air
SKYERS > SKYER
SKYEY *adj* of the sky
SKYF *n* South African slang for a cigarette or substance for smoking ▷ *vb* smoke a cigarette
SKYFED > SKYF
SKYFING > SKYF
SKYFS > SKYF
SKYHOME *n* Australian slang for a sub-penthouse flat in a tall building
SKYHOMES > SKYHOME
SKYHOOK *n* hook hung from helicopter
SKYHOOKS > SKYHOOK
SKYIER > SKYEY
SKYIEST > SKYEY
SKYING > SKY
SKYISH > SKY
SKYJACK *vb* hijack (an aircraft)
SKYJACKED > SKYJACK
SKYJACKER > SKYJACK
SKYJACKS > SKYJACK
SKYLAB *n* orbiting space station
SKYLABS > SKYLAB
SKYLARK *n* lark that sings while soaring at a great height ▷ *vb* play or frolic
SKYLARKED > SKYLARK
SKYLARKER > SKYLARK
SKYLARKS > SKYLARK
SKYLIGHT *n* window in a roof or ceiling
SKYLIGHTS > SKYLIGHT
SKYLIKE > SKY
SKYLINE *n* outline of buildings, trees, etc against the sky
SKYLINES > SKYLINE
SKYLIT *adj* having skylight
SKYMAN *n* paratrooper
SKYMEN > SKYMAN
SKYPHOI > SKYPHOS
SKYPHOS *n* ancient Greek drinking cup
SKYR *n* Scandinavian cheese
SKYRE *vb* Scots word meaning shine
SKYRED > SKYRE
SKYRES > SKYRE
SKYRING > SKYRE
SKYROCKET *vb* rise very quickly
SKYRS > SKYR
SKYSAIL *n* square sail set above the royal on a square-rigger

SKYSAILS > SKYSAIL
SKYSCAPE *n* painting, drawing, photograph, etc, representing or depicting the sky
SKYSCAPES > SKYSCAPE
SKYSURF *vb* perform freefall aerobatics
SKYSURFED > SKYSURF
SKYSURFER *n* someone who performs stunts with a small board attached to his or her feet while in free fall
SKYSURFS > SKYSURF
SKYTE *vb* Scots word meaning slide
SKYTED > SKYTE
SKYTES > SKYTE
SKYTING > SKYTE
SKYWALK *n* tightrope walk at great height
SKYWALKS > SKYWALK
SKYWARD *adj* towards the sky ▷ *adv* towards the sky
SKYWARDS *same as* > SKYWARD
SKYWAY *n* air route
SKYWAYS > SKYWAY
SKYWRITE *vb* write message in sky with smoke from aircraft
SKYWRITER > SKYWRITE
SKYWRITES > SKYWRITE
SKYWROTE > SKYWRITE
SLAB *n* broad flat piece ▷ *vb* cut or make into a slab or slabs
SLABBED > SLAB
SLABBER *vb* dribble from the mouth
SLABBERED > SLABBER
SLABBERER > SLABBER
SLABBERS > SLABBER
SLABBERY > SLABBER
SLABBIER > SLAB
SLABBIEST > SLAB
SLABBING > SLAB
SLABBY > SLAB
SLABLIKE > SLAB
SLABS > SLAB
SLABSTONE *n* flagstone
SLACK *same as* > SLAKE
SLACKED > SLACK
SLACKEN *vb* make or become slack
SLACKENED > SLACKEN
SLACKENER > SLACKEN
SLACKENS > SLACKEN
SLACKER *n* person who evades work or duty
SLACKERS > SLACKER
SLACKEST > SLACK
SLACKING > SLACK
SLACKLY > SLACK
SLACKNESS > SLACK
SLACKS *pl n* casual trousers
SLADANG *n* Malayan tapir
SLADANGS > SLADANG
SLADE *n* little valley
SLADES > SLADE
SLAE *Scots word for* > SLOE
SLAES > SLAE
SLAG *n* waste left after metal is smelted ▷ *vb* criticize
SLAGGED > SLAG
SLAGGIER > SLAG

SLAGGIEST > SLAG
SLAGGING > SLAG
SLAGGINGS > SLAG
SLAGGY > SLAG
SLAGS > SLAG
SLAID *vb* Scots word for 'slid'
SLAIN > SLAY
SLAINTE *interj* cheers!
SLAIRG *Scots word for* > SPREAD
SLAIRGED > SLAIRG
SLAIRGING > SLAIRG
SLAIRGS > SLAIRG
SLAISTER *vb* cover with a sloppy mess ▷ *n* sloppy mess
SLAISTERS > SLAISTER
SLAISTERY > SLAISTER
SLAKABLE > SLAKE
SLAKE *vb* satisfy (thirst or desire)
SLAKEABLE > SLAKE
SLAKED > SLAKE
SLAKELESS *adj* impossible to slake
SLAKER > SLAKE
SLAKERS > SLAKE
SLAKES > SLAKE
SLAKING > SLAKE
SLALOM *n* skiing or canoeing race over a winding course ▷ *vb* take part in a slalom
SLALOMED > SLALOM
SLALOMER > SLALOM
SLALOMERS > SLALOM
SLALOMING > SLALOM
SLALOMIST > SLALOM
SLALOMS > SLALOM
SLAM *vb* shut, put down, or hit violently and noisily ▷ *n* act or sound of slamming
SLAMDANCE *vb* dance aggressively, bumping into others
SLAMMAKIN *n* woman's loose dress
SLAMMED > SLAM
SLAMMER *n* prison
SLAMMERS > SLAMMER
SLAMMING > SLAM
SLAMMINGS > SLAM
SLAMS > SLAM
SLANDER *n* false and malicious statement about a person ▷ *vb* utter slander about
SLANDERED > SLANDER
SLANDERER > SLANDER
SLANDERS > SLANDER
SLANE *n* spade for cutting turf
SLANES > SLANE
SLANG *n* very informal language ▷ *vb* use insulting language to (someone)
SLANGED > SLANG
SLANGER *n* street vendor
SLANGERS > SLANGER
SLANGIER > SLANG
SLANGIEST > SLANG
SLANGILY > SLANG
SLANGING > SLANG
SLANGINGS > SLANG
SLANGISH > SLANG
SLANGS > SLANG

SLANGUAGE *n* language using slang
SLANGULAR *adj* of or using slang
SLANGY > SLANG
SLANK *dialect word for* > LANK
SLANT *vb* lean at an angle, slope ▷ *n* slope
SLANTED > SLANT
SLANTER *same as* > SLINTER
SLANTERS > SLANTER
SLANTING > SLANT
SLANTLY > SLANT
SLANTS > SLANT
SLANTWAYS *same as* > SLANTWISE
SLANTWISE *adj* in a slanting or oblique direction
SLANTY *adj* slanting
SLAP *n* blow with the open hand or a flat object ▷ *vb* strike with the open hand or a flat object
SLAPDASH *adj* careless and hasty ▷ *adv* carelessly or hastily ▷ *n* slapdash activity or work
SLAPHAPPY *adj* cheerfully irresponsible or careless
SLAPHEAD *n* derogatory term for a bald person
SLAPHEADS > SLAPHEAD
SLAPJACK *n* simple card game
SLAPJACKS > SLAPJACK
SLAPPED > SLAP
SLAPPER > SLAP
SLAPPERS > SLAP
SLAPPING > SLAP
SLAPS > SLAP
SLAPSHOT *n* hard, fast, often wild, shot executed with a powerful downward swing
SLAPSHOTS > SLAPSHOT
SLAPSTICK *n* boisterous knockabout comedy
SLART *vb* spill (something)
SLARTED > SLART
SLARTING > SLART
SLARTS > SLART
SLASH *vb* cut with a sweeping stroke ▷ *n* sweeping stroke
SLASHED > SLASH
SLASHER *n* tool or tractor-drawn machine used for cutting scrub or undergrowth in the bush
SLASHERS > SLASHER
SLASHES > SLASH
SLASHFEST *n* film or computer game that features bloody killings involving blades
SLASHING *adj* aggressively critical ▷ *n* act of slashing
SLASHINGS > SLASHING
SLAT *n* narrow strip of wood or metal ▷ *vb* provide with slats
SLATCH *n* slack part of rope
SLATCHES > SLATCH
SLATE *n* rock which splits easily into thin layers ▷ *vb* cover with slates ▷ *adj*

dark grey
SLATED > SLATE
SLATELIKE > SLATE
SLATER n person trained in laying roof slates
SLATERS > SLATER
SLATES > SLATE
SLATEY adj slightly mad
SLATHER vb spread quickly or lavishly
SLATHERED > SLATHER
SLATHERS > SLATHER
SLATIER > SLATY
SLATIEST > SLATY
SLATINESS > SLATY
SLATING n act or process of laying slates
SLATINGS > SLATING
SLATS > SLAT
SLATTED > SLAT
SLATTER vb be slovenly
SLATTERED > SLATTER
SLATTERN n slovenly woman
SLATTERNS > SLATTERN
SLATTERS > SLATTER
SLATTERY adj slovenly
SLATTING > SLAT
SLATTINGS > SLAT
SLATY adj consisting of or resembling slate
SLAUGHTER vb kill (animals) for food ▷ n slaughtering
SLAVE n person owned by another for whom he or she has to work ▷ vb work like a slave
SLAVED > SLAVE
SLAVER n person or ship engaged in the slave trade ▷ vb dribble saliva from the mouth
SLAVERED > SLAVER
SLAVERER > SLAVER
SLAVERERS > SLAVER
SLAVERIES > SLAVERY
SLAVERING > SLAVER
SLAVERS > SLAVER
SLAVERY n state or condition of being a slave
SLAVES > SLAVE
SLAVEY n female general servant
SLAVEYS > SLAVEY
SLAVING > SLAVE
SLAVISH adj of or like a slave
SLAVISHLY > SLAVISH
SLAVOCRAT n US slaveholder before the Civil War
SLAVOPHIL n person who admires the Slavs or their cultures
SLAW short for > COLESLAW
SLAWS > SLAW
SLAY vb kill
SLAYABLE > SLAY
SLAYED > SLAY
SLAYER > SLAY
SLAYERS > SLAY
SLAYING > SLAY
SLAYS > SLAY
SLEAVE n tangled thread ▷ vb disentangle (twisted thread, etc)
SLEAVED > SLEAVE

SLEAVES > SLEAVE
SLEAVING > SLEAVE
SLEAZE n behaviour in public life considered immoral, dishonest, or disreputable
SLEAZEBAG n disgusting person
SLEAZES > SLEAZE
SLEAZIER > SLEAZY
SLEAZIEST > SLEAZY
SLEAZILY > SLEAZY
SLEAZO n sleazy person
SLEAZOID n sleazy person
SLEAZOIDS > SLEAZOID
SLEAZY adj run-down or sordid
SLED same as > SLEDGE
SLEDDED > SLED
SLEDDER > SLED
SLEDDERS > SLED
SLEDDING > SLED
SLEDDINGS > SLED
SLEDED > SLED
SLEDGE n carriage on runners for sliding on snow ▷ vb travel by sledge
SLEDGED > SLEDGE
SLEDGER > SLEDGE
SLEDGERS > SLEDGE
SLEDGES > SLEDGE
SLEDGING > SLEDGE
SLEDGINGS > SLEDGE
SLEDS > SLED
SLEE Scots word for > SLY
SLEECH n slippery mud
SLEECHES > SLEECH
SLEECHIER > SLEECH
SLEECHY > SLEECH
SLEEK adj glossy, smooth, and shiny ▷ vb make smooth and glossy, as by grooming, etc
SLEEKED > SLEEK
SLEEKEN vb make sleek
SLEEKENED > SLEEKEN
SLEEKENS > SLEEKEN
SLEEKER > SLEEK
SLEEKERS > SLEEK
SLEEKEST > SLEEK
SLEEKIER > SLEEK
SLEEKIEST > SLEEK
SLEEKING > SLEEK
SLEEKINGS > SLEEK
SLEEKIT adj smooth
SLEEKLY > SLEEK
SLEEKNESS > SLEEK
SLEEKS > SLEEK
SLEEKY > SLEEK
SLEEP n state of rest characterized by unconsciousness ▷ vb be in or as if in a state of sleep
SLEEPAWAY n camp for teenagers
SLEEPER n railway car fitted for sleeping in
SLEEPERS > SLEEPER
SLEEPERY Scots word for > SLEEPY
SLEEPIER > SLEEPY
SLEEPIEST > SLEEPY
SLEEPILY > SLEEPY
SLEEPING > SLEEP
SLEEPINGS > SLEEP
SLEEPLESS adj (of a night) one during which one does

not sleep
SLEEPLIKE > SLEEP
SLEEPOUT n small building for sleeping in
SLEEPOUTS > SLEEPOUT
SLEEPOVER n occasion when a person stays overnight at a friend's house
SLEEPRY Scots word for > SLEEPY
SLEEPS > SLEEP
SLEEPSUIT n baby's sleeping garment
SLEEPWALK vb walk while asleep
SLEEPWEAR n clothes for sleeping in
SLEEPY adj needing sleep
SLEER > SLEE
SLEEST > SLEE
SLEET n rain and snow or hail falling together ▷ vb fall as sleet
SLEETED > SLEET
SLEETIER > SLEET
SLEETIEST > SLEET
SLEETING > SLEET
SLEETS > SLEET
SLEETY > SLEET
SLEEVE n part of a garment which covers the arm
SLEEVED > SLEEVE
SLEEVEEN n sly obsequious smooth-tongued person
SLEEVEENS > SLEEVEEN
SLEEVELET n protective covering for forearm
SLEEVER n old beer measure
SLEEVERS > SLEEVER
SLEEVES > SLEEVE
SLEEVING n tubular flexible insulation into which bare wire can be inserted
SLEEVINGS > SLEEVING
SLEEZIER > SLEEZY
SLEEZIEST > SLEEZY
SLEEZY adj sleazy
SLEIDED adj old word meaning separated
SLEIGH same as > SLEDGE
SLEIGHED > SLEIGH
SLEIGHER > SLEIGH
SLEIGHERS > SLEIGH
SLEIGHING > SLEIGH
SLEIGHS > SLEIGH
SLEIGHT n skill or cunning
SLEIGHTS > SLEIGHT
SLENDER adj slim
SLENDERER > SLENDER
SLENDERLY > SLENDER
SLENTER same as > SLINTER
SLENTERS > SLENTER
SLEPT > SLEEP
SLEUTH n detective ▷ vb track or follow
SLEUTHED > SLEUTH
SLEUTHING > SLEUTH
SLEUTHS > SLEUTH
SLEW vb twist sideways, esp awkwardly
SLEWED > SLEW
SLEWING > SLEW
SLEWS > SLEW
SLEY n weaver's tool for separating threads

SLEYS > SLEY
SLICE n thin flat piece cut from something ▷ vb cut into slices
SLICEABLE > SLICE
SLICED > SLICE
SLICER > SLICE
SLICERS > SLICE
SLICES > SLICE
SLICING > SLICE
SLICINGS > SLICE
SLICK adj persuasive and glib ▷ n patch of oil on water ▷ vb make smooth or sleek
SLICKED > SLICK
SLICKEN vb make smooth
SLICKENED > SLICKEN
SLICKENER > SLICKEN
SLICKENS > SLICKEN
SLICKER n sly or untrustworthy person
SLICKERED adj wearing a waterproof jacket
SLICKERS > SLICKER
SLICKEST > SLICK
SLICKING > SLICK
SLICKINGS > SLICK
SLICKLY > SLICK
SLICKNESS > SLICK
SLICKROCK n weathered and smooth sandstone or other rock
SLICKS > SLICK
SLICKSTER n dishonest person
SLID > SLIDE
SLIDABLE > SLIDE
SLIDDEN > SLIDE
SLIDDER vb slip
SLIDDERED > SLIDDER
SLIDDERS > SLIDDER
SLIDDERY adj slippery
SLIDE vb slip smoothly along (a surface) ▷ n sliding
SLIDED > SLIDE
SLIDER > SLIDE
SLIDERS > SLIDE
SLIDES > SLIDE
SLIDEWAY n sloping channel down which things are slid
SLIDEWAYS > SLIDEWAY
SLIDING > SLIDE
SLIDINGLY > SLIDE
SLIDINGS > SLIDE
SLIER > SLY
SLIEST > SLY
SLIEVE n Irish mountain
SLIEVES > SLIEVE
SLIGHT adj small in quantity or extent ▷ n snub ▷ vb insult (someone) by behaving rudely
SLIGHTED > SLIGHT
SLIGHTER > SLIGHT
SLIGHTERS > SLIGHT
SLIGHTEST > SLIGHT
SLIGHTING adj characteristic of a slight
SLIGHTISH > SLIGHT
SLIGHTLY adv in small measure or degree
SLIGHTS > SLIGHT
SLILY > SLY

S

SLIM *adj* not heavy or stout, thin ▷*vb* make or become slim by diet and exercise
SLIMDOWN *n* instance of an organization cutting staff
SLIMDOWNS > SLIMDOWN
SLIME *n* unpleasant thick slippery substance ▷*vb* cover with slime
SLIMEBALL *n* odious and contemptible person
SLIMED > SLIME
SLIMES > SLIME
SLIMIER > SLIMY
SLIMIEST > SLIMY
SLIMILY > SLIMY
SLIMINESS > SLIMY
SLIMING > SLIME
SLIMLINE *adj* slim
SLIMLY > SLIM
SLIMMED > SLIM
SLIMMER > SLIM
SLIMMERS > SLIM
SLIMMEST > SLIM
SLIMMING > SLIM
SLIMMINGS > SLIM
SLIMMISH > SLIM
SLIMNESS > SLIM
SLIMPSIER > SLIMPSY
SLIMPSY *adj* thin and flimsy
SLIMS > SLIM
SLIMSIER > SLIMSY
SLIMSIEST > SLIMSY
SLIMSY *adj* frail
SLIMY *adj* of, like, or covered with slime
SLING *n* bandage hung from the neck to support an injured hand or arm ▷*vb* throw
SLINGBACK *n* shoe with a strap that goes around the back of the heel
SLINGER > SLING
SLINGERS > SLING
SLINGING > SLING
SLINGS > SLING
SLINGSHOT *n* Y-shaped implement with a loop of elastic fastened to the ends of the two prongs, used for shooting small stones, etc
SLINK *vb* move furtively or guiltily ▷*n* animal, esp a calf, born prematurely
SLINKED > SLINK
SLINKER > SLINK
SLINKERS > SLINK
SLINKIER > SLINKY
SLINKIEST > SLINKY
SLINKILY > SLINKY
SLINKING > SLINK
SLINKS > SLINK
SLINKSKIN *n* skin of premature calf
SLINKWEED *n* plant believed to make cow give birth prematurely
SLINKY *adj* (of clothes) figure-hugging
SLINTER *n* dodge, trick, or stratagem
SLINTERS > SLINTER
SLIOTAR *n* ball used in hurling
SLIOTARS > SLIOTAR
SLIP *vb* lose balance by

sliding ▷*n* slipping
SLIPCASE *n* protective case for a book that is open at one end so that only the spine of the book is visible
SLIPCASED *adj* having a slipcase
SLIPCASES > SLIPCASE
SLIPCOVER *n* fitted but easily removable cloth cover for a chair, sofa, etc
SLIPDRESS *n* silky sleeveless dress
SLIPE *n* wool removed from the pelt of a slaughtered sheep by immersion in a chemical bath ▷*vb* remove skin
SLIPED > SLIPE
SLIPES > SLIPE
SLIPFORM *n* mould used in building
SLIPFORMS > SLIPFORM
SLIPING > SLIPE
SLIPKNOT *n* knot tied so that it will slip along the rope round which it is made
SLIPKNOTS > SLIPKNOT
SLIPLESS > SLIP
SLIPNOOSE *n* noose made with a slipknot, so that it tightens when pulled
SLIPOUT *n* instance of slipping out
SLIPOUTS > SLIPOUT
SLIPOVER *adj* of or denoting a garment that can be put on easily over the head ▷*n* such a garment, esp a sleeveless pullover
SLIPOVERS > SLIPOVER
SLIPPAGE *n* act or an instance of slipping
SLIPPAGES > SLIPPAGE
SLIPPED > SLIP
SLIPPER *n* light shoe for indoor wear ▷*vb* hit or beat with a slipper
SLIPPERED > SLIPPER
SLIPPERS > SLIPPER
SLIPPERY *adj* so smooth or wet as to cause slipping or be difficult to hold
SLIPPIER > SLIPPY
SLIPPIEST > SLIPPY
SLIPPILY > SLIPPY
SLIPPING > SLIP
SLIPPY *adj* slippery
SLIPRAIL *n* rail in a fence that can be slipped out of place to make an opening
SLIPRAILS > SLIPRAIL
SLIPS > SLIP
SLIPSHEET *n* sheet of paper that is interleaved between freshly printed sheets
SLIPSHOD *adj* (of an action) careless
SLIPSLOP *n* weak or unappetizing food or drink
SLIPSLOPS > SLIPSLOP
SLIPSOLE *n* separate sole on shoe
SLIPSOLES > SLIPSOLE
SLIPT *vb* old form of slipped
SLIPUP *n* mistake or

mishap
SLIPUPS > SLIPUP
SLIPWARE *n* pottery that has been decorated with slip
SLIPWARES > SLIPWARE
SLIPWAY *n* launching slope on which ships are built or repaired
SLIPWAYS > SLIPWAY
SLISH *n* old word meaning cut
SLISHES > SLISH
SLIT *n* long narrow cut or opening ▷*vb* make a long straight cut in
SLITHER *vb* slide unsteadily ▷*n* slithering movement
SLITHERED > SLITHER
SLITHERS > SLITHER
SLITHERY *adj* moving with a slithering motion
SLITLESS > SLIT
SLITLIKE > SLIT
SLITS > SLIT
SLITTED > SLIT
SLITTER > SLIT
SLITTERS > SLIT
SLITTIER > SLIT
SLITTIEST > SLIT
SLITTING > SLIT
SLITTY > SLIT
SLIVE *vb* slip
SLIVED > SLIVE
SLIVEN > SLIVE
SLIVER *n* small thin piece ▷*vb* cut into slivers
SLIVERED > SLIVER
SLIVERER > SLIVER
SLIVERERS > SLIVER
SLIVERING > SLIVER
SLIVERS > SLIVER
SLIVES > SLIVE
SLIVING > SLIVE
SLIVOVIC *n* plum brandy
SLIVOVICA *n* plum brandy
SLIVOVITZ *n* plum brandy from E Europe
SLIVOWITZ *n* plum brandy
SLOAN *n* severe telling-off
SLOANS > SLOAN
SLOB *n* lazy and untidy person
SLOBBER *vb* dribble or drool ▷*n* liquid or saliva spilt from the mouth
SLOBBERED > SLOBBER
SLOBBERER > SLOBBER
SLOBBERS > SLOBBER
SLOBBERY > SLOBBER
SLOBBIER > SLOB
SLOBBIEST > SLOB
SLOBBISH > SLOB
SLOBBY > SLOB
SLOBLAND *n* muddy ground
SLOBLANDS > SLOBLAND
SLOBS > SLOB
SLOCKEN *vb* Scots word meaning slake
SLOCKENED > SLOCKEN
SLOCKENS > SLOCKEN
SLOE *n* sour blue-black fruit
SLOEBUSH *n* bush on which sloes grow
SLOES > SLOE
SLOETHORN *n* sloe plant
SLOETREE *n* sloe plant

SLOETREES > SLOETREE
SLOG *vb* work hard and steadily ▷*n* long and exhausting work or walk
SLOGAN *n* catchword or phrase used in politics or advertising
SLOGANEER *n* person who coins or employs slogans frequently ▷*vb* coin or employ slogans so as to sway opinion
SLOGANISE *same as* > SLOGANIZE
SLOGANIZE *vb* use slogans
SLOGANS > SLOGAN
SLOGGED > SLOG
SLOGGER > SLOG
SLOGGERS > SLOG
SLOGGING > SLOG
SLOGS > SLOG
SLOID *n* Swedish woodwork
SLOIDS > SLOID
SLOJD *n* Swedish woodwork
SLOJDS > SLOJD
SLOKEN *vb* Scots word meaning slake
SLOKENED > SLOKEN
SLOKENING > SLOKEN
SLOKENS > SLOKEN
SLOMMOCK *vb* walk assertively with a hip-rolling gait
SLOMMOCKS > SLOMMOCK
SLOOM *vb* slumber
SLOOMED > SLOOM
SLOOMIER > SLOOM
SLOOMIEST > SLOOM
SLOOMING > SLOOM
SLOOMS > SLOOM
SLOOMY > SLOOM
SLOOP *n* small single-masted ship
SLOOPS > SLOOP
SLOOSH *vb* wash with water
SLOOSHED > SLOOSH
SLOOSHES > SLOOSH
SLOOSHING > SLOOSH
SLOOT *n* ditch for irrigation or drainage
SLOOTS > SLOOT
SLOP *vb* splash or spill ▷*n* spilt liquid
SLOPE *vb* slant ▷*n* sloping surface
SLOPED > SLOPE
SLOPER > SLOPE
SLOPERS > SLOPE
SLOPES > SLOPE
SLOPEWISE > SLOPE
SLOPIER > SLOPE
SLOPIEST > SLOPE
SLOPING > SLOPE
SLOPINGLY > SLOPE
SLOPPED > SLOP
SLOPPIER > SLOPPY
SLOPPIEST > SLOPPY
SLOPPILY > SLOPPY
SLOPPING > SLOP
SLOPPY *adj* careless or untidy
SLOPS > SLOP
SLOPWORK *n* manufacture of cheap shoddy clothing or the clothes so produced

SLOPWORKS > SLOPWORK
SLOPY > SLOPE
SLORM vb wipe carelessly
SLORMED > SLORM
SLORMING > SLORM
SLORMS > SLORM
SLOSH vb pour carelessly
▷ n splashing sound
SLOSHED > SLOSH
SLOSHES > SLOSH
SLOSHIER > SLOSH
SLOSHIEST > SLOSH
SLOSHING > SLOSH
SLOSHINGS > SLOSH
SLOSHY > SLOSH
SLOT n narrow opening for
inserting something ▷ vb
make a slot or slots in
SLOTBACK n American
football player
SLOTBACKS > SLOTBACK
SLOTH n slow-moving
animal of tropical America
▷ vb be lazy
SLOTHED > SLOTH
SLOTHFUL adj lazy or idle
SLOTHING > SLOTH
SLOTHS > SLOTH
SLOTS > SLOT
SLOTTED > SLOT
SLOTTER > SLOT
SLOTTERS > SLOT
SLOTTING > SLOT
SLOUCH vb sit, stand, or
move with a drooping
posture ▷ n drooping
posture
SLOUCHED > SLOUCH
SLOUCHER > SLOUCH
SLOUCHERS > SLOUCH
SLOUCHES > SLOUCH
SLOUCHIER > SLOUCHY
SLOUCHILY > SLOUCHY
SLOUCHING > SLOUCH
SLOUCHY adj slouching
SLOUGH n bog ▷ vb (of a
snake) shed (its skin)
SLOUGHED > SLOUGH
SLOUGHIER > SLOUGH
SLOUGHING > SLOUGH
SLOUGHS > SLOUGH
SLOUGHY > SLOUGH
SLOVE > SLIVE
SLOVEN n habitually dirty or
untidy person
SLOVENLY adj dirty or
untidy ▷ adv in a slovenly
manner
SLOVENRY n quality of being
slovenly
SLOVENS > SLOVEN
SLOW adj taking a longer
time than is usual or
expected ▷ adv slowly ▷ vb
reduce the speed (of)
SLOWBACK n lazy person
SLOWBACKS > SLOWBACK
SLOWCOACH n person who
moves or works slowly
SLOWDOWN n any slackening
of pace
SLOWDOWNS > SLOWDOWN
SLOWED > SLOW
SLOWER > SLOW
SLOWEST > SLOW
SLOWING > SLOW
SLOWINGS > SLOW

SLOWISH > SLOW
SLOWLY > SLOW
SLOWNESS > SLOW
SLOWPOKE same
as > SLOWCOACH
SLOWPOKES > SLOWPOKE
SLOWS > SLOW
SLOWWORM n small legless
lizard
SLOWWORMS > SLOWWORM
SLOYD n Swedish
woodwork
SLOYDS > SLOYD
SLUB n lump in yarn
or fabric, often made
intentionally to give a
knobbly effect ▷ vb draw
out and twist (a sliver
of fibre) preparatory
to spinning ▷ adj (of
material) having an
irregular appearance
SLUBB same as > SLUB
SLUBBED > SLUB
SLUBBER vb smear
SLUBBERED > SLUBBER
SLUBBERS > SLUBBER
SLUBBIER > SLUB
SLUBBIEST > SLUB
SLUBBING > SLUB
SLUBBINGS > SLUB
SLUBBS > SLUBB
SLUBBY > SLUB
SLUBS > SLUB
SLUDGE n thick mud
SLUDGED > SLUDGE
SLUDGES > SLUDGE
SLUDGIER > SLUDGY
SLUDGIEST > SLUDGY
SLUDGING > SLUDGE
SLUDGY adj consisting of,
containing, or like sludge
SLUE same as > SLEW
SLUED > SLUE
SLUEING > SLUE
SLUES > SLUE
SLUFF same as > SLOUGH
SLUFFED > SLUFF
SLUFFING > SLUFF
SLUFFS > SLUFF
SLUG n land snail with no
shell ▷ vb hit hard
SLUGABED n person who
remains in bed through
laziness
SLUGABEDS > SLUGABED
SLUGFEST n fist fight
SLUGFESTS > SLUGFEST
SLUGGABED same
as > SLUGABED
SLUGGARD n lazy person
▷ adj lazy
SLUGGARDS > SLUGGARD
SLUGGED > SLUG
SLUGGER n (esp in boxing,
baseball, etc) a person who
strikes hard
SLUGGERS > SLUGGER
SLUGGING > SLUG
SLUGGISH adj slow-moving,
lacking energy
SLUGHORN same as > SLOGAN
SLUGHORNE same
as > SLOGAN
SLUGHORNS > SLUGHORN
SLUGS > SLUG
SLUICE n channel that

carries a rapid current of
water ▷ vb drain water by
means of a sluice
SLUICED > SLUICE
SLUICES > SLUICE
SLUICEWAY same as > SLUICE
SLUICIER > SLUICE
SLUICIEST > SLUICE
SLUICING > SLUICE
SLUICY > SLUICE
SLUING > SLUE
SLUIT n water channel in
South Africa
SLUITS > SLUIT
SLUM n squalid
overcrowded house or
area ▷ vb temporarily and
deliberately experience
poorer places or conditions
than usual
SLUMBER n sleep ▷ vb sleep
SLUMBERED > SLUMBER
SLUMBERER > SLUMBER
SLUMBERS > SLUMBER
SLUMBERY adj sleepy
SLUMBROUS adj sleepy
SLUMBRY same
as > SLUMBERY
SLUMGUM n material left
after wax is extracted from
honeycomb
SLUMGUMS > SLUMGUM
SLUMISM n existence of
slums
SLUMISMS > SLUMISM
SLUMLORD n absentee
landlord of slum property,
esp one who profiteers
SLUMLORDS > SLUMLORD
SLUMMED > SLUM
SLUMMER > SLUM
SLUMMERS > SLUM
SLUMMIER > SLUM
SLUMMIEST > SLUM
SLUMMING > SLUM
SLUMMINGS > SLUM
SLUMMOCK vb move slowly
and heavily
SLUMMOCKS > SLUMMOCK
SLUMMY > SLUM
SLUMP vb (of prices or
demand) decline suddenly
▷ n sudden decline in
prices or demand
SLUMPED > SLUMP
SLUMPIER > SLUMPY
SLUMPIEST > SLUMPY
SLUMPING > SLUMP
SLUMPS > SLUMP
SLUMPY adj boggy
SLUMS > SLUM
SLUNG > SLING
SLUNGSHOT n weight
attached to the end of a
cord and used as a weapon
SLUNK > SLINK
SLUR vb pronounce or utter
(words) indistinctly ▷ n
slurring of words
SLURB n suburban slum
SLURBAN > SLURB
SLURBS > SLURB
SLURP vb eat or drink noisily
▷ n slurping sound
SLURPED > SLURP
SLURPER > SLURP
SLURPERS > SLURP

SLURPING > SLURP
SLURPS > SLURP
SLURRED > SLUR
SLURRIED > SLURRY
SLURRIES > SLURRY
SLURRING > SLUR
SLURRY n muddy liquid
mixture ▷ vb spread slurry
SLURRYING > SLURRY
SLURS > SLUR
SLUSE same as > SLUICE
SLUSES > SLUICE
SLUSH n watery muddy
substance ▷ vb make
one's way through or as if
through slush
SLUSHED > SLUSH
SLUSHES > SLUSH
SLUSHIER > SLUSHY
SLUSHIES > SLUSHY
SLUSHIEST > SLUSHY
SLUSHILY > SLUSHY
SLUSHING > SLUSH
SLUSHY adj of, resembling,
or consisting of slush ▷ n
unskilled kitchen assistant
SLUT n derogatory term for
a dirty or immoral woman
SLUTCH n mud
SLUTCHES > SLUTCH
SLUTCHIER > SLUTCH
SLUTCHY > SLUTCH
SLUTS > SLUT
SLUTTERY n state of being
slut
SLUTTIER > SLUT
SLUTTIEST > SLUT
SLUTTISH > SLUT
SLUTTY > SLUT
SLY adj crafty
SLYBOOTS pl n person who
is sly
SLYER > SLY
SLYEST > SLY
SLYISH > SLY
SLYLY > SLY
SLYNESS > SLY
SLYNESSES > SLY
SLYPE n covered
passageway in a church
that connects the transept
to the chapterhouse
SLYPES > SLYPE
SMA Scots word for > SMALL
SMAAK vb South African
slang for like or love
SMAAKED > SMAAK
SMAAKING > SMAAK
SMAAKS > SMAAK
SMACK vb slap sharply ▷ n
sharp slap ▷ adv squarely
or directly
SMACKED > SMACK
SMACKER n loud kiss
SMACKERS > SMACKER
SMACKHEAD n person who is
addicted to heroin
SMACKING adj brisk
SMACKINGS > SMACKING
SMACKS > SMACK
SMAIK n Scots word
meaning rascal
SMAIKS > SMAIK
SMALL adj not large in size,
number, or amount ▷ n
narrow part of the lower
back ▷ adv into small

pieces ▷ *vb* make small
SMALLAGE *n* wild celery
SMALLAGES > SMALLAGE
SMALLBOY *n* steward's assistant or deputy steward in European households in W Africa
SMALLBOYS > SMALLBOY
SMALLED > SMALL
SMALLER > SMALL
SMALLEST > SMALL
SMALLING > SMALL
SMALLISH > SMALL
SMALLNESS > SMALL
SMALLPOX *n* contagious disease with blisters that leave scars
SMALLS > SMALL
SMALLSAT *n* small communications satellite
SMALLSATS > SMALLSAT
SMALLTIME *adj* unimportant
SMALM *same as* > SMARM
SMALMED > SMALM
SMALMILY > SMALMY
SMALMING > SMALM
SMALMS > SMALM
SMALMY *same as* > SMARMY
SMALT *n* type of silica glass coloured deep blue with cobalt oxide
SMALTI > SMALTO
SMALTINE *n* mineral containing cobalt
SMALTINES > SMALTINE
SMALTITE *n* silver-white to greyish mineral
SMALTITES > SMALTITE
SMALTO *n* coloured glass, etc, used in mosaics
SMALTOS > SMALTO
SMALTS > SMALT
SMARAGD *n* any green gemstone, such as the emerald
SMARAGDE *same as* > SMARAGD
SMARAGDES > SMARAGDE
SMARAGDS > SMARAGD
SMARM *vb* bring (oneself) into favour (with) ▷ *n* obsequious flattery
SMARMED > SMARM
SMARMIER > SMARMY
SMARMIEST > SMARMY
SMARMILY > SMARMY
SMARMING > SMARM
SMARMS > SMARM
SMARMY *adj* unpleasantly suave or flattering
SMART *adj* well-kept and neat ▷ *vb* feel or cause stinging pain ▷ *n* stinging pain ▷ *adv* in a smart manner
SMARTARSE *n* derogatory term for a clever person, esp one who parades his knowledge offensively
SMARTASS *same as* > SMARTARSE
SMARTED > SMART
SMARTEN *vb* make or become smart
SMARTENED > SMARTEN
SMARTENS > SMARTEN

SMARTER > SMART
SMARTEST > SMART
SMARTIE *same as* > SMARTY
SMARTIES > SMARTY
SMARTING > SMART
SMARTISH > SMART
SMARTLY > SMART
SMARTNESS > SMART
SMARTS *pl n* know-how, intelligence, or wits
SMARTWEED *n* grass with acrid smell
SMARTY *n* would-be clever person
SMASH *vb* break violently and noisily ▷ *n* act or sound of smashing ▷ *adv* with a smash
SMASHABLE > SMASH
SMASHED *adj* completely intoxicated with alcohol
SMASHER *n* attractive person or thing
SMASHEROO *n* excellent person or thing
SMASHERS > SMASHER
SMASHES > SMASH
SMASHING *adj* excellent
SMASHINGS > SMASHING
SMASHUP *n* bad collision of cars
SMASHUPS > SMASHUP
SMATCH *less common word for* > SMACK
SMATCHED > SMATCH
SMATCHES > SMATCH
SMATCHING > SMATCH
SMATTER *n* smattering ▷ *vb* prattle
SMATTERED > SMATTER
SMATTERER > SMATTER
SMATTERS > SMATTER
SMAZE *n* smoky haze, less damp than fog
SMAZES > SMAZE
SMEAR *vb* spread with a greasy or sticky substance ▷ *n* dirty mark or smudge
SMEARCASE *n* American type of cottage cheese
SMEARED > SMEAR
SMEARER > SMEAR
SMEARERS > SMEAR
SMEARIER > SMEARY
SMEARIEST > SMEARY
SMEARILY > SMEARY
SMEARING > SMEAR
SMEARS > SMEAR
SMEARY *adj* smeared, dirty
SMEATH *n* duck
SMEATHS > SMEATH
SMECTIC *adj* (of a substance) existing in state in which the molecules are oriented in layers
SMECTITE *n* type of clay mineral
SMECTITES > SMECTITE
SMECTITIC > SMECTITE
SMEDDUM *n* any fine powder
SMEDDUMS > SMEDDUM
SMEE *n* duck
SMEECH *Southwest English dialect form of* > SMOKE
SMEECHED > SMEECH
SMEECHES > SMEECH
SMEECHING > SMEECH

SMEEK *vb* smoke
SMEEKED > SMEEK
SMEEKING > SMEECH
SMEEKS > SMEECH
SMEES > SMEE
SMEETH *n* duck
SMEETHS > SMEETH
SMEGMA *n* whitish sebaceous secretion that accumulates beneath the prepuce
SMEGMAS > SMEGMA
SMELL *vb* perceive (a scent or odour) by means of the nose ▷ *n* ability to perceive odours by the nose
SMELLED > SMELL
SMELLER > SMELL
SMELLERS > SMELL
SMELLIER > SMELLY
SMELLIES *pl n* pleasant-smelling products such as perfumes, body lotions, bath salts, etc
SMELLIEST > SMELLY
SMELLING > SMELL
SMELLINGS > SMELL
SMELLS > SMELL
SMELLY *adj* having a nasty smell
SMELT *vb* extract metal from an ore
SMELTED > SMELL
SMELTER *n* industrial plant where smelting is carried out
SMELTERS > SMELTER
SMELTERY *variant of* > SMELTER
SMELTING > SMELL
SMELTINGS > SMELL
SMELTS > SMELL
SMERK *same as* > SMIRK
SMERKED > SMERK
SMERKING > SMERK
SMERKS > SMERK
SMEUSE *n* way through hedge
SMEUSES > SMEUSE
SMEW *n* duck of N Europe and Asia
SMEWS > SMEW
SMICKER *vb* look at someone amorously
SMICKERED > SMICKER
SMICKERS > SMICKER
SMICKET *n* smock
SMICKETS > SMICKET
SMICKLY *adv* amorously
SMIDDIED > SMIDDY
SMIDDIES > SMIDDY
SMIDDY *Scots word for* > SMITHY
SMIDDYING > SMIDDY
SMIDGE *n* very small amount or part
SMIDGEN *n* very small amount or part
SMIDGENS > SMIDGEN
SMIDGEON *same as* > SMIDGEN
SMIDGEONS > SMIDGEON
SMIDGES > SMIDGE
SMIDGIN *same as* > SMIDGEN
SMIDGINS > SMIDGIN
SMIERCASE *same as* > SMEARCASE

SMIGHT *same as* > SMITE
SMIGHTING > SMIGHT
SMIGHTS > SMIGHT
SMILAX *n* type of climbing shrub
SMILAXES > SMILAX
SMILE *n* turning up of the corners of the mouth to show pleasure or friendliness ▷ *vb* give a smile
SMILED > SMILE
SMILEFUL *adj* full of smiles
SMILELESS > SMILE
SMILER > SMILE
SMILERS > SMILE
SMILES > SMILE
SMILET *n* little smile
SMILETS > SMILET
SMILEY *n* symbol depicting a smile or other facial expression, used in e-mail ▷ *adj* cheerful
SMILEYS > SMILEY
SMILING > SMILE
SMILINGLY > SMILE
SMILINGS > SMILE
SMILODON *n* extinct sabre-toothed tiger
SMILODONS > SMILODON
SMIR *n* drizzly rain ▷ *vb* drizzle lightly
SMIRCH *n* stain ▷ *vb* disgrace
SMIRCHED > SMIRCH
SMIRCHER > SMIRCH
SMIRCHERS > SMIRCH
SMIRCHES > SMIRCH
SMIRCHING > SMIRCH
SMIRK *n* smug smile ▷ *vb* give a smirk
SMIRKED > SMIRK
SMIRKER > SMIRK
SMIRKERS > SMIRK
SMIRKIER > SMIRK
SMIRKIEST > SMIRK
SMIRKILY > SMIRK
SMIRKING > SMIRK
SMIRKS > SMIRK
SMIRKY > SMIRK
SMIRR *same as* > SMIR
SMIRRED > SMIRR
SMIRRIER > SMIRR
SMIRRIEST > SMIRR
SMIRRING > SMIRR
SMIRRS > SMIRR
SMIRRY > SMIRR
SMIRS > SMIR
SMIRTING *n* flirting amongst those smoking outside a non-smoking office, pub, etc
SMIRTINGS > SMIRTING
SMIT > SMITE
SMITE *vb* strike hard
SMITER > SMITE
SMITERS > SMITE
SMITES > SMITE
SMITH *n* worker in metal ▷ *vb* work in metal
SMITHED > SMITH
SMITHERS *pl n* little shattered pieces
SMITHERY *n* trade or craft of a blacksmith
SMITHIED > SMITHY
SMITHIES > SMITHY

SMITHING > SMITH

SMITHS > SMITH

SMITHY *n* blacksmith's workshop ▷*vb* work as a smith

SMITHYING > SMITHY

SMITING > SMITE

SMITS > SMIT

SMITTED > SMIT

SMITTEN > SMITE

SMITTING > SMIT

SMITTLE *adj* infectious

SMOCK *n* loose overall ▷*vb* gather (material) by sewing in a honeycomb pattern

SMOCKED > SMOCK

SMOCKING *n* ornamental needlework used to gather material

SMOCKINGS > SMOCKING

SMOCKLIKE > SMOCK

SMOCKS > SMOCK

SMOG *n* mixture of smoke and fog

SMOGGIER > SMOG

SMOGGIEST > SMOG

SMOGGY > SMOG

SMOGLESS > SMOG

SMOGS > SMOG

SMOILE *same as* > SMILE

SMOILED > SMOILE

SMOILES > SMOILE

SMOILING > SMOILE

SMOKABLE > SMOKE

SMOKE *n* cloudy mass that rises from something burning ▷*vb* give off smoke or treat with smoke

SMOKEABLE > SMOKE

SMOKEBUSH *n* plant with small light flowers

SMOKED > SMOKE

SMOKEHO *same as* > SMOKO

SMOKEHOOD *n* hood worn to keep out smoke

SMOKEHOS > SMOKEHO

SMOKEJACK *n* device formerly used for turning a roasting spit, operated by the movement of ascending gases in a chimney

SMOKELESS *adj* having or producing little or no smoke

SMOKELIKE > SMOKE

SMOKEPOT *n* device for producing smoke

SMOKEPOTS > SMOKEPOT

SMOKER *n* person who habitually smokes tobacco

SMOKERS > SMOKER

SMOKES > SMOKE

SMOKETREE *n* shrub with clusters of yellowish flowers

SMOKEY *same as* > SMOKY

SMOKIER > SMOKY

SMOKIES > SMOKY

SMOKIEST > SMOKY

SMOKILY > SMOKY

SMOKINESS > SMOKY

SMOKING > SMOKE

SMOKINGS > SMOKING

SMOKO *n* short break from work for tea or a cigarette

SMOKOS > SMOKO

SMOKY *adj* filled with or giving off smoke, sometimes excessively ▷*n* haddock that has been smoked

SMOLDER *same as* > SMOULDER

SMOLDERED > SMOLDER

SMOLDERS > SMOLDER

SMOLT *n* young salmon at the stage when it migrates to the sea

SMOLTS > SMOLT

SMOOCH *vb* kiss and cuddle ▷*n* smooching

SMOOCHED > SMOOCH

SMOOCHER > SMOOCH

SMOOCHERS > SMOOCH

SMOOCHES > SMOOCH

SMOOCHING > SMOOCH

SMOOCHY *adj* romantic

SMOODGE *same as* > SMOOCH

SMOODGED > SMOODGE

SMOODGES > SMOODGE

SMOODGING > SMOODGE

SMOOGE *same as* > SMOOCH

SMOOGED > SMOOGE

SMOOGES > SMOOGE

SMOOGING > SMOOGE

SMOOR *vb* Scots word meaning put out fire

SMOORED > SMOOR

SMOORING > SMOOR

SMOORS > SMOOR

SMOOSH *vb* paint to give softened look

SMOOSHED > SMOOSH

SMOOSHES > SMOOSH

SMOOSHING > SMOOSH

SMOOT *vb* work as printer

SMOOTED > SMOOT

SMOOTH *adj* even in surface, texture, or consistency ▷*vb* make smooth ▷*adv* in a smooth manner ▷*n* smooth part of something

SMOOTHED > SMOOTH

SMOOTHEN *vb* make or become smooth

SMOOTHENS > SMOOTHEN

SMOOTHER > SMOOTH

SMOOTHERS > SMOOTH

SMOOTHES > SMOOTH

SMOOTHEST > SMOOTH

SMOOTHIE *n* slang, usu derogatory term for a charming but possibly insincere man

SMOOTHIES > SMOOTHY

SMOOTHING > SMOOTH

SMOOTHISH > SMOOTH

SMOOTHLY > SMOOTH

SMOOTHS > SMOOTH

SMOOTHY *same as* > SMOOTHIE

SMOOTING > SMOOT

SMOOTS > SMOOT

SMORBROD *n* Danish hors d'oeuvre

SMORBRODS > SMORBROD

SMORE *same as* > SMOOR

SMORED > SMORE

SMORES > SMORE

SMORING > SMORE

SMORZANDO *adv* musical instruction meaning fading away gradually

SMORZATO *same as* > SMORZANDO

SMOTE > SMITE

SMOTHER *vb* suffocate or stifle ▷*n* anything, such as a cloud of smoke, that stifles

SMOTHERED > SMOTHER

SMOTHERER > SMOTHER

SMOTHERS > SMOTHER

SMOTHERY > SMOTHER

SMOUCH *vb* kiss

SMOUCHED > SMOUCH

SMOUCHES > SMOUCH

SMOUCHING > SMOUCH

SMOULDER *vb* burn slowly with smoke but no flame ▷*n* dense smoke, as from a smouldering fire

SMOULDERS > SMOULDER

SMOULDRY *adj* smouldering

SMOUSE *vb* South African word meaning peddle

SMOUSED > SMOUSE

SMOUSER > SMOUSE

SMOUSERS > SMOUSE

SMOUSES > SMOUSE

SMOUSING > SMOUSE

SMOUT *n* child or undersized person ▷*vb* creep or sneak

SMOUTED > SMOUT

SMOUTING > SMOUT

SMOUTS > SMOUT

SMOWT *same as* > SMOUT

SMOWTS > SMOWT

SMOYLE *same as* > SMILE

SMOYLED > SMOYLE

SMOYLES > SMOYLE

SMOYLING > SMOYLE

SMRITI *n* class of Hindu sacred literature derived from the Vedas

SMRITIS > SMRITI

SMUDGE *vb* make or become smeared or soiled ▷*n* dirty mark

SMUDGED > SMUDGE

SMUDGEDLY > SMUDGE

SMUDGER > SMUDGE

SMUDGERS > SMUDGE

SMUDGES > SMUDGE

SMUDGIER > SMUDGY

SMUDGIEST > SMUDGY

SMUDGILY > SMUDGE

SMUDGING > SMUDGE

SMUDGINGS > SMUDGE

SMUDGY *adj* smeared, blurred, or soiled, or likely to become so

SMUG *adj* self-satisfied ▷*vb* make neat

SMUGGED > SMUG

SMUGGER > SMUG

SMUGGERY *n* condition or an instance of being smug

SMUGGEST > SMUG

SMUGGING > SMUG

SMUGGLE *vb* import or export (goods) secretly and illegally

SMUGGLED > SMUGGLE

SMUGGLER > SMUGGLE

SMUGGLERS > SMUGGLE

SMUGGLES > SMUGGLE

SMUGGLING > SMUGGLE

SMUGLY > SMUG

SMUGNESS > SMUG

SMUGS > SMUG

SMUR *same as* > SMIR

SMURFING *n* intentionally flooding and overwhelming a computer network with messages by means of a program

SMURFINGS > SMURFING

SMURRED > SMUR

SMURRIER > SMUR

SMURRIEST > SMUR

SMURRING > SMUR

SMURRY > SMUR

SMURS > SMUR

SMUSH *vb* crush

SMUSHED > SMUSH

SMUSHES > SMUSH

SMUSHING > SMUSH

SMUT *n* obscene jokes, pictures, etc ▷*vb* mark or become marked or smudged, as with soot

SMUTCH *vb* smudge ▷*n* mark

SMUTCHED > SMUTCH

SMUTCHES > SMUTCH

SMUTCHIER > SMUTCH

SMUTCHING > SMUTCH

SMUTCHY > SMUTCH

SMUTS > SMUT

SMUTTED > SMUT

SMUTTIER > SMUT

SMUTTIEST > SMUT

SMUTTILY > SMUT

SMUTTING > SMUT

SMUTTY > SMUT

SMYTRIE *n* Scots word meaning collection

SMYTRIES > SMYTRIE

SNAB *same as* > SNOB

SNABBLE *same as* > SNAFFLE

SNABBLED > SNABBLE

SNABBLES > SNABBLE

SNABBLING > SNABBLE

SNABS > SNAB

SNACK *n* light quick meal ▷*vb* eat a snack

SNACKED > SNACK

SNACKER > SNACK

SNACKERS > SNACK

SNACKETTE *n* snack bar

SNACKING > SNACK

SNACKS > SNACK

SNAFFLE *n* jointed bit for a horse ▷*vb* steal

SNAFFLED > SNAFFLE

SNAFFLES > SNAFFLE

SNAFFLING > SNAFFLE

SNAFU *n* confusion or chaos regarded as the normal state ▷*adj* confused or muddled up, as usual ▷*vb* throw into chaos

SNAFUED > SNAFU

SNAFUING > SNAFU

SNAFUS > SNAFU

SNAG *n* difficulty or disadvantage ▷*vb* catch or tear on a point

SNAGGED > SNAG

SNAGGIER > SNAGGY

SNAGGIEST > SNAGGY

SNAGGING > SNAG

SNAGGY *adj* having sharp protuberances

SNAGLIKE > SNAG

S

SNAGS > SNAG
SNAIL n slow-moving mollusc with a spiral shell ▷ vb move slowly
SNAILED > SNAIL
SNAILERY n place where snails are bred
SNAILFISH n sea snail
SNAILIER > SNAIL
SNAILIEST > SNAIL
SNAILING > SNAIL
SNAILLIKE adj resembling a snail
SNAILS > SNAIL
SNAILY > SNAIL
SNAKE n long thin scaly limbless reptile ▷ vb move in a winding course like a snake
SNAKEBIRD n darter bird
SNAKEBIT adj bitten by snake
SNAKEBITE n bite of a snake
SNAKED > SNAKE
SNAKEFISH n fish resembling snake
SNAKEHEAD n Chinese criminal involved in the illegal transport of Chinese citizens to other parts of the world
SNAKELIKE > SNAKE
SNAKEPIT n pit filled with snakes
SNAKEPITS > SNAKEPIT
SNAKEROOT n any of various North American plants
SNAKES > SNAKE
SNAKESKIN n skin of a snake, esp when made into a leather valued for handbags, shoes, etc
SNAKEWEED same as > SNAKEROOT
SNAKEWISE adv in snakelike way
SNAKEWOOD n South American tree
SNAKEY same as > SNAKY
SNAKIER > SNAKY
SNAKIEST > SNAKY
SNAKILY > SNAKY
SNAKINESS > SNAKY
SNAKING > SNAKE
SNAKISH > SNAKE
SNAKY adj twisted or winding
SNAP vb break suddenly ▷ n act or sound of snapping ▷ adj made on the spur of the moment ▷ adv with a snap
SNAPBACK n sudden rebound or change in direction
SNAPBACKS > SNAPBACK
SNAPHANCE n flintlock gun
SNAPLESS > SNAP
SNAPLINK n metal link used in mountaineering
SNAPLINKS > SNAPLINK
SNAPPABLE > SNAP
SNAPPED > SNAP
SNAPPER n food fish of Australia and New Zealand ▷ vb stumble
SNAPPERED > SNAPPER

SNAPPERS > SNAPPER
SNAPPIER > SNAPPY
SNAPPIEST > SNAPPY
SNAPPILY > SNAPPY
SNAPPING > SNAP
SNAPPINGS > SNAP
SNAPPISH same as > SNAPPY
SNAPPY adj irritable
SNAPS > SNAP
SNAPSHOT n informal photograph
SNAPSHOTS > SNAPSHOT
SNAPTIN n container for food
SNAPTINS > SNAPTIN
SNAPWEED n impatiens
SNAPWEEDS > SNAPWEED
SNAR same as > SNARL
SNARE n trap with a noose ▷ vb catch in or as if in a snare
SNARED > SNARE
SNARELESS > SNARE
SNARER > SNARE
SNARERS > SNARE
SNARES > SNARE
SNARF vb eat or drink greedily
SNARFED > SNARF
SNARFING > SNARF
SNARFS > SNARF
SNARIER > SNARE
SNARIEST > SNARE
SNARING > SNARE
SNARINGS > SNARE
SNARK n imaginary creature in Lewis Carroll's poetry
SNARKIER > SNARKY
SNARKIEST > SNARKY
SNARKILY > SNARKY
SNARKS > SNARK
SNARKY adj unpleasant and scornful
SNARL vb (of an animal) growl with bared teeth ▷ n act or sound of snarling
SNARLED > SNARL
SNARLER > SNARL
SNARLERS > SNARL
SNARLIER > SNARL
SNARLIEST > SNARL
SNARLING > SNARL
SNARLINGS > SNARL
SNARLS > SNARL
SNARLY > SNARL
SNARRED > SNAR
SNARRING > SNAR
SNARS > SNAR
SNARY > SNARE
SNASH vb Scots word meaning speak cheekily
SNASHED > SNASH
SNASHES > SNASH
SNASHING > SNASH
SNASTE n candle wick
SNASTES > SNASTE
SNATCH vb seize or try to seize suddenly ▷ n snatching
SNATCHED > SNATCH
SNATCHER > SNATCH
SNATCHERS > SNATCH
SNATCHES > SNATCH
SNATCHIER > SNATCHY
SNATCHILY > SNATCHY
SNATCHING > SNATCH
SNATCHY adj disconnected

or spasmodic
SNATH n handle of a scythe
SNATHE same as > SNATH
SNATHES > SNATHE
SNATHS > SNATH
SNAW Scots variant of > SNOW
SNAWED > SNAW
SNAWING > SNAW
SNAWS > SNAW
SNAZZIER > SNAZZY
SNAZZIEST > SNAZZY
SNAZZILY > SNAZZY
SNAZZY adj stylish and flashy
SNEAD n scythe handle
SNEADS > SNEAD
SNEAK vb move furtively ▷ n cowardly or underhand person ▷ adj without warning
SNEAKED > SNEAK
SNEAKER n soft shoe
SNEAKERED adj wearing sneakers
SNEAKERS pl n canvas shoes with rubber soles
SNEAKEUP n sneaky person
SNEAKEUPS > SNEAKEUP
SNEAKIER > SNEAK
SNEAKIEST > SNEAK
SNEAKILY > SNEAK
SNEAKING adj slight but persistent
SNEAKISH adj typical of sneak
SNEAKS > SNEAK
SNEAKSBY n sneak
SNEAKY > SNEAK
SNEAP vb nip
SNEAPED > SNEAP
SNEAPING > SNEAP
SNEAPS > SNEAP
SNEATH same as > SNATH
SNEATHS > SNEATH
SNEB same as > SNIB
SNEBBE same as > SNUB
SNEBBED > SNEB
SNEBBES > SNEBBE
SNEBBING > SNEB
SNEBS > SNEB
SNECK n small squared stone used in a rubble wall to fill spaces between stones ▷ vb fasten (a latch)
SNECKED > SNECK
SNECKING > SNECK
SNECKS > SNECK
SNED vb prune or trim
SNEDDED > SNED
SNEDDING > SNED
SNEDS > SNED
SNEE vb cut
SNEED > SNEE
SNEEING > SNEE
SNEER n contemptuous expression or remark ▷ vb show contempt by a sneer
SNEERED > SNEER
SNEERER > SNEER
SNEERERS > SNEER
SNEERFUL > SNEER
SNEERIER > SNEERY
SNEERIEST > SNEERY
SNEERING > SNEER
SNEERINGS > SNEER
SNEERS > SNEER
SNEERY adj contemptuous

or scornful
SNEES > SNEE
SNEESH n Scots word meaning pinch of snuff
SNEESHAN n Scots word meaning pinch of snuff
SNEESHANS > SNEESHAN
SNEESHES > SNEESH
SNEESHIN same as > SNEESHAN
SNEESHING same as > SNEESHAN
SNEESHINS > SNEESHIN
SNEEZE vb expel air from the nose suddenly, involuntarily, and noisily ▷ n act or sound of sneezing
SNEEZED > SNEEZE
SNEEZER > SNEEZE
SNEEZERS > SNEEZE
SNEEZES > SNEEZE
SNEEZIER > SNEEZE
SNEEZIEST > SNEEZE
SNEEZING > SNEEZE
SNEEZINGS > SNEEZE
SNEEZY > SNEEZE
SNELL adj biting ▷ vb attach hook to fishing line
SNELLED > SNELL
SNELLER > SNELL
SNELLEST > SNELL
SNELLING > SNELL
SNELLS > SNELL
SNELLY > SNELL
SNIB n catch of a door or window ▷ vb bolt or fasten (a door)
SNIBBED > SNIB
SNIBBING > SNIB
SNIBS > SNIB
SNICK n (make) a small cut or notch ▷ vb make a small cut or notch in (something)
SNICKED > SNICK
SNICKER same as > SNIGGER
SNICKERED > SNICKER
SNICKERER > SNICKER
SNICKERS > SNICKER
SNICKERY > SNICKER
SNICKET n passageway between walls or fences
SNICKETS > SNICKET
SNICKING > SNICK
SNICKS > SNICK
SNIDE adj critical in an unfair and nasty way ▷ n sham jewellery ▷ vb fill or load
SNIDED > SNIDE
SNIDELY > SNIDE
SNIDENESS > SNIDE
SNIDER > SNIDE
SNIDES > SNIDE
SNIDEST > SNIDE
SNIDEY same as > SNIDE
SNIDIER > SNIDEY
SNIDIEST > SNIDEY
SNIDING > SNIDE
SNIES > SNY
SNIFF vb inhale through the nose in short audible breaths ▷ n act or sound of sniffing
SNIFFABLE > SNIFF
SNIFFED > SNIFF
SNIFFER n device for

detecting hidden substances such as drugs or explosives, esp by their odour

SNIFFERS > SNIFFER

SNIFFIER > SNIFFY

SNIFFIEST > SNIFFY

SNIFFILY > SNIFFY

SNIFFING > SNIFF

SNIFFINGS > SNIFF

SNIFFISH *adj* disdainful

SNIFFLE *vb* sniff repeatedly, as when suffering from a cold ▷*n* slight cold

SNIFFLED > SNIFFLE

SNIFFLER > SNIFFLE

SNIFFLERS > SNIFFLE

SNIFFLES > SNIFFLE

SNIFFLIER > SNIFFLE

SNIFFLING > SNIFFLE

SNIFFLY > SNIFFLE

SNIFFS > SNIFF

SNIFFY *adj* contemptuous or scornful

SNIFT *same as* > SNIFF

SNIFTED > SNIFT

SNIFTER *n* small quantity of alcoholic drink ▷*vb* sniff

SNIFTERED > SNIFTER

SNIFTERS > SNIFTER

SNIFTIER > SNIFTY

SNIFTIEST > SNIFTY

SNIFTING > SNIFT

SNIFTS > SNIFT

SNIFTY *adj* slang word meaning excellent

SNIG *vb* drag (a felled log) by a chain or cable

SNIGGED > SNIG

SNIGGER *n* a sly laugh ▷*vb* laugh slyly

SNIGGERED > SNIGGER

SNIGGERER > SNIGGER

SNIGGERS > SNIGGER

SNIGGING > SNIG

SNIGGLE *vb* fish for eels by dangling or thrusting a baited hook into cavities ▷*n* baited hook used for sniggling eels

SNIGGLED > SNIGGLE

SNIGGLER > SNIGGLE

SNIGGLERS > SNIGGLE

SNIGGLES > SNIGGLE

SNIGGLING > SNIGGLE

SNIGLET *n* invented word

SNIGLETS > SNIGLET

SNIGS > SNIG

SNIP *vb* cut in small quick strokes with scissors or shears ▷*n* bargain ▷*interj* representation of the sound of scissors or shears closing

SNIPE *n* wading bird with a long straight bill ▷*vb* shoot at (a person) from cover

SNIPED > SNIPE

SNIPEFISH *n* any teleost fish of the family *Macrorhamphosidae*

SNIPELIKE > SNIPE

SNIPER *n* person who shoots at someone from cover

SNIPERS > SNIPER

SNIPES > SNIPE

SNIPIER > SNIPY

SNIPIEST > SNIPY

SNIPING > SNIPE

SNIPINGS > SNIPE

SNIPPED > SNIP

SNIPPER > SNIP

SNIPPERS > SNIP

SNIPPET *n* small piece

SNIPPETS > SNIPPET

SNIPPETY > SNIPPET

SNIPPIER > SNIPPY

SNIPPIEST > SNIPPY

SNIPPILY > SNIPPY

SNIPPING > SNIP

SNIPPINGS > SNIP

SNIPPY *adj* scrappy

SNIPS > SNIP

SNIPY *adj* like a snipe

SNIRT *n* Scots word meaning suppressed laugh

SNIRTLE *vb* Scots word meaning snicker

SNIRTLED > SNIRTLE

SNIRTLES > SNIRTLE

SNIRTLING > SNIRTLE

SNIRTS > SNIRT

SNIT *n* fit of temper

SNITCH *vb* act as an informer ▷*n* informer

SNITCHED > SNITCH

SNITCHER > SNITCH

SNITCHERS > SNITCH

SNITCHES > SNITCH

SNITCHIER > SNITCHY

SNITCHING > SNITCH

SNITCHY *adj* bad-tempered or irritable

SNITS > SNIT

SNIVEL *vb* cry in a whining way ▷*n* act of snivelling

SNIVELED > SNIVEL

SNIVELER > SNIVEL

SNIVELERS > SNIVEL

SNIVELING > SNIVEL

SNIVELLED > SNIVEL

SNIVELLER > SNIVEL

SNIVELLY > SNIVEL

SNIVELS > SNIVEL

SNOB *n* person who judges others by social rank

SNOBBERY > SNOB

SNOBBIER > SNOB

SNOBBIEST > SNOB

SNOBBILY > SNOB

SNOBBISH > SNOB

SNOBBISM > SNOB

SNOBBISMS > SNOB

SNOBBY > SNOB

SNOBLING *n* little snob

SNOBLINGS > SNOBLING

SNOBS > SNOB

SNOD *vb* Scots word meaning make tidy

SNODDED > SNOD

SNODDER > SNOD

SNODDEST > SNOD

SNODDING > SNOD

SNODDIT > SNOD

SNODS > SNOD

SNOEK *n* edible marine fish

SNOEKS > SNOEK

SNOEP *adj* mean or tight-fisted

SNOG *vb* kiss and cuddle ▷*n* act of kissing and cuddling

SNOGGED > SNOG

SNOGGING > SNOG

SNOGS > SNOG

SNOKE *same as* > SNOOK

SNOKED > SNOKE

SNOKES > SNOKE

SNOKING > SNOKE

SNOOD *n* pouch, often of net, loosely holding a woman's hair at the back ▷*vb* hold (the hair) in a snood

SNOODED > SNOOD

SNOODING > SNOOD

SNOODS > SNOOD

SNOOK *n* any of several large game fishes ▷*vb* lurk

SNOOKED > SNOOK

SNOOKER *n* game played on a billiard table ▷*vb* leave (a snooker opponent) in a position such that another ball blocks the target ball

SNOOKERED > SNOOKER

SNOOKERS > SNOOKER

SNOOKING > SNOOK

SNOOKS > SNOOK

SNOOL *vb* Scots word meaning dominate

SNOOLED > SNOOL

SNOOLING > SNOOL

SNOOLS > SNOOL

SNOOP *vb* pry ▷*n* snooping

SNOOPED > SNOOP

SNOOPER *n* person who snoops

SNOOPERS > SNOOPER

SNOOPIER > SNOOP

SNOOPIEST > SNOOP

SNOOPILY > SNOOP

SNOOPING > SNOOP

SNOOPS > SNOOP

SNOOPY > SNOOP

SNOOT *n* nose ▷*vb* look contemptuously at

SNOOTED > SNOOT

SNOOTFUL *n* enough alcohol to make someone drunk

SNOOTFULS > SNOOTFUL

SNOOTIER > SNOOTY

SNOOTIEST > SNOOTY

SNOOTILY > SNOOTY

SNOOTING > SNOOT

SNOOTS > SNOOT

SNOOTY *adj* haughty

SNOOZE *vb* take a brief light sleep ▷*n* brief light sleep

SNOOZED > SNOOZE

SNOOZER > SNOOZE

SNOOZERS > SNOOZE

SNOOZES > SNOOZE

SNOOZIER > SNOOZE

SNOOZIEST > SNOOZE

SNOOZING > SNOOZE

SNOOZLE *vb* cuddle and sleep

SNOOZLED > SNOOZLE

SNOOZLES > SNOOZLE

SNOOZLING > SNOOZLE

SNOOZY > SNOOZE

SNORE *vb* make snorting sounds while sleeping ▷*n* sound of snoring

SNORED > SNORE

SNORER > SNORE

SNORERS > SNORE

SNORES > SNORE

SNORING > SNORE

SNORINGS > SNORE

SNORKEL *n* tube allowing a swimmer to breathe while face down on the surface of the water ▷*vb* swim using a snorkel

SNORKELED > SNORKEL

SNORKELER > SNORKEL

SNORKELS > SNORKEL

SNORT *vb* exhale noisily through the nostrils ▷*n* act or sound of snorting

SNORTED > SNORT

SNORTER *n* person or animal that snorts

SNORTERS > SNORTER

SNORTIER > SNORT

SNORTIEST > SNORT

SNORTING > SNORT

SNORTINGS > SNORT

SNORTS > SNORT

SNORTY > SNORT

SNOT *n* mucus from the nose ▷*vb* blow one's nose

SNOTS > SNOT

SNOTTED > SNOT

SNOTTER *vb* breathe through obstructed nostrils

SNOTTERED > SNOTTER

SNOTTERS > SNOTTER

SNOTTERY *n* snot

SNOTTIE *n* midshipman

SNOTTIER > SNOTTY

SNOTTIES > SNOTTY

SNOTTIEST > SNOTTY

SNOTTILY > SNOTTY

SNOTTING > SNOT

SNOTTY *adj* covered with mucus from the nose

SNOUT *n* animal's projecting nose and jaws ▷*vb* have or give a snout

SNOUTED > SNOUT

SNOUTIER > SNOUT

SNOUTIEST > SNOUT

SNOUTING > SNOUT

SNOUTISH > SNOUT

SNOUTLESS > SNOUT

SNOUTLIKE > SNOUT

SNOUTS > SNOUT

SNOUTY > SNOUT

SNOW *n* frozen vapour falling from the sky in flakes ▷*vb* fall as or like snow

SNOWBALL *n* snow pressed into a ball for throwing ▷*vb* increase rapidly

SNOWBALLS > SNOWBALL

SNOWBANK *n* bank of snow

SNOWBANKS > SNOWBANK

SNOWBELL *n* Asian shrub

SNOWBELLS > SNOWBELL

SNOWBELT *n* northern states of USA

SNOWBELTS > SNOWBELT

SNOWBERRY *n* shrub grown for its white berries

SNOWBIRD *n* person addicted to cocaine, or sometimes heroin

SNOWBIRDS > SNOWBIRD

SNOWBLINK *n* whitish glare in the sky reflected from snow

SNOWBOARD *n* board on which a person stands to

s

slide across the snow

SNOWBOOT *n* boot for walking in snow

SNOWBOOTS > SNOWBOOT

SNOWBOUND *adj* shut in by snow

SNOWBRUSH *n* brush for clearing snow

SNOWBUSH *n* North American plant

SNOWCAP *n* cap of snow on top of a mountain

SNOWCAPS > SNOWCAP

SNOWCAT *n* tracked vehicle for travelling over snow

SNOWCATS > SNOWCAT

SNOWDRIFT *n* bank of deep snow

SNOWDROP *n* small white bell-shaped spring flower

SNOWDROPS > SNOWDROP

SNOWED *adj* under the influence of narcotic drugs

SNOWFALL *n* fall of snow

SNOWFALLS > SNOWFALL

SNOWFIELD *n* large area of permanent snow

SNOWFLAKE *n* single crystal of snow

SNOWFLECK *n* snow bunting

SNOWFLICK *same as* > SNOWFLECK

SNOWIER > SNOWY

SNOWIEST > SNOWY

SNOWILY > SNOWY

SNOWINESS > SNOWY

SNOWING > SNOW

SNOWISH *adj* like snow

SNOWK *same as* > SNOOK

SNOWKED > SNOWK

SNOWKING > SNOWK

SNOWKS > SNOWK

SNOWLAND *n* area where snow lies

SNOWLANDS > SNOWLAND

SNOWLESS > SNOW

SNOWLIKE > SNOW

SNOWLINE *n* limit of permanent snow

SNOWLINES > SNOWLINE

SNOWMAKER *n* machine making artificial snow

SNOWMAN *n* figure shaped out of snow

SNOWMELT *n* melting of snow in spring

SNOWMELTS > SNOWMELT

SNOWMEN > SNOWMAN

SNOWMOLD *n* fungus growing on grass under snow

SNOWMOLDS > SNOWMOLD

SNOWPACK *n* body of hard-packed snow

SNOWPACKS > SNOWPACK

SNOWPLOW *n* implement or vehicle for clearing snow away

SNOWPLOWS > SNOWPLOW

SNOWS > SNOW

SNOWSCAPE *n* snow-covered landscape

SNOWSHED *n* shelter built over an exposed section of railway track to prevent its blockage by snow

SNOWSHEDS > SNOWSHED

SNOWSHOE *n* racket-shaped frame with a network of thongs stretched across it, worn on the feet to make walking on snow less difficult ▷ *vb* walk or go using snowshoes

SNOWSHOED > SNOWSHOE

SNOWSHOER > SNOWSHOE

SNOWSHOES > SNOWSHOE

SNOWSLIDE *n* snow avalanche

SNOWSLIP *n* small snow avalanche

SNOWSLIPS > SNOWSLIP

SNOWSTORM *n* storm with heavy snow

SNOWSUIT *n* one-piece winter outer garment for child

SNOWSUITS > SNOWSUIT

SNOWY *adj* covered with or abounding in snow

SNUB *vb* insult deliberately ▷ *n* deliberate insult ▷ *adj* (of a nose) short and blunt

SNUBBE *n* stub

SNUBBED > SNUB

SNUBBER > SNUB

SNUBBERS > SNUB

SNUBBES > SNUBBE

SNUBBIER > SNUB

SNUBBIEST > SNUB

SNUBBING > SNUB

SNUBBINGS > SNUB

SNUBBISH > SNUB

SNUBBY > SNUB

SNUBNESS > SNUB

SNUBS > SNUB

SNUCK *past tense and past participle of* > SNEAK

SNUDGE *vb* be miserly

SNUDGED > SNUDGE

SNUDGES > SNUDGE

SNUDGING > SNUDGE

SNUFF *n* powdered tobacco for sniffing up the nostrils ▷ *vb* extinguish (a candle)

SNUFFBOX *n* small container for holding snuff

SNUFFED > SNUFF

SNUFFER > SNUFF

SNUFFERS > SNUFF

SNUFFIER > SNUFFY

SNUFFIEST > SNUFFY

SNUFFILY > SNUFFY

SNUFFING > SNUFF

SNUFFINGS > SNUFF

SNUFFLE *vb* breathe noisily or with difficulty ▷ *n* act or the sound of snuffling

SNUFFLED > SNUFFLE

SNUFFLER > SNUFFLE

SNUFFLERS > SNUFFLE

SNUFFLES *same as* > SNIFFLES

SNUFFLIER > SNUFFLE

SNUFFLING > SNUFFLE

SNUFFLY > SNUFFLE

SNUFFS > SNUFF

SNUFFY *adj* of, relating to, or resembling snuff

SNUG *adj* warm and comfortable ▷ *n* (in Britain and Ireland) small room in a pub ▷ *vb* make or become comfortable and warm

SNUGGED > SNUG

SNUGGER > SNUG

SNUGGERIE *n* small bar in pub

SNUGGERY *n* cosy and comfortable place or room

SNUGGEST > SNUG

SNUGGIES *pl n* specially warm underwear

SNUGGING > SNUG

SNUGGLE *vb* nestle into a person or thing for warmth or from affection ▷ *n* act of snuggling

SNUGGLED > SNUGGLE

SNUGGLES > SNUGGLE

SNUGGLING > SNUGGLE

SNUGLY > SNUG

SNUGNESS > SNUG

SNUGS > SNUG

SNUSH *vb* take snuff

SNUSHED > SNUSH

SNUSHES > SNUSH

SNUSHING > SNUSH

SNUZZLE *vb* root in ground

SNUZZLED > SNUZZLE

SNUZZLES > SNUZZLE

SNUZZLING > SNUZZLE

SNY *same as* > SNYE

SNYE *n* side channel of a river

SNYES > SNYE

SO *adv* such an extent ▷ *interj* exclamation of surprise, triumph, or realization

SOAK *vb* make wet ▷ *n* soaking

SOAKAGE *n* process or a period in which a permeable substance is soaked in a liquid

SOAKAGES > SOAKAGE

SOAKAWAY *n* pit filled with rubble, etc, into which rain or waste water drains

SOAKAWAYS > SOAKAWAY

SOAKED > SOAK

SOAKEN > SOAK

SOAKER > SOAK

SOAKERS > SOAK

SOAKING > SOAK

SOAKINGLY > SOAK

SOAKINGS > SOAK

SOAKS > SOAK

SOAP *n* compound of alkali and fat, used with water as a cleaning agent ▷ *vb* apply soap to

SOAPBARK *n* W South American rosaceous tree

SOAPBARKS > SOAPBARK

SOAPBERRY *n* any of various chiefly tropical American sapindaceous trees

SOAPBOX *n* crate used as a platform for speech-making ▷ *vb* deliver a speech from a soapbox

SOAPBOXED > SOAPBOX

SOAPBOXES > SOAPBOX

SOAPED > SOAP

SOAPER *n* soap opera

SOAPERS > SOAPER

SOAPIE *n* soap opera

SOAPIER > SOAPY

SOAPIES > SOAPIE

SOAPIEST > SOAPY

SOAPILY > SOAPY

SOAPINESS > SOAPY

SOAPING > SOAP

SOAPLAND *n* Japanese massage parlour and brothel

SOAPLANDS > SOAPLAND

SOAPLESS > SOAP

SOAPLIKE > SOAP

SOAPROOT *n* plant with roots used as soap substitute

SOAPROOTS > SOAPROOT

SOAPS > SOAP

SOAPSTONE *n* soft mineral used for making table tops and ornaments

SOAPSUDS *pl n* foam or lather produced when soap is mixed with water

SOAPSUDSY > SOAPSUDS

SOAPWORT *n* Eurasian plant with clusters of fragrant pink or white flowers

SOAPWORTS > SOAPWORT

SOAPY *adj* covered with soap

SOAR *vb* rise or fly upwards ▷ *n* act of soaring

SOARAWAY *adj* exceedingly successful

SOARE *n* young hawk

SOARED > SOAR

SOARER > SOAR

SOARERS > SOAR

SOARES > SOARE

SOARING > SOAR

SOARINGLY > SOAR

SOARINGS > SOAR

SOARS > SOAR

SOAVE *n* dry white Italian wine

SOAVES > SOAVE

SOB *vb* weep with convulsive gasps ▷ *n* act or sound of sobbing

SOBA *n* (in Japanese cookery) noodles made from buckwheat flour

SOBAS > SOBA

SOBBED > SOB

SOBBER > SOB

SOBBERS > SOB

SOBBING > SOB

SOBBINGLY > SOB

SOBBINGS > SOB

SOBEIT *conj* provided that

SOBER *adj* not drunk ▷ *vb* make or become sober

SOBERED > SOBER

SOBERER > SOBER

SOBEREST > SOBER

SOBERING > SOBER

SOBERISE *same as* > SOBERIZE

SOBERISED > SOBERISE

SOBERISES > SOBERISE

SOBERIZE *vb* make sober

SOBERIZED > SOBERIZE

SOBERIZES > SOBERIZE

SOBERLY > SOBER

SOBERNESS > SOBER

SOBERS > SOBER

SOBFUL *adj* tearful

SOBOLE *n* creeping

underground stem that produces roots and buds

SOBOLES > SOBOLE

SOBRIETY n state of being sober

SOBRIQUET n nickname

SOBS > SOB

SOC n feudal right to hold court

SOCA n mixture of soul and calypso music popular in the E Caribbean

SOCAGE n tenure of land by certain services, esp of an agricultural nature

SOCAGER > SOCAGE

SOCAGERS > SOCAGE

SOCAGES > SOCAGE

SOCAS > SOCA

SOCCAGE same as > SOCAGE

SOCCAGES > SOCCAGE

SOCCER n football played by two teams of eleven kicking a spherical ball

SOCCERS > SOCCER

SOCIABLE adj friendly or companionable ▷ n type of open carriage with two seats facing each other

SOCIABLES > SOCIABLE

SOCIABLY > SOCIABLE

SOCIAL adj living in a community ▷ n informal gathering

SOCIALISE same as > SOCIALIZE

SOCIALISM n political system which advocates public ownership of industries, resources, and transport

SOCIALIST n supporter or advocate of socialism ▷ adj of or relating to socialism

SOCIALITE n member of fashionable society

SOCIALITY n tendency of groups and persons to develop social links and live in communities

SOCIALIZE vb meet others socially

SOCIALLY > SOCIAL

SOCIALS > SOCIAL

SOCIATE n associate

SOCIATES > SOCIATE

SOCIATION n plant community

SOCIATIVE adj of association

SOCIETAL adj of or relating to society, esp human society or social relations

SOCIETIES > SOCIETY

SOCIETY n human beings considered as a group

SOCIOGRAM n chart showing social relationships

SOCIOLECT n language spoken by particular social class

SOCIOLOGY n study of human societies

SOCIOPATH n person with a personality disorder characterized

by a tendency to commit antisocial acts without any feelings of guilt

SOCK n knitted covering for the foot ▷ vb hit hard

SOCKED > SOCK

SOCKET n hole or recess into which something fits ▷ vb furnish with or place into a socket

SOCKETED > SOCKET

SOCKETING > SOCKET

SOCKETS > SOCKET

SOCKETTE n sock not covering ankle

SOCKETTES > SOCKETTE

SOCKEYE n Pacific salmon with red flesh

SOCKEYES > SOCKEYE

SOCKING > SOCK

SOCKLESS > SOCK

SOCKMAN same as > SOCMAN

SOCKMEN > SOCKMAN

SOCKO adj excellent

SOCKS > SOCK

SOCLE another name for > PLINTH

SOCLES > SOCLE

SOCMAN n tenant holding land by socage

SOCMEN > SOCMAN

SOCS > SOC

SOD n (piece of) turf ▷ vb cover with sods

SODA n compound of sodium

SODAIC adj containing soda

SODAIN same as > SUDDEN

SODAINE same as > SUDDEN

SODALESS > SODA

SODALIST n member of sodality

SODALISTS > SODALIST

SODALITE n blue, grey, yellow, or colourless mineral

SODALITES > SODALITE

SODALITY n religious or charitable society

SODAMIDE n white crystalline compound used as a dehydrating agent

SODAMIDES > SODAMIDE

SODAS > SODA

SODBUSTER n farmer who grows crops

SODDED > SOD

SODDEN adj soaked ▷ vb make or become sodden

SODDENED > SODDEN

SODDENING > SODDEN

SODDENLY > SODDEN

SODDENS > SODDEN

SODDIER > SODDY

SODDIES > SODDY

SODDIEST > SODDY

SODDING > SOD

SODDY adj covered with turf

SODGER dialect variant of > SOLDIER

SODGERED > SODGER

SODGERING > SODGER

SODGERS > SODGER

SODIC adj containing sodium

SODICITY > SODIC

SODIUM n silvery-white

metallic element

SODIUMS > SODIUM

SODOM n person who performs sodomy

SODOMIES > SODOMY

SODOMISE same as > SODOMIZE

SODOMISED > SODOMISE

SODOMISES > SODOMISE

SODOMIST > SODOMY

SODOMISTS > SODOMY

SODOMITE n person who practises sodomy

SODOMITES > SODOMITE

SODOMITIC > SODOMY

SODOMIZE vb be the active partner in anal intercourse

SODOMIZED > SODOMIZE

SODOMIZES > SODOMIZE

SODOMS > SODOM

SODOMY n anal intercourse

SODS > SOD

SOEVER adv in any way at all

SOFA n couch

SOFABED n sofa that converts into a bed

SOFABEDS > SOFABED

SOFAR n system for determining a position at sea

SOFARS > SOFAR

SOFAS > SOFA

SOFFIONI n holes in volcano that emit steam

SOFFIT n underside of a part of a building or a structural component

SOFFITS > SOFFIT

SOFT adj easy to shape or cut ▷ adv softly ▷ vb soften

SOFTA n Muslim student of divinity and jurisprudence, esp in Turkey

SOFTAS > SOFTA

SOFTBACK n paperback

SOFTBACKS > SOFTBACK

SOFTBALL n game similar to baseball, played using a larger softer ball

SOFTBALLS > SOFTBALL

SOFTBOUND adj having paperback binding

SOFTCORE adj not explicit

SOFTCOVER n book with paper covers

SOFTED > SOFT

SOFTEN vb make or become soft or softer

SOFTENED > SOFTEN

SOFTENER n substance added to another substance to increase its softness

SOFTENERS > SOFTENER

SOFTENING > SOFTEN

SOFTENS > SOFTEN

SOFTER > SOFT

SOFTEST > SOFT

SOFTGOODS n clothing and soft furniture

SOFTHEAD n half-witted person

SOFTHEADS > SOFTHEAD

SOFTIE n person who is easily upset

SOFTIES > SOFTY

SOFTING > SOFT

SOFTISH > SOFT

SOFTLING n weakling

SOFTLINGS > SOFTLING

SOFTLY > SOFT

SOFTNESS n quality or an instance of being soft

SOFTPASTE n artifical porcelain made from clay

SOFTS > SOFT

SOFTSHELL n crab or turtle with a soft shell

SOFTWARE n computer programs

SOFTWARES > SOFTWARE

SOFTWOOD n wood of a coniferous tree

SOFTWOODS > SOFTWOOD

SOFTY same as > SOFTIE

SOG vb soak

SOGER same as > SODGER

SOGERS > SOGER

SOGGED > SOG

SOGGIER > SOGGY

SOGGIEST > SOGGY

SOGGILY > SOGGY

SOGGINESS > SOGGY

SOGGING > SOG

SOGGINGS > SOG

SOGGY adj soaked

SOGS > SOG

SOH n (in tonic sol-fa) fifth degree of any major scale

SOHO interj exclamation announcing the sighting of a hare

SOHS > SOH

SOIGNE adj well-groomed, elegant

SOIGNEE variant of > SOIGNE

SOIL n top layer of earth ▷ vb make or become dirty

SOILAGE n green fodder, esp when freshly cut and fed to livestock in a confined area

SOILAGES > SOILAGE

SOILBORNE adj carried in soil

SOILED > SOIL

SOILIER > SOIL

SOILIEST > SOIL

SOILINESS > SOIL

SOILING > SOIL

SOILINGS > SOIL

SOILLESS > SOIL

SOILS > SOIL

SOILURE n act of soiling or the state of being soiled

SOILURES > SOILURE

SOILY > SOIL

SOIREE n evening party or gathering

SOIREES > SOIREE

SOJA same as > SOYA

SOJAS > SOJA

SOJOURN n temporary stay ▷ vb stay temporarily

SOJOURNED > SOJOURN

SOJOURNER > SOJOURN

SOJOURNS > SOJOURN

SOKAH same as > SOCA

SOKAHS > SOKAH

SOKAIYA n Japanese extortionist

SOKE n right to hold a local court

SOKEMAN *same as* > SOCMAN
SOKEMANRY *n* feudal tenure by socage
SOKEMEN > SOKEMAN
SOKEN *n* feudal district
SOKENS > SOKEN
SOKES > SOKE
SOKOL *n* Czech gymnastic association
SOKOLS > SOKOL
SOL *n* liquid colloidal solution
SOLA > SOLUM
SOLACE *vb* comfort in distress ▷ *n* comfort in misery or disappointment
SOLACED > SOLACE
SOLACER > SOLACE
SOLACERS > SOLACE
SOLACES > SOLACE
SOLACING > SOLACE
SOLACIOUS *adj* providing solace
SOLAH *n* Indian plant
SOLAHS > SOLAH
SOLAN *archaic name for* > GANNET
SOLAND *n* solan goose
SOLANDER *n* box for botanical specimens, maps, etc, made in the form of a book, the front cover being the lid
SOLANDERS > SOLANDER
SOLANDS > SOLAND
SOLANIN *same as* > SOLANINE
SOLANINE *n* poisonous alkaloid found in various solanaceous plants
SOLANINES > SOLANINE
SOLANINS > SOLANIN
SOLANO *n* hot wind in Spain
SOLANOS > SOLANO
SOLANS > SOLAN
SOLANUM *n* any plant of the mainly tropical genus that includes the potato, aubergine, and certain nightshades
SOLANUMS > SOLANUM
SOLAR *adj* of the sun
SOLARIA > SOLARIUM
SOLARISE *same as* > SOLARIZE
SOLARISED > SOLARISE
SOLARISES > SOLARISE
SOLARISM *n* explanation of myths in terms of the movements and influence of the sun
SOLARISMS > SOLARISM
SOLARIST > SOLARISM
SOLARISTS > SOLARISM
SOLARIUM *n* place with beds and ultraviolet lights used for acquiring an artificial suntan
SOLARIUMS > SOLARIUM
SOLARIZE *vb* treat by exposure to the sun's rays
SOLARIZED > SOLARIZE
SOLARIZES > SOLARIZE
SOLARS > SOLUM
SOLAS > SOLUM
SOLATE *vb* change from gel to liquid

SOLATED > SOLATE
SOLATES > SOLATE
SOLATIA > SOLATIUM
SOLATING > SOLATE
SOLATION *n* liquefaction of a gel
SOLATIONS > SOLATION
SOLATIUM *n* compensation awarded for injury to the feelings
SOLD *n* obsolete word for salary
SOLDADO *n* soldier
SOLDADOS > SOLDADO
SOLDAN *archaic word for* > SULTAN
SOLDANS > SOLDAN
SOLDE *n* wages
SOLDER *n* soft alloy used to join two metal surfaces ▷ *vb* join with solder
SOLDERED > SOLDER
SOLDERER > SOLDER
SOLDERERS > SOLDER
SOLDERING > SOLDER
SOLDERS > SOLDER
SOLDES > SOLDE
SOLDI > SOLDO
SOLDIER *n* member of an army ▷ *vb* serve in an army
SOLDIERED > SOLDIER
SOLDIERLY *adj* of or befitting a good soldier
SOLDIERS > SOLDIER
SOLDIERY *n* soldiers collectively
SOLDO *n* former Italian copper coin worth one twentieth of a lira
SOLDS > SOLD
SOLE *adj* one and only ▷ *n* underside of the foot ▷ *vb* provide (a shoe) with a sole
SOLECISE *variant of* > SOLECIZE
SOLECISED > SOLECISE
SOLECISES > SOLECISE
SOLECISM *n* minor grammatical mistake
SOLECISMS > SOLECISM
SOLECIST > SOLECISM
SOLECISTS > SOLECISM
SOLECIZE *vb* commit a solecism
SOLECIZED *same as* > SOLECIZE
SOLECIZES > SOLECIZE
SOLED > SOLE
SOLEI > SOLEUS
SOLEIN *same as* > SULLEN
SOLELESS > SOLE
SOLELY *adv* only, completely
SOLEMN *adj* serious, deeply sincere
SOLEMNER > SOLEMN
SOLEMNESS > SOLEMN
SOLEMNEST > SOLEMN
SOLEMNIFY *vb* make serious or grave
SOLEMNISE *same as* > SOLEMNIZE
SOLEMNITY *n* state or quality of being solemn
SOLEMNIZE *vb* celebrate or perform (a ceremony)
SOLEMNLY > SOLEMN

SOLENESS > SOLE
SOLENETTE *n* small European sole
SOLENODON *n* either of two rare shrewlike nocturnal mammals of the Caribbean
SOLENOID *n* coil of wire magnetized by passing a current through it
SOLENOIDS > SOLENOID
SOLEPLATE *n* joist forming the lowest member of a timber frame
SOLEPRINT *n* print of sole of foot
SOLER *same as* > SOLE
SOLERA *n* system for aging sherry and other fortified wines
SOLERAS > SOLERA
SOLERET *n* armour for foot
SOLERETS > SOLERET
SOLERS > SOLER
SOLES > SOLE
SOLEUS *n* muscle in calf of leg
SOLEUSES > SOLEUS
SOLFATARA *n* volcanic vent emitting only sulphurous gases and water vapour or sometimes hot mud
SOLFEGE *variant of* > SOLFEGGIO
SOLFEGES > SOLFEGE
SOLFEGGI > SOLFEGGIO
SOLFEGGIO *n* voice exercise in which runs, scales, etc, are sung to the same syllable or syllables
SOLFERINO *n* moderate purplish-red colour
SOLGEL *adj* changing between sol and gel
SOLI *adv* (of a piece or passage) to be performed by or with soloists
SOLICIT *vb* request
SOLICITED > SOLICIT
SOLICITOR *n* lawyer who advises clients and prepares documents and cases
SOLICITS > SOLICIT
SOLICITY *n* act of making a request
SOLID *adj* (of a substance) keeping its shape ▷ *n* three-dimensional shape
SOLIDAGO *n* any plant of the chiefly American genus *Solidago*
SOLIDAGOS > SOLIDAGO
SOLIDARE *n* old coin
SOLIDARES > SOLIDARE
SOLIDARY *adj* marked by unity of interests, responsibilities, etc
SOLIDATE *vb* consolidate
SOLIDATED > SOLIDATE
SOLIDATES > SOLIDATE
SOLIDER > SOLID
SOLIDEST > SOLID
SOLIDI > SOLIDUS
SOLIDIFY *vb* make or become solid or firm
SOLIDISH > SOLID
SOLIDISM *n* belief that

diseases spring from damage to solid parts of body
SOLIDISMS > SOLIDISM
SOLIDIST > SOLIDISM
SOLIDISTS > SOLIDISM
SOLIDITY > SOLID
SOLIDLY > SOLID
SOLIDNESS > SOLID
SOLIDS > SOLID
SOLIDUM *n* part of pedestal
SOLIDUMS > SOLIDUM
SOLIDUS *same as* > SLASH
SOLILOQUY *n* speech made by a person while alone, esp in a play
SOLING > SOLE
SOLION *n* amplifier used in chemistry
SOLIONS > SOLION
SOLIPED *n* animal whose hooves are not cloven
SOLIPEDS > SOLIPED
SOLIPSISM *n* doctrine that the self is the only thing known to exist
SOLIPSIST > SOLIPSISM
SOLIQUID *n* semi-solid, semi-liquid solution
SOLIQUIDS > SOLIQUID
SOLITAIRE *n* game for one person played with pegs set in a board
SOLITARY *adj* alone, single ▷ *n* hermit
SOLITO *adv* musical instruction meaning play in usual manner
SOLITON *n* type of isolated particle-like wave
SOLITONS > SOLITON
SOLITUDE *n* state of being alone
SOLITUDES > SOLITUDE
SOLIVE *n* type of joist
SOLIVES > SOLIVE
SOLLAR *n* archaic word meaning attic
SOLLARS > SOLLAR
SOLLER *same as* > SOLLAR
SOLLERET *n* protective covering for the foot consisting of riveted plates of armour
SOLLERETS > SOLLERET
SOLLERS > SOLLER
SOLLICKER *n* something very large
SOLO *n* music for one performer ▷ *adj* done alone ▷ *adv* by oneself, alone ▷ *vb* undertake a venture alone, esp to operate an aircraft alone or climb alone
SOLOED > SOLO
SOLOING > SOLO
SOLOIST *n* person who performs a solo
SOLOISTIC > SOLOIST
SOLOISTS > SOLOIST
SOLON *n* US congressman
SOLONCHAK *n* type of intrazonal soil of arid regions with a greyish surface crust
SOLONETS *same*

as > SOLONETZ

SOLONETZ *n* type of intrazonal soil with a high saline content characterized by leaching

SOLONS > SOLON

SOLOS > SOLO

SOLPUGID *n* venomous arachnid

SOLPUGIDS > SOLPUGID

SOLS > SOL

SOLSTICE *n* either the shortest (in winter) or longest (in summer) day of the year

SOLSTICES > SOLSTICE

SOLUBLE *adj* able to be dissolved ▷ *n* soluble substance

SOLUBLES > SOLUBLE

SOLUBLY > SOLUBLE

SOLUM *n* upper layers of the soil profile, affected by climate and vegetation

SOLUMS > SOLUM

SOLUNAR *adj* relating to sun and moon

SOLUS *adj* alone

SOLUTE *n* substance in a solution that is dissolved ▷ *adj* loose or unattached

SOLUTES > SOLUTE

SOLUTION *n* answer to a problem

SOLUTIONS > SOLUTION

SOLUTIVE *adj* dissolving

SOLVABLE *adj* capable of being solved

SOLVATE *vb* undergo, cause to undergo, or partake in solvation

SOLVATED > SOLVATE

SOLVATES > SOLVATE

SOLVATING > SOLVATE

SOLVATION *n* type of chemical process

SOLVE *vb* find the answer to (a problem)

SOLVED > SOLVE

SOLVENCY *n* ability to pay all debts

SOLVENT *adj* having enough money to pay one's debts ▷ *n* liquid capable of dissolving other substances

SOLVENTLY > SOLVENT

SOLVENTS > SOLVENT

SOLVER > SOLVE

SOLVERS > SOLVE

SOLVES > SOLVE

SOLVING > SOLVE

SOM *n* currency of Kyrgyzstan and Uzbekistan

SOMA *n* body of an organism, esp an animal, as distinct from the germ cells

SOMAN *n* organophosphorus compound developed as a nerve gas in Germany during World War II

SOMANS > SOMAN

SOMAS > SOMA

SOMASCOPE *n* instrument for inspecting internal organs

SOMATA > SOMA

SOMATIC *adj* of the body, as distinct from the mind

SOMATISM *n* materialism

SOMATISMS > SOMATISM

SOMATIST > SOMATISM

SOMATISTS > SOMATISM

SOMBER *adj* (in the US) sombre ▷ *vb* (in the US) make sombre

SOMBERED > SOMBER

SOMBERER > SOMBER

SOMBEREST > SOMBER

SOMBERING > SOMBER

SOMBERLY > SOMBER

SOMBERS > SOMBER

SOMBRE *adj* dark, gloomy ▷ *vb* make sombre

SOMBRED > SOMBRE

SOMBRELY > SOMBRE

SOMBRER > SOMBRE

SOMBRERO *n* wide-brimmed Mexican hat

SOMBREROS > SOMBRERO

SOMBRES > SOMBRE

SOMBREST > SOMBRE

SOMBRING > SOMBRE

SOMBROUS > SOMBRE

SOME *adj* unknown or unspecified ▷ *pron* certain unknown or unspecified people or things ▷ *adv* approximately ▷ *determiner* (a) certain unknown or unspecified

SOMEBODY *pron* some person ▷ *n* important person

SOMEDAY *adv* at some unspecified time in the future

SOMEDEAL *adv* to some extent

SOMEDELE *same as* > SOMEDEAL

SOMEGATE *adv* Scots word meaning somehow

SOMEHOW *adv* in some unspecified way

SOMEONE *pron* somebody ▷ *n* significant or important person

SOMEONES > SOMEONE

SOMEPLACE *adv* in, at, or to some unspecified place or region

SOMERSET *variant of* > SOMERSAULT

SOMERSETS > SOMERSET

SOMETHING *pron* unknown or unspecified thing or amount ▷ *n* impressive or important person or thing

SOMETIME *adv* at some unspecified time ▷ *adj* former

SOMETIMES *adv* from time to time, now and then

SOMEWAY *adv* in some unspecified manner

SOMEWAYS *same as* > SOMEWAY

SOMEWHAT *adv* some extent, rather ▷ *n* vague amount

SOMEWHATS > SOMEWHAT

SOMEWHEN *adv* at some time

SOMEWHERE *adv* in, to, or at some unspecified or

unknown place

SOMEWHILE *adv* sometimes

SOMEWHY *adv* for some reason

SOMEWISE *adv* in some way or to some degree

SOMITAL > SOMITE

SOMITE *n* any of a series of dorsal paired segments of mesoderm occurring along the notochord in vertebrate embryos

SOMITES > SOMITE

SOMITIC > SOMITE

SOMMELIER *n* wine steward in a restaurant or hotel

SOMNIAL *adj* of dreams

SOMNIATE *vb* dream

SOMNIATED > SOMNIATE

SOMNIATES > SOMNIATE

SOMNIFIC *adj* inducing sleep

SOMNOLENT *adj* drowsy

SOMONI *n* monetary unit of Tajikistan

SOMS > SOM

SOMY > SOM

SON *n* male offspring

SONANCE > SONANT

SONANCES > SONANT

SONANCIES > SONANT

SONANCY > SONANT

SONANT *n* voiced sound able to form a syllable or syllable nucleus ▷ *adj* denoting a voiced sound like this

SONANTAL > SONANT

SONANTIC > SONANT

SONANTS > SONANT

SONAR *n* device for detecting underwater objects by the reflection of sound waves

SONARMAN *n* sonar operator

SONARMEN > SONARMAN

SONARS > SONAR

SONATA *n* piece of music in several movements for one instrument with or without piano

SONATAS > SONATA

SONATINA *n* short sonata

SONATINAS > SONATINA

SONATINE *same as* > SONATINA

SONCE *n* Scots word meaning good luck

SONCES > SONCE

SONDAGE *n* deep trial trench for inspecting stratigraphy

SONDAGES > SONDAGE

SONDE *n* rocket, balloon, or probe used for observing in the upper atmosphere

SONDELI *n* Indian shrew

SONDELIS > SONDELI

SONDER *n* yacht category

SONDERS > SONDER

SONDES > SONDE

SONE *n* subjective unit of loudness

SONERI *n* Indian cloth of gold

SONERIS > SONERI

SONES > SONE

SONG *n* music for the voice

SONGBIRD *n* any bird with a

musical call

SONGBIRDS > SONGBIRD

SONGBOOK *n* book of songs

SONGBOOKS > SONGBOOK

SONGCRAFT *n* art of songwriting

SONGFEST *n* event with many songs

SONGFESTS > SONGFEST

SONGFUL *adj* tuneful

SONGFULLY > SONGFUL

SONGKOK *n* (in Malaysia and Indonesia) a kind of oval brimless hat, resembling a skull

SONGKOKS > SONGKOK

SONGLESS > SONG

SONGLIKE > SONG

SONGMAN *n* singer

SONGMEN > SONGMAN

SONGOLOLO *n* kind of millipede

SONGS > SONG

SONGSMITH *n* person who writes songs

SONGSTER *n* singer

SONGSTERS > SONGSTER

SONHOOD > SON

SONHOODS > SON

SONIC *adj* of or producing sound

SONICALLY > SONIC

SONICATE *vb* subject to sound waves

SONICATED > SONICATE

SONICATES > SONICATE

SONICATOR > SONICATE

SONICS *n* study of mechanical vibrations in matter

SONLESS > SON

SONLIKE > SON

SONLY *adj* like a son

SONNE *same as* > SON

SONNES > SONNE

SONNET *n* fourteen-line poem with a fixed rhyme scheme ▷ *vb* compose sonnets

SONNETARY > SONNET

SONNETED > SONNET

SONNETEER *n* writer of sonnets

SONNETING > SONNET

SONNETISE *same as* > SONNETIZE

SONNETIZE *vb* write sonnets

SONNETS > SONNET

SONNETTED > SONNET

SONNIES > SONNY

SONNY *n* term of address to a boy

SONOBUOY *n* buoy equipped to detect underwater noises and transmit them by radio

SONOBUOYS > SONOBUOY

SONOGRAM *n* three-dimensional representation of a sound signal

SONOGRAMS > SONOGRAM

SONOGRAPH *n* device for scanning sound

SONOMETER *same as* > MONOCHORD

S

SONORANT *n* type of frictionless continuant or nasal
SONORANTS > SONORANT
SONORITY > SONOROUS
SONOROUS *adj* (of sound) deep or resonant
SONOVOX *n* device used to alter sound of human voice in music recordings
SONOVOXES > SONOVOX
SONS > SON
SONSE *same as* > SONCE
SONSES > SONSE
SONSHIP > SON
SONSHIPS > SON
SONSIE *same as* > SONSY
SONSIER > SONSY
SONSIEST > SONSY
SONSY *adj* plump
SONTAG *n* type of knitted women's cape
SONTAGS > SONTAG
SONTIES *n* Shakespearian oath
SOOCHONG *same as* > SOUCHONG
SOOCHONGS > SOOCHONG
SOOEY *interj* call used to summon pigs
SOOGEE *vb* clean ship using a special solution
SOOGEED > SOOGEE
SOOGEEING > SOOGEE
SOOGEES > SOOGEE
SOOGIE *same as* > SOUGEE
SOOGIED > SOOGIE
SOOGIEING > SOOGIE
SOOGIES > SOOGIE
SOOJEY *same as* > SOOGEE
SOOJEYS > SOOJEY
SOOK *n* baby ▷ *vb* suck
SOOKED > SOOK
SOOKING > SOOK
SOOKS > SOOK
SOOL *vb* incite (a dog) to attack
SOOLE *same as* > SOOL
SOOLED > SOOL
SOOLES > SOOLE
SOOLING > SOOL
SOOLS > SOOL
SOOM *Scots word for* > SWIM
SOOMED > SOOM
SOOMING > SOOM
SOOMS > SOOM
SOON *adv* in a short time
SOONER *adv* rather ▷ *n* native of Oklahoma
SOONERS > SOONER
SOONEST *adv* as soon as possible
SOOP *Scots word for* > SWEEP
SOOPED > SOOP
SOOPING > SOOP
SOOPINGS > SOOP
SOOPS > SOOP
SOOPSTAKE *adv* sweeping up all stakes
SOOT *n* black powder formed by the incomplete burning of an organic substance ▷ *vb* cover with soot
SOOTE *n* sweet
SOOTED > SOOT
SOOTERKIN *n* mythical black afterbirth of Dutch women that was believed to result from their warming themselves on stoves
SOOTES > SOOT
SOOTFLAKE *n* speck of soot
SOOTH *n* truth or reality ▷ *adj* true or real
SOOTHE *vb* make calm
SOOTHED > SOOTHE
SOOTHER > SOOTHE *vb* flatter
SOOTHERED > SOOTHE
SOOTHERS > SOOTHE
SOOTHES > SOOTHE
SOOTHEST > SOOTH
SOOTHFAST *adj* truthful
SOOTHFUL *adj* truthful
SOOTHING *adj* having a calming, assuaging, or relieving effect
SOOTHINGS > SOOTHING
SOOTHLICH *adv* truly
SOOTHLY > SOOTH
SOOTHS > SOOTH
SOOTHSAID > SOOTHSAY
SOOTHSAY *vb* predict the future
SOOTHSAYS > SOOTHSAY
SOOTIER > SOOTY
SOOTIEST > SOOTY
SOOTILY > SOOTY
SOOTINESS > SOOTY
SOOTING > SOOT
SOOTLESS > SOOT
SOOTS > SOOT
SOOTY *adj* covered with soot
SOP *n* concession to pacify someone ▷ *vb* mop up or absorb (liquid)
SOPAPILLA *n* Mexican deep-fried pastry
SOPH *shortened form of* > SOPHOMORE
SOPHERIC > SOPHERIM
SOPHERIM *n* Jewish scribes
SOPHIES > SOPHY
SOPHISM *n* argument that seems reasonable but is actually false and misleading
SOPHISMS > SOPHISM
SOPHIST *n* person who uses clever but invalid arguments
SOPHISTER *n* (esp formerly) a second-year undergraduate at certain British universities
SOPHISTIC *adj* of or relating to sophists or sophistry
SOPHISTRY *n* clever but invalid argument
SOPHISTS > SOPHIST
SOPHOMORE *n* student in second year at college
SOPHS > SOPH
SOPHY *n* title of the Persian monarchs
SOPITE *vb* lull to sleep
SOPITED > SOPITE
SOPITES > SOPITE
SOPITING > SOPITE
SOPOR *n* abnormally deep sleep

SOPORIFIC *adj* causing sleep ▷ *n* drug that causes sleep
SOPOROSE *adj* sleepy
SOPOROUS *same as* > SOPOROSE
SOPORS > SOPOR
SOPPED > SOP
SOPPIER > SOPPY
SOPPIEST > SOPPY
SOPPILY > SOPPY
SOPPINESS > SOPPY
SOPPING > SOP
SOPPINGS > SOP
SOPPY *adj* oversentimental
SOPRA *adv* musical instruction meaning above
SOPRANI > SOPRANO
SOPRANINI > SOPRANINO
SOPRANINO *n* instrument with the highest possible pitch in a family of instruments
SOPRANIST *n* soprano
SOPRANO *n* singer with the highest female or boy's voice ▷ *adj* of a musical instrument that is the highest or second highest pitched in its family
SOPRANOS > SOPRANO
SOPS > SOP
SORA *n* North American rail with a yellow bill
SORAGE *n* first year in hawk's life
SORAGES > SORAGE
SORAL > SORUS
SORAS > SORA
SORB *n* any of various related trees, esp the mountain ash ▷ *vb* absorb or adsorb
SORBABLE > SORB
SORBARIA *n* Asian shrub
SORBARIAS > SORBARIA
SORBATE *n* salt of sorbic acid
SORBATES > SORBATE
SORBED > SORB
SORBENT > SORB
SORBENTS > SORB
SORBET *same as* > SHERBET
SORBETS > SORBET
SORBIC > SORB
SORBING > SORB
SORBITE *n* mineral found in steel
SORBITES > SORBITE
SORBITIC > SORBITE
SORBITISE *same as* > SORBITIZE
SORBITIZE *vb* turn metal into form containing sorbite
SORBITOL *n* white water-soluble crystalline alcohol with a sweet taste
SORBITOLS > SORBITOL
SORBO *as in* *sorbo rubber* spongy form of rubber
SORBOSE *n* sweet-tasting hexose sugar derived from the berries of the mountain ash
SORBOSES > SORBOSE
SORBS > SORB

SORBUS *n* rowan or related tree
SORBUSES > SORBUS
SORCERER *n* magician
SORCERERS > SORCERER
SORCERESS *same as* > SORCERER
SORCERIES > SORCERY
SORCEROUS > SORCERY
SORCERY *n* witchcraft or magic
SORD *n* flock of mallard ducks
SORDA *n* deaf woman
SORDES *pl n* dark incrustations on the lips and teeth of patients with prolonged fever
SORDID *adj* dirty, squalid
SORDIDER > SORDID
SORDIDEST > SORDID
SORDIDLY > SORDID
SORDINE *same as* > SORDINO
SORDINES > SORDINE
SORDINI > SORDINO
SORDINO *n* mute for a stringed or brass musical instrument
SORDO *n* deaf man
SORDOR *n* sordidness
SORDORS > SORDOR
SORDS > SORD
SORE *adj* painful ▷ *n* painful area on the body ▷ *adv* greatly ▷ *vb* make sore
SORED > SORE
SOREDIA > SOREDIUM
SOREDIAL > SOREDIUM
SOREDIATE > SOREDIUM
SOREDIUM *n* organ of vegetative reproduction in lichens
SOREE *same as* > SORA
SOREES > SOREE
SOREHEAD *n* peevish or disgruntled person
SOREHEADS > SOREHEAD
SOREHON *n* old Irish feudal right
SOREHONS > SOREHON
SOREL *variant of* > SORREL
SORELL *same as* > SORREL
SORELLS > SORELL
SORELS > SOREL
SORELY *adv* greatly
SORENESS > SORE
SORER > SORE
SORES > SORE
SOREST > SORE
SOREX *n* shrew or related animal
SOREXES > SOREX
SORGHO *same as* > SORGO
SORGHOS > SORGHO
SORGHUM *n* kind of grass cultivated for grain
SORGHUMS > SORGHUM
SORGO *n* any of several varieties of sorghum that have watery sweet juice
SORGOS > SORGO
SORI > SORUS
SORICINE *adj* of or resembling a shrew
SORICOID *same as* > SORICINE
SORING > SORE

SORINGS > SORE

SORITES *n* polysyllogism in which the premises are arranged so that intermediate conclusions are omitted, being understood, and only the final conclusion is stated

SORITIC > SORITES

SORITICAL > SORITES

SORN *vb* obtain food, lodging, etc, from another person by presuming on his or her generosity

SORNED > SORN

SORNER > SORN

SORNERS > SORE

SORNING > SORN

SORNINGS > SORN

SORNS > SORN

SOROBAN *n* Japanese abacus

SOROBANS > SOROBAN

SOROCHE *n* altitude sickness

SOROCHES > SOROCHE

SORORAL *adj* of sister

SORORALLY > SORORAL

SORORATE *n* custom in some societies of a widower marrying his deceased wife's younger sister

SORORATES > SORORATE

SORORIAL *same as* > SORORAL

SORORISE *same as* > SORORIZE

SORORISED > SORORISE

SORORISES > SORORISE

SORORITY *n* society for female students

SORORIZE *vb* socialize in sisterly way

SORORIZED > SORORIZE

SORORIZES > SORORIZE

SOROSES > SOROSIS

SOROSIS *n* fleshy multiple fruit

SOROSISES > SOROSIS

SORPTION *n* process in which one substance takes up or holds another

SORPTIONS > SORPTION

SORPTIVE > SORPTION

SORRA *Irish word for* > SORROW

SORRAS > SORRA

SORREL *n* bitter-tasting plant

SORRELS > SORREL

SORRIER > SORRY

SORRIEST > SORRY

SORRILY > SORRY

SORRINESS > SORRY

SORROW *n* grief or sadness ▷ *vb* grieve

SORROWED > SORROW

SORROWER > SORROW

SORROWERS > SORROW

SORROWFUL > SORROW

SORROWING > SORROW

SORROWS > SORROW

SORRY *adj* feeling pity or regret ▷ *interj* exclamation expressing apology or asking someone to repeat what he or she has said

SORRYISH > SORRY

SORT *n* group all sharing certain qualities or characteristics ▷ *vb* arrange according to kind

SORTA *adv* phonetic representation of 'sort of'

SORTABLE > SORT

SORTABLY > SORT

SORTAL *n* type of logical or linguistic concept

SORTALS > SORTAL

SORTANCE *n* suitableness

SORTANCES > SORTANCE

SORTATION *n* act of sorting

SORTED *interj* exclamation of satisfaction, approval, etc ▷ *adj* possessing the desired recreational drugs

SORTER > SORT

SORTERS > SORT

SORTES *n* divination by opening book at random

SORTIE *n* relatively short return trip ▷ *vb* make a sortie

SORTIED > SORTIE

SORTIEING > SORTIE

SORTIES > SORTIE

SORTILEGE *n* act or practice of divination by drawing lots

SORTILEGY *same as* > SORTILEGE

SORTING > SORT

SORTINGS > SORT

SORTITION *n* act of casting lots

SORTMENT *n* assortment

SORTMENTS > SORTMENT

SORTS > SORT

SORUS *n* cluster of sporangia on the undersurface of certain fern leaves

SOS > SO

SOSATIE *n* skewer of curried meat pieces

SOSATIES > SOSATIE

SOSS *vb* make dirty or muddy

SOSSED > SOSS

SOSSES > SOSS

SOSSING > SOSS

SOSSINGS > SOSS

SOSTENUTI > SOSTENUTO

SOSTENUTO *adv* to be performed in a smooth sustained manner

SOT *n* habitual drunkard ▷ *adv* indeed: used to contradict a negative statement ▷ *vb* be a drunkard

SOTERIAL *adj* of salvation

SOTH *archaic variant of* > SOOTH

SOTHS > SOTH

SOTOL *n* American plant related to agave

SOTOLS > SOTOL

SOTS > SOT

SOTTED > SOT

SOTTEDLY > SOT

SOTTING > SOT

SOTTINGS > SOT

SOTTISH > SOT

SOTTISHLY > SOT

SOTTISIER *n* collection of jokes

SOU *n* former French coin

SOUARI *n* tree of tropical America

SOUARIS > SOUARI

SOUBISE *n* purée of onions mixed into a thick white sauce and served over eggs, fish, etc

SOUBISES > SOUBISE

SOUBRETTE *n* minor female role in comedy, often that of a pert maid

SOUCAR *n* Indian banker

SOUCARS > SOUCAR

SOUCE *same as* > SOUSE

SOUCED > SOUCE

SOUCES > SOUCE

SOUCHONG *n* black tea with large leaves

SOUCHONGS > SOUCHONG

SOUCING > SOUCE

SOUCT > SOUCE

SOUDAN *obsolete variant of* > SULTAN

SOUDANS > SOUDAN

SOUFFLE *n* light fluffy dish made with beaten egg whites and other ingredients ▷ *adj* made light and puffy, as by beating and cooking

SOUFFLED > SOUFFLE

SOUFFLEED > SOUFFLE

SOUFFLES > SOUFFLE

SOUGH *vb* (of the wind) make a sighing sound ▷ *n* soft continuous murmuring sound

SOUGHED > SOUGH

SOUGHING > SOUGH

SOUGHS > SOUGH

SOUGHT > SEEK

SOUK *same as* > SOOK

SOUKED > SOUK

SOUKING > SOUK

SOUKOUS *n* style of African popular music characterized by syncopated rhythms and intricate contrasting guitar melodies

SOUKOUSES > SOUKOUS

SOUKS > SOUK

SOUL *n* spiritual and immortal part of a human being

SOULDAN *same as* > SOLDAN

SOULDANS > SOULDAN

SOULDIER *same as* > SOLDIER

SOULDIERS > SOULDIER

SOULED *adj* having soul

SOULFUL *adj* full of emotion

SOULFULLY > SOULFUL

SOULLESS *adj* lacking human qualities, mechanical

SOULLIKE *adj* resembling a soul

SOULMATE *n* person with whom one has most affinity

SOULMATES > SOULMATE

SOULS > SOUL

SOUM *vb* decide how many animals can graze particular pasture

SOUMED > SOUM

SOUMING > SOUM

SOUMINGS > SOUM

SOUMS > SOUM

SOUND *n* something heard, noise ▷ *vb* make or cause to make a sound ▷ *adj* in good condition ▷ *adv* soundly

SOUNDABLE > SOUND

SOUNDBITE *n* short pithy sentence or phrase extracted from a longer speech

SOUNDBOX *n* resonating chamber of the hollow body of a violin, guitar, etc

SOUNDCARD *n* component giving computer sound effects

SOUNDED > SOUND

SOUNDER *n* electromagnetic device formerly used in telegraphy to convert electric signals into audible sounds

SOUNDERS > SOUNDER

SOUNDEST > SOUND

SOUNDING *adj* resounding

SOUNDINGS > SOUNDING

SOUNDLESS *adj* extremely still or silent

SOUNDLY > SOUND

SOUNDMAN *n* sound recorder in television crew

SOUNDMEN > SOUNDMAN

SOUNDNESS > SOUND

SOUNDPOST *n* small post on guitars, violins, etc, that joins the front surface to the back and allows the whole body of the instrument to vibrate

SOUNDS > SOUND

SOUP *n* liquid food made from meat, vegetables, etc ▷ *vb* give soup to

SOUPCON *n* small amount

SOUPCONS > SOUPCON

SOUPED > SOUP

SOUPER *n* person dispensing soup

SOUPERS > SOUPER

SOUPFIN *n* Pacific requiem shark valued for its fins

SOUPFINS > SOUPFIN

SOUPIER > SOUPY

SOUPIEST > SOUPY

SOUPING > SOUP

SOUPLE *same as* > SUPPLE

SOUPLED > SOUPLE

SOUPLES > SOUPLE

SOUPLESS > SOUP

SOUPLIKE > SOUP

SOUPLING > SOUPLE

SOUPS > SOUP

SOUPSPOON *n* spoon for eating soup

SOUPY *adj* having the appearance or consistency of soup

SOUR *adj* sharp-tasting ▷ *vb* make or become sour

SOURBALL *n* tart-flavoured boiled sweet

S

SOURBALLS > SOURBALL
SOURCE *n* origin or starting point ▷ *vb* establish a supplier of (a product, etc)
SOURCED > SOURCE
SOURCEFUL *adj* offering useful things
SOURCES > SOURCE
SOURCING > SOURCE
SOURCINGS > SOURCE
SOURDINE *n* soft stop on an organ or harmonium
SOURDINES > SOURDINE
SOURDOUGH *adj* (of bread) made with fermented dough used as a leaven ▷ *n* (in Western US, Canada, and Alaska) an old-time prospector or pioneer
SOURED > SOUR
SOURER > SOUR
SOUREST > SOUR
SOURING > SOUR
SOURINGS > SOUR
SOURISH > SOUR
SOURISHLY > SOUR
SOURLY > SOUR
SOURNESS > SOUR
SOUROCK *n* Scots word for sorrel plant
SOUROCKS > SOUROCK
SOURPUSS *n* person who is always gloomy, pessimistic, or bitter
SOURS > SOUR
SOURSE *same as* > SOURCE
SOURSES > SOURSE
SOURSOP *n* small West Indian tree
SOURSOPS > SOURSOP
SOURWOOD *n* sorrel tree
SOURWOODS > SOURWOOD
SOUS > SOU
SOUSE *vb* plunge (something) into liquid ▷ *n* liquid used in pickling
SOUSED > SOUSE
SOUSES > SOUSE
SOUSING > SOUSE
SOUSINGS > SOUSE
SOUSLIK *same as* > SUSLIK
SOUSLIKS > SOUSLIK
SOUT *same as* > SOOT
SOUTACHE *n* narrow braid used as a decorative trimming
SOUTACHES > SOUTACHE
SOUTANE *n* Roman Catholic priest's cassock
SOUTANES > SOUTANE
SOUTAR *same as* > SOUTER
SOUTARS > SOUTAR
SOUTENEUR *n* pimp
SOUTER *n* shoemaker or cobbler
SOUTERLY > SOUTER
SOUTERS > SOUTER
SOUTH *n* direction towards the South Pole, opposite north ▷ *adj* or in the south ▷ *adv* in, to, or towards the south ▷ *vb* turn south
SOUTHEAST *adv* (in or to) direction between south and east ▷ *n* point of the compass or the direction midway between south

and east ▷ *adj* of or denoting the southeastern part of a specified country, area, etc
SOUTHED > SOUTH
SOUTHER *n* strong wind or storm from the south ▷ *vb* turn south
SOUTHERED > SOUTHER
SOUTHERLY *adj* of or in the south ▷ *adv* towards the south ▷ *n* wind from the south
SOUTHERN *adj* situated in or towards the south ▷ *n* southerner
SOUTHERNS > SOUTHERN
SOUTHERS > SOUTHER
SOUTHING *n* movement, deviation, or distance covered in a southerly direction
SOUTHINGS > SOUTHING
SOUTHLAND *n* southern part of country
SOUTHMOST *adj* situated or occurring farthest south
SOUTHPAW *n* left-handed person, esp a boxer ▷ *adj* left-handed
SOUTHPAWS > SOUTHPAW
SOUTHRON *n* southerner
SOUTHRONS > SOUTHRON
SOUTHS > SOUTH
SOUTHSAID > SOUTHSAY
SOUTHSAY *same as* > SOOTHSAY
SOUTHSAYS > SOUTHSAY
SOUTHWARD *adv* towards the south
SOUTHWEST *adv* (in or to) direction between south and west ▷ *n* point of the compass or the direction midway between west and south ▷ *adj* of or denoting the southwestern part of a specified country, area, etc
SOUTIE *same as* > SOUTPIEL
SOUTIES > SOUTIE
SOUTPIEL *n* South African derogatory slang for an English-speaking South African
SOUTPIELS > SOUTPIEL
SOUTS > SOUT
SOUVENIR *n* keepsake, memento ▷ *vb* steal or keep (something, esp a small article) for one's own use
SOUVENIRS > SOUVENIR
SOUVLAKI *same as* > SOUVLAKIA
SOUVLAKIA *n* Greek dish of kebabs, esp made with lamb
SOUVLAKIS > SOUVLAKI
SOV *shortening of* > SOVEREIGN
SOVENANCE *n* memory
SOVEREIGN *n* king or queen ▷ *adj* (of a state) independent
SOVIET *n* formerly, elected council at various levels of government in the USSR

▷ *adj* of the former USSR
SOVIETIC > SOVIET
SOVIETISE *same as* > SOVIETIZE
SOVIETISM *n* principle or practice of government through soviets
SOVIETIST > SOVIETISM
SOVIETIZE *vb* bring (a country, person, etc) under Soviet control or influence
SOVIETS > SOVIET
SOVKHOZ *n* (in the former Soviet Union) a large mechanized farm owned by the state
SOVKHOZES > SOVKHOZ
SOVKHOZY > SOVKHOZ
SOVRAN *literary word for* > SOVEREIGN
SOVRANLY > SOVRAN
SOVRANS > SOVRAN
SOVRANTY > SOVRAN
SOVS > SOV
SOW *vb* scatter or plant (seed) in or on (the ground) ▷ *n* female adult pig
SOWABLE > SOW
SOWANS *same as* > SOWENS
SOWAR *n* Indian cavalryman
SOWARREE *n* Indian mounted escort
SOWARREES > SOWARREE
SOWARRIES > SOWARRY
SOWARRY *same as* > SOWARREE
SOWARS > SOWAR
SOWBACK *another name for* > HOGBACK
SOWBACKS > SOWBACK
SOWBELLY *n* salt pork from pig's belly
SOWBREAD *n* S European primulaceous plant
SOWBREADS > SOWBREAD
SOWCAR *same as* > SOUCAR
SOWCARS > SOWCAR
SOWCE *same as* > SOUSE
SOWCED > SOWCE
SOWCES > SOWCE
SOWCING > SOWCE
SOWED > SOW
SOWENS *n* pudding made from oatmeal husks steeped and boiled
SOWER > SOW
SOWERS > SOW
SOWF *same as* > SOWTH
SOWFED > SOWF
SOWFF *same as* > SOWTH
SOWFFED > SOWFF
SOWFFING > SOWFF
SOWFFS > SOWFF
SOWFING > SOWF
SOWFS > SOWF
SOWING > SOW
SOWINGS > SOW
SOWL *same as* > SOLE
SOWLE *same as* > SOLE
SOWLED > SOWL
SOWLES > SOWLE
SOWLING > SOWL
SOWLS > SOWL
SOWM *same as* > SOUM
SOWMED > SOWM
SOWMING > SOWM
SOWMS > SOWM

SOWN > SOW
SOWND *vb* wield
SOWNDED > SOWND
SOWNDING > SOWND
SOWNDS > SOWND
SOWNE *same as* > SOUND
SOWNES > SOWNE
SOWP *n* spoonful
SOWPS > SOWP
SOWS > SOW
SOWSE *same as* > SOUSE
SOWSED > SOWSE
SOWSES > SOWSE
SOWSING > SOWSE
SOWSSE *same as* > SOUSE
SOWSSED > SOWSSE
SOWSSES > SOWSSE
SOWSSING > SOWSSE
SOWTER *same as* > SOUTER
SOWTERS > SOWTER
SOWTH *vb* Scots word meaning whistle
SOWTHED > SOWTH
SOWTHING > SOWTH
SOWTHS > SOWTH
SOX *pl n* informal spelling of 'socks'
SOY *as in soy sauce* salty dark brown sauce made from soya beans, used in Chinese and Japanese cookery
SOYA *n* plant whose edible bean is used for food and as a source of oil
SOYAS > SOYA
SOYBEAN *n* soya bean
SOYBEANS > SOYBEAN
SOYLE *n* body
SOYLES > SOYLE
SOYMILK *n* milk substitute made from soya
SOYMILKS > SOYMILK
SOYS > SOY
SOYUZ *n* Russian spacecraft used to ferry crew to and from space stations
SOYUZES > SOYUZ
SOZIN *n* form of protein
SOZINE *same as* > SOZIN
SOZINES > SOZINE
SOZINS > SOZIN
SOZZLE *vb* make wet
SOZZLED *adj* drunk
SOZZLES > SOZZLE
SOZZLIER > SOZZLY
SOZZLIEST > SOZZLY
SOZZLING > SOZZLE
SOZZLY *adj* wet
SPA *n* resort with a mineral-water spring ▷ *vb* visit a spa
SPACE *n* unlimited expanse in which all objects exist and move ▷ *vb* place at intervals
SPACEBAND *n* device on a linecaster for evening up the spaces between words
SPACED > SPACE
SPACELAB *n* laboratory in space where scientific experiments are performed
SPACELABS > SPACELAB
SPACELESS *adj* having no limits in space
SPACEMAN *n* person who

travels in space

SPACEMEN > SPACEMAN

SPACEPORT n base equipped to launch, maintain, and test spacecraft

SPACER n piece of material used to create or maintain a space between two things

SPACERS > SPACER

SPACES > SPACE

SPACESHIP n (in science fiction) a spacecraft used for travel between planets and galaxies

SPACESUIT n sealed pressurized suit worn by an astronaut

SPACEWALK n instance of floating and manoeuvring in space, outside but attached by a lifeline to a spacecraft ▷vb float and manoeuvre in space while outside but attached to a spacecraft

SPACEWARD adv into space

SPACEY adj vague and dreamy, as if under the influence of drugs

SPACIAL same as > SPATIAL

SPACIALLY > SPACIAL

SPACIER > SPACEY

SPACIEST > SPACEY

SPACINESS > SPACEY

SPACING n arrangement of letters, words, etc, on a page in order to achieve legibility

SPACINGS > SPACING.

SPACIOUS adj having a large capacity or area

SPACKLE vb fill holes in plaster

SPACKLED > SPACKLE

SPACKLES > SPACKLE

SPACKLING > SPACKLE

SPACY same as > SPACEY

SPADASSIN n swordsman

SPADE n tool for digging

SPADED > SPADE

SPADEFISH n type of spiny-finned food fish

SPADEFUL n amount spade will hold

SPADEFULS > SPADEFUL

SPADELIKE > SPADE

SPADEMAN n man who works with spade

SPADEMEN > SPADEMAN

SPADER > SPADE

SPADERS > SPADE

SPADES > SPADE

SPADESMAN same as > SPADEMAN

SPADESMEN > SPADEMAN

SPADEWORK n hard preparatory work

SPADGER n sparrow

SPADGERS > SPADGER

SPADICES > SPADIX

SPADILLE n (in ombre and quadrille) the ace of spades

SPADILLES > SPADILLE

SPADILLIO same as > SPADILLE

SPADILLO same as > SPADILLE

SPADILLOS > SPADILLO

SPADING > SPADE

SPADIX n spike of small flowers on a fleshy stem

SPADIXES > SPADIX

SPADO n neutered animal

SPADOES > SPADO

SPADONES > SPADO

SPADOS > SPADO

SPADROON n type of sword

SPADROONS > SPADROON

SPAE vb foretell (the future)

SPAED > SPAE

SPAEING > SPAE

SPAEINGS > SPAE

SPAEMAN n man who foretells future

SPAEMEN > SPAEMAN

SPAER > SPAE

SPAERS > SPAE

SPAES > SPAE

SPAETZLE n German noodle dish

SPAETZLES > SPAETZLE

SPAEWIFE n woman who can supposedly foretell the future

SPAEWIVES > SPAEWIFE

SPAG vb (of a cat) to scratch (a person) with the claws ▷n Australian offensive slang for an Italian

SPAGERIC same as > SPAGYRIC

SPAGERICS > SPAGERIC

SPAGERIST > SPAGERIC

SPAGGED > SPAG

SPAGGING > SPAG

SPAGHETTI n pasta in the form of long strings

SPAGIRIC same as > SPAGYRIC

SPAGIRICS > SPAGIRIC

SPAGIRIST > SPAGIRIC

SPAGS > SPAG

SPAGYRIC adj of or relating to alchemy ▷n alchemist

SPAGYRICS > SPAGYRIC

SPAGYRIST > SPAGYRIC

SPAHEE same as > SPAHI

SPAHEES > SPAHEE

SPAHI n (formerly) an irregular cavalryman in the Turkish armed forces

SPAHIS > SPAHI

SPAIL Scots word for > SPALL

SPAILS > SPAIL

SPAIN variant of > SPANE

SPAINED > SPAIN

SPAING > SPA

SPAINGS > SPA

SPAINING > SPAIN

SPAINS > SPAIN

SPAIRGE Scots word for > SPARGE

SPAIRGED > SPAIRGE

SPAIRGES > SPAIRGE

SPAIRGING > SPAIRGE

SPAIT same as > SPATE

SPAITS > SPAIT

SPAKE past tense of > SPEAK

SPALD same as > SPAULD

SPALDEEN n ball used in street game

SPALDEENS > SPALDEEN

SPALDS > SPALD

SPALE Scots word for > SPALL

SPALES > SPALE

SPALL n splinter or chip of ore, rock, or stone ▷vb split or cause to split into such fragments

SPALLABLE > SPALL

SPALLE same as > SPAULD

SPALLED > SPALL

SPALLER > SPALL

SPALLERS > SPALL

SPALLES > SPALLE

SPALLING > SPALL

SPALLINGS > SPALL

SPALLS > SPALL

SPALPEEN n itinerant seasonal labourer

SPALPEENS > SPALPEEN

SPALT vb split

SPALTED > SPALT

SPALTING > SPALT

SPALTS > SPALT

SPAM vb send unsolicited e-mail simultaneously to a number of newsgroups on the internet ▷n unsolicited electronic mail or text messages sent in this way

SPAMBOT n computer programme that identifies email addresses to send spam to

SPAMBOTS > SPAMBOT

SPAMMED > SPAM

SPAMMER > SPAM

SPAMMERS > SPAM

SPAMMIE n love bite

SPAMMIER > SPAMMY

SPAMMIES > SPAMMIE

SPAMMIEST > SPAMMY

SPAMMING > SPAM

SPAMMINGS > SPAM

SPAMMY adj bland

SPAMS > SPAM

SPAN n space between two points ▷vb stretch or extend across

SPANAEMIA n lack of red corpuscles in blood

SPANAEMIC > SPANAEMIA

SPANCEL n length of rope for hobbling an animal, esp a horse or cow ▷vb hobble (an animal) with a loose rope

SPANCELED > SPANCEL

SPANCELS > SPANCEL

SPANDEX n type of synthetic stretch fabric made from polyurethane fibre

SPANDEXES > SPANDEX

SPANDREL n triangular surface bounded by the outer curve of an arch and the adjacent wall

SPANDRELS > SPANDREL

SPANDRIL same as > SPANDREL

SPANDRILS > SPANDRIL

SPANE vb Scots word meaning wean

SPANED > SPANE

SPANES > SPANE

SPANG adv exactly, firmly, or straight ▷vb dash

SPANGED > SPANG

SPANGHEW vb throw in air

SPANGHEWS > SPANGHEW

SPANGING > SPANG

SPANGLE n small shiny metallic ornament ▷vb decorate with spangles

SPANGLED > SPANGLE

SPANGLER > SPANGLE

SPANGLERS > SPANGLE

SPANGLES > SPANGLE

SPANGLET n little spangle

SPANGLETS > SPANGLET

SPANGLIER > SPANGLE

SPANGLING > SPANGLE

SPANGLY > SPANGLE

SPANGS > SPANG

SPANIEL n dog with long ears and silky hair

SPANIELS > SPANIEL

SPANING > SPANE

SPANK vb slap with the open hand, on the buttocks or legs ▷n such a slap

SPANKED > SPANK

SPANKER n fore-and-aft sail or a mast that is aftermost in a sailing vessel

SPANKERS > SPANKER

SPANKING adj outstandingly fine or smart ▷n series of spanks, usually as a punishment for children

SPANKINGS > SPANKING

SPANKS > SPANK

SPANLESS adj impossible to span

SPANNED > SPAN

SPANNER n tool for gripping and turning a nut or bolt

SPANNERS > SPANNER

SPANNING > SPAN

SPANS > SPAN

SPANSPEK n cantaloupe melon

SPANSPEKS > SPANSPEK

SPANSULE n modified-release capsule of a drug

SPANSULES > SPANSULE

SPANWORM n larva of a type of moth

SPANWORMS > SPANWORM

SPAR n pole used as a ship's mast, boom, or yard ▷vb box or fight using light blows for practice

SPARABLE n small nail with no head, used for fixing the soles and heels of shoes

SPARABLES > SPARABLE

SPARAXIS n type of plant with dainty spikes of star-shaped purple, red, or orange flowers

SPARD > SPARE

SPARE adj extra ▷n duplicate kept in case of damage or loss ▷vb refrain from punishing or harming

SPAREABLE > SPARE

SPARED > SPARE

SPARELESS adj merciless

SPARELY > SPARE

SPARENESS > SPARE

SPARER > SPARE

SPARERIB *n* cut of pork ribs with most of the meat trimmed off
SPARERIBS > SPARERIB
SPARERS > SPARE
SPARES > SPARE
SPAREST > SPARE
SPARGE *vb* sprinkle or scatter (something)
SPARGED > SPARGE
SPARGER > SPARGE
SPARGERS > SPARGE
SPARGES > SPARGE
SPARGING > SPARGE
SPARID *n* type of marine percoid fish ▷ *adj* of or belonging to this family of fish
SPARIDS > SPARID
SPARING *adj* economical
SPARINGLY > SPARING
SPARK *n* fiery particle thrown out from a fire or caused by friction ▷ *vb* give off sparks
SPARKE *n* weapon
SPARKED > SPARK
SPARKER > SPARK
SPARKERS > SPARK
SPARKES > SPARKE
SPARKIE *n* electrician
SPARKIER > SPARKY
SPARKIES > SPARKIE
SPARKIEST > SPARKY
SPARKILY > SPARKY
SPARKING > SPARK
SPARKISH > SPARK
SPARKLE *vb* glitter with many points of light ▷ *n* sparkling points of light
SPARKLED > SPARKLE
SPARKLER *n* hand-held firework that emits sparks
SPARKLERS > SPARKLER
SPARKLES > SPARKLE
SPARKLESS > SPARK
SPARKLET *n* little spark
SPARKLETS > SPARKLET
SPARKLIER > SPARKLY
SPARKLIES > SPARKLY
SPARKLING *adj* (of wine or mineral water) slightly fizzy
SPARKLY *adj* sparkling ▷ *n* sparkling thing
SPARKPLUG *n* device in an engine that ignites the fuel
SPARKS *n* electrician
SPARKY *adj* lively
SPARLIKE > SPAR
SPARLING *n* European smelt
SPARLINGS > SPARLING
SPAROID *same as* > SPARID
SPAROIDS > SPAROID
SPARRE *same as* > SPAR
SPARRED > SPAR
SPARRER > SPAR
SPARRERS > SPAR
SPARRES > SPARRE
SPARRIER > SPARRY
SPARRIEST > SPARRY
SPARRING > SPAR
SPARRINGS > SPAR
SPARROW *n* small brownish bird
SPARROWS > SPARROW

SPARRY *adj* (of minerals) containing, relating to, or resembling spar
SPARS > SPAR
SPARSE *adj* thinly scattered
SPARSEDLY > SPARSE
SPARSELY > SPARSE
SPARSER > SPARSE
SPARSEST > SPARSE
SPARSITY > SPARSE
SPART *n* esparto
SPARTAN *adj* strict and austere ▷ *n* disciplined or brave person
SPARTANS > SPARTAN
SPARTEINE *n* viscous oily alkaloid extracted from the broom plant and lupin seeds
SPARTERIE *n* things made from esparto
SPARTH *n* type of battle-axe
SPARTHE *same as* > SPARTH
SPARTHES > SPARTHE
SPARTHS > SPARTH
SPARTINA *n* grass growing in salt marshes
SPARTINAS > SPARTINA
SPARTS > SPART
SPASM *n* involuntary muscular contraction ▷ *vb* go into spasm
SPASMATIC > SPASM
SPASMED > SPASM
SPASMIC > SPASM
SPASMING > SPASM
SPASMODIC *adj* occurring in spasms
SPASMS > SPASM
SPASTIC *n* offensive slang for a person with cerebral palsy ▷ *adj* suffering from cerebral palsy
SPASTICS > SPASTIC
SPAT *vb* have a quarrel
SPATE *n* large number of things happening within a period of time
SPATES > SPATE
SPATFALL *n* mass of larvae on sea bed
SPATFALLS > SPATFALL
SPATHAL > SPATHE
SPATHE *n* large sheathlike leaf enclosing a flower cluster
SPATHED > SPATHE
SPATHES > SPATHE
SPATHIC *adj* (of minerals) resembling spar, esp in having good cleavage
SPATHOSE *same as* > SPATHIC
SPATIAL *adj* of or in space
SPATIALLY > SPATIAL
SPATLESE *n* type of German wine, usu white
SPATLESEN > SPATLESE
SPATLESES > SPATLESE
SPATS > SPAT
SPATTED > SPAT
SPATTEE *n* type of gaiter
SPATTEES > SPATTEE
SPATTER *vb* scatter or be scattered in drops over (something) ▷ *n* spattering sound

SPATTERED > SPATTER
SPATTERS > SPATTER
SPATTING > SPIT
SPATULA *n* utensil with a broad flat blade for spreading or stirring
SPATULAR > SPATULA
SPATULAS > SPATULA
SPATULATE *adj* shaped like a spatula
SPATULE *n* spatula
SPATULES > SPATULE
SPATZLE *same as* > SPAETZLE
SPATZLES > SPATZLE
SPAUL *same as* > SPAULD
SPAULD *n* shoulder
SPAULDS > SPAULD
SPAULS > SPAUL
SPAVIE *Scots variant of* > SPAVIN
SPAVIES > SPAVIE
SPAVIET *adj* Scots word meaning spavined
SPAVIN *n* enlargement of the hock of a horse by a bony growth
SPAVINED *adj* affected with spavin
SPAVINS > SPAVIN
SPAW *same as* > SPA
SPAWL *vb* spit
SPAWLED > SPAWL
SPAWLING > SPAWL
SPAWLS > SPAWL
SPAWN *n* jelly-like mass of eggs of fish, frogs, or molluscs ▷ *vb* (of fish, frogs, or molluscs) lay eggs
SPAWNED > SPAWN
SPAWNER > SPAWN
SPAWNERS > SPAWN
SPAWNIER > SPAWNY
SPAWNIEST > SPAWNY
SPAWNING > SPAWN
SPAWNINGS > SPAWN
SPAWNS > SPAWN
SPAWNY *adj* like spawn
SPAWS > SPAW
SPAY *vb* remove the ovaries from (a female animal)
SPAYAD *n* male deer
SPAYADS > SPAYAD
SPAYD *same as* > SPAYAD
SPAYDS > SPAYD
SPAYED > SPAY
SPAYING > SPAY
SPAYS > SPAY
SPAZ *vb* offensive slang meaning lose self-control
SPAZA *as in spaza shop* South African slang for a small shop in a township
SPAZZ *same as* > SPAZ
SPAZZED > SPAZ
SPAZZES > SPAZ
SPAZZING > SPAZ
SPEAK *vb* say words, talk
SPEAKABLE > SPEAK
SPEAKEASY *n* place where alcoholic drink was sold illegally during Prohibition
SPEAKER *n* person who speaks, esp at a formal occasion
SPEAKERS > SPEAKER
SPEAKING > SPEAK
SPEAKINGS > SPEAK

SPEAKOUT *n* firm or brave statement of one's beliefs
SPEAKOUTS > SPEAKOUT
SPEAKS > SPEAK
SPEAL *same as* > SPULE
SPEALS > SPEAL
SPEAN *same as* > SPANE
SPEANED > SPEAN
SPEANING > SPEAN
SPEANS > SPEAN
SPEAR *n* weapon consisting of a long shaft with a sharp point ▷ *vb* pierce with or as if with a spear
SPEARED > SPEAR
SPEARER > SPEAR
SPEARERS > SPEAR
SPEARFISH *n* another name for > MARLIN
SPEARGUN *n* device for shooting spears underwater
SPEARGUNS > SPEARGUN
SPEARHEAD *vb* lead (an attack or campaign) ▷ *n* leading force in an attack or campaign
SPEARIER > SPEAR
SPEARIEST > SPEAR
SPEARING > SPEAR
SPEARLIKE > SPEAR
SPEARMAN *n* soldier armed with a spear
SPEARMEN > SPEARMAN
SPEARMINT *n* type of mint
SPEARS > SPEAR
SPEARWORT *n* any of several Eurasian ranunculaceous plants
SPEARY > SPEAR
SPEAT *same as* > SPATE
SPEATS > SPEAT
SPEC *vb* set specifications
SPECCED > SPEC
SPECCIES > SPECCY
SPECCING > SPEC
SPECCY *n* person wearing spectacles
SPECIAL *adj* distinguished from others of its kind ▷ *n* product, programme, etc which is only available at a certain time ▷ *vb* advertise and sell (an item) at a reduced price
SPECIALER > SPECIAL
SPECIALLY > SPECIAL
SPECIALS > SPECIAL
SPECIALTY *n* special interest or skill
SPECIATE *vb* form or develop into a new biological species
SPECIATED > SPECIATE
SPECIATES > SPECIATE
SPECIE *n* coins as distinct from paper money
SPECIES *n* group of plants or animals that are related closely enough to interbreed naturally
SPECIFIC *adj* particular, definite ▷ *n* drug used to treat a particular disease
SPECIFICS > SPECIFIC
SPECIFIED > SPECIFY
SPECIFIER > SPECIFY

SPECIFIES > SPECIFY
SPECIFY *vb* refer to or state specifically
SPECIMEN *n* individual or part typifying a whole
SPECIMENS > SPECIMEN
SPECIOUS *adj* apparently true, but actually false
SPECK *n* small spot or particle ▷ *vb* mark with specks or spots
SPECKED > SPECK
SPECKIER > SPECKY
SPECKIEST > SPECKY
SPECKING > SPECK
SPECKLE *n* small spot ▷ *vb* mark with speckles
SPECKLED > SPECKLE
SPECKLES > SPECKLE
SPECKLESS > SPECK
SPECKLING > SPECKLE
SPECKS > SPECK
SPECKY *same as* > SPECCY
SPECS *pl n* spectacles
SPECTACLE *n* strange, interesting, or ridiculous sight
SPECTATE *vb* watch
SPECTATED > SPECTATE
SPECTATES > SPECTATE
SPECTATOR *n* person viewing anything, onlooker
SPECTER *same as* > SPECTRE
SPECTERS > SPECTER
SPECTRA > SPECTRUM
SPECTRAL *adj* of or like a spectre
SPECTRE *n* ghost
SPECTRES > SPECTRE
SPECTRIN *n* any one of a class of fibrous proteins found in the membranes of red blood cells
SPECTRINS > SPECTRIN
SPECTRUM *n* range of different colours, radio waves, etc in order of their wavelengths
SPECTRUMS > SPECTRUM
SPECULA > SPECULUM
SPECULAR *adj* of, relating to, or having the properties of a mirror
SPECULATE *vb* guess, conjecture
SPECULUM *n* medical instrument for examining body cavities
SPECULUMS > SPECULUM
SPED > SPEED
SPEECH *n* act, power, or manner of speaking ▷ *vb* make a speech
SPEECHED > SPEECH
SPEECHES > SPEECH
SPEECHFUL > SPEECH
SPEECHIFY *vb* make speeches, esp boringly
SPEECHING > SPEECH
SPEED *n* swiftness ▷ *vb* go quickly
SPEEDBALL *n* mixture of heroin with amphetamine or cocaine
SPEEDBOAT *n* light fast motorboat
SPEEDED > SPEED

SPEEDER > SPEED
SPEEDERS > SPEED
SPEEDFUL > SPEED
SPEEDIER > SPEEDY
SPEEDIEST > SPEEDY
SPEEDILY > SPEEDY
SPEEDING > SPEED
SPEEDINGS > SPEED
SPEEDLESS > SPEED
SPEEDO *n* speedometer
SPEEDOS > SPEEDO
SPEEDREAD *vb* read very quickly
SPEEDS > SPEED
SPEEDSTER *n* fast car, esp a sports model
SPEEDUP *n* acceleration
SPEEDUPS > SPEEDUP
SPEEDWAY *n* track for motorcycle racing
SPEEDWAYS > SPEEDWAY
SPEEDWELL *n* plant with small blue flowers
SPEEDY *adj* prompt
SPEEL *n* splinter of wood ▷ *vb* Scots word meaning climb
SPEELED > SPEEL
SPEELER > SPEEL
SPEELERS > SPEEL
SPEELING > SPEEL
SPEELS > SPEEL
SPEER *same as* > SPEIR
SPEERED > SPEER
SPEERING > SPEER
SPEERINGS > SPEER
SPEERS > SPEER
SPEIL *dialect word for* > CLIMB
SPEILED > SPEIL
SPEILING > SPEIL
SPEILS > SPEIL
SPEIR *vb* ask
SPEIRED > SPEIR
SPEIRING > SPEIR
SPEIRINGS > SPEIR
SPEIRS > SPEIR
SPEISE *same as* > SPEISS
SPEISES > SPEISE
SPEISS *n* arsenides and antimonides that form when ores containing arsenic or antimony are smelted
SPEISSES > SPEISS
SPEK *n* bacon, fat, or fatty pork used for larding venison or other game
SPEKBOOM *n* South African shrub
SPEKBOOMS > SPEKBOOM
SPEKS > SPEK
SPELAEAN *adj* of, found in, or inhabiting caves
SPELD *vb* Scots word meaning spread
SPELDED > SPELD
SPELDER *same as* > SPELD
SPELDERED > SPELDER
SPELDERS > SPELDER
SPELDIN *n* fish split and dried
SPELDING *same as* > SPELDIN
SPELDINGS > SPELDING
SPELDINS > SPELDIN
SPELDRIN > VARIANT OF > SPELDIN

SPELDRING *same as* > SPELDIN
SPELDRINS > SPELDRIN
SPELDS > SPELD
SPELEAN *same as* > SPELAEAN
SPELK *n* splinter of wood
SPELKS > SPELK
SPELL *vb* give in correct order the letters that form (a word) ▷ *n* formula of words supposed to have magic power
SPELLABLE > SPELL
SPELLBIND *vb* cause to be spellbound
SPELLDOWN *n* spelling competition
SPELLED > SPELL
SPELLER *n* person who spells words in the manner specified
SPELLERS > SPELLER
SPELLFUL *adj* magical
SPELLICAN *same as* > SPILLIKIN
SPELLING > SPELL
SPELLINGS > SPELL
SPELLS > SPELL
SPELT > SPELL
SPELTER *n* impure zinc, usually containing about 3 per cent of lead and other impurities
SPELTERS > SPELTER
SPELTS > SPELL
SPELTZ *n* wheat variety
SPELTZES > SPELTZ
SPELUNK *vb* explore caves
SPELUNKED > SPELUNK
SPELUNKER *n* person whose hobby is the exploration and study of caves
SPELUNKS > SPELUNK
SPENCE *n* larder or pantry
SPENCER *n* short fitted coat or jacket
SPENCERS > SPENCER
SPENCES > SPENCE
SPEND *vb* pay out (money)
SPENDABLE > SPEND
SPENDALL *n* spendthrift
SPENDALLS > SPENDALL
SPENDER *n* person who spends money in a manner specified
SPENDERS > SPENDER
SPENDIER > SPENDY
SPENDIEST > SPENDY
SPENDING > SPEND
SPENDINGS > SPEND
SPENDS > SPEND
SPENDY *adj* expensive
SPENSE *same as* > SPENCE
SPENSES > SPENSE
SPENT > SPEND
SPEOS *n* (esp in ancient Egypt) a temple or tomb cut into a rock face
SPEOSES > SPEOS
SPERLING *same as* > SPARLING
SPERLINGS > SPERLING
SPERM *n* male reproductive cell released in semen during ejaculation
SPERMARIA *pl n* spermaries

SPERMARY *n* any organ in which spermatozoa are produced, esp a testis
SPERMATIA *pl n* male reproductive cells in red algae and some fungi
SPERMATIC *adj* of or relating to spermatozoa
SPERMATID *n* any of four immature male gametes that are formed from a spermatocyte
SPERMIC *same as* > SPERMATIC
SPERMINE *n* colourless basic water-soluble amine that is found in semen, sputum, and animal tissues
SPERMINES > SPERMINE
SPERMOUS *same as* > SPERMATIC
SPERMS > SPERM
SPERRE *vb* bolt
SPERRED > SPERRE
SPERRES > SPERRE
SPERRING > SPERRE
SPERSE *vb* disperse
SPERSED > SPERSE
SPERSES > SPERSE
SPERSING > SPERSE
SPERST > SPERSE
SPERTHE *same as* > SPARTH
SPERTHES > SPERTHE
SPET *same as* > SPIT
SPETCH *n* piece of animal skin
SPETCHES > SPETCH
SPETS > SPET
SPETSNAZ *n* Soviet intelligence force
SPETTING > SPET
SPETZNAZ *same as* > SPETSNAZ
SPEUG *n* sparrow
SPEUGS > SPEUG
SPEW *vb* vomit ▷ *n* something ejected from the mouth
SPEWED > SPEW
SPEWER > SPEW
SPEWERS > SPEW
SPEWIER > SPEWY
SPEWIEST > SPEWY
SPEWINESS > SPEWY
SPEWING > SPEW
SPEWS > SPEW
SPEWY *adj* marshy
SPHACELUS *n* death of living tissue
SPHAER *same as* > SPHERE
SPHAERE *same as* > SPHERE
SPHAERES > SPHAERE
SPHAERITE *n* aluminium phosphate
SPHAERS > SPHAERE
SPHAGNOUS > SPHAGNUM
SPHAGNUM *n* moss found in bogs
SPHAGNUMS > SPHAGNUM
SPHAIREE *n* game resembling tennis played with wooden bats and a perforated plastic ball
SPHAIREES > SPHAIREE
SPHEAR *same as* > SPHERE
SPHEARE *same as* > SPHERE

SPHEARES > SPHEARE
SPHEARS > SPHEAR
SPHENDONE n ancient Greek headband
SPHENE n brown, yellow, green, or grey lustrous mineral
SPHENES > SPHENE
SPHENIC adj having the shape of a wedge
SPHENODON technical name for the > TUATARA
SPHENOID adj wedge-shaped ▷ n wedge-shaped thing
SPHENOIDS > SPHENOID
SPHERAL adj of or shaped like a sphere
SPHERE n perfectly round solid object ▷ vb surround or encircle
SPHERED > SPHERE
SPHERES > SPHERE
SPHERIC same as > SPHERICAL
SPHERICAL adj shaped like a sphere
SPHERICS n geometry and trigonometry of figures on the surface of a sphere
SPHERIER > SPHERY
SPHERIEST > SPHERY
SPHERING > SPHERE
SPHEROID n solid figure that is almost but not exactly a sphere
SPHEROIDS > SPHEROID
SPHERULAR > SPHERULE
SPHERULE n very small sphere or globule
SPHERULES > SPHERULE
SPHERY adj resembling a sphere
SPHINCTER n ring of muscle which controls the opening and closing of a hollow organ
SPHINGES > SPHINX
SPHINGID n hawk moth
SPHINGIDS > SPHINGID
SPHINX n one of the huge statues built by the ancient Egyptians, with the body of a lion and the head of a man
SPHINXES > SPHINX
SPHYGMIC adj of or relating to the pulse
SPHYGMOID adj resembling the pulse
SPHYGMUS n person's pulse
SPHYNX n breed of cat
SPHYNXES > SPHYNX
SPIAL n observation
SPIALS > SPIAL
SPIC n derogatory word for a Spanish-speaking person
SPICA n spiral bandage formed by a series of overlapping figure-of-eight turns
SPICAE > SPICA
SPICAS > SPICA
SPICATE adj having, arranged in, or relating to spikes
SPICATED same as > SPICATE

SPICCATO n style of playing a bowed stringed instrument in which the bow bounces lightly off the strings ▷ adv be played in this manner
SPICCATOS > SPICCATO
SPICE n aromatic substance used as flavouring ▷ vb flavour with spices
SPICEBUSH n North American lauraceous shrub
SPICED > SPICE
SPICELESS > SPICE
SPICER > SPICE
SPICERIES > SPICERY
SPICERS > SPICE
SPICERY n spices collectively
SPICES > SPICE
SPICEY same as > SPICY
SPICIER > SPICY
SPICIEST > SPICY
SPICILEGE n anthology
SPICILY > SPICY
SPICINESS > SPICY
SPICING > SPICE
SPICK adj neat and clean ▷ n spic
SPICKER > SPICK
SPICKEST > SPICK
SPICKNEL same as > SPIGNEL
SPICKNELS > SPICKNEL
SPICKS > SPICK
SPICS > SPIC
SPICULA > SPICULUM
SPICULAE > SPICULUM
SPICULAR > SPICULUM
SPICULATE > SPICULE
SPICULE n small slender pointed structure or crystal
SPICULES > SPICULE
SPICULUM same as > SPICULE
SPICY adj flavoured with spices
SPIDE n Irish derogatory slang for a young working-class man who dresses in casual sports clothes
SPIDER n small eight-legged creature which spins a web to catch insects for food
SPIDERIER > SPIDERY
SPIDERISH > SPIDER
SPIDERMAN n person who erects the steel structure of a building
SPIDERMEN > SPIDERMAN
SPIDERS > SPIDER
SPIDERWEB n spider's web
SPIDERY adj thin and angular like a spider's legs
SPIDES > SPIDE
SPIE same as > SPY
SPIED > SPY
SPIEGEL n manganese-rich pig iron
SPIEGELS > SPIEGEL
SPIEL n speech made to persuade someone to do something ▷ vb deliver a prepared spiel
SPIELED > SPIEL
SPIELER > SPIEL
SPIELERS > SPIEL

SPIELING > SPIEL
SPIELS > SPIEL
SPIER variant of > SPEIR
SPIERED > SPIER
SPIERING > SPIER
SPIERS > SPIER
SPIES > SPY
SPIF n postage stamp perforated with the initials of a firm to avoid theft by employees
SPIFF vb make smart
SPIFFED > SPIFF
SPIFFIED > SPIFFY
SPIFFIER > SPIFFY
SPIFFIES > SPIFFY
SPIFFIEST > SPIFFY
SPIFFILY > SPIFFY
SPIFFING adj excellent
SPIFFS > SPIFF
SPIFFY adj smart ▷ n smart thing or person
SPIFFYING > SPIFFY
SPIFS > SPIF
SPIGHT same as > SPITE
SPIGHTED > SPIGHT
SPIGHTING > SPIGHT
SPIGHTS > SPIGHT
SPIGNEL n European umbelliferous plant
SPIGNELS > SPIGNEL
SPIGOT n stopper for, or tap fitted to, a cask
SPIGOTS > SPIGOT
SPIK same as > SPIC
SPIKE n sharp point ▷ vb put spikes on
SPIKED > SPIKE
SPIKEFISH n large sea fish
SPIKELET n unit of a grass inflorescence
SPIKELETS > SPIKELET
SPIKELIKE > SPIKE
SPIKENARD n fragrant Indian plant with rose-purple flowers
SPIKER > SPIKE
SPIKERIES > SPIKERY
SPIKERS > SPIKE
SPIKERY n High-Church Anglicanism
SPIKES > SPIKE
SPIKEY same as > SPIKY
SPIKIER > SPIKY
SPIKIEST > SPIKY
SPIKILY > SPIKY
SPIKINESS > SPIKY
SPIKING > SPIKE
SPIKS > SPIK
SPIKY adj resembling a spike
SPILE n heavy timber stake or pile ▷ vb provide or support with a spile
SPILED > SPILE
SPILES > SPILE
SPILIKIN same as > SPILLIKIN
SPILIKINS > SPILIKIN
SPILING > SPILE
SPILINGS > SPILE
SPILITE n type of igneous rock
SPILITES > SPILITE
SPILITIC > SPILITE
SPILL vb pour from or as if from a container ▷ n fall

SPILLABLE > SPILL
SPILLAGE n instance or the process of spilling
SPILLAGES > SPILLAGE
SPILLED > SPILL
SPILLER > SPILL
SPILLERS > SPILL
SPILLIKIN n thin strip of wood, cardboard, or plastic used in spillikins
SPILLING > SPILL
SPILLINGS > SPILL
SPILLOVER n act of spilling over
SPILLS > SPILL
SPILLWAY n channel that carries away surplus water, as from a dam
SPILLWAYS > SPILLWAY
SPILOSITE n form of slate
SPILT > SPILL
SPILTH n something spilled
SPILTHS > SPILTH
SPIM n unsolicited commercial communications received on a computer via an instant-messaging system
SPIMS > SPIM
SPIN vb revolve or cause to revolve rapidly ▷ n revolving motion
SPINA n spine
SPINACENE n type of vaccine
SPINACH n dark green leafy vegetable
SPINACHES > SPINACH
SPINACHY > SPINACH
SPINAE > SPINA
SPINAGE same as > SPINACH
SPINAGES > SPINAGE
SPINAL adj of the spine ▷ n anaesthetic administered in the spine
SPINALLY > SPINAL
SPINALS > SPINAL
SPINAR n fast-spinning star
SPINARS > SPINAR
SPINAS > SPINA
SPINATE adj having a spine
SPINDLE n rotating rod that acts as an axle ▷ vb form into a spindle or equip with spindles
SPINDLED > SPINDLE
SPINDLER > SPINDLE
SPINDLERS > SPINDLE
SPINDLES > SPINDLE
SPINDLIER > SPINDLY
SPINDLING adj long and slender, esp disproportionately so ▷ n spindling person or thing
SPINDLY adj long, slender, and frail
SPINDRIFT n spray blown up from the sea
SPINE n backbone
SPINED > SPINE
SPINEL n any of a group of hard glassy minerals of variable colour
SPINELESS adj lacking courage
SPINELIKE > SPINE
SPINELLE same as > SPINEL

SPINELLES > SPINELLE
SPINELS > SPINEL
SPINES > SPINE
SPINET *n* small harpsichord
SPINETS > SPINET
SPINETTE *same as* > SPINET
SPINETTES > SPINETTE
SPINIER > SPINY
SPINIEST > SPINY
SPINIFEX *n* coarse spiny Australian grass
SPINIFORM *adj* like a thorn
SPININESS > SPINY
SPINK *n* finch
SPINKS > SPINK
SPINLESS > SPIN
SPINNAKER *n* large sail on a racing yacht
SPINNER *n* bowler who specializes in spinning the ball to make it change direction when it bounces or strikes the bat
SPINNERET *n* organ through which silk threads come out of a spider
SPINNERS > SPINNER
SPINNERY *n* spinning mill
SPINNET *same as* > SPINET
SPINNETS > SPINNET
SPINNEY *n* small wood
SPINNEYS > SPINNEY
SPINNIES > SPINNY
SPINNING > SPIN
SPINNINGS > SPIN
SPINNY *same as* > SPINNEY
SPINODE *another name for* > CUSP
SPINODES > SPINODE
SPINOFF *n* development derived incidentally from an existing enterprise
SPINOFFS > SPINOFF
SPINONE *as in Italian spinone* wiry-coated gun dog
SPINONI > SPINONE
SPINOR *n* type of mathematical object
SPINORS > SPINOR
SPINOSE *adj* (esp of plants) bearing many spines
SPINOSELY > SPINOSE
SPINOSITY > SPINOSE
SPINOUS *adj* resembling a spine or thorn
SPINOUT *n* spinning skid that causes a car to run off the road
SPINOUTS > SPINOUT
SPINS > SPIN
SPINSTER *n* unmarried woman
SPINSTERS > SPINSTER
SPINTEXT *n* preacher
SPINTEXTS > SPINTEXT
SPINTO *n* lyrical singing voice
SPINTOS > SPINTO
SPINULA *n* small spine
SPINULAE > SPINULA
SPINULATE *adj* like a spine
SPINULE *n* very small spine, thorn, or prickle
SPINULES > SPINULE
SPINULOSE > SPINULE
SPINULOUS > SPINULE
SPINY *adj* covered with

spines
SPIRACLE *n* small blowhole for breathing through, such as that of a whale
SPIRACLES > SPIRACLE
SPIRACULA *pl n* spiracles
SPIRAEA *n* plant with small white or pink flowers
SPIRAEAS > SPIRAEA
SPIRAL *n* continuous curve formed by a point winding about a central axis at an ever-increasing distance from it ▷ *vb* move in a spiral ▷ *adj* having the form of a spiral
SPIRALED > SPIRAL
SPIRALING > SPIRAL
SPIRALISM *n* ascent in spiral structure
SPIRALIST > SPIRALISM
SPIRALITY > SPIRAL
SPIRALLED > SPIRAL
SPIRALLY > SPIRAL
SPIRALS > SPIRAL
SPIRANT *n* fricative consonant
SPIRANTS > SPIRANT
SPIRASTER *n* part of living sponge
SPIRATED *adj* twisted in spiral
SPIRATION *n* breathing
SPIRE *n* pointed part of a steeple ▷ *vb* assume the shape of a spire
SPIREA *same as* > SPIRAEA
SPIREAS > SPIREA
SPIRED > SPIRE
SPIRELESS > SPIRE
SPIRELET *another name for* > FLECHE
SPIRELETS > SPIRELET
SPIREM *same as* > SPIREME
SPIREME *n* tangled mass of chromatin threads into which the nucleus of a cell is resolved at the start of mitosis
SPIREMES > SPIREME
SPIREMS > SPIREM
SPIRES > SPIRE
SPIREWISE > SPIRE
SPIRIC *n* type of curve
SPIRICS > SPIRIC
SPIRIER > SPIRE
SPIRIEST > SPIRE
SPIRILLA > SPIRILLUM
SPIRILLAR > SPIRILLUM
SPIRILLUM *n* any bacterium having a curved or spirally twisted rodlike body
SPIRING > SPIRE
SPIRIT *n* nonphysical aspect of a person concerned with profound thoughts ▷ *vb* carry away mysteriously
SPIRITED *adj* lively
SPIRITFUL > SPIRIT
SPIRITING > SPIRIT
SPIRITISM *n* belief that the spirits of the dead can communicate with the living
SPIRITIST > SPIRITISM

SPIRITOSO *adv* to be played in a spirited or animated manner
SPIRITOUS *adj* high-spirited
SPIRITS > SPIRIT
SPIRITUAL *adj* relating to the spirit ▷ *n* type of religious folk song originating among Black slaves in America
SPIRITUEL *adj* having a refined and lively mind or wit
SPIRITUS *n* spirit
SPIRITY *adj* spirited
SPIRLING *same as* > SPARLING
SPIRLINGS > SPIRLING
SPIROGRAM *n* record made by spirograph
SPIROGYRA *n* green freshwater plant that floats on the surface of ponds and ditches
SPIROID *adj* resembling a spiral or displaying a spiral form
SPIRT *same as* > SPURT
SPIRTED > SPIRT
SPIRTING > SPIRT
SPIRTLE *same as* > SPURTLE
SPIRTLES > SPIRTLE
SPIRTS > SPIRT
SPIRULA *n* tropical cephalopod mollusc
SPIRULAE > SPIRULA
SPIRULAS > SPIRULA
SPIRULINA *n* any filamentous cyanobacterium of the genus *Spirulina*
SPIRY > SPIRE
SPIT *vb* eject (saliva or food) from the mouth ▷ *n* saliva
SPITAL *n* hospital, esp for the needy sick
SPITALS > SPITAL
SPITBALL *n* small missile made from chewed paper
SPITBALLS > SPITBALL
SPITCHER *adj* doomed
SPITE *n* deliberate nastiness ▷ *vb* annoy or hurt from spite
SPITED > SPITE
SPITEFUL *adj* full of or motivated by spite
SPITES > SPITE
SPITFIRE *n* person with a fiery temper
SPITFIRES > SPITFIRE
SPITING > SPITE
SPITS > SPIT
SPITTED > SPIT
SPITTEN > SPIT
SPITTER > SPIT
SPITTERS > SPIT
SPITTING > SPIT
SPITTINGS > SPIT
SPITTLE *n* fluid produced in the mouth, saliva
SPITTLES > SPITTLE
SPITTOON *n* bowl to spit into
SPITTOONS > SPITTOON

SPITZ *n* stockily built dog with a pointed face, erect ears, and a tightly curled tail
SPITZES > SPITZ
SPIV *n* smartly dressed man who makes a living by shady dealings
SPIVS > SPIV
SPIVVERY *n* behaviour of spivs
SPIVVIER > SPIV
SPIVVIEST > SPIV
SPIVVY > SPIV
SPLAKE *n* type of hybrid trout bred by Canadian zoologists
SPLAKES > SPLAKE
SPLASH *vb* scatter liquid on (something) ▷ *n* splashing sound
SPLASHED > SPLASH
SPLASHER *n* anything used for protection against splashes
SPLASHERS > SPLASHER
SPLASHES > SPLASH
SPLASHIER > SPLASHY
SPLASHILY > SPLASHY
SPLASHING > SPLASH
SPLASHY *adj* having irregular marks
SPLAT *n* wet slapping sound ▷ *vb* make wet slapping sound
SPLATCH *vb* splash
SPLATCHED > SPLATCH
SPLATCHES > SPLATCH
SPLATS > SPLAT
SPLATTED > SPLAT
SPLATTER *n* splash ▷ *vb* splash (something or someone) with small blobs
SPLATTERS > SPLATTER
SPLATTING > SPLAT
SPLAY *vb* spread out, with ends spreading in different directions ▷ *adj* spread out ▷ *n* surface of a wall that forms an oblique angle to the main flat surfaces
SPLAYED > SPLAY
SPLAYFEET > SPLAYFOOT
SPLAYFOOT *n* foot of which the toes are spread out
SPLAYING > SPLAY
SPLAYS > SPLAY
SPLEEN *n* abdominal organ which filters bacteria from the blood
SPLEENFUL *adj* bad-tempered or irritable
SPLEENIER > SPLEEN
SPLEENISH > SPLEEN
SPLEENS > SPLEEN
SPLEENY > SPLEEN
SPLENDENT *adj* shining brightly
SPLENDID *adj* excellent
SPLENDOR *same as* > SPLENDOUR
SPLENDORS > SPLENDOR
SPLENDOUR *n* state or quality of being splendid
SPLENETIC *adj* spiteful or irritable ▷ *n* spiteful or irritable person

SPLENIA > SPLENIUM
SPLENIAL > SPLENIUS
SPLENIC adj of, relating to, or in the spleen
SPLENII > SPLENIUS
SPLENITIS n inflammation of the spleen
SPLENIUM n structure in brain
SPLENIUMS > SPLENIUM
SPLENIUS n either of two flat muscles situated at the back of the neck
SPLENT same as > SPLINT
SPLENTS > SPLENT
SPLEUCHAN n pouch for tobacco
SPLICE vb join by interweaving or overlapping ends
SPLICED > SPLICE
SPLICER > SPLICE
SPLICERS > SPLICE
SPLICES > SPLICE
SPLICING > SPLICE
SPLIFF n cannabis, used as a drug
SPLIFFS > SPLIFF
SPLINE n type of narrow key around a shaft that fits into a corresponding groove ▷ vb provide (a shaft, part, etc) with splines
SPLINED > SPLINE
SPLINES > SPLINE
SPLINING > SPLINE
SPLINT n rigid support for a broken bone ▷ vb apply a splint to (a broken arm, etc)
SPLINTED > SPLINT
SPLINTER n thin sharp piece broken off, esp from wood ▷ vb break into fragments
SPLINTERS > SPLINTER
SPLINTERY adj liable to produce or break into splinters
SPLINTING > SPLINT
SPLINTS > SPLINT
SPLIT vb break into separate pieces ▷ n splitting
SPLITS > SPLIT
SPLITTED > SPLIT
SPLITTER > SPLIT
SPLITTERS > SPLIT
SPLITTING > SPLIT
SPLODGE n large uneven spot or stain ▷ vb mark (something) with a splodge or splodges
SPLODGED > SPLODGE
SPLODGES > SPLODGE
SPLODGIER > SPLODGE
SPLODGILY > SPLODGE
SPLODGING > SPLODGE
SPLODGY > SPLODGE
SPLOOSH vb splash or cause to splash about uncontrollably ▷ n instance or sound of splooshing
SPLOOSHED > SPLOOSH
SPLOOSHES > SPLOOSH
SPLORE n revel

SPLORES > SPLORE
SPLOSH vb scatter (liquid) vigorously about in blobs ▷ n instance or sound of sploshing
SPLOSHED > SPLOSH
SPLOSHES > SPLOSH
SPLOSHING > SPLOSH
SPLOTCH vb splash, daub
SPLOTCHED > SPLOTCH
SPLOTCHES > SPLOTCH
SPLOTCHY > SPLOTCH
SPLURGE vb spend money extravagantly ▷ n bout of extravagance
SPLURGED > SPLURGE
SPLURGER > SPLURGE
SPLURGERS > SPLURGE
SPLURGES > SPLURGE
SPLURGIER > SPLURGE
SPLURGING > SPLURGE
SPLURGY > SPLURGE
SPLUTTER vb utter with spitting or choking sounds ▷ n spluttering
SPLUTTERS > SPLUTTER
SPLUTTERY > SPLUTTER
SPOD n boring, unattractive, or overstudious person
SPODDIER > SPOD
SPODDIEST > SPOD
SPODDY > SPOD
SPODE n type of English china or porcelain
SPODES > SPODE
SPODIUM n black powder
SPODIUMS > SPODIUM
SPODOGRAM n ash from plant used in studying it
SPODOSOL n ashy soil
SPODOSOLS > SPODOSOL
SPODS > SPOD
SPODUMENE n greyish-white, green, or lilac pyroxene mineral
SPOFFISH adj officious
SPOFFY same as > SPOFFISH
SPOIL vb damage
SPOILABLE > SPOIL
SPOILAGE n amount of material that has been spoilt
SPOILAGES > SPOILAGE
SPOILED > SPOIL
SPOILER n device on an aircraft or car to increase drag
SPOILERS > SPOILER
SPOILFIVE n card game for two or more players with five cards each
SPOILFUL adj taking spoils
SPOILING > SPOIL
SPOILS > SPOIL
SPOILSMAN n person who shares in the spoils of office or advocates the spoils system
SPOILSMEN > SPOILSMAN
SPOILT > SPOIL
SPOKE n radial member of a wheel ▷ vb equip with spokes
SPOKED > SPOKE
SPOKEN > SPEAK
SPOKES > SPOKE
SPOKESMAN n person

chosen to speak on behalf of a group
SPOKESMEN > SPOKESMAN
SPOKEWISE > SPEAK
SPOKING > SPOKE
SPOLIATE less common word for > DESPOIL
SPOLIATED > SPOLIATE
SPOLIATES > SPOLIATE
SPOLIATOR > SPOLIATE
SPONDAIC adj of, relating to, or consisting of spondees ▷ n spondaic line
SPONDAICS > SPONDAIC
SPONDEE n metrical foot of two long syllables
SPONDEES > SPONDEE
SPONDULIX n money
SPONDYL n vertebra
SPONDYLS > SPONDYL
SPONGE n sea animal with a porous absorbent skeleton ▷ vb wipe with a sponge
SPONGEBAG n small bag for holding toiletries when travelling
SPONGED > SPONGE
SPONGEOUS adj spongy
SPONGER n person who sponges on others
SPONGERS > SPONGER
SPONGES > SPONGE
SPONGIER > SPONGY
SPONGIEST > SPONGY
SPONGILY > SPONGY
SPONGIN n fibrous horny protein that forms the skeletal framework of the bath sponge and related sponges
SPONGING > SPONGE
SPONGINS > SPONGIN
SPONGIOSE > SPONGE
SPONGIOUS > SPONGE
SPONGOID > SPONGE
SPONGY adj of or resembling a sponge
SPONSAL n marriage
SPONSALIA n marriage ceremony
SPONSIBLE adj responsible
SPONSING same as > SPONSON
SPONSINGS > SPONSING
SPONSION n act or process of becoming surety
SPONSIONS > SPONSION
SPONSON n outboard support for a gun enabling it to fire fore and aft
SPONSONS > SPONSON
SPONSOR n person who promotes something ▷ vb act as a sponsor for
SPONSORED > SPONSOR
SPONSORS > SPONSOR
SPONTOON n form of halberd carried by some junior infantry officers in the 18th and 19th centuries
SPONTOONS > SPONTOON
SPOOF n mildly satirical parody ▷ vb fool (a person) with a trick or deception
SPOOFED > SPOOF
SPOOFER > SPOOF
SPOOFERS > SPOOF

SPOOFERY > SPOOF
SPOOFING > SPOOF
SPOOFINGS > SPOOF
SPOOFS > SPOOF
SPOOFY > SPOOF
SPOOK n ghost ▷ vb frighten
SPOOKED > SPOOK
SPOOKERY n spooky events
SPOOKIER > SPOOKY
SPOOKIEST > SPOOKY
SPOOKILY > SPOOKY
SPOOKING > SPOOK
SPOOKISH > SPOOK
SPOOKS > SPOOK
SPOOKY adj ghostly or eerie
SPOOL n cylinder round which something can be wound ▷ vb wind or be wound onto a spool or reel
SPOOLED > SPOOL
SPOOLER > SPOOL
SPOOLERS > SPOOL
SPOOLING > SPOOL
SPOOLINGS > SPOOL
SPOOLS > SPOOL
SPOOM vb sail fast before wind
SPOOMED > SPOOM
SPOOMING > SPOOM
SPOOMS > SPOOM
SPOON n shallow bowl attached to a handle for eating, stirring, or serving food ▷ vb lift with a spoon
SPOONBAIT n type of lure used in angling
SPOONBILL n wading bird of warm regions with a long flat bill
SPOONED > SPOON
SPOONEY same as > SPOONY
SPOONEYS > SPOONEY
SPOONFED adj having been given someone else's opinions
SPOONFUL n amount that a spoon is able to hold
SPOONFULS > SPOONFUL
SPOONIER > SPOONY
SPOONIES > SPOONY
SPOONIEST > SPOONY
SPOONILY > SPOONY
SPOONING > SPOONY
SPOONS > SPOON
SPOONSFUL > SPOONFUL
SPOONWAYS adv like spoons
SPOONWISE same as > SPOONWAYS
SPOONY adj foolishly or stupidly amorous ▷ n fool or silly person, esp one in love
SPOOR n trail of an animal ▷ vb track (an animal) by following its trail
SPOORED > SPOOR
SPOORER > SPOOR
SPOORERS > SPOOR
SPOORING > SPOOR
SPOORS > SPOOR
SPOOT n razor shell
SPOOTS > SPOOT
SPORADIC adj intermittent, scattered
SPORAL > SPORE
SPORANGIA pl n organs

in fungi in which asexual spores are produced

SPORE *n* minute reproductive body of some plants ▷ *vb* produce, carry, or release spores

SPORED > SPORE

SPORES > SPORE

SPORICIDE *n* substance killing spores

SPORIDESM *n* group of spores

SPORIDIA > SPORIDIUM

SPORIDIAL > SPORIDIUM

SPORIDIUM *n* type of spore

SPORING > SPORE

SPOROCARP *n* specialized leaf branch in certain aquatic ferns that encloses the sori

SPOROCYST *n* thick-walled rounded structure produced by sporozoan protozoans

SPOROCYTE *n* diploid cell that divides by meiosis to produce four haploid spores

SPOROGENY *n* process of spore formation in plants and animals

SPOROGONY *n* process in sporozoans by which sporozoites are formed

SPOROID *adj* of or like a spore

SPOROPHYL *n* leaf in ferns that bears the sporangia

SPOROZOA *n* class of microscopic creature

SPOROZOAL > SPOROZOA

SPOROZOAN *n* any parasitic protozoan of the phylum *Apicomplexa* ▷ *adj* of or relating to sporozoans

SPOROZOIC > SPOROZOA

SPOROZOON *same as* > SPOROZOAN

SPORRAN *n* pouch worn in front of a kilt

SPORRANS > SPORRAN

SPORT *n* activity for pleasure, competition, or exercise ▷ *vb* wear proudly

SPORTABLE *adj* playful

SPORTANCE *n* playing

SPORTED > SPORT

SPORTER > SPORT

SPORTERS > SPORT

SPORTFUL > SPORT

SPORTIER > SPORTY

SPORTIES > SPORTY

SPORTIEST > SPORTY

SPORTIF *adj* sporty

SPORTILY > SPORTY

SPORTING *adj* of sport

SPORTIVE *adj* playful

SPORTLESS > SPORT

SPORTS *adj* of or used in sports ▷ *n* meeting held at a school or college for competitions in athletic events

SPORTSMAN *n* person who plays sports

SPORTSMEN > SPORTSMAN

SPORTY *adj* (of a person)

interested in sport ▷ *n* young person who typically wears sportswear, is competitive about sport, and takes an interest in his or her fitness

SPORULAR > SPORULE

SPORULATE *vb* produce spores, esp by multiple fission

SPORULE *n* spore, esp a very small spore

SPORULES > SPORULE

SPOSH *n* slush

SPOSHES > SPOSH

SPOSHIER > SPOSH

SPOSHIEST > SPOSH

SPOSHY > SPOSH

SPOT *n* small mark on a surface ▷ *vb* notice

SPOTLESS *adj* absolutely clean

SPOTLIGHT *n* powerful light illuminating a small area ▷ *vb* draw attention to

SPOTLIT > SPOTLIGHT

SPOTS > SPOT

SPOTTABLE > SPOT

SPOTTED > SPOT

SPOTTER *n* person whose hobby is watching for and noting numbers or types of trains or planes

SPOTTERS > SPOTTER

SPOTTIE *n* young deer of up to three months of age

SPOTTIER > SPOTTY

SPOTTIES > SPOTTIE

SPOTTIEST > SPOTTY

SPOTTILY > SPOTTY

SPOTTING > SPOT

SPOTTINGS > SPOT

SPOTTY *adj* with spots

SPOUSAGE *n* marriage

SPOUSAGES > SPOUSAGE

SPOUSAL *n* marriage ceremony ▷ *adj* of or relating to marriage

SPOUSALLY > SPOUSAL

SPOUSALS > SPOUSAL

SPOUSE *n* husband or wife ▷ *vb* marry

SPOUSED > SPOUSE

SPOUSES > SPOUSE

SPOUSING > SPOUSE

SPOUT *vb* pour out in a stream or jet ▷ *n* projecting tube or lip for pouring liquids

SPOUTED > SPOUT

SPOUTER > SPOUT

SPOUTERS > SPOUT

SPOUTIER > SPOUT

SPOUTIEST > SPOUT

SPOUTING *n* rainwater downpipe on the outside of a building

SPOUTINGS > SPOUTING

SPOUTLESS > SPOUT

SPOUTS > SPOUT

SPOUTY > SPOUT

SPRACK *adj* vigorous

SPRACKLE *vb* clamber

SPRACKLED > SPRACKLE

SPRACKLES > SPRACKLE

SPRAD > SPREAD

SPRADDLE *n* disease of fowl

preventing them from standing

SPRADDLED *adj* affected by spraddle

SPRADDLES > SPRADDLE

SPRAG *n* chock or steel bar used to prevent a vehicle from running backwards on an incline ▷ *vb* use sprag to prevent vehicle from moving

SPRAGGED > SPRAG

SPRAGGING > SPRAG

SPRAGS > SPRAG

SPRAID *vb* chapped

SPRAIN *vb* injure (a joint) by a sudden twist ▷ *n* such an injury

SPRAINED > SPRAIN

SPRAINING > SPRAIN

SPRAINS > SPRAIN

SPRAINT *n* piece of otter's dung

SPRAINTS > SPRAINT

SPRANG *n* branch

SPRANGLE *vb* sprawl

SPRANGLED > SPRANGLE

SPRANGLES > SPRANGLE

SPRANGS > SPRANG

SPRAT *n* small sea fish

SPRATS > SPRAT

SPRATTLE *vb* scramble

SPRATTLED > SPRATTLE

SPRATTLES > SPRATTLE

SPRAUCHLE *same as* > SPRACKLE

SPRAUNCY *adj* smart

SPRAWL *vb* lie or sit with the limbs spread out ▷ *n* part of a city that has spread untidily over a large area

SPRAWLED > SPRAWL

SPRAWLER > SPRAWL

SPRAWLERS > SPRAWL

SPRAWLIER > SPRAWL

SPRAWLING > SPRAWL

SPRAWLS > SPRAWL

SPRAWLY > SPRAWL

SPRAY *n* (device for producing) fine drops of liquid ▷ *vb* scatter in fine drops

SPRAYED > SPRAY

SPRAYER > SPRAY

SPRAYERS > SPRAY

SPRAYEY > SPRAY

SPRAYIER > SPRAY

SPRAYIEST > SPRAY

SPRAYING > SPRAY

SPRAYINGS > SPRAY

SPRAYS > SPRAY

SPREAD *vb* open out or be displayed to the fullest extent ▷ *n* spreading ▷ *adj* extended or stretched out, esp to the fullest extent

SPREADER *n* machine or device used for scattering bulk materials over a relatively wide area

SPREADERS > SPREADER

SPREADING > SPREAD

SPREADS > SPREAD

SPREAGH *n* cattle raid

SPREAGHS > SPREAGH

SPREATHE *vb* chap

SPREATHED *adj* sore

SPREATHES > SPREATHE

SPREAZE *same as* > SPREATHE

SPREAZED *same as* > SPREATHED

SPREAZES > SPREAZE

SPREAZING > SPREAZE

SPRECHERY *n* theft of cattle

SPRECKLED *adj* speckled

SPRED *same as* > SPREAD

SPREDD *same as* > SPREAD

SPREDDE *same as* > SPREAD

SPREDDEN > SPREDDE

SPREDDES > SPREDDE

SPREDDING > SPREDDE

SPREDDS > SPREDD

SPREDS > SPRED

SPREE *n* session of overindulgence, usu in drinking or spending money ▷ *vb* go on a spree

SPREED > SPREE

SPREEING > SPREE

SPREES > SPREE

SPREETHE *same as* > SPREATHE

SPREETHED > SPREETHE

SPREETHES > SPREETHE

SPREEZE *same as* > SPREATHE

SPREEZED > SPREEZE

SPREEZES > SPREEZE

SPREEZING > SPREEZE

SPREKELIA *n* bulbous plant grown for its striking crimson or white pendent flowers

SPRENT > SPRINKLE

SPREW *same as* > SPRUE

SPREWS > SPREW

SPRIER > SPRY

SPRIEST > SPRY

SPRIG *n* twig or shoot ▷ *vb* fasten or secure with sprigs

SPRIGGED > SPRIG

SPRIGGER > SPRIG

SPRIGGERS > SPRIG

SPRIGGIER > SPRIG

SPRIGGING > SPRIG

SPRIGGY > SPRIG

SPRIGHT *same as* > SPRITE

SPRIGHTED > SPRIGHT

SPRIGHTLY *adj* lively and brisk ▷ *adv* in a lively manner

SPRIGHTS > SPRIGHT

SPRIGS > SPRIG

SPRIGTAIL *n* species of duck

SPRING *vb* move suddenly upwards or forwards in a single motion, jump ▷ *n* season between winter and summer

SPRINGAL *n* young man

SPRINGALD *same as* > SPRINGAL

SPRINGALS > SPRINGAL

SPRINGBOK *n* S African antelope

SPRINGE *n* type of snare for catching small wild animals or birds ▷ *vb* set such a snare

SPRINGED > SPRINGE

SPRINGER *n* small spaniel

SPRINGERS > SPRINGER

SPRINGES > SPRINGE
SPRINGIER > SPRINGY
SPRINGILY > SPRINGY
SPRINGING > SPRING
SPRINGLE *same as* > SPRINGE
SPRINGLES > SPRINGE
SPRINGLET *n* small spring
SPRINGS > SPRING
SPRINGY *adj* elastic
SPRINKLE *vb* scatter (liquid or powder) in tiny drops or particles over (something) ▷ *n* act or an instance of sprinkling or a quantity that is sprinkled
SPRINKLED > SPRINKLE
SPRINKLER *n* device with small holes that is attached to a garden hose or watering can and used to spray water
SPRINKLES > SPRINKLE
SPRINT *n* short race run at top speed ▷ *vb* run a short distance at top speed
SPRINTED > SPRINT
SPRINTER > SPRINT
SPRINTERS > SPRINT
SPRINTING > SPRINT
SPRINTS > SPRINT
SPRIT *n* small spar set diagonally across a sail to extend it
SPRITE *n* elf
SPRITEFUL > SPRITE
SPRITELY *same as* > SPRIGHTLY
SPRITES > SPRITE
SPRITS > SPRIT
SPRITSAIL *n* sail extended by a sprit
SPRITZ *vb* spray liquid
SPRITZED > SPRITZ
SPRITZER *n* tall drink of wine and soda water
SPRITZERS > SPRITZER
SPRITZES > SPRITZ
SPRITZIG *adj* (of wine) sparkling ▷ *n* sparkling wine
SPRITZIGS > SPRITZIG
SPRITZING > SPRITZ
SPROCKET *n* wheel with teeth on the rim, that drives or is driven by a chain
SPROCKETS > SPROCKET
SPROD *n* young salmon
SPRODS > SPROD
SPROG *n* child
SPROGS > SPROG
SPRONG > SPRING
SPROUT *vb* put forth shoots ▷ *n* shoot
SPROUTED > SPROUT
SPROUTING > SPROUT
SPROUTS > SPROUT
SPRUCE *n* kind of fir ▷ *adj* neat and smart
SPRUCED > SPRUCE
SPRUCELY > SPRUCE
SPRUCER > SPRUCE
SPRUCES > SPRUCE
SPRUCEST > SPRUCE
SPRUCIER > SPRUCE
SPRUCIEST > SPRUCE
SPRUCING > SPRUCE

SPRUCY > SPRUCE
SPRUE *n* vertical channel in a mould through which plastic or molten metal is poured
SPRUES > SPRUE
SPRUG *n* sparrow
SPRUGS > SPRUG
SPRUIK *vb* speak in public (used esp of a showman or salesman)
SPRUIKED > SPRUIK
SPRUIKER > SPRUIK
SPRUIKERS > SPRUIK
SPRUIKING > SPRUIK
SPRUIKS > SPRUIK
SPRUIT *n* small tributary stream or watercourse
SPRUITS > SPRUIT
SPRUNG > SPRING
SPRUSH *Scots form of* > SPRUCE
SPRUSHED > SPRUSH
SPRUSHES > SPRUSH
SPRUSHING > SPRUSH
SPRY *adj* active or nimble
SPRYER > SPRY
SPRYEST > SPRY
SPRYLY > SPRY
SPRYNESS > SPRY
SPUD *n* potato ▷ *vb* remove (bark) or eradicate (weeds) with a spud
SPUDDED > SPUD
SPUDDER *same as* > SPUD
SPUDDERS > SPUDDER
SPUDDIER > SPUDDY
SPUDDIEST > SPUDDY
SPUDDING > SPUD
SPUDDINGS > SPUD
SPUDDLE *n* feeble movement
SPUDDLES > SPUDDLE
SPUDDY *adj* short and fat
SPUDS > SPUD
SPUE *same as* > SPEW
SPUED > SPUE
SPUEING > SPUE
SPUER > SPUE
SPUERS > SPUE
SPUES > SPUE
SPUG *same as* > SPUGGY
SPUGGIES > SPUGGY
SPUGGY *n* house sparrow
SPUGS > SPUG
SPUILZIE *vb* plunder
SPUILZIED > SPUILZIE
SPUILZIES > SPUILZIE
SPUING > SPUE
SPULE *Scots word for* > SHOULDER
SPULES > SPULE
SPULYE *same as* > SPUILZIE
SPULYED > SPULYE
SPULYEING > SPULYE
SPULYES > SPULYE
SPULYIE *same as* > SPUILZIE
SPULYIED > SPULYIE
SPULYIES > SPULYIE
SPULZIE *same as* > SPUILZIE
SPULZIED > SPULZIE
SPULZIES > SPULZIE
SPUMANTE *n* Italian sparkling wine
SPUMANTES > SPUMANTE
SPUME *vb* froth ▷ *n* foam or froth on the sea

SPUMED > SPUME
SPUMES > SPUME
SPUMIER > SPUM
SPUMIEST > SPUM
SPUMING > SPUME
SPUMONE *n* creamy Italian ice cream
SPUMONES > SPUMONE
SPUMONI *same as* > SPUMONE
SPUMONIS > SPUMONI
SPUMOUS > SPUME
SPUMY > SPUME
SPUN > SPIN
SPUNGE *same as* > SPONGE
SPUNGES > SPUNGE
SPUNK *n* courage, spirit ▷ *vb* catch fire
SPUNKED > SPUNK
SPUNKIE *n* will-o'-the-wisp
SPUNKIER > SPUNK
SPUNKIES > SPUNKIE
SPUNKIEST > SPUNK
SPUNKILY > SPUNK
SPUNKING > SPUNK
SPUNKS > SPUNK
SPUNKY > SPUNK
SPUNYARN *n* small stuff made from rope yarns twisted together
SPUNYARNS > SPUNYARN
SPUR *n* stimulus or incentive ▷ *vb* urge on, incite (someone)
SPURGALL *vb* prod with spur
SPURGALLS > SPURGALL
SPURGE *n* plant with milky sap
SPURGES > SPURGE
SPURIAE *n* type of bird feathers
SPURIOUS *adj* not genuine
SPURLESS > SPUR
SPURLING *same as* > SPARLING
SPURLINGS > SPURLING
SPURN *vb* reject with scorn ▷ *n* instance of spurning
SPURNE *vb* spur
SPURNED > SPURN
SPURNER > SPURN
SPURNERS > SPURN
SPURNES > SPURNE
SPURNING > SPURN
SPURNINGS > SPURN
SPURNS > SPURN
SPURRED > SPUR
SPURRER > SPUR
SPURRERS > SPUR
SPURREY *n* any of several low-growing European plants
SPURREYS > SPURREY
SPURRIER *n* maker of spurs
SPURRIERS > SPURRIER
SPURRIES > SPURRY
SPURRIEST > SPURRY
SPURRING > SPUR
SPURRINGS > SPUR
SPURRY *n* spurrey ▷ *adj* resembling a spur
SPURS > SPUR
SPURT *vb* gush or cause to gush out in a jet ▷ *n* short sudden burst of activity or speed
SPURTED > SPURT

SPURTER > SPURT
SPURTERS > SPURT
SPURTING > SPURT
SPURTLE *n* wooden spoon for stirring porridge
SPURTLES > SPURTLE
SPURTS > SPURT
SPURWAY *n* path used by riders
SPURWAYS > SPURWAY
SPUTA > SPUTUM
SPUTNIK *n* early Soviet artificial satellite
SPUTNIKS > SPUTNIK
SPUTTER *n* splutter ▷ *vb* splutter
SPUTTERED > SPUTTER
SPUTTERER > SPUTTER
SPUTTERS > SPUTTER
SPUTTERY > SPUTTER
SPUTUM *n* spittle, usu mixed with mucus
SPY *n* person employed to obtain secret information ▷ *vb* act as a spy
SPYAL *n* spy
SPYALS > SPYAL
SPYGLASS *n* small telescope
SPYHOLE *n* small hole in a door, etc through which one may watch secretly
SPYHOLES > SPYHOLE
SPYING > SPY
SPYINGS > SPY
SPYMASTER *n* person who controls spy network
SPYPLANE *n* military aeroplane used to spy on enemy
SPYPLANES > SPYPLANE
SPYRE *same as* > SPIRE
SPYRES > SPYRE
SPYWARE *n* software installed via the internet on a computer without the user's knowledge and used to gain information about the user
SPYWARES > SPYWARE
SQUAB *n* young bird yet to leave the nest ▷ *adj* (of birds) recently hatched and still unfledged ▷ *vb* fall
SQUABASH *vb* crush
SQUABBED > SQUAB
SQUABBER > SQUAB
SQUABBEST > SQUAB
SQUABBIER > SQUAB
SQUABBING > SQUAB
SQUABBISH > SQUAB
SQUABBLE *n* (engage in) a petty or noisy quarrel ▷ *vb* quarrel over a small matter
SQUABBLED > SQUABBLE
SQUABBLER > SQUABBLE
SQUABBLES > SQUABBLE
SQUABBY > SQUAB
SQUABS > SQUAB
SQUACCO *n* S European heron
SQUACCOS > SQUACCO
SQUAD *n* small group of people working or training together ▷ *vb* set up squads
SQUADDED > SQUAD
SQUADDIE *n* private soldier

SQUADDIES > SQUADDY

SQUADDING > SQUAD

SQUADDY *same as* > SQUADDIE

SQUADRON *n* division of an air force, fleet, or cavalry regiment ▷ *vb* assign to squadrons

SQUADRONE *n* former Scottish political party

SQUADRONS > SQUADRON

SQUADS > SQUAD

SQUAIL *vb* throw sticks at

SQUAILED > SQUAIL

SQUAILER > SQUAIL

SQUAILERS > SQUAIL

SQUAILING > SQUAIL

SQUAILS > SQUAIL

SQUALENE *n* terpene first found in the liver of sharks

SQUALENES > SQUALENE

SQUALID *adj* dirty and unpleasant

SQUALIDER > SQUALID

SQUALIDLY > SQUALID

SQUALL *n* sudden strong wind ▷ *vb* cry noisily, yell

SQUALLED > SQUALL

SQUALLER > SQUALL

SQUALLERS > SQUALL

SQUALLIER > SQUALL

SQUALLING > SQUALL

SQUALLISH > SQUALL

SQUALLS > SQUALL

SQUALLY > SQUALL

SQUALOID *adj* of or like a shark

SQUALOR *n* disgusting dirt and filth

SQUALORS > SQUALOR

SQUAMA *n* scale or scalelike structure

SQUAMAE > SQUAMA

SQUAMATE > SQUAMA

SQUAMATES > SQUAMA

SQUAME *same as* > SQUAMA

SQUAMELLA *n* small scale

SQUAMES > SQUAME

SQUAMOSAL *n* thin platelike paired bone in the skull of vertebrates ▷ *adj* of or relating to this bone

SQUAMOSE *same as* > SQUAMOUS

SQUAMOUS *adj* (of epithelium) consisting of one or more layers of flat platelike cells

SQUAMULA *same as* > SQUAMELLA

SQUAMULAS > SQUAMULA

SQUAMULE *same as* > SQUAMELLA

SQUAMULES > SQUAMULE

SQUANDER *vb* waste (money or resources) ▷ *n* extravagance or dissipation

SQUANDERS > SQUANDER

SQUARE *n* geometric figure with four equal sides and four right angles ▷ *adj* square in shape ▷ *vb* multiply (a number) by itself ▷ *adv* squarely, directly

SQUARED > SQUARE

SQUARELY *adv* in a direct way

SQUARER > SQUARE

SQUARERS > SQUARE

SQUARES > SQUARE

SQUAREST > SQUARE

SQUARIAL *n* type of square dish for receiving satellite television

SQUARIALS > SQUARIAL

SQUARING > SQUARE

SQUARINGS > SQUARE

SQUARISH > SQUARE

SQUARK *n* hypothetical boson partner of a quark

SQUARKS > SQUARK

SQUARROSE *adj* having a rough surface

SQUARSON *n* clergyman who is also landowner

SQUARSONS > SQUARSON

SQUASH *vb* crush flat ▷ *n* sweet fruit drink diluted with water

SQUASHED > SQUASH

SQUASHER > SQUASH

SQUASHERS > SQUASH

SQUASHES > SQUASH

SQUASHIER > SQUASHY

SQUASHILY > SQUASHY

SQUASHING > SQUASH

SQUASHY *adj* soft and easily squashed

SQUAT *vb* crouch with the knees bent and the weight on the feet ▷ *n* place where squatters live ▷ *adj* short and broad

SQUATLY > SQUAT

SQUATNESS > SQUAT

SQUATS > SQUAT

SQUATTED > SQUAT

SQUATTER *n* illegal occupier of unused premises

SQUATTERS > SQUATTER

SQUATTEST > SQUAT

SQUATTIER > SQUATTY

SQUATTILY > SQUATTY

SQUATTING > SQUAT

SQUATTLE *vb* squat

SQUATTLED > SQUATTLE

SQUATTLES > SQUATTLE

SQUATTY *adj* short and broad

SQUAW *n* offensive term for a Native American woman

SQUAWBUSH *n* American shrub

SQUAWFISH *n* North American minnow

SQUAWK *n* loud harsh cry ▷ *vb* utter a squawk

SQUAWKED > SQUAWK

SQUAWKER > SQUAWK

SQUAWKERS > SQUAWK

SQUAWKIER > SQUAWK

SQUAWKING > SQUAWK

SQUAWKS > SQUAWK

SQUAWKY > SQUAWK

SQUAWMAN *n* offensive term for a White man married to a Native American woman

SQUAWMEN > SQUAWMAN

SQUAWROOT *n* North American parasitic plant

SQUAWS > SQUAW

SQUEAK *n* short shrill cry or sound ▷ *vb* make or utter a squeak

SQUEAKED > SQUEAK

SQUEAKER > SQUEAK

SQUEAKERS > SQUEAK

SQUEAKERY > SQUEAK

SQUEAKIER > SQUEAK

SQUEAKILY > SQUEAK

SQUEAKING > SQUEAK

SQUEAKS > SQUEAK

SQUEAKY > SQUEAK

SQUEAL *n* long shrill cry or sound ▷ *vb* make or utter a squeal

SQUEALED > SQUEAL

SQUEALER > SQUEAL

SQUEALERS > SQUEAL

SQUEALING > SQUEAL

SQUEALS > SQUEAL

SQUEAMISH *adj* easily sickened or shocked

SQUEEGEE *n* tool with a rubber blade for clearing water from a surface ▷ *vb* remove (water or other liquid) from (something) by use of a squeegee

SQUEEGEED > SQUEEGEE

SQUEEGEES > SQUEEGEE

SQUEEZE *vb* grip or press firmly ▷ *n* squeezing

SQUEEZED > SQUEEZE

SQUEEZER > SQUEEZE

SQUEEZERS > SQUEEZE

SQUEEZES > SQUEEZE

SQUEEZIER > SQUEEZE

SQUEEZING > SQUEEZE

SQUEEZY > SQUEEZE

SQUEG *vb* oscillate

SQUEGGED > SQUEG

SQUEGGER > SQUEG

SQUEGGERS > SQUEG

SQUEGGING > SQUEG

SQUEGS > SQUEG

SQUELCH *vb* make a wet sucking sound, as by walking through mud ▷ *n* squelching sound

SQUELCHED > SQUELCH

SQUELCHER > SQUELCH

SQUELCHES > SQUELCH

SQUELCHY > SQUELCH

SQUIB *n* small firework that hisses before exploding

SQUIBBED > SQUIB

SQUIBBING > SQUIB

SQUIBS > SQUIB

SQUID *n* sea creature with a long soft body and ten tentacles ▷ *vb* (of a parachute) to assume an elongated squidlike shape owing to excess air pressure

SQUIDDED > SQUID

SQUIDDING > SQUID

SQUIDGE *vb* squash

SQUIDGED > SQUIDGE

SQUIDGES > SQUIDGE

SQUIDGIER > SQUIDGY

SQUIDGING > SQUIDGE

SQUIDGY *adj* soft, moist, and squashy

SQUIDS > SQUID

SQUIER *same as* > SQUIRE

SQUIERS > SQUIER

SQUIFF *same as* > SQUIFFY

SQUIFFED *same as* > SQUIFFY

SQUIFFER *n* concertina

SQUIFFERS > SQUIFFER

SQUIFFIER > SQUIFFY

SQUIFFY *adj* slightly drunk

SQUIGGLE *n* wavy line ▷ *vb* wriggle

SQUIGGLED > SQUIGGLE

SQUIGGLER > SQUIGGLE

SQUIGGLES > SQUIGGLE

SQUIGGLY > SQUIGGLE

SQUILGEE *same as* > SQUEEGEE

SQUILGEED > SQUILGEE

SQUILGEES > SQUILGEE

SQUILL *n* Mediterranean plant of the lily family

SQUILLA *n* any mantis shrimp of the genus *Squilla*

SQUILLAE > SQUILLA

SQUILLAS > SQUILLA

SQUILLION *n* extremely large but unspecified number, quantity, or amount

SQUILLS > SQUILL

SQUINANCY *same as* > QUINSY

SQUINCH *n* small arch across an internal corner of a tower, used to support a superstructure such as a spire ▷ *vb* squeeze

SQUINCHED > SQUINCH

SQUINCHES > SQUINCH

SQUINIED > SQUINY

SQUINIES > SQUINY

SQUINNIED > SQUINNY

SQUINNIER > SQUINNY

SQUINNIES > SQUINNY

SQUINNY *vb* squint ▷ *adj* squint

SQUINT *vb* have eyes which face in different directions ▷ *n* squinting condition of the eye ▷ *adj* crooked

SQUINTED > SQUINT

SQUINTER > SQUINT

SQUINTERS > SQUINT

SQUINTEST > SQUINT

SQUINTIER > SQUINT

SQUINTING > SQUINT

SQUINTS > SQUINT

SQUINTY > SQUINT

SQUINY *same as* > SQUINNY

SQUINYING > SQUINY

SQUIRAGE *n* body of squires

SQUIRAGES > SQUIRAGE

SQUIRALTY *same as* > SQUIRAGE

SQUIRARCH *n* person who believes in government by squires

SQUIRE *n* country gentleman, usu the main landowner in a community ▷ *vb* (of a man) escort (a woman)

SQUIREAGE *same as* > SQUIRAGE

SQUIRED > SQUIRE

SQUIREDOM > SQUIRE

SQUIREEN *n* petty squire

SQUIREENS > SQUIREEN

SQUIRELY > SQUIRE

SQUIRES > SQUIRE

SQUIRESS *n* wife of squire

SQUIRING > SQUIRE
SQUIRISH > SQUIRE
SQUIRM *vb* wriggle, writhe ▷ *n* wriggling movement
SQUIRMED > SQUIRM
SQUIRMER > SQUIRM
SQUIRMERS > SQUIRM
SQUIRMIER > SQUIRMY
SQUIRMING > SQUIRM
SQUIRMS > SQUIRM
SQUIRMY *adj* moving with a wriggling motion
SQUIRR *same as* > SKIRR
SQUIRRED > SQUIRR
SQUIRREL *n* small bushy-tailed tree-living animal ▷ *vb* store for future use
SQUIRRELS > SQUIRREL
SQUIRRELY > SQUIRREL
SQUIRRING > SQUIRR
SQUIRRS > SQUIRR
SQUIRT *vb* force (a liquid) or (of a liquid) be forced out of a narrow opening ▷ *n* jet of liquid
SQUIRTED > SQUIRT
SQUIRTER > SQUIRT
SQUIRTERS > SQUIRT
SQUIRTING > SQUIRT
SQUIRTS > SQUIRT
SQUISH *n* (make) a soft squelching sound ▷ *vb* crush (something) with a soft squelching sound
SQUISHED > SQUISH
SQUISHES > SQUISH
SQUISHIER > SQUISHY
SQUISHING > SQUISH
SQUISHY *adj* soft and yielding to the touch
SQUIT *n* insignificant person
SQUITCH *n* couch grass
SQUITCHES > SQUITCH
SQUITS > SQUIT
SQUIZ *n* look or glance, esp an inquisitive one
SQUIZZES > SQUIZ
SQUOOSH *vb* squash
SQUOOSHED > SQUOOSH
SQUOOSHES > SQUOOSH
SQUOOSHY > SQUOOSH
SQUUSH *same as* > SQUOOSH
SQUUSHED > SQUUSH
SQUUSHES > SQUUSH
SQUUSHING > SQUUSH
SRADDHA *n* Hindu offering to ancestor
SRADDHAS > SRADDHA
SRADHA *same as* > SRADHA
SRADHAS > SRADHA
SRI *n* title of respect used when addressing a Hindu
SRIS > SRI
ST *interj* exclamation to attract attention
STAB *vb* pierce with something pointed ▷ *n* stabbing
STABBED > STAB
STABBER > STAB
STABBERS > STAB
STABBING > STAB
STABBINGS > STAB
STABILATE *n* preserved collection of tiny animals
STABILE *n* stationary

abstract construction, usually of wire, metal, wood, etc ▷ *adj* fixed
STABILES > STABILE
STABILISE *same as* > STABILIZE
STABILITY *n* quality of being stable
STABILIZE *vb* make or become stable
STABLE *n* building in which horses are kept ▷ *vb* put or keep (a horse) in a stable ▷ *adj* firmly fixed or established
STABLEBOY *n* boy or man who works in a stable
STABLED > STABLE
STABLEMAN *same as* > STABLEBOY
STABLEMEN > STABLEMAN
STABLER *n* stable owner
STABLERS > STABLER
STABLES > STABLE
STABLEST > STABLE
STABLING *n* stable buildings or accommodation
STABLINGS > STABLING
STABLISH *archaic variant of* > ESTABLISH
STABLY > STABLE
STABS > STAB
STACCATI > STACCATO
STACCATO *adv* with the notes sharply separated ▷ *adj* consisting of short abrupt sounds ▷ *n* staccato note
STACCATOS > STACCATO
STACHYS *n* any plant of the genus *Stachys*
STACHYSES > STACHYS
STACK *n* ordered pile ▷ *vb* pile in a stack
STACKABLE > STACK
STACKED > STACK
STACKER > STACK
STACKERS > STACK
STACKET *n* fence of wooden posts
STACKETS > STACKET
STACKING *n* arrangement of aircraft traffic in busy flight lanes
STACKINGS > STACKING
STACKLESS > STACK
STACKROOM *n* area of library where books are not on open shelves
STACKS > STACK
STACKUP *n* number of aircraft waiting to land
STACKUPS > STACKUP
STACKYARD *n* place where livestock are kept
STACTE *n* one of several sweet-smelling spices used in incense
STACTES > STACTE
STADDA *n* type of saw
STADDAS > STADDA
STADDLE *n* type of support or prop
STADDLES > STADDLE
STADE *same as* > STADIUM
STADES > STADE

STADIA *n* instrument used in surveying
STADIAL *n* stage in development of glacier
STADIALS > STADIAL
STADIAS > STADIA
STADIUM *n* sports arena with tiered seats for spectators
STADIUMS > STADIUM
STAFF *n* people employed in an organization ▷ *vb* supply with personnel
STAFFAGE *n* ornamentation in work of art
STAFFAGES > STAFFAGE
STAFFED > STAFF
STAFFER *n* member of staff, esp, in journalism, of editorial staff
STAFFERS > STAFFER
STAFFING > STAFF
STAFFMAN *n* person who holds the levelling staff when a survey is being made
STAFFMEN > STAFFMAN
STAFFROOM *n* common room for teachers
STAFFS > STAFF
STAG *n* adult male deer ▷ *adv* without a female escort ▷ *vb* apply for (shares in a new issue) with the intention of selling them for a quick profit
STAGE *n* step or period of development ▷ *vb* put (a play) on stage
STAGEABLE > STAGE
STAGED > STAGE
STAGEFUL *n* amount that can appear on stage
STAGEFULS > STAGEFUL
STAGEHAND *n* person who moves props and scenery on a stage
STAGELIKE > STAGE
STAGER *n* person of experience
STAGERIES > STAGERY
STAGERS > STAGER
STAGERY *n* theatrical effects or techniques
STAGES > STAGE
STAGEY *same as* > STAGY
STAGGARD *n* male red deer in the fourth year of life
STAGGARDS > STAGGARD
STAGGART *same as* > STAGGARD
STAGGARTS > STAGGART
STAGGED > STAG
STAGGER *vb* walk unsteadily ▷ *n* staggering
STAGGERED > STAGGER
STAGGERER > STAGGER
STAGGERS *n* disease of horses and other domestic animals that causes staggering
STAGGERY > STAGGER
STAGGIE *n* little stag
STAGGIER > STAG
STAGGIES > STAGGIE
STAGGIEST > STAG
STAGGING > STAG

STAGGY > STAG
STAGHORN *as in staghorn fern* type of fern with fronds that resemble antlers
STAGHOUND *n* breed of hound similar in appearance to the foxhound but larger
STAGIER > STAGY
STAGIEST > STAGY
STAGILY > STAGY
STAGINESS > STAGY
STAGING *n* temporary support used in building
STAGINGS > STAGING
STAGNANCE > STAGNANT
STAGNANCY > STAGNANT
STAGNANT *adj* (of water or air) stale from not moving
STAGNATE *vb* be stagnant
STAGNATED > STAGNATE
STAGNATES > STAGNATE
STAGS > STAG
STAGY *adj* too theatrical or dramatic
STAID *adj* sedate, serious, and rather dull
STAIDER > STAID
STAIDEST > STAID
STAIDLY > STAID
STAIDNESS > STAID
STAIG *Scots variant of* > STAG
STAIGS > STAIG
STAIN *vb* discolour, mark ▷ *n* discoloration or mark
STAINABLE > STAIN
STAINED > STAIN
STAINER > STAIN
STAINERS > STAIN
STAINING > STAIN
STAININGS > STAIN
STAINLESS *adj* resistant to discoloration, esp discoloration resulting from corrosion ▷ *n* stainless steel
STAINS > STAIN
STAIR *n* one step in a flight of stairs
STAIRCASE *n* flight of stairs with a handrail or banisters ▷ *vb* buy other houses in same building
STAIRED *adj* having stairs
STAIRFOOT *n* place at foot of stairs
STAIRHEAD *n* top of a flight of stairs
STAIRLESS > STAIR
STAIRLIFT *n* wall-mounted lifting device to carry person up stairs
STAIRLIKE > STAIR
STAIRS *pl n* flight of steps between floors, usu indoors
STAIRSTEP *n* one of the steps in a staircase
STAIRWAY *n* staircase
STAIRWAYS > STAIRWAY
STAIRWELL *n* vertical shaft in a building that contains a staircase
STAIRWISE *adv* by steps
STAIRWORK *n* unseen plotting
STAITH *same as* > STAITHE

STAITHE n wharf
STAITHES > STAITHE
STAITHS > STAITH
STAKE n pointed stick or post driven into the ground as a support or marker ▷ vb support or mark out with stakes
STAKED > STAKE
STAKEOUT n police surveillance of an area or house ▷ vb keep an area or house under surveillance
STAKEOUTS > STAKEOUT
STAKES > STAKE
STAKING > STAKE
STALACTIC adj relating to the masses of calcium carbonate hanging from the roofs of limestone caves
STALAG n German prisoner-of-war camp in World War II
STALAGS > STALAG
STALE adj not fresh ▷ vb make or become stale ▷ n urine of horses or cattle
STALED > STALE
STALELY > STALE
STALEMATE n (in chess) position in which any of a player's moves would put his king in check, resulting in a draw ▷ vb subject to a stalemate
STALENESS > STALE
STALER > STALE
STALES > STALE
STALEST > STALE
STALING > STALE
STALK n plant's stem ▷ vb follow or approach stealthily
STALKED > STALK
STALKER > STALK
STALKERS > STALK
STALKIER > STALKY
STALKIEST > STALKY
STALKILY > STALKY
STALKING > STALK
STALKINGS > STALK
STALKLESS > STALK
STALKLIKE > STALK
STALKO n idle gentleman
STALKOES > STALKO
STALKS > STALK
STALKY adj like a stalk
STALL n small stand for the display and sale of goods ▷ vb stop (a motor vehicle or engine) or (of a motor vehicle or engine) stop accidentally
STALLAGE n rent paid for market stall
STALLAGES > STALLAGE
STALLED > STALL
STALLING > STALL
STALLINGS > STALL
STALLION n uncastrated male horse
STALLIONS > STALLION
STALLMAN n keeper of a stall
STALLMEN > STALLMAN
STALLS > STALL
STALWART adj strong and

sturdy ▷ n stalwart person
STALWARTS > STALWART
STALWORTH n stalwart person
STAMEN n pollen-producing part of a flower
STAMENED adj having stamen
STAMENS > STAMEN
STAMINA n enduring energy and strength
STAMINAL > STAMINA
STAMINAS > STAMINA
STAMINATE adj (of plants) having stamens, esp having stamens but no carpels
STAMINEAL adj having a stamen
STAMINODE n stamen that produces no pollen
STAMINODY n development of any of various plant organs into stamens
STAMINOID adj like a stamen
STAMMEL n coarse woollen cloth in former use for undergarments
STAMMELS > STAMMEL
STAMMER vb speak or say with involuntary pauses or repetition of syllables ▷ n tendency to stammer
STAMMERED > STAMMER
STAMMERER > STAMMER
STAMMERS > STAMMER
STAMNOI > STAMNOS
STAMNOS n ancient Greek jar
STAMP n piece of gummed paper stuck to an envelope or parcel to show that the postage has been paid ▷ vb bring (one's foot) down forcefully
STAMPED > STAMP
STAMPEDE n sudden rush of frightened animals or of a crowd ▷ vb (cause to) take part in a stampede
STAMPEDED > STAMPEDE
STAMPEDER > STAMPEDE
STAMPEDES > STAMPEDE
STAMPEDO same as > STAMPEDE
STAMPEDOS > STAMPEDO
STAMPER > STAMP
STAMPERS > STAMP
STAMPING > STAMP
STAMPINGS > STAMP
STAMPLESS > STAMP
STAMPS > STAMP
STANCE n attitude
STANCES > STANCE
STANCH vb stem the flow of (a liquid, esp blood) ▷ adj loyal and dependable
STANCHED > STANCH
STANCHEL same as > STANCHION
STANCHELS > STANCHEL
STANCHER > STANCH
STANCHERS > STANCH
STANCHES > STANCH
STANCHEST > STANCH
STANCHING > STANCH
STANCHION n upright bar

used as a support ▷ vb provide or support with a stanchion or stanchions
STANCHLY > STANCH
STANCK adj faint
STAND vb be in, rise to, or place in an upright position ▷ n stall for the sale of goods
STANDARD n level of quality ▷ adj usual, regular, or average
STANDARDS > STANDARD
STANDAWAY adj erect
STANDBY n person or thing that is ready for use
STANDBYS > STANDBY
STANDDOWN n return to normal after alert
STANDEE n person who stands, esp when there are no vacant seats
STANDEES > STANDEE
STANDEN > STAND
STANDER > STAND
STANDERS > STAND
STANDFAST n reliable person or thing
STANDGALE same as > STANIEL
STANDING > STAND
STANDINGS > STAND
STANDISH n stand, usually of metal, for pens, ink bottles, etc
STANDOFF n act or an instance of standing off or apart ▷ vb stay at a distance
STANDOFFS > STANDOFF
STANDOUT n distinctive or outstanding person or thing
STANDOUTS > STANDOUT
STANDOVER n threatening or intimidating act
STANDPAT n (in poker) refusal to change one's card
STANDPIPE n tap attached to a water main to provide a public water supply
STANDS > STAND
STANDUP n comedian who performs solo
STANDUPS > STANDUP
STANE Scot word for > STONE
STANED > STANE
STANES > STANE
STANG vb sting
STANGED > STANG
STANGING > STANG
STANGS > STANG
STANHOPE n light one-seater carriage with two or four wheels
STANHOPES > STANHOPE
STANIEL n kestrel
STANIELS > STANIEL
STANINE n scale of nine levels
STANINES > STANINE
STANING > STANE
STANK vb dam
STANKED > STINK
STANKING > STINK
STANKS > STINK
STANNARY n place or region

where tin is mined or worked
STANNATE n salt of stannic acid
STANNATES > STANNATE
STANNATOR n member of old Cornish parliament
STANNEL same as > STANIEL
STANNELS > STANNEL
STANNIC adj of or containing tin, esp in the tetravalent state
STANNITE n grey metallic mineral
STANNITES > STANNITE
STANNOUS adj of or containing tin, esp in the divalent state
STANNUM n tin (the metal)
STANNUMS > STANNUM
STANOL n drug taken to prevent heart disease
STANOLS > STANOL
STANYEL same as > STANIEL
STANYELS > STANYEL
STANZA n verse of a poem
STANZAED > STANZA
STANZAIC > STANZA
STANZAS > STANZA
STANZE same as > STANZA
STANZES > STANZE
STANZO same as > STANZA
STANZOES > STANZO
STANZOS > STANZO
STAP same as > STOP
STAPEDES > STAPES
STAPEDIAL > STAPES
STAPEDII > STAPEDIUS
STAPEDIUS n muscle in stapes
STAPELIA n fleshy cactus-like leafless African plant
STAPELIAS > STAPELIA
STAPES n stirrup-shaped bone that is the innermost of three small bones in the middle ear of mammals
STAPH n staphylococcus
STAPHS > STAPH
STAPLE n U-shaped piece of metal used to fasten papers or secure things ▷ vb fasten with staples ▷ adj of prime importance, principal
STAPLED > STAPLE
STAPLER n small device for fastening papers together
STAPLERS > STAPLER
STAPLES > STAPLE
STAPLING > STAPLE
STAPPED > STAP
STAPPING > STAP
STAPPLE same as > STOPPLE
STAPPLES > STAPPLE
STAPS > STAP
STAR n hot gaseous mass in space, visible in the night sky as a point of light ▷ vb feature or be featured as a star ▷ adj leading, famous
STARAGEN n tarragon
STARAGENS > STARAGEN
STARBOARD n right-hand side of a ship, when facing forward ▷ adj of or on this side ▷ vb turn or be turned

towards the starboard

STARBURST n pattern of rays or lines radiating from a light source

STARCH n carbohydrate forming the main food element in bread, potatoes, etc, and used mixed with water for stiffening fabric ▷ vb stiffen (fabric) with starch ▷ adj (of a person) formal

STARCHED > STARCH

STARCHER > STARCH

STARCHERS > STARCH

STARCHES > STARCH

STARCHIER > STARCHY

STARCHILY > STARCHY

STARCHING > STARCH

STARCHY adj containing starch

STARDOM n status of a star in the entertainment or sports world

STARDOMS > STARDOM

STARDRIFT n regular movement of stars

STARDUST n dusty material found between the stars

STARDUSTS > STARDUST

STARE vb look or gaze fixedly (at) ▷ n fixed gaze

STARED > STARE

STARER > STARE

STARERS > STARE

STARES > STARE

STARETS n Russian holy man

STARETSES > STARETS

STARETZ same as > STARETZ

STARETZES > STARETZ

STARFISH n star-shaped sea creature

STARFRUIT n tree with edible yellow fruit which is star-shaped on cross section

STARGAZE vb observe the stars

STARGAZED > STARGAZE

STARGAZER > STARGAZE

STARGAZES > STARGAZE

STARING > STARE

STARINGLY > STARE

STARINGS > STARE

STARK adj harsh, unpleasant, and plain ▷ adv completely ▷ vb stiffen

STARKED > STARK

STARKEN vb become or make stark

STARKENED > STARKEN

STARKENS > STARKEN

STARKER > STARK

STARKERS adj completely naked

STARKEST > STARK

STARKING > STARK

STARKLY > STARK

STARKNESS > STARK

STARKS > STARK

STARLESS > STAR

STARLET n young actress presented as a future star

STARLETS > STARLET

STARLIGHT n light that

comes from the stars ▷ adj of or like starlight

STARLIKE > STAR

STARLING n songbird with glossy black speckled feathers

STARLINGS > STARLING

STARLIT same as > STARLIGHT

STARN same as > STERN

STARNED > STARN

STARNIE n Scots word for little star

STARNIES > STARNIE

STARNING > STARN

STARNOSE n American mole with starlike nose

STARNOSES > STARNOSE

STARNS > STARN

STAROSTA n headman of Russian village

STAROSTAS > STAROSTA

STAROSTY n estate of Polish nobleman

STARR n (in Judaism) release from a debt

STARRED > STAR

STARRIER > STARRY

STARRIEST > STARRY

STARRILY > STARRY

STARRING > STAR

STARRINGS > STARE

STARRS > STARR

STARRY adj full of or like stars

STARS > STAR

STARSHINE n starlight

STARSHIP n spacecraft in science fiction

STARSHIPS > STARSHIP

STARSPOT n dark patch on surface of star

STARSPOTS > STARSPOT

STARSTONE n precious stone reflecting light in starlike pattern

START vb take the first step, begin ▷ n first part of something

STARTED > START

STARTER n first course of a meal

STARTERS > STARTER

STARTFUL adj tending to start

STARTING > START

STARTINGS > START

STARTISH same as > STARTFUL

STARTLE vb slightly surprise or frighten

STARTLED > STARTLE

STARTLER > STARTLE

STARTLERS > STARTLE

STARTLES > STARTLE

STARTLING adj causing surprise or fear

STARTLISH adj easily startled

STARTLY same as > STARTLISH

STARTS > START

STARTSY > STARETS

STARTUP n business enterprise that has been launched recently

STARTUPS > STARTUP

STARVE vb die or suffer or cause to die or suffer from hunger

STARVED > STARVE

STARVER > STARVE

STARVERS > STARVE

STARVES > STARVE

STARVING > STARVE

STARVINGS > STARVE

STARWORT n plant with star-shaped flowers

STARWORTS > STARWORT

STASES > STASIS

STASH vb store in a secret place ▷ n secret store

STASHED > STASH

STASHES > STASH

STASHIE same as > STUSHIE

STASHIES > STASHIE

STASHING > STASH

STASIDION n stall in Greek church

STASIMA > STASIMON

STASIMON n ode sung in Greek tragedy

STASIS n stagnation in the normal flow of bodily fluids, such as the blood or urine

STAT n statistic

STATABLE > STATE

STATAL adj of a federal state

STATANT adj (of an animal) in profile with all four feet on the ground

STATE n condition of a person or thing ▷ adj of or concerning the State ▷ vb express in words

STATEABLE > STATE

STATED adj (esp of a sum) determined by agreement

STATEDLY > STATED

STATEHOOD > STATE

STATELESS adj not belonging to any country

STATELET n small state

STATELETS > STATELET

STATELIER > STATELY

STATELILY > STATELY

STATELY adj dignified or grand ▷ adv in a stately manner

STATEMENT n something stated ▷ vb assess (a pupil) with regard to his or her special educational needs

STATER n any of various usually silver coins of ancient Greece

STATEROOM n private cabin on a ship

STATERS > STATER

STATES > STATE

STATESIDE adv of, in, to, or towards the US

STATESMAN n experienced and respected political leader

STATESMEN > STATESMAN

STATEWIDE adj throughout a state

STATIC adj stationary or inactive ▷ n crackling sound or speckled picture caused by interference in radio or television

reception

STATICAL > STATIC

STATICE n plant name formerly used for both thrift and sea lavender

STATICES > STATICE

STATICKY > STATIC

STATICS n branch of mechanics dealing with the forces producing a state of equilibrium

STATIM adv right away

STATIN n type of drug that lowers the levels of low-density lipoproteins in the blood

STATING > STATE

STATINS > STATIN

STATION n place where trains stop for passengers ▷ vb assign (someone) to a particular place

STATIONAL > STATION

STATIONED > STATION

STATIONER n dealer in stationery

STATIONS > STATION

STATISM n theory or practice of concentrating economic and political power in the state

STATISMS > STATISM

STATIST n advocate of statism ▷ adj of, characteristic of, advocating, or relating to statism

STATISTIC n numerical fact collected and classified systematically

STATISTS > STATIST

STATIVE adj denoting a verb describing a state rather than an activity, act, or event ▷ n stative verb

STATIVES > STATIVE

STATOCYST n organ of balance in some invertebrates

STATOLITH n any of the granules of calcium carbonate occurring in a statocyst

STATOR n stationary part of a rotary machine or device, esp of a motor or generator

STATORS > STATOR

STATS > STAT

STATUA same as > STATUE

STATUARY n statues collectively ▷ adj of, relating to, or suitable for statues

STATUAS > STATUA

STATUE n large sculpture of a human or animal figure

STATUED adj decorated with or portrayed in a statue or statues

STATUES > STATUE

STATUETTE n small statue

STATURE n person's height

STATURED adj having stature

STATURES > STATURE

STATUS n social position

STATUSES > STATUS

STATUSY *adj* conferring or having status

STATUTE *n* written law

STATUTES > STATUTE

STATUTORY *adj* required or authorized by law

STAUMREL *n* stupid person

STAUMRELS > STAUMREL

STAUN *Scot word for* > STAND

STAUNCH *same as* > STANCH

STAUNCHED > STAUNCH

STAUNCHER > STAUNCH

STAUNCHES > STAUNCH

STAUNCHLY > STAUNCH

STAUNING > STAUN

STAUNS > STAUN

STAVE *same as* > STAFF

STAVED > STAVE

STAVES > STAVE

STAVING > STAVE

STAVUDINE *n* drug used to treat HIV

STAW *Scots form of* > STALL

STAWED > STAW

STAWING > STAW

STAWS > STAW

STAY *vb* remain in a place or condition ▷ *n* period of staying in a place

STAYAWAY *n* strike in South Africa

STAYAWAYS > STAYAWAY

STAYED > STAY

STAYER *n* person or thing that stays

STAYERS > STAYER

STAYING > STAY

STAYLESS *adj* with no stays or support

STAYMAKER *n* corset maker

STAYNE *same as* > STAIN

STAYNED > STAYNE

STAYNES > STAYNE

STAYNING > STAYNE

STAYRE *same as* > STAIR

STAYRES > STAYRE

STAYS *pl n* old-fashioned corsets with bones in them

STAYSAIL *n* sail fastened on a stay

STAYSAILS > STAYSAIL

STEAD *n* place or function that should be taken by another ▷ *vb* help or benefit

STEADED > STEAD

STEADFAST *adj* firm, determined

STEADICAM *n* tradename for a mechanism for steadying a hand-held camera

STEADIED > STEADY

STEADIER > STEADY

STEADIERS > STEADY

STEADIES > STEADY

STEADIEST > STEADY

STEADILY > STEADY

STEADING *n* farmstead

STEADINGS > STEADING

STEADS > STEAD

STEADY *adj* not shaky or wavering ▷ *vb* make steady ▷ *adv* in a steady manner

STEADYING > STEADY

STEAK *n* thick slice of meat,

esp beef

STEAKS > STEAK

STEAL *vb* take unlawfully or without permission

STEALABLE > STEAL

STEALAGE *n* theft

STEALAGES > STEALAGE

STEALE *n* handle

STEALED > STEAL

STEALER *n* person who steals something

STEALERS > STEALER

STEALES > STEALE

STEALING > STEAL

STEALINGS > STEAL

STEALS > STEAL

STEALT > STEAL

STEALTH *n* moving carefully and quietly ▷ *adj* (of technology) able to render an aircraft almost invisible to radar ▷ *vb* approach undetected

STEALTHED > STEALTH

STEALTHS > STEALTH

STEALTHY *adj* characterized by great caution, secrecy, etc

STEAM *n* vapour into which water changes when boiled ▷ *vb* give off steam

STEAMBOAT *n* boat powered by a steam engine

STEAMED > STEAM

STEAMER *n* steam-propelled ship ▷ *vb* travel by steamer

STEAMERED > STEAMER

STEAMERS > STEAMER

STEAMIE *n* public wash house

STEAMIER > STEAMY

STEAMIES > STEAMIE

STEAMIEST > STEAMY

STEAMILY > STEAMY

STEAMING *adj* very hot ▷ *n* robbery, esp of passengers in a railway carriage or bus, by a large gang of armed youths

STEAMINGS > STEAMING

STEAMROLL *vb* crush (opposition) by overpowering force

STEAMS > STEAM

STEAMSHIP *n* ship powered by steam engines

STEAMY *adj* full of steam

STEAN *n* earthenware vessel

STEANE *same as* > STEEN

STEANED > STEANE

STEANES > STEANE

STEANING > STEANE

STEANINGS > STEANE

STEANS > STEAN

STEAPSIN *n* pancreatic lipase

STEAPSINS > STEAPSIN

STEAR *same as* > STEER

STEARAGE *same as* > STEERAGE

STEARAGES > STEARAGE

STEARATE *n* any salt or ester of stearic acid

STEARATES > STEARATE

STEARD > STEAR

STEARE *same as* > STEER

STEARED > STEARE

STEARES > STEARE

STEARIC *adj* of or relating to suet or fat

STEARIN *n* colourless crystalline ester of glycerol and stearic acid

STEARINE *same as* > STEARIN

STEARINES > STEARINE

STEARING > STEAR

STEARINS > STEARIN

STEARS > STEAR

STEARSMAN *same as* > STEERSMAN

STEARSMEN > STEARSMAN

STEATITE *same as* > SOAPSTONE

STEATITES > STEATITE

STEATITIC > STEATITE

STEATOMA *n* tumour of sebaceous gland

STEATOMAS > STEATOMA

STEATOSES > STEATOSIS

STEATOSIS *n* abnormal accumulation of fat

STED *same as* > STEAD

STEDD *same as* > STEAD

STEDDE *same as* > STEAD

STEDDED > STED

STEDDES > STEDDE

STEDDIED > STEDDY

STEDDIES > STEDDY

STEDDING > STED

STEDDS > STEDD

STEDDY *same as* > STEADY

STEDDYING > STEDDY

STEDE *same as* > STEAD

STEDED > STEDE

STEDES > STEDE

STEDFAST *same as* > STEADFAST

STEDING > STEDE

STEDS > STED

STEED *same as* > STEAD

STEEDED > STEED

STEEDIED > STEEDY

STEEDIES > STEEDY

STEEDING > STEED

STEEDLIKE > STEED

STEEDS > STEED

STEEDY *same as* > STEADY

STEEDYING > STEEDY

STEEK *vb* Scots word meaning shut

STEEKED > STEEK

STEEKING > STEEK

STEEKIT > STEEK

STEEKS > STEEK

STEEL *n* hard malleable alloy of iron and carbon ▷ *vb* prepare (oneself) for something unpleasant

STEELBOW *n* material lent to tenant by landlord

STEELBOWS > STEELBOW

STEELD > STEEL

STEELED > STEEL

STEELHEAD *n* silvery North Pacific variety of the rainbow trout

STEELIE *n* steel ball bearing used as marble

STEELIER > STEEL

STEELIES > STEELIE

STEELIEST > STEELIE

STEELING > STEEL

STEELINGS > STEEL

STEELMAN *n* person working in steel industry

STEELMEN > STEELMAN

STEELS *pl n* shares and bonds of steel companies

STEELWARE *n* things made of steel

STEELWORK *n* frame, foundation, building, or article made of steel

STEELY > STEEL

STEELYARD *n* portable balance consisting of a pivoted bar with two unequal arms

STEEM *variant of* > ESTEEM

STEEMED > STEEM

STEEMING > STEEM

STEEMS > STEEM

STEEN *vb* line with stone

STEENBOK *n* small antelope of central and southern Africa

STEENBOKS > STEENBOK

STEENBRAS *n* variety of sea bream

STEENBUCK *same as* > STEENBOK

STEENED > STEEN

STEENING > STEEN

STEENINGS > STEEN

STEENKIRK *n* type of cravat

STEENS > STEEN

STEEP *adj* sloping sharply ▷ *vb* soak or be soaked in liquid ▷ *n* instance or the process of steeping or the condition of being steeped

STEEPED > STEEP

STEEPEN *vb* become or cause (something) to become steep or steeper

STEEPENED > STEEPEN

STEEPENS > STEEPEN

STEEPER > STEEP

STEEPERS > STEEP

STEEPEST > STEEP

STEEPEUP *adj* very steep

STEEPIER > STEEPY

STEEPIEST > STEEPY

STEEPING > STEEP

STEEPISH > STEEP

STEEPLE *same as* > SPIRE

STEEPLED > STEEPLE

STEEPLES > STEEPLE

STEEPLY > STEEP

STEEPNESS > STEEP

STEEPS > STEEP

STEEPUP *adj* very steep

STEEPY *same as* > STEEP

STEER *vb* direct the course of (a vehicle or ship) ▷ *n* castrated male ox

STEERABLE > STEER

STEERAGE *n* cheapest accommodation on a passenger ship

STEERAGES > STEERAGE

STEERED > STEER

STEERER > STEER

STEERERS > STEER

STEERIES > STEERY

STEERING > STEER

STEERINGS > STEER

STEERLING *n* young steer

STEERS > STEER

STEERSMAN *n* person who

steers a vessel
STEERSMEN > STEERSMAN
STEERY n commotion
STEEVE n spar having a
pulley block at one end,
used for stowing cargo on
a ship ▷ vb stow (cargo)
securely in the hold of a
ship
STEEVED > STEEVE
STEEVELY > STEEVE
STEEVER > STEEVE
STEEVES > STEEVE
STEEVEST > STEEVE
STEEVING > STEEVE
STEEVINGS > STEEVE
STEGNOSES > STEGNOSIS
STEGNOSIS n constriction
of bodily pores
STEGNOTIC > STEGNOSIS
STEGODON n mammal of
Pliocene to Pleistocene
times, similar to the
mastodon
STEGODONS > STEGODON
STEGODONT same
as > STEGODON
STEGOMYIA former name
for > AEDES
STEGOSAUR n quadrupedal
herbivorous dinosaur
STEIL same as > STEAL
STEILS > STEIL
STEIN same as > STEEN
STEINBOCK another name
for > IBEX
STEINBOK same
as > STEENBOK
STEINBOKS > STEINBOK
STEINED > STEIN
STEINING > STEIN
STEININGS > STEIN
STEINKIRK same
as > STEENKIRK
STEINS > STEIN
STELA same as > STELE
STELAE > STELE
STELAI > STELE
STELAR > STELE
STELE n upright stone slab
or column decorated with
figures or inscriptions
STELENE > STELE
STELES > STELE
STELIC > STELE
STELL n shelter for cattle
or sheep built on moorland
or hillsides ▷ vb position
or place
STELLA n star or something
star-shaped
STELLAR adj of stars
STELLAS > STELLA
STELLATE adj resembling a
star in shape
STELLATED same
as > STELLATE
STELLED > STELL
STELLERID n starfish
STELLIFY vb change or be
changed into a star
STELLING > STELL
STELLION n Mediterranean
lizard
STELLIONS > STELLION
STELLITE n tradename
for any of various

alloys containing
cobalt, chromium,
carbon, tungsten, and
molybdenum
STELLITES > STELLITE
STELLS > STELL
STELLULAR adj displaying
or abounding in small stars
STEM vb stop (the flow of
something) ▷ n main axis
of a plant, which bears the
leaves, axillary buds, and
flowers
STEMBOK same
as > STEENBOK
STEMBOKS > STEMBOK
STEMBUCK same
as > STEENBOK
STEMBUCKS > STEMBUCK
STEME same as > STEAM
STEMED > STEME
STEMES > STEME
STEMHEAD n head of the
stem of a vessel
STEMHEADS > STEMHEAD
STEMING > STEME
STEMLESS > STEM
STEMLET n little stem
STEMLETS > STEMLET
STEMLIKE > STEM
STEMMA n family tree
STEMMAS > STEMMA
STEMMATA > STEMMA
STEMMATIC > STEMMA
STEMME archaic variant
of > STEM
STEMMED > STEM
STEMMER > STEM
STEMMERS > STEM
STEMMERY n tobacco
factory
STEMMES > STEMME
STEMMIER > STEMMY
STEMMIEST > STEMMY
STEMMING > STEM
STEMMINGS > STEM
STEMMY adj (of wine) young
and raw
STEMPEL n timber support
STEMPELS > STEMPEL
STEMPLE same as > STEMPEL
STEMPLES > STEMPLE
STEMS > STEM
STEMSON n curved timber
scarfed into or bolted to
the stem and keelson at the
bow of a wooden vessel
STEMSONS > STEMSON
STEMWARE n collective term
for glasses, goblets, etc,
with stems
STEMWARES > STEMWARE
STEN vb stride
STENCH n foul smell ▷ vb
cause to smell
STENCHED > STENCH
STENCHES > STENCH
STENCHFUL > STENCH
STENCHIER > STENCH
STENCHING > STENCH
STENCHY > STENCH
STENCIL n thin sheet with
cut-out pattern through
which ink or paint passes
to form the pattern on the
surface below ▷ vb make
(a pattern) with a stencil

STENCILED > STENCIL
STENCILER > STENCIL
STENCILS > STENCIL
STEND vb Scots word
meaning bound
STENDED > STEND
STENDING > STEND
STENDS > STEND
STENGAH same as > STINGER
STENGAHS > STENGAH
STENLOCK n fish of northern
seas
STENLOCKS > STENLOCK
STENNED > STEN
STENNING > STEN
STENO n stenographer
STENOBATH n stenobathic
organism
STENOKIES > STENOKY
STENOKOUS adj able to
live in narrow range of
environments
STENOKY n life and survival
that is dependent on
conditions remaining
within a narrow range of
variables
STENOPAIC adj having
narrow opening
STENOS > STENO
STENOSED adj abnormally
contracted
STENOSES > STENOSIS
STENOSIS n abnormal
narrowing of a bodily canal
or passage
STENOTIC > STENOSIS
STENOTYPE n machine with
a keyboard for recording
speeches in a phonetic
shorthand
STENOTYPY n form of
shorthand in which
alphabetic combinations
are used to represent
groups of sounds or short
common words
STENS > STEN
STENT n surgical implant
used to keep an artery
open ▷ vb assess
STENTED > STENT
STENTING > STENT
STENTOR n person with an
unusually loud voice
STENTORS > STENTOR
STENTOUR n tax assessor
STENTOURS > STENTOUR
STENTS > STENT
STEP vb move and set down
the foot, as when walking
▷ n stepping
STEPBAIRN Scots word
for > STEPCHILD
STEPCHILD n stepson or
stepdaughter
STEPDAME n woman
married to one's father
STEPDAMES > STEPDAME
STEPHANE n ancient Greek
headdress
STEPHANES > STEPHANE
STEPLIKE > STEP
STEPNEY n spare wheel
STEPNEYS > STEPNEY
STEPPE n extensive grassy
plain usually without trees

STEPPED > STEP
STEPPER n person who or
animal that steps, esp a
horse or a dancer
STEPPERS > STEPPER
STEPPES > STEPPE
STEPPING > STEP
STEPS > STEP
STEPSON n son of one's
husband or wife by an
earlier relationship
STEPSONS > STEPSON
STEPSTOOL n stool able to
be used as step
STEPT > STEP
STEPWISE adj arranged
in the manner of or
resembling steps
▷ adv with the form or
appearance of steps
STERADIAN n SI unit of solid
angle
STERCORAL adj relating to
excrement
STERCULIA n dietary fibre
used as a food stabilizer
and denture adhesive
STERE n unit used to
measure volumes of
stacked timber
STEREO n stereophonic
record player ▷ adj (of
a sound system) using
two or more separate
microphones to feed two
or more loudspeakers
through separate channels
▷ vb make stereophonic
STEREOED > STEREO
STEREOING > STEREO
STEREOME n tissue of a plant
that provides mechanical
support
STEREOMES > STEREOME
STEREOS > STEREO
STERES > STERE
STERIC adj of or caused by
the spatial arrangement of
atoms in a molecule
STERICAL same as > STERIC
STERIGMA n minute stalk
bearing a spore or chain of
spores in certain fungi
STERIGMAS > STERIGMA
STERILANT n any
substance or agent used in
sterilization
STERILE adj free from
germs
STERILELY > STERILE
STERILISE same
as > STERILIZE
STERILITY > STERILE
STERILIZE vb make sterile
STERLET n small sturgeon
of seas and rivers in N Asia
and E Europe
STERLETS > STERLET
STERLING n British money
system ▷ adj genuine and
reliable
STERLINGS > STERLING
STERN adj severe, strict ▷ n
rear part of a ship ▷ vb row
boat backward
STERNA > STERNUM
STERNAGE n sterns

STERNAGES > STERNAGE

STERNAL > STERNUM

STERNEBRA n part of breastbone

STERNED > STERN

STERNER > STERN

STERNEST > STERN

STERNFAST n rope for securing boat at stern

STERNING > STERN

STERNITE n part of arthropod

STERNITES > STERNITE

STERNITIC > STERNITE

STERNLY > STERN

STERNMOST adj farthest to the stern

STERNNESS > STERN

STERNPORT n opening in stern of ship

STERNPOST n main upright timber or structure at the stern of a vessel

STERNS > STERN

STERNSON n timber scarfed into or bolted to the sternpost and keelson at the stern of a wooden vessel

STERNSONS > STERNSON

STERNUM n long flat bone in the front of the body, to which the collarbone and most of the ribs are attached

STERNUMS > STERNUM

STERNWARD adv towards the stern

STERNWAY n movement of a vessel sternforemost

STERNWAYS > STERNWAY

STEROID n organic compound containing a carbon ring system, such as many hormones

STEROIDAL > STEROID

STEROIDS > STEROID

STEROL n natural insoluble alcohol such as cholesterol and ergosterol

STEROLS > STEROL

STERTOR n laborious or noisy breathing caused by obstructed air passages

STERTORS > STERTOR

STERVE same as > STARVE

STERVED > STERVE

STERVES > STERVE

STERVING > STERVE

STET interj instruction to ignore an alteration previously made by a proofreader ▷ vb indicate to a printer that certain deleted matter is to be kept ▷ n word or mark indicating that certain deleted written matter is to be retained

STETS > STET

STETSON n cowboy hat

STETSONS > STETSON

STETTED > STET

STETTING > STET

STEVEDORE n person who loads and unloads ships ▷ vb load or unload (a ship, ship's cargo, etc)

STEVEN n voice

STEVENS > STEVEN

STEW n food cooked slowly in a closed pot ▷ vb cook slowly in a closed pot

STEWABLE > STEW

STEWARD n person who looks after passengers on a ship or aircraft ▷ vb act as a steward (of)

STEWARDED > STEWARD

STEWARDRY n office of steward

STEWARDS > STEWARD

STEWARTRY variant of > STEWARDRY

STEWBUM n drunkard

STEWBUMS > STEWBUM

STEWED adj (of food) cooked by stewing

STEWER > STEW

STEWERS > STEW

STEWIER > STEW

STEWIEST > STEW

STEWING > STEW

STEWINGS > STEW

STEWPAN n pan used for making stew

STEWPANS > STEWPAN

STEWPOND n fishpond

STEWPONDS > STEWPOND

STEWPOT n pot used for making stew

STEWPOTS > STEWPOT

STEWS > STEW

STEWY > STEW

STEY adj Scots word meaning steep

STEYER > STEY

STEYEST > STEY

STHENIA n abnormal strength

STHENIAS > STHENIA

STHENIC adj abounding in energy or bodily strength

STIBBLE Scots form of > STUBBLE

STIBBLER n horse allowed to eat stubble

STIBBLERS > STIBBLE

STIBBLES > STIBBLE

STIBIAL > STIBIUM

STIBINE n colourless slightly soluble poisonous gas

STIBINES > STIBINE

STIBIUM obsolete name for > ANTIMONY

STIBIUMS > STIBIUM

STIBNITE n soft greyish mineral

STIBNITES > STIBNITE

STICCADO n type of xylophone

STICCADOS > STICCADO

STICCATO same as > STICCADO

STICCATOS > STICCATO

STICH n line of poetry

STICHARIA pl n priest's robes of the Greek Church

STICHERA > STICHERON

STICHERON n short hymn in Greek Church

STICHIC > STICH

STICHIDIA pl n seaweed branches

STICHOI > STICHOS

STICHOS n line of poem

STICHS > STICH

STICK n long thin piece of wood ▷ vb push (a pointed object) into (something)

STICKABLE > STICK

STICKBALL n form of baseball played in street

STICKED > STICK

STICKER n adhesive label or sign ▷ vb put stickers on

STICKERED > STICKER

STICKERS > STICKER

STICKFUL > STICK

STICKFULS > STICK

STICKIED > STICKY

STICKIER > STICKY

STICKIES > STICKY

STICKIEST > STICKY

STICKILY > STICKY

STICKING > STICK

STICKINGS > STICK

STICKIT Scots form of > STUCK

STICKJAW n stodgy food

STICKJAWS > STICKJAW

STICKLE vb dispute stubbornly, esp about minor points

STICKLED > STICKLE

STICKLER n person who insists on something

STICKLERS > STICKLER

STICKLES > STICKLE

STICKLIKE > STICK

STICKLING > STICKLE

STICKMAN n human figure drawn in thin strokes

STICKMEN > STICKMAN

STICKOUT n conspicuous person or thing

STICKOUTS > STICKOUT

STICKPIN n tiepin

STICKPINS > STICKPIN

STICKS > STICK

STICKSEED n type of Eurasian and North American plant

STICKUM n adhesive

STICKUMS > STICKUM

STICKUP n robbery at gun-point

STICKUPS > STICKUP

STICKWEED n any of several plants that have clinging fruits or seeds, esp the ragweed

STICKWORK n use of stick in hockey

STICKY adj covered with an adhesive substance ▷ vb make sticky ▷ n inquisitive look or stare

STICKYING > STICKY

STICTION n frictional force to be overcome to set one object in motion when it is in contact with another

STICTIONS > STICTION

STIDDIE same as > STITHY

STIDDIED > STIDDIE

STIDDIES > STIDDIE

STIE same as > STY

STIED > STY

STIES > STY

STIEVE same as > STEEVE

STIEVELY > STIEVE

STIEVER > STIEVE

STIEVEST > STIEVE

STIFF adj not easily bent or moved ▷ n corpse ▷ adv completely or utterly ▷ vb fail completely

STIFFED > STIFF

STIFFEN vb make or become stiff

STIFFENED > STIFFEN

STIFFENER > STIFFEN

STIFFENS > STIFFEN

STIFFER > STIFF

STIFFEST > STIFF

STIFFIE n erection of the penis

STIFFIES > STIFFIE

STIFFING > STIFF

STIFFISH > STIFF

STIFFLY > STIFF

STIFFNESS > STIFF

STIFFS > STIFF

STIFFWARE n computer software that is hard to modify

STIFFY n erection of the penis

STIFLE vb suppress ▷ n joint in the hind leg of a horse, dog, etc, between the femur and tibia

STIFLED > STIFLE

STIFLER > STIFLE

STIFLERS > STIFLE

STIFLES > STIFLE

STIFLING adj uncomfortably hot and stuffy

STIFLINGS > STIFLING

STIGMA n mark of social disgrace

STIGMAL adj of part of insect wing

STIGMAS > STIGMA

STIGMATA > STIGMA

STIGMATIC adj relating to or having a stigma or stigmata ▷ n person marked with the stigmata

STIGME n dot in Greek punctuation

STIGMES > STIGME

STILB n unit of luminance equal to 1 candela per square centimetre.

STILBENE n colourless or slightly yellow crystalline hydrocarbon used in the manufacture of dyes

STILBENES > STILBENE

STILBITE n white or yellow zeolite mineral

STILBITES > STILBITE

STILBS > STILB

STILE same as > STYLE

STILED > STILE

STILES > STILE

STILET same as > STYLET

STILETS > STILET

STILETTO n high narrow heel on a woman's shoe ▷ vb stab with a stiletto

STILETTOS > STILETTO

STILING > STILE

STILL adv now or in the

future as before ▷ *adj* motionless ▷ *n* calmness; apparatus for distillation ▷ *vb* make still
STILLAGE *n* frame or stand for keeping things off the ground, such as casks in a brewery
STILLAGES > STILLAGE
STILLBORN *adj* born dead ▷ *n* stillborn fetus or baby
STILLED > STILL
STILLER > STILL
STILLERS > STILL
STILLEST > STILL
STILLIER > STILLY
STILLIEST > STILLY
STILLING > STILL
STILLINGS > STILL
STILLION *n* stand for cask
STILLIONS > STILLION
STILLMAN *n* someone involved in the operation of a still
STILLMEN > STILLMAN
STILLNESS > STILL
STILLROOM *n* room in which distilling is carried out
STILLS > STILL
STILLY *adv* quietly or calmly ▷ *adj* still, quiet, or calm
STILT *n* either of a pair of long poles with footrests for walking raised from the ground ▷ *vb* raise or place on or as if on stilts
STILTBIRD *n* long-legged wading bird
STILTED *adj* stiff and formal in manner
STILTEDLY > STILTED
STILTER > STILT
STILTERS > STILT
STILTIER > STILT
STILTIEST > STILT
STILTING > STILT
STILTINGS > STILT
STILTISH > STILT
STILTS > STILT
STILTY > STILT
STIM *n* very small amount
STIME *same as* > STYME
STIMED > STIME
STIMES > STIME
STIMIE *same as* > STYMIE
STIMIED > STIMIE
STIMIES > STIMIE
STIMING > STIME
STIMS > STIM
STIMULANT *n* something, such as a drug, that acts as a stimulus ▷ *adj* stimulating
STIMULATE *vb* act as a stimulus (on)
STIMULI > STIMULUS
STIMULUS *n* something that rouses a person or thing to activity
STIMY *same as* > STYMIE
STIMYING > STIMY
STING *vb* (of certain animals or plants) wound by injecting with poison ▷ *n* wound or pain caused by or as if by stinging

STINGAREE *popular name for* > STINGRAY
STINGBULL *n* spiny fish
STINGED > STING
STINGER *n* person, plant, animal, etc, that stings or hurts
STINGERS > STINGER
STINGFISH *same as* > STINGBULL
STINGIER > STINGY
STINGIES > STINGY
STINGIEST > STINGY
STINGILY > STINGY
STINGING > STING
STINGINGS > STING
STINGLESS > STING
STINGO *n* strong alcohol
STINGOS > STINGO
STINGRAY *n* flatfish capable of inflicting painful wounds
STINGRAYS > STINGRAY
STINGS > STING
STINGY *adj* mean or miserly ▷ *n* stinging nettle
STINK *n* strong unpleasant smell ▷ *vb* give off a strong unpleasant smell
STINKARD *n* smelly person
STINKARDS > STINKARD
STINKBUG *n* type of insect that releases an unpleasant odour
STINKBUGS > STINKBUG
STINKER *n* difficult or unpleasant person or thing
STINKEROO *n* bad or contemptible person or thing
STINKERS > STINKER
STINKHORN *n* type of fungus with an offensive odour
STINKIER > STINKY
STINKIEST > STINKY
STINKING > STINK
STINKINGS > STINK
STINKO *adj* drunk
STINKPOT *n* person or thing that stinks
STINKPOTS > STINKPOT
STINKS > STINK
STINKWEED *n* plant that has a disagreeable smell when bruised
STINKWOOD *n* any of various trees having offensive-smelling wood
STINKY *adj* having a foul smell
STINT *vb* be miserly with (something) ▷ *n* allotted amount of work
STINTED > STINT
STINTEDLY > STINT
STINTER > STINT
STINTERS > STINT
STINTIER > STINT
STINTIEST > STINT
STINTING > STINT
STINTINGS > STINT
STINTLESS > STINT
STINTS > STINT
STINTY > STINT
STIPA *n* variety of grass
STIPAS > STIPA
STIPE *n* stalk in plants that bears reproductive

structures
STIPED *same as* > STIPITATE
STIPEL *n* small paired leaflike structure at the base of certain leaflets
STIPELS > STIPEL
STIPEND *n* regular allowance or salary, esp that paid to a clergyman
STIPENDS > STIPEND
STIPES *n* second maxillary segment in insects and crustaceans
STIPIFORM > STIPES
STIPITATE *adj* possessing or borne on the end of a stipe
STIPITES > STIPES
STIPPLE *vb* paint, draw, or engrave using dots ▷ *n* technique of stippling or a picture produced by or using stippling
STIPPLED > STIPPLE
STIPPLER > STIPPLE
STIPPLERS > STIPPLE
STIPPLES > STIPPLE
STIPPLING > STIPPLE
STIPULAR > STIPULE
STIPULARY > STIPULE
STIPULATE *vb* specify as a condition of an agreement ▷ *adj* (of a plant) having stipules
STIPULE *n* small paired usually leaflike outgrowth occurring at the base of a leaf or its stalk
STIPULED > STIPULE
STIPULES > STIPULE
STIR *vb* mix up (a liquid) by moving a spoon etc around in it ▷ *n* stirring
STIRABOUT *n* kind of porridge orginally made in Ireland
STIRE *same as* > STEER
STIRED > STIRE
STIRES > STIRE
STIRING > STIRE
STIRK *n* heifer of 6 to 12 months old
STIRKS > STIRK
STIRLESS > STIR
STIRP *same as* > STIRPS
STIRPES > STIRPS
STIRPS *n* line of descendants from an ancestor
STIRRA *same as* > SIRRA
STIRRABLE > STIR
STIRRAH *same as* > SIRRAH
STIRRAHS > STIRRAH
STIRRAS > STIRRA
STIRRE *same as* > STEER
STIRRED > STIR
STIRRER *n* person who deliberately causes trouble
STIRRERS > STIRRER
STIRRES > STIRRE
STIRRING > STIR
STIRRINGS > STIR
STIRRUP *n* metal loop attached to a saddle for supporting a rider's foot
STIRRUPS > STIRRUP
STIRS > STIR

STISHIE *same as* > STUSHIE
STISHIES > STISHIE
STITCH *n* link made by drawing thread through material with a needle ▷ *vb* sew
STITCHED > STITCH
STITCHER > STITCH
STITCHERS > STITCH
STITCHERY *n* needlework, esp modern embroidery
STITCHES > STITCH
STITCHING > STITCH
STITHIED > STITHY
STITHIES > STITHY
STITHY *n* forge or anvil ▷ *vb* forge on an anvil
STITHYING > STITHY
STIVE *vb* stifle
STIVED > STIVE
STIVER *n* former Dutch coin worth one twentieth of a guilder
STIVERS > STIVER
STIVES > STIVE
STIVIER > STIVY
STIVIEST > STIVY
STIVING > STIVE
STIVY *adj* stuffy
STOA *n* covered walk that has a colonnade on one or both sides, esp as used in ancient Greece
STOAE > STOA
STOAI > STOA
STOAS > STOA
STOAT *n* small mammal of the weasel family, with brown fur that turns white in winter
STOATS > STOAT
STOB *same as* > STAB
STOBBED > STOB
STOBBING > STOB
STOBS > STOB
STOCCADO *n* fencing thrust
STOCCADOS > STOCCADO
STOCCATA *same as* > STOCCADO
STOCCATAS > STOCCATA
STOCIOUS *same as* > STOTIOUS
STOCK *n* total amount of goods available for sale in a shop ▷ *adj* kept in stock, standard ▷ *vb* keep for sale or future use
STOCKADE *n* enclosure or barrier made of stakes ▷ *vb* surround with a stockade
STOCKADED > STOCKADE
STOCKADES > STOCKADE
STOCKAGE *n* livestock put to graze on crops
STOCKAGES > STOCKAGE
STOCKCAR *n* car that has been strengthened for a form of racing in which the cars often collide
STOCKCARS > STOCKCAR
STOCKED > STOCK
STOCKER > STOCK
STOCKERS > STOCK
STOCKFISH *n* fish, such as cod or haddock, cured by splitting and drying in the air

STOCKHORN n instrument made from animal horn
STOCKIER > STOCKY
STOCKIEST > STOCKY
STOCKILY > STOCKY
STOCKINET n machine-knitted elastic fabric
STOCKING n close-fitting covering for the foot and leg
STOCKINGS > STOCKING
STOCKISH adj stupid or dull
STOCKIST n dealer who stocks a particular product
STOCKISTS > STOCKIST
STOCKLESS > STOCK
STOCKLIST n list of items in stock
STOCKLOCK n lock that is enclosed in a wooden case
STOCKMAN n man engaged in the rearing or care of farm livestock, esp cattle
STOCKMEN > STOCKMAN
STOCKPILE vb store a large quantity of (something) for future use ▷ n accumulated store
STOCKPOT n pot in which stock for soup is made
STOCKPOTS > STOCKPOT
STOCKROOM n room in which a stock of goods is kept in a shop or factory
STOCKS pl n instrument of punishment consisting of a heavy wooden frame with holes in which the feet, hands, or head of an offender were locked
STOCKTAKE vb take stock
STOCKTOOK > STOCKTAKE
STOCKWORK n group of veins in mine
STOCKY adj (of a person) broad and sturdy
STOCKYARD n yard where farm animals are sold
STODGE n heavy starchy food ▷ vb stuff (oneself or another) with food
STODGED > STODGE
STODGER n dull person
STODGERS > STODGER
STODGES > STODGE
STODGIER > STODGY
STODGIEST > STODGY
STODGILY > STODGY
STODGING > STODGE
STODGY adj (of food) heavy and starchy
STOEP n verandah
STOEPS > STOEP
STOGEY same as > STOGY
STOGEYS > STOGEY
STOGIE same as > STOGY
STOGIES > STOGY
STOGY n any long cylindrical inexpensive cigar
STOIC n person who suffers hardship without showing his or her feelings ▷ adj suffering hardship without showing one's feelings
STOICAL adj suffering great difficulties without showing one's feelings

STOICALLY > STOICAL
STOICISM n indifference to pleasure and pain
STOICISMS > STOICISM
STOICS > STOIC
STOIT vb bounce
STOITED > STOIT
STOITER vb stagger
STOITERED > STOITER
STOITERS > STOITER
STOITING > STOIT
STOITS > STOIT
STOKE vb feed and tend (a fire or furnace)
STOKED adj very pleased
STOKEHOLD n hold for a ship's boilers
STOKEHOLE n hole in a furnace through which it is stoked
STOKER n person employed to tend a furnace on a ship or train powered by steam
STOKERS > STOKER
STOKES n cgs unit of kinematic viscosity
STOKESIA n American flowering plant
STOKESIAS > STOKESIA
STOKING > STOKE
STOKVEL n (in S Africa) informal savings pool or syndicate
STOKVELS > STOKVEL
STOLE n long scarf or shawl
STOLED adj wearing a stole
STOLEN > STEAL
STOLES > STOLE
STOLID adj showing little emotion or interest
STOLIDER > STOLID
STOLIDEST > STOLID
STOLIDITY > STOLID
STOLIDLY > STOLID
STOLLEN n rich sweet bread containing nuts, raisins, etc
STOLLENS > STOLLEN
STOLN > STEAL
STOLON n long horizontal stem that grows along the surface of the soil and propagates by producing roots and shoots at the nodes or tip
STOLONATE adj having a stolon
STOLONIC > STOLON
STOLONS > STOLON
STOLPORT n airport for short take-off aircraft
STOLPORTS > STOLPORT
STOMA n pore in a plant leaf that controls the passage of gases into and out of the plant
STOMACH n organ in the body which digests food ▷ vb put up with
STOMACHAL > STOMACH
STOMACHED > STOMACH
STOMACHER n decorative V-shaped panel of stiff material worn over the chest and stomach
STOMACHIC adj stimulating gastric activity ▷ n

stomachic medicine
STOMACHS > STOMACH
STOMACHY adj having a large belly
STOMACK as in have a stomack (in E Africa) be pregnant
STOMACKS > STOMACK
STOMAL > STOMA
STOMAS > STOMA
STOMATA > STOMA
STOMATAL adj of, relating to, or possessing stomata or a stoma
STOMATE n opening on leaf through which water evaporates
STOMATES > STOMATE
STOMATIC adj of or relating to a mouth or mouthlike part
STOMATOUS same as > STOMATAL
STOMIA > STOMIUM
STOMIUM n part of the sporangium of ferns that ruptures to release the spores
STOMIUMS > STOMIUM
STOMODAEA > STOMODEUM
STOMODEA > STOMODEUM
STOMODEAL > STOMODEUM
STOMODEUM n oral cavity of a vertebrate embryo
STOMP vb tread heavily ▷ n rhythmic stamping jazz dance
STOMPED > STOMP
STOMPER n rock or jazz song with a particularly strong and danceable beat
STOMPERS > STOMPER
STOMPIE n cigarette butt
STOMPIES > STOMPIE
STOMPING > STOMP
STOMPS > STOMP
STONABLE > STONE
STOND same as > STAND
STONDS > STOND
STONE n material of which rocks are made ▷ vb throw stones at
STONEABLE > STONE
STONEBOAT n type of sleigh used for moving rocks from fields
STONECAST n short distance
STONECHAT n songbird that has black feathers and a reddish-brown breast
STONECROP n type of plant with fleshy leaves and red, yellow, or white flowers
STONED adj under the influence of alcohol or drugs
STONEFISH n venomous tropical marine scorpaenid fish
STONEFLY n any insect of the order Plecoptera, in which the larvae are aquatic
STONEHAND n type of compositor
STONELESS > STONE

STONELIKE > STONE
STONEN adj of stone
STONER n device for removing stones from fruit
STONERAG n type of lichen
STONERAGS > STONERAG
STONERAW same as > STONERAG
STONERAWS > STONERAW
STONERN same as > STONEN
STONERS > STONER
STONES > STONE
STONESHOT n stone's throw
STONEWALL vb obstruct or hinder discussion
STONEWARE n hard kind of pottery fired at a very high temperature ▷ adj made of stoneware
STONEWASH vb wash with stones to give worn appearance
STONEWORK n part of a building made of stone
STONEWORT n any of various green algae which grow in brackish or fresh water
STONEY same as > STONY
STONG > STING
STONIED > STONY
STONIER > STONY
STONIES > STONY
STONIEST > STONY
STONILY > STONY
STONINESS > STONY
STONING > STONE
STONINGS > STONE
STONISH same as > ASTONISH
STONISHED > STONISH
STONISHES > STONISH
STONK vb bombard (soldiers, buildings, etc) with artillery ▷ n concentrated bombardment by artillery
STONKED > STONK
STONKER vb destroy
STONKERED adj completely exhausted or beaten
STONKERS > STONKER
STONKING > STONK
STONKS > STONK
STONN same as > STUN
STONNE same as > STUN
STONNED > STONNE
STONNES > STONNE
STONNING > STONN
STONNS > STONN
STONY adj of or like stone ▷ vb astonish
STONYING > STONY
STOOD > STAND
STOODEN > STAND
STOOGE n actor who feeds lines to a comedian or acts as the butt of his jokes ▷ vb act as a stooge
STOOGED > STOOGE
STOOGES > STOOGE
STOOGING > STOOGE
STOOK n number of sheaves set upright in a field to dry with their heads together ▷ vb set up (sheaves) in stooks
STOOKED > STOOK

S

STOOKER > STOOK
STOOKERS > STOOK
STOOKIE n stucco
STOOKIES > STOOKIE
STOOKING > STOOK
STOOKS > STOOK
STOOL n chair without arms or back ▷ vb (of a plant) send up shoots from the base of the stem
STOOLBALL n game resembling cricket played by girls
STOOLED > STOOL
STOOLIE n police informer
STOOLIES > STOOLIE
STOOLING > STOOL
STOOLS > STOOL
STOOP vb bend forward and downward
STOOPBALL n American street game
STOOPE same as > STOUP
STOOPED > STOOP
STOOPER > STOOP
STOOPERS > STOOP
STOOPES > STOOPE
STOOPING > STOOP
STOOPS > STOOP
STOOR same as > STOUR
STOORS > STOOR
STOOSHIE same as > STUSHIE
STOOSHIES > STOOSHIE
STOP vb cease or cause to cease from doing (something) ▷ n stopping or being stopped
STOPBANK n embankment to prevent flooding
STOPBANKS > STOPBANK
STOPCOCK n valve to control or stop the flow of fluid in a pipe
STOPCOCKS > STOPCOCK
STOPE n steplike excavation made in a mine to extract ore ▷ vb mine (ore, etc) by cutting stopes
STOPED > STOPE
STOPER n drill used in mining
STOPERS > STOPER
STOPES > STOPE
STOPGAP n temporary substitute
STOPGAPS > STOPGAP
STOPING n process by which country rock is broken up and engulfed by the upward movement of magma
STOPINGS > STOPING
STOPLESS > STOP
STOPLIGHT n red light on a traffic signal indicating that vehicles coming towards it should stop
STOPOFF n break in a journey
STOPOFFS > STOPOFF
STOPOVER n short break in a journey ▷ vb make a stopover
STOPOVERS > STOPOVER
STOPPABLE > STOP
STOPPAGE n act of stopping

something or the state of being stopped
STOPPAGES > STOPPAGE
STOPPED > STOP
STOPPER n plug for closing a bottle etc ▷ vb close or fit with a stopper
STOPPERED > STOPPER
STOPPERS > STOPPER
STOPPING > STOP
STOPPINGS > STOP
STOPPLE same as > STOPPER
STOPPLED > STOPPLE
STOPPLES > STOPPLE
STOPPLING > STOPPLE
STOPS > STOP
STOPT > STOP
STOPWATCH n watch which can be stopped instantly for exact timing of a sporting event
STOPWORD n common word not used in computer search engines
STOPWORDS > STOPWORD
STORABLE > STORE
STORABLES > STORE
STORAGE n storing
STORAGES > STORAGE
STORAX n type of tree or shrub with drooping showy white flowers
STORAXES > STORAX
STORE vb collect and keep (things) for future use ▷ n shop
STORED > STORE
STOREMAN n man looking after storeroom
STOREMEN > STOREMAN
STORER > STORE
STOREROOM n room in which things are stored
STORERS > STORE
STORES pl n supply or stock of food and other essentials for a journey
STORESHIP n ship carrying naval stores
STOREWIDE adj throughout stores
STOREY n floor or level of a building
STOREYED adj having a storey or storeys
STOREYS > STOREY
STORGE n affection
STORGES > STORGE
STORIATED adj decorated with flowers or animals
STORIED > STORY
STORIES > STORY
STORIETTE n short story
STORING > STORE
STORK n large wading bird
STORKS > STORK
STORM n violent weather with wind, rain, or snow ▷ vb attack or capture (a place) suddenly
STORMBIRD n petrel
STORMED > STORM
STORMER n outstanding example of its kind
STORMERS > STORMER
STORMFUL > STORM
STORMIER > STORMY

STORMIEST > STORMY
STORMILY > STORMY
STORMING adj characterized by or displaying dynamism, speed, and energy
STORMINGS > STORM
STORMLESS > STORM
STORMLIKE > STORM
STORMS > STORM
STORMY adj characterized by storms
STORNELLI > STORNELLO
STORNELLO n type of Italian poem
STORY n narration of a chain of events ▷ vb decorate with scenes from history
STORYBOOK n book containing stories for children ▷ adj better or happier than in real life
STORYETTE n short story
STORYING > STORY
STORYINGS > STORY
STORYLINE n plot of a book, film, play, etc
STOSS adj (of the side of a hill) facing the onward flow of a glacier ▷ n hillside facing glacier flow
STOSSES > STOSS
STOT n bullock ▷ vb bounce or cause to bounce
STOTIN n monetary unit of Slovenia, worth one hundredth of a tolar
STOTINKA n monetary unit of Bulgaria, worth one hundredth of a lev
STOTINKI > STOTINKA
STOTINOV > STOTIN
STOTINS > STOTIN
STOTIOUS adj drunk
STOTS > STOT
STOTT same as > STOT
STOTTED > STOT
STOTTER same as > STOT
STOTTERED > STOTTER
STOTTERS > STOTTER
STOTTIE n wedge of bread cut from a flat round loaf that has been split and filled with meat, cheese, etc
STOTTIES > STOTTIE
STOTTING > STOT
STOTTS > STOTT
STOUN same as > STUN
STOUND n short while ▷ vb ache
STOUNDED > STOUND
STOUNDING > STOUND
STOUNDS > STOUND
STOUNING > STOUN
STOUNS > STOUN
STOUP n small basin for holy water
STOUPS > STOUP
STOUR n turmoil or conflict
STOURE same as > STOUR
STOURES > STOURE
STOURIE same as > STOURY
STOURIER > STOURY
STOURIEST > STOURY
STOURS > STOUR
STOURY adj dusty
STOUSH vb hit or punch

(someone) ▷ n fighting or violence
STOUSHED > STOUSH
STOUSHES > STOUSH
STOUSHIE same as > STUSHIE
STOUSHIES > STOUSHIE
STOUSHING > STOUSH
STOUT adj fat ▷ n strong dark beer
STOUTEN vb make or become stout
STOUTENED > STOUTEN
STOUTENS > STOUTEN
STOUTER > STOUT
STOUTEST > STOUT
STOUTH n Scots word meaning theft
STOUTHS > STOUTH
STOUTISH > STOUT
STOUTLY > STOUT
STOUTNESS > STOUT
STOUTS > STOUT
STOVAINE n anaesthetic drug
STOVAINES > STOVAINE
STOVE n apparatus for cooking or heating ▷ vb process (ceramics, metalwork, etc) by heating in a stove
STOVED > STOVE
STOVEPIPE n pipe that takes fumes and smoke away from a stove
STOVER n fodder
STOVERS > STOVER
STOVES > STOVE
STOVETOP US word for > HOB
STOVETOPS > STOVETOP
STOVIES pl n potatoes stewed with onions
STOVING > STOVE
STOVINGS > STOVE
STOW vb pack or store
STOWABLE > STOW
STOWAGE n space or charge for stowing goods
STOWAGES > STOWAGE
STOWAWAY n person who hides on a ship or aircraft in order to travel free ▷ vb travel in such a way
STOWAWAYS > STOWAWAY
STOWDOWN n packing of ship's hold
STOWDOWNS > STOWDOWN
STOWED > STOW
STOWER > STOW
STOWERS > STOW
STOWING > STOW
STOWINGS > STOW
STOWLINS adv stealthily
STOWN > STEAL
STOWND same as > STOUND
STOWNDED > STOWND
STOWNDING > STOWND
STOWNDS > STOWND
STOWNLINS same as > STOWLINS
STOWP same as > STOUP
STOWPS > STOWP
STOWRE same as > STOUR
STOWRES > STOWRE
STOWS > STOW
STRABISM n abnormal alignment of one or both

eyes

STRABISMS > STRABISM

STRAD *n* violin made by Stradivarius

STRADDLE *vb* have one leg or part on each side of (something) ▷ *n* act or position of straddling

STRADDLED > STRADDLE

STRADDLER > STRADDLE

STRADDLES > STRADDLE

STRADIOT *n* Venetian cavalryman

STRADIOTS > STRADIOT

STRADS > STRAD

STRAE *Scots form of* > STRAW

STRAES > STRAE

STRAFE *vb* attack (an enemy) with machine guns from the air ▷ *n* act or instance of strafing

STRAFED > STRAFE

STRAFER > STRAFE

STRAFERS > STRAFE

STRAFES > STRAFE

STRAFF *same as* > STRAFE

STRAFFED > STRAFF

STRAFFING > STRAFF

STRAFFS > STRAFF

STRAFING > STRAFE

STRAG *n* straggler

STRAGGLE *vb* go or spread in a rambling or irregular way

STRAGGLED > STRAGGLE

STRAGGLER > STRAGGLE

STRAGGLES > STRAGGLE

STRAGGLY > STRAGGLE

STRAGS > STRAG

STRAICHT *Scots word for* > STRAIGHT

STRAIGHT *adj* not curved or crooked ▷ *adv* in a straight line ▷ *n* straight part, esp of a racetrack ▷ *vb* tighten

STRAIGHTS > STRAIGHT

STRAIK *Scots word for* > STROKE

STRAIKED > STRAIK

STRAIKING > STRAIK

STRAIKS > STRAIK

STRAIN *vb* subject to mental tension ▷ *n* tension or tiredness

STRAINED *adj* not natural, forced

STRAINER *n* sieve

STRAINERS > STRAINER

STRAINING > STRAIN

STRAINS > STRAIN

STRAINT *n* pressure

STRAINTS > STRAINT

STRAIT *n* narrow channel connecting two areas of sea ▷ *adj* (of spaces, etc) affording little room ▷ *vb* tighten

STRAITED > STRAIT

STRAITEN *vb* embarrass or distress, esp financially

STRAITENS > STRAITEN

STRAITER > STRAIT

STRAITEST > STRAIT

STRAITING > STRAIT

STRAITLY > STRAIT

STRAITS > STRAIT

STRAKE *n* curved metal plate forming part of the

metal rim on a wooden wheel

STRAKED *adj* having a strake

STRAKES > STRAKE

STRAMACON *same as* > STRAMAZON

STRAMASH *n* uproar ▷ *vb* destroy

STRAMAZON *n* downward fencing stroke

STRAMMEL *same as* > STRUMMEL

STRAMMELS > STRAMMEL

STRAMONY *n* former asthma medicine made from the dried leaves and flowers of the thorn apple

STRAMP *Scots variant of* > TRAMP

STRAMPED > STRAMP

STRAMPING > STRAMP

STRAMPS > STRAMP

STRAND *vb* run aground ▷ *n* shore

STRANDED > STRAND

STRANDER > STRAND

STRANDERS > STRAND

STRANDING > STRAND

STRANDS > STRAND

STRANG *dialect variant of* > STRONG

STRANGE *adj* odd or unusual ▷ *n* odd or unfamiliar person or thing

STRANGELY > STRANGE

STRANGER *n* person who is not known or is new to a place or experience

STRANGERS > STRANGER

STRANGES > STRANGE

STRANGEST > STRANGE

STRANGLE *vb* kill by squeezing the throat

STRANGLED > STRANGLE

STRANGLER *n* person or thing that strangles

STRANGLES *n* acute bacterial disease of horses

STRANGURY *n* painful excretion of urine caused by muscular spasms of the urinary tract

STRAP *n* strip of flexible material for lifting or holding in place ▷ *vb* fasten with a strap or straps

STRAPHANG *vb* travel standing on public transport

STRAPHUNG > STRAPHANG

STRAPLESS *adj* (of women's clothes) without straps over the shoulders

STRAPLINE *n* subheading in a newspaper or magazine article or in any advertisement

STRAPPADO *n* system of torture in which a victim was hoisted by a rope tied to his wrists and then allowed to drop until his fall was suddenly checked by the rope ▷ *vb* subject to strappado

STRAPPED > STRAP

STRAPPER *n* strapping person

STRAPPERS > STRAPPER

STRAPPIER > STRAPPY

STRAPPING > STRAP

STRAPPY *adj* having straps

STRAPS > STRAP

STRAPWORT *n* plant with leaves like straps

STRASS *another word for* > PASTE

STRASSES > STRASS

STRATA > STRATUM

STRATAGEM *n* clever plan, trick

STRATAL > STRATUM

STRATAS > STRATUM

STRATEGIC *adj* advantageous

STRATEGY *n* overall plan

STRATH *n* flat river valley

STRATHS > STRATH

STRATI > STRATUS

STRATIFY *vb* form or be formed in layers or strata

STRATONIC *adj* of army

STRATOSE *adj* formed in strata

STRATOUS *adj* of stratus

STRATUM *n* layer, esp of rock

STRATUMS > STRATUM

STRATUS *n* grey layer cloud

STRAUCHT *Scots word for* > STRETCH

STRAUCHTS > STRAUCHT

STRAUGHT *same as* > STRAUCHT

STRAUGHTS > STRAUGHT

STRAUNGE *same as* > STRANGE

STRAVAGE *same as* > STRAVAIG

STRAVAGED > STRAVAGE

STRAVAGES > STRAVAGE

STRAVAIG *vb* wander aimlessly

STRAVAIGS > STRAVAIG

STRAW *n* dried stalks of grain ▷ *vb* spread around

STRAWED > STRAW

STRAWEN *adj* of straw

STRAWHAT *adj* of summer dramatic performance

STRAWIER > STRAWY

STRAWIEST > STRAWY

STRAWING > STRAW

STRAWLESS > STRAW

STRAWLIKE > STRAW

STRAWN > STREW

STRAWS > STRAW

STRAWWORM *n* aquatic larva of a caddis fly

STRAWY *adj* containing straw, or like straw in colour or texture

STRAY *vb* wander ▷ *adj* having strayed ▷ *n* stray animal

STRAYED > STRAY

STRAYER > STRAY

STRAYERS > STRAY

STRAYING > STRAY

STRAYINGS > STRAY

STRAYLING *n* stray

STRAYS > STRAY

STRAYVE *vb* wander aimlessly

STRAYVED > STRAYVE

STRAYVES > STRAYVE

STRAYVING > STRAYVE

STREAK *n* long band of contrasting colour or substance ▷ *vb* mark with streaks

STREAKED > STREAK

STREAKER > STREAK

STREAKERS > STREAK

STREAKIER > STREAKY

STREAKILY > STREAKY

STREAKING > STREAK

STREAKS > STREAK

STREAKY *adj* marked with streaks

STREAM *n* small river ▷ *vb* flow steadily

STREAMBED *n* bottom of stream

STREAMED > STREAM

STREAMER *n* strip of coloured paper that unrolls when tossed

STREAMERS > STREAMER

STREAMIER > STREAMY

STREAMING > STREAM

STREAMLET > STREAM

STREAMS > STREAM

STREAMY *adj* (of an area, land, etc) having many streams

STREEK *Scots word for* > STRETCH

STREEKED > STREEK

STREEKER > STREEK

STREEKERS > STREEK

STREEKING > STREEK

STREEKS > STREEK

STREEL *n* slovenly woman ▷ *vb* trail

STREELED > STREEL

STREELING > STREEL

STREELS > STREEL

STREET *n* public road, usu lined with buildings ▷ *vb* lay out a street or streets

STREETAGE *n* toll charged for using a street

STREETBOY *n* boy living on the street

STREETCAR *n* tram

STREETED > STREET

STREETFUL *n* amount of people or things street can hold

STREETIER > STREETY

STREETING > STREET

STREETS > STREET

STREETY *adj* of streets

STREIGHT *same as* > STRAIT

STREIGHTS > STREIGHT

STREIGNE *same as* > STRAIN

STREIGNED > STREIGNE

STREIGNES > STREIGNE

STRELITZ *n* former Russian soldier

STRELITZI > STRELITZ

STRENE *same as* > STRAIN

STRENES > STRENE

STRENGTH *n* quality of being strong

STRENGTHS > STRENGTH

STRENUITY > STRENUOUS

STRENUOUS *adj* requiring great energy or effort

STREP *n* streptococcus

STREPENT *adj* noisy
STREPS > STREP
STRESS *n* tension or strain ▷ *vb* emphasize
STRESSED > STRESS
STRESSES > STRESS
STRESSFUL > STRESS
STRESSING > STRESS
STRESSOR *n* event, experience, etc, that causes stress
STRESSORS > STRESSOR
STRETCH *vb* extend or be extended ▷ *n* stretching
STRETCHED > STRETCH
STRETCHER *n* frame covered with canvas, on which an injured person is carried ▷ *vb* transport (a sick or injured person) on a stretcher
STRETCHES > STRETCH
STRETCHY *adj* characterized by elasticity
STRETTA *same as* > STRETTO
STRETTAS > STRETTA
STRETTE > STRETTO
STRETTI > STRETTO
STRETTO *n* (in a fugue) the close overlapping of two parts or voices
STRETTOS > STRETTO
STREUSEL *n* crumbly topping for rich pastries
STREUSELS > STREUSEL
STREW *vb* scatter (things) over a surface
STREWAGE > STREW
STREWAGES > STREW
STREWED > STREW
STREWER > STREW
STREWERS > STREW
STREWING > STREW
STREWINGS > STREW
STREWMENT *n* strewing
STREWN > STREW
STREWS > STREW
STREWTH *interj* expression of surprise or alarm
STRIA *n* scratch or groove on the surface of a rock crystal
STRIAE > STRIA
STRIATA > STRIATUM
STRIATE *adj* marked with striae ▷ *vb* mark with striae
STRIATED *adj* having a pattern of scratches or grooves
STRIATES > STRIATE
STRIATING > STRIATE
STRIATION *same as* > STRIA
STRIATUM *n* part of brain
STRIATUMS > STRIATUM
STRIATURE *n* way something is striated
STRICH *n* screech owl
STRICHES > STRICH
STRICK *n* any bast fibres preparatory to being made into slivers
STRICKEN *adj* seriously affected by disease, grief, pain, etc
STRICKLE *n* board used for sweeping off excess

material in a container ▷ *vb* level, form, or sharpen with a strickle
STRICKLED > STRICKLE
STRICKLES > STRICKLE
STRICKS > STRICK
STRICT *adj* stern or severe
STRICTER > STRICT
STRICTEST > STRICT
STRICTION *n* act of restricting
STRICTISH > STRICT
STRICTLY > STRICT
STRICTURE *n* severe criticism
STRIDDEN > STRIDE
STRIDDLE *same as* > STRADDLE
STRIDDLED > STRIDDLE
STRIDDLES > STRIDDLE
STRIDE *vb* walk with long steps ▷ *n* long step
STRIDENCE > STRIDENT
STRIDENCY > STRIDENT
STRIDENT *adj* loud and harsh
STRIDER > STRIDE
STRIDERS > STRIDE
STRIDES > STRIDE
STRIDING > STRIDE
STRIDLING *adv* astride
STRIDOR *n* high-pitched whistling sound made during respiration
STRIDORS > STRIDOR
STRIFE *n* conflict, quarrelling
STRIFEFUL > STRIFE
STRIFES > STRIFE
STRIFT *n* struggle
STRIFTS > STRIFT
STRIG *vb* remove stalk from
STRIGA *same as* > STRIA
STRIGAE > STRIGA
STRIGATE *adj* streaked
STRIGGED > STRIG
STRIGGING > STRIG
STRIGIL *n* curved blade used by the ancient Romans and Greeks to scrape the body after bathing
STRIGILS > STRIGIL
STRIGINE *adj* of or like owl
STRIGOSE *adj* bearing stiff hairs or bristles
STRIGS > STRIG
STRIKE *vb* cease work as a protest ▷ *n* stoppage of work as a protest
STRIKEOUT *n* dismissal in baseball due to three successive failures to hit the ball
STRIKER *n* striking worker
STRIKERS > STRIKER
STRIKES > STRIKE
STRIKING > STRIKE
STRIKINGS > STRIKE
STRING *n* thin cord used for tying ▷ *vb* provide with a string or strings
STRINGED *adj* (of a musical instrument) having strings that are plucked or played with a bow
STRINGENT *adj* strictly

controlled or enforced
STRINGER *n* journalist retained by a newspaper to cover a particular town or area
STRINGERS > STRINGER
STRINGIER > STRINGY
STRINGILY > STRINGY
STRINGING > STRING
STRINGS > STRING
STRINGY *adj* like string
STRINKLE *Scots variant of* > SPRINKLE
STRINKLED > STRINKLE
STRINKLES > STRINKLE
STRIP *vb* take (the covering or clothes) off ▷ *n* act of stripping
STRIPE *n* long narrow band of contrasting colour or substance ▷ *vb* mark (something) with stripes
STRIPED *adj* marked or decorated with stripes
STRIPER *n* officer who has a stripe or stripes on his uniform, esp in the navy
STRIPERS > STRIPER
STRIPES > STRIPE
STRIPEY *same as* > STRIPY
STRIPIER > STRIPY
STRIPIEST > STRIPY
STRIPING > STRIPE
STRIPINGS > STRIPE
STRIPLING *n* youth
STRIPPED > STRIP
STRIPPER *n* person who performs a striptease
STRIPPERS > STRIPPER
STRIPPING > STRIP
STRIPS > STRIP
STRIPT > STRIP
STRIPY *adj* marked by or with stripes
STRIVE *vb* make a great effort
STRIVED > STRIVE
STRIVEN > STRIVE
STRIVER > STRIVE
STRIVERS > STRIVE
STRIVES > STRIVE
STRIVING > STRIVE
STRIVINGS > STRIVE
STROAM *vb* wander
STROAMED > STROAM
STROAMING > STROAM
STROAMS > STROAM
STROBE *n* high intensity flashing beam of light ▷ *vb* give the appearance of slow motion by using a strobe
STROBED > STROBE
STROBES > STROBE
STROBIC *adj* spinning or appearing to spin
STROBIL *n* scaly multiple fruit
STROBILA *n* body of a tapeworm, consisting of a string of similar segments
STROBILAE > STROBILA
STROBILAR > STROBILA
STROBILE *same as* > STROBILUS
STROBILES > STROBILE
STROBILI > STROBILUS

STROBILS > STROBIL
STROBILUS *technical name for* > CONE
STROBING > STROBE
STROBINGS > STROBE
STRODDLE *same as* > STRADDLE
STRODDLED > STRODDLE
STRODDLES > STRODDLE
STRODE > STRIDE
STRODLE *same as* > STRADDLE
STRODLED > STRODLE
STRODLES > STRODLE
STRODLING > STRODLE
STROKE *vb* touch or caress lightly with the hand ▷ *n* light touch or caress with the hand
STROKED > STROKE
STROKEN > STRIKE
STROKER > STROKE
STROKERS > STROKE
STROKES > STROKE
STROKING > STROKE
STROKINGS > STROKE
STROLL *vb* walk in a leisurely manner ▷ *n* leisurely walk
STROLLED > STROLL
STROLLER *n* chair-shaped carriage for a baby
STROLLERS > STROLLER
STROLLING > STROLL
STROLLS > STROLL
STROMA *n* gel-like matrix of chloroplasts and certain cells
STROMAL > STROMA
STROMATA > STROMA
STROMATIC > STROMA
STROMB *n* shellfish like a whelk
STROMBS > STROMB
STROMBUS *same as* > STROMB
STROND *same as* > STRAND
STRONDS > STROND
STRONG *adj* having physical power
STRONGARM *adj* involving physical force
STRONGBOX *n* box in which valuables are locked for safety
STRONGER > STRONG
STRONGEST > STRONG
STRONGISH > STRONG
STRONGLY > STRONG
STRONGMAN *n* performer, esp one in a circus, who performs feats of strength
STRONGMEN > STRONGMAN
STRONGYL *same as* > STRONGYLE
STRONGYLE *n* type of parasitic worm chiefly occurring in the intestines of horses
STRONGYLS > STRONGYL
STRONTIA > STRONTIUM
STRONTIAN *n* type of white mineral
STRONTIAS > STRONTIA
STRONTIC > STRONTIUM
STRONTIUM *n* silvery-white metallic element

STROOK > STRIKE
STROOKE n stroke
STROOKEN same
as > STRICKEN
STROOKES > STROOKE
STROP n leather strap for
sharpening razors ▷ vb
sharpen (a razor, etc) on a
strop
STROPHE n first of two
movements made by
a chorus during the
performance of a choral
ode
STROPHES > STROPHE
STROPHIC adj of, relating
to, or employing a strophe
or strophes
STROPHOID n type of curve
on graph
STROPHULI pl n skin
inflammations seen
primarily on small children
STROPPED > STROP
STROPPER > STROP
STROPPERS > STROP
STROPPIER > STROPPY
STROPPILY > STROPPY
STROPPING > STROP
STROPPY adj angry or
awkward
STROPS > STROP
STROSSERS same
as > TROUSERS
STROUD n coarse woollen
fabric
STROUDING n woolly
material for making
strouds
STROUDS > STROUD
STROUP Scots word
for > SPOUT
STROUPACH n cup of tea
STROUPAN same
as > STROUPACH
STROUPANS > STROUPAN
STROUPS > STROUP
STROUT vb bulge
STROUTED > STROUT
STROUTING > STROUT
STROUTS > STROUT
STROVE > STRIVE
STROW archaic variant
of > STREW
STROWED > STROW
STROWER > STROW
STROWERS > STROW
STROWING > STROW
STROWINGS > STROW
STROWN > STROW
STROWS > STROW
STROY archaic variant
of > DESTROY
STROYED > STROY
STROYER > STROY
STROYERS > STROY
STROYING > STROY
STROYS > STROY
STRUCK > STRIKE
STRUCKEN same
as > STRICKEN
STRUCTURE n complex
construction ▷ vb give a
structure to
STRUDEL n thin sheet of
filled dough rolled up and
baked, usu with an apple

filling
STRUDELS > STRUDEL
STRUGGLE vb work, strive,
or make one's way with
difficulty ▷ n striving
STRUGGLED > STRUGGLE
STRUGGLER > STRUGGLE
STRUGGLES > STRUGGLE
STRUM vb play (a guitar or
banjo) by sweeping the
thumb or a plectrum across
the strings
STRUMA n abnormal
enlargement of the thyroid
gland
STRUMAE > STRUMA
STRUMAS > STRUMA
STRUMATIC > STRUMA
STRUMITIS n inflammation
of thyroid gland
STRUMMED > STRUM
STRUMMEL n straw
STRUMMELS > STRUMMEL
STRUMMER > STRUM
STRUMMERS > STRUM
STRUMMING > STRUM
STRUMOSE > STRUMA
STRUMOUS > STRUMA
STRUMPET n prostitute ▷ vb
turn into a strumpet
STRUMPETS > STRUMPET
STRUMS > STRUM
STRUNG > STRING
STRUNT Scots word
for > STRUT
STRUNTED > STRUNT
STRUNTING > STRUNT
STRUNTS > STRUNT
STRUT vb walk pompously,
swagger ▷ n bar
supporting a structure
STRUTS > STRUT
STRUTTED > STRUT
STRUTTER > STRUT
STRUTTERS > STRUT
STRUTTING > STRUT
STRYCHNIA n strychnine
STRYCHNIC adj of, relating
to, or derived from
strychnine
STUB n short piece left after
use ▷ vb strike (the toe)
painfully against an object
STUBBED > STUB
STUBBIE same as > STUBBY
STUBBIER > STUBBY
STUBBIES > STUBBY
STUBBIEST > STUBBY
STUBBILY > STUBBY
STUBBING > STUB
STUBBLE n short stalks of
grain left in a field after
reaping
STUBBLED adj having the
stubs of stalks left after
a crop has been cut and
harvested
STUBBLES > STUBBLE
STUBBLIER > STUBBLE
STUBBLY > STUBBLE
STUBBORN adj refusing to
agree or give in ▷ vb make
stubborn
STUBBORNS > STUBBORN
STUBBY adj short and broad
▷ n small bottle of beer
STUBS > STUB

STUCCO n plaster used for
coating or decorating walls
▷ vb apply stucco to (a
building)
STUCCOED > STUCCO
STUCCOER > STUCCO
STUCCOERS > STUCCO
STUCCOES > STUCCO
STUCCOING > STUCCO
STUCCOS > STUCCO
STUCK n thrust
STUCKS > STUCK
STUD n small piece of metal
attached to a surface for
decoration ▷ vb set with
studs
STUDBOOK n written
record of the pedigree of
a purebred stock, esp of
racehorses
STUDBOOKS > STUDBOOK
STUDDED > STUD
STUDDEN > STAND
STUDDIE Scots word
for > ANVIL
STUDDIES > STUDDIE
STUDDING > STUD
STUDDINGS > STUD
STUDDLE n post
STUDDLES > STUDDLE
STUDENT n person who
studies a subject, esp at
university
STUDENTRY n body of
students
STUDENTS > STUDENT
STUDENTY adj informal,
sometimes derogatory
term denoting the
characteristics
believed typical of an
undergraduate student
STUDFARM n farm where
horses are bred
STUDFARMS > STUDFARM
STUDFISH n American
minnow
STUDHORSE another word
for > STALLION
STUDIED adj carefully
practised
STUDIEDLY > STUDIED
STUDIER > STUDY
STUDIERS > STUDY
STUDIES > STUDY
STUDIO n workroom of an
artist or photographer
STUDIOS > STUDIO
STUDIOUS adj fond of study
STUDLIER > STUDLY
STUDLIEST > STUDLY
STUDLY adj strong and virile
STUDS > STUD
STUDWORK n work
decorated with studs
STUDWORKS > STUDWORK
STUDY vb be engaged in
learning (a subject) ▷ n act
or process of studying
STUDYING > STUDY
STUFF n substance or
material ▷ vb pack, cram,
or fill completely
STUFFED > STUFF
STUFFER > STUFF
STUFFERS > STUFF
STUFFIER > STUFFY

STUFFIEST > STUFFY
STUFFILY > STUFFY
STUFFING n seasoned
mixture with which food is
stuffed
STUFFINGS > STUFFING
STUFFLESS > STUFF
STUFFS > STUFF
STUFFY adj lacking fresh air
STUGGIER > STUGGY
STUGGIEST > STUGGY
STUGGY adj stout
STUIVER same as > STIVER
STUIVERS > STUIVER
STUKKEND adj South
African slang for broken or
wrecked
STULL n timber prop or
platform in a stope
STULLS > STULL
STULM n shaft
STULMS > STULM
STULTIFY vb dull (the mind)
by boring routine
STUM n partly fermented
wine added to fermented
wine as a preservative ▷ vb
preserve (wine) by adding
stum
STUMBLE vb trip and nearly
fall ▷ n stumbling
STUMBLED > STUMBLE
STUMBLER > STUMBLE
STUMBLERS > STUMBLE
STUMBLES > STUMBLE
STUMBLIER > STUMBLY
STUMBLING > STUMBLE
STUMBLY adj tending to
stumble
STUMER n forgery or cheat
STUMERS > STUMER
STUMM same as > SHTOOM
STUMMED > STUM
STUMMEL n bowl of pipe
STUMMELS > STUMMEL
STUMMING > STUM
STUMP n base of a tree left
when the main trunk has
been cut away ▷ vb baffle
STUMPAGE n standing
timber or its value
STUMPAGES > STUMPAGE
STUMPED > STUMP
STUMPER > STUMP
STUMPERS > STUMP
STUMPIER > STUMPY
STUMPIES > STUMPY
STUMPIEST > STUMPY
STUMPILY > STUMPY
STUMPING > STUMP
STUMPS > STUMP
STUMPWORK n type of
embroidery featuring
raised figures, padded with
cotton wool or hair
STUMPY adj short and thick
▷ n stumpy thing
STUMS > STUM
STUN vb shock or
overwhelm ▷ n state or
effect of being stunned
STUNG > STING
STUNK > STINK
STUNKARD adj sulky
STUNNED > STUN
STUNNER n beautiful person
or thing

STUNNERS > STUNNER
STUNNING > STUN
STUNNINGS > STUN
STUNS > STUN
STUNSAIL n type of light auxiliary sail
STUNSAILS > STUNSAIL
STUNT vb prevent or impede the growth of ▷ n acrobatic or dangerous action
STUNTED > STUNT
STUNTING > STUNT
STUNTMAN n person who performs dangerous acts in a film, etc in place of an actor
STUNTMEN > STUNTMAN
STUNTS > STUNT
STUPA n domed edifice housing Buddhist or Jain relics
STUPAS > STUPA
STUPE n hot damp cloth applied to the body to relieve pain ▷ vb treat with a stupe
STUPED > STUPE
STUPEFIED > STUPEFY
STUPEFIER > STUPEFY
STUPEFIES > STUPEFY
STUPEFY vb make insensitive or lethargic
STUPENT adj astonished
STUPES > STUPE
STUPID adj lacking intelligence ▷ n stupid person
STUPIDER > STUPID
STUPIDEST > STUPID
STUPIDITY n quality or state of being stupid
STUPIDLY > STUPID
STUPIDS > STUPID
STUPING > STUPE
STUPOR n dazed or unconscious state
STUPOROUS > STUPOR
STUPORS > STUPOR
STUPRATE vb ravish
STUPRATED > STUPRATE
STUPRATES > STUPRATE
STURDIED > STURDY
STURDIER > STURDY
STURDIES > STURDY
STURDIEST > STURDY
STURDILY > STURDY
STURDY adj healthy and robust ▷ n disease of sheep
STURE same as > STOOR
STURGEON n fish from which caviar is obtained
STURGEONS > STURGEON
STURMER n type of eating apple with pale green skin
STURMERS > STURMER
STURNINE > STURNUS
STURNOID > STURNUS
STURNUS n bird of starling family
STURNUSES > STURNUS
STURT vb bother
STURTED > STURT
STURTING > STURT
STURTS > STURT
STUSHIE n commotion,

rumpus, or row
STUSHIES > STUSHIE
STUTTER vb speak with repetition of initial consonants ▷ n tendency to stutter
STUTTERED > STUTTER
STUTTERER > STUTTER
STUTTERS > STUTTER
STY vb climb
STYE n inflammation at the base of an eyelash
STYED > STYE
STYES > STYE
STYGIAN adj dark, gloomy, or hellish
STYING > STY
STYLAR > STYLUS
STYLATE adj having style
STYLE n shape or design ▷ vb shape or design
STYLEBOOK n book containing rules of punctuation, etc, for the use of writers, editors, and printers
STYLED > STYLE
STYLELESS > STYLE
STYLER > STYLE
STYLERS > STYLE
STYLES > STYLE
STYLET n wire for insertion into a flexible cannula or catheter to maintain its rigidity during passage
STYLETS > STYLET
STYLI > STYLUS
STYLIE adj fashion-conscious
STYLIER > STYLIE
STYLIEST > STYLIE
STYLIFORM adj shaped like a stylus or bristle
STYLING > STYLE
STYLINGS > STYLE
STYLISE same as > STYLIZE
STYLISED > STYLISE
STYLISER > STYLISE
STYLISERS > STYLISE
STYLISES > STYLISE
STYLISH adj smart, elegant, and fashionable
STYLISHLY > STYLISH
STYLISING > STYLISE
STYLIST n hairdresser
STYLISTIC adj of literary or artistic style
STYLISTS > STYLIST
STYLITE n one of a class of recluses who in ancient times lived on the top of high pillars
STYLITES > STYLITE
STYLITIC > STYLITE
STYLITISM > STYLITE
STYLIZE vb cause to conform to an established stylistic form
STYLIZED > STYLIZE
STYLIZER > STYLIZE
STYLIZERS > STYLIZE
STYLIZES > STYLIZE
STYLIZING > STYLIZE
STYLO n type of fountain pen
STYLOBATE n continuous horizontal course of

masonry that supports a colonnade
STYLOID adj resembling a stylus ▷ n spiny growth
STYLOIDS > STYLOID
STYLOLITE n any of the small striated columnar or irregular structures within the strata of some limestones
STYLOPES > STYLOPS
STYLOPISE same as > STYLOPIZE
STYLOPIZE vb (of a stylops) to parasitize (a host)
STYLOPS n type of insect that lives as a parasite in other insects
STYLOS > STYLO
STYLUS n needle-like device on a record player that rests in the groove of the record and picks up the sound signals
STYLUSES > STYLUS
STYME vb peer
STYMED > STYME
STYMES > STYME
STYMIE vb hinder or thwart
STYMIED > STYMY
STYMIEING > STYMIE
STYMIES > STYMY
STYMING > STYME
STYMY same as > STYMIE
STYMYING > STYMY
STYPSIS n action, application, or use of a styptic
STYPSISES > STYPSIS
STYPTIC adj (drug) used to stop bleeding ▷ n styptic drug
STYPTICAL > STYPTIC
STYPTICS > STYPTIC
STYRAX n type of tropical or subtropical tree
STYRAXES > STYRAX
STYRE same as > STIR
STYRED > STYRE
STYRENE n colourless oily volatile flammable water-insoluble liquid
STYRENES > STYRENE
STYRES > STYRE
STYRING > STYRE
STYROFOAM n tradename for a light expanded polystyrene plastic
STYTE vb bounce
STYTED > STYTE
STYTES > STYTE
STYTING > STYTE
SUABILITY > SUABLE
SUABLE adj liable to be sued in a court
SUABLY > SUABLE
SUASIBLE > SUASION
SUASION n persuasion
SUASIONS > SUASION
SUASIVE > SUASION
SUASIVELY > SUASION
SUASORY > SUASION
SUAVE adj smooth and sophisticated in manner
SUAVELY > SUAVE
SUAVENESS > SUAVE
SUAVER > SUAVE

SUAVEST > SUAVE
SUAVITIES > SUAVE
SUAVITY > SUAVE
SUB n subeditor ▷ vb act as a substitute
SUBA n shepherd's cloak
SUBABBOT n abbot who is subordinate to another abbot
SUBABBOTS > SUBABBOT
SUBACID adj (esp of some fruits) moderately acid or sour
SUBACIDLY > SUBACID
SUBACRID adj slightly acrid
SUBACT vb subdue
SUBACTED > SUBACT
SUBACTING > SUBACT
SUBACTION > SUBACT
SUBACTS > SUBACT
SUBACUTE adj intermediate between acute and chronic
SUBADAR n (formerly) the chief native officer of a company of Indian soldiers in the British service
SUBADARS > SUBADAR
SUBADULT n animal not quite at adult stage
SUBADULTS > SUBADULT
SUBAERIAL adj in open air
SUBAGENCY n agency employed by larger agency
SUBAGENT n agent who is subordinate to another agent
SUBAGENTS > SUBAGENT
SUBAH same as > SUBADAR
SUBAHDAR same as > SUBADAR
SUBAHDARS > SUBAHDAR
SUBAHDARY n office of subahdar
SUBAHS > SUBAH
SUBAHSHIP > SUBAH
SUBALAR adj below a wing
SUBALPINE adj situated in or relating to the regions at the foot of mountains
SUBALTERN n British army officer below the rank of captain ▷ adj of inferior position or rank
SUBAPICAL adj below an apex
SUBAQUA adj of or relating to underwater sport
SUBARCTIC adj of or relating to latitudes immediately south of the Arctic Circle
SUBAREA n area within a larger area
SUBAREAS > SUBAREA
SUBARID adj receiving slightly more rainfall than arid regions
SUBAS > SUBA
SUBASTRAL adj terrestrial
SUBATOM n part of an atom
SUBATOMIC adj of or being one of the particles which make up an atom
SUBATOMS > SUBATOM
SUBAUDIO adj (of sound) low frequency
SUBAURAL adj below the ear

SUBAXIAL *adj* below an axis of the body

SUBBASAL > SUBBASE

SUBBASE *same as* > SUBBASS

SUBBASES > SUBBASE

SUBBASIN *n* geographical basin within larger basin

SUBBASINS > SUBBASIN

SUBBASS *another name for* > BOURDON

SUBBASSES > SUBBASS

SUBBED > SUB

SUBBIE *n* subcontractor

SUBBIES > SUBBIE

SUBBING > SUB

SUBBINGS > SUB

SUBBLOCK *n* part of mathematical matrix

SUBBLOCKS > SUBBLOCK

SUBBRANCH *n* branch within another branch

SUBBREED *n* breed within a larger breed

SUBBREEDS > SUBBREED

SUBBUREAU *n* bureau subordinate to the main bureau

SUBBY *same as* > SUBBIE

SUBCANTOR *n* deputy to a cantor

SUBCASTE *n* subdivision of a caste

SUBCASTES > SUBCASTE

SUBCAUDAL *adj* below a tail

SUBCAUSE *n* factor less important than a cause

SUBCAUSES > SUBCAUSE

SUBCAVITY *n* cavity within a larger cavity

SUBCELL *n* cell within a larger cell

SUBCELLAR *n* cellar below another cellar

SUBCELLS > SUBCELL

SUBCENTER *n* secondary center

SUBCHASER *n* anti-submarine warship

SUBCHIEF *n* chief below the main chief

SUBCHIEFS > SUBCHIEF

SUBCHORD *n* part of a curve

SUBCHORDS > SUBCHORD

SUBCLAIM *n* claim that is part of a larger claim

SUBCLAIMS > SUBCLAIM

SUBCLAN *n* clan within a larger clan

SUBCLANS > SUBCLAN

SUBCLASS *n* principal subdivision of a class ▷ *vb* assign to a subclass

SUBCLAUSE *n* subordinate section of a larger clause in a document

SUBCLERK *n* clerk who is subordinate to another clerk

SUBCLERKS > SUBCLERK

SUBCLIMAX *n* community in which development has been arrested before climax has been attained

SUBCODE *n* computer tag identifying data

SUBCODES > SUBCODE

SUBCOLONY *n* colony

established by existing colony

SUBCONSUL *n* assistant to a consul

SUBCOOL *vb* make colder

SUBCOOLED > SUBCOOL

SUBCOOLS > SUBCOOL

SUBCORTEX *n* matter of the brain situated beneath the cerebral cortex

SUBCOSTA *n* vein in insect wing

SUBCOSTAE > SUBCOSTA

SUBCOSTAL *adj* below the rib

SUBCOUNTY *n* division of a county

SUBCRUST *n* secondary crust below main crust

SUBCRUSTS > SUBCRUST

SUBCULT *n* cult within larger cult

SUBCULTS > SUBCULT

SUBCUTES > SUBCUTIS

SUBCUTIS *n* layer of tissue beneath outer skin

SUBDEACON *n* cleric who assists at High Mass

SUBDEALER *n* dealer who buys from other dealer

SUBDEAN *n* deputy of dean

SUBDEANS > SUBDEAN

SUBDEB *n* young woman who is not yet a debutante

SUBDEBS > SUBDEB

SUBDEPOT *n* depot within a larger depot

SUBDEPOTS > SUBDEPOT

SUBDEPUTY *n* assistant to a deputy

SUBDERMAL *adj* below the skin

SUBDEW *same as* > SUBDUE

SUBDEWED > SUBDEW

SUBDEWING > SUBDEW

SUBDEWS > SUBDEW

SUBDIVIDE *vb* divide (a part of something) into smaller parts

SUBDOLOUS *adj* clever

SUBDORSAL *adj* situated close to the back

SUBDUABLE > SUBDUE

SUBDUABLY > SUBDUE

SUBDUAL > SUBDUE

SUBDUALS > SUBDUE

SUBDUCE *vb* withdraw

SUBDUCED > SUBDUCE

SUBDUCES > SUBDUCE

SUBDUCING > SUBDUCE

SUBDUCT *vb* draw or turn (the eye, etc) downwards

SUBDUCTED > SUBDUCT

SUBDUCTS > SUBDUCT

SUBDUE *vb* overcome

SUBDUED *adj* cowed, passive, or shy

SUBDUEDLY > SUBDUED

SUBDUER > SUBDUE

SUBDUERS > SUBDUE

SUBDUES > SUBDUE

SUBDUING > SUBDUE

SUBDUPLE *adj* in proportion of one to two

SUBDURAL *adj* between the dura mater and the arachnoid

SUBDWARF *n* star smaller than a dwarf star

SUBDWARFS > SUBDWARF

SUBECHO *n* echo resonating more quietly than another echo

SUBECHOES > SUBECHO

SUBEDAR *same as* > SUBADAR

SUBEDARS > SUBEDAR

SUBEDIT *vb* edit and correct (written or printed material)

SUBEDITED > SUBEDIT

SUBEDITOR *n* person who checks and edits text for a newspaper or magazine

SUBEDITS > SUBEDIT

SUBENTIRE *adj* slightly indented

SUBENTRY *n* entry within another entry

SUBEPOCH *n* epoch within another epoch

SUBEPOCHS > SUBEPOCH

SUBEQUAL *adj* not quite equal

SUBER *n* cork

SUBERATE *n* salt of suberic acid

SUBERATES > SUBERATE

SUBERECT *adj* not quite erect

SUBEREOUS *same as* > SUBEROSE

SUBERIC *same as* > SUBEROSE

SUBERIN *n* fatty or waxy substance that is present in the walls of cork cells

SUBERINS > SUBERIN

SUBERISE *same as* > SUBERIZE

SUBERISED > SUBERISE

SUBERISES > SUBERISE

SUBERIZE *vb* impregnate (cell walls) with suberin during the formation of corky tissue

SUBERIZED > SUBERIZE

SUBERIZES > SUBERIZE

SUBEROSE *adj* relating to, resembling, or consisting of cork

SUBEROUS *same as* > SUBEROSE

SUBERS > SUBER

SUBFAMILY *n* taxonomic group that is a subdivision of a family

SUBFEU *vb* grant feu to vassal

SUBFEUED > SUBFEU

SUBFEUING > SUBFEU

SUBFEUS > SUBFEU

SUBFIELD *n* subdivision of a field

SUBFIELDS > SUBFIELD

SUBFILE *n* file within another file

SUBFILES > SUBFILE

SUBFIX *n* suffix

SUBFIXES > SUBFIX

SUBFLOOR *n* rough floor that forms a base for a finished floor

SUBFLOORS > SUBFLOOR

SUBFLUID *adj* viscous

SUBFOSSIL *n* something partly fossilized

SUBFRAME *n* frame on which car body is built

SUBFRAMES > SUBFRAME

SUBFUSC *adj* devoid of brightness or appeal ▷ *n* (at Oxford University) formal academic dress

SUBFUSCS > SUBFUSC

SUBFUSK *same as* > SUBFUSC

SUBFUSKS > SUBFUSK

SUBGENERA > SUBGENUS

SUBGENRE *n* genre within a larger genre

SUBGENRES > SUBGENRE

SUBGENUS *n* taxonomic group that is a subdivision of a genus but of higher rank than a species

SUBGOAL *n* secondary goal

SUBGOALS > SUBGOAL

SUBGRADE *n* ground beneath a roadway or pavement

SUBGRADES > SUBGRADE

SUBGRAPH *n* graph sharing vertices of other graph

SUBGRAPHS > SUBGRAPH

SUBGROUP *n* small group that is part of a larger group

SUBGROUPS > SUBGROUP

SUBGUM *n* Chinese dish

SUBGUMS > SUBGUM

SUBHA *n* string of beads used in praying and meditating

SUBHAS > SUBHA

SUBHEAD *n* heading of a subsection in a printed work

SUBHEADS > SUBHEAD

SUBHEDRAL *adj* with some characteristics of crystal

SUBHUMAN *adj* less than human

SUBHUMANS > SUBHUMAN

SUBHUMID *adj* not wet enough for trees to grow

SUBIDEA *n* secondary idea

SUBIDEAS > SUBIDEA

SUBIMAGO *n* first winged stage of the mayfly

SUBIMAGOS > SUBIMAGO

SUBINCISE *vb* perform subincision

SUBINDEX *same as* > SUBSCRIPT

SUBINFEUD *vb* grant by feudal tenant to further tenant

SUBITEM *n* item that is less important than another item

SUBITEMS > SUBITEM

SUBITISE *same as* > SUBITIZE

SUBITISED > SUBITISE

SUBITISES > SUBITISE

SUBITIZE *vb* perceive the number of (a group of items) at a glance and without counting

SUBITIZED > SUBITIZE

SUBITIZES > SUBITIZE

SUBITO *adv* (preceding

or following a dynamic marking, etc) suddenly

SUBJACENT *adj* forming a foundation

SUBJECT *n* person or thing being dealt with or studied ▷ *adj* being under the rule of a monarch or government ▷ *vb* cause to undergo

SUBJECTED > SUBJECT

SUBJECTS > SUBJECT

SUBJOIN *vb* add or attach at the end of something spoken, written, etc

SUBJOINED > SUBJOIN

SUBJOINS > SUBJOIN

SUBJUGATE *vb* bring (a group of people) under one's control

SUBLATE *vb* deny

SUBLATED > SUBLATE

SUBLATES > SUBLATE

SUBLATING > SUBLATE

SUBLATION > SUBLATE

SUBLEASE *n* lease of property made by a person who is himself or herself a lessee or tenant of that property ▷ *vb* grant a sublease of (property)

SUBLEASED > SUBLEASE

SUBLEASES > SUBLEASE

SUBLESSEE > SUBLEASE

SUBLESSOR > SUBLEASE

SUBLET *vb* rent out (property rented from someone else) ▷ *n* sublease

SUBLETHAL *adj* not strong enough to kill

SUBLETS > SUBLET

SUBLETTER > SUBLET

SUBLEVEL *n* subdivision of a level

SUBLEVELS > SUBLEVEL

SUBLIMATE *vb* direct the energy of (a strong desire, esp a sexual one) into socially acceptable activities ▷ *n* material obtained when a substance is sublimed ▷ *adj* exalted or purified

SUBLIME *adj* of high moral, intellectual, or spiritual value ▷ *vb* change from a solid to a vapour without first melting

SUBLIMED > SUBLIME

SUBLIMELY > SUBLIME

SUBLIMER > SUBLIME

SUBLIMERS > SUBLIME

SUBLIMES > SUBLIME

SUBLIMEST > SUBLIME

SUBLIMING > SUBLIME

SUBLIMISE *same as* > SUBLIMIZE

SUBLIMIT *n* limit on a subcategory

SUBLIMITS > SUBLIMIT

SUBLIMITY > SUBLIME

SUBLIMIZE *vb* make sublime

SUBLINE *n* secondary headline

SUBLINEAR *adj* beneath a line

SUBLINES > SUBLINE

SUBLOT *n* subdivision of a lot

SUBLOTS > SUBLOT

SUBLUNAR *same as* > SUBLUNARY

SUBLUNARY *adj* situated between the moon and the earth

SUBLUNATE *adj* almost crescent-shaped

SUBLUXATE *vb* partially dislocate

SUBMAN *n* primitive form of human

SUBMARINE *n* vessel which can operate below the surface of the sea ▷ *adj* below the surface of the sea ▷ *vb* slide beneath seatbelt in car crash

SUBMARKET *n* specialized market within larger market

SUBMATRIX *n* part of matrix

SUBMEN > SUBMAN

SUBMENTA > SUBMENTUM

SUBMENTAL *adj* situated beneath the chin

SUBMENTUM *n* base of insect lip

SUBMENU *n* further list of options within computer menu

SUBMENUS > SUBMENU

SUBMERGE *vb* put or go below the surface of water or other liquid

SUBMERGED *adj* (of plants or plant parts) growing beneath the surface of the water

SUBMERGES > SUBMERGE

SUBMERSE *same as* > SUBMERGE

SUBMERSED *same as* > SUBMERGED

SUBMERSES > SUBMERSE

SUBMICRON *n* object only visible through powerful microscope

SUBMISS *adj* docile

SUBMISSLY *adv* submissively

SUBMIT *vb* surrender

SUBMITS > SUBMIT

SUBMITTAL > SUBMIT

SUBMITTED > SUBMIT

SUBMITTER > SUBMIT

SUBMUCOSA *n* connective tissue beneath a mucous membrane

SUBMUCOUS > SUBMUCOSA

SUBNASAL *adj* beneath nose

SUBNET *n* part of network

SUBNETS > SUBNET

SUBNEURAL *adj* beneath a nerve centre

SUBNICHE *n* subdivision of a niche

SUBNICHES > SUBNICHE

SUBNIVEAL *adj* beneath the snow

SUBNIVEAN *same as* > SUBNIVEAL

SUBNODAL *adj* below the

level of a node

SUBNORMAL *adj* less than normal, esp in intelligence ▷ *n* subnormal person

SUBNUCLEI *pl n* plural of subnucleus, secondary nucleus

SUBOCEAN *adj* beneath the ocean

SUBOCTAVE *n* octave below another

SUBOCULAR *adj* below the eye

SUBOFFICE *n* office that is subordinate to another office

SUBOPTIC *adj* below the eye

SUBORAL *adj* not quite oral

SUBORDER *n* taxonomic group that is a subdivision of an order

SUBORDERS > SUBORDER

SUBORN *vb* bribe or incite (a person) to commit a wrongful act

SUBORNED > SUBORN

SUBORNER > SUBORN

SUBORNERS > SUBORN

SUBORNING > SUBORN

SUBORNS > SUBORN

SUBOSCINE *adj* belonging to a subfamily of birds

SUBOVAL *adj* not quite oval

SUBOVATE *adj* almost egg-shaped

SUBOXIDE *n* oxide of an element containing less oxygen than the common oxide formed by the element

SUBOXIDES > SUBOXIDE

SUBPANEL *n* panel that is part of larger panel

SUBPANELS > SUBPANEL

SUBPAR *adj* not up to standard

SUBPART *n* part within another part

SUBPARTS > SUBPART

SUBPENA *same as* > SUBPOENA

SUBPENAED > SUBPENA

SUBPENAS > SUBPENA

SUBPERIOD *n* subdivision of time period

SUBPHASE *n* subdivision of phase

SUBPHASES > SUBPHASE

SUBPHYLA > SUBPHYLUM

SUBPHYLAR > SUBPHYLUM

SUBPHYLUM *n* taxonomic group that is a subdivision of a phylum

SUBPLOT *n* secondary plot in a novel, play, or film

SUBPLOTS > SUBPLOT

SUBPOENA *n* writ requiring a person to appear before a lawcourt ▷ *vb* summon (someone) with a subpoena

SUBPOENAS > SUBPOENA

SUBPOLAR *adj* not quite polar

SUBPOTENT *adj* not at full strength

SUBPRIOR *n* monk junior to

a prior

SUBPRIORS > SUBPRIOR

SUBPUBIC *adj* beneath the pubic bone

SUBRACE *n* race of people considered to be inferior

SUBRACES > SUBRACE

SUBREGION *n* subdivision of a region, esp a zoogeographical or ecological region

SUBRENT *n* rent paid to renter who rents to another

SUBRENTS > SUBRENT

SUBRING *n* mathematical ring that is a subset of another ring

SUBRINGS > SUBRING

SUBROGATE *vb* put (one person or thing) in the place of another in respect of a right or claim

SUBRULE *n* rule within another rule

SUBRULES > SUBRULE

SUBS > SUB

SUBSACRAL *adj* below the sacrum

SUBSALE *n* sale carried out within the process of a larger sale

SUBSALES > SUBSALE

SUBSAMPLE *vb* take further sample from existing sample

SUBSCALE *n* scale within a scale

SUBSCALES > SUBSCALE

SUBSCHEMA *n* part of computer database used by an individual

SUBSCRIBE *vb* pay (a subscription)

SUBSCRIPT *adj* (character) printed below the line ▷ *n* subscript character

SUBSEA *adj* undersea

SUBSECIVE *adj* left over

SUBSECT *n* sect within a larger sect

SUBSECTOR *n* subdivision of sector

SUBSECTS > SUBSECT

SUBSELLIA *pl n* ledges underneath the hinged seats in a church

SUBSENSE *n* definition that is division of wider definition

SUBSENSES > SUBSENSE

SUBSERE *n* secondary sere arising when the progress of a sere towards its climax has been interrupted

SUBSERES > SUBSERE

SUBSERIES *n* series within a larger series

SUBSERVE *vb* be helpful or useful to

SUBSERVED > SUBSERVE

SUBSERVES > SUBSERVE

SUBSET *n* mathematical set contained within a larger set

SUBSETS > SUBSET

SUBSHAFT *n* secondary

shaft in mine

SUBSHAFTS > SUBSHAFT

SUBSHELL *n* part of a shell of an atom

SUBSHELLS > SUBSHELL

SUBSHRUB *n* small bushy plant that is woody except for the tips of the branches

SUBSHRUBS > SUBSHRUB

SUBSIDE *vb* become less intense

SUBSIDED > SUBSIDE

SUBSIDER > SUBSIDE

SUBSIDERS > SUBSIDE

SUBSIDES > SUBSIDE

SUBSIDIES > SUBSIDY

SUBSIDING > SUBSIDE

SUBSIDISE *same as* > SUBSIDIZE

SUBSIDIZE *vb* help financially

SUBSIDY *n* financial aid

SUBSIST *vb* manage to live

SUBSISTED > SUBSIST

SUBSISTER > SUBSIST

SUBSISTS > SUBSIST

SUBSITE *n* location within a website

SUBSITES > SUBSITE

SUBSIZAR *n* type of undergraduate at Cambridge

SUBSIZARS > SUBSIZAR

SUBSKILL *n* element of a wider skill

SUBSKILLS > SUBSKILL

SUBSOCIAL *adj* lacking a complex or definite social structure

SUBSOIL *n* earth just below the surface soil ▷ *vb* plough (land) to a depth below the normal ploughing level

SUBSOILED > SUBSOIL

SUBSOILER > SUBSOIL

SUBSOILS > SUBSOIL

SUBSOLAR *adj* (of a point on the earth) directly below the sun

SUBSONG *n* subdued form of birdsong modified from the full territorial song

SUBSONGS > SUBSONG

SUBSONIC *adj* moving at a speed less than that of sound

SUBSPACE *n* part of a mathematical matrix

SUBSPACES > SUBSPACE

SUBSTAGE *n* part of a microscope below the stage

SUBSTAGES > SUBSTAGE

SUBSTANCE *n* physical composition of something

SUBSTATE *n* subdivision of state

SUBSTATES > SUBSTATE

SUBSTRACT *same as* > SUBTRACT

SUBSTRATA *pl n* layers lying underneath other layers

SUBSTRATE *n* substance upon which an enzyme acts

SUBSTRUCT *vb* build as a

foundation

SUBSTYLAR > SUBSTYLE

SUBSTYLE *n* line on a dial

SUBSTYLES > SUBSTYLE

SUBSULTUS *n* abnormal twitching

SUBSUME *vb* include (an idea, case, etc) under a larger classification or group

SUBSUMED > SUBSUME

SUBSUMES > SUBSUME

SUBSUMING > SUBSUME

SUBSYSTEM *n* system operating within a larger system

SUBTACK *Scots word for* > SUBLEASE

SUBTACKS > SUBTACK

SUBTASK *n* task that is part of a larger task

SUBTASKS > SUBTASK

SUBTAXA > SUBTAXON

SUBTAXON *n* supplementary piece of identifying information in plant or animal scientific name

SUBTAXONS > SUBTAXON

SUBTEEN *n* young person who has not yet become a teenager

SUBTEENS > SUBTEEN

SUBTENANT *n* person who rents property from a tenant

SUBTEND *vb* be opposite (an angle or side)

SUBTENDED > SUBTEND

SUBTENDS > SUBTEND

SUBTENSE *n* line that subtends

SUBTENSES > SUBTENSE

SUBTENURE *n* tenancy given by other tenant

SUBTEST *n* test that is part of larger test

SUBTESTS > SUBTEST

SUBTEXT *n* underlying theme in a piece of writing

SUBTEXTS > SUBTEXT

SUBTHEME *n* secondary theme

SUBTHEMES > SUBTHEME

SUBTIDAL *adj* below the level of low tide

SUBTIL *same as* > SUBTLE

SUBTILE *rare spelling of* > SUBTLE

SUBTILELY > SUBTILE

SUBTILER > SUBTILE

SUBTILEST > SUBTILE

SUBTILIN *n* antibiotic drug

SUBTILINS > SUBTILIN

SUBTILISE *same as* > SUBTILIZE

SUBTILITY > SUBTILE

SUBTILIZE *vb* bring to a purer state

SUBTILTY > SUBTILE

SUBTITLE *n* secondary title of a book ▷ *vb* provide with a subtitle or subtitles

SUBTITLED > SUBTITLE

SUBTITLES > SUBTITLE

SUBTLE *adj* not immediately obvious

SUBTLER > SUBTLE

SUBTLEST > SUBTLE

SUBTLETY *n* fine distinction

SUBTLY > SUBTLE

SUBTONE *n* subdivision of a tone

SUBTONES > SUBTONE

SUBTONIC *n* seventh degree of a major or minor scale

SUBTONICS > SUBTONIC

SUBTOPIA *n* suburban development that encroaches on rural areas yet appears to offer the attractions of country life to suburban dwellers

SUBTOPIAN > SUBTOPIA

SUBTOPIAS > SUBTOPIA

SUBTOPIC *n* topic within a larger topic

SUBTOPICS > SUBTOPIC

SUBTORRID *same as* > SUBTROPIC

SUBTOTAL *n* total made up by a column of figures, forming part of the total made up by a larger column or group ▷ *vb* establish or work out a subtotal for (a column, group, etc)

SUBTOTALS > SUBTOTAL

SUBTRACT *vb* take (one number or quantity) from another

SUBTRACTS > SUBTRACT

SUBTREND *n* minor trend

SUBTRENDS > SUBTREND

SUBTRIBE *n* tribe within a larger tribe

SUBTRIBES > SUBTRIBE

SUBTRIST *adj* slightly sad

SUBTROPIC *adj* relating to the region lying between the tropics and the temperate lands

SUBTRUDE *vb* intrude stealthily

SUBTRUDED > SUBTRUDE

SUBTRUDES > SUBTRUDE

SUBTUNIC *adj* below membrane ▷ *n* garment worn under a tunic

SUBTUNICS > SUBTUNIC

SUBTYPE *n* secondary or subordinate type or genre

SUBTYPES > SUBTYPE

SUBUCULA *n* ancient Roman man's undergarment

SUBUCULAS > SUBUCULA

SUBULATE *adj* (esp of plant parts) tapering to a point

SUBUNIT *n* distinct part or component of something larger

SUBUNITS > SUBUNIT

SUBURB *n* residential area on the outskirts of a city

SUBURBAN *adj* mildly derogatory term for inhabiting a suburb ▷ *n* mildly derogatory term for a person who lives in a suburb

SUBURBANS > SUBURBAN

SUBURBED > SUBURB

SUBURBIA *n* suburbs and their inhabitants

SUBURBIAS > SUBURBIA

SUBURBS > SUBURB

SUBURSINE *adj* of a bear subspecies

SUBVASSAL *n* vassal of a vassal

SUBVENE *vb* happen in such a way as to be of assistance, esp in preventing something

SUBVENED > SUBVENE

SUBVENES > SUBVENE

SUBVENING > SUBVENE

SUBVERSAL > SUBVERT

SUBVERSE *same as* > SUBVERT

SUBVERSED > SUBVERSE

SUBVERSES > SUBVERSE

SUBVERST > SUBVERSE

SUBVERT *vb* overthrow the authority of

SUBVERTED > SUBVERT

SUBVERTER > SUBVERT

SUBVERTS > SUBVERT

SUBVICAR *n* assistant to a vicar

SUBVICARS > SUBVICAR

SUBVIRAL *adj* of, caused by, or denoting a part of the structure of a virus

SUBVIRUS *n* organism smaller than a virus

SUBVISUAL *adj* not visible to the naked eye

SUBVOCAL *adj* formed in mind without being spoken aloud

SUBWARDEN *n* assistant to a warden

SUBWAY *n* passage under a road or railway ▷ *vb* travel by subway

SUBWAYED > SUBWAY

SUBWAYING > SUBWAY

SUBWAYS > SUBWAY

SUBWOOFER *n* loudspeaker for very low tones

SUBWORLD *n* underworld

SUBWORLDS > SUBWORLD

SUBWRITER *n* person carrying out writing tasks for other writer

SUBZERO *adj* lower than zero

SUBZONAL > SUBZONE

SUBZONE *n* subdivision of a zone

SUBZONES > SUBZONE

SUCCADE *n* piece of candied fruit

SUCCADES > SUCCADE

SUCCAH *same as* > SUKKAH

SUCCAHS > SUCCAH

SUCCEDENT *adj* following

SUCCEED *vb* accomplish an aim

SUCCEEDED > SUCCEED

SUCCEEDER > SUCCEED

SUCCEEDS > SUCCEED

SUCCENTOR *n* deputy of the precentor of a cathedral that has retained its statutes from pre-Reformation days

SUCCES *French word for* > SUCCESS

SUCCESS *n* achievement of something attempted

SUCCESSES > SUCCESS
SUCCESSOR n person who succeeds someone in a position
SUCCI > SUCCUS
SUCCINATE n any salt or ester of succinic acid
SUCCINCT adj brief and clear
SUCCINIC adj of, relating to, or obtained from amber
SUCCINITE n type of amber
SUCCINYL n constituent of succinic acid
SUCCINYLS > SUCCINYL
SUCCISE adj ending abruptly, as if cut off
SUCCOR same as > SUCCOUR
SUCCORED > SUCCOR
SUCCORER > SUCCOR
SUCCORERS > SUCCOR
SUCCORIES > SUCCORY
SUCCORING > SUCCOR
SUCCORS > SUCCOR
SUCCORY another name for > CHICORY
SUCCOS same as > SUCCOTH
SUCCOSE > SUCCUS
SUCCOT same as > SUKKOTH
SUCCOTASH n mixture of cooked sweet corn kernels and lima beans, served as a vegetable
SUCCOTH variant of > SUKKOTH
SUCCOUR n help in distress ▷ vb give aid to (someone in time of difficulty)
SUCCOURED > SUCCOUR
SUCCOURER > SUCCOUR
SUCCOURS > SUCCOUR
SUCCOUS > SUCCUS
SUCCUBA same as > SUCCUBUS
SUCCUBAE > SUCCUBA
SUCCUBAS > SUCCUBA
SUCCUBI > SUCCUBUS
SUCCUBINE > SUCCUBUS
SUCCUBOUS adj having the leaves arranged so that the upper margin of each leaf is covered by the lower margin of the next leaf along
SUCCUBUS n female demon believed to have sex with sleeping men
SUCCULENT adj juicy and delicious ▷ n succulent plant
SUCCUMB vb give way (to something overpowering)
SUCCUMBED > SUCCUMB
SUCCUMBER > SUCCUMB
SUCCUMBS > SUCCUMB
SUCCURSAL adj (esp of a religious establishment) subsidiary ▷ n subsidiary establishment
SUCCUS n fluid
SUCCUSS vb shake (a patient) to detect the sound of fluid in the thoracic or another bodily cavity
SUCCUSSED > SUCCUSS
SUCCUSSES > SUCCUSS

SUCH adj of the kind specified ▷ pron such things
SUCHLIKE pron such or similar things ▷ n such or similar things ▷ adj of such a kind
SUCHNESS > SUCH
SUCHWISE > SUCH
SUCK vb draw (liquid or air) into the mouth ▷ n sucking
SUCKED > SUCK
SUCKEN Scots word for > DISTRICT
SUCKENER n tenant
SUCKENERS > SUCKENER
SUCKENS > SUCKEN
SUCKER n person who is easily deceived or swindled ▷ vb strip off the suckers from (a plant)
SUCKERED > SUCKER
SUCKERING > SUCKER
SUCKERS > SUCKER
SUCKET same as > SUCCADE
SUCKETS > SUCKET
SUCKFISH n type of spiny-finned marine fish
SUCKIER > SUCKY
SUCKIEST > SUCKY
SUCKING adj not yet weaned
SUCKINGS > SUCKING
SUCKLE vb feed at the breast
SUCKLED > SUCKLE
SUCKLER > SUCKLE
SUCKLERS > SUCKLE
SUCKLES > SUCKLE
SUCKLESS > SUCK
SUCKLING n unweaned baby or young animal
SUCKLINGS > SUCKLING
SUCKS interj expression of disappointment
SUCKY adj despicable
SUCRALOSE n artificial sweetener
SUCRASE another name for > INVERTASE
SUCRASES > SUCRASE
SUCRE n former standard monetary unit of Ecuador
SUCRES > SUCRE
SUCRIER n small container for sugar at table
SUCRIERS > SUCRIER
SUCROSE same as > SUGAR
SUCROSES > SUCROSE
SUCTION n sucking ▷ vb subject to suction
SUCTIONAL > SUCTION
SUCTIONED > SUCTION
SUCTIONS > SUCTION
SUCTORIAL adj specialized for sucking or adhering
SUCTORIAN n microscopic creature
SUCURUJU n anaconda
SUCURUJUS > SUCURUJU
SUD singular of > SUDS
SUDAMEN n small cavity in the skin
SUDAMINA > SUDAMEN
SUDAMINAL > SUDAMEN
SUDARIA > SUDARIUM

SUDARIES > SUDARY
SUDARIUM n room in a Roman bathhouse where sweating is induced by heat
SUDARY same as > SUDARIUM
SUDATE vb sweat
SUDATED > SUDATE
SUDATES > SUDATE
SUDATING > SUDATE
SUDATION > SUDATE
SUDATIONS > SUDATE
SUDATORIA same as > SUDARIA
SUDATORY > SUDORIUM
SUDD n floating masses of reeds and weeds that occur on the White Nile
SUDDEN adj done or occurring quickly and unexpectedly
SUDDENLY adv quickly and without warning
SUDDENS > SUDDEN
SUDDENTY n suddenness
SUDDER n supreme court in India
SUDDERS > SUDDER
SUDDS > SUDD
SUDOR technical name for > SWEAT
SUDORAL > SUDOR
SUDORIFIC adj (drug) causing sweating ▷ n drug that causes sweating
SUDOROUS > SUDOR
SUDORS > SUDOR
SUDS pl n froth of soap and water, lather ▷ vb wash in suds
SUDSED > SUDS
SUDSER n soap opera
SUDSERS > SUDSER
SUDSES > SUDS
SUDSIER > SUDS
SUDSIEST > SUDS
SUDSING > SUDS
SUDSLESS > SUDS
SUDSY > SUDS
SUE vb start legal proceedings against
SUEABLE > SUE
SUED > SUE
SUEDE n leather with a velvety finish on one side ▷ vb give a suede finish to
SUEDED > SUEDE
SUEDES > SUEDE
SUEDETTE n imitation suede fabric
SUEDETTES > SUEDETTE
SUEDING > SUEDE
SUENT adj smooth
SUER > SUE
SUERS > SUE
SUES > SUE
SUET n hard fat obtained from sheep and cattle, used in cooking
SUETIER > SUET
SUETIEST > SUET
SUETS > SUET
SUETTIER > SUET
SUETTIEST > SUET
SUETTY > SUET
SUETY > SUET
SUFFARI same as > SAFARI
SUFFARIS > SUFFARI

SUFFECT adj additional
SUFFER vb undergo or be subjected to
SUFFERED > SUFFER
SUFFERER > SUFFER
SUFFERERS > SUFFER
SUFFERING n pain, misery, or loss experienced by a person who suffers
SUFFERS > SUFFER
SUFFETE n official in ancient Carthage
SUFFETES > SUFFETE
SUFFICE vb be enough for a purpose
SUFFICED > SUFFICE
SUFFICER > SUFFICE
SUFFICERS > SUFFICE
SUFFICES > SUFFICE
SUFFICING > SUFFICE
SUFFIX n letter or letters added to the end of a word to form another word ▷ vb add (a letter or letters) to the end of a word to form another word
SUFFIXAL > SUFFIX
SUFFIXED > SUFFIX
SUFFIXES > SUFFIX
SUFFIXING > SUFFIX
SUFFIXION > SUFFIX
SUFFLATE archaic word for > INFLATE
SUFFLATED > SUFFLATE
SUFFLATES > SUFFLATE
SUFFOCATE vb kill or be killed by deprivation of oxygen
SUFFRAGAN n bishop appointed to assist an archbishop ▷ adj (of any bishop of a diocese) subordinate to and assisting his superior archbishop
SUFFRAGE n right to vote in public elections
SUFFRAGES > SUFFRAGE
SUFFUSE vb spread through or over (something)
SUFFUSED > SUFFUSE
SUFFUSES > SUFFUSE
SUFFUSING > SUFFUSE
SUFFUSION > SUFFUSE
SUFFUSIVE > SUFFUSE
SUGAN n straw rope
SUGANS > SUGAN
SUGAR n sweet crystalline carbohydrate used to sweeten food and drinks ▷ vb sweeten or cover with sugar
SUGARALLY n liquorice
SUGARBUSH n area covered in sugar maple trees
SUGARCANE n coarse grass that yields sugar
SUGARCOAT vb cover with sugar
SUGARED adj made sweeter or more appealing with or as with sugar
SUGARER > SUGAR
SUGARERS > SUGAR
SUGARIER > SUGARY
SUGARIEST > SUGARY
SUGARING n method of

removing unwanted body hair

SUGARINGS > SUGARING

SUGARLESS > SUGAR

SUGARLIKE > SUGAR

SUGARLOAF n large conical mass of unrefined sugar

SUGARPLUM n crystallized plum

SUGARS > SUGAR

SUGARY adj of, like, or containing sugar

SUGGEST vb put forward (an idea) for consideration

SUGGESTED > SUGGEST

SUGGESTER > SUGGEST

SUGGESTS > SUGGEST

SUGGING n practice of selling products under the pretence of conducting market research

SUGGINGS > SUGGING

SUGH same as > SOUGH

SUGHED > SUGH

SUGHING > SUGH

SUGHS > SUGH

SUI adj of itself

SUICIDAL adj liable to commit suicide

SUICIDE n killing oneself intentionally ▷ vb commit suicide

SUICIDED > SUICIDE

SUICIDES > SUICIDE

SUICIDING > SUICIDE

SUID n pig or related animal

SUIDIAN > SUID

SUIDIANS > SUID

SUIDS > SUID

SUILLINE adj of or like a pig

SUING > SUE

SUINGS > SUE

SUINT n water-soluble substance found in the fleece of sheep

SUINTS > SUINT

SUIPLAP n South African slang for a drunkard

SUIPLAPS > SUIPLAP

SUIT n set of clothes designed to be worn together ▷ vb be appropriate for

SUITABLE adj appropriate or proper

SUITABLY > SUITABLE

SUITCASE n portable travelling case for clothing

SUITCASES > SUITCASE

SUITE n set of connected rooms in a hotel

SUITED > SUIT

SUITER n piece of luggage for carrying suits and dresses

SUITERS > SUITER

SUITES > SUITE

SUITING n fabric used for suits

SUITINGS > SUITING

SUITLIKE > SUIT

SUITOR n man who is courting a woman ▷ vb act as a suitor

SUITORED > SUITOR

SUITORING > SUITOR

SUITORS > SUITOR

SUITRESS n female suitor

SUITS > SUIT

SUIVANTE n lady's maid

SUIVANTES > SUIVANTE

SUIVEZ vb musical direction meaning follow

SUJEE same as > SOOGEE

SUJEES > SUJEE

SUK same as > SOUK

SUKH same as > SOUK

SUKHS > SUKH

SUKIYAKI n Japanese dish consisting of very thinly sliced beef, vegetables, and seasonings cooked together quickly

SUKIYAKIS > SUKIYAKI

SUKKAH n temporary structure with a roof of branches in which orthodox Jews eat and, if possible, sleep during the festival of Sukkoth

SUKKAHS > SUKKAH

SUKKOS same as > SUKKOTH

SUKKOT same as > SUKKOTH

SUKKOTH n eight-day Jewish harvest festival

SUKS > SUK

SULCAL > SULCUS

SULCALISE same as > SULCALIZE

SULCALIZE vb furrow

SULCATE adj marked with longitudinal parallel grooves

SULCATED same as > SULCATE

SULCATION > SULCATE

SULCI > SULCUS

SULCUS n linear groove, furrow, or slight depression

SULDAN same as > SULTAN

SULDANS > SULDAN

SULFA same as > SULPHA

SULFAS > SULFA

SULFATASE n type of enzyme

SULFATE same as > SULPHATE

SULFATED > SULFATE

SULFATES > SULFATE

SULFATIC adj relating to sulphate

SULFATING > SULFATE

SULFATION > SULFATE

SULFID same as > SULPHIDE

SULFIDE same as > SULPHIDE

SULFIDES > SULFIDE

SULFIDS > SULFID

SULFINYL same as > SULPHINYL

SULFINYLS > SULFINYL

SULFITE same as > SULPHITE

SULFITES > SULFITE

SULFITIC > SULFITE

SULFO same as > SULPHONIC

SULFONATE n salt or ester of sulphonic acid

SULFONE same as > SULPHONE

SULFONES > SULFONE

SULFONIC > SULFONE

SULFONIUM n one of a type of salts

SULFONYL same as > SULPHURYL

SULFONYLS > SULFONYL

SULFOXIDE n compound containing sulphur

SULFUR variant of > SULPHUR

SULFURATE vb treat with sulphur

SULFURED > SULFUR

SULFURET same as > SULPHURET

SULFURETS > SULFURET

SULFURIC > SULFUR

SULFURING > SULFUR

SULFURISE variant of > SULFURIZE

SULFURIZE vb combine or treat with sulphur

SULFUROUS adj resembling sulphur

SULFURS > SULFUR

SULFURY > SULFUR

SULFURYL same as > SULPHURYL

SULFURYLS > SULFURYL

SULK vb be silent and sullen because of resentment or bad temper ▷ n resentful or sullen mood

SULKED > SULK

SULKER same as > SULK

SULKERS > SULKER

SULKIER > SULKY

SULKIES > SULKY

SULKIEST > SULKY

SULKILY > SULKY

SULKINESS > SULKY

SULKING > SULK

SULKS > SULK

SULKY adj moody or silent because of anger or resentment ▷ n light two-wheeled vehicle for one person, usually drawn by one horse

SULLAGE n filth or waste, esp sewage

SULLAGES > SULLAGE

SULLEN adj unwilling to talk or be sociable ▷ n sullen mood

SULLENER > SULLEN

SULLENEST > SULLEN

SULLENLY > SULLEN

SULLENS > SULLEN

SULLIABLE > SULLY

SULLIED > SULLY

SULLIES > SULLY

SULLY vb ruin (someone's reputation) ▷ n stain

SULLYING > SULLY

SULPHA n any of a group of sulphonamides that prevent the growth of bacteria

SULPHAS > SULPHA

SULPHATE n salt or ester of sulphuric acid ▷ vb treat with a sulphate or convert into a sulphate

SULPHATED > SULPHATE

SULPHATES > SULPHATE

SULPHATIC > SULPHATE

SULPHID same as > SULPHIDE

SULPHIDE n compound of sulphur with another

element

SULPHIDES > SULPHIDE

SULPHIDS > SULPHID

SULPHINYL another term for > THIONYL

SULPHITE n salt or ester of sulphurous acid

SULPHITES > SULPHITE

SULPHITIC > SULPHITE

SULPHONE n type of organic compound

SULPHONES > SULPHONE

SULPHONIC as in sulphonic acid type of strong organic acid

SULPHONYL same as > SULPHURYL

SULPHUR n pale yellow nonmetallic element ▷ vb treat with sulphur

SULPHURED > SULPHUR

SULPHURET vb treat or combine with sulphur

SULPHURIC > SULPHUR

SULPHURS > SULPHUR

SULPHURY > SULPHUR

SULPHURYL n particular chemical divalent group

SULTAN n sovereign of a Muslim country

SULTANA n kind of raisin

SULTANAS > SULTANA

SULTANATE n territory of a sultan

SULTANESS same as > SULTANA

SULTANIC > SULTAN

SULTANS > SULTAN

SULTRIER > SULTRY

SULTRIEST > SULTRY

SULTRILY > SULTRY

SULTRY adj (of weather or climate) hot and humid

SULU n type of sarong worn in Fiji

SULUS > SULU

SUM n result of addition, total ▷ vb add or form a total of (something)

SUMAC same as > SUMACH

SUMACH n type of temperate or subtropical shrub or small tree

SUMACHS > SUMACH

SUMACS > SUMAC

SUMATRA n violent storm blowing from the direction of Sumatra

SUMATRAS > SUMATRA

SUMLESS adj uncountable

SUMMA n compendium of theology, philosophy, or canon law, or sometimes of all three together

SUMMABLE > SUM

SUMMAE > SUMMA

SUMMAND n number or quantity forming part of a sum

SUMMANDS > SUMMAND

SUMMAR Scots variant of > SUMMER

SUMMARIES > SUMMARY

SUMMARILY > SUMMARY

SUMMARISE same as > SUMMARIZE

SUMMARIST > SUMMARIZE

SUMMARIZE vb make or be a summary of (something)

SUMMARY n brief account giving the main points of something ▷ adj done quickly, without formalities

SUMMAS > SUMMA

SUMMAT pron something ▷ n impressive or important person or thing

SUMMATE vb add up

SUMMATED > SUMMATE

SUMMATES > SUMMATE

SUMMATING > SUMMATE

SUMMATION n summary

SUMMATIVE > SUMMATION

SUMMATS > SUMMAT

SUMMED > SUM

SUMMER n warmest season of the year, between spring and autumn ▷ vb spend the summer (at a place)

SUMMERED > SUMMER

SUMMERIER > SUMMER

SUMMERING > SUMMER

SUMMERLY > SUMMER

SUMMERS > SUMMER

SUMMERSET n somersault

SUMMERY > SUMMER

SUMMING > SUM

SUMMINGS > SUM

SUMMIST n writer of summae

SUMMISTS > SUMMIST

SUMMIT n top of a mountain or hill ▷ vb reach summit

SUMMITAL > SUMMIT

SUMMITED > SUMMIT

SUMMITEER n person who participates in a summit conference

SUMMITING > SUMMIT

SUMMITRY n practice of conducting international negotiations by summit conferences

SUMMITS > SUMMIT

SUMMON vb order (someone) to come

SUMMONED > SUMMON

SUMMONER > SUMMON

SUMMONERS > SUMMON

SUMMONING > SUMMON

SUMMONS n command summoning someone ▷ vb order (someone) to appear in court

SUMMONSED > SUMMONS

SUMMONSES > SUMMONS

SUMO n Japanese style of wrestling

SUMOIST > SUMO

SUMOISTS > SUMO

SUMOS > SUMO

SUMOTORI n sumo wrestler

SUMOTORIS > SUMOTORI

SUMP n container in an internal-combustion engine into which oil can drain

SUMPH n stupid person

SUMPHISH > SUMPH

SUMPHS > SUMPH

SUMPIT n Malay blowpipe

SUMPITAN same as > SUMPIT

SUMPITANS > SUMPITAN

SUMPITS > SUMPIT

SUMPS > SUMP

SUMPSIMUS n correct form of expression

SUMPTER n packhorse, mule, or other beast of burden

SUMPTERS > SUMPTER

SUMPTUARY adj controlling expenditure or extravagant use of resources

SUMPTUOUS adj lavish, magnificent

SUMPWEED n American weed

SUMPWEEDS > SUMPWEED

SUMS > SUM

SUMY pl n the monetary units of Uzbekistan

SUN n star around which the earth and other planets revolve ▷ vb expose (oneself) to the sun's rays

SUNBACK adj (of dress) cut low at back

SUNBAKE vb sunbathe, esp in order to become tanned ▷ n period of sunbaking

SUNBAKED adj (esp of roads, etc) dried or cracked by the sun's heat

SUNBAKES > SUNBAKE

SUNBAKING > SUNBAKE

SUNBATH n exposure of the body to the sun to get a suntan

SUNBATHE vb lie in the sunshine in order to get a suntan

SUNBATHED > SUNBATHE

SUNBATHER > SUNBATHE

SUNBATHES > SUNBATHE

SUNBATHS > SUNBATH

SUNBEAM n ray of sun

SUNBEAMED > SUNBEAM

SUNBEAMS > SUNBEAM

SUNBEAMY > SUNBEAM

SUNBEAT adj exposed to sun

SUNBEATEN same as > SUNBEAT

SUNBED n machine for giving an artificial tan

SUNBEDS > SUNBED

SUNBELT n southern states of the US

SUNBELTS > SUNBELT

SUNBERRY n red fruit like the blackberry

SUNBIRD n any small songbird of the family Nectariniidae

SUNBIRDS > SUNBIRD

SUNBLIND n blind that shades a room from the sun's glare

SUNBLINDS > SUNBLIND

SUNBLOCK n cream applied to the skin to protect it from the sun's rays

SUNBLOCKS > SUNBLOCK

SUNBONNET n hat that shades the face and neck from the sun

SUNBOW n bow of prismatic colours similar to a rainbow, produced when sunlight shines through spray

SUNBOWS > SUNBOW

SUNBRIGHT adj bright as the sun

SUNBURN n painful reddening of the skin caused by overexposure to the sun ▷ vb become sunburnt

SUNBURNED > SUNBURN

SUNBURNS > SUNBURN

SUNBURNT > SUNBURN

SUNBURST n burst of sunshine, as through a break in the clouds

SUNBURSTS > SUNBURST

SUNCHOKE n Jerusalem artichoke

SUNCHOKES > SUNCHOKE

SUNDAE n ice cream topped with fruit etc

SUNDAES > SUNDAE

SUNDARI n Indian tree

SUNDARIS > SUNDARI

SUNDECK n upper open deck on a passenger ship

SUNDECKS > SUNDECK

SUNDER vb break apart

SUNDERED > SUNDER

SUNDERER > SUNDER

SUNDERERS > SUNDER

SUNDERING > SUNDER

SUNDERS > SUNDER

SUNDEW n any of several bog plants of the genus Drosera

SUNDEWS > SUNDEW

SUNDIAL n device showing the time by means of a pointer that casts a shadow on a marked dial

SUNDIALS > SUNDIAL

SUNDOG n small rainbow or halo near the horizon

SUNDOGS > SUNDOG

SUNDOWN same as > SUNSET

SUNDOWNED > SUNDOWN

SUNDOWNER n tramp, esp one who seeks food and lodging at sundown when it is too late to work

SUNDOWNS > SUNDOWN

SUNDRA same as > SUNDARI

SUNDRAS > SUNDRA

SUNDRESS n dress for hot weather that exposes the shoulders, arms, and back, esp one with straps over the shoulders

SUNDRI same as > SUNDARI

SUNDRIES > SUNDRY

SUNDRILY > SUNDRY

SUNDRIS > SUNDRI

SUNDROPS n American primrose

SUNDRY adj several, various

SUNFAST adj not fading in sunlight

SUNFISH n large sea fish with a rounded body

SUNFISHES > SUNFISH

SUNFLOWER n tall plant with large golden flowers

SUNG > SING

SUNGAR same as > SANGAR

SUNGARS > SUNGAR

SUNGLASS n convex lens used to focus the sun's rays and thus produce heat or ignition

SUNGLOW n pinkish glow often seen in the sky before sunrise or after sunset

SUNGLOWS > SUNGLOW

SUNGREBE another name for > FINFOOT

SUNGREBES > SUNGREBE

SUNHAT n hat that shades the face and neck from the sun

SUNHATS > SUNHAT

SUNK n bank or pad

SUNKEN adj unhealthily hollow

SUNKET n something good to eat

SUNKETS > SUNKET

SUNKIE n little stool

SUNKIES > SUNKIE

SUNKS > SUNK

SUNLAMP n lamp that generates ultraviolet rays

SUNLAMPS > SUNLAMP

SUNLAND n sunny area

SUNLANDS > SUNLAND

SUNLESS adj without sun or sunshine

SUNLESSLY > SUNLESS

SUNLIGHT n light that comes from the sun

SUNLIGHTS > SUNLIGHT

SUNLIKE > SUN

SUNLIT > SUNLIGHT

SUNN n leguminous plant of the East Indies, having yellow flowers

SUNNA n body of traditional Islamic law

SUNNAH same as > SUNNA

SUNNAHS > SUNNAH

SUNNAS > SUNNA

SUNNED > SUN

SUNNIER > SUNNY

SUNNIES pl n pair of sunglasses

SUNNIEST > SUNNY

SUNNILY > SUNNY

SUNNINESS > SUNNY

SUNNING > SUN

SUNNS > SUNN

SUNNY adj full of or exposed to sunlight

SUNPORCH n porch for sunbathing on

SUNPROOF > SUN

SUNRAY n ray of light from the sun

SUNRAYS > SUNRAY

SUNRISE n daily appearance of the sun above the horizon

SUNRISES > SUNRISE

SUNRISING same as > SUNRISE

SUNROOF n panel in the roof of a car that opens to let in air

SUNROOFS > SUNROOF

SUNROOM n room or glass-enclosed porch designed to display beautiful views

SUNROOMS > SUNROOM

SUNS > SUN

SUNSCALD n sun damage on tomato plants

SUNSCALDS > SUNSCALD

SUNSCREEN *n* cream or lotion applied to exposed skin to protect it from the ultraviolet rays of the sun

SUNSEEKER *n* person looking for sunny weather

SUNSET *n* daily disappearance of the sun below the horizon

SUNSETS > SUNSET

SUNSHADE *n* anything used to shade people from the sun, such as a parasol or awning

SUNSHADES > SUNSHADE

SUNSHINE *n* light and warmth from the sun

SUNSHINES > SUNSHINE

SUNSHINY > SUNSHINE

SUNSPOT *n* dark patch appearing temporarily on the sun's surface

SUNSPOTS > SUNSPOT

SUNSTAR *n* any starfish of the genus *Solaster*, having up to 13 arms radiating from a central disc

SUNSTARS > SUNSTAR

SUNSTONE *n* type of translucent feldspar with reddish-gold speckles

SUNSTONES > SUNSTONE

SUNSTROKE *n* illness caused by prolonged exposure to intensely hot sunlight

SUNSTRUCK *adj* suffering from sunstroke

SUNSUIT *n* child's outfit consisting of a brief top and shorts or a short skirt

SUNSUITS > SUNSUIT

SUNTAN *n* browning of the skin caused by exposure to the sun

SUNTANNED > SUNTAN

SUNTANS > SUNTAN

SUNTRAP *n* very sunny sheltered place

SUNTRAPS > SUNTRAP

SUNUP *same as* > SUNRISE

SUNUPS > SUNUP

SUNWARD *same as* > SUNWARDS

SUNWARDS *adv* towards the sun

SUNWISE *adv* moving in the same direction as the sun

SUP *same as* > SUPINE

SUPAWN *same as* > SUPPAWN

SUPAWNS > SUPAWN

SUPE *n* superintendent

SUPER *adj* excellent ▷ *n* superannuation ▷ *interj* enthusiastic expression of approval or assent ▷ *vb* work as superintendent

SUPERABLE *adj* able to be surmounted or overcome

SUPERABLY > SUPERABLE

SUPERADD *vb* add (something) to something that has already been added

SUPERADDS > SUPERADD

SUPERATE *vb* overcome

SUPERATED > SUPERATE

SUPERATES > SUPERATE

SUPERATOM *n* cluster of atoms behaving like a single atom

SUPERB *adj* excellent, impressive, or splendid

SUPERBAD *adj* exceptionally bad

SUPERBANK *n* bank that owns other banks

SUPERBER > SUPERB

SUPERBEST > SUPERB

SUPERBIKE *n* high-performance motorcycle

SUPERBITY > SUPERB

SUPERBLY > SUPERB

SUPERBOLD *adj* exceptionally bold

SUPERBOMB *n* large bomb

SUPERBRAT *n* exceptionally unpleasant child

SUPERBUG *n* bacterium resistant to antibiotics

SUPERBUGS > SUPERBUG

SUPERCAR *n* very expensive fast or powerful car with a centrally located engine

SUPERCARS > SUPERCAR

SUPERCEDE *former variant of* > SUPERSEDE

SUPERCHIC *adj* highly chic

SUPERCITY *n* very large city

SUPERCLUB *n* large and important club

SUPERCOIL *vb* form a complex coil

SUPERCOLD *adj* very cold

SUPERCOOL *vb* cool or be cooled to a temperature below that at which freezing or crystallization should occur

SUPERCOP *n* high-ranking police officer

SUPERCOPS > SUPERCOP

SUPERCOW *n* dairy cow that produces a very high milk yield

SUPERCOWS > SUPERCOW

SUPERCUTE *adj* very cute

SUPERED > SUPER

SUPEREGO *n* that part of the unconscious mind that governs ideas about what is right and wrong

SUPEREGOS > SUPEREGO

SUPERETTE *n* small store or dairy laid out along the lines of a supermarket

SUPERFAN *n* very devoted fan

SUPERFANS > SUPERFAN

SUPERFARM *n* very large farm

SUPERFAST *adj* very fast

SUPERFINE *adj* of exceptional fineness or quality

SUPERFIRM *adj* very firm

SUPERFIT *adj* highly fit

SUPERFIX *n* linguistic feature distinguishing the meaning of one word that of another

SUPERFLUX *n* superfluity

SUPERFUND *n* large fund

SUPERFUSE *vb* pour or be poured so as to cover

something

SUPERGENE *n* cluster of genes

SUPERGLUE *n* extremely strong and quick-drying glue ▷ *vb* fix with superglue

SUPERGOOD *adj* very good

SUPERGUN *n* large powerful gun

SUPERGUNS > SUPERGUN

SUPERHEAT *vb* heat (a vapour, esp steam) to a temperature above its saturation point for a given pressure

SUPERHERO *n* any of various comic-strip characters with superhuman abilities or magical powers

SUPERHET *n* type of radio receiver

SUPERHETS > SUPERHET

SUPERHIGH *adj* extremely high

SUPERHIT *n* very popular hit

SUPERHITS > SUPERHIT

SUPERHIVE *n* upper part of beehive

SUPERHOT *adj* very hot

SUPERHYPE *n* exaggerated hype

SUPERING > SUPER

SUPERIOR *adj* greater in quality, quantity, or merit ▷ *n* person of greater rank or status

SUPERIORS > SUPERIOR

SUPERJET *n* supersonic aircraft

SUPERJETS > SUPERJET

SUPERJOCK *n* very athletic person

SUPERLAIN > SUPERLIE

SUPERLAY > SUPERLIE

SUPERLIE *vb* lie above

SUPERLIES > SUPERLIE

SUPERLOAD *n* variable weight on a structure

SUPERLONG *adj* very long

SUPERLOO *n* automated public toilet

SUPERLOOS > SUPERLOO

SUPERMALE *former name for* > METAMALE

SUPERMAN *n* man with great physical or mental powers

SUPERMART *n* large self-service store selling food and household supplies

SUPERMAX *n* having or relating to the very highest levels of security

SUPERMEN > SUPERMAN

SUPERMIND *n* very powerful brain

SUPERMINI *n* small car, usually a hatchback, that is economical to run but has a high level of performance

SUPERMOM *n* very capable and busy mother

SUPERMOMS > SUPERMOM

SUPERMOTO *n* form of motorcycle racing over part-tarmac and part-dirt

circuits

SUPERNAL *adj* of or from the world of the divine

SUPERNATE *n* liquid lying above a sediment

SUPERNOVA *n* star that explodes and briefly becomes exceptionally bright

SUPERPIMP *n* pimp controlling many prostitutes

SUPERPLUS *n* surplus

SUPERPORT *n* large port

SUPERPOSE *vb* transpose (the coordinates of one geometric figure) to coincide with those of another

SUPERPRO *n* person regarded as a real professional

SUPERPROS > SUPERPRO

SUPERRACE *n* important race

SUPERREAL *adj* surreal

SUPERRICH *adj* exceptionally wealthy

SUPERROAD *n* very large road

SUPERS > SUPER

SUPERSAFE *adj* very safe

SUPERSALE *n* large sale

SUPERSALT *n* acid salt

SUPERSAUR *n* very large dinosaur

SUPERSEDE *vb* replace, supplant

SUPERSELL *vb* sell in very large numbers

SUPERSEX *n* sterile organism in which the ratio between the sex chromosomes is disturbed

SUPERSHOW *n* very impressive show

SUPERSIZE *vb* make larger

SUPERSOFT *adj* very soft

SUPERSOLD > SUPERSELL

SUPERSPY *n* highly accomplished spy

SUPERSTAR *n* very famous entertainer or sportsperson

SUPERSTUD *n* highly virile man

SUPERTAX *n* extra tax on incomes above a certain level

SUPERTHIN *adj* very thin

SUPERVENE *vb* occur as an unexpected development

SUPERVISE *vb* watch over to direct or check

SUPERWAIF *n* very young and very thin supermodel

SUPERWAVE *n* large wave

SUPERWEED *n* hybrid plant that contains genes for herbicide resistance

SUPERWIDE *n* very wide lens

SUPERWIFE *n* highly accomplished wife

SUPES > SUPE

SUPINATE *vb* turn (the hand and forearm) so that the palm faces up or forwards

SUPINATED > SUPINATE
SUPINATES > SUPINATE
SUPINATOR n muscle of the forearm that can produce the motion of supination
SUPINE adj lying flat on one's back ▷ n noun form derived from a verb in Latin
SUPINELY > SUPINE
SUPINES > SUPINE
SUPLEX n wrestling hold in which a wrestler grasps his opponent round the waist from behind and carries him backwards
SUPLEXES > SUPLEX
SUPPAWN n kind of porridge
SUPPAWNS > SUPPAWN
SUPPEAGO same as > SERPIGO
SUPPED > SUP
SUPPER n light evening meal ▷ vb eat supper
SUPPERED > SUPPER
SUPPERING > SUPPER
SUPPERS > SUPPER
SUPPING > SUP
SUPPLANT vb take the place of, oust
SUPPLANTS > SUPPLANT
SUPPLE adj (of a person) moving and bending easily and gracefully ▷ vb make or become supple
SUPPLED > SUPPLE
SUPPLELY same as > SUPPLY
SUPPLER > SUPPLE
SUPPLES > SUPPLE
SUPPLEST > SUPPLE
SUPPLIAL n instance of supplying
SUPPLIALS > SUPPLIAL
SUPPLIANT n person who requests humbly
SUPPLICAT n university petition
SUPPLIED > SUPPLY
SUPPLIER > SUPPLY
SUPPLIERS > SUPPLY
SUPPLIES > SUPPLY
SUPPLING > SUPPLE
SUPPLY vb provide with something required ▷ n supplying ▷ adj acting as a temporary substitute ▷ adv in a supple manner
SUPPLYING > SUPPLY
SUPPORT vb bear the weight of ▷ n supporting
SUPPORTED > SUPPORT
SUPPORTER n person who supports a team, principle, etc
SUPPORTS > SUPPORT
SUPPOSAL n supposition
SUPPOSALS > SUPPOSAL
SUPPOSE vb presume to be true
SUPPOSED adj presumed to be true without proof, doubtful
SUPPOSER > SUPPOSE
SUPPOSERS > SUPPOSE
SUPPOSES > SUPPOSE
SUPPOSING > SUPPOSE
SUPPRESS vb put an end to
SUPPURATE vb (of a wound

etc) produce pus
SUPRA adv above, esp referring to earlier parts of a book etc
SUPREMACY n supreme power
SUPREME adj highest in authority, rank, or degree ▷ n rich velouté sauce made with a base of veal or chicken stock, with cream or egg yolks added
SUPREMELY > SUPREME
SUPREMER > SUPREME
SUPREMES > SUPREME
SUPREMEST > SUPREME
SUPREMITY n supremeness
SUPREMO n person in overall authority
SUPREMOS > SUPREMO
SUPS > SUP
SUQ same as > SOUK
SUQS > SUQ
SUR prep above
SURA n any of the 114 chapters of the Koran
SURAH n twill-weave fabric of silk or rayon, used for dresses, blouses, etc
SURAHS > SURAH
SURAL adj of or relating to the calf of the leg
SURAMIN n drug used in treating sleeping sickness
SURAMINS > SURAMIN
SURANCE same as > ASSURANCE
SURANCES > SURANCE
SURAS > SURA
SURAT n (formerly) a cotton fabric from the Surat area of India
SURATS > SURAT
SURBAHAR n Indian string instrument
SURBAHARS > SURBAHAR
SURBASE n uppermost part, such as a moulding, of a pedestal, base, or skirting
SURBASED adj having a surbase
SURBASES > SURBASE
SURBATE vb make feet sore through walking
SURBATED > SURBATE
SURBATES > SURBATE
SURBATING > SURBATE
SURBED vb put something on its edge
SURBEDDED > SURBED
SURBEDS > SURBED
SURBET > SURBATE
SURCEASE n cessation or intermission ▷ vb desist from (some action)
SURCEASED > SURCEASE
SURCEASES > SURCEASE
SURCHARGE n additional charge ▷ vb charge (someone) an additional sum or tax
SURCINGLE n girth for a horse which goes around the body, used esp with a racing saddle ▷ vb put a surcingle on or over (a horse)

SURCOAT n tunic worn by a knight over his armour during the Middle Ages
SURCOATS > SURCOAT
SURCULI > SURCULUS
SURCULOSE adj (of a plant) bearing suckers
SURCULUS n sucker on plant
SURD n number that cannot be expressed in whole numbers ▷ adj of or relating to a surd
SURDITIES > SURDITY
SURDITY n deafness
SURDS > SURD
SURE adj free from uncertainty or doubt ▷ interj certainly ▷ vb archaic form of sewer
SURED > SURE
SUREFIRE adj certain to succeed
SURELY adv it must be true that
SURENESS > SURE
SURER > SURE
SURES > SURE
SUREST > SURE
SURETIED > SURETY
SURETIES > SURETY
SURETY n person who takes responsibility for the fulfilment of another's obligation ▷ vb be surety for
SURETYING > SURETY
SURF n foam caused by waves breaking on the shore ▷ vb take part in surfing
SURFABLE > SURF
SURFACE n outside or top of an object ▷ vb become apparent
SURFACED > SURFACE
SURFACER > SURFACE
SURFACERS > SURFACE
SURFACES > SURFACE
SURFACING > SURFACE
SURFBIRD n American shore bird
SURFBIRDS > SURFBIRD
SURFBOARD n long smooth board used in surfing
SURFBOAT n boat with a high bow and stern and flotation chambers
SURFBOATS > SURFBOAT
SURFED > SURF
SURFEIT n excessive amount ▷ vb supply or feed excessively
SURFEITED > SURFEIT
SURFEITER > SURFEIT
SURFEITS > SURFEIT
SURFER > SURFING
SURFERS > SURFING
SURFFISH n fish of American coastal seas
SURFICIAL adj superficial
SURFIE n young person whose main interest is in surfing
SURFIER > SURF
SURFIES > SURFIE
SURFIEST > SURF
SURFING n sport of riding

towards the shore on a surfboard on the crest of a wave
SURFINGS > SURFING
SURFLIKE > SURF
SURFMAN n sailor skilled in sailing through surf
SURFMEN > SURFMAN
SURFPERCH n type of marine fish of North American Pacific coastal waters
SURFRIDER > SURFING
SURFS > SURF
SURFSIDE adj next to the sea
SURFY > SURF
SURGE n sudden powerful increase ▷ vb increase suddenly
SURGED > SURGE
SURGEFUL > SURGE
SURGELESS > SURGE
SURGENT > SURGE
SURGEON n doctor who specializes in surgery
SURGEONCY n office, duties, or position of a surgeon, esp in the army or navy
SURGEONS > SURGEON
SURGER > SURGE
SURGERIES > SURGERY
SURGERS > SURGE
SURGERY n treatment in which the patient's body is cut open in order to treat the affected part
SURGES > SURGE
SURGICAL adj involving or used in surgery
SURGIER > SURGE
SURGIEST > SURGE
SURGING > SURGE
SURGINGS > SURGE
SURGY > SURGE
SURICATE n type of meerkat
SURICATES > SURICATE
SURIMI n blended seafood product made from precooked fish, restructured into stick shapes
SURIMIS > SURIMI
SURING > SURE
SURLIER > SURLY
SURLIEST > SURLY
SURLILY > SURLY
SURLINESS > SURLY
SURLOIN same as > SIRLOIN
SURLOINS > SURLOIN
SURLY adj ill-tempered and rude
SURMASTER n deputy headmaster
SURMISAL > SURMISE
SURMISALS > SURMISE
SURMISE n guess, conjecture ▷ vb guess (something) from incomplete or uncertain evidence
SURMISED > SURMISE
SURMISER > SURMISE
SURMISERS > SURMISE
SURMISES > SURMISE
SURMISING > SURMISE

SURMOUNT vb overcome (a problem)
SURMOUNTS > SURMOUNT
SURMULLET n red mullet
SURNAME n family name ▷ vb furnish with or call by a surname
SURNAMED > SURNAME
SURNAMER > SURNAME
SURNAMERS > SURNAME
SURNAMES > SURNAME
SURNAMING > SURNAME
SURPASS vb be greater than or superior to
SURPASSED > SURPASS
SURPASSER > SURPASS
SURPASSES > SURPASS
SURPLICE n loose white robe worn by clergymen and choristers
SURPLICED > SURPLICE
SURPLICES > SURPLICE
SURPLUS n amount left over in excess of what is required ▷ adj extra ▷ vb be left over in excess of what is required
SURPLUSED > SURPLUS
SURPLUSES > SURPLUS
SURPRINT vb print (additional matter) over something already printed ▷ n marks, printed matter, etc, that have been surprinted
SURPRINTS > SURPRINT
SURPRISAL > SURPRISE
SURPRISE n unexpected event ▷ vb cause to feel amazement or wonder
SURPRISED > SURPRISE
SURPRISER > SURPRISE
SURPRISES > SURPRISE
SURPRIZE same as > SURPRISE
SURPRIZED > SURPRIZE
SURPRIZES > SURPRIZE
SURQUEDRY n arrogance
SURQUEDY same as > SURQUEDRY
SURRA n tropical febrile disease of animals
SURRAS > SURRA
SURREAL adj bizarre ▷ n atmosphere or qualities evoked by surrealism
SURREALLY > SURREAL
SURREBUT vb give evidence to support the surrebutter
SURREBUTS > SURREBUT
SURREINED adj (of horse) ridden too much
SURREJOIN vb reply to legal rejoinder
SURRENDER vb give oneself up ▷ n surrendering
SURRENDRY same as > SURRENDER
SURREY n light four-wheeled horse-drawn carriage having two or four seats
SURREYS > SURREY
SURROGACY > SURROGATE
SURROGATE n substitute ▷ adj acting as a substitute ▷ vb put in another's

position as a deputy, substitute, etc
SURROUND vb be, come, or place all around (a person or thing) ▷ n border or edging
SURROUNDS > SURROUND
SURROYAL n high point on stag's horns
SURROYALS > SURROYAL
SURTAX n extra tax on incomes above a certain level ▷ vb assess for liability to surtax
SURTAXED > SURTAX
SURTAXES > SURTAX
SURTAXING > SURTAX
SURTITLE singular of > SURTITLE
SURTITLES pl n brief translations of the text of an opera or play projected above the stage
SURTOUT n man's overcoat resembling a frock coat, popular in the late 19th century
SURTOUTS > SURTOUT
SURUCUCU n South American snake
SURUCUCUS > SURUCUCU
SURVEIL same as > SURVEILLE
SURVEILED > SURVEIL
SURVEILLE vb observe closely
SURVEILS > SURVEIL
SURVEY vb view or consider in a general way ▷ n surveying
SURVEYAL > SURVEY
SURVEYALS > SURVEY
SURVEYED > SURVEY
SURVEYING n practice of measuring altitudes, angles, and distances on the land surface so that they can be accurately plotted on a map
SURVEYOR n person whose occupation is to survey land or buildings
SURVEYORS > SURVEYOR
SURVEYS > SURVEY
SURVIEW vb survey
SURVIEWED > SURVIEW
SURVIEWS > SURVIEW
SURVIVAL n condition of having survived ▷ adj of, relating to, or assisting the act of surviving
SURVIVALS > SURVIVAL
SURVIVE vb continue to live or exist after (a difficult experience)
SURVIVED > SURVIVE
SURVIVER same as > SURVIVOR
SURVIVERS > SURVIVER
SURVIVES > SURVIVE
SURVIVING > SURVIVE
SURVIVOR n person or thing that survives
SURVIVORS > SURVIVOR
SUS same as > SUSS
SUSCEPTOR n sponsor
SUSCITATE vb excite

SUSES > SUS
SUSHI n Japanese dish of small cakes of cold rice with a topping of raw fish
SUSHIS > SUSHI
SUSLIK n central Eurasian ground squirrel
SUSLIKS > SUSLIK
SUSPECT vb believe (someone) to be guilty without having any proof ▷ adj not to be trusted ▷ n person who is suspected
SUSPECTED > SUSPECT
SUSPECTER > SUSPECT
SUSPECTS > SUSPECT
SUSPENCE same as > SUSPENSE
SUSPEND vb hang from a high place
SUSPENDED > SUSPEND
SUSPENDER n elastic strap for holding up women's stockings
SUSPENDS > SUSPEND
SUSPENS same as > SUSPENSE
SUSPENSE n state of uncertainty while awaiting news, an event, etc
SUSPENSER n film that creates a feeling of suspense
SUSPENSES > SUSPENSE
SUSPENSOR n ligament or muscle that holds a part in position
SUSPICION n feeling of not trusting a person or thing
SUSPIRE vb sigh or utter with a sigh
SUSPIRED > SUSPIRE
SUSPIRES > SUSPIRE
SUSPIRING > SUSPIRE
SUSS vb attempt to work out (a situation, etc), using one's intuition ▷ n sharpness of mind
SUSSED > SUSS
SUSSES > SUSS
SUSSING > SUSS
SUSTAIN vb maintain or prolong ▷ n prolongation of a note, by playing technique or electronics
SUSTAINED > SUSTAIN
SUSTAINER n rocket engine that maintains the velocity of a space vehicle after the booster has been jettisoned
SUSTAINS > SUSTAIN
SUSTINENT adj sustaining
SUSU n (in the Caribbean) savings fund shared by friends
SUSURRANT > SUSURRATE
SUSURRATE vb make a soft rustling sound
SUSURROUS adj full of murmuring sounds
SUSURRUS > SUSURRATE
SUSUS > SUSU
SUTILE adj involving sewing
SUTLER n (formerly) a merchant who

accompanied an army in order to sell provisions to the soldiers
SUTLERIES > SUTLER
SUTLERS > SUTLER
SUTLERY > SUTLER
SUTOR n cobbler
SUTORIAL > SUTOR
SUTORIAN > SUTOR
SUTORS > SUTOR
SUTRA n Sanskrit sayings or collections of sayings
SUTRAS > SUTRA
SUTTA n Buddhist scripture
SUTTAS > SUTTA
SUTTEE n former Hindu custom whereby a widow burnt herself to death on her husband's funeral pyre
SUTTEEISM > SUTTEE
SUTTEES > SUTTEE
SUTTLE vb work as sutler
SUTTLED > SUTTLE
SUTTLES > SUTTLE
SUTTLETIE same as > SUBTLETY
SUTTLING > SUTTLE
SUTTLY > SUBTLE
SUTURAL > SUTURE
SUTURALLY > SUTURE
SUTURE n stitch joining the edges of a wound ▷ vb join (the edges of a wound, etc) by means of sutures
SUTURED > SUTURE
SUTURES > SUTURE
SUTURING > SUTURE
SUZERAIN n state or sovereign with limited authority over another self-governing state
SUZERAINS > SUZERAIN
SVARAJ same as > SWARAJ
SVARAJES > SVARAJ
SVASTIKA same as > SWASTIKA
SVASTIKAS > SVASTIKA
SVEDBERG n unit used in physics
SVEDBERGS > SVEDBERG
SVELTE adj attractively or gracefully slim
SVELTELY > SVELTE
SVELTER > SVELTE
SVELTEST > SVELTE
SWAB n small piece of cotton wool used to apply medication, clean a wound, etc ▷ vb clean (a wound) with a swab
SWABBED > SWAB
SWABBER n person who uses a swab
SWABBERS > SWABBER
SWABBIE same as > SWABBY
SWABBIES > SWABBY
SWABBING > SWAB
SWABBY n seaman
SWABS > SWAB
SWACK adj flexible
SWACKED adj in a state of intoxication, stupor, or euphoria induced by drugs or alcohol
SWAD n loutish person
SWADDIE same as > SWADDY
SWADDIES > SWADDY

SWADDLE vb wrap (a baby) in swaddling clothes ▷ n swaddling clothes
SWADDLED > SWADDLE
SWADDLER > SWADDLE
SWADDLERS > SWADDLE
SWADDLES > SWADDLE
SWADDLING > SWADDLE
SWADDY n private soldier
SWADS > SWADDLE
SWAG n stolen property ▷ vb sway from side to side
SWAGE n shaped tool or die used in forming cold metal by hammering ▷ vb form (metal) with a swage
SWAGED > SWAGE
SWAGER > SWAGE
SWAGERS > SWAGE
SWAGES > SWAGE
SWAGGED > SWAG
SWAGGER vb walk or behave arrogantly ▷ n arrogant walk or manner ▷ adj elegantly fashionable
SWAGGERED > SWAGGER
SWAGGERER > SWAGGER
SWAGGERS > SWAGGER
SWAGGIE same as > SWAGGER
SWAGGIES > SWAGGIE
SWAGGING > SWAG
SWAGING > SWAGE
SWAGMAN n tramp who carries his belongings in a bundle on his back
SWAGMEN > SWAGMAN
SWAGS > SWAG
SWAGSHOP n shop selling cheap goods
SWAGSHOPS > SWAGSHOP
SWAGSMAN same as > SWAGMAN
SWAGSMEN > SWAGSMAN
SWAIL same as > SWALE
SWAILS > SWAIL
SWAIN n suitor
SWAINING n acting as suitor
SWAININGS > SWAINING
SWAINISH > SWAIN
SWAINS > SWAIN
SWALE n moist depression in a tract of land, usually with rank vegetation ▷ vb sway
SWALED > SWALE
SWALES > SWALE
SWALIER > SWALE
SWALIEST > SWALE
SWALING > SWALE
SWALINGS > SWALE
SWALLET n hole where water goes underground
SWALLETS > SWALLET
SWALLOW vb cause to pass down one's throat ▷ n swallowing
SWALLOWED > SWALLOW
SWALLOWER > SWALLOW
SWALLOWS > SWALLOW
SWALY > SWALE
SWAM > SWIM
SWAMI n Hindu religious teacher
SWAMIES > SWAMI
SWAMIS > SWAMI
SWAMP n watery area of land, bog ▷ vb cause (a boat) to fill with water and

sink
SWAMPED > SWAMP
SWAMPER n person who lives or works in a swampy region, esp in the southern US
SWAMPERS > SWAMPER
SWAMPIER > SWAMP
SWAMPIEST > SWAMP
SWAMPING > SWAMP
SWAMPISH > SWAMP
SWAMPLAND n permanently waterlogged area
SWAMPLESS > SWAMP
SWAMPS > SWAMP
SWAMPY > SWAMP
SWAMY same as > SWAMI
SWAN n large usu white water bird with a long graceful neck ▷ vb wander about idly
SWANG > SWING
SWANHERD n person who herds swans
SWANHERDS > SWANHERD
SWANK vb show off or boast ▷ n showing off or boasting
SWANKED > SWANK
SWANKER > SWANK
SWANKERS > SWANK
SWANKEST > SWANK
SWANKEY same as > SWANKY
SWANKEYS > SWANKY
SWANKIE same as > SWANKY
SWANKIER > SWANKY
SWANKIES > SWANKY
SWANKIEST > SWANKY
SWANKILY > SWANKY
SWANKING > SWANK
SWANKPOT same as > SWANK
SWANKPOTS > SWANKPOT
SWANKS > SWANK
SWANKY adj expensive and showy, stylish ▷ n lively person
SWANLIKE > SWAN
SWANNED > SWAN
SWANNERY n place where swans are kept and bred
SWANNIE n (in NZ) type of all-weather heavy woollen shirt
SWANNIER > SWANNY
SWANNIES > SWANNIE
SWANNIEST > SWANNY
SWANNING > SWAN
SWANNINGS > SWAN
SWANNY adj swanlike
SWANPAN n Chinese abacus
SWANPANS > SWANPAN
SWANS > SWAN
SWANSDOWN n fine soft feathers of a swan
SWANSKIN n skin of a swan with the feathers attached
SWANSKINS > SWANSKIN
SWAP vb exchange (something) for something else ▷ n exchange
SWAPPED > SWAP
SWAPPER > SWAP
SWAPPERS > SWAP
SWAPPING > SWAP
SWAPPINGS > SWAP
SWAPS > SWAP
SWAPT > SWAP

SWAPTION another name for > SWAP
SWAPTIONS > SWAPTION
SWARAJ n (in British India) self-government
SWARAJES > SWARAJ
SWARAJISM > SWARAJ
SWARAJIST > SWARAJ
SWARD n stretch of short grass ▷ vb cover or become covered with grass
SWARDED > SWARD
SWARDIER > SWARDY
SWARDIEST > SWARDY
SWARDING > SWARD
SWARDS > SWARD
SWARDY adj covered with sward
SWARE > SWEAR
SWARF n material removed by cutting tools in the machining of metals, stone, etc ▷ vb faint
SWARFED > SWARF
SWARFING > SWARF
SWARFS > SWARF
SWARM n large group of bees or other insects ▷ vb move in a swarm
SWARMED > SWARM
SWARMER > SWARM
SWARMERS > SWARM
SWARMING > SWARM
SWARMINGS > SWARM
SWARMS > SWARM
SWART adj swarthy
SWARTH same as > SWART
SWARTHIER > SWARTHY
SWARTHILY > SWARTHY
SWARTHS > SWARTH
SWARTHY adj dark-complexioned
SWARTNESS > SWART
SWARTY > SWART
SWARVE same as > SWARF
SWARVED > SWARF
SWARVES > SWARF
SWARVING > SWARF
SWASH n rush of water up a beach following each break of the waves ▷ vb (esp of water or things in water) to wash or move with noisy splashing
SWASHED > SWASH
SWASHER n braggart
SWASHERS > SWASHER
SWASHES > SWASH
SWASHIER > SWASHY
SWASHIEST > SWASHY
SWASHING > SWASH
SWASHINGS > SWASH
SWASHWORK n type of work done on lathe
SWASHY adj slushy
SWASTICA same as > SWASTIKA
SWASTICAS > SWASTICA
SWASTIKA n symbol in the shape of a cross with the arms bent at right angles, used as the emblem of Nazi Germany
SWASTIKAS > SWASTIKA
SWAT vb strike or hit sharply ▷ n swatter
SWATCH n sample of cloth

SWATCHES > SWATCH
SWATH n width of one sweep of a scythe or of the blade of a mowing machine
SWATHABLE > SWATHE
SWATHE vb bandage or wrap completely ▷ n bandage or wrapping
SWATHED > SWATHE
SWATHER > SWATHE
SWATHERS > SWATHE
SWATHES > SWATHE
SWATHIER > SWATH
SWATHIEST > SWATH
SWATHING > SWATHE
SWATHS > SWATH
SWATHY > SWATH
SWATS > SWAT
SWATTED > SWAT
SWATTER n device for killing insects, esp a meshed flat attached to a handle ▷ vb splash
SWATTERED > SWATTER
SWATTERS > SWATTER
SWATTING > SWAT
SWATTINGS > SWAT
SWAY vb swing to and fro or from side to side ▷ n power or influence
SWAYABLE > SWAY
SWAYBACK n abnormal sagging in the spine of older horses
SWAYBACKS > SWAYBACK
SWAYED > SWAY
SWAYER > SWAY
SWAYERS > SWAY
SWAYFUL > SWAY
SWAYING > SWAY
SWAYINGS > SWAY
SWAYL same as > SWEAL
SWAYLED > SWAYL
SWAYLING > SWAYL
SWAYLINGS > SWAYL
SWAYLS > SWAYL
SWAYS > SWAY
SWAZZLE n small metal instrument used to produce a shrill voice
SWAZZLES > SWAZZLE
SWEAL vb scorch
SWEALED > SWEAL
SWEALING > SWEAL
SWEALINGS > SWEAL
SWEALS > SWEAL
SWEAR vb use obscene or blasphemous language
SWEARD same as > SWORD
SWEARDS > SWEARD
SWEARER > SWEAR
SWEARERS > SWEAR
SWEARING > SWEAR
SWEARINGS > SWEAR
SWEARS > SWEAR
SWEARWORD n word considered obscene or blasphemous
SWEAT n salty liquid given off through the pores of the skin ▷ vb have sweat coming through the pores
SWEATBAND n strip of cloth tied around the forehead or wrist to absorb sweat
SWEATBOX n device for causing tobacco leaves,

fruit, or hides to sweat

SWEATED *adj* made by exploited labour

SWEATER *n* (woollen) garment for the upper part of the body

SWEATERS > SWEATER

SWEATIER > SWEATY

SWEATIEST > SWEATY

SWEATILY > SWEATY

SWEATING > SWEAT

SWEATINGS > SWEAT

SWEATLESS > SWEAT

SWEATS > SWEAT

SWEATSHOP *n* place where employees work long hours in poor conditions for low pay

SWEATSUIT *n* knitted suit worn by athletes for training

SWEATY *adj* covered with sweat

SWEDE *n* kind of turnip

SWEDES > SWEDE

SWEDGER *n* Scots dialect word for sweet

SWEDGERS > SWEDGER

SWEE *vb* sway

SWEED > SWEE

SWEEING > SWEE

SWEEL *same as* > SWEAL

SWEELED > SWEEL

SWEELING > SWEEL

SWEELS > SWEEL

SWEENEY *n* police flying squad

SWEENEYS > SWEENEY

SWEENIES > SWEENY

SWEENY *n* wasting of the shoulder muscles of a horse

SWEEP *vb* remove dirt from (a floor) with a broom ▷ *n* sweeping

SWEEPBACK *n* rearward inclination of a component or surface

SWEEPER *n* device used to sweep carpets, consisting of a long handle attached to a revolving brush

SWEEPERS > SWEEPER

SWEEPIER > SWEEP

SWEEPIEST > SWEEP

SWEEPING > SWEEP

SWEEPINGS *pl n* debris, litter, or refuse

SWEEPS > SWEEP

SWEEPY > SWEEP

SWEER *variant of* > SWEIR

SWEERED > SWEER

SWEERING > SWEER

SWEERS > SWEER

SWEERT > SWEER

SWEES > SWEE

SWEET *adj* tasting of or like sugar ▷ *n* shaped piece of food consisting mainly of sugar ▷ *vb* sweeten

SWEETCORN *n* variety of maize, the kernels of which are eaten when young

SWEETED > SWEET

SWEETEN *vb* make (food or drink) sweet or sweeter

SWEETENED > SWEETEN

SWEETENER *n* sweetening

agent that does not contain sugar

SWEETENS > SWEETEN

SWEETER > SWEET

SWEETEST > SWEET

SWEETFISH *n* small Japanese fish

SWEETIE *n* lovable person

SWEETIES > SWEETIE

SWEETING *n* variety of sweet apple

SWEETINGS > SWEETING

SWEETISH > SWEET

SWEETLY > SWEET

SWEETMAN *n* (in the Caribbean) a man kept by a woman

SWEETMEAL *adj* (of biscuits) sweet and wholemeal

SWEETMEAT *n* sweet delicacy such as a small cake

SWEETMEN > SWEETMAN

SWEETNESS > SWEET

SWEETPEA *n* climbing plant with fragrant flowers of delicate pastel colours

SWEETPEAS > SWEETPEA

SWEETS > SWEET

SWEETSHOP *n* shop selling confectionery

SWEETSOP *n* small West Indian tree

SWEETSOPS > SWEETSOP

SWEETWOOD *n* tropical tree

SWEETY *same as* > SWEETIE

SWEIR *vb* swear ▷ *adj* lazy

SWEIRED > SWEIR

SWEIRER > SWEIR

SWEIREST > SWEIR

SWEIRING > SWEIR

SWEIRNESS > SWEIR

SWEIRS > SWEIR

SWEIRT > SWEIR

SWELCHIE *n* whirlpool in Orkney

SWELCHIES > SWELCHIE

SWELL *vb* expand or increase ▷ *n* swelling or being swollen ▷ *adj* excellent or fine

SWELLDOM *n* fashionable society

SWELLDOMS > SWELLDOM

SWELLED > SWELL

SWELLER > SWELL

SWELLERS > SWELL

SWELLEST > SWELL

SWELLFISH *popular name for* > PUFFER

SWELLHEAD *n* conceited person

SWELLING > SWELL

SWELLINGS > SWELL

SWELLISH > SWELL

SWELLS > SWELL

SWELT *vb* die

SWELTED > SWELT

SWELTER *vb* feel uncomfortably hot ▷ *n* hot and uncomfortable condition

SWELTERED > SWELTER

SWELTERS > SWELTER

SWELTING > SWELT

SWELTRIER > SWELTRY

SWELTRY *adj* sultry

SWELTS > SWELT

SWEPT > SWEEP

SWEPTBACK *adj* (of an aircraft wing) having the leading edge inclined backwards towards the rear

SWEPTWING *adj* (of an aircraft) having wings swept backwards

SWERF *same as* > SWARF

SWERFED > SWERF

SWERFING > SWERF

SWERFS > SWERF

SWERVABLE > SWERVE

SWERVE *vb* turn aside from a course sharply or suddenly ▷ *n* swerving

SWERVED > SWERVE

SWERVER > SWERVE

SWERVERS > SWERVE

SWERVES > SWERVE

SWERVING > SWERVE

SWERVINGS > SWERVE

SWEVEN *n* vision or dream

SWEVENS > SWEVEN

SWEY *same as* > SWEE

SWEYED > SWEY

SWEYING > SWEY

SWEYS > SWEY

SWIDDEN *n* area of land where slash-and-burn techniques have been used to prepare it for cultivation

SWIDDENS > SWIDDEN

SWIES > SWY

SWIFT *adj* moving or able to move quickly ▷ *n* fast-flying bird with pointed wings ▷ *adv* swiftly or quickly ▷ *vb* make tight

SWIFTED > SWIFT

SWIFTER *n* line run around the ends of capstan bars to prevent their falling out of their sockets

SWIFTERS > SWIFTER

SWIFTEST > SWIFT

SWIFTIE *n* trick, ruse, or deception

SWIFTIES > SWIFTY

SWIFTING > SWIFT

SWIFTLET *n* type of small Asian swift

SWIFTLETS > SWIFTLET

SWIFTLY > SWIFT

SWIFTNESS > SWIFT

SWIFTS > SWIFT

SWIFTY *same as* > SWIFTIE

SWIG *n* large mouthful of drink ▷ *vb* drink in large mouthfuls

SWIGGED > SWIG

SWIGGER > SWIG

SWIGGERS > SWIG

SWIGGING > SWIG

SWIGS > SWIG

SWILER *n* (in Newfoundland) a seal hunter

SWILERS > SWILER

SWILL *vb* drink greedily ▷ *n* sloppy mixture containing waste food, fed to pigs

SWILLED > SWILL

SWILLER > SWILL

SWILLERS > SWILL

SWILLING > SWILL

SWILLINGS > SWILL

SWILLS > SWILL

SWIM *vb* move along in water by movements of the limbs ▷ *n* act or period of swimming

SWIMMABLE > SWIM

SWIMMER > SWIM

SWIMMERET *n* any of the small paired appendages on the abdomen of crustaceans

SWIMMERS *pl n* swimming costume

SWIMMIER > SWIMMY

SWIMMIEST > SWIMMY

SWIMMILY > SWIMMY

SWIMMING > SWIM

SWIMMINGS > SWIM

SWIMMY *adj* dizzy

SWIMS > SWIM

SWIMSUIT *n* woman's swimming garment that leaves the arms and legs bare

SWIMSUITS > SWIMSUIT

SWIMWEAR *n* swimming costumes

SWIMWEARS > SWIMWEAR

SWINDGE *same as* > SWINGE

SWINDGED > SWINDGE

SWINDGES > SWINDGE

SWINDGING > SWINDGE

SWINDLE *vb* cheat (someone) out of money ▷ *n* instance of swindling

SWINDLED > SWINDLE

SWINDLER > SWINDLE

SWINDLERS > SWINDLE

SWINDLES > SWINDLE

SWINDLING > SWINDLE

SWINE *n* contemptible person

SWINEHERD *n* person who looks after pigs

SWINEHOOD > SWINE

SWINELIKE > SWINE

SWINEPOX *n* acute infectious viral disease of pigs

SWINERIES > SWINERY

SWINERY *n* pig farm

SWINES > SWINE

SWING *vb* move to and fro, sway ▷ *n* swinging

SWINGBEAT *n* type of modern dance music that combines soul, rhythm and blues, and hip-hop

SWINGBOAT *n* piece of fairground equipment consisting of a boat-shaped carriage for swinging in

SWINGBY *n* act of spacecraft passing close to planet

SWINGBYS > SWINGBY

SWINGE *vb* beat, flog, or punish

SWINGED > SWINGE

SWINGEING > SWINGE

SWINGER *n* person regarded as being modern and lively

SWINGERS > SWINGER

SWINGES > SWINGE

SWINGIER > SWINGY

S

SWINGIEST > SWINGY

SWINGING > SWING

SWINGINGS > SWING

SWINGISM n former resistance to use of agricultural machines

SWINGISMS > SWINGISM

SWINGLE n flat-bladed wooden instrument used for beating and scraping flax ▷ vb use a swingle on

SWINGLED > SWINGLE

SWINGLES > SWINGLE

SWINGLING > SWINGLE

SWINGMAN n musician specializing in swing music

SWINGMEN > SWINGMAN

SWINGS > SWING

SWINGTREE n crossbar in a horse's harness

SWINGY adj lively and modern

SWINISH > SWINE

SWINISHLY > SWINE

SWINK vb toil or drudge ▷ n toil or drudgery

SWINKED > SWINK

SWINKER > SWINK

SWINKERS > SWINK

SWINKING > SWINK

SWINKS > SWINK

SWINNEY variant of > SWEENY

SWINNEYS > SWINNEY

SWIPE vb strike (at) with a sweeping blow ▷ n hard blow

SWIPED > SWIPE

SWIPER > SWIPE

SWIPERS > SWIPE

SWIPES pl n beer, esp when poor or weak

SWIPEY adj drunk

SWIPIER > SWIPEY

SWIPIEST > SWIPEY

SWIPING > SWIPE

SWIPLE same as > SWIPPLE

SWIPLES > SWIPLE

SWIPPLE n part of a flail that strikes the grain

SWIPPLES > SWIPPLE

SWIRE n neck

SWIRES > SWIRE

SWIRL vb turn with a whirling motion ▷ n whirling motion

SWIRLED > SWIRL

SWIRLIER > SWIRL

SWIRLIEST > SWIRL

SWIRLING > SWIRL

SWIRLS > SWIRL

SWIRLY > SWIRL

SWISH vb move with a whistling or hissing sound ▷ n whistling or hissing sound ▷ adj fashionable, smart

SWISHED > SWISH

SWISHER > SWISH

SWISHERS > SWISH

SWISHES > SWISH

SWISHEST > SWISH

SWISHIER > SWISHY

SWISHIEST > SWISHY

SWISHING > SWISH

SWISHINGS > SWISH

SWISHY adj moving with a

swishing sound

SWISS n type of muslin

SWISSES > SWISS

SWISSING n method of treating cloth

SWISSINGS > SWISSING

SWITCH n device for opening and closing an electric circuit ▷ vb change abruptly

SWITCHED > SWITCH

SWITCHEL n type of beer

SWITCHELS > SWITCHEL

SWITCHER > SWITCH

SWITCHERS > SWITCH

SWITCHES > SWITCH

SWITCHIER > SWITCH

SWITCHING > SWITCH

SWITCHMAN n person who operates railway points

SWITCHMEN > SWITCHMAN

SWITCHY > SWITCH

SWITH adv swiftly

SWITHE same as > SWITH

SWITHER vb hesitate or be indecisive ▷ n state of hesitation or uncertainty

SWITHERED > SWITHER

SWITHERS > SWITHER

SWITHLY > SWITH

SWITS same as > SWITCH

SWITSES > SWITS

SWIVE vb have sexual intercourse with (a person)

SWIVED > SWIVE

SWIVEL vb turn on a central point ▷ n coupling device that allows an attached object to turn freely

SWIVELED > SWIVEL

SWIVELING > SWIVEL

SWIVELLED > SWIVEL

SWIVELS > SWIVEL

SWIVES > SWIVE

SWIVET n nervous state

SWIVETS > SWIVET

SWIVING > SWIVE

SWIZ n swindle or disappointment

SWIZZ same as > SWIZ

SWIZZED > SWIZZ

SWIZZES > SWIZZ

SWIZZING > SWIZZ

SWIZZLE n unshaken cocktail ▷ vb stir a swizzle stick in (a drink)

SWIZZLED > SWIZZLE

SWIZZLER > SWIZZLE

SWIZZLERS > SWIZZLE

SWIZZLES > SWIZZLE

SWIZZLING > SWIZZLE

SWOB less common word for > SWAB

SWOBBED > SWOB

SWOBBER > SWOB

SWOBBERS > SWOB

SWOBBING > SWOB

SWOBS > SWOB

SWOFFER > SWOFFING

SWOFFERS > SWOFFING

SWOFFING n sport of saltwater fly-fishing

SWOFFINGS > SWOFFING

SWOLLEN > SWELL

SWOLLENLY > SWELL

SWOLN > SWELL

SWONE archaic variant

of > SWOON

SWONES > SWONE

SWOON n faint ▷ vb faint because of shock or strong emotion

SWOONED > SWOON

SWOONER > SWOON

SWOONERS > SWOON

SWOONIER > SWOONY

SWOONIEST > SWOONY

SWOONING > SWOON

SWOONINGS > SWOON

SWOONS > SWOON

SWOONY adj romantic or sexy

SWOOP vb sweep down or pounce on suddenly ▷ n swooping

SWOOPED > SWOOP

SWOOPER > SWOOP

SWOOPERS > SWOOP

SWOOPIER > SWOOP

SWOOPIEST > SWOOP

SWOOPING > SWOOP

SWOOPS > SWOOP

SWOOPY > SWOOP

SWOOSH vb make a swirling or rustling sound when moving or pouring out ▷ n swirling or rustling sound or movement

SWOOSHED > SWOOSH

SWOOSHES > SWOOSH

SWOOSHING > SWOOSH

SWOP same as > SWAP

SWOPPED > SWOP

SWOPPER > SWOP

SWOPPERS > SWOP

SWOPPING > SWOP

SWOPPINGS > SWOP

SWOPS > SWOP

SWOPT > SWOP

SWORD n weapon with a long sharp blade ▷ vb bear a sword

SWORDBILL n South American hummingbird

SWORDED > SWORD

SWORDER n fighter with sword

SWORDERS > SWORDER

SWORDFISH n large fish with a very long upper jaw

SWORDING > SWORD

SWORDLESS > SWORD

SWORDLIKE > SWORD

SWORDMAN same as > SWORDSMAN

SWORDMEN > SWORDMAN

SWORDPLAY n action or art of fighting with a sword

SWORDS > SWORD

SWORDSMAN n person skilled in the use of a sword

SWORDSMEN > SWORDSMAN

SWORDTAIL n type of small freshwater fish of Central America

SWORE > SWEAR

SWORN > SWEAR

SWOT vb study (a subject) intensively ▷ n person who studies hard

SWOTS > SWOT

SWOTTED > SWOT

SWOTTER same as > SWOT

SWOTTERS > SWOT

SWOTTIER > SWOTTY

SWOTTIEST > SWOTTY

SWOTTING > SWOT

SWOTTINGS > SWOT

SWOTTY adj given to studying hard, esp to the exclusion of other activities

SWOUN same as > SWOON

SWOUND same as > SWOON

SWOUNDED > SWOUND

SWOUNDING > SWOUND

SWOUNDS less common spellings of > ZOUNDS

SWOUNE same as > SWOON

SWOUNED > SWOUNE

SWOUNES > SWOUNE

SWOUNING > SWOUNE

SWOUNS > SWOUN

SWOWND same as > SWOON

SWOWNDS > SWOWND

SWOWNE same as > SWOON

SWOWNES > SWOWNE

SWOZZLE same as > SWAZZLE

SWOZZLES > SWOZZLE

SWUM > SWIM

SWUNG > SWING

SWY n Australian gambling game involving two coins

SYBARITE n lover of luxury ▷ adj luxurious or sensuous

SYBARITES > SYBARITE

SYBARITIC > SYBARITE

SYBBE same as > SIB

SYBBES > SYBBE

SYBIL same as > SIBYL

SYBILS > SYBIL

SYBO n spring onion

SYBOE same as > SYBO

SYBOES > SYBOE

SYBOTIC adj of a swineherd

SYBOTISM > SYBOTIC

SYBOTISMS > SYBOTIC

SYBOW same as > SYBO

SYBOWS > SYBOW

SYCAMINE n mulberry tree mentioned in the Bible, thought to be the black mulberry

SYCAMINES > SYCAMINE

SYCAMORE n tree with five-pointed leaves and two-winged fruits

SYCAMORES > SYCAMORE

SYCE n (formerly, in India) a servant employed to look after horses, etc

SYCEE n silver ingots formerly used as a medium of exchange in China

SYCEES > SYCEE

SYCES > SYCE

SYCOMORE same as > SYCAMORE

SYCOMORES > SYCOMORE

SYCONIA > SYCONIUM

SYCONIUM n fleshy fruit of the fig

SYCOPHANT n person who uses flattery to win favour from people with power or influence

SYCOSES > SYCOSIS

SYCOSIS n chronic inflammation of the hair follicles

SYE vb strain

SYED > SYE

SYEING > SYE

SYEN *same as* > SCION

SYENITE *n* light-coloured coarse-grained plutonic igneous rock

SYENITES > SYENITE

SYENITIC > SYENITE

SYENS > SYEN

SYES > SYE

SYKE *same as* > SIKE

SYKER *adv* surely

SYKES > SYKE

SYLI *n* Finnish unit of volume

SYLIS > SYLI

SYLLABARY *n* table or list of syllables

SYLLABI > SYLLABUS

SYLLABIC *adj* of or relating to syllables ▷ *n* syllabic consonant

SYLLABICS > SYLLABIC

SYLLABIFY *vb* divide (a word) into syllables

SYLLABISE *same as* > SYLLABIZE

SYLLABISM *n* use of a writing system consisting of characters for syllables

SYLLABIZE *vb* divide into syllables

SYLLABLE *n* part of a word pronounced as a unit

SYLLABLED > SYLLABLE

SYLLABLES > SYLLABLE

SYLLABUB *n* dessert of beaten cream, sugar, and wine

SYLLABUBS > SYLLABUB

SYLLABUS *n* list of subjects for a course of study

SYLLEPSES > SYLLEPSIS

SYLLEPSIS *n* (in grammar or rhetoric) the use of a single sentence construction in which a verb, adjective, etc is made to cover two syntactical functions

SYLLEPTIC > SYLLEPSIS

SYLLOGISE *same as* > SYLLOGIZE

SYLLOGISM *n* form of logical reasoning consisting of two premises and a conclusion

SYLLOGIST > SYLLOGISM

SYLLOGIZE *vb* reason or infer by using syllogisms

SYLPH *n* slender graceful girl or woman

SYLPHIC *sylph*

SYLPHID *n* little sylph

SYLPHIDE *same as* > SYLPHID

SYLPHIDES > SYLPHIDE

SYLPHIDS > SYLPHID

SYLPHIER > SYLPH

SYLPHIEST > SYLPH

SYLPHINE > SYLPH

SYLPHISH > SYLPH

SYLPHLIKE > SYLPH

SYLPHS > SYLPH

SYLPHY > SYLPH

SYLVA *n* trees growing in a particular region

SYLVAE > SYLVA

SYLVAN *adj* relating to woods and trees ▷ *n* inhabitant of the woods, esp a spirit

SYLVANER *n* German variety of grape

SYLVANERS > SYLVANER

SYLVANITE *n* silver-white mineral

SYLVANS > SYLVAN

SYLVAS > SYLVA

SYLVATIC *adj* growing, living, or occurring in a wood or beneath a tree

SYLVIA *n* songbird

SYLVIAS > SYLVIA

SYLVIINE > SYLVIA

SYLVIN *same as* > SYLVITE

SYLVINE *same as* > SYLVITE

SYLVINES > SYLVINE

SYLVINITE *n* rock containing sylvine

SYLVINS > SYLVIN

SYLVITE *n* soluble colourless, white, or coloured mineral

SYLVITES > SYLVITE

SYMAR *same as* > CYMAR

SYMARS > SYMAR

SYMBION *same as* > SYMBIONT

SYMBIONS > SYMBION

SYMBIONT *n* organism living in a state of symbiosis

SYMBIONTS > SYMBIONT

SYMBIOSES > SYMBIOSIS

SYMBIOSIS *n* close association of two species living together to their mutual benefit

SYMBIOT *same as* > SYMBIONT

SYMBIOTE *same as* > SYMBIONT

SYMBIOTES > SYMBIOTE

SYMBIOTIC > SYMBIOSIS

SYMBIOTS > SYMBIOT

SYMBOL *n* sign or thing that stands for something else ▷ *vb* be a symbol

SYMBOLE *same as* > CYMBAL

SYMBOLED > SYMBOL

SYMBOLES > SYMBOLE

SYMBOLIC *adj* of or relating to a symbol or symbols

SYMBOLICS *n* study of beliefs

SYMBOLING > SYMBOL

SYMBOLISE *same as* > SYMBOLIZE

SYMBOLISM *n* representation of something by symbols

SYMBOLIST *n* person who uses or can interpret symbols ▷ *adj* of, relating to, or characterizing symbolism or symbolists

SYMBOLIZE *vb* be a symbol of

SYMBOLLED > SYMBOL

SYMBOLOGY *n* use, study, or interpretation of symbols

SYMBOLS > SYMBOL

SYMITAR *same as* > SCIMITAR

SYMITARE *same as* > SCIMITAR

SYMITARES > SYMITARE

SYMITARS > SYMITAR

SYMMETRAL > SYMMETRY

SYMMETRIC *adj* (of a disease) affecting both sides of the body

SYMMETRY *n* state of having two halves that are mirror images of each other

SYMPATHIN *n* substance released at certain sympathetic nerve endings

SYMPATHY *n* compassion for someone's pain or distress

SYMPATICO *adj* nice

SYMPATRIC *adj* (of biological speciation or species) existing in the same geographical areas

SYMPATRY *n* existing of organisms together without interbreeding

SYMPETALY *n* quality of having petals that are united

SYMPHILE *n* insect that lives in the nests of social insects and is fed and reared by the inmates

SYMPHILES > SYMPHILE

SYMPHILY *n* presence of different kinds of animal in ants' nests

SYMPHONIC > SYMPHONY

SYMPHONY *n* composition for orchestra, with several movements

SYMPHYSES > SYMPHYSIS

SYMPHYSIS *n* growing together of parts or structures

SYMPHYTIC > SYMPHYSIS

SYMPLAST *n* continuous system of protoplasts, linked by plasmodesmata and bounded by the cell wall

SYMPLASTS > SYMPLAST

SYMPLOCE *n* word repetition in successive clauses

SYMPLOCES > SYMPLOCE

SYMPODIA > SYMPODIUM

SYMPODIAL > SYMPODIUM

SYMPODIUM *n* main axis of growth in the grapevine and similar plants

SYMPOSIA > SYMPOSIUM

SYMPOSIAC *adj* of, suitable for, or occurring at a symposium

SYMPOSIAL > SYMPOSIUM

SYMPOSIUM *n* conference for discussion of a particular topic

SYMPTOM *n* sign indicating the presence of an illness

SYMPTOMS > SYMPTOM

SYMPTOSES > SYMPTOSIS

SYMPTOSIS *n* wasting condition

SYMPTOTIC > SYMPTOSIS

SYN *adv Scots word for* > SINCE

SYNAGOG *same as* > SYNAGOGUE

SYNAGOGAL > SYNAGOGUE

SYNAGOGS > SYNAGOG

SYNAGOGUE *n* Jewish place of worship and religious instruction

SYNALEPHA *n* elision of vowels in speech

SYNANDRIA *pl n* peculiar bunchings of stamens

SYNANGIA > SYNANGIUM

SYNANGIUM *n* junction between arteries

SYNANON *n* type of therapy given to drug addicts

SYNANONS > SYNANON

SYNANTHIC > SYNANTHY

SYNANTHY *n* abnormal joining between flowers

SYNAPHEA *n* continuity in metre of verses of poem

SYNAPHEAS > SYNAPHEA

SYNAPHEIA *same as* > SYNAPHEA

SYNAPSE *n* gap where nerve impulses pass between two nerve cells ▷ *vb* create a synapse

SYNAPSED > SYNAPSE

SYNAPSES > SYNAPSIS

SYNAPSID *n* prehistoric mammal-like reptile

SYNAPSIDS > SYNAPSID

SYNAPSING > SYNAPSE

SYNAPSIS *n* association in pairs of homologous chromosomes at the start of meiosis

SYNAPTASE *n* type of enzyme

SYNAPTE *n* litany in Greek Orthodox Church

SYNAPTES > SYNAPTE

SYNAPTIC *adj* of or relating to a synapse

SYNARCHY *n* joint rule

SYNASTRY *n* coincidence of astrological influences

SYNAXARIA *pl n* readings in the Greek Orthodox Church

SYNAXES > SYNAXIS

SYNAXIS *n* early Christian meeting

SYNC *n* synchronization ▷ *vb* synchronize

SYNCARP *n* fleshy multiple fruit

SYNCARPS > SYNCARP

SYNCARPY *n* quality of consisting of united carpels

SYNCED > SYNC

SYNCH *same as* > SYNC

SYNCHED > SYNCH

SYNCHING > SYNCH

SYNCHRO *n* type of electrical device

SYNCHRONY *n* state of being synchronous

SYNCHROS > SYNCHRO

SYNCHS > SYNCH

SYNCHYSES > SYNCHYSIS

SYNCHYSIS *n* muddled meaning

SYNCING > SYNC

SYNCLINAL > SYNCLINE

SYNCLINE *n* downward slope of stratified rock in which the layers dip towards each other from either side

SYNCLINES > SYNCLINE

SYNCOM n communications satellite in stationary orbit

SYNCOMS > SYNCOM

SYNCOPAL > SYNCOPE

SYNCOPATE vb stress the weak beats in (a rhythm) instead of the strong ones

SYNCOPE n omission of one or more sounds or letters from the middle of a word

SYNCOPES > SYNCOPE

SYNCOPIC > SYNCOPE

SYNCOPTIC > SYNCOPE

SYNCRETIC adj of the tendency of languages to reduce their use of inflection

SYNCS > SYNC

SYNCYTIA > SYNCYTIUM

SYNCYTIAL > SYNCYTIUM

SYNCYTIUM n mass of cytoplasm containing many nuclei and enclosed in a cell membrane

SYND same as > SYNE

SYNDACTYL adj (of certain animals) having two or more digits growing fused together ▷ n animal with this arrangement of digits

SYNDED > SYND

SYNDESES > SYNDESIS

SYNDESIS n use of syndetic constructions

SYNDET n synthetic detergent

SYNDETIC adj denoting a grammatical construction in which two clauses are connected by a conjunction

SYNDETON n syndetic construction

SYNDETONS > SYNDETON

SYNDETS > SYNDET

SYNDIC n business or legal agent of some universities or other institutions

SYNDICAL adj relating to the theory that syndicates of workers should seize the means of production

SYNDICATE n group of people or firms undertaking a joint business project ▷ vb publish (material) in several newspapers

SYNDICS > SYNDIC

SYNDING > SYND

SYNDINGS > SYND

SYNDROME n combination of symptoms indicating a particular disease

SYNDROMES > SYNDROME

SYNDROMIC > SYNDROME

SYNDS > SYND

SYNE vb rinse ▷ n rinse ▷ adv since

SYNECHIA n abnormality of the eye

SYNECHIAS > SYNECHIA

SYNECIOUS adj having male and female organs together on a branch

SYNECTIC > SYNECTICS

SYNECTICS n method of identifying and solving problems that depends on creative thinking

SYNED > SYNE

SYNEDRIA > SYNEDRION

SYNEDRIAL > SYNEDRION

SYNEDRION n assembly of judges

SYNEDRIUM same as > SYNEDRION

SYNERESES > SYNERESIS

SYNERESIS n process in which a gel contracts on standing and exudes liquid

SYNERGIA same as > SYNERGY

SYNERGIAS > SYNERGIA

SYNERGIC > SYNERGY

SYNERGID n type of cell in embryo

SYNERGIDS > SYNERGID

SYNERGIES > SYNERGY

SYNERGISE same as > SYNERGIZE

SYNERGISM same as > SYNERGY

SYNERGIST n drug, muscle, etc, that increases the action of another ▷ adj of or relating to synergism

SYNERGIZE vb act in synergy

SYNERGY n working together of two or more people, substances, or things to produce an effect greater than the sum of their individual effects

SYNES > SYNE

SYNESES > SYNESIS

SYNESIS n grammatical construction in which the inflection or form of a word is conditioned by the meaning rather than the syntax

SYNESISES > SYNESIS

SYNFUEL n synthetic fuel

SYNFUELS > SYNFUEL

SYNGAMIC > SYNGAMY

SYNGAMIES > SYNGAMY

SYNGAMOUS > SYNGAMY

SYNGAMY n sexual reproduction

SYNGAS n mixture of carbon monoxide and hydrogen

SYNGASES > SYNGAS

SYNGASSES > SYNGAS

SYNGENEIC adj with identical genes

SYNGENIC adj with the same genetic makeup

SYNGRAPH n document signed by several parties

SYNGRAPHS > SYNGRAPH

SYNING > SYNE

SYNIZESES > SYNIZESIS

SYNIZESIS n contraction of two vowels originally belonging to separate syllables into a single syllable

SYNKARYA > SYNKARYON

SYNKARYON n nucleus of a fertilized egg

SYNOD n church council

SYNODAL adj of or relating to a synod n money paid to a bishop by less senior members of the clergy at a synod

SYNODALS > SYNOD

SYNODIC adj relating to or involving a conjunction or two successive conjunctions of the same star, planet, or satellite

SYNODICAL > SYNOD

SYNODS > SYNOD

SYNODSMAN n layman at synod

SYNODSMEN > SYNODSMAN

SYNOECETE same as > SYNOEKETE

SYNOECISE same as > SYNOECIZE

SYNOECISM n union

SYNOECIZE vb unite

SYNOEKETE n insect that lives in the nests of social insects without receiving any attentions from the inmates

SYNOICOUS variant of > SYNECIOUS

SYNONYM n word with the same meaning as another

SYNONYME same as > SYNONYM

SYNONYMES > SYNONYME

SYNONYMIC > SYNONYM

SYNONYMS > SYNONYM

SYNONYMY n study of synonyms

SYNOPSES > SYNOPSIS

SYNOPSIS n summary or outline

SYNOPSISE same as > SYNOPSIZE

SYNOPSIZE vb make a synopsis of

SYNOPTIC adj of or relating to a synopsis ▷ n any of the three synoptic Gospels

SYNOPTICS > SYNOPTIC

SYNOPTIST > SYNOPTIC

SYNOVIA n clear thick fluid that lubricates the body joints

SYNOVIAL adj of or relating to the synovia

SYNOVIAS > SYNOVIA

SYNOVITIC > SYNOVITIS

SYNOVITIS n inflammation of the membrane surrounding a joint

SYNROC n titanium-ceramic substance that can incorporate nuclear waste in its crystals

SYNROCS > SYNROC

SYNTACTIC adj relating to or determined by syntax

SYNTAGM same as > SYNTAGMA

SYNTAGMA n syntactic unit or a word or phrase forming a syntactic unit

SYNTAGMAS > SYNTAGMA

SYNTAGMIC > SYNTAGMA

SYNTAGMS > SYNTAGMA

SYNTAN n synthetic tanning substance

SYNTANS > SYNTAN

SYNTAX n way in which words are arranged to form phrases and sentences

SYNTAXES > SYNTAX

SYNTECTIC > SYNTEXIS

SYNTENIC > SYNTENY

SYNTENIES > SYNTENY

SYNTENY n presence of two or more genes on the same chromosome

SYNTEXIS n liquefaction

SYNTH n type of electrophonic musical instrument operated by a keyboard and pedals

SYNTHESES > SYNTHESIS

SYNTHESIS n combination of objects or ideas into a whole

SYNTHETIC adj (of a substance) made artificially ▷ n synthetic substance or material

SYNTHON n molecule used in synthesis

SYNTHONS > SYNTHON

SYNTHPOP n pop music using synthesizers

SYNTHPOPS > SYNTHPOP

SYNTHRONI pl n combined thrones for bishops and their subordinates

SYNTHS > SYNTH

SYNTONIC adj emotionally in harmony with one's environment

SYNTONIES > SYNTONY

SYNTONIN n substance in muscle

SYNTONINS > SYNTONIN

SYNTONISE same as > SYNTONIZE

SYNTONIZE vb make frequencies match

SYNTONOUS same as > SYNTONIC

SYNTONY n matching of frequencies

SYNURA n variety of microbe

SYNURAE > SYNURA

SYPE same as > SIPE

SYPED > SYPE

SYPES > SYPE

SYPH shortening of > SYPHILIS

SYPHER vb lap (a chamfered edge of one plank over that of another) in order to form a flush surface

SYPHERED > SYPHER

SYPHERING > SYPHER

SYPHERS > SYPHER

SYPHILIS n serious sexually transmitted disease

SYPHILISE same as > SYPHILIZE

SYPHILIZE vb infect with syphilis

SYPHILOID > SYPHILIS

SYPHILOMA n tumour or gumma caused by infection with syphilis

SYPHON same as > SIPHON

SYPHONED > SYPHON

SYPHONING > SYPHON

SYPHONS > SYPHON

SYPHS > SYPH

SYPING > SYPE

SYRAH *n* type of French red wine

SYRAHS > SYRAH

SYREN *same as* > SIREN

SYRENS > SYREN

SYRETTE *n* small disposable syringe

SYRETTES > SYRETTE

SYRINGA *n* mock orange or lilac

SYRINGAS > SYRINGA

SYRINGE *n* device for withdrawing or injecting fluids, consisting of a hollow cylinder, a piston, and a hollow needle ▷ *vb* wash out or inject with a syringe

SYRINGEAL > SYRINX

SYRINGED > SYRINGE

SYRINGES > SYRINX

SYRINGING > SYRINGE

SYRINX *n* vocal organ of a bird, which is situated in the lower part of the trachea

SYRINXES > SYRINX

SYRPHIAN *same as* > SYRPHID

SYRPHIANS > SYRPHIAN

SYRPHID *n* type of fly

SYRPHIDS > SYRPHID

SYRTES > SYRTIS

SYRTIS *n* area of quicksand

SYRUP *n* solution of sugar in water ▷ *vb* bring to the consistency of syrup

SYRUPED > SYRUP

SYRUPIER > SYRUPY

SYRUPIEST > SYRUPY

SYRUPING > SYRUP

SYRUPLIKE > SYRUP

SYRUPS > SYRUP

SYRUPY *adj* thick and sweet

SYSADMIN *n* computer system administrator

SYSADMINS > SYSADMIN

SYSOP *n* person who runs a system or network

SYSOPS > SYSOP

SYSSITIA *n* ancient Spartan communal meal

SYSSITIAS > SYSSITIA

SYSTALTIC *adj* (esp of the action of the heart) characterized by alternate contractions and dilations

SYSTEM *n* method or set of methods

SYSTEMED *adj* having system

SYSTEMIC *adj* affecting the entire animal or body ▷ *n* systemic pesticide, fungicide, etc

SYSTEMICS > SYSTEMIC

SYSTEMISE *same as* > SYSTEMIZE

SYSTEMIZE *vb* give a system to

SYSTEMS > SYSTEM

SYSTOLE *n* regular contraction of the heart as it pumps blood

SYSTOLES > SYSTOLE

SYSTOLIC > SYSTOLE

SYSTYLE *n* building with different types of columns

SYSTYLES > SYSTYLE

SYTHE *same as* > SITH

SYTHES > SYTHE

SYVER *n* street drain or the grating over it

SYVERS > SYVER

SYZYGAL > SYZYGY

SYZYGETIC > SYZYGY

SYZYGIAL > SYZYGY

SYZYGIES > SYZYGY

SYZYGY *n* either of the two positions of a celestial body when sun, earth, and the body lie in a straight line

Tt

TA *interj* thank you

TAAL *n* language: usually, by implication, Afrikaans

TAALS > TAAL

TAATA *child's word for* > FATHER

TAATAS > TAATA

TAB *n* small flap or projecting label ▷ *vb* supply with a tab

TABANID *n* stout-bodied fly, the females of which have mouthparts specialized for sucking blood

TABANIDS > TABANID

TABARD *n* short sleeveless tunic decorated with a coat of arms, worn in medieval times

TABARDED *adj* wearing a tabard

TABARDS > TABARD

TABARET *n* hard-wearing fabric of silk or similar cloth with stripes of satin or moire, used esp for upholstery

TABARETS > TABARET

TABASHEER *n* dried bamboo sap, used medicinally

TABASHIR *same as* > TABASHEER

TABASHIRS > TABASHIR

TABBED > TAB

TABBIED > TABBY

TABBIES > TABBY

TABBINET *same as* > TABINET

TABBINETS > TABBINET

TABBING > TAB

TABBIS *n* silken cloth

TABBISES > TABBIS

TABBOULEH *n* kind of Middle Eastern salad made with cracked wheat, mint, parsley, and usually cucumber

TABBOULI *same as* > TABBOULEH

TABBOULIS > TABBOULI

TABBY *vb* make (eg a material) appear wavy ▷ *n* female domestic cat

TABBYHOOD *n* spinsterhood

TABBYING > TABBY

TABEFIED > TABEFY

TABEFIES > TABEFY

TABEFY *vb* emaciate or become emaciated

TABEFYING > TABEFY

TABELLION *n* scribe or notary authorized by the Roman Empire

TABER *old variant of* > TABOR

TABERD *same as* > TABARD

TABERDAR *n* holder of a scholarship at Queen's College, Oxford

TABERDARS > TABERDAR

TABERDS > TABERD

TABERED > TABER

TABERING > TABER

TABERS > TABER

TABES *n* wasting of a bodily organ or part

TABESCENT *adj* progressively emaciating

TABETIC > TABES

TABETICS > TABES

TABI *n* thick-soled Japanese sock, worn with sandals

TABID *adj* emaciated

TABINET *n* type of tabbied fabric

TABINETS > TABINET

TABIS > TABI

TABLA *n* one of a pair of Indian drums played with the hands

TABLAS > TABLA

TABLATURE *n* any of a number of forms of musical notation, esp for playing the lute, consisting of letters and signs indicating rhythm and fingering

TABLE *n* piece of furniture with a flat top supported by legs ▷ *vb* submit (a motion) for discussion by a meeting

TABLEAU *n* silent motionless group arranged to represent some scene

TABLEAUS > TABLEAU

TABLEAUX > TABLEAU

TABLED > TABLE

TABLEFUL > TABLE

TABLEFULS > TABLE

TABLELAND *n* high plateau

TABLELESS > TABLE

TABLEMATE *n* someone with whom one shares a table

TABLES > TABLE

TABLESFUL > TABLE

TABLET *n* medicinal pill ▷ *vb* make (something) into a tablet

TABLETED > TABLET

TABLETING > TABLET

TABLETOP *n* upper surface of a table

TABLETOPS > TABLETOP

TABLETS > TABLET

TABLETTED > TABLET

TABLEWARE *n* articles such as dishes, plates, knives, forks, etc, used at meals

TABLEWISE *adv* in the form of a table

TABLIER *n* (formerly) part of a dress resembling an apron

TABLIERS > TABLIER

TABLING > TABLE

TABLINGS > TABLE

TABLOID *n* small-sized newspaper with many photographs and a concise, usu sensational style

TABLOIDS > TABLOID

TABLOIDY *adj* characteristic of a tabloid newspaper; trashy

TABOGGAN *same as* > TOBOGGAN

TABOGGANS > TABOGGAN

TABOO *n* prohibition resulting from religious or social conventions ▷ *adj* forbidden by a taboo ▷ *vb* place under a taboo

TABOOED > TABOO

TABOOING > TABOO

TABOOLEY *variant of* > TABBOULEH

TABOOLEYS > TABOOLEY

TABOOS > TABOO

TABOR *vb* play the tabor

TABORED > TABOR

TABORER > TABOR

TABORERS > TABOR

TABORET *n* low stool, originally in the shape of a drum

TABORETS > TABORET

TABORIN *same as* > TABORET

TABORINE *same as* > TABOURIN

TABORINES > TABORINE

TABORING > TABOR

TABORINS > TABORIN

TABORS > TABOR

TABOULEH *variant of* > TABBOULEH

TABOULEHS > TABOULEH

TABOULI *same as* > TABBOULEH

TABOULIS > TABOULI

TABOUR *same as* > TABOR

TABOURED > TABOUR

TABOURER > TABOUR

TABOURERS > TABOUR

TABOURET *same as* > TABORET

TABOURETS > TABOURET

TABOURIN *same as* > TABORET

TABOURING > TABOUR

TABOURINS > TABOURIN

TABOURS > TABOUR

TABRERE *same as* > TABOR

TABRERES > TABRERE

TABRET *n* smaller version of a tabor

TABRETS > TABRET

TABS > TAB

TABU *same as* > TABOO

TABUED > TABU

TABUING > TABU

TABULA *n* tablet for writing on

TABULABLE > TABULATE

TABULAE > TABULA

TABULAR *adj* arranged in a table

TABULARLY > TABULAR

TABULATE *vb* arrange (information) in a table ▷ *adj* having a flat surface

TABULATED > TABULATE

TABULATES > TABULATE

TABULATOR *n* key on a typewriter or word processor that sets stops so that data can be arranged and presented in columns

TABULI *variant of* > TABBOULEH

TABULIS > TABULI

TABUN *n* organic compound used in chemical warfare as a lethal nerve gas

TABUNS > TABUN

TABUS > TABU

TACAHOUT *n* abnormal outgrowth on the tamarisk

plant

TACAHOUTS > TACAHOUT

TACAMAHAC *n* any of several strong-smelling resinous gums obtained from certain trees, used in making ointments, incense, etc

TACAN *n* electronic ultrahigh-frequency navigation system for aircraft which gives a continuous indication of bearing and distance from a transmitting station

TACANS > TACAN

TACE *same as* > TASSET

TACES > TACE

TACET *n* direction on a musical score indicating that a particular instrument or singer does not take part in a movement or part of a movement

TACETS > TACET

TACH *n* device for measuring speed

TACHE *n* buckle, clasp, or hook

TACHES > TACHE

TACHINA *as in tachina fly* bristly fly

TACHINID *n* type of fly

TACHINIDS > TACHINID

TACHISM *same as* > TACHISME

TACHISME *n* type of action painting evolved in France in which haphazard dabs and blots of colour are treated as a means of instinctive or unconscious expression

TACHISMES > TACHISME

TACHISMS > TACHISM

TACHIST > TACHISM

TACHISTE > TACHISME

TACHISTES > TACHISME

TACHISTS > TACHIST

TACHO *same as* > TACHOGRAM

TACHOGRAM *n* graphical record of readings

TACHOS > TACHO

TACHS > TACH

TACHYLITE *same as* > TACHYLYTE

TACHYLYTE *n* black basaltic glass often found on the edges of intrusions of basalt

TACHYON *n* hypothetical elementary particle capable of travelling faster than the velocity of light

TACHYONIC > TACHYON

TACHYONS > TACHYON

TACHYPNEA *n* abnormally rapid breathing

TACIT *adj* implied but not spoken

TACITLY > TACIT

TACITNESS > TACIT

TACITURN *adj* habitually uncommunicative

TACK *n* short nail with a large head ▷ *vb* fasten with tacks

TACKBOARD *n* noticeboard

TACKED > TACK

TACKER > TACK

TACKERS > TACK

TACKET *n* nail, esp a hobnail

TACKETS > TACKET

TACKETY > TACKET

TACKEY *same as* > TACKY

TACKIER > TACKY

TACKIES *pl n* tennis shoes or plimsolls

TACKIEST > TACKY

TACKIFIED > TACKIFY

TACKIFIER > TACKIFY

TACKIFIES > TACKIFY

TACKIFY *vb* give (eg rubber) a sticky feel

TACKILY > TACKY

TACKINESS > TACKY

TACKING > TACK

TACKINGS > TACK

TACKLE *vb* deal with (a task) ▷ *n* act of tackling an opposing player

TACKLED > TACKLE

TACKLER > TACKLE

TACKLERS > TACKLE

TACKLES > TACKLE

TACKLESS > TACK

TACKLING > TACKLE

TACKLINGS > TACKLE

TACKS > TACK

TACKSMAN *n* leaseholder, esp a tenant in the Highlands who sublets

TACKSMEN > TACKSMAN

TACKY *adj* slightly sticky

TACMAHACK *same as* > TACAMAHAC

TACNODE *n* in maths, point at which two branches of a curve have a common tangent, each branch extending in both directions of the tangent

TACNODES > TACNODE

TACO *n* tortilla fried until crisp, served with a filling

TACONITE *n* fine-grained sedimentary rock containing magnetite, haematite, and silica, which occurs in the Lake Superior region: a low-grade iron ore

TACONITES > TACONITE

TACOS > TACO

TACRINE *n* drug used to treat Alzheimer's disease

TACRINES > TACRINE

TACT *n* skill in avoiding giving offence

TACTFUL > TACT

TACTFULLY > TACT

TACTIC *n* method or plan to achieve an end

TACTICAL *adj* of or employing tactics

TACTICIAN > TACTICS

TACTICITY *n* quality of regularity in the arrangement of repeated units within a polymer chain

TACTICS *n* art of directing military forces in battle

TACTILE *adj* of or having the sense of touch

TACTILELY > TACTILE

TACTILIST *n* artist whose work strives to appeal to the sense of touch

TACTILITY > TACTILE

TACTION *n* act of touching

TACTIONS > TACTION

TACTISM *another word for* > TAXIS

TACTISMS > TACTISM

TACTLESS > TACT

TACTS > TACT

TACTUAL *adj* caused by touch

TACTUALLY > TACTUAL

TAD *n* small bit or piece

TADDIE *short for* > TADPOLE

TADDIES > TADDIE

TADPOLE *n* limbless tailed larva of a frog or toad

TADPOLES > TADPOLE

TADS > TAD

TADVANCE *vb* Spenserian form of advance

TAE *Scots form of the verb* > TOE

TAED > TAE

TAEDIUM *archaic spelling of* > TEDIUM

TAEDIUMS > TAEDIUM

TAEING > TAE

TAEKWONDO *n* Korean martial art

TAEL *n* unit of weight, used in the Far East, having various values between one to two and a half ounces

TAELS > TAEL

TAENIA *n* (in ancient Greece) a narrow fillet or headband for the hair

TAENIAE > TAENIA

TAENIAS > TAENIA

TAENIASES > TAENIASIS

TAENIASIS *n* infestation with tapeworms

TAENIATE *adj* ribbon-like

TAENIOID *adj* ribbon-like

TAES > TAE

TAFFAREL *same as* > TAFFRAIL

TAFFARELS > TAFFAREL

TAFFEREL *same as* > TAFFRAIL

TAFFERELS > TAFFEREL

TAFFETA *n* shiny silk or rayon fabric

TAFFETAS *same as* > TAFFETA

TAFFETIES > TAFFETY

TAFFETY *same as* > TAFFETA

TAFFIA *same as* > TAFIA

TAFFIAS > TAFFIA

TAFFIES > TAFFY

TAFFRAIL *n* rail at the back of a ship or boat

TAFFRAILS > TAFFRAIL

TAFFY *same as* > TOFFEE

TAFIA *n* type of rum, esp from Guyana or the Caribbean

TAFIAS > TAFIA

TAG *n* label bearing information ▷ *vb* attach a tag to

TAGALONG *n* one who trails behind, esp uninvited; a hanger-on

TAGALONGS > TAGALONG

TAGAREEN *n* junk shop

TAGAREENS > TAGAREEN

TAGBOARD *n* sturdy form of cardboard

TAGBOARDS > TAGBOARD

TAGETES *n* any of a genus of plants with yellow or orange flowers, including the French and African marigolds

TAGGANT *n* microscopic material added to substance to identify it

TAGGANTS > TAGGANT

TAGGED > TAG

TAGGEE *n* one who has been made to wear a tag

TAGGEES > TAGGEE

TAGGER *n* one who marks with a tag

TAGGERS > TAGGER

TAGGIER > TAGGY

TAGGIEST > TAGGY

TAGGING > TAG

TAGGINGS > TAG

TAGGY *adj* (of wool, hair, etc) matted

TAGHAIRM *n* form of divination once practised in the Highlands of Scotland

TAGHAIRMS > TAGHAIRM

TAGINE *n* large, heavy N African cooking pot with a conical lid

TAGINES > TAGINE

TAGLIKE *adj* resembling a tag

TAGLINE *n* funny line of joke

TAGLINES > TAGLINE

TAGLIONI *n* type of coat

TAGLIONIS > TAGLIONI

TAGMA *n* distinct region of the body of an arthropod, such as the head, thorax, or abdomen of an insect

TAGMATA > TAGMA

TAGMEME *n* class of speech elements all of which may fulfil the same grammatical role in a sentence

TAGMEMES > TAGMEME

TAGMEMIC > TAGMEME

TAGMEMICS > TAGMEME

TAGRAG *same as* > RAGTAG

TAGRAGS > TAGRAG

TAGS > TAG

TAGUAN *n* large nocturnal flying squirrel of high forests in the East Indies that uses its long tail as a rudder

TAGUANS > TAGUAN

TAHA *n* type of South African bird

TAHAS > TAHA

TAHINA *same as* > TAHINI

TAHINAS > TAHINA

TAHINI *n* paste made from ground sesame seeds, used esp in Middle Eastern cookery

TAHINIS > TAHINI

Section 1: Words between 2 and 9 letters in length

TAHOU *same as* > SILVEREYE

TAHOUS > TAHOU

TAHR *n* goatlike bovid mammal of mountainous regions of S and SW Asia, having a shaggy coat and curved horns

TAHRS > TAHR

TAHSIL *n* administrative division of a zila in certain states in India

TAHSILDAR *n* officer in charge of the collection of revenues, etc, in a tahsil

TAHSILS > TAHSIL

TAI as in *tai chi chuan* Chinese system of callisthenics characterized by coordinated and rhythmic movements

TAIAHA *n* carved weapon in the form of a staff, now used in Māori ceremonial oratory

TAIAHAS > TAIAHA

TAIG *n* often derogatory term for Roman Catholic

TAIGA *n* belt of coniferous forest extending across much of subarctic North America, Europe, and Asia

TAIGAS > TAIGA

TAIGLACH *same as* > TEIGLACH

TAIGLE *vb* entangle or impede

TAIGLED > TAIGLE

TAIGLES > TAIGLE

TAIGLING > TAIGLE

TAIGS > TAIG

TAIHOA *interj* hold on! no hurry!

TAIKONAUT *n* astronaut from the People's Republic of China

TAIL *n* rear part of an animal's body, usu forming a flexible appendage ▷ *adj* at the rear ▷ *vb* follow (someone) secretly

TAILARD *n* one having a tail

TAILARDS > TAILARD

TAILBACK *n* queue of traffic stretching back from an obstruction

TAILBACKS > TAILBACK

TAILBOARD *n* removable or hinged rear board on a truck etc

TAILBONE *nontechnical name for* > COCCYX

TAILBONES > TAILBONE

TAILCOAT *n* man's black coat having a horizontal cut over the hips and a tapering tail with a vertical slit up to the waist

TAILCOATS > TAILCOAT

TAILED > TAIL

TAILENDER *n* (in cricket) the batter last in the batting order

TAILER *n* one that tails

TAILERON *n* aileron located on the tailplane of an aircraft

TAILERONS > TAILERON

TAILERS > TAILER

TAILFAN *n* fanned structure at the hind end of a lobster or related crustacean, formed from the telson and uropods

TAILFANS > TAILFAN

TAILFIN *n* decorative projection at back of car

TAILFINS > TAILFIN

TAILFLIES > TAILFLY

TAILFLY *n* in angling, the lowest fly on a wet-fly cast

TAILGATE *n* door at the rear of a hatchback vehicle ▷ *vb* drive very close behind (a vehicle)

TAILGATED > TAILGATE

TAILGATER > TAILGATE

TAILGATES > TAILGATE

TAILING *n* part of a beam, rafter, projecting brick or stone, etc, embedded in a wall

TAILINGS *pl n* waste left over after certain processes, such as from an ore-crushing plant or in milling grain

TAILLAMP *n* rear light

TAILLAMPS > TAILLAMP

TAILLE *n* (in France before 1789) a tax levied by a king or overlord on his subjects

TAILLES > TAILLE

TAILLESS > TAIL

TAILLEUR *n* woman's suit

TAILLEURS > TAILLEUR

TAILLIE *n* (in law) the limitation of an estate or interest to a person and the heirs of his body

TAILLIES > TAILLIE

TAILLIGHT *same as* > TAILLAMP

TAILLIKE *adj* resembling a tail

TAILOR *n* person who makes men's clothes ▷ *vb* cut or style (a garment) to specific requirements

TAILORED > TAILOR

TAILORESS *n* female tailor

TAILORING > TAILOR

TAILORS > TAILOR

TAILPIECE *n* piece added at the end of something, for example a report

TAILPIPE *vb* attach an object, esp a tin can, to the tail of an animal

TAILPIPED > TAILPIPE

TAILPIPES > TAILPIPE

TAILPLANE *n* small stabilizing wing at the rear of an aircraft

TAILRACE *n* channel that carries water away from a water wheel, turbine, etc

TAILRACES > TAILRACE

TAILS *adv* with the side of a coin that does not have a portrait of a head on it uppermost

TAILSKID *n* runner under the tail of an aircraft

TAILSKIDS > TAILSKID

TAILSLIDE *n* backwards descent of an aeroplane after stalling while in an upward trajectory

TAILSPIN *n* uncontrolled spinning dive of an aircraft

TAILSPINS > TAILSPIN

TAILSTOCK *n* casting that slides on the bed of a lathe in alignment with the headstock and is locked in position to support the free end of a workpiece

TAILWATER *n* water flowing in a tailrace

TAILWHEEL *n* wheel fitted to the rear of a vehicle, esp the landing wheel under the tail of an aircraft

TAILWIND *n* wind coming from the rear

TAILWINDS > TAILWIND

TAILYE *same as* > TAILLIE

TAILYES > TAILYE

TAILZIE *same as* > TAILLIE

TAILZIES > TAILZIE

TAIN *n* tinfoil used in backing mirrors

TAINS > TAIN

TAINT *vb* spoil with a small amount of decay, contamination, or other bad quality ▷ *n* something that taints

TAINTED > TAINT

TAINTING > TAINT

TAINTLESS > TAINT

TAINTS > TAINT

TAINTURE *n* contamination; staining

TAINTURES > TAINTURE

TAIPAN *n* large poisonous Australian snake

TAIPANS > TAIPAN

TAIRA *same as* > TAYRA

TAIRAS > TAIRA

TAIS > TAI

TAISCH *n* (in Scotland) apparition of a person whose death is imminent

TAISCHES > TAISCH

TAISH *same as* > TAISCH

TAISHES > TAISH

TAIT *same as* > TATE

TAITS > TAIT

TAIVER *same as* > TAVER

TAIVERED > TAIVER

TAIVERING > TAIVER

TAIVERS > TAIVER

TAIVERT *adj* Scots word meaning confused or bewildered

TAJ *n* tall conical cap worn as a mark of distinction by Muslims

TAJES > TAJ

TAJINE *same as* > TAGINE

TAJINES > TAJINE

TAK *Scots variant spelling of* > TAKE

TAKA *n* standard monetary unit of Bangladesh, divided into 100 paise

TAKABLE > TAKE

TAKAHE *n* very rare flightless New Zealand bird

TAKAHES > TAKAHE

TAKAMAKA *same as* > TACAMAHAC

TAKAMAKAS > TAKAMAKA

TAKAS > TAKA

TAKE *vb* remove from a place ▷ *n* one of a series of recordings from which the best will be used

TAKEABLE > TAKE

TAKEAWAY *adj* (of food) sold for consumption away from the premises ▷ *n* shop or restaurant selling meals for eating elsewhere

TAKEAWAYS > TAKEAWAY

TAKEDOWN *n* disassembly

TAKEDOWNS > TAKEDOWN

TAKEN > TAKE

TAKEOFF *n* act or process of making an aircraft airborne

TAKEOFFS > TAKEOFF

TAKEOUT *n* shop or restaurant that sells such food

TAKEOUTS > TAKEOUT

TAKEOVER *n* act of taking control of a company by buying a large number of its shares

TAKEOVERS > TAKEOVER

TAKER *n* person who agrees to take something that is offered

TAKERS > TAKER

TAKES > TAKE

TAKEUP *n* the claiming or acceptance of something, esp a state benefit, that is due or available

TAKEUPS > TAKEUP

TAKHI *n* type of wild Mongolian horse

TAKHIS > TAKHI

TAKI *same as* > TAKHIW

TAKIER > TAKY

TAKIEST > TAKY

TAKIN *n* massive bovid mammal of mountainous regions of S Asia, having a shaggy coat, short legs, and horns that point backwards and upwards

TAKING > TAKE

TAKINGLY > TAKE

TAKINGS > TAKE

TAKINS > TAKIN

TAKIS > TAKI

TAKKIES *same as* > TACKIES

TAKS > TAK

TAKY *adj* appealing

TALA *n* standard monetary unit of Samoa, divided into 100 sene

TALAK *same as* > TALAQ

TALAKS > TALAK

TALANT *old variant of* > TALON

TALANTS > TALANT

TALAPOIN *n* smallest of the guenon monkeys of swampy central W African forests, having olive-green fur and slightly webbed digits

TALAPOINS > TALAPOIN

TALAQ *n* Muslim form of divorce

TALAQS > TALAQ

TALAR *n* ankle-length robe

TALARIA *pl n* winged sandals, such as those worn by Hermes

TALARS > TALAR

TALAS > TALA

TALAUNT *old variant of* > TALON

TALAUNTS > TALAUNT

TALAYOT *n* ancient Balearic stone tower

TALAYOTS > TALAYOT

TALBOT *n* (formerly) an ancient breed of large hound, usually white or light-coloured, having pendulous ears and strong powers of scent

TALBOTS > TALBOT

TALBOTYPE *n* early type of photographic process (invented by W H Fox Talbot) or a photograph produced using it

TALC *n* talcum powder ▷ *vb* apply talc to ▷ *adj* of, or relating to, talc

TALCED > TALC

TALCIER > TALCY

TALCIEST > TALCY

TALCING > TALC

TALCKED > TALCKY

TALCKIER > TALCKY

TALCKIEST > TALCKY

TALCKING > TALCKY

TALCKY *same as* > TALCY

TALCOSE > TALC

TALCOUS > TALC

TALCS > TALC

TALCUM *n* white, grey, brown, or pale green mineral, found in metamorphic rocks. It is used in the manufacture of talcum powder and electrical insulatorsr

TALCUMS > TALCUM

TALCY *adj* like, containing, or covered in talc

TALE *n* story

TALEA *n* rhythmic pattern in certain mediaeval choral compositions

TALEAE > TALEA

TALEFUL *adj* having many tales

TALEGALLA *n* brush turkey, of New Guinea and Australia

TALEGGIO *n* Italian cheese

TALEGGIOS > TALEGGIO

TALENT *n* natural ability

TALENTED > TALENT

TALENTS > TALENT

TALER *same as* > THALER

TALERS > TALER

TALES *n* group of persons summoned from among those present in court or from bystanders to fill vacancies on a jury panel

TALESMAN > TALES

TALESMEN > TALES

TALEYSIM > TALLITH

TALI > TALUS

TALIGRADE *adj* (of

mammals) walking on the outer side of the foot

TALION *n* system or legal principle of making the punishment correspond to the crime

TALIONIC *adj* of or relating to talion

TALIONS > TALION

TALIPAT *same as* > TALIPOT

TALIPATS > TALIPAT

TALIPED *adj* having a club foot ▷ *n* club-footed person

TALIPEDS > TALIPED

TALIPES *n* congenital deformity of the foot by which it is twisted in any of various positions

TALIPOT *n* palm tree of the East Indies, having large leaves that are used for fans, thatching houses, etc

TALIPOTS > TALIPOT

TALISMAN *n* object believed to have magic power

TALISMANS > TALISMAN

TALK *vb* express ideas or feelings by means of speech ▷ *n* speech or lecture

TALKABLE > TALK

TALKATHON *n* epic bout of discussion or speechifying

TALKATIVE *adj* fond of talking

TALKBACK *n* broadcast in which telephone comments or questions from the public are transmitted live

TALKBACKS > TALKBACK

TALKBOX *n* voice box

TALKBOXES > TALKBOX

TALKED > TALK

TALKER > TALK

TALKERS > TALK

TALKFEST *n* lengthy discussion

TALKFESTS > TALKFEST

TALKIE *n* early film with a soundtrack

TALKIER > TALKY

TALKIES > TALKIE

TALKIEST > TALKY

TALKINESS *n* quality or condition of being talky

TALKING *n* speech; the act of speaking

TALKINGS > TALKING

TALKS > TALK

TALKY *adj* containing too much dialogue or inconsequential talk

TALL *adj* higher than average

TALLAGE *n* tax levied by the Norman and early Angevin kings on their Crown lands and royal towns ▷ *vb* levy a tax (upon)

TALLAGED > TALLAGE

TALLAGES > TALLAGE

TALLAGING > TALLAGE

TALLAISIM > TALLITH

TALLAT *same as* > TALLET

TALLATS > TALLAT

TALLBOY *n* high chest of drawers

TALLBOYS > TALLBOY

TALLENT *n* plenty

TALLENTS > TALLENT

TALLER > TALL

TALLEST > TALL

TALLET *n* loft

TALLETS > TALLET

TALLGRASS *n* long grass in North American prairie

TALLIABLE *adj* taxable

TALLIATE *vb* levy a tax

TALLIATED > TALLIATE

TALLIATES > TALLIATE

TALLIED > TALLY

TALLIER > TALLY

TALLIERS > TALLY

TALLIES > TALLY

TALLIS *variant of* > TALLITH

TALLISES > TALLIS

TALLISH *adj* quite tall

TALLISIM > TALLITH

TALLIT *variant of* > TALLITH

TALLITES > TALLIT

TALLITH *n* white shawl with fringed corners worn over the head and shoulders by Jewish males during religious services

TALLITHES > TALLITH

TALLITHIM > TALLITH

TALLITHS > TALLITH

TALLITIM > TALLIT

TALLITOT > TALLIT

TALLITOTH > TALLITH

TALLITS > TALLIT

TALLNESS > TALL

TALLOL *n* oily liquid used for making soaps, lubricants, etc

TALLOLS > TALLOL

TALLOT *same as* > TALLET

TALLOTS > TALLOT

TALLOW *n* hard animal fat used to make candles ▷ *vb* cover or smear with tallow

TALLOWED > TALLOW

TALLOWING > TALLOW

TALLOWISH > TALLOW

TALLOWS > TALLOW

TALLOWY > TALLOW

TALLS > TALL

TALLY *vb* (of two things) correspond ▷ *n* record of a debt or score

TALLYHO *n* cry of a participant at a hunt to encourage the hounds when the quarry is sighted ▷ *vb* to make the cry of tallyho

TALLYHOED > TALLYHO

TALLYHOS > TALLYHO

TALLYING > TALLY

TALLYMAN *n* scorekeeper or recorder

TALLYMEN > TALLYMAN

TALLYSHOP *n* shop that allows customers to pay in instalments

TALMA *n* short cloak

TALMAS > TALMA

TALMUD *n* primary source of Jewish religious law, consisting of the Mishnah and the Gemara

TALMUDIC > TALMUD

TALMUDISM > TALMUD

TALMUDS > TALMUD

TALON *n* bird's hooked claw

TALONED > TALON

TALONS > TALON

TALOOKA *same as* > TALUK

TALOOKAS > TALOOKA

TALPA *n* sebaceous cyst

TALPAE > TALPA

TALPAS > TALPA

TALUK *n* subdivision of a district

TALUKA *same as* > TALUK

TALUKAS > TALUKA

TALUKDAR *n* person in charge of a taluk

TALUKDARS > TALUKDAR

TALUKS > TALUK

TALUS *n* bone of the ankle that articulates with the leg bones to form the ankle joint

TALUSES > TALUS

TALWEG *same as* > THALWEG

TALWEGS > TALWEG

TAM *n* tam-o'-shanter

TAMABLE > TAME

TAMAL *same as* > TAMALE

TAMALE *n* Mexican dish made of minced meat mixed with crushed maize and seasonings, wrapped in maize husks and steamed

TAMALES > TAMALE

TAMALS > TAMAL

TAMANDU *same as* > TAMANDUA

TAMANDUA *n* small arboreal edentate mammal

TAMANDUAS > TAMANDUA

TAMANDUS > TAMANDU

TAMANOIR *n* anteater

TAMANOIRS > TAMANOIR

TAMANU *n* poon tree

TAMANUS > TAMANU

TAMARA *n* powder consisting of cloves, cinnamon, fennel, coriander, etc, used in certain cuisines

TAMARACK *n* North American larch, with reddish-brown bark, bluish-green needle-like leaves, and shiny oval cones

TAMARACKS > TAMARACK

TAMARAO *same as* > TAMARAU

TAMARAOS > TAMARAO

TAMARAS > TAMARA

TAMARAU *n* small rare member of the cattle tribe of lowland areas of Mindoro in the Philippines

TAMARAUS > TAMARAU

TAMARI *n* Japanese variety of soy sauce

TAMARILLO *n* shrub with a red oval edible fruit

TAMARIN *n* small monkey of South and Central American forests

TAMARIND *n* tropical tree

TAMARINDS > TAMARIND

TAMARINS > TAMARIN

TAMARIS > TAMARI

TAMARISK n evergreen shrub with slender branches and feathery flower clusters

TAMARISKS > TAMARISK

TAMASHA n (in India) a show

TAMASHAS > TAMASHA

TAMBAC same as > TOMBAC

TAMBACS > TAMBAC

TAMBAK same as > TOMBAC

TAMBAKS > TAMBAK

TAMBALA n unit of Malawian currency

TAMBALAS > TAMBALA

TAMBER same as > TIMBRE

TAMBERS > TAMBER

TAMBOUR n embroidery frame, consisting of two hoops over which the fabric is stretched while being worked ▷ vb embroider (fabric or a design) on a tambour

TAMBOURA n instrument with a long neck, four strings, and no frets, used in Indian music to provide a drone

TAMBOURAS > TAMBOURA

TAMBOURED > TAMBOUR

TAMBOURER n one who embroiders on a tambour

TAMBOURIN n 18th-century Provençal folk dance

TAMBOURS > TAMBOUR

TAMBUR n old Turkish stringed instrument

TAMBURA n Middle-Eastern stringed instrument with a long neck, related to the tambur

TAMBURAS > TAMBURA

TAMBURIN same as > TAMBURIN

TAMBURINS > TAMBURIN

TAMBURS > TAMBUR

TAME adj (of animals) brought under human control ▷ vb make tame

TAMEABLE > TAME

TAMED > TAME

TAMEIN n Burmese skirt

TAMEINS > TAMEIN

TAMELESS > TAME

TAMELY > TAME

TAMENESS > TAME

TAMER > TAME

TAMERS > TAME

TAMES > TAME

TAMEST > TAME

TAMIN n thin woollen fabric

TAMINE same as > TAMIN

TAMINES > TAMINE

TAMING n act of making (something) tame

TAMINGS > TAMING

TAMINS > TAMIN

TAMIS same as > TAMMY

TAMISE n type of thin cloth

TAMISES > TAMIS

TAMMAR n small scrub wallaby of Australia, with a thick dark-coloured coat

TAMMARS > TAMMAR

TAMMIE n short for tam-o'shanter, a traditional

Scottish hat

TAMMIED > TAMMY

TAMMIES > TAMMY

TAMMY n glazed woollen or mixed fabric, used for linings, undergarments, etc ▷ vb (esp formerly) to strain (sauce, soup, etc) through a tammy

TAMMYING > TAMMY

TAMOXIFEN n drug that antagonizes the action of oestrogen and is used to treat breast cancer and some types of infertility in women

TAMP vb pack down by repeated taps

TAMPALA n Asian plant (Amaranthus tricolor), eaten as food

TAMPALAS > TAMPALA

TAMPAN n biting mite

TAMPANS > TAMPAN

TAMPED > TAMP

TAMPER vb interfere ▷ n person or thing that tamps, esp an instrument for packing down tobacco in a pipe

TAMPERED > TAMPER

TAMPERER > TAMPER

TAMPERERS > TAMPER

TAMPERING > TAMPER

TAMPERS > TAMPER

TAMPING adj very angry ▷ n act or instance of tamping

TAMPINGS > TAMPING

TAMPION n plug placed in a gun's muzzle when the gun is not in use to keep out moisture and dust

TAMPIONS > TAMPION

TAMPON n absorbent plug of cotton wool inserted into the vagina during menstruation ▷ vb use a tampon

TAMPONADE > TAMPON

TAMPONAGE > TAMPON

TAMPONED > TAMPON

TAMPONING > TAMPON

TAMPONS > TAMPON

TAMPS > TAMP

TAMS > TAM

TAMWORTH n any of a hardy rare breed of long-bodied reddish pigs

TAMWORTHS > TAMWORTH

TAN n brown coloration of the skin from exposure to sunlight ▷ vb (of skin) go brown from exposure to sunlight ▷ adj yellowish-brown

TANA n small Madagascan lemur

TANADAR n commanding officer of an Indian police station

TANADARS > TANADAR

TANAGER n any American songbird of the family Thraupidae, having a short thick bill and a brilliantly coloured male plumage

TANAGERS > TANAGER

TANAGRA n type of tanager

TANAGRAS > TANAGRA

TANAGRINE adj of or relating to the tanager

TANAISTE n prime minister of the Republic of Ireland

TANAISTES > TANAISTE

TANALISED adj having been treated with the trademarked timber preservative Tanalith

TANALIZED same as > TANALISED

TANAS > TANA

TANBARK n bark of certain trees, esp the oak and hemlock, used as a source of tannin

TANBARKS > TANBARK

TANDEM n bicycle for two riders, one behind the other

TANDEMS > TANDEM

TANDOOR n type of Indian clay oven

TANDOORI adj (of food) cooked in an Indian clay oven ▷ n Indian method of cooking meat or vegetables on a spit in a clay oven

TANDOORIS > TANDOORI

TANDOORS > TANDOOR

TANE old Scottish variant of > TAKEN

TANG n strong taste or smell ▷ vb cause to ring

TANGA n triangular loincloth worn by indigenous peoples in tropical America

TANGAS > TANGA

TANGED > TANG

TANGELO n hybrid produced by crossing a tangerine tree with a grapefruit tree

TANGELOS > TANGELO

TANGENCE n touching

TANGENCES > TANGENCE

TANGENCY > TANGENT

TANGENT n line that touches a curve without intersecting it

TANGENTAL > TANGENT

TANGENTS > TANGENT

TANGERINE n small orange-like fruit of an Asian citrus tree ▷ adj reddish-orange

TANGHIN n strong poison formerly used in Madagascar to determine the guilt or otherwise of crime suspects

TANGHININ n active ingredient in tanghin

TANGHINS > TANGHIN

TANGI n Māori funeral ceremony

TANGIBLE adj able to be touched ▷ n tangible thing or asset

TANGIBLES > TANGIBLE

TANGIBLY > TANGIBLE

TANGIE n water spirit of Orkney, appearing as a figure draped in seaweed, or as a seahorse

TANGIER > TANGY

TANGIES > TANGIE

TANGIEST > TANGY

TANGINESS > TANGY

TANGING > TANG

TANGIS > TANGI

TANGLE n confused mass or situation ▷ vb twist together in a tangle

TANGLED > TANGLE

TANGLER > TANGLE

TANGLERS > TANGLE

TANGLES > TANGLE

TANGLIER > TANGLE

TANGLIEST > TANGLE

TANGLING n act or condition of tangling

TANGLINGS > TANGLING

TANGLY > TANGLE

TANGO n S American dance ▷ vb dance a tango

TANGOED > TANGO

TANGOING > TANGO

TANGOIST > TANGO

TANGOISTS > TANGO

TANGOLIKE > TANGO

TANGOS > TANGO

TANGRAM n Chinese puzzle in which a square, cut into a parallelogram, a square, and five triangles, is formed into figures

TANGRAMS > TANGRAM

TANGS > TANG

TANGUN n small and sturdy Tibetan pony

TANGUNS > TANGUN

TANGY adj having a pungent, fresh, or briny flavour or aroma

TANH n hyperbolic tangent

TANHS > TANH

TANIST n heir apparent of a Celtic chieftain chosen by election during the chief's lifetime: usually the worthiest of his kin

TANISTRY > TANIST

TANISTS > TANIST

TANIWHA n mythical Māori monster that lives in water

TANIWHAS > TANIWHA

TANK n container for liquids or gases ▷ vb put or keep in a tank

TANKA n Japanese verse form consisting of five lines, the first and third having five syllables, the others seven

TANKAGE n capacity or contents of a tank or tanks

TANKAGES > TANKAGE

TANKARD n large beer-mug, often with a hinged lid

TANKARDS > TANKARD

TANKAS > TANKA

TANKED > TANK

TANKER n ship or truck for carrying liquid in bulk

TANKERS > TANKER

TANKFUL n quantity contained in a tank

TANKFULS > TANKFUL

TANKIA n type of boat used in Canton

TANKIAS > TANKIA

TANKIES > TANKY

TANKING *n* heavy defeat

TANKINGS > TANKING

TANKINI *n* woman's two-piece swimming costume consisting of a vest or camisole top and bikini briefs

TANKINIS > TANKINI

TANKLESS > TANK

TANKLIKE > TANK

TANKS > TANK

TANKSHIP *same as* > TANKER

TANKSHIPS > TANKSHIP

TANKY *n* die-hard communist

TANLING *n* suntanned person

TANLINGS > TANLING

TANNA *n* Indian police station or army base

TANNABLE > TAN

TANNAGE *n* act or process of tanning

TANNAGES > TANNAGE

TANNAH *same as* > TANNA

TANNAHS > TANNAH

TANNAS > TANNA

TANNATE *n* any salt or ester of tannic acid

TANNATES > TANNATE

TANNED > TAN

TANNER > TAN

TANNERIES > TANNERY

TANNERS > TAN

TANNERY *n* place where hides are tanned

TANNEST > TAN

TANNIC *adj* of, containing, or produced from tannin or tannic acid

TANNIE *n* in S Africa, title of respect used to refer to an elderly woman

TANNIES > TANNIE

TANNIN *n* vegetable substance used in tanning

TANNING > TAN

TANNINGS > TAN

TANNINS > TANNIN

TANNISH > TAN

TANNOY *n* sound-amplifying apparatus used as a public-address system esp in a large building, such as a university ▷ *vb* announce (something) using a Tannoy system

TANNOYED > TANNOY

TANNOYING > TANNOY

TANNOYS > TANNOY

TANREC *same as* > TENREC

TANRECS > TANREC

TANS > TAN

TANSIES > TANSY

TANSY *n* yellow-flowered plant

TANTALATE *n* any of various salts of tantalic acid formed when the pentoxide of tantalum dissolves in an alkali

TANTALIC *adj* of or containing tantalum, esp in the pentavalent state

TANTALISE *same as* > TANTALIZE

TANTALISM > TANTALISE

TANTALITE *n* heavy brownish mineral consisting of a tantalum oxide of iron and manganese in orthorhombic crystalline form

TANTALIZE *vb* torment by showing but withholding something desired

TANTALOUS *adj* of or containing tantalum in the trivalent state

TANTALUM *n* hard greyish-white metallic element

TANTALUMS > TANTALUM

TANTALUS *n* case in which bottles of wine and spirits may be locked with their contents tantalizingly visible

TANTARA *n* blast, as on a trumpet or horn

TANTARARA *same as* > TANTARA

TANTARAS > TANTARA

TANTI *adj* old word for worthwhile

TANTIVIES > TANTIVY

TANTIVY *adv* at full speed ▷ *interj* hunting cry, esp at full gallop

TANTO *adv* too much

TANTONIES > TANTONY

TANTONY *n* runt

TANTRA *n* sacred books of Tantrism, written between the 7th and 17th centuries AD, mainly in the form of a dialogue between Siva and his wife

TANTRAS > TANTRA

TANTRIC > TANTRA

TANTRISM *n* teaching of tantra

TANTRISMS > TANTRISM

TANTRUM *n* childish outburst of temper

TANTRUMS > TANTRUM

TANUKI *n* animal similar to a raccoon, found in Japan

TANUKIS > TANUKI

TANYARD *n* part of a tannery

TANYARDS > TANYARD

TANZANITE *n* blue gemstone

TAO *n* (in Confucian philosophy) the correct course of action

TAOISEACH *n* prime minister of the Republic of Ireland

TAONGA *n* treasure

TAONGAS > TAONGA

TAOS > TAO

TAP *vb* knock lightly and usu repeatedly ▷ *n* light knock

TAPA *n* inner bark of the paper mulberry

TAPACOLO *n* small bird of Chile and Argentina

TAPACOLOS > TAPACOLO

TAPACULO *same as* > TAPACOLO

TAPACULOS > TAPACULO

TAPADERA *n* leather covering for the stirrup on an American saddle

TAPADERAS > TAPADERA

TAPADERO *same as* > TAPADERA

TAPADEROS > TAPADERO

TAPALO *n* Latin American scarf, often patterned and brightly coloured

TAPALOS > TAPALO

TAPAS *pl n* (in Spanish cookery) light snacks or appetizers, usually eaten with drinks

TAPE *n* narrow long strip of material ▷ *vb* record on magnetic tape

TAPEABLE > TAPE

TAPED > TAPE

TAPELESS > TAPE

TAPELIKE > TAPE

TAPELINE *n* tape or length of metal marked off in inches, centimetres, etc, used principally for measuring and fitting garments

TAPELINES > TAPELINE

TAPEN *adj* made of tape

TAPENADE *n* savoury paste made from capers, olives, and anchovies, with olive oil and lemon juice

TAPENADES > TAPENADE

TAPER > TAPE

TAPERED > TAPE

TAPERER > TAPE

TAPERERS > TAPE

TAPERING > TAPE

TAPERINGS > TAPE

TAPERNESS *n* state or quality of being tapered

TAPERS > TAPE

TAPERWISE *adv* in the manner of a taper

TAPES > TAPE

TAPESTRY *n* fabric decorated with coloured woven designs ▷ *vb* portray in tapestry

TAPET *n* example of tapestry

TAPETA > TAPETUM

TAPETAL > TAPETUM

TAPETI *n* forest rabbit of Brazil

TAPETIS > TAPETI

TAPETS > TAPET

TAPETUM *n* layer of nutritive cells in the sporangia of ferns and anthers of flowering plants that surrounds developing spore cells

TAPEWORM *n* long flat parasitic worm living in the intestines of vertebrates

TAPEWORMS > TAPEWORM

TAPHOLE *n* hole in a furnace for running off molten metal or slag

TAPHOLES > TAPHOLE

TAPHONOMY *n* study of the processes affecting an organism after death that result in its fossilization

TAPHOUSE *n* inn or bar

TAPHOUSES > TAPHOUSE

TAPING > TAPE

TAPIOCA *n* beadlike starch made from cassava root, used in puddings

TAPIOCAS > TAPIOCA

TAPIR *n* piglike mammal of tropical America and SE Asia, with a long snout

TAPIROID > TAPIR

TAPIRS > TAPIR

TAPIS *n* tapestry or carpeting, esp as formerly used to cover a table in a council chamber

TAPISES > TAPIS

TAPIST *n* person who records (read out) printed matter in an audio format for the benefit of visually impaired people

TAPISTS > TAPIST

TAPLASH *n* dregs of beer

TAPLASHES > TAPLASH

TAPPA *same as* > TAPA

TAPPABLE > TAP

TAPPAS > TAPPA

TAPPED > TAP

TAPPER *n* person who taps

TAPPERS > TAPPER

TAPPET *n* short steel rod in an engine, transferring motion from one part to another

TAPPETS > TAPPET

TAPPICE *vb* hide

TAPPICED > TAPPICE

TAPPICES > TAPPICE

TAPPICING > TAPPICE

TAPPING > TAP

TAPPINGS > TAP

TAPPIT *adj* crested; topped

TAPROOM *n* public bar in a hotel or pub

TAPROOMS > TAPROOM

TAPROOT *n* main root of a plant, growing straight down

TAPROOTED > TAPROOT

TAPROOTS > TAPROOT

TAPS > TAP

TAPSMAN *n* old word for a barman

TAPSMEN > TAPSMAN

TAPSTER *n* barman

TAPSTERS > TAPSTER

TAPSTRESS > TAPSTER

TAPSTRY *adj* relating to tapestry

TAPU *adj* sacred ▷ *n* Māori religious or superstitious restriction on something ▷ *vb* put a tapu on something

TAPUED > TAPU

TAPUING > TAPU

TAPUS > TAPU

TAQUERIA *n* restaurant specializing in tacos

TAQUERIAS > TAQUERIA

TAR *n* thick black liquid distilled from coal etc ▷ *vb* coat with tar

TARA *same as* > TARO

TARAIRE *n* type of New Zealand tree

TARAKIHI *n* common edible sea fish of New Zealand

waters

TARAKIHIS > TARAKIHI

TARAMA n cod roe

TARAMAS > TARAMA

TARAMEA n variety of New Zealand speargrass

TARAMEAS > TARAMEA

TARAND n northern animal of legend, now supposed to have been the reindeer

TARANDS > TARAND

TARANTARA same as > TANTARA

TARANTAS same as > TARANTASS

TARANTASS n large horse-drawn four-wheeled Russian carriage without springs

TARANTISM n nervous disorder marked by uncontrollable bodily movement, widespread in S Italy during the 15th to 17th centuries: popularly thought to be caused by the bite of a tarantula

TARANTIST > TARANTISM

TARANTULA n large hairy spider with a poisonous bite

TARAS > TARA

TARAXACUM n perennial plant with dense heads of small yellow flowers and seeds with a feathery attachment

TARBOGGIN same as > TOBOGGAN

TARBOOSH n felt or cloth brimless cap, usually red and often with a silk tassel, formerly worn by Muslim men

TARBOUCHE same as > TARBOOSH

TARBOUSH same as > TARBOOSH

TARBOY n boy who applies tar to the skin of sheep cut during shearing

TARBOYS > TARBOY

TARBUSH same as > TARBOOSH

TARBUSHES > TARBUSH

TARCEL same as > TARCEL

TARCELS > TARCEL

TARDIED > TARDY

TARDIER > TARDY

TARDIES > TARDY

TARDIEST > TARDY

TARDILY > TARDY

TARDINESS > TARDY

TARDIVE adj tending to develop late

TARDO adj (of music) slow; to be played slowly

TARDY adj slow or late ▷ vb delay or impede (something or someone)

TARDYING > TARDY

TARDYON n particle travelling slower than the speed of light

TARDYONS > TARDYON

TARE n weight of the wrapping or container

of goods ▷ vb weigh (a package, etc) in order to calculate the amount of tare

TARED > TARE

TARES > TARE

TARGE vb interrogate

TARGED > TARGE

TARGES > TARGE

TARGET n object or person a missile is aimed at ▷ vb aim or direct

TARGETED > TARGET

TARGETEER n soldier armed with a small round shield

TARGETING > TARGET

TARGETS > TARGET

TARGING > TARGE

TARIFF n tax levied on imports ▷ vb impose punishment for a criminal offence

TARIFFED > TARIFF

TARIFFING > TARIFF

TARIFFS > TARIFF

TARING > TARE

TARINGS > TARE

TARLATAN n open-weave cotton fabric, used for stiffening garments

TARLATANS > TARLATAN

TARLETAN same as > TARLATAN

TARLETANS > TARLETAN

TARMAC See also > MACADAM

TARMACKED > TARMAC

TARMACS > TARMAC

TARN n small mountain lake

TARNAL adj damned ▷ adv extremely

TARNALLY > TARNAL

TARNATION euphemism for > DAMNATION

TARNISH vb make or become stained or less bright ▷ n discoloration or blemish

TARNISHED > TARNISH

TARNISHER > TARNISH

TARNISHES > TARNISH

TARNS > TARN

TARO n plant with a large edible rootstock

TAROC old variant of > TAROT

TAROCS > TAROC

TAROK old variant of > TAROT

TAROKS > TAROK

TAROS > TARO

TAROT n special pack of cards used mainly in fortune-telling ▷ adj relating to tarot cards

TAROTS > TAROT

TARP informal word for > TARPAULIN

TARPAN n European wild horse common in prehistoric times but now extinct

TARPANS > TARPAN

TARPAPER n paper coated or impregnated with tar

TARPAPERS > TARPAPER

TARPAULIN n (sheet of) heavy waterproof fabric

TARPON n large silvery clupeoid game fish found in

warm Atlantic waters

TARPONS > TARPON

TARPS > TARP

TARRAGON n aromatic herb

TARRAGONS > TARRAGON

TARRAS same as > TRASS

TARRASES > TARRAS

TARRE vb old word meaning to provoke or goad

TARRED > TAR

TARRES > TARRE

TARRIANCE archaic word for > DELAY

TARRIED > TARRY

TARRIER > TARRY

TARRIERS > TARRY

TARRIES > TARRY

TARRIEST > TARRY

TARRINESS > TAR

TARRING > TAR

TARRINGS > TAR

TARROCK n seabird

TARROCKS > TARROCK

TARROW vb exhibit reluctance

TARROWED > TARROW

TARROWING > TARROW

TARROWS > TARROW

TARRY vb linger or delay ▷ n stay ▷ adj covered in or resembling tar

TARRYING > TARRY

TARS > TAR

TARSAL adj of the tarsus or tarsi ▷ n tarsal bone

TARSALGIA n pain in the tarsus

TARSALS > TARSAL

TARSEAL n bitumen surface of a road

TARSEALS > TARSEAL

TARSEL same as > TERCEL

TARSELS > TARSEL

TARSI > TARSUS

TARSIA another term for > INTARSIA

TARSIAS > TARSIA

TARSIER n small nocturnal primate of the E Indies, which has very large eyes

TARSIERS > TARSIER

TARSIOID adj resembling a tarsier

TARSIPED n generic term for a number of marsupials

TARSIPEDS > TARSIPED

TARSUS n bones of the heel and ankle collectively

TART n pie or flan with a sweet filling ▷ adj sharp or bitter ▷ adj (of a flavour, food, etc) sour, acid, or astringent ▷ vb (of food, drink, etc) become tart (sour)

TARTAN n design of straight lines crossing at right angles, esp one associated with a Scottish clan

TARTANA n small Mediterranean sailing boat

TARTANAS > TARTANA

TARTANE same as > TARTANA

TARTANED > TARTAN

TARTANES > TARTANE

TARTANRY n derogatory term for excessive use of

tartan and other Scottish imagery to produce a distorted sentimental view of Scotland and its history

TARTANS > TARTAN

TARTAR n hard deposit on the teeth

TARTARE n mayonnaise sauce mixed with hard-boiled egg yolks, chopped herbs, capers, and gherkins

TARTARES > TARTARE

TARTARIC adj of or derived from tartar or tartaric acid

TARTARISE same as > TARTARIZE

TARTARIZE vb impregnate or treat with tartar or tartar emetic

TARTARLY adj resembling a tartar

TARTAROUS adj consisting of, containing, or resembling tartar

TARTARS > TARTAR

TARTED > TART

TARTER > TART

TARTEST > TART

TARTIER > TARTY

TARTIEST > TARTY

TARTILY > TARTY

TARTINE n slice of bread with butter or jam spread on it

TARTINES > TARTINE

TARTINESS > TARTY

TARTING > TART

TARTISH > TART

TARTISHLY > TART

TARTLET n individual pastry case with a filling of fruit or other sweet or savoury mixture

TARTLETS > TARTLET

TARTLY > TART

TARTNESS > TART

TARTRATE n any salt or ester of tartaric acid

TARTRATED adj being in the form of a tartrate

TARTRATES > TARTRATE

TARTS > TART

TARTUFE same as > TARTUFFE

TARTUFES > TARTUFE

TARTUFFE n person who hypocritically pretends to be deeply pious

TARTUFFES > TARTUFFE

TARTY adj resembling a promiscuous woman; provocative in a cheap and bawdy way

TARWEED n resinous Californian plant with a pungent scent

TARWEEDS > TARWEED

TARWHINE n bream of E Australia, silver in colour with gold streaks

TARWHINES > TARWHINE

TARZAN n man with great physical strength, agility, and virility

TARZANS > TARZAN

TAS old form of > TASS

TASAR same as > TUSSORE

TASARS > TASAR
TASER *vb* use a Taser (trademark) stun gun on (someone)
TASERED > TASER
TASERING > TASER
TASERS > TASER
TASH *vb* stain or besmirch
TASHED > TASH
TASHES > TASH
TASHING > TASH
TASIMETER *n* device for measuring small temperature changes. It depends on the changes of pressure resulting from expanding or contracting solids
TASIMETRY > TASIMETER
TASK *n* piece of work to be done ▷ *vb* give someone a task to do
TASKBAR *n* area of computer screen showing what programs are running
TASKBARS > TASKBAR
TASKED > TASK
TASKER > TASK
TASKERS > TASK
TASKING > TASK
TASKINGS > TASK
TASKLESS > TASK
TASKS > TASK
TASKWORK *n* hard or unpleasant work
TASKWORKS > TASKWORK
TASLET *same as* > TASSET
TASLETS > TASLET
TASS *n* cup, goblet, or glass
TASSE *same as* > TASSET
TASSEL *n* decorative fringed knot of threads ▷ *vb* adorn with a tassel or tassels
TASSELED > TASSEL
TASSELING > TASSEL
TASSELL *same as* > TASSEL
TASSELLED > TASSEL
TASSELLS > TASSELL
TASSELLY > TASSEL
TASSELS > TASSEL
TASSES > TASSE
TASSET *n* piece of armour consisting of one or more plates fastened on to the bottom of a cuirass to protect the thigh
TASSETS > TASSET
TASSIE *same as* > TASS
TASSIES > TASSIE
TASSWAGE *vb* old poetic contraction of "to assuage"
TASTABLE > TASTE
TASTE *n* sense by which the flavour of a substance is distinguished in the mouth ▷ *vb* distinguish the taste of (a substance)
TASTEABLE > TASTE
TASTED > TASTE
TASTEFUL *adj* having or showing good taste
TASTELESS *adj* bland or insipid
TASTER *n* person employed to test the quality of food or drink by tasting it

TASTERS > TASTER
TASTES > TASTE
TASTEVIN *n* small shallow cup for wine tasting
TASTEVINS > TASTEVIN
TASTIER > TASTY
TASTIEST > TASTY
TASTILY > TASTY
TASTINESS > TASTY
TASTING > TASTE
TASTINGS > TASTE
TASTY *adj* pleasantly flavoured
TAT *n* tatty or tasteless article(s) ▷ *vb* make (something) by tatting
TATAHASH *n* stew containing potatoes and cheap cuts of meat
TATAMI *n* thick rectangular mat of woven straw, used as a standard to measure a Japanese room
TATAMIS > TATAMI
TATAR *n* brutal person
TATARS > TATAR
TATE *n* small tuft of fibre
TATER *n* potato
TATERS > TATER
TATES > TATE
TATH *vb* (of cattle) to defecate
TATHED > TATH
TATHING > TATH
TATHS > TATH
TATIE *same as* > TATTIE
TATIES > TATIE
TATLER *old variant of* > TATTLER
TATLERS > TATLER
TATOU *n* armadillo
TATOUAY *n* large armadillo of South America
TATOUAYS > TATOUAY
TATOUS > TATOU
TATS > TAT
TATSOI *n* variety of Chinese cabbage
TATSOIS > TATSOI
TATT *same as* > TAT
TATTED > TAT
TATTER *vb* make or become torn
TATTERED > TATTER
TATTERING > TATTER
TATTERS > TATTER
TATTERY *same as* > TATTERED
TATTIE *Scot or dialect word for* > POTATO
TATTIER > TATTY
TATTIES > TATTIE
TATTIEST > TATTY
TATTILY > TATTY
TATTINESS > TATTY
TATTING > TAT
TATTINGS > TAT
TATTLE *n* gossip or chatter ▷ *vb* gossip or chatter
TATTLED > TATTLE
TATTLER *n* person who tattles
TATTLERS > TATTLER
TATTLES > TATTLE
TATTLING > TATTLE
TATTLINGS > TATTLE
TATTOO *n* pattern made on

the body by pricking the skin and staining it with indelible inks ▷ *vb* make such a pattern on the skin
TATTOOED > TATTOO
TATTOOER > TATTOO
TATTOOERS > TATTOO
TATTOOING > TATTOO
TATTOOIST > TATTOO
TATTOOS > TATTOO
TATTOW *old variant of* > TATTOO
TATTOWED > TATTOW
TATTOWING > TATTOW
TATTOWS > TATTOW
TATTS > TATT
TATTY *adj* worn out, shabby, tawdry, or unkempt
TATU *old variant of* > TATTOO
TATUED > TATU
TATUING > TATU
TATUS > TATU
TAU *n* 19th letter in the Greek alphabet
TAUBE *n* type of German aeroplane
TAUBES > TAUBE
TAUGHT > TEACH
TAUHINU *New Zealand name for* > POPLAR
TAUHINUS > TAUHINU
TAUHOU *same as* > SILVEREYE
TAUIWI *n* Māori term for the non-Māori people of New Zealand
TAUIWIS > TAUIWI
TAULD *vb* old Scots variant of told
TAUNT *vb* tease with jeers ▷ *n* jeering remark ▷ *adj* (of the mast or masts of a sailing vessel) unusually tall
TAUNTED > TAUNT
TAUNTER > TAUNT
TAUNTERS > TAUNT
TAUNTING > TAUNT
TAUNTINGS > TAUNT
TAUNTS > TAUNT
TAUON *n* negatively charged elementary particle
TAUONS > TAUON
TAUPATA *n* New Zealand shrub or tree, with shiny dark green leaves
TAUPE *adj* brownish-grey ▷ *n* brownish-grey colour
TAUPES > TAUPE
TAUPIE *same as* > TAWPIE
TAUPIES > TAUPIE
TAUREAN *adj* born under or characteristic of Taurus
TAURIC *same as* > TAUREAN
TAURIFORM *adj* in the form of a bull
TAURINE *adj* of, relating to, or resembling a bull ▷ *n* derivative of the amino acid, cysteine, obtained from the bile of animals
TAURINES > TAURINE
TAUS > TAU
TAUT *adj* drawn tight ▷ *vb* Scots word meaning to tangle
TAUTAUG *same as* > TAUTOG

TAUTAUGS > TAUTAUG
TAUTED > TAUT
TAUTEN *vb* make or become taut
TAUTENED > TAUTEN
TAUTENING > TAUTEN
TAUTENS > TAUTEN
TAUTER > TAUT
TAUTEST > TAUT
TAUTING > TAUT
TAUTIT *adj* Scots word meaning tangled
TAUTLY > TAUT
TAUTNESS > TAUT
TAUTOG *n* large dark-coloured wrasse, used as a food fish
TAUTOGS > TAUTOG
TAUTOLOGY *n* use of words which merely repeat something already stated
TAUTOMER *n* either of the two forms of a chemical compound that exhibits tautomerism
TAUTOMERS > TAUTOMER
TAUTONYM *n* taxonomic name in which the generic and specific components are the same
TAUTONYMS > TAUTONYM
TAUTONYMY > TAUTONYM
TAUTS > TAUT
TAV *n* 23rd and last letter in the Hebrew alphabet
TAVA *n* thick Indian frying pan
TAVAH *variant of* > TAVA
TAVAHS > TAVAH
TAVAS > TAVA
TAVER *vb* wander about
TAVERED > TAVER
TAVERING > TAVER
TAVERN *n* pub
TAVERNA *n* (in Greece) a guesthouse that has its own bar
TAVERNAS > TAVERNA
TAVERNER *n* keeper of a tavern
TAVERNERS > TAVERNER
TAVERNS > TAVERN
TAVERS > TAVER
TAVERT *adj* bewildered or confused
TAVS > TAV
TAW *vb* convert skins into leather
TAWA *n* tall timber tree from New Zealand, with edible purple berries
TAWAI *n* any of various species of beech of the genus *Nothofagus* of New Zealand, originally called "birches" by the settlers
TAWAIS > TAWAI
TAWAS > TAWA
TAWDRIER > TAWDRY
TAWDRIES > TAWDRY
TAWDRIEST > TAWDRY
TAWDRILY > TAWDRY
TAWDRY *adj* cheap, showy, and of poor quality ▷ *n* gaudy finery of poor quality
TAWED > TAW
TAWER > TAW

TAWERIES > TAWERY
TAWERS > TAW
TAWERY n place where tawing is carried out
TAWHAI same as > TAWAI
TAWHAIS > TAWHAI
TAWHIRI n small New Zealand tree with wavy green glossy leaves
TAWIE adj easily persuaded or managed
TAWIER > TAWIE
TAWIEST > TAWIE
TAWING > TAW
TAWINGS > TAW
TAWNEY same as > TAWNY
TAWNEYS > TAWNEY
TAWNIER > TAWNY
TAWNIES > TAWNY
TAWNIEST > TAWNY
TAWNILY > TAWNY
TAWNINESS > TAWNY
TAWNY adj yellowish-brown ▷ n light brown to brownish-orange colour
TAWPIE n foolish or maladroit girl
TAWPIES > TAWPIE
TAWS same as > TAWSE
TAWSE n leather strap with one end cut into thongs, formerly used by schoolteachers to hit children who had misbehaved ▷ vb punish (someone) with or as if with a tawse
TAWSED > TAWSE
TAWSES > TAWSE
TAWSING > TAWSE
TAWT same as > TAUT
TAWTED > TAWT
TAWTIE > TAWT
TAWTIER > TAWT
TAWTIEST > TAWT
TAWTING > TAWT
TAWTS > TAWT
TAX n compulsory payment levied by a government on income, property, etc to raise revenue ▷ vb levy a tax on
TAXA > TAXON
TAXABLE adj capable of being taxed ▷ n person, income, property, etc, that is subject to tax
TAXABLES > TAXABLE
TAXABLY > TAXABLE
TAXACEOUS adj of, relating to, or belonging to the Taxaceae, a family of coniferous trees that includes the yews
TAXAMETER old variant of > TAXIMETER
TAXATION n levying of taxes
TAXATIONS > TAXATION
TAXATIVE > TAXATION
TAXED > TAX
TAXEME n any element of speech that may differentiate one utterance from another with a different meaning
TAXEMES > TAXEME
TAXEMIC > TAXEME

TAXER > TAX
TAXERS > TAX
TAXES > TAX
TAXI n car with a driver that may be hired to take people to any specified destination ▷ vb (of an aircraft) run along the ground before taking off or after landing
TAXIARCH n soldier in charge of a Greek taxis
TAXIARCHS > TAXIARCH
TAXICAB same as > TAXI
TAXICABS > TAXICAB
TAXIDERMY n art of stuffing and mounting animal skins to give them a lifelike appearance
TAXIED > TAXI
TAXIES > TAXIS
TAXIING > TAXI
TAXIMAN n taxi driver
TAXIMEN > TAXIMAN
TAXIMETER n meter fitted to a taxi to register the fare, based on the length of the journey
TAXING adj demanding, onerous
TAXINGLY > TAXING
TAXINGS > TAX
TAXIPLANE n aircraft that is available for hire
TAXIS n movement of a cell or organism in a particular direction in response to an external stimulus ancient Greek army unit
TAXITE n type of volcanic rock
TAXITES > TAXITE
TAXITIC > TAXITE
TAXIWAY n marked path along which aircraft taxi to or from a runway, parking area, etc
TAXIWAYS > TAXIWAY
TAXLESS > TAX
TAXMAN n collector of taxes
TAXMEN > TAXMAN
TAXOL n trademarked anti-cancer drug
TAXOLS > TAXOL
TAXON n any taxonomic group or rank
TAXONOMER > TAXONOMY
TAXONOMIC > TAXONOMY
TAXONOMY n classification of plants and animals into groups
TAXONS > TAXON
TAXOR > TAX
TAXORS > TAX
TAXPAID adj (of taxable products, esp wine) having had the applicable tax paid already
TAXPAYER n person or organization that pays taxes
TAXPAYERS > TAXPAYER
TAXPAYING > TAXPAYER
TAXUS n genus of conifers
TAXWISE adv regarding tax
TAXYING > TAXI
TAY Irish dialect word for > TEA

TAYASSUID n peccary
TAYBERRY n hybrid shrub produced by crossing a blackberry, raspberry, and loganberry
TAYRA n large arboreal musteline mammal, of Central and South America, with a dark brown body and paler head
TAYRAS > TAYRA
TAYS > TAY
TAZZA n wine cup with a shallow bowl and a circular foot
TAZZAS > TAZZA
TAZZE > TAZZA
TCHICK vb make a click by creating a vacuum in the mouth with the tongue pressed againt the palate then suddenly breaking the seal by withdrawing part of the tongue from the palate
TCHICKED > TCHICK
TCHICKING > TCHICK
TCHICKS > TCHICK
TCHOTCHKE n trinket
TE n (in tonic sol-fa) seventh degree of any major scale
TEA n drink made from infusing the dried leaves of an Asian bush in boiling water ▷ vb take tea
TEABERRY n berry of the wintergreen
TEABOARD n tea tray
TEABOARDS > TEABOARD
TEABOWL n small bowl used (instead of a teacup) for serving tea
TEABOWLS > TEABOWL
TEABOX n box for storing tea
TEABOXES > TEABOX
TEABREAD n loaf-shaped cake that contains dried fruit which has been steeped in cold tea before baking: served sliced and buttered
TEABREADS > TEABREAD
TEACAKE n flat bun, usually eaten toasted and buttered
TEACAKES > TEACAKE
TEACART n trolley from which tea is served
TEACARTS > TEACART
TEACH vb tell or show (someone) how to do something
TEACHABLE > TEACH
TEACHABLY > TEACH
TEACHER n person who teaches, esp in a school
TEACHERLY > TEACHER
TEACHERS > TEACHER
TEACHES > TEACH
TEACHIE old form of > TETCHY
TEACHING > TEACH
TEACHINGS > TEACH
TEACHLESS adj unable to be taught
TEACUP n cup out of which tea may be drunk
TEACUPFUL n amount a teacup will hold, about four

fluid ounces
TEACUPS > TEACUP
TEAD old word for > TORCH
TEADE same as > TEAD
TEADES > TEADE
TEADS > TEAD
TEAED > TEA
TEAGLE vb raise or hoist using a tackle
TEAGLED > TEAGLE
TEAGLES > TEAGLE
TEAGLING > TEAGLE
TEAHOUSE n restaurant, esp in Japan or China, where tea and light refreshments are served
TEAHOUSES > TEAHOUSE
TEAING > TEA
TEAK n very hard wood of an E Indian tree
TEAKETTLE n kettle for boiling water to make tea
TEAKS > TEAK
TEAKWOOD another word for > TEAK
TEAKWOODS > TEAKWOOD
TEAL n kind of small duck
TEALIKE adj resembling tea
TEALS > TEAL
TEAM n group of people forming one side in a game ▷ vb make or cause to make a team
TEAMAKER n person or thing that makes tea
TEAMAKERS > TEAMAKER
TEAMED > TEAM
TEAMER > TEAM
TEAMERS > TEAM
TEAMING > TEAM
TEAMINGS > TEAM
TEAMMATE n fellow member of a team
TEAMMATES > TEAMMATE
TEAMS > TEAM
TEAMSTER n commercial vehicle driver
TEAMSTERS > TEAMSTER
TEAMWISE adv in respect of a team; in the manner of a team
TEAMWORK n cooperative work by a team
TEAMWORKS > TEAMWORK
TEAPOT n container with a lid, spout, and handle for making and serving tea
TEAPOTS > TEAPOT
TEAPOY n small table or stand with a tripod base
TEAPOYS > TEAPOY
TEAR n drop of fluid appearing in and falling from the eye ▷ vb rip a hole in ▷ vb shed tears
TEARABLE > TEAR
TEARAWAY n wild or unruly person
TEARAWAYS > TEARAWAY
TEARDOWN n demolition; disassembly
TEARDOWNS > TEARDOWN
TEARDROP same as > TEAR
TEARDROPS > TEARDROP
TEARED > TEAR
TEARER > TEAR
TEARERS > TEAR

TEARFUL *adj* weeping or about to weep
TEARFULLY > TEARFUL
TEARGAS *n* gas or vapour that makes the eyes smart and water ▷ *vb* deploy teargas against
TEARGASES > TEARGAS
TEARIER > TEARY
TEARIEST > TEARY
TEARILY > TEARY
TEARINESS > TEARY
TEARING > TEAR
TEARLESS > TEAR
TEAROOM *same as* > TEASHOP
TEAROOMS > TEAROOM
TEARS > TEAR
TEARSHEET *n* page in a newspaper or periodical that is cut or perforated so that it can be easily torn out
TEARSTAIN *n* stain or streak left by tears
TEARSTRIP *n* part of packaging torn to open it
TEARY *adj* characterized by, covered with, or secreting tears
TEAS > TEA
TEASABLE > TEASE
TEASE *vb* make fun of (someone) in a provoking or playful way ▷ *n* person who teases
TEASED > TEASE
TEASEL *n* plant with prickly leaves and flowers ▷ *vb* tease (a fabric)
TEASELED > TEASEL
TEASELER > TEASEL
TEASELERS > TEASEL
TEASELING > TEASEL
TEASELLED > TEASEL
TEASELLER > TEASEL
TEASELS > TEASEL
TEASER *n* annoying or difficult problem
TEASERS > TEASER
TEASES > TEASE
TEASHOP *n* restaurant where tea and light refreshments are served
TEASHOPS > TEASHOP
TEASING > TEASE
TEASINGLY > TEASE
TEASINGS > TEASE
TEASPOON *n* small spoon for stirring tea
TEASPOONS > TEASPOON
TEAT *n* nipple of a breast or udder
TEATASTER *n* person assessing teas by tasting them
TEATED > TEAT
TEATIME *n* late afternoon
TEATIMES > TEATIME
TEATS > TEAT
TEAWARE *n* implements and vessels for brewing and serving tea
TEAWARES > TEAWARE
TEAZE *old variant of* > TEASE
TEAZED > TEAZE
TEAZEL *same as* > TEASEL
TEAZELED > TEAZEL

TEAZELING > TEAZEL
TEAZELLED > TEAZEL
TEAZELS > TEAZEL
TEAZES > TEAZE
TEAZING > TEAZE
TEAZLE *same as* > TEASEL
TEAZLED > TEAZLE
TEAZLES > TEAZLE
TEAZLING > TEAZLE
TEBBAD *n* sandstorm
TEBBADS > TEBBAD
TEC *short for* > DETECTIVE
TECH *n* technical college
TECHED *adj* showing slight insanity
TECHIE *n* person who is skilled in the use of technology ▷ *adj* relating to or skilled in the use of technology
TECHIER > TECHY
TECHIES > TECHIE
TECHIEST > TECHY
TECHILY > TECHY
TECHINESS > TECHY
TECHNIC *another word for* > TECHNIQUE
TECHNICAL *adj* of or specializing in industrial, practical, or mechanical arts and applied sciences ▷ *n* small armed military truck
TECHNICS *n* study or theory of industry and industrial arts
TECHNIKON *n* technical college
TECHNIQUE *n* method or skill used for a particular task
TECHNO *n* type of electronic dance music with a very fast beat
TECHNOPOP *n* pop music sharing certain features with techno
TECHNOS > TECHNO
TECHS > TECH
TECHY *same as* > TECHIE
TECKEL *n* dachshund
TECKELS > TECKEL
TECS > TEC
TECTA > TECTUM
TECTAL > TECTUM
TECTIFORM *adj* in the form of a roof
TECTITE *same as* > TEKTITE
TECTITES > TECTITE
TECTONIC *adj* denoting or relating to construction or building
TECTONICS *n* study of the earth's crust and the forces affecting it
TECTONISM > TECTONIC
TECTORIAL *as in* *tectorial membrane* membrane in the inner ear that covers the organ of Corti
TECTRICES > TECTRIX
TECTRIX *another name for* > COVERT
TECTUM *n* any roof-like structure in the body, esp the dorsal area of the midbrain

TECTUMS > TECTUM
TED *vb* shake out (hay), so as to dry it
TEDDED > TED
TEDDER *n* machine equipped with a series of small rotating forks for tedding hay
TEDDERED > TEDDER
TEDDERING > TEDDER
TEDDERS > TEDDER
TEDDIE *same as* > TEDDY
TEDDIES > TEDDY
TEDDING > TED
TEDDY *n* teddy bear
TEDESCA *adj* (of a piece of music) in German style
TEDESCHE > TEDESCA
TEDESCHI > TEDESCO
TEDESCO *adj* German
TEDIER > TEDY
TEDIEST > TEDY
TEDIOSITY > TEDIOUS
TEDIOUS *adj* causing fatigue or boredom
TEDIOUSLY > TEDIOUS
TEDISOME *old Scottish variant of* > TEDIOUS
TEDIUM *n* monotony
TEDIUMS > TEDIUM
TEDS > TED
TEDY *same as* > TEDIOUS
TEE *n* small peg from which a golf ball can be played at the start of each hole ▷ *vb* position (the ball) ready for striking, on or as if on a tee
TEED > TEE
TEEING > TEE
TEEK *adj* in Indian English, well
TEEL *same as* > SESAME
TEELS > TEEL
TEEM *vb* be full of
TEEMED > TEEM
TEEMER > TEEM
TEEMERS > TEEM
TEEMFUL > TEEM
TEEMING > TEEM
TEEMINGLY > TEEM
TEEMLESS > TEEM
TEEMS > TEEM
TEEN *n* affliction or woe ▷ *n* teenager ▷ *vb* set alight
TEENAGE *adj* (of a person) aged between 13 and 19 ▷ *n* this period of time
TEENAGED *adj* (of a person) aged between 13 and 19
TEENAGER *n* person aged between 13 and 19
TEENAGERS > TEENAGER
TEEND *same as* > TIND
TEENDED > TEEND
TEENDING > TEEND
TEENDS > TEEND
TEENE *same as* > TEEN
TEENED > TEEN
TEENER > TEEN
TEENERS > TEEN
TEENES > TEENE
TEENFUL > TEEN
TEENIER > TEENY
TEENIEST > TEENY
TEENING > TEEN
TEENS > TEEN
TEENSIER > TEENSY

TEENSIEST > TEENSY
TEENSY *same as* > TEENY
TEENTIER > TEENTY
TEENTIEST > TEENTY
TEENTSIER > TEENTSY
TEENTSY *same as* > TEENY
TEENTY *same as* > TEENY
TEENY *adj* extremely small
TEENYBOP *adj* of, or relating to, a young teenager who avidly follows fashions in music and clothes
TEEPEE *same as* > TEPEE
TEEPEES > TEEPEE
TEER *vb* smear; daub
TEERED > TEER
TEERING > TEER
TEERS > TEER
TEES > TEE
TEETER *vb* wobble or move unsteadily
TEETERED > TEETER
TEETERING > TEETER
TEETERS > TEETER
TEETH > TOOTH
TEETHE *vb* (of a baby) grow his or her first teeth
TEETHED > TEETHE
TEETHER *n* object for an infant to bite on during teething
TEETHERS > TEETHER
TEETHES > TEETHE
TEETHING > TEETHE
TEETHINGS > TEETHING
TEETHLESS > TEETH
TEETOTAL *adj* drinking no alcohol ▷ *vb* advocate total abstinence from alcohol
TEETOTALS > TEETOTAL
TEETOTUM *n* spinning top bearing letters of the alphabet on its four sides
TEETOTUMS > TEETOTUM
TEF *n* annual grass, of NE Africa, grown for its grain
TEFF *same as* > TEF
TEFFS > TEFF
TEFILLAH *n* either of the pair of blackened square cases containing parchments inscribed with biblical passages, bound by leather thongs to the head and left arm, and worn by Jewish men during weekday morning prayers
TEFILLIN > TEFILLAH
TEFLON *n* a trademark for polytetrafluoroethylene when used in nonstick cooking vessels
TEFLONS > TEFLON
TEFS > TEF
TEG *n* two-year-old sheep
TEGG *same as* > TEG
TEGGS > TEGG
TEGMEN *n* either of the leathery forewings of the cockroach and related insects
TEGMENTA > TEGMENTUM
TEGMENTAL > TEGMENTUM
TEGMENTUM *n* one of the hard protective sometimes hairy or

resinous specialized leaves surrounding the buds of certain plants

TEGMINA > TEGMEN

TEGMINAL > TEGMEN

TEGS > TEG

TEGU n large South American lizard

TEGUA n type of moccasin

TEGUAS > TEGUA

TEGUEXIN same as > TEGU

TEGUEXINS > TEGUEXIN

TEGULA n one of a pair of coverings of the forewings of certain insects

TEGULAE > TEGULA

TEGULAR adj of, relating to, or resembling a tile or tiles

TEGULARLY > TEGULAR

TEGULATED adj overlapping in the manner of roof tiles

TEGUMEN same as > TEGMEN

TEGUMENT n protective layer around an ovule

TEGUMENTS > TEGUMENT

TEGUMINA > TEGUMEN

TEGUS > TEGU

TEHR same as > TAHR

TEHRS > TEHR

TEIGLACH n dish consisting of morsels of dough boiled in honey

TEIID n member of the Teiidae family of lizards

TEIIDS > TEIID

TEIL n lime tree

TEILS > TEIL

TEIND Scot and northern English word for > TITHE

TEINDED > TEIND

TEINDING > TEIND

TEINDS > TEIND

TEKKIE variant of > TECHIE

TEKKIES > TEKKIE

TEKNONYMY n practice of naming a child after his or her parent

TEKTITE n small dark glassy object found in several areas around the world, thought to be a product of meteorite impact

TEKTITES > TEKTITE

TEKTITIC > TEKTITE

TEL same as > TELL

TELA n any delicate tissue or weblike structure

TELAE > TELA

TELAMON n column in the form of a male figure, used to support an entablature

TELAMONES > TELAMON

TELAMONS > TELAMON

TELARY adj capable of spinning a web

TELCO n telecommunications company

TELCOS > TELCO

TELD same as > TAULD

TELE same as > TELLY

TELECAST vb broadcast by television ▷ n television broadcast

TELECASTS > TELECAST

TELECHIR n robot arm controlled by a human operator

TELECHIRS > TELECHIR

TELECINE n apparatus for producing a television signal from cinematograph film

TELECINES > TELECINE

TELECOM n telecommunications

TELECOMS same as > TELECOM

TELEDU n badger of SE Asia and Indonesia, having dark brown hair with a white stripe along the back and producing a fetid secretion from the anal glands when attacked

TELEDUS > TELEDU

TELEFAX another word for > FAX

TELEFAXED > TELEFAX

TELEFAXES > TELEFAX

TELEFILM n TV movie

TELEFILMS > TELEFILM

TELEGA n rough four-wheeled cart used in Russia

TELEGAS > TELEGA

TELEGENIC adj having or showing a pleasant television image

TELEGONIC > TELEGONY

TELEGONY n supposed influence of a previous sire on offspring borne by a female to other sires

TELEGRAM n formerly, a message sent by telegraph ▷ vb send a telegram

TELEGRAMS > TELEGRAM

TELEGRAPH n formerly, a system for sending messages over a distance along a cable ▷ vb communicate by telegraph

TELEMAN n noncommissioned officer in the US navy, usually charged with communications duties

TELEMARK n turn in which one ski is placed far forward of the other and turned gradually inwards ▷ vb perform a telemark turn

TELEMARKS > TELEMARK

TELEMATIC adj of, or relating to, the branch of science concerned with the use of technological devices to transmit information over long distances

TELEMEN > TELEMAN

TELEMETER n any device for recording or measuring a distant event and transmitting the data to a receiver or observer ▷ vb obtain and transmit (data) from a distant source, esp from a spacecraft

TELEMETRY n use of electronic devices to record or measure a distant event and transmit the data to a receiver

TELEOLOGY n belief that all things have a predetermined purpose

TELEONOMY n condition of having a fundamental purpose

TELEOSAUR n type of crocodile from the Jurassic period

TELEOST n bony fish with rayed fins and a swim bladder ▷ adj of, relating to, or belonging to this type of fish

TELEOSTS > TELEOST

TELEPATH n person who is telepathic ▷ vb practise telepathy

TELEPATHS > TELEPATH

TELEPATHY n direct communication between minds

TELEPHEME n any message sent by telephone

TELEPHONE n device for transmitting sound over a distance along wires ▷ vb call or talk to (a person) by telephone ▷ adj of or using a telephone

TELEPHONY n system of telecommunications for the transmission of speech or other sounds

TELEPHOTO n short for telephoto lens: a compound camera lens that produces a magnified image of distant objects

TELEPLAY n play written for television

TELEPLAYS > TELEPLAY

TELEPOINT n system providing a place where a cordless telephone can be connected to a telephone network

TELEPORT vb (in science fiction) to transport (a person or object) across a distance instantaneously

TELEPORTS > TELEPORT

TELERAN n electronic navigational aid in which the image of a ground-based radar system is televised to aircraft in flight so that a pilot can see the position of his aircraft in relation to others

TELERANS > TELERAN

TELERGIC > TELERGY

TELERGIES > TELERGY

TELERGY n name for the form of energy supposedly transferred during telepathy

TELES > TELE

TELESALE > TELESALES

TELESALES n selling of a product or service by telephone

TELESCOPE n optical instrument for magnifying distant objects ▷ vb shorten

TELESCOPY n branch of astronomy concerned with the use and design of telescopes

TELESEME n old-fashioned electric signalling system

TELESEMES > TELESEME

TELESES > TELESIS

TELESHOP vb buy goods by telephone or Internet

TELESHOPS > TELESHOP

TELESIS n purposeful use of natural and social processes to obtain specific social goals

TELESM n talisman

TELESMS > TELESM

TELESTIC adj relating to a hierophant

TELESTICH n short poem in which the last letters of each successive line form a word

TELESTICS n ancient pseudoscientific art of animating statues, idols, etc, or causing them to be inhabited by a diety

TELETEX n international means of communicating text between a variety of terminals

TELETEXES > TELETEX

TELETEXT n system which shows information and news on television screens

TELETEXTS > TELETEXT

TELETHON n lengthy television programme to raise charity funds, etc

TELETHONS > TELETHON

TELETRON n system for showing enlarged televisual images in eg sports stadiums

TELETRONS > TELETRON

TELETYPE vb send typed message by telegraph

TELETYPED > TELETYPE

TELETYPES > TELETYPE > TELETYPESETTING

TELEVIEW vb watch television

TELEVIEWS > TELEVIEW

TELEVISE vb broadcast on television

TELEVISED > TELEVISE

TELEVISER > TELEVISE

TELEVISES > TELEVISE

TELEVISOR n apparatus through which one transmits or receives televisual images

TELEX n international communication service using teleprinters ▷ vb transmit by telex

TELEXED > TELEX

TELEXES > TELEX

TELEXING > TELEX

TELFER same as > TELPHERAGE

TELFERAGE n overhead transport system in which an electrically driven truck runs along a single rail or cable, the load being suspended in a separate car beneath

TELFERED > TELFER

TELFERIC > TELFER

TELFERING > TELFER

TELFERS > TELFER

TELFORD *n* road built using a method favoured by Thomas Telford (1757-1834)

TELFORDS > TELFORD

TELIA > TELIUM

TELIAL > TELIUM

TELIC *adj* directed or moving towards some goal

TELICALLY > TELIC

TELIUM *n* spore-producing body of some rust fungi in which the teliospores are formed

TELL *vb* make known in words ▷ *n* large mound resulting from the accumulation of rubbish on a long-settled site, esp one with mudbrick buildings, particularly in the Middle East

TELLABLE > TELL

TELLAR *same as* > TILLER

TELLARED > TELLAR

TELLARING > TELLAR

TELLARS > TELLAR

TELLEN *same as* > TELLIN

TELLENS > TELLEN

TELLER *n* narrator ▷ *vb* (of a plant) to produce tillers

TELLERED > TELLER

TELLERING > TELLER

TELLERS > TELLER

TELLIES > TELLY

TELLIN *n* slim marine bivalve molluscs that live in intertidal sand

TELLING > TELL

TELLINGLY > TELL

TELLINGS > TELL

TELLINOID > TELLIN

TELLINS > TELLIN

TELLS > TELL

TELLTALE *n* person who reveals secrets ▷ *adj* revealing

TELLTALES > TELLTALE

TELLURAL *adj* tellurial; of or relating to the earth

TELLURATE *n* any salt or ester of telluric acid

TELLURIAN *same as* > TELLURION

TELLURIC *adj* of, relating to, or originating on or in the earth or soil

TELLURIDE *n* any compound of tellurium, esp one formed between tellurium and a more electropositive element or group

TELLURION *n* instrument that shows how day and night and the seasons result from the tilt of the earth, its rotation on its axis, and its revolution around the sun

TELLURISE *same as* > TELLURIZE

TELLURITE *n* any salt or ester of tellurous acid

TELLURIUM *n* brittle silvery-white nonmetallic element

TELLURIZE *vb* mix or combine with tellurium

TELLUROUS *adj* of or containing tellurium, esp in a low valence state

TELLUS *n* earth

TELLUSES > TELLUS

TELLY *n* television

TELLYS > TELLY

TELNET *n* computer system allowing one user to access remotely other computers on the same network ▷ *vb* use a telnet system

TELNETED > TELNET

TELNETING > TELNET

TELNETS > TELNET

TELNETTED > TELNET

TELOI > TELOS

TELOME *n* fundamental unit of a plant's structure

TELOMERE *n* either of the ends of a chromosome

TELOMERES > TELOMERE

TELOMES > TELOME

TELOMIC > TELOME

TELOPHASE *n* final stage of mitosis, during which a set of chromosomes is present at each end of the cell and a nuclear membrane forms around each, producing two new nuclei

TELOS *n* objective; ultimate purpose

TELOSES > TELOS

TELOTAXES > TELOTAXIS

TELOTAXIS *n* movement of an organism in response to one particular stimulus, overriding any response to other stimuli present

TELPHER *same as* > TELFERAGE

TELPHERED > TELPHER

TELPHERIC > TELPHER

TELPHERS > TELPHER

TELS > TEL

TELSON *n* last segment or an appendage on the last segment of the body of crustaceans and arachnids

TELSONIC > TELSON

TELSONS > TELSON

TELT *same as* > TAULD

TEMAZEPAM *n* sedative in the form of a gel-like capsule, which is taken orally or melted and injected by drug users

TEMBLOR *n* earthquake or earth tremor

TEMBLORES > TEMBLOR

TEMBLORS > TEMBLOR

TEME *old variant of* > TEAM

TEMED > TEME

TEMENE > TEMENOS

TEMENOS *n* sacred area, esp one surrounding a temple

TEMERITY *n* boldness or audacity

TEMEROUS > TEMERITY

TEMES > TEME

TEMP *same as* > TEMPORARY

TEMPED > TEMP

TEMPEH *n* fermented soya beans

TEMPEHS > TEMPEH

TEMPER *n* outburst of anger ▷ *vb* make less extreme

TEMPERA *n* painting medium for powdered pigments

TEMPERAS > TEMPERA

TEMPERATE *adj* (of climate) not extreme ▷ *vb* temper

TEMPERED *adj* (of a scale) having the frequency differences between notes adjusted in accordance with the system of equal temperament

TEMPERER > TEMPER

TEMPERERS > TEMPER

TEMPERING > TEMPER

TEMPERS > TEMPER

TEMPEST *n* violent storm ▷ *vb* agitate or disturb violently

TEMPESTED > TEMPEST

TEMPESTS > TEMPEST

TEMPI > TEMPO

TEMPING > TEMP

TEMPLAR *n* lawyer, esp a barrister, who lives or has chambers in the Inner or Middle Temple in London

TEMPLARS > TEMPLAR

TEMPLATE *n* pattern used to cut out shapes accurately

TEMPLATES > TEMPLATE

TEMPLE *n* building for worship

TEMPLED > TEMPLE

TEMPLES > TEMPLE

TEMPLET *same as* > TEMPLATE

TEMPLETS > TEMPLET

TEMPO *n* rate or pace

TEMPORAL *adj* of time ▷ *n* any body part relating to or near the temple or temples

TEMPORALS > TEMPORAL

TEMPORARY *adj* lasting only for a short time ▷ *n* person, esp a secretary or other office worker, employed on a temporary basis

TEMPORE *adv* in the time of

TEMPORISE *same as* > TEMPORIZE

TEMPORIZE *vb* gain time by negotiation or evasiveness

TEMPOS > TEMPO

TEMPS > TEMP

TEMPT *vb* entice (a person) to do something wrong

TEMPTABLE > TEMPT

TEMPTED > TEMPT

TEMPTER > TEMPT

TEMPTERS > TEMPT

TEMPTING *adj* attractive or inviting

TEMPTINGS > TEMPTING

TEMPTRESS *n* woman who sets out to allure or seduce a man or men

TEMPTS > TEMPT

TEMPURA *n* Japanese dish of seafood or vegetables dipped in batter and deep-fried, often at the table

TEMPURAS > TEMPURA

TEMS *same as* > TEMSE

TEMSE *vb* sieve

TEMSED > TEMSE

TEMSES > TEMSE

TEMSING > TEMSE

TEMULENCE *n* drunkenness

TEMULENCY *same as* > TEMULENCE

TEMULENT > TEMULENCE

TEN *n* one more than nine ▷ *adj* amounting to ten

TENABLE *adj* able to be upheld or maintained

TENABLY > TENABLE

TENACE *n* holding of two nonconsecutive high cards of a suit, such as the ace and queen

TENACES > TENACE

TENACIOUS *adj* holding fast

TENACITY > TENACIOUS

TENACULA > TENACULUM

TENACULUM *n* surgical or dissecting instrument for grasping and holding parts, consisting of a slender hook mounted in a handle

TENAIL *same as* > TENAILLE

TENAILLE *n* low outwork in the main ditch between two bastions

TENAILLES > TENAILLE

TENAILLON *n* outwork shoring up a ravelin

TENAILS > TENAIL

TENANCIES > TENANCY

TENANCY *n* temporary possession or use of lands or property owned by somebody else, in return for payment

TENANT *n* person who rents land or a building ▷ *vb* hold (land or property) as a tenant

TENANTED > TENANT

TENANTING > TENANT

TENANTRY *n* tenants collectively

TENANTS > TENANT

TENCH *n* freshwater game fish of the carp family

TENCHES > TENCH

TEND *vb* be inclined

TENDANCE *n* care and attention

TENDANCES > TENDANCE

TENDED > TEND

TENDENCE *same as* > TENDENCY

TENDENCES > TENDENCE > TENDENCIOUSNESS

TENDENCY *n* inclination to act in a certain way

TENDENZ *same as* > TENDENCY

TENDENZEN > TENDENZ

TENDER *adj* not tough ▷ *vb* offer ▷ *n* such an offer

TENDERED > TENDER

TENDERER > TENDER

TENDERERS > TENDER

t

TENDEREST > TENDER
TENDERING > TENDER
TENDERISE same
as > TENDERIZE
TENDERIZE vb soften
(meat) by pounding or
treatment with a special
substance
TENDERLY > TENDER
TENDERS > TENDER
TENDING > TEND
TENDINOUS adj of, relating
to, possessing, or
resembling tendons
TENDON n strong tissue
attaching a muscle to a
bone
TENDONS > TENDON
TENDRE n care
TENDRES > TENDRE
TENDRESSE n feeling of
love; tenderness
TENDRIL n slender stem
by which a climbing plant
clings
TENDRILED > TENDRIL
TENDRILS > TENDRIL
TENDRON n shoot
TENDRONS > TENDRON
TENDS > TEND
TENDU n position in ballet
TENDUS > TENDU
TENE same as > TEEN
TENEBRAE n darkness
TENEBRIO n type of small
mealworm
TENEBRIOS > TENEBRIO
> TENEBRIOUSNESS
TENEBRISM n school, style,
or method of painting,
adopted chiefly by
17th-century Spanish and
Neapolitan painters, esp
Caravaggio, characterized
by large areas of dark
colours, usually relieved
with a shaft of light
TENEBRIST > TENEBRISM
TENEBRITY n darkness;
gloominess
TENEBROSE same
as > TENEBROUS
TENEBROUS adj gloomy,
shadowy, or dark
TENEMENT n (esp in
Scotland or the US)
building divided into
several flats
TENEMENTS > TENEMENT
TENENDUM n part of a deed
that specifies the terms of
tenure
TENENDUMS > TENENDUM
TENES > TENE
TENESMIC > TENESMUS
TENESMUS n bowel disorder
TENET n doctrine or belief
TENETS > TENET
TENFOLD n one tenth
TENFOLDS > TENFOLD
TENGE n standard monetary
unit of Kazakhstan, divided
into 100 tiyn
TENGES > TENGE
TENIA same as > TAENIA
TENIACIDE n substance,
esp a drug, that kills

tapeworms
TENIAE > TENIA
TENIAFUGE same
as > TENIACIDE
TENIAS > TENIA
TENIASES > TENIASIS
TENIASIS same
as > TAENIASIS
TENIOID > TENIA
TENNE n tawny colour
TENNER n ten-pound note
TENNERS > TENNER
TENNES > TENNE
TENNIES > TENNY
TENNIS n game in which
players use rackets to hit
a ball back and forth over
a net
TENNISES > TENNIS
TENNIST n tennis player
TENNISTS > TENNIST
TENNO n formal title of the
Japanese emperor, esp
when regarded as a divine
religious leader
TENNOS > TENNO
TENNY same as > TENNE
TENON n projecting end on a
piece of wood fitting into a
slot in another ▷ vb form a
tenon on (a piece of wood)
TENONED > TENON
TENONER > TENON
TENONERS > TENON
TENONING > TENON
TENONS > TENON
TENOR n (singer with)
the second highest male
voice ▷ adj (of a voice or
instrument) between alto
and baritone
TENORIST n musician
playing any tenor
instrument
TENORISTS > TENORIST
TENORITE n black mineral
found in copper deposits
and consisting of copper
oxide in the form of either
metallic scales or earthy
masses. Formula: CuO
TENORITES > TENORITE
TENORLESS > TENOR
TENOROON n tenor bassoon
TENOROONS > TENOROON
TENORS > TENOR
TENOTOMY n surgical
division of a tendon
TENOUR old variant
of > TENOR
TENOURS > TENOUR
TENPENCE n sum of money
equivalent to ten pennies
TENPENCES > TENPENCE
TENPENNY adj (of a nail)
three inches in length
TENPIN n one of the pins
used in tenpin bowling
TENPINS > TENPIN
TENREC n small mammal
resembling hedgehogs or
shrews
TENRECS > TENREC
TENS > TEN
TENSE adj emotionally
strained ▷ vb make or
become tense ▷ n form of

a verb showing the time of
action
TENSED > TENSE
TENSELESS > TENSE
TENSELY > TENSE
TENSENESS > TENSE
TENSER > TENSE
TENSES > TENSE
TENSEST > TENSE
TENSIBLE adj capable of
being stretched
TENSIBLY > TENSIBLE
TENSILE adj of tension
TENSILELY > TENSILE
TENSILITY > TENSILE
TENSING > TENSE
TENSION n hostility or
suspense ▷ vb tighten
TENSIONAL > TENSION
TENSIONED > TENSION
TENSIONER > TENSION
TENSIONS > TENSION
TENSITIES > TENSITY
TENSITY rare word
for > TENSION
TENSIVE adj of or causing
tension or strain
TENSON n type of French
lyric poem
TENSONS > TENSON
TENSOR n any muscle that
can cause a part to become
firm or tense
TENSORIAL > TENSOR
TENSORS > TENSOR
TENT n portable canvas
shelter ▷ vb camp in a tent
TENTACLE n flexible organ
of many invertebrates,
used for grasping, feeding,
etc
TENTACLED > TENTACLE
TENTACLES > TENTACLE
TENTACULA > TENTACLE
TENTAGE n tents collectively
TENTAGES > TENTAGE
TENTATION n method
of achieving the
correct adjustment of a
mechanical device by a
series of trials
TENTATIVE adj provisional
or experimental ▷ n
investigative attempt
TENTED > TENT
TENTER > TENT
TENTERED > TENT
TENTERING > TENT
TENTERS > TENT
TENTFUL n number of
people or objects that can
fit in a tent
TENTFULS > TENTFUL
TENTH n (of) number ten in
a series ▷ adj coming after
the ninth in numbering or
counting order, position,
time, etc ▷ adv after the
ninth person, position,
event, etc
TENTHLY same as > TENTH
TENTHS > TENTH
TENTIE adj wary
TENTIER > TENTIE
TENTIEST > TENTIE
TENTIGO n morbid
preoccupation with sex

TENTIGOS > TENTIGO
TENTING > TENT
TENTINGS > TENT
TENTLESS > TENT
TENTLIKE > TENT
TENTMAKER n maker of
tents
TENTORIA > TENTORIUM
TENTORIAL > TENTORIUM
TENTORIUM n tough
membrane covering
the upper part of the
cerebellum
TENTS > TENT
TENTWISE adv in the
manner of a tent
TENTY same as > TENTIE
TENUE n deportment
TENUES > TENUIS
TENUIOUS same
as > TENUOUS
TENUIS n (in the grammar
of classical Greek) any
of the voiceless stops as
represented by kappa, pi,
or tau (k, p, t)
TENUITIES > TENUOUS
TENUITY > TENUOUS
TENUOUS adj slight or flimsy
TENUOUSLY > TENUOUS
TENURABLE > TENURE
TENURE n (period of) the
holding of an office or
position
TENURED adj having tenure
of office
TENURES > TENURE
TENURIAL > TENURE
TENURING n process of
making tenured
TENUTI > TENUTO
TENUTO adv (of a note) to
be held for or beyond its
full time value ▷ vb note
sustained thus
TENUTOS > TENUTO
TENZON same as > TENSON
TENZONS > TENZON
TEOCALLI n any of various
truncated pyramids built
by the Aztecs as bases for
their temples
TEOCALLIS > TEOCALLI
TEOPAN n enclosure
surrounding a teocalli
TEOPANS > TEOPAN
TEOSINTE n tall Central
American annual grass,
related to maize and grown
for forage in the southern
US
TEOSINTES > TEOSINTE
TEPA n type of tree native to
South America
TEPAL n any of the
subdivisions of a perianth
that is not clearly
differentiated into calyx
and corolla
TEPALS > TEPAL
TEPAS > TEPA
TEPEE n cone-shaped tent,
formerly used by Native
Americans
TEPEES > TEPEE
TEPEFIED > TEPEFY
TEPEFIES > TEPEFY

TEPEFY *vb* make or become tepid

TEPEFYING > TEPEFY

TEPHIGRAM *n* chart depicting variations in atmospheric conditions relative to altitude

TEPHILLAH *same as* > TEFILLAH

TEPHILLIN > TEPHILLAH

TEPHRA *n* solid matter ejected during a volcanic eruption

TEPHRAS > TEPHRA

TEPHRITE *n* variety of basalt

TEPHRITES > TEPHRITE

TEPHRITIC > TEPHRITE

TEPHROITE *n* manganese silicate

TEPID *adj* slightly warm

TEPIDARIA *pl n* in Ancient Rome, the warm rooms of the baths

TEPIDER > TEPID

TEPIDEST > TEPID

TEPIDITY > TEPID

TEPIDLY > TEPID

TEPIDNESS > TEPID

TEPOY *same as* > TEAPOY

TEPOYS > TEPOY

TEQUILA *n* Mexican alcoholic drink

TEQUILAS > TEQUILA

TEQUILLA *same as* > TEQUILA

TEQUILLAS > TEQUILLA

TERABYTE *n* large unit of computer memory

TERABYTES > TERABYTE

TERAFLOP *n* measure of processing speed, consisting of a thousand billion floating-point operations a second

TERAFLOPS > TERAFLOP

TERAGLIN *n* edible marine fish of Australia which has fine scales and is blue in colour

TERAGLINS > TERAGLIN

TERAHERTZ *n* large unit of electrical frequency

TERAI *n* felt hat with a wide brim worn in subtropical regions

TERAIS > TERAI

TERAKIHI *same as* > TARAKIHI

TERAKIHIS > TERAKIHI

TERAOHM *n* unit of resistance equal to 10^{12}ohms

TERAOHMS > TERAOHM

TERAPH *n* any of various small household gods or images venerated by ancient Semitic peoples

TERAPHIM > TERAPH

TERAPHIMS > TERAPH

TERAS *n* monstrosity; teratism

TERATA > TERAS

TERATISM *n* malformed animal or human, esp in the fetal stage

TERATISMS > TERATISM

TERATOGEN *n* any substance, organism, or process that causes malformations in a fetus

TERATOID *adj* resembling a monster

TERATOMA *n* tumour or group of tumours composed of tissue foreign to the site of growth

TERATOMAS > TERATOMA

TERAWATT *n* unit of power equal to one million megawatts

TERAWATTS > TERAWATT

TERBIA *n* amorphous white insoluble powder

TERBIAS > TERBIA

TERBIC > TERBIUM

TERBIUM *n* rare metallic element

TERBIUMS > TERBIUM

TERCE *n* third of the seven canonical hours of the divine office, originally fixed at the third hour of the day, about 9 am

TERCEL *n* male falcon or hawk, esp as used in falconry

TERCELET *same as* > TERCEL

TERCELETS > TERCELET

TERCELS > TERCEL

TERCES > TERCE

TERCET *n* group of three lines of verse that rhyme together or are connected by rhyme with adjacent groups of three lines

TERCETS > TERCET

TERCIO *n* regiment of Spanish or Italian infantry

TERCIOS > TERCIO

TEREBENE *n* mixture of hydrocarbons prepared from oil of turpentine and sulphuric acid, used to make paints and varnishes and medicinally as an expectorant and antiseptic

TEREBENES > TEREBENE

TEREBIC *as in* *terebic acid* white crystalline carboxylic acid produced by the action of nitric acid on turpentin

TEREBINTH *n* small anacardiaceous tree with winged leafstalks and clusters of small flowers, and yielding a turpentine

TEREBRA *n* ancient Roman device used for boring holes in defensive walls

TEREBRAE > TEREBRA

TEREBRANT *n* type of hymenopterous insect

TEREBRAS > TEREBRA

TEREBRATE *adj* (of animals, esp insects) having a boring or penetrating organ, such as a sting ▷ *vb* bore

TEREDINES > TEREDO

TEREDO *n* marine mollusc that bores into and destroys submerged timber

TEREDOS > TEREDO

TEREFA *same as* > TREF

TEREFAH *same as* > TREF

TEREK *n* type of sandpiper

TEREKS > TEREK

TERES *n* shoulder muscle

TERETE *adj* (esp of plant parts) smooth and usually cylindrical and tapering

TERETES > TERETE

TERF *old variant of* > TURF

TERFE *old variant of* > TURF

TERFES > TERFE

TERFS > TERF

TERGA > TERGUM

TERGAL > TERGUM

TERGITE *n* constituent part of a tergum

TERGITES > TERGITE

TERGUM *n* cuticular plate covering the dorsal surface of a body segment of an arthropod

TERIYAKI *adj* basted with soy sauce and rice wine and broiled over an open fire ▷ *n* dish prepared in this way

TERIYAKIS > TERIYAKI

TERM *n* word or expression ▷ *vb* name or designate

TERMAGANT *n* unpleasant and bad-tempered woman

TERMED > TERM

TERMER *same as* > TERMOR

TERMERS > TERMER

TERMINAL *adj* (of an illness) ending in death ▷ *n* place where people or vehicles begin or end a journey

TERMINALS > TERMINAL

TERMINATE *vb* bring or come to an end

TERMINER *n* person or thing that limits or determines

TERMINERS > TERMINER

TERMING > TERM

TERMINI > TERMINUS

TERMINISM *n* philosophical theory

TERMINIST > TERMINISM

TERMINUS *n* railway or bus station at the end of a line

TERMITARY *n* termite nest

TERMITE *n* white antlike insect that destroys timber

TERMITES > TERMITE

TERMITIC > TERMITE

TERMLESS *adj* without limit or boundary

TERMLIES > TERMLY

TERMLY *n* publication issued once a term

TERMOR *n* person who holds an estate for a term of years or until he dies

TERMORS > TERMOR

TERMS > TERM

TERMTIME *n* time during a term, esp a school or university term

TERMTIMES > TERMTIME

TERN *n* gull-like sea bird with a forked tail and pointed wings

TERNAL > TERN

TERNARIES > TERNARY

TERNARY *adj* consisting of three parts ▷ *n* group of three

TERNATE *adj* (esp of a leaf) consisting of three leaflets or other parts

TERNATELY > TERNATE

TERNE *n* alloy of lead containing tin (10–20 per cent) and antimony (1.5–2 per cent) ▷ *vb* coat with this alloy

TERNED > TERNE

TERNES > TERNE

TERNING > TERNE

TERNION *n* group of three

TERNIONS > TERNION

TERNS > TERN

TERPENE *n* any one of a class of unsaturated hydrocarbons, such as the carotenes, that are found in the essential oils of many plants

TERPENES > TERPENE

TERPENIC > TERPENE

TERPENOID > TERPENE

TERPINEOL *n* terpene alcohol with an odour of lilac, present in several essential oils

TERPINOL *same as* > TERPINEOL

TERPINOLS > TERPINOL

TERRA *n* (in legal contexts) earth or land

TERRACE *n* row of houses built as one block ▷ *vb* form into or provide with a terrace

TERRACED > TERRACE

TERRACES > TERRACE

TERRACING *n* series of terraces, esp one dividing a slope into a steplike system of flat narrow fields

TERRAE > TERRA

TERRAFORM *vb* engage in planetary engineering to enhance the capacity of an extraterrestrial planetary environment to sustain life

TERRAIN *same as* > TERRANE

TERRAINS > TERRAIN

TERRAMARA *n* neolithic Italian pile-dwelling

TERRAMARE > TERRAMARA

TERRANE *n* series of rock formations, esp one having a prevalent type of rock

TERRANES > TERRANE

TERRAPIN *n* small turtle-like reptile

TERRAPINS > TERRAPIN

TERRARIA > TERRARIUM

TERRARIUM *n* enclosed container for small plants or animals

TERRAS *same as* > TRASS

TERRASES > TERRAS

TERRAZZO *n* floor of marble chips set in mortar and polished

TERRAZZOS > TERRAZZO

TERREEN *old variant of* > TUREEN

TERREENS > TERREEN

TERRELLA *n* magnetic globe designed to simulate and

demonstrate the earth's magnetic fields

TERRELLAS > TERRELLA

TERRENE *adj* of or relating to the earth ▷ *n* land

TERRENELY > TERRENE

TERRENES > TERRENE > TERRESTRIAL

TERRET *n* either of the two metal rings on a harness saddle through which the reins are passed

TERRETS > TERRET

TERRIBLE *adj* very serious ▷ *n* something terrible

TERRIBLES > TERRIBLE

TERRIBLY *adv* in a terrible manner

TERRICOLE *n* plant or animal living on land

TERRIER *n* any of various breeds of small active dog

TERRIERS > TERRIER

TERRIES > TERRY

TERRIFIC *adj* great or intense

TERRIFIED > TERRIFY

TERRIFIER > TERRIFY

TERRIFIES > TERRIFY

TERRIFY *vb* fill with fear

TERRINE *n* earthenware dish with a lid

TERRINES > TERRINE

TERRIT *same as* > TERRET

TERRITORY *n* district

TERRITS > TERRIT

TERROIR *n* combination of factors, including soil, climate, and environment, that gives a wine its distinctive character

TERROIRS > TERROIR

TERROR *n* great fear

TERRORFUL > TERROR

TERRORISE *same as* > TERRORIZE

TERRORISM *n* use of violence and intimidation to achieve political ends

TERRORIST *n* person who employs terror or terrorism, esp as a political weapon

TERRORIZE *vb* force or oppress by fear or violence

TERRORS > TERROR

TERRY *n* fabric with small loops covering both sides, used esp for making towels

TERSE *adj* neat and concise

TERSELY > TERSE

TERSENESS > TERSE

TERSER > TERSE

TERSEST > TERSE

TERSION *n* action of rubbing off or wiping

TERSIONS > TERSION

TERTIA *same as* > TERCIO

TERTIAL *same as* > TERTIARY

TERTIALS > TERTIAL

TERTIAN *adj* (of a fever or the symptoms of a disease, esp malaria) occurring every other day ▷ *n* tertian fever or symptoms

TERTIANS > TERTIAN

TERTIARY *adj* third in

degree, order, etc ▷ *n* any of the tertiary feathers

TERTIAS > TERTIA

TERTIUM as in *tertium quid* unknown or indefinite thing related in some way to two known or definite things, but distinct from both

TERTIUS *n* third (in a group)

TERTIUSES > TERTIUS

TERTS *n* card game using 32 cards

TERVALENT *same as* > TRIVALENT

TERYLENE *n* tradename for a synthetic polyester fibre or fabric based on terephthalic acid, characterized by lightness and crease resistance and used for clothing, sheets, ropes, sails, etc

TERYLENES > TERYLENE

TERZETTA *n* tercet

TERZETTAS > TERZETTA

TERZETTI > TERZETTO

TERZETTO *n* trio, esp a vocal one

TERZETTOS > TERZETTO

TES > TE

TESLA *n* derived SI unit of magnetic flux density equal to a flux of 1 weber in an area of 1 square metre.

TESLAS > TESLA

TESSELATE *vb* cover with small tiles

TESSELLA *n* little tessera

TESSELLAE > TESSELLA

TESSELLAR *adj* of or relating to tessellae

TESSERA *n* small square tile used in mosaics

TESSERACT *n* cube inside another cube

TESSERAE > TESSERA

TESSERAL > TESSERA

TESSITURA *n* general pitch level of a piece of vocal music

TESSITURE > TESSITURA

TEST *vb* try out to ascertain the worth, capability, or endurance of ▷ *n* critical examination

TESTA *n* hard outer layer of a seed

TESTABLE > TEST

TESTACEAN *n* microscopic animal with hard shell

TESTACIES > TESTATE

TESTACY > TESTATE

TESTAE > TESTA

TESTAMENT *n* proof or tribute

TESTAMUR *n* certificate proving an examination has been passed

TESTAMURS > TESTAMUR

TESTATE *adj* having left a valid will ▷ *n* person who dies and leaves a legally valid will

TESTATES > TESTATE

TESTATION > TESTATOR

TESTATOR *n* maker of a will

TESTATORS > TESTATOR

TESTATRIX *same as* > TESTATOR

TESTATUM *n* part of a purchase deed

TESTATUMS > TESTATUM

TESTCROSS *vb* subject to a testcross, a genetic test for ascertaining whether an individual is homozygous or heterozygous

TESTE *n* witness

TESTED > TEST

TESTEE *n* person subjected to a test

TESTEES > TESTEE

TESTER *n* person or thing that tests or is used for testing

TESTERN *vb* give (someone) a teston

TESTERNED > TESTERN

TESTERNS > TESTERN

TESTERS > TESTER

TESTES > TESTIS

TESTICLE *n* either of the two male reproductive glands

TESTICLES > TESTICLE

TESTIER > TESTY

TESTIEST > TESTY

TESTIFIED > TESTIFY

TESTIFIER > TESTIFY

TESTIFIES > TESTIFY

TESTIFY *vb* give evidence under oath

TESTILY > TESTY

TESTIMONY *n* declaration of truth or fact ▷ *vb* testify

TESTINESS > TESTY

TESTING > TEST

TESTINGS > TEST

TESTIS *same as* > TESTICLE

TESTON *n* French silver coin of the 16th century

TESTONS > TESTON

TESTOON *same as* > TESTON

TESTOONS > TESTOON

TESTRIL *same as* > TESTRILL

TESTRILL *n* sixpence

TESTRILLS > TESTRILL

TESTRILS > TESTRIL

TESTS > TEST

TESTUDO *n* form of shelter used by the ancient Roman Army for protection against attack from above, consisting either of a mobile arched structure or of overlapping shields held by the soldiers over their heads

TESTUDOS > TESTUDO

TESTY *adj* irritable or touchy

TET *same as* > TETH

TETANAL > TETANUS

TETANIC *adj* of, relating to, or producing tetanus or the spasms of tetanus ▷ *n* tetanic drug or agent

TETANICAL > TETANUS

TETANICS > TETANIC

TETANIES > TETANY

TETANISE *same as* > TETANIZE

TETANISED > TETANISE

TETANISES > TETANISE

TETANIZE *vb* induce tetanus in (a muscle)

TETANIZED > TETANIZE

TETANIZES > TETANIZE

TETANOID > TETANIZE

TETANUS *n* acute infectious disease producing muscular spasms and convulsions

TETANUSES > TETANUS

TETANY *n* abnormal increase in the excitability of nerves and muscles resulting in spasms of the arms and legs, caused by a deficiency of parathyroid secretion

TETCHED *same as* > TECHED

TETCHIER > TETCHY

TETCHIEST > TETCHY

TETCHILY > TETCHY

TETCHY *adj* cross and irritable

TETE *n* elaborate hairstyle

TETES > TETE

TETH *n* ninth letter of the Hebrew alphabet transliterated as *t* and pronounced more or less like English *t* with pharyngeal articulation

TETHER *n* rope or chain for tying an animal to a spot ▷ *vb* tie up with rope

TETHERED > TETHER

TETHERING > TETHER

TETHERS > TETHER

TETHS > TETH

TETOTUM *same as* > TEETOTUM

TETOTUMS > TETOTUM

TETRA *n* brightly coloured tropical freshwater fish

TETRACID *adj* (of a base) capable of reacting with four molecules of a monobasic acid

TETRACIDS > TETRACID

TETRACT *n* sponge spicule with four rays

TETRACTS > TETRACT

TETRAD *n* group or series of four

TETRADIC > TETRAD

TETRADITE *n* person who believes that the number four has supernatural significance

TETRADS > TETRAD

TETRAGON *n* figure with four angles and four sides > TETRAGONAL

TETRAGONS > TETRAGON

TETRAGRAM *n* any word of four letters

TETRALOGY *n* series of four related works

TETRAMER *n* four-molecule polymer

TETRAMERS > TETRAMER

TETRAPLA *n* book containing versions of the same text in four languages

TETRAPLAS > TETRAPLA

TETRAPOD *n* any vertebrate that has four limbs

TETRAPODS > TETRAPOD
TETRAPODY *n* metrical unit consisting of four feet
TETRARCH *n* ruler of one fourth of a country
TETRARCHS > TETRARCH
TETRARCHY > TETRARCH
TETRAS > TETRA
TETRAXON *n* four-pointed spicule
TETRAXONS > TETRAXON
TETRI *n* currency unit of Georgia
TETRIS > TETRI
TETRODE *n* electronic valve having four electrodes, namely a cathode, control grid, screen grid, and anode
TETRODES > TETRODE
TETRONAL *n* sedative drug
TETRONALS > TETRONAL
TETROXID *same as* > TETROXIDE
TETROXIDE *n* any oxide that contains four oxygen atoms per molecule
TETROXIDS > TETROXID
TETRYL *n* yellow crystalline explosive solid used in detonators
TETRYLS > TETRYL
TETS > TET
TETTER *n* blister or pimple ▷ *vb* cause a tetter to erupt (on)
TETTERED > TETTER
TETTERING > TETTER
TETTEROUS > TETTER
TETTERS > TETTER
TETTIX *n* cicada
TETTIXES > TETTIX
TEUCH *Scots variant of* > TOUGH
TEUCHAT *Scots variant of* > TEWIT
TEUCHATS > TEUCHAT
TEUCHER > TEUCH
TEUCHEST > TEUCH
TEUCHTER *n* in Scotland, derogatory word used by Lowlanders for a Highlander
TEUCHTERS > TEUCHTER
TEUGH *same as* > TEUCH
TEUGHER > TEUGH
TEUGHEST > TEUGH
TEUGHLY > TEUGH
TEUTONISE *same as* > TEUTONIZE
TEUTONIZE *vb* make or become German or Germanic
TEVATRON *n* machine used in nuclear research
TEVATRONS > TEVATRON
TEW *vb* work hard
TEWART *same as* > TUART
TEWARTS > TEWART
TEWED > TEW
TEWEL *n* horse's rectum
TEWELS > TEWEL
TEWHIT *same as* > TEWIT
TEWHITS > TEWHIT
TEWING > TEW
TEWIT *n* lapwing
TEWITS > TEWIT
TEWS > TEW

TEX *n* unit of weight used to measure yarn density
TEXAS *n* structure on the upper deck of a paddle-steamer containing the officers' quarters and the wheelhouse
TEXASES > TEXAS
TEXES > TEX
TEXT *n* main body of a book as distinct from illustrations etc ▷ *vb* send a text message to (someone)
TEXTBOOK *n* standard book on a particular subject ▷ *adj* perfect
TEXTBOOKS > TEXTBOOK
TEXTED > TEXT
TEXTER *n* person who communicates by text messaging
TEXTERS > TEXTER
TEXTILE *n* fabric or cloth, esp woven ▷ *adj* of (the making of) fabrics
TEXTILES > TEXTILE
TEXTING > TEXT
TEXTLESS > TEXT
TEXTORIAL *adj* of or relating to weaving or weavers
TEXTPHONE *n* phone designed to translate speech into text and vice versa
TEXTS > TEXT
TEXTUAL *adj* of, based on, or relating to, a text or texts
TEXTUALLY > TEXTUAL
TEXTUARY *adj* of, relating to, or contained in a text ▷ *n* textual critic
TEXTURAL > TEXTURE
TEXTURE *n* structure, feel, or consistency ▷ *vb* give a distinctive texture to (something)
TEXTURED > TEXTURE
TEXTURES > TEXTURE
TEXTURING > TEXTURE
TEXTURISE *same as* > TEXTURIZE
TEXTURIZE *vb* texture
THACK *Scots word for* > THATCH
THACKED > THACK
THACKING > THACK
THACKS > THACK
THAE *Scots word for* > THOSE
THAGI *same as* > THUGGEE
THAGIS > THAGI
THAIM *Scots variant of* > THEM
THAIRM *n* catgut
THAIRMS > THAIRM
THALAMI > THALAMUS
THALAMIC > THALAMUS
THALAMUS *n* either of the two contiguous egg-shaped masses of grey matter at the base of the brain
THALASSIC *adj* of or relating to the sea
THALER *n* former German, Austrian, or Swiss silver coin

THALERS > THALER
THALI *n* meal consisting of several small meat or vegetable dishes accompanied by rice, bread, etc, and sometimes by a starter or a sweet
THALIAN *adj* of or relating to comedy
THALIS > THALI
THALLI > THALLUS
THALLIC *adj* of or containing thallium, esp in the trivalent state
THALLINE > THALLUS
THALLIOUS > THALLIUM
THALLIUM *n* highly toxic metallic element
THALLIUMS > THALLIUM
THALLOID > THALLUS
THALLOUS *adj* of or containing thallium, esp in the monovalent state
THALLUS *n* undifferentiated vegetative body of algae, fungi, and lichens
THALLUSES > THALLUS
THALWEG *n* longitudinal outline of a riverbed from source to mouth
THALWEGS > THALWEG
THAN *prep* used to introduce the second element of a comparison ▷ *n* old variant of "then" (that time)
THANA *same as* > TANA
THANADAR *same as* > TANADAR
THANADARS > THANADAR
THANAGE *n* state of being a thane
THANAGES > THANAGE
THANAH *same as* > TANA
THANAHS > THANAH
THANAS > THANA
THANATISM *n* belief that the soul ceases to exist when the body dies
THANATIST > THANATISM
THANATOID *adj* like death
THANATOS *n* Greek personification of death
THANE *n* Anglo-Saxon or medieval Scottish nobleman
THANEDOM > THANE
THANEDOMS > THANE
THANEHOOD > THANE
THANES > THANE
THANESHIP > THANE
THANGKA *n* (in Tibetan Buddhism) a religious painting on a scroll
THANGKAS > THANGKA
THANK *vb* express gratitude to
THANKED > THANK
THANKEE *interj* thank you
THANKER > THANK
THANKERS > THANK
THANKFUL *adj* grateful
THANKING > THANK
THANKINGS > THANK
THANKLESS *adj* unrewarding or unappreciated

THANKS *pl n* words of gratitude ▷ *interj* polite expression of gratitude
THANKYOU *n* conventional expression of gratitude
THANKYOUS > THANKYOU
THANNA *same as* > TANA
THANNAH *same as* > TANA
THANNAHS > THANNAH
THANNAS > THANNA
THANS > THAN
THAR *same as* > TAHR
THARM *n* stomach
THARMS > THARM
THARS > THAR
THAT *pron* used to refer to something already mentioned or familiar, or further away
THATAWAY *adv* that way
THATCH *n* roofing material of reeds or straw ▷ *vb* roof (a house) with reeds or straw
THATCHED > THATCH
THATCHER > THATCH
THATCHERS > THATCH
THATCHES > THATCH
THATCHIER > THATCH
THATCHING > THATCH
THATCHT *old variant of* > THATCHED
THATCHY > THATCH
THATNESS *n* state or quality of being 'that'
THAUMATIN *n* type of natural sweetener
THAW *vb* make or become unfrozen ▷ *n* thawing
THAWED > THAW
THAWER > THAW
THAWERS > THAW
THAWIER > THAWY
THAWIEST > THAWY
THAWING > THAW
THAWINGS > THAW
THAWLESS > THAW
THAWS > THAW
THAWY *adj* tending to thaw
THE *determiner* definite article, used before a noun
THEACEOUS *adj* of, relating to, or belonging to the *Theaceae*, a family of evergreen trees and shrubs of tropical and warm regions: includes the tea plant
THEANDRIC *adj* both divine and human
THEARCHIC > THEARCHY
THEARCHY *n* rule or government by God or gods
THEATER *same as* > THEATRE
THEATERS > THEATER
THEATRAL *adj* of or relating to the theatre
THEATRE *n* place where plays etc are performed
THEATRES > THEATRE
THEATRIC *adj* of or relating to the theatre
THEATRICS *n* art of staging plays
THEAVE *n* young ewe
THEAVES > THEAVE

t

THEBAINE n poisonous white crystalline alkaloid, found in opium but without opioid actions

THEBAINES > THEBAINE

THEBE n inner satellite of Jupiter discovered in 1979

THEBES > THEBE

THECA n enclosing organ, cell, or spore case, esp the capsule of a moss

THECAE > THECA

THECAL > THECA

THECATE > THECA

THECODONT adj (of mammals and certain reptiles) having teeth that grow in sockets ▷ n extinct reptile

THEE pron refers to the person addressed: used mainly by members of the Society of Friends ▷ vb use the word "thee"

THEED > THEE

THEEING > THEE

THEEK Scots variant of > THATCH

THEEKED > THEEK

THEEKING > THEEK

THEEKS > THEEK

THEELIN trade name for > ESTRONE

THEELINS > THEELIN

THEELOL n estriol

THEELOLS > THEELOL

THEES > THEE

THEFT n act or an instance of stealing

THEFTLESS > THEFT

THEFTS > THEFT

THEFTUOUS adj tending to commit theft

THEGITHER Scots variant of > TOGETHER

THEGN same as > THANE

THEGNLY > THEGN

THEGNS > THEGN

THEIC n person who drinks excessive amounts of tea

THEICS > THEIC

THEIN old variant of > THANE

THEINE another name for > CAFFEINE

THEINES > THEINE

THEINS > THEIN

THEIR determiner of, belonging to, or associated in some way with them

THEIRS pron (thing or person) belonging to them

THEIRSELF pron dialect form of themselves: reflexive form of they or them

THEISM n belief in a God or gods

THEISMS > THEISM

THEIST > THEISM

THEISTIC > THEISM

THEISTS > THEISM

THELEMENT n old contraction of "the element"

THELF n old contraction of "the element"

THELITIS n inflammation

of the nipple

THELVES > THELF

THELYTOKY n type of reproduction resulting in female offspring only

THEM pron refers to people or things other than the speaker or those addressed

THEMA n theme

THEMATA > THEMA

THEMATIC adj of, relating to, or consisting of a theme or themes ▷ n thematic vowel

THEMATICS > THEMATIC

THEME n main idea or subject being discussed ▷ vb design, decorate, arrange, etc, in accordance with a theme

THEMED > THEME

THEMELESS > THEME

THEMES > THEME

THEMING > THEME

THEMSELF pron reflexive form of one, whoever, anybody

THEN adv at that time ▷ pron that time ▷ adj existing or functioning at that time ▷ n that time

THENABOUT adv around then

THENAGE old variant of > THANAGE

THENAGES > THENAGE

THENAL adj of or relating to the thenar

THENAR n palm of the hand ▷ adj of or relating to the palm or the region at the base of the thumb

THENARS > THENAR

THENCE adv from that place or time

THENS > THEN

THEOCRACY n government by a god or priests

THEOCRASY n mingling into one of deities or divine attributes previously regarded as distinct

THEOCRAT > THEOCRACY

THEOCRATS > THEOCRACY

THEODICY n branch of theology concerned with defending the attributes of God against objections resulting from physical and moral evil

THEOGONIC > THEOGONY

THEOGONY n origin and descent of the gods

THEOLOG same as > THEOLOGUE

THEOLOGER n theologian

THEOLOGIC > THEOLOGY

THEOLOGS > THEOLOG

THEOLOGUE n theologian

THEOLOGY n study of religions and religious beliefs

THEOMACHY n battle among the gods or against them

THEOMANCY n divination or prophecy by an oracle or by people directly inspired

by a god

THEOMANIA n religious madness, esp when it takes the form of believing oneself to be a god

THEONOMY n state of being governed by God

THEOPATHY n religious emotion engendered by the contemplation of or meditation upon God

THEOPHAGY n sacramental eating of a god

THEOPHANY n manifestation of a deity to man in a form that, though visible, is not necessarily material

THEORBIST > THEORBO

THEORBO n obsolete form of the lute, having two necks, one above the other, the second neck carrying a set of unstopped sympathetic bass strings

THEORBOS > THEORBO

THEOREM n proposition that can be proved by reasoning

THEOREMIC > THEOREM

THEOREMS > THEOREM

THEORETIC adj of, or based on, a theory

THEORIC n theory; conjecture

THEORICS > THEORIC

THEORIES > THEORY

THEORIQUE same as > THEORIC

THEORISE same as > THEORIZE

THEORISED > THEORISE

THEORISER > THEORISE

THEORISES > THEORISE

THEORIST n originator of a theory

THEORISTS > THEORIST

THEORIZE vb form theories, speculate

THEORIZED > THEORIZE

THEORIZER > THEORIZE

THEORIZES > THEORIZE

THEORY n set of ideas to explain something

THEOSOPH n proponent of theosophy

THEOSOPHS > THEOSOPH

THEOSOPHY n religious or philosophical system claiming to be based on intuitive insight into the divine nature

THEOTOKOI > THEOTOKOS

THEOTOKOS n mother of God

THEOW n slave in Anglo-Saxon Britain

THEOWS > THEOW

THERALITE n type of igneous rock

THERAPIES > THERAPY

THERAPIST n person skilled in a particular type of therapy

THERAPSID n extinct reptile: considered to be the ancestors of mammals

THERAPY n curing treatment

THERBLIG n basic unit of work in an industrial process

THERBLIGS > THERBLIG

THERE adv in or to that place ▷ n that place

THEREAT adv at that point or time

THEREAWAY adv in that direction

THEREBY adv by that means

THEREFOR adv for this, that, or it

THEREFORE adv consequently, that being so

THEREFROM adv from that or there

THEREIN adv in or into that place or thing

THEREINTO adv into that place, circumstance, etc

THEREMIN n electronic musical instrument, played by moving the hands through electromagnetic fields created by two metal rods

THEREMINS > THEREMIN

THERENESS n quality of having existence

THEREOF adv of or concerning that or it

THEREON archaic word for > THEREUPON

THEREOUT another word for > THEREFROM

THERES > THERE

THERETO adv that or it

THEREUNTO adv to that

THEREUPON adv immediately after that

THEREWITH adv with or in addition to that

THERIAC n ointment or potion of varying composition, used as an antidote to a poison

THERIACA same as > THERIAC

THERIACAL > THERIAC

THERIACAS > THERIACA

THERIACS > THERIAC

THERIAN n animal of the class Theria, a subclass of mammals

THERIANS > THERIAN

THERM n unit of measurement of heat public bath

THERMAE pl n public baths or hot springs, esp in ancient Greece or Rome

THERMAL adj of heat ▷ n rising current of warm air

THERMALLY > THERMAL

THERMALS > THERMAL

THERME old variant of > THERM

THERMEL n type of thermometer measuring temperature by means of thermoelectric current

THERMELS > THERMEL

THERMES > THERME

THERMETTE n device, used outdoors, for boiling water rapidly

THERMIC *same as* > THERMAL

THERMICAL *same as* > THERMAL

THERMIDOR *as in lobster thermidor* dish of cooked lobster

THERMION *n* electron or ion emitted by a body at high temperature

THERMIONS > THERMION

THERMIT *variant of* > THERMITE

THERMITE *as in thermite process* process for reducing metallic oxides

THERMITES > THERMITE

THERMITS > THERMIT

THERMOS *n* trademark term for a type of stoppered vacuum flask used to preserve the temperature of its contents

THERMOSES > THERMOS

THERMOSET *n* material (esp a synthetic plastic or resin) that hardens permanently after one application of heat and pressure

THERMOTIC *adj* of or because of heat

THERMS > THERM

THEROID *adj* of, relating to, or resembling a beast

THEROLOGY *n* study of mammals

THEROPOD *n* bipedal carnivorous saurischian dinosaur with strong hind legs and grasping hands

THEROPODS > THEROPOD

THESAURAL > THESAURUS

THESAURI > THESAURUS

THESAURUS *n* book containing lists of synonyms and related words

THESE *determiner* form of this used before a plural noun

THESES > THESIS

THESIS *n* written work submitted for a degree

THESP *short for* > THESPIAN

THESPIAN *adj* of or relating to drama and the theatre ▷ *n* actor or actress

THESPIANS > THESPIAN

THESPS > THESP

THETA *n* eighth letter of the Greek alphabet

THETAS > THETA

THETCH *old variant spelling of* > THATCH

THETCHED > THETCH

THETCHES > THETCH

THETCHING > THETCH

THETE *n* member of the lowest order of freeman in ancient Athens

THETES > THETE

THETHER *old variant of* > THITHER

THETIC *adj* (in classical prosody) of, bearing, or relating to a metrical stress

THETICAL *another word for* > THETIC

THEURGIC > THEURGY

THEURGIES > THEURGY

THEURGIST > THEURGY

THEURGY *n* intervention of a divine or supernatural agency in the affairs of man

THEW *n* muscle, esp if strong or well-developed

THEWED *adj* strong; muscular

THEWES > THEW

THEWIER > THEW

THEWIEST > THEW

THEWLESS > THEW

THEWS > THEW

THEWY > THEW

THEY *pron* people or things other than the speaker or people addressed

THIAMIN *same as* > THIAMINE

THIAMINE *n* vitamin found in the outer coat of rice and other grains

THIAMINES > THIAMINE

THIAMINS > THIAMIN

THIASUS *n* congregation of people who have gathered to sing and dance in honour of a god

THIASUSES > THIASUS

THIAZIDE *n* diuretic drug

THIAZIDES > THIAZIDE

THIAZIN *same as* > THIAZINE

THIAZINE *n* any of a group of organic compounds containing a ring system composed of four carbon atoms, a sulphur atom, and a nitrogen atom

THIAZINES > THIAZINE

THIAZINS > THIAZIN

THIAZOL *same as* > THIAZOLE

THIAZOLE *n* colourless liquid with a pungent smell that contains a ring system composed of three carbon atoms, a sulphur atom, and a nitrogen atom

THIAZOLES > THIAZOLE

THIAZOLS > THIAZOL

THIBET *n* coloured woollen cloth

THIBETS > THIBET

THIBLE *n* stick for stirring porridge

THIBLES > THIBLE

THICK *adj* of great or specified extent from one side to the other ▷ *vb* thicken

THICKED > THICK

THICKEN *vb* make or become thick or thicker

THICKENED > THICKEN

THICKENER > THICKEN

THICKENS > THICKEN

THICKER > THICK

THICKEST > THICK

THICKET *n* dense growth of small trees

THICKETED *adj* covered in thicket

THICKETS > THICKET

THICKETY > THICKET

THICKHEAD *n* stupid or ignorant person

THICKIE *same as* > THICKO

THICKIES > THICKY

THICKING > THICK

THICKISH > THICK

THICKLEAF *n* succulent plant with sessile or short-stalked fleshy leaves

THICKLY > THICK

THICKNESS *n* state of being thick

THICKO *n* slow-witted unintelligent person

THICKOES > THICKO

THICKOS > THICKO

THICKS > THICK

THICKSET *adj* stocky in build

THICKSETS > THICKSET

THICKSKIN *n* insensitive person

THICKY *same as* > THICKO

THIEF *n* person who steals

THIEVE *vb* steal

THIEVED > THIEVE

THIEVERY > THIEVE

THIEVES > THIEVE

THIEVING *adj* given to stealing other people's possessions

THIEVINGS > THIEVING

THIEVISH > THIEF

THIG *vb* beg

THIGGER > THIG

THIGGERS > THIG

THIGGING > THIG

THIGGINGS > THIG

THIGGIT *Scots inflection of* > THIG

THIGH *n* upper part of the human leg

THIGHBONE *same as* > FEMUR

THIGHED *adj* having thighs

THIGHS > THIGH

THIGS > THIG

THILK *pron* that same

THILL *another word for* > SHAFT

THILLER *n* horse that goes between the thills of a (cart

THILLERS > THILLER

THILLS > THILL

THIMBLE *n* cap protecting the end of the finger (when sewing ▷ *vb* use a thimble

THIMBLED > THIMBLE

THIMBLES > THIMBLE

THIMBLING > THIMBLE

THIN *adj* not thick ▷ *vb* make or become thin ▷ *adv* in order to produce something thin

THINCLAD *n* track-and-field athlete

THINCLADS > THINCLAD

THINDOWN *n* reduction in the amount of particles, esp protons, of very high energy reaching and penetrating the earth's atmosphere from outer space

THINDOWNS > THINDOWN

THINE *adj* (something) of or associated with you (thou) ▷ *pron* something belonging to you (thou)

▷ *determiner* of, belonging to, or associated in some way with you (thou)

THING *n* material object

THINGAMY *n* person or thing the name of which is unknown

THINGHOOD *n* existence; state or condition of being a thing

THINGIER > THINGY

THINGIES > THINGY

THINGIEST > THINGY

THINGNESS *n* state of being a thing

THINGS > THING

THINGUMMY *n* person or thing the name of which is unknown, temporarily forgotten, or deliberately overlooked

THINGY *adj* existing in reality; actual

THINK *vb* consider, judge, or believe

THINKABLE *adj* able to be conceived or considered

THINKABLY > THINKABLE

THINKER > THINK

THINKERS > THINK

THINKING > THINK

THINKINGS > THINK

THINKS > THINK

THINLY > THIN

THINNED > THIN

THINNER > THIN

THINNERS > THIN

THINNESS > THIN

THINNEST > THIN

THINNING > THIN

THINNINGS > THIN

THINNISH > THIN

THINS > THIN

THIO *adj* of, or relating to, sulphur

THIOFURAN *another name for* > THIOPHEN

THIOL *n* any of a class of sulphur-containing organic compounds with the formula RSH, where R is an organic group

THIOLIC > THIOL

THIOLS > THIOL

THIONATE *n* any salt or ester of thionic acid

THIONATES > THIONATE

THIONIC *adj* of, relating to, or containing sulphur

THIONIN *same as* > THIONINE

THIONINE *n* crystalline derivative of thiazine used as a violet dye to stain microscope specimens

THIONINES > THIONINE

THIONINS > THIONIN

THIONYL *n* of, consisting of, or containing the divalent group SO

THIONYLS > THIONYL

THIOPHEN *n* colourless liquid heterocyclic compound found in the benzene fraction of coal tar and manufactured from butane and sulphur

t

THIOPHENE same as > THIOPHEN

THIOPHENS > THIOPHEN

THIOPHIL adj having an attraction to sulphur

THIOTEPA n drug used in chemotherapy

THIOTEPAS > THIOTEPA

THIOUREA n white water-soluble crystalline substance with a bitter taste

THIOUREAS > THIOUREA

THIR Scots word for > THESE

THIRAM n antifungal agent

THIRAMS > THIRAM

THIRD adj of number three in a series ▷n one of three equal parts ▷adv in the third place ▷vb divide (something) by three

THIRDED > THIRD

THIRDHAND adv from the second of two intermediaries

THIRDING > THIRD

THIRDINGS > THIRD

THIRDLY > THIRD

THIRDS > THIRD

THIRDSMAN n intermediary

THIRDSMEN > THIRDSMAN

THIRL vb bore or drill

THIRLAGE n obligation imposed upon tenants of certain lands requiring them to have their grain ground at a specified mill

THIRLAGES > THIRLAGE

THIRLED > THIRL

THIRLING > THIRL

THIRLS > THIRL

THIRST n desire to drink ▷vb feel thirst

THIRSTED > THIRST

THIRSTER > THIRST

THIRSTERS > THIRSTER

THIRSTFUL > THIRST

THIRSTIER > THIRSTY

THIRSTILY > THIRSTY

THIRSTING > THIRST

THIRSTS > THIRST

THIRSTY adj feeling a desire to drink

THIRTEEN n three plus ten ▷adj amounting to thirteen ▷determiner amounting to thirteen

THIRTEENS > THIRTEEN

THIRTIES > THIRTY

THIRTIETH adj being the ordinal number of thirty in counting order, position, time, etc: often written 30th ▷n one of 30 approximately equal parts of something

THIRTY n three times ten ▷adj amounting to thirty ▷determiner amounting to thirty

THIRTYISH adj around thirty years of age

THIS pron used to refer to a thing or person nearby, just mentioned, or about to be mentioned ▷adj used to refer to the present time

THISAWAY adv this way

THISNESS n state or quality of being this

THISTLE n prickly plant with dense flower heads

THISTLES > THISTLE

THISTLIER > THISTLE

THISTLY > THISTLE

THITHER adv or towards that place

THITHERTO adv until that time

THIVEL same as > THIBLE

THIVELS > THIVEL

THLIPSES > THLIPSIS

THLIPSIS n compression, esp of part of the body

THO short for > THOUGH

THOFT n bench (in a boat) upon which a rower sits

THOFTS > THOFT

THOLE n wooden pin set in the side of a rowing boat to serve as a fulcrum for rowing ▷vb bear or put up with

THOLED > THOLE

THOLEIITE n type of volcanic rock

THOLEPIN same as > THOLE

THOLEPINS > THOLEPIN

THOLES > THOLE

THOLI > THOLUS

THOLING > THOLE

THOLOBATE n structure supporting a dome

THOLOI > THOLOS

THOLOS n dry-stone beehive-shaped tomb associated with the Mycenaean culture of Greece in the 16th to the 12th century BC

THOLUS n domed tomb

THON Scot word for > YON

THONDER Scot word for > YONDER

THONG n thin strip of leather etc

THONGED adj fastened with a thong

THONGS > THONG

THORACAL another word for > THORACIC

THORACES > THORAX

THORACIC adj of, near, or relating to the thorax

THORAX n part of the body between the neck and the abdomen

THORAXES > THORAX

THORIA > THORIUM

THORIAS > THORIUM

THORIC > THORIUM

THORITE n yellow, brownish, or black radioactive mineral consisting of tetragonal thorium silicate. It occurs in coarse granite and is a source of thorium

THORITES > THORITE

THORIUM n radioactive metallic element

THORIUMS > THORIUM

THORN n prickle on a plant ▷vb jag or prick

(something) as if with a thorn

THORNBACK n European ray with a row of spines along the back and tail

THORNBILL n South American hummingbirds

THORNBUSH n tree, shrub, or bush with thorns

THORNED > THORN

THORNIER > THORNY

THORNIEST > THORNY

THORNILY > THORNY

THORNING > THORN

THORNLESS > THORN

THORNLIKE > THORN

THORNS > THORN

THORNSET adj set with thorns

THORNTREE n tree with thorns

THORNY adj covered with thorns

THORO (nonstandard) variant spelling of > THOROUGH

THORON n radioisotope of radon that is a decay product of thorium

THORONS > THORON

THOROUGH adj complete ▷n passage

THOROUGHS > THOROUGH

THORP n small village

THORPE same as > THORP

THORPES > THORPE

THORPS > THORP

THOSE determiner form of that used before a plural noun

THOTHER pron old contraction of the other

THOU pron used when talking to one person ▷n one thousandth of an inch ▷vb use the word thou

THOUED > THOU

THOUGH adv nevertheless

THOUGHT > THINK

THOUGHTED adj with thoughts

THOUGHTEN adj convinced

THOUGHTS > THINK

THOUING > THOU

THOUS > THOU

THOUSAND n ten hundred ▷adj amounting to a thousand ▷determiner amounting to a thousand

THOUSANDS > THOUSAND

THOWEL old variant of > THOLE

THOWELS > THOWEL

THOWL old variant of > THOLE

THOWLESS adj lacking in vigour

THOWLS > THOWEL

THRAE same as > FRAE

THRAIPING n thrashing

THRALDOM same as > THRALL

THRALDOMS > THRALDOM

THRALL n state of being in the power of another person ▷vb enslave or dominate

THRALLDOM same as > THRALL

THRALLED > THRALL

THRALLING > THRALL

THRALLS > THRALL

THRANG n throng ▷vb throng ▷adj crowded

THRANGED > THRANG

THRANGING > THRANG

THRANGS > THRANG

THRAPPLE n throat or windpipe ▷vb throttle

THRAPPLED > THRAPPLE

THRAPPLES > THRAPPLE

THRASH vb beat, esp with a stick or whip ▷n party

THRASHED > THRASH

THRASHER same as > THRESHER

THRASHERS > THRASHER

THRASHES > THRASH

THRASHING n severe beating

THRASONIC adj bragging or boastful

THRAVE n twenty-four sheaves of corn

THRAVES > THRAVE

THRAW vb twist (something); make something thrawn

THRAWARD adj contrary or stubborn

THRAWART same as > THRAWARD

THRAWED > THRAW

THRAWING > THRAW

THRAWN adj crooked or twisted

THRAWNLY > THRAWN

THRAWS > THRAW

THREAD n fine strand or yarn ▷vb pass thread through

THREADED > THREAD

THREADEN adj made of thread

THREADER > THREAD

THREADERS > THREAD

THREADFIN n spiny-finned tropical marine fish

THREADIER > THREADY

THREADING > THREAD

THREADS slang word for > CLOTHES

THREADY adj of, relating to, or resembling a thread or threads

THREAP vb scold

THREAPED > THREAP

THREAPER > THREAP

THREAPERS > THREAP

THREAPING > THREAP

THREAPIT variant past participle of > THREAP

THREAPS > THREAP

THREAT n declaration of intent to harm

THREATED > THREAT

THREATEN vb make or be a threat to

THREATENS > THREATEN

THREATFUL > THREAT

THREATING > THREAT

THREATS > THREAT

THREAVE same as > THRAVE

THREAVES > THREAVE

THREE n one more than two ▷adj amounting to three ▷determiner amounting to three

THREEFOLD adv (having) three times as many or as much ▷ adj having three times as many or as much

THREENESS n state or quality of being three

THREEP same as > THREAP

THREEPED > THREEP

THREEPER > THREAP

THREEPERS > THREAP

THREEPING > THREEP

THREEPIT variant past participle of > THREEP

THREEPS > THREEP

THREES > THREE

THREESOME n group of three

THRENE n dirge; threnody

THRENES > THRENE

THRENETIC > THRENE

THRENODE same as > THRENODY

THRENODES > THRENODE

THRENODIC > THRENODY

THRENODY n lament for the dead

THRENOS n threnody; lamentation

THRENOSES > THRENOS

THREONINE n essential amino acid that occurs in certain proteins

THRESH vb beat (wheat etc) to separate the grain from the husks and straw ▷ n act of threshing

THRESHED > THRESH

THRESHEL n flail

THRESHELS > THRESHEL

THRESHER n any of a genus of large sharks occurring in tropical and temperate seas. They have a very long whiplike tail

THRESHERS > THRESHER

THRESHES > THRESH

THRESHING > THRESH

THRESHOLD n bar forming the bottom of a doorway

THRETTIES > THRETTY

THRETTY nonstandard variant of > THIRTY

THREW > THROW

THRICE adv three times

THRID old variant of > THREAD

THRIDACE n sedative made from lettuce juice

THRIDACES > THRIDACE

THRIDDED > THRID

THRIDDING > THRID

THRIDS > THRID

THRIFT n wisdom and caution with money

THRIFTIER > THRIFTY

THRIFTILY > THRIFTY

THRIFTS > THRIFT

THRIFTY adj not wasteful with money

THRILL n sudden feeling of excitement ▷ vb (cause to) feel a thrill

THRILLANT another word for > THRILLING

THRILLED > THRILL

THRILLER n book, film, etc with an atmosphere of mystery or suspense

THRILLERS > THRILLER

THRILLIER > THRILLY

THRILLING adj very exciting or stimulating

THRILLS > THRILL

THRILLY adj causing thrills

THRIMSA same as > THRYMSA

THRIMSAS > THRIMSA

THRIP same as > THRIPS

THRIPS n small slender-bodied insect with piercing mouthparts that feeds on plant sap

THRIPSES > THRIPS

THRISSEL Scots variant of > THISTLE

THRISSELS > THRISSEL

THRIST old variant of > THIRST

THRISTED > THRIST

THRISTING > THRIST

THRISTLE Scots variant of > THISTLE

THRISTLES > THRISTLE

THRISTS > THRIST

THRISTY > THRIST

THRIVE vb flourish or prosper

THRIVED > THRIVE

THRIVEN > THRIVE

THRIVER > THRIVE

THRIVERS > THRIVE

THRIVES > THRIVE

THRIVING > THRIVE

THRIVINGS > THRIVE

THRO same as > THROUGH

THROAT n passage from the mouth and nose to the stomach and lungs ▷ vb vocalize in the throat

THROATED > THROAT

THROATIER > THROATY

THROATILY > THROATY

THROATING > THROAT

THROATS > THROAT

THROATY adj (of the voice) hoarse

THROB vb pulsate repeatedly ▷ n throbbing

THROBBED > THROB

THROBBER > THROB

THROBBERS > THROB

THROBBING > THROB

THROBLESS > THROB

THROBS > THROB

THROE n pang or pain ▷ n endure throes

THROED > THROE

THROEING > THROE

THROES pl n violent pangs or pains

THROMBI > THROMBUS

THROMBIN n enzyme that acts on fibrinogen in blood causing it to clot

THROMBINS > THROMBIN

THROMBOSE vb become or affect with a thrombus

THROMBUS n clot of coagulated blood that forms within a blood vessel or inside the heart and remains at the site of its formation, often impeding the flow of blood

THRONE n ceremonial seat of a monarch or bishop

▷ vb place or be placed on a throne

THRONED > THRONE

THRONES > THRONE

THRONG vb crowd ▷ n great number of people or things crowded together ▷ adj busy

THRONGED > THRONG

THRONGFUL > THRONG

THRONGING > THRONG

THRONGS > THRONG

THRONING > THRONE

THRONNER n person who is good at doing odd jobs

THRONNERS > THRONNER

THROPPLE vb strangle or choke

THROPPLED > THROPPLE

THROPPLES > THROPPLE

THROSTLE n song thrush

THROSTLES > THROSTLE

THROTTLE n device controlling the amount of fuel entering an engine ▷ vb strangle

THROTTLED > THROTTLE

THROTTLER > THROTTLE

THROTTLES > THROTTLE

THROUGH prep from end to end or side to side of ▷ adj finished

THROUGHLY adv thoroughly

THROVE > THRIVE

THROW vb hurl through the air ▷ n throwing

THROWAWAY adj done or said casually ▷ vb get rid of or discard ▷ n handbill or advertisement distributed in a public place

THROWBACK n person or thing that reverts to an earlier type ▷ vb remind someone of (something he or she said or did previously) in order to upset him or her

THROWE old variant of > THROE

THROWER > THROW

THROWERS > THROW

THROWES > THROWE

THROWING > THROW

THROWINGS > THROW

THROWN > THROW

THROWS > THROW

THROWSTER n person who twists silk or other fibres into yarn

THRU same as > THROUGH

THRUM vb strum rhythmically but without expression on (a musical instrument) ▷ n in textiles, unwoven ends of warp thread

THRUMMED > THRUM

THRUMMER > THRUM

THRUMMERS > THRUM

THRUMMIER > THRUMMY

THRUMMING > THRUM

THRUMMY adj made of thrums

THRUMS > THRUM

THRUPENNY as in thrupenny bit twelve-sided British

coin of nickel-brass, valued at three old pence, obsolete since 1971

THRUPUT n quantity of raw material or information processed in a given period

THRUPUTS > THRUPUT

THRUSH n brown songbird

THRUSHES > THRUSH

THRUST vb push forcefully ▷ n forceful stab

THRUSTED > THRUST

THRUSTER n person or thing that thrusts

THRUSTERS > THRUSTER

THRUSTFUL > THRUST

THRUSTING > THRUST

THRUSTOR variant of > THRUSTER

THRUSTORS > THRUSTOR

THRUSTS > THRUST

THRUTCH n narrow, fast-moving stream ▷ vb thrust

THRUTCHED > THRUTCH

THRUTCHES > THRUTCH

THRUWAY n thoroughfare

THRUWAYS > THRUWAY

THRYMSA n gold coin used in Anglo-Saxon England

THRYMSAS > THRYMSA

THUD n dull heavy sound ▷ vb make such a sound

THUDDED > THUD

THUDDING > THUD

THUDS > THUD

THUG n violent man, esp a criminal

THUGGEE n methods and practices of the thugs of India

THUGGEES > THUGGEE

THUGGERY > THUG

THUGGISH > THUG

THUGGISM > THUG

THUGGISMS > THUG

THUGGO n tough and violent person

THUGGOS > THUGGO

THUGS > THUG

THUJA n coniferous tree of North America and East Asia, with scalelike leaves, small cones, and an aromatic wood

THUJAS > THUJA

THULIA n oxide of thulium

THULIAS > THULIA

THULITE n rose-coloured zoisite sometimes incorporated into jewellery

THULITES > THULITE

THULIUM n malleable ductile silvery-grey element

THULIUMS > THULIUM

THUMB n short thick finger set apart from the others ▷ vb touch or handle with the thumb

THUMBED > THUMB

THUMBHOLE n hole for putting the thumb into

THUMBIER > THUMBY

THUMBIEST > THUMBY

THUMBING > THUMB

THUMBKIN same as > THUMBKIN

THUMBKINS *n* thumbscrew
THUMBLESS > THUMB
THUMBLIKE > THUMB
THUMBLING *n* extremely small person
THUMBNAIL *n* nail of the thumb ▷ *adj* concise and brief
THUMBNUT *n* nut with projections enabling it to be turned by the thumb and forefinger
THUMBNUTS > THUMBNUT
THUMBPOT *n* tiny flowerpot
THUMBPOTS > THUMBPOT
THUMBS > THUMB
THUMBTACK *n* short tack with a broad smooth head for fastening papers to a drawing board, etc
THUMBY *adj* clumsy; uncoordinated
THUMP *n* (sound of) a dull heavy blow ▷ *vb* strike heavily
THUMPED > THUMP
THUMPER > THUMP
THUMPERS > THUMP
THUMPING *adj* huge or excessive
THUMPS > THUMP
THUNDER *n* loud noise accompanying lightning ▷ *vb* rumble with thunder
THUNDERED > THUNDER
THUNDERER > THUNDER
THUNDERS > THUNDER
THUNDERY > THUNDER
THUNDROUS > THUNDER
THUNK *another word for* > THUD
THUNKED > THUNK
THUNKING > THUNK
THUNKS > THUNK
THURIBLE *same as* > CENSER
THURIBLES > THURIBLE
THURIFER *n* person appointed to carry the censer at religious ceremonies
THURIFERS > THURIFER
THURIFIED > THURIFY
THURIFIES > THURIFY
THURIFY *vb* burn incense near or before an altar, shrine, etc
THURL *same as* > THIRL
THURLS > THURL
THUS *adv* in this manner ▷ *n* aromatic gum resin
THUSES > THUS
THUSLY *adv* in such a way; thus
THUSNESS *n* state or quality of being *thus*
THUSWISE *adj* in this way; thus
THUYA *same as* > THUJA
THUYAS > THUYA
THWACK *n* whack ▷ *vb* beat with something flat ▷ *interj* exclamation imitative of this sound
THWACKED > THWACK
THWACKER > THWACK
THWACKERS > THWACK
THWACKING > THWACK

THWACKS > THWACK
THWAITE *n* piece of land cleared from forest or reclaimed from wasteland
THWAITES > THWAITE
THWART *vb* foil or frustrate ▷ *n* seat across a boat ▷ *adj* passing or being situated across ▷ *adv* across
THWARTED > THWART
THWARTER > THWART
THWARTERS > THWART
THWARTING > THWART
THWARTLY > THWART
THWARTS > THWART
THY *adj* of or associated with you (thou) ▷ *determiner* belonging to or associated in some way with you (thou)
THYINE *adj* of relating to the sandarac tree
THYLACINE *n* extinct doglike Tasmanian marsupial
THYLAKOID *n* small membranous sac within a chloroplast
THYLOSE *old variant of* > TYLOSIS
THYLOSES > THYLOSIS
THYLOSIS *same as* > TYLOSIS
THYME *n* aromatic herb
THYMES > THYME
THYMEY > THYME
THYMI > THYMUS
THYMIC *adj* of or relating to the thymus
THYMIDINE *n* crystalline nucleoside of thymine, found in DNA
THYMIER > THYME
THYMIEST > THYME
THYMINE *n* white crystalline pyrimidine base found in DNA
THYMINES > THYMINE
THYMOCYTE *n* lymphocyte found in the thymus
THYMOL *n* substance obtained from thyme, used as an antiseptic
THYMOLS > THYMOL
THYMOSIN *n* hormone secreted by the thymus
THYMOSINS > THYMOSIN
THYMUS *n* small gland at the base of the neck
THYMUSES > THYMUS
THYMY > THYME
THYRATRON *n* gas-filled tube that has three electrodes and can be switched between an 'off' state and an 'on' state. It has been superseded, except for application involving high-power switching, by the thyristor
THYREOID *same as* > THYROID
THYREOIDS > THYREOID
THYRISTOR *n* any of a group of semiconductor devices, such as the silicon-controlled rectifier, that can be switched between

two states
THYROID *n* (of) a gland in the neck controlling body growth ▷ *adj* of or relating to the thyroid gland
THYROIDAL > THYROID
THYROIDS > THYROID
THYROXIN *same as* > THYROXINE
THYROXINE *n* principal hormone produced by the thyroid gland
THYROXINS > THYROXIN
THYRSE *n* type of inflorescence, occurring in the lilac and grape, in which the main branch is racemose and the lateral branches cymose
THYRSES > THYRSE
THYRSI > THYRSUS
THYRSOID > THYRSE
THYRSUS *same as* > THYRSE
THYSELF *pron* reflexive form of thou
TI *same as* > TE
TIAR *same as* > TIARA
TIARA *n* semicircular jewelled headdress
TIARAED > TIARA
TIARAS > TIARA
TIARS > TIAR
TIBIA *n* inner bone of the lower leg
TIBIAE > TIBIA
TIBIAL > TIBIA
TIBIAS > TIBIA
TIC *n* spasmodic muscular twitch
TICAL *n* former standard monetary unit of Thailand, replaced by the baht in 1928
TICALS > TICAL
TICCA *adj* (of a thing or the services of a person) having been acquired for temporary use in exchange for payment
TICCED > TIC
TICCING > TIC
TICE *vb* tempt or allure; entice
TICED > TICE
TICES > TICE
TICH *same as* > TITCH
TICHES > TICH
TICHIER > TICHY
TICHIEST > TICHY
TICHY *same as* > TITCHY
TICING > TICE
TICK *n* mark (✓) used to check off or indicate the correctness of something ▷ *vb* mark with a tick
TICKED > TICK
TICKEN *same as* > TICKING
TICKENS > TICKEN
TICKER *n* heart
TICKERS > TICKER
TICKET *n* card or paper entitling the holder to admission, travel, etc ▷ *vb* attach or issue a ticket to
TICKETED > TICKET
TICKETING > TICKET
TICKETS *pl n* death or ruin
TICKEY *n* South African

threepenny piece, which was replaced by the five-cent coin in 1961
TICKEYS > TICKEY
TICKIES > TICKY
TICKING *n* strong material for mattress covers
TICKINGS > TICKING
TICKLACE *n* (in Newfoundland) a kittiwake
TICKLACES > TICKLACE
TICKLE *vb* touch or stroke (a person) to produce laughter ▷ *n* tickling
TICKLED > TICKLE
TICKLER *n* difficult or delicate problem
TICKLERS > TICKLER
TICKLES > TICKLE
TICKLIER > TICKLE
TICKLIEST > TICKLE
TICKLING > TICKLE
TICKLINGS > TICKLE
TICKLISH *adj* sensitive to tickling
TICKLY > TICKLE
TICKS > TICK
TICKSEED *another name for* > COREOPSIS
TICKSEEDS > TICKSEED
TICKTACK *n* bookmakers' sign language ▷ *vb* make a ticking sound
TICKTACKS > TICKTACK
TICKTOCK *n* ticking sound made by a clock ▷ *vb* make a ticking sound
TICKTOCKS > TICKTOCK
TICKY *same as* > TICKEY
TICS > TIC
TICTAC *same as* > TICKTACK
TICTACKED > TICTAC
TICTACS > TICTAC
TICTOC *same as* > TICKTOCK
TICTOCKED > TICTOC
TICTOCS > TICTOC
TID *n* girl
TIDAL *adj* (of a river, lake, or sea) having tides
TIDALLY > TIDAL
TIDBIT *same as* > TITBIT
TIDBITS > TIDBIT
TIDDIER > TIDDY
TIDDIES > TIDDY
TIDDIEST > TIDDY
TIDDLE *vb* busy oneself with inconsequential tasks
TIDDLED > TIDDLE
TIDDLER *n* very small fish
TIDDLERS > TIDDLER
TIDDLES > TIDDLE
TIDDLEY *same as* > TIDDLY
TIDDLEYS > TIDDLEY
TIDDLIER > TIDDLY
TIDDLIES > TIDDLY
TIDDLIEST > TIDDLY
TIDDLING > TIDDLE
TIDDLY *adj* tiny ▷ *n* alcoholic beverage
TIDDY *n* four of trumps in the card game gleek
TIDE *n* rise and fall of the sea caused by the gravitational pull of the sun and moon ▷ *vb* carry or be carried with or as if with the tide

TIDED > TIDE

TIDELAND n land between high-water and low-water marks

TIDELANDS > TIDELAND

TIDELESS > TIDE

TIDELIKE > TIDE

TIDEMARK n mark left by the highest or lowest point of a tide

TIDEMARKS > TIDEMARK

TIDEMILL n watermill powered by the force of the tide

TIDEMILLS > TIDEMILL

TIDERIP same as > RIPTIDE

TIDERIPS > TIDERIP

TIDES > TIDE

TIDESMAN n customs official at a port

TIDESMEN > TIDESMAN

TIDEWATER n water that advances and recedes with the tide

TIDEWAVE n undulation of the earth's water levels as the tide moves around it

TIDEWAVES > TIDEWAVE

TIDEWAY n strong tidal current or its channel, esp the tidal part of a river

TIDEWAYS > TIDEWAY

TIDIED > TIDY

TIDIER > TIDY

TIDIERS > TIDY

TIDIES > TIDY

TIDIEST > TIDY

TIDILY > TIDY

TIDINESS > TIDY

TIDING > TIDE

TIDINGS pl n news

TIDIVATE same as > TITIVATE

TIDIVATED > TITIVATE

TIDIVATES > TITIVATE

TIDS > TID

TIDY adj neat and orderly ▷ vb put in order ▷ n small container for odds and ends

TIDYING > TIDY

TIDYTIPS n herb with flowers resembling those of the daisy

TIE vb fasten or be fastened with string, rope, etc ▷ n long narrow piece of material worn knotted round the neck

TIEBACK n length of cord, ribbon, or other fabric used for tying a curtain to one side

TIEBACKS > TIEBACK

TIEBREAK n deciding game in drawn match

TIEBREAKS > TIEBREAK

TIECLASP n clip, often ornamental, which holds a tie in place against a shirt

TIECLASPS > TIECLASP

TIED > TIE

TIEING same as > TIE

TIELESS > TIE

TIEPIN n ornamental pin used to pin the two ends of a tie to a shirt

TIEPINS > TIEPIN

TIER n one of a set of rows placed one above and behind the other ▷ vb be or arrange in tiers

TIERCE same as > TERCE

TIERCED adj (of a shield) divided into three sections of similar size but different colour

TIERCEL same as > TERCEL

TIERCELET another name for > TERCEL

TIERCELS > TIERCEL

TIERCERON n (in Gothic architecture) a type of rib on a vault

TIERCES > TIERCE

TIERCET same as > TERCET

TIERCETS > TIERCET

TIERED > TIER

TIERING > TIER

TIEROD n any rod- or bar-shaped structural member designed to prevent the separation of two parts, as in a vehicle

TIERODS > TIEROD

TIERS > TIER

TIES > TIE

TIETAC n fastener for holding a tie in place

TIETACK same as > TIETAC

TIETACKS > TIETACK

TIETACS > TIETAC

TIFF n petty quarrel ▷ vb have or be in a tiff

TIFFANIES > TIFFANY

TIFFANY n sheer fine gauzy fabric

TIFFED > TIFF

TIFFIN n (in India) a light meal, esp at midday ▷ vb take tiffin

TIFFINED > TIFFIN

TIFFING > TIFF

TIFFINGS > TIFF

TIFFINING > TIFFIN

TIFFINS > TIFFIN

TIFFS > TIFF

TIFOSI > TIFOSO

TIFOSO n fanatical fan (esp an Italian F1 fan)

TIFT (Scots) variant of > TIFF

TIFTED > TIFT

TIFTING > TIFT

TIFTS > TIFT

TIG n child's game

TIGE n trunk of an architectural column

TIGER n large yellow-and-black striped Asian cat

TIGEREYE n golden brown silicified variety of crocidolite, used as an ornamental stone

TIGEREYES > TIGEREYE

TIGERISH > TIGER

TIGERISM n arrogant and showy manner

TIGERISMS > TIGERISM

TIGERLIKE adj resembling a tiger

TIGERLY adj of or like a tiger

TIGERS > TIGER

TIGERY > TIGER

TIGES > TIGE

TIGGED > TIG

TIGGING > TIG

TIGHT adj stretched or drawn taut ▷ adv in a close, firm, or secure way

TIGHTASS n inhibited or excessively self-controlled person

TIGHTEN vb make or become tight or tighter

TIGHTENED > TIGHTEN

TIGHTENER > TIGHTEN

TIGHTENS > TIGHTEN

TIGHTER > TIGHT

TIGHTEST > TIGHT

TIGHTISH > TIGHT

TIGHTKNIT adj closely integrated

TIGHTLY > TIGHT

TIGHTNESS > TIGHT

TIGHTROPE n rope stretched taut on which acrobats perform

TIGHTS pl n one-piece clinging garment covering the body from the waist to the feet

TIGHTWAD n stingy person

TIGHTWADS > TIGHTWAD

TIGHTWIRE n wire tightrope

TIGLIC as in tiglic acid syrupy liquid or crystalline colourless unsaturated carboxylic acid

TIGLON same as > TIGON

TIGLONS > TIGLON

TIGON n hybrid offspring of a male tiger and a female lion

TIGONS > TIGON

TIGRESS n female tiger

TIGRESSES > TIGRESS

TIGRIDIA n type of tropical American plant

TIGRIDIAS > TIGRIDIA

TIGRINE adj of, characteristic of, or resembling a tiger

TIGRISH > TIGER

TIGRISHLY > TIGER

TIGROID adj resembling a tiger

TIGS > TIG

TIKA same as > TIKKA

TIKANGA n Māori ways or customs

TIKANGAS > TIKANGA

TIKAS > TIKA

TIKE same as > TYKE

TIKES > TIKE

TIKI n small carving of a grotesque person worn as a pendant ▷ vb take a scenic tour around an area

TIKIED > TIKI

TIKIING > TIKI

TIKIS > TIKI

TIKKA adj marinated in spices and dry-roasted ▷ n act of marking a tikka on the forehead

TIKKAS > TIKKA

TIKOLOSHE same as > TOKOLOSHE

TIL another name for > SESAME

TILAK n coloured spot or mark worn by Hindus, esp on the forehead, often indicating membership of a religious sect, caste, etc, or (in the case of a woman) marital status

TILAKS > TILAK

TILAPIA n type of fish

TILAPIAS > TILAPIA

TILBURIES > TILBURY

TILBURY n light two-wheeled horse-drawn open carriage, seating two people

TILDE n mark (~) used in Spanish to indicate that the letter 'n' is to be pronounced in a particular way

TILDES > TILDE

TILE n flat piece of ceramic, plastic, etc used to cover a roof, floor, or wall ▷ vb cover with tiles

TILED > TILE

TILEFISH n large brightly coloured deep-sea percoid food fish

TILELIKE adj like a tile

TILER > TILE

TILERIES > TILERY

TILERS > TILE

TILERY n place where tiles are produced

TILES > TILE

TILING n tiles collectively

TILINGS > TILING

TILL prep until ▷ vb cultivate (land) ▷ n drawer for money, usu in a cash register ▷ n unstratified glacial deposit consisting of rock fragments of various sizes

TILLABLE > TILL

TILLAGE n act, process, or art of tilling

TILLAGES > TILLAGE

TILLED > TILL

TILLER n on boats, a handle fixed to the top of a rudderpost to serve as a lever in steering ▷ vb use a tiller

TILLERED > TILLER

TILLERING > TILLER

TILLERMAN n one working a tiller

TILLERMEN > TILLERMAN

TILLERS > TILL

TILLICUM n (in the Pacific Northwest) a friend

TILLICUMS > TILLICUM

TILLIER > TILL

TILLIEST > TILL

TILLING > TILL

TILLINGS > TILL

TILLITE n rock formed from hardened till

TILLITES > TILLITE

TILLS > TILL

TILLY > TILL

TILS > TIL

TILT vb slant at an angle ▷ n slope

TILTABLE > TILT

TILTED > TILT

TILTER > TILT

TILTERS > TILT

TILTH n (condition of) land that has been tilled

TILTHS > TILTH

TILTING > TILT

TILTINGS > TILT

TILTMETER n instrument for measuring the tilt of the earth's surface

TILTROTOR n aircraft with rotors that can be tilted

TILTS > TILT

TILTYARD n (formerly) an enclosed area for tilting

TILTYARDS > TILTYARD

TIMARAU same as > TAMARAU

TIMARAUS > TIMARAU

TIMARIOT n one holding a fief in feudal Turkey

TIMARIOTS > TIMARIOT

TIMBAL n type of kettledrum

TIMBALE n mixture of meat, fish, etc, in a rich sauce, cooked in a mould lined with potato or pastry

TIMBALES > TIMBALE

TIMBALS > TIMBAL

TIMBER n wood as a building material ▷ adj made out of timber ▷ vb provide with timbers ▷ interj lumberjack's shouted warning when a tree is about to fall

TIMBERED adj made of or containing timber or timbers

TIMBERING n timbers collectively

TIMBERMAN n any of various longicorn beetles that have destructive wood-eating larvae

TIMBERMEN > TIMBERMAN

TIMBERS > TIMBER

TIMBERY > TIMBER

TIMBO n Amazonian vine from which a useful insecticide can be derived

TIMBOS > TIMBO

TIMBRAL adj relating to timbre

TIMBRE n distinctive quality of sound of a voice or instrument

TIMBREL n tambourine

TIMBRELS > TIMBREL

TIMBRES > TIMBRE

TIME n past, present, and future as a continuous whole ▷ vb note the time taken by

TIMEBOMB n bomb containing a timing mechanism that determines the time it will detonate

TIMEBOMBS > TIMEBOMB

TIMECARD n card used with a time clock

TIMECARDS > TIMECARD

TIMED > TIME

TIMEFRAME n period of time within which certain events are scheduled to occur

TIMELESS adj unaffected by time

TIMELIER > TIMELY

TIMELIEST > TIMELY

TIMELINE n graphic representation showing the passage of time as a line

TIMELINES > TIMELINE

TIMELY adj at the appropriate time ▷ adv at the right or an appropriate time

TIMENOGUY n taut rope on a ship

TIMEOUS adj in good time

TIMEOUSLY > TIMEOUS

TIMEOUT n in sport, interruption in play during which players rest, discuss tactics, or make substitutions

TIMEOUTS > TIMEOUT

TIMEPASS n way of passing the time ▷ vb pass the time

TIMEPIECE n watch or clock

TIMER n device for measuring time, esp a switch or regulator that causes a mechanism to operate at a specific time

TIMERS > TIMER

TIMES > TIME

TIMESAVER n something that saves time

TIMESCALE n period of time within which events occur or are due to occur

TIMETABLE n plan showing the times when something takes place, the departure and arrival times of trains or buses, etc ▷ vb set a time when a particular thing should be done

TIMEWORK n work paid for by the length of time taken, esp by the hour or the day

TIMEWORKS > TIMEWORK

TIMEWORN adj showing the adverse effects of overlong use or of old age

TIMID adj easily frightened

TIMIDER > TIMID

TIMIDEST > TIMID

TIMIDITY > TIMID

TIMIDLY > TIMID

TIMIDNESS > TIMID

TIMING n ability to judge when to do or say something so as to make the best effect

TIMINGS > TIMING

TIMIST n one concerned with time

TIMISTS > TIMIST

TIMOCRACY n political unit or system in which possession of property serves as the first requirement for participation in government

TIMOLOL n relaxant medicine used (for

example) to reduce blood pressure

TIMOLOLS > TIMOLOL

TIMON n apparatus by which a vessel is steered

TIMONEER n helmsman; tillerman

TIMONEERS > TIMONEER

TIMONS > TIMON

TIMOROUS adj timid

TIMORSOME adj timorous; timid

TIMOTHIES > TIMOTHY

TIMOTHY as in timothy grass perennial grass of temperate regions, having erect stiff stems and cylindrical flower spikes: grown for hay and pasture

TIMOUS same as > TIMEOUS

TIMOUSLY > TIMOUS

TIMPANA n traditional Maltese baked pasta and pastry dish

TIMPANI pl n set of kettledrums

TIMPANIST > TIMPANI

TIMPANO n kettledrum

TIMPANUM same as > TYMPANUM

TIMPANUMS > TIMPANUM

TIMPS same as > TIMPANI

TIN n soft metallic element ▷ vb put (food) into tins

TINAJA n large jar for cooling water

TINAJAS > TINAJA

TINAMOU n any bird of the order Tinamiformes of Central and South America, having small wings, a heavy body, and an inconspicuous plumage

TINAMOUS > TINAMOU

TINCAL another name for > BORAX

TINCALS > TINCAL

TINCHEL n in Scotland, a circle of deer hunters who gradually close in on their quarry

TINCHELS > TINCHEL

TINCT vb tint ▷ adj tinted or coloured

TINCTED > TINCT

TINCTING > TINCT

TINCTS > TINCT

TINCTURE n medicinal extract in a solution of alcohol ▷ vb give a tint or colour to

TINCTURED > TINCTURE

TINCTURES > TINCTURE

TIND vb set alight

TINDAL n petty officer

TINDALS > TINDAL

TINDED > TIND

TINDER n dry easily-burning material used to start a fire

TINDERBOX n formerly, small box for tinder, esp one fitted with a flint and steel

TINDERS > TINDER

TINDERY > TINDER

TINDING > TIND

TINDS > TIND

TINE n prong of a fork or antler ▷ vb lose

TINEA n any fungal skin disease, esp ringworm

TINEAL > TINEA

TINEAS > TINEA

TINED > TINE

TINEID n any moth of the family Tineidae, which includes the clothes moths ▷ adj of, relating to, or belonging to the family Tineidae

TINEIDS > TINEID

TINES > TINE

TINFOIL n paper-thin sheet of metal, used for wrapping foodstuffs

TINFOILS > TINFOIL

TINFUL n contents of a tin or the amount a tin will hold

TINFULS > TINFUL

TING same as > THING

TINGE n slight tint ▷ vb give a slight tint or trace to

TINGED > TINGE

TINGEING > TINGE

TINGES > TINGE

TINGING > TINGE

TINGLE n (feel) a prickling or stinging sensation ▷ vb feel a mild prickling or stinging sensation, as from cold or excitement

TINGLED > TINGLE

TINGLER > TINGLE

TINGLERS > TINGLE

TINGLES > TINGLE

TINGLIER > TINGLE

TINGLIEST > TINGLE

TINGLING > TINGLE

TINGLINGS > TINGLE

TINGLISH adj exciting

TINGLY > TINGLE

TINGS > TING

TINGUAITE n type of igneous rock

TINHORN n cheap pretentious person, esp a gambler with extravagant claims ▷ adj cheap and showy

TINHORNS > TINHORN

TINIER > TINY

TINIES pl n small children

TINIEST > TINY

TINILY > TINY

TININESS > TINY

TINING > TINE

TINK shortened form of > TINKER

TINKED > TINK

TINKER n derogatory term for travelling mender of pots and pans ▷ vb fiddle with (an engine etc) in an attempt to repair it

TINKERED > TINKER

TINKERER > TINKER

TINKERERS > TINKER

TINKERING > TINKER

TINKERS > TINKER

TINKERTOY n children's construction set

TINKING > TINK

TINKLE vb ring with a high

tinny sound like a small bell ▷ *n* this sound or action

TINKLED > TINKLE

TINKLER *same as* > TINKER

TINKLERS > TINKLER

TINKLES > TINKLE

TINKLIER > TINKLE

TINKLIEST > TINKLE

TINKLING > TINKLE

TINKLINGS > TINKLE

TINKLY > TINKLE

TINKS > TINK

TINLIKE > TIN

TINMAN *n* one who works with tin or tin plate

TINMEN > TINMAN

TINNED > TIN

TINNER *n* tin miner

TINNERS > TINNER

TINNIE *same as* > TINNY

TINNIER > TINNY

TINNIES > TINNY

TINNIEST > TINNY

TINNILY > TINNY

TINNINESS > TINNY

TINNING > TIN

TINNINGS > TIN

TINNITUS *n* ringing, hissing, or booming sensation in one or both ears, caused by infection of the middle or inner ear, a side effect of certain drugs, etc

TINNY *adj* (of sound) thin and metallic ▷ *n* can of beer

TINPLATE *n* thin steel sheet coated with a layer of tin that protects the steel from corrosion ▷ *vb* coat (a metal or object) with a layer of tin, usually either by electroplating or by dipping in a bath of molten tin

TINPLATED > TINPLATE

TINPLATES > TINPLATE

TINPOT *adj* worthless or unimportant ▷ *n* pot made of tin

TINPOTS > TINPOT

TINS > TIN

TINSEL *n* decorative metallic strips or threads ▷ *adj* made of or decorated with tinsel ▷ *vb* decorate with or as if with tinsel

TINSELED > TINSEL

TINSELING > TINSEL

TINSELLED > TINSEL

TINSELLY > TINSEL

TINSELRY *n* tinsel-like material

TINSELS > TINSEL

TINSEY *old variant of* > TINSEL

TINSEYS > TINSEY

TINSMITH *n* person who works with tin or tin plate

TINSMITHS > TINSMITH

TINSNIPS *n* metal cutters

TINSTONE *n* black or brown stone

TINSTONES > TINSTONE

TINT *n* (pale) shade of a colour ▷ *vb* give a tint to

TINTACK *n* tin-plated tack

TINTACKS > TINTACK

TINTED > TINT

TINTER > TINT

TINTERS > TINT

TINTIER > TINTY

TINTIEST > TINTY

TINTINESS > TINTY

TINTING > TINT

TINTINGS > TINT

TINTLESS > TINT

TINTOOKIE *n* in informal Australian English, fawning or servile person

TINTS > TINT

TINTY *adj* having many tints

TINTYPE *another name for* > FERROTYPE

TINTYPES > TINTYPE

TINWARE *n* objects made of tin plate

TINWARES > TINWARE

TINWORK *n* objects made of tin

TINWORKS *n* place where tin is mined, smelted, or rolled

TINY *adj* very small

TIP *n* narrow or pointed end of anything ▷ *vb* put a tip on

TIPCART *n* cart that can be tipped to empty out its contents

TIPCARTS > TIPCART

TIPCAT *n* game in which a short sharp-ended piece of wood (the cat) is tipped in the air with a stick

TIPCATS > TIPCAT

TIPI *variant spelling of* > TEPEE

TIPIS > TIPI

TIPLESS > TIP

TIPOFF *n* warning or hint, esp given confidentially and based on inside information

TIPOFFS > TIPOFF

TIPPABLE > TIP

TIPPED > TIP

TIPPEE *n* person who receives a tip, esp regarding share prices

TIPPEES > TIPPEE

TIPPER *n* person who gives or leaves a tip

TIPPERS > TIPPER

TIPPET *n* scarflike piece of fur, often made from a whole animal skin, worn, esp formerly, round a woman's shoulders

TIPPETS > TIPPET

TIPPIER > TIPPY

TIPPIEST > TIPPY

TIPPING > TIP

TIPPINGS > TIP

TIPPLE *vb* drink alcohol habitually, esp in small quantities ▷ *n* alcoholic drink

TIPPLED > TIPPLE

TIPPLER > TIPPLE

TIPPLERS > TIPPLE

TIPPLES > TIPPLE

TIPPLING > TIPPLE

TIPPY *adj* extremely fashionable or stylish

TIPPYTOE *same as* > TIPTOE

TIPPYTOED > TIPPYTOE

TIPPYTOES > TIPPYTOE

TIPS > TIP

TIPSHEET *n* list of advice or instructions

TIPSHEETS > TIPSHEET

TIPSIER > TIPSY

TIPSIEST > TIPSY

TIPSIFIED > TIPSIFY

TIPSIFIES > TIPSIFY

TIPSIFY *vb* make tipsy

TIPSILY > TIPSY

TIPSINESS > TIPSY

TIPSTAFF *n* court official

TIPSTAFFS > TIPSTAFF

TIPSTAVES > TIPSTAFF

TIPSTER *n* person who sells tips about races

TIPSTERS > TIPSTER

TIPSTOCK *n* detachable section of a gunstock, usually gripped by the left hand of the user

TIPSTOCKS > TIPSTOCK

TIPSY *adj* slightly drunk

TIPT > TIP

TIPTOE *vb* walk quietly with the heels off the ground

TIPTOED > TIPTOE

TIPTOEING > TIPTOE

TIPTOES > TIPTOE

TIPTOP *adj* of the highest quality or condition ▷ *adv* of the highest quality or condition ▷ *n* best in quality ▷ *n* very top; pinnacle

TIPTOPS > TIPTOP

TIPTRONIC *n* type of gearbox that has both automatic and manual options

TIPULA *n* crane fly

TIPULAS > TIPULA

TIPUNA *n* ancestor

TIPUNAS > TIPUNA

TIRADE *n* long angry speech

TIRADES > TIRADE

TIRAGE *n* drawing of wine from a barrel prior to bottling

TIRAGES > TIRAGE

TIRAMISU *n* Italian dessert made with sponge soaked in coffee and Marsala, topped with soft cheese and powdered chocolate

TIRAMISUS > TIRAMISU

TIRASSE *n* mechanism in an organ connecting two pedals, so that both may be depressed at once

TIRASSES > TIRASSE

TIRE *vb* reduce the energy of, as by exertion

TIRED *adj* exhausted

TIREDER > TIRED

TIREDEST > TIRED

TIREDLY > TIRED

TIREDNESS > TIRED

TIRELESS *adj* energetic and determined

TIRELING *n* fatigued person or animal

TIRELINGS > TIRELING

TIRES > TIRE

TIRESOME *adj* boring and irritating

TIREWOMAN *n* an obsolete term for lady's maid

TIREWOMEN > TIREWOMAN

TIRING > TIRE

TIRINGS > TIRE

TIRITI *n* another name for the Treaty of Waitangi

TIRITIS > TIRITI

TIRL *vb* turn

TIRLED > TIRL

TIRLING > TIRL

TIRLS > TIRL

TIRO *same as* > TYRO

TIROES > TIRO

TIRONIC *variant of* > TYRONIC

TIROS > TIRO

TIRR *vb* strip or denude

TIRRED > TIRR

TIRRING > TIRR

TIRRIT *n* panic; scare

TIRRITS > TIRRIT

TIRRIVEE *n* outburst of bad temper; rumpus

TIRRIVEES > TIRRIVEE

TIRRIVIE *same as* > TIRRIVEE

TIRRIVIES > TIRRIVIE

TIRRS > TIRR

TIS > TI

TISANE *n* infusion of dried or fresh leaves or flowers, as camomile

TISANES > TISANE

TISICK *n* splutter; cough

TISICKS > TISICK

TISSUAL *adj* relating to tissue

TISSUE *n* substance of an animal body or plant ▷ *vb* weave into tissue

TISSUED > TISSUE

TISSUES > TISSUE

TISSUEY > TISSUE

TISSUING > TISSUE

TISSULAR *adj* relating to tissue

TISWAS *n* state of anxiety or excitement

TISWASES > TISWAS

TIT *n* any of various small songbirds; informal term for a female breast ▷ *vb* jerk or tug

TITAN *n* person who is huge, strong, or very important

TITANATE *n* any salt or ester of titanic acid

TITANATES > TITANATE

TITANESS *n* person who is huge, strong, or very important

TITANIA > TITANIUM

TITANIAS > TITANIA

TITANIC *adj* huge or very important

TITANIS *n* large predatory flightless prehistoric bird

TITANISES > TITANIS

TITANISM *n* titanic power

TITANISMS > TITANISM

TITANITE *another name*

for > SPHENE

TITANITES > TITANITE

TITANIUM *n* strong light metallic element used to make alloys

TITANIUMS > TITANIUM

TITANOUS *adj* of or containing titanium, esp in the trivalent state

TITANS > TITAN

TITBIT *n* tasty piece of food

TITBITS > TITBIT

TITCH *n* small person

TITCHES > TITCH

TITCHIER > TITCHY

TITCHIEST > TITCHY

TITCHY *adj* very small

TITE *adj* immediately

TITELY *adv* immediately

TITER *same as* > TITRE

TITERS > TITER

TITFER *n* hat

TITFERS > TITFER

TITHABLE *adj* (until 1936) liable to pay tithes

TITHE *n* esp formerly, one tenth of one's income or produce paid to the church as a tax ▷ *vb* charge or pay a tithe

TITHED > TITHE

TITHER > TITHE

TITHERS > TITHE

TITHES > TITHE

TITHING > TITHE

TITHINGS > TITHING

TITHONIA *n* Central American herb with flowers resembling sunflowers

TITHONIAS > TITHONIA

TITI *n* small omnivorous New World monkey of South America, with long beautifully coloured fur and a long nonprehensile tail

TITIAN *n* reddish gold colour

TITIANS > TITIAN

TITILLATE *vb* excite or stimulate pleasurably

TITIS > TITI

TITIVATE *vb* smarten up

TITIVATED > TITIVATE

TITIVATES > TITIVATE

TITIVATOR > TITIVATE

TITLARK *another name for* > PIPIT

TITLARKS > TITLARK

TITLE *n* name of a book, film, etc ▷ *vb* give a title to

TITLED *adj* aristocratic

TITLELESS > TITLE

TITLER *n* one who writes titles

TITLERS > TITLE

TITLES > TITLE

TITLING > TITLE

TITLINGS > TITLE

TITLIST *n* titleholder

TITLISTS > TITLIST

TITMAN *n* (of pigs) the runt of a litter

TITMEN > TITMAN

TITMICE > TITMOUSE

TITMOSE *old spelling*

of > TITMOUSE

TITMOUSE *n* any small active songbird

TITOKI *n* New Zealand evergreen tree with a spreading crown and glossy green leaves

TITOKIS > TITOKI

TITRABLE > TITRATE

TITRANT *n* solution in a titration that is added from a burette to a measured quantity of another solution

TITRANTS > TITRANT

TITRATE *vb* measure the volume or concentration of (a solution) by titration

TITRATED > TITRATE

TITRATES > TITRATE

TITRATING > TITRATE

TITRATION *n* operation in which a measured amount of one solution is added to a known quantity of another solution until the reaction between the two is complete

TITRATOR *n* device used to perform titration

TITRATORS > TITRATOR

TITRE *n* concentration of a solution as determined by titration

TITRES > TITRE

TITS > TIT

TITTED > TIT

TITTER *vb* laugh in a suppressed way ▷ *n* suppressed laugh

TITTERED > TITTER

TITTERER > TITTER

TITTERERS > TITTER

TITTERING > TITTER

TITTERS > TITTER

TITTIE *n* sister; young woman

TITTIES > TITTIE

TITTING > TIT

TITTISH *adj* testy

TITTIVATE *same as* > TITIVATE

TITTLE *n* very small amount ▷ *vb* chatter; tattle

TITTLEBAT *n* child's name for the stickleback fish

TITTLED > TITTLE

TITTLES > TITTLE

TITTLING > TITTLE

TITTUP *vb* prance or frolic ▷ *n* caper

TITTUPED > TITTUP

TITTUPING > TITTUP

TITTUPPED > TITTUP

TITTUPPY *same as* > TITTUPY

TITTUPS > TITTUP

TITTUPY *adj* spritely; lively

TITTY *same as* > TITTIE

TITUBANCY *n* staggering or stumbling

TITUBANT *adj* staggering

TITUBATE *vb* stagger

TITUBATED > TITUBATE

TITUBATES > TITUBATE

TITULAR *adj* in name only ▷ *n* bearer of a title

TITULARLY > TITULAR

TITULARS > TITULAR

TITULARY *same as* > TITULAR

TITULE *same as* > TITLE

TITULED > TITULE

TITULES > TITULE

TITULI > TITULUS

TITULING > TITULE

TITULUS *n* (in crucifixion) a sign attached to the top of the cross on which were written the condemned man's name and crime

TITUP *same as* > TITTUP

TITUPED > TITUP

TITUPING > TITUP

TITUPPED > TITUP

TITUPPING > TITUP

TITUPS > TITUP

TITUPY *same as* > TITTUPY

TIVY *same as* > TANTIVY

TIX *pl n* tickets

TIZWAS *same as* > TISWAS

TIZWASES > TIZWAS

TIZZ *same as* > TIZZY

TIZZES > TIZZ

TIZZIES > TIZZY

TIZZY *n* confused or agitated state

TJANTING *n* pen-like tool used in batik for applying molten wax to fabric

TJANTINGS > TJANTING

TMESES > TMESIS

TMESIS *n* interpolation of a word or group of words between the parts of a compound word

TO *prep* indicating movement towards, equality or comparison, etc ▷ *adv* a closed position

TOAD *n* animal like a large frog

TOADEATER *rare word for* > TOADY

TOADFISH *n* spiny-finned bottom-dwelling marine fish of tropical and temperate seas, with a flattened tapering body and a wide mouth

TOADFLAX *n* plant with narrow leaves and yellow-orange flowers

TOADGRASS *another name for* > TOADRUSH

TOADIED > TOADY

TOADIES > TOADY

TOADISH > TOAD

TOADLESS *adj* having no toads

TOADLIKE > TOAD

TOADRUSH *n* annual rush growing in damp lowlands

TOADS > TOAD

TOADSTONE *n* amygdaloidal basalt occurring in the limestone regions of Derbyshire

TOADSTOOL *n* poisonous fungus like a mushroom

TOADY *n* ingratiating person ▷ *vb* be ingratiating

TOADYING > TOADY

TOADYISH > TOADY

TOADYISM > TOADY

TOADYISMS > TOADY

TOAST *n* sliced bread browned by heat ▷ *vb* brown (bread) by heat

TOASTED > TOAST

TOASTER > TOAST

TOASTERS > TOAST

TOASTIE *same as* > TOASTY

TOASTIER > TOASTY

TOASTIES > TOASTY

TOASTIEST > TOASTY

TOASTING > TOAST

TOASTINGS > TOAST

TOASTS > TOAST

TOASTY *n* toasted sandwich ▷ *adj* tasting or smelling like toast

TOAZE *variant spelling of* > TOZE

TOAZED > TOAZE

TOAZES > TOAZE

TOAZING > TOAZE

TOBACCO *n* plant with large leaves dried for smoking

TOBACCOES > TOBACCO

TOBACCOS > TOBACCO

TOBIES > TOBY

TOBOGGAN *n* narrow sledge for sliding over snow ▷ *vb* ride a toboggan

TOBOGGANS > TOBOGGAN

TOBOGGIN *variant spelling of* > TOBOGGAN

TOBOGGINS > TOBOGGIN

TOBY *n* water stopcock at the boundary of a street and house section

TOC *n* in communications code, signal for letter t

TOCCATA *n* rapid piece of music for a keyboard instrument

TOCCATAS > TOCCATA

TOCCATE > TOCCATA

TOCCATINA *n* short toccata

TOCHER *n* dowry ▷ *vb* give a dowry to

TOCHERED > TOCHER

TOCHERING > TOCHER

TOCHERS > TOCHER

TOCK *n* sound made by a clock ▷ *vb* (of a clock) make such a sound

TOCKED > TOCK

TOCKIER > TOCKY

TOCKIEST > TOCKY

TOCKING > TOCK

TOCKLEY *slang word for* > PENIS

TOCKLEYS > TOCKLEY

TOCKS > TOCK

TOCKY *adj* muddy

TOCO *n* punishment

TOCOLOGY *n* branch of medicine concerned with childbirth

TOCOS > TOCO

TOCS > TOC

TOCSIN *n* warning signal

TOCSINS > TOCSIN

TOD *n* unit of weight, used for wool, etc, usually equal to 28 pounds ▷ *vb* produce a tod

TODAY *n* this day ▷ *adv* on this day

TODAYS > TODAY

TODDE *same as* > TOD

TODDED > TOD

TODDES > TODDE

TODDIES > TODDY

TODDING > TOD

TODDLE *vb* walk with short unsteady steps ▷ *n* act or an instance of toddling

TODDLED > TODDLE

TODDLER *n* child beginning to walk

TODDLERS > TODDLER

TODDLES > TODDLE

TODDLING > TODDLE

TODDY *n* sweetened drink of spirits and hot water

TODIES > TODY

TODS > TOD

TODY *n* small bird of the Caribbean, with a red-and-green plumage and long straight bill

TOE *n* digit of the foot ▷ *vb* touch or kick with the toe

TOEA *n* monetary unit of Papua New Guinea, worth one-hundredth of a kina

TOEAS > TOEA

TOEBIE *n* South African slang for sandwich

TOEBIES > TOEBIE

TOECAP *n* strengthened covering for the toe of a shoe

TOECAPS > TOECAP

TOECLIP *n* clip on a bicycle pedal into which the toes are inserted to prevent the foot from slipping

TOECLIPS > TOECLIP

TOED > TOE

TOEHOLD *n* small space on a mountain for supporting the toe of the foot in climbing

TOEHOLDS > TOEHOLD

TOEIER > TOEY

TOEIEST > TOEY

TOEING > TOE

TOELESS *adj* not having toes

TOELIKE > TOE

TOENAIL *n* thin hard clear plate covering part of the upper surface of the end of each toe ▷ *vb* join (beams) by driving nails obliquely

TOENAILED > TOENAIL

TOENAILS > TOENAIL

TOEPIECE *n* part of a shoe that covers the toes

TOEPIECES > TOEPIECE

TOEPLATE *n* metal reinforcement of the part of the sole of a shoe or boot underneath the toes

TOEPLATES > TOEPLATE

TOERAG *n* contemptible person

TOERAGGER *same as* > TOERAG

TOERAGS > TOERAG

TOES > TOE

TOESHOE *n* ballet pump with padded toes

TOESHOES > TOESHOE

TOETOE *same as* > TOITOI

TOETOES > TOETOE

TOEY *adj* (of a person) nervous or anxious

TOFF *n* well-dressed or upper-class person

TOFFEE *n* chewy sweet made of boiled sugar

TOFFEES > TOFFEE

TOFFIER > TOFFY

TOFFIES > TOFFY

TOFFIEST > TOFFY

TOFFISH *adj* belonging to or characteristic of the upper class

TOFFS *adj* like a toff

TOFFY *same as* > TOFFEE

TOFORE *prep* before

TOFT *n* homestead

TOFTS > TOFT

TOFU *n* soft food made from soya-bean curd

TOFUS > TOFU

TOFUTTI *n* tradename for any of a variety of nondairy, soya-based food products, esp frozen desserts

TOFUTTIS > TOFUTTI

TOG *n* unit for measuring the insulating power of duvets ▷ *vb* dress oneself, esp in smart clothes

TOGA *n* garment worn by citizens of ancient Rome ▷ *vb* wear a toga

TOGAE > TOGA

TOGAED > TOGA

TOGAS > TOGA

TOGATE *adj* clad in a toga

TOGATED *same as* > TOGATE

TOGAVIRUS *n* one of family of viruses

TOGE *old variant of* > TOGA

TOGED > TOGE

TOGES > TOGE

TOGETHER *adv* in company ▷ *adj* organized

TOGGED > TOG

TOGGER *vb* play football ▷ *n* football player

TOGGERED > TOGGER

TOGGERIES > TOGGERY

TOGGERING > TOGGER

TOGGERS > TOGGER

TOGGERY *n* clothes

TOGGING > TOG

TOGGLE *n* small bar-shaped button inserted through a loop for fastening ▷ *vb* supply or fasten with a toggle or toggles

TOGGLED > TOGGLE

TOGGLER > TOGGLE

TOGGLERS > TOGGLE

TOGGLES > TOGGLE

TOGGLING > TOGGLE

TOGS > TOG

TOGUE *n* large North American freshwater game fish

TOGUES > TOGUE

TOHEROA *n* large edible mollusc of New Zealand with a distinctive flavour

TOHEROAS > TOHEROA

TOHO *n* (to a hunting dog) an instruction to stop

TOHOS > TOHO

TOHUNGA *n* Māori priest

TOHUNGAS > TOHUNGA

TOIL *n* hard work ▷ *vb* work hard

TOILE *n* transparent linen or cotton fabric

TOILED > TOIL

TOILER > TOIL

TOILERS > TOIL

TOILES > TOILE

TOILET *n* a bowl connected to a drain for receiving and disposing of urine and faeces ▷ *vb* go to the toilet

TOILETED > TOILET

TOILETING > TOILET

TOILETRY *n* object or cosmetic used to clean or groom oneself

TOILETS > TOILET

TOILETTE *same as* > TOILET

TOILETTES > TOILETTE

TOILFUL *same as* > TOILSOME

TOILFULLY > TOILFUL

TOILINET *n* type of fabric with a woollen weft and a cotton or silk warp

TOILINETS > TOILINET

TOILING > TOIL

TOILINGS > TOIL

TOILLESS > TOIL

TOILS > TOIL

TOILSOME *adj* requiring hard work

TOILWORN *adj* fatigued, wearied by work

TOING *as in* *toing and froing* state of going back and forth

TOINGS > TOING

TOISE *n* obsolete French unit of length roughly equal to 2m

TOISEACH *n* ancient Celtic nobleman

TOISEACHS > TOISEACH

TOISECH *same as* > TOISEACH

TOISECHS > TOISECH

TOISES > TOISE

TOISON *n* fleece

TOISONS > TOISON

TOIT *vb* walk or move in an unsteady manner, as from old age

TOITED > TOIT

TOITING > TOIT

TOITOI *n* tall grasses with feathery fronds

TOITOIS > TOITOI

TOITS > TOIT

TOKAMAK *n* reactor used in thermonuclear experiments

TOKAMAKS > TOKAMAK

TOKAY *n* small gecko of S and SE Asia, having a retractile claw at the tip of each digit

TOKAYS > TOKAY

TOKE *n* draw on a cannabis cigarette ▷ *vb* take a draw on a cannabis cigarette

TOKED > TOKE

TOKEN *n* sign or symbol ▷ *adj* nominal or slight

TOKENED > TOKEN

TOKENING > TOKEN

TOKENISM *n* policy of making only a token effort, esp to comply with a law

TOKENISMS > TOKENISM

TOKENS > TOKEN

TOKER > TOKE

TOKERS > TOKE

TOKES > TOKE

TOKING > TOKE

TOKO *same as* > TOCO

TOKOLOGY *same as* > TOCOLOGY

TOKOLOSHE *n* (in Bantu folklore) a malevolent mythical manlike animal of short stature

TOKOLOSHI *variant of* > TOKOLOSHE

TOKOMAK *variant spelling of* > TOKAMAK

TOKOMAKS > TOKOMAK

TOKONOMA *n* recess off a living room

TOKONOMAS > TOKONOMA

TOKOS > TOKO

TOKOTOKO *n* ceremonial carved Māori walking stick

TOKOTOKOS > TOKOTOKO

TOKTOKKIE *n* large South African beetle

TOLA *n* unit of weight, used in India, equal to 180 ser or 180 grains

TOLAN *n* white crystalline derivative of acetylene

TOLANE *same as* > TOLAN

TOLANES > TOLANE

TOLANS > TOLAN

TOLAR *n* standard monetary unit of Slovenia, divided into 100 stotin

TOLARJEV > TOLAR

TOLARJI > TOLAR

TOLARS > TOLAR

TOLAS > TOLA

TOLBOOTH *same as* > TOLLBOOTH

TOLBOOTHS > TOLBOOTH

TOLD > TELL

TOLE *same as* > TOLL

TOLED > TOLE

TOLEDO *n* type of sword originally made in Toledo

TOLEDOS > TOLEDO

TOLERABLE *adj* bearable

TOLERABLY > TOLERABLE

TOLERANCE *n* acceptance of other people's rights to their own opinions or actions

TOLERANT *adj* able to tolerate the beliefs, actions, opinions, etc, of others

TOLERATE *vb* allow to exist or happen

TOLERATED > TOLERATE

TOLERATES > TOLERATE

TOLERATOR > TOLERATE

TOLES > TOLE

TOLEWARE *n* enamelled or lacquered metal ware, usually gilded

TOLEWARES > TOLEWARE

TOLIDIN *same as* > TOLIDINE

TOLIDINE *n* compound

used in dying and in chemical analysis, esp as an indicator of the presence of free chlorine in water

TOLIDINES > TOLIDINE

TOLIDINS > TOLIDIN

TOLING > TOLE

TOLINGS > TOLE

TOLL vb ring (a bell) slowly and regularly, esp to announce a death ▷ n tolling

TOLLABLE > TOLL

TOLLAGE same as > TOLL

TOLLAGES > TOLLAGE

TOLLBAR n bar blocking passage of a thoroughfare, raised on payment of a toll

TOLLBARS > TOLLBAR

TOLLBOOTH n booth or kiosk at which a toll is collected

TOLLDISH n dish used to measure out the portion of grain given to a miller as payment for his or her work

TOLLED > TOLL

TOLLER > TOLL

TOLLERS > TOLLER

TOLLGATE n gate across a toll road or bridge at which travellers must pay

TOLLGATES > TOLLGATE

TOLLHOUSE n small house at a tollgate occupied by a toll collector

TOLLIE same as > TOLLY

TOLLIES > TOLLY

TOLLING > TOLL

TOLLINGS > TOLL

TOLLMAN n man who collects tolls

TOLLMEN > TOLLMAN

TOLLS > TOLL

TOLLWAY n road on which users must pay tolls to travel

TOLLWAYS > TOLLWAY

TOLLY n castrated calf

TOLSEL n tolbooth

TOLSELS > TOLSEL

TOLSEY n tolbooth

TOLSEYS > TOLBOOTH

TOLT n type of obsolete English writ

TOLTER vb struggle or move with difficulty, as in mud

TOLTERED > TOLTER

TOLTERING > TOLTER

TOLTERS > TOLTER

TOLTS > TOLT

TOLU n sweet-smelling balsam obtained from a South American tree, used in medicine and perfume

TOLUATE n any salt or ester of any of the three isomeric forms of toluic acid

TOLUATES > TOLUATE

TOLUENE n colourless volatile flammable liquid obtained from petroleum and coal tar

TOLUENES > TOLUENE

TOLUIC as in toluic acid white crystalline derivative of toluene existing in three

isomeric forms

TOLUID n white crystalline derivative of glycocoll

TOLUIDE variant of > TOLUID

TOLUIDES > TOLUIDE

TOLUIDIDE n chemical deriving from toluene

TOLUIDIN n type of dye

TOLUIDINE n compound used in dye production

TOLUIDINS > TOLUIDIN

TOLUIDS > TOLUID

TOLUOL another name for > TOLUENE

TOLUOLE another name for > TOLUENE

TOLUOLES > TOLUOLE

TOLUOLS > TOLUOL

TOLUS > TOLU

TOLUYL n of, consisting of, or containing any of three isomeric groups $CH_3C_6H_4CO-$, derived from a toluic acid by removal of the hydroxyl group

TOLUYLS > TOLUYL

TOLYL n of, consisting of, or containing any of three isomeric groups, $CH_3C_6H_4-$, derived from toluene

TOLYLS > TOLYL

TOLZEY n tolbooth

TOLZEYS > TOLZEY

TOM n male cat ▷ adj (of an animal) male ▷ vb prostitute oneself

TOMAHAWK n fighting axe of the Native Americans

TOMAHAWKS > TOMAHAWK

TOMALLEY n fat from a lobster, called "liver", and eaten as a delicacy

TOMALLEYS > TOMALLEY

TOMAN n gold coin formerly issued in Persia

TOMANS > TOMAN

TOMATILLO n Mexican plant bearing edible berries of the same name

TOMATO n red fruit used in salads and as a vegetable

TOMATOES > TOMATO

TOMATOEY > TOMATO

TOMB n grave

TOMBAC n any of various brittle alloys containing copper and zinc and sometimes tin and arsenic: used for making cheap jewellery, etc

TOMBACK variant spelling of > TOMBAC

TOMBACKS > TOMBAC

TOMBACS > TOMBAC

TOMBAK same as > TOMBAC

TOMBAKS > TOMBAK

TOMBAL adj like or relating to a tomb

TOMBED > TOMB

TOMBIC adj of or relating to tombs

TOMBING > TOMB

TOMBLESS > TOMB

TOMBLIKE > TOMB

TOMBOC n weapon

TOMBOCS > TOMBOC

TOMBOLA n lottery with

tickets drawn from a revolving drum

TOMBOLAS > TOMBOLA

TOMBOLO n narrow sand or shingle bar linking a small island with another island or the mainland

TOMBOLOS > TOMBOLO

TOMBOY n girl who acts or dresses like a boy

TOMBOYISH > TOMBOY

TOMBOYS > TOMBOY

TOMBS > TOMB

TOMBSTONE n gravestone

TOMCAT vb (of a man) to be promiscuous

TOMCATS > TOMCAT

TOMCATTED > TOMCAT

TOMCOD n small fish resembling the cod

TOMCODS > TOMCOD

TOME n large heavy book

TOMENTA > TOMENTUM

TOMENTOSE > TOMENTUM

TOMENTOUS > TOMENTUM

TOMENTUM n feltlike covering of downy hairs on leaves and other plant parts

TOMES > TOME

TOMFOOL n fool ▷ vb act the fool

TOMFOOLED > TOMFOOL

TOMFOOLS > TOMFOOL

TOMIA > TOMIUM

TOMIAL > TOMIUM

TOMIUM n sharp edge of a bird's beak

TOMMED > TOM

TOMMIED > TOMMY

TOMMIES > TOMMY

TOMMING > TOM

TOMMY n private in the British Army ▷ vb (formerly) to exploit workers by paying them in goods rather than in money

TOMMYING > TOMMY

TOMMYROT n utter nonsense

TOMMYROTS > TOMMYROT

TOMO n shaft formed by the action of water on limestone or volcanic rock

TOMOGRAM n x-ray photograph of a selected plane section of the human body or some other solid object

TOMOGRAMS > TOMOGRAM

TOMOGRAPH n device for making tomograms

TOMORROW n (on) the day after today ▷ adv on the day after today

TOMORROWS > TOMORROW

TOMOS > TOMO

TOMPION same as > TAMPION

TOMPIONS > TOMPION

TOMPON same as > TAMPON

TOMPONED > TOMPON

TOMPONING > TOMPON

TOMPONS > TOMPON

TOMS > TOM

TOMTIT n small European bird that eats insects and seeds

TOMTITS > TOMTIT

TON n unit of weight equal to 2240 pounds or 1016 kilograms (long ton) or, in the US, 2000 pounds or 907 kilograms (short ton); style, distinction

TONAL adj written in a key

TONALITE n igneous rock found in the Italian Alps

TONALITES > TONALITE

TONALITY n presence of a musical key in a composition

TONALLY > TONAL

TONANT adj very loud

TONDI > TONDO

TONDINI > TONDINO

TONDINO n small tondo

TONDINOS > TONDINO

TONDO n circular easel painting or relief carving

TONDOS > TONDO

TONE n sound with reference to its pitch, volume, etc ▷ vb harmonize (with)

TONEARM same as > PICKUP

TONEARMS > TONEARM

TONED > TONE

TONELESS adj having no tone

TONEME n phoneme that is distinguished from another phoneme only by its tone

TONEMES > TONEME

TONEMIC > TONEME

TONEPAD n keypad used to transmit information by generating tones that can be recognised by a central system as corresponding to particular digits

TONEPADS > TONEPAD

TONER n cosmetic applied to the skin to reduce oiliness

TONERS > TONER

TONES > TONE

TONETIC adj (of a language) distinguishing words semantically by distinction of tone as well as by other sounds

TONETICS pl n area of linguistics concentrating on the use of tone to distinguish words semantically

TONETTE n small musical instrument resembling a recorder

TONETTES > TONETTE

TONEY variant spelling of > TONY

TONG n (formerly) a secret society of Chinese Americans ▷ vb gather or seize with tongs ▷ n (formerly) a Chinese secret society

TONGA n light two-wheeled vehicle used in rural areas of India

TONGAS > TONGA

TONGED > TONG

TONGER n one who uses tongs to gather oysters

TONGERS > TONGER

TONGING > TONG

TONGMAN *another word for* > TONGER

TONGMEN > TONGMAN

TONGS *pl n* large pincers for grasping and lifting

TONGSTER *n* tong member

TONGSTERS > TONGSTER

TONGUE *n* muscular organ in the mouth, used in speaking and tasting ▷ *vb* use the tongue

TONGUED > TONGUE

TONGUELET *n* small tongue

TONGUES > TONGUE

TONGUING > TONGUE

TONGUINGS > TONGUE

TONIC *n* medicine to improve body tone ▷ *adj* invigorating

TONICALLY > TONIC

TONICITY *n* state, condition, or quality of being tonic

TONICS > TONIC

TONIER > TONY

TONIES > TONY

TONIEST > TONY

TONIGHT *n* (in or during) the night or evening of this day ▷ *adv* in or during the night or evening of this day

TONIGHTS > TONIGHT

TONING > TONE

TONINGS > TONE

TONISH > TON

TONISHLY > TON

TONITE *n* explosive used in quarrying

TONITES > TONITE

TONK *vb* strike with a heavy blow ▷ *n* effete or effeminate man

TONKA as in *tonka bean* tall leguminous tree of tropical America, having fragrant black almond-shaped seeds

TONKED > TONK

TONKER > TONK

TONKERS > TONK

TONKING > TONK

TONKS > TONK

TONLET *n* skirt of a suit of armour, consisting of overlapping metal bands

TONLETS > TONLET

TONNAG *n* type of (usually tartan) shawl

TONNAGE *n* weight capacity of a ship

TONNAGES > TONNAGE

TONNAGS > TONNAG

TONNE *same as* > TON

TONNEAU *n* detachable cover to protect the rear part of an open car when it is not carrying passengers

TONNEAUS > TONNEAU

TONNEAUX > TONNEAU

TONNELL *old spelling of* > TUNNEL

TONNELLS > TONNELL

TONNER *n* something, for example a vehicle, that weighs one ton

TONNERS > TONNE

TONNES > TONNE

TONNISH > TON

TONNISHLY > TON

TONOMETER *n* instrument for measuring the pitch of a sound, esp one consisting of a set of tuning forks

TONOMETRY > TONOMETER

TONOPLAST *n* membrane enclosing a vacuole in a plant cell

TONS > TON

TONSIL *n* small gland in the throat

TONSILAR > TONSIL

TONSILLAR > TONSIL

TONSILS > TONSIL

TONSOR *n* barber

TONSORIAL *adj* of a barber or his trade

TONSORS > TONSOR

TONSURE *n* shaving of all or the top of the head as a religious or monastic practice ▷ *vb* shave the head of

TONSURED > TONSURE

TONSURES > TONSURE

TONSURING > TONSURE

TONTINE *n* annuity scheme by which several subscribers accumulate and invest a common fund out of which they receive an annuity that increases as subscribers die until the last survivor takes the whole

TONTINER *n* subscriber to a tontine

TONTINERS > TONTINER

TONTINES > TONTINE

TONUS *n* normal tension of a muscle at rest

TONUSES > TONUS

TONY *adj* stylish or distinctive ▷ *n* stylish or distinctive person

TOO *adv* also, as well

TOOART *variant spelling of* > TUART

TOOARTS > TOOART

TOOK > TAKE

TOOL *n* implement used by hand ▷ *vb* work on with a tool

TOOLBAG *n* bag for storing or carrying tools

TOOLBAGS > TOOLBAG

TOOLBAR *n* horizontal row or vertical column of selectable buttons displayed on a computer screen, allowing the user to select a variety of functions

TOOLBARS > TOOLBAR

TOOLBOX *n* box for storing or carrying tools

TOOLBOXES > TOOLBOX

TOOLED > TOOL

TOOLER > TOOL

TOOLERS > TOOL

TOOLHEAD *n* adjustable attachment for a machine tool that holds the tool in position

TOOLHEADS > TOOLHEAD

TOOLHOUSE *another word for* > TOOLSHED

TOOLING *n* any decorative work done with a tool, esp a design stamped onto a book cover, piece of leatherwork, etc

TOOLINGS > TOOLING

TOOLKIT *n* set of tools designed to be used together or for a particular purpose

TOOLKITS > TOOLKIT

TOOLLESS *adj* having no tools

TOOLMAKER *n* person who makes tools

TOOLMAN *n* person who works with tools

TOOLMEN > TOOLMAN

TOOLROOM *n* room, as in a machine shop, where tools are made or stored

TOOLROOMS > TOOLROOM

TOOLS > TOOL

TOOLSET *n* set of predefined tools associated with a particular computer application

TOOLSETS > TOOLSET

TOOLSHED *n* small shed in the garden or yard of a house used for storing tools, esp those for gardening

TOOLSHEDS > TOOLSHED

TOOM *vb* empty (something) ▷ *adj* empty

TOOMED > TOOM

TOOMER > TOOM

TOOMEST > TOOM

TOOMING > TOOM

TOOMS > TOOM

TOON *n* large meliaceous tree of the East Indies and Australia, having clusters of flowers from which a dye is obtained

TOONIE *n* Canadian two-dollar coin

TOONIES > TOONIE

TOONS > TOON

TOORIE *n* tassel or bobble on a bonnet

TOORIES > TOORIE

TOOSHIE *adj* angry

TOOT *n* short hooting sound ▷ *vb* (cause to) make such a sound

TOOTED > TOOT

TOOTER > TOOT

TOOTERS > TOOT

TOOTH *n* bonelike projection in the jaws of most vertebrates for biting and chewing

TOOTHACHE *n* pain in or near a tooth

TOOTHCOMB *n* comb with fine teeth set closely together

TOOTHED *adj* having a tooth or teeth

TOOTHFISH as in *Patagonian toothfish* Chilean sea bass

TOOTHFUL *n* little (esp alcoholic) drink

TOOTHFULS > TOOTHFUL

TOOTHIER > TOOTHY

TOOTHIEST > TOOTHY

TOOTHILY > TOOTHY

TOOTHING > TOOTH

TOOTHINGS > TOOTH

TOOTHLESS > TOOTH

TOOTHLIKE > TOOTH

TOOTHPICK *n* small stick for removing scraps of food from between the teeth

TOOTHS > TOOTH

TOOTHSOME *adj* delicious or appetizing in appearance, flavour, or smell

TOOTHWASH *n* tooth-cleaning liquid

TOOTHWORT *n* parasitic plant

TOOTHY *adj* having or showing numerous, large, or prominent teeth

TOOTING > TOOT

TOOTLE *vb* hoot softly or repeatedly ▷ *n* soft hoot or series of hoots

TOOTLED > TOOTLE

TOOTLER > TOOTLE

TOOTLERS > TOOTLE

TOOTLES > TOOTLE

TOOTLING > TOOTLE

TOOTS *Scots version of* > TUT

TOOTSED > TOOTS

TOOTSES > TOOTS

TOOTSIE *same as* > TOOTSY

TOOTSIES > TOOTSY

TOOTSING > TOOTS

TOOTSY *same as* > TOOTS

TOP *n* highest point or part ▷ *adj* at or of the top ▷ *vb* form a top on

TOPALGIA *n* pain restricted to a particular spot: a neurotic or hysterical symptom

TOPALGIAS > TOPALGIA

TOPARCH *n* ruler of a small state or realm

TOPARCHS > TOPARCH

TOPARCHY > TOPARCH

TOPAZ *n* semiprecious stone in various colours

TOPAZES > TOPAZ

TOPAZINE *adj* like topaz

TOPCOAT *n* overcoat

TOPCOATS > TOPCOAT

TOPCROSS *n* class of hybrid

TOPE *vb* drink alcohol regularly ▷ *n* small European shark

TOPECTOMY *n* (formerly) the surgical removal of part of the cerebral cortex to relieve certain psychiatric disorders

TOPED > TOPE

TOPEE *n* lightweight hat worn in tropical countries

TOPEES > TOPEE

TOPEK *same as* > TUPIK

TOPEKS > TOPEK

TOPER > TOPE

TOPERS > TOPE

TOPES > TOPE

TOPFLIGHT *adj* superior or excellent quality;

outstanding

TOPFUL *variant spelling of* > TOPFULL

TOPFULL *adj* full to the top

TOPH *n* variety of sandstone

TOPHE *variant spelling of* > TOPH

TOPHES > TOPHE

TOPHI > TOPHUS

TOPHS > TOPH

TOPHUS *n* deposit of sodium urate in the helix of the ear or surrounding a joint

TOPI *same as* > TOPEE

TOPIARIAN > TOPIARY

TOPIARIES > TOPIARY

TOPIARIST > TOPIARY

TOPIARY *n* art of trimming trees and bushes into decorative shapes ▷ *adj* of or relating to topiary

TOPIC *n* subject of a conversation, book, etc

TOPICAL *adj* relating to current events

TOPICALLY > TOPICAL

TOPICS > TOPIC

TOPING > TOPE

TOPIS > TOPI

TOPKICK *n* (formerly) sergeant

TOPKICKS > TOPKICK

TOPKNOT *n* crest, tuft, decorative bow, etc, on the top of the head

TOPKNOTS > TOPKNOT

TOPLESS *adj* (of a costume or woman) with no covering for the breasts

TOPLINE *vb* headline; be the main focus of a newspaper story

TOPLINED > TOPLINE

TOPLINER > TOPLINE

TOPLINERS > TOPLINE

TOPLINES > TOPLINE

TOPLINING > TOPLINE

TOPLOFTY *adj* haughty or pretentious

TOPMAKER *n* wool dealer

TOPMAKERS > TOPMAKER

TOPMAKING > TOPMAKER

TOPMAN *n* sailor positioned in the rigging of the topsail

TOPMAST *n* mast next above a lower mast on a sailing vessel

TOPMASTS > TOPMAST

TOPMEN > TOPMAN

TOPMINNOW *n* small American freshwater cyprinodont fish

TOPMOST *adj* highest or best

TOPNOTCH *adj* excellent

TOPO *n* picture of a mountain with details of climbing routes superimposed on it

TOPOGRAPH *n* type of x-ray photograph

TOPOI > TOPO

TOPOLOGIC > TOPOLOGY

TOPOLOGY *n* geometry of the properties of a shape which are unaffected by continuous distortion

TOPONYM *n* name of a place

TOPONYMAL > TOPONYMY

TOPONYMIC > TOPONYMY

TOPONYMS > TOPONYM

TOPONYMY *n* study of place names

TOPOS > TOPO

TOPOTYPE *n* specimen plant or animal taken from an area regarded as the typical habitat

TOPOTYPES > TOPOTYPE

TOPPED > TOP

TOPPER *n* top hat

TOPPERS > TOPPER

TOPPING > TOP

TOPPINGLY > TOP

TOPPINGS > TOP

TOPPLE *vb* (cause to) fall over

TOPPLED > TOPPLE

TOPPLES > TOPPLE

TOPPLING > TOPPLE

TOPS > TOP

TOPSAIL *n* square sail carried on a yard set on a topmast

TOPSAILS > TOPSAIL

TOPSIDE *n* lean cut of beef from the thigh containing no bone

TOPSIDER *n* person in charge

TOPSIDERS > TOPSIDER

TOPSIDES > TOPSIDE

TOPSMAN *n* chief drover

TOPSMEN > TOPSMAN

TOPSOIL *n* surface layer of soil ▷ *vb* spread topsoil on (land)

TOPSOILED > TOPSOIL

TOPSOILS > TOPSOIL

TOPSPIN *n* spin imparted to make a ball bounce or travel exceptionally far, high, or quickly, as by hitting it with a sharp forward and upward stroke

TOPSPINS > TOPSPIN

TOPSTITCH *vb* stitch a line the outside of a garment, running close to a seam

TOPSTONE *n* stone forming the top of something

TOPSTONES > TOPSTONE

TOPWORK *vb* graft shoots or twigs onto the main branches of (for example, a fruit tree) to modify its yield

TOPWORKED > TOPWORK

TOPWORKS > TOPWORK

TOQUE *same as* > TUQUE

TOQUES > TOQUE

TOQUET *same as* > TOQUE

TOQUETS > TOQUET

TOQUILLA *another name for* > JIPIJAPA

TOQUILLAS > TOQUILLA

TOR *n* high rocky hill

TORA *variant spelling of* > TORAH

TORAH *n* whole body of traditional Jewish teaching, including the Oral Law

TORAHS > TORAH

TORAN *n* (in Indian architecture) an archway,

usually wooden and often ornately carved

TORANA *same as* > TORAN

TORANAS > TORANA

TORANS > TORAN

TORAS > TORA

TORBANITE *n* type of oil shale

TORC *same as* > TORQUE

TORCH *n* small portable battery-powered lamp ▷ *vb* deliberately set (a building) on fire

TORCHABLE > TORCH

TORCHED > TORCH

TORCHER > TORCH

TORCHERE *n* tall narrow stand for holding a candelabrum

TORCHERES > TORCHERE

TORCHERS > TORCH

TORCHES > TORCH

TORCHIER *n* standing lamp with a bowl for casting light upwards and so giving all-round indirect illumination

TORCHIERE *same as* > TORCHIER

TORCHIERS > TORCHIER

TORCHIEST > TORCHY

TORCHING > TORCH

TORCHINGS > TORCH

TORCHLIKE > TORCH

TORCHON *as in torchon lace* coarse linen or cotton lace with a simple openwork pattern

TORCHONS > TORCHON

TORCHWOOD *n* rutaceous tree or shrub of Florida and the Caribbean, with hard resinous wood used for torches

TORCHY *adj* sentimental; maudlin; characteristic of a torch song

TORCS > TORC

TORCULAR *n* tourniquet

TORCULARS > TORCULAR

TORDION *n* old triple-time dance for two people

TORDIONS > TORDION

TORE *same as* > TORUS

TOREADOR *n* bullfighter

TOREADORS > TOREADOR

TORERO *n* bullfighter, esp one on foot

TOREROS > TORERO

TORES > TORE

TOREUTIC > TOREUTICS

TOREUTICS *n* art of making detailed ornamental reliefs, esp in metal, by embossing and chasing

TORGOCH *n* type of char

TORGOCHS > TORGOCH

TORI > TORUS

TORIC *adj* of, relating to, or having the form of a torus

TORICS > TORIC

TORIES > TORY

TORII *n* gateway, esp one at the entrance to a Japanese Shinto temple

TORMENT *vb* cause (someone) great suffering

▷ *n* great suffering

TORMENTA > TORMENTUM

TORMENTED > TORMENT

TORMENTER *same as* > TORMENTOR

TORMENTIL *n* creeping plant with yellow four-petalled flowers

TORMENTOR *n* person or thing that torments

TORMENTS > TORMENT

TORMENTUM *n* type of Roman catapult

TORMINA *n* complaints

TORMINAL > TORMINA

TORMINOUS > TORMINA

TORN > TEAR

TORNADE *same as* > TORNADO

TORNADES > TORNADE

TORNADIC > TORNADO

TORNADO *n* violent whirlwind

TORNADOES > TORNADO

TORNADOS > TORNADO

TORNILLO *n* shrub found in Mexico and some southwestern states of the US

TORNILLOS > TORNILLO

TORO *n* bull

TOROID *n* surface generated by rotating a closed plane curve about a coplanar line that does not intersect the curve

TOROIDAL > TOROID

TOROIDS > TOROID

TOROS > TORO

TOROSE *adj* (of a cylindrical part) having irregular swellings

TOROSITY > TOROSE

TOROT > TORAH

TOROTH > TORAH

TOROUS *same as* > TOROSE

TORPEDO *n* self-propelled underwater missile ▷ *vb* attack or destroy with or as if with torpedoes

TORPEDOED > TORPEDO

TORPEDOER > TORPEDO

TORPEDOES > TORPEDO

TORPEDOS > TORPEDO

TORPEFIED > TORPEFY

TORPEFIES > TORPEFY

TORPEFY *n* make torpid

TORPID *adj* sluggish and inactive

TORPIDITY > TORPID

TORPIDLY > TORPID

TORPIDS *n* series of boat races held at Oxford University during Lent

TORPITUDE *another word for* > TORPOR

TORPOR *n* torpid state

TORPORS > TORPOR

TORQUATE > TORQUES

TORQUATED > TORQUES

TORQUE *n* force causing rotation ▷ *vb* apply torque to (something)

TORQUED > TORQUE

TORQUER > TORQUE

TORQUERS > TORQUE

TORQUES *n* distinctive band of hair, feathers, skin, or colour around the neck of an animal

TORQUESES > TORQUES

TORQUING > TORQUE

TORR n unit of pressure equal to one millimetre of mercury (133.3 newtons per square metre)

TORREFIED > TORREFY

TORREFIES > TORREFY

TORREFY vb dry (drugs, ores, etc) by subjection to intense heat

TORRENT n rushing stream ▷ adj like or relating to a torrent

TORRENTS > TORRENT

TORRET same as > TERRET

TORRETS > TORRET

TORRID adj very hot and dry

TORRIDER > TORRID

TORRIDEST > TORRID

TORRIDITY > TORRID

TORRIDLY > TORRID

TORRIFIED > TORRIEFY

TORRIFIES > TORRIFY

TORRIFY same as > TORREFY

TORRS > TORR

TORS > TOR

TORSADE n ornamental twist or twisted cord, as on hats

TORSADES > TORSADE

TORSE same as > TORSO

TORSEL n wooden beam along the top of a wall for distributing the weight of something laid upon it

TORSELS > TORSEL

TORSES > TORSE

TORSI > TORSO

TORSION n twisting of a part by equal forces being applied at both ends but in opposite directions

TORSIONAL > TORSION

TORSIONS > TORSION

TORSIVE adj twisted

TORSK n fish with a single long dorsal fin

TORSKS > TORSK

TORSO n trunk of the human body

TORSOS > TORSO

TORT n civil wrong or injury for which damages may be claimed

TORTA n (in mining) a flat circular pile of silver ore

TORTAS > TORTA

TORTE n rich cake, originating in Austria, usually decorated or filled with cream, fruit, nuts, and jam

TORTEN > TORTE

TORTES > TORTE

TORTILE adj twisted or coiled

TORTILITY > TORTILE

TORTILLA n thin Mexican pancake

TORTILLAS > TORTILLA

TORTILLON another word for > STUMP

TORTIOUS adj having the nature of or involving a tort

TORTIVE adj twisted

TORTOISE n slow-moving land reptile with a dome-shaped shell

TORTOISES > TORTOISE

TORTONI n rich ice cream often flavoured with sherry

TORTONIS > TORTONI

TORTRICES > TORTRIX

TORTRICID n small moth of the chiefly temperate family *Tortricidae*, ▷ adj of, relating to, or belonging to the family *Tortricidae*

TORTRIX n type of moth

TORTRIXES > TORTRIX

TORTS > TORT

TORTUOUS adj winding or twisting

TORTURE vb cause (someone) severe pain or mental anguish ▷ n severe physical or mental pain

TORTURED > TORTURE

TORTURER > TORTURE

TORTURERS > TORTURE

TORTURES > TORTURE

TORTURING > TORTURE

TORTUROUS > TORTURE

TORULA n species of fungal microorganisms

TORULAE > TORULA

TORULAS > TORULA

TORULI > TORULUS

TORULIN n vitamin found in yeast

TORULINS > TORULIN

TORULOSE adj (of something cylindrical) alternately swollen and pinched along its length

TORULOSES > TORULOSIS

TORULOSIS n infection by one of the torula

TORULUS n socket in an insect's head in which its antenna is attached

TORUS n large convex moulding approximately semicircular in cross section, esp one used on the base of a classical column

TORY n ultraconservative or reactionary person ▷ adj ultraconservative or reactionary

TOSA n large reddish dog, originally bred for fighting

TOSAS > TOSA

TOSE same as > TOZE

TOSED > TOSE

TOSES > TOSE

TOSH n nonsense ▷ vb tidy or trim

TOSHACH n military leader of a clan

TOSHACHS > TOSHACH

TOSHED > TOSH

TOSHER > TOSH

TOSHERS > TOSH

TOSHES > TOSH

TOSHIER > TOSHY

TOSHIEST > TOSHY

TOSHING > TOSH

TOSHY adj neat; trim

TOSING > TOSE

TOSS vb throw lightly ▷ n tossing

TOSSED > TOSS

TOSSEN old past participle of > TOSS

TOSSER n stupid or despicable person

TOSSERS > TOSSER

TOSSES > TOSS

TOSSIER > TOSSY

TOSSIEST > TOSSY

TOSSILY > TOSSY

TOSSING > TOSS

TOSSINGS > TOSS

TOSSPOT n habitual drinker

TOSSPOTS > TOSSPOT

TOSSUP n an instance of tossing up a coin

TOSSUPS > TOSSUP

TOSSY adj impudent

TOST old past participle of > TOSS

TOSTADA n crispy deep-fried tortilla topped with meat, cheese, and refried beans

TOSTADAS > TOSTADA

TOSTADO same as > TOSTADA

TOSTADOS > TOSTADO

TOT n small child ▷ vb total

TOTABLE > TOTE

TOTAL n whole, esp a sum of parts ▷ adj complete ▷ vb amount to

TOTALED > TOTAL

TOTALING > TOTAL

TOTALISE same as > TOTALIZE

TOTALISED > TOTALISE

TOTALISER > TOTALISE

TOTALISES > TOTALISE

TOTALISM n practice of a dictatorial one party state that regulates every form of life

TOTALISMS > TOTALISM

TOTALIST > TOTALISM

TOTALISTS > TOTALISM

TOTALITY n whole amount

TOTALIZE vb combine or make into a total

TOTALIZED > TOTALIZE

TOTALIZER > TOTALIZE

TOTALIZES > TOTALIZE

TOTALLED > TOTAL

TOTALLING > TOTAL

TOTALLY > TOTAL

TOTALS > TOTAL

TOTANUS another name for > REDSHANK

TOTANUSES > TOTANUS

TOTAQUINE n mixture of quinine and other alkaloids derived from cinchona bark, used as a substitute for quinine in treating malaria

TOTARA n tall coniferous forest tree of New Zealand, with a hard durable wood

TOTARAS > TOTARA

TOTE vb carry (a gun etc) ▷ n act of or an instance of toting

TOTEABLE > TOTE

TOTED > TOTE

TOTEM n tribal badge or emblem

TOTEMIC > TOTEM

TOTEMISM n belief in kinship of groups or individuals having a common totem

TOTEMISMS > TOTEMISM

TOTEMIST > TOTEMISM

TOTEMISTS > TOTEMISM

TOTEMITE > TOTEMISM

TOTEMITES > TOTEMITE

TOTEMS > TOTEM

TOTER > TOTE

TOTERS > TOTE

TOTES > TOTE

TOTHER n other

TOTIENT n quantity of numbers less than, and sharing no common factors with, a given number

TOTIENTS > TOTIENT

TOTING > TOTE

TOTITIVE n number less than, and having no common factors with, a given number

TOTITIVES > TOTITIVE

TOTS > TOT

TOTTED > TOT

TOTTER vb move unsteadily ▷ n act or an instance of tottering

TOTTERED > TOTTER

TOTTERER > TOTTER

TOTTERERS > TOTTER

TOTTERING > TOTTER

TOTTERS > TOTTER

TOTTERY > TOTTER

TOTTIE adj very small

TOTTIER > TOTTY

TOTTIES > TOTTY

TOTTIEST > TOTTY

TOTTING > TOT

TOTTINGS > TOT

TOTTY n people, esp women, collectively considered as sexual objects ▷ adj very small

TOUCAN n tropical American bird with a large bill

TOUCANET n type of small toucan

TOUCANETS > TOUCAN

TOUCANS > TOUCAN

TOUCH vb come into contact with ▷ n sense by which an object's qualities are perceived when they come into contact with part of the body ▷ adj of a non-contact version of particular sport

TOUCHABLE > TOUCH

TOUCHBACK n play in which the ball is put down by a player behind his own goal line when the ball has been put across the goal line by an opponent

TOUCHDOWN n moment at which a landing aircraft or spacecraft comes into contact with the landing surface ▷ vb (of an aircraft or spacecraft) to land

TOUCHE interj acknowledgment of the striking home of a remark or witty reply

TOUCHED *adj* emotionally moved

TOUCHER > TOUCH

TOUCHERS > TOUCH

TOUCHES > TOUCH

TOUCHHOLE *n* hole in the breech of early cannon and firearms through which the charge was ignited

TOUCHIER > TOUCHY

TOUCHIEST > TOUCHY

TOUCHILY > TOUCHY

TOUCHING *adj* emotionally moving ▷ *prep* relating to or concerning

TOUCHINGS > TOUCH

TOUCHLESS > TOUCH

TOUCHLINE *n* side line of the pitch in some games

TOUCHMARK *n* maker's mark stamped on pewter objects

TOUCHPAD *n* part of laptop computer functioning like mouse

TOUCHPADS > TOUCHPAD

TOUCHTONE *adj* of or relating to a telephone dialling system in which each of the buttons pressed generates a tone of a different pitch, which is transmitted to the exchange

TOUCHUP *n* renovation or retouching, as of a painting

TOUCHUPS > TOUCHUP

TOUCHWOOD *n* something, esp dry wood, used as tinder

TOUCHY *adj* easily offended

TOUGH *adj* strong or resilient ▷ *n* rough violent person

TOUGHED > TOUGH

TOUGHEN *vb* make or become tough or tougher

TOUGHENED > TOUGHEN

TOUGHENER > TOUGHEN

TOUGHENS > TOUGHEN

TOUGHER > TOUGH

TOUGHEST > TOUGH

TOUGHIE *n* person who is tough

TOUGHIES > TOUGHIE

TOUGHING > TOUGH

TOUGHISH > TOUGH

TOUGHLY > TOUGH

TOUGHNESS *n* quality or an instance of being tough

TOUGHS > TOUGH

TOUGHY *same as* > TOUGHIE

TOUK *same as* > TUCK

TOUKED > TOUK

TOUKING > TOUK

TOUKS > TOUK

TOUN *n* town

TOUNS > TOUN

TOUPEE *n* small wig

TOUPEES > TOUPEE

TOUPET *same as* > TOUPEE

TOUPETS > TOUPET

TOUR *n* journey visiting places of interest along the way ▷ *vb* make a tour (of)

TOURACO *n* any brightly coloured crested arboreal African bird of the family *Musophagidae*: order

Cuculiformes (cuckoos, etc)

TOURACOS > TOURACO

TOURED > TOUR

TOURER *n* large open car with a folding top, usually seating a driver and four passengers

TOURERS > TOURER

TOURIE *same as* > TOORIE

TOURIES > TOURIE

TOURING > TOUR

TOURINGS > TOUR

TOURISM *n* tourist travel as an industry

TOURISMS > TOURISM

TOURIST *n* person travelling for pleasure ▷ *adj* of or relating to tourists or tourism

TOURISTA *variant of* > TOURIST

TOURISTAS > TOURISTA

TOURISTED *adj* busy with tourists

TOURISTIC > TOURIST

TOURISTS > TOURIST

TOURISTY *adj* informal term for full of tourists or tourist attractions

TOURNEDOS *n* thick round steak of beef

TOURNEY *n* knightly tournament ▷ *vb* engage in a tourney

TOURNEYED > TOURNEY

TOURNEYER > TOURNEY

TOURNEYS > TOURNEY

TOURNURE *n* outline or contour

TOURNURES > TOURNURE

TOURS > TOUR

TOURTIERE *n* type of meat pie

TOUSE *vb* tangle, ruffle, or disarrange; treat roughly

TOUSED > TOUSE

TOUSER > TOUSE

TOUSERS > TOUSE

TOUSES > TOUSE

TOUSIER > TOUSY

TOUSIEST > TOUSY

TOUSING > TOUSE

TOUSINGS > TOUSE

TOUSLE *vb* make (hair or clothes) ruffled and untidy ▷ *n* disorderly, tangled, or rumpled state

TOUSLED > TOUSLE

TOUSLES > TOUSLE

TOUSLING > TOUSLE

TOUSTIE *adj* irritable; testy

TOUSTIER > TOUSTIE

TOUSTIEST > TOUSTIE

TOUSY *adj* tousled

TOUT *vb* seek business in a persistent manner ▷ *n* person who sells tickets for a popular event at inflated prices

TOUTED > TOUT

TOUTER > TOUT

TOUTERS > TOUT

TOUTIE childishly irritable or sullen

TOUTIER > TOUTIE

TOUTIEST > TOUTIE

TOUTING > TOUT

TOUTS > TOUT

TOUZE *variant spelling of* > TOUSE

TOUZED > TOUZE

TOUZES > TOUZE

TOUZIER > TOUZY

TOUZIEST > TOUZY

TOUZING > TOUZE

TOUZLE *rare spelling of* > TOUSLE

TOUZLED > TOUZLE

TOUZLES > TOUZLE

TOUZLING > TOUZLE

TOUZY *variant spelling of* > TOUSY

TOVARICH *same as* > TOVARISCH

TOVARISCH *n* comrade: a term of address

TOVARISH *same as* > TOVARISCH

TOW *vb* drag, esp by means of a rope ▷ *n* towing

TOWABLE > TOW

TOWAGE *n* charge made for towing

TOWAGES > TOWAGE

TOWARD *same as* > TOWARDS

TOWARDLY *adj* compliant

TOWARDS *prep* in the direction of

TOWAWAY *n* vehicle which has been towed away (because, for example, it was illegally parked)

TOWAWAYS > TOWAWAY

TOWBAR *n* metal bar on a car for towing vehicles

TOWBARS > TOWBAR

TOWBOAT *n* another word for tug (the boat)

TOWBOATS > TOWBOAT

TOWED > TOW

TOWEL *n* cloth for drying things ▷ *vb* dry or wipe with a towel

TOWELED > TOWEL

TOWELETTE *n* paper towel

TOWELHEAD *n* offensive term for someone who wears a turban

TOWELING > TOWEL

TOWELINGS > TOWEL

TOWELLED > TOWEL

TOWELLING *n* material used for making towels

TOWELS > TOWEL

TOWER *n* tall structure, often forming part of a larger building

TOWERED *adj* having a tower or towers

TOWERIER > TOWERY

TOWERIEST > TOWERY

TOWERING *adj* very tall or impressive

TOWERLESS *adj* not having a tower

TOWERLIKE *adj* like a tower

TOWERS > TOWER

TOWERY *adj* with towers

TOWHEAD *n* often disparaging term for a person with blond or yellowish hair

TOWHEADED *adj* having blonde or yellowish hair

TOWHEADS > TOWHEAD

TOWHEE *n* any of various North American brownish-coloured sparrows of the genera *Pipilo* and *Chlorura*

TOWHEES > TOWHEE

TOWIE *n* truck used for towing

TOWIER > TOW

TOWIES > TOWIE

TOWIEST > TOW

TOWING > TOW

TOWINGS > TOW

TOWKAY *n* sir

TOWKAYS > TOWKAY

TOWLINE *same as* > TOWROPE

TOWLINES > TOWLINE

TOWMON *same as* > TOWMOND

TOWMOND *n* old word for year

TOWMONDS > TOWMOND

TOWMONS > TOWMON

TOWMONT *same as* > TOWMOND

TOWMONTS > TOWMONT

TOWN *n* group of buildings larger than a village

TOWNEE *same as* > TOWNIE

TOWNEES > TOWNEE

TOWNFOLK *same as* > TOWNSFOLK

TOWNHALL *n* chief building in which municipal business is transacted, often with a hall for public meetings

TOWNHOME *another word for* > TOWNHOUSE

TOWNHOMES > TOWNHOME

TOWNHOUSE *n* terraced house in an urban area, esp a fashionable one, often having the main living room on the first floor with an integral garage on the ground floor

TOWNIE *n* often disparaging term for a resident in a town, esp as distinct from country dwellers

TOWNIER > TOWNY

TOWNIES > TOWNY

TOWNIEST > TOWNY

TOWNISH > TOWN

TOWNLAND *n* division of land of various sizes

TOWNLANDS > TOWNLAND

TOWNLESS > TOWN

TOWNLET *n* small town

TOWNLETS > TOWNLET

TOWNLIER > TOWNLY

TOWNLIEST > TOWNLY

TOWNLING *n* person who lives in a town

TOWNLINGS > TOWNLING

TOWNLY *adj* characteristic of a town

TOWNS > TOWN

TOWNSCAPE *n* view of an urban scene

TOWNSFOLK *n* people of a town

TOWNSHIP *n* small town

TOWNSHIPS > TOWNSHIP

TOWNSKIP *n* old term for a mischievous and roguish child who frequents city streets

TOWNSKIPS > TOWNSKIP

TOWNSMAN *n* inhabitant of a town

TOWNSMEN > TOWNSMAN

TOWNWEAR *n* clothes suitable for wearing while persuing activities usually associated with towns

TOWNY *adj* characteristic of a town

TOWPATH *n* path beside a canal or river, originally for horses towing boats

TOWPATHS > TOWPATH

TOWPLANE *n* aeroplane that tows gliders

TOWPLANES > TOWPLANE

TOWROPE *n* rope or cable used for towing a vehicle or vessel

TOWROPES > TOWROPE

TOWS > TOW

TOWSACK *n* sack made from tow

TOWSACKS > TOWSACK

TOWSE *same as* > TOUSE

TOWSED > TOWSE

TOWSER > TOWSE

TOWSERS > TOWSE

TOWSES > TOWSE

TOWSIER > TOWSY

TOWSIEST > TOWSY

TOWSING > TOWSE

TOWSY *same as* > TOUSY

TOWT *vb* sulk

TOWTED > TOWT

TOWTING > TOWT

TOWTS > TOWT

TOWY > TOW

TOWZE *same as* > TOUSE

TOWZED > TOWZE

TOWZES > TOWZE

TOWZIER > TOWZY

TOWZIEST > TOWZY

TOWZING > TOWZE

TOWZY *same as* > TOUSY

TOXAEMIA *n* blood poisoning

TOXAEMIAS > TOXAEMIA

TOXAEMIC > TOXAEMIA

TOXAPHENE *n* amber waxy solid with a pleasant pine odour, consisting of chlorinated terpenes, esp chlorinated camphene: used as an insecticide

TOXEMIA *same as* > TOXAEMIA

TOXEMIAS > TOXEMIA

TOXEMIC > TOXAEMIA

TOXIC *adj* poisonous ▷ *n* toxic substance

TOXICAL *adj* toxic

TOXICALLY > TOXIC

TOXICANT *n* toxic substance ▷ *adj* poisonous

TOXICANTS > TOXICANT

TOXICITY *n* degree of strength of a poison

TOXICOSES > TOXICOSIS

TOXICOSIS *n* any disease or condition caused by poisoning

TOXICS > TOXIC

TOXIGENIC *adj* producing poison

TOXIN *n* poison of bacterial origin

TOXINE *nonstandard variant spelling of* > TOXIN

TOXINES > TOXINE

TOXINS > TOXIN

TOXOCARA *n* parasitic worm infesting the intestines of cats and dogs

TOXOCARAS > TOXOCARA

TOXOID *n* toxin that has been treated to reduce its toxicity and is used in immunization to stimulate production of antitoxins

TOXOIDS > TOXOID

TOXOPHILY *n* archer

TOY *n* something designed to be played with ▷ *adj* designed to be played with ▷ *vb* play, fiddle, or flirt

TOYED > TOY

TOYER > TOY

TOYERS > TOY

TOYING > TOY

TOYINGS > TOY

TOYISH *adj* resembling a toy

TOYISHLY > TOYISH

TOYLESOME *old spelling of* > TOILSOME

TOYLESS > TOY

TOYLIKE > TOY

TOYLSOM *old spelling of* > TOILSOME

TOYMAN *n* man who sells toys

TOYMEN > TOYMAN

TOYO *n* Japanese straw-like material made out of rice paper and used to make hats

TOYON *n* shrub related to the rose

TOYONS > TOYON

TOYOS > TOYO

TOYS > TOY

TOYSHOP *n* shop selling toys

TOYSHOPS > TOYSHOP

TOYSOME *adj* playful

TOYTOWN *adj* having an unreal and picturesque appearance

TOYWOMAN *n* woman who sells toys

TOYWOMEN > TOYWOMAN

TOZE *vb* tease out; (of wool, etc) card

TOZED > TOZE

TOZES > TOZE

TOZIE *n* type of shawl

TOZIES > TOZIE

TOZING > TOZE

TRABEATE *same as* > TRABEATED

TRABEATED *adj* constructed with horizontal beams as opposed to arches

TRABECULA *n* any of various rod-shaped structures that divide organs into separate chambers

TRABS *pl n* training shoes

TRACE *vb* locate or work out (the cause of something) ▷ *n* track left by something

TRACEABLE > TRACE

TRACEABLY > TRACE

TRACED > TRACE

TRACELESS > TRACE

TRACER *n* projectile which leaves a visible trail

TRACERIED > TRACERY

TRACERIES > TRACERY

TRACERS > TRACER

TRACERY *n* pattern of interlacing lines

TRACES > TRACE

TRACEUR *n* parkour participant

TRACEURS > TRACEUR

TRACHEA *n* windpipe

TRACHEAE > TRACHEA

TRACHEAL > TRACHEA

TRACHEARY *adj* using tracheae to breathe

TRACHEAS > TRACHEA

TRACHEATE > TRACHEA

TRACHEID *n* element of xylem tissue consisting of an elongated lignified cell with tapering ends and large pits

TRACHEIDE *same as* > TRACHEID

TRACHEIDS > TRACHEID

TRACHEOLE *n* small trachea found in some insects

TRACHINUS *n* weever fish

TRACHITIS *n* another spelling of tracheitis (inflammation of the trachea)

TRACHLE *vb* (of hair, clothing, etc) make untidy; dishevel; rumple

TRACHLED > TRACHLE

TRACHLES > TRACHLE

TRACHLING > TRACHLE

TRACHOMA *n* chronic contagious disease of the eye characterized by inflammation of the inner surface of the lids and the formation of scar tissue

TRACHOMAS > TRACHOMA

TRACHYTE *n* light-coloured fine-grained volcanic rock

TRACHYTES > TRACHYTE

TRACHYTIC *adj* (of the texture of certain igneous rocks) characterized by a parallel arrangement of crystals, which mark the flow of the lava when still molten

TRACING *n* traced copy

TRACINGS > TRACING

TRACK *n* rough road or path ▷ *vb* follow the trail or path of

TRACKABLE > TRACK

TRACKAGE *n* collective term for the railway tracks in general, or those in a given area or belonging to a particular company, etc

TRACKAGES > TRACKAGE

TRACKBALL *n* device consisting of a small ball, mounted in a cup, which can be rotated to move the cursor around the screen

TRACKED > TRACK

TRACKER > TRACK

TRACKERS > TRACK

TRACKING *n* act or process of following something or someone

TRACKINGS > TRACKING

TRACKLESS *adj* having or leaving no trace or trail

TRACKMAN *n* workman who lays and maintains railway track

TRACKMEN > TRACKMAN

TRACKPAD *same as* > TOUCHPAD

TRACKPADS > TRACKPAD

TRACKROAD *another word for* > TOWPATH

TRACKS > TRACK

TRACKSIDE *n* area alongside a track

TRACKSUIT *n* warm loose-fitting suit worn by athletes etc, esp during training

TRACKWAY *n* path or track

TRACKWAYS > TRACKWAY

TRACT *n* wide area ▷ *vb* track

TRACTABLE *adj* easy to manage or control

TRACTABLY > TRACTABLE

TRACTATE *n* short tract

TRACTATES > TRACTATE

TRACTATOR *n* person who writes tracts

TRACTED > TRACT

TRACTILE *adj* capable of being drawn out

TRACTING > TRACT

TRACTION *n* pulling, esp by engine power

TRACTIONS > TRACTION

TRACTIVE > TRACTION

TRACTOR *n* motor vehicle with large rear wheels for pulling farm machinery

TRACTORS > TRACTOR

TRACTRIX *n* (in geometry) type of curve

TRACTS > TRACT

TRACTUS *n* anthem sung in some RC masses

TRACTUSES > TRACTUS

TRAD *n* traditional jazz, as revived in the 1950s

TRADABLE > TRADE

TRADE *n* buying, selling, or exchange of goods ▷ *vb* buy and sell ▷ *adj* intended for or available only to people in industry or business

TRADEABLE > TRADE

TRADED > TRADE

TRADEFUL *adj* (of shops, for example) full of trade

TRADELESS > TRADE

TRADEMARK *n* (legally registered) name or symbol used by a firm to distinguish its goods ▷ *vb* label with a trademark

TRADENAME *n* name used by a trade to refer to a commodity, service, etc

TRADEOFF *n* exchange, esp as a compromise

TRADEOFFS > TRADEOFF

TRADER *n* person who

engages in trade

TRADERS > TRADER

TRADES > TRADE

TRADESMAN *n* skilled worker

TRADESMEN > TRADESMAN

TRADING > TRADE

TRADINGS > TRADE

TRADITION *n* handing down from generation to generation of customs and beliefs

TRADITIVE *adj* traditional

TRADITOR *n* Christian who betrayed his fellow Christians at the time of the Roman persecutions

TRADITORS > TRADITOR

TRADS > TRAD

TRADUCE *vb* slander

TRADUCED > TRADUCE

TRADUCER > TRADUCE

TRADUCERS > TRADUCE

TRADUCES > TRADUCE

TRADUCIAN > TRADUCE

TRADUCING > TRADUCE

TRAFFIC *n* vehicles coming and going on a road ▷ *vb* trade, usu illicitly

TRAFFICKY *adj* (of a street, area, town, etc) busy with motor vehicles

TRAFFICS > TRAFFIC

TRAGAL > TRAGUS

TRAGEDIAN *n* person who acts in or writes tragedies

TRAGEDIES > TRAGEDY

TRAGEDY *n* shocking or sad event

TRAGELAPH *n* mythical animal: a cross between a goat and a stag

TRAGI > TRAGUS

TRAGIC *adj* of or like a tragedy ▷ *n* tragedian

TRAGICAL *same as* > TRAGIC

TRAGICS > TRAGIC

TRAGOPAN *n* pheasant of S and SE Asia, with a brilliant plumage and brightly coloured fleshy processes on the head

TRAGOPANS > TRAGOPAN

TRAGULE *n* mouse deer

TRAGULES > TRAGULE

TRAGULINE *adj* like or characteristic of a tragule

TRAGUS *n* cartilaginous fleshy projection that partially covers the entrance to the external ear

TRAHISON *n* treason

TRAHISONS > TRAHISON

TRAIK *vb* trudge; trek with difficulty

TRAIKED > TRAIK

TRAIKING > TRAIK

TRAIKIT > TRAIK

TRAIKS > TRAIK

TRAIL *n* path, track, or road ▷ *vb* drag along the ground

TRAILABLE *adj* capable of being trailed

TRAILED > TRAIL

TRAILER *n* vehicle designed to be towed by another vehicle ▷ *vb* use a trailer to

advertise (something)

TRAILERED > TRAILER

TRAILERS > TRAILER

TRAILHEAD *n* place where a trail begins

TRAILING *adj* (of a plant) having a long stem which spreads over the ground or hangs loosely

TRAILLESS *adj* without trail

TRAILS > TRAIL

TRAILSIDE *adj* beside a trail

TRAIN *vb* instruct in a skill ▷ *n* line of railway coaches or wagons drawn by an engine

TRAINABLE > TRAIN

TRAINBAND *n* company of English militia from the 16th to the 18th century

TRAINED > TRAIN

TRAINEE *n* person being trained ▷ *adj* (of a person) undergoing training

TRAINEES > TRAINEE

TRAINER *n* person who trains an athlete or sportsman

TRAINERS *pl n* shoes in the style of those used for sports training

TRAINFUL *n* quantity of people or cargo that would be capable of filling a train

TRAINFULS > TRAINFUL

TRAINING *n* process of bringing a person to an agreed standard of proficiency by practice and instruction

TRAININGS > TRAINING

TRAINLESS > TRAIN

TRAINLOAD *n* quantity of people or cargo sufficient to fill a train

TRAINMAN *n* man who works on a train

TRAINMEN > TRAINMAN

TRAINS > TRAIN

TRAINWAY *n* railway track; channel in a built-up area through which a train passes

TRAINWAYS > TRAINWAY

TRAIPSE *vb* walk wearily ▷ *n* long or tiring walk

TRAIPSED > TRAIPSE

TRAIPSES > TRAIPSE

TRAIPSING > TRAIPSE

TRAIT *n* characteristic feature

TRAITOR *n* person guilty of treason or treachery

TRAITORLY *adj* of or characteristic of a traitor

TRAITORS > TRAITOR

TRAITRESS > TRAITOR

TRAITS > TRAIT

TRAJECT *vb* transport or transmit

TRAJECTED > TRAJECT

TRAJECTS > TRAJECT

TRAM *same as* > TRAMMEL

TRAMCAR *same as* > TRAM

TRAMCARS > TRAMCAR

TRAMEL *variant spelling of* > TRAMMEL

TRAMELED > TRAMEL

TRAMELING > TRAMEL

TRAMELL *variant spelling of* > TRAMMEL

TRAMELLED > TRAMELL

TRAMELLS > TRAMELL

TRAMELS > TRAMEL

TRAMLESS > TRAM

TRAMLINE *n* tracks on which a tram runs

TRAMLINED *adj* having tramlines

TRAMLINES > TRAMLINE

TRAMMED > TRAM

TRAMMEL *n* hindrance to free action or movement ▷ *vb* hinder or restrain

TRAMMELED > TRAMMEL

TRAMMELER > TRAMMEL

TRAMMELS > TRAMMEL

TRAMMIE *n* conductor or driver of a tram

TRAMMIES > TRAMMIE

TRAMMING > TRAM

TRAMP *vb* travel on foot, hike ▷ *n* homeless person who travels on foot

TRAMPED > TRAMP

TRAMPER *n* person who tramps

TRAMPERS > TRAMPER

TRAMPET *variant spelling of* > TRAMPETTE

TRAMPETS > TRAMPET

TRAMPETTE *n* small trampoline

TRAMPIER > TRAMPY

TRAMPIEST > TRAMPY

TRAMPING > TRAMP

TRAMPINGS > TRAMP

TRAMPISH > TRAMP

TRAMPLE *vb* tread on and crush ▷ *n* action or sound of trampling

TRAMPLED > TRAMPLE

TRAMPLER > TRAMPLE

TRAMPLERS > TRAMPLE

TRAMPLES > TRAMPLE

TRAMPLING > TRAMPLE

TRAMPOLIN *n* variant of trampoline: a tough canvass sheet suspended by springs from a frame, used by acrobats, gymnasts, etc

TRAMPS > TRAMP

TRAMPY *adj* (of woman) disreputable

TRAMROAD *same as* > TRAMWAY

TRAMROADS > TRAMROAD

TRAMS > TRAM

TRAMWAY *same as* > TRAMLINE

TRAMWAYS > TRAMWAY

TRANCE *n* unconscious or dazed state ▷ *vb* put into or as into a trance

TRANCED > TRANCE

TRANCEDLY > TRANCE

TRANCES > TRANCE

TRANCHE *n* portion of something large, esp a sum of money

TRANCHES > TRANCHE

TRANCHET *n* stoneage cutting tool

TRANCHETS > TRANCHET

TRANCING > TRANCE

TRANECT *n* ferry

TRANECTS > TRANECT

TRANGAM *n* bauble or trinket

TRANGAMS > TRANGAM

TRANGLE *n* (in heraldry) a small fesse

TRANGLES > TRANGLE

TRANK *n* short form of tranquillizer: drug that calms a person

TRANKS > TRANK

TRANKUM *same as* > TRANGAM

TRANKUMS > TRANKUM

TRANNIE *n* transistor radio

TRANNIES > TRANNY

TRANNY *same as* > TRANNIE

TRANQ *same as* > TRANK

TRANQS > TRANQ

TRANQUIL *adj* calm and quiet

TRANS *n* short from of translation

TRANSACT *vb* conduct or negotiate (a business deal)

TRANSACTS > TRANSACT

TRANSAXLE *n* combined axle and gearbox

TRANSCEND *vb* rise above

TRANSDUCE *vb* change one form of energy to another

TRANSE *n* way through; passage

TRANSECT *n* sample strip of land used to monitor plant distribution and animal populations within a given area ▷ *vb* cut or divide crossways

TRANSECTS > TRANSECT

TRANSENNA *n* screen around a shrine

TRANSEPT *n* either of the two shorter wings of a cross-shaped church

TRANSEPTS > TRANSEPT

TRANSES > TRANSE

TRANSEUNT *adj* (of a mental act) causing effects outside the mind

TRANSFARD *old past participle of* > TRANSFER

TRANSFECT *vb* transfer genetic material isolated from a cell or virus into another cell

TRANSFER *vb* move or send from one person or place to another ▷ *n* transferring

TRANSFERS > TRANSFER

TRANSFIX *vb* astound or stun

TRANSFIXT > TRANSFIX

TRANSFORM *vb* change the shape or character of ▷ *n* result of a mathematical transformation

TRANSFUSE *vb* give a transfusion to

TRANSGENE *n* gene that is transferred from an organism of one species to an organism of another species by genetic engineering

TRANSHIP *same*

as > TRANSSHIP
TRANSHIPS > TRANSHIP
TRANSHUME *vb* (of livestock) move to suitable grazing grounds according to the season
TRANSIENT *same as* > TRANSEUNT
TRANSIRE *n* document allowing goods to pass through customs
TRANSIRES > TRANSIRE
TRANSIT *n* passage or conveyance of goods or people ▷ *vb* make transit
TRANSITED > TRANSIT
TRANSITS > TRANSIT
TRANSLATE *vb* turn from one language into another
TRANSMEW *old variant of* > TRANSMUTE
TRANSMEWS > TRANSMEW
TRANSMIT *vb* pass (something) from one person or place to another
TRANSMITS > TRANSMIT
> TRANSMITTIVITY
TRANSMOVE *vb* change the form, character, or substance of
TRANSMUTE *vb* change the form or nature of
TRANSOM *n* horizontal bar across a window
TRANSOMED > TRANSOM
TRANSOMS > TRANSOM
TRANSONIC *adj* of or relating to conditions when travelling at or near the speed of sound
TRANSPIRE *vb* become known
TRANSPORT *vb* convey from one place to another ▷ *n* business or system of transporting
TRANSPOSE *vb* interchange two things ▷ *n* matrix resulting from interchanging the rows and columns of a given matrix
TRANSSHIP *vb* transfer or be transferred from one ship or vehicle to another
TRANSUDE *vb* (of a fluid) ooze or pass through interstices, pores, or small holes
TRANSUDED > TRANSUDE
TRANSUDES > TRANSUDE
TRANSUME *vb* make an official transcription of
TRANSUMED > TRANSUME
TRANSUMES > TRANSUME
TRANSUMPT *n* official transcription
TRANSVEST *vb* wear clothes traditionally associated with the opposite sex
TRANT *vb* travel from place to place selling goods
TRANTED > TRANT
TRANTER > TRANT
TRANTERS > TRANT
TRANTING > TRANT
TRANTS > TRANT

TRAP *n* device for catching animals ▷ *vb* catch
TRAPAN *same as* > TREPAN
TRAPANNED > TRAPAN
TRAPANNER > TRAPAN
TRAPANS > TRAPAN
TRAPBALL *n* old ball game in which a ball is placed in a see-saw device called a trap, flicked up by a batsman hitting one end of the trap, and then hit with a bat
TRAPBALLS > TRAPBALL
TRAPDOOR *n* door in floor or roof
TRAPDOORS > TRAPDOOR
TRAPE *same as* > TRAIPSE
TRAPED > TRAPE
TRAPES *same as* > TRAIPSE
TRAPESED > TRAPES
TRAPESES > TRAPES
TRAPESING > TRAPES
TRAPEZE *n* horizontal bar suspended from two ropes, used by circus acrobats ▷ *vb* swing on a trapeze
TRAPEZED > TRAPEZE
TRAPEZES > TRAPEZE
TRAPEZIA > TRAPEZIUM
TRAPEZIAL > TRAPEZIUM
TRAPEZII > TRAPEZIUS
TRAPEZING > TRAPEZE
TRAPEZIST *n* trapeze artist
TRAPEZIUM *same as* > TRAPEZOID
TRAPEZIUS *n* either of two flat triangular muscles, one covering each side of the back and shoulders, that rotate the shoulder blades
TRAPEZOID *same as* > TRAPEZIUM
TRAPING > TRAPE
TRAPLIKE > TRAP
TRAPLINE *n* line of traps
TRAPLINES > TRAPLINE
TRAPNEST *n* nest that holds a hen in place so that the number of eggs it alone produces can be counted
TRAPNESTS > TRAPNEST
TRAPPEAN *adj* of, relating to, or consisting of igneous rock, esp a basalt
TRAPPED > TRAP
TRAPPER *n* person who traps animals for their fur
TRAPPERS > TRAPPER
TRAPPIER > TRAPPY
TRAPPIEST > TRAPPY
TRAPPING > TRAP
TRAPPINGS *pl n* accessories that symbolize an office or position
TRAPPOSE *adj* of or relating to traprock
TRAPPOUS *same as* > TRAPPOSE
TRAPPY *adj* having many traps
TRAPROCK *another name for* > TRAP
TRAPROCKS > TRAPROCK
TRAPS > TRAP
TRAPT *old past participle of* > TRAP

TRAPUNTO *n* type of quilting that is only partly padded in a design
TRAPUNTOS > TRAPUNTO
TRASH *n* anything worthless ▷ *vb* attack or destroy maliciously
TRASHCAN *n* dustbin
TRASHCANS > TRASHCAN
TRASHED *adj* drunk
TRASHER > TRASH
TRASHERS > TRASH
TRASHERY > TRASH
TRASHES > TRASH
TRASHIER > TRASHY
TRASHIEST > TRASHY
TRASHILY > TRASHY
TRASHING > TRASH
TRASHMAN *another name for* > BINMAN
TRASHMEN > TRASHMAN
TRASHTRIE *n* trash
TRASHY *adj* cheap, worthless, or badly made
TRASS *n* variety of the volcanic rock tuff, used to make a hydraulic cement
TRASSES > TRASS
TRAT *n* type of fishing line holding a series of baited hooks
TRATS > TRAT
TRATT *short for* > TRATTORIA
TRATTORIA *n* Italian restaurant
TRATTORIE > TRATTORIA
TRATTS > TRATT
TRAUCHLE *n* work or a task that is tiring, monotonous, and lengthy ▷ *vb* walk or work slowly and wearily
TRAUCHLED *adj* exhausted by long hard work or concern
TRAUCHLES > TRAUCHLE
TRAUMA *n* emotional shock
TRAUMAS > TRAUMA
TRAUMATA > TRAUMA
TRAUMATIC > TRAUMA
TRAVAIL *n* labour or toil ▷ *vb* suffer or labour painfully, esp in childbirth
TRAVAILED > TRAVAIL
TRAVAILS > TRAVAIL
TRAVE *n* stout wooden cage in which difficult horses are shod
TRAVEL *vb* go from one place to another, through an area, or for a specified distance ▷ *n* travelling, esp as a tourist
TRAVELED *same as* > TRAVELLED
TRAVELER *same as* > TRAVELLER
TRAVELERS > TRAVELER
TRAVELING > TRAVEL
TRAVELLED *adj* having experienced or undergone much travelling
TRAVELLER *n* person who makes a journey or travels a lot
TRAVELOG *n* film, lecture, or brochure on travel
TRAVELOGS > TRAVELOG

TRAVELS > TRAVEL
TRAVERSAL > TRAVERSE
TRAVERSE *vb* pass or go over
TRAVERSED > TRAVERSE
TRAVERSER > TRAVERSE
TRAVERSES > TRAVERSE
TRAVERTIN *n* porous rock
TRAVES > TRAVE
TRAVESTY *n* grotesque imitation or mockery ▷ *vb* make or be a travesty of
TRAVIS *same as* > TREVISS
TRAVISES > TRAVIS
TRAVOIS *n* sled used for dragging logs
TRAVOISE *same as* > TRAVOIS
TRAVOISES > TRAVOISE
TRAWL *n* net dragged at deep levels behind a fishing boat ▷ *vb* fish with such a net
TRAWLED > TRAWL
TRAWLER *n* trawling boat
TRAWLERS > TRAWLER
TRAWLEY *same as* > TROLLEY
TRAWLEYS > TRAWLEY
TRAWLING > TRAWL
TRAWLINGS > TRAWL
TRAWLNET *n* large net, usually in the shape of a sock or bag, drawn at deep levels behind special boats (trawlers)
TRAWLNETS > TRAWLNET
TRAWLS > TRAWL
TRAY *n* flat board, usu with a rim, for carrying things
TRAYBIT *n* threepenny bit
TRAYBITS > TRAYBIT
TRAYFUL *n* as many or as much as will fit on a tray
TRAYFULS > TRAYFUL
TRAYNE *old spelling of* > TRAIN
TRAYNED > TRAIN
TRAYNES > TRAYNE
TRAYNING > TRAYNE
TRAYS > TRAY
TRAZODONE *n* drug used to treat depression
TREACHER *n* traitor; treacherous person
TREACHERS > TREACHER
TREACHERY *n* wilful betrayal
TREACHOUR *same as* > TREACHER
TREACLE *n* thick dark syrup produced when sugar is refined ▷ *vb* add treacle to
TREACLED > TREACLE
TREACLES > TREACLE
TREACLIER > TREACLE
TREACLING > TREACLE
TREACLY > TREACLE
TREAD *vb* set one's foot on ▷ *n* way of walking or dancing
TREADED > TREAD
TREADER > TREAD
TREADERS > TREAD
TREADING > TREAD
TREADINGS > TREAD
TREADLE *n* lever worked by the foot to turn a wheel ▷ *vb* work (a machine) with a treadle

TREADLED > TREADLE

TREADLER > TREADLE

TREADLERS > TREADLE

TREADLES > TREADLE

TREADLESS *adj* (of a tyre, for example) having no tread

TREADLING > TREADLE

TREADMILL *n* cylinder turned by treading on steps projecting from it

TREADS > TREAD

TREAGUE *n* agreement to stop fighting

TREAGUES > TREAGUE

TREASON *n* betrayal of one's sovereign or country

TREASONS > TREASON

TREASURE *n* collection of wealth, esp gold or jewels ▷ *vb* prize or cherish

TREASURED > TREASURE

TREASURER *n* official in charge of funds

TREASURES > TREASURE

TREASURY *n* storage place for treasure

TREAT *vb* deal with or regard in a certain manner ▷ *n* pleasure, entertainment, etc given or paid for by someone else

TREATABLE > TREAT

TREATED > TREAT

TREATER > TREAT

TREATERS > TREAT

TREATIES > TREATY

TREATING > TREAT

TREATINGS > TREAT

TREATISE *n* formal piece of writing on a particular subject

TREATISES > TREATISE

TREATMENT *n* medical care

TREATS > TREAT

TREATY *n* signed contract between states

TREBBIANO *n* grape used to make wine

TREBLE *adj* triple ▷ *n* (singer with or part for) a soprano voice ▷ *vb* increase three times

TREBLED > TREBLE

TREBLES > TREBLE

TREBLING > TREBLE

TREBLY > TREBLE

TREBUCHET *n* large medieval siege engine for hurling missiles consisting of a sling on a pivoted wooden arm set in motion by the fall of a weight

TREBUCKET *same as* > TREBUCHET

TRECENTO *n* 14th century, esp with reference to Italian art and literature

TRECENTOS > TRECENTO

TRECK *same as* > TREK

TRECKED > TRECK

TRECKING > TRECK

TRECKS > TRECK

TREDDLE *variant spelling of* > TREADLE

TREDDLED > TREDDLE

TREDDLES > TREDDLE

TREDDLING > TREDDLE

TREDILLE *same as* > TREDRILLE

TREDILLES > TREDILLE

TREDRILLE *n* card game for three players

TREE *n* large perennial plant with a woody trunk

TREED > TREE

TREEHOUSE *n* house built in tree

TREEING > TREE

TREELAWN *n* narrow band of grass between a road and a pavement, usually planted with trees

TREELAWNS > TREELAWN

TREELESS > TREE

TREELIKE > TREE

TREEN *adj* made of wood ▷ *n* art of making treenware

TREENAIL *n* dowel used for pinning planks or timbers together

TREENAILS > TREENAIL

TREENS > TREEN

TREENWARE *n* dishes and other household utensils made of wood, as by pioneers in North America

TREES > TREE

TREESHIP *n* state of being a tree

TREESHIPS > TREESHIP

TREETOP *n* top of a tree

TREETOPS > TREETOP

TREEWARE *n* books, magazines, or other reading materials that are printed on paper made from wood pulp as opposed to texts in the form of computer software, CD-ROM, audio books, etc

TREEWARES > TREEWARE

TREEWAX *n* yellowish wax secreted by an oriental scale insect

TREEWAXES > TREEWAX

TREF *adj* in Judaism, ritually unfit to be eaten

TREFA *same as* > TREF

TREFAH *same as* > TREF

TREFOIL *n* plant, such as clover, with a three-lobed leaf

TREFOILED > TREFOIL

TREFOILS > TREFOIL

TREGETOUR *n* juggler

TREHALA *n* edible sugary substance obtained from the pupal cocoon of an Asian weevil

TREHALAS > TREHALA

TREHALOSE *n* white crystalline disaccharide that occurs in yeast and certain fungi

TREIF *same as* > TREF

TREIFA *same as* > TREF

TREILLAGE *n* latticework

TREILLE *another word for* > TRELLIS

TREILLES > TREILLE

TREK *n* long difficult journey, esp on foot ▷ *vb* make such a journey

TREKKED > TREK

TREKKER > TREK

TREKKERS > TREK

TREKKING > TREK

TREKS > TREK

TRELLIS *n* framework of horizontal and vertical strips of wood ▷ *vb* interweave (strips of wood, etc) to make a trellis

TRELLISED > TRELLIS

TRELLISES > TRELLIS

TREMA *n* mark consisting of two dots placed over the second of two adjacent vowels to indicate it is to be pronounced separately rather than forming a diphthong with the first

TREMAS > TREMA

TREMATIC *adj* relating to the gills

TREMATODE *n* parasitic flatworm

TREMATOID > TREMATODE

TREMBLANT *adj* (of jewels) set in such a way that they shake when the wearer moves

TREMBLE *vb* shake or quiver ▷ *n* trembling

TREMBLED > TREMBLE

TREMBLER *n* device that vibrates to make or break an electrical circuit

TREMBLERS > TREMBLER

TREMBLES *n* disease of cattle and sheep characterized by muscular incoordination and tremor, caused by ingestion of white snakeroot or rayless goldenrod

TREMBLIER > TREMBLE

TREMBLING > TREMBLE

TREMBLY > TREMBLE

TREMIE *n* large metal hopper and pipe used to distribute freshly mixed concrete over an underwater site.

TREMIES > TREMIE

TREMOLANT *another word for* > TREMOLO

TREMOLITE *n* white or pale green mineral of the amphibole group consisting of calcium magnesium silicate

TREMOLO *n* quivering effect in singing or playing

TREMOLOS > TREMOLO

TREMOR *n* involuntary shaking ▷ *vb* tremble

TREMORED > TREMOR

TREMORING > TREMOR

TREMOROUS > TREMOR

TREMORS > TREMOR

TREMULANT *n* device on an organ by which the wind stream is made to fluctuate in intensity producing a tremolo effect

TREMULATE *vb* produce a tremulous sound

TREMULOUS *adj* trembling, as from fear or excitement

TRENAIL *same as* > TREENAIL

TRENAILS > TRENAIL

TRENCH *n* long narrow ditch, esp one used as a shelter in war ▷ *adj* of or involving military trenches ▷ *vb* make a trench in (a place)

TRENCHAND *old variant of* > TRENCHANT

TRENCHANT *adj* incisive

TRENCHARD *same as* > TRENCHER

TRENCHED > TRENCH

TRENCHER *n* wooden plate for serving food

TRENCHERS > TRENCHER

TRENCHES > TRENCH

TRENCHING > TRENCH

TREND *n* general tendency or direction ▷ *vb* take a certain trend

TRENDED > TREND

TRENDIER > TRENDY

TRENDIES > TRENDY

TRENDIEST > TRENDY

TRENDIFY *vb* render fashionable

TRENDILY > TRENDY

TRENDING > TREND

TRENDOID *n* follower of trends

TRENDOIDS > TRENDOID

TRENDS > TREND

TRENDY *n* consciously fashionable (person) ▷ *adj* consciously fashionable

TRENDYISM > TRENDY

TRENISE *n* one of the figures in a quadrille

TRENISES > TRENISE

TRENTAL *n* mass said in remembrance of a person 30 days after his or her death

TRENTALS > TRENTAL

TREPAN *same as* > TREPHINE

TREPANG *n* any of various large sea cucumbers of tropical Oriental seas, the body walls of which are used as food by the Japanese and Chinese

TREPANGS > TREPANG

TREPANNED > TREPAN

TREPANNER > TREPAN

TREPANS > TREPAN

TREPHINE *n* surgical sawlike instrument for removing circular sections of bone, esp from the skull ▷ *vb* remove a circular section of bone from (esp the skull)

TREPHINED > TREPHINE

TREPHINER > TREPHINE

TREPHINES > TREPHINE

TREPID *adj* trembling

TREPIDANT *adj* trembling

TREPONEMA *n* anaerobic spirochaete bacterium that causes syphilis

TREPONEME *same as* > TREPONEMA

TRES *adj* very

TRESPASS *vb* go onto

t

another's property without permission ▷ n trespassing

TRESS n lock of hair, esp a long lock of woman's hair ▷ vb arrange in tresses

TRESSED adj having a tress or tresses as specified

TRESSEL variant spelling of > TRESTLE

TRESSELS > TRESSEL

TRESSES > TRESS

TRESSIER > TRESS

TRESSIEST > TRESS

TRESSING > TRESS

TRESSOUR same as > TRESSURE

TRESSOURS > TRESSOUR

TRESSURE n narrow inner border on a shield, usually decorated with fleurs-de-lys

TRESSURED > TRESSURE

TRESSURES > TRESSURE

TRESSY > TRESS

TREST old variant of > TRESTLE

TRESTLE n board fixed on pairs of spreading legs, used as a support

TRESTLES > TRESTLE

TRESTS > TREST

TRET n (formerly) an allowance according to weight granted to purchasers for waste due to transportation

TRETINOIN n retinoid drug used to treat certain skin conditions

TRETS > TRET

TREVALLY n any of various food and game fishes

TREVALLYS > TREVALLY

TREVET same as > TRIVET

TREVETS > TREVET

TREVIS variant spelling of > TREVISS

TREVISES > TREVIS

TREVISS n partition in a stable for keeping animals apart

TREVISSES > TREVISS

TREW old variant spelling of > TRUE

TREWS pl n close-fitting tartan trousers

TREWSMAN n Highlander

TREWSMEN > TREWSMAN

TREY n any card or dice throw with three spots

TREYBIT same as > TRAYBIT

TREYBITS > TREYBIT

TREYS > TREY

TREZ same as > TREY

TREZES > TREZ

TRIABLE adj liable to be tried judicially

TRIAC n device for regulating the amount of electric current allowed to reach a circuit

TRIACID adj (of a base) capable of reacting with three molecules of a monobasic acid

TRIACIDS > TRIACID

TRIACS > TRIAC

TRIACT adj having three rays

TRIACTINE same as > TRIACT

TRIAD n group of three

TRIADIC n something that has the characteristics of a triad

TRIADICS > TRIADIC

TRIADISM > TRIAD

TRIADISMS > TRIAD

TRIADIST > TRIAD

TRIADISTS > TRIAD

TRIADS > TRIAD

TRIAGE n (in a hospital) the principle or practice of sorting emergency patients into categories of priority for treatment ▷ vb sort (patients) into categories of priority for treatment

TRIAGED > TRIAGE

TRIAGES > TRIAGE

TRIAGING > TRIAGE

TRIAL n investigation of a case before a judge

TRIALISM n belief that man consists of body, soul, and spirit

TRIALISMS > TRIALISM

TRIALIST same as > TRIALLIST

TRIALISTS > TRIALIST

TRIALITY > TRIALISM

TRIALLED > TRIAL

TRIALLING > TRIAL

TRIALLIST n person who takes part in a competition

TRIALOGUE n dialogue between three people

TRIALS > TRIAL

TRIALWARE n computer software that can be used without charge for a limited evaluation period

TRIANGLE n geometric figure with three sides

TRIANGLED > TRIANGLE

TRIANGLES > TRIANGLE

TRIAPSAL adj (of a church) having three apses

TRIARCH n one of three rulers of a triarchy

TRIARCHS > TRIARCH

TRIARCHY n government by three people

TRIASSIC adj of, denoting, or formed in the first period of the Mesozoic era

TRIATHLON n athletic contest in which each athlete competes in three different events: swimming, cycling, and running

TRIATIC n rope between a ship's mastheads

TRIATICS > TRIATIC

TRIATOMIC adj a molecule having three atoms

TRIAXIAL adj having three axes ▷ n sponge spicule with three axes

TRIAXIALS > TRIAXIAL

TRIAXON another name for > TRIAXIAL

TRIAXONS > TRIAXON

TRIAZIN same as > TRIAZINE

TRIAZINE n any of three azines that contain three nitrogen atoms in their molecules

TRIAZINES > TRIAZINE

TRIAZINS > TRIAZIN

TRIAZOLE n heterocyclic compound

TRIAZOLES > TRIAZOLE

TRIAZOLIC > TRIAZOLE

TRIBADE n lesbian, esp one who practises tribadism

TRIBADES > TRIBADE

TRIBADIC > TRIBADE

TRIBADIES > TRIBADY

TRIBADISM n lesbian practice in which one partner lies on top of the other and simulates the male role in heterosexual intercourse

TRIBADY another word for > TRIBADISM

TRIBAL adj of or denoting a tribe or tribes

TRIBALISM n loyalty to a tribe

TRIBALIST > TRIBALISM

TRIBALLY > TRIBAL

TRIBALS > TRIBAL

TRIBASIC adj (of an acid) containing three replaceable hydrogen atoms in the molecule

TRIBBLE n frame for drying paper

TRIBBLES > TRIBBLE

TRIBE n group of clans or families believed to have a common ancestor

TRIBELESS > TRIBE

TRIBES > TRIBE

TRIBESMAN n member of a tribe

TRIBESMEN > TRIBESMAN

TRIBLET n spindle or mandrel used in making rings, tubes, etc

TRIBLETS > TRIBLET

TRIBOLOGY n study of friction, lubrication, and wear between moving surfaces

TRIBRACH n metrical foot of three short syllables

TRIBRACHS > TRIBRACH

TRIBULATE vb trouble

TRIBUNAL n board appointed to inquire into a specific matter

TRIBUNALS > TRIBUNAL

TRIBUNARY > TRIBUNE

TRIBUNATE n office or rank of a tribune

TRIBUNE n people's representative, esp in ancient Rome

TRIBUNES > TRIBUNE

TRIBUTARY n stream or river flowing into a larger one ▷ adj (of a stream or river) flowing into a larger one

TRIBUTE n sign of respect or admiration

TRIBUTER n miner

TRIBUTERS > TRIBUTER

TRIBUTES > TRIBUTE

TRICAR n car with three wheels

TRICARS > TRICAR

TRICE n moment ▷ vb haul up or secure

TRICED > TRICE

TRICEP same as > TRICEPS

TRICEPS n muscle at the back of the upper arm

TRICEPSES > TRICEPS

TRICERION n candlestick with three arms

TRICES > TRICE

TRICHINA n parasitic nematode worm, occurring in the intestines of pigs, rats, and man and producing larvae that form cysts in skeletal muscle

TRICHINAE > TRICHINA

TRICHINAL > TRICHINA

TRICHINAS > TRICHINA

TRICHITE n any of various needle-shaped crystals that occur in some glassy volcanic rocks

TRICHITES > TRICHITE

TRICHITIC > TRICHITE

TRICHOID adj resembling a hair

TRICHOME n any hairlike outgrowth from the surface of a plant

TRICHOMES > TRICHOME

TRICHOMIC > TRICHOME

TRICHORD n musical instrument with three strings

TRICHORDS > TRICHORD

TRICHOSES > TRICHOSIS

TRICHOSIS n any abnormal condition or disease of the hair

TRICHROIC n state of having three colours

TRICHROME adj three-coloured

TRICING > TRICE

TRICK n deceitful or cunning action or plan ▷ vb cheat or deceive

TRICKED > TRICK

TRICKER > TRICK

TRICKERS > TRICK

TRICKERY n practice or an instance of using tricks

TRICKIE Scots form of > TRICKY

TRICKIER > TRICKY

TRICKIEST > TRICKY

TRICKILY > TRICKY

TRICKING > TRICK

TRICKINGS > TRICK

TRICKISH same as > TRICKY

TRICKLE vb (cause to) flow in a thin stream or drops ▷ n gradual flow

TRICKLED > TRICKLE

TRICKLES > TRICKLE

TRICKLESS > TRICK

TRICKLET n tiny trickle

TRICKLETS > TRICKLET

TRICKLIER > TRICKLE

TRICKLING > TRICKLE

TRICKLY > TRICKLE

TRICKS > TRICK

TRICKSIER > TRICKSY

TRICKSOME adj full of tricks

TRICKSTER n person who deceives or plays tricks

TRICKSY adj playing tricks habitually

TRICKY adj difficult, needing careful handling

TRICLAD n type of worm having a tripartite intestine

TRICLADS > TRICLAD

TRICLINIA n plural of triclinium: in Ancient Rome, reclining couch

TRICLINIC adj relating to or belonging to the crystal system characterized by three unequal axes, no pair of which are perpendicular

TRICLOSAN n drug used to treat skin infections

TRICOLOR same as > TRICOLOUR

TRICOLORS > TRICOLOR

TRICOLOUR n three-coloured striped flag ▷ adj having or involving three colours

TRICORN n cocked hat with opposing brims turned back and caught in three places ▷ adj having three horns or corners

TRICORNE same as > TRICORN

TRICORNES > TRICORNE

TRICORNS > TRICORN

TRICOT n thin rayon or nylon fabric knitted or resembling knitting, used for dresses, etc

TRICOTINE n twill-weave woollen fabric resembling gabardine

TRICOTS > TRICOT

TRICROTIC adj (of the pulse) having a tracing characterized by three elevations with each beat

TRICTRAC n game similar to backgammon

TRICTRACS > TRICTRAC

TRICUSPID adj having three points, cusps, or segments ▷ n tooth having three cusps

TRICYCLE n three-wheeled cycle ▷ vb ride a tricycle

TRICYCLED > TRICYCLE

TRICYCLER > TRICYCLE

TRICYCLES > TRICYCLE

TRICYCLIC adj (of a chemical compound) containing three rings in the molecular structure ▷ n antidepressant drug having a tricyclic molecular structure

TRIDACNA n giant clam

TRIDACNAS > TRIDACNA

TRIDACTYL adj having three digits on one hand or foot

TRIDARN n sideboard with three levels

TRIDARNS > TRIDARN

TRIDE old spelling of the past tense of > TRY

TRIDENT n three-pronged spear ▷ adj having three prongs

TRIDENTAL adj having three prongs, teeth, etc

TRIDENTED adj having three prongs

TRIDENTS > TRIDENT

TRIDUAN adj three days long

TRIDUUM n period of three days for prayer before a feast

TRIDUUMS > TRIDUUM

TRIDYMITE n form of silica

TRIE old spelling of > TRY

TRIECIOUS adj (of a plant) having male, female, and hermaphroditic flowers

TRIED > TRY

TRIELLA n three nominated horse races in which the punter bets on selecting the three winners

TRIELLAS > TRIELLA

TRIENE n chemical compound containing three double bonds

TRIENES > TRIENE

TRIENNIA > TRIENNIUM

TRIENNIAL adj happening every three years ▷ n relating to, lasting for, or occurring every three years

TRIENNIUM n period or cycle of three years

TRIENS n Byzantine gold goin worth one third of a solidus

TRIENTES > TRIENS

TRIER n person or thing that tries

TRIERARCH n citizen responsible for fitting out a state trireme, esp in Athens

TRIERS > TRIER

TRIES > TRY

TRIETERIC adj occurring once every two years

TRIETHYL adj consisting of three groups of ethyls

TRIFACIAL adj relating to the trigeminal nerve

TRIFECTA n form of betting in which the punter selects the first three place-winners in a horse race in the correct order

TRIFECTAS > TRIFECTA

TRIFF adj terrific; very good indeed

TRIFFER > TRIFF

TRIFFEST > TRIFF

TRIFFIC adj terrific; very good indeed

TRIFFID n any of a species of fictional plants that supposedly grew to a gigantic size, were capable of moving about, and could kill humans

TRIFFIDS > TRIFFID

TRIFFIDY adj resembling a triffid

TRIFID adj divided or split into three parts or lobes

TRIFLE n insignificant thing or amount ▷ vb deal (with) as if worthless

TRIFLED > TRIFLE

TRIFLER > TRIFLE

TRIFLERS > TRIFLE

TRIFLES > TRIFLE

TRIFLING adj insignificant

TRIFLINGS > TRIFLE

TRIFOCAL adj having three focuses ▷ n glasses that have trifocal lenses

TRIFOCALS > TRIFOCAL

TRIFOLD less common word for > TRIPLE

TRIFOLIES > TRIFOLY

TRIFOLIUM n leguminous plant with leaves divided into three leaflets and dense heads of small white, yellow, red, or purple flowers

TRIFOLY same as > TREFOIL

TRIFORIA > TRIFORIUM

TRIFORIAL > TRIFORIUM

TRIFORIUM n arcade above the arches of the nave, choir, or transept of a church

TRIFORM adj having three parts

TRIFORMED same as > TRIFORM

TRIG adj neat or spruce ▷ vb make or become spruce

TRIGAMIES > TRIGAMY

TRIGAMIST > TRIGAMY

TRIGAMOUS > TRIGAMY

TRIGAMY n condition of having three spouses

TRIGGED > TRIG

TRIGGER n small lever releasing a catch on a gun or machine ▷ vb set (an action or process) in motion

TRIGGERED > TRIGGER

TRIGGERS > TRIGGER

TRIGGEST > TRIG

TRIGGING > TRIG

TRIGLOT n person who can speak three languages

TRIGLOTS > TRIGLOT

TRIGLY > TRIG

TRIGLYPH n stone block in a Doric frieze, having three vertical channels

TRIGLYPHS > TRIGLYPH

TRIGNESS > TRIG

TRIGO n wheat field

TRIGON n (in classical Greece or Rome) a triangular harp or lyre

TRIGONAL adj triangular

TRIGONIC > TRIGON

TRIGONOUS adj (of stems, seeds, and similar parts) having a triangular cross section

TRIGONS > TRIGON

TRIGOS > TRIGO

TRIGRAM n three-letter inscription

TRIGRAMS > TRIGRAM

TRIGRAPH n combination of three letters used to represent a single speech sound or phoneme, such as eau in French beau

TRIGRAPHS > TRIGRAPH

TRIGS > TRIG

TRIGYNIAN adj relating to the Trigynia order of plants

TRIGYNOUS adj (of a plant) having three pistils

TRIHEDRA > TRIHEDRON

TRIHEDRAL adj having or formed by three plane faces meeting at a point ▷ n figure formed by the intersection of three lines in different planes

TRIHEDRON n figure determined by the intersection of three planes

TRIHYBRID n hybrid that differs from its parents in three genetic traits

TRIHYDRIC adj (of an alcohol or similar compound) containing three hydroxyl groups

TRIJET n jet with three engines

TRIJETS > TRIJET

TRIJUGATE adj in three pairs

TRIJUGOUS same as > TRIJUGATE

TRIKE n tricycle

TRIKES > TRIKE

TRILBIES > TRILBY

TRILBY n man's soft felt hat

TRILBYS > TRILBY

TRILD old past tense of > TRILL

TRILEMMA n quandary posed by three alternative courses of action

TRILEMMAS > TRILEMMA

TRILINEAR adj consisting of, bounded by, or relating to three lines

TRILITH same as > TRILITHON

TRILITHIC > TRILITHON

TRILITHON n structure consisting of two upright stones with a third placed across the top, such as those of Stonehenge

TRILITHS > TRILITH

TRILL n rapid alternation between two notes ▷ vb play or sing a trill

TRILLED > TRILL

TRILLER > TRILL

TRILLERS > TRILL

TRILLING > TRILL

TRILLINGS > TRILL

TRILLION n one million million ▷ adj amounting to a trillion

TRILLIONS > TRILLION

TRILLIUM n plant of Asia and North America that has three leaves at the top of the stem with a single white, pink, or purple three-petalled flower

TRILLIUMS > TRILLIUM

TRILLO n (in music) a trill

TRILLOES > TRILL

TRILLS > TRILL

TRILOBAL > TRILOBE
TRILOBATE adj (esp of a leaf) consisting of or having three lobes or parts
TRILOBE n three-lobed thing
TRILOBED adj having three lobes
TRILOBES > TRILOBE
TRILOBITE n small prehistoric sea animal
TRILOGIES > TRILOGY
TRILOGY n series of three related books, plays, etc
TRIM adj neat and smart ▷ vb cut or prune into good shape ▷ n decoration
TRIMARAN n three-hulled boat
TRIMARANS > TRIMARAN
TRIMER n polymer or a molecule of a polymer consisting of three identical monomers
TRIMERIC > TRIMER
TRIMERISM > TRIMER
TRIMEROUS adj (of plants) having parts arranged in groups of three
TRIMERS > TRIMER
TRIMESTER n period of three months
TRIMETER n verse line consisting of three metrical feet ▷ adj designating such a line
TRIMETERS > TRIMETER
TRIMETHYL adj having three methyl groups
TRIMETRIC adj of, relating to, or consisting of a trimeter or trimeters
TRIMLY > TRIM
TRIMMED > TRIM
TRIMMER > TRIM
TRIMMERS > TRIM
TRIMMEST > TRIM
TRIMMING > TRIM
TRIMMINGS > TRIM
TRIMNESS > TRIM
TRIMORPH n substance, esp a mineral, that exists in three distinct forms
TRIMORPHS > TRIMORPH
TRIMOTOR n vehicle with three motors
TRIMOTORS > TRIMOTOR
TRIMS > TRIM
TRIMTAB n small control surface attached to the trailing edge of a main control surface to enable the pilot to balance an aircraft
TRIMTABS > TRIMTAB
TRIN n triplet
TRINAL > TRINE
TRINARY adj made up of three parts
TRINDLE vb move heavily on (or as if on) wheels
TRINDLED > TRINDLE
TRINDLES > TRINDLE
TRINDLING > TRINDLE
TRINE n aspect of 120° between two planets, an orb of 8° being allowed

▷ adj of or relating to a trine ▷ vb put in a trine aspect
TRINED > TRINE
TRINES > TRINE
TRINGLE n slim rod
TRINGLES > TRINGLE
TRINING > TRINE
TRINITIES > TRINITY
TRINITRIN n pale yellow viscous explosive liquid substance made from glycerol and nitric and sulphuric acids
TRINITY n group of three
TRINKET n small or worthless ornament or piece of jewellery ▷ vb ornament with trinkets
TRINKETED > TRINKET
TRINKETER > TRINKET
TRINKETRY > TRINKET
TRINKETS > TRINKET
TRINKUM n trinket or bauble
TRINKUMS > TRINKUM
TRINODAL adj having three nodes
TRINOMIAL adj consisting of or relating to three terms ▷ n polynomial consisting of three terms, such as $ax^2 + bx + c$
TRINS > TRIN
TRIO n group of three
TRIODE n electronic valve having three electrodes, a cathode, an anode, and a grid
TRIODES > TRIODE
TRIOL n any of a class of alcohols that have three hydroxyl groups per molecule
TRIOLEIN n naturally occurring glyceride of oleic acid, found in fats and oils
TRIOLEINS > TRIOLEIN
TRIOLET n verse form of eight lines
TRIOLETS > TRIOLET
TRIOLS > TRIOL
TRIONES n seven stars of the constellation Ursa Major
TRIONYM another name for > TRINOMIAL
TRIONYMAL > TRIONYM
TRIONYMS > TRIONYM
TRIOR old form of > TRIER
TRIORS > TRIOR
TRIOS > TRIO
TRIOSE n simple monosaccharide produced by the oxidation of glycerol
TRIOSES > TRIOSE
TRIOXID same as > TRIOXIDE
TRIOXIDE n any oxide that contains three oxygen atoms per molecule
TRIOXIDES > TRIOXIDE
TRIOXIDS > TRIOXIDE
TRIOXYGEN technical name for > OXYGEN
TRIP n journey to a place and back, esp for pleasure ▷ vb (cause to) stumble
TRIPACK n pack of three

TRIPACKS > TRIPACK
TRIPART adj composed of three parts
TRIPE n stomach of a cow used as food
TRIPEDAL adj having three feet
TRIPERIES > TRIPERY
TRIPERY n place where tripe is prepared
TRIPES > TRIPE
TRIPEY > TRIPE
TRIPHASE adj having three phases
TRIPHONE n group of three phonemes
TRIPHONES > TRIPHONE
TRIPIER > TRIPE
TRIPIEST > TRIPE
TRIPITAKA n three collections of books making up the Buddhist canon of scriptures
TRIPLANE n aeroplane having three wings arranged one above the other
TRIPLANES > TRIPLANE
TRIPLE adj having three parts ▷ vb increase three times ▷ n something that is, or contains, three times as much as normal
TRIPLED > TRIPLE
TRIPLES > TRIPLE
TRIPLET n one of three babies born at one birth
TRIPLETS > TRIPLET
TRIPLEX n building divided into three separate dwellings
TRIPLEXES > TRIPLEX
TRIPLIED > TRIPLY
TRIPLIES > TRIPLY
TRIPLING > TRIPLE
TRIPLINGS > TRIPLE
TRIPLITE n brownish-red phosphate
TRIPLITES > TRIPLITE
TRIPLOID adj having or relating to three times the haploid number of chromosomes ▷ n triploid organism
TRIPLOIDS > TRIPLOID
TRIPLOIDY n triploid state
TRIPLY vb give a reply to a duply
TRIPLYING > TRIPLY
TRIPOD n three-legged stand, stool, etc
TRIPODAL > TRIPOD
TRIPODIC > TRIPOD
TRIPODIES > TRIPODY
TRIPODS > TRIPOD
TRIPODY n metrical unit consisting of three feet
TRIPOLI n lightweight porous siliceous rock derived by weathering and used in a powdered form as a polish, filter, etc
TRIPOLIS > TRIPOLI
TRIPOS n final examinations for an honours degree at Cambridge University

TRIPOSES > TRIPOS
TRIPPANT adj (in heraldry) in the process of tripping
TRIPPED > TRIP
TRIPPER n tourist
TRIPPERS > TRIPPER
TRIPPERY adj like a tripper
TRIPPET n any mechanism that strikes or is struck at regular intervals, as by a cam
TRIPPETS > TRIPPET
TRIPPIER > TRIPPY
TRIPPIEST > TRIPPY
TRIPPING > TRIP
TRIPPINGS > TRIP
TRIPPLE vb canter
TRIPPLED > TRIPPLE
TRIPPLER > TRIPPLE
TRIPPLERS > TRIPPLE
TRIPPLES > TRIPPLE
TRIPPLING > TRIPPLE
TRIPPY adj suggestive of or resembling the effect produced by a hallucinogenic drug
TRIPS > TRIP
TRIPSES > TRIPSIS
TRIPSIS n act of kneading the body to promote circulation, suppleness, etc
TRIPTAN n drug used to treat migraine
TRIPTANE n colourless highly flammable liquid
TRIPTANES > TRIPTANE
TRIPTANS > TRIPTAN
TRIPTOTE n word that has only three cases
TRIPTOTES > TRIPTOTE
TRIPTYCA variant of > TRIPTYCH
TRIPTYCAS > TRIPTYCA
TRIPTYCH n painting or carving on three hinged panels, often forming an altarpiece
TRIPTYCHS > TRIPTYCH
TRIPTYQUE n customs permit for the temporary importation of a motor vehicle
TRIPUDIA > TRIPUDIUM
TRIPUDIUM n ancient religious dance
TRIPWIRE n wire that activates a trap, mine, etc, when tripped over
TRIPWIRES > TRIPWIRE
TRIPY > TRIPE
TRIQUETRA n ornament in the shape of three intersecting ellipses roughly forming a triangle
TRIRADIAL adj having or consisting of three rays or radiating branches
TRIREME n ancient Greek warship with three rows of oars on each side
TRIREMES > TRIREME
TRISAGION n old hymn
TRISCELE variant spelling of > TRISKELE
TRISCELES > TRISCELE
TRISECT vb divide into three parts, esp three equal

t

parts

TRISECTED > TRISECT

TRISECTOR > TRISECT

TRISECTS > TRISECT

TRISEME n metrical foot of a length equal to three short syllables

TRISEMES > TRISEME

TRISEMIC > TRISEME

TRISERIAL adj arranged in three rows or series

TRISHAW another name for > RICKSHAW

TRISHAWS > TRISHAW

TRISKELE n three-limbed symbol

TRISKELES > TRISKELE

TRISKELIA n plural of singular triskelion: three-limbed symbol

TRISMIC > TRISMUS

TRISMUS n state of being unable to open the mouth because of sustained contractions of the jaw muscles, caused by tetanus

TRISMUSES > TRISMUS

TRISODIUM adj containing three sodium atoms

TRISOME n chromosome occurring three times (rather than twice) in a cell

TRISOMES > TRISOME

TRISOMIC > TRISOMY

TRISOMICS n study of trisomy

TRISOMIES > TRISOMY

TRISOMY n condition of having one chromosome of the set represented three times in an otherwise diploid organism, cell, etc

TRIST variant spelling of > TRISTE

TRISTATE adj (of a digital computer chip) having high, low, and floating output states

TRISTE adj sad

TRISTESSE n sadness

TRISTEZA n disease affecting citrus trees

TRISTEZAS > TRISTEZA

TRISTFUL same as > TRISTE

TRISTICH n poem, stanza, or strophe that consists of three lines

TRISTICHS > TRISTICH

TRISUL n trident symbol of Siva

TRISULA same as > TRISUL

TRISULAS > TRISULA

TRISULS > TRISUL

TRITE adj (of a remark or idea) commonplace and unoriginal ▷ n (on a lyre) the third string from the highest in pitch

TRITELY > TRITE

TRITENESS > TRITE

TRITER > TRITE

TRITES > TRITE

TRITEST > TRITE

TRITHEISM n belief in three gods, esp in the Trinity as consisting of three distinct gods

TRITHEIST > TRITHEISM

TRITHING n tripartition

TRITHINGS > TRITHING

TRITIATE vb replace normal hydrogen atoms in (a compound) by those of tritium

TRITIATED > TRITIATE

TRITIATES > TRITIATE

TRITICAL n trite; hackneyed

TRITICALE n fertile hybrid cereal

TRITICISM n something trite

TRITICUM n any annual cereal grass of the genus Triticum, which includes the wheats

TRITICUMS > TRITICUM

TRITIDE n tritium compound

TRITIDES > TRITIDE

TRITIUM n radioactive isotope of hydrogen

TRITIUMS > TRITIUM

TRITOMA another name for > KNIPHOFIA

TRITOMAS > TRITOMA

TRITON n any of various chiefly tropical marine gastropod molluscs, having large beautifully-coloured spiral shells

TRITONE n musical interval consisting of three whole tones

TRITONES > TRITONE

TRITONIA n any plant of the perennial cormous S. African genus Tritonia, with typically scarlet or orange flowers

TRITONIAS > TRITONIA

TRITONS > TRITON

TRITURATE vb grind or rub into a fine powder or pulp ▷ n powder or pulp resulting from this grinding

TRIUMPH n (happiness caused by) victory or success ▷ vb be victorious or successful

TRIUMPHAL adj celebrating a triumph

TRIUMPHED > TRIUMPH

TRIUMPHER > TRIUMPH

TRIUMPHS > TRIUMPH

TRIUMVIR n (esp in ancient Rome) a member of a triumvirate

TRIUMVIRI > TRIUMVIR

TRIUMVIRS > TRIUMVIR

TRIUMVIRY n triumvirate

TRIUNE adj constituting three in one, esp the three persons in one God of the Trinity ▷ n group of three

TRIUNES > TRIUNE

TRIUNITY > TRIUNE

TRIVALENT adj having a valency of three

TRIVALVE n animal having three valves

TRIVALVED adj having three valves

TRIVALVES > TRIVALVE

TRIVET n metal stand for a pot or kettle

TRIVETS > TRIVET

TRIVIA pl n trivial things or details

TRIVIAL adj of little importance

TRIVIALLY > TRIVIAL

TRIVIUM n (in medieval learning) the lower division of the seven liberal arts, consisting of grammar, rhetoric, and logic

TRIVIUMS > TRIVIUM

TRIWEEKLY adv every three weeks ▷ n triweekly publication

TRIZONAL > TRIZONE

TRIZONE n area comprising three zones

TRIZONES > TRIZONE

TROAD same as > TROD

TROADE same as > TROD

TROADES > TROADE

TROADS > TROAD

TROAK old form of > TRUCK

TROAKED > TROAK

TROAKING > TROAK

TROAKS > TROAK

TROAT vb (of a rutting buck) to call or bellow

TROATED > TROAT

TROATING > TROAT

TROATS > TROAT

TROCAR n surgical instrument for removing fluid from bodily cavities, consisting of a puncturing device situated inside a tube

TROCARS > TROCAR

TROCHAIC adj of, relating to, or consisting of trochees ▷ n verse composed of trochees

TROCHAICS > TROCHAIC

TROCHAL adj shaped like a wheel

TROCHAR old variant spelling of > TROCAR

TROCHARS > TROCHAR

TROCHE another name for > LOZENGE

TROCHEE n metrical foot of one long and one short syllable

TROCHEES > TROCHEE

TROCHES > TROCHE

TROCHI > TROCHUS

TROCHIL same as > TROCHILUS

TROCHILI > TROCHILUS

TROCHILIC adj relating to the movement of a hummingbird's wings

TROCHILS > TROCHIL

TROCHILUS n any of several Old World warblers

TROCHISK another word for > TROCHE

TROCHISKS > TROCHISK

TROCHITE n joint of a crinoid

TROCHITES > TROCHITE

TROCHLEA n any bony or cartilaginous part with a grooved surface over which a bone, tendon, etc, may slide or articulate

TROCHLEAE > TROCHLEA

TROCHLEAR as in trochlear nerve either one of the fourth pair of cranial nerves, which supply the superior oblique muscle of the eye

TROCHLEAS > TROCHLEA

TROCHOID n curve described by a fixed point on the radius or extended radius of a circle as the circle rolls along a straight line ▷ adj rotating or capable of rotating about a central axis

TROCHOIDS > TROCHOID

TROCHUS n hoop (used in exercise)

TROCHUSES > TROCHUS

TROCK same as > TRUCK

TROCKED > TROCK

TROCKEN adj dry (used of wine, esp German wine)

TROCKING > TROCK

TROCKS > TROCK

TROD vb past participle of tread ▷ n path

TRODDEN > TREAD

TRODE same as > TROD

TRODES > TRODE

TRODS > TROD

TROELIE same as > TROOLIE

TROELIES > TROELIE

TROELY same as > TROOLIE

TROFFER n trough-like fixture for holding in place and reflecting light from a fluorescent tube

TROFFERS > TROFFER

TROG vb walk, esp aimlessly or heavily

TROGGED > TROG

TROGGING > TROG

TROGGS n loyalty; fidelity

TROGON n bird of tropical and subtropical regions of America, Africa, and Asia. They have a brilliant plumage, short hooked bill, and long tail

TROGONS > TROGON

TROGS > TROG

TROIKA n Russian vehicle drawn by three horses abreast

TROIKAS > TROIKA

TROILISM n sexual activity involving three people

TROILISMS > TROILISM

TROILIST > TROILISM

TROILISTS > TROILISM

TROILITE n iron sulphide present in most meteorites

TROILITES > TROILITE

TROILUS n type of large butterfly

TROILUSES > TROILUS

TROIS Scots form of > TROY

TROKE same as > TRUCK

TROKED > TROKE

TROKES > TROKE

TROKING > TROKE

TROLAND n unit of light intensity in the eye

TROLANDS > TROLAND

TROLL *n* giant or dwarf in Scandinavian folklore ▷ *vb* fish by dragging a lure through the water

TROLLED > TROLL

TROLLER > TROLL

TROLLERS > TROLL

TROLLEY *n* small wheeled table for food and drink ▷ *vb* transport on a trolley

TROLLEYED > TROLLEY

TROLLEYS *pl n* men's underpants

TROLLIED > TROLLY

TROLLIES > TROLLY

TROLLING > TROLL

TROLLINGS > TROLL

TROLLIUS *n* plant with globe-shaped flowers

TROLLOP *n* promiscuous or slovenly woman ▷ *vb* behave like a trollop

TROLLOPED > TROLLOP

TROLLOPEE *n* loose dress or gown

TROLLOPS > TROLLOP

TROLLOPY > TROLLOP

TROLLS > TROLL

TROLLY *same as* > TROLLEY

TROLLYING > TROLLY

TROMBONE *n* brass musical instrument with a sliding tube

TROMBONES > TROMBONE

TROMINO *n* shape made from three squares, each joined to the next along one full side

TROMINOES > TROMINO

TROMINOS > TROMINO

TROMMEL *n* revolving cylindrical sieve used to screen crushed ore

TROMMELS > TROMMEL

TROMP *vb* trample

TROMPE *n* apparatus for supplying the blast of air in a forge, consisting of a thin column down which water falls, drawing in air through side openings

TROMPED > TROMP

TROMPES > TROMPE

TROMPING > TROMP

TROMPS > TROMP

TRON *n* public weighing machine

TRONA *n* greyish mineral that consists of hydrated sodium carbonate and occurs in salt deposits

TRONAS > TRONA

TRONC *n* pool into which waiters, waitresses, hotel workers, etc, pay their tips

TRONCS > TRONC

TRONE *same as* > TRON

TRONES > TRONE

TRONK *n* jail

TRONKS > TRONK

TRONS > TRON

TROOLIE *n* large palm leaf

TROOLIES > TROOLIE

TROOP *n* large group ▷ *vb* move in a crowd

TROOPED > TROOP

TROOPER *n* cavalry soldier

TROOPERS > TROOPER

TROOPIAL *same as* > TROUPIAL

TROOPIALS > TROOPIAL

TROOPING > TROOP

TROOPS > TROOP

TROOPSHIP *n* ship used to transport military personnel

TROOSTITE *n* reddish or greyish mineral that is a variety of willemite in which some of the zinc is replaced by manganese

TROOZ *same as* > TREWS

TROP *adv* too, too much

TROPAEOLA *n* plural of singular tropaeolum (a garden plant)

TROPARIA > TROPARION

TROPARION *n* short hymn

TROPE *n* figure of speech ▷ *vb* use tropes (in speech or writing)

TROPED > TROPE

TROPEOLIN *n* type of dye

TROPES > TROPE

TROPHESY *n* disorder of the nerves relating to nutrition

TROPHI *n* collective term for the mandibles other parts of an insect's mouth

TROPHIC *adj* of or relating to nutrition

TROPHIED > TROPHY

TROPHIES > TROPHY

TROPHY *n* cup, shield, etc given as a prize ▷ *adj* regraded as a highly desirable symbol of wealth or success ▷ *vb* award a trophy to (someone)

TROPHYING > TROPHY

TROPIC *n* either of two lines of latitude at 23½°N (tropic of Cancer) or 23½°S (tropic of Capricorn)

TROPICAL *adj* of or in the tropics ▷ *n* tropical thing or place

TROPICALS > TROPICAL

TROPICS > TROPIC

TROPIN *n* andrenal androgen

TROPINE *n* white crystalline poisonous hygroscopic alkaloid obtained by heating atropine or hyoscyamine with barium hydroxide

TROPINES > TROPINE

TROPING > TROPE

TROPINS > TROPIN

TROPISM *n* tendency of a plant or animal to turn or curve in response to an external stimulus

TROPISMS > TROPISM

TROPIST > TROPISM

TROPISTIC > TROPISM

TROPISTS > TROPISM

TROPOLOGY *n* use of figurative language in speech or writing

TROPONIN *n* muscle-tissue protein involved in the controlling of muscle contraction

TROPONINS > TROPONIN

TROPPO *adv* too much ▷ *adj* mentally affected by a tropical climate

TROSSERS *old form of* > TROUSERS

TROT *vb* (of a horse) move at a medium pace, lifting the feet in diagonal pairs ▷ *n* trotting

TROTH *n* pledge of devotion, esp a betrothal ▷ *vb* promise to marry (someone)

TROTHED > TROTH

TROTHFUL > TROTH

TROTHING > TROTH

TROTHLESS > TROTH

TROTHS > TROTH

TROTLINE *n* long line suspended across a stream, river, etc, to which shorter hooked and baited lines are attached

TROTLINES > TROTLINE

TROTS > TROT

TROTTED > TROT

TROTTER *n* pig's foot

TROTTERS > TROTTER

TROTTING > TROT

TROTTINGS > TROT

TROTTOIR *n* pavement

TROTTOIRS > TROTTOIR

TROTYL *n* trinitrotoluene; a yellow solid: used chiefly as a high explosive and is also an intermediate in the manufacture of dyestuffs

TROTYLS > TROTYL

TROUBLE *n* (cause of) distress or anxiety ▷ *vb* (cause to) worry

TROUBLED > TROUBLE

TROUBLER > TROUBLE

TROUBLERS > TROUBLE

TROUBLES > TROUBLE

TROUBLING > TROUBLE

TROUBLOUS *adj* unsettled or agitated

TROUCH *n* rubbish

TROUCHES > TROUCH

TROUGH *n* long open container, esp for animals' food or water ▷ *vb* eat, consume, or take greedily

TROUGHED > TROUGH

TROUGHING > TROUGH

TROUGHS > TROUGH

TROULE *old variant of* > TROLL

TROULED > TROULE

TROULES > TROULE

TROULING > TROULE

TROUNCE *vb* defeat utterly

TROUNCED > TROUNCE

TROUNCER > TROUNCE

TROUNCERS > TROUNCE

TROUNCES > TROUNCE

TROUNCING > TROUNCE

TROUPE *n* company of performers ▷ *vb* (esp of actors) to move or travel in a group

TROUPED > TROUPE

TROUPER *n* member of a troupe

TROUPERS > TROUPER

TROUPES > TROUPE

TROUPIAL *n* any of various American orioles

TROUPIALS > TROUPIAL

TROUPING > TROUPE

TROUSE *pl n* close-fitting breeches worn in Ireland

TROUSER *adj* of trousers ▷ *vb* take (something, esp money), often surreptitiously or unlawfully ▷ *n* of or relating to trousers

TROUSERED > TROUSERS

TROUSERS *pl n* two-legged outer garment with legs reaching usu to the ankles

TROUSES > TROUSE

TROUSSEAU *n* bride's collection of clothing etc for her marriage

TROUT *n* game fish related to the salmon ▷ *vb* fish for trout

TROUTER > TROUT

TROUTERS > TROUT

TROUTFUL *adj* (of a body of water) full of trout

TROUTIER > TROUT

TROUTIEST > TROUT

TROUTING > TROUT

TROUTINGS > TROUT

TROUTLESS > TROUT

TROUTLET *n* small trout

TROUTLETS > TROUTLET

TROUTLING *n* small trout

TROUTS > TROUT

TROUTY > TROUT

TROUVERE *n* any of a group of poets of N France during the 12th and 13th centuries who composed chiefly narrative works

TROUVERES > TROUVERE

TROUVEUR *same as* > TROUVERE

TROUVEURS > TROUVEUR

TROVE *as in treasure-trove* valuable articles, such as coins, bullion, etc, found hidden in the earth or elsewhere and of unknown ownership

TROVER *n* (formerly) the act of wrongfully assuming proprietary rights over personal goods or property belonging to another

TROVERS > TROVER

TROVES > TROVE

TROW *vb* think, believe, or trust

TROWED > TROW

TROWEL *n* hand tool with a wide blade for spreading mortar, lifting plants, etc ▷ *vb* use a trowel on (plaster, soil, etc)

TROWELED > TROWEL

TROWELER > TROWEL

TROWELERS > TROWEL

TROWELING > TROWEL

TROWELLED > TROWEL

TROWELLER > TROWEL

TROWELS > TROWEL

t

TROWING > TROW

TROWS > TROW

TROWSERS old spelling of > TROUSERS

TROWTH variant spelling of > TROTH

TROWTHS > TROWTH

TROY as in troy weight system of weights used for precious metals and gemstones, based on the grain, which is identical to the avoirdupois grain

TROYS > TROY

TRUANCIES > TRUANT

TRUANCY > TRUANT

TRUANT n pupil who stays away from school without permission ▷ adj being or relating to a truant ▷ vb play truant

TRUANTED > TRUANT

TRUANTING > TRUANT

TRUANTLY > TRUANT

TRUANTRY > TRUANT

TRUANTS > TRUANT

TRUCAGE n art forgery

TRUCAGES > TRUCAGE

TRUCE n temporary agreement to stop fighting ▷ vb make a truce

TRUCED > TRUCE

TRUCELESS > TRUCE

TRUCES > TRUCE

TRUCHMAN n interpreter; translator

TRUCHMANS > TRUCHMAN

TRUCHMEN > TRUCHMAN

TRUCIAL > TRUCE

TRUCING > TRUCE

TRUCK n railway goods wagon ▷ vb exchange (goods); barter

TRUCKABLE > TRUCK

TRUCKAGE n conveyance of cargo by truck

TRUCKAGES > TRUCKAGE

TRUCKED > TRUCK

TRUCKER n truck driver

TRUCKERS > TRUCKER

TRUCKFUL n amount of something that can be conveyed in a truck

TRUCKFULS > TRUCKFUL

TRUCKIE n truck driver

TRUCKIES > TRUCKIE

TRUCKING n transportation of goods by lorry

TRUCKINGS > TRUCKING

TRUCKLE vb yield weakly or give in ▷ n small wheel

TRUCKLED > TRUCKLE

TRUCKLER > TRUCKLE

TRUCKLERS > TRUCKLE

TRUCKLES > TRUCKLE

TRUCKLINE n organisation that conveys freight by truck

TRUCKLING > TRUCKLE

TRUCKLOAD n amount carried by a truck

TRUCKMAN n truck driver

TRUCKMEN > TRUCKMAN

TRUCKS > TRUCK

TRUCKSTOP n place providing fuel, oil, and often service facilities for

truck drivers

TRUCULENT adj aggressively defiant

TRUDGE vb walk heavily or wearily ▷ n long tiring walk

TRUDGED > TRUDGE

TRUDGEN n type of swimming stroke that uses overarm action, as in the crawl, and a scissors kick

TRUDGENS > TRUDGEN

TRUDGEON nonstandard variant of > TRUDGEN

TRUDGEONS > TRUDGEON

TRUDGER > TRUDGE

TRUDGERS > TRUDGE

TRUDGES > TRUDGE

TRUDGING > TRUDGE

TRUDGINGS > TRUDGE

TRUE adj in accordance with facts

TRUEBLUE n staunch royalist or Conservative

TRUEBLUES > TRUEBLUE

TRUEBORN adj being such by birth

TRUEBRED adj thoroughbred

TRUED > TRUE

TRUEING > TRUE

TRUELOVE n person that one loves

TRUELOVES > TRUELOVE

TRUEMAN n honest person

TRUEMEN > TRUEMAN

TRUENESS > TRUE

TRUEPENNY n truthful person

TRUER > TRUE

TRUES > TRUE

TRUEST > TRUE

TRUFFE rare word for > TRUFFLE

TRUFFES > TRUFFE

TRUFFLE n edible underground fungus ▷ vb hunt for truffles

TRUFFLED > TRUFFLE

TRUFFLES > TRUFFLE

TRUFFLING > TRUFFLE

TRUG n long shallow basket used by gardeners

TRUGO n game similar to croquet, originally improvised in Victoria from the rubber discs used as buffers on railway carriages

TRUGOS > TRUGO

TRUGS > TRUG

TRUING > TRUE

TRUISM n self-evident truth

TRUISMS > TRUISM

TRUISTIC > TRUISM

TRULL n prostitute

TRULLS > TRULL

TRULY adv in a true manner

TRUMEAU n section of a wall or pillar between two openings

TRUMEAUX > TRUMEAU

TRUMP adj (card) of the suit outranking the others ▷ vb play a trump card on (another card) ▷ pl n suit outranking the others

TRUMPED > TRUMP

TRUMPERY n something useless or worthless ▷ adj useless or worthless

TRUMPET n valved brass instrument with a flared tube ▷ vb proclaim loudly

TRUMPETED > TRUMPET

TRUMPETER n person who plays the trumpet, esp one whose duty it is to play fanfares, signals, etc

TRUMPETS > TRUMPET

TRUMPING > TRUMP

TRUMPINGS > TRUMP

TRUMPLESS > TRUMP

TRUMPS > TRUMP

TRUNCAL adj of or relating to the trunk

TRUNCATE vb cut short ▷ adj cut short

TRUNCATED adj (of a cone, pyramid, prism, etc) having an apex or end removed by a plane intersection that is usually nonparallel to the base

TRUNCATES > TRUNCATE

TRUNCHEON n club formerly carried by a policeman ▷ vb beat with a truncheon

TRUNDLE vb move heavily on wheels ▷ n act or an instance of trundling

TRUNDLED > TRUNDLE

TRUNDLER n golf or shopping trolley

TRUNDLERS > TRUNDLER

TRUNDLES > TRUNDLE

TRUNDLING > TRUNDLE

TRUNK n main stem of a tree ▷ vb lop or truncate

TRUNKED > TRUNK

TRUNKFISH n tropical fish, having the body encased in bony plates with openings for the fins, eyes, mouth, etc

TRUNKFUL > TRUNK

TRUNKFULS > TRUNK

TRUNKING n cables that take a common route through an exchange building linking ranks of selectors

TRUNKINGS > TRUNKING

TRUNKLESS > TRUNK

TRUNKS pl n shorts worn by a man for swimming

TRUNNEL same as > TREENAIL

TRUNNELS > TRUNNEL

TRUNNION n one of a pair of coaxial projections attached to opposite sides of a container, cannon, etc, to provide a support about which it can turn in a vertical

TRUNNIONS > TRUNNION

TRUQUAGE variant of > TRUCAGE

TRUQUAGES > TRUQUAGE

TRUQUEUR n art forger

TRUQUEURS > TRUQUEUR

TRUSS vb tie or bind up ▷ n device for holding a hernia, etc in place

TRUSSED > TRUSS

TRUSSER > TRUSS

TRUSSERS > TRUSS

TRUSSES > TRUSS

TRUSSING n system of trusses, esp for strengthening or reinforcing a structure

TRUSSINGS > TRUSSING

TRUST vb believe in and rely on ▷ n confidence in the truth, reliability, etc of a person or thing ▷ adj of or relating to a trust or trusts

TRUSTABLE > TRUST

TRUSTED > TRUST

TRUSTEE n person holding property on another's behalf ▷ vb act as a trustee

TRUSTEED > TRUSTEE

TRUSTEES > TRUSTEE

TRUSTER > TRUST

TRUSTERS > TRUST

TRUSTFUL adj inclined to trust others

TRUSTIER > TRUSTY

TRUSTIES > TRUSTY

TRUSTIEST > TRUSTY

TRUSTILY > TRUSTY

TRUSTING same as > TRUSTFUL

TRUSTLESS adj untrustworthy

TRUSTOR n person who sets up a trust

TRUSTORS > TRUSTOR

TRUSTS > TRUST

TRUSTY adj faithful or reliable ▷ n trustworthy convict to whom special privileges are granted

TRUTH n state of being true

TRUTHFUL adj honest

TRUTHIER > TRUTHY

TRUTHIEST > TRUTHY

TRUTHLESS > TRUTH

TRUTHLIKE n truthful

TRUTHS > TRUTH

TRUTHY adj truthful

TRY vb make an effort or attempt ▷ n attempt or effort

TRYE adj very good; select

TRYER variant of > TRIER

TRYERS > TRYER

TRYING > TRY

TRYINGLY > TRY

TRYINGS > TRY

TRYKE variant spelling of > TRIKE

TRYKES > TRYKE

TRYMA n drupe produced by the walnut and similar plants, in which the endocarp is a hard shell and the epicarp is dehiscent

TRYMATA > TRYMA

TRYOUT n a trial or test, as of an athlete or actor

TRYOUTS > TRYOUT

TRYP n parasitic protozoan

TRYPAN as in trypan blue dye obtained from tolidine that is absorbed by the macrophages of the reticuloendothelial system and is therefore used for staining cells in biological

research
TRYPS > TRYP
TRYPSIN n enzyme occurring in pancreatic juice
TRYPSINS > TRYPSIN
TRYPTIC > TRYPSIN
TRYSAIL n small fore-and-aft sail set on a sailing vessel to help keep her head to the wind in a storm
TRYSAILS > TRYSAIL
TRYST n arrangement to meet ▷ vb meet at or arrange a tryst
TRYSTE variant spelling of > TRYST
TRYSTED > TRYST
TRYSTER > TRYST
TRYSTERS > TRYST
TRYSTES > TRYSTE
TRYSTING > TRYST
TRYSTS > TRYST
TRYWORKS n furnace for rendering blubber
TSADDIK variant of > ZADDIK
TSADDIKIM > TSADDIK
TSADDIKS > TSADDIK
TSADDIQ variant of > ZADDIK
TSADDIQIM > TSADDIQ
TSADDIQS > TSADDIQ
TSADE variant spelling of > SADHE
TSADES > TSADE
TSADI variant of > SADHE
TSADIS > TSADI
TSAMBA n Tibetan dish made from roasted barley and tea
TSAMBAS > TSAMBA
TSANTSA n (among the Shuar subgroup of the Jivaro people of Ecuador) shrunken head of an enemy kept as a trophy
TSANTSAS > TSANTSA
TSAR n Russian emperor
TSARDOM > TSAR
TSARDOMS > TSAR
TSAREVICH n tsar's son
TSAREVNA n daughter of a Russian tsar
TSAREVNAS > TSAREVNA
TSARINA n wife of a Russian tsar
TSARINAS > TSARINA
TSARISM n system of government by a tsar, esp in Russia until 1917
TSARISMS > TSARISM
TSARIST > TSARISM
TSARISTS > TSARISM
TSARITSA same as > TSARINA
TSARITSAS > TSARITSA
TSARITZA variant spelling of > TSARITSA
TSARITZAS > TSARITZA
TSARS > TSAR
TSATSKE variant of > TCHOTCHKE
TSATSKES > TSATSKE
TSESSEBE South African variant of > SASSABY
TSESSEBES > TSESSEBE
TSETSE n any of various bloodsucking African dipterous flies which

transmit the pathogens of various diseases
TSETSES > TSETSE
TSIGANE variant of > TZIGANE
TSIGANES > TSIGANE
TSIMMES variant spelling of > TZIMMES
TSITSITH n tassels or fringes of thread attached to the four corners of the tallith
TSK vb utter the sound "tsk", usu in disapproval
TSKED > TSK
TSKING > TSK
TSKS > TSK
TSKTSK same as > TSK
TSKTSKED > TSKTSK
TSKTSKING > TSKTSK
TSKTSKS > TSKTSK
TSOORIS variant of > TSURIS
TSORES variant of > TSURIS
TSORIS variant of > TSURIS
TSORRISS variant of > TSURIS
TSOTSI n Black street thug or gang member
TSOTSIS > TSOTSI
TSOURIS variant of > TSURIS
TSOURISES > TSOURIS
TSUBA n sword guard of a Japanese sword
TSUBAS > TSUBA
TSUNAMI n tidal wave, usu caused by an earthquake under the sea
TSUNAMIC > TSUNAMI
TSUNAMIS > TSUNAMI
TSURIS n grief or strife
TSURISES > TSURIS
TSUTSUMU n Japanese art of wrapping gifts
TSUTSUMUS > TSUTSUMU
TUAN n lord
TUANS > TUAN
TUART n eucalyptus tree of Australia, yielding a very durable light-coloured timber
TUARTS > TUART
TUATARA n large lizard-like New Zealand reptile
TUATARAS > TUATARA
TUATERA variant spelling of > TUATARA
TUATERAS > TUATERA
TUATH n territory of an ancient Irish tribe
TUATHS > TUATH
TUATUA n edible marine bivalve of New Zealand waters
TUB n open, usu round container ▷ vb wash (oneself or another) in a tub
TUBA n valved low-pitched brass instrument
TUBAE > TUBA
TUBAGE n insertion of a tube
TUBAGES > TUBAGE
TUBAIST > TUBA
TUBAISTS > TUBA
TUBAL adj of or relating to a tube
TUBAR another word for > TUBULAR

TUBAS > TUBA
TUBATE less common word for > TUBULAR
TUBBABLE > TUB
TUBBED > TUB
TUBBER > TUB
TUBBERS > TUB
TUBBIER > TUBBY
TUBBIEST > TUBBY
TUBBINESS > TUBBY
TUBBING > TUB
TUBBINGS > TUB
TUBBISH adj fat
TUBBY adj (of a person) short and fat
TUBE n hollow cylinder
TUBECTOMY n excision of the Fallopian tubes
TUBED > TUBE
TUBEFUL n quantity (of something) that a tube can hold
TUBEFULS > TUBEFUL
TUBELESS adj without a tube
TUBELIKE adj resembling a tube
TUBENOSE n seabird with tubular nostrils on its beak
TUBENOSES > TUBENOSE
TUBER n fleshy underground root of a plant such as a potato
TUBERCLE n small rounded swelling
TUBERCLED adj having tubercles
TUBERCLES > TUBERCLE
TUBERCULA n plural of tuberculum (another name for "turbercle")
TUBERCULE variant of > TUBERCLE
TUBEROID adj resembling a tuber
TUBEROSE same as > TUBEROUS
TUBEROSES > TUBEROSE
TUBEROUS adj (of plants) forming, bearing, or resembling a tuber or tubers
TUBERS > TUBER
TUBES > TUBE
TUBEWORK n collective term for tubes or tubing
TUBEWORKS > TUBEWORK
TUBEWORM n undersea worm
TUBEWORMS > TUBEWORM
TUBFAST n period of fasting and sweating in a tub, intended as a cure for disease
TUBFASTS > TUBFAST
TUBFISH another name for > GURNARD
TUBFISHES > TUBFISH
TUBFUL n amount a tub will hold
TUBFULS > TUBFUL
TUBICOLAR adj tube-dwelling
TUBICOLE n tube-dwelling creature
TUBICOLES > TUBICOLE
TUBIFEX n any small

reddish freshwater oligochaete worm of the genus Tubifex
TUBIFEXES > TUBIFEX
TUBIFICID n type of threadlike annelid worm
TUBIFORM same as > TUBULAR
TUBING n length of tube
TUBINGS > TUBING
TUBIST > TUBA
TUBISTS > TUBA
TUBLIKE > TUB
TUBS > TUB
TUBULAR adj of or shaped like a tube
TUBULARLY > TUBULAR
TUBULATE vb form or shape into a tube
TUBULATED > TUBULATE
TUBULATES > TUBULATE
TUBULATOR > TUBULATE
TUBULE n any small tubular structure, esp in an animal or plant
TUBULES > TUBULE
TUBULIN n protein forming the basis of microtubules
TUBULINS > TUBULIN
TUBULOSE adj tube-shaped; consisting of tubes
TUBULOUS adj tube-shaped
TUBULURE n tube leading into a retort or other receptacle
TUBULURES > TUBULURE
TUCHUN n (formerly) a Chinese military governor or warlord
TUCHUNS > TUCHUN
TUCK vb push or fold into a small space ▷ n stitched fold ▷ vb touch or strike
TUCKAHOE n type of edible root
TUCKAHOES > TUCKAHOE
TUCKED > TUCK
TUCKER n food ▷ vb weary or tire completely
TUCKERBAG n in Australia, bag or box used for carrying food
TUCKERBOX same as > TUCKERBAG
TUCKERED > TUCKER
TUCKERING > TUCKER
TUCKERS > TUCKER
TUCKET n flourish on a trumpet
TUCKETS > TUCKET
TUCKING > TUCK
TUCKS > TUCK
TUCKSHOP n shop, esp one in or near a school, where food such as cakes and sweets are sold
TUCKSHOPS > TUCKSHOP
TUCOTUCO n colonial burrowing South American rodent
TUCOTUCOS > TUCOTUCO
TUCUTUCO variant spelling of > TUCOTUCO
TUCUTUCOS > TUCOTUCO
TUCUTUCU same as > TUCOTUCO
TUCUTUCUS > TUCUTUCU

TUFA n porous rock formed as a deposit from springs
TUFACEOUS > TUFA
TUFAS > TUFA
TUFF n porous rock formed from volcanic dust or ash
TUFFE old form of > TUFT
TUFFES > TUFFE
TUFFET n small mound or seat
TUFFETS > TUFFET
TUFFS > TUFF
TUFOLI n type of tubular pasta
TUFT n bunch of feathers, grass, hair, etc held or growing together at the base ▷ vb provide or decorate with a tuft or tufts
TUFTED adj having a tuft or tufts
TUFTER > TUFT
TUFTERS > TUFT
TUFTIER > TUFT
TUFTIEST > TUFT
TUFTILY > TUFT
TUFTING > TUFT
TUFTINGS > TUFT
TUFTS > TUFT
TUFTY > TUFT
TUG vb pull hard ▷ n hard pull
TUGBOAT same as > TUG
TUGBOATS > TUGBOAT
TUGGED > TUG
TUGGER > TUG
TUGGERS > TUG
TUGGING > TUG
TUGGINGLY > TUG
TUGGINGS > TUG
TUGHRA n Turkish Sultan's official emblem
TUGHRAS > TUGHRA
TUGHRIK same as > TUGRIK
TUGHRIKS > TUGHRIK
TUGLESS > TUG
TUGRA variant of > TUGHRA
TUGRAS > TUGRA
TUGRIK n standard monetary unit of Mongolia, divided into 100 möngös
TUGRIKS > TUGRIK
TUGS > TUG
TUI n New Zealand honeyeater that mimics human speech and the songs of other birds
TUILLE n (in a suit of armour) hanging plate protecting the thighs
TUILLES > TUILLE
TUILLETTE n little tuille
TUILYIE vb fight
TUILYIED > TUILYIE
TUILYIES > TUILYIE
TUILZIE variant form of > TUILYIE
TUILZIED > TUILZIE
TUILZIES > TUILZIE
TUINA n form of massage originating in China
TUINAS > TUINA
TUIS > TUI
TUISM n practice of putting the interests of another

before one's own
TUISMS > TUISM
TUITION n instruction, esp received individually or in a small group
TUITIONAL > TUITION
TUITIONS > TUITION
TUKTOO same as > TUKTU
TUKTOOS > TUKTOO
TUKTU (in Canada) another name for > CARIBOU
TUKTUS > TUKTU
TULADI n large trout found in Canada and northern areas of the US
TULADIS > TULADI
TULAREMIA n infectious disease of rodents
TULAREMIC > TULAREMIA
TULBAN old form of > TURBAN
TULBANS > TULBAN
TULCHAN n skin of a calf placed next to a cow to induce it to give milk
TULCHANS > TULCHAN
TULE n type of bulrush found in California
TULES > TULE
TULIP n plant with bright cup-shaped flowers
TULIPANT n turban
TULIPANTS > TULIPANT
TULIPLIKE > TULIP
TULIPS > TULIP
TULIPWOOD n light soft wood of the tulip tree, used in making furniture and veneer
TULLE n fine net fabric of silk etc
TULLES > TULLE
TULLIBEE n cisco of the Great Lakes of Canada
TULLIBEES > TULLIBEE
TULPA n being or object created through willpower and visualization techniques
TULPAS > TULPA
TULWAR n Indian sabre
TULWARS > TULWAR
TUM informal or childish word for > STOMACH
TUMBLE vb (cause to) fall, esp awkwardly or violently ▷ n fall
TUMBLEBUG n type of dung beetle
TUMBLED > TUMBLE
TUMBLER n stemless drinking glass
TUMBLERS > TUMBLER
TUMBLES > TUMBLE
TUMBLESET n somersault
TUMBLING > TUMBLE
TUMBLINGS > TUMBLING
TUMBREL n farm cart for carrying dung, esp one that tilts backwards to deposit its load
TUMBRELS > TUMBREL
TUMBRIL same as > TUMBREL
TUMBRILS > TUMBRIL
TUMEFIED > TUMEFY
TUMEFIES > TUMEFY
TUMEFY vb make or become tumid

TUMEFYING > TUMEFY
TUMESCE vb swell
TUMESCED > TUMESCE
TUMESCENT adj swollen or becoming swollen
TUMESCES > TUMESCE
TUMESCING > TUMESCE
TUMID adj (of an organ or part of the body) enlarged or swollen
TUMIDITY > TUMID
TUMIDLY > TUMID
TUMIDNESS > TUMID
TUMMIES > TUMMY
TUMMLER n comedian or other entertainer employed to encourage audience participation or to encourage guests at a resort to take part in communal activities
TUMMLERS > TUMMLER
TUMMY n stomach
TUMOR same as > TUMOUR
TUMORAL > TUMOUR
TUMORLIKE > TUMOUR
TUMOROUS > TUMOUR
TUMORS > TUMOR
TUMOUR n abnormal growth in or on the body
TUMOURS > TUMOUR
TUMP n small mound or clump ▷ vb make a tump around
TUMPED > TUMP
TUMPHIES > TUMPHY
TUMPHY n dolt; fool
TUMPIER > TUMP
TUMPIEST > TUMP
TUMPING > TUMP
TUMPLINE n (in the US and Canada, esp formerly) leather or cloth band strung across the forehead or chest and attached to a pack or load in order to support it
TUMPLINES > TUMPLINE
TUMPS > TUMP
TUMPY > TUMP
TUMS > TUM
TUMSHIE n turnip
TUMSHIES > TUMSHIE
TUMULAR adj of, relating to, or like a mound
TUMULARY same as > TUMULAR
TUMULI > TUMULUS
TUMULOSE adj abounding in small hills or mounds
TUMULOUS same as > TUMULOSE
TUMULT n uproar or commotion ▷ vb stir up a commotion
TUMULTED > TUMULT
TUMULTING > TUMULT
TUMULTS > TUMULT
TUMULUS n burial mound
TUMULUSES > TUMULUS
TUN n large beer cask ▷ vb put into or keep in tuns
TUNA n large marine food fish
TUNABLE adj able to be tuned
TUNABLY > TUNABLE

TUNAS > TUNA
TUNBELLY n large round belly
TUND vb beat; strike
TUNDED > TUND
TUNDING > TUND
TUNDISH n type of funnel
TUNDISHES > TUNDISH
TUNDRA n vast treeless Arctic region with permanently frozen subsoil
TUNDRAS > TUNDRA
TUNDS > TUND
TUNDUN n wooden instrument used by Native Australians in religious rites
TUNDUNS > TUNDUN
TUNE n (pleasing) sequence of musical notes ▷ vb adjust (a musical instrument) so that it is in tune
TUNEABLE same as > TUNABLE
TUNEABLY > TUNEABLE
TUNED > TUNE
TUNEFUL adj having a pleasant tune
TUNEFULLY > TUNEFUL
TUNELESS adj having no melody or tune
TUNER n part of a radio or television receiver for selecting channels
TUNERS > TUNER
TUNES > TUNE
TUNESMITH n composer of light or popular music and songs
TUNEUP n adjustments made to an engine to improve its performance
TUNEUPS > TUNEUP
TUNG as in tung oil fast-drying oil obtained from the seeds of a central Asian euphorbiaceous tree, used in paints, varnishes, etc, as a drying agent and to give a water-resistant finish
TUNGS > TUNG
TUNGSTATE n salt of tungstic acid
TUNGSTEN n greyish-white metal
TUNGSTENS > TUNGSTEN
TUNGSTIC adj of or containing tungsten, esp in a high valence state
TUNGSTITE n yellow earthy rare secondary mineral that consists of tungsten oxide and occurs with tungsten ores
TUNGSTOUS adj of or containing tungsten in a low valence state
TUNIC n close-fitting jacket forming part of some uniforms
TUNICA n tissue forming a layer or covering of an organ or part, such as any of the tissue layers of a blood vessel wall
TUNICAE > TUNICA

TUNICATE *n* minute primitive marine chordate animal ▷ *adj* of, relating to this animal ▷ *vb* wear a tunic

TUNICATED > TUNICATE

TUNICATES > TUNICATE

TUNICIN *n* cellulose-like substance found in tunicates

TUNICINS > TUNICIN

TUNICKED *adj* wearing a tunic

TUNICLE *n* liturgical vestment worn by the subdeacon and bishops at High Mass and other religious ceremonies

TUNICLES > TUNICLE

TUNICS > TUNIC

TUNIER > TUNY

TUNIEST > TUNY

TUNING *n* set of pitches to which the open strings of a guitar, violin, etc, are tuned

TUNINGS > TUNING

TUNNAGE *same as* > TONNAGE

TUNNAGES > TUNNAGE

TUNNED > TUN

TUNNEL *n* underground passage ▷ *vb* make a tunnel (through)

TUNNELED > TUNNEL

TUNNELER > TUNNEL

TUNNELERS > TUNNEL

TUNNELING > TUNNEL

TUNNELLED > TUNNEL

TUNNELLER > TUNNEL

TUNNELS > TUNNEL

TUNNIES > TUNNY

TUNNING > TUN

TUNNINGS > TUN

TUNNY *same as* > TUNA

TUNS > TUN

TUNY *adj* having an easily discernable melody

TUP *n* male sheep ▷ *vb* cause (a ram) to mate with a ewe, or (of a ram) to mate with (a ewe)

TUPEK *same as* > TUPIK

TUPEKS > TUPEK

TUPELO *n* large tree of deep swamps and rivers of the southern US

TUPELOS > TUPELO

TUPIK *n* tent of seal or caribou skin used for shelter by the Inuit in summer

TUPIKS > TUPIK

TUPLE *n* row of values in a relational database

TUPLES > TUPLE

TUPPED > TUP

TUPPENCE *same as* > TWOPENCE

TUPPENCES > TUPPENCE

TUPPENNY *same as* > TWOPENNY

TUPPING > TUP

TUPS > TUP

TUPTOWING *n* study of Greek grammar

TUPUNA *same as* > TIPUNA

TUPUNAS > TUPUNA

TUQUE *n* knitted cap with a long tapering end

TUQUES > TUQUE

TURACIN *n* red pigment found in touraco feathers

TURACINS > TURACIN

TURACO *same as* > TOURACO

TURACOS > TURACO

TURACOU *variant of* > TOURACO

TURACOUS > TURACOU

TURBAN *n* Muslim, Hindu, or Sikh man's head covering, made by winding cloth round the head

TURBAND *old variant of* > TURBAN

TURBANDS > TURBAND

TURBANED > TURBAN

TURBANNED > TURBAN

TURBANS > TURBAN

TURBANT *old variant of* > TURBAN

TURBANTS > TURBANT

TURBARIES > TURBARY

TURBARY *n* land where peat or turf is cut or has been cut

TURBETH *variant of* > TURPETH

TURBETHS > TURBETH

TURBID *adj* muddy, not clear

TURBIDITE *n* sediment deposited by a turbidity current

TURBIDITY > TURBID

TURBIDLY > TURBID

TURBINAL *same as* > TURBINATE

TURBINALS > TURBINAL

TURBINATE *adj* of or relating to any of the thin scroll-shaped bones situated on the walls of the nasal passages ▷ *n* turbinate bone

TURBINE *n* machine or generator driven by gas, water, etc turning blades

TURBINED *adj* having a turbine

TURBINES > TURBINE

TURBIT *n* crested breed of domestic pigeon

TURBITH *variant of* > TURPETH

TURBITHS > TURBITH

TURBITS > TURBIT

TURBO *n* compressor in an engine

TURBOCAR *n* car driven by a gas turbine

TURBOCARS > TURBOCAR

TURBOFAN *n* engine in which a large fan driven by a turbine forces air rearwards to increase the thrust

TURBOFANS > TURBOFAN

TURBOJET *n* gas turbine in which the exhaust gases provide the propulsive thrust to drive an aircraft

TURBOJETS > TURBOJET

TURBOND *old variant of* > TURBAN

TURBONDS > TURBOND

TURBOPROP *n* gas turbine for driving an aircraft propeller

TURBOS > TURBO

TURBOT *n* large European edible flatfish

TURBOTS > TURBOT

TURBULENT *adj* involving a lot of sudden changes and conflicting elements

TURCOPOLE *n* lightly armed and highly mobile class of Crusader

TURD *n* piece of excrement

TURDINE *adj* of, relating to, or characteristic of thrushes

TURDION *variant of* > TORDION

TURDIONS > TURDION

TURDOID *same as* > TURDINE

TURDS > TURD

TUREEN *n* serving dish for soup

TUREENS > TUREEN

TURF *n* short thick even grass ▷ *vb* cover with turf

TURFED > TURF

TURFEN *adj* made of turf

TURFGRASS *n* grass grown for lawns

TURFIER > TURFY

TURFIEST > TURFY

TURFINESS > TURFY

TURFING > TURF

TURFINGS > TURF

TURFITE *same as* > TURFMAN

TURFITES > TURFITE

TURFLESS > TURF

TURFLIKE > TURF

TURFMAN *n* person devoted to horse racing

TURFMEN > TURFMAN

TURFS > TURF

TURFSKI *n* ski down a grassy hill on skis modified with integral wheels

TURFSKIS > TURFSKI

TURFY *adj* of, covered with, or resembling turf

TURGENCY > TURGENT

TURGENT *obsolete word for* > TURGID

TURGENTLY > TURGENT

TURGID *adj* (of language) pompous

TURGIDER > TURGID

TURGIDEST > TURGID

TURGIDITY > TURGID

TURGIDLY > TURGID

TURGITE *n* red or black mineral consisting of hydrated ferric oxide

TURGITES > TURGITE

TURGOR *n* normal rigid state of a cell, caused by pressure of the cell contents against the cell wall or membrane

TURGORS > TURGOR

TURION *n* perennating bud produced by many aquatic plants

TURIONS > TURION

TURISTA *n* traveller's diarrhoea

TURISTAS > TURISTA

TURK *n* obsolete derogatory term for a violent, brutal, or domineering person

TURKEY *n* large bird bred for food

TURKEYS > TURKEY

TURKIES *old form of* > TURQUOISE

TURKIESES > TURKIES

TURKIS *old form of* > TURQUOISE

TURKISES > TURKIS

TURKOIS *old form of* > TURQUOISE

TURKOISES > TURKOIS

TURKS > TURK

TURLOUGH *n* seasonal lake or pond

TURLOUGHS > TURLOUGH

TURM *n* troop of horsemen

TURME *variant of* > TURM

TURMERIC *n* yellow spice obtained from the root of an Asian plant

TURMERICS > TURMERIC

TURMES > TURME

TURMOIL *n* agitation or confusion ▷ *vb* make or become turbulent

TURMOILED > TURMOIL

TURMOILS > TURMOIL

TURMS > TURM

TURN *vb* change the position or direction (of) ▷ *n* turning

TURNABLE > TURN

TURNABOUT *n* act of turning so as to face a different direction

TURNAGAIN *n* revolution

TURNBACK *n* one who turns back (from a challenge, for example)

TURNBACKS > TURNBACK

TURNCOAT *n* person who deserts one party or cause to join another

TURNCOATS > TURNCOAT

TURNCOCK *n* (formerly) official employed to turn on the water for the mains supply

TURNCOCKS > TURNCOCK

TURNDOWN *adj* capable of being or designed to be folded or doubled down ▷ *n* instance of turning down

TURNDOWNS > TURNDOWN

TURNDUN *another name for* > TUNDUN

TURNDUNS > TURNDUN

TURNED > TURN

TURNER *n* person or thing that turns, esp a person who operates a lathe

TURNERIES > TURNERY

TURNERS > TURNER

TURNERY *n* objects made on a lathe

TURNHALL *n* building in which gymnastics is taught and practised

TURNHALLS > TURNHALL

TURNING *n* road or path leading off a main route

TURNINGS > TURNING

TURNIP *n* root vegetable

Section 1: Words between 2 and 9 letters in length

with orange or white flesh ▷ vb sow (a field) with turnips

TURNIPED > TURNIP

TURNIPING > TURNIP

TURNIPS > TURNIP

TURNKEY n jailer ▷ adj denoting a project, as in civil engineering, in which a single contractor has responsibility for the complete job from the start to the time of installation or occupancy

TURNKEYS > TURNKEY

TURNOFF road or other way branching off from the main

TURNOFFS > TURNOFF

TURNON n something sexually exciting

TURNONS > TURNON

TURNOUT n number of people appearing at a gathering

TURNOUTS > TURNOUT

TURNOVER n total sales made by a business over a certain period

TURNOVERS > TURNOVER

TURNPIKE n road where a toll is collected at barriers

TURNPIKES > TURNPIKE

TURNROUND n act or process in which a ship, aircraft, etc, unloads passengers and freight at end of a trip and reloads for next trip

TURNS > TURN

TURNSKIN n old name for a werewolf

TURNSKINS > TURNSKIN

TURNSOLE n any of various plants having flowers that are said to turn towards the sun

TURNSOLES > TURNSOLE

TURNSPIT n (formerly) a servant or small dog whose job was to turn the spit on which meat, poultry, etc, was roasting

TURNSPITS > TURNSPIT

TURNSTILE n revolving gate for admitting one person at a time

TURNSTONE n shore bird

TURNTABLE n revolving platform

TURNUP n the turned-up fold at the bottom of some trouser legs

TURNUPS > TURNUP

TUROPHILE n person who loves cheese

TURPETH n convolvulaceous plant of the East Indies, having roots with purgative properties

TURPETHS > TURPETH

TURPITUDE n wickedness

TURPS n colourless, flammable liquid

TURQUOIS variant of > TURQUOISE

TURQUOISE adj blue-green ▷ n blue-green precious

stone

TURRET n small tower

TURRETED adj having or resembling a turret or turrets

TURRETS > TURRET

TURRIBANT old variant of > TURBAN

TURRICAL adj of, relating to, or resembling a turret

TURTLE n sea tortoise

TURTLED > TURTLE

TURTLER > TURTLE

TURTLERS > TURTLE

TURTLES > TURTLE

TURTLING > TURTLE

TURTLINGS > TURTLE

TURVES > TURF

TUSCHE n substance used in lithography for drawing the design and as a resist in silk-screen printing and lithography

TUSCHES > TUSCHE

TUSH interj exclamation of disapproval or contempt ▷ n small tusk ▷ vb utter the interjection "tush"

TUSHED > TUSH

TUSHERIES > TUSHERY

TUSHERY n use of affectedly archaic language in novels, etc

TUSHES > TUSH

TUSHIE n pair of buttocks

TUSHIES > TUSHIE

TUSHING > TUSH

TUSHKAR variant of > TUSKAR

TUSHKARS > TUSHKAR

TUSHKER variant of > TUSKAR

TUSHKERS > TUSHKER

TUSHY variant of > TUSHIE

TUSK n long pointed tooth of an elephant, walrus, etc ▷ vb stab, tear, or gore with the tusks

TUSKAR n peat-cutting spade

TUSKARS > TUSKAR

TUSKED > TUSK

TUSKER n any animal with prominent tusks, esp a wild boar or elephant

TUSKERS > TUSKER

TUSKIER > TUSK

TUSKIEST > TUSK

TUSKING > TUSK

TUSKINGS > TUSK

TUSKLESS > TUSK

TUSKLIKE > TUSK

TUSKS > TUSK

TUSKY > TUSK

TUSSAH same as > TUSSORE

TUSSAHS > TUSSAH

TUSSAL > TUSSIS

TUSSAR variant of > TUSSORE

TUSSARS > TUSSAR

TUSSEH variant of > TUSSORE

TUSSEHS > TUSSEH

TUSSER same as > TUSSORE

TUSSERS > TUSSER

TUSSES > TUSS

TUSSIS technical name for a > COUGH

TUSSISES > TUSSIS

TUSSIVE > TUSSIS

TUSSLE vb fight or scuffle

▷ n energetic fight, struggle, or argument

TUSSLED > TUSSLE

TUSSLES > TUSSLE

TUSSLING > TUSSLE

TUSSOCK n tuft of grass

TUSSOCKED adj having tussocks

TUSSOCKS > TUSSOCK

TUSSOCKY > TUSSOCK

TUSSOR variant of > TUSSORE

TUSSORE n strong coarse brownish Indian silk obtained from the cocoons of an Oriental saturniid silkworm

TUSSORES > TUSSORE

TUSSORS > TUSSOR

TUSSUCK variant of > TUSSOCK

TUSSUCKS > TUSSUCK

TUSSUR variant of > TUSSORE

TUSSURS > TUSSUR

TUT interj an exclamation of mild reprimand, disapproval, or surprise ▷ vb express disapproval by the exclamation of "tut-tut." ▷ n payment system based on measurable work done rather that time spent doing it

TUTANIA n alloy of low melting point containing tin, antimony, copper and used mostly for decorative purposes

TUTANIAS > TUTANIA

TUTEE n one who is tutored, esp in a university

TUTEES > TUTEE

TUTELAGE n instruction or guidance, esp by a tutor

TUTELAGES > TUTELAGE

TUTELAR same as > TUTELARY

TUTELARS > TUTELAR

TUTELARY adj having the role of guardian or protector ▷ n tutelary person, deity, or saint

TUTENAG n zinc alloy

TUTENAGS > TUTENAG

TUTIORISM n (in Roman Catholic moral theology) the doctrine that in cases of moral doubt it is best to follow the safer course or that in agreement with the law

TUTIORIST > TUTIORISM

TUTMAN n one who does tutwork

TUTMEN > TUTMAN

TUTOR n person teaching individuals or small groups ▷ vb act as a tutor to

TUTORAGE > TUTOR

TUTORAGES > TUTOR

TUTORED > TUTOR

TUTORESS n female tutor

TUTORIAL n period of instruction with a tutor ▷ adj of or relating to a tutor

TUTORIALS > TUTORIAL

TUTORING > TUTOR

TUTORINGS > TUTOR

TUTORISE variant spelling of > TUTORIZE

TUTORISED > TUTORISE

TUTORISES > TUTORISE

TUTORISM > TUTOR

TUTORISMS > TUTOR

TUTORIZE vb tutor

TUTORIZED > TUTOR

TUTORIZES > TUTOR

TUTORS > TUTOR

TUTORSHIP > TUTOR

TUTOYED > TUTOY

TUTOYER vb speak to someone on familiar terms

TUTOYERED > TUTOYER

TUTOYERS > TUTOYER

TUTRESS same as > TUTORESS

TUTRESSES > TUTRESS

TUTRICES > TUTRIX

TUTRIX n female tutor; tutoress

TUTRIXES > TUTRIX

TUTS Scots version of > TUT

TUTSAN n woodland shrub of Europe and W Asia

TUTSANS > TUTSAN

TUTSED > TUTS

TUTSES > TUTS

TUTSING > TUTS

TUTTED > TUT

TUTTI adv be performed by the whole orchestra or choir ▷ n piece of tutti music

TUTTIES > TUTTY

TUTTING > TUT

TUTTINGS > TUT

TUTTIS > TUTTI

TUTTY n finely powdered impure zinc oxide obtained from the flues of zinc-smelting furnaces and used as a polishing powder

TUTU n short stiff skirt worn by ballerinas

TUTUED adj wearing tutu

TUTUS > TUTU

TUTWORK n work paid using a tut system

TUTWORKER > TUTWORK

TUTWORKS > TUTWORK

TUX short for > TUXEDO

TUXEDO n dinner jacket

TUXEDOED adj wearing a tuxedo

TUXEDOES > TUXEDO

TUXEDOS > TUXEDO

TUXES > TUX

TUYER variant of > TUYERE

TUYERE n water-cooled nozzle through which air is blown into a cupola, blast furnace, or forge

TUYERES > TUYERE

TUYERS > TUYER

TUZZ n tuft or clump of hair

TUZZES > TUZZ

TWA Scots word for > TWO

TWADDLE n silly or pretentious talk or writing ▷ vb talk or write in a silly or pretentious way

TWADDLED > TWADDLE

TWADDLER > TWADDLE

TWADDLERS > TWADDLE

TWADDLES > TWADDLE
TWADDLIER > TWADDLE
TWADDLING > TWADDLE
TWADDLY > TWADDLE
TWAE *same as* > TWA
TWAES > TWAE
TWAFALD *Scots variant of* > TWOFOLD
TWAIN *n* two
TWAINS > TWAIN
TWAITE *n* herring-like food fish
TWAITES > TWAITE
TWAL *n* twelve
TWALPENNY *n* shilling
TWALS > TWAL
TWANG *n* sharp ringing sound ▷ *vb* (cause to) make a twang
TWANGED > TWANG
TWANGER > TWANG
TWANGERS > TWANG
TWANGIER > TWANG
TWANGIEST > TWANG
TWANGING > TWANG
TWANGINGS > TWANG
TWANGLE *vb* make a continuous loose twanging sound (on a musical instrument, for example)
TWANGLED > TWANGLE
TWANGLER > TWANGLE
TWANGLERS > TWANGLE
TWANGLES > TWANGLE
TWANGLING > TWANGLE
TWANGS > TWANG
TWANGY > TWANG
TWANK *vb* make an sharply curtailed twang
TWANKAY *n* variety of Chinese green tea
TWANKAYS > TWANKAY
TWANKIES > TWANKY
TWANKS > TWANK
TWANKY *same as* > TWANKAY
TWAS > TWA
TWASOME *same as* > TWOSOME
TWASOMES > TWASOME
TWAT *n* taboo term for female genitals
TWATS > TWAT
TWATTLE *rare word for* > TWADDLE
TWATTLED > TWATTLE
TWATTLER > TWATTLE
TWATTLERS > TWATTLE
TWATTLES > TWATTLE
TWATTLING > TWATTLE
TWAY *old variant of* > TWAIN
TWAYBLADE *n* type of orchid
TWAYS > TWAY
TWEAK *vb* pinch or twist sharply ▷ *n* tweaking
TWEAKED > TWEAK
TWEAKER *n* engineer's small screwdriver, used for fine adjustments
TWEAKERS > TWEAKER
TWEAKIER > TWEAK
TWEAKIEST > TWEAK
TWEAKING > TWEAK
TWEAKINGS > TWEAK
TWEAKS > TWEAK
TWEAKY > TWEAK
TWEE *adj* too sentimental, sweet, or pretty

TWEED *n* thick woollen cloth
TWEEDIER > TWEEDY
TWEEDIEST > TWEEDY
TWEEDLE *vb* improvise aimlessly on a musical instrument
TWEEDLED > TWEEDLE
TWEEDLER > TWEEDLE
TWEEDLERS > TWEEDLE
TWEEDLES > TWEEDLE
TWEEDLING > TWEEDLE
TWEEDS > TWEED
TWEEDY *adj* of or made of tweed
TWEEL *variant of* > TWILL
TWEELED > TWEEL
TWEELING > TWEEL
TWEELS > TWEEL
TWEELY > TWEE
TWEEN *same as* > BETWEEN
TWEENAGER *n* child of approximately eight to fourteen years of age
TWEENER *same as* > TWEENAGER
TWEENERS > TWEENER
TWEENESS > TWEE
TWEENIE *same as* > TWEENY
TWEENIES > TWEENY
TWEENS > TWEEN
TWEENY *n* maid who assists both cook and housemaid
TWEER *variant of* > TWIRE
TWEERED > TWEER
TWEERING > TWEER
TWEERS > TWEER
TWEEST > TWEE
TWEET *vb* chirp ▷ *interj* imitation of the thin chirping sound made by small birds
TWEETED > TWEET
TWEETER *n* loudspeaker reproducing high-frequency sounds
TWEETERS > TWEETER
TWEETING > TWEET
TWEETS > TWEET
TWEEZE *vb* take hold of or pluck (hair, small objects, etc) with or as if with tweezers
TWEEZED > TWEEZE
TWEEZER *same as* > TWEEZERS
TWEEZERS *pl n* small pincer-like tool
TWEEZES > TWEEZE
TWEEZING > TWEEZE
TWELFTH *n* (of) number twelve in a series ▷ *adj* of or being number twelve in a series
TWELFTHLY *adv* after the eleventh person, position, event, etc
TWELFTHS > TWELFTH
TWELVE *n* two more than ten ▷ *adj* amounting to twelve ▷ *determiner* amounting to twelve
TWELVEMO *another word for* > DUODECIMO
TWELVEMOS > TWELVEMO
TWELVES > TWELVE
TWENTIES > TWENTY
TWENTIETH *adj* coming

after the nineteenth in numbering or counting order, position, time, etc ▷ *n* one of 20 approximately equal parts of something
TWENTY *n* two times ten ▷ *adj* amounting to twenty ▷ *determiner* amounting to twenty
TWENTYISH *adj* around 20
TWERP *n* silly person
TWERPIER > TWERP
TWERPIEST > TWERP
TWERPS > TWERP
TWERPY > TWERP
TWIBIL *same as* > TWIBILL
TWIBILL *n* mattock with a blade shaped like an adze at one end and like an axe at the other
TWIBILLS > TWIBILL
TWIBILS > TWIBIL
TWICE *adv* two times
TWICER *n* someone who does something twice
TWICERS > TWICER
TWICHILD *n* person in his or her dotage
TWIDDLE *vb* fiddle or twirl in an idle way ▷ *n* act or instance of twiddling
TWIDDLED > TWIDDLE
TWIDDLER > TWIDDLE
TWIDDLERS > TWIDDLE
TWIDDLES > TWIDDLE
TWIDDLIER > TWIDDLE
TWIDDLING > TWIDDLE
TWIDDLY > TWIDDLE
TWIER *variant of* > TUYERE
TWIERS > TWIER
TWIFOLD *variant of* > TWOFOLD
TWIFORKED *adj* having two forks; bifurcate
TWIFORMED *adj* having two forms
TWIG *n* small branch or shoot ▷ *vb* realize or understand
TWIGGED > TWIG
TWIGGEN *adj* made of twigs
TWIGGER > TWIG
TWIGGERS > TWIG
TWIGGIER > TWIGGY
TWIGGIEST > TWIGGY
TWIGGING > TWIG
TWIGGY *adj* of or relating to a twig or twigs
TWIGHT *old variant of* > TWIT
TWIGHTED > TWIGHT
TWIGHTING > TWIGHT
TWIGHTS > TWIGHT
TWIGLESS > TWIG
TWIGLIKE > TWIG
TWIGLOO *n* temporary shelter made from twigs, branches, leaves, etc
TWIGLOOS > TWIGLOO
TWIGS > TWIG
TWIGSOME *adj* covered with twigs; twiggy
TWILIGHT *n* soft dim light just after sunset ▷ *adj* of or relating to the period towards the end of the day
TWILIGHTS > TWILIGHT

TWILIT > TWILIGHT
TWILL *n* fabric woven to produce parallel ridges ▷ *adj* (in textiles) of or designating a weave in which the weft yarns are worked around two or more warp yarns to produce an effect of parallel diagonal lines or ribs ▷ *vb* weave in this fashion
TWILLED > TWILL
TWILLIES > TWILLY
TWILLING > TWILL
TWILLINGS > TWILL
TWILLS > TWILL
TWILLY *n* machine having a system of revolving spikes for opening and cleaning raw textile fibres
TWILT *variant of* > QUILT
TWILTED > TWILT
TWILTING > TWILT
TWILTS > TWILT
TWIN *n* one of a pair, esp of two children born at one birth ▷ *vb* pair or be paired
TWINBERRY *n* creeping wooden plant
TWINBORN *adj* born as a twin
TWINE *n* string or cord ▷ *vb* twist or coil round
TWINED > TWINE
TWINER > TWINE
TWINERS > TWINE
TWINES > TWINE
TWINGE *n* sudden sharp pain or emotional pang ▷ *vb* have or cause to have a twinge
TWINGED > TWINGE
TWINGEING > TWINGE
TWINGES > TWINGE
TWINGING > TWINGE
TWINIER > TWINE
TWINIEST > TWINE
TWINIGHT *adj* (of a baseball double-header) held in the late afternoon and evening
TWINING > TWINE
TWININGLY > TWINE
TWININGS > TWINE
TWINJET *n* jet aircraft with two engines
TWINJETS > TWINJET
TWINK *n* white correction fluid for deleting written text ▷ *vb* twinkle
TWINKED > TWINK
TWINKIE *n* stupid person
TWINKIES > TWINKIE
TWINKING > TWINK
TWINKLE *vb* shine brightly but intermittently ▷ *n* flickering brightness
TWINKLED > TWINKLE
TWINKLER > TWINKLE
TWINKLERS > TWINKLE
TWINKLES > TWINKLE
TWINKLING *n* very short time
TWINKLY > TWINKLE
TWINKS > TWINK
TWINLING *old name for* > TWIN
TWINLINGS > TWINLING

TWINNED > TWIN

TWINNING > TWIN

TWINNINGS > TWIN

TWINS > TWIN

TWINSET *n* matching jumper and cardigan

TWINSETS > TWINSET

TWINSHIP *n* condition of being a twin or twins

TWINSHIPS > TWIN

TWINTER *n* animal that is 2 years old

TWINTERS > TWINTER

TWINY > TWINE

TWIRE *vb* look intently at with (or as if with) difficulty

TWIRED > TWIRE

TWIRES > TWIRE

TWIRING > TWIRE

TWIRL *vb* turn or spin around quickly ▷ *n* whirl or twist

TWIRLED > TWIRL

TWIRLER > TWIRL

TWIRLERS > TWIRL

TWIRLIER > TWIRL

TWIRLIEST > TWIRL

TWIRLING > TWIRL

TWIRLS > TWIRL

TWIRLY > TWIRL

TWIRP *same as* > TWERP

TWIRPIER > TWIRP

TWIRPIEST > TWIRP

TWIRPS > TWIRP

TWIRPY > TWIRP

TWISCAR *variant of* > TUSKAR

TWISCARS > TWISCAR

TWIST *vb* turn out of the natural position ▷ *n* twisting

TWISTABLE > TWIST

TWISTED > TWIST

TWISTER *n* swindler

TWISTERS > TWISTER

TWISTIER > TWIST

TWISTIEST > TWIST

TWISTING > TWIST

TWISTINGS > TWIST

TWISTOR *n* variable corresponding to the coordinates of a point in space and time

TWISTORS > TWISTOR

TWISTS > TWIST

TWISTY > TWIST

TWIT *vb* poke fun at (someone) ▷ *n* foolish person

TWITCH *vb* move spasmodically ▷ *n* nervous muscular spasm

TWITCHED > TWITCH

TWITCHER *n* bird-watcher who tries to spot as many rare varieties as possible

TWITCHERS > TWITCHER

TWITCHES > TWITCH

TWITCHIER > TWITCHY

TWITCHILY > TWITCHY

TWITCHING > TWITCH

TWITCHY *adj* nervous, worried, and ill-at-ease

TWITE *n* N European finch with a brown streaked plumage

TWITES > TWITE

TWITS > TWIT

TWITTED > TWIT

TWITTEN *n* narrow alleyway

TWITTENS > TWITTEN

TWITTER *vb* (of birds) utter chirping sounds ▷ *n* act or sound of twittering

TWITTERED > TWITTER

TWITTERER > TWITTER

TWITTERS > TWITTER

TWITTERY > TWITTER

TWITTING > TWIT

TWITTINGS > TWIT

TWIXT *same as* > BETWIXT

TWIZZLE *vb* spin around

TWIZZLED > TWIZZLE

TWIZZLES > TWIZZLE

TWIZZLING > TWIZZLE

TWO *n* one more than one

TWOCCER > TWOCCING

TWOCCERS > TWOCCING

TWOCCING *n* act of breaking into a motor vehicle and driving it away

TWOCCINGS > TWOCCING

TWOCKER > TWOCCING

TWOCKERS > TWOCCING

TWOCKING *same as* > TWOCCING

TWOCKINGS > TWOCKING

TWOER *n* (in a game) something that scores two

TWOERS > TWOER

TWOFER *n* single ticket allowing the buyer entrance to two events, attractions, etc, for substantially less than the cost were he or she to pay for each individually

TWOFERS > TWOFER

TWOFOLD *adj* having twice as many or as much ▷ *adv* by twice as many or as much ▷ *n* folding piece of theatrical scenery

TWOFOLDS > TWOFOLD

TWONESS *n* state or condition of being two

TWONESSES > TWONESS

TWONIE *same as* > TOONIE

TWONIES > TWONIE

TWOONIE *variant of* > TOONIE

TWOONIES > TWOONIE

TWOPENCE *n* sum of two pennies

TWOPENCES > TWOPENCE

TWOPENNY *adj* cheap or tawdry

TWOS > TWO

TWOSEATER *n* vehicle providing seats for two people

TWOSOME *n* group of two people

TWOSOMES > TWOSOME

TWOSTROKE *adj* relating to or designating an internal-combustion engine whose piston makes two strokes for every explosion

TWP *adj* stupid

TWYER *same as* > TUYERE

TWYERE *variant of* > TUYERE

TWYERES > TWYERE

TWYERS > TWYER

TWYFOLD *adj* twofold

TYCHISM *n* theory that chance is an objective reality at work in the universe, esp in evolutionary adaptations

TYCHISMS > TYCHISM

TYCOON *n* powerful wealthy businessman; shogun

TYCOONATE *n* office or rule of a tycoon

TYCOONERY > TYCOON

TYCOONS > TYCOON

TYDE *old variant of the past participle of* > TIE

TYE *n* trough used in mining to separate valuable material from dross ▷ *vb* (in mining) isolate valuable material from dross using a tye

TYED > TYE

TYEE *n* large northern Pacific salmon

TYEES > TYEE

TYEING > TYE

TYER > TYE

TYERS > TYE

TYES > TYE

TYG *n* mug with two handles

TYGS > TYG

TYIN *variant of* > TYIYN

TYING > TIE

TYIYN *n* money unit of Kyrgyzstan

TYKE *n* often offensive term for small cheeky child

TYKES > TYKE

TYKISH > TYKE

TYLECTOMY *n* excision of a breast tumour

TYLER *variant of* > TILER

TYLERS > TYLER

TYLOPOD *n* mammal with padded feet, such as a camel or llama

TYLOPODS > TYLOPOD

TYLOSES > TYLOSIS

TYLOSIN *n* broad spectrum antibiotic

TYLOSINS > TYLOSIN

TYLOSIS *n* bladder-like outgrowth from certain cells in woody tissue that extends into and blocks adjacent conducting xylem cells

TYLOTE *n* knobbed sponge spicule

TYLOTES > TYLOTE

TYMBAL *same as* > TIMBAL

TYMBALS > TYMBAL

TYMP *n* blast furnace outlet through which molten metal flows

TYMPAN *same as* > TYMPANUM

TYMPANA > TYMPANUM

TYMPANAL *adj* relating to the tympanum

TYMPANI *same as* > TIMPANI

TYMPANIC *adj* of, relating to, or having a tympanum ▷ *n* part of the temporal bone in the mammalian skull that surrounds the auditory canal

TYMPANICS > TYMPANIC

TYMPANIES > TYMPANY

TYMPANIST > TIMPANI

TYMPANO > TYMPANI

TYMPANS > TYMPAN

TYMPANUM *n* cavity of the middle ear

TYMPANUMS > TYMPANUM

TYMPANY *n* distention of the abdomen

TYMPS > TYMP

TYND *variant of* > TIND

TYNDE *variant of* > TIND

TYNE *variant of* > TINE

TYNED *variant of* > TYNE

TYNES > TYNE

TYNING > TYNE

TYPABLE > TYPE

TYPAL *rare word for* > TYPICAL

TYPE *n* class or category ▷ *vb* print with a typewriter or word processor

TYPEABLE > TYPE

TYPEBAR *n* one of the bars in a typewriter that carry the type and are operated by keys

TYPEBARS > TYPEBAR

TYPECASE *n* compartmental tray for storing printer's type

TYPECASES > TYPECASE

TYPECAST *vb* continually cast (an actor or actress) in similar roles

TYPECASTS > TYPECAST

TYPED > TYPE

TYPEFACE *n* style of the type

TYPEFACES > TYPEFACE

TYPES > TYPE

TYPESET *vb* set (text for printing) in type

TYPESETS > TYPESET

TYPESTYLE *another word for* > TYPEFACE

TYPEWRITE *vb* write by means of a typewriter

TYPEWROTE > TYPEWRITE

TYPEY *variant of* > TYPY

TYPHLITIC > TYPHLITIS

TYPHLITIS *n* inflammation of the caecum

TYPHOID *adj* of or relating to typhoid fever

TYPHOIDAL > TYPHOID

TYPHOIDIN *n* culture of dead typhoid bacillus for injection into the skin to test for typhoid fever

TYPHOIDS > TYPHOID

TYPHON *n* whirlwind

TYPHONIAN > TYPHON

TYPHONIC > TYPHOON

TYPHONS > TYPHON

TYPHOON *n* violent tropical storm

TYPHOONS > TYPHOON

TYPHOSE *adj* relating to typhoid

TYPHOUS > TYPHUS

TYPHUS *n* infectious feverish disease

TYPHUSES > TYPHUS

TYPIC *same as* > TYPICAL

TYPICAL *adj* true to type, characteristic

TYPICALLY > TYPICAL

TYPIER > TYPY

TYPIEST > TYPY

TYPIFIED > TYPIFY

TYPIFIER > TYPIFY

TYPIFIERS > TYPIFY

TYPIFIES > TYPIFY

TYPIFY vb be typical of

TYPIFYING > TYPIFY

TYPING n work or activity of using a typewriter or word processor

TYPINGS > TYPING

TYPIST n person who types with a typewriter or word processor

TYPISTS > TYPIST

TYPO n typographical error

TYPOGRAPH n person skilled in the art of composing type and printing from it

TYPOLOGIC > TYPOLOGY

TYPOLOGY n doctrine or study of types or of the correspondence between them and the realities which they typify

TYPOMANIA n obsession with typology

TYPOS > TYPO

TYPP n unit of thickness of yarn

TYPPS > TYPP

TYPTO vb learn Greek conjugations

TYPTOED > TYPTO

TYPTOING > TYPTO

TYPTOS > TYPTO

TYPY adj (of an animal) typifying the breed

TYRAMINE n colourless crystalline amine derived from phenol

TYRAMINES > TYRAMINE

TYRAN vb act as a tyrant

TYRANED > TYRAN

TYRANING > TYRAN

TYRANNE variant of > TYRAN

TYRANNED > TYRANNE

TYRANNES > TYRANNE

TYRANNESS n female tyrant

TYRANNIC > TYRANNY

TYRANNIES > TYRANNY

TYRANNING > TYRANNE

TYRANNIS n tyrannical government

TYRANNISE same as > TYRANNIZE

TYRANNIZE vb exert power (over) oppressively or cruelly

TYRANNOUS > TYRANNY

TYRANNY n tyrannical rule

TYRANS > TYRAN

TYRANT n oppressive or cruel ruler ▷ vb act the tyrant

TYRANTED > TYRANT

TYRANTING > TYRANT

TYRANTS > TYRANT

TYRE n rubber ring, usu inflated, over the rim of a vehicle's wheel to grip the road ▷ vb fit a tyre or tyres to (a wheel, vehicle, etc)

TYRED > TYRE

TYRELESS > TYRE

TYRES > TYRE

TYRING > TYRE

TYRO n novice or beginner

TYROCIDIN n antibiotic

TYROES > TYRO

TYRONES > TYRO

TYRONIC > TYRO

TYROPITTA n Greek cheese pie

TYROS > TYRO

TYROSINE n aromatic nonessential amino acid

TYROSINES > TYROSINE

TYSTIE n black guillemot

TYSTIES > TYSTIE

TYTE variant spelling of > TITE

TYTHE variant of > TITHE

TYTHED > TYTHE

TYTHES > TYTHE

TYTHING > TYTHE

TZADDIK variant of > ZADDIK

TZADDIKIM > TZADDIK

TZADDIKS > TZADDIK

TZADDIQ variant of > ZADDIK

TZADDIQIM > TZADDIQ

TZADDIQS > TZADDIQ

TZAR same as > TSAR

TZARDOM > TZAR

TZARDOMS > TZAR

TZAREVNA variant of > TSAREVNA

TZAREVNAS > TZAREVNA

TZARINA variant of > TSARINA

TZARINAS > TZARINA

TZARISM variant of > TSARISM

TZARISMS > TZARISM

TZARIST > TZARISM

TZARISTS > TZARISM

TZARITZA variant of > TSARITSA

TZARITZAS > TZARITZA

TZARS > TZAR

TZATZIKI n Greek dip made from yogurt, chopped cucumber, and mint

TZATZIKIS > TZATZIKI

TZETSE variant of > TSETSE

TZETSES > TZETSE

TZETZE variant of > TSETSE

TZETZES > TZETZE

TZIGANE n type of Gypsy music

TZIGANES > TZIGANE

TZIGANIES > TZIGANY

TZIGANY variant of > TZIGANE

TZIMMES n traditional Jewish stew

TZITZIS variant of > TSITSITH

TZITZIT variant of > TZITZIT

TZITZITH variant of > TSITSITH

TZURIS variant of > TSURIS

Uu

UAKARI n type of monkey
UAKARIS > UAKARI
UBEROUS adj abundant
UBERTIES > UBERTY
UBERTY n abundance
UBIETIES > UBIETY
UBIETY n condition of being in a particular place
UBIQUE adv everywhere
UBIQUITIN n type of polypeptide
UBIQUITY n state of apparently being everywhere at once; omnipresence
UCKERS n type of naval game
UDAL n form of freehold possession of land existing in northern Europe before the introduction of the feudal system and still used in Orkney and Shetland
UDALLER n person possessing a udal
UDALLERS > UDALLER
UDALS > UDAL
UDDER n large baglike milk-producing gland of cows, sheep, or goats
UDDERED > UDDER
UDDERFUL > UDDER
UDDERLESS > UDDER
UDDERS > UDDER
UDO n stout perennial plant of Japan and China with berry-like black fruits and young shoots that are edible when blanched
UDOMETER n archaic term for an instrument for measuring rainfall or snowfall
UDOMETERS > UDOMETER
UDOMETRIC > UDOMETER
UDOMETRY > UDOMETER
UDON n (in Japanese cookery) large noodles made of wheat flour
UDONS > UDON
UDOS > UDO
UDS interj God's or God save
UEY n u-turn
UEYS > UEY
UFO n flying saucer
UFOLOGIES > UFOLOGY
UFOLOGIST > UFOLOGY

UFOLOGY n study of UFOs
UFOS > UFO
UG vb hate
UGALI n type of stiff porridge made by mixing corn meal with boiling water: the basic starch constituent of a meal
UGALIS > UGALI
UGGED > UG
UGGING > UG
UGH interj exclamation of disgust ▷ n sound made to indicate disgust
UGHS > UGH
UGLIED > UGLY
UGLIER > UGLY
UGLIES > UGLY
UGLIEST > UGLY
UGLIFIED > UGLIFY
UGLIFIER > UGLIFY
UGLIFIERS > UGLIFY
UGLIFIES > UGLIFY
UGLIFY vb make or become ugly or more ugly
UGLIFYING > UGLIFY
UGLILY > UGLY
UGLINESS > UGLY
UGLY adj of unpleasant appearance ▷ vb make ugly
UGLYING > UGLY
UGS > UG
UGSOME adj loathsome
UH interj used to express hesitation
UHLAN n member of a body of lancers first employed in the Polish army and later in W European armies
UHLANS > UHLAN
UHURU n national independence
UHURUS > UHURU
UILLEAN as in uillean pipes bagpipes developed in Ireland and operated by squeezing bellows under the arm
UINTAHITE same as > UINTAITE
UINTAITE n variety of asphalt
UINTAITES > UINTAITE
UITLANDER n foreigner
UJAMAA as in ujamaa village communally organized

village in Tanzania
UJAMAAS > UJAMAA
UKASE n (in imperial Russia) a decree from the tsar
UKASES > UKASE
UKE short form of > UKULELE
UKELELE same as > UKULELE
UKELELES > UKELELE
UKES > UKE
UKULELE n small guitar with four strings
UKULELES > UKULELE
ULAMA n body of Muslim scholars or religious leaders
ULAMAS > ULAMA
ULAN same as > UHLAN
ULANS > ULAN
ULCER n open sore on the surface of the skin or mucous membrane. ▷ vb make or become ulcerous
ULCERATE vb make or become ulcerous
ULCERATED > ULCERATE
ULCERATES > ULCERATE
ULCERED > ULCER
ULCERING > ULCER
ULCEROUS adj of, like, or characterized by ulcers
ULCERS > ULCER
ULE n rubber tree
ULEMA same as > ULAMA
ULEMAS > ULEMA
ULES > ULE
ULEX n variety of shrub
ULEXES > ULEX
ULEXITE n type of mineral
ULEXITES > ULEXITE
ULICON same as > EULACHON
ULICONS > ULICON
ULIGINOSE same as > ULIGINOUS
ULIGINOUS adj marshy
ULIKON same as > EULACHON
ULIKONS > ULIKON
ULITIS n gingivitis
ULITISES > ULITIS
ULLAGE n volume by which a liquid container falls short of being full ▷ vb create ullage in
ULLAGED > ULLAGE
ULLAGES > ULLAGE
ULLAGING > ULLAGE
ULLING n process of filling
ULLINGS > ULLING

ULMACEOUS adj of, relating to, or belonging to the Ulmaceae, a temperate and tropical family of deciduous trees and shrubs having scaly buds, simple serrated leaves, and typically winged fruits: includes the elms
ULMIN n substance found in decaying vegetation
ULMINS > ULMIN
ULNA n inner and longer of the two bones of the human forearm
ULNAD adv towards the ulna
ULNAE > ULNA
ULNAR > ULNA
ULNARE n bone in the wrist
ULNARIA > ULNARE
ULNAS > ULNA
ULOSES > ULOSIS
ULOSIS n formation of a scar
ULOTRICHY n state of having woolly or curly hair
ULPAN n Israeli study centre
ULPANIM > ULPAN
ULSTER n man's heavy double-breasted overcoat
ULSTERED adj wearing an ulster
ULSTERS > ULSTER
ULTERIOR adj (of an aim, reason, etc) concealed or hidden
ULTIMA n final syllable of a word
ULTIMACY > ULTIMATE
ULTIMAS > ULTIMA
ULTIMATA > ULTIMATUM
ULTIMATE adj final in a series or process ▷ n most significant, highest, furthest, or greatest thing ▷ vb end
ULTIMATED > ULTIMATE
ULTIMATES > ULTIMATE
ULTIMATUM n final warning stating that action will be taken unless certain conditions are met
ULTIMO adv in or during the previous month
ULTION n vengeance
ULTIONS > ULTION
ULTRA n person who has

extreme or immoderate beliefs or opinions ▷ *adj* extreme or immoderate, esp in beliefs or opinions
ULTRACHIC *adj* extremely chic
ULTRACOLD *adj* extremely cold
ULTRACOOL *adj* extremely cool
ULTRADRY *adj* extremely dry
ULTRAFAST *adj* extremely fast
ULTRAFINE *adj* extremely fine
ULTRAHEAT *vb* sterilize through extreme heat treatment
ULTRAHIGH as in *ultrahigh frequency* radio-frequency band or radio frequency lying between 3000 and 300 megahertz
ULTRAHIP *adj* extremely trendy
ULTRAHOT *adj* extremely hot
ULTRAISM *n* extreme philosophy, belief, or action
ULTRAISMS > ULTRAISM
ULTRAIST > ULTRAISM
ULTRAISTS > ULTRAISM
ULTRALEFT *adj* of the extreme political Left or extremely radical
ULTRALOW *adj* extremely low
ULTRAPOSH *adj* extremely posh
ULTRAPURE *adj* extremely pure
ULTRARARE *adj* extremely rare
ULTRARED *obsolete word for* > INFRARED
ULTRAREDS > ULTRARED
ULTRARICH *adj* extremely rich
ULTRAS > ULTRA
ULTRASAFE *adj* extremely safe
ULTRASLOW *adj* extremely slow
ULTRASOFT *adj* extremely soft
ULTRATHIN *adj* extremely thin
ULTRATINY *adj* extremely small
ULTRAWIDE *adj* extremely wide
ULU *n* type of knife
ULULANT > ULULATE
ULULATE *vb* howl or wail
ULULATED > ULULATE
ULULATES > ULULATE
ULULATING > ULULATE
ULULATION > ULULATE
ULUS > ULU
ULVA *n* genus of seaweed
ULVAS > ULVA
ULYIE *Scots variant of* > OIL
ULYIES > ULYIE
ULZIE *Scots variant of* > OIL
ULZIES > ULZIE
UM *interj* representation of a common sound made when hesitating in speech

UMAMI *n* savoury flavour
UMAMIS > UMAMI
UMANGITE *n* type of mineral
UMANGITES > UMANGITE
UMBEL *n* umbrella-like flower cluster with the stalks springing from the central point
UMBELED *same as* > UMBELLED
UMBELLAR > UMBEL
UMBELLATE > UMBEL
UMBELLED *adj* having umbels
UMBELLET *same as* > UMBELLULE
UMBELLETS > UMBELLET
UMBELLULE *n* any of the small secondary umbels that make up a compound umbel
UMBELS > UMBEL
UMBER *adj* dark brown to reddish-brown ▷ *n* type of dark brown earth containing ferric oxide (rust) ▷ *vb* stain with umber
UMBERED > UMBER
UMBERING > UMBER
UMBERS > UMBER
UMBERY > UMBER
UMBILICAL *adj* of the navel
UMBILICI > UMBILICUS
UMBILICUS *n* navel
UMBLE as in *umble pie* (formerly) a pie made from the heart, entrails, etc, of a deer
UMBLES *another term for* > NUMBLES
UMBO *n* small hump projecting from the centre of the cap in certain mushrooms
UMBONAL > UMBO
UMBONATE > UMBO
UMBONES > UMBO
UMBONIC > UMBO
UMBOS > UMBO
UMBRA *n* shadow, esp the shadow cast by the moon onto the earth during a solar eclipse
UMBRACULA *pl n* umbrella-like structures
UMBRAE > UMBRA
UMBRAGE *n* displeasure or resentment ▷ *vb* shade
UMBRAGED > UMBRAGE
UMBRAGES > UMBRAGE
UMBRAGING > UMBRAGE
UMBRAL > UMBRA
UMBRAS > UMBRA
UMBRATED *adj* shown in a faint manner
UMBRATIC > UMBRA
UMBRATILE *adj* shadowy
UMBRE *same as* > UMBRETTE
UMBREL *n* umbrella
UMBRELLA *n* portable device used for protection against rain, consisting of a folding frame covered in material attached to a central rod ▷ *adj* containing or covering many different

organizations, ideas, etc
UMBRELLAS > UMBRELLA
UMBRELLO *same as* > UMBRELLA
UMBRELLOS > UMBRELLO
UMBRELS > UMBREL
UMBRERE *n* helmet visor
UMBRERES > UMBRERE
UMBRES > UMBRE
UMBRETTE *n* African wading bird
UMBRETTES > UMBRETTE
UMBRIERE *same as* > UMBRERE
UMBRIERES > UMBRIERE
UMBRIL *same as* > UMBRERE
UMBRILS > UMBRIL
UMBROSE *same as* > UMBROUS
UMBROUS *adj* shady
UMFAZI *n* African married woman
UMFAZIS > UMFAZI
UMIAC *variant of* > UMIAK
UMIACK *variant of* > UMIAK
UMIACKS > UMIACK
UMIACS > UMIAC
UMIAK *n* Inuit boat made of skins
UMIAKS > UMIAK
UMIAQ *same as* > UMIAK
UMIAQS > UMIAQ
UMLAUT *n* mark (¨) placed over a vowel, esp in German, to indicate a change in its sound ▷ *vb* modify by umlaut
UMLAUTED > UMLAUT
UMLAUTING > UMLAUT
UMLAUTS > UMLAUT
UMLUNGU *n* White man: used esp as a term of address
UMLUNGUS > UMLUNGU
UMM *same as* > UM
UMP *short for* > UMPIRE
UMPED > UMP
UMPH *same as* > HUMPH
UMPIE *informal word for* > UMPIRE
UMPIES > UMPY
UMPING > UMP
UMPIRAGE > UMPIRE
UMPIRAGES > UMPIRE
UMPIRE *n* official who rules on the playing of a game ▷ *vb* act as umpire in (a game)
UMPIRED > UMPIRE
UMPIRES > UMPIRE
UMPIRING > UMPIRE
UMPS > UMP
UMPTEEN *adj* very many ▷ *determiner* very many
UMPTEENTH *n* latest in a tediously long series
UMPTIETH *same as* > UMPTEENTH
UMPTY *same as* > UMPTEEN
UMPY *same as* > UMPIE
UMQUHILE *adv* formerly
UMTEENTH *same as* > UMPTEENTH
UMU *n* type of oven
UMWELT *n* environmental factors, collectively, that are capable of affecting the behaviour of an animal or

individual
UMWELTS > UMWELT
UMWHILE *same as* > UMQUHILE
UN *pron* spelling of 'one' intended to reflect a dialectal or informal pronunciation
UNABASHED *adj* not ashamed or embarrassed
UNABATED *adv* without any reduction in force ▷ *adj* without losing any original force or violence
UNABATING *adj* not growing less in strength
UNABETTED *adj* without assistance
UNABIDING *adj* not lasting
UNABJURED *adj* not denied
UNABLE *adj* lacking the necessary power, ability, or authority (to do something)
UNABORTED *adj* not aborted
UNABRADED *adj* not eroded
UNABUSED *adj* not abused
UNABUSIVE *adj* not abusive
UNACCRUED *adj* not accrued
UNACCUSED *adj* not charged with wrongdoing
UNACERBIC *adj* not acerbic
UNACHING *adj* not aching
UNACIDIC *adj* not acidic
UNACTABLE *adj* unable to be acted
UNACTED *adj* not acted or performed
UNACTIVE *adj* inactive
UNADAPTED *adj* not adapted
UNADDED *adj* not added
UNADEPT *adj* not adept
UNADEPTLY > UNADEPT
UNADMIRED *adj* not admired
UNADOPTED *adj* (of a road) not maintained by a local authority
UNADORED *adj* not adored
UNADORNED *adj* not decorated
UNADULT *adj* not mature
UNADVISED *adj* rash or unwise
UNAFRAID *adj* not frightened or nervous
UNAGED *adj* not old
UNAGEING *adj* not ageing
UNAGILE *adj* not agile
UNAGING *same as* > UNAGEING
UNAGREED *adj* not agreed
UNAI *same as* > UNAU
UNAIDABLE *adj* unable to be helped
UNAIDED *adv* without any help or assistance ▷ *adj* without having received any help
UNAIDEDLY > UNAIDED
UNAIMED *adj* not aimed or specifically targeted
UNAIRED *adj* not aired
UNAIS > UNAI
UNAKIN *adj* not related
UNAKING *Shakespearean form of* > UNACHING
UNAKITE *n* type of mineral

u

UNAKITES > UNAKITE
UNALARMED adj not alarmed
UNALERTED adj not alerted
UNALIGNED adj not aligned
UNALIKE adj not similar
UNALIST n priest holding
   only one benefice
UNALISTS > UNALIST
UNALIVE adj unaware
UNALLAYED adj not allayed
UNALLEGED adj not alleged
UNALLIED adj not allied
UNALLOWED adj not allowed
UNALLOYED adj not spoiled
   by being mixed with
   anything else
UNALTERED adj not altered
UNAMASSED adj not
   amassed
UNAMAZED adj not greatly
   surprised
UNAMENDED adj not
   amended
UNAMERCED adj not amerced
UNAMIABLE adj not amiable
UNAMUSED adj not
   entertained, diverted, or
   laughing
UNAMUSING adj not
   entertaining
UNANCHOR vb remove
   anchor
UNANCHORS > UNANCHOR
UNANELED adj not having
   received extreme unction
UNANIMITY > UNANIMOUS
UNANIMOUS adj in complete
   agreement
UNANNEXED adj not annexed
UNANNOYED adj not annoyed
UNANXIOUS adj not anxious
UNAPPAREL vb undress
UNAPPLIED adj not applied
UNAPT adj not suitable or
   qualified
UNAPTLY > UNAPT
UNAPTNESS > UNAPT
UNARCHED adj not arched
UNARGUED adj not debated
UNARISEN adj not having
   risen
UNARM less common word
   for > DISARM
UNARMED adj without
   weapons
UNARMING > UNARM
UNARMORED adj without
   armour
UNARMS > UNARM
UNAROUSED adj not aroused
UNARRAYED adj not arrayed
UNARTFUL adj not artful
UNARY adj consisting of, or
   affecting, a single element
   or component
UNASHAMED adj not
   embarrassed, esp when
   doing something some
   people might find offensive
UNASKED adv without being
   asked to do something
   ▷ adj (of a question)
   not asked, although
   sometimes implied
UNASSAYED adj untried
UNASSUMED adj not
   assumed

UNASSURED adj insecure
UNATONED adj not atoned
   for
UNATTIRED adj unclothed
UNATTUNED adj
   unaccustomed
UNAU n two-toed sloth
UNAUDITED adj not having
   been audited
UNAUS > UNAU
UNAVENGED adj not avenged
UNAVERAGE adj not average
UNAVERTED adj not averted
UNAVOIDED adj not avoided
UNAVOWED adj not openly
   admitted
UNAWAKE adj not awake
UNAWAKED adj not aroused
UNAWARDED adj not
   awarded
UNAWARE adj not aware
   or conscious ▷ adv by
   surprise
UNAWARELY > UNAWARE
UNAWARES adv by surprise
UNAWED adj not awed
UNAWESOME adj not
   awesome
UNAXED adj not axed
UNBACKED adj (of a book,
   chair, etc) not having a
   back
UNBAFFLED adj not baffled
UNBAG vb take out of a bag
UNBAGGED > UNBAG
UNBAGGING > UNBAG
UNBAGS > UNBAG
UNBAITED adj not baited
UNBAKED adj not having
   been baked
UNBALANCE vb upset the
   equilibrium or balance of
   ▷ n imbalance or instability
UNBALE vb remove from
   bale
UNBALED > UNBALE
UNBALES > UNBALE
UNBALING > UNBALE
UNBAN vb stop banning or
   permit again
UNBANDAGE vb remove
   bandage from
UNBANDED adj not fastened
   with a band
UNBANKED adj not having
   been banked
UNBANNED > UNBAN
UNBANNING > UNBAN
UNBANS > UNBAN
UNBAPTISE same
   as > UNBAPTIZE
UNBAPTIZE vb remove the
   effect of baptism
UNBAR vb take away a bar or
   bars from
UNBARBED adj without
   barbs
UNBARE vb expose
UNBARED > UNBARE
UNBARES > UNBARE
UNBARING > UNBARE
UNBARK vb strip bark from
UNBARKED > UNBARK
UNBARKING > UNBARK
UNBARKS > UNBARK
UNBARRED > UNBAR
UNBARRING > UNBAR

UNBARS > UNBAR
UNBASED adj not having a
   base
UNBASHFUL adj not shy
UNBASTED adj not basted
UNBATED adj (of a sword,
   lance, etc) not covered
   with a protective button
UNBATHED adj unwashed
UNBE vb make non-existent
UNBEAR vb release (horse)
   from the bearing rein
UNBEARDED adj not having
   a beard
UNBEARED > UNBEAR
UNBEARING > UNBEAR
UNBEARS > UNBEAR
UNBEATEN adj having
   suffered no defeat
UNBED vb remove from bed
UNBEDDED > UNBED
UNBEDDING > UNBED
UNBEDS > UNBED
UNBEEN > UNBE
UNBEGET vb deprive of
   existence
UNBEGETS > UNBEGET
UNBEGGED adj not obtained
   by begging
UNBEGOT adj unbegotten
UNBEGUILE vb undeceive
UNBEGUN adj not
   commenced
UNBEING n non-existence
UNBEINGS > UNBEING
UNBEKNOWN adv without the
   knowledge (of a person)
   ▷ adj not known (to)
UNBELIEF n disbelief or
   rejection of belief
UNBELIEFS > UNBELIEF
UNBELIEVE vb disbelieve
UNBELOVED adj unhappy
   in love
UNBELT vb unbuckle the
   belt of (a garment)
UNBELTED > UNBELT
UNBELTING > UNBELT
UNBELTS > UNBELT
UNBEMUSED adj not
   bemused
UNBEND vb become less
   strict or more informal
   in one's attitudes or
   behaviour
UNBENDED > UNBEND
UNBENDING adj rigid or
   inflexible
UNBENDS > UNBEND
UNBENIGN adj not benign
UNBENT adj not bent or
   bowed
UNBEREFT adj not bereft
UNBERUFEN adj not called
   for
UNBESEEM vb be unbefitting
   to
UNBESEEMS > UNBESEEM
UNBESPEAK vb annul
UNBESPOKE adj not
   bespoken
UNBIAS vb free from
   prejudice
UNBIASED adj not having
   or showing prejudice or
   favouritism
UNBIASES > UNBIAS

UNBIASING > UNBIAS
UNBIASSED same
   as > UNBIASED
UNBIASSES > UNBIAS
UNBID same as > UNBIDDEN
UNBIDDEN adj not ordered
   or asked
UNBIGOTED adj not bigoted
UNBILLED adj not having
   been billed
UNBIND vb set free from
   bonds or chains
UNBINDING > UNBIND
UNBINDS > UNBIND
UNBISHOP vb remove from
   the position of bishop
UNBISHOPS > UNBISHOP
UNBITT vb remove (cable)
   from the bitts
UNBITTED > UNBITT
UNBITTEN adj not having
   been bitten
UNBITTER adj not bitter
UNBITTING > UNBITT
UNBITTS > UNBITT
UNBLAMED vb not blamed
UNBLENDED adj not blended
UNBLENT same
   as > UNBLENDED
UNBLESS vb deprive of a
   blessing
UNBLESSED adj deprived of
   blessing
UNBLESSES > UNBLESS
UNBLEST same
   as > UNBLESSED
UNBLIND vb rid of blindness
UNBLINDED > UNBLIND
UNBLINDS > UNBLIND
UNBLOCK vb remove a
   blockage from
UNBLOCKED > UNBLOCK
UNBLOCKS > UNBLOCK
UNBLOODED adj not bloodied
UNBLOODY adj not covered
   with blood
UNBLOTTED adj not blotted
UNBLOWED same
   as > UNBLOWN
UNBLOWN adj (of a flower)
   still in the bud
UNBLUNTED adj not blunted
UNBLURRED adj not blurred
UNBOARDED adj not boarded
UNBOBBED adj not bobbed
UNBODIED adj having no
   body
UNBODING adj having no
   presentiment
UNBOILED adj not boiled
UNBOLT vb unfasten a bolt
   of (a door)
UNBOLTED adj (of grain,
   meal, or flour) not sifted
UNBOLTING > UNBOLT
UNBOLTS > UNBOLT
UNBONDED adj not bonded
UNBONE vb remove bone
   from
UNBONED adj (of meat, fish,
   etc) not having had the
   bones removed
UNBONES > UNBONE
UNBONING > UNBONE
UNBONNET vb remove the
   bonnet from
UNBONNETS > UNBONNET

UNBOOKED adj not reserved
UNBOOKISH adj not studious
UNBOOT vb remove boots from
UNBOOTED > UNBOOT
UNBOOTING > UNBOOT
UNBOOTS > UNBOOT
UNBORE adj unborn
UNBORN adj not yet born
UNBORNE adj not borne
UNBOSOM vb relieve (oneself) of (secrets or feelings) by telling someone
UNBOSOMED > UNBOSOM
UNBOSOMER > UNBOSOM
UNBOSOMS > UNBOSOM
UNBOTTLE vb allow out of bottle
UNBOTTLED > UNBOTTLE
UNBOTTLES > UNBOTTLE
UNBOUGHT adj not purchased
UNBOUNCY adj not bouncy
UNBOUND adj (of a book) not bound within a cover
UNBOUNDED adj having no boundaries or limits
UNBOWED adj not giving in or submitting
UNBOWING adj not bowing
UNBOX vb empty a box
UNBOXED > UNBOX
UNBOXES > UNBOX
UNBOXING > UNBOX
UNBRACE vb remove tension or strain from
UNBRACED > UNBRACE
UNBRACES > UNBRACE
UNBRACING > UNBRACE
UNBRAID vb remove braids from
UNBRAIDED > UNBRAID
UNBRAIDS > UNBRAID
UNBRAKE vb stop reducing speed by releasing brake
UNBRAKED > UNBRAKE
UNBRAKES > UNBRAKE
UNBRAKING > UNBRAKE
UNBRANDED adj not having a brand name
UNBRASTE archaic past form of > UNBRACE
UNBRED adj not taught or instructed
UNBREECH vb remove breech from
UNBRIDGED adj not spanned by a bridge
UNBRIDLE vb remove the bridle from (a horse)
UNBRIDLED adj (of feelings or behaviour) not controlled in any way
UNBRIDLES > UNBRIDLE
UNBRIEFED adj not instructed
UNBRIGHT adj not bright
UNBRIZZED same as > UNBRUISED
UNBROILED adj not broiled
UNBROKE same as > UNBROKEN
UNBROKEN adj complete or whole
UNBROWNED adj not browned
UNBRUISED adj not bruised

UNBRUSED same as > UNBRUISED
UNBRUSHED adj not brushed
UNBUCKLE vb undo the buckle or buckles of
UNBUCKLED > UNBUCKLE
UNBUCKLES > UNBUCKLE
UNBUDDED adj not having buds
UNBUDGING adj not moving
UNBUILD vb destroy
UNBUILDS > UNBUILD
UNBUILT > UNBUILD
UNBULKY adj not bulky
UNBUNDLE vb separate (hardware from software) for sales purposes
UNBUNDLED > UNBUNDLE
UNBUNDLER > UNBUNDLE
UNBUNDLES > UNBUNDLE
UNBURDEN vb relieve (one's mind or oneself) of a worry by confiding in someone
UNBURDENS > UNBURDEN
UNBURIED > UNBURY
UNBURIES > UNBURY
UNBURNED same as > UNBURNT
UNBURNT adj not burnt
UNBURROW vb remove from a burrow
UNBURROWS > UNBURROW
UNBURTHEN same as > UNBURDEN
UNBURY vb unearth
UNBURYING > UNBURY
UNBUSTED adj unbroken
UNBUSY adj not busy
UNBUTTON vb undo by unfastening the buttons of (a garment)
UNBUTTONS > UNBUTTON
UNCAGE vb release from a cage
UNCAGED adj at liberty
UNCAGES > UNCAGE
UNCAGING > UNCAGE
UNCAKE vb remove compacted matter from
UNCAKED > UNCAKE
UNCAKES > UNCAKE
UNCAKING > UNCAKE
UNCALLED adj not called
UNCANDID adj not frank
UNCANDLED adj not illuminated by candle
UNCANDOUR n lack of candour
UNCANNED adj not canned
UNCANNIER > UNCANNY
UNCANNILY > UNCANNY
UNCANNY adj weird or mysterious
UNCANONIC adj unclerical
UNCAP vb remove a cap or top from (a container)
UNCAPABLE same as > INCAPABLE
UNCAPE vb remove the cape from
UNCAPED > UNCAPE
UNCAPES > UNCAPE
UNCAPING > UNCAPE
UNCAPPED > UNCAP
UNCAPPING > UNCAP
UNCAPS > UNCAP
UNCARDED adj not carded

UNCAREFUL adj careless
UNCARING adj thoughtless
UNCART vb remove from a cart
UNCARTED > UNCART
UNCARTING > UNCART
UNCARTS > UNCART
UNCARVED adj not carved
UNCASE vb display
UNCASED > UNCASE
UNCASES > UNCASE
UNCASHED adj not cashed
UNCASING > UNCASE
UNCASKED adj removed from a cask
UNCAST adj not cast
UNCATCHY adj not catchy
UNCATE same as > UNCINATE
UNCATERED adj not catered
UNCAUGHT adj not caught
UNCAUSED adj not brought into existence by any cause
UNCE same as > OUNCE
UNCEASING adj continuing without a break
UNCEDED adj not ceded
UNCERTAIN adj not able to be accurately known or predicted
UNCES > UNCE
UNCESSANT same as > INCESSANT
UNCHAIN vb remove a chain or chains from
UNCHAINED > UNCHAIN
UNCHAINS > UNCHAIN
UNCHAIR vb unseat from chair
UNCHAIRED > UNCHAIR
UNCHAIRS > UNCHAIR
UNCHANCY adj unlucky, ill-omened, or dangerous
UNCHANGED adj remaining the same
UNCHARGE vb unload
UNCHARGED adj (of land or other property) not subject to a charge
UNCHARGES > UNCHARGE
UNCHARITY n lack of charity
UNCHARM vb disenchant
UNCHARMED > UNCHARM
UNCHARMS > UNCHARM
UNCHARNEL vb exhume
UNCHARRED adj not charred
UNCHARTED adj (of an area of sea or land) not having had a map made of it, esp because it is unexplored
UNCHARY adj not cautious
UNCHASTE adj not chaste
UNCHASTER > UNCHASTE
UNCHECK vb remove check mark from
UNCHECKED adj not prevented from continuing or growing ▷ adv without being stopped or hindered
UNCHECKS > UNCHECK
UNCHEERED adj miserable
UNCHEWED adj not chewed
UNCHIC adj not chic
UNCHICLY > UNCHIC
UNCHILD vb deprive of children
UNCHILDED > UNCHILD
UNCHILDS > UNCHILD

UNCHILLED adj not chilled
UNCHOKE vb unblock
UNCHOKED > UNCHOKE
UNCHOKES > UNCHOKE
UNCHOKING > UNCHOKE
UNCHOSEN adj not chosen
UNCHRISOM adj unchristened
UNCHURCH vb excommunicate
UNCI > UNCUS
UNCIA n twelfth part
UNCIAE > UNCIA
UNCIAL adj of or written in letters that resemble modern capitals, as used in Greek and Latin manuscripts of the third to ninth centuries ▷ n uncial letter or manuscript
UNCIALLY > UNCIAL
UNCIALS > UNCIAL
UNCIFORM adj having the shape of a hook ▷ n any hook-shaped structure or part, esp a small bone of the wrist
UNCIFORMS > UNCIFORM
UNCINAL same as > UNCINATE
UNCINARIA same as > HOOKWORM
UNCINATE adj shaped like a hook
UNCINATED > UNCINATE
UNCINI > UNCINUS
UNCINUS n small hooked structure, such as any of the hooked chaetae of certain polychaete worms
UNCIPHER vb decode
UNCIPHERS > UNCIPHER
UNCITED adj not quoted
UNCIVIL adj impolite, rude or bad-mannered
UNCIVILLY > UNCIVIL
UNCLAD adj having no clothes on
UNCLAIMED adj not having been claimed
UNCLAMP vb remove clamp from
UNCLAMPED > UNCLAMP
UNCLAMPS > UNCLAMP
UNCLARITY adj lack of clarity
UNCLASP vb unfasten the clasp of (something)
UNCLASPED > UNCLASP
UNCLASPS > UNCLASP
UNCLASSED adj not divided into classes
UNCLASSY adj not classy
UNCLAWED adj not clawed
UNCLE n brother of one's father or mother ▷ vb refer to as uncle
UNCLEAN adj lacking moral, spiritual, or physical cleanliness
UNCLEANED adj not cleaned
UNCLEANER > UNCLEAN
UNCLEANLY adv in an unclean manner ▷ adj characterized by an absence of cleanliness
UNCLEAR adj confusing or

hard to understand

UNCLEARED adj not cleared

UNCLEARER > UNCLEAR

UNCLEARLY > UNCLEAR

UNCLED > UNCLE

UNCLEFT adj not cleft

UNCLENCH vb relax from a clenched position

UNCLES > UNCLE

UNCLESHIP n position of an uncle

UNCLEW vb undo

UNCLEWED > UNCLEW

UNCLEWING > UNCLEW

UNCLEWS > UNCLEW

UNCLICHED adj not cliched

UNCLINCH same as > UNCLENCH

UNCLING > UNCLE

UNCLIP vb remove clip from

UNCLIPPED > UNCLIP

UNCLIPS > UNCLIP

UNCLIPT archaic past form of > UNCLIP

UNCLOAK vb remove cloak from

UNCLOAKED > UNCLOAK

UNCLOAKS > UNCLOAK

UNCLOG vb remove an obstruction from (a drain, etc)

UNCLOGGED > UNCLOG

UNCLOGS > UNCLOG

UNCLOSE vb open or cause to open

UNCLOSED > UNCLOSE

UNCLOSES > UNCLOSE

UNCLOSING > UNCLOSE

UNCLOTHE vb take off garments from

UNCLOTHED > UNCLOTHE

UNCLOTHES > UNCLOTHE

UNCLOUD vb clear clouds from

UNCLOUDED > UNCLOUD

UNCLOUDS > UNCLOUD

UNCLOUDY adj not cloudy

UNCLOVEN adj not cleaved

UNCLOYED adj not cloyed

UNCLOYING adj not cloying

UNCLUTCH vb open from tight grip

UNCLUTTER vb tidy and straighten up

UNCO adj awkward ▷ n awkward or clumsy person

UNCOATED adj not covered with a layer

UNCOATING n process whereby a virus exposes its genome in order to replicate

UNCOBBLED adj not cobbled

UNCOCK vb remove from a cocked position

UNCOCKED > UNCOCK

UNCOCKING > UNCOCK

UNCOCKS > UNCOCK

UNCODED adj not coded

UNCOER > UNCO

UNCOERCED adj unforced

UNCOES > UNCO

UNCOEST > UNCO

UNCOFFIN vb take out of a coffin

UNCOFFINS > UNCOFFIN

UNCOIL vb unwind or

untwist

UNCOILED > UNCOIL

UNCOILING > UNCOIL

UNCOILS > UNCOIL

UNCOINED adj (of a metal) not made into coin

UNCOLORED adj not coloured

UNCOLT vb divest of a horse

UNCOLTED > UNCOLT

UNCOLTING > UNCOLT

UNCOLTS > UNCOLT

UNCOMBED adj not combed

UNCOMBINE vb break apart

UNCOMELY adj not attractive

UNCOMIC adj not comical

UNCOMMON adj not happening or encountered often

UNCONCERN n apathy or indifference

UNCONFINE vb remove restrictions from

UNCONFORM adj dissimilar

UNCONFUSE vb remove confusion from

UNCONGEAL vb become liquid again

UNCOOKED adj raw

UNCOOL adj unsophisticated

UNCOOLED adj not cooled

UNCOPE vb unmuzzle

UNCOPED > UNCOPE

UNCOPES > UNCOPE

UNCOPING > UNCOPE

UNCORD vb release from cords

UNCORDED > UNCORD

UNCORDIAL adj unfriendly

UNCORDING > UNCORD

UNCORDS > UNCORD

UNCORK vb remove the cork from (a bottle)

UNCORKED > UNCORK

UNCORKING > UNCORK

UNCORKS > UNCORK

UNCORRUPT adj not corrupt

UNCOS > UNCO

UNCOSTLY adj inexpensive

UNCOUNTED adj unable to be counted

UNCOUPLE vb disconnect or become disconnected

UNCOUPLED > UNCOUPLE

UNCOUPLER > UNCOUPLE

UNCOUPLES > UNCOUPLE

UNCOURTLY adj not courtly

UNCOUTH adj lacking in good manners, refinement, or grace

UNCOUTHER > UNCOUTH

UNCOUTHLY > UNCOUTH

UNCOVER vb reveal or disclose

UNCOVERED adj not covered

UNCOVERS > UNCOVER

UNCOWL vb remove hood from

UNCOWLED > UNCOWL

UNCOWLING > UNCOWL

UNCOWLS > UNCOWL

UNCOY adj not modest

UNCOYNED same as > UNCOINED

UNCRACKED adj not cracked

UNCRATE vb remove from a crate

UNCRATED > UNCRATE

UNCRATES > UNCRATE

UNCRATING > UNCRATE

UNCRAZY adj not crazy

UNCREATE vb unmake

UNCREATED > UNCREATE

UNCREATES > UNCREATE

UNCREWED adj not crewed

UNCROPPED adj not cropped

UNCROSS vb cease to cross

UNCROSSED > UNCROSS

UNCROSSES > UNCROSS

UNCROWDED adj (of a confined space, area, etc) not containing too many people or things

UNCROWN vb take the crown from

UNCROWNED adj having the powers, but not the title, of royalty

UNCROWNS > UNCROWN

UNCRUDDED adj uncurdled

UNCRUMPLE vb remove creases from

UNCRUSHED adj not crushed

UNCTION n act of anointing with oil in sacramental ceremonies

UNCTIONS > UNCTION

UNCTUOUS adj pretending to be kind and concerned

UNCUFF vb remove handcuffs from

UNCUFFED > UNCUFF

UNCUFFING > UNCUFF

UNCUFFS > UNCUFF

UNCULLED adj not culled

UNCURABLE same as > INCURABLE

UNCURABLY > UNCURABLE

UNCURB vb remove curbs from (a horse)

UNCURBED > UNCURB

UNCURBING > UNCURB

UNCURBS > UNCURB

UNCURDLED adj not curdled

UNCURED adj not cured

UNCURIOUS adj not curious

UNCURL vb move or cause to move out of a curled or rolled up position

UNCURLED > UNCURL

UNCURLING > UNCURL

UNCURLS > UNCURL

UNCURRENT adj not current

UNCURSE vb remove curse from

UNCURSED > UNCURSE

UNCURSES > UNCURSE

UNCURSING > UNCURSE

UNCURTAIN vb reveal

UNCURVED adj not curved

UNCUS n hooked part or process, as in the human cerebrum

UNCUT adj not shortened or censored

UNCUTE adj not cute

UNCYNICAL adj not cynical

UNDAM vb free from a dam

UNDAMAGED adj not spoilt or damaged

UNDAMMED > UNDAM

UNDAMMING > UNDAM

UNDAMNED adj not damned

UNDAMPED adj (of an

oscillating system) having unrestricted motion

UNDAMS > UNDAM

UNDARING adj not daring

UNDASHED adj not dashed

UNDATABLE adj not able to be dated

UNDATE vb remove date from

UNDATED adj (of a manuscript, letter, etc) not having an identifying date

UNDAUNTED adj not put off, discouraged, or beaten

UNDAWNING adj not dawning

UNDAZZLE vb recover from a daze

UNDAZZLED > UNDAZZLE

UNDAZZLES > UNDAZZLE

UNDE same as > UNDEE

UNDEAD adj alive

UNDEAF vb restore hearing to

UNDEAFED > UNDEAF

UNDEAFING > UNDEAF

UNDEAFS > UNDEAF

UNDEALT adj not dealt (with)

UNDEAR adj not dear

UNDEBASED adj not debased

UNDEBATED adj not debated

UNDECAGON n polygon having eleven sides

UNDECAYED adj not rotten

UNDECEIVE vb reveal the truth to (someone previously misled or deceived)

UNDECENT same as > INDECENT

UNDECIDED adj not having made up one's mind

UNDECIMAL adj based on the number 11

UNDECK vb remove decorations from

UNDECKED > UNDECK

UNDECKING > UNDECK

UNDECKS > UNDECK

UNDEE adj wavy

UNDEEDED adj not transferred by deed

UNDEFACED adj not spoilt

UNDEFIDE same as > UNDEFIED

UNDEFIED adj not challenged

UNDEFILED adj not defiled

UNDEFINED adj not defined or made clear

UNDEIFIED > UNDEIFY

UNDEIFIES > UNDEIFY

UNDEIFY vb strip of the status of a deity

UNDELAYED adj not delayed

UNDELETED adj not deleted, or restored after being deleted

UNDELIGHT n absence of delight

UNDELUDED adj not deluded

UNDENIED adj not denied

UNDENTED adj not dented

UNDER adv indicating movement to or position beneath the underside or base ▷ *prep* less than

UNDERACT *vb* play (a role) without adequate emphasis

UNDERACTS > UNDERACT

UNDERAGE *adj* below the required or standard age ▷ *n* shortfall

UNDERAGED *adj* not old enough

UNDERAGES > UNDERAGE

UNDERARM *adj* denoting a style of throwing, bowling, or serving in which the hand is swung below shoulder level ▷ *adv* in an underarm style ▷ *n* armpit

UNDERARMS > UNDERARM

UNDERATE > UNDEREAT

UNDERBAKE *vb* bake insufficiently

UNDERBEAR *vb* endure

UNDERBID *vb* submit a bid lower than that of (others)

UNDERBIDS > UNDERBID

UNDERBIT > UNDERBITE

UNDERBITE *vb* use insufficient acid in etching

UNDERBODY *n* underpart of a body, as of an animal or motor vehicle

UNDERBORE > UNDERBEAR

UNDERBOSS *n* person who is second in command

UNDERBRED *adj* of impure stock

UNDERBRIM *n* part of a hat

UNDERBUD *vb* produce fewer buds than expected

UNDERBUDS > UNDERBUD

UNDERBUSH *n* undergrowth or underbrush

UNDERBUY *vb* buy (stock in trade) in amounts lower than required

UNDERBUYS > UNDERBUY

UNDERCARD *n* event supporting a main event

UNDERCART *n* aircraft undercarriage

UNDERCAST *vb* cast beneath

UNDERCLAD *adj* not wearing enough clothes

UNDERCLAY *n* grey or whitish clay rock containing fossilized plant roots and occurring beneath coal seams. When used as a refractory, it is known as fireclay

UNDERCLUB *vb* use a golf club that will not hit the ball as far as required

UNDERCOAT *n* coat of paint applied before the final coat ▷ *vb* apply an undercoat to a surface

UNDERCOOK *vb* cook for too short a time or at too low a temperature

UNDERCOOL *vb* cool insufficiently

UNDERCUT *vb* charge less than (a competitor) to obtain trade ▷ *n* act or an instance of cutting underneath

UNDERCUTS > UNDERCUT

UNDERDAKS *pl n* underpants

UNDERDECK *n* lower deck of a vessel

UNDERDID > UNDERDO

UNDERDO *vb* do (something) inadequately

UNDERDOER > UNDERDO

UNDERDOES > UNDERDO

UNDERDOG *n* person or team in a weak or underprivileged position

UNDERDOGS > UNDERDOG

UNDERDONE *adj* not cooked enough

UNDERDOSE *vb* give insufficient dose

UNDERDRAW *vb* sketch the subject before painting it on the same surface

UNDERDREW > UNDERDRAW

UNDEREAT *vb* not eat enough

UNDEREATS > UNDEREAT

UNDERFED > UNDERFEED

UNDERFEED *vb* give too little food to ▷ *n* apparatus by which fuel, etc, is supplied from below

UNDERFELT *n* thick felt laid under a carpet to increase insulation

UNDERFIRE *vb* bake insufficiently

UNDERFISH *vb* catch fewer fish than the permitted maximum amount

UNDERFLOW *n* undercurrent

UNDERFONG *vb* receive

UNDERFOOT *adv* under the feet

UNDERFUND *vb* provide insufficient funding

UNDERFUR *n* layer of dense soft fur occurring beneath the outer coarser fur in certain mammals, such as the otter and seal

UNDERFURS > UNDERFUR

UNDERGIRD *vb* strengthen or reinforce by passing a rope, cable, or chain around the underside of (an object, load, etc)

UNDERGIRT > UNDERGIRD

UNDERGO *vb* experience, endure, or sustain

UNDERGOD *n* subordinate god

UNDERGODS > UNDERGOD

UNDERGOER > UNDERGO

UNDERGOES > UNDERGO

UNDERGONE > UNDERGO

UNDERGOWN *n* gown worn under another article of clothing

UNDERGRAD *n* person studying for a first degree; undergraduate

UNDERHAIR *n* lower layer of animal's hair

UNDERHAND *adj* sly, deceitful, and secretive ▷ *adv* in an underhand manner or style

UNDERHEAT *vb* heat insufficiently

UNDERHUNG *adj* (of the lower jaw) projecting beyond the upper jaw

UNDERIVED *adj* not derived

UNDERJAW *n* lower jaw

UNDERJAWS > UNDERJAW

UNDERKEEP *vb* suppress

UNDERKEPT > UNDERKEEP

UNDERKILL *n* less force than is needed to defeat enemy

UNDERKING *n* ruler subordinate to a king

UNDERLAID *adj* laid underneath

UNDERLAIN > UNDERLIE

UNDERLAP *vb* project under the edge of

UNDERLAPS > UNDERLAP

UNDERLAY *n* felt or rubber laid beneath a carpet to increase insulation and resilience ▷ *vb* place (something) under or beneath

UNDERLAYS > UNDERLAY

UNDERLEAF *n* (in liverworts) any of the leaves forming a row on the underside of the stem: usually smaller than the two rows of lateral leaves and sometimes absent

UNDERLET *vb* let for a price lower than expected or justified

UNDERLETS > UNDERLET

UNDERLIE *vb* lie or be placed under

UNDERLIER > UNDERLIE

UNDERLIES > UNDERLIE

UNDERLINE *vb* draw a line under ▷ *n* line underneath, esp under written matter

UNDERLING *n* subordinate

UNDERLIP *n* lower lip

UNDERLIPS > UNDERLIP

UNDERLIT *adj* lit from beneath

UNDERLOAD *vb* load incompletely

UNDERMAN *vb* supply with insufficient staff ▷ *n* subordinate man

UNDERMANS > UNDERMAN

UNDERMEN > UNDERMAN

UNDERMINE *vb* weaken gradually

UNDERMOST *adj* being the furthest under ▷ *adv* in the lowest place

UNDERN *n* time between sunrise and noon

UNDERNOTE *n* undertone

UNDERNS > UNDERN

UNDERPAID *adj* not paid as much as the job deserves

UNDERPART *n* lower part or underside of something such as an animal

UNDERPASS *n* section of a road that passes under another road or a railway line

UNDERPAY *vb* pay someone insufficiently

UNDERPAYS > UNDERPAY

UNDERPEEP *vb* peep under

UNDERPIN *vb* give strength or support to

UNDERPINS > UNDERPIN

UNDERPLAY *vb* achieve (an effect) by deliberate lack of emphasis

UNDERPLOT *n* subsidiary plot in a literary or dramatic work

UNDERPROP *vb* prop up from beneath

UNDERRAN > UNDERRUN

UNDERRATE *vb* underestimate

UNDERRIPE *adj* not quite ripe

UNDERRUN *vb* run beneath

UNDERRUNS > UNDERRUN

UNDERSAID > UNDERSAY

UNDERSAY *vb* say by way of response

UNDERSAYS > UNDERSAY

UNDERSEA *adv* below the surface of the sea

UNDERSEAL *n* coating of tar etc applied to the underside of a motor vehicle to prevent corrosion ▷ *vb* apply such a coating to a motor vehicle

UNDERSEAS *same as* > UNDERSEA

UNDERSELF *n* subconscious or person within

UNDERSELL *vb* sell at a price lower than that of another seller

UNDERSET *n* ocean undercurrent ▷ *vb* support from underneath

UNDERSETS > UNDERSET

UNDERSHOT *adj* (of the lower jaw) projecting beyond the upper jaw

UNDERSIDE *n* bottom or lower surface

UNDERSIGN *vb* sign the bottom (of a document)

UNDERSIZE *adj* smaller than normal

UNDERSKY *n* lower sky

UNDERSOIL *another word for* > SUBSOIL

UNDERSOLD > UNDERSELL

UNDERSONG *n* accompanying secondary melody

UNDERSPIN *n* backspin

UNDERTAKE *vb* agree or commit oneself to (something) or to do (something)

UNDERTANE *Shakespearean past participle of* > UNDERTAKE

UNDERTAX *vb* tax insufficiently

UNDERTIME *n* time spent by an employee at work in non-work-related activities like socializing, surfing the internet, making personal telephone calls, etc

UNDERTINT *n* slight, subdued, or delicate tint

UNDERTONE *n* quiet tone of

voice
UNDERTOOK *past tense of* > UNDERTAKE
UNDERTOW n strong undercurrent flowing in a different direction from the surface current
UNDERTOWS > UNDERTOW
UNDERUSE vb use less than normal
UNDERUSED > UNDERUSE
UNDERUSES > UNDERUSE
UNDERVEST *another name for* > VEST
UNDERVOTE n vote cast but invalid
UNDERWAY adj in progress ▷ adv in progress
UNDERWEAR n clothing worn under the outer garments and next to the skin
UNDERWENT *past tense of* > UNDERGO
UNDERWING n hind wing of an insect, esp when covered by the forewing
UNDERWIRE vb support with wire underneath
UNDERWIT n half-wit
UNDERWITS > UNDERWIT
UNDERWOOD n small trees, bushes, ferns, etc growing beneath taller trees in a wood or forest
UNDERWOOL n lower layer of an animal's coat
UNDERWORK vb do less work than expected
UNDESERT n lack of worth
UNDESERTS > UNDESERT
UNDESERVE vb fail to deserve
UNDESIRED adj not desired
UNDEVOUT adj not devout
UNDID > UNDO
UNDIES pl n underwear, esp women's
UNDIGHT vb remove
UNDIGHTS > UNDIGHT
UNDIGNIFY vb divest of dignity
UNDILUTED adj (of a liquid) not having any water added to it
UNDIMMED adj (of eyes, light, etc) still bright or shining
UNDINE n female water spirit
UNDINES > UNDINE
UNDINISM n obsession with water
UNDINISMS > UNDINISM
UNDINTED adj not dinted
UNDIPPED adj not dipped
UNDIVIDED adj total and whole-hearted
UNDIVINE adj not divine
UNDO vb open, unwrap
UNDOABLE adj impossible
UNDOCILE adj not docile
UNDOCK vb take out of a dock
UNDOCKED > UNDOCK
UNDOCKING > UNDOCK
UNDOCKS > UNDOCK
UNDOER > UNDO
UNDOERS > UNDO

UNDOES > UNDO
UNDOING n cause of someone's downfall
UNDOINGS > UNDOING
UNDONE adj not done or completed
UNDOOMED adj not doomed
UNDOTTED adj not dotted
UNDOUBLE vb stretch out
UNDOUBLED > UNDOUBLE
UNDOUBLES > UNDOUBLE
UNDOUBTED adj certain or indisputable
UNDRAINED adj not drained
UNDRAPE vb remove drapery from
UNDRAPED > UNDRAPE
UNDRAPES > UNDRAPE
UNDRAPING > UNDRAPE
UNDRAW vb open (curtains)
UNDRAWING > UNDRAW
UNDRAWN > UNDRAW
UNDRAWS > UNDRAW
UNDREADED adj not feared
UNDREAMED adj not thought of or imagined
UNDREAMT *same as* > UNDREAMED
UNDRESS vb take off clothes from (oneself or another) ▷ n partial or complete nakedness ▷ adj characterized by or requiring informal or normal working dress or uniform
UNDRESSED adj partially or completely naked
UNDRESSES > UNDRESS
UNDREST *same as* > UNDRESSED
UNDREW > UNDRAW
UNDRIED adj not dried
UNDRILLED adj not drilled
UNDRIVEN adj not driven
UNDROSSY adj pure
UNDROWNED adj not drowned
UNDRUNK adj not drunk
UNDUBBED adj (of a film, etc) not dubbed
UNDUE adj greater than is reasonable; excessive
UNDUG adj not having been dug
UNDULANCE > UNDULANT
UNDULANCY > UNDULANT
UNDULANT adj resembling waves
UNDULAR > UNDULATE
UNDULATE vb move in waves ▷ adj having a wavy or rippled appearance, margin, or form
UNDULATED > UNDULATE
UNDULATES > UNDULATE
UNDULATOR > UNDULATE
UNDULLED adj not dulled
UNDULOSE *same as* > UNDULOUS
UNDULOUS adj undulate
UNDULY adv excessively
UNDUTEOUS *same as* > UNDUTIFUL
UNDUTIFUL adj not dutiful
UNDY *same as* > UNDEE
UNDYED adj not dyed

UNDYING adj never ending, eternal
UNDYINGLY > UNDYING
UNDYNAMIC adj not dynamic
UNEAGER adj nonchalant
UNEAGERLY > UNEAGER
UNEARED adj not ploughed
UNEARNED adj not deserved
UNEARTH vb reveal or discover by searching
UNEARTHED > UNEARTH
UNEARTHLY adj ghostly or eerie
UNEARTHS > UNEARTH
UNEASE > UNEASY
UNEASES > UNEASY
UNEASIER > UNEASY
UNEASIEST > UNEASY
UNEASILY > UNEASY
UNEASY adj (of a person) anxious or apprehensive
UNEATABLE adj (of food) so rotten or unattractive as to be unfit to eat
UNEATEN adj (of food) not having been consumed
UNEATH adv not easily
UNEATHES > UNEATH
UNEDGE vb take the edge off
UNEDGED > UNEDGE
UNEDGES > UNEDGE
UNEDGING > UNEDGE
UNEDIBLE *variant of* > INEDIBLE
UNEDITED adj not edited
UNEFFACED adj not destroyed
UNELATED adj not elated
UNELECTED adj not elected
UNEMPTIED adj not emptied
UNENDED adj without end
UNENDING adj not showing any signs of ever stopping
UNENDOWED adj not endowed
UNENGAGED adj not engaged
UNENJOYED adj not enjoyed
UNENSURED adj not ensured
UNENTERED adj not having been entered previously
UNENVIED adj not envied
UNENVIOUS adj not envious
UNENVYING adj not envying
UNEQUABLE adj unstable
UNEQUAL adj not equal in quantity, size, rank, value, etc ▷ n person who is not equal
UNEQUALED adj (in US English) not equalled
UNEQUALLY > UNEQUAL
UNEQUALS > UNEQUAL
UNERASED adj not rubbed out
UNEROTIC adj not erotic
UNERRING adj never mistaken, consistently accurate
UNESPIED adj unnoticed
UNESSAYED adj untried
UNESSENCE vb deprive of being
UNETH *same as* > UNEATH
UNETHICAL adj morally wrong
UNEVADED adj not evaded
UNEVEN adj not level or flat

UNEVENER > UNEVEN
UNEVENEST > UNEVEN
UNEVENLY > UNEVEN
UNEVOLVED adj not evolved
UNEXALTED adj not exalted
UNEXCITED adj not aroused to pleasure, interest, agitation, etc
UNEXCUSED adj not excused
UNEXOTIC adj not exotic
UNEXPERT *same as* > INEXPERT
UNEXPIRED adj not having expired
UNEXPOSED adj not having been exhibited or brought to public notice
UNEXTINCT adj not extinct
UNEXTREME adj not extreme
UNEYED adj unseen
UNFABLED adj not fictitious
UNFACT n event or thing not provable
UNFACTS > UNFACT
UNFADABLE adj incapable of fading
UNFADED adj not faded
UNFADING adj not fading
UNFAILING adj continuous or reliable
UNFAIR adj not right, fair, or just ▷ vb disfigure
UNFAIRED > UNFAIR
UNFAIRER > UNFAIR
UNFAIREST > UNFAIR
UNFAIRING > UNFAIR
UNFAIRLY > UNFAIR
UNFAIRS > UNFAIR
UNFAITH n lack of faith
UNFAITHS > UNFAITH
UNFAKED adj not faked
UNFALLEN adj not fallen
UNFAMED adj not famous
UNFAMOUS adj not famous
UNFANCY adj not fancy
UNFANNED adj not fanned
UNFASTEN vb undo, untie, or open or become undone, untied, or opened
UNFASTENS > UNFASTEN
UNFAULTY adj not faulty
UNFAVORED adj (in US English) not favoured
UNFAZED adj not disconcerted
UNFEARED adj unafraid
UNFEARFUL adj not scared
UNFEARING adj having no fear
UNFED adj not fed
UNFEED adj unpaid
UNFEELING adj without sympathy
UNFEIGNED adj not feigned
UNFELLED adj not cut down
UNFELT adj not felt
UNFELTED adj not felted
UNFENCE vb remove a fence from
UNFENCED adj not enclosed by a fence
UNFENCES > UNFENCE
UNFENCING > UNFENCE
UNFERTILE *same as* > INFERTILE
UNFETTER vb release from fetters, bonds, etc

UNFETTERS > UNFETTER
UNFEUDAL *adj* not feudal
UNFEUED *adj* not feued
UNFIGURED *adj* not numbered
UNFILDE *archaic form of* > UNFILED
UNFILED *adj* not filed
UNFILIAL *adj* not filial
UNFILLED *adj* (of a container, receptacle, etc) not having become or been made full
UNFILMED *adj* not filmed
UNFINE *adj* not fine
UNFIRED *adj* not fired
UNFIRM *adj* soft or unsteady
UNFISHED *adj* not used for fishing
UNFIT *adj* unqualified or unsuitable ▷ *vb* make unfit
UNFITLY *adv* in an unfit way
UNFITNESS > UNFIT
UNFITS > UNFIT
UNFITTED *adj* unsuitable
UNFITTER > UNFIT
UNFITTEST > UNFIT
UNFITTING *adj* not fitting
UNFIX *vb* unfasten, detach, or loosen
UNFIXED *adj* not fixed
UNFIXES > UNFIX
UNFIXING > UNFIX
UNFIXITY *n* instability
UNFIXT *variant of* > UNFIXED
UNFLAPPED *adj* not agitated or excited
UNFLASHY *adj* not flashy
UNFLAWED *adj* perfect
UNFLEDGED *adj* (of a young bird) not having developed adult feathers
UNFLESH *vb* remove flesh from
UNFLESHED > UNFLESH
UNFLESHES > UNFLESH
UNFLESHLY *adj* immaterial
UNFLEXED *adj* unbent
UNFLOORED *adj* without flooring
UNFLUSH *vb* lose the colour caused by flushing
UNFLUSHED > UNFLUSH
UNFLUSHES > UNFLUSH
UNFLUTED *adj* not fluted
UNFLYABLE *adj* unable to be flown
UNFOCUSED *adj* blurry
UNFOILED *adj* not thwarted
UNFOLD *vb* open or spread out from a folded state
UNFOLDED > UNFOLD
UNFOLDER > UNFOLD
UNFOLDERS > UNFOLD
UNFOLDING > UNFOLD
UNFOLDS > UNFOLD
UNFOND *adj* not fond
UNFOOL *vb* undeceive
UNFOOLED > UNFOOL
UNFOOLING > UNFOOL
UNFOOLS > UNFOOL
UNFOOTED *adj* untrodden
UNFORBID *adj* archaic word meaning unforbidden
UNFORCED *adj* not forced or having been forced
UNFORGED *adj* genuine

UNFORGOT *adj* archaic word meaning unforgotten
UNFORKED *adj* not forked
UNFORM *vb* make formless
UNFORMAL *same as* > INFORMAL
UNFORMED *adj* in an early stage of development
UNFORMING > UNFORM
UNFORMS > UNFORM
UNFORTUNE *n* misfortune
UNFOUGHT *adj* not fought
UNFOUND *adj* not found
UNFOUNDED *adj* not based on facts or evidence
UNFRAMED *adj* not framed
UNFRANKED *adj* not franked
UNFRAUGHT *adj* not fraught
UNFREE *vb* remove freedom from
UNFREED > UNFREE
UNFREEDOM *n* lack of freedom
UNFREEING > UNFREE
UNFREEMAN *n* person who is not a freeman
UNFREEMEN > UNFREEMAN
UNFREES > UNFREE
UNFREEZE *vb* thaw or cause to thaw
UNFREEZES > UNFREEZE
UNFRETTED *adj* not worried
UNFRIEND *n* enemy
UNFRIENDS > UNFRIEND
UNFROCK *vb* deprive (a priest in holy orders) of his or her priesthood
UNFROCKED > UNFROCK
UNFROCKS > UNFROCK
UNFROZE > UNFREEZE
UNFROZEN > UNFREEZE
UNFUELLED *adj* not fuelled
UNFUMED *adj* not fumigated
UNFUNDED *adj* not funded
UNFUNNY *adj* not funny
UNFURL *vb* unroll or unfold
UNFURLED > UNFURL
UNFURLING > UNFURL
UNFURLS > UNFURL
UNFURNISH *vb* clear
UNFURRED *adj* not adorned with fur
UNFUSED *adj* not fused
UNFUSSIER > UNFUSSY
UNFUSSILY > UNFUSSY
UNFUSSY *adj* not characterized by overelaborate detail
UNGAG *vb* restore freedom of speech to
UNGAGGED > UNGAG
UNGAGGING > UNGAG
UNGAGS > UNGAG
UNGAIN *adj* inconvenient
UNGAINFUL > UNGAIN
UNGAINLY *adj* lacking grace when moving ▷ *adv* clumsily
UNGALLANT *adj* not gallant
UNGALLED *adj* not annoyed
UNGARBED *adj* undressed
UNGARBLED *adj* clear
UNGATED *adj* without gate
UNGAUGED *adj* not measured
UNGAZING *adj* not gazing
UNGEAR *vb* disengage
UNGEARED > UNGEAR

UNGEARING > UNGEAR
UNGEARS > UNGEAR
UNGELDED *adj* not gelded
UNGENIAL *adj* unfriendly
UNGENTEEL *adj* impolite
UNGENTLE *adj* not gentle
UNGENTLY > UNGENTLE
UNGENUINE *adj* false
UNGERMANE *adj* inappropriate
UNGET *vb* get rid of
UNGETS > UNGET
UNGETTING > UNGET
UNGHOSTLY *adj* not ghostly
UNGIFTED *adj* not talented
UNGILD *vb* remove gilding from
UNGILDED > UNGILD
UNGILDING > UNGILD
UNGILDS > UNGILD
UNGILT > UNGILD
UNGIRD *vb* remove belt from
UNGIRDED > UNGIRD
UNGIRDING > UNGIRD
UNGIRDS > UNGIRD
UNGIRT *adj* not belted
UNGIRTH *vb* release from a girth
UNGIRTHED > UNGIRTH
UNGIRTHS > UNGIRTH
UNGIVING *adj* inflexible
UNGLAD *adj* not glad
UNGLAZED *adj* not glazed
UNGLOSSED *adj* not glossed
UNGLOVE *vb* remove glove(s)
UNGLOVED > UNGLOVE
UNGLOVES > UNGLOVE
UNGLOVING > UNGLOVE
UNGLUE *vb* remove adhesive from
UNGLUED > UNGLUE
UNGLUES > UNGLUE
UNGLUING > UNGLUE
UNGOD *vb* remove status of being a god from
UNGODDED > UNGOD
UNGODDING > UNGOD
UNGODLIER > UNGODLY
UNGODLIKE *adj* not godlike
UNGODLILY > UNGODLY
UNGODLY *adj* unreasonable or outrageous
UNGODS > UNGOD
UNGORD *same as* > UNGORED
UNGORED *adj* not gored
UNGORGED *same as* > UNGORED
UNGOT *same as* > UNGOTTEN
UNGOTTEN *adj* not obtained or won
UNGOWN *vb* remove gown (from)
UNGOWNED > UNGOWN
UNGOWNING > UNGOWN
UNGOWNS > UNGOWN
UNGRACED *adj* not graced
UNGRADED *adj* not graded
UNGRASSED *adj* not covered with grass
UNGRAVELY *adj* in a light-hearted manner
UNGRAZED *adj* not grazed
UNGREASED *adj* not greased
UNGREEDY *adj* not greedy
UNGROOMED *adj* not groomed
UNGROUND *adj* not crushed

UNGROUPED *adj* not placed in a group
UNGROWN *adj* not fully developed
UNGRUDGED *adj* not grudged
UNGUAL *adj* of, relating to, or affecting the fingernails or toenails
UNGUARD *vb* expose (to attack)
UNGUARDED *adj* not protected
UNGUARDS > UNGUARD
UNGUENT *n* ointment
UNGUENTA > UNGUENTUM
UNGUENTS > UNGUENT
UNGUENTUM *same as* > UNGUENT
UNGUES > UNGUIS
UNGUESSED *adj* unexpected
UNGUIDED *adj* (of a missile, bomb, etc) not having a flight path controlled either by radio signals or internal preset or self-actuating homing devices
UNGUIFORM *adj* shaped like a nail or claw
UNGUILTY *adj* innocent
UNGUINOUS *adj* fatty
UNGUIS *n* nail, claw, or hoof, or the part of the digit giving rise to it
UNGULA *n* truncated cone, cylinder, etc
UNGULAE > UNGULA
UNGULAR > UNGULA
UNGULATE *n* hoofed mammal
UNGULATES > UNGULATE
UNGULED *adj* hoofed
UNGUM *vb* remove adhesive from
UNGUMMED > UNGUM
UNGUMMING > UNGUM
UNGUMS > UNGUM
UNGYVE *vb* release from shackles
UNGYVED > UNGYVE
UNGYVES > UNGYVE
UNGYVING > UNGYVE
UNHABLE *same as* > UNABLE
UNHACKED *adj* not hacked
UNHAILED *adj* not hailed
UNHAIR *vb* remove the hair from (a hide)
UNHAIRED > UNHAIR
UNHAIRER > UNHAIR
UNHAIRERS > UNHAIR
UNHAIRING > UNHAIR
UNHAIRS > UNHAIR
UNHALLOW *vb* desecrate
UNHALLOWS > UNHALLOW
UNHALSED *adj* not hailed
UNHALVED *adj* not divided in half
UNHAND *vb* release from one's grasp
UNHANDED > UNHAND
UNHANDIER > UNHANDY
UNHANDILY > UNHANDY
UNHANDING > UNHAND
UNHANDLED *adj* not handled
UNHANDS > UNHAND
UNHANDY *adj* not skilful with one's hands
UNHANG *vb* take down from

hanging position

UNHANGED *adj* not executed by hanging

UNHANGING > UNHANG

UNHANGS > UNHANG

UNHAPPIED > UNHAPPY

UNHAPPIER > UNHAPPY

UNHAPPIES > UNHAPPY

UNHAPPILY > UNHAPPY

UNHAPPY *adj* sad or depressed ▷ *vb* make unhappy

UNHARBOUR *vb* force out of shelter

UNHARDY *adj* fragile

UNHARMED *adj* not hurt or damaged in any way

UNHARMFUL *adj* not harmful

UNHARMING *adj* not capable of harming

UNHARNESS *vb* remove the harness from (a horse, etc)

UNHARRIED *adj* not harried

UNHASP *vb* unfasten

UNHASPED > UNHASP

UNHASPING > UNHASP

UNHASPS > UNHASP

UNHASTING *adj* not rushing

UNHASTY *adj* not speedy

UNHAT *vb* doff one's hat

UNHATCHED *adj* (of an egg) not having broken to release the fully developed young

UNHATS > UNHAT

UNHATTED > UNHAT

UNHATTING > UNHAT

UNHAUNTED *adj* not haunted

UNHEAD *vb* remove the head from

UNHEADED *adj* not having a heading

UNHEADING > UNHEAD

UNHEADS > UNHEAD

UNHEAL *vb* expose

UNHEALED *adj* not having healed physically, mentally, or emotionally

UNHEALING *adj* not healing

UNHEALS > UNHEAL

UNHEALTH *n* illness

UNHEALTHS > UNHEALTH

UNHEALTHY *adj* likely to cause poor health

UNHEARD *adj* not listened to

UNHEARSE *vb* remove from a hearse

UNHEARSED > UNHEARSE

UNHEARSES > UNHEARSE

UNHEART *vb* discourage

UNHEARTED > UNHEART

UNHEARTS > UNHEART

UNHEATED *adj* not having been warmed up

UNHEDGED *adj* unprotected

UNHEEDED *adj* noticed but ignored

UNHEEDFUL *adj* not heedful

UNHEEDILY *adv* carelessly

UNHEEDING *adj* not heeding

UNHEEDY *adj* not heedful

UNHELE *same as* > UNHEAL

UNHELED > UNHELE

UNHELES > UNHELE

UNHELING > UNHELE

UNHELM *vb* remove the helmet of (oneself or

another)

UNHELMED > UNHELM

UNHELMING > UNHELM

UNHELMS > UNHELM

UNHELPED *adj* without help

UNHELPFUL *adj* doing nothing to improve a situation

UNHEPPEN *adj* awkward

UNHEROIC *adj* not heroic

UNHERST *archaic past form of* > UNHEARSE

UNHEWN *adj* not hewn

UNHIDDEN *adj* not hidden

UNHINGE *vb* derange or unbalance (a person or his or her mind)

UNHINGED > UNHINGE

UNHINGES > UNHINGE

UNHINGING > UNHINGE

UNHIP *adj* not at all fashionable or up to date

UNHIPPER > UNHIP

UNHIPPEST > UNHIP

UNHIRABLE *adj* not fit to be hired

UNHIRED *adj* not hired

UNHITCH *vb* unfasten or detach

UNHITCHED > UNHITCH

UNHITCHES > UNHITCH

UNHIVE *vb* remove from a hive

UNHIVED > UNHIVE

UNHIVES > UNHIVE

UNHIVING > UNHIVE

UNHOARD *vb* remove from a hoard

UNHOARDED > UNHOARD

UNHOARDS > UNHOARD

UNHOLIER > UNHOLY

UNHOLIEST > UNHOLY

UNHOLILY > UNHOLY

UNHOLPEN *same as* > UNHELPED

UNHOLY *adj* immoral or wicked

UNHOMELY *adj* not homely

UNHONEST *same as* > DISHONEST

UNHONORED *adj* not honoured

UNHOOD *vb* remove hood from

UNHOODED > UNHOOD

UNHOODING > UNHOOD

UNHOODS > UNHOOD

UNHOOK *vb* unfasten the hooks of (a garment)

UNHOOKED > UNHOOK

UNHOOKING > UNHOOK

UNHOOKS > UNHOOK

UNHOOP *vb* remove hoop(s) from

UNHOOPED > UNHOOP

UNHOOPING > UNHOOP

UNHOOPS > UNHOOP

UNHOPED *adj* unhoped-for

UNHOPEFUL *adj* not hopeful

UNHORSE *vb* knock or throw from a horse

UNHORSED > UNHORSE

UNHORSES > UNHORSE

UNHORSING > UNHORSE

UNHOSTILE *adj* not hostile

UNHOUSE *vb* remove from a house

UNHOUSED > UNHOUSE

UNHOUSES > UNHOUSE

UNHOUSING > UNHOUSE

UNHUMAN *adj* inhuman or not human

UNHUMANLY > UNHUMAN

UNHUMBLED *adj* not humbled

UNHUNG > UNHANG

UNHUNTED *adj* not hunted

UNHURRIED *adj* done at a leisurely pace, without any rush or anxiety

UNHURT *adj* not injured in an accident, attack, etc

UNHURTFUL *adj* not hurtful

UNHUSK *vb* remove the husk from

UNHUSKED > UNHUSK

UNHUSKING > UNHUSK

UNHUSKS > UNHUSK

UNI *n* (in informal English) university

UNIALGAL *adj* microbiological term

UNIAXIAL *adj* (esp of plants) having an unbranched main axis

UNIBODY *n* vehicle in which frame and body are one unit

UNIBROW *n* informal word for eyebrows that meet above the nose

UNIBROWS > UNIBROW

UNICITIES > UNICITY

UNICITY *n* oneness

UNICOLOR *same as* > UNICOLOUR

UNICOLOUR *adj* of one colour

UNICORN *n* imaginary horselike creature with one horn growing from its forehead

UNICORNS > UNICORN

UNICYCLE *n* one-wheeled vehicle driven by pedals, used in a circus ▷ *vb* ride a unicycle

UNICYCLED > UNICYCLE

UNICYCLES > UNICYCLE

UNIDEAED *adj* not having ideas

UNIDEAL *adj* not ideal

UNIFACE *n* type of tool

UNIFACES > UNIFACE

UNIFIABLE > UNIFY

UNIFIC *adj* unifying

UNIFIED > UNIFY

UNIFIER > UNIFY

UNIFIERS > UNIFY

UNIFIES > UNIFY

UNIFILAR *adj* composed of, having, or using only one wire, thread, filament, etc

UNIFORM *n* special identifying set of clothes for the members of an organization, such as soldiers ▷ *adj* regular and even throughout, unvarying ▷ *vb* fit out (a body of soldiers, etc) with uniforms

UNIFORMED > UNIFORM

UNIFORMER > UNIFORM

UNIFORMLY > UNIFORM

UNIFORMS > UNIFORM

UNIFY *vb* make or become one

UNIFYING > UNIFY

UNIFYINGS > UNIFY

UNIJUGATE *adj* (of a compound leaf) having only one pair of leaflets

UNILINEAL *same as* > UNILINEAR

UNILINEAR *adj* developing in a progressive sequence

UNILLUMED *adj* not illuminated

UNILOBAR *adj* having one lobe

UNILOBED *same as* > UNILOBAR

UNIMBUED *adj* not imbued

UNIMPEDED *adj* not stopped or disrupted by anything

UNIMPOSED *adj* not imposed

UNINCITED *adj* unprovoked

UNINDEXED *adj* not indexed

UNINJURED *adj* not having sustained any injury

UNINSTALL *vb* remove from a computer system

UNINSURED *adj* not covered by insurance

UNINURED *adj* unaccustomed

UNINVITED *adj* not having been asked ▷ *adv* without having been asked

UNINVOKED *adj* not invoked

UNION *n* uniting or being united ▷ *adj* of a trade union

UNIONISE *same as* > UNIONIZE

UNIONISED > UNIONISE

UNIONISER > UNIONISE

UNIONISES > UNIONISE

UNIONISM *n* principles of trade unions

UNIONISMS > UNIONISM

UNIONIST *n* member or supporter of a trade union ▷ *adj* of or relating to union or unionism, esp trade unionism

UNIONISTS > UNIONIST

UNIONIZE *vb* organize (workers) into a trade union

UNIONIZED > UNIONIZE

UNIONIZER > UNIONIZE

UNIONIZES > UNIONIZE

UNIONS > UNION

UNIPAROUS *adj* (of certain animals) producing a single offspring at each birth

UNIPED *n* person or thing with one foot

UNIPEDS > UNIPED

UNIPLANAR *adj* situated in one plane

UNIPOD *n* one-legged support, as for a camera

UNIPODS > UNIPOD

UNIPOLAR *adj* of, concerned with, or having a single magnetic or electric pole

UNIPOTENT *adj* able to form only one type of cell

Section 1: Words between 2 and 9 letters in length

UNIQUE n person or thing that is unique
UNIQUELY > UNIQUE
UNIQUER > UNIQUE
UNIQUES > UNIQUE
UNIQUEST > UNIQUE
UNIRAMOSE same as > UNIRAMOUS
UNIRAMOUS adj (esp of the appendages of crustaceans) consisting of a single branch
UNIRONED adj not ironed
UNIRONIC adj not ironic
UNIS > UNI
UNISERIAL adj in or relating to a single series
UNISEX adj designed for use by both sexes ▷ n condition of seeming not to belong obviously either to one sex or the other from the way one behaves or dresses
UNISEXES > UNISEX
UNISEXUAL adj of one sex only
UNISIZE adj in one size only
UNISON n complete agreement
UNISONAL > UNISON
UNISONANT > UNISON
UNISONOUS > UNISON
UNISONS > UNISON
UNISSUED adj not issued
UNIT n single undivided entity or whole
UNITAGE > UNIT
UNITAGES > UNIT
UNITAL > UNIT
UNITARD n all-in-one skintight suit
UNITARDS > UNITARD
UNITARIAN n supporter of unity or centralization ▷ adj of or relating to unity or centralization
UNITARILY > UNITARY
UNITARY adj consisting of a single undivided whole
UNITE vb make or become an integrated whole ▷ n English gold coin minted in the Stuart period, originally worth 20 shillings
UNITED adj produced by two or more people or things in combination
UNITEDLY > UNITED
UNITER > UNITE
UNITERS > UNITE
UNITES > UNITE
UNITIES > UNITY
UNITING > UNITE
UNITINGS > UNITE
UNITION n joining
UNITIONS > UNITION
UNITISE same as > UNITIZE
UNITISED > UNITISE
UNITISER same as > UNITIZER
UNITISERS > UNITISER
UNITISES > UNITISE
UNITISING > UNITISE
UNITIVE adj tending to unite or capable of uniting

UNITIVELY > UNITIVE
UNITIZE vb convert (an investment trust) into a unit trust
UNITIZED > UNITIZE
UNITIZER n person or thing that arranges units into batches
UNITIZERS > UNITIZER
UNITIZES > UNITIZE
UNITIZING > UNITIZE
UNITRUST n type of income-producing trust fund
UNITRUSTS > UNITRUST
UNITS > UNIT
UNITY n state of being one
UNIVALENT adj (of a chromosome during meiosis) not paired with its homologue
UNIVALVE adj relating to, designating, or possessing a mollusc shell that consists of a single piece (valve) ▷ n gastropod mollusc or its shell
UNIVALVED > UNIVALVE
UNIVALVES > UNIVALVE
UNIVERSAL adj of or typical of the whole of mankind or of nature ▷ n something which exists or is true in all places and all situations
UNIVERSE n whole of all existing matter, energy, and space
UNIVERSES > UNIVERSE
UNIVOCAL adj unambiguous or unmistakable ▷ n word or term that has only one meaning
UNIVOCALS > UNIVOCAL
UNJADED adj not jaded
UNJAM vb remove blockage from
UNJAMMED > UNJAM
UNJAMMING > UNJAM
UNJAMS > UNJAM
UNJEALOUS adj not jealous
UNJOINED adj not joined
UNJOINT vb disjoint
UNJOINTED > UNJOINT
UNJOINTS > UNJOINT
UNJOYFUL adj not joyful
UNJOYOUS adj not joyous
UNJUDGED adj not judged
UNJUST adj not fair or just
UNJUSTER > UNJUST
UNJUSTEST > UNJUST
UNJUSTLY > UNJUST
UNKED adj alien
UNKEELED adj without a keel
UNKEMPT adj (of the hair) not combed
UNKEMPTLY > UNKEMPT
UNKEND same as > UNKENNED
UNKENNED adj unknown
UNKENNEL vb release from a kennel
UNKENNELS > UNKENNEL
UNKENT same as > UNKENNED
UNKEPT adj not kept
UNKET same as > UNKED
UNKID same as > UNKED

UNKIND adj unsympathetic or cruel
UNKINDER > UNKIND
UNKINDEST > UNKIND
UNKINDLED adj not kindled
UNKINDLY > UNKIND
UNKING vb strip of sovereignty
UNKINGED > UNKING
UNKINGING > UNKING
UNKINGLY adj not kingly
UNKINGS > UNKING
UNKINK vb straighten out
UNKINKED > UNKINK
UNKINKING > UNKINK
UNKINKS > UNKINK
UNKISS vb cancel (a previous action) with a kiss
UNKISSED adj not kissed
UNKISSES > UNKISS
UNKISSING > UNKISS
UNKNELLED adj not tolled
UNKNIGHT vb strip of knighthood
UNKNIGHTS > UNKNIGHT
UNKNIT vb make or become undone, untied, or unravelled
UNKNITS > UNKNIT
UNKNITTED > UNKNIT
UNKNOT vb disentangle or undo a knot or knots in
UNKNOTS > UNKNOT
UNKNOTTED > UNKNOT
UNKNOWING adj unaware or ignorant
UNKNOWN adj not known ▷ n unknown person, quantity, or thing
UNKNOWNS > UNKNOWN
UNKOSHER adj not conforming to Jewish religious law
UNLABELED adj not labelled
UNLABORED adj not laboured
UNLACE vb loosen or undo the lacing of (shoes, garments, etc)
UNLACED adj not laced
UNLACES > UNLACE
UNLACING > UNLACE
UNLADE less common word for > UNLOAD
UNLADED > UNLADE
UNLADEN adj not laden
UNLADES > UNLADE
UNLADING > UNLADE
UNLADINGS > UNLADE
UNLAID > UNLAY
UNLASH vb untie or unfasten
UNLASHED > UNLASH
UNLASHES > UNLASH
UNLASHING > UNLASH
UNLAST archaic variant of > UNLACED
UNLASTE archaic variant of > UNLACED
UNLATCH vb open or unfasten or come open or unfastened by the lifting or release of a latch
UNLATCHED > UNLATCH
UNLATCHES > UNLATCH
UNLAW vb penalize
UNLAWED > UNLAW
UNLAWFUL adj not

permitted by law
UNLAWING > UNLAW
UNLAWS > UNLAW
UNLAY vb untwist (a rope or cable) to separate its strands
UNLAYING > UNLAY
UNLAYS > UNLAY
UNLEAD vb strip off lead
UNLEADED adj (of petrol) containing less tetraethyl lead, in order to reduce environmental pollution ▷ n petrol containing a reduced amount of tetraethyl lead
UNLEADEDS > UNLEADED
UNLEADING > UNLEAD
UNLEADS > UNLEAD
UNLEAL adj treacherous
UNLEARN vb try to forget something learnt or to discard accumulated knowledge
UNLEARNED same as > UNLEARNT
UNLEARNS > UNLEARN
UNLEARNT adj denoting knowledge or skills innately present rather than learnt
UNLEASED adj not leased
UNLEASH vb set loose or cause (something bad)
UNLEASHED > UNLEASH
UNLEASHES > UNLEASH
UNLED adj not led
UNLESS conj except under the circumstances that ▷ prep except
UNLET adj not rented
UNLETHAL adj not deadly
UNLETTED adj unimpeded
UNLEVEL adj not level ▷ vb make unbalanced
UNLEVELED > UNLEVEL
UNLEVELS > UNLEVEL
UNLEVIED adj not levied
UNLICH Spenserian form of > UNLIKE
UNLICKED adj not licked
UNLID vb remove lid from
UNLIDDED > UNLID
UNLIDDING > UNLID
UNLIDS > UNLID
UNLIGHTED adj not lit
UNLIKABLE adj not likable
UNLIKE adj dissimilar or different ▷ prep not like or typical of ▷ n person or thing that is unlike another
UNLIKED adj not liked
UNLIKELY adj improbable
UNLIKES > UNLIKE
UNLIMBER vb disengage (a gun) from its limber
UNLIMBERS > UNLIMBER
UNLIME vb detach
UNLIMED > UNLIME
UNLIMES > UNLIME
UNLIMING > UNLIME
UNLIMITED adj apparently endless
UNLINE vb remove the lining from
UNLINEAL adj not lineal
UNLINED adj not having any

u

lining
UNLINES > UNLINE
UNLINING > UNLINE
UNLINK vb undo the link or links between
UNLINKED > UNLINK
UNLINKING > UNLINK
UNLINKS > UNLINK
UNLISTED adj not entered on a list
UNLIT adj (of a fire, cigarette, etc) not lit and therefore not burning
UNLIVABLE adj not fit for living in
UNLIVE vb live so as to nullify, undo, or live down (past events or times)
UNLIVED > UNLIVE
UNLIVELY adj lifeless
UNLIVES > UNLIVE
UNLIVING > UNLIVE
UNLOAD vb remove (cargo) from (a ship, truck, or plane)
UNLOADED > UNLOAD
UNLOADER > UNLOAD
UNLOADERS > UNLOAD
UNLOADING > UNLOAD
UNLOADS > UNLOAD
UNLOBED adj without lobes
UNLOCATED adj not located
UNLOCK vb unfasten (a lock or door)
UNLOCKED adj not locked
UNLOCKING > UNLOCK
UNLOCKS > UNLOCK
UNLOGICAL same as > ILLOGICAL
UNLOOKED adj not looked (at)
UNLOOSE vb set free or release
UNLOOSED > UNLOOSE
UNLOOSEN same as > UNLOOSE
UNLOOSENS > UNLOOSEN
UNLOOSES > UNLOOSE
UNLOOSING > UNLOOSE
UNLOPPED adj not chopped off
UNLORD vb remove from position of being lord
UNLORDED > UNLORD
UNLORDING > UNLORD
UNLORDLY adv not in a lordlike manner
UNLORDS > UNLORD
UNLOSABLE adj unable to be lost
UNLOST adj not lost
UNLOVABLE adj too unpleasant or unattractive to be loved
UNLOVE vb stop loving
UNLOVED adj not loved by anyone
UNLOVELY adj unpleasant in appearance or character
UNLOVES > UNLOVE
UNLOVING adj not feeling or showing love and affection
UNLUCKIER > UNLUCKY
UNLUCKILY > UNLUCKY
UNLUCKY adj having bad luck, unfortunate
UNLYRICAL adj not lyrical

UNMACHO adj not macho
UNMADE adj (of a bed) with the bedclothes not smoothed and tidied
UNMAILED adj not sent by post
UNMAIMED adj not injured
UNMAKABLE adj unable to be made
UNMAKE vb undo or destroy
UNMAKER > UNMAKE
UNMAKERS > UNMAKE
UNMAKES > UNMAKE
UNMAKING > UNMAKE
UNMAKINGS > UNMAKE
UNMAN vb cause to lose courage or nerve
UNMANACLE vb release from manacles
UNMANAGED adj not managed
UNMANFUL adj unmanly
UNMANLIER > UNMANLY
UNMANLIKE adj not worthy of a man
UNMANLY adj not masculine or virile
UNMANNED adj having no personnel or crew
UNMANNING > UNMAN
UNMANNISH adj not mannish
UNMANS > UNMAN
UNMANTLE vb remove mantle from
UNMANTLED > UNMANTLE
UNMANTLES > UNMANTLE
UNMANURED adj not treated with manure
UNMAPPED adj not charted
UNMARD same as > UNMARRED
UNMARKED adj having no signs of damage or injury
UNMARRED adj not marred
UNMARRIED adj not married
UNMARRIES > UNMARRY
UNMARRY vb divorce
UNMASK vb remove the mask or disguise from
UNMASKED > UNMASK
UNMASKER > UNMASK
UNMASKERS > UNMASK
UNMASKING > UNMASK
UNMASKS > UNMASK
UNMATCHED adj not equalled or surpassed
UNMATED adj not mated
UNMATTED adj not matted
UNMATURED adj not matured
UNMEANING adj having no meaning
UNMEANT adj unintentional
UNMEEK adj not submissive
UNMEET adj not meet
UNMEETLY > UNMEET
UNMELLOW adj not mellow
UNMELTED adj not melted
UNMENDED adj not mended
UNMERITED adj not merited or deserved
UNMERRY adj not merry
UNMESH vb release from mesh
UNMESHED > UNMESH
UNMESHES > UNMESH
UNMESHING > UNMESH

UNMET adj unfulfilled
UNMETED adj unmeasured
UNMEW vb release from confinement
UNMEWED > UNMEW
UNMEWING > UNMEW
UNMEWS > UNMEW
UNMILKED adj not milked
UNMILLED adj not milled
UNMINDED adj disregarded
UNMINDFUL adj careless, heedless, or forgetful
UNMINED adj not mined
UNMINGLE vb separate
UNMINGLED > UNMINGLE
UNMINGLES > UNMINGLE
UNMIRY adj not swampy
UNMISSED adj unnoticed
UNMITER same as > UNMITRE
UNMITERED > UNMITER
UNMITERS > UNMITER
UNMITRE vb divest of a mitre
UNMITRED > UNMITRE
UNMITRES > UNMITRE
UNMITRING > UNMITRE
UNMIX vb separate
UNMIXABLE adj incapable of being mixed
UNMIXED > UNMIX
UNMIXEDLY > UNMIXED
UNMIXES > UNMIX
UNMIXING > UNMIX
UNMIXT same as > UNMIX
UNMOANED adj unmourned
UNMODISH adj passé
UNMOLD same as > UNMOULD
UNMOLDED > UNMOLD
UNMOLDING > UNMOLD
UNMOLDS > UNMOLD
UNMOLTEN adj not molten
UNMONEYED adj poor
UNMONIED same as > UNMONEYED
UNMOOR vb weigh the anchor or drop the mooring of (a vessel)
UNMOORED > UNMOOR
UNMOORING > UNMOOR
UNMOORS > UNMOOR
UNMORAL adj outside morality
UNMORALLY > UNMORAL
UNMORTISE vb release from mortise
UNMOTIVED adj without motive
UNMOULD vb change shape of
UNMOULDED > UNMOULD
UNMOULDS > UNMOULD
UNMOUNT vb dismount
UNMOUNTED > UNMOUNT
UNMOUNTS > UNMOUNT
UNMOURNED adj not mourned
UNMOVABLE adj not movable
UNMOVABLY > UNMOVABLE
UNMOVED adj not affected by emotion, indifferent
UNMOVEDLY > UNMOVED
UNMOVING adj still and motionless
UNMOWN adj not mown
UNMUFFLE vb remove a muffle or muffles from
UNMUFFLED > UNMUFFLE
UNMUFFLES > UNMUFFLE

UNMUSICAL adj (of a person) unable to appreciate or play music
UNMUZZLE vb take the muzzle off (a dog, etc)
UNMUZZLED > UNMUZZLE
UNMUZZLES > UNMUZZLE
UNNAIL vb unfasten by removing nails
UNNAILED > UNNAIL
UNNAILING > UNNAIL
UNNAILS > UNNAIL
UNNAMABLE adj that cannot or must not be named
UNNAMED adj not mentioned by name
UNNANELD same as > UNANELED
UNNATIVE adj not native
UNNATURAL adj strange and frightening because not usual
UNNEATH adj archaic word for underneath
UNNEEDED adj not needed
UNNEEDFUL adj not needful
UNNERVE vb cause to lose courage, confidence, or self-control
UNNERVED > UNNERVE
UNNERVES > UNNERVE
UNNERVING > UNNERVE
UNNEST vb remove from a nest
UNNESTED > UNNEST
UNNESTING > UNNEST
UNNESTS > UNNEST
UNNETHES same as > UNNEATH
UNNETTED adj not having or not enclosed in a net
UNNOBLE vb strip of nobility
UNNOBLED > UNNOBLE
UNNOBLES > UNNOBLE
UNNOBLING > UNNOBLE
UNNOISY adj quiet
UNNOTED adj not noted
UNNOTICED adj without being seen or noticed
UNNUANCED adj without nuances
UNOBEYED adj not obeyed
UNOBVIOUS adj unapparent
UNOFFERED adj not offered
UNOFTEN adv infrequently
UNOILED adj not lubricated with oil
UNOPEN adj not open
UNOPENED adj closed, barred, or sealed
UNOPPOSED adj not opposed
UNORDER vb cancel an order
UNORDERED adj not ordered
UNORDERLY adj not orderly or disorderly
UNORDERS > UNORDER
UNORNATE same as > INORNATE
UNOWED same as > UNOWNED
UNOWNED adj not owned
UNPACED adj without the aid of a pacemaker
UNPACK vb remove the contents of (a suitcase, trunk, etc)
UNPACKED > UNPACK
UNPACKER > UNPACK

UNPACKERS > UNPACK
UNPACKING > UNPACK
UNPACKS > UNPACK
UNPADDED adj not padded
UNPAGED adj (of a book) having no page numbers
UNPAID adj without a salary or wage
UNPAINED adj not suffering pain
UNPAINFUL adj painless
UNPAINT vb remove paint from
UNPAINTED > UNPAINT
UNPAINTS > UNPAINT
UNPAIRED adj not paired up
UNPALSIED adj not affected with palsy
UNPANEL vb unsaddle
UNPANELS > UNPANEL
UNPANGED adj without pain or sadness
UNPANNEL same
   as > UNPANEL
UNPANNELS > UNPANNEL
UNPAPER vb remove paper from
UNPAPERED > UNPAPER
UNPAPERS > UNPAPER
UNPARED adj not pared
UNPARTED adj not parted
UNPARTIAL same
   as > IMPARTIAL
UNPATCHED adj not patched
UNPATHED adj not having a path
UNPAVED adj not covered in paving
UNPAY vb undo
UNPAYABLE adj incapable of being paid
UNPAYING > UNPAY
UNPAYS > UNPAY
UNPEELED adj not peeled
UNPEERED adj unparalleled
UNPEG vb remove the peg or pegs from, esp to unfasten
UNPEGGED > UNPEG
UNPEGGING > UNPEG
UNPEGS > UNPEG
UNPEN vb release from a pen
UNPENNED > UNPEN
UNPENNIED adj not having pennies
UNPENNING > UNPEN
UNPENS > UNPEN
UNPENT archaic past form of > UNPEN
UNPEOPLE vb empty of people
UNPEOPLED > UNPEOPLE
UNPEOPLES > UNPEOPLE
UNPERCH vb remove from a perch
UNPERCHED > UNPERCH
UNPERCHES > UNPERCH
UNPERFECT same
   as > IMPERFECT
UNPERPLEX vb remove confusion from
UNPERSON n person whose existence is officially denied or ignored
UNPERSONS > UNPERSON
UNPERVERT vb free (someone) from perversion
UNPICK vb undo (the

stitches) of (a piece of sewing)
UNPICKED adj (of knitting, sewing, etc) having been unravelled or picked out
UNPICKING > UNPICK
UNPICKS > UNPICK
UNPIERCED adj not pierced
UNPILE vb remove from a pile
UNPILED > UNPILE
UNPILES > UNPILE
UNPILING > UNPILE
UNPILOTED adj unguided
UNPIN vb remove a pin or pins from
UNPINKED adj not decorated with a perforated pattern
UNPINKT same
   as > UNPINKED
UNPINNED > UNPIN
UNPINNING > UNPIN
UNPINS > UNPIN
UNPITIED adj not pitied
UNPITIFUL adj pitiless
UNPITTED adj not having had pits removed
UNPITYING adj not pitying
UNPLACE same as > DISPLACE
UNPLACED adj not given or put in a particular place
UNPLACES > UNPLACE
UNPLACING > UNPLACE
UNPLAGUED adj not plagued
UNPLAINED adj unmourned
UNPLAIT vb remove plaits from
UNPLAITED > UNPLAIT
UNPLAITS > UNPLAIT
UNPLANKED adj not planked
UNPLANNED adj not intentional or deliberate
UNPLANTED adj not planted
UNPLAYED adj not played
UNPLEASED adj not pleased or displeased
UNPLEATED adj not pleated
UNPLEDGED adj not pledged
UNPLIABLE adj not easily bent
UNPLIABLY > UNPLIABLE
UNPLIANT adj not pliant
UNPLOWED adj not ploughed
UNPLUCKED adj not plucked
UNPLUG vb disconnect (a piece of electrical equipment) by taking the plug out of the socket
UNPLUGGED adj using acoustic rather than electric instruments
UNPLUGS > UNPLUG
UNPLUMB vb remove lead from
UNPLUMBED adj not measured
UNPLUMBS > UNPLUMB
UNPLUME vb remove feathers from
UNPLUMED > UNPLUME
UNPLUMES > UNPLUME
UNPLUMING > UNPLUME
UNPOETIC adj not poetic
UNPOINTED adj not pointed
UNPOISED adj not poised
UNPOISON vb extract poison

from
UNPOISONS > UNPOISON
UNPOLICED adj without police control
UNPOLISH vb remove polish from
UNPOLITE same
   as > IMPOLITE
UNPOLITIC another word for > IMPOLITIC
UNPOLLED adj not included in an opinion poll
UNPOPE vb strip of popedom
UNPOPED > UNPOPE
UNPOPES > UNPOPE
UNPOPING > UNPOPE
UNPOPULAR adj generally disliked or disapproved of
UNPOSED adj not posed
UNPOSTED adj not sent by post
UNPOTABLE adj undrinkable
UNPOTTED adj not planted in a pot
UNPRAISE vb withhold praise from
UNPRAISED > UNPRAISE
UNPRAISES > UNPRAISE
UNPRAY vb withdraw (a prayer)
UNPRAYED > UNPRAY
UNPRAYING > UNPRAY
UNPRAYS > UNPRAY
UNPREACH vb retract (a sermon)
UNPRECISE same
   as > IMPRECISE
UNPREDICT vb retract (a previous prediction)
UNPREPARE vb make unprepared
UNPRESSED adj not pressed
UNPRETTY adj unattractive
UNPRICED adj having no fixed or marked price
UNPRIEST vb strip of priesthood
UNPRIESTS > UNPRIEST
UNPRIMED adj not primed
UNPRINTED adj not printed
UNPRISON vb release from prison
UNPRISONS > UNPRISON
UNPRIZED adj not treasured
UNPROBED adj not examined
UNPROP vb remove support from
UNPROPER same
   as > IMPROPER
UNPROPPED > UNPROP
UNPROPS > UNPROP
UNPROVED adj not having been established as true, valid, or possible
UNPROVEN adj not established as true by evidence or demonstration
UNPROVIDE vb fail to supply requirements for
UNPROVOKE vb remove provocation from
UNPRUNED adj not pruned
UNPUCKER vb remove wrinkles from
UNPUCKERS > UNPUCKER
UNPULLED adj not pulled
UNPURE same as > IMPURE

UNPURELY > UNPURE
UNPURGED adj not purged
UNPURSE vb relax (lips) from pursed position
UNPURSED > UNPURSE
UNPURSES > UNPURSE
UNPURSING > UNPURSE
UNPURSUED adj not followed
UNPUZZLE vb figure out
UNPUZZLED > UNPUZZLE
UNPUZZLES > UNPUZZLE
UNQUAKING adj not quaking
UNQUALIFY vb disqualify
UNQUEEN vb depose from the position of queen
UNQUEENED > UNQUEEN
UNQUEENLY adv not in a queenlike manner
UNQUEENS > UNQUEEN
UNQUELLED adj not quelled
UNQUIET adj anxious or uneasy ▷ n state of unrest ▷ vb disquiet
UNQUIETED > UNQUIET
UNQUIETER > UNQUIET
UNQUIETLY > UNQUIET
UNQUIETS > UNQUIET
UNQUOTE interj expression used to indicate the end of a quotation that was introduced with the word 'quote' ▷ vb close (a quotation), esp in printing
UNQUOTED > UNQUOTE
UNQUOTES > UNQUOTE
UNQUOTING > UNQUOTE
UNRACED adj not raced
UNRACKED adj not stretched
UNRAISED adj not raised
UNRAKE vb unearth through raking
UNRAKED adj not raked
UNRAKES > UNRAKE
UNRAKING > UNRAKE
UNRANKED adj not ranked
UNRATED adj not rated
UNRAVAGED adj not ravaged
UNRAVEL vb reduce (something knitted or woven) to separate strands
UNRAVELED > UNRAVEL
UNRAVELS > UNRAVEL
UNRAZED adj not razed
UNRAZORED adj unshaven
UNREACHED adj not reached
UNREAD adj (of a book or article) not yet read
UNREADIER > UNREADY
UNREADILY > UNREADY
UNREADY adj not ready or prepared
UNREAL adj (as if) existing only in the imagination
UNREALISE same
   as > UNREALIZE
UNREALISM n abstractionism
UNREALITY n quality or state of being unreal, fanciful, or impractical
UNREALIZE vb make unreal
UNREALLY > UNREAL
UNREAPED adj not reaped
UNREASON n irrationality or madness ▷ vb deprive of reason
UNREASONS > UNREASON

u

UNREAVE vb unwind
UNREAVED > UNREAVE
UNREAVES > UNREAVE
UNREAVING > UNREAVE
UNREBATED adj not
refunded
UNREBUKED adj not rebuked
UNRECKED adj disregarded
UNRED same as > UNREAD
UNREDREST adj not
redressed
UNREDUCED adj not reduced
UNREDY same as > UNREADY
UNREEL vb unwind from
a reel
UNREELED > UNREEL
UNREELER n machine that
unwinds something from
a reel
UNREELERS > UNREELER
UNREELING > UNREEL
UNREELS > UNREEL
UNREEVE vb withdraw
(a rope) from a block,
thimble, etc
UNREEVED > UNREEVE
UNREEVES > UNREEVE
UNREEVING > UNREEVE
UNREFINED adj (of
substances such as
petroleum, ores, and
sugar) not processed into a
pure or usable form
UNREFUTED adj not refuted
UNREIN vb free from reins
UNREINED > UNREIN
UNREINING > UNREIN
UNREINS > UNREIN
UNRELATED adj not
connected with each other
UNRELAXED adj not relaxed
UNREMOVED adj not
removed
UNRENEWED adj not renewed
UNRENT adj not torn
UNRENTED adj not rented
UNREPAID adj not repaid
UNREPAIR less common word
for > DISREPAIR
UNREPAIRS > UNREPAIR
UNRESERVE n candour
UNREST n rebellious state of
discontent
UNRESTED adj not rested
UNRESTFUL adj restless
UNRESTING adj not resting
UNRESTS > UNREST
UNRETIRE vb resume work
after retiring
UNRETIRED > UNRETIRE
UNRETIRES > UNRETIRE
UNREVISED adj not revised
UNREVOKED adj not revoked
UNRHYMED adj not rhymed
UNRIBBED adj not ribbed
UNRID adj unridden
UNRIDABLE adj not capable
of being ridden
UNRIDDEN adj not or never
ridden
UNRIDDLE vb solve or puzzle
out
UNRIDDLED > UNRIDDLE
UNRIDDLER > UNRIDDLE
UNRIDDLES > UNRIDDLE
UNRIFLED adj (of a firearm
or its bore) not rifled

UNRIG vb strip (a vessel)
of standing and running
rigging
UNRIGGED > UNRIG
UNRIGGING > UNRIG
UNRIGHT n wrong
UNRIGHTS > UNRIGHT
UNRIGS > UNRIG
UNRIMED same
as > UNRHYMED
UNRINGED adj not having or
wearing a ring
UNRINSED adj not rinsed
UNRIP vb rip open
UNRIPE adj not fully
matured
UNRIPELY > UNRIPE
UNRIPENED same
as > UNRIPE
UNRIPER > UNRIPE
UNRIPEST > UNRIPE
UNRIPPED > UNRIP
UNRIPPING > UNRIP
UNRIPS > UNRIP
UNRISEN adj not risen
UNRIVALED adj (in US
English) matchless or
unrivalled
UNRIVEN adj not torn apart
UNRIVET vb remove rivets
from
UNRIVETED > UNRIVET
UNRIVETS > UNRIVET
UNROASTED adj not roasted
UNROBE same as > DISROBE
UNROBED > UNROBE
UNROBES > UNROBE
UNROBING > UNROBE
UNROLL vb open out or
unwind (something rolled
or coiled) or (of something
rolled or coiled) become
opened out or unwound
UNROLLED > UNROLL
UNROLLING > UNROLL
UNROLLS > UNROLL
UNROOF vb remove the roof
from
UNROOFED > UNROOF
UNROOFING > UNROOF
UNROOFS > UNROOF
UNROOST vb remove from
a perch
UNROOSTED > UNROOST
UNROOSTS > UNROOST
UNROOT less common word
for > UPROOT
UNROOTED > UNROOT
UNROOTING > UNROOT
UNROOTS > UNROOT
UNROPE vb release from a
rope
UNROPED > UNROPE
UNROPES > UNROPE
UNROPING > UNROPE
UNROSINED adj not coated
with rosin
UNROTTED adj not rotted
UNROTTEN adj not rotten
UNROUGED adj not coloured
with rouge
UNROUGH adj not rough
UNROUND vb release (lips)
from a rounded position
UNROUNDED adj articulated
with the lips spread
UNROUNDS > UNROUND

UNROUSED adj not roused
UNROVE > UNREEVE
UNROVEN > UNREEVE
UNROYAL adj not royal
UNROYALLY > UNROYAL
UNRUBBED adj not rubbed
UNRUDE adj not rude
UNRUFFE same
as > UNROUGH
UNRUFFLE vb calm
UNRUFFLED adj calm and
unperturbed
UNRUFFLES > UNRUFFLE
UNRULE n lack of authority
UNRULED adj not ruled
UNRULES > UNRULE
UNRULIER > UNRULY
UNRULIEST > UNRULY
UNRULY adj difficult to
control or organize
UNRUMPLED adj neat
UNRUSHED adj unhurried
UNRUSTED adj not rusted
UNS > UN
UNSADDLE vb remove the
saddle from (a horse)
UNSADDLED > UNSADDLE
UNSADDLES > UNSADDLE
UNSAFE adj dangerous
UNSAFELY > UNSAFE
UNSAFER > UNSAFE
UNSAFEST > UNSAFE
UNSAFETY n lack of safety
UNSAID adj not said or
expressed
UNSAILED adj not sailed
UNSAINED adj not blessed
UNSAINT vb remove status
of being a saint from
UNSAINTED > UNSAINT
UNSAINTLY adj not saintly
UNSAINTS > UNSAINT
UNSALABLE adj not capable
of being sold
UNSALABLY > UNSALABLE
UNSALTED adj not
seasoned, preserved, or
treated with salt
UNSALUTED adj not saluted
UNSAMPLED adj not sampled
UNSAPPED adj not
undermined
UNSASHED adj not furnished
with a sash
UNSATABLE adj not able to
be sated; insatiable
UNSATED adj not sated
UNSATIATE same
as > INSATIABLE
UNSATING adj not satisfying
UNSAVED adj not saved
UNSAVORY same
as > UNSAVOURY
UNSAVOURY adj distasteful
or objectionable
UNSAWED same as > UNSAWN
UNSAWN adj not cut with a
saw
UNSAY vb retract or
withdraw (something said
or written)
UNSAYABLE adj that cannot
be said
UNSAYING > UNSAY
UNSAYS > UNSAY
UNSCALE same as > DESCALE
UNSCALED > UNSCALE

UNSCALES > UNSCALE
UNSCALING > UNSCALE
UNSCANNED adj not scanned
UNSCARRED adj not scarred
UNSCARY adj not scary
UNSCATHED adj not harmed
or injured
UNSCENTED adj not filled or
impregnated with odour or
fragrance
UNSCOURED adj not scoured
UNSCREW vb loosen (a screw
or lid) by turning it
UNSCREWED > UNSCREW
UNSCREWS > UNSCREW
UNSCYTHED adj not cut with
a scythe
UNSEAL vb remove or break
the seal of
UNSEALED > UNSEAL
UNSEALING > UNSEAL
UNSEALS > UNSEAL
UNSEAM vb open or undo the
seam of
UNSEAMED > UNSEAM
UNSEAMING > UNSEAM
UNSEAMS > UNSEAM
UNSEARED adj not seared
UNSEASON vb affect
unfavourably
UNSEASONS > UNSEASON
UNSEAT vb throw or displace
from a seat or saddle
UNSEATED > UNSEAT
UNSEATING > UNSEAT
UNSEATS > UNSEAT
UNSECRET adj not secret
UNSECULAR adj not secular
UNSECURED adj (of a loan,
etc) secured only against
general assets and not
against a specific asset
UNSEDUCED adj not seduced
UNSEEABLE adj not able to
be seen
UNSEEDED adj (of a player
in a sport) not given a
top player's position in
the opening rounds of a
tournament
UNSEEING adj not noticing
or looking at anything
UNSEEL vb undo seeling
UNSEELED > UNSEEL
UNSEELIE pl n evil
malevolent fairies ▷ adj
of or belonging to the
unseelie
UNSEELING > UNSEEL
UNSEELS > UNSEEL
UNSEEMING adj unseemly
UNSEEMLY adj not according
to expected standards
of behaviour ▷ adv in an
unseemly manner
UNSEEN adj hidden or
invisible ▷ adv without
being seen ▷ n passage
which is given to students
for translation without
them having seen it in
advance
UNSEENS > UNSEEN
UNSEIZED adj not seized
UNSELDOM adv frequently
UNSELF vb remove self-
centredness from ▷ n lack

of self
UNSELFED > UNSELF
UNSELFING > UNSELF
UNSELFISH adj concerned about other people's wishes and needs rather than one's own
UNSELFS > UNSELF
UNSELL vb speak unfavourably and off-puttingly of (something or someone)
UNSELLING > UNSELL
UNSELLS > UNSELL
UNSELVES > UNSELF
UNSENSE vb remove sense from
UNSENSED > UNSENSE
UNSENSES > UNSENSE
UNSENSING > UNSENSE
UNSENT adj not sent
UNSERIOUS adj not serious
UNSERVED adj not served
UNSET adj not yet solidified or firm ▷ vb displace
UNSETS > UNSET
UNSETTING > UNSET
UNSETTLE vb change or become changed from a fixed or settled condition
UNSETTLED adj lacking order or stability
UNSETTLES > UNSETTLE
UNSEVERED adj not severed
UNSEW vb undo stitching of
UNSEWED same as > UNSEW
UNSEWING > UNSEW
UNSEWN > UNSEW
UNSEWS > UNSEW
UNSEX vb deprive (a person) of the attributes of his or her sex, esp to make a woman more callous
UNSEXED > UNSEX
UNSEXES > UNSEX
UNSEXING > UNSEX
UNSEXIST adj not sexist
UNSEXUAL adj not sexual
UNSEXY adj not sexually attractive
UNSHACKLE vb release from shackles
UNSHADED adj not shaded
UNSHADOW vb remove shadow from
UNSHADOWS > UNSHADOW
UNSHAKED same as > UNSHAKEN
UNSHAKEN adj (of faith or feelings) not having been weakened
UNSHALE vb expose
UNSHALED > UNSHALE
UNSHALES > UNSHALE
UNSHALING > UNSHALE
UNSHAMED same as > UNASHAMED
UNSHAPE vb make shapeless
UNSHAPED > UNSHAPE
UNSHAPELY adj not shapely
UNSHAPEN adj having no definite shape
UNSHAPES > UNSHAPE
UNSHAPING > UNSHAPE
UNSHARED adj not shared
UNSHARP adj not sharp
UNSHAVED adj not shaved

UNSHAVEN adj (of a man who does not have a beard) having stubble on his chin because he has not shaved recently
UNSHEATHE vb pull (a weapon) from a sheath
UNSHED adj not shed
UNSHELL vb remove from a shell
UNSHELLED > UNSHELL
UNSHELLS > UNSHELL
UNSHENT adj undamaged
UNSHEWN adj unshown
UNSHIFT vb release the shift key on a keyboard
UNSHIFTED > UNSHIFT
UNSHIFTS > UNSHIFT
UNSHIP vb be or cause to be unloaded, discharged, or disembarked from a ship
UNSHIPPED > UNSHIP
UNSHIPS > UNSHIP
UNSHIRTED adj not wearing a shirt
UNSHOCKED adj not shocked
UNSHOD adj not wearing shoes
UNSHOE vb remove shoes from
UNSHOED same as > UNSHOD
UNSHOEING > UNSHOE
UNSHOES > UNSHOE
UNSHOOT Shakespearean variant of > UNSHOUT
UNSHOOTED > UNSHOOT
UNSHOOTS > UNSHOOT
UNSHORN adj not cut
UNSHOT adj not shot
UNSHOUT vb revoke (an earlier statement) by shouting a contrary one
UNSHOUTED > UNSHOUT
UNSHOUTS > UNSHOUT
UNSHOWN adj not shown
UNSHOWY adj not showy
UNSHRIVED same as > UNSHRIVEN
UNSHRIVEN adj not shriven
UNSHROUD vb uncover
UNSHROUDS > UNSHROUD
UNSHRUBD adj not having shrubs
UNSHRUNK adj not shrunk
UNSHUNNED adj not shunned
UNSHUT vb open
UNSHUTS > UNSHUT
UNSHUTTER vb remove shutters from
UNSICKER adj unsettled
UNSICKLED adj not cut with a sickle
UNSIFTED adj not strained
UNSIGHING adj not lamented
UNSIGHT vb obstruct vision of
UNSIGHTED adj not sighted
UNSIGHTLY adj unpleasant to look at
UNSIGHTS > UNSIGHT
UNSIGNED adj (of a letter etc) anonymous
UNSILENT adj not silent
UNSIMILAR adj not similar
UNSINEW vb weaken
UNSINEWED > UNSINEW

UNSINEWS > UNSINEW
UNSINFUL adj without sin
UNSISTING adj Shakespearean term, possibly meaning insisting
UNSIZABLE adj of inadequate size
UNSIZED adj not made or sorted according to size
UNSKILFUL adj lacking dexterity or proficiency
UNSKILLED adj not having or requiring any special skill or training
UNSKIMMED adj not skimmed
UNSKINNED adj not skinned
UNSLAIN adj not killed
UNSLAKED adj not slaked
UNSLICED adj not sliced
UNSLICK adj not slick
UNSLING vb remove or release from a slung position
UNSLINGS > UNSLING
UNSLUICE vb let flow
UNSLUICED > UNSLUICE
UNSLUICES > UNSLUICE
UNSLUNG > UNSLING
UNSMART adj not smart
UNSMILING adj not wearing or assuming a smile
UNSMITTEN adj not smitten
UNSMOKED adj not smoked
UNSMOOTH vb roughen
UNSMOOTHS > UNSMOOTH
UNSMOTE same as > UNSMITTEN
UNSNAG vb remove snags from
UNSNAGGED > UNSNAG
UNSNAGS > UNSNAG
UNSNAP vb unfasten (the snap or catch) of (something)
UNSNAPPED > UNSNAP
UNSNAPS > UNSNAP
UNSNARL vb free from a snarl or tangle
UNSNARLED > UNSNARL
UNSNARLS > UNSNARL
UNSNECK vb unlatch
UNSNECKED > UNSNECK
UNSNECKS > UNSNECK
UNSNUFFED adj not snuffed
UNSOAKED adj not soaked
UNSOAPED adj not rubbed with soap
UNSOBER adj not sober
UNSOBERLY > UNSOBER
UNSOCIAL adj avoiding the company of other people
UNSOCKET vb remove from a socket
UNSOCKETS > UNSOCKET
UNSOD same as > UNSODDEN
UNSODDEN adj not soaked
UNSOFT adj hard
UNSOILED adj not soiled
UNSOLACED adj not comforted
UNSOLD adj not sold
UNSOLDER vb remove soldering from
UNSOLDERS > UNSOLDER
UNSOLEMN adj unceremonious

UNSOLID adj not solid
UNSOLIDLY > UNSOLID
UNSOLVED adj not having been solved or explained
UNSONCY same as > UNSONSY
UNSONSIE same as > UNSONSY
UNSONSY adj unfortunate
UNSOOTE adj not sweet
UNSOOTHED adj not soothed
UNSORTED adj not sorted
UNSOUGHT adj not sought after
UNSOUL vb cause to be soulless
UNSOULED > UNSOUL
UNSOULING > UNSOUL
UNSOULS > UNSOUL
UNSOUND adj unhealthy or unstable
UNSOUNDED adj not sounded
UNSOUNDER > UNSOUND
UNSOUNDLY > UNSOUND
UNSOURCED adj without a source
UNSOURED adj not soured
UNSOWED same as > UNSOWN
UNSOWN adj not sown
UNSPAR vb open
UNSPARED adj not spared
UNSPARING adj very generous
UNSPARRED > UNSPAR
UNSPARS > UNSPAR
UNSPEAK obsolete word for > UNSAY
UNSPEAKS > UNSPEAK
UNSPED adj not achieved
UNSPELL vb release from a spell
UNSPELLED > UNSPELL
UNSPELLS > UNSPELL
UNSPENT adj not spent
UNSPHERE vb remove from its, one's, etc, sphere or place
UNSPHERED > UNSPHERE
UNSPHERES > UNSPHERE
UNSPIDE same as > UNSPIED
UNSPIED adj unnoticed
UNSPILLED same as > UNSPILT
UNSPILT adj not spilt
UNSPLIT adj not split
UNSPOILED adj not damaged or harmed
UNSPOILT same as > UNSPOILED
UNSPOKE > UNSPEAK
UNSPOKEN adj not openly expressed
UNSPOOL vb unwind from spool
UNSPOOLED > UNSPOOL
UNSPOOLS > UNSPOOL
UNSPOTTED adj without spots or stains
UNSPRAYED adj not sprayed
UNSPRUNG adj without springs
UNSPUN adj not spun
UNSQUARED adj not made into a square shape
UNSTABLE adj lacking stability or firmness
UNSTABLER > UNSTABLE
UNSTABLY > UNSTABLE

UNSTACK *vb* remove from a stack
UNSTACKED > UNSTACK
UNSTACKS > UNSTACK
UNSTAID *adj* not staid
UNSTAINED *adj* not stained
UNSTALKED *adj* without a stalk
UNSTAMPED *adj* not stamped
UNSTARCH *vb* remove starch from
UNSTARRED *adj* not marked with a star
UNSTARRY *adj* not resembling or characteristic of a star from the entertainment world
UNSTATE *vb* deprive of state
UNSTATED *adj* not having been articulated or uttered
UNSTATES > UNSTATE
UNSTATING > UNSTATE
UNSTAYED *adj* unhindered
UNSTAYING *adj* nonstop
UNSTEADY *adj* not securely fixed ▷ *vb* make unsteady
UNSTEEL *vb* make (the heart, feelings, etc) more gentle or compassionate
UNSTEELED > UNSTEEL
UNSTEELS > UNSTEEL
UNSTEMMED *adj* without a stem
UNSTEP *vb* remove (a mast) from its step
UNSTEPPED > UNSTEP
UNSTEPS > UNSTEP
UNSTERILE *adj* not free from living, esp pathogenic, microorganisms
UNSTICK *vb* free or loosen (something stuck)
UNSTICKS > UNSTICK
UNSTIFLED *adj* not suppressed
UNSTILLED *adj* not reduced
UNSTINTED *adj* not stinted
UNSTIRRED *adj* not stirred
UNSTITCH *vb* remove stitching from
UNSTOCK *vb* remove stock from
UNSTOCKED *adj* without stock
UNSTOCKS > UNSTOCK
UNSTONED *adj* not stoned
UNSTOP *vb* remove the stop or stopper from
UNSTOPPED *adj* not obstructed or stopped up
UNSTOPPER *vb* unplug
UNSTOPS > UNSTOP
UNSTOW *vb* remove from storage
UNSTOWED > UNSTOW
UNSTOWING > UNSTOW
UNSTOWS > UNSTOW
UNSTRAP *vb* undo the straps fastening (something) in position
UNSTRAPS > UNSTRAP
UNSTRESS *n* weak syllable
UNSTRING *vb* remove the strings of
UNSTRINGS > UNSTRING

UNSTRIP *vb* strip
UNSTRIPED *adj* (esp of smooth muscle) not having stripes
UNSTRIPS > UNSTRIP
UNSTRUCK *adj* not struck
UNSTRUNG *adj* emotionally distressed
UNSTUCK *adj* freed from being stuck, glued, fastened, etc
UNSTUDIED *adj* natural or spontaneous
UNSTUFFED *adj* not stuffed
UNSTUFFY *adj* well-ventilated
UNSTUFT *same as* > UNSTUFFED
UNSTUNG *adj* not stung
UNSTYLISH *adj* unfashionable
UNSUBDUED *adj* not subdued
UNSUBJECT *adj* not subject
UNSUBTLE *adj* not subtle
UNSUBTLY > UNSUBTLE
UNSUCCESS *n* failure
UNSUCKED *adj* not sucked
UNSUIT *vb* make unsuitable
UNSUITED *adj* not appropriate for a particular task or situation
UNSUITING > UNSUIT
UNSUITS > UNSUIT
UNSULLIED *adj* (of a reputation, etc) not stained or tarnished
UNSUMMED *adj* not calculated
UNSUNG *adj* not acclaimed or honoured
UNSUNK *adj* not sunken
UNSUNNED *adj* not subjected to sunlight
UNSUNNY *adj* not sunny
UNSUPPLE *adj* rigid
UNSURE *adj* lacking assurance or self-confidence
UNSURED *adj* not assured
UNSURELY > UNSURE
UNSURER > UNSURE
UNSUREST > UNSURE
UNSUSPECT *adj* not open to suspicion
UNSWADDLE *same as* > UNSWATHE
UNSWATHE *vb* unwrap
UNSWATHED > UNSWATHE
UNSWATHES > UNSWATHE
UNSWAYED *adj* not swayed
UNSWEAR *vb* retract or revoke (a sworn oath)
UNSWEARS > UNSWEAR
UNSWEET *adj* not sweet
UNSWEPT *adj* not swept
UNSWOLLEN *adj* not swollen
UNSWORE > UNSWEAR
UNSWORN > UNSWEAR
UNTACK *vb* remove saddle and harness, etc, from
UNTACKED > UNTACK
UNTACKING > UNTACK
UNTACKLE *vb* remove tackle from
UNTACKLED > UNTACKLE
UNTACKLES > UNTACKLE
UNTACKS > UNTACK

UNTACTFUL *adj* not tactful
UNTAGGED *adj* without a label
UNTAILED *adj* tailless
UNTAINTED *adj* not tarnished, contaminated, or polluted
UNTAKEN *adj* not taken
UNTAMABLE *adj* (of an animal or person) not capable of being tamed, subdued, or made obedient
UNTAMABLY > UNTAMABLE
UNTAME *vb* undo the taming of
UNTAMED *adj* not brought under human control
UNTAMES > UNTAME
UNTAMING > UNTAME
UNTANGLE *vb* free from tangles or confusion
UNTANGLED > UNTANGLE
UNTANGLES > UNTANGLE
UNTANNED *adj* not tanned
UNTAPPED *adj* not yet used
UNTARRED *adj* not coated with tar
UNTASTED *adj* not tasted
UNTAUGHT *adj* without training or education
UNTAX *vb* stop taxing
UNTAXED *adj* not subject to taxation
UNTAXES > UNTAX
UNTAXING > UNTAX
UNTEACH *vb* cause to disbelieve (teaching)
UNTEACHES > UNTEACH
UNTEAM *vb* disband a team
UNTEAMED > UNTEAM
UNTEAMING > UNTEAM
UNTEAMS > UNTEAM
UNTEMPER *vb* soften
UNTEMPERS > UNTEMPER
UNTEMPTED *adj* not tempted
UNTENABLE *adj* (of a theory, idea, etc) incapable of being defended
UNTENABLY > UNTENABLE
UNTENANT *vb* remove (a tenant)
UNTENANTS > UNTENANT
UNTENDED *adj* not cared for or attended to
UNTENDER *adj* not tender
UNTENT *vb* remove from a tent
UNTENTED > UNTENT
UNTENTING > UNTENT
UNTENTS > UNTENT
UNTENTY *adj* inattentive
UNTENURED *adj* not having tenure
UNTESTED *adj* not having been tested or examined
UNTETHER *vb* untie
UNTETHERS > UNTETHER
UNTHANKED *adj* not thanked
UNTHATCH *vb* remove the thatch from
UNTHAW *same as* > THAW
UNTHAWED *adj* not thawed
UNTHAWING > UNTHAW
UNTHAWS > UNTHAW
UNTHINK *vb* reverse one's opinion about
UNTHINKS > UNTHINK

UNTHOUGHT > UNTHINK
UNTHREAD *vb* draw out the thread or threads from (a needle, etc)
UNTHREADS > UNTHREAD
UNTHRIFT *n* unthrifty person
UNTHRIFTS > UNTHRIFT
UNTHRIFTY *adj* careless with money
UNTHRONE *less common word for* > DETHRONE
UNTHRONED > UNTHRONE
UNTHRONES > UNTHRONE
UNTIDIED > UNTIDY
UNTIDIER > UNTIDY
UNTIDIES > UNTIDY
UNTIDIEST > UNTIDY
UNTIDILY > UNTIDY
UNTIDY *adj* messy and disordered ▷ *vb* make untidy
UNTIDYING > UNTIDY
UNTIE *vb* open or free (something that is tied)
UNTIED > UNTIE
UNTIEING > UNTIE
UNTIES > UNTIE
UNTIL *prep* in or throughout the period before
UNTILE *vb* strip tiles from
UNTILED > UNTILE
UNTILES > UNTILE
UNTILING > UNTILE
UNTILLED *adj* not tilled
UNTILTED *adj* not tilted
UNTIMED *adj* not timed
UNTIMELY *adj* occurring before the expected or normal time ▷ *adv* prematurely or inopportunely
UNTIMEOUS *same as* > UNTIMELY
UNTIN *vb* remove tin from
UNTINGED *adj* not tinged
UNTINNED > UNTIN
UNTINNING > UNTIN
UNTINS > UNTIN
UNTIPPED *adj* not tipped
UNTIRABLE *adj* not able to be fatigued
UNTIRED *adj* not tired
UNTIRING *adj* (of a person or their actions) continuing or persisting without declining in strength or vigour
UNTITLED *adj* without a title
UNTO *prep* to
UNTOILING *adj* not labouring
UNTOLD *adj* incapable of description
UNTOMB *vb* exhume
UNTOMBED > UNTOMB
UNTOMBING > UNTOMB
UNTOMBS > UNTOMB
UNTONED *adj* not toned
UNTORN *adj* not torn
UNTOUCHED *adj* not changed, moved, or affected
UNTOWARD *adj* causing misfortune or annoyance
UNTRACE *vb* remove traces

from
UNTRACED *adj* not traced
UNTRACES > UNTRACE
UNTRACING > UNTRACE
UNTRACK *vb* remove from track
UNTRACKED *adj* not tracked
UNTRACKS > UNTRACK
UNTRADED *adj* not traded
UNTRAINED *adj* without formal or adequate training or education
UNTRAPPED *adj* not trapped
UNTREAD *vb* retrace (a course, path, etc)
UNTREADED > UNTREAD
UNTREADS > UNTREAD
UNTREATED *adj* (of an illness, etc) not having been dealt with
UNTRENDY *adj* not trendy
UNTRESSED *adj* not having a tress
UNTRIDE *same as* > UNTRIED
UNTRIED *adj* not yet used, done, or tested
UNTRIM *vb* deprive of elegance or adornment
UNTRIMMED > UNTRIM
UNTRIMS > UNTRIM
UNTROD > UNTREAD
UNTRODDEN > UNTREAD
UNTRUE *adj* incorrect or false
UNTRUER > UNTRUE
UNTRUEST > UNTRUE
UNTRUISM *n* something that is false
UNTRUISMS > UNTRUISM
UNTRULY > UNTRUE
UNTRUSS *vb* release from or as if from a truss
UNTRUSSED > UNTRUSS
UNTRUSSER *n* person who untrusses
UNTRUSSES > UNTRUSS
UNTRUST *n* mistrust
UNTRUSTS > UNTRUST
UNTRUSTY *adj* not trusty
UNTRUTH *n* statement that is not true, lie
UNTRUTHS > UNTRUTH
UNTUCK *vb* become or cause to become loose or not tucked in
UNTUCKED > UNTUCK
UNTUCKING > UNTUCK
UNTUCKS > UNTUCK
UNTUFTED *adj* not having tufts
UNTUMBLED *adj* not tumbled
UNTUNABLE *adj* not tuneful
UNTUNABLY > UNTUNABLE
UNTUNE *vb* make out of tune
UNTUNED > UNTUNE
UNTUNEFUL *adj* not tuneful
UNTUNES > UNTUNE
UNTUNING > UNTUNE
UNTURBID *adj* clear
UNTURF *vb* remove turf from
UNTURFED > UNTURF
UNTURFING > UNTURF
UNTURFS > UNTURF
UNTURN *vb* turn in a reverse direction
UNTURNED *adj* not turned
UNTURNING > UNTURN

UNTURNS > UNTURN
UNTUTORED *adj* without formal education
UNTWILLED *adj* not twilled
UNTWINE *vb* untwist, unravel, and separate
UNTWINED > UNTWINE
UNTWINES > UNTWINE
UNTWINING > UNTWINE
UNTWIST *vb* twist apart and loosen
UNTWISTED > UNTWIST
UNTWISTS > UNTWIST
UNTYING > UNTIE
UNTYINGS > UNTIE
UNTYPABLE *adj* incapable of being typed
UNTYPICAL *adj* not representative or characteristic of a particular type, person, etc
UNUNBIUM *n* chemical element
UNUNBIUMS > UNUNBIUM
UNUNITED *adj* separated
UNUNUNIUM *n* chemical element
UNURGED *adj* not urged
UNUSABLE *adj* not in good enough condition to be used
UNUSABLY > UNUSABLE
UNUSED *adj* not being or never having been used
UNUSEFUL *adj* useless
UNUSHERED *adj* not escorted
UNUSUAL *adj* uncommon or extraordinary
UNUSUALLY > UNUSUAL
UNUTTERED *adj* not uttered
UNVAIL *same as* > UNVEIL
UNVAILE *same as* > UNVEIL
UNVAILED > UNVAIL
UNVAILES > UNVAIL
UNVAILING > UNVAIL
UNVAILS > UNVAIL
UNVALUED *adj* not appreciated or valued
UNVARIED *adj* not varied
UNVARYING *adj* always staying the same
UNVEIL *vb* ceremonially remove the cover from (a new picture, plaque, etc)
UNVEILED > UNVEIL
UNVEILER *n* person who removes a veil
UNVEILERS > UNVEILER
UNVEILING *n* ceremony involving the removal of a veil covering a statue
UNVEILS > UNVEIL
UNVEINED *adj* without veins
UNVENTED *adj* not vented
UNVERSED *adj* not versed
UNVESTED *adj* not vested
UNVETTED *adj* not thoroughly examined
UNVEXED *adj* not annoyed
UNVEXT *same as* > UNVEXED
UNVIABLE *adj* not capable of succeeding, esp financially
UNVIEWED *adj* not viewed
UNVIRTUE *n* state of having no virtue

UNVIRTUES > UNVIRTUE
UNVISITED *adj* not visited
UNVISOR *vb* remove visor from
UNVISORED > UNVISOR
UNVISORS > UNVISOR
UNVITAL *adj* not vital
UNVIZARD *same as* > UNVISOR
UNVIZARDS > UNVIZARD
UNVOCAL *adj* not vocal
UNVOICE *vb* pronounce without vibration of the vocal cords
UNVOICED *adj* not expressed or spoken
UNVOICES > UNVOICE
UNVOICING > UNVOICE
UNVULGAR *adj* not vulgar
UNWAGED *adj* (of a person) not having a paid job
UNWAKED *same as* > UNWAKENED
UNWAKENED *adj* not roused from sleep
UNWALLED *adj* not surrounded by walls
UNWANING *adj* not waning
UNWANTED *adj* not wanted or welcome
UNWARDED *adj* not warded
UNWARE *same as* > UNAWARE
UNWARELY > UNWARE
UNWARES *same as* > UNAWARES
UNWARIE *same as* > UNWARY
UNWARIER > UNWARY
UNWARIEST > UNWARY
UNWARILY > UNWARY
UNWARLIKE *adj* not warlike
UNWARMED *adj* not warmed
UNWARNED *adj* not warned
UNWARPED *adj* not warped
UNWARY *adj* not careful or cautious and therefore likely to be harmed
UNWASHED *adj* not washed ▷ *pl n* the masses
UNWASHEDS > UNWASHED
UNWASHEN *same as* > UNWASHED
UNWASTED *adj* not wasted
UNWASTING *adj* not wasting
UNWATCHED *adj* (of an automatic device, such as a beacon) not manned
UNWATER *vb* dry out
UNWATERED > UNWATER
UNWATERS > UNWATER
UNWATERY *adj* not watery
UNWAXED *adj* not treated with wax, esp of oranges or lemons, not sprayed with a protective coating of wax
UNWAYED *adj* having no routes
UNWEAL *n* ill or sorrow
UNWEALS > UNWEAL
UNWEANED *adj* not weaned
UNWEAPON *vb* disarm
UNWEAPONS > UNWEAPON
UNWEARIED *adj* not abating or tiring
UNWEARY *adj* not weary
UNWEAVE *vb* undo (weaving)
UNWEAVES > UNWEAVE
UNWEAVING > UNWEAVE

UNWEBBED *adj* not webbed
UNWED *adj* not wed
UNWEDDED *adj* not wedded
UNWEEDED *adj* not weeded
UNWEENED *adj* unknown
UNWEETING *same as* > UNWITTING
UNWEIGHED *adj* (of quantities purchased, etc) not measured for weight
UNWEIGHT *vb* remove weight from
UNWEIGHTS > UNWEIGHT
UNWELCOME *adj* unpleasant and unwanted
UNWELDED *adj* not welded
UNWELDY *same as* > UNWIELDY
UNWELL *adj* not healthy, ill
UNWEPT *adj* not wept for or lamented
UNWET *adj* not wet
UNWETTED *same as* > UNWET
UNWHIPPED *adj* not whipped
UNWHIPT *same as* > UNWHIPPED
UNWHITE *adj* not white
UNWIELDLY *same as* > UNWIELDY
UNWIELDY *adj* too heavy, large, or awkward to be easily handled
UNWIFELY *adj* not like a wife
UNWIGGED *adj* without a wig
UNWILFUL *adj* complaisant
UNWILL *vb* will the reversal of (something that has already occurred)
UNWILLED *adj* not intentional
UNWILLING *adj* reluctant
UNWILLS > UNWILL
UNWIND *vb* relax after a busy or tense time
UNWINDER > UNWIND
UNWINDERS > UNWIND
UNWINDING > UNWIND
UNWINDS > UNWIND
UNWINGED *adj* without wings
UNWINKING *adj* vigilant
UNWIPED *adj* not wiped
UNWIRE *vb* remove wiring from
UNWIRED > UNWIRE
UNWIRES > UNWIRE
UNWIRING > UNWIRE
UNWISDOM *n* imprudence
UNWISDOMS > UNWISDOM
UNWISE *adj* foolish
UNWISELY > UNWISE
UNWISER > UNWISE
UNWISEST > UNWISE
UNWISH *vb* retract or revoke (a wish)
UNWISHED *adj* not desired
UNWISHES > UNWISH
UNWISHFUL *adj* not wishful
UNWISHING > UNWISH
UNWIST *adj* unknown
UNWIT *vb* divest of wit
UNWITCH *vb* release from witchcraft
UNWITCHED > UNWITCH
UNWITCHES > UNWITCH
UNWITS > UNWIT

u

UNWITTED > UNWIT
UNWITTILY > UNWITTY
UNWITTING adj not intentional
UNWITTY adj not clever and amusing
UNWIVE vb remove a wife from
UNWIVED > UNWIVE
UNWIVES > UNWIVE
UNWIVING > UNWIVE
UNWOMAN vb remove womanly qualities from
UNWOMANED > UNWOMAN
UNWOMANLY adj not womanly
UNWOMANS > UNWOMAN
UNWON adj not won
UNWONT adj unaccustomed
UNWONTED adj out of the ordinary
UNWOODED adj not wooded
UNWOOED adj not wooed
UNWORDED adj not expressed in words
UNWORK vb destroy (work previously done)
UNWORKED adj not worked
UNWORKING > UNWORK
UNWORKS > UNWORK
UNWORLDLY adj not concerned with material values or pursuits
UNWORMED adj not rid of worms
UNWORN adj not having deteriorated through use or age
UNWORRIED adj not bothered or perturbed
UNWORTH n lack of value
UNWORTHS > UNWORTH
UNWORTHY adj not deserving or worthy
UNWOUND past tense and past participle of > UNWIND
UNWOUNDED adj not wounded
UNWOVE > UNWEAVE
UNWOVEN > UNWEAVE
UNWRAP vb remove the wrapping from (something)
UNWRAPPED > UNWRAP
UNWRAPS > UNWRAP
UNWREAKED adj unavenged
UNWREATHE vb untwist from a wreathed shape
UNWRINKLE vb remove wrinkles from
UNWRITE vb cancel (what has been written)
UNWRITES > UNWRITE
UNWRITING > UNWRITE
UNWRITTEN adj not printed or in writing
UNWROTE > UNWRITE
UNWROUGHT adj not worked
UNWRUNG adj not twisted
UNYEANED adj not having given birth
UNYOKE vb release (an animal, etc) from a yoke
UNYOKED > UNYOKE
UNYOKES > UNYOKE
UNYOKING > UNYOKE
UNYOUNG adj not young

UNZEALOUS adj unenthusiastic
UNZIP vb unfasten the zip of (a garment) or (of a zip or a garment with a zip) to become unfastened
UNZIPPED > UNZIP
UNZIPPING > UNZIP
UNZIPS > UNZIP
UNZONED adj not divided into zones
UP adv indicating movement to or position at a higher place ▷ adj of a high or higher position ▷ vb increase or raise
UPADAISY same as > UPSADAISY
UPAITHRIC adj without a roof
UPAS n large Javan tree with whitish bark and poisonous milky sap
UPASES > UPAS
UPBEAR vb sustain
UPBEARER > UPBEAR
UPBEARERS > UPBEAR
UPBEARING > UPBEAR
UPBEARS > UPBEAR
UPBEAT adj cheerful and optimistic ▷ n unaccented beat
UPBEATS > UPBEAT
UPBIND vb bind up
UPBINDING > UPBIND
UPBINDS > UPBIND
UPBLEW > UPBLOW
UPBLOW vb inflate
UPBLOWING > UPBLOW
UPBLOWN > UPBLOW
UPBLOWS > UPBLOW
UPBOIL vb boil up
UPBOILED > UPBOIL
UPBOILING > UPBOIL
UPBOILS > UPBOIL
UPBORE > UPBEAR
UPBORNE adj held up
UPBOUND adj travelling upwards
UPBOUNDEN same as > UPBOUND
UPBOW n stroke of the bow from its tip to its nut on a stringed instrument
UPBOWS > UPBOW
UPBRAID vb scold or reproach
UPBRAIDED > UPBRAID
UPBRAIDER > UPBRAID
UPBRAIDS > UPBRAID
UPBRAST same as > UPBURST
UPBRAY vb shame
UPBRAYED > UPBRAY
UPBRAYING > UPBRAY
UPBRAYS > UPBRAY
UPBREAK vb escape upwards
UPBREAKS > UPBREAK
UPBRING vb rear
UPBRINGS > UPBRING
UPBROKE > UPBREAK
UPBROKEN > UPBREAK
UPBROUGHT > UPBRING
UPBUILD vb build up
UPBUILDER > UPBUILD
UPBUILDS > UPBUILD
UPBUILT > UPBUILD

UPBURNING adj burning upwards
UPBURST vb burst upwards
UPBURSTS > UPBURST
UPBY same as > UPBYE
UPBYE adv yonder
UPCAST n material cast or thrown up ▷ adj directed or thrown upwards ▷ vb throw or cast up
UPCASTING > UPCAST
UPCASTS > UPCAST
UPCATCH vb catch up
UPCATCHES > UPCATCH
UPCAUGHT > UPCATCH
UPCHEER vb cheer up
UPCHEERED > UPCHEER
UPCHEERS > UPCHEER
UPCHUCK vb vomit
UPCHUCKED > UPCHUCK
UPCHUCKS > UPCHUCK
UPCLIMB vb ascend
UPCLIMBED > UPCLIMB
UPCLIMBS > UPCLIMB
UPCLOSE vb close up
UPCLOSED > UPCLOSE
UPCLOSES > UPCLOSE
UPCLOSING > UPCLOSE
UPCOAST adv up the coast
UPCOIL vb make into a coil
UPCOILED > UPCOIL
UPCOILING > UPCOIL
UPCOILS > UPCOIL
UPCOME vb come up
UPCOMES > UPCOME
UPCOMING adj coming soon
UPCOUNTRY adj of or from the interior of a country ▷ adv towards or in the interior of a country ▷ n interior part of a region or country
UPCOURT adv up basketball court
UPCURL vb curl up
UPCURLED > UPCURL
UPCURLING > UPCURL
UPCURLS > UPCURL
UPCURVE vb curve upwards
UPCURVED > UPCURVE
UPCURVES > UPCURVE
UPCURVING > UPCURVE
UPDART vb dart upwards
UPDARTED > UPDART
UPDARTING > UPDART
UPDARTS > UPDART
UPDATE vb bring up to date ▷ n act of updating or something that is updated
UPDATED > UPDATE
UPDATER > UPDATE
UPDATERS > UPDATE
UPDATES > UPDATE
UPDATING > UPDATE
UPDIVE vb leap upwards
UPDIVED > UPDIVE
UPDIVES > UPDIVE
UPDIVING > UPDIVE
UPDO n type of hairstyle
UPDOS > UPDO
UPDOVE > UPDIVE
UPDRAFT n upwards air current
UPDRAFTS > UPDRAFT
UPDRAG vb drag up
UPDRAGGED > UPDRAG
UPDRAGS > UPDRAG

UPDRAUGHT n upward movement of air or other gas
UPDRAW vb draw up
UPDRAWING > UPDRAW
UPDRAWN > UPDRAW
UPDRAWS > UPDRAW
UPDREW > UPDRAW
UPDRIED > UPDRY
UPDRIES > UPDRY
UPDRY vb dry up
UPDRYING > UPDRY
UPEND vb turn or set (something) on its end
UPENDED > UPEND
UPENDING > UPEND
UPENDS > UPEND
UPFIELD adj in sport, away from the defending team's goal
UPFILL vb fill up
UPFILLED > UPFILL
UPFILLING > UPFILL
UPFILLS > UPFILL
UPFLING vb throw upwards
UPFLINGS > UPFLING
UPFLOW vb flow upwards
UPFLOWED > UPFLOW
UPFLOWING > UPFLOW
UPFLOWS > UPFLOW
UPFLUNG > UPFLING
UPFOLD vb fold up
UPFOLDED > UPFOLD
UPFOLDING > UPFOLD
UPFOLDS > UPFOLD
UPFOLLOW vb follow
UPFOLLOWS > UPFOLLOW
UPFRONT adj open and frank ▷ adv (of money) paid out at the beginning of a business arrangement
UPFURL vb roll up
UPFURLED > UPFURL
UPFURLING > UPFURL
UPFURLS > UPFURL
UPGANG n climb
UPGANGS > UPGANG
UPGATHER vb draw together
UPGATHERS > UPGATHER
UPGAZE vb gaze upwards
UPGAZED > UPGAZE
UPGAZES > UPGAZE
UPGAZING > UPGAZE
UPGIRD vb belt up
UPGIRDED > UPGIRD
UPGIRDING > UPGIRD
UPGIRDS > UPGIRD
UPGIRT > UPGIRD
UPGO vb ascend
UPGOES > UPGO
UPGOING > UPGO
UPGOINGS > UPGO
UPGONE > UPGO
UPGRADE vb promote (a person or job) to a higher rank
UPGRADED > UPGRADE
UPGRADER > UPGRADE
UPGRADERS > UPGRADE
UPGRADES > UPGRADE
UPGRADING > UPGRADE
UPGREW > UPGROW
UPGROW vb grow up
UPGROWING > UPGROW
UPGROWN > UPGROW
UPGROWS > UPGROW
UPGROWTH n process of

developing or growing upwards
UPGROWTHS > UPGROWTH
UPGUSH *vb* flow upwards
UPGUSHED > UPGUSH
UPGUSHES > UPGUSH
UPGUSHING > UPGUSH
UPHAND *adj* lifted by hand
UPHANG *vb* hang up
UPHANGING > UPHANG
UPHANGS > UPHANG
UPHAUD *Scots variant of* > UPHOLD
UPHAUDING > UPHAUD
UPHAUDS > UPHAUD
UPHEAP *vb* computing term
UPHEAPED > UPHEAP
UPHEAPING > UPHEAP
UPHEAPS > UPHEAP
UPHEAVAL *n* strong, sudden, or violent disturbance
UPHEAVALS > UPHEAVAL
UPHEAVE *vb* heave or rise upwards
UPHEAVED > UPHEAVE
UPHEAVER > UPHEAVE
UPHEAVERS > UPHEAVE
UPHEAVES > UPHEAVE
UPHEAVING > UPHEAVE
UPHELD > UPHOLD
UPHILD *archaic past form of* > UPHOLD
UPHILL *adj* sloping or leading upwards ▷ *adv* up a slope ▷ *n* difficulty
UPHILLS > UPHILL
UPHOARD *vb* hoard up
UPHOARDED > UPHOARD
UPHOARDS > UPHOARD
UPHOIST *vb* raise
UPHOISTED > UPHOIST
UPHOISTS > UPHOIST
UPHOLD *vb* maintain or defend against opposition
UPHOLDER > UPHOLD
UPHOLDERS > UPHOLD
UPHOLDING > UPHOLD
UPHOLDS > UPHOLD
UPHOLSTER *vb* fit (a chair or sofa) with padding, springs, and covering
UPHOORD *vb* heap up
UPHOORDED > UPHOORD
UPHOORDS > UPHOORD
UPHOVE > UPHEAVE
UPHROE *variant spelling of* > EUPHROE
UPHROES > UPHROE
UPHUDDEN > UPHAUD
UPHUNG > UPHANG
UPHURL *vb* throw upwards
UPHURLED > UPHURL
UPHURLING > UPHURL
UPHURLS > UPHURL
UPJET *vb* stream upwards
UPJETS > UPJET
UPJETTED > UPJET
UPJETTING > UPJET
UPKEEP *n* act, process, or cost of keeping something in good repair
UPKEEPS > UPKEEP
UPKNIT *vb* bind
UPKNITS > UPKNIT
UPKNITTED > UPKNIT
UPLAID > UPLAY
UPLAND *adj* of or in an area

of high or relatively high ground ▷ *n* area of high or relatively high ground
UPLANDER *n* person hailing from the uplands
UPLANDERS > UPLANDER
UPLANDISH > UPLAND
UPLANDS > UPLAND
UPLAY *vb* stash
UPLAYING > UPLAY
UPLAYS > UPLAY
UPLEAD *vb* lead upwards
UPLEADING > UPLEAD
UPLEADS > UPLEAD
UPLEAN *vb* lean on something
UPLEANED > UPLEAN
UPLEANING > UPLEAN
UPLEANS > UPLEAN
UPLEANT > UPLEAN
UPLEAP *vb* jump upwards
UPLEAPED > UPLEAP
UPLEAPING > UPLEAP
UPLEAPS > UPLEAP
UPLEAPT > UPLEAP
UPLED > UPLEAD
UPLIFT *vb* raise or lift up ▷ *n* act or process of improving moral, social, or cultural conditions ▷ *adj* (of a bra) designed to lift and support the breasts
UPLIFTED > UPLIFT
UPLIFTER > UPLIFT
UPLIFTERS > UPLIFT
UPLIFTING *adj* acting to raise moral, spiritual, cultural, etc, levels
UPLIFTS > UPLIFT
UPLIGHT *n* lamp or wall light designed or positioned to cast its light upwards ▷ *vb* light in an upward direction
UPLIGHTED > UPLIGHT
UPLIGHTER *n* lamp or wall light designed or positioned to cast its light upwards
UPLIGHTS > UPLIGHT
UPLINK *n* transmitter on the ground that sends signals up to a communications satellite ▷ *vb* send (data) to a communications satellite
UPLINKED > UPLINK
UPLINKING > UPLINK
UPLINKS > UPLINK
UPLIT > UPLIGHT
UPLOAD *vb* transfer (data or a program) from one's own computer into the memory of another computer
UPLOADED > UPLOAD
UPLOADING > UPLOAD
UPLOADS > UPLOAD
UPLOCK *vb* lock up
UPLOCKED > UPLOCK
UPLOCKING > UPLOCK
UPLOCKS > UPLOCK
UPLOOK *vb* look up
UPLOOKED > UPLOOK
UPLOOKING > UPLOOK
UPLOOKS > UPLOOK
UPLYING *adj* raised
UPMAKE *vb* make up

UPMAKER > UPMAKE
UPMAKERS > UPMAKE
UPMAKES > UPMAKE
UPMAKING > UPMAKE
UPMAKINGS > UPMAKE
UPMANSHIP *n* one-upmanship
UPMARKET *adj* expensive and of superior quality
UPMOST *another word for* > UPPERMOST
UPO *prep* upon
UPON *prep* on
UPPED > UP
UPPER *adj* higher or highest in physical position, wealth, rank, or status ▷ *n* part of a shoe above the sole
UPPERCASE *adj* capitalized ▷ *vb* capitalize or print in capitals
UPPERCUT *n* short swinging upward punch delivered to the chin ▷ *vb* hit (an opponent) with an uppercut
UPPERCUTS > UPPERCUT
UPPERMOST *adj* highest in position, power, or importance ▷ *adv* in or into the highest place or position
UPPERPART *n* highest part
UPPERS > UPPER
UPPILE *vb* pile up
UPPILED > UPPILE
UPPILES > UPPILE
UPPILING > UPPILE
UPPING > UP
UPPINGS > UP
UPPISH *adj* snobbish, arrogant, or presumptuous
UPPISHLY > UPPISH
UPPITY *adj* snobbish, arrogant, or presumptuous
UPPROP *vb* support
UPPROPPED > UPPROP
UPPROPS > UPPROP
UPRAISE *vb* lift up
UPRAISED > UPRAISE
UPRAISER > UPRAISE
UPRAISERS > UPRAISE
UPRAISES > UPRAISE
UPRAISING > UPRAISE
UPRAN > UPRUN
UPRATE *vb* raise the value, rate, or size of, upgrade
UPRATED > UPRATE
UPRATES > UPRATE
UPRATING > UPRATE
UPREACH *vb* reach up
UPREACHED > UPREACH
UPREACHES > UPREACH
UPREAR *vb* lift up
UPREARED > UPREAR
UPREARING > UPREAR
UPREARS > UPREAR
UPREST *n* uprising
UPRESTS > UPREST
UPRIGHT *adj* vertical or erect ▷ *adv* vertically or in an erect position ▷ *n* vertical support, such as a post ▷ *vb* make upright
UPRIGHTED > UPRIGHT
UPRIGHTLY > UPRIGHT

UPRIGHTS > UPRIGHT
UPRISAL > UPRISE
UPRISALS > UPRISE
UPRISE *vb* rise up
UPRISEN > UPRISE
UPRISER > UPRISE
UPRISERS > UPRISE
UPRISES > UPRISE
UPRISING *n* rebellion or revolt
UPRISINGS > UPRISING
UPRIST *same as* > UPREST
UPRISTS > UPRIST
UPRIVER *adv* towards or near the source of a river ▷ *n* area located upstream
UPRIVERS > UPRIVER
UPROAR *n* disturbance characterized by loud noise and confusion ▷ *vb* cause an uproar
UPROARED > UPROAR
UPROARING > UPROAR
UPROARS > UPROAR
UPROLL *vb* roll up
UPROLLED > UPROLL
UPROLLING > UPROLL
UPROLLS > UPROLL
UPROOT *vb* pull up by or as if by the roots
UPROOTAL > UPROOT
UPROOTALS > UPROOT
UPROOTED > UPROOT
UPROOTER > UPROOT
UPROOTERS > UPROOT
UPROOTING > UPROOT
UPROOTS > UPROOT
UPROSE > UPRISE
UPROUSE *vb* rouse or stir up
UPROUSED > UPROUSE
UPROUSES > UPROUSE
UPROUSING > UPROUSE
UPRUN *vb* run up
UPRUNNING > UPRUN
UPRUNS > UPRUN
UPRUSH *n* upward rush, as of consciousness ▷ *vb* rush upwards
UPRUSHED > UPRUSH
UPRUSHES > UPRUSH
UPRUSHING > UPRUSH
UPRYST *same as* > UPREST
UPS > UP
UPSADAISY *interj* expression of reassurance often uttered when someone stumbles or is lifted up
UPSCALE *adj* of or for the upper end of an economic or social scale ▷ *vb* upgrade
UPSCALED > UPSCALE
UPSCALES > UPSCALE
UPSCALING > UPSCALE
UPSEE *n* drunken revel
UPSEES > UPSEE
UPSEND *vb* send up
UPSENDING > UPSEND
UPSENDS > UPSEND
UPSENT > UPSEND
UPSET *adj* emotionally or physically disturbed or distressed ▷ *vb* tip over ▷ *n* unexpected defeat or reversal
UPSETS > UPSET

UPSETTER > UPSET
UPSETTERS > UPSET
UPSETTING > UPSET
UPSEY *same as* > UPSEE
UPSEYS > UPSEY
UPSHIFT *vb* move up (a gear)
UPSHIFTED > UPSHIFT
UPSHIFTS > UPSHIFT
UPSHOOT *vb* shoot upwards
UPSHOOTS > UPSHOOT
UPSHOT *n* final result or conclusion
UPSHOTS > UPSHOT
UPSIDE *n* upper surface or part
UPSIDES > UPSIDE
UPSIES > UPSY
UPSILON *n* 20th letter in the Greek alphabet
UPSILONS > UPSILON
UPSITTING *n* sitting up of a woman after childbirth
UPSIZE *vb* increase in size
UPSIZED > UPSIZE
UPSIZES > UPSIZE
UPSIZING > UPSIZE
UPSKILL *vb* improve the aptitude for work of (a person) by additional training
UPSKILLED > UPSKILL
UPSKILLS > UPSKILL
UPSLOPE *adv* up a or the slope
UPSOAR *vb* soar up
UPSOARED > UPSOAR
UPSOARING > UPSOAR
UPSOARS > UPSOAR
UPSPAKE > UPSPEAK
UPSPEAK *vb* speak with rising intonation
UPSPEAKS > UPSPEAK
UPSPEAR *vb* grow upwards in a spear-like manner
UPSPEARED > UPSPEAR
UPSPEARS > UPSPEAR
UPSPOKE > UPSPEAK
UPSPOKEN > UPSPEAK
UPSPRANG > UPSPRING
UPSPRING *vb* spring up or come into existence ▷ *n* leap forwards or upwards
UPSPRINGS > UPSPRING
UPSPRUNG > UPSPRING
UPSTAGE *adj* at the back half of the stage ▷ *vb* draw attention to oneself from (someone else) ▷ *adv* on, at, or to the rear of the stage ▷ *n* back half of the stage
UPSTAGED > UPSTAGE
UPSTAGER > UPSTAGE
UPSTAGERS > UPSTAGE
UPSTAGES > UPSTAGE
UPSTAGING > UPSTAGE
UPSTAIR *same as* > UPSTAIRS
UPSTAIRS *adv* or on an upper floor of a building ▷ *n* upper floor ▷ *adj* situated on an upper floor
UPSTAND *vb* rise
UPSTANDS > UPSTAND
UPSTARE *vb* stare upwards
UPSTARED > UPSTARE
UPSTARES > UPSTARE

UPSTARING > UPSTARE
UPSTART *n* person who has risen suddenly to a position of power and behaves arrogantly ▷ *vb* start up, as in surprise, etc
UPSTARTED > UPSTART
UPSTARTS > UPSTART
UPSTATE *adv* towards, in, from, or relating to the outlying or northern sections of a state, esp of New York State ▷ *n* outlying, esp northern, sections of a state
UPSTATER > UPSTATE
UPSTATERS > UPSTATE
UPSTATES > UPSTATE
UPSTAY *vb* support
UPSTAYED > UPSTAY
UPSTAYING > UPSTAY
UPSTAYS > UPSTAY
UPSTEP *n* type of vocal intonation
UPSTEPPED > UPSTEP
UPSTEPS > UPSTEP
UPSTIR *vb* stir up ▷ *n* commotion
UPSTIRRED > UPSTIR
UPSTIRS > UPSTIR
UPSTOOD > UPSTAND
UPSTREAM *adj* in or towards the higher part of a stream ▷ *vb* stream upwards
UPSTREAMS > UPSTREAM
UPSTROKE *n* upward stroke or movement, as of a pen or brush
UPSTROKES > UPSTROKE
UPSURGE *n* rapid rise or swell ▷ *vb* surge up
UPSURGED > UPSURGE
UPSURGES > UPSURGE
UPSURGING > UPSURGE
UPSWARM *vb* rise in a swarm
UPSWARMED > UPSWARM
UPSWARMS > UPSWARM
UPSWAY *vb* swing in the air
UPSWAYED > UPSWAY
UPSWAYING > UPSWAY
UPSWAYS > UPSWAY
UPSWEEP *n* curve or sweep upwards ▷ *vb* sweep, curve, or brush or be swept, curved, or brushed upwards
UPSWEEPS > UPSWEEP
UPSWELL *vb* swell up or cause to swell up
UPSWELLED > UPSWELL
UPSWELLS > UPSWELL
UPSWEPT > UPSWEEP
UPSWING *n* recovery period in the trade cycle ▷ *vb* swing or move up
UPSWINGS > UPSWING
UPSWOLLEN > UPSWELL
UPSWUNG > UPSWING
UPSY *same as* > UPSEE
UPTA *same as* > UPTER
UPTAK *same as* > UPTAKE
UPTAKE *n* numbers taking up something such as an offer or the act of taking it up ▷ *vb* take up
UPTAKEN > UPTAKE
UPTAKES > UPTAKE

UPTAKING > UPTAKE
UPTAKS > UPTAK
UPTALK *n* style of speech in which every sentence ends with a rising tone, as if the speaker is always asking a question ▷ *vb* talk in this manner
UPTALKED > UPTALK
UPTALKING > UPTALK
UPTALKS > UPTALK
UPTEAR *vb* tear up
UPTEARING > UPTEAR
UPTEARS > UPTEAR
UPTEMPO *adj* fast ▷ *n* uptempo piece
UPTEMPOS > UPTEMPO
UPTER *adj* of poor quality
UPTHREW > UPTHROW
UPTHROW *n* upward movement of rocks on one side of a fault plane relative to rocks on the other side ▷ *vb* throw upwards
UPTHROWN > UPTHROW
UPTHROWS > UPTHROW
UPTHRUST *n* upward push
UPTHRUSTS > UPTHRUST
UPTHUNDER *vb* make a noise like thunder
UPTICK *n* rise or increase
UPTICKS > UPTICK
UPTIE *vb* tie up
UPTIED > UPTIE
UPTIES > UPTIE
UPTIGHT *adj* nervously tense, irritable, or angry
UPTIGHTER > UPTIGHT
UPTILT *vb* tilt up
UPTILTED > UPTILT
UPTILTING > UPTILT
UPTILTS > UPTILT
UPTIME *n* time during which a machine, such as a computer, actually operates
UPTIMES > UPTIME
UPTITLING *n* practice of conferring grandiose job titles to employees performing relatively menial jobs
UPTOOK > UPTAKE
UPTORE > UPTEAR
UPTORN > UPTEAR
UPTOSS *vb* throw upwards
UPTOSSED > UPTOSS
UPTOSSES > UPTOSS
UPTOSSING > UPTOSS
UPTOWN *adv* towards, in, or relating to some part of a town that is away from the centre ▷ *n* such a part of town, esp a residential part
UPTOWNER > UPTOWN
UPTOWNERS > UPTOWN
UPTOWNS > UPTOWN
UPTRAIN *vb* train up
UPTRAINED > UPTRAIN
UPTRAINS > UPTRAIN
UPTREND *n* upward trend
UPTRENDS > UPTREND
UPTRILLED *adj* trilled high
UPTURN *n* upward trend or improvement ▷ *vb* turn or cause to turn over or upside down

UPTURNED > UPTURN
UPTURNING > UPTURN
UPTURNS > UPTURN
UPTYING > UPTIE
UPVALUE *vb* raise the value of
UPVALUED > UPVALUE
UPVALUES > UPVALUE
UPVALUING > UPVALUE
UPWAFT *vb* waft upwards
UPWAFTED > UPWAFT
UPWAFTING > UPWAFT
UPWAFTS > UPWAFT
UPWARD *same as* > UPWARDS
UPWARDLY > UPWARD
UPWARDS *adv* from a lower to a higher place, level, condition, etc
UPWELL *vb* well up
UPWELLED > UPWELL
UPWELLING > UPWELL
UPWELLS > UPWELL
UPWENT > UPGO
UPWHIRL *vb* spin upwards
UPWHIRLED > UPWHIRL
UPWHIRLS > UPWHIRL
UPWIND *adv* into or against the wind ▷ *adj* going against the wind ▷ *vb* wind up
UPWINDING > UPWIND
UPWINDS > UPWIND
UPWOUND > UPWIND
UPWRAP *vb* wrap up
UPWRAPS > UPWRAP
UPWROUGHT *adj* wrought up
UR *interj* hesitant utterance used to fill gaps in talking
URACHI > URACHUS
URACHUS *n* cord of tissue connected to the bladder
URACHUSES > URACHUS
URACIL *n* pyrimidine present in all living cells, usually in a combined form, as in RNA
URACILS > URACIL
URAEI > URAEUS
URAEMIA *n* accumulation of waste products, normally excreted in the urine, in the blood: causes severe headaches, vomiting, etc
URAEMIAS > URAEMIA
URAEMIC > URAEMIA
URAEUS *n* sacred serpent represented on the headdresses of ancient Egyptian kings and gods
URAEUSES > URAEUS
URALI *n* type of plant
URALIS > URALI
URALITE *n* amphibole mineral, similar to hornblende, that replaces pyroxene in some igneous and metamorphic rocks
URALITES > URALITE
URALITIC > URALITE
URALITISE *same as* > URALITIZE
URALITIZE *vb* turn into uralite
URANIA *n* uranium dioxide
URANIAN *adj* heavenly
URANIAS > URANIA
URANIC *adj* of or containing

uranium, esp in a high valence state

URANIDE *n* any element having an atomic number greater than that of protactinium

URANIDES > URANIDE

URANIN *n* type of alkaline substance

URANINITE *n* blackish heavy radioactive mineral consisting of uranium oxide in cubic crystalline form together with radium, lead, helium, etc: occurs in coarse granite

URANINS > URANIN

URANISCI > URANISCUS

URANISCUS *n* palate

URANISM *n* homosexuality

URANISMS > URANISM

URANITE *n* any of various minerals containing uranium, esp torbernite or autunite

URANITES > URANITE

URANITIC > URANITE

URANIUM *n* radioactive silvery-white metallic element, used chiefly as a source of nuclear energy

URANIUMS > URANIUM

URANOLOGY *n* study of the universe and planets

URANOUS *adj* of or containing uranium, esp in a low valence state

URANYL *n* of, consisting of, or containing the divalent ion UO_2^{2+} or the group $-UO_2$

URANYLIC > URANYL

URANYLS > URANYL

URAO *n* type of mineral

URAOS > URAO

URARE *same as* > URALI

URARES > URARE

URARI *same as* > URALI

URARIS > URARI

URASE *same as* > UREASE

URASES > URASE

URATE *n* any salt or ester of uric acid

URATES > URATE

URATIC > URATE

URB *n* urban area

URBAN *adj* of or living in a city or town

URBANE *adj* characterized by courtesy, elegance, and sophistication

URBANELY > URBANE

URBANER > URBANE

URBANEST > URBANE

URBANISE *same as* > URBANIZE

URBANISED > URBANISE

URBANISES > URBANISE

URBANISM *n* character of city life

URBANISMS > URBANISM

URBANIST *n* person who studies towns and cities

URBANISTS > URBANIST

URBANITE *n* resident of an urban community

URBANITES > URBANITE

URBANITY *n* quality of being urbane

URBANIZE *vb* make (a rural area) more industrialized and urban

URBANIZED > URBANIZE

URBANIZES > URBANIZE

URBIA *n* urban area

URBIAS > URBIA

URBS > URB

URCEOLATE *adj* shaped like an urn or pitcher

URCEOLI > URCEOLUS

URCEOLUS *n* organ of a plant

URCHIN *n* mischievous child

URCHINS > URCHIN

URD *n* type of plant with edible seeds

URDE *adj* (in heraldry) having points

URDEE > URDE

URDS > URD

URDY *n* heraldic line pattern

URE *same as* > AUROCHS

UREA *n* white soluble crystalline compound found in urine

UREAL > UREA

UREAS > UREA

UREASE *n* enzyme occurring in many plants, esp fungi, that converts urea to ammonium carbonate

UREASES > UREASE

UREDIA > UREDIUM

UREDIAL > UREDIUM

UREDINE > UREDO

UREDINES > UREDO

UREDINIA > UREDINIUM

UREDINIAL > UREDINIUM

UREDINIUM *same as* > UREDIUM

UREDINOUS > UREDO

UREDIUM *n* spore-producing body of some rust fungi in which uredospores are formed

UREDO *less common name for* > URTICARIA

UREDOS > UREDO

UREDOSORI *pl n* spore-producing bodies of some rust fungi in which uredospores are formed; uredia

UREIC > UREA

UREIDE *n* any of a class of organic compounds derived from urea by replacing one or more of its hydrogen atoms by organic groups

UREIDES > UREIDE

UREMIA *same as* > URAEMIA

UREMIAS > UREMIA

UREMIC > UREMIA

URENA *n* plant genus

URENAS > URENA

URENT *adj* burning

UREOTELIC *adj* excreting urea

URES > URE

URESES > URESIS

URESIS *n* urination

URETER *n* tube that conveys urine from the kidney to the bladder

URETERAL > URETER

URETERIC > URETER

URETERS > URETER

URETHAN *same as* > URETHANE

URETHANE *n* short for the synthetic material polyurethane

URETHANES > URETHANE

URETHANS > URETHAN

URETHRA *n* canal that carries urine from the bladder out of the body

URETHRAE > URETHRA

URETHRAL > URETHRA

URETHRAS > URETHRA

URETIC *adj* of or relating to the urine

URGE *n* strong impulse, inner drive, or yearning ▷ *vb* plead with or press (a person to do something)

URGED > URGE

URGENCE > URGENT

URGENCES > URGENT

URGENCIES > URGENT

URGENCY > URGENT

URGENT *adj* requiring speedy action or attention

URGENTLY > URGENT

URGER > URGE

URGERS > URGE

URGES > URGE

URGING > URGE

URGINGLY > URGE

URGINGS > URGE

URIAL *n* type of sheep

URIALS > URIAL

URIC *adj* of or derived from urine

URICASE *n* type of enzyme

URICASES > URICASE

URIDINE *n* nucleoside present in all living cells in a combined form, esp in RNA

URIDINES > URIDINE

URIDYLIC *as in uridylic acid* nucleotide consisting of uracil, ribose, and a phosphate group. It is a constituent of RNA

URINAL *n* sanitary fitting used by men for urination

URINALS > URINAL

URINANT *adj* having the head downwards

URINARIES > URINARY

URINARY *adj* of urine or the organs that secrete and pass urine ▷ *n* reservoir for urine

URINATE *vb* discharge urine

URINATED > URINATE

URINATES > URINATE

URINATING > URINATE

URINATION > URINATE

URINATIVE > URINATE

URINATOR > URINATE

URINATORS > URINATE

URINE *n* pale yellow fluid excreted by the kidneys to the bladder and passed as waste from the body ▷ *vb* urinate

URINED > URINE

URINEMIA *same as* > UREMIA

URINEMIAS > URINEMIA

URINEMIC > URINEMIA

URINES > URINE

URINING > URINE

URINOLOGY *same as* > UROLOGY

URINOSE *same as* > URINOUS

URINOUS *adj* of, resembling, or containing urine

URITE *n* part of the abdomen

URITES > URITE

URMAN *n* forest

URMANS > URMAN

URN *n* vase used as a container for the ashes of the dead ▷ *vb* put in an urn

URNAL > URN

URNED > URN

URNFIELD *n* cemetery full of individual cremation urns ▷ *adj* (of a number of Bronze Age cultures) characterized by cremation in urns, which began in E Europe about the second millennium BC and by the seventh century BC had covered almost all of mainland Europe

URNFIELDS > URNFIELD

URNFUL *n* capacity of an urn

URNFULS > URNFUL

URNING *n* homosexual man

URNINGS > URNING

URNLIKE > URN

URNS > URN

UROBILIN *n* brownish pigment found in faeces and sometimes in urine

UROBILINS > UROBILIN

UROCHORD *n* notochord of a larval tunicate, typically confined to the tail region

UROCHORDS > UROCHORD

UROCHROME *n* yellowish pigment that colours urine

URODELAN > URODELE

URODELANS > URODELAN

URODELE *n* any amphibian of the order *Urodela*, having a long body and tail and four short limbs: includes the salamanders and newts ▷ *adj* of, relating to, or belonging to the *Urodela*

URODELES > URODELE

URODELOUS > URODELE

UROGENOUS *adj* producing or derived from urine

UROGRAPHY *n* branch of radiology concerned with X-ray examination of the kidney and associated structures

UROKINASE *n* biochemical catalyst

UROLAGNIA *n* sexual arousal involving urination

UROLITH *n* calculus in the urinary tract

UROLITHIC > UROLITH

UROLITHS > UROLITH

UROLOGIC > UROLOGY

UROLOGIES > UROLOGY

UROLOGIST > UROLOGY

UROLOGY *n* branch of medicine concerned with

the urinary system and its diseases

UROMERE *n* part of the abdomen

UROMERES > UROMERE

UROPOD *n* paired appendage that arises from the last segment of the body in lobsters and related crustaceans and forms part of the tail fan

UROPODAL > UROPOD

UROPODOUS > UROPOD

UROPODS > UROPOD

UROPYGIA > UROPYGIUM

UROPYGIAL > UROPYGIUM

UROPYGIUM *n* hindmost part of a bird's body, from which the tail feathers grow

UROSCOPIC > UROSCOPY

UROSCOPY *n* examination of the urine

UROSES > UROSIS

UROSIS *n* urinary disease

UROSOME *n* abdomen of arthropods

UROSOMES > UROSOME

UROSTEGE *n* part of a serpent's tail

UROSTEGES > UROSTEGE

UROSTOMY *n* type of urinary surgery

UROSTYLE *n* bony rod forming the last segment of the vertebral column of frogs, toads, and related amphibians

UROSTYLES > UROSTYLE

URP *dialect word for* > VOMIT

URPED > URP

URPING > URP

URPS > URP

URSA *n* she-bear

URSAE > URSA

URSID *n* meteor

URSIDS > URSID

URSIFORM *adj* bear-shaped or bearlike in form

URSINE *adj* of or like a bear

URSON *n* type of porcupine

URSONS > URSON

URTEXT *n* earliest form of a text as established by linguistic scholars as a basis for variants in later texts still in existence

URTEXTS > URTEXT

URTICA *n* type of nettle

URTICANT *n* something that causes itchiness and irritation

URTICANTS > URTICANT

URTICARIA *n* skin condition characterized by the formation of itchy red or whitish raised patches, usually caused by an allergy

URTICAS > URTICA

URTICATE *adj* characterized by the presence of weals ▷ *vb* sting

URTICATED > URTICATE

URTICATES > URTICATE

URUBU *n* type of bird

URUBUS > URUBU

URUS *another name for*

the > AUROCHS

URUSES > URUS

URUSHIOL *n* poisonous pale yellow liquid occurring in poison ivy and the lacquer tree

URUSHIOLS > URUSHIOL

URVA *n* Indian mongoose

URVAS > URVA

US *pron* refers to the speaker or writer and another person or other people

USABILITY > USABLE

USABLE *adj* able to be used

USABLY > USABLE

USAGE *n* regular or constant use

USAGER *n* person who has the use of something in trust

USAGERS > USAGER

USAGES > USAGE

USANCE *n* period of time permitted by commercial usage for the redemption of foreign bills of exchange

USANCES > USANCE

USAUNCE *same as* > USANCE

USAUNCES > USAUNCE

USE *vb* put into service or action ▷ *n* using or being used

USEABLE *same as* > USABLE

USEABLY > USABLE

USED *adj* second-hand

USEFUL *adj* able to be used advantageously or for several different purposes ▷ *n* odd-jobman or general factotum

USEFULLY > USEFUL

USEFULS > USEFUL

USELESS *adj* having no practical use

USELESSLY > USELESS

USER *n* continued exercise, use, or enjoyment of a right, esp in property

USERNAME *n* name given by computer user to gain access

USERNAMES > USERNAME

USERS > USER

USES > USE

USHER *n* official who shows people to their seats, as in a church ▷ *vb* conduct or escort

USHERED > USHER

USHERESS *n* female usher

USHERETTE *n* female assistant in a cinema who shows people to their seats

USHERING > USHER

USHERINGS > USHER

USHERS > USHER

USHERSHIP > USHER

USING > USE

USNEA *n* type of lichen

USNEAS > USNEA

USQUABAE *n* whisky

USQUABAES > USQUABAE

USQUE *n* whisky

USQUEBAE *same as* > USQUABAE

USQUEBAES > USQUEBAE

USQUES > USQUE

USTION *n* burning

USTIONS > USTION

USTULATE *adj* charred

USUAL *adj* of the most normal, frequent, or regular type ▷ *n* ordinary or commonplace events

USUALLY *adv* most often, in most cases

USUALNESS > USUAL

USUALS > USUAL

USUCAPION *n* method of acquiring property

USUCAPT > USUCAPION

USUCAPTED > USUCAPION

USUCAPTS > USUCAPION

USUFRUCT *n* right to use and derive profit from a piece of property belonging to another, provided the property itself remains undiminished and uninjured in any way

USUFRUCTS > USUFRUCT

USURE *vb* be involved in usury

USURED > USURE

USURER *n* person who lends funds at an exorbitant rate of interest

USURERS > USURER

USURES > USURE

USURESS *n* female usurer

USURESSES > USURESS

USURIES > USURY

USURING > USURE

USURIOUS > USURY

USUROUS > USURY

USURP *vb* seize (a position or power) without authority

USURPED > USURP

USURPEDLY > USURP

USURPER > USURP

USURPERS > USURP

USURPING > USURP

USURPINGS > USURP

USURPS > USURP

USURY *n* practice of lending money at an extremely high rate of interest

USWARD *adv* towards us

USWARDS *same as* > USWARD

UT *n* syllable used in the fixed system of solmization for the note C

UTA *n* side-blotched lizard

UTAS *n* eighth day of a festival

UTASES > UTAS

UTE *same as* > UTILITY

UTENSIL *n* tool or container for practical use

UTENSILS > UTENSIL

UTERI > UTERUS

UTERINE *adj* of or affecting the womb

UTERITIS *n* inflammation of the womb

UTEROTOMY *n* surgery on the uterus

UTERUS *n* womb

UTERUSES > UTERUS

UTES > UTE

UTILE *obsolete word for* > USEFUL

UTILIDOR *n* above-ground insulated casing

for pipes carrying water, sewerage and electricity in permafrost regions

UTILIDORS > UTILIDOR

UTILISE *same as* > UTILIZE

UTILISED > UTILISE

UTILISER > UTILISE

UTILISERS > UTILISE

UTILISES > UTILISE

UTILISING > UTILISE

UTILITIES > UTILITY

UTILITY *n* usefulness ▷ *adj* designed for use rather than beauty

UTILIZE *vb* make practical use of

UTILIZED > UTILIZE

UTILIZER > UTILIZE

UTILIZERS > UTILIZE

UTILIZES > UTILIZE

UTILIZING > UTILIZE

UTIS *n* uproar

UTISES > UTIS

UTMOST *n* the greatest possible degree or amount ▷ *adj* of the greatest possible degree or amount

UTMOSTS > UTMOST

UTOPIA *n* real or imaginary society, place, state, etc, considered to be perfect or ideal

UTOPIAN *adj* of or relating to a perfect or ideal existence ▷ *n* idealistic social reformer

UTOPIANS > UTOPIAN

UTOPIAS > UTOPIA

UTOPIAST > UTOPIA

UTOPIASTS > UTOPIA

UTOPISM > UTOPIA

UTOPISMS > UTOPIA

UTOPIST > UTOPIA

UTOPISTIC > UTOPIA

UTOPISTS > UTOPIA

UTRICLE *n* larger of the two parts of the membranous labyrinth of the internal ear

UTRICLES > UTRICLE

UTRICULAR > UTRICLE

UTRICULI > UTRICULUS

UTRICULUS *same as* > UTRICLE

UTS > UT

UTTER *vb* express (something) in sounds or words ▷ *adj* total or absolute

UTTERABLE > UTTER

UTTERANCE *n* something uttered

UTTERED > UTTER

UTTERER > UTTER

UTTERERS > UTTER

UTTEREST > UTTER

UTTERING > UTTER

UTTERINGS > UTTER

UTTERLESS > UTTER

UTTERLY *adv* extrremely

UTTERMOST *same as* > UTMOST

UTTERNESS > UTTER

UTTERS > UTTER

UTU *n* reward

UTUS > UTU

UVA *n* grape or fruit resembling this

UVAE > UVA

UVAROVITE n emerald-green garnet found in chromium deposits: consists of calcium chromium silicate

UVAS > UVA

UVEA n part of the eyeball consisting of the iris, ciliary body, and choroid

UVEAL > UVEA

UVEAS > UVEA

UVEITIC > UVEITIS

UVEITIS n inflammation of the uvea

UVEITISES > UVEITIS

UVEOUS > UVEA

UVULA n small fleshy part of the soft palate that hangs in the back of the throat

UVULAE > UVULA

UVULAR adj of or relating to the uvula ▷ n uvular consonant

UVULARLY > UVULAR

UVULARS > UVULAR

UVULAS > UVULA

UVULITIS n inflammation of the uvula

UXORIAL adj of or relating to a wife

UXORIALLY > UXORIAL

UXORICIDE n act of killing one's wife

UXORIOUS adj excessively fond of or dependent on one's wife

Vv

VAC *vb* clean with a vacuum cleaner
VACANCE *n* vacant period
VACANCES > VACANCE
VACANCIES > VACANCY
VACANCY *n* unfilled job
VACANT *adj* (of a toilet, room, etc) unoccupied
VACANTLY > VACANT
VACATABLE > VACATE
VACATE *vb* cause (something) to be empty by leaving
VACATED > VACATE
VACATES > VACATE
VACATING > VACATE
VACATION *n* time when universities and law courts are closed ▷ *vb* take a vacation
VACATIONS > VACATION
VACATUR *n* annulment
VACATURS > VACATUR
VACCINA *same as* > VACCINIA
VACCINAL *adj* of or relating to vaccine or vaccination
VACCINAS > VACCINA
VACCINATE *vb* inject with a vaccine
VACCINE *n* substance designed to cause a mild form of a disease to make a person immune to the disease itself
VACCINEE *n* person who has been vaccinated
VACCINEES > VACCINEE
VACCINES > VACCINE
VACCINIA *technical name for* > COWPOX
VACCINIAL > VACCINIA
VACCINIAS > VACCINIA
VACCINIUM *n* shrub genus
VACHERIN *n* soft cheese made from cows' milk
VACHERINS > VACHERIN
VACILLANT *adj* indecisive
VACILLATE *vb* keep changing one's mind or opinions
VACKED > VAC
VACKING > VAC
VACS > VAC
VACUA > VACUUM
VACUATE *vb* empty
VACUATED > VACUATE
VACUATES > VACUATE

VACUATING > VACUATE
VACUATION > VACUATE
VACUIST *n* person believing in the existence of vacuums in nature
VACUISTS > VACUIST
VACUITIES > VACUITY
VACUITY *n* absence of intelligent thought or ideas
VACUOLAR > VACUOLE
VACUOLATE > VACUOLE
VACUOLE *n* fluid-filled cavity in the cytoplasm of a cell
VACUOLES > VACUOLE
VACUOUS *adj* not expressing intelligent thought
VACUOUSLY > VACUOUS
VACUUM *n* empty space from which all or most air or gas has been removed ▷ *vb* clean with a vacuum cleaner
VACUUMED > VACUUM
VACUUMING > VACUUM
VACUUMS > VACUUM
VADE *vb* fade
VADED > VADE
VADES > VADE
VADING > VADE
VADOSE *adj* of or derived from water occurring above the water table
VAE *same as* > VOE
VAES > VAE
VAG *n* vagrant
VAGABOND *n* person with no fixed home, esp a beggar
VAGABONDS > VAGABOND
VAGAL *adj* of, relating to, or affecting the vagus nerve
VAGALLY > VAGAL
VAGARIES > VAGARY
VAGARIOUS *adj* characterized or caused by vagaries
VAGARISH > VAGARY
VAGARY *n* unpredictable change
VAGGED > VAG
VAGGING > VAG
VAGI > VAGUS
VAGILE *adj* able to move freely
VAGILITY > VAGILE
VAGINA *n* (in female mammals) passage from the womb to the external

genitals
VAGINAE > VAGINA
VAGINAL > VAGINA
VAGINALLY > VAGINA
VAGINANT *adj* sheathing
VAGINAS > VAGINA
VAGINATE *adj* (esp of plant parts) having a sheath
VAGINATED > VAGINATE
VAGINITIS *n* inflammation of the vagina
VAGINOSES > VAGINOSIS
VAGINOSIS *n* bacterial vaginal infection
VAGINULA *n* little sheath
VAGINULAE > VAGINULA
VAGINULE *same as* > VAGINULA
VAGINULES > VAGINULE
VAGITUS *n* new-born baby's cry
VAGITUSES > VAGITUS
VAGOTOMY *n* surgical division of the vagus nerve
VAGOTONIA *n* pathological overactivity of the vagus nerve
VAGOTONIC > VAGOTONIA
VAGRANCY *n* state or condition of being a vagrant
VAGRANT *n* person with no settled home ▷ *adj* wandering
VAGRANTLY > VAGRANT
VAGRANTS > VAGRANT
VAGROM *same as* > VAGRANT
VAGS > VAG
VAGUE *adj* not clearly explained ▷ *vb* wander
VAGUED > VAGUE
VAGUELY > VAGUE
VAGUENESS > VAGUE
VAGUER > VAGUE
VAGUES > VAGUE
VAGUEST > VAGUE
VAGUING > VAGUE
VAGUS *n* tenth cranial nerve, which supplies the heart, lungs, and viscera
VAHANA *n* vehicle
VAHANAS > VAHANA
VAHINE *n* Polynesian woman
VAHINES > VAHINE
VAIL *vb* lower (something, such as a weapon), esp

as a sign of deference or submission
VAILED > VAIL
VAILING > VAIL
VAILS > VAIL
VAIN *adj* excessively proud, esp of one's appearance
VAINER > VAIN
VAINESSE *n* vainness
VAINESSES > VAINESSE
VAINEST > VAIN
VAINGLORY *n* boastfulness or vanity
VAINLY > VAIN
VAINNESS > VAIN
VAIR *n* fur, probably Russian squirrel, used to trim robes in the Middle Ages
VAIRE *same as* > VAIR
VAIRIER > VAIR
VAIRIEST > VAIR
VAIRS > VAIR
VAIRY > VAIR
VAIVODE *n* European ruler
VAIVODES > VAIVODE
VAKASS *n* type of cloak
VAKASSES > VAKASS
VAKEEL *n* ambassador
VAKEELS > VAKEEL
VAKIL *same as* > VAKEEL
VAKILS > VAKIL
VALANCE *n* piece of drapery round the edge of a bed ▷ *vb* provide with a valance
VALANCED > VALANCE
VALANCES > VALANCE
VALANCING > VALANCE
VALE *n* valley ▷ *sentence substitute* farewell
VALENCE *same as* > VALENCY
VALENCES > VALENCE
VALENCIA *n* type of fabric
VALENCIAS > VALENCIA
VALENCIES > VALENCY
VALENCY *n* power of an atom to make molecular bonds
VALENTINE *n* (person to whom one sends) a romantic card on Saint Valentine's Day, 14th February
VALERATE *n* salt of valeric acid
VALERATES > VALERATE
VALERIAN *n* herb used as a

sedative

VALERIANS > VALERIAN

VALERIC adj of, relating to, or derived from valerian

VALES > VALE

VALET n man's personal male servant ▷ vb act as a valet (for)

VALETA n old-time dance in triple time

VALETAS > VALETA

VALETE n farewell

VALETED > VALET

VALETES > VALETE

VALETING > VALET

VALETINGS > VALET

VALETS > VALET

VALGOID > VALGUS

VALGOUS same as > VALGUS

VALGUS adj denoting a deformity of a limb ▷ n abnormal position of a limb

VALGUSES > VALGUS

VALI n Turkish civil governor

VALIANCE > VALIANT

VALIANCES > VALIANT

VALIANCY > VALIANT

VALIANT adj brave or courageous ▷ n brave person

VALIANTLY > VALIANT

VALIANTS > VALIANT

VALID adj soundly reasoned

VALIDATE vb make valid

VALIDATED > VALIDATE

VALIDATES > VALIDATE

VALIDER > VALID

VALIDEST > VALID

VALIDITY > VALID

VALIDLY > VALID

VALIDNESS > VALID

VALINE n essential amino acid

VALINES > VALINE

VALIS > VALI

VALISE n small suitcase

VALISES > VALISE

VALKYR variant of > VALKYRIE

VALKYRIE n (in Norse mythology) beatiful maiden who collects dead heroes on the battlefield to take to Valhalla

VALKYRIES > VALKYRIES

VALKYRS > VALKYR

VALLAR adj pertaining to a rampart

VALLARY > VALLAR

VALLATE adj surrounded with a wall

VALLATION n act or process of building fortifications

VALLECULA n any of various natural depressions or crevices

VALLEY n low area between hills, often with a river running through it

VALLEYED adj having a valley

VALLEYS > VALLEY

VALLHUND as in Swedish vallhund breed of dog

VALLHUNDS > VALLHUND

VALLONIA same

VALLONIAS > VALLONIA

VALLUM n Roman rampart or earthwork

VALLUMS > VALLUM

VALONEA same as > VALONIA

VALONEAS > VALONEA

VALONIA n acorn cups and unripe acorns of a particular oak

VALONIAS > VALONIA

VALOR same as > VALOUR

VALORISE same as > VALORIZE

VALORISED > VALORISE

VALORISES > VALORISE

VALORIZE vb fix and maintain an artificial price for (a commodity) by governmental action

VALORIZED > VALORIZE

VALORIZES > VALORIZE

VALOROUS > VALOUR

VALORS > VALOR

VALOUR n bravery ▷ n courageous person

VALOURS > VALOUR

VALPROATE n medicament derived from valproic acid

VALPROIC as in valproic acid synthetic crystalline compound, used as an anticonvulsive

VALSE another word for > WALTZ

VALSED > VALSE

VALSES > VALSE

VALSING > VALSE

VALUABLE adj having great worth ▷ n valuable article of personal property, esp jewellery

VALUABLES > VALUABLE

VALUABLY > VALUABLE

VALUATE vb value or evaluate

VALUATED > VALUATE

VALUATES > VALUATE

VALUATING > VALUATE

VALUATION n assessment of worth

VALUATOR n person who estimates the value of objects, paintings, etc

VALUATORS > VALUATOR

VALUE n importance, usefulness ▷ vb assess the worth or desirability of

VALUED > VALUE

VALUELESS adj having or possessing no value

VALUER > VALUE

VALUERS > VALUE

VALUES > VALUE

VALUING > VALUE

VALUTA n value of one currency in terms of its exchange rate with another

VALUTAS > VALUTA

VALVAL same as > VALVULAR

VALVAR same as > VALVULAR

VALVASSOR same as > VAVASOR

VALVATE adj furnished with a valve or valves

VALVE n device to control

the movement of fluid through a pipe ▷ vb provide with a valve

VALVED > VALVE

VALVELESS > VALVE

VALVELET same as > VALVULE

VALVELETS > VALVELET

VALVELIKE > VALVE

VALVES > VALVE

VALVING > VALVE

VALVULA same as > VALVULE

VALVULAE > VALVULA

VALVULAR adj of or having valves

VALVULE n small valve or a part resembling one

VALVULES > VALVULE

VAMBRACE n piece of armour used to protect the arm

VAMBRACED > VAMBRACE

VAMBRACES > VAMBRACE

VAMOOSE vb leave a place hurriedly

VAMOOSED > VAMOSE

VAMOOSES > VAMOSE

VAMOOSING > VAMOSE

VAMOSE same as > VAMOOSE

VAMOSED > VAMOSE

VAMOSES > VAMOSE

VAMOSING > VAMOSE

VAMP n sexually attractive woman who seduces men ▷ vb (of a woman) to seduce (a man)

VAMPED > VAMP

VAMPER > VAMP

VAMPERS > VAMP

VAMPIER > VAMP

VAMPIEST > VAMP

VAMPING > VAMP

VAMPINGS > VAMP

VAMPIRE n (in folklore) corpse that rises at night to drink the blood of the living ▷ vb assail

VAMPIRED > VAMPIRE

VAMPIRES > VAMPIRE

VAMPIRIC > VAMPIRE

VAMPIRING > VAMPIRE

VAMPIRISE same as > VAMPIRIZE

VAMPIRISH > VAMPIRE

VAMPIRISM n belief in the existence of vampires

VAMPIRIZE vb suck blood from

VAMPISH > VAMP

VAMPISHLY > VAMP

VAMPLATE n piece of metal mounted on a lance to protect the hand

VAMPLATES > VAMPLATE

VAMPS > VAMP

VAMPY > VAMP

VAN n motor vehicle for transporting goods ▷ vb send in a van

VANADATE n any salt or ester of a vanadic acid

VANADATES > VANADATE

VANADIATE same as > VANADATE

VANADIC adj of or containing vanadium, esp in a trivalent or pentavalent state

VANADIUM n metallic element, used in steel

VANADIUMS > VANADIUM

VANADOUS adj of or containing vanadium

VANASPATI n hydrogenated vegetable fat commonly used in India as a substitute for butter

VANDA n type of orchid

VANDAL n person who deliberately damages property

VANDALIC > VANDAL

VANDALISE same as > VANDALIZE

VANDALISH > VANDAL

VANDALISM n wanton or deliberate destruction caused by a vandal or an instance of such destruction

VANDALIZE vb cause damage to (personal or public property) deliberately

VANDALS > VANDAL

VANDAS > VANDA

VANDYKE n short pointed beard ▷ vb cut with deep zigzag indentations

VANDYKED > VANDYKE

VANDYKES > VANDYKE

VANDYKING > VANDYKE

VANE n flat blade on a rotary device such as a weathercock or propeller

VANED > VANE

VANELESS > VANE

VANES > VANE

VANESSA n type of butterfly

VANESSAS > VANESSA

VANESSID n type of butterfly ▷ adj relating to this butterfly

VANESSIDS > VANESSID

VANG n type of rope or tackle on a sailing ship

VANGS > VANG

VANGUARD n unit of soldiers leading an army

VANGUARDS > VANGUARD

VANILLA n seed pod of a tropical climbing orchid, used for flavouring ▷ adj flavoured with vanilla

VANILLAS > VANILLA

VANILLIC adj of, resembling, containing, or derived from vanilla or vanillin

VANILLIN n white crystalline aldehyde found in vanilla

VANILLINS > VANILLIN

VANISH vb disappear suddenly or mysteriously ▷ n second and weaker of the two vowels in a falling diphthong

VANISHED > VANISH

VANISHER > VANISH

VANISHERS > VANISH

VANISHES > VANISH

VANISHING > VANISH

VANITAS n type of Dutch painting

v

VANITASES > VANITAS
VANITIED adj with vanity units or mirrors
VANITIES > VANITY
VANITORY n vanity unit
VANITY n (display of) excessive pride
VANLOAD n amount van will carry
VANLOADS > VANLOAD
VANMAN n man in control of a van
VANMEN > VANMAN
VANNED > VAN
VANNER n horse used to pull delivery vehicles
VANNERS > VANNER
VANNING > VAN
VANNINGS > VAN
VANPOOL n van-sharing group
VANPOOLS > VANPOOL
VANQUISH vb defeat (someone) utterly
VANS > VAN
VANT archaic word for > VANGUARD
VANTAGE n state, position, or opportunity offering advantage ▷ vb benefit
VANTAGED > VANTAGE
VANTAGES > VANTAGE
VANTAGING > VANTAGE
VANTBRACE n armour for the arm
VANTS > VANT
VANWARD adv in or towards the front
VAPID adj lacking character, dull
VAPIDER > VAPID
VAPIDEST > VAPID
VAPIDITY > VAPID
VAPIDLY > VAPID
VAPIDNESS > VAPID
VAPOR same as > VAPOUR
VAPORABLE > VAPOR
VAPORED > VAPOR
VAPORER > VAPOR
VAPORERS > VAPOR
VAPORETTI > VAPORETTO
VAPORETTO n steam-powered passenger boat, as used on the canals in Venice
VAPORIFIC adj producing, causing, or tending to produce vapour
VAPORING > VAPOR
VAPORINGS > VAPOR
VAPORISE same as > VAPORIZE
VAPORISED > VAPORISE
VAPORISER same as > VAPORIZER
VAPORISES > VAPORISE
VAPORISH > VAPOR
VAPORIZE vb change into a vapour
VAPORIZED > VAPORIZE
VAPORIZER n substance that vaporizes or a device that causes vaporization
VAPORIZES > VAPORIZE
VAPORLESS > VAPOR
VAPORLIKE > VAPOR
VAPOROUS same

as > VAPORIFIC
VAPORS > VAPOR
VAPORWARE n new software that has not yet been produced
VAPORY > VAPOUR
VAPOUR n moisture suspended in air as steam or mist ▷ vb evaporate
VAPOURED > VAPOUR
VAPOURER > VAPOUR
VAPOURERS > VAPOUR
VAPOURING > VAPOUR
VAPOURISH > VAPOUR
VAPOURS > VAPOUR
VAPOURY > VAPOUR
VAPULATE vb strike
VAPULATED > VAPULATE
VAPULATES > VAPULATE
VAQUERO n cattlehand
VAQUEROS > VAQUERO
VAR n unit of reactive power of an alternating current
VARA n unit of length used in Spain, Portugal, and South America
VARACTOR n semiconductor diode that acts as a voltage-dependent capacitor
VARACTORS > VARACTOR
VARAN n type of lizard
VARANS > VARAN
VARAS > VARA
VARDIES > VARDY
VARDY n verdict
VARE n rod
VAREC n ash obtained from kelp
VARECH same as > VAREC
VARECHS > VARECH
VARECS > VAREC
VARES > VARE
VAREUSE n type of coat
VAREUSES > VAREUSE
VARGUENO n type of Spanish cabinet
VARGUENOS > VARGUENO
VARIA n collection or miscellany, esp of literary works
VARIABLE adj not always the same, changeable ▷ n something that is subject to variation
VARIABLES > VARIABLE
VARIABLY > VARIABLE
VARIANCE n act of varying
VARIANCES > VARIANCE
VARIANT adj differing from a standard or type ▷ n something that differs from a standard or type
VARIANTS > VARIANT
VARIAS > VARIA
VARIATE n random variable or a numerical value taken by it ▷ vb vary
VARIATED > VARIATE
VARIATES > VARIATE
VARIATING > VARIATE
VARIATION n something presented in a slightly different form
VARIATIVE > VARIATE
VARICELLA n chickenpox
VARICES > VARIX

VARICOID same as > CIRSOID
VARICOSE adj of or resulting from varicose veins
VARICOSED same as > VARICOSE
VARICOSES > VARICOSIS
VARICOSIS n any condition characterized by distension of the veins
VARIED > VARY
VARIEDLY > VARY
VARIEGATE vb alter the appearance of, esp by adding different colours
VARIER n person who varies
VARIERS > VARIER
VARIES > VARY
VARIETAL adj of or forming a variety, esp a biological variety ▷ n wine labelled with the name of the grape from which it is pressed
VARIETALS > VARIETAL
VARIETIES > VARIETY
VARIETY n state of being diverse or various
VARIFOCAL adj gradated to permit any length of vision between near and distant ▷ n lens of this type
VARIFORM adj varying in form or shape
VARIOLA n smallpox
VARIOLAR > VARIOLA
VARIOLAS > VARIOLA
VARIOLATE vb inoculate with the smallpox virus ▷ adj marked or pitted with or as if with the scars of smallpox
VARIOLE n any of the rounded masses that make up the rock variolite
VARIOLES > VARIOLE
VARIOLITE n type of basic igneous rock
VARIOLOID adj resembling smallpox ▷ n mild form of smallpox occurring in persons with partial immunity
VARIOLOUS adj relating to or resembling smallpox
VARIORUM adj containing notes by various scholars or critics or various versions of the text ▷ n edition or text of this kind
VARIORUMS > VARIORUM
VARIOUS adj of several kinds
VARIOUSLY > VARIOUS
VARISCITE n green secondary mineral
VARISIZED adj of different sizes
VARISTOR n type of semiconductor device
VARISTORS > VARISTOR
VARITYPE vb produce (copy) on a Varityper ▷ n copy produced on a Varityper
VARITYPED > VARITYPE
VARITYPES > VARITYPE
VARIX n tortuous dilated vein
VARLET n menial servant

VARLETESS n female varlet
VARLETRY n the rabble
VARLETS > VARLET
VARLETTO same as > VARLET
VARLETTOS > VARLETTO
VARMENT same as > VARMINT
VARMENTS > VARMENT
VARMINT n irritating or obnoxious person or animal
VARMINTS > VARMINT
VARNA n any of the four Hindu castes
VARNAS > VARNA
VARNISH n solution of oil and resin, put on a surface to make it hard and glossy ▷ vb apply varnish to
VARNISHED > VARNISH
VARNISHER > VARNISH
VARNISHES > VARNISH
VARNISHY > VARNISH
VAROOM same as > VROOM
VAROOMED same as > VAROOM
VAROOMING same as > VAROOM
VAROOMS same as > VAROOM
VARROA n small parasite
VARROAS > VARROA
VARS > VAR
VARSAL adj universal
VARSITIES > VARSITY
VARSITY n university
VARTABED n position in the Armenian church
VARTABEDS > VARTABED
VARUS adj denoting a deformity of a limb ▷ n abnormal position of a limb
VARUSES > VARUS
VARVE n typically thin band of sediment deposited annually in glacial lakes
VARVED adj having layers of sedimentary deposit
VARVEL n piece of falconry equipment
VARVELLED adj having varvels
VARVELS > VARVEL
VARVES > VARVE
VARY vb change
VARYING > VARY
VARYINGLY > VARY
VARYINGS > VARY
VAS n vessel or tube that carries a fluid
VASA > VAS
VASAL > VAS
VASCULA > VASCULUM
VASCULAR adj relating to vessels
VASCULUM n metal box used by botanists in the field for carrying botanical specimens
VASCULUMS > VASCULUM
VASE n ornamental jar, esp for flowers
VASECTOMY n surgical removal of part of the vas deferens, as a contraceptive method
VASELIKE > VASE
VASELINE n translucent gelatinous substance

obtained from petroleum

VASELINES > VASELINE

VASES > VASE

VASIFORM > VAS

VASOMOTOR *adj* (of a drug, agent, nerve, etc) affecting the diameter of blood vessels

VASOSPASM *n* sudden contraction of a blood vessel

VASOTOCIN *n* chemical found in birds, reptiles, and some amphibians

VASOTOMY *n* surgery on the vas deferens

VASOVAGAL *adj* relating to blood vessels and the vagus nerve

VASSAIL *archaic variant of* > VASSAL

VASSAILS > VASSAIL

VASSAL *n* man given land by a lord in return for military service ▷ *adj* of or relating to a vassal ▷ *vb* vassalize

VASSALAGE *n* condition of being a vassal or the obligations to which a vassal was liable

VASSALESS > VASSAL

VASSALISE *same as* > VASSALIZE

VASSALIZE *vb* make a vassal of

VASSALLED > VASSAL

VASSALRY *n* vassalage

VASSALS > VASSAL

VAST *adj* extremely large ▷ *n* immense or boundless space

VASTER > VAST

VASTEST > VAST

VASTIDITY *n* vastness

VASTIER > VASTY

VASTIEST > VASTY

VASTITIES > VAST

VASTITUDE *n* condition or quality of being vast

VASTITY > VAST

VASTLY > VAST

VASTNESS > VAST

VASTS > VAST

VASTY *archaic or poetic word for* > VAST

VAT *n* large container for liquids ▷ *vb* place, store, or treat in a vat

VATABLE *adj* subject to VAT

VATFUL *n* amount enough to fill a vat

VATFULS > VATFUL

VATIC *adj* of, relating to, or characteristic of a prophet

VATICAL *same as* > VATIC

VATICIDE *n* murder of a prophet

VATICIDES > VATICIDE

VATICINAL *adj* foretelling or prophesying

VATMAN *n* Customs and Excise employee

VATMEN > VATMAN

VATS > VAT

VATTED > VAT

VATTER *n* person who works with vats; blender

VATTERS > VATTER

VATTING > VAT

VATU *n* standard monetary unit of Vanuatu

VATUS > VATU

VAU *same as* > VAV

VAUCH *vb* move fast

VAUCHED > VAUCH

VAUCHES > VAUCH

VAUCHING > VAUCH

VAUDOO *same as* > VOODOO

VAUDOOS > VAUDOO

VAUDOUX *same as* > VOODOO

VAULT *n* secure room for storing valuables ▷ *vb* jump over (something) by resting one's hand(s) on it.

VAULTAGE *n* group of vaults

VAULTAGES > VAULTAGE

VAULTED > VAULT

VAULTER > VAULT

VAULTERS > VAULT

VAULTIER > VAULTY

VAULTIEST > VAULTY

VAULTING *n* arrangement of ceiling vaults in a building ▷ *adj* excessively confident

VAULTINGS > VAULTING

VAULTLIKE > VAULT

VAULTS > VAULT

VAULTY *adj* arched

VAUNCE > ADVANCE

VAUNCED > VAUNCE

VAUNCES > VAUNCE

VAUNCING > VAUNCE

VAUNT *vb* describe or display (success or possessions) boastfully ▷ *n* boast

VAUNTAGE *archaic variant of* > VANTAGE

VAUNTAGES > VAUNTAGE

VAUNTED > VAUNT

VAUNTER > VAUNT

VAUNTERS > VAUNT

VAUNTERY *n* bravado

VAUNTFUL > VAUNT

VAUNTIE *same as* > VAUNTY

VAUNTIER > VAUNT

VAUNTIEST > VAUNT

VAUNTING > VAUNT

VAUNTINGS > VAUNT

VAUNTS > VAUNT

VAUNTY *adj* proud

VAURIEN *n* rascal

VAURIENS > VAURIEN

VAUS > VAU

VAUT *same as* > VAULT

VAUTE *same as* > VAULT

VAUTED > VAUTE

VAUTES > VAUTE

VAUTING > VAUT

VAUTS > VAUT

VAV *n* sixth letter of the Hebrew alphabet

VAVASOR *n* (in feudal society) vassal who also has vassals himself

VAVASORS > VAVASOR

VAVASORY *n* lands held by a vavasor

VAVASOUR *same as* > VAVASOR

VAVASOURS > VAVASOUR

VAVASSOR *same as* > VAVASOR

VAVASSORS > VAVASSOR

VAVS > VAV

VAW *n* Hebrew letter

VAWARD *n* vanguard

VAWARDS > VAWARD

VAWNTIE > VAUNT

VAWS > VAW

VAWTE *same as* > VAULT

VAWTED > VAWTE

VAWTES > VAWTE

VAWTING > VAWTE

VEAL *n* calf meat ▷ *vb* cover with a veil

VEALE *same as* > VEIL

VEALED > VEAL

VEALER *n* young bovine animal of up to 14 months old grown for veal

VEALERS > VEALER

VEALES > VEALE

VEALIER > VEAL

VEALIEST > VEAL

VEALING > VEAL

VEALS > VEAL

VEALY > VEAL

VECTOR *n* quantity that has size and direction, such as force ▷ *vb* direct or guide (a pilot) by directions transmitted by radio

VECTORED > VECTOR

VECTORIAL > VECTOR

VECTORING > VECTOR

VECTORISE *same as* > VECTORIZE

VECTORIZE *vb* computing term

VECTORS > VECTOR

VEDALIA *n* Australian ladybird which is a pest of citrus fruits

VEDALIAS > VEDALIA

VEDETTE *n* small patrol vessel

VEDETTES > VEDETTE

VEDUTA *n* painting of a town or city

VEDUTE > VEDUTA

VEDUTISTA *n* artist who creates vedutas

VEDUTISTI > VEDUTISTA

VEE *n* letter 'v'

VEEJAY *n* video jockey

VEEJAYS > VEEJAY

VEENA *same as* > VINA

VEENAS > VEENA

VEEP *n* vice president

VEEPEE *n* vice president

VEEPEES > VEEPEE

VEEPS > VEEP

VEER *vb* change direction suddenly ▷ *n* change of course or direction

VEERED > VEER

VEERIES > VEERY

VEERING > VEER

VEERINGLY > VEER

VEERINGS > VEER

VEERS > VEER

VEERY *n* tawny brown North American thrush

VEES > VEE

VEG *n* vegetable or vegetables ▷ *vb* relax

VEGA *n* tobacco plantation

VEGAN *n* person who eats no meat, fish, eggs, or dairy products ▷ *adj* suitable for

a vegan

VEGANIC *adj* farmed without the use of animal products or byproducts

VEGANISM > VEGAN

VEGANISMS > VEGAN

VEGANS > VEGAN

VEGAS > VEGA

VEGELATE *n* type of chocolate

VEGELATES > VEGELATE

VEGEMITE *n* informal word for a child

VEGEMITES > VEGEMITE

VEGES > VEG

VEGETABLE *n* edible plant ▷ *adj* of or like plants or vegetables

VEGETABLY > VEGETABLE

VEGETAL *adj* of or relating to plant life ▷ *n* vegetable

VEGETALLY > VEGETAL

VEGETALS > VEGETAL

VEGETANT *adj* causing growth or vegetation-like

VEGETATE *vb* live a dull boring life with no mental stimulation

VEGETATED > VEGETATE

VEGETATES > VEGETATE

VEGETE *adj* lively

VEGETIST *n* vegetable cultivator or enthusiast

VEGETISTS > VEGETIST

VEGETIVE *adj* dull or passive ▷ *n* vegetable

VEGETIVES > VEGETIVE

VEGGED > VEG

VEGGES > VEG

VEGGIE *n* vegetable ▷ *adj* vegetarian

VEGGIES > VEGGIE

VEGGING > VEG

VEGIE *variant of* > VEGGIE

VEGIES > VEGIE

VEGO *adj* vegetarian ▷ *n* vegetarian

VEGOS > VEGO

VEHEMENCE > VEHEMENT

VEHEMENCY > VEHEMENT

VEHEMENT *adj* expressing strong feelings

VEHICLE *n* machine for carrying people or objects

VEHICLES > VEHICLE

VEHICULAR > VEHICLE

VEHM *n* type of medieval German court

VEHME > VEHM

VEHMIC > VEHM

VEHMIQUE > VEHM

VEIL *n* piece of thin cloth covering the head or face ▷ *vb* cover with or as if with a veil

VEILED *adj* disguised

VEILEDLY > VEILED

VEILER > VEIL

VEILERS > VEIL

VEILIER > VEIL

VEILIEST > VEIL

VEILING *n* veil or the fabric used for veils

VEILINGS > VEILING

VEILLESS > VEIL

VEILLEUSE *n* small night-light

VEILLIKE > VEIL
VEILS > VEIL
VEILY > VEIL
VEIN n tube that takes blood to the heart ▷ vb diffuse over or cause to diffuse over in streaked patterns
VEINAL > VEIN
VEINED > VEIN
VEINER n wood-carving tool
VEINERS > VEINER
VEINIER > VEIN
VEINIEST > VEIN
VEINING n pattern or network of veins or streaks
VEININGS > VEINING
VEINLESS > VEIN
VEINLET n any small vein or venule
VEINLETS > VEINLET
VEINLIKE > VEIN
VEINOUS > VEIN
VEINS > VEIN
VEINSTONE another word for > GANGUE
VEINSTUFF another word for same as > GANGUE
VEINULE less common spelling of > VENULE
VEINULES > VEINULE
VEINULET same as > VEINLET
VEINULETS > VEINULET
VEINY > VEIN
VELA > VELUM
VELAMEN n thick layer of dead cells that covers the aerial roots of certain orchids
VELAMINA > VELAMEN
VELAR adj of, relating to, or attached to a velum ▷ n velar sound
VELARIA > VELARIUM
VELARIC > VELAR
VELARISE same as > VELARIZE
VELARISED > VELARISE
VELARISES > VELARISE
VELARIUM n awning used to protect the audience in ancient Roman theatres and amphitheatres
VELARIZE vb pronounce or supplement the pronunciation of (a speech sound) with articulation at the soft palate
VELARIZED > VELARIZE
VELARIZES > VELARIZE
VELARS > VELAR
VELATE adj having or covered with velum
VELATED same as > VELATE
VELATURA n overglaze
VELATURAS > VELATURA
VELCRO n tradename for a fastening consisting of two strips of nylon fabric that form a strong bond when pressed together
VELCROS > VELCRO
VELD n high grassland in southern Africa
VELDS > VELD
VELDSKOEN n leather ankle boot

VELDT same as > VELD
VELDTS > VELDT
VELE same as > VEIL
VELES > VELE
VELETA same as > VALETA
VELETAS > VELETA
VELIGER n free-swimming larva of many molluscs
VELIGERS > VELIGER
VELITES pl n light-armed troops in ancient Rome, drawn from the poorer classes
VELL vb cut turf
VELLEITY n weakest level of desire or volition
VELLENAGE n (in Medieval Europe) status of being a villein
VELLET n velvet
VELLETS > VELLET
VELLICATE vb twitch, pluck, or pinch
VELLON n silver and copper alloy used in old Spanish coins
VELLONS > VELLON
VELLS > VELL
VELLUM n fine calfskin parchment ▷ adj made of or resembling vellum
VELLUMS > VELLUM
VELOCE adv be played rapidly
VELOCITY n speed of movement in a given direction
VELODROME n arena with a banked track for cycle racing
VELOUR n fabric similar to velvet
VELOURS same as > VELOUR
VELOUTE n rich white sauce or soup made from stock, egg yolks, and cream
VELOUTES > VELOUTE
VELOUTINE n type of velvety fabric
VELSKOEN n type of shoe
VELSKOENS > VELSKOEN
VELUM n any of various membranous structures
VELURE n velvet or a similar fabric ▷ vb cover with velure
VELURED > VELURE
VELURES > VELURE
VELURING > VELURE
VELVERET n type of velvet-like fabric
VELVERETS > VELVERET
VELVET n fabric with a thick soft pile ▷ vb cover with velvet
VELVETED > VELVET
VELVETEEN n cotton velvet
VELVETIER > VELVET
VELVETING > VELVET
VELVETS > VELVET
VELVETY > VELVET
VENA n vein in the body
VENAE > VENA
VENAL adj easily bribed
VENALITY > VENAL
VENALLY > VENAL

VENATIC adj of, relating to, or used in hunting
VENATICAL same as > VENATIC
VENATION n arrangement of the veins in a leaf or in the wing of an insect
VENATIONS > VENATION
VENATOR n hunter
VENATORS > VENATOR
VEND vb sell
VENDABLE > VEND
VENDABLES > VEND
VENDACE n either of two small whitefish occurring in lakes in Scotland and NW England
VENDACES > VENDACE
VENDAGE n vintage
VENDAGES > VENDAGE
VENDANGE same as > VENDAGE
VENDANGES > VENDANGE
VENDED > VEND
VENDEE n person to whom something, esp real property, is sold
VENDEES > VENDEE
VENDER same as > VENDOR
VENDERS > VENDER
VENDETTA n long-lasting quarrel between people in which they attempt to harm each other
VENDETTAS > VENDETTA
VENDEUSE n female salesperson
VENDEUSES > VENDEUSE
VENDIBLE adj saleable or marketable ▷ n saleable object
VENDIBLES > VENDIBLE
VENDIBLY > VENDIBLE
VENDING > VEND
VENDINGS > VEND
VENDIS same as > VENDACE
VENDISES > VENDIS
VENDISS same as > VENDACE
VENDISSES > VENDIS
VENDITION > VEND
VENDOR n person who sells goods such as newspapers or hamburgers from a stall or cart
VENDORS > VENDOR
VENDS > VEND
VENDUE n public sale
VENDUES > VENDUE
VENEER n thin layer of wood etc covering a cheaper material ▷ vb cover (a surface) with a veneer
VENEERED > VENEER
VENEERER > VENEER
VENEERERS > VENEER
VENEERING n material used as veneer or a veneered surface
VENEERS > VENEER
VENEFIC adj having poisonous effects
VENEFICAL same as > VENEFIC
VENENATE vb poison
VENENATED > VENENATE
VENENATES > VENENATE
VENENE n medicine from

snake venom
VENENES > VENENE
VENENOSE adj poisonous
VENERABLE adj worthy of deep respect
VENERABLY > VENERABLE
VENERATE vb hold (a person) in deep respect
VENERATED > VENERATE
VENERATES > VENERATE
VENERATOR > VENERATE
VENEREAL adj transmitted by sexual intercourse
VENEREAN n sex addict
VENEREANS > VENEREAN
VENEREOUS adj libidinous
VENERER n hunter
VENERERS > VENERER
VENERIES > VENERY
VENERY n pursuit of sexual gratification
VENETIAN n Venetian blind
VENETIANS > VENETIAN
VENEWE same as > VENUE
VENEWES > VENEWE
VENEY n thrust
VENEYS > VENEY
VENGE vb avenge
VENGEABLE > VENGE
VENGEABLY > VENGE
VENGEANCE n revenge
VENGED > VENGE
VENGEFUL adj wanting revenge
VENGEMENT > VENGE
VENGER > VENGE
VENGERS > VENGE
VENGES > VENGE
VENGING > VENGE
VENIAL adj (of a sin or fault) easily forgiven
VENIALITY > VENIAL
VENIALLY > VENIAL
VENIDIUM n genus of flowering plants
VENIDIUMS > VENIDIUM
VENIN n any of the poisonous constituents of animal venoms
VENINE same as > VENIN
VENINES > VENINE
VENINS > VENIN
VENIRE n list from which jurors are selected
VENIREMAN n person summoned for jury service
VENIREMEN > VENIREMAN
VENIRES > VENIRE
VENISON n deer meat
VENISONS > VENISON
VENITE n musical setting for the 95th psalm
VENITES > VENITE
VENNEL n lane
VENNELS > VENNEL
VENOGRAM n X-ray of a vein
VENOGRAMS > VENOGRAM
VENOLOGY n study of veins
VENOM n malice or spite ▷ vb poison
VENOMED > VENOM
VENOMER > VENOM
VENOMERS > VENOM
VENOMING > VENOM
VENOMLESS > VENOM
VENOMOUS > VENOM
VENOMS > VENOM

VENOSE *adj* having veins
VENOSITY *n* excessive quantity of blood in the venous system or in an organ or part
VENOUS *adj* of veins
VENOUSLY > VENOUS
VENT *n* outlet releasing fumes or fluid ▷ *vb* express (an emotion) freely
VENTAGE *n* small opening
VENTAGES > VENTAGE
VENTAIL *n* (in medieval armour) a covering for the lower part of the face
VENTAILE *same as* > VENTAIL
VENTAILES > VENTAILE
VENTAILS > VENTAIL
VENTANA *n* window
VENTANAS > VENTANA
VENTAYLE *same as* > VENTAIL
VENTAYLES > VENTAYLE
VENTED > VENT
VENTER > VENT
VENTERS > VENT
VENTIDUCT *n* air pipe
VENTIFACT *n* pebble that has been shaped by wind-blown sand
VENTIGE *same as* > VENTAGE
VENTIGES > VENTIGE
VENTIL *n* valve on a musical instrument
VENTILATE *vb* let fresh air into
VENTILS > VENTIL
VENTING > VENT
VENTINGS > VENT
VENTLESS > VENT
VENTOSE *adj* full of wind
VENTOSITY *n* flatulence
VENTOUSE *n* apparatus sometimes used to assist the delivery of a baby
VENTOUSES > VENTOUSE
VENTRAL *adj* relating to the front of the body ▷ *n* ventral fin
VENTRALLY > VENTRAL
VENTRALS > VENTRAL
VENTRE *same as* > VENTURE
VENTRED > VENTRE
VENTRES > VENTRE
VENTRICLE *n* cavity in an organ such as the heart
VENTRING > VENTRE
VENTRINGS > VENTRE
VENTROUS > VENTRE
VENTS > VENT
VENTURE *n* risky undertaking, esp in business ▷ *vb* do something risky
VENTURED > VENTURE
VENTURER > VENTURE
VENTURERS > VENTURE
VENTURES > VENTURE
VENTURI *n* tube used to control the flow of fluid
VENTURING > VENTURE
VENTURIS > VENTURI
VENTUROUS *adj* adventurous
VENUE *n* place where an organized gathering is held
VENUES > VENUE
VENULAR > VENULE

VENULE *n* any of the small branches of a vein
VENULES > VENULE
VENULOSE > VENULE
VENULOUS > VENULE
VENUS *n* type of marine bivalve mollusc
VENUSES > VENUS
VENVILLE *n* type of parish tenure
VENVILLES > VENVILLE
VERA as in *aloe vera* plant substance used in skin and hair preparations
VERACIOUS *adj* habitually truthful
VERACITY *n* truthfulness
VERANDA *n* porch or portico along the outside of a building
VERANDAED > VERANDA
VERANDAH *same as* > VERANDA
VERANDAHS > VERANDAH
VERANDAS > VERANDA
VERAPAMIL *n* calcium-channel blocker used in the treatment of some types of irregular heart rhythm
VERATRIA *same as* > VERATRINE
VERATRIAS > VERATRIA
VERATRIN *same as* > VERATRINE
VERATRINE *n* white poisonous mixture obtained from the seeds of sabadilla
VERATRINS > VERATRIN
VERATRUM *n* genus of herbs
VERATRUMS > VERATRUM
VERB *n* word that expresses the idea of action, happening, or being
VERBAL *adj* spoken ▷ *n* abuse or invective ▷ *vb* implicate (someone) in a crime by quoting alleged admission of guilt in court
VERBALISE *same as* > VERBALIZE
VERBALISM *n* exaggerated emphasis on the importance of words
VERBALIST *n* person who deals with words alone, rather than facts, ideas, feeling, etc
VERBALITY > VERBAL
VERBALIZE *vb* express (something) in words
VERBALLED > VERBAL
VERBALLY > VERBAL
VERBALS > VERBAL
VERBARIAN *n* inventor of words
VERBASCUM *See* > MULLEIN
VERBATIM *adj* word for word ▷ *adv* using exactly the same words
VERBENA *n* plant with sweet-smelling flowers
VERBENAS > VERBENA
VERBERATE *vb* lash
VERBIAGE *n* excessive use of words
VERBIAGES > VERBIAGE

VERBICIDE *n* person who destroys a word
VERBID *n* any nonfinite form of a verb or any nonverbal word derived from a verb
VERBIDS > VERBID
VERBIFIED > VERBIFY
VERBIFIES > VERBIFY
VERBIFY *another word for* > VERBALIZE
VERBILE *n* person who is best stimulated by words
VERBILES > VERBILE
VERBING *n* use of nouns as verbs
VERBINGS > VERBING
VERBLESS > VERB
VERBOSE *adj* speaking at tedious length
VERBOSELY > VERBOSE
VERBOSER > VERBOSE
VERBOSEST > VERBOSE
VERBOSITY > VERBOSE
VERBOTEN *adj* forbidden
VERBS > VERB
VERD as in *verd antique* dark green mottled impure variety of serpentine marble
VERDANCY > VERDANT
VERDANT *adj* covered in green vegetation
VERDANTLY > VERDANT
VERDELHO *n* type of grape
VERDELHOS > VERDELHO
VERDERER *n* judicial officer responsible for the maintenance of law and order in the royal forests
VERDERERS > VERDERER
VERDEROR *same as* > VERDERER
VERDERORS > VERDEROR
VERDET *n* type of verdigris
VERDETS > VERDET
VERDICT *n* decision of a jury
VERDICTS > VERDICT
VERDIGRIS *n* green film on copper, brass, or bronze
VERDIN *n* small W North American tit having grey plumage with a yellow head
VERDINS > VERDIN
VERDIT *same as* > VERDICT
VERDITE *n* type of rock used in jewellery
VERDITER *n* blue-green pigment made from copper
VERDITERS > VERDITER
VERDITES > VERDITE
VERDITS > VERDIT
VERDOY *n* floral or leafy shield decoration
VERDURE *n* flourishing green vegetation
VERDURED > VERDURE
VERDURES > VERDURE
VERDUROUS > VERDURE
VERECUND *adj* shy or modest
VERGE *n* grass border along a road ▷ *vb* move in a specified direction
VERGED > VERGE
VERGENCE *n* inward or outward turning

movement of the eyes in convergence or divergence
VERGENCES > VERGENCE
VERGENCY *adj* inclination
VERGER *n* church caretaker
VERGERS > VERGER
VERGES > VERGE
VERGING > VERGE
VERGLAS *n* thin film of ice on rock
VERGLASES > VERGLAS
VERIDIC *same as* > VERIDICAL
VERIDICAL *adj* truthful
VERIER > VERY
VERIEST > VERY
VERIFIED > VERIFY
VERIFIER > VERIFY
VERIFIERS > VERIFY
VERIFIES > VERIFY
VERIFY *vb* check the truth or accuracy of
VERIFYING > VERIFY
VERILY *adv* in truth
VERISM *n* extreme naturalism in art or literature
VERISMO *n* school of composition that originated in Italian opera
VERISMOS > VERISMO
VERISMS > VERISM
VERIST > VERISM
VERISTIC > VERISM
VERISTS > VERISM
VERITABLE *adj* rightly called, without exaggeration
VERITABLY > VERITABLE
VERITAS *n* truth
VERITATES > VERITAS
VERITE *adj* involving a high degree of realism or naturalism ▷ *n* this kind of realism in film
VERITES > VERITE
VERITIES > VERITY
VERITY *n* true statement or principle
VERJUICE *n* acid juice of unripe grapes, apples, or crab apples ▷ *vb* make sour
VERJUICED > VERJUICE
VERJUICES > VERJUICE
VERKRAMP *adj* bigoted or illiberal
VERLAN *n* variety of French slang in which the syllables are inverted
VERLANS > VERLAN
VERLIG *adj* enlightened
VERLIGTE *n* (during apartheid) a White political liberal
VERLIGTES > VERLIGTE
VERMAL > VERMIS
VERMEIL *n* gilded silver, bronze, or other metal, used esp in the 19th century ▷ *vb* decorate with vermeil ▷ *adj* vermilion
VERMEILED > VERMEIL
VERMEILLE *variant of* > VERMEIL
VERMEILS > VERMEIL
VERMELL *same as* > VERMEIL

VERMELLS > VERMELL
VERMES > VERMIS
VERMIAN > VERMIS
VERMICIDE n any substance used to kill worms
VERMICULE n small worm
VERMIFORM adj shaped like a worm
VERMIFUGE n any drug or agent able to destroy or expel intestinal worms
VERMIL same as > VERMEIL
VERMILIES > VERMILY
VERMILION adj orange-red ▷ n mercuric sulphide, used as an orange-red pigment
VERMILLED > VERMIL
VERMILS > VERMIL
VERMILY > VERMEIL
VERMIN pl n animals, esp insects and rodents, that spread disease or cause damage
VERMINATE vb breed vermin
VERMINED adj plagued with vermin
VERMINOUS adj relating to, infested with, or suggestive of vermin
VERMINS > VERMIN
VERMINY > VERMIN
VERMIS n middle lobe connecting the two halves of the cerebellum
VERMOULU adj worm-eaten
VERMOUTH n wine flavoured with herbs
VERMOUTHS > VERMOUTH
VERMUTH same as > VERMOUTH
VERMUTHS > VERMUTH
VERNACLE same as > VERNICLE
VERNACLES > VERNACLE
VERNAL adj occurring in spring
VERNALISE same as > VERNALIZE
VERNALITY > VERNAL
VERNALIZE vb subject (ungerminated or germinating seeds) to low temperatures
VERNALLY > VERNAL
VERNANT > VERNAL
VERNATION n way in which leaves are arranged in the bud
VERNICLE n veronica
VERNICLES > VERNICLE
VERNIER n movable scale on a graduated measuring instrument for taking readings in fractions
VERNIERS > VERNIER
VERNIX n white substance covering the skin of a foetus
VERNIXES > VERNIX
VERONAL n a long-acting barbiturate used medicinally
VERONALS > VERONAL
VERONICA n plant with small blue, pink, or white flowers

VERONICAS > VERONICA
VERONIQUE adj (of a dish) garnished with seedless white grapes
VERQUERE n type of backgammon game
VERQUERES > VERQUERE
VERQUIRE variant of > VERQUERE
VERQUIRES > VERQUIRE
VERRA Scot word for > VERY
VERREL n ferrule
VERRELS > VERREL
VERREY same as > VAIR
VERRUCA n wart, usu on the foot
VERRUCAE > VERRUCA
VERRUCAS > VERRUCA
VERRUCOSE adj covered with warts
VERRUCOUS same as > VERRUCOSE
VERRUGA same as > VERRUCA
VERRUGAS > VERRUGA
VERRY same as > VAIR
VERS n verse
VERSAL n embellished letter
VERSALS > VERSAL
VERSANT n side or slope of a mountain or mountain range
VERSANTS > VERSANT
VERSATILE adj having many skills or uses
VERSE n group of lines forming part of a song or poem ▷ vb write verse
VERSED adj thoroughly knowledgeable (about)
VERSELET n small verse
VERSELETS > VERSELET
VERSEMAN n man who writes verse
VERSEMEN > VERSEMAN
VERSER n versifier
VERSERS > VERSER
VERSES > VERSE
VERSET n short, often sacred, verse
VERSETS > VERSET
VERSICLE n short verse
VERSICLES > VERSICLE
VERSIFIED > VERSIFY
VERSIFIER > VERSIFY
VERSIFIES > VERSIFY
VERSIFORM adj changing in form
VERSIFY vb write in verse
VERSIN same as > VERSINE
VERSINE n mathematical term
VERSINES > VERSINE
VERSING > VERSE
VERSINGS > VERSE
VERSINS > VERSIN
VERSION n form of something, such as a piece of writing, with some differences from other forms
VERSIONAL > VERSION
VERSIONER n translator
VERSIONS > VERSION
VERSO n left-hand page of a book
VERSOS > VERSO
VERST n unit of length used

in Russia
VERSTE same as > VERST
VERSTES > VERSTE
VERSTS > VERST
VERSUS prep in opposition to or in contrast with
VERSUTE adj cunning
VERT n right to cut green wood in a forest ▷ vb turn
VERTEBRA n one of the bones that form the spine
VERTEBRAE > VERTEBRA
VERTEBRAL > VERTEBRA
VERTEBRAS > VERTEBRA
VERTED > VERT
VERTEX n point on a geometric figure where the sides form an angle
VERTEXES > VERTEX
VERTICAL adj straight up and down ▷ n vertical direction
VERTICALS > VERTICAL
VERTICES > VERTEX
VERTICIL n circular arrangement of parts about an axis, esp leaves around a stem
VERTICILS > VERTICIL
VERTICITY n ability to turn
VERTIGO n dizziness, usu when looking down from a high place
VERTIGOES > VERTIGO
VERTIGOS > VERTIGO
VERTING > VERT
VERTIPORT n type of airport
VERTS > VERT
VERTU same as > VIRTU
VERTUE same as > VIRTU
VERTUES > VERTUE
VERTUOUS > VERTU
VERTUS > VERTU
VERVAIN n plant with spikes of blue, purple, or white flowers
VERVAINS > VERVAIN
VERVE n enthusiasm or liveliness
VERVEL same as > VARVEL
VERVELLED > VERVEL
VERVELS > VERVEL
VERVEN same as > VERVAIN
VERVENS > VERVEN
VERVES > VERVE
VERVET n variety of a South African guenon monkey
VERVETS > VERVET
VERY adv more than usually, extremely ▷ adj absolute, exact
VESICA n bladder
VESICAE > VESICA
VESICAL adj of or relating to a vesica, esp the urinary bladder
VESICANT n any substance that causes blisters ▷ adj acting as a vesicant
VESICANTS > VESICANT
VESICATE vb blister
VESICATED > VESICATE
VESICATES > VESICATE
VESICLE n sac or small cavity, esp one containing fluid
VESICLES > VESICLE

VESICULA n vesicle
VESICULAE > VESICULA
VESICULAR > VESICLE
VESPA n type of wasp
VESPAS > VESPA
VESPER n evening prayer, service, or hymn
VESPERAL n liturgical book containing the prayers, psalms, and hymns used at vespers
VESPERALS > VESPERAL
VESPERS pl n service of evening prayer
VESPIARY n nest or colony of social wasps or hornets
VESPID n insect of the family that includes the common wasp and hornet ▷ adj of or belonging to this family
VESPIDS > VESPID
VESPINE adj of, relating to, or resembling a wasp or wasps
VESPOID adj like a wasp
VESSAIL archaic variant of > VESSEL
VESSAILS > VESSAIL
VESSEL n container or ship ▷ adj contained in a vessel
VESSELED > VESSEL
VESSELS > VESSEL
VEST n undergarment worn on the top half of the body ▷ vb give (authority) to (someone)
VESTA n short friction match, usually of wood
VESTAL adj pure, chaste ▷ n chaste woman
VESTALLY > VESTAL
VESTALS > VESTAL
VESTAS > VESTA
VESTED adj having an existing right to the immediate or future possession of property
VESTEE n person having a vested interest something
VESTEES > VESTEE
VESTIARY n room for storing clothes or dressing in, such as a vestry ▷ adj of or relating to clothes
VESTIBULA > VESTIBULE
VESTIBULE n small entrance hall
VESTIGE n small amount or trace
VESTIGES > VESTIGE
VESTIGIA > VESTIGIUM
VESTIGIAL adj remaining after a larger or more important thing has gone
VESTIGIUM n trace
VESTIMENT same as > VESTMENT
VESTING > VEST
VESTINGS > VEST
VESTITURE n investiture
VESTLESS > VEST
VESTLIKE > VEST
VESTMENT n garment or robe, esp one denoting office, authority, or rank
VESTMENTS > VESTMENT

VESTRAL > VESTRY

VESTRIES > VESTRY

VESTRY *n* room in a church used as an office by the priest or minister

VESTRYMAN *n* member of a church vestry

VESTRYMEN > VESTRYMAN

VESTS > VEST

VESTURAL > VESTURE

VESTURE *n* garment or something that seems like a garment ▷ *vb* clothe

VESTURED > VESTURE

VESTURER *n* person in charge of church vestments

VESTURERS > VESTURER

VESTURES > VESTURE

VESTURING > VESTURE

VESUVIAN *n* match for lighting cigars

VESUVIANS > VESUVIAN

VET *vb* check the suitability of ▷ *n* military veteran

VETCH *n* climbing plant with a beanlike fruit used as fodder

VETCHES > VETCH

VETCHIER > VETCHY

VETCHIEST > VETCHY

VETCHLING *n* type of climbing plant

VETCHY *adj* consisting of vetches

VETERAN *n* person with long experience in a particular activity, esp military service ▷ *adj* long-serving

VETERANS > VETERAN

VETIVER *n* tall hairless grass of tropical and subtropical Asia

VETIVERS > VETIVER

VETIVERT *n* oil from the vetiver

VETIVERTS > VETIVERT

VETKOEK *n* South African cake

VETKOEKS > VETKOEK

VETO *n* official power to cancel a proposal ▷ *vb* enforce a veto against

VETOED > VETO

VETOER > VETO

VETOERS > VETO

VETOES > VETO

VETOING > VETO

VETOLESS > VETO

VETS > VET

VETTED > VET

VETTER > VET

VETTERS > VET

VETTING > VET

VETTURA *n* Italian mode of transport

VETTURAS > VETTURA

VETTURINI > VETTURINO

VETTURINO *n* person who drives a vettura

VEX *vb* frustrate, annoy

VEXATION *n* something annoying

VEXATIONS > VEXATION

VEXATIOUS *adj* vexing

VEXATORY > VEX

VEXED *adj* annoyed and puzzled

VEXEDLY > VEXED

VEXEDNESS > VEXED

VEXER > VEX

VEXERS > VEX

VEXES > VEX

VEXIL *same as* > VEXILLUM

VEXILLA > VEXILLUM

VEXILLAR > VEXILLUM

VEXILLARY > VEXILLUM

VEXILLATE > VEXILLUM

VEXILLUM *n* vane of a feather

VEXILS > VEXIL

VEXING > VEX

VEXINGLY > VEX

VEXINGS > VEX

VEXT *same as* > VEXED

VEZIR *same as* > VIZIER

VEZIRS > VEZIR

VIA *prep* by way of ▷ *n* road

VIABILITY > VIABLE

VIABLE *adj* able to be put into practice

VIABLY > VIABLE

VIADUCT *n* bridge over a valley

VIADUCTS > VIADUCT

VIAE > VIA

VIAL *n* small bottle for liquids ▷ *vb* put into a vial

VIALED > VIAL

VIALFUL > VIAL

VIALFULS > VIAL

VIALING > VIAL

VIALLED > VIAL

VIALLING > VIAL

VIALS > VIAL

VIAMETER *n* device to measure distance travelled

VIAMETERS > VIAMETER

VIAND *n* type of food, esp a delicacy

VIANDS > VIAND

VIAS > VIA

VIATIC *same as* > VIATICAL

VIATICA > VIATICUM

VIATICAL *adj* of or denoting a road or a journey ▷ *n* purchase of a terminal patient's life assurance policy so that he or she may make use of the proceeds

VIATICALS > VIATICAL

VIATICUM *n* Holy Communion given to a person who is dying or in danger of death

VIATICUMS > VIATICUM

VIATOR *n* traveller

VIATORES > VIATOR

VIATORIAL *adj* pertaining to travelling

VIATORS > VIATOR

VIBE *n* feeling or flavour of the kind specified

VIBES *pl n* vibrations

VIBEX *n* mark under the skin

VIBEY *adj* lively and vibrant

VIBICES > VIBEX

VIBIER > VIBEY

VIBIEST > VIBEY

VIBIST *n* person who plays a vibraphone in a jazz band or group

VIBISTS > VIBIST

VIBRACULA *pl n* bristle-like polyps in certain bryozoans

VIBRAHARP *n* type of percussion instrument

VIBRANCE *n* vibrancy

VIBRANCES > VIBRANCE

VIBRANCY > VIBRANT

VIBRANT *adj* vigorous in appearance, energetic ▷ *n* trilled or rolled speech sound

VIBRANTLY > VIBRANT

VIBRANTS > VIBRANT

VIBRATE *vb* move back and forth rapidly

VIBRATED > VIBRATE

VIBRATES > VIBRATE

VIBRATILE > VIBRATE

VIBRATING > VIBRATE

VIBRATION *n* vibrating

VIBRATIVE > VIBRATE

VIBRATO *n* rapid fluctuation in the pitch of a note

VIBRATOR *n* device that produces vibratory motion

VIBRATORS > VIBRATOR

VIBRATORY > VIBRATE

VIBRATOS > VIBRATO

VIBRIO *n* curved or spiral rodlike bacterium

VIBRIOID > VIBRIO

VIBRION *same as* > VIBRIO

VIBRIONIC > VIBRIO

VIBRIONS > VIBRION

VIBRIOS > VIBRIO

VIBRIOSES > VIBRIOSIS

VIBRIOSIS *n* bacterial disease

VIBRISSA *n* any of the bristle-like sensitive hairs on the face of many mammals

VIBRISSAE > VIBRISSA

VIBRISSAL > VIBRISSA

VIBRONIC *adj* of, concerned with, or involving both electronic and vibrational energy levels of a molecule

VIBS *pl n* type of climbing shoes

VIBURNUM *n* subtropical shrub with white flowers and berry-like fruits

VIBURNUMS > VIBURNUM

VICAR *n* member of the clergy in charge of a parish

VICARAGE *n* vicar's house

VICARAGES > VICARAGE

VICARATE *same as* > VICARIATE

VICARATES > VICARATE

VICARESS *n* rank of nun

VICARIAL *adj* of or relating to a vicar, vicars, or a vicariate

VICARIANT *n* any of several closely related species, etc, each of which exists in a separate geographical area

VICARIATE *n* office, rank, or authority of a vicar

VICARIES > VICARY

VICARIOUS *adj* felt indirectly by imagining what another person experiences

VICARLY > VICAR

VICARS > VICAR

VICARSHIP *same as* > VICARIATE

VICARY *n* office of a vicar

VICE *n* immoral or evil habit or action ▷ *adj* serving in place of ▷ *vb* grip (something) with or as if with a vice ▷ *prep* instead of

VICED > VICE

VICEGERAL *adj* of or relating to a person who deputizes for another

VICELESS > VICE

VICELIKE > VICE

VICENARY *adj* relating to or consisting of 20

VICENNIAL *adj* occurring every 20 years

VICEREGAL *adj* of a viceroy

VICEREINE *n* wife of a viceroy

VICEROY *n* governor of a colony who represents the monarch

VICEROYS > VICEROY

VICES > VICE

VICESIMAL *same as* > VIGESIMAL

VICHIES > VICHY

VICHY *n* French mineral water

VICIATE *same as* > VITIATE

VICIATED > VICIATE

VICIATES > VICIATE

VICIATING > VICIATE

VICINAGE *n* residents of a particular neighbourhood

VICINAGES > VICINAGE

VICINAL *adj* neighbouring

VICING > VICE

VICINITY *n* surrounding area

VICIOSITY *same as* > VITIOSITY

VICIOUS *adj* cruel and violent

VICIOUSLY > VICIOUS

VICOMTE *n* French nobleman

VICOMTES > VICOMTE

VICTIM *n* person or thing harmed or killed

VICTIMISE *same as* > VICTIMIZE

VICTIMIZE *vb* punish unfairly

VICTIMS > VICTIM

VICTOR *n* person who has defeated an opponent, esp in war or in sport

VICTORESS *same as* > VICTRESS

VICTORIA *n* large sweet plum, red and yellow in colour

VICTORIAS > VICTORIA

VICTORIES > VICTORY

VICTORINE *n* woman's article of clothing

VICTORS > VICTOR

VICTORY *n* winning of a battle or contest

VICTRESS *n* female victor

VICTRIX *same as* > VICTRESS

V

VICTRIXES > VICTRIX
VICTROLLA n type of gramophone
VICTUAL vb supply with or obtain victuals
VICTUALED > VICTUAL
VICTUALER > VICTUAL
VICTUALS pl n food and drink
VICUGNA same as > VICUNA
VICUGNAS > VICUGNA
VICUNA n S American animal like the llama
VICUNAS > VICUNA
VID same as > VIDEO
VIDAME n French nobleman
VIDAMES > VIDAME
VIDE interj look
VIDELICET adv namely: used to specify items
VIDENDA > VIDENDUM
VIDENDUM n that which is to be seen
VIDEO vb record (a TV programme or event) on video ▷ adj relating to or used in producing television images ▷ n recording and showing of films and events using a television set, video tapes, and a video recorder
VIDEODISC variant of > VIDEODISK
VIDEODISK n disk on which information is stored in digital form
VIDEOED > VIDEO
VIDEOFIT n computer-generated picture of a person sought by the police
VIDEOFITS > VIDEOFIT
VIDEOGRAM n audiovisual recording
VIDEOING > VIDEO
VIDEOLAND n world of television and televised images
VIDEOS > VIDEO
VIDEOTAPE vb record (a TV programme) on video tape
VIDEOTEX n information system that displays data from a distant computer on a screen
VIDEOTEXT n means of representing on a TV screen information that is held in a computer
VIDETTE same as > VEDETTE
VIDETTES > VIDETTE
VIDICON n small television camera tube used in closed-circuit television
VIDICONS > VIDICON
VIDIMUS n inspection
VIDIMUSES > VIDIMUS
VIDS > VID
VIDUAGE n widows collectively
VIDUAGES > VIDUAGE
VIDUAL adj widowed
VIDUITIES > VIDUITY
VIDUITY n widowhood
VIDUOUS adj empty
VIE vb compete (with someone)

VIED > VIE
VIELLE n stringed musical instrument
VIELLES > VIELLE
VIER > VIE
VIERS > VIE
VIES > VIE
VIEW n opinion or belief ▷ vb think of (something) in a particular way
VIEWABLE > VIEW
VIEWDATA n interactive form of videotext
VIEWDATAS > VIEWDATA
VIEWED > VIEW
VIEWER n person who watches television
VIEWERS > VIEWER
VIEWIER > VIEWY
VIEWIEST > VIEWY
VIEWINESS > VIEWY
VIEWING n act of watching television
VIEWINGS > VIEWING
VIEWLESS adj (of windows, etc) not affording a view
VIEWLY adj pleasant on the eye
VIEWPHONE n videophone
VIEWPOINT n person's attitude towards something
VIEWS > VIEW
VIEWY adj having fanciful opinions or ideas
VIFDA same as > VIVDA
VIFDAS > VIFDA
VIG n interest on a loan that is paid to a moneylender
VIGA n rafter
VIGAS > VIGA
VIGESIMAL adj relating to or based on the number 20
VIGIA n navigational hazard marked on a chart although its existence has not been confirmed
VIGIAS > VIGIA
VIGIL n night-time period of staying awake to look after a sick person, pray, etc
VIGILANCE n careful attention
VIGILANT adj watchful in case of danger
VIGILANTE n person who takes it upon himself or herself to enforce the law
VIGILS > VIGIL
VIGNERON n person who grows grapes for winemaking
VIGNERONS > VIGNERON
VIGNETTE n small illustration placed at the beginning or end of a chapter or book ▷ vb portray in a vignette
VIGNETTED > VIGNETTE
VIGNETTER n device used in printing vignettes
VIGNETTES > VIGNETTE
VIGOR same as > VIGOUR
VIGORISH n type of commission
VIGORO n women's game similar to cricket

VIGOROS > VIGORO
VIGOROSO adv in music, emphatically
VIGOROUS adj having physical or mental energy
VIGORS > VIGOR
VIGOUR n physical or mental energy
VIGOURS > VIGOUR
VIGS > VIG
VIHARA n type of Buddhist temple
VIHARAS > VIHARA
VIHUELA n obsolete plucked stringed instrument of Spain, related to the guitar
VIHUELAS > VIHUELA
VIKING n Dane, Norwegian, or Swede who raided by sea most of N and W Europe between the 8th and 11th centuries
VIKINGISM > VIKING
VIKINGS > VIKING
VILAYET n major administrative division of Turkey
VILAYETS > VILAYET
VILD same as > VILE
VILDE same as > VILE
VILDLY > VILD
VILDNESS > VILD
VILE adj very wicked
VILELY > VILE
VILENESS > VILE
VILER > VILE
VILEST > VILE
VILIACO n scoundrel
VILIACOES > VILIACO
VILIACOS > VILIACO
VILIAGO same as > VILIACO
VILIAGOES > VILIAGO
VILIAGOS > VILIAGO
VILIFIED > VILIFY
VILIFIER > VILIFY
VILIFIERS > VILIFY
VILIFIES > VILIFY
VILIFY vb attack the character of
VILIFYING > VILIFY
VILIPEND vb treat or regard with contempt
VILIPENDS > VILIPEND
VILL n township
VILLA n large house with gardens
VILLADOM > VILLA
VILLADOMS > VILLA
VILLAE > VILLA
VILLAGE n small group of houses in a country area
VILLAGER n inhabitant of a village ▷ adj backward, unsophisticated, or illiterate
VILLAGERS > VILLAGER
VILLAGERY n villages
VILLAGES > VILLAGE
VILLAGIO same as > VILIACO
VILLAGIOS > VILLAGIO
VILLAGREE variant of > VILLAGERY
VILLAIN n wicked person
VILLAINS > VILLAIN
VILLAINY n evil or vicious behaviour
VILLAN same as > VILLEIN

VILLANAGE > VILLAN
VILLANIES > VILLANY
VILLANOUS > VILLAIN
VILLANS > VILLAN
VILLANY same as > VILLAINY
VILLAR > VILL
VILLAS > VILLA
VILLATIC adj of or relating to a villa, village, or farm
VILLEIN n peasant bound in service to his lord
VILLEINS > VILLEIN
VILLENAGE n villein's status
VILLI > VILLUS
VILLIAGO same as > VILIACO
VILLIAGOS > VILLIAGO
VILLIFORM adj having the form of a villus or a series of villi
VILLOSE same as > VILLOUS
VILLOSITY n state of being villous
VILLOUS adj (of plant parts) covered with long hairs
VILLOUSLY > VILLOUS
VILLS > VILL
VILLUS n one of the finger-like projections in the small intestine of many vertebrates
VIM n force, energy
VIMANA n Indian mythological chariot of the gods
VIMANAS > VIMANA
VIMEN n long flexible shoot that occurs in certain plants
VIMINA > VIMEN
VIMINAL > VIMEN
VIMINEOUS adj having, producing, or resembling long flexible shoots
VIMS > VIM
VIN n French wine
VINA n stringed musical instrument related to the sitar
VINACEOUS adj of, relating to, or containing wine
VINAL n type of manmade fibre
VINALS > VINAL
VINAS > VINA
VINASSE n residue left in a still after distilling spirits, esp brandy
VINASSES > VINASSE
VINCA n type of trailing plant with blue flowers
VINCAS > VINCA
VINCIBLE adj capable of being defeated or overcome
VINCIBLY > VINCIBLE
VINCULA > VINCULUM
VINCULUM n horizontal line drawn above a group of mathematical terms
VINCULUMS > VINCULUM
VINDALOO n type of very hot Indian curry
VINDALOOS > VINDALOO
VINDEMIAL adj relating to a grape harvest
VINDICATE vb clear (someone) of guilt

VINE *n* climbing plant, esp one producing grapes ▷ *vb* form like a vine

VINEAL *adj* relating to wines

VINED > VINE

VINEGAR *n* acid liquid made from wine, beer, or cider ▷ *vb* apply vinegar to

VINEGARED > VINEGAR

VINEGARS > VINEGAR

VINEGARY *adj* containing vinegar

VINELESS > VINE

VINELIKE > VINE

VINER *n* vinedresser

VINERIES > VINERY

VINERS > VINER

VINERY *n* hothouse for growing grapes

VINES > VINE

VINEW *vb* become mouldy

VINEWED > VINEW

VINEWING > VINEW

VINEWS > VINEW

VINEYARD *n* plantation of grape vines, esp for making wine

VINEYARDS > VINEYARD

VINIC *adj* of, relating to, or contained in wine

VINIER > VINE

VINIEST > VINE

VINIFERA *n* species of vine

VINIFERAS > VINIFERA

VINIFIED > VINIFY

VINIFIES > VINIFY

VINIFY *vb* convert into wine

VINIFYING > VINIFY

VINING > VINE

VINO *n* wine

VINOLENT *adj* drunken

VINOLOGY *n* scientific study of vines

VINOS > VINO

VINOSITY *n* distinctive and essential quality and flavour of wine

VINOUS *adj* of or characteristic of wine

VINOUSLY > VINOUS

VINS > VIN

VINT *vb* sell (wine)

VINTAGE *n* wine from a particular harvest of grapes ▷ *adj* best and most typical ▷ *vb* gather (grapes) or make (wine)

VINTAGED > VINTAGE

VINTAGER *n* grape harvester

VINTAGERS > VINTAGER

VINTAGES > VINTAGE

VINTAGING > VINTAGE

VINTED > VINT

VINTING > VINT

VINTNER *n* dealer in wine

VINTNERS > VINTNER

VINTRIES > VINTRY

VINTRY *n* place where wine is sold

VINTS > VINT

VINY > VINE

VINYL *n* type of plastic, used in mock leather and records ▷ *adj* of or containing a particular group of atoms

VINYLIC > VINYL

VINYLS > VINYL

VIOL *n* early stringed instrument preceding the violin

VIOLA *n* stringed instrument lower in pitch than a violin

VIOLABLE > VIOLATE

VIOLABLY > VIOLATE

VIOLAS > VIOLA

VIOLATE *vb* break (a law or agreement) ▷ *adj* violated or dishonoured

VIOLATED > VIOLATE

VIOLATER > VIOLATE

VIOLATERS > VIOLATE

VIOLATES > VIOLATE

VIOLATING > VIOLATE

VIOLATION > VIOLATE

VIOLATIVE > VIOLATE

VIOLATOR > VIOLATE

VIOLATORS > VIOLATE

VIOLD *archaic or poetic past form of* > VIAL

VIOLENCE *n* use of physical force, usu intended to cause injury or destruction

VIOLENCES > VIOLENCE

VIOLENT *adj* using or involving physical force with the intention of causing injury or destruction ▷ *vb* coerce

VIOLENTED > VIOLENT

VIOLENTLY > VIOLENT

VIOLENTS > VIOLENT

VIOLER *n* person who plays the viol

VIOLERS > VIOLER

VIOLET *n* plant with bluish-purple flowers ▷ *adj* bluish-purple

VIOLETS > VIOLET

VIOLIN *n* small four-stringed musical instrument played with a bow.

VIOLINIST *n* person who plays the violin

VIOLINS > VIOLIN

VIOLIST *n* person who plays the viola

VIOLISTS > VIOLIST

VIOLONE *n* double-bass member of the viol family

VIOLONES > VIOLONE

VIOLS > VIOL

VIOMYCIN *n* type of antibiotic

VIOMYCINS > VIOMYCIN

VIOSTEROL *n* type of vitamin

VIPER *n* poisonous snake

VIPERFISH *n* predatory deep-sea fish

VIPERINE *same as* > VIPEROUS

VIPERISH *same as* > VIPEROUS

VIPEROUS *adj* of, relating to, or resembling a viper

VIPERS > VIPER

VIRAEMIA *n* condition in which virus particles circulate and reproduce in the bloodstream

VIRAEMIAS > VIRAEMIA

VIRAEMIC > VIRAEMIA

VIRAGO *n* aggressive woman

VIRAGOES > VIRAGO

VIRAGOISH > VIRAGO

VIRAGOS > VIRAGO

VIRAL *adj* of or caused by a virus

VIRALLY > VIRAL

VIRANDA *same as* > VERANDA

VIRANDAS > VIRANDA

VIRANDO *same as* > VERANDA

VIRANDOS > VIRANDO

VIRE *vb* turn

VIRED > VIRE

VIRELAI *same as* > VIRELAY

VIRELAIS > VIRELAI

VIRELAY *n* old French verse form

VIRELAYS > VIRELAY

VIREMENT *n* administrative transfer of funds from one part of a budget to another

VIREMENTS > VIREMENT

VIREMIA *same as* > VIRAEMIA

VIREMIAS > VIREMIA

VIREMIC > VIREMIA

VIRENT *adj* green

VIREO *n* American songbird

VIREONINE > VIREO

VIREOS > VIREO

VIRES > VIRE

VIRESCENT *adj* greenish or becoming green

VIRETOT *as in on the viretot* in a rush

VIRETOTS > VIRETOT

VIRGA *n* wisps of rain or snow that evaporate before reaching the earth

VIRGAS > VIRGA

VIRGATE *adj* long, straight, and thin ▷ *n* obsolete measure of land area, usually taken as equivalent to 30 acres

VIRGATES > VIRGATE

VIRGE *n* rod

VIRGER *n* rod-bearer

VIRGERS > VIRGER

VIRGES > VIRGE

VIRGIN *n* person, esp a woman, who has not had sexual intercourse ▷ *adj* not having had sexual intercourse ▷ *vb* behave like a virgin

VIRGINAL *adj* like a virgin ▷ *n* early keyboard instrument like a small harpsichord

VIRGINALS > VIRGINAL

VIRGINED > VIRGIN

VIRGINIA *n* type of flue-cured tobacco grown originally in Virginia

VIRGINIAS > VIRGINIA

VIRGINING > VIRGIN

VIRGINITY *n* condition or fact of being a virgin

VIRGINIUM *former name for* > FRANCIUM

VIRGINLY > VIRGIN

VIRGINS > VIRGIN

VIRGULATE *adj* rod-shaped or rodlike

VIRGULE *another name for* > SLASH

VIRGULES > VIRGULE

VIRICIDAL > VIRICIDE

VIRICIDE *n* substance that destroys viruses

VIRICIDES > VIRICIDE

VIRID *adj* verdant

VIRIDIAN *n* green pigment consisting of a hydrated form of chromic oxide

VIRIDIANS > VIRIDIAN

VIRIDITE *n* greenish mineral

VIRIDITES > VIRIDITE

VIRIDITY *n* quality or state of being green

VIRILE *adj* having the traditional male characteristics of physical strength and a high sex drive

VIRILELY > VIRILE

VIRILISE *same as* > VIRILIZE

VIRILISED > VIRILISE

VIRILISES > VIRILISE

VIRILISM *n* abnormal development in a woman of male secondary sex characteristics

VIRILISMS > VIRILISM

VIRILITY > VIRILE

VIRILIZE *vb* cause male characteristics to appear in female

VIRILIZED > VIRILIZE

VIRILIZES > VIRILIZE

VIRILOCAL *adj* living with husband's family

VIRING > VIRE

VIRINO *n* entity postulated to be the causative agent of BSE

VIRINOS > VIRINO

VIRION *n* virus in infective form, consisting of an RNA particle within a protein covering

VIRIONS > VIRION

VIRL *same as* > FERRULE

VIRLS > VIRL

VIROGENE *n* type of viral gene

VIROGENES > VIROGENE

VIROID *n* any of various infective RNA particles

VIROIDS > VIROID

VIROLOGIC > VIROLOGY

VIROLOGY *n* study of viruses

VIROSE *adj* poisonous

VIROSES > VIROSIS

VIROSIS *n* viral disease

VIROUS *same as* > VIROSE

VIRTU *n* taste or love for curios or works of fine art

VIRTUAL *adj* having the effect but not the form of

VIRTUALLY *adv* practically, almost

VIRTUE *n* moral goodness

VIRTUES > VIRTUE

VIRTUOSA *n* female virtuoso

VIRTUOSAS > VIRTUOSA

VIRTUOSE > VIRTUOSA
VIRTUOSI > VIRTUOSO
VIRTUOSIC > VIRTUOSO
VIRTUOSO n person with impressive esp musical skill ▷ adj showing exceptional skill or brilliance
VIRTUOSOS > VIRTUOSO
VIRTUOUS adj morally good
VIRTUS > VIRTU
VIRUCIDAL > VIRUCIDE
VIRUCIDE same as > VIRICIDE
VIRUCIDES > VIRUCIDE
VIRULENCE n quality of being virulent
VIRULENCY same as > VIRULENCE
VIRULENT adj extremely bitter or hostile
VIRUS n microorganism that causes disease in humans, animals, and plants
VIRUSES > VIRUS
VIRUSLIKE > VIRUS
VIRUSOID n small plant virus
VIRUSOIDS > VIRUSOID
VIS n power, force, or strength
VISA n permission to enter a country, shown by a stamp on the passport ▷ vb enter a visa into (a passport)
VISAED > VISA
VISAGE n face
VISAGED > VISAGE
VISAGES > VISAGE
VISAGIST same as > VISAGISTE
VISAGISTE n person who designs and applies face make-up
VISAGISTS > VISAGIST
VISAING > VISA
VISARD same as > VIZARD
VISARDS > VISARD
VISAS > VISA
VISCACHA n South American rodent
VISCACHAS > VISCACHA
VISCARIA n type of perennial plant
VISCARIAS > VISCARIA
VISCERA pl n large abdominal organs
VISCERAL adj instinctive
VISCERATE vb disembowel
VISCID adj sticky
VISCIDITY > VISCID
VISCIDLY > VISCID
VISCIN n sticky substance found on plants
VISCINS > VISCIN
VISCOID adj (of a fluid) somewhat viscous
VISCOIDAL same as > VISCOID
VISCOSE same as > VISCOUS
VISCOSES > VISCOSE
VISCOSITY n state of being viscous
VISCOUNT n British nobleman ranking between an earl and a baron

VISCOUNTS > VISCOUNT
VISCOUNTY > VISCOUNT
VISCOUS adj thick and sticky
VISCOUSLY > VISCOUS
VISCUM n shrub genus
VISCUMS > VISCUM
VISCUS n internal organ
VISE vb advise or award a visa to ▷ n (in US English) vice
VISED > VISE
VISEED > VISE
VISEING > VISE
VISELIKE > VICE
VISES > VISE
VISIBLE adj able to be seen ▷ n visible item of trade
VISIBLES > VISIBLE
VISIBLY > VISIBLE
VISIE same as > VIZY
VISIED > VISIE
VISIEING > VISIE
VISIER > VISIE
VISIERS > VISIE
VISIES > VISIE
VISILE n person best stimulated by vision
VISILES > VISILE
VISING > VISE
VISION n ability to see ▷ vb see or show in or as if in a vision
VISIONAL adj of, relating to, or seen in a vision, apparition, etc
VISIONARY adj showing foresight ▷ n visionary person
VISIONED > VISION
VISIONER n visionary
VISIONERS > VISIONER
VISIONING > VISION
VISIONIST n type of visionary
VISIONS > VISION
VISIT vb go or come to see ▷ n instance of visiting
VISITABLE > VISIT
VISITANT n ghost or apparition ▷ adj paying a visit
VISITANTS > VISITANT
VISITATOR n official visitor
VISITE n type of cape
VISITED > VISIT
VISITEE n person who is visited
VISITEES > VISITEE
VISITER variant of > VISITOR
VISITERS > VISITER
VISITES > VISITE
VISITING > VISIT
VISITINGS > VISIT
VISITOR n person who visits a person or place
VISITORS > VISITOR
VISITRESS n female visitor
VISITS > VISIT
VISIVE adj visual
VISNE n neighbourhood
VISNES > VISNE
VISNOMIE same as > VISNOMY
VISNOMIES > VISNOMY
VISNOMY n method of

judging character from facial features
VISON n type of mink
VISONS > VISON
VISOR n transparent part of a helmet that pulls down over the face ▷ vb cover, provide, or protect with a visor
VISORED > VISOR
VISORING > VISOR
VISORLESS > VISOR
VISORS > VISOR
VISTA n (beautiful) extensive view ▷ vb make into vistas
VISTAED > VISTA
VISTAING > VISTA
VISTAL > VISTA
VISTALESS > VISTA
VISTAS > VISTA
VISTO same as > VISTA
VISTOS > VISTO
VISUAL adj done by or used in seeing ▷ n sketch to show the proposed layout of an advertisement, as in a newspaper
VISUALISE same as > VISUALIZE
VISUALIST n visualiser
VISUALITY > VISUAL
VISUALIZE vb form a mental image of
VISUALLY > VISUAL
VISUALS > VISUAL
VITA n curriculum vitae
VITACEOUS adj of a family of flowering plants that includes the grapevine
VITAE > VITA
VITAL adj essential or highly important ▷ n bodily organs that are necessary to maintain life
VITALISE same as > VITALIZE
VITALISED > VITALISE
VITALISER > VITALISE
VITALISES > VITALISE
VITALISM n philosophical doctrine that the phenomena of life cannot be explained in purely mechanical terms
VITALISMS > VITALISM
VITALIST > VITALISM
VITALISTS > VITALISM
VITALITY n physical or mental energy
VITALIZE vb fill with life or vitality
VITALIZED > VITALIZE
VITALIZER > VITALIZE
VITALIZES > VITALIZE
VITALLY > VITAL
VITALNESS > VITAL
VITALS > VITAL
VITAMER n type of chemical
VITAMERS > VITAMER
VITAMIN n one of a group of substances that are essential in the diet for specific body processes
VITAMINE same as > VITAMIN
VITAMINES > VITAMINE
VITAMINIC > VITAMIN

VITAMINS > VITAMIN
VITAS > VITA
VITASCOPE n early type of film projector
VITATIVE adj fond of life
VITE adv musical direction
VITELLARY > VITELLUS
VITELLI > VITELLUS
VITELLIN n phosphoprotein that is the major protein in egg yolk
VITELLINE adj of or relating to the yolk of an egg
VITELLINS > VITELLIN
VITELLUS n yolk of an egg
VITESSE n speed
VITESSES > VITESSE
VITEX n type of herb
VITEXES > VITEX
VITIABLE > VITIATE
VITIATE vb spoil the effectiveness of
VITIATED > VITIATE
VITIATES > VITIATE
VITIATING > VITIATE
VITIATION > VITIATE
VITIATOR > VITIATE
VITIATORS > VITIATE
VITICETA > VITICETUM
VITICETUM n place where vines are cultivated
VITICIDE n vine killer
VITICIDES > VITICIDE
VITILIGO n area of skin that is white from albinism or loss of melanin pigmentation
VITILIGOS > VITILIGO
VITIOSITY n viciousness
VITRAGE n light fabric
VITRAGES > VITRAGE
VITRAIL n stained glass
VITRAIN n type of coal occurring as horizontal glassy bands of a nonsoiling friable material
VITRAINS > VITRAIN
VITRAUX > VITRAIL
VITREOUS adj like or made from glass
VITREUM n vitreous body
VITREUMS > VITREUM
VITRIC adj of, relating to, resembling, or having the nature of glass
VITRICS n glassware
VITRIFIED > VITRIFY
VITRIFIES > VITRIFY
VITRIFORM adj having the form or appearance of glass
VITRIFY vb change or be changed into glass or a glassy substance
VITRINE n glass display case or cabinet for works of art, curios, etc
VITRINES > VITRINE
VITRIOL n language expressing bitterness and hatred ▷ vb attack or injure with or as if with vitriol
VITRIOLED > VITRIOL
VITRIOLIC adj (of language) severely bitter

or harsh
VITRIOLS > VITRIOL
VITTA n tubelike cavity containing oil that occurs in the fruits of certain plants
VITTAE > VITTA
VITTATE > VITTA
VITTLE obsolete or dialect spelling of > VICTUAL
VITTLED > VITTLE
VITTLES obsolete or dialect spelling of > VICTUALS
VITTLING > VITTLE
VITULAR same as > VITULINE
VITULINE adj of or resembling a calf or veal
VIVA interj long live (a person or thing) ▷ n examination in the form of an interview ▷ vb examine (a candidate) in a spoken interview
VIVACE adv in a lively manner ▷ adj be performed in a lively manner ▷ n piece of music to be performed in this way
VIVACES > VIVACE
VIVACIOUS adj full of energy and enthusiasm
VIVACITY n quality of being vivacious
VIVAED > VIVA
VIVAING > VIVA
VIVAMENTE adv in a lively manner
VIVANDIER n sutler
VIVARIA > VIVARIUM
VIVARIES > VIVARY
VIVARIUM n place where animals are kept in natural conditions
VIVARIUMS > VIVARIUM
VIVARY same as > VIVARIUM
VIVAS > VIVA
VIVAT interj long live ▷ n expression of acclamation
VIVATS > VIVAT
VIVDA n method of drying meat
VIVDAS > VIVDA
VIVE interj long live
VIVELY adv in a lively manner
VIVENCIES > VIVENCY
VIVENCY n physical or mental energy
VIVER n fish pond
VIVERRA n civet genus
VIVERRAS > VIVERRA
VIVERRID > VIVERRINE
VIVERRIDS > VIVERRINE
VIVERRINE n type of mammal of Eurasia and Africa ▷ adj of this family of mammals
VIVERS > VIVER
VIVES n disease found in horses
VIVIANITE n type of mineral
VIVID adj very bright
VIVIDER > VIVID
VIVIDEST > VIVID
VIVIDITY > VIVID
VIVIDLY > VIVID

VIVIDNESS > VIVID
VIVIFIC adj giving life
VIVIFIED > VIVIFY
VIVIFIER > VIVIFY
VIVIFIERS > VIVIFY
VIVIFIES > VIVIFY
VIVIFY vb animate, inspire
VIVIFYING > VIVIFY
VIVIPARA n animal that produces offspring that develop as embryos within the female parent
VIVIPARY n act of giving birth producing offspring that have developed as embryos
VIVISECT vb subject (an animal) to vivisection
VIVISECTS > VIVISECT
VIVO adv with life and vigour
VIVRES n provisions
VIXEN n female fox
VIXENISH > VIXEN
VIXENLY > VIXEN
VIXENS > VIXEN
VIZAMENT n consultation
VIZAMENTS > VIZAMENT
VIZARD n means of disguise ▷ vb conceal by means of a disguise
VIZARDED > VIZARD
VIZARDING > VIZARD
VIZARDS > VIZARD
VIZCACHA same as > VISCACHA
VIZCACHAS > VIZCACHA
VIZIED > VIZY
VIZIER n high official in certain Muslim countries
VIZIERATE n position, rank, or authority of a vizier
VIZIERIAL > VIZIER
VIZIERS > VIZIER
VIZIES > VIZY
VIZIR same as > VIZIER
VIZIRATE > VIZIR
VIZIRATES > VIZIR
VIZIRIAL > VIZIR
VIZIRS > VIZIR
VIZIRSHIP > VIZIR
VIZOR same as > VISOR
VIZORED > VIZOR
VIZORING > VIZOR
VIZORLESS > VIZOR
VIZORS > VIZOR
VIZSLA n breed of Hungarian hunting dog with a smooth rusty-gold coat
VIZSLAS > VIZSLA
VIZY vb look
VIZYING > VIZY
VIZZIE same as > VIZY
VIZZIED > VIZZIE
VIZZIEING > VIZZIE
VIZZIES > VIZZIE
VLEI n area of low marshy ground, esp one that feeds a stream
VLEIS > VLEI
VLIES > VLY
VLY same as > VLEI
VOAR n spring
VOARS > VOAR
VOCAB n vocabulary
VOCABLE n word regarded

simply as a sequence of letters or spoken sounds ▷ adj capable of being uttered
VOCABLES > VOCABLE
VOCABLY > VOCABLE
VOCABS > VOCAB
VOCABULAR > VOCABLE
VOCAL adj relating to the voice ▷ n piece of jazz or pop music that is sung
VOCALESE n style of jazz singing
VOCALESES > VOCALESE
VOCALIC adj of, relating to, or containing a vowel or vowels
VOCALICS n non-verbal aspects of voice
VOCALION n type of musical instrument
VOCALIONS > VOCALION
VOCALISE same as > VOCALIZE
VOCALISED > VOCALISE
VOCALISER > VOCALISE
VOCALISES > VOCALISE
VOCALISM n exercise of the voice, as in singing or speaking
VOCALISMS > VOCALISM
VOCALIST n singer
VOCALISTS > VOCALIST
VOCALITY > VOCAL
VOCALIZE vb express with the voice
VOCALIZED > VOCALIZE
VOCALIZER > VOCALIZE
VOCALIZES > VOCALIZE
VOCALLY > VOCAL
VOCALNESS > VOCAL
VOCALS > VOCAL
VOCATION n profession or trade
VOCATIONS > VOCATION
VOCATIVE n (in some languages) case of nouns used when addressing a person ▷ adj relating to, used in, or characterized by calling
VOCATIVES > VOCATIVE
VOCES > VOX
VOCODER n type of synthesizer that uses the human voice as an oscillator
VOCODERS > VOCODER
VOCULAR > VOCULE
VOCULE n faint noise made when articulating certain sounds
VOCULES > VOCULE
VODKA n (Russian) spirit distilled from potatoes or grain
VODKAS > VODKA
VODOU variant of > VOODOO
VODOUN same as > VODUN
VODOUNS > VODOUN
VODOUS > VODOU
VODUN n voodoo
VODUNS > VODUN
VOE n (in Orkney and Shetland) a small bay or narrow creek
VOEMA n vigour or energy

VOEMAS > VOEMA
VOERTSAK variant of > VOETSEK
VOERTSEK variant of > VOETSEK
VOES > VOE
VOETSAK same as > VOETSEK
VOETSEK interj S African offensive expression of rejection
VOGIE adj conceited
VOGIER > VOGIE
VOGIEST > VOGIE
VOGUE n popular style ▷ adj popular or fashionable ▷ vb bring into vogue
VOGUED > VOGUE
VOGUEING n dance style of the late 1980s
VOGUEINGS > VOGUEING
VOGUER > VOGUE
VOGUERS > VOGUE
VOGUES > VOGUE
VOGUEY > VOGUE
VOGUIER > VOGUE
VOGUIEST > VOGUE
VOGUING same as > VOGUEING
VOGUINGS > VOGUING
VOGUISH > VOGUE
VOGUISHLY > VOGUE
VOICE n (quality of) sound made when speaking or singing ▷ vb express verbally
VOICED adj articulated with accompanying vibration of the vocal cords
VOICEFUL > VOICE
VOICELESS adj without a voice
VOICEMAIL n facility of leaving recorded message by telephone
VOICEOVER n spoken commentary by unseen narrator on film
VOICER > VOICE
VOICERS > VOICE
VOICES > VOICE
VOICING > VOICE
VOICINGS > VOICE
VOID adj not legally binding ▷ n feeling of deprivation ▷ vb make invalid
VOIDABLE adj capable of being voided
VOIDANCE n annulment, as of a contract
VOIDANCES > VOIDANCE
VOIDED adj (of a design) with a hole in the centre of the same shape as the design
VOIDEE n light meal eaten before bed
VOIDEES > VOIDEE
VOIDER > VOID
VOIDERS > VOID
VOIDING > VOID
VOIDINGS > VOID
VOIDNESS > VOID
VOIDS > VOID
VOILA interj word used to express satisfaction
VOILE n light semitransparent fabric

VOILES > VOILE
VOISINAGE n district or neighbourhood
VOITURE n type of vehicle
VOITURES > VOITURE
VOITURIER n driver of a voiture
VOIVODE n type of military leader
VOIVODES > VOIVODE
VOL n volume
VOLA n palm of hand or sole of foot
VOLABLE adj quick-witted
VOLAE > VOLA
VOLAGE adj changeable
VOLANT adj in a flying position
VOLANTE n Spanish horse carriage
VOLANTES > VOLANTE
VOLAR adj of or relating to the palm of the hand or the sole of the foot
VOLARIES > VOLARY
VOLARY n large bird enclosure
VOLATIC adj flying
VOLATILE adj liable to sudden change, esp in behaviour ▷ n volatile substance
VOLATILES > VOLATILE
VOLCANIAN same as > VOLCANIC
VOLCANIC adj of or relating to volcanoes
VOLCANICS n types of rock
VOLCANISE same as > VOLCANIZE
VOLCANISM n processes that result in the formation of volcanoes
VOLCANIST n person who studies volcanoes
VOLCANIZE vb subject to the effects of or change by volcanic heat
VOLCANO n mountain with a vent through which lava is ejected
VOLCANOES > VOLCANO
VOLCANOS > VOLCANO
VOLE n small rodent ▷ vb to win by taking all the tricks in a deal
VOLED > VOLE
VOLENS as in nolens volens whether willing or unwilling
VOLERIES > VOLERY
VOLERY same as > VOLARY
VOLES > VOLE
VOLET n type of veil
VOLETS > VOLET
VOLING > VOLE
VOLITANT adj flying or moving about rapidly
VOLITATE vb flutter
VOLITATED > VOLITATE
VOLITATES > VOLITATE
VOLITIENT > VOLITION
VOLITION n ability to decide things for oneself
VOLITIONS > VOLITION
VOLITIVE adj of, relating to, or emanating from

the will ▷ n (in some languages) a verb form or mood used to express a wish or desire
VOLITIVES > VOLITIVE
VOLK n people or nation, esp the nation of Afrikaners
VOLKS > VOLK
VOLKSLIED n German folk song
VOLKSRAAD n Boer assembly in South Africa in the 19th century
VOLLEY n simultaneous discharge of ammunition ▷ vb discharge (ammunition) in a volley
VOLLEYED > VOLLEY
VOLLEYER > VOLLEY
VOLLEYERS > VOLLEY
VOLLEYING > VOLLEY
VOLLEYS > VOLLEY
VOLOST n (in the former Soviet Union) a rural soviet
VOLOSTS > VOLOST
VOLPINO n Italian breed of dog
VOLPINOS > VOLPINO
VOLPLANE vb glide in an aeroplane
VOLPLANED > VOLPLANE
VOLPLANES > VOLPLANE
VOLS > VOL
VOLT n unit of electric potential
VOLTA n quick-moving Italian dance popular during the 16th and 17th centuries
VOLTAGE n electric potential difference expressed in volts
VOLTAGES > VOLTAGE
VOLTAIC adj producing an electric current
VOLTAISM another name for > GALVANISM
VOLTAISMS > VOLTAISM
VOLTE same as > VOLT
VOLTES > VOLTE
VOLTI adv musical direction
VOLTIGEUR n French infantry member
VOLTINISM n number of annual broods of an animal
VOLTMETER n instrument for measuring voltage
VOLTS > VOLT
VOLUBIL same as > VOLUBLE
VOLUBLE adj talking easily and at length
VOLUBLY > VOLUBLE
VOLUCRINE adj relating to birds
VOLUME n size of the space occupied by something ▷ vb billow or surge in volume
VOLUMED > VOLUME
VOLUMES > VOLUME
VOLUMETER n any instrument for measuring the volume of a solid, liquid, or gas
VOLUMETRY n act of measuring by volume
VOLUMINAL > VOLUME

VOLUMING > VOLUME
VOLUMISE same as > VOLUMIZE
VOLUMISED > VOLUMISE
VOLUMISES > VOLUMISE
VOLUMIST n author
VOLUMISTS > VOLUMIST
VOLUMIZE vb create volume in something
VOLUMIZED > VOLUMIZE
VOLUMIZES > VOLUMIZE
VOLUNTARY adj done by choice ▷ n organ solo in a church service
VOLUNTEER n person who offers voluntarily to do something ▷ vb offer one's services
VOLUSPA n Icelandic mythological poem
VOLUSPAS > VOLUSPA
VOLUTE n spiral or twisting turn, form, or object ▷ adj having the form of a volute
VOLUTED > VOLUTE
VOLUTES > VOLUTE
VOLUTIN n granular substance found in cells
VOLUTINS > VOLUTIN
VOLUTION n rolling, revolving, or spiral form or motion
VOLUTIONS > VOLUTION
VOLUTOID > VOLUTE
VOLVA n cup-shaped structure that sheathes the base of the stalk of certain mushrooms
VOLVAE > VOLVA
VOLVAS > VOLVA
VOLVATE > VOLVA
VOLVE vb turn over
VOLVED > VOLVE
VOLVES > VOLVE
VOLVING > VOLVE
VOLVOX n freshwater protozoan
VOLVOXES > VOLVOX
VOLVULI > VOLVULUS
VOLVULUS n abnormal twisting of the intestines causing obstruction
VOMER n thin flat bone forming part of the separation between the nasal passages in mammals
VOMERINE > VOMER
VOMERS > VOMER
VOMICA n pus-containing cavity
VOMICAE > VOMICA
VOMICAS > VOMICA
VOMIT vb eject (the contents of the stomach) through the mouth ▷ n matter vomited
VOMITED > VOMIT
VOMITER > VOMIT
VOMITERS > VOMIT
VOMITING > VOMIT
VOMITINGS > VOMIT
VOMITIVE same as > VOMITORY
VOMITIVES > VOMITIVE
VOMITO n form of yellow fever

VOMITORIA n entrances in an amphitheatre
VOMITORY adj causing vomiting ▷ n vomitory agent
VOMITOS > VOMITO
VOMITOUS adj arousing feelings of disgust
VOMITS > VOMIT
VOMITUS n matter that has been vomited
VOMITUSES > VOMITUS
VOODOO n religion involving ancestor worship and witchcraft ▷ adj of or relating to voodoo ▷ vb affect by or as if by the power of voodoo
VOODOOED > VOODOO
VOODOOING > VOODOO
VOODOOISM same as > VOODOO
VOODOOIST > VOODOO
VOODOOS > VOODOO
VOORKAMER n front room of a house
VOORSKOT n advance payment made to a farmer for crops
VOORSKOTS > VOORSKOT
VOR vb (in dialect) warn
VORACIOUS adj craving great quantities of food
VORACITY > VORACIOUS
VORAGO n chasm
VORAGOES > VORAGO
VORANT adj devouring
VORLAGE n skiing position
VORLAGES > VORLAGE
VORPAL adj sharp
VORRED > VOR
VORRING > VOR
VORS > VOR
VORTEX n whirlpool
VORTEXES > VORTEX
VORTICAL > VORTEX
VORTICES > VORTEX
VORTICISM n art movement in 20th-century England
VORTICIST > VORTICISM
VORTICITY n rotational spin in a fluid
VORTICOSE adj rotating quickly
VOSTRO as in vostro account bank account held by a foreign bank with a British bank
VOTABLE > VOTE
VOTARESS n female votary
VOTARIES > VOTARY
VOTARIST variant of > VOTARY
VOTARISTS > VOTARIST
VOTARY n person dedicated to religion or to a cause ▷ adj ardently devoted to the services or worship of God
VOTE n choice made by a participant in a shared decision ▷ vb make a choice by a vote
VOTEABLE > VOTE
VOTED > VOTE
VOTEEN n devotee

VOTEENS > VOTEEN
VOTELESS > VOTE
VOTER *n* person who can or does vote
VOTERS > VOTER
VOTES > VOTE
VOTING > VOTE
VOTINGS > VOTE
VOTIVE *adj* done or given to fulfil a vow ▷*n* votive offering
VOTIVELY > VOTIVE
VOTIVES > VOTIVE
VOTRESS > VOTARESS
VOTRESSES > VOTRESS
VOUCH *vb* give personal assurance ▷*n* act of vouching
VOUCHED > VOUCH
VOUCHEE *n* person summoned to court to defend a title
VOUCHEES > VOUCHEE
VOUCHER *n* ticket used instead of money to buy specified goods ▷*vb* summon someone to court as a vouchee
VOUCHERED > VOUCHER
VOUCHERS > VOUCHER
VOUCHES > VOUCH
VOUCHING > VOUCH
VOUCHSAFE *vb* give, entrust
VOUDON *variant of* > VOODOO
VOUDONS > VOUDON
VOUDOU *same as* > VOODOO
VOUDOUED > VOUDOU
VOUDOUING > VOUDOU
VOUDOUN *variant of* > VOODOO
VOUDOUNS > VOUDOUN
VOUDOUS > VOUDOU
VOUGE *n* form of pike used by foot soldiers in the 14th century and later
VOUGES > VOUGE
VOULGE *n* type of medieval weapon
VOULGES > VOULGE
VOULU *adj* deliberate
VOUSSOIR *n* wedge-shaped stone or brick that is used with others to construct an arch
VOUSSOIRS > VOUSSOIR
VOUTSAFE *same as* > VOUCHSAFE
VOUTSAFED > VOUTSAFE
VOUTSAFES > VOUTSAFE
VOUVRAY *n* dry white French wine
VOUVRAYS > VOUVRAY
VOW *n* solemn and binding promise ▷*vb* promise

solemnly
VOWED > VOW
VOWEL *n* speech sound made without obstructing the flow of breath ▷*vb* say as a vowel
VOWELISE *same as* > VOWELIZE
VOWELISED > VOWELISE
VOWELISES > VOWELISE
VOWELIZE *vb* mark the vowel points in (a Hebrew word or text)
VOWELIZED > VOWELIZE
VOWELIZES > VOWELIZE
VOWELLED > VOWEL
VOWELLESS > VOWEL
VOWELLING > VOWEL
VOWELLY > VOWEL
VOWELS > VOWEL
VOWER > VOW
VOWERS > VOW
VOWESS *n* nun
VOWESSES > VOWESS
VOWING > VOW
VOWLESS > VOW
VOWS > VOW
VOX *n* voice or sound
VOXEL *n* term used in computing imaging
VOXELS > VOXEL
VOYAGE *n* long journey by sea or in space ▷*vb* make a voyage
VOYAGED > VOYAGE
VOYAGER > VOYAGE
VOYAGERS > VOYAGE
VOYAGES > VOYAGE
VOYAGEUR *n* French canoeman who transported furs from trading posts in the North American interior
VOYAGEURS > VOYAGEUR
VOYAGING > VOYAGE
VOYEUR *n* person who obtains pleasure from watching people undressing or having sex
VOYEURISM > VOYEUR
VOYEURS > VOYEUR
VOZHD *n* Russian leader
VOZHDS > VOZHD
VRAIC *n* type of seaweed
VRAICKER *n* person who gathers vraic
VRAICKERS > VRAICKER
VRAICKING *n* act of gathering vraic
VRAICS > VRAIC
VRIL *n* life force
VRILS > VRIL
VROOM *interj* exclamation imitative of a car engine

revving up ▷*vb* move noisily and at high speed
VROOMED > VROOM
VROOMING > VROOM
VROOMS > VROOM
VROT *adj* South African slang for rotten
VROU *n* Afrikaner woman, esp a married woman
VROUS > VROU
VROUW *n* woman
VROUWS > VROUW
VROW *same as* > VROUW
VROWS > VROW
VUG *n* small cavity in a rock or vein, usually lined with crystals
VUGG *same as* > VUG
VUGGIER > VUG
VUGGIEST > VUG
VUGGS > VUGG
VUGGY > VUG
VUGH *same as* > VUG
VUGHIER > VUGH
VUGHIEST > VUGH
VUGHS > VUGH
VUGHY > VUG
VUGS > VUG
VULCAN *n* blacksmith
VULCANIAN *adj* of or relating to a volcanic eruption
VULCANIC *same as* > VOLCANIC
VULCANISE *same as* > VULCANIZE
VULCANISM *same as* > VOLCANISM
VULCANIST *same as* > VOLCANIST
VULCANITE *n* vulcanized rubber
VULCANIZE *vb* strengthen (rubber) by treating it with sulphur
VULCANS > VULCAN
VULGAR *adj* showing lack of good taste, decency, or refinement ▷*n* common and ignorant person
VULGARER > VULGAR
VULGAREST > VULGAR
VULGARIAN *n* vulgar (rich) person
VULGARISE *same as* > VULGARIZE
VULGARISM *n* coarse word or phrase
VULGARITY *n* condition of being vulgar
VULGARIZE *vb* make vulgar or too common
VULGARLY > VULGAR
VULGARS > VULGAR

VULGATE *n* commonly recognized text or version ▷*adj* generally accepted
VULGATES > VULGATE
VULGO *adv* generally
VULGUS *n* the common people
VULGUSES > VULGUS
VULN *vb* wound
VULNED > VULN
VULNERARY *adj* of, relating to, or used to heal a wound ▷*n* vulnerary drug or agent
VULNERATE *vb* wound
VULNING > VULN
VULNS > VULN
VULPICIDE *n* person who kills foxes
VULPINE *adj* of or like a fox
VULPINISM > VULPINE
VULPINITE *n* type of granular anhydrite
VULSELLA *n* forceps
VULSELLAE > VULSELLA
VULSELLUM *variant of* > VULSELLA
VULTURE *n* large bird that feeds on the flesh of dead animals
VULTURES > VULTURE
VULTURINE *adj* of, relating to, or resembling a vulture
VULTURISH > VULTURE
VULTURISM *n* greed
VULTURN *n* type of turkey
VULTURNS > VULTURN
VULTUROUS *same as* > VULTURINE
VULVA *n* woman's external genitals
VULVAE > VULVA
VULVAL > VULVA
VULVAR > VULVA
VULVAS > VULVA
VULVATE > VULVA
VULVIFORM > VULVA
VULVITIS *n* inflammation of the vulva
VUM *vb* swear
VUMMED > VUM
VUMMING > VUM
VUMS > VUM
VUTTIER > VUTTY
VUTTIEST > VUTTY
VUTTY *adj* dirty
VUVUZELA *n* South African instrument blown by football fans
VUVUZELAS > VUVUZELA
VYING > VIE
VYINGLY > VIE
VYINGS > VIE

Ww

WAAC n (formerly) member of the Women's Auxiliary Army Corp

WAACS > WAAC

WAB n offensive term for Mexican living in US

WABAIN same as > OUABAIN

WABAINS > WABAIN

WABBIT adj weary

WABBLE same as > WOBBLE

WABBLED > WABBLE

WABBLER > WABBLE

WABBLERS > WABBLE

WABBLES > WABBLE

WABBLIER > WABBLE

WABBLIEST > WABBLE

WABBLING > WABBLE

WABBLY > WABBLE

WABOOM another word for > WAGENBOOM

WABOOMS > WABOOM

WABS > WAB

WABSTER Scots form of > WEBSTER

WABSTERS > WABSTER

WACK n friend

WACKE n any of various soft earthy rocks that resemble or are derived from basaltic rocks

WACKER same as > WACK

WACKERS > WACKER

WACKES > WACKE

WACKEST > WACK

WACKIER > WACKY

WACKIEST > WACKY

WACKILY > WACKY

WACKINESS > WACKY

WACKO adj mad or eccentric ⊳n mad or eccentric person

WACKOS > WACKO

WACKS > WACK

WACKY adj eccentric or funny

WAD n black earthy ore of manganese ⊳n small mass of soft material ⊳vb form (something) into a wad

WADABLE > WADE

WADD same as > WAD

WADDED > WAD

WADDER > WAD

WADDERS > WAD

WADDIE same as > WADDY

WADDIED > WADDY

WADDIES > WADDY

WADDING > WAD

WADDINGS > WAD

WADDLE vb walk with short swaying steps ⊳n swaying walk

WADDLED > WADDLE

WADDLER > WADDLE

WADDLERS > WADDLE

WADDLES > WADDLE

WADDLIER > WADDLE

WADDLIEST > WADDLE

WADDLING > WADDLE

WADDLY > WADDLE

WADDS > WADD

WADDY n heavy wooden club used by Australian Aborigines ⊳vb hit with a waddy

WADDYING > WADDY

WADE vb walk with difficulty through water or mud ⊳n act or an instance of wading

WADEABLE > WADE

WADED > WADE

WADER n long-legged water bird

WADERS pl n long waterproof boots which completely cover the legs, worn by anglers for standing in water

WADES > WADE

WADI n (in N Africa and Arabia) river which is dry except in the wet season

WADIES > WADY

WADING > WADE

WADINGS > WADE

WADIS > WADI

WADMAAL same as > WADMAL

WADMAALS > WADMAAL

WADMAL n coarse thick woollen fabric, formerly woven esp in Orkney and Shetland, for outer garments

WADMALS > WADMAL

WADMEL same as > WADMAL

WADMELS > WADMEL

WADMOL same as > WADMAL

WADMOLL same as > WADMAL

WADMOLLS > WADMOLL

WADMOLS > WADMOL

WADS > WAD

WADSET vb pledge or mortgage

WADSETS > WADSET

WADSETT same as > WADSET

WADSETTED > WADSET

WADSETTER > WADSET

WADSETTS > WADSETT

WADT same as > WAD

WADTS > WADT

WADY same as > WADI

WAE old form of > WOE

WAEFUL old form of > WOEFUL

WAENESS n sorrow

WAENESSES > WAENESS

WAES > WAE

WAESOME adj sorrowful

WAESUCK interj alas

WAESUCKS interj alas

WAFER n thin crisp biscuit ⊳vb seal, fasten, or attach with a wafer

WAFERED > WAFER

WAFERING > WAFER

WAFERS > WAFER

WAFERY > WAFER

WAFF n gust or puff of air ⊳vb flutter or cause to flutter

WAFFED > WAFF

WAFFIE n person regarded as having little worth to society

WAFFIES > WAFFIE

WAFFING > WAFF

WAFFLE vb speak or write in a vague wordy way ⊳n vague wordy talk or writing

WAFFLED > WAFFLE

WAFFLER > WAFFLE

WAFFLERS > WAFFLE

WAFFLES > WAFFLE

WAFFLIER > WAFFLE

WAFFLIEST > WAFFLE

WAFFLING > WAFFLE

WAFFLINGS > WAFFLE

WAFFLY > WAFFLE

WAFFS > WAFF

WAFT vb drift or carry gently through the air ⊳n something wafted

WAFTAGE > WAFT

WAFTAGES > WAFT

WAFTED > WAFT

WAFTER n device that causes a draught

WAFTERS > WAFTER

WAFTING > WAFT

WAFTINGS > WAFT

WAFTS > WAFT

WAFTURE n act of wafting or waving

WAFTURES > WAFTURE

WAG vb move rapidly from side to side ⊳n wagging movement

WAGE n payment for work done, esp when paid weekly ⊳vb engage in (an activity)

WAGED > WAGE

WAGELESS > WAGE

WAGENBOOM n S African tree

WAGER vb bet on the outcome of something ⊳n bet on the outcome of an event or activity

WAGERED > WAGER

WAGERER > WAGER

WAGERERS > WAGER

WAGERING > WAGER

WAGERS > WAGER

WAGES > WAGE

WAGGA n blanket or bed covering made out of sacks stitched together

WAGGAS > WAGGA

WAGGED > WAG

WAGGER > WAG

WAGGERIES > WAGGERY

WAGGERS > WAG

WAGGERY n quality of being humorous

WAGGING > WAG

WAGGISH adj jocular or humorous

WAGGISHLY > WAGGISH

WAGGLE vb move with a rapid shaking or wobbling motion ⊳n rapid shaking or wobbling motion

WAGGLED > WAGGLE

WAGGLER n float only the bottom of which is attached to the fishing line

WAGGLERS > WAGGLER

WAGGLES > WAGGLE

WAGGLIER > WAGGLE

WAGGLIEST > WAGGLE

WAGGLING > WAGGLE

WAGGLY > WAGGLE

WAGGON same as > WAGON

WAGGONED > WAGGON

WAGGONER same as > WAGONER

WAGGONERS > WAGGONER

WAGGONING > WAGGON

WAGGONS > WAGGON

WAGHALTER n person likely to be hanged

WAGING > WAGE

WAGMOIRE obsolete word for > QUAGMIRE

WAGMOIRES > WAGMOIRE

WAGON n four-wheeled vehicle for heavy loads ▷ vb transport by wagon

WAGONAGE n money paid for transport by wagon

WAGONAGES > WAGONAGE

WAGONED > WAGON

WAGONER n person who drives a wagon

WAGONERS > WAGONER

WAGONETTE n light four-wheeled horse-drawn vehicle with two lengthwise seats facing each other behind a crosswise driver's seat

WAGONFUL > WAGON

WAGONFULS > WAGON

WAGONING > WAGON

WAGONLESS > WAGON

WAGONLOAD n load that is or can be carried by a wagon

WAGONS > WAGON

WAGS > WAG

WAGSOME another word for > WAGGISH

WAGTAIL n small long-tailed bird

WAGTAILS > WAGTAIL

WAHCONDA n supreme being

WAHCONDAS > WAHCONDA

WAHINE n Māori woman, esp a wife

WAHINES > WAHINE

WAHOO n food and game fish of tropical seas

WAHOOS > WAHOO

WAI n in New Zealand, water

WAIATA n Māori song

WAIATAS > WAIATA

WAID > WEIGH

WAIDE > WEIGH

WAIF n young person who is, or seems, homeless or neglected ▷ vb treat as a waif

WAIFED > WAIF

WAIFING > WAIF

WAIFISH > WAIF

WAIFLIKE > WAIF

WAIFS > WAIF

WAIFT n piece of lost property found by someone other than the owner

WAIFTS > WAIFT

WAIL vb cry out in pain or misery ▷ n mournful cry

WAILED > WAIL

WAILER > WAIL

WAILERS > WAIL

WAILFUL > WAIL

WAILFULLY > WAIL

WAILING > WAIL

WAILINGLY > WAIL

WAILINGS > WAIL

WAILS > WAIL

WAILSOME > WAIL

WAIN vb transport ▷ n farm wagon

WAINAGE n carriages, etc, for transportation of goods

WAINAGES > WAINAGE

WAINED > WAIN

WAINING > WAIN

WAINS > WAIN

WAINSCOT n wooden lining of the lower part of the walls of a room ▷ vb line (a wall of a room) with a wainscot

WAINSCOTS > WAINSCOT

WAIR vb spend

WAIRED > WAIR

WAIRING > WAIR

WAIRS > WAIR

WAIRSH variant spelling of > WERSH

WAIRSHER > WAIRSH

WAIRSHEST > WAIRSH

WAIRUA n in New Zealand, spirit or soul

WAIRUAS > WAIRUA

WAIS > WAI

WAIST n part of the trunk between the ribs and the hips

WAISTBAND n band of material sewn on to the waist of a garment to strengthen it

WAISTBELT n belt

WAISTCOAT n sleeveless garment which buttons up the front, usu worn over a shirt and under a jacket

WAISTED adj having a waist or waistlike part

WAISTER n sailor performing menial duties

WAISTERS > WAISTER

WAISTING n act of wasting

WAISTINGS > WAISTING

WAISTLESS > WAIST

WAISTLINE n (size of) the waist of a person or garment

WAISTS > WAIST

WAIT vb remain inactive in expectation (of something) ▷ n act or period of waiting

WAITE old form of > WAIT

WAITED > WAIT

WAITER n man who serves in a restaurant etc ▷ vb serve at table

WAITERAGE n service

WAITERED > WAITER

WAITERING n act of serving at table

WAITERS > WAITER

WAITES > WAITE

WAITING > WAIT

WAITINGLY > WAIT

WAITINGS > WAIT

WAITLIST n waiting list

WAITLISTS > WAITLIST

WAITRESS n woman who serves people with food and drink in a restaurant ▷ vb work as a waitress

WAITRON n waiter or waitress

WAITRONS > WAITRON

WAITS > WAIT

WAITSTAFF n waiters and waitresses collectively

WAIVE vb refrain from enforcing (a law, right, etc)

WAIVED > WAIVE

WAIVER n act or instance of voluntarily giving up a claim, right, etc

WAIVERS > WAIVER

WAIVES > WAIVE

WAIVING > WAIVE

WAIVODE same as > VOIVODE

WAIVODES > WAIVODE

WAIWODE same as > VOIVODE

WAIWODES > WAIWODE

WAKA n Māori canoe

WAKAME n edible seaweed

WAKAMES > WAKAME

WAKANDA n supernatural quality said by Native American people to be held by natural objects

WAKANDAS > WAKANDA

WAKANE n type of seaweed

WAKANES > WAKANE

WAKAS > WAKA

WAKE vb rouse from sleep or inactivity ▷ n vigil beside a corpse the night before the funeral

WAKEBOARD n short surfboard for a rider towed behind a motorboat

WAKED > WAKE

WAKEFUL adj unable to sleep

WAKEFULLY > WAKEFUL

WAKELESS adj (of sleep) deep or unbroken

WAKEMAN n watchman

WAKEMEN > WAKEMAN

WAKEN vb wake

WAKENED > WAKEN

WAKENER > WAKEN

WAKENERS > WAKEN

WAKENING > WAKEN

WAKENINGS > WAKEN

WAKENS > WAKEN

WAKER > WAKE

WAKERIFE adj watchful

WAKERS > WAKE

WAKES > WAKE

WAKF same as > WAQF

WAKFS > WAKF

WAKIKI n Melanesian shell currency

WAKIKIS > WAKIKI

WAKING > WAKE

WAKINGS > WAKE

WALD Scots form of > WELD

WALDFLUTE n organ flute stop

WALDGRAVE n (in medieval Germany) an officer with jurisdiction over a royal forest

WALDHORN n organ reed stop

WALDHORNS > WALDHORN

WALDO n gadget for manipulating objects by remote control

WALDOES > WALDO

WALDOS > WALDO

WALDRAPP n type of ibis

WALDRAPPS > WALDRAPP

WALDS > WALD

WALE same as > WEAL

WALED > WALE

WALER > WALE

WALERS > WALE

WALES > WALE

WALI same as > VALI

WALIER > WALY

WALIES > WALY

WALIEST > WALY

WALING > WALE

WALIS > WALI

WALISE same as > VALISE

WALISES > WALISE

WALK vb move on foot with at least one foot always on the ground ▷ n short journey on foot, usu for pleasure

WALKABLE > WALK

WALKABOUT n informal walk among the public by royalty etc

WALKATHON n long walk done, esp for charity

WALKAWAY n easily achieved victory

WALKAWAYS > WALKAWAY

WALKED > WALK

WALKER n person who walks

WALKERS > WALKER

WALKING adj (of a person) considered to possess the qualities of something inanimate as specified ▷ n act of walking

WALKINGS > WALKING

WALKMILL same as > WAULKMILL

WALKMILLS > WALKMILL

WALKOUT n strike

WALKOUTS > WALKOUT

WALKOVER n easy victory

WALKOVERS > WALKOVER

WALKS > WALK

WALKUP n building with stairs to upper floors

WALKUPS > WALKUP

WALKWAY n path designed for use by pedestrians

WALKWAYS > WALKWAY

WALKYRIE variant of > VALKYRIE

WALKYRIES > WALKYRIE

WALL n structure of brick, stone, etc used to enclose, divide, or support ▷ vb enclose or seal with a wall or walls

WALLA same as > WALLAH

WALLABA n type of S American tree

WALLABAS > WALLABA

WALLABIES > WALLABY

WALLABY n marsupial like a small kangaroo

WALLAH n person involved with or in charge of a specified thing

WALLAHS > WALLAH

WALLAROO n large stocky Australian kangaroo of rocky regions

WALLAROOS > WALLAROO

WALLAS > WALLA

WALLBOARD n thin board made of materials, such as compressed wood fibres or gypsum plaster, between

stiff paper, and used to cover walls, partitions, etc
WALLCHART *n* chart on wall
WALLED > WALL
WALLER > WALL
WALLERS > WALL
WALLET *n* small folding case for paper money, documents, etc
WALLETS > WALLET
WALLEYE *n* fish with large staring eyes
WALLEYED > WALLEYE
WALLEYES > WALLEYE
WALLFISH *n* snail
WALLIE *same as* > WALLY
WALLIER > WALLY
WALLIES > WALLY
WALLIEST > WALLY
WALLING > WALL
WALLINGS > WALL
WALLOP *vb* hit hard ▷ *n* hard blow
WALLOPED > WALLOP
WALLOPER *n* person or thing that wallops
WALLOPERS > WALLOPER
WALLOPING *n* thrashing ▷ *adj* large or great
WALLOPS > WALLOP
WALLOW *vb* revel in an emotion ▷ *n* act or instance of wallowing
WALLOWED > WALLOW
WALLOWER > WALLOW
WALLOWERS > WALLOW
WALLOWING > WALLOW
WALLOWS > WALLOW
WALLPAPER *n* decorative paper to cover interior walls ▷ *vb* cover (walls) with wallpaper
WALLS > WALL
WALLSEND *n* type of coal
WALLSENDS > WALLSEND
WALLWORT *n* type of plant
WALLWORTS > WALLWORT
WALLY *n* stupid person ▷ *adj* fine, pleasing, or splendid
WALLYBALL *n* ball game played on court
WALLYDRAG *n* worthless person or animal
WALNUT *n* edible nut with a wrinkled shell ▷ *adj* made from the wood of a walnut tree
WALNUTS > WALNUT
WALRUS *n* large sea mammal with long tusks
WALRUSES > WALRUS
WALTIER > WALTY
WALTIEST > WALTY
WALTY *adj* (of a ship) likely to roll over
WALTZ *n* ballroom dance ▷ *vb* dance a waltz
WALTZED > WALTZ
WALTZER *n* person who waltzes
WALTZERS > WALTZER
WALTZES > WALTZ
WALTZING > WALTZ
WALTZINGS > WALTZ
WALTZLIKE > WALTZ
WALY *same as* > WALLY
WAMBENGER *another name*

for > TUAN
WAMBLE *vb* move unsteadily ▷ *n* unsteady movement
WAMBLED > WAMBLE
WAMBLES > WAMBLE
WAMBLIER > WAMBLE
WAMBLIEST > WAMBLE
WAMBLING > WAMBLE
WAMBLINGS > WAMBLE
WAMBLY > WAMBLE
WAME *n* belly, abdomen, or womb
WAMED > WAME
WAMEFOU *Scots variant of* > WAMEFUL
WAMEFOUS
WAMEFUL *n* bellyful
WAMEFULS > WAMEFUL
WAMES > WAME
WAMMUL *n* dog
WAMMULS > WAMMUL
WAMMUS *same as* > WAMUS
WAMMUSES > WAMMUS
WAMPEE *n* type of Asian fruit tree
WAMPEES > WAMPEE
WAMPISH *vb* wave
WAMPISHED > WAMPISH
WAMPISHES > WAMPISH
WAMPUM *n* shells woven together, formerly used by Native Americans for money and ornament
WAMPUMS > WAMPUM
WAMPUS *same as* > WAMUS
WAMPUSES > WAMPUS
WAMUS *n* type of cardigan or jacket
WAMUSES > WAMUS
WAN *adj* pale and sickly looking ▷ *vb* make or become wan
WANCHANCY *adj* infelicitous
WAND *n* thin rod, esp one used in performing magic tricks
WANDER *vb* move about without a definite destination or aim ▷ *n* act or instance of wandering
WANDERED > WANDER
WANDERER > WANDER
WANDERERS > WANDER
WANDERING > WANDER
WANDEROO *n* macaque monkey of India and Sri Lanka, having black fur with a ruff of long greyish fur on each side of the face
WANDEROOS > WANDEROO
WANDERS > WANDER
WANDLE *adj* supple
WANDLIKE > WAND
WANDOO *n* eucalyptus tree of W Australia, having white bark and durable wood
WANDOOS > WANDOO
WANDS > WAND
WANE *vb* decrease gradually in size or strength
WANED > WANE
WANES > WANE
WANEY > WANE
WANG *n* cheekbone
WANGAN *same as* > WANIGAN
WANGANS > WANGAN
WANGLE *vb* get by devious

methods ▷ *n* act or an instance of wangling
WANGLED > WANGLE
WANGLER > WANGLE
WANGLERS > WANGLE
WANGLES > WANGLE
WANGLING > WANGLE
WANGLINGS > WANGLE
WANGS > WANG
WANGUN *same as* > WANIGAN
WANGUNS > WANGUN
WANHOPE *n* delusion
WANHOPES > WANHOPE
WANIER > WANY
WANIEST > WANY
WANIGAN *n* provisions for camp
WANIGANS > WANIGAN
WANING > WANE
WANINGS > WANE
WANION *n* vehemence
WANIONS > WANION
WANK *vb* slang word for masturbate ▷ *n* instance of masturbating ▷ *adj* bad, useless, or worthless
WANKED > WANK
WANKER *n* slang word for worthless or stupid person
WANKERS > WANKER
WANKIER > WANKY
WANKIEST > WANKY
WANKING > WANK
WANKLE *adj* unstable
WANKS > WANK
WANKSTA *n* derogatory slang word for a person who acts or dresses like a gangster but who is not involved in crime
WANKSTAS > WANKSTA
WANKY *adj* slang word for pretentious
WANLE *same as* > WANDLE
WANLY > WAN
WANNA *vb* spelling of **want to** intended to reflect a dialectal or informal pronunciation
WANNABE *adj* wanting to be, or be like, a particular person or thing ▷ *n* person who wants to be, or be like, a particular person or thing
WANNABEE *same as* > WANNABE
WANNABEES > WANNABEE
WANNABES > WANNABE
WANNED > WAN
WANNEL *same as* > WANDLE
WANNER > WAN
WANNESS > WAN
WANNESSES > WAN
WANNEST > WAN
WANNIGAN *same as* > WANIGAN
WANNIGANS > WANNIGAN
WANNING > WAN
WANNISH *adj* rather wan
WANS > WAN
WANT *vb* need or long for ▷ *n* act or instance of wanting
WANTAGE *n* shortage
WANTAGES > WANTAGE
WANTED > WANT
WANTER > WANT
WANTERS > WANT

WANTHILL *n* molehill
WANTHILLS > WANTHILL
WANTIES > WANTY
WANTING *adj* lacking ▷ *prep* without
WANTINGS > WANT
WANTON *adj* without motive, provocation, or justification ▷ *n* sexually unrestrained or immodest woman ▷ *vb* behave in a wanton manner
WANTONED > WANTON
WANTONER > WANTON
WANTONERS > WANTON
WANTONEST > WANTON
WANTONING > WANTON
WANTONISE *same as* > WANTONIZE
WANTONIZE *vb* behave wantonly
WANTONLY > WANTON
WANTONS > WANTON
WANTS > WANT
WANTY *adj* belt
WANWORDY *adj* without merit
WANWORTH *n* inexpensive purchase
WANWORTHS > WANWORTH
WANY > WANE
WANZE *vb* wane
WANZED > WANZE
WANZES > WANZE
WANZING > WANZE
WAP *vb* strike
WAPENSHAW *n* showing of weapons
WAPENTAKE *n* subdivision of certain shires or counties, esp in the Midlands and North of England
WAPINSHAW *same as* > WAPENSHAW
WAPITI *n* large N American deer, now also common in New Zealand
WAPITIS > WAPITI
WAPPED > WAP
WAPPEND *adj* tired
WAPPER *vb* blink
WAPPERED > WAPPER
WAPPERING > WAPPER
WAPPERS > WAPPER
WAPPING > WAP
WAPS > WAP
WAQF *n* endowment in Muslim law
WAQFS > WAQF
WAR *n* fighting between nations ▷ *adj* of, like, or caused by war ▷ *vb* conduct a war
WARAGI *n* Ugandan alcoholic drink made from bananas
WARAGIS > WARAGI
WARATAH *n* Australian shrub with crimson flowers
WARATAHS > WARATAH
WARB *n* dirty or insignificant person
WARBIER > WARB
WARBIEST > WARB
WARBLE *vb* sing in a trilling voice ▷ *n* act or an instance of warbling

WARBLED > WARBLE

WARBLER *n* any of various small songbirds

WARBLERS > WARBLER

WARBLES > WARBLE

WARBLING > WARBLE

WARBLINGS > WARBLE

WARBONNET *n* headband with trailing feathers worn by certain North American Indian warriors

WARBS > WARB

WARBY > WARB

WARCRAFT *n* skill in warfare

WARCRAFTS > WARCRAFT

WARD *n* room in a hospital for patients needing a similar kind of care ▷ *vb* guard or protect

WARDCORN *n* payment of corn

WARDCORNS > WARDCORN

WARDED > WARD

WARDEN *n* person in charge of a building and its occupants ▷ *vb* act as a warden

WARDENED > WARDEN

WARDENING > WARDEN

WARDENRY > WARDEN

WARDENS > WARDEN

WARDER *vb* guard ▷ *n* prison officer

WARDERED > WARDER

WARDERING > WARDER

WARDERS > WARDER

WARDIAN as in *wardian case* type of glass container for housing delicate plants

WARDING > WARD

WARDINGS > WARD

WARDLESS > WARD

WARDMOTE *n* assembly of the citizens or liverymen of an area

WARDMOTES > WARDMOTE

WARDOG *n* veteran warrior

WARDOGS > WARDOG

WARDRESS *n* female officer in charge of prisoners in a jail

WARDROBE *n* cupboard for hanging clothes in

WARDROBED > WARDROBE

WARDROBER *n* person in charge of someone's wardrobe

WARDROBES > WARDROBE

WARDROOM *n* officers' quarters on a warship

WARDROOMS > WARDROOM

WARDROP *obsolete form of* > WARDROBE

WARDROPS > WARDROP

WARDS > WARD

WARDSHIP *n* state of being a ward

WARDSHIPS > WARDSHIP

WARE *n* articles of a specified type or material ▷ *vb* spend or squander

WARED > WARE

WAREHOU *n* any of several edible saltwater New Zealand fish

WAREHOUSE *n* building for storing goods prior to sale

or distribution ▷ *vb* store or place in a warehouse, esp a bonded warehouse

WARELESS *adj* careless

WAREROOM *n* store-room

WAREROOMS > WAREROOM

WARES *pl n* goods for sale

WAREZ *pl n* illegally copied computer software which has had its protection codes de-activated

WARFARE *vb* engage in war ▷ *n* fighting or hostilities

WARFARED > WARFARE

WARFARER > WARFARE

WARFARERS > WARFARE

WARFARES > WARFARE

WARFARIN *n* crystalline compound, used as a medical anticoagulant

WARFARING > WARFARE

WARFARINS > WARFARIN

WARHABLE *adj* able to fight in war

WARHEAD *n* explosive front part of a missile

WARHEADS > WARHEAD

WARHORSE *n* (formerly) a horse used in battle

WARHORSES > WARHORSE

WARIBASHI *n* disposable chopsticks

WARIER > WARY

WARIEST > WARY

WARILY > WARY

WARIMENT *n* caution

WARIMENTS > WARIMENT

WARINESS > WARY

WARING > WARE

WARISON *n* (esp formerly) a bugle note used as an order to a military force to attack

WARISONS > WARISON

WARK *Scots form of* > WORK

WARKED > WARK

WARKING > WARK

WARKS > WARK

WARLESS > WAR

WARLIKE *adj* of or relating to war

WARLING *n* one who is not liked

WARLINGS > WARLING

WARLOCK *n* man who practises black magic

WARLOCKRY *n* witchcraft

WARLOCKS > WARLOCK

WARLORD *n* military leader of a nation or part of a nation

WARLORDS > WARLORD

WARM *adj* moderately hot ▷ *vb* make or become warm ▷ *n* warm place or area

WARMAKER *n* one who wages war

WARMAKERS > WARMAKER

WARMAN *n* one experienced in warfare

WARMBLOOD *n* type of horse

WARMED > WARM

WARMEN > WARMAN

WARMER > WARM

WARMERS > WARM

WARMEST > WARM

WARMING > WARM

WARMINGS > WARM

WARMISH > WARM

WARMLY > WARM

WARMNESS > WARM

WARMONGER *n* person who encourages war

WARMOUTH *n* type of fish

WARMOUTHS > WARMOUTH

WARMS > WARM

WARMTH *n* mild heat

WARMTHS > WARMTH

WARMUP *n* preparatory exercise routine

WARMUPS > WARMUP

WARN *vb* make aware of possible danger or harm

WARNED > WARN

WARNER > WARN

WARNERS > WARN

WARNING *n* something that warns ▷ *adj* giving or serving as a warning

WARNINGLY > WARNING

WARNINGS > WARNING

WARNS > WARN

WARP *vb* twist out of shape ▷ *n* state of being warped

WARPAGE > WARP

WARPAGES > WARP

WARPATH *n* route taken by Native Americans on a warlike expedition

WARPATHS > WARPATH

WARPED > WARP

WARPER > WARP

WARPERS > WARP

WARPING > WARP

WARPINGS > WARP

WARPLANE *n* any aircraft designed for and used in warfare

WARPLANES > WARPLANE

WARPOWER *n* ability to wage war

WARPOWERS > WARPOWER

WARPS > WARP

WARPWISE *adv* (weaving) in the direction of the warp

WARRAGAL *same as* > WARRIGAL

WARRAGALS > WARRAGAL

WARRAGLE *same as* > WARRIGAL

WARRAGLES > WARRAGLE

WARRAGUL *same as* > WARRIGAL

WARRAGULS > WARRAGUL

WARRAN *same as* > WARRANT

WARRAND *same as* > WARRANT

WARRANDED > WARRAND

WARRANDS > WARRAND

WARRANED > WARRAN

WARRANING > WARRAN

WARRANS > WARRAN

WARRANT *n* (document giving) official authorization ▷ *vb* make necessary

WARRANTED > WARRANT

WARRANTEE *n* person to whom a warranty is given

WARRANTER > WARRANT

WARRANTOR *n* person or company that provides a warranty

WARRANTS > WARRANT

WARRANTY *n* (document giving) a guarantee

WARRAY *vb* wage war on

WARRAYED > WARRAY

WARRAYING > WARRAY

WARRAYS > WARRAY

WARRE *same as* > WAR

WARRED > WAR

WARREN *n* series of burrows in which rabbits live

WARRENER *n* gamekeeper or keeper of a warren

WARRENERS > WARRENER

WARRENS > WARREN

WARREY *same as* > WARRAY

WARREYED > WARREY

WARREYING > WARREY

WARREYS > WARREY

WARRIGAL *n* dingo ▷ *adj* wild

WARRIGALS > WARRIGAL

WARRING > WAR

WARRIOR *n* person who fights in a war

WARRIORS > WARRIOR

WARRISON *same as* > WARISON

WARRISONS > WARRISON

WARS > WAR

WARSAW *n* type of grouper fish

WARSAWS > WARSAW

WARSHIP *n* ship designed and equipped for naval combat

WARSHIPS > WARSHIP

WARSLE *dialect word for* > WRESTLE

WARSLED > WARSLE

WARSLER > WARSLE

WARSLERS > WARSLE

WARSLES > WARSLE

WARSLING > WARSLE

WARST *obsolete form of* > WORST

WARSTLE *dialect form of* > WRESTLE

WARSTLED > WARSTLE

WARSTLER > WARSTLE

WARSTLERS > WARSTLE

WARSTLES > WARSTLE

WARSTLING > WARSTLE

WART *n* small hard growth on the skin

WARTED > WART

WARTHOG *n* wild African pig with heavy tusks, wartlike lumps on the face, and a mane of coarse hair

WARTHOGS > WARTHOG

WARTIER > WART

WARTIEST > WART

WARTIME *n* time of war ▷ *adj* of or in a time of war

WARTIMES > WARTIME

WARTLESS > WART

WARTLIKE > WART

WARTS > WART

WARTWEED *n* type of plant

WARTWEEDS > WARTWEED

WARTWORT *another word for* > WARTWEED

WARTWORTS > WARTWORT

WARTY > WART

WARWOLF *n* Roman engine of war

WARWOLVES > WARWOLF

WARWORK *n* work contributing to war effort

WARWORKS > WARWORK

WARWORN adj worn down by war

WARY adj watchful or cautious

WARZONE n area where a war is taking place or there is some other violent conflict

WARZONES > WARZONE

WAS vb form of the subjunctive mood used in place of were, esp in conditional sentences

WASABI n Japanese cruciferous plant cultivated for its thick green pungent root

WASABIS > WASABI

WASE n pad to relieve pressure of load carried on head

WASES > WASE

WASH vb clean (oneself, clothes, etc) with water and usu soap ▷ n act or process of washing

WASHABLE n thing that can be washed ▷ adj (esp of fabrics or clothes) capable of being washed without deteriorating

WASHABLES > WASHABLE

WASHAWAY another word for > WASHOUT

WASHAWAYS > WASHAWAY

WASHBALL n ball of soap

WASHBALLS > WASHBALL

WASHBASIN n basin for washing the face and hands

WASHBOARD n board having a surface, usually of corrugated metal, on which esp formerly, clothes were scrubbed

WASHBOWL same as > WASHBASIN

WASHBOWLS > WASHBOWL

WASHCLOTH n small piece of cloth used to wash the face and hands

WASHDAY n day on which clothes and linen are washed, often the same day each week

WASHDAYS > WASHDAY

WASHED > WASH

WASHEN > WASH

WASHER n ring put under a nut or bolt or in a tap as a seal ▷ vb fit with a washer

WASHERED > WASHER

WASHERIES > WASHERY

WASHERING > WASHER

WASHERMAN n man who washes clothes for a living

WASHERMEN > WASHERMAN

WASHERS > WASHER

WASHERY n plant at a mine where water or other liquid is used to remove dirt from a mineral, esp coal

WASHES > WASH

WASHHOUSE n (formerly) building in which laundry was done

WASHIER > WASHY

WASHIEST > WASHY

WASHILY > WASHY

WASHIN n increase in the angle of attack of an aircraft wing towards the wing tip

WASHINESS > WASHY

WASHING n clothes to be washed

WASHINGS > WASHING

WASHINS > WASHIN

WASHLAND n frequently-flooded plain

WASHLANDS > WASHLAND

WASHOUT n complete failure

WASHOUTS > WASHOUT

WASHPOT n pot for washing things in

WASHPOTS > WASHPOT

WASHRAG same as > WASHCLOTH

WASHRAGS > WASHRAG

WASHROOM n toilet

WASHROOMS > WASHROOM

WASHSTAND n piece of furniture designed to hold a basin for washing the face and hands in

WASHTUB n tub or large container used for washing anything, esp clothes

WASHTUBS > WASHTUB

WASHUP n outcome of a process

WASHUPS > WASHUP

WASHWIPE n windscreen spray-cleaning mechanism

WASHWIPES > WASHWIPE

WASHWOMAN n woman who washes clothes for a living

WASHWOMEN > WASHWOMAN

WASHY adj overdiluted or weak

WASM n obsolete belief

WASMS > WASM

WASP n stinging insect with a slender black-and-yellow striped body

WASPIE n tight-waited corset

WASPIER > WASP

WASPIES > WASPIE

WASPIEST > WASP

WASPILY > WASP

WASPINESS > WASP

WASPISH adj bad-tempered

WASPISHLY > WASPISH

WASPLIKE > WASP

WASPNEST n nest of wasp

WASPNESTS > WASPNEST

WASPS > WASP

WASPY > WASP

WASSAIL n formerly, festivity when much drinking took place ▷ vb drink health of (a person) at a wassail

WASSAILED > WASSAIL

WASSAILER > WASSAIL

WASSAILRY > WASSAIL

WASSAILS > WASSAIL

WASSERMAN n man-shaped sea monster

WASSERMEN > WASSERMAN

WASSUP sentence substitute what is happening?

WAST singular form of the past tense of > BE

WASTABLE > WASTE

WASTAGE n loss by wear or waste

WASTAGES > WASTAGE

WASTE vb use pointlessly or thoughtlessly ▷ n act of wasting or state of being wasted ▷ adj rejected as worthless or surplus to requirements

WASTED > WASTE

WASTEFUL adj extravagant

WASTEL n fine bread or cake

WASTELAND n barren or desolate area of land

WASTELOT n piece of waste ground in a city

WASTELOTS > WASTELOT

WASTELS > WASTEL

WASTENESS > WASTE

WASTER vb waste ▷ n layabout

WASTERED > WASTER

WASTERFUL Scots variant of > WASTEFUL

WASTERIE same as > WASTERY

WASTERIES > WASTERIE

WASTERING > WASTER

WASTERS > WASTER

WASTERY n extravagance

WASTES > WASTE

WASTEWAY n open ditch

WASTEWAYS > WASTEWAY

WASTEWEIR another name for > SPILLWAY

WASTFULL obsolete form of > WASTEFUL

WASTING adj reducing the vitality and strength of the body

WASTINGLY > WASTING

WASTINGS > WASTE

WASTNESS n obsolete form of wasteness

WASTREL n lazy or worthless person

WASTRELS > WASTREL

WASTRIE same as > WASTERY

WASTRIES > WASTRIE

WASTRIFE n wastefulness

WASTRIFES > WASTRIFE

WASTRY n wastefulness

WASTS > WAST

WAT n Thai Buddhist monastery or temple

WATAP n stringy thread made by Native Americans from the roots of conifers

WATAPE same as > WATAP

WATAPES > WATAPE

WATAPS > WATAP

WATCH vb look at closely ▷ n portable timepiece for the wrist or pocket

WATCHABLE adj interesting, enjoyable, or entertaining

WATCHBAND n watch strap

WATCHBOX n sentry's box

WATCHCASE n protective case for a watch, generally of metal such as gold, silver, brass, or gunmetal

WATCHCRY n slogan used to rally support

WATCHDOG n dog kept to guard property

WATCHDOGS > WATCHDOG

WATCHED > WATCH

WATCHER n person who watches

WATCHERS > WATCHER

WATCHES > WATCH

WATCHET n shade of blue

WATCHETS > WATCHET

WATCHEYE n eye with a light-coloured iris

WATCHEYES > WATCHEYE

WATCHFUL adj vigilant or alert

WATCHING > WATCH

WATCHLIST n list of things to be monitored

WATCHMAN n man employed to guard a building or property

WATCHMEN > WATCHMAN

WATCHOUT n lookout

WATCHOUTS > WATCHOUT

WATCHWORD n word or phrase that sums up the attitude of a particular group

WATE > WIT

WATER n clear colourless tasteless liquid that falls as rain and forms rivers etc ▷ vb put water on or into

WATERAGE n transportation of cargo by means of ships, or the charges for such transportation

WATERAGES > WATERAGE

WATERBED n watertight mattress filled with water

WATERBEDS > WATERBED

WATERBIRD n any aquatic bird

WATERBUCK n any of various antelopes of the swampy areas of Africa, having long curved ridged horns

WATERBUS n boat offering regular transport service

WATERDOG n dog trained to hunt in water

WATERDOGS > WATERDOG

WATERED > WATER

WATERER > WATER

WATERERS > WATER

WATERFALL n place where the waters of a river drop vertically

WATERFOWL n bird that swims on water, such as a duck or swan

WATERHEAD n source of river

WATERHEN another name for > GALLINULE

WATERHENS > WATERHEN

WATERIER > WATERY

WATERIEST > WATERY

WATERILY > WATERY

WATERING > WATER

WATERINGS > WATER

WATERISH > WATER

WATERJET n jet of water

WATERJETS > WATERJET

WATERLEAF n carved column design

WATERLESS > WATER

WATERLILY n any of various

aquatic plants having large leaves and showy flowers that float on the surface of the water

WATERLINE n level to which a ship's hull will be immersed when afloat

WATERLOG vb flood with water

WATERLOGS > WATERLOG

WATERLOO n total defeat

WATERLOOS > WATERLOO

WATERMAN n skilled boatman

WATERMARK n faint translucent design in a sheet of paper ▷ vb mark (paper) with a watermark

WATERMEN > WATERMAN

WATERPOX n chickenpox

WATERS > WATER

WATERSHED n important period or factor serving as a dividing line

WATERSIDE n area of land beside a river or lake

WATERSKI vb ski on water towed behind motorboat

WATERSKIS > WATERSKI

WATERWAY n river, canal, or other navigable channel used as a means of travel or transport

WATERWAYS > WATERWAY

WATERWEED n any of various weedy aquatic plants

WATERWORK n machinery, etc for storing, purifying, and distributing water

WATERWORN adj worn smooth by the action or passage of water

WATERY adj of, like, or containing water

WATERZOOI n type of Flemish stew

WATS > WAT

WATT n unit of power

WATTAGE n electrical power expressed in watts

WATTAGES > WATTAGE

WATTAPE same as > WATAP

WATTAPES > WATTAPE

WATTER > WAT

WATTEST > WAT

WATTHOUR n unit of energy equal to the power of one watt operating for an hour

WATTHOURS > WATTHOUR

WATTLE n branches woven over sticks to make a fence ▷ adj made of, formed by, or covered with wattle ▷ vb construct from wattle

WATTLED > WATTLE

WATTLES > WATTLE

WATTLESS > WATT

WATTLING > WATTLE

WATTLINGS > WATTLE

WATTMETER n meter for measuring electric power in watts

WATTS > WATT

WAUCHT same as > WAUGHT

WAUCHTED > WAUCHT

WAUCHTING > WAUCHT

WAUCHTS > WAUCHT

WAUFF same as > WAFF

WAUFFED > WAUFF

WAUFFING > WAUFF

WAUFFS > WAUFF

WAUGH vb bark

WAUGHED > WAUGH

WAUGHING > WAUGH

WAUGHS > WAUGH

WAUGHT vb drink in large amounts

WAUGHTED > WAUGHT

WAUGHTING > WAUGHT

WAUGHTS > WAUGHT

WAUK vb full (cloth)

WAUKED > WAUK

WAUKER > WAUK

WAUKERS > WAUK

WAUKING > WAUK

WAUKMILL same as > WAULKMILL

WAUKMILLS > WAUKMILL

WAUKRIFE variant of > WAKERIFE

WAUKS > WAUK

WAUL vb cry or wail plaintively like a cat

WAULED > WAUL

WAULING > WAUL

WAULINGS > WAUL

WAULK same as > WAUK

WAULKED > WAULK

WAULKER > WAULK

WAULKERS > WAULK

WAULKING > WAULK

WAULKMILL n cloth-fulling mill

WAULKS > WAULK

WAULS > WAUL

WAUR obsolete form of > WAR

WAURED > WAUR

WAURING > WAUR

WAURS > WAUR

WAURST > WAUR

WAVE vb move the hand to and fro as a greeting or signal ▷ n moving ridge on water

WAVEBAND n range of wavelengths or frequencies used for a particular type of radio transmission

WAVEBANDS > WAVEBAND

WAVED > WAVE

WAVEFORM n shape of the graph of a wave or oscillation obtained by plotting the value of some changing quantity against time

WAVEFORMS > WAVEFORM

WAVEFRONT n surface associated with a propagating wave and passing through all points in the wave that have the same phase

WAVEGUIDE n solid rod of dielectric or a hollow metal tube, usually of rectangular cross section, used as a path to guide microwaves

WAVELESS > WAVE

WAVELET n small wave

WAVELETS > WAVELET

WAVELIKE > WAVE

WAVELLITE n greyish-white, yellow, or brown mineral

WAVEMETER n instrument for measuring the frequency or wavelength of radio waves

WAVEOFF n signal or instruction to an aircraft not to land

WAVEOFFS > WAVEOFF

WAVER vb hesitate or be irresolute ▷ n act or an instance of wavering

WAVERED > WAVER

WAVERER > WAVER

WAVERERS > WAVER

WAVERIER > WAVERY

WAVERIEST > WAVERY

WAVERING > WAVER

WAVERINGS > WAVER

WAVEROUS same as > WAVERY

WAVERS > WAVER

WAVERY adj lacking firmness

WAVES > WAVE

WAVESHAPE another word for > WAVEFORM

WAVESON n goods floating on waves after shipwreck

WAVESONS > WAVESON

WAVEY n snow goose or other wild goose

WAVEYS > WAVEY

WAVICLE n origin of wave

WAVICLES > WAVICLE

WAVIER > WAVY

WAVIES > WAVY

WAVIEST > WAVY

WAVILY > WAVY

WAVINESS > WAVY

WAVING > WAVE

WAVINGS > WAVE

WAVY adj having curves ▷ n snow goose or other wild goose

WAW another name for > VAV

WAWA n speech ▷ vb speak

WAWAED > WAWA

WAWAING > WAWA

WAWAS > WAWA

WAWE same as > WAW

WAWES > WAWE

WAWL same as > WAUL

WAWLED > WAWL

WAWLING > WAWL

WAWLINGS > WAWL

WAWLS > WAWL

WAWS > WAW

WAX n solid shiny fatty or oily substance used for sealing, making candles, etc ▷ vb coat or polish with wax

WAXABLE > WAX

WAXBERRY n waxy fruit of the wax myrtle or the snowberry

WAXBILL n any of various chiefly African finchlike weaverbirds

WAXBILLS > WAXBILL

WAXCLOTH another name for > OILCLOTH

WAXCLOTHS > WAXCLOTH

WAXED > WAX

WAXEN adj made of or like wax

WAXER > WAX

WAXERS > WAX

WAXES > WAX

WAXEYE n small New Zealand bird with a white circle round its eye

WAXEYES > WAXEYE

WAXFLOWER n any of various plants with waxy flowers

WAXIER > WAXY

WAXIEST > WAXY

WAXILY > WAXY

WAXINESS > WAXY

WAXING > WAX

WAXINGS > WAX

WAXLIKE > WAX

WAXPLANT n climbing shrub of E Asia and Australia

WAXPLANTS > WAXPLANT

WAXWEED n type of wild flower

WAXWEEDS > WAXWEED

WAXWING n type of songbird

WAXWINGS > WAXWING

WAXWORK n lifelike wax model of a (famous) person

WAXWORKER > WAXWORK

WAXWORKS > WAXWORK

WAXWORM n waxmoth larva

WAXWORMS > WAXWORM

WAXY adj resembling wax in colour, appearance, or texture

WAY n manner or method ▷ vb travel

WAYBILL n document stating the nature, origin, and destination of goods being transported

WAYBILLS > WAYBILL

WAYBOARD n thin geological seam separating larger strata

WAYBOARDS > WAYBOARD

WAYBREAD n plantain

WAYBREADS > WAYBREAD

WAYED > WAY

WAYFARE vb travel

WAYFARED > WAYFARE

WAYFARER n traveller

WAYFARERS > WAYFARER

WAYFARES > WAYFARE

WAYFARING > WAYFARE

WAYGOING n leaving

WAYGOINGS > WAYGOING

WAYGONE adj travel-weary

WAYGOOSE same as > WAYZGOOSE

WAYGOOSES > WAYGOOSE

WAYING > WAY

WAYLAID > WAYLAY

WAYLAY vb lie in wait for and accost or attack

WAYLAYER > WAYLAY

WAYLAYERS > WAYLAY

WAYLAYING > WAYLAY

WAYLAYS > WAYLAY

WAYLEAVE n access to property granted by a landowner for payment

WAYLEAVES > WAYLEAVE

WAYLEGGO interj away here! let go!

WAYLESS > WAY

WAYMARK n symbol or signpost marking the route of a footpath ▷ vb mark out with waymarks

WAYMARKED > WAYMARK

WAYMARKS > WAYMARK

w

WAYMENT vb express grief
WAYMENTED > WAYMENT
WAYMENTS > WAYMENT
WAYPOINT n stopping point on route
WAYPOINTS > WAYPOINT
WAYPOST n signpost
WAYPOSTS > WAYPOST
WAYS > WAY
WAYSIDE n side of a road
WAYSIDES > WAYSIDE
WAYWARD adj erratic, selfish, or stubborn
WAYWARDLY > WAYWARD
WAYWISER n device for measuring distance
WAYWISERS > WAYWISER
WAYWODE n Slavonic governor
WAYWODES > WAYWODE
WAYWORN adj worn or tired by travel
WAYZGOOSE n works outing made annually by a printing house
WAZIR another word for > VIZIER
WAZIRS > WAZIR
WAZOO n slang word for person's bottom
WAZOOS > WAZOO
WAZZOCK n foolish or annoying person
WAZZOCKS > WAZZOCK
WE pron speaker or writer and one or more others
WEAK adj lacking strength
WEAKEN vb make or become weak
WEAKENED > WEAKEN
WEAKENER > WEAKEN
WEAKENERS > WEAKEN
WEAKENING > WEAKEN
WEAKENS > WEAKEN
WEAKER > WEAK
WEAKEST > WEAK
WEAKFISH n any of several sea trouts
WEAKISH > WEAK
WEAKISHLY > WEAK
WEAKLIER > WEAKLY
WEAKLIEST > WEAKLY
WEAKLING n feeble person or animal
WEAKLINGS > WEAKLING
WEAKLY adv feebly ▷ adj weak or sickly
WEAKNESS n being weak
WEAKON n subatomic particle
WEAKONS > WEAKON
WEAKSIDE n (in basketball) side of court away from ball
WEAKSIDES > WEAKSIDE
WEAL n raised mark left on the skin by a blow
WEALD n open or forested country
WEALDS > WEALD
WEALS > WEAL
WEALSMAN n statesman
WEALSMEN > WEALSMAN
WEALTH n state of being rich
WEALTHIER > WEALTHY
WEALTHILY > WEALTHY
WEALTHS > WEALTH
WEALTHY adj possessing wealth

WEAMB same as > WAME
WEAMBS > WEAMB
WEAN vb accustom (a baby or young mammal) to food other than mother's milk
WEANED > WEAN
WEANEL n recently-weaned child or animal
WEANELS > WEANEL
WEANER n person or thing that weans
WEANERS > WEANER
WEANING > WEAN
WEANINGS > WEAN
WEANLING n child or young animal recently weaned
WEANLINGS > WEANLING
WEANS > WEAN
WEAPON vb arm ▷ n object used in fighting
WEAPONED > WEAPON
WEAPONEER n person associated with the use or maintenance of weapons, esp nuclear weapons
WEAPONING > WEAPON
WEAPONISE same as > WEAPONIZE
WEAPONIZE vb adapt (a chemical, bacillus, etc) in such a way that it can be used as a weapon
WEAPONRY n weapons collectively
WEAPONS > WEAPON
WEAR vb have on the body as clothing or ornament ▷ n clothes suitable for a particular time or purpose
WEARABLE adj suitable for wear or able to be worn ▷ n any garment that can be worn
WEARABLES > WEARABLE
WEARED > WEAR
WEARER > WEAR
WEARERS > WEAR
WEARIED > WEARY
WEARIER > WEARY
WEARIES > WEARY
WEARIEST > WEARY
WEARIFUL same as > WEARISOME
WEARILESS adj not wearied or able to be wearied
WEARILY > WEARY
WEARINESS > WEARY
WEARING adj tiring ▷ n act of wearing
WEARINGLY > WEARING
WEARINGS > WEAR
WEARISH adj withered
WEARISOME adj tedious
WEARPROOF adj resistant to damage from normal wear or usage
WEARS > WEAR
WEARY adj tired or exhausted ▷ vb make or become weary
WEARYING > WEARY
WEASAND former name for the > TRACHEA
WEASANDS > WEASAND
WEASEL n small carnivorous mammal with a long body

and short legs ▷ vb use ambiguous language to avoid speaking directly or honestly
WEASELED > WEASEL
WEASELER > WEASEL
WEASELERS > WEASEL
WEASELING > WEASEL
WEASELLED > WEASEL
WEASELLER > WEASEL
WEASELLY > WEASEL
WEASELS > WEASEL
WEASELY > WEASEL
WEASON Scots form of > WEASAND
WEASONS > WEASON
WEATHER n day-to-day atmospheric conditions of a place ▷ vb (cause to) be affected by the weather
WEATHERED adj affected by exposure to the action of the weather
WEATHERER > WEATHER
WEATHERLY adj (of a sailing vessel) making very little leeway when close-hauled, even in a stiff breeze
WEATHERS > WEATHER
WEAVE vb make (fabric) by interlacing (yarn) on a loom
WEAVED > WEAVE
WEAVER n person who weaves, esp as a means of livelihood
WEAVERS > WEAVER
WEAVES > WEAVE
WEAVING > WEAVE
WEAVINGS > WEAVE
WEAZAND same as > WEASAND
WEAZANDS > WEAZAND
WEAZEN same as > WIZEN
WEAZENED > WEAZEN
WEAZENING > WEAZEN
WEAZENS > WEAZEN
WEB n net spun by a spider ▷ vb cover with or as if with a web
WEBBED > WEB
WEBBIE n person who is well versed in the use the World Wide Web
WEBBIER > WEBBY
WEBBIES > WEBBIE
WEBBIEST > WEBBY
WEBBING n anything that forms a web
WEBBINGS > WEBBING
WEBBY adj of, relating to, resembling, or consisting of a web
WEBCAM n camera that transmits images over the internet
WEBCAMS > WEBCAM
WEBCAST n broadcast of an event over the internet ▷ vb make such a broadcast
WEBCASTED > WEBCAST
WEBCASTER > WEBCAST
WEBCASTS > WEBCAST
WEBER n SI unit of magnetic flux
WEBERS > WEBER
WEBFED adj (of printing press) printing from rolls

of paper
WEBFEET > WEBFOOT
WEBFOOT n foot having the toes connected by folds of skin
WEBFOOTED > WEBFOOT
WEBINAR n interactive seminar conducted over the World Wide Web
WEBINARS > WEBINAR
WEBLESS > WEB
WEBLIKE > WEB
WEBLISH n shorthand form of English that is used in text messaging, chat rooms, etc
WEBLISHES > WEBLISH
WEBLOG n person's online journal
WEBLOGGER > WEBLOG
WEBLOGS > WEBLOG
WEBMAIL n system of electronic mail that allows account holders to access their mail via an internet site rather than downloading it
WEBMAILS > WEBMAIL
WEBMASTER n person responsible for the administration of a website on the World Wide Web
WEBPAGE n page on website
WEBPAGES > WEBPAGE
WEBS > WEB
WEBSITE n group of connected pages on the World Wide Web
WEBSITES > WEBSITE
WEBSTER archaic word for > WEAVER
WEBSTERS > WEBSTER
WEBWHEEL n wheel containing a plate or web instead of spokes
WEBWHEELS > WEBWHEEL
WEBWORK n work done using the World Wide Web
WEBWORKS > WEBWORK
WEBWORM n type of caterpillar
WEBWORMS > WEBWORM
WECHT n agricultural tool
WECHTS > WECHT
WED vb marry
WEDDED > WED
WEDDER dialect form of > WEATHER
WEDDERED > WEDDER
WEDDERING > WEDDER
WEDDERS > WEDDER
WEDDING > WED
WEDDINGS > WEDDING
WEDEL variant of > WEDELN
WEDELED > WEDEL
WEDELING > WEDEL
WEDELN n succession of high-speed turns performed in skiing ▷ vb perform a wedeln
WEDELNED > WEDELN
WEDELNING > WEDELN
WEDELNS > WEDELN
WEDELS > WEDEL
WEDGE n piece of material thick at one end and thin at the other ▷ vb fasten or

split with a wedge
WEDGED > WEDGE
WEDGELIKE > WEDGE
WEDGES > WEDGE
WEDGEWISE *adv* in manner of a wedge
WEDGIE *n* wedge-heeled shoe
WEDGIER > WEDGE
WEDGIES > WEDGIE
WEDGIEST > WEDGE
WEDGING > WEDGE
WEDGINGS > WEDGE
WEDGY > WEDGE
WEDLOCK *n* marriage
WEDLOCKS > WEDLOCK
WEDS > WED
WEE *adj* small or short ▷ *n* instance of urinating ▷ *vb* urinate
WEED *n* plant growing where undesired ▷ *vb* clear of weeds
WEEDED > WEED
WEEDER > WEED
WEEDERIES > WEEDERY
WEEDERS > WEED
WEEDERY *n* weed-ridden area
WEEDICIDE *n* weed-killer
WEEDIER > WEEDY
WEEDIEST > WEEDY
WEEDILY > WEEDY
WEEDINESS > WEEDY
WEEDING > WEED
WEEDINGS > WEED
WEEDLESS > WEED
WEEDLIKE > WEED
WEEDS *pl n* widow's mourning clothes
WEEDY *adj* (of a person) thin and weak
WEEING > WEE
WEEK *n* period of seven days, esp one beginning on a Sunday ▷ *adv* seven days before or after a specified day
WEEKDAY *n* any day of the week except Saturday or Sunday
WEEKDAYS > WEEKDAY
WEEKE *same as* > WICK
WEEKEND *n* Saturday and Sunday ▷ *vb* spend or pass a weekend
WEEKENDED > WEEKEND
WEEKENDER *n* person spending a weekend holiday in a place, esp habitually
WEEKENDS *adv* at the weekend, esp regularly or during every weekend
WEEKES > WEEKE
WEEKLIES > WEEKLY
WEEKLONG *adj* lasting a week
WEEKLY *adv* happening, done, etc once a week ▷ *n* newspaper or magazine published once a week ▷ *adj* happening once a week or every week
WEEKNIGHT *n* evening or night of a weekday
WEEKS > WEEK

WEEL *Scot word for* > WELL
WEELS > WEEL
WEEM *n* underground home
WEEMS > WEEM
WEEN *vb* think or imagine (something)
WEENED > WEEN
WEENIE *adj* very small ▷ *n* wiener
WEENIER > WEENY
WEENIES > WEENIE
WEENIEST > WEENY
WEENING > WEEN
WEENS > WEEN
WEENSIER > WEENSY
WEENSIEST > WEENSY
WEENSY *same as* > WEENY
WEENY *adj* very small
WEEP *vb* shed tears ▷ *n* spell of weeping
WEEPER *n* person who weeps, esp a hired mourner
WEEPERS > WEEPER
WEEPHOLE *n* small drain hole in wall
WEEPHOLES > WEEPHOLE
WEEPIE > WEEPY
WEEPIER > WEEPY
WEEPIES > WEEPY
WEEPIEST > WEEPY
WEEPILY > WEEPY
WEEPINESS > WEEPY
WEEPING *adj* (of plants) having slender hanging branches
WEEPINGLY > WEEPING
WEEPINGS > WEEPING
WEEPS > WEEP
WEEPY *adj* liable to cry ▷ *n* sentimental film or book
WEER > WEE
WEES > WEE
WEEST > WEE
WEET *dialect form of* > WET
WEETE *same as* > WIT
WEETED > WEETE
WEETEN *same as* > WIT
WEETER > WEET
WEETEST > WEET
WEETING > WEET
WEETINGLY > WEET
WEETLESS *obsolete variant of* > WITLESS
WEETS > WEET
WEEVER *n* type of small fish
WEEVERS > WEEVER
WEEVIL *n* small beetle that eats grain etc
WEEVILED *same as* > WEEVILLED
WEEVILLED *adj* weevil-ridden
WEEVILLY *another word for* > WEEVILLED
WEEVILS > WEEVIL
WEEVILY *another word for* > WEEVILLED
WEEWEE *vb* urinate
WEEWEED > WEEWEE
WEEWEEING > WEEWEE
WEEWEES > WEEWEE
WEFT *n* cross threads in weaving ▷ *vb* form weft
WEFTAGE *n* texture
WEFTAGES > WEFTAGE
WEFTE *n* forsaken child
WEFTED > WEFT

WEFTES > WEFTE
WEFTING > WEFT
WEFTS > WEFT
WEFTWISE *adv* in the direction of the weft
WEID *n* sudden illness
WEIDS > WEID
WEIGELA *n* type of shrub
WEIGELAS > WEIGELA
WEIGELIA *same as* > WEIGELA
WEIGELIAS > WEIGELIA
WEIGH *vb* have a specified weight
WEIGHABLE > WEIGH
WEIGHAGE *n* duty paid for weighing goods
WEIGHAGES > WEIGHAGE
WEIGHED > WEIGH
WEIGHER > WEIGH
WEIGHERS > WEIGH
WEIGHING > WEIGH
WEIGHINGS > WEIGH
WEIGHMAN *n* person responsible for weighing goods
WEIGHMEN > WEIGHMAN
WEIGHS > WEIGH
WEIGHT *n* heaviness of an object ▷ *vb* add weight to
WEIGHTED > WEIGHT
WEIGHTER > WEIGHT
WEIGHTERS > WEIGHT
WEIGHTIER > WEIGHTY
WEIGHTILY > WEIGHTY
WEIGHTING *n* extra allowance paid in special circumstances
WEIGHTS > WEIGHT
WEIGHTY *adj* important or serious
WEIL *n* whirlpool
WEILS > WEIL
WEINER *same as* > WIENER
WEINERS > WEINER
WEIR *vb* ward off ▷ *n* river dam
WEIRD *adj* strange or bizarre ▷ *vb* warn beforehand
WEIRDED > WEIRD
WEIRDER > WEIRD
WEIRDEST > WEIRD
WEIRDIE *same as* > WEIRDO
WEIRDIES > WEIRDIE
WEIRDING > WEIRD
WEIRDLY > WEIRD
WEIRDNESS > WEIRD
WEIRDO *n* peculiar person
WEIRDOES > WEIRDO
WEIRDOS > WEIRDO
WEIRDS > WEIRD
WEIRDY *n* weird person
WEIRED > WEIR
WEIRING > WEIR
WEIRS > WEIR
WEISE *same as* > WISE
WEISED > WEISE
WEISES > WEISE
WEISING > WEISE
WEIZE *same as* > WISE
WEIZED > WEIZE
WEIZES > WEIZE
WEIZING > WEIZE
WEKA *n* flightless New Zealand rail
WEKAS > WEKA
WELAWAY *same*

as > WELLAWAY
WELCH *same as* > WELSH
WELCHED > WELCH
WELCHER > WELCH
WELCHERS > WELCH
WELCHES > WELCH
WELCHING > WELCH
WELCOME *vb* greet with pleasure ▷ *n* kindly greeting ▷ *adj* received gladly
WELCOMED > WELCOME
WELCOMELY > WELCOME
WELCOMER > WELCOME
WELCOMERS > WELCOME
WELCOMES > WELCOME
WELCOMING > WELCOME
WELD *vb* join (pieces of metal or plastic) by softening with heat ▷ *n* welded joint
WELDABLE > WELD
WELDED > WELD
WELDER > WELD
WELDERS > WELD
WELDING > WELD
WELDINGS > WELD
WELDLESS > WELD
WELDMENT *n* unit composed of welded pieces
WELDMENTS > WELDMENT
WELDMESH *n* type of metal fencing
WELDOR > WELD
WELDORS > WELDOR
WELDS > WELD
WELFARE *n* wellbeing
WELFARES > WELFARE
WELFARISM *n* policies or attitudes associated with a welfare state
WELFARIST > WELFARISM
WELK *vb* wither; dry up
WELKE *obsolete form of* > WELK
WELKED > WELK
WELKES > WELKE
WELKIN *n* sky, heavens, or upper air
WELKING > WELK
WELKINS > WELKIN
WELKS > WELK
WELKT *adj* twisted
WELL *adv* satisfactorily ▷ *adj* in good health ▷ *interj* exclamation of surprise, interrogation, etc ▷ *n* hole sunk into the earth to reach water, oil, or gas ▷ *vb* flow upwards or outwards
WELLADAY *interj* alas
WELLADAYS *interj* alas
WELLANEAR *interj* alas
WELLAWAY *interj* alas!
WELLAWAYS *interj* alas
WELLBEING *n* state of being well, happy, or prosperous
WELLBORN *adj* having been born into a wealthy family
WELLCURB *n* stone surround at top of well
WELLCURBS > WELLCURB
WELLDOER *n* moral person
WELLDOERS > WELLDOER
WELLED > WELL
WELLHEAD *n* source of a well or stream
WELLHEADS > WELLHEAD

W

WELLHOLE *n* well shaft
WELLHOLES > WELLHOLE
WELLHOUSE *n* housing for well
WELLIE *n* wellington boot
WELLIES > WELLY
WELLING > WELL
WELLINGS > WELL
WELLNESS *n* state of being in good physical and mental health
WELLS > WELL
WELLSITE *n* site of well
WELLSITES > WELLSITE
WELLY *n* energy or commitment
WELSH *vb* fail to pay a debt or fulfil an obligation
WELSHED > WELSH
WELSHER > WELSH
WELSHERS > WELSH
WELSHES > WELSH
WELSHING > WELSH
WELT *same as* > WEAL
WELTED > WELT
WELTER *n* jumbled mass ▷ *vb* roll about, writhe, or wallow
WELTERED > WELTER
WELTERING > WELTER
WELTERS > WELTER
WELTING > WELT
WELTINGS > WELT
WELTS > WELT
WEM *same as* > WAME
WEMB *same as* > WAME
WEMBS > WEMB
WEMS > WEM
WEN *n* cyst on the scalp
WENA *n* South African word for you
WENCH *n* young woman ▷ *vb* frequent the company of prostitutes
WENCHED > WENCH
WENCHER > WENCH
WENCHERS > WENCH
WENCHES > WENCH
WENCHING > WENCH
WEND *vb* go or travel
WENDED > WEND
WENDIGO *n* evil spirit or cannibal
WENDIGOS > WENDIGO
WENDING > WEND
WENDS > WEND
WENGE *n* type of tree found in central and West Africa
WENGES > WENGE
WENNIER > WEN
WENNIEST > WEN
WENNISH > WEN
WENNY > WEN
WENS > WEN
WENT *n* path
WENTS > WENT
WEPT > WEEP
WERE *vb* form of the past tense of **be** used after *we*, *you*, *they*, or a plural noun
WEREGILD *same as* > WERGILD
WEREGILDS > WEREGILD
WEREWOLF *n* (in folklore) person who can turn into a wolf
WERGELD *same as* > WERGILD

WERGELDS > WERGELD
WERGELT *same as* > WERGELD
WERGELTS > WERGELT
WERGILD *n* price set on a man's life in successive Anglo-Saxon and Germanic law codes, to be paid as compensation by his slayer
WERGILDS > WERGILD
WERNERITE *another name for* > SCAPOLITE
WERO *n* challenge made by an armed Māori warrior to a visitor to a marae
WEROS > WERO
WERRIS *slang word for* > URINATION
WERRISES > WERRIS
WERSH *adj* tasteless
WERSHER > WERSH
WERSHEST > WERSH
WERT *singular form of the past tense of* > BE
WERWOLF *same as* > WEREWOLF
WERWOLVES > WERWOLF
WESAND *same as* > WEASAND
WESANDS > WESAND
WESKIT *informal word for* > WAISTCOAT
WESKITS > WESKIT
WESSAND *same as* > WEASAND
WESSANDS > WESSAND
WEST *n* part of the horizon where the sun sets ▷ *adj* or in the west ▷ *adv* in, to, or towards the west ▷ *vb* move in westerly direction
WESTBOUND *adj* going towards the west
WESTED > WEST
WESTER *vb* move or appear to move towards the west ▷ *n* strong wind or storm from the west
WESTERED > WESTER
WESTERING > WESTER
WESTERLY *adj* of or in the west ▷ *adv* towards the west ▷ *n* wind blowing from the west
WESTERN *adj* of or in the west ▷ *n* film or story about cowboys in the western US
WESTERNER *n* person from the west of a country or area
WESTERNS > WESTERN
WESTERS > WESTER
WESTIE *n* informal word for a young working-class person from the western suburbs of Sydney
WESTIES > WESTIE
WESTING *n* movement, deviation, or distance covered in a westerly direction
WESTINGS > WESTING
WESTLIN *Scots word for* > WESTERN
WESTLINS *adv* to or in west
WESTMOST *adj* most western
WESTS > WEST
WESTWARD *adv* towards the west ▷ *n* westward part

or direction ▷ *adj* moving, facing, or situated in the west
WESTWARDS *same as* > WESTWARD
WET *adj* covered or soaked with water or another liquid ▷ *n* moisture or rain ▷ *vb* make wet
WETA *n* type of wingless insect
WETAS > WETA
WETBACK *n* Mexican labourer who enters the US illegally
WETBACKS > WETBACK
WETHER *n* male sheep, esp a castrated one
WETHERS > WETHER
WETLAND *n* area of marshy land
WETLANDS > WETLAND
WETLY > WET
WETNESS > WET
WETNESSES > WET
WETPROOF *adj* waterproof
WETS > WET
WETSUIT *n* body suit for diving
WETSUITS > WETSUIT
WETTABLE > WET
WETTED > WET
WETTER > WET
WETTERS > WET
WETTEST > WET
WETTIE *n* wetsuit
WETTIES > WETTIE
WETTING > WET
WETTINGS > WET
WETTISH > WET
WETWARE *n* humorous term for the brain
WETWARES > WETWARE
WEX *obsolete form of* > WAX
WEXE *obsolete form of* > WAX
WEXED > WEX
WEXES > WEX
WEXING > WEX
WEY *n* measurement of weight
WEYARD *obsolete form of* > WEIRD
WEYS > WEY
WEYWARD *obsolete form of* > WEIRD
WEZAND *obsolete form of* > WEASAND
WEZANDS > WEZAND
WHA *Scot word for* > WHO
WHACK *vb* strike with a resounding blow ▷ *n* such a blow
WHACKED > WHACK
WHACKER > WHACK
WHACKERS > WHACK
WHACKIER > WHACKY
WHACKIEST > WHACKY
WHACKING *adj* huge ▷ *n* severe beating ▷ *adv* extremely
WHACKINGS > WHACKING
WHACKO *n* mad person
WHACKOES > WHACKO
WHACKOS > WHACKO
WHACKS > WHACK
WHACKY *variant spelling of* > WACKY

WHAE *same as* > WHA
WHAISLE *Scots form of* > WHEEZE
WHAISLED > WHAISLE
WHAISLES > WHAISLE
WHAISLING > WHAISLE
WHAIZLE *same as* > WHAISLE
WHAIZLED > WHAIZLE
WHAIZLES > WHAIZLE
WHAIZLING > WHAIZLE
WHAKAIRO *n* art of carving
WHAKAIROS > WHAKAIRO
WHAKAPAPA *n* genealogy
WHALE *n* large fish-shaped sea mammal ▷ *vb* hunt for whales
WHALEBACK *n* something shaped like the back of a whale
WHALEBOAT *n* narrow boat from 20 to 30 feet long having a sharp prow and stern, formerly used in whaling
WHALEBONE *n* horny substance hanging from the upper jaw of toothless whales
WHALED > WHALE
WHALELIKE > WHALE
WHALEMAN *n* person employed in whaling
WHALEMEN > WHALEMAN
WHALER *n* ship or person involved in whaling
WHALERIES > WHALERY
WHALERS > WHALER
WHALERY *n* whaling
WHALES > WHALE
WHALING *n* hunting of whales for food and oil ▷ *adv* extremely
WHALINGS > WHALING
WHALLY *adj* (of eyes) with light-coloured irises
WHAM *interj* expression indicating suddenness or forcefulness ▷ *n* forceful blow or impact or the sound produced by such a blow or impact ▷ *vb* strike or cause to strike with great force
WHAMMED > WHAM
WHAMMIES > WHAMMY
WHAMMING > WHAM
WHAMMO *n* sound of a sudden collision
WHAMMOS > WHAMMO
WHAMMY *n* devastating setback
WHAMO *same as* > WHAMMO
WHAMPLE *n* strike
WHAMPLES > WHAMPLE
WHAMS > WHAM
WHANAU *n* (in Māori societies) a family, esp an extended family
WHANAUS > WHANAU
WHANG *vb* strike or be struck so as to cause a resounding noise ▷ *n* resounding noise produced by a heavy blow
WHANGAM *n* imaginary creature
WHANGAMS > WHANGAM
WHANGED > WHANG

WHANGEE n tall woody grass grown for its stems, which are used for bamboo canes
WHANGEES > WHANGEE
WHANGING > WHANG
WHANGS > WHANG
WHAP same as > WHOP
WHAPPED > WHAP
WHAPPER same as > WHOPPER
WHAPPERS > WHAPPER
WHAPPING > WHAP
WHAPS > WHAP
WHARE n Māori hut or dwelling place
WHARENUI n (in New Zealand) meeting house
WHARENUIS > WHARENUI
WHAREPUNI n (in a Māori community) a tall carved building used as a guesthouse
WHARES > WHARE
WHARF n platform at a harbour for loading and unloading ships ▷ vb put (goods, etc) on a wharf
WHARFAGE n accommodation for ships at wharves
WHARFAGES > WHARFAGE
WHARFED > WHARF
WHARFIE n person employed to load and unload ships
WHARFIES > WHARFIE
WHARFING > WHARF
WHARFINGS > WHARF
WHARFS > WHARF
WHARVE n wooden disc or wheel on a shaft serving as a flywheel or pulley
WHARVES > WHARVE
WHAT pron which thing ▷ interj exclamation of anger, surprise, etc ▷ adv in which way, how much ▷ n part; portion
WHATA n building on stilts or a raised platform for storing provisions
WHATAS > WHATA
WHATEN adj what; what kind of
WHATEVER pron everything or anything that ▷ adj intensive form of what ▷ determiner intensive form of what ▷ interj expression used to show indifference or dismissal
whatna another word for > WHATEN
WHATNESS n what something is
WHATNOT n similar unspecified thing
WHATNOTS > WHATNOT
WHATS > WHAT
WHATSIS US form of > WHATSIT
WHATSISES > WHATSIS
WHATSIT n person or thing the name of which is unknown, temporarily forgotten, or deliberately overlooked

WHATSITS > WHATSIT
WHATSO n of whatever kind
WHATTEN same as > WHATEN
WHAUP n curlew
WHAUPS > WHAUP
WHAUR Scot word for > WHERE
WHAURS > WHAUR
WHEAL same as > WEAL
WHEALS > WHEAL
WHEAR obsolete variant of > WHERE
WHEARE obsolete variant of > WHERE
WHEAT n grain used in making flour, bread, and pasta
WHEATEAR n small songbird
WHEATEARS > WHEATEAR
WHEATEN n type of dog ▷ adj made of the grain or flour of wheat
WHEATENS > WHEATEN
WHEATIER > WHEATY
WHEATIEST > WHEATY
WHEATLAND n region where wheat is grown
WHEATLESS > WHEAT
WHEATMEAL n brown, but not wholemeal, flour
WHEATS > WHEAT
WHEATWORM n parasitic nematode worm that forms galls in the seeds of wheat
WHEATY adj having a wheat-like taste
WHEE interj exclamation of joy, thrill, etc
WHEECH vb move quickly
WHEECHED > WHEECH
WHEECHING > WHEECH
WHEECHS > WHEECH
WHEEDLE vb coax or cajole
WHEEDLED > WHEEDLE
WHEEDLER > WHEEDLE
WHEEDLERS > WHEEDLE
WHEEDLES > WHEEDLE
WHEEDLING > WHEEDLE
WHEEL n disc that revolves on an axle ▷ vb push or pull (something with wheels)
WHEELBASE n distance between a vehicle's front and back axles
WHEELED adj having or equipped with a wheel or wheels
WHEELER n horse or other draught animal nearest the wheel
WHEELERS > WHEELER
WHEELIE n manoeuvre on a bike in which the front wheel is raised off the ground
WHEELIER > WHEELY
WHEELIES > WHEELIE
WHEELIEST > WHEELY
WHEELING > WHEEL
WHEELINGS > WHEEL
WHEELLESS adj having no wheels
WHEELMAN n helmsman
WHEELMEN > WHEELMAN
WHEELS > WHEEL
WHEELSMAN same as > WHEELMAN

WHEELSMEN > WHEELSMAN
WHEELWORK n arrangement of wheels in a machine, esp a train of gears
WHEELY adj resembling a wheel
WHEEN n few
WHEENGE Scots form of > WHINGE
WHEENGED > WHEENGE
WHEENGES > WHEENGE
WHEENGING > WHEENGE
WHEENS > WHEEN
WHEEP vb fly quickly and lightly
WHEEPED > WHEEP
WHEEPING > WHEEP
WHEEPLE vb whistle weakly
WHEEPLED > WHEEPLE
WHEEPLES > WHEEPLE
WHEEPLING > WHEEPLE
WHEEPS > WHEEP
WHEESH vb silence (a person, noise, etc) or be silenced
WHEESHED > WHEESH
WHEESHES > WHEESH
WHEESHING > WHEESH
WHEESHT same as > WHEESH
WHEESHTED > WHEESHT
WHEESHTS > WHEESHT
WHEEZE vb breathe with a hoarse whistling noise ▷ n wheezing sound
WHEEZED > WHEEZE
WHEEZER > WHEEZE
WHEEZERS > WHEEZE
WHEEZES > WHEEZE
WHEEZIER > WHEEZE
WHEEZIEST > WHEEZE
WHEEZILY > WHEEZE
WHEEZING > WHEEZE
WHEEZINGS > WHEEZE
WHEEZLE vb make hoarse breathing sound
WHEEZLED > WHEEZLE
WHEEZLES > WHEEZLE
WHEEZLING > WHEEZLE
WHEEZY > WHEEZE
WHEFT same as > WAFT
WHEFTS > WHEFT
WHELK n edible snail-like shellfish
WHELKED adj having or covered with whelks
WHELKIER > WHELK
WHELKIEST > WHELK
WHELKS > WHELK
WHELKY > WHELK
WHELM vb engulf entirely with or as if with water
WHELMED > WHELM
WHELMING > WHELM
WHELMS > WHELM
WHELP n pup or cub ▷ vb (of an animal) give birth
WHELPED > WHELP
WHELPING > WHELP
WHELPLESS > WHELP
WHELPS > WHELP
WHEMMLE vb overturn
WHEMMLED > WHEMMLE
WHEMMLES > WHEMMLE
WHEMMLING > WHEMMLE
WHEN adv at what time? ▷ pron at which time ▷ n question of when
WHENAS conj while;

inasmuch as
WHENCE n point of origin ▷ adv from what place or source ▷ pron from what place, cause, or origin
WHENCES > WHENCE
WHENCEVER adv out of whatsoever place, cause or origin
WHENEVER adv at whatever time
WHENS > WHEN
WHENUA n land
WHENUAS > WHENUA
WHENWE n White immigrant from Zimbabwe, caricatured as being tiresomely over-reminiscent of happier times
WHENWES > WHENWE
WHERE adv in, at, or to what place? ▷ pron in, at, or to which place ▷ n question as to the position, direction, or destination of something
WHEREAS n testimonial introduced by whereas
WHEREASES > WHEREAS
WHEREAT adv at or to which place
WHEREBY pron by which ▷ adv how? by what means?
WHEREFOR adv for which
WHEREFORE adv why ▷ n explanation or reason
WHEREFROM adv from what or where? whence? ▷ pron from which place
WHEREIN adv in what place or respect? ▷ pron in which place or thing
WHEREINTO adv into what place? ▷ pron into which place
WHERENESS n state of having a place
WHEREOF adv of what or which person or thing? ▷ pron of which person or thing
WHEREON adv on what thing or place? ▷ pron on which thing, place, etc
WHEREOUT adv out of which
WHERES > WHERE
WHERESO adv in or to unspecified place
WHERETO adv towards what (place, end, etc)? ▷ pron which
WHEREUNTO same as > WHERETO
WHEREUPON adv upon what?
WHEREVER adv at whatever place ▷ pron at, in, or to every place or point which
WHEREWITH pron with or by which ▷ adv with what?
WHERRET vb strike (someone) a blow ▷ n blow, esp a slap on the face
WHERRETED > WHERRET
WHERRETS > WHERRET
WHERRIED > WHERRY

w

WHERRIES > WHERRY

WHERRIT vb worry or cause to worry

WHERRITED > WHERRIT

WHERRITS > WHERRIT

WHERRY n any of certain kinds of half-decked commercial boats, such as barges, used in Britain ▷ vb travel in a wherry

WHERRYING > WHERRY

WHERRYMAN > WHERRY

WHERRYMEN > WHERRY

WHERVE same as > WHARVE

WHERVES > WHERVE

WHET vb sharpen (a tool) ▷ n act of whetting

WHETHER conj used to introduce any indirect question

WHETS > WHET

WHETSTONE n stone for sharpening tools

WHETTED > WHET

WHETTER > WHET

WHETTERS > WHET

WHETTING > WHET

WHEUGH same as > WHEW

WHEUGHED > WHEUGH

WHEUGHING > WHEUGH

WHEUGHS > WHEUGH

WHEW interj exclamation expressing relief, delight, etc ▷ vb express relief

WHEWED > WHEW

WHEWING > WHEW

WHEWS > WHEW

WHEY n watery liquid that separates from the curd when milk is clotted

WHEYEY > WHEY

WHEYFACE n pale bloodless face

WHEYFACED > WHEYFACE

WHEYFACES > WHEYFACE

WHEYIER > WHEY

WHEYIEST > WHEY

WHEYISH > WHEY

WHEYLIKE > WHEY

WHEYS > WHEY

WHICH pron used to request or refer to a choice from different possibilities ▷ adj used with a noun in requesting that the particular thing being referred to is further identified or distinguished

WHICHEVER pron any out of several ▷ adj any out of several ▷ determiner any (one, two, etc, out of several)

WHICKER vb (of a horse) to whinny or neigh

WHICKERED > WHICKER

WHICKERS > WHICKER

WHID vb move quickly

WHIDAH same as > WHYDAH

WHIDAHS > WHIDAH

WHIDDED > WHID

WHIDDER vb move with force

WHIDDERED > WHIDDER

WHIDDERS > WHIDDER

WHIDDING > WHID

WHIDS > WHID

WHIFF n puff of air or odour ▷ vb come, convey, or go in whiffs

WHIFFED > WHIFF

WHIFFER > WHIFF

WHIFFERS > WHIFF

WHIFFET n insignificant person

WHIFFETS > WHIFFET

WHIFFIER > WHIFFY

WHIFFIEST > WHIFFY

WHIFFING > WHIFF

WHIFFINGS > WHIFF

WHIFFLE vb think or behave in an erratic or unpredictable way

WHIFFLED > WHIFFLE

WHIFFLER n person who whiffles

WHIFFLERS > WHIFFLER

WHIFFLERY n frivolity

WHIFFLES > WHIFFLE

WHIFFLING > WHIFFLE

WHIFFS > WHIFF

WHIFFY adj smelly

WHIFT n brief emission of air

WHIFTS > WHIFT

WHIG vb go quickly

WHIGGED > WHIG

WHIGGING > WHIG

WHIGS > WHIG

WHILE n period of time

WHILED > WHILE

WHILERE adv a while ago

WHILES adv at times

WHILING > WHILE

WHILK archaic and dialect word for > WHICH

WHILLIED > WHILLY

WHILLIES > WHILLY

WHILLY vb influence by flattery

WHILLYING > WHILLY

WHILLYWHA variant of > WHILLY

WHILOM adv formerly ▷ adj one-time

WHILST same as > WHILE

WHIM n sudden fancy ▷ vb have a whim

WHIMBERRY n whortleberry

WHIMBREL n small European curlew with a striped head

WHIMBRELS > WHIMBREL

WHIMMED > WHIM

WHIMMIER > WHIMMY

WHIMMIEST > WHIMMY

WHIMMING > WHIM

WHIMMY adj having whims

WHIMPER vb cry in a soft whining way ▷ n soft plaintive whine

WHIMPERED > WHIMPER

WHIMPERER > WHIMPER

WHIMPERS > WHIMPER

WHIMPLE same as > WIMPLE

WHIMPLED > WHIMPLE

WHIMPLES > WHIMPLE

WHIMPLING > WHIMPLE

WHIMS > WHIM

WHIMSEY same as > WHIMSY

WHIMSEYS > WHIMSEY

WHIMSICAL adj unusual, playful, and fanciful

WHIMSIED > WHIMSY

WHIMSIER > WHIMSY

WHIMSIES > WHIMSY

WHIMSIEST > WHIMSY

WHIMSILY > WHIMSY

WHIMSY n capricious idea ▷ adj quaint, comical, or unusual, often in a tasteless way

WHIN n gorse

WHINBERRY same as > WHIMBERRY

WHINCHAT n type of songbird

WHINCHATS > WHINCHAT

WHINE n high-pitched plaintive cry ▷ vb make such a sound

WHINED > WHINE

WHINER > WHINE

WHINERS > WHINE

WHINES > WHINE

WHINEY same as > WHINY

WHINGDING same as > WINGDING

WHINGE vb complain ▷ n complaint

WHINGED > WHINGE

WHINGEING > WHINGE

WHINGER > WHINGE

WHINGERS > WHINGE

WHINGES > WHINGE

WHINGING > WHINGE

WHINIARD same as > WHINYARD

WHINIARDS > WHINIARD

WHINIER > WHINY

WHINIEST > WHINY

WHININESS > WHINY

WHINING > WHINE

WHININGLY > WHINE

WHININGS > WHINE

WHINNIED > WHINNY

WHINNIER > WHINNY

WHINNIES > WHINNY

WHINNIEST > WHINNY

WHINNY vb neigh softly ▷ n soft neigh ▷ adj covered in whin

WHINNYING > WHINNY

WHINS > WHIN

WHINSTONE n any dark hard fine-grained rock, such as basalt

WHINY adj high-pitched and plaintive

WHINYARD n sword

WHINYARDS > WHINYARD

WHIO n New Zealand mountain duck with blue plumage

WHIP n cord attached to a handle, used for beating animals or people ▷ vb strike with a whip, strap, or cane

WHIPBIRD n any of several birds having a whistle ending in a whipcrack note

WHIPBIRDS > WHIPBIRD

WHIPCAT n tailor

WHIPCATS > WHIPCAT

WHIPCORD n strong worsted or cotton fabric with a diagonally ribbed surface

WHIPCORDS > WHIPCORD

WHIPCORDY adj whipcord-like

WHIPJACK n beggar imitating a sailor

WHIPJACKS > WHIPJACK

WHIPLASH n quick lash of a whip

WHIPLIKE > WHIP

WHIPPED > WHIP

WHIPPER > WHIP

WHIPPERS > WHIP

WHIPPET n racing dog like a small greyhound

WHIPPETS > WHIPPET

WHIPPIER > WHIPPY

WHIPPIEST > WHIPPY

WHIPPING > WHIP

WHIPPINGS > WHIP

WHIPPY adj springy

WHIPRAY n stingray

WHIPRAYS > WHIPRAY

WHIPS > WHIP

WHIPSAW n any saw with a flexible blade, such as a bandsaw ▷ vb saw with a whipsaw

WHIPSAWED > WHIPSAW

WHIPSAWN > WHIPSAW

WHIPSAWS > WHIPSAW

WHIPSNAKE n thin snake like leather whip

WHIPSTAFF n ship's steering bar

WHIPSTALL n stall in which an aircraft goes into a nearly vertical climb, pauses, slips backwards momentarily, and drops suddenly with its nose down

WHIPSTER n insignificant but pretentious or cheeky person, esp a young one

WHIPSTERS > WHIPSTER

WHIPSTOCK n handle of a whip

WHIPT old past tense of > WHIP

WHIPTAIL n type of lizard

WHIPTAILS > WHIPTAIL

WHIPWORM n parasitic worm living in the intestines of mammals

WHIPWORMS > WHIPWORM

WHIR n prolonged soft swish or buzz, as of a motor working or wings flapping ▷ vb make or cause to make a whir

WHIRL vb spin or revolve ▷ n whirling movement

WHIRLBAT n thing moved with a whirl

WHIRLBATS > WHIRLBAT

WHIRLED > WHIRL

WHIRLER > WHIRL

WHIRLERS > WHIRL

WHIRLIER > WHIRLY

WHIRLIES n illness induced by excessive use of alcohol or drugs

WHIRLIEST > WHIRLY

WHIRLIGIG same as > WINDMILL

WHIRLING > WHIRL

WHIRLINGS > WHIRL

WHIRLPOOL n strong circular current of water

WHIRLS > WHIRL

WHIRLWIND n column of air whirling violently upwards

in a spiral ▷ *adj* much quicker than normal

WHIRLY *adj* characterized by whirling

WHIRR *same as* > WHIR

WHIRRED > WHIR

WHIRRET *vb* strike with sharp blow

WHIRRETED > WHIRRET

WHIRRETS > WHIRRET

WHIRRIED > WHIRRY

WHIRRIES > WHIRRY

WHIRRING > WHIR

WHIRRINGS > WHIR

WHIRRS > WHIRR

WHIRRY *vb* move quickly

WHIRRYING > WHIRRY

WHIRS > WHIR

WHIRTLE *same as* > WORTLE

WHIRTLES > WHIRTLE

WHISH *less common word for* > SWISH

WHISHED > WHISH

WHISHES > WHISH

WHISHING > WHISH

WHISHT *interj* hush! be quiet! ▷ *adj* silent or still ▷ *vb* make or become silent

WHISHTED > WHISHT

WHISHTING > WHISHT

WHISHTS > WHISHT

WHISK *vb* move or remove quickly ▷ *n* quick movement

WHISKED > WHISK

WHISKER *n* any of the long stiff hairs on the face of a cat or other mammal

WHISKERED *adj* having whiskers

WHISKERS > WHISKER

WHISKERY *adj* having whiskers

WHISKET *same as* > WISKET

WHISKETS > WHISKET

WHISKEY *n* Irish or American whisky

WHISKEYS > WHISKEY

WHISKIES > WHISKY

WHISKING > WHISK

WHISKS > WHISK

WHISKY *n* spirit distilled from fermented cereals

WHISPER *vb* speak softly, without vibration of the vocal cords ▷ *n* soft voice

WHISPERED > WHISPER

WHISPERER *n* person or thing that whispers

WHISPERS > WHISPER

WHISPERY > WHISPER

WHISS *vb* hiss

WHISSED > WHISS

WHISSES > WHISS

WHISSING > WHISS

WHIST *same as* > WHISHT

WHISTED > WHIST

WHISTING > WHIST

WHISTLE *vb* produce a shrill sound, esp by forcing the breath through pursed lips ▷ *n* whistling sound

WHISTLED > WHISTLE

WHISTLER *n* person or thing that whistles

WHISTLERS > WHISTLER

WHISTLES > WHISTLE

WHISTLING > WHISTLE

WHISTS > WHIST

WHIT *n* smallest particle

WHITE *adj* of the colour of snow ▷ *n* colour of snow

WHITEBAIT *n* small edible fish

WHITEBASS *n* type of fish

WHITEBEAM *n* type of tree

WHITECAP *n* wave with a white broken crest

WHITECAPS > WHITECAP

WHITECOAT *n* person who wears a white coat

WHITECOMB *n* fungal disease infecting the combs of certain fowls

WHITED *as in* *whited sepulchre* hypocrite

WHITEDAMP *n* mixture of poisonous gases, mainly carbon monoxide, occurring in coal mines

WHITEFACE *n* white stage make-up

WHITEFISH *n* type of fish

WHITEFLY *n* tiny whitish insect that is harmful to greenhouse plants

WHITEHEAD *n* type of pimple with a white head

WHITELY > WHITE

WHITEN *vb* make or become white or whiter

WHITENED > WHITEN

WHITENER *n* substance that makes something white or whiter

WHITENERS > WHITENER

WHITENESS > WHITE

WHITENING > WHITEN

WHITENS > WHITEN

WHITEOUT *n* atmospheric condition in which blizzards or low clouds make it very difficult to see

WHITEOUTS > WHITEOUT

WHITEPOT *n* custard or milk pudding

WHITEPOTS > WHITEPOT

WHITER > WHITE

WHITES *pl n* white clothes, as worn for playing cricket

WHITEST > WHITE

WHITETAIL *n* type of deer

WHITEWALL *n* pneumatic tyre having white sidewalls

WHITEWARE *n* white ceramics

WHITEWASH *n* substance for whitening walls ▷ *vb* cover with whitewash

WHITEWING *n* type of bird

WHITEWOOD *n* light-coloured wood often prepared for staining

WHITEY *same as* > WHITY

WHITEYS > WHITEY

WHITHER *same as* > WUTHER

WHITHERED > WHITHER

WHITHERS > WHITHER

WHITIER > WHITY

WHITIES > WHITY

WHITIEST > WHITY

WHITING *n* edible sea fish

WHITINGS > WHITING

WHITISH > WHITE

WHITLING *n* type of trout

WHITLINGS > WHITLING

WHITLOW *n* inflamed sore on a finger or toe, esp round a nail

WHITLOWS > WHITLOW

WHITRACK *n* weasel or stoat

WHITRACKS > WHITRACK

WHITRET *n* variant of whittret

WHITRETS > WHITRET

WHITRICK *n* dialect word for a male weasel

WHITRICKS > WHITRICK

WHITS > WHIT

WHITSTER *n* person who whitens clothes

WHITSTERS > WHITSTER

WHITTAW *same as* > WHITTAWER

WHITTAWER *n* person who treats leather

WHITTAWS > WHITTAW

WHITTER *variant spelling of* > WITTER

WHITTERED > WHITTER

WHITTERS > WHITTER

WHITTLE *vb* cut or carve (wood) with a knife ▷ *n* knife, esp a large one

WHITTLED > WHITTLE

WHITTLER > WHITTLE

WHITTLERS > WHITTLE

WHITTLES > WHITTLE

WHITTLING > WHITTLE

WHITTRET *n* male weasel

WHITTRETS > WHITTRET

WHITY *adj* of a white colour ▷ *n* derogatory term for a White person

WHIZ *same as* > WHIZZ

WHIZBANG *n* small-calibre shell

WHIZBANGS > WHIZBANG

WHIZZ *vb* make a loud buzzing sound ▷ *n* loud buzzing sound

WHIZZBANG *same as* > WHIZBANG

WHIZZED > WHIZZ

WHIZZER > WHIZZ

WHIZZERS > WHIZZ

WHIZZES > WHIZZ

WHIZZIER > WHIZZY

WHIZZIEST > WHIZZY

WHIZZING > WHIZZ

WHIZZINGS > WHIZZ

WHIZZY *adj* using sophisticated technology to produce vivid effects

WHO *pron* which person

WHOA *interj* command used, esp to horses, to stop or slow down

WHODUNIT *same as* > WHODUNNIT

WHODUNITS > WHODUNIT

WHODUNNIT *n* detective story, play, or film

WHOEVER *pron* any person who

WHULE *adj* containing all the elements or parts ▷ *n* complete thing or system

WHOLEFOOD *n* food that has been processed as little as possible ▷ *adj* of or

relating to wholefood

WHOLEMEAL *adj* (of flour) made from the whole wheat grain

WHOLENESS > WHOLE

WHOLES > WHOLE

WHOLESALE *adv* dealing by selling goods in large quantities to retailers ▷ *n* business of selling goods in large quantities and at lower prices to retailers for resale

WHOLESOME *adj* physically or morally beneficial

WHOLISM *same as* > HOLISM

WHOLISMS > WHOLISM

WHOLIST *same as* > HOLIST

WHOLISTIC *same as* > HOLISTIC

WHOLISTS > WHOLIST

WHOLLY *adv* completely or totally

WHOM *pron* objective form of *who*

WHOMBLE *same as* > WHEMMLE

WHOMBLED > WHOMBLE

WHOMBLES > WHOMBLE

WHOMBLING > WHOMBLE

WHOMEVER *pron* objective form of *whoever*

WHOMMLE *same as* > WHEMMLE

WHOMMLED > WHOMMLE

WHOMMLES > WHOMMLE

WHOMMLING > WHOMMLE

WHOMP *vb* strike; thump

WHOMPED > WHOMP

WHOMPING > WHOMP

WHOMPS > WHOMP

WHOMSO *pron* whom; whomever

WHOOBUB *same as* > HUBBUB

WHOOBUBS > WHOOBUB

WHOOF *same as* > WOOF

WHOOFED > WHOOF

WHOOFING > WHOOF

WHOOFS > WHOOF

WHOOP *n* shout or cry to express excitement ▷ *vb* emit a whoop

WHOOPED > WHOOP

WHOOPEE *n* cry of joy

WHOOPEES > WHOOPEE

WHOOPER *n* type of swan

WHOOPERS > WHOOPER

WHOOPIE *same as* > WHOOPEE

WHOOPIES > WHOOPIE

WHOOPING > WHOOP

WHOOPINGS > WHOOPING

WHOOPLA *n* commotion; fuss

WHOOPLAS > WHOOPLA

WHOOPS *interj* exclamation of surprise or of apology

WHOOPSIE *n* animal excrement

WHOOPSIES > WHOOPSIE

WHOOSH *n* hissing or rushing sound ▷ *vb* make or move with a hissing or rushing sound

WHOOSHED > WHOOSH

WHOOSHES > WHOOSH

WHOOSHING > WHOOSH

WHOOSIS *n* thingamajig

WHOOSISES > WHOOSIS

WHOOT *obsolete variant of* > HOOT

WHOOTED > WHOOT

WHOOTING > WHOOT

WHOOTS > WHOOT

WHOP *vb* strike, beat, or thrash ▷ *n* heavy blow or the sound made by such a blow

WHOPPED > WHOP

WHOPPER *n* anything unusually large

WHOPPERS > WHOPPER

WHOPPING *n* beating as punishment ▷ *adj* unusually large ▷ *adv* extremely

WHOPPINGS > WHOPPING

WHOPS > WHOP

WHORE *n* prostitute ▷ *vb* be or act as a prostitute

WHORED > WHORE

WHOREDOM *n* activity of whoring or state of being a whore

WHOREDOMS > WHOREDOM

WHORES > WHORE

WHORESON *n* bastard ▷ *adj* vile or hateful

WHORESONS > WHORESON

WHORING > WHORE

WHORISH > WHORE

WHORISHLY > WHORE

WHORL *n* ring of leaves or petals

WHORLBAT *same as* > WHIRLBAT

WHORLBATS > WHORLBAT

WHORLED > WHORL

WHORLS > WHORL

WHORT *n* small shrub bearing blackish edible sweet berries

WHORTLE *n* whortleberry

WHORTLES > WHORTLE

WHORTS > WHORT

WHOSE *pron* of whom or of which ▷ *determiner* of whom? belonging to whom?

WHOSEVER *pron* belonging to whoever

WHOSIS *n* thingamajig

WHOSISES > WHOSIS

WHOSO *archaic word for* > WHOEVER

WHOSOEVER *same as* > WHOEVER

WHOT *obsolete variant of* > HOT

WHOW *interj* wow

WHUMMLE *vb* variant of whemmle

WHUMMLED > WHUMMLE

WHUMMLES > WHUMMLE

WHUMMLING > WHUMMLE

WHUMP *vb* make a dull thud ▷ *n* dull thud

WHUMPED > WHUMP

WHUMPING > WHUMP

WHUMPS > WHUMP

WHUNSTANE *Scots variant of* > WHINSTONE

WHUP *vb* defeat totally

WHUPPED > WHUP

WHUPPING > WHUP

WHUPS > WHUP

WHY *adv* for what reason ▷ *pron* because of which ▷ *n* reason, purpose, or cause of something

WHYDAH *n* type of black African bird

WHYDAHS > WHYDAH

WHYDUNIT *same as* > WHYDUNNIT

WHYDUNITS > WHYDUNIT

WHYDUNNIT *n* novel, film, etc, concerned with the motives of the criminal rather than his or her identity

WHYEVER *adv* for whatever reason

WHYS > WHY

WIBBLE *vb* wobble

WIBBLED > WIBBLE

WIBBLES > WIBBLE

WIBBLING > WIBBLE

WICCA *n* cult or practice of witchcraft

WICCAN *n* member of wicca

WICCANS > WICCAN

WICCAS > WICCA

WICE *Scots form of* > WISE

WICH *n* variant of wych

WICHES > WICH

WICK *n* cord through a lamp or candle which carries fuel to the flame ▷ *adj* lively or active ▷ *vb* (of a material) draw in (water, fuel, etc)

WICKAPE *same as* > WICOPY

WICKAPES > WICKAPE

WICKED *adj* morally bad ▷ *n* wicked person

WICKEDER > WICKED

WICKEDEST > WICKED

WICKEDLY > WICKED

WICKEDS > WICKED

WICKEN *same as* > QUICKEN

WICKENS > WICKEN

WICKER *adj* made of woven cane ▷ *n* slender flexible twig or shoot, esp of willow

WICKERED > WICKER

WICKERS > WICKER

WICKET *n* set of three cricket stumps and two bails

WICKETS > WICKET

WICKIES > WICKY

WICKING > WICK

WICKINGS > WICK

WICKIUP *n* crude shelter made of brushwood, mats, or grass and having an oval frame

WICKIUPS > WICKIUP

WICKLESS > WICK

WICKS > WICK

WICKTHING *n* creeping animal, such as a woodlouse

WICKY *same as* > QUICKEN

WICKYUP *same as* > WICKIUP

WICKYUPS > WICKYUP

WICOPIES > WICOPY

WICOPY *n* any of various North American trees, shrubs, or herbaceous plants

WIDDER *same as* > WIDOW

WIDDERS > WIDDER

WIDDIE *same as* > WIDDY

WIDDIES > WIDDY

WIDDLE *vb* urinate ▷ *n* urine

WIDDLED > WIDDLE

WIDDLES > WIDDLE

WIDDLING > WIDDLE

WIDDY *vb* rope made of twigs

WIDE *adj* large from side to side ▷ *adv* the full extent ▷ *n* (in cricket) a bowled ball ruled to be outside a batsman's reach

WIDEAWAKE *n* hat with a low crown and a very wide brim

WIDEBAND *n* wide bandwidth transmission medium

WIDEBODY *n* aircraft with a wide fuselage

WIDELY > WIDE

WIDEN *vb* make or become wider

WIDENED > WIDEN

WIDENER > WIDEN

WIDENERS > WIDEN

WIDENESS > WIDE

WIDENING > WIDEN

WIDENS > WIDEN

WIDEOUT *n* footballer who catches passes from the quarterback

WIDEOUTS > WIDEOUT

WIDER > WIDE

WIDES > WIDE

WIDEST > WIDE

WIDGEON *same as* > WIGEON

WIDGEONS > WIDGEON

WIDGET *n* any small device, the name of which is unknown or forgotten

WIDGETS > WIDGET

WIDGIE *n* female larrikin or bodgie

WIDGIES > WIDGIE

WIDISH > WIDE

WIDOW *n* woman whose husband is dead and who has not remarried ▷ *vb* cause to become a widow

WIDOWBIRD *n* whydah

WIDOWED > WIDOW

WIDOWER *n* man whose wife is dead and who has not remarried

WIDOWERED > WIDOWER

WIDOWERS > WIDOWER

WIDOWHOOD > WIDOW

WIDOWING > WIDOW

WIDOWMAN *n* widower

WIDOWMEN > WIDOWMAN

WIDOWS > WIDOW

WIDTH *n* distance from side to side

WIDTHS > WIDTH

WIDTHWAY *adj* across the width

WIDTHWAYS *same as* > WIDTHWISE

WIDTHWISE *adv* in the direction of the width

WIEL *same as* > WEEL

WIELD *vb* hold and use (a weapon)

WIELDABLE > WIELD

WIELDED > WIELD

WIELDER > WIELD

WIELDERS > WIELD

WIELDIER > WIELDY

WIELDIEST > WIELDY

WIELDING > WIELD

WIELDLESS *adj* unwieldy

WIELDS > WIELD

WIELDY *adj* easily handled, used, or managed

WIELS > WIEL

WIENER *n* kind of smoked beef or pork sausage, similar to a frankfurter

WIENERS > WIENER

WIENIE *same as* > WIENER

WIENIES > WIENIE

WIFE *n* woman to whom a man is married ▷ *vb* marry

WIFED > WIFE

WIFEDOM *n* state of being a wife

WIFEDOMS > WIFEDOM

WIFEHOOD > WIFE

WIFEHOODS > WIFE

WIFELESS > WIFE

WIFELIER > WIFE

WIFELIEST > WIFE

WIFELIKE > WIFE

WIFELY > WIFE

WIFES > WIFE

WIFEY *n* wife

WIFEYS > WIFEY

WIFIE *n* woman

WIFIES > WIFIE

WIFING > WIFE

WIFTIER > WIFTY

WIFTIEST > WIFTY

WIFTY *adj* scatterbrained

WIG *n* artificial head of hair ▷ *vb* furnish with a wig

WIGAN *n* stiff fabric

WIGANS > WIGAN

WIGEON *n* duck found in marshland

WIGEONS > WIGEON

WIGGA *same as* > WIGGER

WIGGAS > WIGGA

WIGGED > WIG

WIGGER *n* white youth who adopts Black youth culture

WIGGERIES > WIGGERY

WIGGERS > WIGGER

WIGGERY *n* wigs

WIGGIER > WIGGY

WIGGIEST > WIGGY

WIGGING > WIG

WIGGINGS > WIG

WIGGLE *vb* move jerkily from side to side ▷ *n* wiggling movement

WIGGLED > WIGGLE

WIGGLER > WIGGLE

WIGGLERS > WIGGLE

WIGGLES > WIGGLE

WIGGLIER > WIGGLE

WIGGLIEST > WIGGLE

WIGGLING > WIGGLE

WIGGLY > WIGGLE

WIGGY *adj* eccentric

WIGHT *vb* blame ▷ *n* human being ▷ *adj* strong and brave

WIGHTED > WIGHT

WIGHTING > WIGHT

WIGHTLY *adv* swiftly

WIGHTS > WIGHT
WIGLESS > WIG
WIGLET n small wig
WIGLETS > WIGLET
WIGLIKE > WIG
WIGMAKER n person who makes wigs
WIGMAKERS > WIGMAKER
WIGS > WIG
WIGWAG vb move (something) back and forth ▷ n system of communication by flag semaphore
WIGWAGGED > WIGWAG
WIGWAGGER > WIGWAG
WIGWAGS > WIGWAG
WIGWAM n Native American's tent
WIGWAMS > WIGWAM
WIKIUP same as > WICKIUP
WIKIUPS > WIKIUP
WILCO interj expression in telecommunications etc, indicating that the message just received will be complied with
WILD same as > WIELD
WILDCARD n person given entry to competition without qualifying
WILDCARDS > WILDCARD
WILDCAT n European wild animal like a large domestic cat ▷ adj risky and financially unsound ▷ vb drill for petroleum or natural gas in an area having no known reserves
WILDCATS > WILDCAT
WILDED > WILD
WILDER vb lead or be led astray
WILDERED > WILDER
WILDERING > WILDER
WILDERS > WILDER
WILDEST > WILD
WILDFIRE n highly flammable material, such as Greek fire, formerly used in warfare
WILDFIRES > WILDFIRE
WILDFOWL n wild bird that is hunted for sport or food
WILDFOWLS > WILDFOWL
WILDGRAVE same as > WALDGRAVE
WILDING n uncultivated plant, esp the crab apple, or a cultivated plant that has become wild
WILDINGS > WILDING
WILDISH > WILD
WILDLAND n land which has not been cultivated
WILDLANDS > WILDLAND
WILDLIFE n wild animals and plants collectively
WILDLIFES > WILDLIFE
WILDLING same as > WILDING
WILDLINGS > WILDLING
WILDLY > WILD
WILDNESS > WILD
WILDS > WILD
WILDWOOD n wood or forest growing in a natural

uncultivated state
WILDWOODS > WILDWOOD
WILE n trickery, cunning, or craftiness ▷ vb lure, beguile, or entice
WILED > WILE
WILEFUL adj deceitful
WILES > WILE
WILFUL adj headstrong or obstinate
WILFULLY > WILFUL
WILGA n small drought-resistant tree of Australia
WILGAS > WILGA
WILI n spirit
WILIER > WILY
WILIEST > WILY
WILILY > WILY
WILINESS > WILY
WILING > WILE
WILIS > WILI
WILJA n variety of potato
WILJAS > WILJA
WILL vb used as an auxiliary to form the future tense or to indicate intention, ability, or expectation ▷ n strong determination
WILLABLE adj able to be wished or determined by the will
WILLED adj having a will as specified
WILLEMITE n secondary mineral consisting of zinc silicate
WILLER > WILL
WILLERS > WILL
WILLEST > WILL
WILLET n large American shore bird
WILLETS > WILLET
WILLEY same as > WILLY
WILLEYED > WILLEY
WILLEYING > WILLEY
WILLEYS > WILLEY
WILLFUL same as > WILFUL
WILLFULLY > WILLFUL
WILLIAM as in sweet william flowering plant
WILLIAMS > WILLIAM
WILLIE n informal word for a penis
WILLIED > WILLY
WILLIES > WILLY
WILLING adj ready or inclined (to do something)
WILLINGER > WILLING
WILLINGLY > WILLING
WILLIWAU same as > WILLIWAW
WILLIWAUS > WILLIWAU
WILLIWAW n sudden strong gust of cold wind blowing offshore from a mountainous coast
WILLIWAWS > WILLIWAW
WILLOW n tree with thin flexible branches ▷ vb (of raw textile fibres) to open and clean in a machine having a system of rotating spikes
WILLOWED > WILLOW
WILLOWER n willow
WILLOWERS > WILLOWER
WILLOWIER > WILLOWY

WILLOWING > WILLOW
WILLOWISH > WILLOW
WILLOWS > WILLOW
WILLOWY adj slender and graceful
WILLPOWER n ability to control oneself and one's actions
WILLS > WILL
WILLY vb clean in willowing-machine
WILLYARD adj timid
WILLYART same as > WILLYARD
WILLYING > WILLY
WILLYWAW same as > WILLIWAW
WILLYWAWS > WILLYWAW
WILT vb (cause to) become limp or lose strength ▷ n act of wilting or state of becoming wilted
WILTED > WILT
WILTING > WILT
WILTJA n Aboriginal shelter
WILTJAS > WILTJA
WILTS > WILT
WILY adj crafty or sly
WIMBLE n any of a number of hand tools, such as a brace and bit or a gimlet, used for boring holes ▷ vb bore (a hole) with or as if with a wimble
WIMBLED > WIMBLE
WIMBLES > WIMBLE
WIMBLING > WIMBLE
WIMBREL same as > WHIMBREL
WIMBRELS > WIMBREL
WIMMIN n common intentional literary misspelling of 'women'
WIMP n feeble ineffectual person ▷ vb fail to complete something through fear
WIMPED > WIMP
WIMPIER > WIMP
WIMPIEST > WIMP
WIMPINESS > WIMP
WIMPING > WIMP
WIMPISH > WIMP
WIMPISHLY > WIMP
WIMPLE n garment framing the face, worn by medieval women and now by nuns ▷ vb ripple or cause to ripple or undulate
WIMPLED > WIMPLE
WIMPLES > WIMPLE
WIMPLING > WIMPLE
WIMPS > WIMP
WIMPY > WIMP
WIN vb come first in (a competition, fight, etc) ▷ n victory, esp in a game
WINCE vb draw back, as if in pain ▷ n wincing
WINCED > WINCE
WINCER > WINCE
WINCERS > WINCE
WINCES > WINCE
WINCEY n plain- or twill-weave cloth, usually having a cotton or linen warp and

a wool filling
WINCEYS > WINCEY
WINCH n machine for lifting or hauling using a cable or chain wound round a drum ▷ vb lift or haul using a winch
WINCHED > WINCH
WINCHER > WINCH
WINCHERS > WINCH
WINCHES > WINCH
WINCHING > WINCH
WINCHMAN n man who operates winch
WINCHMEN > WINCHMAN
WINCING > WINCE
WINCINGS > WINCE
WINCOPIPE n type of plant
WIND n current of air ▷ vb render short of breath
WINDABLE n able to be wound
WINDAC same as > WINDAS
WINDACS > WINDAC
WINDAGE n deflection of a projectile as a result of the effect of the wind
WINDAGES > WINDAGE
WINDAS n windlass
WINDASES > WINDAS
WINDBAG n person who talks much but uninterestingly
WINDBAGS > WINDBAG
WINDBELL n light bell made to be sounded by wind
WINDBELLS > WINDBELL
WINDBILL n bill of exchange cosigned by a guarantor
WINDBILLS > WINDBILL
WINDBLAST n strong gust of wind
WINDBLOW n trees uprooted by wind
WINDBLOWN adj blown about by the wind
WINDBLOWS > WINDBLOW
WINDBORNE adj (of plant seeds, etc) borne on the wind
WINDBOUND adj (of a sailing vessel) prevented from sailing by an unfavourable wind
WINDBREAK n fence or line of trees providing shelter from the wind
WINDBURN n irritation and redness of the skin caused by prolonged exposure to winds of high velocity
WINDBURNS > WINDBURN
WINDBURNT > WINDBURN
WINDCHILL n chilling effect of wind and low temperature
WINDED > WIND
WINDER n person or device that winds, as an engine for hoisting the cages in a mine shaft
WINDERS > WINDER
WINDFALL n unexpected good luck
WINDFALLS > WINDFALL
WINDFLAW n squall
WINDFLAWS > WINDFLAW

WINDGALL *n* soft swelling in the area of the fetlock joint of a horse

WINDGALLS > WINDGALL

WINDGUN *n* air gun

WINDGUNS > WINDGUN

WINDHOVER *dialect name for* > KESTREL

WINDIER > WINDY

WINDIEST > WINDY

WINDIGO *same as* > WENDIGO

WINDIGOS > WINDIGO

WINDILY > WINDY

WINDINESS > WINDY

WINDING > WIND

WINDINGLY > WINDING

WINDINGS > WIND

WINDLASS *n* winch worked by a crank ▷ *vb* raise or haul (a weight, etc) by means of a windlass

WINDLE *vb* wind something round continuously

WINDLED > WINDLE

WINDLES > WINDLE

WINDLESS > WIND

WINDLING > WINDLE

WINDLINGS > WINDLE

WINDMILL *n* machine for grinding or pumping driven by sails turned by the wind ▷ *vb* move or cause to move like the arms of a windmill

WINDMILLS > WINDMILL

WINDOCK *same as* > WINNOCK

WINDOCKS > WINDOCK

WINDORE *n* window

WINDORES > WINDORE

WINDOW *n* opening in a wall to let in light or air ▷ *vb* furnish with windows

WINDOWED > WINDOW

WINDOWING > WINDOW

WINDOWS > WINDOW

WINDOWY > WINDOW

WINDPIPE *n* tube linking the throat and the lungs

WINDPIPES > WINDPIPE

WINDPROOF *n* wind-resistant

WINDRING *adj* winding

WINDROSE *n* diagram with radiating lines showing the strength and frequency of winds from each direction affecting a specific place

WINDROSES > WINDROSE

WINDROW *n* long low ridge or line of hay or a similar crop, designed to achieve the best conditions for drying or curing ▷ *vb* put (hay or a similar crop) into windrows

WINDROWED > WINDROW

WINDROWER > WINDROW

WINDROWS > WINDROW

WINDS > WIND

WINDSAIL *n* sail rigged as an air scoop over a hatch or companionway to catch breezes and divert them below

WINDSAILS > WINDSAIL

WINDSES *pl n* ventilation shafts within mines

WINDSHAKE *n* crack between the annual rings in wood

WINDSHIP *n* ship propelled by wind

WINDSHIPS > WINDSHIP

WINDSOCK *n* cloth cone on a mast at an airfield to indicate wind direction

WINDSOCKS > WINDSOCK

WINDSTORM *n* storm consisting of violent winds

WINDSURF *vb* sail standing on a board equipped with a mast, sail, and boom

WINDSURFS > WINDSURF

WINDSWEPT *adj* exposed to the wind

WINDTHROW *n* uprooting of trees by wind

WINDTIGHT *adj* impenetrable by wind

WINDUP *n* prank or hoax

WINDUPS > WINDUP

WINDWARD *n* direction from which the wind is blowing ▷ *adj* of or in the direction from which the wind blows ▷ *adv* towards the wind

WINDWARDS *adv* in the direction of the wind

WINDWAY *n* part of wind instrument

WINDWAYS > WINDWAY

WINDY *adj* denoting a time or conditions in which there is a strong wind

WINE *n* alcoholic drink made from fermented grapes ▷ *adj* of a dark purplish-red colour ▷ *vb* give wine to

WINEBERRY *another name for* > MAKO

WINED > WINE

WINEGLASS *n* glass for wine, usually with a small bowl on a stem with a flared base

WINELESS > WINE

WINEMAKER *n* maker of wine

WINEPRESS *n* any equipment used for squeezing the juice from grapes in order to make wine

WINERIES > WINERY

WINERY *n* place where wine is made

WINES > WINE

WINESAP *n* variety of apple

WINESAPS > WINESAP

WINESHOP *n* shop where wine is sold

WINESHOPS > WINESHOP

WINESKIN *n* skin of a sheep or goat sewn up and used as a holder for wine

WINESKINS > WINESKIN

WINESOP *n* old word for an alcoholic

WINESOPS > WINESOP

WINEY *adj* having the taste or qualities of wine

WING *n* one of the limbs or organs of a bird, insect, or bat that are used for flying ▷ *vb* fly

WINGBACK *n* football position

WINGBACKS > WINGBACK

WINGBEAT *n* complete cycle of moving the wing by a bird in flight

WINGBEATS > WINGBEAT

WINGBOW *n* distinctive band of colour marking the wing of a bird

WINGBOWS > WINGBOW

WINGCHAIR *n* chair with forward projections from back

WINGDING *n* noisy lively party or festivity

WINGDINGS > WINGDING

WINGE *same as* > WHINGE

WINGED *adj* furnished with wings

WINGEDLY > WINGED

WINGEING > WINGE

WINGER *n* player positioned on a wing

WINGERS > WINGER

WINGES > WINGE

WINGIER > WINGY

WINGIEST > WINGY

WINGING > WING

WINGLESS *adj* having no wings or vestigial wings

WINGLET *n* small wing

WINGLETS > WINGLET

WINGLIKE > WING

WINGMAN *n* player in the wing position in Australian Rules

WINGMEN > WINGMAN

WINGOVER *n* manoeuvre in which the direction of flight of an aircraft is reversed by putting it into a climbing turn until nearly stalled, the nose then being allowed to fall while continuing the turn

WINGOVERS > WINGOVER

WINGS > WING

WINGSPAN *n* distance between the wing tips of an aircraft, bird, or insect

WINGSPANS > WINGSPAN

WINGSUIT *n* type of skydiving suit

WINGSUITS > WINGSUIT

WINGTIP *n* outermost edge of a wing

WINGTIPS > WINGTIP

WINGY *adj* having wings

WINIER > WINY

WINIEST > WINY

WINING > WINE

WINISH > WINE

WINK *vb* close and open (an eye) quickly as a signal ▷ *n* winking

WINKED > WINK

WINKER *n* person or thing that winks

WINKERS > WINKER

WINKING > WINK

WINKINGLY > WINK

WINKINGS > WINK

WINKLE *n* shellfish with a spiral shell ▷ *vb* extract or prise out

WINKLED > WINKLE

WINKLER *n* one who forces person or thing out

WINKLERS > WINKLER

WINKLES > WINKLE

WINKLING > WINKLE

WINKS > WINK

WINLESS *adj* not having won anything

WINN *n* penny

WINNA *vb* will not

WINNABLE > WIN

WINNARD *n* heron

WINNARDS > WINNARD

WINNED > WIN

WINNER *n* person or thing that wins

WINNERS > WINNER

WINNING *adj* (of a person) charming, attractive, etc

WINNINGLY > WINNING

WINNINGS > WIN

WINNLE *same as* > WINNLE

WINNLES > WINNLE

WINNOCK *n* window

WINNOCKS > WINNOCK

WINNOW *vb* separate (chaff) from (grain) ▷ *n* device for winnowing

WINNOWED > WINNOW

WINNOWER > WINNOW

WINNOWERS > WINNOW

WINNOWING > WINNOW

WINNOWS > WINNOW

WINNS > WINN

WINO *n* destitute person who habitually drinks cheap wine

WINOES > WINO

WINOS > WINO

WINS > WIN

WINSEY *same as* > WINCEY

WINSEYS > WINSEY

WINSOME *adj* charming or winning

WINSOMELY > WINSOME

WINSOMER > WINSOME

WINSOMEST > WINSOME

WINTER *n* coldest season ▷ *vb* spend the winter

WINTERED > WINTER

WINTERER > WINTER

WINTERERS > WINTER

WINTERFED *vb* past tense of 'winterfeed' (to feed (livestock) in winter when the grazing is not rich enough)

WINTERIER > WINTERY

WINTERING > WINTER

WINTERISE *same as* > WINTERIZE

WINTERISH > WINTER

WINTERIZE *vb* prepare (a house, car, etc) to withstand winter conditions

WINTERLY *same as* > WINTRY

WINTERS > WINTER

WINTERY *same as* > WINTRY

WINTLE *vb* reel; stagger

WINTLED > WINTLE

WINTLES > WINTLE

WINTLING > WINTLE

WINTRIER > WINTRY

WINTRIEST > WINTRY

WINTRILY > WINTRY

WINTRY *adj* of or like winter

WINY *same as* > WINEY

WINZE *n* steeply inclined shaft, as for ventilation between levels
WINZES > WINZE
WIPE *vb* clean or dry by rubbing ▷ *n* wiping
WIPED > WIPE
WIPEOUT *n* instance of wiping out
WIPEOUTS > WIPEOUT
WIPER *n* any piece of cloth, such as a handkerchief, towel, etc, used for wiping
WIPERS > WIPER
WIPES > WIPE
WIPING > WIPE
WIPINGS > WIPE
WIPPEN *n* part of hammer action in piano
WIPPENS > WIPPEN
WIRABLE *adj* that can be wired
WIRE *n* thin flexible strand of metal ▷ *vb* fasten with wire
WIRED *adj* excited or nervous
WIREDRAW *vb* convert (metal) into wire by drawing through successively smaller dies
WIREDRAWN > WIREDRAW
WIREDRAWS > WIREDRAW
WIREDREW > WIREDRAW
WIREGRASS *n* fine variety of grass
WIREHAIR *n* type of terrier
WIREHAIRS > WIREHAIR
WIRELESS *adj* (of a computer network) connected by radio rather than by cables or fibre optics ▷ *n* old-fashioned name for radio ▷ *vb* send by wireless
WIRELIKE > WIRE
WIREMAN *n* person who installs and maintains electric wiring, cables, etc
WIREMEN > WIREMAN
WIREPHOTO *n* facsimile of a photograph transmitted electronically via a telephone system
WIRER *n* person who sets or uses wires to snare rabbits and similar animals
WIRERS > WIRER
WIRES > WIRE
WIRETAP *vb* make a connection to a telegraph or telephone wire in order to obtain information secretly
WIRETAPS > WIRETAP
WIREWAY *n* tube for electric wires
WIREWAYS > WIREWAY
WIREWORK *n* functional or decorative work made of wire
WIREWORKS *n* factory where wire or articles of wire are made
WIREWORM *n* destructive wormlike beetle larva
WIREWORMS > WIREWORM

WIREWOVE *adj* woven out of wire
WIRIER > WIRY
WIRIEST > WIRY
WIRILDA *n* acacia tree, *Acacia retinoides*, of SE Australia with edible seeds
WIRILDAS > WIRILDA
WIRILY > WIRY
WIRINESS > WIRY
WIRING *n* system of wires ▷ *adj* used in wiring
WIRINGS > WIRING
WIRRA *interj* exclamation of sorrow or deep concern
WIRRAH *n* saltwater fish, *Acanthistius serratus*, of Australia, with bright blue spots
WIRRAHS > WIRRAH
WIRRICOW *same as* > WORRICOW
WIRRICOWS > WIRRICOW
WIRY *adj* lean and tough
WIS *vb* know or suppose (something)
WISARD *obsolete spelling of* > WIZARD
WISARDS > WISARD
WISDOM *n* good sense and judgment
WISDOMS > WISDOM
WISE *vb* guide ▷ *adj* having wisdom ▷ *n* manner
WISEACRE *n* person who wishes to seem wise
WISEACRES > WISEACRE
WISEASS *n* person who thinks he or she is being witty or clever
WISEASSES > WISEASS
WISECRACK *n* clever, sometimes unkind, remark ▷ *vb* make a wisecrack
WISED > WISE
WISEGUY *n* person who wants to seem clever
WISEGUYS > WISEGUY
WISELIER > WISE
WISELIEST > WISE
WISELING *n* one who claims to be wise
WISELINGS > WISELING
WISELY > WISE
WISENESS > WISE
WISENT *n* European bison
WISENTS > WISENT
WISER > WISE
WISES > WISE
WISEST > WISE
WISEWOMAN *n* witch
WISEWOMEN > WISEWOMAN
WISH *vb* want or desire ▷ *n* expression of a desire
WISHA *interj* expression of surprise
WISHBONE *n* V-shaped bone above the breastbone of a fowl
WISHBONES > WISHBONE
WISHED > WISH
WISHER > WISH
WISHERS > WISH
WISHES > WISH
WISHFUL *adj* too optimistic
WISHFULLY > WISHFUL
WISHING > WISH

WISHINGS > WISH
WISHLESS > WISH
WISHT *variant of* > WHISHT
WISING > WISE
WISKET *n* basket
WISKETS > WISKET
WISP *n* light delicate streak ▷ *vb* move or act like a wisp
WISPED > WISP
WISPIER > WISPY
WISPIEST > WISPY
WISPILY > WISPY
WISPINESS > WISPY
WISPING > WISP
WISPISH > WISP
WISPLIKE > WISP
WISPS > WISP
WISPY *adj* thin, fine, or delicate
WISS *vb* urinate
WISSED > WIS
WISSES > WIS
WISSING > WIS
WIST *vb* know
WISTARIA *same as* > WISTERIA
WISTARIAS > WISTARIA
WISTED > WIST
WISTERIA *n* climbing shrub with blue or purple flowers
WISTERIAS > WISTERIA
WISTFUL *adj* sadly longing
WISTFULLY > WISTFUL
WISTING > WIST
WISTITI *n* marmoset
WISTITIS > WISTITI
WISTLY *adv* intently
WISTS > WIST
WIT *vb* detect ▷ *n* ability to use words or ideas in a clever and amusing way
WITAN *n* assembly of higher ecclesiastics and important laymen, including king's thegns, that met to counsel the king on matters such as judicial problems
WITANS > WITAN
WITBLITS *n* illegally distilled strong alcoholic drink
WITCH *n* person, usu female, who practises (black) magic ▷ *vb* cause or change by or as if by witchcraft
WITCHED > WITCH
WITCHEN *n* rowan tree
WITCHENS > WITCHEN
WITCHERY *n* practice of witchcraft
WITCHES > WITCH
WITCHETTY *n* edible larva of certain Australian moths and beetles
WITCHHOOD > WITCH
WITCHIER > WITCHY
WITCHIEST > WITCHY
WITCHING *adj* relating to or appropriate for witchcraft ▷ *n* witchcraft
WITCHINGS > WITCHING
WITCHKNOT *n* knot in hair
WITCHLIKE > WITCH
WITCHWEED *n* any of several scrophulariaceous plants

of the genus *Striga*, esp *S. hermonthica*, that are serious pests of grain crops in parts of Africa and Asia
WITCHY *adj* like a witch
WITE *vb* blame
WITED > WITE
WITELESS *adj* witless
WITES > WITE
WITGAT *n* type of S African tree
WITGATS > WITGAT
WITH *prep* indicating presence alongside, possession, means of performance, characteristic manner, etc ▷ *n* division between flues in chimney
WITHAL *adv* as well
WITHDRAW *vb* take or move out or away
WITHDRAWN *adj* unsociable
WITHDRAWS > WITHDRAW
WITHDREW *past tense of* > WITHDRAW
WITHE *n* strong flexible twig, esp of willow, suitable for binding things together ▷ *vb* bind with withes
WITHED > WITHE
WITHER *vb* wilt or dry up
WITHERED > WITHER
WITHERER > WITHER
WITHERERS > WITHER
WITHERING > WITHER
WITHERITE *n* white, grey, or yellowish mineral
WITHEROD *n* American shrub
WITHERODS > WITHEROD
WITHERS *pl n* ridge between a horse's shoulder blades
WITHES > WITHE
WITHHAULT > WITHHOLD
WITHHELD > WITHHOLD
WITHHOLD *vb* refrain from giving
WITHHOLDS > WITHHOLD
WITHIER > WITHY
WITHIES > WITHY
WITHIEST > WITHY
WITHIN *adv* in or inside ▷ *prep* in or inside ▷ *n* something that is within
WITHING > WITHE
WITHINS > WITHIN
WITHOUT *prep* not accompanied by, using, or having ▷ *adv* outside ▷ *n* person who is without
WITHOUTEN *obsolete form of* > WITHOUT
WITHOUTS > WITHOUT
WITHS > WITH
WITHSTAND *vb* oppose or resist successfully
WITHSTOOD > WITHSTAND
WITHWIND *n* bindweed
WITHWINDS > WITHWIND
WITHY *n* willow tree, esp an osier ▷ *adj* (of people) tough and agile
WITHYWIND *same as* > WITHWIND
WITING > WITE

WITLESS *adj* foolish
WITLESSLY > WITLESS
WITLING *n* person who thinks himself witty
WITLINGS > WITLING
WITLOOF *n* chicory
WITLOOFS > WITLOOF
WITNESS *n* person who has seen something happen ▷ *vb* see at first hand
WITNESSED > WITNESS
WITNESSER > WITNESS
WITNESSES > WITNESS
WITNEY *n* type of blanket; heavy cloth
WITNEYS > WITNEY
WITS > WIT
WITTED *adj* having wit
WITTER *vb* chatter pointlessly or at unnecessary length ▷ *n* pointless chat
WITTERED > WITTER
WITTERING > WITTER
WITTERS > WITTER
WITTICISM *n* witty remark
WITTIER > WITTY
WITTIEST > WITTY
WITTILY > WITTY
WITTINESS > WITTY
WITTING *adj* deliberate
WITTINGLY > WITTING
WITTINGS > WIT
WITTOL *n* man who tolerates his wife's unfaithfulness
WITTOLLY > WITTOL
WITTOLS > WITTOL
WITTY *adj* clever and amusing
WITWALL *n* golden oriole
WITWALLS > WITWALL
WITWANTON *n* be disrespectfully witty
WIVE *vb* marry (a woman)
WIVED > WIVE
WIVEHOOD *obsolete variant of* > WIFEHOOD
WIVEHOODS > WIVEHOOD
WIVER *another word for* > WIVERN
WIVERN *same as* > WYVERN
WIVERNS > WIVERN
WIVERS > WIVER
WIVES > WIFE
WIVING > WIVE
WIZ *shortened form of* > WIZARD
WIZARD *n* magician ▷ *adj* superb
WIZARDLY > WIZARD
WIZARDRY *n* magic or sorcery
WIZARDS > WIZARD
WIZEN *vb* make or become shrivelled ▷ *n* archaic word for 'weasand' (the gullet)
WIZENED *adj* shrivelled or wrinkled
WIZENING > WIZEN
WIZENS > WIZEN
WIZES > WIZ
WIZIER *same as* > VIZIER
WIZIERS > WIZIER
WIZZEN *same as* > WIZEN
WIZZENS > WIZEN

WIZZES > WIZ
WO *archaic spelling of* > WOE
WOAD *n* blue dye obtained from a plant, used by the ancient Britons as a body dye
WOADED *adj* coloured blue with woad
WOADS > WOAD
WOADWAX *n* small Eurasian leguminous shrub
WOADWAXEN *n* small leguminous shrub with yellow flowers producing a yellow dye
WOADWAXES > WOADWAX
WOALD *same as* > WELD
WOALDS > WOALD
WOBBEGONG *n* Australian shark with brown-and-white skin
WOBBLE *vb* move unsteadily ▷ *n* wobbling movement or sound
WOBBLED > WOBBLE
WOBBLER > WOBBLE
WOBBLERS > WOBBLE
WOBBLES > WOBBLE
WOBBLIER > WOBBLY
WOBBLIES > WOBBLY
WOBBLIEST > WOBBLY
WOBBLING > WOBBLE
WOBBLINGS > WOBBLE
WOBBLY *adj* unsteady ▷ *n* temper tantrum
WOBEGONE *same as* > WOEBEGONE
WOCK *same as* > WOK
WOCKS > WOCK
WODGE *n* thick lump or chunk
WODGES > WODGE
WOE *n* grief
WOEBEGONE *adj* looking miserable
WOEFUL *adj* extremely sad
WOEFULLER > WOEFUL
WOEFULLY > WOEFUL
WOENESS > WOE
WOENESSES > WOE
WOES > WOE
WOESOME *adj* woeful
WOF *n* fool
WOFS > WOF
WOFUL *same as* > WOEFUL
WOFULLER > WOFUL
WOFULLEST > WOFUL
WOFULLY > WOFUL
WOFULNESS > WOFUL
WOG *n* derogatory word for a foreigner, esp one who is not White
WOGGISH > WOG
WOGGLE *n* ring of leather through which a Scout neckerchief is threaded
WOGGLES > WOGGLE
WOGS > WOG
WOIWODE *same as* > VOIVODE
WOIWODES > WOIWODE
WOK *n* bowl-shaped Chinese cooking pan, used for stir-frying
WOKE > WAKE
WOKEN > WAKE
WOKKA *as in* *wokka board* wobble board: a piece

of fibreboard used as a musical instrument
WOKS > WOK
WOLD *same as* > WELD
WOLDS > WOLD
WOLF *n* wild predatory canine mammal ▷ *vb* eat ravenously
WOLFBERRY *n* type of shrub
WOLFED > WOLF
WOLFER *same as* > WOLVER
WOLFERS > WOLFER
WOLFFISH *n* any large northern deep-sea blennioid fish of the family *Anarhichadidae* with large sharp teeth and no pelvic fins
WOLFHOUND *n* very large breed of dog
WOLFING > WOLF
WOLFINGS > WOLF
WOLFISH > WOLF
WOLFISHLY > WOLF
WOLFKIN *n* young wolf
WOLFKINS > WOLFKIN
WOLFLIKE > WOLF
WOLFLING *n* young wolf
WOLFLINGS > WOLFLING
WOLFRAM *another name for* > TUNGSTEN
WOLFRAMS > WOLFRAM
WOLFS > WOLF
WOLFSBANE *n* any of several poisonous N temperate plants of the ranunculaceous genus *Aconitum*, esp *A. lycoctonum*, which has yellow hoodlike flowers
WOLFSKIN *n* skin of wolf used for clothing, etc
WOLFSKINS > WOLFSKIN
WOLLIES > WOLLY
WOLLY *n* pickled cucumber or olive
WOLVE *vb* hunt for wolves
WOLVED > WOLVE
WOLVER *n* person who hunts wolves
WOLVERENE *same as* > WOLVERINE
WOLVERINE *n* carnivorous mammal of Arctic regions
WOLVERS > WOLVER
WOLVES > WOLF
WOLVING > WOLVE
WOLVINGS > WOLVE
WOLVISH *same as* > WOLFISH
WOLVISHLY > WOLVISH
WOMAN *n* adult human female ▷ *adj* female ▷ *vb* provide with a woman or women
WOMANED > WOMAN
WOMANHOOD *n* state of being a woman
WOMANING > WOMAN
WOMANISE *same as* > WOMANIZE
WOMANISED > WOMANISE
WOMANISER > WOMANISE
WOMANISES > WOMANISE
WOMANISH *adj* effeminate
WOMANISM *n* feminism among black women
WOMANISMS > WOMANISM

WOMANIST > WOMANISM
WOMANISTS > WOMANISM
WOMANIZE *vb* (of a man) to indulge in many casual affairs with women
WOMANIZED > WOMANIZE
WOMANIZER > WOMANIZE
WOMANIZES > WOMANIZE
WOMANKIND *n* all women considered as a group
WOMANLESS > WOMAN
WOMANLIER > WOMANLY
WOMANLIKE *adj* like a woman
WOMANLY *adj* having qualities traditionally associated with a woman
WOMANNESS > WOMAN
WOMANS > WOMAN
WOMB *vb* enclose ▷ *n* hollow organ in female mammals where babies are conceived and develop
WOMBAT *n* small heavily-built burrowing Australian marsupial
WOMBATS > WOMBAT
WOMBED > WOMB
WOMBIER > WOMBY
WOMBIEST > WOMBY
WOMBING > WOMB
WOMBLIKE > WOMB
WOMBS > WOMB
WOMBY *adj* hollow; spacious
WOMEN > WOMAN
WOMENFOLK *pl n* women collectively
WOMENKIND *same as* > WOMANKIND
WOMERA *same as* > WOOMERA
WOMERAS > WOMERA
WOMMERA *same as* > WOOMERA
WOMMERAS > WOMMERA
WOMMIT *n* foolish person
WOMMITS > WOMMIT
WOMYN *same as* > WOMAN
WON *n* standard monetary unit of North Korea, divided into 100 chon ▷ *vb* live or dwell
WONDER *vb* be curious about ▷ *n* wonderful thing ▷ *adj* spectacularly successful
WONDERED > WONDER
WONDERER > WONDER
WONDERERS > WONDER
WONDERFUL *adj* very fine
WONDERING > WONDER
WONDERKID *n* informal word for an exceptionally successful young person
WONDEROUS *obsolete variant of* > WONDROUS
WONDERS > WONDER
WONDRED *adj* splendid
WONDROUS *adj* wonderful ▷ *adv* (intensifier)
WONGA *n* money
WONGAS > WONGA
WONGI *vb* talk informally
WONGIED > WONGI
WONGIING > WONGI
WONGIS > WONGI
WONING > WON
WONINGS > WON
WONK *n* person who is

obsessively interested in a specified subject

WONKIER > WONKY

WONKIEST > WONKY

WONKS > WONK

WONKY *adj* shaky or unsteady

WONNED > WON

WONNER > WON

WONNERS > WON

WONNING > WON

WONNINGS > WON

WONS > WON

WONT *adj* accustomed ▷ *n* custom ▷ *vb* become or cause to become accustomed

WONTED *adj* accustomed or habituated (to doing something)

WONTEDLY > WONTED

WONTING > WONT

WONTLESS > WONT

WONTON *n* dumpling filled with spiced minced pork

WONTONS > WONTON

WONTS > WONT

WOO *vb* seek the love or affection of (a woman)

WOOBUT *same as* > WOUBIT

WOOBUTS > WOOBUT

WOOD *n* substance trees are made of, used in carpentry and as fuel ▷ *adj* made of or using wood ▷ *vb* (of land) plant with trees

WOODBIN *n* box for firewood

WOODBIND *same as* > WOODBINE

WOODBINDS > WOODBIND

WOODBINE *n* honeysuckle

WOODBINES > WOODBINE

WOODBINS > WOODBIN

WOODBLOCK *n* hollow block of wood used as a percussion instrument

WOODBORER *n* any of various beetles of the families *Anobiidae, Buprestidae*, etc, the larvae of which bore into and damage wood

WOODBOX *n* box for firewood

WOODBOXES > WOODBOX

WOODCHAT *n* songbird, *Lanius senator*, of Europe and N Africa, having a black-and-white plumage with a reddish-brown crown and a hooked bill

WOODCHATS > WOODCHAT

WOODCHIP *n* textured wallpaper

WOODCHIPS > WOODCHIP

WOODCHOP *n* wood-chopping competition, esp at a show

WOODCHOPS > WOODCHOP

WOODCHUCK *n* North American marmot, *Marmota monax*, having coarse reddish-brown fur

WOODCOCK *n* game bird

WOODCOCKS > WOODCOCK

WOODCRAFT *n* ability and experience in matters concerned with living in a wood or forest

WOODCUT *n* (print made from) an engraved block of wood

WOODCUTS > WOODCUT

WOODED *adj* covered with trees

WOODEN *adj* made of wood ▷ *vb* fell or kill (a person or animal)

WOODENED > WOODEN

WOODENER > WOODEN

WOODENEST > WOODEN

WOODENING > WOODEN

WOODENLY > WOODEN

WOODENS > WOODEN

WOODENTOP *n* dull, foolish, or unintelligent person

WOODFREE *adj* (of high-quality paper) made from pulp that has been treated chemically, removing impurities

WOODGRAIN *n* grain in wood

WOODHEN *another name for* > WEKA

WOODHENS > WOODHEN

WOODHOLE *n* store area for wood

WOODHOLES > WOODHOLE

WOODHORSE *n* frame for holding wood being sawn

WOODHOUSE *n* shed for firewood

WOODIE *n* gallows rope

WOODIER > WOODY

WOODIES > WOODIE

WOODIEST > WOODY

WOODINESS > WOODY

WOODING > WOOD

WOODLAND *n* forest ▷ *adj* living in woods

WOODLANDS > WOODLAND

WOODLARK *n* Old World lark, *Lullula arborea*, similar to but slightly smaller than the skylark

WOODLARKS > WOODLARK

WOODLESS > WOOD

WOODLICE > WOODLOUSE

WOODLORE *n* woodcraft skills

WOODLORES > WOODLORE

WOODLOT *n* area restricted to the growing of trees

WOODLOTS > WOODLOT

WOODLOUSE *n* small insect-like creature with many legs

WOODMAN *same as* > WOODSMAN

WOODMEAL *n* sawdust powder

WOODMEALS > WOODMEAL

WOODMEN > WOODMAN

WOODMICE > WOODMOUSE

WOODMOUSE *n* field mouse

WOODNESS > WOOD

WOODNOTE *n* natural musical note or song, like that of a wild bird

WOODNOTES > WOODNOTE

WOODPILE *n* heap of firewood

WOODPILES > WOODPILE

WOODPRINT *another name for* > WOODCUT

WOODREEVE *n* steward

responsible for wood

WOODROOF *same as* > WOODRUFF

WOODROOFS > WOODROOF

WOODRUFF *n* plant with small sweet-smelling white flowers and sweet-smelling leaves

WOODRUFFS > WOODRUFF

WOODRUSH *n* any of various juncaceous plants of the genus *Luzula*, chiefly of cold and temperate regions of the N hemisphere, having grasslike leaves and small brown flowers

WOODS *pl n* closely packed trees forming a forest or wood

WOODSCREW *n* metal screw that tapers to a point so that it can be driven into wood by a screwdriver

WOODSHED *n* small outbuilding where firewood, garden tools, etc, are stored

WOODSHEDS > WOODSHED

WOODSHOCK *n* type of bird

WOODSIA *n* any small fern of the genus *Woodsia*, of temperate and cold regions, having tufted rhizomes and numerous wiry fronds

WOODSIAS > WOODSIA

WOODSIER > WOODSY

WOODSIEST > WOODSY

WOODSKIN *n* canoe made of bark

WOODSKINS > WOODSKIN

WOODSMAN *n* person who lives in a wood or who is skilled at woodwork or carving

WOODSMEN > WOODSMAN

WOODSPITE *n* green woodpecker

WOODSTONE *n* type of stone resembling wood

WOODSTOVE *n* wood-burning stove

WOODSY *adj* of, reminiscent of, or connected with woods

WOODTONE *n* colour matching that of wood

WOODTONES > WOODTONE

WOODWALE *n* green woodpecker

WOODWALES > WOODWALE

WOODWARD *n* person in charge of a forest or wood

WOODWARDS > WOODWARD

WOODWAX *same as* > WOODWAXEN

WOODWAXEN *same as* > WOADWAXEN

WOODWAXES > WOODWAX

WOODWIND *n* (of) a type of wind instrument made of wood ▷ *adj* of or denoting a type of wind instrument, such as the oboe

WOODWINDS > WOODWIND

WOODWORK *n* parts of a room or building made of wood

WOODWORKS > WOODWORK

WOODWORM *n* insect larva that bores into wood

WOODWORMS > WOODWORM

WOODWOSE *n* hairy wildman of the woods

WOODWOSES > WOODWOSE

WOODY *adj* (of a plant) having a very hard stem

WOODYARD *n* place where timber is cut and stored

WOODYARDS > WOODYARD

WOOED > WOO

WOOER > WOO

WOOERS > WOO

WOOF *vb* (of dogs) bark or growl

WOOFED > WOOF

WOOFER *n* loudspeaker reproducing low-frequency sounds

WOOFERS > WOOFER

WOOFIER > WOOFY

WOOFIEST > WOOFY

WOOFING > WOOF

WOOFS > WOOF

WOOFTER *n* derogatory term for a male homosexual

WOOFTERS > WOOFTER

WOOFY *adj* with close, dense texture

WOOING > WOO

WOOINGLY > WOO

WOOINGS > WOO

WOOL *n* soft hair of sheep, goats, etc

WOOLD *vb* wind (rope)

WOOLDED > WOOLD

WOOLDER *n* stick for winding rope

WOOLDERS > WOOLDER

WOOLDING > WOOLD

WOOLDINGS > WOOLD

WOOLDS > WOOLD

WOOLED *same as* > WOOLLED

WOOLEN *same as* > WOOLLEN

WOOLENS > WOOLEN

WOOLER *same as* > WOOLDER

WOOLERS > WOOLER

WOOLFAT *same as* > LANOLIN

WOOLFATS > WOOLFAT

WOOLFELL *n* skin of a sheep or similar animal with the fleece still attached

WOOLFELLS > WOOLFELL

WOOLHAT *n* poor white person in S States

WOOLHATS > WOOLHAT

WOOLIE *n* wool garment

WOOLIER > WOOLY

WOOLIES > WOOLY

WOOLIEST > WOOLY

WOOLINESS > WOOLY

WOOLLED *adj* (of animals) having wool

WOOLLEN *adj* relating to or consisting partly or wholly of wool ▷ *n* garment or piece of cloth made wholly or partly of wool, esp a knitted one

WOOLLENS > WOOLLEN

WOOLLIER > WOOLLY

WOOLLIES > WOOLLY

WOOLLIEST > WOOLLY

WOOLLIKE > WOOL

WOOLLILY > WOOLLY

WOOLLY *adj* of or like wool ▷ *n* knitted woollen garment
WOOLMAN *n* wool trader
WOOLMEN > WOOLMAN
WOOLPACK *n* cloth or canvas wrapping used to pack a bale of wool
WOOLPACKS > WOOLPACK
WOOLS > WOOL
WOOLSACK *n* sack containing or intended to contain wool
WOOLSACKS > WOOLSACK
WOOLSEY *n* cotton and wool blend
WOOLSEYS > WOOLSEY
WOOLSHED *n* large building in which sheep shearing takes place
WOOLSHEDS > WOOLSHED
WOOLSKIN *n* sheepskin with wool still on
WOOLSKINS > WOOLSKIN
WOOLWARD *adv* with woollen side touching the skin
WOOLWORK *n* embroidery with wool
WOOLWORKS > WOOLWORK
WOOLY *same as* > WOOLLY
WOOMERA *n* notched stick used by Australian Aborigines to aid the propulsion of a spear
WOOMERANG *same as* > WOOMERA
WOOMERAS > WOOMERA
WOON *same as* > WON
WOONED > WOON
WOONING > WOON
WOONS > WOON
WOOPIE *n* well-off older person
WOOPIES > WOOPIE
WOOPS *vb* (esp of small child) vomit
WOOPSED > WOOPS
WOOPSES > WOOPS
WOOPSING > WOOPS
WOORALI *less common name for* > CURARE
WOORALIS > WOORALI
WOORARA *same as* > WOURALI
WOORARAS > WOORARA
WOORARI *same as* > WOURALI
WOORARIS > WOORARI
WOOS > WOO
WOOSE *same as* > WUSS
WOOSEL *same as* > OUZEL
WOOSELL *same as* > OUZEL
WOOSELLS > WOOSELL
WOOSELS > WOOSEL
WOOSES > WOOSE
WOOSH *same as* > WHOOSH
WOOSHED > WOOSH
WOOSHES > WOOSH
WOOSHING > WOOSH
WOOT *vb* wilt thou?
WOOTZ *n* Middle-Eastern steel
WOOTZES > WOOTZ
WOOZIER > WOOZY
WOOZIEST > WOOZY
WOOZILY > WOOZY
WOOZINESS > WOOZY
WOOZY *adj* weak, dizzy, and confused

WOP *same as* > WHOP
WOPPED > WOP
WOPPING > WOP
WOPS > WOP
WORCESTER *n* type of woollen fabric
WORD *n* smallest single meaningful unit of speech or writing ▷ *vb* express in words
WORDAGE *n* words considered collectively, esp a quantity of words
WORDAGES > WORDAGE
WORDBOOK *n* book containing words, usually with their meanings
WORDBOOKS > WORDBOOK
WORDBOUND *adj* unable to find words to express sth
WORDBREAK *n* point at which a word is divided when it runs over from one line of print to the next
WORDED > WORD
WORDGAME *n* any game involving the formation, discovery, or alteration of a word or words
WORDGAMES > WORDGAME
WORDIER > WORDY
WORDIEST > WORDY
WORDILY > WORDY
WORDINESS > WORDY
WORDING *n* choice and arrangement of words
WORDINGS > WORDING
WORDISH *adj* talkative
WORDLESS *adj* inarticulate or silent
WORDLORE *n* knowledge about words
WORDLORES > WORDLORE
WORDPLAY *n* verbal wit based on the meanings and ambiguities of words
WORDPLAYS > WORDPLAY
WORDS > WORD
WORDSMITH *n* person skilled in using words
WORDY *adj* using too many words
WORE > WEAR
WORK *n* physical or mental effort directed to making or doing something ▷ *adj* of or for work ▷ *vb* (cause to) do work
WORKABLE *adj* able to operate efficiently
WORKABLY > WORKABLE
WORKADAY *n* working day ▷ *adj* ordinary
WORKADAYS > WORKADAY
WORKBAG *n* container for implements, tools, or materials, esp sewing equipment
WORKBAGS > WORKBAG
WORKBENCH *n* heavy table at which a craftsman or mechanic works
WORKBOAT *n* boat used for tasks
WORKBOATS > WORKBOAT
WORKBOOK *n* exercise book or textbook used for study,

esp a textbook with spaces for answers
WORKBOOKS > WORKBOOK
WORKBOX *same as* > WORKBAG
WORKBOXES > WORKBOX
WORKDAY *another word for* > WORKADAY
WORKDAYS > WORKDAY
WORKED *adj* made or decorated with evidence of workmanship
WORKER *n* person who works in a specified way
WORKERIST *n* supporter of working-class politics
WORKERS > WORKER
WORKFARE *n* scheme under which the government of a country requires unemployed people to do community work or undergo job training in return for social-security payments
WORKFARES > WORKFARE
WORKFLOW *n* rate of progress of work
WORKFLOWS > WORKFLOW
WORKFOLK *pl n* working people, esp labourers on a farm
WORKFOLKS *same as* > WORKFOLK
WORKFORCE *n* total number of workers
WORKFUL *adj* hardworking
WORKGIRL *n* young female manual worker
WORKGIRLS > WORKGIRL
WORKGROUP *n* collection of networked computers
WORKHORSE *n* person or thing that does a lot of dull or routine work
WORKHOUR *n* time set aside for work
WORKHOURS > WORKHOUR
WORKHOUSE *n* (in England, formerly) institution where the poor were given food and lodgings in return for work
WORKING *n* operation or mode of operation of something ▷ *adj* relating to or concerned with a person or thing that works
WORKINGS > WORKING
WORKLESS > WORK
WORKLOAD *n* amount of work to be done, esp in a specified period
WORKLOADS > WORKLOAD
WORKMAN *n* manual worker
WORKMANLY *adj* appropriate to or befitting a good workman
WORKMATE *n* person who works with another person
WORKMATES > WORKMATE
WORKMEN > WORKMAN
WORKOUT *n* session of physical exercise for training or fitness
WORKOUTS > WORKOUT
WORKPIECE *n* piece of metal

or other material that is in the process of being worked on or made or has actually been cut or shaped by a hand tool or machine
WORKPLACE *n* place, such as a factory or office, where people work
WORKPRINT *n* unfinished print of cinema film
WORKROOM *n* room in which work, usually manual labour, is done
WORKROOMS > WORKROOM
WORKS > WORK
WORKSHEET *n* sheet of paper containing exercises to be completed by a student
WORKSHOP *n* room or building for a manufacturing process ▷ *vb* perform (a play) with no costumes, set, or musical accompaniment
WORKSHOPS > WORKSHOP
WORKSHY *adj* not inclined to work
WORKSOME *adj* hardworking
WORKSPACE *n* area set aside for work
WORKTABLE *n* table at which writing, sewing, or other work may be done
WORKTOP *n* surface in a kitchen, used for food preparation
WORKTOPS > WORKTOP
WORKUP *n* medical examination
WORKUPS > WORKUP
WORKWEAR *n* clothes, such as overalls, as worn for work in a factory, shop, etc
WORKWEARS > WORKWEAR
WORKWEEK *n* number of hours or days in a week actually or officially allocated to work
WORKWEEKS > WORKWEEK
WORKWOMAN *n* female manual worker
WORKWOMEN > WORKWOMAN
WORLD *n* planet earth ▷ *adj* of the whole world
WORLDBEAT *n* popular music from outside western mainstream
WORLDED *adj* incorporating worlds
WORLDLIER > WORLDLY
WORLDLING *n* person who is primarily concerned with worldly matters or material things
WORLDLY *adj* not spiritual ▷ *adv* in a worldly manner
WORLDS > WORLD
WORLDVIEW *n* comprehensive view of human life and the universe
WORLDWIDE *adj* applying or extending throughout the world
WORM *n* small limbless invertebrate animal ▷ *vb* rid of worms

w

WORMCAST n coil of earth excreted by a burrowing worm

WORMCASTS > WORMCAST

WORMED > WORM

WORMER > WORM

WORMERIES > WORMERY

WORMERS > WORM

WORMERY n piece of apparatus, having a glass side or sides, in which worms are kept for study

WORMFLIES > WORMFLY

WORMFLY n type of lure dressed on a double hook, the barbs of which sit one above the other and back-to-back

WORMGEAR n gear with screw thread

WORMGEARS > WORMGEAR

WORMHOLE n hole made by a worm in timber, plants, or fruit

WORMHOLED > WORMHOLE

WORMHOLES > WORMHOLE

WORMIER > WORMY

WORMIEST > WORMY

WORMIL n burrowing larva of type of fly

WORMILS > WORMIL

WORMINESS > WORMY

WORMING > WORM

WORMISH > WORM

WORMLIKE > WORM

WORMROOT n plant used to cure worms

WORMROOTS > WORMROOT

WORMS n disease caused by parasitic worms living in the intestines

WORMSEED n any of various plants having seeds or other parts used in medicine to treat worm infestation

WORMSEEDS > WORMSEED

WORMWOOD n bitter plant

WORMWOODS > WORMWOOD

WORMY adj infested with or eaten by worms

WORN > WEAR

WORNNESS n quality or condition of being worn

WORRAL n type of lizard

WORRALS > WORRAL

WORREL same as > WORRAL

WORRELS > WORREL

WORRICOW n frightening creature

WORRICOWS > WORRICOW

WORRIED > WORRY

WORRIEDLY > WORRY

WORRIER > WORRY

WORRIERS > WORRY

WORRIES > WORRY

WORRIMENT n anxiety or the trouble that causes it

WORRISOME adj causing worry

WORRIT vb tease or worry

WORRITED > WORRIT

WORRITING > WORRIT

WORRITS > WORRIT

WORRY vb (cause to) be anxious or uneasy ▷ n (cause of) anxiety or concern

WORRYCOW same as > WORRICOW

WORRYCOWS > WORRYCOW

WORRYGUTS n person who tends to worry, esp about insignificant matters

WORRYING > WORRY

WORRYINGS > WORRY

WORRYWART same as > WORRYGUTS

WORSE vb defeat

WORSED > WORSE

WORSEN vb make or grow worse

WORSENED > WORSEN

WORSENESS n state or condition of being worse

WORSENING > WORSEN

WORSENS > WORSEN

WORSER archaic or nonstandard word for > WORSE

WORSES > WORSE

WORSET n worsted fabric

WORSETS > WORSET

WORSHIP vb show religious devotion to ▷ n act or instance of worshipping

WORSHIPED > WORSHIP

WORSHIPER same as > WORSHIPPER

WORSHIPS > WORSHIP

WORSING > WORSE

WORST n worst thing ▷ vb defeat

WORSTED n type of woollen yarn or fabric

WORSTEDS > WORSTED

WORSTING > WORST

WORSTS > WORST

WORT n any of various unrelated plants, esp ones formerly used to cure diseases

WORTH prep having a value of ▷ n value or price ▷ vb happen or betide

WORTHED > WORTH

WORTHFUL adj worthy

WORTHIED > WORTHY

WORTHIER > WORTHY

WORTHIES > WORTHY

WORTHIEST > WORTHY

WORTHILY > WORTHY

WORTHING > WORTH

WORTHLESS adj without value or usefulness

WORTHS > WORTH

WORTHY adj deserving admiration or respect ▷ n notable person ▷ vb make worthy

WORTHYING > WORTHY

WORTLE n plate with holes for drawing wire through

WORTLES > WORTLE

WORTS > WORT

WOS > WO

WOSBIRD n illegitimate child

WOSBIRDS > WOSBIRD

WOST obsolete 2nd pers sing of wit, to know

WOT form of the present tense (indicative mood) of wit, to know

WOTCHER sentence substitute slang term of greeting

WOTS > WOT

WOTTED > WOT

WOTTEST > WOT

WOTTETH > WOT

WOTTING > WOT

WOUBIT n type of caterpillar

WOUBITS > WOUBIT

WOULD > WILL

WOULDEST same as > WOULDST

WOULDS same as > WOULDST

WOULDST singular form of the past tense of > WILL

WOUND vb injure ▷ n injury

WOUNDABLE > WOUND

WOUNDED adj suffering from wounds

WOUNDEDLY > WOUNDED

WOUNDER > WOUND

WOUNDERS > WOUND

WOUNDILY > WOUNDY

WOUNDING > WOUND

WOUNDINGS > WOUND

WOUNDLESS > WOUND

WOUNDS > WOUND

WOUNDWORT n type of plant formerly used for dressing wounds

WOUNDY adj extreme

WOURALI n plant from which curare is obtained

WOURALIS > WOURALI

WOVE > WEAVE

WOVEN n article made from woven cloth

WOVENS > WOVEN

WOW interj exclamation of astonishment ▷ n astonishing person or thing ▷ vb be a great success with

WOWED > WOW

WOWEE stronger form of > WOW

WOWF adj mad

WOWFER > WOWF

WOWFEST > WOWF

WOWING > WOW

WOWS > WOW

WOWSER n puritanical person

WOWSERS > WOWSER

WOX > WAX

WOXEN > WAX

WRACK n seaweed ▷ vb strain or shake (something) violently

WRACKED > WRACK

WRACKFUL n ruinous

WRACKING > WRACK

WRACKS > WRACK

WRAITH n ghost

WRAITHS > WRAITH

WRANG Scot word for > WRONG

WRANGED > WRANG

WRANGING > WRANG

WRANGLE vb argue noisily ▷ n noisy argument

WRANGLED > WRANGLE

WRANGLER n one who wrangles

WRANGLERS > WRANGLER

WRANGLES > WRANGLE

WRANGLING > WRANGLE

WRANGS > WRANG

WRAP vb fold (something) round (a person or thing) so as to cover ▷ n garment wrapped round the shoulders

WRAPOVER adj (of a garment, esp a skirt) not sewn up at one side, but worn wrapped round the body and fastened so that the open edges overlap ▷ n such a garment

WRAPOVERS > WRAPOVER

WRAPPAGE n material for wrapping

WRAPPAGES > WRAPPAGE

WRAPPED > WRAP

WRAPPER vb cover with wrapping ▷ n cover for a product

WRAPPERED > WRAPPER

WRAPPERS > WRAPPER

WRAPPING > WRAP

WRAPPINGS > WRAP

WRAPROUND same as > WRAPOVER

WRAPS > WRAP

WRAPT same as > RAPT

WRASSE n colourful sea fish

WRASSES > WRASSE

WRASSLE same as > WRESTLE

WRASSLED > WRASSLE

WRASSLES > WRASSLE

WRASSLING > WRASSLE

WRAST same as > WREST

WRASTED > WRAST

WRASTING > WRAST

WRASTLE same as > WRESTLE

WRASTLED > WRASTLE

WRASTLES > WRASTLE

WRASTLING > WRASTLE

WRASTS > WRAST

WRATE > WRITE

WRATH n intense anger ▷ adj incensed ▷ vb make angry

WRATHED > WRATH

WRATHFUL adj full of wrath

WRATHIER > WRATHY

WRATHIEST > WRATHY

WRATHILY > WRATHY

WRATHING > WRATH

WRATHLESS > WRATH

WRATHS > WRATH

WRATHY same as > WRATHFUL

WRAWL vb howl

WRAWLED > WRAWL

WRAWLING > WRAWL

WRAWLS > WRAWL

WRAXLE vb wrestle

WRAXLED > WRAXLE

WRAXLES > WRAXLE

WRAXLING > WRAXLE

WRAXLINGS > WRAXLE

WREAK vb inflict (vengeance, etc) or to cause (chaos, etc)

WREAKED > WREAK

WREAKER > WREAK

WREAKERS > WREAK

WREAKFUL adj seeking revenge

WREAKING > WREAK

WREAKLESS adj unrevengeful

WREAKS > WREAK

WREATH n twisted ring or band of flowers or leaves used as a memorial or tribute

WREATHE *vb* form into or take the form of a wreath by intertwining or twisting together

WREATHED > WREATHE

WREATHEN *adj* twisted into wreath

WREATHER > WREATHE

WREATHERS > WREATHE

WREATHES > WREATHE

WREATHIER > WREATHY

WREATHING > WREATHE

WREATHS > WREATH

WREATHY *adj* twisted into wreath

WRECK *vb* destroy ▷ *n* remains of something that has been destroyed or badly damaged, esp a ship

WRECKAGE *n* wrecked remains

WRECKAGES > WRECKAGE

WRECKED *adj* in a state of intoxication, stupor, or euphoria, induced by drugs or alcohol

WRECKER *n* formerly, person who lured ships onto the rocks in order to plunder them

WRECKERS > WRECKER

WRECKFISH *n* large sea perch

WRECKFUL *adj* causing wreckage

WRECKING > WRECK

WRECKINGS > WRECK

WRECKS > WRECK

WREN *n* small brown songbird

WRENCH *vb* twist or pull violently ▷ *n* violent twist or pull

WRENCHED > WRENCH

WRENCHER > WRENCH

WRENCHERS > WRENCH

WRENCHES > WRENCH

WRENCHING > WRENCH

WRENS > WREN

WREST *vb* twist violently ▷ *n* act or an instance of wresting

WRESTED > WREST

WRESTER > WREST

WRESTERS > WREST

WRESTING > WREST

WRESTLE *vb* fight, esp as a sport, by grappling with and trying to throw down an opponent ▷ *n* act of wrestling

WRESTLED > WRESTLE

WRESTLER > WRESTLE

WRESTLERS > WRESTLE

WRESTLES > WRESTLE

WRESTLING *n* sport in which each contestant tries to overcome the other either by throwing or pinning him or her to the ground or by forcing a submission

WRESTS > WREST

WRETCH *n* despicable person

WRETCHED *adj* miserable or unhappy

WRETCHES > WRETCH

WRETHE *same as* > WREATHE

WRETHED > WRETHE

WRETHES > WRETHE

WRETHING > WRETHE

WRICK *variant spelling (chiefly Brit) of* > RICK

WRICKED > WRICK

WRICKING > WRICK

WRICKS > WRICK

WRIED > WRY

WRIER > WRY

WRIES > WRY

WRIEST > WRY

WRIGGLE *vb* move with a twisting action ▷ *n* wriggling movement

WRIGGLED > WRIGGLE

WRIGGLER > WRIGGLE

WRIGGLERS > WRIGGLE

WRIGGLES > WRIGGLE

WRIGGLIER > WRIGGLE

WRIGGLING > WRIGGLE

WRIGGLY > WRIGGLE

WRIGHT *n* maker

WRIGHTS > WRIGHT

WRING *vb* twist, esp to squeeze liquid out of

WRINGED > WRING

WRINGER *same as* > MANGLE

WRINGERS > WRINGER

WRINGING > WRING

WRINGINGS > WRING

WRINGS > WRING

WRINKLE *n* slight crease, esp one in the skin due to age ▷ *vb* make or become slightly creased

WRINKLED > WRINKLE

WRINKLES > WRINKLE

WRINKLIER > WRINKLE

WRINKLIES *pl n* derogatory word for old people

WRINKLING > WRINKLE

WRINKLY > WRINKLE

WRIST *n* joint between the hand and the arm

WRISTBAND *n* band around the wrist, esp one attached to a watch or forming part of a long sleeve

WRISTIER > WRISTY

WRISTIEST > WRISTY

WRISTLET *n* band or bracelet worn around the wrist

WRISTLETS > WRISTLET

WRISTLOCK *n* wrestling hold in which a wrestler seizes his opponent's wrist and exerts pressure against the joints of his hand, arm, or shoulder

WRISTS > WRIST

WRISTY *adj* (of a player's style of hitting the ball in cricket, tennis, etc) characterized by considerable movement of the wrist

WRIT *n* written legal command

WRITABLE > WRITE

WRITATIVE *adj* inclined to write a lot

WRITE *vb* mark paper etc with symbols or words

WRITEABLE > WRITE

WRITER *n* author

WRITERESS *n* female writer

WRITERLY *adj* of or characteristic of a writer

WRITERS > WRITER

WRITES > WRITE

WRITHE *vb* twist or squirm in or as if in pain ▷ *n* act or an instance of writhing

WRITHED > WRITHE

WRITHEN *adj* twisted

WRITHER > WRITHE

WRITHERS > WRITHE

WRITHES > WRITHE

WRITHING > WRITHE

WRITHINGS > WRITHE

WRITHLED *adj* wrinkled

WRITING > WRITE

WRITINGS > WRITE

WRITS > WRIT

WRITTEN > WRITE

WRIZLED *adj* wrinkled

WROATH *n* unforeseen trouble

WROATHS > WROATH

WROKE > WREAK

WROKEN > WREAK

WRONG *adj* incorrect or mistaken ▷ *adv* in a wrong manner ▷ *n* something immoral or unjust ▷ *vb* treat unjustly

WRONGDOER *n* person who acts immorally or illegally

WRONGED > WRONG

WRONGER > WRONG

WRONGERS > WRONG

WRONGEST > WRONG

WRONGFUL *adj* unjust or illegal

WRONGING > WRONG

WRONGLY > WRONG

WRONGNESS > WRONG

WRONGOUS *adj* unfair

WRONGS > WRONG

WROOT *obsolete form of* > ROOT

WROOTED > WROOT

WROOTING > WROOT

WROOTS > WROOT

WROTE > WRITE

WROTH *adj* angry

WROTHFUL *same as* > WRATHFUL

WROUGHT *adj* (of metals) shaped by hammering or beating

WRUNG > WRING

WRY *adj* drily humorous ▷ *vb* twist or contort

WRYBILL *n* New Zealand plover whose bill is bent to one side enabling it to search for food beneath stones

WRYBILLS > WRYBILL

WRYER *same as* > WRY

WRYEST *same as* > WRY

WRYING > WRY

WRYLY > WRY

WRYNECK *n* woodpecker that has a habit of twisting its neck round

WRYNECKS > WRYNECK

WRYNESS > WRY

WRYNESSES > WRY

WRYTHEN *adj* twisted

WUD *Scots form of* > WOOD

WUDDED > WUD

WUDDING > WUD

WUDJULA *n* Australian word for a non-Aboriginal person

WUDJULAS > WUDJULA

WUDS > WUD

WUDU *n* practice of ritual washing before daily prayer

WUDUS > WUDU

WUKKAS *pl n* Australian taboo slang expression for no problems

WULFENITE *n* yellow, orange, red, or grey lustrous secondary mineral

WULL *obsolete form of* > WILL

WULLED > WILL

WULLING > WILL

WULLS > WILL

WUNNER *same as* > ONER

WUNNERS > WUNNER

WURLEY *n* Aboriginal hut

WURLEYS > WURLEY

WURLIE *same as* > WURLEY

WURLIES > WURLIE

WURST *n* large sausage, esp of a type made in Germany, Austria, etc

WURSTS > WURST

WURTZITE *n* zinc sulphide

WURTZITES > WURTZITE

WURZEL *n* root

WURZELS > WURZEL

WUS *n* casual term of address

WUSES > WUS

WUSHU *n* Chinese martial arts

WUSHUS > WUSHU

WUSS *n* feeble or effeminate person

WUSSES > WUSS

WUSSIER > WUSSY

WUSSIES > WUSSY

WUSSIEST > WUSSY

WUSSY *adj* feeble or effeminate ▷ *n* feeble person

WUTHER *vb* (of wind) blow and roar

WUTHERED > WUTHER

WUTHERING *adj* (of a wind) blowing strongly with a roaring sound

WUTHERS > WUTHER

WUXIA *n* genre of Chinese fiction and film, concerning the adventures of sword-wielding chivalrous heroes

WUXIAS > WUXIA

WUZZLE *vb* mix up

WUZZLED > WUZZLE

WUZZLES > WUZZLE

WUZZLING > WUZZLE

WYANDOTTE *n* heavy American breed of domestic fowl

WYCH *n* type of tree having flexible branches

WYCHES > WYCH

WYE *n* y-shaped pipe

WYES > WYE

WYLE *vb* entice

WYLED > WYLE

WYLES > WYLE

WYLIECOAT *n* petticoat

WYLING > WYLE
WYN *n* rune equivalent to English 'w'
WYND *n* narrow lane or alley
WYNDS > WYND
WYNN *same as* > WYN

WYNNS > WYNN
WYNS > WYN
WYSIWYG *adj* (of text and images displayed on a computer screen) being the same as what will be

printed out
WYTE *vb* blame
WYTED > WYTE
WYTES > WYTE
WYTING > WYTE
WYVERN *n* heraldic beast

having a serpent's tail and a dragon's head and a body with wings and two legs
WYVERNS > WYVERN

Xx

XANTHAM *n* acacia gum
XANTHAMS > XANTHAM
XANTHAN *same as* > XANTHAM
XANTHANS > XANTHAN
XANTHATE *n* any salt or ester of xanthic acid
XANTHATES > XANTHATE
XANTHEIN *n* soluble part of the yellow pigment that is found in the cell sap of some flowers
XANTHEINS > XANTHEIN
XANTHENE *n* yellowish crystalline heterocyclic compound used as a fungicide
XANTHENES > XANTHENE
XANTHIC *adj* of, containing, or derived from xanthic acid
XANTHIN *n* any of a group of yellow or orange carotene derivatives that occur in the fruit and flowers of certain plants
XANTHINE *n* crystalline compound related in structure to uric acid and found in urine, blood, certain plants, and certain animal tissues
XANTHINES > XANTHINE
XANTHINS > XANTHIN
XANTHISM *n* condition of skin, fur, or feathers in which yellow coloration predominates
XANTHISMS > XANTHISM
XANTHOMA *n* presence in the skin of fatty yellow or brownish plaques or nodules, esp on the eyelids, caused by a disorder of lipid metabolism
XANTHOMAS > XANTHOMA
XANTHONE *n* crystalline compound
XANTHONES > XANTHONE
XANTHOUS *adj* of, relating to, or designating races with yellowish hair and a light complexion
XANTHOXYL *n* South American plant
XEBEC *n* small three-masted Mediterranean vessel with both square and lateen sails, formerly used by Algerian pirates and later used for commerce
XEBECS > XEBEC
XENIA *n* influence of pollen upon the form of the fruit developing after pollination
XENIAL > XENIA
XENIAS > XENIA
XENIC *adj* denoting the presence of bacteria
XENIUM *n* diplomatic gift
XENOBLAST *n* type of mineral deposit
XENOCRYST *n* crystal included within an igneous rock as the magma cooled but not formed from it
XENOGAMY *n* fertilization by the fusion of male and female gametes from different individuals of the same species
XENOGENIC *adj* relating to the supposed production of offspring completely unlike either parent
XENOGENY *n* offspring unlike either parent
XENOGRAFT *n* tissue graft obtained from a donor of a different species from the recipient
XENOLITH *n* fragment of rock differing in origin, composition, structure, etc, from the igneous rock enclosing it
XENOLITHS > XENOLITH
XENOMANIA *n* passion for foreign things
XENOMENIA *n* menstruation from unusual orifices
XENON *n* colourless odourless gas found in very small quantities in the air
XENONS > XENON
XENOPHILE *n* person who likes foreigners or things foreign
XENOPHOBE *n* person who hates or fears foreigners or strangers
XENOPHOBY *n* hatred or fear of foreigners or strangers
XENOPHYA *n* parts of shell or skeleton formed by foreign bodies
XENOPUS *n* African frog
XENOPUSES > XENOPUS
XENOTIME *n* yellow-brown mineral
XENOTIMES > XENOTIME
XENURINE *adj* relating to a type of armadillo
XERAFIN *n* Indian coin
XERAFINS > XERAFIN
XERANSES > XERANSIS
XERANSIS *n* gradual loss of tissue moisture
XERANTIC > XERANSIS
XERAPHIM *same as* > XERAFIN
XERAPHIMS > XERAPHIM
XERARCH *adj* (of a sere) having its origin in a dry habitat
XERASIA *n* dryness of the hair
XERASIAS > XERASIA
XERIC *adj* of, relating to, or growing in dry conditions
XERICALLY > XERIC
XERISCAPE *n* landscape designed to conserve water
XEROCHASY *n* release of seeds or pollen on drying
XERODERMA *n* any abnormal dryness of the skin as the result of diminished secretions from the sweat or sebaceous glands
XEROMA *n* excessive dryness of the cornea
XEROMAS > XEROMA
XEROMATA > XEROMA
XEROMORPH *n* xerophilous plant
XEROPHAGY *n* fasting by eating only dry food
XEROPHILE *n* plant or animal who likes living in dry surroundings
XEROPHILY > XEROPHILE
XEROPHYTE *n* xerophilous plant, such as a cactus
XEROSERE *n* sere that originates in dry surroundings
XEROSERES > XEROSERE
XEROSES > XEROSIS
XEROSIS *n* abnormal dryness of bodily tissues, esp the skin, eyes, or mucous membranes
XEROSTOMA *n* abnormal lack of saliva; dryness of the mouth
XEROTES *same as* > XEROSIS
XEROTIC > XEROSIS
XEROX *n* tradename for a machine employing a xerographic copying process ▷ *vb* produce a copy (of a document, etc) using such a machine
XEROXED > XEROX
XEROXES > XEROX
XEROXING > XEROX
XERUS *n* ground squirrel
XERUSES > XERUS
XI *n* 14th letter in the Greek alphabet
XIPHOID *adj* shaped like a sword ▷ *n* part of the sternum
XIPHOIDAL > XIPHOID
XIPHOIDS > XIPHOID
XIPHOPAGI *n* Siamese twins joined at the lower sternum
XIS > XI
XOANA > XOANON
XOANON *n* primitive image of a god, carved, esp originally, in wood, and supposed to have fallen from heaven
XU *n* Vietnamese currency unit
XYLAN *n* yellow polysaccharide consisting of xylose units: occurs in straw husks and other woody tissue
XYLANS > XYLAN
XYLEM *n* plant tissue that conducts water and minerals from the roots to all other parts
XYLEMS > XYLEM
XYLENE *n* type of hydrocarbon
XYLENES > XYLENE
XYLENOL *n* synthetic resin made from xylene
XYLENOLS > XYLENOL**

XYLIC > XYLEM

XYLIDIN *same as* > XYLIDINE

XYLIDINE *n* mixture of six isomeric amines derived from xylene and used in dyes

XYLIDINES > XYLIDINE

XYLIDINS > XYLIDIN

XYLITOL *n* crystalline alcohol used as sweetener

XYLITOLS > XYLITOL

XYLOCARP *n* fruit, such as a coconut, having a hard woody pericarp

XYLOCARPS > XYLOCARP

XYLOGEN *same as* > XYLEM

XYLOGENS > XYLOGEN

XYLOGRAPH *n* engraving in wood ▷*vb* print (a design, illustration, etc) from a wood engraving

XYLOID *adj* of, relating to, or resembling wood

XYLOIDIN *n* type of explosive

XYLOIDINE *same as* > XYLOIDIN

XYLOIDINS > XYLOIDIN

XYLOL *another name (not in technical usage) for* > XYLENE

XYLOLOGY *n* study of the composition of wood

XYLOLS > XYLOL

XYLOMA *n* hard growth in fungi

XYLOMAS > XYLOMA

XYLOMATA > XYLOMA

XYLOMETER *n* device for measuring the specific gravity of wood

XYLONIC *adj* denoting an acid formed from xylose

XYLONITE *n* type of plastic

XYLONITES > XYLONITE

XYLOPHAGE *n* creature that eats wood

XYLOPHONE *n* musical instrument made of a row of wooden bars played with hammers

XYLORIMBA *n* large xylophone with an extended range of five octaves

XYLOSE *n* white crystalline dextrorotatory sugar found in the form of xylan in wood and straw

XYLOSES > XYLOSE

XYLOTOMY *n* preparation of sections of wood for examination by microscope

XYLYL *n* group of atoms

XYLYLS > XYLYL

XYST *n* long portico, esp one used in ancient Greece for athletics

XYSTER *n* surgical instrument for scraping bone

XYSTERS > XYSTER

XYSTI > XYSTUS

XYSTOI > XYSTOS

XYSTOS *same as* > XYST

XYSTS > XYST

XYSTUS *same as* > XYST

Yy

YA *pron* you

YAAR *n* in informal Indian English, a friend

YAARS > YAAR

YABA *n* informal word for 'yet another bloody acronym'

YABBA *n* form of methamphetamine

YABBAS > YABBA

YABBER *vb* talk or jabber ▷ *n* talk or jabber

YABBERED > YABBER

YABBERING > YABBER

YABBERS > YABBER

YABBIE *same as* > YABBY

YABBIED > YABBY

YABBIES > YABBY

YABBY *n* small freshwater crayfish ▷ *vb* go out to catch yabbies

YABBYING > YABBY

YACCA *n* Australian plant with a woody stem, stiff grasslike leaves, and a spike of small white flowers

YACCAS > YACCA

YACHT *n* large boat with sails or an engine, used for racing or pleasure cruising ▷ *vb* sail in a yacht

YACHTED > YACHT

YACHTER > YACHT

YACHTERS > YACHT

YACHTIE *n* yachtsman

YACHTIES > YACHTIE

YACHTING *n* sport or practice of navigating a yacht

YACHTINGS > YACHTING

YACHTMAN *same as* > YACHTSMAN

YACHTMEN > YACHTMAN

YACHTS > YACHT

YACHTSMAN *n* person who sails a yacht

YACHTSMEN > YACHTSMAN

YACK *same as* > YAK

YACKA *same as* > YACCA

YACKAS > YACKA

YACKED > YACK

YACKER *same as* > YAKKA

YACKERS > YACKER

YACKING > YACK

YACKS > YACK

YAD *n* hand-held pointer used for reading the sefer torah

YADS > YAD

YAE *same as* > AE

YAFF *vb* bark

YAFFED > YAFF

YAFFING > YAFF

YAFFLE *n* woodpecker with a green back and wings, and a red crown

YAFFLES > YAFFLE

YAFFS > YAFF

YAG *n* artificial crystal

YAGER *same as* > JAEGER

YAGERS > YAGER

YAGGER *n* pedlar

YAGGERS > YAGGER

YAGI *n* type of highly directional aerial

YAGIS > YAGI

YAGS > YAG

YAH *interj* exclamation of derision or disgust ▷ *n* affected upper-class person

YAHOO *n* crude coarse person

YAHOOISM > YAHOO

YAHOOISMS > YAHOO

YAHOOS > YAHOO

YAHRZEIT *n* (in Judaism) the anniversary of the death of a close relative, on which it is customary to kindle a light and recite the Kaddish

YAHRZEITS > YAHRZEIT

YAHS > YAH

YAIRD *Scots form of* > YARD

YAIRDS > YAIRD

YAK *n* Tibetan ox with long shaggy hair ▷ *vb* talk continuously about unimportant matters

YAKHDAN *n* box for carrying ice on a pack animal

YAKHDANS > YAKHDAN

YAKIMONO *n* grilled food

YAKIMONOS > YAKIMONO

YAKITORI *n* Japanese dish consisting of small pieces of chicken skewered and grilled

YAKITORIS > YAKITORI

YAKKA *n* work

YAKKAS > YAKKA

YAKKED > YAK

YAKKER *same as* > YAKKA

YAKKERS > YAKKER

YAKKING > YAK

YAKOW *n* animal bred from a male yak and a domestic cow

YAKOWS > YAKOW

YAKS > YAK

YAKUZA *n* Japanese criminal organization involved in illegal gambling, extortion, gun-running, etc

YALD *adj* vigorous

YALE *n* mythical beast with the body of an antelope (or similar animal) and swivelling horns

YALES > YALE

YAM *n* tropical root vegetable

YAMALKA *same as* > YARMULKE

YAMALKAS > YAMALKA

YAMEN *n* (in imperial China) the office or residence of a public official

YAMENS > YAMEN

YAMMER *vb* whine in a complaining manner ▷ *n* yammering sound

YAMMERED > YAMMER

YAMMERER > YAMMER

YAMMERERS > YAMMER

YAMMERING > YAMMER

YAMMERS > YAMMER

YAMPIES > YAMPY

YAMPY *n* foolish person

YAMS > YAM

YAMULKA *same as* > YARMULKE

YAMULKAS > YAMULKA

YAMUN *same as* > YAMEN

YAMUNS > YAMUN

YANG *n* (in Chinese philosophy) one of two complementary principles maintaining harmony in the universe

YANGS > YANG

YANK *vb* pull or jerk suddenly ▷ *n* sudden pull or jerk

YANKED > YANK

YANKER > YANK

YANKERS > YANK

YANKIE *n* shrewish woman

YANKIES > YANKIE

YANKING > YANK

YANKS > YANK

YANQUI *n* slang word for American

YANQUIS > YANQUI

YANTRA *n* diagram used in meditation

YANTRAS > YANTRA

YAOURT *n* yoghurt

YAOURTS > YAOURT

YAP *vb* bark with a high-pitched sound ▷ *n* high-pitched bark ▷ *interj* imitation or representation of the sound of a dog yapping or people jabbering

YAPOCK *same as* > YAPOK

YAPOCKS > YAPOCK

YAPOK *n* type of opossum

YAPOKS > YAPOK

YAPON *same as* > YAUPON

YAPONS > YAPON

YAPP *n* type of book binding

YAPPED > YAP

YAPPER > YAP

YAPPERS > YAP

YAPPIE *n* young aspiring professional

YAPPIER > YAP

YAPPIES > YAPPIE

YAPPIEST > YAP

YAPPING > YAP

YAPPINGLY > YAP

YAPPS > YAPP

YAPPY > YAP

YAPS > YAP

YAPSTER > YAP

YAPSTERS > YAP

YAQONA *n* Polynesian shrub

YAQONAS > YAQONA

YAR *adj* nimble

YARCO *n* derogatory dialect word for a young working-class person who wears casual sports clothes

YARCOS > YARCO

YARD *n* unit of length equal to 36 inches or about 91.4 centimetres ▷ *vb* draft (animals), esp to a saleyard

YARDAGE *n* length measured in yards

YARDAGES > YARDAGE

YARDANG *n* ridge formed by wind erosion

YARDANGS > YARDANG

YARDARM *n* outer end of a ship's yard

YARDARMS > YARDARM

YARDBIRD n inexperienced, untrained, or clumsy soldier, esp one employed on menial duties

YARDBIRDS > YARDBIRD

YARDED > YARD

YARDER > YARD

YARDERS > YARD

YARDING n group of animals displayed for sale

YARDINGS > YARDING

YARDLAND n archaic unit of land

YARDLANDS > YARDLAND

YARDMAN n farm overseer

YARDMEN > YARDMAN

YARDS > YARD

YARDSTICK n standard against which to judge other people or things

YARDWAND same as > YARDSTICK

YARDWANDS > YARDWAND

YARDWORK n garden work

YARDWORKS > YARDWORK

YARE adj ready, brisk, or eager ▷ adv readily or eagerly

YARELY > YARE

YARER > YARE

YAREST > YARE

YARFA n peat

YARFAS > YARFA

YARK vb make ready

YARKED > YARK

YARKING > YARK

YARKS > YARK

YARMELKE same as > YARMULKE

YARMELKES > YARMELKE

YARMULKA same as > YARMULKE

YARMULKAS > YARMULKA

YARMULKE n skullcap worn by Jewish men

YARMULKES > YARMULKE

YARN n thread used for knitting or making cloth ▷ vb thread with yarn

YARNED > YARN

YARNER > YARN

YARNERS > YARN

YARNING > YARN

YARNS > YARN

YARPHA n peat

YARPHAS > YARPHA

YARR n wild white flower

YARRAMAN n horse

YARRAMANS > YARRAMAN

YARRAMEN > YARRAMAN

YARRAN n small hardy tree, *Acacia homalophylla*, of inland Australia

YARRANS > YARRAN

YARROW n wild plant with flat clusters of white flowers

YARROWS > YARROW

YARRS > YARR

YARTA Shetland word for > HEART

YARTAS > YARTA

YARTO same as > YARTA

YARTOS > YARTO

YASHMAC same as > YASHMAK

YASHMACS > YASHMAC

YASHMAK n veil worn by a Muslim woman to cover her face in public

YASHMAKS > YASHMAK

YASMAK same as > YASHMAK

YASMAKS > YASHMAK

YATAGAN same as > YATAGHAN

YATAGANS > YATAGAN

YATAGHAN n Turkish sword with a curved single-edged blade

YATAGHANS > YATAGHAN

YATE n any of several small eucalyptus trees, esp *Eucalyptus cornuta*, yielding a very hard timber

YATES > YATE

YATTER vb talk at length ▷ n continuous chatter

YATTERED > YATTER

YATTERING > YATTER

YATTERS > YATTER

YAUD Scots word for > MARE

YAUDS > YAUD

YAULD adj alert, spritely, or nimble

YAUP variant spelling of > YAWP

YAUPED > YAUP

YAUPER > YAUP

YAUPERS > YAUP

YAUPING > YAUP

YAUPON n southern US evergreen holly shrub, *Ilex vomitoria*, with spreading branches, scarlet fruits, and oval leaves

YAUPONS > YAUPON

YAUPS > YAUP

YAUTIA n any of several Caribbean aroid plants of the genus *Xanthosoma*, cultivated for their edible leaves and underground stems

YAUTIAS > YAUTIA

YAW vb (of an aircraft or ship) turn to one side or from side to side while moving ▷ n act or movement of yawing

YAWED > YAW

YAWEY > YAWS

YAWING > YAW

YAWL n two-masted sailing boat ▷ vb howl, weep, or scream harshly

YAWLED > YAWL

YAWLING > YAWL

YAWLS > YAWL

YAWMETER n instrument for measuring an aircraft's yaw

YAWMETERS > YAWMETER

YAWN vb open the mouth wide and take in air deeply, often when sleepy or bored ▷ n act of yawning

YAWNED > YAWN

YAWNER > YAWN

YAWNERS > YAWN

YAWNIER > YAWN

YAWNIEST > YAWN

YAWNING > YAWN

YAWNINGLY > YAWN

YAWNINGS > YAWN

YAWNS > YAWN

YAWNY > YAWN

YAWP vb gape or yawn, esp audibly ▷ n shout, bark, yelp, or cry

YAWPED > YAWP

YAWPER > YAWP

YAWPERS > YAWP

YAWPING > YAWP

YAWPINGS > YAWP

YAWPS > YAWP

YAWS n infectious tropical skin disease

YAWY > YAWS

YAY interj exclamation indicating approval, congratulation, or triumph ▷ n cry of approval

YAYS > YAY

YBET archaic past participle of > BEAT

YBLENT archaic past participle of > BLEND

YBORE archaic past participle of > BEAR

YBOUND archaic past participle of > BIND

YBOUNDEN archaic past participle of > BIND

YBRENT archaic past participle of > BURN

YCLAD archaic past participle of > CLOTHE

YCLED archaic past participle of > CLOTHE

YCLEEPE archaic form of > CLEPE

YCLEEPED > YCLEEPE

YCLEEPES > YCLEEPE

YCLEEPING > YCLEEPE

YCLEPED same as > YCLEPT

YCLEPT adj having the name of

YCOND archaic past participle of > CON

YDRAD archaic past participle of > DREAD

YDRED archaic past participle of > DREAD

YE pron you ▷ adj the

YEA interj yes ▷ adv indeed or truly ▷ sentence substitute aye ▷ n cry of agreement

YEAD vb proceed

YEADING > YEAD

YEADS > YEAD

YEAH n positive affirmation

YEAHS > YEAH

YEALDON n fuel

YEALDONS > YEALDON

YEALING n person of the same age as oneself

YEALINGS > YEALING

YEALM vb prepare for thatching

YEALMED > YEALM

YEALMING > YEALM

YEALMS > YEALM

YEAN vb (of a sheep or goat) to give birth to (offspring)

YEANED > YEAN

YEANING > YEAN

YEANLING n young of a goat or sheep

YEANLINGS > YEANLING

YEANS > YEAN

YEAR n time taken for the earth to make one revolution around the sun, about 365 days

YEARBOOK n reference book published annually containing details of the previous year's events

YEARBOOKS > YEARBOOK

YEARD vb bury

YEARDED > YEARD

YEARDING > YEARD

YEARDS > YEARD

YEAREND n end of the year

YEARENDS > YEAREND

YEARLIES > YEARLY

YEARLING n animal between one and two years old ▷ adj being a year old

YEARLINGS > YEARLING

YEARLONG adj throughout a whole year

YEARLY adv (happening) every year or once a year ▷ adj occurring, done, or appearing once a year or every year ▷ n publication, event, etc, that occurs once a year

YEARN vb want (something) very much

YEARNED > YEARN

YEARNER > YEARN

YEARNERS > YEARN

YEARNING n intense or overpowering longing, desire, or need

YEARNINGS > YEARNING

YEARNS > YEARN

YEARS > YEAR

YEAS > YEA

YEASAYER n person who usually agrees with proposals

YEASAYERS > YEASAYER

YEAST n fungus used to make bread rise and to ferment alcoholic drinks ▷ vb froth or foam

YEASTED > YEAST

YEASTIER > YEASTY

YEASTIEST > YEASTY

YEASTILY > YEASTY

YEASTING > YEAST

YEASTLESS > YEAST

YEASTLIKE > YEAST

YEASTS > YEAST

YEASTY adj of, resembling, or containing yeast

YEBO interj yes ▷ sentence substitute expression of affirmation

YECCH same as > YECH

YECCHS > YECCH

YECH n expression of disgust

YECHS > YECH

YECHY > YECH

YEDE same as > YEAD

YEDES > YEDE

YEDING > YEDE

YEED same as > YEAD

YEEDING > YEED

YEEDS > YEED

YEELIN n person of the same age as oneself

YEELINS > YEELIN

Section 1: Words between 2 and 9 letters in length

YEGG *n* burglar or safe-breaker
YEGGMAN *same as* > YEGG
YEGGMEN > YEGGMAN
YEGGS > YEGG
YEH *same as* > YEAH
YELD *adj* (of an animal) barren or too young to bear young
YELDRING *n* yellowhammer (bird)
YELDRINGS > YELDRING
YELDROCK *same as* > YELDRING
YELDROCKS > YELDROCK
YELK *n* yolk of an egg
YELKS > YELK
YELL *vb* shout or scream in a loud or piercing way ▷ *n* loud cry of pain, anger, or fear
YELLED > YELL
YELLER > YELL
YELLERS > YELL
YELLING > YELL
YELLINGS > YELL
YELLOCH *vb* yell
YELLOCHED > YELLOCH
YELLOCHS > YELLOCH
YELLOW *n* colour of gold, a lemon, etc ▷ *adj* of this colour ▷ *vb* make or become yellow
YELLOWED > YELLOW
YELLOWER > YELLOW
YELLOWEST > YELLOW
YELLOWFIN *n* type of tuna
YELLOWIER > YELLOW
YELLOWING > YELLOW
YELLOWISH > YELLOW
YELLOWLY > YELLOW
YELLOWS *n* any of various fungal or viral diseases of plants, characterized by yellowish discoloration and stunting
YELLOWY > YELLOW
YELLS > YELL
YELM *same as* > YEALM
YELMED > YELM
YELMING > YELM
YELMS > YELM
YELP *n* a short sudden cry ▷ *vb* utter a sharp or high-pitched cry of pain
YELPED > YELP
YELPER > YELP
YELPERS > YELP
YELPING > YELP
YELPINGS > YELP
YELPS > YELP
YELT *n* young sow
YELTS > YELT
YEMMER *southwest English form of* > EMBER
YEMMERS > YEMMER
YEN *n* monetary unit of Japan ▷ *vb* have a longing
YENNED > YEN
YENNING > YEN
YENS > YEN
YENTA *n* meddlesome woman
YENTAS > YENTA
YENTE *same as* > YENTA
YENTES > YENTE
YEOMAN *n* farmer owning

and farming his own land
YEOMANLY *adj* of, relating to, or like a yeoman ▷ *adv* in a yeomanly manner, as in being brave, staunch, or loyal
YEOMANRY *n* yeomen
YEOMEN > YEOMAN
YEP *n* affirmative statement
YEPS > YEP
YERBA *n* stimulating South American drink made from dried leaves
YERBAS > YERBA
YERD *vb* bury
YERDED > YERD
YERDING > YERD
YERDS > YERD
YERK *vb* tighten stitches
YERKED > YERK
YERKING > YERK
YERKS > YERK
YERSINIA *n* plague bacterium
YERSINIAE > YERSINIA
YERSINIAS > YERSINIA
YES *interj* expresses consent, agreement, or approval ▷ *n* answer or vote of yes ▷ *sentence substitute* used to express acknowledgment, affirmation, consent, agreement, or approval or to answer when one is addressed ▷ *vb* reply in the affirmative
YESES > YES
YESHIVA *n* traditional Jewish school devoted chiefly to the study of rabbinic literature and the Talmud
YESHIVAH *same as* > YESHIVA
YESHIVAHS > YESHIVAH
YESHIVAS > YESHIVA
YESHIVOT > YESHIVA
YESHIVOTH > YESHIVA
YESK *vb* hiccup
YESKED > YESK
YESKING > YESK
YESKS > YESK
YESSED > YES
YESSES > YES
YESSING > YES
YEST *archaic form of* > YEAST
YESTER *adj* of or relating to yesterday
YESTERDAY *n* the day before today ▷ *adv* on or during the day before today
YESTEREVE *n* yesterday evening
YESTERN *same as* > YESTER
YESTREEN *n* yesterday evening
YESTREENS > YESTREEN
YESTS > YEST
YESTY *archaic form of* > YEASTY
YET *adv* up until then or now
YETI *n* large legendary manlike creature alleged to inhabit the Himalayan Mountains

YETIS > YETI
YETT *n* gate or door
YETTIE *n* young, entrepreneurial, and technology-based (person)
YETTIES > YETTIE
YETTS > YETT
YEUK *vb* itch
YEUKED > YEUK
YEUKING > YEUK
YEUKS > YEUK
YEUKY > YEUK
YEVE *vb* give
YEVEN > YEVE
YEVES > YEVE
YEVING > YEVE
YEW *n* evergreen tree with needle-like leaves and red berries
YEWEN *adj* made of yew
YEWS > YEW
YEX *vb* hiccup
YEXED > YEX
YEXES > YEX
YEXING > YEX
YFERE *adv* together
YGLAUNST *archaic past participle of* > GLANCE
YGO *archaic past participle of* > GO
YGOE *archaic past participle of* > GO
YIBBLES *adv* perhaps
YICKER *vb* squeal or squeak
YICKERED > YICKER
YICKERING > YICKER
YICKERS > YICKER
YID *n* offensive word for a Jew
YIDAKI *n* long wooden wind instrument played by the Aboriginal peoples of Arnhem Land
YIDAKIS > YIDAKI
YIDS > YID
YIELD *vb* produce or bear ▷ *n* amount produced
YIELDABLE > YIELD
YIELDED > YIELD
YIELDER > YIELD
YIELDERS > YIELD
YIELDING *adj* submissive
YIELDINGS > YIELD
YIELDS > YIELD
YIKE *n* argument, squabble, or fight ▷ *vb* argue, squabble, or fight
YIKED > YIKE
YIKES *interj* expression of surprise, fear, or alarm
YIKING > YIKE
YIKKER *vb* squeal or squeak
YIKKERED > YIKKER
YIKKERING > YIKKER
YIKKERS > YIKKER
YILL *n* ale
YILLS > YILL
YIN *Scots word for* > ONE
YINCE *Scots form of* > ONCE
YINS > YIN
YIP *n* emit a high-pitched bark
YIPE *same as* > YIPES
YIPES *interj* expression of surprise, fear, or alarm
YIPPED > YIP
YIPPEE *interj* exclamation

of joy or pleasure
YIPPER *n* golfer who suffers from a failure of nerve
YIPPERS > YIPPER
YIPPIE *n* young person sharing hippy ideals
YIPPIES > YIPPIE
YIPPING > YIP
YIPPY *same as* > YIPPIE
YIPS > YIP
YIRD *vb* bury
YIRDED > YIRD
YIRDING > YIRD
YIRDS > YIRD
YIRK *same as* > YERK
YIRKED > YIRK
YIRKING > YIRK
YIRKS > YIRK
YIRR *vb* snarl, growl, or yell
YIRRED > YIRR
YIRRING > YIRR
YIRRS > YIRR
YIRTH *n* earth
YIRTHS > YIRTH
YITE *n* European bunting with a yellowish head and body and brown streaked wings and tail
YITES > YITE
YITIE *same as* > YITE
YITIES > YITIE
YITTEN *adj* frightened
YLEM *n* original matter from which the basic elements are said to have been formed following the explosion postulated in the big bang theory of cosmology
YLEMS > YLEM
YLIKE *Spenserian form of* > ALIKE
YLKE *archaic spelling of* > ILK
YLKES > YLKE
YMOLT *Spenserian past participle of* > MELT
YMOLTEN *Spenserian past participle of* > MELT
YMPE *Spenserian form of* > IMP
YMPES > YMPE
YMPING > YMPE
YMPT > YMPE
YNAMBU *n* South American bird
YNAMBUS > YNAMBU
YO *interj* expression used as a greeting or to attract someone's attention ▷ *sentence substitute* expression used as a greeting, to attract someone's attention, etc ▷ *n* cry of greeting
YOB *n* bad-mannered aggressive youth
YOBBERIES > YOBBERY
YOBBERY *n* behaviour typical of aggressive surly youths
YOBBISH *adj* typical of aggressive surly youths
YOBBISHLY > YOBBISH
YOBBISM > YOB
YOBBISMS > YOB
YOBBO *same as* > YOB
YOBBOES > YOBBO

YOBBOS > YOBBO
YOBS > YOB
YOCK vb chuckle
YOCKED > YOCK
YOCKING > YOCK
YOCKS > YOCK
YOD n tenth letter in the Hebrew alphabet
YODE > YEAD
YODEL vb sing with abrupt changes between a normal and a falsetto voice ▷ n act or sound of yodelling
YODELED > YODEL
YODELER > YODEL
YODELERS > YODEL
YODELING > YODEL
YODELLED > YODEL
YODELLER > YODEL
YODELLERS > YODEL
YODELLING > YODEL
YODELS > YODEL
YODH same as > YOD
YODHS > YODH
YODLE variant spelling of > YODEL
YODLED > YODLE
YODLER > YODLE
YODLERS > YODLE
YODLES > YODLE
YODLING > YODLE
YODS > YOD
YOGA n Hindu method of exercise and discipline aiming at spiritual, mental, and physical wellbeing
YOGAS > YOGA
YOGEE same as > YOGI
YOGEES > YOGEE
YOGH n character used in Old and Middle English to represent a palatal fricative
YOGHOURT variant form of > YOGURT
YOGHOURTS > YOGHOURT
YOGHS > YOGH
YOGHURT same as > YOGURT
YOGHURTS > YOGHURT
YOGI n person who practises yoga
YOGIC > YOGA
YOGIN same as > YOGI
YOGINI > YOGI
YOGINIS > YOGI
YOGINS > YOGIN
YOGIS > YOGI
YOGISM > YOGI
YOGISMS > YOGI
YOGURT n slightly sour custard-like food made from milk that has had bacteria added to it, often sweetened and flavoured with fruit
YOGURTS > YOGURT
YOHIMBE n bark used in herbal medicine
YOHIMBES > YOHIMBE
YOHIMBINE n alkaloid found in the bark of the tree Corynanthe yohimbe
YOICK vb urge on foxhounds
YOICKED > YOICK
YOICKING > YOICK
YOICKS interj cry used by huntsmen to urge on the hounds to the fox ▷ vb

urge on foxhounds
YOICKSED > YOICKS
YOICKSES > YOICKS
YOICKSING > YOICKS
YOJAN n Indian unit of distance
YOJANA same as > YOJAN
YOJANAS > YOJANA
YOJANS > YOJAN
YOK vb chuckle
YOKE n wooden bar put across the necks of two animals to hold them together ▷ vb put a yoke on
YOKED > YOKE
YOKEL n derogatory term for a person who lives in the country and is usu simple and old-fashioned
YOKELESS > YOKE
YOKELISH > YOKEL
YOKELS > YOKEL
YOKEMATE n colleague
YOKEMATES > YOKEMATE
YOKER > YOKE
YOKERS > YOKE
YOKES > YOKE
YOKING > YOKE
YOKINGS > YOKE
YOKKED > YOK
YOKKING > YOK
YOKOZUNA n grand champion sumo wrestler
YOKOZUNAS > YOKOZUNA
YOKS > YOK
YOKUL Shetland word for > YES
YOLD archaic past participle of > YIELD
YOLDRING n yellowhammer (bird)
YOLDRINGS > YOLDRING
YOLK n yellow part of an egg that provides food for the developing embryo
YOLKED > YOLK
YOLKIER > YOLK
YOLKIEST > YOLK
YOLKLESS > YOLK
YOLKS > YOLK
YOLKY > YOLK
YOM n day
YOMIM > YOM
YOMP vb walk or trek laboriously, esp heavily laden and over difficult terrain
YOMPED > YOMP
YOMPING > YOMP
YOMPS > YOMP
YON adj that or those over there ▷ adv yonder ▷ pron that person or thing
YOND same as > YON
YONDER adv over there ▷ adj situated over there ▷ determiner being at a distance, either within view or as if within view ▷ n person
YONDERLY > YONDER
YONDERS > YONDER
YONI n female genitalia, regarded as a divine symbol of sexual pleasure
YONIC adj resembling a

vulva
YONIS > YONI
YONKER same as > YOUNKER
YONKERS > YONKER
YONKS pl n very long time
YONNIE n stone
YONNIES > YONNIE
YONT same as > YON
YOOF n non-standard spelling of youth, used humorously or facetiously
YOOFS > YOOF
YOOP n sob
YOOPS > YOOP
YOPPER n (formerly in Britain) a youth employed under the Youth Opportunities Programme)
YOPPERS > YOPPER
YORE n time long past ▷ adv in the past
YORES > YORE
YORK vb bowl or try to bowl (a batsman) by pitching the ball under or just beyond the bat
YORKED > YORK
YORKER n ball that pitches just under the bat
YORKERS > YORKER
YORKIE n Yorkshire terrier
YORKIES > YORKIE
YORKING > YORK
YORKS > YORK
YORP vb shout
YORPED > YORP
YORPING > YORP
YORPS > YORP
YOS > YO
YOTTABYTE n very large unit of computer memory
YOU pron person or people addressed ▷ n personality of the person being addressed
YOUK vb itch
YOUKED > YOUK
YOUKING > YOUK
YOUKS > YOUK
YOUNG adj in an early stage of life or growth ▷ n young people in general; offspring
YOUNGER > YOUNG
YOUNGERS n young people
YOUNGEST > YOUNG
YOUNGISH > YOUNG
YOUNGLING n young person, animal, or plant
YOUNGLY adv youthfully
YOUNGNESS > YOUNG
YOUNGS > YOUNG
YOUNGSTER n young person
YOUNGTH n youth
YOUNGTHLY adj youthful
YOUNGTHS > YOUNGTH
YOUNKER n young man
YOUNKERS > YOUNKER
YOUPON same as > YAUPON
YOUPONS > YOUPON
YOUR adj of, belonging to, or associated with you
YOURN dialect form of > YOURS
YOURS pron something belonging to you
YOURSELF pron reflexive

form of you
YOURT same as > YURT
YOURTS > YOURT
YOUS pron refers to more than one person including the person or persons addressed but not including the speaker
YOUSE same as > YOUS
YOUTH n time of being young
YOUTHEN vb render more youthful-seeming
YOUTHENED > YOUTHEN
YOUTHENS > YOUTHEN
YOUTHFUL adj vigorous or active
YOUTHHEAD same as > YOUTHHOOD
YOUTHHOOD n youth
YOUTHIER > YOUTHY
YOUTHIEST > YOUTHY
YOUTHLESS > YOUTH
YOUTHLY adv young
YOUTHS > YOUTH
YOUTHSOME archaic variant of > YOUTHFUL
YOUTHY Scots word for > YOUNG
YOW vb howl
YOWE Scot word for > EWE
YOWED > YOW
YOWES > YOW
YOWIE n legendary Australian apelike creature
YOWIES > YOWIE
YOWING > YOW
YOWL n loud mournful cry ▷ vb produce a loud mournful wail or cry
YOWLED > YOWL
YOWLER > YOWL
YOWLERS > YOWL
YOWLEY n yellowhammer (bird)
YOWLEYS > YOWLEY
YOWLING > YOWL
YOWLINGS > YOWL
YOWLS > YOWL
YOWS > YOW
YPERITE n mustard gas
YPERITES > YPERITE
YPIGHT archaic past participle of > PITCH
YPLAST archaic past participle of > PLACE
YPLIGHT archaic past participle of > PLIGHT
YPSILOID > YPSILON
YPSILON same as > UPSILON
YPSILONS > YPSILON
YRAPT Spenserian form of > RAPT
YRAVISHED archaic past participle of > RAVISH
YRENT archaic past participle of > REND
YRIVD archaic past participle of > RIVE
YRNEH n unit of reciprocal inductance
YRNEHS > YRNEH
YSAME Spenserian word for > TOGETHER
YSHEND Spenserian form of > SHEND
YSHENDING > YSHEND

YSHENDS > YSHEND
YSHENT > YSHEND
YSLAKED *archaic past participle of* > SLAKE
YTOST *archaic past participle of* > TOSS
YTTERBIA *n* colourless hygroscopic substance used in certain alloys and ceramics
YTTERBIAS > YTTERBIA
YTTERBIC > YTTERBIUM
YTTERBITE *n* rare mineral
YTTERBIUM *n* soft silvery element
YTTERBOUS > YTTERBIUM
YTTRIA *n* insoluble solid used mainly in incandescent mantles
YTTRIAS > YTTRIA
YTTRIC > YTTRIUM
YTTRIOUS > YTTRIUM
YTTRIUM *n* silvery metallic element used in various alloys
YTTRIUMS > YTTRIUM
YU *n* jade
YUAN *n* standard monetary unit of the People's Republic of China
YUANS > YUAN
YUCA *same as* > YUCCA
YUCAS > YUCA
YUCCA *n* tropical plant with spikes of white leaves
YUCCAS > YUCCA
YUCCH *interj* expression of disgust
YUCH *interj* expression of disgust

YUCK *interj* exclamation indicating contempt, dislike, or disgust ▷ *vb* chuckle
YUCKED > YUCK
YUCKER > YUCK
YUCKERS > YUCK
YUCKIER > YUCKY
YUCKIEST > YUCKY
YUCKINESS > YUCKY
YUCKING > YUCK
YUCKO *adj* disgusting ▷ *interj* exclamation of disgust
YUCKS > YUCK
YUCKY *adj* disgusting, nasty
YUFT *n* Russia leather
YUFTS > YUFT
YUG *same as* > YUGA
YUGA *n* (in Hindu cosmology) one of the four ages of mankind
YUGARIE *variant spelling of* > EUGARIE
YUGARIES > YUGARIE
YUGAS > YUGA
YUGS > YUG
YUK *same as* > YUCK
YUKATA *n* light kimono
YUKATAS > YUKATA
YUKE *vb* itch
YUKED > YUKE
YUKES > YUKE
YUKIER > YUKY
YUKIEST > YUKY
YUKING > YUKE
YUKKED > YUK
YUKKIER > YUKKY
YUKKIEST > YUKKY
YUKKING > YUK

YUKKY *same as* > YUCKY
YUKO *n* score of five points in judo
YUKOS > YUKO
YUKS > YUK
YUKY *adj* itchy
YULAN *n* Chinese magnolia, *Magnolia denudata*, that is often cultivated for its showy white flowers
YULANS > YULAN
YULE *n* Christmas, the Christmas season, or Christmas festivities
YULES > YULE
YULETIDE *n* Christmas season
YULETIDES > YULETIDE
YUM *interj* expression of delight
YUMMIER > YUMMY
YUMMIES > YUMMY
YUMMIEST > YUMMY
YUMMINESS > YUMMY
YUMMO *adj* tasty ▷ *interj* exclamation of delight or approval
YUMMY *adj* delicious ▷ *interj* exclamation indicating pleasure or delight, as in anticipation of delicious food ▷ *n* delicious food item
YUMP *vb* leave the ground when driving over a ridge
YUMPED > YUMP
YUMPIE *n* young upwardly mobile person
YUMPIES > YUMPIE
YUMPING > YUMP

YUMPS > YUMP
YUNX *n* wryneck
YUNXES > YUNX
YUP *n* informal affirmative statement
YUPON *same as* > YAUPON
YUPONS > YUPON
YUPPIE *n* young highly-paid professional person, esp one who has a materialistic way of life ▷ *adj* typical of or reflecting the values of yuppies
YUPPIEDOM > YUPPIE
YUPPIEISH > YUPPIE
YUPPIES > YUPPY
YUPPIFIED > YUPPIFY
YUPPIFIES > YUPPIFY
YUPPIFY *vb* make yuppie in nature
YUPPY *same as* > YUPPIE
YUPS > YUP
YURT *n* circular tent consisting of a framework of poles covered with felt or skins, used by Mongolian and Turkic nomads of E and central Asia
YURTA *same as* > YURT
YURTAS > YURT
YURTS > YURT
YUS > YU
YUTZ *n* Yiddish word meaning fool
YUTZES > YUTZ
YUZU *n* type of citrus fruit
YUZUS > YUZU
YWIS *adv* certainly
YWROKE *archaic past participle of* > WREAK

Zz

ZA *n* pizza

ZABAIONE *n* light foamy dessert

ZABAIONES > ZABAIONE

ZABAJONE *same as* > ZABAIONE

ZABAJONES > ZABAJONE

ZABETA *n* tariff

ZABETAS > ZABETA

ZABRA *n* small sailing vessel

ZABRAS > ZABRA

ZABTIEH *n* Turkish police officer

ZABTIEHS > ZABTIEH

ZACATON *n* coarse grass

ZACATONS > ZACATON

ZACK *n* Australian five-cent piece

ZACKS > ZACK

ZADDICK *adj* righteous

ZADDIK *n* Hasidic Jewish leader

ZADDIKIM > ZADDIK

ZADDIKS > ZADDIK

ZAFFAR *same as* > ZAFFER

ZAFFARS > ZAFFAR

ZAFFER *n* impure cobalt oxide, used to impart a blue colour to enamels

ZAFFERS > ZAFFER

ZAFFIR *same as* > ZAFFER

ZAFFIRS > ZAFFIR

ZAFFRE *same as* > ZAFFER

ZAFFRES > ZAFFRE

ZAFTIG *adj* ripe or curvaceous

ZAG *vb* change direction sharply

ZAGGED > ZAG

ZAGGING > ZAG

ZAGS > ZAG

ZAIBATSU *n* group or combine comprising a few wealthy families that controls industry, business, and finance in Japan

ZAIKAI *n* Japanese business community

ZAIKAIS > ZAIKAI

ZAIRE *n* currency used in the former Zaïre

ZAIRES > ZAIRE

ZAITECH *n* investment in financial markets by a company to supplement its main income

ZAITECHS > ZAITECH

ZAKAT *n* annual tax on Muslims to aid the poor in the Muslim community

ZAKATS > ZAKAT

ZAKOUSKA > ZAKOUSKI

ZAKOUSKI *same as* > ZAKUSKI

ZAKUSKA > ZAKUSKI

ZAKUSKI *pl n* hors d'oeuvres, consisting of tiny open sandwiches spread with caviar, smoked sausage, etc

ZAMAN *n* tropical tree

ZAMANG *same as* > ZAMAN

ZAMANGS > ZAMANG

ZAMANS > ZAMAN

ZAMARRA *n* sheepskin coat

ZAMARRAS > ZAMARRA

ZAMARRO *same as* > ZAMARRA

ZAMARROS > ZAMARRO

ZAMBO *n* offensive word for a Black person

ZAMBOMBA *n* drum-like musical instrument

ZAMBOMBAS > ZAMBOMBA

ZAMBOORAK *n* small swivel-mounted cannon

ZAMBOS > ZAMBO

ZAMBUCK *n* St John ambulance attendant, esp at a sports meeting

ZAMBUCKS > ZAMBUCK

ZAMBUK *same as* > ZAMBUCK

ZAMBUKS > ZAMBUK

ZAMIA *n* any cycadaceous plant of the genus *Zamia*, of tropical and subtropical America, having a short thick trunk, palmlike leaves, and short stout cones

ZAMIAS > ZAMIA

ZAMINDAR *n* (in India) the owner of an agricultural estate

ZAMINDARI *n* (in India) a large agricultural estate

ZAMINDARS > ZAMINDAR

ZAMINDARY *same as* > ZAMINDARI

ZAMOUSE *n* West African buffalo

ZAMOUSES > ZAMOUSE

ZAMPOGNA *n* Italian bagpipes

ZAMPOGNAS > ZAMPOGNA

ZAMPONE *n* sausage made

from pig's trotters

ZAMPONI > ZAMPONE

ZAMZAWED *adj* (of tea) having been left in the pot to stew

ZANANA *same as* > ZENANA

ZANANAS > ZANANA

ZANDER *n* freshwater teleost pikeperch of Europe, *Stizostedion lucioperca*, valued as a food fish

ZANDERS > ZANDER

ZANELLA *n* twill fabric

ZANELLAS > ZANELLA

ZANIED > ZANY

ZANIER > ZANY

ZANIES > ZANY

ZANIEST > ZANY

ZANILY > ZANY

ZANINESS > ZANY

ZANJA *n* irrigation canal

ZANJAS > ZANJA

ZANJERO *n* irrigation supervisor

ZANJEROS > ZANJERO

ZANTE *n* type of wood

ZANTES > ZANTE

ZANTHOXYL *variant spelling of* > XANTHOXYL

ZANY *adj* comical in an endearing way ▷ *n* clown or buffoon, esp one in old comedies who imitated other performers with ludicrous effect ▷ *vb* clown

ZANYING > ZANY

ZANYISH > ZANY

ZANYISM > ZANY

ZANYISMS > ZANY

ZANZA *same as* > ZANZE

ZANZAS > ZANZA

ZANZE *n* African musical instrument

ZANZES > ZANZE

ZAP *vb* kill (by shooting) ▷ *n* energy, vigour, or pep ▷ *interj* exclamation used to express sudden or swift action

ZAPATA *adj* (of a moustache) drooping

ZAPATEADO *n* Spanish dance with stamping and very fast footwork

ZAPATEO *n* Cuban folk dance

ZAPATEOS > ZAPATEO

ZAPOTILLA *n* shoe

ZAPPED > ZAP

ZAPPER *n* remote control for a television etc

ZAPPERS > ZAPPER

ZAPPIER > ZAPPY

ZAPPIEST > ZAPPY

ZAPPING > ZAP

ZAPPY *adj* energetic

ZAPS > ZAP

ZAPTIAH *same as* > ZAPTIEH

ZAPTIAHS > ZAPTIAH

ZAPTIEH *n* Turkish police officer

ZAPTIEHS > ZAPTIEH

ZARAPE *n* blanket-like shawl

ZARAPES > ZARAPE

ZARATITE *n* green amorphous mineral

ZARATITES > ZARATITE

ZAREBA *n* stockade or enclosure of thorn bushes around a village or campsite

ZAREBAS > ZAREBA

ZAREEBA *same as* > ZAREBA

ZAREEBAS > ZAREEBA

ZARF *n* (esp in the Middle East) a holder, usually ornamental, for a hot coffee cup

ZARFS > ZARF

ZARIBA *same as* > ZAREBA

ZARIBAS > ZARIBA

ZARNEC *n* sulphide of arsenic

ZARNECS > ZARNEC

ZARNICH *same as* > ZARNEC

ZARNICHS > ZARNICH

ZARZUELA *n* type of Spanish vaudeville or operetta, usually satirical in nature

ZARZUELAS > ZARZUELA

ZAS > ZA

ZASTRUGA *variant spelling of* > SASTRUGA

ZASTRUGI > ZASTRUGA

ZATI *n* type of macaque

ZATIS > ZATI

ZAX *variant of* > SAX

ZAXES > ZAX

ZAYIN *n* seventh letter of the Hebrew alphabet

ZAYINS > ZAYIN

ZAZEN *n* (in Zen Buddhism)

deep meditation undertaken whilst sitting upright with legs crossed

ZAZENS > ZAZEN

ZEA n corn silk

ZEAL n great enthusiasm or eagerness

ZEALANT archaic variant of > ZEALOT

ZEALANTS > ZEALANT

ZEALFUL > ZEAL

ZEALLESS > ZEAL

ZEALOT n fanatic or extreme enthusiast

ZEALOTISM > ZEALOT

ZEALOTRY n extreme or excessive zeal or devotion

ZEALOTS > ZEALOT

ZEALOUS adj extremely eager or enthusiastic

ZEALOUSLY > ZEALOUS

ZEALS > ZEAL

ZEAS > ZEAL

ZEATIN n cytokinin derived from corn

ZEATINS > ZEATIN

ZEBEC variant spelling of > XEBEC

ZEBECK same as > ZEBEC

ZEBECKS > ZEBECK

ZEBECS > ZEBEC

ZEBRA n black-and-white striped African animal of the horse family

ZEBRAFISH n striped tropical fish

ZEBRAIC adj like a zebra

ZEBRANO n type of striped wood

ZEBRANOS > ZEBRANO

ZEBRAS > ZEBRA

ZEBRASS n offspring of a male zebra and a female ass

ZEBRASSES > ZEBRASS

ZEBRAWOOD n tree yielding striped hardwood used in cabinetwork

ZEBRINA n trailing herbaceous plant

ZEBRINAS > ZEBRINA

ZEBRINE > ZEBRA

ZEBRINES > ZEBRA

ZEBRINNY n offspring of a male horse and a female zebra

ZEBROID > ZEBRA

ZEBRULA n offspring of a male zebra and a female horse

ZEBRULAS > ZEBRULA

ZEBRULE same as > ZEBRULA

ZEBRULES > ZEBRULE

ZEBU n Asian ox with a humped back and long horns

ZEBUB n large African fly

ZEBUBS > ZEBUB

ZEBUS > ZEBU

ZECCHIN same as > ZECCHINO

ZECCHINE same as > ZECCHINO

ZECCHINES > ZECCHINE

ZECCHINI > ZECCHINO

ZECCHINO n former gold coin

ZECCHINOS > ZECCHINO

ZECCHINS > ZECCHIN

ZECHIN same as > ZECCHINO

ZECHINS > ZECHIN

ZED n British and New Zealand spoken form of the letter z

ZEDOARIES > ZEDOARY

ZEDOARY n dried rhizome of the tropical Asian plant *Curcuma zedoaria*, used as a stimulant and a condiment

ZEDS > ZED

ZEE same as > ZED

ZEES > ZEE

ZEIN n protein occurring in maize and used in the manufacture of plastics

ZEINS > ZEIN

ZEITGEBER n agent or event that sets or resets the biological clock

ZEITGEIST n spirit or attitude of a specific time or period

ZEK n Soviet prisoner

ZEKS > ZEK

ZEL n Turkish cymbal

ZELANT alternative form of > ZEALANT

ZELANTS > ZELANT

ZELATOR same as > ZELATRIX

ZELATORS > ZELATOR

ZELATRICE same as > ZELATRIX

ZELATRIX n nun who monitors the behaviour of younger nuns

ZELKOVA n type of elm tree

ZELKOVAS > ZELKOVA

ZELOSO adv with zeal

ZELOTYPIA n morbid zeal

ZELS > ZEL

ZEMINDAR same as > ZAMINDAR

ZEMINDARI > ZEMINDAR

ZEMINDARS > ZEMINDAR

ZEMINDARY n jurisdiction of a zemindar

ZEMSTVA > ZEMSTVO

ZEMSTVO n (in tsarist Russia) an elective provincial or district council established in most provinces of Russia by Alexander II in 1864 as part of his reform policy

ZEMSTVOS > ZEMSTVO

ZENAIDA n dove

ZENAIDAS > ZENAIDA

ZENANA n (in the East, esp in Muslim and Hindu homes) part of a house reserved for the women and girls of a household

ZENANAS > ZENANA

ZENDIK n unbeliever or heretic

ZENDIKS > ZENDIK

ZENITH n highest point of success or power

ZENITHAL > ZENITH

ZENITHS > ZENITH

ZEOLITE n any of a large group of glassy secondary minerals

ZEOLITES > ZEOLITE

ZEOLITIC > ZEOLITE

ZEP n type of long sandwich

ZEPHYR n soft gentle breeze

ZEPHYRS > ZEPHYR

ZEPPELIN n large cylindrical airship

ZEPPELINS > ZEPPELIN

ZEPPOLE n Italian fritter

ZEPPOLES > ZEPPOLE

ZEPPOLI > ZEPPOLE

ZEPS > ZEP

ZERDA n fennec

ZERDAS > ZERDA

ZEREBA same as > ZAREBA

ZEREBAS > ZEREBA

ZERIBA same as > ZAREBA

ZERIBAS > ZERIBA

ZERK n grease fitting

ZERKS > ZERK

ZERO n (symbol representing) the number 0 ▷ adj having no measurable quantity or size ▷ vb adjust (an instrument or scale) so as to read zero ▷ determiner no (thing) at all

ZEROED > ZERO

ZEROES > ZERO

ZEROING > ZERO

ZEROS > ZERO

ZEROTH adj denoting a term in a series that precedes the term otherwise regarded as the first term

ZERUMBET n plant stem used as stimulant and condiment

ZERUMBETS > ZERUMBET

ZEST n enjoyment or excitement ▷ vb give flavour, interest, or piquancy to

ZESTED > ZEST

ZESTER n kitchen utensil used to scrape fine shreds of peel from citrus fruits

ZESTERS > ZESTER

ZESTFUL > ZEST

ZESTFULLY > ZEST

ZESTIER > ZEST

ZESTIEST > ZEST

ZESTILY > ZEST

ZESTING > ZEST

ZESTLESS > ZEST

ZESTS > ZEST

ZESTY > ZEST

ZETA n sixth letter in the Greek alphabet, a consonant, transliterated as z

ZETAS > ZETA

ZETETIC adj proceeding by inquiry ▷ n investigation

ZETETICS > ZETETIC

ZETTABYTE n 10^{21} or 2^{70} bytes

ZEUGMA n figure of speech in which a word is used to modify or govern two or more words although appropriate to only one of them or making a different sense with each, as in the sentence *Mr Pickwick took his hat and his leave* (Charles Dickens)

ZEUGMAS > ZEUGMA

ZEUGMATIC > ZEUGMA

ZEUXITE n ferriferous mineral

ZEUXITES > ZEUXITE

ZEX n tool for cutting roofing slate

ZEXES > ZEX

ZEZE n stringed musical instrument

ZEZES > ZEZE

ZHO same as > ZO

ZHOMO n female zho

ZHOMOS > ZHOMO

ZHOS > ZHO

ZIBELINE n sable or the fur of this animal ▷ adj of, relating to, or resembling a sable

ZIBELINES > ZIBELINE

ZIBELLINE same as > ZIBELINE

ZIBET n large civet of S and SE Asia, having tawny fur marked with black spots and stripes

ZIBETH same as > ZIBET

ZIBETHS > ZIBETH

ZIBETS > ZIBET

ZIFF n beard

ZIFFIUS n sea monster

ZIFFIUSES > ZIFFIUS

ZIFFS > ZIFF

ZIG same as > ZAG

ZIGAN n gypsy

ZIGANKA n Russian dance

ZIGANKAS > ZIGANKA

ZIGANS > ZIGAN

ZIGGED > ZIG

ZIGGING > ZIG

ZIGGURAT n (in ancient Mesopotamia) a temple in the shape of a pyramid

ZIGGURATS > ZIGGURAT

ZIGS > ZIG

ZIGZAG n line or course having sharp turns in alternating directions ▷ vb move in a zigzag ▷ adj formed in or proceeding in a zigzag ▷ adv in a zigzag manner

ZIGZAGGED > ZIGZAG

ZIGZAGGER > ZIGZAG

ZIGZAGGY > ZIGZAG

ZIGZAGS > ZIGZAG

ZIKKURAT same as > ZIGGURAT

ZIKKURATS > ZIKKURAT

ZIKURAT same as > ZIGGURAT

ZIKURATS > ZIKURAT

ZILA n administrative district in India

ZILAS > ZILA

ZILCH n nothing

ZILCHES > ZILCH

ZILL n finger cymbal

ZILLA same as > ZILA

ZILLAH same as > ZILA

ZILLAHS > ZILLAH

ZILLAS > ZILLA

ZILLION n extremely large but unspecified number

ZILLIONS > ZILLION

ZILLIONTH > ZILLION

ZILLS > ZILL

ZIMB same as > ZEBUB

ZIMBI n cowrie shell used as money

ZIMBIS > ZIMBI

ZIMBS > ZIMB

ZIMMER n tradename for a kind of walking frame

ZIMMERS > ZIMMER

ZIMOCCA n bath sponge

ZIMOCCAS > ZIMOCCA

ZIN short form of > ZINFANDEL

ZINC n bluish-white metallic element used in alloys and to coat metal ▷ vb coat with zinc

ZINCATE n any of a class of salts derived from the amphoteric hydroxide of zinc

ZINCATES > ZINCATE

ZINCED > ZINC

ZINCIC > ZINC

ZINCIER > ZINC

ZINCIEST > ZINC

ZINCIFIED > ZINCIFY

ZINCIFIES > ZINCIFY

ZINCIFY vb coat with zinc

ZINCING > ZINC

ZINCITE n red or yellow mineral consisting of zinc oxide in hexagonal crystalline form

ZINCITES > ZINCITE

ZINCKED > ZINC

ZINCKIER > ZINC

ZINCKIEST > ZINC

ZINCKIFY same as > ZINCIFY

ZINCKING > ZINC

ZINCKY > ZINC

ZINCO n printing plate made from zincography

ZINCODE n positive electrode

ZINCODES > ZINCODE

ZINCOID > ZINC

ZINCOS > ZINCO

ZINCOUS > ZINC

ZINCS > ZINC

ZINCY > ZINC

ZINDABAD vb long live: used as part of a slogan in India, Pakistan, etc

ZINE n magazine or fanzine

ZINEB n organic insecticide

ZINEBS > ZINEB

ZINES > ZINE

ZINFANDEL n type of Californian wine

ZING n quality in something that makes it lively or interesting ▷ vb make or move with or as if with a high-pitched buzzing sound

ZINGANI > ZINGANO

ZINGANO n gypsy

ZINGARA same as > ZINGARO

ZINGARE > ZINGARA

ZINGARI > ZINGARO

ZINGARO n Italian Gypsy

ZINGED > ZING

ZINGEL n small freshwater perch

ZINGELS > ZINGEL

ZINGER > ZING

ZINGERS > ZING

ZINGIBER n ginger plant

ZINGIBERS > ZINGIBER

ZINGIER > ZINGY

ZINGIEST > ZINGY

ZINGING > ZING

ZINGS > ZING

ZINGY adj vibrant

ZINKE n cornett

ZINKED > ZINC

ZINKENITE n steel-grey metallic mineral consisting of a sulphide of lead and antimony

ZINKES > ZINKE

ZINKIER > ZINC

ZINKIEST > ZINC

ZINKIFIED > ZINKIFY

ZINKIFIES > ZINKIFY

ZINKIFY vb coat with zinc

ZINKING > ZINC

ZINKY > ZINC

ZINNIA n plant of tropical and subtropical America, with solitary heads of brightly coloured flowers

ZINNIAS > ZINNIA

ZINS > ZIN

ZIP same as > ZIPPER

ZIPLESS > ZIP

ZIPLOCK adj fastened with interlocking plastic strips

ZIPPED > ZIP

ZIPPER n fastening device operating by means of two parallel rows of metal or plastic teeth on either side of a closure that are interlocked by a sliding tab ▷ vb fasten with a zipper

ZIPPERED adj provided or fastened with a zip

ZIPPERING > ZIPPER

ZIPPERS > ZIPPER

ZIPPIER > ZIPPY

ZIPPIEST > ZIPPY

ZIPPING > ZIP

ZIPPO n nothing

ZIPPOS > ZIPPO

ZIPPY adj full of energy

ZIPS > ZIP

ZIPTOP adj (of a bag) closed with a zip

ZIRAM n industrial fungicide

ZIRAMS > ZIRAM

ZIRCALLOY n alloy of zirconium containing small amounts of tin, chromium, and nickel. It is used in pressurized-water reactors

ZIRCALOY same as > ZIRCALLOY

ZIRCALOYS > ZIRCALOY

ZIRCON n mineral used as a gemstone and in industry

ZIRCONIA n white oxide of zirconium, used as a pigment for paints, a catalyst, and an abrasive

ZIRCONIAS > ZIRCONIA

ZIRCONIC > ZIRCONIUM

ZIRCONIUM n greyish-white metallic element that is resistant to corrosion

ZIRCONS > ZIRCON

ZIT n spot or pimple

ZITE same as > ZITI

ZITHER n musical instrument consisting of strings stretched over a flat box and plucked to produce musical notes

ZITHERIST > ZITHER

ZITHERN same as > ZITHER

ZITHERNS > ZITHERN

ZITHERS > ZITHER

ZITI n type of pasta

ZITIS > ZITI

ZITS > ZIT

ZIZ same as > ZIZZ

ZIZANIA n aquatic grass

ZIZANIAS > ZIZANIA

ZIZEL n chipmunk

ZIZELS > ZIZEL

ZIZIT same as > ZIZITH

ZIZITH variant spelling of > TSITSITH

ZIZYPHUS n jubejube tree

ZIZZ n short sleep ▷ vb take a short sleep, snooze

ZIZZED > ZIZZ

ZIZZES > ZIZZ

ZIZZING > ZIZZ

ZIZZLE vb sizzle

ZIZZLED > ZIZZLE

ZIZZLES > ZIZZLE

ZIZZLING > ZIZZLE

ZLOTE > ZLOTY

ZLOTIES > ZLOTY

ZLOTY n monetary unit of Poland

ZLOTYCH same as > ZLOTY

ZLOTYS > ZLOTY

ZO n Tibetan breed of cattle, developed by crossing the yak with common cattle

ZOA > ZOON

ZOAEA same as > ZOEA

ZOAEAE > ZOAEA

ZOAEAS > ZOAEA

ZOARIA > ZOARIUM

ZOARIAL > ZOARIUM

ZOARIUM n colony of zooids

ZOBO same as > ZO

ZOBOS > ZOBO

ZOBU same as > ZO

ZOBUS > ZOBU

ZOCALO n plaza in Mexico

ZOCALOS > ZOCALO

ZOCCO n plinth

ZOCCOLO same as > ZOCCO

ZOCCOLOS > ZOCCOLO

ZOCCOS > ZOCCO

ZODIAC n imaginary belt in the sky within which the sun, moon, and planets appear to move, divided into twelve equal areas, called signs of the zodiac, each named after a constellation

ZODIACAL > ZODIAC

ZODIACS > ZODIAC

ZOEA n free-swimming larva of a crab or related crustacean, which has well-developed abdominal appendages and may bear one or more spines

ZOEAE > ZOEA

ZOEAL > ZOEA

ZOEAS > ZOAEA

ZOECHROME same as > ZOETROPE

ZOECIA > ZOECIUM

ZOECIUM same as > ZOOECIUM

ZOEFORM > ZOEA

ZOETIC adj pertaining to life

ZOETROPE n cylinder-shaped toy with a sequence of pictures on its inner surface which, when viewed through the vertical slits spaced regularly around it while the toy is rotated, produce an illusion of animation

ZOETROPES > ZOETROPE

ZOETROPIC > ZOETROPE

ZOFTIG adj ripe or curvaceous

ZOIATRIA n veterinary surgery

ZOIATRIAS > ZOIATRIA

ZOIATRICS n veterinary surgery

ZOIC adj relating to or having animal life

ZOISITE n grey, brown, or pink mineral

ZOISITES > ZOISITE

ZOISM n belief in magical animal powers

ZOISMS > ZOISM

ZOIST > ZOISM

ZOISTS > ZOISM

ZOL n South African slang for a cannabis cigarette

ZOLS > ZOL

ZOMBI same as > ZOMBIE

ZOMBIE n person who appears to be lifeless, apathetic, or totally lacking in independent judgment

ZOMBIES > ZOMBIE

ZOMBIFIED > ZOMBIFY

ZOMBIFIES > ZOMBIFY

ZOMBIFY vb turn into a zombie

ZOMBIISM > ZOMBIE

ZOMBIISMS > ZOMBIE

ZOMBIS > ZOMBI

ZOMBORUK n small swivel-mounted cannon

ZOMBORUKS > ZOMBORUK

ZONA n zone or belt

ZONAE > ZONA

ZONAL adj of, relating to, or of the nature of a zone

ZONALLY > ZONAL

ZONARY same as > ZONAL

ZONATE adj marked with, divided into, or arranged in zones

ZONATED same as > ZONATE

ZONATION n arrangement in zones

ZONATIONS > ZONATION

ZONDA n South American wind

ZONDAS > ZONDA

ZONE n area with particular features or properties ▷ vb divide into zones

ZONED > ZONE

ZONELESS > ZONE

ZONER n something which divides other things into zones

ZONERS > ZONER

ZONES > ZONE

ZONETIME n standard time

of the time zone in which a ship is located at sea, each zone extending 7½° to each side of a meridian

ZONETIMES > ZONETIME

ZONING > ZONE

ZONINGS > ZONE

ZONK vb strike resoundingly

ZONKED adj highly intoxicated with drugs or alcohol

ZONKING > ZONK

ZONKS > ZONK

ZONOID adj resembling a zone

ZONULA n small zone or belt

ZONULAE > ZONULA

ZONULAR > ZONULE

ZONULAS > ZONULA

ZONULE n small zone, band, or area

ZONULES > ZONULE

ZONULET n small belt

ZONULETS > ZONULET

ZONURE n lizard with ringed tail

ZONURES > ZONURE

ZOO n place where live animals are kept for show

ZOOBIOTIC adj parasitic on or living in association with an animal

ZOOBLAST n animal cell

ZOOBLASTS > ZOOBLAST

ZOOCHORE n plant with the spores or seeds dispersed by animals

ZOOCHORES > ZOOCHORE

ZOOCHORY > ZOOCHORE

ZOOCYTIA > ZOOCYTIUM

ZOOCYTIUM n outer sheath of some social infusorians

ZOOEA same as > ZOEA

ZOOEAE > ZOOEA

ZOOEAL > ZOOEA

ZOOEAS > ZOOEA

ZOOECIA > ZOOECIUM

ZOOECIUM n part of a polyzoan colony that houses the feeding zooids

ZOOEY > ZOO

ZOOGAMETE n gamete that can move independently

ZOOGAMIES > ZOOGAMY

ZOOGAMOUS > ZOOGAMY

ZOOGAMY n sexual reproduction in animals

ZOOGENIC adj produced from animals

ZOOGENIES > ZOOGENY

ZOOGENOUS same as > ZOOGENIC

ZOOGENY n doctrine of formation of animals

ZOOGLEA same as > ZOOGLOEA

ZOOGLEAE > ZOOGLEA

ZOOGLEAL > ZOOGLEA

ZOOGLEAS > ZOOGLEA

ZOOGLOEA n mass of bacteria adhering together by a jelly-like substance derived from their cell walls

ZOOGLOEAE > ZOOGLOEA

ZOOGLOEAL > ZOOGLOEA

ZOOGLOEAS > ZOOGLOEA

ZOOGLOEIC > ZOOGLOEA

ZOOGONIES > ZOOGONY

ZOOGONOUS > ZOOGONY

ZOOGONY same as > ZOOGENY

ZOOGRAFT n animal tissue grafted onto a human body

ZOOGRAFTS > ZOOGRAFT

ZOOGRAPHY n branch of zoology concerned with the description of animals

ZOOID n any independent animal body, such as an individual of a coral colony

ZOOIDAL > ZOOID

ZOOIDS > ZOOID

ZOOIER > ZOO

ZOOIEST > ZOO

ZOOKEEPER n person who cares for animals in a zoo

ZOOKS short form of > GADZOOKS

ZOOLATER > ZOOLATRY

ZOOLATERS > ZOOLATRY

ZOOLATRIA same as > ZOOLATRY

ZOOLATRY n (esp in ancient or primitive religions) the worship of animals as the incarnations of certain deities, symbols of particular qualities or natural forces, etc

ZOOLITE n fossilized animal

ZOOLITES > ZOOLITE

ZOOLITH n fossilized animal

ZOOLITHIC > ZOOLITH

ZOOLITHS > ZOOLITH

ZOOLITIC > ZOOLITE

ZOOLOGIC > ZOOLOGY

ZOOLOGIES > ZOOLOGY

ZOOLOGIST > ZOOLOGY

ZOOLOGY n study of animals

ZOOM vb move or rise very rapidly ▷ n sound or act of zooming

ZOOMANCY n divination through observing the actions of animals

ZOOMANIA n extreme or excessive devotion to animals

ZOOMANIAS > ZOOMANIA

ZOOMANTIC > ZOOMANCY

ZOOMED > ZOOM

ZOOMETRIC > ZOOMETRY

ZOOMETRY n branch of zoology concerned with the relative length or size of the different parts of an animal or animals

ZOOMING > ZOOM

ZOOMORPH n representation of an animal form

ZOOMORPHS > ZOOMORPH

ZOOMORPHY > ZOOMORPH

ZOOMS > ZOOM

ZOON less common term for > ZOOID vb zoom

ZOONAL > ZOON

ZOONED > ZOON

ZOONIC adj concerning animals

ZOONING > ZOON

ZOONITE n segment of an articulated animal

ZOONITES > ZOONITE

ZOONITIC > ZOONITE

ZOONOMIA same

as > ZOONOMY

ZOONOMIAS > ZOONOMIA

ZOONOMIC > ZOONOMY

ZOONOMIES > ZOONOMY

ZOONOMIST > ZOONOMY

ZOONOMY n science of animal life

ZOONOSES > ZOONOSIS

ZOONOSIS n any infection or disease that is transmitted to man from lower vertebrates

ZOONOTIC > ZOONOSIS

ZOONS > ZOON

ZOOPATHY n science of animal diseases

ZOOPERAL > ZOOPERY

ZOOPERIES > ZOOPERY

ZOOPERIST > ZOOPERY

ZOOPERY n experimentation on animals

ZOOPHAGAN n carnivore

ZOOPHAGY n eating other animals

ZOOPHILE n person who is devoted to animals and their protection from practices such as vivisection

ZOOPHILES > ZOOPHILE

ZOOPHILIA n morbid condition in which a person has a sexual attraction to animals

ZOOPHILIC > ZOOPHILE

ZOOPHILY same as > ZOOPHILIA

ZOOPHOBE > ZOOPHOBIA

ZOOPHOBES > ZOOPHOBIA

ZOOPHOBIA n unusual or morbid dread of animals

ZOOPHORI > ZOOPHORUS

ZOOPHORIC > ZOOPHORUS

ZOOPHORUS n frieze with animal figures

ZOOPHYTE n any animal resembling a plant, such as a sea anemone

ZOOPHYTES > ZOOPHYTE

ZOOPHYTIC > ZOOPHYTE

ZOOPLASTY n surgical transplantation to man of animal tissues

ZOOS > ZOO

ZOOSCOPIC > ZOOSCOPY

ZOOSCOPY n condition causing hallucinations of animals

ZOOSPERM n any of the male reproductive cells released in the semen during ejaculation

ZOOSPERMS > ZOOSPERM

ZOOSPORE n asexual spore of some algae and fungi that moves by means of flagella

ZOOSPORES > ZOOSPORE

ZOOSPORIC > ZOOSPORE

ZOOSTEROL n any of a group of animal sterols, such as cholesterol

ZOOT as in zoot suit man's suit consisting of baggy trousers with tapered bottoms and a long jacket with wide padded

shoulders

ZOOTAXIES > ZOOTAXY

ZOOTAXY n science of the classification of animals

ZOOTECHNY n science of breeding animals

ZOOTHECIA n outer layers of certain protozoans

ZOOTHEISM n treatment of an animal as a god

ZOOTHOME n group of zooids

ZOOTHOMES > ZOOTHOME

ZOOTIER > ZOOTY

ZOOTIEST > ZOOTY

ZOOTOMIC > ZOOTOMY

ZOOTOMIES > ZOOTOMY

ZOOTOMIST > ZOOTOMY

ZOOTOMY n branch of zoology concerned with the dissection and anatomy of animals

ZOOTOXIC > ZOOTOXIN

ZOOTOXIN n toxin, such as snake venom, that is produced by an animal

ZOOTOXINS > ZOOTOXIN

ZOOTROPE same as > ZOETROPE

ZOOTROPES > ZOOTROPE

ZOOTROPHY n nourishment of animals

ZOOTY adj showy

ZOOTYPE n animal figure used as a symbol

ZOOTYPES > ZOOTYPE

ZOOTYPIC > ZOOTYPE

ZOOZOO n wood pigeon

ZOOZOOS > ZOOZOO

ZOPILOTE n small American vulture

ZOPILOTES > ZOPILOTE

ZOPPA adj syncopated

ZOPPO same as > ZOPPA

ZORBING n activity of travelling downhill inside a large air-cushioned hollow ball

ZORBINGS > ZORBING

ZORBONAUT n person who engages in the activity of zorbing

ZORGITE n copper-lead selenide

ZORGITES > ZORGITE

ZORI n Japanese sandal

ZORIL same as > ZORILLA

ZORILLA n skunk-like African musteline mammal having a long black-and-white coat

ZORILLAS > ZORILLA

ZORILLE same as > ZORILLA

ZORILLES > ZORILLE

ZORILLO same as > ZORILLE

ZORILLOS > ZORILLO

ZORILS > ZORIL

ZORINO n skunk fur

ZORINOS > ZORINO

ZORIS > ZORI

ZORRO n hoary fox

ZORROS > ZORRO

ZOS > ZO

ZOSTER n shingles; herpes zoster

ZOSTERS > ZOSTER

ZOUAVE n (formerly) member of a body of

French infantry composed of Algerian recruits

ZOUAVES > ZOUAVE

ZOUK n style of dance music that combines African and Latin American rhythms and uses electronic instruments and modern studio technology

ZOUKS > ZOUK

ZOUNDS interj mild oath indicating surprise or indignation

ZOWIE interj expression of pleasurable surprise

ZOYSIA n any creeping perennial grass of the genus Zoysia, of warm dry regions, having short stiffly pointed leaves: often used for lawns

ZOYSIAS > ZOYSIA

ZUCCHETTI > ZUCCHETTO

ZUCCHETTO n small round skullcap worn by clergymen and varying in colour according to the rank of the wearer

ZUCCHINI n courgette

ZUCCHINIS > ZUCCHINI

ZUCHETTA same as > ZUCCHETTO

ZUCHETTAS > ZUCHETTA

ZUCHETTO same as > ZUCCHETTO

ZUCHETTOS > ZUCHETTO

ZUFFOLI > ZUFFOLO

ZUFFOLO same as > ZUFOLO

ZUFOLI > ZUFOLO

ZUFOLO n small flute

ZUGZWANG n (in chess) position in which one player can move only with loss or severe disadvantage ▷ vb manoeuvre (one's opponent) into a zugzwang

ZUGZWANGS > ZUGZWANG

ZULU n (in the NATO phonetic alphabet) used to represent z

ZULUS > ZULU

ZUMBOORUK n small swivel-mounted cannon

ZUPA n confederation of Serbian villages

ZUPAN n head of a zupa

ZUPANS > ZUPAN

ZUPAS > ZUPA

ZURF same as > ZARF

ZURFS > ZURF

ZUZ n ancient Hebrew silver coin

ZUZIM > ZUZ

ZWIEBACK n small type of rusk, which has been baked first as a loaf, then sliced and toasted, usually bought ready-made

ZWIEBACKS > ZWIEBACK

ZYDECO n type of Black Cajun music

ZYDECOS > ZYDECO

ZYGA > ZYGON

ZYGAENID adj of the burnet moth genus

ZYGAENOID same as > ZYGAENID

ZYGAL > ZYGON

ZYGANTRA > ZYGANTRUM

ZYGANTRUM n vertebral articulation in snakes and some lizards

ZYGOCACTI n branching cactuses

ZYGODONT adj possessing paired molar cusps

ZYGOID same as > DIPLOID

ZYGOMA n slender arch of bone that forms a bridge between the cheekbone and the temporal bone on each side of the skull of mammals

ZYGOMAS > ZYGOMA

ZYGOMATA > ZYGOMA

ZYGOMATIC adj of or relating to the zygoma

ZYGON n brain fissure

ZYGOPHYTE n plant that reproduces by means of zygospores

ZYGOSE > ZYGOSIS

ZYGOSES > ZYGOSIS

ZYGOSIS n (in bacteria) the direct transfer of DNA between two cells that are temporarily joined

ZYGOSITY > ZYGOSIS

ZYGOSPERM same as > ZYGOSPORE

ZYGOSPORE n thick-walled sexual spore formed from the zygote of some fungi and algae

ZYGOTE n fertilized egg cell

ZYGOTENE n second stage of the prophase of meiosis, during which homologous chromosomes become associated in pairs (bivalents)

ZYGOTENES > ZYGOTENE

ZYGOTES > ZYGOTE

ZYGOTIC > ZYGOTE

ZYLONITE variant spelling of > XYLONITE

ZYLONITES > ZYLONITE

ZYMASE n mixture of enzymes that is obtained as an extract from yeast and ferments sugars

ZYMASES > ZYMASE

ZYME n ferment

ZYMES > ZYME

ZYMIC > ZYME

ZYMITE n priest who uses leavened bread during communion

ZYMITES > ZYMITE

ZYMOGEN n any of a group of compounds that are inactive precursors of enzymes and are activated by a kinase

ZYMOGENE same as > ZYMOGEN

ZYMOGENES > ZYMOGENE

ZYMOGENIC adj of, or relating to a zymogen

ZYMOGENS > ZYMOGEN

ZYMOGRAM n band of electrophoretic medium showing a pattern of enzymes following electrophoresis

ZYMOGRAMS > ZYMOGRAM

ZYMOID adj relating to a ferment

ZYMOLOGIC > ZYMOLOGY

ZYMOLOGY n chemistry of fermentation

ZYMOLYSES > ZYMOLYSIS

ZYMOLYSIS n process of fermentation

ZYMOLYTIC > ZYMOLYSIS

ZYMOME n glutinous substance that is insoluble in alcohol

ZYMOMES > ZYMOME

ZYMOMETER n instrument for estimating the degree of fermentation

ZYMOSAN n insoluble carbohydrate found in yeast

ZYMOSANS > ZYMOSAN

ZYMOSES > ZYMOSIS

ZYMOSIS same as > ZYMOLYSIS

ZYMOTIC adj of, relating to, or causing fermentation ▷ n disease

ZYMOTICS > ZYMOTIC

ZYMURGIES > ZYMURGY

ZYMURGY n branch of chemistry concerned with fermentation processes in brewing, etc

ZYTHUM n Ancient Egyptian beer

ZYTHUMS > ZYTHUM

ZYZZYVA n American weevil

ZYZZYVAS > ZYZZYVA

ZZZ n informal word for sleep

ZZZS > ZZZ

A Quick Guide to Scrabble

Barry Grossman

Contents

1 Introducing Scrabble

Games are strange things. Some, like chess and backgammon, look terribly complicated to an onlooker who doesn't know the rules. It seems that you must have to be some sort of expert to play these games. Scrabble is different somehow.

Even if someone had never seen the game in their life before, it probably wouldn't take them long to pick up the general idea if they watched a game being played. The scoring might take them a little longer but, fundamentally, it's easy enough – just place the letters on the board to form words, like in a crossword. This makes most people think that once they've grasped that, they know all they need to know – perhaps all there is to know – about the game.

This is very far from the truth. Scrabble, like chess, backgammon or bridge, has a high skill factor. And that doesn't just mean knowing lots of words. A strong player will certainly know a lot of words that the average person, even the **AVERAGE** reasonably well-educated person, will never have heard of. But you have to know the right words. A professor of English will find it no help at all in Scrabble to know words like **CATACHRESTICAL** or **SOMNILOQUENCE**. You can beat the Prof. if you know words like **OURIE** and **ZAX**.

> *Scrabble facts – In 1985, two Royal Marines on a training exercise on Brabant Island, Antarctica, fell down a crevasse; luckily, one of them had a Scrabble set in his kit-bag and they passed the five days that they waited to be rescued playing Scrabble.*

Increasing your enjoyment

A game of Scrabble is basically a series of problems. How many times have you yelled in frustration at picking too many vowels or consonants, or cursed the fates for giving you an unwanted **J**, **Q**, **X** or **Z**? How often have you looked at the tiles on your rack and thought, 'I bet these make a seven-letter word', but not been able to work out what it was? How much more fun would the game be if you knew how to deal with these situations?

> *Scrabble facts – In a two-person game, most people playing with family and friends will average between 180 and 300 points per game. Stronger players can average more than 400 points.*

Making the most of 'good' tiles on your rack and limiting the damage from 'bad' ones is what makes your game more enjoyable, and improves your chances of winning. And that's what this book is all about.

> *Scrabble facts – The highest-ever score for a single word was 392 for **CAZIQUES**, played by Karl Khoshnaw of Richmond, Surrey, in 1982. The highest score for a game is a massive 1049 by Phil Appleby of Lymington, Hampshire.*

It won't happen automatically. It'll take a bit of concentration, a bit of practice, a bit of memory work. But if you enjoy Scrabble already, reading this book and taking on board what it suggests will bring you a lot more success at the game, and – more importantly – a lot more pleasure.

Who invented Scrabble?

Alfred Butts was an architect, but in the 1930s he was unemployed as a result of the Great Depression. He was also a word-game enthusiast, doing crosswords and tinkering with anagrams.

First there was Lexiko

Hoping to make some money, he developed a game called Lexiko. This involved players drawing seven tiles, then simply taking turns to discard tiles and draw new ones until they could make a seven-letter word. The first player to do so won. There was no board, no points and no element of interlocking your word with what had already been played. No games manufacturer was interested in producing it, partly because in the Depression most people presumably had little money to spend on games, but partly, one suspects, because it sounds a bit boring.

> *Scrabble facts – Early names for Scrabble included Lexiko, Criss-Crosswords and It.*

Butts then introduced point values for the different letters. When a player had won a round by playing a seven-letter word, the others could play whatever words they could make from their hand, and lose the point values of the remaining tiles.

Determined as ever, Alfred tried again to have the game produced commercially, but still with no success. As an architect, Butts would have known that everything takes time, whether building a house or perfecting a game. He kept refining his invention, and eventually added the board, the premium squares and the crossword-style building up of words that we know from the game today.

Scrabble is born

By now, you might think that the manufacturers would have been falling over themselves to produce the game, but still Butts had no success. In 1939 he met James Brunot, a civil servant with an entrepreneurial streak. Brunot was immediately intrigued by the game. He played around with the idea, refined it a bit more and, like Butts, tried to get it onto the market. But it was now the early 1940s, and the world had more pressing matters to attend to. Finally, in 1949,

Brunot formed his own business, the Production and Marketing Company, and the game – by now, after a few more name changes, called Scrabble – was finally ready to go into the shops.

> *Scrabble facts – Butts based the frequency of letters in the Scrabble set on how often each occurred in headlines in the* New York Times, *the* Herald Tribune *and the* Evening Post.

Unfortunately, even after 18 years or so of development, Scrabble was still no overnight success. Sales were slow, and Brunot was losing money. In the first three years, no more than 20,000 sets were sold. Things were looking grim for Alfred and James, and Scrabble might well have faded away there and then. Then Jack Strauss went on holiday.

Holiday success

Strauss was a shopkeeper, and he discovered Scrabble while on a summer break with some friends. He loved the game and, on his return to work, promptly placed an order and organized a major promotion for the game in the store. This might not have mattered much if Jack Strauss had just been any shopkeeper. In fact, he was the chairman of Macy's, one of the largest department stores in New York. With that kind of power to push it, Scrabble was well and truly on its way. Sales in the low thousands were transformed into millions, and Brunot's and Butts' long struggle was over.

> *Scrabble facts – There are daily or weekly puzzles or columns based on Scrabble in* The Times, Daily Telegraph, Daily Mail *and* Daily Express.
>
> *Because its Orthodox readers cannot write on a Saturday, the* Jewish Chronicle *has a weekly crossword designed to be done by placing tiles on a Scrabble board.*

Scrabble around the world

Scrabble soon spread through the English-speaking world, and it wasn't long until the game was being produced in foreign languages too. Of course, this required a re-evaluation of the point values and frequency of each tile for every new language.

- If you struggle without an **E**, spare a thought for the Dutch, who are such **E** addicts that they have a whopping 18 of them in a set, but only 20 other vowels in total.
- A Russian set has 33 different letters plus two blanks. Not surprisingly all these letters cannot fit into 98 tiles, so Russian Scrabble has a mighty 126 tiles per set, including the blanks.

> *Scrabble facts – Amongst the languages you can play Scrabble in are:*
> *Afrikaans, Arabic, Danish, Dutch, Finnish, Portuguese, Russian, Yiddish*

Scrabble is now played by millions of people across the world, and it regularly tops the chart of best-selling games. About 100 million sets have been sold worldwide since it all started in 1948! Walk into any house in Britain, and there's a 50 per cent chance that it will have a Scrabble set lurking somewhere. The game is said to be popular in homes ranging from Buckingham Palace to prisons.

> *Scrabble facts – Kylie Minogue is a big fan. Snooker players use it to relax in the long intervals between matches – Steve Davis and James Wattana are reported to be particularly hot, clearly masters of the **Q** as well as the cue.*

Parents can introduce young children to the game with **My First Scrabble**, and then they can move on to **Junior Scrabble** when they are a little older. There is also a Braille version of the game, with raised dots on the tiles and the premium squares.

And nowadays, of course, no range is complete without the computer version. You can buy a CD-ROM to play against your computer, choosing an appropriate skill level so that you always (luck permitting) get a good, close game. But be warned, the computer version of the game is addictive.

> *Scrabble facts – To celebrate the game's 50th anniversary in 1998, two teams from the Army and the Navy played a game on the pitch at Wembley Stadium. The side of each tile was 1.25 metres (4 feet) and the side of the board was over 18.5 metres (60 feet)!*

Alfred Butts died in 1993, so he lived long enough to see the worldwide success the game had become. Millions of sets, addicts by the tens of thousands, even Scrabble clubs and World Championships – could he have dreamt of what he was starting when he came up with his curious little game, back in those dark, depressed days of 1931?

2 The rules of the game

Every Scrabble set contains a copy of the rules, but just in case you've lost yours, or you haven't actually got yourself a Scrabble set yet, this chapter gives you a quick guide.

Setting up the game

1 Open out the board and give each player one of the tile racks. The bag containing the tiles should be placed to one side of the board, within easy reach of all the players.

2 One player acts as score-keeper for all the players, and will need a pen and paper. (Alternatively, all players can keep score as a check.) See Rules 7 to 11 for more details about scoring.

3 Each player draws one tile from the bag. The nearest to the beginning of the alphabet starts. In the event of a tie, the tied players draw again. A blank beats an **A**. The letters are then put back in the bag and the bag is shaken.

4 The player who starts picks seven tiles from the bag, and places them on his or her rack without letting the other players see them. Passing to the left, the other players in turn also pick seven tiles and place them on their rack.

The first move

5 The first player makes a word from two to seven of his or her letters and places that word on the board, either across (from left to right) or down (from top to bottom). One letter must go on the centre square (in most sets this is marked with a star or similar marker). The player counts his or her score (the first word counts as a double word score, see scoring, below) and announces it. He or she then takes as many tiles from the bag as have just been played, thus giving seven tiles on the rack again.

Second and subsequent moves

6 Play passes to the left. Each player makes his or her move by adding from one to seven of their own tiles to those already on the board. The letters played, either across or down, must themselves form a valid word, and they must interlock with the letters already on the board, crossword-style, so that all additional words formed are also valid words. Again, the move is completed by the counting and announcing of the score, and the replenishment of the rack back to seven tiles by picking from the bag.

Scoring

7 The basic score for each tile is shown by a small number, from one to ten, printed in the bottom right-hand corner of the tile. The following list shows the score for each letter.

Letter	No. in set	Score
A	9	1
B	2	3
C	2	3
D	4	2
E	12	1
F	2	4
G	3	2
H	2	4
I	9	1
J	1	8
K	1	5
L	4	1
M	2	3

Letter	No. in set	Score
N	6	1
O	8	1
P	2	3
Q	1	10
R	6	1
S	4	1
T	6	1
U	4	1
V	2	4
W	2	4
X	1	8
Y	2	4
Z	1	10
BLANK	2	0

8 The board contains a number of special scoring squares.

- A letter placed on a **Double Letter** square has its value doubled.
- A letter placed on a **Triple Letter** square has its value tripled.
- If any letter of a word has been placed on a **Double Word** square the complete word has its entire score doubled.
- If any letter of a word has been placed on a **Triple Word** square then the word has its entire score tripled.

9 When two or more words are formed in one move, each is scored. The common letter is counted (with full premium values, if any) in the score for each word.

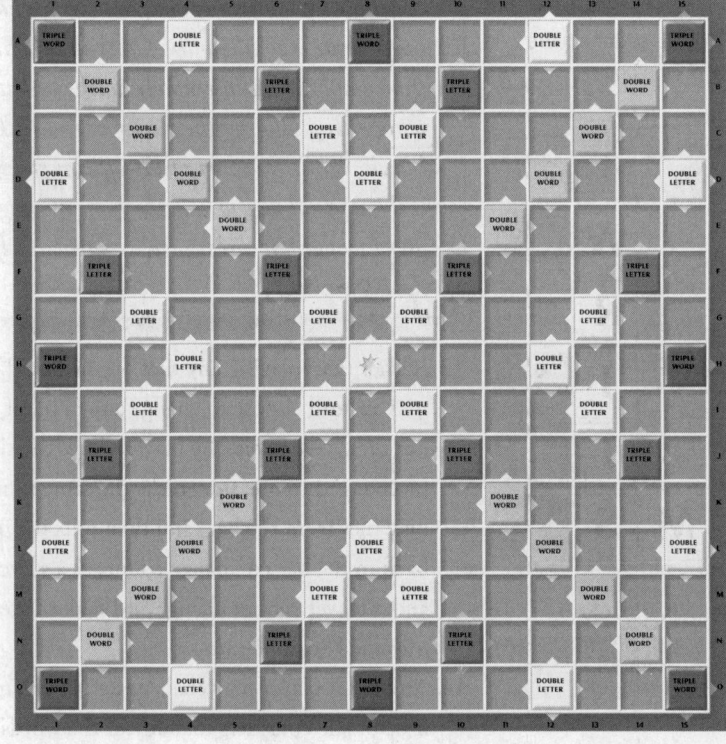

DOUBLE LETTER

TRIPLE WORD

DOUBLE WORD

TRIPLE LETTER

MOTIF = (3 + 1 + 1 + 1 + (4 x 2)) x 2 = 28
F is on a Double Letter square. **M** is on a Double Word square. The total letter score is added up first and then multiplied by 2 because of the Double Word square.
FIRM = 4 + 1 + 1 + 3 = 9
Only the tile value of **F** is used. The Double Letter square only benefits the player who placed **F** on the board.

FIRMS = (4 + 1 + 1 + 3 + 1) x 2 = 20
WRITS = ((4 x 2) + 1 + 1 + 1 + 1) x 2 = 24
Total score = 44 The **S** is on a Double Word square so both **FIRMS** and **WRITS** score double. **W** is on a Double Letter square.

10 Premium squares are only counted in the move in which they are covered. If the word is modified in a subsequent move, tiles on premium squares count at face value only.

11 Any player playing all seven of his or her tiles in one move scores a **bonus** of 50 points in addition to the regular score for the move.

Miscellaneous

12 There are two blank tiles in the set, which may be used as any letter. When a blank is played, the player must nominate which letter the blank represents. The blank then remains as that letter for the rest of the game. A blank tile has a score of zero, but if a blank is placed on a Double Word or Triple Word square, the word is still doubled or tripled, as appropriate.

> *Scrabble tip — Another rule some people like to incorporate is to allow the blank to be lifted from the board and replaced with the letter it represents, allowing the player to re-use the blank. While not part of the official rules, this is a useful way to keep the game moving, and I would not discourage it, particularly for beginners.*

13 Rather than playing any tiles on the board, a player may instead choose to change any or all of his or her tiles. To do this, the player places the tiles to be changed to one side, picks the same number of new tiles from the bag, and then puts the old tiles back in the bag. A change counts as a score of zero, and a player cannot change and make a scoring move in the same turn.

14 Any other player may challenge a player's move, if he or she considers that any of the words made are not valid words. A challenge must be made before the player has picked and looked at any of the replacement tiles. The word should then be checked in a dictionary or an official Scrabble word

source. If the word is wrong, the player must take back his or her tiles from that move, and gets a score of zero.

Scrabble tip – Some 'house rules' allow players to consult a dictionary before playing their move, but most keen players do not favour this. It can be useful to have a dictionary around if a player challenges a word after it has been played. It's a good idea to use this dictionary because it gives all plurals and different verb forms.

Ending the game

15 When there are no tiles left in the bag, play continues until one player has used all the tiles on his or her rack. Every other player then has the total value of their unplayed tiles deducted from their score, and the player who has played all his or her tiles has the total value of all unplayed tiles added to his or her score. If no player can play off all their tiles, each player has the value of their unplayed tiles deducted from their score.

Some example moves

To help get you under way, follow through the moves shown on the boards on the following spread.

You may not spot words like **BIOGRAPHER**, **HONESTY** and **TENSILE** right away, but these moves have been shown to demonstrate the variety of ways you can 'build' a move within the basic rules, and how to score them.

Knowing if a word is allowed

It's very annoying when you play a word, only to have it disallowed by those you are playing with. Use this book to adjudicate on any challenges. This lists every allowable word in strict alphabetical order, except that very long words, those with ten letters or more, are confined to a separate section at the end. No arguing about the plural of octopus or whether you can have **SUBLIMER** or **HONESTEST**.

If you haven't got this book or *Collins Scrabble Lists*, you and your fellow-players will have to do a bit of adjudicating from time to time. Dictionaries will generally list only a base word, such as **TABLE** and will not specifically show **TABLES**, **TABLED**, **TABLING** or **TABLINGS**. Before starting play it's worth agreeing a few guidelines as to what you're going to allow and what you aren't. If you want to find out more, look at the section at the back of the book on allowable word forms.

Scrabble tip – By using the most recent edition of this book, the allowable word list stays up to date; new words are being coined or accepted into English all the time, and you don't want to be prevented from playing **EMAIL**, **EURO**, **CHAV**, **ZIT**, **BIRYANI** or any of a host of others.

Using a large word source is the only way to bring into play the wealth of fascinating words which we will be looking at throughout this book, and which your own dictionary may not have. Some people feel that the more words are allowed in the game, the more it becomes just a memory exercise. Learning the words is certainly important, but having a large number of words at your disposal allows you to display a fuller range of Scrabble skills than would otherwise be the case.

Scrabble facts – It's difficult to assess how many words the average English speaker knows or uses, but estimates range from 40,000 to 75,000. Yet there are a whopping 267,633 words eligible for Scrabble in English!
Lots to learn then…

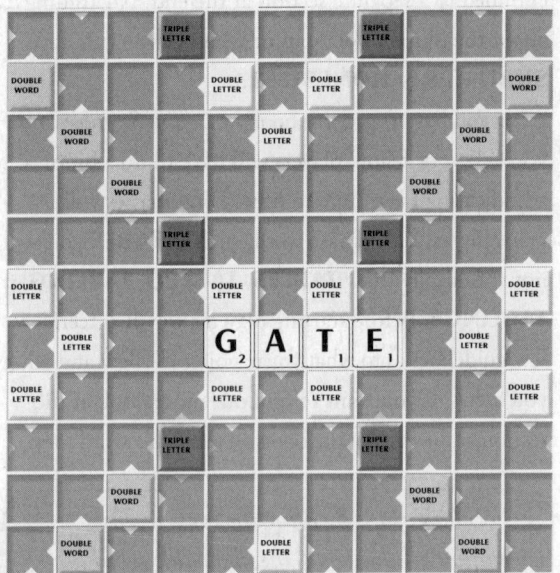

Move 1

GATE scores 5, doubled, scores 10 points.

Move 2

PITCH, with the **I** and **C** doubled, scores 16 points.

Move 3

GLARED, with the **G** and **E** tripled, score 14,
plus 6 for **AGATE**, scores 20 points.

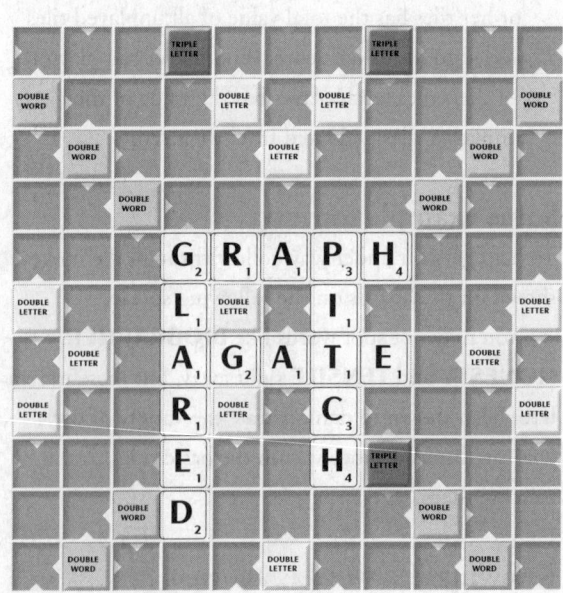

Move 4

GRAPH, with the **H** tripled, scores 19 points.

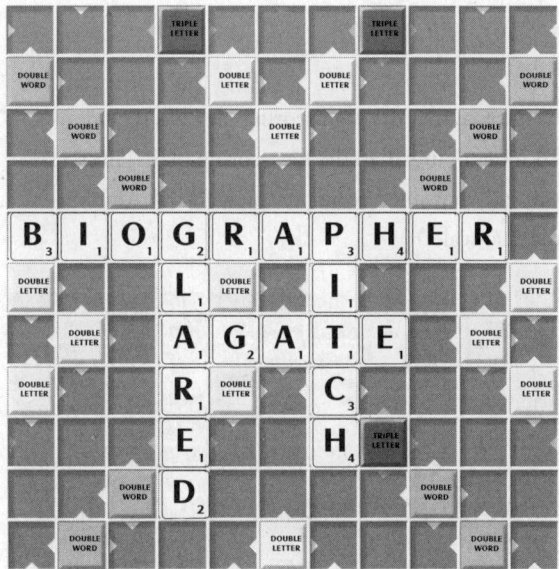

Move 5

BIOGRAPHER scores 18 points.
(Note the **H** is not re-tripled.)

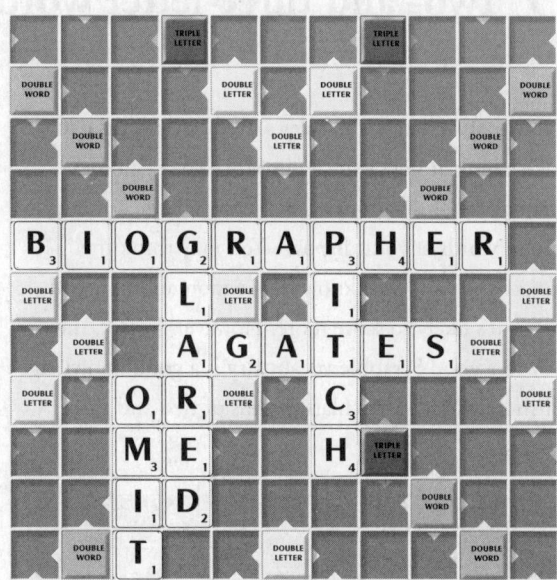

Move 6

OMIT scores 6 and **ID** scores 3, both doubled, making 18.
ME scores 4 and **OR** 2, for a total score of 24 points.

Move 7

doubled then redoubled, scoring 7 × 4 = 28,
plus 7 for **AGATES**, scores 35 points.

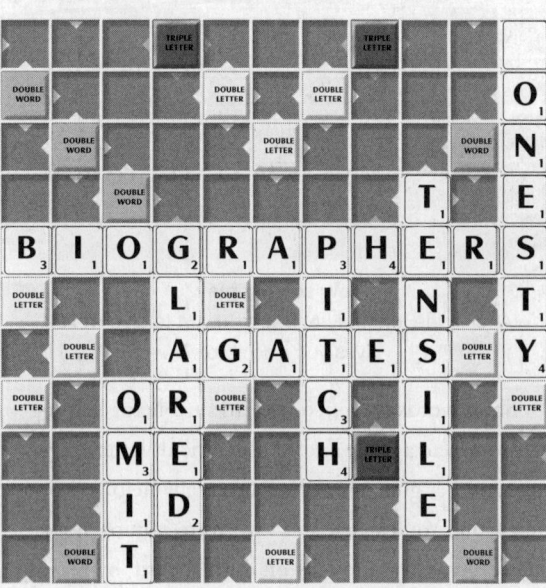

Move 8

The **T** of **HONESTY** is doubled, then the whole word is
doubled, scoring 20 (with the **H** as a blank scoring zero).
Add 19 for **BIOGRAPHERS**, plus the 50-point bonus for
using all seven tiles, for a total score of 89 points.

3 Two- and three-letter words

Now that we've got the rules sorted out, it's time to take a look at how you can improve your game. A major part of that consists of having a large armoury of useful words at your disposal. You may think the longer the word you know is, the more useful it will be, as it's likely to score more. However, in fact, the key to a good Scrabble vocabulary is a good knowledge of short words, particularly words of two and three letters.

Low scoring play
Adding the letters **F**, **A**, **R**, **E** to **TEAM** to give **AFTER** gives you a score of 7.

Short words are, of course, invaluable for helping you complete a game and to use difficult letters. They have another great use, which can really help you boost your score. You can use short words to join or 'hook' the word you want to play on to the board, by playing parallel to another word. You will usually make more than one word each turn and so make a higher score than just by crossing over another word. Look at the two different ways of playing on the two boards shown here.

Notice that the high scoring play has scored 18 more points than the low scoring play. This score was only possible because of the word **FA** (think musical scales).

High scoring play
Adding the letters **F**, **A**, **R**, **E** to **TEAM** to gives a score of 25.

Two-letter words

Here is the first, essential thing you have to know to improve your game: *know all the allowable two-letter words*. There are 124 of them in *Collins Official Scrabble Dictionary*, but to make the list more manageable, you can divide them into three groups:
- The ones you already know.
- The ones you already know, but may not have realized were words.
- The ones you probably don't know.

Commonly known two-letter words

Here are the words you most likely know and which will appear in most dictionaries:

AH	AM	AN	AS	AT	AX	AY
BE	BY				
DO					
EH					
GO					
HA	HE	HI	HO		
ID	IF	IN	IS	IT	
LA	LO				
MA	ME	MY			
NO					
OF	OH	ON	OR	OX	
PA					
SO					
TO					
UP	US				
WE					
YE					

Less well-known two-letter words

There are then a good selection of words that you probably know but were unsure whether they were allowable Scrabble words. As we enter less familiar areas, it is useful to know the meaning of the special words you use, not least so you can convince those you are playing with that the words are for real.

Contracted words

AD	advertisement
BI	bisexual
MO	moment
OP	operation
PO	chamberpot
RE	regarding
TA	thank you

Exclamations and interjections

AW	variant of **ALL**
ER	sound made when hesitating in conversation
HM	sound made to express hesitation or doubt
MM	expression of enjoyment of taste or smell
OI, OY	shout to attract attention
OW	exclamation of pain
OY	shout to attract attention (*or* grandchild)
SH	exclamation to request silence or quiet (*or used instead of* **SHILLING**)
ST	used to attract attention
UH, UM, UR	used to express hesitation or uncertainty in speech
YA	*variant of* **YOU**
YO	used as a greeting or to attract someone's attention

Then there are letters of the alphabet when spelt out. At the end of the list are some names for some Greek letters.

Letters of the alphabet

AR	letter **R**
EF	letter **F**
EL	letter **L** *or* an abbreviated version of **ELEVATED RAILWAY**, as in Chicago
EM	letter **M** *or* a standard unit of measurement in typography
EN	letter **N** *or* a unit of measurement that is half an em
ES	letter **S**
EX	letter **X** *or* a preposition meaning not including or an informal name for a former husband or wife
PE	letter **P**
TE	letter **T**

MU, **NU**, **PI** and **XI** are all Greek letters

Unfamiliar two-letter words

The third group of words will be less familiar, but, as a result, likely to be very useful once you have remembered them. They are listed below, and then some explanations follow.

AA	AB	AE	AG	AI	AL
BA	BO				
CH					
DA	DE	DI			
EA	ED	EE	ET		
FA	FE	FY			
GI	GU				
IO					
JA	JO				
KA	KI	KO	KY		
LI					
MI					
NA	NE	NY			
OB	OD	OE	OM	OO	OS	OU
QI					
SI					
TI					
UG	UN	UT			
WO					
XU					
YU					
ZA	ZO				

If all this looks a bit gobbledygookish, you may be surprised to know that even some of these are more familiar to you than you might realise:

- An **AB** is an abdominal muscle, as in toning up your abs and your pecs.
- **OM** is what Buddhists chant as part of their prayers.
- **AA** is a word from Hawaiian, meaning a rough volcanic rock. Its opposite, smooth volcanic rock, is called **PAHOEHOE**.

- **ZO** is a Himalayan cross-breed of a yak and a cow, also spelt **ZHO**, **DZO**, **DZHO** or **DSO**, useful Scrabble words every man-jack of them.

Just to help you along, here are a list of meanings for the rest of them.

AE	one
AG	agriculture
AI	shaggy-coated slow-moving South American animal
AL	Asian shrub or tree
BA	Ancient Egyptian symbol for the soul
BO	exclamation used to startle or surprise someone
CH	archaic form of **EKE** (to lengthen or stretch)
DA	Burmese knife
DE	of, from
DI	plural of **DEUS** (god)
EA	river
ED	editor
EE	eye (*Scots*)
ET	ate (*dialect*)
FA	fourth degree of any major scale (*music*)
FE	fee
FY	exclamation of disapproval
GI	loose-fitting white suit worn in judo and karate
GU	type of violin used in Shetland
IO	type of moth
JA	yes (*in South Africa*)
JO	sweetheart (*Scots*)
KA	spirit dwelling as a vital force in man or a statue
KI	Japanese martial art
KO	traditional digging tool (*in New Zealand*)
KY	cows (*Scots*)
LI	Chinese measurement of distance
MI	third degree of any major scale (*music*)

NA	no (*Scots*)
NE	nor
NY	near
OB	expression of opposition
OD	hypothetical force formerly thought to be responsible for many natural phenomena
OE	grandchild
OO	wool (*Scots*)
OS	mouthlike opening
OU	man, chap
QI	vital life force (*in Oriental medicine and martial arts*)
SI	seventh degree of any major scale (*music*)
TI	seventh degree of any major scale (*music*)
UG	to hate
UN	one
UT	the note C
WO	woe
XU	Vietnamese currency unit
YU	jade
ZA	pizza

Have a look back at the two-letter words every so often as you're going through the book. Once you're happy with the first two groups (i.e. the common ones, the contractions, the interjections and the letters), have a real go at mastering the unusual ones. They really are the essential first step to improving your game.

Three-letter words

But it doesn't end there. ***Three-letter words are almost as important as the twos*** for helping you build up your moves – and there are a lot more of them. Unless you have a lot of time and aptitude to study lists, or have a photographic memory, it will take you a few months to get to grips fully with the threes. Take them gradually, starting with the ones containing **J**, **Q**, **X** and **Z**. You won't need to know all of them before your game starts to improve.

Here are some of the most useful threes:

Containing **J**

GJU	type of violin used in Shetland
JAP	to splash
JEE	mild exclamation of surprise
JIZ	wig
JOE	sweetheart (*Scots*)
RAJ	British government in India before 1947
TAJ	tall conical cap worn as a mark of distinction by Muslims

Containing **Q**

QAT	evergreen shrubs
QIS	plural of **QI** (*vital life force*)
QUA	in the capacity of
SUQ	open-air market place, e.g. in North Africa

Containing **X**

DEX	dextroamphetamine
GOX	gaseous oxygen
HOX	to hamstring
KEX	any of several large hollow-stemmed umbelliferous plants, such as chervil
RAX	to stretch or extend
REX	king
VOX	voice
WEX	wax
WOX	wax
XIS	plural of **XI** (*14th letter in the Greek alphabet*)
ZAX	axe

Containing **Z**

You can remember some of the **Z**-threes in sets of two and three:

BEZ	part of a deer's horn
BIZ	business
CAZ	casual

COZ, CUZ
  cousin
FEZ tasselled cap
FIZ fizz
MIZ misery
MOZ hex
SAZ Middle Eastern stringed instrument
SEZ informal spelling of 'says'
ZIG, ZAG
  to change direction sharply

Other useful Z-threes

ADZ tool with cutting blade at right angles to
  the handle
DZO animal that is a cross between a cow and
  a yak
JIZ wig
ZAX axe
ZEP type of long sandwich
ZOA independent animal bodies (*plural of*
  ZOON)
ZOS plural of **ZO** (*animal that is a cross
  between a cow and a yak*)

These lists are not exhaustive, but they will get you started. You won't always be able to fit in a **QUIVER**, a **ZEBRA** or an **ANNEX**, so you need to know a good selection of these shorter words to help you play your high-scoring letters – preferably for a more than face-value score.

Threes containing awkward letters

Other useful three-letter words are those that can help you get rid of awkward letters like **U** and **V**, or which allow you to use excess vowels. You should try to remember:

AIA female servant, usually Indian or Malay
AUA yellow-eye mullet (*Maori*)
AUE Maori exclamation of pain or astonishment

AYU small Japanese fish
EAU river
UVA grape
VAU, VAV
  sixth letter of the Hebrew alphabet

Threes as 'hooks'

By 'hooks', we mean words which can be formed by adding one letter at the beginning or end of another word. Threes which are hooks of frequently used twos can be very helpful. You'll find that you play **ZO** fairly often now that you know it, which is why it's especially good to know **AZO**, **DZO** and **ZOA** – so that you can add the extra letter to an already-played **ZO**, making another word at right angles while you're doing it.

If you look back at the example moves shown in the previous chapter, notice that we didn't just add an **A** to **GATE** to make **AGATE** – we made a whole new word, **GLARED**, as well. This is why these hook-words of any length are so useful. The lists of useful **J**, **Q**, **X** and **Z** words above have been compiled partly with hooks in mind. Here are a few more commonly played twos with the threes you can make from them:

AA:	AAH	AAL	AAS	BAA	CAA
	FAA	MAA			
CH:	ACH	CHA	CHE	CHI	ECH
	ICH	OCH			
HM:	HMM	OHM			
KY:	KYE	KYU	SKY		

By now, you're no doubt wondering what these odd-looking words mean. As with the twos, some are more familiar than you might realize – **BAA** and **MAA** are the cries of a sheep and a goat respectively, **CHA** is tea, **ACH** and **OCH** are what you say in Scotland when you're annoyed, **HMM** is what you say if you're puzzled, and **AAS** is the plural of the rough volcanic rock **AA**. Here are some more meanings:

AAH	to exclaim in surprise
AAL	Asian shrub or tree
CAA	to call (*Scots*)
FAA	to fall (*Scots*)
CHE	dialect form of I
CHI	22nd letter of the Greek alphabet
ECH, ICH	to eke out
KYE	Korean fundraising meeting
KYU	in judo, one of the five grades for inexperienced competitors
OHM	unit of electrical resistance

> *Scrabble facts – The only letter which does not feature in any two-letter word is **V**. There are no twos ending in **C**, **J**, **K**, **Q** or **Z**.*

Don't worry about meanings

A word of advice – don't get too hung-up on meanings. It's a familiar, plaintive cry when someone new to a Scrabble club has an unfamiliar word played against them: 'What does that mean?'. It only adds to their bafflement when, as often as not, the answer comes back, 'I don't know'. It comes back to what has been said before – it's not knowing lots of words that wins you games, it's knowing the right words.

Experienced players build up a stockpile of words that they know will prove useful to them again and again. Sometimes the words have interesting meanings which can help you remember them. But often it's just

another fish or plant, or a word Shakespeare used, and which has lain, dusty and unloved, at the back of the cupboard of English words ever since. Until, that is, Scrabble players came along, blew the dust off and started using it. Some of the meanings worth knowing are given in this book, but there is no rule that says you have to know the meaning of every word you play and, at the risk of incurring the wrath of the purists, I would suggest that it's very often all right just to know the word because it's good for Scrabble and not to worry about the meaning.

Another reason it is not *de rigueur* to ask about meanings during a game is that you might seem to be fishing for useful information, such as whether the word is a noun, verb or adjective, and therefore whether you can put an **S** or some other letter after it. The time to ask about meanings is after a game, not during it.

> *Scrabble tip – You can get rid of excess **I**s and **U**s with **IWI** (a Maori tribe), **ULU** (type of knife) and **UTU** (a reward). You can then use hooks to turn them into **KIWI**, **ZULU** and **TUTU**.*

When you are ready, you can find complete lists of three-letter words on the internet. In the meantime, you will be doing fine if you learn the twos and make a start on the threes highlighted in this chapter. You'll soon wonder how you ever managed to play without **AIA**, **AUA**, **WEX** or **WOX**.

4 Dealing with J, Q, X and Z

Many players don't like to pick 'the big tiles' – **J**, **Q**, **X** and **Z**. They think that because there are fewer words in which to play them, they'll be hard to get rid of, and perhaps will even end up on their rack at the end of the game, costing them a handful of points. This is wrong. The big tiles are, *usually*, good tiles to pick.

The big tiles

You have already seen the two-letter words and some of the threes containing **J**, **Q**, **X** and **Z**. Right away you have an armoury of words that will help you play these tiles.

Get points with short words

The good thing about these small words is that they may well help you play a big tile for a worthwhile score. Remind yourself of the twos containing 'the big four':

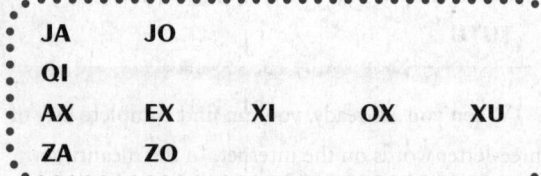

JA	**JO**
QI	
AX	**EX**	**XI**	**OX**	**XU**
ZA	**ZO**

Have a look at the section of a board in play opposite:

You could play **QUITE** using the **T** on the board, scoring 16. But with your new-found knowledge of **QI**, you can play **QI** both ways, slotting in another two-letter word, **ID**, as well for a very healthy 65 points.

In a similar way, how would you score more than 60 points with this board and rack?

You should see right away that the Triple Letter square is the one which is going to pay the dividend. Playing the **J** alone to make **JO** scores 25. But can you play a word downwards as well to get the **J** tripled again? **JO** doesn't fit in this case because you can't have

Your rack: **D E I K L Q U**

Playing **QI** scores 65 points.

OTE, but there's no problem with **ATE**. So play **JA** downwards, also making **JO** and **ATE**, and you're getting somewhere – 53 points for doing very little. Even better, add the **P** to the end of **JA** making **JAP**,

Your rack: **A D F I J O P**

turning **LATE** into **PLATE**, and you've bagged yourself another 10 – 63 for the move which is shown in the next column.

Always be on the lookout for these small but profitable moves when you have one of the big tiles. The **X**, which forms two-letter words with all the vowels (**AX EX XI OX XU**), is particularly useful for this tactic.

> *Scrabble tip – Always try to play the **J**, **Q**, **X** and **Z** tiles on premium squares for extra points.*

Get points with longer words

Another great way to get big scores with the big tiles is to look for 'double-letter–double-word' slots, or, even better, 'triple-letter–double-word' or 'double-letter–triple-word'. It works like this. Remember that if one of the letters in your word covers a Premium *Letter* square, and another covers a Premium *Word* square, the appropriate letter is doubled or tripled before the whole word. So it's another way of making a letter count for a mighty *six times* its face value. You need to make sure that it's a high-scoring tile that gets the six-times treatment.

Playing **JAP** scores 63.

Look at the situation on the board shown below. On your rack you have **E E I N O S** plus one of the big tiles. Can you see where you could get your big tile doubled then redoubled, or doubled then tripled, or tripled then doubled, if it was a **J**, a **Q** or a **Z**?

With a rack of **E E I N O S** plus a **J**, **Q**, or **Z**, there are opportunities for multiple scores

Of course, you need to think here of rather longer words than the two- and three-letter ones we have been using up to now. There are plenty of common five- and six-letter words, even with the big tiles in them, and none of the words you are looking for here is unusual. The following boards show you some possible solutions.

JOINS scores 63

ZONES scores 75

QUINS scores 48

SNEEZE scores 75

Score with **J**, **Q**, **X** or **Z** on the Triple Word square

If no opportunities like the ones shown above present themselves when you have a big tile, you can often get a good score simply by mopping up a handy Triple Word square.

Look at the position on the board shown below. Ordinarily it wouldn't be worth much to use this Triple Word square. Low-scoring tiles will not score much and, if the left-hand row is usable all the way to the top or bottom, you could be opening a good place for your opponent to play a high-scoring bonus. But if you can slot in **JET**, **QAT** or **ZIT**, you pocket a handy 30 or 36 points, and you would be very unlucky if your opponent was ready to move in with an eight-letter word beginning or ending with the high-scoring tile you have provided. If your opponent does use the high-scorer to make a word that isn't a 50-point bonus, it would be most unlikely to score as many as yours just has. It would quite likely score no more than 12 or 14 points – a big net profit for you.

On this board use the Triple Word square for a high-score.

Useful four- and five-letter words with **J**, **Q**, **X** and **Z**

JUGA	plural of **JUGUM**, a small process at the base of each forewing in certain insects
JORAM	large drinking bowl
JORUM	large drinking bowl
AFLAJ	plural of **FALAJ**
FALAJ	water channel
AQUA	water
QUATE	fortune
QUINE	a young, unmarried woman or girl (*Scots*)
TRANQ	tranquiliser
IXIA	southern African plant of the iris family
PREX	US college president
SOREX	a shrew or related animal
XENIA	influence of pollen upon the form of the fruit that develops after pollination
ZEIN	protein occurring in maize
ZILA	administrative district in India
ZAIRE	currency used in the former Zaire

But the big tiles aren't always good

There are times when you don't want to pull one of these high-scorers out of the bag: when you're close to a bonus, and, sometimes, when you're close to the end of a game.

Breaking up a bonus word

If you have six low-scoring tiles, well balanced between vowels and consonants, and with not too many duplicates, you should be well on your way to making a seven-letter bonus word. Picking **J**, **Q**, **X** or **Z** at that stage just screws the whole thing up, unless you're lucky enough to pick, say, a **Z** to a rack of **A E I**

N S T, which you can then arrange into **ZANIEST**. Usually you just have to play the high-scorer as quickly as possible for a low score, such as using the **Z** to make **ZO** for 11 points.

Pulling out a **Q** in such circumstances can be a real challenge. You need to know that there are some words that use a **Q** without a **U**, many of Arabic origin. Here are some examples of allowed words:

QI	vital life force (*in Oriental medicine and martial arts*)
QAT	white-flowered evergreen shrub whose leaves have narcotic properties
QADI	judge in a Muslim country
QAID	chief
QOPH	19th letter of the Hebrew alphabet
WAQF	religious or charitable endowment in Muslim law
FAQIR	Muslim who spurns worldly possessions
QANAT	underground irrigation channel
QIBLA	direction of Mecca, to which Muslims turn in prayer
TALAQ	Muslim form of divorce

Sometimes you are faced with the dilemma of whether to break up your promising combination (**A E I N S T** or whatever) for the sake of getting around 20 points for your high scorer rather than about 11 or so. How much easier if you had drawn an **R** for **RETAINS** or **G** for **SEATING**.

At the end of a game

The other time you may not want to see a big tile arriving on your rack is towards the end of the game. It depends on whether there is somewhere to play it for at least 20 points or so. If there is, it can win you a close game. If not, you either have to play it off for what you can (possibly giving your opponent a chance to play out and leave you with the rest of your letters on your rack), or conversely, get rid of the rest of your letters for whatever you can and perhaps be stuck with the biggie. In some cases, if the board is blocked, you might not be able to get rid of it at all.

5 Using the S

Although **S** is only worth one point, it's much more valuable than you might think, because it can help you form seven-letter words and score 50 bonus points.

If you look at a game played between two good club players, and one between two less experienced players, a few differences will quickly be obvious.

- The stronger players will have played plenty of those unusual two- and three-letter words we have already looked at.
- There will be more parallel plays, resulting in solid blocks of tiles, rather than words which criss-cross through each other.
- There will be more seven- and eight-letter words played for 50-point bonuses.

This chapter will focus on the third of these, and in particular, how to use four of the six best tiles in the set – the four **S**s. The other two tiles, the two blanks, will be covered in the next chapter.

Why is the S so useful?

Look around you and come up with the first few words that come into your head. You might think of **CHAIR**, **TABLE**, **BOOK**, **SIT** and **READ**. Depending on who's in the room with you, you could come up with **MAN**, **WOMAN**, **HUSBAND**, **WIFE**, **BOY**, **GIRL**.

And what does every one of those words have in common? Yes, you can put an **S** at the end of all of them. Even **MAN** (he mans the lifeboat), **WOMAN** (to act like a woman or to staff with women) and **WIFE** (to become a wife or take a wife) are verbs which can have **S** after them (or 'take an **S**', as Scrabble players tend to say). In fact, nearly every noun and verb in the English language can take an **S**. Many of the smaller words take S, and not always because of their status as a noun or verb – **DI** is a noun

but is plural already (plural of **DEUS**, a god), but you can have **DIS**, teenage slang meaning to disrespect.

> *Scrabble tip* – *Some unexpected words that take an* **S** *(i.e. they can have an* **S** *put at the end of them):*
> **EROTIC   ERRATIC   MALTED   PRY   TELLY   TRILBY   WICKED**

Even a lot of words that end in S take an **S** – **PRINCES** (to give **PRINCESS**), **POSSES** (to give **POSSESS**), **BRAS** (to give **BRASS**), **NEEDLES** (to give **NEEDLESS**) and indeed **DIS** (to give **DISS**, to treat with contempt). **ZEBRAS** can become **ZEBRASS** (a cross between a zebra and an ass), and if you're ever in a game where **DEADLINE** is played, then someone makes it **DEADLINES**, you could well and truly flabbergast your opponent by turning that into **DEADLINESS**.

> *Scrabble facts* – *Don't forget that there are four* **S** *tiles in a set, so there's a reasonably high chance that you'll get one at some point in the game.*

Using your S

The relevance of all this to the **S** on your Scrabble rack is twofold. Firstly, if you can make a six-letter word with the other six letters, the chances are you'll be able to stick an **S** on the end of it and, you've got a seven-letter word. So you've only got six letters to worry about manipulating. That means, assuming no blanks or duplicates, you only have 720 different ways to arrange your tiles which, while it might sound quite a lot, is a lot easier than the 5,040 ways you can arrange seven different tiles.

Of course, you may have a seven-letter word with an **S** in it, but the **S** isn't at the end. For example, with a rack of **I L N O R S T**, it may only be after coming up with wrong 'uns like *litrons* and *trinols* that you finally sniff out **NOSTRIL**. However, it's worth putting your **S** at the end of the rack and thinking around the other six to start with, and only if that fails, should you need to be more imaginative.

Secondly, once you've found your bonus word, you have a high chance of being able to fit it in. What can match the desolation of working out a splendid seven and then not being able to get it down? But with all those other words already on the board, most of them taking an **S**, you will usually have a couple of positions onto which you can hook your brilliant bonus.

It is worth stressing that you should not necessarily hang onto an **S** until you can get a bonus with it. Its usefulness for hooking means you can often get a good score without using it in a bonus word. Watch especially for positions where you can get two words doubled with the addition of an **S**. Look at the board opposite with a Double Word square next to **FIRM**.

If you have an **S** in this position, you should be looking to make whatever word you can with it, and use it to turn **FIRM** into **FIRMS**. If you can get a high-scorer on the Double Letter square, so much the better. Something like **WRITS**, coming down to also make **FIRMS**, would score 44 (see opposite).

To summarize, the **S** can:

- Allow you to play a word, hooking an existing word, and thus scoring for both.
- Increase your chance of finding a seven-letter word.
- Taking 1 and 2 together, it can increase your chance of finding a playable seven-letter word.

You should expect to score at least 20 for an **S**, preferably more than 25.

A good board for playing an **S**.

Using the **S** to get down **WRITS** scores 44.

The two Ss problem

If one **S** is good, it follows that two on your rack at the same time must be twice as good. Right? Wrong!

Why? Well, quite simply, two of anything on your rack tends to weaken it (leaving aside blanks, which we'll come to in the next chapter). It's all to do with those different combinations again – you have far fewer separate ways of arranging your letters if you have a duplicate.

Two **E**s are usually alright, because **E** is such a common letter in English. And two **S**s are certainly better than some other duplicates; the dreaded duplicate **V** or **U** are real killers. But a second **S** has basically lost its advantage of being an **S** – its essential 'essness' (no, not a valid word). If you put one **S** to one side, hoping to make a word with the other six letters, and then stick the **S** at the end of it to make a seven, what has happened is that your second **S** has turned into just another letter. You're not really very likely to pick the letters for **ZEBRASS**, and your opponent would be amazed if you got all four **S**s for **POSSESS**.

As it happens, the most common initial letter for a word in this book is **S**, and by quite a long way. So yes, there are lots of words, many of them seven- and eight-letter words, that begin and end with an **S**. Then there are armies of words ending in –**ISES** and –**ISTS**. So it's far from impossible to get a bonus word with two **S**s. It's just not twice as easy as getting one with one **S**.

Generally, the thing to do with a duplicate **S** is play one, hooking it onto a word already on the board, making another word at the same time, preferably using your higher-scoring tiles – you should be getting the hang of it by now – and then you're still left with one **S** and your lower-scoring tiles with which, fingers crossed, to get a bonus next time.

S at the beginning

As well as being an 'end hook' (going on the end of a word), the **S** is frequently also a 'front hook'; which means that it can be placed at the front of a word to form another word. You can often put an **S** at the front of words beginning with:

C: **(S)CAM**, **(S)CAMP**, **(S)CABBY**, **(S)CANNER**, **(S)CURRIED**, and many more, including unusual words like **(S)CAMEL** and **(S)COPULATE**.

H: **(S)HOD**, **(S)HALL**, **(S)HATTER**, **(S)HEATH**, **(S)HELLFIRE** and, more surprisingly, **(S)HADDOCK** and **(S)HOOKS**.

L: **(S)LAP**, **(S)LINK**, **(S)LOUGH**, **(S)LIPPY**, **(S)LIGHTLY** and nice words like **(S)LOWDOWN** and **(S)LAUGHTER**.

P: **(S)PUD**, **(S)PRAY**, **(S)PRINT**, **(S)PRIEST**, **(S)PLATTER** and the more unexpected **(S)PINK** and **(S)PROD**.

T: **(S)TRAP**, **(S)TANNIC**, **(S)TICKER**, **(S)TAKEOUT** and **TATUS**, the plural of an old spelling of tattoo, converts rather pleasingly into **STATUS**.

S-CAMEL   Shakespearian word of uncertain meaning

S-COPULATE   of or like the small tufts of dense hair on the legs of some spiders

S-DEIGN   old form of disdain

S-GRAFFITI   ceramic objects that are decorated with patterns incised in to the top layer of the glaze to reveal parts of the ground

S-HADDOCK   edible yellow fruit that is a bit like a grapefruit

S-HOOK   set of parts ready for assembly

S-PINK   finch

S-PROD   young salmon

Words beginning with **M**, **N**, **W** and even **Q** are also good to check for **S** front-hooks. And of course, like most other consonants, it will often go before a word starting with a vowel (**S-ADDER**, **S-EVEN**, **S-IRE**, **S-ODIUM**, **S-UNDRESS**). Add in exotica like **S-DEIGN** and **S-GRAFFITI** and you might almost start to think an **S** was as likely to go before a word as after it. It is, however, its power as an end hook that makes the **S** such a potent weapon to have on your rack.

6 Using the blank

Sometimes a very inexperienced player will feel hard done by when they pick the blank, because it doesn't score anything. Wrong, wrong, wrong!

If you pick a blank, your heart should leap like a March hare on a trampoline. So long as there is an opening on the board somewhere, a blank should set you on your way to being able to play a bonus word, maybe not immediately, but reasonably soon.

Why? It's those combinations again. The larger the number of different ways you can form your rack into seven letters, the more likely it is that one of them will be a seven-letter word. We've already noted that a straightforward rack of seven different letters can be arranged 5,040 different ways. But six different letters plus a blank can be arranged in a massive 115,920 ways, counting the blank as each possible letter in each separate position. That's 23 times as many; picking a blank is like having 23 tickets in the lottery instead of just one.

> *Scrabble facts – Don't forget that the blank has no value, whatever letter it is standing in for.*

How to use the blank

You could try painstakingly working your way through all 115,920 combinations to find if you have a seven-letter word. At, say, 10 seconds per combination, that would take about 13½ days, assuming you don't stop for sleeping, eating or other essentials. Your opponent may get a tad restless. Happily, your brain will automatically shut out consideration of the vast number of these combinations that are obviously fruitless. In addition, the following will help you work at the challenge:

1 If some of your letters form a useful combination such as –**ING** or –**ATE**, put the blank with the other letters and see if any words suggest themselves. **G H I L N R ?** (**?** represents a blank) might look a bit of a mishmash. But make it **H L R ? + I N G** and it should immediately resolve itself into **HURLING**.

2 If there are no such handy combinations on your rack, go through the alphabet, making the blank each letter in turn. **D F I M N U ?** may not immediately look like anything, but once you try making the blank an **L**, **MINDFUL** might pop into your head.

3 Perhaps the blank will become the last letter in one of those useful combinations. **G H I L R U ?** also makes **HURLING**, even though you can't immediately isolate –**ING**.

4 You may be able to save a bit of time and mental energy by eliminating several possibilities for the blank:

- If you have five consonants, one vowel and a blank, the blank is almost certainly going to have to be a vowel if you are using it to make a seven-letter word.

- More obviously, with five bonus-friendly tiles (i.e. mainly one-pointers with a good vowel–consonant balance) plus a blank and a **Q**, there's really only one letter you need to think about making the blank. If you don't have a **U**, that's almost certainly what the blank is going to have to be if you are going for a bonus.

Play your blank with care

You must avoid the ultimate Scrabble crime of wasting your blank for a low score. Don't just stick it into a four- or five-letter word for a few points, even if you can't see anything else. Hold onto the blank and get rid of some of your more awkward tiles, even for a lower score this time round, and some bonus possibilities ought to start revealing themselves within one or two moves.

In club and tournament Scrabble, the blank will rarely be played other than in a bonus move, unless the blank is picked right at the end of the game, when it may be too late to knock the rest of the rack into shape or there may be nowhere to play a bonus.

You may also be able to use the blank to get a move as good as a bonus, even if not an actual one. Remember we talked about getting a **J**, **Q**, **X** or **Z** on a Premium Letter square, at the same time as getting the word on a Premium Word square. Such a move can easily score 60–70 points or more, and could be well worth using a blank for.

> *Scrabble tip* – *Do you ever feel the blank in the Scrabble bag? Mattel produce special tile sets for tournaments where every tile is smooth.*

As a general rule, you should be looking to score at least 50 for a blank.

Two blanks

Even some quite experienced club players claim to dislike getting two blanks at the same time. The mesmerizingly high number of different combinations that can be made throws some people into confusion, and they say they 'just can't think', or even, appropriately enough, 'go blank'. This is a bit like people who say that being rich doesn't make you happy. It may be true, but you wouldn't mind giving it a try anyway.

The fact is that with two blanks you should be well on your way to making a bonus, unless the board is extremely blocked. If you find a double blank difficult to cope with, try thinking of one of them as the most useful letter it could be (bearing in mind your other five tiles) if it was not a blank. With a rack of, say, **A A C I P ? ?**, given that you have three vowels, at least one of your blanks is going to be a consonant. So think of it as one of those one-point, bonus-friendly consonants like **N** or **T**, and words like **CAPTAIN** and **CAPITAL** should soon start suggesting themselves to you. If you have **H O R T X ? ?**, make the rack more manageable by calling one blank an **E**, and **EXHORTS** suddenly becomes much easier to find.

However, with a rack like that, you may be able to play your **X**, perhaps with one of the blanks, for around 40 points, and still have a good chance of the bonus next turn. Unless you can play **EXHORTS** (or whatever) for a real stonker of a score – I would suggest at least 80 – a rack with lots of goodies like that should be good for two high scores.

Never change a blank

Above all, never change a blank. Why give your opponent the chance of picking it later? The only possible time you might want to try breaking that rule is if you are over 100 behind, and thus need two bonuses to come back. You could try putting a blank back in the hope of picking it later and getting bonuses with both of them. But this is an unwise tactic – particularly as by changing you waste a turn and fall even further behind.

7 Finding the bonus words

Once you have mastered (and I do mean mastered) the twos, started learning some useful threes, lost your fear of **J**, **Q**, **X** and **Z**, and realized the value of the **S** and the blank, the next step on your road to being an accomplished Scrabble player is to be able to play bonus words; in other words, play out all seven of your letters in one go for that lovely, satisfying, game-changing, onlooker-impressing, opponent-shattering 50-point bonus.

Making bonus words

You may manage the occasional bonus now, but if you can get up to playing a regular one per game, then two per game, you will soon see your average score rocketing out of the sub-200 doldrums and into the stratosphere of 300+ and even 400+ (based on a two-player game).

So how is it done? Essentially, there are two keys to playing bonuses regularly: **managing your rack** and **knowing the words**. In this chapter we will look first at the various ways of managing your rack and then at how to form words through the use of **prefixes and suffixes** and by creating **compound words**.

Rack management

It's not just knowing words, it's knowing the right words that counts. There is no point in the random learning of seven-letter words. **PUPUNHA**, **MUNDIFY** or **THRUTCH** may just show up on someone's rack somewhere between now and the next millennium, but that's not the way to bet. Better by far to get familiar with words which, on the balance of probabilities, will come up on your rack with reasonable regularity.

Rack management essentially means knowing which letters to keep and which letters to get rid of to maximize your chances of a good score next time –

preferably a bonus. Just as a good snooker player doesn't take a whack at the first ball he sees but tries to make sure he leaves himself an easy shot for next time, so should a Scrabble player have an eye to what he or she is storing up for the future.

Rack management: keep the right letters

The first thing to know when working out which letters to keep and which to play is the distribution of the tiles in a set. In other words, how many **A**s are there, how many **B**s, etc. Happily, many Scrabble boards actually list this distribution down one side of the board. We list them in Chapter 2. If your board doesn't, it's fairly easy to have a rough idea of how many of a particular letter are in the set by its point value:

> **Scrabble tip** – *Know the distribution of tiles in the set by point value.*
>
> | Point value | Number in set |
> | --- | --- |
> | 1 | 4–12 |
> | 2 | 3–4 |
> | 3–4 | 2 |
> | 5–10 | 1 |

Clearly, the fewer points a letter scores, the more there are of them. There are lots of the common letters to help you make words, but they don't score so much. There are fewer of the less common letters because they're harder to use, but they are worth more points.

This means a rack is going to tend towards having a lot of the one-point tiles: 68 of the 98 tiles (leaving aside the blanks) are worth one point. So the best bonus words to learn must be the ones consisting wholly or mainly of one-point letters.

Rack management: one-point letters

So which are the one-point letters? There are 10 of them: the five vowels **A E I O U**, plus five consonants, **L N R S T**.

Are these the 10 commonest letters in the language? A statistical analysis of over a million words of English covering newspaper reports, scientific and religious writing and general fiction concluded that the most frequently used letters, in order, were:

E T A O I N S R H L

So nine of our 10 commonest letters in the Scrabble set agree with this study. The rogue interloper in the study is **H**, but its frequency can be explained by the number of short, very common words in which it appears:

THE	THAT	THIS	THESE	THOSE
HE	SHE	THEY	HIM	HER
THEM	HIS	HERS	THEIR	WHICH
WHAT	WHO	HOW	WHY	

Thus the letter **H** appears in a passage of written or spoken English much more often than it would in a random collection of unconnected words.

The letter U

So the missing letter from our 'Scrabble Top Ten', the **U**, presumably came 11th in the statistical survey? Actually, it came 13th, behind **D** and **C**.

So why are there so many **U**s in the Scrabble set? Scrabble's creator, Alfred Butts, decided on the number of each letter by counting the frequency with which each appeared in three newspapers, the *New York Times*, the *Herald Tribune* and the *Evening Post*. But it seems clear that he must have made some judicious adjustments after his mammoth count. He would have had to iron out the **H** problem, for one. And he also realized that there had to be a reasonable number of **U**s so that players could play the **Q**. (**QI**, **QAT**, **QADI** and the other non-**U** words would not have been part of his thinking at that time.) Four **U**s would be enough

to give a reasonable chance of shedding the awkward **Q**, but not so many that players would be overburdened with a letter which, apart from **Q** duty, is not particularly helpful.

Rack management: the right vowels

The vowels have a fairly clear hierarchy of usefulness. **E** is the biggie. It's difficult (far from impossible, but difficult) to get a bonus without an **E**. As you may have discovered yourself, it can be hard playing any good move without an **E**. **A** and **I** come next, about equally useful, closely followed by **O**. As the ideal vowel–consonant split is three vowels and four consonants, it follows that the vowels you want on your rack are **A E I**. Even though our million-word analysis placed **O** above **I**, experience in Scrabble shows that the **I** is easier to work with.

> **Scrabble tip** – In Scrabble **I** is more useful than **O**. It can be used in lots of suffixes:–
> **–ING**, **–IER**, **–IEST**, **–ISE**, **–IZE**, **–ISM** and **–IST**.

So do you try to keep **A E I** on your rack, and play any **O** or **U** that you have? Maybe, but it's not always quite that simple.

How to manage duplicate vowels

The problem of duplicated letters can easily come to haunt you with vowels, especially the **A** and **I**. You don't want two of either of these letters on your rack, because comparatively few words have two **A**s or two **I**s in them. Yes, there are all the words ending in **–ING**, thus giving **AIMING**, **BOILING**, **CHIDING** and lots of others, or the **–IER** and **–IEST** words – **DIRTIER**, **FIERIER**, **GIDDIEST**, etc., and no doubt you can rattle off a dozen words off the top of your head with two **A**s as well. However, duplicates radically diminish the number of different ways you can arrange the letters on your rack, and that constricts the number of useful moves you can make.

Tracking the letters played

For this reason, it is always a good idea to keep track of how many **A**s and **I**s have been played. Let's say it's about halfway through the game, with about 45 or 50 letters on the board. There are six **A**s on the board and two **I**s. You also have one of each on your rack. You can see that you are far more likely to pick another **I** than another **A**, so it makes sense to play the **I** if you can, but not be so concerned about ditching the **A**.

> **Scrabble facts** – *The distribution of vowels in a set is:*
> *twelve* **E**s   *nine* **A**s   *nine* **I**s
> *eight* **O**s   *four* **U**s

This should not take precedence over any really good move you can make that involves keeping the **I** and playing the **A**. But, other things being equal, play the **I**. A choice between **BAD** and **BID**? Go for **BID**. Wondering about **CARP**? Perhaps with a judicious reshuffle you could make it **PRIG** instead.

If you play bridge or poker, you will know the value of remembering the cards that have been played or folded. In poker, you don't try for the third six to go with your pair if both the other sixes are gone. In bridge, the king of trumps must win a trick if the ace is gone. We are using the exact same principle here in Scrabble. You use your knowledge of what has already been played to help you predict what will happen next. Except it's easier in Scrabble because you don't need to remember – the 'discarded' letters are all there face up on the board in front of you, so all you need to do is count them. (You might not even need to do that – in a later chapter, we'll look at the concept of tile-tracking, which shows you at a glance how many of each letter are still to come.)

The **E**, as we have already seen, is a sufficiently useful letter that to hold two of them is no bad thing. And there are plenty of four-letter words with a double **O** in the middle if you want to get rid of a couple of **O**s – but four-letter words with two **A**s or two **I**s are considerably thinner on the ground. Of course, you don't need to get rid of both your duplicates to alleviate your problem, as you only need to play one – but there is a comfort in having those double-**O** words available if you need them.

So, we have the apparently contradictory situation that one **A** or one **I** on your rack is better than one **O**, because **A** and **I** are commoner letters, especially for bonuses. But two **O**s are better than two **A**s or two **I**s, because they're easier to get rid of in short words.

An example

It's halfway through a game, there are four **A**s, four **I**s and four **O**s to come, and you have one of each on your rack.

Do you play **BID**, **BAD** or **BOD**?

The answer is, probably, play **BOD**.

The extra strength of **A** and **I** over **O** just about overrides the fear of picking a duplicate. But much would depend on other factors.

For example, if you have –**TION** on your rack, is it worth holding this useful suffix and playing the A? It could be, but you need to be aware that –**TION** is mainly useful for eight-letter bonuses; there are not many seven-letter words ending in –**TION**. So don't build your hopes up of getting a –**TION** bonus unless there are places on the board where an eight-letter word is playable.

If you think this is all starting to sound a bit technical, well, you're right. But that's the trouble with Scrabble racks – there is not always a clear-cut answer. It's like walking through a wood. This path is more overgrown, that one is muddier, a third goes uphill, and the fourth one looks pretty but there's a strange growling noise coming from its vicinity. Which one do you take? Hitting on the right one is a mixture of experience, common sense, instinct and luck.

Conclusion

We have established in general that **E** is the best vowel, **A** and **I** come next, **O** a little behind but with some points in its favour, and **U** the least useful. But even the humble **U** can be worth hanging onto if it is towards the end of the game and the **Q** hasn't appeared yet, especially if there are no handy places to slot in a **QI** or a **QAT**. So the distribution of vowels in Scrabble turns out to be about right. Well done, Alfred Butts!

Rack management: the right consonants

So what about consonants? Remember the one-point tiles, **L N R S T**. Holding on to these and discarding the rest is generally the quickest way to a bonus word. But as always, there are complications.

We will now consider each of these one-point consonants in turn.

The letter L

Of these five consonants, **L** is unquestionably the least useful. It should really be worth one and a half points. Hang on to it if you like but have no qualms about playing it away if you have a good move in which to play it.

The letter S

The **S** is a special case which we have already discussed in Chapter 5. If your rack is your afternoon tea-break, the **S** is a cream cake – great to have, but two are no better than one and might leave you feeling sick.

The letter N

The **N** is a common letter and is useful for forming words with **–ING**, **–TION** and **–SION**. But a word of warning about the **N** – it's a terrible letter for beginning words with. Try this little experiment: take your dictionary or this book, and hold the 'N' section between your thumb and forefinger. Look how skimpy it is. There are more words beginning with **W** than beginning with **N**. So if you have an **N** and you're

trying to use it to start an eight-letter word for a bonus, my advice is – try something else, fast.

The letter R

Now, how about the **R**? Another useful letter, but again there's a catch. The **R** really needs an **E** to give it much value. It comes into its own because of the large number of words with the prefix **RE–**, or the suffix **–ER** (whether in its agent noun sense, e.g. **COUNTER**, **BUILDER**, or as a comparative of an adjective, e.g. **BLACKER**, **NEEDIER**). And it will not have escaped your notice that the one letter in both **RE–** and **–ER**, apart from **R**, is **E**. So if you don't have an **E**, and there aren't so many left that you're likely to pick one any time soon, don't bust a gut to hold on to an **R**.

The letter T

Which leaves the **T**. I am a **T** fan – apart from a blank, **S** or **E**, no letter gives me more comfort to hold on my rack than a **T**. The only trouble is, the statistics don't back up my enthusiasm as far as seven-and eight-letter words are concerned – the **N** and the **R** are slightly better, because of all those **–ING**s, **RE–**s, and **–ER**s. But that may be the point – the **T** is not dependent on specific other letters to make it useful, and my gut feeling is that its versatility makes it more valuable. A duplicate **T** is also far less of a handicap than a duplicate **N** or **R**. Cherish your **T**s, try not to play them unless you have no reasonable alternative, and a fair percentage of them will help you on the way to that elusive bonus.

I could analyse my games and try to produce statistics to back this up, but the trouble is that it would be something of a self-fulfilling prophecy. If I (generally) hold onto a **T** until I can make a bonus word with it, then I will obviously be able to count my bonuses and announce triumphantly that 50 per cent of them (or whatever) have a **T** in them, which wouldn't prove anything. But the **T** is a cheerful, sociable letter that will fit in with pretty much any rack it finds itself on, so if it knocks on your door, invite it in and make it comfortable. More often than not, it will reward your hospitality.

Rack management: the right balance

It goes without saying that if you've got a rack of **L N R S S T T** or **A E E I O O U**, then you haven't got a bonus. In fact, you haven't got much of a move at all. It's essential to maintain a balance of vowels and consonants, and we will look at what this means on the next page.

An example

Let's say your opponent has started the game with **CLOT**, and your rack is as shown. Your first thought might be to play **FLOWN** through the **O**. That would get the high-scoring **F** on a Triple Letter square and net you an acceptable 21. But look what you've left yourself with on your rack: **I O U**. You may well pick at least two vowels among your four replacement tiles, leaving you with a vowel-heavy rack and little hope of a decent score next time.

You could still play **FLOWN**, but using the **L** on the board rather than the **O**. That only gets you 16 points, but leaves you with a more acceptable **I L U**. Still a bit too vowelly – ideally, if playing four tiles, you want to leave yourself two consonants and a vowel.

> **Scrabble tip** – *For good rack management the golden rule is that, where possible, you should leave yourself with either the same number of vowels as consonants, or one or two more consonants than vowels.*

FLOUT, using the **T**, would give you the desired two-consonants, one-vowel outcome, and also scores 16. The main disadvantage of **FLOUT** is that **O** next to the Triple Letter square; although you have to play your own game and not worry too much about what your opponent might have. On this occasion the pesky blighter only needs a **Z** and an **O** up his or her sleeve to score 65 points, leaving you with a disheartening deficit at this stage of proceedings.

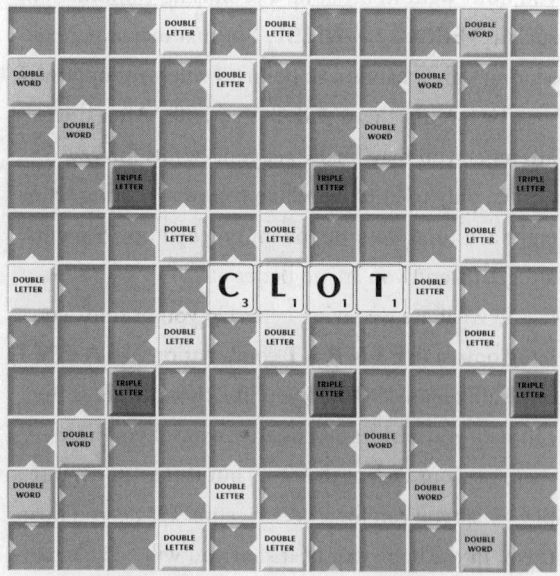

The right balance: your rack is **F I L N O U W**

FLOUT scores 16,
but leaves a Triple Letter square next to the **O**.

Remembering that you should also be trying for **parallel** rather than **crosswise** plays, you might try **FOWL**. Not bad, scoring 18 points, though you are left with two vowels and one consonant. Pity about the **L** on the Double Letter square, rather than a higher-scoring letter. Hang on – how about **WOLF** in the same position? Now you score 21, the same as for **FLOWN**, and a more acceptable leave of **I N U**. (Scrabble players refer to the letters left on their rack after a move as the '*leave*'.)

As so often in Scrabble, there is no clear-cut answer. **WOLF** and **FLOUT** both have something to recommend them, and personally I would go for **WOLF**. But they're both a big improvement on **FLOWN**, because of the better leave – we have given ourselves a better chance of a balanced rack for our next move.

Rack management: keep letters that go together

It's not just a case of keeping **A E I** and **N R S T** and maintaining a good vowel–consonant balance. Often you'll have to keep some other letters as well – you may

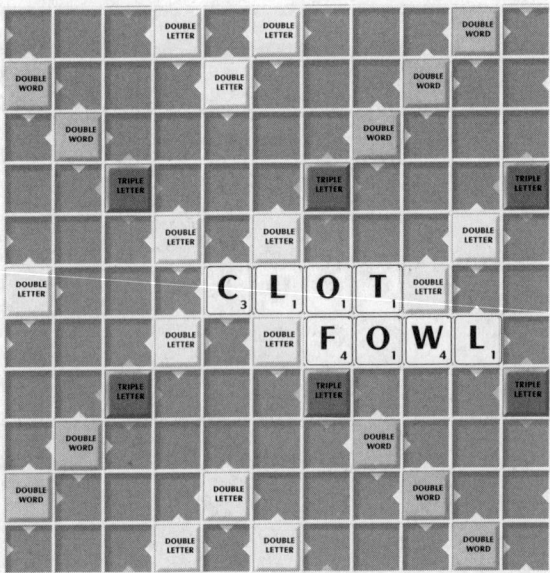

Playing **FOWL** in parallel is another option – and **WOLF** performs even better.

not have many of **A E I N R S T**, so you have to decide what else to offload. Again, much will depend on what good scores are available – never lose sight of the fact that that is the object of the exercise. But it will often be worth accepting a less than optimal score to give yourself that all-important optimal leave. If you have a rack **C D G K W** and two vowels, you don't want to leave yourself with incompatible letters like **G K W**, which are unlikely to combine together in a profitable way next time. Far better to play **G W**, probably along with a vowel, and leave yourself with **C D K**, a much happier combination, especially if you draw (or already have) an **E** to go with them.

Some Scrabble players refer to combinations like **C D K** as having better synergy than ones like **G K W**, although others just say that the letters go together, which is every bit as good.

Strategy and rack management

One of the most difficult things in Scrabble is when you know you're close to a seven-letter bonus but you haven't quite got one (or can't quite find it if you have). You are loath to play more than one or two of your tiles, because you don't want to break up a promising combination, such as **–ERING** or **–NIEST**. But that means you are scoring only a handful of points, while your opponent may be forging ahead with 20s and 30s. After three attempts, you may finally get your bonus for, say, 65 points, only to find that while you were scoring six or eight at a time, your opponent notched up 75 points altogether and you are no better off.

So what are we saying here? Do you or don't you hang onto a **A E I N R S T** combination like **A E N T**, or a suffix like **–ISH**? Do you just check to see if they can help you make a seven-letter word if you have them on your rack at the time, but if they don't, just play what you can for a decent score? Or do you hoard them, in the hope that next shot you will be able to put down that satisfying, opponent-demoralizing bonus?

There is no easy answer. Among the things to take into account are:

1 **The score**
   If you are appreciably behind, you may have no alternative but to go for a bonus.
   If you're ahead, try to keep your score moving along and don't worry so much about bonus-hunting.

2 **The state of the board**
   Are there places to play a bonus word if you do get one?

3 **Are there bonus letters left to come?**
   There is little point in trying for a bonus if the unseen letters are mainly **O**s, **U**s and higher-scoring consonants.

Remember that the extra 50 points from a bonus gives you such a powerful propulsion of points that it is worth devoting a lot of time to learning how to get them. If your rack is even starting to look as if it might make a bonus, and the board has openings or spaces where you can create openings, then it has to be worth considering.

Prefixes and suffixes

You should now be aware of the need to hold on to a reasonable balance of vowels and consonants and to keep the letters **N R S T** and **A E I** (think of the word **RETAINS**), as long as you are scoring reasonably in the meantime. When you keep other letters, you are trying to make sure they are compatible with each other. But the seven-letter words are unlikely to just turn up on your rack with all the letters in the right order. You still have to sort the letters out.

> *Scrabble tip* – It's rarely worth worrying about hyphens with bonus words. Words like **REEJECT**, **CODRIVE** and **NONOILY** are all valid. North American words are included in this book, and the hyphen appears to be virtually obsolete in America. Indeed, **CODRIVE** gives rise to the distinctly odd-looking (to British eyes) **CODRIVER** – not a river full of cod, but someone who shares the driving.

So how do you find the seven-letter word that may be sitting on your rack and earn those 50 lovely bonus points? The first things to check for are **prefixes** and **suffixes**.

Suffixes

Remember that some of these suffixes can do a double duty. **–ER** can form an *agent noun* (**BUILDER** from **BUILD**) or a *comparative adjective* (**SHORTER** from **SHORT**). **–ISH** can go after an adjective or noun to mean 'somewhat' or 'somewhat like' (**WARMISH**, **HAWKISH**). If you have an **F**, you could also try and catch one of the many available **FISH** which may be swimming around, such as **CATFISH**, **DOGFISH** or the rather unimaginatively named **FINFISH**.

> *Scrabble tip* – Here are some suffixes that will help you form seven-letter words:
> –ING   –ED   –ISH   –IST
> –ISE (or –IZE *if you're holding the* **Z**)
> –EST *and* –EST (*especially* –IER *and* –IEST)
> –ABLE   –AGE   –ATE   –ANT
> –ENT   –MAN   –MEN   –LESS
> –NESS   –LIKE   –TION   –LY

Be careful about –ING

A quick word of warning about –ING. It's very tempting to hang onto these letters if you get them, come what may, in the expectation that they are bound to combine with almost any other four letters to form a seven-letter word. Well, sometimes they will and sometimes they won't, but it doesn't happen as often as you might think. In the meantime you are effectively trying to play with only your other four letters, drastically minimizing your potential score. And if and when you do get an –ING word, the double-consonant –NG can make it difficult to fit into a parallel play, so you may well not be able to get it down on the board.

Prefixes

The kings of the prefix world are **RE**– and **UN**–. A quick glance through the **RE**– and **UN**– sections of Section 2 of this book might suggest that you can put either of these two pairs of letters before almost any word. You will quickly be disabused of this notion if you start trying to do so during a game. There are many, many words, some of which look perfectly reasonable, that cannot be formed in this way.

> *Scrabble tip* – *Not all* **RE**– *words are valid, even if you think they look right. You CANNOT play:*
> **RECLAMP   RECOACH   RESLUMP**
> **RESTAND   RETRICK**
> *any of which look as feasible as some words which are valid, such as:*
> **REVICTUAL   RESPLICE**
> **REEDIFY** *(hyphen not compulsory).*

Remember, Scrabble players didn't write this book, lexicographers did. They will be able to cite examples of usage for all the words in their dictionary, and have excluded those for which they could find no examples. Fine, but it doesn't help you much when you're trying

to work out whether to risk **REHAPPEN** or **UNSEXY** (the latter is valid, the former not).

> *Scrabble tip* – *Not all* **UN**– *words are valid either. This book does NOT allow:*
> **UNLIGHT   UNDARK   UNRUNG**
> **UNHAIRY   UNSAD**
> *but does approve of:*
> **UNBRIGHT   UNHEARSE   UNHONEST**
> **UNMELLOW**

So **UN**– and **RE**– are useful to remember, and well worth putting to one side of your rack to see whether they'll help you towards a bonus, but the frequency with which they can be used makes it all the more heartbreaking when they let you down when you need them most. There are lots of other common prefixes which can ease your path towards that elusive seven-letter word.

> *Scrabble tip* – *Watch out for these prefixes to help you towards a bonus word:*
> **PRE–   PRO–   ANTI–   DIS–   MIS–**
> **OUT–   OVER–   DE–   EN–   IN–**
> **CON–   SUB–   UP–**

Using S

Apart from prefixes and suffixes, how else can we discover seven-letter words on our rack? We have covered the obvious one of words ending in **S** in Chapter 5. If you have an **S**, always pop it to the end of your rack, and see if your other six letters can make a six-letter word that your **S** might go on the end of to make a seven.

Compound words

Something else to watch for is **compound words**. This can often pay dividends even if you have higher-scoring letters on your rack. Does your rack divide into a three-letter word and a four-letter word? If so, they just might combine to form a seven. There are lots of examples:

> **PAYBACK** **AIRLINE** **MANHUNT**
> **FOOTPAD** **SEAFOOD** **REDCOAT**
> **SUNTRAP** **WARSHIP** **HATBAND**
> **KEYHOLE**

This technique may lead you to an eight-letter word (using a letter on the board) giving you to a 4–4, 3–5 or 5–3 compound word:

> **AIRTIGHT** **WORMWOOD** **BLUEBIRD**
> **PAYCHECK** **CAUSEWAY**

Always look at your letters in as many different ways as you can. A word with a **Q** doesn't have to begin with a **Q**. Words can begin with vowels, or end with vowels other than **E**.

> *Scrabble tip – Some three-and four-letter words are particularly good for creating compound words, such as:* **AIR, FISH, MAN, MEN, SEA, SHIP, WARD, WOOD, WORK** *and some colours such as* **RED** *and* **BLUE**.

A bonus-word challenge

Try and unravel these 20 teasers using the words shown below:

Five take unexpected letters before them to form other words.
Five take unexpected letters after them.
Five end with **A**, **I**, **O** *or* **U**.
And five have a **J**, **Q**, **X** *or* **Z**, *but where it comes in the word is up to you to discover.*

> **SIPRAIN**   **RAJTHING**   **CANTHEN**
> **AIMSTRAP**   **QUARPET**   **THRIVEON**
> **FLYWAUL**   **SHEISVAL**   **FILMNAG**
> **IPLOTSEX**   **AIHOOTS**   **DRAWPLOY**
> **AACEHUT**   **RUEPHONE**   **ZELEGAL**
> **PLUMTILE**   **IMAPLOD**   **HATEDEER**
> **ILOVAIR**   **ZREFEREE**

Some will be compound words or will use prefixes or suffixes. The answers are given at the back of the book.

When you've got them, work out which 10 have the unexpected 'hooks' – and see if you can find them. For example, if the answer was **BRIDGES**, the hook would be **ABRIDGES**. For a hook at the end, **ELEVATOR** would become **ELEVATORY** (as well as the obvious **ELEVATORS**).

How to look for bonus words

The only other advice I can give in spotting bonus words is simply to look for them. Obvious, I know – but it's easy to get into the habit of playing that reasonable move for 20 points or so, or that word which will leave you a perfectly balanced and compatible rack, while all the time the seven-letter word is hiding in there somewhere. The more you play, the more you will develop a feel for whether a rack is likely to contain a bonus.

Have a look at these racks:

> **A C D E H I R**   **A B I N O P T**   **A E L M N S V**
> **E E F G L O R**   **A E I N O S T**

First, without trying to work out what the seven-letter words might be, decide which combinations are likely to make a seven-letter word. Then, try and figure out the words. Let's look at them one at a time:

A C D E H I R

- The **C** and **H** might go together.
- And there's an **RE/ER**, in fact an **IER**, with other possibilities like **ED** and **IC. CHADIER, DACHIER** – nothing there.
- **CHAIDER, REDAICH** – the **RE** and **ER** don't appear to be much help.
- Maybe **IC** at the end – **HERADIC**? No, but a usable **L** on the board would give **HERALDIC**.
- A compound, perhaps – **ICEHARD, HARDICE**? **ICEHARD** sounds feasibly poetic but I haven't actually seen it anywhere, so it's a big risk.
- Finally, with the simple expedient of trying **ED** at the end to see if there might be a nice, simple past tense, and keeping our compatible **CH** together, we find the answer – **CHAIRED**.

A B I N O P T

- There is a **TION** in there but the only way the other three letters might go with them is **BAPTION** – not a word.
- No compounds suggest themselves.
- Nothing ending with **ANT**.
- The **ANTI** prefix likewise leads nowhere, unless someone who doesn't like dancing could be **ANTIBOP** – which is getting into the realms of fantasy.
- **BIOPTAN** sounds vaguely scientific but that doesn't make it a word.
- Finally, we correctly conclude that there is no seven-letter word here.

A E L M N S V

- Like **A B I N O P T**, it has five one-point tiles.
- It has an **S**, and both **MAN** and **MEN**.
- Any six-letter words from **A E L M N V** that the **S** might go after? **MALVEN, VELMAN, MENVAL** – all rubbish.
- **ELSV** doesn't combine with **MAN**, nor **ALSV** with **MEN**.
- The **A E L M N S** make a nice start and would go with various other letters to form a seven, but the **V** fouls things up – once again, regretfully, no seven-letter word.

E E F G L O R

- Not too promising on the face of it.
- **E F G L O** doesn't match up with **RE** or **ER** – **GEFOLER, REFLOGE**? Not a chance.
- **GOLFER** is in there but we have an **E** left over – still, it could be worth playing if we can get it on at least a Double Word for 20 or so.
- Any compounds? **EELFROG**? **LOGFREE**? **FOREGEL**? Hang on – **FORELEG**. The 4–3 split, using the fairly common **FORE** prefix, brings us to the seven-letter word.
- We got there mainly by technique, but with just that last little mental jump to finish the job.

AEINOST

- Now this looks good. Six of our **RETAINS** letters, and the seventh is a fairly acceptable **O**.

- A slight excess of vowels, but we have an S and there are prefixes and suffixes galore: **–(I)EST**, **–ATE**, **–ISE**, **–TION**, **–SION**, **IN–**, **EN–**, **ANTI–**.

- So what's the word? Well, there is one, but you could probably shuffle your tiles for ever and you wouldn't find it. It's **ATONIES**, the plural of **ATONY**, which means lack of muscle tone. It's an awkward, obscure word which not one person in a hundred will come across outside the confines of a Scrabble board. But **ATONY** is in this book, and since the rule used in compiling this book is that all nouns have a plural, that means **ATONIES** gets in as well.

Learning bonus words

And that brings us on to one more method of getting bonuses. It might not sound much fun, it might not be your idea of the spirit of a game, but there are many words which will keep coming up on your rack because they are composed of the common letters, and you just have to learn them. Sometimes games do require a bit of work. Ask a chess player who's memorized 50 standard openings up to the 20th move. Ask a footballer who's just completed a punishing two-hour training session in a downpour.

8 Ending the game

So, you've learned your twos, most of your threes, and some useful fours. You've got maximum value from whatever high-value tiles you picked up, you've used your new-found confidence in using an **S** or a blank, to make a couple of bonus words, and you have increased your vocabulary from the great variety of world English. The only problem is, your opponent, being one of those annoying people, has done the exact same thing.

Final pointers

You are now approaching the end of the game, and the scores are close. Whether it's about 200 each or 400 each doesn't matter. Your score as such has become irrelevant. You want to win the game.

It won't always happen this way. In a game between two evenly matched players, one can get all the luck, or just that little bit when it matters, and run out the winner by 200 or 300 points. A weaker player can often beat a stronger one over one game. That's why tournament players always like to settle important tournaments over a number of matches – not necessarily all against the same player, but against a number of players of similar standard. Then the cream tends to rise to the top. A one-off win proves nothing.

But let's assume you are playing a game now and, with few or no tiles left in the bag, the scores are close. How do you find that vital edge?

Essentially, what you are now trying to do is not just maximize your own score but also minimize your opponent's. And to do that, you need to know what letters your opponent has got, or know as nearly as is possible. You do this by tile-tracking.

The need for tile-tracking

Back at the beginning of the book we talked about counting up whether more **A**s or **I**s had been played.

If given a choice, you could then play whichever there were more of left in the bag, making you less likely to be left with an awkward duplicate. *Tile-tracking* is an extension of this tactic, and relies on the fact that you know exactly how many of each letter were in the bag at the start of the game. You also know what's been played – it's all there in front of you. And you know what's on your rack. It's simple arithmetic to work out what's left – and that must be what is on your opponent's rack or still in the bag.

I'll repeat again what I said about the **A**s and **I**s. A card player – such as in bridge or poker – will always try to remember what cards have been turned over and are therefore not in the hands of the other players or still in the pack to be dealt. It's an accepted – indeed essential – part of good play. So it is in Scrabble, but with the advantage that all that tough memory work is eliminated. Everything that's been played in Scrabble is face up. It's hard enough remembering over 200,000 allowable words without remembering whether or not somebody played the second **F** twenty minutes ago. Fortunately you don't have to. Just look at the board.

Using a tile-tracking sheet

Even better, look at your tile-tracking sheet. A tile-tracking sheet is a pre-prepared list or grid of letters, which you cross off as each tile is played. At the end of the game, what you haven't crossed off is what's still to come.

Different people use different types of tracking sheet. Some list the letters **A–Z**, plus blank, down one side of the sheet, and mark a tick against each as it is played (see Tile-Tracking Sheet 1 on the next page). Towards the end of the game, if there are only eight ticks against the letter **A**, you know there is one to come, as there are nine in the set.

Some make the relevant number of ticks against

each letter at the start of the game and then cross them off, so the number of ticks left is the number of that letter still to be played (see Tile-Tracking Sheet 2 below). Some write out all hundred letters and cross them through as they are played (see Tile-Tracking Sheet 3 opposite).

Three different styles of tile-tracking sheet, each shown part way through a game are shown here.

Tile-Tracking Sheet 1

A	✓✓✓✓✓✓	O	✓✓✓✓✓
B	✓	P	✓✓
C	✓✓	Q	✓
D	✓✓✓	R	✓✓✓✓
E	✓✓✓✓✓✓✓	S	✓✓
F	✓	T	✓✓✓✓✓
G	✓	U	✓✓✓
H	✓✓	V	
I	✓✓✓✓	W	✓✓
J	✓	X	✓
K		Y	✓
L	✓✓✓	Z	✓
M	✓	?	✓
N	✓✓✓✓		

Tile-Tracking Sheet 2

A	✗✗✗✗✓✓✓✓	O	✗✗✗✗✓✓✓✓
B	✗✓	P	✗✓
C	✗✓	Q	✗
D	✗✗✗✓	R	✗✗✗✓✓✓
E	✗✗✗✗✗✗✓✓✓✓✓✓	S	✗✓✓✓
F	✓✓	T	✗✗✓✓✓✓
G	✗✗✓	U	✗✗✓✓
H	✗✗	V	✗✓
I	✗✗✗✗✓✓✓✓	W	✗✗
J	✓	X	✓
K	✗	Y	✗✓
L	✗✗✓✓	Z	✓
M	✗✗	?	✗✗
N	✗✗✗✓✓✓		

Tile-Tracking Sheet 3

ᴀᴀᴀᴀᴀᴀᴀᴀᴀ	J K Q X Z̷
E̷E̷E̷E̷E̷E̷E̷E̷E̷EEEE	BB C̷C̷ D̷D̷D̷D
I̷I̷I̷I̷I̷I̷I̷III	F̷F GG̷G̷ H̷H
O̷O̷O̷O̷O̷OOO	L̷L̷LL MM M̷M̷M̷M̷M̷N
U̷U̷U̷U	P̷P
	R̷R̷R̷R̷R
	S̷S̷S̷S
	T̷T̷T̷TTT
	VV WW X̷Y
	Y̷Y̷

Of course, if you have access to a computer or photocopier, you only need to write or type your tracking sheet out once and then print off a whole batch of them.

Many people still think of tile-tracking as somehow cheating. Coming back to the cards analogy, it has been pointed out that you can't pre-prepare a grid of cards and cross them off as they are played. I certainly wouldn't try it in the local bridge club or poker casino. But in Scrabble, given that you have pen and paper in front of you to keep the score, it would be perverse not to allow it. If I've got seven tiles left on my rack and you've got the last five, there is a far greater level of skill attached to winning the game if each of us knows what the other is holding, rather than both just shooting in the dark.

Note that you shouldn't cross tiles off your tracking sheet when you pick them; you may decide to change, so only eliminate them when they are actually played. If tile-tracking is new to you, you may find you forget to track the occasional move – usually after a bonus – but with the majority crossed off, you can usually rescue the situation with a quick count. If both the **B**s have been played and you discover you have only crossed off one, chances are that it's one of the moves in which a **B** was played that you forgot about.

Predicting what your opponent will do

So, you know what your opponent has on his final rack. (To avoid a lot of tiresome uses of 'he or she' and 'his or her', let's say in this instance that the opponent is male.) Try to work out what his highest move is, especially if he has a high-scoring tile. If his next-highest move is substantially less, play something to block the high-scoring move – unless by doing so you deny yourself a sufficiently high score for your own highest move. Do the arithmetic. If I score 16 here, he gets 32 there. But if I block his 32, even though it only scores me 12 (so I'm 'down four'), he can only get 20, so he's 'down 12'. So it must be worth it to block his 32 point move.

Playing out

The other main consideration in endgame play is playing out (i.e. getting rid of all your tiles to finish the game) as quickly as possible. When you're down to your final tiles, try to play a move which will allow you to play all your remaining tiles in the next move. That means you need two places to play out, so that even if your opponent blocks one, you still have the other. Conversely, you must look to see if your opponent only has one place to play out – and if so, block it.

It's surprising how often it's worth accepting a score that might be lower than your optimal score by quite a few points, if it enables you to play out at your next move. You deny your opponent another score, and get the value of his remaining tiles added to your score, and he gets the same value deducted. That usually adds up to a sizable swing that can make all the difference in a tight game.

Playing an end game

Have a look at this board from my good friend and Scrabble genius Phil Appleby. You are 13 points behind, and, having tile-tracked, you know your opponent has **D E K O R**. What points do you need to consider for your next move? What would you play? Take a few minutes to examine the board and decide what you would do.

Your rack: **I I N O S S T**

Your opponent has one place to play out – by playing **FORKED** using the floating **F** near the bottom left-hand corner. You must block this play, and play something that will enable you to play out in the following move. Look for his next-best score, and work out whether you can score enough to win the game. If not, look again.

Assuming your opponent has a good knowledge of three- and four-letter words, he can play **KEB** or **KOB** on the top left Triple Word square, for 27. **DREK** or **DEEK**, using the **E** of **OYEZ** and also making **KO**, notches up 25. His best score is **ROED**, played directly under the **AINE** of **MORAINE**, also making **AR**, **IO**, **NE** and **JOBED**, which scores 33.

Endgame problems can get very complex, and computer power (not available during a real game, obviously) has to be harnessed to be sure of getting the optimal path for each player. One good play for you would be **MOIST**, using the **M** of **MORAINE** and making four two-letter words. That scores you 27, and blocks your opponent's **FORKED**. If he now plays his next-best **ROED**, you go down to the bottom-right Triple Word square and play out with **SIN/WARDENS/GI**, which would give you a 14-point win.

If your opponent, rather than playing **ROED**, blocks your **SIN** outplay, such as by playing **GO/OD**, he gets a much smaller score and you can win by playing **SIN** elsewhere, such as making **SIN/JOBES**.

The two important things here are that you blocked his **FORKED**, and you left yourself more than one place to play out your remaining letters. And unlike other Scrabble situations, where the best move is all about the balance of probabilities, maximizing your chances, seeing which way the wind's blowing and hoping for the best, the working out of a winning endgame can, if you can find the right path, give you a guaranteed win without trusting to luck. It's an immensely satisfying feeling to get it right and know you've won a game that, with a little less care, you could have lost.

Developing endgame strategy

Endgames need a lot of practice. As you can see in the example above, they also need a good knowledge of the shorter words. And one further difficulty – it's much harder working out what your opponent might do, even if you know what tiles he is holding, when you can't physically see those tiles in front of you.

In a recent game, I worked out that my opponent's final tiles were **D E E E M R T**, and duly blocked what I thought was her best score (probably something like **ME** for 20) while making sure I could play out next move. What I completely missed was that she had the word **METERED**, which she duly played with great glee for around 70 points to win the game. I wouldn't have missed **METERED** if I'd had those tiles in front of me on my own rack (or at least I hope I wouldn't), but it's that much harder when you're looking at the letters scribbled in a corner of a crowded piece of paper.

There are other elements to endgame strategy. For example, if you have a high-scoring tile which you can't score much with on the board as it stands, you might be able to set yourself up an unblockable high score with it next time.

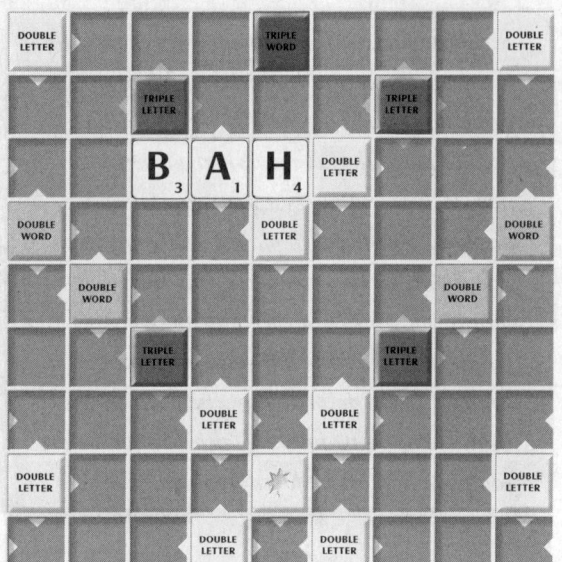

Your rack: **A A C D E I X**
Opponent's rack: **N R U Y**

The outcome from preparing an unblockable high score.

Without showing the whole board, let's assume there is nowhere for you to score much with your **X**. If you play **ACID** in the second-top row, also making **AA** and **CH**, you can then play out in the next move with **AXE** along the top row, also making **ACH/XI/ED** and scoring 66 points. If your opponent uses the **D** to make **DUN** or **DRY**, you still get 60 for **AX** – not an outplay,

but probably enough to win even a semi-close game.

It will rarely, if ever, work out quite as neatly as that, but always see if you can use your perfect knowledge of your opponent's rack to set yourself up a move like this if you have a high-scoring tile on your rack at the endgame.

9 Other forms of Scrabble

Over the years, some players have taken to experimenting with other ways of playing Scrabble, apart from sitting facing your opponent across a table and playing to the standard rules of the game. Various ideas have come and gone. Some take hold and become popular alternatives, others vanish almost as soon as they appear.

Junior Scrabble

Many people will have had their first introduction to the game in the form of Junior Scrabble or some other children's version of the game. Junior Scrabble has a board with preprinted words in a Scrabble game format, and players have to pick tiles which match the letters on the board and play them in the appropriate squares. The back of the board has yet another version of the game, somewhat more challenging than Junior Scrabble but not quite up to the complexity of the real thing.

Simpsons Scrabble

Mattel currently produce a range of Scrabble games for younger players, including Simpsons Scrabble, which involves among other things Bart stealing Triple Word squares from an ever more exasperated Homer. This author has not had the pleasure of playing Simpsons Scrabble yet, but it sounds immense fun.

Computer Scrabble

No game would be complete today without its computer version. There are various forms of Computer Scrabble for sale, most of which have features such as allowing you to play the computer at different levels, thus putting your opponent at a standard of anything from beginner to expert.

You can set the computer to tell you what it would have played with your letters, and, being a computer, it has the annoying property, when set at the top level, of never missing a seven-letter word or other good play, thus gradually shredding your confidence as it points out all the bonuses you missed. Happily you can always switch it off, an option I would dearly love to have with certain human opponents I can think of.

Duplicate Scrabble

Another way of playing the game is Duplicate Scrabble. This is a method used for large tournaments, and involves all the players sitting at their own individual table with their own set. You do not have an opponent – or rather, everyone else in the room is your opponent. A Master of Ceremonies will draw seven tiles, and all players then have a set time to come up with the highest-scoring move they can make with those tiles. Each player scores according to his or her move, but then the highest-scoring move is announced, and all the players who did not play that move remove their own play from their board, and substitute the highest-scoring move.

Play continues with the MC drawing as many tiles as are necessary to replenish the rack to seven in the normal way, and all the players, using the tiles which are already on the board and their new rack of seven tiles, again have to find the highest-scoring move they can. This process goes on until all the tiles have been used or no further plays are possible, with the player achieving the highest total for the game being the winner.

Pros and cons of Duplicate Scrabble

The advantage of Duplicate is that the luck element is eliminated; every player has the exact same rack and the exact same board at every move; thus, in theory, the best player should always win. While this is a big advantage, there are a number of downsides to Duplicate. The skills of rack management, such as accepting a lower score this time in the hope of a much higher one next time, do not apply. You are simply looking for the highest score you can every time; if you can get one extra point for adding an **S**, you do so. There is no question of playing in certain positions to try to open up the board or close it off. Only the score for that move is important.

Duplicate Scrabble also loses an important social aspect of the game. There is less to talk about afterwards. The 'If-only-I'd-played-this-you-wouldn't-have-been-able-to-play-that' type of conversation so beloved of Scrabble players doesn't take place. No clever play such as holding back a **U** because there are only half a dozen tiles left in the bag and the **Q** has not yet been played. If you need that **U** to obtain the highest possible score now, you have to play it.

Duplicate is the form of the game used for tournaments in France. It has been tried a few times in the UK but has never proved popular, and you will be most unlikely to come across it unless you cross the Channel (where they will sneakily place you at the additional disadvantage of having to play in French).

If Only

A few other unofficial variations of Scrabble have emerged. If Only allows you to turn one of your tiles over each shot and use it as a blank, as long as you score at least 50. You can then replace that 'blank' later with the letter it represents, and reuse the original tile. For instance, you play **SQUEEZE** with the **Z** represented by a tile turned over to look like a blank. You, but not your opponent, know that the tile is really a **K**. Later in the game, your rack reads **J H U C Z L E**. You place the **Z**, right way up, in **SQUEEZE**, lifting the **K**. Then you turn your **J** over to look like a

blank, call it a **C**, and hey presto – the semantic mishmash of **J H U C Z L E** becomes **CHUCKLE**.

If Only is a fast, open form of the game with bonuses aplenty and very high scores. It's useful for honing your bonus-finding skills, and as players generally enjoy this aspect of the game more than the board-blocking negative side, If Only friendlies are often played at tournaments at the end of the day as a wind-down from the rigours of the official games.

Super Scrabble

Some time ago, an Australian player came up with **Super Scrabble**. He cut a number of Scrabble boards into sections and created a larger board, something like 25 x 25 as against the standard 15 x 15. He added Quadruple and even Quintuple Letter and Word squares, and played with two or perhaps three full sets of tiles. I believe there was even a 'wrap-around' option, where, if you came to the end of the row or bottom of the column, you could continue your word by going back to the beginning of the row or top of the column, if the space was free. A version of Super Scrabble is available but not in most shops. It's best to master the standard game before you worry about going Super.

Scrabble Poker

Finally, I can add my own modest creation to the panoply of Scrabble-related games with Scrabble Poker, a combination of Scrabble and my other favourite game, though one at which I remain distressingly and impoverishingly inept, poker. Each player picks, or is dealt, two tiles face down and one face up. There is then a round of betting in normal poker fashion, with each player calling, raising or folding as he or she sees fit. Another four tiles are dealt to each player, face up, with a further round of betting at the conclusion of each round of dealing.

When each player has seven tiles, five open and the other two known only to the holder, there is a final round of betting. The winner is the player who can make the longest word from his or her seven tiles (unlike real poker, you can use all seven to make your hand, not just your best five). In the event of two or more players making words of equal length, the winner is the one whose word has the highest face value.

It may never take the casinos or the on-line poker sites by storm, but I and a few of my friends like it as an occasional alternative to the Full Scrabble Monty, as it were. The civilizing influence of Scrabble tends to ensure stakes stay as pennies rather than pounds, and it's another good exercise in bonus-spotting, as well as giving practice in five- and six-letter words, which can sometimes get rather swept aside in the real game in the rush to master twos, threes, and fours, and to learn large numbers of ever more unlikely sevens.

None of these alternatives will ever usurp the genuine article from its position of supremacy, remaining rather the boisterous offspring of a serene and untroubled mother. Difficult enough to be challenging, yet not so arcane as to be open only to a select few, sociable, with the right combination of luck and skill, it can be tinkered with, but not improved upon. It is a tribute to the original game that it can admit so many other versions yet still remain effortlessly superior to all of them.

10 Taking it further

So, you've had your appetite whetted for trying to move your Scrabble game up a level or two. You want to squeeze more points out of every move with neat little parallel plays using two- and three-letter words, you want to play some impressive bonuses, and then eke out a win with a well-thought-out endgame. The only problem is, if your Scrabble-playing friends and relatives don't want to come on this journey with you, you are pitched into an endless round of 'What does that mean?' and 'That's not a proper word'.

Even showing Auntie Mary that **XU**, **JIZ** or **ETESIAN** is there in black and white in this book is unlikely to appease her. Learning useful words and good techniques to improve your game is seen as unsportsmanlike, almost cheating. So your next move has to be to take a deep breath and move into the wonderful world of your local Scrabble club.

Clubs and tournaments

People can have some odd ideas about Scrabble clubs – that's if they realize they exist at all. They are assumed to be patronized solely by either elderly ladies in pink cardigans or geeky guys taking an evening off from working out the square root of minus one. While I can't quite guarantee you won't meet anyone at all like that, most Scrabble club members are normal, well-adjusted people who want nothing more than a sociable evening out and a good game of Scrabble.

> *Scrabble facts – There are about 330 Scrabble clubs in Britain, and a further 200 or so in schools.*

You can find the whereabouts of your local Scrabble club by writing to:

Scrabble Clubs UK
Mattel House
Vanwall Business Park
Vanwall Road
Maidenhead
Berkshire
SL6 4UB.

Or if you're of a more technological turn of mind, try putting 'Scrabble' and your home town into your internet search engine and see what comes up.

What happens at a Scrabble Club?

It's impossible to be definitive, as each will be run in a slightly different way. Some will have a very informal approach, where you just turn up and play anyone else who is waiting for a game. Others are more structured, where you all start at the same time and the organizer tells you who to play. Others again have a league table where you have to play everyone, or everyone in your division, once or twice in a season (however long a season may be), but within that you arrange your own games at times to suit.

However, a few things are pretty much universal at any Scrabble club in the country (and, I imagine, the world). There will be a meeting place and a regular evening when the club meets (although the large and venerable London Scrabble League, of which I have had the honour of being chairman, arranges four-player fixtures in members' homes). There will either be tables about the size of card tables for individual games, or longer trestle tables that can accommodate a few games at a time. Players generally supply their own Scrabble sets and other paraphernalia, so take yours if possible. Crucially, tea and coffee will be supplied either as part of your entry fee or subscription, or for a small charge.

There are a few other ways in which playing at a club may be different from how you are used to playing at home.

De luxe sets

Most clubs insist on, or at least give preference to, de luxe sets; these have boards which are on a turntable so that they can be moved to face each player, and tiles that click into the square on which they are played so that they don't move around when the board is turned, accidentally nudged or otherwise moved. Nothing detracts more from the pleasure of the game than continually having to realign the tiles so that you can read the words properly, or having to twist your neck to try to read the board upside-down. You don't read a book or newspaper upside-down, so why try to do it with a Scrabble board?

Smooth tiles

As you now know, the most valuable tiles in the bag are the blanks. For that reason, it is slightly unsatisfactory that you can sometimes, accidentally or deliberately, feel that a tile in the bag is a blank. Smooth tiles prevent any suspicion that a player has been feeling in the bag for a blank tile. The newest sets do contain smooth tiles. However, there are many older sets around which do not contain smooth tiles. Some Clubs insist that you play with smooth tiles.

Playing one opponent at a time

Quite simply, Scrabble is a game for two players. The rules that come with your set may say you can play with up to four, but the two-person game is far superior. You cannot form a strategy, nor can you plan ahead in any way, if there are two or even three more people to play between your last turn and your next one. Apart from that, it's just boring playing with three or four players – you are only involved in the game a

third or a quarter of the time, and if one or two of your opponents are slow, you can have an interminable wait till it comes round to you again. Sure, you can be looking for what you might play when it eventually becomes your turn, but only to a limited extent. You have no way of knowing if your opponents' plays will drive a coach and horses through the place you were going to make your move – or if they might give you a better one.

In club and tournament play, if the numbers are odd, one person will sit out for a round. Alternatively, one player may take on two players at once, but in two completely separate games on two separate boards. This is an excellent way of sharpening up your Scrabble reflexes, rather like a chess simul, a form of chess match where one (usually superior) player takes on a number of others simultaneously.

Playing to win

As I've emphasized throughout this book, it's not what you score that counts, it's whether you score more than your opponent. It's a statement of the obvious, surely. Don't we always play a game to win?

In the early days of the National Scrabble Championship (NSC), the winner was the person with the highest total score over a set number of games. It didn't matter whether you actually won the games or not. So if you could score 500 points or so in all your games, even if you lost one or two, this was better than plodding along scoring 300–400 but making sure you always won. This led to a highly artificial form of the game where your opponent effectively became your partner where you played a very open game, which means you tried to make lots of places on the board where bonus words would fit in.

Matchplay Scrabble

Eventually most players realized this was a silly way to play, and what was called Matchplay Scrabble took over. Quite simply, this meant playing to win: scoring

500 is pointless if your opponent gets 501. At the end of the tournament, the player who had won the most games was the winner.

Having said that, you can't afford to neglect the possibility of high scores, because players on the same number of wins are ranked according to their 'spread'. This is the total points scored by you minus the total points scored by all your opponents – the equivalent of goal difference in football. So, at least at the beginning of a tournament or club competition, and at the end if you're in contention, it's nice to stick in a really high score, as long as your opponent doesn't score almost as much (or even more). Note that spread is a very different thing from score. Spread takes into account not just your score but also what your opponent scores against you, so you must always be alert to denying chances to your opponent as well as getting a good score yourself.

So what all that boils down to for you is this. Don't just think of your move as a score of a certain number of points. See how it affects the board before you play it. Check if it opens up any high-scoring opportunities, which your opponent is almost bound to take. If it does, try to find an alternative, less risky move elsewhere.

Both players keep the score

If you are playing to win, it follows that you need to know whether you are winning or losing, and by how much, at any particular time. If you're behind, you may need to take a bit of a risk and make some openings. If you're ahead, you should be trying to close things up. So make sure you keep the score. If your opponent is of a like mind – fine, both of you can then keep the score. In any case, it's useful to have a check – mistakes are easily made.

When you try all these things for yourself at a club, as well as involving yourself in the higher standard of play, you will be rewarded by finding Scrabble suddenly just feels like a better game.

The playing of **CARE** would be a risky move here, as you have opened a triple-word chance for your opponent if he has an **S**, **D**, **R**, **T** or even **X** for **CAREX**.

Differences between club and home play

There are a few other ways in which club play and home play differ. The moment when your shot is over is defined carefully. If timers are being used, it's the moment you press the button to stop your own timer and start your opponent's; without timers, it's the moment you announce your score. Until that point of no return is passed, you can take your tiles back and change your mind.

Challenging

From this, it follows that you shouldn't challenge your opponent's move until he has pressed the timer or announced that score; by doing so, you alert him to the fact that you think the word is wrong, and he may take the opportunity to think again.

Lifting the tile-bag

Another thing newcomers to a club find quite odd is the sight of players lifting the bag well clear of the table when they pick new tiles. The rule is that the bag should be lifted to shoulder height, thus precluding any possibility of cheating by having a sly look in the bag as it lies on the table. As with the 'feelable blanks', this is not to say that cheating was rife before this rule was introduced; merely that it is better to eliminate the possibility of cheating rather than having any unwarranted suspicions lingering around the name of an honest player.

No late changes

Apart from a few details introduced mainly to facilitate the use of timers, the actual rules of the game at a club are exactly the same as you are used to at home – with one exception: you can't change when there are fewer than seven tiles left in the bag.

This rule was introduced back in the dark days when a **Q** picked late in the game was likely to be unplayable. It prevented a player throwing a **Q** back into the bag at the last moment, in an attempt to foist it on his opponent. Nowadays, with **QI**, **QAT** and so on at our disposal, a last-minute **Q** is not such a nightmare, but the rule persists. It may be fair to say that you shouldn't be allowed to put a **Q**, a **J**, a **V**, or some other unplayable letter back in the bag at the very end, forcing your opponent to pick it if he wants to make a move. On the other hand, a more hard-nosed player may think it should all be part of the game. At the moment, once there are six tiles in the bag or fewer, whatever you've got on your rack is what you're stuck with.

Tournament play

This has the same rules as club play, but it's a difference of atmosphere more than anything else. Everyone is trying that bit harder and their play is that bit sharper.

Tournaments are generally divided into divisions, so that you play people roughly of your own standard. Also, tournaments are usually played under the Swiss system, which means that, as far as possible, you play someone on the same number of wins as yourself.

However they are arranged, everyone plays in every round, so there is no danger of travelling half the length of the country and only playing one game because you lose in the first round.

A one-day tournament will normally be held over six rounds. Weekend tournaments over two days can have between 11 and 16 rounds. Sometimes, usually on a holiday weekend, they are played over three days, with between 17 and 19 rounds. Occasionally there are even weeklong tournaments. If you fancy having a go at a tournament, get in touch with the Association of British Scrabble Players. The ABSP regulates tournament play in the UK, and you'll find a very useful calendar of events on their website, **www.absp.org.uk**

Reaching for the top

One of the best aspects of getting involved in the Scrabble club and tournament scene is that, even if you don't immediately feel ready to take on the very best players, you can still mix with them, get to know them, and learn from them. With most competitions being divided into divisions, you can rub shoulders with the top players without the risk to your ego of actually having to play them. Go along to some tournaments, especially the bigger ones and you will find that restaurant, bar, and tea-room are a mix of potential world champions, the greenest of newcomers, and everything in between.

Once you've taken that first step of venturing along to a local club, the whole vista of how to get more out of Scrabble starts to open out for you. You will find out where to get hold of the better equipment that adds so much to the game but may not be available in your local shops. Many players now have personalized boards made to their own design (so much classier than a personalized number plate). Round boards, which can be turned without knocking over racks, cups of tea, etc., are particularly popular. Someone will tell you about computer programs, electronic pocket gizmos of various kinds, or even good old-fashioned books, any or all of which you can use to improve your word power and check where you might have done better in an actual game.

At this stage in developing your Scrabble skills, don't worry about tournaments but just concentrate on getting a good grip of some of the basics in this book, such as the twos, the threes, making good use of **JQXZ**, trying for bonuses by balancing your rack between vowels and consonants, keeping those bonus-friendly tiles (especially blank and **S**) and learning some of the sevens and eights that they make. Then either get your regular opponents to do the same, or join a Scrabble club. I wish you many hours of happy and stimulating Scrabble playing.

Allowable word forms

Plurals

Nouns, fairly obviously, have a plural. But all nouns? If you watch *Countdown* you will have become familiar with the concept of 'count nouns' and 'mass nouns'. A count noun is something you can have more than one of, and therefore the noun takes a plural. **MAN**, **HORSE** and **BANANA** are all count nouns with obvious plurals. It needn't be a thing you can touch – **DAY**, **LIE** and **FEELING** are also count nouns.

The problems start, if you allow them to, with the mass noun. Can you pluralize words like **TENNIS**, **CALCITE** and **FLU**? *Countdown* will often say 'no', declaring that they are mass nouns, so you can't have more than one of them. My advice about this is – forget it. Any noun can have a plural. Go ahead and allow **TENNISES**, **CALCITES** and **FLUS**. This book certainly does.

What is not always so easy to work out is what the plural actually is. We know that it is usually formed by adding –s. There are some well-known exceptions – so well-known, in fact, that you barely register them. Nouns ending in –s, –ch or –sh all add –es, for example **TENNISES**, **CHURCHES** and **BRUSHES**. (As usual, there are exceptions to the exceptions – words ending in the Scottish ch, like **LOCH**, just add –s in the plural).

Words ending in –y preceded by a consonant change the –y to –ies, so we have **FLIES**, **BERRIES**, etc. And of course we have **MEN**, **MICE**, **SHEEP** and plenty of other common irregular plurals.

But what is the plural of **TROUT**? Usually it would just be **TROUT**, as in 'I caught six trout.' But could it ever be valid to say **TROUTS**? Remember **TROUT** has an informal meaning of a silly or unpleasant person. 'The neighbours round here are a right bunch of trout'. That sounds odd. 'A right bunch of trouts', surely. And sometimes you need a bit more technical knowledge. Is **RADIUSES** an acceptable alternative to

RADII as the plural of **RADIUS**? It's at moments like these that you do need to go to the dictionary – preferably always the same one. For the record, this book allows **TROUTS** and **RADIUSES**.

Verbs

What about verbs? Again, it's fairly simple on the face of it. We have the –s, –ed and –ing endings; thus **CONTAIN** leads to **CONTAINS**, **CONTAINED** and **CONTAINING**. If the verb ends in –e, drop the e before adding –ed or –ing, as in **STROKED**, **STROKING**. And we have a similar –y adjustment to the one we have with nouns, as in **MARRIES**, **MARRIED**. Then there is the doubling, in certain circumstances, of a final consonant before –ed and –ing, as in **STRUMMED**, **STRUMMING**. That's quite a few exceptions already, all of which we handle in normal speech and writing without a moment's thought. But if we think of short, simple verbs, there seem to be more exceptions than adherents to the rule – **RUN**, **SWIM**, **BUILD**, **TAKE**, **GO**, **DO**, **SPEAK**, **PAY**, **EAT**, **DRINK** and **MAKE** all deviate from the –ed form. Again, there is no substitute for a good dictionary if you want to be sure of the irregularities.

Adjectives

Now for the adjectives. Before the advent of Collins' Scrabble dictionaries, no element of word adjudication caused more problems than whether you could add –er and –est to an adjective. **POLITER**, **STERILEST**, **WHOLER**, **HONESTEST**, **UNFITTER**, **LIVEST**, **DEADEST** – these and many like them caused hours of harmless merriment, and the occasional tantrum, as their acceptability or otherwise was debated. There is no doubt now which ones are not allowed (**STERILEST** and **WHOLER**).

Glossary of terms

Only terms used in this book are included.

ABSP   The Association of British Scrabble Players, the official organization which regulates tournament play and carries out other associated functions.

affix   A prefix or suffix.

anagram   A word which comprises the same letters as another word, but in a different order.

big tiles   The high-scoring tiles – **J**, **Q**, **X** and **Z**. In some contexts also includes the **S**s and blanks.

blank   One of two tiles in the set which the holder may use to represent any letter.

block   To play a move which prevents an opponent from playing in that part of the board.

blocked board *or* **game**   A board with few positions where moves are possible. Opposite of open board or game.

blocker   A move which prevents an opponent from playing, either a specific move or in a particular part of the board; a word which cannot be extended either at the front or the back.

bonus   The extra 50 points awarded for playing all seven tiles in one move; or a move which achieves this.

break up   To play some of a promising combination of letters.

challenge   To query the validity of a word played by an opponent. The word must then be checked in a dictionary or this book.

change   To use one's turn by putting unwanted tiles back into the bag and picking new ones, rather than by placing a move on the board.

combination   Any stated group of letters.

common letter   A low-scoring letter of which there are several in the set; or a letter which is part of a word on the board both horizontally and vertically.

compound word   A word made out of two smaller words, which combines the meanings of both of them.

consonant-heavy   Describes a rack with too many consonants.

contraction   A word formed from a longer word, but with some of the letters omitted, although the meaning is unchanged.

count noun   A noun representing something of which there can be one or more than one, e.g. table. *Opposite* of mass noun.

Criss-Crosswords   The name of an early version of Scrabble.

crosswise play   The playing of a move which creates only one new word on the board. *Opposite* of parallel play.

discard (tiles)   To replace unwanted tiles in the bag, in order to draw new ones.

distribution   The frequency with which each letter appears in a standard set of tiles.

Double Letter square (score)   A square, on most boards coloured light blue, which doubles the point value of any tile played on it.

Double Word square (score)   A square, on most boards coloured pink, which doubles the point value of any word which has one of its letters on it.

draw (tiles)   To pick tiles from the bag.

duplicate   The same letter appearing two or more times on the same rack.

endgame   The final stages of a game, when knowledge of the letters which are or may be on an opponent's rack affects the moves a player makes.

end hook   A letter which can be placed at the end of a word to make another word.

face value   The number of points scored by any tile, word or move, unaffected by Premium squares.

floater   A tile on the board, in such a position that it can be used as part of another word.

frequency   The number of times a given letter appears in a standard set.

front hook   A letter which can be placed at the beginning of a word to make another word.

hook   A letter which can be placed at the beginning or end of a word to make another word; to play a move which uses a letter in this way.

interlocking   Joining tiles to those already on the board to make new words; all moves in a game except the opening move must be interlocking.

It   The name of an early version of Scrabble.

leave (the)   The tiles left on a player's rack, after playing a move but before picking fresh tiles from the bag.

Lexiko   The name of the original version of Scrabble.

mass noun   A noun representing something which cannot be counted, e.g. fairness. *Opposite* of count noun.

Matchplay   Playing solely to win the game, without relevance to the score achieved.

one-pointer   A tile worth one point, i.e. the commonest letters most useful for making bonus words – **A E I L N O R S T U**.

open board *or* **game**   A board with several positions where moves, especially high-scoring moves, are possible. *Opposite of* blocked board or game.

outplay   A move which enables a player to play all his or her remaining tiles, there being no more tiles left in the bag – therefore, the last move of the game.

parallel play   A move in which a word is placed parallel to another word or words on the board, thus also forming one or more vertical words if the main word is played horizontally, and vice versa. *Opposite of* crosswise play.

play out   To play all one's remaining tiles, there being no more tiles left in the bag, thus playing the last move of the game.

point value   The number of points scored by a given tile.

prefix   A combination of letters which can often be found at the beginning of a word.

Premium square   A square on the board which awards more than face value to a letter or word played on it – a Double Letter, Double Word, Triple Letter, or Triple Word score.

rack   The wooden or plastic stand on which a player places his or her tiles; the letters held by a player at any particular time.

rack management   The playing of tiles in such a way as to increase one's chances of having a bonus word, or other high-scoring move, on the next or subsequent turn.

'six plus one' list   A list of seven-letter words which can be formed by the addition of one other letter to a particular combination of six letters. Similarly 'six plus two' list or 'seven plus one' list.

spread   In a game or tournament, the total number of points scored by a player, minus the total points scored against him or her. A spread may therefore be positive or negative.

suffix   A combination of letters which can often be found at the end of a word.

Swiss system   A method of organizing fixtures at large tournaments, where each player is, as far as possible, matched against another on the same number of wins.

synergy   The property of certain combinations of letters of combining well with each other to form words.

take   A word is said to take a particular letter when that letter can be added to the word to form another word. A word may take a letter at the front or at the end.

tile   Any of the one hundred pieces, each (except the two blanks) representing a letter, which are used to play the game by forming words on the board.

tile-tracking Noting which tiles have been played, and modifying one's play accordingly to take account of which tiles are likely to be picked or which tiles the opponent is, or may be, holding.

Triple Letter square (score) A square, on most boards coloured dark blue, which triples the point value of any letter played on it.

Triple Word square (score) A square, on most boards coloured red, which triples the point value of any word which has one of its letters on it.

vowel–consonant balance *or* **vowel–consonant split** The number of vowels and consonants on the rack, or remaining in the bag, at any particular time.

vowel-heavy Describes a rack with too many vowels.

Z-three A three-letter word containing a **Z**.

Quick reference lists

Alphabetical list of all two-letter words

AA	AB	AD	AE	AG	AH	AI	AL	AM	AN	AR	AS	AT	AW	AX	AY
BA	BE	BI	BO	BY										
CH														
DA	DE	DI	DO											
EA	ED	EE	EF	EH	EL	EM	EN	ER	ES	ET	EX			
FA	FE	FY												
GI	GO	GU												
HA	HE	HI	HM	HO										
ID	IF	IN	IO	IS	IT									
JA	JO													
KA	KI	KO	KY											
LA	LI	LO												
MA	ME	MI	MM	MO	MU	MY								
NA	NE	NO	NU	NY										
OB	OD	OE	OF	OH	OI	OM	ON	OO	OP	OR	OS	OU	OW	OX	OY
PA	PE	PI	PO											
QI														
RE														
SH	SI	SO	ST											
TA	TE	TI	TO											
UG	UH	UM	UN	UP	UR	US	UT							
WE	WO													
XI	XU													
YA	YE	YO	YU											
ZA	ZO													

Alphabetical list of useful three-letter words appearing in this book

AAH	AAL	AAS	ACH	ADZ	AIA	AUA	AUE	AYU
BAA	BEZ	BIZ						
CAA	CAZ	CHA	CHE	CHI	COZ	CUZ		
DEX	DZO							
EAU	ECH							
FAA	FEZ	FIZ						
GJU	GOX							
HMM	HOX							
ICH								
JAP	JEE	JIZ	JOE					
KEX	KYE	KYU						
MAA	MIZ	MOZ						
OCH	OHM							
QAT	QIS	QUA						
RAJ	RAX	REX						
SAZ	SEZ	SKY	SUQ					
TAJ								
UVA								
VAU	VAV	VOX						
WEX	WOX							
XIS								
ZAG	ZAX	ZEP	ZIG	ZOA	ZOS			

AFLAJ	AQUA	AX	AXE					
EX								
FALAJ	FAQIR							
IXIA								
JA	JO	JORAM	JORUM	JUGA				
OX								
PREX								
QADI	QAID	QANAT	QAT	QI	QIBLA	QOPH	QUATE	QUINE
SOREX								
TALAQ	TRANQ							
WAQF								
XENIA								
XI	XU							
ZA	ZAIRE	ZEIN	ZILA	ZO				

Scrabble® Trivia

- In a two-person game, most people playing with family and friends will average between 180 and 300 points per game. Stronger players can average more than 400 points.
- The highest-ever score for a single word was 392 for **CAZIQUES**, played by Karl Khoshnaw of Richmond, Surrey in 1982. The highest score for a game is a massive 1049 by Phil Appleby of Lymington, Hampshire.
- In 1985, two Royal Marines on a training exercise on Brabant Island, Antarctica, fell down a crevasse; luckily, one of them had a Scrabble set in his kitbag and they passed the five days that they waited to be rescued playing Scrabble.
- Scrabble has previously been known as Lexiko, Criss-Crosswords and It.
- Other foreign languages in which Scrabble is available include: Afrikaans, Arabic, Danish, Finnish, Portuguese, Yiddish.

- In 1998, to celebrate the game's 50th anniversary, two teams from the Army and the Navy played a game on the pitch at Wembley Stadium. The board was $30m^2$ and each tile was $1.5m^2$.
- It's difficult to assess how many words the average English speaker knows or uses, but estimates range from 40,000 to 75,000. Yet there are a whopping 267,633 words eligible for Scrabble in English!
- Sometimes you can feel the blank tiles in the Scrabble bag by their smoothness and take them intentionally, giving you an unfair advantage. Therefore, Mattel produce special tile sets for tournaments where every tile is smooth.
- Statistically, the seven-letter word you are most likely to pick out of a standard bag of tiles is OTARINE, the adjective from OTARY. An otary is any member of the seal family *with ears*.
- There are about 330 Scrabble clubs in Britain, and a further 200 or so in schools.

World Scrabble® Champions

1991	London	Peter Morris (USA)
1993	New York	Mark Nyman (UK)
1995	London	David Boys (Canada)
1997	Washington DC	Joel Sherman (USA)
1999	Melbourne Joel	Wapnick (Canada)
2001	Las Vegas Brian	Cappelletto (USA)
2003	Kuala Lumpur	Panupol Sujjayakorn (Thailand)
2005	London	Adam Logan (Canada)
2007	Mumbai	Nigel Richards (New Zealand)

Aa

AARDWOLVES
ABACTERIAL
ABACTINALLY
ABANDONEDLY
ABANDONEES
ABANDONERS
ABANDONING
ABANDONMENT
ABANDONMENTS
ABANDONWARE
ABANDONWARES
ABASEMENTS
ABASHMENTS
ABATEMENTS
ABBOTSHIPS
ABBREVIATE
ABBREVIATED
ABBREVIATES
ABBREVIATING
ABBREVIATION
ABBREVIATIONS
ABBREVIATOR
ABBREVIATORS
ABBREVIATORY
ABBREVIATURE
ABBREVIATURES
ABCOULOMBS
ABDICATING
ABDICATION
ABDICATIONS
ABDICATIVE
ABDICATORS
ABDOMINALLY
ABDOMINALS
ABDOMINOPLASTY
ABDOMINOUS
ABDUCENTES
ABDUCTIONS
ABDUCTORES
ABECEDARIAN
ABECEDARIANS
ABERDEVINE
ABERDEVINES
ABERNETHIES
ABERRANCES
ABERRANCIES
ABERRANTLY
ABERRATING
ABERRATION
ABERRATIONAL
ABERRATIONS
ABEYANCIES
ABHOMINABLE
ABHORRENCE
ABHORRENCES
ABHORRENCIES
ABHORRENCY
ABHORRENTLY
ABHORRINGS
ABIOGENESES
ABIOGENESIS
ABIOGENETIC
ABIOGENETICALLY
ABIOGENICALLY
ABIOGENIST
ABIOGENISTS
ABIOLOGICAL

ABIOTICALLY
ABIOTROPHIC
ABIOTROPHIES
ABIOTROPHY
ABIRRITANT
ABIRRITANTS
ABIRRITATE
ABIRRITATED
ABIRRITATES
ABIRRITATING
ABITURIENT
ABITURIENTS
ABJECTIONS
ABJECTNESS
ABJECTNESSES
ABJOINTING
ABJUNCTION
ABJUNCTIONS
ABJURATION
ABJURATIONS
ABLACTATION
ABLACTATIONS
ABLATITIOUS
ABLATIVELY
ABLUTIONARY
ABLUTOMANE
ABLUTOMANES
ABNEGATING
ABNEGATION
ABNEGATIONS
ABNEGATORS
ABNORMALISM
ABNORMALISMS
ABNORMALITIES
ABNORMALITY
ABNORMALLY
ABNORMITIES
ABODEMENTS
ABOLISHABLE
ABOLISHERS
ABOLISHING
ABOLISHMENT
ABOLISHMENTS
ABOLITIONAL
ABOLITIONARY
ABOLITIONISM
ABOLITIONISMS
ABOLITIONIST
ABOLITIONISTS
ABOLITIONS
ABOMASUSES
ABOMINABLE
ABOMINABLENESS
ABOMINABLY
ABOMINATED
ABOMINATES
ABOMINATING
ABOMINATION
ABOMINATIONS
ABOMINATOR
ABOMINATORS
ABONDANCES
ABONNEMENT
ABONNEMENTS
ABORIGINAL
ABORIGINALISM
ABORIGINALISMS

ABORIGINALITIES
ABORIGINALITY
ABORIGINALLY
ABORIGINALS
ABORIGINES
ABORTICIDE
ABORTICIDES
ABORTIFACIENT
ABORTIFACIENTS
ABORTIONAL
ABORTIONIST
ABORTIONISTS
ABORTIVELY
ABORTIVENESS
ABORTIVENESSES
ABORTUARIES
ABOVEBOARD
ABOVEGROUND
ABRACADABRA
ABRACADABRAS
ABRANCHIAL
ABRANCHIATE
ABRASIVELY
ABRASIVENESS
ABRASIVENESSES
ABREACTING
ABREACTION
ABREACTIONS
ABREACTIVE
ABRIDGABLE
ABRIDGEABLE
ABRIDGEMENT
ABRIDGEMENTS
ABRIDGMENT
ABRIDGMENTS
ABROGATING
ABROGATION
ABROGATIONS
ABROGATIVE
ABROGATORS
ABRUPTIONS
ABRUPTNESS
ABRUPTNESSES
ABSCESSING
ABSCINDING
ABSCISSINS
ABSCISSION
ABSCISSIONS
ABSCONDENCE
ABSCONDENCES
ABSCONDERS
ABSCONDING
ABSEILINGS
ABSENTEEISM
ABSENTEEISMS
ABSENTMINDED
ABSENTMINDEDLY
ABSINTHIATED
ABSINTHISM
ABSINTHISMS
ABSOLUTELY
ABSOLUTENESS
ABSOLUTENESSES
ABSOLUTEST
ABSOLUTION
ABSOLUTIONS
ABSOLUTISE

ABSOLUTISED
ABSOLUTISES
ABSOLUTISING
ABSOLUTISM
ABSOLUTISMS
ABSOLUTIST
ABSOLUTISTIC
ABSOLUTISTS
ABSOLUTIVE
ABSOLUTIZE
ABSOLUTIZED
ABSOLUTIZES
ABSOLUTIZING
ABSOLUTORY
ABSOLVABLE
ABSOLVENTS
ABSOLVITOR
ABSOLVITORS
ABSORBABILITIES
ABSORBABILITY
ABSORBABLE
ABSORBANCE
ABSORBANCES
ABSORBANCIES
ABSORBANCY
ABSORBANTS
ABSORBATES
ABSORBEDLY
ABSORBEFACIENT
ABSORBEFACIENTS
ABSORBENCIES
ABSORBENCY
ABSORBENTS
ABSORBINGLY
ABSORPTANCE
ABSORPTANCES
ABSORPTIOMETER
ABSORPTIOMETERS
ABSORPTION
ABSORPTIONS
ABSORPTIVE
ABSORPTIVENESS
ABSORPTIVITIES
ABSORPTIVITY
ABSQUATULATE
ABSQUATULATED
ABSQUATULATES
ABSQUATULATING
ABSTAINERS
ABSTAINING
ABSTEMIOUS
ABSTEMIOUSLY
ABSTEMIOUSNESS
ABSTENTION
ABSTENTIONISM
ABSTENTIONISMS
ABSTENTIONIST
ABSTENTIONISTS
ABSTENTIONS
ABSTENTIOUS
ABSTERGENT
ABSTERGENTS
ABSTERGING
ABSTERSION
ABSTERSIONS
ABSTERSIVE
ABSTERSIVES

ABSTINENCE
ABSTINENCES
ABSTINENCIES
ABSTINENCY
ABSTINENTLY
ABSTRACTABLE
ABSTRACTED
ABSTRACTEDLY
ABSTRACTEDNESS
ABSTRACTER
ABSTRACTERS
ABSTRACTEST
ABSTRACTING
ABSTRACTION
ABSTRACTIONAL
ABSTRACTIONISM
ABSTRACTIONISMS
ABSTRACTIONIST
ABSTRACTIONISTS
ABSTRACTIONS
ABSTRACTIVE
ABSTRACTIVELY
ABSTRACTIVES
ABSTRACTLY
ABSTRACTNESS
ABSTRACTNESSES
ABSTRACTOR
ABSTRACTORS
ABSTRICTED
ABSTRICTING
ABSTRICTION
ABSTRICTIONS
ABSTRUSELY
ABSTRUSENESS
ABSTRUSENESSES
ABSTRUSEST
ABSTRUSITIES
ABSTRUSITY
ABSURDISMS
ABSURDISTS
ABSURDITIES
ABSURDNESS
ABSURDNESSES
ABUNDANCES
ABUNDANCIES
ABUNDANTLY
ABUSIVENESS
ABUSIVENESSES
ABYSSOPELAGIC
ACADEMICAL
ACADEMICALISM
ACADEMICALISMS
ACADEMICALLY
ACADEMICALS
ACADEMICIAN
ACADEMICIANS
ACADEMICISM
ACADEMICISMS
ACADEMISMS
ACADEMISTS
ACALCULIAS
ACALEPHANS
ACANACEOUS
ACANTHACEOUS
ACANTHOCEPHALAN
ACANTHUSES
ACARICIDAL

ACARICIDES
ACARIDEANS
ACARIDIANS
ACARIDOMATIA
ACARIDOMATIUM
ACARODOMATIA
ACARODOMATIUM
ACAROLOGIES
ACAROLOGIST
ACAROLOGISTS
ACAROPHILIES
ACAROPHILY
ACARPELLOUS
ACARPELOUS
ACATALECTIC
ACATALECTICS
ACATALEPSIES
ACATALEPSY
ACATALEPTIC
ACATALEPTICS
ACATAMATHESIA
ACATAMATHESIAS
ACAULESCENT
ACCEDENCES
ACCELERABLE
ACCELERANDO
ACCELERANDOS
ACCELERANT
ACCELERANTS
ACCELERATE
ACCELERATED
ACCELERATES
ACCELERATING
ACCELERATINGLY
ACCELERATION
ACCELERATIONS
ACCELERATIVE
ACCELERATOR
ACCELERATORS
ACCELERATORY
ACCELEROMETER
ACCELEROMETERS
ACCENSIONS
ACCENTLESS
ACCENTUALITIES
ACCENTUALITY
ACCENTUALLY
ACCENTUATE
ACCENTUATED
ACCENTUATES
ACCENTUATING
ACCENTUATION
ACCENTUATIONS
ACCEPTABILITIES
ACCEPTABILITY
ACCEPTABLE
ACCEPTABLENESS
ACCEPTABLY
ACCEPTANCE
ACCEPTANCES
ACCEPTANCIES
ACCEPTANCY
ACCEPTANTS
ACCEPTATION
ACCEPTATIONS
ACCEPTEDLY
ACCEPTILATION

ACCEPTILATIONS
ACCEPTINGLY
ACCEPTINGNESS
ACCEPTINGNESSES
ACCEPTIVITIES
ACCEPTIVITY
ACCESSARIES
ACCESSARILY
ACCESSARINESS
ACCESSARINESSES
ACCESSIBILITIES
ACCESSIBILITY
ACCESSIBLE
ACCESSIBLENESS
ACCESSIBLY
ACCESSIONAL
ACCESSIONED
ACCESSIONING
ACCESSIONS
ACCESSORIAL
ACCESSORIES
ACCESSORII
ACCESSORILY
ACCESSORINESS
ACCESSORINESSES
ACCESSORISE
ACCESSORISED
ACCESSORISES
ACCESSORISING
ACCESSORIUS
ACCESSORIZE
ACCESSORIZED
ACCESSORIZES
ACCESSORIZING
ACCIACCATURA
ACCIACCATURAS
ACCIACCATURE
ACCIDENCES
ACCIDENTAL
ACCIDENTALISM
ACCIDENTALISMS
ACCIDENTALITIES
ACCIDENTALITY
ACCIDENTALLY
ACCIDENTALNESS
ACCIDENTALS
ACCIDENTED
ACCIDENTLY
ACCIDENTOLOGIES
ACCIDENTOLOGY
ACCIPITERS
ACCIPITRAL
ACCIPITRINE
ACCIPITRINES
ACCLAIMERS
ACCLAIMING
ACCLAMATION
ACCLAMATIONS
ACCLAMATORY
ACCLIMATABLE
ACCLIMATATION
ACCLIMATATIONS
ACCLIMATED
ACCLIMATES
ACCLIMATING
ACCLIMATION
ACCLIMATIONS
ACCLIMATISABLE
ACCLIMATISATION
ACCLIMATISE
ACCLIMATISED
ACCLIMATISER
ACCLIMATISERS
ACCLIMATISES
ACCLIMATISING
ACCLIMATIZABLE
ACCLIMATIZATION
ACCLIMATIZE
ACCLIMATIZED
ACCLIMATIZER
ACCLIMATIZERS
ACCLIMATIZES
ACCLIMATIZING

ACCLIVITIES
ACCLIVITOUS
ACCOASTING
ACCOLADING
ACCOMMODABLE
ACCOMMODATE
ACCOMMODATED
ACCOMMODATES
ACCOMMODATING
ACCOMMODATINGLY
ACCOMMODATION
ACCOMMODATIONAL
ACCOMMODATIONS
ACCOMMODATIVE
ACCOMMODATOR
ACCOMMODATORS
ACCOMPANIED
ACCOMPANIER
ACCOMPANIERS
ACCOMPANIES
ACCOMPANIMENT
ACCOMPANIMENTS
ACCOMPANIST
ACCOMPANISTS
ACCOMPANYING
ACCOMPANYIST
ACCOMPANYISTS
ACCOMPLICE
ACCOMPLICES
ACCOMPLISH
ACCOMPLISHABLE
ACCOMPLISHED
ACCOMPLISHER
ACCOMPLISHERS
ACCOMPLISHES
ACCOMPLISHING
ACCOMPLISHMENT
ACCOMPLISHMENTS
ACCOMPTABLE
ACCOMPTANT
ACCOMPTANTS
ACCOMPTING
ACCORAGING
ACCORDABLE
ACCORDANCE
ACCORDANCES
ACCORDANCIES
ACCORDANCY
ACCORDANTLY
ACCORDINGLY
ACCORDIONIST
ACCORDIONISTS
ACCORDIONS
ACCOSTABLE
ACCOUCHEMENT
ACCOUCHEMENTS
ACCOUCHEUR
ACCOUCHEURS
ACCOUCHEUSE
ACCOUCHEUSES
ACCOUNTABILITY
ACCOUNTABLE
ACCOUNTABLENESS
ACCOUNTABLY
ACCOUNTANCIES
ACCOUNTANCY
ACCOUNTANT
ACCOUNTANTS
ACCOUNTANTSHIP
ACCOUNTANTSHIPS
ACCOUNTING
ACCOUNTINGS
ACCOUPLEMENT
ACCOUPLEMENTS
ACCOURAGED
ACCOURAGES
ACCOURAGING
ACCOURTING
ACCOUSTREMENT
ACCOUSTREMENTS
ACCOUTERED
ACCOUTERING
ACCOUTERMENT

ACCOUTERMENTS
ACCOUTREMENT
ACCOUTREMENTS
ACCOUTRING
ACCREDITABLE
ACCREDITATION
ACCREDITATIONS
ACCREDITED
ACCREDITING
ACCRESCENCE
ACCRESCENCES
ACCRESCENT
ACCRETIONARY
ACCRETIONS
ACCRUEMENT
ACCRUEMENTS
ACCUBATION
ACCUBATIONS
ACCULTURAL
ACCULTURATE
ACCULTURATED
ACCULTURATES
ACCULTURATING
ACCULTURATION
ACCULTURATIONAL
ACCULTURATIONS
ACCULTURATIVE
ACCUMBENCIES
ACCUMBENCY
ACCUMULABLE
ACCUMULATE
ACCUMULATED
ACCUMULATES
ACCUMULATING
ACCUMULATION
ACCUMULATIONS
ACCUMULATIVE
ACCUMULATIVELY
ACCUMULATOR
ACCUMULATORS
ACCURACIES
ACCURATELY
ACCURATENESS
ACCURATENESSES
ACCURSEDLY
ACCURSEDNESS
ACCURSEDNESSES
ACCUSATION
ACCUSATIONS
ACCUSATIVAL
ACCUSATIVE
ACCUSATIVELY
ACCUSATIVES
ACCUSATORIAL
ACCUSATORY
ACCUSEMENT
ACCUSEMENTS
ACCUSINGLY
ACCUSTOMARY
ACCUSTOMATION
ACCUSTOMATIONS
ACCUSTOMED
ACCUSTOMEDNESS
ACCUSTOMING
ACCUSTREMENT
ACCUSTREMENTS
ACEPHALOUS
ACERACEOUS
ACERBATING
ACERBICALLY
ACERBITIES
ACERVATELY
ACERVATION
ACERVATIONS
ACESCENCES
ACESCENCIES
ACETABULAR
ACETABULUM
ACETABULUMS
ACETALDEHYDE
ACETALDEHYDES
ACETAMIDES
ACETAMINOPHEN

ACETAMINOPHENS
ACETANILID
ACETANILIDE
ACETANILIDES
ACETANILIDS
ACETAZOLAMIDE
ACETAZOLAMIDES
ACETIFICATION
ACETIFICATIONS
ACETIFIERS
ACETIFYING
ACETOMETER
ACETOMETERS
ACETONAEMIA
ACETONAEMIAS
ACETONEMIA
ACETONEMIAS
ACETONITRILE
ACETONITRILES
ACETONURIA
ACETONURIAS
ACETOPHENETIDIN
ACETYLATED
ACETYLATES
ACETYLATING
ACETYLATION
ACETYLATIONS
ACETYLATIVE
ACETYLCHOLINE
ACETYLCHOLINES
ACETYLENES
ACETYLENIC
ACETYLIDES
ACETYLSALICYLIC
ACHAENIUMS
ACHAENOCARP
ACHAENOCARPS
ACHALASIAS
ACHIEVABLE
ACHIEVEMENT
ACHIEVEMENTS
ACHINESSES
ACHLAMYDEOUS
ACHLORHYDRIA
ACHLORHYDRIAS
ACHLORHYDRIC
ACHONDRITE
ACHONDRITES
ACHONDRITIC
ACHONDROPLASIA
ACHONDROPLASIAS
ACHONDROPLASTIC
ACHROMATIC
ACHROMATICALLY
ACHROMATICITIES
ACHROMATICITY
ACHROMATIN
ACHROMATINS
ACHROMATISATION
ACHROMATISE
ACHROMATISED
ACHROMATISES
ACHROMATISING
ACHROMATISM
ACHROMATISMS
ACHROMATIZATION
ACHROMATIZE
ACHROMATIZED
ACHROMATIZES
ACHROMATIZING
ACHROMATOPSIA
ACHROMATOPSIAS
ACHROMATOUS
ACICULATED
ACIDANTHERA
ACIDANTHERAS
ACIDFREAKS
ACIDIFIABLE
ACIDIFICATION
ACIDIFICATIONS
ACIDIFIERS
ACIDIFYING
ACIDIMETER

ACIDIMETERS
ACIDIMETRIC
ACIDIMETRICAL
ACIDIMETRICALLY
ACIDIMETRIES
ACIDIMETRY
ACIDNESSES
ACIDOMETER
ACIDOMETERS
ACIDOPHILE
ACIDOPHILES
ACIDOPHILIC
ACIDOPHILOUS
ACIDOPHILS
ACIDOPHILUS
ACIDOPHILUSES
ACIDULATED
ACIDULATES
ACIDULATING
ACIDULATION
ACIDULATIONS
ACIERATING
ACIERATION
ACIERATIONS
ACINACEOUS
ACINACIFORM
ACKNOWLEDGE
ACKNOWLEDGEABLE
ACKNOWLEDGEABLY
ACKNOWLEDGED
ACKNOWLEDGEDLY
ACKNOWLEDGEMENT
ACKNOWLEDGER
ACKNOWLEDGERS
ACKNOWLEDGES
ACKNOWLEDGING
ACKNOWLEDGMENT
ACKNOWLEDGMENTS
ACOELOMATE
ACOELOMATES
ACOLOUTHIC
ACOLOUTHITE
ACOLOUTHITES
ACOLOUTHOS
ACOLOUTHOSES
ACONITINES
ACOTYLEDON
ACOTYLEDONOUS
ACOTYLEDONS
ACOUSTICAL
ACOUSTICALLY
ACOUSTICIAN
ACOUSTICIANS
ACQUAINTANCE
ACQUAINTANCES
ACQUAINTED
ACQUAINTING
ACQUIESCED
ACQUIESCENCE
ACQUIESCENCES
ACQUIESCENT
ACQUIESCENTLY
ACQUIESCENTS
ACQUIESCES
ACQUIESCING
ACQUIESCINGLY
ACQUIGHTING
ACQUIRABILITIES
ACQUIRABILITY
ACQUIRABLE
ACQUIREMENT
ACQUIREMENTS
ACQUISITION
ACQUISITIONAL
ACQUISITIONS
ACQUISITIVE
ACQUISITIVELY
ACQUISITIVENESS
ACQUISITOR
ACQUISITORS
ACQUITMENT
ACQUITMENTS
ACQUITTALS

ACQUITTANCE
ACQUITTANCED
ACQUITTANCES
ACQUITTANCING
ACQUITTERS
ACQUITTING
ACRIDITIES
ACRIDNESSES
ACRIFLAVIN
ACRIFLAVINE
ACRIFLAVINES
ACRIFLAVINS
ACRIMONIES
ACRIMONIOUS
ACRIMONIOUSLY
ACRIMONIOUSNESS
ACRITARCHS
ACROAMATIC
ACROAMATICAL
ACROBATICALLY
ACROBATICS
ACROBATISM
ACROBATISMS
ACROCARPOUS
ACROCENTRIC
ACROCENTRICS
ACROCYANOSES
ACROCYANOSIS
ACRODROMOUS
ACROGENOUS
ACROGENOUSLY
ACROLITHIC
ACROMEGALIC
ACROMEGALICS
ACROMEGALIES
ACROMEGALY
ACRONICALLY
ACRONYCALLY
ACRONYCHAL
ACRONYCHALLY
ACRONYMANIA
ACRONYMANIAS
ACRONYMICALLY
ACRONYMOUS
ACROPARESTHESIA
ACROPETALLY
ACROPHOBES
ACROPHOBIA
ACROPHOBIAS
ACROPHOBIC
ACROPHONETIC
ACROPHONIC
ACROPHONIES
ACROPOLISES
ACROSPIRES
ACROSTICAL
ACROSTICALLY
ACROTERIAL
ACROTERION
ACROTERIUM
ACROTERIUMS
ACRYLAMIDE
ACRYLAMIDES
ACRYLONITRILE
ACRYLONITRILES
ACTABILITIES
ACTABILITY
ACTINICALLY
ACTINIFORM
ACTINOBACILLI
ACTINOBACILLUS
ACTINOBIOLOGIES
ACTINOBIOLOGY
ACTINOCHEMISTRY
ACTINOLITE
ACTINOLITES
ACTINOMERE
ACTINOMERES
ACTINOMETER
ACTINOMETERS
ACTINOMETRIC
ACTINOMETRICAL
ACTINOMETRIES

ACTINOMETRY	ADAPTIVENESSES	ADIPOSITIES	ADMISSIBILITIES	ADULTERATED	ADVERSARINESSES
ACTINOMORPHIC	ADAPTIVITIES	ADJACENCES	ADMISSIBILITY	ADULTERATES	ADVERSATIVE
ACTINOMORPHIES	ADAPTIVITY	ADJACENCIES	ADMISSIBLE	ADULTERATING	ADVERSATIVELY
ACTINOMORPHOUS	ADAPTOGENIC	ADJACENTLY	ADMISSIBLENESS	ADULTERATION	ADVERSATIVES
ACTINOMORPHY	ADAPTOGENS	ADJECTIVAL	ADMISSIONS	ADULTERATIONS	ADVERSENESS
ACTINOMYCES	ADDERSTONE	ADJECTIVALLY	ADMITTABLE	ADULTERATOR	ADVERSENESSES
ACTINOMYCETE	ADDERSTONES	ADJECTIVELY	ADMITTANCE	ADULTERATORS	ADVERSITIES
ACTINOMYCETES	ADDERWORTS	ADJECTIVES	ADMITTANCES	ADULTERERS	ADVERTENCE
ACTINOMYCETOUS	ADDICTEDNESS	ADJOURNING	ADMITTEDLY	ADULTERESS	ADVERTENCES
ACTINOMYCIN	ADDICTEDNESSES	ADJOURNMENT	ADMIXTURES	ADULTERESSES	ADVERTENCIES
ACTINOMYCINS	ADDICTIONS	ADJOURNMENTS	ADMONISHED	ADULTERIES	ADVERTENCY
ACTINOMYCOSES	ADDITAMENT	ADJUDGEMENT	ADMONISHER	ADULTERINE	ADVERTENTLY
ACTINOMYCOSIS	ADDITAMENTS	ADJUDGEMENTS	ADMONISHERS	ADULTERINES	ADVERTISED
ACTINOMYCOTIC	ADDITIONAL	ADJUDGMENT	ADMONISHES	ADULTERISE	ADVERTISEMENT
ACTINOPODS	ADDITIONALITIES	ADJUDGMENTS	ADMONISHING	ADULTERISED	ADVERTISEMENTS
ACTINOTHERAPIES	ADDITIONALITY	ADJUDICATE	ADMONISHINGLY	ADULTERISES	ADVERTISER
ACTINOTHERAPY	ADDITIONALLY	ADJUDICATED	ADMONISHMENT	ADULTERISING	ADVERTISERS
ACTINOURANIUM	ADDITITIOUS	ADJUDICATES	ADMONISHMENTS	ADULTERIZE	ADVERTISES
ACTINOURANIUMS	ADDITIVELY	ADJUDICATING	ADMONITION	ADULTERIZED	ADVERTISING
ACTINOZOAN	ADDITIVITIES	ADJUDICATION	ADMONITIONS	ADULTERIZES	ADVERTISINGS
ACTIONABLE	ADDITIVITY	ADJUDICATIONS	ADMONITIVE	ADULTERIZING	ADVERTIZED
ACTIONABLY	ADDLEMENTS	ADJUDICATIVE	ADMONITORILY	ADULTEROUS	ADVERTIZEMENT
ACTIONISTS	ADDLEPATED	ADJUDICATOR	ADMONITORS	ADULTEROUSLY	ADVERTIZEMENTS
ACTIONLESS	ADDRESSABILITY	ADJUDICATORS	ADMONITORY	ADULTESCENT	ADVERTIZER
ACTIVATING	ADDRESSABLE	ADJUDICATORY	ADNOMINALS	ADULTESCENTS	ADVERTIZERS
ACTIVATION	ADDRESSEES	ADJUNCTION	ADOLESCENCE	ADULTHOODS	ADVERTIZES
ACTIVATIONS	ADDRESSERS	ADJUNCTIONS	ADOLESCENCES	ADULTNESSES	ADVERTIZING
ACTIVATORS	ADDRESSING	ADJUNCTIVE	ADOLESCENT	ADULTRESSES	ADVERTORIAL
ACTIVENESS	ADDRESSORS	ADJUNCTIVELY	ADOLESCENTLY	ADUMBRATED	ADVERTORIALS
ACTIVENESSES	ADDUCEABLE	ADJURATION	ADOLESCENTS	ADUMBRATES	ADVISABILITIES
ACTIVISING	ADDUCTIONS	ADJURATIONS	ADOPTABILITIES	ADUMBRATING	ADVISABILITY
ACTIVISTIC	ADELANTADO	ADJURATORY	ADOPTABILITY	ADUMBRATION	ADVISABLENESS
ACTIVITIES	ADELANTADOS	ADJUSTABILITIES	ADOPTIANISM	ADUMBRATIONS	ADVISABLENESSES
ACTIVIZING	ADEMPTIONS	ADJUSTABILITY	ADOPTIANISMS	ADUMBRATIVE	ADVISATORY
ACTOMYOSIN	ADENECTOMIES	ADJUSTABLE	ADOPTIANIST	ADUMBRATIVELY	ADVISEDNESS
ACTOMYOSINS	ADENECTOMY	ADJUSTABLY	ADOPTIANISTS	ADUNCITIES	ADVISEDNESSES
ACTUALISATION	ADENITISES	ADJUSTMENT	ADOPTIONISM	ADVANCEMENT	ADVISEMENT
ACTUALISATIONS	ADENOCARCINOMA	ADJUSTMENTAL	ADOPTIONISMS	ADVANCEMENTS	ADVISEMENTS
ACTUALISED	ADENOCARCINOMAS	ADJUSTMENTS	ADOPTIONIST	ADVANCINGLY	ADVISERSHIP
ACTUALISES	ADENOHYPOPHYSES	ADJUTANCIES	ADOPTIONISTS	ADVANTAGEABLE	ADVISERSHIPS
ACTUALISING	ADENOHYPOPHYSIS	ADJUVANCIES	ADOPTIVELY	ADVANTAGED	ADVISORATE
ACTUALISTS	ADENOIDECTOMIES	ADMEASURED	ADORABILITIES	ADVANTAGEOUS	ADVISORATES
ACTUALITES	ADENOIDECTOMY	ADMEASUREMENT	ADORABILITY	ADVANTAGEOUSLY	ADVISORIES
ACTUALITIES	ADENOMATOUS	ADMEASUREMENTS	ADORABLENESS	ADVANTAGES	ADVOCACIES
ACTUALIZATION	ADENOPATHIES	ADMEASURES	ADORABLENESSES	ADVANTAGING	ADVOCATING
ACTUALIZATIONS	ADENOPATHY	ADMEASURING	ADORATIONS	ADVECTIONS	ADVOCATION
ACTUALIZED	ADENOSINES	ADMINICLES	ADORNMENTS	ADVENTITIA	ADVOCATIONS
ACTUALIZES	ADENOVIRAL	ADMINICULAR	ADPRESSING	ADVENTITIAL	ADVOCATIVE
ACTUALIZING	ADENOVIRUS	ADMINICULATE	ADRENALECTOMIES	ADVENTITIAS	ADVOCATORS
ACTUARIALLY	ADENOVIRUSES	ADMINICULATED	ADRENALECTOMY	ADVENTITIOUS	ADVOCATORY
ACTUATIONS	ADEPTNESSES	ADMINICULATES	ADRENALINE	ADVENTITIOUSLY	ADVOUTRERS
ACUMINATED	ADEQUACIES	ADMINICULATING	ADRENALINES	ADVENTIVES	ADVOUTRIES
ACUMINATES	ADEQUATELY	ADMINISTER	ADRENALINS	ADVENTURED	AECIDIOSPORE
ACUMINATING	ADEQUATENESS	ADMINISTERED	ADRENALISED	ADVENTUREFUL	AECIDIOSPORES
ACUMINATION	ADEQUATENESSES	ADMINISTERING	ADRENALIZED	ADVENTURER	AECIDOSPORE
ACUMINATIONS	ADEQUATIVE	ADMINISTERS	ADRENERGIC	ADVENTURERS	AECIDOSPORES
ACUPRESSURE	ADHERENCES	ADMINISTRABLE	ADRENERGICALLY	ADVENTURES	AECIOSPORE
ACUPRESSURES	ADHERENTLY	ADMINISTRANT	ADRENOCHROME	ADVENTURESOME	AECIOSPORES
ACUPUNCTURAL	ADHESIONAL	ADMINISTRANTS	ADRENOCHROMES	ADVENTURESS	AEDILESHIP
ACUPUNCTURE	ADHESIVELY	ADMINISTRATE	ADRENOCORTICAL	ADVENTURESSES	AEDILESHIPS
ACUPUNCTURES	ADHESIVENESS	ADMINISTRATED	ADRIAMYCIN	ADVENTURING	AEOLIPILES
ACUPUNCTURIST	ADHESIVENESSES	ADMINISTRATES	ADRIAMYCINS	ADVENTURISM	AEOLIPYLES
ACUPUNCTURISTS	ADHIBITING	ADMINISTRATING	ADROITNESS	ADVENTURISMS	AEOLOTROPIC
ACUTENESSES	ADHIBITION	ADMINISTRATION	ADROITNESSES	ADVENTURIST	AEOLOTROPIES
ACYCLOVIRS	ADHIBITIONS	ADMINISTRATIONS	ADSCITITIOUS	ADVENTURISTIC	AEOLOTROPY
ACYLATIONS	ADHOCRACIES	ADMINISTRATIVE	ADSCITITIOUSLY	ADVENTURISTS	AEPYORNISES
ADACTYLOUS	ADIABATICALLY	ADMINISTRATOR	ADSCRIPTION	ADVENTUROUS	AERENCHYMA
ADAMANCIES	ADIABATICS	ADMINISTRATORS	ADSCRIPTIONS	ADVENTUROUSLY	AERENCHYMAS
ADAMANTEAN	ADIACTINIC	ADMINISTRATRIX	ADSORBABILITIES	ADVENTUROUSNESS	AERENCHYMATOUS
ADAMANTINE	ADIAPHORISM	ADMIRABILITIES	ADSORBABILITY	ADVERBIALISE	AERIALISTS
ADAPTABILITIES	ADIAPHORISMS	ADMIRABILITY	ADSORBABLE	ADVERBIALISED	AERIALITIES
ADAPTABILITY	ADIAPHORIST	ADMIRABLENESS	ADSORBATES	ADVERBIALISES	AERIFICATION
ADAPTABLENESS	ADIAPHORISTIC	ADMIRABLENESSES	ADSORBENTS	ADVERBIALISING	AERIFICATIONS
ADAPTABLENESSES	ADIAPHORISTS	ADMIRALSHIP	ADSORPTION	ADVERBIALIZE	AEROACOUSTICS
ADAPTATION	ADIAPHORON	ADMIRALSHIPS	ADSORPTIONS	ADVERBIALIZED	AEROBALLISTICS
ADAPTATIONAL	ADIAPHOROUS	ADMIRALTIES	ADSORPTIVE	ADVERBIALIZES	AEROBATICS
ADAPTATIONALLY	ADIATHERMANCIES	ADMIRANCES	ADULARESCENCE	ADVERBIALIZING	AEROBICALLY
ADAPTATIONS	ADIATHERMANCY	ADMIRATION	ADULARESCENCES	ADVERBIALLY	AEROBICISE
ADAPTATIVE	ADIATHERMANOUS	ADMIRATIONS	ADULARESCENT	ADVERBIALS	AEROBICISED
ADAPTEDNESS	ADIATHERMIC	ADMIRATIVE	ADULATIONS	ADVERSARIA	AEROBICISES
ADAPTEDNESSES	ADIPOCERES	ADMIRAUNCE	ADULTERANT	ADVERSARIAL	AEROBICISING
ADAPTIVELY	ADIPOCEROUS	ADMIRAUNCES	ADULTERANTS	ADVERSARIES	AEROBICIST
ADAPTIVENESS	ADIPOCYTES	ADMIRINGLY	ADULTERATE	ADVERSARINESS	AEROBICISTS

AEROBICIZE
AEROBICIZED
AEROBICIZES
AEROBICIZING
AEROBIOLOGICAL
AEROBIOLOGIES
AEROBIOLOGIST
AEROBIOLOGISTS
AEROBIOLOGY
AEROBIONTS
AEROBIOSES
AEROBIOSIS
AEROBIOTIC
AEROBIOTICALLY
AEROBRAKED
AEROBRAKES
AEROBRAKING
AEROBRAKINGS
AEROBUSSES
AERODONETICS
AERODROMES
AERODYNAMIC
AERODYNAMICAL
AERODYNAMICALLY
AERODYNAMICIST
AERODYNAMICISTS
AERODYNAMICS
AEROELASTIC
AEROELASTICIAN
AEROELASTICIANS
AEROELASTICITY
AEROEMBOLISM
AEROEMBOLISMS
AEROGENERATOR
AEROGENERATORS
AEROGRAMME
AEROGRAMMES
AEROGRAPHIES
AEROGRAPHS
AEROGRAPHY
AEROHYDROPLANE
AEROHYDROPLANES
AEROLITHOLOGIES
AEROLITHOLOGY
AEROLOGICAL
AEROLOGIES
AEROLOGIST
AEROLOGISTS
AEROMAGNETIC
AEROMANCIES
AEROMECHANIC
AEROMECHANICAL
AEROMECHANICS
AEROMEDICAL
AEROMEDICINE
AEROMEDICINES
AEROMETERS
AEROMETRIC
AEROMETRIES
AEROMOTORS
AERONAUTIC
AERONAUTICAL
AERONAUTICALLY
AERONAUTICS
AERONEUROSES
AERONEUROSIS
AERONOMERS
AERONOMICAL
AERONOMIES
AERONOMIST
AERONOMISTS
AEROPAUSES
AEROPHAGIA
AEROPHAGIAS
AEROPHAGIES
AEROPHOBES
AEROPHOBIA
AEROPHOBIAS
AEROPHOBIC
AEROPHONES
AEROPHORES
AEROPHYTES
AEROPLANES

AEROPLANKTON
AEROPLANKTONS
AEROPULSES
AEROSCOPES
AEROSHELLS
AEROSIDERITE
AEROSIDERITES
AEROSOLISATION
AEROSOLISATIONS
AEROSOLISE
AEROSOLISED
AEROSOLISES
AEROSOLISING
AEROSOLIZATION
AEROSOLIZATIONS
AEROSOLIZE
AEROSOLIZED
AEROSOLIZES
AEROSOLIZING
AEROSPACES
AEROSPHERE
AEROSPHERES
AEROSTATIC
AEROSTATICAL
AEROSTATICS
AEROSTATION
AEROSTATIONS
AEROSTRUCTURE
AEROSTRUCTURES
AEROTACTIC
AEROTRAINS
AEROTROPIC
AEROTROPISM
AEROTROPISMS
AERUGINOUS
AESTHESIAS
AESTHESIOGEN
AESTHESIOGENIC
AESTHESIOGENS
AESTHETICAL
AESTHETICALLY
AESTHETICIAN
AESTHETICIANS
AESTHETICISE
AESTHETICISED
AESTHETICISES
AESTHETICISING
AESTHETICISM
AESTHETICISMS
AESTHETICIST
AESTHETICISTS
AESTHETICIZE
AESTHETICIZED
AESTHETICIZES
AESTHETICIZING
AESTHETICS
AESTIVATED
AESTIVATES
AESTIVATING
AESTIVATION
AESTIVATIONS
AESTIVATOR
AESTIVATORS
AETHEREALITIES
AETHEREALITY
AETHEREALLY
AETHRIOSCOPE
AETHRIOSCOPES
AETIOLOGICAL
AETIOLOGICALLY
AETIOLOGIES
AETIOLOGIST
AETIOLOGISTS
AFFABILITIES
AFFABILITY
AFFECTABILITIES
AFFECTABILITY
AFFECTABLE
AFFECTATION
AFFECTATIONS
AFFECTEDLY
AFFECTEDNESS
AFFECTEDNESSES

AFFECTINGLY
AFFECTIONAL
AFFECTIONALLY
AFFECTIONATE
AFFECTIONATELY
AFFECTIONED
AFFECTIONING
AFFECTIONLESS
AFFECTIONS
AFFECTIVELY
AFFECTIVENESS
AFFECTIVENESSES
AFFECTIVITIES
AFFECTIVITY
AFFECTLESS
AFFECTLESSNESS
AFFEERMENT
AFFEERMENTS
AFFENPINSCHER
AFFENPINSCHERS
AFFERENTLY
AFFETTUOSO
AFFETTUOSOS
AFFIANCING
AFFICIONADO
AFFICIONADOS
AFFIDAVITS
AFFILIABLE
AFFILIATED
AFFILIATES
AFFILIATING
AFFILIATION
AFFILIATIONS
AFFINITIES
AFFINITIVE
AFFIRMABLE
AFFIRMANCE
AFFIRMANCES
AFFIRMANTS
AFFIRMATION
AFFIRMATIONS
AFFIRMATIVE
AFFIRMATIVELY
AFFIRMATIVES
AFFIRMATORY
AFFIRMINGLY
AFFIXATION
AFFIXATIONS
AFFIXMENTS
AFFIXTURES
AFFLATIONS
AFFLATUSES
AFFLICTERS
AFFLICTING
AFFLICTINGS
AFFLICTION
AFFLICTIONS
AFFLICTIVE
AFFLICTIVELY
AFFLUENCES
AFFLUENCIES
AFFLUENTIAL
AFFLUENTIALS
AFFLUENTLY
AFFLUENTNESS
AFFLUENTNESSES
AFFLUENZAS
AFFLUXIONS
AFFOORDING
AFFORCEMENT
AFFORCEMENTS
AFFORDABILITIES
AFFORDABILITY
AFFORDABLE
AFFORDABLY
AFFORESTABLE
AFFORESTATION
AFFORESTATIONS
AFFORESTED
AFFORESTING
AFFRANCHISE
AFFRANCHISED
AFFRANCHISEMENT

AFFRANCHISES
AFFRANCHISING
AFFRAPPING
AFFREIGHTMENT
AFFREIGHTMENTS
AFFRICATED
AFFRICATES
AFFRICATING
AFFRICATION
AFFRICATIONS
AFFRICATIVE
AFFRICATIVES
AFFRIGHTED
AFFRIGHTEDLY
AFFRIGHTEN
AFFRIGHTENED
AFFRIGHTENING
AFFRIGHTENS
AFFRIGHTFUL
AFFRIGHTING
AFFRIGHTMENT
AFFRIGHTMENTS
AFFRONTING
AFFRONTINGLY
AFFRONTINGS
AFFRONTIVE
AFICIONADA
AFICIONADAS
AFICIONADO
AFICIONADOS
AFLATOXINS
AFOREMENTIONED
AFORETHOUGHT
AFORETHOUGHTS
AFRORMOSIA
AFRORMOSIAS
AFTERBIRTH
AFTERBIRTHS
AFTERBODIES
AFTERBRAIN
AFTERBRAINS
AFTERBURNER
AFTERBURNERS
AFTERBURNING
AFTERBURNINGS
AFTERCARES
AFTERCLAPS
AFTERDAMPS
AFTERDECKS
AFTEREFFECT
AFTEREFFECTS
AFTEREYEING
AFTEREYING
AFTERGAMES
AFTERGLOWS
AFTERGRASS
AFTERGRASSES
AFTERGROWTH
AFTERGROWTHS
AFTERHEATS
AFTERIMAGE
AFTERIMAGES
AFTERLIFES
AFTERLIVES
AFTERMARKET
AFTERMARKETS
AFTERMATHS
AFTERNOONS
AFTERPAINS
AFTERPEAKS
AFTERPIECE
AFTERPIECES
AFTERSALES
AFTERSENSATION
AFTERSENSATIONS
AFTERSHAFT
AFTERSHAFTS
AFTERSHAVE
AFTERSHAVES
AFTERSHOCK
AFTERSHOCKS
AFTERSHOWS
AFTERSUPPER

AFTERSUPPERS
AFTERSWARM
AFTERSWARMS
AFTERTASTE
AFTERTASTES
AFTERTHOUGHT
AFTERTHOUGHTS
AFTERTIMES
AFTERWARDS
AFTERWORDS
AFTERWORLD
AFTERWORLDS
AGALACTIAS
AGALMATOLITE
AGALMATOLITES
AGAMICALLY
AGAMOGENESES
AGAMOGENESIS
AGAMOGENETIC
AGAMOGONIES
AGAMOSPERMIES
AGAMOSPERMY
AGAPANTHUS
AGAPANTHUSES
AGARICACEOUS
AGATEWARES
AGATHODAIMON
AGATHODAIMONS
AGEDNESSES
AGELESSNESS
AGELESSNESSES
AGENDALESS
AGENTIVITIES
AGENTIVITY
AGGIORNAMENTI
AGGIORNAMENTO
AGGIORNAMENTOS
AGGLOMERATE
AGGLOMERATED
AGGLOMERATES
AGGLOMERATING
AGGLOMERATION
AGGLOMERATIONS
AGGLOMERATIVE
AGGLUTINABILITY
AGGLUTINABLE
AGGLUTINANT
AGGLUTINANTS
AGGLUTINATE
AGGLUTINATED
AGGLUTINATES
AGGLUTINATING
AGGLUTINATION
AGGLUTINATIONS
AGGLUTINATIVE
AGGLUTININ
AGGLUTININS
AGGLUTINOGEN
AGGLUTINOGENIC
AGGLUTINOGENS
AGGRADATION
AGGRADATIONS
AGGRANDISE
AGGRANDISED
AGGRANDISEMENT
AGGRANDISEMENTS
AGGRANDISER
AGGRANDISERS
AGGRANDISES
AGGRANDISING
AGGRANDIZE
AGGRANDIZED
AGGRANDIZEMENT
AGGRANDIZEMENTS
AGGRANDIZER
AGGRANDIZERS
AGGRANDIZES
AGGRANDIZING
AGGRAVATED
AGGRAVATES
AGGRAVATING
AGGRAVATINGLY
AGGRAVATION

AGGRAVATIONS
AGGREGATED
AGGREGATELY
AGGREGATENESS
AGGREGATENESSES
AGGREGATES
AGGREGATING
AGGREGATION
AGGREGATIONAL
AGGREGATIONS
AGGREGATIVE
AGGREGATIVELY
AGGREGATOR
AGGREGATORS
AGGRESSING
AGGRESSION
AGGRESSIONS
AGGRESSIVE
AGGRESSIVELY
AGGRESSIVENESS
AGGRESSIVITIES
AGGRESSIVITY
AGGRESSORS
AGGRIEVEDLY
AGGRIEVEMENT
AGGRIEVEMENTS
AGGRIEVING
AGILENESSES
AGISTMENTS
AGITATEDLY
AGITATIONAL
AGITATIONS
AGNATICALLY
AGNOIOLOGIES
AGNOIOLOGY
AGNOSTICISM
AGNOSTICISMS
AGONISEDLY
AGONISINGLY
AGONISTICAL
AGONISTICALLY
AGONISTICS
AGONIZEDLY
AGONIZINGLY
AGONOTHETES
AGORAPHOBE
AGORAPHOBES
AGORAPHOBIA
AGORAPHOBIAS
AGORAPHOBIC
AGORAPHOBICS
AGRANULOCYTE
AGRANULOCYTES
AGRANULOCYTOSES
AGRANULOCYTOSIS
AGRANULOSES
AGRANULOSIS
AGRARIANISM
AGRARIANISMS
AGREEABILITIES
AGREEABILITY
AGREEABLENESS
AGREEABLENESSES
AGREEMENTS
AGREGATION
AGREGATIONS
AGRIBUSINESS
AGRIBUSINESSES
AGRIBUSINESSMAN
AGRIBUSINESSMEN
AGRICHEMICAL
AGRICHEMICALS
AGRICULTURAL
AGRICULTURALIST
AGRICULTURALLY
AGRICULTURE
AGRICULTURES
AGRICULTURIST
AGRICULTURISTS
AGRIMONIES
AGRIOLOGIES
AGRIPRODUCT
AGRIPRODUCTS

AGRITOURISM	AIRCOACHES	ALBUMINIZES	ALERTNESSES	ALKALINISE	ALLEVIATORS
AGRITOURISMS	AIRCRAFTMAN	ALBUMINIZING	ALEXANDERS	ALKALINISED	ALLEVIATORY
AGRITOURIST	AIRCRAFTMEN	ALBUMINOID	ALEXANDERSES	ALKALINISES	ALLHALLOND
AGRITOURISTS	AIRCRAFTSMAN	ALBUMINOIDS	ALEXANDRINE	ALKALINISING	ALLHALLOWEN
AGROBIOLOGICAL	AIRCRAFTSMEN	ALBUMINOUS	ALEXANDRINES	ALKALINITIES	ALLHALLOWN
AGROBIOLOGIES	AIRCRAFTSWOMAN	ALBUMINURIA	ALEXANDRITE	ALKALINITY	ALLHOLLOWN
AGROBIOLOGIST	AIRCRAFTSWOMEN	ALBUMINURIAS	ALEXANDRITES	ALKALINIZATION	ALLIACEOUS
AGROBIOLOGISTS	AIRCRAFTWOMAN	ALBUMINURIC	ALEXIPHARMAKON	ALKALINIZATIONS	ALLICHOLIES
AGROBIOLOGY	AIRCRAFTWOMEN	ALBUTEROLS	ALEXIPHARMAKONS	ALKALINIZE	ALLIGARTAS
AGROBUSINESS	AIRDROPPED	ALCAICERIA	ALEXIPHARMIC	ALKALINIZED	ALLIGATING
AGROBUSINESSES	AIRDROPPING	ALCAICERIAS	ALEXIPHARMICS	ALKALINIZES	ALLIGATION
AGROCHEMICAL	AIRFREIGHT	ALCARRAZAS	ALFILARIAS	ALKALINIZING	ALLIGATIONS
AGROCHEMICALS	AIRFREIGHTED	ALCATRASES	ALFILERIAS	ALKALISABLE	ALLIGATORS
AGRODOLCES	AIRFREIGHTING	ALCHEMICAL	ALGAECIDES	ALKALISERS	ALLINEATION
AGROFORESTER	AIRFREIGHTS	ALCHEMICALLY	ALGARROBAS	ALKALISING	ALLINEATIONS
AGROFORESTERS	AIRINESSES	ALCHEMISED	ALGARROBOS	ALKALIZABLE	ALLITERATE
AGROFORESTRIES	AIRLESSNESS	ALCHEMISES	ALGEBRAICAL	ALKALIZERS	ALLITERATED
AGROFORESTRY	AIRLESSNESSES	ALCHEMISING	ALGEBRAICALLY	ALKALIZING	ALLITERATES
AGROINDUSTRIAL	AIRLIFTING	ALCHEMISTIC	ALGEBRAIST	ALKALOIDAL	ALLITERATING
AGROINDUSTRIES	AIRMAILING	ALCHEMISTICAL	ALGEBRAISTS	ALKYLATING	ALLITERATION
AGROINDUSTRY	AIRMANSHIP	ALCHEMISTS	ALGIDITIES	ALKYLATION	ALLITERATIONS
AGROLOGICAL	AIRMANSHIPS	ALCHEMIZED	ALGIDNESSES	ALKYLATIONS	ALLITERATIVE
AGROLOGIES	AIRPROOFED	ALCHEMIZES	ALGOLAGNIA	ALLANTOIDAL	ALLITERATIVELY
AGROLOGIST	AIRPROOFING	ALCHEMIZING	ALGOLAGNIAC	ALLANTOIDES	ALLNIGHTER
AGROLOGISTS	AIRSICKNESS	ALCHERINGA	ALGOLAGNIACS	ALLANTOIDS	ALLNIGHTERS
AGRONOMIAL	AIRSICKNESSES	ALCHERINGAS	ALGOLAGNIAS	ALLANTOINS	ALLOANTIBODIES
AGRONOMICAL	AIRSTREAMS	ALCOHOLICALLY	ALGOLAGNIC	ALLANTOISES	ALLOANTIBODY
AGRONOMICALLY	AIRSTRIKES	ALCOHOLICITIES	ALGOLAGNIST	ALLARGANDO	ALLOANTIGEN
AGRONOMICS	AIRTIGHTNESS	ALCOHOLICITY	ALGOLAGNISTS	ALLAYMENTS	ALLOANTIGENS
AGRONOMIES	AIRTIGHTNESSES	ALCOHOLICS	ALGOLOGICAL	ALLEGATION	ALLOCARPIES
AGRONOMIST	AIRWORTHIER	ALCOHOLISATION	ALGOLOGICALLY	ALLEGATIONS	ALLOCATABLE
AGRONOMISTS	AIRWORTHIEST	ALCOHOLISATIONS	ALGOLOGIES	ALLEGEANCE	ALLOCATING
AGROSTEMMA	AIRWORTHINESS	ALCOHOLISE	ALGOLOGIST	ALLEGEANCES	ALLOCATION
AGROSTEMMAS	AIRWORTHINESSES	ALCOHOLISED	ALGOLOGISTS	ALLEGIANCE	ALLOCATIONS
AGROSTEMMATA	AITCHBONES	ALCOHOLISES	ALGOMETERS	ALLEGIANCES	ALLOCATORS
AGROSTOLOGICAL	AKATHISIAS	ALCOHOLISING	ALGOMETRIES	ALLEGIANTS	ALLOCHEIRIA
AGROSTOLOGIES	AKOLOUTHOS	ALCOHOLISM	ALGOPHOBIA	ALLEGORICAL	ALLOCHEIRIAS
AGROSTOLOGIST	AKOLOUTHOSES	ALCOHOLISMS	ALGOPHOBIAS	ALLEGORICALLY	ALLOCHIRIA
AGROSTOLOGISTS	AKOLUTHOSES	ALCOHOLIZATION	ALGORISMIC	ALLEGORICALNESS	ALLOCHIRIAS
AGROSTOLOGY	ALABAMINES	ALCOHOLIZATIONS	ALGORITHMIC	ALLEGORIES	ALLOCHTHONOUS
AGROTERRORISM	ALABANDINE	ALCOHOLIZE	ALGORITHMICALLY	ALLEGORISATION	ALLOCUTION
AGROTERRORISMS	ALABANDINES	ALCOHOLIZED	ALGORITHMS	ALLEGORISATIONS	ALLOCUTIONS
AGROTOURISM	ALABANDITE	ALCOHOLIZES	ALIENABILITIES	ALLEGORISE	ALLOGAMIES
AGROTOURISMS	ALABANDITES	ALCOHOLIZING	ALIENABILITY	ALLEGORISED	ALLOGAMOUS
AGROTOURIST	ALABASTERS	ALCOHOLOMETER	ALIENATING	ALLEGORISER	ALLOGENEIC
AGROTOURISTS	ALABASTRINE	ALCOHOLOMETERS	ALIENATION	ALLEGORISERS	ALLOGRAFTED
AGRYPNOTIC	ALABLASTER	ALCOHOLOMETRIES	ALIENATIONS	ALLEGORISES	ALLOGRAFTING
AGRYPNOTICS	ALABLASTERS	ALCOHOLOMETRY	ALIENATORS	ALLEGORISING	ALLOGRAFTS
AGTERSKOTS	ALACRITIES	ALCYONARIAN	ALIENNESSES	ALLEGORIST	ALLOGRAPHIC
AGUARDIENTE	ALACRITOUS	ALCYONARIANS	ALIGHTMENT	ALLEGORISTS	ALLOGRAPHS
AGUARDIENTES	ALARMINGLY	ALDERFLIES	ALIGHTMENTS	ALLEGORIZATION	ALLOIOSTROPHOS
AHISTORICAL	ALBARELLOS	ALDERMANIC	ALIGNMENTS	ALLEGORIZATIONS	ALLOMERISM
AHORSEBACK	ALBATROSSES	ALDERMANITIES	ALIKENESSES	ALLEGORIZE	ALLOMERISMS
AICHMOPHOBIA	ALBERTITES	ALDERMANITY	ALIMENTARY	ALLEGORIZED	ALLOMEROUS
AICHMOPHOBIAS	ALBESCENCE	ALDERMANLIKE	ALIMENTATION	ALLEGORIZER	ALLOMETRIC
AIGUILLETTE	ALBESCENCES	ALDERMANLY	ALIMENTATIONS	ALLEGORIZERS	ALLOMETRIES
AIGUILLETTES	ALBESPINES	ALDERMANRIES	ALIMENTATIVE	ALLEGORIZES	ALLOMORPHIC
AILANTHUSES	ALBESPYNES	ALDERMANRY	ALIMENTING	ALLEGORIZING	ALLOMORPHISM
AILOUROPHILE	ALBINESSES	ALDERMANSHIP	ALIMENTIVENESS	ALLEGRETTO	ALLOMORPHISMS
AILOUROPHILES	ALBINISTIC	ALDERMANSHIPS	ALINEATION	ALLEGRETTOS	ALLOMORPHS
AILOUROPHILIA	ALBINOISMS	ALDERWOMAN	ALINEATIONS	ALLELOMORPH	ALLONYMOUS
AILOUROPHILIAS	ALBITISING	ALDERWOMEN	ALINEMENTS	ALLELOMORPHIC	ALLOPATHIC
AILOUROPHILIC	ALBITIZING	ALDOHEXOSE	ALISMACEOUS	ALLELOMORPHISM	ALLOPATHICALLY
AILOUROPHOBE	ALBUGINEOUS	ALDOHEXOSES	ALITERACIES	ALLELOMORPHISMS	ALLOPATHIES
AILOUROPHOBES	ALBUMBLATT	ALDOLISATION	ALITERATES	ALLELOMORPHS	ALLOPATHIST
AILOUROPHOBIA	ALBUMBLATTER	ALDOLISATIONS	ALIVENESSES	ALLELOPATHIC	ALLOPATHISTS
AILOUROPHOBIAS	ALBUMBLATTS	ALDOLIZATION	ALIZARINES	ALLELOPATHIES	ALLOPATRIC
AILOUROPHOBIC	ALBUMENISE	ALDOLIZATIONS	ALKAHESTIC	ALLELOPATHY	ALLOPATRICALLY
AILUROPHILE	ALBUMENISED	ALDOPENTOSE	ALKALESCENCE	ALLELUIAHS	ALLOPATRIES
AILUROPHILES	ALBUMENISES	ALDOPENTOSES	ALKALESCENCES	ALLEMANDES	ALLOPHANES
AILUROPHILIA	ALBUMENISING	ALDOSTERONE	ALKALESCENCIES	ALLERGENIC	ALLOPHONES
AILUROPHILIAS	ALBUMENIZE	ALDOSTERONES	ALKALESCENCY	ALLERGENICITIES	ALLOPHONIC
AILUROPHILIC	ALBUMENIZED	ALDOSTERONISM	ALKALESCENT	ALLERGENICITY	ALLOPLASMIC
AILUROPHOBE	ALBUMENIZES	ALDOSTERONISMS	ALKALIFIED	ALLERGISTS	ALLOPLASMS
AILUROPHOBES	ALBUMENIZING	ALEATORIES	ALKALIFIES	ALLETHRINS	ALLOPLASTIC
AILUROPHOBIA	ALBUMINATE	ALEBENCHES	ALKALIFYING	ALLEVIANTS	ALLOPOLYPLOID
AILUROPHOBIAS	ALBUMINATES	ALECTRYONS	ALKALIMETER	ALLEVIATED	ALLOPOLYPLOIDS
AILUROPHOBIC	ALBUMINISE	ALEGGEAUNCE	ALKALIMETERS	ALLEVIATES	ALLOPOLYPLOIDY
AIMLESSNESS	ALBUMINISED	ALEGGEAUNCES	ALKALIMETRIC	ALLEVIATING	ALLOPURINOL
AIMLESSNESSES	ALBUMINISES	ALEMBICATED	ALKALIMETRIES	ALLEVIATION	ALLOPURINOLS
AIRBRUSHED	ALBUMINISING	ALEMBICATION	ALKALIMETRY	ALLEVIATIONS	ALLOSAURUS
AIRBRUSHES	ALBUMINIZE	ALEMBICATIONS	ALKALINISATION	ALLEVIATIVE	ALLOSAURUSES
AIRBRUSHING	ALBUMINIZED	ALEMBROTHS	ALKALINISATIONS	ALLEVIATOR	ALLOSTERIC

ALLOSTERICALLY
ALLOSTERIES
ALLOTETRAPLOID
ALLOTETRAPLOIDS
ALLOTETRAPLOIDY
ALLOTHEISM
ALLOTHEISMS
ALLOTMENTS
ALLOTRIOMORPHIC
ALLOTROPES
ALLOTROPIC
ALLOTROPICALLY
ALLOTROPIES
ALLOTROPISM
ALLOTROPISMS
ALLOTROPOUS
ALLOTTERIES
ALLOTYPICALLY
ALLOTYPIES
ALLOWABILITIES
ALLOWABILITY
ALLOWABLENESS
ALLOWABLENESSES
ALLOWABLES
ALLOWANCED
ALLOWANCES
ALLOWANCING
ALLUREMENT
ALLUREMENTS
ALLURINGLY
ALLUSIVELY
ALLUSIVENESS
ALLUSIVENESSES
ALLYCHOLLIES
ALLYCHOLLY
ALMACANTAR
ALMACANTARS
ALMANDINES
ALMANDITES
ALMIGHTILY
ALMIGHTINESS
ALMIGHTINESSES
ALMSGIVERS
ALMSGIVING
ALMSGIVINGS
ALMSHOUSES
ALMUCANTAR
ALMUCANTARS
ALOGICALLY
ALONENESSES
ALONGSHORE
ALONGSHOREMAN
ALONGSHOREMEN
ALOOFNESSES
ALPARGATAS
ALPENGLOWS
ALPENHORNS
ALPENSTOCK
ALPENSTOCKS
ALPESTRINE
ALPHABETARIAN
ALPHABETARIANS
ALPHABETED
ALPHABETIC
ALPHABETICAL
ALPHABETICALLY
ALPHABETIFORM
ALPHABETING
ALPHABETISATION
ALPHABETISE
ALPHABETISED
ALPHABETISER
ALPHABETISERS
ALPHABETISES
ALPHABETISING
ALPHABETIZATION
ALPHABETIZE
ALPHABETIZED
ALPHABETIZER
ALPHABETIZERS
ALPHABETIZES
ALPHABETIZING
ALPHAMERIC

ALPHAMERICAL
ALPHAMERICALLY
ALPHAMETIC
ALPHAMETICS
ALPHANUMERIC
ALPHANUMERICAL
ALPHANUMERICS
ALPHASORTED
ALPHASORTING
ALPHASORTS
ALPHOSISES
ALSTROEMERIA
ALSTROEMERIAS
ALTALTISSIMO
ALTALTISSIMOS
ALTARPIECE
ALTARPIECES
ALTAZIMUTH
ALTAZIMUTHS
ALTERABILITIES
ALTERABILITY
ALTERATION
ALTERATIONS
ALTERATIVE
ALTERATIVES
ALTERCATED
ALTERCATES
ALTERCATING
ALTERCATION
ALTERCATIONS
ALTERCATIVE
ALTERITIES
ALTERNANCE
ALTERNANCES
ALTERNANTS
ALTERNATED
ALTERNATELY
ALTERNATES
ALTERNATIM
ALTERNATING
ALTERNATION
ALTERNATIONS
ALTERNATIVE
ALTERNATIVELY
ALTERNATIVENESS
ALTERNATIVES
ALTERNATOR
ALTERNATORS
ALTIGRAPHS
ALTIMETERS
ALTIMETRICAL
ALTIMETRICALLY
ALTIMETRIES
ALTIPLANOS
ALTISONANT
ALTITONANT
ALTITUDINAL
ALTITUDINARIAN
ALTITUDINARIANS
ALTITUDINOUS
ALTOCUMULI
ALTOCUMULUS
ALTOGETHER
ALTOGETHERS
ALTORUFFLED
ALTOSTRATI
ALTOSTRATUS
ALTRICIALS
ALTRUISTIC
ALTRUISTICALLY
ALUMINATES
ALUMINIFEROUS
ALUMINISED
ALUMINISES
ALUMINISING
ALUMINIUMS
ALUMINIZED
ALUMINIZES
ALUMINIZING
ALUMINOSILICATE
ALUMINOSITIES
ALUMINOSITY
ALUMINOTHERMIES

ALUMINOTHERMY
ALUMSTONES
ALVEOLARLY
ALVEOLATION
ALVEOLATIONS
ALVEOLITIS
ALVEOLITISES
ALYCOMPAINE
ALYCOMPAINES
AMAKWEREKWERE
AMALGAMATE
AMALGAMATED
AMALGAMATES
AMALGAMATING
AMALGAMATION
AMALGAMATIONS
AMALGAMATIVE
AMALGAMATOR
AMALGAMATORS
AMANTADINE
AMANTADINES
AMANUENSES
AMANUENSIS
AMARACUSES
AMARANTACEOUS
AMARANTHACEOUS
AMARANTHINE
AMARANTINE
AMARYLLIDACEOUS
AMARYLLIDS
AMARYLLISES
AMASSMENTS
AMATEURISH
AMATEURISHLY
AMATEURISHNESS
AMATEURISM
AMATEURISMS
AMATEURSHIP
AMATEURSHIPS
AMATIVENESS
AMATIVENESSES
AMATORIALLY
AMATORIOUS
AMAZEDNESS
AMAZEDNESSES
AMAZEMENTS
AMAZONIANS
AMAZONITES
AMAZONSTONE
AMAZONSTONES
AMBAGITORY
AMBASSADOR
AMBASSADORIAL
AMBASSADORS
AMBASSADORSHIP
AMBASSADORSHIPS
AMBASSADRESS
AMBASSADRESSES
AMBASSAGES
AMBERGRISES
AMBERJACKS
AMBIDENTATE
AMBIDEXTER
AMBIDEXTERITIES
AMBIDEXTERITY
AMBIDEXTEROUS
AMBIDEXTERS
AMBIDEXTROUS
AMBIDEXTROUSLY
AMBIGUITIES
AMBIGUOUSLY
AMBIGUOUSNESS
AMBIGUOUSNESSES
AMBILATERAL
AMBIOPHONIES
AMBIOPHONY
AMBISEXUAL
AMBISEXUALITIES
AMBISEXUALITY
AMBISEXUALS
AMBISONICS
AMBITIONED
AMBITIONING

AMBITIONLESS
AMBITIOUSLY
AMBITIOUSNESS
AMBITIOUSNESSES
AMBIVALENCE
AMBIVALENCES
AMBIVALENCIES
AMBIVALENCY
AMBIVALENT
AMBIVALENTLY
AMBIVERSION
AMBIVERSIONS
AMBLYGONITE
AMBLYGONITES
AMBLYOPIAS
AMBOCEPTOR
AMBOCEPTORS
AMBOSEXUAL
AMBROSIALLY
AMBROTYPES
AMBULACRAL
AMBULACRUM
AMBULANCEMAN
AMBULANCEMEN
AMBULANCES
AMBULANCEWOMAN
AMBULANCEWOMEN
AMBULATING
AMBULATION
AMBULATIONS
AMBULATORIES
AMBULATORILY
AMBULATORS
AMBULATORY
AMBULETTES
AMBUSCADED
AMBUSCADER
AMBUSCADERS
AMBUSCADES
AMBUSCADING
AMBUSCADOES
AMBUSCADOS
AMBUSHMENT
AMBUSHMENTS
AMEBOCYTES
AMELIORABLE
AMELIORANT
AMELIORANTS
AMELIORATE
AMELIORATED
AMELIORATES
AMELIORATING
AMELIORATION
AMELIORATIONS
AMELIORATIVE
AMELIORATOR
AMELIORATORS
AMELIORATORY
AMELOBLAST
AMELOBLASTS
AMELOGENESES
AMELOGENESIS
AMENABILITIES
AMENABILITY
AMENABLENESS
AMENABLENESSES
AMENAUNCES
AMENDATORY
AMENDMENTS
AMENORRHEA
AMENORRHEAS
AMENORRHEIC
AMENORRHOEA
AMENORRHOEAS
AMENTACEOUS
AMENTIFEROUS
AMERCEABLE
AMERCEMENT
AMERCEMENTS
AMERCIABLE
AMERCIAMENT
AMERCIAMENTS
AMERICIUMS

AMETABOLIC
AMETABOLISM
AMETABOLISMS
AMETABOLOUS
AMETHYSTINE
AMETROPIAS
AMIABILITIES
AMIABILITY
AMIABLENESS
AMIABLENESSES
AMIANTHINE
AMIANTHOID
AMIANTHOIDAL
AMIANTHUSES
AMIANTUSES
AMICABILITIES
AMICABILITY
AMICABLENESS
AMICABLENESSES
AMINOACIDURIA
AMINOACIDURIAS
AMINOBENZOIC
AMINOBUTENE
AMINOBUTENES
AMINOPEPTIDASE
AMINOPEPTIDASES
AMINOPHENAZONE
AMINOPHENAZONES
AMINOPHENOL
AMINOPHENOLS
AMINOPHYLLINE
AMINOPHYLLINES
AMINOPTERIN
AMINOPTERINS
AMINOPYRINE
AMINOPYRINES
AMISSIBILITIES
AMISSIBILITY
AMITOTICALLY
AMITRIPTYLINE
AMITRIPTYLINES
AMITRYPTYLINE
AMITRYPTYLINES
AMMOCOETES
AMMONIACAL
AMMONIACUM
AMMONIACUMS
AMMONIATED
AMMONIATES
AMMONIATING
AMMONIATION
AMMONIATIONS
AMMONIFICATION
AMMONIFICATIONS
AMMONIFIED
AMMONIFIES
AMMONIFYING
AMMONOLYSES
AMMONOLYSIS
AMMOPHILOUS
AMMUNITION
AMMUNITIONED
AMMUNITIONING
AMMUNITIONS
AMNESTYING
AMNIOCENTESES
AMNIOCENTESIS
AMNIOTOMIES
AMOBARBITAL
AMOBARBITALS
AMOEBIASES
AMOEBIASIS
AMOEBIFORM
AMOEBOCYTE
AMOEBOCYTES
AMONTILLADO
AMONTILLADOS
AMORALISMS
AMORALISTS
AMORALITIES
AMOROSITIES
AMOROUSNESS
AMOROUSNESSES

AMORPHISMS
AMORPHOUSLY
AMORPHOUSNESS
AMORPHOUSNESSES
AMORTISABLE
AMORTISATION
AMORTISATIONS
AMORTISEMENT
AMORTISEMENTS
AMORTISING
AMORTIZABLE
AMORTIZATION
AMORTIZATIONS
AMORTIZEMENT
AMORTIZEMENTS
AMORTIZING
AMOURETTES
AMOXICILLIN
AMOXICILLINS
AMOXYCILLIN
AMOXYCILLINS
AMPELOGRAPHIES
AMPELOGRAPHY
AMPELOPSES
AMPELOPSIS
AMPEROMETRIC
AMPERSANDS
AMPERZANDS
AMPHETAMINE
AMPHETAMINES
AMPHIARTHROSES
AMPHIARTHROSIS
AMPHIASTER
AMPHIASTERS
AMPHIBIANS
AMPHIBIOTIC
AMPHIBIOUS
AMPHIBIOUSLY
AMPHIBIOUSNESS
AMPHIBLASTIC
AMPHIBLASTULA
AMPHIBLASTULAE
AMPHIBOLES
AMPHIBOLIC
AMPHIBOLIES
AMPHIBOLITE
AMPHIBOLITES
AMPHIBOLOGICAL
AMPHIBOLOGIES
AMPHIBOLOGY
AMPHIBOLOUS
AMPHIBRACH
AMPHIBRACHIC
AMPHIBRACHS
AMPHICHROIC
AMPHICHROMATIC
AMPHICOELOUS
AMPHICTYON
AMPHICTYONIC
AMPHICTYONIES
AMPHICTYONS
AMPHICTYONY
AMPHIDENTATE
AMPHIDIPLOID
AMPHIDIPLOIDIES
AMPHIDIPLOIDS
AMPHIDIPLOIDY
AMPHIGASTRIA
AMPHIGASTRIUM
AMPHIGORIC
AMPHIGORIES
AMPHIGOURI
AMPHIGOURIS
AMPHIMACER
AMPHIMACERS
AMPHIMICTIC
AMPHIMIXES
AMPHIMIXIS
AMPHIOXUSES
AMPHIPATHIC
AMPHIPHILE
AMPHIPHILES
AMPHIPHILIC

AMPHIPLOID	AMYLOPSINS	ANAESTHETIZING	ANANDAMIDES	ANATOMIZERS	ANDROPAUSES
AMPHIPLOIDIES	AMYOTONIAS	ANAGENESES	ANAPAESTIC	ANATOMIZES	ANDROPHORE
AMPHIPLOIDS	AMYOTROPHIC	ANAGENESIS	ANAPAESTICAL	ANATOMIZING	ANDROPHORES
AMPHIPLOIDY	AMYOTROPHIES	ANAGLYPHIC	ANAPESTICS	ANATROPIES	ANDROSPHINGES
AMPHIPODOUS	AMYOTROPHY	ANAGLYPHICAL	ANAPHORESES	ANATROPOUS	ANDROSPHINX
AMPHIPROSTYLAR	ANABANTIDS	ANAGLYPHIES	ANAPHORESIS	ANCESTORED	ANDROSPHINXES
AMPHIPROSTYLE	ANABAPTISE	ANAGLYPTIC	ANAPHORICAL	ANCESTORING	ANDROSTERONE
AMPHIPROSTYLES	ANABAPTISED	ANAGLYPTICAL	ANAPHORICALLY	ANCESTRALLY	ANDROSTERONES
AMPHIPROTIC	ANABAPTISES	ANAGNORISES	ANAPHRODISIA	ANCESTRESS	ANECDOTAGE
AMPHISBAENA	ANABAPTISING	ANAGNORISIS	ANAPHRODISIAC	ANCESTRESSES	ANECDOTAGES
AMPHISBAENAE	ANABAPTISM	ANAGOGICAL	ANAPHRODISIACS	ANCESTRIES	ANECDOTALISM
AMPHISBAENAS	ANABAPTISMS	ANAGOGICALLY	ANAPHRODISIAS	ANCHORAGES	ANECDOTALISMS
AMPHISBAENIC	ANABAPTIST	ANAGRAMMATIC	ANAPHYLACTIC	ANCHORESSES	ANECDOTALIST
AMPHISCIAN	ANABAPTISTIC	ANAGRAMMATICAL	ANAPHYLACTOID	ANCHORETIC	ANECDOTALISTS
AMPHISCIANS	ANABAPTISTS	ANAGRAMMATISE	ANAPHYLAXES	ANCHORETICAL	ANECDOTALLY
AMPHISTOMATAL	ANABAPTIZE	ANAGRAMMATISED	ANAPHYLAXIES	ANCHORETTE	ANECDOTICAL
AMPHISTOMATIC	ANABAPTIZED	ANAGRAMMATISES	ANAPHYLAXIS	ANCHORETTES	ANECDOTICALLY
AMPHISTOMOUS	ANABAPTIZES	ANAGRAMMATISING	ANAPHYLAXY	ANCHORITES	ANECDOTIST
AMPHISTYLAR	ANABAPTIZING	ANAGRAMMATISM	ANAPLASIAS	ANCHORITIC	ANECDOTISTS
AMPHISTYLARS	ANABLEPSES	ANAGRAMMATISMS	ANAPLASMOSES	ANCHORITICAL	ANELASTICITIES
AMPHITHEATER	ANABOLISMS	ANAGRAMMATIST	ANAPLASMOSIS	ANCHORITICALLY	ANELASTICITY
AMPHITHEATERS	ANABOLITES	ANAGRAMMATISTS	ANAPLASTIC	ANCHORLESS	ANEMICALLY
AMPHITHEATRAL	ANABOLITIC	ANAGRAMMATIZE	ANAPLASTIES	ANCHORPEOPLE	ANEMOCHORE
AMPHITHEATRE	ANABRANCHES	ANAGRAMMATIZED	ANAPLEROSES	ANCHORPERSON	ANEMOCHORES
AMPHITHEATRES	ANACARDIACEOUS	ANAGRAMMATIZES	ANAPLEROSIS	ANCHORPERSONS	ANEMOCHOROUS
AMPHITHEATRIC	ANACARDIUM	ANAGRAMMATIZING	ANAPLEROTIC	ANCHORWOMAN	ANEMOGRAMS
AMPHITHEATRICAL	ANACARDIUMS	ANAGRAMMED	ANAPTYCTIC	ANCHORWOMEN	ANEMOGRAPH
AMPHITHECIA	ANACATHARSES	ANAGRAMMER	ANAPTYCTICAL	ANCHOVETAS	ANEMOGRAPHIC
AMPHITHECIUM	ANACATHARSIS	ANAGRAMMERS	ANARCHICAL	ANCHOVETTA	ANEMOGRAPHIES
AMPHITRICHA	ANACATHARTIC	ANAGRAMMING	ANARCHICALLY	ANCHOVETTAS	ANEMOGRAPHS
AMPHITRICHOUS	ANACATHARTICS	ANALEMMATA	ANARCHISED	ANCHYLOSED	ANEMOGRAPHY
AMPHITROPOUS	ANACHARISES	ANALEMMATIC	ANARCHISES	ANCHYLOSES	ANEMOLOGIES
AMPHOLYTES	ANACHORISM	ANALEPTICS	ANARCHISING	ANCHYLOSING	ANEMOMETER
AMPHOTERIC	ANACHORISMS	ANALGESIAS	ANARCHISMS	ANCHYLOSIS	ANEMOMETERS
AMPICILLIN	ANACHRONIC	ANALGESICS	ANARCHISTIC	ANCHYLOTIC	ANEMOMETRIC
AMPICILLINS	ANACHRONICAL	ANALGETICS	ANARCHISTS	ANCIENTEST	ANEMOMETRICAL
AMPLENESSES	ANACHRONICALLY	ANALOGICAL	ANARCHIZED	ANCIENTNESS	ANEMOMETRIES
AMPLEXICAUL	ANACHRONISM	ANALOGICALLY	ANARCHIZES	ANCIENTNESSES	ANEMOMETRY
AMPLEXUSES	ANACHRONISMS	ANALOGISED	ANARCHIZING	ANCIENTRIES	ANEMOPHILIES
AMPLIATION	ANACHRONISTIC	ANALOGISES	ANARTHRIAS	ANCILLARIES	ANEMOPHILOUS
AMPLIATIONS	ANACHRONOUS	ANALOGISING	ANARTHROUS	ANCIPITOUS	ANEMOPHILY
AMPLIATIVE	ANACHRONOUSLY	ANALOGISMS	ANARTHROUSLY	ANCYLOSTOMIASES	ANEMOPHOBIA
AMPLIDYNES	ANACLASTIC	ANALOGISTS	ANARTHROUSNESS	ANCYLOSTOMIASIS	ANEMOPHOBIAS
AMPLIFIABLE	ANACOLUTHA	ANALOGIZED	ANASARCOUS	ANDALUSITE	ANEMOSCOPE
AMPLIFICATION	ANACOLUTHIA	ANALOGIZES	ANASTIGMAT	ANDALUSITES	ANEMOSCOPES
AMPLIFICATIONS	ANACOLUTHIAS	ANALOGIZING	ANASTIGMATIC	ANDANTINOS	ANENCEPHALIA
AMPLIFIERS	ANACOLUTHIC	ANALOGOUSLY	ANASTIGMATISM	ANDOUILLES	ANENCEPHALIAS
AMPLIFYING	ANACOLUTHICALLY	ANALOGOUSNESS	ANASTIGMATISMS	ANDOUILLETTE	ANENCEPHALIC
AMPLITUDES	ANACOLUTHON	ANALOGOUSNESSES	ANASTIGMATS	ANDOUILLETTES	ANENCEPHALIES
AMPLOSOMES	ANACOLUTHONS	ANALPHABET	ANASTOMOSE	ANDRADITES	ANENCEPHALY
AMPULLACEAL	ANACOUSTIC	ANALPHABETE	ANASTOMOSED	ANDROCENTRIC	ANESTHESIA
AMPULLACEOUS	ANACREONTIC	ANALPHABETES	ANASTOMOSES	ANDROCENTRISM	ANESTHESIAS
AMPULLOSITIES	ANACREONTICALLY	ANALPHABETIC	ANASTOMOSING	ANDROCENTRISMS	ANESTHESIOLOGY
AMPULLOSITY	ANACREONTICS	ANALPHABETICS	ANASTOMOSIS	ANDROCEPHALOUS	ANESTHETIC
AMPUTATING	ANACRUSTIC	ANALPHABETISM	ANASTOMOTIC	ANDROCLINIA	ANESTHETICALLY
AMPUTATION	ANADIPLOSES	ANALPHABETISMS	ANASTROPHE	ANDROCLINIUM	ANESTHETICS
AMPUTATIONS	ANADIPLOSIS	ANALPHABETS	ANASTROPHES	ANDRODIOECIOUS	ANESTHETISE
AMPUTATORS	ANADROMOUS	ANALYSABLE	ANASTROZOLE	ANDRODIOECISM	ANESTHETISED
AMRITATTVA	ANADYOMENE	ANALYSANDS	ANASTROZOLES	ANDRODIOECISMS	ANESTHETISES
AMRITATTVAS	ANAEROBICALLY	ANALYSATION	ANATHEMATA	ANDROECIAL	ANESTHETISING
AMSINCKIAS	ANAEROBIONT	ANALYSATIONS	ANATHEMATICAL	ANDROECIUM	ANESTHETIST
AMUSEMENTS	ANAEROBIONTS	ANALYTICAL	ANATHEMATISE	ANDROECIUMS	ANESTHETISTS
AMUSINGNESS	ANAEROBIOSES	ANALYTICALLY	ANATHEMATISED	ANDROGENESES	ANESTHETIZATION
AMUSINGNESSES	ANAEROBIOSIS	ANALYTICITIES	ANATHEMATISES	ANDROGENESIS	ANESTHETIZE
AMUSIVENESS	ANAEROBIOTIC	ANALYTICITY	ANATHEMATISING	ANDROGENETIC	ANESTHETIZED
AMUSIVENESSES	ANAEROBIUM	ANALYZABILITIES	ANATHEMATIZE	ANDROGENIC	ANESTHETIZES
AMYGDALACEOUS	ANAESTHESES	ANALYZABILITY	ANATHEMATIZED	ANDROGENOUS	ANESTHETIZING
AMYGDALATE	ANAESTHESIA	ANALYZABLE	ANATHEMATIZES	ANDROGYNES	ANEUPLOIDIES
AMYGDALINE	ANAESTHESIAS	ANALYZATION	ANATHEMATIZING	ANDROGYNIES	ANEUPLOIDS
AMYGDALINS	ANAESTHESIOLOGY	ANALYZATIONS	ANATOMICAL	ANDROGYNOPHORE	ANEUPLOIDY
AMYGDALOID	ANAESTHESIS	ANAMNESTIC	ANATOMICALLY	ANDROGYNOPHORES	ANEURISMAL
AMYGDALOIDAL	ANAESTHETIC	ANAMNESTICALLY	ANATOMISATION	ANDROGYNOUS	ANEURISMALLY
AMYGDALOIDS	ANAESTHETICALLY	ANAMNIOTES	ANATOMISATIONS	ANDROLOGIES	ANEURISMATIC
AMYLACEOUS	ANAESTHETICS	ANAMNIOTIC	ANATOMISED	ANDROLOGIST	ANEURYSMAL
AMYLOIDOSES	ANAESTHETISE	ANAMORPHIC	ANATOMISER	ANDROLOGISTS	ANEURYSMALLY
AMYLOIDOSIS	ANAESTHETISED	ANAMORPHISM	ANATOMISERS	ANDROMEDAS	ANEURYSMATIC
AMYLOLYSES	ANAESTHETISES	ANAMORPHISMS	ANATOMISES	ANDROMEDOTOXIN	ANFRACTUOSITIES
AMYLOLYSIS	ANAESTHETISING	ANAMORPHOSCOPE	ANATOMISING	ANDROMEDOTOXINS	ANFRACTUOSITY
AMYLOLYTIC	ANAESTHETIST	ANAMORPHOSCOPES	ANATOMISTS	ANDROMONOECIOUS	ANFRACTUOUS
AMYLOPECTIN	ANAESTHETISTS	ANAMORPHOSES	ANATOMIZATION	ANDROMONOECISM	ANGASHORES
AMYLOPECTINS	ANAESTHETIZE	ANAMORPHOSIS	ANATOMIZATIONS	ANDROMONOECISMS	ANGELFISHES
AMYLOPLAST	ANAESTHETIZED	ANAMORPHOUS	ANATOMIZED	ANDROPAUSE	ANGELHOODS
AMYLOPLASTS	ANAESTHETIZES	ANANDAMIDE	ANATOMIZER	ANDROPAUSES	ANGELICALLY

ANGELOLATRIES
ANGELOLATRY
ANGELOLOGIES
ANGELOLOGIST
ANGELOLOGISTS
ANGELOLOGY
ANGELOPHANIES
ANGELOPHANY
ANGIOCARPOUS
ANGIOGENESES
ANGIOGENESIS
ANGIOGENIC
ANGIOGRAMS
ANGIOGRAPHIC
ANGIOGRAPHIES
ANGIOGRAPHY
ANGIOLOGIES
ANGIOMATOUS
ANGIOPLASTIES
ANGIOPLASTY
ANGIOSARCOMA
ANGIOSARCOMAS
ANGIOSARCOMATA
ANGIOSPERM
ANGIOSPERMAL
ANGIOSPERMOUS
ANGIOSPERMS
ANGIOSTOMATOUS
ANGIOSTOMOUS
ANGIOTENSIN
ANGIOTENSINS
ANGLEBERRIES
ANGLEBERRY
ANGLEDOZER
ANGLEDOZERS
ANGLERFISH
ANGLERFISHES
ANGLESITES
ANGLETWITCH
ANGLETWITCHES
ANGLEWORMS
ANGLICISATION
ANGLICISATIONS
ANGLICISED
ANGLICISES
ANGLICISING
ANGLICISMS
ANGLICISTS
ANGLICIZATION
ANGLICIZATIONS
ANGLICIZED
ANGLICIZES
ANGLICIZING
ANGLIFYING
ANGLISTICS
ANGLOMANIA
ANGLOMANIAC
ANGLOMANIACS
ANGLOMANIAS
ANGLOPHILE
ANGLOPHILES
ANGLOPHILIA
ANGLOPHILIAS
ANGLOPHILIC
ANGLOPHILS
ANGLOPHOBE
ANGLOPHOBES
ANGLOPHOBIA
ANGLOPHOBIAC
ANGLOPHOBIAS
ANGLOPHOBIC
ANGLOPHONE
ANGLOPHONES
ANGLOPHONIC
ANGOPHORAS
ANGOSTURAS
ANGRINESSES
ANGUIFAUNA
ANGUIFAUNAE
ANGUIFAUNAS
ANGUILLIFORM
ANGUISHING
ANGULARITIES

ANGULARITY
ANGULARNESS
ANGULARNESSES
ANGULATING
ANGULATION
ANGULATIONS
ANGUSTIFOLIATE
ANGUSTIROSTRATE
ANGWANTIBO
ANGWANTIBOS
ANHARMONIC
ANHEDONIAS
ANHELATION
ANHELATIONS
ANHIDROSES
ANHIDROSIS
ANHIDROTIC
ANHIDROTICS
ANHUNGERED
ANHYDRASES
ANHYDRIDES
ANHYDRITES
ANICONISMS
ANICONISTS
ANILINCTUS
ANILINCTUSES
ANILINGUSES
ANIMADVERSION
ANIMADVERSIONS
ANIMADVERT
ANIMADVERTED
ANIMADVERTER
ANIMADVERTERS
ANIMADVERTING
ANIMADVERTS
ANIMALCULA
ANIMALCULAR
ANIMALCULE
ANIMALCULES
ANIMALCULISM
ANIMALCULISMS
ANIMALCULIST
ANIMALCULISTS
ANIMALCULUM
ANIMALIERS
ANIMALISATION
ANIMALISATIONS
ANIMALISED
ANIMALISES
ANIMALISING
ANIMALISMS
ANIMALISTIC
ANIMALISTS
ANIMALITIES
ANIMALIZATION
ANIMALIZATIONS
ANIMALIZED
ANIMALIZES
ANIMALIZING
ANIMALLIKE
ANIMATEDLY
ANIMATENESS
ANIMATENESSES
ANIMATINGLY
ANIMATIONS
ANIMATISMS
ANIMATISTS
ANIMATRONIC
ANIMATRONICALLY
ANIMATRONICS
ANIMOSITIES
ANISEIKONIA
ANISEIKONIAS
ANISEIKONIC
ANISOCERCAL
ANISODACTYL
ANISODACTYLOUS
ANISODACTYLS
ANISOGAMIES
ANISOGAMOUS
ANISOMERIC
ANISOMEROUS
ANISOMETRIC

ANISOMETROPIA
ANISOMETROPIAS
ANISOMETROPIC
ANISOMORPHIC
ANISOPHYLLIES
ANISOPHYLLOUS
ANISOPHYLLY
ANISOTROPIC
ANISOTROPICALLY
ANISOTROPIES
ANISOTROPISM
ANISOTROPISMS
ANISOTROPY
ANKLEBONES
ANKYLOSAUR
ANKYLOSAURS
ANKYLOSAURUS
ANKYLOSAURUSES
ANKYLOSING
ANKYLOSTOMIASES
ANKYLOSTOMIASIS
ANNABERGITE
ANNABERGITES
ANNALISING
ANNALISTIC
ANNALIZING
ANNEALINGS
ANNELIDANS
ANNEXATION
ANNEXATIONAL
ANNEXATIONISM
ANNEXATIONISMS
ANNEXATIONIST
ANNEXATIONISTS
ANNEXATIONS
ANNEXMENTS
ANNIHILABLE
ANNIHILATE
ANNIHILATED
ANNIHILATES
ANNIHILATING
ANNIHILATION
ANNIHILATIONISM
ANNIHILATIONS
ANNIHILATIVE
ANNIHILATOR
ANNIHILATORS
ANNIHILATORY
ANNIVERSARIES
ANNIVERSARY
ANNOTATABLE
ANNOTATING
ANNOTATION
ANNOTATIONS
ANNOTATIVE
ANNOTATORS
ANNOUNCEMENT
ANNOUNCEMENTS
ANNOUNCERS
ANNOUNCING
ANNOYANCES
ANNOYINGLY
ANNUALISED
ANNUALISES
ANNUALISING
ANNUALIZED
ANNUALIZES
ANNUALIZING
ANNUITANTS
ANNULARITIES
ANNULARITY
ANNULATION
ANNULATIONS
ANNULLABLE
ANNULMENTS
ANNUNCIATE
ANNUNCIATED
ANNUNCIATES
ANNUNCIATING
ANNUNCIATION
ANNUNCIATIONS
ANNUNCIATIVE
ANNUNCIATOR

ANNUNCIATORS
ANNUNCIATORY
ANNUNTIATE
ANNUNTIATED
ANNUNTIATES
ANNUNTIATING
ANODICALLY
ANODISATION
ANODISATIONS
ANODIZATION
ANODIZATIONS
ANODONTIAS
ANOESTROUS
ANOINTMENT
ANOINTMENTS
ANOMALISTIC
ANOMALISTICAL
ANOMALISTICALLY
ANOMALOUSLY
ANOMALOUSNESS
ANOMALOUSNESSES
ANONACEOUS
ANONYMISED
ANONYMISES
ANONYMISING
ANONYMITIES
ANONYMIZED
ANONYMIZES
ANONYMIZING
ANONYMOUSLY
ANONYMOUSNESS
ANONYMOUSNESSES
ANOPHELINE
ANOPHELINES
ANORECTICS
ANOREXIGENIC
ANORTHITES
ANORTHITIC
ANORTHOSITE
ANORTHOSITES
ANORTHOSITIC
ANOTHERGUESS
ANOVULANTS
ANOVULATORY
ANOXAEMIAS
ANSWERABILITIES
ANSWERABILITY
ANSWERABLE
ANSWERABLENESS
ANSWERABLY
ANSWERLESS
ANSWERPHONE
ANSWERPHONES
ANTAGONISABLE
ANTAGONISATION
ANTAGONISATIONS
ANTAGONISE
ANTAGONISED
ANTAGONISES
ANTAGONISING
ANTAGONISM
ANTAGONISMS
ANTAGONIST
ANTAGONISTIC
ANTAGONISTS
ANTAGONIZABLE
ANTAGONIZATION
ANTAGONIZATIONS
ANTAGONIZE
ANTAGONIZED
ANTAGONIZES
ANTAGONIZING
ANTALKALIES
ANTALKALINE
ANTALKALINES
ANTALKALIS
ANTAPHRODISIAC
ANTAPHRODISIACS
ANTARTHRITIC
ANTARTHRITICS
ANTASTHMATIC
ANTASTHMATICS
ANTEBELLUM

ANTECEDENCE
ANTECEDENCES
ANTECEDENT
ANTECEDENTLY
ANTECEDENTS
ANTECEDING
ANTECESSOR
ANTECESSORS
ANTECHAMBER
ANTECHAMBERS
ANTECHAPEL
ANTECHAPELS
ANTECHOIRS
ANTEDATING
ANTEDILUVIAL
ANTEDILUVIALLY
ANTEDILUVIAN
ANTEDILUVIANS
ANTEMERIDIAN
ANTEMORTEM
ANTEMUNDANE
ANTENATALLY
ANTENATALS
ANTENNIFEROUS
ANTENNIFORM
ANTENNULAR
ANTENNULES
ANTENUPTIAL
ANTEORBITAL
ANTEPENDIA
ANTEPENDIUM
ANTEPENDIUMS
ANTEPENULT
ANTEPENULTIMA
ANTEPENULTIMAS
ANTEPENULTIMATE
ANTEPENULTS
ANTEPOSITION
ANTEPOSITIONS
ANTEPRANDIAL
ANTERIORITIES
ANTERIORITY
ANTERIORLY
ANTEROGRADE
ANTEVERSION
ANTEVERSIONS
ANTEVERTED
ANTEVERTING
ANTHELICES
ANTHELIONS
ANTHELIXES
ANTHELMINTHIC
ANTHELMINTHICS
ANTHELMINTIC
ANTHELMINTICS
ANTHEMWISE
ANTHERIDIA
ANTHERIDIAL
ANTHERIDIUM
ANTHEROZOID
ANTHEROZOIDS
ANTHEROZOOID
ANTHEROZOOIDS
ANTHERSMUT
ANTHERSMUTS
ANTHOCARPOUS
ANTHOCARPS
ANTHOCHLORE
ANTHOCHLORES
ANTHOCYANIN
ANTHOCYANINS
ANTHOCYANS
ANTHOLOGICAL
ANTHOLOGIES
ANTHOLOGISE
ANTHOLOGISED
ANTHOLOGISER
ANTHOLOGISERS
ANTHOLOGISES
ANTHOLOGISING
ANTHOLOGIST
ANTHOLOGISTS
ANTHOLOGIZE

ANTHOLOGIZED
ANTHOLOGIZER
ANTHOLOGIZERS
ANTHOLOGIZES
ANTHOLOGIZING
ANTHOMANIA
ANTHOMANIAC
ANTHOMANIACS
ANTHOMANIAS
ANTHOPHILOUS
ANTHOPHORE
ANTHOPHORES
ANTHOPHYLLITE
ANTHOPHYLLITES
ANTHOTAXIES
ANTHOXANTHIN
ANTHOXANTHINS
ANTHOZOANS
ANTHRACENE
ANTHRACENES
ANTHRACITE
ANTHRACITES
ANTHRACITIC
ANTHRACNOSE
ANTHRACNOSES
ANTHRACOID
ANTHRACOSES
ANTHRACOSIS
ANTHRANILATE
ANTHRANILATES
ANTHRAQUINONE
ANTHRAQUINONES
ANTHROPICAL
ANTHROPOBIOLOGY
ANTHROPOCENTRIC
ANTHROPOGENESES
ANTHROPOGENESIS
ANTHROPOGENETIC
ANTHROPOGENIC
ANTHROPOGENIES
ANTHROPOGENY
ANTHROPOGONIES
ANTHROPOGONY
ANTHROPOGRAPHY
ANTHROPOID
ANTHROPOIDAL
ANTHROPOIDS
ANTHROPOLATRIES
ANTHROPOLATRY
ANTHROPOLOGICAL
ANTHROPOLOGIES
ANTHROPOLOGIST
ANTHROPOLOGISTS
ANTHROPOLOGY
ANTHROPOMETRIC
ANTHROPOMETRIES
ANTHROPOMETRIST
ANTHROPOMETRY
ANTHROPOMORPH
ANTHROPOMORPHIC
ANTHROPOMORPHS
ANTHROPOPATHIC
ANTHROPOPATHIES
ANTHROPOPATHISM
ANTHROPOPATHY
ANTHROPOPHAGI
ANTHROPOPHAGIC
ANTHROPOPHAGIES
ANTHROPOPHAGITE
ANTHROPOPHAGOUS
ANTHROPOPHAGUS
ANTHROPOPHAGY
ANTHROPOPHOBIA
ANTHROPOPHOBIAS
ANTHROPOPHOBIC
ANTHROPOPHOBICS
ANTHROPOPHUISM
ANTHROPOPHUISMS
ANTHROPOPHYTE
ANTHROPOPHYTES
ANTHROPOPSYCHIC
ANTHROPOSOPHIC
ANTHROPOSOPHIES

ANTHROPOSOPHIST	ANTICHRISTIANLY	ANTIDIABETIC	ANTIHELMINTHIC	ANTIMILITARISTS	ANTIPASTOS
ANTHROPOSOPHY	ANTICHRISTS	ANTIDIARRHEAL	ANTIHELMINTHICS	ANTIMILITARY	ANTIPATHETIC
ANTHROPOTOMIES	ANTICHTHONES	ANTIDIARRHEALS	ANTIHEROES	ANTIMISSILE	ANTIPATHETICAL
ANTHROPOTOMY	ANTICHURCH	ANTIDILUTION	ANTIHEROIC	ANTIMISSILES	ANTIPATHIC
ANTHURIUMS	ANTICIGARETTE	ANTIDIURETIC	ANTIHEROINE	ANTIMITOTIC	ANTIPATHIES
ANTIABORTION	ANTICIPANT	ANTIDIURETICS	ANTIHEROINES	ANTIMITOTICS	ANTIPATHIST
ANTIABORTIONIST	ANTICIPANTS	ANTIDOGMATIC	ANTIHERPES	ANTIMNEMONIC	ANTIPATHISTS
ANTIACADEMIC	ANTICIPATABLE	ANTIDOTALLY	ANTIHIJACK	ANTIMNEMONICS	ANTIPERIODIC
ANTIADITIS	ANTICIPATE	ANTIDOTING	ANTIHISTAMINE	ANTIMODERN	ANTIPERIODICS
ANTIADITISES	ANTICIPATED	ANTIDROMIC	ANTIHISTAMINES	ANTIMODERNIST	ANTIPERISTALSES
ANTIAGGRESSION	ANTICIPATES	ANTIDROMICALLY	ANTIHISTAMINIC	ANTIMODERNISTS	ANTIPERISTALSIS
ANTIAIRCRAFT	ANTICIPATING	ANTIDUMPING	ANTIHISTAMINICS	ANTIMONARCHICAL	ANTIPERISTALTIC
ANTIAIRCRAFTS	ANTICIPATION	ANTIECONOMIC	ANTIHISTORICAL	ANTIMONARCHIST	ANTIPERISTASES
ANTIALCOHOL	ANTICIPATIONS	ANTIEDUCATIONAL	ANTIHOMOSEXUAL	ANTIMONARCHISTS	ANTIPERISTASIS
ANTIALCOHOLISM	ANTICIPATIVE	ANTIEGALITARIAN	ANTIHUMANISM	ANTIMONATE	ANTIPERSONNEL
ANTIALCOHOLISMS	ANTICIPATIVELY	ANTIELECTRON	ANTIHUMANISMS	ANTIMONATES	ANTIPERSPIRANT
ANTIALLERGENIC	ANTICIPATOR	ANTIELECTRONS	ANTIHUMANISTIC	ANTIMONIAL	ANTIPERSPIRANTS
ANTIANEMIA	ANTICIPATORILY	ANTIELITES	ANTIHUNTER	ANTIMONIALS	ANTIPESTICIDE
ANTIANXIETY	ANTICIPATORS	ANTIELITISM	ANTIHUNTING	ANTIMONIATE	ANTIPETALOUS
ANTIAPARTHEID	ANTICIPATORY	ANTIELITISMS	ANTIHYDROGEN	ANTIMONIATES	ANTIPHLOGISTIC
ANTIAPHRODISIAC	ANTICISING	ANTIELITIST	ANTIHYDROGENS	ANTIMONIDE	ANTIPHLOGISTICS
ANTIARRHYTHMIC	ANTICIVISM	ANTIEMETIC	ANTIHYSTERIC	ANTIMONIDES	ANTIPHONAL
ANTIARRHYTHMICS	ANTICIVISMS	ANTIEMETICS	ANTIHYSTERICS	ANTIMONIES	ANTIPHONALLY
ANTIARTHRITIC	ANTICIZING	ANTIENTROPIC	ANTIJACOBIN	ANTIMONIOUS	ANTIPHONALS
ANTIARTHRITICS	ANTICLASSICAL	ANTIEPILEPSY	ANTIJACOBINS	ANTIMONITE	ANTIPHONARIES
ANTIARTHRITIS	ANTICLASTIC	ANTIEPILEPTIC	ANTIJAMMING	ANTIMONITES	ANTIPHONARY
ANTIASTHMA	ANTICLERICAL	ANTIEPILEPTICS	ANTIJAMMINGS	ANTIMONOPOLIST	ANTIPHONER
ANTIASTHMATIC	ANTICLERICALISM	ANTIEROTIC	ANTIKICKBACK	ANTIMONOPOLISTS	ANTIPHONERS
ANTIASTHMATICS	ANTICLERICALS	ANTIESTROGEN	ANTIKNOCKS	ANTIMONOPOLY	ANTIPHONIC
ANTIAUTHORITY	ANTICLIMACTIC	ANTIESTROGENS	ANTILEGOMENA	ANTIMONOUS	ANTIPHONICAL
ANTIAUXINS	ANTICLIMACTICAL	ANTIEVOLUTION	ANTILEPROSY	ANTIMONYLS	ANTIPHONICALLY
ANTIBACCHII	ANTICLIMAX	ANTIFAMILY	ANTILEPTON	ANTIMOSQUITO	ANTIPHONIES
ANTIBACCHIUS	ANTICLIMAXES	ANTIFASCISM	ANTILEPTONS	ANTIMUSICAL	ANTIPHRASES
ANTIBACKLASH	ANTICLINAL	ANTIFASCISMS	ANTILEUKEMIC	ANTIMUSICS	ANTIPHRASIS
ANTIBACTERIAL	ANTICLINALS	ANTIFASCIST	ANTILIBERAL	ANTIMUTAGEN	ANTIPHRASTIC
ANTIBACTERIALS	ANTICLINES	ANTIFASCISTS	ANTILIBERALISM	ANTIMUTAGENS	ANTIPHRASTICAL
ANTIBALLISTIC	ANTICLINORIA	ANTIFASHION	ANTILIBERALISMS	ANTIMYCINS	ANTIPIRACY
ANTIBARBARUS	ANTICLINORIUM	ANTIFASHIONABLE	ANTILIBERALS	ANTIMYCOTIC	ANTIPLAGUE
ANTIBARBARUSES	ANTICLINORIUMS	ANTIFASHIONS	ANTILIBERTARIAN	ANTINARRATIVE	ANTIPLAQUE
ANTIBARYON	ANTICLOCKWISE	ANTIFATIGUE	ANTILIFERS	ANTINARRATIVES	ANTIPLEASURE
ANTIBARYONS	ANTICLOTTING	ANTIFEBRILE	ANTILITERATE	ANTINATIONAL	ANTIPOACHING
ANTIBILIOUS	ANTICOAGULANT	ANTIFEBRILES	ANTILITTER	ANTINATIONALIST	ANTIPODALS
ANTIBILLBOARD	ANTICOAGULANTS	ANTIFEDERALIST	ANTILITTERING	ANTINATURAL	ANTIPODEAN
ANTIBIOSES	ANTICODONS	ANTIFEDERALISTS	ANTILOGARITHM	ANTINATURE	ANTIPODEANS
ANTIBIOSIS	ANTICOINCIDENCE	ANTIFEMALE	ANTILOGARITHMIC	ANTINAUSEA	ANTIPOETIC
ANTIBIOTIC	ANTICOLLISION	ANTIFEMININE	ANTILOGARITHMS	ANTINEOPLASTIC	ANTIPOLICE
ANTIBIOTICALLY	ANTICOLONIAL	ANTIFEMINISM	ANTILOGICAL	ANTINEPHRITIC	ANTIPOLITICAL
ANTIBIOTICS	ANTICOLONIALISM	ANTIFEMINISMS	ANTILOGIES	ANTINEPHRITICS	ANTIPOLITICS
ANTIBLACKISM	ANTICOLONIALIST	ANTIFEMINIST	ANTILOGOUS	ANTINEPOTISM	ANTIPOLLUTION
ANTIBLACKISMS	ANTICOMMERCIAL	ANTIFEMINISTS	ANTILOPINE	ANTINEUTRINO	ANTIPOLLUTIONS
ANTIBODIES	ANTICOMMUNISM	ANTIFERROMAGNET	ANTILYNCHING	ANTINEUTRINOS	ANTIPOPULAR
ANTIBOURGEOIS	ANTICOMMUNISMS	ANTIFERTILITY	ANTIMACASSAR	ANTINEUTRON	ANTIPORNOGRAPHY
ANTIBOYCOTT	ANTICOMMUNIST	ANTIFILIBUSTER	ANTIMACASSARS	ANTINEUTRONS	ANTIPOVERTY
ANTIBURGLAR	ANTICOMMUNISTS	ANTIFOAMING	ANTIMAGNETIC	ANTINOMIAN	ANTIPREDATOR
ANTIBURGLARY	ANTICOMPETITIVE	ANTIFOGGING	ANTIMALARIA	ANTINOMIANISM	ANTIPROGRESSIVE
ANTIBUSERS	ANTICONSUMER	ANTIFORECLOSURE	ANTIMALARIAL	ANTINOMIANISMS	ANTIPROTON
ANTIBUSINESS	ANTICONVULSANT	ANTIFOREIGN	ANTIMALARIALS	ANTINOMIANS	ANTIPROTONS
ANTIBUSING	ANTICONVULSANTS	ANTIFOREIGNER	ANTIMANAGEMENT	ANTINOMICAL	ANTIPRURITIC
ANTICAKING	ANTICONVULSIVE	ANTIFORMALIST	ANTIMARIJUANA	ANTINOMICALLY	ANTIPRURITICS
ANTICANCER	ANTICONVULSIVES	ANTIFOULING	ANTIMARKET	ANTINOMIES	ANTIPSYCHIATRY
ANTICAPITALISM	ANTICORPORATE	ANTIFOULINGS	ANTIMASQUE	ANTINOVELIST	ANTIPSYCHOTIC
ANTICAPITALISMS	ANTICORROSION	ANTIFREEZE	ANTIMASQUES	ANTINOVELISTS	ANTIPSYCHOTICS
ANTICAPITALIST	ANTICORROSIVE	ANTIFREEZES	ANTIMATERIALISM	ANTINOVELS	ANTIPYRESES
ANTICAPITALISTS	ANTICORROSIVES	ANTIFRICTION	ANTIMATERIALIST	ANTINUCLEAR	ANTIPYRESIS
ANTICARCINOGEN	ANTICORRUPTION	ANTIFUNGAL	ANTIMATTER	ANTINUCLEARIST	ANTIPYRETIC
ANTICARCINOGENS	ANTICREATIVE	ANTIFUNGALS	ANTIMATTERS	ANTINUCLEARISTS	ANTIPYRETICS
ANTICARIES	ANTICRUELTY	ANTIGAMBLING	ANTIMECHANIST	ANTINUCLEON	ANTIPYRINE
ANTICATALYST	ANTICULTURAL	ANTIGENICALLY	ANTIMECHANISTS	ANTINUCLEONS	ANTIPYRINES
ANTICATALYSTS	ANTICYCLONE	ANTIGENICITIES	ANTIMERGER	ANTINUKERS	ANTIQUARIAN
ANTICATHODE	ANTICYCLONES	ANTIGENICITY	ANTIMERISM	ANTIOBESITY	ANTIQUARIANISM
ANTICATHODES	ANTICYCLONIC	ANTIGLOBULIN	ANTIMERISMS	ANTIOBSCENITY	ANTIQUARIANISMS
ANTICATHOLIC	ANTIDANDRUFF	ANTIGLOBULINS	ANTIMETABOLE	ANTIODONTALGIC	ANTIQUARIANS
ANTICELLULITE	ANTIDAZZLE	ANTIGOVERNMENT	ANTIMETABOLES	ANTIODONTALGICS	ANTIQUARIES
ANTICENSORSHIP	ANTIDEFAMATION	ANTIGRAVITIES	ANTIMETABOLIC	ANTIOXIDANT	ANTIQUARKS
ANTICHLORISTIC	ANTIDEMOCRATIC	ANTIGRAVITY	ANTIMETABOLITE	ANTIOXIDANTS	ANTIQUATED
ANTICHLORS	ANTIDEPRESSANT	ANTIGROPELOES	ANTIMETABOLITES	ANTIOZONANT	ANTIQUATEDNESS
ANTICHOICE	ANTIDEPRESSANTS	ANTIGROPELOS	ANTIMETATHESES	ANTIOZONANTS	ANTIQUATES
ANTICHOICER	ANTIDEPRESSION	ANTIGROWTH	ANTIMETATHESIS	ANTIPARALLEL	ANTIQUATING
ANTICHOICERS	ANTIDERIVATIVE	ANTIGUERRILLA	ANTIMICROBIAL	ANTIPARALLELS	ANTIQUATION
ANTICHOLESTEROL	ANTIDERIVATIVES	ANTIHALATION	ANTIMICROBIALS	ANTIPARASITIC	ANTIQUATIONS
ANTICHOLINERGIC	ANTIDESICCANT	ANTIHALATIONS	ANTIMILITARISM	ANTIPARTICLE	ANTIQUENESS
ANTICHRIST	ANTIDESICCANTS	ANTIHELICES	ANTIMILITARISMS	ANTIPARTICLES	ANTIQUENESSES
ANTICHRISTIAN	ANTIDEVELOPMENT	ANTIHELIXES	ANTIMILITARIST	ANTIPARTIES	ANTIQUITARIAN

ANTIQUITARIANS	ANTISMOKING	ANTIVENENES	APICULTURES	APOLOGIZED	APOSTROPHIZES
ANTIQUITIES	ANTISMUGGLING	ANTIVENINS	APICULTURIST	APOLOGIZER	APOSTROPHIZING
ANTIRABIES	ANTISOCIAL	ANTIVENOMS	APICULTURISTS	APOLOGIZERS	APOSTROPHUS
ANTIRACHITIC	ANTISOCIALISM	ANTIVIOLENCE	APIOLOGIES	APOLOGIZES	APOSTROPHUSES
ANTIRACHITICS	ANTISOCIALISMS	ANTIVIRUSES	APISHNESSES	APOLOGIZING	APOTHECARIES
ANTIRACISM	ANTISOCIALIST	ANTIVITAMIN	APITHERAPIES	APOMICTICAL	APOTHECARY
ANTIRACISMS	ANTISOCIALISTS	ANTIVITAMINS	APITHERAPY	APOMICTICALLY	APOTHECIAL
ANTIRACIST	ANTISOCIALITIES	ANTIVIVISECTION	APLACENTAL	APOMORPHIA	APOTHECIUM
ANTIRACISTS	ANTISOCIALITY	ANTIWELFARE	APLANATICALLY	APOMORPHIAS	APOTHEGMATIC
ANTIRADARS	ANTISOCIALLY	ANTIWHALING	APLANATISM	APOMORPHINE	APOTHEGMATICAL
ANTIRADICAL	ANTISPASMODIC	ANTIWORLDS	APLANATISMS	APOMORPHINES	APOTHEGMATISE
ANTIRADICALISM	ANTISPASMODICS	ANTIWRINKLE	APLANOGAMETE	APONEUROSES	APOTHEGMATISED
ANTIRADICALISMS	ANTISPASTIC	ANTONINIANUS	APLANOGAMETES	APONEUROSIS	APOTHEGMATISES
ANTIRATIONAL	ANTISPASTS	ANTONINIANUSES	APLANOSPORE	APONEUROTIC	APOTHEGMATISING
ANTIRATIONALISM	ANTISPECULATION	ANTONOMASIA	APLANOSPORES	APOPEMPTIC	APOTHEGMATIST
ANTIRATIONALIST	ANTISPECULATIVE	ANTONOMASIAS	APOAPSIDES	APOPHLEGMATIC	APOTHEGMATISTS
ANTIRATIONALITY	ANTISPENDING	ANTONOMASTIC	APOCALYPSE	APOPHLEGMATICS	APOTHEGMATIZE
ANTIREALISM	ANTISTATIC	ANTONYMIES	APOCALYPSES	APOPHONIES	APOTHEGMATIZED
ANTIREALISMS	ANTISTATICS	ANTONYMOUS	APOCALYPTIC	APOPHTHEGM	APOTHEGMATIZES
ANTIREALIST	ANTISTORIES	ANTRORSELY	APOCALYPTICAL	APOPHTHEGMATIC	APOTHEGMATIZING
ANTIREALISTS	ANTISTRESS	ANTSINESSES	APOCALYPTICALLY	APOPHTHEGMATISE	APOTHEOSES
ANTIRECESSION	ANTISTRIKE	ANUCLEATED	APOCALYPTICISM	APOPHTHEGMATIST	APOTHEOSIS
ANTIREFLECTION	ANTISTROPHE	ANXIOLYTIC	APOCALYPTICISMS	APOPHTHEGMATIZE	APOTHEOSISE
ANTIREFLECTIVE	ANTISTROPHES	ANXIOLYTICS	APOCALYPTISM	APOPHTHEGMS	APOTHEOSISED
ANTIREFORM	ANTISTROPHIC	ANXIOUSNESS	APOCALYPTISMS	APOPHYLLITE	APOTHEOSISES
ANTIREGULATORY	ANTISTROPHON	ANXIOUSNESSES	APOCALYPTIST	APOPHYLLITES	APOTHEOSISING
ANTIREJECTION	ANTISTROPHONS	ANYTHINGARIAN	APOCALYPTISTS	APOPHYSATE	APOTHEOSIZE
ANTIRELIGION	ANTISTUDENT	ANYTHINGARIANS	APOCARPIES	APOPHYSEAL	APOTHEOSIZED
ANTIRELIGIOUS	ANTISTYLES	ANYWHITHER	APOCARPOUS	APOPHYSIAL	APOTHEOSIZES
ANTIREPUBLICAN	ANTISUBMARINE	AORISTICALLY	APOCATASTASES	APOPLECTIC	APOTHEOSIZING
ANTIREPUBLICANS	ANTISUBSIDY	AORTITISES	APOCATASTASIS	APOPLECTICAL	APOTROPAIC
ANTIRHEUMATIC	ANTISUBVERSION	AORTOGRAPHIC	APOCHROMAT	APOPLECTICALLY	APOTROPAICALLY
ANTIRHEUMATICS	ANTISUBVERSIVE	AORTOGRAPHIES	APOCHROMATIC	APOPLECTICS	APOTROPAISM
ANTIRITUALISM	ANTISUICIDE	AORTOGRAPHY	APOCHROMATISM	APOPLEXIES	APOTROPAISMS
ANTIRITUALISMS	ANTISYMMETRIC	APAGOGICAL	APOCHROMATISMS	APOPLEXING	APOTROPOUS
ANTIROMANTIC	ANTISYPHILITIC	APAGOGICALLY	APOCHROMATS	APOPROTEIN	APPALLINGLY
ANTIROMANTICISM	ANTISYPHILITICS	APARTHEIDS	APOCOPATED	APOPROTEINS	APPALOOSAS
ANTIROMANTICS	ANTISYZYGIES	APARTHOTEL	APOCOPATES	APOSEMATIC	APPARATCHIK
ANTIROYALIST	ANTISYZYGY	APARTHOTELS	APOCOPATING	APOSEMATICALLY	APPARATCHIKI
ANTIROYALISTS	ANTITAKEOVER	APARTMENTAL	APOCOPATION	APOSIOPESES	APPARATCHIKS
ANTIRRHINUM	ANTITARNISH	APARTMENTS	APOCOPATIONS	APOSIOPESIS	APPARATUSES
ANTIRRHINUMS	ANTITECHNOLOGY	APARTNESSES	APOCRYPHAL	APOSIOPETIC	APPARELING
ANTISATELLITE	ANTITERRORISM	APATHATONS	APOCRYPHALLY	APOSPORIES	APPARELLED
ANTISCIANS	ANTITERRORISMS	APATHETICAL	APOCRYPHALNESS	APOSPOROUS	APPARELLING
ANTISCIENCE	ANTITERRORIST	APATHETICALLY	APOCRYPHON	APOSTACIES	APPARELMENT
ANTISCIENCES	ANTITERRORISTS	APATOSAURS	APOCYNACEOUS	APOSTASIES	APPARELMENTS
ANTISCIENTIFIC	ANTITHALIAN	APATOSAURUS	APOCYNTHION	APOSTATICAL	APPARENCIES
ANTISCORBUTIC	ANTITHEISM	APATOSAURUSES	APOCYNTHIONS	APOSTATISE	APPARENTLY
ANTISCORBUTICS	ANTITHEISMS	APERIODICALLY	APODEICTIC	APOSTATISED	APPARENTNESS
ANTISCRIPTURAL	ANTITHEIST	APERIODICITIES	APODEICTICAL	APOSTATISES	APPARENTNESSES
ANTISECRECY	ANTITHEISTIC	APERIODICITY	APODEICTICALLY	APOSTATISING	APPARITION
ANTISEGREGATION	ANTITHEISTS	APERITIVES	APODICTICAL	APOSTATIZE	APPARITIONAL
ANTISEIZURE	ANTITHEORETICAL	APERTNESSES	APODICTICALLY	APOSTATIZED	APPARITIONS
ANTISENTIMENTAL	ANTITHESES	APFELSTRUDEL	APODYTERIUM	APOSTATIZES	APPARITORS
ANTISEPALOUS	ANTITHESIS	APFELSTRUDELS	APODYTERIUMS	APOSTATIZING	APPARTEMENT
ANTISEPARATIST	ANTITHETIC	APHAERESES	APOENZYMES	APOSTILLES	APPARTEMENTS
ANTISEPARATISTS	ANTITHETICAL	APHAERESIS	APOGAMOUSLY	APOSTLESHIP	APPASSIONATO
ANTISEPSES	ANTITHETICALLY	APHAERETIC	APOGEOTROPIC	APOSTLESHIPS	APPEACHING
ANTISEPSIS	ANTITHROMBIN	APHANIPTEROUS	APOGEOTROPISM	APOSTOLATE	APPEACHMENT
ANTISEPTIC	ANTITHROMBINS	APHELANDRA	APOGEOTROPISMS	APOSTOLATES	APPEACHMENTS
ANTISEPTICALLY	ANTITHROMBOTIC	APHELANDRAS	APOLAUSTIC	APOSTOLICAL	APPEALABILITIES
ANTISEPTICISE	ANTITHROMBOTICS	APHELIOTROPIC	APOLAUSTICS	APOSTOLICALLY	APPEALABILITY
ANTISEPTICISED	ANTITHYROID	APHELIOTROPISM	APOLIPOPROTEIN	APOSTOLICISM	APPEALABLE
ANTISEPTICISES	ANTITOBACCO	APHELIOTROPISMS	APOLIPOPROTEINS	APOSTOLICISMS	APPEALINGLY
ANTISEPTICISING	ANTITOXINS	APHETICALLY	APOLITICAL	APOSTOLICITIES	APPEALINGNESS
ANTISEPTICISM	ANTITRADES	APHETISING	APOLITICALITIES	APOSTOLICITY	APPEALINGNESSES
ANTISEPTICISMS	ANTITRADITIONAL	APHETIZING	APOLITICALITY	APOSTOLISE	APPEARANCE
ANTISEPTICIZE	ANTITRAGUS	APHIDICIDE	APOLITICALLY	APOSTOLISED	APPEARANCES
ANTISEPTICIZED	ANTITRANSPIRANT	APHIDICIDES	APOLITICISM	APOSTOLISES	APPEASABLE
ANTISEPTICIZES	ANTITRINITARIAN	APHORISERS	APOLITICISMS	APOSTOLISING	APPEASEMENT
ANTISEPTICIZING	ANTITRUSTER	APHORISING	APOLLONIAN	APOSTOLIZE	APPEASEMENTS
ANTISEPTICS	ANTITRUSTERS	APHORISTIC	APOLLONICON	APOSTOLIZED	APPEASINGLY
ANTISERUMS	ANTITRUSTS	APHORISTICALLY	APOLLONICONS	APOSTOLIZES	APPELLANTS
ANTISEXIST	ANTITUBERCULAR	APHORIZERS	APOLOGETIC	APOSTOLIZING	APPELLATION
ANTISEXISTS	ANTITUBERCULOUS	APHORIZING	APOLOGETICAL	APOSTROPHE	APPELLATIONAL
ANTISEXUAL	ANTITUMORAL	APHRODISIA	APOLOGETICALLY	APOSTROPHES	APPELLATIONS
ANTISEXUALITIES	ANTITUMORS	APHRODISIAC	APOLOGETICS	APOSTROPHIC	APPELLATIVE
ANTISEXUALITY	ANTITUSSIVE	APHRODISIACAL	APOLOGISED	APOSTROPHISE	APPELLATIVELY
ANTISHOCKS	ANTITUSSIVES	APHRODISIACS	APOLOGISER	APOSTROPHISED	APPELLATIVES
ANTISHOPLIFTING	ANTITYPHOID	APHRODISIAS	APOLOGISERS	APOSTROPHISES	APPENDAGES
ANTISLAVERY	ANTITYPICAL	APHRODITES	APOLOGISES	APOSTROPHISING	APPENDANTS
ANTISMOKER	ANTITYPICALLY	APICULTURAL	APOLOGISING	APOSTROPHIZE	APPENDECTOMIES
ANTISMOKERS	ANTIVENENE	APICULTURE	APOLOGISTS	APOSTROPHIZED	APPENDECTOMY

a

APPENDENTS	APPORTIONABLE	APPROPINQUED	AQUAPLANERS	ARBITRABLE	ARCHANGELIC
APPENDICECTOMY	APPORTIONED	APPROPINQUES	AQUAPLANES	ARBITRAGED	ARCHANGELS
APPENDICES	APPORTIONER	APPROPINQUING	AQUAPLANING	ARBITRAGER	ARCHBISHOP
APPENDICITIS	APPORTIONERS	APPROPINQUITIES	AQUAPLANINGS	ARBITRAGERS	ARCHBISHOPRIC
APPENDICITISES	APPORTIONING	APPROPINQUITY	AQUAPORINS	ARBITRAGES	ARCHBISHOPRICS
APPENDICLE	APPORTIONMENT	APPROPRIABLE	AQUARELLES	ARBITRAGEUR	ARCHBISHOPS
APPENDICLES	APPORTIONMENTS	APPROPRIACIES	AQUARELLIST	ARBITRAGEURS	ARCHDEACON
APPENDICULAR	APPORTIONS	APPROPRIACY	AQUARELLISTS	ARBITRAGING	ARCHDEACONRIES
APPENDICULARIAN	APPOSITELY	APPROPRIATE	AQUARIISTS	ARBITRAMENT	ARCHDEACONRY
APPENDICULATE	APPOSITENESS	APPROPRIATED	AQUAROBICS	ARBITRAMENTS	ARCHDEACONS
APPENDIXES	APPOSITENESSES	APPROPRIATELY	AQUATICALLY	ARBITRARILY	ARCHDIOCESAN
APPERCEIVE	APPOSITION	APPROPRIATENESS	AQUATINTAS	ARBITRARINESS	ARCHDIOCESE
APPERCEIVED	APPOSITIONAL	APPROPRIATES	AQUATINTED	ARBITRARINESSES	ARCHDIOCESES
APPERCEIVES	APPOSITIONS	APPROPRIATING	AQUATINTER	ARBITRATED	ARCHDUCHESS
APPERCEIVING	APPOSITIVE	APPROPRIATION	AQUATINTERS	ARBITRATES	ARCHDUCHESSES
APPERCEPTION	APPOSITIVELY	APPROPRIATIONS	AQUATINTING	ARBITRATING	ARCHDUCHIES
APPERCEPTIONS	APPOSITIVES	APPROPRIATIVE	AQUATINTIST	ARBITRATION	ARCHDUKEDOM
APPERCEPTIVE	APPRAISABLE	APPROPRIATOR	AQUATINTISTS	ARBITRATIONAL	ARCHDUKEDOMS
APPERCIPIENT	APPRAISALS	APPROPRIATORS	AQUICULTURAL	ARBITRATIONS	ARCHEGONIA
APPERTAINANCE	APPRAISEES	APPROVABLE	AQUICULTURE	ARBITRATIVE	ARCHEGONIAL
APPERTAINANCES	APPRAISEMENT	APPROVABLY	AQUICULTURES	ARBITRATOR	ARCHEGONIATE
APPERTAINED	APPRAISEMENTS	APPROVANCE	AQUICULTURIST	ARBITRATORS	ARCHEGONIATES
APPERTAINING	APPRAISERS	APPROVANCES	AQUICULTURISTS	ARBITRATRICES	ARCHEGONIUM
APPERTAINMENT	APPRAISING	APPROVINGLY	AQUIFEROUS	ARBITRATRIX	ARCHENEMIES
APPERTAINMENTS	APPRAISINGLY	APPROXIMAL	AQUIFOLIACEOUS	ARBITRATRIXES	ARCHENTERA
APPERTAINS	APPRAISIVE	APPROXIMATE	AQUILEGIAS	ARBITREMENT	ARCHENTERIC
APPERTINENT	APPRAISIVELY	APPROXIMATED	AQUILINITIES	ARBITREMENTS	ARCHENTERON
APPERTINENTS	APPRECIABLE	APPROXIMATELY	AQUILINITY	ARBITRESSES	ARCHENTERONS
APPETEEZEMENT	APPRECIABLY	APPROXIMATES	ARABESQUED	ARBITRIUMS	ARCHEOASTRONOMY
APPETEEZEMENTS	APPRECIATE	APPROXIMATING	ARABESQUES	ARBLASTERS	ARCHEOBOTANIES
APPETENCES	APPRECIATED	APPROXIMATION	ARABICISATION	ARBORACEOUS	ARCHEOBOTANIST
APPETENCIES	APPRECIATES	APPROXIMATIONS	ARABICISATIONS	ARBOREALLY	ARCHEOBOTANISTS
APPETISEMENT	APPRECIATING	APPROXIMATIVE	ARABICISED	ARBORESCENCE	ARCHEOBOTANY
APPETISEMENTS	APPRECIATION	APPULSIVELY	ARABICISES	ARBORESCENCES	ARCHEOLOGICAL
APPETISERS	APPRECIATIONS	APPURTENANCE	ARABICISING	ARBORESCENT	ARCHEOLOGICALLY
APPETISING	APPRECIATIVE	APPURTENANCES	ARABICIZATION	ARBORETUMS	ARCHEOLOGIES
APPETISINGLY	APPRECIATIVELY	APPURTENANT	ARABICIZATIONS	ARBORICULTURAL	ARCHEOLOGIST
APPETITION	APPRECIATOR	APPURTENANTS	ARABICIZED	ARBORICULTURE	ARCHEOLOGISTS
APPETITIONS	APPRECIATORILY	APRICATING	ARABICIZES	ARBORICULTURES	ARCHEOLOGY
APPETITIVE	APPRECIATORS	APRICATION	ARABICIZING	ARBORICULTURIST	ARCHEOMAGNETISM
APPETIZERS	APPRECIATORY	APRICATIONS	ARABILITIES	ARBORISATION	ARCHEOMETRIES
APPETIZING	APPREHENDED	APRIORISMS	ARABINOSES	ARBORISATIONS	ARCHEOMETRY
APPETIZINGLY	APPREHENDING	APRIORISTS	ARABINOSIDE	ARBORISING	ARCHEOZOOLOGIES
APPLAUDABLE	APPREHENDS	APRIORITIES	ARABINOSIDES	ARBORIZATION	ARCHEOZOOLOGIST
APPLAUDABLY	APPREHENSIBLE	APSIDIOLES	ARABISATION	ARBORIZATIONS	ARCHEOZOOLOGY
APPLAUDERS	APPREHENSIBLY	APTERYGIAL	ARABISATIONS	ARBORIZING	ARCHERESSES
APPLAUDING	APPREHENSION	APTITUDINAL	ARABIZATION	ARBORVITAE	ARCHERFISH
APPLAUDINGLY	APPREHENSIONS	APTITUDINALLY	ARABIZATIONS	ARBORVITAES	ARCHERFISHES
APPLAUSIVE	APPREHENSIVE	AQUABATICS	ARACHIDONIC	ARBOVIRUSES	ARCHESPORE
APPLAUSIVELY	APPREHENSIVELY	AQUABOARDS	ARACHNIDAN	ARBUSCULAR	ARCHESPORES
APPLECARTS	APPRENTICE	AQUACEUTICAL	ARACHNIDANS	ARCANENESS	ARCHESPORIA
APPLEDRAIN	APPRENTICED	AQUACEUTICALS	ARACHNOIDAL	ARCANENESSES	ARCHESPORIAL
APPLEDRAINS	APPRENTICEHOOD	AQUACULTURAL	ARACHNOIDITIS	ARCCOSINES	ARCHESPORIUM
APPLEJACKS	APPRENTICEHOODS	AQUACULTURE	ARACHNOIDITISES	ARCHAEBACTERIA	ARCHETYPAL
APPLERINGIE	APPRENTICEMENT	AQUACULTURES	ARACHNOIDS	ARCHAEBACTERIUM	ARCHETYPALLY
APPLERINGIES	APPRENTICEMENTS	AQUACULTURIST	ARACHNOLOGICAL	ARCHAEOBOTANIES	ARCHETYPES
APPLESAUCE	APPRENTICES	AQUACULTURISTS	ARACHNOLOGIES	ARCHAEOBOTANIST	ARCHETYPICAL
APPLESAUCES	APPRENTICESHIP	AQUADROMES	ARACHNOLOGIST	ARCHAEOBOTANY	ARCHETYPICALLY
APPLIANCES	APPRENTICESHIPS	AQUAEROBICS	ARACHNOLOGISTS	ARCHAEOLOGICAL	ARCHFIENDS
APPLICABILITIES	APPRENTICING	AQUAFARMED	ARACHNOLOGY	ARCHAEOLOGIES	ARCHGENETHLIAC
APPLICABILITY	APPRESSING	AQUAFARMING	ARACHNOPHOBE	ARCHAEOLOGIST	ARCHGENETHLIACS
APPLICABLE	APPRESSORIA	AQUAFITNESS	ARACHNOPHOBES	ARCHAEOLOGISTS	ARCHICARPS
APPLICABLENESS	APPRESSORIUM	AQUAFITNESSES	ARACHNOPHOBIA	ARCHAEOLOGY	ARCHIDIACONAL
APPLICABLY	APPRISINGS	AQUAFORTIS	ARACHNOPHOBIAS	ARCHAEOMETRIC	ARCHIDIACONATE
APPLICANTS	APPRIZINGS	AQUAFORTISES	ARAEOMETER	ARCHAEOMETRIES	ARCHIDIACONATES
APPLICATION	APPROACHABILITY	AQUAFORTIST	ARAEOMETERS	ARCHAEOMETRIST	ARCHIEPISCOPACY
APPLICATIONS	APPROACHABLE	AQUAFORTISTS	ARAEOMETRIC	ARCHAEOMETRISTS	ARCHIEPISCOPAL
APPLICATIVE	APPROACHED	AQUALEATHER	ARAEOMETRICAL	ARCHAEOMETRY	ARCHIEPISCOPATE
APPLICATIVELY	APPROACHES	AQUALEATHERS	ARAEOMETRIES	ARCHAEOPTERYX	ARCHILOWES
APPLICATOR	APPROACHING	AQUAMANALE	ARAEOMETRY	ARCHAEOPTERYXES	ARCHIMAGES
APPLICATORS	APPROBATED	AQUAMANALES	ARAEOSTYLE	ARCHAEORNIS	ARCHIMANDRITE
APPLICATORY	APPROBATES	AQUAMANILE	ARAEOSTYLES	ARCHAEORNISES	ARCHIMANDRITES
APPLIQUEING	APPROBATING	AQUAMANILES	ARAEOSYSTYLE	ARCHAEOZOOLOGY	ARCHIPELAGIAN
APPOGGIATURA	APPROBATION	AQUAMARINE	ARAEOSYSTYLES	ARCHAEZOOLOGIES	ARCHIPELAGIC
APPOGGIATURAS	APPROBATIONS	AQUAMARINES	ARAGONITES	ARCHAEZOOLOGY	ARCHIPELAGO
APPOGGIATURE	APPROBATIVE	AQUANAUTICS	ARAGONITIC	ARCHAICALLY	ARCHIPELAGOES
APPOINTEES	APPROBATORY	AQUAPHOBES	ARALIACEOUS	ARCHAICISM	ARCHIPELAGOS
APPOINTERS	APPROPINQUATE	AQUAPHOBIA	ARAUCARIAN	ARCHAICISMS	ARCHIPHONEME
APPOINTING	APPROPINQUATED	AQUAPHOBIAS	ARAUCARIAS	ARCHAISERS	ARCHIPHONEMES
APPOINTIVE	APPROPINQUATES	AQUAPHOBIC	ARBALESTER	ARCHAISING	ARCHIPLASM
APPOINTMENT	APPROPINQUATING	AQUAPHOBICS	ARBALESTERS	ARCHAISTIC	ARCHIPLASMIC
APPOINTMENTS	APPROPINQUATION	AQUAPLANED	ARBALISTER	ARCHAIZERS	ARCHIPLASMS
APPOINTORS	APPROPINQUE	AQUAPLANER	ARBALISTERS	ARCHAIZING	ARCHITECTED

ARCHITECTING	ARGUMENTIVE	ARQUEBUSIERS	ARTFULNESSES	ARTOCARPUS	ASHLERINGS
ARCHITECTONIC	ARGUMENTUM	ARRACACHAS	ARTHRALGIA	ARTOCARPUSES	ASHRAMITES
ARCHITECTONICS	ARGUMENTUMS	ARRAGONITE	ARTHRALGIAS	ARTSINESSES	ASININITIES
ARCHITECTS	ARGUTENESS	ARRAGONITES	ARTHRALGIC	ARUNDINACEOUS	ASKEWNESSES
ARCHITECTURAL	ARGUTENESSES	ARRAIGNERS	ARTHRECTOMIES	ARVICOLINE	ASPARAGINASE
ARCHITECTURALLY	ARGYRODITE	ARRAIGNING	ARTHRECTOMY	ARYBALLOID	ASPARAGINASES
ARCHITECTURE	ARGYRODITES	ARRAIGNINGS	ARTHRITICALLY	ARYBALLOSES	ASPARAGINE
ARCHITECTURES	ARHATSHIPS	ARRAIGNMENT	ARTHRITICS	ARYTAENOID	ASPARAGINES
ARCHITRAVE	ARHYTHMIAS	ARRAIGNMENTS	ARTHRITIDES	ARYTAENOIDS	ASPARAGUSES
ARCHITRAVED	ARIBOFLAVINOSES	ARRANGEABLE	ARTHRITISES	ARYTENOIDAL	ASPARTAMES
ARCHITRAVES	ARIBOFLAVINOSIS	ARRANGEMENT	ARTHRODESES	ARYTENOIDS	ASPARTATES
ARCHITYPES	ARIDNESSES	ARRANGEMENTS	ARTHRODESIS	ASAFETIDAS	ASPECTABLE
ARCHIVISTS	ARISTOCRACIES	ARRAYMENTS	ARTHRODIAE	ASAFOETIDA	ASPERATING
ARCHIVOLTS	ARISTOCRACY	ARREARAGES	ARTHRODIAL	ASAFOETIDAS	ASPERGATION
ARCHNESSES	ARISTOCRAT	ARRESTABLE	ARTHROGRAPHIES	ASARABACCA	ASPERGATIONS
ARCHOLOGIES	ARISTOCRATIC	ARRESTANTS	ARTHROGRAPHY	ASARABACCAS	ASPERGILLA
ARCHONSHIP	ARISTOCRATICAL	ARRESTATION	ARTHROMERE	ASBESTIFORM	ASPERGILLI
ARCHONSHIPS	ARISTOCRATISM	ARRESTATIONS	ARTHROMERES	ASBESTOSES	ASPERGILLOSES
ARCHONTATE	ARISTOCRATISMS	ARRESTINGLY	ARTHROMERIC	ASBESTOSIS	ASPERGILLOSIS
ARCHONTATES	ARISTOCRATS	ARRESTMENT	ARTHROPATHIES	ASBESTUSES	ASPERGILLS
ARCHOPLASM	ARISTOLOCHIA	ARRESTMENTS	ARTHROPATHY	ASCARIASES	ASPERGILLUM
ARCHOPLASMIC	ARISTOLOCHIAS	ARRHENOTOKIES	ARTHROPLASTIES	ASCARIASIS	ASPERGILLUMS
ARCHOPLASMS	ARISTOLOGIES	ARRHENOTOKY	ARTHROPLASTY	ASCENDABLE	ASPERGILLUS
ARCHOSAURIAN	ARISTOLOGY	ARRHYTHMIA	ARTHROPODAL	ASCENDANCE	ASPERITIES
ARCHOSAURS	ARISTOTLES	ARRHYTHMIAS	ARTHROPODAN	ASCENDANCES	ASPERSIONS
ARCHPRIEST	ARITHMETIC	ARRHYTHMIC	ARTHROPODOUS	ASCENDANCIES	ASPERSIVELY
ARCHPRIESTHOOD	ARITHMETICAL	ARRIVANCES	ARTHROPODS	ASCENDANCY	ASPERSOIRS
ARCHPRIESTHOODS	ARITHMETICALLY	ARRIVANCIES	ARTHROSCOPE	ASCENDANTLY	ASPERSORIA
ARCHPRIESTS	ARITHMETICIAN	ARRIVEDERCI	ARTHROSCOPES	ASCENDANTS	ASPERSORIES
ARCHPRIESTSHIP	ARITHMETICIANS	ARRIVISMES	ARTHROSCOPIC	ASCENDENCE	ASPERSORIUM
ARCHPRIESTSHIPS	ARITHMETICS	ARRIVISTES	ARTHROSCOPIES	ASCENDENCES	ASPERSORIUMS
ARCHRIVALS	ARITHMOMANIA	ARROGANCES	ARTHROSCOPY	ASCENDENCIES	ASPHALTERS
ARCOGRAPHS	ARITHMOMANIAS	ARROGANCIES	ARTHROSPORE	ASCENDENCY	ASPHALTING
ARCOLOGIES	ARITHMOMETER	ARROGANTLY	ARTHROSPORES	ASCENDENTS	ASPHALTITE
ARCSECONDS	ARITHMOMETERS	ARROGATING	ARTHROSPORIC	ASCENDEURS	ASPHALTITES
ARCTANGENT	ARITHMOPHOBIA	ARROGATION	ARTHROSPOROUS	ASCENDIBLE	ASPHALTUMS
ARCTANGENTS	ARITHMOPHOBIAS	ARROGATIONS	ARTICHOKES	ASCENSIONAL	ASPHERICAL
ARCTICALLY	ARMADILLOS	ARROGATIVE	ARTICULABLE	ASCENSIONIST	ASPHETERISE
ARCTOPHILE	ARMAMENTARIA	ARROGATORS	ARTICULACIES	ASCENSIONISTS	ASPHETERISED
ARCTOPHILES	ARMAMENTARIUM	ARRONDISSEMENT	ARTICULACY	ASCENSIONS	ASPHETERISES
ARCTOPHILIA	ARMAMENTARIUMS	ARRONDISSEMENTS	ARTICULATE	ASCERTAINABLE	ASPHETERISING
ARCTOPHILIAS	ARMATURING	ARROWGRASS	ARTICULATED	ASCERTAINABLY	ASPHETERISM
ARCTOPHILIES	ARMIGEROUS	ARROWGRASSES	ARTICULATELY	ASCERTAINED	ASPHETERISMS
ARCTOPHILIST	ARMILLARIA	ARROWHEADS	ARTICULATENESS	ASCERTAINING	ASPHETERIZE
ARCTOPHILISTS	ARMILLARIAS	ARROWROOTS	ARTICULATES	ASCERTAINMENT	ASPHETERIZED
ARCTOPHILS	ARMIPOTENCE	ARROWWOODS	ARTICULATING	ASCERTAINMENTS	ASPHETERIZES
ARCTOPHILY	ARMIPOTENCES	ARROWWORMS	ARTICULATION	ASCERTAINS	ASPHETERIZING
ARCUATIONS	ARMIPOTENT	ARSENIATES	ARTICULATIONS	ASCETICALLY	ASPHYXIANT
ARCUBALIST	ARMISTICES	ARSENICALS	ARTICULATIVE	ASCETICISM	ASPHYXIANTS
ARCUBALISTS	ARMLOCKING	ARSENOPYRITE	ARTICULATOR	ASCETICISMS	ASPHYXIATE
ARDUOUSNESS	ARMORIALLY	ARSENOPYRITES	ARTICULATORS	ASCITITIOUS	ASPHYXIATED
ARDUOUSNESSES	ARMOURLESS	ARSMETRICK	ARTICULATORY	ASCLEPIADACEOUS	ASPHYXIATES
ARECOLINES	AROMATASES	ARSMETRICKS	ARTIFACTUAL	ASCLEPIADS	ASPHYXIATING
AREFACTION	AROMATHERAPIES	ARSPHENAMINE	ARTIFICERS	ASCLEPIASES	ASPHYXIATION
AREFACTIONS	AROMATHERAPIST	ARSPHENAMINES	ARTIFICIAL	ASCOCARPIC	ASPHYXIATIONS
ARENACEOUS	AROMATHERAPISTS	ARTEFACTUAL	ARTIFICIALISE	ASCOGONIUM	ASPHYXIATOR
ARENATIONS	AROMATHERAPY	ARTEMISIAS	ARTIFICIALISED	ASCOMYCETE	ASPHYXIATORS
ARENICOLOUS	AROMATICALLY	ARTEMISININ	ARTIFICIALISES	ASCOMYCETES	ASPIDISTRA
AREOCENTRIC	AROMATICITIES	ARTEMISININS	ARTIFICIALISING	ASCOMYCETOUS	ASPIDISTRAS
AREOGRAPHIC	AROMATICITY	ARTERIALISATION	ARTIFICIALITIES	ASCORBATES	ASPIRATING
AREOGRAPHIES	AROMATISATION	ARTERIALISE	ARTIFICIALITY	ASCOSPORES	ASPIRATION
AREOGRAPHY	AROMATISATIONS	ARTERIALISED	ARTIFICIALIZE	ASCOSPORIC	ASPIRATIONAL
AREOLATION	AROMATISED	ARTERIALISES	ARTIFICIALIZED	ASCRIBABLE	ASPIRATIONS
AREOLATIONS	AROMATISES	ARTERIALISING	ARTIFICIALIZES	ASCRIPTION	ASPIRATORS
AREOLOGIES	AROMATISING	ARTERIALIZATION	ARTIFICIALIZING	ASCRIPTIONS	ASPIRATORY
AREOMETERS	AROMATIZATION	ARTERIALIZE	ARTIFICIALLY	ASCRIPTIVE	ASPIRINGLY
AREOSTYLES	AROMATIZATIONS	ARTERIALIZED	ARTIFICIALNESS	ASEPTICALLY	ASPIRINGNESS
AREOSYSTILE	AROMATIZED	ARTERIALIZES	ARTILLERIES	ASEPTICISE	ASPIRINGNESSES
AREOSYSTILES	AROMATIZES	ARTERIALIZING	ARTILLERIST	ASEPTICISED	ASPLANCHNIC
ARFVEDSONITE	AROMATIZING	ARTERIALLY	ARTILLERISTS	ASEPTICISES	ASPLENIUMS
ARFVEDSONITES	ARPEGGIATE	ARTERIOGRAM	ARTILLERYMAN	ASEPTICISING	ASPORTATION
ARGENTIFEROUS	ARPEGGIATED	ARTERIOGRAMS	ARTILLERYMEN	ASEPTICISM	ASPORTATIONS
ARGENTINES	ARPEGGIATES	ARTERIOGRAPHIC	ARTINESSES	ASEPTICISMS	ASSAFETIDA
ARGENTITES	ARPEGGIATING	ARTERIOGRAPHIES	ARTIODACTYL	ASEPTICIZE	ASSAFETIDAS
ARGILLACEOUS	ARPEGGIATION	ARTERIOGRAPHY	ARTIODACTYLOUS	ASEPTICIZED	ASSAFOETIDA
ARGILLIFEROUS	ARPEGGIATIONS	ARTERIOLAR	ARTIODACTYLS	ASEPTICIZES	ASSAFOETIDAS
ARGILLITES	ARPEGGIONE	ARTERIOLES	ARTISANSHIP	ASEPTICIZING	ASSAGAIING
ARGILLITIC	ARPEGGIONES	ARTERIOTOMIES	ARTISANSHIPS	ASEXUALITIES	ASSAILABLE
ARGONAUTIC	ARPILLERAS	ARTERIOTOMY	ARTISTICAL	ASEXUALITY	ASSAILANTS
ARGUMENTATION	ARQUEBUSADE	ARTERIOVENOUS	ARTISTICALLY	ASHAMEDNESS	ASSAILMENT
ARGUMENTATIONS	ARQUEBUSADES	ARTERITIDES	ARTISTRIES	ASHAMEDNESSES	ASSAILMENTS
ARGUMENTATIVE	ARQUEBUSES	ARTERITISES	ARTLESSNESS	ASHINESSES	ASSASSINATE
ARGUMENTATIVELY	ARQUEBUSIER	ARTFULNESS	ARTLESSNESSES	ASHLARINGS	ASSASSINATED

a

ASSASSINATES
ASSASSINATING
ASSASSINATION
ASSASSINATIONS
ASSASSINATOR
ASSASSINATORS
ASSAULTERS
ASSAULTING
ASSAULTIVE
ASSAULTIVELY
ASSAULTIVENESS
ASSEGAAIED
ASSEGAAIING
ASSEGAIING
ASSEMBLAGE
ASSEMBLAGES
ASSEMBLAGIST
ASSEMBLAGISTS
ASSEMBLANCE
ASSEMBLANCES
ASSEMBLAUNCE
ASSEMBLAUNCES
ASSEMBLERS
ASSEMBLIES
ASSEMBLING
ASSEMBLYMAN
ASSEMBLYMEN
ASSEMBLYWOMAN
ASSEMBLYWOMEN
ASSENTANEOUS
ASSENTATION
ASSENTATIONS
ASSENTATOR
ASSENTATORS
ASSENTIENT
ASSENTIENTS
ASSENTINGLY
ASSENTIVENESS
ASSENTIVENESSES
ASSERTABLE
ASSERTEDLY
ASSERTIBLE
ASSERTIONS
ASSERTIVELY
ASSERTIVENESS
ASSERTIVENESSES
ASSERTORIC
ASSESSABLE
ASSESSMENT
ASSESSMENTS
ASSESSORIAL
ASSESSORSHIP
ASSESSORSHIPS
ASSEVERATE
ASSEVERATED
ASSEVERATES
ASSEVERATING
ASSEVERATINGLY
ASSEVERATION
ASSEVERATIONS
ASSEVERATIVE
ASSEVERING
ASSIBILATE
ASSIBILATED
ASSIBILATES
ASSIBILATING
ASSIBILATION
ASSIBILATIONS
ASSIDUITIES
ASSIDUOUSLY
ASSIDUOUSNESS
ASSIDUOUSNESSES
ASSIGNABILITIES
ASSIGNABILITY
ASSIGNABLE
ASSIGNABLY
ASSIGNATION
ASSIGNATIONS
ASSIGNMENT
ASSIGNMENTS
ASSIMILABILITY
ASSIMILABLE
ASSIMILABLY

ASSIMILATE
ASSIMILATED
ASSIMILATES
ASSIMILATING
ASSIMILATION
ASSIMILATIONISM
ASSIMILATIONIST
ASSIMILATIONS
ASSIMILATIVE
ASSIMILATIVELY
ASSIMILATOR
ASSIMILATORS
ASSIMILATORY
ASSISTANCE
ASSISTANCES
ASSISTANTS
ASSISTANTSHIP
ASSISTANTSHIPS
ASSOCIABILITIES
ASSOCIABILITY
ASSOCIABLE
ASSOCIATED
ASSOCIATES
ASSOCIATESHIP
ASSOCIATESHIPS
ASSOCIATING
ASSOCIATION
ASSOCIATIONAL
ASSOCIATIONISM
ASSOCIATIONISMS
ASSOCIATIONIST
ASSOCIATIONISTS
ASSOCIATIONS
ASSOCIATIVE
ASSOCIATIVELY
ASSOCIATIVITIES
ASSOCIATIVITY
ASSOCIATOR
ASSOCIATORS
ASSOCIATORY
ASSOILMENT
ASSOILMENTS
ASSOILZIED
ASSOILZIEING
ASSOILZIES
ASSONANCES
ASSONANTAL
ASSONATING
ASSORTATIVE
ASSORTATIVELY
ASSORTEDNESS
ASSORTEDNESSES
ASSORTMENT
ASSORTMENTS
ASSUAGEMENT
ASSUAGEMENTS
ASSUAGINGS
ASSUBJUGATE
ASSUBJUGATED
ASSUBJUGATES
ASSUBJUGATING
ASSUEFACTION
ASSUEFACTIONS
ASSUETUDES
ASSUMABILITIES
ASSUMABILITY
ASSUMINGLY
ASSUMPSITS
ASSUMPTION
ASSUMPTIONS
ASSUMPTIVE
ASSUMPTIVELY
ASSURANCES
ASSUREDNESS
ASSUREDNESSES
ASSURGENCIES
ASSURGENCY
ASSYTHMENT
ASSYTHMENTS
ASTACOLOGICAL
ASTACOLOGIES
ASTACOLOGIST
ASTACOLOGISTS

ASTACOLOGY
ASTARBOARD
ASTATICALLY
ASTATICISM
ASTATICISMS
ASTEREOGNOSES
ASTEREOGNOSIS
ASTERIATED
ASTERIDIAN
ASTERIDIANS
ASTERISKED
ASTERISKING
ASTERISKLESS
ASTEROIDAL
ASTEROIDEAN
ASTEROIDEANS
ASTHENOPIA
ASTHENOPIAS
ASTHENOPIC
ASTHENOSPHERE
ASTHENOSPHERES
ASTHENOSPHERIC
ASTHMATICAL
ASTHMATICALLY
ASTHMATICS
ASTIGMATIC
ASTIGMATICALLY
ASTIGMATICS
ASTIGMATISM
ASTIGMATISMS
ASTOMATOUS
ASTONISHED
ASTONISHES
ASTONISHING
ASTONISHINGLY
ASTONISHMENT
ASTONISHMENTS
ASTOUNDING
ASTOUNDINGLY
ASTOUNDMENT
ASTOUNDMENTS
ASTRACHANS
ASTRAGALUS
ASTRAGALUSES
ASTRAKHANS
ASTRANTIAS
ASTRAPHOBIA
ASTRAPHOBIAS
ASTRAPHOBIC
ASTRAPOPHOBIA
ASTRAPOPHOBIAS
ASTRICTING
ASTRICTION
ASTRICTIONS
ASTRICTIVE
ASTRICTIVELY
ASTRINGENCE
ASTRINGENCES
ASTRINGENCIES
ASTRINGENCY
ASTRINGENT
ASTRINGENTLY
ASTRINGENTS
ASTRINGERS
ASTRINGING
ASTROBIOLOGIES
ASTROBIOLOGIST
ASTROBIOLOGISTS
ASTROBIOLOGY
ASTROBLEME
ASTROBLEMES
ASTROBOTANIES
ASTROBOTANY
ASTROCHEMISTRY
ASTROCOMPASS
ASTROCOMPASSES
ASTROCYTES
ASTROCYTIC
ASTROCYTOMA
ASTROCYTOMAS
ASTROCYTOMATA
ASTRODOMES
ASTRODYNAMICIST

ASTRODYNAMICS
ASTROFELLS
ASTROGEOLOGIES
ASTROGEOLOGIST
ASTROGEOLOGISTS
ASTROGEOLOGY
ASTROHATCH
ASTROHATCHES
ASTROLABES
ASTROLATRIES
ASTROLATRY
ASTROLOGER
ASTROLOGERS
ASTROLOGIC
ASTROLOGICAL
ASTROLOGICALLY
ASTROLOGIES
ASTROLOGIST
ASTROLOGISTS
ASTROMETRIC
ASTROMETRICAL
ASTROMETRIES
ASTROMETRY
ASTRONAUTIC
ASTRONAUTICAL
ASTRONAUTICALLY
ASTRONAUTICS
ASTRONAUTS
ASTRONAVIGATION
ASTRONAVIGATOR
ASTRONAVIGATORS
ASTRONOMER
ASTRONOMERS
ASTRONOMIC
ASTRONOMICAL
ASTRONOMICALLY
ASTRONOMIES
ASTRONOMISE
ASTRONOMISED
ASTRONOMISES
ASTRONOMISING
ASTRONOMIZE
ASTRONOMIZED
ASTRONOMIZES
ASTRONOMIZING
ASTROPHELS
ASTROPHOBIA
ASTROPHOBIAS
ASTROPHOBIC
ASTROPHOTOGRAPH
ASTROPHYSICAL
ASTROPHYSICALLY
ASTROPHYSICIST
ASTROPHYSICISTS
ASTROPHYSICS
ASTROSPHERE
ASTROSPHERES
ASTROTOURISM
ASTROTOURISMS
ASTROTOURIST
ASTROTOURISTS
ASTUCIOUSLY
ASTUCITIES
ASTUTENESS
ASTUTENESSES
ASYMMETRIC
ASYMMETRICAL
ASYMMETRICALLY
ASYMMETRIES
ASYMPTOMATIC
ASYMPTOTES
ASYMPTOTIC
ASYMPTOTICAL
ASYMPTOTICALLY
ASYNARTETE
ASYNARTETES
ASYNARTETIC
ASYNCHRONIES
ASYNCHRONISM
ASYNCHRONISMS
ASYNCHRONOUS
ASYNCHRONOUSLY
ASYNCHRONY

ASYNDETICALLY
ASYNDETONS
ASYNERGIAS
ASYNERGIES
ASYNTACTIC
ASYSTOLISM
ASYSTOLISMS
ATACAMITES
ATARACTICS
ATAVISTICALLY
ATCHIEVING
ATELECTASES
ATELECTASIS
ATELECTATIC
ATELEIOSES
ATELEIOSIS
ATHANASIES
ATHEISTICAL
ATHEISTICALLY
ATHEMATICALLY
ATHENAEUMS
ATHEOLOGICAL
ATHEOLOGIES
ATHEORETICAL
ATHERMANCIES
ATHERMANCY
ATHERMANOUS
ATHEROGENESES
ATHEROGENESIS
ATHEROGENIC
ATHEROMATA
ATHEROMATOUS
ATHEROSCLEROSES
ATHEROSCLEROSIS
ATHEROSCLEROTIC
ATHETISING
ATHETIZING
ATHLETICALLY
ATHLETICISM
ATHLETICISMS
ATHROCYTES
ATHROCYTOSES
ATHROCYTOSIS
ATHWARTSHIP
ATHWARTSHIPS
ATMOLOGIES
ATMOLOGIST
ATMOLOGISTS
ATMOLYSING
ATMOLYZING
ATMOMETERS
ATMOMETRIES
ATMOSPHERE
ATMOSPHERED
ATMOSPHERES
ATMOSPHERIC
ATMOSPHERICAL
ATMOSPHERICALLY
ATMOSPHERICS
ATOMICALLY
ATOMICITIES
ATOMISATION
ATOMISATIONS
ATOMISTICAL
ATOMISTICALLY
ATOMIZATION
ATOMIZATIONS
ATONALISMS
ATONALISTS
ATONALITIES
ATONEMENTS
ATONICITIES
ATRABILIAR
ATRABILIOUS
ATRABILIOUSNESS
ATRACURIUM
ATRACURIUMS
ATRAMENTAL
ATRAMENTOUS
ATROCIOUSLY
ATROCIOUSNESS
ATROCIOUSNESSES
ATROCITIES

ATROPHYING
ATTACHABLE
ATTACHMENT
ATTACHMENTS
ATTACKABLE
ATTAINABILITIES
ATTAINABILITY
ATTAINABLE
ATTAINABLENESS
ATTAINDERS
ATTAINMENT
ATTAINMENTS
ATTAINTING
ATTAINTMENT
ATTAINTMENTS
ATTAINTURE
ATTAINTURES
ATTEMPERED
ATTEMPERING
ATTEMPERMENT
ATTEMPERMENTS
ATTEMPTABILITY
ATTEMPTABLE
ATTEMPTERS
ATTEMPTING
ATTENDANCE
ATTENDANCES
ATTENDANCIES
ATTENDANCY
ATTENDANTS
ATTENDEMENT
ATTENDEMENTS
ATTENDINGS
ATTENDMENT
ATTENDMENTS
ATTENTIONAL
ATTENTIONS
ATTENTIVELY
ATTENTIVENESS
ATTENTIVENESSES
ATTENUANTS
ATTENUATED
ATTENUATES
ATTENUATING
ATTENUATION
ATTENUATIONS
ATTENUATOR
ATTENUATORS
ATTESTABLE
ATTESTANTS
ATTESTATION
ATTESTATIONS
ATTESTATIVE
ATTESTATOR
ATTESTATORS
ATTICISING
ATTICIZING
ATTIREMENT
ATTIREMENTS
ATTITUDINAL
ATTITUDINALLY
ATTITUDINARIAN
ATTITUDINARIANS
ATTITUDINISE
ATTITUDINISED
ATTITUDINISER
ATTITUDINISERS
ATTITUDINISING
ATTITUDINISINGS
ATTITUDINIZE
ATTITUDINIZED
ATTITUDINIZER
ATTITUDINIZERS
ATTITUDINIZES
ATTITUDINIZING
ATTITUDINIZINGS
ATTOLASERS
ATTOLLENTS
ATTOPHYSICS
ATTORNEYDOM
ATTORNEYDOMS
ATTORNEYED

ATTORNEYING	AUDIOLOGISTS	AUSTRALITE	AUTOCEPHALY	AUTOIONISATIONS	AUTOPHYTICALLY
ATTORNEYISM	AUDIOMETER	AUSTRALITES	AUTOCHANGER	AUTOIONIZATION	AUTOPILOTS
ATTORNEYISMS	AUDIOMETERS	AUSTRINGER	AUTOCHANGERS	AUTOIONIZATIONS	AUTOPISTAS
ATTORNEYSHIP	AUDIOMETRIC	AUSTRINGERS	AUTOCHTHON	AUTOJUMBLE	AUTOPLASTIC
ATTORNEYSHIPS	AUDIOMETRICALLY	AUTARCHICAL	AUTOCHTHONAL	AUTOJUMBLES	AUTOPLASTIES
ATTORNMENT	AUDIOMETRICIAN	AUTARCHIES	AUTOCHTHONES	AUTOKINESES	AUTOPLASTY
ATTORNMENTS	AUDIOMETRICIANS	AUTARCHIST	AUTOCHTHONIC	AUTOKINESIS	AUTOPOINTS
ATTRACTABLE	AUDIOMETRIES	AUTARCHISTS	AUTOCHTHONIES	AUTOKINETIC	AUTOPOLYPLOID
ATTRACTANCE	AUDIOMETRIST	AUTARKICAL	AUTOCHTHONISM	AUTOLATRIES	AUTOPOLYPLOIDS
ATTRACTANCES	AUDIOMETRISTS	AUTARKISTS	AUTOCHTHONISMS	AUTOLOADING	AUTOPOLYPLOIDY
ATTRACTANCIES	AUDIOMETRY	AUTECOLOGIC	AUTOCHTHONOUS	AUTOLOGIES	AUTOPSISTS
ATTRACTANCY	AUDIOPHILE	AUTECOLOGICAL	AUTOCHTHONOUSLY	AUTOLOGOUS	AUTOPSYING
ATTRACTANT	AUDIOPHILES	AUTECOLOGIES	AUTOCHTHONS	AUTOLYSATE	AUTOPTICAL
ATTRACTANTS	AUDIOPHILS	AUTECOLOGY	AUTOCHTHONY	AUTOLYSATES	AUTOPTICALLY
ATTRACTERS	AUDIOTAPED	AUTEURISMS	AUTOCLAVED	AUTOLYSING	AUTORADIOGRAM
ATTRACTING	AUDIOTAPES	AUTEURISTS	AUTOCLAVES	AUTOLYSINS	AUTORADIOGRAMS
ATTRACTINGLY	AUDIOTAPING	AUTHENTICAL	AUTOCLAVING	AUTOLYZATE	AUTORADIOGRAPH
ATTRACTION	AUDIOTYPING	AUTHENTICALLY	AUTOCOPROPHAGY	AUTOLYZATES	AUTORADIOGRAPHS
ATTRACTIONS	AUDIOTYPINGS	AUTHENTICATE	AUTOCORRELATION	AUTOLYZING	AUTORADIOGRAPHY
ATTRACTIVE	AUDIOTYPIST	AUTHENTICATED	AUTOCRACIES	AUTOMAKERS	AUTORICKSHAW
ATTRACTIVELY	AUDIOTYPISTS	AUTHENTICATES	AUTOCRATIC	AUTOMATABLE	AUTORICKSHAWS
ATTRACTIVENESS	AUDIOVISUAL	AUTHENTICATING	AUTOCRATICAL	AUTOMATICAL	AUTOROTATE
ATTRACTORS	AUDIOVISUALLY	AUTHENTICATION	AUTOCRATICALLY	AUTOMATICALLY	AUTOROTATED
ATTRAHENTS	AUDIOVISUALS	AUTHENTICATIONS	AUTOCRIMES	AUTOMATICITIES	AUTOROTATES
ATTRAPPING	AUDIPHONES	AUTHENTICATOR	AUTOCRITIQUE	AUTOMATICITY	AUTOROTATING
ATTRIBUTABLE	AUDITIONED	AUTHENTICATORS	AUTOCRITIQUES	AUTOMATICS	AUTOROTATION
ATTRIBUTED	AUDITIONER	AUTHENTICITIES	AUTOCROSSES	AUTOMATING	AUTOROTATIONS
ATTRIBUTER	AUDITIONERS	AUTHENTICITY	AUTOCUTIES	AUTOMATION	AUTOROUTES
ATTRIBUTERS	AUDITIONING	AUTHIGENIC	AUTOCYCLES	AUTOMATIONS	AUTOSCHEDIASM
ATTRIBUTES	AUDITORIAL	AUTHORCRAFT	AUTODESTRUCT	AUTOMATISATION	AUTOSCHEDIASMS
ATTRIBUTING	AUDITORIES	AUTHORCRAFTS	AUTODESTRUCTED	AUTOMATISATIONS	AUTOSCHEDIASTIC
ATTRIBUTION	AUDITORILY	AUTHORESSES	AUTODESTRUCTING	AUTOMATISE	AUTOSCHEDIAZE
ATTRIBUTIONAL	AUDITORIUM	AUTHORINGS	AUTODESTRUCTIVE	AUTOMATISED	AUTOSCHEDIAZED
ATTRIBUTIONS	AUDITORIUMS	AUTHORISABLE	AUTODESTRUCTS	AUTOMATISES	AUTOSCHEDIAZES
ATTRIBUTIVE	AUDITORSHIP	AUTHORISATION	AUTODIDACT	AUTOMATISING	AUTOSCHEDIAZING
ATTRIBUTIVELY	AUDITORSHIPS	AUTHORISATIONS	AUTODIDACTIC	AUTOMATISM	AUTOSCOPIC
ATTRIBUTIVENESS	AUDITRESSES	AUTHORISED	AUTODIDACTICISM	AUTOMATISMS	AUTOSCOPIES
ATTRIBUTIVES	AUGMENTABLE	AUTHORISER	AUTODIDACTS	AUTOMATIST	AUTOSEXING
ATTRIBUTOR	AUGMENTATION	AUTHORISERS	AUTOECIOUS	AUTOMATISTS	AUTOSOMALLY
ATTRIBUTORS	AUGMENTATIONS	AUTHORISES	AUTOECIOUSLY	AUTOMATIZATION	AUTOSPORES
ATTRISTING	AUGMENTATIVE	AUTHORISING	AUTOECISMS	AUTOMATIZATIONS	AUTOSTABILITIES
ATTRITIONAL	AUGMENTATIVELY	AUTHORISMS	AUTOEROTIC	AUTOMATIZE	AUTOSTABILITY
ATTRITIONS	AUGMENTATIVES	AUTHORITARIAN	AUTOEROTICISM	AUTOMATIZED	AUTOSTRADA
ATTRITTING	AUGMENTERS	AUTHORITARIANS	AUTOEROTICISMS	AUTOMATIZES	AUTOSTRADAS
ATTUITIONAL	AUGMENTING	AUTHORITATIVE	AUTOEROTISM	AUTOMATIZING	AUTOSTRADE
ATTUITIONS	AUGMENTORS	AUTHORITATIVELY	AUTOEROTISMS	AUTOMATONS	AUTOSUGGEST
ATTUITIVELY	AUGURSHIPS	AUTHORITIES	AUTOEXPOSURE	AUTOMATOUS	AUTOSUGGESTED
ATTUNEMENT	AUGUSTNESS	AUTHORIZABLE	AUTOEXPOSURES	AUTOMETERS	AUTOSUGGESTING
ATTUNEMENTS	AUGUSTNESSES	AUTHORIZATION	AUTOFLARES	AUTOMOBILE	AUTOSUGGESTION
ATYPICALITIES	AURALITIES	AUTHORIZATIONS	AUTOFOCUSES	AUTOMOBILED	AUTOSUGGESTIONS
ATYPICALITY	AUREATENESS	AUTHORIZED	AUTOGAMIES	AUTOMOBILES	AUTOSUGGESTIVE
ATYPICALLY	AUREATENESSES	AUTHORIZER	AUTOGAMOUS	AUTOMOBILIA	AUTOSUGGESTS
AUBERGINES	AURICULARLY	AUTHORIZERS	AUTOGENESES	AUTOMOBILING	AUTOTELLER
AUBERGISTE	AURICULARS	AUTHORIZES	AUTOGENESIS	AUTOMOBILISM	AUTOTELLERS
AUBERGISTES	AURICULATE	AUTHORIZING	AUTOGENETIC	AUTOMOBILISMS	AUTOTETRAPLOID
AUBRIETIAS	AURICULATED	AUTHORLESS	AUTOGENICS	AUTOMOBILIST	AUTOTETRAPLOIDS
AUCTIONARY	AURICULATELY	AUTHORSHIP	AUTOGENIES	AUTOMOBILISTS	AUTOTETRAPLOIDY
AUCTIONEER	AURIFEROUS	AUTHORSHIPS	AUTOGENOUS	AUTOMOBILITIES	AUTOTHEISM
AUCTIONEERED	AURISCOPES	AUTISTICALLY	AUTOGENOUSLY	AUTOMOBILITY	AUTOTHEISMS
AUCTIONEERING	AURISCOPIC	AUTOALLOGAMIES	AUTOGRAFTED	AUTOMORPHIC	AUTOTHEIST
AUCTIONEERS	AUSCULTATE	AUTOALLOGAMY	AUTOGRAFTING	AUTOMORPHICALLY	AUTOTHEISTS
AUCTIONING	AUSCULTATED	AUTOANTIBODIES	AUTOGRAFTS	AUTOMORPHISM	AUTOTIMERS
AUDACIOUSLY	AUSCULTATES	AUTOANTIBODY	AUTOGRAPHED	AUTOMORPHISMS	AUTOTOMIES
AUDACIOUSNESS	AUSCULTATING	AUTOBAHNEN	AUTOGRAPHIC	AUTOMOTIVE	AUTOTOMISE
AUDACIOUSNESSES	AUSCULTATION	AUTOBIOGRAPHER	AUTOGRAPHICAL	AUTONOMICAL	AUTOTOMISED
AUDACITIES	AUSCULTATIONS	AUTOBIOGRAPHERS	AUTOGRAPHICALLY	AUTONOMICALLY	AUTOTOMISES
AUDIBILITIES	AUSCULTATIVE	AUTOBIOGRAPHIC	AUTOGRAPHIES	AUTONOMICS	AUTOTOMISING
AUDIBILITY	AUSCULTATOR	AUTOBIOGRAPHIES	AUTOGRAPHING	AUTONOMIES	AUTOTOMIZE
AUDIBLENESS	AUSCULTATORS	AUTOBIOGRAPHY	AUTOGRAPHS	AUTONOMIST	AUTOTOMIZED
AUDIBLENESSES	AUSCULTATORY	AUTOBUSSES	AUTOGRAPHY	AUTONOMISTS	AUTOTOMIZES
AUDIENCIAS	AUSFORMING	AUTOCATALYSE	AUTOGRAVURE	AUTONOMOUS	AUTOTOMIZING
AUDIOBOOKS	AUSLANDERS	AUTOCATALYSED	AUTOGRAVURES	AUTONOMOUSLY	AUTOTOMOUS
AUDIOCASSETTE	AUSPICATED	AUTOCATALYSES	AUTOGUIDES	AUTOPHAGIA	AUTOTOXAEMIA
AUDIOCASSETTES	AUSPICATES	AUTOCATALYSING	AUTOHYPNOSES	AUTOPHAGIAS	AUTOTOXAEMIAS
AUDIOGENIC	AUSPICATING	AUTOCATALYSIS	AUTOHYPNOSIS	AUTOPHAGIES	AUTOTOXEMIA
AUDIOGRAMS	AUSPICIOUS	AUTOCATALYTIC	AUTOHYPNOTIC	AUTOPHAGOUS	AUTOTOXEMIAS
AUDIOGRAPH	AUSPICIOUSLY	AUTOCATALYZE	AUTOIMMUNE	AUTOPHANOUS	AUTOTOXINS
AUDIOGRAPHS	AUSPICIOUSNESS	AUTOCATALYZED	AUTOIMMUNITIES	AUTOPHOBIA	AUTOTRANSFORMER
AUDIOLOGIC	AUSTENITES	AUTOCATALYZES	AUTOIMMUNITY	AUTOPHOBIAS	AUTOTRANSFUSION
AUDIOLOGICAL	AUSTENITIC	AUTOCATALYZING	AUTOINFECTION	AUTOPHOBIES	AUTOTROPHIC
AUDIOLOGICALLY	AUSTERENESS	AUTOCEPHALIC	AUTOINFECTIONS	AUTOPHONIES	AUTOTROPHICALLY
AUDIOLOGIES	AUSTERENESSES	AUTOCEPHALIES	AUTOINOCULATION	AUTOPHYTES	AUTOTROPHIES
AUDIOLOGIST	AUSTERITIES	AUTOCEPHALOUS	AUTOIONISATION	AUTOPHYTIC	AUTOTROPHS

AUTOTROPHY
AUTOTYPIES
AUTOTYPING
AUTOTYPOGRAPHY
AUTOWINDER
AUTOWINDERS
AUTOWORKER
AUTOWORKERS
AUTOXIDATION
AUTOXIDATIONS
AUTUMNALLY
AUXANOMETER
AUXANOMETERS
AUXILIARIES
AUXOCHROME
AUXOCHROMES
AUXOMETERS
AUXOSPORES
AUXOTROPHIC
AUXOTROPHIES
AUXOTROPHS
AUXOTROPHY
AVAILABILITIES
AVAILABILITY
AVAILABLENESS
AVAILABLENESSES
AVAILINGLY
AVALANCHED
AVALANCHES
AVALANCHING

AVANTURINE
AVANTURINES
AVARICIOUS
AVARICIOUSLY
AVARICIOUSNESS
AVASCULARITIES
AVASCULARITY
AVENACEOUS
AVENGEMENT
AVENGEMENTS
AVENGERESS
AVENGERESSES
AVENTAILES
AVENTURINE
AVENTURINES
AVENTURINS
AVERAGENESS
AVERAGENESSES
AVERAGINGS
AVERRUNCATE
AVERRUNCATED
AVERRUNCATES
AVERRUNCATING
AVERRUNCATION
AVERRUNCATIONS
AVERRUNCATOR
AVERRUNCATORS
AVERSENESS
AVERSENESSES
AVERSIVELY

AVERSIVENESS
AVERSIVENESSES
AVERTIMENT
AVERTIMENTS
AVGOLEMONO
AVGOLEMONOS
AVIANISING
AVIANIZING
AVIATRESSES
AVIATRICES
AVIATRIXES
AVICULTURE
AVICULTURES
AVICULTURIST
AVICULTURISTS
AVIDNESSES
AVISANDUMS
AVISEMENTS
AVITAMINOSES
AVITAMINOSIS
AVITAMINOTIC
AVIZANDUMS
AVOCATIONAL
AVOCATIONALLY
AVOCATIONS
AVOIDANCES
AVOIRDUPOIS
AVOIRDUPOISES
AVOUCHABLE
AVOUCHMENT

AVOUCHMENTS
AVOUTERERS
AVOWABLENESS
AVOWABLENESSES
AVUNCULARITIES
AVUNCULARITY
AVUNCULARLY
AVUNCULATE
AVUNCULATES
AVVOGADORE
AVVOGADORES
AWAKENINGS
AWARENESSES
AWAYNESSES
AWELESSNESS
AWELESSNESSES
AWESOMENESS
AWESOMENESSES
AWESTRICKEN
AWESTRIKES
AWESTRIKING
AWFULNESSES
AWKWARDEST
AWKWARDISH
AWKWARDNESS
AWKWARDNESSES
AXENICALLY
AXEROPHTHOL
AXEROPHTHOLS
AXIALITIES

AXILLARIES
AXINOMANCIES
AXINOMANCY
AXIOLOGICAL
AXIOLOGICALLY
AXIOLOGIES
AXIOLOGIST
AXIOLOGISTS
AXIOMATICAL
AXIOMATICALLY
AXIOMATICS
AXIOMATISATION
AXIOMATISATIONS
AXIOMATISE
AXIOMATISED
AXIOMATISES
AXIOMATISING
AXIOMATIZATION
AXIOMATIZATIONS
AXIOMATIZE
AXIOMATIZED
AXIOMATIZES
AXIOMATIZING
AXISYMMETRIC
AXISYMMETRICAL
AXISYMMETRIES
AXISYMMETRY
AXOLEMMATA
AXONOMETRIC
AXONOMETRIES

AXONOMETRY
AXOPLASMIC
AYAHUASCAS
AYAHUASCOS
AYATOLLAHS
AYUNTAMIENTO
AYUNTAMIENTOS
AYURVEDICS
AZATHIOPRINE
AZATHIOPRINES
AZEDARACHS
AZEOTROPES
AZEOTROPIC
AZEOTROPIES
AZIDOTHYMIDINE
AZIDOTHYMIDINES
AZIMUTHALLY
AZOBENZENE
AZOBENZENES
AZOOSPERMIA
AZOOSPERMIAS
AZOOSPERMIC
AZOTAEMIAS
AZOTOBACTER
AZOTOBACTERS
AZYGOSPORE
AZYGOSPORES

Bb

BAALEBATIM
BABACOOTES
BABBITRIES
BABBITTING
BABBITTRIES
BABBLATIVE
BABBLEMENT
BABBLEMENTS
BABELESQUE
BABESIASES
BABESIASIS
BABESIOSES
BABESIOSIS
BABINGTONITE
BABINGTONITES
BABIROUSSA
BABIROUSSAS
BABIRUSSAS
BABOONERIES
BABYPROOFED
BABYPROOFING
BABYPROOFS
BABYSITTING
BACCALAUREAN
BACCALAUREATE
BACCALAUREATES
BACCHANALIA
BACCHANALIAN
BACCHANALIANISM
BACCHANALIANS
BACCHANALS
BACCHANTES
BACCIFEROUS
BACCIVOROUS
BACHARACHS
BACHELORDOM
BACHELORDOMS
BACHELORETTE
BACHELORETTES
BACHELORHOOD
BACHELORHOODS
BACHELORISM
BACHELORISMS
BACHELORSHIP
BACHELORSHIPS
BACILLAEMIA
BACILLAEMIAS
BACILLEMIA
BACILLEMIAS
BACILLICIDE
BACILLICIDES
BACILLIFORM
BACILLURIA
BACILLURIAS
BACITRACIN
BACITRACINS
BACKBENCHER
BACKBENCHERS
BACKBENCHES
BACKBITERS
BACKBITING
BACKBITINGS
BACKBITTEN
BACKBLOCKER
BACKBLOCKERS
BACKBLOCKS
BACKBOARDS

BACKBONELESS
BACKBREAKER
BACKBREAKERS
BACKBREAKING
BACKBURNED
BACKBURNING
BACKCHATTED
BACKCHATTING
BACKCHECKED
BACKCHECKING
BACKCHECKS
BACKCLOTHS
BACKCOMBED
BACKCOMBING
BACKCOUNTRIES
BACKCOUNTRY
BACKCOURTMAN
BACKCOURTMEN
BACKCOURTS
BACKCROSSED
BACKCROSSES
BACKCROSSING
BACKDATING
BACKDRAFTS
BACKDRAUGHT
BACKDRAUGHTS
BACKDROPPED
BACKDROPPING
BACKFIELDS
BACKFILLED
BACKFILLING
BACKFIRING
BACKFISCHES
BACKFITTED
BACKFITTING
BACKFITTINGS
BACKFLIPPED
BACKFLIPPING
BACKGAMMON
BACKGAMMONED
BACKGAMMONING
BACKGAMMONS
BACKGROUND
BACKGROUNDED
BACKGROUNDER
BACKGROUNDERS
BACKGROUNDING
BACKGROUNDS
BACKHANDED
BACKHANDEDLY
BACKHANDEDNESS
BACKHANDER
BACKHANDERS
BACKHANDING
BACKHAULED
BACKHAULING
BACKHOEING
BACKHOUSES
BACKLASHED
BACKLASHER
BACKLASHERS
BACKLASHES
BACKLASHING
BACKLIGHTED
BACKLIGHTING
BACKLIGHTS
BACKLISTED

BACKLISTING
BACKLOADED
BACKLOADING
BACKLOGGED
BACKLOGGING
BACKMARKER
BACKMARKERS
BACKPACKED
BACKPACKER
BACKPACKERS
BACKPACKING
BACKPACKINGS
BACKPEDALED
BACKPEDALING
BACKPEDALLED
BACKPEDALLING
BACKPEDALS
BACKPIECES
BACKRUSHES
BACKSCATTER
BACKSCATTERED
BACKSCATTERING
BACKSCATTERINGS
BACKSCATTERS
BACKSCRATCH
BACKSCRATCHED
BACKSCRATCHER
BACKSCRATCHERS
BACKSCRATCHES
BACKSCRATCHING
BACKSCRATCHINGS
BACKSHEESH
BACKSHEESHED
BACKSHEESHES
BACKSHEESHING
BACKSHISHED
BACKSHISHES
BACKSHISHING
BACKSHORES
BACKSIGHTS
BACKSLAPPED
BACKSLAPPER
BACKSLAPPERS
BACKSLAPPING
BACKSLASHES
BACKSLIDDEN
BACKSLIDER
BACKSLIDERS
BACKSLIDES
BACKSLIDING
BACKSLIDINGS
BACKSPACED
BACKSPACER
BACKSPACERS
BACKSPACES
BACKSPACING
BACKSPEERED
BACKSPEERING
BACKSPEERS
BACKSPEIRED
BACKSPEIRING
BACKSPEIRS
BACKSPLASH
BACKSPLASHES
BACKSTABBED
BACKSTABBER
BACKSTABBERS

BACKSTABBING
BACKSTABBINGS
BACKSTAGES
BACKSTAIRS
BACKSTALLS
BACKSTAMPED
BACKSTAMPING
BACKSTAMPS
BACKSTARTING
BACKSTITCH
BACKSTITCHED
BACKSTITCHES
BACKSTITCHING
BACKSTOPPED
BACKSTOPPING
BACKSTORIES
BACKSTREET
BACKSTREETS
BACKSTRETCH
BACKSTRETCHES
BACKSTROKE
BACKSTROKES
BACKSWINGS
BACKSWORDMAN
BACKSWORDMEN
BACKSWORDS
BACKSWORDSMAN
BACKSWORDSMEN
BACKTRACKED
BACKTRACKING
BACKTRACKINGS
BACKTRACKS
BACKVELDER
BACKVELDERS
BACKWARDATION
BACKWARDATIONS
BACKWARDLY
BACKWARDNESS
BACKWARDNESSES
BACKWASHED
BACKWASHES
BACKWASHING
BACKWATERS
BACKWOODSMAN
BACKWOODSMEN
BACKWOODSY
BACKWORKER
BACKWORKERS
BACTERAEMIA
BACTERAEMIAS
BACTEREMIA
BACTEREMIAS
BACTEREMIC
BACTERIALLY
BACTERIALS
BACTERICIDAL
BACTERICIDALLY
BACTERICIDE
BACTERICIDES
BACTERIOCIN
BACTERIOCINS
BACTERIOID
BACTERIOIDS
BACTERIOLOGIC
BACTERIOLOGICAL
BACTERIOLOGIES
BACTERIOLOGIST

BACTERIOLOGISTS
BACTERIOLOGY
BACTERIOLYSES
BACTERIOLYSIN
BACTERIOLYSINS
BACTERIOLYSIS
BACTERIOLYTIC
BACTERIOPHAGE
BACTERIOPHAGES
BACTERIOPHAGIC
BACTERIOPHAGIES
BACTERIOPHAGOUS
BACTERIOPHAGY
BACTERIOSES
BACTERIOSIS
BACTERIOSTASES
BACTERIOSTASIS
BACTERIOSTAT
BACTERIOSTATIC
BACTERIOSTATS
BACTERIOTOXIN
BACTERIOTOXINS
BACTERISATION
BACTERISATIONS
BACTERISED
BACTERISES
BACTERISING
BACTERIURIA
BACTERIURIAS
BACTERIZATION
BACTERIZATIONS
BACTERIZED
BACTERIZES
BACTERIZING
BACTEROIDS
BACTERURIA
BACTERURIAS
BACULIFORM
BACULOVIRUS
BACULOVIRUSES
BADDELEVITE
BADDELEVITES
BADDERLOCK
BADDERLOCKS
BADINAGING
BADINERIES
BADMINTONS
BADMOUTHED
BADMOUTHING
BAFFLEGABS
BAFFLEMENT
BAFFLEMENTS
BAFFLINGLY
BAGASSOSES
BAGASSOSIS
BAGATELLES
BAGGINESSES
BAGPIPINGS
BAGSWINGER
BAGSWINGERS
BAHUVRIHIS
BAIGNOIRES
BAILIESHIP
BAILIESHIPS
BAILIFFSHIP
BAILIFFSHIPS
BAILIWICKS

BAILLIAGES
BAILLIESHIP
BAILLIESHIPS
BAIRNLIEST
BAISEMAINS
BAITFISHES
BAKEAPPLES
BAKEBOARDS
BAKEHOUSES
BAKESTONES
BAKHSHISHED
BAKHSHISHES
BAKHSHISHING
BAKSHEESHED
BAKSHEESHES
BAKSHEESHING
BAKSHISHED
BAKSHISHES
BAKSHISHING
BALACLAVAS
BALALAIKAS
BALANCEABLE
BALANCINGS
BALANITISES
BALBRIGGAN
BALBRIGGANS
BALBUTIENT
BALCONETTE
BALCONETTES
BALDACHINO
BALDACHINOS
BALDACHINS
BALDAQUINS
BALDERDASH
BALDERDASHES
BALDERLOCKS
BALDERLOCKSES
BALDHEADED
BALDICOOTS
BALDMONEYS
BALDNESSES
BALECTIONS
BALEFULNESS
BALEFULNESSES
BALIBUNTAL
BALIBUNTALS
BALKANISATION
BALKANISATIONS
BALKANISED
BALKANISES
BALKANISING
BALKANIZATION
BALKANIZATIONS
BALKANIZED
BALKANIZES
BALKANIZING
BALKINESSES
BALLABILES
BALLADEERED
BALLADEERING
BALLADEERS
BALLADINES
BALLADISTS
BALLADMONGER
BALLADMONGERS
BALLADRIES
BALLANTING

BALLANWRASSE
BALLANWRASSES
BALLASTERS
BALLASTING
BALLBREAKER
BALLBREAKERS
BALLCARRIER
BALLCARRIERS
BALLERINAS
BALLETICALLY
BALLETOMANE
BALLETOMANES
BALLETOMANIA
BALLETOMANIAS
BALLFLOWER
BALLFLOWERS
BALLHANDLING
BALLHANDLINGS
BALLICATTER
BALLICATTERS
BALLISTICALLY
BALLISTICS
BALLISTITE
BALLISTITES
BALLISTOSPORE
BALLISTOSPORES
BALLOCKSED
BALLOCKSES
BALLOCKSING
BALLOONING
BALLOONINGS
BALLOONIST
BALLOONISTS
BALLOTTEMENT
BALLOTTEMENTS
BALLPLAYER
BALLPLAYERS
BALLPOINTS
BALLSINESS
BALLSINESSES
BALLYHOOED
BALLYHOOING
BALLYRAGGED
BALLYRAGGING
BALMACAANS
BALMINESSES
BALMORALITIES
BALMORALITY
BALNEARIES
BALNEATION
BALNEATIONS
BALNEOLOGICAL
BALNEOLOGIES
BALNEOLOGIST
BALNEOLOGISTS
BALNEOLOGY
BALNEOTHERAPIES
BALNEOTHERAPY
BALSAMIFEROUS
BALSAMINACEOUS
BALSAWOODS
BALTHASARS
BALTHAZARS
BALUSTERED
BALUSTRADE
BALUSTRADED
BALUSTRADES
BALZARINES
BAMBOOZLED
BAMBOOZLEMENT
BAMBOOZLEMENTS
BAMBOOZLER
BAMBOOZLERS
BAMBOOZLES
BAMBOOZLING
BANALISATION
BANALISATIONS
BANALISING
BANALITIES
BANALIZATION
BANALIZATIONS
BANALIZING
BANCASSURANCE

BANCASSURANCES
BANCASSURER
BANCASSURERS
BANDALORES
BANDBRAKES
BANDEIRANTE
BANDEIRANTES
BANDELIERS
BANDERILLA
BANDERILLAS
BANDERILLERO
BANDERILLEROS
BANDEROLES
BANDERSNATCH
BANDERSNATCHES
BANDICOOTED
BANDICOOTING
BANDICOOTS
BANDINESSES
BANDITRIES
BANDLEADER
BANDLEADERS
BANDMASTER
BANDMASTERS
BANDOBASTS
BANDOBUSTS
BANDOLEERED
BANDOLEERS
BANDOLEONS
BANDOLEROS
BANDOLIERED
BANDOLIERS
BANDOLINED
BANDOLINES
BANDOLINING
BANDONEONS
BANDONIONS
BANDSHELLS
BANDSPREADING
BANDSPREADINGS
BANDSTANDS
BANDWAGONS
BANDWIDTHS
BANEBERRIES
BANEFULNESS
BANEFULNESSES
BANGSRINGS
BANISHMENT
BANISHMENTS
BANISTERED
BANJULELES
BANKABILITIES
BANKABILITY
BANKROLLED
BANKROLLER
BANKROLLERS
BANKROLLING
BANKRUPTCIES
BANKRUPTCY
BANKRUPTED
BANKRUPTING
BANNERALLS
BANNERETTE
BANNERETTES
BANNISTERS
BANQUETEER
BANQUETEERS
BANQUETERS
BANQUETING
BANQUETINGS
BANQUETTES
BANTAMWEIGHT
BANTAMWEIGHTS
BANTERINGLY
BANTERINGS
BANTINGISM
BANTINGISMS
BAPHOMETIC
BAPTISMALLY
BAPTISTERIES
BAPTISTERY
BAPTISTRIES
BARAESTHESIA

BARAESTHESIAS
BARAGOUINS
BARASINGAS
BARASINGHA
BARASINGHAS
BARATHRUMS
BARBARESQUE
BARBARIANISM
BARBARIANISMS
BARBARIANS
BARBARICALLY
BARBARISATION
BARBARISATIONS
BARBARISED
BARBARISES
BARBARISING
BARBARISMS
BARBARITIES
BARBARIZATION
BARBARIZATIONS
BARBARIZED
BARBARIZES
BARBARIZING
BARBAROUSLY
BARBAROUSNESS
BARBAROUSNESSES
BARBASCOES
BARBASTELLE
BARBASTELLES
BARBASTELS
BARBECUERS
BARBECUING
BARBELLATE
BARBEQUING
BARBERRIES
BARBERSHOP
BARBERSHOPS
BARBITONES
BARBITURATE
BARBITURATES
BARBITURIC
BARBOTINES
BARCAROLES
BARCAROLLE
BARCAROLLES
BARDOLATER
BARDOLATERS
BARDOLATRIES
BARDOLATROUS
BARDOLATRY
BAREBACKED
BAREBACKING
BAREFACEDLY
BAREFACEDNESS
BAREFACEDNESSES
BAREFOOTED
BAREHANDED
BAREHANDING
BAREHEADED
BARELEGGED
BARENESSES
BARESTHESIA
BARESTHESIAS
BARGAINERS
BARGAINING
BARGAININGS
BARGANDERS
BARGEBOARD
BARGEBOARDS
BARGEMASTER
BARGEMASTERS
BARGEPOLES
BARHOPPING
BARKANTINE
BARKANTINES
BARKEEPERS
BARKENTINE
BARKENTINES
BARLEYCORN
BARLEYCORNS
BARMBRACKS
BARMINESSES
BARMITSVAH

BARMITSVAHS
BARMITZVAH
BARMITZVAHS
BARNBRACKS
BARNSBREAKING
BARNSBREAKINGS
BARNSTORMED
BARNSTORMER
BARNSTORMERS
BARNSTORMING
BARNSTORMINGS
BARNSTORMS
BAROCEPTOR
BAROCEPTORS
BARODYNAMICS
BAROGNOSES
BAROGNOSIS
BAROGRAPHIC
BAROGRAPHS
BAROMETERS
BAROMETRIC
BAROMETRICAL
BAROMETRICALLY
BAROMETRIES
BAROMETZES
BARONESSES
BARONETAGE
BARONETAGES
BARONETCIES
BARONETESS
BARONETESSES
BARONETICAL
BAROPHILES
BAROPHILIC
BAROPHORESES
BAROPHORESIS
BARORECEPTOR
BARORECEPTORS
BAROSCOPES
BAROSCOPIC
BAROTRAUMA
BAROTRAUMAS
BAROTRAUMATA
BARPERSONS
BARQUANTINE
BARQUANTINES
BARQUENTINE
BARQUENTINES
BARQUETTES
BARRACKERS
BARRACKING
BARRACKINGS
BARRACOONS
BARRACOOTA
BARRACOOTAS
BARRACOUTA
BARRACOUTAS
BARRACUDAS
BARRAMUNDA
BARRAMUNDAS
BARRAMUNDI
BARRAMUNDIES
BARRAMUNDIS
BARRATRIES
BARRATROUS
BARRATROUSLY
BARRELAGES
BARRELFULS
BARRELHEAD
BARRELHEADS
BARRELHOUSE
BARRELHOUSES
BARRELLING
BARRELSFUL
BARRENNESS
BARRENNESSES
BARRENWORT
BARRENWORTS
BARRETRIES
BARRETROUS
BARRETROUSLY
BARRETTERS
BARRICADED

BARRICADER
BARRICADERS
BARRICADES
BARRICADING
BARRICADOED
BARRICADOES
BARRICADOING
BARRICADOS
BARRIERING
BARRISTERIAL
BARRISTERS
BARRISTERSHIP
BARRISTERSHIPS
BARROWFULS
BARTENDERS
BARTENDING
BARTIZANED
BARYCENTRE
BARYCENTRES
BARYCENTRIC
BAROMETERS
BARYSPHERE
BARYSPHERES
BASALTWARE
BASALTWARES
BASEBALLER
BASEBALLERS
BASEBOARDS
BASEBURNER
BASEBURNERS
BASELESSLY
BASELESSNESS
BASELESSNESSES
BASELINERS
BASEMENTLESS
BASENESSES
BASEPLATES
BASERUNNER
BASERUNNERS
BASERUNNING
BASERUNNINGS
BASHAWISMS
BASHAWSHIP
BASHAWSHIPS
BASHFULNESS
BASHFULNESSES
BASHIBAZOUK
BASHIBAZOUKS
BASICITIES
BASICRANIAL
BASIDIOCARP
BASIDIOCARPS
BASIDIOMYCETE
BASIDIOMYCETES
BASIDIOMYCETOUS
BASIDIOSPORE
BASIDIOSPORES
BASIDIOSPOROUS
BASIFICATION
BASIFICATIONS
BASILICONS
BASIPETALLY
BASKETBALL
BASKETBALLS
BASKETFULS
BASKETLIKE
BASKETRIES
BASKETSFUL
BASKETWEAVE
BASKETWEAVER
BASKETWEAVERS
BASKETWEAVES
BASKETWORK
BASKETWORKS
BASMITZVAH
BASMITZVAHS
BASOPHILES
BASOPHILIA
BASOPHILIAS
BASOPHILIC
BASSETTING
BASSNESSES
BASSOONIST
BASSOONISTS

BASTARDIES
BASTARDISATION
BASTARDISATIONS
BASTARDISE
BASTARDISED
BASTARDISES
BASTARDISING
BASTARDISM
BASTARDISMS
BASTARDIZATION
BASTARDIZATIONS
BASTARDIZE
BASTARDIZED
BASTARDIZES
BASTARDIZING
BASTARDRIES
BASTINADED
BASTINADES
BASTINADING
BASTINADOED
BASTINADOES
BASTINADOING
BASTNAESITE
BASTNAESITES
BASTNASITE
BASTNASITES
BATFOWLERS
BATFOWLING
BATFOWLINGS
BATHETICALLY
BATHHOUSES
BATHMITSVAH
BATHMITSVAHS
BATHMITZVAH
BATHMITZVAHS
BATHMIZVAH
BATHMIZVAHS
BATHOCHROME
BATHOCHROMES
BATHOCHROMIC
BATHOLITES
BATHOLITHIC
BATHOLITHS
BATHOLITIC
BATHOMETER
BATHOMETERS
BATHOMETRIC
BATHOMETRICALLY
BATHOMETRIES
BATHOMETRY
BATHOPHILOUS
BATHOPHOBIA
BATHOPHOBIAS
BATHWATERS
BATHYBIUSES
BATHYGRAPHICAL
BATHYLIMNETIC
BATHYLITES
BATHYLITHIC
BATHYLITHS
BATHYLITIC
BATHYMETER
BATHYMETERS
BATHYMETRIC
BATHYMETRICAL
BATHYMETRICALLY
BATHYMETRIES
BATHYMETRY
BATHYPELAGIC
BATHYSCAPE
BATHYSCAPES
BATHYSCAPH
BATHYSCAPHE
BATHYSCAPHES
BATHYSCAPHS
BATHYSPHERE
BATHYSPHERES
BATMITZVAH
BATMITZVAHS
BATOLOGICAL
BATOLOGIES
BATOLOGIST
BATOLOGISTS

BATRACHIAN	BEANFEASTS	BECUDGELING	BEFINGERED	BEKNIGHTING	BELTCOURSE
BATRACHIANS	BEANSTALKS	BECUDGELLED	BEFINGERING	BEKNOTTING	BELTCOURSES
BATRACHOPHOBIA	BEARABILITIES	BECUDGELLING	BEFITTINGLY	BELABORING	BELVEDERES
BATRACHOPHOBIAS	BEARABILITY	BEDABBLING	BEFLAGGING	BELABOURED	BEMADAMING
BATRACHOPHOBIC	BEARABLENESS	BEDAGGLING	BEFLECKING	BELABOURING	BEMADDENED
BATSMANSHIP	BEARABLENESSES	BEDARKENED	BEFLOWERED	BELAMOURES	BEMADDENING
BATSMANSHIPS	BEARBAITING	BEDARKENING	BEFLOWERING	BELATEDNESS	BEMEDALLED
BATTAILOUS	BEARBAITINGS	BEDAZZLEMENT	BEFLUMMING	BELATEDNESSES	BEMEDALLING
BATTALIONS	BEARBERRIES	BEDAZZLEMENTS	BEFOREHAND	BELEAGUERED	BEMINGLING
BATTEILANT	BEARDEDNESS	BEDAZZLING	BEFORETIME	BELEAGUERING	BEMOANINGS
BATTELLING	BEARDEDNESSES	BEDCHAMBER	BEFORTUNED	BELEAGUERMENT	BEMONSTERED
BATTEMENTS	BEARDLESSNESS	BEDCHAMBERS	BEFORTUNES	BELEAGUERMENTS	BEMONSTERING
BATTENINGS	BEARDLESSNESSES	BEDCLOTHES	BEFORTUNING	BELEAGUERS	BEMONSTERS
BATTERINGS	BEARDTONGUE	BEDCOVERING	BEFOULMENT	BELEMNITES	BEMOUTHING
BATTILLING	BEARDTONGUES	BEDCOVERINGS	BEFOULMENTS	BELIEFLESS	BEMUDDLING
BATTINESSES	BEARGRASSES	BEDEAFENED	BEFRETTING	BELIEVABILITIES	BEMUFFLING
BATTLEBUSES	BEARISHNESS	BEDEAFENING	BEFRIENDED	BELIEVABILITY	BEMURMURED
BATTLEBUSSES	BEARISHNESSES	BEDEHOUSES	BEFRIENDER	BELIEVABLE	BEMURMURING
BATTLEDOOR	BEARNAISES	BEDELLSHIP	BEFRIENDERS	BELIEVABLY	BEMUSEMENT
BATTLEDOORS	BEASTHOODS	BEDELLSHIPS	BEFRIENDING	BELIEVINGLY	BEMUSEMENTS
BATTLEDORE	BEASTLIEST	BEDELSHIPS	BEFRINGING	BELIEVINGS	BEMUZZLING
BATTLEDORES	BEASTLINESS	BEDEVILING	BEFUDDLEMENT	BELIQUORED	BENCHERSHIP
BATTLEDRESS	BEASTLINESSES	BEDEVILLED	BEFUDDLEMENTS	BELIQUORING	BENCHERSHIPS
BATTLEDRESSES	BEATIFICAL	BEDEVILLING	BEFUDDLING	BELITTLEMENT	BENCHLANDS
BATTLEFIELD	BEATIFICALLY	BEDEVILMENT	BEGGARDOMS	BELITTLEMENTS	BENCHMARKED
BATTLEFIELDS	BEATIFICATION	BEDEVILMENTS	BEGGARHOOD	BELITTLERS	BENCHMARKING
BATTLEFRONT	BEATIFICATIONS	BEDFELLOWS	BEGGARHOODS	BELITTLING	BENCHMARKINGS
BATTLEFRONTS	BEATIFYING	BEDIAPERED	BEGGARLINESS	BELITTLINGLY	BENCHMARKS
BATTLEGROUND	BEATITUDES	BEDIAPERING	BEGGARLINESSES	BELLADONNA	BENCHWARMER
BATTLEGROUNDS	BEAUJOLAIS	BEDIGHTING	BEGGARWEED	BELLADONNAS	BENCHWARMERS
BATTLEMENT	BEAUJOLAISES	BEDIMMINGS	BEGGARWEEDS	BELLAMOURE	BENEDICITE
BATTLEMENTED	BEAUMONTAGE	BEDIMPLING	BEGINNINGLESS	BELLAMOURES	BENEDICITES
BATTLEMENTS	BEAUMONTAGES	BEDIRTYING	BEGINNINGS	BELLARMINE	BENEDICTION
BATTLEPIECE	BEAUMONTAGUE	BEDIZENING	BEGIRDLING	BELLARMINES	BENEDICTIONAL
BATTLEPIECES	BEAUMONTAGUES	BEDIZENMENT	BEGLADDING	BELLETRISM	BENEDICTIONS
BATTLEPLANE	BEAUTEOUSLY	BEDIZENMENTS	BEGLAMORED	BELLETRISMS	BENEDICTIVE
BATTLEPLANES	BEAUTEOUSNESS	BEDLAMISMS	BEGLAMORING	BELLETRIST	BENEDICTORY
BATTLESHIP	BEAUTEOUSNESSES	BEDLAMITES	BEGLAMOURED	BELLETRISTIC	BENEDICTUS
BATTLESHIPS	BEAUTICIAN	BEDPRESSER	BEGLAMOURING	BELLETRISTICAL	BENEDICTUSES
BATTLEWAGON	BEAUTICIANS	BEDPRESSERS	BEGLAMOURS	BELLETRISTS	BENEFACTED
BATTLEWAGONS	BEAUTIFICATION	BEDRAGGLED	BEGLERBEGS	BELLETTRIST	BENEFACTING
BATTOLOGICAL	BEAUTIFICATIONS	BEDRAGGLES	BEGLOOMING	BELLETTRISTS	BENEFACTION
BATTOLOGIES	BEAUTIFIED	BEDRAGGLING	BEGRIMMING	BELLFLOWER	BENEFACTIONS
BAUDRICKES	BEAUTIFIER	BEDRENCHED	BEGROANING	BELLFLOWERS	BENEFACTOR
BAUDRONSES	BEAUTIFIERS	BEDRENCHES	BEGRUDGERIES	BELLFOUNDER	BENEFACTORS
BAULKINESS	BEAUTIFIES	BEDRENCHING	BEGRUDGERS	BELLFOUNDERS	BENEFACTORY
BAULKINESSES	BEAUTIFULLER	BEDRIVELED	BEGRUDGERY	BELLFOUNDRIES	BENEFACTRESS
BAVARDAGES	BEAUTIFULLEST	BEDRIVELING	BEGRUDGING	BELLFOUNDRY	BENEFACTRESSES
BAVAROISES	BEAUTIFULLY	BEDRIVELLED	BEGRUDGINGLY	BELLHANGER	BENEFICENCE
BAWDINESSES	BEAUTIFULNESS	BEDRIVELLING	BEGUILEMENT	BELLHANGERS	BENEFICENCES
BAWDYHOUSE	BEAUTIFULNESSES	BEDROPPING	BEGUILEMENTS	BELLIBONES	BENEFICENT
BAWDYHOUSES	BEAUTIFYING	BEDRUGGING	BEGUILINGLY	BELLICOSELY	BENEFICENTIAL
BAYBERRIES	BEAVERBOARD	BEDSITTERS	BEGUINAGES	BELLICOSITIES	BENEFICENTLY
BAYONETING	BEAVERBOARDS	BEDSITTING	BEHAPPENED	BELLICOSITY	BENEFICIAL
BAYONETTED	BEBEERINES	BEDSPREADS	BEHAPPENING	BELLIGERATI	BENEFICIALLY
BAYONETTING	BEBLOODING	BEDSPRINGS	BEHAVIORAL	BELLIGERENCE	BENEFICIALNESS
BAZILLIONS	BEBLUBBERED	BEDWARFING	BEHAVIORALLY	BELLIGERENCES	BENEFICIALS
BEACHBALLS	BECARPETED	BEDWARMERS	BEHAVIORISM	BELLIGERENCIES	BENEFICIARIES
BEACHCOMBED	BECARPETING	BEDWETTERS	BEHAVIORISMS	BELLIGERENCY	BENEFICIARY
BEACHCOMBER	BECCACCIAS	BEECHDROPS	BEHAVIORIST	BELLIGERENT	BENEFICIATE
BEACHCOMBERS	BECCAFICOS	BEECHMASTS	BEHAVIORISTIC	BELLIGERENTLY	BENEFICIATED
BEACHCOMBING	BECHALKING	BEECHWOODS	BEHAVIORISTS	BELLIGERENTS	BENEFICIATES
BEACHCOMBINGS	BECHANCING	BEEFBURGER	BEHAVIOURAL	BELLOCKING	BENEFICIATING
BEACHCOMBS	BECHARMING	BEEFBURGERS	BEHAVIOURALLY	BELLPUSHES	BENEFICIATION
BEACHFRONT	BECKONINGS	BEEFEATERS	BEHAVIOURISM	BELLWETHER	BENEFICIATIONS
BEACHFRONTS	BECLAMORED	BEEFINESSES	BEHAVIOURISMS	BELLWETHERS	BENEFICING
BEACHGOERS	BECLAMORING	BEEFSTEAKS	BEHAVIOURIST	BELLYACHED	BENEFITERS
BEACHHEADS	BECLASPING	BEEKEEPERS	BEHAVIOURISTIC	BELLYACHER	BENEFITING
BEADBLASTED	BECLOAKING	BEEKEEPING	BEHAVIOURISTS	BELLYACHERS	BENEFITTED
BEADBLASTER	BECLOGGING	BEEKEEPINGS	BEHAVIOURS	BELLYACHES	BENEFITTING
BEADBLASTERS	BECLOTHING	BEERINESSES	BEHEADINGS	BELLYACHING	BENEPLACITO
BEADBLASTING	BECLOUDING	BEESWAXING	BEHIGHTING	BELLYBANDS	BENEVOLENCE
BEADBLASTS	BECLOWNING	BEESWINGED	BEHINDHAND	BELLYBUTTON	BENEVOLENCES
BEADHOUSES	BECOMINGLY	BEETLEBRAIN	BEHOLDINGS	BELLYBUTTONS	BENEVOLENT
BEADINESSES	BECOMINGNESS	BEETLEBRAINED	BEINGNESSES	BELOMANCIES	BENEVOLENTLY
BEADLEDOMS	BECOMINGNESSES	BEETLEBRAINS	BEINNESSES	BELONGINGNESS	BENEVOLENTNESS
BEADLEHOOD	BECOWARDED	BEETLEHEAD	BEJESUITED	BELONGINGNESSES	BENGALINES
BEADLEHOODS	BECOWARDING	BEETLEHEADED	BEJESUITING	BELONGINGS	BENIGHTEDLY
BEADLESHIP	BECQUERELS	BEETLEHEADS	BEJEWELING	BELOWDECKS	BENIGHTEDNESS
BEADLESHIPS	BECRAWLING	BEETMASTER	BEJEWELLED	BELOWGROUND	BENIGHTEDNESSES
BEADSWOMAN	BECROWDING	BEETMASTERS	BEJEWELLING	BELOWSTAIRS	BENIGHTENED
BEADSWOMEN	BECRUSTING	BEETMISTER	BEJUMBLING	BELSHAZZAR	BENIGHTENING
BEAMINESSES	BECUDGELED	BEETMISTERS	BEKNIGHTED	BELSHAZZARS	BENIGHTENINGS

BENIGHTENS	BERIBBONED	BESPECKLING	BETTERMOST	BIBLIOPHILES	BIENNIALLY
BENIGHTERS	BERKELIUMS	BESPECTACLED	BETTERNESS	BIBLIOPHILIC	BIENSEANCE
BENIGHTING	BERRYFRUIT	BESPEEDING	BETTERNESSES	BIBLIOPHILIES	BIENSEANCES
BENIGHTINGS	BERRYFRUITS	BESPITTING	BETULACEOUS	BIBLIOPHILISM	BIERKELLER
BENIGHTMENT	BERSAGLIERE	BESPORTING	BETWEENBRAIN	BIBLIOPHILISMS	BIERKELLERS
BENIGHTMENTS	BERSAGLIERI	BESPOTTEDNESS	BETWEENBRAINS	BIBLIOPHILIST	BIFACIALLY
BENIGNANCIES	BERSERKERS	BESPOTTEDNESSES	BETWEENITIES	BIBLIOPHILISTIC	BIFARIOUSLY
BENIGNANCY	BERTILLONAGE	BESPOTTING	BETWEENITY	BIBLIOPHILISTS	BIFIDITIES
BENIGNANTLY	BERTILLONAGES	BESPOUSING	BETWEENNESS	BIBLIOPHILS	BIFLAGELLATE
BENIGNITIES	BERYLLIOSES	BESPOUTING	BETWEENNESSES	BIBLIOPHILY	BIFOLIOLATE
BENTGRASSES	BERYLLIOSIS	BESPREADING	BETWEENTIME	BIBLIOPHOBIA	BIFUNCTIONAL
BENTHOPELAGIC	BERYLLIUMS	BESPRINKLE	BETWEENTIMES	BIBLIOPHOBIAS	BIFURCATED
BENTHOSCOPE	BESAINTING	BESPRINKLED	BETWEENWHILES	BIBLIOPOLE	BIFURCATES
BENTHOSCOPES	BESCATTERED	BESPRINKLES	BEVELLINGS	BIBLIOPOLES	BIFURCATING
BENTONITES	BESCATTERING	BESPRINKLING	BEVELMENTS	BIBLIOPOLIC	BIFURCATION
BENTONITIC	BESCATTERS	BESTAINING	BEVOMITING	BIBLIOPOLICAL	BIFURCATIONS
BENUMBEDNESS	BESCORCHED	BESTARRING	BEWAILINGLY	BIBLIOPOLIES	BIGAMOUSLY
BENUMBEDNESSES	BESCORCHES	BESTEADING	BEWAILINGS	BIBLIOPOLIST	BIGARREAUS
BENUMBINGLY	BESCORCHING	BESTIALISE	BEWEARYING	BIBLIOPOLISTS	BIGEMINIES
BENUMBMENT	BESCOURING	BESTIALISED	BEWELTERED	BIBLIOPOLY	BIGFOOTING
BENUMBMENTS	BESCRAWLED	BESTIALISES	BEWHISKERED	BIBLIOTHECA	BIGHEADEDLY
BENZALDEHYDE	BESCRAWLING	BESTIALISING	BEWILDERED	BIBLIOTHECAE	BIGHEADEDNESS
BENZALDEHYDES	BESCREENED	BESTIALISM	BEWILDEREDLY	BIBLIOTHECAL	BIGHEADEDNESSES
BENZANTHRACENE	BESCREENING	BESTIALISMS	BEWILDEREDNESS	BIBLIOTHECARIES	BIGHEARTED
BENZANTHRACENES	BESCRIBBLE	BESTIALITIES	BEWILDERING	BIBLIOTHECARY	BIGHEARTEDLY
BENZENECARBONYL	BESCRIBBLED	BESTIALITY	BEWILDERINGLY	BIBLIOTHECAS	BIGHEARTEDNESS
BENZENOIDS	BESCRIBBLES	BESTIALIZE	BEWILDERMENT	BIBLIOTHERAPIES	BIGMOUTHED
BENZIDINES	BESCRIBBLING	BESTIALIZED	BEWILDERMENTS	BIBLIOTHERAPY	BIGNONIACEOUS
BENZIMIDAZOLE	BESEECHERS	BESTIALIZES	BEWITCHERIES	BIBLIOTICS	BIGUANIDES
BENZIMIDAZOLES	BESEECHING	BESTIALIZING	BEWITCHERS	BIBLIOTIST	BIJECTIONS
BENZOAPYRENE	BESEECHINGLY	BESTIARIES	BEWITCHERY	BIBLIOTISTS	BIJOUTERIE
BENZOAPYRENES	BESEECHINGNESS	BESTICKING	BEWITCHING	BIBULOUSLY	BIJOUTERIES
BENZOCAINE	BESEECHINGS	BESTILLING	BEWITCHINGLY	BIBULOUSNESS	BILATERALISM
BENZOCAINES	BESEEMINGLY	BESTIRRING	BEWITCHMENT	BIBULOUSNESSES	BILATERALISMS
BENZODIAZEPINE	BESEEMINGNESS	BESTORMING	BEWITCHMENTS	BICAMERALISM	BILATERALLY
BENZODIAZEPINES	BESEEMINGNESSES	BESTOWMENT	BEWORRYING	BICAMERALISMS	BILBERRIES
BENZOFURAN	BESEEMINGS	BESTOWMENTS	BEWRAPPING	BICAMERALIST	BILDUNGSROMAN
BENZOFURANS	BESETMENTS	BESTRADDLE	BHIKKHUNIS	BICAMERALISTS	BILDUNGSROMANS
BENZOLINES	BESHADOWED	BESTRADDLED	BIANNUALLY	BICAPSULAR	BILECTIONS
BENZOPHENONE	BESHADOWING	BESTRADDLES	BIANNULATE	BICARBONATE	BILESTONES
BENZOPHENONES	BESHIVERED	BESTRADDLING	BIASNESSES	BICARBONATES	BILGEWATER
BENZOQUINONE	BESHIVERING	BESTRAUGHT	BIATHLETES	BICARPELLARY	BILGEWATERS
BENZOQUINONES	BESHOUTING	BESTREAKED	BIAURICULAR	BICENTENARIES	BILHARZIAL
BENZPYRENE	BESHREWING	BESTREAKING	BIAURICULATE	BICENTENARY	BILHARZIAS
BENZPYRENES	BESHROUDED	BESTREWING	BIBLICALLY	BICENTENNIAL	BILHARZIASES
BENZYLIDINE	BESHROUDING	BESTRIDABLE	BIBLICISMS	BICENTENNIALS	BILHARZIASIS
BENZYLIDINES	BESIEGEMENT	BESTRIDDEN	BIBLICISTS	BICEPHALOUS	BILHARZIOSES
BEPAINTING	BESIEGEMENTS	BESTRIDING	BIBLIOGRAPHER	BICHLORIDE	BILHARZIOSIS
BEPEARLING	BESIEGINGLY	BESTROWING	BIBLIOGRAPHERS	BICHLORIDES	BILIMBINGS
BEPEPPERED	BESIEGINGS	BESTSELLER	BIBLIOGRAPHIC	BICHROMATE	BILINGUALISM
BEPEPPERING	BESLAVERED	BESTSELLERDOM	BIBLIOGRAPHICAL	BICHROMATED	BILINGUALISMS
BEPESTERED	BESLAVERING	BESTSELLERDOMS	BIBLIOGRAPHIES	BICHROMATES	BILINGUALLY
BEPESTERING	BESLOBBERED	BESTSELLERS	BIBLIOGRAPHY	BICKERINGS	BILINGUALS
BEPIMPLING	BESLOBBERING	BESTSELLING	BIBLIOLATER	BICOLLATERAL	BILINGUIST
BEPLASTERED	BESLOBBERS	BESTUDDING	BIBLIOLATERS	BICOLOURED	BILINGUISTS
BEPLASTERING	BESLUBBERED	BESWARMING	BIBLIOLATRIES	BICOMPONENT	BILIOUSNESS
BEPLASTERS	BESLUBBERING	BETACAROTENE	BIBLIOLATRIST	BICONCAVITIES	BILIOUSNESSES
BEPOMMELLED	BESLUBBERS	BETACAROTENES	BIBLIOLATRISTS	BICONCAVITY	BILIRUBINS
BEPOMMELLING	BESMEARERS	BETACYANIN	BIBLIOLATROUS	BICONDITIONAL	BILIVERDIN
BEPOWDERED	BESMEARING	BETACYANINS	BIBLIOLATRY	BICONDITIONALS	BILIVERDINS
BEPOWDERING	BESMIRCHED	BETATTERED	BIBLIOLOGICAL	BICONVEXITIES	BILLABONGS
BEPRAISING	BESMIRCHES	BETATTERING	BIBLIOLOGIES	BICONVEXITY	BILLBOARDED
BEQUEATHABLE	BESMIRCHING	BETHANKING	BIBLIOLOGIST	BICORNUATE	BILLBOARDING
BEQUEATHAL	BESMOOTHED	BETHANKITS	BIBLIOLOGISTS	BICORPORATE	BILLBOARDS
BEQUEATHALS	BESMOOTHING	BETHINKING	BIBLIOLOGY	BICULTURAL	BILLFISHES
BEQUEATHED	BESMUDGING	BETHORNING	BIBLIOMANCIES	BICULTURALISM	BILLINGSGATE
BEQUEATHER	BESMUTCHED	BETHRALLED	BIBLIOMANCY	BICULTURALISMS	BILLINGSGATES
BEQUEATHERS	BESMUTCHES	BETHRALLING	BIBLIOMANE	BICUSPIDATE	BILLIONAIRE
BEQUEATHING	BESMUTCHING	BETHUMBING	BIBLIOMANES	BICUSPIDATES	BILLIONAIRES
BEQUEATHMENT	BESMUTTING	BETHUMPING	BIBLIOMANIA	BICYCLICAL	BILLIONTHS
BEQUEATHMENTS	BESOOTHING	BETHWACKED	BIBLIOMANIAC	BICYCLISTS	BILLOWIEST
BERASCALED	BESOTTEDLY	BETHWACKING	BIBLIOMANIACAL	BIDDABILITIES	BILLOWINESS
BERASCALING	BESOTTEDNESS	BETOKENING	BIBLIOMANIACS	BIDDABILITY	BILLOWINESSES
BERBERIDACEOUS	BESOTTEDNESSES	BETREADING	BIBLIOMANIAS	BIDDABLENESS	BILLOWINGS
BERBERINES	BESPANGLED	BETRIMMING	BIBLIOPEGIC	BIDDABLENESSES	BILLPOSTER
BERBERISES	BESPANGLES	BETROTHALS	BIBLIOPEGIES	BIDENTATED	BILLPOSTERS
BEREAVEMENT	BESPANGLING	BETROTHEDS	BIBLIOPEGIST	BIDIALECTAL	BILLPOSTING
BEREAVEMENTS	BESPATTERED	BETROTHING	BIBLIOPEGISTS	BIDIALECTALISM	BILLPOSTINGS
BERGAMASKS	BESPATTERING	BETROTHMENT	BIBLIOPEGY	BIDIALECTALISMS	BILLSTICKER
BERGANDERS	BESPATTERS	BETROTHMENTS	BIBLIOPHAGIST	BIDIRECTIONAL	BILLSTICKERS
BERGOMASKS	BESPEAKING	BETTERINGS	BIBLIOPHAGISTS	BIDIRECTIONALLY	BILLSTICKING
BERGSCHRUND	BESPECKLED	BETTERMENT	BIBLIOPHIL	BIDONVILLE	BILLSTICKINGS
BERGSCHRUNDS	BESPECKLES	BETTERMENTS	BIBLIOPHILE	BIDONVILLES	BILLYCOCKS

BILOCATION	BIOCONTROLS	BIOLOGICALS	BIOSOCIALLY	BIRDHOUSES	BITTERLINGS
BILOCATIONS	BIOCONVERSION	BIOLOGISMS	BIOSPHERES	BIRDLIMING	BITTERNESS
BILOCULATE	BIOCONVERSIONS	BIOLOGISTIC	BIOSPHERIC	BIRDWATCHED	BITTERNESSES
BIMANUALLY	BIODEGRADABLE	BIOLOGISTS	BIOSTATICALLY	BIRDWATCHER	BITTERNUTS
BIMESTRIAL	BIODEGRADATION	BIOLUMINESCENCE	BIOSTATICS	BIRDWATCHERS	BITTERROOT
BIMESTRIALLY	BIODEGRADATIONS	BIOLUMINESCENT	BIOSTATISTICAL	BIRDWATCHES	BITTERROOTS
BIMETALLIC	BIODEGRADE	BIOMAGNETICS	BIOSTATISTICIAN	BIRDWATCHING	BITTERSWEET
BIMETALLICS	BIODEGRADED	BIOMARKERS	BIOSTATISTICS	BIREFRINGENCE	BITTERSWEETLY
BIMETALLISM	BIODEGRADES	BIOMATERIAL	BIOSTRATIGRAPHY	BIREFRINGENCES	BITTERSWEETNESS
BIMETALLISMS	BIODEGRADING	BIOMATERIALS	BIOSTROMES	BIREFRINGENT	BITTERSWEETS
BIMETALLIST	BIODESTRUCTIBLE	BIOMATHEMATICAL	BIOSURGERIES	BIROSTRATE	BITTERWEED
BIMETALLISTIC	BIODIESELS	BIOMATHEMATICS	BIOSURGERY	BIRTHMARKS	BITTERWEEDS
BIMETALLISTS	BIODIVERSITIES	BIOMECHANICAL	BIOSYNTHESES	BIRTHNAMES	BITTERWOOD
BIMILLENARIES	BIODIVERSITY	BIOMECHANICALLY	BIOSYNTHESIS	BIRTHNIGHT	BITTERWOODS
BIMILLENARY	BIODYNAMIC	BIOMECHANICS	BIOSYNTHETIC	BIRTHNIGHTS	BITTINESSES
BIMILLENNIA	BIODYNAMICAL	BIOMEDICAL	BIOSYSTEMATIC	BIRTHPLACE	BITUMINATE
BIMILLENNIAL	BIODYNAMICS	BIOMEDICINE	BIOSYSTEMATICS	BIRTHPLACES	BITUMINATED
BIMILLENNIALS	BIOECOLOGICAL	BIOMEDICINES	BIOSYSTEMATIST	BIRTHRATES	BITUMINATES
BIMILLENNIUM	BIOECOLOGICALLY	BIOMETEOROLOGY	BIOSYSTEMATISTS	BIRTHRIGHT	BITUMINATING
BIMILLENNIUMS	BIOECOLOGIES	BIOMETRICAL	BIOTECHNICAL	BIRTHRIGHTS	BITUMINISATION
BIMODALITIES	BIOECOLOGIST	BIOMETRICALLY	BIOTECHNOLOGIES	BIRTHROOTS	BITUMINISATIONS
BIMODALITY	BIOECOLOGISTS	BIOMETRICIAN	BIOTECHNOLOGIST	BIRTHSTONE	BITUMINISE
BIMOLECULAR	BIOECOLOGY	BIOMETRICIANS	BIOTECHNOLOGY	BIRTHSTONES	BITUMINISED
BIMOLECULARLY	BIOELECTRIC	BIOMETRICS	BIOTELEMETRIC	BIRTHWORTS	BITUMINISES
BIMONTHLIES	BIOELECTRICAL	BIOMETRIES	BIOTELEMETRIES	BISECTIONAL	BITUMINISING
BIMORPHEMIC	BIOELECTRICITY	BIOMIMETIC	BIOTELEMETRY	BISECTIONALLY	BITUMINIZATION
BINATIONAL	BIOENERGETIC	BIOMIMETICS	BIOTERRORS	BISECTIONS	BITUMINIZATIONS
BINAURALLY	BIOENERGETICS	BIOMIMICRIES	BIOTICALLY	BISECTRICES	BITUMINIZE
BINDINGNESS	BIOENGINEER	BIOMIMICRY	BIOTURBATION	BISEXUALISM	BITUMINIZED
BINDINGNESSES	BIOENGINEERED	BIOMININGS	BIOTURBATIONS	BISEXUALISMS	BITUMINIZES
BINOCULARITIES	BIOENGINEERING	BIOMOLECULAR	BIOWEAPONS	BISEXUALITIES	BITUMINIZING
BINOCULARITY	BIOENGINEERINGS	BIOMOLECULE	BIPARENTAL	BISEXUALITY	BITUMINOUS
BINOCULARLY	BIOENGINEERS	BIOMOLECULES	BIPARENTALLY	BISEXUALLY	BIUNIQUENESS
BINOCULARS	BIOETHICAL	BIOMORPHIC	BIPARIETAL	BISHOPBIRD	BIUNIQUENESSES
BINOMIALLY	BIOETHICIST	BIONOMICALLY	BIPARTISAN	BISHOPBIRDS	BIVALENCES
BINOMINALS	BIOETHICISTS	BIONOMISTS	BIPARTISANISM	BISHOPDOMS	BIVALENCIES
BINTURONGS	BIOFEEDBACK	BIOPARENTS	BIPARTISANISMS	BISHOPESSES	BIVALVULAR
BINUCLEATE	BIOFEEDBACKS	BIOPESTICIDAL	BIPARTISANSHIP	BISHOPRICS	BIVARIANTS
BINUCLEATED	BIOFLAVONOID	BIOPESTICIDE	BIPARTISANSHIPS	BISHOPWEED	BIVARIATES
BIOACCUMULATE	BIOFLAVONOIDS	BIOPESTICIDES	BIPARTITELY	BISHOPWEEDS	BIVOUACKED
BIOACCUMULATED	BIOFOULERS	BIOPHILIAS	BIPARTITION	BISMUTHINITE	BIVOUACKING
BIOACCUMULATES	BIOFOULING	BIOPHYSICAL	BIPARTITIONS	BISMUTHINITES	BIWEEKLIES
BIOACCUMULATING	BIOFOULINGS	BIOPHYSICALLY	BIPEDALISM	BISMUTHOUS	BIZARRENESS
BIOACCUMULATION	BIOGENESES	BIOPHYSICIST	BIPEDALISMS	BISOCIATION	BIZARRENESSES
BIOACOUSTICS	BIOGENESIS	BIOPHYSICISTS	BIPEDALITIES	BISOCIATIONS	BIZARRERIE
BIOACTIVITIES	BIOGENETIC	BIOPHYSICS	BIPEDALITY	BISOCIATIVE	BIZARRERIES
BIOACTIVITY	BIOGENETICAL	BIOPIRACIES	BIPETALOUS	BISPHOSPHONATE	BLABBERING
BIOAERATION	BIOGENETICALLY	BIOPIRATES	BIPINNARIA	BISPHOSPHONATES	BLABBERMOUTH
BIOAERATIONS	BIOGENETICS	BIOPLASMIC	BIPINNARIAS	BISSEXTILE	BLABBERMOUTHS
BIOAERONAUTICS	BIOGEOCHEMICAL	BIOPOIESES	BIPINNATELY	BISSEXTILES	BLACKAMOOR
BIOASSAYED	BIOGEOCHEMICALS	BIOPOIESIS	BIPOLARISATION	BISTOURIES	BLACKAMOORS
BIOASSAYING	BIOGEOCHEMISTRY	BIOPOLYMER	BIPOLARISATIONS	BISULFATES	BLACKBALLED
BIOASTRONAUTICS	BIOGEOGRAPHER	BIOPOLYMERS	BIPOLARISE	BISULFIDES	BLACKBALLING
BIOAVAILABILITY	BIOGEOGRAPHERS	BIOPROSPECTING	BIPOLARISED	BISULFITES	BLACKBALLINGS
BIOAVAILABLE	BIOGEOGRAPHIC	BIOPROSPECTINGS	BIPOLARISES	BISULPHATE	BLACKBALLS
BIOCATALYST	BIOGEOGRAPHICAL	BIOPSYCHOLOGIES	BIPOLARISING	BISULPHATES	BLACKBANDS
BIOCATALYSTS	BIOGEOGRAPHIES	BIOPSYCHOLOGY	BIPOLARITIES	BISULPHIDE	BLACKBERRIED
BIOCATALYTIC	BIOGEOGRAPHY	BIOREACTOR	BIPOLARITY	BISULPHIDES	BLACKBERRIES
BIOCELLATE	BIOGRAPHED	BIOREACTORS	BIPOLARIZATION	BISULPHITE	BLACKBERRY
BIOCENOLOGIES	BIOGRAPHEE	BIOREAGENT	BIPOLARIZATIONS	BISULPHITES	BLACKBERRYING
BIOCENOLOGY	BIOGRAPHEES	BIOREAGENTS	BIPOLARIZE	BISYMMETRIC	BLACKBERRYINGS
BIOCENOSES	BIOGRAPHER	BIOREGIONAL	BIPOLARIZED	BISYMMETRICAL	BLACKBIRDED
BIOCENOSIS	BIOGRAPHERS	BIOREGIONALISM	BIPOLARIZES	BISYMMETRICALLY	BLACKBIRDER
BIOCENOTIC	BIOGRAPHIC	BIOREGIONALISMS	BIPOLARIZING	BISYMMETRIES	BLACKBIRDERS
BIOCHEMICAL	BIOGRAPHICAL	BIOREGIONALIST	BIPROPELLANT	BISYMMETRY	BLACKBIRDING
BIOCHEMICALLY	BIOGRAPHICALLY	BIOREGIONALISTS	BIPROPELLANTS	BITARTRATE	BLACKBIRDINGS
BIOCHEMICALS	BIOGRAPHIES	BIOREGIONS	BIPYRAMIDAL	BITARTRATES	BLACKBIRDS
BIOCHEMIST	BIOGRAPHING	BIOREMEDIATION	BIPYRAMIDS	BITCHERIES	BLACKBOARD
BIOCHEMISTRIES	BIOGRAPHISE	BIOREMEDIATIONS	BIQUADRATE	BITCHFESTS	BLACKBOARDS
BIOCHEMISTRY	BIOGRAPHISED	BIORHYTHMIC	BIQUADRATES	BITCHINESS	BLACKBODIES
BIOCHEMISTS	BIOGRAPHISES	BIORHYTHMICALLY	BIQUADRATIC	BITCHINESSES	BLACKBUCKS
BIOCLASTIC	BIOGRAPHISING	BIORHYTHMICS	BIQUADRATICS	BITEPLATES	BLACKBUTTS
BIOCLIMATIC	BIOGRAPHIZE	BIORHYTHMS	BIQUARTERLY	BITMAPPING	BLACKCOCKS
BIOCLIMATOLOGY	BIOGRAPHIZED	BIOSAFETIES	BIQUINTILE	BITONALITIES	BLACKCURRANT
BIOCOENOLOGIES	BIOGRAPHIZES	BIOSATELLITE	BIQUINTILES	BITONALITY	BLACKCURRANTS
BIOCOENOLOGY	BIOGRAPHIZING	BIOSATELLITES	BIRACIALISM	BITSTREAMS	BLACKDAMPS
BIOCOENOSES	BIOHAZARDOUS	BIOSCIENCE	BIRACIALISMS	BITTERBARK	BLACKENERS
BIOCOENOSIS	BIOHAZARDS	BIOSCIENCES	BIRACIALLY	BITTERBARKS	BLACKENING
BIOCOENOTIC	BIOINDUSTRIES	BIOSCIENTIFIC	BIRADICALS	BITTERBRUSH	BLACKENINGS
BIOCOMPATIBLE	BIOINDUSTRY	BIOSCIENTIST	BIRDBRAINED	BITTERBRUSHES	BLACKFACED
BIOCOMPUTING	BIOINFORMATICS	BIOSCIENTISTS	BIRDBRAINS	BITTERCRESS	BLACKFACES
BIOCOMPUTINGS	BIOLOGICAL	BIOSCOPIES	BIRDDOGGED	BITTERCRESSES	BLACKFISHES
BIOCONTROL	BIOLOGICALLY	BIOSENSORS	BIRDDOGGING	BITTERLING	BLACKFLIES

b

BLACKGAMES
BLACKGUARD
BLACKGUARDED
BLACKGUARDING
BLACKGUARDISM
BLACKGUARDISMS
BLACKGUARDLY
BLACKGUARDS
BLACKHANDER
BLACKHANDERS
BLACKHEADED
BLACKHEADS
BLACKHEART
BLACKHEARTS
BLACKISHLY
BLACKJACKED
BLACKJACKING
BLACKJACKS
BLACKLANDS
BLACKLEADS
BLACKLEGGED
BLACKLEGGING
BLACKLISTED
BLACKLISTER
BLACKLISTERS
BLACKLISTING
BLACKLISTINGS
BLACKLISTS
BLACKMAILED
BLACKMAILER
BLACKMAILERS
BLACKMAILING
BLACKMAILS
BLACKNESSES
BLACKPOLLS
BLACKSMITH
BLACKSMITHING
BLACKSMITHINGS
BLACKSMITHS
BLACKSNAKE
BLACKSNAKES
BLACKSTRAP
BLACKTAILS
BLACKTHORN
BLACKTHORNS
BLACKTOPPED
BLACKTOPPING
BLACKWASHED
BLACKWASHES
BLACKWASHING
BLACKWATER
BLACKWATERS
BLACKWOODS
BLADDERLIKE
BLADDERNOSE
BLADDERNOSES
BLADDERNUT
BLADDERNUTS
BLADDERWORT
BLADDERWORTS
BLADDERWRACK
BLADDERWRACKS
BLADEWORKS
BLAEBERRIES
BLAMABLENESS
BLAMABLENESSES
BLAMEABLENESS
BLAMEABLENESSES
BLAMEFULLY
BLAMEFULNESS
BLAMEFULNESSES
BLAMELESSLY
BLAMELESSNESS
BLAMELESSNESSES
BLAMEWORTHINESS
BLAMEWORTHY
BLANCHISSEUSE
BLANCHISSEUSES
BLANCMANGE
BLANCMANGES
BLANDISHED
BLANDISHER
BLANDISHERS

BLANDISHES
BLANDISHING
BLANDISHMENT
BLANDISHMENTS
BLANDNESSES
BLANKETFLOWER
BLANKETFLOWERS
BLANKETIES
BLANKETING
BLANKETINGS
BLANKETLIKE
BLANKETWEED
BLANKETWEEDS
BLANKNESSES
BLANQUETTE
BLANQUETTES
BLARNEYING
BLASPHEMED
BLASPHEMER
BLASPHEMERS
BLASPHEMES
BLASPHEMIES
BLASPHEMING
BLASPHEMOUS
BLASPHEMOUSLY
BLASPHEMOUSNESS
BLASTEMATA
BLASTEMATIC
BLASTMENTS
BLASTOCHYLE
BLASTOCHYLES
BLASTOCOEL
BLASTOCOELE
BLASTOCOELES
BLASTOCOELIC
BLASTOCOELS
BLASTOCYST
BLASTOCYSTS
BLASTODERM
BLASTODERMIC
BLASTODERMS
BLASTODISC
BLASTODISCS
BLASTOGENESES
BLASTOGENESIS
BLASTOGENETIC
BLASTOGENIC
BLASTOMATA
BLASTOMERE
BLASTOMERES
BLASTOMERIC
BLASTOMYCOSES
BLASTOMYCOSIS
BLASTOPORAL
BLASTOPORE
BLASTOPORES
BLASTOPORIC
BLASTOPORS
BLASTOSPHERE
BLASTOSPHERES
BLASTOSPORE
BLASTOSPORES
BLASTULATION
BLASTULATIONS
BLATANCIES
BLATHERERS
BLATHERING
BLATHERSKITE
BLATHERSKITES
BLATTERING
BLAXPLOITATION
BLAXPLOITATIONS
BLAZONINGS
BLAZONRIES
BLEACHABLE
BLEACHERIES
BLEACHERITE
BLEACHERITES
BLEACHINGS
BLEAKNESSES
BLEARINESS
BLEARINESSES
BLEMISHERS

BLEMISHING
BLEMISHMENT
BLEMISHMENTS
BLENNIOIDS
BLENNORRHEA
BLENNORRHEAS
BLENNORRHOEA
BLENNORRHOEAS
BLEPHARISM
BLEPHARISMS
BLEPHARITIC
BLEPHARITIS
BLEPHARITISES
BLEPHAROPLAST
BLEPHAROPLASTS
BLEPHAROPLASTY
BLEPHAROSPASM
BLEPHAROSPASMS
BLESSEDEST
BLESSEDNESS
BLESSEDNESSES
BLETHERANSKATE
BLETHERANSKATES
BLETHERATION
BLETHERATIONS
BLETHERERS
BLETHERING
BLETHERINGS
BLETHERSKATE
BLETHERSKATES
BLIGHTINGLY
BLIGHTINGS
BLIMPISHLY
BLIMPISHNESS
BLIMPISHNESSES
BLINDFISHES
BLINDFOLDED
BLINDFOLDING
BLINDFOLDS
BLINDINGLY
BLINDNESSES
BLINDSIDED
BLINDSIDES
BLINDSIDING
BLINDSIGHT
BLINDSIGHTS
BLINDSTOREY
BLINDSTOREYS
BLINDSTORIES
BLINDSTORY
BLINDWORMS
BLINGLISHES
BLINKERING
BLISSFULLY
BLISSFULNESS
BLISSFULNESSES
BLISTERIER
BLISTERIEST
BLISTERING
BLISTERINGLY
BLITHENESS
BLITHENESSES
BLITHERING
BLITHESOME
BLITHESOMELY
BLITHESOMENESS
BLITZKRIEG
BLITZKRIEGS
BLIZZARDLY
BLOATEDNESS
BLOATEDNESSES
BLOATWARES
BLOCKADERS
BLOCKADING
BLOCKBOARD
BLOCKBOARDS
BLOCKBUSTED
BLOCKBUSTER
BLOCKBUSTERS
BLOCKBUSTING
BLOCKBUSTINGS
BLOCKBUSTS
BLOCKHEADED

BLOCKHEADEDLY
BLOCKHEADEDNESS
BLOCKHEADS
BLOCKHOLES
BLOCKHOUSE
BLOCKHOUSES
BLOCKINESS
BLOCKINESSES
BLOCKISHLY
BLOCKISHNESS
BLOCKISHNESSES
BLOCKWORKS
BLOKEISHNESS
BLOKEISHNESSES
BLOKISHNESS
BLOKISHNESSES
BLONDENESS
BLONDENESSES
BLONDINING
BLONDNESSES
BLOODBATHS
BLOODCURDLING
BLOODCURDLINGLY
BLOODGUILT
BLOODGUILTINESS
BLOODGUILTS
BLOODGUILTY
BLOODHEATS
BLOODHOUND
BLOODHOUNDS
BLOODINESS
BLOODINESSES
BLOODLESSLY
BLOODLESSNESS
BLOODLESSNESSES
BLOODLETTER
BLOODLETTERS
BLOODLETTING
BLOODLETTINGS
BLOODLINES
BLOODLUSTS
BLOODMOBILE
BLOODMOBILES
BLOODROOTS
BLOODSHEDS
BLOODSPRENT
BLOODSTAIN
BLOODSTAINED
BLOODSTAINS
BLOODSTOCK
BLOODSTOCKS
BLOODSTONE
BLOODSTONES
BLOODSTREAM
BLOODSTREAMS
BLOODSUCKER
BLOODSUCKERS
BLOODSUCKING
BLOODTHIRSTIER
BLOODTHIRSTIEST
BLOODTHIRSTILY
BLOODTHIRSTY
BLOODWOODS
BLOODWORMS
BLOODWORTS
BLOOMERIES
BLOQUISTES
BLOSSOMING
BLOSSOMINGS
BLOSSOMLESS
BLOTCHIEST
BLOTCHINESS
BLOTCHINESSES
BLOTCHINGS
BLOTTESQUE
BLOTTESQUES
BLOVIATING
BLOVIATION
BLOVIATIONS
BLOWFISHES
BLOWINESSES
BLOWKARTING
BLOWKARTINGS

BLOWSINESS
BLOWSINESSES
BLOWTORCHED
BLOWTORCHES
BLOWTORCHING
BLOWZINESS
BLOWZINESSES
BLUBBERERS
BLUBBERIER
BLUBBERIEST
BLUBBERING
BLUDGEONED
BLUDGEONER
BLUDGEONERS
BLUDGEONING
BLUEBEARDS
BLUEBERRIES
BLUEBLOODS
BLUEBONNET
BLUEBONNETS
BLUEBOTTLE
BLUEBOTTLES
BLUEBREAST
BLUEBREASTS
BLUEBUSHES
BLUEFISHES
BLUEGRASSES
BLUEISHNESS
BLUEISHNESSES
BLUEJACKET
BLUEJACKETS
BLUEJACKING
BLUEJACKINGS
BLUELINERS
BLUENESSES
BLUEPOINTS
BLUEPRINTED
BLUEPRINTING
BLUEPRINTS
BLUESHIFTED
BLUESHIFTS
BLUESNARFING
BLUESNARFINGS
BLUESTOCKING
BLUESTOCKINGS
BLUESTONES
BLUETHROAT
BLUETHROATS
BLUETONGUE
BLUETONGUES
BLUFFNESSES
BLUISHNESS
BLUISHNESSES
BLUNDERBUSS
BLUNDERBUSSES
BLUNDERERS
BLUNDERING
BLUNDERINGLY
BLUNDERINGS
BLUNTHEADS
BLUNTNESSES
BLURREDNESS
BLURREDNESSES
BLURRINESS
BLURRINESSES
BLURRINGLY
BLUSHINGLY
BLUSHLESSLY
BLUSTERERS
BLUSTERIER
BLUSTERIEST
BLUSTERING
BLUSTERINGLY
BLUSTERINGS
BLUSTEROUS
BLUSTEROUSLY
BLUTWURSTS
BOARDINGHOUSE
BOARDINGHOUSES
BOARDROOMS
BOARDSAILING
BOARDSAILINGS
BOARDSAILOR

BOARDSAILORS
BOARDWALKS
BOARFISHES
BOARHOUNDS
BOARISHNESS
BOARISHNESSES
BOASTFULLY
BOASTFULNESS
BOASTFULNESSES
BOASTINGLY
BOATBUILDER
BOATBUILDERS
BOATBUILDING
BOATBUILDINGS
BOATHOUSES
BOATLIFTED
BOATLIFTING
BOATSWAINS
BOBBEJAANS
BOBBITTING
BOBBYSOCKS
BOBBYSOXER
BOBBYSOXERS
BOBSLEDDED
BOBSLEDDER
BOBSLEDDERS
BOBSLEDDING
BOBSLEDDINGS
BOBSLEIGHED
BOBSLEIGHING
BOBSLEIGHS
BOBTAILING
BOBWEIGHTS
BOCCONCINI
BODACIOUSLY
BODDHISATTVA
BODDHISATTVAS
BODEGUEROS
BODHISATTVA
BODHISATTVAS
BODYBOARDED
BODYBOARDING
BODYBOARDINGS
BODYBOARDS
BODYBUILDER
BODYBUILDERS
BODYBUILDING
BODYBUILDINGS
BODYCHECKED
BODYCHECKING
BODYCHECKS
BODYGUARDED
BODYGUARDING
BODYGUARDS
BODYSHELLS
BODYSURFED
BODYSURFER
BODYSURFERS
BODYSURFING
BODYSURFINGS
BODYWORKER
BODYWORKERS
BOEREMUSIEK
BOEREMUSIEKS
BOEREWORSES
BOGGINESSES
BOGTROTTER
BOGTROTTERS
BOGTROTTING
BOGTROTTINGS
BOGUSNESSES
BOHEMIANISM
BOHEMIANISMS
BOILERMAKER
BOILERMAKERS
BOILERPLATE
BOILERPLATED
BOILERPLATES
BOILERPLATING
BOILERSUIT
BOILERSUITS
BOISTEROUS
BOISTEROUSLY

BOISTEROUSNESS	BONESETTER	BOOTMAKING	BOULDERINGS	BOYCOTTERS	BRAGADISMES
BOKMAKIERIE	BONESETTERS	BOOTMAKINGS	BOULEVARDIER	BOYCOTTING	BRAGGADOCIO
BOKMAKIERIES	BONESHAKER	BOOTSTRAPPED	BOULEVARDIERS	BOYFRIENDS	BRAGGADOCIOS
BOLDFACING	BONESHAKERS	BOOTSTRAPPING	BOULEVARDS	BOYISHNESS	BRAGGADOCIOUS
BOLDNESSES	BONHOMMIES	BOOTSTRAPS	BOULEVERSEMENT	BOYISHNESSES	BRAGGARTISM
BOLECTIONS	BONILASSES	BOOTYLICIOUS	BOULEVERSEMENTS	BOYSENBERRIES	BRAGGARTISMS
BOLIVIANOS	BONINESSES	BOOZINESSES	BOULLEWORK	BOYSENBERRY	BRAGGARTLY
BOLLETRIES	BONKBUSTER	BORAGINACEOUS	BOULLEWORKS	BRAAIVLEIS	BRAGGINGLY
BOLLOCKING	BONKBUSTERS	BORBORYGMAL	BOUNCINESS	BRAAIVLEISES	BRAHMANISM
BOLLOCKINGS	BONNIBELLS	BORBORYGMI	BOUNCINESSES	BRABBLEMENT	BRAHMANISMS
BOLLOCKSED	BONNILASSE	BORBORYGMIC	BOUNCINGLY	BRABBLEMENTS	BRAHMANIST
BOLLOCKSES	BONNILASSES	BORBORYGMUS	BOUNDARIES	BRACHIATED	BRAHMANISTS
BOLLOCKSING	BONNINESSES	BORBORYGMUSES	BOUNDEDNESS	BRACHIATES	BRAHMINISM
BOLOGRAPHS	BONNYCLABBER	BORDEREAUX	BOUNDEDNESSES	BRACHIATING	BRAHMINISMS
BOLOMETERS	BONNYCLABBERS	BORDERLAND	BOUNDERISH	BRACHIATION	BRAHMINIST
BOLOMETRIC	BOOBIALLAS	BORDERLANDS	BOUNDLESSLY	BRACHIATIONS	BRAHMINISTS
BOLOMETRICALLY	BOOBOISIES	BORDERLESS	BOUNDLESSNESS	BRACHIATOR	BRAILLEWRITER
BOLOMETRIES	BOOKBINDER	BORDERLINE	BOUNDLESSNESSES	BRACHIATORS	BRAILLEWRITERS
BOLSHEVIKI	BOOKBINDERIES	BORDERLINES	BOUNDNESSES	BRACHIOCEPHALIC	BRAILLISTS
BOLSHEVIKS	BOOKBINDERS	BORDRAGING	BOUNTEOUSLY	BRACHIOPOD	BRAINBOXES
BOLSHEVISE	BOOKBINDERY	BORDRAGINGS	BOUNTEOUSNESS	BRACHIOPODS	BRAINCASES
BOLSHEVISED	BOOKBINDING	BORESCOPES	BOUNTEOUSNESSES	BRACHIOSAURUS	BRAINCHILD
BOLSHEVISES	BOOKBINDINGS	BORGHETTOS	BOUNTIFULLY	BRACHIOSAURUSES	BRAINCHILDREN
BOLSHEVISING	BOOKCROSSING	BORINGNESS	BOUNTIFULNESS	BRACHISTOCHRONE	BRAINFARTS
BOLSHEVISM	BOOKCROSSINGS	BORINGNESSES	BOUNTIFULNESSES	BRACHYAXES	BRAININESS
BOLSHEVISMS	BOOKISHNESS	BOROHYDRIDE	BOUNTYHEDS	BRACHYAXIS	BRAININESSES
BOLSHEVIST	BOOKISHNESSES	BOROHYDRIDES	BOUQUETIERE	BRACHYCEPHAL	BRAINLESSLY
BOLSHEVISTS	BOOKKEEPER	BOROSILICATE	BOUQUETIERES	BRACHYCEPHALIC	BRAINLESSNESS
BOLSHEVIZE	BOOKKEEPERS	BOROSILICATES	BOURASQUES	BRACHYCEPHALICS	BRAINLESSNESSES
BOLSHEVIZED	BOOKKEEPING	BORROWINGS	BOURBONISM	BRACHYCEPHALIES	BRAINPOWER
BOLSHEVIZES	BOOKKEEPINGS	BOSBERAADS	BOURBONISMS	BRACHYCEPHALISM	BRAINPOWERS
BOLSHEVIZING	BOOKLIGHTS	BOSCHVARKS	BOURGEOISE	BRACHYCEPHALOUS	BRAINSICKLY
BOLSTERERS	BOOKMAKERS	BOSCHVELDS	BOURGEOISES	BRACHYCEPHALS	BRAINSICKNESS
BOLSTERING	BOOKMAKING	BOSKINESSES	BOURGEOISIE	BRACHYCEPHALY	BRAINSICKNESSES
BOLSTERINGS	BOOKMAKINGS	BOSSINESSES	BOURGEOISIES	BRACHYCEROUS	BRAINSTEMS
BOMBACACEOUS	BOOKMARKED	BOSSYBOOTS	BOURGEOISIFIED	BRACHYDACTYL	BRAINSTORM
BOMBARDERS	BOOKMARKER	BOTANICALLY	BOURGEOISIFIES	BRACHYDACTYLIC	BRAINSTORMED
BOMBARDIER	BOOKMARKERS	BOTANICALS	BOURGEOISIFY	BRACHYDACTYLIES	BRAINSTORMER
BOMBARDIERS	BOOKMARKING	BOTANISERS	BOURGEOISIFYING	BRACHYDACTYLISM	BRAINSTORMERS
BOMBARDING	BOOKMOBILE	BOTANISING	BOURGEONED	BRACHYDACTYLOUS	BRAINSTORMING
BOMBARDMENT	BOOKMOBILES	BOTANIZERS	BOURGEONING	BRACHYDACTYLY	BRAINSTORMINGS
BOMBARDMENTS	BOOKPLATES	BOTANIZING	BOURGUIGNON	BRACHYDIAGONAL	BRAINSTORMS
BOMBARDONS	BOOKSELLER	BOTANOMANCIES	BOURGUIGNONNE	BRACHYDIAGONALS	BRAINTEASER
BOMBASINES	BOOKSELLERS	BOTANOMANCY	BOUSINGKEN	BRACHYDOME	BRAINTEASERS
BOMBASTERS	BOOKSELLING	BOTCHERIES	BOUSINGKENS	BRACHYDOMES	BRAINWASHED
BOMBASTICALLY	BOOKSELLINGS	BOTCHINESS	BOUSTROPHEDON	BRACHYGRAPHIES	BRAINWASHER
BOMBASTING	BOOKSHELVES	BOTCHINESSES	BOUSTROPHEDONIC	BRACHYGRAPHY	BRAINWASHERS
BOMBAZINES	BOOKSTALLS	BOTHERATION	BOUSTROPHEDONS	BRACHYLOGIES	BRAINWASHES
BOMBILATED	BOOKSTANDS	BOTHERATIONS	BOUTONNIERE	BRACHYLOGOUS	BRAINWASHING
BOMBILATES	BOOKSTORES	BOTHERSOME	BOUTONNIERES	BRACHYLOGY	BRAINWASHINGS
BOMBILATING	BOOMERANGED	BOTRYOIDAL	BOUVARDIAS	BRACHYODONT	BRAINWAVES
BOMBILATION	BOOMERANGING	BOTRYTISES	BOVINITIES	BRACHYPINAKOID	BRAMBLIEST
BOMBILATIONS	BOOMERANGS	BOTTLEBRUSH	BOWDLERISATION	BRACHYPINAKOIDS	BRAMBLINGS
BOMBINATED	BOOMSLANGS	BOTTLEBRUSHES	BOWDLERISATIONS	BRACHYPRISM	BRANCHERIES
BOMBINATES	BOONDOGGLE	BOTTLEFULS	BOWDLERISE	BRACHYPRISMS	BRANCHIATE
BOMBINATING	BOONDOGGLED	BOTTLENECK	BOWDLERISED	BRACHYPTERISM	BRANCHIEST
BOMBINATION	BOONDOGGLER	BOTTLENECKED	BOWDLERISER	BRACHYPTERISMS	BRANCHINGS
BOMBINATIONS	BOONDOGGLERS	BOTTLENECKING	BOWDLERISERS	BRACHYPTEROUS	BRANCHIOPOD
BOMBPROOFED	BOONDOGGLES	BOTTLENECKS	BOWDLERISES	BRACHYTHERAPIES	BRANCHIOPODS
BOMBPROOFING	BOONDOGGLING	BOTTLENOSE	BOWDLERISING	BRACHYTHERAPY	BRANCHIOSTEGAL
BOMBPROOFS	BOONGARIES	BOTTOMLAND	BOWDLERISM	BRACHYURAL	BRANCHLESS
BOMBSHELLS	BOORISHNESS	BOTTOMLANDS	BOWDLERISMS	BRACHYURAN	BRANCHLETS
BOMBSIGHTS	BOORISHNESSES	BOTTOMLESS	BOWDLERIZATION	BRACHYURANS	BRANCHLIKE
BONAMIASES	BOOSTERISH	BOTTOMLESSLY	BOWDLERIZATIONS	BRACHYUROUS	BRANCHLINE
BONAMIASIS	BOOSTERISM	BOTTOMLESSNESS	BOWDLERIZE	BRACKETING	BRANCHLINES
BONASSUSES	BOOSTERISMS	BOTTOMMOST	BOWDLERIZED	BRACKETINGS	BRANDERING
BONBONNIERE	BOOTBLACKS	BOTTOMNESS	BOWDLERIZER	BRACKISHNESS	BRANDISHED
BONBONNIERES	BOOTLEGGED	BOTTOMNESSES	BOWDLERIZERS	BRACKISHNESSES	BRANDISHER
BONDHOLDER	BOOTLEGGER	BOTTOMRIES	BOWDLERIZES	BRACTEATES	BRANDISHERS
BONDHOLDERS	BOOTLEGGERS	BOTULINUMS	BOWDLERIZING	BRACTEOLATE	BRANDISHES
BONDMANSHIP	BOOTLEGGING	BOTULINUSES	BOWERBIRDS	BRACTEOLES	BRANDISHING
BONDMANSHIPS	BOOTLEGGINGS	BOUGAINVILIA	BOWERWOMAN	BRADYCARDIA	BRANDLINGS
BONDSERVANT	BOOTLESSLY	BOUGAINVILIAS	BOWERWOMEN	BRADYCARDIAC	BRANDRETHS
BONDSERVANTS	BOOTLESSNESS	BOUGAINVILLAEA	BOWHUNTERS	BRADYCARDIAS	BRANFULNESS
BONDSTONES	BOOTLESSNESSES	BOUGAINVILLAEAS	BOWSTRINGED	BRADYKINESIA	BRANFULNESSES
BONDSWOMAN	BOOTLICKED	BOUGAINVILLEA	BOWSTRINGING	BRADYKINESIAS	BRANGLINGS
BONDSWOMEN	BOOTLICKER	BOUGAINVILLEAS	BOWSTRINGS	BRADYKININ	BRANKURSINE
BONEBLACKS	BOOTLICKERS	BOUILLABAISSE	BOXBERRIES	BRADYKININS	BRANKURSINES
BONEFISHES	BOOTLICKING	BOUILLABAISSES	BOXERCISES	BRADYPEPTIC	BRANNIGANS
BONEFISHING	BOOTLICKINGS	BOUILLOTTE	BOXHAULING	BRADYPEPTICS	BRASHINESS
BONEFISHINGS	BOOTLOADER	BOUILLOTTES	BOXINESSES	BRADYSEISM	BRASHINESSES
BONEHEADED	BOOTLOADERS	BOULDERERS	BOXKEEPERS	BRADYSEISMS	BRASHNESSES
BONEHEADEDNESS	BOOTMAKERS	BOULDERING	BOXWALLAHS	BRAGADISME	BRASILEINS

b

BRASSBOUND
BRASSERIES
BRASSFOUNDER
BRASSFOUNDERS
BRASSFOUNDING
BRASSFOUNDINGS
BRASSICACEOUS
BRASSIERES
BRASSINESS
BRASSINESSES
BRASSWARES
BRATPACKER
BRATPACKERS
BRATTICING
BRATTICINGS
BRATTINESS
BRATTINESSES
BRATTISHED
BRATTISHES
BRATTISHING
BRATTISHINGS
BRATTLINGS
BRATWURSTS
BRAUNCHING
BRAUNSCHWEIGER
BRAUNSCHWEIGERS
BRAVADOING
BRAVENESSES
BRAVISSIMO
BRAWNINESS
BRAWNINESSES
BRAZENNESS
BRAZENNESSES
BRAZENRIES
BRAZIERIES
BRAZILEINS
BRAZILWOOD
BRAZILWOODS
BREADBASKET
BREADBASKETS
BREADBERRIES
BREADBERRY
BREADBOARD
BREADBOARDED
BREADBOARDING
BREADBOARDS
BREADBOXES
BREADCRUMB
BREADCRUMBED
BREADCRUMBING
BREADCRUMBS
BREADFRUIT
BREADFRUITS
BREADHEADS
BREADLINES
BREADROOMS
BREADROOTS
BREADSTICKS
BREADSTUFF
BREADSTUFFS
BREADTHWAYS
BREADTHWISE
BREADWINNER
BREADWINNERS
BREADWINNING
BREADWINNINGS
BREAKABLENESS
BREAKABLENESSES
BREAKABLES
BREAKAWAYS
BREAKBEATS
BREAKDANCE
BREAKDANCED
BREAKDANCER
BREAKDANCERS
BREAKDANCES
BREAKDANCING
BREAKDANCINGS
BREAKDOWNS
BREAKEVENS
BREAKFASTED
BREAKFASTER
BREAKFASTERS

BREAKFASTING
BREAKFASTS
BRETTICING
BREAKFRONT
BREAKFRONTS
BREAKPOINT
BREAKPOINTS
BREAKTHROUGH
BREAKTHROUGHS
BREAKTIMES
BREAKWALLS
BREAKWATER
BREAKWATERS
BREASTBONE
BREASTBONES
BREASTFEED
BREASTFEEDING
BREASTFEEDS
BREASTPINS
BREASTPLATE
BREASTPLATES
BREASTPLOUGH
BREASTPLOUGHS
BREASTRAIL
BREASTRAILS
BREASTSTROKE
BREASTSTROKER
BREASTSTROKERS
BREASTSTROKES
BREASTSUMMER
BREASTSUMMERS
BREASTWORK
BREASTWORKS
BREATHABILITIES
BREATHABILITY
BREATHABLE
BREATHALYSE
BREATHALYSED
BREATHALYSER
BREATHALYSERS
BREATHALYSES
BREATHALYSING
BREATHALYZE
BREATHALYZED
BREATHALYZER
BREATHALYZERS
BREATHALYZES
BREATHALYZING
BREATHARIAN
BREATHARIANISM
BREATHARIANISMS
BREATHARIANS
BREATHIEST
BREATHINESS
BREATHINESSES
BREATHINGS
BREATHLESS
BREATHLESSLY
BREATHLESSNESS
BREATHTAKING
BREATHTAKINGLY
BRECCIATED
BRECCIATES
BRECCIATING
BRECCIATION
BRECCIATIONS
BREECHBLOCK
BREECHBLOCKS
BREECHCLOTH
BREECHCLOTHS
BREECHCLOUT
BREECHCLOUTS
BREECHINGS
BREECHLESS
BREECHLOADER
BREECHLOADERS
BREEZELESS
BREEZEWAYS
BREEZINESS
BREEZINESSES
BREMSSTRAHLUNG
BREMSSTRAHLUNGS
BRESSUMMER
BRESSUMMERS

BRETASCHES
BRETTICING
BREUNNERITE
BREUNNERITES
BREVETCIES
BREVETTING
BREVIARIES
BREVIPENNATE
BREWMASTER
BREWMASTERS
BRIARROOTS
BRIARWOODS
BRICABRACS
BRICKCLAYS
BRICKEARTH
BRICKEARTHS
BRICKFIELD
BRICKFIELDER
BRICKFIELDERS
BRICKFIELDS
BRICKKILNS
BRICKLAYER
BRICKLAYERS
BRICKLAYING
BRICKLAYINGS
BRICKMAKER
BRICKMAKERS
BRICKMAKING
BRICKMAKINGS
BRICKSHAPED
BRICKWALLS
BRICKWORKS
BRICKYARDS
BRICOLAGES
BRIDECAKES
BRIDEGROOM
BRIDEGROOMS
BRIDEMAIDEN
BRIDEMAIDENS
BRIDEMAIDS
BRIDESMAID
BRIDESMAIDS
BRIDEWEALTH
BRIDEWEALTHS
BRIDEWELLS
BRIDGEABLE
BRIDGEBOARD
BRIDGEBOARDS
BRIDGEHEAD
BRIDGEHEADS
BRIDGELESS
BRIDGEWORK
BRIDGEWORKS
BRIDLEWAYS
BRIDLEWISE
BRIEFCASES
BRIEFNESSES
BRIERROOTS
BRIERWOODS
BRIGADIERS
BRIGANDAGE
BRIGANDAGES
BRIGANDINE
BRIGANDINES
BRIGANDRIES
BRIGANTINE
BRIGANTINES
BRIGHTENED
BRIGHTENER
BRIGHTENERS
BRIGHTENING
BRIGHTNESS
BRIGHTNESSES
BRIGHTSOME
BRIGHTWORK
BRIGHTWORKS
BRILLIANCE
BRILLIANCES
BRILLIANCIES
BRILLIANCY
BRILLIANTE
BRILLIANTED
BRILLIANTINE

BRILLIANTINES
BRILLIANTING
BRILLIANTLY
BRILLIANTNESS
BRILLIANTNESSES
BRILLIANTS
BRIMFULLNESS
BRIMFULLNESSES
BRIMFULNESS
BRIMFULNESSES
BRIMSTONES
BRINELLING
BRINELLINGS
BRINGDOWNS
BRININESSES
BRINJARRIES
BRINKMANSHIP
BRINKMANSHIPS
BRINKSMANSHIP
BRINKSMANSHIPS
BRIOLETTES
BRIQUETTED
BRIQUETTES
BRIQUETTING
BRISKENING
BRISKNESSES
BRISTLECONE
BRISTLECONES
BRISTLELIKE
BRISTLETAIL
BRISTLETAILS
BRISTLIEST
BRISTLINESS
BRISTLINESSES
BRITANNIAS
BRITSCHKAS
BRITTANIAS
BRITTLENESS
BRITTLENESSES
BROADBANDS
BROADBEANS
BROADBILLS
BROADBRIMS
BROADBRUSH
BROADCASTED
BROADCASTER
BROADCASTERS
BROADCASTING
BROADCASTINGS
BROADCASTS
BROADCLOTH
BROADCLOTHS
BROADENERS
BROADENING
BROADLEAVES
BROADLINES
BROADLOOMS
BROADMINDED
BROADMINDEDLY
BROADMINDEDNESS
BROADNESSES
BROADPIECE
BROADPIECES
BROADSCALE
BROADSHEET
BROADSHEETS
BROADSIDED
BROADSIDES
BROADSIDING
BROADSWORD
BROADSWORDS
BROADTAILS
BROBDINGNAGIAN
BROCATELLE
BROCATELLES
BROCHETTES
BROGUERIES
BROIDERERS
BROIDERIES
BROIDERING
BROIDERINGS
BROKENHEARTED
BROKENHEARTEDLY

BROKENNESS
BROKENNESSES
BROKERAGES
BROKERINGS
BROMEGRASS
BROMEGRASSES
BROMELAINS
BROMELIACEOUS
BROMELIADS
BROMEOSINS
BROMHIDROSES
BROMHIDROSIS
BROMIDROSES
BROMIDROSIS
BROMINATED
BROMINATES
BROMINATING
BROMINATION
BROMINATIONS
BROMINISMS
BROMOCRIPTINE
BROMOCRIPTINES
BROMOFORMS
BROMOURACIL
BROMOURACILS
BRONCHIALLY
BRONCHIECTASES
BRONCHIECTASIS
BRONCHIOLAR
BRONCHIOLE
BRONCHIOLES
BRONCHIOLITIS
BRONCHIOLITISES
BRONCHITIC
BRONCHITICS
BRONCHITIS
BRONCHITISES
BRONCHODILATOR
BRONCHODILATORS
BRONCHOGENIC
BRONCHOGRAPHIES
BRONCHOGRAPHY
BRONCHOSCOPE
BRONCHOSCOPES
BRONCHOSCOPIC
BRONCHOSCOPICAL
BRONCHOSCOPIES
BRONCHOSCOPIST
BRONCHOSCOPISTS
BRONCHOSCOPY
BRONCHOSPASM
BRONCHOSPASMS
BRONCHOSPASTIC
BRONCOBUSTER
BRONCOBUSTERS
BRONDYRONS
BRONTOBYTE
BRONTOBYTES
BRONTOSAUR
BRONTOSAURS
BRONTOSAURUS
BRONTOSAURUSES
BRONZIFIED
BRONZIFIES
BRONZIFYING
BROODINESS
BROODINESSES
BROODINGLY
BROODMARES
BROOKLIMES
BROOKWEEDS
BROOMBALLER
BROOMBALLERS
BROOMBALLS
BROOMCORNS
BROOMRAPES
BROOMSTAFF
BROOMSTAFFS
BROOMSTICK
BROOMSTICKS
BROTHERHOOD
BROTHERHOODS
BROTHERING

BROTHERLIKE
BROTHERLINESS
BROTHERLINESSES
BROUGHTASES
BROWALLIAS
BROWBEATEN
BROWBEATER
BROWBEATERS
BROWBEATING
BROWBEATINGS
BROWNFIELD
BROWNFIELDS
BROWNNESSES
BROWNNOSED
BROWNNOSER
BROWNNOSERS
BROWNNOSES
BROWNNOSING
BROWNSHIRT
BROWNSHIRTS
BROWNSTONE
BROWNSTONES
BROWRIDGES
BROWSABLES
BRUCELLOSES
BRUCELLOSIS
BRUGMANSIA
BRUGMANSIAS
BRUMMAGEMS
BRUSCHETTA
BRUSCHETTAS
BRUSCHETTE
BRUSHABILITIES
BRUSHABILITY
BRUSHBACKS
BRUSHFIRES
BRUSHLANDS
BRUSHMARKS
BRUSHWHEEL
BRUSHWHEELS
BRUSHWOODS
BRUSHWORKS
BRUSQUENESS
BRUSQUENESSES
BRUSQUERIE
BRUSQUERIES
BRUTALISATION
BRUTALISATIONS
BRUTALISED
BRUTALISES
BRUTALISING
BRUTALISMS
BRUTALISTS
BRUTALITIES
BRUTALIZATION
BRUTALIZATIONS
BRUTALIZED
BRUTALIZES
BRUTALIZING
BRUTENESSES
BRUTIFYING
BRUTISHNESS
BRUTISHNESSES
BRYOLOGICAL
BRYOLOGIES
BRYOLOGIST
BRYOLOGISTS
BRYOPHYLLUM
BRYOPHYLLUMS
BRYOPHYTES
BRYOPHYTIC
BUBBLEGUMS
BUBBLEHEAD
BUBBLEHEADED
BUBBLEHEADS
BUBONOCELE
BUBONOCELES
BUCCANEERED
BUCCANEERING
BUCCANEERINGS
BUCCANEERISH
BUCCANEERS
BUCCANIERED

b

BUCCANIERING	BULLDOGGERS	BUMFREEZER	BURGLARISES	BUSHMASTERS	BUTTERFLYERS
BUCCANIERS	BULLDOGGING	BUMFREEZERS	BURGLARISING	BUSHRANGER	BUTTERFLYING
BUCCINATOR	BULLDOGGINGS	BUMFUZZLED	BURGLARIZE	BUSHRANGERS	BUTTERIEST
BUCCINATORS	BULLDOZERS	BUMFUZZLES	BURGLARIZED	BUSHRANGING	BUTTERINES
BUCCINATORY	BULLDOZING	BUMFUZZLING	BURGLARIZES	BUSHRANGINGS	BUTTERINESS
BUCELLASES	BULLETINED	BUMMALOTIS	BURGLARIZING	BUSHWALKED	BUTTERINESSES
BUCENTAURS	BULLETINING	BUMPINESSES	BURGLARPROOF	BUSHWALKER	BUTTERLESS
BUCKBOARDS	BULLETPROOF	BUMPKINISH	BURGOMASTER	BUSHWALKERS	BUTTERMILK
BUCKBRUSHES	BULLETPROOFED	BUMPOLOGIES	BURGOMASTERS	BUSHWALKING	BUTTERMILKS
BUCKETFULS	BULLETPROOFING	BUMPSADAISY	BURGUNDIES	BUSHWALKINGS	BUTTERNUTS
BUCKETINGS	BULLETPROOFS	BUMPTIOUSLY	BURLADEROS	BUSHWHACKED	BUTTERSCOTCH
BUCKETSFUL	BULLETRIES	BUMPTIOUSNESS	BURLESQUED	BUSHWHACKER	BUTTERSCOTCHES
BUCKHOUNDS	BULLETWOOD	BUMPTIOUSNESSES	BURLESQUELY	BUSHWHACKERS	BUTTERWEED
BUCKJUMPER	BULLETWOODS	BUMSUCKERS	BURLESQUER	BUSHWHACKING	BUTTERWEEDS
BUCKJUMPERS	BULLFIGHTER	BUMSUCKING	BURLESQUERS	BUSHWHACKINGS	BUTTERWORT
BUCKJUMPING	BULLFIGHTERS	BUMSUCKINGS	BURLESQUES	BUSHWHACKS	BUTTERWORTS
BUCKJUMPINGS	BULLFIGHTING	BUNCHBERRIES	BURLESQUING	BUSINESSES	BUTTINSKIES
BUCKLERING	BULLFIGHTINGS	BUNCHBERRY	BURLEYCUES	BUSINESSLIKE	BUTTINSKIS
BUCKRAMING	BULLFIGHTS	BUNCHGRASS	BURLINESSES	BUSINESSMAN	BUTTOCKING
BUCKSHISHED	BULLFINCHES	BUNCHGRASSES	BURNETTISE	BUSINESSMEN	BUTTONBALL
BUCKSHISHES	BULLHEADED	BUNCHINESS	BURNETTISED	BUSINESSPEOPLE	BUTTONBALLS
BUCKSHISHING	BULLHEADEDLY	BUNCHINESSES	BURNETTISES	BUSINESSPERSON	BUTTONBUSH
BUCKSKINNED	BULLHEADEDNESS	BUNDOBUSTS	BURNETTISING	BUSINESSPERSONS	BUTTONBUSHES
BUCKTHORNS	BULLIONIST	BUNGALOIDS	BURNETTIZE	BUSINESSWOMAN	BUTTONHELD
BUCKTOOTHED	BULLIONISTS	BUNGLESOME	BURNETTIZED	BUSINESSWOMEN	BUTTONHOLD
BUCKWHEATS	BULLISHNESS	BUNGLINGLY	BURNETTIZES	BUSTICATED	BUTTONHOLDING
BUCKYBALLS	BULLISHNESSES	BUNKHOUSES	BURNETTIZING	BUSTICATES	BUTTONHOLDS
BUCKYTUBES	BULLMASTIFF	BUOYANCIES	BURNISHABLE	BUSTICATING	BUTTONHOLE
BUCOLICALLY	BULLMASTIFFS	BUOYANTNESS	BURNISHERS	BUSTINESSES	BUTTONHOLED
BUDGERIGAR	BULLNECKED	BUOYANTNESSES	BURNISHING	BUSTLINGLY	BUTTONHOLER
BUDGERIGARS	BULLOCKIES	BUPIVACAINE	BURNISHINGS	BUSYBODIED	BUTTONHOLERS
BUDGETEERS	BULLOCKING	BUPIVACAINES	BURNISHMENT	BUSYBODIES	BUTTONHOLES
BUFFALOBERRIES	BULLROARER	BUPRENORPHINE	BURNISHMENTS	BUSYBODYING	BUTTONHOLING
BUFFALOBERRY	BULLROARERS	BUPRENORPHINES	BURRAMUNDI	BUSYBODYINGS	BUTTONHOOK
BUFFALOFISH	BULLRUSHES	BUPRESTIDS	BURRAMUNDIS	BUSYNESSES	BUTTONHOOKED
BUFFALOFISHES	BULLSHITTED	BURDENSOME	BURRAMYSES	BUTADIENES	BUTTONHOOKING
BUFFALOING	BULLSHITTER	BUREAUCRACIES	BURRAWANGS	BUTCHERBIRD	BUTTONHOOKS
BUFFETINGS	BULLSHITTERS	BUREAUCRACY	BURROWSTOWN	BUTCHERBIRDS	BUTTONLESS
BUFFLEHEAD	BULLSHITTING	BUREAUCRAT	BURROWSTOWNS	BUTCHERERS	BUTTONMOULD
BUFFLEHEADS	BULLSHITTINGS	BUREAUCRATESE	BURRSTONES	BUTCHERIES	BUTTONMOULDS
BUFFOONERIES	BULLSNAKES	BUREAUCRATESES	BURSARSHIP	BUTCHERING	BUTTONWOOD
BUFFOONERY	BULLTERRIER	BUREAUCRATIC	BURSARSHIPS	BUTCHERINGS	BUTTONWOODS
BUFFOONISH	BULLTERRIERS	BUREAUCRATISE	BURSERACEOUS	BUTCHNESSES	BUTTRESSED
BUFOTALINS	BULLWADDIE	BUREAUCRATISED	BURSICULATE	BUTENEDIOIC	BUTTRESSES
BUFOTENINE	BULLWADDIES	BUREAUCRATISES	BURSITISES	BUTEONINES	BUTTRESSING
BUFOTENINES	BULLWHACKED	BUREAUCRATISING	BURTHENING	BUTLERAGES	BUTTSTOCKS
BUGGINESSES	BULLWHACKING	BUREAUCRATISM	BURTHENSOME	BUTLERSHIP	BUTYLATING
BUGLEWEEDS	BULLWHACKS	BUREAUCRATISMS	BUSHBABIES	BUTLERSHIPS	BUTYLATION
BUHRSTONES	BULLWHIPPED	BUREAUCRATIST	BUSHBASHING	BUTTERBALL	BUTYLATIONS
BUILDDOWNS	BULLWHIPPING	BUREAUCRATISTS	BUSHBASHINGS	BUTTERBALLS	BUTYRACEOUS
BUIRDLIEST	BULLYRAGGED	BUREAUCRATIZE	BUSHCRAFTS	BUTTERBURS	BUTYRALDEHYDE
BULBIFEROUS	BULLYRAGGING	BUREAUCRATIZED	BUSHELLERS	BUTTERCUPS	BUTYRALDEHYDES
BULBOSITIES	BULWADDEES	BUREAUCRATIZES	BUSHELLING	BUTTERDOCK	BUTYROPHENONE
BULBOUSNESS	BULWADDIES	BUREAUCRATIZING	BUSHELLINGS	BUTTERDOCKS	BUTYROPHENONES
BULBOUSNESSES	BULWARKING	BUREAUCRATS	BUSHELWOMAN	BUTTERFATS	BUXOMNESSES
BULGINESSES	BUMBAILIFF	BURGEONING	BUSHELWOMEN	BUTTERFINGERED	BYPRODUCTS
BULKINESSES	BUMBAILIFFS	BURGLARIES	BUSHHAMMER	BUTTERFINGERS	BYSSACEOUS
BULLBAITING	BUMBERSHOOT	BURGLARING	BUSHHAMMERS	BUTTERFISH	BYSSINOSES
BULLBAITINGS	BUMBERSHOOTS	BURGLARIOUS	BUSHINESSES	BUTTERFISHES	BYSSINOSIS
BULLBRIERS	BUMBLEBEES	BURGLARIOUSLY	BUSHMANSHIP	BUTTERFLIED	BYSTANDERS
BULLDOGGED	BUMBLEDOMS	BURGLARISE	BUSHMANSHIPS	BUTTERFLIES	BYTOWNITES
BULLDOGGER	BUMBLINGLY	BURGLARISED	BUSHMASTER	BUTTERFLYER	

Cc

CABALETTAS
CABALISTIC
CABALISTICAL
CABALLEROS
CABBAGETOWN
CABBAGETOWNS
CABBAGEWORM
CABBAGEWORMS
CABBALISMS
CABBALISTIC
CABBALISTICAL
CABBALISTS
CABDRIVERS
CABINETMAKER
CABINETMAKERS
CABINETMAKING
CABINETMAKINGS
CABINETRIES
CABINETWORK
CABINETWORKS
CABINMATES
CABLECASTED
CABLECASTING
CABLECASTS
CABLEGRAMS
CABLEVISION
CABLEVISIONS
CABRIOLETS
CACAFUEGOS
CACCIATORA
CACCIATORE
CACHAEMIAS
CACHECTICAL
CACHINNATE
CACHINNATED
CACHINNATES
CACHINNATING
CACHINNATION
CACHINNATIONS
CACHINNATORY
CACHOLONGS
CACIQUISMS
CACKERMANDER
CACKERMANDERS
CACKLEBERRIES
CACKLEBERRY
CACODAEMON
CACODAEMONS
CACODEMONIC
CACODEMONS
CACODOXIES
CACOEPISTIC
CACOGASTRIC
CACOGENICS
CACOGRAPHER
CACOGRAPHERS
CACOGRAPHIC
CACOGRAPHICAL
CACOGRAPHIES
CACOGRAPHY
CACOLOGIES
CACOMISTLE
CACOMISTLES
CACOMIXLES
CACONYMIES
CACOPHONIC
CACOPHONICAL

CACOPHONICALLY
CACOPHONIES
CACOPHONIOUS
CACOPHONOUS
CACOPHONOUSLY
CACOTOPIAN
CACOTOPIAS
CACOTROPHIES
CACOTROPHY
CACTACEOUS
CACTOBLASTES
CACTOBLASTIS
CACUMINALS
CACUMINOUS
CADASTRALLY
CADAVERINE
CADAVERINES
CADAVEROUS
CADAVEROUSLY
CADAVEROUSNESS
CADDISFLIES
CADDISHNESS
CADDISHNESSES
CADDISWORM
CADDISWORMS
CADETSHIPS
CADUCITIES
CAECILIANS
CAECITISES
CAENOGENESES
CAENOGENESIS
CAENOGENETIC
CAESALPINOID
CAESAREANS
CAESARIANS
CAESARISMS
CAESAROPAPISM
CAESAROPAPISMS
CAESPITOSE
CAESPITOSELY
CAFETERIAS
CAFETIERES
CAFETORIUM
CAFETORIUMS
CAFFEINATED
CAFFEINISM
CAFFEINISMS
CAGEYNESSES
CAGINESSES
CAGMAGGING
CAGYNESSES
CAILLEACHS
CAILLIACHS
CAINOGENESES
CAINOGENESIS
CAINOGENETIC
CAIRNGORMS
CAJOLEMENT
CAJOLEMENTS
CAJOLERIES
CAJOLINGLY
CAKEWALKED
CAKEWALKER
CAKEWALKERS
CAKEWALKING
CAKINESSES
CALABASHES

CALABOGUSES
CALABOOSES
CALABRESES
CALAMANCOES
CALAMANCOS
CALAMANDER
CALAMANDERS
CALAMARIES
CALAMINING
CALAMITIES
CALAMITOUS
CALAMITOUSLY
CALAMITOUSNESS
CALAMONDIN
CALAMONDINS
CALANDRIAS
CALAVANCES
CALAVERITE
CALAVERITES
CALCAREOUS
CALCAREOUSLY
CALCARIFEROUS
CALCARIFORM
CALCEAMENTA
CALCEAMENTUM
CALCEATING
CALCEDONIES
CALCEDONIO
CALCEDONIOS
CALCEIFORM
CALCEOLARIA
CALCEOLARIAS
CALCEOLATE
CALCICOLES
CALCICOLOUS
CALCIFEROL
CALCIFEROLS
CALCIFEROUS
CALCIFICATION
CALCIFICATIONS
CALCIFUGAL
CALCIFUGES
CALCIFUGOUS
CALCIFYING
CALCIGEROUS
CALCIMINED
CALCIMINES
CALCIMINING
CALCINABLE
CALCINATION
CALCINATIONS
CALCINOSES
CALCINOSIS
CALCITONIN
CALCITONINS
CALCSINTER
CALCSINTERS
CALCULABILITIES
CALCULABILITY
CALCULABLE
CALCULABLY
CALCULATED
CALCULATEDLY
CALCULATEDNESS
CALCULATES
CALCULATING
CALCULATINGLY

CALCULATION
CALCULATIONAL
CALCULATIONS
CALCULATIVE
CALCULATOR
CALCULATORS
CALCULUSES
CALEFACIENT
CALEFACIENTS
CALEFACTION
CALEFACTIONS
CALEFACTIVE
CALEFACTOR
CALEFACTORIES
CALEFACTORS
CALEFACTORY
CALEMBOURS
CALENDARED
CALENDARER
CALENDARERS
CALENDARING
CALENDARISATION
CALENDARISE
CALENDARISED
CALENDARISES
CALENDARISING
CALENDARIST
CALENDARISTS
CALENDARIZATION
CALENDARIZE
CALENDARIZED
CALENDARIZES
CALENDARIZING
CALENDERED
CALENDERER
CALENDERERS
CALENDERING
CALENDERINGS
CALENDRERS
CALENDRICAL
CALENDRIES
CALENDULAS
CALENTURES
CALESCENCE
CALESCENCES
CALFDOZERS
CALIATOURS
CALIBRATED
CALIBRATER
CALIBRATERS
CALIBRATES
CALIBRATING
CALIBRATION
CALIBRATIONS
CALIBRATOR
CALIBRATORS
CALIDITIES
CALIFORNIUM
CALIFORNIUMS
CALIGINOSITIES
CALIGINOSITY
CALIGINOUS
CALIOLOGIES
CALIPASHES
CALIPERING
CALIPHATES
CALISTHENIC

CALISTHENICS
CALLBOARDS
CALLIATURE
CALLIATURES
CALLIDITIES
CALLIGRAMME
CALLIGRAMMES
CALLIGRAMS
CALLIGRAPHER
CALLIGRAPHERS
CALLIGRAPHIC
CALLIGRAPHICAL
CALLIGRAPHIES
CALLIGRAPHIST
CALLIGRAPHISTS
CALLIGRAPHY
CALLIOPSIS
CALLIPASHES
CALLIPERED
CALLIPERING
CALLIPYGEAN
CALLIPYGIAN
CALLIPYGOUS
CALLISTEMON
CALLISTEMONS
CALLISTHENIC
CALLISTHENICS
CALLITHUMP
CALLITHUMPIAN
CALLITHUMPS
CALLOSITIES
CALLOUSING
CALLOUSNESS
CALLOUSNESSES
CALLOWNESS
CALLOWNESSES
CALMATIVES
CALMNESSES
CALMODULIN
CALMODULINS
CALMSTONES
CALORESCENCE
CALORESCENCES
CALORESCENT
CALORICALLY
CALORICITIES
CALORICITY
CALORIFICALLY
CALORIFICATION
CALORIFICATIONS
CALORIFIER
CALORIFIERS
CALORIMETER
CALORIMETERS
CALORIMETRIC
CALORIMETRICAL
CALORIMETRIES
CALORIMETRY
CALORISING
CALORIZING
CALOTYPIST
CALOTYPISTS
CALUMNIABLE
CALUMNIATE
CALUMNIATED
CALUMNIATES
CALUMNIATING

CALUMNIATION
CALUMNIATIONS
CALUMNIATOR
CALUMNIATORS
CALUMNIATORY
CALUMNIOUS
CALUMNIOUSLY
CALVADOSES
CALVARIUMS
CALYCANTHEMIES
CALYCANTHEMY
CALYCANTHUS
CALYCANTHUSES
CALYCIFORM
CALYCOIDEOUS
CALYCULATE
CALYPSONIAN
CALYPSONIANS
CALYPTERAS
CALYPTRATE
CALYPTROGEN
CALYPTROGENS
CAMANACHDS
CAMARADERIE
CAMARADERIES
CAMARILLAS
CAMBERINGS
CAMBISTRIES
CAMCORDERS
CAMELBACKS
CAMELEOPARD
CAMELEOPARDS
CAMELHAIRS
CAMELOPARD
CAMELOPARDS
CAMERAPERSON
CAMERAPERSONS
CAMERATION
CAMERATIONS
CAMERAWOMAN
CAMERAWOMEN
CAMERAWORK
CAMERAWORKS
CAMERLENGO
CAMERLENGOS
CAMERLINGO
CAMERLINGOS
CAMIKNICKERS
CAMIKNICKS
CAMISADOES
CAMORRISTA
CAMORRISTI
CAMORRISTS
CAMOUFLAGE
CAMOUFLAGEABLE
CAMOUFLAGED
CAMOUFLAGES
CAMOUFLAGIC
CAMOUFLAGING
CAMOUFLETS
CAMOUFLEUR
CAMOUFLEURS
CAMPAIGNED
CAMPAIGNER
CAMPAIGNERS
CAMPAIGNING
CAMPANEROS

CAMPANIFORM
CAMPANILES
CAMPANISTS
CAMPANOLOGER
CAMPANOLOGERS
CAMPANOLOGICAL
CAMPANOLOGIES
CAMPANOLOGIST
CAMPANOLOGISTS
CAMPANOLOGY
CAMPANULACEOUS
CAMPANULAR
CAMPANULAS
CAMPANULATE
CAMPCRAFTS
CAMPEADORS
CAMPESINOS
CAMPESTRAL
CAMPESTRIAN
CAMPGROUND
CAMPGROUNDS
CAMPHORACEOUS
CAMPHORATE
CAMPHORATED
CAMPHORATES
CAMPHORATING
CAMPIMETRIES
CAMPIMETRY
CAMPINESSES
CAMPNESSES
CAMPODEIDS
CAMPODEIFORM
CAMPSHIRTS
CAMPSTOOLS
CAMPYLOBACTER
CAMPYLOBACTERS
CAMPYLOTROPOUS
CAMSTEERIE
CANALBOATS
CANALICULAR
CANALICULATE
CANALICULATED
CANALICULI
CANALICULUS
CANALISATION
CANALISATIONS
CANALISING
CANALIZATION
CANALIZATIONS
CANALIZING
CANCELABLE
CANCELATION
CANCELATIONS
CANCELEERED
CANCELEERING
CANCELEERS
CANCELIERED
CANCELIERING
CANCELIERS
CANCELLABLE
CANCELLARIAL
CANCELLARIAN
CANCELLARIATE
CANCELLARIATES
CANCELLATE
CANCELLATED
CANCELLATION
CANCELLATIONS
CANCELLERS
CANCELLING
CANCELLOUS
CANCERATED
CANCERATES
CANCERATING
CANCERATION
CANCERATIONS
CANCEROPHOBIA
CANCEROPHOBIAS
CANCEROUSLY
CANCERPHOBIA
CANCERPHOBIAS
CANCIONERO
CANCIONEROS

CANCRIFORM
CANCRIZANS
CANDELABRA
CANDELABRAS
CANDELABRUM
CANDELABRUMS
CANDELILLA
CANDELILLAS
CANDESCENCE
CANDESCENCES
CANDESCENT
CANDESCENTLY
CANDIDACIES
CANDIDATES
CANDIDATESHIP
CANDIDATESHIPS
CANDIDATURE
CANDIDATURES
CANDIDIASES
CANDIDIASIS
CANDIDNESS
CANDIDNESSES
CANDLEBERRIES
CANDLEBERRY
CANDLEFISH
CANDLEFISHES
CANDLEHOLDER
CANDLEHOLDERS
CANDLELIGHT
CANDLELIGHTED
CANDLELIGHTER
CANDLELIGHTERS
CANDLELIGHTS
CANDLENUTS
CANDLEPINS
CANDLEPOWER
CANDLEPOWERS
CANDLESNUFFER
CANDLESNUFFERS
CANDLESTICK
CANDLESTICKS
CANDLEWICK
CANDLEWICKS
CANDLEWOOD
CANDLEWOODS
CANDYFLOSS
CANDYFLOSSES
CANDYGRAMS
CANDYTUFTS
CANEBRAKES
CANEFRUITS
CANEPHORAS
CANEPHORES
CANEPHORUS
CANEPHORUSES
CANESCENCE
CANESCENCES
CANINITIES
CANISTERED
CANISTERING
CANISTERISATION
CANISTERISE
CANISTERISED
CANISTERISES
CANISTERISING
CANISTERIZATION
CANISTERIZE
CANISTERIZED
CANISTERIZES
CANISTERIZING
CANKEREDLY
CANKEREDNESS
CANKEREDNESSES
CANKERWORM
CANKERWORMS
CANNABINOID
CANNABINOIDS
CANNABINOL
CANNABINOLS
CANNABISES
CANNELLINI
CANNELLONI
CANNELURES

CANNIBALISATION
CANNIBALISE
CANNIBALISED
CANNIBALISES
CANNIBALISING
CANNIBALISM
CANNIBALISMS
CANNIBALISTIC
CANNIBALIZATION
CANNIBALIZE
CANNIBALIZED
CANNIBALIZES
CANNIBALIZING
CANNIBALLY
CANNINESSES
CANNISTERS
CANNONADED
CANNONADES
CANNONADING
CANNONBALL
CANNONBALLED
CANNONBALLING
CANNONBALLS
CANNONEERS
CANNONIERS
CANNONRIES
CANNULATED
CANNULATES
CANNULATING
CANNULATION
CANNULATIONS
CANOEWOODS
CANONESSES
CANONICALLY
CANONICALS
CANONICATE
CANONICATES
CANONICITIES
CANONICITY
CANONISATION
CANONISATIONS
CANONISERS
CANONISING
CANONISTIC
CANONIZATION
CANONIZATIONS
CANONIZERS
CANONIZING
CANOODLERS
CANOODLING
CANOPHILIA
CANOPHILIAS
CANOPHILIST
CANOPHILISTS
CANOPHOBIA
CANOPHOBIAS
CANOROUSLY
CANOROUSNESS
CANOROUSNESSES
CANTABANKS
CANTABILES
CANTALOUPE
CANTALOUPES
CANTALOUPS
CANTANKEROUS
CANTANKEROUSLY
CANTATRICE
CANTATRICES
CANTATRICI
CANTERBURIES
CANTERBURY
CANTERBURYS
CANTHARIDAL
CANTHARIDES
CANTHARIDIAN
CANTHARIDIC
CANTHARIDIN
CANTHARIDINE
CANTHARIDINES
CANTHARIDINS
CANTHARIDS
CANTHAXANTHIN
CANTHAXANTHINE

CANTHAXANTHINES
CANTHAXANTHINS
CANTHITISES
CANTICOING
CANTICOYED
CANTICOYING
CANTILENAS
CANTILEVER
CANTILEVERED
CANTILEVERING
CANTILEVERS
CANTILLATE
CANTILLATED
CANTILLATES
CANTILLATING
CANTILLATION
CANTILLATIONS
CANTILLATORY
CANTINESSES
CANTONISATION
CANTONISATIONS
CANTONISED
CANTONISES
CANTONISING
CANTONIZATION
CANTONIZATIONS
CANTONIZED
CANTONIZES
CANTONIZING
CANTONMENT
CANTONMENTS
CANULATING
CANULATION
CANULATIONS
CANVASBACK
CANVASBACKS
CANVASLIKE
CANVASSERS
CANVASSING
CANVASSINGS
CANYONEERS
CANYONINGS
CANZONETTA
CANZONETTAS
CANZONETTE
CAOUTCHOUC
CAOUTCHOUCS
CAPABILITIES
CAPABILITY
CAPABLENESS
CAPABLENESSES
CAPACIOUSLY
CAPACIOUSNESS
CAPACIOUSNESSES
CAPACITANCE
CAPACITANCES
CAPACITATE
CAPACITATED
CAPACITATES
CAPACITATING
CAPACITATION
CAPACITATIONS
CAPACITIES
CAPACITIVE
CAPACITIVELY
CAPACITORS
CAPARISONED
CAPARISONING
CAPARISONS
CAPELLINES
CAPELLMEISTER
CAPELLMEISTERS
CAPERCAILLIE
CAPERCAILLIES
CAPERCAILZIE
CAPERCAILZIES
CAPERINGLY
CAPERNOITED
CAPERNOITIE
CAPERNOITIES
CAPERNOITY
CAPILLACEOUS
CAPILLAIRE

CAPILLAIRES
CAPILLARIES
CAPILLARITIES
CAPILLARITY
CAPILLITIA
CAPILLITIUM
CAPILLITIUMS
CAPITALISATION
CAPITALISATIONS
CAPITALISE
CAPITALISED
CAPITALISES
CAPITALISING
CAPITALISM
CAPITALISMS
CAPITALIST
CAPITALISTIC
CAPITALISTS
CAPITALIZATION
CAPITALIZATIONS
CAPITALIZE
CAPITALIZED
CAPITALIZES
CAPITALIZING
CAPITATION
CAPITATIONS
CAPITATIVE
CAPITELLUM
CAPITOLIAN
CAPITOLINE
CAPITULANT
CAPITULANTS
CAPITULARIES
CAPITULARLY
CAPITULARS
CAPITULARY
CAPITULATE
CAPITULATED
CAPITULATES
CAPITULATING
CAPITULATION
CAPITULATIONS
CAPITULATOR
CAPITULATORS
CAPITULATORY
CAPNOMANCIES
CAPNOMANCY
CAPOCCHIAS
CAPODASTRO
CAPODASTROS
CAPONIERES
CAPONISING
CAPONIZING
CAPOTASTOS
CAPPARIDACEOUS
CAPPELLETTI
CAPPERNOITIES
CAPPERNOITY
CAPPUCCINO
CAPPUCCINOS
CAPREOLATE
CAPRICCIOS
CAPRICCIOSO
CAPRICIOUS
CAPRICIOUSLY
CAPRICIOUSNESS
CAPRIFICATION
CAPRIFICATIONS
CAPRIFOILS
CAPRIFOLES
CAPRIFOLIACEOUS
CAPRIFYING
CAPRIOLING
CAPROLACTAM
CAPROLACTAMS
CAPRYLATES
CAPSAICINS
CAPSIZABLE
CAPSOMERES
CAPSULATED
CAPSULATION
CAPSULATIONS
CAPSULISED

CAPSULISES
CAPSULISING
CAPSULIZED
CAPSULIZES
CAPSULIZING
CAPTAINCIES
CAPTAINING
CAPTAINRIES
CAPTAINSHIP
CAPTAINSHIPS
CAPTIONING
CAPTIONLESS
CAPTIOUSLY
CAPTIOUSNESS
CAPTIOUSNESSES
CAPTIVANCE
CAPTIVANCES
CAPTIVATED
CAPTIVATES
CAPTIVATING
CAPTIVATINGLY
CAPTIVATION
CAPTIVATIONS
CAPTIVATOR
CAPTIVATORS
CAPTIVAUNCE
CAPTIVAUNCES
CAPTIVITIES
CAPTOPRILS
CARABINEER
CARABINEERS
CARABINERO
CARABINEROS
CARABINERS
CARABINIER
CARABINIERE
CARABINIERI
CARABINIERS
CARACOLERS
CARACOLING
CARACOLLED
CARACOLLING
CARAGEENAN
CARAGEENANS
CARAMBOLAS
CARAMBOLED
CARAMBOLES
CARAMBOLING
CARAMELISATION
CARAMELISATIONS
CARAMELISE
CARAMELISED
CARAMELISES
CARAMELISING
CARAMELIZATION
CARAMELIZATIONS
CARAMELIZE
CARAMELIZED
CARAMELIZES
CARAMELIZING
CARAMELLED
CARAMELLING
CARANGOIDS
CARAPACIAL
CARAVANCES
CARAVANEER
CARAVANEERS
CARAVANERS
CARAVANETTE
CARAVANETTES
CARAVANING
CARAVANINGS
CARAVANNED
CARAVANNER
CARAVANNERS
CARAVANNING
CARAVANNINGS
CARAVANSARAI
CARAVANSARAIS
CARAVANSARIES
CARAVANSARY
CARAVANSERAI
CARAVANSERAIS

CARAVELLES
CARBACHOLS
CARBAMATES
CARBAMAZEPINE
CARBAMAZEPINES
CARBAMIDES
CARBAMIDINE
CARBAMIDINES
CARBAMOYLS
CARBANIONS
CARBAZOLES
CARBIMAZOLE
CARBIMAZOLES
CARBINEERS
CARBINIERS
CARBOCYCLIC
CARBOHYDRASE
CARBOHYDRASES
CARBOHYDRATE
CARBOHYDRATES
CARBOLATED
CARBOLISED
CARBOLISES
CARBOLISING
CARBOLIZED
CARBOLIZES
CARBOLIZING
CARBONACEOUS
CARBONADES
CARBONADOED
CARBONADOES
CARBONADOING
CARBONADOS
CARBONARAS
CARBONATED
CARBONATES
CARBONATING
CARBONATION
CARBONATIONS
CARBONATITE
CARBONATITES
CARBONETTE
CARBONETTES
CARBONIFEROUS
CARBONISATION
CARBONISATIONS
CARBONISED
CARBONISER
CARBONISERS
CARBONISES
CARBONISING
CARBONIUMS
CARBONIZATION
CARBONIZATIONS
CARBONIZED
CARBONIZER
CARBONIZERS
CARBONIZES
CARBONIZING
CARBONLESS
CARBONNADE
CARBONNADES
CARBONYLATE
CARBONYLATED
CARBONYLATES
CARBONYLATING
CARBONYLATION
CARBONYLATIONS
CARBONYLIC
CARBOXYLASE
CARBOXYLASES
CARBOXYLATE
CARBOXYLATED
CARBOXYLATES
CARBOXYLATING
CARBOXYLATION
CARBOXYLATIONS
CARBOXYLIC
CARBUNCLED
CARBUNCLES
CARBUNCULAR
CARBURATED
CARBURATES

CARBURATING
CARBURATION
CARBURATIONS
CARBURETED
CARBURETER
CARBURETERS
CARBURETING
CARBURETION
CARBURETIONS
CARBURETOR
CARBURETORS
CARBURETTED
CARBURETTER
CARBURETTERS
CARBURETTING
CARBURETTOR
CARBURETTORS
CARBURISATION
CARBURISATIONS
CARBURISED
CARBURISES
CARBURISING
CARBURIZATION
CARBURIZATIONS
CARBURIZED
CARBURIZES
CARBURIZING
CARBYLAMINE
CARBYLAMINES
CARCASSING
CARCINOGEN
CARCINOGENESES
CARCINOGENESIS
CARCINOGENIC
CARCINOGENICITY
CARCINOGENS
CARCINOIDS
CARCINOLOGICAL
CARCINOLOGIES
CARCINOLOGIST
CARCINOLOGISTS
CARCINOLOGY
CARCINOMAS
CARCINOMATA
CARCINOMATOID
CARCINOMATOSES
CARCINOMATOSIS
CARCINOMATOUS
CARCINOSARCOMA
CARCINOSARCOMAS
CARCINOSES
CARCINOSIS
CARDAMINES
CARDBOARDS
CARDBOARDY
CARDCASTLE
CARDCASTLES
CARDHOLDER
CARDHOLDERS
CARDIALGIA
CARDIALGIAS
CARDIALGIC
CARDIALGIES
CARDIGANED
CARDINALATE
CARDINALATES
CARDINALATIAL
CARDINALITIAL
CARDINALITIES
CARDINALITY
CARDINALLY
CARDINALSHIP
CARDINALSHIPS
CARDIOCENTESES
CARDIOCENTESIS
CARDIOGENIC
CARDIOGRAM
CARDIOGRAMS
CARDIOGRAPH
CARDIOGRAPHER
CARDIOGRAPHERS
CARDIOGRAPHIC
CARDIOGRAPHICAL

CARDIOGRAPHIES
CARDIOGRAPHS
CARDIOGRAPHY
CARDIOLOGICAL
CARDIOLOGIES
CARDIOLOGIST
CARDIOLOGISTS
CARDIOLOGY
CARDIOMEGALIES
CARDIOMEGALY
CARDIOMOTOR
CARDIOMYOPATHY
CARDIOPATHIES
CARDIOPATHY
CARDIOPLEGIA
CARDIOPLEGIAS
CARDIOPULMONARY
CARDIOTHORACIC
CARDIOTONIC
CARDIOTONICS
CARDIOVASCULAR
CARDITISES
CARDOPHAGI
CARDOPHAGUS
CARDPHONES
CARDPLAYER
CARDPLAYERS
CARDPUNCHES
CARDSHARPER
CARDSHARPERS
CARDSHARPING
CARDSHARPINGS
CARDSHARPS
CARDUACEOUS
CAREENAGES
CAREERISMS
CAREERISTS
CAREFREENESS
CAREFREENESSES
CAREFULLER
CAREFULLEST
CAREFULNESS
CAREFULNESSES
CAREGIVERS
CAREGIVING
CAREGIVINGS
CARELESSLY
CARELESSNESS
CARELESSNESSES
CARESSINGLY
CARESSINGS
CARESSIVELY
CARETAKERS
CARETAKING
CARETAKINGS
CAREWORKER
CAREWORKERS
CARFUFFLED
CARFUFFLES
CARFUFFLING
CARHOPPING
CARICATURA
CARICATURAL
CARICATURAS
CARICATURE
CARICATURED
CARICATURES
CARICATURING
CARICATURIST
CARICATURISTS
CARILLONED
CARILLONING
CARILLONIST
CARILLONISTS
CARILLONNED
CARILLONNEUR
CARILLONNEURS
CARILLONNING
CARIOGENIC
CARIOSITIES
CARIOUSNESS
CARIOUSNESSES
CARJACKERS

CARJACKING
CARJACKINGS
CARMAGNOLE
CARMAGNOLES
CARMELITES
CARMINATIVE
CARMINATIVES
CARNAHUBAS
CARNALISED
CARNALISES
CARNALISING
CARNALISMS
CARNALISTS
CARNALITIES
CARNALIZED
CARNALIZES
CARNALIZING
CARNALLING
CARNALLITE
CARNALLITES
CARNAPTIOUS
CARNAROLIS
CARNASSIAL
CARNASSIALS
CARNATIONED
CARNATIONS
CARNELIANS
CARNIFEXES
CARNIFICATION
CARNIFICATIONS
CARNIFICIAL
CARNIFYING
CARNITINES
CARNIVALESQUE
CARNIVORES
CARNIVORIES
CARNIVOROUS
CARNIVOROUSLY
CARNIVOROUSNESS
CARNOSAURS
CARNOSITIES
CARNOTITES
CAROLLINGS
CAROMELLED
CAROMELLING
CAROTENOID
CAROTENOIDS
CAROTINOID
CAROTINOIDS
CAROUSINGLY
CARPACCIOS
CARPELLARY
CARPELLATE
CARPELLATES
CARPENTARIA
CARPENTARIAS
CARPENTERED
CARPENTERING
CARPENTERS
CARPENTRIES
CARPETBAGGED
CARPETBAGGER
CARPETBAGGERIES
CARPETBAGGERS
CARPETBAGGERY
CARPETBAGGING
CARPETBAGS
CARPETINGS
CARPETMONGER
CARPETMONGERS
CARPETWEED
CARPETWEEDS
CARPHOLOGIES
CARPHOLOGY
CARPOGONIA
CARPOGONIAL
CARPOGONIUM
CARPOLOGICAL
CARPOLOGIES
CARPOLOGIST
CARPOLOGISTS
CARPOMETACARPI
CARPOMETACARPUS

CARPOOLERS
CARPOOLING
CARPOPHAGOUS
CARPOPHORE
CARPOPHORES
CARPOSPORE
CARPOSPORES
CARRAGEENAN
CARRAGEENANS
CARRAGEENIN
CARRAGEENINS
CARRAGEENS
CARRAGHEEN
CARRAGHEENAN
CARRAGHEENANS
CARRAGHEENIN
CARRAGHEENINS
CARRAGHEENS
CARREFOURS
CARRIAGEABLE
CARRIAGEWAY
CARRIAGEWAYS
CARRITCHES
CARRIWITCHET
CARRIWITCHETS
CARRONADES
CARROTIEST
CARROTTOPPED
CARROTTOPS
CARROUSELS
CARRYBACKS
CARRYFORWARD
CARRYFORWARDS
CARRYOVERS
CARRYTALES
CARSICKNESS
CARSICKNESSES
CARTELISATION
CARTELISATIONS
CARTELISED
CARTELISES
CARTELISING
CARTELISMS
CARTELISTS
CARTELIZATION
CARTELIZATIONS
CARTELIZED
CARTELIZES
CARTELIZING
CARTHAMINE
CARTHAMINES
CARTHORSES
CARTILAGES
CARTILAGINOUS
CARTOGRAMS
CARTOGRAPHER
CARTOGRAPHERS
CARTOGRAPHIC
CARTOGRAPHICAL
CARTOGRAPHIES
CARTOGRAPHY
CARTOLOGICAL
CARTOLOGIES
CARTOMANCIES
CARTOMANCY
CARTONAGES
CARTONNAGE
CARTONNAGES
CARTOONING
CARTOONINGS
CARTOONISH
CARTOONISHLY
CARTOONIST
CARTOONISTS
CARTOONLIKE
CARTOPHILE
CARTOPHILES
CARTOPHILIC
CARTOPHILIES
CARTOPHILIST
CARTOPHILISTS
CARTOPHILY
CARTOPPERS

CARTOUCHES
CARTRIDGES
CARTULARIES
CARTWHEELED
CARTWHEELER
CARTWHEELERS
CARTWHEELING
CARTWHEELS
CARTWRIGHT
CARTWRIGHTS
CARUNCULAR
CARUNCULATE
CARUNCULATED
CARVACROLS
CARYATIDAL
CARYATIDEAN
CARYATIDES
CARYATIDIC
CARYOPSIDES
CARYOPTERIS
CARYOPTERISES
CASCADURAS
CASCARILLA
CASCARILLAS
CASEATIONS
CASEBEARER
CASEBEARERS
CASEINATES
CASEINOGEN
CASEINOGENS
CASEMAKERS
CASEMENTED
CASEWORKER
CASEWORKERS
CASHIERERS
CASHIERING
CASHIERINGS
CASHIERMENT
CASHIERMENTS
CASHPOINTS
CASINGHEAD
CASINGHEADS
CASKSTANDS
CASSAREEPS
CASSATIONS
CASSEROLED
CASSEROLES
CASSEROLING
CASSIMERES
CASSINGLES
CASSIOPEIUM
CASSIOPEIUMS
CASSITERITE
CASSITERITES
CASSOLETTE
CASSOLETTES
CASSONADES
CASSOULETS
CASSOWARIES
CASSUMUNAR
CASSUMUNARS
CASTABILITIES
CASTABILITY
CASTANOSPERMINE
CASTELLANS
CASTELLATED
CASTELLATION
CASTELLATIONS
CASTELLUMS
CASTIGATED
CASTIGATES
CASTIGATING
CASTIGATION
CASTIGATIONS
CASTIGATOR
CASTIGATORS
CASTIGATORY
CASTOREUMS
CASTRAMETATION
CASTRAMETATIONS
CASTRATERS
CASTRATING

CASTRATION	CATALOGUISE	CATECHESIS	CATHARIZED	CAULIFLOWERS	CELEBRANTS
CASTRATIONS	CATALOGUISED	CATECHETIC	CATHARIZES	CAULIGENOUS	CELEBRATED
CASTRATORS	CATALOGUISES	CATECHETICAL	CATHARIZING	CAUMSTONES	CELEBRATEDNESS
CASTRATORY	CATALOGUISING	CATECHETICALLY	CATHARTICAL	CAUSABILITIES	CELEBRATES
CASUALISATION	CATALOGUIST	CATECHETICS	CATHARTICALLY	CAUSABILITY	CELEBRATING
CASUALISATIONS	CATALOGUISTS	CATECHISATION	CATHARTICS	CAUSALGIAS	CELEBRATION
CASUALISED	CATALOGUIZE	CATECHISATIONS	CATHECTING	CAUSALITIES	CELEBRATIONS
CASUALISES	CATALOGUIZED	CATECHISED	CATHEDRALS	CAUSATIONAL	CELEBRATIVE
CASUALISING	CATALOGUIZES	CATECHISER	CATHEDRATIC	CAUSATIONISM	CELEBRATOR
CASUALISMS	CATALOGUIZING	CATECHISERS	CATHEPSINS	CAUSATIONISMS	CELEBRATORS
CASUALIZATION	CATALYSERS	CATECHISES	CATHETERISATION	CAUSATIONIST	CELEBRATORY
CASUALIZATIONS	CATALYSING	CATECHISING	CATHETERISE	CAUSATIONISTS	CELEBRITIES
CASUALIZED	CATALYTICAL	CATECHISINGS	CATHETERISED	CAUSATIONS	CELERITIES
CASUALIZES	CATALYTICALLY	CATECHISMAL	CATHETERISES	CAUSATIVELY	CELESTIALLY
CASUALIZING	CATALYZERS	CATECHISMS	CATHETERISING	CAUSATIVENESS	CELESTIALS
CASUALNESS	CATALYZING	CATECHISTIC	CATHETERISM	CAUSATIVENESSES	CELESTINES
CASUALNESSES	CATAMARANS	CATECHISTICAL	CATHETERISMS	CAUSATIVES	CELESTITES
CASUALTIES	CATAMENIAL	CATECHISTICALLY	CATHETERIZATION	CAUSELESSLY	CELIBACIES
CASUARINAS	CATAMOUNTAIN	CATECHISTS	CATHETERIZE	CAUSELESSNESS	CELIBATARIAN
CASUISTICAL	CATAMOUNTAINS	CATECHIZATION	CATHETERIZED	CAUSELESSNESSES	CELLARAGES
CASUISTICALLY	CATAMOUNTS	CATECHIZATIONS	CATHETERIZES	CAUSEWAYED	CELLARETTE
CASUISTRIES	CATANANCHE	CATECHIZED	CATHETERIZING	CAUSEWAYING	CELLARETTES
CATABOLICALLY	CATANANCHES	CATECHIZER	CATHETOMETER	CAUSTICALLY	CELLARISTS
CATABOLISE	CATAPHONIC	CATECHIZERS	CATHETOMETERS	CAUSTICITIES	CELLARWAYS
CATABOLISED	CATAPHONICS	CATECHIZES	CATHETUSES	CAUSTICITY	CELLBLOCKS
CATABOLISES	CATAPHORAS	CATECHIZING	CATHODALLY	CAUSTICNESS	CELLENTANI
CATABOLISING	CATAPHORESES	CATECHIZINGS	CATHODICAL	CAUSTICNESSES	CELLENTANIS
CATABOLISM	CATAPHORESIS	CATECHOLAMINE	CATHODICALLY	CAUTERANTS	CELLIFEROUS
CATABOLISMS	CATAPHORETIC	CATECHOLAMINES	CATHODOGRAPH	CAUTERISATION	CELLOBIOSE
CATABOLITE	CATAPHORIC	CATECHUMEN	CATHODOGRAPHER	CAUTERISATIONS	CELLOBIOSES
CATABOLITES	CATAPHRACT	CATECHUMENAL	CATHODOGRAPHERS	CAUTERISED	CELLOIDINS
CATABOLIZE	CATAPHRACTIC	CATECHUMENATE	CATHODOGRAPHIES	CAUTERISES	CELLOPHANE
CATABOLIZED	CATAPHRACTS	CATECHUMENATES	CATHODOGRAPHS	CAUTERISING	CELLOPHANES
CATABOLIZES	CATAPHYLLARY	CATECHUMENICAL	CATHODOGRAPHY	CAUTERISMS	CELLPHONES
CATABOLIZING	CATAPHYLLS	CATECHUMENISM	CATHOLICALLY	CAUTERIZATION	CELLULARITIES
CATACAUSTIC	CATAPHYSICAL	CATECHUMENISMS	CATHOLICATE	CAUTERIZATIONS	CELLULARITY
CATACAUSTICS	CATAPLASIA	CATECHUMENS	CATHOLICATES	CAUTERIZED	CELLULASES
CATACHRESES	CATAPLASIAS	CATECHUMENSHIP	CATHOLICISATION	CAUTERIZES	CELLULATED
CATACHRESIS	CATAPLASMS	CATECHUMENSHIPS	CATHOLICISE	CAUTERIZING	CELLULIFEROUS
CATACHRESTIC	CATAPLASTIC	CATEGOREMATIC	CATHOLICISED	CAUTIONARY	CELLULITES
CATACHRESTICAL	CATAPLECTIC	CATEGORIAL	CATHOLICISES	CAUTIONERS	CELLULITIS
CATACLASES	CATAPLEXIES	CATEGORIALLY	CATHOLICISING	CAUTIONING	CELLULITISES
CATACLASIS	CATAPULTED	CATEGORICAL	CATHOLICISM	CAUTIONRIES	CELLULOIDS
CATACLASMIC	CATAPULTIC	CATEGORICALLY	CATHOLICISMS	CAUTIOUSLY	CELLULOLYTIC
CATACLASMS	CATAPULTIER	CATEGORICALNESS	CATHOLICITIES	CAUTIOUSNESS	CELLULOSES
CATACLASTIC	CATAPULTIERS	CATEGORIES	CATHOLICITY	CAUTIOUSNESSES	CELLULOSIC
CATACLINAL	CATAPULTING	CATEGORISATION	CATHOLICIZATION	CAVALCADED	CELLULOSICS
CATACLYSMAL	CATARACTOUS	CATEGORISATIONS	CATHOLICIZE	CAVALCADES	CELSITUDES
CATACLYSMIC	CATARRHALLY	CATEGORISE	CATHOLICIZED	CAVALCADING	CEMBALISTS
CATACLYSMICALLY	CATARRHINE	CATEGORISED	CATHOLICIZES	CAVALIERED	CEMENTATION
CATACLYSMS	CATARRHINES	CATEGORISES	CATHOLICIZING	CAVALIERING	CEMENTATIONS
CATACOUSTICS	CATARRHOUS	CATEGORISING	CATHOLICLY	CAVALIERISH	CEMENTATORY
CATACUMBAL	CATASTASES	CATEGORIST	CATHOLICOI	CAVALIERISM	CEMENTITES
CATADIOPTRIC	CATASTASIS	CATEGORISTS	CATHOLICON	CAVALIERISMS	CEMENTITIOUS
CATADIOPTRICAL	CATASTROPHE	CATEGORIZATION	CATHOLICONS	CAVALIERLY	CEMETERIES
CATADROMOUS	CATASTROPHES	CATEGORIZATIONS	CATHOLICOS	CAVALLETTI	CENESTHESES
CATAFALCOES	CATASTROPHIC	CATEGORIZE	CATHOLICOSES	CAVALRYMAN	CENESTHESIA
CATAFALQUE	CATASTROPHISM	CATEGORIZED	CATHOLYTES	CAVALRYMEN	CENESTHESIAS
CATAFALQUES	CATASTROPHISMS	CATEGORIZES	CATILINARIAN	CAVEFISHES	CENESTHESIS
CATALECTIC	CATASTROPHIST	CATEGORIZING	CATIONICALLY	CAVENDISHES	CENESTHETIC
CATALECTICS	CATASTROPHISTS	CATENACCIO	CATNAPPERS	CAVERNICOLOUS	CENOBITICAL
CATALEPSIES	CATATONIAS	CATENACCIOS	CATNAPPING	CAVERNOUSLY	CENOGENESES
CATALEPTIC	CATATONICALLY	CATENARIAN	CATOPTRICAL	CAVERNULOUS	CENOGENESIS
CATALEPTICALLY	CATATONICS	CATENARIES	CATOPTRICS	CAVILLATION	CENOGENETIC
CATALEPTICS	CATATONIES	CATENATING	CATTINESSES	CAVILLATIONS	CENOGENETICALLY
CATALLACTIC	CATCALLERS	CATENATION	CATTISHNESS	CAVILLINGS	CENOSPECIES
CATALLACTICALLY	CATCALLING	CATENATIONS	CATTISHNESSES	CAVITATING	CENOTAPHIC
CATALLACTICS	CATCHCRIES	CATENULATE	CAUCHEMARS	CAVITATION	CENSORABLE
CATALOGERS	CATCHFLIES	CATERCORNER	CAUCUSSING	CAVITATIONS	CENSORIOUS
CATALOGING	CATCHINESS	CATERCORNERED	CAUDATIONS	CEANOTHUSES	CENSORIOUSLY
CATALOGISE	CATCHINESSES	CATERESSES	CAUDILLISMO	CEASEFIRES	CENSORIOUSNESS
CATALOGISED	CATCHMENTS	CATERPILLAR	CAUDILLISMOS	CEASELESSLY	CENSORSHIP
CATALOGISES	CATCHPENNIES	CATERPILLARS	CAULESCENT	CEASELESSNESS	CENSORSHIPS
CATALOGISING	CATCHPENNY	CATERWAULED	CAULICOLOUS	CEASELESSNESSES	CENSURABILITIES
CATALOGIZE	CATCHPHRASE	CATERWAULER	CAULICULATE	CEBADILLAS	CENSURABILITY
CATALOGIZED	CATCHPHRASES	CATERWAULERS	CAULICULUS	CECUTIENCIES	CENSURABLE
CATALOGIZES	CATCHPOLES	CATERWAULING	CAULICULUSES	CECUTIENCY	CENSURABLENESS
CATALOGIZING	CATCHPOLLS	CATERWAULINGS	CAULIFLORIES	CEDARBIRDS	CENSURABLY
CATALOGUED	CATCHWATER	CATERWAULS	CAULIFLOROUS	CEDARWOODS	CENTAUREAS
CATALOGUER	CATCHWEEDS	CATFACINGS	CAULIFLORY	CEDRELACEOUS	CENTAURIAN
CATALOGUERS	CATCHWEIGHT	CATHARISED	CAULIFLOWER	CEILOMETER	CENTAURIES
CATALOGUES	CATCHWORDS	CATHARISES	CAULIFLOWERET	CEILOMETERS	CENTENARIAN
CATALOGUING	CATECHESES	CATHARISING	CAULIFLOWERETS	CELANDINES	CENTENARIANISM

C

CENTENARIANISMS	CENTRICALNESSES	CEPHALOSPORIN	CERTIFICATES	CHAIRPERSON	CHAMPERTIES
CENTENARIANS	CENTRICITIES	CEPHALOSPORINS	CERTIFICATING	CHAIRPERSONS	CHAMPERTOUS
CENTENARIES	CENTRICITY	CEPHALOTHIN	CERTIFICATION	CHAIRWOMAN	CHAMPIGNON
CENTENIERS	CENTRIFUGAL	CEPHALOTHINS	CERTIFICATIONS	CHAIRWOMEN	CHAMPIGNONS
CENTENNIAL	CENTRIFUGALISE	CEPHALOTHORACES	CERTIFICATORIES	CHAISELESS	CHAMPIONED
CENTENNIALLY	CENTRIFUGALISED	CEPHALOTHORACIC	CERTIFICATORY	CHAKALAKAS	CHAMPIONESS
CENTENNIALS	CENTRIFUGALISES	CEPHALOTHORAX	CERTIFIERS	CHALAZIONS	CHAMPIONESSES
CENTERBOARD	CENTRIFUGALIZE	CEPHALOTHORAXES	CERTIFYING	CHALAZOGAMIC	CHAMPIONING
CENTERBOARDS	CENTRIFUGALIZED	CEPHALOTOMIES	CERTIORARI	CHALAZOGAMIES	CHAMPIONSHIP
CENTEREDNESS	CENTRIFUGALIZES	CEPHALOTOMY	CERTIORARIS	CHALAZOGAMY	CHAMPIONSHIPS
CENTEREDNESSES	CENTRIFUGALLY	CERAMICIST	CERTITUDES	CHALCANTHITE	CHAMPLEVES
CENTERFOLD	CENTRIFUGALS	CERAMICISTS	CERULOPLASMIN	CHALCANTHITES	CHANCELESS
CENTERFOLDS	CENTRIFUGATION	CERAMOGRAPHIES	CERULOPLASMINS	CHALCEDONIC	CHANCELLERIES
CENTERINGS	CENTRIFUGATIONS	CERAMOGRAPHY	CERUMINOUS	CHALCEDONIES	CHANCELLERY
CENTERLESS	CENTRIFUGE	CERARGYRITE	CERUSSITES	CHALCEDONY	CHANCELLOR
CENTERLINE	CENTRIFUGED	CERARGYRITES	CERVELASES	CHALCEDONYX	CHANCELLORIES
CENTERLINES	CENTRIFUGENCE	CERASTIUMS	CERVICITIS	CHALCEDONYXES	CHANCELLORS
CENTERPIECE	CENTRIFUGENCES	CERATITISES	CERVICITISES	CHALCOCITE	CHANCELLORSHIP
CENTERPIECES	CENTRIFUGES	CERATODUSES	CERVICOGRAPHIES	CHALCOCITES	CHANCELLORSHIPS
CENTESIMAL	CENTRIFUGING	CERATOPSIAN	CERVICOGRAPHY	CHALCOGENIDE	CHANCELLORY
CENTESIMALLY	CENTRIOLES	CERATOPSIANS	CESAREVICH	CHALCOGENIDES	CHANCERIES
CENTESIMALS	CENTRIPETAL	CERATOPSID	CESAREVICHES	CHALCOGENS	CHANCINESS
CENTESIMOS	CENTRIPETALISM	CERATOPSIDS	CESAREVITCH	CHALCOGRAPHER	CHANCINESSES
CENTIGRADE	CENTRIPETALISMS	CERCARIANS	CESAREVITCHES	CHALCOGRAPHERS	CHANCROIDAL
CENTIGRAMME	CENTRIPETALLY	CERCOPITHECID	CESAREVNAS	CHALCOGRAPHIC	CHANCROIDS
CENTIGRAMMES	CENTROBARIC	CERCOPITHECIDS	CESAREWICH	CHALCOGRAPHICAL	CHANDELIER
CENTIGRAMS	CENTROCLINAL	CERCOPITHECOID	CESAREWICHES	CHALCOGRAPHIES	CHANDELIERED
CENTILITER	CENTROIDAL	CERCOPITHECOIDS	CESAREWITCH	CHALCOGRAPHIST	CHANDELIERS
CENTILITERS	CENTROLECITHAL	CEREALISTS	CESAREWITCHES	CHALCOGRAPHISTS	CHANDELLED
CENTILITRE	CENTROMERE	CEREBELLAR	CESPITOSELY	CHALCOGRAPHY	CHANDELLES
CENTILITRES	CENTROMERES	CEREBELLIC	CESSATIONS	CHALCOLITHIC	CHANDELLING
CENTILLION	CENTROMERIC	CEREBELLOUS	CESSIONARIES	CHALCOPYRITE	CHANDLERIES
CENTILLIONS	CENTROSOME	CEREBELLUM	CESSIONARY	CHALCOPYRITES	CHANDLERING
CENTILLIONTH	CENTROSOMES	CEREBELLUMS	CESTOIDEAN	CHALICOTHERE	CHANDLERINGS
CENTILLIONTHS	CENTROSOMIC	CEREBRALISM	CESTOIDEANS	CHALICOTHERES	CHANDLERLY
CENTIMETER	CENTROSPHERE	CEREBRALISMS	CETEOSAURUS	CHALKBOARD	CHANGEABILITIES
CENTIMETERS	CENTROSPHERES	CEREBRALIST	CETEOSAURUSES	CHALKBOARDS	CHANGEABILITY
CENTIMETRE	CENTROSYMMETRIC	CEREBRALISTS	CETOLOGICAL	CHALKFACES	CHANGEABLE
CENTIMETRES	CENTUMVIRATE	CEREBRALLY	CETOLOGIES	CHALKINESS	CHANGEABLENESS
CENTIMETRIC	CENTUMVIRATES	CEREBRATED	CETOLOGIST	CHALKINESSES	CHANGEABLY
CENTIMORGAN	CENTUMVIRI	CEREBRATES	CETOLOGISTS	CHALKSTONE	CHANGEFULLY
CENTIMORGANS	CENTUPLICATE	CEREBRATING	CETRIMIDES	CHALKSTONES	CHANGEFULNESS
CENTINELLS	CENTUPLICATED	CEREBRATION	CEVADILLAS	CHALLANING	CHANGEFULNESSES
CENTIPEDES	CENTUPLICATES	CEREBRATIONS	CEYLANITES	CHALLENGEABLE	CHANGELESS
CENTIPOISE	CENTUPLICATING	CEREBRIFORM	CEYLONITES	CHALLENGED	CHANGELESSLY
CENTIPOISES	CENTUPLICATION	CEREBRITIS	CHABAZITES	CHALLENGER	CHANGELESSNESS
CENTONELLS	CENTUPLICATIONS	CEREBRITISES	CHAENOMELES	CHALLENGERS	CHANGELING
CENTONISTS	CENTUPLING	CEREBROSIDE	CHAENOMELESES	CHALLENGES	CHANGELINGS
CENTRALEST	CENTURIATION	CEREBROSIDES	CHAETIFEROUS	CHALLENGING	CHANGEOVER
CENTRALISATION	CENTURIATIONS	CEREBROSPINAL	CHAETODONS	CHALLENGINGLY	CHANGEOVERS
CENTRALISATIONS	CENTURIATOR	CEREBROTONIA	CHAETOGNATH	CHALUMEAUS	CHANGEROUND
CENTRALISE	CENTURIATORS	CEREBROTONIAS	CHAETOGNATHS	CHALUMEAUX	CHANGEROUNDS
CENTRALISED	CENTURIONS	CEREBROTONIC	CHAETOPODS	CHALYBEATE	CHANNELERS
CENTRALISER	CEPHALAGRA	CEREBROVASCULAR	CHAFFERERS	CHALYBEATES	CHANNELING
CENTRALISERS	CEPHALAGRAS	CERECLOTHS	CHAFFERIES	CHALYBITES	CHANNELISATION
CENTRALISES	CEPHALALGIA	CEREMONIAL	CHAFFERING	CHAMAELEON	CHANNELISATIONS
CENTRALISING	CEPHALALGIAS	CEREMONIALISM	CHAFFINCHES	CHAMAELEONS	CHANNELISE
CENTRALISM	CEPHALALGIC	CEREMONIALISMS	CHAFFINGLY	CHAMAEPHYTE	CHANNELISED
CENTRALISMS	CEPHALEXIN	CEREMONIALIST	CHAGRINING	CHAMAEPHYTES	CHANNELISES
CENTRALIST	CEPHALEXINS	CEREMONIALISTS	CHAGRINNED	CHAMBERERS	CHANNELISING
CENTRALISTIC	CEPHALICALLY	CEREMONIALLY	CHAGRINNING	CHAMBERHAND	CHANNELIZATION
CENTRALISTS	CEPHALISATION	CEREMONIALS	CHAINBRAKE	CHAMBERHANDS	CHANNELIZATIONS
CENTRALITIES	CEPHALISATIONS	CEREMONIES	CHAINBRAKES	CHAMBERING	CHANNELIZE
CENTRALITY	CEPHALITIS	CEREMONIOUS	CHAINFALLS	CHAMBERINGS	CHANNELIZED
CENTRALIZATION	CEPHALITISES	CEREMONIOUSLY	CHAINPLATE	CHAMBERLAIN	CHANNELIZES
CENTRALIZATIONS	CEPHALIZATION	CEREMONIOUSNESS	CHAINPLATES	CHAMBERLAINS	CHANNELIZING
CENTRALIZE	CEPHALIZATIONS	CERIFEROUS	CHAINSAWED	CHAMBERLAINSHIP	CHANNELLED
CENTRALIZED	CEPHALOCELE	CEROGRAPHIC	CHAINSAWING	CHAMBERMAID	CHANNELLER
CENTRALIZER	CEPHALOCELES	CEROGRAPHICAL	CHAINSHOTS	CHAMBERMAIDS	CHANNELLERS
CENTRALIZERS	CEPHALOCHORDATE	CEROGRAPHIES	CHAINSTITCH	CHAMBERPOT	CHANNELLING
CENTRALIZES	CEPHALOMETER	CEROGRAPHIST	CHAINSTITCHES	CHAMBERPOTS	CHANSONETTE
CENTRALIZING	CEPHALOMETERS	CEROGRAPHISTS	CHAINWHEEL	CHAMBRANLE	CHANSONETTES
CENTREBOARD	CEPHALOMETRIC	CEROGRAPHS	CHAINWHEELS	CHAMBRANLES	CHANSONNIER
CENTREBOARDS	CEPHALOMETRIES	CEROGRAPHY	CHAINWORKS	CHAMELEONIC	CHANSONNIERS
CENTREFOLD	CEPHALOMETRY	CEROMANCIES	CHAIRBORNE	CHAMELEONLIKE	CHANTARELLE
CENTREFOLDS	CEPHALOPOD	CEROPLASTIC	CHAIRBOUND	CHAMELEONS	CHANTARELLES
CENTREINGS	CEPHALOPODAN	CEROPLASTICS	CHAIRLIFTS	CHAMFERERS	CHANTECLER
CENTRELINE	CEPHALOPODANS	CERTAINEST	CHAIRMANED	CHAMFERING	CHANTECLERS
CENTRELINES	CEPHALOPODIC	CERTAINTIES	CHAIRMANING	CHAMFRAINS	CHANTERELLE
CENTREPIECE	CEPHALOPODOUS	CERTIFIABLE	CHAIRMANNED	CHAMOISING	CHANTERELLES
CENTREPIECES	CEPHALOPODS	CERTIFIABLY	CHAIRMANNING	CHAMOMILES	CHANTEUSES
CENTRICALLY	CEPHALORIDINE	CERTIFICATE	CHAIRMANSHIP	CHAMPAGNES	CHANTICLEER
CENTRICALNESS	CEPHALORIDINES	CERTIFICATED	CHAIRMANSHIPS	CHAMPAIGNS	CHANTICLEERS

CHANTINGLY
CHANTRESSES
CHANUKIAHS
CHAOLOGIES
CHAOLOGIST
CHAOLOGISTS
CHAOTICALLY
CHAPARAJOS
CHAPAREJOS
CHAPARRALS
CHAPATTIES
CHAPELRIES
CHAPERONAGE
CHAPERONAGES
CHAPERONED
CHAPERONES
CHAPERONING
CHAPFALLEN
CHAPLAINCIES
CHAPLAINCY
CHAPLAINRIES
CHAPLAINRY
CHAPLAINSHIP
CHAPLAINSHIPS
CHAPMANSHIP
CHAPMANSHIPS
CHAPPESSES
CHAPRASSIES
CHAPRASSIS
CHAPSTICKS
CHAPTALISATION
CHAPTALISATIONS
CHAPTALISE
CHAPTALISED
CHAPTALISES
CHAPTALISING
CHAPTALIZATION
CHAPTALIZATIONS
CHAPTALIZE
CHAPTALIZED
CHAPTALIZES
CHAPTALIZING
CHAPTERHOUSE
CHAPTERHOUSES
CHAPTERING
CHARABANCS
CHARACINOID
CHARACTERED
CHARACTERFUL
CHARACTERIES
CHARACTERING
CHARACTERISABLE
CHARACTERISE
CHARACTERISED
CHARACTER'SER
CHARACTERISERS
CHARACTERISES
CHARACTERISING
CHARACTERISM
CHARACTERISMS
CHARACTERISTIC
CHARACTERISTICS
CHARACTERIZABLE
CHARACTERIZE
CHARACTERIZED
CHARACTERIZER
CHARACTERIZERS
CHARACTERIZES
CHARACTERIZING
CHARACTERLESS
CHARACTEROLOGY
CHARACTERS
CHARACTERY
CHARBROILED
CHARBROILER
CHARBROILERS
CHARBROILING
CHARBROILS
CHARCOALED
CHARCOALING
CHARCUTERIE
CHARCUTERIES
CHARDONNAY

CHARDONNAYS
CHARGEABILITIES
CHARGEABILITY
CHARGEABLE
CHARGEABLENESS
CHARGEABLY
CHARGEHAND
CHARGEHANDS
CHARGELESS
CHARGENURSE
CHARGENURSES
CHARGESHEET
CHARGESHEETS
CHARGRILLED
CHARGRILLING
CHARGRILLS
CHARINESSES
CHARIOTEER
CHARIOTEERED
CHARIOTEERING
CHARIOTEERS
CHARIOTING
CHARISMATA
CHARISMATIC
CHARISMATICS
CHARITABLE
CHARITABLENESS
CHARITABLY
CHARIVARIED
CHARIVARIING
CHARIVARIS
CHARLADIES
CHARLATANIC
CHARLATANICAL
CHARLATANISM
CHARLATANISMS
CHARLATANISTIC
CHARLATANRIES
CHARLATANRY
CHARLATANS
CHARLESTON
CHARLESTONED
CHARLESTONING
CHARLESTONS
CHARLOTTES
CHARMEUSES
CHARMINGER
CHARMINGEST
CHARMINGLY
CHARMLESSLY
CHARMONIUM
CHAROSETHS
CHARTACEOUS
CHARTERERS
CHARTERING
CHARTERPARTIES
CHARTERPARTY
CHARTHOUSE
CHARTHOUSES
CHARTOGRAPHER
CHARTOGRAPHERS
CHARTOGRAPHIC
CHARTOGRAPHICAL
CHARTOGRAPHIES
CHARTOGRAPHY
CHARTREUSE
CHARTREUSES
CHARTULARIES
CHARTULARY
CHASEPORTS
CHASMOGAMIC
CHASMOGAMIES
CHASMOGAMOUS
CHASMOGAMY
CHASSEPOTS
CHASTENERS
CHASTENESS
CHASTENESSES
CHASTENING
CHASTENINGLY
CHASTENMENT
CHASTENMENTS
CHASTISABLE

CHASTISEMENT
CHASTISEMENTS
CHASTISERS
CHASTISING
CHASTITIES
CHATEAUBRIAND
CHATEAUBRIANDS
CHATELAINE
CHATELAINES
CHATELAINS
CHATOYANCE
CHATOYANCES
CHATOYANCIES
CHATOYANCY
CHATOYANTS
CHATTERATI
CHATTERBOX
CHATTERBOXES
CHATTERERS
CHATTERING
CHATTERINGS
CHATTINESS
CHATTINESSES
CHAUDFROID
CHAUDFROIDS
CHAUFFEURED
CHAUFFEURING
CHAUFFEURS
CHAUFFEUSE
CHAUFFEUSED
CHAUFFEUSES
CHAUFFEUSING
CHAULMOOGRA
CHAULMOOGRAS
CHAULMUGRA
CHAULMUGRAS
CHAUNTRESS
CHAUNTRESSES
CHAUNTRIES
CHAUSSURES
CHAUTAUQUA
CHAUTAUQUAS
CHAUVINISM
CHAUVINISMS
CHAUVINIST
CHAUVINISTIC
CHAUVINISTS
CHAVENDERS
CHAVTASTIC
CHAWBACONS
CHEAPENERS
CHEAPENING
CHEAPISHLY
CHEAPJACKS
CHEAPNESSES
CHEAPSKATE
CHEAPSKATES
CHEATERIES
CHEATINGLY
CHECHAKOES
CHECHAQUOS
CHECKBOOKS
CHECKCLERK
CHECKCLERKS
CHECKERBERRIES
CHECKERBERRY
CHECKERBLOOM
CHECKERBLOOMS
CHECKERBOARD
CHECKERBOARDS
CHECKERING
CHECKLATON
CHECKLATONS
CHECKLISTED
CHECKLISTING
CHECKLISTS
CHECKMARKED
CHECKMARKING
CHECKMARKS
CHECKMATED
CHECKMATES
CHECKMATING
CHECKPOINT

CHECKPOINTS
CHECKRAILS
CHECKREINS
CHECKROOMS
CHECKROWED
CHECKROWING
CHECKWEIGHER
CHECKWEIGHERS
CHEECHAKOES
CHEECHAKOS
CHEECHALKO
CHEECHALKOES
CHEECHALKOS
CHEEKBONES
CHEEKINESS
CHEEKINESSES
CHEEKPIECE
CHEEKPIECES
CHEEKPOUCH
CHEEKPOUCHES
CHEEKTEETH
CHEEKTOOTH
CHEERFULLER
CHEERFULLEST
CHEERFULLY
CHEERFULNESS
CHEERFULNESSES
CHEERINESS
CHEERINESSES
CHEERINGLY
CHEERISHNESS
CHEERISHNESSES
CHEERLEADER
CHEERLEADERS
CHEERLEADING
CHEERLEADS
CHEERLESSLY
CHEERLESSNESS
CHEERLESSNESSES
CHEESEBOARD
CHEESEBOARDS
CHEESEBURGER
CHEESEBURGERS
CHEESECAKE
CHEESECAKES
CHEESECLOTH
CHEESECLOTHS
CHEESECUTTER
CHEESECUTTERS
CHEESEHOPPER
CHEESEHOPPERS
CHEESEMITE
CHEESEMITES
CHEESEMONGER
CHEESEMONGERS
CHEESEPARER
CHEESEPARERS
CHEESEPARING
CHEESEPARINGS
CHEESEPRESS
CHEESEPRESSES
CHEESETASTER
CHEESETASTERS
CHEESEVATS
CHEESEWIRE
CHEESEWIRES
CHEESEWOOD
CHEESEWOODS
CHEESEWRING
CHEESEWRINGS
CHEESINESS
CHEESINESSES
CHEILITISES
CHELASHIPS
CHELATABLE
CHELATIONS
CHELICERAE
CHELICERAL
CHELICERATE
CHELICERATES
CHELIFEROUS
CHELONIANS
CHELUVIATION

CHELUVIATIONS
CHEMAUTOTROPH
CHEMAUTOTROPHIC
CHEMAUTOTROPHS
CHEMIATRIC
CHEMICALLY
CHEMICKING
CHEMIOSMOSES
CHEMIOSMOSIS
CHEMIOSMOTIC
CHEMISETTE
CHEMISETTES
CHEMISORBED
CHEMISORBING
CHEMISORBS
CHEMISORPTION
CHEMISORPTIONS
CHEMISTRIES
CHEMITYPES
CHEMITYPIES
CHEMOATTRACTANT
CHEMOAUTOTROPH
CHEMOAUTOTROPHS
CHEMOAUTOTROPHY
CHEMOAUTROPH
CHEMOAUTROPHS
CHEMOCEPTOR
CHEMOCEPTORS
CHEMOKINES
CHEMOKINESES
CHEMOKINESIS
CHEMOLITHOTROPH
CHEMONASTIES
CHEMONASTY
CHEMOPSYCHIATRY
CHEMORECEPTION
CHEMORECEPTIONS
CHEMORECEPTIVE
CHEMORECEPTOR
CHEMORECEPTORS
CHEMOSMOSES
CHEMOSMOSIS
CHEMOSMOTIC
CHEMOSORBED
CHEMOSORBING
CHEMOSORBS
CHEMOSPHERE
CHEMOSPHERES
CHEMOSPHERIC
CHEMOSTATS
CHEMOSURGERIES
CHEMOSURGERY
CHEMOSURGICAL
CHEMOSYNTHESES
CHEMOSYNTHESIS
CHEMOSYNTHETIC
CHEMOTACTIC
CHEMOTACTICALLY
CHEMOTAXES
CHEMOTAXIS
CHEMOTAXONOMIC
CHEMOTAXONOMIES
CHEMOTAXONOMIST
CHEMOTAXONOMY
CHEMOTHERAPIES
CHEMOTHERAPIST
CHEMOTHERAPISTS
CHEMOTHERAPY
CHEMOTROPIC
CHEMOTROPICALLY
CHEMOTROPISM
CHEMOTROPISMS
CHEMPADUKS
CHEMURGICAL
CHEMURGIES
CHENOPODIACEOUS
CHEONGSAMS
CHEQUEBOOK
CHEQUEBOOKS
CHEQUERBOARD
CHEQUERBOARDS
CHEQUERING
CHEQUERWISE

CHEQUERWORK
CHEQUERWORKS
CHERALITES
CHERIMOYAS
CHERIMOYER
CHERIMOYERS
CHERISHABLE
CHERISHERS
CHERISHING
CHERISHINGLY
CHERISHMENT
CHERISHMENTS
CHERNOZEMIC
CHERNOZEMS
CHERRYLIKE
CHERRYSTONE
CHERRYSTONES
CHERSONESE
CHERSONESES
CHERUBICAL
CHERUBICALLY
CHERUBIMIC
CHERUBLIKE
CHERVONETS
CHESSBOARD
CHESSBOARDS
CHESSPIECE
CHESSPIECES
CHESSYLITE
CHESSYLITES
CHESTERFIELD
CHESTERFIELDS
CHESTINESS
CHESTINESSES
CHEVALIERS
CHEVELURES
CHEVESAILE
CHEVESAILES
CHEVISANCE
CHEVISANCES
CHEVRETTES
CHEVROTAIN
CHEVROTAINS
CHEWINESSES
CHIACKINGS
CHIAROSCURISM
CHIAROSCURISMS
CHIAROSCURIST
CHIAROSCURISTS
CHIAROSCURO
CHIAROSCUROS
CHIASMATIC
CHIASTOLITE
CHIASTOLITES
CHIBOUQUES
CHICALOTES
CHICANERIES
CHICANINGS
CHICCORIES
CHICKABIDDIES
CHICKABIDDY
CHICKADEES
CHICKAREES
CHICKENHEARTED
CHICKENING
CHICKENPOX
CHICKENPOXES
CHICKENSHIT
CHICKENSHITS
CHICKLINGS
CHICKORIES
CHICKWEEDS
CHICNESSES
CHIEFERIES
CHIEFESSES
CHIEFLINGS
CHIEFSHIPS
CHIEFTAINCIES
CHIEFTAINCY
CHIEFTAINESS
CHIEFTAINESSES
CHIEFTAINRIES
CHIEFTAINRY

CHIEFTAINS
CHIEFTAINSHIP
CHIEFTAINSHIPS
CHIFFCHAFF
CHIFFCHAFFS
CHIFFONADE
CHIFFONADES
CHIFFONIER
CHIFFONIERS
CHIFFONNIER
CHIFFONNIERS
CHIFFOROBE
CHIFFOROBES
CHIHUAHUAS
CHILBLAINED
CHILBLAINS
CHILDBEARING
CHILDBEARINGS
CHILDBIRTH
CHILDBIRTHS
CHILDCARES
CHILDCROWING
CHILDCROWINGS
CHILDERMAS
CHILDERMASES
CHILDHOODS
CHILDISHLY
CHILDISHNESS
CHILDISHNESSES
CHILDLESSNESS
CHILDLESSNESSES
CHILDLIEST
CHILDLIKENESS
CHILDLIKENESSES
CHILDMINDER
CHILDMINDERS
CHILDNESSES
CHILDPROOF
CHILIAGONS
CHILIAHEDRA
CHILIAHEDRON
CHILIAHEDRONS
CHILIARCHIES
CHILIARCHS
CHILIARCHY
CHILIASTIC
CHILLINESS
CHILLINESSES
CHILLINGLY
CHILLNESSES
CHILOPODAN
CHILOPODANS
CHILOPODOUS
CHILTEPINS
CHIMAERISM
CHIMAERISMS
CHIMERICAL
CHIMERICALLY
CHIMERICALNESS
CHIMERISMS
CHIMICHANGA
CHIMICHANGAS
CHIMNEYBOARD
CHIMNEYBOARDS
CHIMNEYBREAST
CHIMNEYBREASTS
CHIMNEYING
CHIMNEYLIKE
CHIMNEYPIECE
CHIMNEYPIECES
CHIMNEYPOT
CHIMNEYPOTS
CHIMPANZEE
CHIMPANZEES
CHINABERRIES
CHINABERRY
CHINACHINA
CHINACHINAS
CHINAROOTS
CHINAWARES
CHINCAPINS
CHINCHERINCHEE
CHINCHERINCHEES

CHINCHIEST
CHINCHILLA
CHINCHILLAS
CHINCOUGHS
CHINKAPINS
CHINKERINCHEE
CHINKERINCHEES
CHINOISERIE
CHINOISERIES
CHINOVNIKS
CHINQUAPIN
CHINQUAPINS
CHINSTRAPS
CHINTZIEST
CHINWAGGED
CHINWAGGING
CHIONODOXA
CHIONODOXAS
CHIPBOARDS
CHIPOCHIAS
CHIPOLATAS
CHIPPERING
CHIPPINESS
CHIPPINESSES
CHIQUICHIQUI
CHIQUICHIQUIS
CHIRAGRICAL
CHIRALITIES
CHIRIMOYAS
CHIROGNOMIES
CHIROGNOMY
CHIROGRAPH
CHIROGRAPHER
CHIROGRAPHERS
CHIROGRAPHIC
CHIROGRAPHICAL
CHIROGRAPHIES
CHIROGRAPHIST
CHIROGRAPHISTS
CHIROGRAPHS
CHIROGRAPHY
CHIROLOGIES
CHIROLOGIST
CHIROLOGISTS
CHIROMANCER
CHIROMANCERS
CHIROMANCIES
CHIROMANCY
CHIROMANTIC
CHIROMANTICAL
CHIRONOMER
CHIRONOMERS
CHIRONOMIC
CHIRONOMID
CHIRONOMIDS
CHIRONOMIES
CHIROPODIAL
CHIROPODIES
CHIROPODIST
CHIROPODISTS
CHIROPRACTIC
CHIROPRACTICS
CHIROPRACTOR
CHIROPRACTORS
CHIROPTERAN
CHIROPTERANS
CHIROPTEROUS
CHIROPTERS
CHIRPINESS
CHIRPINESSES
CHIRRUPERS
CHIRRUPING
CHIRURGEON
CHIRURGEONLY
CHIRURGEONS
CHIRURGERIES
CHIRURGERY
CHIRURGICAL
CHISELLERS
CHISELLING
CHISELLINGS
CHITARRONE
CHITARRONI

CHITCHATTED
CHITCHATTING
CHITTAGONG
CHITTAGONGS
CHITTERING
CHITTERINGS
CHITTERLING
CHITTERLINGS
CHIVALRIES
CHIVALROUS
CHIVALROUSLY
CHIVALROUSNESS
CHIVAREEING
CHIVARIING
CHIYOGAMIS
CHLAMYDATE
CHLAMYDEOUS
CHLAMYDIAE
CHLAMYDIAL
CHLAMYDIAS
CHLAMYDOMONADES
CHLAMYDOMONAS
CHLAMYDOSPORE
CHLAMYDOSPORES
CHLOANTHITE
CHLOANTHITES
CHLOASMATA
CHLORACETIC
CHLORACNES
CHLORALISM
CHLORALISMS
CHLORALOSE
CHLORALOSED
CHLORALOSES
CHLORAMBUCIL
CHLORAMBUCILS
CHLORAMINE
CHLORAMINES
CHLORAMPHENICOL
CHLORARGYRITE
CHLORARGYRITES
CHLORDANES
CHLORELLAS
CHLORENCHYMA
CHLORENCHYMAS
CHLORHEXIDINE
CHLORHEXIDINES
CHLORIDATE
CHLORIDATED
CHLORIDATES
CHLORIDATING
CHLORIDISE
CHLORIDISED
CHLORIDISES
CHLORIDISING
CHLORIDIZE
CHLORIDIZED
CHLORIDIZES
CHLORIDIZING
CHLORIMETER
CHLORIMETERS
CHLORIMETRIC
CHLORIMETRIES
CHLORIMETRY
CHLORINATE
CHLORINATED
CHLORINATES
CHLORINATING
CHLORINATION
CHLORINATIONS
CHLORINATOR
CHLORINATORS
CHLORINISE
CHLORINISED
CHLORINISES
CHLORINISING
CHLORINITIES
CHLORINITY
CHLORINIZE
CHLORINIZED
CHLORINIZES
CHLORINIZING
CHLORITISATION

CHLORITISATIONS
CHLORITIZATION
CHLORITIZATIONS
CHLOROACETIC
CHLOROARGYRITE
CHLOROBENZENE
CHLOROBENZENES
CHLOROBROMIDE
CHLOROBROMIDES
CHLOROCRUORIN
CHLOROCRUORINS
CHLORODYNE
CHLORODYNES
CHLOROFORM
CHLOROFORMED
CHLOROFORMER
CHLOROFORMERS
CHLOROFORMING
CHLOROFORMIST
CHLOROFORMISTS
CHLOROFORMS
CHLOROHYDRIN
CHLOROHYDRINS
CHLOROMETER
CHLOROMETERS
CHLOROMETHANE
CHLOROMETHANES
CHLOROMETRIC
CHLOROMETRIES
CHLOROMETRY
CHLOROPHYL
CHLOROPHYLL
CHLOROPHYLLOID
CHLOROPHYLLOUS
CHLOROPHYLLS
CHLOROPHYLS
CHLOROPHYTUM
CHLOROPHYTUMS
CHLOROPICRIN
CHLOROPICRINS
CHLOROPLAST
CHLOROPLASTAL
CHLOROPLASTIC
CHLOROPLASTS
CHLOROPRENE
CHLOROPRENES
CHLOROQUIN
CHLOROQUINE
CHLOROQUINES
CHLOROQUINS
CHLOROTHIAZIDE
CHLOROTHIAZIDES
CHLORPICRIN
CHLORPICRINS
CHLORPROMAZINE
CHLORPROMAZINES
CHLORPROPAMIDE
CHLORPROPAMIDES
CHLORTHALIDONE
CHLORTHALIDONES
CHOANOCYTE
CHOANOCYTES
CHOCAHOLIC
CHOCAHOLICS
CHOCKABLOCK
CHOCKSTONE
CHOCKSTONES
CHOCOHOLIC
CHOCOHOLICS
CHOCOLATES
CHOCOLATEY
CHOCOLATIER
CHOCOLATIERS
CHOCOLATIEST
CHOICENESS
CHOICENESSES
CHOIRGIRLS
CHOIRMASTER
CHOIRMASTERS
CHOIRSCREEN
CHOIRSCREENS
CHOIRSTALLS
CHOKEBERRIES

CHOKEBERRY
CHOKEBORES
CHOKECHERRIES
CHOKECHERRY
CHOKECOILS
CHOKEDAMPS
CHOKEHOLDS
CHOLAEMIAS
CHOLAGOGIC
CHOLAGOGUE
CHOLAGOGUES
CHOLANGIOGRAM
CHOLANGIOGRAMS
CHOLANGIOGRAPHY
CHOLECALCIFEROL
CHOLECYSTECTOMY
CHOLECYSTITIS
CHOLECYSTITISES
CHOLECYSTOKININ
CHOLECYSTOSTOMY
CHOLECYSTOTOMY
CHOLECYSTS
CHOLELITHIASES
CHOLELITHIASIS
CHOLELITHS
CHOLERICALLY
CHOLERICLY
CHOLESTASES
CHOLESTASIS
CHOLESTATIC
CHOLESTERIC
CHOLESTERIN
CHOLESTERINS
CHOLESTEROL
CHOLESTEROLEMIA
CHOLESTEROLS
CHOLESTYRAMINE
CHOLESTYRAMINES
CHOLIAMBIC
CHOLIAMBICS
CHOLINERGIC
CHOLINERGICALLY
CHOLINESTERASE
CHOLINESTERASES
CHOMOPHYTE
CHOMOPHYTES
CHONDRICHTHYAN
CHONDRICHTHYANS
CHONDRIFICATION
CHONDRIFIED
CHONDRIFIES
CHONDRIFYING
CHONDRIOSOMAL
CHONDRIOSOME
CHONDRIOSOMES
CHONDRITES
CHONDRITIC
CHONDRITIS
CHONDRITISES
CHONDROBLAST
CHONDROBLASTS
CHONDROCRANIA
CHONDROCRANIUM
CHONDROCRANIUMS
CHONDROGENESES
CHONDROGENESIS
CHONDROITIN
CHONDROITINS
CHONDROMAS
CHONDROMATA
CHONDROMATOSES
CHONDROMATOSIS
CHONDROMATOUS
CHONDROPHORINE
CHONDROPHORINES
CHONDROSKELETON
CHONDROSTIAN
CHONDROSTIANS
CHONDRULES
CHOPFALLEN
CHOPHOUSES
CHOPLOGICS
CHOPPERING

CHOPPINESS
CHOPPINESSES
CHOPSOCKIES
CHOPSTICKS
CHORAGUSES
CHORALISTS
CHORDAMESODERM
CHORDAMESODERMS
CHORDOPHONE
CHORDOPHONES
CHORDOPHONIC
CHORDOTOMIES
CHORDOTOMY
CHOREGRAPH
CHOREGRAPHED
CHOREGRAPHER
CHOREGRAPHERS
CHOREGRAPHIC
CHOREGRAPHIES
CHOREGRAPHING
CHOREGRAPHS
CHOREGRAPHY
CHOREGUSES
CHOREIFORM
CHOREODRAMA
CHOREODRAMAS
CHOREOGRAPH
CHOREOGRAPHED
CHOREOGRAPHER
CHOREOGRAPHERS
CHOREOGRAPHIC
CHOREOGRAPHIES
CHOREOGRAPHING
CHOREOGRAPHS
CHOREOGRAPHY
CHOREOLOGIES
CHOREOLOGIST
CHOREOLOGISTS
CHOREOLOGY
CHOREPISCOPAL
CHORIAMBIC
CHORIAMBICS
CHORIAMBUS
CHORIAMBUSES
CHORIOALLANTOIC
CHORIOALLANTOIS
CHORIOCARCINOMA
CHORISATION
CHORISATIONS
CHORISTERS
CHORIZATION
CHORIZATIONS
CHORIZONTIST
CHORIZONTISTS
CHORIZONTS
CHOROGRAPHER
CHOROGRAPHERS
CHOROGRAPHIC
CHOROGRAPHICAL
CHOROGRAPHIES
CHOROGRAPHY
CHOROIDITIS
CHOROIDITISES
CHOROLOGICAL
CHOROLOGIES
CHOROLOGIST
CHOROLOGISTS
CHOROPLETH
CHOROPLETHS
CHORUSMASTER
CHORUSMASTERS
CHORUSSING
CHOUCROUTE
CHOUCROUTES
CHOULTRIES
CHOUNTERED
CHOUNTERING
CHOWDERHEAD
CHOWDERHEADED
CHOWDERHEADS
CHOWDERING
CHOWHOUNDS
CHOWKIDARS

CHREMATIST
CHREMATISTIC
CHREMATISTICS
CHREMATISTS
CHRESTOMATHIC
CHRESTOMATHICAL
CHRESTOMATHIES
CHRESTOMATHY
CHRISMATION
CHRISMATIONS
CHRISMATORIES
CHRISMATORY
CHRISTCROSS
CHRISTCROSSES
CHRISTENED
CHRISTENER
CHRISTENERS
CHRISTENING
CHRISTENINGS
CHRISTIANIA
CHRISTIANIAS
CHRISTIANISE
CHRISTIANISED
CHRISTIANISER
CHRISTIANISERS
CHRISTIANISES
CHRISTIANISING
CHRISTIANIZE
CHRISTIANIZED
CHRISTIANIZER
CHRISTIANIZERS
CHRISTIANIZES
CHRISTIANIZING
CHRISTIANS
CHRISTINGLE
CHRISTINGLES
CHRISTOPHANIES
CHRISTOPHANY
CHROMAFFIN
CHROMAKEYS
CHROMATICALLY
CHROMATICISM
CHROMATICISMS
CHROMATICITIES
CHROMATICITY
CHROMATICNESS
CHROMATICNESSES
CHROMATICS
CHROMATIDS
CHROMATINIC
CHROMATINS
CHROMATIST
CHROMATISTS
CHROMATOGRAM
CHROMATOGRAMS
CHROMATOGRAPH
CHROMATOGRAPHED
CHROMATOGRAPHER
CHROMATOGRAPHIC
CHROMATOGRAPHS
CHROMATOGRAPHY
CHROMATOID
CHROMATOLOGIES
CHROMATOLOGIST
CHROMATOLOGISTS
CHROMATOLOGY
CHROMATOLYSES
CHROMATOLYSIS
CHROMATOLYTIC
CHROMATOPHORE
CHROMATOPHORES
CHROMATOPHORIC
CHROMATOPHOROUS
CHROMATOPSIA
CHROMATOPSIAS
CHROMATOSPHERE
CHROMATOSPHERES
CHROMATYPE
CHROMATYPES
CHROMIDIUM
CHROMINANCE
CHROMINANCES
CHROMISING

CHROMIZING
CHROMOCENTER
CHROMOCENTERS
CHROMODYNAMICS
CHROMOGENIC
CHROMOGENS
CHROMOGRAM
CHROMOGRAMS
CHROMOMERE
CHROMOMERES
CHROMOMERIC
CHROMONEMA
CHROMONEMAL
CHROMONEMATA
CHROMONEMATIC
CHROMONEMIC
CHROMOPHIL
CHROMOPHILIC
CHROMOPHOBE
CHROMOPHONIC
CHROMOPHORE
CHROMOPHORES
CHROMOPHORIC
CHROMOPHOROUS
CHROMOPLAST
CHROMOPLASTS
CHROMOPROTEIN
CHROMOPROTEINS
CHROMOSCOPE
CHROMOSCOPES
CHROMOSOMAL
CHROMOSOMALLY
CHROMOSOME
CHROMOSOMES
CHROMOSPHERE
CHROMOSPHERES
CHROMOSPHERIC
CHROMOTHERAPIES
CHROMOTHERAPY
CHROMOTYPE
CHROMOTYPES
CHROMOXYLOGRAPH
CHRONAXIES
CHRONICALLY
CHRONICITIES
CHRONICITY
CHRONICLED
CHRONICLER
CHRONICLERS
CHRONICLES
CHRONICLING
CHRONOBIOLOGIC
CHRONOBIOLOGIES
CHRONOBIOLOGIST
CHRONOBIOLOGY
CHRONOGRAM
CHRONOGRAMMATIC
CHRONOGRAMS
CHRONOGRAPH
CHRONOGRAPHER
CHRONOGRAPHERS
CHRONOGRAPHIC
CHRONOGRAPHIES
CHRONOGRAPHS
CHRONOGRAPHY
CHRONOLOGER
CHRONOLOGERS
CHRONOLOGIC
CHRONOLOGICAL
CHRONOLOGICALLY
CHRONOLOGIES
CHRONOLOGISE
CHRONOLOGISED
CHRONOLOGISES
CHRONOLOGISING
CHRONOLOGIST
CHRONOLOGISTS
CHRONOLOGIZE
CHRONOLOGIZED
CHRONOLOGIZES
CHRONOLOGIZING
CHRONOLOGY
CHRONOMETER

CHRONOMETERS
CHRONOMETRIC
CHRONOMETRICAL
CHRONOMETRIES
CHRONOMETRY
CHRONOSCOPE
CHRONOSCOPES
CHRONOSCOPIC
CHRONOTHERAPIES
CHRONOTHERAPY
CHRONOTRON
CHRONOTRONS
CHRYSALIDAL
CHRYSALIDES
CHRYSALIDS
CHRYSALISES
CHRYSANTHEMUM
CHRYSANTHEMUMS
CHRYSANTHS
CHRYSAROBIN
CHRYSAROBINS
CHRYSOBERYL
CHRYSOBERYLS
CHRYSOCOLLA
CHRYSOCOLLAS
CHRYSOCRACIES
CHRYSOCRACY
CHRYSOLITE
CHRYSOLITES
CHRYSOLITIC
CHRYSOMELID
CHRYSOMELIDS
CHRYSOPHAN
CHRYSOPHANS
CHRYSOPHILITE
CHRYSOPHILITES
CHRYSOPHYTE
CHRYSOPHYTES
CHRYSOPRASE
CHRYSOPRASES
CHRYSOTILE
CHRYSOTILES
CHUBBINESS
CHUBBINESSES
CHUCKAWALLA
CHUCKAWALLAS
CHUCKHOLES
CHUCKLEHEAD
CHUCKLEHEADED
CHUCKLEHEADS
CHUCKLESOME
CHUCKLINGLY
CHUCKLINGS
CHUCKWALLA
CHUCKWALLAS
CHUFFINESS
CHUFFINESSES
CHUGALUGGED
CHUGALUGGING
CHUMMINESS
CHUMMINESSES
CHUNDERING
CHUNDEROUS
CHUNKINESS
CHUNKINESSES
CHUNNERING
CHUNTERING
CHUPATTIES
CHUPRASSIES
CHURCHGOER
CHURCHGOERS
CHURCHGOING
CHURCHGOINGS
CHURCHIANITIES
CHURCHIANITY
CHURCHIEST
CHURCHINGS
CHURCHISMS
CHURCHLESS
CHURCHLIER
CHURCHLIEST
CHURCHLINESS
CHURCHLINESSES

CHURCHMANLY
CHURCHMANSHIP
CHURCHMANSHIPS
CHURCHPEOPLE
CHURCHWARD
CHURCHWARDEN
CHURCHWARDENS
CHURCHWARDS
CHURCHWAYS
CHURCHWOMAN
CHURCHWOMEN
CHURCHYARD
CHURCHYARDS
CHURLISHLY
CHURLISHNESS
CHURLISHNESSES
CHURNMILKS
CHURRIGUERESCO
CHURRIGUERESQUE
CHYLACEOUS
CHYLIFEROUS
CHYLIFICATION
CHYLIFICATIONS
CHYLIFYING
CHYLOMICRON
CHYLOMICRONS
CHYMIFEROUS
CHYMIFICATION
CHYMIFICATIONS
CHYMIFYING
CHYMISTRIES
CHYMOTRYPSIN
CHYMOTRYPSINS
CHYMOTRYPTIC
CIBACHROME
CIBACHROMES
CICADELLID
CICADELLIDS
CICATRICES
CICATRICHULE
CICATRICHULES
CICATRICIAL
CICATRICLE
CICATRICLES
CICATRICOSE
CICATRICULA
CICATRICULAS
CICATRISANT
CICATRISATION
CICATRISATIONS
CICATRISED
CICATRISER
CICATRISERS
CICATRISES
CICATRISING
CICATRIXES
CICATRIZANT
CICATRIZATION
CICATRIZATIONS
CICATRIZED
CICATRIZER
CICATRIZERS
CICATRIZES
CICATRIZING
CICERONEING
CICHORACEOUS
CICINNUSES
CICISBEISM
CICISBEISMS
CICLATOUNS
CICLOSPORIN
CICLOSPORINS
CIGARETTES
CIGARILLOS
CIGUATERAS
CILIATIONS
CIMETIDINE
CIMETIDINES
CINCHONACEOUS
CINCHONIDINE
CINCHONIDINES
CINCHONINE
CINCHONINES

CINCHONINIC
CINCHONISATION
CINCHONISATIONS
CINCHONISE
CINCHONISED
CINCHONISES
CINCHONISING
CINCHONISM
CINCHONISMS
CINCHONIZATION
CINCHONIZATIONS
CINCHONIZE
CINCHONIZED
CINCHONIZES
CINCHONIZING
CINCINNATE
CINCINNUSES
CINCTURING
CINEANGIOGRAPHY
CINEMAGOER
CINEMAGOERS
CINEMATHEQUE
CINEMATHEQUES
CINEMATICALLY
CINEMATISE
CINEMATISED
CINEMATISES
CINEMATISING
CINEMATIZE
CINEMATIZED
CINEMATIZES
CINEMATIZING
CINEMATOGRAPH
CINEMATOGRAPHED
CINEMATOGRAPHER
CINEMATOGRAPHIC
CINEMATOGRAPHS
CINEMATOGRAPHY
CINEMICROGRAPHY
CINEPHILES
CINEPLEXES
CINERARIAS
CINERARIUM
CINERATION
CINERATIONS
CINERATORS
CINERITIOUS
CINGULATED
CINNABARIC
CINNABARINE
CINNAMONIC
CINNARIZINE
CINNARIZINES
CINQUECENTIST
CINQUECENTISTS
CINQUECENTO
CINQUECENTOS
CINQUEFOIL
CINQUEFOILS
CIPHERINGS
CIPHERTEXT
CIPHERTEXTS
CIPOLLINOS
CIPROFLOXACIN
CIPROFLOXACINS
CIRCASSIAN
CIRCASSIANS
CIRCASSIENNE
CIRCASSIENNES
CIRCENSIAL
CIRCENSIAN
CIRCINATELY
CIRCUITEER
CIRCUITEERS
CIRCUITIES
CIRCUITING
CIRCUITOUS
CIRCUITOUSLY
CIRCUITOUSNESS
CIRCUITRIES
CIRCULABLE
CIRCULARISATION
CIRCULARISE

CIRCULARISED
CIRCULARISER
CIRCULARISERS
CIRCULARISES
CIRCULARISING
CIRCULARITIES
CIRCULARITY
CIRCULARIZATION
CIRCULARIZE
CIRCULARIZED
CIRCULARIZER
CIRCULARIZERS
CIRCULARIZES
CIRCULARIZING
CIRCULARLY
CIRCULARNESS
CIRCULARNESSES
CIRCULATABLE
CIRCULATED
CIRCULATES
CIRCULATING
CIRCULATINGS
CIRCULATION
CIRCULATIONS
CIRCULATIVE
CIRCULATOR
CIRCULATORS
CIRCULATORY
CIRCUMAMBAGES
CIRCUMAMBAGIOUS
CIRCUMAMBIENCE
CIRCUMAMBIENCES
CIRCUMAMBIENCY
CIRCUMAMBIENT
CIRCUMAMBIENTLY
CIRCUMAMBULATE
CIRCUMAMBULATED
CIRCUMAMBULATES
CIRCUMAMBULATOR
CIRCUMBENDIBUS
CIRCUMCENTER
CIRCUMCENTERS
CIRCUMCENTRE
CIRCUMCENTRES
CIRCUMCIRCLE
CIRCUMCIRCLES
CIRCUMCISE
CIRCUMCISED
CIRCUMCISER
CIRCUMCISERS
CIRCUMCISES
CIRCUMCISING
CIRCUMCISION
CIRCUMCISIONS
CIRCUMDUCE
CIRCUMDUCED
CIRCUMDUCES
CIRCUMDUCING
CIRCUMDUCT
CIRCUMDUCTED
CIRCUMDUCTING
CIRCUMDUCTION
CIRCUMDUCTIONS
CIRCUMDUCTORY
CIRCUMDUCTS
CIRCUMFERENCE
CIRCUMFERENCES
CIRCUMFERENTIAL
CIRCUMFERENTOR
CIRCUMFERENTORS
CIRCUMFLECT
CIRCUMFLECTED
CIRCUMFLECTING
CIRCUMFLECTS
CIRCUMFLEX
CIRCUMFLEXES
CIRCUMFLEXION
CIRCUMFLEXIONS
CIRCUMFLUENCE
CIRCUMFLUENCES
CIRCUMFLUENT
CIRCUMFLUOUS
CIRCUMFORANEAN

CIRCUMFORANEOUS	CIRCUMVENTED	CIVILIZATIONAL	CLAPPERBOY	CLAUSTROPHOBIAS	CLERGYWOMEN
CIRCUMFUSE	CIRCUMVENTER	CIVILIZATIONS	CLAPPERBOYS	CLAUSTROPHOBIC	CLERICALISM
CIRCUMFUSED	CIRCUMVENTERS	CIVILIZERS	CLAPPERCLAW	CLAVATIONS	CLERICALISMS
CIRCUMFUSES	CIRCUMVENTING	CIVILIZING	CLAPPERCLAWED	CLAVECINIST	CLERICALIST
CIRCUMFUSILE	CIRCUMVENTION	CIVILNESSES	CLAPPERCLAWER	CLAVECINISTS	CLERICALISTS
CIRCUMFUSING	CIRCUMVENTIONS	CLABBERING	CLAPPERCLAWERS	CLAVICEMBALO	CLERICALLY
CIRCUMFUSION	CIRCUMVENTIVE	CLACKBOXES	CLAPPERCLAWING	CLAVICEMBALOS	CLERICATES
CIRCUMFUSIONS	CIRCUMVENTOR	CLACKDISHES	CLAPPERCLAWS	CLAVICHORD	CLERICITIES
CIRCUMGYRATE	CIRCUMVENTORS	CLADISTICALLY	CLAPPERING	CLAVICHORDIST	CLERKESSES
CIRCUMGYRATED	CIRCUMVENTS	CLADISTICS	CLAPPERINGS	CLAVICHORDISTS	CLERKLIEST
CIRCUMGYRATES	CIRCUMVOLUTION	CLADOCERAN	CLAPTRAPPERIES	CLAVICHORDS	CLERKLINESS
CIRCUMGYRATING	CIRCUMVOLUTIONS	CLADOCERANS	CLAPTRAPPERY	CLAVICORNS	CLERKLINESSES
CIRCUMGYRATION	CIRCUMVOLUTORY	CLADOGENESES	CLARABELLA	CLAVICULAE	CLERKLINGS
CIRCUMGYRATIONS	CIRCUMVOLVE	CLADOGENESIS	CLARABELLAS	CLAVICULAR	CLERKSHIPS
CIRCUMGYRATORY	CIRCUMVOLVED	CLADOGENETIC	CLARENDONS	CLAVICULATE	CLEROMANCIES
CIRCUMINCESSION	CIRCUMVOLVES	CLADOGRAMS	CLARIBELLA	CLAVICYTHERIA	CLEROMANCY
CIRCUMINSESSION	CIRCUMVOLVING	CLADOPHYLL	CLARIBELLAS	CLAVICYTHERIUM	CLERUCHIAL
CIRCUMJACENCIES	CIRRHIPEDE	CLADOPHYLLS	CLARICHORD	CLAVIERIST	CLERUCHIAS
CIRCUMJACENCY	CIRRHIPEDES	CLADOSPORIA	CLARICHORDS	CLAVIERISTIC	CLERUCHIES
CIRCUMJACENT	CIRRHOTICS	CLADOSPORIUM	CLARIFICATION	CLAVIERISTS	CLEVERALITIES
CIRCUMLITTORAL	CIRRIGRADE	CLADOSPORIUMS	CLARIFICATIONS	CLAVIGEROUS	CLEVERALITY
CIRCUMLOCUTE	CIRRIPEDES	CLAIRAUDIENCE	CLARIFIERS	CLAWHAMMER	CLEVERDICK
CIRCUMLOCUTED	CIRROCUMULI	CLAIRAUDIENCES	CLARIFYING	CLAYMATION	CLEVERDICKS
CIRCUMLOCUTES	CIRROCUMULUS	CLAIRAUDIENT	CLARINETIST	CLAYMATIONS	CLEVERNESS
CIRCUMLOCUTING	CIRROSTRATI	CLAIRAUDIENTLY	CLARINETISTS	CLAYSTONES	CLEVERNESSES
CIRCUMLOCUTION	CIRROSTRATIVE	CLAIRAUDIENTS	CLARINETTIST	CLAYTONIAS	CLIANTHUSES
CIRCUMLOCUTIONS	CIRROSTRATUS	CLAIRCOLLE	CLARINETTISTS	CLEANABILITIES	CLICKETING
CIRCUMLOCUTORY	CISMONTANE	CLAIRCOLLES	CLARIONETS	CLEANABILITY	CLICKSTREAM
CIRCUMLUNAR	CISPLATINS	CLAIRSCHACH	CLARIONING	CLEANHANDED	CLICKSTREAMS
CIRCUMMURE	CISPONTINE	CLAIRSCHACHS	CLARTHEADS	CLEANLIEST	CLIENTAGES
CIRCUMMURED	CISTACEOUS	CLAIRVOYANCE	CLASHINGLY	CLEANLINESS	CLIENTELES
CIRCUMMURES	CITATIONAL	CLAIRVOYANCES	CLASSICALISM	CLEANLINESSES	CLIENTLESS
CIRCUMMURING	CITHARISTIC	CLAIRVOYANCIES	CLASSICALISMS	CLEANNESSES	CLIENTSHIP
CIRCUMNAVIGABLE	CITHARISTS	CLAIRVOYANCY	CLASSICALIST	CLEANSABLE	CLIENTSHIPS
CIRCUMNAVIGATE	CITIFICATION	CLAIRVOYANT	CLASSICALISTS	CLEANSINGS	CLIFFHANGER
CIRCUMNAVIGATED	CITIFICATIONS	CLAIRVOYANTLY	CLASSICALITIES	CLEANSKINS	CLIFFHANGERS
CIRCUMNAVIGATES	CITIZENESS	CLAIRVOYANTS	CLASSICALITY	CLEARANCES	CLIFFHANGING
CIRCUMNAVIGATOR	CITIZENESSES	CLAMANCIES	CLASSICALLY	CLEARCOLED	CLIFFHANGINGS
CIRCUMNUTATE	CITIZENISE	CLAMATORIAL	CLASSICALNESS	CLEARCOLES	CLIFFHANGS
CIRCUMNUTATED	CITIZENISED	CLAMBERERS	CLASSICALNESSES	CLEARCOLING	CLIMACTERIC
CIRCUMNUTATES	CITIZENISES	CLAMBERING	CLASSICALS	CLEARCUTTING	CLIMACTERICAL
CIRCUMNUTATING	CITIZENISING	CLAMJAMFRIES	CLASSICISE	CLEARHEADED	CLIMACTERICALLY
CIRCUMNUTATION	CITIZENIZE	CLAMJAMFRY	CLASSICISED	CLEARHEADEDLY	CLIMACTERICS
CIRCUMNUTATIONS	CITIZENIZED	CLAMJAMPHRIE	CLASSICISES	CLEARHEADEDNESS	CLIMACTICAL
CIRCUMNUTATORY	CITIZENIZES	CLAMJAMPHRIES	CLASSICISING	CLEARINGHOUSE	CLIMACTICALLY
CIRCUMPOLAR	CITIZENIZING	CLAMMINESS	CLASSICISM	CLEARINGHOUSES	CLIMATICAL
CIRCUMPOSE	CITIZENRIES	CLAMMINESSES	CLASSICISMS	CLEARNESSES	CLIMATICALLY
CIRCUMPOSED	CITIZENSHIP	CLAMOROUSLY	CLASSICIST	CLEARSKINS	CLIMATISED
CIRCUMPOSES	CITIZENSHIPS	CLAMOROUSNESS	CLASSICISTIC	CLEARSTORIED	CLIMATISES
CIRCUMPOSING	CITRICULTURE	CLAMOROUSNESSES	CLASSICISTS	CLEARSTORIES	CLIMATISING
CIRCUMPOSITION	CITRICULTURES	CLAMOURERS	CLASSICIZE	CLEARSTORY	CLIMATIZED
CIRCUMPOSITIONS	CITRICULTURIST	CLAMOURING	CLASSICIZED	CLEARWEEDS	CLIMATIZES
CIRCUMSCISSILE	CITRICULTURISTS	CLAMPDOWNS	CLASSICIZES	CLEARWINGS	CLIMATIZING
CIRCUMSCRIBABLE	CITRONELLA	CLAMPERING	CLASSICIZING	CLEAVABILITIES	CLIMATOGRAPHIES
CIRCUMSCRIBE	CITRONELLAL	CLAMSHELLS	CLASSIFIABLE	CLEAVABILITY	CLIMATOGRAPHY
CIRCUMSCRIBED	CITRONELLALS	CLANDESTINE	CLASSIFICATION	CLEAVABLENESS	CLIMATOLOGIC
CIRCUMSCRIBER	CITRONELLAS	CLANDESTINELY	CLASSIFICATIONS	CLEAVABLENESSES	CLIMATOLOGICAL
CIRCUMSCRIBERS	CITRONELLOL	CLANDESTINENESS	CLASSIFICATORY	CLEISTOGAMIC	CLIMATOLOGIES
CIRCUMSCRIBES	CITRONELLOLS	CLANDESTINITIES	CLASSIFIED	CLEISTOGAMIES	CLIMATOLOGIST
CIRCUMSCRIBING	CITRULLINE	CLANDESTINITY	CLASSIFIER	CLEISTOGAMOUS	CLIMATOLOGISTS
CIRCUMSCRIPTION	CITRULLINES	CLANGBOXES	CLASSIFIERS	CLEISTOGAMOUSLY	CLIMATOLOGY
CIRCUMSCRIPTIVE	CITYFICATION	CLANGORING	CLASSIFIES	CLEISTOGAMY	CLIMATURES
CIRCUMSOLAR	CITYFICATIONS	CLANGOROUS	CLASSIFYING	CLEMATISES	CLIMAXLESS
CIRCUMSPECT	CITYSCAPES	CLANGOROUSLY	CLASSINESS	CLEMENCIES	CLIMBDOWNS
CIRCUMSPECTION	CIVILIANISATION	CLANGOURED	CLASSINESSES	CLEMENTINE	CLINANDRIA
CIRCUMSPECTIONS	CIVILIANISE	CLANGOURING	CLASSLESSNESS	CLEMENTINES	CLINANDRIUM
CIRCUMSPECTIVE	CIVILIANISED	CLANJAMFRAY	CLASSLESSNESSES	CLENBUTEROL	CLINCHINGLY
CIRCUMSPECTLY	CIVILIANISES	CLANJAMFRAYS	CLASSMATES	CLENBUTEROLS	CLINDAMYCIN
CIRCUMSPECTNESS	CIVILIANISING	CLANKINGLY	CLASSROOMS	CLEOPATRAS	CLINDAMYCINS
CIRCUMSTANCE	CIVILIANIZATION	CLANNISHLY	CLASSWORKS	CLEPSYDRAE	CLINGFILMS
CIRCUMSTANCED	CIVILIANIZE	CLANNISHNESS	CLATHRATES	CLEPSYDRAS	CLINGFISHES
CIRCUMSTANCES	CIVILIANIZED	CLANNISHNESSES	CLATTERERS	CLEPTOCRACIES	CLINGINESS
CIRCUMSTANCING	CIVILIANIZES	CLANSWOMAN	CLATTERING	CLEPTOCRACY	CLINGINESSES
CIRCUMSTANTIAL	CIVILIANIZING	CLANSWOMEN	CLATTERINGLY	CLEPTOMANIA	CLINGINGLY
CIRCUMSTANTIALS	CIVILISABLE	CLAPBOARDED	CLAUCHTING	CLEPTOMANIAC	CLINGINGNESS
CIRCUMSTANTIATE	CIVILISATION	CLAPBOARDING	CLAUDICATION	CLEPTOMANIACS	CLINGINGNESSES
CIRCUMSTELLAR	CIVILISATIONAL	CLAPBOARDS	CLAUDICATIONS	CLEPTOMANIAS	CLINGSTONE
CIRCUMVALLATE	CIVILISATIONS	CLAPBREADS	CLAUGHTING	CLERESTORIED	CLINGSTONES
CIRCUMVALLATED	CIVILISERS	CLAPOMETER	CLAUSTRATION	CLERESTORIES	CLINICALLY
CIRCUMVALLATES	CIVILISING	CLAPOMETERS	CLAUSTRATIONS	CLERESTORY	CLINICALNESS
CIRCUMVALLATING	CIVILITIES	CLAPPERBOARD	CLAUSTROPHOBE	CLERGIABLE	CLINICALNESSES
CIRCUMVALLATION	CIVILIZABLE	CLAPPERBOARDS	CLAUSTROPHOBES	CLERGYABLE	CLINICIANS
CIRCUMVENT	CIVILIZATION	CLAPPERBOARDS	CLAUSTROPHOBIA	CLERGYWOMAN	CLINKERING

CLINKSTONE	CLOSEDOWNS	COACERVATION	COARCTATES	COCHAIRPERSONS	COCONSCIOUSES
CLINKSTONES	CLOSEFISTED	COACERVATIONS	COARCTATING	COCHAIRWOMAN	COCONSCIOUSNESS
CLINOCHLORE	CLOSEHEADS	COACHBUILDER	COARCTATION	COCHAIRWOMEN	COCONSPIRATOR
CLINOCHLORES	CLOSEMOUTHED	COACHBUILDERS	COARCTATIONS	COCHAMPION	COCONSPIRATORS
CLINODIAGONAL	CLOSENESSES	COACHBUILDING	COARSENESS	COCHAMPIONS	COCOONERIES
CLINODIAGONALS	CLOSESTOOL	COACHBUILDINGS	COARSENESSES	COCHINEALS	COCOONINGS
CLINOMETER	CLOSESTOOLS	COACHBUILT	COARSENING	COCHLEARES	COCOUNSELED
CLINOMETERS	CLOSETFULS	COACHLINES	COASSISTED	COCHLEARIFORM	COCOUNSELING
CLINOMETRIC	CLOSTRIDIA	COACHLOADS	COASSISTING	COCHLEATED	COCOUNSELLED
CLINOMETRICAL	CLOSTRIDIAL	COACHWHIPS	COASSUMING	COCKABULLIES	COCOUNSELLING
CLINOMETRIES	CLOSTRIDIAN	COACHWOODS	COASTEERING	COCKABULLY	COCOUNSELS
CLINOMETRY	CLOSTRIDIUM	COACHWORKS	COASTEERINGS	COCKALEEKIE	COCOZELLES
CLINOPINACOID	CLOSTRIDIUMS	COACTIVELY	COASTGUARD	COCKALEEKIES	COCREATING
CLINOPINACOIDS	CLOTHBOUND	COACTIVITIES	COASTGUARDMAN	COCKALORUM	COCREATORS
CLINOPINAKOID	CLOTHESHORSE	COACTIVITY	COASTGUARDMEN	COCKALORUMS	COCULTIVATE
CLINOPINAKOIDS	CLOTHESHORSES	COADAPTATION	COASTGUARDS	COCKAMAMIE	COCULTIVATED
CLINOPYROXENE	CLOTHESLINE	COADAPTATIONS	COASTGUARDSMAN	COCKATEELS	COCULTIVATES
CLINOPYROXENES	CLOTHESLINED	COADJACENCIES	COASTGUARDSMEN	COCKATIELS	COCULTIVATING
CLINOSTATS	CLOTHESLINES	COADJACENCY	COASTLANDS	COCKATRICE	COCULTIVATION
CLINQUANTS	CLOTHESLINING	COADJACENT	COASTLINES	COCKATRICES	COCULTIVATIONS
CLINTONIAS	CLOTHESPIN	COADJUTANT	COASTWARDS	COCKBILLED	COCULTURED
CLIOMETRIC	CLOTHESPINS	COADJUTANTS	COATDRESSES	COCKBILLING	COCULTURES
CLIOMETRICAL	CLOTHESPRESS	COADJUTORS	COATIMUNDI	COCKCHAFER	COCULTURING
CLIOMETRICIAN	CLOTHESPRESSES	COADJUTORSHIP	COATIMUNDIS	COCKCHAFERS	COCURATORS
CLIOMETRICIANS	CLOTTERING	COADJUTORSHIPS	COATSTANDS	COCKCROWING	COCURRICULAR
CLIOMETRICS	CLOTTINESS	COADJUTRESS	COATTENDED	COCKCROWINGS	COCUSWOODS
CLIPBOARDS	CLOTTINESSES	COADJUTRESSES	COATTENDING	COCKERNONIES	CODECLINATION
CLIPSHEARS	CLOUDBERRIES	COADJUTRICES	COATTESTED	COCKERNONY	CODECLINATIONS
CLIPSHEETS	CLOUDBERRY	COADJUTRIX	COATTESTING	COCKEYEDLY	CODEFENDANT
CLIQUINESS	CLOUDBURST	COADJUTRIXES	COAUTHORED	COCKEYEDNESS	CODEFENDANTS
CLIQUINESSES	CLOUDBURSTS	COADMIRING	COAUTHORING	COCKEYEDNESSES	CODEPENDENCE
CLIQUISHLY	CLOUDINESS	COADMITTED	COAUTHORSHIP	COCKFIGHTING	CODEPENDENCES
CLIQUISHNESS	CLOUDINESSES	COADMITTING	COAUTHORSHIPS	COCKFIGHTINGS	CODEPENDENCIES
CLIQUISHNESSES	CLOUDLANDS	COADUNATED	COBALAMINS	COCKFIGHTS	CODEPENDENCY
CLISHMACLAVER	CLOUDLESSLY	COADUNATES	COBALTIFEROUS	COCKHORSES	CODEPENDENT
CLISHMACLAVERS	CLOUDLESSNESS	COADUNATING	COBALTINES	COCKIELEEKIE	CODEPENDENTS
CLISTOGAMIES	CLOUDLESSNESSES	COADUNATION	COBALTITES	COCKIELEEKIES	CODERIVING
CLISTOGAMY	CLOUDSCAPE	COADUNATIONS	COBBLERIES	COCKINESSES	CODESIGNED
CLITICISED	CLOUDSCAPES	COADUNATIVE	COBBLESTONE	COCKLEBOAT	CODESIGNING
CLITICISES	CLOUDTOWNS	COAGENCIES	COBBLESTONED	COCKLEBOATS	CODETERMINATION
CLITICISING	CLOVEPINKS	COAGULABILITIES	COBBLESTONES	COCKLEBURS	CODEVELOPED
CLITICIZED	CLOVERGRASS	COAGULABILITY	COBBLESTONING	COCKLEERTS	CODEVELOPER
CLITICIZES	CLOVERGRASSES	COAGULABLE	COBELLIGERENT	COCKLESHELL	CODEVELOPERS
CLITICIZING	CLOVERLEAF	COAGULANTS	COBELLIGERENTS	COCKLESHELLS	CODEVELOPING
CLITORECTOMIES	CLOVERLEAFS	COAGULASES	COBWEBBERIES	COCKMATCHES	CODEVELOPS
CLITORECTOMY	CLOVERLEAVES	COAGULATED	COBWEBBERY	COCKNEYDOM	CODICILLARY
CLITORIDECTOMY	CLOWNERIES	COAGULATES	COBWEBBIER	COCKNEYDOMS	CODICOLOGICAL
CLITORIDES	CLOWNISHLY	COAGULATING	COBWEBBIEST	COCKNEYFICATION	CODICOLOGIES
CLITORISES	CLOWNISHNESS	COAGULATION	COBWEBBING	COCKNEYFIED	CODICOLOGY
CLITTERING	CLOWNISHNESSES	COAGULATIONS	COCAINISATION	COCKNEYFIES	CODIFIABILITIES
CLOACALINE	CLOXACILLIN	COAGULATIVE	COCAINISATIONS	COCKNEYFYING	CODIFIABILITY
CLOACITISES	CLOXACILLINS	COAGULATOR	COCAINISED	COCKNEYISH	CODIFICATION
CLOAKROOMS	CLOZAPINES	COAGULATORS	COCAINISES	COCKNEYISM	CODIFICATIONS
CLOBBERING	CLUBABILITIES	COAGULATORY	COCAINISING	COCKNEYISMS	CODIRECTED
CLOCKMAKER	CLUBABILITY	COALESCENCE	COCAINISMS	COCKNIFICATION	CODIRECTING
CLOCKMAKERS	CLUBBABILITIES	COALESCENCES	COCAINIZED	COCKNIFICATIONS	CODIRECTION
CLOCKWORKS	CLUBBABILITY	COALESCENT	COCAINIZES	COCKNIFIED	CODIRECTIONS
CLODDISHLY	CLUBBINESS	COALESCING	COCAINIZING	COCKNIFIES	CODIRECTOR
CLODDISHNESS	CLUBBINESSES	COALFIELDS	COCAPTAINED	COCKNIFYING	CODIRECTORS
CLODDISHNESSES	CLUBFOOTED	COALFISHES	COCAPTAINING	COCKROACHES	CODISCOVER
CLODHOPPER	CLUBHAULED	COALHOUSES	COCAPTAINS	COCKSCOMBS	CODISCOVERED
CLODHOPPERS	CLUBHAULING	COALIFICATION	COCARBOXYLASE	COCKSFOOTS	CODISCOVERER
CLODHOPPING	CLUBHOUSES	COALIFICATIONS	COCARBOXYLASES	COCKSINESS	CODISCOVERERS
CLOFIBRATE	CLUBMANSHIP	COALIFYING	COCARCINOGEN	COCKSINESSES	CODISCOVERING
CLOFIBRATES	CLUBMANSHIPS	COALITIONAL	COCARCINOGENIC	COCKSUCKER	CODISCOVERS
CLOGDANCES	CLUBMASTER	COALITIONER	COCARCINOGENS	COCKSUCKERS	CODOLOGIES
CLOGGINESS	CLUBMASTERS	COALITIONERS	COCATALYST	COCKSURELY	CODOMINANCE
CLOGGINESSES	CLUBRUSHES	COALITIONISM	COCATALYSTS	COCKSURENESS	CODOMINANCES
CLOISONNAGE	CLUMPINESS	COALITIONISMS	COCCIDIOSES	COCKSURENESSES	CODOMINANT
CLOISONNAGES	CLUMPINESSES	COALITIONIST	COCCIDIOSIS	COCKSWAINED	CODOMINANTS
CLOISONNES	CLUMSINESS	COALITIONISTS	COCCIDIOSTAT	COCKSWAINING	CODSWALLOP
CLOISTERED	CLUMSINESSES	COALITIONS	COCCIDIOSTATS	COCKSWAINS	CODSWALLOPS
CLOISTERER	CLUSTERING	COALMASTER	COCCIFEROUS	COCKTAILED	COEDUCATION
CLOISTERERS	CLUSTERINGLY	COALMASTERS	COCCINEOUS	COCKTAILING	COEDUCATIONAL
CLOISTERING	CLUTTERING	COALMINERS	COCCOLITES	COCKTEASER	COEDUCATIONALLY
CLOISTRESS	CLYPEIFORM	COANCHORED	COCCOLITHS	COCKTEASERS	COEDUCATIONS
CLOISTRESSES	CNIDARIANS	COANCHORING	COCHAIRING	COCKTHROWING	COEFFICIENT
CLOMIPHENE	CNIDOBLAST	COANNEXING	COCHAIRMAN	COCKTHROWINGS	COEFFICIENTS
CLOMIPHENES	CNIDOBLASTS	COAPPEARED	COCHAIRMEN	COCKYLEEKIES	COELACANTH
CLONAZEPAM	COACERVATE	COAPPEARING	COCHAIRPERSON	COCKYLEEKY	COELACANTHIC
CLONAZEPAMS	COACERVATED	COAPTATION	COCHAIRS	COCOMPOSER	COELACANTHS
CLONICITIES	COACERVATES	COAPTATIONS	COCHAIRWOMAN	COCOMPOSERS	COELANAGLYPHIC
CLONIDINES	COACERVATING	COARCTATED	COCHAIRPERSON	COCONSCIOUS	COELENTERA

COELENTERATE	COEXISTING	COHESIONLESS	COLEOPTERIST	COLLECTIVES	COLLOCUTOR
COELENTERATES	COEXTENDED	COHESIVELY	COLEOPTERISTS	COLLECTIVISE	COLLOCUTORS
COELENTERIC	COEXTENDING	COHESIVENESS	COLEOPTERON	COLLECTIVISED	COLLOCUTORY
COELENTERON	COEXTENSION	COHESIVENESSES	COLEOPTERONS	COLLECTIVISES	COLLODIONS
COELOMATES	COEXTENSIONS	COHIBITING	COLEOPTEROUS	COLLECTIVISING	COLLODIUMS
COELOMATIC	COEXTENSIVE	COHIBITION	COLEOPTERS	COLLECTIVISM	COLLOGUING
COELOSTATS	COEXTENSIVELY	COHIBITIONS	COLEOPTILE	COLLECTIVISMS	COLLOIDALITIES
COELUROSAUR	COFAVORITE	COHIBITIVE	COLEOPTILES	COLLECTIVIST	COLLOIDALITY
COELUROSAURS	COFAVORITES	COHOBATING	COLEORHIZA	COLLECTIVISTIC	COLLOIDALLY
COEMBODIED	COFEATURED	COHOMOLOGICAL	COLEORHIZAE	COLLECTIVISTS	COLLOQUIAL
COEMBODIES	COFEATURES	COHOMOLOGIES	COLEORHIZAS	COLLECTIVITIES	COLLOQUIALISM
COEMBODYING	COFEATURING	COHOMOLOGY	COLEORRHIZA	COLLECTIVITY	COLLOQUIALISMS
COEMPLOYED	COFFEEHOUSE	COHORTATIVE	COLEORRHIZAS	COLLECTIVIZE	COLLOQUIALIST
COEMPLOYING	COFFEEHOUSES	COHORTATIVES	COLESTIPOL	COLLECTIVIZED	COLLOQUIALISTS
COEMPTIONS	COFFEEMAKER	COHOSTESSED	COLESTIPOLS	COLLECTIVIZES	COLLOQUIALITIES
COENACTING	COFFEEMAKERS	COHOSTESSES	COLICKIEST	COLLECTIVIZING	COLLOQUIALITY
COENAESTHESES	COFFEEPOTS	COHOSTESSING	COLICROOTS	COLLECTORATE	COLLOQUIALLY
COENAESTHESIA	COFFERDAMS	COHOUSINGS	COLICWEEDS	COLLECTORATES	COLLOQUIALNESS
COENAESTHESIAS	COFFINITES	COHYPONYMS	COLINEARITIES	COLLECTORS	COLLOQUIALS
COENAESTHESIS	COFINANCED	COIFFEUSES	COLINEARITY	COLLECTORSHIP	COLLOQUIED
COENAMORED	COFINANCES	COILABILITIES	COLIPHAGES	COLLECTORSHIPS	COLLOQUIES
COENAMORING	COFINANCING	COILABILITY	COLLABORATE	COLLEGIALISM	COLLOQUING
COENDURING	COFOUNDERS	COINCIDENCE	COLLABORATED	COLLEGIALISMS	COLLOQUISE
COENENCHYMA	COFOUNDING	COINCIDENCES	COLLABORATES	COLLEGIALITIES	COLLOQUISED
COENENCHYMAS	COFUNCTION	COINCIDENCIES	COLLABORATING	COLLEGIALITY	COLLOQUISES
COENENCHYMATA	COFUNCTIONS	COINCIDENCY	COLLABORATION	COLLEGIALLY	COLLOQUISING
COENESTHESES	COGENERATION	COINCIDENT	COLLABORATIONS	COLLEGIANER	COLLOQUIST
COENESTHESIA	COGENERATIONS	COINCIDENTAL	COLLABORATIVE	COLLEGIANERS	COLLOQUISTS
COENESTHESIAS	COGENERATOR	COINCIDENTALLY	COLLABORATIVELY	COLLEGIANS	COLLOQUIUM
COENESTHESIS	COGENERATORS	COINCIDENTLY	COLLABORATIVES	COLLEGIATE	COLLOQUIUMS
COENESTHETIC	COGITATING	COINCIDING	COLLABORATOR	COLLEGIATELY	COLLOQUIZE
COENOBITES	COGITATINGLY	COINFECTED	COLLABORATORS	COLLEGIATES	COLLOQUIZED
COENOBITIC	COGITATION	COINFECTING	COLLAGENASE	COLLEGIUMS	COLLOQUIZES
COENOBITICAL	COGITATIONS	COINFERRED	COLLAGENASES	COLLEMBOLAN	COLLOQUIZING
COENOBITISM	COGITATIVE	COINFERRING	COLLAGENIC	COLLEMBOLANS	COLLOQUYING
COENOBITISMS	COGITATIVELY	COINHERENCE	COLLAGENOUS	COLLEMBOLOUS	COLLOTYPES
COENOCYTES	COGITATIVENESS	COINHERENCES	COLLAGISTS	COLLENCHYMA	COLLOTYPIC
COENOCYTIC	COGITATORS	COINHERING	COLLAPSABILITY	COLLENCHYMAS	COLLOTYPIES
COENOSARCS	COGNATENESS	COINHERITANCE	COLLAPSABLE	COLLENCHYMATA	COLLUCTATION
COENOSPECIES	COGNATENESSES	COINHERITANCES	COLLAPSARS	COLLENCHYMATOUS	COLLUCTATIONS
COENOSTEUM	COGNATIONS	COINHERITOR	COLLAPSIBILITY	COLLETERIAL	COLLUSIONS
COENOSTEUMS	COGNISABLE	COINHERITORS	COLLAPSIBLE	COLLICULUS	COLLUSIVELY
COENZYMATIC	COGNISABLY	COINSTANTANEITY	COLLAPSING	COLLICULUSES	COLLUVIUMS
COENZYMATICALLY	COGNISANCE	COINSTANTANEOUS	COLLARBONE	COLLIERIES	COLLYRIUMS
COEQUALITIES	COGNISANCES	COINSURANCE	COLLARBONES	COLLIESHANGIE	COLLYWOBBLES
COEQUALITY	COGNITIONAL	COINSURANCES	COLLARETTE	COLLIESHANGIES	COLOBOMATA
COEQUALNESS	COGNITIONS	COINSURERS	COLLARETTES	COLLIGATED	COLOCATING
COEQUALNESSES	COGNITIVELY	COINSURING	COLLARLESS	COLLIGATES	COLOCYNTHS
COEQUATING	COGNITIVISM	COINTERRED	COLLATABLE	COLLIGATING	COLOGARITHM
COERCIMETER	COGNITIVISMS	COINTERRING	COLLATERAL	COLLIGATION	COLOGARITHMS
COERCIMETERS	COGNITIVITIES	COINTREAUS	COLLATERALISE	COLLIGATIONS	COLOMBARDS
COERCIONIST	COGNITIVITY	COINVENTED	COLLATERALISED	COLLIGATIVE	COLONELCIES
COERCIONISTS	COGNIZABLE	COINVENTING	COLLATERALISES	COLLIMATED	COLONELLING
COERCIVELY	COGNIZABLY	COINVENTOR	COLLATERALISING	COLLIMATES	COLONELLINGS
COERCIVENESS	COGNIZANCE	COINVENTORS	COLLATERALITIES	COLLIMATING	COLONELSHIP
COERCIVENESSES	COGNIZANCES	COINVESTIGATOR	COLLATERALITY	COLLIMATION	COLONELSHIPS
COERCIVITIES	COGNOMINAL	COINVESTIGATORS	COLLATERALIZE	COLLIMATIONS	COLONIALISE
COERCIVITY	COGNOMINALLY	COINVESTOR	COLLATERALIZED	COLLIMATOR	COLONIALISED
COERECTING	COGNOMINATE	COINVESTORS	COLLATERALIZES	COLLIMATORS	COLONIALISES
COESSENTIAL	COGNOMINATED	COKULORISES	COLLATERALIZING	COLLINEARITIES	COLONIALISING
COESSENTIALITY	COGNOMINATES	COLATITUDE	COLLATERALLY	COLLINEARITY	COLONIALISM
COESSENTIALLY	COGNOMINATING	COLATITUDES	COLLATERALS	COLLINEARLY	COLONIALISMS
COESSENTIALNESS	COGNOMINATION	COLCANNONS	COLLATIONS	COLLINSIAS	COLONIALIST
COETANEOUS	COGNOMINATIONS	COLCHICINE	COLLEAGUED	COLLIQUABLE	COLONIALISTIC
COETANEOUSLY	COGNOSCENTE	COLCHICINES	COLLEAGUES	COLLIQUANT	COLONIALISTS
COETANEOUSNESS	COGNOSCENTI	COLCHICUMS	COLLEAGUESHIP	COLLIQUATE	COLONIALIZE
COETERNALLY	COGNOSCIBLE	COLCOTHARS	COLLEAGUESHIPS	COLLIQUATED	COLONIALIZED
COETERNITIES	COGNOSCING	COLDBLOODS	COLLEAGUING	COLLIQUATES	COLONIALIZES
COETERNITY	COHABITANT	COLDCOCKED	COLLECTABLE	COLLIQUATING	COLONIALIZING
COEVALITIES	COHABITANTS	COLDCOCKING	COLLECTABLES	COLLIQUATION	COLONIALLY
COEVOLUTION	COHABITATION	COLDHEARTED	COLLECTANEA	COLLIQUATIONS	COLONIALNESS
COEVOLUTIONARY	COHABITATIONS	COLDHEARTEDLY	COLLECTEDLY	COLLIQUATIVE	COLONIALNESSES
COEVOLUTIONS	COHABITEES	COLDHEARTEDNESS	COLLECTEDNESS	COLLIQUESCENCE	COLONISABLE
COEVOLVING	COHABITERS	COLDHOUSES	COLLECTEDNESSES	COLLIQUESCENCES	COLONISATION
COEXECUTOR	COHABITING	COLDNESSES	COLLECTIBLE	COLLISIONAL	COLONISATIONIST
COEXECUTORS	COHABITORS	COLECTOMIES	COLLECTIBLES	COLLISIONALLY	COLONISATIONS
COEXECUTRICES	COHEIRESSES	COLEMANITE	COLLECTING	COLLISIONS	COLONISERS
COEXECUTRIX	COHERENCES	COLEMANITES	COLLECTINGS	COLLOCATED	COLONISING
COEXECUTRIXES	COHERENCIES	COLEOPTERA	COLLECTION	COLLOCATES	COLONITISES
COEXERTING	COHERENTLY	COLEOPTERAL	COLLECTIONS	COLLOCATING	COLONIZABLE
COEXISTENCE	COHERITORS	COLEOPTERAN	COLLECTIVE	COLLOCATION	COLONIZATION
COEXISTENCES	COHESIBILITIES	COLEOPTERANS	COLLECTIVELY	COLLOCATIONAL	COLONIZATIONIST
COEXISTENT	COHESIBILITY		COLLECTIVENESS	COLLOCATIONS	COLONIZATIONS

COLONIZERS
COLONIZING
COLONNADED
COLONNADES
COLONOSCOPE
COLONOSCOPES
COLONOSCOPIES
COLONOSCOPY
COLOPHONIES
COLOQUINTIDA
COLOQUINTIDAS
COLORATION
COLORATIONS
COLORATURA
COLORATURAS
COLORATURE
COLORATURES
COLORBREED
COLORBREEDING
COLORBREEDS
COLORCASTED
COLORCASTING
COLORCASTS
COLORECTAL
COLORFASTNESS
COLORFASTNESSES
COLORFULLY
COLORFULNESS
COLORFULNESSES
COLORIMETER
COLORIMETERS
COLORIMETRIC
COLORIMETRICAL
COLORIMETRIES
COLORIMETRY
COLORISATION
COLORISATIONS
COLORISERS
COLORISING
COLORISTIC
COLORISTICALLY
COLORIZATION
COLORIZATIONS
COLORIZERS
COLORIZING
COLORLESSLY
COLORLESSNESS
COLORLESSNESSES
COLORPOINT
COLORPOINTS
COLOSSALLY
COLOSSEUMS
COLOSSUSES
COLOSTOMIES
COLOSTROUS
COLOSTRUMS
COLOTOMIES
COLOURABILITIES
COLOURABILITY
COLOURABLE
COLOURABLENESS
COLOURABLY
COLOURANTS
COLOURATION
COLOURATIONS
COLOURFAST
COLOURFASTNESS
COLOURFULLY
COLOURFULNESS
COLOURFULNESSES
COLOURINGS
COLOURISATION
COLOURISATIONS
COLOURISED
COLOURISES
COLOURISING
COLOURISTIC
COLOURISTS
COLOURIZATION
COLOURIZATIONS
COLOURIZED
COLOURIZES
COLOURIZING

COLOURLESS
COLOURLESSLY
COLOURLESSNESS
COLOURPOINT
COLOURPOINTS
COLOURWASH
COLOURWASHED
COLOURWASHES
COLOURWASHING
COLOURWAYS
COLPITISES
COLPORTAGE
COLPORTAGES
COLPORTEUR
COLPORTEURS
COLPOSCOPE
COLPOSCOPES
COLPOSCOPICAL
COLPOSCOPICALLY
COLPOSCOPIES
COLPOSCOPY
COLPOTOMIES
COLTISHNESS
COLTISHNESSES
COLTSFOOTS
COLUBRIADS
COLUBRIFORM
COLUMBARIA
COLUMBARIES
COLUMBARIUM
COLUMBATES
COLUMBINES
COLUMBITES
COLUMBIUMS
COLUMELLAE
COLUMELLAR
COLUMNARITIES
COLUMNARITY
COLUMNATED
COLUMNIATED
COLUMNIATION
COLUMNIATIONS
COLUMNISTIC
COLUMNISTS
COMANAGEMENT
COMANAGEMENTS
COMANAGERS
COMANAGING
COMANCHERO
COMANCHEROS
COMATOSELY
COMATULIDS
COMBATABLE
COMBATANTS
COMBATIVELY
COMBATIVENESS
COMBATIVENESSES
COMBATTING
COMBINABILITIES
COMBINABILITY
COMBINABLE
COMBINATION
COMBINATIONAL
COMBINATIONS
COMBINATIVE
COMBINATORIAL
COMBINATORIALLY
COMBINATORICS
COMBINATORY
COMBININGS
COMBRETUMS
COMBURGESS
COMBURGESSES
COMBUSTIBILITY
COMBUSTIBLE
COMBUSTIBLENESS
COMBUSTIBLES
COMBUSTIBLY
COMBUSTING
COMBUSTION
COMBUSTIONS
COMBUSTIOUS
COMBUSTIVE

COMBUSTIVES
COMBUSTORS
COMEDDLING
COMEDICALLY
COMEDIENNE
COMEDIENNES
COMEDIETTA
COMEDIETTAS
COMEDOGENIC
COMELINESS
COMELINESSES
COMESTIBLE
COMESTIBLES
COMETOGRAPHIES
COMETOGRAPHY
COMETOLOGIES
COMETOLOGY
COMEUPPANCE
COMEUPPANCES
COMFINESSES
COMFITURES
COMFORTABLE
COMFORTABLENESS
COMFORTABLY
COMFORTERS
COMFORTING
COMFORTINGLY
COMFORTLESS
COMFORTLESSLY
COMFORTLESSNESS
COMICALITIES
COMICALITY
COMICALNESS
COMICALNESSES
COMINGLING
COMITADJIS
COMITATIVE
COMITATIVES
COMITATUSES
COMMANDABLE
COMMANDANT
COMMANDANTS
COMMANDANTSHIP
COMMANDANTSHIPS
COMMANDEER
COMMANDEERED
COMMANDEERING
COMMANDEERS
COMMANDERIES
COMMANDERS
COMMANDERSHIP
COMMANDERSHIPS
COMMANDERY
COMMANDING
COMMANDINGLY
COMMANDMENT
COMMANDMENTS
COMMANDOES
COMMEASURABLE
COMMEASURE
COMMEASURED
COMMEASURES
COMMEASURING
COMMEMORABLE
COMMEMORATE
COMMEMORATED
COMMEMORATES
COMMEMORATING
COMMEMORATION
COMMEMORATIONAL
COMMEMORATIONS
COMMEMORATIVE
COMMEMORATIVELY
COMMEMORATIVES
COMMEMORATOR
COMMEMORATORS
COMMEMORATORY
COMMENCEMENT
COMMENCEMENTS
COMMENCERS
COMMENCING
COMMENDABLE
COMMENDABLENESS

COMMENDABLY
COMMENDAMS
COMMENDATION
COMMENDATIONS
COMMENDATOR
COMMENDATORS
COMMENDATORY
COMMENDERS
COMMENDING
COMMENSALISM
COMMENSALISMS
COMMENSALITIES
COMMENSALITY
COMMENSALLY
COMMENSALS
COMMENSURABLE
COMMENSURABLY
COMMENSURATE
COMMENSURATELY
COMMENSURATION
COMMENSURATIONS
COMMENTARIAL
COMMENTARIAT
COMMENTARIATS
COMMENTARIES
COMMENTARY
COMMENTATE
COMMENTATED
COMMENTATES
COMMENTATING
COMMENTATION
COMMENTATIONS
COMMENTATOR
COMMENTATORIAL
COMMENTATORS
COMMENTERS
COMMENTING
COMMENTORS
COMMERCIAL
COMMERCIALESE
COMMERCIALESES
COMMERCIALISE
COMMERCIALISED
COMMERCIALISES
COMMERCIALISING
COMMERCIALISM
COMMERCIALISMS
COMMERCIALIST
COMMERCIALISTIC
COMMERCIALISTS
COMMERCIALITIES
COMMERCIALITY
COMMERCIALIZE
COMMERCIALIZED
COMMERCIALIZES
COMMERCIALIZING
COMMERCIALLY
COMMERCIALS
COMMERCING
COMMERGING
COMMINATED
COMMINATES
COMMINATING
COMMINATION
COMMINATIONS
COMMINATIVE
COMMINATORY
COMMINGLED
COMMINGLES
COMMINGLING
COMMINUTED
COMMINUTES
COMMINUTING
COMMINUTION
COMMINUTIONS
COMMISERABLE
COMMISERATE
COMMISERATED
COMMISERATES
COMMISERATING
COMMISERATINGLY
COMMISERATION
COMMISERATIONS

COMMISERATIVE
COMMISERATIVELY
COMMISERATOR
COMMISERATORS
COMMISSAIRE
COMMISSAIRES
COMMISSARIAL
COMMISSARIAT
COMMISSARIATS
COMMISSARIES
COMMISSARS
COMMISSARY
COMMISSARYSHIP
COMMISSARYSHIPS
COMMISSION
COMMISSIONAIRE
COMMISSIONAIRES
COMMISSIONAL
COMMISSIONARY
COMMISSIONED
COMMISSIONER
COMMISSIONERS
COMMISSIONING
COMMISSIONS
COMMISSURAL
COMMISSURE
COMMISSURES
COMMITMENT
COMMITMENTS
COMMITTABLE
COMMITTALS
COMMITTEEMAN
COMMITTEEMEN
COMMITTEES
COMMITTEESHIP
COMMITTEESHIPS
COMMITTEEWOMAN
COMMITTEEWOMEN
COMMITTERS
COMMITTING
COMMIXTION
COMMIXTIONS
COMMIXTURE
COMMIXTURES
COMMODIFICATION
COMMODIFIED
COMMODIFIES
COMMODIFYING
COMMODIOUS
COMMODIOUSLY
COMMODIOUSNESS
COMMODITIES
COMMODITISE
COMMODITISED
COMMODITISES
COMMODITISING
COMMODITIZE
COMMODITIZED
COMMODITIZES
COMMODITIZING
COMMODORES
COMMONABLE
COMMONAGES
COMMONALITIES
COMMONALITY
COMMONALTIES
COMMONALTY
COMMONHOLD
COMMONHOLDS
COMMONINGS
COMMONNESS
COMMONNESSES
COMMONPLACE
COMMONPLACED
COMMONPLACENESS
COMMONPLACES
COMMONPLACING
COMMONSENSE
COMMONSENSIBLE
COMMONSENSICAL
COMMONWEAL
COMMONWEALS
COMMONWEALTH

COMMONWEALTHS
COMMORANTS
COMMORIENTES
COMMOTIONAL
COMMOTIONS
COMMUNALISATION
COMMUNALISE
COMMUNALISED
COMMUNALISER
COMMUNALISERS
COMMUNALISES
COMMUNALISING
COMMUNALISM
COMMUNALISMS
COMMUNALIST
COMMUNALISTIC
COMMUNALISTS
COMMUNALITIES
COMMUNALITY
COMMUNALIZATION
COMMUNALIZE
COMMUNALIZED
COMMUNALIZER
COMMUNALIZERS
COMMUNALIZES
COMMUNALIZING
COMMUNALLY
COMMUNARDS
COMMUNAUTAIRE
COMMUNAUTAIRES
COMMUNICABILITY
COMMUNICABLE
COMMUNICABLY
COMMUNICANT
COMMUNICANTS
COMMUNICATE
COMMUNICATED
COMMUNICATEE
COMMUNICATEES
COMMUNICATES
COMMUNICATING
COMMUNICATION
COMMUNICATIONAL
COMMUNICATIONS
COMMUNICATIVE
COMMUNICATIVELY
COMMUNICATOR
COMMUNICATORS
COMMUNICATORY
COMMUNINGS
COMMUNIONAL
COMMUNIONALLY
COMMUNIONS
COMMUNIQUE
COMMUNIQUES
COMMUNISATION
COMMUNISATIONS
COMMUNISED
COMMUNISES
COMMUNISING
COMMUNISMS
COMMUNISTIC
COMMUNISTICALLY
COMMUNISTS
COMMUNITAIRE
COMMUNITAIRES
COMMUNITARIAN
COMMUNITARIANS
COMMUNITIES
COMMUNIZATION
COMMUNIZATIONS
COMMUNIZED
COMMUNIZES
COMMUNIZING
COMMUTABILITIES
COMMUTABILITY
COMMUTABLE
COMMUTABLENESS
COMMUTATED
COMMUTATES
COMMUTATING
COMMUTATION
COMMUTATIONS

COMMUTATIVE
COMMUTATIVELY
COMMUTATIVITIES
COMMUTATIVITY
COMMUTATOR
COMMUTATORS
COMONOMERS
COMPACTEDLY
COMPACTEDNESS
COMPACTEDNESSES
COMPACTERS
COMPACTEST
COMPACTIBLE
COMPACTIFIED
COMPACTIFIES
COMPACTIFY
COMPACTIFYING
COMPACTING
COMPACTION
COMPACTIONS
COMPACTNESS
COMPACTNESSES
COMPACTORS
COMPACTURE
COMPACTURES
COMPAGINATE
COMPAGINATED
COMPAGINATES
COMPAGINATING
COMPAGINATION
COMPAGINATIONS
COMPANDERS
COMPANDING
COMPANDORS
COMPANIABLE
COMPANIONABLE
COMPANIONABLY
COMPANIONATE
COMPANIONED
COMPANIONHOOD
COMPANIONHOODS
COMPANIONING
COMPANIONLESS
COMPANIONS
COMPANIONSHIP
COMPANIONSHIPS
COMPANIONWAY
COMPANIONWAYS
COMPANYING
COMPARABILITIES
COMPARABILITY
COMPARABLE
COMPARABLENESS
COMPARABLY
COMPARATIST
COMPARATISTS
COMPARATIVE
COMPARATIVELY
COMPARATIVENESS
COMPARATIVES
COMPARATIVIST
COMPARATIVISTS
COMPARATOR
COMPARATORS
COMPARISON
COMPARISONS
COMPARTING
COMPARTMENT
COMPARTMENTAL
COMPARTMENTALLY
COMPARTMENTED
COMPARTMENTING
COMPARTMENTS
COMPASSABLE
COMPASSING
COMPASSINGS
COMPASSION
COMPASSIONABLE
COMPASSIONATE
COMPASSIONATED
COMPASSIONATELY
COMPASSIONATES
COMPASSIONATING

COMPASSIONED
COMPASSIONING
COMPASSIONLESS
COMPASSIONS
COMPATIBILITIES
COMPATIBILITY
COMPATIBLE
COMPATIBLENESS
COMPATIBLES
COMPATIBLY
COMPATRIOT
COMPATRIOTIC
COMPATRIOTISM
COMPATRIOTISMS
COMPATRIOTS
COMPEARANCE
COMPEARANCES
COMPEARANT
COMPEARANTS
COMPEARING
COMPEERING
COMPELLABLE
COMPELLABLY
COMPELLATION
COMPELLATIONS
COMPELLATIVE
COMPELLATIVES
COMPELLERS
COMPELLING
COMPELLINGLY
COMPENDIOUS
COMPENDIOUSLY
COMPENDIOUSNESS
COMPENDIUM
COMPENDIUMS
COMPENSABILITY
COMPENSABLE
COMPENSATE
COMPENSATED
COMPENSATES
COMPENSATING
COMPENSATION
COMPENSATIONAL
COMPENSATIONS
COMPENSATIVE
COMPENSATOR
COMPENSATORS
COMPENSATORY
COMPESCING
COMPETENCE
COMPETENCES
COMPETENCIES
COMPETENCY
COMPETENTLY
COMPETENTNESS
COMPETENTNESSES
COMPETITION
COMPETITIONS
COMPETITIVE
COMPETITIVELY
COMPETITIVENESS
COMPETITOR
COMPETITORS
COMPILATION
COMPILATIONS
COMPILATOR
COMPILATORS
COMPILATORY
COMPILEMENT
COMPILEMENTS
COMPLACENCE
COMPLACENCES
COMPLACENCIES
COMPLACENCY
COMPLACENT
COMPLACENTLY
COMPLAINANT
COMPLAINANTS
COMPLAINED
COMPLAINER
COMPLAINERS
COMPLAINING
COMPLAININGLY

COMPLAININGS
COMPLAINTS
COMPLAISANCE
COMPLAISANCES
COMPLAISANT
COMPLAISANTLY
COMPLANATE
COMPLANATION
COMPLANATIONS
COMPLECTED
COMPLECTING
COMPLEMENT
COMPLEMENTAL
COMPLEMENTALLY
COMPLEMENTARIES
COMPLEMENTARILY
COMPLEMENTARITY
COMPLEMENTARY
COMPLEMENTATION
COMPLEMENTED
COMPLEMENTING
COMPLEMENTISER
COMPLEMENTISERS
COMPLEMENTIZER
COMPLEMENTIZERS
COMPLEMENTS
COMPLETABLE
COMPLETELY
COMPLETENESS
COMPLETENESSES
COMPLETERS
COMPLETEST
COMPLETING
COMPLETION
COMPLETIONS
COMPLETIST
COMPLETISTS
COMPLETIVE
COMPLETORY
COMPLEXATION
COMPLEXATIONS
COMPLEXEDNESS
COMPLEXEDNESSES
COMPLEXEST
COMPLEXIFIED
COMPLEXIFIES
COMPLEXIFY
COMPLEXIFYING
COMPLEXING
COMPLEXION
COMPLEXIONAL
COMPLEXIONED
COMPLEXIONLESS
COMPLEXIONS
COMPLEXITIES
COMPLEXITY
COMPLEXNESS
COMPLEXNESSES
COMPLEXOMETRIC
COMPLEXONE
COMPLEXONES
COMPLEXUSES
COMPLIABLE
COMPLIABLENESS
COMPLIABLY
COMPLIANCE
COMPLIANCES
COMPLIANCIES
COMPLIANCY
COMPLIANTLY
COMPLIANTNESS
COMPLIANTNESSES
COMPLICACIES
COMPLICACY
COMPLICANT
COMPLICATE
COMPLICATED
COMPLICATEDLY
COMPLICATEDNESS
COMPLICATES
COMPLICATING
COMPLICATION
COMPLICATIONS

COMPLICATIVE
COMPLICITIES
COMPLICITOUS
COMPLICITY
COMPLIMENT
COMPLIMENTAL
COMPLIMENTARILY
COMPLIMENTARY
COMPLIMENTED
COMPLIMENTER
COMPLIMENTERS
COMPLIMENTING
COMPLIMENTS
COMPLISHED
COMPLISHES
COMPLISHING
COMPLOTTED
COMPLOTTER
COMPLOTTERS
COMPLOTTING
COMPLUVIUM
COMPLUVIUMS
COMPONENCIES
COMPONENCY
COMPONENTAL
COMPONENTIAL
COMPONENTS
COMPORTANCE
COMPORTANCES
COMPORTING
COMPORTMENT
COMPORTMENTS
COMPOSEDLY
COMPOSEDNESS
COMPOSEDNESSES
COMPOSITED
COMPOSITELY
COMPOSITENESS
COMPOSITENESSES
COMPOSITES
COMPOSITING
COMPOSITION
COMPOSITIONAL
COMPOSITIONALLY
COMPOSITIONS
COMPOSITIVE
COMPOSITOR
COMPOSITORIAL
COMPOSITORS
COMPOSITOUS
COMPOSSIBILITY
COMPOSSIBLE
COMPOSTABLE
COMPOSTERS
COMPOSTING
COMPOSTURE
COMPOSTURED
COMPOSTURES
COMPOSTURING
COMPOSURES
COMPOTATION
COMPOTATIONS
COMPOTATIONSHIP
COMPOTATOR
COMPOTATORS
COMPOTATORY
COMPOTIERS
COMPOUNDABLE
COMPOUNDED
COMPOUNDER
COMPOUNDERS
COMPOUNDING
COMPRADORE
COMPRADORES
COMPRADORS
COMPREHEND
COMPREHENDED
COMPREHENDIBLE
COMPREHENDING
COMPREHENDS
COMPREHENSIBLE
COMPREHENSIBLY
COMPREHENSION

COMPREHENSIONS
COMPREHENSIVE
COMPREHENSIVELY
COMPREHENSIVES
COMPREHENSIVISE
COMPREHENSIVIZE
COMPRESSED
COMPRESSEDLY
COMPRESSES
COMPRESSIBILITY
COMPRESSIBLE
COMPRESSIBLY
COMPRESSING
COMPRESSION
COMPRESSIONAL
COMPRESSIONS
COMPRESSIVE
COMPRESSIVELY
COMPRESSOR
COMPRESSORS
COMPRESSURE
COMPRESSURES
COMPRIMARIO
COMPRIMARIOS
COMPRINTED
COMPRINTING
COMPRISABLE
COMPRISALS
COMPRISING
COMPRIZING
COMPROMISE
COMPROMISED
COMPROMISER
COMPROMISERS
COMPROMISES
COMPROMISING
COMPROMISINGLY
COMPROVINCIAL
COMPTROLLED
COMPTROLLER
COMPTROLLERS
COMPTROLLERSHIP
COMPTROLLING
COMPTROLLS
COMPULSATIVE
COMPULSATORY
COMPULSING
COMPULSION
COMPULSIONIST
COMPULSIONISTS
COMPULSIONS
COMPULSITOR
COMPULSITORS
COMPULSIVE
COMPULSIVELY
COMPULSIVENESS
COMPULSIVES
COMPULSIVITIES
COMPULSIVITY
COMPULSORIES
COMPULSORILY
COMPULSORINESS
COMPULSORY
COMPUNCTION
COMPUNCTIONS
COMPUNCTIOUS
COMPUNCTIOUSLY
COMPURGATION
COMPURGATIONS
COMPURGATOR
COMPURGATORIAL
COMPURGATORS
COMPURGATORY
COMPURSION
COMPURSIONS
COMPUTABILITIES
COMPUTABILITY
COMPUTABLE
COMPUTANTS
COMPUTATION
COMPUTATIONAL
COMPUTATIONALLY
COMPUTATIONS

COMPUTATIVE
COMPUTATOR
COMPUTATORS
COMPUTERATE
COMPUTERDOM
COMPUTERDOMS
COMPUTERESE
COMPUTERESES
COMPUTERISABLE
COMPUTERISATION
COMPUTERISE
COMPUTERISED
COMPUTERISES
COMPUTERISING
COMPUTERIST
COMPUTERISTS
COMPUTERIZABLE
COMPUTERIZATION
COMPUTERIZE
COMPUTERIZED
COMPUTERIZES
COMPUTERIZING
COMPUTERLESS
COMPUTERLIKE
COMPUTERNIK
COMPUTERNIKS
COMPUTERPHOBE
COMPUTERPHOBES
COMPUTERPHOBIA
COMPUTERPHOBIAS
COMPUTERPHOBIC
COMPUTISTS
COMRADELINESS
COMRADELINESSES
COMRADERIES
COMRADESHIP
COMRADESHIPS
COMSTOCKER
COMSTOCKERIES
COMSTOCKERS
COMSTOCKERY
COMSTOCKISM
COMSTOCKISMS
CONACREISM
CONACREISMS
CONATIONAL
CONCANAVALIN
CONCANAVALINS
CONCATENATE
CONCATENATED
CONCATENATES
CONCATENATING
CONCATENATION
CONCATENATIONS
CONCAVENESS
CONCAVENESSES
CONCAVITIES
CONCEALABLE
CONCEALERS
CONCEALING
CONCEALINGLY
CONCEALMENT
CONCEALMENTS
CONCEDEDLY
CONCEITEDLY
CONCEITEDNESS
CONCEITEDNESSES
CONCEITFUL
CONCEITING
CONCEITLESS
CONCEIVABILITY
CONCEIVABLE
CONCEIVABLENESS
CONCEIVABLY
CONCEIVERS
CONCEIVING
CONCELEBRANT
CONCELEBRANTS
CONCELEBRATE
CONCELEBRATED
CONCELEBRATES
CONCELEBRATING
CONCELEBRATION

CONCELEBRATIONS	CONCERTISING	CONCOCTIONS	CONCUSSIVE	CONDUCTIBLE	CONFESSIONAL
CONCENTERED	CONCERTIZE	CONCOCTIVE	CONCYCLICALLY	CONDUCTIMETRIC	CONFESSIONALISM
CONCENTERING	CONCERTIZED	CONCOCTORS	CONDEMNABLE	CONDUCTING	CONFESSIONALIST
CONCENTERS	CONCERTIZES	CONCOLORATE	CONDEMNABLY	CONDUCTIOMETRIC	CONFESSIONALIST
CONCENTRATE	CONCERTIZING	CONCOLOROUS	CONDEMNATION	CONDUCTION	CONFESSIONALS
CONCENTRATED	CONCERTMASTER	CONCOMITANCE	CONDEMNATIONS	CONDUCTIONAL	CONFESSIONARIES
CONCENTRATEDLY	CONCERTMASTERS	CONCOMITANCES	CONDEMNATORY	CONDUCTIONS	CONFESSIONARY
CONCENTRATES	CONCERTMEISTER	CONCOMITANCIES	CONDEMNERS	CONDUCTIVE	CONFESSIONS
CONCENTRATING	CONCERTMEISTERS	CONCOMITANCY	CONDEMNING	CONDUCTIVELY	CONFESSORESS
CONCENTRATION	CONCERTSTUCK	CONCOMITANT	CONDEMNINGLY	CONDUCTIVITIES	CONFESSORESSES
CONCENTRATIONS	CONCERTSTUCKS	CONCOMITANTLY	CONDEMNORS	CONDUCTIVITY	CONFESSORS
CONCENTRATIVE	CONCESSIBLE	CONCOMITANTS	CONDENSABILITY	CONDUCTOMETRIC	CONFESSORSHIP
CONCENTRATIVELY	CONCESSION	CONCORDANCE	CONDENSABLE	CONDUCTORIAL	CONFESSORSHIPS
CONCENTRATOR	CONCESSIONAIRE	CONCORDANCES	CONDENSATE	CONDUCTORS	CONFIDANTE
CONCENTRATORS	CONCESSIONAIRES	CONCORDANT	CONDENSATED	CONDUCTORSHIP	CONFIDANTES
CONCENTRED	CONCESSIONAL	CONCORDANTLY	CONDENSATES	CONDUCTORSHIPS	CONFIDANTS
CONCENTRES	CONCESSIONARIES	CONCORDATS	CONDENSATING	CONDUCTRESS	CONFIDENCE
CONCENTRIC	CONCESSIONARY	CONCORDIAL	CONDENSATION	CONDUCTRESSES	CONFIDENCES
CONCENTRICAL	CONCESSIONER	CONCORDING	CONDENSATIONAL	CONDUPLICATE	CONFIDENCIES
CONCENTRICALLY	CONCESSIONERS	CONCORPORATE	CONDENSATIONS	CONDUPLICATION	CONFIDENCY
CONCENTRICITIES	CONCESSIONIST	CONCORPORATED	CONDENSERIES	CONDUPLICATIONS	CONFIDENTIAL
CONCENTRICITY	CONCESSIONISTS	CONCORPORATES	CONDENSERS	CONDYLOMAS	CONFIDENTIALITY
CONCENTRING	CONCESSIONNAIRE	CONCORPORATING	CONDENSERY	CONDYLOMATA	CONFIDENTIALLY
CONCEPTACLE	CONCESSIONS	CONCOURSES	CONDENSIBILITY	CONDYLOMATOUS	CONFIDENTLY
CONCEPTACLES	CONCESSIVE	CONCREATED	CONDENSIBLE	CONEFLOWER	CONFIDENTS
CONCEPTION	CONCESSIVELY	CONCREATES	CONDENSING	CONEFLOWERS	CONFIDINGLY
CONCEPTIONAL	CONCETTISM	CONCREATING	CONDESCEND	CONFABBING	CONFIDINGNESS
CONCEPTIONS	CONCETTISMS	CONCREMATION	CONDESCENDED	CONFABULAR	CONFIDINGNESSES
CONCEPTIOUS	CONCETTIST	CONCREMATIONS	CONDESCENDENCE	CONFABULATE	CONFIGURATE
CONCEPTIVE	CONCETTISTS	CONCRESCENCE	CONDESCENDENCES	CONFABULATED	CONFIGURATED
CONCEPTUAL	CONCHIFEROUS	CONCRESCENCES	CONDESCENDING	CONFABULATES	CONFIGURATES
CONCEPTUALISE	CONCHIFORM	CONCRESCENT	CONDESCENDINGLY	CONFABULATING	CONFIGURATING
CONCEPTUALISED	CONCHIGLIE	CONCRETELY	CONDESCENDS	CONFABULATION	CONFIGURATION
CONCEPTUALISER	CONCHIOLIN	CONCRETENESS	CONDESCENSION	CONFABULATIONS	CONFIGURATIONAL
CONCEPTUALISERS	CONCHIOLINS	CONCRETENESSES	CONDESCENSIONS	CONFABULATOR	CONFIGURATIONS
CONCEPTUALISES	CONCHITISES	CONCRETING	CONDIDDLED	CONFABULATORS	CONFIGURATIVE
CONCEPTUALISING	CONCHOIDAL	CONCRETION	CONDIDDLES	CONFABULATORY	CONFIGURED
CONCEPTUALISM	CONCHOIDALLY	CONCRETIONARY	CONDIDDLING	CONFARREATE	CONFIGURES
CONCEPTUALISMS	CONCHOLOGICAL	CONCRETIONS	CONDIGNNESS	CONFARREATION	CONFIGURING
CONCEPTUALIST	CONCHOLOGIES	CONCRETISATION	CONDIGNNESSES	CONFARREATIONS	CONFINABLE
CONCEPTUALISTIC	CONCHOLOGIST	CONCRETISATIONS	CONDIMENTAL	CONFECTING	CONFINEABLE
CONCEPTUALISTS	CONCHOLOGISTS	CONCRETISE	CONDIMENTED	CONFECTION	CONFINEDLY
CONCEPTUALITIES	CONCHOLOGY	CONCRETISED	CONDIMENTING	CONFECTIONARIES	CONFINEDNESS
CONCEPTUALITY	CONCIERGES	CONCRETISES	CONDIMENTS	CONFECTIONARY	CONFINEDNESSES
CONCEPTUALIZE	CONCILIABLE	CONCRETISING	CONDISCIPLE	CONFECTIONER	CONFINELESS
CONCEPTUALIZED	CONCILIARLY	CONCRETISM	CONDISCIPLES	CONFECTIONERIES	CONFINEMENT
CONCEPTUALIZER	CONCILIARY	CONCRETISMS	CONDITIONABLE	CONFECTIONERS	CONFINEMENTS
CONCEPTUALIZERS	CONCILIATE	CONCRETIST	CONDITIONAL	CONFECTIONERY	CONFIRMABILITY
CONCEPTUALIZES	CONCILIATED	CONCRETISTS	CONDITIONALITY	CONFECTIONS	CONFIRMABLE
CONCEPTUALIZING	CONCILIATES	CONCRETIVE	CONDITIONALLY	CONFEDERACIES	CONFIRMAND
CONCEPTUALLY	CONCILIATING	CONCRETIVELY	CONDITIONALS	CONFEDERACY	CONFIRMANDS
CONCEPTUSES	CONCILIATION	CONCRETIZATION	CONDITIONATE	CONFEDERAL	CONFIRMATION
CONCERNANCIES	CONCILIATIONS	CONCRETIZATIONS	CONDITIONATED	CONFEDERATE	CONFIRMATIONAL
CONCERNANCY	CONCILIATIVE	CONCRETIZE	CONDITIONATES	CONFEDERATED	CONFIRMATIONS
CONCERNEDLY	CONCILIATOR	CONCRETIZED	CONDITIONATING	CONFEDERATES	CONFIRMATIVE
CONCERNEDNESS	CONCILIATORILY	CONCRETIZES	CONDITIONED	CONFEDERATING	CONFIRMATOR
CONCERNEDNESSES	CONCILIATORS	CONCRETIZING	CONDITIONER	CONFEDERATION	CONFIRMATORS
CONCERNING	CONCILIATORY	CONCREWING	CONDITIONERS	CONFEDERATIONS	CONFIRMATORY
CONCERNMENT	CONCINNITIES	CONCUBINAGE	CONDITIONING	CONFEDERATIVE	CONFIRMEDLY
CONCERNMENTS	CONCINNITY	CONCUBINAGES	CONDITIONINGS	CONFERENCE	CONFIRMEDNESS
CONCERTANTE	CONCINNOUS	CONCUBINARIES	CONDITIONS	CONFERENCES	CONFIRMEDNESSES
CONCERTANTES	CONCIPIENCIES	CONCUBINARY	CONDOLATORY	CONFERENCIER	CONFIRMEES
CONCERTANTI	CONCIPIENCY	CONCUBINES	CONDOLEMENT	CONFERENCIERS	CONFIRMERS
CONCERTEDLY	CONCIPIENT	CONCUBITANCIES	CONDOLEMENTS	CONFERENCING	CONFIRMING
CONCERTEDNESS	CONCISENESS	CONCUBITANCY	CONDOLENCE	CONFERENCINGS	CONFIRMINGS
CONCERTEDNESSES	CONCISENESSES	CONCUBITANT	CONDOLENCES	CONFERENTIAL	CONFIRMORS
CONCERTGOER	CONCISIONS	CONCUBITANTS	CONDOLINGLY	CONFERMENT	CONFISCABLE
CONCERTGOERS	CONCLAMATION	CONCUPISCENCE	CONDOMINIUM	CONFERMENTS	CONFISCATABLE
CONCERTGOING	CONCLAMATIONS	CONCUPISCENCES	CONDOMINIUMS	CONFERRABLE	CONFISCATE
CONCERTGOINGS	CONCLAVIST	CONCUPISCENT	CONDONABLE	CONFERRALS	CONFISCATED
CONCERTINA	CONCLAVISTS	CONCUPISCIBLE	CONDONATION	CONFERREES	CONFISCATES
CONCERTINAED	CONCLUDERS	CONCURRENCE	CONDONATIONS	CONFERRENCE	CONFISCATING
CONCERTINAING	CONCLUDING	CONCURRENCES	CONDOTTIERE	CONFERRENCES	CONFISCATION
CONCERTINAS	CONCLUSION	CONCURRENCIES	CONDOTTIERI	CONFERRERS	CONFISCATIONS
CONCERTING	CONCLUSIONARY	CONCURRENCY	CONDUCEMENT	CONFERRING	CONFISCATOR
CONCERTINI	CONCLUSIONS	CONCURRENT	CONDUCEMENTS	CONFERVOID	CONFISCATORS
CONCERTINIST	CONCLUSIVE	CONCURRENTLY	CONDUCIBLE	CONFERVOIDS	CONFISCATORY
CONCERTINISTS	CONCLUSIVELY	CONCURRENTS	CONDUCINGLY	CONFESSABLE	CONFISERIE
CONCERTINO	CONCLUSIVENESS	CONCURRING	CONDUCIVENESS	CONFESSANT	CONFISERIES
CONCERTINOS	CONCLUSORY	CONCURRINGLY	CONDUCIVENESSES	CONFESSANTS	CONFISEURS
CONCERTISE	CONCOCTERS	CONCUSSING	CONDUCTANCE	CONFESSEDLY	CONFITEORS
CONCERTISED	CONCOCTING	CONCUSSION	CONDUCTANCES	CONFESSING	CONFITURES
CONCERTISES	CONCOCTION	CONCUSSIONS	CONDUCTIBILITY	CONFESSION	CONFLAGRANT

CONFLAGRATE
CONFLAGRATED
CONFLAGRATES
CONFLAGRATING
CONFLAGRATION
CONFLAGRATIONS
CONFLAGRATIVE
CONFLATING
CONFLATION
CONFLATIONS
CONFLICTED
CONFLICTFUL
CONFLICTING
CONFLICTINGLY
CONFLICTION
CONFLICTIONS
CONFLICTIVE
CONFLICTORY
CONFLICTUAL
CONFLUENCE
CONFLUENCES
CONFLUENTLY
CONFLUENTS
CONFOCALLY
CONFORMABILITY
CONFORMABLE
CONFORMABLENESS
CONFORMABLY
CONFORMANCE
CONFORMANCES
CONFORMATION
CONFORMATIONAL
CONFORMATIONS
CONFORMERS
CONFORMING
CONFORMINGLY
CONFORMISM
CONFORMISMS
CONFORMIST
CONFORMISTS
CONFORMITIES
CONFORMITY
CONFOUNDABLE
CONFOUNDED
CONFOUNDEDLY
CONFOUNDEDNESS
CONFOUNDER
CONFOUNDERS
CONFOUNDING
CONFOUNDINGLY
CONFRATERNAL
CONFRATERNITIES
CONFRATERNITY
CONFRERIES
CONFRONTAL
CONFRONTALS
CONFRONTATION
CONFRONTATIONAL
CONFRONTATIONS
CONFRONTED
CONFRONTER
CONFRONTERS
CONFRONTING
CONFRONTMENT
CONFRONTMENTS
CONFUSABILITIES
CONFUSABILITY
CONFUSABLE
CONFUSABLES
CONFUSEDLY
CONFUSEDNESS
CONFUSEDNESSES
CONFUSIBLE
CONFUSIBLES
CONFUSINGLY
CONFUSIONAL
CONFUSIONS
CONFUTABLE
CONFUTATION
CONFUTATIONS
CONFUTATIVE
CONFUTEMENT
CONFUTEMENTS

CONGEALABLE
CONGEALABLENESS
CONGEALERS
CONGEALING
CONGEALMENT
CONGEALMENTS
CONGELATION
CONGELATIONS
CONGENERIC
CONGENERICAL
CONGENERICS
CONGENEROUS
CONGENETIC
CONGENIALITIES
CONGENIALITY
CONGENIALLY
CONGENIALNESS
CONGENIALNESSES
CONGENITAL
CONGENITALLY
CONGENITALNESS
CONGESTIBLE
CONGESTING
CONGESTION
CONGESTIONS
CONGESTIVE
CONGIARIES
CONGLOBATE
CONGLOBATED
CONGLOBATES
CONGLOBATING
CONGLOBATION
CONGLOBATIONS
CONGLOBING
CONGLOBULATE
CONGLOBULATED
CONGLOBULATES
CONGLOBULATING
CONGLOBULATION
CONGLOBULATIONS
CONGLOMERATE
CONGLOMERATED
CONGLOMERATES
CONGLOMERATEUR
CONGLOMERATEURS
CONGLOMERATIC
CONGLOMERATING
CONGLOMERATION
CONGLOMERATIONS
CONGLOMERATIVE
CONGLOMERATOR
CONGLOMERATORS
CONGLUTINANT
CONGLUTINATE
CONGLUTINATED
CONGLUTINATES
CONGLUTINATING
CONGLUTINATION
CONGLUTINATIONS
CONGLUTINATIVE
CONGLUTINATOR
CONGLUTINATORS
CONGRATTERS
CONGRATULABLE
CONGRATULANT
CONGRATULANTS
CONGRATULATE
CONGRATULATED
CONGRATULATES
CONGRATULATING
CONGRATULATION
CONGRATULATIONS
CONGRATULATIVE
CONGRATULATOR
CONGRATULATORS
CONGRATULATORY
CONGREEING
CONGREETED
CONGREETING
CONGREGANT
CONGREGANTS
CONGREGATE
CONGREGATED

CONGREGATES
CONGREGATING
CONGREGATION
CONGREGATIONAL
CONGREGATIONS
CONGREGATIVE
CONGREGATOR
CONGREGATORS
CONGRESSED
CONGRESSES
CONGRESSING
CONGRESSIONAL
CONGRESSIONALLY
CONGRESSMAN
CONGRESSMEN
CONGRESSPEOPLE
CONGRESSPERSON
CONGRESSPERSONS
CONGRESSWOMAN
CONGRESSWOMEN
CONGRUENCE
CONGRUENCES
CONGRUENCIES
CONGRUENCY
CONGRUENTLY
CONGRUITIES
CONGRUOUSLY
CONGRUOUSNESS
CONGRUOUSNESSES
CONICITIES
CONIDIOPHORE
CONIDIOPHORES
CONIDIOPHOROUS
CONIDIOSPORE
CONIDIOSPORES
CONIFEROUS
CONIOLOGIES
CONIROSTRAL
CONJECTING
CONJECTURABLE
CONJECTURABLY
CONJECTURAL
CONJECTURALLY
CONJECTURE
CONJECTURED
CONJECTURER
CONJECTURERS
CONJECTURES
CONJECTURING
CONJOINERS
CONJOINING
CONJOINTLY
CONJUGABLE
CONJUGALITIES
CONJUGALITY
CONJUGALLY
CONJUGANTS
CONJUGATED
CONJUGATELY
CONJUGATENESS
CONJUGATENESSES
CONJUGATES
CONJUGATING
CONJUGATINGS
CONJUGATION
CONJUGATIONAL
CONJUGATIONALLY
CONJUGATIONS
CONJUGATIVE
CONJUGATOR
CONJUGATORS
CONJUNCTION
CONJUNCTIONAL
CONJUNCTIONALLY
CONJUNCTIONS
CONJUNCTIVA
CONJUNCTIVAE
CONJUNCTIVAL
CONJUNCTIVAS
CONJUNCTIVE
CONJUNCTIVELY
CONJUNCTIVENESS
CONJUNCTIVES

CONJUNCTIVITIS
CONJUNCTLY
CONJUNCTURAL
CONJUNCTURE
CONJUNCTURES
CONJURATION
CONJURATIONS
CONJURATOR
CONJURATORS
CONJUREMENT
CONJUREMENTS
CONJURINGS
CONNASCENCE
CONNASCENCES
CONNASCENCIES
CONNASCENCY
CONNASCENT
CONNATENESS
CONNATENESSES
CONNATIONS
CONNATURAL
CONNATURALISE
CONNATURALISED
CONNATURALISES
CONNATURALISING
CONNATURALITIES
CONNATURALITY
CONNATURALIZE
CONNATURALIZED
CONNATURALIZES
CONNATURALIZING
CONNATURALLY
CONNATURALNESS
CONNATURES
CONNECTABLE
CONNECTEDLY
CONNECTEDNESS
CONNECTEDNESSES
CONNECTERS
CONNECTIBLE
CONNECTING
CONNECTION
CONNECTIONAL
CONNECTIONISM
CONNECTIONISMS
CONNECTIONS
CONNECTIVE
CONNECTIVELY
CONNECTIVES
CONNECTIVITIES
CONNECTIVITY
CONNECTORS
CONNEXIONAL
CONNEXIONS
CONNIPTION
CONNIPTIONS
CONNIVANCE
CONNIVANCES
CONNIVANCIES
CONNIVANCY
CONNIVENCE
CONNIVENCES
CONNIVENCIES
CONNIVENCY
CONNIVENTLY
CONNIVERIES
CONNIVINGLY
CONNOISSEUR
CONNOISSEURS
CONNOISSEURSHIP
CONNOTATED
CONNOTATES
CONNOTATING
CONNOTATION
CONNOTATIONAL
CONNOTATIONS
CONNOTATIVE
CONNOTATIVELY
CONNOTIVELY
CONNUBIALISM
CONNUBIALISMS
CONNUBIALITIES
CONNUBIALITY

CONNUBIALLY
CONNUMERATE
CONNUMERATED
CONNUMERATES
CONNUMERATING
CONNUMERATION
CONNUMERATIONS
CONOIDALLY
CONOIDICAL
CONOMINEES
CONOSCENTE
CONOSCENTI
CONQUERABLE
CONQUERABLENESS
CONQUERERS
CONQUERESS
CONQUERESSES
CONQUERING
CONQUERINGLY
CONQUERORS
CONQUISTADOR
CONQUISTADORES
CONQUISTADORS
CONSANGUINE
CONSANGUINEOUS
CONSANGUINITIES
CONSANGUINITY
CONSCIENCE
CONSCIENCELESS
CONSCIENCES
CONSCIENTIOUS
CONSCIENTIOUSLY
CONSCIENTISE
CONSCIENTISED
CONSCIENTISES
CONSCIENTISING
CONSCIENTIZE
CONSCIENTIZED
CONSCIENTIZES
CONSCIENTIZING
CONSCIONABLE
CONSCIONABLY
CONSCIOUSES
CONSCIOUSLY
CONSCIOUSNESS
CONSCIOUSNESSES
CONSCRIBED
CONSCRIBES
CONSCRIBING
CONSCRIPTED
CONSCRIPTING
CONSCRIPTION
CONSCRIPTIONAL
CONSCRIPTIONIST
CONSCRIPTIONS
CONSCRIPTS
CONSECRATE
CONSECRATED
CONSECRATEDNESS
CONSECRATES
CONSECRATING
CONSECRATION
CONSECRATIONS
CONSECRATIVE
CONSECRATOR
CONSECRATORS
CONSECRATORY
CONSECTANEOUS
CONSECTARIES
CONSECTARY
CONSECUTION
CONSECUTIONS
CONSECUTIVE
CONSECUTIVELY
CONSECUTIVENESS
CONSENESCENCE
CONSENESCENCES
CONSENESCENCIES
CONSENESCENCY
CONSENSION
CONSENSIONS
CONSENSUAL
CONSENSUALLY

CONSENSUSES
CONSENTANEITIES
CONSENTANEITY
CONSENTANEOUS
CONSENTANEOUSLY
CONSENTERS
CONSENTIENCE
CONSENTIENCES
CONSENTIENT
CONSENTING
CONSENTINGLY
CONSEQUENCE
CONSEQUENCED
CONSEQUENCES
CONSEQUENCING
CONSEQUENT
CONSEQUENTIAL
CONSEQUENTIALLY
CONSEQUENTLY
CONSEQUENTS
CONSERVABLE
CONSERVANCIES
CONSERVANCY
CONSERVANT
CONSERVATION
CONSERVATIONAL
CONSERVATIONIST
CONSERVATIONS
CONSERVATISE
CONSERVATISED
CONSERVATISES
CONSERVATISING
CONSERVATISM
CONSERVATISMS
CONSERVATIVE
CONSERVATIVELY
CONSERVATIVES
CONSERVATIZE
CONSERVATIZED
CONSERVATIZES
CONSERVATIZING
CONSERVATOIRE
CONSERVATOIRES
CONSERVATOR
CONSERVATORIA
CONSERVATORIAL
CONSERVATORIES
CONSERVATORIUM
CONSERVATORIUMS
CONSERVATORS
CONSERVATORSHIP
CONSERVATORY
CONSERVATRICES
CONSERVATRIX
CONSERVATRIXES
CONSERVERS
CONSERVING
CONSIDERABLE
CONSIDERABLES
CONSIDERABLY
CONSIDERANCE
CONSIDERANCES
CONSIDERATE
CONSIDERATELY
CONSIDERATENESS
CONSIDERATION
CONSIDERATIONS
CONSIDERATIVE
CONSIDERATIVELY
CONSIDERED
CONSIDERER
CONSIDERERS
CONSIDERING
CONSIDERINGLY
CONSIGLIERE
CONSIGLIERI
CONSIGNABLE
CONSIGNATION
CONSIGNATIONS
CONSIGNATORIES
CONSIGNATORY
CONSIGNEES
CONSIGNERS

CONSIGNIFIED
CONSIGNIFIES
CONSIGNIFY
CONSIGNIFYING
CONSIGNING
CONSIGNMENT
CONSIGNMENTS
CONSIGNORS
CONSILIENCE
CONSILIENCES
CONSILIENT
CONSIMILAR
CONSIMILARITIES
CONSIMILARITY
CONSIMILITIES
CONSIMILITUDE
CONSIMILITUDES
CONSIMILITY
CONSISTENCE
CONSISTENCES
CONSISTENCIES
CONSISTENCY
CONSISTENT
CONSISTENTLY
CONSISTING
CONSISTORIAL
CONSISTORIAN
CONSISTORIES
CONSISTORY
CONSOCIATE
CONSOCIATED
CONSOCIATES
CONSOCIATING
CONSOCIATION
CONSOCIATIONAL
CONSOCIATIONS
CONSOLABLE
CONSOLATED
CONSOLATES
CONSOLATING
CONSOLATION
CONSOLATIONS
CONSOLATORIES
CONSOLATORY
CONSOLATRICES
CONSOLATRIX
CONSOLATRIXES
CONSOLEMENT
CONSOLEMENTS
CONSOLIDATE
CONSOLIDATED
CONSOLIDATES
CONSOLIDATING
CONSOLIDATION
CONSOLIDATIONS
CONSOLIDATIVE
CONSOLIDATOR
CONSOLIDATORS
CONSOLINGLY
CONSONANCE
CONSONANCES
CONSONANCIES
CONSONANCY
CONSONANTAL
CONSONANTALLY
CONSONANTLY
CONSONANTS
CONSORTABLE
CONSORTERS
CONSORTIAL
CONSORTING
CONSORTISM
CONSORTISMS
CONSORTIUM
CONSORTIUMS
CONSPECIFIC
CONSPECIFICS
CONSPECTUITIES
CONSPECTUITY
CONSPECTUS
CONSPECTUSES
CONSPICUITIES
CONSPICUITY

CONSPICUOUS
CONSPICUOUSLY
CONSPICUOUSNESS
CONSPIRACIES
CONSPIRACY
CONSPIRANT
CONSPIRATION
CONSPIRATIONAL
CONSPIRATIONS
CONSPIRATOR
CONSPIRATORIAL
CONSPIRATORS
CONSPIRATORY
CONSPIRATRESS
CONSPIRATRESSES
CONSPIRERS
CONSPIRING
CONSPIRINGLY
CONSPURCATION
CONSPURCATIONS
CONSTABLES
CONSTABLESHIP
CONSTABLESHIPS
CONSTABLEWICK
CONSTABLEWICKS
CONSTABULARIES
CONSTABULARY
CONSTANCIES
CONSTANTAN
CONSTANTANS
CONSTANTLY
CONSTATATION
CONSTATATIONS
CONSTATING
CONSTATIVE
CONSTATIVES
CONSTELLATE
CONSTELLATED
CONSTELLATES
CONSTELLATING
CONSTELLATION
CONSTELLATIONAL
CONSTELLATIONS
CONSTELLATORY
CONSTERING
CONSTERNATE
CONSTERNATED
CONSTERNATES
CONSTERNATING
CONSTERNATION
CONSTERNATIONS
CONSTIPATE
CONSTIPATED
CONSTIPATES
CONSTIPATING
CONSTIPATION
CONSTIPATIONS
CONSTITUENCIES
CONSTITUENCY
CONSTITUENT
CONSTITUENTLY
CONSTITUENTS
CONSTITUTE
CONSTITUTED
CONSTITUTER
CONSTITUTERS
CONSTITUTES
CONSTITUTING
CONSTITUTION
CONSTITUTIONAL
CONSTITUTIONALS
CONSTITUTIONIST
CONSTITUTIONS
CONSTITUTIVE
CONSTITUTIVELY
CONSTITUTOR
CONSTITUTORS
CONSTRAINABLE
CONSTRAINED
CONSTRAINEDLY
CONSTRAINER
CONSTRAINERS
CONSTRAINING

CONSTRAINS
CONSTRAINT
CONSTRAINTS
CONSTRICTED
CONSTRICTING
CONSTRICTION
CONSTRICTIONS
CONSTRICTIVE
CONSTRICTIVELY
CONSTRICTOR
CONSTRICTORS
CONSTRICTS
CONSTRINGE
CONSTRINGED
CONSTRINGENCE
CONSTRINGENCES
CONSTRINGENCIES
CONSTRINGENCY
CONSTRINGENT
CONSTRINGES
CONSTRINGING
CONSTRUABILITY
CONSTRUABLE
CONSTRUALS
CONSTRUCTABLE
CONSTRUCTED
CONSTRUCTER
CONSTRUCTERS
CONSTRUCTIBLE
CONSTRUCTING
CONSTRUCTION
CONSTRUCTIONAL
CONSTRUCTIONISM
CONSTRUCTIONIST
CONSTRUCTIONS
CONSTRUCTIVE
CONSTRUCTIVELY
CONSTRUCTIVISM
CONSTRUCTIVISMS
CONSTRUCTIVIST
CONSTRUCTIVISTS
CONSTRUCTOR
CONSTRUCTORS
CONSTRUCTS
CONSTRUCTURE
CONSTRUCTURES
CONSTRUERS
CONSTRUING
CONSTUPRATE
CONSTUPRATED
CONSTUPRATES
CONSTUPRATING
CONSTUPRATION
CONSTUPRATIONS
CONSUBSIST
CONSUBSISTED
CONSUBSISTING
CONSUBSISTS
CONSUBSTANTIAL
CONSUBSTANTIATE
CONSUETUDE
CONSUETUDES
CONSUETUDINARY
CONSULAGES
CONSULATES
CONSULSHIP
CONSULSHIPS
CONSULTABLE
CONSULTANCIES
CONSULTANCY
CONSULTANT
CONSULTANTS
CONSULTANTSHIP
CONSULTANTSHIPS
CONSULTATION
CONSULTATIONS
CONSULTATIVE
CONSULTATIVELY
CONSULTATORY
CONSULTEES
CONSULTERS
CONSULTING
CONSULTIVE

CONSULTORS
CONSULTORY
CONSUMABLE
CONSUMABLES
CONSUMEDLY
CONSUMERISM
CONSUMERISMS
CONSUMERIST
CONSUMERISTIC
CONSUMERISTS
CONSUMERSHIP
CONSUMERSHIPS
CONSUMINGLY
CONSUMINGS
CONSUMMATE
CONSUMMATED
CONSUMMATELY
CONSUMMATES
CONSUMMATING
CONSUMMATION
CONSUMMATIONS
CONSUMMATIVE
CONSUMMATOR
CONSUMMATORS
CONSUMMATORY
CONSUMPTION
CONSUMPTIONS
CONSUMPTIVE
CONSUMPTIVELY
CONSUMPTIVENESS
CONSUMPTIVES
CONSUMPTIVITIES
CONSUMPTIVITY
CONTABESCENCE
CONTABESCENCES
CONTABESCENT
CONTACTABLE
CONTACTEES
CONTACTING
CONTACTORS
CONTACTUAL
CONTACTUALLY
CONTADINAS
CONTAGIONIST
CONTAGIONISTS
CONTAGIONS
CONTAGIOUS
CONTAGIOUSLY
CONTAGIOUSNESS
CONTAINABLE
CONTAINERBOARD
CONTAINERBOARDS
CONTAINERISE
CONTAINERISED
CONTAINERISES
CONTAINERISING
CONTAINERIZE
CONTAINERIZED
CONTAINERIZES
CONTAINERIZING
CONTAINERLESS
CONTAINERPORT
CONTAINERPORTS
CONTAINERS
CONTAINERSHIP
CONTAINERSHIPS
CONTAINING
CONTAINMENT
CONTAINMENTS
CONTAMINABLE
CONTAMINANT
CONTAMINANTS
CONTAMINATE
CONTAMINATED
CONTAMINATES
CONTAMINATING
CONTAMINATION
CONTAMINATIONS
CONTAMINATIVE
CONTAMINATOR
CONTAMINATORS
CONTANGOED
CONTANGOES

CONTANGOING
CONTEMNERS
CONTEMNIBLE
CONTEMNIBLY
CONTEMNING
CONTEMNORS
CONTEMPERATION
CONTEMPERATIONS
CONTEMPERATURE
CONTEMPERATURES
CONTEMPERED
CONTEMPERING
CONTEMPERS
CONTEMPLABLE
CONTEMPLANT
CONTEMPLANTS
CONTEMPLATE
CONTEMPLATED
CONTEMPLATES
CONTEMPLATING
CONTEMPLATION
CONTEMPLATIONS
CONTEMPLATIST
CONTEMPLATISTS
CONTEMPLATIVE
CONTEMPLATIVELY
CONTEMPLATIVES
CONTEMPLATOR
CONTEMPLATORS
CONTEMPORANEAN
CONTEMPORANEANS
CONTEMPORANEITY
CONTEMPORANEOUS
CONTEMPORARIES
CONTEMPORARILY
CONTEMPORARY
CONTEMPORISE
CONTEMPORISED
CONTEMPORISES
CONTEMPORISING
CONTEMPORIZE
CONTEMPORIZED
CONTEMPORIZES
CONTEMPORIZING
CONTEMPTIBILITY
CONTEMPTIBLE
CONTEMPTIBLY
CONTEMPTUOUS
CONTEMPTUOUSLY
CONTENDENT
CONTENDENTS
CONTENDERS
CONTENDING
CONTENDINGLY
CONTENDINGS
CONTENEMENT
CONTENEMENTS
CONTENTATION
CONTENTATIONS
CONTENTEDLY
CONTENTEDNESS
CONTENTEDNESSES
CONTENTING
CONTENTION
CONTENTIONS
CONTENTIOUS
CONTENTIOUSLY
CONTENTIOUSNESS
CONTENTLESS
CONTENTMENT
CONTENTMENTS
CONTERMINALLY
CONTERMINAL
CONTERMINANT
CONTERMINATE
CONTERMINOUS
CONTERMINOUSLY
CONTESSERATION
CONTESSERATIONS
CONTESTABILITY
CONTESTABLE
CONTESTABLENESS
CONTESTABLY

CONTESTANT
CONTESTANTS
CONTESTATION
CONTESTATIONS
CONTESTERS
CONTESTING
CONTESTINGLY
CONTEXTLESS
CONTEXTUAL
CONTEXTUALISE
CONTEXTUALISED
CONTEXTUALISES
CONTEXTUALISING
CONTEXTUALIZE
CONTEXTUALIZED
CONTEXTUALIZES
CONTEXTUALIZING
CONTEXTUALLY
CONTEXTURAL
CONTEXTURE
CONTEXTURES
CONTIGNATION
CONTIGNATIONS
CONTIGUITIES
CONTIGUITY
CONTIGUOUS
CONTIGUOUSLY
CONTIGUOUSNESS
CONTINENCE
CONTINENCES
CONTINENCIES
CONTINENCY
CONTINENTAL
CONTINENTALISM
CONTINENTALISMS
CONTINENTALIST
CONTINENTALISTS
CONTINENTALLY
CONTINENTALS
CONTINENTLY
CONTINENTS
CONTINGENCE
CONTINGENCES
CONTINGENCIES
CONTINGENCY
CONTINGENT
CONTINGENTLY
CONTINGENTS
CONTINUABLE
CONTINUALITIES
CONTINUALITY
CONTINUALLY
CONTINUALNESS
CONTINUALNESSES
CONTINUANCE
CONTINUANCES
CONTINUANT
CONTINUANTS
CONTINUATE
CONTINUATION
CONTINUATIONS
CONTINUATIVE
CONTINUATIVELY
CONTINUATIVES
CONTINUATOR
CONTINUATORS
CONTINUEDLY
CONTINUEDNESS
CONTINUEDNESSES
CONTINUERS
CONTINUING
CONTINUINGLY
CONTINUITIES
CONTINUITY
CONTINUOUS
CONTINUOUSLY
CONTINUOUSNESS
CONTINUUMS
CONTORNIATE
CONTORNIATES
CONTORTEDLY
CONTORTEDNESS
CONTORTEDNESSES

CONTORTING
CONTORTION
CONTORTIONAL
CONTORTIONATE
CONTORTIONED
CONTORTIONISM
CONTORTIONISMS
CONTORTIONIST
CONTORTIONISTIC
CONTORTIONISTS
CONTORTIONS
CONTORTIVE
CONTOURING
CONTRABAND
CONTRABANDISM
CONTRABANDISMS
CONTRABANDIST
CONTRABANDISTS
CONTRABANDS
CONTRABASS
CONTRABASSES
CONTRABASSI
CONTRABASSIST
CONTRABASSISTS
CONTRABASSO
CONTRABASSOON
CONTRABASSOONS
CONTRABASSOS
CONTRABBASSI
CONTRABBASSO
CONTRABBASSOS
CONTRACEPTION
CONTRACEPTIONS
CONTRACEPTIVE
CONTRACEPTIVES
CONTRACLOCKWISE
CONTRACTABILITY
CONTRACTABLE
CONTRACTED
CONTRACTEDLY
CONTRACTEDNESS
CONTRACTIBILITY
CONTRACTIBLE
CONTRACTIBLY
CONTRACTILE
CONTRACTILITIES
CONTRACTILITY
CONTRACTING
CONTRACTION
CONTRACTIONAL
CONTRACTIONARY
CONTRACTIONS
CONTRACTIVE
CONTRACTIVELY
CONTRACTIVENESS
CONTRACTOR
CONTRACTORS
CONTRACTUAL
CONTRACTUALLY
CONTRACTURAL
CONTRACTURE
CONTRACTURES
CONTRACYCLICAL
CONTRADANCE
CONTRADANCES
CONTRADICT
CONTRADICTABLE
CONTRADICTED
CONTRADICTER
CONTRADICTERS
CONTRADICTING
CONTRADICTION
CONTRADICTIONS
CONTRADICTIOUS
CONTRADICTIVE
CONTRADICTIVELY
CONTRADICTOR
CONTRADICTORIES
CONTRADICTORILY
CONTRADICTORS
CONTRADICTORY
CONTRADICTS
CONTRAFAGOTTO

CONTRAFAGOTTOS
CONTRAFLOW
CONTRAFLOWS
CONTRAGESTION
CONTRAGESTIONS
CONTRAGESTIVE
CONTRAGESTIVES
CONTRAHENT
CONTRAHENTS
CONTRAINDICANT
CONTRAINDICANTS
CONTRAINDICATE
CONTRAINDICATED
CONTRAINDICATES
CONTRALATERAL
CONTRALTOS
CONTRANATANT
CONTRAOCTAVE
CONTRAOCTAVES
CONTRAPLEX
CONTRAPOSITION
CONTRAPOSITIONS
CONTRAPOSITIVE
CONTRAPOSITIVES
CONTRAPPOSTO
CONTRAPPOSTOS
CONTRAPROP
CONTRAPROPELLER
CONTRAPROPS
CONTRAPTION
CONTRAPTIONS
CONTRAPUNTAL
CONTRAPUNTALIST
CONTRAPUNTALLY
CONTRAPUNTIST
CONTRAPUNTISTS
CONTRARIAN
CONTRARIANS
CONTRARIED
CONTRARIES
CONTRARIETIES
CONTRARIETY
CONTRARILY
CONTRARINESS
CONTRARINESSES
CONTRARIOUS
CONTRARIOUSLY
CONTRARIOUSNESS
CONTRARIWISE
CONTRARYING
CONTRASEXUAL
CONTRASEXUALS
CONTRASTABLE
CONTRASTABLY
CONTRASTED
CONTRASTING
CONTRASTIVE
CONTRASTIVELY
CONTRATERRENE
CONTRAVALLATION
CONTRAVENE
CONTRAVENED
CONTRAVENER
CONTRAVENERS
CONTRAVENES
CONTRAVENING
CONTRAVENTION
CONTRAVENTIONS
CONTRAYERVA
CONTRAYERVAS
CONTRECOUP
CONTRECOUPS
CONTREDANCE
CONTREDANCES
CONTREDANSE
CONTREDANSES
CONTRETEMPS
CONTRIBUTABLE
CONTRIBUTARIES
CONTRIBUTARY
CONTRIBUTE
CONTRIBUTED
CONTRIBUTES

CONTRIBUTING
CONTRIBUTION
CONTRIBUTIONS
CONTRIBUTIVE
CONTRIBUTIVELY
CONTRIBUTOR
CONTRIBUTORIES
CONTRIBUTORS
CONTRIBUTORY
CONTRISTATION
CONTRISTATIONS
CONTRISTED
CONTRISTING
CONTRITELY
CONTRITENESS
CONTRITENESSES
CONTRITION
CONTRITIONS
CONTRITURATE
CONTRITURATED
CONTRITURATES
CONTRITURATING
CONTRIVABLE
CONTRIVANCE
CONTRIVANCES
CONTRIVEMENT
CONTRIVEMENTS
CONTRIVERS
CONTRIVING
CONTROLLABILITY
CONTROLLABLE
CONTROLLABLY
CONTROLLED
CONTROLLER
CONTROLLERS
CONTROLLERSHIP
CONTROLLERSHIPS
CONTROLLING
CONTROLMENT
CONTROLMENTS
CONTROULED
CONTROULING
CONTROVERSE
CONTROVERSES
CONTROVERSIAL
CONTROVERSIALLY
CONTROVERSIES
CONTROVERSY
CONTROVERT
CONTROVERTED
CONTROVERTER
CONTROVERTERS
CONTROVERTIBLE
CONTROVERTIBLY
CONTROVERTING
CONTROVERTIST
CONTROVERTISTS
CONTROVERTS
CONTUBERNAL
CONTUBERNYAL
CONTUMACIES
CONTUMACIOUS
CONTUMACIOUSLY
CONTUMACITIES
CONTUMACITY
CONTUMELIES
CONTUMELIOUS
CONTUMELIOUSLY
CONTUNDING
CONTUSIONED
CONTUSIONS
CONUNDRUMS
CONURBATION
CONURBATIONS
CONVALESCE
CONVALESCED
CONVALESCENCE
CONVALESCENCES
CONVALESCENCIES
CONVALESCENCY
CONVALESCENT
CONVALESCENTLY
CONVALESCENTS

CONVALESCES
CONVALESCING
CONVECTING
CONVECTION
CONVECTIONAL
CONVECTIONS
CONVECTIVE
CONVECTORS
CONVENABLE
CONVENANCE
CONVENANCES
CONVENERSHIP
CONVENERSHIPS
CONVENIENCE
CONVENIENCES
CONVENIENCIES
CONVENIENCY
CONVENIENT
CONVENIENTLY
CONVENORSHIP
CONVENORSHIPS
CONVENTICLE
CONVENTICLED
CONVENTICLER
CONVENTICLERS
CONVENTICLES
CONVENTICLING
CONVENTING
CONVENTION
CONVENTIONAL
CONVENTIONALISE
CONVENTIONALISM
CONVENTIONALIST
CONVENTIONALITY
CONVENTIONALIZE
CONVENTIONALLY
CONVENTIONALS
CONVENTIONARY
CONVENTIONEER
CONVENTIONEERS
CONVENTIONER
CONVENTIONERS
CONVENTIONIST
CONVENTIONISTS
CONVENTIONS
CONVENTUAL
CONVENTUALLY
CONVENTUALS
CONVERGENCE
CONVERGENCES
CONVERGENCIES
CONVERGENCY
CONVERGENT
CONVERGING
CONVERSABLE
CONVERSABLENESS
CONVERSABLY
CONVERSANCE
CONVERSANCES
CONVERSANCIES
CONVERSANCY
CONVERSANT
CONVERSANTLY
CONVERSATION
CONVERSATIONAL
CONVERSATIONISM
CONVERSATIONIST
CONVERSATIONS
CONVERSATIVE
CONVERSAZIONE
CONVERSAZIONES
CONVERSAZIONI
CONVERSELY
CONVERSERS
CONVERSING
CONVERSION
CONVERSIONAL
CONVERSIONARY
CONVERSIONS
CONVERTAPLANE
CONVERTAPLANES
CONVERTEND
CONVERTENDS

CONVERTERS
CONVERTIBILITY
CONVERTIBLE
CONVERTIBLENESS
CONVERTIBLES
CONVERTIBLY
CONVERTING
CONVERTIPLANE
CONVERTIPLANES
CONVERTITE
CONVERTITES
CONVERTIVE
CONVERTOPLANE
CONVERTOPLANES
CONVERTORS
CONVEXEDLY
CONVEXITIES
CONVEXNESS
CONVEXNESSES
CONVEYABLE
CONVEYANCE
CONVEYANCER
CONVEYANCERS
CONVEYANCES
CONVEYANCING
CONVEYANCINGS
CONVEYORISATION
CONVEYORISE
CONVEYORISED
CONVEYORISES
CONVEYORISING
CONVEYORIZATION
CONVEYORIZE
CONVEYORIZED
CONVEYORIZES
CONVEYORIZING
CONVICINITIES
CONVICINITY
CONVICTABLE
CONVICTIBLE
CONVICTING
CONVICTION
CONVICTIONAL
CONVICTIONS
CONVICTISM
CONVICTISMS
CONVICTIVE
CONVICTIVELY
CONVINCEMENT
CONVINCEMENTS
CONVINCERS
CONVINCIBLE
CONVINCING
CONVINCINGLY
CONVINCINGNESS
CONVIVIALIST
CONVIVIALISTS
CONVIVIALITIES
CONVIVIALITY
CONVIVIALLY
CONVOCATED
CONVOCATES
CONVOCATING
CONVOCATION
CONVOCATIONAL
CONVOCATIONIST
CONVOCATIONISTS
CONVOCATIONS
CONVOCATIVE
CONVOCATOR
CONVOCATORS
CONVOLUTED
CONVOLUTEDLY
CONVOLUTEDNESS
CONVOLUTELY
CONVOLUTES
CONVOLUTING
CONVOLUTION
CONVOLUTIONAL
CONVOLUTIONARY
CONVOLUTIONS
CONVOLVING
CONVOLVULACEOUS

CONVOLVULI
CONVOLVULUS
CONVOLVULUSES
CONVULSANT
CONVULSANTS
CONVULSIBLE
CONVULSING
CONVULSION
CONVULSIONAL
CONVULSIONARIES
CONVULSIONARY
CONVULSIONIST
CONVULSIONISTS
CONVULSIONS
CONVULSIVE
CONVULSIVELY
CONVULSIVENESS
COOKHOUSES
COOKSHACKS
COOKSTOVES
COOLHEADED
COOLHOUSES
COOLINGNESS
COOLINGNESSES
COOLNESSES
COOMCEILED
COONHOUNDS
COOPERAGES
COOPERATED
COOPERATES
COOPERATING
COOPERATION
COOPERATIONIST
COOPERATIONISTS
COOPERATIONS
COOPERATIVE
COOPERATIVELY
COOPERATIVENESS
COOPERATIVES
COOPERATIVITIES
COOPERATIVITY
COOPERATOR
COOPERATORS
COOPERINGS
COOPTATION
COOPTATIONS
COOPTATIVE
COORDINANCE
COORDINANCES
COORDINATE
COORDINATED
COORDINATELY
COORDINATENESS
COORDINATES
COORDINATING
COORDINATION
COORDINATIONS
COORDINATIVE
COORDINATOR
COORDINATORS
COPARCENARIES
COPARCENARY
COPARCENER
COPARCENERIES
COPARCENERS
COPARCENERY
COPARCENIES
COPARENTED
COPARENTING
COPARTNERED
COPARTNERIES
COPARTNERING
COPARTNERS
COPARTNERSHIP
COPARTNERSHIPS
COPARTNERY
COPATRIOTS
COPAYMENTS
COPESETTIC
COPESTONES
COPINGSTONE
COPINGSTONES
COPIOUSNESS

COPIOUSNESSES
COPLANARITIES
COPLANARITY
COPLOTTING
COPOLYMERIC
COPOLYMERISE
COPOLYMERISED
COPOLYMERISES
COPOLYMERISING
COPOLYMERIZE
COPOLYMERIZED
COPOLYMERIZES
COPOLYMERIZING
COPOLYMERS
COPPERASES
COPPERHEAD
COPPERHEADS
COPPERINGS
COPPERPLATE
COPPERPLATES
COPPERSKIN
COPPERSKINS
COPPERSMITH
COPPERSMITHS
COPPERWORK
COPPERWORKS
COPPERWORM
COPPERWORMS
COPPICINGS
COPRESENCE
COPRESENCES
COPRESENTED
COPRESENTING
COPRESENTS
COPRESIDENT
COPRESIDENTS
COPRINCIPAL
COPRINCIPALS
COPRISONER
COPRISONERS
COPROCESSING
COPROCESSOR
COPROCESSORS
COPRODUCED
COPRODUCER
COPRODUCERS
COPRODUCES
COPRODUCING
COPRODUCTION
COPRODUCTIONS
COPRODUCTS
COPROLALIA
COPROLALIAC
COPROLALIAS
COPROLITES
COPROLITHS
COPROLITIC
COPROLOGIES
COPROMOTER
COPROMOTERS
COPROPHAGAN
COPROPHAGANS
COPROPHAGIC
COPROPHAGIES
COPROPHAGIST
COPROPHAGISTS
COPROPHAGOUS
COPROPHAGY
COPROPHILIA
COPROPHILIAC
COPROPHILIACS
COPROPHILIAS
COPROPHILIC
COPROPHILOUS
COPROPRIETOR
COPROPRIETORS
COPROSPERITIES
COPROSPERITY
COPROSTEROL
COPROSTEROLS
COPSEWOODS
COPUBLISHED
COPUBLISHER

COPUBLISHERS
COPUBLISHES
COPUBLISHING
COPULATING
COPULATION
COPULATIONS
COPULATIVE
COPULATIVELY
COPULATIVES
COPULATORY
COPURIFIED
COPURIFIES
COPURIFYING
COPYCATTED
COPYCATTING
COPYEDITED
COPYEDITING
COPYGRAPHS
COPYHOLDER
COPYHOLDERS
COPYREADER
COPYREADERS
COPYREADING
COPYREADINGS
COPYRIGHTABLE
COPYRIGHTED
COPYRIGHTER
COPYRIGHTERS
COPYRIGHTING
COPYRIGHTS
COPYTAKERS
COPYWRITER
COPYWRITERS
COPYWRITING
COPYWRITINGS
COQUELICOT
COQUELICOTS
COQUETRIES
COQUETTING
COQUETTISH
COQUETTISHLY
COQUETTISHNESS
COQUIMBITE
COQUIMBITES
CORACIIFORM
CORADICATE
CORALBELLS
CORALBERRIES
CORALBERRY
CORALLACEOUS
CORALLIFEROUS
CORALLIFORM
CORALLIGENOUS
CORALLINES
CORALLITES
CORALLOIDAL
CORALROOTS
CORALWORTS
CORBEILLES
CORBELINGS
CORBELLING
CORBELLINGS
CORBICULAE
CORBICULATE
CORDECTOMIES
CORDECTOMY
CORDELLING
CORDGRASSES
CORDIALISE
CORDIALISED
CORDIALISES
CORDIALISING
CORDIALITIES
CORDIALITY
CORDIALIZE
CORDIALIZED
CORDIALIZES
CORDIALIZING
CORDIALNESS
CORDIALNESSES
CORDIERITE
CORDIERITES
CORDILLERA

CORDILLERAN
CORDILLERAS
CORDLESSES
CORDOCENTESES
CORDOCENTESIS
CORDONNETS
CORDOTOMIES
CORDUROYED
CORDUROYING
CORDWAINER
CORDWAINERIES
CORDWAINERS
CORDWAINERY
CORDYLINES
CORECIPIENT
CORECIPIENTS
COREDEEMED
COREDEEMING
COREFERENTIAL
COREGONINE
CORELATING
CORELATION
CORELATIONS
CORELATIVE
CORELATIVES
CORELIGIONIST
CORELIGIONISTS
COREOPSISES
COREPRESSOR
COREPRESSORS
COREQUISITE
COREQUISITES
CORESEARCHER
CORESEARCHERS
CORESIDENT
CORESIDENTIAL
CORESIDENTS
CORESPONDENT
CORESPONDENTS
CORFHOUSES
CORIACEOUS
CORIANDERS
CORINTHIANISE
CORINTHIANISED
CORINTHIANISES
CORINTHIANISING
CORINTHIANIZE
CORINTHIANIZED
CORINTHIANIZES
CORINTHIANIZING
CORIVALLED
CORIVALLING
CORIVALRIES
CORIVALSHIP
CORIVALSHIPS
CORKBOARDS
CORKBORERS
CORKINESSES
CORKSCREWED
CORKSCREWING
CORKSCREWS
CORMOPHYTE
CORMOPHYTES
CORMOPHYTIC
CORMORANTS
CORNACEOUS
CORNBORERS
CORNBRAIDED
CORNBRAIDING
CORNBRAIDS
CORNBRANDIES
CORNBRANDY
CORNBRASHES
CORNBREADS
CORNCOCKLE
CORNCOCKLES
CORNCRAKES
CORNEITISES
CORNELIANS
CORNEMUSES
CORNERBACK
CORNERBACKS
CORNERSTONE

CORNERSTONES
CORNERWAYS
CORNERWISE
CORNETCIES
CORNETISTS
CORNETTINO
CORNETTINOS
CORNETTIST
CORNETTISTS
CORNFIELDS
CORNFLAKES
CORNFLOURS
CORNFLOWER
CORNFLOWERS
CORNHUSKER
CORNHUSKERS
CORNHUSKING
CORNHUSKINGS
CORNICHONS
CORNICULATE
CORNICULUM
CORNICULUMS
CORNIFEROUS
CORNIFICATION
CORNIFICATIONS
CORNIFYING
CORNIGEROUS
CORNINESSES
CORNOPEANS
CORNROWING
CORNSTALKS
CORNSTARCH
CORNSTARCHES
CORNSTONES
CORNUCOPIA
CORNUCOPIAN
CORNUCOPIAS
COROLLACEOUS
COROLLARIES
COROLLIFLORAL
COROLLIFLOROUS
COROLLIFORM
COROMANDEL
COROMANDELS
CORONAGRAPH
CORONAGRAPHS
CORONARIES
CORONATING
CORONATION
CORONATIONS
CORONAVIRUS
CORONAVIRUSES
CORONERSHIP
CORONERSHIPS
CORONOGRAPH
CORONOGRAPHS
COROTATING
COROTATION
COROTATIONS
CORPORALES
CORPORALITIES
CORPORALITY
CORPORALLY
CORPORALSHIP
CORPORALSHIPS
CORPORASES
CORPORATELY
CORPORATENESS
CORPORATENESSES
CORPORATES
CORPORATION
CORPORATIONS
CORPORATISE
CORPORATISED
CORPORATISES
CORPORATISING
CORPORATISM
CORPORATISMS
CORPORATIST
CORPORATISTS
CORPORATIVE
CORPORATIVISM
CORPORATIVISMS

CORPORATIZE
CORPORATIZED
CORPORATIZES
CORPORATIZING
CORPORATOR
CORPORATORS
CORPOREALISE
CORPOREALISED
CORPOREALISES
CORPOREALISING
CORPOREALISM
CORPOREALISMS
CORPOREALIST
CORPOREALISTS
CORPOREALITIES
CORPOREALITY
CORPOREALIZE
CORPOREALIZED
CORPOREALIZES
CORPOREALIZING
CORPOREALLY
CORPOREALNESS
CORPOREALNESSES
CORPOREITIES
CORPOREITY
CORPORIFICATION
CORPORIFIED
CORPORIFIES
CORPORIFYING
CORPOSANTS
CORPULENCE
CORPULENCES
CORPULENCIES
CORPULENCY
CORPULENTLY
CORPUSCLES
CORPUSCULAR
CORPUSCULARIAN
CORPUSCULARIANS
CORPUSCULARITY
CORPUSCULE
CORPUSCULES
CORRALLING
CORRASIONS
CORRECTABLE
CORRECTEST
CORRECTIBLE
CORRECTING
CORRECTION
CORRECTIONAL
CORRECTIONER
CORRECTIONERS
CORRECTIONS
CORRECTITUDE
CORRECTITUDES
CORRECTIVE
CORRECTIVELY
CORRECTIVES
CORRECTNESS
CORRECTNESSES
CORRECTORS
CORRECTORY
CORREGIDOR
CORREGIDORS
CORRELATABLE
CORRELATED
CORRELATES
CORRELATING
CORRELATION
CORRELATIONAL
CORRELATIONS
CORRELATIVE
CORRELATIVELY
CORRELATIVENESS
CORRELATIVES
CORRELATIVITIES
CORRELATIVITY
CORRELATOR
CORRELATORS
CORRELIGIONIST
CORRELIGIONISTS
CORREPTION
CORREPTIONS

CORRESPOND
CORRESPONDED
CORRESPONDENCE
CORRESPONDENCES
CORRESPONDENCY
CORRESPONDENT
CORRESPONDENTLY
CORRESPONDENTS
CORRESPONDING
CORRESPONDINGLY
CORRESPONDS
CORRESPONSIVE
CORRIGENDA
CORRIGENDUM
CORRIGENTS
CORRIGIBILITIES
CORRIGIBILITY
CORRIGIBLE
CORRIGIBLY
CORRIVALLED
CORRIVALLING
CORRIVALRIES
CORRIVALRY
CORRIVALSHIP
CORRIVALSHIPS
CORROBORABLE
CORROBORANT
CORROBORATE
CORROBORATED
CORROBORATES
CORROBORATING
CORROBORATION
CORROBORATIONS
CORROBORATIVE
CORROBORATIVELY
CORROBORATIVES
CORROBORATOR
CORROBORATORS
CORROBORATORY
CORROBOREE
CORROBOREED
CORROBOREEING
CORROBOREES
CORRODANTS
CORRODENTS
CORRODIBILITIES
CORRODIBILITY
CORRODIBLE
CORROSIBILITIES
CORROSIBILITY
CORROSIBLE
CORROSIONS
CORROSIVELY
CORROSIVENESS
CORROSIVENESSES
CORROSIVES
CORRUGATED
CORRUGATES
CORRUGATING
CORRUGATION
CORRUGATIONS
CORRUGATOR
CORRUGATORS
CORRUPTERS
CORRUPTEST
CORRUPTIBILITY
CORRUPTIBLE
CORRUPTIBLENESS
CORRUPTIBLY
CORRUPTING
CORRUPTION
CORRUPTIONIST
CORRUPTIONISTS
CORRUPTIONS
CORRUPTIVE
CORRUPTIVELY
CORRUPTNESS
CORRUPTNESSES
CORRUPTORS
CORSELETTE
CORSELETTES
CORSETIERE
CORSETIERES

C

CORSETIERS	COSMODROMES	COTERMINOUSLY	COUNSELLORSHIPS	COUNTERCLAIMANT	COUNTERMOTION
CORSETRIES	COSMOGENIC	COTILLIONS	COUNSELORS	COUNTERCLAIMED	COUNTERMOTIONS
CORTICALLY	COSMOGENIES	COTONEASTER	COUNSELORSHIP	COUNTERCLAIMING	COUNTERMOVE
CORTICATED	COSMOGONAL	COTONEASTERS	COUNSELORSHIPS	COUNTERCLAIMS	COUNTERMOVED
CORTICATION	COSMOGONIC	COTRANSDUCE	COUNTABILITIES	COUNTERCOUP	COUNTERMOVEMENT
CORTICATIONS	COSMOGONICAL	COTRANSDUCED	COUNTABILITY	COUNTERCOUPS	COUNTERMOVES
CORTICOIDS	COSMOGONIES	COTRANSDUCES	COUNTBACKS	COUNTERCRIES	COUNTERMOVING
CORTICOLOUS	COSMOGONIST	COTRANSDUCING	COUNTDOWNS	COUNTERCRY	COUNTERMURE
CORTICOSTEROID	COSMOGONISTS	COTRANSDUCTION	COUNTENANCE	COUNTERCULTURAL	COUNTERMURED
CORTICOSTEROIDS	COSMOGRAPHER	COTRANSDUCTIONS	COUNTENANCED	COUNTERCULTURE	COUNTERMURES
CORTICOSTERONE	COSMOGRAPHERS	COTRANSFER	COUNTENANCER	COUNTERCULTURES	COUNTERMURING
CORTICOSTERONES	COSMOGRAPHIC	COTRANSFERS	COUNTENANCERS	COUNTERCURRENT	COUNTERMYTH
CORTICOTROPHIC	COSMOGRAPHICAL	COTRANSPORT	COUNTENANCES	COUNTERCURRENTS	COUNTERMYTHS
CORTICOTROPHIN	COSMOGRAPHIES	COTRANSPORTED	COUNTENANCING	COUNTERCYCLICAL	COUNTEROFFER
CORTICOTROPHINS	COSMOGRAPHIST	COTRANSPORTING	COUNTERACT	COUNTERDEMAND	COUNTEROFFERS
CORTICOTROPIC	COSMOGRAPHISTS	COTRANSPORTS	COUNTERACTED	COUNTERDEMANDS	COUNTERORDER
CORTICOTROPIN	COSMOGRAPHY	COTRUSTEES	COUNTERACTING	COUNTERDRAW	COUNTERORDERED
CORTICOTROPINS	COSMOLATRIES	COTTABUSES	COUNTERACTION	COUNTERDRAWING	COUNTERORDERING
CORTISONES	COSMOLATRY	COTTAGINGS	COUNTERACTIONS	COUNTERDRAWN	COUNTERORDERS
CORUSCATED	COSMOLINED	COTTERLESS	COUNTERACTIVE	COUNTERDRAWS	COUNTERPACE
CORUSCATES	COSMOLINES	COTTIERISM	COUNTERACTIVELY	COUNTERDREW	COUNTERPACES
CORUSCATING	COSMOLINING	COTTIERISMS	COUNTERACTS	COUNTEREFFORT	COUNTERPANE
CORUSCATION	COSMOLOGIC	COTTONADES	COUNTERAGENT	COUNTEREFFORTS	COUNTERPANES
CORUSCATIONS	COSMOLOGICAL	COTTONMOUTH	COUNTERAGENTS	COUNTEREVIDENCE	COUNTERPART
CORVETTING	COSMOLOGICALLY	COTTONMOUTHS	COUNTERARGUE	COUNTEREXAMPLE	COUNTERPARTIES
CORYBANTES	COSMOLOGIES	COTTONOCRACIES	COUNTERARGUED	COUNTEREXAMPLES	COUNTERPARTS
CORYBANTIC	COSMOLOGIST	COTTONOCRACY	COUNTERARGUES	COUNTERFACTUAL	COUNTERPARTY
CORYBANTISM	COSMOLOGISTS	COTTONSEED	COUNTERARGUING	COUNTERFACTUALS	COUNTERPEISE
CORYBANTISMS	COSMONAUTICS	COTTONSEEDS	COUNTERARGUMENT	COUNTERFECT	COUNTERPEISED
CORYDALINE	COSMONAUTS	COTTONTAIL	COUNTERASSAULT	COUNTERFEISANCE	COUNTERPEISES
CORYDALINES	COSMOPLASTIC	COTTONTAILS	COUNTERASSAULTS	COUNTERFEIT	COUNTERPEISING
CORYDALISES	COSMOPOLIS	COTTONWEED	COUNTERATTACK	COUNTERFEITED	COUNTERPETITION
CORYLOPSES	COSMOPOLISES	COTTONWEEDS	COUNTERATTACKED	COUNTERFEITER	COUNTERPICKET
CORYLOPSIS	COSMOPOLITAN	COTTONWOOD	COUNTERATTACKER	COUNTERFEITERS	COUNTERPICKETED
CORYMBOSELY	COSMOPOLITANISM	COTTONWOODS	COUNTERATTACKS	COUNTERFEITING	COUNTERPICKETS
CORYNEBACTERIA	COSMOPOLITANS	COTURNIXES	COUNTERBALANCE	COUNTERFEITLY	COUNTERPLAN
CORYNEBACTERIAL	COSMOPOLITE	COTYLEDONAL	COUNTERBALANCED	COUNTERFEITS	COUNTERPLANS
CORYNEBACTERIUM	COSMOPOLITES	COTYLEDONARY	COUNTERBALANCES	COUNTERFESAUNCE	COUNTERPLAY
CORYNEFORM	COSMOPOLITIC	COTYLEDONOID	COUNTERBASE	COUNTERFIRE	COUNTERPLAYER
CORYPHAEUS	COSMOPOLITICAL	COTYLEDONOUS	COUNTERBASES	COUNTERFIRES	COUNTERPLAYERS
CORYPHENES	COSMOPOLITICS	COTYLEDONS	COUNTERBID	COUNTERFLOW	COUNTERPLAYS
COSCINOMANCIES	COSMOPOLITISM	COTYLIFORM	COUNTERBIDDER	COUNTERFLOWS	COUNTERPLEA
COSCINOMANCY	COSMOPOLITISMS	COTYLOIDAL	COUNTERBIDDERS	COUNTERFOIL	COUNTERPLEAD
COSCRIPTED	COSMORAMAS	COTYLOIDALS	COUNTERBIDS	COUNTERFOILS	COUNTERPLEADED
COSCRIPTING	COSMORAMIC	COTYLOSAUR	COUNTERBLAST	COUNTERFORCE	COUNTERPLEADING
COSEISMALS	COSMOSPHERE	COTYLOSAURS	COUNTERBLASTS	COUNTERFORCES	COUNTERPLEADS
COSEISMICS	COSMOSPHERES	COUCHETTES	COUNTERBLOCKADE	COUNTERFORT	COUNTERPLEAS
COSENTIENT	COSMOTHEISM	COULIBIACA	COUNTERBLOW	COUNTERFORTS	COUNTERPLED
COSHERINGS	COSMOTHEISMS	COULIBIACAS	COUNTERBLOWS	COUNTERGLOW	COUNTERPLOT
COSIGNATORIES	COSMOTHETIC	COULIBIACS	COUNTERBLUFF	COUNTERGLOWS	COUNTERPLOTS
COSIGNATORY	COSMOTHETICAL	COULOMBMETER	COUNTERBLUFFS	COUNTERGUERILLA	COUNTERPLOTTED
COSIGNIFICATIVE	COSMOTRONS	COULOMBMETERS	COUNTERBOND	COUNTERIMAGE	COUNTERPLOTTING
COSINESSES	COSPONSORED	COULOMETER	COUNTERBONDS	COUNTERIMAGES	COUNTERPLOY
COSMECEUTICAL	COSPONSORING	COULOMETERS	COUNTERBORE	COUNTERING	COUNTERPLOYS
COSMECEUTICALS	COSPONSORS	COULOMETRIC	COUNTERBORED	COUNTERINSTANCE	COUNTERPOINT
COSMETICAL	COSPONSORSHIP	COULOMETRICALLY	COUNTERBORES	COUNTERION	COUNTERPOINTED
COSMETICALLY	COSPONSORSHIPS	COULOMETRIES	COUNTERBORING	COUNTERIONS	COUNTERPOINTING
COSMETICIAN	COSTALGIAS	COULOMETRY	COUNTERBRACE	COUNTERIRRITANT	COUNTERPOINTS
COSMETICIANS	COSTARDMONGER	COUMARILIC	COUNTERBRACED	COUNTERLIGHT	COUNTERPOISE
COSMETICISE	COSTARDMONGERS	COUMARONES	COUNTERBRACES	COUNTERLIGHTS	COUNTERPOISED
COSMETICISED	COSTARRING	COUNCILLOR	COUNTERBRACING	COUNTERMAN	COUNTERPOISES
COSMETICISES	COSTEANING	COUNCILLORS	COUNTERBUFF	COUNTERMAND	COUNTERPOISING
COSMETICISING	COSTEANINGS	COUNCILLORSHIP	COUNTERBUFFED	COUNTERMANDABLE	COUNTERPOSE
COSMETICISM	COSTERMONGER	COUNCILLORSHIPS	COUNTERBUFFING	COUNTERMANDED	COUNTERPOSED
COSMETICISMS	COSTERMONGERS	COUNCILMAN	COUNTERBUFFS	COUNTERMANDING	COUNTERPOSES
COSMETICIZE	COSTIVENESS	COUNCILMANIC	COUNTERCAMPAIGN	COUNTERMANDS	COUNTERPOSING
COSMETICIZED	COSTIVENESSES	COUNCILMEN	COUNTERCHANGE	COUNTERMARCH	COUNTERPOWER
COSMETICIZES	COSTLESSLY	COUNCILORS	COUNTERCHANGED	COUNTERMARCHED	COUNTERPOWERS
COSMETICIZING	COSTLINESS	COUNCILORSHIP	COUNTERCHANGES	COUNTERMARCHES	COUNTERPRESSURE
COSMETICOLOGIES	COSTLINESSES	COUNCILORSHIPS	COUNTERCHANGING	COUNTERMARCHING	COUNTERPROJECT
COSMETICOLOGY	COSTMARIES	COUNCILWOMAN	COUNTERCHARGE	COUNTERMARK	COUNTERPROJECTS
COSMETOLOGIES	COSTOTOMIES	COUNCILWOMEN	COUNTERCHARGED	COUNTERMARKS	COUNTERPROOF
COSMETOLOGIST	COSTUMERIES	COUNSELABLE	COUNTERCHARGES	COUNTERMEASURE	COUNTERPROOFS
COSMETOLOGISTS	COSTUMIERS	COUNSELEES	COUNTERCHARGING	COUNTERMEASURES	COUNTERPROPOSAL
COSMETOLOGY	COSURFACTANT	COUNSELING	COUNTERCHARM	COUNTERMELODIES	COUNTERPROTEST
COSMICALLY	COSURFACTANTS	COUNSELINGS	COUNTERCHARMED	COUNTERMELODY	COUNTERPROTESTS
COSMOCHEMICAL	COTANGENTIAL	COUNSELLABLE	COUNTERCHARMING	COUNTERMEMO	COUNTERPUNCH
COSMOCHEMIST	COTANGENTS	COUNSELLED	COUNTERCHARMS	COUNTERMEMOS	COUNTERPUNCHED
COSMOCHEMISTRY	COTELETTES	COUNSELLING	COUNTERCHECK	COUNTERMEN	COUNTERPUNCHER
COSMOCHEMISTS	COTEMPORANEOUS	COUNSELLINGS	COUNTERCHECKED	COUNTERMINE	COUNTERPUNCHERS
COSMOCRATIC	COTEMPORARY	COUNSELLOR	COUNTERCHECKING	COUNTERMINED	COUNTERPUNCHES
COSMOCRATS	COTENANCIES	COUNSELLORS	COUNTERCHECKS	COUNTERMINES	COUNTERPUNCHING
COSMODROME	COTERMINOUS	COUNSELLORSHIP	COUNTERCLAIM	COUNTERMINING	COUNTERQUESTION

COUNTERRAID	COUNTERTRADE	COURTHOUSES	COXCOMBICALLY	CRANIOLOGY	CREAMERIES
COUNTERRAIDS	COUNTERTRADED	COURTIERISM	COXCOMBRIES	CRANIOMETER	CREAMINESS
COUNTERRALLIED	COUNTERTRADES	COURTIERISMS	COXCOMICAL	CRANIOMETERS	CREAMINESSES
COUNTERRALLIES	COUNTERTRADING	COURTIERLIKE	COXINESSES	CRANIOMETRIC	CREAMPUFFS
COUNTERRALLY	COUNTERTREND	COURTIERLY	COXSWAINED	CRANIOMETRICAL	CREAMWARES
COUNTERRALLYING	COUNTERTRENDS	COURTLIEST	COXSWAINING	CRANIOMETRIES	CREASELESS
COUNTERREACTION	COUNTERTYPE	COURTLINESS	COYISHNESS	CRANIOMETRIST	CREASOTING
COUNTERREFORM	COUNTERTYPES	COURTLINESSES	COYISHNESSES	CRANIOMETRISTS	CREATIANISM
COUNTERREFORMER	COUNTERVAIL	COURTLINGS	COYOTILLOS	CRANIOMETRY	CREATIANISMS
COUNTERREFORMS	COUNTERVAILABLE	COURTMARTIALLED	COZINESSES	CRANIOPAGI	CREATININE
COUNTERRESPONSE	COUNTERVAILED	COURTROOMS	CRABAPPLES	CRANIOPAGUS	CREATININES
COUNTERSANK	COUNTERVAILING	COURTSHIPS	CRABBEDNESS	CRANIOSACRAL	CREATIONAL
COUNTERSCARP	COUNTERVAILS	COURTSIDES	CRABBEDNESSES	CRANIOSCOPIES	CREATIONISM
COUNTERSCARPS	COUNTERVIEW	COURTYARDS	CRABBINESS	CRANIOSCOPIST	CREATIONISMS
COUNTERSEAL	COUNTERVIEWS	COUSCOUSES	CRABBINESSES	CRANIOSCOPISTS	CREATIONIST
COUNTERSEALED	COUNTERVIOLENCE	COUSCOUSOU	CRABEATERS	CRANIOSCOPY	CREATIONISTIC
COUNTERSEALING	COUNTERWEIGH	COUSCOUSOUS	CRABGRASSES	CRANIOTOMIES	CREATIONISTS
COUNTERSEALS	COUNTERWEIGHED	COUSINAGES	CRABSTICKS	CRANIOTOMY	CREATIVELY
COUNTERSHADING	COUNTERWEIGHING	COUSINHOOD	CRACKAJACK	CRANKCASES	CREATIVENESS
COUNTERSHADINGS	COUNTERWEIGHS	COUSINHOODS	CRACKAJACKS	CRANKHANDLE	CREATIVENESSES
COUNTERSHAFT	COUNTERWEIGHT	COUSINRIES	CRACKBACKS	CRANKHANDLES	CREATIVITIES
COUNTERSHAFTS	COUNTERWEIGHTED	COUSINSHIP	CRACKBERRIES	CRANKINESS	CREATIVITY
COUNTERSHOT	COUNTERWEIGHTS	COUSINSHIPS	CRACKBERRY	CRANKINESSES	CREATORSHIP
COUNTERSHOTS	COUNTERWORD	COUTURIERE	CRACKBRAIN	CRANKNESSES	CREATORSHIPS
COUNTERSIGN	COUNTERWORDS	COUTURIERES	CRACKBRAINED	CRANKSHAFT	CREATRESSES
COUNTERSIGNED	COUNTERWORK	COUTURIERS	CRACKBRAINS	CRANKSHAFTS	CREATRIXES
COUNTERSIGNING	COUNTERWORKED	COVALENCES	CRACKDOWNS	CRANREUCHS	CREATUREHOOD
COUNTERSIGNS	COUNTERWORKER	COVALENCIES	CRACKERJACK	CRAPEHANGER	CREATUREHOODS
COUNTERSINK	COUNTERWORKERS	COVALENTLY	CRACKERJACKS	CRAPEHANGERS	CREATURELINESS
COUNTERSINKING	COUNTERWORKING	COVARIANCE	CRACKHEADS	CRAPEHANGING	CREATURELY
COUNTERSINKS	COUNTERWORKS	COVARIANCES	CRACKLEWARE	CRAPEHANGINGS	CREATURESHIP
COUNTERSNIPER	COUNTERWORLD	COVARIANTS	CRACKLEWARES	CRAPSHOOTER	CREATURESHIPS
COUNTERSNIPERS	COUNTERWORLDS	COVARIATES	CRACKLIEST	CRAPSHOOTERS	CREDENTIAL
COUNTERSPELL	COUNTESSES	COVARIATION	CRACKLINGS	CRAPSHOOTS	CREDENTIALED
COUNTERSPELLS	COUNTINGHOUSE	COVARIATIONS	CRACOVIENNE	CRAPULENCE	CREDENTIALING
COUNTERSPIES	COUNTINGHOUSES	COVELLINES	CRACOVIENNES	CRAPULENCES	CREDENTIALISM
COUNTERSPY	COUNTLESSLY	COVELLITES	CRADLESONG	CRAPULENTLY	CREDENTIALISMS
COUNTERSPYING	COUNTLINES	COVENANTAL	CRADLESONGS	CRAPULOSITIES	CREDENTIALLED
COUNTERSPYINGS	COUNTRIFIED	COVENANTALLY	CRADLEWALK	CRAPULOSITY	CREDENTIALLING
COUNTERSTAIN	COUNTROLLED	COVENANTED	CRADLEWALKS	CRAPULOUSLY	CREDENTIALS
COUNTERSTAINED	COUNTROLLING	COVENANTEE	CRAFTINESS	CRAPULOUSNESS	CREDIBILITIES
COUNTERSTAINING	COUNTRYFIED	COVENANTEES	CRAFTINESSES	CRAPULOUSNESSES	CREDIBILITY
COUNTERSTAINS	COUNTRYISH	COVENANTER	CRAFTMANSHIP	CRAQUELURE	CREDIBLENESS
COUNTERSTATE	COUNTRYMAN	COVENANTERS	CRAFTMANSHIPS	CRAQUELURES	CREDIBLENESSES
COUNTERSTATED	COUNTRYMEN	COVENANTING	CRAFTSMANLIKE	CRASHINGLY	CREDITABILITIES
COUNTERSTATES	COUNTRYSEAT	COVENANTOR	CRAFTSMANLY	CRASHLANDED	CREDITABILITY
COUNTERSTATING	COUNTRYSEATS	COVENANTORS	CRAFTSMANSHIP	CRASHLANDING	CREDITABLE
COUNTERSTEP	COUNTRYSIDE	COVERALLED	CRAFTSMANSHIPS	CRASHLANDS	CREDITABLENESS
COUNTERSTEPS	COUNTRYSIDES	COVERMOUNT	CRAFTSPEOPLE	CRASHWORTHINESS	CREDITABLY
COUNTERSTRATEGY	COUNTRYWIDE	COVERMOUNTED	CRAFTSPERSON	CRASHWORTHY	CREDITLESS
COUNTERSTREAM	COUNTRYWOMAN	COVERMOUNTING	CRAFTSPERSONS	CRASSAMENTA	CREDITWORTHY
COUNTERSTREAMS	COUNTRYWOMEN	COVERMOUNTS	CRAFTSWOMAN	CRASSAMENTUM	CREDULITIES
COUNTERSTRICKEN	COUNTSHIPS	COVERSINES	CRAFTSWOMEN	CRASSITUDE	CREDULOUSLY
COUNTERSTRIKE	COUPLEDOMS	COVERSLIPS	CRAFTWORKS	CRASSITUDES	CREDULOUSNESS
COUNTERSTRIKES	COUPLEMENT	COVERTNESS	CRAGGEDNESS	CRASSNESSES	CREDULOUSNESSES
COUNTERSTRIKING	COUPLEMENTS	COVERTNESSES	CRAGGEDNESSES	CRASSULACEAN	CREEPINESS
COUNTERSTROKE	COUPONINGS	COVERTURES	CRAGGINESS	CRASSULACEOUS	CREEPINESSES
COUNTERSTROKES	COURAGEFUL	COVETINGLY	CRAGGINESSES	CRATERIFORM	CREEPINGLY
COUNTERSTRUCK	COURAGEOUS	COVETIVENESS	CRAIGFLUKE	CRATERINGS	CREEPMOUSE
COUNTERSTYLE	COURAGEOUSLY	COVETIVENESSES	CRAIGFLUKES	CRATERLESS	CREESHIEST
COUNTERSTYLES	COURAGEOUSNESS	COVETOUSLY	CRAKEBERRIES	CRATERLETS	CREMAILLERE
COUNTERSUBJECT	COURANTOES	COVETOUSNESS	CRAKEBERRY	CRATERLIKE	CREMAILLERES
COUNTERSUBJECTS	COURBARILS	COVETOUSNESSES	CRAMBOCLINK	CRAUNCHABLE	CREMASTERS
COUNTERSUE	COURBETTES	COWARDICES	CRAMBOCLINKS	CRAUNCHIER	CREMATIONISM
COUNTERSUED	COURGETTES	COWARDLINESS	CRAMOISIES	CRAUNCHIEST	CREMATIONISMS
COUNTERSUES	COURIERING	COWARDLINESSES	CRAMPBARKS	CRAUNCHINESS	CREMATIONIST
COUNTERSUING	COURSEBOOK	COWARDRIES	CRAMPFISHES	CRAUNCHINESSES	CREMATIONISTS
COUNTERSUIT	COURSEBOOKS	COWARDSHIP	CRAMPONING	CRAUNCHING	CREMATIONS
COUNTERSUITS	COURSEWARE	COWARDSHIPS	CRANBERRIES	CRAVATTING	CREMATORIA
COUNTERSUNK	COURSEWARES	COWBERRIES	CRANEFLIES	CRAVENNESS	CREMATORIAL
COUNTERTACTIC	COURSEWORK	COWCATCHER	CRANESBILL	CRAVENNESSES	CREMATORIES
COUNTERTACTICS	COURSEWORKS	COWCATCHERS	CRANESBILLS	CRAWDADDIES	CREMATORIUM
COUNTERTENDENCY	COURTCRAFT	COWERINGLY	CRANIECTOMIES	CRAWFISHED	CREMATORIUMS
COUNTERTENOR	COURTCRAFTS	COWFEEDERS	CRANIECTOMY	CRAWFISHES	CREMOCARPS
COUNTERTENORS	COURTEOUSLY	COWFETERIA	CRANIOCEREBRAL	CRAWFISHING	CRENATIONS
COUNTERTERROR	COURTEOUSNESS	COWFETERIAS	CRANIOFACIAL	CRAWLINGLY	CRENATURES
COUNTERTERRORS	COURTEOUSNESSES	COWGRASSES	CRANIOGNOMIES	CRAYFISHES	CRENELATED
COUNTERTHREAT	COURTESANS	COWLSTAFFS	CRANIOGNOMY	CRAYONISTS	CRENELATES
COUNTERTHREATS	COURTESIED	COWLSTAVES	CRANIOLOGICAL	CRAZINESSES	CRENELATING
COUNTERTHRUST	COURTESIES	COWPUNCHER	CRANIOLOGICALLY	CRAZYWEEDS	CRENELATION
COUNTERTHRUSTS	COURTESYING	COWPUNCHERS	CRANIOLOGIES	CREAKINESS	CRENELATIONS
COUNTERTOP	COURTEZANS	COXCOMBICAL	CRANIOLOGIST	CREAKINESSES	CRENELLATE
COUNTERTOPS	COURTHOUSE	COXCOMBICALITY	CRANIOLOGISTS	CREAKINGLY	CRENELLATED

c

CRENELLATES	CRIMINALISTS	CRITICISER	CROSSCLAIMS	CRUISEWAYS	CRYPTANALYSTS
CRENELLATING	CRIMINALITIES	CRITICISERS	CROSSCOURT	CRUISEWEAR	CRYPTANALYTIC
CRENELLATION	CRIMINALITY	CRITICISES	CROSSCURRENT	CRUISEWEARS	CRYPTANALYTICAL
CRENELLATIONS	CRIMINALIZATION	CRITICISING	CROSSCURRENTS	CRUMBCLOTH	CRYPTARITHM
CRENELLING	CRIMINALIZE	CRITICISINGLY	CROSSCUTTING	CRUMBCLOTHS	CRYPTARITHMS
CRENULATED	CRIMINALIZED	CRITICISMS	CROSSCUTTINGS	CRUMBLIEST	CRYPTESTHESIA
CRENULATION	CRIMINALIZES	CRITICIZABLE	CROSSETTES	CRUMBLINESS	CRYPTESTHESIAS
CRENULATIONS	CRIMINALIZING	CRITICIZED	CROSSFALLS	CRUMBLINESSES	CRYPTICALLY
CREOLISATION	CRIMINALLY	CRITICIZER	CROSSFIELD	CRUMBLINGS	CRYPTOBIONT
CREOLISATIONS	CRIMINATED	CRITICIZERS	CROSSFIRES	CRUMMINESS	CRYPTOBIONTS
CREOLISING	CRIMINATES	CRITICIZES	CROSSFISHES	CRUMMINESSES	CRYPTOBIOSES
CREOLIZATION	CRIMINATING	CRITICIZING	CROSSHAIRS	CRUMPLIEST	CRYPTOBIOSIS
CREOLIZATIONS	CRIMINATION	CRITICIZINGLY	CROSSHATCH	CRUMPLINGS	CRYPTOCLASTIC
CREOLIZING	CRIMINATIONS	CRITIQUING	CROSSHATCHED	CRUNCHABLE	CRYPTOCOCCAL
CREOPHAGIES	CRIMINATIVE	CROAKINESS	CROSSHATCHES	CRUNCHIEST	CRYPTOCOCCI
CREOPHAGOUS	CRIMINATOR	CROAKINESSES	CROSSHATCHING	CRUNCHINESS	CRYPTOCOCCOSES
CREOSOTING	CRIMINATORS	CROCHETERS	CROSSHATCHINGS	CRUNCHINESSES	CRYPTOCOCCOSIS
CREPEHANGER	CRIMINATORY	CROCHETING	CROSSHEADS	CRUNCHINGS	CRYPTOCOCCUS
CREPEHANGERS	CRIMINOGENIC	CROCHETINGS	CROSSJACKS	CRUSHABILITIES	CRYPTOGAMIAN
CREPEHANGING	CRIMINOLOGIC	CROCIDOLITE	CROSSLIGHT	CRUSHABILITY	CRYPTOGAMIC
CREPEHANGINGS	CRIMINOLOGICAL	CROCIDOLITES	CROSSLIGHTS	CRUSHINGLY	CRYPTOGAMIES
CREPINESSES	CRIMINOLOGIES	CROCKERIES	CROSSLINGUISTIC	CRUSHPROOF	CRYPTOGAMIST
CREPITATED	CRIMINOLOGIST	CROCODILES	CROSSNESSES	CRUSTACEAN	CRYPTOGAMISTS
CREPITATES	CRIMINOLOGISTS	CROCODILIAN	CROSSOPTERYGIAN	CRUSTACEANS	CRYPTOGAMOUS
CREPITATING	CRIMINOLOGY	CROCODILIANS	CROSSOVERS	CRUSTACEOUS	CRYPTOGAMS
CREPITATION	CRIMINOUSNESS	CROCOISITE	CROSSPATCH	CRUSTATION	CRYPTOGAMY
CREPITATIONS	CRIMINOUSNESSES	CROCOISITES	CROSSPATCHES	CRUSTATIONS	CRYPTOGENIC
CREPITATIVE	CRIMSONING	CROCOSMIAS	CROSSPIECE	CRUSTINESS	CRYPTOGRAM
CREPITUSES	CRIMSONNESS	CROISSANTS	CROSSPIECES	CRUSTINESSES	CRYPTOGRAMS
CREPOLINES	CRIMSONNESSES	CROKINOLES	CROSSROADS	CRUTCHINGS	CRYPTOGRAPH
CREPUSCLES	CRINGELING	CROOKBACKED	CROSSRUFFED	CRYMOTHERAPIES	CRYPTOGRAPHER
CREPUSCULAR	CRINGELINGS	CROOKBACKS	CROSSRUFFING	CRYMOTHERAPY	CRYPTOGRAPHERS
CREPUSCULE	CRINGEWORTHY	CROOKEDEST	CROSSRUFFS	CRYOBIOLOGICAL	CRYPTOGRAPHIC
CREPUSCULES	CRINGINGLY	CROOKEDNESS	CROSSTALKS	CRYOBIOLOGIES	CRYPTOGRAPHICAL
CREPUSCULOUS	CRINICULTURAL	CROOKEDNESSES	CROSSTREES	CRYOBIOLOGIST	CRYPTOGRAPHIES
CRESCENDOED	CRINIGEROUS	CROOKERIES	CROSSWALKS	CRYOBIOLOGISTS	CRYPTOGRAPHIST
CRESCENDOES	CRINKLEROOT	CROOKNECKS	CROSSWINDS	CRYOBIOLOGY	CRYPTOGRAPHISTS
CRESCENDOING	CRINKLEROOTS	CROPDUSTER	CROSSWORDS	CRYOCABLES	CRYPTOGRAPHS
CRESCENDOS	CRINKLIEST	CROPDUSTERS	CROSSWORTS	CRYOCONITE	CRYPTOGRAPHY
CRESCENTADE	CRINOIDEAN	CROQUANTES	CROTALARIA	CRYOCONITES	CRYPTOLOGIC
CRESCENTADES	CRINOIDEANS	CROQUETING	CROTALARIAS	CRYOGENICALLY	CRYPTOLOGICAL
CRESCENTED	CRINOLETTE	CROQUETTES	CROTALISMS	CRYOGENICS	CRYPTOLOGIES
CRESCENTIC	CRINOLETTES	CROQUIGNOLE	CROTCHETED	CRYOGENIES	CRYPTOLOGIST
CRESCIVELY	CRINOLINED	CROQUIGNOLES	CROTCHETEER	CRYOGLOBULIN	CRYPTOLOGISTS
CRESCOGRAPH	CRINOLINES	CROSSABILITIES	CROTCHETEERS	CRYOGLOBULINS	CRYPTOLOGY
CRESCOGRAPHS	CRIPPLEDOM	CROSSABILITY	CROTCHETIER	CRYOHYDRATE	CRYPTOMERIA
CRESTFALLEN	CRIPPLEDOMS	CROSSANDRA	CROTCHETIEST	CRYOHYDRATES	CRYPTOMERIAS
CRESTFALLENLY	CRIPPLEWARE	CROSSANDRAS	CROTCHETINESS	CRYOMETERS	CRYPTOMETER
CRESTFALLENNESS	CRIPPLEWARES	CROSSBANDED	CROTCHETINESSES	CRYOMETRIC	CRYPTOMETERS
CRETACEOUS	CRIPPLINGLY	CROSSBANDING	CROTONBUGS	CRYOMETRIES	CRYPTOMNESIA
CRETACEOUSES	CRIPPLINGS	CROSSBANDINGS	CROUPINESS	CRYOPHILIC	CRYPTOMNESIAS
CRETACEOUSLY	CRISPATION	CROSSBANDS	CROUPINESSES	CRYOPHORUS	CRYPTOMNESIC
CRETINISED	CRISPATIONS	CROSSBARRED	CROUSTADES	CRYOPHORUSES	CRYPTONYMOUS
CRETINISES	CRISPATURE	CROSSBARRING	CROWBARRED	CRYOPHYSICS	CRYPTONYMS
CRETINISING	CRISPATURES	CROSSBEAMS	CROWBARRING	CRYOPHYTES	CRYPTOPHYTE
CRETINISMS	CRISPBREAD	CROSSBEARER	CROWBERRIES	CRYOPLANKTON	CRYPTOPHYTES
CRETINIZED	CRISPBREADS	CROSSBEARERS	CROWDEDNESS	CRYOPLANKTONS	CRYPTOPHYTIC
CRETINIZES	CRISPENING	CROSSBENCH	CROWDEDNESSES	CRYOPRECIPITATE	CRYPTORCHID
CRETINIZING	CRISPHEADS	CROSSBENCHER	CROWKEEPER	CRYOPRESERVE	CRYPTORCHIDISM
CRETINOIDS	CRISPINESS	CROSSBENCHERS	CROWKEEPERS	CRYOPRESERVED	CRYPTORCHIDISMS
CREVASSING	CRISPINESSES	CROSSBENCHES	CROWNLANDS	CRYOPRESERVES	CRYPTORCHIDS
CREWELISTS	CRISPNESSES	CROSSBILLS	CROWNPIECE	CRYOPRESERVING	CRYPTORCHISM
CREWELLERIES	CRISSCROSS	CROSSBIRTH	CROWNPIECES	CRYOPROBES	CRYPTORCHISMS
CREWELLERY	CRISSCROSSED	CROSSBIRTHS	CROWNWORKS	CRYOPROTECTANT	CRYPTOSPORIDIA
CREWELLING	CRISSCROSSES	CROSSBITES	CROWSTEPPED	CRYOPROTECTANTS	CRYPTOSPORIDIUM
CREWELWORK	CRISSCROSSING	CROSSBITING	CRUCIATELY	CRYOPROTECTIVE	CRYPTOZOIC
CREWELWORKS	CRISTIFORM	CROSSBITTEN	CRUCIFEROUS	CRYOSCOPES	CRYPTOZOITE
CRIBRATION	CRISTOBALITE	CROSSBONES	CRUCIFIERS	CRYOSCOPIC	CRYPTOZOITES
CRIBRATIONS	CRISTOBALITES	CROSSBOWER	CRUCIFIXES	CRYOSCOPIES	CRYPTOZOOLOGIES
CRIBRIFORM	CRITERIONS	CROSSBOWERS	CRUCIFIXION	CRYOSTATIC	CRYPTOZOOLOGIST
CRICKETERS	CRITERIUMS	CROSSBOWMAN	CRUCIFIXIONS	CRYOSURGEON	CRYPTOZOOLOGY
CRICKETING	CRITHIDIAL	CROSSBOWMEN	CRUCIFORMLY	CRYOSURGEONS	CRYSTALISABLE
CRICKETINGS	CRITHOMANCIES	CROSSBREDS	CRUCIFORMS	CRYOSURGERIES	CRYSTALISATION
CRIMEWAVES	CRITHOMANCY	CROSSBREED	CRUCIFYING	CRYOSURGERY	CRYSTALISATIONS
CRIMINALESE	CRITICALITIES	CROSSBREEDING	CRUCIVERBAL	CRYOSURGICAL	CRYSTALISE
CRIMINALESES	CRITICALITY	CROSSBREEDINGS	CRUCIVERBALISM	CRYOTHERAPIES	CRYSTALISED
CRIMINALISATION	CRITICALLY	CROSSBREEDS	CRUCIVERBALISMS	CRYOTHERAPY	CRYSTALISER
CRIMINALISE	CRITICALNESS	CROSSBUCKS	CRUCIVERBALIST	CRYPTAESTHESIA	CRYSTALISERS
CRIMINALISED	CRITICALNESSES	CROSSCHECK	CRUCIVERBALISTS	CRYPTAESTHESIAS	CRYSTALISES
CRIMINALISES	CRITICASTER	CROSSCHECKED	CRUDENESSES	CRYPTAESTHETIC	CRYSTALISING
CRIMINALISING	CRITICASTERS	CROSSCHECKING	CRUELNESSES	CRYPTANALYSES	CRYSTALIZABLE
CRIMINALIST	CRITICISABLE	CROSSCHECKS	CRUISERWEIGHT	CRYPTANALYSIS	CRYSTALIZATION
CRIMINALISTICS	CRITICISED	CROSSCLAIM	CRUISERWEIGHTS	CRYPTANALYST	CRYSTALIZATIONS

CRYSTALIZE	CULMIFEROUS	CUPFERRONS	CURSORINESS	CUTINIZING	CYCADOPHYTE
CRYSTALIZED	CULMINATED	CUPIDINOUS	CURSORINESSES	CUTTHROATS	CYCADOPHYTES
CRYSTALIZER	CULMINATES	CUPIDITIES	CURSTNESSES	CUTTLEBONE	CYCLAMATES
CRYSTALIZERS	CULMINATING	CUPRAMMONIUM	CURTAILERS	CUTTLEBONES	CYCLANDELATE
CRYSTALIZES	CULMINATION	CUPRAMMONIUMS	CURTAILING	CUTTLEFISH	CYCLANDELATES
CRYSTALIZING	CULMINATIONS	CUPRESSUSES	CURTAILMENT	CUTTLEFISHES	CYCLANTHACEOUS
CRYSTALLINE	CULPABILITIES	CUPRIFEROUS	CURTAILMENTS	CYANAMIDES	CYCLAZOCINE
CRYSTALLINES	CULPABILITY	CUPRONICKEL	CURTAINING	CYANIDATION	CYCLAZOCINES
CRYSTALLINITIES	CULPABLENESS	CUPRONICKELS	CURTAINLESS	CYANIDATIONS	CYCLICALITIES
CRYSTALLINITY	CULPABLENESSES	CUPULIFEROUS	CURTALAXES	CYANIDINGS	CYCLICALITY
CRYSTALLISABLE	CULTISHNESS	CURABILITIES	CURTATIONS	CYANOACETYLENE	CYCLICALLY
CRYSTALLISATION	CULTISHNESSES	CURABILITY	CURTILAGES	CYANOACETYLENES	CYCLICISMS
CRYSTALLISE	CULTIVABILITIES	CURABLENESS	CURTNESSES	CYANOACRYLATE	CYCLICITIES
CRYSTALLISED	CULTIVABILITY	CURABLENESSES	CURTSEYING	CYANOACRYLATES	CYCLISATION
CRYSTALLISER	CULTIVABLE	CURANDERAS	CURVACEOUS	CYANOBACTERIA	CYCLISATIONS
CRYSTALLISERS	CULTIVATABLE	CURANDEROS	CURVACEOUSLY	CYANOBACTERIUM	CYCLIZATION
CRYSTALLISES	CULTIVATED	CURARISATION	CURVACIOUS	CYANOCOBALAMIN	CYCLIZATIONS
CRYSTALLISING	CULTIVATES	CURARISATIONS	CURVATIONS	CYANOCOBALAMINE	CYCLIZINES
CRYSTALLITE	CULTIVATING	CURARISING	CURVATURES	CYANOCOBALAMINS	CYCLOADDITION
CRYSTALLITES	CULTIVATION	CURARIZATION	CURVEBALLED	CYANOETHYLATE	CYCLOADDITIONS
CRYSTALLITIC	CULTIVATIONS	CURARIZATIONS	CURVEBALLING	CYANOETHYLATED	CYCLOALIPHATIC
CRYSTALLITIS	CULTIVATOR	CURARIZING	CURVEBALLS	CYANOETHYLATES	CYCLOALKANE
CRYSTALLITISES	CULTIVATORS	CURATESHIP	CURVEDNESS	CYANOETHYLATING	CYCLOALKANES
CRYSTALLIZABLE	CULTRIFORM	CURATESHIPS	CURVEDNESSES	CYANOETHYLATION	CYCLOBARBITONE
CRYSTALLIZATION	CULTURABLE	CURATIVELY	CURVETTING	CYANOGENAMIDE	CYCLOBARBITONES
CRYSTALLIZE	CULTURALLY	CURATIVENESS	CURVICAUDATE	CYANOGENAMIDES	CYCLODEXTRIN
CRYSTALLIZED	CULTURELESS	CURATIVENESSES	CURVICOSTATE	CYANOGENESES	CYCLODEXTRINS
CRYSTALLIZER	CULTURISTS	CURATORIAL	CURVIFOLIATE	CYANOGENESIS	CYCLODIALYSES
CRYSTALLIZERS	CULVERINEER	CURATORSHIP	CURVILINEAL	CYANOGENETIC	CYCLODIALYSIS
CRYSTALLIZES	CULVERINEERS	CURATORSHIPS	CURVILINEAR	CYANOGENIC	CYCLODIENE
CRYSTALLIZING	CULVERTAGE	CURATRIXES	CURVILINEARITY	CYANOHYDRIN	CYCLODIENES
CRYSTALLOGRAPHY	CULVERTAGES	CURBSTONES	CURVILINEARLY	CYANOHYDRINS	CYCLOGENESES
CRYSTALLOID	CULVERTAILED	CURCUMINES	CURVIROSTRAL	CYANOMETER	CYCLOGENESIS
CRYSTALLOIDAL	CUMBERBUND	CURDINESSES	CUSHINESSES	CYANOMETERS	CYCLOGIROS
CRYSTALLOIDS	CUMBERBUNDS	CURETTAGES	CUSHIONETS	CYANOPHYTE	CYCLOGRAPH
CRYSTALLOMANCY	CUMBERLESS	CURETTEMENT	CUSHIONING	CYANOPHYTES	CYCLOGRAPHIC
CTENOPHORAN	CUMBERMENT	CURETTEMENTS	CUSHIONLESS	CYANOTYPES	CYCLOGRAPHS
CTENOPHORANS	CUMBERMENTS	CURFUFFLED	CUSPIDATED	CYANURATES	CYCLOHEXANE
CTENOPHORE	CUMBERSOME	CURFUFFLES	CUSPIDATION	CYATHIFORM	CYCLOHEXANES
CTENOPHORES	CUMBERSOMELY	CURFUFFLING	CUSPIDATIONS	CYBERATHLETE	CYCLOHEXANONE
CUADRILLAS	CUMBERSOMENESS	CURIALISMS	CUSPIDORES	CYBERATHLETES	CYCLOHEXANONES
CUBANELLES	CUMBRANCES	CURIALISTIC	CUSSEDNESS	CYBERATHLETICS	CYCLOHEXIMIDE
CUBBYHOLES	CUMBROUSLY	CURIALISTS	CUSSEDNESSES	CYBERCAFES	CYCLOHEXIMIDES
CUBICALNESS	CUMBROUSNESS	CURIETHERAPIES	CUSTODIANS	CYBERCASTS	CYCLOHEXYLAMINE
CUBICALNESSES	CUMBROUSNESSES	CURIETHERAPY	CUSTODIANSHIP	CYBERCRIME	CYCLOIDALLY
CUBICITIES	CUMMERBUND	CURIOSITIES	CUSTODIANSHIPS	CYBERCRIMES	CYCLOIDIAN
CUBISTICALLY	CUMMERBUNDS	CURIOUSEST	CUSTODIERS	CYBERCRIMINAL	CYCLOIDIANS
CUCKOLDING	CUMMINGTONITE	CURIOUSNESS	CUSTOMABLE	CYBERCRIMINALS	CYCLOLITHS
CUCKOLDISE	CUMMINGTONITES	CURIOUSNESSES	CUSTOMARIES	CYBERNATED	CYCLOMETER
CUCKOLDISED	CUMULATELY	CURLICUING	CUSTOMARILY	CYBERNATES	CYCLOMETERS
CUCKOLDISES	CUMULATING	CURLIEWURLIE	CUSTOMARINESS	CYBERNATING	CYCLOMETRIES
CUCKOLDISING	CUMULATION	CURLIEWURLIES	CUSTOMARINESSES	CYBERNATION	CYCLOMETRY
CUCKOLDIZE	CUMULATIONS	CURLINESSES	CUSTOMHOUSE	CYBERNATIONS	CYCLONICAL
CUCKOLDIZED	CUMULATIVE	CURLPAPERS	CUSTOMHOUSES	CYBERNAUTS	CYCLONICALLY
CUCKOLDIZES	CUMULATIVELY	CURMUDGEON	CUSTOMISATION	CYBERNETIC	CYCLONITES
CUCKOLDIZING	CUMULATIVENESS	CURMUDGEONLY	CUSTOMISATIONS	CYBERNETICAL	CYCLOOLEFIN
CUCKOLDOMS	CUMULIFORM	CURMUDGEONS	CUSTOMISED	CYBERNETICALLY	CYCLOOLEFINIC
CUCKOLDRIES	CUMULOCIRRI	CURMURRING	CUSTOMISER	CYBERNETICIAN	CYCLOOLEFINS
CUCKOOFLOWER	CUMULOCIRRUS	CURMURRINGS	CUSTOMISERS	CYBERNETICIANS	CYCLOPAEDIA
CUCKOOFLOWERS	CUMULONIMBI	CURNAPTIOUS	CUSTOMISES	CYBERNETICIST	CYCLOPAEDIAS
CUCKOOPINT	CUMULONIMBUS	CURRAJONGS	CUSTOMISING	CYBERNETICISTS	CYCLOPAEDIC
CUCKOOPINTS	CUMULONIMBUSES	CURRANTIER	CUSTOMIZATION	CYBERNETICS	CYCLOPAEDIST
CUCULIFORM	CUMULOSTRATI	CURRANTIEST	CUSTOMIZATIONS	CYBERPHOBIA	CYCLOPAEDISTS
CUCULLATED	CUMULOSTRATUS	CURRAWONGS	CUSTOMIZED	CYBERPHOBIAS	CYCLOPARAFFIN
CUCULLATELY	CUNCTATION	CURREJONGS	CUSTOMIZER	CYBERPHOBIC	CYCLOPARAFFINS
CUCUMIFORM	CUNCTATIONS	CURRENCIES	CUSTOMIZERS	CYBERPORNS	CYCLOPEDIA
CUCURBITACEOUS	CUNCTATIOUS	CURRENTNESS	CUSTOMIZES	CYBERPUNKS	CYCLOPEDIAS
CUCURBITAL	CUNCTATIVE	CURRENTNESSES	CUSTOMIZING	CYBERSECURITIES	CYCLOPEDIC
CUDDLESOME	CUNCTATORS	CURRICULAR	CUSTOMSHOUSE	CYBERSECURITY	CYCLOPEDIST
CUDGELLERS	CUNCTATORY	CURRICULUM	CUSTOMSHOUSES	CYBERSEXES	CYCLOPEDISTS
CUDGELLING	CUNEIFORMS	CURRICULUMS	CUSTUMARIES	CYBERSPACE	CYCLOPENTADIENE
CUDGELLINGS	CUNNILINCTUS	CURRIERIES	CUTABILITIES	CYBERSPACES	CYCLOPENTANE
CUFFUFFLES	CUNNILINCTUSES	CURRIJONGS	CUTABILITY	CYBERSQUATTER	CYCLOPENTANES
CUIRASSIER	CUNNILINGUS	CURRISHNESS	CUTANEOUSLY	CYBERSQUATTERS	CYCLOPENTOLATE
CUIRASSIERS	CUNNILINGUSES	CURRISHNESSES	CUTCHERIES	CYBERSQUATTING	CYCLOPENTOLATES
CUIRASSING	CUNNINGEST	CURRYCOMBED	CUTCHERRIES	CYBERSQUATTINGS	CYCLOPLEGIA
CUISINARTS	CUNNINGNESS	CURRYCOMBING	CUTENESSES	CYBERTERRORISM	CYCLOPLEGIAS
CUISINIERS	CUNNINGNESSES	CURRYCOMBS	CUTGRASSES	CYBERTERRORISMS	CYCLOPLEGIC
CULICIFORM	CUPBEARERS	CURSEDNESS	CUTINISATION	CYBERTERRORIST	CYCLOPROPANE
CULINARIAN	CUPBOARDED	CURSEDNESSES	CUTINISATIONS	CYBERTERRORISTS	CYCLOPROPANES
CULINARIANS	CUPBOARDING	CURSELARIE	CUTINISING	CYBRARIANS	CYCLORAMAS
CULINARILY	CUPELLATION	CURSIVENESS	CUTINIZATION	CYCADACEOUS	CYCLORAMIC
CULLENDERS	CUPELLATIONS	CURSIVENESSES	CUTINIZATIONS	CYCADEOIDS	CYCLOSERINE

CYCLOSERINES	CYLINDRICALITY	CYNOPHILIST	CYSTINURIA	CYTODIAGNOSIS	CYTOPATHOLOGIES
CYCLOSPERMOUS	CYLINDRICALLY	CYNOPHILISTS	CYSTINURIAS	CYTOGENESES	CYTOPATHOLOGY
CYCLOSPORIN	CYLINDRICALNESS	CYNOPHOBIA	CYSTITIDES	CYTOGENESIS	CYTOPENIAS
CYCLOSPORINE	CYLINDRICITIES	CYNOPHOBIAS	CYSTITISES	CYTOGENETIC	CYTOPHILIC
CYCLOSPORINES	CYLINDRICITY	CYNOPODOUS	CYSTOCARPIC	CYTOGENETICAL	CYTOPHOTOMETRIC
CYCLOSPORINS	CYLINDRIFORM	CYPERACEOUS	CYSTOCARPS	CYTOGENETICALLY	CYTOPHOTOMETRY
CYCLOSTOMATE	CYLINDRITE	CYPRINODONT	CYSTOCELES	CYTOGENETICIST	CYTOPLASMIC
CYCLOSTOMATOUS	CYLINDRITES	CYPRINODONTS	CYSTOGENOUS	CYTOGENETICISTS	CYTOPLASMICALLY
CYCLOSTOME	CYLINDROID	CYPRINOIDS	CYSTOGRAPHIES	CYTOGENETICS	CYTOPLASMS
CYCLOSTOMES	CYLINDROIDS	CYPRIPEDIA	CYSTOGRAPHY	CYTOGENIES	CYTOPLASTIC
CYCLOSTOMOUS	CYMAGRAPHS	CYPRIPEDIUM	CYSTOLITHIASES	CYTOKINESES	CYTOPLASTS
CYCLOSTYLE	CYMBALEERS	CYPRIPEDIUMS	CYSTOLITHIASIS	CYTOKINESIS	CYTOSKELETAL
CYCLOSTYLED	CYMBALISTS	CYPROHEPTADINE	CYSTOLITHS	CYTOKINETIC	CYTOSKELETON
CYCLOSTYLES	CYMBIDIUMS	CYPROHEPTADINES	CYSTOSCOPE	CYTOKININS	CYTOSKELETONS
CYCLOSTYLING	CYMIFEROUS	CYPROTERONE	CYSTOSCOPES	CYTOLOGICAL	CYTOSTATIC
CYCLOTHYME	CYMOGRAPHIC	CYPROTERONES	CYSTOSCOPIC	CYTOLOGICALLY	CYTOSTATICALLY
CYCLOTHYMES	CYMOGRAPHS	CYSTEAMINE	CYSTOSCOPIES	CYTOLOGIES	CYTOSTATICS
CYCLOTHYMIA	CYMOPHANES	CYSTEAMINES	CYSTOSCOPY	CYTOLOGIST	CYTOTAXONOMIC
CYCLOTHYMIAC	CYMOPHANOUS	CYSTECTOMIES	CYSTOSTOMIES	CYTOLOGISTS	CYTOTAXONOMIES
CYCLOTHYMIACS	CYMOTRICHIES	CYSTECTOMY	CYSTOSTOMY	CYTOLYSINS	CYTOTAXONOMIST
CYCLOTHYMIAS	CYMOTRICHOUS	CYSTICERCI	CYSTOTOMIES	CYTOMEGALIC	CYTOTAXONOMISTS
CYCLOTHYMIC	CYMOTRICHY	CYSTICERCOID	CYTOCHALASIN	CYTOMEGALOVIRUS	CYTOTAXONOMY
CYCLOTHYMICS	CYNGHANEDD	CYSTICERCOIDS	CYTOCHALASINS	CYTOMEMBRANE	CYTOTECHNOLOGY
CYCLOTOMIC	CYNGHANEDDS	CYSTICERCOSES	CYTOCHEMICAL	CYTOMEMBRANES	CYTOTOXICITIES
CYCLOTRONS	CYNICALNESS	CYSTICERCOSIS	CYTOCHEMISTRIES	CYTOMETERS	CYTOTOXICITY
CYLINDERED	CYNICALNESSES	CYSTICERCUS	CYTOCHEMISTRY	CYTOMETRIC	CYTOTOXINS
CYLINDERING	CYNOMOLGUS	CYSTIDEANS	CYTOCHROME	CYTOMETRIES	CZAREVICHES
CYLINDRACEOUS	CYNOPHILIA	CYSTINOSES	CYTOCHROMES	CYTOPATHIC	CZAREVITCH
CYLINDRICAL	CYNOPHILIAS	CYSTINOSIS	CYTODIAGNOSES	CYTOPATHOGENIC	CZAREVITCHES

Dd

DABBLINGLY
DACHSHUNDS
DACOITAGES
DACQUOISES
DACTYLICALLY
DACTYLIOGRAPHY
DACTYLIOLOGIES
DACTYLIOLOGY
DACTYLIOMANCIES
DACTYLIOMANCY
DACTYLISTS
DACTYLOGRAM
DACTYLOGRAMS
DACTYLOGRAPHER
DACTYLOGRAPHERS
DACTYLOGRAPHIC
DACTYLOGRAPHIES
DACTYLOGRAPHY
DACTYLOLOGIES
DACTYLOLOGY
DACTYLOSCOPIES
DACTYLOSCOPY
DAFFADOWNDILLY
DAFFINESSES
DAFFODILLIES
DAFFODILLY
DAFTNESSES
DAGGERBOARD
DAGGERBOARDS
DAGGERLIKE
DAGUERREAN
DAGUERREOTYPE
DAGUERREOTYPED
DAGUERREOTYPER
DAGUERREOTYPERS
DAGUERREOTYPES
DAGUERREOTYPIES
DAGUERREOTYPING
DAGUERREOTYPIST
DAGUERREOTYPY
DAHABEEAHS
DAHABEEYAH
DAHABEEYAHS
DAHABIYAHS
DAHABIYEHS
DAILINESSES
DAILYNESSES
DAINTINESS
DAINTINESSES
DAIRYMAIDS
DAISYWHEEL
DAISYWHEELS
DALLIANCES
DALMATIANS
DALTONISMS
DAMAGEABILITIES
DAMAGEABILITY
DAMAGEABLE
DAMAGINGLY
DAMASCEENE
DAMASCEENED
DAMASCEENES
DAMASCEENING
DAMASCENED
DAMASCENES
DAMASCENING
DAMASCENINGS

DAMASKEENED
DAMASKEENING
DAMASKEENS
DAMASKINED
DAMASKINING
DAMASQUINED
DAMASQUINING
DAMASQUINS
DAMINOZIDE
DAMINOZIDES
DAMNABILITIES
DAMNABILITY
DAMNABLENESS
DAMNABLENESSES
DAMNATIONS
DAMNEDESTS
DAMNIFICATION
DAMNIFICATIONS
DAMNIFYING
DAMOISELLE
DAMOISELLES
DAMPCOURSE
DAMPCOURSES
DAMPISHNESS
DAMPISHNESSES
DAMPNESSES
DAMSELFISH
DAMSELFISHES
DAMSELFLIES
DANCEHALLS
DANDELIONS
DANDIFICATION
DANDIFICATIONS
DANDIFYING
DANDIPRATS
DANDYFUNKS
DANDYISHLY
DANDYPRATS
DANGERLESS
DANGEROUSLY
DANGEROUSNESS
DANGEROUSNESSES
DANGLINGLY
DANKNESSES
DANNEBROGS
DANTHONIAS
DAPPERLING
DAPPERLINGS
DAPPERNESS
DAPPERNESSES
DAREDEVILRIES
DAREDEVILRY
DAREDEVILS
DAREDEVILTRIES
DAREDEVILTRY
DARINGNESS
DARINGNESSES
DARKNESSES
DARLINGNESS
DARLINGNESSES
DARNATIONS
DARNEDESTS
DARRAIGNED
DARRAIGNES
DARRAIGNING
DARRAIGNMENT
DARRAIGNMENTS

DARRAINING
DARRAYNING
DARTBOARDS
DASHBOARDS
DASTARDIES
DASTARDLINESS
DASTARDLINESSES
DASTARDNESS
DASTARDNESSES
DASYMETERS
DASYPAEDAL
DASYPHYLLOUS
DATABASING
DATABUSSES
DATAGLOVES
DATAMATION
DATAMATIONS
DATEDNESSES
DATELINING
DAUGHTERHOOD
DAUGHTERHOODS
DAUGHTERLESS
DAUGHTERLINESS
DAUGHTERLING
DAUGHTERLINGS
DAUGHTERLY
DAUNDERING
DAUNOMYCIN
DAUNOMYCINS
DAUNORUBICIN
DAUNORUBICINS
DAUNTINGLY
DAUNTLESSLY
DAUNTLESSNESS
DAUNTLESSNESSES
DAUNTONING
DAUPHINESS
DAUPHINESSES
DAVENPORTS
DAWDLINGLY
DAWSONITES
DAYCENTRES
DAYDREAMED
DAYDREAMER
DAYDREAMERS
DAYDREAMING
DAYDREAMLIKE
DAYFLOWERS
DAYLIGHTED
DAYLIGHTING
DAYLIGHTINGS
DAYSPRINGS
DAYWORKERS
DAZEDNESSES
DAZZLEMENT
DAZZLEMENTS
DAZZLINGLY
DEACIDIFICATION
DEACIDIFIED
DEACIDIFIES
DEACIDIFYING
DEACONESSES
DEACONHOOD
DEACONHOODS
DEACONRIES
DEACONSHIP
DEACONSHIPS

DEACTIVATE
DEACTIVATED
DEACTIVATES
DEACTIVATING
DEACTIVATION
DEACTIVATIONS
DEACTIVATOR
DEACTIVATORS
DEADENINGLY
DEADENINGS
DEADHEADED
DEADHEADING
DEADHOUSES
DEADLIFTED
DEADLIFTING
DEADLIGHTS
DEADLINESS
DEADLINESSES
DEADLINING
DEADLOCKED
DEADLOCKING
DEADNESSES
DEADPANNED
DEADPANNER
DEADPANNERS
DEADPANNING
DEADSTOCKS
DEADSTROKE
DEADWEIGHT
DEADWEIGHTS
DEAERATING
DEAERATION
DEAERATIONS
DEAERATORS
DEAFENINGLY
DEAFENINGS
DEAFNESSES
DEALATIONS
DEALBATION
DEALBATIONS
DEALERSHIP
DEALERSHIPS
DEALFISHES
DEAMBULATORIES
DEAMBULATORY
DEAMINASES
DEAMINATED
DEAMINATES
DEAMINATING
DEAMINATION
DEAMINATIONS
DEAMINISATION
DEAMINISATIONS
DEAMINISED
DEAMINISES
DEAMINISING
DEAMINIZATION
DEAMINIZATIONS
DEAMINIZED
DEAMINIZES
DEAMINIZING
DEARBOUGHT
DEARNESSES
DEARTICULATE
DEARTICULATED
DEARTICULATES
DEARTICULATING

DEASPIRATE
DEASPIRATED
DEASPIRATES
DEASPIRATING
DEASPIRATION
DEASPIRATIONS
DEATHBLOWS
DEATHLESSLY
DEATHLESSNESS
DEATHLESSNESSES
DEATHLIEST
DEATHLINESS
DEATHLINESSES
DEATHTRAPS
DEATHWARDS
DEATHWATCH
DEATHWATCHES
DEATTRIBUTE
DEATTRIBUTED
DEATTRIBUTES
DEATTRIBUTING
DEBAGGINGS
DEBARCATION
DEBARCATIONS
DEBARKATION
DEBARKATIONS
DEBARMENTS
DEBARRASSED
DEBARRASSES
DEBARRASSING
DEBASEDNESS
DEBASEDNESSES
DEBASEMENT
DEBASEMENTS
DEBASINGLY
DEBATEABLE
DEBATEMENT
DEBATEMENTS
DEBATINGLY
DEBAUCHEDLY
DEBAUCHEDNESS
DEBAUCHEDNESSES
DEBAUCHEES
DEBAUCHERIES
DEBAUCHERS
DEBAUCHERY
DEBAUCHING
DEBAUCHMENT
DEBAUCHMENTS
DEBEARDING
DEBENTURED
DEBENTURES
DEBILITATE
DEBILITATED
DEBILITATES
DEBILITATING
DEBILITATION
DEBILITATIONS
DEBILITATIVE
DEBILITIES
DEBONAIRLY
DEBONAIRNESS
DEBONAIRNESSES
DEBONNAIRE
DEBOUCHING
DEBOUCHMENT
DEBOUCHMENTS

DEBOUCHURE
DEBOUCHURES
DEBRIDEMENT
DEBRIDEMENTS
DEBRIEFERS
DEBRIEFING
DEBRIEFINGS
DEBRUISING
DEBUTANTES
DECACHORDS
DECADENCES
DECADENCIES
DECADENTLY
DECAFFEINATE
DECAFFEINATED
DECAFFEINATES
DECAFFEINATING
DECAGONALLY
DECAGRAMME
DECAGRAMMES
DECAGYNIAN
DECAGYNOUS
DECAHEDRAL
DECAHEDRON
DECAHEDRONS
DECALCIFICATION
DECALCIFIED
DECALCIFIER
DECALCIFIERS
DECALCIFIES
DECALCIFYING
DECALCOMANIA
DECALCOMANIAS
DECALESCENCE
DECALESCENCES
DECALESCENT
DECALITERS
DECALITRES
DECALOGIST
DECALOGUES
DECAMERONIC
DECAMEROUS
DECAMETERS
DECAMETHONIUM
DECAMETHONIUMS
DECAMETRES
DECAMETRIC
DECAMPMENT
DECAMPMENTS
DECANDRIAN
DECANDROUS
DECANEDIOIC
DECANICALLY
DECANTATED
DECANTATES
DECANTATING
DECANTATION
DECANTATIONS
DECAPITALISE
DECAPITALISED
DECAPITALISES
DECAPITALISING
DECAPITALIZE
DECAPITALIZED
DECAPITALIZES
DECAPITALIZING

d

DECAPITATE	DECELERATED	DECIGRAMMES	DECLASSIFIABLE	DECOLOURED	DECONTAMINANTS
DECAPITATED	DECELERATES	DECILITERS	DECLASSIFIED	DECOLOURING	DECONTAMINATE
DECAPITATES	DECELERATING	DECILITRES	DECLASSIFIES	DECOLOURISATION	DECONTAMINATED
DECAPITATING	DECELERATION	DECILLIONS	DECLASSIFY	DECOLOURISE	DECONTAMINATES
DECAPITATION	DECELERATIONS	DECILLIONTH	DECLASSIFYING	DECOLOURISED	DECONTAMINATING
DECAPITATIONS	DECELERATOR	DECILLIONTHS	DECLASSING	DECOLOURISES	DECONTAMINATION
DECAPITATOR	DECELERATORS	DECIMALISATION	DECLENSION	DECOLOURISING	DECONTAMINATIVE
DECAPITATORS	DECELEROMETER	DECIMALISATIONS	DECLENSIONAL	DECOLOURIZATION	DECONTAMINATOR
DECAPODANS	DECELEROMETERS	DECIMALISE	DECLENSIONALLY	DECOLOURIZE	DECONTAMINATORS
DECAPODOUS	DECELERONS	DECIMALISED	DECLENSIONS	DECOLOURIZED	DECONTROLLED
DECAPSULATE	DECEMVIRAL	DECIMALISES	DECLINABLE	DECOLOURIZES	DECONTROLLING
DECAPSULATED	DECEMVIRATE	DECIMALISING	DECLINATION	DECOLOURIZING	DECONTROLS
DECAPSULATES	DECEMVIRATES	DECIMALISM	DECLINATIONAL	DECOMMISSION	DECORATING
DECAPSULATING	DECENARIES	DECIMALISMS	DECLINATIONS	DECOMMISSIONED	DECORATION
DECAPSULATION	DECENNARIES	DECIMALIST	DECLINATOR	DECOMMISSIONER	DECORATIONS
DECAPSULATIONS	DECENNIALLY	DECIMALISTS	DECLINATORS	DECOMMISSIONERS	DECORATIVE
DECARBONATE	DECENNIALS	DECIMALIZATION	DECLINATORY	DECOMMISSIONING	DECORATIVELY
DECARBONATED	DECENNIUMS	DECIMALIZATIONS	DECLINATURE	DECOMMISSIONS	DECORATIVENESS
DECARBONATES	DECENNOVAL	DECIMALIZE	DECLINATURES	DECOMMITTED	DECORATORS
DECARBONATING	DECENTERED	DECIMALIZED	DECLINISTS	DECOMMITTING	DECOROUSLY
DECARBONATION	DECENTERING	DECIMALIZES	DECLINOMETER	DECOMPENSATE	DECOROUSNESS
DECARBONATIONS	DECENTNESS	DECIMALIZING	DECLINOMETERS	DECOMPENSATED	DECOROUSNESSES
DECARBONATOR	DECENTNESSES	DECIMATING	DECLIVITIES	DECOMPENSATES	DECORTICATE
DECARBONATORS	DECENTRALISE	DECIMATION	DECLIVITOUS	DECOMPENSATING	DECORTICATED
DECARBONISATION	DECENTRALISED	DECIMATIONS	DECLUTCHED	DECOMPENSATION	DECORTICATES
DECARBONISE	DECENTRALISES	DECIMATORS	DECLUTCHES	DECOMPENSATIONS	DECORTICATING
DECARBONISED	DECENTRALISING	DECIMETERS	DECLUTCHING	DECOMPOSABILITY	DECORTICATION
DECARBONISER	DECENTRALIST	DECIMETRES	DECLUTTERED	DECOMPOSABLE	DECORTICATIONS
DECARBONISERS	DECENTRALISTS	DECIMETRIC	DECLUTTERING	DECOMPOSED	DECORTICATOR
DECARBONISES	DECENTRALIZE	DECINORMAL	DECLUTTERS	DECOMPOSER	DECORTICATORS
DECARBONISING	DECENTRALIZED	DECIPHERABILITY	DECOCTIBLE	DECOMPOSERS	DECOUPAGED
DECARBONIZATION	DECENTRALIZES	DECIPHERABLE	DECOCTIONS	DECOMPOSES	DECOUPAGES
DECARBONIZE	DECENTRALIZING	DECIPHERED	DECOCTURES	DECOMPOSING	DECOUPAGING
DECARBONIZED	DECENTRING	DECIPHERER	DECOHERENCE	DECOMPOSITE	DECOUPLERS
DECARBONIZER	DECEPTIBILITIES	DECIPHERERS	DECOHERENCES	DECOMPOSITION	DECOUPLING
DECARBONIZERS	DECEPTIBILITY	DECIPHERING	DECOHERERS	DECOMPOSITIONS	DECOUPLINGS
DECARBONIZES	DECEPTIBLE	DECIPHERMENT	DECOLLATED	DECOMPOUND	DECRASSIFIED
DECARBONIZING	DECEPTIONAL	DECIPHERMENTS	DECOLLATES	DECOMPOUNDABLE	DECRASSIFIES
DECARBOXYLASE	DECEPTIONS	DECISIONAL	DECOLLATING	DECOMPOUNDED	DECRASSIFY
DECARBOXYLASES	DECEPTIOUS	DECISIONED	DECOLLATION	DECOMPOUNDING	DECRASSIFYING
DECARBOXYLATE	DECEPTIVELY	DECISIONING	DECOLLATIONS	DECOMPOUNDS	DECREASING
DECARBOXYLATED	DECEPTIVENESS	DECISIVELY	DECOLLATOR	DECOMPRESS	DECREASINGLY
DECARBOXYLATES	DECEPTIVENESSES	DECISIVENESS	DECOLLATORS	DECOMPRESSED	DECREEABLE
DECARBOXYLATING	DECEREBRATE	DECISIVENESSES	DECOLLETAGE	DECOMPRESSES	DECREMENTAL
DECARBOXYLATION	DECEREBRATED	DECISTERES	DECOLLETAGES	DECOMPRESSING	DECREMENTED
DECARBURATION	DECEREBRATES	DECITIZENISE	DECOLLETES	DECOMPRESSION	DECREMENTING
DECARBURATIONS	DECEREBRATING	DECITIZENISED	DECOLONISATION	DECOMPRESSIONS	DECREMENTS
DECARBURISATION	DECEREBRATION	DECITIZENISES	DECOLONISATIONS	DECOMPRESSIVE	DECREPITATE
DECARBURISE	DECEREBRATIONS	DECITIZENISING	DECOLONISE	DECOMPRESSOR	DECREPITATED
DECARBURISED	DECEREBRISE	DECITIZENIZE	DECOLONISED	DECOMPRESSORS	DECREPITATES
DECARBURISES	DECEREBRISED	DECITIZENIZED	DECOLONISES	DECONCENTRATE	DECREPITATING
DECARBURISING	DECEREBRISES	DECITIZENIZES	DECOLONISING	DECONCENTRATED	DECREPITATION
DECARBURIZATION	DECEREBRISING	DECITIZENIZING	DECOLONIZATION	DECONCENTRATES	DECREPITATIONS
DECARBURIZE	DECEREBRIZE	DECIVILISE	DECOLONIZATIONS	DECONCENTRATING	DECREPITLY
DECARBURIZED	DECEREBRIZED	DECIVILISED	DECOLONIZE	DECONCENTRATION	DECREPITNESS
DECARBURIZES	DECEREBRIZES	DECIVILISING	DECOLONIZED	DECONDITION	DECREPITNESSES
DECARBURIZING	DECEREBRIZING	DECIVILIZE	DECOLONIZES	DECONDITIONED	DECREPITUDE
DECASTERES	DECERTIFICATION	DECIVILIZED	DECOLONIZING	DECONDITIONING	DECREPITUDES
DECASTICHS	DECERTIFIED	DECIVILIZES	DECOLORANT	DECONDITIONS	DECRESCENCE
DECASTYLES	DECERTIFIES	DECIVILIZING	DECOLORANTS	DECONGESTANT	DECRESCENCES
DECASUALISATION	DECERTIFYING	DECKCHAIRS	DECOLORATE	DECONGESTANTS	DECRESCENDO
DECASUALIZATION	DECESSIONS	DECKHOUSES	DECOLORATED	DECONGESTED	DECRESCENDOS
DECASYLLABIC	DECHEANCES	DECLAIMANT	DECOLORATES	DECONGESTING	DECRESCENT
DECASYLLABICS	DECHLORINATE	DECLAIMANTS	DECOLORATING	DECONGESTION	DECRETALIST
DECASYLLABLE	DECHLORINATED	DECLAIMERS	DECOLORATION	DECONGESTIONS	DECRETALISTS
DECASYLLABLES	DECHLORINATES	DECLAIMING	DECOLORATIONS	DECONGESTIVE	DECRETISTS
DECATHLETE	DECHLORINATING	DECLAIMINGS	DECOLORING	DECONGESTS	DECRIMINALISE
DECATHLETES	DECHLORINATION	DECLAMATION	DECOLORISATION	DECONSECRATE	DECRIMINALISED
DECATHLONS	DECHLORINATIONS	DECLAMATIONS	DECOLORISATIONS	DECONSECRATED	DECRIMINALISES
DECAUDATED	DECHRISTIANISE	DECLAMATORILY	DECOLORISE	DECONSECRATES	DECRIMINALISING
DECAUDATES	DECHRISTIANISED	DECLAMATORY	DECOLORISED	DECONSECRATING	DECRIMINALIZE
DECAUDATING	DECHRISTIANISES	DECLARABLE	DECOLORISER	DECONSECRATION	DECRIMINALIZED
DECEITFULLY	DECHRISTIANIZE	DECLARANTS	DECOLORISERS	DECONSECRATIONS	DECRIMINALIZES
DECEITFULNESS	DECHRISTIANIZED	DECLARATION	DECOLORISES	DECONSTRUCT	DECRIMINALIZING
DECEITFULNESSES	DECHRISTIANIZES	DECLARATIONS	DECOLORISING	DECONSTRUCTED	DECROWNING
DECEIVABILITIES	DECIDABILITIES	DECLARATIVE	DECOLORIZATION	DECONSTRUCTING	DECRUSTATION
DECEIVABILITY	DECIDABILITY	DECLARATIVELY	DECOLORIZATIONS	DECONSTRUCTION	DECRUSTATIONS
DECEIVABLE	DECIDABILITY	DECLARATOR	DECOLORIZE	DECONSTRUCTIONS	DECRYPTING
DECEIVABLENESS	DECIDEDNESS	DECLARATORILY	DECOLORIZED	DECONSTRUCTIVE	DECRYPTION
DECEIVABLY	DECIDEDNESSES	DECLARATORY	DECOLORIZER	DECONSTRUCTOR	DECRYPTIONS
DECEIVINGLY	DECIDUOUSLY	DECLARATORS	DECOLORIZERS	DECONSTRUCTORS	DECUMBENCE
DECEIVINGS	DECIDUOUSNESS	DECLARATORY	DECOLORIZES	DECONSTRUCTS	DECUMBENCES
DECELERATE	DECIDUOUSNESSES	DECLAREDLY	DECOLORIZING	DECONTAMINANT	DECUMBENCIES
	DECIGRAMME				

DECUMBENCY	DEFALCATORS	DEFERVESCENCY	DEFLATIONARY	DEFRAUDERS	DEGRINGOLADE
DECUMBENTLY	DEFAMATION	DEFEUDALISE	DEFLATIONIST	DEFRAUDING	DEGRINGOLADED
DECUMBITURE	DEFAMATIONS	DEFEUDALISED	DEFLATIONISTS	DEFRAUDMENT	DEGRINGOLADES
DECUMBITURES	DEFAMATORILY	DEFEUDALISES	DEFLATIONS	DEFRAUDMENTS	DEGRINGOLADING
DECURIONATE	DEFAMATORY	DEFEUDALISING	DEFLECTABLE	DEFRAYABLE	DEGRINGOLER
DECURIONATES	DEFAULTERS	DEFEUDALIZE	DEFLECTING	DEFRAYMENT	DEGRINGOLERED
DECURRENCIES	DEFAULTING	DEFEUDALIZED	DEFLECTION	DEFRAYMENTS	DEGRINGOLERING
DECURRENCY	DEFEASANCE	DEFEUDALIZES	DEFLECTIONAL	DEFREEZING	DEGRINGOLERS
DECURRENTLY	DEFEASANCED	DEFEUDALIZING	DEFLECTIONS	DEFROCKING	DEGUSTATED
DECURSIONS	DEFEASANCES	DEFIANTNESS	DEFLECTIVE	DEFROSTERS	DEGUSTATES
DECURSIVELY	DEFEASIBILITIES	DEFIANTNESSES	DEFLECTORS	DEFROSTING	DEGUSTATING
DECURVATION	DEFEASIBILITY	DEFIBRILLATE	DEFLEXIONAL	DEFTNESSES	DEGUSTATION
DECURVATIONS	DEFEASIBLE	DEFIBRILLATED	DEFLEXIONS	DEFUELLING	DEGUSTATIONS
DECUSSATED	DEFEASIBLENESS	DEFIBRILLATES	DEFLEXURES	DEFUNCTION	DEGUSTATORY
DECUSSATELY	DEFEATISMS	DEFIBRILLATING	DEFLOCCULANT	DEFUNCTIONS	DEHISCENCE
DECUSSATES	DEFEATISTS	DEFIBRILLATION	DEFLOCCULANTS	DEFUNCTIVE	DEHISCENCES
DECUSSATING	DEFEATURED	DEFIBRILLATIONS	DEFLOCCULATE	DEFUNCTNESS	DEHORTATION
DECUSSATION	DEFEATURES	DEFIBRILLATOR	DEFLOCCULATED	DEFUNCTNESSES	DEHORTATIONS
DECUSSATIONS	DEFEATURING	DEFIBRILLATORS	DEFLOCCULATES	DEGARNISHED	DEHORTATIVE
DEDICATEDLY	DEFECATING	DEFIBRINATE	DEFLOCCULATING	DEGARNISHES	DEHORTATORY
DEDICATEES	DEFECATION	DEFIBRINATED	DEFLOCCULATION	DEGARNISHING	DEHUMANISATION
DEDICATING	DEFECATIONS	DEFIBRINATES	DEFLOCCULATIONS	DEGAUSSERS	DEHUMANISATIONS
DEDICATION	DEFECATORS	DEFIBRINATING	DEFLORATED	DEGAUSSING	DEHUMANISE
DEDICATIONAL	DEFECTIBILITIES	DEFIBRINATION	DEFLORATES	DEGEARINGS	DEHUMANISED
DEDICATIONS	DEFECTIBILITY	DEFIBRINATIONS	DEFLORATING	DEGENDERED	DEHUMANISES
DEDICATIVE	DEFECTIBLE	DEFIBRINISE	DEFLORATION	DEGENDERING	DEHUMANISING
DEDICATORIAL	DEFECTIONIST	DEFIBRINISED	DEFLORATIONS	DEGENERACIES	DEHUMANIZATION
DEDICATORS	DEFECTIONISTS	DEFIBRINISES	DEFLOWERED	DEGENERACY	DEHUMANIZATIONS
DEDICATORY	DEFECTIONS	DEFIBRINISING	DEFLOWERER	DEGENERATE	DEHUMANIZE
DEDIFFERENTIATE	DEFECTIVELY	DEFIBRINIZE	DEFLOWERERS	DEGENERATED	DEHUMANIZED
DEDRAMATISE	DEFECTIVENESS	DEFIBRINIZED	DEFLOWERING	DEGENERATELY	DEHUMANIZES
DEDRAMATISED	DEFECTIVENESSES	DEFIBRINIZES	DEFLUXIONS	DEGENERATENESS	DEHUMANIZING
DEDRAMATISES	DEFECTIVES	DEFIBRINIZING	DEFOCUSING	DEGENERATES	DEHUMIDIFIED
DEDRAMATISING	DEFEMINISATION	DEFICIENCE	DEFOCUSSED	DEGENERATING	DEHUMIDIFIER
DEDRAMATIZE	DEFEMINISATIONS	DEFICIENCES	DEFOCUSSES	DEGENERATION	DEHUMIDIFIERS
DEDRAMATIZED	DEFEMINISE	DEFICIENCIES	DEFOCUSSING	DEGENERATIONIST	DEHUMIDIFIES
DEDRAMATIZES	DEFEMINISED	DEFICIENCY	DEFOLIANTS	DEGENERATIONS	DEHUMIDIFY
DEDRAMATIZING	DEFEMINISES	DEFICIENTLY	DEFOLIATED	DEGENERATIVE	DEHUMIDIFYING
DEDUCEMENT	DEFEMINISING	DEFICIENTNESS	DEFOLIATES	DEGENEROUS	DEHYDRATED
DEDUCEMENTS	DEFEMINIZATION	DEFICIENTNESSES	DEFOLIATING	DEGLACIATED	DEHYDRATER
DEDUCIBILITIES	DEFEMINIZATIONS	DEFICIENTS	DEFOLIATION	DEGLACIATION	DEHYDRATERS
DEDUCIBILITY	DEFEMINIZE	DEFILADING	DEFOLIATIONS	DEGLACIATIONS	DEHYDRATES
DEDUCIBLENESS	DEFEMINIZED	DEFILEMENT	DEFOLIATOR	DEGLAMORISATION	DEHYDRATING
DEDUCIBLENESSES	DEFEMINIZES	DEFILEMENTS	DEFOLIATORS	DEGLAMORISE	DEHYDRATION
DEDUCTIBILITIES	DEFEMINIZING	DEFILIATION	DEFORCEMENT	DEGLAMORISED	DEHYDRATIONS
DEDUCTIBILITY	DEFENCELESS	DEFILIATIONS	DEFORCEMENTS	DEGLAMORISES	DEHYDRATOR
DEDUCTIBLE	DEFENCELESSLY	DEFINABILITIES	DEFORCIANT	DEGLAMORISING	DEHYDRATORS
DEDUCTIBLES	DEFENCELESSNESS	DEFINABILITY	DEFORCIANTS	DEGLAMORIZATION	DEHYDROGENASE
DEDUCTIONS	DEFENCEMAN	DEFINEMENT	DEFORCIATION	DEGLAMORIZE	DEHYDROGENASES
DEDUCTIVELY	DEFENCEMEN	DEFINEMENTS	DEFORCIATIONS	DEGLAMORIZED	DEHYDROGENATE
DEEMSTERSHIP	DEFENDABLE	DEFINIENDA	DEFORESTATION	DEGLAMORIZES	DEHYDROGENATED
DEEMSTERSHIPS	DEFENDANTS	DEFINIENDUM	DEFORESTATIONS	DEGLAMORIZING	DEHYDROGENATES
DEEPFREEZE	DEFENESTRATE	DEFINIENTIA	DEFORESTED	DEGLUTINATE	DEHYDROGENATING
DEEPFREEZES	DEFENESTRATED	DEFINITELY	DEFORESTER	DEGLUTINATED	DEHYDROGENATION
DEEPFREEZING	DEFENESTRATES	DEFINITENESS	DEFORESTERS	DEGLUTINATES	DEHYDROGENISE
DEEPFROZEN	DEFENESTRATING	DEFINITENESSES	DEFORESTING	DEGLUTINATING	DEHYDROGENISED
DEEPNESSES	DEFENESTRATION	DEFINITION	DEFORMABILITIES	DEGLUTINATION	DEHYDROGENISES
DEEPWATERMAN	DEFENESTRATIONS	DEFINITIONAL	DEFORMABILITY	DEGLUTINATIONS	DEHYDROGENISING
DEEPWATERMEN	DEFENSATIVE	DEFINITIONS	DEFORMABLE	DEGLUTITION	DEHYDROGENIZE
DEERBERRIES	DEFENSATIVES	DEFINITISE	DEFORMALISE	DEGLUTITIONS	DEHYDROGENIZED
DEERGRASSES	DEFENSELESS	DEFINITISED	DEFORMALISED	DEGLUTITIVE	DEHYDROGENIZES
DEERHOUNDS	DEFENSELESSLY	DEFINITISES	DEFORMALISES	DEGLUTITORY	DEHYDROGENIZING
DEERSTALKER	DEFENSELESSNESS	DEFINITISING	DEFORMALISING	DEGRADABILITIES	DEHYDRORETINOL
DEERSTALKERS	DEFENSEMAN	DEFINITIVE	DEFORMALIZE	DEGRADABILITY	DEHYDRORETINOLS
DEERSTALKING	DEFENSEMEN	DEFINITIVELY	DEFORMALIZED	DEGRADABLE	DEHYPNOTISATION
DEERSTALKINGS	DEFENSIBILITIES	DEFINITIVENESS	DEFORMALIZES	DEGRADATION	DEHYPNOTISE
DEFACEABLE	DEFENSIBILITY	DEFINITIVES	DEFORMALIZING	DEGRADATIONS	DEHYPNOTISED
DEFACEMENT	DEFENSIBLE	DEFINITIZE	DEFORMATION	DEGRADATIVE	DEHYPNOTISES
DEFACEMENTS	DEFENSIBLENESS	DEFINITIZED	DEFORMATIONAL	DEGRADEDLY	DEHYPNOTISING
DEFACINGLY	DEFENSIBLY	DEFINITIZES	DEFORMATIONS	DEGRADINGLY	DEHYPNOTIZATION
DEFAECATED	DEFENSIVELY	DEFINITIZING	DEFORMATIVE	DEGRADINGNESS	DEHYPNOTIZE
DEFAECATES	DEFENSIVENESS	DEFINITUDE	DEFORMEDLY	DEGRADINGNESSES	DEHYPNOTIZED
DEFAECATING	DEFENSIVENESSES	DEFINITUDES	DEFORMEDNESS	DEGRANULATION	DEHYPNOTIZES
DEFAECATION	DEFENSIVES	DEFLAGRABILITY	DEFORMEDNESSES	DEGRANULATIONS	DEHYPNOTIZING
DEFAECATIONS	DEFERENCES	DEFLAGRABLE	DEFORMITIES	DEGREASANT	DEICTICALLY
DEFAECATOR	DEFERENTIAL	DEFLAGRATE	DEFRAGGERS	DEGREASANTS	DEIFICATION
DEFAECATORS	DEFERENTIALLY	DEFLAGRATED	DEFRAGGING	DEGREASERS	DEIFICATIONS
DEFALCATED	DEFERMENTS	DEFLAGRATES	DEFRAGMENT	DEGREASING	DEINDEXING
DEFALCATES	DEFERRABLE	DEFLAGRATING	DEFRAGMENTED	DEGREELESS	DEINDIVIDUATION
DEFALCATING	DEFERRABLES	DEFLAGRATION	DEFRAGMENTING	DEGRESSION	DEINDUSTRIALISE
DEFALCATION	DEFERVESCENCE	DEFLAGRATIONS	DEFRAGMENTS	DEGRESSIONS	DEINDUSTRIALIZE
DEFALCATIONS	DEFERVESCENCES	DEFLAGRATOR	DEFRAUDATION	DEGRESSIVE	DEINONYCHUS
DEFALCATOR	DEFERVESCENCIES	DEFLAGRATORS	DEFRAUDATIONS	DEGRESSIVELY	DEINONYCHUSES

d

DEINOSAURS	DELIBERATORS	DELOCALIZES	DEMENTEDLY	DEMOCRATIST	DEMONOLOGIES
DEINOTHERE	DELICACIES	DELOCALIZING	DEMENTEDNESS	DEMOCRATISTS	DEMONOLOGIST
DEINOTHERES	DELICATELY	DELPHICALLY	DEMENTEDNESSES	DEMOCRATIZATION	DEMONOLOGISTS
DEINOTHERIUM	DELICATENESS	DELPHINIUM	DEMERGERED	DEMOCRATIZE	DEMONOLOGY
DEINOTHERIUMS	DELICATENESSES	DELPHINIUMS	DEMERGERING	DEMOCRATIZED	DEMONOMANIA
DEIONISATION	DELICATESSEN	DELPHINOID	DEMERITING	DEMOCRATIZER	DEMONOMANIAS
DEIONISATIONS	DELICATESSENS	DELTIOLOGIES	DEMERITORIOUS	DEMOCRATIZERS	DEMONSTRABILITY
DEIONISERS	DELICIOUSLY	DELTIOLOGIST	DEMERITORIOUSLY	DEMOCRATIZES	DEMONSTRABLE
DEIONISING	DELICIOUSNESS	DELTIOLOGISTS	DEMERSIONS	DEMOCRATIZING	DEMONSTRABLY
DEIONIZATION	DELICIOUSNESSES	DELTIOLOGY	DEMIBASTION	DEMODULATE	DEMONSTRATE
DEIONIZATIONS	DELIGATION	DELTOIDEUS	DEMIBASTIONS	DEMODULATED	DEMONSTRATED
DEIONIZERS	DELIGATIONS	DELUDINGLY	DEMICANTON	DEMODULATES	DEMONSTRATES
DEIONIZING	DELIGHTEDLY	DELUNDUNGS	DEMICANTONS	DEMODULATING	DEMONSTRATING
DEIPNOSOPHIST	DELIGHTEDNESS	DELUSIONAL	DEMIGODDESS	DEMODULATION	DEMONSTRATION
DEIPNOSOPHISTS	DELIGHTEDNESSES	DELUSIONARY	DEMIGODDESSES	DEMODULATIONS	DEMONSTRATIONAL
DEISTICALLY	DELIGHTERS	DELUSIONIST	DEMIGRATION	DEMODULATOR	DEMONSTRATIONS
DEJECTEDLY	DELIGHTFUL	DELUSIONISTS	DEMIGRATIONS	DEMODULATORS	DEMONSTRATIVE
DEJECTEDNESS	DELIGHTFULLY	DELUSIVELY	DEMILITARISE	DEMOGRAPHER	DEMONSTRATIVELY
DEJECTEDNESSES	DELIGHTFULNESS	DELUSIVENESS	DEMILITARISED	DEMOGRAPHERS	DEMONSTRATIVES
DEJECTIONS	DELIGHTING	DELUSIVENESSES	DEMILITARISES	DEMOGRAPHIC	DEMONSTRATOR
DEKALITERS	DELIGHTLESS	DELUSTERED	DEMILITARISING	DEMOGRAPHICAL	DEMONSTRATORS
DEKALITRES	DELIGHTSOME	DELUSTERING	DEMILITARIZE	DEMOGRAPHICALLY	DEMONSTRATORY
DEKALOGIES	DELIMITATE	DELUSTRANT	DEMILITARIZED	DEMOGRAPHICS	DEMORALISATION
DEKAMETERS	DELIMITATED	DELUSTRANTS	DEMILITARIZES	DEMOGRAPHIES	DEMORALISATIONS
DEKAMETRES	DELIMITATES	DEMAGNETISATION	DEMILITARIZING	DEMOGRAPHIST	DEMORALISE
DEKAMETRIC	DELIMITATING	DEMAGNETISE	DEMIMONDAINE	DEMOGRAPHISTS	DEMORALISED
DELAMINATE	DELIMITATION	DEMAGNETISED	DEMIMONDAINES	DEMOGRAPHY	DEMORALISER
DELAMINATED	DELIMITATIONS	DEMAGNETISER	DEMIMONDES	DEMOISELLE	DEMORALISERS
DELAMINATES	DELIMITATIVE	DEMAGNETISERS	DEMINERALISE	DEMOISELLES	DEMORALISES
DELAMINATING	DELIMITERS	DEMAGNETISES	DEMINERALISED	DEMOLISHED	DEMORALISING
DELAMINATION	DELIMITING	DEMAGNETISING	DEMINERALISER	DEMOLISHER	DEMORALISINGLY
DELAMINATIONS	DELINEABLE	DEMAGNETIZATION	DEMINERALISERS	DEMOLISHERS	DEMORALIZATION
DELAPSIONS	DELINEATED	DEMAGNETIZE	DEMINERALISES	DEMOLISHES	DEMORALIZATIONS
DELASSEMENT	DELINEATES	DEMAGNETIZED	DEMINERALISING	DEMOLISHING	DEMORALIZE
DELASSEMENTS	DELINEATING	DEMAGNETIZER	DEMINERALIZE	DEMOLISHMENT	DEMORALIZED
DELAYERING	DELINEATION	DEMAGNETIZERS	DEMINERALIZED	DEMOLISHMENTS	DEMORALIZER
DELAYERINGS	DELINEATIONS	DEMAGNETIZES	DEMINERALIZER	DEMOLITION	DEMORALIZERS
DELAYINGLY	DELINEATIVE	DEMAGNETIZING	DEMINERALIZERS	DEMOLITIONIST	DEMORALIZES
DELECTABILITIES	DELINEATOR	DEMAGOGICAL	DEMINERALIZES	DEMOLITIONISTS	DEMORALIZING
DELECTABILITY	DELINEATORS	DEMAGOGICALLY	DEMINERALIZING	DEMOLITIONS	DEMORALIZINGLY
DELECTABLE	DELINEAVIT	DEMAGOGIES	DEMIPIQUES	DEMOLOGIES	DEMOTICIST
DELECTABLENESS	DELINQUENCIES	DEMAGOGING	DEMIRELIEF	DEMONESSES	DEMOTICISTS
DELECTABLES	DELINQUENCY	DEMAGOGISM	DEMIRELIEFS	DEMONETARISE	DEMOTIVATE
DELECTABLY	DELINQUENT	DEMAGOGISMS	DEMIREPDOM	DEMONETARISED	DEMOTIVATED
DELECTATED	DELINQUENTLY	DEMAGOGUED	DEMIREPDOMS	DEMONETARISES	DEMOTIVATES
DELECTATES	DELINQUENTS	DEMAGOGUERIES	DEMISEMIQUAVER	DEMONETARISING	DEMOTIVATING
DELECTATING	DELIQUESCE	DEMAGOGUERY	DEMISEMIQUAVERS	DEMONETARIZE	DEMOUNTABLE
DELECTATION	DELIQUESCED	DEMAGOGUES	DEMISSIONS	DEMONETARIZED	DEMOUNTING
DELECTATIONS	DELIQUESCENCE	DEMAGOGUING	DEMITASSES	DEMONETARIZES	DEMULCENTS
DELEGACIES	DELIQUESCENCES	DEMAGOGUISM	DEMIURGEOUS	DEMONETARIZING	DEMULSIFICATION
DELEGATEES	DELIQUESCENT	DEMAGOGUISMS	DEMIURGICAL	DEMONETISATION	DEMULSIFIED
DELEGATING	DELIQUESCES	DEMANDABLE	DEMIURGICALLY	DEMONETISATIONS	DEMULSIFIER
DELEGATION	DELIQUESCING	DEMANDANTS	DEMIURGUSES	DEMONETISE	DEMULSIFIERS
DELEGATIONS	DELIQUIUMS	DEMANDINGLY	DEMIVEGGES	DEMONETISED	DEMULSIFIES
DELEGATORS	DELIRATION	DEMANDINGNESS	DEMIVIERGE	DEMONETISES	DEMULSIFYING
DELEGITIMATION	DELIRATIONS	DEMANDINGNESSES	DEMIVIERGES	DEMONETISING	DEMULTIPLEXER
DELEGITIMATIONS	DELIRIFACIENT	DEMANNINGS	DEMIVOLTES	DEMONETIZATION	DEMULTIPLEXERS
DELEGITIMISE	DELIRIFACIENTS	DEMANTOIDS	DEMIWORLDS	DEMONETIZATIONS	DEMURENESS
DELEGITIMISED	DELIRIOUSLY	DEMARCATED	DEMOBILISATION	DEMONETIZE	DEMURENESSES
DELEGITIMISES	DELIRIOUSNESS	DEMARCATES	DEMOBILISATIONS	DEMONETIZED	DEMURRABLE
DELEGITIMISING	DELIRIOUSNESSES	DEMARCATING	DEMOBILISE	DEMONETIZES	DEMURRAGES
DELEGITIMIZE	DELITESCENCE	DEMARCATION	DEMOBILISED	DEMONETIZING	DEMUTUALISATION
DELEGITIMIZED	DELITESCENCES	DEMARCATIONS	DEMOBILISES	DEMONIACAL	DEMUTUALISE
DELEGITIMIZES	DELITESCENT	DEMARCATOR	DEMOBILISING	DEMONIACALLY	DEMUTUALISED
DELEGITIMIZING	DELIVERABILITY	DEMARCATORS	DEMOBILIZATION	DEMONIACISM	DEMUTUALISES
DELETERIOUS	DELIVERABLE	DEMARKATION	DEMOBILIZATIONS	DEMONIACISMS	DEMUTUALISING
DELETERIOUSLY	DELIVERANCE	DEMARKATIONS	DEMOBILIZE	DEMONIANISM	DEMUTUALIZATION
DELETERIOUSNESS	DELIVERANCES	DEMARKETED	DEMOBILIZED	DEMONIANISMS	DEMUTUALIZE
DELFTWARES	DELIVERERS	DEMARKETING	DEMOBILIZES	DEMONICALLY	DEMUTUALIZED
DELIBATING	DELIVERIES	DEMATERIALISE	DEMOBILIZING	DEMONISATION	DEMUTUALIZES
DELIBATION	DELIVERING	DEMATERIALISED	DEMOCRACIES	DEMONISATIONS	DEMUTUALIZING
DELIBATIONS	DELIVERYMAN	DEMATERIALISES	DEMOCRATIC	DEMONISING	DEMYELINATE
DELIBERATE	DELIVERYMEN	DEMATERIALISING	DEMOCRATICAL	DEMONIZATION	DEMYELINATED
DELIBERATED	DELOCALISATION	DEMATERIALIZE	DEMOCRATICALLY	DEMONIZATIONS	DEMYELINATES
DELIBERATELY	DELOCALISATIONS	DEMATERIALIZED	DEMOCRATIES	DEMONIZING	DEMYELINATING
DELIBERATENESS	DELOCALISE	DEMATERIALIZES	DEMOCRATIFIABLE	DEMONOCRACIES	DEMYELINATION
DELIBERATES	DELOCALISED	DEMATERIALIZING	DEMOCRATISATION	DEMONOCRACY	DEMYELINATIONS
DELIBERATING	DELOCALISES	DEMEANOURS	DEMOCRATISE	DEMONOLATER	DEMYSTIFICATION
DELIBERATION	DELOCALISING	DEMEASNURE	DEMOCRATISED	DEMONOLATERS	DEMYSTIFIED
DELIBERATIONS	DELOCALIZATION	DEMEASNURES	DEMOCRATISER	DEMONOLATRIES	DEMYSTIFIES
DELIBERATIVE	DELOCALIZATIONS	DEMENTATED	DEMOCRATISERS	DEMONOLATRY	DEMYSTIFYING
DELIBERATIVELY	DELOCALIZE	DEMENTATES	DEMOCRATISES	DEMONOLOGIC	DEMYTHOLOGISE
DELIBERATOR	DELOCALIZED	DEMENTATING	DEMOCRATISING	DEMONOLOGICAL	DEMYTHOLOGISED

DEMYTHOLOGISER
DEMYTHOLOGISERS
DEMYTHOLOGISES
DEMYTHOLOGISING
DEMYTHOLOGIZE
DEMYTHOLOGIZED
DEMYTHOLOGIZER
DEMYTHOLOGIZERS
DEMYTHOLOGIZES
DEMYTHOLOGIZING
DENATIONALISE
DENATIONALISED
DENATIONALISES
DENATIONALISING
DENATIONALIZE
DENATIONALIZED
DENATIONALIZES
DENATIONALIZING
DENATURALISE
DENATURALISED
DENATURALISES
DENATURALISING
DENATURALIZE
DENATURALIZED
DENATURALIZES
DENATURALIZING
DENATURANT
DENATURANTS
DENATURATION
DENATURATIONS
DENATURING
DENATURISE
DENATURISED
DENATURISES
DENATURISING
DENATURIZE
DENATURIZED
DENATURIZES
DENATURIZING
DENAZIFICATION
DENAZIFICATIONS
DENAZIFIED
DENAZIFIES
DENAZIFYING
DENDRACHATE
DENDRACHATES
DENDRIFORM
DENDRIMERS
DENDRITICAL
DENDRITICALLY
DENDROBIUM
DENDROBIUMS
DENDROGLYPH
DENDROGLYPHS
DENDROGRAM
DENDROGRAMS
DENDROIDAL
DENDROLATRIES
DENDROLATRY
DENDROLOGIC
DENDROLOGICAL
DENDROLOGIES
DENDROLOGIST
DENDROLOGISTS
DENDROLOGOUS
DENDROLOGY
DENDROMETER
DENDROMETERS
DENDROPHIS
DENDROPHISES
DENEGATION
DENEGATIONS
DENERVATED
DENERVATES
DENERVATING
DENERVATION
DENERVATIONS
DENIABILITIES
DENIABILITY
DENIGRATED
DENIGRATES
DENIGRATING
DENIGRATION

DENIGRATIONS
DENIGRATIVE
DENIGRATOR
DENIGRATORS
DENIGRATORY
DENISATION
DENISATIONS
DENITRATED
DENITRATES
DENITRATING
DENITRATION
DENITRATIONS
DENITRIFICATION
DENITRIFICATOR
DENITRIFICATORS
DENITRIFIED
DENITRIFIER
DENITRIFIERS
DENITRIFIES
DENITRIFYING
DENIZATION
DENIZATIONS
DENIZENING
DENIZENSHIP
DENIZENSHIPS
DENOMINABLE
DENOMINATE
DENOMINATED
DENOMINATES
DENOMINATING
DENOMINATION
DENOMINATIONAL
DENOMINATIONS
DENOMINATIVE
DENOMINATIVELY
DENOMINATIVES
DENOMINATOR
DENOMINATORS
DENOTATING
DENOTATION
DENOTATIONS
DENOTATIVE
DENOTATIVELY
DENOTEMENT
DENOTEMENTS
DENOUEMENT
DENOUEMENTS
DENOUNCEMENT
DENOUNCEMENTS
DENOUNCERS
DENOUNCING
DENSENESSES
DENSIFICATION
DENSIFICATIONS
DENSIFIERS
DENSIFYING
DENSIMETER
DENSIMETERS
DENSIMETRIC
DENSIMETRIES
DENSIMETRY
DENSITOMETER
DENSITOMETERS
DENSITOMETRIC
DENSITOMETRIES
DENSITOMETRY
DENTALITIES
DENTALIUMS
DENTATIONS
DENTICULATE
DENTICULATED
DENTICULATELY
DENTICULATION
DENTICULATIONS
DENTIFRICE
DENTIFRICES
DENTIGEROUS
DENTILABIAL
DENTILINGUAL
DENTILINGUALS
DENTIROSTRAL
DENTISTRIES
DENTITIONS

DENTURISTS
DENUCLEARISE
DENUCLEARISED
DENUCLEARISES
DENUCLEARISING
DENUCLEARIZE
DENUCLEARIZED
DENUCLEARIZES
DENUCLEARIZING
DENUDATING
DENUDATION
DENUDATIONS
DENUDEMENT
DENUDEMENTS
DENUMERABILITY
DENUMERABLE
DENUMERABLY
DENUNCIATE
DENUNCIATED
DENUNCIATES
DENUNCIATING
DENUNCIATION
DENUNCIATIONS
DENUNCIATIVE
DENUNCIATOR
DENUNCIATORS
DENUNCIATORY
DEOBSTRUENT
DEOBSTRUENTS
DEODORANTS
DEODORISATION
DEODORISATIONS
DEODORISED
DEODORISER
DEODORISERS
DEODORISES
DEODORISING
DEODORIZATION
DEODORIZATIONS
DEODORIZED
DEODORIZER
DEODORIZERS
DEODORIZES
DEODORIZING
DEONTOLOGICAL
DEONTOLOGIES
DEONTOLOGIST
DEONTOLOGISTS
DEONTOLOGY
DEOPPILATE
DEOPPILATED
DEOPPILATES
DEOPPILATING
DEOPPILATION
DEOPPILATIONS
DEOPPILATIVE
DEORBITING
DEOXIDATED
DEOXIDATES
DEOXIDATING
DEOXIDATION
DEOXIDATIONS
DEOXIDISATION
DEOXIDISATIONS
DEOXIDISED
DEOXIDISER
DEOXIDISERS
DEOXIDISES
DEOXIDISING
DEOXIDIZATION
DEOXIDIZATIONS
DEOXIDIZED
DEOXIDIZER
DEOXIDIZERS
DEOXIDIZES
DEOXIDIZING
DEOXYCORTONE
DEOXYCORTONES
DEOXYGENATE
DEOXYGENATED
DEOXYGENATES
DEOXYGENATING
DEOXYGENATION

DEOXYGENATIONS
DEOXYGENISE
DEOXYGENISED
DEOXYGENISES
DEOXYGENISING
DEOXYGENIZE
DEOXYGENIZED
DEOXYGENIZES
DEOXYGENIZING
DEOXYRIBOSE
DEOXYRIBOSES
DEPAINTING
DEPANNEURS
DEPARTEMENT
DEPARTEMENTS
DEPARTINGS
DEPARTMENT
DEPARTMENTAL
DEPARTMENTALISE
DEPARTMENTALISM
DEPARTMENTALIZE
DEPARTMENTALLY
DEPARTMENTS
DEPARTURES
DEPASTURED
DEPASTURES
DEPASTURING
DEPAUPERATE
DEPAUPERATED
DEPAUPERATES
DEPAUPERATING
DEPAUPERISE
DEPAUPERISED
DEPAUPERISES
DEPAUPERISING
DEPAUPERIZE
DEPAUPERIZED
DEPAUPERIZES
DEPAUPERIZING
DEPEINCTED
DEPEINCTING
DEPENDABILITIES
DEPENDABILITY
DEPENDABLE
DEPENDABLENESS
DEPENDABLY
DEPENDACIE
DEPENDACIES
DEPENDANCE
DEPENDANCES
DEPENDANCY
DEPENDANTS
DEPENDENCE
DEPENDENCES
DEPENDENCIES
DEPENDENCY
DEPENDENTLY
DEPENDENTS
DEPENDINGLY
DEPEOPLING
DEPERSONALISE
DEPERSONALISED
DEPERSONALISES
DEPERSONALISING
DEPERSONALIZE
DEPERSONALIZED
DEPERSONALIZES
DEPERSONALIZING
DEPHLEGMATE
DEPHLEGMATED
DEPHLEGMATES
DEPHLEGMATING
DEPHLEGMATION
DEPHLEGMATIONS
DEPHLEGMATOR
DEPHLEGMATORS
DEPHLOGISTICATE
DEPHOSPHORYLATE
DEPICTIONS
DEPICTURED
DEPICTURES
DEPICTURING

DEPIGMENTATION
DEPIGMENTATIONS
DEPILATING
DEPILATION
DEPILATIONS
DEPILATORIES
DEPILATORS
DEPILATORY
DEPLETABLE
DEPLETIONS
DEPLORABILITIES
DEPLORABILITY
DEPLORABLE
DEPLORABLENESS
DEPLORABLY
DEPLORATION
DEPLORATIONS
DEPLORINGLY
DEPLOYABLE
DEPLOYMENT
DEPLOYMENTS
DEPLUMATION
DEPLUMATIONS
DEPOLARISATION
DEPOLARISATIONS
DEPOLARISE
DEPOLARISED
DEPOLARISER
DEPOLARISERS
DEPOLARISES
DEPOLARISING
DEPOLARIZATION
DEPOLARIZATIONS
DEPOLARIZE
DEPOLARIZED
DEPOLARIZER
DEPOLARIZERS
DEPOLARIZES
DEPOLARIZING
DEPOLISHED
DEPOLISHES
DEPOLISHING
DEPOLITICISE
DEPOLITICISED
DEPOLITICISES
DEPOLITICISING
DEPOLITICIZE
DEPOLITICIZED
DEPOLITICIZES
DEPOLITICIZING
DEPOLYMERISE
DEPOLYMERISED
DEPOLYMERISES
DEPOLYMERISING
DEPOLYMERIZE
DEPOLYMERIZED
DEPOLYMERIZES
DEPOLYMERIZING
DEPOPULATE
DEPOPULATED
DEPOPULATES
DEPOPULATING
DEPOPULATION
DEPOPULATIONS
DEPOPULATOR
DEPOPULATORS
DEPORTABLE
DEPORTATION
DEPORTATIONS
DEPORTMENT
DEPORTMENTS
DEPOSITARIES
DEPOSITARY
DEPOSITATION
DEPOSITATIONS
DEPOSITING
DEPOSITION
DEPOSITIONAL
DEPOSITIONS
DEPOSITIVE
DEPOSITORIES
DEPOSITORS
DEPOSITORY

DEPRAVATION
DEPRAVATIONS
DEPRAVEDLY
DEPRAVEDNESS
DEPRAVEDNESSES
DEPRAVEMENT
DEPRAVEMENTS
DEPRAVINGLY
DEPRAVITIES
DEPRECABLE
DEPRECATED
DEPRECATES
DEPRECATING
DEPRECATINGLY
DEPRECATION
DEPRECATIONS
DEPRECATIVE
DEPRECATIVELY
DEPRECATOR
DEPRECATORILY
DEPRECATORS
DEPRECATORY
DEPRECIABLE
DEPRECIATE
DEPRECIATED
DEPRECIATES
DEPRECIATING
DEPRECIATINGLY
DEPRECIATION
DEPRECIATIONS
DEPRECIATIVE
DEPRECIATOR
DEPRECIATORS
DEPRECIATORY
DEPREDATED
DEPREDATES
DEPREDATING
DEPREDATION
DEPREDATIONS
DEPREDATOR
DEPREDATORS
DEPREDATORY
DEPREHENDED
DEPREHENDING
DEPREHENDS
DEPRESSANT
DEPRESSANTS
DEPRESSIBLE
DEPRESSING
DEPRESSINGLY
DEPRESSION
DEPRESSIONS
DEPRESSIVE
DEPRESSIVELY
DEPRESSIVENESS
DEPRESSIVES
DEPRESSOMOTOR
DEPRESSOMOTORS
DEPRESSORS
DEPRESSURISE
DEPRESSURISED
DEPRESSURISES
DEPRESSURISING
DEPRESSURIZE
DEPRESSURIZED
DEPRESSURIZES
DEPRESSURIZING
DEPRIVABLE
DEPRIVATION
DEPRIVATIONS
DEPRIVATIVE
DEPRIVEMENT
DEPRIVEMENTS
DEPROGRAMED
DEPROGRAMING
DEPROGRAMME
DEPROGRAMMED
DEPROGRAMMER
DEPROGRAMMERS
DEPROGRAMMES
DEPROGRAMMING
DEPROGRAMS
DEPURATING

d

DEPURATION	DEREQUISITION	DESACRALISATION	DESECRATOR	DESIGNATION	DESPICABILITIES
DEPURATIONS	DEREQUISITIONED	DESACRALISE	DESECRATORS	DESIGNATIONS	DESPICABILITY
DEPURATIVE	DEREQUISITIONS	DESACRALISED	DESEGREGATE	DESIGNATIVE	DESPICABLE
DEPURATIVES	DERESTRICT	DESACRALISES	DESEGREGATED	DESIGNATOR	DESPICABLENESS
DEPURATORS	DERESTRICTED	DESACRALISING	DESEGREGATES	DESIGNATORS	DESPICABLY
DEPURATORY	DERESTRICTING	DESACRALIZATION	DESEGREGATING	DESIGNATORY	DESPIRITUALISE
DEPUTATION	DERESTRICTION	DESACRALIZE	DESEGREGATION	DESIGNEDLY	DESPIRITUALISED
DEPUTATIONS	DERESTRICTIONS	DESACRALIZED	DESEGREGATIONS	DESIGNINGLY	DESPIRITUALISES
DEPUTISATION	DERESTRICTS	DESACRALIZES	DESELECTED	DESIGNINGS	DESPIRITUALIZE
DEPUTISATIONS	DERIDINGLY	DESACRALIZING	DESELECTING	DESIGNLESS	DESPIRITUALIZED
DEPUTISING	DERISIVELY	DESAGREMENT	DESELECTION	DESIGNMENT	DESPIRITUALIZES
DEPUTIZATION	DERISIVENESS	DESAGREMENTS	DESELECTIONS	DESIGNMENTS	DESPISABLE
DEPUTIZATIONS	DERISIVENESSES	DESALINATE	DESENSITISATION	DESILVERED	DESPISEDNESS
DEPUTIZING	DERIVATION	DESALINATED	DESENSITISE	DESILVERING	DESPISEDNESSES
DERACIALISE	DERIVATIONAL	DESALINATES	DESENSITISED	DESILVERISATION	DESPISEMENT
DERACIALISED	DERIVATIONIST	DESALINATING	DESENSITISER	DESILVERISE	DESPISEMENTS
DERACIALISES	DERIVATIONISTS	DESALINATION	DESENSITISERS	DESILVERISED	DESPITEFUL
DERACIALISING	DERIVATIONS	DESALINATIONS	DESENSITISES	DESILVERISES	DESPITEFULLY
DERACIALIZE	DERIVATISATION	DESALINATOR	DESENSITISING	DESILVERISING	DESPITEFULNESS
DERACIALIZED	DERIVATISATIONS	DESALINATORS	DESENSITIZATION	DESILVERIZATION	DESPITEOUS
DERACIALIZES	DERIVATISE	DESALINISATION	DESENSITIZE	DESILVERIZE	DESPITEOUSLY
DERACIALIZING	DERIVATISED	DESALINISATIONS	DESENSITIZED	DESILVERIZED	DESPOILERS
DERACINATE	DERIVATISES	DESALINISE	DESENSITIZER	DESILVERIZES	DESPOILING
DERACINATED	DERIVATISING	DESALINISED	DESENSITIZERS	DESILVERIZING	DESPOILMENT
DERACINATES	DERIVATIVE	DESALINISES	DESENSITIZES	DESINENCES	DESPOILMENTS
DERACINATING	DERIVATIVELY	DESALINISING	DESENSITIZING	DESINENTIAL	DESPOLIATION
DERACINATION	DERIVATIVENESS	DESALINIZATION	DESERPIDINE	DESIPIENCE	DESPOLIATIONS
DERACINATIONS	DERIVATIVES	DESALINIZATIONS	DESERPIDINES	DESIPIENCES	DESPONDENCE
DERAIGNING	DERIVATIZATION	DESALINIZE	DESERTIFICATION	DESIPRAMINE	DESPONDENCES
DERAIGNMENT	DERIVATIZATIONS	DESALINIZED	DESERTIFIED	DESIPRAMINES	DESPONDENCIES
DERAIGNMENTS	DERIVATIZE	DESALINIZES	DESERTIFIES	DESIRABILITIES	DESPONDENCY
DERAILLEUR	DERIVATIZED	DESALINIZING	DESERTIFYING	DESIRABILITY	DESPONDENT
DERAILLEURS	DERIVATIZES	DESALTINGS	DESERTIONS	DESIRABLENESS	DESPONDENTLY
DERAILMENT	DERIVATIZING	DESATURATION	DESERTISATION	DESIRABLENESSES	DESPONDING
DERAILMENTS	DERMABRASION	DESATURATIONS	DESERTISATIONS	DESIRABLES	DESPONDINGLY
DERANGEMENT	DERMABRASIONS	DESCANTERS	DESERTIZATION	DESIRELESS	DESPONDINGS
DERANGEMENTS	DERMAPTERAN	DESCANTING	DESERTIZATIONS	DESIROUSLY	DESPOTATES
DERATIONED	DERMAPTERANS	DESCENDABLE	DESERTLESS	DESIROUSNESS	DESPOTICAL
DERATIONING	DERMATITIS	DESCENDANT	DESERVEDLY	DESIROUSNESSES	DESPOTICALLY
DEREALISATION	DERMATITISES	DESCENDANTS	DESERVEDNESS	DESISTANCE	DESPOTICALNESS
DEREALISATIONS	DERMATOGEN	DESCENDENT	DESERVEDNESSES	DESISTANCES	DESPOTISMS
DEREALIZATION	DERMATOGENS	DESCENDENTS	DESERVINGLY	DESISTENCE	DESPOTOCRACIES
DEREALIZATIONS	DERMATOGLYPHIC	DESCENDERS	DESERVINGNESS	DESISTENCES	DESPOTOCRACY
DERECOGNISE	DERMATOGLYPHICS	DESCENDEUR	DESERVINGNESSES	DESKILLING	DESPUMATED
DERECOGNISED	DERMATOGRAPHIA	DESCENDEURS	DESERVINGS	DESKILLINGS	DESPUMATES
DERECOGNISES	DERMATOGRAPHIAS	DESCENDIBLE	DESEXUALISATION	DESMODIUMS	DESPUMATING
DERECOGNISING	DERMATOGRAPHIC	DESCENDING	DESEXUALISE	DESMODROMIC	DESPUMATION
DERECOGNITION	DERMATOGRAPHIES	DESCENDINGS	DESEXUALISED	DESMOSOMAL	DESPUMATIONS
DERECOGNITIONS	DERMATOGRAPHY	DESCENSION	DESEXUALISES	DESMOSOMES	DESQUAMATE
DERECOGNIZE	DERMATOLOGIC	DESCENSIONAL	DESEXUALISING	DESNOODING	DESQUAMATED
DERECOGNIZED	DERMATOLOGICAL	DESCENSIONS	DESEXUALIZATION	DESOBLIGEANTE	DESQUAMATES
DERECOGNIZES	DERMATOLOGIES	DESCHOOLED	DESEXUALIZE	DESOBLIGEANTES	DESQUAMATING
DERECOGNIZING	DERMATOLOGIST	DESCHOOLER	DESEXUALIZED	DESOLATELY	DESQUAMATION
DEREGISTER	DERMATOLOGISTS	DESCHOOLERS	DESEXUALIZES	DESOLATENESS	DESQUAMATIONS
DEREGISTERED	DERMATOLOGY	DESCHOOLING	DESEXUALIZING	DESOLATENESSES	DESQUAMATIVE
DEREGISTERING	DERMATOMAL	DESCHOOLINGS	DESHABILLE	DESOLATERS	DESQUAMATORY
DEREGISTERS	DERMATOMES	DESCRAMBLE	DESHABILLES	DESOLATING	DESSERTSPOON
DEREGISTRATION	DERMATOMIC	DESCRAMBLED	DESICCANTS	DESOLATINGLY	DESSERTSPOONFUL
DEREGISTRATIONS	DERMATOMYOSITIS	DESCRAMBLER	DESICCATED	DESOLATION	DESSERTSPOONS
DEREGULATE	DERMATOPHYTE	DESCRAMBLERS	DESICCATES	DESOLATIONS	DESSIATINE
DEREGULATED	DERMATOPHYTES	DESCRAMBLES	DESICCATING	DESOLATORS	DESSIATINES
DEREGULATES	DERMATOPHYTIC	DESCRAMBLING	DESICCATION	DESOLATORY	DESSIGNMENT
DEREGULATING	DERMATOPHYTOSES	DESCRIBABLE	DESICCATIONS	DESORIENTE	DESSIGNMENTS
DEREGULATION	DERMATOPHYTOSIS	DESCRIBERS	DESICCATIVE	DESORPTION	DESSYATINE
DEREGULATIONS	DERMATOPLASTIC	DESCRIBING	DESICCATIVES	DESORPTIONS	DESSYATINES
DEREGULATOR	DERMATOPLASTIES	DESCRIPTION	DESICCATOR	DESOXYRIBOSE	DESTABILISATION
DEREGULATORS	DERMATOPLASTY	DESCRIPTIONS	DESICCATORS	DESOXYRIBOSES	DESTABILISE
DEREGULATORY	DERMATOSES	DESCRIPTIVE	DESIDERATA	DESPAIRERS	DESTABILISED
DERELICTION	DERMATOSIS	DESCRIPTIVELY	DESIDERATE	DESPAIRFUL	DESTABILISER
DERELICTIONS	DERMESTIDS	DESCRIPTIVENESS	DESIDERATED	DESPAIRING	DESTABILISERS
DERELIGIONISE	DERMOGRAPHIES	DESCRIPTIVISM	DESIDERATES	DESPAIRINGLY	DESTABILISES
DERELIGIONISED	DERMOGRAPHY	DESCRIPTIVISMS	DESIDERATING	DESPATCHED	DESTABILISING
DERELIGIONISES	DEROGATELY	DESCRIPTIVIST	DESIDERATION	DESPATCHER	DESTABILIZATION
DERELIGIONISING	DEROGATING	DESCRIPTOR	DESIDERATIONS	DESPATCHERS	DESTABILIZE
DERELIGIONIZE	DEROGATION	DESCRIPTORS	DESIDERATIVE	DESPATCHES	DESTABILIZED
DERELIGIONIZED	DEROGATIONS	DESCRIVING	DESIDERATIVES	DESPATCHING	DESTABILIZER
DERELIGIONIZES	DEROGATIVE	DESECRATED	DESIDERATUM	DESPERADOES	DESTABILIZERS
DERELIGIONIZING	DEROGATIVELY	DESECRATER	DESIDERIUM	DESPERADOS	DESTABILIZES
DEREPRESSED	DEROGATORILY	DESECRATERS	DESIDERIUMS	DESPERATELY	DESTABILIZING
DEREPRESSES	DEROGATORINESS	DESECRATES	DESIGNABLE	DESPERATENESS	DESTAINING
DEREPRESSING	DEROGATORY	DESECRATING	DESIGNATED	DESPERATENESSES	DESTEMPERED
DEREPRESSION	DERRICKING	DESECRATION	DESIGNATES	DESPERATION	DESTEMPERING
DEREPRESSIONS	DERRINGERS	DESECRATIONS	DESIGNATING	DESPERATIONS	DESTEMPERS

DESTINATED
DESTINATES
DESTINATING
DESTINATION
DESTINATIONS
DESTITUTED
DESTITUTENESS
DESTITUTENESSES
DESTITUTES
DESTITUTING
DESTITUTION
DESTITUTIONS
DESTOCKING
DESTROYABLE
DESTROYERS
DESTROYING
DESTRUCTED
DESTRUCTIBILITY
DESTRUCTIBLE
DESTRUCTING
DESTRUCTION
DESTRUCTIONAL
DESTRUCTIONIST
DESTRUCTIONISTS
DESTRUCTIONS
DESTRUCTIVE
DESTRUCTIVELY
DESTRUCTIVENESS
DESTRUCTIVES
DESTRUCTIVIST
DESTRUCTIVISTS
DESTRUCTIVITIES
DESTRUCTIVITY
DESTRUCTOR
DESTRUCTORS
DESTRUCTOS
DESUETUDES
DESUGARING
DESULFURED
DESULFURING
DESULFURISATION
DESULFURISE
DESULFURISED
DESULFURISES
DESULFURISING
DESULFURIZATION
DESULFURIZE
DESULFURIZED
DESULFURIZES
DESULFURIZING
DESULPHURATE
DESULPHURATED
DESULPHURATES
DESULPHURATING
DESULPHURATION
DESULPHURATIONS
DESULPHURED
DESULPHURING
DESULPHURISE
DESULPHURISED
DESULPHURISER
DESULPHURISERS
DESULPHURISES
DESULPHURISING
DESULPHURIZE
DESULPHURIZED
DESULPHURIZER
DESULPHURIZERS
DESULPHURIZES
DESULPHURIZING
DESULPHURS
DESULTORILY
DESULTORINESS
DESULTORINESSES
DETACHABILITIES
DETACHABILITY
DETACHABLE
DETACHABLY
DETACHEDLY
DETACHEDNESS
DETACHEDNESSES
DETACHMENT
DETACHMENTS

DETAILEDLY
DETAILEDNESS
DETAILEDNESSES
DETAILINGS
DETAINABLE
DETAINMENT
DETAINMENTS
DETASSELED
DETASSELING
DETASSELLED
DETASSELLING
DETECTABILITIES
DETECTABILITY
DETECTABLE
DETECTIBLE
DETECTIONS
DETECTIVELIKE
DETECTIVES
DETECTIVIST
DETECTIVISTS
DETECTOPHONE
DETECTOPHONES
DETECTORIST
DETECTORISTS
DETENTIONS
DETENTISTS
DETERGENCE
DETERGENCES
DETERGENCIES
DETERGENCY
DETERGENTS
DETERIORATE
DETERIORATED
DETERIORATES
DETERIORATING
DETERIORATION
DETERIORATIONS
DETERIORATIVE
DETERIORISM
DETERIORISMS
DETERIORITIES
DETERIORITY
DETERMENTS
DETERMINABILITY
DETERMINABLE
DETERMINABLY
DETERMINACIES
DETERMINACY
DETERMINANT
DETERMINANTAL
DETERMINANTS
DETERMINATE
DETERMINATED
DETERMINATELY
DETERMINATENESS
DETERMINATES
DETERMINATING
DETERMINATION
DETERMINATIONS
DETERMINATIVE
DETERMINATIVELY
DETERMINATIVES
DETERMINATOR
DETERMINATORS
DETERMINED
DETERMINEDLY
DETERMINEDNESS
DETERMINENTALLY
DETERMINER
DETERMINERS
DETERMINES
DETERMINING
DETERMINISM
DETERMINISMS
DETERMINIST
DETERMINISTIC
DETERMINISTS
DETERRABILITIES
DETERRABILITY
DETERRABLE
DETERRENCE
DETERRENCES
DETERRENTLY
DETERRENTS

DETERSIONS
DETERSIVES
DETESTABILITIES
DETESTABILITY
DETESTABLE
DETESTABLENESS
DETESTABLY
DETESTATION
DETESTATIONS
DETHATCHED
DETHATCHES
DETHATCHING
DETHRONEMENT
DETHRONEMENTS
DETHRONERS
DETHRONING
DETHRONINGS
DETONABILITIES
DETONABILITY
DETONATABLE
DETONATING
DETONATION
DETONATIONS
DETONATIVE
DETONATORS
DETORSIONS
DETORTIONS
DETOXICANT
DETOXICANTS
DETOXICATE
DETOXICATED
DETOXICATES
DETOXICATING
DETOXICATION
DETOXICATIONS
DETOXIFICATION
DETOXIFICATIONS
DETOXIFIED
DETOXIFIES
DETOXIFYING
DETRACTING
DETRACTINGLY
DETRACTINGS
DETRACTION
DETRACTIONS
DETRACTIVE
DETRACTIVELY
DETRACTORS
DETRACTORY
DETRACTRESS
DETRACTRESSES
DETRAINING
DETRAINMENT
DETRAINMENTS
DETRAQUEES
DETRIBALISATION
DETRIBALISE
DETRIBALISED
DETRIBALISES
DETRIBALISING
DETRIBALIZATION
DETRIBALIZE
DETRIBALIZED
DETRIBALIZES
DETRIBALIZING
DETRIMENTAL
DETRIMENTALLY
DETRIMENTALS
DETRIMENTS
DETRITIONS
DETRITOVORE
DETRITOVORES
DETRUNCATE
DETRUNCATED
DETRUNCATES
DETRUNCATING
DETRUNCATION
DETRUNCATIONS
DETRUSIONS
DETUMESCENCE
DETUMESCENCES
DETUMESCENT
DEUTERAGONIST

DEUTERAGONISTS
DEUTERANOMALIES
DEUTERANOMALOUS
DEUTERANOMALY
DEUTERANOPE
DEUTERANOPES
DEUTERANOPIA
DEUTERANOPIAS
DEUTERANOPIC
DEUTERATED
DEUTERATES
DEUTERATING
DEUTERATION
DEUTERATIONS
DEUTERIDES
DEUTERIUMS
DEUTEROGAMIES
DEUTEROGAMIST
DEUTEROGAMISTS
DEUTEROGAMY
DEUTEROPLASM
DEUTEROPLASMS
DEUTEROSCOPIC
DEUTEROSCOPIES
DEUTEROSCOPY
DEUTEROSTOME
DEUTEROSTOMES
DEUTEROTOKIES
DEUTEROTOKY
DEUTOPLASM
DEUTOPLASMIC
DEUTOPLASMS
DEUTOPLASTIC
DEVALORISATION
DEVALORISATIONS
DEVALORISE
DEVALORISED
DEVALORISES
DEVALORISING
DEVALORIZATION
DEVALORIZATIONS
DEVALORIZE
DEVALORIZED
DEVALORIZES
DEVALORIZING
DEVALUATED
DEVALUATES
DEVALUATING
DEVALUATION
DEVALUATIONS
DEVANAGARI
DEVANAGARIS
DEVASTATED
DEVASTATES
DEVASTATING
DEVASTATINGLY
DEVASTATION
DEVASTATIONS
DEVASTATIVE
DEVASTATOR
DEVASTATORS
DEVASTAVIT
DEVASTAVITS
DEVELOPABLE
DEVELOPERS
DEVELOPING
DEVELOPMENT
DEVELOPMENTAL
DEVELOPMENTALLY
DEVELOPMENTS
DEVELOPPES
DEVERBATIVE
DEVERBATIVES
DEVIANCIES
DEVIATIONISM
DEVIATIONISMS
DEVIATIONIST
DEVIATIONISTS
DEVIATIONS
DEVILESSES
DEVILFISHES
DEVILISHLY
DEVILISHNESS

DEVILISHNESSES
DEVILMENTS
DEVILSHIPS
DEVILTRIES
DEVILWOODS
DEVIOUSNESS
DEVIOUSNESSES
DEVITALISATION
DEVITALISATIONS
DEVITALISE
DEVITALISED
DEVITALISES
DEVITALISING
DEVITALIZATION
DEVITALIZATIONS
DEVITALIZE
DEVITALIZED
DEVITALIZES
DEVITALIZING
DEVITRIFICATION
DEVITRIFIED
DEVITRIFIES
DEVITRIFYING
DEVOCALISE
DEVOCALISED
DEVOCALISES
DEVOCALISING
DEVOCALIZE
DEVOCALIZED
DEVOCALIZES
DEVOCALIZING
DEVOLUTION
DEVOLUTIONARY
DEVOLUTIONIST
DEVOLUTIONISTS
DEVOLUTIONS
DEVOLVEMENT
DEVOLVEMENTS
DEVONPORTS
DEVOTEDNESS
DEVOTEDNESSES
DEVOTEMENT
DEVOTEMENTS
DEVOTIONAL
DEVOTIONALIST
DEVOTIONALISTS
DEVOTIONALITIES
DEVOTIONALITY
DEVOTIONALLY
DEVOTIONALNESS
DEVOTIONALS
DEVOTIONIST
DEVOTIONISTS
DEVOURINGLY
DEVOURMENT
DEVOURMENTS
DEVOUTNESS
DEVOUTNESSES
DEVVELLING
DEWATERERS
DEWATERING
DEWATERINGS
DEWBERRIES
DEWINESSES
DEXAMETHASONE
DEXAMETHASONES
DEXAMPHETAMINE
DEXAMPHETAMINES
DEXIOTROPIC
DEXTERITIES
DEXTEROUSLY
DEXTEROUSNESS
DEXTEROUSNESSES
DEXTERWISE
DEXTRALITIES
DEXTRALITY
DEXTRANASE
DEXTRANASES
DEXTROCARDIA
DEXTROCARDIAC
DEXTROCARDIACS
DEXTROCARDIAS
DEXTROGLUCOSE

DEXTROGLUCOSES
DEXTROGYRATE
DEXTROGYRE
DEXTROPHOSPHATE
DEXTROROTARY
DEXTROROTATION
DEXTROROTATIONS
DEXTROROTATORY
DEXTRORSAL
DEXTRORSELY
DEXTROUSLY
DEXTROUSNESS
DEXTROUSNESSES
DEZINCKING
DHARMSALAS
DHARMSHALA
DHARMSHALAS
DIABETICAL
DIABETOGENIC
DIABETOLOGIST
DIABETOLOGISTS
DIABLERIES
DIABOLICAL
DIABOLICALLY
DIABOLICALNESS
DIABOLISED
DIABOLISES
DIABOLISING
DIABOLISMS
DIABOLISTS
DIABOLIZED
DIABOLIZES
DIABOLIZING
DIABOLOGIES
DIABOLOLOGIES
DIABOLOLOGY
DIACATHOLICON
DIACATHOLICONS
DIACAUSTIC
DIACAUSTICS
DIACHRONIC
DIACHRONICALLY
DIACHRONIES
DIACHRONISM
DIACHRONISMS
DIACHRONISTIC
DIACHRONOUS
DIACHYLONS
DIACHYLUMS
DIACODIONS
DIACODIUMS
DIACONATES
DIACONICON
DIACONICONS
DIACOUSTIC
DIACOUSTICS
DIACRITICAL
DIACRITICALLY
DIACRITICS
DIACTINISM
DIACTINISMS
DIADELPHOUS
DIADOCHIES
DIADROMOUS
DIAGENESES
DIAGENESIS
DIAGENETIC
DIAGENETICALLY
DIAGEOTROPIC
DIAGEOTROPISM
DIAGEOTROPISMS
DIAGNOSABILITY
DIAGNOSABLE
DIAGNOSEABLE
DIAGNOSING
DIAGNOSTIC
DIAGNOSTICAL
DIAGNOSTICALLY
DIAGNOSTICIAN
DIAGNOSTICIANS
DIAGNOSTICS
DIAGOMETER
DIAGOMETERS

d

DIAGONALISABLE
DIAGONALISATION
DIAGONALISE
DIAGONALISED
DIAGONALISES
DIAGONALISING
DIAGONALIZABLE
DIAGONALIZATION
DIAGONALIZE
DIAGONALIZED
DIAGONALIZES
DIAGONALIZING
DIAGONALLY
DIAGRAMING
DIAGRAMMABLE
DIAGRAMMATIC
DIAGRAMMATICAL
DIAGRAMMED
DIAGRAMMING
DIAGRAPHIC
DIAHELIOTROPIC
DIAHELIOTROPISM
DIAKINESES
DIAKINESIS
DIALECTALLY
DIALECTICAL
DIALECTICALLY
DIALECTICIAN
DIALECTICIANS
DIALECTICISM
DIALECTICISMS
DIALECTICS
DIALECTOLOGICAL
DIALECTOLOGIES
DIALECTOLOGIST
DIALECTOLOGISTS
DIALECTOLOGY
DIALLAGOID
DIALOGICAL
DIALOGICALLY
DIALOGISED
DIALOGISES
DIALOGISING
DIALOGISMS
DIALOGISTIC
DIALOGISTICAL
DIALOGISTS
DIALOGITES
DIALOGIZED
DIALOGIZES
DIALOGIZING
DIALOGUERS
DIALOGUING
DIALYPETALOUS
DIALYSABILITIES
DIALYSABILITY
DIALYSABLE
DIALYSATES
DIALYSATION
DIALYSATIONS
DIALYTICALLY
DIALYZABILITIES
DIALYZABILITY
DIALYZABLE
DIALYZATES
DIALYZATION
DIALYZATIONS
DIAMAGNETIC
DIAMAGNETICALLY
DIAMAGNETISM
DIAMAGNETISMS
DIAMAGNETS
DIAMANTIFEROUS
DIAMANTINE
DIAMETRALLY
DIAMETRICAL
DIAMETRICALLY
DIAMONDBACK
DIAMONDBACKS
DIAMONDIFEROUS
DIAMONDING
DIAMORPHINE
DIAMORPHINES

DIANTHUSES
DIAPASONAL
DIAPASONIC
DIAPAUSING
DIAPEDESES
DIAPEDESIS
DIAPEDETIC
DIAPERINGS
DIAPHANEITIES
DIAPHANEITY
DIAPHANOMETER
DIAPHANOMETERS
DIAPHANOUS
DIAPHANOUSLY
DIAPHANOUSNESS
DIAPHONIES
DIAPHORASE
DIAPHORASES
DIAPHORESES
DIAPHORESIS
DIAPHORETIC
DIAPHORETICS
DIAPHOTOTROPIC
DIAPHOTOTROPIES
DIAPHOTOTROPISM
DIAPHOTOTROPY
DIAPHRAGMAL
DIAPHRAGMATIC
DIAPHRAGMATITIS
DIAPHRAGMED
DIAPHRAGMING
DIAPHRAGMS
DIAPHYSEAL
DIAPHYSIAL
DIAPIRISMS
DIAPOPHYSES
DIAPOPHYSIAL
DIAPOPHYSIS
DIAPOSITIVE
DIAPOSITIVES
DIAPYETICS
DIARCHICAL
DIARRHETIC
DIARRHOEAL
DIARRHOEAS
DIARRHOEIC
DIARTHRODIAL
DIARTHROSES
DIARTHROSIS
DIASCORDIUM
DIASCORDIUMS
DIASKEUAST
DIASKEUASTS
DIASTALSES
DIASTALSIS
DIASTALTIC
DIASTEMATA
DIASTEMATIC
DIASTEREOISOMER
DIASTEREOMER
DIASTEREOMERIC
DIASTEREOMERS
DIASTROPHIC
DIASTROPHICALLY
DIASTROPHISM
DIASTROPHISMS
DIATESSARON
DIATESSARONS
DIATHERMACIES
DIATHERMACY
DIATHERMAL
DIATHERMANCIES
DIATHERMANCY
DIATHERMANEITY
DIATHERMANOUS
DIATHERMIA
DIATHERMIAS
DIATHERMIC
DIATHERMIES
DIATHERMOUS
DIATOMACEOUS
DIATOMICITIES
DIATOMICITY

DIATOMISTS
DIATOMITES
DIATONICALLY
DIATONICISM
DIATONICISMS
DIATRETUMS
DIATRIBIST
DIATRIBISTS
DIATROPISM
DIATROPISMS
DIAZEUCTIC
DIAZOMETHANE
DIAZOMETHANES
DIAZONIUMS
DIAZOTISATION
DIAZOTISATIONS
DIAZOTISED
DIAZOTISES
DIAZOTISING
DIAZOTIZATION
DIAZOTIZATIONS
DIAZOTIZED
DIAZOTIZES
DIAZOTIZING
DIBASICITIES
DIBASICITY
DIBENZOFURAN
DIBENZOFURANS
DIBRANCHIATE
DIBRANCHIATES
DIBROMIDES
DICACITIES
DICACITY
DICACODYLS
DICARBOXYLIC
DICARPELLARY
DICASTERIES
DICENTRICS
DICEPHALISM
DICEPHALISMS
DICEPHALOUS
DICHASIALLY
DICHLAMYDEOUS
DICHLORACETIC
DICHLORIDE
DICHLORIDES
DICHLOROBENZENE
DICHLOROETHANE
DICHLOROETHANES
DICHLOROMETHANE
DICHLORVOS
DICHLORVOSES
DICHOGAMIC
DICHOGAMIES
DICHOGAMOUS
DICHONDRAS
DICHOTICALLY
DICHOTOMIC
DICHOTOMIES
DICHOTOMISATION
DICHOTOMISE
DICHOTOMISED
DICHOTOMISES
DICHOTOMISING
DICHOTOMIST
DICHOTOMISTS
DICHOTOMIZATION
DICHOTOMIZE
DICHOTOMIZED
DICHOTOMIZES
DICHOTOMIZING
DICHOTOMOUS
DICHOTOMOUSLY
DICHOTOMOUSNESS
DICHROISCOPE
DICHROISCOPES
DICHROISCOPIC
DICHROISMS
DICHROITES
DICHROITIC
DICHROMATE
DICHROMATES
DICHROMATIC
DICHROMATICISM

DICHROMATICISMS
DICHROMATICS
DICHROMATISM
DICHROMATISMS
DICHROMATS
DICHROMISM
DICHROMISMS
DICHROOSCOPE
DICHROOSCOPES
DICHROOSCOPIC
DICHROSCOPE
DICHROSCOPES
DICHROSCOPIC
DICKCISSEL
DICKCISSELS
DICKEYBIRD
DICKEYBIRDS
DICKYBIRDS
DICLINISMS
DICOTYLEDON
DICOTYLEDONOUS
DICOTYLEDONS
DICOUMARIN
DICOUMARINS
DICOUMAROL
DICOUMAROLS
DICROTISMS
DICTATIONAL
DICTATIONS
DICTATORIAL
DICTATORIALLY
DICTATORIALNESS
DICTATORSHIP
DICTATORSHIPS
DICTATRESS
DICTATRESSES
DICTATRICES
DICTATRIXES
DICTATURES
DICTIONALLY
DICTIONARIES
DICTIONARY
DICTYOGENS
DICTYOPTERAN
DICTYOPTERANS
DICTYOSOME
DICTYOSOMES
DICTYOSTELE
DICTYOSTELES
DICUMAROLS
DICYNODONT
DICYNODONTS
DIDACTICAL
DIDACTICALLY
DIDACTICISM
DIDACTICISMS
DIDACTYLISM
DIDACTYLISMS
DIDACTYLOUS
DIDASCALIC
DIDELPHIAN
DIDELPHIDS
DIDELPHINE
DIDELPHOUS
DIDGERIDOO
DIDGERIDOOS
DIDJERIDOO
DIDJERIDOOS
DIDJERIDUS
DIDRACHMAS
DIDYNAMIAN
DIDYNAMIES
DIDYNAMOUS
DIECIOUSLY
DIECIOUSNESS
DIECIOUSNESSES
DIEFFENBACHIA
DIEFFENBACHIAS
DIELECTRIC
DIELECTRICALLY
DIELECTRICS
DIENCEPHALA
DIENCEPHALIC

DIENCEPHALON
DIENCEPHALONS
DIESELINGS
DIESELISATION
DIESELISATIONS
DIESELISED
DIESELISES
DIESELISING
DIESELIZATION
DIESELIZATIONS
DIESELIZED
DIESELIZES
DIESELIZING
DIESINKERS
DIESTRUSES
DIETARIANS
DIETETICAL
DIETETICALLY
DIETHYLAMIDE
DIETHYLAMIDES
DIETHYLAMINE
DIETHYLAMINES
DIETHYLENE
DIETHYLENES
DIETICIANS
DIETITIANS
DIFFARREATION
DIFFARREATIONS
DIFFERENCE
DIFFERENCED
DIFFERENCES
DIFFERENCIED
DIFFERENCIES
DIFFERENCING
DIFFERENCY
DIFFERENCYING
DIFFERENTIA
DIFFERENTIABLE
DIFFERENTIAE
DIFFERENTIAL
DIFFERENTIALLY
DIFFERENTIALS
DIFFERENTIATE
DIFFERENTIATED
DIFFERENTIATES
DIFFERENTIATING
DIFFERENTIATION
DIFFERENTIATOR
DIFFERENTIATORS
DIFFERENTLY
DIFFERENTNESS
DIFFERENTNESSES
DIFFICULTIES
DIFFICULTLY
DIFFICULTY
DIFFIDENCE
DIFFIDENCES
DIFFIDENTLY
DIFFORMITIES
DIFFORMITY
DIFFRACTED
DIFFRACTING
DIFFRACTION
DIFFRACTIONS
DIFFRACTIVE
DIFFRACTIVELY
DIFFRACTIVENESS
DIFFRACTOMETER
DIFFRACTOMETERS
DIFFRACTOMETRIC
DIFFRACTOMETRY
DIFFRANGIBILITY
DIFFRANGIBLE
DIFFUSEDLY
DIFFUSEDNESS
DIFFUSEDNESSES
DIFFUSENESS
DIFFUSENESSES
DIFFUSIBILITIES
DIFFUSIBILITY
DIFFUSIBLE
DIFFUSIBLENESS
DIFFUSIONAL

DIFFUSIONISM
DIFFUSIONISMS
DIFFUSIONIST
DIFFUSIONISTS
DIFFUSIONS
DIFFUSIVELY
DIFFUSIVENESS
DIFFUSIVENESSES
DIFFUSIVITIES
DIFFUSIVITY
DIFUNCTIONAL
DIFUNCTIONALS
DIGASTRICS
DIGESTANTS
DIGESTEDLY
DIGESTIBILITIES
DIGESTIBILITY
DIGESTIBLE
DIGESTIBLENESS
DIGESTIBLY
DIGESTIONAL
DIGESTIONS
DIGESTIVELY
DIGESTIVES
DIGITALINS
DIGITALISATION
DIGITALISATIONS
DIGITALISE
DIGITALISED
DIGITALISES
DIGITALISING
DIGITALISM
DIGITALISMS
DIGITALIZATION
DIGITALIZATIONS
DIGITALIZE
DIGITALIZED
DIGITALIZES
DIGITALIZING
DIGITATELY
DIGITATION
DIGITATIONS
DIGITIFORM
DIGITIGRADE
DIGITIGRADES
DIGITISATION
DIGITISATIONS
DIGITISERS
DIGITISING
DIGITIZATION
DIGITIZATIONS
DIGITIZERS
DIGITIZING
DIGITONINS
DIGITORIUM
DIGITORIUMS
DIGITOXIGENIN
DIGITOXIGENINS
DIGITOXINS
DIGLADIATE
DIGLADIATED
DIGLADIATES
DIGLADIATING
DIGLADIATION
DIGLADIATIONS
DIGLADIATOR
DIGLADIATORS
DIGLOSSIAS
DIGLYCERIDE
DIGLYCERIDES
DIGNIFICATION
DIGNIFICATIONS
DIGNIFIEDLY
DIGNIFIEDNESS
DIGNIFIEDNESSES
DIGNIFYING
DIGNITARIES
DIGONEUTIC
DIGONEUTISM
DIGONEUTISMS
DIGRAPHICALLY
DIGRESSERS
DIGRESSING

DIGRESSION
DIGRESSIONAL
DIGRESSIONARY
DIGRESSIONS
DIGRESSIVE
DIGRESSIVELY
DIGRESSIVENESS
DIHYBRIDISM
DIHYBRIDISMS
DIHYDROGEN
DIJUDICATE
DIJUDICATED
DIJUDICATES
DIJUDICATING
DIJUDICATION
DIJUDICATIONS
DILACERATE
DILACERATED
DILACERATES
DILACERATING
DILACERATION
DILACERATIONS
DILAPIDATE
DILAPIDATED
DILAPIDATES
DILAPIDATING
DILAPIDATION
DILAPIDATIONS
DILAPIDATOR
DILAPIDATORS
DILATABILITIES
DILATABILITY
DILATABLENESS
DILATABLENESSES
DILATANCIES
DILATATION
DILATATIONAL
DILATATIONS
DILATATORS
DILATOMETER
DILATOMETERS
DILATOMETRIC
DILATOMETRIES
DILATOMETRY
DILATORILY
DILATORINESS
DILATORINESSES
DILEMMATIC
DILETTANTE
DILETTANTEISH
DILETTANTEISM
DILETTANTEISMS
DILETTANTES
DILETTANTI
DILETTANTISH
DILETTANTISM
DILETTANTISMS
DILIGENCES
DILIGENTLY
DILLYDALLIED
DILLYDALLIES
DILLYDALLY
DILLYDALLYING
DILTIAZEMS
DILUCIDATE
DILUCIDATED
DILUCIDATES
DILUCIDATING
DILUCIDATION
DILUCIDATIONS
DILUTABLES
DILUTENESS
DILUTENESSES
DILUTIONARY
DILUVIALISM
DILUVIALISMS
DILUVIALIST
DILUVIALISTS
DIMENHYDRINATE
DIMENHYDRINATES
DIMENSIONAL
DIMENSIONALITY
DIMENSIONALLY

DIMENSIONED
DIMENSIONING
DIMENSIONLESS
DIMENSIONS
DIMERCAPROL
DIMERCAPROLS
DIMERISATION
DIMERISATIONS
DIMERISING
DIMERIZATION
DIMERIZATIONS
DIMERIZING
DIMETHOATE
DIMETHOATES
DIMETHYLAMINE
DIMETHYLAMINES
DIMETHYLANILINE
DIMIDIATED
DIMIDIATES
DIMIDIATING
DIMIDIATION
DIMIDIATIONS
DIMINISHABLE
DIMINISHED
DIMINISHES
DIMINISHING
DIMINISHINGLY
DIMINISHINGS
DIMINISHMENT
DIMINISHMENTS
DIMINUENDO
DIMINUENDOES
DIMINUENDOS
DIMINUTION
DIMINUTIONS
DIMINUTIVAL
DIMINUTIVE
DIMINUTIVELY
DIMINUTIVENESS
DIMINUTIVES
DIMORPHISM
DIMORPHISMS
DIMORPHOUS
DIMPLEMENT
DIMPLEMENTS
DINANDERIE
DINANDERIES
DINARCHIES
DINGDONGED
DINGDONGING
DINGINESSES
DINGLEBERRIES
DINGLEBERRY
DINITROBENZENE
DINITROBENZENES
DINITROGEN
DINITROPHENOL
DINITROPHENOLS
DINNERLESS
DINNERTIME
DINNERTIMES
DINNERWARE
DINNERWARES
DINOCERASES
DINOFLAGELLATE
DINOFLAGELLATES
DINOMANIAS
DINOSAURIAN
DINOSAURIC
DINOTHERES
DINOTHERIUM
DINOTHERIUMS
DINOTURBATION
DINOTURBATIONS
DINUCLEOTIDE
DINUCLEOTIDES
DIOECIOUSLY
DIOECIOUSNESS
DIOECIOUSNESSES
DIOESTRUSES
DIOICOUSLY
DIOICOUSNESS
DIOICOUSNESSES

DIOPHYSITE
DIOPHYSITES
DIOPTOMETER
DIOPTOMETERS
DIOPTOMETRIES
DIOPTOMETRY
DIOPTRICAL
DIOPTRICALLY
DIORISTICAL
DIORISTICALLY
DIORTHOSES
DIORTHOSIS
DIORTHOTIC
DIOSCOREACEOUS
DIOSGENINS
DIOTHELETE
DIOTHELETES
DIOTHELETIC
DIOTHELETICAL
DIOTHELISM
DIOTHELISMS
DIOTHELITE
DIOTHELITES
DIOXONITRIC
DIPEPTIDASE
DIPEPTIDASES
DIPEPTIDES
DIPETALOUS
DIPHENHYDRAMINE
DIPHENYLAMINE
DIPHENYLAMINES
DIPHENYLENIMINE
DIPHENYLKETONE
DIPHENYLKETONES
DIPHOSGENE
DIPHOSGENES
DIPHOSPHATE
DIPHOSPHATES
DIPHTHERIA
DIPHTHERIAL
DIPHTHERIAS
DIPHTHERIC
DIPHTHERITIC
DIPHTHERITIS
DIPHTHERITISES
DIPHTHEROID
DIPHTHEROIDS
DIPHTHONGAL
DIPHTHONGALLY
DIPHTHONGED
DIPHTHONGIC
DIPHTHONGING
DIPHTHONGISE
DIPHTHONGISED
DIPHTHONGISES
DIPHTHONGISING
DIPHTHONGIZE
DIPHTHONGIZED
DIPHTHONGIZES
DIPHTHONGIZING
DIPHTHONGS
DIPHYCERCAL
DIPHYLETIC
DIPHYLLOUS
DIPHYODONT
DIPHYODONTS
DIPHYSITES
DIPHYSITISM
DIPHYSITISMS
DIPLEIDOSCOPE
DIPLEIDOSCOPES
DIPLOBIONT
DIPLOBIONTIC
DIPLOBIONTS
DIPLOBLASTIC
DIPLOCARDIAC
DIPLOCOCCAL
DIPLOCOCCI
DIPLOCOCCIC
DIPLOCOCCUS
DIPLODOCUS
DIPLODOCUSES
DIPLOGENESES

DIPLOGENESIS
DIPLOIDIES
DIPLOMACIES
DIPLOMAING
DIPLOMATED
DIPLOMATES
DIPLOMATESE
DIPLOMATESES
DIPLOMATIC
DIPLOMATICAL
DIPLOMATICALLY
DIPLOMATICS
DIPLOMATING
DIPLOMATISE
DIPLOMATISED
DIPLOMATISES
DIPLOMATISING
DIPLOMATIST
DIPLOMATISTS
DIPLOMATIZE
DIPLOMATIZED
DIPLOMATIZES
DIPLOMATIZING
DIPLOMATOLOGIES
DIPLOMATOLOGY
DIPLONEMAS
DIPLOPHASE
DIPLOPHASES
DIPLOSTEMONOUS
DIPLOTENES
DIPNETTING
DIPPERFULS
DIPPINESSES
DIPRIONIDIAN
DIPROPELLANT
DIPROPELLANTS
DIPROTODON
DIPROTODONS
DIPROTODONT
DIPROTODONTID
DIPROTODONTIDS
DIPROTODONTS
DIPSOMANIA
DIPSOMANIAC
DIPSOMANIACAL
DIPSOMANIACS
DIPSOMANIAS
DIPTERISTS
DIPTEROCARP
DIPTEROCARPOUS
DIPTEROCARPS
DIPTEROSES
DIRECTEDNESS
DIRECTEDNESSES
DIRECTIONAL
DIRECTIONALITY
DIRECTIONLESS
DIRECTIONS
DIRECTIVES
DIRECTIVITIES
DIRECTIVITY
DIRECTNESS
DIRECTNESSES
DIRECTORATE
DIRECTORATES
DIRECTORIAL
DIRECTORIALLY
DIRECTORIES
DIRECTORSHIP
DIRECTORSHIPS
DIRECTRESS
DIRECTRESSES
DIRECTRICE
DIRECTRICES
DIRECTRIXES
DIREFULNESS
DIREFULNESSES
DIREMPTING
DIREMPTION
DIREMPTIONS
DIRENESSES
DIRIGIBILITIES
DIRIGIBILITY

DIRIGIBLES
DIRIGISMES
DIRTINESSES
DISABILITIES
DISABILITY
DISABLEMENT
DISABLEMENTS
DISABUSALS
DISABUSING
DISACCHARID
DISACCHARIDASE
DISACCHARIDASES
DISACCHARIDE
DISACCHARIDES
DISACCHARIDS
DISACCOMMODATE
DISACCOMMODATED
DISACCOMMODATES
DISACCORDANT
DISACCORDED
DISACCORDING
DISACCORDS
DISACCREDIT
DISACCREDITED
DISACCREDITING
DISACCREDITS
DISACCUSTOM
DISACCUSTOMED
DISACCUSTOMING
DISACCUSTOMS
DISACKNOWLEDGE
DISACKNOWLEDGED
DISACKNOWLEDGES
DISADORNED
DISADORNING
DISADVANCE
DISADVANCED
DISADVANCES
DISADVANCING
DISADVANTAGE
DISADVANTAGED
DISADVANTAGEOUS
DISADVANTAGES
DISADVANTAGING
DISADVENTURE
DISADVENTURES
DISADVENTUROUS
DISAFFECTED
DISAFFECTEDLY
DISAFFECTEDNESS
DISAFFECTING
DISAFFECTION
DISAFFECTIONATE
DISAFFECTIONS
DISAFFECTS
DISAFFILIATE
DISAFFILIATED
DISAFFILIATES
DISAFFILIATING
DISAFFILIATION
DISAFFILIATIONS
DISAFFIRMANCE
DISAFFIRMANCES
DISAFFIRMATION
DISAFFIRMATIONS
DISAFFIRMED
DISAFFIRMING
DISAFFIRMS
DISAFFOREST
DISAFFORESTED
DISAFFORESTING
DISAFFORESTMENT
DISAFFORESTS
DISAGGREGATE
DISAGGREGATED
DISAGGREGATES
DISAGGREGATING
DISAGGREGATION
DISAGGREGATIONS
DISAGGREGATIVE
DISAGREEABILITY
DISAGREEABLE
DISAGREEABLES

DISAGREEABLY
DISAGREEING
DISAGREEMENT
DISAGREEMENTS
DISALLOWABLE
DISALLOWANCE
DISALLOWANCES
DISALLOWED
DISALLOWING
DISALLYING
DISAMBIGUATE
DISAMBIGUATED
DISAMBIGUATES
DISAMBIGUATING
DISAMBIGUATION
DISAMBIGUATIONS
DISAMENITIES
DISAMENITY
DISANALOGIES
DISANALOGOUS
DISANALOGY
DISANCHORED
DISANCHORING
DISANCHORS
DISANIMATE
DISANIMATED
DISANIMATES
DISANIMATING
DISANNEXED
DISANNEXES
DISANNEXING
DISANNULLED
DISANNULLER
DISANNULLERS
DISANNULLING
DISANNULLINGS
DISANNULMENT
DISANNULMENTS
DISANOINTED
DISANOINTING
DISANOINTS
DISAPPAREL
DISAPPARELLED
DISAPPARELLING
DISAPPARELS
DISAPPEARANCE
DISAPPEARANCES
DISAPPEARED
DISAPPEARING
DISAPPEARS
DISAPPLICATION
DISAPPLICATIONS
DISAPPLIED
DISAPPLIES
DISAPPLYING
DISAPPOINT
DISAPPOINTED
DISAPPOINTEDLY
DISAPPOINTING
DISAPPOINTINGLY
DISAPPOINTMENT
DISAPPOINTMENTS
DISAPPOINTS
DISAPPROBATION
DISAPPROBATIONS
DISAPPROBATIVE
DISAPPROBATORY
DISAPPROPRIATE
DISAPPROPRIATED
DISAPPROPRIATES
DISAPPROVAL
DISAPPROVALS
DISAPPROVE
DISAPPROVED
DISAPPROVER
DISAPPROVERS
DISAPPROVES
DISAPPROVING
DISAPPROVINGLY
DISARMAMENT
DISARMAMENTS
DISARMINGLY
DISARRANGE

d

DISARRANGED	DISBENCHES	DISCHURCHING	DISCOMMENDED	DISCONTINUED	DISCREPANT
DISARRANGEMENT	DISBENCHING	DISCIPLESHIP	DISCOMMENDING	DISCONTINUER	DISCREPANTLY
DISARRANGEMENTS	DISBENEFIT	DISCIPLESHIPS	DISCOMMENDS	DISCONTINUERS	DISCRETELY
DISARRANGES	DISBENEFITS	DISCIPLINABLE	DISCOMMISSION	DISCONTINUES	DISCRETENESS
DISARRANGING	DISBOSOMED	DISCIPLINAL	DISCOMMISSIONED	DISCONTINUING	DISCRETENESSES
DISARRAYED	DISBOSOMING	DISCIPLINANT	DISCOMMISSIONS	DISCONTINUITIES	DISCRETEST
DISARRAYING	DISBOWELED	DISCIPLINANTS	DISCOMMODE	DISCONTINUITY	DISCRETION
DISARTICULATE	DISBOWELING	DISCIPLINARIAN	DISCOMMODED	DISCONTINUOUS	DISCRETIONAL
DISARTICULATED	DISBOWELLED	DISCIPLINARIANS	DISCOMMODES	DISCONTINUOUSLY	DISCRETIONALLY
DISARTICULATES	DISBOWELLING	DISCIPLINARILY	DISCOMMODING	DISCOPHILE	DISCRETIONARILY
DISARTICULATING	DISBRANCHED	DISCIPLINARITY	DISCOMMODIOUS	DISCOPHILES	DISCRETIONARY
DISARTICULATION	DISBRANCHES	DISCIPLINARIUM	DISCOMMODIOUSLY	DISCOPHORAN	DISCRETIONS
DISARTICULATOR	DISBRANCHING	DISCIPLINARIUMS	DISCOMMODITIES	DISCOPHORANS	DISCRETIVE
DISARTICULATORS	DISBUDDING	DISCIPLINARY	DISCOMMODITY	DISCOPHOROUS	DISCRETIVELY
DISASSEMBLE	DISBURDENED	DISCIPLINE	DISCOMMONED	DISCORDANCE	DISCRIMINABLE
DISASSEMBLED	DISBURDENING	DISCIPLINED	DISCOMMONING	DISCORDANCES	DISCRIMINABLY
DISASSEMBLER	DISBURDENMENT	DISCIPLINER	DISCOMMONS	DISCORDANCIES	DISCRIMINANT
DISASSEMBLERS	DISBURDENMENTS	DISCIPLINERS	DISCOMMUNITIES	DISCORDANCY	DISCRIMINANTS
DISASSEMBLES	DISBURDENS	DISCIPLINES	DISCOMMUNITY	DISCORDANT	DISCRIMINATE
DISASSEMBLIES	DISBURSABLE	DISCIPLING	DISCOMPOSE	DISCORDANTLY	DISCRIMINATED
DISASSEMBLING	DISBURSALS	DISCIPLINING	DISCOMPOSED	DISCORDFUL	DISCRIMINATELY
DISASSEMBLY	DISBURSEMENT	DISCIPULAR	DISCOMPOSEDLY	DISCORDING	DISCRIMINATES
DISASSIMILATE	DISBURSEMENTS	DISCISSION	DISCOMPOSES	DISCORPORATE	DISCRIMINATING
DISASSIMILATED	DISBURSERS	DISCISSIONS	DISCOMPOSING	DISCOTHEQUE	DISCRIMINATION
DISASSIMILATES	DISBURSING	DISCLAIMED	DISCOMPOSINGLY	DISCOTHEQUES	DISCRIMINATIONS
DISASSIMILATING	DISBURTHEN	DISCLAIMER	DISCOMPOSURE	DISCOUNSEL	DISCRIMINATIVE
DISASSIMILATION	DISBURTHENED	DISCLAIMERS	DISCOMPOSURES	DISCOUNSELLED	DISCRIMINATOR
DISASSIMILATIVE	DISBURTHENING	DISCLAIMING	DISCOMYCETE	DISCOUNSELLING	DISCRIMINATORS
DISASSOCIATE	DISBURTHENS	DISCLAMATION	DISCOMYCETES	DISCOUNSELS	DISCRIMINATORY
DISASSOCIATED	DISCALCEATE	DISCLAMATIONS	DISCOMYCETOUS	DISCOUNTABLE	DISCROWNED
DISASSOCIATES	DISCALCEATES	DISCLIMAXES	DISCONCERT	DISCOUNTED	DISCROWNING
DISASSOCIATING	DISCANDERING	DISCLOSERS	DISCONCERTED	DISCOUNTENANCE	DISCULPATE
DISASSOCIATION	DISCANDERINGS	DISCLOSING	DISCONCERTEDLY	DISCOUNTENANCED	DISCULPATED
DISASSOCIATIONS	DISCANDIED	DISCLOSURE	DISCONCERTING	DISCOUNTENANCES	DISCULPATES
DISASTROUS	DISCANDIES	DISCLOSURES	DISCONCERTINGLY	DISCOUNTER	DISCULPATING
DISASTROUSLY	DISCANDYING	DISCOBOLOS	DISCONCERTION	DISCOUNTERS	DISCUMBERED
DISATTIRED	DISCANDYINGS	DISCOBOLUS	DISCONCERTIONS	DISCOUNTING	DISCUMBERING
DISATTIRES	DISCANTERS	DISCOBOLUSES	DISCONCERTMENT	DISCOURAGE	DISCUMBERS
DISATTIRING	DISCANTING	DISCOGRAPHER	DISCONCERTMENTS	DISCOURAGEABLE	DISCURSION
DISATTRIBUTION	DISCAPACITATE	DISCOGRAPHERS	DISCONCERTS	DISCOURAGED	DISCURSIONS
DISATTRIBUTIONS	DISCAPACITATED	DISCOGRAPHIC	DISCONFIRM	DISCOURAGEMENT	DISCURSIST
DISATTUNED	DISCAPACITATES	DISCOGRAPHICAL	DISCONFIRMATION	DISCOURAGEMENTS	DISCURSISTS
DISATTUNES	DISCAPACITATING	DISCOGRAPHIES	DISCONFIRMED	DISCOURAGER	DISCURSIVE
DISATTUNING	DISCARDABLE	DISCOGRAPHY	DISCONFIRMING	DISCOURAGERS	DISCURSIVELY
DISAUTHORISE	DISCARDERS	DISCOLOGIES	DISCONFIRMS	DISCOURAGES	DISCURSIVENESS
DISAUTHORISED	DISCARDING	DISCOLOGIST	DISCONFORMABLE	DISCOURAGING	DISCURSORY
DISAUTHORISES	DISCARDMENT	DISCOLOGISTS	DISCONFORMITIES	DISCOURAGINGLY	DISCURSUSES
DISAUTHORISING	DISCARDMENTS	DISCOLORATION	DISCONFORMITY	DISCOURAGINGS	DISCUSSABLE
DISAUTHORIZE	DISCARNATE	DISCOLORATIONS	DISCONNECT	DISCOURING	DISCUSSANT
DISAUTHORIZED	DISCEPTATION	DISCOLORED	DISCONNECTED	DISCOURSAL	DISCUSSANTS
DISAUTHORISES	DISCEPTATIONS	DISCOLORING	DISCONNECTEDLY	DISCOURSED	DISCUSSERS
DISAUTHORIZING	DISCEPTATIOUS	DISCOLORMENT	DISCONNECTER	DISCOURSER	DISCUSSIBLE
DISAVAUNCE	DISCEPTATOR	DISCOLORMENTS	DISCONNECTERS	DISCOURSERS	DISCUSSING
DISAVAUNCED	DISCEPTATORIAL	DISCOLOURATION	DISCONNECTING	DISCOURSES	DISCUSSION
DISAVAUNCES	DISCEPTATORS	DISCOLOURATIONS	DISCONNECTION	DISCOURSING	DISCUSSIONAL
DISAVAUNCING	DISCEPTING	DISCOLOURED	DISCONNECTIONS	DISCOURSIVE	DISCUSSIONS
DISAVENTROUS	DISCERNABLE	DISCOLOURING	DISCONNECTIVE	DISCOURTEISE	DISCUSSIVE
DISAVENTURE	DISCERNABLY	DISCOLOURMENT	DISCONNECTS	DISCOURTEOUS	DISCUTIENT
DISAVENTURES	DISCERNERS	DISCOLOURMENTS	DISCONNEXION	DISCOURTEOUSLY	DISCUTIENTS
DISAVOUCHED	DISCERNIBLE	DISCOLOURS	DISCONNEXIONS	DISCOURTESIES	DISDAINFUL
DISAVOUCHES	DISCERNIBLY	DISCOMBOBERATE	DISCONSENT	DISCOURTESY	DISDAINFULLY
DISAVOUCHING	DISCERNING	DISCOMBOBERATED	DISCONSENTED	DISCOVERABLE	DISDAINFULNESS
DISAVOWABLE	DISCERNINGLY	DISCOMBOBERATES	DISCONSENTING	DISCOVERED	DISDAINING
DISAVOWALS	DISCERNMENT	DISCOMBOBULATE	DISCONSENTS	DISCOVERER	DISEASEDNESS
DISAVOWEDLY	DISCERNMENTS	DISCOMBOBULATED	DISCONSOLATE	DISCOVERERS	DISEASEDNESSES
DISAVOWERS	DISCERPIBILITY	DISCOMBOBULATES	DISCONSOLATELY	DISCOVERIES	DISEASEFUL
DISAVOWING	DISCERPIBLE	DISCOMEDUSAN	DISCONSOLATION	DISCOVERING	DISECONOMIES
DISBANDING	DISCERPING	DISCOMEDUSANS	DISCONSOLATIONS	DISCOVERTURE	DISECONOMY
DISBANDMENT	DISCERPTIBLE	DISCOMFITED	DISCONTENT	DISCOVERTURES	DISEMBARKATION
DISBANDMENTS	DISCERPTION	DISCOMFITER	DISCONTENTED	DISCREDITABLE	DISEMBARKATIONS
DISBARKING	DISCERPTIONS	DISCOMFITERS	DISCONTENTEDLY	DISCREDITABLY	DISEMBARKED
DISBARMENT	DISCERPTIVE	DISCOMFITING	DISCONTENTFUL	DISCREDITED	DISEMBARKING
DISBARMENTS	DISCHARGEABLE	DISCOMFITS	DISCONTENTING	DISCREDITING	DISEMBARKMENT
DISBARRING	DISCHARGED	DISCOMFITURE	DISCONTENTMENT	DISCREDITS	DISEMBARKMENTS
DISBELIEFS	DISCHARGEE	DISCOMFITURES	DISCONTENTMENTS	DISCREETER	DISEMBARKS
DISBELIEVE	DISCHARGEES	DISCOMFORT	DISCONTENTS	DISCREETEST	DISEMBARRASS
DISBELIEVED	DISCHARGER	DISCOMFORTABLE	DISCONTIGUITIES	DISCREETLY	DISEMBARRASSED
DISBELIEVER	DISCHARGERS	DISCOMFORTED	DISCONTIGUITY	DISCREETNESS	DISEMBARRASSES
DISBELIEVERS	DISCHARGES	DISCOMFORTING	DISCONTIGUOUS	DISCREETNESSES	DISEMBARRASSING
DISBELIEVES	DISCHARGING	DISCOMFORTS	DISCONTINUANCE	DISCREPANCE	DISEMBELLISH
DISBELIEVING	DISCHUFFED	DISCOMMEND	DISCONTINUANCES	DISCREPANCES	DISEMBELLISHED
DISBELIEVINGLY	DISCHURCHED	DISCOMMENDABLE	DISCONTINUATION	DISCREPANCIES	DISEMBELLISHES
DISBENCHED	DISCHURCHES	DISCOMMENDATION	DISCONTINUE	DISCREPANCY	DISEMBELLISHING

d

DISEMBITTER	DISENDOWING	DISENVIRON	DISGESTING	DISHEARTENMENTS	DISINCENTIVES
DISEMBITTERED	DISENDOWMENT	DISENVIRONED	DISGESTION	DISHEARTENS	DISINCLINATION
DISEMBITTERING	DISENDOWMENTS	DISENVIRONING	DISGESTIONS	DISHELMING	DISINCLINATIONS
DISEMBITTERS	DISENFRANCHISE	DISENVIRONS	DISGLORIFIED	DISHERISON	DISINCLINE
DISEMBODIED	DISENFRANCHISED	DISEPALOUS	DISGLORIFIES	DISHERISONS	DISINCLINED
DISEMBODIES	DISENFRANCHISES	DISEQUILIBRATE	DISGLORIFY	DISHERITED	DISINCLINES
DISEMBODIMENT	DISENGAGED	DISEQUILIBRATED	DISGLORIFYING	DISHERITING	DISINCLINING
DISEMBODIMENTS	DISENGAGEDNESS	DISEQUILIBRATES	DISGORGEMENT	DISHERITOR	DISINCLOSE
DISEMBODYING	DISENGAGEMENT	DISEQUILIBRIA	DISGORGEMENTS	DISHERITORS	DISINCLOSED
DISEMBOGUE	DISENGAGEMENTS	DISEQUILIBRIUM	DISGORGERS	DISHEVELED	DISINCLOSES
DISEMBOGUED	DISENGAGES	DISEQUILIBRIUMS	DISGORGING	DISHEVELING	DISINCLOSING
DISEMBOGUEMENT	DISENGAGING	DISESPOUSE	DISGOSPELLING	DISHEVELLED	DISINCORPORATE
DISEMBOGUEMENTS	DISENNOBLE	DISESPOUSED	DISGOWNING	DISHEVELLING	DISINCORPORATED
DISEMBOGUES	DISENNOBLED	DISESPOUSES	DISGRACEFUL	DISHEVELMENT	DISINCORPORATES
DISEMBOGUING	DISENNOBLES	DISESPOUSING	DISGRACEFULLY	DISHEVELMENTS	DISINFECTANT
DISEMBOSOM	DISENNOBLING	DISESTABLISH	DISGRACEFULNESS	DISHONESTIES	DISINFECTANTS
DISEMBOSOMED	DISENROLLED	DISESTABLISHED	DISGRACERS	DISHONESTLY	DISINFECTED
DISEMBOSOMING	DISENROLLING	DISESTABLISHES	DISGRACING	DISHONESTY	DISINFECTING
DISEMBOSOMS	DISENSHROUD	DISESTABLISHING	DISGRACIOUS	DISHONORABLE	DISINFECTION
DISEMBOWEL	DISENSHROUDED	DISESTEEMED	DISGRADATION	DISHONORABLY	DISINFECTIONS
DISEMBOWELED	DISENSHROUDING	DISESTEEMING	DISGRADATIONS	DISHONORARY	DISINFECTOR
DISEMBOWELING	DISENSHROUDS	DISESTEEMS	DISGRADING	DISHONORED	DISINFECTORS
DISEMBOWELLED	DISENSLAVE	DISESTIMATION	DISGREGATION	DISHONORER	DISINFECTS
DISEMBOWELLING	DISENSLAVED	DISESTIMATIONS	DISGREGATIONS	DISHONORERS	DISINFESTANT
DISEMBOWELMENT	DISENSLAVES	DISFAVORED	DISGRUNTLE	DISHONORING	DISINFESTANTS
DISEMBOWELMENTS	DISENSLAVING	DISFAVORING	DISGRUNTLED	DISHONOURABLE	DISINFESTATION
DISEMBOWELS	DISENTAILED	DISFAVOURED	DISGRUNTLEMENT	DISHONOURABLY	DISINFESTATIONS
DISEMBRANGLE	DISENTAILING	DISFAVOURER	DISGRUNTLEMENTS	DISHONOURED	DISINFESTED
DISEMBRANGLED	DISENTAILMENT	DISFAVOURERS	DISGRUNTLES	DISHONOURER	DISINFESTING
DISEMBRANGLES	DISENTAILMENTS	DISFAVOURING	DISGRUNTLING	DISHONOURERS	DISINFESTS
DISEMBRANGLING	DISENTAILS	DISFAVOURS	DISGUISABLE	DISHONOURING	DISINFLATION
DISEMBROIL	DISENTANGLE	DISFEATURE	DISGUISEDLY	DISHONOURS	DISINFLATIONARY
DISEMBROILED	DISENTANGLED	DISFEATURED	DISGUISEDNESS	DISHORNING	DISINFLATIONS
DISEMBROILING	DISENTANGLEMENT	DISFEATUREMENT	DISGUISEDNESSES	DISHORSING	DISINFORMATION
DISEMBROILS	DISENTANGLES	DISFEATUREMENTS	DISGUISELESS	DISHOUSING	DISINFORMATIONS
DISEMBURDEN	DISENTANGLING	DISFEATURES	DISGUISEMENT	DISHTOWELS	DISINFORMED
DISEMBURDENED	DISENTHRAL	DISFEATURING	DISGUISEMENTS	DISHUMOURED	DISINFORMING
DISEMBURDENING	DISENTHRALL	DISFELLOWSHIP	DISGUISERS	DISHUMOURING	DISINFORMS
DISEMBURDENS	DISENTHRALLED	DISFELLOWSHIPS	DISGUISING	DISHUMOURS	DISINGENUITIES
DISEMPLOYED	DISENTHRALLING	DISFIGURATION	DISGUISINGS	DISHWASHER	DISINGENUITY
DISEMPLOYING	DISENTHRALLMENT	DISFIGURATIONS	DISGUSTEDLY	DISHWASHERS	DISINGENUOUS
DISEMPLOYMENT	DISENTHRALLS	DISFIGURED	DISGUSTEDNESS	DISHWATERS	DISINGENUOUSLY
DISEMPLOYMENTS	DISENTHRALMENT	DISFIGUREMENT	DISGUSTEDNESSES	DISILLUDED	DISINHERISON
DISEMPLOYS	DISENTHRALMENTS	DISFIGUREMENTS	DISGUSTFUL	DISILLUDES	DISINHERISONS
DISEMPOWER	DISENTHRALS	DISFIGURER	DISGUSTFULLY	DISILLUDING	DISINHERIT
DISEMPOWERED	DISENTHRONE	DISFIGURERS	DISGUSTFULNESS	DISILLUMINATE	DISINHERITANCE
DISEMPOWERING	DISENTHRONED	DISFIGURES	DISGUSTING	DISILLUMINATED	DISINHERITANCES
DISEMPOWERMENT	DISENTHRONES	DISFIGURING	DISGUSTINGLY	DISILLUMINATES	DISINHERITED
DISEMPOWERMENTS	DISENTHRONING	DISFLESHED	DISGUSTINGNESS	DISILLUMINATING	DISINHERITING
DISEMPOWERS	DISENTITLE	DISFLESHES	DISHABILITATE	DISILLUSION	DISINHERITS
DISENABLED	DISENTITLED	DISFLESHING	DISHABILITATED	DISILLUSIONARY	DISINHIBIT
DISENABLEMENT	DISENTITLES	DISFLUENCIES	DISHABILITATES	DISILLUSIONED	DISINHIBITED
DISENABLEMENTS	DISENTITLING	DISFLUENCY	DISHABILITATING	DISILLUSIONING	DISINHIBITING
DISENABLES	DISENTOMBED	DISFORESTATION	DISHABILITATION	DISILLUSIONISE	DISINHIBITION
DISENABLING	DISENTOMBING	DISFORESTATIONS	DISHABILLE	DISILLUSIONISED	DISINHIBITIONS
DISENCHAIN	DISENTOMBS	DISFORESTED	DISHABILLES	DISILLUSIONISES	DISINHIBITORY
DISENCHAINED	DISENTRAIL	DISFORESTING	DISHABITED	DISILLUSIONIZE	DISINHIBITS
DISENCHAINING	DISENTRAILED	DISFORESTS	DISHABITING	DISILLUSIONIZED	DISINHUMED
DISENCHAINS	DISENTRAILING	DISFORMING	DISHABLING	DISILLUSIONIZES	DISINHUMES
DISENCHANT	DISENTRAILS	DISFRANCHISE	DISHALLOWED	DISILLUSIONMENT	DISINHUMING
DISENCHANTED	DISENTRAIN	DISFRANCHISED	DISHALLOWING	DISILLUSIONS	DISINTEGRABLE
DISENCHANTER	DISENTRAINED	DISFRANCHISES	DISHALLOWS	DISILLUSIVE	DISINTEGRATE
DISENCHANTERS	DISENTRAINING	DISFRANCHISING	DISHARMONIC	DISIMAGINE	DISINTEGRATED
DISENCHANTING	DISENTRAINMENT	DISFROCKED	DISHARMONIES	DISIMAGINED	DISINTEGRATES
DISENCHANTINGLY	DISENTRAINMENTS	DISFROCKING	DISHARMONIOUS	DISIMAGINES	DISINTEGRATING
DISENCHANTMENT	DISENTRAINS	DISFUNCTION	DISHARMONIOUSLY	DISIMAGINING	DISINTEGRATION
DISENCHANTMENTS	DISENTRANCE	DISFUNCTIONS	DISHARMONISE	DISIMMURED	DISINTEGRATIONS
DISENCHANTRESS	DISENTRANCED	DISFURNISH	DISHARMONISED	DISIMMURES	DISINTEGRATIVE
DISENCHANTS	DISENTRANCEMENT	DISFURNISHED	DISHARMONISES	DISIMMURING	DISINTEGRATOR
DISENCLOSE	DISENTRANCES	DISFURNISHES	DISHARMONISING	DISIMPASSIONED	DISINTEGRATORS
DISENCLOSED	DISENTRANCING	DISFURNISHING	DISHARMONIZE	DISIMPRISON	DISINTEREST
DISENCLOSES	DISENTRAYLE	DISFURNISHMENT	DISHARMONIZED	DISIMPRISONED	DISINTERESTED
DISENCLOSING	DISENTRAYLED	DISFURNISHMENTS	DISHARMONIZES	DISIMPRISONING	DISINTERESTEDLY
DISENCUMBER	DISENTRAYLES	DISGARNISH	DISHARMONIZING	DISIMPRISONMENT	DISINTERESTING
DISENCUMBERED	DISENTRAYLING	DISGARNISHED	DISHARMONY	DISIMPRISONS	DISINTERESTS
DISENCUMBERING	DISENTWINE	DISGARNISHES	DISHCLOTHS	DISIMPROVE	DISINTERMENT
DISENCUMBERMENT	DISENTWINED	DISGARNISHING	DISHCLOUTS	DISIMPROVED	DISINTERMENTS
DISENCUMBERS	DISENTWINES	DISGARRISON	DISHDASHAS	DISIMPROVES	DISINTERRED
DISENCUMBRANCE	DISENTWINING	DISGARRISONED	DISHEARTEN	DISIMPROVING	DISINTERRING
DISENCUMBRANCES	DISENVELOP	DISGARRISONING	DISHEARTENED	DISINCARCERATE	DISINTHRAL
DISENDOWED	DISENVELOPED	DISGARRISONS	DISHEARTENING	DISINCARCERATED	DISINTHRALLED
DISENDOWER	DISENVELOPING	DISGAVELLED	DISHEARTENINGLY	DISINCARCERATES	DISINTHRALLING
DISENDOWERS	DISENVELOPS	DISGAVELLING	DISHEARTENMENT	DISINCENTIVE	DISINTHRALS

DISINTOXICATE
DISINTOXICATED
DISINTOXICATES
DISINTOXICATING
DISINTOXICATION
DISINTRICATE
DISINTRICATED
DISINTRICATES
DISINTRICATING
DISINURING
DISINVESTED
DISINVESTING
DISINVESTITURE
DISINVESTITURES
DISINVESTMENT
DISINVESTMENTS
DISINVESTS
DISINVIGORATE
DISINVIGORATED
DISINVIGORATES
DISINVIGORATING
DISINVITED
DISINVITES
DISINVITING
DISINVOLVE
DISINVOLVED
DISINVOLVES
DISINVOLVING
DISJECTING
DISJECTION
DISJECTIONS
DISJOINABLE
DISJOINING
DISJOINTED
DISJOINTEDLY
DISJOINTEDNESS
DISJOINTING
DISJUNCTION
DISJUNCTIONS
DISJUNCTIVE
DISJUNCTIVELY
DISJUNCTIVES
DISJUNCTOR
DISJUNCTORS
DISJUNCTURE
DISJUNCTURES
DISLEAFING
DISLEAVING
DISLIKABLE
DISLIKEABLE
DISLIKEFUL
DISLIKENED
DISLIKENESS
DISLIKENESSES
DISLIKENING
DISLIMBING
DISLIMNING
DISLINKING
DISLOADING
DISLOCATED
DISLOCATEDLY
DISLOCATES
DISLOCATING
DISLOCATION
DISLOCATIONS
DISLODGEMENT
DISLODGEMENTS
DISLODGING
DISLODGMENT
DISLODGMENTS
DISLOIGNED
DISLOIGNING
DISLOYALLY
DISLOYALTIES
DISLOYALTY
DISLUSTRED
DISLUSTRES
DISLUSTRING
DISMALITIES
DISMALLEST
DISMALNESS
DISMALNESSES
DISMANNING

DISMANTLED
DISMANTLEMENT
DISMANTLEMENTS
DISMANTLER
DISMANTLERS
DISMANTLES
DISMANTLING
DISMASKING
DISMASTING
DISMASTMENT
DISMASTMENTS
DISMAYEDNESS
DISMAYEDNESSES
DISMAYFULLY
DISMAYINGLY
DISMAYLING
DISMEMBERED
DISMEMBERER
DISMEMBERERS
DISMEMBERING
DISMEMBERMENT
DISMEMBERMENTS
DISMEMBERS
DISMISSALS
DISMISSIBLE
DISMISSING
DISMISSION
DISMISSIONS
DISMISSIVE
DISMISSIVELY
DISMISSORY
DISMOUNTABLE
DISMOUNTED
DISMOUNTING
DISMUTATION
DISMUTATIONS
DISNATURALISE
DISNATURALISED
DISNATURALISES
DISNATURALISING
DISNATURALIZE
DISNATURALIZED
DISNATURALIZES
DISNATURALIZING
DISNATURED
DISNESTING
DISOBEDIENCE
DISOBEDIENCES
DISOBEDIENT
DISOBEDIENTLY
DISOBEYERS
DISOBEYING
DISOBLIGATION
DISOBLIGATIONS
DISOBLIGATORY
DISOBLIGED
DISOBLIGEMENT
DISOBLIGEMENTS
DISOBLIGES
DISOBLIGING
DISOBLIGINGLY
DISOBLIGINGNESS
DISOPERATION
DISOPERATIONS
DISORDERED
DISORDEREDLY
DISORDEREDNESS
DISORDERING
DISORDERLIES
DISORDERLINESS
DISORDERLY
DISORDINATE
DISORDINATELY
DISORGANIC
DISORGANISATION
DISORGANISE
DISORGANISED
DISORGANISER
DISORGANISERS
DISORGANISES
DISORGANISING
DISORGANIZATION
DISORGANIZE

DISORGANIZED
DISORGANIZER
DISORGANIZERS
DISORGANIZES
DISORGANIZING
DISORIENTATE
DISORIENTATED
DISORIENTATES
DISORIENTATING
DISORIENTATION
DISORIENTATIONS
DISORIENTED
DISORIENTING
DISORIENTS
DISOWNMENT
DISOWNMENTS
DISPARAGED
DISPARAGEMENT
DISPARAGEMENTS
DISPARAGER
DISPARAGERS
DISPARAGES
DISPARAGING
DISPARAGINGLY
DISPARATELY
DISPARATENESS
DISPARATENESSES
DISPARATES
DISPARITIES
DISPARKING
DISPARTING
DISPASSION
DISPASSIONATE
DISPASSIONATELY
DISPASSIONS
DISPATCHED
DISPATCHER
DISPATCHERS
DISPATCHES
DISPATCHFUL
DISPATCHING
DISPATHIES
DISPAUPERED
DISPAUPERING
DISPAUPERISE
DISPAUPERISED
DISPAUPERISES
DISPAUPERISING
DISPAUPERIZE
DISPAUPERIZED
DISPAUPERIZES
DISPAUPERIZING
DISPAUPERS
DISPELLERS
DISPELLING
DISPENCING
DISPENDING
DISPENSABILITY
DISPENSABLE
DISPENSABLENESS
DISPENSABLY
DISPENSARIES
DISPENSARY
DISPENSATION
DISPENSATIONAL
DISPENSATIONS
DISPENSATIVE
DISPENSATIVELY
DISPENSATOR
DISPENSATORIES
DISPENSATORILY
DISPENSATORS
DISPENSATORY
DISPENSERS
DISPENSING
DISPEOPLED
DISPEOPLES
DISPEOPLING
DISPERMOUS
DISPERSALS
DISPERSANT
DISPERSANTS
DISPERSEDLY

DISPERSEDNESS
DISPERSEDNESSES
DISPERSERS
DISPERSIBLE
DISPERSING
DISPERSION
DISPERSIONS
DISPERSIVE
DISPERSIVELY
DISPERSIVENESS
DISPERSOID
DISPERSOIDS
DISPIRITED
DISPIRITEDLY
DISPIRITEDNESS
DISPIRITING
DISPIRITINGLY
DISPIRITMENT
DISPIRITMENTS
DISPITEOUS
DISPITEOUSLY
DISPITEOUSNESS
DISPLACEABLE
DISPLACEMENT
DISPLACEMENTS
DISPLACERS
DISPLACING
DISPLANTATION
DISPLANTATIONS
DISPLANTED
DISPLANTING
DISPLAYABLE
DISPLAYERS
DISPLAYING
DISPLEASANCE
DISPLEASANCES
DISPLEASANT
DISPLEASED
DISPLEASEDLY
DISPLEASEDNESS
DISPLEASES
DISPLEASING
DISPLEASINGLY
DISPLEASINGNESS
DISPLEASURE
DISPLEASURED
DISPLEASURES
DISPLEASURING
DISPLENISH
DISPLENISHED
DISPLENISHES
DISPLENISHING
DISPLENISHMENT
DISPLENISHMENTS
DISPLODING
DISPLOSION
DISPLOSIONS
DISPLUMING
DISPONDAIC
DISPONDEES
DISPONGING
DISPORTING
DISPORTMENT
DISPORTMENTS
DISPOSABILITIES
DISPOSABILITY
DISPOSABLE
DISPOSABLENESS
DISPOSABLES
DISPOSEDLY
DISPOSINGLY
DISPOSINGS
DISPOSITION
DISPOSITIONAL
DISPOSITIONED
DISPOSITIONS
DISPOSITIVE
DISPOSITIVELY
DISPOSITOR
DISPOSITORS
DISPOSSESS
DISPOSSESSED
DISPOSSESSES

DISPOSSESSING
DISPOSSESSION
DISPOSSESSIONS
DISPOSSESSOR
DISPOSSESSORS
DISPOSSESSORY
DISPOSTING
DISPOSURES
DISPRAISED
DISPRAISER
DISPRAISERS
DISPRAISES
DISPRAISING
DISPRAISINGLY
DISPREADING
DISPREDDEN
DISPREDDING
DISPRINCED
DISPRISONED
DISPRISONING
DISPRISONS
DISPRIVACIED
DISPRIVILEGE
DISPRIVILEGED
DISPRIVILEGES
DISPRIVILEGING
DISPRIZING
DISPROFESS
DISPROFESSED
DISPROFESSES
DISPROFESSING
DISPROFITS
DISPROOVED
DISPROOVES
DISPROOVING
DISPROPERTIED
DISPROPERTIES
DISPROPERTY
DISPROPERTYING
DISPROPORTION
DISPROPORTIONAL
DISPROPORTIONED
DISPROPORTIONS
DISPROPRIATE
DISPROPRIATED
DISPROPRIATES
DISPROPRIATING
DISPROVABLE
DISPROVALS
DISPROVERS
DISPROVIDE
DISPROVIDED
DISPROVIDES
DISPROVIDING
DISPROVING
DISPURSING
DISPURVEYANCE
DISPURVEYANCES
DISPURVEYED
DISPURVEYING
DISPURVEYS
DISPUTABILITIES
DISPUTABILITY
DISPUTABLE
DISPUTABLENESS
DISPUTABLY
DISPUTANTS
DISPUTATION
DISPUTATIONS
DISPUTATIOUS
DISPUTATIOUSLY
DISPUTATIVE
DISPUTATIVELY
DISPUTATIVENESS
DISQUALIFIABLE
DISQUALIFIED
DISQUALIFIER
DISQUALIFIERS
DISQUALIFIES
DISQUALIFY
DISQUALIFYING
DISQUANTITIED

DISQUANTITIES
DISQUANTITY
DISQUANTITYING
DISQUIETED
DISQUIETEDLY
DISQUIETEDNESS
DISQUIETEN
DISQUIETENED
DISQUIETENING
DISQUIETENS
DISQUIETFUL
DISQUIETING
DISQUIETINGLY
DISQUIETIVE
DISQUIETLY
DISQUIETNESS
DISQUIETNESSES
DISQUIETOUS
DISQUIETUDE
DISQUIETUDES
DISQUISITION
DISQUISITIONAL
DISQUISITIONARY
DISQUISITIONS
DISQUISITIVE
DISQUISITORY
DISRANKING
DISREGARDED
DISREGARDER
DISREGARDERS
DISREGARDFUL
DISREGARDFULLY
DISREGARDING
DISREGARDS
DISRELATED
DISRELATION
DISRELATIONS
DISRELISHED
DISRELISHES
DISRELISHING
DISREMEMBER
DISREMEMBERED
DISREMEMBERING
DISREMEMBERS
DISREPAIRS
DISREPUTABILITY
DISREPUTABLE
DISREPUTABLY
DISREPUTATION
DISREPUTATIONS
DISREPUTES
DISRESPECT
DISRESPECTABLE
DISRESPECTED
DISRESPECTFUL
DISRESPECTFULLY
DISRESPECTING
DISRESPECTS
DISROBEMENT
DISROBEMENTS
DISROOTING
DISRUPTERS
DISRUPTING
DISRUPTION
DISRUPTIONS
DISRUPTIVE
DISRUPTIVELY
DISRUPTIVENESS
DISRUPTORS
DISSATISFACTION
DISSATISFACTORY
DISSATISFIED
DISSATISFIEDLY
DISSATISFIES
DISSATISFY
DISSATISFYING
DISSAVINGS
DISSEATING
DISSECTIBLE
DISSECTING
DISSECTINGS
DISSECTION
DISSECTIONS

d

DISSECTIVE	DISSHIVERED	DISSOLUTIVE	DISTILLERIES	DISTRIBUTED	DITHELETIC
DISSECTORS	DISSHIVERING	DISSOLVABILITY	DISTILLERS	DISTRIBUTEE	DITHELETICAL
DISSEISEES	DISSHIVERS	DISSOLVABLE	DISTILLERY	DISTRIBUTEES	DITHELETISM
DISSEISING	DISSIDENCE	DISSOLVABLENESS	DISTILLING	DISTRIBUTER	DITHELETISMS
DISSEISINS	DISSIDENCES	DISSOLVENT	DISTILLINGS	DISTRIBUTERS	DITHELISMS
DISSEISORS	DISSIDENTLY	DISSOLVENTS	DISTILMENT	DISTRIBUTES	DITHELITISM
DISSEIZEES	DISSIDENTS	DISSOLVERS	DISTILMENTS	DISTRIBUTING	DITHELITISMS
DISSEIZING	DISSILIENCE	DISSOLVING	DISTINCTER	DISTRIBUTION	DITHERIEST
DISSEIZINS	DISSILIENCES	DISSOLVINGS	DISTINCTEST	DISTRIBUTIONAL	DITHIOCARBAMATE
DISSEIZORS	DISSILIENT	DISSONANCE	DISTINCTION	DISTRIBUTIONS	DITHIONATE
DISSELBOOM	DISSIMILAR	DISSONANCES	DISTINCTIONS	DISTRIBUTIVE	DITHIONATES
DISSELBOOMS	DISSIMILARITIES	DISSONANCIES	DISTINCTIVE	DISTRIBUTIVELY	DITHIONITE
DISSEMBLANCE	DISSIMILARITY	DISSONANCY	DISTINCTIVELY	DISTRIBUTIVES	DITHIONITES
DISSEMBLANCES	DISSIMILARLY	DISSONANTLY	DISTINCTIVENESS	DISTRIBUTIVITY	DITHIONOUS
DISSEMBLED	DISSIMILARS	DISSUADABLE	DISTINCTIVES	DISTRIBUTOR	DITHYRAMBIC
DISSEMBLER	DISSIMILATE	DISSUADERS	DISTINCTLY	DISTRIBUTORS	DITHYRAMBICALLY
DISSEMBLERS	DISSIMILATED	DISSUADING	DISTINCTNESS	DISTRICTED	DITHYRAMBIST
DISSEMBLES	DISSIMILATES	DISSUASION	DISTINCTNESSES	DISTRICTING	DITHYRAMBISTS
DISSEMBLIES	DISSIMILATING	DISSUASIONS	DISTINCTURE	DISTRINGAS	DITHYRAMBS
DISSEMBLING	DISSIMILATION	DISSUASIVE	DISTINCTURES	DISTRINGASES	DITRANSITIVE
DISSEMBLINGLY	DISSIMILATIONS	DISSUASIVELY	DISTINGUEE	DISTROUBLE	DITRANSITIVES
DISSEMBLINGS	DISSIMILATIVE	DISSUASIVENESS	DISTINGUISH	DISTROUBLED	DITRIGLYPH
DISSEMINATE	DISSIMILATORY	DISSUASIVES	DISTINGUISHABLE	DISTROUBLES	DITRIGLYPHIC
DISSEMINATED	DISSIMILES	DISSUASORIES	DISTINGUISHABLY	DISTROUBLING	DITRIGLYPHS
DISSEMINATES	DISSIMILITUDE	DISSUASORY	DISTINGUISHED	DISTRUSTED	DITROCHEAN
DISSEMINATING	DISSIMILITUDES	DISSUNDERED	DISTINGUISHER	DISTRUSTER	DITROCHEES
DISSEMINATION	DISSIMULATE	DISSUNDERING	DISTINGUISHERS	DISTRUSTERS	DITSINESSES
DISSEMINATIONS	DISSIMULATED	DISSUNDERS	DISTINGUISHES	DISTRUSTFUL	DITTANDERS
DISSEMINATIVE	DISSIMULATES	DISSYLLABIC	DISTINGUISHING	DISTRUSTFULLY	DITTOGRAPHIC
DISSEMINATOR	DISSIMULATING	DISSYLLABLE	DISTINGUISHMENT	DISTRUSTFULNESS	DITTOGRAPHIES
DISSEMINATORS	DISSIMULATION	DISSYLLABLES	DISTORTEDLY	DISTRUSTING	DITTOGRAPHY
DISSEMINULE	DISSIMULATIONS	DISSYMMETRIC	DISTORTEDNESS	DISTRUSTLESS	DITTOLOGIES
DISSEMINULES	DISSIMULATIVE	DISSYMMETRICAL	DISTORTEDNESSES	DISTURBANCE	DITZINESSES
DISSENSION	DISSIMULATOR	DISSYMMETRIES	DISTORTERS	DISTURBANCES	DIURETICALLY
DISSENSIONS	DISSIMULATORS	DISSYMMETRY	DISTORTING	DISTURBANT	DIURETICALNESS
DISSENSUSES	DISSIPABLE	DISTAINING	DISTORTION	DISTURBANTS	DIURNALIST
DISSENTERISH	DISSIPATED	DISTANCELESS	DISTORTIONAL	DISTURBATIVE	DIURNALISTS
DISSENTERISM	DISSIPATEDLY	DISTANCING	DISTORTIONS	DISTURBERS	DIUTURNITIES
DISSENTERISMS	DISSIPATEDNESS	DISTANTNESS	DISTORTIVE	DISTURBING	DIUTURNITY
DISSENTERS	DISSIPATER	DISTANTNESSES	DISTRACTABLE	DISTURBINGLY	DIVAGATING
DISSENTIENCE	DISSIPATERS	DISTASTEFUL	DISTRACTED	DISUBSTITUTED	DIVAGATION
DISSENTIENCES	DISSIPATES	DISTASTEFULLY	DISTRACTEDLY	DISULFATES	DIVAGATIONS
DISSENTIENCIES	DISSIPATING	DISTASTEFULNESS	DISTRACTEDNESS	DISULFIDES	DIVALENCES
DISSENTIENCY	DISSIPATION	DISTASTING	DISTRACTER	DISULFIRAM	DIVALENCIES
DISSENTIENT	DISSIPATIONS	DISTELFINK	DISTRACTERS	DISULFIRAMS	DIVARICATE
DISSENTIENTLY	DISSIPATIVE	DISTELFINKS	DISTRACTIBILITY	DISULFOTON	DIVARICATED
DISSENTIENTS	DISSIPATOR	DISTEMPERATE	DISTRACTIBLE	DISULFOTONS	DIVARICATELY
DISSENTING	DISSIPATORS	DISTEMPERATURE	DISTRACTING	DISULPHATE	DIVARICATES
DISSENTINGLY	DISSOCIABILITY	DISTEMPERATURES	DISTRACTINGLY	DISULPHATES	DIVARICATING
DISSENTION	DISSOCIABLE	DISTEMPERED	DISTRACTION	DISULPHIDE	DIVARICATINGLY
DISSENTIONS	DISSOCIABLENESS	DISTEMPERING	DISTRACTIONS	DISULPHIDES	DIVARICATION
DISSENTIOUS	DISSOCIABLY	DISTEMPERS	DISTRACTIVE	DISULPHURET	DIVARICATIONS
DISSEPIMENT	DISSOCIALISE	DISTENDERS	DISTRACTIVELY	DISULPHURETS	DIVARICATOR
DISSEPIMENTAL	DISSOCIALISED	DISTENDING	DISTRAINABLE	DISULPHURIC	DIVARICATORS
DISSEPIMENTS	DISSOCIALISES	DISTENSIBILITY	DISTRAINED	DISUNIONIST	DIVEBOMBED
DISSERTATE	DISSOCIALISING	DISTENSIBLE	DISTRAINEE	DISUNIONISTS	DIVEBOMBING
DISSERTATED	DISSOCIALITIES	DISTENSILE	DISTRAINEES	DISUNITERS	DIVELLICATE
DISSERTATES	DISSOCIALITY	DISTENSION	DISTRAINER	DISUNITIES	DIVELLICATED
DISSERTATING	DISSOCIALIZE	DISTENSIONS	DISTRAINERS	DISUNITING	DIVELLICATES
DISSERTATION	DISSOCIALIZED	DISTENSIVE	DISTRAINING	DISUTILITIES	DIVELLICATING
DISSERTATIONAL	DISSOCIALIZES	DISTENTION	DISTRAINMENT	DISUTILITY	DIVERGEMENT
DISSERTATIONIST	DISSOCIALIZING	DISTENTIONS	DISTRAINMENTS	DISVALUING	DIVERGEMENTS
DISSERTATIONS	DISSOCIATE	DISTHRONED	DISTRAINOR	DISVOUCHED	DIVERGENCE
DISSERTATIVE	DISSOCIATED	DISTHRONES	DISTRAINORS	DISVOUCHES	DIVERGENCES
DISSERTATOR	DISSOCIATES	DISTHRONING	DISTRAINTS	DISVOUCHING	DIVERGENCIES
DISSERTATORS	DISSOCIATING	DISTHRONISE	DISTRAUGHT	DISWORSHIP	DIVERGENCY
DISSERTING	DISSOCIATION	DISTHRONISED	DISTRAUGHTLY	DISWORSHIPS	DIVERGENTLY
DISSERVICE	DISSOCIATIONS	DISTHRONISES	DISTRESSED	DISYLLABIC	DIVERGINGLY
DISSERVICEABLE	DISSOCIATIVE	DISTHRONISING	DISTRESSER	DISYLLABIFIED	DIVERSENESS
DISSERVICES	DISSOLUBILITIES	DISTHRONIZE	DISTRESSERS	DISYLLABIFIES	DIVERSENESSES
DISSERVING	DISSOLUBILITY	DISTHRONIZED	DISTRESSES	DISYLLABIFY	DIVERSIFIABLE
DISSEVERANCE	DISSOLUBLE	DISTHRONIZES	DISTRESSFUL	DISYLLABIFYING	DIVERSIFICATION
DISSEVERANCES	DISSOLUBLENESS	DISTHRONIZING	DISTRESSFULLY	DISYLLABISM	DIVERSIFIED
DISSEVERATION	DISSOLUTELY	DISTICHOUS	DISTRESSFULNESS	DISYLLABISMS	DIVERSIFIER
DISSEVERATIONS	DISSOLUTENESS	DISTICHOUSLY	DISTRESSING	DISYLLABLE	DIVERSIFIERS
DISSEVERED	DISSOLUTENESSES	DISTILLABLE	DISTRESSINGLY	DISYLLABLES	DIVERSIFIES
DISSEVERING	DISSOLUTES	DISTILLAND	DISTRESSINGS	DITCHDIGGER	DIVERSIFORM
DISSEVERMENT	DISSOLUTION	DISTILLANDS	DISTRIBUEND	DITCHDIGGERS	DIVERSIFYING
DISSEVERMENTS	DISSOLUTIONISM	DISTILLATE	DISTRIBUENDS	DITCHWATER	DIVERSIONAL
DISSHEATHE	DISSOLUTIONISMS	DISTILLATES	DISTRIBUTABLE	DITCHWATERS	DIVERSIONARY
DISSHEATHED	DISSOLUTIONIST	DISTILLATION	DISTRIBUTARIES	DITHEISTIC	DIVERSIONIST
DISSHEATHES	DISSOLUTIONISTS	DISTILLATIONS	DISTRIBUTARY	DITHEISTICAL	DIVERSIONISTS
DISSHEATHING	DISSOLUTIONS	DISTILLATORY	DISTRIBUTE	DITHELETES	DIVERSIONS

DIVERSITIES	DOBSONFLIES	DODECAHEDRAL	DOLICHOSAURUS	DOMICILIATION	DORSIFLEXIONS
DIVERTIBILITIES	DOCENTSHIP	DODECAHEDRON	DOLICHOSAURUSES	DOMICILIATIONS	DORSIGRADE
DIVERTIBILITY	DOCENTSHIPS	DODECAHEDRONS	DOLICHOSES	DOMICILING	DORSIVENTRAL
DIVERTIBLE	DOCHMIACAL	DODECANDROUS	DOLICHURUS	DOMINANCES	DORSIVENTRALITY
DIVERTICULA	DOCHMIUSES	DODECANOIC	DOLICHURUSES	DOMINANCIES	DORSIVENTRALLY
DIVERTICULAR	DOCIBILITIES	DODECAPHONIC	DOLLARBIRD	DOMINANTLY	DORSOLATERAL
DIVERTICULATE	DOCIBILITY	DODECAPHONIES	DOLLARBIRDS	DOMINATING	DORSOLUMBAR
DIVERTICULATED	DOCIBLENESS	DODECAPHONISM	DOLLARFISH	DOMINATINGLY	DORSOVENTRAL
DIVERTICULITIS	DOCIBLENESSES	DODECAPHONISMS	DOLLARFISHES	DOMINATION	DORSOVENTRALITY
DIVERTICULOSES	DOCILITIES	DODECAPHONIST	DOLLARISATION	DOMINATIONS	DORSOVENTRALLY
DIVERTICULOSIS	DOCIMASIES	DODECAPHONISTS	DOLLARISATIONS	DOMINATIVE	DORTINESSES
DIVERTICULUM	DOCIMASTIC	DODECAPHONY	DOLLARISED	DOMINATORS	DOSEMETERS
DIVERTIMENTI	DOCIMOLOGIES	DODECASTYLE	DOLLARISES	DOMINATRICES	DOSIMETERS
DIVERTIMENTO	DOCIMOLOGY	DODECASTYLES	DOLLARISING	DOMINATRIX	DOSIMETRIC
DIVERTIMENTOS	DOCKISATION	DODECASYLLABIC	DOLLARIZATION	DOMINATRIXES	DOSIMETRICIAN
DIVERTINGLY	DOCKISATIONS	DODECASYLLABLE	DOLLARIZATIONS	DOMINEERED	DOSIMETRICIANS
DIVERTISEMENT	DOCKIZATION	DODECASYLLABLES	DOLLARIZED	DOMINEERING	DOSIMETRIES
DIVERTISEMENTS	DOCKIZATIONS	DODGEBALLS	DOLLARIZES	DOMINEERINGLY	DOSIMETRIST
DIVERTISSEMENT	DOCKMASTER	DODGINESSES	DOLLARIZING	DOMINEERINGNESS	DOSIMETRISTS
DIVERTISSEMENTS	DOCKMASTERS	DOGARESSAS	DOLLARLESS	DOMINICKER	DOSIOLOGIES
DIVESTIBLE	DOCKWORKER	DOGBERRIES	DOLLAROCRACIES	DOMINICKERS	DOSOLOGIES
DIVESTITURE	DOCKWORKERS	DOGBERRYISM	DOLLAROCRACY	DOMINIQUES	DOSSHOUSES
DIVESTITURES	DOCQUETING	DOGBERRYISMS	DOLLARSHIP	DONATARIES	DOTCOMMERS
DIVESTMENT	DOCTORANDS	DOGCATCHER	DOLLARSHIPS	DONATISTIC	DOTTINESSES
DIVESTMENTS	DOCTORATED	DOGCATCHERS	DOLLHOUSES	DONATISTICAL	DOUBLEHEADER
DIVESTURES	DOCTORATES	DOGFIGHTING	DOLLINESSES	DONATORIES	DOUBLEHEADERS
DIVIDEDNESS	DOCTORATING	DOGGEDNESS	DOLLISHNESS	DONENESSES	DOUBLENESS
DIVIDEDNESSES	DOCTORESSES	DOGGEDNESSES	DOLLISHNESSES	DONKEYWORK	DOUBLENESSES
DIVIDENDLESS	DOCTORLESS	DOGGINESSES	DOLLYBIRDS	DONKEYWORKS	DOUBLESPEAK
DIVINATION	DOCTORSHIP	DOGGISHNESS	DOLOMITISATION	DONNICKERS	DOUBLESPEAKER
DIVINATIONS	DOCTORSHIPS	DOGGISHNESSES	DOLOMITISATIONS	DONNISHNESS	DOUBLESPEAKERS
DIVINATORIAL	DOCTRESSES	DOGGONEDER	DOLOMITISE	DONNISHNESSES	DOUBLESPEAKS
DIVINATORS	DOCTRINAIRE	DOGGONEDEST	DOLOMITISED	DONNYBROOK	DOUBLETHINK
DIVINATORY	DOCTRINAIRES	DOGLEGGING	DOLOMITISES	DONNYBROOKS	DOUBLETHINKS
DIVINENESS	DOCTRINAIRISM	DOGMATICAL	DOLOMITISING	DONORSHIPS	DOUBLETONS
DIVINENESSES	DOCTRINAIRISMS	DOGMATICALLY	DOLOMITIZATION	DOODLEBUGS	DOUBLETREE
DIVINERESS	DOCTRINALITIES	DOGMATICALNESS	DOLOMITIZATIONS	DOOHICKEYS	DOUBLETREES
DIVINERESSES	DOCTRINALITY	DOGMATISATION	DOLOMITIZE	DOOHICKIES	DOUBTFULLY
DIVINIFIED	DOCTRINALLY	DOGMATISATIONS	DOLOMITIZED	DOOMSAYERS	DOUBTFULNESS
DIVINIFIES	DOCTRINARIAN	DOGMATISED	DOLOMITIZES	DOOMSAYING	DOUBTFULNESSES
DIVINIFYING	DOCTRINARIANISM	DOGMATISER	DOLOMITIZING	DOOMSAYINGS	DOUBTINGLY
DIVINISATION	DOCTRINARIANS	DOGMATISERS	DOLORIFEROUS	DOOMSDAYER	DOUBTLESSLY
DIVINISATIONS	DOCTRINARISM	DOGMATISES	DOLORIMETRIES	DOOMSDAYERS	DOUBTLESSNESS
DIVINISING	DOCTRINARISMS	DOGMATISING	DOLORIMETRY	DOOMWATCHED	DOUBTLESSNESSES
DIVINITIES	DOCTRINISM	DOGMATISMS	DOLOROUSLY	DOOMWATCHER	DOUCENESSES
DIVINIZATION	DOCTRINISMS	DOGMATISTS	DOLOROUSNESS	DOOMWATCHERS	DOUCEPERES
DIVINIZATIONS	DOCTRINIST	DOGMATIZATION	DOLOROUSNESSES	DOOMWATCHES	DOUCHEBAGS
DIVINIZING	DOCTRINISTS	DOGMATIZATIONS	DOLOSTONES	DOOMWATCHING	DOUGHFACED
DIVISIBILITIES	DOCUDRAMAS	DOGMATIZED	DOLPHINARIA	DOOMWATCHINGS	DOUGHFACES
DIVISIBILITY	DOCUMENTABLE	DOGMATIZER	DOLPHINARIUM	DOORFRAMES	DOUGHINESS
DIVISIBLENESS	DOCUMENTAL	DOGMATIZERS	DOLPHINARIUMS	DOORKEEPER	DOUGHINESSES
DIVISIBLENESSES	DOCUMENTALIST	DOGMATIZES	DOLPHINETS	DOORKEEPERS	DOUGHNUTLIKE
DIVISIONAL	DOCUMENTALISTS	DOGMATIZING	DOLPHINFISH	DOORKNOCKED	DOUGHNUTTED
DIVISIONALLY	DOCUMENTARIAN	DOGMATOLOGIES	DOLPHINFISHES	DOORKNOCKER	DOUGHNUTTING
DIVISIONARY	DOCUMENTARIANS	DOGMATOLOGY	DOLTISHNESS	DOORKNOCKERS	DOUGHNUTTINGS
DIVISIONISM	DOCUMENTARIES	DOGNAPINGS	DOLTISHNESSES	DOORKNOCKING	DOUGHTIEST
DIVISIONISMS	DOCUMENTARILY	DOGNAPPERS	DOMESTICABLE	DOORKNOCKS	DOUGHTINESS
DIVISIONIST	DOCUMENTARISE	DOGNAPPING	DOMESTICAL	DOORPLATES	DOUGHTINESSES
DIVISIONISTS	DOCUMENTARISED	DOGNAPPINGS	DOMESTICALLY	DOORSTEPPED	DOULOCRACIES
DIVISIVELY	DOCUMENTARISES	DOGROBBERS	DOMESTICATE	DOORSTEPPER	DOULOCRACY
DIVISIVENESS	DOCUMENTARISING	DOGSBODIED	DOMESTICATED	DOORSTEPPERS	DOUPPIONIS
DIVISIVENESSES	DOCUMENTARIST	DOGSBODIES	DOMESTICATES	DOORSTEPPING	DOURNESSES
DIVORCEABLE	DOCUMENTARISTS	DOGSBODYING	DOMESTICATING	DOORSTEPPINGS	DOUROUCOULI
DIVORCEMENT	DOCUMENTARIZE	DOGSLEDDED	DOMESTICATION	DOORSTONES	DOUROUCOULIS
DIVORCEMENTS	DOCUMENTARIZED	DOGSLEDDER	DOMESTICATIONS	DOPAMINERGIC	DOVEISHNESS
DIVULGATED	DOCUMENTARIZES	DOGSLEDDERS	DOMESTICATIVE	DOPESHEETS	DOVEISHNESSES
DIVULGATER	DOCUMENTARIZING	DOGSLEDDING	DOMESTICATOR	DOPEYNESSES	DOVETAILED
DIVULGATERS	DOCUMENTARY	DOGTROTTED	DOMESTICATORS	DOPINESSES	DOVETAILING
DIVULGATES	DOCUMENTATION	DOGTROTTING	DOMESTICISE	DOPPELGANGER	DOVETAILINGS
DIVULGATING	DOCUMENTATIONAL	DOGWATCHES	DOMESTICISED	DOPPELGANGERS	DOVISHNESS
DIVULGATION	DOCUMENTATIONS	DOLABRIFORM	DOMESTICISES	DOPPLERITE	DOVISHNESSES
DIVULGATIONS	DOCUMENTED	DOLCELATTE	DOMESTICISING	DOPPLERITES	DOWDINESSES
DIVULGATOR	DOCUMENTER	DOLCELATTES	DOMESTICITIES	DORBEETLES	DOWELLINGS
DIVULGATORS	DOCUMENTERS	DOLCEMENTE	DOMESTICITY	DORKINESSES	DOWFNESSES
DIVULGEMENT	DOCUMENTING	DOLEFULLER	DOMESTICIZE	DORMANCIES	DOWITCHERS
DIVULGEMENTS	DODDERIEST	DOLEFULLEST	DOMESTICIZED	DORMITIONS	DOWNBURSTS
DIVULGENCE	DODDIPOLLS	DOLEFULNESS	DOMESTICIZES	DORMITIVES	DOWNCOMERS
DIVULGENCES	DODDYPOLLS	DOLEFULNESSES	DOMESTICIZING	DORMITORIES	DOWNDRAFTS
DIVULSIONS	DODECAGONAL	DOLESOMELY	DOMICILIARY	DORONICUMS	DOWNDRAUGHT
DIZENMENTS	DODECAGONS	DOLICHOCEPHAL	DOMICILIATE	DORSIBRANCHIATE	DOWNDRAUGHTS
DIZZINESSES	DODECAGYNIAN	DOLICHOCEPHALIC	DOMICILIATED	DORSIFEROUS	DOWNFALLEN
DIZZYINGLY	DODECAGYNOUS	DOLICHOCEPHALS	DOMICILIATES	DORSIFIXED	DOWNFORCES
DJELLABAHS	DODECAHEDRA	DOLICHOCEPHALY	DOMICILIATING	DORSIFLEXION	DOWNGRADED

DOWNGRADES	DRACONTIASIS	DRAUGHTINESS	DRILLABILITY	DRUMBEATER	DUMFOUNDERED
DOWNGRADING	DRACUNCULUS	DRAUGHTINESSES	DRILLMASTER	DRUMBEATERS	DUMFOUNDERING
DOWNHEARTED	DRACUNCULUSES	DRAUGHTING	DRILLMASTERS	DRUMBEATING	DUMFOUNDERS
DOWNHEARTEDLY	DRAFTINESS	DRAUGHTMAN	DRILLSHIPS	DRUMBEATINGS	DUMFOUNDING
DOWNHEARTEDNESS	DRAFTINESSES	DRAUGHTMEN	DRILLSTOCK	DRUMBLEDOR	DUMMELHEAD
DOWNHILLER	DRAFTSMANSHIP	DRAUGHTSMAN	DRILLSTOCKS	DRUMBLEDORS	DUMMELHEADS
DOWNHILLERS	DRAFTSMANSHIPS	DRAUGHTSMANSHIP	DRINKABILITIES	DRUMBLEDRANE	DUMMINESSES
DOWNINESSES	DRAFTSPERSON	DRAUGHTSWOMAN	DRINKABILITY	DRUMBLEDRANES	DUMORTIERITE
DOWNLIGHTER	DRAFTSPERSONS	DRAUGHTSWOMEN	DRINKABLENESS	DRUMFISHES	DUMORTIERITES
DOWNLIGHTERS	DRAGGINGLY	DRAWBRIDGE	DRINKABLENESSES	DRUMSTICKS	DUMOSITIES
DOWNLIGHTS	DRAGGLETAILED	DRAWBRIDGES	DRINKABLES	DRUNKATHON	DUMPINESSES
DOWNLINKED	DRAGHOUNDS	DRAWERFULS	DRIPSTONES	DRUNKATHONS	DUMPISHNESS
DOWNLINKING	DRAGONESSES	DRAWKNIVES	DRIVABILITIES	DRUNKENNESS	DUMPISHNESSES
DOWNLOADABLE	DRAGONFLIES	DRAWLINGLY	DRIVABILITY	DRUNKENNESSES	DUMPTRUCKS
DOWNLOADED	DRAGONHEAD	DRAWLINGNESS	DRIVEABILITIES	DRUPACEOUS	DUNDERFUNK
DOWNLOADING	DRAGONHEADS	DRAWLINGNESSES	DRIVEABILITY	DRYASDUSTS	DUNDERFUNKS
DOWNLOOKED	DRAGONISED	DRAWNWORKS	DRIVELINES	DRYBEATING	DUNDERHEAD
DOWNPLAYED	DRAGONISES	DRAWPLATES	DRIVELLERS	DRYOPITHECINE	DUNDERHEADED
DOWNPLAYING	DRAGONISING	DRAWSHAVES	DRIVELLING	DRYOPITHECINES	DUNDERHEADISM
DOWNREGULATION	DRAGONISMS	DRAWSTRING	DRIVENNESS	DRYSALTERIES	DUNDERHEADISMS
DOWNREGULATIONS	DRAGONIZED	DRAWSTRINGS	DRIVENNESSES	DRYSALTERS	DUNDERHEADS
DOWNRIGHTLY	DRAGONIZES	DRAYHORSES	DRIVERLESS	DRYSALTERY	DUNDERPATE
DOWNRIGHTNESS	DRAGONIZING	DREADFULLY	DRIVESHAFT	DRYWALLING	DUNDERPATES
DOWNRIGHTNESSES	DRAGONLIKE	DREADFULNESS	DRIVESHAFTS	DUALISTICALLY	DUNDREARIES
DOWNRUSHES	DRAGONNADE	DREADFULNESSES	DRIVETHROUGH	DUBIOSITIES	DUNGEONERS
DOWNSCALED	DRAGONNADED	DREADLESSLY	DRIVETHROUGHS	DUBIOUSNESS	DUNGEONING
DOWNSCALES	DRAGONNADES	DREADLESSNESS	DRIVETRAIN	DUBIOUSNESSES	DUNIEWASSAL
DOWNSCALING	DRAGONNADING	DREADLESSNESSES	DRIVETRAINS	DUBITANCIES	DUNIEWASSALS
DOWNSHIFTED	DRAGONROOT	DREADLOCKS	DRIZZLIEST	DUBITATING	DUNIWASSAL
DOWNSHIFTER	DRAGONROOTS	DREADNAUGHT	DRIZZLINGLY	DUBITATION	DUNIWASSALS
DOWNSHIFTERS	DRAGOONAGE	DREADNAUGHTS	DROICHIEST	DUBITATIONS	DUNNIEWASSAL
DOWNSHIFTING	DRAGOONAGES	DREADNOUGHT	DROLLERIES	DUBITATIVE	DUNNIEWASSALS
DOWNSHIFTINGS	DRAGOONING	DREADNOUGHTS	DROLLNESSES	DUBITATIVELY	DUODECENNIAL
DOWNSHIFTS	DRAGSTRIPS	DREAMBOATS	DROMEDARES	DUCHESSING	DUODECILLION
DOWNSIZING	DRAINLAYER	DREAMERIES	DROMEDARIES	DUCKBOARDS	DUODECILLIONS
DOWNSLIDES	DRAINLAYERS	DREAMFULLY	DROMOPHOBIA	DUCKSHOVED	DUODECIMAL
DOWNSPOUTS	DRAINPIPES	DREAMFULNESS	DROMOPHOBIAS	DUCKSHOVER	DUODECIMALLY
DOWNSTAGES	DRAKESTONE	DREAMFULNESSES	DRONISHNESS	DUCKSHOVERS	DUODECIMALS
DOWNSTAIRS	DRAKESTONES	DREAMHOLES	DRONISHNESSES	DUCKSHOVES	DUODECIMOS
DOWNSTAIRSES	DRAMATICAL	DREAMINESS	DRONKVERDRIET	DUCKSHOVING	DUODENECTOMIES
DOWNSTATER	DRAMATICALLY	DREAMINESSES	DROOPINESS	DUCKWALKED	DUODENECTOMY
DOWNSTATERS	DRAMATICISM	DREAMINGLY	DROOPINESSES	DUCKWALKING	DUODENITIS
DOWNSTATES	DRAMATICISMS	DREAMLANDS	DROOPINGLY	DUCTILENESS	DUODENITISES
DOWNSTREAM	DRAMATISABLE	DREAMLESSLY	DROPCLOTHS	DUCTILENESSES	DUOPOLISTIC
DOWNSTROKE	DRAMATISATION	DREAMLESSNESS	DROPFORGED	DUCTILITIES	DUOPSONIES
DOWNSTROKES	DRAMATISATIONS	DREAMLESSNESSES	DROPFORGES	DUENNASHIP	DUPABILITIES
DOWNSWINGS	DRAMATISED	DREAMTIMES	DROPFORGING	DUENNASHIPS	DUPABILITY
DOWNTHROWS	DRAMATISER	DREAMWHILE	DROPKICKER	DUFFERDOMS	DUPLEXITIES
DOWNTOWNER	DRAMATISERS	DREAMWHILES	DROPKICKERS	DUFFERISMS	DUPLICABILITIES
DOWNTOWNERS	DRAMATISES	DREAMWORLD	DROPLIGHTS	DUIKERBOKS	DUPLICABILITY
DOWNTRENDED	DRAMATISING	DREAMWORLDS	DROPPERFUL	DUKKERIPEN	DUPLICABLE
DOWNTRENDING	DRAMATISTS	DREARIHEAD	DROPPERFULS	DUKKERIPENS	DUPLICANDS
DOWNTRENDS	DRAMATIZABLE	DREARIHEADS	DROPPERSFUL	DULCAMARAS	DUPLICATED
DOWNTRODDEN	DRAMATIZATION	DREARIHOOD	DROPSICALLY	DULCETNESS	DUPLICATELY
DOWNTURNED	DRAMATIZATIONS	DREARIHOODS	DROPSONDES	DULCETNESSES	DUPLICATES
DOWNWARDLY	DRAMATIZED	DREARIMENT	DROPSTONES	DULCIFICATION	DUPLICATING
DOWNWARDNESS	DRAMATIZER	DREARIMENTS	DROSERACEOUS	DULCIFICATIONS	DUPLICATION
DOWNWARDNESSES	DRAMATIZERS	DREARINESS	DROSOMETER	DULCIFLUOUS	DUPLICATIONS
DOWNWASHES	DRAMATIZES	DREARINESSES	DROSOMETERS	DULCIFYING	DUPLICATIVE
DOWNZONING	DRAMATIZING	DREARISOME	DROSOPHILA	DULCILOQUIES	DUPLICATOR
DOXOGRAPHER	DRAMATURGE	DRECKSILLS	DROSOPHILAE	DULCILOQUY	DUPLICATORS
DOXOGRAPHERS	DRAMATURGES	DREGGINESS	DROSOPHILAS	DULCIMORES	DUPLICATURE
DOXOGRAPHIC	DRAMATURGIC	DREGGINESSES	DROSSINESS	DULCITUDES	DUPLICATURES
DOXOGRAPHIES	DRAMATURGICAL	DREIKANTER	DROSSINESSES	DULLNESSES	DUPLICIDENT
DOXOGRAPHY	DRAMATURGICALLY	DREIKANTERS	DROUGHTIER	DULLSVILLE	DUPLICITIES
DOXOLOGICAL	DRAMATURGIES	DRENCHINGS	DROUGHTIEST	DULLSVILLES	DUPLICITOUS
DOXOLOGICALLY	DRAMATURGIST	DREPANIUMS	DROUGHTINESS	DULOCRACIES	DUPLICITOUSLY
DOXOLOGIES	DRAMATURGISTS	DRERIHEADS	DROUGHTINESSES	DUMBFOUNDED	DURABILITIES
DOXORUBICIN	DRAMATURGS	DRESSGUARD	DROUTHIEST	DUMBFOUNDER	DURABILITY
DOXORUBICINS	DRAMATURGY	DRESSGUARDS	DROUTHINESS	DUMBFOUNDERED	DURABLENESS
DOXYCYCLINE	DRAPABILITIES	DRESSINESS	DROUTHINESSES	DUMBFOUNDERING	DURABLENESSES
DOXYCYCLINES	DRAPABILITY	DRESSINESSES	DROWSIHEAD	DUMBFOUNDERS	DURALUMINIUM
DOZINESSES	DRAPEABILITIES	DRESSMAKER	DROWSIHEADS	DUMBFOUNDING	DURALUMINIUMS
DRABBINESS	DRAPEABILITY	DRESSMAKERS	DROWSIHEDS	DUMBFOUNDS	DURALUMINS
DRABBINESSES	DRAPERYING	DRESSMAKES	DROWSINESS	DUMBLEDORE	DURATIONAL
DRABBLINGS	DRASTICALLY	DRESSMAKES	DROWSINESSES	DUMBLEDORES	DURCHKOMPONIERT
DRABNESSES	DRATCHELLS	DRESSMAKING	DRUCKENNESS	DUMBNESSES	DURCHKOMPONIRT
DRACONIANISM	DRAUGHTBOARD	DRESSMAKINGS	DRUCKENNESSES	DUMBSTRICKEN	DURICRUSTS
DRACONIANISMS	DRAUGHTBOARDS	DRIBBLIEST	DRUDGERIES	DUMBSTRUCK	DUROMETERS
DRACONICALLY	DRAUGHTERS	DRICKSIEST	DRUDGINGLY	DUMBWAITER	DUSKINESSES
DRACONISMS	DRAUGHTIER	DRIFTINGLY	DRUGMAKERS	DUMBWAITERS	DUSKISHNESS
DRACONITES	DRAUGHTIEST	DRIFTWOODS	DRUGSTORES	DUMFOUNDED	DUSKISHNESSES
DRACONTIASES	DRAUGHTILY	DRILLABILITIES	DRUIDESSES	DUMFOUNDER	DUSKNESSES

d

DUSTCOVERS	DYNAMICIST	DYNORPHINS	DYSCRASITE	DYSMENORRHOEAS	DYSPROSIUM
DUSTINESSES	DYNAMICISTS	DYOPHYSITE	DYSCRASITES	DYSMENORRHOEIC	DYSPROSIUMS
DUSTSHEETS	DYNAMISING	DYOPHYSITES	DYSENTERIC	DYSMORPHIC	DYSRHYTHMIA
DUSTSTORMS	DYNAMISTIC	DYOTHELETE	DYSENTERIES	DYSMORPHOPHOBIA	DYSRHYTHMIAS
DUTEOUSNESS	DYNAMITARD	DYOTHELETES	DYSFUNCTION	DYSPAREUNIA	DYSRHYTHMIC
DUTEOUSNESSES	DYNAMITARDS	DYOTHELETIC	DYSFUNCTIONAL	DYSPAREUNIAS	DYSSYNERGIA
DUTIABILITIES	DYNAMITERS	DYOTHELETICAL	DYSFUNCTIONS	DYSPATHETIC	DYSSYNERGIAS
DUTIABILITY	DYNAMITING	DYOTHELETISM	DYSGENESES	DYSPATHIES	DYSTELEOLOGICAL
DUTIFULNESS	DYNAMIZING	DYOTHELETISMS	DYSGENESIS	DYSPEPSIAS	DYSTELEOLOGIES
DUTIFULNESSES	DYNAMOELECTRIC	DYOTHELISM	DYSGRAPHIA	DYSPEPSIES	DYSTELEOLOGIST
DUUMVIRATE	DYNAMOGENESES	DYOTHELISMS	DYSGRAPHIAS	DYSPEPTICAL	DYSTELEOLOGISTS
DUUMVIRATES	DYNAMOGENESIS	DYOTHELITE	DYSGRAPHIC	DYSPEPTICALLY	DYSTELEOLOGY
DWARFISHLY	DYNAMOGENIES	DYOTHELITES	DYSHARMONIC	DYSPEPTICS	DYSTHESIAS
DWARFISHNESS	DYNAMOGENY	DYOTHELITIC	DYSKINESIA	DYSPHAGIAS	DYSTHYMIAC
DWARFISHNESSES	DYNAMOGRAPH	DYOTHELITICAL	DYSKINESIAS	DYSPHAGIES	DYSTHYMIACS
DWARFNESSES	DYNAMOGRAPHS	DYSAESTHESIA	DYSKINETIC	DYSPHASIAS	DYSTHYMIAS
DWINDLEMENT	DYNAMOMETER	DYSAESTHESIAS	DYSLECTICS	DYSPHASICS	DYSTHYMICS
DWINDLEMENTS	DYNAMOMETERS	DYSAESTHETIC	DYSLOGISTIC	DYSPHEMISM	DYSTOPIANS
DYADICALLY	DYNAMOMETRIC	DYSARTHRIA	DYSLOGISTICALLY	DYSPHEMISMS	DYSTROPHIA
DYARCHICAL	DYNAMOMETRICAL	DYSARTHRIAS	DYSMENORRHEA	DYSPHEMISTIC	DYSTROPHIAS
DYEABILITIES	DYNAMOMETRIES	DYSBINDINS	DYSMENORRHEAL	DYSPHONIAS	DYSTROPHIC
DYEABILITY	DYNAMOMETRY	DYSCALCULIA	DYSMENORRHEAS	DYSPHORIAS	DYSTROPHIES
DYINGNESSES	DYNAMOTORS	DYSCALCULIAS	DYSMENORRHEIC	DYSPLASIAS	DYSTROPHIN
DYNAMETERS	DYNASTICAL	DYSCHROIAS	DYSMENORRHOEA	DYSPLASTIC	DYSTROPHINS
DYNAMICALLY	DYNASTICALLY	DYSCRASIAS	DYSMENORRHOEAL	DYSPRAXIAS	DZIGGETAIS

Ee

EAGERNESSES
EAGLEHAWKS
EAGLESTONE
EAGLESTONES
EAGLEWOODS
EARBASHERS
EARBASHING
EARBASHINGS
EARLIERISE
EARLIERISED
EARLIERISES
EARLIERISING
EARLIERIZE
EARLIERIZED
EARLIERIZES
EARLIERIZING
EARLINESSES
EARLYWOODS
EARMARKING
EARNESTNESS
EARNESTNESSES
EARSPLITTING
EARTHBOUND
EARTHENWARE
EARTHENWARES
EARTHFALLS
EARTHFLAXES
EARTHINESS
EARTHINESSES
EARTHLIEST
EARTHLIGHT
EARTHLIGHTS
EARTHLINESS
EARTHLINESSES
EARTHLINGS
EARTHMOVER
EARTHMOVERS
EARTHMOVING
EARTHMOVINGS
EARTHQUAKE
EARTHQUAKED
EARTHQUAKES
EARTHQUAKING
EARTHRISES
EARTHSHAKER
EARTHSHAKERS
EARTHSHAKING
EARTHSHAKINGLY
EARTHSHATTERING
EARTHSHINE
EARTHSHINES
EARTHSTARS
EARTHWARDS
EARTHWAXES
EARTHWOLVES
EARTHWOMAN
EARTHWOMEN
EARTHWORKS
EARTHWORMS
EARWIGGING
EARWIGGINGS
EARWITNESS
EARWITNESSES
EASEFULNESS
EASEFULNESSES
EASINESSES
EASSELGATE

EASSELWARD
EASTERLIES
EASTERLING
EASTERLINGS
EASTERMOST
EASTERNERS
EASTERNMOST
EASTWARDLY
EASYGOINGNESS
EASYGOINGNESSES
EAVESDRIPS
EAVESDROPPED
EAVESDROPPER
EAVESDROPPERS
EAVESDROPPING
EAVESDROPPINGS
EAVESDROPS
EAVESTROUGH
EAVESTROUGHS
EBIONISING
EBIONITISM
EBIONITISMS
EBIONIZING
EBOULEMENT
EBOULEMENTS
EBRACTEATE
EBRACTEOLATE
EBRILLADES
EBRIOSITIES
EBULLIENCE
EBULLIENCES
EBULLIENCIES
EBULLIENCY
EBULLIENTLY
EBULLIOMETER
EBULLIOMETERS
EBULLIOMETRIES
EBULLIOMETRY
EBULLIOSCOPE
EBULLIOSCOPES
EBULLIOSCOPIC
EBULLIOSCOPICAL
EBULLIOSCOPIES
EBULLIOSCOPY
EBULLITION
EBULLITIONS
EBURNATION
EBURNATIONS
EBURNIFICATION
EBURNIFICATIONS
ECARDINATE
ECBLASTESES
ECBLASTESIS
ECCALEOBION
ECCALEOBIONS
ECCENTRICAL
ECCENTRICALLY
ECCENTRICITIES
ECCENTRICITY
ECCENTRICS
ECCHYMOSED
ECCHYMOSES
ECCHYMOSIS
ECCHYMOTIC
ECCLESIARCH
ECCLESIARCHS
ECCLESIAST

ECCLESIASTIC
ECCLESIASTICAL
ECCLESIASTICISM
ECCLESIASTICS
ECCLESIASTS
ECCLESIOLATER
ECCLESIOLATERS
ECCLESIOLATRIES
ECCLESIOLATRY
ECCLESIOLOGICAL
ECCLESIOLOGIES
ECCLESIOLOGIST
ECCLESIOLOGISTS
ECCLESIOLOGY
ECCOPROTIC
ECCOPROTICS
ECCREMOCARPUS
ECCREMOCARPUSES
ECCRINOLOGIES
ECCRINOLOGY
ECDYSIASTS
ECHELONING
ECHEVERIAS
ECHIDNINES
ECHINACEAS
ECHINOCOCCI
ECHINOCOCCOSES
ECHINOCOCCOSIS
ECHINOCOCCUS
ECHINODERM
ECHINODERMAL
ECHINODERMATOUS
ECHINODERMS
ECHIUROIDS
ECHOCARDIOGRAM
ECHOCARDIOGRAMS
ECHOGRAPHIES
ECHOGRAPHY
ECHOLALIAS
ECHOLOCATION
ECHOLOCATIONS
ECHOPRAXES
ECHOPRAXIA
ECHOPRAXIAS
ECHOPRAXIS
ECHOVIRUSES
ECLAIRCISSEMENT
ECLAMPSIAS
ECLAMPSIES
ECLECTICALLY
ECLECTICISM
ECLECTICISMS
ECLIPSISES
ECLIPTICALLY
ECOCATASTROPHE
ECOCATASTROPHES
ECOCENTRIC
ECOCLIMATE
ECOCLIMATES
ECOFEMINISM
ECOFEMINISMS
ECOFEMINIST
ECOFEMINISTS
ECOFRIENDLY
ECOLOGICAL
ECOLOGICALLY
ECOLOGISTS

ECOMMERCES
ECONOBOXES
ECONOMETRIC
ECONOMETRICAL
ECONOMETRICALLY
ECONOMETRICIAN
ECONOMETRICIANS
ECONOMETRICS
ECONOMETRIST
ECONOMETRISTS
ECONOMICAL
ECONOMICALLY
ECONOMISATION
ECONOMISATIONS
ECONOMISED
ECONOMISER
ECONOMISERS
ECONOMISES
ECONOMISING
ECONOMISMS
ECONOMISTIC
ECONOMISTS
ECONOMIZATION
ECONOMIZATIONS
ECONOMIZED
ECONOMIZER
ECONOMIZERS
ECONOMIZES
ECONOMIZING
ECOPHOBIAS
ECOPHYSIOLOGIES
ECOPHYSIOLOGY
ECOREGIONS
ECOSPECIES
ECOSPECIFIC
ECOSPHERES
ECOSSAISES
ECOSYSTEMS
ECOTERRORISM
ECOTERRORISMS
ECOTERRORIST
ECOTERRORISTS
ECOTOURISM
ECOTOURISMS
ECOTOURIST
ECOTOURISTS
ECOTOXICOLOGIES
ECOTOXICOLOGIST
ECOTOXICOLOGY
ECOTYPICALLY
ECPHONESES
ECPHONESIS
ECPHRACTIC
ECPHRACTICS
ECRITOIRES
ECSTASISED
ECSTASISES
ECSTASISING
ECSTASIZED
ECSTASIZES
ECSTASIZING
ECSTASYING
ECSTATICALLY
ECTHLIPSES
ECTHLIPSIS
ECTOBLASTIC
ECTOBLASTS

ECTOCRINES
ECTODERMAL
ECTODERMIC
ECTOENZYME
ECTOENZYMES
ECTOGENESES
ECTOGENESIS
ECTOGENETIC
ECTOGENICALLY
ECTOGENIES
ECTOGENOUS
ECTOMORPHIC
ECTOMORPHIES
ECTOMORPHS
ECTOMORPHY
ECTOMYCORRHIZA
ECTOMYCORRHIZAE
ECTOMYCORRHIZAS
ECTOPARASITE
ECTOPARASITES
ECTOPARASITIC
ECTOPHYTES
ECTOPHYTIC
ECTOPICALLY
ECTOPLASMIC
ECTOPLASMS
ECTOPLASTIC
ECTOPROCTS
ECTOSARCOUS
ECTOTHERMIC
ECTOTHERMS
ECTOTROPHIC
ECTROPIONS
ECTROPIUMS
ECTYPOGRAPHIES
ECTYPOGRAPHY
ECUMENICAL
ECUMENICALISM
ECUMENICALISMS
ECUMENICALLY
ECUMENICISM
ECUMENICISMS
ECUMENICIST
ECUMENICISTS
ECUMENICITIES
ECUMENICITY
ECUMENISMS
ECUMENISTS
ECZEMATOUS
EDACIOUSLY
EDACIOUSNESS
EDACIOUSNESSES
EDAPHICALLY
EDAPHOLOGIES
EDAPHOLOGY
EDELWEISSES
EDENTULATE
EDENTULOUS
EDGINESSES
EDIBILITIES
EDIBILITY
EDIBLENESS
EDIBLENESSES
EDIFICATION
EDIFICATIONS
EDIFICATORY
EDIFYINGLY
EDITIONING

EDITORIALISE
EDITORIALISED
EDITORIALISER
EDITORIALISERS
EDITORIALISES
EDITORIALISING
EDITORIALIST
EDITORIALISTS
EDITORIALIZE
EDITORIALIZED
EDITORIALIZER
EDITORIALIZERS
EDITORIALIZES
EDITORIALIZING
EDITORIALLY
EDITORIALS
EDITORSHIP
EDITORSHIPS
EDITRESSES
EDRIOPHTHALMIAN
EDRIOPHTHALMIC
EDRIOPHTHALMOUS
EDUCABILITIES
EDUCABILITY
EDUCATABILITIES
EDUCATABILITY
EDUCATABLE
EDUCATEDNESS
EDUCATEDNESSES
EDUCATIONAL
EDUCATIONALIST
EDUCATIONALISTS
EDUCATIONALLY
EDUCATIONESE
EDUCATIONESES
EDUCATIONIST
EDUCATIONISTS
EDUCATIONS
EDUCEMENTS
EDULCORANT
EDULCORATE
EDULCORATED
EDULCORATES
EDULCORATING
EDULCORATION
EDULCORATIONS
EDULCORATIVE
EDULCORATOR
EDULCORATORS
EDUSKUNTAS
EDUTAINMENT
EDUTAINMENTS
EELGRASSES
EERINESSES
EFFACEABLE
EFFACEMENT
EFFACEMENTS
EFFECTIBLE
EFFECTIVELY
EFFECTIVENESS
EFFECTIVENESSES
EFFECTIVES
EFFECTIVITIES
EFFECTIVITY
EFFECTLESS
EFFECTUALITIES
EFFECTUALITY

EFFECTUALLY
EFFECTUALNESS
EFFECTUALNESSES
EFFECTUATE
EFFECTUATED
EFFECTUATES
EFFECTUATING
EFFECTUATION
EFFECTUATIONS
EFFEMINACIES
EFFEMINACY
EFFEMINATE
EFFEMINATED
EFFEMINATELY
EFFEMINATENESS
EFFEMINATES
EFFEMINATING
EFFEMINISE
EFFEMINISED
EFFEMINISES
EFFEMINISING
EFFEMINIZE
EFFEMINIZED
EFFEMINIZES
EFFEMINIZING
EFFERENCES
EFFERENTLY
EFFERVESCE
EFFERVESCED
EFFERVESCENCE
EFFERVESCENCES
EFFERVESCENCIES
EFFERVESCENCY
EFFERVESCENT
EFFERVESCENTLY
EFFERVESCES
EFFERVESCIBLE
EFFERVESCING
EFFERVESCINGLY
EFFETENESS
EFFETENESSES
EFFICACIES
EFFICACIOUS
EFFICACIOUSLY
EFFICACIOUSNESS
EFFICACITIES
EFFICACITY
EFFICIENCE
EFFICIENCES
EFFICIENCIES
EFFICIENCY
EFFICIENTLY
EFFICIENTS
EFFIERCING
EFFIGURATE
EFFIGURATION
EFFIGURATIONS
EFFLEURAGE
EFFLEURAGED
EFFLEURAGES
EFFLEURAGING
EFFLORESCE
EFFLORESCED
EFFLORESCENCE
EFFLORESCENCES
EFFLORESCENT
EFFLORESCES
EFFLORESCING
EFFLUENCES
EFFLUVIUMS
EFFLUXIONS
EFFORTFULLY
EFFORTFULNESS
EFFORTFULNESSES
EFFORTLESS
EFFORTLESSLY
EFFORTLESSNESS
EFFRONTERIES
EFFRONTERY
EFFULGENCE
EFFULGENCES
EFFULGENTLY
EFFUSIOMETER

EFFUSIOMETERS
EFFUSIVELY
EFFUSIVENESS
EFFUSIVENESSES
EGALITARIAN
EGALITARIANISM
EGALITARIANISMS
EGALITARIANS
EGAREMENTS
EGGBEATERS
EGGHEADEDNESS
EGGHEADEDNESSES
EGLANDULAR
EGLANDULOSE
EGLANTINES
EGOCENTRIC
EGOCENTRICALLY
EGOCENTRICITIES
EGOCENTRICITY
EGOCENTRICS
EGOCENTRISM
EGOCENTRISMS
EGOISTICAL
EGOISTICALLY
EGOMANIACAL
EGOMANIACALLY
EGOMANIACS
EGOTHEISMS
EGOTISTICAL
EGOTISTICALLY
EGREGIOUSLY
EGREGIOUSNESS
EGREGIOUSNESSES
EGRESSIONS
EGURGITATE
EGURGITATED
EGURGITATES
EGURGITATING
EICOSANOID
EICOSANOIDS
EIDERDOWNS
EIDETICALLY
EIDOGRAPHS
EIGENFREQUENCY
EIGENFUNCTION
EIGENFUNCTIONS
EIGENMODES
EIGENTONES
EIGENVALUE
EIGENVALUES
EIGENVECTOR
EIGENVECTORS
EIGHTBALLS
EIGHTEENMO
EIGHTEENMOS
EIGHTEENTH
EIGHTEENTHLY
EIGHTEENTHS
EIGHTFOILS
EIGHTIETHS
EIGHTPENCE
EIGHTPENCES
EIGHTPENNY
EIGHTSCORE
EIGHTSCORES
EIGHTSOMES
EINSTEINIUM
EINSTEINIUMS
EIRENICALLY
EIRENICONS
EISTEDDFOD
EISTEDDFODAU
EISTEDDFODIC
EISTEDDFODS
EJACULATED
EJACULATES
EJACULATING
EJACULATION
EJACULATIONS
EJACULATIVE
EJACULATOR
EJACULATORS
EJACULATORY

EJECTAMENTA
EJECTIVELY
EJECTMENTS
EKISTICIAN
EKISTICIANS
ELABORATED
ELABORATELY
ELABORATENESS
ELABORATENESSES
ELABORATES
ELABORATING
ELABORATION
ELABORATIONS
ELABORATIVE
ELABORATOR
ELABORATORIES
ELABORATORS
ELABORATORY
ELAEOLITES
ELAEOPTENE
ELAEOPTENES
ELAIOSOMES
ELASMOBRANCH
ELASMOBRANCHS
ELASMOSAUR
ELASMOSAURS
ELASTANCES
ELASTICALLY
ELASTICATE
ELASTICATED
ELASTICATES
ELASTICATING
ELASTICATION
ELASTICATIONS
ELASTICISE
ELASTICISED
ELASTICISES
ELASTICISING
ELASTICITIES
ELASTICITY
ELASTICIZE
ELASTICIZED
ELASTICIZES
ELASTICIZING
ELASTICNESS
ELASTICNESSES
ELASTOMERIC
ELASTOMERS
ELATEDNESS
ELATEDNESSES
ELATERITES
ELATERIUMS
ELBOWROOMS
ELDERBERRIES
ELDERBERRY
ELDERCARES
ELDERLINESS
ELDERLINESSES
ELDERSHIPS
ELECAMPANE
ELECAMPANES
ELECTABILITIES
ELECTABILITY
ELECTIONEER
ELECTIONEERED
ELECTIONEERER
ELECTIONEERERS
ELECTIONEERING
ELECTIONEERINGS
ELECTIONEERS
ELECTIVELY
ELECTIVENESS
ELECTIVENESSES
ELECTIVITIES
ELECTIVITY
ELECTORALLY
ELECTORATE
ELECTORATES
ELECTORESS
ELECTORESSES
ELECTORIAL
ELECTORSHIP
ELECTORSHIPS

ELECTRESSES
ELECTRICAL
ELECTRICALLY
ELECTRICIAN
ELECTRICIANS
ELECTRICITIES
ELECTRICITY
ELECTRIFIABLE
ELECTRIFICATION
ELECTRIFIED
ELECTRIFIER
ELECTRIFIERS
ELECTRIFIES
ELECTRIFYING
ELECTRISATION
ELECTRISATIONS
ELECTRISED
ELECTRISES
ELECTRISING
ELECTRIZATION
ELECTRIZATIONS
ELECTRIZED
ELECTRIZES
ELECTRIZING
ELECTROACOUSTIC
ELECTROACTIVE
ELECTROACTIVITY
ELECTROANALYSES
ELECTROANALYSIS
ELECTROANALYTIC
ELECTROBIOLOGY
ELECTROCAUTERY
ELECTROCEMENT
ELECTROCEMENTS
ELECTROCHEMIC
ELECTROCHEMICAL
ELECTROCHEMIST
ELECTROCHEMISTS
ELECTROCLASH
ELECTROCLASHES
ELECTROCULTURE
ELECTROCULTURES
ELECTROCUTE
ELECTROCUTED
ELECTROCUTES
ELECTROCUTING
ELECTROCUTION
ELECTROCUTIONS
ELECTROCYTE
ELECTROCYTES
ELECTRODEPOSIT
ELECTRODEPOSITS
ELECTRODERMAL
ELECTRODES
ELECTRODIALYSES
ELECTRODIALYSIS
ELECTRODIALYTIC
ELECTRODYNAMIC
ELECTRODYNAMICS
ELECTROFISHING
ELECTROFISHINGS
ELECTROFLUOR
ELECTROFLUORS
ELECTROFORM
ELECTROFORMED
ELECTROFORMING
ELECTROFORMINGS
ELECTROFORMS
ELECTROGEN
ELECTROGENESES
ELECTROGENESIS
ELECTROGENIC
ELECTROGENS
ELECTROGILDING
ELECTROGILDINGS
ELECTROGRAM
ELECTROGRAMS
ELECTROGRAPH
ELECTROGRAPHIC
ELECTROGRAPHIES
ELECTROGRAPHS
ELECTROGRAPHY
ELECTROING

ELECTROJET
ELECTROJETS
ELECTROKINETIC
ELECTROKINETICS
ELECTROLESS
ELECTROLIER
ELECTROLIERS
ELECTROLOGIES
ELECTROLOGIST
ELECTROLOGISTS
ELECTROLOGY
ELECTROLYSATION
ELECTROLYSE
ELECTROLYSED
ELECTROLYSER
ELECTROLYSERS
ELECTROLYSES
ELECTROLYSING
ELECTROLYSIS
ELECTROLYTE
ELECTROLYTES
ELECTROLYTIC
ELECTROLYTICS
ELECTROLYZATION
ELECTROLYZE
ELECTROLYZED
ELECTROLYZER
ELECTROLYZERS
ELECTROLYZES
ELECTROLYZING
ELECTROMAGNET
ELECTROMAGNETIC
ELECTROMAGNETS
ELECTROMER
ELECTROMERIC
ELECTROMERISM
ELECTROMERISMS
ELECTROMERS
ELECTROMETER
ELECTROMETERS
ELECTROMETRIC
ELECTROMETRICAL
ELECTROMETRIES
ELECTROMETRY
ELECTROMOTANCE
ELECTROMOTANCES
ELECTROMOTIVE
ELECTROMOTOR
ELECTROMOTORS
ELECTROMYOGRAM
ELECTROMYOGRAMS
ELECTROMYOGRAPH
ELECTRONEGATIVE
ELECTRONIC
ELECTRONICA
ELECTRONICALLY
ELECTRONICAS
ELECTRONICS
ELECTRONVOLT
ELECTRONVOLTS
ELECTROOSMOSES
ELECTROOSMOSIS
ELECTROOSMOTIC
ELECTROPHILE
ELECTROPHILES
ELECTROPHILIC
ELECTROPHONE
ELECTROPHONES
ELECTROPHONIC
ELECTROPHORESE
ELECTROPHORESED
ELECTROPHORESES
ELECTROPHORESIS
ELECTROPHORETIC
ELECTROPHORI
ELECTROPHORUS
ELECTROPHORUSES
ELECTROPLATE
ELECTROPLATED
ELECTROPLATER
ELECTROPLATERS
ELECTROPLATES
ELECTROPLATING

ELECTROPLATINGS
ELECTROPOLAR
ELECTROPOSITIVE
ELECTRORECEPTOR
ELECTRORHEOLOGY
ELECTROSCOPE
ELECTROSCOPES
ELECTROSCOPIC
ELECTROSHOCK
ELECTROSHOCKS
ELECTROSONDE
ELECTROSONDES
ELECTROSTATIC
ELECTROSTATICS
ELECTROSURGERY
ELECTROSURGICAL
ELECTROTECHNICS
ELECTROTHERAPY
ELECTROTHERMAL
ELECTROTHERMIC
ELECTROTHERMICS
ELECTROTHERMIES
ELECTROTHERMY
ELECTROTINT
ELECTROTINTS
ELECTROTONIC
ELECTROTONUS
ELECTROTONUSES
ELECTROTYPE
ELECTROTYPED
ELECTROTYPER
ELECTROTYPERS
ELECTROTYPES
ELECTROTYPIC
ELECTROTYPIES
ELECTROTYPING
ELECTROTYPIST
ELECTROTYPISTS
ELECTROTYPY
ELECTROVALENCE
ELECTROVALENCES
ELECTROVALENCY
ELECTROVALENT
ELECTROVALENTLY
ELECTROWEAK
ELECTROWINNING
ELECTROWINNINGS
ELECTUARIES
ELEDOISINS
ELEEMOSYNARY
ELEGANCIES
ELEGIACALLY
ELEMENTALISM
ELEMENTALISMS
ELEMENTALLY
ELEMENTALS
ELEMENTARILY
ELEMENTARINESS
ELEMENTARY
ELEOPTENES
ELEPHANTIASES
ELEPHANTIASIC
ELEPHANTIASIS
ELEPHANTINE
ELEPHANTOID
ELEUTHERARCH
ELEUTHERARCHS
ELEUTHERIAN
ELEUTHEROCOCCI
ELEUTHEROCOCCUS
ELEUTHERODACTYL
ELEUTHEROMANIA
ELEUTHEROMANIAS
ELEUTHEROPHOBIA
ELEUTHEROPHOBIC
ELEVATIONAL
ELEVATIONS
ELEVENTHLY
ELFISHNESS
ELFISHNESSES
ELICITABLE
ELICITATION
ELICITATIONS

ELIGIBILITIES
ELIGIBILITY
ELIMINABILITIES
ELIMINABILITY
ELIMINABLE
ELIMINANTS
ELIMINATED
ELIMINATES
ELIMINATING
ELIMINATION
ELIMINATIONS
ELIMINATIVE
ELIMINATOR
ELIMINATORS
ELIMINATORY
ELLIPSOGRAPH
ELLIPSOGRAPHS
ELLIPSOIDAL
ELLIPSOIDS
ELLIPTICAL
ELLIPTICALLY
ELLIPTICALNESS
ELLIPTICALS
ELLIPTICITIES
ELLIPTICITY
ELOCUTIONARY
ELOCUTIONIST
ELOCUTIONISTS
ELOCUTIONS
ELOIGNMENT
ELOIGNMENTS
ELOINMENTS
ELONGATING
ELONGATION
ELONGATIONS
ELOPEMENTS
ELOQUENCES
ELOQUENTLY
ELSEWHITHER
ELUCIDATED
ELUCIDATES
ELUCIDATING
ELUCIDATION
ELUCIDATIONS
ELUCIDATIVE
ELUCIDATOR
ELUCIDATORS
ELUCIDATORY
ELUCUBRATE
ELUCUBRATED
ELUCUBRATES
ELUCUBRATING
ELUCUBRATION
ELUCUBRATIONS
ELUSIVENESS
ELUSIVENESSES
ELUSORINESS
ELUSORINESSES
ELUTRIATED
ELUTRIATES
ELUTRIATING
ELUTRIATION
ELUTRIATIONS
ELUTRIATOR
ELUTRIATORS
ELUVIATING
ELUVIATION
ELUVIATIONS
ELVISHNESS
ELVISHNESSES
ELYTRIFORM
ELYTRIGEROUS
EMACIATING
EMACIATION
EMACIATIONS
EMALANGENI
EMANATIONS
EMANATISTS
EMANCIPATE
EMANCIPATED
EMANCIPATES
EMANCIPATING

EMANCIPATION
EMANCIPATIONIST
EMANCIPATIVE
EMANCIPATOR
EMANCIPATORS
EMANCIPATORY
EMANCIPIST
EMANCIPISTS
EMARGINATE
EMARGINATED
EMARGINATELY
EMARGINATES
EMARGINATING
EMARGINATION
EMARGINATIONS
EMASCULATE
EMASCULATED
EMASCULATES
EMASCULATING
EMASCULATION
EMASCULATIONS
EMASCULATIVE
EMASCULATOR
EMASCULATORS
EMASCULATORY
EMBALLINGS
EMBALMINGS
EMBALMMENT
EMBALMMENTS
EMBANKMENT
EMBANKMENTS
EMBARCADERO
EMBARCADEROS
EMBARCATION
EMBARCATIONS
EMBARGOING
EMBARKATION
EMBARKATIONS
EMBARKMENT
EMBARKMENTS
EMBARQUEMENT
EMBARQUEMENTS
EMBARRASSABLE
EMBARRASSED
EMBARRASSEDLY
EMBARRASSES
EMBARRASSING
EMBARRASSINGLY
EMBARRASSMENT
EMBARRASSMENTS
EMBARRINGS
EMBASEMENT
EMBASEMENTS
EMBASSADES
EMBASSADOR
EMBASSADORS
EMBASSAGES
EMBATTLEMENT
EMBATTLEMENTS
EMBATTLING
EMBAYMENTS
EMBEDDINGS
EMBEDMENTS
EMBELLISHED
EMBELLISHER
EMBELLISHERS
EMBELLISHES
EMBELLISHING
EMBELLISHINGLY
EMBELLISHMENT
EMBELLISHMENTS
EMBEZZLEMENT
EMBEZZLEMENTS
EMBEZZLERS
EMBEZZLING
EMBITTERED
EMBITTERER
EMBITTERERS
EMBITTERING
EMBITTERINGS
EMBITTERMENT
EMBITTERMENTS

EMBLAZONED
EMBLAZONER
EMBLAZONERS
EMBLAZONING
EMBLAZONMENT
EMBLAZONMENTS
EMBLAZONRIES
EMBLAZONRY
EMBLEMATIC
EMBLEMATICAL
EMBLEMATICALLY
EMBLEMATISE
EMBLEMATISED
EMBLEMATISES
EMBLEMATISING
EMBLEMATIST
EMBLEMATISTS
EMBLEMATIZE
EMBLEMATIZED
EMBLEMATIZES
EMBLEMATIZING
EMBLEMENTS
EMBLEMISED
EMBLEMISES
EMBLEMISING
EMBLEMIZED
EMBLEMIZES
EMBLEMIZING
EMBLOOMING
EMBLOSSOMED
EMBLOSSOMING
EMBLOSSOMS
EMBODIMENT
EMBODIMENTS
EMBOITEMENT
EMBOITEMENTS
EMBOLDENED
EMBOLDENER
EMBOLDENERS
EMBOLDENING
EMBOLECTOMIES
EMBOLECTOMY
EMBOLISATION
EMBOLISATIONS
EMBOLISING
EMBOLISMAL
EMBOLISMIC
EMBOLIZATION
EMBOLIZATIONS
EMBOLIZING
EMBONPOINT
EMBONPOINTS
EMBORDERED
EMBORDERING
EMBOSCATAS
EMBOSOMING
EMBOSSABLE
EMBOSSMENT
EMBOSSMENTS
EMBOTHRIUM
EMBOTHRIUMS
EMBOUCHURE
EMBOUCHURES
EMBOUNDING
EMBOURGEOISE
EMBOURGEOISED
EMBOURGEOISES
EMBOURGEOISING
EMBOWELING
EMBOWELLED
EMBOWELLING
EMBOWELMENT
EMBOWELMENTS
EMBOWERING
EMBOWERMENT
EMBOWERMENTS
EMBOWMENTS
EMBRACEABLE
EMBRACEMENT
EMBRACEMENTS
EMBRACEORS
EMBRACERIES
EMBRACINGLY

EMBRACINGNESS
EMBRACINGNESSES
EMBRAIDING
EMBRANCHMENT
EMBRANCHMENTS
EMBRANGLED
EMBRANGLEMENT
EMBRANGLEMENTS
EMBRANGLES
EMBRANGLING
EMBRASURED
EMBRASURES
EMBRAZURES
EMBREADING
EMBREATHED
EMBREATHES
EMBREATHING
EMBRITTLED
EMBRITTLEMENT
EMBRITTLEMENTS
EMBRITTLES
EMBRITTLING
EMBROCATED
EMBROCATES
EMBROCATING
EMBROCATION
EMBROCATIONS
EMBROGLIOS
EMBROIDERED
EMBROIDERER
EMBROIDERERS
EMBROIDERIES
EMBROIDERING
EMBROIDERS
EMBROIDERY
EMBROILERS
EMBROILING
EMBROILMENT
EMBROILMENTS
EMBROWNING
EMBRUEMENT
EMBRUEMENTS
EMBRYECTOMIES
EMBRYECTOMY
EMBRYOGENESES
EMBRYOGENESIS
EMBRYOGENETIC
EMBRYOGENIC
EMBRYOGENIES
EMBRYOGENY
EMBRYOLOGIC
EMBRYOLOGICAL
EMBRYOLOGICALLY
EMBRYOLOGIES
EMBRYOLOGIST
EMBRYOLOGISTS
EMBRYOLOGY
EMBRYONATE
EMBRYONATED
EMBRYONICALLY
EMBRYOPHYTE
EMBRYOPHYTES
EMBRYOTOMIES
EMBRYOTOMY
EMBRYULCIA
EMBRYULCIAS
EMENDATING
EMENDATION
EMENDATIONS
EMENDATORS
EMENDATORY
EMERGENCES
EMERGENCIES
EMERGENTLY
EMETICALLY
EMETOPHOBIA
EMETOPHOBIAS
EMICATIONS
EMIGRATING
EMIGRATION
EMIGRATIONAL
EMIGRATIONIST
EMIGRATIONISTS

EMIGRATIONS
EMIGRATORY
EMINENCIES
EMINENTIAL
EMISSARIES
EMISSIVITIES
EMISSIVITY
EMITTANCES
EMMARBLING
EMMENAGOGIC
EMMENAGOGUE
EMMENAGOGUES
EMMENOLOGIES
EMMENOLOGY
EMMETROPES
EMMETROPIA
EMMETROPIAS
EMMETROPIC
EMOLLESCENCE
EMOLLESCENCES
EMOLLIATED
EMOLLIATES
EMOLLIATING
EMOLLIENCE
EMOLLIENCES
EMOLLIENTS
EMOLLITION
EMOLLITIONS
EMOLUMENTAL
EMOLUMENTARY
EMOLUMENTS
EMOTIONABLE
EMOTIONALISE
EMOTIONALISED
EMOTIONALISES
EMOTIONALISING
EMOTIONALISM
EMOTIONALISMS
EMOTIONALIST
EMOTIONALISTIC
EMOTIONALISTS
EMOTIONALITIES
EMOTIONALITY
EMOTIONALIZE
EMOTIONALIZED
EMOTIONALIZES
EMOTIONALIZING
EMOTIONALLY
EMOTIONLESS
EMOTIONLESSLY
EMOTIONLESSNESS
EMOTIVENESS
EMOTIVENESSES
EMOTIVISMS
EMOTIVITIES
EMPACKETED
EMPACKETING
EMPALEMENT
EMPALEMENTS
EMPANELING
EMPANELLED
EMPANELLING
EMPANELMENT
EMPANELMENTS
EMPANOPLIED
EMPANOPLIES
EMPANOPLYING
EMPARADISE
EMPARADISED
EMPARADISES
EMPARADISING
EMPARLAUNCE
EMPARLAUNCES
EMPASSIONATE
EMPASSIONED
EMPATHETIC
EMPATHETICALLY
EMPATHICALLY
EMPATHISED
EMPATHISES
EMPATHISING
EMPATHISTS
EMPATHIZED

EMPATHIZES
EMPATHIZING
EMPATRONED
EMPATRONING
EMPEACHING
EMPENNAGES
EMPEOPLING
EMPERISHED
EMPERISHES
EMPERISHING
EMPERISING
EMPERIZING
EMPERORSHIP
EMPERORSHIPS
EMPHASISED
EMPHASISES
EMPHASISING
EMPHASIZED
EMPHASIZES
EMPHASIZING
EMPHATICAL
EMPHATICALLY
EMPHATICALNESS
EMPHRACTIC
EMPHRACTICS
EMPHYSEMAS
EMPHYSEMATOUS
EMPHYSEMIC
EMPHYSEMICS
EMPHYTEUSES
EMPHYTEUSIS
EMPHYTEUTIC
EMPIECEMENT
EMPIECEMENTS
EMPIERCING
EMPIRICALLY
EMPIRICALNESS
EMPIRICALNESSES
EMPIRICISM
EMPIRICISMS
EMPIRICIST
EMPIRICISTS
EMPIRICUTIC
EMPLACEMENT
EMPLACEMENTS
EMPLASTERED
EMPLASTERING
EMPLASTERS
EMPLASTICS
EMPLASTRON
EMPLASTRONS
EMPLASTRUM
EMPLASTRUMS
EMPLEACHED
EMPLEACHES
EMPLEACHING
EMPLECTONS
EMPLECTUMS
EMPLONGING
EMPLOYABILITIES
EMPLOYABILITY
EMPLOYABLE
EMPLOYABLES
EMPLOYMENT
EMPLOYMENTS
EMPOISONED
EMPOISONING
EMPOISONMENT
EMPOISONMENTS
EMPOLDERED
EMPOLDERING
EMPOVERISH
EMPOVERISHED
EMPOVERISHER
EMPOVERISHERS
EMPOVERISHES
EMPOVERISHING
EMPOVERISHMENT
EMPOVERISHMENTS
EMPOWERING
EMPOWERMENT
EMPOWERMENTS
EMPRESSEMENT

e

EMPRESSEMENTS
EMPTINESSES
EMPURPLING
EMPYREUMATA
EMPYREUMATIC
EMPYREUMATICAL
EMPYREUMATISE
EMPYREUMATISED
EMPYREUMATISES
EMPYREUMATISING
EMPYREUMATIZE
EMPYREUMATIZED
EMPYREUMATIZES
EMPYREUMATIZING
EMULATIONS
EMULATIVELY
EMULATRESS
EMULATRESSES
EMULGENCES
EMULOUSNESS
EMULOUSNESSES
EMULSIFIABLE
EMULSIFICATION
EMULSIFICATIONS
EMULSIFIED
EMULSIFIER
EMULSIFIERS
EMULSIFIES
EMULSIFYING
EMULSIONISE
EMULSIONISED
EMULSIONISES
EMULSIONISING
EMULSIONIZE
EMULSIONIZED
EMULSIONIZES
EMULSIONIZING
EMULSOIDAL
EMUNCTIONS
EMUNCTORIES
ENABLEMENT
ENABLEMENTS
ENACTMENTS
ENALAPRILS
ENAMELISTS
ENAMELLERS
ENAMELLING
ENAMELLINGS
ENAMELLIST
ENAMELLISTS
ENAMELWARE
ENAMELWARES
ENAMELWORK
ENAMELWORKS
ENAMORADOS
ENAMOURING
ENANTIODROMIA
ENANTIODROMIAS
ENANTIODROMIC
ENANTIOMER
ENANTIOMERIC
ENANTIOMERS
ENANTIOMORPH
ENANTIOMORPHIC
ENANTIOMORPHIES
ENANTIOMORPHISM
ENANTIOMORPHOUS
ENANTIOMORPHS
ENANTIOMORPHY
ENANTIOPATHIES
ENANTIOPATHY
ENANTIOSES
ENANTIOSIS
ENANTIOSTYLIES
ENANTIOSTYLOUS
ENANTIOSTYLY
ENANTIOTROPIC
ENANTIOTROPIES
ENANTIOTROPY
ENARRATION
ENARRATIONS
ENARTHRODIAL
ENARTHROSES

ENARTHROSIS
ENCAMPMENT
ENCAMPMENTS
ENCANTHISES
ENCAPSULATE
ENCAPSULATED
ENCAPSULATES
ENCAPSULATING
ENCAPSULATION
ENCAPSULATIONS
ENCAPSULED
ENCAPSULES
ENCAPSULING
ENCARNALISE
ENCARNALISED
ENCARNALISES
ENCARNALISING
ENCARNALIZE
ENCARNALIZED
ENCARNALIZES
ENCARNALIZING
ENCARPUSES
ENCASEMENT
ENCASEMENTS
ENCASHABLE
ENCASHMENT
ENCASHMENTS
ENCAUSTICALLY
ENCAUSTICS
ENCEPHALALGIA
ENCEPHALALGIAS
ENCEPHALIC
ENCEPHALIN
ENCEPHALINE
ENCEPHALINES
ENCEPHALINS
ENCEPHALITIC
ENCEPHALITIDES
ENCEPHALITIS
ENCEPHALITISES
ENCEPHALITOGEN
ENCEPHALITOGENS
ENCEPHALOCELE
ENCEPHALOCELES
ENCEPHALOGRAM
ENCEPHALOGRAMS
ENCEPHALOGRAPH
ENCEPHALOGRAPHS
ENCEPHALOGRAPHY
ENCEPHALOID
ENCEPHALOMA
ENCEPHALOMAS
ENCEPHALOMATA
ENCEPHALON
ENCEPHALONS
ENCEPHALOPATHIC
ENCEPHALOPATHY
ENCEPHALOTOMIES
ENCEPHALOTOMY
ENCEPHALOUS
ENCHAINING
ENCHAINMENT
ENCHAINMENTS
ENCHANTERS
ENCHANTING
ENCHANTINGLY
ENCHANTMENT
ENCHANTMENTS
ENCHANTRESS
ENCHANTRESSES
ENCHARGING
ENCHARMING
ENCHEASONS
ENCHEERING
ENCHEIRIDION
ENCHEIRIDIONS
ENCHILADAS
ENCHIRIDIA
ENCHIRIDION
ENCHIRIDIONS
ENCHONDROMA
ENCHONDROMAS
ENCHONDROMATA

ENCHONDROMATOUS
ENCINCTURE
ENCINCTURED
ENCINCTURES
ENCINCTURING
ENCIPHERED
ENCIPHERER
ENCIPHERERS
ENCIPHERING
ENCIPHERMENT
ENCIPHERMENTS
ENCIRCLEMENT
ENCIRCLEMENTS
ENCIRCLING
ENCIRCLINGS
ENCLASPING
ENCLITICALLY
ENCLOISTER
ENCLOISTERED
ENCLOISTERING
ENCLOISTERS
ENCLOSABLE
ENCLOSURES
ENCLOTHING
ENCLOUDING
ENCODEMENT
ENCODEMENTS
ENCOIGNURE
ENCOIGNURES
ENCOLOURED
ENCOLOURING
ENCOLPIONS
ENCOLPIUMS
ENCOMENDERO
ENCOMENDEROS
ENCOMIASTIC
ENCOMIASTICAL
ENCOMIASTICALLY
ENCOMIASTS
ENCOMIENDA
ENCOMIENDAS
ENCOMPASSED
ENCOMPASSES
ENCOMPASSING
ENCOMPASSMENT
ENCOMPASSMENTS
ENCOPRESES
ENCOPRESIS
ENCOPRETIC
ENCOUNTERED
ENCOUNTERER
ENCOUNTERERS
ENCOUNTERING
ENCOUNTERS
ENCOURAGED
ENCOURAGEMENT
ENCOURAGEMENTS
ENCOURAGER
ENCOURAGERS
ENCOURAGES
ENCOURAGING
ENCOURAGINGLY
ENCOURAGINGS
ENCRADLING
ENCREASING
ENCRIMSONED
ENCRIMSONING
ENCRIMSONS
ENCRINITAL
ENCRINITES
ENCRINITIC
ENCRINITIC
ENCROACHED
ENCROACHER
ENCROACHERS
ENCROACHES
ENCROACHING
ENCROACHINGLY
ENCROACHMENT
ENCROACHMENTS
ENCRUSTATION
ENCRUSTATIONS
ENCRUSTING
ENCRUSTMENT

ENCRUSTMENTS
ENCRYPTING
ENCRYPTION
ENCRYPTIONS
ENCULTURATE
ENCULTURATED
ENCULTURATES
ENCULTURATING
ENCULTURATION
ENCULTURATIONS
ENCULTURATIVE
ENCUMBERED
ENCUMBERING
ENCUMBERINGLY
ENCUMBERMENT
ENCUMBERMENTS
ENCUMBRANCE
ENCUMBRANCER
ENCUMBRANCERS
ENCUMBRANCES
ENCURTAINED
ENCURTAINING
ENCURTAINS
ENCYCLICAL
ENCYCLICALS
ENCYCLOPAEDIA
ENCYCLOPAEDIAS
ENCYCLOPAEDIC
ENCYCLOPAEDISM
ENCYCLOPAEDISMS
ENCYCLOPAEDIST
ENCYCLOPAEDISTS
ENCYCLOPEDIA
ENCYCLOPEDIAN
ENCYCLOPEDIAS
ENCYCLOPEDIC
ENCYCLOPEDICAL
ENCYCLOPEDISM
ENCYCLOPEDISMS
ENCYCLOPEDIST
ENCYCLOPEDISTS
ENCYSTATION
ENCYSTATIONS
ENCYSTMENT
ENCYSTMENTS
ENDAMAGEMENT
ENDAMAGEMENTS
ENDAMAGING
ENDAMOEBAE
ENDAMOEBAS
ENDANGERED
ENDANGERER
ENDANGERERS
ENDANGERING
ENDANGERMENT
ENDANGERMENTS
ENDARCHIES
ENDARTERECTOMY
ENDEARINGLY
ENDEARINGNESS
ENDEARINGNESSES
ENDEARMENT
ENDEARMENTS
ENDEAVORED
ENDEAVORER
ENDEAVORERS
ENDEAVORING
ENDEAVOURED
ENDEAVOURER
ENDEAVOURERS
ENDEAVOURING
ENDEAVOURMENT
ENDEAVOURMENTS
ENDEAVOURS
ENDECAGONS
ENDEIXISES
ENDEMICALLY
ENDEMICITIES
ENDEMICITY
ENDEMIOLOGIES
ENDEMIOLOGY
ENDENIZENED
ENDENIZENING

ENDENIZENS
ENDERGONIC
ENDERMICAL
ENDERMICAL
ENDLESSNESS
ENDLESSNESSES
ENDOBIOTIC
ENDOBLASTIC
ENDOBLASTS
ENDOCARDIA
ENDOCARDIAC
ENDOCARDIAL
ENDOCARDITIC
ENDOCARDITIS
ENDOCARDITISES
ENDOCARDIUM
ENDOCARPAL
ENDOCARPIC
ENDOCENTRIC
ENDOCHONDRAL
ENDOCHYLOUS
ENDOCRANIA
ENDOCRANIAL
ENDOCRANIUM
ENDOCRINAL
ENDOCRINES
ENDOCRINIC
ENDOCRINOLOGIC
ENDOCRINOLOGIES
ENDOCRINOLOGIST
ENDOCRINOLOGY
ENDOCRINOPATHIC
ENDOCRINOPATHY
ENDOCRINOUS
ENDOCRITIC
ENDOCUTICLE
ENDOCUTICLES
ENDOCYTOSES
ENDOCYTOSIS
ENDOCYTOTIC
ENDODERMAL
ENDODERMIC
ENDODERMIS
ENDODERMISES
ENDODONTAL
ENDODONTIC
ENDODONTICALLY
ENDODONTICS
ENDODONTIST
ENDODONTISTS
ENDOENZYME
ENDOENZYMES
ENDOGAMIES
ENDOGAMOUS
ENDOGENIES
ENDOGENOUS
ENDOGENOUSLY
ENDOLITHIC
ENDOLYMPHATIC
ENDOLYMPHS
ENDOMETRIA
ENDOMETRIAL
ENDOMETRIOSES
ENDOMETRIOSIS
ENDOMETRITIS
ENDOMETRITISES
ENDOMETRIUM
ENDOMITOSES
ENDOMITOSIS
ENDOMITOTIC
ENDOMIXISES
ENDOMORPHIC
ENDOMORPHIES
ENDOMORPHISM
ENDOMORPHISMS
ENDOMORPHS
ENDOMORPHY
ENDOMYCORRHIZA
ENDONEURIA
ENDONEURIUM
ENDONUCLEASE
ENDONUCLEASES
ENDONUCLEOLYTIC

ENDOPARASITE
ENDOPARASITES
ENDOPARASITIC
ENDOPARASITISM
ENDOPARASITISMS
ENDOPEPTIDASE
ENDOPEPTIDASES
ENDOPEROXIDE
ENDOPEROXIDES
ENDOPHAGIES
ENDOPHAGOUS
ENDOPHYLLOUS
ENDOPHYTES
ENDOPHYTIC
ENDOPHYTICALLY
ENDOPLASMIC
ENDOPLASMS
ENDOPLASTIC
ENDOPLEURA
ENDOPLEURAS
ENDOPODITE
ENDOPODITES
ENDOPOLYPLOID
ENDOPOLYPLOIDY
ENDOPROCTS
ENDORADIOSONDE
ENDORADIOSONDES
ENDORHIZAL
ENDORPHINS
ENDORSABLE
ENDORSEMENT
ENDORSEMENTS
ENDOSCOPES
ENDOSCOPIC
ENDOSCOPICALLY
ENDOSCOPIES
ENDOSCOPIST
ENDOSCOPISTS
ENDOSKELETAL
ENDOSKELETON
ENDOSKELETONS
ENDOSMOMETER
ENDOSMOMETERS
ENDOSMOMETRIC
ENDOSMOSES
ENDOSMOSIS
ENDOSMOTIC
ENDOSMOTICALLY
ENDOSPERMIC
ENDOSPERMS
ENDOSPORES
ENDOSPOROUS
ENDOSTEALLY
ENDOSTOSES
ENDOSTOSIS
ENDOSTYLES
ENDOSULFAN
ENDOSULFANS
ENDOSYMBIONT
ENDOSYMBIONTS
ENDOSYMBIOSES
ENDOSYMBIOSIS
ENDOSYMBIOTIC
ENDOTHECIA
ENDOTHECIAL
ENDOTHECIUM
ENDOTHELIA
ENDOTHELIAL
ENDOTHELIOID
ENDOTHELIOMA
ENDOTHELIOMAS
ENDOTHELIOMATA
ENDOTHELIUM
ENDOTHERMAL
ENDOTHERMIC
ENDOTHERMICALLY
ENDOTHERMIES
ENDOTHERMISM
ENDOTHERMISMS
ENDOTHERMS
ENDOTHERMY
ENDOTOXINS
ENDOTRACHEAL

ENDOTROPHIC
ENDOWMENTS
ENDPLAYING
ENDUNGEONED
ENDUNGEONING
ENDUNGEONS
ENDURABILITIES
ENDURABILITY
ENDURABLENESS
ENDURABLENESSES
ENDURANCES
ENDURINGLY
ENDURINGNESS
ENDURINGNESSES
ENERGETICAL
ENERGETICALLY
ENERGETICS
ENERGISATION
ENERGISATIONS
ENERGISERS
ENERGISING
ENERGIZATION
ENERGIZATIONS
ENERGIZERS
ENERGIZING
ENERGUMENS
ENERVATING
ENERVATION
ENERVATIONS
ENERVATIVE
ENERVATORS
ENFACEMENT
ENFACEMENTS
ENFEEBLEMENT
ENFEEBLEMENTS
ENFEEBLERS
ENFEEBLING
ENFELONING
ENFEOFFING
ENFEOFFMENT
ENFEOFFMENTS
ENFESTERED
ENFETTERED
ENFETTERING
ENFEVERING
ENFIERCING
ENFILADING
ENFLESHING
ENFLEURAGE
ENFLEURAGES
ENFLOWERED
ENFLOWERING
ENFOLDMENT
ENFOLDMENTS
ENFORCEABILITY
ENFORCEABLE
ENFORCEDLY
ENFORCEMENT
ENFORCEMENTS
ENFORESTED
ENFORESTING
ENFOULDERED
ENFRAMEMENT
ENFRAMEMENTS
ENFRANCHISE
ENFRANCHISED
ENFRANCHISEMENT
ENFRANCHISER
ENFRANCHISERS
ENFRANCHISES
ENFRANCHISING
ENFREEDOMED
ENFREEDOMING
ENFREEDOMS
ENFREEZING
ENGAGEMENT
ENGAGEMENTS
ENGAGINGLY
ENGAGINGNESS
ENGAGINGNESSES
ENGARLANDED
ENGARLANDING
ENGARLANDS

ENGARRISON
ENGARRISONED
ENGARRISONING
ENGARRISONS
ENGENDERED
ENGENDERER
ENGENDERERS
ENGENDERING
ENGENDERMENT
ENGENDERMENTS
ENGENDRURE
ENGENDRURES
ENGENDURES
ENGINEERED
ENGINEERING
ENGINEERINGS
ENGINERIES
ENGIRDLING
ENGISCOPES
ENGLACIALLY
ENGLISHING
ENGLOOMING
ENGLUTTING
ENGORGEMENT
ENGORGEMENTS
ENGOUEMENT
ENGOUEMENTS
ENGOUMENTS
ENGRAFFING
ENGRAFTATION
ENGRAFTATIONS
ENGRAFTING
ENGRAFTMENT
ENGRAFTMENTS
ENGRAILING
ENGRAILMENT
ENGRAILMENTS
ENGRAINEDLY
ENGRAINEDNESS
ENGRAINEDNESSES
ENGRAINERS
ENGRAINING
ENGRAMMATIC
ENGRASPING
ENGRAVERIES
ENGRAVINGS
ENGRENAGES
ENGRIEVING
ENGROOVING
ENGROSSEDLY
ENGROSSERS
ENGROSSING
ENGROSSINGLY
ENGROSSMENT
ENGROSSMENTS
ENGUARDING
ENGULFMENT
ENGULFMENTS
ENGULPHING
ENGYSCOPES
ENHANCEMENT
ENHANCEMENTS
ENHARMONIC
ENHARMONICAL
ENHARMONICALLY
ENHEARSING
ENHEARTENED
ENHEARTENING
ENHEARTENS
ENHUNGERED
ENHUNGERING
ENHYDRITES
ENHYDRITIC
ENHYDROSES
ENHYPOSTASIA
ENHYPOSTASIAS
ENHYPOSTATIC
ENHYPOSTATISE
ENHYPOSTATISED
ENHYPOSTATISES
ENHYPOSTATISING
ENHYPOSTATIZE
ENHYPOSTATIZED

ENHYPOSTATIZES
ENHYPOSTATIZING
ENIGMATICAL
ENIGMATICALLY
ENIGMATISE
ENIGMATISED
ENIGMATISES
ENIGMATISING
ENIGMATIST
ENIGMATISTS
ENIGMATIZE
ENIGMATIZED
ENIGMATIZES
ENIGMATIZING
ENIGMATOGRAPHY
ENJAMBEMENT
ENJAMBEMENTS
ENJAMBMENT
ENJAMBMENTS
ENJOINDERS
ENJOINMENT
ENJOINMENTS
ENJOYABLENESS
ENJOYABLENESSES
ENJOYMENTS
ENKEPHALIN
ENKEPHALINE
ENKEPHALINES
ENKEPHALINS
ENKERNELLED
ENKERNELLING
ENKINDLERS
ENKINDLING
ENLACEMENT
ENLACEMENTS
ENLARGEABLE
ENLARGEDLY
ENLARGEDNESS
ENLARGEDNESSES
ENLARGEMENT
ENLARGEMENTS
ENLARGENED
ENLARGENING
ENLEVEMENT
ENLEVEMENTS
ENLIGHTENED
ENLIGHTENER
ENLIGHTENERS
ENLIGHTENING
ENLIGHTENMENT
ENLIGHTENMENTS
ENLIGHTENS
ENLIGHTING
ENLISTMENT
ENLISTMENTS
ENLIVENERS
ENLIVENING
ENLIVENMENT
ENLIVENMENTS
ENLUMINING
ENMESHMENT
ENMESHMENTS
ENNEAGONAL
ENNEAHEDRA
ENNEAHEDRAL
ENNEAHEDRON
ENNEAHEDRONS
ENNEANDRIAN
ENNEANDROUS
ENNEASTYLE
ENNOBLEMENT
ENNOBLEMENTS
ENOKIDAKES
ENOKITAKES
ENOLOGICAL
ENOLOGISTS
ENORMITIES
ENORMOUSLY
ENORMOUSNESS
ENORMOUSNESSES
ENOUNCEMENT
ENOUNCEMENTS
ENPHYTOTIC

ENQUIRATION
ENQUIRATIONS
ENRAGEMENT
ENRAGEMENTS
ENRANCKLED
ENRANCKLES
ENRANCKLING
ENRAPTURED
ENRAPTURES
ENRAPTURING
ENRAUNGING
ENRAVISHED
ENRAVISHES
ENRAVISHING
ENREGIMENT
ENREGIMENTED
ENREGIMENTING
ENREGIMENTS
ENREGISTER
ENREGISTERED
ENREGISTERING
ENREGISTERS
ENRHEUMING
ENRICHMENT
ENRICHMENTS
ENROLLMENT
ENROLLMENTS
ENROLMENTS
ENROUGHING
ENROUNDING
ENSAMPLING
ENSANGUINATED
ENSANGUINE
ENSANGUINED
ENSANGUINES
ENSANGUINING
ENSCHEDULE
ENSCHEDULED
ENSCHEDULES
ENSCHEDULING
ENSCONCING
ENSCROLLED
ENSCROLLING
ENSEPULCHRE
ENSEPULCHRED
ENSEPULCHRES
ENSEPULCHRING
ENSERFMENT
ENSERFMENTS
ENSHEATHED
ENSHEATHES
ENSHEATHING
ENSHELLING
ENSHELTERED
ENSHELTERING
ENSHELTERS
ENSHIELDED
ENSHIELDING
ENSHRINEES
ENSHRINEMENT
ENSHRINEMENTS
ENSHRINING
ENSHROUDED
ENSHROUDING
ENSIGNCIES
ENSIGNSHIP
ENSIGNSHIPS
ENSILABILITIES
ENSILABILITY
ENSILAGEING
ENSILAGING
ENSLAVEMENT
ENSLAVEMENTS
ENSNAREMENT
ENSNAREMENTS
ENSNARLING
ENSORCELED
ENSORCELING
ENSORCELLED
ENSORCELLING
ENSORCELLMENT
ENSORCELLMENTS
ENSORCELLS

ENSOULMENT
ENSOULMENTS
ENSPHERING
ENSTAMPING
ENSTATITES
ENSTEEPING
ENSTRUCTURED
ENSWATHEMENT
ENSWATHEMENTS
ENSWATHING
ENSWEEPING
ENTABLATURE
ENTABLATURES
ENTABLEMENT
ENTABLEMENTS
ENTAILMENT
ENTAILMENTS
ENTAMOEBAE
ENTAMOEBAS
ENTANGLEMENT
ENTANGLEMENTS
ENTANGLERS
ENTANGLING
ENTELECHIES
ENTELLUSES
ENTENDERED
ENTENDERING
ENTERCHAUNGE
ENTERCHAUNGED
ENTERCHAUNGES
ENTERCHAUNGING
ENTERDEALE
ENTERDEALED
ENTERDEALES
ENTERDEALING
ENTERECTOMIES
ENTERECTOMY
ENTERITIDES
ENTERITISES
ENTEROBACTERIA
ENTEROBACTERIAL
ENTEROBACTERIUM
ENTEROBIASES
ENTEROBIASIS
ENTEROCELE
ENTEROCELES
ENTEROCENTESES
ENTEROCENTESIS
ENTEROCOCCAL
ENTEROCOCCI
ENTEROCOCCUS
ENTEROCOEL
ENTEROCOELE
ENTEROCOELES
ENTEROCOELIC
ENTEROCOELOUS
ENTEROCOELS
ENTEROCOLITIS
ENTEROCOLITISES
ENTEROGASTRONE
ENTEROGASTRONES
ENTEROHEPATITIS
ENTEROKINASE
ENTEROKINASES
ENTEROLITH
ENTEROLITHS
ENTEROPATHIES
ENTEROPATHY
ENTEROPNEUST
ENTEROPNEUSTAL
ENTEROPNEUSTS
ENTEROPTOSES
ENTEROPTOSIS
ENTEROSTOMAL
ENTEROSTOMIES
ENTEROSTOMY
ENTEROTOMIES
ENTEROTOMY
ENTEROTOXIN
ENTEROTOXINS
ENTEROVIRAL
ENTEROVIRUS
ENTEROVIRUSES

ENTERPRISE
ENTERPRISED
ENTERPRISER
ENTERPRISERS
ENTERPRISES
ENTERPRISING
ENTERPRISINGLY
ENTERTAINED
ENTERTAINER
ENTERTAINERS
ENTERTAINING
ENTERTAININGLY
ENTERTAININGS
ENTERTAINMENT
ENTERTAINMENTS
ENTERTAINS
ENTERTAKEN
ENTERTAKES
ENTERTAKING
ENTERTISSUED
ENTHALPIES
ENTHRALDOM
ENTHRALDOMS
ENTHRALLED
ENTHRALLER
ENTHRALLERS
ENTHRALLING
ENTHRALLMENT
ENTHRALLMENTS
ENTHRALMENT
ENTHRALMENTS
ENTHRONEMENT
ENTHRONEMENTS
ENTHRONING
ENTHRONISATION
ENTHRONISATIONS
ENTHRONISE
ENTHRONISED
ENTHRONISES
ENTHRONISING
ENTHRONIZATION
ENTHRONIZATIONS
ENTHRONIZE
ENTHRONIZED
ENTHRONIZES
ENTHRONIZING
ENTHUSIASM
ENTHUSIASMS
ENTHUSIAST
ENTHUSIASTIC
ENTHUSIASTICAL
ENTHUSIASTS
ENTHYMEMATIC
ENTHYMEMATICAL
ENTHYMEMES
ENTICEABLE
ENTICEMENT
ENTICEMENTS
ENTICINGLY
ENTICINGNESS
ENTICINGNESSES
ENTIRENESS
ENTIRENESSES
ENTIRETIES
ENTITATIVE
ENTITLEMENT
ENTITLEMENTS
ENTOBLASTIC
ENTOBLASTS
ENTODERMAL
ENTODERMIC
ENTOILMENT
ENTOILMENTS
ENTOMBMENT
ENTOMBMENTS
ENTOMOFAUNA
ENTOMOFAUNAE
ENTOMOFAUNAS
ENTOMOLOGIC
ENTOMOLOGICAL
ENTOMOLOGICALLY
ENTOMOLOGIES
ENTOMOLOGISE

e

e

ENTOMOLOGISED	ENUCLEATED	ENZYMOLYTIC	EPICONDYLE	EPIGRAMMATISED	EPIPHYSIAL
ENTOMOLOGISES	ENUCLEATES	EOHIPPUSES	EPICONDYLES	EPIGRAMMATISER	EPIPHYTICAL
ENTOMOLOGISING	ENUCLEATING	EOSINOPHIL	EPICONDYLITIS	EPIGRAMMATISERS	EPIPHYTICALLY
ENTOMOLOGIST	ENUCLEATION	EOSINOPHILE	EPICONDYLITISES	EPIGRAMMATISES	EPIPHYTISM
ENTOMOLOGISTS	ENUCLEATIONS	EOSINOPHILES	EPICONTINENTAL	EPIGRAMMATISING	EPIPHYTISMS
ENTOMOLOGIZE	ENUMERABILITIES	EOSINOPHILIA	EPICRANIUM	EPIGRAMMATISM	EPIPHYTOLOGIES
ENTOMOLOGIZED	ENUMERABILITY	EOSINOPHILIAS	EPICUREANISM	EPIGRAMMATISMS	EPIPHYTOLOGY
ENTOMOLOGIZES	ENUMERABLE	EOSINOPHILIC	EPICUREANISMS	EPIGRAMMATIST	EPIPHYTOTIC
ENTOMOLOGIZING	ENUMERATED	EOSINOPHILOUS	EPICUREANS	EPIGRAMMATISTS	EPIPHYTOTICS
ENTOMOLOGY	ENUMERATES	EOSINOPHILS	EPICURISED	EPIGRAMMATIZE	EPIPLASTRA
ENTOMOPHAGIES	ENUMERATING	EPAGOMENAL	EPICURISES	EPIGRAMMATIZED	EPIPLASTRAL
ENTOMOPHAGOUS	ENUMERATION	EPANADIPLOSES	EPICURISING	EPIGRAMMATIZER	EPIPLASTRON
ENTOMOPHAGY	ENUMERATIONS	EPANADIPLOSIS	EPICURISMS	EPIGRAMMATIZERS	EPIPOLISMS
ENTOMOPHILIES	ENUMERATIVE	EPANALEPSES	EPICURIZED	EPIGRAMMATIZES	EPIROGENETIC
ENTOMOPHILOUS	ENUMERATOR	EPANALEPSIS	EPICURIZES	EPIGRAMMATIZING	EPIROGENIC
ENTOMOPHILY	ENUMERATORS	EPANALEPTIC	EPICURIZING	EPIGRAPHED	EPIROGENIES
ENTOMOSTRACAN	ENUNCIABLE	EPANAPHORA	EPICUTICLE	EPIGRAPHER	EPIRRHEMAS
ENTOMOSTRACANS	ENUNCIATED	EPANAPHORAL	EPICUTICLES	EPIGRAPHERS	EPIRRHEMATIC
ENTOMOSTRACOUS	ENUNCIATES	EPANAPHORAS	EPICUTICULAR	EPIGRAPHIC	EPISCOPACIES
ENTOPHYTAL	ENUNCIATING	EPANODOSES	EPICYCLICAL	EPIGRAPHICAL	EPISCOPACY
ENTOPHYTES	ENUNCIATION	EPANORTHOSES	EPICYCLOID	EPIGRAPHICALLY	EPISCOPALIAN
ENTOPHYTIC	ENUNCIATIONS	EPANORTHOSIS	EPICYCLOIDAL	EPIGRAPHIES	EPISCOPALIANISM
ENTOPHYTOUS	ENUNCIATIVE	EPANORTHOTIC	EPICYCLOIDS	EPIGRAPHING	EPISCOPALIANS
ENTOPLASTRA	ENUNCIATIVELY	EPARCHATES	EPIDEICTIC	EPIGRAPHIST	EPISCOPALISM
ENTOPLASTRAL	ENUNCIATOR	EPAULEMENT	EPIDEICTICAL	EPIGRAPHISTS	EPISCOPALISMS
ENTOPLASTRON	ENUNCIATORS	EPAULEMENTS	EPIDEMICAL	EPILATIONS	EPISCOPALLY
ENTOPROCTS	ENUNCIATORY	EPAULETTED	EPIDEMICALLY	EPILEPSIES	EPISCOPANT
ENTOURAGES	ENUREDNESS	EPAULETTES	EPIDEMICITIES	EPILEPTICAL	EPISCOPANTS
ENTRAILING	ENUREDNESSES	EPEIROGENESES	EPIDEMICITY	EPILEPTICALLY	EPISCOPATE
ENTRAINEMENT	ENUREMENTS	EPEIROGENESIS	EPIDEMIOLOGIC	EPILEPTICS	EPISCOPATED
ENTRAINEMENTS	ENURESISES	EPEIROGENETIC	EPIDEMIOLOGICAL	EPILEPTIFORM	EPISCOPATES
ENTRAINERS	ENVASSALLED	EPEIROGENIC	EPIDEMIOLOGIES	EPILEPTOGENIC	EPISCOPATING
ENTRAINING	ENVASSALLING	EPEIROGENICALLY	EPIDEMIOLOGIST	EPILEPTOID	EPISCOPIES
ENTRAINMENT	ENVAULTING	EPEIROGENIES	EPIDEMIOLOGISTS	EPILIMNION	EPISCOPISE
ENTRAINMENTS	ENVEIGLING	EPEIROGENY	EPIDEMIOLOGY	EPILIMNIONS	EPISCOPISED
ENTRAMMELLED	ENVELOPERS	EPENCEPHALA	EPIDENDRONE	EPILOBIUMS	EPISCOPISES
ENTRAMMELLING	ENVELOPING	EPENCEPHALIC	EPIDENDRONES	EPILOGISED	EPISCOPISING
ENTRAMMELS	ENVELOPMENT	EPENCEPHALON	EPIDENDRUM	EPILOGISES	EPISCOPIZE
ENTRANCEMENT	ENVELOPMENTS	EPENCEPHALONS	EPIDENDRUMS	EPILOGISING	EPISCOPIZED
ENTRANCEMENTS	ENVENOMING	EPENTHESES	EPIDERMISES	EPILOGISTIC	EPISCOPIZES
ENTRANCEWAY	ENVENOMISATION	EPENTHESIS	EPIDERMOID	EPILOGISTS	EPISCOPIZING
ENTRANCEWAYS	ENVENOMISATIONS	EPENTHETIC	EPIDERMOLYSES	EPILOGIZED	EPISEMATIC
ENTRANCING	ENVENOMIZATION	EPEOLATRIES	EPIDERMOLYSIS	EPILOGIZES	EPISEPALOUS
ENTRAPMENT	ENVENOMIZATIONS	EPEXEGESES	EPIDIASCOPE	EPILOGIZING	EPISIOTOMIES
ENTRAPMENTS	ENVERMEILED	EPEXEGESIS	EPIDIASCOPES	EPILOGUING	EPISIOTOMY
ENTRAPPERS	ENVERMEILING	EPEXEGETIC	EPIDIDYMAL	EPILOGUISE	EPISODICAL
ENTRAPPING	ENVERMEILS	EPEXEGETICAL	EPIDIDYMIDES	EPILOGUISED	EPISODICALLY
ENTREASURE	ENVIABLENESS	EPEXEGETICALLY	EPIDIDYMIS	EPILOGUISES	EPISOMALLY
ENTREASURED	ENVIABLENESSES	EPHEBOPHILIA	EPIDIDYMITIS	EPILOGUISING	EPISPASTIC
ENTREASURES	ENVIOUSNESS	EPHEBOPHILIAS	EPIDIDYMITISES	EPILOGUIZE	EPISPASTICS
ENTREASURING	ENVIOUSNESSES	EPHEDRINES	EPIDIORITE	EPILOGUIZED	EPISTASIES
ENTREATABLE	ENVIRONICS	EPHEMERALITIES	EPIDIORITES	EPILOGUIZES	EPISTAXISES
ENTREATIES	ENVIRONING	EPHEMERALITY	EPIDOSITES	EPILOGUIZING	EPISTEMICALLY
ENTREATING	ENVIRONMENT	EPHEMERALLY	EPIDOTISATION	EPIMELETIC	EPISTEMICS
ENTREATINGLY	ENVIRONMENTAL	EPHEMERALNESS	EPIDOTISATIONS	EPIMERASES	EPISTEMOLOGICAL
ENTREATIVE	ENVIRONMENTALLY	EPHEMERALNESSES	EPIDOTISED	EPIMERISMS	EPISTEMOLOGIES
ENTREATMENT	ENVIRONMENTS	EPHEMERALS	EPIDOTIZATION	EPIMORPHIC	EPISTEMOLOGIST
ENTREATMENTS	ENVISAGEMENT	EPHEMERIDES	EPIDOTIZATIONS	EPIMORPHOSES	EPISTEMOLOGISTS
ENTRECHATS	ENVISAGEMENTS	EPHEMERIDIAN	EPIDOTIZED	EPIMORPHOSIS	EPISTEMOLOGY
ENTRECOTES	ENVISAGING	EPHEMERIDS	EPIGASTRIA	EPINASTICALLY	EPISTERNAL
ENTREMESSE	ENVISIONED	EPHEMERIST	EPIGASTRIAL	EPINASTIES	EPISTERNUM
ENTREMESSES	ENVISIONING	EPHEMERISTS	EPIGASTRIC	EPINEPHRIN	EPISTERNUMS
ENTRENCHED	ENVOYSHIPS	EPHEMERONS	EPIGASTRIUM	EPINEPHRINE	EPISTILBITE
ENTRENCHER	ENWALLOWED	EPHEMEROPTERAN	EPIGENESES	EPINEPHRINES	EPISTILBITES
ENTRENCHERS	ENWALLOWING	EPHEMEROPTERANS	EPIGENESIS	EPINEPHRINS	EPISTOLARIAN
ENTRENCHES	ENWHEELING	EPHEMEROUS	EPIGENESIST	EPINEURIAL	EPISTOLARIANS
ENTRENCHING	ENWRAPMENT	EPHORALTIES	EPIGENESISTS	EPINEURIUM	EPISTOLARIES
ENTRENCHMENT	ENWRAPMENTS	EPIBLASTIC	EPIGENETIC	EPINEURIUMS	EPISTOLARY
ENTRENCHMENTS	ENWRAPPING	EPICALYCES	EPIGENETICALLY	EPINICIONS	EPISTOLATORY
ENTREPRENEUR	ENWRAPPINGS	EPICALYXES	EPIGENETICIST	EPINIKIONS	EPISTOLERS
ENTREPRENEURIAL	ENWREATHED	EPICANTHIC	EPIGENETICISTS	EPIPELAGIC	EPISTOLETS
ENTREPRENEURS	ENWREATHES	EPICANTHUS	EPIGENETICS	EPIPETALOUS	EPISTOLICAL
ENTREPRENEUSE	ENWREATHING	EPICARDIAC	EPIGENISTS	EPIPHANIES	EPISTOLISE
ENTREPRENEUSES	ENZOOTICALLY	EPICARDIAL	EPIGLOTTAL	EPIPHANOUS	EPISTOLISED
ENTROPICALLY	ENZYMATICALLY	EPICARDIUM	EPIGLOTTIC	EPIPHENOMENA	EPISTOLISES
ENTROPIONS	ENZYMICALLY	EPICENISMS	EPIGLOTTIDES	EPIPHENOMENAL	EPISTOLISING
ENTROPIUMS	ENZYMOLOGICAL	EPICENTERS	EPIGLOTTIS	EPIPHENOMENALLY	EPISTOLIST
ENTRUSTING	ENZYMOLOGIES	EPICENTRAL	EPIGLOTTISES	EPIPHENOMENON	EPISTOLISTS
ENTRUSTMENT	ENZYMOLOGIST	EPICENTRES	EPIGNATHOUS	EPIPHONEMA	EPISTOLIZE
ENTRUSTMENTS	ENZYMOLOGISTS	EPICENTRUM	EPIGONISMS	EPIPHONEMAS	EPISTOLIZED
ENTWINEMENT	ENZYMOLOGY	EPICHEIREMA	EPIGRAMMATIC	EPIPHRAGMS	EPISTOLIZES
ENTWINEMENTS	ENZYMOLYSES	EPICHEIREMAS	EPIGRAMMATICAL	EPIPHYLLOUS	EPISTOLIZING
ENTWISTING	ENZYMOLYSIS	EPICHLOROHYDRIN	EPIGRAMMATISE	EPIPHYSEAL	EPISTOLOGRAPHY

e

EPISTROPHE	EPOXIDIZED	EQUINUMEROUS	ERECTILITY	EROTOLOGICAL	ERYTHROSINES
EPISTROPHES	EPOXIDIZES	EQUIPAGING	ERECTNESSES	EROTOLOGIES	ERYTHROSINS
EPITAPHERS	EPOXIDIZING	EQUIPARATE	EREMACAUSES	EROTOLOGIST	ESCADRILLE
EPITAPHIAL	EPROUVETTE	EQUIPARATED	EREMACAUSIS	EROTOLOGISTS	ESCADRILLES
EPITAPHIAN	EPROUVETTES	EQUIPARATES	EREMITICAL	EROTOMANIA	ESCALADERS
EPITAPHING	EPULATIONS	EQUIPARATING	EREMITISMS	EROTOMANIAC	ESCALADING
EPITAPHIST	EPURATIONS	EQUIPARATION	EREMURUSES	EROTOMANIACS	ESCALADOES
EPITAPHISTS	EQUABILITIES	EQUIPARATIONS	ERETHISMIC	EROTOMANIAS	ESCALATING
EPITAXIALLY	EQUABILITY	EQUIPARTITION	ERETHISTIC	EROTOPHOBIA	ESCALATION
EPITHALAMIA	EQUABLENESS	EQUIPARTITIONS	ERGASTOPLASM	EROTOPHOBIAS	ESCALATIONS
EPITHALAMIC	EQUABLENESSES	EQUIPMENTS	ERGASTOPLASMIC	ERRANTRIES	ESCALATORS
EPITHALAMION	EQUALISATION	EQUIPOISED	ERGASTOPLASMS	ERRATICALLY	ESCALATORY
EPITHALAMIUM	EQUALISATIONS	EQUIPOISES	ERGATANDROMORPH	ERRATICISM	ESCALLONIA
EPITHALAMIUMS	EQUALISERS	EQUIPOISING	ERGATANERS	ERRATICISMS	ESCALLONIAS
EPITHELIAL	EQUALISING	EQUIPOLLENCE	ERGATIVITIES	ERRONEOUSLY	ESCALLOPED
EPITHELIALISE	EQUALITARIAN	EQUIPOLLENCES	ERGATIVITY	ERRONEOUSNESS	ESCALLOPING
EPITHELIALISED	EQUALITARIANISM	EQUIPOLLENCIES	ERGATOCRACIES	ERRONEOUSNESSES	ESCALOPING
EPITHELIALISES	EQUALITARIANS	EQUIPOLLENCY	ERGATOCRACY	ERUBESCENCE	ESCAMOTAGE
EPITHELIALISING	EQUALITIES	EQUIPOLLENT	ERGATOGYNE	ERUBESCENCES	ESCAMOTAGES
EPITHELIALIZE	EQUALIZATION	EQUIPOLLENTLY	ERGATOGYNES	ERUBESCENCIES	ESCAPADOES
EPITHELIALIZED	EQUALIZATIONS	EQUIPOLLENTS	ERGATOMORPH	ERUBESCENCY	ESCAPELESS
EPITHELIALIZES	EQUALIZERS	EQUIPONDERANCE	ERGATOMORPHIC	ERUBESCENT	ESCAPEMENT
EPITHELIALIZING	EQUALIZING	EQUIPONDERANCES	ERGATOMORPHS	ERUBESCITE	ESCAPEMENTS
EPITHELIOID	EQUALNESSES	EQUIPONDERANCY	ERGODICITIES	ERUBESCITES	ESCAPOLOGIES
EPITHELIOMA	EQUANIMITIES	EQUIPONDERANT	ERGODICITY	ERUCTATING	ESCAPOLOGIST
EPITHELIOMAS	EQUANIMITY	EQUIPONDERATE	ERGOGRAPHS	ERUCTATION	ESCAPOLOGISTS
EPITHELIOMATA	EQUANIMOUS	EQUIPONDERATED	ERGOMANIAC	ERUCTATIONS	ESCAPOLOGY
EPITHELIOMATOUS	EQUANIMOUSLY	EQUIPONDERATES	ERGOMANIACS	ERUCTATIVE	ESCARMOUCHE
EPITHELISATION	EQUATABILITIES	EQUIPONDERATING	ERGOMANIAS	ERUDITENESS	ESCARMOUCHES
EPITHELISATIONS	EQUATABILITY	EQUIPOTENT	ERGOMETERS	ERUDITENESSES	ESCARPMENT
EPITHELISE	EQUATIONAL	EQUIPOTENTIAL	ERGOMETRIC	ERUDITIONS	ESCARPMENTS
EPITHELISED	EQUATIONALLY	EQUIPROBABILITY	ERGOMETRIES	ERUPTIONAL	ESCHAROTIC
EPITHELISES	EQUATORIAL	EQUIPROBABLE	ERGONOMICALLY	ERUPTIVELY	ESCHAROTICS
EPITHELISING	EQUATORIALLY	EQUISETACEOUS	ERGONOMICS	ERUPTIVENESS	ESCHATOLOGIC
EPITHELIUM	EQUATORIALS	EQUISETIFORM	ERGONOMIST	ERUPTIVENESSES	ESCHATOLOGICAL
EPITHELIUMS	EQUATORWARD	EQUISETUMS	ERGONOMISTS	ERUPTIVITIES	ESCHATOLOGIES
EPITHELIZATION	EQUESTRIAN	EQUITABILITIES	ERGONOVINE	ERUPTIVITY	ESCHATOLOGIST
EPITHELIZATIONS	EQUESTRIANISM	EQUITABILITY	ERGONOVINES	ERVALENTAS	ESCHATOLOGISTS
EPITHELIZE	EQUESTRIANISMS	EQUITABLENESS	ERGOPHOBIA	ERYSIPELAS	ESCHATOLOGY
EPITHELIZED	EQUESTRIANS	EQUITABLENESSES	ERGOPHOBIAS	ERYSIPELASES	ESCHEATABLE
EPITHELIZES	EQUESTRIENNE	EQUITATION	ERGOSTEROL	ERYSIPELATOUS	ESCHEATAGE
EPITHELIZING	EQUESTRIENNES	EQUITATIONS	ERGOSTEROLS	ERYSIPELOID	ESCHEATAGES
EPITHEMATA	EQUIANGULAR	EQUIVALENCE	ERGOTAMINE	ERYSIPELOIDS	ESCHEATING
EPITHERMAL	EQUIANGULARITY	EQUIVALENCES	ERGOTAMINES	ERYTHEMATIC	ESCHEATMENT
EPITHETICAL	EQUIBALANCE	EQUIVALENCIES	ERGOTISING	ERYTHEMATOUS	ESCHEATMENTS
EPITHETING	EQUIBALANCED	EQUIVALENCY	ERGOTIZING	ERYTHORBATE	ESCHEATORS
EPITHETONS	EQUIBALANCES	EQUIVALENT	ERICACEOUS	ERYTHORBATES	ESCHSCHOLTZIA
EPITHYMETIC	EQUIBALANCING	EQUIVALENTLY	ERINACEOUS	ERYTHRAEMIA	ESCHSCHOLTZIAS
EPITOMICAL	EQUICALORIC	EQUIVALENTS	ERIOMETERS	ERYTHRAEMIAS	ESCHSCHOLZIA
EPITOMISATION	EQUIDIFFERENT	EQUIVOCALITIES	ERIOPHOROUS	ERYTHREMIA	ESCHSCHOLZIAS
EPITOMISATIONS	EQUIDISTANCE	EQUIVOCALITY	ERIOPHORUM	ERYTHREMIAS	ESCLANDRES
EPITOMISED	EQUIDISTANCES	EQUIVOCALLY	ERIOPHORUMS	ERYTHRINAS	ESCOPETTES
EPITOMISER	EQUIDISTANT	EQUIVOCALNESS	ERIOPHYIDS	ERYTHRISMAL	ESCORTAGES
EPITOMISERS	EQUIDISTANTLY	EQUIVOCALNESSES	ERIOSTEMON	ERYTHRISMS	ESCRIBANOS
EPITOMISES	EQUILATERAL	EQUIVOCATE	ERIOSTEMONS	ERYTHRISTIC	ESCRITOIRE
EPITOMISING	EQUILATERALLY	EQUIVOCATED	ERISTICALLY	ERYTHRITES	ESCRITOIRES
EPITOMISTS	EQUILATERALS	EQUIVOCATES	ERODIBILITIES	ERYTHRITIC	ESCRITORIAL
EPITOMIZATION	EQUILIBRANT	EQUIVOCATING	ERODIBILITY	ERYTHRITOL	ESCUTCHEON
EPITOMIZATIONS	EQUILIBRANTS	EQUIVOCATINGLY	EROGENEITIES	ERYTHRITOLS	ESCUTCHEONED
EPITOMIZED	EQUILIBRATE	EQUIVOCATION	EROGENEITY	ERYTHROBLAST	ESCUTCHEONS
EPITOMIZER	EQUILIBRATED	EQUIVOCATIONS	EROSIONALLY	ERYTHROBLASTIC	ESEMPLASIES
EPITOMIZERS	EQUILIBRATES	EQUIVOCATOR	EROSIVENESS	ERYTHROBLASTS	ESEMPLASTIC
EPITOMIZES	EQUILIBRATING	EQUIVOCATORS	EROSIVENESSES	ERYTHROCYTE	ESOPHAGEAL
EPITOMIZING	EQUILIBRATION	EQUIVOCATORY	EROSIVITIES	ERYTHROCYTES	ESOPHAGOSCOPE
EPITRACHELION	EQUILIBRATIONS	EQUIVOQUES	EROTICALLY	ERYTHROCYTIC	ESOPHAGOSCOPES
EPITRACHELIONS	EQUILIBRATOR	ERADIATING	EROTICISATION	ERYTHROMELALGIA	ESOPHAGUSES
EPITROCHOID	EQUILIBRATORS	ERADIATION	EROTICISATIONS	ERYTHROMYCIN	ESOTERICALLY
EPITROCHOIDS	EQUILIBRATORY	ERADIATIONS	EROTICISED	ERYTHROMYCINS	ESOTERICISM
EPIZEUXISES	EQUILIBRIA	ERADICABLE	EROTICISES	ERYTHRONIUM	ESOTERICISMS
EPIZOOTICALLY	EQUILIBRIST	ERADICABLY	EROTICISING	ERYTHRONIUMS	ESOTERICIST
EPIZOOTICS	EQUILIBRISTIC	ERADICANTS	EROTICISMS	ERYTHROPENIA	ESOTERICISTS
EPIZOOTIES	EQUILIBRISTS	ERADICATED	EROTICISTS	ERYTHROPENIAS	ESOTERISMS
EPIZOOTIOLOGIC	EQUILIBRITIES	ERADICATES	EROTICIZATION	ERYTHROPHOBIA	ESOTROPIAS
EPIZOOTIOLOGIES	EQUILIBRITY	ERADICATING	EROTICIZATIONS	ERYTHROPHOBIAS	ESPADRILLE
EPIZOOTIOLOGY	EQUILIBRIUM	ERADICATION	EROTICIZED	ERYTHROPOIESES	ESPADRILLES
EPONYCHIUM	EQUILIBRIUMS	ERADICATIONS	EROTICIZES	ERYTHROPOIESIS	ESPAGNOLES
EPONYCHIUMS	EQUIMOLECULAR	ERADICATIVE	EROTICIZING	ERYTHROPOIETIC	ESPAGNOLETTE
EPONYMOUSLY	EQUIMULTIPLE	ERADICATOR	EROTISATION	ERYTHROPOIETIN	ESPAGNOLETTES
EPOXIDATION	EQUIMULTIPLES	ERADICATORS	EROTISATIONS	ERYTHROPOIETINS	ESPALIERED
EPOXIDATIONS	EQUINITIES	ERASABILITIES	EROTIZATION	ERYTHROPSIA	ESPALIERING
EPOXIDISED	EQUINOCTIAL	ERASABILITY	EROTIZATIONS	ERYTHROPSIAS	ESPECIALLY
EPOXIDISES	EQUINOCTIALLY	ERASEMENTS	EROTOGENIC	ERYTHROSIN	ESPERANCES
EPOXIDISING	EQUINOCTIALS	ERECTILITIES	EROTOGENOUS	ERYTHROSINE	ESPIEGLERIE

e

ESPIEGLERIES	ESTRILDIDS	ETHNICALLY	ETYMOLOGISTS	EUHEMERIZING	EUROCURRENCIES
ESPIONAGES	ESTROGENIC	ETHNICISMS	ETYMOLOGIZE	EUKARYOTES	EUROCURRENCY
ESPLANADES	ESTROGENICALLY	ETHNICITIES	ETYMOLOGIZED	EUKARYOTIC	EURODEPOSIT
ESPRESSIVO	ESURIENCES	ETHNOBIOLOGIES	ETYMOLOGIZES	EULOGISERS	EURODEPOSITS
ESQUIRESSES	ESURIENCIES	ETHNOBIOLOGY	ETYMOLOGIZING	EULOGISING	EURODOLLAR
ESSAYETTES	ESURIENTLY	ETHNOBOTANICAL	EUBACTERIA	EULOGISTIC	EURODOLLARS
ESSAYISTIC	ETEPIMELETIC	ETHNOBOTANIES	EUBACTERIUM	EULOGISTICAL	EUROMARKET
ESSENTIALISE	ETERNALISATION	ETHNOBOTANIST	EUCALYPTOL	EULOGISTICALLY	EUROMARKETS
ESSENTIALISED	ETERNALISATIONS	ETHNOBOTANISTS	EUCALYPTOLE	EULOGIZERS	EUROPEANISE
ESSENTIALISES	ETERNALISE	ETHNOBOTANY	EUCALYPTOLES	EULOGIZING	EUROPEANISED
ESSENTIALISING	ETERNALISED	ETHNOCENTRIC	EUCALYPTOLS	EUMELANINS	EUROPEANISES
ESSENTIALISM	ETERNALISES	ETHNOCENTRICITY	EUCALYPTUS	EUNUCHISED	EUROPEANISING
ESSENTIALISMS	ETERNALISING	ETHNOCENTRISM	EUCALYPTUSES	EUNUCHISES	EUROPEANIZE
ESSENTIALIST	ETERNALIST	ETHNOCENTRISMS	EUCARYOTES	EUNUCHISING	EUROPEANIZED
ESSENTIALISTS	ETERNALISTS	ETHNOCIDES	EUCARYOTIC	EUNUCHISMS	EUROPEANIZES
ESSENTIALITIES	ETERNALITIES	ETHNOGENIC	EUCHARISES	EUNUCHIZED	EUROPEANIZING
ESSENTIALITY	ETERNALITY	ETHNOGENIES	EUCHARISTIC	EUNUCHIZES	EUROPHILES
ESSENTIALIZE	ETERNALIZATION	ETHNOGENIST	EUCHARISTICAL	EUNUCHIZING	EUROPHILIA
ESSENTIALIZED	ETERNALIZATIONS	ETHNOGENISTS	EUCHLORINE	EUNUCHOIDISM	EUROPHILIAS
ESSENTIALIZES	ETERNALIZE	ETHNOGRAPHER	EUCHLORINES	EUNUCHOIDISMS	EUROPHOBIA
ESSENTIALIZING	ETERNALIZED	ETHNOGRAPHERS	EUCHLORINS	EUNUCHOIDS	EUROPHOBIAS
ESSENTIALLY	ETERNALIZES	ETHNOGRAPHIC	EUCHOLOGIA	EUONYMUSES	EUROPHOBIC
ESSENTIALNESS	ETERNALIZING	ETHNOGRAPHICA	EUCHOLOGIES	EUPATORIUM	EUROTERMINAL
ESSENTIALNESSES	ETERNALNESS	ETHNOGRAPHICAL	EUCHOLOGION	EUPATORIUMS	EUROTERMINALS
ESSENTIALS	ETERNALNESSES	ETHNOGRAPHIES	EUCHROMATIC	EUPATRIDAE	EURYBATHIC
ESTABLISHABLE	ETERNISATION	ETHNOGRAPHY	EUCHROMATIN	EUPEPTICITIES	EURYHALINE
ESTABLISHED	ETERNISATIONS	ETHNOHISTORIAN	EUCHROMATINS	EUPEPTICITY	EURYPTERID
ESTABLISHER	ETERNISING	ETHNOHISTORIANS	EUCRYPHIAS	EUPHAUSIACEAN	EURYPTERIDS
ESTABLISHERS	ETERNITIES	ETHNOHISTORIC	EUDAEMONIA	EUPHAUSIACEANS	EURYPTEROID
ESTABLISHES	ETERNIZATION	ETHNOHISTORICAL	EUDAEMONIAS	EUPHAUSIDS	EURYPTEROIDS
ESTABLISHING	ETERNIZATIONS	ETHNOHISTORIES	EUDAEMONIC	EUPHAUSIID	EURYTHERMAL
ESTABLISHMENT	ETERNIZING	ETHNOHISTORY	EUDAEMONICS	EUPHAUSIIDS	EURYTHERMIC
ESTABLISHMENTS	ETHAMBUTOL	ETHNOLINGUIST	EUDAEMONIES	EUPHEMISED	EURYTHERMOUS
ESTAFETTES	ETHAMBUTOLS	ETHNOLINGUISTIC	EUDAEMONISM	EUPHEMISER	EURYTHERMS
ESTAMINETS	ETHANEDIOIC	ETHNOLINGUISTS	EUDAEMONISMS	EUPHEMISERS	EURYTHMICAL
ESTANCIERO	ETHANEDIOL	ETHNOLOGIC	EUDAEMONIST	EUPHEMISES	EURYTHMICS
ESTANCIEROS	ETHANEDIOLS	ETHNOLOGICAL	EUDAEMONISTIC	EUPHEMISING	EURYTHMIES
ESTATESMAN	ETHANOATES	ETHNOLOGICALLY	EUDAEMONISTICAL	EUPHEMISMS	EUSPORANGIATE
ESTATESMEN	ETHANOLAMINE	ETHNOLOGIES	EUDAEMONISTS	EUPHEMISTIC	EUSTATICALLY
ESTERIFICATION	ETHANOLAMINES	ETHNOLOGIST	EUDAIMONISM	EUPHEMISTICALLY	EUTECTOIDS
ESTERIFICATIONS	ETHEOSTOMINE	ETHNOLOGISTS	EUDAIMONISMS	EUPHEMISTS	EUTHANASIA
ESTERIFIED	ETHEREALISATION	ETHNOMUSICOLOGY	EUDEMONIAS	EUPHEMIZED	EUTHANASIAS
ESTERIFIES	ETHEREALISE	ETHNOSCIENCE	EUDEMONICS	EUPHEMIZER	EUTHANASIAST
ESTERIFYING	ETHEREALISED	ETHNOSCIENCES	EUDEMONISM	EUPHEMIZERS	EUTHANASIASTS
ESTHESIOGEN	ETHEREALISES	ETHOLOGICAL	EUDEMONISMS	EUPHEMIZES	EUTHANASIC
ESTHESIOGENS	ETHEREALISING	ETHOLOGICALLY	EUDEMONIST	EUPHEMIZING	EUTHANASIES
ESTHESISES	ETHEREALITIES	ETHOLOGIES	EUDEMONISTIC	EUPHONICAL	EUTHANATISE
ESTHETICAL	ETHEREALITY	ETHOLOGIST	EUDEMONISTICAL	EUPHONICALLY	EUTHANATISED
ESTHETICALLY	ETHEREALIZATION	ETHOLOGISTS	EUDEMONISTS	EUPHONIOUS	EUTHANATISES
ESTHETICIAN	ETHEREALIZE	ETHOXYETHANE	EUDIALYTES	EUPHONIOUSLY	EUTHANATISING
ESTHETICIANS	ETHEREALIZED	ETHOXYETHANES	EUDICOTYLEDON	EUPHONIOUSNESS	EUTHANATIZE
ESTHETICISM	ETHEREALIZES	ETHYLAMINE	EUDICOTYLEDONS	EUPHONISED	EUTHANATIZED
ESTHETICISMS	ETHEREALIZING	ETHYLAMINES	EUDIOMETER	EUPHONISES	EUTHANATIZES
ESTIMABLENESS	ETHEREALLY	ETHYLATING	EUDIOMETERS	EUPHONISING	EUTHANATIZING
ESTIMABLENESSES	ETHEREALNESS	ETHYLATION	EUDIOMETRIC	EUPHONISMS	EUTHANISED
ESTIMATING	ETHEREALNESSES	ETHYLATIONS	EUDIOMETRICAL	EUPHONIUMS	EUTHANISES
ESTIMATION	ETHERIFICATION	ETHYLBENZENE	EUDIOMETRICALLY	EUPHONIZED	EUTHANISING
ESTIMATIONS	ETHERIFICATIONS	ETHYLBENZENES	EUDIOMETRIES	EUPHONIZES	EUTHANIZED
ESTIMATIVE	ETHERIFIED	ETIOLATING	EUDIOMETRY	EUPHONIZING	EUTHANIZES
ESTIMATORS	ETHERIFIES	ETIOLATION	EUGENECIST	EUPHORBIACEOUS	EUTHANIZING
ESTIPULATE	ETHERIFYING	ETIOLATIONS	EUGENECISTS	EUPHORBIAS	EUTHENISTS
ESTIVATING	ETHERISATION	ETIOLOGICAL	EUGENICALLY	EUPHORBIUM	EUTHERIANS
ESTIVATION	ETHERISATIONS	ETIOLOGICALLY	EUGENICIST	EUPHORBIUMS	EUTHYROIDS
ESTIVATIONS	ETHERISERS	ETIOLOGIES	EUGENICISTS	EUPHORIANT	EUTRAPELIA
ESTIVATORS	ETHERISING	ETIOLOGIST	EUGEOSYNCLINAL	EUPHORIANTS	EUTRAPELIAS
ESTOPPAGES	ETHERIZATION	ETIOLOGISTS	EUGEOSYNCLINE	EUPHORICALLY	EUTRAPELIES
ESTRADIOLS	ETHERIZATIONS	ETIQUETTES	EUGEOSYNCLINES	EUPHRASIES	EUTROPHICATION
ESTRAMAZONE	ETHERIZERS	ETONOGESTREL	EUGLOBULIN	EUPHUISING	EUTROPHICATIONS
ESTRAMAZONES	ETHERIZING	ETONOGESTRELS	EUGLOBULINS	EUPHUISTIC	EUTROPHIES
ESTRANGEDNESS	ETHEROMANIA	ETOURDERIE	EUHARMONIC	EUPHUISTICAL	EVACUATING
ESTRANGEDNESSES	ETHEROMANIAC	ETOURDERIES	EUHEMERISE	EUPHUISTICALLY	EVACUATION
ESTRANGELO	ETHEROMANIACS	ETRANGERES	EUHEMERISED	EUPHUIZING	EVACUATIONS
ESTRANGELOS	ETHEROMANIAS	ETYMOLOGICA	EUHEMERISES	EUPLASTICS	EVACUATIVE
ESTRANGEMENT	ETHICALITIES	ETYMOLOGICAL	EUHEMERISING	EUPLOIDIES	EVACUATORS
ESTRANGEMENTS	ETHICALITY	ETYMOLOGICALLY	EUHEMERISM	EURHYTHMIC	EVAGATIONS
ESTRANGERS	ETHICALNESS	ETYMOLOGICON	EUHEMERISMS	EURHYTHMICAL	EVAGINATED
ESTRANGHELO	ETHICALNESSES	ETYMOLOGICUM	EUHEMERIST	EURHYTHMICS	EVAGINATES
ESTRANGHELOS	ETHICISING	ETYMOLOGIES	EUHEMERISTIC	EURHYTHMIES	EVAGINATING
ESTRANGING	ETHICIZING	ETYMOLOGISE	EUHEMERISTS	EURHYTHMIST	EVAGINATION
ESTRAPADES	ETHIONAMIDE	ETYMOLOGISED	EUHEMERIZE	EURHYTHMISTS	EVAGINATIONS
ESTREATING	ETHIONAMIDES	ETYMOLOGISES	EUHEMERIZED	EUROCHEQUE	EVALUATING
ESTREPEMENT	ETHIONINES	ETYMOLOGISING	EUHEMERIZES	EUROCHEQUES	EVALUATION
ESTREPEMENTS	ETHNARCHIES	ETYMOLOGIST		EUROCREEPS	EVALUATIONS

EVALUATIVE	EVENTRATES	EXACTINGNESS	EXCEPTIONABLY	EXCOGITATIVE	EXECRATORY
EVALUATORS	EVENTRATING	EXACTINGNESSES	EXCEPTIONAL	EXCOGITATOR	EXECUTABLE
EVANESCENCE	EVENTRATION	EXACTITUDE	EXCEPTIONALISM	EXCOGITATORS	EXECUTABLES
EVANESCENCES	EVENTRATIONS	EXACTITUDES	EXCEPTIONALISMS	EXCOMMUNICABLE	EXECUTANCIES
EVANESCENT	EVENTUALISE	EXACTMENTS	EXCEPTIONALITY	EXCOMMUNICATE	EXECUTANCY
EVANESCENTLY	EVENTUALISED	EXACTNESSES	EXCEPTIONALLY	EXCOMMUNICATED	EXECUTANTS
EVANESCING	EVENTUALISES	EXACTRESSES	EXCEPTIONALNESS	EXCOMMUNICATES	EXECUTARIES
EVANGELIAR	EVENTUALISING	EXAGGERATE	EXCEPTIONALS	EXCOMMUNICATING	EXECUTIONER
EVANGELIARIES	EVENTUALITIES	EXAGGERATED	EXCEPTIONS	EXCOMMUNICATION	EXECUTIONERS
EVANGELIARION	EVENTUALITY	EXAGGERATEDLY	EXCEPTIOUS	EXCOMMUNICATIVE	EXECUTIONS
EVANGELIARIONS	EVENTUALIZE	EXAGGERATEDNESS	EXCEPTLESS	EXCOMMUNICATOR	EXECUTIVELY
EVANGELIARIUM	EVENTUALIZED	EXAGGERATES	EXCERPTERS	EXCOMMUNICATORS	EXECUTIVES
EVANGELIARIUMS	EVENTUALIZES	EXAGGERATING	EXCERPTIBLE	EXCOMMUNICATORY	EXECUTORIAL
EVANGELIARS	EVENTUALIZING	EXAGGERATINGLY	EXCERPTING	EXCOMMUNION	EXECUTORSHIP
EVANGELIARY	EVENTUALLY	EXAGGERATION	EXCERPTINGS	EXCOMMUNIONS	EXECUTORSHIPS
EVANGELICAL	EVENTUATED	EXAGGERATIONS	EXCERPTION	EXCORIATED	EXECUTRESS
EVANGELICALISM	EVENTUATES	EXAGGERATIVE	EXCERPTIONS	EXCORIATES	EXECUTRESSES
EVANGELICALISMS	EVENTUATING	EXAGGERATOR	EXCERPTORS	EXCORIATING	EXECUTRICES
EVANGELICALLY	EVENTUATION	EXAGGERATORS	EXCESSIVELY	EXCORIATION	EXECUTRIES
EVANGELICALNESS	EVENTUATIONS	EXAGGERATORY	EXCESSIVENESS	EXCORIATIONS	EXECUTRIXES
EVANGELICALS	EVERBLOOMING	EXAHERTZES	EXCESSIVENESSES	EXCORTICATE	EXEGETICAL
EVANGELICISM	EVERDURING	EXALBUMINOUS	EXCHANGEABILITY	EXCORTICATED	EXEGETICALLY
EVANGELICISMS	EVERGLADES	EXALTATION	EXCHANGEABLE	EXCORTICATES	EXEGETISTS
EVANGELIES	EVERGREENS	EXALTATIONS	EXCHANGEABLY	EXCORTICATING	EXEMPLARILY
EVANGELISATION	EVERLASTING	EXALTEDNESS	EXCHANGERS	EXCORTICATION	EXEMPLARINESS
EVANGELISATIONS	EVERLASTINGLY	EXALTEDNESSES	EXCHANGING	EXCORTICATIONS	EXEMPLARINESSES
EVANGELISE	EVERLASTINGNESS	EXAMINABILITIES	EXCHEQUERED	EXCREMENTA	EXEMPLARITIES
EVANGELISED	EVERLASTINGS	EXAMINABILITY	EXCHEQUERING	EXCREMENTAL	EXEMPLARITY
EVANGELISER	EVERYDAYNESS	EXAMINABLE	EXCHEQUERS	EXCREMENTITIAL	EXEMPLIFIABLE
EVANGELISERS	EVERYDAYNESSES	EXAMINANTS	EXCIPIENTS	EXCREMENTITIOUS	EXEMPLIFICATION
EVANGELISES	EVERYPLACE	EXAMINATES	EXCISIONAL	EXCREMENTS	EXEMPLIFICATIVE
EVANGELISING	EVERYTHING	EXAMINATION	EXCITABILITIES	EXCREMENTUM	EXEMPLIFIED
EVANGELISM	EVERYWHENCE	EXAMINATIONAL	EXCITABILITY	EXCRESCENCE	EXEMPLIFIER
EVANGELISMS	EVERYWHERE	EXAMINATIONS	EXCITABLENESS	EXCRESCENCES	EXEMPLIFIERS
EVANGELIST	EVERYWHITHER	EXAMINATOR	EXCITABLENESSES	EXCRESCENCIES	EXEMPLIFIES
EVANGELISTARIES	EVERYWOMAN	EXAMINATORS	EXCITANCIES	EXCRESCENCY	EXEMPLIFYING
EVANGELISTARION	EVERYWOMEN	EXAMINERSHIP	EXCITATION	EXCRESCENT	EXEMPTIONS
EVANGELISTARY	EVIDENCING	EXAMINERSHIPS	EXCITATIONS	EXCRESCENTIAL	EXENTERATE
EVANGELISTIC	EVIDENTIAL	EXANIMATION	EXCITATIVE	EXCRESCENTLY	EXENTERATED
EVANGELISTS	EVIDENTIALLY	EXANIMATIONS	EXCITATORY	EXCRETIONS	EXENTERATES
EVANGELIZATION	EVIDENTIARY	EXANTHEMAS	EXCITEDNESS	EXCRETORIES	EXENTERATING
EVANGELIZATIONS	EVILDOINGS	EXANTHEMATA	EXCITEDNESSES	EXCRUCIATE	EXENTERATION
EVANGELIZE	EVILNESSES	EXANTHEMATIC	EXCITEMENT	EXCRUCIATED	EXENTERATIONS
EVANGELIZED	EVINCEMENT	EXANTHEMATOUS	EXCITEMENTS	EXCRUCIATES	EXEQUATURS
EVANGELIZER	EVINCEMENTS	EXARATIONS	EXCITINGLY	EXCRUCIATING	EXERCISABLE
EVANGELIZERS	EVISCERATE	EXARCHATES	EXCLAIMERS	EXCRUCIATINGLY	EXERCISERS
EVANGELIZES	EVISCERATED	EXARCHISTS	EXCLAIMING	EXCRUCIATION	EXERCISING
EVANGELIZING	EVISCERATES	EXASPERATE	EXCLAMATION	EXCRUCIATIONS	EXERCITATION
EVANISHING	EVISCERATING	EXASPERATED	EXCLAMATIONAL	EXCULPABLE	EXERCITATIONS
EVANISHMENT	EVISCERATION	EXASPERATEDLY	EXCLAMATIONS	EXCULPATED	EXERCYCLES
EVANISHMENTS	EVISCERATIONS	EXASPERATER	EXCLAMATIVE	EXCULPATES	EXFOLIANTS
EVANITIONS	EVISCERATOR	EXASPERATERS	EXCLAMATORILY	EXCULPATING	EXFOLIATED
EVAPORABILITIES	EVISCERATORS	EXASPERATES	EXCLAMATORY	EXCULPATION	EXFOLIATES
EVAPORABILITY	EVITATIONS	EXASPERATING	EXCLAUSTRATION	EXCULPATIONS	EXFOLIATING
EVAPORABLE	EVITERNALLY	EXASPERATINGLY	EXCLAUSTRATIONS	EXCULPATORY	EXFOLIATION
EVAPORATED	EVITERNITIES	EXASPERATION	EXCLOSURES	EXCURSIONED	EXFOLIATIONS
EVAPORATES	EVITERNITY	EXASPERATIONS	EXCLUDABILITIES	EXCURSIONING	EXFOLIATIVE
EVAPORATING	EVOCATIONS	EXASPERATIVE	EXCLUDABILITY	EXCURSIONISE	EXFOLIATOR
EVAPORATION	EVOCATIVELY	EXASPERATOR	EXCLUDABLE	EXCURSIONISED	EXFOLIATORS
EVAPORATIONS	EVOCATIVENESS	EXASPERATORS	EXCLUDIBLE	EXCURSIONISES	EXHALATION
EVAPORATIVE	EVOCATIVENESSES	EXCAMBIONS	EXCLUSIONARY	EXCURSIONISING	EXHALATIONS
EVAPORATOR	EVOLUTIONAL	EXCAMBIUMS	EXCLUSIONISM	EXCURSIONIST	EXHAUSTERS
EVAPORATORS	EVOLUTIONARILY	EXCARNATED	EXCLUSIONISMS	EXCURSIONISTS	EXHAUSTIBILITY
EVAPORIMETER	EVOLUTIONARY	EXCARNATES	EXCLUSIONIST	EXCURSIONIZE	EXHAUSTIBLE
EVAPORIMETERS	EVOLUTIONISM	EXCARNATING	EXCLUSIONISTS	EXCURSIONIZED	EXHAUSTING
EVAPORITES	EVOLUTIONISMS	EXCARNATION	EXCLUSIONS	EXCURSIONIZES	EXHAUSTION
EVAPORITIC	EVOLUTIONIST	EXCARNATIONS	EXCLUSIVELY	EXCURSIONIZING	EXHAUSTIONS
EVAPOROGRAPH	EVOLUTIONISTIC	EXCAVATING	EXCLUSIVENESS	EXCURSIONS	EXHAUSTIVE
EVAPOROGRAPHS	EVOLUTIONISTS	EXCAVATION	EXCLUSIVENESSES	EXCURSIVELY	EXHAUSTIVELY
EVAPOROMETER	EVOLUTIONS	EXCAVATIONAL	EXCLUSIVES	EXCURSIVENESS	EXHAUSTIVENESS
EVAPOROMETERS	EVOLVEMENT	EXCAVATIONS	EXCLUSIVISM	EXCURSIVENESSES	EXHAUSTIVITIES
EVASIVENESS	EVOLVEMENTS	EXCAVATORS	EXCLUSIVISMS	EXCURSUSES	EXHAUSTIVITY
EVASIVENESSES	EVONYMUSES	EXCEEDABLE	EXCLUSIVIST	EXCUSABLENESS	EXHAUSTLESS
EVECTIONAL	EVULGATING	EXCEEDINGLY	EXCLUSIVISTS	EXCUSABLENESSES	EXHAUSTLESSLY
EVENEMENTS	EXACERBATE	EXCELLENCE	EXCLUSIVITIES	EXCUSATORY	EXHAUSTLESSNESS
EVENHANDED	EXACERBATED	EXCELLENCES	EXCLUSIVITY	EXECRABLENESS	EXHEREDATE
EVENHANDEDLY	EXACERBATES	EXCELLENCIES	EXCOGITABLE	EXECRABLENESSES	EXHEREDATED
EVENHANDEDNESS	EXACERBATING	EXCELLENCY	EXCOGITATE	EXECRATING	EXHEREDATES
EVENNESSES	EXACERBATION	EXCELLENTLY	EXCOGITATED	EXECRATION	EXHEREDATING
EVENTFULLY	EXACERBATIONS	EXCELSIORS	EXCOGITATES	EXECRATIONS	EXHEREDATION
EVENTFULNESS	EXACERBESCENCE	EXCENTRICS	EXCOGITATING	EXECRATIVE	EXHEREDATIONS
EVENTFULNESSES	EXACERBESCENCES	EXCEPTANTS	EXCOGITATION	EXECRATIVELY	EXHIBITERS
EVENTRATED	EXACTINGLY	EXCEPTIONABLE	EXCOGITATIONS	EXECRATORS	EXHIBITING

e

EXHIBITION
EXHIBITIONER
EXHIBITIONERS
EXHIBITIONISM
EXHIBITIONISMS
EXHIBITIONIST
EXHIBITIONISTIC
EXHIBITIONISTS
EXHIBITIONS
EXHIBITIVE
EXHIBITIVELY
EXHIBITORS
EXHIBITORY
EXHILARANT
EXHILARANTS
EXHILARATE
EXHILARATED
EXHILARATES
EXHILARATING
EXHILARATINGLY
EXHILARATION
EXHILARATIONS
EXHILARATIVE
EXHILARATOR
EXHILARATORS
EXHILARATORY
EXHORTATION
EXHORTATIONS
EXHORTATIVE
EXHORTATORY
EXHUMATING
EXHUMATION
EXHUMATIONS
EXIGENCIES
EXIGUITIES
EXIGUOUSLY
EXIGUOUSNESS
EXIGUOUSNESSES
EXILEMENTS
EXIMIOUSLY
EXISTENCES
EXISTENTIAL
EXISTENTIALISM
EXISTENTIALISMS
EXISTENTIALIST
EXISTENTIALISTS
EXISTENTIALLY
EXOBIOLOGICAL
EXOBIOLOGIES
EXOBIOLOGIST
EXOBIOLOGISTS
EXOBIOLOGY
EXOCENTRIC
EXOCUTICLE
EXOCUTICLES
EXOCYTOSED
EXOCYTOSES
EXOCYTOSING
EXOCYTOSIS
EXOCYTOTIC
EXODERMISES
EXODONTIAS
EXODONTICS
EXODONTIST
EXODONTISTS
EXOENZYMES
EXOERYTHROCYTIC
EXOGENETIC
EXOGENISMS
EXOGENOUSLY
EXONERATED
EXONERATES
EXONERATING
EXONERATION
EXONERATIONS
EXONERATIVE
EXONERATOR
EXONERATORS
EXONUCLEASE
EXONUCLEASES
EXONUMISTS
EXOPARASITE
EXOPARASITES

EXOPARASITIC
EXOPEPTIDASE
EXOPEPTIDASES
EXOPHAGIES
EXOPHAGOUS
EXOPHTHALMIA
EXOPHTHALMIAS
EXOPHTHALMIC
EXOPHTHALMOS
EXOPHTHALMOSES
EXOPHTHALMUS
EXOPHTHALMUSES
EXOPLANETS
EXOPODITES
EXOPODITIC
EXORABILITIES
EXORABILITY
EXORATIONS
EXORBITANCE
EXORBITANCES
EXORBITANCIES
EXORBITANCY
EXORBITANT
EXORBITANTLY
EXORBITATE
EXORBITATED
EXORBITATES
EXORBITATING
EXORCISERS
EXORCISING
EXORCISTIC
EXORCISTICAL
EXORCIZERS
EXORCIZING
EXOSKELETAL
EXOSKELETON
EXOSKELETONS
EXOSPHERES
EXOSPHERIC
EXOSPHERICAL
EXOSPORIUM
EXOSPOROUS
EXOTERICAL
EXOTERICALLY
EXOTERICISM
EXOTERICISMS
EXOTHERMAL
EXOTHERMALLY
EXOTHERMIC
EXOTHERMICALLY
EXOTHERMICITIES
EXOTHERMICITY
EXOTICALLY
EXOTICISMS
EXOTICISTS
EXOTICNESS
EXOTICNESSES
EXOTROPIAS
EXPANDABILITIES
EXPANDABILITY
EXPANDABLE
EXPANSIBILITIES
EXPANSIBILITY
EXPANSIBLE
EXPANSIBLY
EXPANSIONAL
EXPANSIONARY
EXPANSIONISM
EXPANSIONISMS
EXPANSIONIST
EXPANSIONISTIC
EXPANSIONISTS
EXPANSIONS
EXPANSIVELY
EXPANSIVENESS
EXPANSIVENESSES
EXPANSIVITIES
EXPANSIVITY
EXPATIATED
EXPATIATES
EXPATIATING
EXPATIATION
EXPATIATIONS

EXPATIATIVE
EXPATIATOR
EXPATIATORS
EXPATIATORY
EXPATRIATE
EXPATRIATED
EXPATRIATES
EXPATRIATING
EXPATRIATION
EXPATRIATIONS
EXPATRIATISM
EXPATRIATISMS
EXPECTABLE
EXPECTABLY
EXPECTANCE
EXPECTANCES
EXPECTANCIES
EXPECTANCY
EXPECTANTLY
EXPECTANTS
EXPECTATION
EXPECTATIONAL
EXPECTATIONS
EXPECTATIVE
EXPECTATIVES
EXPECTEDLY
EXPECTEDNESS
EXPECTEDNESSES
EXPECTINGLY
EXPECTINGS
EXPECTORANT
EXPECTORANTS
EXPECTORATE
EXPECTORATED
EXPECTORATES
EXPECTORATING
EXPECTORATION
EXPECTORATIONS
EXPECTORATIVE
EXPECTORATOR
EXPECTORATORS
EXPEDIENCE
EXPEDIENCES
EXPEDIENCIES
EXPEDIENCY
EXPEDIENTIAL
EXPEDIENTIALLY
EXPEDIENTLY
EXPEDIENTS
EXPEDITATE
EXPEDITATED
EXPEDITATES
EXPEDITATING
EXPEDITATION
EXPEDITATIONS
EXPEDITELY
EXPEDITERS
EXPEDITING
EXPEDITION
EXPEDITIONARY
EXPEDITIONS
EXPEDITIOUS
EXPEDITIOUSLY
EXPEDITIOUSNESS
EXPEDITIVE
EXPEDITORS
EXPELLABLE
EXPELLANTS
EXPELLENTS
EXPENDABILITIES
EXPENDABILITY
EXPENDABLE
EXPENDABLES
EXPENDITURE
EXPENDITURES
EXPENSIVELY
EXPENSIVENESS
EXPENSIVENESSES
EXPERIENCE
EXPERIENCEABLE
EXPERIENCED
EXPERIENCELESS
EXPERIENCES

EXPERIENCING
EXPERIENTIAL
EXPERIENTIALISM
EXPERIENTIALIST
EXPERIENTIALLY
EXPERIMENT
EXPERIMENTAL
EXPERIMENTALISE
EXPERIMENTALISM
EXPERIMENTALIST
EXPERIMENTALIZE
EXPERIMENTALLY
EXPERIMENTATION
EXPERIMENTATIVE
EXPERIMENTED
EXPERIMENTER
EXPERIMENTERS
EXPERIMENTING
EXPERIMENTIST
EXPERIMENTISTS
EXPERIMENTS
EXPERTISED
EXPERTISES
EXPERTISING
EXPERTISMS
EXPERTIZED
EXPERTIZES
EXPERTIZING
EXPERTNESS
EXPERTNESSES
EXPIATIONS
EXPIRATION
EXPIRATIONS
EXPIRATORY
EXPISCATED
EXPISCATES
EXPISCATING
EXPISCATION
EXPISCATIONS
EXPISCATORY
EXPLAINABLE
EXPLAINERS
EXPLAINING
EXPLANATION
EXPLANATIONS
EXPLANATIVE
EXPLANATIVELY
EXPLANATORILY
EXPLANATORY
EXPLANTATION
EXPLANTATIONS
EXPLANTING
EXPLETIVELY
EXPLETIVES
EXPLICABLE
EXPLICABLY
EXPLICATED
EXPLICATES
EXPLICATING
EXPLICATION
EXPLICATIONS
EXPLICATIVE
EXPLICATIVELY
EXPLICATOR
EXPLICATORS
EXPLICATORY
EXPLICITLY
EXPLICITNESS
EXPLICITNESSES
EXPLOITABLE
EXPLOITAGE
EXPLOITAGES
EXPLOITATION
EXPLOITATIONS
EXPLOITATIVE
EXPLOITATIVELY
EXPLOITERS
EXPLOITING
EXPLOITIVE
EXPLORATION
EXPLORATIONAL
EXPLORATIONIST
EXPLORATIONISTS

EXPLORATIONS
EXPLORATIVE
EXPLORATIVELY
EXPLORATORY
EXPLOSIBLE
EXPLOSIONS
EXPLOSIVELY
EXPLOSIVENESS
EXPLOSIVENESSES
EXPLOSIVES
EXPONENTIAL
EXPONENTIALLY
EXPONENTIALS
EXPONENTIATION
EXPONENTIATIONS
EXPORTABILITIES
EXPORTABILITY
EXPORTABLE
EXPORTATION
EXPORTATIONS
EXPOSEDNESS
EXPOSEDNESSES
EXPOSITING
EXPOSITION
EXPOSITIONAL
EXPOSITIONS
EXPOSITIVE
EXPOSITIVELY
EXPOSITORILY
EXPOSITORS
EXPOSITORY
EXPOSITRESS
EXPOSITRESSES
EXPOSTULATE
EXPOSTULATED
EXPOSTULATES
EXPOSTULATING
EXPOSTULATINGLY
EXPOSTULATION
EXPOSTULATIONS
EXPOSTULATIVE
EXPOSTULATOR
EXPOSTULATORS
EXPOSTULATORY
EXPOSTURES
EXPOUNDERS
EXPOUNDING
EXPRESSAGE
EXPRESSAGES
EXPRESSERS
EXPRESSIBLE
EXPRESSING
EXPRESSION
EXPRESSIONAL
EXPRESSIONISM
EXPRESSIONISMS
EXPRESSIONIST
EXPRESSIONISTIC
EXPRESSIONISTS
EXPRESSIONLESS
EXPRESSIONS
EXPRESSIVE
EXPRESSIVELY
EXPRESSIVENESS
EXPRESSIVITIES
EXPRESSIVITY
EXPRESSMAN
EXPRESSMEN
EXPRESSNESS
EXPRESSNESSES
EXPRESSURE
EXPRESSURES
EXPRESSWAY
EXPRESSWAYS
EXPROBRATE
EXPROBRATED
EXPROBRATES
EXPROBRATING
EXPROBRATION
EXPROBRATIONS
EXPROBRATIVE
EXPROBRATORY
EXPROMISSION

EXPROMISSIONS
EXPROMISSOR
EXPROMISSORS
EXPROPRIABLE
EXPROPRIATE
EXPROPRIATED
EXPROPRIATES
EXPROPRIATING
EXPROPRIATION
EXPROPRIATIONS
EXPROPRIATOR
EXPROPRIATORS
EXPUGNABLE
EXPUGNATION
EXPUGNATIONS
EXPUNCTING
EXPUNCTION
EXPUNCTIONS
EXPURGATED
EXPURGATES
EXPURGATING
EXPURGATION
EXPURGATIONS
EXPURGATOR
EXPURGATORIAL
EXPURGATORS
EXPURGATORY
EXQUISITELY
EXQUISITENESS
EXQUISITENESSES
EXQUISITES
EXSANGUINATE
EXSANGUINATED
EXSANGUINATES
EXSANGUINATING
EXSANGUINATION
EXSANGUINATIONS
EXSANGUINE
EXSANGUINED
EXSANGUINEOUS
EXSANGUINITIES
EXSANGUINITY
EXSANGUINOUS
EXSCINDING
EXSECTIONS
EXSERTIONS
EXSICCATED
EXSICCATES
EXSICCATING
EXSICCATION
EXSICCATIONS
EXSICCATIVE
EXSICCATOR
EXSICCATORS
EXSOLUTION
EXSOLUTIONS
EXSTIPULATE
EXSTROPHIES
EXSUFFLATE
EXSUFFLATED
EXSUFFLATES
EXSUFFLATING
EXSUFFLATION
EXSUFFLATIONS
EXSUFFLICATE
EXTEMPORAL
EXTEMPORALLY
EXTEMPORANEITY
EXTEMPORANEOUS
EXTEMPORARILY
EXTEMPORARINESS
EXTEMPORARY
EXTEMPORES
EXTEMPORISATION
EXTEMPORISE
EXTEMPORISED
EXTEMPORISER
EXTEMPORISERS
EXTEMPORISES
EXTEMPORISING
EXTEMPORIZATION
EXTEMPORIZE

e

EXTEMPORIZED	EXTERIORITY	EXTINGUISHANTS	EXTRADOSES	EXTRATEXTUAL	EXTROVERTS
EXTEMPORIZER	EXTERIORIZATION	EXTINGUISHED	EXTRADOTAL	EXTRATROPICAL	EXTRUDABILITIES
EXTEMPORIZERS	EXTERIORIZE	EXTINGUISHER	EXTRADURAL	EXTRAUTERINE	EXTRUDABILITY
EXTEMPORIZES	EXTERIORIZED	EXTINGUISHERS	EXTRAEMBRYONIC	EXTRAVAGANCE	EXTRUDABLE
EXTEMPORIZING	EXTERIORIZES	EXTINGUISHES	EXTRAFLORAL	EXTRAVAGANCES	EXTRUSIBLE
EXTENDABILITIES	EXTERIORIZING	EXTINGUISHING	EXTRAFORANEOUS	EXTRAVAGANCIES	EXTRUSIONS
EXTENDABILITY	EXTERIORLY	EXTINGUISHMENT	EXTRAGALACTIC	EXTRAVAGANCY	EXTUBATING
EXTENDABLE	EXTERMINABLE	EXTINGUISHMENTS	EXTRAHEPATIC	EXTRAVAGANT	EXUBERANCE
EXTENDEDLY	EXTERMINATE	EXTIRPABLE	EXTRAJUDICIAL	EXTRAVAGANTLY	EXUBERANCES
EXTENDEDNESS	EXTERMINATED	EXTIRPATED	EXTRAJUDICIALLY	EXTRAVAGANZA	EXUBERANCIES
EXTENDEDNESSES	EXTERMINATES	EXTIRPATES	EXTRALEGAL	EXTRAVAGANZAS	EXUBERANCY
EXTENDIBILITIES	EXTERMINATING	EXTIRPATING	EXTRALEGALLY	EXTRAVAGATE	EXUBERANTLY
EXTENDIBILITY	EXTERMINATION	EXTIRPATION	EXTRALIMITAL	EXTRAVAGATED	EXUBERATED
EXTENDIBLE	EXTERMINATIONS	EXTIRPATIONS	EXTRALIMITARY	EXTRAVAGATES	EXUBERATES
EXTENSIBILITIES	EXTERMINATIVE	EXTIRPATIVE	EXTRALINGUISTIC	EXTRAVAGATING	EXUBERATING
EXTENSIBILITY	EXTERMINATOR	EXTIRPATOR	EXTRALITERARY	EXTRAVAGATION	EXUDATIONS
EXTENSIBLE	EXTERMINATORS	EXTIRPATORS	EXTRALITIES	EXTRAVAGATIONS	EXULCERATE
EXTENSIBLENESS	EXTERMINATORY	EXTIRPATORY	EXTRALOGICAL	EXTRAVASATE	EXULCERATED
EXTENSIFICATION	EXTERMINED	EXTOLLINGLY	EXTRAMARITAL	EXTRAVASATED	EXULCERATES
EXTENSIMETER	EXTERMINES	EXTOLMENTS	EXTRAMETRICAL	EXTRAVASATES	EXULCERATING
EXTENSIMETERS	EXTERMINING	EXTORSIVELY	EXTRAMUNDANE	EXTRAVASATING	EXULCERATION
EXTENSIONAL	EXTERNALISATION	EXTORTIONARY	EXTRAMURAL	EXTRAVASATION	EXULCERATIONS
EXTENSIONALISM	EXTERNALISE	EXTORTIONATE	EXTRAMURALLY	EXTRAVASATIONS	EXULTANCES
EXTENSIONALISMS	EXTERNALISED	EXTORTIONATELY	EXTRAMUSICAL	EXTRAVASCULAR	EXULTANCIES
EXTENSIONALITY	EXTERNALISES	EXTORTIONER	EXTRANEITIES	EXTRAVEHICULAR	EXULTANTLY
EXTENSIONALLY	EXTERNALISING	EXTORTIONERS	EXTRANEITY	EXTRAVERSION	EXULTATION
EXTENSIONIST	EXTERNALISM	EXTORTIONIST	EXTRANEOUS	EXTRAVERSIONS	EXULTATIONS
EXTENSIONISTS	EXTERNALISMS	EXTORTIONISTS	EXTRANEOUSLY	EXTRAVERSIVE	EXULTINGLY
EXTENSIONS	EXTERNALIST	EXTORTIONS	EXTRANEOUSNESS	EXTRAVERSIVELY	EXURBANITE
EXTENSITIES	EXTERNALISTS	EXTRABOLDS	EXTRANUCLEAR	EXTRAVERTED	EXURBANITES
EXTENSIVELY	EXTERNALITIES	EXTRACANONICAL	EXTRAORDINAIRE	EXTRAVERTING	EXUVIATING
EXTENSIVENESS	EXTERNALITY	EXTRACELLULAR	EXTRAORDINARIES	EXTRAVERTS	EXUVIATION
EXTENSIVENESSES	EXTERNALIZATION	EXTRACELLULARLY	EXTRAORDINARILY	EXTREMENESS	EXUVIATIONS
EXTENSIVISATION	EXTERNALIZE	EXTRACORPOREAL	EXTRAORDINARY	EXTREMENESSES	EYEBALLING
EXTENSIVIZATION	EXTERNALIZED	EXTRACRANIAL	EXTRAPOLATE	EXTREMISMS	EYEBRIGHTS
EXTENSOMETER	EXTERNALIZES	EXTRACTABILITY	EXTRAPOLATED	EXTREMISTS	EYEBROWING
EXTENSOMETERS	EXTERNALIZING	EXTRACTABLE	EXTRAPOLATES	EXTREMITIES	EYEBROWLESS
EXTENUATED	EXTERNALLY	EXTRACTANT	EXTRAPOLATING	EXTREMOPHILE	EYEDNESSES
EXTENUATES	EXTERNSHIP	EXTRACTANTS	EXTRAPOLATION	EXTREMOPHILES	EYEDROPPER
EXTENUATING	EXTERNSHIPS	EXTRACTIBLE	EXTRAPOLATIONS	EXTRICABLE	EYEDROPPERS
EXTENUATINGLY	EXTEROCEPTIVE	EXTRACTING	EXTRAPOLATIVE	EXTRICATED	EYEGLASSES
EXTENUATINGS	EXTEROCEPTOR	EXTRACTION	EXTRAPOLATOR	EXTRICATES	EYELETEERS
EXTENUATION	EXTEROCEPTORS	EXTRACTIONS	EXTRAPOLATORS	EXTRICATING	EYELETTING
EXTENUATIONS	EXTERRITORIAL	EXTRACTIVE	EXTRAPOLATORY	EXTRICATION	EYEOPENERS
EXTENUATIVE	EXTERRITORIALLY	EXTRACTIVELY	EXTRAPOSED	EXTRICATIONS	EYEPOPPERS
EXTENUATOR	EXTINCTING	EXTRACTIVES	EXTRAPOSES	EXTRINSICAL	EYESHADOWS
EXTENUATORS	EXTINCTION	EXTRACTORS	EXTRAPOSING	EXTRINSICALITY	EYESTRAINS
EXTENUATORY	EXTINCTIONS	EXTRACURRICULAR	EXTRAPOSITION	EXTRINSICALLY	EYESTRINGS
EXTERIORISATION	EXTINCTIVE	EXTRADITABLE	EXTRAPOSITIONS	EXTROVERSION	EYEWITNESS
EXTERIORISE	EXTINCTURE	EXTRADITED	EXTRAPYRAMIDAL	EXTROVERSIONS	EYEWITNESSES
EXTERIORISED	EXTINCTURES	EXTRADITES	EXTRASENSORY	EXTROVERSIVE	
EXTERIORISES	EXTINGUISH	EXTRADITING	EXTRASOLAR	EXTROVERSIVELY	
EXTERIORISING	EXTINGUISHABLE	EXTRADITION	EXTRASYSTOLE	EXTROVERTED	
EXTERIORITIES	EXTINGUISHANT	EXTRADITIONS	EXTRASYSTOLES	EXTROVERTING	

Ff

FABRICANTS
FABRICATED
FABRICATES
FABRICATING
FABRICATION
FABRICATIONS
FABRICATIVE
FABRICATOR
FABRICATORS
FABRICKING
FABULATING
FABULATORS
FABULISING
FABULISTIC
FABULIZING
FABULOSITIES
FABULOSITY
FABULOUSLY
FABULOUSNESS
FABULOUSNESSES
FACECLOTHS
FACELESSNESS
FACELESSNESSES
FACELIFTED
FACELIFTING
FACEPLATES
FACEPRINTS
FACETIOUSLY
FACETIOUSNESS
FACETIOUSNESSES
FACEWORKER
FACEWORKERS
FACILENESS
FACILENESSES
FACILITATE
FACILITATED
FACILITATES
FACILITATING
FACILITATION
FACILITATIONS
FACILITATIVE
FACILITATOR
FACILITATORS
FACILITATORY
FACILITIES
FACINERIOUS
FACINOROUS
FACINOROUSNESS
FACSIMILED
FACSIMILEING
FACSIMILES
FACSIMILIST
FACSIMILISTS
FACTICITIES
FACTIONALISM
FACTIONALISMS
FACTIONALIST
FACTIONALISTS
FACTIONALLY
FACTIONARIES
FACTIONARY
FACTIONIST
FACTIONISTS
FACTIOUSLY
FACTIOUSNESS
FACTIOUSNESSES
FACTITIOUS

FACTITIOUSLY
FACTITIOUSNESS
FACTITIVELY
FACTORABILITIES
FACTORABILITY
FACTORABLE
FACTORAGES
FACTORIALLY
FACTORIALS
FACTORINGS
FACTORISATION
FACTORISATIONS
FACTORISED
FACTORISES
FACTORISING
FACTORIZATION
FACTORIZATIONS
FACTORIZED
FACTORIZES
FACTORIZING
FACTORSHIP
FACTORSHIPS
FACTORYLIKE
FACTSHEETS
FACTUALISM
FACTUALISMS
FACTUALIST
FACTUALISTIC
FACTUALISTS
FACTUALITIES
FACTUALITY
FACTUALNESS
FACTUALNESSES
FACULTATIVE
FACULTATIVELY
FACUNDITIES
FADDINESSES
FADDISHNESS
FADDISHNESSES
FADEDNESSES
FADELESSLY
FADOMETERS
FAGGOTINGS
FAGGOTRIES
FAGOTTISTS
FAINEANCES
FAINEANCIES
FAINEANTISE
FAINEANTISES
FAINNESSES
FAINTHEARTED
FAINTHEARTEDLY
FAINTINGLY
FAINTISHNESS
FAINTISHNESSES
FAINTNESSES
FAIRGROUND
FAIRGROUNDS
FAIRLEADER
FAIRLEADERS
FAIRNESSES
FAIRNITICKLE
FAIRNITICKLES
FAIRNITICLE
FAIRNITICLES
FAIRNYTICKLE
FAIRNYTICKLES

FAIRNYTICLE
FAIRNYTICLES
FAIRYFLOSS
FAIRYFLOSSES
FAIRYHOODS
FAIRYLANDS
FAIRYTALES
FAITHCURES
FAITHFULLY
FAITHFULNESS
FAITHFULNESSES
FAITHLESSLY
FAITHLESSNESS
FAITHLESSNESSES
FAITHWORTHINESS
FAITHWORTHY
FALANGISMS
FALANGISTS
FALCATIONS
FALCONIFORM
FALCONRIES
FALDISTORIES
FALDISTORY
FALDSTOOLS
FALLACIOUS
FALLACIOUSLY
FALLACIOUSNESS
FALLALERIES
FALLALISHLY
FALLBOARDS
FALLFISHES
FALLIBILISM
FALLIBILISMS
FALLIBILIST
FALLIBILISTS
FALLIBILITIES
FALLIBILITY
FALLIBLENESS
FALLIBLENESSES
FALLOWNESS
FALLOWNESSES
FALSEFACES
FALSEHOODS
FALSENESSES
FALSEWORKS
FALSIDICAL
FALSIFIABILITY
FALSIFIABLE
FALSIFICATION
FALSIFICATIONS
FALSIFIERS
FALSIFYING
FALTERINGLY
FALTERINGS
FAMILIARISATION
FAMILIARISE
FAMILIARISED
FAMILIARISER
FAMILIARISERS
FAMILIARISES
FAMILIARISING
FAMILIARITIES
FAMILIARITY
FAMILIARIZATION
FAMILIARIZE
FAMILIARIZED
FAMILIARIZER

FAMILIARIZERS
FAMILIARIZES
FAMILIARIZING
FAMILIARLY
FAMILIARNESS
FAMILIARNESSES
FAMILISTIC
FAMISHMENT
FAMISHMENTS
FAMOUSNESS
FAMOUSNESSES
FANATICALLY
FANATICALNESS
FANATICALNESSES
FANATICISE
FANATICISED
FANATICISES
FANATICISING
FANATICISM
FANATICISMS
FANATICIZE
FANATICIZED
FANATICIZES
FANATICIZING
FANCIFULLY
FANCIFULNESS
FANCIFULNESSES
FANCIFYING
FANCINESSES
FANCYWORKS
FANDANGLES
FANDANGOES
FANFARADES
FANFARONADE
FANFARONADED
FANFARONADES
FANFARONADING
FANFARONAS
FANFOLDING
FANTABULOUS
FANTASISED
FANTASISER
FANTASISERS
FANTASISES
FANTASISING
FANTASISTS
FANTASIZED
FANTASIZER
FANTASIZERS
FANTASIZES
FANTASIZING
FANTASMALLY
FANTASMICALLY
FANTASQUES
FANTASTICAL
FANTASTICALITY
FANTASTICALLY
FANTASTICALNESS
FANTASTICATE
FANTASTICATED
FANTASTICATES
FANTASTICATING
FANTASTICATION
FANTASTICATIONS
FANTASTICISM
FANTASTICISMS
FANTASTICO

FANTASTICOES
FANTASTICS
FANTASTRIES
FANTASYING
FANTASYLAND
FANTASYLANDS
FANTOCCINI
FARADISATION
FARADISATIONS
FARADISERS
FARADISING
FARADIZATION
FARADIZATIONS
FARADIZERS
FARADIZING
FARANDINES
FARANDOLES
FARAWAYNESS
FARAWAYNESSES
FARBOROUGH
FARBOROUGHS
FARCEMEATS
FARCICALITIES
FARCICALITY
FARCICALLY
FARCICALNESS
FARCICALNESSES
FARCIFYING
FAREWELLED
FAREWELLING
FARFETCHEDNESS
FARINACEOUS
FARINOSELY
FARKLEBERRIES
FARKLEBERRY
FARMERESSES
FARMERETTE
FARMERETTES
FARMHOUSES
FARMSTEADS
FARMWORKER
FARMWORKERS
FARNARKELED
FARNARKELING
FARNARKELINGS
FARNARKELS
FARRAGINOUS
FARRANDINE
FARRANDINES
FARRIERIES
FARSIGHTED
FARSIGHTEDLY
FARSIGHTEDNESS
FARTHERMORE
FARTHERMOST
FARTHINGALE
FARTHINGALES
FARTHINGLAND
FARTHINGLANDS
FARTHINGLESS
FARTHINGSWORTH
FARTHINGSWORTHS
FASCIATELY
FASCIATION
FASCIATIONS
FASCICULAR
FASCICULARLY

FASCICULATE
FASCICULATED
FASCICULATELY
FASCICULATION
FASCICULATIONS
FASCICULES
FASCICULUS
FASCIITISES
FASCINATED
FASCINATEDLY
FASCINATES
FASCINATING
FASCINATINGLY
FASCINATION
FASCINATIONS
FASCINATIVE
FASCINATOR
FASCINATORS
FASCIOLIASES
FASCIOLIASIS
FASCISTICALLY
FASCITISES
FASHIONABILITY
FASHIONABLE
FASHIONABLENESS
FASHIONABLES
FASHIONABLY
FASHIONERS
FASHIONING
FASHIONIST
FASHIONISTA
FASHIONISTAS
FASHIONISTS
FASHIONMONGER
FASHIONMONGERS
FASHIONMONGING
FASHIOUSNESS
FASHIOUSNESSES
FASTBALLER
FASTBALLERS
FASTENINGS
FASTIDIOUS
FASTIDIOUSLY
FASTIDIOUSNESS
FASTIGIATE
FASTIGIATED
FASTIGIUMS
FASTNESSES
FATALISTIC
FATALISTICALLY
FATALITIES
FATALNESSES
FATBRAINED
FATEFULNESS
FATEFULNESSES
FATHEADEDLY
FATHEADEDNESS
FATHEADEDNESSES
FATHERHOOD
FATHERHOODS
FATHERINGS
FATHERLAND
FATHERLANDS
FATHERLESS
FATHERLESSNESS
FATHERLIKE
FATHERLINESS

FATHERLINESSES
FATHERSHIP
FATHERSHIPS
FATHOMABLE
FATHOMETER
FATHOMETERS
FATHOMLESS
FATHOMLESSLY
FATHOMLESSNESS
FATIDICALLY
FATIGABILITIES
FATIGABILITY
FATIGABLENESS
FATIGABLENESSES
FATIGATING
FATIGUABLE
FATIGUABLENESS
FATIGUELESS
FATIGUINGLY
FATISCENCE
FATISCENCES
FATSHEDERA
FATSHEDERAS
FATTENABLE
FATTENINGS
FATTINESSES
FATUOUSNESS
FATUOUSNESSES
FAULCHIONS
FAULTFINDER
FAULTFINDERS
FAULTFINDING
FAULTFINDINGS
FAULTINESS
FAULTINESSES
FAULTLESSLY
FAULTLESSNESS
FAULTLESSNESSES
FAUNISTICALLY
FAUXBOURDON
FAUXBOURDONS
FAVORABLENESS
FAVORABLENESSES
FAVOREDNESS
FAVOREDNESSES
FAVORINGLY
FAVORITISM
FAVORITISMS
FAVOURABLE
FAVOURABLENESS
FAVOURABLY
FAVOUREDNESS
FAVOUREDNESSES
FAVOURINGLY
FAVOURITES
FAVOURITISM
FAVOURITISMS
FAVOURLESS
FAWNINGNESS
FAWNINGNESSES
FAZENDEIRO
FAZENDEIROS
FEARFULLER
FEARFULLEST
FEARFULNESS
FEARFULNESSES
FEARLESSLY
FEARLESSNESS
FEARLESSNESSES
FEARNAUGHT
FEARNAUGHTS
FEARNOUGHT
FEARNOUGHTS
FEARSOMELY
FEARSOMENESS
FEARSOMENESSES
FEASIBILITIES
FEASIBILITY
FEASIBLENESS
FEASIBLENESSES
FEATEOUSLY
FEATHERBED
FEATHERBEDDED

FEATHERBEDDING
FEATHERBEDDINGS
FEATHERBEDS
FEATHERBRAIN
FEATHERBRAINED
FEATHERBRAINS
FEATHEREDGE
FEATHEREDGED
FEATHEREDGES
FEATHEREDGING
FEATHERHEAD
FEATHERHEADED
FEATHERHEADS
FEATHERIER
FEATHERIEST
FEATHERINESS
FEATHERINESSES
FEATHERING
FEATHERINGS
FEATHERLESS
FEATHERLIGHT
FEATHERSTITCH
FEATHERSTITCHED
FEATHERSTITCHES
FEATHERWEIGHT
FEATHERWEIGHTS
FEATLINESS
FEATLINESSES
FEATURELESS
FEATURELESSNESS
FEATURETTE
FEATURETTES
FEBRICITIES
FEBRICULAS
FEBRICULES
FEBRIFACIENT
FEBRIFACIENTS
FEBRIFEROUS
FEBRIFUGAL
FEBRIFUGES
FEBRILITIES
FECKLESSLY
FECKLESSNESS
FECKLESSNESSES
FECULENCES
FECULENCIES
FECUNDATED
FECUNDATES
FECUNDATING
FECUNDATION
FECUNDATIONS
FECUNDATOR
FECUNDATORS
FECUNDATORY
FECUNDITIES
FEDERACIES
FEDERALESE
FEDERALESES
FEDERALISATION
FEDERALISATIONS
FEDERALISE
FEDERALISED
FEDERALISES
FEDERALISING
FEDERALISM
FEDERALISMS
FEDERALIST
FEDERALISTIC
FEDERALISTS
FEDERALIZATION
FEDERALIZATIONS
FEDERALIZE
FEDERALIZED
FEDERALIZES
FEDERALIZING
FEDERARIES
FEDERATING
FEDERATION
FEDERATIONS
FEDERATIVE
FEDERATIVELY
FEDERATORS
FEEBLEMINDED

FEEBLEMINDEDLY
FEEBLENESS
FEEBLENESSES
FEEDGRAINS
FEEDINGSTUFF
FEEDINGSTUFFS
FEEDSTOCKS
FEEDSTUFFS
FEEDTHROUGH
FEEDTHROUGHS
FEEDWATERS
FEELINGLESS
FEELINGNESS
FEELINGNESSES
FEIGNEDNESS
FEIGNEDNESSES
FEIGNINGLY
FEISTINESS
FEISTINESSES
FELDSCHARS
FELDSCHERS
FELDSPATHIC
FELDSPATHOID
FELDSPATHOIDS
FELDSPATHOSE
FELDSPATHS
FELICITATE
FELICITATED
FELICITATES
FELICITATING
FELICITATION
FELICITATIONS
FELICITATOR
FELICITATORS
FELICITIES
FELICITOUS
FELICITOUSLY
FELICITOUSNESS
FELINENESS
FELINENESSES
FELINITIES
FELLATIONS
FELLATRICES
FELLATRIXES
FELLMONGER
FELLMONGERED
FELLMONGERIES
FELLMONGERING
FELLMONGERINGS
FELLMONGERS
FELLMONGERY
FELLNESSES
FELLOWSHIP
FELLOWSHIPED
FELLOWSHIPING
FELLOWSHIPPED
FELLOWSHIPPING
FELLOWSHIPS
FELLWALKER
FELLWALKERS
FELONIOUSLY
FELONIOUSNESS
FELONIOUSNESSES
FELSPATHIC
FELSPATHOID
FELSPATHOIDS
FELSPATHOSE
FEMALENESS
FEMALENESSES
FEMALITIES
FEMETARIES
FEMINACIES
FEMINALITIES
FEMINALITY
FEMINEITIES
FEMINILITIES
FEMINILITY
FEMININELY
FEMININENESS
FEMININENESSES
FEMINISM
FEMININISMS
FEMININITIES

FEMININITY
FEMINISATION
FEMINISATIONS
FEMINISING
FEMINISTIC
FEMINITIES
FEMINIZATION
FEMINIZATIONS
FEMINIZING
FEMTOSECOND
FEMTOSECONDS
FENCELESSNESS
FENCELESSNESSES
FENDERLESS
FENESTELLA
FENESTELLAE
FENESTELLAS
FENESTRALS
FENESTRATE
FENESTRATED
FENESTRATION
FENESTRATIONS
FENNELFLOWER
FENNELFLOWERS
FENUGREEKS
FEOFFMENTS
FERACITIES
FERETORIES
FERMENTABILITY
FERMENTABLE
FERMENTATION
FERMENTATIONS
FERMENTATIVE
FERMENTATIVELY
FERMENTERS
FERMENTESCIBLE
FERMENTING
FERMENTITIOUS
FERMENTIVE
FERMENTORS
FERNITICKLE
FERNITICKLES
FERNITICLE
FERNITICLES
FERNTICKLE
FERNTICKLED
FERNTICKLES
FERNTICLED
FERNTICLES
FERNYTICKLE
FERNYTICKLES
FERNYTICLE
FERNYTICLES
FEROCIOUSLY
FEROCIOUSNESS
FEROCIOUSNESSES
FEROCITIES
FERRANDINE
FERRANDINES
FERREDOXIN
FERREDOXINS
FERRELLING
FERRETINGS
FERRICYANIC
FERRICYANIDE
FERRICYANIDES
FERRICYANOGEN
FERRICYANOGENS
FERRIFEROUS
FERRIMAGNET
FERRIMAGNETIC
FERRIMAGNETISM
FERRIMAGNETISMS
FERRIMAGNETS
FERROCENES
FERROCHROME
FERROCHROMES
FERROCHROMIUM
FERROCHROMIUMS
FERROCONCRETE
FERROCONCRETES
FERROCYANIC
FERROCYANIDE

FERROCYANIDES
FERROCYANOGEN
FERROCYANOGENS
FERROELECTRIC
FERROELECTRICS
FERROGRAMS
FERROGRAPHIES
FERROGRAPHY
FERROMAGNESIAN
FERROMAGNET
FERROMAGNETIC
FERROMAGNETISM
FERROMAGNETISMS
FERROMAGNETS
FERROMANGANESE
FERROMANGANESES
FERROMOLYBDENUM
FERRONICKEL
FERRONICKELS
FERRONIERE
FERRONIERES
FERRONNIERE
FERRONNIERES
FERROPRUSSIATE
FERROPRUSSIATES
FERROSILICON
FERROSILICONS
FERROSOFERRIC
FERROTYPED
FERROTYPES
FERROTYPING
FERRUGINEOUS
FERRUGINOUS
FERRYBOATS
FERTIGATED
FERTIGATES
FERTIGATING
FERTIGATION
FERTIGATIONS
FERTILENESS
FERTILENESSES
FERTILISABLE
FERTILISATION
FERTILISATIONS
FERTILISED
FERTILISER
FERTILISERS
FERTILISES
FERTILISING
FERTILITIES
FERTILIZABLE
FERTILIZATION
FERTILIZATIONS
FERTILIZED
FERTILIZER
FERTILIZERS
FERTILIZES
FERTILIZING
FERULACEOUS
FERVENCIES
FERVENTEST
FERVENTNESS
FERVENTNESSES
FERVESCENT
FERVIDITIES
FERVIDNESS
FERVIDNESSES
FESCENNINE
FESTILOGIES
FESTINATED
FESTINATELY
FESTINATES
FESTINATING
FESTINATION
FESTINATIONS
FESTIVALGOER
FESTIVALGOERS
FESTIVENESS
FESTIVENESSES
FESTIVITIES
FESTOLOGIES
FESTOONERIES
FESTOONERY

FESTOONING
FESTSCHRIFT
FESTSCHRIFTEN
FESTSCHRIFTS
FETCHINGLY
FETICHISED
FETICHISES
FETICHISING
FETICHISMS
FETICHISTIC
FETICHISTS
FETICHIZED
FETICHIZES
FETICHIZING
FETIDITIES
FETIDNESSES
FETIPAROUS
FETISHISATION
FETISHISATIONS
FETISHISED
FETISHISES
FETISHISING
FETISHISMS
FETISHISTIC
FETISHISTICALLY
FETISHISTS
FETISHIZATION
FETISHIZATIONS
FETISHIZED
FETISHIZES
FETISHIZING
FETOLOGIES
FETOLOGIST
FETOLOGISTS
FETOPROTEIN
FETOPROTEINS
FETOSCOPES
FETOSCOPIES
FETTERLESS
FETTERLOCK
FETTERLOCKS
FETTUCCINE
FETTUCCINES
FETTUCCINI
FETTUCINES
FETTUCINIS
FEUDALISATION
FEUDALISATIONS
FEUDALISED
FEUDALISES
FEUDALISING
FEUDALISMS
FEUDALISTIC
FEUDALISTS
FEUDALITIES
FEUDALIZATION
FEUDALIZATIONS
FEUDALIZED
FEUDALIZES
FEUDALIZING
FEUDATORIES
FEUILLETES
FEUILLETON
FEUILLETONISM
FEUILLETONISMS
FEUILLETONIST
FEUILLETONISTIC
FEUILLETONISTS
FEUILLETONS
FEVERISHLY
FEVERISHNESS
FEVERISHNESSES
FEVEROUSLY
FEVERROOTS
FEVERWEEDS
FEVERWORTS
FIANCAILLES
FIANCHETTI
FIANCHETTO
FIANCHETTOED
FIANCHETTOES
FIANCHETTOING
FIANCHETTOS

FIBERBOARD	FICTIONEER	FIGURATION	FINALISING	FIREBREAKS	FISTFIGHTS
FIBERBOARDS	FICTIONEERING	FIGURATIONS	FINALISTIC	FIREBRICKS	FISTICUFFS
FIBERFILLS	FICTIONEERINGS	FIGURATIVE	FINALITIES	FIREBUSHES	FITFULNESS
FIBERGLASS	FICTIONEERS	FIGURATIVELY	FINALIZATION	FIRECRACKER	FITFULNESSES
FIBERGLASSED	FICTIONISATION	FIGURATIVENESS	FINALIZATIONS	FIRECRACKERS	FITTINGNESS
FIBERGLASSES	FICTIONISATIONS	FIGUREHEAD	FINALIZERS	FIRECRESTS	FITTINGNESSES
FIBERGLASSING	FICTIONISE	FIGUREHEADS	FINALIZING	FIREDRAGON	FIVEFINGER
FIBERISATION	FICTIONISED	FIGURELESS	FINANCIALIST	FIREDRAGONS	FIVEFINGERS
FIBERISATIONS	FICTIONISES	FIGUREWORK	FINANCIALISTS	FIREDRAKES	FIVEPENCES
FIBERISING	FICTIONISING	FIGUREWORKS	FINANCIALLY	FIREFANGED	FIXEDNESSES
FIBERIZATION	FICTIONIST	FILAGREEING	FINANCIERED	FIREFANGING	FIXTURELESS
FIBERIZATIONS	FICTIONISTS	FILAMENTARY	FINANCIERING	FIREFIGHTER	FIZGIGGING
FIBERIZING	FICTIONIZATION	FILAMENTOUS	FINANCIERS	FIREFIGHTERS	FIZZENLESS
FIBERSCOPE	FICTIONIZATIONS	FILARIASES	FINANCINGS	FIREFIGHTING	FIZZINESSES
FIBERSCOPES	FICTIONIZE	FILARIASIS	FINEABLENESS	FIREFIGHTINGS	FLABBERGAST
FIBREBOARD	FICTIONIZED	FILATORIES	FINEABLENESSES	FIREFIGHTS	FLABBERGASTED
FIBREBOARDS	FICTIONIZES	FILCHINGLY	FINENESSES	FIREFLOATS	FLABBERGASTING
FIBREFILLS	FICTIONIZING	FILEFISHES	FINESSINGS	FIREFLOODS	FLABBERGASTS
FIBREGLASS	FICTITIOUS	FILIALNESS	FINGERBOARD	FIREGUARDS	FLABBINESS
FIBREGLASSES	FICTITIOUSLY	FILIALNESSES	FINGERBOARDS	FIREHOUSES	FLABBINESSES
FIBREOPTIC	FICTITIOUSNESS	FILIATIONS	FINGERBOWL	FIRELIGHTER	FLABELLATE
FIBRESCOPE	FICTIVENESS	FILIBUSTER	FINGERBOWLS	FIRELIGHTERS	FLABELLATION
FIBRESCOPES	FICTIVENESSES	FILIBUSTERED	FINGERBREADTH	FIRELIGHTS	FLABELLATIONS
FIBRILLARY	FIDDIOUSED	FILIBUSTERER	FINGERBREADTHS	FIREPLACED	FLABELLIFORM
FIBRILLATE	FIDDIOUSES	FILIBUSTERERS	FINGERGLASS	FIREPLACES	FLABELLUMS
FIBRILLATED	FIDDIOUSING	FILIBUSTERING	FINGERGLASSES	FIREPOWERS	FLACCIDEST
FIBRILLATES	FIDDLEBACK	FILIBUSTERINGS	FINGERGUARD	FIREPROOFED	FLACCIDITIES
FIBRILLATING	FIDDLEBACKS	FILIBUSTERISM	FINGERGUARDS	FIREPROOFING	FLACCIDITY
FIBRILLATION	FIDDLEDEDEE	FILIBUSTERISMS	FINGERHOLD	FIREPROOFINGS	FLACCIDNESS
FIBRILLATIONS	FIDDLEDEEDEE	FILIBUSTEROUS	FINGERHOLDS	FIREPROOFS	FLACCIDNESSES
FIBRILLIFORM	FIDDLEHEAD	FILIBUSTERS	FINGERHOLE	FIRESCREEN	FLACKERIES
FIBRILLINS	FIDDLEHEADS	FILICINEAN	FINGERHOLES	FIRESCREENS	FLACKERING
FIBRILLOSE	FIDDLENECK	FILIGRAINS	FINGERINGS	FIRESTONES	FLAFFERING
FIBRILLOUS	FIDDLENECKS	FILIGRANES	FINGERLESS	FIRESTORMS	FLAGELLANT
FIBRINOGEN	FIDDLESTICK	FILIGREEING	FINGERLIKE	FIRETHORNS	FLAGELLANTISM
FIBRINOGENIC	FIDDLESTICKS	FILIOPIETISTIC	FINGERLING	FIRETRUCKS	FLAGELLANTISMS
FIBRINOGENOUS	FIDDLEWOOD	FILIPENDULOUS	FINGERLINGS	FIREWARDEN	FLAGELLANTS
FIBRINOGENS	FIDDLEWOODS	FILLAGREED	FINGERMARK	FIREWARDENS	FLAGELLATE
FIBRINOIDS	FIDEICOMMISSA	FILLAGREEING	FINGERMARKS	FIREWATERS	FLAGELLATED
FIBRINOLYSES	FIDEICOMMISSARY	FILLAGREES	FINGERNAIL	FIRMAMENTAL	FLAGELLATES
FIBRINOLYSIN	FIDEICOMMISSUM	FILLESTERS	FINGERNAILS	FIRMAMENTS	FLAGELLATING
FIBRINOLYSINS	FIDELISMOS	FILLIPEENS	FINGERPICK	FIRMNESSES	FLAGELLATION
FIBRINOLYSIS	FIDELISTAS	FILLISTERS	FINGERPICKED	FIRSTBORNS	FLAGELLATIONS
FIBRINOLYTIC	FIDELITIES	FILMICALLY	FINGERPICKING	FIRSTFRUITS	FLAGELLATOR
FIBRINOPEPTIDE	FIDGETIEST	FILMINESSES	FINGERPICKINGS	FIRSTLINGS	FLAGELLATORS
FIBRINOPEPTIDES	FIDGETINESS	FILMMAKERS	FINGERPICKS	FIRSTNESSES	FLAGELLATORY
FIBROBLAST	FIDGETINESSES	FILMMAKING	FINGERPLATE	FISCALISTS	FLAGELLIFEROUS
FIBROBLASTIC	FIDGETINGLY	FILMMAKINGS	FINGERPLATES	FISHABILITIES	FLAGELLIFORM
FIBROBLASTS	FIDUCIALLY	FILMOGRAPHIES	FINGERPOST	FISHABILITY	FLAGELLINS
FIBROCARTILAGE	FIDUCIARIES	FILMOGRAPHY	FINGERPOSTS	FISHBURGER	FLAGELLOMANIA
FIBROCARTILAGES	FIDUCIARILY	FILMSETTER	FINGERPRINT	FISHBURGERS	FLAGELLOMANIAC
FIBROCEMENT	FIELDBOOTS	FILMSETTERS	FINGERPRINTED	FISHERFOLK	FLAGELLOMANIACS
FIBROCEMENTS	FIELDCRAFT	FILMSETTING	FINGERPRINTING	FISHERWOMAN	FLAGELLOMANIAS
FIBROCYSTIC	FIELDCRAFTS	FILMSETTINGS	FINGERPRINTINGS	FISHERWOMEN	FLAGELLUMS
FIBROCYTES	FIELDFARES	FILMSTRIPS	FINGERPRINTS	FISHFINGER	FLAGEOLETS
FIBROLINES	FIELDMOUSE	FILOPLUMES	FINGERSTALL	FISHFINGERS	FLAGGINESS
FIBROLITES	FIELDPIECE	FILOPODIUM	FINGERSTALLS	FISHIFYING	FLAGGINESSES
FIBROMATOUS	FIELDPIECES	FILOSELLES	FINGERTIPS	FISHINESSES	FLAGGINGLY
FIBROMYALGIA	FIELDSTONE	FILOVIRUSES	FINICALITIES	FISHMONGER	FLAGITATED
FIBROMYALGIAS	FIELDSTONES	FILTERABILITIES	FINICALITY	FISHMONGERS	FLAGITATES
FIBRONECTIN	FIELDSTRIP	FILTERABILITY	FINICALNESS	FISHPLATES	FLAGITATING
FIBRONECTINS	FIELDSTRIPPED	FILTERABLE	FINICALNESSES	FISHTAILED	FLAGITATION
FIBROSARCOMA	FIELDSTRIPPING	FILTERABLENESS	FINICKETIER	FISHTAILING	FLAGITATIONS
FIBROSARCOMAS	FIELDSTRIPS	FILTHINESS	FINICKETIEST	FISHWIFELY	FLAGITIOUS
FIBROSARCOMATA	FIELDVOLES	FILTHINESSES	FINICKIEST	FISHYBACKS	FLAGITIOUSLY
FIBROSITIS	FIELDWARDS	FILTRABILITIES	FINICKINESS	FISSICOSTATE	FLAGITIOUSNESS
FIBROSITISES	FIELDWORKER	FILTRABILITY	FINICKINESSES	FISSILINGUAL	FLAGRANCES
FIBROUSNESS	FIELDWORKERS	FILTRATABLE	FINICKINGS	FISSILITIES	FLAGRANCIES
FIBROUSNESSES	FIELDWORKS	FILTRATING	FINISHINGS	FISSIONABILITY	FLAGRANTLY
FIBROVASCULAR	FIENDISHLY	FILTRATION	FINITENESS	FISSIONABLE	FLAGRANTNESS
FICKLENESS	FIENDISHNESS	FILTRATIONS	FINITENESSES	FISSIONABLES	FLAGRANTNESSES
FICKLENESSES	FIENDISHNESSES	FIMBRIATED	FINNICKIER	FISSIONING	FLAGSTAFFS
FICTIONALISE	FIERCENESS	FIMBRIATES	FINNICKIEST	FISSIPALMATE	FLAGSTAVES
FICTIONALISED	FIERCENESSES	FIMBRIATING	FINNOCHIOS	FISSIPARISM	FLAGSTICKS
FICTIONALISES	FIERINESSES	FIMBRIATION	FINOCCHIOS	FISSIPARISMS	FLAGSTONES
FICTIONALISING	FIFTEENERS	FIMBRIATIONS	FIORATURAE	FISSIPARITIES	FLAKINESSES
FICTIONALITIES	FIFTEENTHLY	FIMBRILLATE	FIREBALLER	FISSIPARITY	FLAMBEEING
FICTIONALITY	FIFTEENTHS	FIMICOLOUS	FIREBALLERS	FISSIPAROUS	FLAMBOYANCE
FICTIONALIZE	FIGHTBACKS	FINABLENESS	FIREBALLING	FISSIPAROUSLY	FLAMBOYANCES
FICTIONALIZED	FIGURABILITIES	FINABLENESSES	FIREBOARDS	FISSIPAROUSNESS	FLAMBOYANCIES
FICTIONALIZES	FIGURABILITY	FINALISATION	FIREBOMBED	FISSIPEDAL	FLAMBOYANCY
FICTIONALIZING	FIGURANTES	FINALISATIONS	FIREBOMBING	FISSIPEDES	FLAMBOYANT
FICTIONALLY	FIGURATELY	FINALISERS	FIREBRANDS	FISSIROSTRAL	FLAMBOYANTE

FLAMBOYANTES
FLAMBOYANTLY
FLAMBOYANTS
FLAMEPROOF
FLAMEPROOFED
FLAMEPROOFER
FLAMEPROOFERS
FLAMEPROOFING
FLAMEPROOFS
FLAMETHROWER
FLAMETHROWERS
FLAMINGOES
FLAMINICAL
FLAMMABILITIES
FLAMMABILITY
FLAMMABLES
FLAMMIFEROUS
FLAMMULATED
FLAMMULATION
FLAMMULATIONS
FLANCHINGS
FLANCONADE
FLANCONADES
FLANGELESS
FLANKERING
FLANNELBOARD
FLANNELBOARDS
FLANNELETS
FLANNELETTE
FLANNELETTES
FLANNELGRAPH
FLANNELGRAPHS
FLANNELING
FLANNELLED
FLANNELLING
FLANNELMOUTHED
FLAPDOODLE
FLAPDOODLES
FLAPPERHOOD
FLAPPERHOODS
FLAPPERISH
FLAPTRACKS
FLAREBACKS
FLASHBACKED
FLASHBACKING
FLASHBACKS
FLASHBOARD
FLASHBOARDS
FLASHBULBS
FLASHCARDS
FLASHCUBES
FLASHFORWARD
FLASHFORWARDED
FLASHFORWARDING
FLASHFORWARDS
FLASHINESS
FLASHINESSES
FLASHLAMPS
FLASHLIGHT
FLASHLIGHTS
FLASHMOBBING
FLASHMOBBINGS
FLASHOVERS
FLASHTUBES
FLATBREADS
FLATFISHES
FLATFOOTED
FLATFOOTING
FLATLANDER
FLATLANDERS
FLATLINERS
FLATLINING
FLATNESSES
FLATSCREEN
FLATSCREENS
FLATSHARES
FLATTENERS
FLATTENING
FLATTERABLE
FLATTERERS
FLATTERIES
FLATTERING
FLATTERINGLY

FLATTEROUS
FLATTEROUSLY
FLATTULENCE
FLATULENCES
FLATULENCIES
FLATULENCY
FLATULENTLY
FLATWASHES
FLAUGHTERED
FLAUGHTERING
FLAUGHTERS
FLAUGHTING
FLAUNCHING
FLAUNCHINGS
FLAUNTIEST
FLAUNTINESS
FLAUNTINESSES
FLAUNTINGLY
FLAVANONES
FLAVESCENT
FLAVIVIRUS
FLAVIVIRUSES
FLAVONOIDS
FLAVOPROTEIN
FLAVOPROTEINS
FLAVOPURPURIN
FLAVOPURPURINS
FLAVORFULLY
FLAVORINGS
FLAVORISTS
FLAVORLESS
FLAVORSOME
FLAVOURDYNAMICS
FLAVOURERS
FLAVOURFUL
FLAVOURFULLY
FLAVOURING
FLAVOURINGS
FLAVOURLESS
FLAVOURSOME
FLAWLESSLY
FLAWLESSNESS
FLAWLESSNESSES
FLEAHOPPER
FLEAHOPPERS
FLEAMARKET
FLEAMARKETS
FLECHETTES
FLECKERING
FLECTIONAL
FLECTIONLESS
FLEDGELING
FLEDGELINGS
FLEDGLINGS
FLEECELESS
FLEECHINGS
FLEECHMENT
FLEECHMENTS
FLEECINESS
FLEECINESSES
FLEERINGLY
FLEETINGLY
FLEETINGNESS
FLEETINGNESSES
FLEETNESSES
FLEHMENING
FLEMISHING
FLESHHOODS
FLESHINESS
FLESHINESSES
FLESHLIEST
FLESHLINESS
FLESHLINESSES
FLESHLINGS
FLESHMENTS
FLESHMONGER
FLESHMONGERS
FLESHWORMS
FLETCHINGS
FLEURETTES
FLEXECUTIVE
FLEXECUTIVES
FLEXIBILITIES

FLEXIBILITY
FLEXIBLENESS
FLEXIBLENESSES
FLEXIHOURS
FLEXIONLESS
FLEXITARIAN
FLEXITARIANISM
FLEXITARIANISMS
FLEXITARIANS
FLEXITIMES
FLEXOGRAPHIC
FLEXOGRAPHIES
FLEXOGRAPHY
FLEXTIMERS
FLEXUOUSLY
FLIBBERTIGIBBET
FLICHTERED
FLICHTERING
FLICKERING
FLICKERINGLY
FLICKERTAIL
FLICKERTAILS
FLIGHTIEST
FLIGHTINESS
FLIGHTINESSES
FLIGHTLESS
FLIMFLAMMED
FLIMFLAMMER
FLIMFLAMMERIES
FLIMFLAMMERS
FLIMFLAMMERY
FLIMFLAMMING
FLIMSINESS
FLIMSINESSES
FLINCHINGLY
FLINCHINGS
FLINDERSIA
FLINDERSIAS
FLINTHEADS
FLINTIFIED
FLINTIFIES
FLINTIFYING
FLINTINESS
FLINTINESSES
FLINTLOCKS
FLIPFLOPPED
FLIPFLOPPING
FLIPPANCIES
FLIPPANTLY
FLIPPANTNESS
FLIPPANTNESSES
FLIRTATION
FLIRTATIONS
FLIRTATIOUS
FLIRTATIOUSLY
FLIRTATIOUSNESS
FLIRTINGLY
FLITTERING
FLITTERMICE
FLITTERMOUSE
FLOATABILITIES
FLOATABILITY
FLOATATION
FLOATATIONS
FLOATINGLY
FLOATPLANE
FLOATPLANES
FLOCCILLATION
FLOCCILLATIONS
FLOCCULANT
FLOCCULANTS
FLOCCULATE
FLOCCULATED
FLOCCULATES
FLOCCULATING
FLOCCULATION
FLOCCULATIONS
FLOCCULATOR
FLOCCULATORS
FLOCCULENCE
FLOCCULENCES
FLOCCULENCIES
FLOCCULENCY

FLOCCULENT
FLOCCULENTLY
FLOODGATES
FLOODLIGHT
FLOODLIGHTED
FLOODLIGHTING
FLOODLIGHTINGS
FLOODLIGHTS
FLOODMARKS
FLOODPLAIN
FLOODPLAINS
FLOODTIDES
FLOODWALLS
FLOODWATER
FLOODWATERS
FLOORBOARD
FLOORBOARDS
FLOORCLOTH
FLOORCLOTHS
FLOORHEADS
FLOORSHOWS
FLOORWALKER
FLOORWALKERS
FLOPHOUSES
FLOPPINESS
FLOPPINESSES
FLORENTINE
FLORENTINES
FLORESCENCE
FLORESCENCES
FLORESCENT
FLORIATION
FLORIATIONS
FLORIBUNDA
FLORIBUNDAS
FLORICANES
FLORICULTURAL
FLORICULTURE
FLORICULTURES
FLORICULTURIST
FLORICULTURISTS
FLORIDEANS
FLORIDEOUS
FLORIDITIES
FLORIDNESS
FLORIDNESSES
FLORIFEROUS
FLORIFEROUSNESS
FLORIGENIC
FLORILEGIA
FLORILEGIUM
FLORISTICALLY
FLORISTICS
FLORISTRIES
FLOSCULOUS
FLOTATIONS
FLOUNCIEST
FLOUNCINGS
FLOUNDERED
FLOUNDERING
FLOURISHED
FLOURISHER
FLOURISHERS
FLOURISHES
FLOURISHING
FLOURISHINGLY
FLOUTINGLY
FLOUTINGSTOCK
FLOUTINGSTOCKS
FLOWCHARTING
FLOWCHARTINGS
FLOWCHARTS
FLOWERAGES
FLOWERBEDS
FLOWERETTE
FLOWERETTES
FLOWERIEST
FLOWERINESS
FLOWERINESSES
FLOWERINGS
FLOWERLESS
FLOWERLIKE
FLOWERPOTS

FLOWINGNESS
FLOWINGNESSES
FLOWMETERS
FLOWSTONES
FLUCTUATED
FLUCTUATES
FLUCTUATING
FLUCTUATION
FLUCTUATIONAL
FLUCTUATIONS
FLUEGELHORN
FLUEGELHORNS
FLUENTNESS
FLUENTNESSES
FLUFFINESS
FLUFFINESSES
FLUGELHORN
FLUGELHORNIST
FLUGELHORNISTS
FLUGELHORNS
FLUIDEXTRACT
FLUIDEXTRACTS
FLUIDIFIED
FLUIDIFIES
FLUIDIFYING
FLUIDISATION
FLUIDISATIONS
FLUIDISERS
FLUIDISING
FLUIDITIES
FLUIDIZATION
FLUIDIZATIONS
FLUIDIZERS
FLUIDIZING
FLUIDNESSES
FLUKINESSES
FLUMMERIES
FLUMMOXING
FLUNITRAZEPAM
FLUNITRAZEPAMS
FLUNKEYDOM
FLUNKEYDOMS
FLUNKEYISH
FLUNKEYISM
FLUNKEYISMS
FLUNKYISMS
FLUORAPATITE
FLUORAPATITES
FLUORESCED
FLUORESCEIN
FLUORESCEINE
FLUORESCEINES
FLUORESCEINS
FLUORESCENCE
FLUORESCENCES
FLUORESCENT
FLUORESCENTS
FLUORESCER
FLUORESCERS
FLUORESCES
FLUORESCING
FLUORIDATE
FLUORIDATED
FLUORIDATES
FLUORIDATING
FLUORIDATION
FLUORIDATIONS
FLUORIDISE
FLUORIDISED
FLUORIDISES
FLUORIDISING
FLUORIDIZE
FLUORIDIZED
FLUORIDIZES
FLUORIDIZING
FLUORIMETER
FLUORIMETERS
FLUORIMETRIC
FLUORIMETRIES
FLUORIMETRY
FLUORINATE
FLUORINATED
FLUORINATES

FLUORINATING
FLUORINATION
FLUORINATIONS
FLUOROACETATE
FLUOROACETATES
FLUOROCARBON
FLUOROCARBONS
FLUOROCHROME
FLUOROCHROMES
FLUOROGRAPHIC
FLUOROGRAPHIES
FLUOROGRAPHY
FLUOROMETER
FLUOROMETERS
FLUOROMETRIC
FLUOROMETRIES
FLUOROMETRY
FLUOROPHORE
FLUOROPHORES
FLUOROSCOPE
FLUOROSCOPED
FLUOROSCOPES
FLUOROSCOPIC
FLUOROSCOPIES
FLUOROSCOPING
FLUOROSCOPIST
FLUOROSCOPISTS
FLUOROSCOPY
FLUOROTYPE
FLUOROTYPES
FLUOROURACIL
FLUOROURACILS
FLUORSPARS
FLUOXETINE
FLUOXETINES
FLUPHENAZINE
FLUPHENAZINES
FLUSHNESSES
FLUSHWORKS
FLUSTEREDLY
FLUSTERING
FLUSTERMENT
FLUSTERMENTS
FLUSTRATED
FLUSTRATES
FLUSTRATING
FLUSTRATION
FLUSTRATIONS
FLUTEMOUTH
FLUTEMOUTHS
FLUTTERBOARD
FLUTTERBOARDS
FLUTTERERS
FLUTTERING
FLUTTERINGLY
FLUVIALIST
FLUVIALISTS
FLUVIATILE
FLUVIOMARINE
FLUVOXAMINE
FLUVOXAMINES
FLUXIONALLY
FLUXIONARY
FLUXIONIST
FLUXIONISTS
FLUXMETERS
FLYBLOWING
FLYBRIDGES
FLYCATCHER
FLYCATCHERS
FLYPITCHER
FLYPITCHERS
FLYPITCHES
FLYPOSTING
FLYPOSTINGS
FLYRODDERS
FLYSCREENS
FLYSPECKED
FLYSPECKING
FLYSTRIKES
FLYSWATTER
FLYSWATTERS
FLYWEIGHTS

FOAMFLOWER
FOAMFLOWERS
FOAMINESSES
FOCALISATION
FOCALISATIONS
FOCALISING
FOCALIZATION
FOCALIZATIONS
FOCALIZING
FOCIMETERS
FOCOMETERS
FODDERINGS
FOEDERATUS
FOETATIONS
FOETICIDAL
FOETICIDES
FOETIDNESS
FOETIDNESSES
FOETIPAROUS
FOETOSCOPIES
FOETOSCOPY
FOGGINESSES
FOGRAMITES
FOGRAMITIES
FOISONLESS
FOLIACEOUS
FOLIATIONS
FOLIATURES
FOLKISHNESS
FOLKISHNESSES
FOLKLORISH
FOLKLORIST
FOLKLORISTIC
FOLKLORISTS
FOLKSINESS
FOLKSINESSES
FOLKSINGER
FOLKSINGERS
FOLKSINGING
FOLKSINGINGS
FOLLICULAR
FOLLICULATE
FOLLICULATED
FOLLICULIN
FOLLICULINS
FOLLICULITIS
FOLLICULITISES
FOLLICULOSE
FOLLICULOUS
FOLLOWABLE
FOLLOWERSHIP
FOLLOWERSHIPS
FOLLOWINGS
FOLLOWSHIP
FOLLOWSHIPS
FOMENTATION
FOMENTATIONS
FONCTIONNAIRE
FONCTIONNAIRES
FONDLINGLY
FONDNESSES
FONTANELLE
FONTANELLES
FONTICULUS
FONTICULUSES
FONTINALIS
FONTINALISES
FOODLESSNESS
FOODLESSNESSES
FOODSTUFFS
FOOLBEGGED
FOOLFISHES
FOOLHARDIER
FOOLHARDIEST
FOOLHARDILY
FOOLHARDINESS
FOOLHARDINESSES
FOOLHARDISE
FOOLHARDISES
FOOLHARDIZE
FOOLHARDIZES
FOOLISHEST
FOOLISHNESS

FOOLISHNESSES
FOOTBALLENE
FOOTBALLENES
FOOTBALLER
FOOTBALLERS
FOOTBALLING
FOOTBALLIST
FOOTBALLISTS
FOOTBOARDS
FOOTBREADTH
FOOTBREADTHS
FOOTBRIDGE
FOOTBRIDGES
FOOTCLOTHS
FOOTDRAGGER
FOOTDRAGGERS
FOOTFAULTED
FOOTFAULTING
FOOTFAULTS
FOOTGUARDS
FOOTLAMBERT
FOOTLAMBERTS
FOOTLESSLY
FOOTLESSNESS
FOOTLESSNESSES
FOOTLIGHTS
FOOTLOCKER
FOOTLOCKERS
FOOTNOTING
FOOTPLATEMAN
FOOTPLATEMEN
FOOTPLATES
FOOTPLATEWOMAN
FOOTPLATEWOMEN
FOOTPRINTS
FOOTSLOGGED
FOOTSLOGGER
FOOTSLOGGERS
FOOTSLOGGING
FOOTSLOGGINGS
FOOTSORENESS
FOOTSORENESSES
FOOTSTALKS
FOOTSTALLS
FOOTSTOCKS
FOOTSTONES
FOOTSTOOLED
FOOTSTOOLS
FOPPISHNESS
FOPPISHNESSES
FORAMINATED
FORAMINIFER
FORAMINIFERA
FORAMINIFERAL
FORAMINIFERAN
FORAMINIFERANS
FORAMINIFEROUS
FORAMINIFERS
FORAMINOUS
FORBEARANCE
FORBEARANCES
FORBEARANT
FORBEARERS
FORBEARING
FORBEARINGLY
FORBIDDALS
FORBIDDANCE
FORBIDDANCES
FORBIDDENLY
FORBIDDERS
FORBIDDING
FORBIDDINGLY
FORBIDDINGNESS
FORBIDDINGS
FORCEDNESS
FORCEDNESSES
FORCEFULLY
FORCEFULNESS
FORCEFULNESSES
FORCEMEATS
FORCEPSLIKE
FORCIBILITIES
FORCIBILITY

FORCIBLENESS
FORCIBLENESSES
FORCIPATED
FORCIPATION
FORCIPATIONS
FOREARMING
FOREBITTER
FOREBITTERS
FOREBODEMENT
FOREBODEMENTS
FOREBODERS
FOREBODIES
FOREBODING
FOREBODINGLY
FOREBODINGNESS
FOREBODINGS
FOREBRAINS
FORECABINS
FORECADDIE
FORECADDIES
FORECARRIAGE
FORECARRIAGES
FORECASTABLE
FORECASTED
FORECASTER
FORECASTERS
FORECASTING
FORECASTLE
FORECASTLES
FORECHECKED
FORECHECKER
FORECHECKERS
FORECHECKING
FORECHECKS
FORECHOSEN
FORECLOSABLE
FORECLOSED
FORECLOSES
FORECLOSING
FORECLOSURE
FORECLOSURES
FORECLOTHS
FORECOURSE
FORECOURSES
FORECOURTS
FOREDAMNED
FOREDATING
FOREDOOMED
FOREDOOMING
FOREFATHER
FOREFATHERLY
FOREFATHERS
FOREFEELING
FOREFEELINGLY
FOREFENDED
FOREFENDING
FOREFINGER
FOREFINGERS
FOREFRONTS
FOREGATHER
FOREGATHERED
FOREGATHERING
FOREGATHERS
FOREGLEAMS
FOREGOINGS
FOREGONENESS
FOREGONENESSES
FOREGROUND
FOREGROUNDED
FOREGROUNDING
FOREGROUNDS
FOREHANDED
FOREHANDEDLY
FOREHANDEDNESS
FOREHANDING
FOREHENTING
FOREHOOVES
FOREIGNERS
FOREIGNISM
FOREIGNISMS
FOREIGNNESS
FOREIGNNESSES
FOREJUDGED

FOREJUDGEMENT
FOREJUDGEMENTS
FOREJUDGES
FOREJUDGING
FOREJUDGMENT
FOREJUDGMENTS
FOREKNOWABLE
FOREKNOWING
FOREKNOWINGLY
FOREKNOWLEDGE
FOREKNOWLEDGES
FORELADIES
FORELAYING
FORELENDING
FORELIFTED
FORELIFTING
FORELOCKED
FORELOCKING
FOREMANSHIP
FOREMANSHIPS
FOREMASTMAN
FOREMASTMEN
FOREMEANING
FOREMENTIONED
FOREMOTHER
FOREMOTHERS
FORENIGHTS
FORENSICALITIES
FORENSICALITY
FORENSICALLY
FOREORDAIN
FOREORDAINED
FOREORDAINING
FOREORDAINMENT
FOREORDAINMENTS
FOREORDAINS
FOREORDINATION
FOREORDINATIONS
FOREPASSED
FOREPAYMENT
FOREPAYMENTS
FOREPLANNED
FOREPLANNING
FOREPOINTED
FOREPOINTING
FOREPOINTS
FOREQUARTER
FOREQUARTERS
FOREREACHED
FOREREACHES
FOREREACHING
FOREREADING
FOREREADINGS
FORERUNNER
FORERUNNERS
FORERUNNING
FORESAYING
FORESEEABILITY
FORESEEABLE
FORESEEING
FORESEEINGLY
FORESHADOW
FORESHADOWED
FORESHADOWER
FORESHADOWERS
FORESHADOWING
FORESHADOWINGS
FORESHADOWS
FORESHANKS
FORESHEETS
FORESHEWED
FORESHEWING
FORESHOCKS
FORESHORES
FORESHORTEN
FORESHORTENED
FORESHORTENING
FORESHORTENINGS
FORESHORTENS
FORESHOWED
FORESHOWING
FORESIGHTED
FORESIGHTEDLY

FORESIGHTEDNESS
FORESIGHTFUL
FORESIGHTLESS
FORESIGHTS
FORESIGNIFIED
FORESIGNIFIES
FORESIGNIFY
FORESIGNIFYING
FORESKIRTS
FORESLACKED
FORESLACKING
FORESLACKS
FORESLOWED
FORESLOWING
FORESPEAKING
FORESPEAKS
FORESPENDING
FORESPENDS
FORESPOKEN
FORESTAGES
FORESTAIRS
FORESTALLED
FORESTALLER
FORESTALLERS
FORESTALLING
FORESTALLINGS
FORESTALLMENT
FORESTALLMENTS
FORESTALLS
FORESTALMENT
FORESTALMENTS
FORESTATION
FORESTATIONS
FORESTAYSAIL
FORESTAYSAILS
FORESTLAND
FORESTLANDS
FORESTLESS
FORESTRIES
FORESWEARING
FORESWEARS
FORETASTED
FORETASTES
FORETASTING
FORETAUGHT
FORETEACHES
FORETEACHING
FORETELLER
FORETELLERS
FORETELLING
FORETHINKER
FORETHINKERS
FORETHINKING
FORETHINKS
FORETHOUGHT
FORETHOUGHTFUL
FORETHOUGHTS
FORETOKENED
FORETOKENING
FORETOKENINGS
FORETOKENS
FORETOPMAN
FORETOPMAST
FORETOPMASTS
FORETOPMEN
FORETRIANGLE
FORETRIANGLES
FOREVERMORE
FOREVERNESS
FOREVERNESSES
FOREVOUCHED
FOREWARNED
FOREWARNER
FOREWARNERS
FOREWARNING
FOREWARNINGLY
FOREWARNINGS
FOREWEIGHED
FOREWEIGHING
FOREWEIGHS
FORFAIRING
FORFAITERS
FORFAITING

FORFAITINGS
FORFEITABLE
FORFEITERS
FORFEITING
FORFEITURE
FORFEITURES
FORFENDING
FORFEUCHEN
FORFICULATE
FORFOUGHEN
FORFOUGHTEN
FORGATHERED
FORGATHERING
FORGATHERS
FORGEABILITIES
FORGEABILITY
FORGETFULLY
FORGETFULNESS
FORGETFULNESSES
FORGETTABLE
FORGETTERIES
FORGETTERS
FORGETTERY
FORGETTING
FORGETTINGLY
FORGETTINGS
FORGIVABLE
FORGIVABLY
FORGIVENESS
FORGIVENESSES
FORGIVINGLY
FORGIVINGNESS
FORGIVINGNESSES
FORGOTTENNESS
FORGOTTENNESSES
FORHAILING
FORHENTING
FORHOOIEING
FORINSECAL
FORISFAMILIATE
FORISFAMILIATED
FORISFAMILIATES
FORJUDGING
FORJUDGMENT
FORJUDGMENTS
FORKEDNESS
FORKEDNESSES
FORKINESSES
FORKLIFTED
FORKLIFTING
FORLENDING
FORLORNEST
FORLORNNESS
FORLORNNESSES
FORMABILITIES
FORMABILITY
FORMALDEHYDE
FORMALDEHYDES
FORMALISABLE
FORMALISATION
FORMALISATIONS
FORMALISED
FORMALISER
FORMALISERS
FORMALISES
FORMALISING
FORMALISMS
FORMALISTIC
FORMALISTICALLY
FORMALISTS
FORMALITER
FORMALITIES
FORMALIZABLE
FORMALIZATION
FORMALIZATIONS
FORMALIZED
FORMALIZER
FORMALIZERS
FORMALIZES
FORMALIZING
FORMALNESS
FORMALNESSES
FORMAMIDES

FORMATIONAL	FORSWINKING	FOSSILISING	FRACTIONALLY	FRANCHISES	FRAXINELLA
FORMATIONS	FORSWORNNESS	FOSSILIZABLE	FRACTIONARY	FRANCHISING	FRAXINELLAS
FORMATIVELY	FORSWORNNESSES	FOSSILIZATION	FRACTIONATE	FRANCHISOR	FREAKERIES
FORMATIVENESS	FORSYTHIAS	FOSSILIZATIONS	FRACTIONATED	FRANCHISORS	FREAKINESS
FORMATIVENESSES	FORTALICES	FOSSILIZED	FRACTIONATES	FRANCISING	FREAKINESSES
FORMATIVES	FORTEPIANIST	FOSSILIZES	FRACTIONATING	FRANCIZING	FREAKISHLY
FORMATTERS	FORTEPIANISTS	FOSSILIZING	FRACTIONATION	FRANCOLINS	FREAKISHNESS
FORMATTING	FORTEPIANO	FOSTERAGES	FRACTIONATIONS	FRANCOMANIA	FREAKISHNESSES
FORMFITTING	FORTEPIANOS	FOSTERINGLY	FRACTIONATOR	FRANCOMANIAS	FRECKLIEST
FORMICARIA	FORTHCOMES	FOSTERINGS	FRACTIONATORS	FRANCOPHIL	FRECKLINGS
FORMICARIES	FORTHCOMING	FOSTERLING	FRACTIONED	FRANCOPHILE	FREEBASERS
FORMICARIUM	FORTHCOMINGNESS	FOSTERLINGS	FRACTIONING	FRANCOPHILES	FREEBASING
FORMICATED	FORTHGOING	FOSTRESSES	FRACTIONISATION	FRANCOPHILS	FREEBOARDS
FORMICATES	FORTHGOINGS	FOTHERGILLA	FRACTIONISE	FRANCOPHOBE	FREEBOOTED
FORMICATING	FORTHINKING	FOTHERGILLAS	FRACTIONISED	FRANCOPHOBES	FREEBOOTER
FORMICATION	FORTHOUGHT	FOUDROYANT	FRACTIONISES	FRANCOPHOBIA	FREEBOOTERIES
FORMICATIONS	FORTHRIGHT	FOUGHTIEST	FRACTIONISING	FRANCOPHOBIAS	FREEBOOTERS
FORMIDABILITIES	FORTHRIGHTLY	FOULBROODS	FRACTIONIZATION	FRANCOPHONE	FREEBOOTERY
FORMIDABILITY	FORTHRIGHTNESS	FOULDERING	FRACTIONIZE	FRANCOPHONES	FREEBOOTIES
FORMIDABLE	FORTHRIGHTS	FOULMOUTHED	FRACTIONIZED	FRANGIBILITIES	FREEBOOTING
FORMIDABLENESS	FORTIFIABLE	FOULNESSES	FRACTIONIZES	FRANGIBILITY	FREEBOOTINGS
FORMIDABLY	FORTIFICATION	FOUNDATION	FRACTIONIZING	FRANGIBLENESS	FREEDIVING
FORMLESSLY	FORTIFICATIONS	FOUNDATIONAL	FRACTIONLET	FRANGIBLENESSES	FREEDIVINGS
FORMLESSNESS	FORTIFIERS	FOUNDATIONALLY	FRACTIONLETS	FRANGIPANE	FREEDWOMAN
FORMLESSNESSES	FORTIFYING	FOUNDATIONARY	FRACTIOUSLY	FRANGIPANES	FREEDWOMEN
FORMULAICALLY	FORTIFYINGLY	FOUNDATIONER	FRACTIOUSNESS	FRANGIPANI	FREEHANDED
FORMULARIES	FORTILAGES	FOUNDATIONERS	FRACTIOUSNESSES	FRANGIPANIS	FREEHANDEDLY
FORMULARISATION	FORTISSIMI	FOUNDATIONLESS	FRACTOCUMULI	FRANGIPANNI	FREEHANDEDNESS
FORMULARISE	FORTISSIMO	FOUNDATIONS	FRACTOCUMULUS	FRANKALMOIGN	FREEHEARTED
FORMULARISED	FORTISSIMOS	FOUNDERING	FRACTOGRAPHIES	FRANKALMOIGNS	FREEHEARTEDLY
FORMULARISER	FORTISSISSIMO	FOUNDEROUS	FRACTOGRAPHY	FRANKFORTS	FREEHOLDER
FORMULARISERS	FORTITUDES	FOUNDLINGS	FRACTOSTRATI	FRANKFURTER	FREEHOLDERS
FORMULARISES	FORTITUDINOUS	FOUNDRESSES	FRACTOSTRATUS	FRANKFURTERS	FREELANCED
FORMULARISING	FORTNIGHTLIES	FOUNTAINED	FRACTURABLE	FRANKFURTS	FREELANCER
FORMULARISTIC	FORTNIGHTLY	FOUNTAINHEAD	FRACTURERS	FRANKINCENSE	FREELANCERS
FORMULARIZATION	FORTNIGHTS	FOUNTAINHEADS	FRACTURING	FRANKINCENSES	FREELANCES
FORMULARIZE	FORTRESSED	FOUNTAINING	FRAGILENESS	FRANKLINITE	FREELANCING
FORMULARIZED	FORTRESSES	FOUNTAINLESS	FRAGILENESSES	FRANKLINITES	FREELOADED
FORMULARIZER	FORTRESSING	FOURCHETTE	FRAGILITIES	FRANKNESSES	FREELOADER
FORMULARIZERS	FORTRESSLIKE	FOURCHETTES	FRAGMENTAL	FRANKPLEDGE	FREELOADERS
FORMULARIZES	FORTUITIES	FOURDRINIER	FRAGMENTALLY	FRANKPLEDGES	FREELOADING
FORMULARIZING	FORTUITISM	FOURDRINIERS	FRAGMENTARILY	FRANSERIAS	FREELOADINGS
FORMULATED	FORTUITISMS	FOURFOLDNESS	FRAGMENTARINESS	FRANTICALLY	FREEMARTIN
FORMULATES	FORTUITIST	FOURFOLDNESSES	FRAGMENTARY	FRANTICNESS	FREEMARTINS
FORMULATING	FORTUITISTS	FOURPENCES	FRAGMENTATE	FRANTICNESSES	FREEMASONIC
FORMULATION	FORTUITOUS	FOURPENNIES	FRAGMENTATED	FRATCHIEST	FREEMASONRIES
FORMULATIONS	FORTUITOUSLY	FOURPLEXES	FRAGMENTATES	FRATERNALISM	FREEMASONRY
FORMULATOR	FORTUITOUSNESS	FOURRAGERE	FRAGMENTATING	FRATERNALISMS	FREEMASONS
FORMULATORS	FORTUNATELY	FOURRAGERES	FRAGMENTATION	FRATERNALLY	FREENESSES
FORMULISED	FORTUNATENESS	FOURSCORTH	FRAGMENTATIONS	FRATERNISATION	FREEPHONES
FORMULISES	FORTUNATENESSES	FOURSQUARE	FRAGMENTED	FRATERNISATIONS	FREESHEETS
FORMULISING	FORTUNATES	FOURSQUARELY	FRAGMENTING	FRATERNISE	FREESTANDING
FORMULISMS	FORTUNELESS	FOURSQUARENESS	FRAGMENTISE	FRATERNISED	FREESTONES
FORMULISTIC	FORTUNISED	FOURTEENER	FRAGMENTISED	FRATERNISER	FREESTYLER
FORMULISTS	FORTUNISES	FOURTEENERS	FRAGMENTISES	FRATERNISERS	FREESTYLERS
FORMULIZED	FORTUNISING	FOURTEENTH	FRAGMENTISING	FRATERNISES	FREESTYLES
FORMULIZES	FORTUNIZED	FOURTEENTHLY	FRAGMENTIZE	FRATERNISING	FREESTYLING
FORMULIZING	FORTUNIZES	FOURTEENTHS	FRAGMENTIZED	FRATERNITIES	FREESTYLINGS
FORNICATED	FORTUNIZING	FOVEOLATED	FRAGMENTIZES	FRATERNITY	FREETHINKER
FORNICATES	FORWANDERED	FOXBERRIES	FRAGMENTIZING	FRATERNIZATION	FREETHINKERS
FORNICATING	FORWANDERING	FOXHUNTERS	FRAGRANCED	FRATERNIZATIONS	FREETHINKING
FORNICATION	FORWANDERS	FOXHUNTING	FRAGRANCES	FRATERNIZE	FREETHINKINGS
FORNICATIONS	FORWARDERS	FOXHUNTINGS	FRAGRANCIES	FRATERNIZED	FREEWHEELED
FORNICATOR	FORWARDEST	FOXINESSES	FRAGRANCING	FRATERNIZER	FREEWHEELER
FORNICATORS	FORWARDING	FOXTROTTED	FRAGRANTLY	FRATERNIZERS	FREEWHEELERS
FORNICATRESS	FORWARDINGS	FOXTROTTING	FRAGRANTNESS	FRATERNIZES	FREEWHEELING
FORNICATRESSES	FORWARDNESS	FOZINESSES	FRAGRANTNESSES	FRATERNIZING	FREEWHEELINGLY
FORSAKENLY	FORWARDNESSES	FRABJOUSLY	FRAICHEURS	FRATRICIDAL	FREEWHEELINGS
FORSAKENNESS	FORWARNING	FRACTALITIES	FRAILNESSES	FRATRICIDE	FREEWHEELS
FORSAKENNESSES	FORWASTING	FRACTALITY	FRAMBESIAS	FRATRICIDES	FREEWRITES
FORSAKINGS	FORWEARIED	FRACTIONAL	FRAMBOESIA	FRAUDFULLY	FREEWRITING
FORSLACKED	FORWEARIES	FRACTIONALISE	FRAMBOESIAS	FRAUDSTERS	FREEWRITINGS
FORSLACKING	FORWEARYING	FRACTIONALISED	FRAMBOISES	FRAUDULENCE	FREEWRITTEN
FORSLOEING	FOSCARNETS	FRACTIONALISES	FRAMESHIFT	FRAUDULENCES	FREEZINGLY
FORSLOWING	FOSSICKERS	FRACTIONALISING	FRAMESHIFTS	FRAUDULENCIES	FREIGHTAGE
FORSPEAKING	FOSSICKING	FRACTIONALISM	FRAMEWORKS	FRAUDULENCY	FREIGHTAGES
FORSPENDING	FOSSICKINGS	FRACTIONALISMS	FRANCHISED	FRAUDULENT	FREIGHTERS
FORSTERITE	FOSSILIFEROUS	FRACTIONALIST	FRANCHISEE	FRAUDULENTLY	FREIGHTING
FORSTERITES	FOSSILISABLE	FRACTIONALISTS	FRANCHISEES	FRAUDULENTNESS	FREIGHTLESS
FORSWEARER	FOSSILISATION	FRACTIONALIZE	FRANCHISEMENT	FRAUGHTAGE	FREMESCENCE
FORSWEARERS	FOSSILISATIONS	FRACTIONALIZED	FRANCHISEMENTS	FRAUGHTAGES	FREMESCENCES
FORSWEARING	FOSSILISED	FRACTIONALIZES	FRANCHISER	FRAUGHTEST	FREMESCENT
FORSWINKED	FOSSILISES	FRACTIONALIZING	FRANCHISERS	FRAUGHTING	FREMITUSES

f

FRENCHIFICATION	FRIGIDNESS	FRONTOGENESIS	FRUITLESSNESS	FUMIGATING	FURBELOWED
FRENCHIFIED	FRIGIDNESSES	FRONTOGENETIC	FRUITLESSNESSES	FUMIGATION	FURBELOWING
FRENCHIFIES	FRIGORIFIC	FRONTOLYSES	FRUITWOODS	FUMIGATIONS	FURBISHERS
FRENCHIFYING	FRIGORIFICO	FRONTOLYSIS	FRUMENTACEOUS	FUMIGATORS	FURBISHING
FRENETICAL	FRIGORIFICOS	FRONTPAGED	FRUMENTARIOUS	FUMIGATORY	FURCATIONS
FRENETICALLY	FRIKKADELS	FRONTPAGES	FRUMENTATION	FUMITORIES	FURCIFEROUS
FRENETICISM	FRILLINESS	FRONTPAGING	FRUMENTATIONS	FUMOSITIES	FURFURACEOUS
FRENETICISMS	FRILLINESSES	FRONTRUNNER	FRUMENTIES	FUNAMBULATE	FURFURACEOUSLY
FRENETICNESS	FRINGELESS	FRONTRUNNERS	FRUMPINESS	FUNAMBULATED	FURFURALDEHYDE
FRENETICNESSES	FRINGILLACEOUS	FRONTRUNNING	FRUMPINESSES	FUNAMBULATES	FURFURALDEHYDES
FRENZIEDLY	FRINGILLID	FRONTRUNNINGS	FRUMPISHLY	FUNAMBULATING	FURFUROLES
FREQUENCES	FRINGILLIFORM	FRONTWARDS	FRUMPISHNESS	FUNAMBULATION	FURIOSITIES
FREQUENCIES	FRINGILLINE	FROSTBITES	FRUMPISHNESSES	FUNAMBULATIONS	FURIOUSNESS
FREQUENTABLE	FRIPONNERIE	FROSTBITING	FRUSEMIDES	FUNAMBULATOR	FURIOUSNESSES
FREQUENTATION	FRIPONNERIES	FROSTBITINGS	FRUSTRATED	FUNAMBULATORS	FURLOUGHED
FREQUENTATIONS	FRIPPERERS	FROSTBITTEN	FRUSTRATER	FUNAMBULATORY	FURLOUGHING
FREQUENTATIVE	FRIPPERIES	FROSTBOUND	FRUSTRATERS	FUNAMBULISM	FURMENTIES
FREQUENTATIVES	FRISKINESS	FROSTFISHES	FRUSTRATES	FUNAMBULISMS	FURNIMENTS
FREQUENTED	FRISKINESSES	FROSTINESS	FRUSTRATING	FUNAMBULIST	FURNISHERS
FREQUENTER	FRISKINGLY	FROSTINESSES	FRUSTRATINGLY	FUNAMBULISTS	FURNISHING
FREQUENTERS	FRITHBORHS	FROSTLINES	FRUSTRATION	FUNCTIONAL	FURNISHINGS
FREQUENTEST	FRITHSOKEN	FROSTWORKS	FRUSTRATIONS	FUNCTIONALISM	FURNISHMENT
FREQUENTING	FRITHSOKENS	FROTHERIES	FRUTESCENCE	FUNCTIONALISMS	FURNISHMENTS
FREQUENTLY	FRITHSTOOL	FROTHINESS	FRUTESCENCES	FUNCTIONALIST	FURNITURES
FREQUENTNESS	FRITHSTOOLS	FROTHINESSES	FRUTESCENT	FUNCTIONALISTIC	FUROSEMIDE
FREQUENTNESSES	FRITILLARIA	FROUGHIEST	FRUTIFYING	FUNCTIONALISTS	FUROSEMIDES
FRESCOINGS	FRITILLARIAS	FROUZINESS	FUCIVOROUS	FUNCTIONALITIES	FURRIERIES
FRESCOISTS	FRITILLARIES	FROUZINESSES	FUCOXANTHIN	FUNCTIONALITY	FURRINESSES
FRESHENERS	FRITILLARY	FROWARDNESS	FUCOXANTHINS	FUNCTIONALLY	FURROWLESS
FRESHENING	FRITTERERS	FROWARDNESSES	FUGACIOUSLY	FUNCTIONALS	FURSHLUGGINER
FRESHERDOM	FRITTERING	FROWNINGLY	FUGACIOUSNESS	FUNCTIONARIES	FURTHCOMING
FRESHERDOMS	FRIVOLITIES	FROWSINESS	FUGACIOUSNESSES	FUNCTIONARY	FURTHCOMINGS
FRESHMANSHIP	FRIVOLLERS	FROWSINESSES	FUGACITIES	FUNCTIONATE	FURTHERANCE
FRESHMANSHIPS	FRIVOLLING	FROWSTIEST	FUGITATION	FUNCTIONATED	FURTHERANCES
FRESHNESSES	FRIVOLOUSLY	FROWSTINESS	FUGITATIONS	FUNCTIONATES	FURTHERERS
FRESHWATER	FRIVOLOUSNESS	FROWSTINESSES	FUGITIVELY	FUNCTIONATING	FURTHERING
FRESHWATERS	FRIVOLOUSNESSES	FROWZINESS	FUGITIVENESS	FUNCTIONED	FURTHERMORE
FRETBOARDS	FRIZZINESS	FROWZINESSES	FUGITIVENESSES	FUNCTIONING	FURTHERMOST
FRETFULNESS	FRIZZINESSES	FROZENNESS	FUGITOMETER	FUNCTIONLESS	FURTHERSOME
FRETFULNESSES	FRIZZLIEST	FROZENNESSES	FUGITOMETERS	FUNDAMENTAL	FURTIVENESS
FRIABILITIES	FRIZZLINESS	FRUCTIFEROUS	FULFILLERS	FUNDAMENTALISM	FURTIVENESSES
FRIABILITY	FRIZZLINESSES	FRUCTIFEROUSLY	FULFILLING	FUNDAMENTALISMS	FURUNCULAR
FRIABLENESS	FROGFISHES	FRUCTIFICATION	FULFILLINGS	FUNDAMENTALIST	FURUNCULOSES
FRIABLENESSES	FROGGERIES	FRUCTIFICATIONS	FULFILLMENT	FUNDAMENTALISTS	FURUNCULOSIS
FRIARBIRDS	FROGHOPPER	FRUCTIFIED	FULFILLMENTS	FUNDAMENTALITY	FURUNCULOUS
FRICANDEAU	FROGHOPPERS	FRUCTIFIER	FULFILMENT	FUNDAMENTALLY	FUSHIONLESS
FRICANDEAUS	FROGMARCHED	FRUCTIFIERS	FULFILMENTS	FUNDAMENTALNESS	FUSIBILITIES
FRICANDEAUX	FROGMARCHES	FRUCTIFIES	FULGENCIES	FUNDAMENTALS	FUSIBILITY
FRICANDOES	FROGMARCHING	FRUCTIFYING	FULGURATED	FUNDAMENTS	FUSIBLENESS
FRICASSEED	FROGMOUTHS	FRUCTIVOROUS	FULGURATES	FUNDHOLDER	FUSIBLENESSES
FRICASSEEING	FROGSPAWNS	FRUCTUARIES	FULGURATING	FUNDHOLDERS	FUSILLADED
FRICASSEES	FROLICKERS	FRUCTUATED	FULGURATION	FUNDHOLDING	FUSILLADES
FRICATIVES	FROLICKING	FRUCTUATES	FULGURATIONS	FUNDRAISED	FUSILLADING
FRICTIONAL	FROLICSOME	FRUCTUATING	FULGURITES	FUNDRAISER	FUSILLATION
FRICTIONALLY	FROLICSOMELY	FRUCTUATION	FULIGINOSITIES	FUNDRAISERS	FUSILLATIONS
FRICTIONLESS	FROLICSOMENESS	FRUCTUATIONS	FULIGINOSITY	FUNDRAISES	FUSIONISMS
FRICTIONLESSLY	FROMENTIES	FRUCTUOUSLY	FULIGINOUS	FUNDRAISING	FUSIONISTS
FRIEDCAKES	FRONDESCENCE	FRUCTUOUSNESS	FULIGINOUSLY	FUNEREALLY	FUSIONLESS
FRIENDINGS	FRONDESCENCES	FRUCTUOUSNESSES	FULIGINOUSNESS	FUNGIBILITIES	FUSSBUDGET
FRIENDLESS	FRONDESCENT	FRUGALISTS	FULLBLOODS	FUNGIBILITY	FUSSBUDGETS
FRIENDLESSNESS	FRONDIFEROUS	FRUGALITIES	FULLERENES	FUNGICIDAL	FUSSBUDGETY
FRIENDLIER	FRONTAGERS	FRUGALNESS	FULLERIDES	FUNGICIDALLY	FUSSINESSES
FRIENDLIES	FRONTALITIES	FRUGALNESSES	FULLERITES	FUNGICIDES	FUSTANELLA
FRIENDLIEST	FRONTALITY	FRUGIFEROUS	FULLMOUTHED	FUNGISTATIC	FUSTANELLAS
FRIENDLILY	FRONTBENCHER	FRUGIVORES	FULLNESSES	FUNGISTATICALLY	FUSTANELLE
FRIENDLINESS	FRONTBENCHERS	FRUGIVOROUS	FULMINANTS	FUNGISTATS	FUSTANELLES
FRIENDLINESSES	FRONTCOURT	FRUITARIAN	FULMINATED	FUNGOSITIES	FUSTIANISE
FRIENDSHIP	FRONTCOURTS	FRUITARIANISM	FULMINATES	FUNICULARS	FUSTIANISED
FRIENDSHIPS	FRONTENISES	FRUITARIANISMS	FULMINATING	FUNICULATE	FUSTIANISES
FRIEZELIKE	FRONTIERED	FRUITARIANS	FULMINATION	FUNKINESSES	FUSTIANISING
FRIGATOONS	FRONTIERING	FRUITCAKES	FULMINATIONS	FUNNELFORM	FUSTIANIST
FRIGHTENED	FRONTIERSMAN	FRUITERERS	FULMINATOR	FUNNELLING	FUSTIANISTS
FRIGHTENER	FRONTIERSMEN	FRUITERESS	FULMINATORS	FUNNINESSES	FUSTIANIZE
FRIGHTENERS	FRONTIERSWOMAN	FRUITERESSES	FULMINATORY	FURACIOUSNESS	FUSTIANIZED
FRIGHTENING	FRONTIERSWOMEN	FRUITERIES	FULMINEOUS	FURACIOUSNESSES	FUSTIANIZES
FRIGHTENINGLY	FRONTISPIECE	FRUITFULLER	FULSOMENESS	FURACITIES	FUSTIANIZING
FRIGHTFULLY	FRONTISPIECED	FRUITFULLEST	FULSOMENESSES	FURALDEHYDE	FUSTIGATED
FRIGHTFULNESS	FRONTISPIECES	FRUITFULLY	FUMATORIES	FURALDEHYDES	FUSTIGATES
FRIGHTFULNESSES	FRONTISPIECING	FRUITFULNESS	FUMATORIUM	FURANOSIDE	FUSTIGATING
FRIGHTSOME	FRONTLESSLY	FRUITFULNESSES	FUMATORIUMS	FURANOSIDES	FUSTIGATION
FRIGIDARIA	FRONTLINES	FRUITINESS	FUMBLINGLY	FURAZOLIDONE	FUSTIGATIONS
FRIGIDARIUM	FRONTLISTS	FRUITINESSES	FUMBLINGNESS	FURAZOLIDONES	FUSTIGATOR
FRIGIDITIES	FRONTOGENESES	FRUITLESSLY	FUMBLINGNESSES	FURBEARERS	FUSTIGATORS

FUSTIGATORY
FUSTILARIAN
FUSTILARIANS
FUSTILIRIAN
FUSTILIRIANS

FUSTILLIRIAN
FUSTILLIRIANS
FUSTINESSES
FUSULINIDS
FUTILENESS

FUTILENESSES
FUTILITARIAN
FUTILITARIANISM
FUTILITARIANS
FUTILITIES

FUTURELESS
FUTURELESSNESS
FUTURISTIC
FUTURISTICALLY
FUTURISTICS

FUTURITIES
FUTURITION
FUTURITIONS
FUTUROLOGICAL
FUTUROLOGIES

FUTUROLOGIST
FUTUROLOGISTS
FUTUROLOGY
FUZZINESSES

GABAPENTIN
GABAPENTINS
GABARDINES
GABBINESSES
GABBLEMENT
GABBLEMENTS
GABBROITIC
GABERDINES
GABERLUNZIE
GABERLUNZIES
GABIONADES
GABIONAGES
GABIONNADE
GABIONNADES
GADGETEERS
GADGETRIES
GADOLINITE
GADOLINITES
GADOLINIUM
GADOLINIUMS
GADROONING
GADROONINGS
GADZOOKERIES
GADZOOKERY
GAELICISED
GAELICISES
GAELICISING
GAELICISMS
GAELICIZED
GAELICIZES
GAELICIZING
GAILLARDIA
GAILLARDIAS
GAINFULNESS
GAINFULNESSES
GAINGIVING
GAINGIVINGS
GAINLESSNESS
GAINLESSNESSES
GAINLINESS
GAINLINESSES
GAINSAYERS
GAINSAYING
GAINSAYINGS
GAINSTRIVE
GAINSTRIVED
GAINSTRIVEN
GAINSTRIVES
GAINSTRIVING
GAINSTROVE
GAITERLESS
GALABIYAHS
GALACTAGOGUE
GALACTAGOGUES
GALACTOMETER
GALACTOMETERS
GALACTOMETRIES
GALACTOMETRY
GALACTOPHOROUS
GALACTOPOIESES
GALACTOPOIESIS
GALACTOPOIETIC
GALACTOPOIETICS
GALACTORRHEA
GALACTORRHEAS
GALACTORRHOEA
GALACTORRHOEAS

GALACTOSAEMIA
GALACTOSAEMIAS
GALACTOSAMINE
GALACTOSAMINES
GALACTOSEMIA
GALACTOSEMIAS
GALACTOSEMIC
GALACTOSES
GALACTOSIDASE
GALACTOSIDASES
GALACTOSIDE
GALACTOSIDES
GALACTOSYL
GALACTOSYLS
GALANTAMINE
GALANTAMINES
GALANTINES
GALAVANTED
GALAVANTING
GALDRAGONS
GALENGALES
GALENICALS
GALEOPITHECINE
GALEOPITHECOID
GALIMATIAS
GALIMATIASES
GALINGALES
GALIONGEES
GALIVANTED
GALIVANTING
GALLABEAHS
GALLABIAHS
GALLABIEHS
GALLABIYAH
GALLABIYAHS
GALLABIYAS
GALLABIYEH
GALLABIYEHS
GALLAMINES
GALLANTEST
GALLANTING
GALLANTNESS
GALLANTNESSES
GALLANTRIES
GALLBLADDER
GALLBLADDERS
GALLEASSES
GALLERISTS
GALLERYGOER
GALLERYGOERS
GALLERYING
GALLERYITE
GALLERYITES
GALLIAMBIC
GALLIAMBICS
GALLIARDISE
GALLIARDISES
GALLIASSES
GALLICISATION
GALLICISATIONS
GALLICISED
GALLICISES
GALLICISING
GALLICISMS
GALLICIZATION
GALLICIZATIONS
GALLICIZED

GALLICIZES
GALLICIZING
GALLIGASKINS
GALLIMAUFRIES
GALLIMAUFRY
GALLINACEAN
GALLINACEANS
GALLINACEOUS
GALLINAZOS
GALLINIPPER
GALLINIPPERS
GALLINULES
GALLISISED
GALLISISES
GALLISISING
GALLISIZED
GALLISIZES
GALLISIZING
GALLIVANTED
GALLIVANTING
GALLIVANTS
GALLIWASPS
GALLOGLASS
GALLOGLASSES
GALLONAGES
GALLOPADED
GALLOPADES
GALLOPADING
GALLOWGLASS
GALLOWGLASSES
GALLOWSNESS
GALLOWSNESSES
GALLSICKNESS
GALLSICKNESSES
GALLSTONES
GALLUMPHED
GALLUMPHING
GALLYGASKINS
GALRAVAGED
GALRAVAGES
GALRAVAGING
GALRAVITCH
GALRAVITCHED
GALRAVITCHES
GALRAVITCHING
GALUMPHERS
GALUMPHING
GALVANICAL
GALVANICALLY
GALVANISATION
GALVANISATIONS
GALVANISED
GALVANISER
GALVANISERS
GALVANISES
GALVANISING
GALVANISMS
GALVANISTS
GALVANIZATION
GALVANIZATIONS
GALVANIZED
GALVANIZER
GALVANIZERS
GALVANIZES
GALVANIZING
GALVANOMETER
GALVANOMETERS

GALVANOMETRIC
GALVANOMETRICAL
GALVANOMETRIES
GALVANOMETRY
GALVANOPLASTIC
GALVANOPLASTIES
GALVANOPLASTY
GALVANOSCOPE
GALVANOSCOPES
GALVANOSCOPIC
GALVANOSCOPIES
GALVANOSCOPY
GALVANOTROPIC
GALVANOTROPISM
GALVANOTROPISMS
GAMAHUCHED
GAMAHUCHES
GAMAHUCHING
GAMARUCHED
GAMARUCHES
GAMARUCHING
GAMBADOING
GAMBOLLING
GAMEBREAKER
GAMEBREAKERS
GAMEKEEPER
GAMEKEEPERS
GAMEKEEPING
GAMEKEEPINGS
GAMENESSES
GAMESMANSHIP
GAMESMANSHIPS
GAMESOMELY
GAMESOMENESS
GAMESOMENESSES
GAMETANGIA
GAMETANGIAL
GAMETANGIUM
GAMETICALLY
GAMETOCYTE
GAMETOCYTES
GAMETOGENESES
GAMETOGENESIS
GAMETOGENIC
GAMETOGENIES
GAMETOGENOUS
GAMETOGENY
GAMETOPHORE
GAMETOPHORES
GAMETOPHORIC
GAMETOPHYTE
GAMETOPHYTES
GAMETOPHYTIC
GAMINERIES
GAMINESQUE
GAMINESSES
GAMMERSTANG
GAMMERSTANGS
GAMMOCKING
GAMMONINGS
GAMOGENESES
GAMOGENESIS
GAMOGENETIC
GAMOGENETICAL
GAMOGENETICALLY
GAMOPETALOUS
GAMOPHYLLOUS

GAMOSEPALOUS
GAMOTROPIC
GAMOTROPISM
GAMOTROPISMS
GAMYNESSES
GANDERISMS
GANGBANGED
GANGBANGER
GANGBANGERS
GANGBANGING
GANGBOARDS
GANGBUSTER
GANGBUSTERS
GANGBUSTING
GANGBUSTINGS
GANGLIATED
GANGLIFORM
GANGLIONATED
GANGLIONIC
GANGLIOSIDE
GANGLIOSIDES
GANGPLANKS
GANGRENING
GANGRENOUS
GANGSHAGGED
GANGSHAGGING
GANGSTERDOM
GANGSTERDOMS
GANGSTERISH
GANGSTERISM
GANGSTERISMS
GANGSTERLAND
GANGSTERLANDS
GANNETRIES
GANNISTERS
GANTELOPES
GANTLETING
GAOLBREAKS
GAOLERESSES
GARAGISTES
GARBAGEMAN
GARBAGEMEN
GARBOLOGIES
GARBOLOGIST
GARBOLOGISTS
GARDENFULS
GARDENINGS
GARDENLESS
GARDEROBES
GARGANTUAN
GARGANTUAS
GARGARISED
GARGARISES
GARGARISING
GARGARISMS
GARGARIZED
GARGARIZES
GARGARIZING
GARGOYLISM
GARGOYLISMS
GARIBALDIS
GARISHNESS
GARISHNESSES
GARLANDAGE
GARLANDAGES
GARLANDING
GARLANDLESS

GARLANDRIES
GARLICKIER
GARLICKIEST
GARLICKING
GARMENTING
GARMENTLESS
GARMENTURE
GARMENTURES
GARNETIFEROUS
GARNIERITE
GARNIERITES
GARNISHEED
GARNISHEEING
GARNISHEEMENT
GARNISHEEMENTS
GARNISHEES
GARNISHERS
GARNISHING
GARNISHINGS
GARNISHMENT
GARNISHMENTS
GARNISHRIES
GARNITURES
GAROTTINGS
GARRETEERS
GARRISONED
GARRISONING
GARROTTERS
GARROTTING
GARROTTINGS
GARRULITIES
GARRULOUSLY
GARRULOUSNESS
GARRULOUSNESSES
GARRYOWENS
GASBAGGING
GASCONADED
GASCONADER
GASCONADERS
GASCONADES
GASCONADING
GASCONISMS
GASEOUSNESS
GASEOUSNESSES
GASHLINESS
GASHLINESSES
GASHOLDERS
GASIFIABLE
GASIFICATION
GASIFICATIONS
GASOMETERS
GASOMETRIC
GASOMETRICAL
GASOMETRIES
GASPEREAUS
GASPEREAUX
GASPINESSES
GASSINESSES
GASTEROPOD
GASTEROPODOUS
GASTEROPODS
GASTIGHTNESS
GASTIGHTNESSES
GASTNESSES
GASTRAEUMS
GASTRALGIA
GASTRALGIAS

GASTRALGIC
GASTRECTOMIES
GASTRECTOMY
GASTRITIDES
GASTRITISES
GASTROCNEMII
GASTROCNEMIUS
GASTROCOLIC
GASTRODUODENAL
GASTROENTERIC
GASTROENTERITIC
GASTROENTERITIS
GASTROLITH
GASTROLITHS
GASTROLOGER
GASTROLOGERS
GASTROLOGICAL
GASTROLOGIES
GASTROLOGIST
GASTROLOGISTS
GASTROLOGY
GASTROMANCIES
GASTROMANCY
GASTRONOME
GASTRONOMER
GASTRONOMERS
GASTRONOMES
GASTRONOMIC
GASTRONOMICAL
GASTRONOMICALLY
GASTRONOMIES
GASTRONOMIST
GASTRONOMISTS
GASTRONOMY
GASTROPODAN
GASTROPODANS
GASTROPODOUS
GASTROPODS
GASTROSCOPE
GASTROSCOPES
GASTROSCOPIC
GASTROSCOPIES
GASTROSCOPIST
GASTROSCOPISTS
GASTROSCOPY
GASTROSOPH
GASTROSOPHER
GASTROSOPHERS
GASTROSOPHIES
GASTROSOPHS
GASTROSOPHY
GASTROSTOMIES
GASTROSTOMY
GASTROTOMIES
GASTROTOMY
GASTROTRICH
GASTROTRICHS
GASTROVASCULAR
GASTRULATE
GASTRULATED
GASTRULATES
GASTRULATING
GASTRULATION
GASTRULATIONS
GATECRASHED
GATECRASHER
GATECRASHERS
GATECRASHES
GATECRASHING
GATEHOUSES
GATEKEEPER
GATEKEEPERS
GATEKEEPING
GATHERABLE
GATHERINGS
GAUCHENESS
GAUCHENESSES
GAUCHERIES
GAUDEAMUSES
GAUDINESSES
GAUFFERING
GAUFFERINGS
GAULEITERS

GAULTHERIA
GAULTHERIAS
GAUNTLETED
GAUNTLETING
GAUNTNESSES
GAUSSMETER
GAUSSMETERS
GAUZINESSES
GAVELKINDS
GAWKIHOODS
GAWKINESSES
GAWKISHNESS
GAWKISHNESSES
GAZEHOUNDS
GAZETTEERED
GAZETTEERING
GAZETTEERISH
GAZETTEERS
GAZILLIONAIRE
GAZILLIONAIRES
GAZILLIONS
GAZUNDERED
GAZUNDERER
GAZUNDERERS
GAZUNDERING
GEALOUSIES
GEANTICLINAL
GEANTICLINE
GEANTICLINES
GEARCHANGE
GEARCHANGES
GEARSHIFTS
GEARWHEELS
GEEKINESSES
GEEKSPEAKS
GEFUFFLING
GEGENSCHEIN
GEGENSCHEINS
GEHLENITES
GEITONOGAMIES
GEITONOGAMOUS
GEITONOGAMY
GELANDESPRUNG
GELANDESPRUNGS
GELATINATE
GELATINATED
GELATINATES
GELATINATING
GELATINATION
GELATINATIONS
GELATINISATION
GELATINISATIONS
GELATINISE
GELATINISED
GELATINISER
GELATINISERS
GELATINISES
GELATINISING
GELATINIZATION
GELATINIZATIONS
GELATINIZE
GELATINIZED
GELATINIZER
GELATINIZERS
GELATINIZES
GELATINIZING
GELATINOID
GELATINOIDS
GELATINOUS
GELATINOUSLY
GELATINOUSNESS
GELIDITIES
GELIDNESSES
GELIGNITES
GELLIFLOWRE
GELLIFLOWRES
GELSEMINES
GELSEMININE
GELSEMININES
GELSEMIUMS
GEMEINSCHAFT
GEMEINSCHAFTEN
GEMEINSCHAFTS

GEMFIBROZIL
GEMFIBROZILS
GEMINATELY
GEMINATING
GEMINATION
GEMINATIONS
GEMMACEOUS
GEMMATIONS
GEMMIFEROUS
GEMMINESSES
GEMMIPAROUS
GEMMIPAROUSLY
GEMMOLOGICAL
GEMMOLOGIES
GEMMOLOGIST
GEMMOLOGISTS
GEMMULATION
GEMMULATIONS
GEMOLOGICAL
GEMOLOGIES
GEMOLOGIST
GEMOLOGISTS
GEMUTLICHKEIT
GEMUTLICHKEITS
GENDARMERIE
GENDARMERIES
GENDARMERY
GENDERISED
GENDERISES
GENDERISING
GENDERIZED
GENDERIZES
GENDERIZING
GENDERLESS
GENEALOGIC
GENEALOGICAL
GENEALOGICALLY
GENEALOGIES
GENEALOGISE
GENEALOGISED
GENEALOGISES
GENEALOGISING
GENEALOGIST
GENEALOGISTS
GENEALOGIZE
GENEALOGIZED
GENEALOGIZES
GENEALOGIZING
GENECOLOGIES
GENECOLOGY
GENERALATE
GENERALATES
GENERALCIES
GENERALISABLE
GENERALISATION
GENERALISATIONS
GENERALISE
GENERALISED
GENERALISER
GENERALISERS
GENERALISES
GENERALISING
GENERALISSIMO
GENERALISSIMOS
GENERALIST
GENERALISTS
GENERALITIES
GENERALITY
GENERALIZABLE
GENERALIZATION
GENERALIZATIONS
GENERALIZE
GENERALIZED
GENERALIZER
GENERALIZERS
GENERALIZES
GENERALIZING
GENERALLED
GENERALLING
GENERALNESS
GENERALNESSES
GENERALSHIP
GENERALSHIPS

GENERATING
GENERATION
GENERATIONAL
GENERATIONALLY
GENERATIONISM
GENERATIONISMS
GENERATIONS
GENERATIVE
GENERATORS
GENERATRICES
GENERATRIX
GENERICALLY
GENERICNESS
GENERICNESSES
GENEROSITIES
GENEROSITY
GENEROUSLY
GENEROUSNESS
GENEROUSNESSES
GENETHLIAC
GENETHLIACAL
GENETHLIACALLY
GENETHLIACON
GENETHLIACONS
GENETHLIACS
GENETHLIALOGIC
GENETHLIALOGIES
GENETHLIALOGY
GENETICALLY
GENETICIST
GENETICISTS
GENETOTROPHIC
GENETRICES
GENETRIXES
GENEVRETTE
GENEVRETTES
GENIALISED
GENIALISES
GENIALISING
GENIALITIES
GENIALIZED
GENIALIZES
GENIALIZING
GENIALNESS
GENIALNESSES
GENICULATE
GENICULATED
GENICULATELY
GENICULATES
GENICULATING
GENICULATION
GENICULATIONS
GENISTEINS
GENITALIAL
GENITIVALLY
GENITIVELY
GENITOURINARY
GENITRICES
GENITRIXES
GENOPHOBIA
GENOPHOBIAS
GENOTYPICAL
GENOTYPICALLY
GENOTYPICITIES
GENOTYPICITY
GENOUILLERE
GENOUILLERES
GENSDARMES
GENTAMICIN
GENTAMICINS
GENTEELEST
GENTEELISE
GENTEELISED
GENTEELISES
GENTEELISH
GENTEELISING
GENTEELISM
GENTEELISMS
GENTEELIZE
GENTEELIZED
GENTEELIZES
GENTEELIZING
GENTEELNESS

GENTEELNESSES
GENTIANACEOUS
GENTIANELLA
GENTIANELLAS
GENTILESSE
GENTILESSES
GENTILHOMME
GENTILISED
GENTILISES
GENTILISING
GENTILISMS
GENTILITIAL
GENTILITIAN
GENTILITIES
GENTILITIOUS
GENTILIZED
GENTILIZES
GENTILIZING
GENTILSHOMMES
GENTLEFOLK
GENTLEFOLKS
GENTLEHOOD
GENTLEHOODS
GENTLEMANHOOD
GENTLEMANHOODS
GENTLEMANLIKE
GENTLEMANLINESS
GENTLEMANLY
GENTLEMANSHIP
GENTLEMANSHIPS
GENTLENESS
GENTLENESSE
GENTLENESSES
GENTLEPERSON
GENTLEPERSONS
GENTLEWOMAN
GENTLEWOMANLY
GENTLEWOMEN
GENTRIFICATION
GENTRIFICATIONS
GENTRIFIED
GENTRIFIER
GENTRIFIERS
GENTRIFIES
GENTRIFYING
GENUFLECTED
GENUFLECTING
GENUFLECTION
GENUFLECTIONS
GENUFLECTOR
GENUFLECTORS
GENUFLECTS
GENUFLEXION
GENUFLEXIONS
GENUINENESS
GENUINENESSES
GEOBOTANIC
GEOBOTANICAL
GEOBOTANIES
GEOBOTANIST
GEOBOTANISTS
GEOCACHING
GEOCACHINGS
GEOCARPIES
GEOCENTRIC
GEOCENTRICAL
GEOCENTRICALLY
GEOCENTRICISM
GEOCENTRICISMS
GEOCHEMICAL
GEOCHEMICALLY
GEOCHEMIST
GEOCHEMISTRIES
GEOCHEMISTRY
GEOCHEMISTS
GEOCHRONOLOGIC
GEOCHRONOLOGIES
GEOCHRONOLOGIST
GEOCHRONOLOGY
GEOCORONAE
GEOCORONAS
GEODEMOGRAPHICS
GEODESICAL

GEODESISTS
GEODETICAL
GEODETICALLY
GEODYNAMIC
GEODYNAMICAL
GEODYNAMICIST
GEODYNAMICISTS
GEODYNAMICS
GEOGNOSIES
GEOGNOSTIC
GEOGNOSTICAL
GEOGNOSTICALLY
GEOGRAPHER
GEOGRAPHERS
GEOGRAPHIC
GEOGRAPHICAL
GEOGRAPHICALLY
GEOGRAPHIES
GEOHYDROLOGIC
GEOHYDROLOGIES
GEOHYDROLOGIST
GEOHYDROLOGISTS
GEOHYDROLOGY
GEOLATRIES
GEOLINGUISTICS
GEOLOGIANS
GEOLOGICAL
GEOLOGICALLY
GEOLOGISED
GEOLOGISES
GEOLOGISING
GEOLOGISTS
GEOLOGIZED
GEOLOGIZES
GEOLOGIZING
GEOMAGNETIC
GEOMAGNETICALLY
GEOMAGNETISM
GEOMAGNETISMS
GEOMAGNETIST
GEOMAGNETISTS
GEOMANCERS
GEOMANCIES
GEOMECHANICS
GEOMEDICAL
GEOMEDICINE
GEOMEDICINES
GEOMETRICAL
GEOMETRICALLY
GEOMETRICIAN
GEOMETRICIANS
GEOMETRICS
GEOMETRIDS
GEOMETRIES
GEOMETRISATION
GEOMETRISATIONS
GEOMETRISE
GEOMETRISED
GEOMETRISES
GEOMETRISING
GEOMETRIST
GEOMETRISTS
GEOMETRIZATION
GEOMETRIZATIONS
GEOMETRIZE
GEOMETRIZED
GEOMETRIZES
GEOMETRIZING
GEOMORPHIC
GEOMORPHOGENIC
GEOMORPHOGENIES
GEOMORPHOGENIST
GEOMORPHOGENY
GEOMORPHOLOGIC
GEOMORPHOLOGIES
GEOMORPHOLOGIST
GEOMORPHOLOGY
GEOPHAGIAS
GEOPHAGIES
GEOPHAGISM
GEOPHAGISMS
GEOPHAGIST
GEOPHAGISTS

GEOPHAGOUS	GERMICIDES	GHETTOISED	GILRAVITCHED	GLAIKITNESS	GLAUCONITIC
GEOPHILOUS	GERMINABILITIES	GHETTOISES	GILRAVITCHES	GLAIKITNESSES	GLAUCOUSLY
GEOPHYSICAL	GERMINABILITY	GHETTOISING	GILRAVITCHING	GLAIRINESS	GLAUCOUSNESS
GEOPHYSICALLY	GERMINABLE	GHETTOIZATION	GILSONITES	GLAIRINESSES	GLAUCOUSNESSES
GEOPHYSICIST	GERMINALLY	GHETTOIZATIONS	GIMBALLING	GLAMORISATION	GLAZIERIES
GEOPHYSICISTS	GERMINATED	GHETTOIZED	GIMCRACKERIES	GLAMORISATIONS	GLAZINESSES
GEOPHYSICS	GERMINATES	GHETTOIZES	GIMCRACKERY	GLAMORISED	GLEEFULNESS
GEOPOLITICAL	GERMINATING	GHETTOIZING	GIMMICKIER	GLAMORISER	GLEEFULNESSES
GEOPOLITICALLY	GERMINATION	GHOSTLIEST	GIMMICKIEST	GLAMORISERS	GLEEMAIDEN
GEOPOLITICIAN	GERMINATIONS	GHOSTLINESS	GIMMICKING	GLAMORISES	GLEEMAIDENS
GEOPOLITICIANS	GERMINATIVE	GHOSTLINESSES	GIMMICKRIES	GLAMORISING	GLEGNESSES
GEOPOLITICS	GERMINATOR	GHOSTWRITE	GINGELLIES	GLAMORIZATION	GLEISATION
GEOPONICAL	GERMINATORS	GHOSTWRITER	GINGERADES	GLAMORIZATIONS	GLEISATIONS
GEOPRESSURED	GERMINESSES	GHOSTWRITERS	GINGERBREAD	GLAMORIZED	GLEIZATION
GEORGETTES	GERMPLASMS	GHOSTWRITES	GINGERBREADED	GLAMORIZER	GLEIZATIONS
GEOSCIENCE	GERONTOCRACIES	GHOSTWRITING	GINGERBREADS	GLAMORIZERS	GLENDOVEER
GEOSCIENCES	GERONTOCRACY	GHOSTWRITTEN	GINGERBREADY	GLAMORIZES	GLENDOVEERS
GEOSCIENTIFIC	GERONTOCRAT	GHOSTWROTE	GINGERLINESS	GLAMORIZING	GLENGARRIES
GEOSCIENTIST	GERONTOCRATIC	GHOULISHLY	GINGERLINESSES	GLAMOROUSLY	GLIBNESSES
GEOSCIENTISTS	GERONTOCRATS	GHOULISHNESS	GINGERROOT	GLAMOROUSNESS	GLIDEPATHS
GEOSPHERES	GERONTOLOGIC	GHOULISHNESSES	GINGERROOTS	GLAMOROUSNESSES	GLIMMERING
GEOSTATICS	GERONTOLOGICAL	GIANTESSES	GINGERSNAP	GLAMOURING	GLIMMERINGLY
GEOSTATIONARY	GERONTOLOGIES	GIANTHOODS	GINGERSNAPS	GLAMOURISE	GLIMMERINGS
GEOSTRATEGIC	GERONTOLOGIST	GIANTLIEST	GINGIVECTOMIES	GLAMOURISED	GLIOBLASTOMA
GEOSTRATEGICAL	GERONTOLOGISTS	GIANTSHIPS	GINGIVECTOMY	GLAMOURISES	GLIOBLASTOMAS
GEOSTRATEGIES	GERONTOLOGY	GIARDIASES	GINGIVITIS	GLAMOURISING	GLIOBLASTOMATA
GEOSTRATEGIST	GERONTOMORPHIC	GIARDIASIS	GINGIVITISES	GLAMOURIZE	GLIOMATOSES
GEOSTRATEGISTS	GERONTOPHIL	GIBBERELLIC	GINGLIMOID	GLAMOURIZED	GLIOMATOSIS
GEOSTRATEGY	GERONTOPHILE	GIBBERELLIN	GIPSYHOODS	GLAMOURIZES	GLIOMATOUS
GEOSTROPHIC	GERONTOPHILES	GIBBERELLINS	GIPSYWORTS	GLAMOURIZING	GLISSADERS
GEOSTROPHICALLY	GERONTOPHILIA	GIBBERISHES	GIRANDOLAS	GLAMOURLESS	GLISSADING
GEOSYNCHRONOUS	GERONTOPHILIAS	GIBBETTING	GIRANDOLES	GLAMOUROUS	GLISSANDOS
GEOSYNCLINAL	GERONTOPHILS	GIBBOSITIES	GIRDLECAKE	GLAMOUROUSLY	GLISTENING
GEOSYNCLINE	GERONTOPHOBE	GIBBOUSNESS	GIRDLECAKES	GLAMOUROUSNESS	GLISTENINGLY
GEOSYNCLINES	GERONTOPHOBES	GIBBOUSNESSES	GIRDLESCONE	GLAMOURPUSS	GLISTERING
GEOTACTICAL	GERONTOPHOBIA	GIDDINESSES	GIRDLESCONES	GLAMOURPUSSES	GLISTERINGLY
GEOTACTICALLY	GERONTOPHOBIAS	GIFTEDNESS	GIRDLESTEAD	GLANCINGLY	GLITCHIEST
GEOTECHNIC	GERRYMANDER	GIFTEDNESSES	GIRDLESTEADS	GLANDEROUS	GLITTERAND
GEOTECHNICAL	GERRYMANDERED	GIFTWRAPPED	GIRLFRIEND	GLANDIFEROUS	GLITTERATI
GEOTECHNICS	GERRYMANDERER	GIFTWRAPPING	GIRLFRIENDS	GLANDIFORM	GLITTERIER
GEOTECHNOLOGIES	GERRYMANDERERS	GIGACYCLES	GIRLISHNESS	GLANDULARLY	GLITTERIEST
GEOTECHNOLOGY	GERRYMANDERING	GIGAHERTZES	GIRLISHNESSES	GLANDULIFEROUS	GLITTERING
GEOTECTONIC	GERRYMANDERINGS	GIGANTESQUE	GIRTHLINES	GLANDULOUS	GLITTERINGLY
GEOTECTONICALLY	GERRYMANDERS	GIGANTICALLY	GISMOLOGIES	GLANDULOUSLY	GLITTERINGS
GEOTECTONICS	GERUNDIVAL	GIGANTICIDE	GITTARONES	GLARINESSES	GLITZINESS
GEOTEXTILE	GERUNDIVELY	GIGANTICIDES	GITTERNING	GLARINGNESS	GLITZINESSES
GEOTEXTILES	GERUNDIVES	GIGANTICNESS	GIVENNESSES	GLARINGNESSES	GLOATINGLY
GEOTHERMAL	GESELLSCHAFT	GIGANTICNESSES	GIZMOLOGIES	GLASNOSTIAN	GLOBALISATION
GEOTHERMALLY	GESELLSCHAFTEN	GIGANTISMS	GLABRESCENT	GLASNOSTIC	GLOBALISATIONS
GEOTHERMIC	GESELLSCHAFTS	GIGANTOLOGIES	GLABROUSNESS	GLASSBLOWER	GLOBALISED
GEOTHERMOMETER	GESNERIADS	GIGANTOLOGY	GLABROUSNESSES	GLASSBLOWERS	GLOBALISES
GEOTHERMOMETERS	GESSAMINES	GIGANTOMACHIA	GLACIALIST	GLASSBLOWING	GLOBALISING
GEOTROPICALLY	GESTALTISM	GIGANTOMACHIAS	GLACIALISTS	GLASSBLOWINGS	GLOBALISMS
GEOTROPISM	GESTALTISMS	GIGANTOMACHIES	GLACIATING	GLASSHOUSE	GLOBALISTS
GEOTROPISMS	GESTALTIST	GIGANTOMACHY	GLACIATION	GLASSHOUSES	GLOBALIZATION
GERANIACEOUS	GESTALTISTS	GIGGLESOME	GLACIATIONS	GLASSIFIED	GLOBALIZATIONS
GERATOLOGICAL	GESTATIONAL	GIGGLINGLY	GLACIOLOGIC	GLASSIFIES	GLOBALIZED
GERATOLOGIES	GESTATIONS	GIGMANITIES	GLACIOLOGICAL	GLASSIFYING	GLOBALIZES
GERATOLOGIST	GESTATORIAL	GILDSWOMAN	GLACIOLOGIES	GLASSINESS	GLOBALIZING
GERATOLOGISTS	GESTICULANT	GILDSWOMEN	GLACIOLOGIST	GLASSINESSES	GLOBEFISHES
GERATOLOGY	GESTICULATE	GILLFLIRTS	GLACIOLOGISTS	GLASSMAKER	GLOBEFLOWER
GERFALCONS	GESTICULATED	GILLIFLOWER	GLACIOLOGY	GLASSMAKERS	GLOBEFLOWERS
GERIATRICIAN	GESTICULATES	GILLIFLOWERS	GLADDENERS	GLASSMAKING	GLOBESITIES
GERIATRICIANS	GESTICULATING	GILLNETTED	GLADDENING	GLASSMAKINGS	GLOBETROTS
GERIATRICS	GESTICULATION	GILLNETTER	GLADFULNESS	GLASSPAPER	GLOBETROTTED
GERIATRIST	GESTICULATIONS	GILLNETTERS	GLADFULNESSES	GLASSPAPERED	GLOBETROTTER
GERIATRISTS	GESTICULATIVE	GILLNETTING	GLADIATORIAL	GLASSPAPERING	GLOBETROTTERS
GERMANDERS	GESTICULATOR	GILLRAVAGE	GLADIATORIAN	GLASSPAPERS	GLOBETROTTING
GERMANENESS	GESTICULATORS	GILLRAVAGED	GLADIATORS	GLASSWARES	GLOBETROTTINGS
GERMANENESSES	GESTICULATORY	GILLRAVAGES	GLADIATORSHIP	GLASSWORKER	GLOBIGERINA
GERMANISATION	GESTURALLY	GILLRAVAGING	GLADIATORSHIPS	GLASSWORKERS	GLOBIGERINAE
GERMANISATIONS	GESUNDHEIT	GILLRAVITCH	GLADIATORY	GLASSWORKS	GLOBIGERINAS
GERMANISED	GETTERINGS	GILLRAVITCHED	GLADIOLUSES	GLASSWORMS	GLOBOSENESS
GERMANISES	GEWURZTRAMINER	GILLRAVITCHES	GLADNESSES	GLASSWORTS	GLOBOSENESSES
GERMANISING	GEWURZTRAMINERS	GILLRAVITCHING	GLADSOMELY	GLASSYHEADED	GLOBOSITIES
GERMANITES	GEYSERITES	GILLYFLOWER	GLADSOMENESS	GLAUBERITE	GLOBULARITIES
GERMANIUMS	GHASTFULLY	GILLYFLOWERS	GLADSOMENESSES	GLAUBERITES	GLOBULARITY
GERMANIZATION	GHASTLIEST	GILRAVAGED	GLADSOMEST	GLAUCESCENCE	GLOBULARLY
GERMANIZATIONS	GHASTLINESS	GILRAVAGER	GLADSTONES	GLAUCESCENCES	GLOBULARNESS
GERMANIZED	GHASTLINESSES	GILRAVAGERS	GLADWRAPPED	GLAUCESCENT	GLOBULARNESSES
GERMANIZES	GHASTNESSES	GILRAVAGES	GLADWRAPPING	GLAUCOMATOUS	GLOBULIFEROUS
GERMANIZING	GHETTOISATION	GILRAVAGING	GLAIKETNESS	GLAUCONITE	GLOBULITES
GERMICIDAL	GHETTOISATIONS	GILRAVITCH	GLAIKETNESSES	GLAUCONITES	GLOCHIDIATE

GLOCHIDIUM	GLUCURONIDES	GLYOXALINES	GODCHILDREN	GONADOTROPHIN	GORGONISES
GLOCKENSPIEL	GLUEYNESSES	GLYPHOGRAPH	GODDAMMING	GONADOTROPHINS	GORGONISING
GLOCKENSPIELS	GLUINESSES	GLYPHOGRAPHER	GODDAMNDEST	GONADOTROPIC	GORGONIZED
GLOMERATED	GLUMACEOUS	GLYPHOGRAPHERS	GODDAMNEDEST	GONADOTROPIN	GORGONIZES
GLOMERATES	GLUMIFEROUS	GLYPHOGRAPHIC	GODDAMNING	GONADOTROPINS	GORGONIZING
GLOMERATING	GLUMNESSES	GLYPHOGRAPHICAL	GODDAUGHTER	GONDOLIERS	GORILLAGRAM
GLOMERATION	GLUTAMATES	GLYPHOGRAPHIES	GODDAUGHTERS	GONENESSES	GORILLAGRAMS
GLOMERATIONS	GLUTAMINASE	GLYPHOGRAPHS	GODDESSHOOD	GONFALONIER	GORINESSES
GLOMERULAR	GLUTAMINASES	GLYPHOGRAPHY	GODDESSHOODS	GONFALONIERS	GORMANDISE
GLOMERULATE	GLUTAMINES	GLYPTODONT	GODFATHERED	GONGORISTIC	GORMANDISED
GLOMERULES	GLUTAMINIC	GLYPTODONTS	GODFATHERING	GONIATITES	GORMANDISER
GLOMERULUS	GLUTARALDEHYDE	GLYPTOGRAPHER	GODFATHERS	GONIATITOID	GORMANDISERS
GLOOMFULLY	GLUTARALDEHYDES	GLYPTOGRAPHERS	GODFORSAKEN	GONIATITOIDS	GORMANDISES
GLOOMINESS	GLUTATHIONE	GLYPTOGRAPHIC	GODLESSNESS	GONIMOBLAST	GORMANDISING
GLOOMINESSES	GLUTATHIONES	GLYPTOGRAPHICAL	GODLESSNESSES	GONIMOBLASTS	GORMANDISINGS
GLORIFIABLE	GLUTETHIMIDE	GLYPTOGRAPHIES	GODLIKENESS	GONIOMETER	GORMANDISM
GLORIFICATION	GLUTETHIMIDES	GLYPTOGRAPHY	GODLIKENESSES	GONIOMETERS	GORMANDISMS
GLORIFICATIONS	GLUTINOSITIES	GLYPTOTHECA	GODLINESSES	GONIOMETRIC	GORMANDIZE
GLORIFIERS	GLUTINOSITY	GLYPTOTHECAE	GODMOTHERED	GONIOMETRICAL	GORMANDIZED
GLORIFYING	GLUTINOUSLY	GMELINITES	GODMOTHERING	GONIOMETRICALLY	GORMANDIZER
GLORIOUSLY	GLUTINOUSNESS	GNAPHALIUM	GODMOTHERS	GONIOMETRIES	GORMANDIZERS
GLORIOUSNESS	GLUTINOUSNESSES	GNAPHALIUMS	GODPARENTS	GONIOMETRY	GORMANDIZES
GLORIOUSNESSES	GLUTTINGLY	GNASHINGLY	GODROONING	GONIOSCOPE	GORMANDIZING
GLOSSARIAL	GLUTTONIES	GNATCATCHER	GODROONINGS	GONIOSCOPES	GORMANDIZINGS
GLOSSARIALLY	GLUTTONISE	GNATCATCHERS	GOFFERINGS	GONOCOCCAL	GOSLARITES
GLOSSARIES	GLUTTONISED	GNATHONICAL	GOGGLEBOXES	GONOCOCCIC	GOSPELISED
GLOSSARIST	GLUTTONISES	GNATHONICALLY	GOITROGENIC	GONOCOCCOID	GOSPELISES
GLOSSARISTS	GLUTTONISH	GNATHOSTOMATOUS	GOITROGENICITY	GONOCOCCUS	GOSPELISING
GLOSSATORS	GLUTTONISING	GNATHOSTOME	GOITROGENS	GONOPHORES	GOSPELIZED
GLOSSECTOMIES	GLUTTONIZE	GNATHOSTOMES	GOLDBEATER	GONOPHORIC	GOSPELIZES
GLOSSECTOMY	GLUTTONIZED	GNEISSITIC	GOLDBEATERS	GONOPHOROUS	GOSPELIZING
GLOSSINESS	GLUTTONIZES	GNETOPHYTE	GOLDBRICKED	GONORRHEAL	GOSPELLERS
GLOSSINESSES	GLUTTONIZING	GNETOPHYTES	GOLDBRICKING	GONORRHEAS	GOSPELLING
GLOSSINGLY	GLUTTONOUS	GNOMICALLY	GOLDBRICKS	GONORRHEIC	GOSPELLISE
GLOSSITISES	GLUTTONOUSLY	GNOMONICAL	GOLDCRESTS	GONORRHOEA	GOSPELLISED
GLOSSODYNIA	GLUTTONOUSNESS	GNOMONICALLY	GOLDENBERRIES	GONORRHOEAL	GOSPELLISES
GLOSSODYNIAS	GLYCAEMIAS	GNOMONOLOGIES	GOLDENBERRY	GONORRHOEAS	GOSPELLISING
GLOSSOGRAPHER	GLYCERALDEHYDE	GNOMONOLOGY	GOLDENEYES	GONORRHOEIC	GOSPELLIZE
GLOSSOGRAPHERS	GLYCERALDEHYDES	GNOSEOLOGIES	GOLDENNESS	GOODFELLOW	GOSPELLIZED
GLOSSOGRAPHICAL	GLYCERIDES	GNOSEOLOGY	GOLDENNESSES	GOODFELLOWS	GOSPELLIZES
GLOSSOGRAPHIES	GLYCERIDIC	GNOSIOLOGIES	GOLDENRODS	GOODFELLOWSHIP	GOSPELLIZING
GLOSSOGRAPHY	GLYCERINATE	GNOSIOLOGY	GOLDENSEAL	GOODFELLOWSHIPS	GOSSIPINGLY
GLOSSOLALIA	GLYCERINATED	GNOSTICALLY	GOLDENSEALS	GOODINESSES	GOSSIPINGS
GLOSSOLALIAS	GLYCERINATES	GNOSTICISM	GOLDFIELDS	GOODLIHEAD	GOSSIPMONGER
GLOSSOLALIST	GLYCERINATING	GNOSTICISMS	GOLDFINCHES	GOODLIHEADS	GOSSIPMONGERS
GLOSSOLALISTS	GLYCERINES	GNOTOBIOLOGICAL	GOLDFINNIES	GOODLINESS	GOSSIPPERS
GLOSSOLOGICAL	GLYCOCOLLS	GNOTOBIOLOGIES	GOLDFISHES	GOODLINESSES	GOSSIPPING
GLOSSOLOGIES	GLYCOGENESES	GNOTOBIOLOGY	GOLDILOCKS	GOODLYHEAD	GOSSIPRIES
GLOSSOLOGIST	GLYCOGENESIS	GNOTOBIOSES	GOLDILOCKSES	GOODLYHEADS	GOTHICALLY
GLOSSOLOGISTS	GLYCOGENETIC	GNOTOBIOSIS	GOLDMINERS	GOODNESSES	GOTHICISED
GLOSSOLOGY	GLYCOGENIC	GNOTOBIOTE	GOLDSINNIES	GOODNIGHTS	GOTHICISES
GLOTTIDEAN	GLYCOGENOLYSES	GNOTOBIOTES	GOLDSMITHERIES	GOOEYNESSES	GOTHICISING
GLOTTOGONIC	GLYCOGENOLYSIS	GNOTOBIOTIC	GOLDSMITHERY	GOOFINESSES	GOTHICISMS
GLOTTOLOGIES	GLYCOGENOLYTIC	GNOTOBIOTICALLY	GOLDSMITHRIES	GOOGLEWHACK	GOTHICIZED
GLOTTOLOGY	GLYCOLIPID	GNOTOBIOTICS	GOLDSMITHRY	GOOGLEWHACKS	GOTHICIZES
GLOWERINGLY	GLYCOLIPIDS	GOALKEEPER	GOLDSMITHS	GOOGOLPLEX	GOTHICIZING
GLOWSTICKS	GLYCOLYSES	GOALKEEPERS	GOLDSPINKS	GOOGOLPLEXES	GOURDINESS
GLUCINIUMS	GLYCOLYSIS	GOALKEEPING	GOLDSTICKS	GOONEYBIRD	GOURDINESSES
GLUCOCORTICOID	GLYCOLYTIC	GOALKEEPINGS	GOLDSTONES	GOONEYBIRDS	GOURMANDISE
GLUCOCORTICOIDS	GLYCONEOGENESES	GOALKICKER	GOLDTHREAD	GOOSANDERS	GOURMANDISED
GLUCOKINASE	GLYCONEOGENESIS	GOALKICKERS	GOLDTHREADS	GOOSEBERRIES	GOURMANDISES
GLUCOKINASES	GLYCOPEPTIDE	GOALKICKING	GOLIARDERIES	GOOSEBERRY	GOURMANDISING
GLUCONATES	GLYCOPEPTIDES	GOALKICKINGS	GOLIARDERY	GOOSEFISHES	GOURMANDISM
GLUCONEOGENESES	GLYCOPHYTE	GOALMOUTHS	GOLIARDIES	GOOSEFLESH	GOURMANDISMS
GLUCONEOGENESIS	GLYCOPHYTES	GOALTENDER	GOLIATHISE	GOOSEFLESHES	GOURMANDIZE
GLUCONEOGENIC	GLYCOPHYTIC	GOALTENDERS	GOLIATHISED	GOOSEFOOTS	GOURMANDIZED
GLUCOPHORE	GLYCOPROTEIN	GOALTENDING	GOLIATHISES	GOOSEGRASS	GOURMANDIZES
GLUCOPHORES	GLYCOPROTEINS	GOALTENDINGS	GOLIATHISING	GOOSEGRASSES	GOURMANDIZING
GLUCOPROTEIN	GLYCOSIDASE	GOATFISHES	GOLIATHIZE	GOOSEHERDS	GOUTINESSES
GLUCOPROTEINS	GLYCOSIDASES	GOATISHNESS	GOLIATHIZED	GOOSENECKED	GOUVERNANTE
GLUCOSAMINE	GLYCOSIDES	GOATISHNESSES	GOLIATHIZES	GOOSENECKS	GOUVERNANTES
GLUCOSAMINES	GLYCOSIDIC	GOATSBEARD	GOLIATHIZING	GOOSINESSES	GOVERNABILITIES
GLUCOSIDAL	GLYCOSIDICALLY	GOATSBEARDS	GOLLIWOGGS	GOPHERWOOD	GOVERNABILITY
GLUCOSIDASE	GLYCOSURIA	GOATSUCKER	GOLOMYNKAS	GOPHERWOODS	GOVERNABLE
GLUCOSIDASES	GLYCOSURIAS	GOATSUCKERS	GOLOPTIOUS	GORBELLIES	GOVERNABLENESS
GLUCOSIDES	GLYCOSURIC	GOBBELINES	GOLUPTIOUS	GORBLIMEYS	GOVERNALLS
GLUCOSIDIC	GLYCOSYLATE	GOBBLEDEGOOK	GOMBEENISM	GOREHOUNDS	GOVERNANCE
GLUCOSURIA	GLYCOSYLATED	GOBBLEDEGOOKS	GOMBEENISMS	GORGEOUSLY	GOVERNANCES
GLUCOSURIAS	GLYCOSYLATES	GOBBLEDYGOOK	GONADECTOMIES	GORGEOUSNESS	GOVERNANTE
GLUCOSURIC	GLYCOSYLATING	GOBBLEDYGOOKS	GONADECTOMISED	GORGEOUSNESSES	GOVERNANTES
GLUCURONIDASE	GLYCOSYLATION	GOBSMACKED	GONADECTOMIZED	GORGONEION	GOVERNESSED
GLUCURONIDASES	GLYCOSYLATIONS	GOBSTOPPER	GONADECTOMY	GORGONIANS	GOVERNESSES
GLUCURONIDE	GLYOXALINE	GOBSTOPPERS	GONADOTROPHIC	GORGONISED	GOVERNESSING

GOVERNESSY
GOVERNMENT
GOVERNMENTAL
GOVERNMENTALISE
GOVERNMENTALISM
GOVERNMENTALIST
GOVERNMENTALIZE
GOVERNMENTALLY
GOVERNMENTESE
GOVERNMENTESES
GOVERNMENTS
GOVERNORATE
GOVERNORATES
GOVERNORSHIP
GOVERNORSHIPS
GOWDSPINKS
GOWPENFULS
GRACEFULLER
GRACEFULLEST
GRACEFULLY
GRACEFULNESS
GRACEFULNESSES
GRACELESSLY
GRACELESSNESS
GRACELESSNESSES
GRACILENESS
GRACILENESSES
GRACILITIES
GRACIOSITIES
GRACIOSITY
GRACIOUSES
GRACIOUSLY
GRACIOUSNESS
GRACIOUSNESSES
GRADABILITIES
GRADABILITY
GRADABLENESS
GRADABLENESSES
GRADATIONAL
GRADATIONALLY
GRADATIONED
GRADATIONS
GRADDANING
GRADELIEST
GRADIENTER
GRADIENTERS
GRADIOMETER
GRADIOMETERS
GRADUALISM
GRADUALISMS
GRADUALIST
GRADUALISTIC
GRADUALISTS
GRADUALITIES
GRADUALITY
GRADUALNESS
GRADUALNESSES
GRADUATESHIP
GRADUATESHIPS
GRADUATING
GRADUATION
GRADUATIONS
GRADUATORS
GRAECISING
GRAECIZING
GRAFFITIED
GRAFFITIING
GRAFFITING
GRAFFITIST
GRAFFITISTS
GRAINFIELD
GRAINFIELDS
GRAININESS
GRAININESSES
GRALLATORIAL
GRALLOCHED
GRALLOCHING
GRAMERCIES
GRAMICIDIN
GRAMICIDINS
GRAMINACEOUS
GRAMINEOUS
GRAMINICOLOUS

GRAMINIVOROUS
GRAMINOLOGIES
GRAMINOLOGY
GRAMMALOGUE
GRAMMALOGUES
GRAMMARIAN
GRAMMARIANS
GRAMMARLESS
GRAMMATICAL
GRAMMATICALITY
GRAMMATICALLY
GRAMMATICALNESS
GRAMMATICASTER
GRAMMATICASTERS
GRAMMATICISE
GRAMMATICISED
GRAMMATICISES
GRAMMATICISING
GRAMMATICISM
GRAMMATICISMS
GRAMMATICIZE
GRAMMATICIZED
GRAMMATICIZES
GRAMMATICIZING
GRAMMATIST
GRAMMATISTS
GRAMMATOLOGIES
GRAMMATOLOGIST
GRAMMATOLOGISTS
GRAMMATOLOGY
GRAMOPHONE
GRAMOPHONES
GRAMOPHONIC
GRAMOPHONICALLY
GRAMOPHONIES
GRAMOPHONIST
GRAMOPHONISTS
GRAMOPHONY
GRANADILLA
GRANADILLAS
GRANDADDIES
GRANDAUNTS
GRANDBABIES
GRANDCHILD
GRANDCHILDREN
GRANDDADDIES
GRANDDADDY
GRANDDAUGHTER
GRANDDAUGHTERS
GRANDEESHIP
GRANDEESHIPS
GRANDFATHER
GRANDFATHERED
GRANDFATHERING
GRANDFATHERLY
GRANDFATHERS
GRANDIFLORA
GRANDIFLORAS
GRANDILOQUENCE
GRANDILOQUENCES
GRANDILOQUENT
GRANDILOQUENTLY
GRANDILOQUOUS
GRANDIOSELY
GRANDIOSENESS
GRANDIOSENESSES
GRANDIOSITIES
GRANDIOSITY
GRANDMAMAS
GRANDMAMMA
GRANDMAMMAS
GRANDMASTER
GRANDMASTERS
GRANDMOTHER
GRANDMOTHERLY
GRANDMOTHERS
GRANDNEPHEW
GRANDNEPHEWS
GRANDNESSES
GRANDNIECE
GRANDNIECES
GRANDPAPAS
GRANDPARENT

GRANDPARENTAL
GRANDPARENTHOOD
GRANDPARENTS
GRANDSIRES
GRANDSTAND
GRANDSTANDED
GRANDSTANDER
GRANDSTANDERS
GRANDSTANDING
GRANDSTANDS
GRANDSTOOD
GRANDUNCLE
GRANDUNCLES
GRANGERISATION
GRANGERISATIONS
GRANGERISE
GRANGERISED
GRANGERISER
GRANGERISERS
GRANGERISES
GRANGERISING
GRANGERISM
GRANGERISMS
GRANGERIZATION
GRANGERIZATIONS
GRANGERIZE
GRANGERIZED
GRANGERIZER
GRANGERIZERS
GRANGERIZES
GRANGERIZING
GRANITELIKE
GRANITEWARE
GRANITEWARES
GRANITIFICATION
GRANITIFORM
GRANITISATION
GRANITISATIONS
GRANITISED
GRANITISES
GRANITISING
GRANITITES
GRANITIZATION
GRANITIZATIONS
GRANITIZED
GRANITIZES
GRANITIZING
GRANIVORES
GRANIVOROUS
GRANNIEING
GRANODIORITE
GRANODIORITES
GRANODIORITIC
GRANOLITHIC
GRANOLITHICS
GRANOLITHS
GRANOPHYRE
GRANOPHYRES
GRANOPHYRIC
GRANTSMANSHIP
GRANTSMANSHIPS
GRANULARITIES
GRANULARITY
GRANULARLY
GRANULATED
GRANULATER
GRANULATERS
GRANULATES
GRANULATING
GRANULATION
GRANULATIONS
GRANULATIVE
GRANULATOR
GRANULATORS
GRANULIFEROUS
GRANULIFORM
GRANULITES
GRANULITIC
GRANULITISATION
GRANULITIZATION
GRANULOCYTE
GRANULOCYTES
GRANULOCYTIC

GRANULOMAS
GRANULOMATA
GRANULOMATOUS
GRANULOSES
GRANULOSIS
GRAPEFRUIT
GRAPEFRUITS
GRAPESEEDS
GRAPESHOTS
GRAPESTONE
GRAPESTONES
GRAPETREES
GRAPEVINES
GRAPHEMICALLY
GRAPHEMICS
GRAPHICACIES
GRAPHICACY
GRAPHICALLY
GRAPHICALNESS
GRAPHICALNESSES
GRAPHICNESS
GRAPHICNESSES
GRAPHITISABLE
GRAPHITISATION
GRAPHITISATIONS
GRAPHITISE
GRAPHITISED
GRAPHITISES
GRAPHITISING
GRAPHITIZABLE
GRAPHITIZATION
GRAPHITIZATIONS
GRAPHITIZE
GRAPHITIZED
GRAPHITIZES
GRAPHITIZING
GRAPHITOID
GRAPHOLECT
GRAPHOLECTS
GRAPHOLOGIC
GRAPHOLOGICAL
GRAPHOLOGIES
GRAPHOLOGIST
GRAPHOLOGISTS
GRAPHOLOGY
GRAPHOMANIA
GRAPHOMANIAS
GRAPHOMOTOR
GRAPHOPHOBIA
GRAPHOPHOBIAS
GRAPINESSES
GRANODIORITE
GRAPLEMENT
GRAPLEMENTS
GRAPPLINGS
GRAPTOLITE
GRAPTOLITES
GRAPTOLITIC
GRASPINGLY
GRASPINGNESS
GRASPINGNESSES
GRASSFINCH
GRASSFINCHES
GRASSHOOKS
GRASSHOPPER
GRASSHOPPERS
GRASSINESS
GRASSINESSES
GRASSLANDS
GRASSPLOTS
GRASSQUITS
GRASSROOTS
GRASSWRACK
GRASSWRACKS
GRATEFULLER
GRATEFULLEST
GRATEFULLY
GRATEFULNESS
GRATEFULNESSES
GRATICULATION
GRATICULATIONS
GRATICULES
GRATIFICATION
GRATIFICATIONS

GRATIFIERS
GRATIFYING
GRATIFYINGLY
GRATILLITIES
GRATILLITY
GRATINATED
GRATINATES
GRATINATING
GRATINEEING
GRATITUDES
GRATUITIES
GRATUITOUS
GRATUITOUSLY
GRATUITOUSNESS
GRATULATED
GRATULATES
GRATULATING
GRATULATION
GRATULATIONS
GRATULATORY
GRAUNCHERS
GRAUNCHING
GRAVADLAXES
GRAVELLING
GRAVENESSES
GRAVEOLENT
GRAVESIDES
GRAVESITES
GRAVESTONE
GRAVESTONES
GRAVEYARDS
GRAVIDITIES
GRAVIDNESS
GRAVIDNESSES
GRAVIMETER
GRAVIMETERS
GRAVIMETRIC
GRAVIMETRICAL
GRAVIMETRICALLY
GRAVIMETRIES
GRAVIMETRY
GRAVIPERCEPTION
GRAVITASES
GRAVITATED
GRAVITATER
GRAVITATERS
GRAVITATES
GRAVITATING
GRAVITATION
GRAVITATIONAL
GRAVITATIONALLY
GRAVITATIONS
GRAVITATIVE
GRAVITINOS
GRAVITOMETER
GRAVITOMETERS
GRAYBEARDED
GRAYBEARDS
GRAYFISHES
GRAYHOUNDS
GRAYNESSES
GRAYWACKES
GRAYWATERS
GREASEBALL
GREASEBALLS
GREASEBAND
GREASEBANDS
GREASEBUSH
GREASEBUSHES
GREASELESS
GREASEPAINT
GREASEPAINTS
GREASEPROOF
GREASEPROOFS
GREASEWOOD
GREASEWOODS
GREASINESS
GREASINESSES
GREATCOATED
GREATCOATS
GREATENING
GREATHEARTED
GREATHEARTEDLY

GREATNESSES
GRECIANISE
GRECIANISED
GRECIANISES
GRECIANISING
GRECIANIZE
GRECIANIZED
GRECIANIZES
GRECIANIZING
GREEDINESS
GREEDINESSES
GREENBACKER
GREENBACKERS
GREENBACKISM
GREENBACKISMS
GREENBACKS
GREENBELTS
GREENBONES
GREENBOTTLE
GREENBOTTLES
GREENBRIER
GREENBRIERS
GREENCLOTH
GREENCLOTHS
GREENERIES
GREENFIELD
GREENFIELDS
GREENFINCH
GREENFINCHES
GREENFLIES
GREENGAGES
GREENGROCER
GREENGROCERIES
GREENGROCERS
GREENGROCERY
GREENHANDS
GREENHEADS
GREENHEART
GREENHEARTS
GREENHORNS
GREENHOUSE
GREENHOUSES
GREENISHNESS
GREENISHNESSES
GREENKEEPER
GREENKEEPERS
GREENLIGHT
GREENLIGHTED
GREENLIGHTING
GREENLIGHTS
GREENLINGS
GREENMAILED
GREENMAILER
GREENMAILERS
GREENMAILING
GREENMAILS
GREENNESSES
GREENOCKITE
GREENOCKITES
GREENROOMS
GREENSANDS
GREENSHANK
GREENSHANKS
GREENSICKNESS
GREENSICKNESSES
GREENSKEEPER
GREENSKEEPERS
GREENSOMES
GREENSPEAK
GREENSPEAKS
GREENSTICK
GREENSTICKS
GREENSTONE
GREENSTONES
GREENSTUFF
GREENSTUFFS
GREENSWARD
GREENSWARDS
GREENWASHED
GREENWASHES
GREENWASHING
GREENWEEDS
GREENWINGS

GREENWOODS
GREGARIANISM
GREGARIANISMS
GREGARINES
GREGARINIAN
GREGARIOUS
GREGARIOUSLY
GREGARIOUSNESS
GREISENISATION
GREISENISATIONS
GREISENISE
GREISENISED
GREISENISES
GREISENISING
GREISENIZATION
GREISENIZATIONS
GREISENIZE
GREISENIZED
GREISENIZES
GREISENIZING
GREMOLATAS
GRENADIERS
GRENADILLA
GRENADILLAS
GRENADINES
GRESSORIAL
GRESSORIOUS
GREVILLEAS
GREWHOUNDS
GREWSOMEST
GREYBEARDED
GREYBEARDS
GREYHOUNDS
GREYLISTED
GREYLISTING
GREYNESSES
GREYSTONES
GREYWACKES
GREYWETHER
GREYWETHERS
GRIDDLEBREAD
GRIDDLEBREADS
GRIDDLECAKE
GRIDDLECAKES
GRIDIRONED
GRIDIRONING
GRIDLOCKED
GRIDLOCKING
GRIEVANCES
GRIEVINGLY
GRIEVOUSLY
GRIEVOUSNESS
GRIEVOUSNESSES
GRIFFINISH
GRIFFINISM
GRIFFINISMS
GRILLERIES
GRILLROOMS
GRILLSTEAK
GRILLSTEAKS
GRILLWORKS
GRIMACINGLY
GRIMALKINS
GRIMINESSES
GRIMLOOKED
GRIMNESSES
GRINDELIAS
GRINDERIES
GRINDHOUSE
GRINDHOUSES
GRINDINGLY
GRINDSTONE
GRINDSTONES
GRINNINGLY
GRIPPINGLY
GRISAILLES
GRISEOFULVIN
GRISEOFULVINS
GRISLINESS
GRISLINESSES
GRISTLIEST
GRISTLINESS
GRISTLINESSES

GRISTMILLS
GRITSTONES
GRITTINESS
GRITTINESSES
GRIVATIONS
GRIZZLIEST
GROANINGLY
GROATSWORTH
GROATSWORTHS
GROCETERIA
GROCETERIAS
GROGGERIES
GROGGINESS
GROGGINESSES
GROMMETING
GROOVELESS
GROOVELIKE
GROSGRAINS
GROSSIERETE
GROSSIERETES
GROSSNESSES
GROSSULARITE
GROSSULARITES
GROSSULARS
GROTESQUELY
GROTESQUENESS
GROTESQUENESSES
GROTESQUER
GROTESQUERIE
GROTESQUERIES
GROTESQUERY
GROTESQUES
GROTESQUEST
GROUCHIEST
GROUCHINESS
GROUCHINESSES
GROUNDAGES
GROUNDBAIT
GROUNDBAITED
GROUNDBAITING
GROUNDBAITS
GROUNDBREAKER
GROUNDBREAKERS
GROUNDBREAKING
GROUNDBREAKINGS
GROUNDBURST
GROUNDBURSTS
GROUNDEDLY
GROUNDFISH
GROUNDFISHES
GROUNDHOGS
GROUNDINGS
GROUNDLESS
GROUNDLESSLY
GROUNDLESSNESS
GROUNDLING
GROUNDLINGS
GROUNDMASS
GROUNDMASSES
GROUNDNUTS
GROUNDOUTS
GROUNDPLOT
GROUNDPLOTS
GROUNDPROX
GROUNDPROXES
GROUNDSELL
GROUNDSELLS
GROUNDSELS
GROUNDSHARE
GROUNDSHARED
GROUNDSHARES
GROUNDSHARING
GROUNDSHEET
GROUNDSHEETS
GROUNDSILL
GROUNDSILLS
GROUNDSKEEPER
GROUNDSKEEPERS
GROUNDSMAN
GROUNDSMEN
GROUNDSPEED
GROUNDSPEEDS
GROUNDSWELL

GROUNDSWELLS
GROUNDWATER
GROUNDWATERS
GROUNDWOOD
GROUNDWOODS
GROUNDWORK
GROUNDWORKS
GROUPTHINK
GROUPTHINKS
GROUPUSCULE
GROUPUSCULES
GROUPWARES
GROUSELIKE
GROVELINGLY
GROVELLERS
GROVELLING
GROVELLINGLY
GROVELLINGS
GROWLERIES
GROWLINESS
GROWLINESSES
GROWLINGLY
GROWTHIEST
GROWTHINESS
GROWTHINESSES
GROWTHISTS
GRUBBINESS
GRUBBINESSES
GRUBSTAKED
GRUBSTAKER
GRUBSTAKERS
GRUBSTAKES
GRUBSTAKING
GRUDGELESS
GRUDGINGLY
GRUELINGLY
GRUELLINGS
GRUESOMELY
GRUESOMENESS
GRUESOMENESSES
GRUESOMEST
GRUFFNESSES
GRUMBLIEST
GRUMBLINGLY
GRUMBLINGS
GRUMMETING
GRUMNESSES
GRUMPINESS
GRUMPINESSES
GRUMPISHLY
GRUMPISHNESS
GRUMPISHNESSES
GRUNTINGLY
GUACAMOLES
GUACHAMOLE
GUACHAMOLES
GUACHAROES
GUANABANAS
GUANAZOLOS
GUANETHIDINE
GUANETHIDINES
GUANIDINES
GUANIFEROUS
GUANOSINES
GUARANTEED
GUARANTEEING
GUARANTEES
GUARANTIED
GUARANTIES
GUARANTORS
GUARANTYING
GUARDEDNESS
GUARDEDNESSES
GUARDHOUSE
GUARDHOUSES
GUARDIANSHIP
GUARDIANSHIPS
GUARDRAILS
GUARDROOMS
GUARDSHIPS
GUARISHING
GUAYABERAS
GUBERNACULA

GUBERNACULAR
GUBERNACULUM
GUBERNATION
GUBERNATIONS
GUBERNATOR
GUBERNATORIAL
GUBERNATORS
GUBERNIYAS
GUDGEONING
GUERDONERS
GUERDONING
GUERILLAISM
GUERILLAISMS
GUERRILLAISM
GUERRILLAISMS
GUERRILLAS
GUERRILLERO
GUERRILLEROS
GUESSINGLY
GUESSTIMATE
GUESSTIMATED
GUESSTIMATES
GUESSTIMATING
GUESSWORKS
GUESTENING
GUESTHOUSE
GUESTHOUSES
GUESTIMATE
GUESTIMATED
GUESTIMATES
GUESTIMATING
GUIDEBOOKS
GUIDELINES
GUIDEPOSTS
GUIDESHIPS
GUIDEWORDS
GUIDWILLIE
GUILDHALLS
GUILDSHIPS
GUILDSWOMAN
GUILDSWOMEN
GUILEFULLY
GUILEFULNESS
GUILEFULNESSES
GUILELESSLY
GUILELESSNESS
GUILELESSNESSES
GUILLEMETS
GUILLEMOTS
GUILLOCHED
GUILLOCHES
GUILLOCHING
GUILLOTINE
GUILLOTINED
GUILLOTINER
GUILLOTINERS
GUILLOTINES
GUILLOTINING
GUILTINESS
GUILTINESSES
GUILTLESSLY
GUILTLESSNESS
GUILTLESSNESSES
GUITARFISH
GUITARFISHES
GUITARISTS
GULLIBILITIES
GULLIBILITY
GULOSITIES
GUMMIFEROUS
GUMMINESSES
GUMMOSITIES
GUMSHIELDS
GUMSHOEING
GUMSUCKERS
GUNCOTTONS
GUNFIGHTER
GUNFIGHTERS
GUNFIGHTING
GUNFIGHTINGS
GUNKHOLING
GUNMANSHIP
GUNMANSHIPS

GUNNERSHIP
GUNNERSHIPS
GUNNYSACKS
GUNPOWDERS
GUNPOWDERY
GUNRUNNERS
GUNRUNNING
GUNRUNNINGS
GUNSLINGER
GUNSLINGERS
GUNSLINGING
GUNSLINGINGS
GUNSMITHING
GUNSMITHINGS
GURGITATION
GURGITATIONS
GUSHINESSES
GUSTATIONS
GUSTATORILY
GUSTINESSES
GUTBUCKETS
GUTLESSNESS
GUTLESSNESSES
GUTSINESSES
GUTTATIONS
GUTTERBLOOD
GUTTERBLOODS
GUTTERINGS
GUTTERSNIPE
GUTTERSNIPES
GUTTERSNIPISH
GUTTIFEROUS
GUTTURALISATION
GUTTURALISE
GUTTURALISED
GUTTURALISES
GUTTURALISING
GUTTURALISM
GUTTURALISMS
GUTTURALITIES
GUTTURALITY
GUTTURALIZATION
GUTTURALIZE
GUTTURALIZED
GUTTURALIZES
GUTTURALIZING
GUTTURALLY
GUTTURALNESS
GUTTURALNESSES
GYMNASIARCH
GYMNASIARCHS
GYMNASIAST
GYMNASIASTS
GYMNASIUMS
GYMNASTICAL
GYMNASTICALLY
GYMNASTICS
GYMNORHINAL
GYMNOSOPHIES
GYMNOSOPHIST
GYMNOSOPHISTS
GYMNOSOPHS
GYMNOSOPHY
GYMNOSPERM
GYMNOSPERMIES
GYMNOSPERMOUS
GYMNOSPERMS
GYMNOSPERMY
GYNAECEUMS
GYNAECOCRACIES
GYNAECOCRACY
GYNAECOCRATIC
GYNAECOLOGIC
GYNAECOLOGICAL
GYNAECOLOGIES
GYNAECOLOGIST
GYNAECOLOGISTS
GYNAECOLOGY
GYNAECOMAST
GYNAECOMASTIA
GYNAECOMASTIAS
GYNAECOMASTIES
GYNAECOMASTS

GYNAECOMASTY
GYNANDRIES
GYNANDRISM
GYNANDRISMS
GYNANDROMORPH
GYNANDROMORPHIC
GYNANDROMORPHS
GYNANDROMORPHY
GYNANDROUS
GYNARCHIES
GYNECOCRACIES
GYNECOCRACY
GYNECOCRATIC
GYNECOLOGIC
GYNECOLOGICAL
GYNECOLOGIES
GYNECOLOGIST
GYNECOLOGISTS
GYNECOLOGY
GYNECOMASTIA
GYNECOMASTIAS
GYNIATRICS
GYNIATRIES
GYNIOLATRIES
GYNIOLATRY
GYNOCRACIES
GYNOCRATIC
GYNODIOECIOUS
GYNODIOECISM
GYNODIOECISMS
GYNOGENESES
GYNOGENESIS
GYNOGENETIC
GYNOMONOECIOUS
GYNOMONOECISM
GYNOMONOECISMS
GYNOPHOBES
GYNOPHOBIA
GYNOPHOBIAS
GYNOPHOBIC
GYNOPHOBICS
GYNOPHORES
GYNOPHORIC
GYNOSTEMIA
GYNOSTEMIUM
GYPSIFEROUS
GYPSOPHILA
GYPSOPHILAS
GYPSYHOODS
GYPSYWORTS
GYRATIONAL
GYRFALCONS
GYROCOMPASS
GYROCOMPASSES
GYROCOPTER
GYROCOPTERS
GYROFREQUENCIES
GYROFREQUENCY
GYROMAGNETIC
GYROMAGNETISM
GYROMAGNETISMS
GYROMANCIES
GYROPILOTS
GYROPLANES
GYROSCOPES
GYROSCOPIC
GYROSCOPICALLY
GYROSCOPICS
GYROSTABILISER
GYROSTABILISERS
GYROSTABILIZER
GYROSTABILIZERS
GYROSTATIC
GYROSTATICALLY
GYROSTATICS
GYROVAGUES

Hh

HAANEPOOTS
HABERDASHER
HABERDASHERIES
HABERDASHERS
HABERDASHERY
HABERDINES
HABERGEONS
HABILATORY
HABILIMENT
HABILIMENTS
HABILITATE
HABILITATED
HABILITATES
HABILITATING
HABILITATION
HABILITATIONS
HABILITATOR
HABILITATORS
HABITABILITIES
HABITABILITY
HABITABLENESS
HABITABLENESSES
HABITATION
HABITATIONAL
HABITATIONS
HABITAUNCE
HABITAUNCES
HABITUALLY
HABITUALNESS
HABITUALNESSES
HABITUATED
HABITUATES
HABITUATING
HABITUATION
HABITUATIONS
HABITUDINAL
HACENDADOS
HACIENDADO
HACIENDADOS
HACKAMORES
HACKBERRIES
HACKBUTEER
HACKBUTEERS
HACKBUTTER
HACKBUTTERS
HACKMATACK
HACKMATACKS
HACKNEYING
HACKNEYISM
HACKNEYISMS
HACKNEYMAN
HACKNEYMEN
HACKSAWING
HACQUETONS
HADROSAURS
HADROSAURUS
HADROSAURUSES
HAECCEITIES
HAEMACHROME
HAEMACHROMES
HAEMACYTOMETER
HAEMACYTOMETERS
HAEMAGGLUTINATE
HAEMAGGLUTININ
HAEMAGGLUTININS
HAEMAGOGUE
HAEMAGOGUES

HAEMANGIOMA
HAEMANGIOMAS
HAEMANGIOMATA
HAEMATEINS
HAEMATEMESES
HAEMATEMESIS
HAEMATINIC
HAEMATINICS
HAEMATITES
HAEMATITIC
HAEMATOBLAST
HAEMATOBLASTIC
HAEMATOBLASTS
HAEMATOCELE
HAEMATOCELES
HAEMATOCRIT
HAEMATOCRITS
HAEMATOCRYAL
HAEMATOGENESES
HAEMATOGENESIS
HAEMATOGENETIC
HAEMATOGENIC
HAEMATOGENOUS
HAEMATOLOGIC
HAEMATOLOGICAL
HAEMATOLOGIES
HAEMATOLOGIST
HAEMATOLOGISTS
HAEMATOLOGY
HAEMATOLYSES
HAEMATOLYSIS
HAEMATOMAS
HAEMATOMATA
HAEMATOPHAGOUS
HAEMATOPOIESES
HAEMATOPOIESIS
HAEMATOPOIETIC
HAEMATOSES
HAEMATOSIS
HAEMATOTHERMAL
HAEMATOXYLIC
HAEMATOXYLIN
HAEMATOXYLINS
HAEMATOXYLON
HAEMATOXYLONS
HAEMATOZOA
HAEMATOZOON
HAEMATURIA
HAEMATURIAS
HAEMATURIC
HAEMOCHROME
HAEMOCHROMES
HAEMOCOELS
HAEMOCONIA
HAEMOCONIAS
HAEMOCYANIN
HAEMOCYANINS
HAEMOCYTES
HAEMOCYTOMETER
HAEMOCYTOMETERS
HAEMODIALYSER
HAEMODIALYSERS
HAEMODIALYSES
HAEMODIALYSIS
HAEMODIALYZER
HAEMODIALYZERS
HAEMOFLAGELLATE

HAEMOGLOBIN
HAEMOGLOBINS
HAEMOGLOBINURIA
HAEMOLYSES
HAEMOLYSIN
HAEMOLYSINS
HAEMOLYSIS
HAEMOLYTIC
HAEMOPHILE
HAEMOPHILES
HAEMOPHILIA
HAEMOPHILIAC
HAEMOPHILIACS
HAEMOPHILIAS
HAEMOPHILIC
HAEMOPHILIOID
HAEMOPOIESES
HAEMOPOIESIS
HAEMOPOIETIC
HAEMOPTYSES
HAEMOPTYSIS
HAEMORRHAGE
HAEMORRHAGED
HAEMORRHAGES
HAEMORRHAGIC
HAEMORRHAGING
HAEMORRHOID
HAEMORRHOIDAL
HAEMORRHOIDS
HAEMOSTASES
HAEMOSTASIA
HAEMOSTASIAS
HAEMOSTASIS
HAEMOSTATIC
HAEMOSTATICS
HAEMOSTATS
HAGBERRIES
HAGBUTEERS
HAGBUTTERS
HAGGADICAL
HAGGADISTIC
HAGGADISTS
HAGGARDNESS
HAGGARDNESSES
HAGGISHNESS
HAGGISHNESSES
HAGIARCHIES
HAGIOCRACIES
HAGIOCRACY
HAGIOGRAPHER
HAGIOGRAPHERS
HAGIOGRAPHIC
HAGIOGRAPHICAL
HAGIOGRAPHIES
HAGIOGRAPHIST
HAGIOGRAPHISTS
HAGIOGRAPHY
HAGIOLATER
HAGIOLATERS
HAGIOLATRIES
HAGIOLATROUS
HAGIOLATRY
HAGIOLOGIC
HAGIOLOGICAL
HAGIOLOGIES
HAGIOLOGIST
HAGIOLOGISTS

HAGIOSCOPE
HAGIOSCOPES
HAGIOSCOPIC
HAILSTONES
HAILSTORMS
HAIRBRAINED
HAIRBREADTH
HAIRBREADTHS
HAIRBRUSHES
HAIRCLOTHS
HAIRCUTTER
HAIRCUTTERS
HAIRCUTTING
HAIRCUTTINGS
HAIRDRESSER
HAIRDRESSERS
HAIRDRESSING
HAIRDRESSINGS
HAIRDRIERS
HAIRDRYERS
HAIRINESSES
HAIRLESSNESS
HAIRLESSNESSES
HAIRPIECES
HAIRSBREADTH
HAIRSBREADTHS
HAIRSPLITTER
HAIRSPLITTERS
HAIRSPLITTING
HAIRSPLITTINGS
HAIRSPRAYS
HAIRSPRING
HAIRSPRINGS
HAIRSTREAK
HAIRSTREAKS
HAIRSTYLES
HAIRSTYLING
HAIRSTYLINGS
HAIRSTYLIST
HAIRSTYLISTS
HAIRWEAVING
HAIRWEAVINGS
HAIRYBACKS
HALACHISTS
HALAKHISTS
HALBERDIER
HALBERDIERS
HALCYONIAN
HALENESSES
HALFENDEALE
HALFHEARTED
HALFHEARTEDLY
HALFHEARTEDNESS
HALFNESSES
HALFPENNIES
HALFPENNYWORTH
HALFPENNYWORTHS
HALFSERIOUSLY
HALFTRACKS
HALFWITTED
HALFWITTEDLY
HALFWITTEDNESS
HALIEUTICS
HALIPLANKTON
HALIPLANKTONS
HALLALLING
HALLEFLINTA

HALLEFLINTAS
HALLELUIAH
HALLELUIAHS
HALLELUJAH
HALLELUJAHS
HALLMARKED
HALLMARKING
HALLOWEDNESS
HALLOWEDNESSES
HALLOYSITE
HALLOYSITES
HALLSTANDS
HALLUCINATE
HALLUCINATED
HALLUCINATES
HALLUCINATING
HALLUCINATION
HALLUCINATIONAL
HALLUCINATIONS
HALLUCINATIVE
HALLUCINATOR
HALLUCINATORS
HALLUCINATORY
HALLUCINOGEN
HALLUCINOGENIC
HALLUCINOGENICS
HALLUCINOGENS
HALLUCINOSES
HALLUCINOSIS
HALOBIONTIC
HALOBIONTS
HALOBIOTIC
HALOCARBON
HALOCARBONS
HALOCLINES
HALOGENATE
HALOGENATED
HALOGENATES
HALOGENATING
HALOGENATION
HALOGENATIONS
HALOGENOID
HALOGENOUS
HALOGETONS
HALOMORPHIC
HALOPERIDOL
HALOPERIDOLS
HALOPHILES
HALOPHILIC
HALOPHILIES
HALOPHILOUS
HALOPHOBES
HALOPHYTES
HALOPHYTIC
HALOPHYTISM
HALOPHYTISMS
HALOTHANES
HALTERBREAK
HALTERBREAKING
HALTERBREAKS
HALTERBROKE
HALTERBROKEN
HALTERNECK
HALTERNECKS
HALTINGNESS
HALTINGNESSES
HAMADRYADES

HAMADRYADS
HAMADRYASES
HAMAMELIDACEOUS
HAMAMELISES
HAMANTASCH
HAMANTASCHEN
HAMARTHRITIS
HAMARTHRITISES
HAMARTIOLOGIES
HAMARTIOLOGY
HAMBURGERS
HAMBURGHER
HAMBURGHERS
HAMESUCKEN
HAMESUCKENS
HAMFATTERED
HAMFATTERING
HAMFATTERS
HAMMERCLOTH
HAMMERCLOTHS
HAMMERHEAD
HAMMERHEADED
HAMMERHEADS
HAMMERINGS
HAMMERKOPS
HAMMERLESS
HAMMERLOCK
HAMMERLOCKS
HAMMERSTONE
HAMMERSTONES
HAMMERTOES
HAMMINESSES
HAMPEREDNESS
HAMPEREDNESSES
HAMSHACKLE
HAMSHACKLED
HAMSHACKLES
HAMSHACKLING
HAMSTRINGED
HAMSTRINGING
HAMSTRINGS
HANDBAGGED
HANDBAGGING
HANDBAGGINGS
HANDBALLED
HANDBALLER
HANDBALLERS
HANDBALLING
HANDBARROW
HANDBARROWS
HANDBASKET
HANDBASKETS
HANDBRAKES
HANDBREADTH
HANDBREADTHS
HANDCLASPS
HANDCRAFTED
HANDCRAFTING
HANDCRAFTS
HANDCRAFTSMAN
HANDCRAFTSMEN
HANDCUFFED
HANDCUFFING
HANDEDNESS
HANDEDNESSES
HANDFASTED
HANDFASTING

HANDFASTINGS
HANDFEEDING
HANDICAPPED
HANDICAPPER
HANDICAPPERS
HANDICAPPING
HANDICRAFT
HANDICRAFTER
HANDICRAFTERS
HANDICRAFTS
HANDICRAFTSMAN
HANDICRAFTSMEN
HANDICUFFS
HANDINESSES
HANDIWORKS
HANDKERCHER
HANDKERCHERS
HANDKERCHIEF
HANDKERCHIEFS
HANDKERCHIEVES
HANDLANGER
HANDLANGERS
HANDLEABLE
HANDLEBARS
HANDLELESS
HANDMAIDEN
HANDMAIDENS
HANDPHONES
HANDPICKED
HANDPICKING
HANDPRESSES
HANDPRINTS
HANDSBREADTH
HANDSBREADTHS
HANDSELING
HANDSELLED
HANDSELLING
HANDSHAKES
HANDSHAKING
HANDSHAKINGS
HANDSOMELY
HANDSOMENESS
HANDSOMENESSES
HANDSOMEST
HANDSPIKES
HANDSPRING
HANDSPRINGS
HANDSTAFFS
HANDSTAMPED
HANDSTAMPING
HANDSTAMPS
HANDSTANDS
HANDSTAVES
HANDSTROKE
HANDSTROKES
HANDSTURNS
HANDTOWELS
HANDWHEELS
HANDWORKED
HANDWORKER
HANDWORKERS
HANDWRINGER
HANDWRINGERS
HANDWRITES
HANDWRITING
HANDWRITINGS
HANDWRITTEN
HANDWROUGHT
HANDYPERSON
HANDYPERSONS
HANDYWORKS
HANGABILITIES
HANGABILITY
HANKERINGS
HANSARDISE
HANSARDISED
HANSARDISES
HANSARDISING
HANSARDIZE
HANSARDIZED
HANSARDIZES
HANSARDIZING
HANSELLING

HANTAVIRUS
HANTAVIRUSES
HAPAXANTHIC
HAPAXANTHOUS
HAPHAZARDLY
HAPHAZARDNESS
HAPHAZARDNESSES
HAPHAZARDRIES
HAPHAZARDRY
HAPHAZARDS
HAPHTARAHS
HAPHTAROTH
HAPLESSNESS
HAPLESSNESSES
HAPLOBIONT
HAPLOBIONTIC
HAPLOBIONTS
HAPLOGRAPHIES
HAPLOGRAPHY
HAPLOIDIES
HAPLOLOGIC
HAPLOLOGIES
HAPLOSTEMONOUS
HAPLOTYPES
HAPPENCHANCE
HAPPENCHANCES
HAPPENINGS
HAPPENSTANCE
HAPPENSTANCES
HAPPINESSES
HAPTOGLOBIN
HAPTOGLOBINS
HAPTOTROPIC
HAPTOTROPISM
HAPTOTROPISMS
HARAMZADAS
HARAMZADIS
HARANGUERS
HARANGUING
HARASSEDLY
HARASSINGLY
HARASSINGS
HARASSMENT
HARASSMENTS
HARBINGERED
HARBINGERING
HARBINGERS
HARBORAGES
HARBORFULS
HARBORLESS
HARBORMASTER
HARBORMASTERS
HARBORSIDE
HARBOURAGE
HARBOURAGES
HARBOURERS
HARBOURING
HARBOURLESS
HARDBACKED
HARDBOARDS
HARDBOUNDS
HARDCOVERS
HARDENINGS
HARDFISTED
HARDGRASSES
HARDHANDED
HARDHEADED
HARDHEADEDLY
HARDHEADEDNESS
HARDHEARTED
HARDHEARTEDLY
HARDHEARTEDNESS
HARDIHEADS
HARDIHOODS
HARDIMENTS
HARDINESSES
HARDINGGRASS
HARDINGGRASSES
HARDLINERS
HARDMOUTHED
HARDNESSES
HARDSCRABBLE

HARDSTANDING
HARDSTANDINGS
HARDSTANDS
HARDWAREMAN
HARDWAREMEN
HARDWIRING
HARDWORKING
HAREBRAINED
HARELIPPED
HARESTAILS
HARIOLATED
HARIOLATES
HARIOLATING
HARIOLATION
HARIOLATIONS
HARLEQUINADE
HARLEQUINADES
HARLEQUINED
HARLEQUINING
HARLEQUINS
HARLOTRIES
HARMALINES
HARMATTANS
HARMDOINGS
HARMFULNESS
HARMFULNESSES
HARMLESSLY
HARMLESSNESS
HARMLESSNESSES
HARMOLODIC
HARMOLODICS
HARMONICAL
HARMONICALLY
HARMONICAS
HARMONICHORD
HARMONICHORDS
HARMONICIST
HARMONICISTS
HARMONICON
HARMONICONS
HARMONIOUS
HARMONIOUSLY
HARMONIOUSNESS
HARMONIPHON
HARMONIPHONE
HARMONIPHONES
HARMONIPHONS
HARMONISABLE
HARMONISATION
HARMONISATIONS
HARMONISED
HARMONISER
HARMONISERS
HARMONISES
HARMONISING
HARMONISTIC
HARMONISTICALLY
HARMONISTS
HARMONIUMIST
HARMONIUMISTS
HARMONIUMS
HARMONIZABLE
HARMONIZATION
HARMONIZATIONS
HARMONIZED
HARMONIZER
HARMONIZERS
HARMONIZES
HARMONIZING
HARMONOGRAM
HARMONOGRAMS
HARMONOGRAPH
HARMONOGRAPHS
HARMONOMETER
HARMONOMETERS
HARMOSTIES
HARMOTOMES
HARNESSERS
HARNESSING
HARNESSLESS
HARPOONEER
HARPOONEERS
HARPOONERS

HARPOONING
HARPSICHORD
HARPSICHORDIST
HARPSICHORDISTS
HARPSICHORDS
HARQUEBUSE
HARQUEBUSES
HARQUEBUSIER
HARQUEBUSIERS
HARQUEBUSS
HARQUEBUSSES
HARROWINGLY
HARROWINGS
HARROWMENT
HARROWMENTS
HARRUMPHED
HARRUMPHING
HARSHENING
HARSHNESSES
HARTBEESES
HARTBEESTS
HARTEBEEST
HARTEBEESTS
HARTSHORNS
HARUMPHING
HARUSPICAL
HARUSPICATE
HARUSPICATED
HARUSPICATES
HARUSPICATING
HARUSPICATION
HARUSPICATIONS
HARUSPICES
HARUSPICIES
HARVESTABLE
HARVESTERS
HARVESTING
HARVESTINGS
HARVESTLESS
HARVESTMAN
HARVESTMEN
HARVESTTIME
HARVESTTIMES
HASENPFEFFER
HASENPFEFFERS
HASHEESHES
HASTEFULLY
HASTINESSES
HATBRUSHES
HATCHABILITIES
HATCHABILITY
HATCHBACKS
HATCHELING
HATCHELLED
HATCHELLER
HATCHELLERS
HATCHELLING
HATCHERIES
HATCHETTITE
HATCHETTITES
HATCHLINGS
HATCHMENTS
HATEFULNESS
HATEFULNESSES
HATELESSNESS
HATELESSNESSES
HATEWORTHY
HATLESSNESS
HATLESSNESSES
HAUBERGEON
HAUBERGEONS
HAUGHTIEST
HAUGHTINESS
HAUGHTINESSES
HAUNTINGLY
HAUSFRAUEN
HAUSSMANNISE
HAUSSMANNISED
HAUSSMANNISES
HAUSSMANNISING
HAUSSMANNIZE
HAUSSMANNIZED
HAUSSMANNIZES

HAUSSMANNIZING
HAUSTELLATE
HAUSTELLUM
HAUSTORIAL
HAUSTORIUM
HAVERSACKS
HAVERSINES
HAWFINCHES
HAWKISHNESS
HAWKISHNESSES
HAWKSBEARD
HAWKSBEARDS
HAWKSBILLS
HAWSEHOLES
HAWSEPIPES
HAYMAKINGS
HAZARDABLE
HAZARDIZES
HAZARDOUSLY
HAZARDOUSNESS
HAZARDOUSNESSES
HAZARDRIES
HAZINESSES
HEADACHIER
HEADACHIEST
HEADBANGED
HEADBANGING
HEADBOARDS
HEADBOROUGH
HEADBOROUGHS
HEADCHAIRS
HEADCHEESE
HEADCHEESES
HEADCLOTHS
HEADCOUNTS
HEADDRESSES
HEADFISHES
HEADFOREMOST
HEADFRAMES
HEADGUARDS
HEADHUNTED
HEADHUNTER
HEADHUNTERS
HEADHUNTING
HEADHUNTINGS
HEADINESSES
HEADLEASES
HEADLESSNESS
HEADLESSNESSES
HEADLIGHTS
HEADLINERS
HEADLINING
HEADMASTER
HEADMASTERLY
HEADMASTERS
HEADMASTERSHIP
HEADMASTERSHIPS
HEADMISTRESS
HEADMISTRESSES
HEADMISTRESSY
HEADPEACES
HEADPHONES
HEADPIECES
HEADQUARTER
HEADQUARTERED
HEADQUARTERING
HEADQUARTERS
HEADREACHED
HEADREACHES
HEADREACHING
HEADSCARVES
HEADSHAKES
HEADSHEETS
HEADSHRINKER
HEADSHRINKERS
HEADSPACES
HEADSPRING
HEADSPRINGS
HEADSQUARE
HEADSQUARES
HEADSTALLS
HEADSTANDS
HEADSTICKS

HEADSTOCKS
HEADSTONES
HEADSTREAM
HEADSTREAMS
HEADSTRONG
HEADSTRONGLY
HEADSTRONGNESS
HEADWAITER
HEADWAITERS
HEADWATERS
HEADWORKER
HEADWORKERS
HEALTHCARE
HEALTHCARES
HEALTHFULLY
HEALTHFULNESS
HEALTHFULNESSES
HEALTHIEST
HEALTHINESS
HEALTHINESSES
HEALTHISMS
HEALTHLESS
HEALTHLESSNESS
HEALTHSOME
HEAPSTEADS
HEARKENERS
HEARKENING
HEARTACHES
HEARTBEATS
HEARTBREAK
HEARTBREAKER
HEARTBREAKERS
HEARTBREAKING
HEARTBREAKINGLY
HEARTBREAKS
HEARTBROKE
HEARTBROKEN
HEARTBROKENLY
HEARTBROKENNESS
HEARTBURNING
HEARTBURNINGS
HEARTBURNS
HEARTENERS
HEARTENING
HEARTENINGLY
HEARTHRUGS
HEARTHSTONE
HEARTHSTONES
HEARTIKINS
HEARTINESS
HEARTINESSES
HEARTLANDS
HEARTLESSLY
HEARTLESSNESS
HEARTLESSNESSES
HEARTLINGS
HEARTRENDING
HEARTRENDINGLY
HEARTSEASE
HEARTSEASES
HEARTSEEDS
HEARTSICKNESS
HEARTSICKNESSES
HEARTSOMELY
HEARTSOMENESS
HEARTSOMENESSES
HEARTSTRING
HEARTSTRINGS
HEARTTHROB
HEARTTHROBS
HEARTWARMING
HEARTWATER
HEARTWATERS
HEARTWOODS
HEARTWORMS
HEATEDNESS
HEATEDNESSES
HEATHBERRIES
HEATHBERRY
HEATHBIRDS
HEATHCOCKS
HEATHENDOM
HEATHENDOMS

HEATHENESSE
HEATHENESSES
HEATHENISE
HEATHENISED
HEATHENISES
HEATHENISH
HEATHENISHLY
HEATHENISHNESS
HEATHENISING
HEATHENISM
HEATHENISMS
HEATHENIZE
HEATHENIZED
HEATHENIZES
HEATHENIZING
HEATHENNESS
HEATHENNESSES
HEATHENRIES
HEATHERIER
HEATHERIEST
HEATHFOWLS
HEATHLANDS
HEATSTROKE
HEATSTROKES
HEAVENLIER
HEAVENLIEST
HEAVENLINESS
HEAVENLINESSES
HEAVENWARD
HEAVENWARDS
HEAVINESSES
HEAVYHEARTED
HEAVYHEARTEDLY
HEAVYWEIGHT
HEAVYWEIGHTS
HEBDOMADAL
HEBDOMADALLY
HEBDOMADAR
HEBDOMADARIES
HEBDOMADARS
HEBDOMADARY
HEBDOMADER
HEBDOMADERS
HEBEPHRENIA
HEBEPHRENIAC
HEBEPHRENIACS
HEBEPHRENIAS
HEBEPHRENIC
HEBEPHRENICS
HEBETATING
HEBETATION
HEBETATIONS
HEBETATIVE
HEBETUDINOSITY
HEBETUDINOUS
HEBRAISATION
HEBRAISATIONS
HEBRAISING
HEBRAIZATION
HEBRAIZATIONS
HEBRAIZING
HECKELPHONE
HECKELPHONES
HECOGENINS
HECTICALLY
HECTOCOTYLI
HECTOCOTYLUS
HECTOGRAMME
HECTOGRAMMES
HECTOGRAMS
HECTOGRAPH
HECTOGRAPHED
HECTOGRAPHIC
HECTOGRAPHIES
HECTOGRAPHING
HECTOGRAPHS
HECTOGRAPHY
HECTOLITER
HECTOLITERS
HECTOLITRE
HECTOLITRES
HECTOMETER
HECTOMETERS

HECTOMETRE
HECTOMETRES
HECTORINGLY
HECTORINGS
HECTORISMS
HECTORSHIP
HECTORSHIPS
HECTOSTERE
HECTOSTERES
HEDGEBILLS
HEDGEHOPPED
HEDGEHOPPER
HEDGEHOPPERS
HEDGEHOPPING
HEDGEHOPPINGS
HEDONICALLY
HEDONISTIC
HEDONISTICALLY
HEDYPHANES
HEEDFULNESS
HEEDFULNESSES
HEEDINESSES
HEEDLESSLY
HEEDLESSNESS
HEEDLESSNESSES
HEELPIECES
HEELPLATES
HEFTINESSES
HEGEMONIAL
HEGEMONICAL
HEGEMONIES
HEGEMONISM
HEGEMONISMS
HEGEMONIST
HEGEMONISTS
HEGUMENIES
HEGUMENOSES
HEIGHTENED
HEIGHTENER
HEIGHTENERS
HEIGHTENING
HEIGHTISMS
HEINOUSNESS
HEINOUSNESSES
HEKTOGRAMS
HELDENTENOR
HELDENTENORS
HELIACALLY
HELIANTHEMUM
HELIANTHEMUMS
HELIANTHUS
HELIANTHUSES
HELIBUSSES
HELICHRYSUM
HELICHRYSUMS
HELICITIES
HELICLINES
HELICOGRAPH
HELICOGRAPHS
HELICOIDAL
HELICOIDALLY
HELICONIAS
HELICOPTED
HELICOPTER
HELICOPTERED
HELICOPTERING
HELICOPTERS
HELICOPTING
HELICTITES
HELIDROMES
HELILIFTED
HELILIFTING
HELIOCENTRIC
HELIOCENTRICISM
HELIOCENTRICITY
HELIOCHROME
HELIOCHROMES
HELIOCHROMIC
HELIOCHROMIES
HELIOCHROMY
HELIOGRAMS
HELIOGRAPH
HELIOGRAPHED

HELIOGRAPHER
HELIOGRAPHERS
HELIOGRAPHIC
HELIOGRAPHICAL
HELIOGRAPHIES
HELIOGRAPHING
HELIOGRAPHS
HELIOGRAPHY
HELIOGRAVURE
HELIOGRAVURES
HELIOLATER
HELIOLATERS
HELIOLATRIES
HELIOLATROUS
HELIOLATRY
HELIOLITHIC
HELIOLOGIES
HELIOMETER
HELIOMETERS
HELIOMETRIC
HELIOMETRICAL
HELIOMETRICALLY
HELIOMETRIES
HELIOMETRY
HELIOPAUSE
HELIOPAUSES
HELIOPHILOUS
HELIOPHOBIC
HELIOPHYTE
HELIOPHYTES
HELIOSCIOPHYTE
HELIOSCIOPHYTES
HELIOSCOPE
HELIOSCOPES
HELIOSCOPIC
HELIOSPHERE
HELIOSPHERES
HELIOSTATIC
HELIOSTATS
HELIOTACTIC
HELIOTAXES
HELIOTAXIS
HELIOTHERAPIES
HELIOTHERAPY
HELIOTROPE
HELIOTROPES
HELIOTROPIC
HELIOTROPICAL
HELIOTROPICALLY
HELIOTROPIES
HELIOTROPIN
HELIOTROPINS
HELIOTROPISM
HELIOTROPISMS
HELIOTROPY
HELIOTYPED
HELIOTYPES
HELIOTYPIC
HELIOTYPIES
HELIOTYPING
HELIOZOANS
HELIPILOTS
HELISPHERIC
HELISPHERICAL
HELLACIOUS
HELLACIOUSLY
HELLBENDER
HELLBENDERS
HELLBROTHS
HELLDIVERS
HELLEBORES
HELLEBORINE
HELLEBORINES
HELLENISATION
HELLENISATIONS
HELLENISED
HELLENISES
HELLENISING
HELLENIZATION
HELLENIZATIONS
HELLENIZED
HELLENIZES
HELLENIZING

HELLGRAMITE
HELLGRAMITES
HELLGRAMMITE
HELLGRAMMITES
HELLHOUNDS
HELLISHNESS
HELLISHNESSES
HELMETLIKE
HELMINTHIASES
HELMINTHIASIS
HELMINTHIC
HELMINTHICS
HELMINTHOID
HELMINTHOLOGIC
HELMINTHOLOGIES
HELMINTHOLOGIST
HELMINTHOLOGY
HELMINTHOUS
HELMSMANSHIP
HELMSMANSHIPS
HELOPHYTES
HELPFULNESS
HELPFULNESSES
HELPLESSLY
HELPLESSNESS
HELPLESSNESSES
HELVETIUMS
HEMACHROME
HEMACHROMES
HEMACYTOMETER
HEMACYTOMETERS
HEMAGGLUTINATE
HEMAGGLUTINATED
HEMAGGLUTINATES
HEMAGGLUTININ
HEMAGGLUTININS
HEMAGOGUES
HEMANGIOMA
HEMANGIOMAS
HEMANGIOMATA
HEMATEMESES
HEMATEMESIS
HEMATINICS
HEMATOBLAST
HEMATOBLASTIC
HEMATOBLASTS
HEMATOCELE
HEMATOCELES
HEMATOCRIT
HEMATOCRITS
HEMATOCRYAL
HEMATOGENESES
HEMATOGENESIS
HEMATOGENETIC
HEMATOGENOUS
HEMATOLOGIC
HEMATOLOGICAL
HEMATOLOGIES
HEMATOLOGIST
HEMATOLOGISTS
HEMATOLOGY
HEMATOLYSES
HEMATOLYSIS
HEMATOMATA
HEMATOPHAGOUS
HEMATOPOIESES
HEMATOPOIESIS
HEMATOPOIETIC
HEMATOPORPHYRIN
HEMATOTHERMAL
HEMATOXYLIN
HEMATOXYLINS
HEMATOZOON
HEMATURIAS
HEMELYTRAL
HEMELYTRON
HEMELYTRUM
HEMERALOPIA
HEMERALOPIAS
HEMERALOPIC
HEMEROCALLIS
HEMEROCALLISES
HEMERYTHRIN

HEMERYTHRINS
HEMIACETAL
HEMIACETALS
HEMIALGIAS
HEMIANOPIA
HEMIANOPIAS
HEMIANOPSIA
HEMIANOPSIAS
HEMIANOPTIC
HEMICELLULOSE
HEMICELLULOSES
HEMICHORDATE
HEMICHORDATES
HEMICRANIA
HEMICRANIAS
HEMICRYPTOPHYTE
HEMICRYSTALLINE
HEMICYCLES
HEMICYCLIC
HEMIELYTRA
HEMIELYTRAL
HEMIELYTRON
HEMIHEDRAL
HEMIHEDRIES
HEMIHEDRISM
HEMIHEDRISMS
HEMIHEDRON
HEMIHEDRONS
HEMIHYDRATE
HEMIHYDRATED
HEMIHYDRATES
HEMIMETABOLOUS
HEMIMORPHIC
HEMIMORPHIES
HEMIMORPHISM
HEMIMORPHISMS
HEMIMORPHITE
HEMIMORPHITES
HEMIMORPHY
HEMIONUSES
HEMIOPSIAS
HEMIPARASITE
HEMIPARASITES
HEMIPARASITIC
HEMIPLEGIA
HEMIPLEGIAS
HEMIPLEGIC
HEMIPLEGICS
HEMIPTERAL
HEMIPTERAN
HEMIPTERANS
HEMIPTERON
HEMIPTERONS
HEMIPTEROUS
HEMISPACES
HEMISPHERE
HEMISPHERES
HEMISPHERIC
HEMISPHERICAL
HEMISPHEROID
HEMISPHEROIDAL
HEMISPHEROIDS
HEMISTICHAL
HEMISTICHS
HEMITERPENE
HEMITERPENES
HEMITROPAL
HEMITROPES
HEMITROPIC
HEMITROPIES
HEMITROPISM
HEMITROPISMS
HEMITROPOUS
HEMIZYGOUS
HEMOCHROMATOSES
HEMOCHROMATOSIS
HEMOCHROME
HEMOCHROMES
HEMOCYANIN
HEMOCYANINS
HEMOCYTOMETER
HEMOCYTOMETERS
HEMODIALYSES

HEMODIALYSIS
HEMODILUTION
HEMODILUTIONS
HEMODYNAMIC
HEMODYNAMICALLY
HEMODYNAMICS
HEMOFLAGELLATE
HEMOFLAGELLATES
HEMOGLOBIN
HEMOGLOBINS
HEMOGLOBINURIA
HEMOGLOBINURIAS
HEMOGLOBINURIC
HEMOLYMPHS
HEMOLYSING
HEMOLYSINS
HEMOLYZING
HEMOPHILES
HEMOPHILIA
HEMOPHILIAC
HEMOPHILIACS
HEMOPHILIAS
HEMOPHILIC
HEMOPHILICS
HEMOPHILIOID
HEMOPOIESES
HEMOPOIESIS
HEMOPOIETIC
HEMOPROTEIN
HEMOPROTEINS
HEMOPTYSES
HEMOPTYSIS
HEMORRHAGE
HEMORRHAGED
HEMORRHAGES
HEMORRHAGIC
HEMORRHAGING
HEMORRHOID
HEMORRHOIDAL
HEMORRHOIDALS
HEMORRHOIDS
HEMOSIDERIN
HEMOSIDERINS
HEMOSTASES
HEMOSTASIA
HEMOSTASIAS
HEMOSTASIS
HEMOSTATIC
HEMOSTATICS
HEMOTOXINS
HEMSTITCHED
HEMSTITCHER
HEMSTITCHERS
HEMSTITCHES
HEMSTITCHING
HENCEFORTH
HENCEFORWARD
HENCEFORWARDS
HENCHPERSON
HENCHPERSONS
HENCHWOMAN
HENCHWOMEN
HENDECAGON
HENDECAGONAL
HENDECAGONS
HENDECAHEDRA
HENDECAHEDRON
HENDECAHEDRONS
HENDECASYLLABIC
HENDECASYLLABLE
HENDIADYSES
HENOTHEISM
HENOTHEISMS
HENOTHEIST
HENOTHEISTIC
HENOTHEISTS
HENPECKERIES
HENPECKERY
HENPECKING
HEORTOLOGICAL
HEORTOLOGIES
HEORTOLOGIST
HEORTOLOGISTS

h

HEORTOLOGY	HERBARIANS	HERMATYPIC	HETAERISTIC	HETEROGONOUSLY	HETEROSTYLED
HEPARINISED	HERBARIUMS	HERMENEUTIC	HETAERISTS	HETEROGONY	HETEROSTYLIES
HEPARINIZED	HERBICIDAL	HERMENEUTICAL	HETAIRISMIC	HETEROGRAFT	HETEROSTYLISM
HEPARINOID	HERBICIDALLY	HERMENEUTICALLY	HETAIRISMS	HETEROGRAFTS	HETEROSTYLISMS
HEPATECTOMIES	HERBICIDES	HERMENEUTICS	HETAIRISTIC	HETEROGRAPHIC	HETEROSTYLOUS
HEPATECTOMISED	HERBIVORES	HERMENEUTIST	HETAIRISTS	HETEROGRAPHICAL	HETEROSTYLY
HEPATECTOMIZED	HERBIVORIES	HERMENEUTISTS	HETERARCHIES	HETEROGRAPHIES	HETEROTACTIC
HEPATECTOMY	HERBIVOROUS	HERMETICAL	HETERARCHY	HETEROGRAPHY	HETEROTACTOUS
HEPATICOLOGICAL	HERBIVOROUSLY	HERMETICALLY	HETERAUXESES	HETEROGYNOUS	HETEROTAXES
HEPATICOLOGIES	HERBIVOROUSNESS	HERMETICISM	HETERAUXESIS	HETEROKARYON	HETEROTAXIA
HEPATICOLOGIST	HERBOLOGIES	HERMETICISMS	HETEROATOM	HETEROKARYONS	HETEROTAXIAS
HEPATICOLOGISTS	HERBORISATION	HERMETICITIES	HETEROATOMS	HETEROKARYOSES	HETEROTAXIC
HEPATICOLOGY	HERBORISATIONS	HERMETICITY	HETEROAUXIN	HETEROKARYOSIS	HETEROTAXIES
HEPATISATION	HERBORISED	HERMETISMS	HETEROAUXINS	HETEROKARYOTIC	HETEROTAXIS
HEPATISATIONS	HERBORISES	HERMETISTS	HETEROBLASTIC	HETEROKONT	HETEROTAXY
HEPATISING	HERBORISING	HERMITAGES	HETEROBLASTIES	HETEROKONTAN	HETEROTHALLIC
HEPATITIDES	HERBORISTS	HERMITESSES	HETEROBLASTY	HETEROKONTS	HETEROTHALLIES
HEPATITISES	HERBORIZATION	HERMITICAL	HETEROCARPOUS	HETEROLECITHAL	HETEROTHALLISM
HEPATIZATION	HERBORIZATIONS	HERMITICALLY	HETEROCERCAL	HETEROLOGIES	HETEROTHALLISMS
HEPATIZATIONS	HERBORIZED	HERMITISMS	HETEROCERCALITY	HETEROLOGOUS	HETEROTHALLY
HEPATIZING	HERBORIZES	HERMITRIES	HETEROCERCIES	HETEROLOGOUSLY	HETEROTHERMAL
HEPATOCELLULAR	HERBORIZING	HERNIATING	HETEROCERCY	HETEROLOGY	HETEROTOPIA
HEPATOCYTE	HERCOGAMIES	HERNIATION	HETEROCHROMATIC	HETEROLYSES	HETEROTOPIAS
HEPATOCYTES	HERCOGAMOUS	HERNIATIONS	HETEROCHROMATIN	HETEROLYSIS	HETEROTOPIC
HEPATOGENOUS	HERCULESES	HERNIORRHAPHIES	HETEROCHROMOUS	HETEROLYTIC	HETEROTOPIES
HEPATOLOGIES	HERCYNITES	HERNIORRHAPHY	HETEROCHRONIC	HETEROMEROUS	HETEROTOPOUS
HEPATOLOGIST	HEREABOUTS	HERNIOTOMIES	HETEROCHRONIES	HETEROMORPHIC	HETEROTOPY
HEPATOLOGISTS	HEREAFTERS	HERNIOTOMY	HETEROCHRONISM	HETEROMORPHIES	HETEROTROPH
HEPATOLOGY	HEREDITABILITY	HEROICALLY	HETEROCHRONISMS	HETEROMORPHISM	HETEROTROPHIC
HEPATOMATA	HEREDITABLE	HEROICALNESS	HETEROCHRONOUS	HETEROMORPHISMS	HETEROTROPHIES
HEPATOMEGALIES	HEREDITABLY	HEROICALNESSES	HETEROCHRONY	HETEROMORPHOUS	HETEROTROPHS
HEPATOMEGALY	HEREDITAMENT	HEROICISED	HETEROCLITE	HETEROMORPHY	HETEROTROPHY
HEPATOPANCREAS	HEREDITAMENTS	HEROICISES	HETEROCLITES	HETERONOMIES	HETEROTYPIC
HEPATOSCOPIES	HEREDITARIAN	HEROICISING	HETEROCLITIC	HETERONOMOUS	HETEROTYPICAL
HEPATOSCOPY	HEREDITARIANISM	HEROICIZED	HETEROCLITOUS	HETERONOMOUSLY	HETEROUSIAN
HEPATOTOXIC	HEREDITARIANIST	HEROICIZES	HETEROCONT	HETERONOMY	HETEROUSIANS
HEPATOTOXICITY	HEREDITARIANS	HEROICIZING	HETEROCONTS	HETERONYMOUS	HETEROZYGOSES
HEPHTHEMIMER	HEREDITARILY	HEROICNESS	HETEROCYCLE	HETERONYMOUSLY	HETEROZYGOSIS
HEPHTHEMIMERAL	HEREDITARINESS	HEROICNESSES	HETEROCYCLES	HETERONYMS	HETEROZYGOSITY
HEPHTHEMIMERS	HEREDITARY	HEROICOMIC	HETEROCYCLIC	HETEROOUSIAN	HETEROZYGOTE
HEPTACHLOR	HEREDITIES	HEROICOMICAL	HETEROCYCLICS	HETEROOUSIANS	HETEROZYGOTES
HEPTACHLORS	HEREDITIST	HEROINISMS	HETEROCYST	HETEROPHIL	HETEROZYGOUS
HEPTACHORD	HEREDITISTS	HERONSHAWS	HETEROCYSTOUS	HETEROPHILE	HETHERWARD
HEPTACHORDS	HEREINABOVE	HERPESVIRUS	HETEROCYSTS	HETEROPHONIES	HETMANATES
HEPTADECANOIC	HEREINAFTER	HERPESVIRUSES	HETERODACTYL	HETEROPHONY	HETMANSHIP
HEPTAGLOTS	HEREINBEFORE	HERPETOFAUNA	HETERODACTYLOUS	HETEROPHYLLIES	HETMANSHIPS
HEPTAGONAL	HEREINBELOW	HERPETOFAUNAE	HETERODACTYLS	HETEROPHYLLOUS	HEULANDITE
HEPTAGYNOUS	HERENESSES	HERPETOFAUNAS	HETERODONT	HETEROPHYLLY	HEULANDITES
HEPTAHEDRA	HERESIARCH	HERPETOLOGIC	HETERODOXIES	HETEROPLASIA	HEURISTICALLY
HEPTAHEDRAL	HERESIARCHS	HERPETOLOGICAL	HETERODOXY	HETEROPLASIAS	HEURISTICS
HEPTAHEDRON	HERESIOGRAPHER	HERPETOLOGIES	HETERODUPLEX	HETEROPLASTIC	HEXACHLORETHANE
HEPTAHEDRONS	HERESIOGRAPHERS	HERPETOLOGIST	HETERODUPLEXES	HETEROPLASTIES	HEXACHLORIDE
HEPTAMEROUS	HERESIOGRAPHIES	HERPETOLOGISTS	HETERODYNE	HETEROPLASTY	HEXACHLORIDES
HEPTAMETER	HERESIOGRAPHY	HERPETOLOGY	HETERODYNED	HETEROPLOID	HEXACHLOROPHANE
HEPTAMETERS	HERESIOLOGIES	HERRENVOLK	HETERODYNES	HETEROPLOIDIES	HEXACHLOROPHENE
HEPTAMETRICAL	HERESIOLOGIST	HERRENVOLKS	HETERODYNING	HETEROPLOIDS	HEXACHORDS
HEPTANDROUS	HERESIOLOGISTS	HERRIMENTS	HETEROECIOUS	HETEROPLOIDY	HEXACOSANOIC
HEPTANGULAR	HERESIOLOGY	HERRINGBONE	HETEROECISM	HETEROPODS	HEXACTINAL
HEPTAPODIC	HERESTHETIC	HERRINGBONED	HETEROECISMS	HETEROPOLAR	HEXACTINELLID
HEPTAPODIES	HERESTHETICAL	HERRINGBONES	HETEROFLEXIBLE	HETEROPOLARITY	HEXACTINELLIDS
HEPTARCHAL	HERESTHETICIAN	HERRINGBONING	HETEROFLEXIBLES	HETEROPTERAN	HEXADACTYLIC
HEPTARCHIC	HERESTHETICIANS	HERRINGERS	HETEROGAMETE	HETEROPTEROUS	HEXADACTYLOUS
HEPTARCHIES	HERESTHETICS	HERRYMENTS	HETEROGAMETES	HETEROSCEDASTIC	HEXADECANE
HEPTARCHIST	HERETICALLY	HERSTORIES	HETEROGAMETIC	HETEROSCIAN	HEXADECANES
HEPTARCHISTS	HERETICATE	HESITANCES	HETEROGAMETIES	HETEROSCIANS	HEXADECANOIC
HEPTASTICH	HERETICATED	HESITANCIES	HETEROGAMETY	HETEROSEXISM	HEXADECIMAL
HEPTASTICHS	HERETICATES	HESITANTLY	HETEROGAMIES	HETEROSEXISMS	HEXADECIMALS
HEPTASYLLABIC	HERETICATING	HESITATERS	HETEROGAMOUS	HETEROSEXIST	HEXAEMERIC
HEPTATHLETE	HERETOFORE	HESITATING	HETEROGAMY	HETEROSEXISTS	HEXAEMERON
HEPTATHLETES	HERETRICES	HESITATINGLY	HETEROGENEITIES	HETEROSEXUAL	HEXAEMERONS
HEPTATHLON	HERETRIXES	HESITATION	HETEROGENEITY	HETEROSEXUALITY	HEXAFLUORIDE
HEPTATHLONS	HERIOTABLE	HESITATIONS	HETEROGENEOUS	HETEROSEXUALLY	HEXAFLUORIDES
HEPTATONIC	HERITABILITIES	HESITATIVE	HETEROGENEOUSLY	HETEROSEXUALS	HEXAGONALLY
HEPTAVALENT	HERITABILITY	HESITATORS	HETEROGENESES	HETEROSOCIAL	HEXAGRAMMOID
HERALDICALLY	HERITABLE	HESITATORY	HETEROGENESIS	HETEROSOCIALITY	HEXAGRAMMOIDS
HERALDISTS	HERITRESSES	HESPERIDIN	HETEROGENETIC	HETEROSOMATOUS	HEXAGYNIAN
HERALDRIES	HERITRICES	HESPERIDINS	HETEROGENIC	HETEROSPECIFIC	HEXAGYNOUS
HERALDSHIP	HERITRIXES	HESPERIDIUM	HETEROGENIES	HETEROSPORIES	HEXAHEDRAL
HERALDSHIPS	HERKOGAMIES	HESPERIDIUMS	HETEROGENOUS	HETEROSPOROUS	HEXAHEDRON
HERBACEOUS	HERMANDADS	HESSONITES	HETEROGENY	HETEROSPORY	HEXAHEDRONS
HERBACEOUSLY	HERMAPHRODITE	HETAERISMIC	HETEROGONIC	HETEROSTROPHIC	HEXAHEMERIC
HERBALISMS	HERMAPHRODITES	HETAERISMS	HETEROGONIES	HETEROSTROPHIES	HEXAHEMERON
HERBALISTS	HERMAPHRODITIC	HETAERISTS	HETEROGONOUS	HETEROSTROPHY	HEXAHEMERONS
	HERMAPHRODITISM				

HEXAHYDRATE	HIDALGOISMS	HIGHBINDERS	HIPPODAMOUS	HISTOGENESES	HOBBLEDEHOYDOMS
HEXAHYDRATED	HIDDENITES	HIGHBLOODED	HIPPODROME	HISTOGENESIS	HOBBLEDEHOYHOOD
HEXAHYDRATES	HIDDENMOST	HIGHBROWED	HIPPODROMES	HISTOGENETIC	HOBBLEDEHOYISH
HEXAMERISM	HIDDENNESS	HIGHBROWISM	HIPPODROMIC	HISTOGENIC	HOBBLEDEHOYISM
HEXAMERISMS	HIDDENNESSES	HIGHBROWISMS	HIPPOGRIFF	HISTOGENICALLY	HOBBLEDEHOYISMS
HEXAMEROUS	HIDEOSITIES	HIGHCHAIRS	HIPPOGRIFFS	HISTOGENIES	HOBBLEDEHOYS
HEXAMETERS	HIDEOUSNESS	HIGHERMOST	HIPPOGRYPH	HISTOGRAMS	HOBBLINGLY
HEXAMETHONIUM	HIDEOUSNESSES	HIGHFALUTIN	HIPPOGRYPHS	HISTOLOGIC	HOBBYHORSE
HEXAMETHONIUMS	HIERACIUMS	HIGHFALUTING	HIPPOLOGIES	HISTOLOGICAL	HOBBYHORSED
HEXAMETRAL	HIERACOSPHINGES	HIGHFALUTINGS	HIPPOLOGIST	HISTOLOGICALLY	HOBBYHORSES
HEXAMETRIC	HIERACOSPHINX	HIGHFALUTINS	HIPPOLOGISTS	HISTOLOGIES	HOBBYHORSING
HEXAMETRICAL	HIERACOSPHINXES	HIGHFLIERS	HIPPOMANES	HISTOLOGIST	HOBGOBLINISM
HEXAMETRISE	HIERARCHAL	HIGHFLYERS	HIPPOPHAGIES	HISTOLOGISTS	HOBGOBLINISMS
HEXAMETRISED	HIERARCHIC	HIGHJACKED	HIPPOPHAGIST	HISTOLYSES	HOBGOBLINRIES
HEXAMETRISES	HIERARCHICAL	HIGHJACKER	HIPPOPHAGISTS	HISTOLYSIS	HOBGOBLINRY
HEXAMETRISING	HIERARCHICALLY	HIGHJACKERS	HIPPOPHAGOUS	HISTOLYTIC	HOBGOBLINS
HEXAMETRIST	HIERARCHIES	HIGHJACKING	HIPPOPHAGY	HISTOLYTICALLY	HOBJOBBERS
HEXAMETRISTS	HIERARCHISE	HIGHLANDER	HIPPOPHILE	HISTOPATHOLOGIC	HOBJOBBING
HEXAMETRIZE	HIERARCHISED	HIGHLANDERS	HIPPOPHILES	HISTOPATHOLOGY	HOBJOBBINGS
HEXAMETRIZED	HIERARCHISES	HIGHLIGHTED	HIPPOPHOBE	HISTOPHYSIOLOGY	HOBNAILING
HEXAMETRIZES	HIERARCHISING	HIGHLIGHTER	HIPPOPHOBES	HISTOPLASMOSES	HOBNOBBERS
HEXAMETRIZING	HIERARCHISM	HIGHLIGHTERS	HIPPOPOTAMI	HISTOPLASMOSIS	HOBNOBBING
HEXANDRIAN	HIERARCHISMS	HIGHLIGHTING	HIPPOPOTAMIAN	HISTORIANS	HOCHMAGANDIES
HEXANDROUS	HIERARCHIZE	HIGHLIGHTS	HIPPOPOTAMIC	HISTORIATED	HOCHMAGANDY
HEXANGULAR	HIERARCHIZED	HIGHNESSES	HIPPOPOTAMUS	HISTORICAL	HODGEPODGE
HEXAPLARIAN	HIERARCHIZES	HIGHTAILED	HIPPOPOTAMUSES	HISTORICALLY	HODGEPODGES
HEXAPLARIC	HIERARCHIZING	HIGHTAILING	HIPPURITES	HISTORICALNESS	HODMANDODS
HEXAPLOIDIES	HIERATICAL	HIGHWAYMAN	HIPPURITIC	HISTORICISE	HODOGRAPHIC
HEXAPLOIDS	HIERATICALLY	HIGHWAYMEN	HIPSTERISM	HISTORICISED	HODOGRAPHS
HEXAPLOIDY	HIERATICAS	HIGHWROUGHT	HIPSTERISMS	HISTORICISES	HODOMETERS
HEXAPODIES	HIEROCRACIES	HILARIOUSLY	HIRCOCERVUS	HISTORICISING	HODOMETRIES
HEXARCHIES	HIEROCRACY	HILARIOUSNESS	HIRCOCERVUSES	HISTORICISM	HODOSCOPES
HEXASTICHAL	HIEROCRATIC	HILARIOUSNESSES	HIRCOSITIES	HISTORICISMS	HOGGISHNESS
HEXASTICHIC	HIEROCRATICAL	HILARITIES	HIRSELLING	HISTORICIST	HOGGISHNESSES
HEXASTICHON	HIEROCRATS	HILLBILLIES	HIRSUTENESS	HISTORICISTS	HOIDENISHNESS
HEXASTICHONS	HIERODULES	HILLCRESTS	HIRSUTENESSES	HISTORICITIES	HOIDENISHNESSES
HEXASTICHS	HIERODULIC	HILLINESSES	HIRSUTISMS	HISTORICITY	HOJATOLESLAM
HEXASTYLES	HIEROGLYPH	HILLSLOPES	HIRUDINEAN	HISTORICIZE	HOJATOLESLAMS
HEXATEUCHAL	HIEROGLYPHED	HILLWALKER	HIRUDINEANS	HISTORICIZED	HOJATOLISLAM
HEXAVALENT	HIEROGLYPHIC	HILLWALKERS	HIRUDINOID	HISTORICIZES	HOJATOLISLAMS
HEXOBARBITAL	HIEROGLYPHICAL	HILLWALKING	HIRUDINOUS	HISTORICIZING	HOKEYNESSES
HEXOBARBITALS	HIEROGLYPHICS	HILLWALKINGS	HISPANICISE	HISTORIETTE	HOKEYPOKEY
HEXOKINASE	HIEROGLYPHING	HINDBERRIES	HISPANICISED	HISTORIETTES	HOKEYPOKEYS
HEXOKINASES	HIEROGLYPHIST	HINDBRAINS	HISPANICISES	HISTORIFIED	HOKINESSES
HEXOSAMINIDASE	HIEROGLYPHISTS	HINDERANCE	HISPANICISING	HISTORIFIES	HOKYPOKIES
HEXOSAMINIDASES	HIEROGLYPHS	HINDERANCES	HISPANICISM	HISTORIFYING	HOLARCHIES
HEXYLRESORCINOL	HIEROGRAMMAT	HINDERINGLY	HISPANICISMS	HISTORIOGRAPHER	HOLDERBATS
HIBAKUSHAS	HIEROGRAMMATE	HINDERINGS	HISPANICIZE	HISTORIOGRAPHIC	HOLDERSHIP
HIBERNACLE	HIEROGRAMMATES	HINDERLAND	HISPANICIZED	HISTORIOGRAPHY	HOLDERSHIPS
HIBERNACLES	HIEROGRAMMATIC	HINDERLANDS	HISPANICIZES	HISTORIOLOGIES	HOLIDAYERS
HIBERNACULA	HIEROGRAMMATIST	HINDERLANS	HISPANICIZING	HISTORIOLOGY	HOLIDAYING
HIBERNACULUM	HIEROGRAMMATS	HINDERLINGS	HISPANIDAD	HISTORISMS	HOLIDAYMAKER
HIBERNATED	HIEROGRAMS	HINDERLINS	HISPANIDADS	HISTORYING	HOLIDAYMAKERS
HIBERNATES	HIEROGRAPH	HINDERMOST	HISPANIOLISE	HISTRIONIC	HOLINESSES
HIBERNATING	HIEROGRAPHER	HINDFOREMOST	HISPANIOLISED	HISTRIONICAL	HOLISTICALLY
HIBERNATION	HIEROGRAPHERS	HINDQUARTER	HISPANIOLISES	HISTRIONICALLY	HOLLANDAISE
HIBERNATIONS	HIEROGRAPHIC	HINDQUARTERS	HISPANIOLISING	HISTRIONICISM	HOLLANDAISES
HIBERNATOR	HIEROGRAPHICAL	HINDRANCES	HISPANIOLIZE	HISTRIONICISMS	HOLLOWARES
HIBERNATORS	HIEROGRAPHIES	HINDSHANKS	HISPANIOLIZED	HISTRIONICS	HOLLOWNESS
HIBERNICISE	HIEROGRAPHS	HINDSIGHTS	HISPANIOLIZES	HISTRIONISM	HOLLOWNESSES
HIBERNICISED	HIEROGRAPHY	HINTERLAND	HISPANIOLIZING	HISTRIONISMS	HOLLOWWARE
HIBERNICISES	HIEROLATRIES	HINTERLANDS	HISPANISMS	HITCHHIKED	HOLLOWWARES
HIBERNICISING	HIEROLATRY	HIPPEASTRUM	HISPIDITIES	HITCHHIKER	HOLLYHOCKS
HIBERNICIZE	HIEROLOGIC	HIPPEASTRUMS	HISTAMINASE	HITCHHIKERS	HOLOBENTHIC
HIBERNICIZED	HIEROLOGICAL	HIPPIATRIC	HISTAMINASES	HITCHHIKES	HOLOBLASTIC
HIBERNICIZES	HIEROLOGIES	HIPPIATRICS	HISTAMINERGIC	HITCHHIKING	HOLOBLASTICALLY
HIBERNICIZING	HIEROLOGIST	HIPPIATRIES	HISTAMINES	HITHERMOST	HOLOCAUSTAL
HIBERNISATION	HIEROLOGISTS	HIPPIATRIST	HISTAMINIC	HITHERSIDE	HOLOCAUSTIC
HIBERNISATIONS	HIEROMANCIES	HIPPIATRISTS	HISTIDINES	HITHERSIDES	HOLOCAUSTS
HIBERNISED	HIEROMANCY	HIPPIEDOMS	HISTIOCYTE	HITHERWARD	HOLOCRYSTALLINE
HIBERNISES	HIEROPHANT	HIPPIENESS	HISTIOCYTES	HITHERWARDS	HOLODISCUS
HIBERNISING	HIEROPHANTIC	HIPPIENESSES	HISTIOCYTIC	HOACTZINES	HOLODISCUSES
HIBERNIZATION	HIEROPHANTS	HIPPINESSES	HISTIOLOGIES	HOARFROSTS	HOLOENZYME
HIBERNIZATIONS	HIEROPHOBIA	HIPPOCAMPAL	HISTIOLOGY	HOARHOUNDS	HOLOENZYMES
HIBERNIZED	HIEROPHOBIAS	HIPPOCAMPI	HISTIOPHOROID	HOARINESSES	HOLOGAMIES
HIBERNIZES	HIEROPHOBIC	HIPPOCAMPUS	HISTOBLAST	HOARSENESS	HOLOGRAPHED
HIBERNIZING	HIEROSCOPIES	HIPPOCENTAUR	HISTOBLASTS	HOARSENESSES	HOLOGRAPHER
HIBISCUSES	HIEROSCOPY	HIPPOCENTAURS	HISTOCHEMICAL	HOARSENING	HOLOGRAPHERS
HICCOUGHED	HIERURGICAL	HIPPOCRASES	HISTOCHEMICALLY	HOBBITRIES	HOLOGRAPHIC
HICCOUGHING	HIERURGIES	HIPPOCREPIAN	HISTOCHEMIST	HOBBLEBUSH	HOLOGRAPHICALLY
HICCUPPING	HIGHBALLED	HIPPODAMES	HISTOCHEMISTRY	HOBBLEBUSHES	HOLOGRAPHIES
HIDALGOISH	HIGHBALLING	HIPPODAMIST	HISTOCHEMISTS	HOBBLEDEHOY	HOLOGRAPHING
HIDALGOISM	HIGHBINDER	HIPPODAMISTS	HISTOCOMPATIBLE	HOBBLEDEHOYDOM	HOLOGRAPHS

h

HOLOGRAPHY
HOLOGYNIES
HOLOHEDRAL
HOLOHEDRISM
HOLOHEDRISMS
HOLOHEDRON
HOLOHEDRONS
HOLOMETABOLIC
HOLOMETABOLISM
HOLOMETABOLISMS
HOLOMETABOLOUS
HOLOMORPHIC
HOLOPHOTAL
HOLOPHOTES
HOLOPHRASE
HOLOPHRASES
HOLOPHRASTIC
HOLOPHYTES
HOLOPHYTIC
HOLOPHYTISM
HOLOPHYTISMS
HOLOPLANKTON
HOLOPLANKTONS
HOLOSTERIC
HOLOTHURIAN
HOLOTHURIANS
HOLSTERING
HOLYSTONED
HOLYSTONES
HOLYSTONING
HOMALOGRAPHIC
HOMALOIDAL
HOMEBIRTHS
HOMEBODIES
HOMEBUYERS
HOMECOMERS
HOMECOMING
HOMECOMINGS
HOMECRAFTS
HOMELESSNESS
HOMELESSNESSES
HOMELINESS
HOMELINESSES
HOMEMAKERS
HOMEMAKING
HOMEMAKINGS
HOMEOBOXES
HOMEOMERIC
HOMEOMERIES
HOMEOMEROUS
HOMEOMORPH
HOMEOMORPHIC
HOMEOMORPHIES
HOMEOMORPHISM
HOMEOMORPHISMS
HOMEOMORPHOUS
HOMEOMORPHS
HOMEOMORPHY
HOMEOPATHIC
HOMEOPATHICALLY
HOMEOPATHIES
HOMEOPATHIST
HOMEOPATHISTS
HOMEOPATHS
HOMEOPATHY
HOMEOSTASES
HOMEOSTASIS
HOMEOSTATIC
HOMEOTELEUTON
HOMEOTELEUTONS
HOMEOTHERM
HOMEOTHERMAL
HOMEOTHERMIC
HOMEOTHERMIES
HOMEOTHERMOUS
HOMEOTHERMS
HOMEOTHERMY
HOMEOTYPIC
HOMEOTYPICAL
HOMEOWNERS
HOMEOWNERSHIP
HOMEOWNERSHIPS
HOMEPLACES

HOMEPORTED
HOMEPORTING
HOMESCHOOL
HOMESCHOOLED
HOMESCHOOLER
HOMESCHOOLERS
HOMESCHOOLING
HOMESCHOOLS
HOMESCREECH
HOMESCREECHES
HOMESICKNESS
HOMESICKNESSES
HOMESTALLS
HOMESTANDS
HOMESTEADED
HOMESTEADER
HOMESTEADERS
HOMESTEADING
HOMESTEADINGS
HOMESTEADS
HOMESTRETCH
HOMESTRETCHES
HOMEWORKER
HOMEWORKERS
HOMEWORKING
HOMEWORKINGS
HOMEYNESSES
HOMICIDALLY
HOMILETICAL
HOMILETICALLY
HOMILETICS
HOMINESSES
HOMINISATION
HOMINISATIONS
HOMINISING
HOMINIZATION
HOMINIZATIONS
HOMINIZING
HOMOBLASTIC
HOMOBLASTIES
HOMOBLASTY
HOMOCENTRIC
HOMOCENTRICALLY
HOMOCERCAL
HOMOCERCIES
HOMOCHLAMYDEOUS
HOMOCHROMATIC
HOMOCHROMATISM
HOMOCHROMATISMS
HOMOCHROMIES
HOMOCHROMOUS
HOMOCHROMY
HOMOCYCLIC
HOMOCYSTEINE
HOMOCYSTEINES
HOMOEOMERIC
HOMOEOMERIES
HOMOEOMEROUS
HOMOEOMERY
HOMOEOMORPH
HOMOEOMORPHIC
HOMOEOMORPHIES
HOMOEOMORPHISM
HOMOEOMORPHISMS
HOMOEOMORPHOUS
HOMOEOMORPHS
HOMOEOMORPHY
HOMOEOPATH
HOMOEOPATHIC
HOMOEOPATHIES
HOMOEOPATHIST
HOMOEOPATHISTS
HOMOEOPATHS
HOMOEOPATHY
HOMOEOSTASES
HOMOEOSTASIS
HOMOEOSTATIC
HOMOEOTELEUTON
HOMOEOTELEUTONS
HOMOEOTHERMAL
HOMOEOTHERMIC
HOMOEOTHERMOUS
HOMOEOTYPIC

HOMOEOTYPICAL
HOMOEROTIC
HOMOEROTICISM
HOMOEROTICISMS
HOMOEROTISM
HOMOEROTISMS
HOMOGAMETIC
HOMOGAMIES
HOMOGAMOUS
HOMOGENATE
HOMOGENATES
HOMOGENEITIES
HOMOGENEITY
HOMOGENEOUS
HOMOGENEOUSLY
HOMOGENEOUSNESS
HOMOGENESES
HOMOGENESIS
HOMOGENETIC
HOMOGENETICAL
HOMOGENIES
HOMOGENISATION
HOMOGENISATIONS
HOMOGENISE
HOMOGENISED
HOMOGENISER
HOMOGENISERS
HOMOGENISES
HOMOGENISING
HOMOGENIZATION
HOMOGENIZATIONS
HOMOGENIZE
HOMOGENIZED
HOMOGENIZER
HOMOGENIZERS
HOMOGENIZES
HOMOGENIZING
HOMOGENOUS
HOMOGONIES
HOMOGONOUS
HOMOGONOUSLY
HOMOGRAFTS
HOMOGRAPHIC
HOMOGRAPHS
HOMOIOMEROUS
HOMOIOTHERM
HOMOIOTHERMAL
HOMOIOTHERMIC
HOMOIOTHERMIES
HOMOIOTHERMS
HOMOIOTHERMY
HOMOIOUSIAN
HOMOIOUSIANS
HOMOLOGATE
HOMOLOGATED
HOMOLOGATES
HOMOLOGATING
HOMOLOGATION
HOMOLOGATIONS
HOMOLOGICAL
HOMOLOGICALLY
HOMOLOGIES
HOMOLOGISE
HOMOLOGISED
HOMOLOGISER
HOMOLOGISERS
HOMOLOGISES
HOMOLOGISING
HOMOLOGIZE
HOMOLOGIZED
HOMOLOGIZER
HOMOLOGIZERS
HOMOLOGIZES
HOMOLOGIZING
HOMOLOGOUMENA
HOMOLOGOUS
HOMOLOGRAPHIC
HOMOLOGUES
HOMOLOGUMENA
HOMOLOSINE
HOMOMORPHIC
HOMOMORPHIES
HOMOMORPHISM

HOMOMORPHISMS
HOMOMORPHOSES
HOMOMORPHOSIS
HOMOMORPHOUS
HOMOMORPHS
HOMOMORPHY
HOMONUCLEAR
HOMONYMIES
HOMONYMITIES
HOMONYMITY
HOMONYMOUS
HOMONYMOUSLY
HOMOOUSIAN
HOMOOUSIANS
HOMOPHILES
HOMOPHOBES
HOMOPHOBIA
HOMOPHOBIAS
HOMOPHOBIC
HOMOPHONES
HOMOPHONIC
HOMOPHONICALLY
HOMOPHONIES
HOMOPHONOUS
HOMOPHYLIES
HOMOPHYLLIC
HOMOPLASIES
HOMOPLASMIES
HOMOPLASMY
HOMOPLASTIC
HOMOPLASTICALLY
HOMOPLASTIES
HOMOPLASTY
HOMOPOLARITIES
HOMOPOLARITY
HOMOPOLYMER
HOMOPOLYMERIC
HOMOPOLYMERS
HOMOPTERAN
HOMOPTERANS
HOMOPTEROUS
HOMORGANIC
HOMOSCEDASTIC
HOMOSEXUAL
HOMOSEXUALISM
HOMOSEXUALISMS
HOMOSEXUALIST
HOMOSEXUALISTS
HOMOSEXUALITIES
HOMOSEXUALITY
HOMOSEXUALLY
HOMOSEXUALS
HOMOSOCIAL
HOMOSOCIALITIES
HOMOSOCIALITY
HOMOSPORIES
HOMOSPOROUS
HOMOSTYLIES
HOMOTAXIAL
HOMOTAXIALLY
HOMOTHALLIC
HOMOTHALLIES
HOMOTHALLISM
HOMOTHALLISMS
HOMOTHALLY
HOMOTHERMAL
HOMOTHERMIC
HOMOTHERMIES
HOMOTHERMOUS
HOMOTHERMY
HOMOTONIES
HOMOTONOUS
HOMOTRANSPLANT
HOMOTRANSPLANTS
HOMOTYPIES
HOMOUSIANS
HOMOZYGOSES
HOMOZYGOSIS
HOMOZYGOSITIES
HOMOZYGOSITY
HOMOZYGOTE
HOMOZYGOTES
HOMOZYGOTIC

HOMOZYGOUS
HOMOZYGOUSLY
HOMUNCULAR
HOMUNCULES
HOMUNCULUS
HONESTNESS
HONESTNESSES
HONEYBUNCH
HONEYBUNCHES
HONEYCOMBED
HONEYCOMBING
HONEYCOMBINGS
HONEYCOMBS
HONEYCREEPER
HONEYCREEPERS
HONEYDEWED
HONEYEATER
HONEYEATERS
HONEYGUIDE
HONEYGUIDES
HONEYMONTH
HONEYMONTHED
HONEYMONTHING
HONEYMONTHS
HONEYMOONED
HONEYMOONER
HONEYMOONERS
HONEYMOONING
HONEYMOONS
HONEYSUCKER
HONEYSUCKERS
HONEYSUCKLE
HONEYSUCKLED
HONEYSUCKLES
HONEYTRAPS
HONORABILITIES
HONORABILITY
HONORABLENESS
HONORABLENESSES
HONORARIES
HONORARILY
HONORARIUM
HONORARIUMS
HONORIFICAL
HONORIFICALLY
HONORIFICS
HONOURABLE
HONOURABLENESS
HONOURABLY
HONOURLESS
HOODEDNESS
HOODEDNESSES
HOODLUMISH
HOODLUMISM
HOODLUMISMS
HOODOOISMS
HOODWINKED
HOODWINKER
HOODWINKERS
HOODWINKING
HOOFPRINTS
HOOKCHECKS
HOOKEDNESS
HOOKEDNESSES
HOOLACHANS
HOOLIGANISM
HOOLIGANISMS
HOOPSKIRTS
HOOTANANNIE
HOOTANANNIES
HOOTANANNY
HOOTENANNIE
HOOTENANNIES
HOOTENANNY
HOOTNANNIE
HOOTNANNIES
HOPEFULNESS
HOPEFULNESSES
HOPELESSLY
HOPELESSNESS
HOPELESSNESSES
HOPLOLOGIES
HOPLOLOGIST

HOPLOLOGISTS
HOPPERCARS
HOPSACKING
HOPSACKINGS
HOPSCOTCHED
HOPSCOTCHES
HOPSCOTCHING
HOREHOUNDS
HORIATIKIS
HORIZONLESS
HORIZONTAL
HORIZONTALITIES
HORIZONTALITY
HORIZONTALLY
HORIZONTALNESS
HORIZONTALS
HORMOGONIA
HORMOGONIUM
HORMONALLY
HORMONELIKE
HORNBLENDE
HORNBLENDES
HORNBLENDIC
HORNEDNESS
HORNEDNESSES
HORNINESSES
HORNLESSNESS
HORNLESSNESSES
HORNSTONES
HORNSWOGGLE
HORNSWOGGLED
HORNSWOGGLES
HORNSWOGGLING
HORNWRACKS
HORNYHEADS
HORNYWINKS
HOROGRAPHER
HOROGRAPHERS
HOROGRAPHIES
HOROGRAPHY
HOROLOGERS
HOROLOGICAL
HOROLOGIES
HOROLOGION
HOROLOGIONS
HOROLOGIST
HOROLOGISTS
HOROLOGIUM
HOROLOGIUMS
HOROMETRICAL
HOROMETRIES
HOROSCOPES
HOROSCOPIC
HOROSCOPIES
HOROSCOPIST
HOROSCOPISTS
HORRENDOUS
HORRENDOUSLY
HORRENDOUSNESS
HORRIBLENESS
HORRIBLENESSES
HORRIDNESS
HORRIDNESSES
HORRIFICALLY
HORRIFICATION
HORRIFICATIONS
HORRIFYING
HORRIFYINGLY
HORRIPILANT
HORRIPILATE
HORRIPILATED
HORRIPILATES
HORRIPILATING
HORRIPILATION
HORRIPILATIONS
HORRISONANT
HORRISONOUS
HORSEBACKS
HORSEBEANS
HORSEBOXES
HORSEFEATHERS
HORSEFLESH
HORSEFLESHES

h

HORSEFLIES	HOTHOUSING	HOUSEWIFESHIP	HUMBUGGERIES	HUNTRESSES	HYDRAGOGUE
HORSEHAIRS	HOTPRESSED	HOUSEWIFESHIPS	HUMBUGGERS	HUNTSMANSHIP	HYDRAGOGUES
HORSEHIDES	HOTPRESSES	HOUSEWIFESKEP	HUMBUGGERY	HUNTSMANSHIPS	HYDRALAZINE
HORSELAUGH	HOTPRESSING	HOUSEWIFESKEPS	HUMBUGGING	HUPAITHRIC	HYDRALAZINES
HORSELAUGHS	HOTTENTOTS	HOUSEWIFEY	HUMDINGERS	HURLBARROW	HYDRANGEAS
HORSELEECH	HOUGHMAGANDIE	HOUSEWIVES	HUMDRUMNESS	HURLBARROWS	HYDRARGYRAL
HORSELEECHES	HOUGHMAGANDIES	HOUSEWORKER	HUMDRUMNESSES	HURRICANES	HYDRARGYRIA
HORSEMANSHIP	HOUNDFISHES	HOUSEWORKERS	HUMDUDGEON	HURRICANOES	HYDRARGYRIAS
HORSEMANSHIPS	HOURGLASSES	HOUSEWORKS	HUMDUDGEONS	HURRIEDNESS	HYDRARGYRIC
HORSEMEATS	HOURPLATES	HOUSTONIAS	HUMECTANTS	HURRIEDNESSES	HYDRARGYRISM
HORSEMINTS	HOUSEBOATER	HOVERCRAFT	HUMECTATED	HURRYINGLY	HYDRARGYRISMS
HORSEPLAYER	HOUSEBOATERS	HOVERCRAFTS	HUMECTATES	HURTFULNESS	HYDRARGYRUM
HORSEPLAYERS	HOUSEBOATS	HOVERFLIES	HUMECTATING	HURTFULNESSES	HYDRARGYRUMS
HORSEPLAYS	HOUSEBOUND	HOVERINGLY	HUMECTATION	HURTLEBERRIES	HYDRARTHROSES
HORSEPONDS	HOUSEBREAK	HOVERPORTS	HUMECTATIONS	HURTLEBERRY	HYDRARTHROSIS
HORSEPOWER	HOUSEBREAKER	HOVERTRAIN	HUMECTIVES	HURTLESSLY	HYDRASTINE
HORSEPOWERS	HOUSEBREAKERS	HOVERTRAINS	HUMGRUFFIAN	HURTLESSNESS	HYDRASTINES
HORSEPOXES	HOUSEBREAKING	HOWLROUNDS	HUMGRUFFIANS	HURTLESSNESSES	HYDRASTININE
HORSERACES	HOUSEBREAKINGS	HOWSOMDEVER	HUMGRUFFIN	HUSBANDAGE	HYDRASTININES
HORSERADISH	HOUSEBREAKS	HOWSOMEVER	HUMGRUFFINS	HUSBANDAGES	HYDRASTISES
HORSERADISHES	HOUSEBROKE	HOWTOWDIES	HUMICOLOUS	HUSBANDERS	HYDRATIONS
HORSESHITS	HOUSEBROKEN	HOYDENHOOD	HUMIDIFICATION	HUSBANDING	HYDRAULICALLY
HORSESHOED	HOUSECARLS	HOYDENHOODS	HUMIDIFICATIONS	HUSBANDLAND	HYDRAULICKED
HORSESHOEING	HOUSECLEAN	HOYDENISHNESS	HUMIDIFIED	HUSBANDLANDS	HYDRAULICKING
HORSESHOEINGS	HOUSECLEANED	HOYDENISHNESSES	HUMIDIFIER	HUSBANDLESS	HYDRAULICS
HORSESHOER	HOUSECLEANING	HOYDENISMS	HUMIDIFIERS	HUSBANDLIKE	HYDRAZIDES
HORSESHOERS	HOUSECLEANINGS	HUBRISTICALLY	HUMIDIFIES	HUSBANDMAN	HYDRAZINES
HORSESHOES	HOUSECLEANS	HUCKABACKS	HUMIDIFYING	HUSBANDMEN	HYDRICALLY
HORSETAILS	HOUSECOATS	HUCKLEBERRIES	HUMIDISTAT	HUSBANDRIES	HYDROACOUSTICS
HORSEWEEDS	HOUSECRAFT	HUCKLEBERRY	HUMIDISTATS	HUSHABYING	HYDROBIOLOGICAL
HORSEWHIPPED	HOUSECRAFTS	HUCKLEBERRYING	HUMIDITIES	HUSHPUPPIES	HYDROBIOLOGIES
HORSEWHIPPER	HOUSEDRESS	HUCKLEBERRYINGS	HUMIDNESSES	HUSKINESSES	HYDROBIOLOGIST
HORSEWHIPPERS	HOUSEDRESSES	HUCKLEBONE	HUMIFICATION	HYACINTHINE	HYDROBIOLOGISTS
HORSEWHIPPING	HOUSEFATHER	HUCKLEBONES	HUMIFICATIONS	HYALINISATION	HYDROBIOLOGY
HORSEWHIPS	HOUSEFATHERS	HUCKSTERAGE	HUMILIATED	HYALINISATIONS	HYDROBROMIC
HORSEWOMAN	HOUSEFLIES	HUCKSTERAGES	HUMILIATES	HYALINISED	HYDROCARBON
HORSEWOMEN	HOUSEFRONT	HUCKSTERED	HUMILIATING	HYALINISES	HYDROCARBONS
HORSINESSES	HOUSEFRONTS	HUCKSTERESS	HUMILIATINGLY	HYALINISING	HYDROCASTS
HORTATIONS	HOUSEGUEST	HUCKSTERESSES	HUMILIATION	HYALINIZATION	HYDROCELES
HORTATIVELY	HOUSEGUESTS	HUCKSTERIES	HUMILIATIONS	HYALINIZATIONS	HYDROCELLULOSE
HORTATORILY	HOUSEHOLDER	HUCKSTERING	HUMILIATIVE	HYALINIZED	HYDROCELLULOSES
HORTICULTURAL	HOUSEHOLDERS	HUCKSTERISM	HUMILIATOR	HYALINIZES	HYDROCEPHALIC
HORTICULTURALLY	HOUSEHOLDERSHIP	HUCKSTERISMS	HUMILIATORS	HYALINIZING	HYDROCEPHALICS
HORTICULTURE	HOUSEHOLDS	HUCKSTRESS	HUMILIATORY	HYALOMELAN	HYDROCEPHALIES
HORTICULTURES	HOUSEHUSBAND	HUCKSTRESSES	HUMILITIES	HYALOMELANE	HYDROCEPHALOID
HORTICULTURIST	HOUSEHUSBANDS	HUDIBRASTIC	HUMMELLERS	HYALOMELANES	HYDROCEPHALOUS
HORTICULTURISTS	HOUSEKEEPER	HUFFINESSES	HUMMELLING	HYALOMELANS	HYDROCEPHALUS
HOSANNAING	HOUSEKEEPERS	HUFFISHNESS	HUMMINGBIRD	HYALONEMAS	HYDROCEPHALUSES
HOSPITABLE	HOUSEKEEPING	HUFFISHNESSES	HUMMINGBIRDS	HYALOPHANE	HYDROCEPHALY
HOSPITABLENESS	HOUSEKEEPINGS	HUGENESSES	HUMMOCKING	HYALOPHANES	HYDROCHLORIC
HOSPITABLY	HOUSEKEEPS	HUGEOUSNESS	HUMORALISM	HYALOPLASM	HYDROCHLORIDE
HOSPITAGES	HOUSELEEKS	HUGEOUSNESSES	HUMORALISMS	HYALOPLASMIC	HYDROCHLORIDES
HOSPITALER	HOUSELESSNESS	HULLABALLOO	HUMORALIST	HYALOPLASMS	HYDROCHORE
HOSPITALERS	HOUSELESSNESSES	HULLABALLOOS	HUMORALISTS	HYALURONIC	HYDROCHORES
HOSPITALES	HOUSELIGHTS	HULLABALOO	HUMORESQUE	HYALURONIDASE	HYDROCHORIC
HOSPITALISATION	HOUSELINES	HULLABALOOS	HUMORESQUES	HYALURONIDASES	HYDROCOLLOID
HOSPITALISE	HOUSELLING	HUMANENESS	HUMORISTIC	HYBRIDISABLE	HYDROCOLLOIDAL
HOSPITALISED	HOUSELLINGS	HUMANENESSES	HUMORLESSLY	HYBRIDISATION	HYDROCOLLOIDS
HOSPITALISES	HOUSEMAIDS	HUMANHOODS	HUMORLESSNESS	HYBRIDISATIONS	HYDROCORAL
HOSPITALISING	HOUSEMASTER	HUMANISATION	HUMORLESSNESSES	HYBRIDISED	HYDROCORALLINE
HOSPITALITIES	HOUSEMASTERS	HUMANISATIONS	HUMOROUSLY	HYBRIDISER	HYDROCORALLINES
HOSPITALITY	HOUSEMATES	HUMANISERS	HUMOROUSNESS	HYBRIDISERS	HYDROCORALS
HOSPITALIZATION	HOUSEMISTRESS	HUMANISING	HUMOROUSNESSES	HYBRIDISES	HYDROCORTISONE
HOSPITALIZE	HOUSEMISTRESSES	HUMANISTIC	HUMOURLESS	HYBRIDISING	HYDROCORTISONES
HOSPITALIZED	HOUSEMOTHER	HUMANISTICALLY	HUMOURLESSNESS	HYBRIDISMS	HYDROCRACK
HOSPITALIZES	HOUSEMOTHERS	HUMANITARIAN	HUMOURSOME	HYBRIDISTS	HYDROCRACKED
HOSPITALIZING	HOUSEPAINTER	HUMANITARIANISM	HUMOURSOMENESS	HYBRIDITIES	HYDROCRACKER
HOSPITALLER	HOUSEPAINTERS	HUMANITARIANIST	HUMPBACKED	HYBRIDIZABLE	HYDROCRACKERS
HOSPITALLERS	HOUSEPARENT	HUMANITARIANS	HUMPINESSES	HYBRIDIZATION	HYDROCRACKING
HOSTELLERS	HOUSEPARENTS	HUMANITIES	HUNCHBACKED	HYBRIDIZATIONS	HYDROCRACKINGS
HOSTELLING	HOUSEPERSON	HUMANIZATION	HUNCHBACKS	HYBRIDIZED	HYDROCRACKS
HOSTELLINGS	HOUSEPERSONS	HUMANIZATIONS	HUNDREDERS	HYBRIDIZER	HYDROCYANIC
HOSTELRIES	HOUSEPLANT	HUMANIZERS	HUNDREDFOLD	HYBRIDIZERS	HYDRODYNAMIC
HOSTESSING	HOUSEPLANTS	HUMANIZING	HUNDREDFOLDS	HYBRIDIZES	HYDRODYNAMICAL
HOSTILITIES	HOUSEROOMS	HUMANKINDS	HUNDREDORS	HYBRIDIZING	HYDRODYNAMICIST
HOTCHPOTCH	HOUSESITTING	HUMANNESSES	HUNDREDTHS	HYBRIDOMAS	HYDRODYNAMICS
HOTCHPOTCHES	HOUSEWARES	HUMBLEBEES	HUNDREDWEIGHT	HYDANTOINS	HYDROELASTIC
HOTDOGGERS	HOUSEWARMING	HUMBLENESS	HUNDREDWEIGHTS	HYDATHODES	HYDROELECTRIC
HOTDOGGING	HOUSEWARMINGS	HUMBLENESSES	HUNGERINGLY	HYDATIDIFORM	HYDROEXTRACTOR
HOTFOOTING	HOUSEWIFELINESS	HUMBLEBEES	HUNGRINESS	HYDNOCARPATE	HYDROEXTRACTORS
HOTHEADEDLY	HOUSEWIFELY	HUMBLINGLY	HUNGRINESSES	HYDNOCARPATES	HYDROFLUORIC
HOTHEADEDNESS	HOUSEWIFERIES	HUMBUCKERS	HUNTIEGOWK	HYDNOCARPIC	HYDROFOILS
HOTHEADEDNESSES	HOUSEWIFERY	HUMBUGGABLE	HUNTIEGOWKS	HYDRAEMIAS	HYDROFORMING

HYDROFORMINGS
HYDROGENASE
HYDROGENASES
HYDROGENATE
HYDROGENATED
HYDROGENATES
HYDROGENATING
HYDROGENATION
HYDROGENATIONS
HYDROGENATOR
HYDROGENATORS
HYDROGENISATION
HYDROGENISE
HYDROGENISED
HYDROGENISES
HYDROGENISING
HYDROGENIZATION
HYDROGENIZE
HYDROGENIZED
HYDROGENIZES
HYDROGENIZING
HYDROGENOLYSES
HYDROGENOLYSIS
HYDROGENOUS
HYDROGEOLOGICAL
HYDROGEOLOGIES
HYDROGEOLOGIST
HYDROGEOLOGISTS
HYDROGEOLOGY
HYDROGRAPH
HYDROGRAPHER
HYDROGRAPHERS
HYDROGRAPHIC
HYDROGRAPHICAL
HYDROGRAPHIES
HYDROGRAPHS
HYDROGRAPHY
HYDROKINETIC
HYDROKINETICAL
HYDROKINETICS
HYDROLASES
HYDROLOGIC
HYDROLOGICAL
HYDROLOGICALLY
HYDROLOGIES
HYDROLOGIST
HYDROLOGISTS
HYDROLYSABLE
HYDROLYSATE
HYDROLYSATES
HYDROLYSATION
HYDROLYSATIONS
HYDROLYSED
HYDROLYSER
HYDROLYSERS
HYDROLYSES
HYDROLYSING
HYDROLYSIS
HYDROLYTES
HYDROLYTIC
HYDROLYTICALLY
HYDROLYZABLE
HYDROLYZATE
HYDROLYZATES
HYDROLYZATION
HYDROLYZATIONS
HYDROLYZED
HYDROLYZER
HYDROLYZERS
HYDROLYZES
HYDROLYZING
HYDROMAGNETIC
HYDROMAGNETICS
HYDROMANCER
HYDROMANCERS
HYDROMANCIES
HYDROMANCY
HYDROMANIA
HYDROMANIAS
HYDROMANTIC
HYDROMECHANICAL
HYDROMECHANICS
HYDROMEDUSA

HYDROMEDUSAE
HYDROMEDUSAN
HYDROMEDUSANS
HYDROMEDUSAS
HYDROMEDUSOID
HYDROMEDUSOIDS
HYDROMETALLURGY
HYDROMETEOR
HYDROMETEORS
HYDROMETER
HYDROMETERS
HYDROMETRIC
HYDROMETRICAL
HYDROMETRICALLY
HYDROMETRIES
HYDROMETRY
HYDROMORPHIC
HYDRONAUTS
HYDRONEPHROSES
HYDRONEPHROSIS
HYDRONEPHROTIC
HYDRONICALLY
HYDRONIUMS
HYDROPATHIC
HYDROPATHICAL
HYDROPATHICALLY
HYDROPATHICS
HYDROPATHIES
HYDROPATHIST
HYDROPATHISTS
HYDROPATHS
HYDROPATHY
HYDROPEROXIDE
HYDROPEROXIDES
HYDROPHANE
HYDROPHANES
HYDROPHANOUS
HYDROPHILE
HYDROPHILES
HYDROPHILIC
HYDROPHILICITY
HYDROPHILIES
HYDROPHILITE
HYDROPHILITES
HYDROPHILOUS
HYDROPHILY
HYDROPHOBIA
HYDROPHOBIAS
HYDROPHOBIC
HYDROPHOBICITY
HYDROPHOBOUS
HYDROPHONE
HYDROPHONES
HYDROPHYTE
HYDROPHYTES
HYDROPHYTIC
HYDROPHYTON
HYDROPHYTONS
HYDROPHYTOUS
HYDROPLANE
HYDROPLANED
HYDROPLANES
HYDROPLANING
HYDROPNEUMATIC
HYDROPOLYP
HYDROPOLYPS
HYDROPONIC
HYDROPONICALLY
HYDROPONICS
HYDROPOWER
HYDROPOWERS
HYDROPSIES
HYDROPULTS
HYDROQUINOL
HYDROQUINOLS
HYDROQUINONE
HYDROQUINONES
HYDROSCOPE
HYDROSCOPES
HYDROSCOPIC
HYDROSCOPICAL
HYDROSERES
HYDROSOLIC

HYDROSOMAL
HYDROSOMATA
HYDROSOMATOUS
HYDROSOMES
HYDROSPACE
HYDROSPACES
HYDROSPHERE
HYDROSPHERES
HYDROSPHERIC
HYDROSTATIC
HYDROSTATICAL
HYDROSTATICALLY
HYDROSTATICS
HYDROSTATS
HYDROSULPHATE
HYDROSULPHATES
HYDROSULPHIDE
HYDROSULPHIDES
HYDROSULPHITE
HYDROSULPHITES
HYDROSULPHURIC
HYDROSULPHUROUS
HYDROTACTIC
HYDROTAXES
HYDROTAXIS
HYDROTHECA
HYDROTHECAE
HYDROTHERAPIC
HYDROTHERAPIES
HYDROTHERAPIST
HYDROTHERAPISTS
HYDROTHERAPY
HYDROTHERMAL
HYDROTHERMALLY
HYDROTHORACES
HYDROTHORACIC
HYDROTHORAX
HYDROTHORAXES
HYDROTROPIC
HYDROTROPICALLY
HYDROTROPISM
HYDROTROPISMS
HYDROVANES
HYDROXIDES
HYDROXONIUM
HYDROXONIUMS
HYDROXYAPATITE
HYDROXYAPATITES
HYDROXYBUTYRATE
HYDROXYLAMINE
HYDROXYLAMINES
HYDROXYLAPATITE
HYDROXYLASE
HYDROXYLASES
HYDROXYLATE
HYDROXYLATED
HYDROXYLATES
HYDROXYLATING
HYDROXYLATION
HYDROXYLATIONS
HYDROXYLIC
HYDROXYPROLINE
HYDROXYPROLINES
HYDROXYUREA
HYDROXYUREAS
HYDROXYZINE
HYDROXYZINES
HYDROZINCITE
HYDROZINCITES
HYDROZOANS
HYETOGRAPH
HYETOGRAPHIC
HYETOGRAPHICAL
HYETOGRAPHIES
HYETOGRAPHS
HYETOGRAPHY
HYETOLOGIES
HYETOMETER
HYETOMETERS
HYETOMETROGRAPH
HYGIENICALLY
HYGIENISTS
HYGRISTORS

HYGROCHASIES
HYGROCHASTIC
HYGROCHASY
HYGRODEIKS
HYGROGRAPH
HYGROGRAPHIC
HYGROGRAPHICAL
HYGROGRAPHS
HYGROLOGIES
HYGROMETER
HYGROMETERS
HYGROMETRIC
HYGROMETRICAL
HYGROMETRICALLY
HYGROMETRIES
HYGROMETRY
HYGROPHILE
HYGROPHILES
HYGROPHILOUS
HYGROPHOBE
HYGROPHYTE
HYGROPHYTES
HYGROPHYTIC
HYGROSCOPE
HYGROSCOPES
HYGROSCOPIC
HYGROSCOPICAL
HYGROSCOPICALLY
HYGROSCOPICITY
HYGROSTATS
HYLOGENESES
HYLOGENESIS
HYLOMORPHIC
HYLOMORPHISM
HYLOMORPHISMS
HYLOPATHISM
HYLOPATHISMS
HYLOPATHIST
HYLOPATHISTS
HYLOPHAGOUS
HYLOPHYTES
HYLOTHEISM
HYLOTHEISMS
HYLOTHEIST
HYLOTHEISTS
HYLOTOMOUS
HYLOZOICAL
HYLOZOISMS
HYLOZOISTIC
HYLOZOISTICALLY
HYLOZOISTS
HYMENEALLY
HYMENOPHORE
HYMENOPHORES
HYMENOPTERAN
HYMENOPTERANS
HYMENOPTERON
HYMENOPTERONS
HYMENOPTEROUS
HYMNODICAL
HYMNODISTS
HYMNOGRAPHER
HYMNOGRAPHERS
HYMNOGRAPHIES
HYMNOGRAPHY
HYMNOLOGIC
HYMNOLOGICAL
HYMNOLOGIES
HYMNOLOGIST
HYMNOLOGISTS
HYOPLASTRA
HYOPLASTRAL
HYOPLASTRON
HYOSCYAMINE
HYOSCYAMINES
HYOSCYAMUS
HYOSCYAMUSES
HYPABYSSAL
HYPABYSSALLY
HYPAESTHESIA
HYPAESTHESIAS
HYPAESTHESIC

HYPAETHRAL
HYPAETHRON
HYPAETHRONS
HYPALGESIA
HYPALGESIAS
HYPALGESIC
HYPALLACTIC
HYPALLAGES
HYPANTHIAL
HYPANTHIUM
HYPERACIDITIES
HYPERACIDITY
HYPERACTION
HYPERACTIONS
HYPERACTIVE
HYPERACTIVES
HYPERACTIVITIES
HYPERACTIVITY
HYPERACUITIES
HYPERACUITY
HYPERACUSES
HYPERACUSIS
HYPERACUTE
HYPERACUTENESS
HYPERADRENALISM
HYPERAEMIA
HYPERAEMIAS
HYPERAEMIC
HYPERAESTHESIA
HYPERAESTHESIAS
HYPERAESTHESIC
HYPERAESTHETIC
HYPERAGGRESSIVE
HYPERALERT
HYPERALGESIA
HYPERALGESIAS
HYPERALGESIC
HYPERAROUSAL
HYPERAROUSALS
HYPERAWARE
HYPERAWARENESS
HYPERBARIC
HYPERBARICALLY
HYPERBATIC
HYPERBATICALLY
HYPERBATON
HYPERBATONS
HYPERBOLAE
HYPERBOLAS
HYPERBOLES
HYPERBOLIC
HYPERBOLICAL
HYPERBOLICALLY
HYPERBOLISE
HYPERBOLISED
HYPERBOLISES
HYPERBOLISING
HYPERBOLISM
HYPERBOLISMS
HYPERBOLIST
HYPERBOLISTS
HYPERBOLIZE
HYPERBOLIZED
HYPERBOLIZES
HYPERBOLIZING
HYPERBOLOID
HYPERBOLOIDAL
HYPERBOLOIDS
HYPERBOREAN
HYPERBOREANS
HYPERCALCAEMIA
HYPERCALCAEMIAS
HYPERCALCEMIA
HYPERCALCEMIAS
HYPERCALCEMIC
HYPERCAPNIA
HYPERCAPNIAS
HYPERCAPNIC
HYPERCARBIA
HYPERCARBIAS
HYPERCATABOLISM
HYPERCATALECTIC
HYPERCATALEXES

HYPERCATALEXIS
HYPERCAUTIOUS
HYPERCHARGE
HYPERCHARGED
HYPERCHARGES
HYPERCHARGING
HYPERCIVILISED
HYPERCIVILIZED
HYPERCOAGULABLE
HYPERCOLOUR
HYPERCOLOURS
HYPERCOMPLEX
HYPERCONSCIOUS
HYPERCORRECT
HYPERCORRECTION
HYPERCORRECTLY
HYPERCRITIC
HYPERCRITICAL
HYPERCRITICALLY
HYPERCRITICISE
HYPERCRITICISED
HYPERCRITICISES
HYPERCRITICISM
HYPERCRITICISMS
HYPERCRITICIZE
HYPERCRITICIZED
HYPERCRITICIZES
HYPERCRITICS
HYPERCUBES
HYPERDACTYL
HYPERDACTYLIES
HYPERDACTYLY
HYPERDORIAN
HYPERDULIA
HYPERDULIAS
HYPERDULIC
HYPERDULICAL
HYPEREFFICIENT
HYPEREMESES
HYPEREMESIS
HYPEREMETIC
HYPEREMIAS
HYPEREMOTIONAL
HYPERENDEMIC
HYPERENERGETIC
HYPERESTHESIA
HYPERESTHESIAS
HYPERESTHETIC
HYPEREUTECTIC
HYPEREUTECTOID
HYPEREXCITABLE
HYPEREXCITED
HYPEREXCITEMENT
HYPEREXCRETION
HYPEREXCRETIONS
HYPEREXTEND
HYPEREXTENDED
HYPEREXTENDING
HYPEREXTENDS
HYPEREXTENSION
HYPEREXTENSIONS
HYPERFASTIDIOUS
HYPERFOCAL
HYPERFUNCTION
HYPERFUNCTIONAL
HYPERFUNCTIONS
HYPERGAMIES
HYPERGAMOUS
HYPERGEOMETRIC
HYPERGLYCAEMIA
HYPERGLYCAEMIAS
HYPERGLYCAEMIC
HYPERGLYCEMIA
HYPERGLYCEMIAS
HYPERGLYCEMIC
HYPERGOLIC
HYPERGOLICALLY
HYPERHIDROSES
HYPERHIDROSIS
HYPERICUMS
HYPERIDROSES
HYPERIDROSIS
HYPERIMMUNE

HYPERIMMUNISE	HYPERPARASITISM	HYPERSONICS	HYPNAGOGIC	HYPOCORISM	HYPOPHOSPHITES
HYPERIMMUNISED	HYPERPHAGIA	HYPERSPACE	HYPNOANALYSES	HYPOCORISMA	HYPOPHOSPHORIC
HYPERIMMUNISES	HYPERPHAGIAS	HYPERSPACES	HYPNOANALYSIS	HYPOCORISMAS	HYPOPHOSPHOROUS
HYPERIMMUNISING	HYPERPHAGIC	HYPERSPATIAL	HYPNOANALYTIC	HYPOCORISMS	HYPOPHRYGIAN
HYPERIMMUNIZE	HYPERPHRYGIAN	HYPERSTATIC	HYPNOGENESES	HYPOCORISTIC	HYPOPHYGES
HYPERIMMUNIZED	HYPERPHYSICAL	HYPERSTHENE	HYPNOGENESIS	HYPOCORISTICAL	HYPOPHYSEAL
HYPERIMMUNIZES	HYPERPHYSICALLY	HYPERSTHENES	HYPNOGENETIC	HYPOCOTYLOUS	HYPOPHYSECTOMY
HYPERIMMUNIZING	HYPERPIGMENTED	HYPERSTHENIA	HYPNOGENIC	HYPOCOTYLS	HYPOPHYSES
HYPERINFLATED	HYPERPITUITARY	HYPERSTHENIAS	HYPNOGENIES	HYPOCRISIES	HYPOPHYSIAL
HYPERINFLATION	HYPERPLANE	HYPERSTHENIC	HYPNOGENOUS	HYPOCRITES	HYPOPHYSIS
HYPERINFLATIONS	HYPERPLANES	HYPERSTHENITE	HYPNOGOGIC	HYPOCRITIC	HYPOPITUITARISM
HYPERINOSES	HYPERPLASIA	HYPERSTHENITES	HYPNOIDISE	HYPOCRITICAL	HYPOPITUITARY
HYPERINOSIS	HYPERPLASIAS	HYPERSTIMULATE	HYPNOIDISED	HYPOCRITICALLY	HYPOPLASIA
HYPERINOTIC	HYPERPLASTIC	HYPERSTIMULATED	HYPNOIDISES	HYPOCRYSTALLINE	HYPOPLASIAS
HYPERINSULINISM	HYPERPLOID	HYPERSTIMULATES	HYPNOIDISING	HYPOCYCLOID	HYPOPLASTIC
HYPERINTENSE	HYPERPLOIDIES	HYPERSTRESS	HYPNOIDIZE	HYPOCYCLOIDAL	HYPOPLASTIES
HYPERINVOLUTION	HYPERPLOIDS	HYPERSTRESSES	HYPNOIDIZED	HYPOCYCLOIDS	HYPOPLASTRA
HYPERIRRITABLE	HYPERPLOIDY	HYPERSURFACE	HYPNOIDIZES	HYPODERMAL	HYPOPLASTRON
HYPERKERATOSES	HYPERPNEAS	HYPERSURFACES	HYPNOIDIZING	HYPODERMAS	HYPOPLASTY
HYPERKERATOSIS	HYPERPNEIC	HYPERTENSE	HYPNOLOGIC	HYPODERMIC	HYPOPLOIDIES
HYPERKERATOTIC	HYPERPNOEA	HYPERTENSION	HYPNOLOGICAL	HYPODERMICALLY	HYPOPLOIDS
HYPERKINESES	HYPERPNOEAS	HYPERTENSIONS	HYPNOLOGIES	HYPODERMICS	HYPOPLOIDY
HYPERKINESIA	HYPERPOLARISE	HYPERTENSIVE	HYPNOLOGIST	HYPODERMIS	HYPOPNOEAS
HYPERKINESIAS	HYPERPOLARISED	HYPERTENSIVES	HYPNOLOGISTS	HYPODERMISES	HYPOSENSITISE
HYPERKINESIS	HYPERPOLARISES	HYPERTEXTS	HYPNOPAEDIA	HYPODIPLOID	HYPOSENSITISED
HYPERKINETIC	HYPERPOLARISING	HYPERTHERMAL	HYPNOPAEDIAS	HYPODIPLOIDIES	HYPOSENSITISES
HYPERLINKED	HYPERPOLARIZE	HYPERTHERMIA	HYPNOPOMPIC	HYPODIPLOIDY	HYPOSENSITISING
HYPERLINKING	HYPERPOLARIZED	HYPERTHERMIAS	HYPNOTHERAPIES	HYPODORIAN	HYPOSENSITIZE
HYPERLINKS	HYPERPOLARIZES	HYPERTHERMIC	HYPNOTHERAPIST	HYPOEUTECTIC	HYPOSENSITIZED
HYPERLIPEMIA	HYPERPOLARIZING	HYPERTHERMIES	HYPNOTHERAPISTS	HYPOEUTECTOID	HYPOSENSITIZES
HYPERLIPEMIAS	HYPERPOWER	HYPERTHERMY	HYPNOTHERAPY	HYPOGAEOUS	HYPOSENSITIZING
HYPERLIPEMIC	HYPERPOWERS	HYPERTHYMIA	HYPNOTICALLY	HYPOGASTRIA	HYPOSPADIAS
HYPERLIPIDAEMIA	HYPERPRODUCER	HYPERTHYMIAS	HYPNOTISABILITY	HYPOGASTRIC	HYPOSPADIASES
HYPERLIPIDEMIA	HYPERPRODUCERS	HYPERTHYROID	HYPNOTISABLE	HYPOGASTRIUM	HYPOSTASES
HYPERLIPIDEMIAS	HYPERPRODUCTION	HYPERTHYROIDISM	HYPNOTISATION	HYPOGENOUS	HYPOSTASIS
HYPERLYDIAN	HYPERPROSEXIA	HYPERTHYROIDS	HYPNOTISATIONS	HYPOGLOSSAL	HYPOSTASISATION
HYPERMANIA	HYPERPROSEXIAS	HYPERTONIA	HYPNOTISED	HYPOGLOSSALS	HYPOSTASISE
HYPERMANIAS	HYPERPYRETIC	HYPERTONIAS	HYPNOTISER	HYPOGLYCAEMIA	HYPOSTASISED
HYPERMANIC	HYPERPYREXIA	HYPERTONIC	HYPNOTISERS	HYPOGLYCAEMIAS	HYPOSTASISES
HYPERMARKET	HYPERPYREXIAL	HYPERTONICITIES	HYPNOTISES	HYPOGLYCAEMIC	HYPOSTASISING
HYPERMARKETS	HYPERPYREXIAS	HYPERTONICITY	HYPNOTISING	HYPOGLYCEMIA	HYPOSTASIZATION
HYPERMARTS	HYPERRATIONAL	HYPERTROPHIC	HYPNOTISMS	HYPOGLYCEMIAS	HYPOSTASIZE
HYPERMASCULINE	HYPERREACTIVE	HYPERTROPHICAL	HYPNOTISTIC	HYPOGLYCEMIC	HYPOSTASIZED
HYPERMEDIA	HYPERREACTIVITY	HYPERTROPHIED	HYPNOTISTS	HYPOGLYCEMICS	HYPOSTASIZES
HYPERMEDIAS	HYPERREACTOR	HYPERTROPHIES	HYPNOTIZABILITY	HYPOGNATHISM	HYPOSTASIZING
HYPERMETABOLIC	HYPERREACTORS	HYPERTROPHOUS	HYPNOTIZABLE	HYPOGNATHISMS	HYPOSTATIC
HYPERMETABOLISM	HYPERREALISM	HYPERTROPHY	HYPNOTIZATION	HYPOGNATHOUS	HYPOSTATICAL
HYPERMETER	HYPERREALISMS	HYPERTROPHYING	HYPNOTIZATIONS	HYPOGYNIES	HYPOSTATICALLY
HYPERMETERS	HYPERREALIST	HYPERTYPICAL	HYPNOTIZED	HYPOGYNOUS	HYPOSTATISATION
HYPERMETRIC	HYPERREALISTIC	HYPERURBANISM	HYPNOTIZER	HYPOKALEMIA	HYPOSTATISE
HYPERMETRICAL	HYPERREALISTS	HYPERURBANISMS	HYPNOTIZERS	HYPOKALEMIAS	HYPOSTATISED
HYPERMETROPIA	HYPERREALITIES	HYPERURICEMIA	HYPNOTIZES	HYPOKALEMIC	HYPOSTATISES
HYPERMETROPIAS	HYPERREALITY	HYPERURICEMIAS	HYPNOTIZING	HYPOLIMNIA	HYPOSTATISING
HYPERMETROPIC	HYPERREALS	HYPERVELOCITIES	HYPOACIDITIES	HYPOLIMNION	HYPOSTATIZATION
HYPERMETROPICAL	HYPERRESPONSIVE	HYPERVELOCITY	HYPOACIDITY	HYPOLIMNIONS	HYPOSTATIZE
HYPERMETROPIES	HYPERROMANTIC	HYPERVENTILATE	HYPOAEOLIAN	HYPOLYDIAN	HYPOSTATIZED
HYPERMETROPY	HYPERROMANTICS	HYPERVENTILATED	HYPOALLERGENIC	HYPOMAGNESAEMIA	HYPOSTATIZES
HYPERMNESIA	HYPERSALINE	HYPERVENTILATES	HYPOBLASTIC	HYPOMAGNESEMIA	HYPOSTATIZING
HYPERMNESIAS	HYPERSALINITIES	HYPERVIGILANCE	HYPOBLASTS	HYPOMAGNESEMIAS	HYPOSTHENIA
HYPERMNESIC	HYPERSALINITY	HYPERVIGILANCES	HYPOCALCEMIA	HYPOMANIAS	HYPOSTHENIAS
HYPERMOBILITIES	HYPERSALIVATION	HYPERVIGILANT	HYPOCALCEMIAS	HYPOMANICS	HYPOSTHENIC
HYPERMOBILITY	HYPERSARCOMA	HYPERVIRULENT	HYPOCALCEMIC	HYPOMENORRHEA	HYPOSTOMES
HYPERMODERN	HYPERSARCOMAS	HYPERVISCOSITY	HYPOCAUSTS	HYPOMENORRHEAS	HYPOSTRESS
HYPERMODERNIST	HYPERSARCOMATA	HYPESTHESIA	HYPOCENTER	HYPOMENORRHOEA	HYPOSTRESSES
HYPERMODERNISTS	HYPERSARCOSES	HYPESTHESIAS	HYPOCENTERS	HYPOMENORRHOEAS	HYPOSTROPHE
HYPERMUTABILITY	HYPERSARCOSIS	HYPESTHESIC	HYPOCENTRAL	HYPOMIXOLYDIAN	HYPOSTROPHES
HYPERMUTABLE	HYPERSECRETION	HYPHENATED	HYPOCENTRE	HYPOMORPHIC	HYPOSTYLES
HYPERNATRAEMIA	HYPERSECRETIONS	HYPHENATES	HYPOCENTRES	HYPOMORPHS	HYPOSULPHATE
HYPERNATRAEMIAS	HYPERSENSITISE	HYPHENATING	HYPOCHLORITE	HYPONASTIC	HYPOSULPHATES
HYPERNOVAE	HYPERSENSITISED	HYPHENATION	HYPOCHLORITES	HYPONASTICALLY	HYPOSULPHITE
HYPERNOVAS	HYPERSENSITISES	HYPHENATIONS	HYPOCHLOROUS	HYPONASTIES	HYPOSULPHITES
HYPERNYMIES	HYPERSENSITIVE	HYPHENISATION	HYPOCHONDRIA	HYPONATRAEMIA	HYPOSULPHURIC
HYPEROPIAS	HYPERSENSITIZE	HYPHENISATIONS	HYPOCHONDRIAC	HYPONATRAEMIAS	HYPOSULPHUROUS
HYPEROREXIA	HYPERSENSITIZED	HYPHENISED	HYPOCHONDRIACAL	HYPONITRITE	HYPOTACTIC
HYPEROREXIAS	HYPERSENSITIZES	HYPHENISES	HYPOCHONDRIACS	HYPONITRITES	HYPOTENSION
HYPEROSMIA	HYPERSENSUAL	HYPHENISING	HYPOCHONDRIAS	HYPONITROUS	HYPOTENSIONS
HYPEROSMIAS	HYPERSEXUAL	HYPHENISMS	HYPOCHONDRIASES	HYPONYMIES	HYPOTENSIVE
HYPEROSTOSES	HYPERSEXUALITY	HYPHENIZATION	HYPOCHONDRIASIS	HYPOPHARYNGES	HYPOTENSIVES
HYPEROSTOSIS	HYPERSOMNIA	HYPHENIZATIONS	HYPOCHONDRIASM	HYPOPHARYNX	HYPOTENUSE
HYPEROSTOTIC	HYPERSOMNIAS	HYPHENIZED	HYPOCHONDRIASMS	HYPOPHARYNXES	HYPOTENUSES
HYPERPARASITE	HYPERSOMNOLENCE	HYPHENIZES	HYPOCHONDRIAST	HYPOPHOSPHATE	HYPOTHALAMI
HYPERPARASITES	HYPERSONIC	HYPHENIZING	HYPOCHONDRIASTS	HYPOPHOSPHATES	HYPOTHALAMIC
HYPERPARASITIC	HYPERSONICALLY	HYPHENLESS	HYPOCHONDRIUM	HYPOPHOSPHITE	HYPOTHALAMUS

HYPOTHECAE
HYPOTHECARY
HYPOTHECATE
HYPOTHECATED
HYPOTHECATES
HYPOTHECATING
HYPOTHECATION
HYPOTHECATIONS
HYPOTHECATOR
HYPOTHECATORS
HYPOTHENUSE
HYPOTHENUSES
HYPOTHERMAL
HYPOTHERMIA
HYPOTHERMIAS
HYPOTHERMIC
HYPOTHESES
HYPOTHESIS
HYPOTHESISE
HYPOTHESISED

HYPOTHESISER
HYPOTHESISERS
HYPOTHESISES
HYPOTHESISING
HYPOTHESIST
HYPOTHESISTS
HYPOTHESIZE
HYPOTHESIZED
HYPOTHESIZER
HYPOTHESIZERS
HYPOTHESIZES
HYPOTHESIZING
HYPOTHETIC
HYPOTHETICAL
HYPOTHETICALLY
HYPOTHETISE
HYPOTHETISED
HYPOTHETISES
HYPOTHETISING
HYPOTHETIZE

HYPOTHETIZED
HYPOTHETIZES
HYPOTHETIZING
HYPOTHYMIA
HYPOTHYMIAS
HYPOTHYROID
HYPOTHYROIDISM
HYPOTHYROIDISMS
HYPOTHYROIDS
HYPOTONIAS
HYPOTONICITIES
HYPOTONICITY
HYPOTROCHOID
HYPOTROCHOIDS
HYPOTYPOSES
HYPOTYPOSIS
HYPOVENTILATION
HYPOXAEMIA
HYPOXAEMIAS
HYPOXAEMIC

HYPOXANTHINE
HYPOXANTHINES
HYPOXEMIAS
HYPSOCHROME
HYPSOCHROMES
HYPSOCHROMIC
HYPSOGRAPHIC
HYPSOGRAPHICAL
HYPSOGRAPHIES
HYPSOGRAPHY
HYPSOMETER
HYPSOMETERS
HYPSOMETRIC
HYPSOMETRICAL
HYPSOMETRICALLY
HYPSOMETRIES
HYPSOMETRIST
HYPSOMETRISTS
HYPSOMETRY
HYPSOPHOBE

HYPSOPHOBES
HYPSOPHOBIA
HYPSOPHOBIAS
HYPSOPHYLL
HYPSOPHYLLARY
HYPSOPHYLLS
HYRACOIDEAN
HYRACOIDEANS
HYSTERANTHOUS
HYSTERECTOMIES
HYSTERECTOMISE
HYSTERECTOMISED
HYSTERECTOMISES
HYSTERECTOMIZE
HYSTERECTOMIZED
HYSTERECTOMIZES
HYSTERECTOMY
HYSTERESES
HYSTERESIAL
HYSTERESIS

HYSTERETIC
HYSTERETICALLY
HYSTERICAL
HYSTERICALLY
HYSTERICKY
HYSTERITIS
HYSTERITISES
HYSTEROGENIC
HYSTEROGENIES
HYSTEROGENY
HYSTEROIDAL
HYSTEROMANIA
HYSTEROMANIAS
HYSTEROTOMIES
HYSTEROTOMY
HYSTRICOMORPH
HYSTRICOMORPHIC
HYSTRICOMORPHS

Ii

IAMBICALLY	ICHTHYOSAURUS	IDEALIZING	IDIOPATHIC	IGNORANTLY	ILLIQUATION
IAMBOGRAPHER	ICHTHYOSAURUSES	IDEALNESSES	IDIOPATHICALLY	IGNORANTNESS	ILLIQUATIONS
IAMBOGRAPHERS	ICHTHYOSES	IDEALOGIES	IDIOPATHIES	IGNORANTNESSES	ILLIQUIDITIES
IATROCHEMICAL	ICHTHYOSIS	IDEALOGUES	IDIOPHONES	IGNORATION	ILLIQUIDITY
IATROCHEMIST	ICHTHYOTIC	IDEATIONAL	IDIOPHONIC	IGNORATIONS	ILLITERACIES
IATROCHEMISTRY	ICKINESSES	IDEATIONALLY	IDIOPLASMATIC	IGUANODONS	ILLITERACY
IATROCHEMISTS	ICONICALLY	IDEMPOTENCIES	IDIOPLASMIC	ILEOSTOMIES	ILLITERATE
IATROGENIC	ICONICITIES	IDEMPOTENCY	IDIOPLASMS	ILLAQUEABLE	ILLITERATELY
IATROGENICALLY	ICONIFYING	IDEMPOTENT	IDIORHYTHMIC	ILLAQUEATE	ILLITERATENESS
IATROGENICITIES	ICONOCLASM	IDEMPOTENTS	IDIORRHYTHMIC	ILLAQUEATED	ILLITERATES
IATROGENICITY	ICONOCLASMS	IDENTICALLY	IDIOSYNCRASIES	ILLAQUEATES	ILLOCUTION
IATROGENIES	ICONOCLAST	IDENTICALNESS	IDIOSYNCRASY	ILLAQUEATING	ILLOCUTIONARY
IBUPROFENS	ICONOCLASTIC	IDENTICALNESSES	IDIOSYNCRATIC	ILLAQUEATION	ILLOCUTIONS
ICEBOATERS	ICONOCLASTS	IDENTIFIABLE	IDIOSYNCRATICAL	ILLAQUEATIONS	ILLOGICALITIES
ICEBOATING	ICONOGRAPHER	IDENTIFIABLY	IDIOTHERMOUS	ILLATIVELY	ILLOGICALITY
ICEBOATINGS	ICONOGRAPHERS	IDENTIFICATION	IDIOTICALLY	ILLAUDABLE	ILLOGICALLY
ICEBREAKER	ICONOGRAPHIC	IDENTIFICATIONS	IDIOTICALNESS	ILLAUDABLY	ILLOGICALNESS
ICEBREAKERS	ICONOGRAPHICAL	IDENTIFIED	IDIOTICALNESSES	ILLEGALISATION	ILLOGICALNESSES
ICEBREAKING	ICONOGRAPHIES	IDENTIFIER	IDIOTICONS	ILLEGALISATIONS	ILLUMINABLE
ICHNEUMONS	ICONOGRAPHY	IDENTIFIERS	IDLENESSES	ILLEGALISE	ILLUMINANCE
ICHNOFOSSIL	ICONOLATER	IDENTIFIES	IDOLATRESS	ILLEGALISED	ILLUMINANCES
ICHNOFOSSILS	ICONOLATERS	IDENTIFYING	IDOLATRESSES	ILLEGALISES	ILLUMINANT
ICHNOGRAPHIC	ICONOLATRIES	IDENTIKITS	IDOLATRIES	ILLEGALISING	ILLUMINANTS
ICHNOGRAPHICAL	ICONOLATROUS	IDENTITIES	IDOLATRISE	ILLEGALITIES	ILLUMINATE
ICHNOGRAPHIES	ICONOLATRY	IDEOGRAMIC	IDOLATRISED	ILLEGALITY	ILLUMINATED
ICHNOGRAPHY	ICONOLOGICAL	IDEOGRAMMATIC	IDOLATRISER	ILLEGALIZATION	ILLUMINATES
ICHNOLITES	ICONOLOGIES	IDEOGRAMMIC	IDOLATRISERS	ILLEGALIZATIONS	ILLUMINATI
ICHNOLOGICAL	ICONOLOGIST	IDEOGRAPHIC	IDOLATRISES	ILLEGALIZE	ILLUMINATING
ICHNOLOGIES	ICONOLOGISTS	IDEOGRAPHICAL	IDOLATRISING	ILLEGALIZED	ILLUMINATINGLY
ICHTHYOCOLLA	ICONOMACHIES	IDEOGRAPHICALLY	IDOLATRIZE	ILLEGALIZES	ILLUMINATION
ICHTHYOCOLLAS	ICONOMACHIST	IDEOGRAPHIES	IDOLATRIZED	ILLEGALIZING	ILLUMINATIONAL
ICHTHYODORULITE	ICONOMACHISTS	IDEOGRAPHS	IDOLATRIZER	ILLEGIBILITIES	ILLUMINATIONS
ICHTHYODORYLITE	ICONOMACHY	IDEOGRAPHY	IDOLATRIZERS	ILLEGIBILITY	ILLUMINATIVE
ICHTHYOFAUNA	ICONOMATIC	IDEOLOGICAL	IDOLATRIZES	ILLEGIBLENESS	ILLUMINATO
ICHTHYOFAUNAE	ICONOMATICISM	IDEOLOGICALLY	IDOLATRIZING	ILLEGIBLENESSES	ILLUMINATOR
ICHTHYOFAUNAL	ICONOMATICISMS	IDEOLOGIES	IDOLATROUS	ILLEGITIMACIES	ILLUMINATORS
ICHTHYOFAUNAS	ICONOMETER	IDEOLOGISE	IDOLATROUSLY	ILLEGITIMACY	ILLUMINERS
ICHTHYOIDAL	ICONOMETERS	IDEOLOGISED	IDOLATROUSNESS	ILLEGITIMATE	ILLUMINING
ICHTHYOIDS	ICONOMETRIES	IDEOLOGISES	IDOLISATION	ILLEGITIMATED	ILLUMINISM
ICHTHYOLATRIES	ICONOMETRY	IDEOLOGISING	IDOLISATIONS	ILLEGITIMATELY	ILLUMINISMS
ICHTHYOLATROUS	ICONOPHILISM	IDEOLOGIST	IDOLIZATION	ILLEGITIMATES	ILLUMINIST
ICHTHYOLATRY	ICONOPHILISMS	IDEOLOGISTS	IDOLIZATIONS	ILLEGITIMATING	ILLUMINISTS
ICHTHYOLITE	ICONOPHILIST	IDEOLOGIZE	IDOLOCLAST	ILLEGITIMATION	ILLUSIONAL
ICHTHYOLITES	ICONOPHILISTS	IDEOLOGIZED	IDOLOCLASTS	ILLEGITIMATIONS	ILLUSIONARY
ICHTHYOLITIC	ICONOSCOPE	IDEOLOGIZES	IDONEITIES	ILLIBERALISE	ILLUSIONED
ICHTHYOLOGIC	ICONOSCOPES	IDEOLOGIZING	IDOXURIDINE	ILLIBERALISED	ILLUSIONISM
ICHTHYOLOGICAL	ICONOSTASES	IDEOLOGUES	IDOXURIDINES	ILLIBERALISES	ILLUSIONISMS
ICHTHYOLOGIES	ICONOSTASIS	IDEOPHONES	IDYLLICALLY	ILLIBERALISING	ILLUSIONIST
ICHTHYOLOGIST	ICOSAHEDRA	IDEOPRAXIST	IFFINESSES	ILLIBERALISM	ILLUSIONISTIC
ICHTHYOLOGISTS	ICOSAHEDRAL	IDEOPRAXISTS	IGNESCENTS	ILLIBERALISMS	ILLUSIONISTS
ICHTHYOLOGY	ICOSAHEDRON	IDIOBLASTIC	IGNIMBRITE	ILLIBERALITIES	ILLUSIVELY
ICHTHYOPHAGIES	ICOSAHEDRONS	IDIOBLASTS	IGNIMBRITES	ILLIBERALITY	ILLUSIVENESS
ICHTHYOPHAGIST	ICOSANDRIAN	IDIOGLOSSIA	IGNIPOTENT	ILLIBERALIZE	ILLUSIVENESSES
ICHTHYOPHAGISTS	ICOSANDROUS	IDIOGLOSSIAS	IGNITABILITIES	ILLIBERALIZED	ILLUSORILY
ICHTHYOPHAGOUS	ICOSITETRAHEDRA	IDIOGRAPHIC	IGNITABILITY	ILLIBERALIZES	ILLUSORINESS
ICHTHYOPHAGY	ICTERICALS	IDIOGRAPHS	IGNITIBILITIES	ILLIBERALIZING	ILLUSORINESSES
ICHTHYOPSID	ICTERITIOUS	IDIOLECTAL	IGNITIBILITY	ILLIBERALLY	ILLUSTRATABLE
ICHTHYOPSIDAN	IDEALISATION	IDIOLECTIC	IGNOBILITIES	ILLIBERALNESS	ILLUSTRATE
ICHTHYOPSIDANS	IDEALISATIONS	IDIOMATICAL	IGNOBILITY	ILLIBERALNESSES	ILLUSTRATED
ICHTHYOPSIDS	IDEALISERS	IDIOMATICALLY	IGNOBLENESS	ILLICITNESS	ILLUSTRATEDS
ICHTHYORNIS	IDEALISING	IDIOMATICALNESS	IGNOBLENESSES	ILLICITNESSES	ILLUSTRATES
ICHTHYORNISES	IDEALISTIC	IDIOMATICNESS	IGNOMINIES	ILLIMITABILITY	ILLUSTRATING
ICHTHYOSAUR	IDEALISTICALLY	IDIOMATICNESSES	IGNOMINIOUS	ILLIMITABLE	ILLUSTRATION
ICHTHYOSAURI	IDEALITIES	IDIOMORPHIC	IGNOMINIOUSNESS	ILLIMITABLENESS	ILLUSTRATIONAL
ICHTHYOSAURIAN	IDEALIZATION	IDIOMORPHICALLY	IGNORAMUSES	ILLIMITABLY	ILLUSTRATIONS
ICHTHYOSAURIANS	IDEALIZATIONS	IDIOMORPHISM	IGNORANCES	ILLIMITATION	ILLUSTRATIVE
ICHTHYOSAURS	IDEALIZERS	IDIOMORPHISMS	IGNORANCES	ILLIMITATIONS	ILLUSTRATIVELY

ILLUSTRATOR	IMMANACLING	IMMINENTNESSES	IMMORTALIZES	IMMUTABILITIES	IMPEACHING
ILLUSTRATORS	IMMANATION	IMMINGLING	IMMORTALIZING	IMMUTABILITY	IMPEACHMENT
ILLUSTRATORY	IMMANATIONS	IMMINUTION	IMMORTALLY	IMMUTABLENESS	IMPEACHMENTS
ILLUSTRIOUS	IMMANENCES	IMMINUTIONS	IMMORTELLE	IMMUTABLENESSES	IMPEARLING
ILLUSTRIOUSLY	IMMANENCIES	IMMISCIBILITIES	IMMORTELLES	IMPACTIONS	IMPECCABILITIES
ILLUSTRIOUSNESS	IMMANENTAL	IMMISCIBILITY	IMMOTILITIES	IMPACTITES	IMPECCABILITY
ILLUSTRISSIMO	IMMANENTISM	IMMISCIBLE	IMMOTILITY	IMPAINTING	IMPECCABLE
ILLUVIATED	IMMANENTISMS	IMMISCIBLY	IMMOVABILITIES	IMPAIRABLE	IMPECCABLY
ILLUVIATES	IMMANENTIST	IMMISERATION	IMMOVABILITY	IMPAIRINGS	IMPECCANCIES
ILLUVIATING	IMMANENTISTIC	IMMISERATIONS	IMMOVABLENESS	IMPAIRMENT	IMPECCANCY
ILLUVIATION	IMMANENTISTS	IMMISERISATION	IMMOVABLENESSES	IMPAIRMENTS	IMPECUNIOSITIES
ILLUVIATIONS	IMMANENTLY	IMMISERISATIONS	IMMOVABLES	IMPALEMENT	IMPECUNIOSITY
IMAGINABLE	IMMANITIES	IMMISERISE	IMMOVEABILITIES	IMPALEMENTS	IMPECUNIOUS
IMAGINABLENESS	IMMANTLING	IMMISERISED	IMMOVEABILITY	IMPALPABILITIES	IMPECUNIOUSLY
IMAGINABLY	IMMARCESCIBLE	IMMISERISES	IMMOVEABLE	IMPALPABILITY	IMPECUNIOUSNESS
IMAGINARIES	IMMARGINATE	IMMISERISING	IMMOVEABLENESS	IMPALPABLE	IMPEDANCES
IMAGINARILY	IMMATERIAL	IMMISERIZATION	IMMOVEABLES	IMPALPABLY	IMPEDIMENT
IMAGINARINESS	IMMATERIALISE	IMMISERIZATIONS	IMMOVEABLY	IMPALUDISM	IMPEDIMENTA
IMAGINARINESSES	IMMATERIALISED	IMMISERIZE	IMMUNIFACIENT	IMPALUDISMS	IMPEDIMENTAL
IMAGINATION	IMMATERIALISES	IMMISERIZED	IMMUNISATION	IMPANATION	IMPEDIMENTARY
IMAGINATIONAL	IMMATERIALISING	IMMISERIZES	IMMUNISATIONS	IMPANATIONS	IMPEDIMENTS
IMAGINATIONS	IMMATERIALISM	IMMISERIZING	IMMUNISERS	IMPANELING	IMPEDINGLY
IMAGINATIVE	IMMATERIALISMS	IMMISSIONS	IMMUNISING	IMPANELLED	IMPEDITIVE
IMAGINATIVELY	IMMATERIALIST	IMMITIGABILITY	IMMUNITIES	IMPANELLING	IMPELLENTS
IMAGINATIVENESS	IMMATERIALISTS	IMMITIGABLE	IMMUNIZATION	IMPANELMENT	IMPENDENCE
IMAGININGS	IMMATERIALITIES	IMMITIGABLY	IMMUNIZATIONS	IMPANELMENTS	IMPENDENCES
IMAGINISTS	IMMATERIALITY	IMMITTANCE	IMMUNIZERS	IMPANNELLED	IMPENDENCIES
IMAGISTICALLY	IMMATERIALIZE	IMMITTANCES	IMMUNIZING	IMPANNELLING	IMPENDENCY
IMBALANCED	IMMATERIALIZED	IMMIXTURES	IMMUNOASSAY	IMPARADISE	IMPENETRABILITY
IMBALANCES	IMMATERIALIZES	IMMOBILISATION	IMMUNOASSAYABLE	IMPARADISED	IMPENETRABLE
IMBECILELY	IMMATERIALIZING	IMMOBILISATIONS	IMMUNOASSAYIST	IMPARADISES	IMPENETRABLY
IMBECILICALLY	IMMATERIALLY	IMMOBILISE	IMMUNOASSAYISTS	IMPARADISING	IMPENETRATE
IMBECILITIES	IMMATERIALNESS	IMMOBILISED	IMMUNOASSAYS	IMPARIDIGITATE	IMPENETRATED
IMBECILITY	IMMATURELY	IMMOBILISER	IMMUNOBLOT	IMPARIPINNATE	IMPENETRATES
IMBIBITION	IMMATURENESS	IMMOBILISERS	IMMUNOBLOTS	IMPARISYLLABIC	IMPENETRATING
IMBIBITIONAL	IMMATURENESSES	IMMOBILISES	IMMUNOBLOTTING	IMPARITIES	IMPENETRATION
IMBIBITIONS	IMMATURITIES	IMMOBILISING	IMMUNOBLOTTINGS	IMPARKATION	IMPENETRATIONS
IMBITTERED	IMMATURITY	IMMOBILISM	IMMUNOCHEMICAL	IMPARKATIONS	IMPENITENCE
IMBITTERING	IMMEASURABILITY	IMMOBILISMS	IMMUNOCHEMIST	IMPARLANCE	IMPENITENCES
IMBOLDENED	IMMEASURABLE	IMMOBILITIES	IMMUNOCHEMISTRY	IMPARLANCES	IMPENITENCIES
IMBOLDENING	IMMEASURABLY	IMMOBILITY	IMMUNOCHEMISTS	IMPARTABLE	IMPENITENCY
IMBORDERED	IMMEASURED	IMMOBILIZATION	IMMUNOCOMPETENT	IMPARTATION	IMPENITENT
IMBORDERING	IMMEDIACIES	IMMOBILIZATIONS	IMMUNOCOMPLEX	IMPARTATIONS	IMPENITENTLY
IMBOSOMING	IMMEDIATELY	IMMOBILIZE	IMMUNOCOMPLEXES	IMPARTIALITIES	IMPENITENTNESS
IMBOWERING	IMMEDIATENESS	IMMOBILIZED	IMMUNODEFICIENT	IMPARTIALITY	IMPENITENTS
IMBRANGLED	IMMEDIATENESSES	IMMOBILIZER	IMMUNODIAGNOSES	IMPARTIALLY	IMPERATIVAL
IMBRANGLES	IMMEDIATISM	IMMOBILIZERS	IMMUNODIAGNOSIS	IMPARTIALNESS	IMPERATIVE
IMBRANGLING	IMMEDIATISMS	IMMOBILIZES	IMMUNODIFFUSION	IMPARTIALNESSES	IMPERATIVELY
IMBRICATED	IMMEDICABLE	IMMOBILIZING	IMMUNOGENESES	IMPARTIBILITIES	IMPERATIVENESS
IMBRICATELY	IMMEDICABLENESS	IMMODERACIES	IMMUNOGENESIS	IMPARTIBILITY	IMPERATIVES
IMBRICATES	IMMEDICABLY	IMMODERACY	IMMUNOGENETIC	IMPARTIBLE	IMPERATORIAL
IMBRICATING	IMMEMORIAL	IMMODERATE	IMMUNOGENETICAL	IMPARTIBLY	IMPERATORIALLY
IMBRICATION	IMMEMORIALLY	IMMODERATELY	IMMUNOGENETICS	IMPARTMENT	IMPERATORS
IMBRICATIONS	IMMENSENESS	IMMODERATENESS	IMMUNOGENIC	IMPARTMENTS	IMPERATORSHIP
IMBROCCATA	IMMENSENESSES	IMMODERATION	IMMUNOGENICALLY	IMPASSABILITIES	IMPERATORSHIPS
IMBROCCATAS	IMMENSITIES	IMMODERATIONS	IMMUNOGENICITY	IMPASSABILITY	IMPERCEABLE
IMBROGLIOS	IMMENSURABILITY	IMMODESTIES	IMMUNOGENS	IMPASSABLE	IMPERCEIVABLE
IMBROWNING	IMMENSURABLE	IMMODESTLY	IMMUNOGLOBULIN	IMPASSABLENESS	IMPERCEPTIBLE
IMBRUEMENT	IMMERGENCE	IMMOLATING	IMMUNOGLOBULINS	IMPASSABLY	IMPERCEPTIBLY
IMBRUEMENTS	IMMERGENCES	IMMOLATION	IMMUNOLOGIC	IMPASSIBILITIES	IMPERCEPTION
IMBUEMENTS	IMMERITOUS	IMMOLATIONS	IMMUNOLOGICAL	IMPASSIBILITY	IMPERCEPTIONS
IMIDAZOLES	IMMERSIBLE	IMMOLATORS	IMMUNOLOGICALLY	IMPASSIBLE	IMPERCEPTIVE
IMINAZOLES	IMMERSIONISM	IMMOMENTOUS	IMMUNOLOGIES	IMPASSIBLENESS	IMPERCEPTIVELY
IMINOUREAS	IMMERSIONISMS	IMMORALISM	IMMUNOLOGIST	IMPASSIBLY	IMPERCEPTIVITY
IMIPRAMINE	IMMERSIONIST	IMMORALISMS	IMMUNOLOGISTS	IMPASSIONATE	IMPERCIPIENCE
IMIPRAMINES	IMMERSIONISTS	IMMORALIST	IMMUNOLOGY	IMPASSIONED	IMPERCIPIENCES
IMITABILITIES	IMMERSIONS	IMMORALISTS	IMMUNOMODULATOR	IMPASSIONEDLY	IMPERCIPIENT
IMITABILITY	IMMETHODICAL	IMMORALITIES	IMMUNOPATHOLOGY	IMPASSIONEDNESS	IMPERFECTIBLE
IMITABLENESS	IMMETHODICALLY	IMMORALITY	IMMUNOPHORESES	IMPASSIONING	IMPERFECTION
IMITABLENESSES	IMMIGRANTS	IMMORTALISATION	IMMUNOPHORESIS	IMPASSIONS	IMPERFECTIONS
IMITANCIES	IMMIGRATED	IMMORTALISE	IMMUNOREACTION	IMPASSIVELY	IMPERFECTIVE
IMITATIONAL	IMMIGRATES	IMMORTALISED	IMMUNOREACTIONS	IMPASSIVENESS	IMPERFECTIVELY
IMITATIONS	IMMIGRATING	IMMORTALISER	IMMUNOREACTIVE	IMPASSIVENESSES	IMPERFECTIVES
IMITATIVELY	IMMIGRATION	IMMORTALISERS	IMMUNOSORBENT	IMPASSIVITIES	IMPERFECTLY
IMITATIVENESS	IMMIGRATIONAL	IMMORTALISES	IMMUNOSORBENTS	IMPASSIVITY	IMPERFECTNESS
IMITATIVENESSES	IMMIGRATIONS	IMMORTALISING	IMMUNOSUPPRESS	IMPASTATION	IMPERFECTNESSES
IMMACULACIES	IMMIGRATOR	IMMORTALITIES	IMMUNOTHERAPIES	IMPASTATIONS	IMPERFECTS
IMMACULACY	IMMIGRATORS	IMMORTALITY	IMMUNOTHERAPY	IMPATIENCE	IMPERFORABLE
IMMACULATE	IMMIGRATORY	IMMORTALIZATION	IMMUNOTOXIC	IMPATIENCES	IMPERFORATE
IMMACULATELY	IMMINENCES	IMMORTALIZE	IMMUNOTOXIN	IMPATIENTLY	IMPERFORATED
IMMACULATENESS	IMMINENCIES	IMMORTALIZED	IMMUNOTOXINS	IMPEACHABILITY	IMPERFORATION
IMMANACLED	IMMINENTLY	IMMORTALIZER	IMMUREMENT	IMPEACHABLE	IMPERFORATIONS
IMMANACLES	IMMINENTNESS	IMMORTALIZERS	IMMUREMENTS	IMPEACHERS	IMPERIALISE

IMPERIALISED	IMPETIGINES	IMPLORATOR	IMPOSTUMATION	IMPRESSMENTS	IMPUDENTNESS
IMPERIALISES	IMPETIGINOUS	IMPLORATORS	IMPOSTUMATIONS	IMPRESSURE	IMPUDENTNESSES
IMPERIALISING	IMPETRATED	IMPLORATORY	IMPOSTUMED	IMPRESSURES	IMPUDICITIES
IMPERIALISM	IMPETRATES	IMPLORINGLY	IMPOSTUMES	IMPRIMATUR	IMPUDICITY
IMPERIALISMS	IMPETRATING	IMPLOSIONS	IMPOSTURES	IMPRIMATURS	IMPUGNABLE
IMPERIALIST	IMPETRATION	IMPLOSIVELY	IMPOSTUROUS	IMPRINTERS	IMPUGNATION
IMPERIALISTIC	IMPETRATIONS	IMPLOSIVES	IMPOTENCES	IMPRINTING	IMPUGNATIONS
IMPERIALISTS	IMPETRATIVE	IMPLUNGING	IMPOTENCIES	IMPRINTINGS	IMPUGNMENT
IMPERIALITIES	IMPETRATOR	IMPOCKETED	IMPOTENTLY	IMPRISONABLE	IMPUGNMENTS
IMPERIALITY	IMPETRATORS	IMPOCKETING	IMPOTENTNESS	IMPRISONED	IMPUISSANCE
IMPERIALIZE	IMPETRATORY	IMPOLDERED	IMPOTENTNESSES	IMPRISONER	IMPUISSANCES
IMPERIALIZED	IMPETUOSITIES	IMPOLDERING	IMPOUNDABLE	IMPRISONERS	IMPUISSANT
IMPERIALIZES	IMPETUOSITY	IMPOLICIES	IMPOUNDAGE	IMPRISONING	IMPULSIONS
IMPERIALIZING	IMPETUOUSLY	IMPOLITELY	IMPOUNDAGES	IMPRISONMENT	IMPULSIVELY
IMPERIALLY	IMPETUOUSNESS	IMPOLITENESS	IMPOUNDERS	IMPRISONMENTS	IMPULSIVENESS
IMPERIALNESS	IMPETUOUSNESSES	IMPOLITENESSES	IMPOUNDING	IMPROBABILITIES	IMPULSIVENESSES
IMPERIALNESSES	IMPICTURED	IMPOLITEST	IMPOUNDMENT	IMPROBABILITY	IMPULSIVITIES
IMPERILING	IMPIERCEABLE	IMPOLITICAL	IMPOUNDMENTS	IMPROBABLE	IMPULSIVITY
IMPERILLED	IMPIGNORATE	IMPOLITICALLY	IMPOVERISH	IMPROBABLENESS	IMPUNDULUS
IMPERILLING	IMPIGNORATED	IMPOLITICLY	IMPOVERISHED	IMPROBABLY	IMPUNITIES
IMPERILMENT	IMPIGNORATES	IMPOLITICNESS	IMPOVERISHER	IMPROBATION	IMPURENESS
IMPERILMENTS	IMPIGNORATING	IMPOLITICNESSES	IMPOVERISHERS	IMPROBATIONS	IMPURENESSES
IMPERIOUSLY	IMPIGNORATION	IMPONDERABILIA	IMPOVERISHES	IMPROBITIES	IMPURITIES
IMPERIOUSNESS	IMPIGNORATIONS	IMPONDERABILITY	IMPOVERISHING	IMPROMPTUS	IMPURPLING
IMPERIOUSNESSES	IMPINGEMENT	IMPONDERABLE	IMPOVERISHMENT	IMPROPERLY	IMPUTABILITIES
IMPERISHABILITY	IMPINGEMENTS	IMPONDERABLES	IMPOVERISHMENTS	IMPROPERNESS	IMPUTABILITY
IMPERISHABLE	IMPIOUSNESS	IMPONDERABLY	IMPOWERING	IMPROPERNESSES	IMPUTABLENESS
IMPERISHABLES	IMPIOUSNESSES	IMPONDEROUS	IMPRACTICABLE	IMPROPRIATE	IMPUTABLENESSES
IMPERISHABLY	IMPISHNESS	IMPORTABILITIES	IMPRACTICABLY	IMPROPRIATED	IMPUTATION
IMPERMANENCE	IMPISHNESSES	IMPORTABILITY	IMPRACTICAL	IMPROPRIATES	IMPUTATIONS
IMPERMANENCES	IMPLACABILITIES	IMPORTABLE	IMPRACTICALITY	IMPROPRIATING	IMPUTATIVE
IMPERMANENCIES	IMPLACABILITY	IMPORTANCE	IMPRACTICALLY	IMPROPRIATION	IMPUTATIVELY
IMPERMANENCY	IMPLACABLE	IMPORTANCES	IMPRACTICALNESS	IMPROPRIATIONS	INABILITIES
IMPERMANENT	IMPLACABLENESS	IMPORTANCIES	IMPRECATED	IMPROPRIATOR	INABSTINENCE
IMPERMANENTLY	IMPLACABLY	IMPORTANCY	IMPRECATES	IMPROPRIATORS	INABSTINENCES
IMPERMEABILITY	IMPLACENTAL	IMPORTANTLY	IMPRECATING	IMPROPRIETIES	INACCESSIBILITY
IMPERMEABLE	IMPLANTABLE	IMPORTATION	IMPRECATION	IMPROPRIETY	INACCESSIBLE
IMPERMEABLENESS	IMPLANTATION	IMPORTATIONS	IMPRECATIONS	IMPROVABILITIES	INACCESSIBLY
IMPERMEABLY	IMPLANTATIONS	IMPORTINGS	IMPRECATORY	IMPROVABILITY	INACCURACIES
IMPERMISSIBLE	IMPLANTERS	IMPORTUNACIES	IMPRECISELY	IMPROVABLE	INACCURACY
IMPERMISSIBLY	IMPLANTING	IMPORTUNACY	IMPRECISENESS	IMPROVABLENESS	INACCURATE
IMPERSCRIPTIBLE	IMPLAUSIBILITY	IMPORTUNATE	IMPRECISENESSES	IMPROVABLY	INACCURATELY
IMPERSEVERANT	IMPLAUSIBLE	IMPORTUNATELY	IMPRECISION	IMPROVEMENT	INACCURATENESS
IMPERSISTENT	IMPLAUSIBLENESS	IMPORTUNATENESS	IMPRECISIONS	IMPROVEMENTS	INACTIVATE
IMPERSONAL	IMPLAUSIBLY	IMPORTUNED	IMPREDICATIVE	IMPROVIDENCE	INACTIVATED
IMPERSONALISE	IMPLEACHED	IMPORTUNELY	IMPREGNABILITY	IMPROVIDENCES	INACTIVATES
IMPERSONALISED	IMPLEACHES	IMPORTUNER	IMPREGNABLE	IMPROVIDENT	INACTIVATING
IMPERSONALISES	IMPLEACHING	IMPORTUNERS	IMPREGNABLENESS	IMPROVIDENTLY	INACTIVATION
IMPERSONALISING	IMPLEADABLE	IMPORTUNES	IMPREGNABLY	IMPROVINGLY	INACTIVATIONS
IMPERSONALITIES	IMPLEADERS	IMPORTUNING	IMPREGNANT	IMPROVISATE	INACTIVELY
IMPERSONALITY	IMPLEADING	IMPORTUNINGS	IMPREGNANTS	IMPROVISATED	INACTIVENESS
IMPERSONALIZE	IMPLEDGING	IMPORTUNITIES	IMPREGNATABLE	IMPROVISATES	INACTIVENESSES
IMPERSONALIZED	IMPLEMENTAL	IMPORTUNITY	IMPREGNATE	IMPROVISATING	INACTIVITIES
IMPERSONALIZES	IMPLEMENTATION	IMPOSINGLY	IMPREGNATED	IMPROVISATION	INACTIVITY
IMPERSONALIZING	IMPLEMENTATIONS	IMPOSINGNESS	IMPREGNATES	IMPROVISATIONAL	INADAPTABLE
IMPERSONALLY	IMPLEMENTED	IMPOSINGNESSES	IMPREGNATING	IMPROVISATIONS	INADAPTATION
IMPERSONATE	IMPLEMENTER	IMPOSITION	IMPREGNATION	IMPROVISATOR	INADAPTATIONS
IMPERSONATED	IMPLEMENTERS	IMPOSITIONS	IMPREGNATIONS	IMPROVISATORE	INADAPTIVE
IMPERSONATES	IMPLEMENTING	IMPOSSIBILISM	IMPREGNATOR	IMPROVISATORES	INADEQUACIES
IMPERSONATING	IMPLEMENTOR	IMPOSSIBILISMS	IMPREGNATORS	IMPROVISATORI	INADEQUACY
IMPERSONATION	IMPLEMENTORS	IMPOSSIBILIST	IMPREGNING	IMPROVISATORIAL	INADEQUATE
IMPERSONATIONS	IMPLEMENTS	IMPOSSIBILISTS	IMPRESARIO	IMPROVISATORS	INADEQUATELY
IMPERSONATOR	IMPLETIONS	IMPOSSIBILITIES	IMPRESARIOS	IMPROVISATORY	INADEQUATENESS
IMPERSONATORS	IMPLEXIONS	IMPOSSIBILITY	IMPRESCRIPTIBLE	IMPROVISATRICES	INADEQUATES
IMPERTINENCE	IMPLEXUOUS	IMPOSSIBLE	IMPRESCRIPTIBLY	IMPROVISATRIX	INADMISSIBILITY
IMPERTINENCES	IMPLICATED	IMPOSSIBLENESS	IMPRESSERS	IMPROVISATRIXES	INADMISSIBLE
IMPERTINENCIES	IMPLICATES	IMPOSSIBLES	IMPRESSIBILITY	IMPROVISED	INADMISSIBLY
IMPERTINENCY	IMPLICATING	IMPOSSIBLY	IMPRESSIBLE	IMPROVISER	INADVERTENCE
IMPERTINENT	IMPLICATION	IMPOSTHUMATE	IMPRESSING	IMPROVISERS	INADVERTENCES
IMPERTINENTLY	IMPLICATIONAL	IMPOSTHUMATED	IMPRESSION	IMPROVISES	INADVERTENCIES
IMPERTURBABLE	IMPLICATIONS	IMPOSTHUMATES	IMPRESSIONABLE	IMPROVISING	INADVERTENCY
IMPERTURBABLY	IMPLICATIVE	IMPOSTHUMATION	IMPRESSIONAL	IMPROVISOR	INADVERTENT
IMPERTURBATION	IMPLICATIVELY	IMPOSTHUMATIONS	IMPRESSIONALLY	IMPROVISORS	INADVERTENTLY
IMPERTURBATIONS	IMPLICATIVENESS	IMPOSTHUME	IMPRESSIONISM	IMPROVVISATORE	INADVISABILITY
IMPERVIABILITY	IMPLICATURE	IMPOSTHUMED	IMPRESSIONISMS	IMPROVVISATORES	INADVISABLE
IMPERVIABLE	IMPLICATURES	IMPOSTHUMES	IMPRESSIONIST	IMPROVVISATRICE	INADVISABLENESS
IMPERVIABLENESS	IMPLICITIES	IMPOSTOROUS	IMPRESSIONISTIC	IMPRUDENCE	INADVISABLY
IMPERVIOUS	IMPLICITLY	IMPOSTROUS	IMPRESSIONISTS	IMPRUDENCES	INALIENABILITY
IMPERVIOUSLY	IMPLICITNESS	IMPOSTUMATE	IMPRESSIONS	IMPRUDENTLY	INALIENABLE
IMPERVIOUSNESS	IMPLICITNESSES	IMPOSTUMATED	IMPRESSIVE	IMPSONITES	INALIENABLENESS
IMPETICOSSED	IMPLODENTS	IMPOSTUMATES	IMPRESSIVELY	IMPUDENCES	INALIENABLY
IMPETICOSSES	IMPLORATION	IMPOSTUMATING	IMPRESSIVENESS	IMPUDENCIES	INALTERABILITY
IMPETICOSSING	IMPLORATIONS	IMPOSTUMATING	IMPRESSMENT	IMPUDENTLY	INALTERABLE

INALTERABLENESS	INBREEDING	INCEDINGLY	INCLEMENCY	INCOMPETENCES	INCONSTANCIES
INALTERABLY	INBREEDINGS	INCENDIARIES	INCLEMENTLY	INCOMPETENCIES	INCONSTANCY
INAMORATAS	INBRINGING	INCENDIARISM	INCLEMENTNESS	INCOMPETENCY	INCONSTANT
INAMORATOS	INBRINGINGS	INCENDIARISMS	INCLEMENTNESSES	INCOMPETENT	INCONSTANTLY
INANENESSES	INCALCULABILITY	INCENDIARY	INCLINABLE	INCOMPETENTLY	INCONSTRUABLE
INANIMATELY	INCALCULABLE	INCENDIVITIES	INCLINABLENESS	INCOMPETENTS	INCONSUMABLE
INANIMATENESS	INCALCULABLY	INCENDIVITY	INCLINATION	INCOMPLETE	INCONSUMABLY
INANIMATENESSES	INCALESCENCE	INCENSATION	INCLINATIONAL	INCOMPLETELY	INCONTESTABLE
INANIMATION	INCALESCENCES	INCENSATIONS	INCLINATIONS	INCOMPLETENESS	INCONTESTABLY
INANIMATIONS	INCALESCENT	INCENSEMENT	INCLINATORIA	INCOMPLETION	INCONTIGUOUS
INANITIONS	INCANDESCE	INCENSEMENTS	INCLINATORIUM	INCOMPLETIONS	INCONTIGUOUSLY
INAPPARENT	INCANDESCED	INCENSORIES	INCLINATORY	INCOMPLIANCE	INCONTINENCE
INAPPARENTLY	INCANDESCENCE	INCENTIVELY	INCLININGS	INCOMPLIANCES	INCONTINENCES
INAPPEASABLE	INCANDESCENCES	INCENTIVES	INCLINOMETER	INCOMPLIANCIES	INCONTINENCIES
INAPPELLABLE	INCANDESCENCIES	INCENTIVISATION	INCLINOMETERS	INCOMPLIANCY	INCONTINENCY
INAPPETENCE	INCANDESCENCY	INCENTIVISE	INCLIPPING	INCOMPLIANT	INCONTINENT
INAPPETENCES	INCANDESCENT	INCENTIVISED	INCLOSABLE	INCOMPLIANTLY	INCONTINENTLY
INAPPETENCIES	INCANDESCENTLY	INCENTIVISES	INCLOSURES	INCOMPOSED	INCONTROLLABLE
INAPPETENCY	INCANDESCENTS	INCENTIVISING	INCLUDABLE	INCOMPOSITE	INCONTROLLABLY
INAPPETENT	INCANDESCES	INCENTIVIZATION	INCLUDEDNESS	INCOMPOSSIBLE	INCONVENIENCE
INAPPLICABILITY	INCANDESCING	INCENTIVIZE	INCLUDEDNESSES	INCOMPREHENSION	INCONVENIENCED
INAPPLICABLE	INCANTATION	INCENTIVIZED	INCLUDIBLE	INCOMPREHENSIVE	INCONVENIENCES
INAPPLICABLY	INCANTATIONAL	INCENTIVIZES	INCLUSIONS	INCOMPRESSIBLE	INCONVENIENCIES
INAPPOSITE	INCANTATIONS	INCENTIVIZING	INCLUSIVELY	INCOMPRESSIBLY	INCONVENIENCING
INAPPOSITELY	INCANTATOR	INCEPTIONS	INCLUSIVENESS	INCOMPUTABILITY	INCONVENIENCY
INAPPOSITENESS	INCANTATORS	INCEPTIVELY	INCLUSIVENESSES	INCOMPUTABLE	INCONVENIENT
INAPPRECIABLE	INCANTATORY	INCEPTIVES	INCLUSIVITIES	INCOMPUTABLY	INCONVENIENTLY
INAPPRECIABLY	INCAPABILITIES	INCERTAINTIES	INCLUSIVITY	INCOMUNICADO	INCONVERSABLE
INAPPRECIATION	INCAPABILITY	INCERTAINTY	INCOAGULABLE	INCONCEIVABLE	INCONVERSANT
INAPPRECIATIONS	INCAPABLENESS	INCERTITUDE	INCOERCIBLE	INCONCEIVABLES	INCONVERTIBLE
INAPPRECIATIVE	INCAPABLENESSES	INCERTITUDES	INCOGITABILITY	INCONCEIVABLY	INCONVERTIBLY
INAPPREHENSIBLE	INCAPABLES	INCESSANCIES	INCOGITABLE	INCONCINNITIES	INCONVINCIBLE
INAPPREHENSION	INCAPACIOUS	INCESSANCY	INCOGITANCIES	INCONCINNITY	INCONVINCIBLY
INAPPREHENSIONS	INCAPACIOUSNESS	INCESSANTLY	INCOGITANCY	INCONCINNOUS	INCOORDINATE
INAPPREHENSIVE	INCAPACITANT	INCESSANTNESS	INCOGITANT	INCONCLUSION	INCOORDINATION
INAPPROACHABLE	INCAPACITANTS	INCESSANTNESSES	INCOGITATIVE	INCONCLUSIONS	INCOORDINATIONS
INAPPROACHABLY	INCAPACITATE	INCESTUOUS	INCOGNISABLE	INCONCLUSIVE	INCORONATE
INAPPROPRIATE	INCAPACITATED	INCESTUOUSLY	INCOGNISANCE	INCONCLUSIVELY	INCORONATED
INAPPROPRIATELY	INCAPACITATES	INCESTUOUSNESS	INCOGNISANCES	INCONDENSABLE	INCORONATION
INAPTITUDE	INCAPACITATING	INCHARITABLE	INCOGNISANT	INCONDENSIBLE	INCORONATIONS
INAPTITUDES	INCAPACITATION	INCHOATELY	INCOGNITAS	INCONDITELY	INCORPORABLE
INAPTNESSES	INCAPACITATIONS	INCHOATENESS	INCOGNITOS	INCONFORMITIES	INCORPORAL
INARGUABLE	INCAPACITIES	INCHOATENESSES	INCOGNIZABLE	INCONFORMITY	INCORPORALL
INARGUABLY	INCAPACITY	INCHOATING	INCOGNIZANCE	INCONGRUENCE	INCORPORATE
INARTICULACIES	INCAPSULATE	INCHOATION	INCOGNIZANCES	INCONGRUENCES	INCORPORATED
INARTICULACY	INCAPSULATED	INCHOATIONS	INCOGNIZANT	INCONGRUENT	INCORPORATES
INARTICULATE	INCAPSULATES	INCHOATIVE	INCOHERENCE	INCONGRUENTLY	INCORPORATING
INARTICULATELY	INCAPSULATING	INCHOATIVELY	INCOHERENCES	INCONGRUITIES	INCORPORATION
INARTICULATES	INCAPSULATION	INCHOATIVES	INCOHERENCIES	INCONGRUITY	INCORPORATIONS
INARTICULATION	INCAPSULATIONS	INCIDENCES	INCOHERENCY	INCONGRUOUS	INCORPORATIVE
INARTICULATIONS	INCARCERATE	INCIDENTAL	INCOHERENT	INCONGRUOUSLY	INCORPORATOR
INARTIFICIAL	INCARCERATED	INCIDENTALLY	INCOHERENTLY	INCONGRUOUSNESS	INCORPORATORS
INARTIFICIALLY	INCARCERATES	INCIDENTALNESS	INCOHERENTNESS	INCONSCIENT	INCORPOREAL
INARTISTIC	INCARCERATING	INCIDENTALS	INCOMBUSTIBLE	INCONSCIENTLY	INCORPOREALITY
INARTISTICALLY	INCARCERATION	INCINERATE	INCOMBUSTIBLES	INCONSCIONABLE	INCORPOREALLY
INATTENTION	INCARCERATIONS	INCINERATED	INCOMBUSTIBLY	INCONSCIOUS	INCORPOREITIES
INATTENTIONS	INCARCERATOR	INCINERATES	INCOMMENSURABLE	INCONSECUTIVE	INCORPOREITY
INATTENTIVE	INCARCERATORS	INCINERATING	INCOMMENSURABLY	INCONSECUTIVELY	INCORPSING
INATTENTIVELY	INCARDINATE	INCINERATION	INCOMMENSURATE	INCONSEQUENCE	INCORRECTLY
INATTENTIVENESS	INCARDINATED	INCINERATIONS	INCOMMISCIBLE	INCONSEQUENCES	INCORRECTNESS
INAUDIBILITIES	INCARDINATES	INCINERATOR	INCOMMODED	INCONSEQUENT	INCORRECTNESSES
INAUDIBILITY	INCARDINATING	INCINERATORS	INCOMMODES	INCONSEQUENTIAL	INCORRIGIBILITY
INAUDIBLENESS	INCARDINATION	INCIPIENCE	INCOMMODING	INCONSEQUENTLY	INCORRIGIBLE
INAUDIBLENESSES	INCARDINATIONS	INCIPIENCES	INCOMMODIOUS	INCONSIDERABLE	INCORRIGIBLES
INAUGURALS	INCARNADINE	INCIPIENCIES	INCOMMODIOUSLY	INCONSIDERABLY	INCORRIGIBLY
INAUGURATE	INCARNADINED	INCIPIENCY	INCOMMODITIES	INCONSIDERATE	INCORRODIBLE
INAUGURATED	INCARNADINES	INCIPIENTLY	INCOMMODITY	INCONSIDERATELY	INCORROSIBLE
INAUGURATES	INCARNADINING	INCISIFORM	INCOMMUNICABLE	INCONSIDERATION	INCORRUPTED
INAUGURATING	INCARNATED	INCISIVELY	INCOMMUNICABLY	INCONSISTENCE	INCORRUPTIBLE
INAUGURATION	INCARNATES	INCISIVENESS	INCOMMUNICADO	INCONSISTENCES	INCORRUPTIBLES
INAUGURATIONS	INCARNATING	INCISIVENESSES	INCOMMUNICATIVE	INCONSISTENCIES	INCORRUPTIBLY
INAUGURATOR	INCARNATION	INCISORIAL	INCOMMUTABILITY	INCONSISTENCY	INCORRUPTION
INAUGURATORS	INCARNATIONS	INCITATION	INCOMMUTABLE	INCONSISTENT	INCORRUPTIONS
INAUGURATORY	INCARVILLEA	INCITATIONS	INCOMMUTABLY	INCONSISTENTLY	INCORRUPTIVE
INAUSPICIOUS	INCARVILLEAS	INCITATIVE	INCOMPARABILITY	INCONSOLABILITY	INCORRUPTLY
INAUSPICIOUSLY	INCASEMENT	INCITATIVES	INCOMPARABLE	INCONSOLABLE	INCORRUPTNESS
INAUTHENTIC	INCASEMENTS	INCITEMENT	INCOMPARABLY	INCONSOLABLY	INCORRUPTNESSES
INAUTHENTICITY	INCATENATION	INCITEMENTS	INCOMPARED	INCONSONANCE	INCRASSATE
INBOUNDING	INCATENATIONS	INCITINGLY	INCOMPATIBILITY	INCONSONANCES	INCRASSATED
INBREATHED	INCAUTIONS	INCIVILITIES	INCOMPATIBLE	INCONSONANT	INCRASSATES
INBREATHES	INCAUTIOUS	INCIVILITY	INCOMPATIBLES	INCONSONANTLY	INCRASSATING
INBREATHING	INCAUTIOUSLY	INCLASPING	INCOMPATIBLY	INCONSPICUOUS	INCRASSATION
INBREEDERS	INCAUTIOUSNESS	INCLEMENCIES	INCOMPETENCE	INCONSPICUOUSLY	INCRASSATIONS

INCRASSATIVE	INCULPATIVE	INDEFINABLES	INDICTIONS	INDISPOSEDNESS	INDOMITABLE
INCREASABLE	INCULPATORY	INDEFINABLY	INDICTMENT	INDISPOSES	INDOMITABLENESS
INCREASEDLY	INCUMBENCIES	INDEFINITE	INDICTMENTS	INDISPOSING	INDOMITABLY
INCREASEFUL	INCUMBENCY	INDEFINITELY	INDIFFERENCE	INDISPOSITION	INDOPHENOL
INCREASERS	INCUMBENTLY	INDEFINITENESS	INDIFFERENCES	INDISPOSITIONS	INDOPHENOLS
INCREASING	INCUMBENTS	INDEFINITES	INDIFFERENCIES	INDISPUTABILITY	INDORSABLE
INCREASINGLY	INCUMBERED	INDEHISCENCE	INDIFFERENCY	INDISPUTABLE	INDORSEMENT
INCREASINGS	INCUMBERING	INDEHISCENCES	INDIFFERENT	INDISPUTABLY	INDORSEMENTS
INCREATELY	INCUMBERINGLY	INDEHISCENT	INDIFFERENTISM	INDISSOCIABLE	INDRAUGHTS
INCREDIBILITIES	INCUMBRANCE	INDELIBILITIES	INDIFFERENTISMS	INDISSOCIABLY	INDRENCHED
INCREDIBILITY	INCUMBRANCES	INDELIBILITY	INDIFFERENTIST	INDISSOLUBILITY	INDRENCHES
INCREDIBLE	INCUNABLES	INDELIBLENESS	INDIFFERENTISTS	INDISSOLUBLE	INDRENCHING
INCREDIBLENESS	INCUNABULA	INDELIBLENESSES	INDIFFERENTLY	INDISSOLUBLY	INDUBITABILITY
INCREDIBLY	INCUNABULAR	INDELICACIES	INDIFFERENTS	INDISSOLVABLE	INDUBITABLE
INCREDULITIES	INCUNABULIST	INDELICACY	INDIGENCES	INDISSUADABLE	INDUBITABLENESS
INCREDULITY	INCUNABULISTS	INDELICATE	INDIGENCIES	INDISSUADABLY	INDUBITABLY
INCREDULOUS	INCUNABULUM	INDELICATELY	INDIGENISATION	INDISTINCT	INDUCEMENT
INCREDULOUSLY	INCURABILITIES	INDELICATENESS	INDIGENISATIONS	INDISTINCTION	INDUCEMENTS
INCREDULOUSNESS	INCURABILITY	INDEMNIFICATION	INDIGENISE	INDISTINCTIONS	INDUCIBILITIES
INCREMATED	INCURABLENESS	INDEMNIFIED	INDIGENISED	INDISTINCTIVE	INDUCIBILITY
INCREMATES	INCURABLENESSES	INDEMNIFIER	INDIGENISES	INDISTINCTIVELY	INDUCTANCE
INCREMATING	INCURABLES	INDEMNIFIERS	INDIGENISING	INDISTINCTLY	INDUCTANCES
INCREMATION	INCURIOSITIES	INDEMNIFIES	INDIGENITIES	INDISTINCTNESS	INDUCTILITIES
INCREMATIONS	INCURIOSITY	INDEMNIFYING	INDIGENITY	INDISTRIBUTABLE	INDUCTILITY
INCREMENTAL	INCURIOUSLY	INDEMNITIES	INDIGENIZATION	INDITEMENT	INDUCTIONAL
INCREMENTALISM	INCURIOUSNESS	INDEMONSTRABLE	INDIGENIZATIONS	INDITEMENTS	INDUCTIONS
INCREMENTALISMS	INCURIOUSNESSES	INDEMONSTRABLY	INDIGENIZE	INDIVERTIBLE	INDUCTIVELY
INCREMENTALIST	INCURRABLE	INDENTATION	INDIGENIZED	INDIVERTIBLY	INDUCTIVENESS
INCREMENTALISTS	INCURRENCE	INDENTATIONS	INDIGENIZES	INDIVIDABLE	INDUCTIVENESSES
INCREMENTALLY	INCURRENCES	INDENTIONS	INDIGENIZING	INDIVIDUAL	INDUCTIVITIES
INCREMENTALS	INCURSIONS	INDENTURED	INDIGENOUS	INDIVIDUALISE	INDUCTIVITY
INCREMENTED	INCURVATED	INDENTURES	INDIGENOUSLY	INDIVIDUALISED	INDULGENCE
INCREMENTING	INCURVATES	INDENTURESHIP	INDIGENOUSNESS	INDIVIDUALISER	INDULGENCED
INCREMENTS	INCURVATING	INDENTURESHIPS	INDIGENTLY	INDIVIDUALISERS	INDULGENCES
INCRESCENT	INCURVATION	INDENTURING	INDIGESTED	INDIVIDUALISES	INDULGENCIES
INCRETIONARY	INCURVATIONS	INDEPENDENCE	INDIGESTIBILITY	INDIVIDUALISING	INDULGENCING
INCRETIONS	INCURVATURE	INDEPENDENCES	INDIGESTIBLE	INDIVIDUALISM	INDULGENCY
INCRIMINATE	INCURVATURES	INDEPENDENCIES	INDIGESTIBLES	INDIVIDUALISMS	INDULGENTLY
INCRIMINATED	INCURVITIES	INDEPENDENCY	INDIGESTIBLY	INDIVIDUALIST	INDULGINGLY
INCRIMINATES	INDAGATING	INDEPENDENT	INDIGESTION	INDIVIDUALISTIC	INDUMENTUM
INCRIMINATING	INDAGATION	INDEPENDENTLY	INDIGESTIONS	INDIVIDUALISTS	INDUMENTUMS
INCRIMINATION	INDAGATIONS	INDEPENDENTS	INDIGESTIVE	INDIVIDUALITIES	INDUPLICATE
INCRIMINATIONS	INDAGATIVE	INDESCRIBABLE	INDIGNANCE	INDIVIDUALITY	INDUPLICATED
INCRIMINATOR	INDAGATORS	INDESCRIBABLES	INDIGNANCES	INDIVIDUALIZE	INDUPLICATION
INCRIMINATORS	INDAGATORY	INDESCRIBABLY	INDIGNANTLY	INDIVIDUALIZED	INDUPLICATIONS
INCRIMINATORY	INDAPAMIDE	INDESIGNATE	INDIGNATION	INDIVIDUALIZER	INDURATING
INCROSSBRED	INDAPAMIDES	INDESTRUCTIBLE	INDIGNATIONS	INDIVIDUALIZERS	INDURATION
INCROSSBREDS	INDEBTEDNESS	INDESTRUCTIBLY	INDIGNIFIED	INDIVIDUALIZES	INDURATIONS
INCROSSBREED	INDEBTEDNESSES	INDETECTABLE	INDIGNIFIES	INDIVIDUALIZING	INDURATIVE
INCROSSBREEDING	INDECENCIES	INDETECTIBLE	INDIGNIFYING	INDIVIDUALLY	INDUSTRIAL
INCROSSBREEDS	INDECENTER	INDETERMINABLE	INDIGNITIES	INDIVIDUALS	INDUSTRIALISE
INCROSSING	INDECENTEST	INDETERMINABLY	INDIGOLITE	INDIVIDUATE	INDUSTRIALISED
INCRUSTANT	INDECENTLY	INDETERMINACIES	INDIGOLITES	INDIVIDUATED	INDUSTRIALISES
INCRUSTANTS	INDECIDUATE	INDETERMINACY	INDIGOTINS	INDIVIDUATES	INDUSTRIALISING
INCRUSTATION	INDECIDUOUS	INDETERMINATE	INDINAVIRS	INDIVIDUATING	INDUSTRIALISM
INCRUSTATIONS	INDECIPHERABLE	INDETERMINATELY	INDIRECTION	INDIVIDUATION	INDUSTRIALISMS
INCRUSTING	INDECIPHERABLY	INDETERMINATION	INDIRECTIONS	INDIVIDUATIONS	INDUSTRIALIST
INCUBATING	INDECISION	INDETERMINED	INDIRECTLY	INDIVIDUATOR	INDUSTRIALISTS
INCUBATION	INDECISIONS	INDETERMINISM	INDIRECTNESS	INDIVIDUATORS	INDUSTRIALIZE
INCUBATIONAL	INDECISIVE	INDETERMINISMS	INDIRECTNESSES	INDIVIDUUM	INDUSTRIALIZED
INCUBATIONS	INDECISIVELY	INDETERMINIST	INDIRUBINS	INDIVISIBILITY	INDUSTRIALIZES
INCUBATIVE	INDECISIVENESS	INDETERMINISTIC	INDISCERNIBLE	INDIVISIBLE	INDUSTRIALIZING
INCUBATORS	INDECLINABLE	INDETERMINISTS	INDISCERNIBLY	INDIVISIBLENESS	INDUSTRIALLY
INCUBATORY	INDECLINABLY	INDEXATION	INDISCERPTIBLE	INDIVISIBLES	INDUSTRIALS
INCULCATED	INDECOMPOSABLE	INDEXATIONS	INDISCIPLINABLE	INDIVISIBLY	INDUSTRIES
INCULCATES	INDECOROUS	INDEXICALS	INDISCIPLINE	INDOCILITIES	INDUSTRIOUS
INCULCATING	INDECOROUSLY	INDEXTERITIES	INDISCIPLINED	INDOCILITY	INDUSTRIOUSLY
INCULCATION	INDECOROUSNESS	INDEXTERITY	INDISCIPLINES	INDOCTRINATE	INDUSTRIOUSNESS
INCULCATIONS	INDECORUMS	INDICATABLE	INDISCOVERABLE	INDOCTRINATED	INDUSTRYWIDE
INCULCATIVE	INDEFATIGABLE	INDICATING	INDISCREET	INDOCTRINATES	INDWELLERS
INCULCATOR	INDEFATIGABLY	INDICATION	INDISCREETLY	INDOCTRINATING	INDWELLING
INCULCATORS	INDEFEASIBILITY	INDICATIONAL	INDISCREETNESS	INDOCTRINATION	INDWELLINGS
INCULCATORY	INDEFEASIBLE	INDICATIONS	INDISCRETE	INDOCTRINATIONS	INEARTHING
INCULPABILITIES	INDEFEASIBLY	INDICATIVE	INDISCRETELY	INDOCTRINATOR	INEBRIANTS
INCULPABILITY	INDEFECTIBILITY	INDICATIVELY	INDISCRETENESS	INDOCTRINATORS	INEBRIATED
INCULPABLE	INDEFECTIBLE	INDICATIVES	INDISCRETION	INDOLEACETIC	INEBRIATES
INCULPABLENESS	INDEFECTIBLY	INDICATORS	INDISCRETIONARY	INDOLEBUTYRIC	INEBRIATING
INCULPABLY	INDEFENSIBILITY	INDICATORY	INDISCRETIONS	INDOLENCES	INEBRIATION
INCULPATED	INDEFENSIBLE	INDICOLITE	INDISCRIMINATE	INDOLENCIES	INEBRIATIONS
INCULPATES	INDEFENSIBLY	INDICOLITES	INDISPENSABLE	INDOLENTLY	INEBRIETIES
INCULPATING	INDEFINABILITY	INDICTABLE	INDISPENSABLES	INDOMETHACIN	INEDIBILITIES
INCULPATION	INDEFINABLE	INDICTABLY	INDISPENSABLY	INDOMETHACINS	INEDIBILITY
INCULPATIONS	INDEFINABLENESS	INDICTIONAL	INDISPOSED	INDOMITABILITY	INEDUCABILITIES

INEDUCABILITY
INEDUCABLE
INEFFABILITIES
INEFFABILITY
INEFFABLENESS
INEFFABLENESSES
INEFFACEABILITY
INEFFACEABLE
INEFFACEABLY
INEFFECTIVE
INEFFECTIVELY
INEFFECTIVENESS
INEFFECTUAL
INEFFECTUALITY
INEFFECTUALLY
INEFFECTUALNESS
INEFFICACIES
INEFFICACIOUS
INEFFICACIOUSLY
INEFFICACITIES
INEFFICACITY
INEFFICACY
INEFFICIENCIES
INEFFICIENCY
INEFFICIENT
INEFFICIENTLY
INEFFICIENTS
INEGALITARIAN
INELABORATE
INELABORATELY
INELASTICALLY
INELASTICITIES
INELASTICITY
INELEGANCE
INELEGANCES
INELEGANCIES
INELEGANCY
INELEGANTLY
INELIGIBILITIES
INELIGIBILITY
INELIGIBLE
INELIGIBLENESS
INELIGIBLES
INELIGIBLY
INELOQUENCE
INELOQUENCES
INELOQUENT
INELOQUENTLY
INELUCTABILITY
INELUCTABLE
INELUCTABLY
INELUDIBILITIES
INELUDIBILITY
INELUDIBLE
INELUDIBLY
INENARRABLE
INEPTITUDE
INEPTITUDES
INEPTNESSES
INEQUALITIES
INEQUALITY
INEQUATION
INEQUATIONS
INEQUIPOTENT
INEQUITABLE
INEQUITABLENESS
INEQUITABLY
INEQUITIES
INEQUIVALVE
INEQUIVALVED
INERADICABILITY
INERADICABLE
INERADICABLY
INERASABLE
INERASABLY
INERASIBLE
INERASIBLY
INERRABILITIES
INERRABILITY
INERRABLENESS
INERRABLENESSES
INERRANCIES
INERTIALLY

INERTNESSES
INESCAPABLE
INESCAPABLY
INESCULENT
INESCUTCHEON
INESCUTCHEONS
INESSENTIAL
INESSENTIALITY
INESSENTIALS
INESTIMABILITY
INESTIMABLE
INESTIMABLENESS
INESTIMABLY
INEVITABILITIES
INEVITABILITY
INEVITABLE
INEVITABLENESS
INEVITABLY
INEXACTITUDE
INEXACTITUDES
INEXACTNESS
INEXACTNESSES
INEXCITABLE
INEXCUSABILITY
INEXCUSABLE
INEXCUSABLENESS
INEXCUSABLY
INEXECRABLE
INEXECUTABLE
INEXECUTION
INEXECUTIONS
INEXHAUSTED
INEXHAUSTIBLE
INEXHAUSTIBLY
INEXHAUSTIVE
INEXISTANT
INEXISTENCE
INEXISTENCES
INEXISTENCIES
INEXISTENCY
INEXISTENT
INEXORABILITIES
INEXORABILITY
INEXORABLE
INEXORABLENESS
INEXORABLY
INEXPANSIBLE
INEXPECTANCIES
INEXPECTANCY
INEXPECTANT
INEXPECTATION
INEXPECTATIONS
INEXPEDIENCE
INEXPEDIENCES
INEXPEDIENCIES
INEXPEDIENCY
INEXPEDIENT
INEXPEDIENTLY
INEXPENSIVE
INEXPENSIVELY
INEXPENSIVENESS
INEXPERIENCE
INEXPERIENCED
INEXPERIENCES
INEXPERTLY
INEXPERTNESS
INEXPERTNESSES
INEXPIABLE
INEXPIABLENESS
INEXPIABLY
INEXPLAINABLE
INEXPLAINABLY
INEXPLICABILITY
INEXPLICABLE
INEXPLICABLY
INEXPLICIT
INEXPLICITLY
INEXPLICITNESS
INEXPRESSIBLE
INEXPRESSIBLES
INEXPRESSIBLY
INEXPRESSIVE
INEXPRESSIVELY

INEXPUGNABILITY
INEXPUGNABLE
INEXPUGNABLY
INEXPUNGIBLE
INEXTENDED
INEXTENSIBILITY
INEXTENSIBLE
INEXTENSION
INEXTENSIONS
INEXTIRPABLE
INEXTRICABILITY
INEXTRICABLE
INEXTRICABLY
INFALLIBILISM
INFALLIBILISMS
INFALLIBILIST
INFALLIBILISTS
INFALLIBILITIES
INFALLIBILITY
INFALLIBLE
INFALLIBLENESS
INFALLIBLES
INFALLIBLY
INFAMISING
INFAMIZING
INFAMONISE
INFAMONISED
INFAMONISES
INFAMONISING
INFAMONIZE
INFAMONIZED
INFAMONIZES
INFAMONIZING
INFAMOUSLY
INFAMOUSNESS
INFAMOUSNESSES
INFANGTHIEF
INFANGTHIEFS
INFANTHOOD
INFANTHOODS
INFANTICIDAL
INFANTICIDE
INFANTICIDES
INFANTILISATION
INFANTILISE
INFANTILISED
INFANTILISES
INFANTILISING
INFANTILISM
INFANTILISMS
INFANTILITIES
INFANTILITY
INFANTILIZATION
INFANTILIZE
INFANTILIZED
INFANTILIZES
INFANTILIZING
INFANTRIES
INFANTRYMAN
INFANTRYMEN
INFARCTION
INFARCTIONS
INFATUATED
INFATUATEDLY
INFATUATES
INFATUATING
INFATUATION
INFATUATIONS
INFEASIBILITIES
INFEASIBILITY
INFEASIBLE
INFEASIBLENESS
INFECTIONS
INFECTIOUS
INFECTIOUSLY
INFECTIOUSNESS
INFECTIVELY
INFECTIVENESS
INFECTIVENESSES
INFECTIVITIES
INFECTIVITY
INFECUNDITIES
INFECUNDITY

INFEFTMENT
INFEFTMENTS
INFELICITIES
INFELICITOUS
INFELICITOUSLY
INFELICITY
INFEOFFING
INFERENCES
INFERENCING
INFERENCINGS
INFERENTIAL
INFERENTIALLY
INFERIORITIES
INFERIORITY
INFERIORLY
INFERNALITIES
INFERNALITY
INFERNALLY
INFERRABLE
INFERRIBLE
INFERTILELY
INFERTILITIES
INFERTILITY
INFESTANTS
INFESTATION
INFESTATIONS
INFEUDATION
INFEUDATIONS
INFIBULATE
INFIBULATED
INFIBULATES
INFIBULATING
INFIBULATION
INFIBULATIONS
INFIDELITIES
INFIDELITY
INFIELDERS
INFIELDSMAN
INFIELDSMEN
INFIGHTERS
INFIGHTING
INFIGHTINGS
INFILLINGS
INFILTRATE
INFILTRATED
INFILTRATES
INFILTRATING
INFILTRATION
INFILTRATIONS
INFILTRATIVE
INFILTRATOR
INFILTRATORS
INFINITANT
INFINITARY
INFINITATE
INFINITATED
INFINITATES
INFINITATING
INFINITELY
INFINITENESS
INFINITENESSES
INFINITESIMAL
INFINITESIMALLY
INFINITESIMALS
INFINITIES
INFINITIVAL
INFINITIVALLY
INFINITIVE
INFINITIVELY
INFINITIVES
INFINITUDE
INFINITUDES
INFIRMARER
INFIRMARERS
INFIRMARIAN
INFIRMARIANS
INFIRMARIES
INFIRMITIES
INFIRMNESS
INFIRMNESSES
INFIXATION
INFIXATIONS
INFLAMABLE

INFLAMINGLY
INFLAMMABILITY
INFLAMMABLE
INFLAMMABLENESS
INFLAMMABLES
INFLAMMABLY
INFLAMMATION
INFLAMMATIONS
INFLAMMATORILY
INFLAMMATORY
INFLATABLE
INFLATABLES
INFLATEDLY
INFLATEDNESS
INFLATEDNESSES
INFLATINGLY
INFLATIONARY
INFLATIONISM
INFLATIONISMS
INFLATIONIST
INFLATIONISTS
INFLATIONS
INFLATUSES
INFLECTABLE
INFLECTEDNESS
INFLECTEDNESSES
INFLECTING
INFLECTION
INFLECTIONAL
INFLECTIONALLY
INFLECTIONLESS
INFLECTIONS
INFLECTIVE
INFLECTORS
INFLEXIBILITIES
INFLEXIBILITY
INFLEXIBLE
INFLEXIBLENESS
INFLEXIBLY
INFLEXIONAL
INFLEXIONALLY
INFLEXIONLESS
INFLEXIONS
INFLEXURES
INFLICTABLE
INFLICTERS
INFLICTING
INFLICTION
INFLICTIONS
INFLICTIVE
INFLICTORS
INFLORESCENCE
INFLORESCENCES
INFLORESCENT
INFLOWINGS
INFLUENCEABLE
INFLUENCED
INFLUENCER
INFLUENCERS
INFLUENCES
INFLUENCING
INFLUENTIAL
INFLUENTIALLY
INFLUENTIALS
INFLUENZAL
INFLUENZAS
INFLUXIONS
INFOLDMENT
INFOLDMENTS
INFOMANIAS
INFOMERCIAL
INFOMERCIALS
INFOPRENEURIAL
INFORMABLE
INFORMALITIES
INFORMALITY
INFORMALLY
INFORMANTS
INFORMATICIAN
INFORMATICIANS
INFORMATICS
INFORMATION
INFORMATIONAL

INFORMATIONALLY
INFORMATIONS
INFORMATIVE
INFORMATIVELY
INFORMATIVENESS
INFORMATORILY
INFORMATORY
INFORMEDLY
INFORMIDABLE
INFORMINGLY
INFORTUNES
INFOSPHERE
INFOSPHERES
INFOTAINMENT
INFOTAINMENTS
INFRACOSTAL
INFRACTING
INFRACTION
INFRACTIONS
INFRACTORS
INFRAGRANT
INFRAHUMAN
INFRAHUMANS
INFRALAPSARIAN
INFRALAPSARIANS
INFRAMAXILLARY
INFRANGIBILITY
INFRANGIBLE
INFRANGIBLENESS
INFRANGIBLY
INFRAORBITAL
INFRAPOSED
INFRAPOSITION
INFRAPOSITIONS
INFRASONIC
INFRASOUND
INFRASOUNDS
INFRASPECIFIC
INFRASTRUCTURAL
INFRASTRUCTURE
INFRASTRUCTURES
INFREQUENCE
INFREQUENCES
INFREQUENCIES
INFREQUENCY
INFREQUENT
INFREQUENTLY
INFRINGEMENT
INFRINGEMENTS
INFRINGERS
INFRINGING
INFRUCTUOUS
INFRUCTUOUSLY
INFUNDIBULA
INFUNDIBULAR
INFUNDIBULATE
INFUNDIBULIFORM
INFUNDIBULUM
INFURIATED
INFURIATELY
INFURIATES
INFURIATING
INFURIATINGLY
INFURIATION
INFURIATIONS
INFUSCATED
INFUSIBILITIES
INFUSIBILITY
INFUSIBLENESS
INFUSIBLENESSES
INFUSIONISM
INFUSIONISMS
INFUSIONIST
INFUSIONISTS
INFUSORIAL
INFUSORIAN
INFUSORIANS
INGATHERED
INGATHERER
INGATHERERS
INGATHERING
INGATHERINGS
INGEMINATE

INGEMINATED
INGEMINATES
INGEMINATING
INGEMINATION
INGEMINATIONS
INGENERATE
INGENERATED
INGENERATES
INGENERATING
INGENERATION
INGENERATIONS
INGENIOUSLY
INGENIOUSNESS
INGENIOUSNESSES
INGENUITIES
INGENUOUSLY
INGENUOUSNESS
INGENUOUSNESSES
INGESTIBLE
INGESTIONS
INGLENEUKS
INGLENOOKS
INGLORIOUS
INGLORIOUSLY
INGLORIOUSNESS
INGRAFTATION
INGRAFTATIONS
INGRAFTING
INGRAFTMENT
INGRAFTMENTS
INGRAINEDLY
INGRAINEDNESS
INGRAINEDNESSES
INGRAINING
INGRATEFUL
INGRATIATE
INGRATIATED
INGRATIATES
INGRATIATING
INGRATIATINGLY
INGRATIATION
INGRATIATIONS
INGRATIATORY
INGRATITUDE
INGRATITUDES
INGRAVESCENCE
INGRAVESCENCES
INGRAVESCENT
INGREDIENT
INGREDIENTS
INGRESSION
INGRESSIONS
INGRESSIVE
INGRESSIVENESS
INGRESSIVES
INGROOVING
INGROSSING
INGROWNNESS
INGROWNNESSES
INGULFMENT
INGULFMENTS
INGULPHING
INGURGITATE
INGURGITATED
INGURGITATES
INGURGITATING
INGURGITATION
INGURGITATIONS
INHABITABILITY
INHABITABLE
INHABITANCE
INHABITANCES
INHABITANCIES
INHABITANCY
INHABITANT
INHABITANTS
INHABITATION
INHABITATIONS
INHABITERS
INHABITING
INHABITIVENESS
INHABITORS
INHABITRESS

INHABITRESSES
INHALATION
INHALATIONAL
INHALATIONS
INHALATORIUM
INHALATORIUMS
INHALATORS
INHARMONIC
INHARMONICAL
INHARMONICITIES
INHARMONICITY
INHARMONICY
INHARMONIES
INHARMONIOUS
INHARMONIOUSLY
INHAUSTING
INHEARSING
INHERENCES
INHERENCIES
INHERENTLY
INHERITABILITY
INHERITABLE
INHERITABLENESS
INHERITABLY
INHERITANCE
INHERITANCES
INHERITING
INHERITORS
INHERITRESS
INHERITRESSES
INHERITRICES
INHERITRIX
INHERITRIXES
INHIBITABLE
INHIBITERS
INHIBITING
INHIBITION
INHIBITIONS
INHIBITIVE
INHIBITORS
INHIBITORY
INHOLDINGS
INHOMOGENEITIES
INHOMOGENEITY
INHOMOGENEOUS
INHOSPITABLE
INHOSPITABLY
INHOSPITALITIES
INHOSPITALITY
INHUMANELY
INHUMANITIES
INHUMANITY
INHUMANNESS
INHUMANNESSES
INHUMATING
INHUMATION
INHUMATIONS
INIMICALITIES
INIMICALITY
INIMICALLY
INIMICALNESS
INIMICALNESSES
INIMICITIOUS
INIMITABILITIES
INIMITABILITY
INIMITABLE
INIMITABLENESS
INIMITABLY
INIQUITIES
INIQUITOUS
INIQUITOUSLY
INIQUITOUSNESS
INITIALERS
INITIALING
INITIALISATION
INITIALISATIONS
INITIALISE
INITIALISED
INITIALISES
INITIALISING
INITIALISM
INITIALISMS
INITIALIZATION
INITIALIZATIONS

INITIALIZE
INITIALIZED
INITIALIZES
INITIALIZING
INITIALLED
INITIALLER
INITIALLERS
INITIALLING
INITIALNESS
INITIALNESSES
INITIATING
INITIATION
INITIATIONS
INITIATIVE
INITIATIVELY
INITIATIVES
INITIATORIES
INITIATORS
INITIATORY
INITIATRESS
INITIATRESSES
INITIATRICES
INITIATRIX
INITIATRIXES
INJECTABLE
INJECTABLES
INJECTANTS
INJECTIONS
INJELLYING
INJOINTING
INJUDICIAL
INJUDICIALLY
INJUDICIOUS
INJUDICIOUSLY
INJUDICIOUSNESS
INJUNCTING
INJUNCTION
INJUNCTIONS
INJUNCTIVE
INJUNCTIVELY
INJURIOUSLY
INJURIOUSNESS
INJURIOUSNESSES
INJUSTICES
INKBERRIES
INKHOLDERS
INKINESSES
INMARRIAGE
INMARRIAGES
INMIGRANTS
INNATENESS
INNATENESSES
INNAVIGABLE
INNAVIGABLY
INNERMOSTS
INNERNESSES
INNERSOLES
INNERSPRING
INNERVATED
INNERVATES
INNERVATING
INNERVATION
INNERVATIONS
INNERWEARS
INNKEEPERS
INNOCENCES
INNOCENCIES
INNOCENTER
INNOCENTEST
INNOCENTLY
INNOCUITIES
INNOCUOUSLY
INNOCUOUSNESS
INNOCUOUSNESSES
INNOMINABLE
INNOMINABLES
INNOMINATE
INNOVATING
INNOVATION
INNOVATIONAL
INNOVATIONIST
INNOVATIONISTS
INNOVATIONS

INNOVATIVE
INNOVATIVELY
INNOVATIVENESS
INNOVATORS
INNOVATORY
INNOXIOUSLY
INNOXIOUSNESS
INNOXIOUSNESSES
INNUENDOED
INNUENDOES
INNUENDOING
INNUMERABILITY
INNUMERABLE
INNUMERABLENESS
INNUMERABLY
INNUMERACIES
INNUMERACY
INNUMERATE
INNUMERATES
INNUMEROUS
INNUTRIENT
INNUTRITION
INNUTRITIONS
INNUTRITIOUS
INOBEDIENCE
INOBEDIENCES
INOBEDIENT
INOBEDIENTLY
INOBSERVABLE
INOBSERVANCE
INOBSERVANCES
INOBSERVANT
INOBSERVANTLY
INOBSERVATION
INOBSERVATIONS
INOBTRUSIVE
INOBTRUSIVELY
INOBTRUSIVENESS
INOCCUPATION
INOCCUPATIONS
INOCULABILITIES
INOCULABILITY
INOCULABLE
INOCULANTS
INOCULATED
INOCULATES
INOCULATING
INOCULATION
INOCULATIONS
INOCULATIVE
INOCULATOR
INOCULATORS
INOCULATORY
INODOROUSLY
INODOROUSNESS
INODOROUSNESSES
INOFFENSIVE
INOFFENSIVELY
INOFFENSIVENESS
INOFFICIOUS
INOFFICIOUSLY
INOFFICIOUSNESS
INOPERABILITIES
INOPERABILITY
INOPERABLE
INOPERABLENESS
INOPERABLY
INOPERATIVE
INOPERATIVENESS
INOPERCULATE
INOPERCULATES
INOPPORTUNE
INOPPORTUNELY
INOPPORTUNENESS
INOPPORTUNITIES
INOPPORTUNITY
INORDINACIES
INORDINACY
INORDINATE
INORDINATELY
INORDINATENESS
INORDINATION
INORDINATIONS

INORGANICALLY
INORGANISATION
INORGANISATIONS
INORGANISED
INORGANIZATION
INORGANIZATIONS
INORGANIZED
INOSCULATE
INOSCULATED
INOSCULATES
INOSCULATING
INOSCULATION
INOSCULATIONS
INPATIENTS
INPAYMENTS
INPOURINGS
INQUIETING
INQUIETUDE
INQUIETUDES
INQUILINES
INQUILINIC
INQUILINICS
INQUILINISM
INQUILINISMS
INQUILINITIES
INQUILINITY
INQUILINOUS
INQUINATED
INQUINATES
INQUINATING
INQUINATION
INQUINATIONS
INQUIRATION
INQUIRATIONS
INQUIRENDO
INQUIRENDOS
INQUIRINGLY
INQUISITION
INQUISITIONAL
INQUISITIONIST
INQUISITIONISTS
INQUISITIONS
INQUISITIVE
INQUISITIVELY
INQUISITIVENESS
INQUISITOR
INQUISITORIAL
INQUISITORIALLY
INQUISITORS
INQUISITRESS
INQUISITRESSES
INQUISITURIENT
INRUSHINGS
INSALIVATE
INSALIVATED
INSALIVATES
INSALIVATING
INSALIVATION
INSALIVATIONS
INSALUBRIOUS
INSALUBRIOUSLY
INSALUBRITIES
INSALUBRITY
INSALUTARY
INSANENESS
INSANENESSES
INSANITARINESS
INSANITARY
INSANITATION
INSANITATIONS
INSANITIES
INSATIABILITIES
INSATIABILITY
INSATIABLE
INSATIABLENESS
INSATIABLY
INSATIATELY
INSATIATENESS
INSATIATENESSES
INSATIETIES
INSCIENCES
INSCONCING
INSCRIBABLE

INSCRIBABLENESS
INSCRIBERS
INSCRIBING
INSCRIPTION
INSCRIPTIONAL
INSCRIPTIONS
INSCRIPTIVE
INSCRIPTIVELY
INSCROLLED
INSCROLLING
INSCRUTABILITY
INSCRUTABLE
INSCRUTABLENESS
INSCRUTABLY
INSCULPING
INSCULPTURE
INSCULPTURED
INSCULPTURES
INSCULPTURING
INSECTARIA
INSECTARIES
INSECTARIUM
INSECTARIUMS
INSECTICIDAL
INSECTICIDALLY
INSECTICIDE
INSECTICIDES
INSECTIFORM
INSECTIFUGE
INSECTIFUGES
INSECTIONS
INSECTIVORE
INSECTIVORES
INSECTIVOROUS
INSECTOLOGIES
INSECTOLOGIST
INSECTOLOGISTS
INSECTOLOGY
INSECURELY
INSECURENESS
INSECURENESSES
INSECURITIES
INSECURITY
INSELBERGE
INSELBERGS
INSEMINATE
INSEMINATED
INSEMINATES
INSEMINATING
INSEMINATION
INSEMINATIONS
INSEMINATOR
INSEMINATORS
INSENSATELY
INSENSATENESS
INSENSATENESSES
INSENSIBILITIES
INSENSIBILITY
INSENSIBLE
INSENSIBLENESS
INSENSIBLY
INSENSITIVE
INSENSITIVELY
INSENSITIVENESS
INSENSITIVITIES
INSENSITIVITY
INSENSUOUS
INSENTIENCE
INSENTIENCES
INSENTIENCIES
INSENTIENCY
INSENTIENT
INSEPARABILITY
INSEPARABLE
INSEPARABLENESS
INSEPARABLES
INSEPARABLY
INSEPARATE
INSERTABLE
INSERTIONAL
INSERTIONS
INSESSORIAL
INSEVERABLE

INSHEATHED
INSHEATHES
INSHEATHING
INSHELLING
INSHELTERED
INSHELTERING
INSHELTERS
INSHIPPING
INSHRINING
INSIDIOUSLY
INSIDIOUSNESS
INSIDIOUSNESSES
INSIGHTFUL
INSIGHTFULLY
INSIGNIFICANCE
INSIGNIFICANCES
INSIGNIFICANCY
INSIGNIFICANT
INSIGNIFICANTLY
INSIGNIFICATIVE
INSINCERELY
INSINCERITIES
INSINCERITY
INSINEWING
INSINUATED
INSINUATES
INSINUATING
INSINUATINGLY
INSINUATION
INSINUATIONS
INSINUATIVE
INSINUATOR
INSINUATORS
INSINUATORY
INSIPIDITIES
INSIPIDITY
INSIPIDNESS
INSIPIDNESSES
INSIPIENCE
INSIPIENCES
INSIPIENTLY
INSISTENCE
INSISTENCES
INSISTENCIES
INSISTENCY
INSISTENTLY
INSISTINGLY
INSNAREMENT
INSNAREMENTS
INSOBRIETIES
INSOBRIETY
INSOCIABILITIES
INSOCIABILITY
INSOCIABLE
INSOCIABLY
INSOLATING
INSOLATION
INSOLATIONS
INSOLENCES
INSOLENTLY
INSOLIDITIES
INSOLIDITY
INSOLUBILISE
INSOLUBILISED
INSOLUBILISES
INSOLUBILISING
INSOLUBILITIES
INSOLUBILITY
INSOLUBILIZE
INSOLUBILIZED
INSOLUBILIZES
INSOLUBILIZING
INSOLUBLENESS
INSOLUBLENESSES
INSOLUBLES
INSOLVABILITIES
INSOLVABILITY
INSOLVABLE
INSOLVABLY
INSOLVENCIES
INSOLVENCY
INSOLVENTS
INSOMNIACS

INSOMNIOUS
INSOMNOLENCE
INSOMNOLENCES
INSOUCIANCE
INSOUCIANCES
INSOUCIANT
INSOUCIANTLY
INSOULMENT
INSOULMENTS
INSPANNING
INSPECTABLE
INSPECTING
INSPECTINGLY
INSPECTION
INSPECTIONAL
INSPECTIONS
INSPECTIVE
INSPECTORAL
INSPECTORATE
INSPECTORATES
INSPECTORIAL
INSPECTORS
INSPECTORSHIP
INSPECTORSHIPS
INSPHERING
INSPIRABLE
INSPIRATION
INSPIRATIONAL
INSPIRATIONALLY
INSPIRATIONISM
INSPIRATIONISMS
INSPIRATIONIST
INSPIRATIONISTS
INSPIRATIONS
INSPIRATIVE
INSPIRATOR
INSPIRATORS
INSPIRATORY
INSPIRINGLY
INSPIRITED
INSPIRITER
INSPIRITERS
INSPIRITING
INSPIRITINGLY
INSPIRITMENT
INSPIRITMENTS
INSPISSATE
INSPISSATED
INSPISSATES
INSPISSATING
INSPISSATION
INSPISSATIONS
INSPISSATOR
INSPISSATORS
INSTABILITIES
INSTABILITY
INSTALLANT
INSTALLANTS
INSTALLATION
INSTALLATIONS
INSTALLERS
INSTALLING
INSTALLMENT
INSTALLMENTS
INSTALMENT
INSTALMENTS
INSTANCIES
INSTANCING
INSTANTANEITIES
INSTANTANEITY
INSTANTANEOUS
INSTANTANEOUSLY
INSTANTIAL
INSTANTIATE
INSTANTIATED
INSTANTIATES
INSTANTIATING
INSTANTIATION
INSTANTIATIONS
INSTANTNESS
INSTANTNESSES
INSTARRING
INSTATEMENT

INSTATEMENTS
INSTAURATION
INSTAURATIONS
INSTAURATOR
INSTAURATORS
INSTIGATED
INSTIGATES
INSTIGATING
INSTIGATINGLY
INSTIGATION
INSTIGATIONS
INSTIGATIVE
INSTIGATOR
INSTIGATORS
INSTILLATION
INSTILLATIONS
INSTILLERS
INSTILLING
INSTILLMENT
INSTILLMENTS
INSTILMENT
INSTILMENTS
INSTINCTIVE
INSTINCTIVELY
INSTINCTIVITIES
INSTINCTIVITY
INSTINCTUAL
INSTINCTUALLY
INSTITORIAL
INSTITUTED
INSTITUTER
INSTITUTERS
INSTITUTES
INSTITUTING
INSTITUTION
INSTITUTIONAL
INSTITUTIONALLY
INSTITUTIONARY
INSTITUTIONS
INSTITUTIST
INSTITUTISTS
INSTITUTIVE
INSTITUTIVELY
INSTITUTOR
INSTITUTORS
INSTREAMING
INSTREAMINGS
INSTRESSED
INSTRESSES
INSTRESSING
INSTRUCTED
INSTRUCTIBLE
INSTRUCTING
INSTRUCTION
INSTRUCTIONAL
INSTRUCTIONS
INSTRUCTIVE
INSTRUCTIVELY
INSTRUCTIVENESS
INSTRUCTOR
INSTRUCTORS
INSTRUCTORSHIP
INSTRUCTORSHIPS
INSTRUCTRESS
INSTRUCTRESSES
INSTRUMENT
INSTRUMENTAL
INSTRUMENTALISM
INSTRUMENTALIST
INSTRUMENTALITY
INSTRUMENTALLY
INSTRUMENTALS
INSTRUMENTATION
INSTRUMENTED
INSTRUMENTING
INSTRUMENTS
INSUBJECTION
INSUBJECTIONS
INSUBORDINATE
INSUBORDINATELY
INSUBORDINATES
INSUBORDINATION
INSUBSTANTIAL

INSUBSTANTIALLY
INSUFFERABLE
INSUFFERABLY
INSUFFICIENCE
INSUFFICIENCES
INSUFFICIENCIES
INSUFFICIENCY
INSUFFICIENT
INSUFFICIENTLY
INSUFFLATE
INSUFFLATED
INSUFFLATES
INSUFFLATING
INSUFFLATION
INSUFFLATIONS
INSUFFLATOR
INSUFFLATORS
INSULARISM
INSULARISMS
INSULARITIES
INSULARITY
INSULATING
INSULATION
INSULATIONS
INSULATORS
INSULINASE
INSULINASES
INSULSITIES
INSULTABLE
INSULTINGLY
INSULTMENT
INSULTMENTS
INSUPERABILITY
INSUPERABLE
INSUPERABLENESS
INSUPERABLY
INSUPPORTABLE
INSUPPORTABLY
INSUPPRESSIBLE
INSUPPRESSIBLY
INSURABILITIES
INSURABILITY
INSURANCER
INSURANCERS
INSURANCES
INSURGENCE
INSURGENCES
INSURGENCIES
INSURGENCY
INSURGENTLY
INSURGENTS
INSURMOUNTABLE
INSURMOUNTABLY
INSURRECTION
INSURRECTIONAL
INSURRECTIONARY
INSURRECTIONISM
INSURRECTIONIST
INSURRECTIONS
INSUSCEPTIBLE
INSUSCEPTIBLY
INSUSCEPTIVE
INSUSCEPTIVELY
INSWATHING
INSWINGERS
INTACTNESS
INTACTNESSES
INTAGLIATED
INTAGLIOED
INTAGLIOING
INTANGIBILITIES
INTANGIBILITY
INTANGIBLE
INTANGIBLENESS
INTANGIBLES
INTANGIBLY
INTEGRABILITIES
INTEGRABILITY
INTEGRABLE
INTEGRALITIES
INTEGRALITY
INTEGRALLY
INTEGRANDS

INTEGRANTS
INTEGRATED
INTEGRATES
INTEGRATING
INTEGRATION
INTEGRATIONIST
INTEGRATIONISTS
INTEGRATIONS
INTEGRATIVE
INTEGRATOR
INTEGRATORS
INTEGRITIES
INTEGUMENT
INTEGUMENTAL
INTEGUMENTARY
INTEGUMENTS
INTELLECTED
INTELLECTION
INTELLECTIONS
INTELLECTIVE
INTELLECTIVELY
INTELLECTS
INTELLECTUAL
INTELLECTUALISE
INTELLECTUALISM
INTELLECTUALIST
INTELLECTUALITY
INTELLECTUALIZE
INTELLECTUALLY
INTELLECTUALS
INTELLIGENCE
INTELLIGENCER
INTELLIGENCERS
INTELLIGENCES
INTELLIGENT
INTELLIGENTIAL
INTELLIGENTLY
INTELLIGENTSIA
INTELLIGENTSIAS
INTELLIGENTZIA
INTELLIGENTZIAS
INTELLIGIBILITY
INTELLIGIBLE
INTELLIGIBLY
INTEMERATE
INTEMERATELY
INTEMERATENESS
INTEMPERANCE
INTEMPERANCES
INTEMPERANT
INTEMPERANTS
INTEMPERATE
INTEMPERATELY
INTEMPERATENESS
INTEMPESTIVE
INTEMPESTIVELY
INTEMPESTIVITY
INTENDANCE
INTENDANCES
INTENDANCIES
INTENDANCY
INTENDANTS
INTENDEDLY
INTENDERED
INTENDERING
INTENDMENT
INTENDMENTS
INTENERATE
INTENERATED
INTENERATES
INTENERATING
INTENERATION
INTENERATIONS
INTENSATED
INTENSATES
INTENSATING
INTENSATIVE
INTENSATIVES
INTENSENESS
INTENSENESSES
INTENSIFICATION
INTENSIFIED
INTENSIFIER

INTENSIFIERS
INTENSIFIES
INTENSIFYING
INTENSIONAL
INTENSIONALITY
INTENSIONALLY
INTENSIONS
INTENSITIES
INTENSITIVE
INTENSITIVES
INTENSIVELY
INTENSIVENESS
INTENSIVENESSES
INTENSIVES
INTENTIONAL
INTENTIONALITY
INTENTIONALLY
INTENTIONED
INTENTIONS
INTENTNESS
INTENTNESSES
INTERABANG
INTERABANGS
INTERACTANT
INTERACTANTS
INTERACTED
INTERACTING
INTERACTION
INTERACTIONAL
INTERACTIONISM
INTERACTIONISMS
INTERACTIONIST
INTERACTIONISTS
INTERACTIONS
INTERACTIVE
INTERACTIVELY
INTERACTIVITIES
INTERACTIVITY
INTERAGENCY
INTERALLELIC
INTERALLIED
INTERAMBULACRA
INTERAMBULACRAL
INTERAMBULACRUM
INTERANIMATION
INTERANIMATIONS
INTERANNUAL
INTERARCHED
INTERARCHES
INTERARCHING
INTERATOMIC
INTERBASIN
INTERBEDDED
INTERBEDDING
INTERBEDDINGS
INTERBEHAVIOR
INTERBEHAVIORAL
INTERBEHAVIORS
INTERBOROUGH
INTERBRAIN
INTERBRAINS
INTERBRANCH
INTERBREED
INTERBREEDING
INTERBREEDINGS
INTERBREEDS
INTERBROKER
INTERCALAR
INTERCALARILY
INTERCALARY
INTERCALATE
INTERCALATED
INTERCALATES
INTERCALATING
INTERCALATION
INTERCALATIONS
INTERCALATIVE
INTERCAMPUS
INTERCASTE
INTERCEDED
INTERCEDENT
INTERCEDER
INTERCEDERS

INTERCEDES
INTERCEDING
INTERCELLULAR
INTERCENSAL
INTERCEPTED
INTERCEPTER
INTERCEPTERS
INTERCEPTING
INTERCEPTION
INTERCEPTIONS
INTERCEPTIVE
INTERCEPTOR
INTERCEPTORS
INTERCEPTS
INTERCESSION
INTERCESSIONAL
INTERCESSIONS
INTERCESSOR
INTERCESSORIAL
INTERCESSORS
INTERCESSORY
INTERCHAIN
INTERCHAINED
INTERCHAINING
INTERCHAINS
INTERCHANGE
INTERCHANGEABLE
INTERCHANGEABLY
INTERCHANGED
INTERCHANGEMENT
INTERCHANGER
INTERCHANGERS
INTERCHANGES
INTERCHANGING
INTERCHANNEL
INTERCHAPTER
INTERCHAPTERS
INTERCHURCH
INTERCIPIENT
INTERCIPIENTS
INTERCLASS
INTERCLAVICLE
INTERCLAVICLES
INTERCLAVICULAR
INTERCLUDE
INTERCLUDED
INTERCLUDES
INTERCLUDING
INTERCLUSION
INTERCLUSIONS
INTERCLUSTER
INTERCOASTAL
INTERCOLLEGIATE
INTERCOLLINE
INTERCOLONIAL
INTERCOLONIALLY
INTERCOLUMNAR
INTERCOMMUNAL
INTERCOMMUNE
INTERCOMMUNED
INTERCOMMUNES
INTERCOMMUNING
INTERCOMMUNION
INTERCOMMUNIONS
INTERCOMMUNITY
INTERCOMPANY
INTERCOMPARE
INTERCOMPARED
INTERCOMPARES
INTERCOMPARING
INTERCOMPARISON
INTERCONNECT
INTERCONNECTED
INTERCONNECTING
INTERCONNECTION
INTERCONNECTOR
INTERCONNECTORS
INTERCONNECTS
INTERCONNEXION
INTERCONNEXIONS
INTERCONVERSION
INTERCONVERT
INTERCONVERTED

INTERCONVERTING
INTERCONVERTS
INTERCOOLED
INTERCOOLER
INTERCOOLERS
INTERCORPORATE
INTERCORRELATE
INTERCORRELATED
INTERCORRELATES
INTERCORTICAL
INTERCOSTAL
INTERCOSTALS
INTERCOUNTRY
INTERCOUNTY
INTERCOUPLE
INTERCOURSE
INTERCOURSES
INTERCRATER
INTERCROPPED
INTERCROPPING
INTERCROPS
INTERCROSS
INTERCROSSED
INTERCROSSES
INTERCROSSING
INTERCRURAL
INTERCULTURAL
INTERCULTURALLY
INTERCULTURE
INTERCURRENCE
INTERCURRENCES
INTERCURRENT
INTERCURRENTLY
INTERCUTTING
INTERDASHED
INTERDASHES
INTERDASHING
INTERDEALER
INTERDEALERS
INTERDEALING
INTERDEALS
INTERDEALT
INTERDENTAL
INTERDENTALLY
INTERDEPEND
INTERDEPENDED
INTERDEPENDENCE
INTERDEPENDENCY
INTERDEPENDENT
INTERDEPENDING
INTERDEPENDS
INTERDIALECTAL
INTERDICTED
INTERDICTING
INTERDICTION
INTERDICTIONS
INTERDICTIVE
INTERDICTIVELY
INTERDICTOR
INTERDICTORS
INTERDICTORY
INTERDICTS
INTERDIFFUSE
INTERDIFFUSED
INTERDIFFUSES
INTERDIFFUSING
INTERDIFFUSION
INTERDIFFUSIONS
INTERDIGITAL
INTERDIGITATE
INTERDIGITATED
INTERDIGITATES
INTERDIGITATING
INTERDIGITATION
INTERDINED
INTERDINES
INTERDINING
INTERDISTRICT
INTERDIVISIONAL
INTERDOMINION
INTERELECTRODE
INTERELECTRON
INTERELECTRONIC

INTEREPIDEMIC
INTERESSED
INTERESSES
INTERESSING
INTERESTED
INTERESTEDLY
INTERESTEDNESS
INTERESTING
INTERESTINGLY
INTERESTINGNESS
INTERETHNIC
INTERFACED
INTERFACES
INTERFACIAL
INTERFACIALLY
INTERFACING
INTERFACINGS
INTERFACULTY
INTERFAITH
INTERFAMILIAL
INTERFAMILY
INTERFASCICULAR
INTERFEMORAL
INTERFERED
INTERFERENCE
INTERFERENCES
INTERFERENTIAL
INTERFERER
INTERFERERS
INTERFERES
INTERFERING
INTERFERINGLY
INTERFEROGRAM
INTERFEROGRAMS
INTERFEROMETER
INTERFEROMETERS
INTERFEROMETRIC
INTERFEROMETRY
INTERFERON
INTERFERONS
INTERFERTILE
INTERFERTILITY
INTERFIBER
INTERFILED
INTERFILES
INTERFILING
INTERFLOWED
INTERFLOWING
INTERFLOWS
INTERFLUENCE
INTERFLUENCES
INTERFLUENT
INTERFLUOUS
INTERFLUVE
INTERFLUVES
INTERFLUVIAL
INTERFOLDED
INTERFOLDING
INTERFOLDS
INTERFOLIATE
INTERFOLIATED
INTERFOLIATES
INTERFOLIATING
INTERFRATERNITY
INTERFRETTED
INTERFRONTAL
INTERFUSED
INTERFUSES
INTERFUSING
INTERFUSION
INTERFUSIONS
INTERGALACTIC
INTERGENERATION
INTERGENERIC
INTERGLACIAL
INTERGLACIALS
INTERGRADATION
INTERGRADATIONS
INTERGRADE
INTERGRADED
INTERGRADES
INTERGRADIENT
INTERGRADING

INTERGRAFT
INTERGRAFTED
INTERGRAFTING
INTERGRAFTS
INTERGRANULAR
INTERGROUP
INTERGROWING
INTERGROWN
INTERGROWS
INTERGROWTH
INTERGROWTHS
INTERINDIVIDUAL
INTERINDUSTRY
INTERINFLUENCE
INTERINFLUENCES
INTERINVOLVE
INTERINVOLVED
INTERINVOLVES
INTERINVOLVING
INTERIONIC
INTERIORISATION
INTERIORISE
INTERIORISED
INTERIORISES
INTERIORISING
INTERIORITIES
INTERIORITY
INTERIORIZATION
INTERIORIZE
INTERIORIZED
INTERIORIZES
INTERIORIZING
INTERIORLY
INTERISLAND
INTERJACENCIES
INTERJACENCY
INTERJACENT
INTERJACULATE
INTERJACULATED
INTERJACULATES
INTERJACULATING
INTERJACULATORY
INTERJECTED
INTERJECTING
INTERJECTION
INTERJECTIONAL
INTERJECTIONARY
INTERJECTIONS
INTERJECTOR
INTERJECTORS
INTERJECTORY
INTERJECTS
INTERJECTURAL
INTERJOINED
INTERJOINING
INTERJOINS
INTERKINESES
INTERKINESIS
INTERKNITS
INTERKNITTED
INTERKNITTING
INTERKNOTS
INTERKNOTTED
INTERKNOTTING
INTERLACED
INTERLACEDLY
INTERLACEMENT
INTERLACEMENTS
INTERLACES
INTERLACING
INTERLACUSTRINE
INTERLAMINAR
INTERLAMINATE
INTERLAMINATED
INTERLAMINATES
INTERLAMINATING
INTERLAMINATION
INTERLAPPED
INTERLAPPING
INTERLARDED
INTERLARDING
INTERLARDS
INTERLAYER

INTERLAYERED
INTERLAYERING
INTERLAYERS
INTERLAYING
INTERLEAVE
INTERLEAVED
INTERLEAVES
INTERLEAVING
INTERLENDING
INTERLENDS
INTERLEUKIN
INTERLEUKINS
INTERLIBRARY
INTERLINEAL
INTERLINEALLY
INTERLINEAR
INTERLINEARLY
INTERLINEARS
INTERLINEATE
INTERLINEATED
INTERLINEATES
INTERLINEATING
INTERLINEATION
INTERLINEATIONS
INTERLINED
INTERLINER
INTERLINERS
INTERLINES
INTERLINGUA
INTERLINGUAL
INTERLINGUALLY
INTERLINGUAS
INTERLINING
INTERLININGS
INTERLINKED
INTERLINKING
INTERLINKS
INTERLOANS
INTERLOBULAR
INTERLOCAL
INTERLOCATION
INTERLOCATIONS
INTERLOCKED
INTERLOCKER
INTERLOCKERS
INTERLOCKING
INTERLOCKS
INTERLOCUTION
INTERLOCUTIONS
INTERLOCUTOR
INTERLOCUTORILY
INTERLOCUTORS
INTERLOCUTORY
INTERLOCUTRESS
INTERLOCUTRICE
INTERLOCUTRICES
INTERLOCUTRIX
INTERLOCUTRIXES
INTERLOOPED
INTERLOOPING
INTERLOOPS
INTERLOPED
INTERLOPER
INTERLOPERS
INTERLOPES
INTERLOPING
INTERLUDED
INTERLUDES
INTERLUDIAL
INTERLUDING
INTERLUNAR
INTERLUNARY
INTERLUNATION
INTERLUNATIONS
INTERMARGINAL
INTERMARRIAGE
INTERMARRIAGES
INTERMARRIED
INTERMARRIES
INTERMARRY
INTERMARRYING
INTERMATTED
INTERMATTING

INTERMAXILLA
INTERMAXILLAE
INTERMAXILLARY
INTERMEDDLE
INTERMEDDLED
INTERMEDDLER
INTERMEDDLERS
INTERMEDDLES
INTERMEDDLING
INTERMEDIA
INTERMEDIACIES
INTERMEDIACY
INTERMEDIAL
INTERMEDIARIES
INTERMEDIARY
INTERMEDIATE
INTERMEDIATED
INTERMEDIATELY
INTERMEDIATES
INTERMEDIATING
INTERMEDIATION
INTERMEDIATIONS
INTERMEDIATOR
INTERMEDIATORS
INTERMEDIATORY
INTERMEDIN
INTERMEDINS
INTERMEDIUM
INTERMEDIUMS
INTERMEMBRANE
INTERMENSTRUAL
INTERMENTS
INTERMESHED
INTERMESHES
INTERMESHING
INTERMETALLIC
INTERMETALLICS
INTERMEZZI
INTERMEZZO
INTERMEZZOS
INTERMIGRATION
INTERMIGRATIONS
INTERMINABILITY
INTERMINABLE
INTERMINABLY
INTERMINGLE
INTERMINGLED
INTERMINGLES
INTERMINGLING
INTERMISSION
INTERMISSIONS
INTERMISSIVE
INTERMITOTIC
INTERMITTED
INTERMITTENCE
INTERMITTENCES
INTERMITTENCIES
INTERMITTENCY
INTERMITTENT
INTERMITTENTLY
INTERMITTER
INTERMITTERS
INTERMITTING
INTERMITTINGLY
INTERMITTOR
INTERMITTORS
INTERMIXED
INTERMIXES
INTERMIXING
INTERMIXTURE
INTERMIXTURES
INTERMODAL
INTERMODULATION
INTERMOLECULAR
INTERMONTANE
INTERMOUNTAIN
INTERMUNDANE
INTERMURED
INTERMURES
INTERMURING
INTERNALISATION
INTERNALISE
INTERNALISED

INTERNALISES
INTERNALISING
INTERNALITIES
INTERNALITY
INTERNALIZATION
INTERNALIZE
INTERNALIZED
INTERNALIZES
INTERNALIZING
INTERNALLY
INTERNALNESS
INTERNALNESSES
INTERNATIONAL
INTERNATIONALLY
INTERNATIONALS
INTERNECINE
INTERNECIVE
INTERNEURAL
INTERNEURON
INTERNEURONAL
INTERNEURONS
INTERNISTS
INTERNMENT
INTERNMENTS
INTERNODAL
INTERNODES
INTERNODIAL
INTERNSHIP
INTERNSHIPS
INTERNUCLEAR
INTERNUCLEON
INTERNUCLEONIC
INTERNUCLEOTIDE
INTERNUNCIAL
INTERNUNCIO
INTERNUNCIOS
INTEROBSERVER
INTEROCEAN
INTEROCEANIC
INTEROCEPTIVE
INTEROCEPTOR
INTEROCEPTORS
INTEROCULAR
INTEROFFICE
INTEROPERABLE
INTEROPERATIVE
INTERORBITAL
INTERORGAN
INTEROSCULANT
INTEROSCULATE
INTEROSCULATED
INTEROSCULATES
INTEROSCULATING
INTEROSCULATION
INTEROSSEAL
INTEROSSEOUS
INTERPAGED
INTERPAGES
INTERPAGING
INTERPANDEMIC
INTERPARIETAL
INTERPARISH
INTERPAROCHIAL
INTERPAROXYSMAL
INTERPARTICLE
INTERPARTY
INTERPELLANT
INTERPELLANTS
INTERPELLATE
INTERPELLATED
INTERPELLATES
INTERPELLATING
INTERPELLATION
INTERPELLATIONS
INTERPELLATOR
INTERPELLATORS
INTERPENETRABLE
INTERPENETRANT
INTERPENETRATE
INTERPENETRATED
INTERPENETRATES
INTERPERCEPTUAL
INTERPERMEATE

INTERPERMEATED
INTERPERMEATES
INTERPERMEATING
INTERPERSONAL
INTERPERSONALLY
INTERPETIOLAR
INTERPHALANGEAL
INTERPHASE
INTERPHASES
INTERPHONE
INTERPHONES
INTERPILASTER
INTERPILASTERS
INTERPLANETARY
INTERPLANT
INTERPLANTED
INTERPLANTING
INTERPLANTS
INTERPLAYED
INTERPLAYING
INTERPLAYS
INTERPLEAD
INTERPLEADED
INTERPLEADER
INTERPLEADERS
INTERPLEADING
INTERPLEADS
INTERPLEURAL
INTERPLUVIAL
INTERPOINT
INTERPOLABLE
INTERPOLAR
INTERPOLATE
INTERPOLATED
INTERPOLATER
INTERPOLATERS
INTERPOLATES
INTERPOLATING
INTERPOLATION
INTERPOLATIONS
INTERPOLATIVE
INTERPOLATOR
INTERPOLATORS
INTERPONED
INTERPONES
INTERPONING
INTERPOPULATION
INTERPOSABLE
INTERPOSAL
INTERPOSALS
INTERPOSED
INTERPOSER
INTERPOSERS
INTERPOSES
INTERPOSING
INTERPOSITION
INTERPOSITIONS
INTERPRETABLE
INTERPRETABLY
INTERPRETATE
INTERPRETATED
INTERPRETATES
INTERPRETATING
INTERPRETATION
INTERPRETATIONS
INTERPRETATIVE
INTERPRETED
INTERPRETER
INTERPRETERS
INTERPRETERSHIP
INTERPRETESS
INTERPRETESSES
INTERPRETING
INTERPRETIVE
INTERPRETIVELY
INTERPRETRESS
INTERPRETRESSES
INTERPRETS
INTERPROVINCIAL
INTERPROXIMAL
INTERPSYCHIC
INTERPUNCTION
INTERPUNCTIONS

INTERPUNCTUATE
INTERPUNCTUATED
INTERPUNCTUATES
INTERPUPILLARY
INTERQUARTILE
INTERRACIAL
INTERRACIALLY
INTERRADIAL
INTERRADIALLY
INTERRADII
INTERRADIUS
INTERRADIUSES
INTERRAILED
INTERRAILER
INTERRAILERS
INTERRAILING
INTERRAILS
INTERRAMAL
INTERREGAL
INTERREGES
INTERREGIONAL
INTERREGNA
INTERREGNAL
INTERREGNUM
INTERREGNUMS
INTERRELATE
INTERRELATED
INTERRELATEDLY
INTERRELATES
INTERRELATING
INTERRELATION
INTERRELATIONS
INTERRELIGIOUS
INTERRENAL
INTERROBANG
INTERROBANGS
INTERROGABLE
INTERROGANT
INTERROGANTS
INTERROGATE
INTERROGATED
INTERROGATEE
INTERROGATEES
INTERROGATES
INTERROGATING
INTERROGATINGLY
INTERROGATION
INTERROGATIONAL
INTERROGATIONS
INTERROGATIVE
INTERROGATIVELY
INTERROGATIVES
INTERROGATOR
INTERROGATORIES
INTERROGATORILY
INTERROGATORS
INTERROGATORY
INTERROGEE
INTERROGEES
INTERRUPTED
INTERRUPTEDLY
INTERRUPTER
INTERRUPTERS
INTERRUPTIBLE
INTERRUPTING
INTERRUPTION
INTERRUPTIONS
INTERRUPTIVE
INTERRUPTIVELY
INTERRUPTOR
INTERRUPTORS
INTERRUPTS
INTERSCAPULAR
INTERSCHOLASTIC
INTERSCHOOL
INTERSCRIBE
INTERSCRIBED
INTERSCRIBES
INTERSCRIBING
INTERSECTED
INTERSECTING
INTERSECTION
INTERSECTIONAL

INTERSECTIONS
INTERSECTS
INTERSEGMENT
INTERSEGMENTAL
INTERSENSORY
INTERSEPTAL
INTERSEPTAL
INTERSERTED
INTERSERTING
INTERSERTS
INTERSERVICE
INTERSESSION
INTERSESSIONS
INTERSEXES
INTERSEXUAL
INTERSEXUALISM
INTERSEXUALISMS
INTERSEXUALITY
INTERSEXUALLY
INTERSIDEREAL
INTERSOCIETAL
INTERSOCIETY
INTERSPACE
INTERSPACED
INTERSPACES
INTERSPACING
INTERSPATIAL
INTERSPATIALLY
INTERSPECIES
INTERSPECIFIC
INTERSPERSAL
INTERSPERSALS
INTERSPERSE
INTERSPERSED
INTERSPERSEDLY
INTERSPERSES
INTERSPERSING
INTERSPERSION
INTERSPERSIONS
INTERSPINAL
INTERSPINOUS
INTERSTADIAL
INTERSTADIALS
INTERSTAGE
INTERSTATE
INTERSTATES
INTERSTATION
INTERSTELLAR
INTERSTELLARY
INTERSTERILE
INTERSTERILITY
INTERSTICE
INTERSTICES
INTERSTIMULUS
INTERSTITIAL
INTERSTITIALLY
INTERSTITIALS
INTERSTRAIN
INTERSTRAND
INTERSTRATIFIED
INTERSTRATIFIES
INTERSTRATIFY
INTERSUBJECTIVE
INTERSYSTEM
INTERTANGLE
INTERTANGLED
INTERTANGLEMENT
INTERTANGLES
INTERTANGLING
INTERTARSAL
INTERTENTACULAR
INTERTERMINAL
INTERTEXTS
INTERTEXTUAL
INTERTEXTUALITY
INTERTEXTUALLY
INTERTEXTURE
INTERTEXTURES
INTERTIDAL
INTERTIDALLY
INTERTILLAGE
INTERTILLAGES
INTERTILLED

INTERTILLING
INTERTILLS
INTERTISSUED
INTERTRAFFIC
INTERTRAFFICS
INTERTRIAL
INTERTRIBAL
INTERTRIGO
INTERTRIGOS
INTERTROOP
INTERTROPICAL
INTERTWINE
INTERTWINED
INTERTWINEMENT
INTERTWINEMENTS
INTERTWINES
INTERTWINING
INTERTWININGLY
INTERTWININGS
INTERTWIST
INTERTWISTED
INTERTWISTING
INTERTWISTINGLY
INTERTWISTS
INTERUNION
INTERUNIONS
INTERUNIVERSITY
INTERURBAN
INTERVALES
INTERVALLEY
INTERVALLIC
INTERVALLUM
INTERVALLUMS
INTERVALOMETER
INTERVALOMETERS
INTERVARSITY
INTERVEINED
INTERVEINING
INTERVEINS
INTERVENED
INTERVENER
INTERVENERS
INTERVENES
INTERVENIENT
INTERVENING
INTERVENOR
INTERVENORS
INTERVENTION
INTERVENTIONAL
INTERVENTIONISM
INTERVENTIONIST
INTERVENTIONS
INTERVENTOR
INTERVENTORS
INTERVERTEBRAL
INTERVIEWED
INTERVIEWEE
INTERVIEWEES
INTERVIEWER
INTERVIEWERS
INTERVIEWING
INTERVIEWS
INTERVILLAGE
INTERVISIBILITY
INTERVISIBLE
INTERVISITATION
INTERVITAL
INTERVOCALIC
INTERVOLVE
INTERVOLVED
INTERVOLVES
INTERVOLVING
INTERWEAVE
INTERWEAVED
INTERWEAVEMENT
INTERWEAVEMENTS
INTERWEAVER
INTERWEAVERS
INTERWEAVES
INTERWEAVING
INTERWINDING
INTERWINDS
INTERWORKED

INTERWORKING
INTERWORKINGS
INTERWORKS
INTERWOUND
INTERWOVEN
INTERWREATHE
INTERWREATHED
INTERWREATHES
INTERWREATHING
INTERWROUGHT
INTERZONAL
INTERZONES
INTESTACIES
INTESTATES
INTESTINAL
INTESTINALLY
INTESTINES
INTHRALLED
INTHRALLING
INTHRONING
INTIFADAHS
INTIFADEHS
INTIMACIES
INTIMATELY
INTIMATENESS
INTIMATENESSES
INTIMATERS
INTIMATING
INTIMATION
INTIMATIONS
INTIMIDATE
INTIMIDATED
INTIMIDATES
INTIMIDATING
INTIMIDATINGLY
INTIMIDATION
INTIMIDATIONS
INTIMIDATOR
INTIMIDATORS
INTIMIDATORY
INTIMISTES
INTIMITIES
INTINCTION
INTINCTIONS
INTITULING
INTOLERABILITY
INTOLERABLE
INTOLERABLENESS
INTOLERABLY
INTOLERANCE
INTOLERANCES
INTOLERANT
INTOLERANTLY
INTOLERANTNESS
INTOLERANTS
INTOLERATION
INTOLERATIONS
INTONATING
INTONATION
INTONATIONAL
INTONATIONS
INTONATORS
INTONINGLY
INTORSIONS
INTORTIONS
INTOXICABLE
INTOXICANT
INTOXICANTS
INTOXICATE
INTOXICATED
INTOXICATEDLY
INTOXICATES
INTOXICATING
INTOXICATINGLY
INTOXICATION
INTOXICATIONS
INTOXICATIVE
INTOXICATOR
INTOXICATORS
INTOXIMETER
INTOXIMETERS
INTRACAPSULAR
INTRACARDIAC

INTRACARDIAL	INTRAVITAL	INTROSPECTS	INUTTERABLE	INVERTIBILITY	INVITINGNESS
INTRACARDIALLY	INTRAVITALLY	INTROSUSCEPTION	INVAGINABLE	INVERTIBLE	INVITINGNESSES
INTRACAVITARY	INTRAVITAM	INTROVERSIBLE	INVAGINATE	INVESTABLE	INVOCATING
INTRACELLULAR	INTRAZONAL	INTROVERSION	INVAGINATED	INVESTIBLE	INVOCATION
INTRACELLULARLY	INTREATFULL	INTROVERSIONS	INVAGINATES	INVESTIGABLE	INVOCATIONAL
INTRACEREBRAL	INTREATING	INTROVERSIVE	INVAGINATING	INVESTIGATE	INVOCATIONS
INTRACEREBRALLY	INTREATINGLY	INTROVERSIVELY	INVAGINATION	INVESTIGATED	INVOCATIVE
INTRACOMPANY	INTREATMENT	INTROVERTED	INVAGINATIONS	INVESTIGATES	INVOCATORS
INTRACRANIAL	INTREATMENTS	INTROVERTING	INVALIDATE	INVESTIGATING	INVOCATORY
INTRACRANIALLY	INTRENCHANT	INTROVERTIVE	INVALIDATED	INVESTIGATION	INVOLUCELLA
INTRACTABILITY	INTRENCHED	INTROVERTS	INVALIDATES	INVESTIGATIONAL	INVOLUCELLATE
INTRACTABLE	INTRENCHER	INTRUDINGLY	INVALIDATING	INVESTIGATIONS	INVOLUCELLATED
INTRACTABLENESS	INTRENCHERS	INTRUSIONAL	INVALIDATION	INVESTIGATIVE	INVOLUCELLUM
INTRACTABLY	INTRENCHES	INTRUSIONIST	INVALIDATIONS	INVESTIGATOR	INVOLUCELS
INTRACUTANEOUS	INTRENCHING	INTRUSIONISTS	INVALIDATOR	INVESTIGATORS	INVOLUCRAL
INTRADERMAL	INTRENCHMENT	INTRUSIONS	INVALIDATORS	INVESTIGATORY	INVOLUCRATE
INTRADERMALLY	INTRENCHMENTS	INTRUSIVELY	INVALIDHOOD	INVESTITIVE	INVOLUCRES
INTRADERMIC	INTREPIDITIES	INTRUSIVENESS	INVALIDHOODS	INVESTITURE	INVOLUCRUM
INTRADERMICALLY	INTREPIDITY	INTRUSIVENESSES	INVALIDING	INVESTITURES	INVOLUNTARILY
INTRADOSES	INTREPIDLY	INTRUSIVES	INVALIDINGS	INVESTMENT	INVOLUNTARINESS
INTRAFALLOPIAN	INTREPIDNESS	INTRUSTING	INVALIDISM	INVESTMENTS	INVOLUNTARY
INTRAFASCICULAR	INTREPIDNESSES	INTRUSTMENT	INVALIDISMS	INVETERACIES	INVOLUTEDLY
INTRAGALACTIC	INTRICACIES	INTRUSTMENTS	INVALIDITIES	INVETERACY	INVOLUTELY
INTRAGENIC	INTRICATELY	INTUBATING	INVALIDITY	INVETERATE	INVOLUTING
INTRAMEDULLARY	INTRICATENESS	INTUBATION	INVALIDNESS	INVETERATELY	INVOLUTION
INTRAMERCURIAL	INTRICATENESSES	INTUBATIONS	INVALIDNESSES	INVETERATENESS	INVOLUTIONAL
INTRAMOLECULAR	INTRIGANTE	INTUITABLE	INVALUABLE	INVIABILITIES	INVOLUTIONS
INTRAMUNDANE	INTRIGANTES	INTUITIONAL	INVALUABLENESS	INVIABILITY	INVOLVEDLY
INTRAMURAL	INTRIGANTS	INTUITIONALISM	INVALUABLY	INVIABLENESS	INVOLVEMENT
INTRAMURALLY	INTRIGUANT	INTUITIONALISMS	INVARIABILITIES	INVIABLENESSES	INVOLVEMENTS
INTRAMUSCULAR	INTRIGUANTE	INTUITIONALIST	INVARIABILITY	INVIDIOUSLY	INVULNERABILITY
INTRAMUSCULARLY	INTRIGUANTES	INTUITIONALISTS	INVARIABLE	INVIDIOUSNESS	INVULNERABLE
INTRANASAL	INTRIGUANTS	INTUITIONALLY	INVARIABLENESS	INVIDIOUSNESSES	INVULNERABLY
INTRANASALLY	INTRIGUERS	INTUITIONISM	INVARIABLES	INVIGILATE	INVULTUATION
INTRANATIONAL	INTRIGUING	INTUITIONISMS	INVARIABLY	INVIGILATED	INVULTUATIONS
INTRANSIGEANCE	INTRIGUINGLY	INTUITIONIST	INVARIANCE	INVIGILATES	INWARDNESS
INTRANSIGEANCES	INTRINSICAL	INTUITIONISTS	INVARIANCES	INVIGILATING	INWARDNESSES
INTRANSIGEANT	INTRINSICALITY	INTUITIONS	INVARIANCIES	INVIGILATION	INWORKINGS
INTRANSIGEANTLY	INTRINSICALLY	INTUITIVELY	INVARIANCY	INVIGILATIONS	INWRAPPING
INTRANSIGEANTS	INTRINSICALNESS	INTUITIVENESS	INVARIANTS	INVIGILATOR	INWREATHED
INTRANSIGENCE	INTRINSICATE	INTUITIVENESSES	INVASIVENESS	INVIGILATORS	INWREATHES
INTRANSIGENCES	INTRODUCED	INTUITIVISM	INVASIVENESSES	INVIGORANT	INWREATHING
INTRANSIGENCIES	INTRODUCER	INTUITIVISMS	INVEAGLING	INVIGORANTS	IODINATING
INTRANSIGENCY	INTRODUCERS	INTUMESCED	INVECTIVELY	INVIGORATE	IODINATION
INTRANSIGENT	INTRODUCES	INTUMESCENCE	INVECTIVENESS	INVIGORATED	IODINATIONS
INTRANSIGENTISM	INTRODUCIBLE	INTUMESCENCES	INVECTIVENESSES	INVIGORATES	IODISATION
INTRANSIGENTIST	INTRODUCING	INTUMESCENCIES	INVECTIVES	INVIGORATING	IODISATIONS
INTRANSIGENTLY	INTRODUCTION	INTUMESCENCY	INVEIGHERS	INVIGORATINGLY	IODIZATION
INTRANSIGENTS	INTRODUCTIONS	INTUMESCENT	INVEIGHING	INVIGORATION	IODIZATIONS
INTRANSITIVE	INTRODUCTIVE	INTUMESCES	INVEIGLEMENT	INVIGORATIONS	IODOMETRIC
INTRANSITIVELY	INTRODUCTORILY	INTUMESCING	INVEIGLEMENTS	INVIGORATIVE	IODOMETRICAL
INTRANSITIVITY	INTRODUCTORY	INTURBIDATE	INVEIGLERS	INVIGORATIVELY	IODOMETRICALLY
INTRANSMISSIBLE	INTROFYING	INTURBIDATED	INVEIGLING	INVIGORATOR	IODOMETRIES
INTRANSMUTABLE	INTROGRESSANT	INTURBIDATES	INVENDIBILITIES	INVIGORATORS	IONICITIES
INTRANUCLEAR	INTROGRESSANTS	INTURBIDATING	INVENDIBILITY	INVINCIBILITIES	IONISATION
INTRAOCULAR	INTROGRESSION	INTUSSUSCEPT	INVENDIBILITY	INVINCIBILITY	IONISATIONS
INTRAOCULARLY	INTROGRESSIONS	INTUSSUSCEPTED	INVENTABLE	INVINCIBLE	IONIZATION
INTRAPARIETAL	INTROGRESSIVE	INTUSSUSCEPTING	INVENTIBLE	INVINCIBLENESS	IONIZATIONS
INTRAPARTUM	INTROITUSES	INTUSSUSCEPTION	INVENTIONAL	INVINCIBLY	IONOPAUSES
INTRAPERITONEAL	INTROJECTED	INTUSSUSCEPTIVE	INVENTIONLESS	INVIOLABILITIES	IONOPHORES
INTRAPERSONAL	INTROJECTING	INTUSSUSCEPTS	INVENTIONS	INVIOLABILITY	IONOPHORESES
INTRAPETIOLAR	INTROJECTION	INTWINEMENT	INVENTIVELY	INVIOLABLE	IONOPHORESIS
INTRAPLATE	INTROJECTIONS	INTWINEMENTS	INVENTIVENESS	INVIOLABLENESS	IONOSONDES
INTRAPOPULATION	INTROJECTIVE	INTWISTING	INVENTIVENESSES	INVIOLABLY	IONOSPHERE
INTRAPRENEUR	INTROJECTS	INUMBRATED	INVENTORIABLE	INVIOLACIES	IONOSPHERES
INTRAPRENEURIAL	INTROMISSIBLE	INUMBRATES	INVENTORIAL	INVIOLATED	IONOSPHERIC
INTRAPRENEURS	INTROMISSION	INUMBRATING	INVENTORIALLY	INVIOLATELY	IONOSPHERICALLY
INTRAPSYCHIC	INTROMISSIONS	INUNCTIONS	INVENTORIED	INVIOLATENESS	IONOTROPIC
INTRASEXUAL	INTROMISSIVE	INUNDATING	INVENTORIES	INVIOLATENESSES	IONOTROPIES
INTRASPECIES	INTROMITTED	INUNDATION	INVENTORYING	INVISIBILITIES	IONTOPHORESES
INTRASPECIFIC	INTROMITTENT	INUNDATIONS	INVENTRESS	INVISIBILITY	IONTOPHORESIS
INTRASTATE	INTROMITTER	INUNDATORS	INVENTRESSES	INVISIBLENESS	IONTOPHORETIC
INTRATELLURIC	INTROMITTERS	INUNDATORY	INVERACITIES	INVISIBLENESSES	IPECACUANHA
INTRATHECAL	INTROMITTING	INURBANELY	INVERACITY	INVISIBLES	IPECACUANHAS
INTRATHECALLY	INTRORSELY	INURBANITIES	INVERITIES	INVITATION	IPRATROPIUM
INTRATHORACIC	INTROSPECT	INURBANITY	INVERNESSES	INVITATIONAL	IPRATROPIUMS
INTRAUTERINE	INTROSPECTED	INUREDNESS	INVERSIONS	INVITATIONALS	IPRINDOLES
INTRAVASATION	INTROSPECTING	INUREDNESSES	INVERTASES	INVITATIONS	IPRONIAZID
INTRAVASATIONS	INTROSPECTION	INUREMENTS	INVERTEBRAL	INVITATORIES	IPRONIAZIDS
INTRAVASCULAR	INTROSPECTIONAL	INURNMENTS	INVERTEBRATE	INVITATORY	IPSELATERAL
INTRAVASCULARLY	INTROSPECTIONS	INUSITATION	INVERTEBRATES	INVITEMENT	IPSILATERAL
INTRAVENOUS	INTROSPECTIVE	INUSITATIONS	INVERTEDLY	INVITEMENTS	IPSILATERALLY
INTRAVENOUSLY	INTROSPECTIVELY	INUTILITIES	INVERTIBILITIES	INVITINGLY	IRACUNDITIES

IRACUNDITY
IRACUNDULOUS
IRASCIBILITIES
IRASCIBILITY
IRASCIBLENESS
IRASCIBLENESSES
IRATENESSES
IREFULNESS
IREFULNESSES
IRENICALLY
IRENICISMS
IRENOLOGIES
IRIDACEOUS
IRIDECTOMIES
IRIDECTOMY
IRIDESCENCE
IRIDESCENCES
IRIDESCENT
IRIDESCENTLY
IRIDISATION
IRIDISATIONS
IRIDIZATION
IRIDIZATIONS
IRIDOCYTES
IRIDOLOGIES
IRIDOLOGIST
IRIDOLOGISTS
IRIDOSMINE
IRIDOSMINES
IRIDOSMIUM
IRIDOSMIUMS
IRIDOTOMIES
IRISATIONS
IRKSOMENESS
IRKSOMENESSES
IRONFISTED
IRONHANDED
IRONHEARTED
IRONICALLY
IRONICALNESS
IRONICALNESSES
IRONMASTER
IRONMASTERS
IRONMONGER
IRONMONGERIES
IRONMONGERS
IRONMONGERY
IRONNESSES
IRONSMITHS
IRONSTONES
IRONWORKER
IRONWORKERS
IRRADIANCE
IRRADIANCES
IRRADIANCIES
IRRADIANCY
IRRADIATED
IRRADIATES
IRRADIATING
IRRADIATION
IRRADIATIONS
IRRADIATIVE
IRRADIATOR
IRRADIATORS
IRRADICABLE
IRRADICABLY
IRRADICATE
IRRADICATED
IRRADICATES
IRRADICATING
IRRATIONAL
IRRATIONALISE
IRRATIONALISED
IRRATIONALISES
IRRATIONALISING
IRRATIONALISM
IRRATIONALISMS
IRRATIONALIST
IRRATIONALISTIC
IRRATIONALISTS
IRRATIONALITIES
IRRATIONALITY
IRRATIONALIZE

IRRATIONALIZED
IRRATIONALIZES
IRRATIONALIZING
IRRATIONALLY
IRRATIONALNESS
IRRATIONALS
IRREALISABLE
IRREALITIES
IRREALIZABLE
IRREBUTTABLE
IRRECEPTIVE
IRRECIPROCAL
IRRECIPROCITIES
IRRECIPROCITY
IRRECLAIMABLE
IRRECLAIMABLY
IRRECOGNISABLE
IRRECOGNITION
IRRECOGNITIONS
IRRECOGNIZABLE
IRRECONCILABLE
IRRECONCILABLES
IRRECONCILABLY
IRRECONCILED
IRRECONCILEMENT
IRRECOVERABLE
IRRECOVERABLY
IRRECUSABLE
IRRECUSABLY
IRREDEEMABILITY
IRREDEEMABLE
IRREDEEMABLES
IRREDEEMABLY
IRREDENTAS
IRREDENTISM
IRREDENTISMS
IRREDENTIST
IRREDENTISTS
IRREDUCIBILITY
IRREDUCIBLE
IRREDUCIBLENESS
IRREDUCIBLY
IRREDUCTIBILITY
IRREDUCTION
IRREDUCTIONS
IRREFLECTION
IRREFLECTIONS
IRREFLECTIVE
IRREFLEXION
IRREFLEXIONS
IRREFLEXIVE
IRREFORMABILITY
IRREFORMABLE
IRREFORMABLY
IRREFRAGABILITY
IRREFRAGABLE
IRREFRAGABLY
IRREFRANGIBLE
IRREFRANGIBLY
IRREFUTABILITY
IRREFUTABLE
IRREFUTABLENESS
IRREFUTABLY
IRREGARDLESS
IRREGULARITIES
IRREGULARITY
IRREGULARLY
IRREGULARS
IRRELATION
IRRELATIONS
IRRELATIVE
IRRELATIVELY
IRRELATIVENESS
IRRELEVANCE
IRRELEVANCES
IRRELEVANCIES
IRRELEVANCY
IRRELEVANT
IRRELEVANTLY
IRRELIEVABLE
IRRELIGION
IRRELIGIONIST
IRRELIGIONISTS

IRRELIGIONS
IRRELIGIOUS
IRRELIGIOUSLY
IRRELIGIOUSNESS
IRREMEABLE
IRREMEABLY
IRREMEDIABLE
IRREMEDIABLY
IRREMISSIBILITY
IRREMISSIBLE
IRREMISSIBLY
IRREMISSION
IRREMISSIONS
IRREMISSIVE
IRREMOVABILITY
IRREMOVABLE
IRREMOVABLENESS
IRREMOVABLY
IRRENOWNED
IRREPAIRABLE
IRREPARABILITY
IRREPARABLE
IRREPARABLENESS
IRREPARABLY
IRREPEALABILITY
IRREPEALABLE
IRREPEALABLY
IRREPLACEABLE
IRREPLACEABLY
IRREPLEVIABLE
IRREPLEVISABLE
IRREPREHENSIBLE
IRREPREHENSIBLY
IRREPRESSIBLE
IRREPRESSIBLY
IRREPROACHABLE
IRREPROACHABLY
IRREPRODUCIBLE
IRREPROVABLE
IRREPROVABLY
IRRESISTANCE
IRRESISTANCES
IRRESISTIBILITY
IRRESISTIBLE
IRRESISTIBLY
IRRESOLUBILITY
IRRESOLUBLE
IRRESOLUBLY
IRRESOLUTE
IRRESOLUTELY
IRRESOLUTENESS
IRRESOLUTION
IRRESOLUTIONS
IRRESOLVABILITY
IRRESOLVABLE
IRRESOLVEDLY
IRRESPECTIVE
IRRESPECTIVELY
IRRESPIRABLE
IRRESPONSIBLE
IRRESPONSIBLES
IRRESPONSIBLY
IRRESPONSIVE
IRRESPONSIVELY
IRRESTRAINABLE
IRRESUSCITABLE
IRRESUSCITABLY
IRRETENTION
IRRETENTIONS
IRRETENTIVE
IRRETENTIVENESS
IRRETRIEVABLE
IRRETRIEVABLY
IRREVERENCE
IRREVERENCES
IRREVERENT
IRREVERENTIAL
IRREVERENTLY
IRREVERSIBILITY
IRREVERSIBLE
IRREVERSIBLY
IRREVOCABILITY
IRREVOCABLE

IRREVOCABLENESS
IRREVOCABLY
IRRIDENTAS
IRRIGATING
IRRIGATION
IRRIGATIONAL
IRRIGATIONS
IRRIGATIVE
IRRIGATORS
IRRITABILITIES
IRRITABILITY
IRRITABLENESS
IRRITABLENESSES
IRRITANCIES
IRRITATING
IRRITATINGLY
IRRITATION
IRRITATIONS
IRRITATIVE
IRRITATORS
IRROTATIONAL
IRRUPTIONS
IRRUPTIVELY
ISABELLINE
ISABELLINES
ISALLOBARIC
ISALLOBARS
ISAPOSTOLIC
ISCHAEMIAS
ISCHURETIC
ISCHURETICS
ISEIKONIAS
ISENTROPIC
ISENTROPICALLY
ISINGLASSES
ISLOMANIAS
ISMATICALNESS
ISMATICALNESSES
ISOAGGLUTININ
ISOAGGLUTININS
ISOALLOXAZINE
ISOALLOXAZINES
ISOAMINILE
ISOAMINILES
ISOANTIBODIES
ISOANTIBODY
ISOANTIGEN
ISOANTIGENIC
ISOANTIGENS
ISOBARISMS
ISOBAROMETRIC
ISOBILATERAL
ISOBUTANES
ISOBUTENES
ISOBUTYLENE
ISOBUTYLENES
ISOCALORIC
ISOCARBOXAZID
ISOCARBOXAZIDS
ISOCHASMIC
ISOCHEIMAL
ISOCHEIMALS
ISOCHEIMENAL
ISOCHEIMENALS
ISOCHEIMIC
ISOCHIMALS
ISOCHROMATIC
ISOCHROMOSOME
ISOCHROMOSOMES
ISOCHRONAL
ISOCHRONALLY
ISOCHRONES
ISOCHRONISE
ISOCHRONISED
ISOCHRONISES
ISOCHRONISING
ISOCHRONISM
ISOCHRONISMS
ISOCHRONIZE
ISOCHRONIZED
ISOCHRONIZES
ISOCHRONIZING
ISOCHRONOUS

ISOCHRONOUSLY
ISOCHROOUS
ISOCLINALS
ISOCLINICS
ISOCRACIES
ISOCRYMALS
ISOCYANATE
ISOCYANATES
ISOCYANIDE
ISOCYANIDES
ISODIAMETRIC
ISODIAMETRICAL
ISODIAPHERE
ISODIAPHERES
ISODIMORPHIC
ISODIMORPHISM
ISODIMORPHISMS
ISODIMORPHOUS
ISODONTALS
ISODYNAMIC
ISODYNAMICS
ISOELECTRIC
ISOELECTRONIC
ISOENZYMATIC
ISOENZYMES
ISOENZYMIC
ISOFLAVONE
ISOFLAVONES
ISOGAMETES
ISOGAMETIC
ISOGENETIC
ISOGEOTHERM
ISOGEOTHERMAL
ISOGEOTHERMALS
ISOGEOTHERMIC
ISOGEOTHERMICS
ISOGEOTHERMS
ISOGLOSSAL
ISOGLOSSES
ISOGLOSSIC
ISOGLOTTAL
ISOGLOTTIC
ISOGRAFTED
ISOGRAFTING
ISOHYETALS
ISOIMMUNISATION
ISOIMMUNIZATION
ISOKINETIC
ISOKONTANS
ISOLABILITIES
ISOLABILITY
ISOLATABLE
ISOLATIONISM
ISOLATIONISMS
ISOLATIONIST
ISOLATIONISTS
ISOLATIONS
ISOLECITHAL
ISOLEUCINE
ISOLEUCINES
ISOMAGNETIC
ISOMAGNETICS
ISOMERASES
ISOMERISATION
ISOMERISATIONS
ISOMERISED
ISOMERISES
ISOMERISING
ISOMERISMS
ISOMERIZATION
ISOMERIZATIONS
ISOMERIZED
ISOMERIZES
ISOMERIZING
ISOMETRICAL
ISOMETRICALLY
ISOMETRICS
ISOMETRIES
ISOMETROPIA
ISOMETROPIAS
ISOMORPHIC
ISOMORPHICALLY
ISOMORPHISM

ISOMORPHISMS
ISOMORPHOUS
ISONIAZIDE
ISONIAZIDES
ISONIAZIDS
ISONITRILE
ISONITRILES
ISOOCTANES
ISOPACHYTE
ISOPACHYTES
ISOPERIMETER
ISOPERIMETERS
ISOPERIMETRICAL
ISOPERIMETRIES
ISOPERIMETRY
ISOPIESTIC
ISOPIESTICALLY
ISOPLETHIC
ISOPOLITIES
ISOPRENALINE
ISOPRENALINES
ISOPRENOID
ISOPROPYLS
ISOPROTERENOL
ISOPROTERENOLS
ISOPTEROUS
ISOPYCNALS
ISOPYCNICS
ISORHYTHMIC
ISOSEISMAL
ISOSEISMALS
ISOSEISMIC
ISOSEISMICS
ISOSMOTICALLY
ISOSPONDYLOUS
ISOSPORIES
ISOSPOROUS
ISOSTACIES
ISOSTASIES
ISOSTATICALLY
ISOSTEMONOUS
ISOSTHENURIA
ISOSTHENURIAS
ISOTENISCOPE
ISOTENISCOPES
ISOTHERALS
ISOTHERMAL
ISOTHERMALLY
ISOTHERMALS
ISOTONICALLY
ISOTONICITIES
ISOTONICITY
ISOTOPICALLY
ISOTRETINOIN
ISOTRETINOINS
ISOTROPICALLY
ISOTROPIES
ISOTROPISM
ISOTROPISMS
ISOTROPOUS
ISOXSUPRINE
ISOXSUPRINES
ISPAGHULAS
ITACOLUMITE
ITACOLUMITES
ITALIANATE
ITALIANATED
ITALIANATES
ITALIANATING
ITALIANISE
ITALIANISED
ITALIANISES
ITALIANISING
ITALIANIZE
ITALIANIZED
ITALIANIZES
ITALIANIZING
ITALICISATION
ITALICISATIONS
ITALICISED
ITALICISES
ITALICISING
ITALICIZATION

ITALICIZATIONS
ITALICIZED
ITALICIZES
ITALICIZING
ITCHINESSES
ITEMISATION
ITEMISATIONS

ITEMIZATION
ITEMIZATIONS
ITERATIONS
ITERATIVELY
ITERATIVENESS
ITERATIVENESSES
ITEROPARITIES

ITEROPARITY
ITEROPAROUS
ITHYPHALLI
ITHYPHALLIC
ITHYPHALLICS
ITHYPHALLUS
ITHYPHALLUSES

ITINERACIES
ITINERANCIES
ITINERANCY
ITINERANTLY
ITINERANTS
ITINERARIES
ITINERATED

ITINERATES
ITINERATING
ITINERATION
ITINERATIONS
IVERMECTIN
IVERMECTINS
IVORYBILLS

IVORYWOODS
IZVESTIYAS

Jj

JABBERINGLY	JAILHOUSES	JAYWALKING	JEWELLERIES	JOINTWORMS	JOYPOPPERS
JABBERINGS	JAILORESSES	JAYWALKINGS	JEWELWEEDS	JOKESMITHS	JOYPOPPING
JABBERWOCK	JAMAHIRIYA	JAZZINESSES	JICKAJOGGED	JOKINESSES	JOYRIDINGS
JABBERWOCKIES	JAMAHIRIYAS	JEALOUSHOOD	JICKAJOGGING	JOLLEYINGS	JUBILANCES
JABBERWOCKS	JAMBALAYAS	JEALOUSHOODS	JIGAJIGGED	JOLLIFICATION	JUBILANCIES
JABBERWOCKY	JAMBOKKING	JEALOUSIES	JIGAJIGGING	JOLLIFICATIONS	JUBILANTLY
JABORANDIS	JAMBOLANAS	JEALOUSING	JIGAJOGGED	JOLLIFYING	JUBILARIAN
JABOTICABA	JANISARIES	JEALOUSNESS	JIGAJOGGING	JOLLIMENTS	JUBILARIANS
JABOTICABAS	JANISSARIES	JEALOUSNESSES	JIGAMAREES	JOLLINESSES	JUBILATING
JACARANDAS	JANITORIAL	JEISTIECOR	JIGGERMAST	JOLLYBOATS	JUBILATION
JACKALLING	JANITORSHIP	JEISTIECORS	JIGGERMASTS	JOLLYHEADS	JUBILATIONS
JACKANAPES	JANITORSHIPS	JEJUNENESS	JIGGUMBOBS	JOLTERHEAD	JUDGEMENTAL
JACKANAPESES	JANITRESSES	JEJUNENESSES	JIGJIGGING	JOLTERHEADS	JUDGEMENTS
JACKAROOED	JANITRIXES	JEJUNITIES	JILLFLIRTS	JONNYCAKES	JUDGESHIPS
JACKAROOING	JANIZARIAN	JEJUNOSTOMIES	JIMPNESSES	JOSEPHINITE	JUDGMATICAL
JACKASSERIES	JANIZARIES	JEJUNOSTOMY	JIMSONWEED	JOSEPHINITES	JUDGMATICALLY
JACKASSERY	JAPANISING	JELLIFICATION	JIMSONWEEDS	JOSTLEMENT	JUDGMENTAL
JACKBOOTED	JAPANIZING	JELLIFICATIONS	JINGOISTIC	JOSTLEMENTS	JUDGMENTALLY
JACKBOOTING	JAPONAISERIE	JELLIFYING	JINGOISTICALLY	JOUISANCES	JUDICATION
JACKEROOED	JAPONAISERIES	JELLYBEANS	JINRICKSHA	JOURNALESE	JUDICATIONS
JACKEROOING	JARDINIERE	JELLYFISHES	JINRICKSHAS	JOURNALESES	JUDICATIVE
JACKETLESS	JARDINIERES	JELLYGRAPH	JINRICKSHAW	JOURNALING	JUDICATORIAL
JACKFISHES	JARGONEERS	JELLYGRAPHED	JINRICKSHAWS	JOURNALISATION	JUDICATORIES
JACKFRUITS	JARGONELLE	JELLYGRAPHING	JINRIKISHA	JOURNALISATIONS	JUDICATORS
JACKHAMMER	JARGONELLES	JELLYGRAPHS	JINRIKISHAS	JOURNALISE	JUDICATORY
JACKHAMMERED	JARGONISATION	JELLYROLLS	JINRIKSHAS	JOURNALISED	JUDICATURE
JACKHAMMERING	JARGONISATIONS	JEMMINESSES	JITTERBUGGED	JOURNALISER	JUDICATURES
JACKHAMMERS	JARGONISED	JENNETINGS	JITTERBUGGING	JOURNALISERS	JUDICIALLY
JACKKNIFED	JARGONISES	JEOPARDERS	JITTERBUGS	JOURNALISES	JUDICIARIES
JACKKNIFES	JARGONISING	JEOPARDIED	JITTERIEST	JOURNALISING	JUDICIOUSLY
JACKKNIFING	JARGONISTIC	JEOPARDIES	JITTERINESS	JOURNALISM	JUDICIOUSNESS
JACKKNIVES	JARGONISTS	JEOPARDING	JITTERINESSES	JOURNALISMS	JUDICIOUSNESSES
JACKLIGHTED	JARGONIZATION	JEOPARDISE	JOBCENTRES	JOURNALIST	JUGGERNAUT
JACKLIGHTING	JARGONIZATIONS	JEOPARDISED	JOBERNOWLS	JOURNALISTIC	JUGGERNAUTS
JACKLIGHTS	JARGONIZED	JEOPARDISES	JOBHOLDERS	JOURNALISTS	JUGGLERIES
JACKPLANES	JARGONIZES	JEOPARDISING	JOBLESSNESS	JOURNALIZATION	JUGGLINGLY
JACKRABBIT	JARGONIZING	JEOPARDIZE	JOBLESSNESSES	JOURNALIZATIONS	JUGLANDACEOUS
JACKRABBITS	JARLSBERGS	JEOPARDIZED	JOBSEEKERS	JOURNALIZE	JUGULATING
JACKROLLED	JAROVISING	JEOPARDIZES	JOBSWORTHS	JOURNALIZED	JUGULATION
JACKROLLING	JAROVIZING	JEOPARDIZING	JOCKEYISMS	JOURNALIZER	JUGULATIONS
JACKSCREWS	JASPERISED	JEOPARDOUS	JOCKEYSHIP	JOURNALIZERS	JUICEHEADS
JACKSHAFTS	JASPERISES	JEOPARDOUSLY	JOCKEYSHIPS	JOURNALIZES	JUICINESSES
JACKSMELTS	JASPERISING	JEOPARDYING	JOCKSTRAPS	JOURNALIZING	JULIENNING
JACKSMITHS	JASPERIZED	JEQUERITIES	JOCKTELEGS	JOURNALLED	JUMBLINGLY
JACKSNIPES	JASPERIZES	JEQUIRITIES	JOCOSENESS	JOURNALLING	JUMBOISING
JACKSTONES	JASPERIZING	JERFALCONS	JOCOSENESSES	JOURNEYERS	JUMBOIZING
JACKSTRAWS	JASPERWARE	JERKINESSES	JOCOSERIOUS	JOURNEYING	JUMHOURIYA
JACQUERIES	JASPERWARES	JERKINHEAD	JOCOSITIES	JOURNEYMAN	JUMHOURIYAS
JACTATIONS	JASPIDEOUS	JERKINHEADS	JOCULARITIES	JOURNEYMEN	JUMPINESSES
JACTITATION	JASPILITES	JERKWATERS	JOCULARITY	JOURNEYWORK	JUNCACEOUS
JACTITATIONS	JAUNDICING	JERRYMANDER	JOCULATORS	JOURNEYWORKS	JUNCTIONAL
JACULATING	JAUNTINESS	JERRYMANDERED	JOCUNDITIES	JOUYSAUNCE	JUNEATINGS
JACULATION	JAUNTINESSES	JERRYMANDERING	JOCUNDNESS	JOUYSAUNCES	JUNGLEGYMS
JACULATIONS	JAUNTINGLY	JERRYMANDERS	JOCUNDNESSES	JOVIALITIES	JUNGLELIKE
JACULATORY	JAVELINING	JESSAMINES	JOHANNESES	JOVIALNESS	JUNIORATES
JADEDNESSES	JAWBATIONS	JESSERANTS	JOHNNYCAKE	JOVIALNESSES	JUNIORITIES
JAGGEDNESS	JAWBONINGS	JESUITICAL	JOHNNYCAKES	JOVIALTIES	JUNKETEERED
JAGGEDNESSES	JAWBREAKER	JESUITICALLY	JOHNSONGRASS	JOVYSAUNCE	JUNKETEERING
JAGGHERIES	JAWBREAKERS	JESUITISMS	JOHNSONGRASSES	JOVYSAUNCES	JUNKETEERS
JAGHIRDARS	JAWBREAKING	JESUITRIES	JOINTEDNESS	JOWLINESSES	JUNKETINGS
JAGUARONDI	JAWBREAKINGLY	JETSTREAMS	JOINTEDNESSES	JOYFULLEST	JUNKETTERS
JAGUARONDIS	JAWBREAKINGS	JETTATURAS	JOINTNESSES	JOYFULNESS	JUNKETTING
JAGUARUNDI	JAWCRUSHER	JETTINESSES	JOINTRESSES	JOYFULNESSES	JUNKINESSES
JAGUARUNDIS	JAWCRUSHERS	JETTISONABLE	JOINTURESS	JOYLESSNESS	JURIDICALLY
JAILBREAKS	JAWDROPPINGLY	JETTISONED	JOINTURESSES	JOYLESSNESSES	JURISCONSULT
JAILERESSES	JAYHAWKERS	JETTISONING	JOINTURING	JOYOUSNESS	JURISCONSULTS
	JAYWALKERS	JEWELFISHES	JOINTWEEDS	JOYOUSNESSES	JURISDICTION

JURISDICTIONAL
JURISDICTIONS
JURISDICTIVE
JURISPRUDENCE
JURISPRUDENCES
JURISPRUDENT
JURISPRUDENTIAL
JURISPRUDENTS

JURISTICAL
JURISTICALLY
JUSTICESHIP
JUSTICESHIPS
JUSTICIABILITY
JUSTICIABLE
JUSTICIALISM
JUSTICIALISMS

JUSTICIARIES
JUSTICIARS
JUSTICIARSHIP
JUSTICIARSHIPS
JUSTICIARY
JUSTIFIABILITY
JUSTIFIABLE
JUSTIFIABLENESS

JUSTIFIABLY
JUSTIFICATION
JUSTIFICATIONS
JUSTIFICATIVE
JUSTIFICATOR
JUSTIFICATORS
JUSTIFICATORY
JUSTIFIERS

JUSTIFYING
JUSTNESSES
JUVENESCENCE
JUVENESCENCES
JUVENESCENT
JUVENILELY
JUVENILENESS
JUVENILENESSES

JUVENILITIES
JUVENILITY
JUXTAPOSED
JUXTAPOSES
JUXTAPOSING
JUXTAPOSITION
JUXTAPOSITIONAL
JUXTAPOSITIONS

Kk

KABALISTIC
KABARAGOYA
KABARAGOYAS
KABBALISMS
KABBALISTIC
KABBALISTS
KABELJOUWS
KADAITCHAS
KAFFEEKLATSCH
KAFFEEKLATSCHES
KAFFIRBOOM
KAFFIRBOOMS
KAHIKATEAS
KAILYAIRDS
KAINOGENESES
KAINOGENESIS
KAINOGENETIC
KAIROMONES
KAISERDOMS
KAISERISMS
KAISERSHIP
KAISERSHIPS
KAKISTOCRACIES
KAKISTOCRACY
KALAMKARIS
KALANCHOES
KALASHNIKOV
KALASHNIKOVS
KALEIDOPHONE
KALEIDOPHONES
KALEIDOSCOPE
KALEIDOSCOPES
KALEIDOSCOPIC
KALENDARED
KALENDARING
KALIPHATES
KALLIKREIN
KALLIKREINS
KALLITYPES
KALSOMINED
KALSOMINES
KALSOMINING
KAMELAUKION
KAMELAUKIONS
KAMERADING
KANAMYCINS
KANGAROOED
KANGAROOING
KANTIKOYED
KANTIKOYING
KAOLINISED
KAOLINISES
KAOLINISING
KAOLINITES
KAOLINITIC
KAOLINIZED
KAOLINIZES
KAOLINIZING
KAOLINOSES
KAOLINOSIS
KAPELLMEISTER
KAPELLMEISTERS
KARABINERS
KARANGAING
KARATEISTS
KARSTIFICATION
KARSTIFICATIONS

KARSTIFIED
KARSTIFIES
KARSTIFYING
KARUHIRUHI
KARYOGAMIC
KARYOGAMIES
KARYOGRAMS
KARYOKINESES
KARYOKINESIS
KARYOKINETIC
KARYOLOGIC
KARYOLOGICAL
KARYOLOGIES
KARYOLOGIST
KARYOLOGISTS
KARYOLYMPH
KARYOLYMPHS
KARYOLYSES
KARYOLYSIS
KARYOLYTIC
KARYOPLASM
KARYOPLASMIC
KARYOPLASMS
KARYOSOMES
KARYOTYPED
KARYOTYPES
KARYOTYPIC
KARYOTYPICAL
KARYOTYPICALLY
KARYOTYPING
KATABOLICALLY
KATABOLISM
KATABOLISMS
KATABOTHRON
KATABOTHRONS
KATADROMOUS
KATATHERMOMETER
KATAVOTHRON
KATAVOTHRONS
KATHAKALIS
KATHAREVOUSA
KATHAREVOUSAS
KATHAROMETER
KATHAROMETERS
KATZENJAMMER
KATZENJAMMERS
KAWANATANGA
KAWANATANGAS
KAZATSKIES
KAZILLIONS
KEELHALING
KEELHAULED
KEELHAULING
KEELHAULINGS
KEELIVINES
KEELYVINES
KEENNESSES
KEEPERLESS
KEEPERSHIP
KEEPERSHIPS
KEESHONDEN
KEFUFFLING
KELYPHITIC
KENNELLING
KENNETTING
KENOGENESES
KENOGENESIS

KENOGENETIC
KENOGENETICALLY
KENOPHOBIA
KENOPHOBIAS
KENOTICIST
KENOTICISTS
KENSPECKLE
KENTLEDGES
KERATECTOMIES
KERATECTOMY
KERATINISATION
KERATINISATIONS
KERATINISE
KERATINISED
KERATINISES
KERATINISING
KERATINIZATION
KERATINIZATIONS
KERATINIZE
KERATINIZED
KERATINIZES
KERATINIZING
KERATINOPHILIC
KERATINOUS
KERATITIDES
KERATITISES
KERATOGENOUS
KERATOMATA
KERATOMETER
KERATOMETERS
KERATOPHYRE
KERATOPHYRES
KERATOPLASTIC
KERATOPLASTIES
KERATOPLASTY
KERATOTOMIES
KERATOTOMY
KERAUNOGRAPH
KERAUNOGRAPHS
KERBSTONES
KERCHIEFED
KERCHIEFING
KERCHIEVES
KERFUFFLED
KERFUFFLES
KERFUFFLING
KERMESITES
KERNELLING
KERNICTERUS
KERNICTERUSES
KERNMANTEL
KERPLUNKED
KERPLUNKING
KERSANTITE
KERSANTITES
KERSEYMERE
KERSEYMERES
KERYGMATIC
KETOGENESES
KETOGENESIS
KETONAEMIA
KETONAEMIAS
KETONEMIAS
KETONURIAS
KETOSTEROID
KETOSTEROIDS
KETTLEDRUM

KETTLEDRUMMER
KETTLEDRUMMERS
KETTLEDRUMS
KETTLEFULS
KETTLESTITCH
KETTLESTITCHES
KEYBOARDED
KEYBOARDER
KEYBOARDERS
KEYBOARDING
KEYBOARDINGS
KEYBOARDIST
KEYBOARDISTS
KEYBUTTONS
KEYLOGGERS
KEYPUNCHED
KEYPUNCHER
KEYPUNCHERS
KEYPUNCHES
KEYPUNCHING
KEYSTONING
KEYSTROKED
KEYSTROKES
KEYSTROKING
KEYSTROKINGS
KHALIFATES
KHANSAMAHS
KHEDIVATES
KHEDIVIATE
KHEDIVIATES
KHIDMUTGAR
KHIDMUTGARS
KHITMUTGAR
KHITMUTGARS
KHUSKHUSES
KIBBITZERS
KIBBITZING
KIBBUTZNIK
KIBBUTZNIKS
KICKABOUTS
KICKAROUND
KICKAROUNDS
KICKBOARDS
KICKBOXERS
KICKBOXING
KICKBOXINGS
KICKSHAWSES
KICKSORTER
KICKSORTERS
KICKSTANDS
KICKSTARTED
KICKSTARTING
KICKSTARTS
KIDDIEWINK
KIDDIEWINKIE
KIDDIEWINKIES
KIDDIEWINKS
KIDDISHNESS
KIDDISHNESSES
KIDDYWINKS
KIDNAPINGS
KIDNAPPEES
KIDNAPPERS
KIDNAPPING
KIDNAPPINGS
KIDNEYLIKE
KIDOLOGIES

KIDOLOGIST
KIDOLOGISTS
KIESELGUHR
KIESELGUHRS
KIESELGURS
KIESERITES
KILDERKINS
KILLIFISHES
KILLIKINICK
KILLIKINICKS
KILOCALORIE
KILOCALORIES
KILOCURIES
KILOCYCLES
KILOGAUSSES
KILOGRAMME
KILOGRAMMES
KILOHERTZES
KILOJOULES
KILOLITERS
KILOLITRES
KILOMETERS
KILOMETRES
KILOMETRIC
KILOMETRICAL
KILOPARSEC
KILOPARSECS
KILOPASCAL
KILOPASCALS
KIMBERLITE
KIMBERLITES
KINAESTHESES
KINAESTHESIA
KINAESTHESIAS
KINAESTHESIS
KINAESTHETIC
KINDERGARTEN
KINDERGARTENER
KINDERGARTENERS
KINDERGARTENS
KINDERGARTNER
KINDERGARTNERS
KINDERSPIEL
KINDERSPIELS
KINDHEARTED
KINDHEARTEDLY
KINDHEARTEDNESS
KINDLESSLY
KINDLINESS
KINDLINESSES
KINDNESSES
KINDREDNESS
KINDREDNESSES
KINDREDSHIP
KINDREDSHIPS
KINEMATICAL
KINEMATICALLY
KINEMATICS
KINEMATOGRAPH
KINEMATOGRAPHER
KINEMATOGRAPHIC
KINEMATOGRAPHS
KINEMATOGRAPHY
KINESCOPED
KINESCOPES
KINESCOPING
KINESIATRIC

KINESIATRICS
KINESIOLOGIES
KINESIOLOGIST
KINESIOLOGISTS
KINESIOLOGY
KINESIPATH
KINESIPATHIC
KINESIPATHIES
KINESIPATHIST
KINESIPATHISTS
KINESIPATHS
KINESIPATHY
KINESITHERAPIES
KINESITHERAPY
KINESTHESES
KINESTHESIA
KINESTHESIAS
KINESTHESIS
KINESTHETIC
KINESTHETICALLY
KINETHEODOLITE
KINETHEODOLITES
KINETICALLY
KINETICIST
KINETICISTS
KINETOCHORE
KINETOCHORES
KINETOGRAPH
KINETOGRAPHS
KINETONUCLEI
KINETONUCLEUS
KINETONUCLEUSES
KINETOPLAST
KINETOPLASTS
KINETOSCOPE
KINETOSCOPES
KINETOSOME
KINETOSOMES
KINGCRAFTS
KINGDOMLESS
KINGFISHER
KINGFISHERS
KINGFISHES
KINGLIHOOD
KINGLIHOODS
KINGLINESS
KINGLINESSES
KINGMAKERS
KINGSNAKES
KINKINESSES
KINNIKINIC
KINNIKINICK
KINNIKINICKS
KINNIKINICS
KINNIKINNICK
KINNIKINNICKS
KIRBIGRIPS
KIRKYAIRDS
KIRSCHWASSER
KIRSCHWASSERS
KISSAGRAMS
KISSOGRAMS
KITCHENALIA
KITCHENALIAS
KITCHENDOM
KITCHENDOMS
KITCHENERS

KITCHENETS
KITCHENETTE
KITCHENETTES
KITCHENING
KITCHENWARE
KITCHENWARES
KITESURFING
KITESURFINGS
KITSCHIEST
KITSCHIFIED
KITSCHIFIES
KITSCHIFYING
KITSCHNESS
KITSCHNESSES
KITTENISHLY
KITTENISHNESS
KITTENISHNESSES
KITTIWAKES
KIWIFRUITS
KIWISPORTS
KLANGFARBE
KLANGFARBES
KLEBSIELLA
KLEBSIELLAS
KLEINHUISIE
KLEINHUISIES
KLENDUSITIES
KLENDUSITY
KLEPHTISMS
KLEPTOCRACIES
KLEPTOCRACY
KLEPTOCRATIC
KLEPTOMANIA
KLEPTOMANIAC

KLEPTOMANIACS
KLEPTOMANIAS
KLETTERSCHUH
KLETTERSCHUHE
KLINOSTATS
KLIPSPRINGER
KLIPSPRINGERS
KLONDIKERS
KLONDIKING
KLONDYKERS
KLONDYKING
KLOOCHMANS
KLOOTCHMAN
KLOOTCHMANS
KLOOTCHMEN
KLUTZINESS
KLUTZINESSES
KNACKERIES
KNACKERING
KNACKINESS
KNACKINESSES
KNACKWURST
KNACKWURSTS
KNAGGINESS
KNAGGINESSES
KNAPSACKED
KNAVESHIPS
KNAVISHNESS
KNAVISHNESSES
KNEECAPPED
KNEECAPPING
KNEECAPPINGS
KNEEPIECES
KNEVELLING

KNICKERBOCKER
KNICKERBOCKERS
KNICKKNACK
KNICKKNACKS
KNICKPOINT
KNICKPOINTS
KNIFEPOINT
KNIFEPOINTS
KNIFERESTS
KNIGHTAGES
KNIGHTHEAD
KNIGHTHEADS
KNIGHTHOOD
KNIGHTHOODS
KNIGHTLESS
KNIGHTLIER
KNIGHTLIEST
KNIGHTLINESS
KNIGHTLINESSES
KNIPHOFIAS
KNOBBINESS
KNOBBINESSES
KNOBBLIEST
KNOBKERRIE
KNOBKERRIES
KNOBSTICKS
KNOCKABOUT
KNOCKABOUTS
KNOCKDOWNS
KNOCKWURST
KNOCKWURSTS
KNOTGRASSES
KNOTTINESS
KNOTTINESSES

KNOWABLENESS
KNOWABLENESSES
KNOWINGEST
KNOWINGNESS
KNOWINGNESSES
KNOWLEDGABILITY
KNOWLEDGABLE
KNOWLEDGABLY
KNOWLEDGEABLE
KNOWLEDGEABLY
KNOWLEDGED
KNOWLEDGES
KNOWLEDGING
KNUBBLIEST
KNUCKLEBALL
KNUCKLEBALLER
KNUCKLEBALLERS
KNUCKLEBALLS
KNUCKLEBONE
KNUCKLEBONES
KNUCKLEDUSTER
KNUCKLEDUSTERS
KNUCKLEHEAD
KNUCKLEHEADED
KNUCKLEHEADS
KNUCKLIEST
KOEKSISTER
KOEKSISTERS
KOHLRABIES
KOHUTUHUTU
KOLINSKIES
KOLKHOZNIK
KOLKHOZNIKI
KOLKHOZNIKS

KOMONDOROCK
KOMONDOROK
KONIMETERS
KONIOLOGIES
KONISCOPES
KOOKABURRA
KOOKABURRAS
KOOKINESSES
KOTAHITANGA
KOTAHITANGAS
KOTTABOSES
KOTUKUTUKU
KOULIBIACA
KOULIBIACAS
KOURBASHED
KOURBASHES
KOURBASHING
KOUSKOUSES
KOWHAIWHAI
KOWHAIWHAIS
KRAKOWIAKS
KREASOTING
KREMLINOLOGIES
KREMLINOLOGIST
KREMLINOLOGISTS
KREMLINOLOGY
KREOSOTING
KRIEGSPIEL
KRIEGSPIELS
KRIEGSSPIEL
KRIEGSSPIELS
KROMESKIES
KRUGERRAND
KRUGERRANDS

KRUMMHORNS
KRYOMETERS
KUMARAHOUS
KUMMERBUND
KUMMERBUNDS
KUNDALINIS
KURBASHING
KURCHATOVIUM
KURCHATOVIUMS
KURDAITCHA
KURDAITCHAS
KURFUFFLED
KURFUFFLES
KURFUFFLING
KURRAJONGS
KURTOSISES
KVETCHIEST
KVETCHINESS
KVETCHINESSES
KWASHIORKOR
KWASHIORKORS
KYANISATION
KYANISATIONS
KYANIZATION
KYANIZATIONS
KYMOGRAPHIC
KYMOGRAPHIES
KYMOGRAPHS
KYMOGRAPHY

k

L1

LABANOTATION	LACERATIONS	LACTOMETER	LAMEBRAINS	LAMPOONISTS	LANDSCAPES
LABANOTATIONS	LACERATIVE	LACTOMETERS	LAMELLARLY	LAMPROPHYRE	LANDSCAPING
LABDACISMS	LACERTIANS	LACTOPROTEIN	LAMELLATED	LAMPROPHYRES	LANDSCAPIST
LABEFACTATION	LACERTILIAN	LACTOPROTEINS	LAMELLATELY	LAMPROPHYRIC	LANDSCAPISTS
LABEFACTATIONS	LACERTILIANS	LACTOSCOPE	LAMELLATION	LAMPSHADES	LANDSHARKS
LABEFACTION	LACHRYMALS	LACTOSCOPES	LAMELLATIONS	LAMPSHELLS	LANDSKIPPED
LABEFACTIONS	LACHRYMARIES	LACTOSURIA	LAMELLIBRANCH	LANCEJACKS	LANDSKIPPING
LABELLISTS	LACHRYMARY	LACTOSURIAS	LAMELLIBRANCHS	LANCEOLATE	LANDSKNECHT
LABIALISATION	LACHRYMATION	LACTOVEGETARIAN	LAMELLICORN	LANCEOLATED	LANDSKNECHTS
LABIALISATIONS	LACHRYMATIONS	LACUNOSITIES	LAMELLICORNS	LANCEOLATELY	LANDSLIDDEN
LABIALISED	LACHRYMATOR	LACUNOSITY	LAMELLIFORM	LANCEWOODS	LANDSLIDES
LABIALISES	LACHRYMATORIES	LACUSTRINE	LAMELLIROSTRAL	LANCINATED	LANDSLIDING
LABIALISING	LACHRYMATORS	LADDERLIKE	LAMELLIROSTRATE	LANCINATES	LANDWAITER
LABIALISMS	LACHRYMATORY	LADDISHNESS	LAMELLOSITIES	LANCINATING	LANDWAITERS
LABIALITIES	LACHRYMOSE	LADDISHNESSES	LAMELLOSITY	LANCINATION	LANGBEINITE
LABIALIZATION	LACHRYMOSELY	LADIESWEAR	LAMENESSES	LANCINATIONS	LANGBEINITES
LABIALIZATIONS	LACHRYMOSITIES	LADIESWEARS	LAMENTABLE	LANDAMMANN	LANGLAUFER
LABIALIZED	LACHRYMOSITY	LADYFINGER	LAMENTABLENESS	LANDAMMANNS	LANGLAUFERS
LABIALIZES	LACINESSES	LADYFINGERS	LAMENTABLY	LANDAMMANS	LANGOSTINO
LABIALIZING	LACINIATED	LADYFISHES	LAMENTATION	LANDAULETS	LANGOSTINOS
LABILITIES	LACINIATION	LADYLIKENESS	LAMENTATIONS	LANDAULETTE	LANGOUSTES
LABIODENTAL	LACINIATIONS	LADYLIKENESSES	LAMENTEDLY	LANDAULETTES	LANGOUSTINE
LABIODENTALS	LACKADAISICAL	LAEOTROPIC	LAMENTINGLY	LANDBOARDING	LANGOUSTINES
LABIONASAL	LACKADAISICALLY	LAEVIGATED	LAMENTINGS	LANDBOARDINGS	LANGRIDGES
LABIONASALS	LACKADAISY	LAEVIGATES	LAMINARIAN	LANDBOARDS	LANGSPIELS
LABIOVELAR	LACKLUSTER	LAEVIGATING	LAMINARIANS	LANDDAMNED	LANGUAGELESS
LABIOVELARS	LACKLUSTERS	LAEVOGYRATE	LAMINARIAS	LANDDAMNES	LANGUAGING
LABORATORIES	LACKLUSTRE	LAEVOROTARY	LAMINARINS	LANDDAMNING	LANGUESCENT
LABORATORY	LACKLUSTRES	LAEVOROTATION	LAMINARISE	LANDDROSES	LANGUETTES
LABOREDNESS	LACONICALLY	LAEVOROTATIONS	LAMINARISED	LANDDROSTS	LANGUIDNESS
LABOREDNESSES	LACONICISM	LAEVOROTATORY	LAMINARISES	LANDFILLED	LANGUIDNESSES
LABORINGLY	LACONICISMS	LAEVULOSES	LAMINARISING	LANDFILLING	LANGUISHED
LABORIOUSLY	LACQUERERS	LAGENIFORM	LAMINARIZE	LANDFILLINGS	LANGUISHER
LABORIOUSNESS	LACQUERING	LAGERPHONE	LAMINARIZED	LANDFORCES	LANGUISHERS
LABORIOUSNESSES	LACQUERINGS	LAGERPHONES	LAMINARIZES	LANDGRAVATE	LANGUISHES
LABORSAVING	LACQUERWARE	LAGGARDNESS	LAMINARIZING	LANDGRAVATES	LANGUISHING
LABOUREDLY	LACQUERWARES	LAGGARDNESSES	LAMINATING	LANDGRAVES	LANGUISHINGLY
LABOUREDNESS	LACQUERWORK	LAGNIAPPES	LAMINATION	LANDGRAVIATE	LANGUISHINGS
LABOUREDNESSES	LACQUERWORKS	LAGOMORPHIC	LAMINATIONS	LANDGRAVIATES	LANGUISHMENT
LABOURINGLY	LACQUEYING	LAGOMORPHOUS	LAMINATORS	LANDGRAVINE	LANGUISHMENTS
LABOURISMS	LACRIMATION	LAGOMORPHS	LAMINECTOMIES	LANDGRAVINES	LANGUOROUS
LABOURISTS	LACRIMATIONS	LAICISATION	LAMINECTOMY	LANDHOLDER	LANGUOROUSLY
LABOURSOME	LACRIMATOR	LAICISATIONS	LAMINGTONS	LANDHOLDERS	LANGUOROUSNESS
LABRADOODLE	LACRIMATORS	LAICIZATION	LAMINITISES	LANDHOLDING	LANIFEROUS
LABRADOODLES	LACRIMATORY	LAICIZATIONS	LAMMERGEIER	LANDHOLDINGS	LANIGEROUS
LABRADORESCENT	LACRYMATOR	LAIRDSHIPS	LAMMERGEIERS	LANDLADIES	LANKINESSES
LABRADORITE	LACRYMATORS	LAKEFRONTS	LAMMERGEYER	LANDLESSNESS	LANKNESSES
LABRADORITES	LACRYMATORY	LAKESHORES	LAMMERGEYERS	LANDLESSNESSES	LANOSITIES
LABYRINTHAL	LACTALBUMIN	LALAPALOOZA	LAMPADARIES	LANDLOCKED	LANSQUENET
LABYRINTHIAN	LACTALBUMINS	LALAPALOOZAS	LAMPADEDROMIES	LANDLOPERS	LANSQUENETS
LABYRINTHIC	LACTARIANS	LALLAPALOOZA	LAMPADEDROMY	LANDLORDISM	LANTERLOOS
LABYRINTHICAL	LACTATIONAL	LALLAPALOOZAS	LAMPADEPHORIA	LANDLORDISMS	LANTERNING
LABYRINTHICALLY	LACTATIONALLY	LALLYGAGGED	LAMPADEPHORIAS	LANDLUBBER	LANTERNIST
LABYRINTHINE	LACTATIONS	LALLYGAGGING	LAMPADISTS	LANDLUBBERLY	LANTERNISTS
LABYRINTHITIS	LACTESCENCE	LAMASERAIS	LAMPADOMANCIES	LANDLUBBERS	LANTHANIDE
LABYRINTHITISES	LACTESCENCES	LAMASERIES	LAMPADOMANCY	LANDLUBBING	LANTHANIDES
LABYRINTHODONT	LACTESCENT	LAMBASTING	LAMPBLACKS	LANDMARKED	LANTHANONS
LABYRINTHODONTS	LACTIFEROUS	LAMBDACISM	LAMPHOLDER	LANDMARKING	LANTHANUMS
LABYRINTHS	LACTIFEROUSNESS	LAMBDACISMS	LAMPHOLDERS	LANDMASSES	LANUGINOSE
LACCOLITES	LACTIFLUOUS	LAMBDOIDAL	LAMPLIGHTER	LANDOWNERS	LANUGINOUS
LACCOLITHIC	LACTOBACILLI	LAMBENCIES	LAMPLIGHTERS	LANDOWNERSHIP	LANUGINOUSNESS
LACCOLITHS	LACTOBACILLUS	LAMBITIVES	LAMPLIGHTS	LANDOWNERSHIPS	LANZKNECHT
LACCOLITIC	LACTOFLAVIN	LAMBREQUIN	LAMPOONERIES	LANDOWNING	LANZKNECHTS
LACERABILITIES	LACTOFLAVINS	LAMBREQUINS	LAMPOONERS	LANDOWNINGS	LAODICEANS
LACERABILITY	LACTOGENIC	LAMBRUSCOS	LAMPOONERY	LANDSCAPED	LAPAROSCOPE
LACERATING	LACTOGLOBULIN	LAMEBRAINED	LAMPOONING	LANDSCAPER	LAPAROSCOPES
LACERATION	LACTOGLOBULINS		LAMPOONIST	LANDSCAPERS	LAPAROSCOPIC

LAPAROSCOPIES	LASTINGNESS	LAUDATIONS	LEADERBOARD	LEERINESSES	LEGITIMISE
LAPAROSCOPIST	LASTINGNESSES	LAUDATIVES	LEADERBOARDS	LEFTWARDLY	LEGITIMISED
LAPAROSCOPISTS	LATCHSTRING	LAUDATORIES	LEADERENES	LEGALISATION	LEGITIMISER
LAPAROSCOPY	LATCHSTRINGS	LAUGHABLENESS	LEADERETTE	LEGALISATIONS	LEGITIMISERS
LAPAROTOMIES	LATECOMERS	LAUGHABLENESSES	LEADERETTES	LEGALISERS	LEGITIMISES
LAPAROTOMY	LATEENRIGGED	LAUGHINGLY	LEADERLESS	LEGALISING	LEGITIMISING
LAPIDARIAN	LATENESSES	LAUGHINGSTOCK	LEADERSHIP	LEGALISTIC	LEGITIMISM
LAPIDARIES	LATENSIFICATION	LAUGHINGSTOCKS	LEADERSHIPS	LEGALISTICALLY	LEGITIMISMS
LAPIDARIST	LATERALING	LAUGHLINES	LEADPLANTS	LEGALITIES	LEGITIMIST
LAPIDARISTS	LATERALISATION	LAUGHWORTHY	LEADSCREWS	LEGALIZATION	LEGITIMISTIC
LAPIDATING	LATERALISATIONS	LAUNCEGAYE	LEAFCUTTER	LEGALIZATIONS	LEGITIMISTS
LAPIDATION	LATERALISE	LAUNCEGAYES	LEAFHOPPER	LEGALIZERS	LEGITIMIZATION
LAPIDATIONS	LATERALISED	LAUNCHPADS	LEAFHOPPERS	LEGALIZING	LEGITIMIZATIONS
LAPIDESCENCE	LATERALISES	LAUNDERERS	LEAFINESSES	LEGATARIES	LEGITIMIZE
LAPIDESCENCES	LATERALISING	LAUNDERETTE	LEAFLESSNESS	LEGATESHIP	LEGITIMIZED
LAPIDESCENT	LATERALITIES	LAUNDERETTES	LEAFLESSNESSES	LEGATESHIPS	LEGITIMIZER
LAPIDICOLOUS	LATERALITY	LAUNDERING	LEAFLETEER	LEGATIONARY	LEGITIMIZERS
LAPIDIFICATION	LATERALIZATION	LAUNDRESSES	LEAFLETEERS	LEGATISSIMO	LEGITIMIZES
LAPIDIFICATIONS	LATERALIZATIONS	LAUNDRETTE	LEAFLETERS	LEGATORIAL	LEGITIMIZING
LAPIDIFIED	LATERALIZE	LAUNDRETTES	LEAFLETING	LEGENDARIES	LEGLESSNESS
LAPIDIFIES	LATERALIZED	LAUNDRYMAN	LEAFLETTED	LEGENDARILY	LEGLESSNESSES
LAPIDIFYING	LATERALIZES	LAUNDRYMEN	LEAFLETTING	LEGENDISED	LEGUMINOUS
LAPILLIFORM	LATERALIZING	LAUNDRYWOMAN	LEAFSTALKS	LEGENDISES	LEGWARMERS
LAPSTRAKES	LATERALLED	LAUNDRYWOMEN	LEAGUERING	LEGENDISING	LEIOMYOMAS
LAPSTREAKS	LATERALLING	LAURACEOUS	LEAKINESSES	LEGENDISTS	LEIOMYOMATA
LARCENISTS	LATERBORNS	LAURDALITE	LEANNESSES	LEGENDIZED	LEIOTRICHIES
LARCENOUSLY	LATERIGRADE	LAURDALITES	LEAPFROGGED	LEGENDIZES	LEIOTRICHOUS
LARDACEOUS	LATERISATION	LAUREATESHIP	LEAPFROGGING	LEGENDIZING	LEIOTRICHY
LARDALITES	LATERISATIONS	LAUREATESHIPS	LEARINESSES	LEGENDRIES	LEISHMANIA
LARGEHEARTED	LATERISING	LAUREATING	LEARNABILITIES	LEGERDEMAIN	LEISHMANIAE
LARGEMOUTH	LATERITIOUS	LAUREATION	LEARNABILITY	LEGERDEMAINIST	LEISHMANIAL
LARGEMOUTHS	LATERIZATION	LAUREATIONS	LEARNEDNESS	LEGERDEMAINISTS	LEISHMANIAS
LARGENESSES	LATERIZATIONS	LAURELLING	LEARNEDNESSES	LEGERDEMAINS	LEISHMANIASES
LARGHETTOS	LATERIZING	LAURUSTINE	LEASEBACKS	LEGERITIES	LEISHMANIASIS
LARGITIONS	LATEROVERSION	LAURUSTINES	LEASEHOLDER	LEGGINESSES	LEISHMANIOSES
LARKINESSES	LATEROVERSIONS	LAURUSTINUS	LEASEHOLDERS	LEGIBILITIES	LEISHMANIOSIS
LARKISHNESS	LATESCENCE	LAURUSTINUSES	LEASEHOLDS	LEGIBILITY	LEISTERING
LARKISHNESSES	LATESCENCES	LAURVIKITE	LEASTAWAYS	LEGIBLENESS	LEISURABLE
LARRIKINISM	LATHERIEST	LAURVIKITES	LEATHERBACK	LEGIBLENESSES	LEISURABLY
LARRIKINISMS	LATHYRISMS	LAVALIERES	LEATHERBACKS	LEGIONARIES	LEISURELINESS
LARVICIDAL	LATHYRITIC	LAVALLIERE	LEATHERETTE	LEGIONELLA	LEISURELINESSES
LARVICIDES	LATHYRUSES	LAVALLIERES	LEATHERETTES	LEGIONELLAE	LEITMOTIFS
LARVIKITES	LATICIFEROUS	LAVATIONAL	LEATHERGOODS	LEGIONNAIRE	LEITMOTIVS
LARVIPAROUS	LATICIFERS	LAVATORIAL	LEATHERHEAD	LEGIONNAIRES	LEMMATISATION
LARYNGEALLY	LATICLAVES	LAVATORIES	LEATHERHEADS	LEGISLATED	LEMMATISATIONS
LARYNGEALS	LATIFUNDIA	LAVENDERED	LEATHERIER	LEGISLATES	LEMMATISED
LARYNGECTOMEE	LATIFUNDIO	LAVENDERING	LEATHERIEST	LEGISLATING	LEMMATISES
LARYNGECTOMEES	LATIFUNDIOS	LAVERBREAD	LEATHERINESS	LEGISLATION	LEMMATISING
LARYNGECTOMIES	LATIFUNDIUM	LAVERBREADS	LEATHERINESSES	LEGISLATIONS	LEMMATIZATION
LARYNGECTOMISED	LATIMERIAS	LAVEROCKED	LEATHERING	LEGISLATIVE	LEMMATIZATIONS
LARYNGECTOMIZED	LATINISATION	LAVEROCKING	LEATHERINGS	LEGISLATIVELY	LEMMATIZED
LARYNGECTOMY	LATINISATIONS	LAVISHMENT	LEATHERJACKET	LEGISLATIVES	LEMMATIZES
LARYNGISMUS	LATINISING	LAVISHMENTS	LEATHERJACKETS	LEGISLATOR	LEMMATIZING
LARYNGISMUSES	LATINITIES	LAVISHNESS	LEATHERLEAF	LEGISLATORIAL	LEMMINGLIKE
LARYNGITIC	LATINIZATION	LAVISHNESSES	LEATHERLEAVES	LEGISLATORS	LEMNISCATE
LARYNGITIS	LATINIZATIONS	LAVOLTAING	LEATHERLIKE	LEGISLATORSHIP	LEMNISCATES
LARYNGITISES	LATINIZING	LAWBREAKER	LEATHERNECK	LEGISLATORSHIPS	LEMONFISHES
LARYNGOLOGIC	LATIROSTRAL	LAWBREAKERS	LEATHERNECKS	LEGISLATRESS	LEMONGRASS
LARYNGOLOGICAL	LATIROSTRATE	LAWBREAKING	LEATHERWOOD	LEGISLATRESSES	LEMONGRASSES
LARYNGOLOGIES	LATISEPTATE	LAWBREAKINGS	LEATHERWOODS	LEGISLATURE	LEMONWOODS
LARYNGOLOGIST	LATITANCIES	LAWFULNESS	LEAVENINGS	LEGISLATURES	LENGTHENED
LARYNGOLOGISTS	LATITATION	LAWFULNESSES	LEBENSRAUM	LEGITIMACIES	LENGTHENER
LARYNGOLOGY	LATITATIONS	LAWGIVINGS	LEBENSRAUMS	LEGITIMACY	LENGTHENERS
LARYNGOPHONIES	LATITUDINAL	LAWLESSNESS	LECHEROUSLY	LEGITIMATE	LENGTHENING
LARYNGOPHONY	LATITUDINALLY	LAWLESSNESSES	LECHEROUSNESS	LEGITIMATED	LENGTHIEST
LARYNGOSCOPE	LATITUDINARIAN	LAWMAKINGS	LECHEROUSNESSES	LEGITIMATELY	LENGTHINESS
LARYNGOSCOPES	LATITUDINARIANS	LAWMONGERS	LECITHINASE	LEGITIMATENESS	LENGTHINESSES
LARYNGOSCOPIC	LATITUDINOUS	LAWNMOWERS	LECITHINASES	LEGITIMATES	LENGTHSMAN
LARYNGOSCOPIES	LATRATIONS	LAWRENCIUM	LECTIONARIES	LEGITIMATING	LENGTHSMEN
LARYNGOSCOPIST	LATROCINIA	LAWRENCIUMS	LECTIONARY	LEGITIMATION	LENGTHWAYS
LARYNGOSCOPISTS	LATROCINIES	LAWYERINGS	LECTISTERNIA	LEGITIMATIONS	LENGTHWISE
LARYNGOSCOPY	LATROCINIUM	LAWYERLIKE	LECTISTERNIUM	LEGITIMATISE	LENIENCIES
LARYNGOSPASM	LATTERMATH	LAXATIVENESS	LECTORATES	LEGITIMATISED	LENITIVELY
LARYNGOSPASMS	LATTERMATHS	LAXATIVENESSES	LECTORSHIP	LEGITIMATISES	LENOCINIUM
LARYNGOTOMIES	LATTERMOST	LAYBACKING	LECTORSHIPS	LEGITIMATISING	LENOCINIUMS
LARYNGOTOMY	LATTICEWORK	LAYPERSONS	LECTOTYPES	LEGITIMATIZE	LENTAMENTE
LASCIVIOUS	LATTICEWORKS	LAZARETTES	LECTRESSES	LEGITIMATIZED	LENTICELLATE
LASCIVIOUSLY	LATTICINGS	LAZARETTOS	LECTURESHIP	LEGITIMATIZES	LENTICULAR
LASCIVIOUSNESS	LATTICINIO	LAZINESSES	LECTURESHIPS	LEGITIMATIZING	LENTICULARLY
LASERDISCS	LAUDABILITIES	LEACHABILITIES	LECYTHIDACEOUS	LEGITIMATOR	LENTICULARS
LASERDISKS	LAUDABILITY	LEACHABILITY	LEDERHOSEN	LEGITIMATORS	LENTICULES
LASERWORTS	LAUDABLENESS	LEADENNESS	LEECHCRAFT	LEGITIMISATION	LENTIGINES
LASSITUDES	LAUDABLENESSES	LEADENNESSES	LEECHCRAFTS	LEGITIMISATIONS	LENTIGINOSE

LENTIGINOUS
LENTISSIMO
LENTIVIRUS
LENTIVIRUSES
LEONTIASES
LEONTIASIS
LEONTOPODIUM
LEONTOPODIUMS
LEOPARDESS
LEOPARDESSES
LEPIDODENDROID
LEPIDODENDROIDS
LEPIDOLITE
LEPIDOLITES
LEPIDOMELANE
LEPIDOMELANES
LEPIDOPTERA
LEPIDOPTERAN
LEPIDOPTERANS
LEPIDOPTERIST
LEPIDOPTERISTS
LEPIDOPTEROLOGY
LEPIDOPTERON
LEPIDOPTERONS
LEPIDOPTEROUS
LEPIDOSIREN
LEPIDOSIRENS
LEPRECHAUN
LEPRECHAUNISH
LEPRECHAUNS
LEPRECHAWN
LEPRECHAWNS
LEPROMATOUS
LEPROSARIA
LEPROSARIUM
LEPROSARIUMS
LEPROSERIE
LEPROSERIES
LEPROSITIES
LEPROUSNESS
LEPROUSNESSES
LEPTOCEPHALI
LEPTOCEPHALIC
LEPTOCEPHALOUS
LEPTOCEPHALUS
LEPTOCERCAL
LEPTODACTYL
LEPTODACTYLOUS
LEPTODACTYLS
LEPTOKURTIC
LEPTOPHOSES
LEPTOPHYLLOUS
LEPTORRHINE
LEPTOSOMATIC
LEPTOSOMES
LEPTOSOMIC
LEPTOSPIRAL
LEPTOSPIRE
LEPTOSPIRES
LEPTOSPIROSES
LEPTOSPIROSIS
LEPTOTENES
LESBIANISM
LESBIANISMS
LESPEDEZAS
LESSEESHIP
LESSEESHIPS
LESSONINGS
LETHALITIES
LETHARGICAL
LETHARGICALLY
LETHARGIED
LETHARGIES
LETHARGISE
LETHARGISED
LETHARGISES
LETHARGISING
LETHARGIZE
LETHARGIZED
LETHARGIZES
LETHARGIZING
LETHIFEROUS
LETTERBOXED

LETTERBOXES
LETTERBOXING
LETTERBOXINGS
LETTERFORM
LETTERFORMS
LETTERHEAD
LETTERHEADS
LETTERINGS
LETTERLESS
LETTERPRESS
LETTERPRESSES
LETTERSETS
LETTERSPACING
LETTERSPACINGS
LEUCAEMIAS
LEUCAEMOGEN
LEUCAEMOGENIC
LEUCAEMOGENS
LEUCHAEMIA
LEUCHAEMIAS
LEUCITOHEDRA
LEUCITOHEDRON
LEUCITOHEDRONS
LEUCOBLAST
LEUCOBLASTS
LEUCOCIDIN
LEUCOCIDINS
LEUCOCRATIC
LEUCOCYTES
LEUCOCYTHAEMIA
LEUCOCYTHAEMIAS
LEUCOCYTIC
LEUCOCYTOLYSES
LEUCOCYTOLYSIS
LEUCOCYTOPENIA
LEUCOCYTOPENIAS
LEUCOCYTOSES
LEUCOCYTOSIS
LEUCOCYTOTIC
LEUCODEPLETED
LEUCODERMA
LEUCODERMAL
LEUCODERMAS
LEUCODERMIA
LEUCODERMIAS
LEUCODERMIC
LEUCOMAINE
LEUCOMAINES
LEUCOPENIA
LEUCOPENIAS
LEUCOPENIC
LEUCOPLAKIA
LEUCOPLAKIAS
LEUCOPLAST
LEUCOPLASTID
LEUCOPLASTIDS
LEUCOPLASTS
LEUCOPOIESES
LEUCOPOIESIS
LEUCOPOIETIC
LEUCORRHOEA
LEUCORRHOEAL
LEUCORRHOEAS
LEUCOTOMES
LEUCOTOMIES
LEUKAEMIAS
LEUKAEMOGENESES
LEUKAEMOGENESIS
LEUKEMOGENESES
LEUKEMOGENESIS
LEUKEMOGENIC
LEUKOBLAST
LEUKOBLASTS
LEUKOCYTES
LEUKOCYTIC
LEUKOCYTOSES
LEUKOCYTOSIS
LEUKOCYTOTIC
LEUKODERMA
LEUKODERMAL
LEUKODERMAS
LEUKODERMIC
LEUKODYSTROPHY

LEUKOPENIA
LEUKOPENIAS
LEUKOPENIC
LEUKOPLAKIA
LEUKOPLAKIAS
LEUKOPLAKIC
LEUKOPOIESES
LEUKOPOIESIS
LEUKOPOIETIC
LEUKORRHEA
LEUKORRHEAL
LEUKORRHEAS
LEUKOTOMIES
LEUKOTRIENE
LEUKOTRIENES
LEVANTINES
LEVELHEADED
LEVELHEADEDNESS
LEVELLINGS
LEVELNESSES
LEVERAGING
LEVIATHANS
LEVIGATING
LEVIGATION
LEVIGATIONS
LEVIGATORS
LEVIRATICAL
LEVIRATION
LEVIRATIONS
LEVITATING
LEVITATION
LEVITATIONAL
LEVITATIONS
LEVITATORS
LEVITICALLY
LEVOROTARY
LEVOROTATORY
LEWDNESSES
LEXICALISATION
LEXICALISATIONS
LEXICALISE
LEXICALISED
LEXICALISES
LEXICALISING
LEXICALITIES
LEXICALITY
LEXICALIZATION
LEXICALIZATIONS
LEXICALIZE
LEXICALIZED
LEXICALIZES
LEXICALIZING
LEXICOGRAPHER
LEXICOGRAPHERS
LEXICOGRAPHIC
LEXICOGRAPHICAL
LEXICOGRAPHIES
LEXICOGRAPHIST
LEXICOGRAPHISTS
LEXICOGRAPHY
LEXICOLOGICAL
LEXICOLOGICALLY
LEXICOLOGIES
LEXICOLOGIST
LEXICOLOGISTS
LEXICOLOGY
LEXIGRAPHIC
LEXIGRAPHICAL
LEXIGRAPHIES
LEXIGRAPHY
LEYLANDIIS
LHERZOLITE
LHERZOLITES
LIABILITIES
LIABLENESS
LIABLENESSES
LIBATIONAL
LIBATIONARY
LIBECCHIOS
LIBELLANTS
LIBELLINGS
LIBELLOUSLY
LIBERALISATION

LIBERALISATIONS
LIBERALISE
LIBERALISED
LIBERALISER
LIBERALISERS
LIBERALISES
LIBERALISING
LIBERALISM
LIBERALISMS
LIBERALIST
LIBERALISTIC
LIBERALISTS
LIBERALITIES
LIBERALITY
LIBERALIZATION
LIBERALIZATIONS
LIBERALIZE
LIBERALIZED
LIBERALIZER
LIBERALIZERS
LIBERALIZES
LIBERALIZING
LIBERALNESS
LIBERALNESSES
LIBERATING
LIBERATION
LIBERATIONISM
LIBERATIONISMS
LIBERATIONIST
LIBERATIONISTS
LIBERATIONS
LIBERATORS
LIBERATORY
LIBERTARIAN
LIBERTARIANISM
LIBERTARIANISMS
LIBERTARIANS
LIBERTICIDAL
LIBERTICIDE
LIBERTICIDES
LIBERTINAGE
LIBERTINAGES
LIBERTINES
LIBERTINISM
LIBERTINISMS
LIBIDINALLY
LIBIDINIST
LIBIDINISTS
LIBIDINOSITIES
LIBIDINOSITY
LIBIDINOUS
LIBIDINOUSLY
LIBIDINOUSNESS
LIBRAIRIES
LIBRARIANS
LIBRARIANSHIP
LIBRARIANSHIPS
LIBRATIONAL
LIBRATIONS
LIBRETTIST
LIBRETTISTS
LICENSABLE
LICENSURES
LICENTIATE
LICENTIATES
LICENTIATESHIP
LICENTIATESHIPS
LICENTIATION
LICENTIATIONS
LICENTIOUS
LICENTIOUSLY
LICENTIOUSNESS
LICHANOSES
LICHENISMS
LICHENISTS
LICHENOLOGICAL
LICHENOLOGIES
LICHENOLOGIST
LICHENOLOGISTS
LICHENOLOGY
LICHTLYING
LICITNESSES
LICKERISHLY

LICKERISHNESS
LICKERISHNESSES
LICKPENNIES
LICKSPITTLE
LICKSPITTLES
LIDOCAINES
LIEBFRAUMILCH
LIEBFRAUMILCHS
LIENTERIES
LIEUTENANCIES
LIEUTENANCY
LIEUTENANT
LIEUTENANTRIES
LIEUTENANTRY
LIEUTENANTS
LIEUTENANTSHIP
LIEUTENANTSHIPS
LIFEBLOODS
LIFEGUARDED
LIFEGUARDING
LIFEGUARDS
LIFELESSLY
LIFELESSNESS
LIFELESSNESSES
LIFELIKENESS
LIFELIKENESSES
LIFEMANSHIP
LIFEMANSHIPS
LIFESAVERS
LIFESAVING
LIFESAVINGS
LIFESTYLER
LIFESTYLERS
LIFESTYLES
LIFEWORLDS
LIGAMENTAL
LIGAMENTARY
LIGAMENTOUS
LIGATURING
LIGHTBULBS
LIGHTENERS
LIGHTENING
LIGHTENINGS
LIGHTERAGE
LIGHTERAGES
LIGHTERING
LIGHTERMAN
LIGHTERMEN
LIGHTFACED
LIGHTFACES
LIGHTFASTNESS
LIGHTFASTNESSES
LIGHTHEARTED
LIGHTHEARTEDLY
LIGHTHOUSE
LIGHTHOUSEMAN
LIGHTHOUSEMEN
LIGHTHOUSES
LIGHTLYING
LIGHTNESSES
LIGHTNINGED
LIGHTNINGS
LIGHTPLANE
LIGHTPLANES
LIGHTPROOF
LIGHTSHIPS
LIGHTSOMELY
LIGHTSOMENESS
LIGHTSOMENESSES
LIGHTTIGHT
LIGHTWEIGHT
LIGHTWEIGHTS
LIGHTWOODS
LIGNICOLOUS
LIGNIFICATION
LIGNIFICATIONS
LIGNIFYING
LIGNIPERDOUS
LIGNIVOROUS
LIGNOCAINE
LIGNOCAINES
LIGNOCELLULOSE
LIGNOCELLULOSES

LIGNOCELLULOSIC
LIGNOSULFONATE
LIGNOSULFONATES
LIGULIFLORAL
LIKABILITIES
LIKABILITY
LIKABLENESS
LIKABLENESSES
LIKEABLENESS
LIKEABLENESSES
LIKELIHOOD
LIKELIHOODS
LIKELINESS
LIKELINESSES
LIKENESSES
LILIACEOUS
LILLIPUTIAN
LILLIPUTIANS
LILTINGNESS
LILTINGNESSES
LIMACIFORM
LIMACOLOGIES
LIMACOLOGIST
LIMACOLOGISTS
LIMACOLOGY
LIMBERNESS
LIMBERNESSES
LIMBURGITE
LIMBURGITES
LIMELIGHTED
LIMELIGHTER
LIMELIGHTERS
LIMELIGHTING
LIMELIGHTS
LIMESCALES
LIMESTONES
LIMEWASHES
LIMEWATERS
LIMICOLINE
LIMICOLOUS
LIMINESSES
LIMITABLENESS
LIMITABLENESSES
LIMITARIAN
LIMITARIANS
LIMITATION
LIMITATIONAL
LIMITATIONS
LIMITATIVE
LIMITEDNESS
LIMITEDNESSES
LIMITINGLY
LIMITLESSLY
LIMITLESSNESS
LIMITLESSNESSES
LIMITROPHE
LIMIVOROUS
LIMNOLOGIC
LIMNOLOGICAL
LIMNOLOGICALLY
LIMNOLOGIES
LIMNOLOGIST
LIMNOLOGISTS
LIMNOPHILOUS
LIMOUSINES
LIMPIDITIES
LIMPIDNESS
LIMPIDNESSES
LIMPNESSES
LINCOMYCIN
LINCOMYCINS
LINCRUSTAS
LINEALITIES
LINEAMENTAL
LINEAMENTS
LINEARISATION
LINEARISATIONS
LINEARISED
LINEARISES
LINEARISING
LINEARITIES
LINEARIZATION
LINEARIZATIONS

LINEARIZED
LINEARIZES
LINEARIZING
LINEATIONS
LINEBACKER
LINEBACKERS
LINEBACKING
LINEBACKINGS
LINEBREEDING
LINEBREEDINGS
LINECASTER
LINECASTERS
LINECASTING
LINECASTINGS
LINEOLATED
LINERBOARD
LINERBOARDS
LINGBERRIES
LINGERINGLY
LINGERINGS
LINGONBERRIES
LINGONBERRY
LINGUIFORM
LINGUISTER
LINGUISTERS
LINGUISTIC
LINGUISTICAL
LINGUISTICALLY
LINGUISTICIAN
LINGUISTICIANS
LINGUISTICS
LINGUISTRIES
LINGUISTRY
LINGULATED
LINISHINGS
LINKSLANDS
LINOLEATES
LINOTYPERS
LINOTYPING
LINTSTOCKS
LINTWHITES
LIONCELLES
LIONFISHES
LIONHEARTED
LIONHEARTEDNESS
LIONISATION
LIONISATIONS
LIONIZATION
LIONIZATIONS
LIPECTOMIES
LIPIDOPLAST
LIPIDOPLASTS
LIPOCHROME
LIPOCHROMES
LIPODYSTROPHIES
LIPODYSTROPHY
LIPOGENESES
LIPOGENESIS
LIPOGRAMMATIC
LIPOGRAMMATISM
LIPOGRAMMATISMS
LIPOGRAMMATIST
LIPOGRAMMATISTS
LIPOGRAPHIES
LIPOGRAPHY
LIPOMATOSES
LIPOMATOSIS
LIPOMATOUS
LIPOPHILIC
LIPOPLASTS
LIPOPROTEIN
LIPOPROTEINS
LIPOSCULPTURE
LIPOSCULPTURES
LIPOSUCKED
LIPOSUCKING
LIPOSUCTION
LIPOSUCTIONS
LIPOTROPIC
LIPOTROPIES
LIPOTROPIN
LIPOTROPINS
LIPPINESSES

LIPPITUDES
LIPREADERS
LIPREADING
LIPREADINGS
LIPSTICKED
LIPSTICKING
LIQUATIONS
LIQUEFACIENT
LIQUEFACIENTS
LIQUEFACTION
LIQUEFACTIONS
LIQUEFACTIVE
LIQUEFIABLE
LIQUEFIERS
LIQUEFYING
LIQUESCENCE
LIQUESCENCES
LIQUESCENCIES
LIQUESCENCY
LIQUESCENT
LIQUESCING
LIQUEURING
LIQUIDAMBAR
LIQUIDAMBARS
LIQUIDATED
LIQUIDATES
LIQUIDATING
LIQUIDATION
LIQUIDATIONS
LIQUIDATOR
LIQUIDATORS
LIQUIDISED
LIQUIDISER
LIQUIDISERS
LIQUIDISES
LIQUIDISING
LIQUIDITIES
LIQUIDIZED
LIQUIDIZER
LIQUIDIZERS
LIQUIDIZES
LIQUIDIZING
LIQUIDNESS
LIQUIDNESSES
LIQUIDUSES
LIQUIFYING
LIQUORICES
LIQUORISHLY
LIQUORISHNESS
LIQUORISHNESSES
LIRIODENDRA
LIRIODENDRON
LIRIODENDRONS
LISSENCEPHALOUS
LISSOMENESS
LISSOMENESSES
LISSOMNESS
LISSOMNESSES
LISSOTRICHOUS
LISTENABILITIES
LISTENABILITY
LISTENABLE
LISTENERSHIP
LISTENERSHIPS
LISTERIOSES
LISTERIOSIS
LISTLESSLY
LISTLESSNESS
LISTLESSNESSES
LITENESSES
LITERACIES
LITERALISATION
LITERALISATIONS
LITERALISE
LITERALISED
LITERALISER
LITERALISERS
LITERALISES
LITERALISING
LITERALISM
LITERALISMS
LITERALIST
LITERALISTIC

LITERALISTS
LITERALITIES
LITERALITY
LITERALIZATION
LITERALIZATIONS
LITERALIZE
LITERALIZED
LITERALIZER
LITERALIZERS
LITERALIZES
LITERALIZING
LITERALNESS
LITERALNESSES
LITERARILY
LITERARINESS
LITERARINESSES
LITERARYISM
LITERARYISMS
LITERATELY
LITERATENESS
LITERATENESSES
LITERATION
LITERATIONS
LITERATORS
LITERATURE
LITERATURED
LITERATURES
LITEROSITIES
LITEROSITY
LITHENESSES
LITHESOMENESS
LITHESOMENESSES
LITHIFICATION
LITHIFICATIONS
LITHIFYING
LITHISTIDS
LITHOCHROMATIC
LITHOCHROMATICS
LITHOCHROMIES
LITHOCHROMY
LITHOCLAST
LITHOCLASTS
LITHOCYSTS
LITHODOMOUS
LITHOGENOUS
LITHOGLYPH
LITHOGLYPHS
LITHOGRAPH
LITHOGRAPHED
LITHOGRAPHER
LITHOGRAPHERS
LITHOGRAPHIC
LITHOGRAPHICAL
LITHOGRAPHIES
LITHOGRAPHING
LITHOGRAPHS
LITHOGRAPHY
LITHOLAPAXIES
LITHOLAPAXY
LITHOLATRIES
LITHOLATROUS
LITHOLATRY
LITHOLOGIC
LITHOLOGICAL
LITHOLOGICALLY
LITHOLOGIES
LITHOLOGIST
LITHOLOGISTS
LITHOMANCIES
LITHOMANCY
LITHOMARGE
LITHOMARGES
LITHOMETEOR
LITHOMETEORS
LITHONTHRYPTIC
LITHONTHRYPTICS
LITHONTRIPTIC
LITHONTRIPTICS
LITHONTRIPTIST
LITHONTRIPTISTS
LITHONTRIPTOR
LITHONTRIPTORS
LITHOPHAGOUS

LITHOPHANE
LITHOPHANES
LITHOPHILOUS
LITHOPHYSA
LITHOPHYSAE
LITHOPHYSE
LITHOPHYSES
LITHOPHYTE
LITHOPHYTES
LITHOPHYTIC
LITHOPONES
LITHOPRINT
LITHOPRINTS
LITHOSPERMUM
LITHOSPERMUMS
LITHOSPHERE
LITHOSPHERES
LITHOSPHERIC
LITHOSTATIC
LITHOTOMES
LITHOTOMIC
LITHOTOMICAL
LITHOTOMIES
LITHOTOMIST
LITHOTOMISTS
LITHOTOMOUS
LITHOTRIPSIES
LITHOTRIPSY
LITHOTRIPTER
LITHOTRIPTERS
LITHOTRIPTIC
LITHOTRIPTICS
LITHOTRIPTIST
LITHOTRIPTISTS
LITHOTRIPTOR
LITHOTRIPTORS
LITHOTRITE
LITHOTRITES
LITHOTRITIC
LITHOTRITICS
LITHOTRITIES
LITHOTRITISE
LITHOTRITISED
LITHOTRITISES
LITHOTRITISING
LITHOTRITIST
LITHOTRITISTS
LITHOTRITIZE
LITHOTRITIZED
LITHOTRITIZES
LITHOTRITIZING
LITHOTRITOR
LITHOTRITORS
LITHOTRITY
LITIGATING
LITIGATION
LITIGATIONS
LITIGATORS
LITIGIOUSLY
LITIGIOUSNESS
LITIGIOUSNESSES
LITTERATEUR
LITTERATEURS
LITTERBAGS
LITTERBUGS
LITTERMATE
LITTERMATES
LITTLENECK
LITTLENECKS
LITTLENESS
LITTLENESSES
LITTLEWORTH
LITURGICAL
LITURGICALLY
LITURGIOLOGIES
LITURGIOLOGIST
LITURGIOLOGISTS
LITURGIOLOGY
LITURGISMS
LITURGISTIC
LITURGISTS
LIVABILITIES
LIVABILITY

LIVABLENESS
LIVABLENESSES
LIVEABILITIES
LIVEABILITY
LIVEABLENESS
LIVEABLENESSES
LIVELIHEAD
LIVELIHEADS
LIVELIHOOD
LIVELIHOODS
LIVELINESS
LIVELINESSES
LIVENESSES
LIVERISHNESS
LIVERISHNESSES
LIVERLEAVES
LIVERWORTS
LIVERWURST
LIVERWURSTS
LIVESTOCKS
LIVETRAPPED
LIVETRAPPING
LIVIDITIES
LIVIDNESSES
LIVINGNESS
LIVINGNESSES
LIVRAISONS
LIXIVIATED
LIXIVIATES
LIXIVIATING
LIXIVIATION
LIXIVIATIONS
LOADMASTER
LOADMASTERS
LOADSAMONEY
LOADSAMONEYS
LOADSAMONIES
LOADSPACES
LOADSTONES
LOAMINESSES
LOANSHIFTS
LOATHEDNESS
LOATHEDNESSES
LOATHFULNESS
LOATHFULNESSES
LOATHINGLY
LOATHLINESS
LOATHLINESSES
LOATHNESSES
LOATHSOMELY
LOATHSOMENESS
LOATHSOMENESSES
LOBECTOMIES
LOBLOLLIES
LOBOTOMIES
LOBOTOMISE
LOBOTOMISED
LOBOTOMISES
LOBOTOMISING
LOBOTOMIZE
LOBOTOMIZED
LOBOTOMIZES
LOBOTOMIZING
LOBSCOUSES
LOBSTERERS
LOBSTERING
LOBSTERINGS
LOBSTERLIKE
LOBSTERMAN
LOBSTERMEN
LOBULATION
LOBULATIONS
LOCALISABILITY
LOCALISABLE
LOCALISATION
LOCALISATIONS
LOCALISERS
LOCALISING
LOCALISTIC
LOCALITIES
LOCALIZABILITY
LOCALIZABLE
LOCALIZATION

LOCALIZATIONS
LOCALIZERS
LOCALIZING
LOCALNESSES
LOCATEABLE
LOCATIONAL
LOCATIONALLY
LOCKHOUSES
LOCKKEEPER
LOCKKEEPERS
LOCKMAKERS
LOCKSMITHERIES
LOCKSMITHERY
LOCKSMITHING
LOCKSMITHINGS
LOCKSMITHS
LOCKSTITCH
LOCKSTITCHED
LOCKSTITCHES
LOCKSTITCHING
LOCOMOBILE
LOCOMOBILES
LOCOMOBILITIES
LOCOMOBILITY
LOCOMOTING
LOCOMOTION
LOCOMOTIONS
LOCOMOTIVE
LOCOMOTIVELY
LOCOMOTIVENESS
LOCOMOTIVES
LOCOMOTIVITIES
LOCOMOTIVITY
LOCOMOTORS
LOCOMOTORY
LOCOPLANTS
LOCORESTIVE
LOCULAMENT
LOCULAMENTS
LOCULATION
LOCULATIONS
LOCULICIDAL
LOCUTIONARY
LOCUTORIES
LODESTONES
LODGEMENTS
LODGEPOLES
LOFTINESSES
LOGAGRAPHIA
LOGAGRAPHIAS
LOGANBERRIES
LOGANBERRY
LOGANIACEOUS
LOGAOEDICS
LOGARITHMIC
LOGARITHMICAL
LOGARITHMICALLY
LOGARITHMS
LOGGERHEAD
LOGGERHEADED
LOGGERHEADS
LOGICALITIES
LOGICALITY
LOGICALNESS
LOGICALNESSES
LOGICISING
LOGICIZING
LOGINESSES
LOGISTICAL
LOGISTICALLY
LOGISTICIAN
LOGISTICIANS
LOGJAMMING
LOGNORMALITIES
LOGNORMALITY
LOGNORMALLY
LOGODAEDALIC
LOGODAEDALIES
LOGODAEDALUS
LOGODAEDALUSES
LOGODAEDALY
LOGOGRAMMATIC
LOGOGRAPHER

LOGOGRAPHERS
LOGOGRAPHIC
LOGOGRAPHICAL
LOGOGRAPHICALLY
LOGOGRAPHIES
LOGOGRAPHS
LOGOGRAPHY
LOGOGRIPHIC
LOGOGRIPHS
LOGOMACHIES
LOGOMACHIST
LOGOMACHISTS
LOGOPAEDIC
LOGOPAEDICS
LOGOPEDICS
LOGOPHILES
LOGORRHEAS
LOGORRHEIC
LOGORRHOEA
LOGORRHOEAS
LOGOTHETES
LOGOTYPIES
LOGROLLERS
LOGROLLING
LOGROLLINGS
LOINCLOTHS
LOITERINGLY
LOITERINGS
LOLLAPALOOZA
LOLLAPALOOZAS
LOLLYGAGGED
LOLLYGAGGING
LOMENTACEOUS
LONELINESS
LONELINESSES
LONENESSES
LONESOMELY
LONESOMENESS
LONESOMENESSES
LONGAEVOUS
LONGANIMITIES
LONGANIMITY
LONGANIMOUS
LONGBOARDS
LONGBOWMAN
LONGBOWMEN
LONGCLOTHS
LONGEVITIES
LONGHAIRED
LONGHEADED
LONGHEADEDNESS
LONGHOUSES
LONGICAUDATE
LONGICORNS
LONGINQUITIES
LONGINQUITY
LONGIPENNATE
LONGIROSTRAL
LONGITUDES
LONGITUDINAL
LONGITUDINALLY
LONGJUMPED
LONGJUMPING
LONGLEAVES
LONGNESSES
LONGPRIMER
LONGPRIMERS
LONGSHOREMAN
LONGSHOREMEN
LONGSHORING
LONGSHORINGS
LONGSIGHTED
LONGSIGHTEDNESS
LONGSOMELY
LONGSOMENESS
LONGSOMENESSES
LONGSUFFERING
LONGSUFFERINGS
LONGWEARING
LOOKALIKES
LOONINESSES

LOOPHOLING
LOOPINESSES
LOOSEBOXES
LOOSENESSES
LOOSESTRIFE
LOOSESTRIFES
LOOYENWORK
LOOYENWORKS
LOPGRASSES
LOPHOBRANCH
LOPHOBRANCHIATE
LOPHOBRANCHS
LOPHOPHORATE
LOPHOPHORE
LOPHOPHORES
LOPSIDEDLY
LOPSIDEDNESS
LOPSIDEDNESSES
LOQUACIOUS
LOQUACIOUSLY
LOQUACIOUSNESS
LOQUACITIES
LORAZEPAMS
LORDLINESS
LORDLINESSES
LORDOLATRIES
LORDOLATRY
LORGNETTES
LORICATING
LORICATION
LORICATIONS
LORNNESSES
LOSABLENESS
LOSABLENESSES
LOSSMAKERS
LOSSMAKING
LOSTNESSES
LOTHNESSES
LOTUSLANDS
LOUDHAILER
LOUDHAILERS
LOUDMOUTHED
LOUDMOUTHS
LOUDNESSES
LOUDSPEAKER
LOUDSPEAKERS
LOUNDERING
LOUNDERINGS
LOUNGEWEAR
LOUNGEWEARS
LOUNGINGLY
LOUSEWORTS
LOUSINESSES
LOUTISHNESS
LOUTISHNESSES
LOVABILITIES
LOVABILITY
LOVABLENESS
LOVABLENESSES
LOVASTATIN
LOVASTATINS
LOVEABILITIES
LOVEABILITY
LOVEABLENESS
LOVEABLENESSES
LOVELESSLY
LOVELESSNESS
LOVELESSNESSES
LOVELIGHTS
LOVELIHEAD
LOVELIHEADS
LOVELINESS
LOVELINESSES
LOVELORNNESS
LOVELORNNESSES
LOVEMAKERS
LOVEMAKING
LOVEMAKINGS
LOVESICKNESS
LOVESICKNESSES
LOVESTRUCK

LOVEWORTHY
LOVINGNESS
LOVINGNESSES
LOWBALLING
LOWBALLINGS
LOWBROWISM
LOWBROWISMS
LOWERCASED
LOWERCASES
LOWERCASING
LOWERCLASSMAN
LOWERCLASSMEN
LOWERINGLY
LOWLANDERS
LOWLIGHTED
LOWLIGHTING
LOWLIHEADS
LOWLINESSES
LOWSENINGS
LOXODROMES
LOXODROMIC
LOXODROMICAL
LOXODROMICALLY
LOXODROMICS
LOXODROMIES
LOYALNESSES
LUBBERLINESS
LUBBERLINESSES
LUBRICANTS
LUBRICATED
LUBRICATES
LUBRICATING
LUBRICATION
LUBRICATIONAL
LUBRICATIONS
LUBRICATIVE
LUBRICATOR
LUBRICATORS
LUBRICIOUS
LUBRICIOUSLY
LUBRICITIES
LUBRICOUSLY
LUBRITORIA
LUBRITORIUM
LUBRITORIUMS
LUCIDITIES
LUCIDNESSES
LUCIFERASE
LUCIFERASES
LUCIFERINS
LUCIFEROUS
LUCIFUGOUS
LUCKENBOOTH
LUCKENBOOTHS
LUCKENGOWAN
LUCKENGOWANS
LUCKINESSES
LUCKLESSLY
LUCKLESSNESS
LUCKLESSNESSES
LUCKPENNIES
LUCRATIVELY
LUCRATIVENESS
LUCRATIVENESSES
LUCTATIONS
LUCUBRATED
LUCUBRATES
LUCUBRATING
LUCUBRATION
LUCUBRATIONS
LUCUBRATOR
LUCUBRATORS
LUCULENTLY
LUDICROUSLY
LUDICROUSNESS
LUDICROUSNESSES
LUETICALLY
LUFTMENSCH
LUFTMENSCHEN
LUGUBRIOUS
LUGUBRIOUSLY

LUGUBRIOUSNESS
LUKEWARMISH
LUKEWARMLY
LUKEWARMNESS
LUKEWARMNESSES
LUKEWARMTH
LUKEWARMTHS
LULLABYING
LUMBAGINOUS
LUMBERINGLY
LUMBERINGNESS
LUMBERINGNESSES
LUMBERINGS
LUMBERJACK
LUMBERJACKET
LUMBERJACKETS
LUMBERJACKS
LUMBERSOME
LUMBERSOMENESS
LUMBERYARD
LUMBERYARDS
LUMBOSACRAL
LUMBRICALES
LUMBRICALIS
LUMBRICALISES
LUMBRICALS
LUMBRICIFORM
LUMBRICOID
LUMBRICUSES
LUMINAIRES
LUMINANCES
LUMINARIAS
LUMINARIES
LUMINARISM
LUMINARISMS
LUMINARIST
LUMINARISTS
LUMINATION
LUMINATIONS
LUMINESCED
LUMINESCENCE
LUMINESCENCES
LUMINESCENT
LUMINESCES
LUMINESCING
LUMINIFEROUS
LUMINOSITIES
LUMINOSITY
LUMINOUSLY
LUMINOUSNESS
LUMINOUSNESSES
LUMISTEROL
LUMISTEROLS
LUMPECTOMIES
LUMPECTOMY
LUMPFISHES
LUMPINESSES
LUMPISHNESS
LUMPISHNESSES
LUMPSUCKER
LUMPSUCKERS
LUNARNAUTS
LUNATICALLY
LUNCHBOXES
LUNCHEONED
LUNCHEONETTE
LUNCHEONETTES
LUNCHEONING
LUNCHMEATS
LUNCHROOMS
LUNCHTIMES
LUNGFISHES
LUNINESSES
LUNKHEADED
LURIDNESSES
LUSCIOUSLY
LUSCIOUSNESS
LUSCIOUSNESSES
LUSHNESSES
LUSKISHNESS
LUSKISHNESSES

LUSTERLESS
LUSTERWARE
LUSTERWARES
LUSTFULNESS
LUSTFULNESSES
LUSTIHEADS
LUSTIHOODS
LUSTINESSES
LUSTRATING
LUSTRATION
LUSTRATIONS
LUSTRATIVE
LUSTRELESS
LUSTREWARE
LUSTREWARES
LUSTROUSLY
LUSTROUSNESS
LUSTROUSNESSES
LUTEINISATION
LUTEINISATIONS
LUTEINISED
LUTEINISES
LUTEINISING
LUTEINIZATION
LUTEINIZATIONS
LUTEINIZED
LUTEINIZES
LUTEINIZING
LUTEOTROPHIC
LUTEOTROPHIN
LUTEOTROPHINS
LUTEOTROPIC
LUTEOTROPIN
LUTEOTROPINS
LUTESTRING
LUTESTRINGS
LUXULIANITE
LUXULIANITES
LUXULLIANITE
LUXULLIANITES
LUXULYANITE
LUXULYANITES
LUXURIANCE
LUXURIANCES
LUXURIANCIES
LUXURIANCY
LUXURIANTLY
LUXURIATED
LUXURIATES
LUXURIATING
LUXURIATION
LUXURIATIONS
LUXURIOUSLY
LUXURIOUSNESS
LUXURIOUSNESSES
LYCANTHROPE
LYCANTHROPES
LYCANTHROPIC
LYCANTHROPES
LYCANTHROPIST
LYCANTHROPISTS
LYCANTHROPY
LYCHNOSCOPE
LYCHNOSCOPES
LYCOPODIUM
LYCOPODIUMS
LYMPHADENITIS
LYMPHADENITISES
LYMPHADENOPATHY
LYMPHANGIAL
LYMPHANGIOGRAM
LYMPHANGIOGRAMS
LYMPHANGITIC
LYMPHANGITIDES
LYMPHANGITIS
LYMPHANGITISES
LYMPHATICALLY
LYMPHATICS
LYMPHOADENOMA
LYMPHOADENOMAS
LYMPHOADENOMATA

LYMPHOBLAST
LYMPHOBLASTIC
LYMPHOBLASTS
LYMPHOCYTE
LYMPHOCYTES
LYMPHOCYTIC
LYMPHOCYTOPENIA
LYMPHOCYTOSES
LYMPHOCYTOSIS
LYMPHOCYTOTIC
LYMPHOGRAM
LYMPHOGRAMS
LYMPHOGRANULOMA
LYMPHOGRAPHIC
LYMPHOGRAPHIES
LYMPHOGRAPHY
LYMPHOKINE
LYMPHOKINES
LYMPHOMATA
LYMPHOMATOID
LYMPHOMATOSES
LYMPHOMATOSIS
LYMPHOMATOUS
LYMPHOPENIA
LYMPHOPENIAS
LYMPHOPOIESES
LYMPHOPOIESIS
LYMPHOPOIETIC
LYMPHOSARCOMA
LYMPHOSARCOMAS
LYMPHOSARCOMATA
LYMPHOTROPHIC
LYOPHILISATION
LYOPHILISATIONS
LYOPHILISE
LYOPHILISED
LYOPHILISER
LYOPHILISERS
LYOPHILISES
LYOPHILISING
LYOPHILIZATION
LYOPHILIZATIONS
LYOPHILIZE
LYOPHILIZED
LYOPHILIZER
LYOPHILIZERS
LYOPHILIZES
LYOPHILIZING
LYOSORPTION
LYOSORPTIONS
LYRICALNESS
LYRICALNESSES
LYRICISING
LYRICIZING
LYSERGIDES
LYSIGENETIC
LYSIGENOUS
LYSIMETERS
LYSIMETRIC
LYSOGENICITIES
LYSOGENICITY
LYSOGENIES
LYSOGENISATION
LYSOGENISATIONS
LYSOGENISE
LYSOGENISED
LYSOGENISES
LYSOGENISING
LYSOGENIZATION
LYSOGENIZATIONS
LYSOGENIZE
LYSOGENIZED
LYSOGENIZES
LYSOGENIZING
LYSOLECITHIN
LYSOLECITHINS
LYTHRACEOUS

Mm

MACABERESQUE
MACADAMIAS
MACADAMISATION
MACADAMISATIONS
MACADAMISE
MACADAMISED
MACADAMISER
MACADAMISERS
MACADAMISES
MACADAMISING
MACADAMIZATION
MACADAMIZATIONS
MACADAMIZE
MACADAMIZED
MACADAMIZER
MACADAMIZERS
MACADAMIZES
MACADAMIZING
MACARISING
MACARIZING
MACARONICALLY
MACARONICS
MACARONIES
MACCARONIES
MACCARONIS
MACCHERONCINI
MACCHERONCINIS
MACCHIATOS
MACEBEARER
MACEBEARERS
MACEDOINES
MACERANDUBA
MACERANDUBAS
MACERATERS
MACERATING
MACERATION
MACERATIONS
MACERATIVE
MACERATORS
MACHAIRODONT
MACHAIRODONTS
MACHIAVELIAN
MACHIAVELIANS
MACHIAVELLIAN
MACHIAVELLIANS
MACHICOLATE
MACHICOLATED
MACHICOLATES
MACHICOLATING
MACHICOLATION
MACHICOLATIONS
MACHINABILITIES
MACHINABILITY
MACHINABLE
MACHINATED
MACHINATES
MACHINATING
MACHINATION
MACHINATIONS
MACHINATOR
MACHINATORS
MACHINEABILITY
MACHINEABLE
MACHINEGUN
MACHINEGUNNED
MACHINEGUNNING
MACHINEGUNS

MACHINELESS
MACHINELIKE
MACHINEMAN
MACHINEMEN
MACHINERIES
MACHININGS
MACHINISTS
MACHMETERS
MACHTPOLITIK
MACHTPOLITIKS
MACINTOSHES
MACKINTOSH
MACKINTOSHES
MACONOCHIE
MACONOCHIES
MACRENCEPHALIA
MACRENCEPHALIAS
MACRENCEPHALIES
MACRENCEPHALY
MACROAGGREGATE
MACROAGGREGATED
MACROAGGREGATES
MACROBIOTA
MACROBIOTE
MACROBIOTES
MACROBIOTIC
MACROBIOTICS
MACROCARPA
MACROCARPAS
MACROCEPHALIA
MACROCEPHALIAS
MACROCEPHALIC
MACROCEPHALIES
MACROCEPHALOUS
MACROCEPHALY
MACROCLIMATE
MACROCLIMATES
MACROCLIMATIC
MACROCODES
MACROCOPIES
MACROCOSMIC
MACROCOSMICALLY
MACROCOSMS
MACROCYCLE
MACROCYCLES
MACROCYCLIC
MACROCYSTS
MACROCYTES
MACROCYTIC
MACROCYTOSES
MACROCYTOSIS
MACRODACTYL
MACRODACTYLIC
MACRODACTYLIES
MACRODACTYLOUS
MACRODACTYLY
MACRODIAGONAL
MACRODIAGONALS
MACRODOMES
MACROECONOMIC
MACROECONOMICS
MACROEVOLUTION
MACROEVOLUTIONS
MACROFAUNA
MACROFLORA
MACROFOSSIL
MACROFOSSILS

MACROGAMETE
MACROGAMETES
MACROGLIAS
MACROGLOBULIN
MACROGLOBULINS
MACROGRAPH
MACROGRAPHIC
MACROGRAPHS
MACROLOGIES
MACROMERES
MACROMOLECULAR
MACROMOLECULE
MACROMOLECULES
MACROMOLES
MACRONUCLEAR
MACRONUCLEI
MACRONUCLEUS
MACRONUTRIENT
MACRONUTRIENTS
MACROPHAGE
MACROPHAGES
MACROPHAGIC
MACROPHAGOUS
MACROPHOTOGRAPH
MACROPHYLA
MACROPHYLUM
MACROPHYSICS
MACROPHYTE
MACROPHYTES
MACROPHYTIC
MACROPINAKOID
MACROPINAKOIDS
MACROPRISM
MACROPRISMS
MACROPSIAS
MACROPTEROUS
MACROSCALE
MACROSCALES
MACROSCOPIC
MACROSCOPICALLY
MACROSOCIOLOGY
MACROSPORANGIA
MACROSPORANGIUM
MACROSPORE
MACROSPORES
MACROSTRUCTURAL
MACROSTRUCTURE
MACROSTRUCTURES
MACROZAMIA
MACROZAMIAS
MACTATIONS
MACULATING
MACULATION
MACULATIONS
MACULATURE
MACULATURES
MADBRAINED
MADDENINGLY
MADDENINGNESS
MADDENINGNESSES
MADEFACTION
MADEFACTIONS
MADELEINES
MADEMOISELLE
MADEMOISELLES
MADERISATION
MADERISATIONS

MADERISING
MADERIZATION
MADERIZATIONS
MADERIZING
MADONNAISH
MADONNAWISE
MADRASSAHS
MADREPORAL
MADREPORES
MADREPORIAN
MADREPORIANS
MADREPORIC
MADREPORITE
MADREPORITES
MADREPORITIC
MADRIGALESQUE
MADRIGALIAN
MADRIGALIST
MADRIGALISTS
MADRILENES
MAELSTROMS
MAENADICALLY
MAENADISMS
MAFFICKERS
MAFFICKING
MAFFICKINGS
MAGALOGUES
MAGAZINIST
MAGAZINISTS
MAGDALENES
MAGGOTIEST
MAGGOTORIA
MAGGOTORIUM
MAGIANISMS
MAGISTERIAL
MAGISTERIALLY
MAGISTERIALNESS
MAGISTERIES
MAGISTERIUM
MAGISTERIUMS
MAGISTRACIES
MAGISTRACY
MAGISTRALITIES
MAGISTRALITY
MAGISTRALLY
MAGISTRALS
MAGISTRAND
MAGISTRANDS
MAGISTRATE
MAGISTRATES
MAGISTRATESHIP
MAGISTRATESHIPS
MAGISTRATIC
MAGISTRATICAL
MAGISTRATICALLY
MAGISTRATURE
MAGISTRATURES
MAGMATISMS
MAGNALIUMS
MAGNANIMITIES
MAGNANIMITY
MAGNANIMOUS
MAGNANIMOUSLY
MAGNANIMOUSNESS
MAGNATESHIP
MAGNATESHIPS
MAGNESITES

MAGNESIUMS
MAGNESSTONE
MAGNESSTONES
MAGNETICAL
MAGNETICALLY
MAGNETICIAN
MAGNETICIANS
MAGNETISABLE
MAGNETISATION
MAGNETISATIONS
MAGNETISED
MAGNETISER
MAGNETISERS
MAGNETISES
MAGNETISING
MAGNETISMS
MAGNETIST
MAGNETISTS
MAGNETITES
MAGNETITIC
MAGNETIZABLE
MAGNETIZATION
MAGNETIZATIONS
MAGNETIZED
MAGNETIZER
MAGNETIZERS
MAGNETIZES
MAGNETIZING
MAGNETOCHEMICAL
MAGNETOELECTRIC
MAGNETOGRAPH
MAGNETOGRAPHS
MAGNETOMETER
MAGNETOMETERS
MAGNETOMETRIC
MAGNETOMETRIES
MAGNETOMETRY
MAGNETOMOTIVE
MAGNETOPAUSE
MAGNETOPAUSES
MAGNETOSPHERE
MAGNETOSPHERES
MAGNETOSPHERIC
MAGNETOSTATIC
MAGNETOSTATICS
MAGNETRONS
MAGNIFIABLE
MAGNIFICAL
MAGNIFICALLY
MAGNIFICAT
MAGNIFICATION
MAGNIFICATIONS
MAGNIFICATS
MAGNIFICENCE
MAGNIFICENCES
MAGNIFICENT
MAGNIFICENTLY
MAGNIFICENTNESS
MAGNIFICOES
MAGNIFICOS
MAGNIFIERS
MAGNIFYING
MAGNILOQUENCE
MAGNILOQUENCES
MAGNILOQUENT
MAGNILOQUENTLY
MAGNITUDES
MAGNITUDINOUS

MAGNOLIACEOUS
MAHARAJAHS
MAHARANEES
MAHARISHIS
MAHATMAISM
MAHATMAISMS
MAHLSTICKS
MAHOGANIES
MAIASAURAS
MAIDENHAIR
MAIDENHAIRS
MAIDENHEAD
MAIDENHEADS
MAIDENHOOD
MAIDENHOODS
MAIDENLIKE
MAIDENLINESS
MAIDENLINESSES
MAIDENWEED
MAIDENWEEDS
MAIDISHNESS
MAIDISHNESSES
MAIDSERVANT
MAIDSERVANTS
MAIEUTICAL
MAILABILITIES
MAILABILITY
MAILCOACHES
MAILGRAMMED
MAILGRAMMING
MAILMERGED
MAILMERGES
MAILMERGING
MAILPOUCHES
MAILSHOTTED
MAILSHOTTING
MAIMEDNESS
MAIMEDNESSES
MAINBRACES
MAINFRAMES
MAINLANDER
MAINLANDERS
MAINLINERS
MAINLINING
MAINLININGS
MAINPERNOR
MAINPERNORS
MAINPRISES
MAINSHEETS
MAINSPRING
MAINSPRINGS
MAINSTREAM
MAINSTREAMED
MAINSTREAMING
MAINSTREAMS
MAINSTREETING
MAINSTREETINGS
MAINTAINABILITY
MAINTAINABLE
MAINTAINED
MAINTAINER
MAINTAINERS
MAINTAINING
MAINTENANCE
MAINTENANCED
MAINTENANCES
MAINTENANCING

MAINTOPMAST
MAINTOPMASTS
MAINTOPSAIL
MAINTOPSAILS
MAISONETTE
MAISONETTES
MAISONNETTE
MAISONNETTES
MAISTERDOME
MAISTERDOMES
MAISTERING
MAISTRINGS
MAJESTICAL
MAJESTICALLY
MAJESTICALNESS
MAJESTICNESS
MAJESTICNESSES
MAJOLICAWARE
MAJOLICAWARES
MAJORDOMOS
MAJORETTES
MAJORETTING
MAJORETTINGS
MAJORITAIRE
MAJORITAIRES
MAJORITARIAN
MAJORITARIANISM
MAJORITARIANS
MAJORITIES
MAJORSHIPS
MAJUSCULAR
MAJUSCULES
MAKEREADIES
MAKESHIFTS
MAKEWEIGHT
MAKEWEIGHTS
MAKUNOUCHI
MAKUNOUCHIS
MALABSORPTION
MALABSORPTIONS
MALACHITES
MALACOLOGICAL
MALACOLOGIES
MALACOLOGIST
MALACOLOGISTS
MALACOLOGY
MALACOPHILIES
MALACOPHILOUS
MALACOPHILY
MALACOPHYLLOUS
MALACOPTERYGIAN
MALACOSTRACAN
MALACOSTRACANS
MALACOSTRACOUS
MALADAPTATION
MALADAPTATIONS
MALADAPTED
MALADAPTIVE
MALADAPTIVELY
MALADDRESS
MALADDRESSES
MALADJUSTED
MALADJUSTIVE
MALADJUSTMENT
MALADJUSTMENTS
MALADMINISTER
MALADMINISTERED
MALADMINISTERS
MALADROITLY
MALADROITNESS
MALADROITNESSES
MALADROITS
MALAGUENAS
MALAGUETTA
MALAGUETTAS
MALAKATOONE
MALAKATOONES
MALAPERTLY
MALAPERTNESS
MALAPERTNESSES
MALAPPORTIONED
MALAPPROPRIATE
MALAPPROPRIATED

MALAPPROPRIATES
MALAPROPIAN
MALAPROPISM
MALAPROPISMS
MALAPROPIST
MALAPROPISTS
MALAPROPOS
MALARIOLOGIES
MALARIOLOGIST
MALARIOLOGISTS
MALARIOLOGY
MALASSIMILATION
MALATHIONS
MALAXATING
MALAXATION
MALAXATIONS
MALAXATORS
MALCONFORMATION
MALCONTENT
MALCONTENTED
MALCONTENTEDLY
MALCONTENTS
MALDEPLOYMENT
MALDEPLOYMENTS
MALDISTRIBUTION
MALEDICENT
MALEDICTED
MALEDICTING
MALEDICTION
MALEDICTIONS
MALEDICTIVE
MALEDICTORY
MALEFACTION
MALEFACTIONS
MALEFACTOR
MALEFACTORS
MALEFACTORY
MALEFACTRESS
MALEFACTRESSES
MALEFFECTS
MALEFICALLY
MALEFICENCE
MALEFICENCES
MALEFICENT
MALEFICIAL
MALENESSES
MALENGINES
MALENTENDU
MALENTENDUS
MALEVOLENCE
MALEVOLENCES
MALEVOLENT
MALEVOLENTLY
MALFEASANCE
MALFEASANCES
MALFEASANT
MALFEASANTS
MALFORMATION
MALFORMATIONS
MALFUNCTION
MALFUNCTIONED
MALFUNCTIONING
MALFUNCTIONINGS
MALFUNCTIONS
MALICIOUSLY
MALICIOUSNESS
MALICIOUSNESSES
MALIGNANCE
MALIGNANCES
MALIGNANCIES
MALIGNANCY
MALIGNANTLY
MALIGNANTS
MALIGNITIES
MALIGNMENT
MALIGNMENTS
MALIMPRINTING
MALIMPRINTINGS
MALINGERED
MALINGERER
MALINGERERS
MALINGERIES

MALINGERING
MALLANDERS
MALLEABILITIES
MALLEABILITY
MALLEABLENESS
MALLEABLENESSES
MALLEATING
MALLEATION
MALLEATIONS
MALLEIFORM
MALLEMAROKING
MALLEMAROKINGS
MALLEMUCKS
MALLENDERS
MALLEOLUSES
MALLOPHAGOUS
MALLOWPUFF
MALLOWPUFFS
MALMSTONES
MALNOURISHED
MALNUTRITION
MALNUTRITIONS
MALOCCLUDED
MALOCCLUSION
MALOCCLUSIONS
MALODOROUS
MALODOROUSLY
MALODOROUSNESS
MALOLACTIC
MALONYLUREA
MALONYLUREAS
MALPIGHIACEOUS
MALPOSITION
MALPOSITIONS
MALPRACTICE
MALPRACTICES
MALPRACTITIONER
MALPRESENTATION
MALTALENTS
MALTINESSES
MALTREATED
MALTREATER
MALTREATERS
MALTREATING
MALTREATMENT
MALTREATMENTS
MALVACEOUS
MALVERSATION
MALVERSATIONS
MALVOISIES
MAMAGUYING
MAMILLATED
MAMILLATION
MAMILLATIONS
MAMILLIFORM
MAMMALIANS
MAMMALIFEROUS
MAMMALITIES
MAMMALOGICAL
MAMMALOGIES
MAMMALOGIST
MAMMALOGISTS
MAMMECTOMIES
MAMMECTOMY
MAMMETRIES
MAMMIFEROUS
MAMMILLARIA
MAMMILLARIAS
MAMMILLARY
MAMMILLATE
MAMMILLATED
MAMMITIDES
MAMMOCKING
MAMMOGENIC
MAMMOGRAMS
MAMMOGRAPH
MAMMOGRAPHIC
MAMMOGRAPHIES
MAMMOGRAPHS
MAMMOGRAPHY
MAMMONISMS
MAMMONISTIC
MAMMONISTS

MAMMONITES
MAMMOPLASTIES
MAMMOPLASTY
MANAGEABILITIES
MANAGEABILITY
MANAGEABLE
MANAGEABLENESS
MANAGEABLY
MANAGEMENT
MANAGEMENTAL
MANAGEMENTS
MANAGERESS
MANAGERESSES
MANAGERIAL
MANAGERIALISM
MANAGERIALISMS
MANAGERIALIST
MANAGERIALISTS
MANAGERIALLY
MANAGERSHIP
MANAGERSHIPS
MANCHESTER
MANCHESTERS
MANCHINEEL
MANCHINEELS
MANCIPATED
MANCIPATES
MANCIPATING
MANCIPATION
MANCIPATIONS
MANCIPATORY
MANDAMUSED
MANDAMUSES
MANDAMUSING
MANDARINATE
MANDARINATES
MANDARINES
MANDARINIC
MANDARINISM
MANDARINISMS
MANDATARIES
MANDATORIES
MANDATORILY
MANDIBULAR
MANDIBULATE
MANDIBULATED
MANDIBULATES
MANDILIONS
MANDIOCCAS
MANDOLINES
MANDOLINIST
MANDOLINISTS
MANDRAGORA
MANDRAGORAS
MANDUCABLE
MANDUCATED
MANDUCATES
MANDUCATING
MANDUCATION
MANDUCATIONS
MANDUCATORY
MANDYLIONS
MANEUVERABILITY
MANEUVERABLE
MANEUVERED
MANEUVERER
MANEUVERERS
MANEUVERING
MANEUVERINGS
MANFULNESS
MANFULNESSES
MANGABEIRA
MANGABEIRAS
MANGALSUTRA
MANGALSUTRAS
MANGANATES
MANGANESES
MANGANESIAN
MANGANIFEROUS
MANGANITES
MANGELWURZEL
MANGELWURZELS
MANGEMANGE

MANGETOUTS
MANGINESSES
MANGOLDWURZEL
MANGOLDWURZELS
MANGOSTANS
MANGOSTEEN
MANGOSTEENS
MANGOUSTES
MANGULATED
MANGULATES
MANGULATING
MANHANDLED
MANHANDLES
MANHANDLING
MANHATTANS
MANHUNTERS
MANIACALLY
MANICOTTIS
MANICURING
MANICURIST
MANICURISTS
MANIFESTABLE
MANIFESTANT
MANIFESTANTS
MANIFESTATION
MANIFESTATIONAL
MANIFESTATIONS
MANIFESTATIVE
MANIFESTED
MANIFESTER
MANIFESTERS
MANIFESTIBLE
MANIFESTING
MANIFESTLY
MANIFESTNESS
MANIFESTNESSES
MANIFESTOED
MANIFESTOES
MANIFESTOING
MANIFESTOS
MANIFOLDED
MANIFOLDER
MANIFOLDERS
MANIFOLDING
MANIFOLDLY
MANIFOLDNESS
MANIFOLDNESSES
MANIPULABILITY
MANIPULABLE
MANIPULARS
MANIPULATABLE
MANIPULATE
MANIPULATED
MANIPULATES
MANIPULATING
MANIPULATION
MANIPULATIONS
MANIPULATIVE
MANIPULATIVELY
MANIPULATOR
MANIPULATORS
MANIPULATORY
MANLINESSES
MANNEQUINS
MANNERISMS
MANNERISTIC
MANNERISTICAL
MANNERISTICALLY
MANNERISTS
MANNERLESS
MANNERLESSNESS
MANNERLINESS
MANNERLINESSES
MANNIFEROUS
MANNISHNESS
MANNISHNESSES
MANOEUVRABILITY
MANOEUVRABLE
MANOEUVRED
MANOEUVRER
MANOEUVRERS
MANOEUVRES
MANOEUVRING

MANOEUVRINGS
MANOMETERS
MANOMETRIC
MANOMETRICAL
MANOMETRICALLY
MANOMETRIES
MANORIALISM
MANORIALISMS
MANOSCOPIES
MANRIKIGUSARI
MANRIKIGUSARIS
MANSERVANT
MANSIONARIES
MANSIONARY
MANSLAUGHTER
MANSLAUGHTERS
MANSLAYERS
MANSONRIES
MANSUETUDE
MANSUETUDES
MANTELLETTA
MANTELLETTAS
MANTELPIECE
MANTELPIECES
MANTELSHELF
MANTELSHELVES
MANTELTREE
MANTELTREES
MANTICALLY
MANTICORAS
MANTICORES
MANTLETREE
MANTLETREES
MANUBRIUMS
MANUFACTORIES
MANUFACTORY
MANUFACTURABLE
MANUFACTURAL
MANUFACTURE
MANUFACTURED
MANUFACTURER
MANUFACTURERS
MANUFACTURES
MANUFACTURING
MANUFACTURINGS
MANUMISSION
MANUMISSIONS
MANUMITTED
MANUMITTER
MANUMITTERS
MANUMITTING
MANURANCES
MANUSCRIPT
MANUSCRIPTS
MANZANILLA
MANZANILLAS
MANZANITAS
MAPMAKINGS
MAPPEMONDS
MAQUILADORA
MAQUILADORAS
MAQUILLAGE
MAQUILLAGES
MAQUISARDS
MARABUNTAS
MARANATHAS
MARASCHINO
MARASCHINOS
MARASMUSES
MARATHONER
MARATHONERS
MARATHONING
MARATHONINGS
MARBELISED
MARBELISES
MARBELISING
MARBELIZED
MARBELIZES
MARBELIZING
MARBLEISED
MARBLEISES
MARBLEISING
MARBLEIZED

MARBLEIZES
MARBLEIZING
MARBLEWOOD
MARBLEWOODS
MARCANTANT
MARCANTANTS
MARCASITES
MARCASITICAL
MARCATISSIMO
MARCELLERS
MARCELLING
MARCESCENCE
MARCESCENCES
MARCESCENT
MARCESCIBLE
MARCHANTIA
MARCHANTIAS
MARCHIONESS
MARCHIONESSES
MARCHLANDS
MARCHPANES
MARCONIGRAM
MARCONIGRAMS
MARCONIGRAPH
MARCONIGRAPHED
MARCONIGRAPHING
MARCONIGRAPHS
MARCONIING
MARESCHALS
MARGARINES
MARGARITAS
MARGARITES
MARGARITIC
MARGARITIFEROUS
MARGENTING
MARGINALIA
MARGINALISATION
MARGINALISE
MARGINALISED
MARGINALISES
MARGINALISING
MARGINALISM
MARGINALISMS
MARGINALIST
MARGINALISTS
MARGINALITIES
MARGINALITY
MARGINALIZATION
MARGINALIZE
MARGINALIZED
MARGINALIZES
MARGINALIZING
MARGINALLY
MARGINATED
MARGINATES
MARGINATING
MARGINATION
MARGINATIONS
MARGRAVATE
MARGRAVATES
MARGRAVIAL
MARGRAVIATE
MARGRAVIATES
MARGRAVINE
MARGRAVINES
MARGUERITE
MARGUERITES
MARIALITES
MARICULTURE
MARICULTURES
MARICULTURIST
MARICULTURISTS
MARIGRAPHS
MARIHUANAS
MARIJUANAS
MARIMBAPHONE
MARIMBAPHONES
MARIMBISTS
MARINADING
MARINATING
MARINATION
MARINATIONS
MARIONBERRIES

MARIONBERRY
MARIONETTE
MARIONETTES
MARISCHALLED
MARISCHALLING
MARISCHALS
MARIVAUDAGE
MARIVAUDAGES
MARKEDNESS
MARKEDNESSES
MARKETABILITIES
MARKETABILITY
MARKETABLE
MARKETABLENESS
MARKETABLY
MARKETEERS
MARKETINGS
MARKETISATION
MARKETISATIONS
MARKETIZATION
MARKETIZATIONS
MARKETPLACE
MARKETPLACES
MARKSMANSHIP
MARKSMANSHIPS
MARKSWOMAN
MARKSWOMEN
MARLACIOUS
MARLINESPIKE
MARLINESPIKES
MARLINGSPIKE
MARLINGSPIKES
MARLINSPIKE
MARLINSPIKES
MARLSTONES
MARMALADES
MARMALISED
MARMALISES
MARMALISING
MARMALIZED
MARMALIZES
MARMALIZING
MARMARISED
MARMARISES
MARMARISING
MARMARIZED
MARMARIZES
MARMARIZING
MARMAROSES
MARMAROSIS
MARMELISED
MARMELISES
MARMELIZED
MARMELIZES
MARMELIZING
MARMOREALLY
MAROONINGS
MARPRELATE
MARPRELATED
MARPRELATES
MARPRELATING
MARQUESSATE
MARQUESSATES
MARQUESSES
MARQUETERIE
MARQUETERIES
MARQUETRIES
MARQUISATE
MARQUISATES
MARQUISETTE
MARQUISETTES
MARRIAGEABILITY
MARRIAGEABLE
MARROWBONE
MARROWBONES
MARROWFATS
MARROWLESS
MARROWSKIED
MARROWSKIES
MARROWSKYING
MARSEILLES
MARSHALCIES

MARSHALERS
MARSHALING
MARSHALLED
MARSHALLER
MARSHALLERS
MARSHALLING
MARSHALLINGS
MARSHALSHIP
MARSHALSHIPS
MARSHBUCKS
MARSHINESS
MARSHINESSES
MARSHLANDER
MARSHLANDERS
MARSHLANDS
MARSHLOCKS
MARSHLOCKSES
MARSHMALLOW
MARSHMALLOWS
MARSHMALLOWY
MARSHWORTS
MARSIPOBRANCH
MARSIPOBRANCHS
MARSQUAKES
MARSUPIALIAN
MARSUPIALIANS
MARSUPIALS
MARSUPIANS
MARSUPIUMS
MARTELLANDO
MARTELLANDOS
MARTELLATO
MARTELLING
MARTENSITE
MARTENSITES
MARTENSITIC
MARTENSITICALLY
MARTIALISM
MARTIALISMS
MARTIALIST
MARTIALISTS
MARTIALNESS
MARTIALNESSES
MARTINETISH
MARTINETISM
MARTINETISMS
MARTINGALE
MARTINGALES
MARTINGALS
MARTYRDOMS
MARTYRISATION
MARTYRISATIONS
MARTYRISED
MARTYRISES
MARTYRISING
MARTYRIZATION
MARTYRIZATIONS
MARTYRIZED
MARTYRIZES
MARTYRIZING
MARTYROLOGIC
MARTYROLOGICAL
MARTYROLOGIES
MARTYROLOGIST
MARTYROLOGISTS
MARTYROLOGY
MARVELLING
MARVELLOUS
MARVELLOUSLY
MARVELLOUSNESS
MARVELOUSLY
MARVELOUSNESS
MARVELOUSNESSES
MASCARAING
MASCARPONE
MASCARPONES
MASCULINELY
MASCULINENESS
MASCULINENESSES
MASCULINES
MASCULINISATION
MASCULINISE
MASCULINISED

MASCULINISES
MASCULINISING
MASCULINIST
MASCULINISTS
MASCULINITIES
MASCULINITY
MASCULINIZATION
MASCULINIZE
MASCULINIZED
MASCULINIZES
MASCULINIZING
MASCULISTS
MASHGICHIM
MASKALLONGE
MASKALLONGES
MASKALONGE
MASKALONGES
MASKANONGE
MASKANONGES
MASKINONGE
MASKINONGES
MASKIROVKA
MASKIROVKAS
MASOCHISMS
MASOCHISTIC
MASOCHISTICALLY
MASOCHISTS
MASONICALLY
MASQUERADE
MASQUERADED
MASQUERADER
MASQUERADERS
MASQUERADES
MASQUERADING
MASSACRERS
MASSACRING
MASSAGISTS
MASSARANDUBA
MASSARANDUBAS
MASSASAUGA
MASSASAUGAS
MASSERANDUBA
MASSERANDUBAS
MASSETERIC
MASSINESSES
MASSIVENESS
MASSIVENESSES
MASSOTHERAPIES
MASSOTHERAPIST
MASSOTHERAPISTS
MASSOTHERAPY
MASSPRIEST
MASSPRIESTS
MASSYMORES
MASTECTOMIES
MASTECTOMY
MASTERATES
MASTERCLASS
MASTERCLASSES
MASTERDOMS
MASTERFULLY
MASTERFULNESS
MASTERFULNESSES
MASTERHOOD
MASTERHOODS
MASTERINGS
MASTERLESS
MASTERLINESS
MASTERLINESSES
MASTERMIND
MASTERMINDED
MASTERMINDING
MASTERMINDS
MASTERPIECE
MASTERPIECES
MASTERSHIP
MASTERSHIPS
MASTERSINGER
MASTERSINGERS
MASTERSTROKE
MASTERSTROKES
MASTERWORK
MASTERWORKS

MASTERWORT
MASTERWORTS
MASTHEADED
MASTHEADING
MASTHOUSES
MASTICABLE
MASTICATED
MASTICATES
MASTICATING
MASTICATION
MASTICATIONS
MASTICATOR
MASTICATORIES
MASTICATORS
MASTICATORY
MASTIGOPHORAN
MASTIGOPHORANS
MASTIGOPHORE
MASTIGOPHORES
MASTIGOPHORIC
MASTIGOPHOROUS
MASTITIDES
MASTITISES
MASTODONIC
MASTODONTIC
MASTODONTS
MASTODYNIA
MASTODYNIAS
MASTOIDECTOMIES
MASTOIDECTOMY
MASTOIDITIS
MASTOIDITISES
MASTOPEXIES
MASTURBATE
MASTURBATED
MASTURBATES
MASTURBATING
MASTURBATION
MASTURBATIONS
MASTURBATOR
MASTURBATORS
MASTURBATORY
MATACHINAS
MATAGOURIS
MATCHBOARD
MATCHBOARDING
MATCHBOARDINGS
MATCHBOARDS
MATCHBOOKS
MATCHBOXES
MATCHLESSLY
MATCHLESSNESS
MATCHLESSNESSES
MATCHLOCKS
MATCHMAKER
MATCHMAKERS
MATCHMAKES
MATCHMAKING
MATCHMAKINGS
MATCHMARKED
MATCHMARKING
MATCHMARKS
MATCHSTICK
MATCHSTICKS
MATCHWOODS
MATELASSES
MATELLASSE
MATELLASSES
MATELOTTES
MATERFAMILIAS
MATERFAMILIASES
MATERIALISATION
MATERIALISE
MATERIALISED
MATERIALISER
MATERIALISERS
MATERIALISES
MATERIALISING
MATERIALISM
MATERIALISMS
MATERIALIST
MATERIALISTIC
MATERIALISTICAL

MATERIALISTS
MATERIALITIES
MATERIALITY
MATERIALIZATION
MATERIALIZE
MATERIALIZED
MATERIALIZER
MATERIALIZERS
MATERIALIZES
MATERIALIZING
MATERIALLY
MATERIALNESS
MATERIALNESSES
MATERNALISM
MATERNALISMS
MATERNALISTIC
MATERNALLY
MATERNITIES
MATEYNESSES
MATGRASSES
MATHEMATIC
MATHEMATICAL
MATHEMATICALLY
MATHEMATICIAN
MATHEMATICIANS
MATHEMATICISE
MATHEMATICISED
MATHEMATICISES
MATHEMATICISING
MATHEMATICISM
MATHEMATICISMS
MATHEMATICIZE
MATHEMATICIZED
MATHEMATICIZES
MATHEMATICIZING
MATHEMATICS
MATHEMATISATION
MATHEMATISE
MATHEMATISED
MATHEMATISES
MATHEMATISING
MATHEMATIZATION
MATHEMATIZE
MATHEMATIZED
MATHEMATIZES
MATHEMATIZING
MATINESSES
MATRESFAMILIAS
MATRIARCHAL
MATRIARCHALISM
MATRIARCHALISMS
MATRIARCHATE
MATRIARCHATES
MATRIARCHIC
MATRIARCHIES
MATRIARCHS
MATRIARCHY
MATRICIDAL
MATRICIDES
MATRICLINIC
MATRICLINOUS
MATRICULANT
MATRICULANTS
MATRICULAR
MATRICULAS
MATRICULATE
MATRICULATED
MATRICULATES
MATRICULATING
MATRICULATION
MATRICULATIONS
MATRICULATOR
MATRICULATORS
MATRICULATORY
MATRIFOCAL
MATRIFOCALITIES
MATRIFOCALITY
MATRILINEAL
MATRILINEALLY
MATRILINEAR
MATRILINIES
MATRILOCAL
MATRILOCALITIES

MATRILOCALITY	MAXIMIZATION	MECHANISTS	MEDICASTER	MEGALOCEPHALOUS	MELANIZATIONS
MATRILOCALLY	MAXIMIZATIONS	MECHANIZABLE	MEDICASTERS	MEGALOCEPHALY	MELANIZING
MATRIMONIAL	MAXIMIZERS	MECHANIZATION	MEDICATING	MEGALOMANIA	MELANOBLAST
MATRIMONIALLY	MAXIMIZING	MECHANIZATIONS	MEDICATION	MEGALOMANIAC	MELANOBLASTS
MATRIMONIES	MAYFLOWERS	MECHANIZED	MEDICATIONS	MEGALOMANIACAL	MELANOCHROI
MATRIOSHKA	MAYONNAISE	MECHANIZER	MEDICATIVE	MEGALOMANIACS	MELANOCHROIC
MATRIOSHKI	MAYONNAISES	MECHANIZERS	MEDICINABLE	MEGALOMANIAS	MELANOCHROOUS
MATROCLINAL	MAYORALTIES	MECHANIZES	MEDICINALLY	MEGALOMANIC	MELANOCYTE
MATROCLINIC	MAYORESSES	MECHANIZING	MEDICINALS	MEGALOPOLIS	MELANOCYTES
MATROCLINIES	MAYORSHIPS	MECHANOCHEMICAL	MEDICINERS	MEGALOPOLISES	MELANOGENESES
MATROCLINOUS	MAYSTERDOME	MECHANOMORPHISM	MEDICINING	MEGALOPOLITAN	MELANOGENESIS
MATROCLINY	MAYSTERDOMES	MECHANORECEPTOR	MEDICOLEGAL	MEGALOPOLITANS	MELANOMATA
MATRONAGES	MAZARINADE	MECHANOTHERAPY	MEDIEVALISM	MEGALOPSES	MELANOPHORE
MATRONHOOD	MAZARINADES	MECHATRONIC	MEDIEVALISMS	MEGALOSAUR	MELANOPHORES
MATRONHOODS	MAZEDNESSES	MECHATRONICS	MEDIEVALIST	MEGALOSAURIAN	MELANOSITIES
MATRONISED	MAZINESSES	MECLIZINES	MEDIEVALISTIC	MEGALOSAURIANS	MELANOSITY
MATRONISES	MEADOWLAND	MECONOPSES	MEDIEVALISTS	MEGALOSAURS	MELANOSOME
MATRONISING	MEADOWLANDS	MECONOPSIS	MEDIEVALLY	MEGALOSAURUS	MELANOSOMES
MATRONIZED	MEADOWLARK	MEDAILLONS	MEDIOCRACIES	MEGALOSAURUSES	MELANOTROPIN
MATRONIZES	MEADOWLARKS	MEDALLIONED	MEDIOCRACY	MEGANEWTON	MELANOTROPINS
MATRONIZING	MEADOWSWEET	MEDALLIONING	MEDIOCRITIES	MEGANEWTONS	MELANTERITE
MATRONLINESS	MEADOWSWEETS	MEDALLIONS	MEDIOCRITY	MEGAPARSEC	MELANTERITES
MATRONLINESSES	MEAGERNESS	MEDDLESOME	MEDITATING	MEGAPARSECS	MELANURIAS
MATRONSHIP	MEAGERNESSES	MEDDLESOMELY	MEDITATION	MEGAPHONED	MELAPHYRES
MATRONSHIPS	MEAGRENESS	MEDDLESOMENESS	MEDITATIONS	MEGAPHONES	MELASTOMACEOUS
MATRONYMIC	MEAGRENESSES	MEDDLINGLY	MEDITATIVE	MEGAPHONIC	MELATONINS
MATRONYMICS	MEALINESSES	MEDEVACING	MEDITATIVELY	MEGAPHONICALLY	MELIACEOUS
MATROYSHKA	MEALYMOUTHED	MEDEVACKED	MEDITATIVENESS	MEGAPHONING	MELICOTTON
MATROYSHKAS	MEANDERERS	MEDEVACKING	MEDITATORS	MEGAPHYLLS	MELICOTTONS
MATRYOSHKA	MEANDERING	MEDIAEVALISM	MEDITERRANEAN	MEGAPIXELS	MELIORABLE
MATRYOSHKAS	MEANDERINGLY	MEDIAEVALISMS	MEDIUMISTIC	MEGAPLEXES	MELIORATED
MATRYOSHKI	MEANINGFUL	MEDIAEVALIST	MEDIUMSHIP	MEGAPROJECT	MELIORATES
MATSUTAKES	MEANINGFULLY	MEDIAEVALISTIC	MEDIUMSHIPS	MEGAPROJECTS	MELIORATING
MATTAMORES	MEANINGFULNESS	MEDIAEVALISTS	MEDIVACING	MEGASCOPES	MELIORATION
MATTERLESS	MEANINGLESS	MEDIAEVALLY	MEDIVACKED	MEGASCOPIC	MELIORATIONS
MATTIFYING	MEANINGLESSLY	MEDIAEVALS	MEDIVACKING	MEGASCOPICALLY	MELIORATIVE
MATTRASSES	MEANINGLESSNESS	MEDIAGENIC	MEDRESSEHS	MEGASPORANGIA	MELIORATIVES
MATTRESSES	MEANNESSES	MEDIASTINA	MEDULLATED	MEGASPORANGIUM	MELIORATOR
MATURATING	MEANWHILES	MEDIASTINAL	MEDULLOBLASTOMA	MEGASPORES	MELIORATORS
MATURATION	MEASLINESS	MEDIASTINUM	MEDUSIFORM	MEGASPORIC	MELIORISMS
MATURATIONAL	MEASLINESSES	MEDIATENESS	MEEKNESSES	MEGASPOROPHYLL	MELIORISTIC
MATURATIONS	MEASURABILITIES	MEDIATENESSES	MEERSCHAUM	MEGASPOROPHYLLS	MELIORISTS
MATURATIVE	MEASURABILITY	MEDIATIONAL	MEERSCHAUMS	MEGASTORES	MELIORITIES
MATURENESS	MEASURABLE	MEDIATIONS	MEETINGHOUSE	MEGASTRUCTURE	MELIPHAGOUS
MATURENESSES	MEASURABLENESS	MEDIATISATION	MEETINGHOUSES	MEGASTRUCTURES	MELISMATIC
MATURITIES	MEASURABLY	MEDIATISATIONS	MEETNESSES	MEGATECHNOLOGY	MELLIFEROUS
MATUTINALLY	MEASUREDLY	MEDIATISED	MEFLOQUINE	MEGATHERES	MELLIFICATION
MAUDLINISM	MEASUREDNESS	MEDIATISES	MEFLOQUINES	MEGATHERIAN	MELLIFICATIONS
MAUDLINISMS	MEASUREDNESSES	MEDIATISING	MEGACEPHALIC	MEGATONNAGE	MELLIFLUENCE
MAUDLINNESS	MEASURELESS	MEDIATIZATION	MEGACEPHALIES	MEGATONNAGES	MELLIFLUENCES
MAUDLINNESSES	MEASURELESSLY	MEDIATIZATIONS	MEGACEPHALOUS	MEGAVERTEBRATE	MELLIFLUENT
MAULSTICKS	MEASURELESSNESS	MEDIATIZED	MEGACEPHALY	MEGAVERTEBRATES	MELLIFLUENTLY
MAUMETRIES	MEASUREMENT	MEDIATIZES	MEGACITIES	MEGAVITAMIN	MELLIFLUOUS
MAUNDERERS	MEASUREMENTS	MEDIATIZING	MEGACORPORATION	MEGAVITAMINS	MELLIFLUOUSLY
MAUNDERING	MEASURINGS	MEDIATORIAL	MEGACURIES	MEIOFAUNAL	MELLIFLUOUSNESS
MAUNDERINGS	MEATINESSES	MEDIATORIALLY	MEGACYCLES	MEIOSPORES	MELLIPHAGOUS
MAUSOLEUMS	MEATLOAVES	MEDIATORSHIP	MEGADEATHS	MEIOTICALLY	MELLIVOROUS
MAVERICKED	MEATPACKING	MEDIATORSHIPS	MEGAFARADS	MEITNERIUM	MELLOPHONE
MAVERICKING	MEATPACKINGS	MEDIATRESS	MEGAFAUNAE	MEITNERIUMS	MELLOPHONES
MAVOURNEEN	MEATSCREEN	MEDIATRESSES	MEGAFAUNAL	MEKOMETERS	MELLOTRONS
MAVOURNEENS	MEATSCREENS	MEDIATRICES	MEGAFAUNAS	MELACONITE	MELLOWNESS
MAVOURNINS	MEATSPACES	MEDIATRIXES	MEGAFLORAE	MELACONITES	MELLOWNESSES
MAWKISHNESS	MECAMYLAMINE	MEDICALISATION	MEGAFLORAS	MELALEUCAS	MELLOWSPEAK
MAWKISHNESSES	MECAMYLAMINES	MEDICALISATIONS	MEGAGAMETE	MELAMPODES	MELLOWSPEAKS
MAWMETRIES	MECHANICAL	MEDICALISE	MEGAGAMETES	MELANAEMIA	MELOCOTONS
MAXILLARIES	MECHANICALISM	MEDICALISED	MEGAGAMETOPHYTE	MELANAEMIAS	MELOCOTOON
MAXILLIPED	MECHANICALISMS	MEDICALISES	MEGAGAUSSES	MELANCHOLIA	MELOCOTOONS
MAXILLIPEDARY	MECHANICALLY	MEDICALISING	MEGAHERBIVORE	MELANCHOLIAC	MELODICALLY
MAXILLIPEDE	MECHANICALNESS	MEDICALIZATION	MEGAHERBIVORES	MELANCHOLIACS	MELODIOUSLY
MAXILLIPEDES	MECHANICALS	MEDICALIZATIONS	MEGAHERTZES	MELANCHOLIAS	MELODIOUSNESS
MAXILLIPEDS	MECHANICIAN	MEDICALIZE	MEGAJOULES	MELANCHOLIC	MELODIOUSNESSES
MAXILLOFACIAL	MECHANICIANS	MEDICALIZED	MEGAKARYOCYTE	MELANCHOLICALLY	MELODISERS
MAXILLULAE	MECHANISABLE	MEDICALIZES	MEGAKARYOCYTES	MELANCHOLICS	MELODISING
MAXIMALIST	MECHANISATION	MEDICALIZING	MEGAKARYOCYTIC	MELANCHOLIES	MELODIZERS
MAXIMALISTS	MECHANISATIONS	MEDICAMENT	MEGALITHIC	MELANCHOLILY	MELODIZING
MAXIMAPHILIES	MECHANISED	MEDICAMENTAL	MEGALITRES	MELANCHOLINESS	MELODRAMAS
MAXIMAPHILY	MECHANISER	MEDICAMENTALLY	MEGALOBLAST	MELANCHOLIOUS	MELODRAMATIC
MAXIMATION	MECHANISERS	MEDICAMENTARY	MEGALOBLASTIC	MELANCHOLY	MELODRAMATICS
MAXIMATIONS	MECHANISES	MEDICAMENTED	MEGALOBLASTS	MELANISATION	MELODRAMATISE
MAXIMISATION	MECHANISING	MEDICAMENTING	MEGALOCARDIA	MELANISATIONS	MELODRAMATISED
MAXIMISATIONS	MECHANISMS	MEDICAMENTOUS	MEGALOCARDIAS	MELANISING	MELODRAMATISES
MAXIMISERS	MECHANISTIC	MEDICAMENTS	MEGALOCEPHALIC	MELANISTIC	MELODRAMATISING
MAXIMISING	MECHANISTICALLY	MEDICAMENTS	MEGALOCEPHALIES	MELANIZATION	MELODRAMATIST

m

MELODRAMATISTS	MENINGITIDES	MERCAPTOPURINES	MEREOLOGICAL	MESMERICAL	MESOTHORACES
MELODRAMATIZE	MENINGITIS	MERCENARIES	MEREOLOGIES	MESMERICALLY	MESOTHORACIC
MELODRAMATIZED	MENINGITISES	MERCENARILY	MERESTONES	MESMERISATION	MESOTHORAX
MELODRAMATIZES	MENINGOCELE	MERCENARINESS	MERETRICIOUS	MESMERISATIONS	MESOTHORAXES
MELODRAMATIZING	MENINGOCELES	MERCENARINESSES	MERETRICIOUSLY	MESMERISED	MESOTHORIUM
MELODRAMES	MENINGOCOCCAL	MERCENARISM	MERGANSERS	MESMERISER	MESOTHORIUMS
MELOMANIAC	MENINGOCOCCI	MERCENARISMS	MERIDIONAL	MESMERISERS	MESOTROPHIC
MELOMANIACS	MENINGOCOCCIC	MERCERISATION	MERIDIONALITIES	MESMERISES	MESQUINERIE
MELOMANIAS	MENINGOCOCCUS	MERCERISATIONS	MERIDIONALITY	MESMERISING	MESQUINERIES
MELONGENES	MENISCECTOMIES	MERCERISED	MERIDIONALLY	MESMERISMS	MESSAGINGS
MELPHALANS	MENISCECTOMY	MERCERISER	MERIDIONALS	MESMERISTS	MESSALINES
MELTABILITIES	MENISCUSES	MERCERISERS	MERISTEMATIC	MESMERIZATION	MESSEIGNEURS
MELTABILITY	MENISPERMACEOUS	MERCERISES	MERISTICALLY	MESMERIZATIONS	MESSENGERED
MELTINGNESS	MENISPERMUM	MERCERISING	MERITOCRACIES	MESMERIZED	MESSENGERING
MELTINGNESSES	MENISPERMUMS	MERCERIZATION	MERITOCRACY	MESMERIZER	MESSENGERS
MELTWATERS	MENOLOGIES	MERCERIZATIONS	MERITOCRAT	MESMERIZERS	MESSIAHSHIP
MELUNGEONS	MENOMINEES	MERCERIZED	MERITOCRATIC	MESMERIZES	MESSIAHSHIPS
MEMBERLESS	MENOPAUSAL	MERCERIZER	MERITOCRATS	MESMERIZING	MESSIANICALLY
MEMBERSHIP	MENOPAUSES	MERCERIZERS	MERITORIOUS	MESNALTIES	MESSIANISM
MEMBERSHIPS	MENOPAUSIC	MERCERIZES	MERITORIOUSLY	MESOAMERICAN	MESSIANISMS
MEMBRANACEOUS	MENOPOLISES	MERCERIZING	MERITORIOUSNESS	MESOBENTHOS	MESSINESSES
MEMBRANEOUS	MENORRHAGIA	MERCHANDISE	MERMAIDENS	MESOBENTHOSES	MESTRANOLS
MEMBRANOUS	MENORRHAGIAS	MERCHANDISED	MEROBLASTIC	MESOBLASTIC	METABOLICALLY
MEMBRANOUSLY	MENORRHAGIC	MERCHANDISER	MEROBLASTICALLY	MESOBLASTS	METABOLIES
MEMOIRISMS	MENORRHEAS	MERCHANDISERS	MEROGENESES	MESOCEPHALIC	METABOLISABLE
MEMOIRISTS	MENORRHOEA	MERCHANDISES	MEROGENESIS	MESOCEPHALICS	METABOLISE
MEMORABILE	MENORRHOEAS	MERCHANDISING	MEROGENETIC	MESOCEPHALIES	METABOLISED
MEMORABILIA	MENSERVANTS	MERCHANDISINGS	MEROGONIES	MESOCEPHALISM	METABOLISES
MEMORABILITIES	MENSTRUALLY	MERCHANDIZE	MEROMORPHIC	MESOCEPHALISMS	METABOLISING
MEMORABILITY	MENSTRUATE	MERCHANDIZED	MEROMYOSIN	MESOCEPHALOUS	METABOLISM
MEMORABLENESS	MENSTRUATED	MERCHANDIZER	MEROMYOSINS	MESOCEPHALY	METABOLISMS
MEMORABLENESSES	MENSTRUATES	MERCHANDIZERS	MERONYMIES	MESOCRANIES	METABOLITE
MEMORANDUM	MENSTRUATING	MERCHANDIZES	MEROPIDANS	MESOCRATIC	METABOLITES
MEMORANDUMS	MENSTRUATION	MERCHANDIZING	MEROPLANKTON	MESOCYCLONE	METABOLIZABLE
MEMORATIVE	MENSTRUATIONS	MERCHANDIZINGS	MEROPLANKTONS	MESOCYCLONES	METABOLIZE
MEMORIALISATION	MENSTRUOUS	MERCHANTABILITY	MEROZOITES	MESODERMAL	METABOLIZED
MEMORIALISE	MENSTRUUMS	MERCHANTABLE	MERPEOPLES	MESODERMIC	METABOLIZES
MEMORIALISED	MENSURABILITIES	MERCHANTED	MERRIMENTS	MESOGASTRIA	METABOLIZING
MEMORIALISER	MENSURABILITY	MERCHANTING	MERRINESSES	MESOGASTRIC	METABOLOME
MEMORIALISERS	MENSURABLE	MERCHANTINGS	MERRYMAKER	MESOGASTRIUM	METABOLOMES
MEMORIALISES	MENSURATION	MERCHANTLIKE	MERRYMAKERS	MESOGLOEAS	METABOLOMICS
MEMORIALISING	MENSURATIONAL	MERCHANTMAN	MERRYMAKING	MESOGNATHIES	METABOTROPIC
MEMORIALIST	MENSURATIONS	MERCHANTMEN	MERRYMAKINGS	MESOGNATHISM	METACARPAL
MEMORIALISTS	MENSURATIVE	MERCHANTRIES	MERRYTHOUGHT	MESOGNATHISMS	METACARPALS
MEMORIALIZATION	MENTALESES	MERCHANTRY	MERRYTHOUGHTS	MESOGNATHOUS	METACARPUS
MEMORIALIZE	MENTALISMS	MERCHILDREN	MERVEILLEUSE	MESOGNATHY	METACENTER
MEMORIALIZED	MENTALISTIC	MERCIFULLY	MERVEILLEUSES	MESOHIPPUS	METACENTERS
MEMORIALIZER	MENTALISTICALLY	MERCIFULNESS	MERVEILLEUX	MESOHIPPUSES	METACENTRE
MEMORIALIZERS	MENTALISTS	MERCIFULNESSES	MERVEILLEUXES	MESOKURTIC	METACENTRES
MEMORIALIZES	MENTALITIES	MERCIFYING	MESALLIANCE	MESOMERISM	METACENTRIC
MEMORIALIZING	MENTATIONS	MERCILESSLY	MESALLIANCES	MESOMERISMS	METACENTRICS
MEMORIALLY	MENTHACEOUS	MERCILESSNESS	MESATICEPHALIC	MESOMORPHIC	METACERCARIA
MEMORISABLE	MENTHOLATED	MERCILESSNESSES	MESATICEPHALIES	MESOMORPHIES	METACERCARIAE
MEMORISATION	MENTICIDES	MERCURATED	MESATICEPHALOUS	MESOMORPHISM	METACERCARIAL
MEMORISATIONS	MENTIONABLE	MERCURATES	MESATICEPHALY	MESOMORPHISMS	METACHROMATIC
MEMORISERS	MENTIONERS	MERCURATING	MESCALINES	MESOMORPHOUS	METACHROMATISM
MEMORISING	MENTIONING	MERCURATION	MESCALISMS	MESOMORPHS	METACHROMATISMS
MEMORIZABLE	MENTONNIERE	MERCURATIONS	MESDEMOISELLES	MESOMORPHY	METACHRONISM
MEMORIZATION	MENTONNIERES	MERCURIALISE	MESENCEPHALA	MESONEPHRIC	METACHRONISMS
MEMORIZATIONS	MENTORINGS	MERCURIALISED	MESENCEPHALIC	MESONEPHROI	METACHROSES
MEMORIZERS	MENTORSHIP	MERCURIALISES	MESENCEPHALON	MESONEPHROS	METACHROSIS
MEMORIZING	MENTORSHIPS	MERCURIALISING	MESENCEPHALONS	MESONEPHROSES	METACINNABARITE
MENACINGLY	MENUISIERS	MERCURIALISM	MESENCHYMAL	MESOPAUSES	METACOGNITION
MENADIONES	MEPACRINES	MERCURIALISMS	MESENCHYMATOUS	MESOPELAGIC	METACOGNITIONS
MENAGERIES	MEPERIDINE	MERCURIALIST	MESENCHYME	MESOPHILES	METACOMPUTER
MENAQUINONE	MEPERIDINES	MERCURIALISTS	MESENCHYMES	MESOPHILIC	METACOMPUTERS
MENAQUINONES	MEPHITICAL	MERCURIALITIES	MESENTERIAL	MESOPHYLLIC	METACOMPUTING
MENARCHEAL	MEPHITICALLY	MERCURIALITY	MESENTERIC	MESOPHYLLOUS	METACOMPUTINGS
MENARCHIAL	MEPHITISES	MERCURIALIZE	MESENTERIES	MESOPHYLLS	METAETHICAL
MENDACIOUS	MEPHITISMS	MERCURIALIZED	MESENTERITIS	MESOPHYTES	METAETHICS
MENDACIOUSLY	MEPROBAMATE	MERCURIALIZES	MESENTERITISES	MESOPHYTIC	METAFEMALE
MENDACIOUSNESS	MEPROBAMATES	MERCURIALIZING	MESENTERON	MESOSCAPHE	METAFEMALES
MENDACITIES	MERBROMINS	MERCURIALLY	MESENTERONIC	MESOSCAPHES	METAFICTION
MENDELEVIUM	MERCANTILE	MERCURIALNESS	MESHUGAASEN	MESOSPHERE	METAFICTIONAL
MENDELEVIUMS	MERCANTILISM	MERCURIALNESSES	MESHUGASEN	MESOSPHERES	METAFICTIONIST
MENDICANCIES	MERCANTILISMS	MERCURIALS	MESHUGGENAH	MESOSPHERIC	METAFICTIONISTS
MENDICANCY	MERCANTILIST	MERCURISED	MESHUGGENAHS	MESOTHELIA	METAFICTIONS
MENDICANTS	MERCANTILISTIC	MERCURISES	MESHUGGENEH	MESOTHELIAL	METAGALACTIC
MENDICITIES	MERCANTILISTS	MERCURISING	MESHUGGENEHS	MESOTHELIOMA	METAGALAXIES
MENINGIOMA	MERCAPTANS	MERCURIZED	MESHUGGENER	MESOTHELIOMAS	METAGALAXY
MENINGIOMAS	MERCAPTIDE	MERCURIZES	MESHUGGENERS	MESOTHELIOMATA	METAGENESES
MENINGIOMATA	MERCAPTIDES	MERCURIZING	MESITYLENE	MESOTHELIUM	METAGENESIS
MENINGITIC	MERCAPTOPURINE	MERDIVOROUS	MESITYLENES	MESOTHELIUMS	METAGENETIC

METAGENETICALLY	METAMATHEMATICS	METASTABILITIES	METEOROLOGIES	METHYLMERCURIES	MEZZALUNAS
METAGNATHISM	METAMERICALLY	METASTABILITY	METEOROLOGIST	METHYLMERCURY	MEZZANINES
METAGNATHISMS	METAMERISM	METASTABLE	METEOROLOGISTS	METHYLPHENIDATE	MEZZOTINTED
METAGNATHOUS	METAMERISMS	METASTABLES	METEOROLOGY	METHYLPHENOL	MEZZOTINTER
METAGRABOLISE	METAMICTISATION	METASTABLY	METESTICKS	METHYLPHENOLS	MEZZOTINTERS
METAGRABOLISED	METAMICTIZATION	METASTASES	METESTROUS	METHYLTHIONINE	MEZZOTINTING
METAGRABOLISES	METAMORPHIC	METASTASIS	METESTRUSES	METHYLTHIONINES	MEZZOTINTO
METAGRABOLISING	METAMORPHICALLY	METASTASISE	METFORMINS	METHYLXANTHINE	MEZZOTINTOS
METAGRABOLIZE	METAMORPHISM	METASTASISED	METHACRYLATE	METHYLXANTHINES	MEZZOTINTS
METAGRABOLIZED	METAMORPHISMS	METASTASISES	METHACRYLATES	METHYSERGIDE	MIAROLITIC
METAGRABOLIZES	METAMORPHIST	METASTASISING	METHACRYLIC	METHYSERGIDES	MIASMATICAL
METAGRABOLIZING	METAMORPHISTS	METASTASIZE	METHADONES	METICULOSITIES	MIASMATOUS
METAGROBOLISE	METAMORPHOSE	METASTASIZED	METHAEMOGLOBIN	METICULOSITY	MIASMICALLY
METAGROBOLISED	METAMORPHOSED	METASTASIZES	METHAEMOGLOBINS	METICULOUS	MICRIFYING
METAGROBOLISES	METAMORPHOSES	METASTASIZING	METHAMPHETAMINE	METICULOUSLY	MICROAEROPHILE
METAGROBOLISING	METAMORPHOSING	METASTATIC	METHANATION	METICULOUSNESS	MICROAEROPHILES
METAGROBOLIZE	METAMORPHOSIS	METASTATICALLY	METHANATIONS	METOESTROUS	MICROAEROPHILIC
METAGROBOLIZED	METAMORPHOUS	METATARSAL	METHANOMETER	METOESTRUS	MICROAMPERE
METAGROBOLIZES	METANALYSES	METATARSALS	METHANOMETERS	METOESTRUSES	MICROAMPERES
METAGROBOLIZING	METANALYSIS	METATARSUS	METHAQUALONE	METONYMICAL	MICROANALYSES
METALANGUAGE	METANEPHRIC	METATHEORETICAL	METHAQUALONES	METONYMICALLY	MICROANALYSIS
METALANGUAGES	METANEPHROI	METATHEORIES	METHEDRINE	METONYMIES	MICROANALYST
METALDEHYDE	METANEPHROS	METATHEORY	METHEDRINES	METOPOSCOPIC	MICROANALYSTS
METALDEHYDES	METAPERIODIC	METATHERIAN	METHEGLINS	METOPOSCOPICAL	MICROANALYTIC
METALEPSES	METAPHASES	METATHERIANS	METHEMOGLOBIN	METOPOSCOPIES	MICROANALYTICAL
METALEPSIS	METAPHORIC	METATHESES	METHEMOGLOBINS	METOPOSCOPIST	MICROANATOMICAL
METALEPTIC	METAPHORICAL	METATHESIS	METHENAMINE	METOPOSCOPISTS	MICROANATOMIES
METALEPTICAL	METAPHORICALLY	METATHESISE	METHENAMINES	METOPOSCOPY	MICROANATOMY
METALHEADS	METAPHORIST	METATHESISED	METHICILLIN	METRALGIAS	MICROARRAY
METALINGUISTIC	METAPHORISTS	METATHESISES	METHICILLINS	METRICALLY	MICROARRAYS
METALINGUISTICS	METAPHOSPHATE	METATHESISING	METHINKETH	METRICATED	MICROBALANCE
METALISING	METAPHOSPHATES	METATHESIZE	METHIONINE	METRICATES	MICROBALANCES
METALIZATION	METAPHOSPHORIC	METATHESIZED	METHIONINES	METRICATING	MICROBAROGRAPH
METALIZATIONS	METAPHRASE	METATHESIZES	METHODICAL	METRICATION	MICROBAROGRAPHS
METALIZING	METAPHRASED	METATHESIZING	METHODICALLY	METRICATIONS	MICROBEAMS
METALLICALLY	METAPHRASES	METATHETIC	METHODICALNESS	METRICIANS	MICROBIOLOGIC
METALLIDING	METAPHRASING	METATHETICAL	METHODISATION	METRICISED	MICROBIOLOGICAL
METALLIDINGS	METAPHRASIS	METATHETICALLY	METHODISATIONS	METRICISES	MICROBIOLOGIES
METALLIFEROUS	METAPHRAST	METATHORACES	METHODISED	METRICISING	MICROBIOLOGIST
METALLINGS	METAPHRASTIC	METATHORACIC	METHODISER	METRICISMS	MICROBIOLOGISTS
METALLISATION	METAPHRASTICAL	METATHORAX	METHODISERS	METRICISTS	MICROBIOLOGY
METALLISATIONS	METAPHRASTS	METATHORAXES	METHODISES	METRICIZED	MICROBIOTA
METALLISED	METAPHYSIC	METATUNGSTIC	METHODISING	METRICIZES	MICROBREWER
METALLISES	METAPHYSICAL	METAVANADIC	METHODISMS	METRICIZING	MICROBREWERIES
METALLISING	METAPHYSICALLY	METAXYLEMS	METHODISTIC	METRIFICATION	MICROBREWERS
METALLISTS	METAPHYSICIAN	METECDYSES	METHODISTS	METRIFICATIONS	MICROBREWERY
METALLIZATION	METAPHYSICIANS	METECDYSIS	METHODIZATION	METRIFIERS	MICROBREWING
METALLIZATIONS	METAPHYSICISE	METEMPIRIC	METHODIZATIONS	METRIFYING	MICROBREWINGS
METALLIZED	METAPHYSICISED	METEMPIRICAL	METHODIZED	METRITISES	MICROBREWS
METALLIZES	METAPHYSICISES	METEMPIRICALLY	METHODIZER	METROLOGIC	MICROBUBBLES
METALLIZING	METAPHYSICISING	METEMPIRICISM	METHODIZERS	METROLOGICAL	MICROBURST
METALLOCENE	METAPHYSICIST	METEMPIRICISMS	METHODIZES	METROLOGICALLY	MICROBURSTS
METALLOCENES	METAPHYSICISTS	METEMPIRICIST	METHODIZING	METROLOGIES	MICROBUSES
METALLOGENETIC	METAPHYSICIZE	METEMPIRICISTS	METHODOLOGICAL	METROLOGIST	MICROBUSSES
METALLOGENIC	METAPHYSICIZED	METEMPIRICS	METHODOLOGIES	METROLOGISTS	MICROCAPSULE
METALLOGENIES	METAPHYSICIZES	METEMPSYCHOSES	METHODOLOGIST	METROMANIA	MICROCAPSULES
METALLOGENY	METAPHYSICIZING	METEMPSYCHOSIS	METHODOLOGISTS	METROMANIAS	MICROCARDS
METALLOGRAPHER	METAPHYSICS	METEMPSYCHOSIST	METHODOLOGY	METRONIDAZOLE	MICROCASSETTE
METALLOGRAPHERS	METAPLASES	METENCEPHALA	METHOMANIA	METRONIDAZOLES	MICROCASSETTES
METALLOGRAPHIC	METAPLASIA	METENCEPHALIC	METHOMANIAS	METRONOMES	MICROCELEBRITY
METALLOGRAPHIES	METAPLASIAS	METENCEPHALON	METHOTREXATE	METRONOMIC	MICROCEPHAL
METALLOGRAPHIST	METAPLASIS	METENCEPHALONS	METHOTREXATES	METRONOMICAL	MICROCEPHALIC
METALLOGRAPHY	METAPLASMIC	METEORICALLY	METHOXIDES	METRONOMICALLY	MICROCEPHALICS
METALLOIDAL	METAPLASMS	METEORISMS	METHOXYBENZENE	METRONYMIC	MICROCEPHALIES
METALLOIDS	METAPLASTIC	METEORISTS	METHOXYBENZENES	METRONYMICS	MICROCEPHALOUS
METALLOPHONE	METAPOLITICAL	METEORITAL	METHOXYCHLOR	METROPLEXES	MICROCEPHALS
METALLOPHONES	METAPOLITICS	METEORITES	METHOXYCHLORS	METROPOLIS	MICROCEPHALY
METALLURGIC	METAPSYCHIC	METEORITIC	METHOXYFLURANE	METROPOLISES	MICROCHEMICAL
METALLURGICAL	METAPSYCHICAL	METEORITICAL	METHOXYFLURANES	METROPOLITAN	MICROCHEMISTRY
METALLURGICALLY	METAPSYCHICS	METEORITICIST	METHYLAMINE	METROPOLITANATE	MICROCHIPPED
METALLURGIES	METAPSYCHOLOGY	METEORITICISTS	METHYLAMINES	METROPOLITANISE	MICROCHIPPING
METALLURGIST	METARCHONS	METEORITICS	METHYLASES	METROPOLITANISM	MICROCHIPS
METALLURGISTS	METASEQUOIA	METEOROGRAM	METHYLATED	METROPOLITANIZE	MICROCIRCUIT
METALLURGY	METASEQUOIAS	METEOROGRAMS	METHYLATES	METROPOLITANS	MICROCIRCUITRY
METALMARKS	METASILICATE	METEOROGRAPH	METHYLATING	METROPOLITICAL	MICROCIRCUITS
METALSMITH	METASILICATES	METEOROGRAPHIC	METHYLATION	METRORRHAGIA	MICROCLIMATE
METALSMITHS	METASILICIC	METEOROGRAPHS	METHYLATIONS	METRORRHAGIAS	MICROCLIMATES
METALWARES	METASOMATA	METEOROIDAL	METHYLATOR	METROSEXUAL	MICROCLIMATIC
METALWORKER	METASOMATIC	METEOROIDS	METHYLATORS	METROSTYLE	MICROCLINE
METALWORKERS	METASOMATISM	METEOROLITE	METHYLCELLULOSE	METROSTYLES	MICROCLINES
METALWORKING	METASOMATISMS	METEOROLITES	METHYLDOPA	METTLESOME	MICROCOCCAL
METALWORKINGS	METASOMATOSES	METEOROLOGIC	METHYLDOPAS	METTLESOMENESS	MICROCOCCI
METALWORKS	METASOMATOSIS	METEOROLOGICAL	METHYLENES	MEZCALINES	MICROCOCCUS

MICROCODES	MICROFLORA	MICROMETRIC	MICROPROCESSING	MICROTECHNICS	MIFFINESSES
MICROCOMPONENT	MICROFLORAE	MICROMETRICAL	MICROPROCESSOR	MICROTECHNIQUE	MIGHTINESS
MICROCOMPONENTS	MICROFLORAL	MICROMETRIES	MICROPROCESSORS	MICROTECHNIQUES	MIGHTINESSES
MICROCOMPUTER	MICROFLORAS	MICROMETRY	MICROPROGRAM	MICROTECHNOLOGY	MIGMATITES
MICROCOMPUTERS	MICROFORMS	MICROMICROCURIE	MICROPROGRAMS	MICROTOMES	MIGNONETTE
MICROCOMPUTING	MICROFOSSIL	MICROMICROFARAD	MICROPROJECTION	MICROTOMIC	MIGNONETTES
MICROCOMPUTINGS	MICROFOSSILS	MICROMILLIMETRE	MICROPROJECTOR	MICROTOMICAL	MIGRAINEUR
MICROCOPIED	MICROFUNGI	MICROMINIATURE	MICROPROJECTORS	MICROTOMIES	MIGRAINEURS
MICROCOPIES	MICROFUNGUS	MICROMINIS	MICROPSIAS	MICROTOMIST	MIGRAINOUS
MICROCOPYING	MICROGAMETE	MICROMOLAR	MICROPTEROUS	MICROTOMISTS	MIGRATIONAL
MICROCOPYINGS	MICROGAMETES	MICROMOLES	MICROPUBLISHER	MICROTONAL	MIGRATIONIST
MICROCOSMIC	MICROGAMETOCYTE	MICROMORPHOLOGY	MICROPUBLISHERS	MICROTONALITIES	MIGRATIONISTS
MICROCOSMICAL	MICROGLIAS	MICRONEEDLE	MICROPUBLISHING	MICROTONALITY	MIGRATIONS
MICROCOSMICALLY	MICROGRAMS	MICRONEEDLES	MICROPULSATION	MICROTONALLY	MILDNESSES
MICROCOSMOS	MICROGRANITE	MICRONISATION	MICROPULSATIONS	MICROTONES	MILEOMETER
MICROCOSMOSES	MICROGRANITES	MICRONISATIONS	MICROPUMPS	MICROTUBULAR	MILEOMETERS
MICROCOSMS	MICROGRANITIC	MICRONISED	MICROPUNCTURE	MICROTUBULE	MILESTONES
MICROCRACK	MICROGRAPH	MICRONISES	MICROPUNCTURES	MICROTUBULES	MILITANCES
MICROCRACKED	MICROGRAPHED	MICRONISING	MICROPYLAR	MICROTUNNELLING	MILITANCIES
MICROCRACKING	MICROGRAPHER	MICRONIZATION	MICROPYLES	MICROVASCULAR	MILITANTLY
MICROCRACKINGS	MICROGRAPHERS	MICRONIZATIONS	MICROPYROMETER	MICROVILLAR	MILITANTNESS
MICROCRACKS	MICROGRAPHIC	MICRONIZED	MICROPYROMETERS	MICROVILLI	MILITANTNESSES
MICROCRYSTAL	MICROGRAPHICS	MICRONIZES	MICROQUAKE	MICROVILLOUS	MILITARIES
MICROCRYSTALS	MICROGRAPHIES	MICRONIZING	MICROQUAKES	MICROVILLUS	MILITARILY
MICROCULTURAL	MICROGRAPHING	MICRONUCLEI	MICRORADIOGRAPH	MICROVOLTS	MILITARISATION
MICROCULTURE	MICROGRAPHS	MICRONUCLEUS	MICROREADER	MICROWATTS	MILITARISATIONS
MICROCULTURES	MICROGRAPHY	MICRONUCLEUSES	MICROREADERS	MICROWAVABLE	MILITARISE
MICROCURIE	MICROGRAVITIES	MICRONUTRIENT	MICROSATELLITE	MICROWAVEABLE	MILITARISED
MICROCURIES	MICROGRAVITY	MICRONUTRIENTS	MICROSATELLITES	MICROWAVED	MILITARISES
MICROCYTES	MICROGROOVE	MICROORGANISM	MICROSCALE	MICROWAVES	MILITARISING
MICROCYTIC	MICROGROOVES	MICROORGANISMS	MICROSCALES	MICROWAVING	MILITARISM
MICRODETECTION	MICROHABITAT	MICROPARASITE	MICROSCOPE	MICROWIRES	MILITARISMS
MICRODETECTIONS	MICROHABITATS	MICROPARASITES	MICROSCOPES	MICROWORLD	MILITARIST
MICRODETECTOR	MICROIMAGE	MICROPARASITIC	MICROSCOPIC	MICROWORLDS	MILITARISTIC
MICRODETECTORS	MICROIMAGES	MICROPARTICLE	MICROSCOPICAL	MICROWRITER	MILITARISTS
MICRODISSECTION	MICROINCHES	MICROPARTICLES	MICROSCOPICALLY	MICROWRITERS	MILITARIZATION
MICRODONTOUS	MICROINJECT	MICROPAYMENT	MICROSCOPIES	MICRURGIES	MILITARIZATIONS
MICRODRIVE	MICROINJECTED	MICROPAYMENTS	MICROSCOPIST	MICTURATED	MILITARIZE
MICRODRIVES	MICROINJECTING	MICROPEGMATITE	MICROSCOPISTS	MICTURATES	MILITARIZED
MICROEARTHQUAKE	MICROINJECTION	MICROPEGMATITES	MICROSCOPY	MICTURATING	MILITARIZES
MICROECONOMIC	MICROINJECTIONS	MICROPEGMATITIC	MICROSECOND	MICTURITION	MILITARIZING
MICROECONOMICS	MICROINJECTS	MICROPHAGE	MICROSECONDS	MICTURITIONS	MILITATING
MICROELECTRODE	MICROLIGHT	MICROPHAGES	MICROSEISM	MIDDELMANNETJIE	MILITATION
MICROELECTRODES	MICROLIGHTING	MICROPHAGOUS	MICROSEISMIC	MIDDENSTEAD	MILITATIONS
MICROELECTRONIC	MICROLIGHTINGS	MICROPHONE	MICROSEISMICAL	MIDDENSTEADS	MILITIAMAN
MICROELEMENT	MICROLIGHTS	MICROPHONES	MICROSEISMICITY	MIDDLEBREAKER	MILITIAMEN
MICROELEMENTS	MICROLITER	MICROPHONIC	MICROSEISMS	MIDDLEBREAKERS	MILKFISHES
MICROEVOLUTION	MICROLITERS	MICROPHONICS	MICROSITES	MIDDLEBROW	MILKINESSES
MICROEVOLUTIONS	MICROLITES	MICROPHOTOGRAPH	MICROSKIRT	MIDDLEBROWED	MILKSHAKES
MICROFARAD	MICROLITHIC	MICROPHOTOMETER	MICROSKIRTS	MIDDLEBROWISM	MILKSOPISM
MICROFARADS	MICROLITHS	MICROPHOTOMETRY	MICROSLEEP	MIDDLEBROWISMS	MILKSOPISMS
MICROFAUNA	MICROLITIC	MICROPHYLL	MICROSLEEPS	MIDDLEBROWS	MILKSOPPING
MICROFAUNAE	MICROLOANS	MICROPHYLLOUS	MICROSMATIC	MIDDLEBUSTER	MILKTOASTS
MICROFAUNAL	MICROLOGIC	MICROPHYLLS	MICROSOMAL	MIDDLEBUSTERS	MILLBOARDS
MICROFAUNAS	MICROLOGICAL	MICROPHYSICAL	MICROSOMES	MIDDLEMOST	MILLEFEUILLE
MICROFELSITIC	MICROLOGICALLY	MICROPHYSICALLY	MICROSPECIES	MIDDLEWEIGHT	MILLEFEUILLES
MICROFIBER	MICROLOGIES	MICROPHYSICS	MICROSPHERE	MIDDLEWEIGHTS	MILLEFIORI
MICROFIBERS	MICROLOGIST	MICROPHYTE	MICROSPHERES	MIDDLINGLY	MILLEFIORIS
MICROFIBRE	MICROLOGISTS	MICROPHYTES	MICROSPHERICAL	MIDFIELDER	MILLEFLEUR
MICROFIBRES	MICROLUCES	MICROPHYTIC	MICROSPORANGIA	MIDFIELDERS	MILLEFLEURS
MICROFIBRIL	MICROLUXES	MICROPIPET	MICROSPORANGIUM	MIDINETTES	MILLENARIAN
MICROFIBRILLAR	MICROMANAGE	MICROPIPETS	MICROSPORE	MIDISKIRTS	MILLENARIANISM
MICROFIBRILS	MICROMANAGED	MICROPIPETTE	MICROSPORES	MIDLATITUDE	MILLENARIANISMS
MICROFICHE	MICROMANAGEMENT	MICROPIPETTES	MICROSPORIC	MIDLATITUDES	MILLENARIANS
MICROFICHES	MICROMANAGER	MICROPLANKTON	MICROSPOROCYTE	MIDLITTORAL	MILLENARIES
MICROFILAMENT	MICROMANAGERS	MICROPLANKTONS	MICROSPOROCYTES	MIDLITTORALS	MILLENARISM
MICROFILAMENTS	MICROMANAGES	MICROPOLIS	MICROSPOROPHYLL	MIDNIGHTLY	MILLENARISMS
MICROFILARIA	MICROMANAGING	MICROPOLISES	MICROSPOROUS	MIDRASHOTH	MILLENNIAL
MICROFILARIAE	MICROMARKETING	MICROPORES	MICROSTATE	MIDSAGITTAL	MILLENNIALISM
MICROFILARIAL	MICROMARKETINGS	MICROPOROSITIES	MICROSTATES	MIDSECTION	MILLENNIALISMS
MICROFILARIAS	MICROMERES	MICROPOROSITY	MICROSTOMATOUS	MIDSECTIONS	MILLENNIALIST
MICROFILING	MICROMESHES	MICROPOROUS	MICROSTOMOUS	MIDSHIPMAN	MILLENNIALISTS
MICROFILINGS	MICROMETEORITE	MICROPOWER	MICROSTRUCTURAL	MIDSHIPMATE	MILLENNIALLY
MICROFILMABLE	MICROMETEORITES	MICROPOWERS	MICROSTRUCTURE	MIDSHIPMATES	MILLENNIANISM
MICROFILMED	MICROMETEORITIC	MICROPRINT	MICROSTRUCTURES	MIDSHIPMEN	MILLENNIANISMS
MICROFILMER	MICROMETEOROID	MICROPRINTED	MICROSURGEON	MIDSTORIES	MILLENNIARISM
MICROFILMERS	MICROMETEOROIDS	MICROPRINTING	MICROSURGEONS	MIDSTREAMS	MILLENNIARISMS
MICROFILMING	MICROMETER	MICROPRINTINGS	MICROSURGERIES	MIDSUMMERS	MILLENNIUM
MICROFILMS	MICROMETERS	MICROPRINTS	MICROSURGERY	MIDWATCHES	MILLENNIUMS
MICROFILTER	MICROMETHOD	MICROPRISM	MICROSURGICAL	MIDWIFERIES	MILLEPEDES
MICROFILTERS	MICROMETHODS	MICROPRISMS	MICROSWITCH	MIDWINTERS	MILLEPORES
MICROFLOPPIES	MICROMETRE	MICROPROBE	MICROSWITCHES	MIFEPRISTONE	MILLERITES
MICROFLOPPY	MICROMETRES	MICROPROBES	MICROTECHNIC	MIFEPRISTONES	MILLESIMAL

MILLESIMALLY
MILLESIMALS
MILLHOUSES
MILLIAMPERE
MILLIAMPERES
MILLIARIES
MILLICURIE
MILLICURIES
MILLIDEGREE
MILLIDEGREES
MILLIGRAMME
MILLIGRAMMES
MILLIGRAMS
MILLIHENRIES
MILLIHENRY
MILLIHENRYS
MILLILAMBERT
MILLILAMBERTS
MILLILITER
MILLILITERS
MILLILITRE
MILLILITRES
MILLILUCES
MILLILUXES
MILLIMETER
MILLIMETERS
MILLIMETRE
MILLIMETRES
MILLIMICRON
MILLIMICRONS
MILLIMOLAR
MILLIMOLES
MILLINERIES
MILLIONAIRE
MILLIONAIRES
MILLIONAIRESS
MILLIONAIRESSES
MILLIONARY
MILLIONFOLD
MILLIONNAIRE
MILLIONNAIRES
MILLIONNAIRESS
MILLIONTHS
MILLIOSMOL
MILLIOSMOLS
MILLIPEDES
MILLIPROBE
MILLIPROBES
MILLIRADIAN
MILLIRADIANS
MILLIROENTGEN
MILLIROENTGENS
MILLISECOND
MILLISECONDS
MILLISIEVERT
MILLISIEVERTS
MILLIVOLTS
MILLIWATTS
MILLOCRACIES
MILLOCRACY
MILLOCRATS
MILLSCALES
MILLSTONES
MILLSTREAM
MILLSTREAMS
MILLWHEELS
MILLWRIGHT
MILLWRIGHTS
MILOMETERS
MILQUETOAST
MILQUETOASTS
MIMEOGRAPH
MIMEOGRAPHED
MIMEOGRAPHING
MIMEOGRAPHS
MIMETICALLY
MIMMICKING
MIMOGRAPHER
MIMOGRAPHERS
MIMOGRAPHIES
MIMOGRAPHY
MIMOSACEOUS
MINACIOUSLY

MINACITIES
MINATORIAL
MINATORIALLY
MINATORILY
MINAUDERIE
MINAUDERIES
MINAUDIERE
MINAUDIERES
MINCEMEATS
MINDBLOWER
MINDBLOWERS
MINDEDNESS
MINDEDNESSES
MINDFULNESS
MINDFULNESSES
MINDLESSLY
MINDLESSNESS
MINDLESSNESSES
MINDSHARES
MINEFIELDS
MINEHUNTER
MINEHUNTERS
MINELAYERS
MINERALISABLE
MINERALISATION
MINERALISATIONS
MINERALISE
MINERALISED
MINERALISER
MINERALISERS
MINERALISES
MINERALISING
MINERALIST
MINERALISTS
MINERALIZABLE
MINERALIZATION
MINERALIZATIONS
MINERALIZE
MINERALIZED
MINERALIZER
MINERALIZERS
MINERALIZES
MINERALIZING
MINERALOGIC
MINERALOGICAL
MINERALOGICALLY
MINERALOGIES
MINERALOGISE
MINERALOGISED
MINERALOGISES
MINERALOGISING
MINERALOGIST
MINERALOGISTS
MINERALOGIZE
MINERALOGIZED
MINERALOGIZES
MINERALOGIZING
MINERALOGY
MINESHAFTS
MINESTONES
MINESTRONE
MINESTRONES
MINESWEEPER
MINESWEEPERS
MINESWEEPING
MINESWEEPINGS
MINGIMINGI
MINGIMINGIS
MINGINESSES
MINGLEMENT
MINGLEMENTS
MINGLINGLY
MINIATIONS
MINIATURED
MINIATURES
MINIATURING
MINIATURISATION
MINIATURISE
MINIATURISED
MINIATURISES
MINIATURISING
MINIATURIST
MINIATURISTIC

MINIATURISTS
MINIATURIZATION
MINIATURIZE
MINIATURIZED
MINIATURIZES
MINIATURIZING
MINIBIKERS
MINIBREAKS
MINIBUDGET
MINIBUDGETS
MINIBUSSES
MINICABBING
MINICABBINGS
MINICOMPUTER
MINICOMPUTERS
MINICOURSE
MINICOURSES
MINIDISHES
MINIDRESSES
MINIFICATION
MINIFICATIONS
MINIFLOPPIES
MINIFLOPPY
MINIMALISM
MINIMALISMS
MINIMALIST
MINIMALISTS
MINIMAXING
MINIMISATION
MINIMISATIONS
MINIMISERS
MINIMISING
MINIMIZATION
MINIMIZATIONS
MINIMIZERS
MINIMIZING
MINIRUGBIES
MINISCHOOL
MINISCHOOLS
MINISCULES
MINISERIES
MINISKIRTED
MINISKIRTS
MINISTATES
MINISTERED
MINISTERIA
MINISTERIAL
MINISTERIALIST
MINISTERIALISTS
MINISTERIALLY
MINISTERING
MINISTERIUM
MINISTERSHIP
MINISTERSHIPS
MINISTRANT
MINISTRANTS
MINISTRATION
MINISTRATIONS
MINISTRATIVE
MINISTRESS
MINISTRESSES
MINISTRIES
MINISTROKE
MINISTROKES
MINITOWERS
MINITRACKS
MINIVOLLEY
MINIVOLLEYS
MINNESINGER
MINNESINGERS
MINNICKING
MINNOCKING
MINORITAIRE
MINORITAIRES
MINORITIES
MINORSHIPS
MINOXIDILS
MINSTRELSIES
MINSTRELSY
MINUSCULAR
MINUSCULES
MINUTENESS
MINUTENESSES

MIRABELLES
MIRABILISES
MIRACIDIAL
MIRACIDIUM
MIRACULOUS
MIRACULOUSLY
MIRACULOUSNESS
MIRANDISED
MIRANDISES
MIRANDISING
MIRANDIZED
MIRANDIZES
MIRANDIZING
MIRIFICALLY
MIRINESSES
MIRKINESSES
MIRRORLIKE
MIRRORWISE
MIRTHFULLY
MIRTHFULNESS
MIRTHFULNESSES
MIRTHLESSLY
MIRTHLESSNESS
MIRTHLESSNESSES
MISACCEPTATION
MISACCEPTATIONS
MISADAPTED
MISADAPTING
MISADDRESS
MISADDRESSED
MISADDRESSES
MISADDRESSING
MISADJUSTED
MISADJUSTING
MISADJUSTS
MISADVENTURE
MISADVENTURED
MISADVENTURER
MISADVENTURERS
MISADVENTURES
MISADVENTUROUS
MISADVERTENCE
MISADVERTENCES
MISADVICES
MISADVISED
MISADVISEDLY
MISADVISEDNESS
MISADVISES
MISADVISING
MISALIGNED
MISALIGNING
MISALIGNMENT
MISALIGNMENTS
MISALLEGED
MISALLEGES
MISALLEGING
MISALLIANCE
MISALLIANCES
MISALLOCATE
MISALLOCATED
MISALLOCATES
MISALLOCATING
MISALLOCATION
MISALLOCATIONS
MISALLOTMENT
MISALLOTMENTS
MISALLOTTED
MISALLOTTING
MISALLYING
MISALTERED
MISALTERING
MISANALYSES
MISANALYSIS
MISANDRIES
MISANDRIST
MISANDRISTS
MISANDROUS
MISANTHROPE
MISANTHROPES
MISANTHROPIC
MISANTHROPICAL
MISANTHROPIES
MISANTHROPIST

MISANTHROPISTS
MISANTHROPOS
MISANTHROPOSES
MISANTHROPY
MISAPPLICATION
MISAPPLICATIONS
MISAPPLIED
MISAPPLIES
MISAPPLYING
MISAPPRAISAL
MISAPPRAISALS
MISAPPRECIATE
MISAPPRECIATED
MISAPPRECIATES
MISAPPRECIATING
MISAPPRECIATION
MISAPPRECIATIVE
MISAPPREHEND
MISAPPREHENDED
MISAPPREHENDING
MISAPPREHENDS
MISAPPREHENSION
MISAPPREHENSIVE
MISAPPROPRIATE
MISAPPROPRIATED
MISAPPROPRIATES
MISARRANGE
MISARRANGED
MISARRANGEMENT
MISARRANGEMENTS
MISARRANGES
MISARRANGING
MISARTICULATE
MISARTICULATED
MISARTICULATES
MISARTICULATING
MISASSAYED
MISASSAYING
MISASSEMBLE
MISASSEMBLED
MISASSEMBLES
MISASSEMBLING
MISASSIGNED
MISASSIGNING
MISASSIGNS
MISASSUMPTION
MISASSUMPTIONS
MISATONING
MISATTRIBUTE
MISATTRIBUTED
MISATTRIBUTES
MISATTRIBUTING
MISATTRIBUTION
MISATTRIBUTIONS
MISAUNTERS
MISAVERRED
MISAVERRING
MISAWARDED
MISAWARDING
MISBALANCE
MISBALANCED
MISBALANCES
MISBALANCING
MISBECOMES
MISBECOMING
MISBECOMINGNESS
MISBEGINNING
MISBEGOTTEN
MISBEHAVED
MISBEHAVER
MISBEHAVERS
MISBEHAVES
MISBEHAVING
MISBEHAVIOR
MISBEHAVIORS
MISBEHAVIOUR
MISBEHAVIOURS
MISBELIEFS
MISBELIEVE
MISBELIEVED
MISBELIEVER
MISBELIEVERS
MISBELIEVES

MISBELIEVING
MISBESEEMED
MISBESEEMING
MISBESEEMS
MISBESTOWAL
MISBESTOWALS
MISBESTOWED
MISBESTOWING
MISBESTOWS
MISBIASING
MISBIASSED
MISBIASSES
MISBIASSING
MISBILLING
MISBINDING
MISBRANDED
MISBRANDING
MISBUILDING
MISBUTTONED
MISBUTTONING
MISBUTTONS
MISCALCULATE
MISCALCULATED
MISCALCULATES
MISCALCULATING
MISCALCULATION
MISCALCULATIONS
MISCALCULATOR
MISCALCULATORS
MISCALLERS
MISCALLING
MISCANTHUS
MISCANTHUSES
MISCAPTION
MISCAPTIONED
MISCAPTIONING
MISCAPTIONS
MISCARRIAGE
MISCARRIAGES
MISCARRIED
MISCARRIES
MISCARRYING
MISCASTING
MISCATALOG
MISCATALOGED
MISCATALOGING
MISCATALOGS
MISCEGENATE
MISCEGENATED
MISCEGENATES
MISCEGENATING
MISCEGENATION
MISCEGENATIONAL
MISCEGENATIONS
MISCEGENATOR
MISCEGENATORS
MISCEGENES
MISCEGENETIC
MISCEGENIST
MISCEGENISTS
MISCEGINES
MISCELLANARIAN
MISCELLANARIANS
MISCELLANEA
MISCELLANEOUS
MISCELLANEOUSLY
MISCELLANIES
MISCELLANIST
MISCELLANISTS
MISCELLANY
MISCHALLENGE
MISCHALLENGES
MISCHANCED
MISCHANCEFUL
MISCHANCES
MISCHANCING
MISCHANNEL
MISCHANNELED
MISCHANNELING
MISCHANNELLED
MISCHANNELLING
MISCHANNELS
MISCHANTER

MISCHANTERS	MISCONTENT	MISDIRECTS	MISFEATURE	MISIMPROVEMENTS	MISMARRIED
MISCHARACTERISE	MISCONTENTED	MISDISTRIBUTION	MISFEATURED	MISIMPROVES	MISMARRIES
MISCHARACTERIZE	MISCONTENTING	MISDIVIDED	MISFEATURES	MISIMPROVING	MISMARRYING
MISCHARGED	MISCONTENTMENT	MISDIVIDES	MISFEATURING	MISINFERRED	MISMATCHED
MISCHARGES	MISCONTENTMENTS	MISDIVIDING	MISFEEDING	MISINFERRING	MISMATCHES
MISCHARGING	MISCONTENTS	MISDIVISION	MISFEIGNED	MISINFORMANT	MISMATCHING
MISCHIEFED	MISCOOKING	MISDIVISIONS	MISFEIGNING	MISINFORMANTS	MISMATCHMENT
MISCHIEFING	MISCOPYING	MISDOUBTED	MISFIELDED	MISINFORMATION	MISMATCHMENTS
MISCHIEVOUS	MISCORRECT	MISDOUBTFUL	MISFIELDING	MISINFORMATIONS	MISMEASURE
MISCHIEVOUSLY	MISCORRECTED	MISDOUBTING	MISFITTING	MISINFORMED	MISMEASURED
MISCHIEVOUSNESS	MISCORRECTING	MISDRAWING	MISFOCUSED	MISINFORMER	MISMEASUREMENT
MISCHMETAL	MISCORRECTION	MISDRAWINGS	MISFOCUSES	MISINFORMERS	MISMEASUREMENTS
MISCHMETALS	MISCORRECTIONS	MISDRIVING	MISFOCUSING	MISINFORMING	MISMEASURES
MISCHOICES	MISCORRECTS	MISEDITING	MISFOCUSSED	MISINFORMS	MISMEASURING
MISCHOOSES	MISCORRELATION	MISEDUCATE	MISFOCUSSES	MISINSTRUCT	MISMEETING
MISCHOOSING	MISCORRELATIONS	MISEDUCATED	MISFOCUSSING	MISINSTRUCTED	MISMETRING
MISCIBILITIES	MISCOUNSEL	MISEDUCATES	MISFORMATION	MISINSTRUCTING	MISNOMERED
MISCIBILITY	MISCOUNSELLED	MISEDUCATING	MISFORMATIONS	MISINSTRUCTION	MISNOMERING
MISCITATION	MISCOUNSELLING	MISEDUCATION	MISFORMING	MISINSTRUCTIONS	MISNUMBERED
MISCITATIONS	MISCOUNSELS	MISEDUCATIONS	MISFORTUNE	MISINSTRUCTS	MISNUMBERING
MISCLAIMED	MISCOUNTED	MISEMPHASES	MISFORTUNED	MISINTELLIGENCE	MISNUMBERS
MISCLAIMING	MISCOUNTING	MISEMPHASIS	MISFORTUNES	MISINTENDED	MISOBSERVANCE
MISCLASSED	MISCREANCE	MISEMPHASISE	MISFRAMING	MISINTENDING	MISOBSERVANCES
MISCLASSES	MISCREANCES	MISEMPHASISED	MISFUNCTION	MISINTENDS	MISOBSERVE
MISCLASSIFIED	MISCREANCIES	MISEMPHASISES	MISFUNCTIONED	MISINTERPRET	MISOBSERVED
MISCLASSIFIES	MISCREANCY	MISEMPHASISING	MISFUNCTIONING	MISINTERPRETED	MISOBSERVES
MISCLASSIFY	MISCREANTS	MISEMPHASIZE	MISFUNCTIONS	MISINTERPRETER	MISOBSERVING
MISCLASSIFYING	MISCREATED	MISEMPHASIZED	MISGAUGING	MISINTERPRETERS	MISOCAPNIC
MISCLASSING	MISCREATES	MISEMPHASIZES	MISGIVINGS	MISINTERPRETING	MISOGAMIES
MISCOINING	MISCREATING	MISEMPHASIZING	MISGOVERNAUNCE	MISINTERPRETS	MISOGAMIST
MISCOLORED	MISCREATION	MISEMPLOYED	MISGOVERNAUNCES	MISINTERRED	MISOGAMISTS
MISCOLORING	MISCREATIONS	MISEMPLOYING	MISGOVERNED	MISINTERRING	MISOGYNIES
MISCOLOURED	MISCREATIVE	MISEMPLOYMENT	MISGOVERNING	MISJOINDER	MISOGYNIST
MISCOLOURING	MISCREATOR	MISEMPLOYMENTS	MISGOVERNMENT	MISJOINDERS	MISOGYNISTIC
MISCOLOURS	MISCREATORS	MISEMPLOYS	MISGOVERNMENTS	MISJOINING	MISOGYNISTICAL
MISCOMPREHEND	MISCREAUNCE	MISENROLLED	MISGOVERNOR	MISJUDGEMENT	MISOGYNISTS
MISCOMPREHENDED	MISCREAUNCES	MISENROLLING	MISGOVERNORS	MISJUDGEMENTS	MISOGYNOUS
MISCOMPREHENDS	MISCREDITED	MISENROLLS	MISGOVERNS	MISJUDGERS	MISOLOGIES
MISCOMPUTATION	MISCREDITING	MISENTERED	MISGRADING	MISJUDGING	MISOLOGIST
MISCOMPUTATIONS	MISCREDITS	MISENTERING	MISGRAFTED	MISJUDGMENT	MISOLOGISTS
MISCOMPUTE	MISCUTTING	MISENTREAT	MISGRAFTING	MISJUDGMENTS	MISONEISMS
MISCOMPUTED	MISDEALERS	MISENTREATED	MISGROWING	MISKEEPING	MISONEISTIC
MISCOMPUTES	MISDEALING	MISENTREATING	MISGROWTHS	MISKENNING	MISONEISTS
MISCOMPUTING	MISDEEMFUL	MISENTREATS	MISGUESSED	MISKICKING	MISORDERED
MISCONCEIT	MISDEEMING	MISENTRIES	MISGUESSES	MISKNOWING	MISORDERING
MISCONCEITED	MISDEEMINGS	MISERABILISM	MISGUESSING	MISKNOWLEDGE	MISORIENTATION
MISCONCEITING	MISDEFINED	MISERABILISMS	MISGUGGLED	MISKNOWLEDGES	MISORIENTATIONS
MISCONCEITS	MISDEFINES	MISERABILIST	MISGUGGLES	MISLABELED	MISORIENTED
MISCONCEIVE	MISDEFINING	MISERABILISTS	MISGUGGLING	MISLABELING	MISORIENTING
MISCONCEIVED	MISDEMEANANT	MISERABLENESS	MISGUIDANCE	MISLABELLED	MISORIENTS
MISCONCEIVER	MISDEMEANANTS	MISERABLENESSES	MISGUIDANCES	MISLABELLING	MISPACKAGE
MISCONCEIVERS	MISDEMEANED	MISERABLES	MISGUIDEDLY	MISLABORED	MISPACKAGED
MISCONCEIVES	MISDEMEANING	MISERABLISM	MISGUIDEDNESS	MISLABORING	MISPACKAGES
MISCONCEIVING	MISDEMEANOR	MISERABLISMS	MISGUIDEDNESSES	MISLEADERS	MISPACKAGING
MISCONCEPTION	MISDEMEANORS	MISERABLIST	MISGUIDERS	MISLEADING	MISPAINTED
MISCONCEPTIONS	MISDEMEANOUR	MISERABLISTS	MISGUIDING	MISLEADINGLY	MISPAINTING
MISCONDUCT	MISDEMEANOURS	MISERICORD	MISHALLOWED	MISLEARNED	MISPARSING
MISCONDUCTED	MISDEMEANS	MISERICORDE	MISHANDLED	MISLEARNING	MISPARTING
MISCONDUCTING	MISDESCRIBE	MISERICORDES	MISHANDLES	MISLEEKING	MISPATCHED
MISCONDUCTS	MISDESCRIBED	MISERICORDS	MISHANDLING	MISLIGHTED	MISPATCHES
MISCONJECTURE	MISDESCRIBES	MISERLIEST	MISHANTERS	MISLIGHTING	MISPATCHING
MISCONJECTURED	MISDESCRIBING	MISERLINESS	MISHAPPENED	MISLIKINGS	MISPENNING
MISCONJECTURES	MISDESCRIPTION	MISERLINESSES	MISHAPPENING	MISLIPPENED	MISPERCEIVE
MISCONJECTURING	MISDESCRIPTIONS	MISESTEEMED	MISHAPPENS	MISLIPPENING	MISPERCEIVED
MISCONNECT	MISDESERTS	MISESTEEMING	MISHAPPING	MISLIPPENS	MISPERCEIVES
MISCONNECTED	MISDEVELOP	MISESTEEMS	MISHEARING	MISLOCATED	MISPERCEIVING
MISCONNECTING	MISDEVELOPED	MISESTIMATE	MISHEGAASEN	MISLOCATES	MISPERCEPTION
MISCONNECTION	MISDEVELOPING	MISESTIMATED	MISHGUGGLE	MISLOCATING	MISPERCEPTIONS
MISCONNECTIONS	MISDEVELOPS	MISESTIMATES	MISHGUGGLED	MISLOCATION	MISPERSUADE
MISCONNECTS	MISDEVOTION	MISESTIMATING	MISHGUGGLES	MISLOCATIONS	MISPERSUADED
MISCONSTER	MISDEVOTIONS	MISESTIMATION	MISHGUGGLING	MISLODGING	MISPERSUADES
MISCONSTERED	MISDIAGNOSE	MISESTIMATIONS	MISHITTING	MISLUCKING	MISPERSUADING
MISCONSTERING	MISDIAGNOSED	MISEVALUATE	MISHMASHES	MISMANAGED	MISPERSUASION
MISCONSTERS	MISDIAGNOSES	MISEVALUATED	MISHMOSHES	MISMANAGEMENT	MISPERSUASIONS
MISCONSTRUCT	MISDIAGNOSING	MISEVALUATES	MISIDENTIFIED	MISMANAGEMENTS	MISPHRASED
MISCONSTRUCTED	MISDIAGNOSIS	MISEVALUATING	MISIDENTIFIES	MISMANAGER	MISPHRASES
MISCONSTRUCTING	MISDIALING	MISEVALUATION	MISIDENTIFY	MISMANAGERS	MISPHRASING
MISCONSTRUCTION	MISDIALLED	MISEVALUATIONS	MISIDENTIFYING	MISMANAGES	MISPICKELS
MISCONSTRUCTS	MISDIALLING	MISFALLING	MISIMPRESSION	MISMANAGING	MISPLACEMENT
MISCONSTRUE	MISDIRECTED	MISFARINGS	MISIMPRESSIONS	MISMANNERS	MISPLACEMENTS
MISCONSTRUED	MISDIRECTING	MISFEASANCE	MISIMPROVE	MISMARKING	MISPLACING
MISCONSTRUES	MISDIRECTION	MISFEASANCES	MISIMPROVED	MISMARRIAGE	MISPLANNED
MISCONSTRUING	MISDIRECTIONS	MISFEASORS	MISIMPROVEMENT	MISMARRIAGES	MISPLANNING

MISPLANTED
MISPLANTING
MISPLAYING
MISPLEADED
MISPLEADING
MISPLEADINGS
MISPLEASED
MISPLEASES
MISPLEASING
MISPOINTED
MISPOINTING
MISPOISING
MISPOSITION
MISPOSITIONED
MISPOSITIONING
MISPOSITIONS
MISPRAISED
MISPRAISES
MISPRAISING
MISPRICING
MISPRINTED
MISPRINTING
MISPRISING
MISPRISION
MISPRISIONS
MISPRIZERS
MISPRIZING
MISPROGRAM
MISPROGRAMED
MISPROGRAMING
MISPROGRAMMED
MISPROGRAMMING
MISPROGRAMS
MISPRONOUNCE
MISPRONOUNCED
MISPRONOUNCES
MISPRONOUNCING
MISPROPORTION
MISPROPORTIONED
MISPROPORTIONS
MISPUNCTUATE
MISPUNCTUATED
MISPUNCTUATES
MISPUNCTUATING
MISPUNCTUATION
MISPUNCTUATIONS
MISQUOTATION
MISQUOTATIONS
MISQUOTERS
MISQUOTING
MISRAISING
MISREADING
MISREADINGS
MISRECKONED
MISRECKONING
MISRECKONINGS
MISRECKONS
MISRECOLLECTION
MISRECORDED
MISRECORDING
MISRECORDS
MISREFERENCE
MISREFERENCES
MISREFERRED
MISREFERRING
MISREGARDS
MISREGISTER
MISREGISTERED
MISREGISTERING
MISREGISTERS
MISREGISTRATION
MISRELATED
MISRELATES
MISRELATING
MISRELATION
MISRELATIONS
MISRELYING
MISREMEMBER
MISREMEMBERED
MISREMEMBERING
MISREMEMBERS
MISRENDERED
MISRENDERING

MISRENDERS
MISREPORTED
MISREPORTER
MISREPORTERS
MISREPORTING
MISREPORTS
MISREPRESENT
MISREPRESENTED
MISREPRESENTER
MISREPRESENTERS
MISREPRESENTING
MISREPRESENTS
MISROUTEING
MISROUTING
MISSAYINGS
MISSEATING
MISSEEMING
MISSEEMINGS
MISSENDING
MISSETTING
MISSHAPENLY
MISSHAPENNESS
MISSHAPENNESSES
MISSHAPERS
MISSHAPING
MISSHEATHED
MISSILEERS
MISSILEMAN
MISSILEMEN
MISSILERIES
MISSILRIES
MISSIOLOGIES
MISSIOLOGY
MISSIONARIES
MISSIONARISE
MISSIONARISED
MISSIONARISES
MISSIONARISING
MISSIONARIZE
MISSIONARIZED
MISSIONARIZES
MISSIONARIZING
MISSIONARY
MISSIONERS
MISSIONING
MISSIONISATION
MISSIONISATIONS
MISSIONISE
MISSIONISED
MISSIONISER
MISSIONISERS
MISSIONISES
MISSIONISING
MISSIONIZATION
MISSIONIZATIONS
MISSIONIZE
MISSIONIZED
MISSIONIZER
MISSIONIZERS
MISSIONIZES
MISSIONIZING
MISSISHNESS
MISSISHNESSES
MISSORTING
MISSOUNDED
MISSOUNDING
MISSPACING
MISSPEAKING
MISSPELLED
MISSPELLING
MISSPELLINGS
MISSPENDER
MISSPENDERS
MISSPENDING
MISSTAMPED
MISSTAMPING
MISSTARTED
MISSTARTING
MISSTATEMENT
MISSTATEMENTS
MISSTATING
MISSTEERED
MISSTEERING

MISSTEPPED
MISSTEPPING
MISSTOPPED
MISSTOPPING
MISSTRICKEN
MISSTRIKES
MISSTRIKING
MISSTYLING
MISSUITING
MISSUMMATION
MISSUMMATIONS
MISTAKABLE
MISTAKABLY
MISTAKEABLE
MISTAKEABLY
MISTAKENLY
MISTAKENNESS
MISTAKENNESSES
MISTAKINGS
MISTEACHES
MISTEACHING
MISTELLING
MISTEMPERED
MISTEMPERING
MISTEMPERS
MISTENDING
MISTERMING
MISTHINKING
MISTHOUGHT
MISTHOUGHTS
MISTHROWING
MISTIGRISES
MISTINESSES
MISTITLING
MISTLETOES
MISTOUCHED
MISTOUCHES
MISTOUCHING
MISTRACING
MISTRAINED
MISTRAINING
MISTRANSCRIBE
MISTRANSCRIBED
MISTRANSCRIBES
MISTRANSCRIBING
MISTRANSLATE
MISTRANSLATED
MISTRANSLATES
MISTRANSLATING
MISTRANSLATION
MISTRANSLATIONS
MISTRAYNED
MISTREADING
MISTREADINGS
MISTREATED
MISTREATING
MISTREATMENT
MISTREATMENTS
MISTRESSED
MISTRESSES
MISTRESSING
MISTRESSLESS
MISTRESSLY
MISTRUSTED
MISTRUSTER
MISTRUSTERS
MISTRUSTFUL
MISTRUSTFULLY
MISTRUSTFULNESS
MISTRUSTING
MISTRUSTINGLY
MISTRUSTLESS
MISTRYSTED
MISTRYSTING
MISTUTORED
MISTUTORING
MISUNDERSTAND
MISUNDERSTANDS
MISUNDERSTOOD
MISUTILISATION
MISUTILISATIONS
MISUTILIZATION
MISUTILIZATIONS

MISVALUING
MISVENTURE
MISVENTURES
MISVENTUROUS
MISVOCALISATION
MISVOCALIZATION
MISWANDRED
MISWEENING
MISWENDING
MISWORDING
MISWORDINGS
MISWORSHIP
MISWORSHIPPED
MISWORSHIPPING
MISWORSHIPS
MISWRITING
MISWRITTEN
MITERWORTS
MITHRADATIC
MITHRIDATE
MITHRIDATES
MITHRIDATIC
MITHRIDATISE
MITHRIDATISED
MITHRIDATISES
MITHRIDATISING
MITHRIDATISM
MITHRIDATISMS
MITHRIDATIZE
MITHRIDATIZED
MITHRIDATIZES
MITHRIDATIZING
MITIGATING
MITIGATION
MITIGATIONS
MITIGATIVE
MITIGATIVES
MITIGATORS
MITIGATORY
MITOCHONDRIA
MITOCHONDRIAL
MITOCHONDRION
MITOGENETIC
MITOGENICITIES
MITOGENICITY
MITOMYCINS
MITOTICALLY
MITRAILLES
MITRAILLEUR
MITRAILLEURS
MITRAILLEUSE
MITRAILLEUSES
MITREWORTS
MITTIMUSES
MIXABILITIES
MIXABILITY
MIXEDNESSES
MIXMASTERS
MIXOBARBARIC
MIXOLOGIES
MIXOLOGIST
MIXOLOGISTS
MIXOLYDIAN
MIXOTROPHIC
MIZENMASTS
MIZZENMAST
MIZZENMASTS
MIZZONITES
MNEMONICAL
MNEMONICALLY
MNEMONISTS
MNEMOTECHNIC
MNEMOTECHNICS
MNEMOTECHNIST
MNEMOTECHNISTS
MOBILISABLE
MOBILISATION
MOBILISATIONS
MOBILISERS
MOBILISING
MOBILITIES
MOBILIZABLE
MOBILIZATION

MOBILIZATIONS
MOBILIZERS
MOBILIZING
MOBLOGGERS
MOBOCRACIES
MOBOCRATIC
MOBOCRATICAL
MOCHINESSES
MOCKERNUTS
MOCKINGBIRD
MOCKINGBIRDS
MOCKUMENTARIES
MOCKUMENTARY
MODALISTIC
MODALITIES
MODELLINGS
MODERATELY
MODERATENESS
MODERATENESSES
MODERATING
MODERATION
MODERATIONS
MODERATISM
MODERATISMS
MODERATORS
MODERATORSHIP
MODERATORSHIPS
MODERATRICES
MODERATRIX
MODERATRIXES
MODERNISATION
MODERNISATIONS
MODERNISED
MODERNISER
MODERNISERS
MODERNISES
MODERNISING
MODERNISMS
MODERNISTIC
MODERNISTICALLY
MODERNISTS
MODERNITIES
MODERNIZATION
MODERNIZATIONS
MODERNIZED
MODERNIZER
MODERNIZERS
MODERNIZES
MODERNIZING
MODERNNESS
MODERNNESSES
MODIFIABILITIES
MODIFIABILITY
MODIFIABLE
MODIFIABLENESS
MODIFICATION
MODIFICATIONS
MODIFICATIVE
MODIFICATORY
MODILLIONS
MODIOLUSES
MODISHNESS
MODISHNESSES
MODULABILITIES
MODULABILITY
MODULARISED
MODULARITIES
MODULARITY
MODULARIZED
MODULATING
MODULATION
MODULATIONS
MODULATIVE
MODULATORS
MODULATORY
MOISTENERS
MOISTENING
MOISTIFIED
MOISTIFIES
MOISTIFYING
MOISTNESSES
MOISTURELESS
MOISTURISE

MOISTURISED
MOISTURISER
MOISTURISERS
MOISTURISES
MOISTURISING
MOISTURIZE
MOISTURIZED
MOISTURIZER
MOISTURIZERS
MOISTURIZES
MOISTURIZING
MOITHERING
MOLALITIES
MOLARITIES
MOLASSESES
MOLDABILITIES
MOLDABILITY
MOLDAVITES
MOLDBOARDS
MOLDINESSES
MOLECATCHER
MOLECATCHERS
MOLECULARITIES
MOLECULARITY
MOLECULARLY
MOLEHUNTER
MOLEHUNTERS
MOLENDINAR
MOLENDINARIES
MOLENDINARS
MOLENDINARY
MOLESTATION
MOLESTATIONS
MOLIMINOUS
MOLLIFIABLE
MOLLIFICATION
MOLLIFICATIONS
MOLLIFIERS
MOLLIFYING
MOLLITIOUS
MOLLUSCANS
MOLLUSCICIDAL
MOLLUSCICIDE
MOLLUSCICIDES
MOLLUSCOID
MOLLUSCOIDAL
MOLLUSCOIDS
MOLLUSCOUS
MOLLUSKANS
MOLLYCODDLE
MOLLYCODDLED
MOLLYCODDLER
MOLLYCODDLERS
MOLLYCODDLES
MOLLYCODDLING
MOLLYHAWKS
MOLLYMAWKS
MOLOCHISED
MOLOCHISES
MOLOCHISING
MOLOCHIZED
MOLOCHIZES
MOLOCHIZING
MOLYBDATES
MOLYBDENITE
MOLYBDENITES
MOLYBDENOSES
MOLYBDENOSIS
MOLYBDENOUS
MOLYBDENUM
MOLYBDENUMS
MOLYBDOSES
MOLYBDOSIS
MOMENTANEOUS
MOMENTARILY
MOMENTARINESS
MOMENTARINESSES
MOMENTOUSLY
MOMENTOUSNESS
MOMENTOUSNESSES
MONACHISMS
MONACHISTS
MONACTINAL

m

MONADELPHOUS	MONGRELIZED	MONOCRACIES	MONOHYDROXY	MONOPHOBICS	MONOSKIERS
MONADICALLY	MONGRELIZER	MONOCRATIC	MONOICOUSLY	MONOPHONIC	MONOSKIING
MONADIFORM	MONGRELIZERS	MONOCRYSTAL	MONOLATERS	MONOPHONICALLY	MONOSKIINGS
MONADISTIC	MONGRELIZES	MONOCRYSTALLINE	MONOLATRIES	MONOPHONIES	MONOSODIUM
MONADNOCKS	MONGRELIZING	MONOCRYSTALS	MONOLATRIST	MONOPHOSPHATE	MONOSOMICS
MONADOLOGIES	MONILIASES	MONOCULARLY	MONOLATRISTS	MONOPHOSPHATES	MONOSOMIES
MONADOLOGY	MONILIASIS	MONOCULARS	MONOLATROUS	MONOPHTHONG	MONOSPACED
MONANDRIES	MONILIFORM	MONOCULOUS	MONOLAYERS	MONOPHTHONGAL	MONOSPECIFIC
MONANDROUS	MONISTICAL	MONOCULTURAL	MONOLINGUAL	MONOPHTHONGISE	MONOSPECIFICITY
MONANTHOUS	MONISTICALLY	MONOCULTURE	MONOLINGUALISM	MONOPHTHONGISED	MONOSPERMAL
MONARCHALLY	MONITORIAL	MONOCULTURES	MONOLINGUALISMS	MONOPHTHONGISES	MONOSPERMOUS
MONARCHIAL	MONITORIALLY	MONOCYCLES	MONOLINGUALS	MONOPHTHONGIZE	MONOSTABLE
MONARCHICAL	MONITORIES	MONOCYCLIC	MONOLINGUIST	MONOPHTHONGIZED	MONOSTELES
MONARCHICALLY	MONITORING	MONOCYTOID	MONOLINGUISTS	MONOPHTHONGIZES	MONOSTELIC
MONARCHIES	MONITORSHIP	MONODACTYLOUS	MONOLITHIC	MONOPHTHONGS	MONOSTELIES
MONARCHISE	MONITORSHIPS	MONODELPHIAN	MONOLITHICALLY	MONOPHYLETIC	MONOSTICHIC
MONARCHISED	MONITRESSES	MONODELPHIC	MONOLOGGED	MONOPHYLIES	MONOSTICHOUS
MONARCHISES	MONKEYGLAND	MONODELPHOUS	MONOLOGGING	MONOPHYLLOUS	MONOSTICHS
MONARCHISING	MONKEYISMS	MONODICALLY	MONOLOGICAL	MONOPHYODONT	MONOSTOMOUS
MONARCHISM	MONKEYPODS	MONODISPERSE	MONOLOGIES	MONOPHYODONTS	MONOSTROPHE
MONARCHISMS	MONKEYPOTS	MONODRAMAS	MONOLOGISE	MONOPHYSITE	MONOSTROPHES
MONARCHIST	MONKEYSHINE	MONODRAMATIC	MONOLOGISED	MONOPHYSITES	MONOSTROPHIC
MONARCHISTIC	MONKEYSHINES	MONOECIOUS	MONOLOGISES	MONOPHYSITIC	MONOSTROPHICS
MONARCHISTS	MONKFISHES	MONOECIOUSLY	MONOLOGISING	MONOPHYSITISM	MONOSTYLAR
MONARCHIZE	MONKISHNESS	MONOECISMS	MONOLOGIST	MONOPHYSITISMS	MONOSTYLOUS
MONARCHIZED	MONKISHNESSES	MONOESTERS	MONOLOGISTS	MONOPLANES	MONOSYLLABIC
MONARCHIZES	MONKSHOODS	MONOFILAMENT	MONOLOGIZE	MONOPLEGIA	MONOSYLLABICITY
MONARCHIZING	MONOACIDIC	MONOFILAMENTS	MONOLOGIZED	MONOPLEGIAS	MONOSYLLABISM
MONASTERIAL	MONOAMINERGIC	MONOGAMIES	MONOLOGIZES	MONOPLEGIC	MONOSYLLABISMS
MONASTERIES	MONOAMINES	MONOGAMIST	MONOLOGIZING	MONOPLOIDS	MONOSYLLABLE
MONASTICAL	MONOATOMIC	MONOGAMISTIC	MONOLOGUED	MONOPODIAL	MONOSYLLABLES
MONASTICALLY	MONOBLEPSES	MONOGAMISTS	MONOLOGUES	MONOPODIALLY	MONOSYMMETRIC
MONASTICISM	MONOBLEPSIS	MONOGAMOUS	MONOLOGUING	MONOPODIES	MONOSYMMETRICAL
MONASTICISMS	MONOCARBOXYLIC	MONOGAMOUSLY	MONOLOGUISE	MONOPODIUM	MONOSYMMETRIES
MONAURALLY	MONOCARDIAN	MONOGAMOUSNESS	MONOLOGUISED	MONOPOLIES	MONOSYMMETRY
MONCHIQUITE	MONOCARPELLARY	MONOGASTRIC	MONOLOGUISES	MONOPOLISATION	MONOSYNAPTIC
MONCHIQUITES	MONOCARPIC	MONOGENEAN	MONOLOGUISING	MONOPOLISATIONS	MONOTELEPHONE
MONDEGREEN	MONOCARPOUS	MONOGENEANS	MONOLOGUIST	MONOPOLISE	MONOTELEPHONES
MONDEGREENS	MONOCEROSES	MONOGENESES	MONOLOGUISTS	MONOPOLISED	MONOTERPENE
MONECIOUSLY	MONOCEROUS	MONOGENESIS	MONOLOGUIZE	MONOPOLISER	MONOTERPENES
MONERGISMS	MONOCHASIA	MONOGENETIC	MONOLOGUIZED	MONOPOLISERS	MONOTHALAMIC
MONESTROUS	MONOCHASIAL	MONOGENICALLY	MONOLOGUIZES	MONOPOLISES	MONOTHALAMOUS
MONETARILY	MONOCHASIUM	MONOGENIES	MONOLOGUIZING	MONOPOLISING	MONOTHECAL
MONETARISM	MONOCHLAMYDEOUS	MONOGENISM	MONOMACHIA	MONOPOLISM	MONOTHECOUS
MONETARISMS	MONOCHLORIDE	MONOGENISMS	MONOMACHIAS	MONOPOLISMS	MONOTHEISM
MONETARIST	MONOCHLORIDES	MONOGENIST	MONOMACHIES	MONOPOLIST	MONOTHEISMS
MONETARISTS	MONOCHORDS	MONOGENISTIC	MONOMANIAC	MONOPOLISTIC	MONOTHEIST
MONETISATION	MONOCHROIC	MONOGENISTS	MONOMANIACAL	MONOPOLISTS	MONOTHEISTIC
MONETISATIONS	MONOCHROICS	MONOGENOUS	MONOMANIACALLY	MONOPOLIZATION	MONOTHEISTICAL
MONETISING	MONOCHROMASIES	MONOGLYCERIDE	MONOMANIACS	MONOPOLIZATIONS	MONOTHEISTS
MONETIZATION	MONOCHROMASY	MONOGLYCERIDES	MONOMANIAS	MONOPOLIZE	MONOTHELETE
MONETIZATIONS	MONOCHROMAT	MONOGONIES	MONOMEROUS	MONOPOLIZED	MONOTHELETES
MONETIZING	MONOCHROMATE	MONOGRAMED	MONOMETALLIC	MONOPOLIZER	MONOTHELETIC
MONEYCHANGER	MONOCHROMATES	MONOGRAMING	MONOMETALLISM	MONOPOLIZERS	MONOTHELETICAL
MONEYCHANGERS	MONOCHROMATIC	MONOGRAMMATIC	MONOMETALLISMS	MONOPOLIZES	MONOTHELETISM
MONEYGRUBBING	MONOCHROMATICS	MONOGRAMMED	MONOMETALLIST	MONOPOLIZING	MONOTHELETISMS
MONEYGRUBBINGS	MONOCHROMATISM	MONOGRAMMER	MONOMETALLISTS	MONOPRIONIDIAN	MONOTHELISM
MONEYLENDER	MONOCHROMATISMS	MONOGRAMMERS	MONOMETERS	MONOPROPELLANT	MONOTHELISMS
MONEYLENDERS	MONOCHROMATOR	MONOGRAMMING	MONOMETRIC	MONOPROPELLANTS	MONOTHELITE
MONEYLENDING	MONOCHROMATORS	MONOGRAPHED	MONOMETRICAL	MONOPSONIES	MONOTHELITES
MONEYLENDINGS	MONOCHROMATS	MONOGRAPHER	MONOMOLECULAR	MONOPSONIST	MONOTHELITISM
MONEYMAKER	MONOCHROME	MONOGRAPHERS	MONOMOLECULARLY	MONOPSONISTIC	MONOTHELITISMS
MONEYMAKERS	MONOCHROMES	MONOGRAPHIC	MONOMORPHEMIC	MONOPSONISTS	MONOTOCOUS
MONEYMAKING	MONOCHROMIC	MONOGRAPHICAL	MONOMORPHIC	MONOPTERAL	MONOTONICALLY
MONEYMAKINGS	MONOCHROMICAL	MONOGRAPHICALLY	MONOMORPHISM	MONOPTEROI	MONOTONICITIES
MONEYSPINNING	MONOCHROMIES	MONOGRAPHIES	MONOMORPHISMS	MONOPTERON	MONOTONICITY
MONEYWORTS	MONOCHROMIST	MONOGRAPHING	MONOMORPHOUS	MONOPTEROS	MONOTONIES
MONGERINGS	MONOCHROMISTS	MONOGRAPHIST	MONOMYARIAN	MONOPTEROSES	MONOTONING
MONGOLISMS	MONOCHROMY	MONOGRAPHISTS	MONONUCLEAR	MONOPTOTES	MONOTONISE
MONGOLOIDS	MONOCLINAL	MONOGRAPHS	MONONUCLEARS	MONOPULSES	MONOTONISED
MONGRELISATION	MONOCLINALLY	MONOGRAPHY	MONONUCLEATE	MONORCHIDISM	MONOTONISES
MONGRELISATIONS	MONOCLINALS	MONOGYNIAN	MONONUCLEATED	MONORCHIDISMS	MONOTONISING
MONGRELISE	MONOCLINES	MONOGYNIES	MONONUCLEOSES	MONORCHIDS	MONOTONIZE
MONGRELISED	MONOCLINIC	MONOGYNIST	MONONUCLEOSIS	MONORCHISM	MONOTONIZED
MONGRELISER	MONOCLINISM	MONOGYNISTS	MONONUCLEOTIDE	MONORCHISMS	MONOTONIZES
MONGRELISERS	MONOCLINISMS	MONOGYNOUS	MONONUCLEOTIDES	MONORHINAL	MONOTONIZING
MONGRELISES	MONOCLINOUS	MONOHYBRID	MONOPETALOUS	MONORHYMED	MONOTONOUS
MONGRELISING	MONOCLONAL	MONOHYBRIDS	MONOPHAGIES	MONORHYMES	MONOTONOUSLY
MONGRELISM	MONOCLONALS	MONOHYDRATE	MONOPHAGOUS	MONOSACCHARIDE	MONOTONOUSNESS
MONGRELISMS	MONOCOQUES	MONOHYDRATED	MONOPHASIC	MONOSACCHARIDES	MONOTREMATOUS
MONGRELIZATION	MONOCOTYLEDON	MONOHYDRATES	MONOPHOBIA	MONOSATURATED	MONOTREMES
MONGRELIZATIONS	MONOCOTYLEDONS	MONOHYDRIC	MONOPHOBIAS	MONOSEMIES	MONOTRICHIC
MONGRELIZE	MONOCOTYLS	MONOHYDROGEN	MONOPHOBIC	MONOSEPALOUS	MONOTRICHOUS

m

Section 2: Words between 10 and 15 letters in length

MONOTROCHS	MOONSHINED	MORPHOGENESES	MOTHBALLED	MOTORTRUCK	MOUTHPIECE
MONOUNSATURATE	MOONSHINER	MORPHOGENESIS	MOTHBALLING	MOTORTRUCKS	MOUTHPIECES
MONOUNSATURATED	MOONSHINERS	MORPHOGENETIC	MOTHERBOARD	MOUCHARABIES	MOUTHWASHES
MONOUNSATURATES	MOONSHINES	MORPHOGENIC	MOTHERBOARDS	MOUCHARABY	MOUTHWATERING
MONOVALENCE	MOONSHINING	MORPHOGENIES	MOTHERCRAFT	MOUDIEWART	MOUTHWATERINGLY
MONOVALENCES	MOONSTONES	MORPHOGENS	MOTHERCRAFTS	MOUDIEWARTS	MOUVEMENTE
MONOVALENCIES	MOONSTRICKEN	MORPHOGENY	MOTHERESES	MOUDIEWORT	MOVABILITIES
MONOVALENCY	MOONSTRIKE	MORPHOGRAPHER	MOTHERFUCKER	MOUDIEWORTS	MOVABILITY
MONOVALENT	MOONSTRIKES	MORPHOGRAPHERS	MOTHERFUCKERS	MOUDIWARTS	MOVABLENESS
MONOXYLONS	MOONSTRUCK	MORPHOGRAPHIES	MOTHERFUCKING	MOUDIWORTS	MOVABLENESSES
MONOXYLOUS	MOONWALKED	MORPHOGRAPHY	MOTHERHOOD	MOULDABILITIES	MOVEABILITIES
MONOZYGOTIC	MOONWALKER	MORPHOLOGIC	MOTHERHOODS	MOULDABILITY	MOVEABILITY
MONOZYGOUS	MOONWALKERS	MORPHOLOGICAL	MOTHERHOUSE	MOULDBOARD	MOVEABLENESS
MONSEIGNEUR	MOONWALKING	MORPHOLOGICALLY	MOTHERHOUSES	MOULDBOARDS	MOVEABLENESSES
MONSIGNORI	MOORBUZZARD	MORPHOLOGIES	MOTHERINGS	MOULDERING	MOVELESSLY
MONSIGNORIAL	MOORBUZZARDS	MORPHOLOGIST	MOTHERLAND	MOULDINESS	MOVELESSNESS
MONSIGNORS	MOOSEBIRDS	MORPHOLOGISTS	MOTHERLANDS	MOULDINESSES	MOVELESSNESSES
MONSTERING	MOOSEWOODS	MORPHOLOGY	MOTHERLESS	MOULDWARPS	MOVIEGOERS
MONSTERINGS	MOOSEYARDS	MORPHOMETRIC	MOTHERLESSNESS	MOULDYWARP	MOVIEGOING
MONSTRANCE	MOOTNESSES	MORPHOMETRICS	MOTHERLINESS	MOULDYWARPS	MOVIEGOINGS
MONSTRANCES	MOPINESSES	MORPHOMETRIES	MOTHERLINESSES	MOUNDBIRDS	MOVIELANDS
MONSTROSITIES	MOPISHNESS	MORPHOMETRY	MOTHERWORT	MOUNTAINBOARD	MOVIEMAKER
MONSTROSITY	MOPISHNESSES	MORPHOPHONEME	MOTHERWORTS	MOUNTAINBOARDER	MOVIEMAKERS
MONSTROUSLY	MORALISATION	MORPHOPHONEMES	MOTHPROOFED	MOUNTAINBOARDS	MOVIEMAKING
MONSTROUSNESS	MORALISATIONS	MORPHOPHONEMIC	MOTHPROOFER	MOUNTAINED	MOVIEMAKINGS
MONSTROUSNESSES	MORALISERS	MORPHOPHONEMICS	MOTHPROOFERS	MOUNTAINEER	MOWBURNING
MONSTRUOSITIES	MORALISING	MORPHOTROPIC	MOTHPROOFING	MOUNTAINEERED	MOWDIEWART
MONSTRUOSITY	MORALISTIC	MORPHOTROPIES	MOTHPROOFS	MOUNTAINEERING	MOWDIEWARTS
MONSTRUOUS	MORALISTICALLY	MORPHOTROPY	MOTILITIES	MOUNTAINEERINGS	MOWDIEWORT
MONTADALES	MORALITIES	MORSELLING	MOTIONISTS	MOUNTAINEERS	MOWDIEWORTS
MONTAGNARD	MORALIZATION	MORTADELLA	MOTIONLESS	MOUNTAINOUS	MOXIBUSTION
MONTAGNARDS	MORALIZATIONS	MORTADELLAS	MOTIONLESSLY	MOUNTAINOUSLY	MOXIBUSTIONS
MONTBRETIA	MORALIZERS	MORTALISED	MOTIONLESSNESS	MOUNTAINOUSNESS	MOYGASHELS
MONTBRETIAS	MORALIZING	MORTALISES	MOTIVATING	MOUNTAINSIDE	MOZZARELLA
MONTELIMAR	MORATORIUM	MORTALISING	MOTIVATION	MOUNTAINSIDES	MOZZARELLAS
MONTELIMARS	MORATORIUMS	MORTALITIES	MOTIVATIONAL	MOUNTAINTOP	MRIDAMGAMS
MONTGOLFIER	MORBIDEZZA	MORTALIZED	MOTIVATIONALLY	MOUNTAINTOPS	MRIDANGAMS
MONTGOLFIERS	MORBIDEZZAS	MORTALIZES	MOTIVATIONS	MOUNTEBANK	MUCEDINOUS
MONTHLINGS	MORBIDITIES	MORTALIZING	MOTIVATIVE	MOUNTEBANKED	MUCHNESSES
MONTICELLITE	MORBIDNESS	MORTARBOARD	MOTIVATORS	MOUNTEBANKERIES	MUCIDITIES
MONTICELLITES	MORBIDNESSES	MORTARBOARDS	MOTIVELESS	MOUNTEBANKERY	MUCIDNESSES
MONTICOLOUS	MORBIFEROUS	MORTARLESS	MOTIVELESSLY	MOUNTEBANKING	MUCIFEROUS
MONTICULATE	MORBIFICALLY	MORTCLOTHS	MOTIVELESSNESS	MOUNTEBANKINGS	MUCILAGINOUS
MONTICULES	MORBILLIFORM	MORTGAGEABLE	MOTIVITIES	MOUNTEBANKISM	MUCILAGINOUSLY
MONTICULOUS	MORBILLIVIRUS	MORTGAGEES	MOTOCROSSES	MOUNTEBANKISMS	MUCINOGENS
MONTICULUS	MORBILLIVIRUSES	MORTGAGERS	MOTONEURON	MOUNTEBANKS	MUCKAMUCKED
MONTICULUSES	MORBILLOUS	MORTGAGING	MOTONEURONAL	MOUNTENANCE	MUCKAMUCKING
MONTMORILLONITE	MORDACIOUS	MORTGAGORS	MOTONEURONS	MOUNTENANCES	MUCKAMUCKS
MONUMENTAL	MORDACIOUSLY	MORTICIANS	MOTORBICYCLE	MOUNTENAUNCE	MUCKENDERS
MONUMENTALISE	MORDACIOUSNESS	MORTIFEROUS	MOTORBICYCLES	MOUNTENAUNCES	MUCKINESSES
MONUMENTALISED	MORDACITIES	MORTIFEROUSNESS	MOTORBIKED	MOURNFULLER	MUCKRAKERS
MONUMENTALISES	MORDANCIES	MORTIFICATION	MOTORBIKES	MOURNFULLEST	MUCKRAKING
MONUMENTALISING	MORDANTING	MORTIFICATIONS	MOTORBIKING	MOURNFULLY	MUCKRAKINGS
MONUMENTALITIES	MORENESSES	MORTIFIERS	MOTORBOATED	MOURNFULNESS	MUCKSPREAD
MONUMENTALITY	MORGANATIC	MORTIFYING	MOTORBOATER	MOURNFULNESSES	MUCKSPREADER
MONUMENTALISE	MORGANATICALLY	MORTIFYINGLY	MOTORBOATERS	MOURNIVALS	MUCKSPREADERS
MONUMENTALIZED	MORGANITES	MORTIFYINGS	MOTORBOATING	MOUSEBIRDS	MUCKSPREADING
MONUMENTALIZES	MORGENSTERN	MORTUARIES	MOTORBOATINGS	MOUSEOVERS	MUCKSPREADS
MONUMENTALIZING	MORGENSTERNS	MORULATION	MOTORBOATS	MOUSEPIECE	MUCKSWEATS
MONUMENTALLY	MORIBUNDITIES	MORULATIONS	MOTORBUSES	MOUSEPIECES	MUCOCUTANEOUS
MONUMENTED	MORIBUNDITY	MOSAICALLY	MOTORBUSSES	MOUSETAILS	MUCOMEMBRANOUS
MONUMENTING	MORIBUNDLY	MOSAICISMS	MOTORCADED	MOUSETRAPPED	MUCOPEPTIDE
MONZONITES	MORIGERATE	MOSAICISTS	MOTORCADES	MOUSETRAPPING	MUCOPEPTIDES
MONZONITIC	MORIGERATION	MOSAICKING	MOTORCADING	MOUSETRAPS	MUCOPROTEIN
MOODINESSES	MORIGERATIONS	MOSAICLIKE	MOTORCOACH	MOUSINESSES	MUCOPROTEINS
MOONCALVES	MORIGEROUS	MOSASAURUS	MOTORCOACHES	MOUSQUETAIRE	MUCOPURULENT
MOONCHILDREN	MORONICALLY	MOSBOLLETJIE	MOTORCYCLE	MOUSQUETAIRES	MUCOSANGUINEOUS
MOONFISHES	MORONITIES	MOSBOLLETJIES	MOTORCYCLED	MOUSSELINE	MUCOSITIES
MOONFLOWER	MOROSENESS	MOSCHATELS	MOTORCYCLES	MOUSSELINES	MUCOVISCIDOSES
MOONFLOWERS	MOROSENESSES	MOSCHIFEROUS	MOTORCYCLING	MOUSTACHED	MUCOVISCIDOSIS
MOONINESSES	MOROSITIES	MOSKONFYTS	MOTORCYCLIST	MOUSTACHES	MUCRONATED
MOONLIGHTED	MORPHACTIN	MOSQUITOES	MOTORCYCLISTS	MOUSTACHIAL	MUCRONATION
MOONLIGHTER	MORPHACTINS	MOSQUITOEY	MOTORHOMES	MOUSTACHIO	MUCRONATIONS
MOONLIGHTERS	MORPHALLAXES	MOSSBACKED	MOTORICALLY	MOUSTACHIOS	MUDCAPPING
MOONLIGHTING	MORPHALLAXIS	MOSSBLUITER	MOTORISATION	MOUTHBREATHER	MUDDINESSES
MOONLIGHTINGS	MORPHEMICALLY	MOSSBLUITERS	MOTORISATIONS	MOUTHBREATHERS	MUDDLEDNESS
MOONLIGHTS	MORPHEMICS	MOSSBUNKER	MOTORISING	MOUTHBREEDER	MUDDLEDNESSES
MOONPHASES	MORPHINISM	MOSSBUNKERS	MOTORIZATION	MOUTHBREEDERS	MUDDLEHEAD
MOONQUAKES	MORPHINISMS	MOSSINESSES	MOTORIZATIONS	MOUTHBROODER	MUDDLEHEADED
MOONRAKERS	MORPHINOMANIA	MOSSPLANTS	MOTORIZING	MOUTHBROODERS	MUDDLEHEADEDLY
MOONRAKING	MORPHINOMANIAC	MOSSTROOPER	MOTORMOUTH	MOUTHFEELS	MUDDLEHEADS
MOONRAKINGS	MORPHINOMANIACS	MOSSTROOPERS	MOTORMOUTHS	MOUTHPARTS	MUDDLEMENT
MOONSCAPES	MORPHINOMANIAS	MOTETTISTS	MOTORSHIPS		MUDDLEMENTS

MUDDLINGLY
MUDLARKING
MUDLOGGERS
MUDLOGGING
MUDLOGGINGS
MUDPUPPIES
MUDSKIPPER
MUDSKIPPERS
MUDSLINGER
MUDSLINGERS
MUDSLINGING
MUDSLINGINGS
MUFFINEERS
MUGEARITES
MUGGINESSES
MUGWUMPERIES
MUGWUMPERY
MUGWUMPISH
MUGWUMPISM
MUGWUMPISMS
MUJAHEDDIN
MUJAHEDEEN
MUJAHIDEEN
MULATTRESS
MULATTRESSES
MULBERRIES
MULIEBRITIES
MULIEBRITY
MULISHNESS
MULISHNESSES
MULLAHISMS
MULLARKIES
MULLIGATAWNIES
MULLIGATAWNY
MULLIGRUBS
MULLIONING
MULTANGULAR
MULTANIMOUS
MULTARTICULATE
MULTEITIES
MULTIACCESS
MULTIACCESSES
MULTIAGENCY
MULTIANGULAR
MULTIARMED
MULTIARTICULATE
MULTIAUTHOR
MULTIAXIAL
MULTIBARREL
MULTIBARRELED
MULTIBILLION
MULTIBLADED
MULTIBRANCHED
MULTIBUILDING
MULTICAMERATE
MULTICAMPUS
MULTICAPITATE
MULTICARBON
MULTICASTS
MULTICAULINE
MULTICAUSAL
MULTICELLED
MULTICELLULAR
MULTICENTER
MULTICENTRAL
MULTICENTRIC
MULTICHAIN
MULTICHAMBERED
MULTICHANNEL
MULTICHARACTER
MULTICIDES
MULTICIPITAL
MULTICLIENT
MULTICOATED
MULTICOLOR
MULTICOLORED
MULTICOLORS
MULTICOLOUR
MULTICOLOURED
MULTICOLOURS
MULTICOLUMN
MULTICOMPONENT
MULTICONDUCTOR

MULTICOSTATE
MULTICOUNTY
MULTICOURSE
MULTICULTURAL
MULTICURIE
MULTICURRENCIES
MULTICURRENCY
MULTICUSPID
MULTICUSPIDATE
MULTICUSPIDS
MULTICYCLE
MULTICYCLES
MULTIDENTATE
MULTIDIALECTAL
MULTIDIGITATE
MULTIDISCIPLINE
MULTIDIVISIONAL
MULTIDOMAIN
MULTIELECTRODE
MULTIELEMENT
MULTIEMPLOYER
MULTIEMPLOYERS
MULTIENGINE
MULTIENZYME
MULTIETHNIC
MULTIETHNICS
MULTIFACED
MULTIFACETED
MULTIFACTOR
MULTIFACTORIAL
MULTIFAMILY
MULTIFARIOUS
MULTIFARIOUSLY
MULTIFIDLY
MULTIFIDOUS
MULTIFILAMENT
MULTIFILAMENTS
MULTIFLASH
MULTIFLORA
MULTIFLOROUS
MULTIFOCAL
MULTIFOILS
MULTIFOLIATE
MULTIFOLIOLATE
MULTIFORMITIES
MULTIFORMITY
MULTIFORMS
MULTIFREQUENCY
MULTIFUNCTION
MULTIFUNCTIONAL
MULTIGENIC
MULTIGRADE
MULTIGRAIN
MULTIGRAVIDA
MULTIGRAVIDAE
MULTIGRAVIDAS
MULTIGROUP
MULTIHEADED
MULTIHOSPITAL
MULTIHULLS
MULTIJUGATE
MULTIJUGOUS
MULTILANES
MULTILATERAL
MULTILATERALISM
MULTILATERALIST
MULTILATERALLY
MULTILAYER
MULTILAYERED
MULTILEVEL
MULTILEVELED
MULTILINEAL
MULTILINEAR
MULTILINGUAL
MULTILINGUALISM
MULTILINGUALLY
MULTILINGUIST
MULTILINGUISTS
MULTILOBATE
MULTILOBED
MULTILOBES
MULTILOBULAR
MULTILOBULATE

MULTILOCATIONAL
MULTILOCULAR
MULTILOCULATE
MULTILOQUENCE
MULTILOQUENCES
MULTILOQUENT
MULTILOQUIES
MULTILOQUOUS
MULTILOQUY
MULTIMANNED
MULTIMEDIA
MULTIMEDIAS
MULTIMEGATON
MULTIMEGAWATT
MULTIMEGAWATTS
MULTIMEMBER
MULTIMETALLIC
MULTIMETER
MULTIMETERS
MULTIMILLENNIAL
MULTIMILLION
MULTIMODAL
MULTIMOLECULAR
MULTINATION
MULTINATIONAL
MULTINATIONALS
MULTINOMIAL
MULTINOMIALS
MULTINOMINAL
MULTINUCLEAR
MULTINUCLEATE
MULTINUCLEATED
MULTINUCLEOLATE
MULTIORGASMIC
MULTIPACKS
MULTIPANED
MULTIPARAE
MULTIPARAMETER
MULTIPARAS
MULTIPARITIES
MULTIPARITY
MULTIPAROUS
MULTIPARTICLE
MULTIPARTITE
MULTIPARTY
MULTIPARTYISM
MULTIPARTYISMS
MULTIPEDES
MULTIPHASE
MULTIPHASIC
MULTIPHOTON
MULTIPICTURE
MULTIPIECE
MULTIPISTON
MULTIPLANE
MULTIPLANES
MULTIPLANT
MULTIPLAYER
MULTIPLAYERS
MULTIPLETS
MULTIPLEXED
MULTIPLEXER
MULTIPLEXERS
MULTIPLEXES
MULTIPLEXING
MULTIPLEXOR
MULTIPLEXORS
MULTIPLIABLE
MULTIPLICABLE
MULTIPLICAND
MULTIPLICANDS
MULTIPLICATE
MULTIPLICATES
MULTIPLICATION
MULTIPLICATIONS
MULTIPLICATIVE
MULTIPLICATOR
MULTIPLICATORS
MULTIPLICITIES
MULTIPLICITY
MULTIPLIED
MULTIPLIER
MULTIPLIERS

MULTIPLIES
MULTIPLYING
MULTIPOLAR
MULTIPOLARITIES
MULTIPOLARITY
MULTIPOLES
MULTIPOTENT
MULTIPOTENTIAL
MULTIPOWER
MULTIPRESENCE
MULTIPRESENCES
MULTIPRESENT
MULTIPROBLEM
MULTIPROCESSING
MULTIPROCESSOR
MULTIPROCESSORS
MULTIPRODUCT
MULTIPRONGED
MULTIPURPOSE
MULTIRACIAL
MULTIRACIALISM
MULTIRACIALISMS
MULTIRAMIFIED
MULTIRANGE
MULTIREGIONAL
MULTIRELIGIOUS
MULTISCIENCE
MULTISCIENCES
MULTISCREEN
MULTISENSE
MULTISENSORY
MULTISEPTATE
MULTISERIAL
MULTISERIATE
MULTISERVICE
MULTISIDED
MULTISKILL
MULTISKILLED
MULTISKILLING
MULTISKILLINGS
MULTISKILLS
MULTISONANT
MULTISOURCE
MULTISPECIES
MULTISPECTRAL
MULTISPEED
MULTISPIRAL
MULTISPORT
MULTISTAGE
MULTISTATE
MULTISTEMMED
MULTISTOREY
MULTISTOREYS
MULTISTORIED
MULTISTORY
MULTISTRANDED
MULTISTRIKE
MULTISTRIKES
MULTISULCATE
MULTISYLLABIC
MULTISYSTEM
MULTITALENTED
MULTITASKED
MULTITASKING
MULTITASKINGS
MULTITASKS
MULTITERMINAL
MULTITHREADING
MULTITHREADINGS
MULTITIERED
MULTITONES
MULTITOWERED
MULTITRACK
MULTITRILLION
MULTITUDES
MULTITUDINARY
MULTITUDINOUS
MULTITUDINOUSLY
MULTIUNION
MULTIVALENCE
MULTIVALENCES
MULTIVALENCIES
MULTIVALENCY

MULTIVALENT
MULTIVALENTS
MULTIVARIABLE
MULTIVARIATE
MULTIVARIOUS
MULTIVERSE
MULTIVERSES
MULTIVERSITIES
MULTIVERSITY
MULTIVIBRATOR
MULTIVIBRATORS
MULTIVIOUS
MULTIVITAMIN
MULTIVITAMINS
MULTIVOCAL
MULTIVOCALS
MULTIVOLTINE
MULTIVOLUME
MULTIWARHEAD
MULTIWAVELENGTH
MULTIWINDOW
MULTIWINDOWS
MULTOCULAR
MULTUNGULATE
MULTUNGULATES
MUMBLEMENT
MUMBLEMENTS
MUMBLETYPEG
MUMBLETYPEGS
MUMBLINGLY
MUMCHANCES
MUMMICHOGS
MUMMIFICATION
MUMMIFICATIONS
MUMMIFYING
MUMPISHNESS
MUMPISHNESSES
MUMPSIMUSES
MUNCHABLES
MUNDANENESS
MUNDANENESSES
MUNDANITIES
MUNDIFICATION
MUNDIFICATIONS
MUNDIFICATIVE
MUNDIFYING
MUNDUNGUSES
MUNICIPALISE
MUNICIPALISED
MUNICIPALISES
MUNICIPALISING
MUNICIPALISM
MUNICIPALISMS
MUNICIPALIST
MUNICIPALISTS
MUNICIPALITIES
MUNICIPALITY
MUNICIPALIZE
MUNICIPALIZED
MUNICIPALIZES
MUNICIPALIZING
MUNICIPALLY
MUNICIPALS
MUNIFICENCE
MUNIFICENCES
MUNIFICENT
MUNIFICENTLY
MUNIFICENTNESS
MUNIFIENCE
MUNIFIENCES
MUNITIONED
MUNITIONEER
MUNITIONEERS
MUNITIONER
MUNITIONERS
MUNITIONETTE
MUNITIONETTES
MUNITIONING
MURDERESSES
MURDEROUSLY
MURDEROUSNESS
MURDEROUSNESSES
MURGEONING

MURKINESSES
MURMURATION
MURMURATIONS
MURMURINGLY
MURMURINGS
MURMUROUSLY
MURTHERERS
MURTHERING
MUSCADELLE
MUSCADELLES
MUSCADINES
MUSCARDINE
MUSCARDINES
MUSCARINES
MUSCARINIC
MUSCATORIA
MUSCATORIUM
MUSCAVADOS
MUSCOLOGIES
MUSCOVADOS
MUSCOVITES
MUSCULARITIES
MUSCULARITY
MUSCULARLY
MUSCULATION
MUSCULATIONS
MUSCULATURE
MUSCULATURES
MUSCULOSKELETAL
MUSEOLOGICAL
MUSEOLOGIES
MUSEOLOGIST
MUSEOLOGISTS
MUSHINESSES
MUSHMOUTHS
MUSHROOMED
MUSHROOMER
MUSHROOMERS
MUSHROOMING
MUSICALISATION
MUSICALISATIONS
MUSICALISE
MUSICALISED
MUSICALISES
MUSICALISING
MUSICALITIES
MUSICALITY
MUSICALIZATION
MUSICALIZATIONS
MUSICALIZE
MUSICALIZED
MUSICALIZES
MUSICALIZING
MUSICALNESS
MUSICALNESSES
MUSICIANER
MUSICIANERS
MUSICIANLY
MUSICIANSHIP
MUSICIANSHIPS
MUSICOLOGICAL
MUSICOLOGICALLY
MUSICOLOGIES
MUSICOLOGIST
MUSICOLOGISTS
MUSICOLOGY
MUSICOTHERAPIES
MUSICOTHERAPY
MUSKELLUNGE
MUSKELLUNGES
MUSKETEERS
MUSKETOONS
MUSKETRIES
MUSKINESSES
MUSKMELONS
MUSQUASHES
MUSQUETOON
MUSQUETOONS
MUSSELCRACKER
MUSSELCRACKERS
MUSSINESSES
MUSSITATED
MUSSITATES

m

MUSSITATING
MUSSITATION
MUSSITATIONS
MUSTACHIOED
MUSTACHIOS
MUSTELINES
MUSTINESSES
MUTABILITIES
MUTABILITY
MUTABLENESS
MUTABLENESSES
MUTAGENESES
MUTAGENESIS
MUTAGENICALLY
MUTAGENICITIES
MUTAGENICITY
MUTAGENISE
MUTAGENISED
MUTAGENISES
MUTAGENISING
MUTAGENIZE
MUTAGENIZED
MUTAGENIZES
MUTAGENIZING
MUTATIONAL
MUTATIONALLY
MUTATIONIST
MUTATIONISTS
MUTENESSES
MUTESSARIF
MUTESSARIFAT
MUTESSARIFATS
MUTESSARIFS
MUTILATING
MUTILATION
MUTILATIONS
MUTILATIVE
MUTILATORS
MUTINEERED
MUTINEERING
MUTINOUSLY
MUTINOUSNESS
MUTINOUSNESSES
MUTOSCOPES
MUTTERATION
MUTTERATIONS
MUTTERINGLY
MUTTERINGS
MUTTONBIRD
MUTTONBIRDS
MUTTONCHOPS
MUTTONFISH
MUTTONFISHES
MUTTONHEAD
MUTTONHEADED
MUTTONHEADS

MUTUALISATION
MUTUALISATIONS
MUTUALISED
MUTUALISES
MUTUALISING
MUTUALISMS
MUTUALISTIC
MUTUALISTS
MUTUALITIES
MUTUALIZATION
MUTUALIZATIONS
MUTUALIZED
MUTUALIZES
MUTUALIZING
MUTUALNESS
MUTUALNESSES
MUZZINESSES
MYASTHENIA
MYASTHENIAS
MYASTHENIC
MYASTHENICS
MYCETOLOGIES
MYCETOLOGY
MYCETOMATA
MYCETOMATOUS
MYCETOPHAGOUS
MYCETOZOAN
MYCETOZOANS
MYCOBACTERIA
MYCOBACTERIAL
MYCOBACTERIUM
MYCOBIONTS
MYCODOMATIA
MYCODOMATIUM
MYCOFLORAE
MYCOFLORAS
MYCOLOGICAL
MYCOLOGICALLY
MYCOLOGIES
MYCOLOGIST
MYCOLOGISTS
MYCOPHAGIES
MYCOPHAGIST
MYCOPHAGISTS
MYCOPHAGOUS
MYCOPHILES
MYCOPLASMA
MYCOPLASMAL
MYCOPLASMAS
MYCOPLASMATA
MYCOPLASMOSES
MYCOPLASMOSIS
MYCORHIZAE
MYCORHIZAL
MYCORHIZAS
MYCORRHIZA

MYCORRHIZAE
MYCORRHIZAL
MYCORRHIZAS
MYCOTOXICOSES
MYCOTOXICOSIS
MYCOTOXINS
MYCOTOXOLOGIES
MYCOTOXOLOGY
MYCOTROPHIC
MYCOVIRUSES
MYDRIATICS
MYELENCEPHALA
MYELENCEPHALIC
MYELENCEPHALON
MYELENCEPHALONS
MYELINATED
MYELITIDES
MYELITISES
MYELOBLAST
MYELOBLASTIC
MYELOBLASTS
MYELOCYTES
MYELOCYTIC
MYELOFIBROSES
MYELOFIBROSIS
MYELOFIBROTIC
MYELOGENOUS
MYELOGRAMS
MYELOGRAPHIES
MYELOGRAPHY
MYELOMATOID
MYELOMATOUS
MYELOPATHIC
MYELOPATHIES
MYELOPATHY
MYIOPHILIES
MYIOPHILOUS
MYLOHYOIDS
MYLONITISATION
MYLONITISATIONS
MYLONITISE
MYLONITISED
MYLONITISES
MYLONITISING
MYLONITIZATION
MYLONITIZATIONS
MYLONITIZE
MYLONITIZED
MYLONITIZES
MYLONITIZING
MYOBLASTIC
MYOCARDIAL
MYOCARDIOGRAPH
MYOCARDIOGRAPHS
MYOCARDIOPATHY
MYOCARDITIS

MYOCARDITISES
MYOCARDIUM
MYOCARDIUMS
MYOCLONUSES
MYOELECTRIC
MYOELECTRICAL
MYOFIBRILLAR
MYOFIBRILS
MYOFILAMENT
MYOFILAMENTS
MYOGLOBINS
MYOGRAPHIC
MYOGRAPHICAL
MYOGRAPHICALLY
MYOGRAPHIES
MYOGRAPHIST
MYOGRAPHISTS
MYOINOSITOL
MYOINOSITOLS
MYOLOGICAL
MYOLOGISTS
MYOMANCIES
MYOMECTOMIES
MYOMECTOMY
MYOPATHIES
MYOPHILIES
MYOPHILOUS
MYOPICALLY
MYOSITISES
MYOSOTISES
MYRIADFOLD
MYRIADFOLDS
MYRIAPODAN
MYRIAPODOUS
MYRINGITIS
MYRINGITISES
MYRINGOSCOPE
MYRINGOSCOPES
MYRINGOTOMIES
MYRINGOTOMY
MYRIORAMAS
MYRIOSCOPE
MYRIOSCOPES
MYRISTICIVOROUS
MYRMECOCHORIES
MYRMECOCHORY
MYRMECOLOGIC
MYRMECOLOGICAL
MYRMECOLOGIES
MYRMECOLOGIST
MYRMECOLOGISTS
MYRMECOLOGY
MYRMECOPHAGOUS
MYRMECOPHILE
MYRMECOPHILES
MYRMECOPHILIES

MYRMECOPHILOUS
MYRMECOPHILY
MYRMIDONES
MYRMIDONIAN
MYROBALANS
MYRTACEOUS
MYSOPHOBIA
MYSOPHOBIAS
MYSTAGOGIC
MYSTAGOGICAL
MYSTAGOGICALLY
MYSTAGOGIES
MYSTAGOGUE
MYSTAGOGUES
MYSTAGOGUS
MYSTAGOGUSES
MYSTERIOUS
MYSTERIOUSLY
MYSTERIOUSNESS
MYSTICALLY
MYSTICALNESS
MYSTICALNESSES
MYSTICETES
MYSTICISMS
MYSTIFICATION
MYSTIFICATIONS
MYSTIFIERS
MYSTIFYING
MYSTIFYINGLY
MYTHICALLY
MYTHICISATION
MYTHICISATIONS
MYTHICISED
MYTHICISER
MYTHICISERS
MYTHICISES
MYTHICISING
MYTHICISMS
MYTHICISTS
MYTHICIZATION
MYTHICIZATIONS
MYTHICIZED
MYTHICIZER
MYTHICIZERS
MYTHICIZES
MYTHICIZING
MYTHMAKERS
MYTHMAKING
MYTHMAKINGS
MYTHOGENESES
MYTHOGENESIS
MYTHOGRAPHER
MYTHOGRAPHERS
MYTHOGRAPHIES
MYTHOGRAPHY
MYTHOLOGER

MYTHOLOGERS
MYTHOLOGIAN
MYTHOLOGIANS
MYTHOLOGIC
MYTHOLOGICAL
MYTHOLOGICALLY
MYTHOLOGIES
MYTHOLOGISATION
MYTHOLOGISE
MYTHOLOGISED
MYTHOLOGISER
MYTHOLOGISERS
MYTHOLOGISES
MYTHOLOGISING
MYTHOLOGIST
MYTHOLOGISTS
MYTHOLOGIZATION
MYTHOLOGIZE
MYTHOLOGIZED
MYTHOLOGIZER
MYTHOLOGIZERS
MYTHOLOGIZES
MYTHOLOGIZING
MYTHOMANES
MYTHOMANIA
MYTHOMANIAC
MYTHOMANIACS
MYTHOMANIAS
MYTHOPOEIA
MYTHOPOEIAS
MYTHOPOEIC
MYTHOPOEISM
MYTHOPOEISMS
MYTHOPOEIST
MYTHOPOEISTS
MYTHOPOESES
MYTHOPOESIS
MYTHOPOETIC
MYTHOPOETICAL
MYTHOPOETS
MYTILIFORM
MYXAMOEBAE
MYXAMOEBAS
MYXEDEMATOUS
MYXOEDEMAS
MYXOEDEMATOUS
MYXOEDEMIC
MYXOMATOSES
MYXOMATOSIS
MYXOMATOUS
MYXOMYCETE
MYXOMYCETES
MYXOMYCETOUS
MYXOVIRUSES

Nn

NABOBERIES	NAPHTHYLAMINES	NASALITIES	NATURALISM	NEARNESSES	NECROLOGIES
NABOBESSES	NAPOLEONITE	NASALIZATION	NATURALISMS	NEARSIGHTED	NECROLOGIST
NACHTMAALS	NAPOLEONITES	NASALIZATIONS	NATURALIST	NEARSIGHTEDLY	NECROLOGISTS
NAFFNESSES	NAPPINESSES	NASALIZING	NATURALISTIC	NEARSIGHTEDNESS	NECROMANCER
NAIFNESSES	NAPRAPATHIES	NASCENCIES	NATURALISTS	NEARTHROSES	NECROMANCERS
NAILBITERS	NAPRAPATHY	NASEBERRIES	NATURALIZATION	NEARTHROSIS	NECROMANCIES
NAILBRUSHES	NARCISSISM	NASOFRONTAL	NATURALIZATIONS	NEATNESSES	NECROMANCY
NAISSANCES	NARCISSISMS	NASOGASTRIC	NATURALIZE	NEBBISHERS	NECROMANIA
NAIVENESSES	NARCISSIST	NASOLACRYMAL	NATURALIZED	NEBENKERNS	NECROMANIAC
NAKEDNESSES	NARCISSISTIC	NASOPHARYNGEAL	NATURALIZES	NEBUCHADNEZZAR	NECROMANIACS
NALBUPHINE	NARCISSISTS	NASOPHARYNGES	NATURALIZING	NEBUCHADNEZZARS	NECROMANIAS
NALBUPHINES	NARCISSUSES	NASOPHARYNX	NATURALNESS	NEBULISATION	NECROMANTIC
NALORPHINE	NARCOANALYSES	NASOPHARYNXES	NATURALNESSES	NEBULISATIONS	NECROMANTICAL
NALORPHINES	NARCOANALYSIS	NASTINESSES	NATURISTIC	NEBULISERS	NECROMANTICALLY
NALTREXONE	NARCOCATHARSES	NASTURTIUM	NATUROPATH	NEBULISING	NECROPHAGOUS
NALTREXONES	NARCOCATHARSIS	NASTURTIUMS	NATUROPATHIC	NEBULIZATION	NECROPHILE
NAMAYCUSHES	NARCOHYPNOSES	NATALITIAL	NATUROPATHIES	NEBULIZATIONS	NECROPHILES
NAMECHECKED	NARCOHYPNOSIS	NATALITIES	NATUROPATHS	NEBULIZERS	NECROPHILIA
NAMECHECKING	NARCOLEPSIES	NATATIONAL	NATUROPATHY	NEBULIZING	NECROPHILIAC
NAMECHECKS	NARCOLEPSY	NATATORIAL	NAUGAHYDES	NEBULOSITIES	NECROPHILIACS
NAMELESSLY	NARCOLEPTIC	NATATORIUM	NAUGHTIEST	NEBULOSITY	NECROPHILIAS
NAMELESSNESS	NARCOLEPTICS	NATATORIUMS	NAUGHTINESS	NEBULOUSLY	NECROPHILIC
NAMELESSNESSES	NARCOSYNTHESES	NATHELESSE	NAUGHTINESSES	NEBULOUSNESS	NECROPHILIES
NAMEPLATES	NARCOSYNTHESIS	NATIONALISATION	NAUMACHIAE	NEBULOUSNESSES	NECROPHILISM
NAMEWORTHY	NARCOTERRORISM	NATIONALISE	NAUMACHIAS	NECESSAIRE	NECROPHILISMS
NANDROLONE	NARCOTERRORISMS	NATIONALISED	NAUMACHIES	NECESSAIRES	NECROPHILOUS
NANDROLONES	NARCOTERRORIST	NATIONALISER	NAUPLIIFORM	NECESSARIAN	NECROPHILS
NANISATION	NARCOTERRORISTS	NATIONALISERS	NAUSEATING	NECESSARIANISM	NECROPHILY
NANISATIONS	NARCOTICALLY	NATIONALISES	NAUSEATINGLY	NECESSARIANISMS	NECROPHOBE
NANIZATION	NARCOTINES	NATIONALISING	NAUSEATION	NECESSARIANS	NECROPHOBES
NANIZATIONS	NARCOTISATION	NATIONALISM	NAUSEATIONS	NECESSARIES	NECROPHOBIA
NANNOPLANKTON	NARCOTISATIONS	NATIONALISMS	NAUSEATIVE	NECESSARILY	NECROPHOBIAS
NANNOPLANKTONS	NARCOTISED	NATIONALIST	NAUSEOUSLY	NECESSARINESS	NECROPHOBIC
NANOGRAMME	NARCOTISES	NATIONALISTIC	NAUSEOUSNESS	NECESSARINESSES	NECROPHOROUS
NANOGRAMMES	NARCOTISING	NATIONALISTS	NAUSEOUSNESSES	NECESSITARIAN	NECROPOLEIS
NANOMATERIAL	NARCOTISMS	NATIONALITIES	NAUTICALLY	NECESSITARIANS	NECROPOLES
NANOMATERIALS	NARCOTISTS	NATIONALITY	NAUTILOIDS	NECESSITATE	NECROPOLIS
NANOMETERS	NARCOTIZATION	NATIONALIZATION	NAUTILUSES	NECESSITATED	NECROPOLISES
NANOMETRES	NARCOTIZATIONS	NATIONALIZE	NAVARCHIES	NECESSITATES	NECROPSIED
NANOPARTICLE	NARCOTIZED	NATIONALIZED	NAVELWORTS	NECESSITATING	NECROPSIES
NANOPARTICLES	NARCOTIZES	NATIONALIZER	NAVICULARE	NECESSITATION	NECROPSYING
NANOPHYSICS	NARCOTIZING	NATIONALIZERS	NAVICULARES	NECESSITATIONS	NECROSCOPIC
NANOPLANKTON	NARGHILIES	NATIONALIZES	NAVICULARS	NECESSITATIVE	NECROSCOPICAL
NANOPLANKTONS	NARGHILLIES	NATIONALIZING	NAVIGABILITIES	NECESSITIED	NECROSCOPIES
NANOSECOND	NARRATABLE	NATIONALLY	NAVIGABILITY	NECESSITIES	NECROSCOPY
NANOSECONDS	NARRATIONAL	NATIONHOOD	NAVIGABLENESS	NECESSITOUS	NECROTISED
NANOTECHNOLOGY	NARRATIONS	NATIONHOODS	NAVIGABLENESSES	NECESSITOUSLY	NECROTISES
NANOTESLAS	NARRATIVELY	NATIONLESS	NAVIGATING	NECESSITOUSNESS	NECROTISING
NANOWORLDS	NARRATIVES	NATIONWIDE	NAVIGATION	NECKCLOTHS	NECROTIZED
NAPHTHALENE	NARRATOLOGICAL	NATIVENESS	NAVIGATIONAL	NECKERCHIEF	NECROTIZES
NAPHTHALENES	NARRATOLOGIES	NATIVENESSES	NAVIGATIONALLY	NECKERCHIEFS	NECROTIZING
NAPHTHALIC	NARRATOLOGIST	NATIVISTIC	NAVIGATIONS	NECKERCHIEVES	NECROTOMIES
NAPHTHALIN	NARRATOLOGISTS	NATIVITIES	NAVIGATORS	NECKLACING	NECROTROPH
NAPHTHALINE	NARRATOLOGY	NATRIURESES	NAYSAYINGS	NECKLACINGS	NECROTROPHIC
NAPHTHALINES	NARROWBAND	NATRIURESIS	NAZIFICATION	NECKPIECES	NECROTROPHS
NAPHTHALINS	NARROWBANDS	NATRIURETIC	NAZIFICATIONS	NECKVERSES	NECTAREOUS
NAPHTHALISE	NARROWCAST	NATRIURETICS	NEANDERTAL	NECROBIOSES	NECTAREOUSNESS
NAPHTHALISED	NARROWCASTED	NATROLITES	NEANDERTALER	NECROBIOSIS	NECTARIFEROUS
NAPHTHALISES	NARROWCASTING	NATTERJACK	NEANDERTALERS	NECROBIOTIC	NECTARINES
NAPHTHALISING	NARROWCASTS	NATTERJACKS	NEANDERTALS	NECROGRAPHER	NECTARIVOROUS
NAPHTHALIZE	NARROWINGS	NATTINESSES	NEANDERTHAL	NECROGRAPHERS	NECTOCALYCES
NAPHTHALIZED	NARROWNESS	NATURALISATION	NEANDERTHALER	NECROLATER	NECTOCALYX
NAPHTHALIZES	NARROWNESSES	NATURALISATIONS	NEANDERTHALERS	NECROLATERS	NEEDCESSITIES
NAPHTHALIZING	NARROWINGS	NATURALISE	NEANDERTHALOID	NECROLATRIES	NEEDCESSITY
NAPHTHENES	NASALISATION	NATURALISED	NEANDERTHALS	NECROLATRY	NEEDFULNESS
NAPHTHENIC	NASALISATIONS	NATURALISES	NEAPOLITAN	NECROLOGIC	NEEDFULNESSES
NAPHTHYLAMINE	NASALISING	NATURALISING	NEAPOLITANS	NECROLOGICAL	NEEDINESSES

n

NEEDLECORD
NEEDLECORDS
NEEDLECRAFT
NEEDLECRAFTS
NEEDLEFISH
NEEDLEFISHES
NEEDLEFULS
NEEDLELIKE
NEEDLEPOINT
NEEDLEPOINTS
NEEDLESSLY
NEEDLESSNESS
NEEDLESSNESSES
NEEDLESTICK
NEEDLEWOMAN
NEEDLEWOMEN
NEEDLEWORK
NEEDLEWORKER
NEEDLEWORKERS
NEEDLEWORKS
NEESBERRIES
NEFARIOUSLY
NEFARIOUSNESS
NEFARIOUSNESSES
NEGATIONAL
NEGATIONIST
NEGATIONISTS
NEGATIVELY
NEGATIVENESS
NEGATIVENESSES
NEGATIVING
NEGATIVISM
NEGATIVISMS
NEGATIVIST
NEGATIVISTIC
NEGATIVISTS
NEGATIVITIES
NEGATIVITY
NEGLECTABLE
NEGLECTEDNESS
NEGLECTEDNESSES
NEGLECTERS
NEGLECTFUL
NEGLECTFULLY
NEGLECTFULNESS
NEGLECTING
NEGLECTINGLY
NEGLECTION
NEGLECTIONS
NEGLECTIVE
NEGLECTORS
NEGLIGEABLE
NEGLIGENCE
NEGLIGENCES
NEGLIGENTLY
NEGLIGIBILITIES
NEGLIGIBILITY
NEGLIGIBLE
NEGLIGIBLENESS
NEGLIGIBLY
NEGOCIANTS
NEGOTIABILITIES
NEGOTIABILITY
NEGOTIABLE
NEGOTIANTS
NEGOTIATED
NEGOTIATES
NEGOTIATING
NEGOTIATION
NEGOTIATIONS
NEGOTIATOR
NEGOTIATORS
NEGOTIATORY
NEGOTIATRESS
NEGOTIATRESSES
NEGOTIATRICES
NEGOTIATRIX
NEGOTIATRIXES
NEGRITUDES
NEGROHEADS
NEGROPHILE
NEGROPHILES
NEGROPHILISM

NEGROPHILISMS
NEGROPHILIST
NEGROPHILISTS
NEGROPHILS
NEGROPHOBE
NEGROPHOBES
NEGROPHOBIA
NEGROPHOBIAS
NEIGHBORED
NEIGHBORHOOD
NEIGHBORHOODS
NEIGHBORING
NEIGHBORLESS
NEIGHBORLINESS
NEIGHBORLY
NEIGHBOURED
NEIGHBOURHOOD
NEIGHBOURHOODS
NEIGHBOURING
NEIGHBOURLESS
NEIGHBOURLINESS
NEIGHBOURLY
NEIGHBOURS
NELUMBIUMS
NEMATHELMINTH
NEMATHELMINTHIC
NEMATHELMINTHS
NEMATICIDAL
NEMATICIDE
NEMATICIDES
NEMATOBLAST
NEMATOBLASTS
NEMATOCIDAL
NEMATOCIDE
NEMATOCIDES
NEMATOCYST
NEMATOCYSTIC
NEMATOCYSTS
NEMATODIRIASES
NEMATODIRIASIS
NEMATODIRUS
NEMATODIRUSES
NEMATOLOGICAL
NEMATOLOGIES
NEMATOLOGIST
NEMATOLOGISTS
NEMATOLOGY
NEMATOPHORE
NEMATOPHORES
NEMERTEANS
NEMERTIANS
NEMERTINES
NEMOPHILAS
NEOANTHROPIC
NEOARSPHENAMINE
NEOCLASSIC
NEOCLASSICAL
NEOCLASSICISM
NEOCLASSICISMS
NEOCLASSICIST
NEOCLASSICISTS
NEOCOLONIAL
NEOCOLONIALISM
NEOCOLONIALISMS
NEOCOLONIALIST
NEOCOLONIALISTS
NEOCONSERVATISM
NEOCONSERVATIVE
NEOCORTEXES
NEOCORTICAL
NEOCORTICES
NEODYMIUMS
NEOGENESES
NEOGENESIS
NEOGENETIC
NEOGOTHICS
NEOGRAMMARIAN
NEOGRAMMARIANS
NEOLIBERAL
NEOLIBERALISM
NEOLIBERALISMS
NEOLIBERALS
NEOLOGIANS

NEOLOGICAL
NEOLOGICALLY
NEOLOGISED
NEOLOGISES
NEOLOGISING
NEOLOGISMS
NEOLOGISTIC
NEOLOGISTICAL
NEOLOGISTICALLY
NEOLOGISTS
NEOLOGIZED
NEOLOGIZES
NEOLOGIZING
NEONATALLY
NEONATICIDE
NEONATICIDES
NEONATOLOGIES
NEONATOLOGIST
NEONATOLOGISTS
NEONATOLOGY
NEONOMIANISM
NEONOMIANISMS
NEONOMIANS
NEOORTHODOX
NEOORTHODOXIES
NEOORTHODOXY
NEOPAGANISE
NEOPAGANISED
NEOPAGANISES
NEOPAGANISING
NEOPAGANISM
NEOPAGANISMS
NEOPAGANIZE
NEOPAGANIZED
NEOPAGANIZES
NEOPAGANIZING
NEOPHILIAC
NEOPHILIACS
NEOPHILIAS
NEOPHILIAS
NEOPHOBIAS
NEOPILINAS
NEOPLASIAS
NEOPLASTIC
NEOPLASTICISM
NEOPLASTICISMS
NEOPLASTICIST
NEOPLASTICISTS
NEOPLASTIES
NEOREALISM
NEOREALISMS
NEOREALIST
NEOREALISTIC
NEOREALISTS
NEOSTIGMINE
NEOSTIGMINES
NEOTEINIAS
NEOTERICAL
NEOTERICALLY
NEOTERICALS
NEOTERISED
NEOTERISES
NEOTERISING
NEOTERISMS
NEOTERISTS
NEOTERIZED
NEOTERIZES
NEOTERIZING
NEOTROPICS
NEOVITALISM
NEOVITALISMS
NEOVITALIST
NEOVITALISTS
NEPENTHEAN
NEPHALISMS
NEPHALISTS
NEPHELINES
NEPHELINIC
NEPHELINITE
NEPHELINITES
NEPHELINITIC
NEPHELITES
NEPHELOMETER
NEPHELOMETERS

NEPHELOMETRIC
NEPHELOMETRIES
NEPHELOMETRY
NEPHOGRAMS
NEPHOGRAPH
NEPHOGRAPHS
NEPHOLOGIC
NEPHOLOGICAL
NEPHOLOGIES
NEPHOLOGIST
NEPHOLOGISTS
NEPHOSCOPE
NEPHOSCOPES
NEPHRALGIA
NEPHRALGIAS
NEPHRALGIC
NEPHRALGIES
NEPHRECTOMIES
NEPHRECTOMISE
NEPHRECTOMISED
NEPHRECTOMISES
NEPHRECTOMISING
NEPHRECTOMIZE
NEPHRECTOMIZED
NEPHRECTOMIZES
NEPHRECTOMIZING
NEPHRECTOMY
NEPHRIDIAL
NEPHRIDIUM
NEPHRITICAL
NEPHRITICS
NEPHRITIDES
NEPHRITISES
NEPHROBLASTOMA
NEPHROBLASTOMAS
NEPHROLEPIS
NEPHROLEPISES
NEPHROLOGICAL
NEPHROLOGIES
NEPHROLOGIST
NEPHROLOGISTS
NEPHROLOGY
NEPHROPATHIC
NEPHROPATHIES
NEPHROPATHY
NEPHROPEXIES
NEPHROPEXY
NEPHROPTOSES
NEPHROPTOSIS
NEPHROSCOPE
NEPHROSCOPES
NEPHROSCOPIES
NEPHROSCOPY
NEPHROSTOME
NEPHROSTOMES
NEPHROTICS
NEPHROTOMIES
NEPHROTOMY
NEPHROTOXIC
NEPHROTOXICITY
NEPOTISTIC
NEPTUNIUMS
NERDINESSES
NERVATIONS
NERVATURES
NERVELESSLY
NERVELESSNESS
NERVELESSNESSES
NERVINESSES
NERVOSITIES
NERVOUSNESS
NERVOUSNESSES
NERVURATION
NERVURATIONS
NESCIENCES
NESHNESSES
NESSELRODE
NESSELRODES
NETBALLERS
NETHERLINGS
NETHERMORE
NETHERMOST
NETHERSTOCK

NETHERSTOCKS
NETHERWARD
NETHERWARDS
NETHERWORLD
NETHERWORLDS
NETIQUETTE
NETIQUETTES
NETMINDERS
NETTLELIKE
NETTLESOME
NETWORKERS
NETWORKING
NETWORKINGS
NEURALGIAS
NEURAMINIDASE
NEURAMINIDASES
NEURASTHENIA
NEURASTHENIAC
NEURASTHENIACS
NEURASTHENIAS
NEURASTHENIC
NEURASTHENICS
NEURATIONS
NEURECTOMIES
NEURECTOMY
NEURILEMMA
NEURILEMMAL
NEURILEMMAS
NEURILITIES
NEURITIDES
NEURITISES
NEUROACTIVE
NEUROANATOMIC
NEUROANATOMICAL
NEUROANATOMIES
NEUROANATOMIST
NEUROANATOMISTS
NEUROANATOMY
NEUROBIOLOGICAL
NEUROBIOLOGIES
NEUROBIOLOGIST
NEUROBIOLOGISTS
NEUROBIOLOGY
NEUROBLAST
NEUROBLASTOMA
NEUROBLASTOMAS
NEUROBLASTOMATA
NEUROBLASTS
NEUROCHEMICAL
NEUROCHEMICALS
NEUROCHEMIST
NEUROCHEMISTRY
NEUROCHEMISTS
NEUROCHIPS
NEUROCOELE
NEUROCOELES
NEUROCOELS
NEUROCOGNITIVE
NEUROCOMPUTER
NEUROCOMPUTERS
NEUROCOMPUTING
NEUROCOMPUTINGS
NEUROENDOCRINE
NEUROETHOLOGIES
NEUROETHOLOGY
NEUROFEEDBACK
NEUROFEEDBACKS
NEUROFIBRIL
NEUROFIBRILAR
NEUROFIBRILLAR
NEUROFIBRILLARY
NEUROFIBRILS
NEUROFIBROMA
NEUROFIBROMAS
NEUROFIBROMATA
NEUROGENESES
NEUROGENESIS
NEUROGENIC
NEUROGENICALLY
NEUROGLIAL
NEUROGLIAS
NEUROGRAMS
NEUROHORMONAL

NEUROHORMONE
NEUROHORMONES
NEUROHUMOR
NEUROHUMORAL
NEUROHUMORS
NEUROHYPNOLOGY
NEUROHYPOPHYSES
NEUROHYPOPHYSIS
NEUROLEMMA
NEUROLEMMAS
NEUROLEPTIC
NEUROLEPTICS
NEUROLINGUIST
NEUROLINGUISTIC
NEUROLINGUISTS
NEUROLOGIC
NEUROLOGICAL
NEUROLOGICALLY
NEUROLOGIES
NEUROLOGIST
NEUROLOGISTS
NEUROLYSES
NEUROLYSIS
NEUROMARKETING
NEUROMARKETINGS
NEUROMASTS
NEUROMATOUS
NEUROMUSCULAR
NEUROPATHIC
NEUROPATHICAL
NEUROPATHICALLY
NEUROPATHIES
NEUROPATHIST
NEUROPATHISTS
NEUROPATHOLOGIC
NEUROPATHOLOGY
NEUROPATHS
NEUROPATHY
NEUROPEPTIDE
NEUROPEPTIDES
NEUROPHYSIOLOGY
NEUROPLASM
NEUROPLASMS
NEUROPSYCHIATRY
NEUROPSYCHOLOGY
NEUROPTERA
NEUROPTERAN
NEUROPTERANS
NEUROPTERIST
NEUROPTERISTS
NEUROPTERON
NEUROPTEROUS
NEURORADIOLOGY
NEUROSCIENCE
NEUROSCIENCES
NEUROSCIENTIFIC
NEUROSCIENTIST
NEUROSCIENTISTS
NEUROSECRETION
NEUROSECRETIONS
NEUROSECRETORY
NEUROSENSORY
NEUROSPORA
NEUROSPORAS
NEUROSURGEON
NEUROSURGEONS
NEUROSURGERIES
NEUROSURGERY
NEUROSURGICAL
NEUROSURGICALLY
NEUROTICALLY
NEUROTICISM
NEUROTICISMS
NEUROTOMIES
NEUROTOMIST
NEUROTOMISTS
NEUROTOXIC
NEUROTOXICITIES
NEUROTOXICITY
NEUROTOXIN
NEUROTOXINS
NEUROTROPHIC
NEUROTROPHIES

n

NEUROTROPHY
NEUROTROPIC
NEUROVASCULAR
NEURULATION
NEURULATIONS
NEURYPNOLOGIES
NEURYPNOLOGY
NEUTRALISATION
NEUTRALISATIONS
NEUTRALISE
NEUTRALISED
NEUTRALISER
NEUTRALISERS
NEUTRALISES
NEUTRALISING
NEUTRALISM
NEUTRALISMS
NEUTRALIST
NEUTRALISTIC
NEUTRALISTS
NEUTRALITIES
NEUTRALITY
NEUTRALIZATION
NEUTRALIZATIONS
NEUTRALIZE
NEUTRALIZED
NEUTRALIZER
NEUTRALIZERS
NEUTRALIZES
NEUTRALIZING
NEUTRALNESS
NEUTRALNESSES
NEUTRETTOS
NEUTRINOLESS
NEUTROPENIA
NEUTROPENIAS
NEUTROPHIL
NEUTROPHILE
NEUTROPHILES
NEUTROPHILIC
NEUTROPHILS
NEVERMINDS
NEVERTHELESS
NEVERTHEMORE
NEWFANGLED
NEWFANGLEDLY
NEWFANGLEDNESS
NEWFANGLENESS
NEWFANGLENESSES
NEWISHNESS
NEWISHNESSES
NEWMARKETS
NEWSAGENCIES
NEWSAGENCY
NEWSAGENTS
NEWSBREAKS
NEWSCASTER
NEWSCASTERS
NEWSCASTING
NEWSCASTINGS
NEWSDEALER
NEWSDEALERS
NEWSFLASHES
NEWSGROUPS
NEWSHOUNDS
NEWSINESSES
NEWSLETTER
NEWSLETTERS
NEWSMAGAZINE
NEWSMAGAZINES
NEWSMAKERS
NEWSMONGER
NEWSMONGERS
NEWSPAPERDOM
NEWSPAPERDOMS
NEWSPAPERED
NEWSPAPERING
NEWSPAPERISM
NEWSPAPERISMS
NEWSPAPERMAN
NEWSPAPERMEN
NEWSPAPERS
NEWSPAPERWOMAN

NEWSPAPERWOMEN
NEWSPEOPLE
NEWSPERSON
NEWSPERSONS
NEWSPRINTS
NEWSREADER
NEWSREADERS
NEWSSTANDS
NEWSTRADES
NEWSWEEKLIES
NEWSWEEKLY
NEWSWORTHINESS
NEWSWORTHY
NEWSWRITING
NEWSWRITINGS
NEXTNESSES
NIACINAMIDE
NIACINAMIDES
NIAISERIES
NIALAMIDES
NIBBLINGLY
NICCOLITES
NICENESSES
NICKELIFEROUS
NICKELINES
NICKELISED
NICKELISES
NICKELISING
NICKELIZED
NICKELIZES
NICKELIZING
NICKELLING
NICKELODEON
NICKELODEONS
NICKNAMERS
NICKNAMING
NICKPOINTS
NICKSTICKS
NICKUMPOOP
NICKUMPOOPS
NICOMPOOPS
NICOTIANAS
NICOTINAMIDE
NICOTINAMIDES
NICOTINISM
NICOTINISMS
NICROSILAL
NICROSILALS
NICTATIONS
NICTITATED
NICTITATES
NICTITATING
NICTITATION
NICTITATIONS
NIDAMENTAL
NIDAMENTUM
NIDDERINGS
NIDDERLING
NIDDERLINGS
NIDERLINGS
NIDICOLOUS
NIDIFICATE
NIDIFICATED
NIDIFICATES
NIDIFICATING
NIDIFICATION
NIDIFICATIONS
NIDIFUGOUS
NIDULATION
NIDULATIONS
NIFEDIPINE
NIFEDIPINES
NIFFNAFFED
NIFFNAFFING
NIFTINESSES
NIGGARDING
NIGGARDISE
NIGGARDISES
NIGGARDIZE
NIGGARDIZES
NIGGARDLINESS
NIGGARDLINESSES
NIGGERDOMS

NIGGERHEAD
NIGGERHEADS
NIGGERISMS
NIGGERLING
NIGGERLINGS
NIGGLINGLY
NIGHNESSES
NIGHTBIRDS
NIGHTBLIND
NIGHTCLASS
NIGHTCLASSES
NIGHTCLOTHES
NIGHTCLUBBED
NIGHTCLUBBER
NIGHTCLUBBERS
NIGHTCLUBBING
NIGHTCLUBBINGS
NIGHTCLUBS
NIGHTDRESS
NIGHTDRESSES
NIGHTFALLS
NIGHTFARING
NIGHTFIRES
NIGHTGEARS
NIGHTGLOWS
NIGHTGOWNS
NIGHTHAWKS
NIGHTINGALE
NIGHTINGALES
NIGHTLIFES
NIGHTLIVES
NIGHTMARES
NIGHTMARISH
NIGHTMARISHLY
NIGHTMARISHNESS
NIGHTPIECE
NIGHTPIECES
NIGHTRIDER
NIGHTRIDERS
NIGHTRIDING
NIGHTRIDINGS
NIGHTSCOPE
NIGHTSCOPES
NIGHTSHADE
NIGHTSHADES
NIGHTSHIRT
NIGHTSHIRTS
NIGHTSIDES
NIGHTSPOTS
NIGHTSTAND
NIGHTSTANDS
NIGHTSTICK
NIGHTSTICKS
NIGHTTIDES
NIGHTTIMES
NIGHTWALKER
NIGHTWALKERS
NIGHTWEARS
NIGRESCENCE
NIGRESCENCES
NIGRESCENT
NIGRIFYING
NIGRITUDES
NIGROMANCIES
NIGROMANCY
NIGROSINES
NIHILISTIC
NIHILITIES
NIKETHAMIDE
NIKETHAMIDES
NILPOTENTS
NIMBLENESS
NIMBLENESSES
NIMBLESSES
NIMBLEWITS
NIMBLEWITTED
NIMBOSTRATI
NIMBOSTRATUS
NIMBYNESSES
NINCOMPOOP
NINCOMPOOPERIES
NINCOMPOOPERY
NINCOMPOOPS

NINEPENCES
NINEPENNIES
NINESCORES
NINETEENTH
NINETEENTHLY
NINETEENTHS
NINETIETHS
NINHYDRINS
NINNYHAMMER
NINNYHAMMERS
NIPCHEESES
NIPPERKINS
NIPPINESSES
NIPPLEWORT
NIPPLEWORTS
NISBERRIES
NITPICKERS
NITPICKIER
NITPICKIEST
NITPICKING
NITRAMINES
NITRANILINE
NITRANILINES
NITRATINES
NITRATIONS
NITRAZEPAM
NITRAZEPAMS
NITRIDINGS
NITRIFIABLE
NITRIFICATION
NITRIFICATIONS
NITRIFIERS
NITRIFYING
NITROBACTERIA
NITROBACTERIUM
NITROBENZENE
NITROBENZENES
NITROCELLULOSE
NITROCELLULOSES
NITROCHLOROFORM
NITROCOTTON
NITROCOTTONS
NITROFURAN
NITROFURANS
NITROGENASE
NITROGENASES
NITROGENISATION
NITROGENISE
NITROGENISED
NITROGENISES
NITROGENISING
NITROGENIZATION
NITROGENIZE
NITROGENIZED
NITROGENIZES
NITROGENIZING
NITROGENOUS
NITROGLYCERIN
NITROGLYCERINE
NITROGLYCERINES
NITROGLYCERINS
NITROMETER
NITROMETERS
NITROMETHANE
NITROMETHANES
NITROMETRIC
NITROPARAFFIN
NITROPARAFFINS
NITROPHILOUS
NITROSAMINE
NITROSAMINES
NITROSATION
NITROSATIONS
NITROTOLUENE
NITROTOLUENES
NITWITTEDNESS
NITWITTEDNESSES
NITWITTERIES
NITWITTERY
NOBBINESSES
NOBILESSES
NOBILITATE
NOBILITATED

NOBILITATES
NOBILITATING
NOBILITATION
NOBILITATIONS
NOBILITIES
NOBLENESSES
NOBLEWOMAN
NOBLEWOMEN
NOCHELLING
NOCICEPTIVE
NOCICEPTOR
NOCICEPTORS
NOCIRECEPTOR
NOCIRECEPTORS
NOCTAMBULATION
NOCTAMBULATIONS
NOCTAMBULISM
NOCTAMBULISMS
NOCTAMBULISTS
NOCTILUCAE
NOCTILUCAS
NOCTILUCENCE
NOCTILUCENCES
NOCTILUCENT
NOCTILUCOUS
NOCTIVAGANT
NOCTIVAGATION
NOCTIVAGATIONS
NOCTIVAGOUS
NOCTUARIES
NOCTURNALITIES
NOCTURNALITY
NOCTURNALLY
NOCTURNALS
NOCUOUSNESS
NOCUOUSNESSES
NODALISING
NODALITIES
NODALIZING
NODOSITIES
NODULATION
NODULATIONS
NOEMATICAL
NOEMATICALLY
NOISELESSLY
NOISELESSNESS
NOISELESSNESSES
NOISEMAKER
NOISEMAKERS
NOISEMAKING
NOISEMAKINGS
NOISINESSES
NOISOMENESS
NOISOMENESSES
NOMADICALLY
NOMADISATION
NOMADISATIONS
NOMADISING
NOMADIZATION
NOMADIZATIONS
NOMADIZING
NOMARCHIES
NOMENCLATIVE
NOMENCLATOR
NOMENCLATORIAL
NOMENCLATORS
NOMENCLATURAL
NOMENCLATURE
NOMENCLATURES
NOMENKLATURA
NOMENKLATURAS
NOMINALISATION
NOMINALISATIONS
NOMINALISE
NOMINALISED
NOMINALISES
NOMINALISING
NOMINALISM
NOMINALISMS
NOMINALIST
NOMINALISTIC
NOMINALISTS

NOMINALIZATION
NOMINALIZATIONS
NOMINALIZE
NOMINALIZED
NOMINALIZES
NOMINALIZING
NOMINATELY
NOMINATING
NOMINATION
NOMINATIONS
NOMINATIVAL
NOMINATIVALLY
NOMINATIVE
NOMINATIVELY
NOMINATIVES
NOMINATORS
NOMOCRACIES
NOMOGENIES
NOMOGRAPHER
NOMOGRAPHERS
NOMOGRAPHIC
NOMOGRAPHICAL
NOMOGRAPHICALLY
NOMOGRAPHIES
NOMOGRAPHS
NOMOGRAPHY
NOMOLOGICAL
NOMOLOGICALLY
NOMOLOGIES
NOMOLOGIST
NOMOLOGISTS
NOMOTHETES
NOMOTHETIC
NOMOTHETICAL
NONABRASIVE
NONABSORBABLE
NONABSORBENT
NONABSORPTIVE
NONABSTRACT
NONACADEMIC
NONACADEMICS
NONACCEPTANCE
NONACCEPTANCES
NONACCIDENTAL
NONACCOUNTABLE
NONACCREDITED
NONACCRUAL
NONACHIEVEMENT
NONACHIEVEMENTS
NONACQUISITIVE
NONACTIONS
NONACTIVATED
NONADAPTIVE
NONADDICTIVE
NONADDICTS
NONADDITIVE
NONADDITIVITIES
NONADDITIVITY
NONADHESIVE
NONADIABATIC
NONADJACENT
NONADMIRER
NONADMIRERS
NONADMISSION
NONADMISSIONS
NONAESTHETIC
NONAFFILIATED
NONAFFLUENT
NONAGENARIAN
NONAGENARIANS
NONAGESIMAL
NONAGESIMALS
NONAGGRESSION
NONAGGRESSIONS
NONAGGRESSIVE
NONAGRICULTURAL
NONALCOHOLIC
NONALIGNED
NONALIGNMENT
NONALIGNMENTS
NONALLELIC
NONALLERGENIC
NONALLERGIC

NONALPHABETIC
NONALUMINUM
NONAMBIGUOUS
NONANALYTIC
NONANATOMIC
NONANSWERS
NONANTAGONISTIC
NONANTIBIOTIC
NONANTIBIOTICS
NONANTIGENIC
NONAPPEARANCE
NONAPPEARANCES
NONAQUATIC
NONAQUEOUS
NONARBITRARY
NONARCHITECT
NONARCHITECTS
NONARCHITECTURE
NONARGUMENT
NONARGUMENTS
NONARISTOCRATIC
NONAROMATIC
NONAROMATICS
NONARTISTIC
NONARTISTS
NONASCETIC
NONASPIRIN
NONASSERTIVE
NONASSOCIATED
NONASTRONOMICAL
NONATHLETE
NONATHLETES
NONATHLETIC
NONATTACHED
NONATTACHMENT
NONATTACHMENTS
NONATTENDANCE
NONATTENDANCES
NONATTENDER
NONATTENDERS
NONAUDITORY
NONAUTHORS
NONAUTOMATED
NONAUTOMATIC
NONAUTOMOTIVE
NONAUTONOMOUS
NONAVAILABILITY
NONBACTERIAL
NONBANKING
NONBARBITURATE
NONBARBITURATES
NONBEARING
NONBEHAVIORAL
NONBELIEFS
NONBELIEVER
NONBELIEVERS
NONBELLIGERENCY
NONBELLIGERENT
NONBELLIGERENTS
NONBETTING
NONBINDING
NONBIOGRAPHICAL
NONBIOLOGICAL
NONBIOLOGICALLY
NONBIOLOGIST
NONBIOLOGISTS
NONBONDING
NONBOTANIST
NONBOTANISTS
NONBREAKABLE
NONBREATHING
NONBREEDER
NONBREEDERS
NONBREEDING
NONBROADCAST
NONBUILDING
NONBURNABLE
NONBUSINESS
NONCABINET
NONCALLABLE
NONCALORIC
NONCANCELABLE
NONCANCEROUS

NONCANDIDACIES
NONCANDIDACY
NONCANDIDATE
NONCANDIDATES
NONCAPITAL
NONCAPITALIST
NONCAPITALISTS
NONCARCINOGEN
NONCARCINOGENIC
NONCARCINOGENS
NONCARDIAC
NONCARRIER
NONCARRIERS
NONCELEBRATION
NONCELEBRATIONS
NONCELEBRITIES
NONCELEBRITY
NONCELLULAR
NONCELLULOSIC
NONCENTRAL
NONCERTIFICATED
NONCERTIFIED
NONCHALANCE
NONCHALANCES
NONCHALANT
NONCHALANTLY
NONCHARACTER
NONCHARACTERS
NONCHARISMATIC
NONCHARISMATICS
NONCHAUVINIST
NONCHEMICAL
NONCHEMICALS
NONCHROMOSOMAL
NONCHURCHGOER
NONCHURCHGOERS
NONCIRCULAR
NONCIRCULATING
NONCITIZEN
NONCITIZENS
NONCLANDESTINE
NONCLASSES
NONCLASSICAL
NONCLASSIFIED
NONCLASSROOM
NONCLERICAL
NONCLINICAL
NONCLOGGING
NONCOERCIVE
NONCOGNITIVE
NONCOGNITIVISM
NONCOGNITIVISMS
NONCOHERENT
NONCOINCIDENCE
NONCOINCIDENCES
NONCOLLECTOR
NONCOLLECTORS
NONCOLLEGE
NONCOLLEGIATE
NONCOLLINEAR
NONCOLORED
NONCOLORFAST
NONCOMBATANT
NONCOMBATANTS
NONCOMBATIVE
NONCOMBUSTIBLE
NONCOMMERCIAL
NONCOMMISSIONED
NONCOMMITMENT
NONCOMMITMENTS
NONCOMMITTAL
NONCOMMITTALLY
NONCOMMITTED
NONCOMMUNIST
NONCOMMUNISTS
NONCOMMUNITY
NONCOMMUTATIVE
NONCOMPARABLE
NONCOMPATIBLE
NONCOMPETITION
NONCOMPETITIVE
NONCOMPETITOR
NONCOMPETITORS

NONCOMPLEX
NONCOMPLIANCE
NONCOMPLIANCES
NONCOMPLICATED
NONCOMPLYING
NONCOMPOSER
NONCOMPOSERS
NONCOMPOUND
NONCOMPRESSIBLE
NONCOMPUTER
NONCOMPUTERISED
NONCOMPUTERIZED
NONCONCEPTUAL
NONCONCERN
NONCONCERNS
NONCONCLUSION
NONCONCLUSIONS
NONCONCURRED
NONCONCURRENCE
NONCONCURRENCES
NONCONCURRENT
NONCONCURRING
NONCONCURS
NONCONDENSABLE
NONCONDITIONED
NONCONDUCTING
NONCONDUCTION
NONCONDUCTIVE
NONCONDUCTOR
NONCONDUCTORS
NONCONFERENCE
NONCONFIDENCE
NONCONFIDENCES
NONCONFIDENTIAL
NONCONFLICTING
NONCONFORM
NONCONFORMANCE
NONCONFORMANCES
NONCONFORMED
NONCONFORMER
NONCONFORMERS
NONCONFORMING
NONCONFORMISM
NONCONFORMISMS
NONCONFORMIST
NONCONFORMISTS
NONCONFORMITIES
NONCONFORMITY
NONCONFORMS
NONCONGRUENT
NONCONJUGATED
NONCONNECTION
NONCONNECTIONS
NONCONSCIOUS
NONCONSECUTIVE
NONCONSENSUAL
NONCONSERVATION
NONCONSERVATIVE
NONCONSOLIDATED
NONCONSTANT
NONCONSTRUCTION
NONCONSTRUCTIVE
NONCONSUMER
NONCONSUMERS
NONCONSUMING
NONCONSUMPTION
NONCONSUMPTIONS
NONCONSUMPTIVE
NONCONTACT
NONCONTAGIOUS
NONCONTEMPORARY
NONCONTIGUOUS
NONCONTINGENT
NONCONTINUOUS
NONCONTRACT
NONCONTRACTUAL
NONCONTRIBUTORY
NONCONTROLLABLE
NONCONTROLLED
NONCONTROLLING
NONCONVENTIONAL
NONCONVERTIBLE
NONCOOPERATION

NONCOOPERATIONS
NONCOOPERATIVE
NONCOOPERATOR
NONCOOPERATORS
NONCOPLANAR
NONCORPORATE
NONCORRELATION
NONCORRELATIONS
NONCORRODIBLE
NONCORRODING
NONCORROSIVE
NONCOUNTRY
NONCOVERAGE
NONCOVERAGES
NONCREATIVE
NONCREATIVITIES
NONCREATIVITY
NONCREDENTIALED
NONCRIMINAL
NONCRIMINALS
NONCRITICAL
NONCROSSOVER
NONCRUSHABLE
NONCRYSTALLINE
NONCULINARY
NONCULTIVATED
NONCULTIVATION
NONCULTIVATIONS
NONCULTURAL
NONCUMULATIVE
NONCURRENT
NONCUSTODIAL
NONCUSTOMER
NONCUSTOMERS
NONCYCLICAL
NONDANCERS
NONDECEPTIVE
NONDECISION
NONDECISIONS
NONDECREASING
NONDEDUCTIBLE
NONDEDUCTIVE
NONDEFENSE
NONDEFERRABLE
NONDEFORMING
NONDEGENERATE
NONDEGRADABLE
NONDELEGATE
NONDELEGATES
NONDELIBERATE
NONDELINQUENT
NONDELINQUENTS
NONDELIVERIES
NONDELIVERY
NONDEMANDING
NONDEMANDS
NONDEMOCRATIC
NONDEPARTMENTAL
NONDEPENDENT
NONDEPENDENTS
NONDEPLETABLE
NONDEPLETING
NONDEPOSITION
NONDEPOSITIONS
NONDEPRESSED
NONDERIVATIVE
NONDESCRIPT
NONDESCRIPTIVE
NONDESCRIPTLY
NONDESCRIPTNESS
NONDESCRIPTS
NONDESTRUCTIVE
NONDETACHABLE
NONDEVELOPMENT
NONDEVELOPMENTS
NONDEVIANT
NONDIABETIC
NONDIABETICS
NONDIALYSABLE
NONDIALYZABLE
NONDIAPAUSING
NONDIDACTIC
NONDIFFUSIBLE

NONDIMENSIONAL
NONDIPLOMATIC
NONDIRECTED
NONDIRECTIONAL
NONDIRECTIVE
NONDISABLED
NONDISCLOSURE
NONDISCLOSURES
NONDISCOUNT
NONDISCURSIVE
NONDISJUNCTION
NONDISJUNCTIONS
NONDISPERSIVE
NONDISRUPTIVE
NONDISTINCTIVE
NONDIVERSIFIED
NONDIVIDING
NONDOCTORS
NONDOCTRINAIRE
NONDOCUMENTARY
NONDOGMATIC
NONDOMESTIC
NONDOMICILED
NONDOMINANT
NONDORMANT
NONDRAMATIC
NONDRINKER
NONDRINKERS
NONDRINKING
NONDRIVERS
NONDURABLE
NONEARNING
NONECONOMIC
NONECONOMIST
NONECONOMISTS
NONEDIBLES
NONEDITORIAL
NONEDUCATION
NONEDUCATIONAL
NONEFFECTIVE
NONEFFECTIVES
NONELASTIC
NONELECTED
NONELECTION
NONELECTIONS
NONELECTIVE
NONELECTRIC
NONELECTRICAL
NONELECTROLYTE
NONELECTROLYTES
NONELECTRONIC
NONELEMENTARY
NONEMERGENCIES
NONEMERGENCY
NONEMOTIONAL
NONEMPHATIC
NONEMPIRICAL
NONEMPLOYEE
NONEMPLOYEES
NONEMPLOYMENT
NONEMPLOYMENTS
NONENCAPSULATED
NONENFORCEMENT
NONENFORCEMENTS
NONENGAGEMENT
NONENGAGEMENTS
NONENGINEERING
NONENTITIES
NONENTRIES
NONENZYMATIC
NONENZYMIC
NONEQUILIBRIA
NONEQUILIBRIUM
NONEQUILIBRIUMS
NONEQUIVALENCE
NONEQUIVALENCES
NONEQUIVALENT
NONESSENTIAL
NONESSENTIALS
NONESTABLISHED
NONESTERIFIED
NONESUCHES
NONETHELESS

NONETHICAL
NONETHNICS
NONEVALUATIVE
NONEVIDENCE
NONEVIDENCES
NONEXCLUSIVE
NONEXECUTIVE
NONEXECUTIVES
NONEXEMPTS
NONEXISTENCE
NONEXISTENCES
NONEXISTENT
NONEXISTENTIAL
NONEXPENDABLE
NONEXPERIMENTAL
NONEXPERTS
NONEXPLANATORY
NONEXPLOITATION
NONEXPLOITATIVE
NONEXPLOITIVE
NONEXPLOSIVE
NONEXPOSED
NONFACTORS
NONFACTUAL
NONFACULTY
NONFAMILIAL
NONFAMILIES
NONFARMERS
NONFATTENING
NONFEASANCE
NONFEASANCES
NONFEDERAL
NONFEDERATED
NONFEMINIST
NONFEMINISTS
NONFERROUS
NONFICTION
NONFICTIONAL
NONFICTIONALLY
NONFICTIONS
NONFIGURATIVE
NONFILAMENTOUS
NONFILTERABLE
NONFINANCIAL
NONFISSIONABLE
NONFLAMMABILITY
NONFLAMMABLE
NONFLOWERING
NONFLUENCIES
NONFLUENCY
NONFLUORESCENT
NONFORFEITABLE
NONFORFEITURE
NONFORFEITURES
NONFREEZING
NONFRIVOLOUS
NONFULFILLMENT
NONFULFILLMENTS
NONFUNCTIONAL
NONFUNCTIONING
NONGASEOUS
NONGENETIC
NONGENITAL
NONGEOMETRICAL
NONGLAMOROUS
NONGOLFERS
NONGONOCOCCAL
NONGOVERNMENT
NONGOVERNMENTAL
NONGRADUATE
NONGRADUATES
NONGRAMMATICAL
NONGRANULAR
NONGREGARIOUS
NONGROWING
NONHALOGENATED
NONHANDICAPPED
NONHAPPENING
NONHAPPENINGS
NONHARMONIC
NONHAZARDOUS
NONHEMOLYTIC
NONHEREDITARY

NONHIERARCHICAL
NONHISTONE
NONHISTORICAL
NONHOMOGENEOUS
NONHOMOLOGOUS
NONHOMOSEXUAL
NONHOMOSEXUALS
NONHORMONAL
NONHOSPITAL
NONHOSPITALISED
NONHOSPITALIZED
NONHOSTILE
NONHOUSING
NONHUNTERS
NONHUNTING
NONHYGROSCOPIC
NONHYSTERICAL
NONIDENTICAL
NONIDENTITIES
NONIDENTITY
NONIDEOLOGICAL
NONILLIONS
NONILLIONTH
NONILLIONTHS
NONIMITATIVE
NONIMMIGRANT
NONIMMIGRANTS
NONIMPLICATION
NONIMPLICATIONS
NONIMPORTATION
NONIMPORTATIONS
NONINCLUSION
NONINCLUSIONS
NONINCREASING
NONINCUMBENT
NONINCUMBENTS
NONINDEPENDENCE
NONINDIGENOUS
NONINDIVIDUAL
NONINDUCTIVE
NONINDUSTRIAL
NONINDUSTRY
NONINFECTED
NONINFECTIOUS
NONINFECTIVE
NONINFESTED
NONINFLAMMABLE
NONINFLAMMATORY
NONINFLATIONARY
NONINFLECTIONAL
NONINFLUENCE
NONINFLUENCES
NONINFORMATION
NONINFORMATIONS
NONINFRINGEMENT
NONINITIAL
NONINITIATE
NONINITIATES
NONINSECTICIDAL
NONINSECTS
NONINSTALLMENT
NONINSTALLMENTS
NONINSTRUMENTAL
NONINSURANCE
NONINSURED
NONINTEGRAL
NONINTEGRATED
NONINTELLECTUAL
NONINTERACTING
NONINTERACTIVE
NONINTERCOURSE
NONINTERCOURSES
NONINTEREST
NONINTERFERENCE
NONINTERSECTING
NONINTERVENTION
NONINTIMIDATING
NONINTOXICANT
NONINTOXICANTS
NONINTOXICATING
NONINTRUSIVE
NONINTUITIVE
NONINVASIVE

NONINVOLVED
NONINVOLVEMENT
NONINVOLVEMENTS
NONIONIZING
NONIRRADIATED
NONIRRIGATED
NONIRRITANT
NONIRRITANTS
NONIRRITATING
NONJOINDER
NONJOINDERS
NONJOINERS
NONJUDGEMENTAL
NONJUDGMENTAL
NONJUDICIAL
NONJUSTICIABLE
NONKOSHERS
NONLANDOWNER
NONLANDOWNERS
NONLANGUAGE
NONLANGUAGES
NONLAWYERS
NONLEGUMES
NONLEGUMINOUS
NONLEXICAL
NONLIBRARIAN
NONLIBRARIANS
NONLIBRARY
NONLINEARITIES
NONLINEARITY
NONLINGUISTIC
NONLIQUIDS
NONLITERAL
NONLITERARY
NONLITERATE
NONLITERATES
NONLIVINGS
NONLOGICAL
NONLUMINOUS
NONMAGNETIC
NONMAINSTREAM
NONMALIGNANT
NONMALLEABLE
NONMANAGEMENT
NONMANAGERIAL
NONMARITAL
NONMARKETS
NONMATERIAL
NONMATHEMATICAL
NONMATRICULATED
NONMEANINGFUL
NONMEASURABLE
NONMECHANICAL
NONMECHANISTIC
NONMEDICAL
NONMEETING
NONMEETINGS
NONMEMBERS
NONMEMBERSHIP
NONMEMBERSHIPS
NONMERCURIAL
NONMETALLIC
NONMETAMERIC
NONMETAPHORICAL
NONMETRICAL
NONMETROPOLITAN
NONMICROBIAL
NONMIGRANT
NONMIGRATORY
NONMILITANT
NONMILITANTS
NONMILITARY
NONMIMETIC
NONMINORITIES
NONMINORITY
NONMODERNS
NONMOLECULAR
NONMONETARIST
NONMONETARISTS
NONMONETARY
NONMONOGAMOUS
NONMORTALS
NONMOTILITIES

NONMOTILITY
NONMOTORISED
NONMOTORIZED
NONMUNICIPAL
NONMUSICAL
NONMUSICALS
NONMUSICIAN
NONMUSICIANS
NONMUTANTS
NONMYELINATED
NONMYSTICAL
NONNARRATIVE
NONNATIONAL
NONNATIONALS
NONNATIVES
NONNATURAL
NONNECESSITIES
NONNECESSITY
NONNEGATIVE
NONNEGLIGENT
NONNEGOTIABLE
NONNEGOTIABLES
NONNETWORK
NONNITROGENOUS
NONNORMATIVE
NONNUCLEAR
NONNUCLEATED
NONNUMERICAL
NONNUTRITIOUS
NONNUTRITIVE
NONOBJECTIVE
NONOBJECTIVISM
NONOBJECTIVISMS
NONOBJECTIVIST
NONOBJECTIVISTS
NONOBJECTIVITY
NONOBSCENE
NONOBSERVANCE
NONOBSERVANCES
NONOBSERVANT
NONOBVIOUS
NONOCCUPATIONAL
NONOCCURRENCE
NONOCCURRENCES
NONOFFICIAL
NONOFFICIALS
NONOPERATIC
NONOPERATING
NONOPERATIONAL
NONOPERATIVE
NONOPTIMAL
NONORGANIC
NONORGASMIC
NONORTHODOX
NONOVERLAPPING
NONOXIDISING
NONOXIDIZING
NONPAPISTS
NONPARALLEL
NONPARAMETRIC
NONPARASITIC
NONPAREILS
NONPARENTS
NONPARITIES
NONPARTICIPANT
NONPARTICIPANTS
NONPARTIES
NONPARTISAN
NONPARTISANSHIP
NONPARTIZAN
NONPARTIZANSHIP
NONPASSERINE
NONPASSIVE
NONPATHOGENIC
NONPAYMENT
NONPAYMENTS
NONPERFORMANCE
NONPERFORMANCES
NONPERFORMER
NONPERFORMERS
NONPERFORMING
NONPERISHABLE
NONPERISHABLES

NONPERMANENT
NONPERMISSIVE
NONPERSISTENT
NONPERSONAL
NONPERSONS
NONPETROLEUM
NONPHILOSOPHER
NONPHILOSOPHERS
NONPHONEMIC
NONPHONETIC
NONPHOSPHATE
NONPHOTOGRAPHIC
NONPHYSICAL
NONPHYSICIAN
NONPHYSICIANS
NONPLASTIC
NONPLASTICS
NONPLAYERS
NONPLAYING
NONPLUSING
NONPLUSSED
NONPLUSSES
NONPLUSSING
NONPOISONOUS
NONPOLARISABLE
NONPOLARIZABLE
NONPOLITICAL
NONPOLITICALLY
NONPOLITICIAN
NONPOLITICIANS
NONPOLLUTING
NONPOSSESSION
NONPOSSESSIONS
NONPRACTICAL
NONPRACTICING
NONPRACTISING
NONPREGNANT
NONPRESCRIPTION
NONPROBLEM
NONPROBLEMS
NONPRODUCING
NONPRODUCTIVE
NONPRODUCTIVITY
NONPROFESSIONAL
NONPROFESSORIAL
NONPROFITS
NONPROGRAM
NONPROGRAMMER
NONPROGRAMMERS
NONPROGRESSIVE
NONPROPRIETARY
NONPROSSED
NONPROSSES
NONPROSSING
NONPROTEIN
NONPSYCHIATRIC
NONPSYCHIATRIST
NONPSYCHOTIC
NONPUNITIVE
NONPURPOSIVE
NONQUANTIFIABLE
NONQUANTITATIVE
NONRACIALLY
NONRADIOACTIVE
NONRAILROAD
NONRANDOMNESS
NONRANDOMNESSES
NONRATIONAL
NONREACTIVE
NONREACTOR
NONREACTORS
NONREADERS
NONREADING
NONREALISTIC
NONRECEIPT
NONRECEIPTS
NONRECIPROCAL
NONRECOGNITION
NONRECOGNITIONS
NONRECOMBINANT
NONRECOMBINANTS
NONRECOURSE
NONRECURRENT

NONRECURRING
NONRECYCLABLE
NONRECYCLABLES
NONREDUCING
NONREDUNDANT
NONREFILLABLE
NONREFLECTING
NONREFLEXIVE
NONREFUNDABLE
NONREGULATED
NONREGULATION
NONRELATIVE
NONRELATIVES
NONRELATIVISTIC
NONRELEVANT
NONRELIGIOUS
NONRENEWABLE
NONRENEWAL
NONREPAYABLE
NONREPRODUCTIVE
NONRESIDENCE
NONRESIDENCES
NONRESIDENCIES
NONRESIDENCY
NONRESIDENT
NONRESIDENTIAL
NONRESIDENTS
NONRESISTANCE
NONRESISTANCES
NONRESISTANT
NONRESISTANTS
NONRESONANT
NONRESPONDENT
NONRESPONDENTS
NONRESPONDER
NONRESPONDERS
NONRESPONSE
NONRESPONSES
NONRESPONSIVE
NONRESTRICTED
NONRESTRICTIVE
NONRETRACTILE
NONRETROACTIVE
NONRETURNABLE
NONRETURNABLES
NONREUSABLE
NONREVERSIBLE
NONRHOTICITIES
NONRHOTICITY
NONRIOTERS
NONRIOTING
NONROTATING
NONROUTINE
NONRUMINANT
NONRUMINANTS
NONSALABLE
NONSAPONIFIABLE
NONSCHEDULED
NONSCIENCE
NONSCIENCES
NONSCIENTIFIC
NONSCIENTIST
NONSCIENTISTS
NONSEASONAL
NONSECRETOR
NONSECRETORS
NONSECRETORY
NONSECRETS
NONSECTARIAN
NONSEDIMENTABLE
NONSEGREGATED
NONSEGREGATION
NONSEGREGATIONS
NONSELECTED
NONSELECTIVE
NONSENSATIONAL
NONSENSICAL
NONSENSICALITY
NONSENSICALLY
NONSENSICALNESS
NONSENSITIVE
NONSENSUOUS
NONSENTENCE

NONSENTENCES
NONSEPTATE
NONSEQUENTIAL
NONSERIALS
NONSERIOUS
NONSHRINKABLE
NONSIGNERS
NONSIGNIFICANT
NONSIMULTANEOUS
NONSINKABLE
NONSKATERS
NONSKELETAL
NONSMOKERS
NONSMOKING
NONSOCIALIST
NONSOCIALISTS
NONSOLUTION
NONSOLUTIONS
NONSPATIAL
NONSPEAKER
NONSPEAKERS
NONSPEAKING
NONSPECIALIST
NONSPECIALISTS
NONSPECIFIC
NONSPECIFICALLY
NONSPECTACULAR
NONSPECULAR
NONSPECULATIVE
NONSPHERICAL
NONSPORTING
NONSTANDARD
NONSTAPLES
NONSTARTER
NONSTARTERS
NONSTATIONARY
NONSTATISTICAL
NONSTATIVE
NONSTATIVES
NONSTEROID
NONSTEROIDAL
NONSTEROIDS
NONSTORIES
NONSTRATEGIC
NONSTRIATED
NONSTRUCTURAL
NONSTRUCTURED
NONSTUDENT
NONSTUDENTS
NONSUBJECT
NONSUBJECTIVE
NONSUBJECTS
NONSUBSIDISED
NONSUBSIDIZED
NONSUCCESS
NONSUCCESSES
NONSUITING
NONSUPERVISORY
NONSUPPORT
NONSUPPORTS
NONSURGICAL
NONSWIMMER
NONSWIMMERS
NONSYLLABIC
NONSYMBOLIC
NONSYMMETRIC
NONSYMMETRICAL
NONSYNCHRONOUS
NONSYSTEMATIC
NONSYSTEMIC
NONSYSTEMS
NONTALKERS
NONTAXABLE
NONTEACHING
NONTECHNICAL
NONTEMPORAL
NONTENURED
NONTERMINAL
NONTERMINALS
NONTERMINATING
NONTHEATRICAL
NONTHEISTIC
NONTHEISTS

n

NONTHEOLOGICAL
NONTHEORETICAL
NONTHERAPEUTIC
NONTHERMAL
NONTHINKING
NONTHREATENING
NONTOBACCO
NONTOTALITARIAN
NONTRADITIONAL
NONTRANSFERABLE
NONTRANSITIVE
NONTREATMENT
NONTREATMENTS
NONTRIVIAL
NONTROPICAL
NONTURBULENT
NONTYPICAL
NONUNANIMOUS
NONUNIFORM
NONUNIFORMITIES
NONUNIFORMITY
NONUNIONISED
NONUNIONISM
NONUNIONISMS
NONUNIONIST
NONUNIONISTS
NONUNIONIZED
NONUNIQUENESS
NONUNIQUENESSES
NONUNIVERSAL
NONUNIVERSITY
NONUTILITARIAN
NONUTILITIES
NONUTILITY
NONUTOPIAN
NONVALIDITIES
NONVALIDITY
NONVANISHING
NONVASCULAR
NONVECTORS
NONVEGETARIAN
NONVEGETARIANS
NONVENOMOUS
NONVERBALLY
NONVETERAN
NONVETERANS
NONVIEWERS
NONVINTAGE
NONVIOLENCE
NONVIOLENCES
NONVIOLENT
NONVIOLENTLY
NONVIRGINS
NONVISCOUS
NONVOCATIONAL
NONVOLATILE
NONVOLCANIC
NONVOLUNTARY
NONWINNING
NONWORKERS
NONWORKING
NONWRITERS
NONYELLOWING
NOODLEDOMS
NOOGENESES
NOOGENESIS
NOOMETRIES
NOOSPHERES
NOOTROPICS
NORADRENALIN
NORADRENALINE
NORADRENALINES
NORADRENALINS
NORADRENERGIC
NOREPINEPHRINE
NOREPINEPHRINES
NORETHINDRONE
NORETHINDRONES
NORETHISTERONE
NORETHISTERONES
NORMALCIES
NORMALISABLE
NORMALISATION

NORMALISATIONS
NORMALISED
NORMALISER
NORMALISERS
NORMALISING
NORMALITIES
NORMALIZABLE
NORMALIZATION
NORMALIZATIONS
NORMALIZED
NORMALIZER
NORMALIZERS
NORMALIZES
NORMALIZING
NORMATIVELY
NORMATIVENESS
NORMATIVENESSES
NORMOTENSIVE
NORMOTENSIVES
NORMOTHERMIA
NORMOTHERMIAS
NORMOTHERMIC
NORSELLERS
NORSELLING
NORTHBOUND
NORTHCOUNTRYMAN
NORTHCOUNTRYMEN
NORTHEASTER
NORTHEASTERLIES
NORTHEASTERLY
NORTHEASTERN
NORTHEASTERS
NORTHEASTS
NORTHEASTWARD
NORTHEASTWARDLY
NORTHEASTWARDS
NORTHERING
NORTHERLIES
NORTHERLINESS
NORTHERLINESSES
NORTHERMOST
NORTHERNER
NORTHERNERS
NORTHERNISE
NORTHERNISED
NORTHERNISES
NORTHERNISING
NORTHERNISM
NORTHERNISMS
NORTHERNIZE
NORTHERNIZED
NORTHERNIZES
NORTHERNIZING
NORTHERNMOST
NORTHLANDS
NORTHWARDLY
NORTHWARDS
NORTHWESTER
NORTHWESTERLIES
NORTHWESTERLY
NORTHWESTERN
NORTHWESTERS
NORTHWESTS
NORTHWESTWARD
NORTHWESTWARDLY
NORTHWESTWARDS
NORTRIPTYLINE
NORTRIPTYLINES
NOSEBANDED
NOSEBLEEDING
NOSEBLEEDINGS
NOSEBLEEDS
NOSEDIVING
NOSEGUARDS
NOSEPIECES
NOSEWHEELS
NOSINESSES
NOSOCOMIAL
NOSOGRAPHER
NOSOGRAPHERS
NOSOGRAPHIC
NOSOGRAPHIES

NOSOGRAPHY
NOSOLOGICAL
NOSOLOGICALLY
NOSOLOGIES
NOSOLOGIST
NOSOLOGISTS
NOSOPHOBIA
NOSOPHOBIAS
NOSTALGIAS
NOSTALGICALLY
NOSTALGICS
NOSTALGIST
NOSTALGISTS
NOSTOLOGIC
NOSTOLOGICAL
NOSTOLOGIES
NOSTOMANIA
NOSTOMANIAS
NOSTOPATHIES
NOSTOPATHY
NOSTRADAMIC
NOTABILITIES
NOTABILITY
NOTABLENESS
NOTABLENESSES
NOTAPHILIC
NOTAPHILIES
NOTAPHILISM
NOTAPHILISMS
NOTAPHILIST
NOTAPHILISTS
NOTARIALLY
NOTARISATION
NOTARISATIONS
NOTARISING
NOTARIZATION
NOTARIZATIONS
NOTARIZING
NOTARYSHIP
NOTARYSHIPS
NOTATIONAL
NOTCHBACKS
NOTCHELLED
NOTCHELLING
NOTEDNESSES
NOTEPAPERS
NOTEWORTHILY
NOTEWORTHINESS
NOTEWORTHY
NOTHINGARIAN
NOTHINGARIANISM
NOTHINGARIANS
NOTHINGISM
NOTHINGISMS
NOTHINGNESS
NOTHINGNESSES
NOTICEABILITIES
NOTICEABILITY
NOTICEABLE
NOTICEABLY
NOTIFIABLE
NOTIFICATION
NOTIFICATIONS
NOTIONALIST
NOTIONALISTS
NOTIONALITIES
NOTIONALITY
NOTIONALLY
NOTIONISTS
NOTOCHORDAL
NOTOCHORDS
NOTODONTID
NOTODONTIDS
NOTONECTAL
NOTORIETIES
NOTORIOUSLY
NOTORIOUSNESS
NOTORIOUSNESSES
NOTORNISES
NOTOTHERIUM
NOTOTHERIUMS
NOTOUNGULATE
NOTOUNGULATES

NOTUNGULATE
NOTUNGULATES
NOTWITHSTANDING
NOUMENALISM
NOUMENALISMS
NOUMENALIST
NOUMENALISTS
NOUMENALITIES
NOUMENALITY
NOUMENALLY
NOURISHABLE
NOURISHERS
NOURISHING
NOURISHINGLY
NOURISHMENT
NOURISHMENTS
NOURITURES
NOURRITURE
NOURRITURES
NOUSELLING
NOVACULITE
NOVACULITES
NOVELETTES
NOVELETTISH
NOVELETTIST
NOVELETTISTS
NOVELISATION
NOVELISATIONS
NOVELISERS
NOVELISING
NOVELISTIC
NOVELISTICALLY
NOVELIZATION
NOVELIZATIONS
NOVELIZERS
NOVELIZING
NOVEMDECILLION
NOVEMDECILLIONS
NOVENARIES
NOVICEHOOD
NOVICEHOODS
NOVICESHIP
NOVICESHIPS
NOVICIATES
NOVITIATES
NOVOBIOCIN
NOVOBIOCINS
NOVOCAINES
NOVOCENTENARIES
NOVOCENTENARY
NOVODAMUSES
NOWCASTING
NOWCASTINGS
NOXIOUSNESS
NOXIOUSNESSES
NUBBINESSES
NUBIFEROUS
NUBIGENOUS
NUBILITIES
NUCIFEROUS
NUCIVOROUS
NUCLEARISATION
NUCLEARISATIONS
NUCLEARISE
NUCLEARISED
NUCLEARISES
NUCLEARISING
NUCLEARIZATION
NUCLEARIZATIONS
NUCLEARIZE
NUCLEARIZED
NUCLEARIZES
NUCLEARIZING
NUCLEATING
NUCLEATION
NUCLEATIONS
NUCLEATORS
NUCLEOCAPSID
NUCLEOCAPSIDS
NUCLEOLATE
NUCLEOLATED
NUCLEONICALLY
NUCLEONICS

NUCLEOPHILE
NUCLEOPHILES
NUCLEOPHILIC
NUCLEOPHILICITY
NUCLEOPLASM
NUCLEOPLASMATIC
NUCLEOPLASMIC
NUCLEOPLASMS
NUCLEOPROTEIN
NUCLEOPROTEINS
NUCLEOSIDE
NUCLEOSIDES
NUCLEOSOMAL
NUCLEOSOME
NUCLEOSOMES
NUCLEOSYNTHESES
NUCLEOSYNTHESIS
NUCLEOSYNTHETIC
NUCLEOTIDASE
NUCLEOTIDASES
NUCLEOTIDE
NUCLEOTIDES
NUDENESSES
NUDIBRANCH
NUDIBRANCHIATE
NUDIBRANCHIATES
NUDIBRANCHS
NUDICAUDATE
NUDICAULOUS
NUGATORINESS
NUGATORINESSES
NUGGETTING
NUISANCERS
NULLIFICATION
NULLIFICATIONS
NULLIFIDIAN
NULLIFIDIANS
NULLIFIERS
NULLIFYING
NULLIPARAE
NULLIPARAS
NULLIPARITIES
NULLIPARITY
NULLIPAROUS
NULLIPORES
NULLNESSES
NUMBERABLE
NUMBERINGS
NUMBERLESS
NUMBERLESSLY
NUMBERLESSNESS
NUMBERPLATE
NUMBERPLATES
NUMBFISHES
NUMBNESSES
NUMBSKULLS
NUMERABILITIES
NUMERABILITY
NUMERACIES
NUMERAIRES
NUMERATING
NUMERATION
NUMERATIONS
NUMERATIVE
NUMERATORS
NUMERICALLY
NUMEROLOGICAL
NUMEROLOGIES
NUMEROLOGIST
NUMEROLOGISTS
NUMEROLOGY
NUMEROSITIES
NUMEROSITY
NUMEROUSLY
NUMEROUSNESS
NUMEROUSNESSES
NUMINOUSES
NUMINOUSNESS
NUMINOUSNESSES
NUMISMATIC
NUMISMATICALLY
NUMISMATICS
NUMISMATIST

NUMISMATISTS
NUMISMATOLOGIES
NUMISMATOLOGIST
NUMISMATOLOGY
NUMMULATED
NUMMULATION
NUMMULATIONS
NUMMULITES
NUMMULITIC
NUMSKULLED
NUNCIATURE
NUNCIATURES
NUNCUPATED
NUNCUPATES
NUNCUPATING
NUNCUPATION
NUNCUPATIONS
NUNCUPATIVE
NUNCUPATORY
NUNNATIONS
NUNNISHNESS
NUNNISHNESSES
NUPTIALITIES
NUPTIALITY
NURSEHOUND
NURSEHOUNDS
NURSELINGS
NURSEMAIDED
NURSEMAIDING
NURSEMAIDS
NURSERYMAID
NURSERYMAIDS
NURSERYMAN
NURSERYMEN
NURTURABLE
NURTURANCE
NURTURANCES
NUTATIONAL
NUTBUTTERS
NUTCRACKER
NUTCRACKERS
NUTGRASSES
NUTHATCHES
NUTJOBBERS
NUTMEGGING
NUTPECKERS
NUTRACEUTICAL
NUTRACEUTICALS
NUTRIMENTAL
NUTRIMENTS
NUTRITIONAL
NUTRITIONALLY
NUTRITIONARY
NUTRITIONIST
NUTRITIONISTS
NUTRITIONS
NUTRITIOUS
NUTRITIOUSLY
NUTRITIOUSNESS
NUTRITIVELY
NUTRITIVES
NUTTINESSES
NYCHTHEMERAL
NYCHTHEMERON
NYCHTHEMERONS
NYCTAGINACEOUS
NYCTALOPES
NYCTALOPIA
NYCTALOPIAS
NYCTALOPIC
NYCTANTHOUS
NYCTINASTIC
NYCTINASTIES
NYCTINASTY
NYCTITROPIC
NYCTITROPISM
NYCTITROPISMS
NYCTOPHOBIA
NYCTOPHOBIAS
NYCTOPHOBIC
NYMPHAEACEOUS
NYMPHAEUMS
NYMPHALIDS

n

NYMPHETTES   NYMPHOLEPT   NYMPHOMANIA   NYMPHOMANIACS   NYSTAGMUSES
NYMPHOLEPSIES   NYMPHOLEPTIC   NYMPHOMANIAC   NYMPHOMANIAS
NYMPHOLEPSY   NYMPHOLEPTS   NYMPHOMANIACAL   NYSTAGMOID

Oo

o

OAFISHNESS	OBJECTLESS	OBSCENENESSES	OBSOLESCES	OBTRUNCATES	OCCULTNESSES
OAFISHNESSES	OBJECTLESSNESS	OBSCENITIES	OBSOLESCING	OBTRUNCATING	OCCUPANCES
OAKENSHAWS	OBJURATION	OBSCURANTIC	OBSOLETELY	OBTRUSIONS	OCCUPANCIES
OARSMANSHIP	OBJURATIONS	OBSCURANTISM	OBSOLETENESS	OBTRUSIVELY	OCCUPANCIES
OARSMANSHIPS	OBJURGATED	OBSCURANTISMS	OBSOLETENESSES	OBTRUSIVENESS	OCCUPATING
OASTHOUSES	OBJURGATES	OBSCURANTIST	OBSOLETING	OBTRUSIVENESSES	OCCUPATION
OBBLIGATOS	OBJURGATING	OBSCURANTISTS	OBSOLETION	OBTUNDENTS	OCCUPATIONAL
OBCOMPRESSED	OBJURGATION	OBSCURANTS	OBSOLETIONS	OBTUNDITIES	OCCUPATIONALLY
OBDURACIES	OBJURGATIONS	OBSCURATION	OBSOLETISM	OBTURATING	OCCUPATIONS
OBDURATELY	OBJURGATIVE	OBSCURATIONS	OBSOLETISMS	OBTURATION	OCCUPATIVE
OBDURATENESS	OBJURGATOR	OBSCUREMENT	OBSTETRICAL	OBTURATIONS	OCCURRENCE
OBDURATENESSES	OBJURGATORS	OBSCUREMENTS	OBSTETRICALLY	OBTURATORS	OCCURRENCES
OBDURATING	OBJURGATORY	OBSCURENESS	OBSTETRICIAN	OBTUSENESS	OCCURRENTS
OBDURATION	OBLANCEOLATE	OBSCURENESSES	OBSTETRICIANS	OBTUSENESSES	OCEANARIUM
OBDURATIONS	OBLATENESS	OBSCURITIES	OBSTETRICS	OBTUSITIES	OCEANARIUMS
OBEDIENCES	OBLATENESSES	OBSECRATED	OBSTINACIES	OBUMBRATED	OCEANFRONT
OBEDIENTIAL	OBLATIONAL	OBSECRATES	OBSTINATELY	OBUMBRATES	OCEANFRONTS
OBEDIENTIARIES	OBLIGATELY	OBSECRATING	OBSTINATENESS	OBUMBRATING	OCEANGOING
OBEDIENTIARY	OBLIGATING	OBSECRATION	OBSTINATENESSES	OBUMBRATION	OCEANOGRAPHER
OBEDIENTLY	OBLIGATION	OBSECRATIONS	OBSTIPATION	OBUMBRATIONS	OCEANOGRAPHERS
OBEISANCES	OBLIGATIONAL	OBSEQUIOUS	OBSTIPATIONS	OBVENTIONS	OCEANOGRAPHIC
OBEISANTLY	OBLIGATIONS	OBSEQUIOUSLY	OBSTREPERATE	OBVERSIONS	OCEANOGRAPHICAL
OBELISCOID	OBLIGATIVE	OBSEQUIOUSNESS	OBSTREPERATED	OBVIATIONS	OCEANOGRAPHIES
OBELISKOID	OBLIGATORILY	OBSERVABILITIES	OBSTREPERATES	OBVIOUSNESS	OCEANOGRAPHY
OBESENESSES	OBLIGATORINESS	OBSERVABILITY	OBSTREPERATING	OBVIOUSNESSES	OCEANOLOGICAL
OBFUSCATED	OBLIGATORS	OBSERVABLE	OBSTREPEROUS	OBVOLUTION	OCEANOLOGIES
OBFUSCATES	OBLIGATORY	OBSERVABLENESS	OBSTREPEROUSLY	OBVOLUTIONS	OCEANOLOGIST
OBFUSCATING	OBLIGEMENT	OBSERVABLES	OBSTRICTION	OBVOLUTIVE	OCEANOLOGISTS
OBFUSCATION	OBLIGEMENTS	OBSERVABLY	OBSTRICTIONS	OCCASIONAL	OCEANOLOGY
OBFUSCATIONS	OBLIGINGLY	OBSERVANCE	OBSTROPALOUS	OCCASIONALISM	OCELLATION
OBFUSCATORY	OBLIGINGNESS	OBSERVANCES	OBSTROPULOUS	OCCASIONALISMS	OCELLATIONS
OBITUARIES	OBLIGINGNESSES	OBSERVANCIES	OBSTRUCTED	OCCASIONALIST	OCHLOCRACIES
OBITUARIST	OBLIQUATION	OBSERVANCY	OBSTRUCTER	OCCASIONALISTS	OCHLOCRACY
OBITUARISTS	OBLIQUATIONS	OBSERVANTLY	OBSTRUCTERS	OCCASIONALITIES	OCHLOCRATIC
OBJECTIFICATION	OBLIQUENESS	OBSERVANTS	OBSTRUCTING	OCCASIONALITY	OCHLOCRATICAL
OBJECTIFIED	OBLIQUENESSES	OBSERVATION	OBSTRUCTION	OCCASIONALLY	OCHLOCRATICALLY
OBJECTIFIES	OBLIQUITIES	OBSERVATIONAL	OBSTRUCTIONAL	OCCASIONED	OCHLOCRATS
OBJECTIFYING	OBLIQUITOUS	OBSERVATIONALLY	OBSTRUCTIONALLY	OCCASIONER	OCHLOPHOBIA
OBJECTIONABLE	OBLITERATE	OBSERVATIONS	OBSTRUCTIONISM	OCCASIONERS	OCHLOPHOBIAC
OBJECTIONABLY	OBLITERATED	OBSERVATIVE	OBSTRUCTIONISMS	OCCASIONING	OCHLOPHOBIACS
OBJECTIONS	QBLITERATES	OBSERVATOR	OBSTRUCTIONIST	OCCIDENTAL	OCHLOPHOBIAS
OBJECTIVAL	OBLITERATING	OBSERVATORIES	OBSTRUCTIONISTS	OCCIDENTALISE	OCHLOPHOBIC
OBJECTIVATE	OBLITERATION	OBSERVATORS	OBSTRUCTIONS	OCCIDENTALISED	OCHRACEOUS
OBJECTIVATED	OBLITERATIONS	OBSERVATORY	OBSTRUCTIVE	OCCIDENTALISES	OCHROLEUCOUS
OBJECTIVATES	OBLITERATIVE	OBSERVINGLY	OBSTRUCTIVELY	OCCIDENTALISING	OCTACHORDAL
OBJECTIVATING	OBLITERATOR	OBSESSIONAL	OBSTRUCTIVENESS	OCCIDENTALISM	OCTACHORDS
OBJECTIVATION	OBLITERATORS	OBSESSIONALLY	OBSTRUCTIVES	OCCIDENTALISMS	OCTAGONALLY
OBJECTIVATIONS	OBLIVIOUSLY	OBSESSIONIST	OBSTRUCTOR	OCCIDENTALIST	OCTAHEDRAL
OBJECTIVELY	OBLIVIOUSNESS	OBSESSIONISTS	OBSTRUCTORS	OCCIDENTALISTS	OCTAHEDRALLY
OBJECTIVENESS	OBLIVIOUSNESSES	OBSESSIONS	OBSTRUENTS	OCCIDENTALIZE	OCTAHEDRITE
OBJECTIVENESSES	OBLIVISCENCE	OBSESSIVELY	OBTAINABILITIES	OCCIDENTALIZED	OCTAHEDRITES
OBJECTIVES	OBLIVISCENCES	OBSESSIVENESS	OBTAINABILITY	OCCIDENTALIZES	OCTAHEDRON
OBJECTIVISE	OBMUTESCENCE	OBSESSIVENESSES	OBTAINABLE	OCCIDENTALIZING	OCTAHEDRONS
OBJECTIVISED	OBMUTESCENCES	OBSESSIVES	OBTAINMENT	OCCIDENTALLY	OCTAMEROUS
OBJECTIVISES	OBMUTESCENT	OBSIDIONAL	OBTAINMENTS	OCCIDENTALS	OCTAMETERS
OBJECTIVISING	OBNOXIOUSLY	OBSIDIONARY	OBTEMPERATE	OCCIPITALLY	OCTANDRIAN
OBJECTIVISM	OBNOXIOUSNESS	OBSIGNATED	OBTEMPERATED	OCCIPITALS	OCTANDROUS
OBJECTIVISMS	OBNOXIOUSNESSES	OBSIGNATES	OBTEMPERATES	OCCLUDENTS	OCTANEDIOIC
OBJECTIVIST	OBNUBILATE	OBSIGNATING	OBTEMPERATING	OCCLUSIONS	OCTANGULAR
OBJECTIVISTIC	OBNUBILATED	OBSIGNATION	OBTEMPERED	OCCLUSIVENESS	OCTAPEPTIDE
OBJECTIVISTS	OBNUBILATES	OBSIGNATIONS	OBTEMPERING	OCCLUSIVENESSES	OCTAPEPTIDES
OBJECTIVITIES	OBNUBILATING	OBSIGNATORY	OBTENTIONS	OCCLUSIVES	OCTAPLOIDIES
OBJECTIVITY	OBNUBILATION	OBSOLESCED	OBTESTATION	OCCULTATION	OCTAPLOIDS
OBJECTIVIZE	OBNUBILATIONS	OBSOLESCENCE	OBTESTATIONS	OCCULTATIONS	OCTAPLOIDY
OBJECTIVIZED	OBREPTIONS	OBSOLESCENCES	OBTRUDINGS	OCCULTISMS	OCTAPODIES
OBJECTIVIZES	OBREPTITIOUS	OBSOLESCENT	OBTRUNCATE	OCCULTISTS	OCTARCHIES
OBJECTIVIZING	OBSCENENESS	OBSOLESCENTLY	OBTRUNCATED	OCCULTNESS	OCTASTICHON
					OCTASTICHONS

OCTASTICHOUS
OCTASTICHS
OCTASTROPHIC
OCTASTYLES
OCTAVALENT
OCTENNIALLY
OCTILLIONS
OCTILLIONTH
OCTILLIONTHS
OCTINGENARIES
OCTINGENARY
OCTINGENTENARY
OCTOCENTENARIES
OCTOCENTENARY
OCTODECILLION
OCTODECILLIONS
OCTODECIMO
OCTODECIMOS
OCTOGENARIAN
OCTOGENARIANS
OCTOGENARIES
OCTOGENARY
OCTOGYNOUS
OCTOHEDRON
OCTOHEDRONS
OCTONARIAN
OCTONARIANS
OCTONARIES
OCTONARIUS
OCTONOCULAR
OCTOPETALOUS
OCTOPLOIDS
OCTOPODANS
OCTOPODOUS
OCTOPUSHER
OCTOPUSHERS
OCTOPUSHES
OCTOSEPALOUS
OCTOSTICHOUS
OCTOSTYLES
OCTOSYLLABIC
OCTOSYLLABICS
OCTOSYLLABLE
OCTOSYLLABLES
OCTOTHORPS
OCTUPLICATE
OCTUPLICATES
OCULARISTS
OCULOMOTOR
ODALISQUES
ODDSMAKERS
ODIOUSNESS
ODIOUSNESSES
ODOMETRIES
ODONATISTS
ODONATOLOGIES
ODONATOLOGIST
ODONATOLOGISTS
ODONATOLOGY
ODONTALGIA
ODONTALGIAS
ODONTALGIC
ODONTALGIES
ODONTOBLAST
ODONTOBLASTIC
ODONTOBLASTS
ODONTOCETE
ODONTOCETES
ODONTOGENIC
ODONTOGENIES
ODONTOGENY
ODONTOGLOSSUM
ODONTOGLOSSUMS
ODONTOGRAPH
ODONTOGRAPHIES
ODONTOGRAPHS
ODONTOGRAPHY
ODONTOLITE
ODONTOLITES
ODONTOLOGIC
ODONTOLOGICAL
ODONTOLOGIES
ODONTOLOGIST

ODONTOLOGISTS
ODONTOLOGY
ODONTOMATA
ODONTOMATOUS
ODONTOPHOBIA
ODONTOPHOBIAS
ODONTOPHORAL
ODONTOPHORAN
ODONTOPHORE
ODONTOPHORES
ODONTOPHOROUS
ODONTORHYNCHOUS
ODONTORNITHES
ODONTOSTOMATOUS
ODORIFEROUS
ODORIFEROUSLY
ODORIFEROUSNESS
ODORIMETRIES
ODORIMETRY
ODORIPHORE
ODORIPHORES
ODOROUSNESS
ODOROUSNESSES
OECOLOGICAL
OECOLOGICALLY
OECOLOGIES
OECOLOGIST
OECOLOGISTS
OECUMENICAL
OECUMENICALLY
OEDEMATOSE
OEDEMATOUS
OEDOMETERS
OENOLOGICAL
OENOLOGIES
OENOLOGIST
OENOLOGISTS
OENOMANCIES
OENOMANIAS
OENOMETERS
OENOPHILES
OENOPHILIES
OENOPHILIST
OENOPHILISTS
OENOTHERAS
OESOPHAGEAL
OESOPHAGITIS
OESOPHAGITISES
OESOPHAGOSCOPE
OESOPHAGOSCOPES
OESOPHAGOSCOPY
OESOPHAGUS
OESTRADIOL
OESTRADIOLS
OESTROGENIC
OESTROGENICALLY
OESTROGENS
OFFENCEFUL
OFFENCELESS
OFFENDEDLY
OFFENDRESS
OFFENDRESSES
OFFENSELESS
OFFENSIVELY
OFFENSIVENESS
OFFENSIVENESSES
OFFENSIVES
OFFERTORIES
OFFHANDEDLY
OFFHANDEDNESS
OFFHANDEDNESSES
OFFICEHOLDER
OFFICEHOLDERS
OFFICERING
OFFICIALDOM
OFFICIALDOMS
OFFICIALESE
OFFICIALESES
OFFICIALISM
OFFICIALISMS
OFFICIALITIES
OFFICIALITY
OFFICIALLY

OFFICIALTIES
OFFICIALTY
OFFICIANTS
OFFICIARIES
OFFICIATED
OFFICIATES
OFFICIATING
OFFICIATION
OFFICIATIONS
OFFICIATOR
OFFICIATORS
OFFICINALLY
OFFICINALS
OFFICIOUSLY
OFFICIOUSNESS
OFFICIOUSNESSES
OFFISHNESS
OFFISHNESSES
OFFLOADING
OFFPRINTED
OFFPRINTING
OFFSADDLED
OFFSADDLES
OFFSADDLING
OFFSCOURING
OFFSCOURINGS
OFFSEASONS
OFFSETABLE
OFFSETTING
OFFSHORING
OFFSHORINGS
OFFSPRINGS
OFTENNESSES
OFTENTIMES
OILINESSES
OINOLOGIES
OLDFANGLED
OLEAGINOUS
OLEAGINOUSLY
OLEAGINOUSNESS
OLEANDOMYCIN
OLEANDOMYCINS
OLECRANONS
OLEIFEROUS
OLEOGRAPHIC
OLEOGRAPHIES
OLEOGRAPHS
OLEOGRAPHY
OLEOMARGARIN
OLEOMARGARINE
OLEOMARGARINES
OLEOMARGARINS
OLEOPHILIC
OLEORESINOUS
OLEORESINS
OLERACEOUS
OLFACTIBLE
OLFACTIONS
OLFACTOLOGIES
OLFACTOLOGIST
OLFACTOLOGISTS
OLFACTOLOGY
OLFACTOMETER
OLFACTOMETERS
OLFACTOMETRIES
OLFACTOMETRY
OLFACTORIES
OLFACTRONICS
OLIGAEMIAS
OLIGARCHAL
OLIGARCHIC
OLIGARCHICAL
OLIGARCHICALLY
OLIGARCHIES
OLIGOCHAETE
OLIGOCHAETES
OLIGOCHROME
OLIGOCHROMES
OLIGOCLASE
OLIGOCLASES
OLIGOCYTHAEMIA
OLIGOCYTHAEMIAS
OLIGODENDROCYTE

OLIGODENDROGLIA
OLIGOGENES
OLIGOMERIC
OLIGOMERISATION
OLIGOMERIZATION
OLIGOMEROUS
OLIGONUCLEOTIDE
OLIGOPEPTIDE
OLIGOPEPTIDES
OLIGOPHAGIES
OLIGOPHAGOUS
OLIGOPHAGY
OLIGOPOLIES
OLIGOPOLISTIC
OLIGOPSONIES
OLIGOPSONISTIC
OLIGOPSONY
OLIGOSACCHARIDE
OLIGOSPERMIA
OLIGOSPERMIAS
OLIGOTROPHIC
OLIGOTROPHIES
OLIGOTROPHY
OLIGURESES
OLIGURESIS
OLIGURETIC
OLIVACEOUS
OLIVENITES
OLIVINITIC
OLOGOANING
OLOLIUQUIS
OMBROGENOUS
OMBROMETER
OMBROMETERS
OMBROPHILE
OMBROPHILES
OMBROPHILOUS
OMBROPHILS
OMBROPHOBE
OMBROPHOBES
OMBROPHOBOUS
OMBUDSMANSHIP
OMBUDSMANSHIPS
OMINOUSNESS
OMINOUSNESSES
OMISSIVENESS
OMISSIVENESSES
OMITTANCES
OMMATIDIAL
OMMATIDIUM
OMMATOPHORE
OMMATOPHORES
OMMATOPHOROUS
OMNIBENEVOLENCE
OMNIBENEVOLENT
OMNIBUSSES
OMNICOMPETENCE
OMNICOMPETENCES
OMNICOMPETENT
OMNIDIRECTIONAL
OMNIFARIOUS
OMNIFARIOUSLY
OMNIFARIOUSNESS
OMNIFEROUS
OMNIFICENCE
OMNIFICENCES
OMNIFICENT
OMNIFORMITIES
OMNIFORMITY
OMNIGENOUS
OMNIPARITIES
OMNIPARITY
OMNIPAROUS
OMNIPATIENT
OMNIPOTENCE
OMNIPOTENCES
OMNIPOTENCIES
OMNIPOTENCY
OMNIPOTENT
OMNIPOTENTLY
OMNIPOTENTS
OMNIPRESENCE
OMNIPRESENCES

OMNIPRESENT
OMNIRANGES
OMNISCIENCE
OMNISCIENCES
OMNISCIENT
OMNISCIENTLY
OMNIVORIES
OMNIVOROUS
OMNIVOROUSLY
OMNIVOROUSNESS
OMOPHAGIAS
OMOPHAGIES
OMOPHAGOUS
OMOPHORION
OMOPLATOSCOPIES
OMOPLATOSCOPY
OMPHACITES
OMPHALOMANCIES
OMPHALOMANCY
OMPHALOSKEPSES
OMPHALOSKEPSIS
ONAGRACEOUS
ONCHOCERCIASES
ONCHOCERCIASIS
ONCOGENESES
ONCOGENESIS
ONCOGENETICIST
ONCOGENETICISTS
ONCOGENICITIES
ONCOGENICITY
ONCOGENOUS
ONCOLOGICAL
ONCOLOGIES
ONCOLOGIST
ONCOLOGISTS
ONCOLYTICS
ONCOMETERS
ONCORNAVIRUS
ONCORNAVIRUSES
ONCOTOMIES
ONCOVIRUSES
ONDOGRAPHS
ONEIRICALLY
ONEIROCRITIC
ONEIROCRITICAL
ONEIROCRITICISM
ONEIROCRITICS
ONEIRODYNIA
ONEIRODYNIAS
ONEIROLOGIES
ONEIROLOGY
ONEIROMANCER
ONEIROMANCERS
ONEIROMANCIES
ONEIROMANCY
ONEIROSCOPIES
ONEIROSCOPIST
ONEIROSCOPISTS
ONEIROSCOPY
ONEROUSNESS
ONEROUSNESSES
ONGOINGNESS
ONGOINGNESSES
ONIONSKINS
ONOCENTAUR
ONOCENTAURS
ONOMASIOLOGIES
ONOMASIOLOGY
ONOMASTICALLY
ONOMASTICIAN
ONOMASTICIANS
ONOMASTICON
ONOMASTICONS
ONOMASTICS
ONOMATOLOGIES
ONOMATOLOGIST
ONOMATOLOGISTS
ONOMATOLOGY
ONOMATOPOEIA
ONOMATOPOEIAS
ONOMATOPOEIC
ONOMATOPOESES
ONOMATOPOESIS

ONOMATOPOETIC
ONOMATOPOIESES
ONOMATOPOIESIS
ONSETTINGS
ONSHORINGS
ONSLAUGHTS
ONTOGENESES
ONTOGENESIS
ONTOGENETIC
ONTOGENETICALLY
ONTOGENICALLY
ONTOGENIES
ONTOLOGICAL
ONTOLOGICALLY
ONTOLOGIES
ONTOLOGIST
ONTOLOGISTS
ONYCHITISES
ONYCHOCRYPTOSES
ONYCHOCRYPTOSIS
ONYCHOMANCIES
ONYCHOMANCY
ONYCHOPHAGIES
ONYCHOPHAGIST
ONYCHOPHAGISTS
ONYCHOPHAGY
ONYCHOPHORAN
ONYCHOPHORANS
OOPHORECTOMIES
OOPHORECTOMISE
OOPHORECTOMISED
OOPHORECTOMISES
OOPHORECTOMIZE
OOPHORECTOMIZED
OOPHORECTOMIZES
OOPHORECTOMY
OOPHORITIC
OOPHORITIS
OOPHORITISES
OOZINESSES
OPACIFIERS
OPACIFYING
OPALESCENCE
OPALESCENCES
OPALESCENT
OPALESCENTLY
OPALESCING
OPAQUENESS
OPAQUENESSES
OPEIDOSCOPE
OPEIDOSCOPES
OPENABILITIES
OPENABILITY
OPENHANDED
OPENHANDEDLY
OPENHANDEDNESS
OPENHEARTED
OPENHEARTEDLY
OPENHEARTEDNESS
OPENMOUTHED
OPENMOUTHEDLY
OPENMOUTHEDNESS
OPENNESSES
OPERABILITIES
OPERABILITY
OPERAGOERS
OPERAGOING
OPERAGOINGS
OPERATICALLY
OPERATIONAL
OPERATIONALISM
OPERATIONALISMS
OPERATIONALIST
OPERATIONALISTS
OPERATIONALLY
OPERATIONISM
OPERATIONISMS
OPERATIONIST
OPERATIONISTS
OPERATIONS
OPERATISED
OPERATISES
OPERATISING

OPERATIVELY
OPERATIVENESS
OPERATIVENESSES
OPERATIVES
OPERATIVITIES
OPERATIVITY
OPERATIZED
OPERATIZES
OPERATIZING
OPERATORLESS
OPERCULARS
OPERCULATE
OPERCULATED
OPERCULUMS
OPERETTIST
OPERETTISTS
OPEROSENESS
OPEROSENESSES
OPEROSITIES
OPHICALCITE
OPHICALCITES
OPHICLEIDE
OPHICLEIDES
OPHIDIARIA
OPHIDIARIUM
OPHIDIARIUMS
OPHIOLATER
OPHIOLATERS
OPHIOLATRIES
OPHIOLATROUS
OPHIOLATRY
OPHIOLITES
OPHIOLITIC
OPHIOLOGIC
OPHIOLOGICAL
OPHIOLOGIES
OPHIOLOGIST
OPHIOLOGISTS
OPHIOMORPH
OPHIOMORPHIC
OPHIOMORPHOUS
OPHIOMORPHS
OPHIOPHAGOUS
OPHIOPHILIST
OPHIOPHILISTS
OPHIUROIDS
OPHTHALMIA
OPHTHALMIAS
OPHTHALMIC
OPHTHALMIST
OPHTHALMISTS
OPHTHALMITIS
OPHTHALMITISES
OPHTHALMOLOGIC
OPHTHALMOLOGIES
OPHTHALMOLOGIST
OPHTHALMOLOGY
OPHTHALMOMETER
OPHTHALMOMETERS
OPHTHALMOMETRY
OPHTHALMOPHOBIA
OPHTHALMOPLEGIA
OPHTHALMOSCOPE
OPHTHALMOSCOPES
OPHTHALMOSCOPIC
OPHTHALMOSCOPY
OPINICUSES
OPINIONATED
OPINIONATEDLY
OPINIONATEDNESS
OPINIONATELY
OPINIONATIVE
OPINIONATIVELY
OPINIONATOR
OPINIONATORS
OPINIONIST
OPINIONISTS
OPISOMETER
OPISOMETERS
OPISTHOBRANCH
OPISTHOBRANCHS
OPISTHOCOELIAN
OPISTHOCOELOUS

OPISTHODOMOI
OPISTHODOMOS
OPISTHOGLOSSAL
OPISTHOGNATHISM
OPISTHOGNATHOUS
OPISTHOGRAPH
OPISTHOGRAPHIC
OPISTHOGRAPHIES
OPISTHOGRAPHS
OPISTHOGRAPHY
OPISTHOSOMA
OPISTHOSOMATA
OPISTHOTONIC
OPISTHOTONOS
OPISTHOTONOSES
OPOBALSAMS
OPODELDOCS
OPOPANAXES
OPOTHERAPIES
OPOTHERAPY
OPPIGNERATE
OPPIGNERATED
OPPIGNERATES
OPPIGNERATING
OPPIGNORATE
OPPIGNORATED
OPPIGNORATES
OPPIGNORATING
OPPIGNORATION
OPPIGNORATIONS
OPPILATING
OPPILATION
OPPILATIONS
OPPILATIVE
OPPONENCIES
OPPORTUNELY
OPPORTUNENESS
OPPORTUNENESSES
OPPORTUNISM
OPPORTUNISMS
OPPORTUNIST
OPPORTUNISTIC
OPPORTUNISTS
OPPORTUNITIES
OPPORTUNITY
OPPOSABILITIES
OPPOSABILITY
OPPOSELESS
OPPOSINGLY
OPPOSITELY
OPPOSITENESS
OPPOSITENESSES
OPPOSITION
OPPOSITIONAL
OPPOSITIONIST
OPPOSITIONISTS
OPPOSITIONLESS
OPPOSITIONS
OPPOSITIVE
OPPRESSING
OPPRESSINGLY
OPPRESSION
OPPRESSIONS
OPPRESSIVE
OPPRESSIVELY
OPPRESSIVENESS
OPPRESSORS
OPPROBRIOUS
OPPROBRIOUSLY
OPPROBRIOUSNESS
OPPROBRIUM
OPPROBRIUMS
OPPUGNANCIES
OPPUGNANCY
OPPUGNANTLY
OPPUGNANTS
OPSIMATHIES
OPSIOMETER
OPSIOMETERS
OPSOMANIAC
OPSOMANIACS
OPSOMANIAS
OPSONIFICATION

OPSONIFICATIONS
OPSONIFIED
OPSONIFIES
OPSONIFYING
OPSONISATION
OPSONISATIONS
OPSONISING
OPSONIZATION
OPSONIZATIONS
OPSONIZING
OPTATIVELY
OPTIMALISATION
OPTIMALISATIONS
OPTIMALISE
OPTIMALISED
OPTIMALISES
OPTIMALISING
OPTIMALITIES
OPTIMALITY
OPTIMALIZATION
OPTIMALIZATIONS
OPTIMALIZE
OPTIMALIZED
OPTIMALIZES
OPTIMALIZING
OPTIMISATION
OPTIMISATIONS
OPTIMISERS
OPTIMISING
OPTIMISTIC
OPTIMISTICAL
OPTIMISTICALLY
OPTIMIZATION
OPTIMIZATIONS
OPTIMIZERS
OPTIMIZING
OPTIONALITIES
OPTIONALITY
OPTIONALLY
OPTOACOUSTIC
OPTOELECTRONIC
OPTOELECTRONICS
OPTOKINETIC
OPTOLOGIES
OPTOLOGIST
OPTOLOGISTS
OPTOMETERS
OPTOMETRIC
OPTOMETRICAL
OPTOMETRIES
OPTOMETRIST
OPTOMETRISTS
OPTOPHONES
OPULENCIES
ORACULARITIES
ORACULARITY
ORACULARLY
ORACULARNESS
ORACULARNESSES
ORACULOUSLY
ORACULOUSNESS
ORACULOUSNESSES
ORANGEADES
ORANGERIES
ORANGEWOOD
ORANGEWOODS
ORANGUTANS
ORATORIANS
ORATORICAL
ORATORICALLY
ORATRESSES
ORBICULARES
ORBICULARIS
ORBICULARITIES
ORBICULARITY
ORBICULARLY
ORBICULATE
ORBICULATED
ORCHARDING
ORCHARDINGS
ORCHARDIST
ORCHARDISTS
ORCHARDMAN

ORCHARDMEN
ORCHESOGRAPHIES
ORCHESOGRAPHY
ORCHESTICS
ORCHESTRAL
ORCHESTRALIST
ORCHESTRALISTS
ORCHESTRALLY
ORCHESTRAS
ORCHESTRATE
ORCHESTRATED
ORCHESTRATER
ORCHESTRATERS
ORCHESTRATES
ORCHESTRATING
ORCHESTRATION
ORCHESTRATIONAL
ORCHESTRATIONS
ORCHESTRATOR
ORCHESTRATORS
ORCHESTRIC
ORCHESTRINA
ORCHESTRINAS
ORCHESTRION
ORCHESTRIONS
ORCHIDACEOUS
ORCHIDECTOMIES
ORCHIDECTOMY
ORCHIDEOUS
ORCHIDISTS
ORCHIDLIKE
ORCHIDOLOGIES
ORCHIDOLOGIST
ORCHIDOLOGISTS
ORCHIDOLOGY
ORCHIDOMANIA
ORCHIDOMANIAC
ORCHIDOMANIACS
ORCHIDOMANIAS
ORCHIECTOMIES
ORCHIECTOMY
ORCHITISES
ORDAINABLE
ORDAINMENT
ORDAINMENTS
ORDERLINESS
ORDERLINESSES
ORDINAIRES
ORDINANCES
ORDINARIER
ORDINARIES
ORDINARIEST
ORDINARILY
ORDINARINESS
ORDINARINESSES
ORDINATELY
ORDINATING
ORDINATION
ORDINATIONS
ORDONNANCE
ORDONNANCES
ORECCHIETTE
ORECCHIETTI
OREOGRAPHIC
OREOGRAPHICAL
OREOGRAPHIES
OREOGRAPHY
OREOLOGICAL
OREOLOGIES
OREOLOGIST
OREOLOGISTS
OREPEARCHED
OREPEARCHES
OREPEARCHING
ORGANELLES
ORGANICALLY
ORGANICISM
ORGANICISMS
ORGANICIST
ORGANICISTIC
ORGANICISTS
ORGANICITIES
ORGANICITY

ORGANISABILITY
ORGANISABLE
ORGANISATION
ORGANISATIONAL
ORGANISATIONS
ORGANISERS
ORGANISING
ORGANISMAL
ORGANISMALLY
ORGANISMIC
ORGANISMICALLY
ORGANISTRUM
ORGANISTRUMS
ORGANITIES
ORGANIZABILITY
ORGANIZABLE
ORGANIZATION
ORGANIZATIONAL
ORGANIZATIONS
ORGANIZERS
ORGANIZING
ORGANOCHLORINE
ORGANOCHLORINES
ORGANOGENESES
ORGANOGENESIS
ORGANOGENETIC
ORGANOGENIES
ORGANOGENY
ORGANOGRAM
ORGANOGRAMS
ORGANOGRAPHIC
ORGANOGRAPHICAL
ORGANOGRAPHIES
ORGANOGRAPHIST
ORGANOGRAPHISTS
ORGANOGRAPHY
ORGANOLEPTIC
ORGANOLOGICAL
ORGANOLOGIES
ORGANOLOGIST
ORGANOLOGISTS
ORGANOLOGY
ORGANOMERCURIAL
ORGANOMETALLIC
ORGANOMETALLICS
ORGANOPHOSPHATE
ORGANOSOLS
ORGANOTHERAPIES
ORGANOTHERAPY
ORGANZINES
ORGIASTICALLY
ORICALCHES
ORICHALCEOUS
ORIENTALISE
ORIENTALISED
ORIENTALISES
ORIENTALISING
ORIENTALISM
ORIENTALISMS
ORIENTALIST
ORIENTALISTS
ORIENTALITIES
ORIENTALITY
ORIENTALIZE
ORIENTALIZED
ORIENTALIZES
ORIENTALIZING
ORIENTALLY
ORIENTATED
ORIENTATES
ORIENTATING
ORIENTATION
ORIENTATIONAL
ORIENTATIONALLY
ORIENTATIONS
ORIENTATOR
ORIENTATORS
ORIENTEERED
ORIENTEERING
ORIENTEERINGS
ORIENTEERS
ORIFLAMMES
ORIGINALITIES

ORIGINALITY
ORIGINALLY
ORIGINATED
ORIGINATES
ORIGINATING
ORIGINATION
ORIGINATIONS
ORIGINATIVE
ORIGINATIVELY
ORIGINATOR
ORIGINATORS
ORINASALLY
ORISMOLOGICAL
ORISMOLOGIES
ORISMOLOGY
ORNAMENTAL
ORNAMENTALLY
ORNAMENTALS
ORNAMENTATION
ORNAMENTATIONS
ORNAMENTED
ORNAMENTER
ORNAMENTERS
ORNAMENTING
ORNAMENTIST
ORNAMENTISTS
ORNATENESS
ORNATENESSES
ORNERINESS
ORNERINESSES
ORNITHICHNITE
ORNITHICHNITES
ORNITHINES
ORNITHISCHIAN
ORNITHISCHIANS
ORNITHODELPHIAN
ORNITHODELPHIC
ORNITHODELPHOUS
ORNITHOGALUM
ORNITHOGALUMS
ORNITHOLOGIC
ORNITHOLOGICAL
ORNITHOLOGIES
ORNITHOLOGIST
ORNITHOLOGISTS
ORNITHOLOGY
ORNITHOMANCIES
ORNITHOMANCY
ORNITHOMANTIC
ORNITHOMORPH
ORNITHOMORPHIC
ORNITHOMORPHS
ORNITHOPHILIES
ORNITHOPHILOUS
ORNITHOPHILY
ORNITHOPHOBIA
ORNITHOPHOBIAS
ORNITHOPOD
ORNITHOPODS
ORNITHOPTER
ORNITHOPTERS
ORNITHORHYNCHUS
ORNITHOSAUR
ORNITHOSAURS
ORNITHOSCOPIES
ORNITHOSCOPY
ORNITHOSES
ORNITHOSIS
OROBANCHACEOUS
OROGENESES
OROGENESIS
OROGENETIC
OROGENETICALLY
OROGENICALLY
OROGRAPHER
OROGRAPHERS
OROGRAPHIC
OROGRAPHICAL
OROGRAPHICALLY
OROGRAPHIES
OROLOGICAL
OROLOGICALLY
OROLOGISTS

OROPHARYNGEAL
OROPHARYNGES
OROPHARYNX
OROPHARYNXES
OROROTUNDITIES
OROROTUNDITY
OROTUNDITIES
OROTUNDITY
ORPHANAGES
ORPHANHOOD
ORPHANHOODS
ORPHANISMS
ORPHARIONS
ORPHEOREON
ORPHEOREONS
ORPHICALLY
ORRISROOTS
ORTANIQUES
ORTHOBORATE
ORTHOBORATES
ORTHOBORIC
ORTHOCAINE
ORTHOCAINES
ORTHOCENTER
ORTHOCENTERS
ORTHOCENTRE
ORTHOCENTRES
ORTHOCEPHALIC
ORTHOCEPHALIES
ORTHOCEPHALOUS
ORTHOCEPHALY
ORTHOCHROMATIC
ORTHOCHROMATISM
ORTHOCLASE
ORTHOCLASES
ORTHOCOUSINS
ORTHODIAGONAL
ORTHODIAGONALS
ORTHODONTIA
ORTHODONTIAS
ORTHODONTIC
ORTHODONTICALLY
ORTHODONTICS
ORTHODONTIST
ORTHODONTISTS
ORTHODOXES
ORTHODOXIES
ORTHODOXLY
ORTHODROMIC
ORTHODROMICS
ORTHODROMIES
ORTHODROMY
ORTHOEPICAL
ORTHOEPICALLY
ORTHOEPIES
ORTHOEPIST
ORTHOEPISTS
ORTHOGENESES
ORTHOGENESIS
ORTHOGENETIC
ORTHOGENIC
ORTHOGENICALLY
ORTHOGENICS
ORTHOGNATHIC
ORTHOGNATHIES
ORTHOGNATHISM
ORTHOGNATHISMS
ORTHOGNATHOUS
ORTHOGNATHY
ORTHOGONAL
ORTHOGONALISE
ORTHOGONALISED
ORTHOGONALISES
ORTHOGONALISING
ORTHOGONALITIES
ORTHOGONALITY
ORTHOGONALIZE
ORTHOGONALIZED
ORTHOGONALIZES
ORTHOGONALIZING
ORTHOGONALLY
ORTHOGRADE
ORTHOGRAPH

ORTHOGRAPHER
ORTHOGRAPHERS
ORTHOGRAPHIC
ORTHOGRAPHICAL
ORTHOGRAPHIES
ORTHOGRAPHIST
ORTHOGRAPHISTS
ORTHOGRAPHS
ORTHOGRAPHY
ORTHOHYDROGEN
ORTHOHYDROGENS
ORTHOMOLECULAR
ORTHOMORPHIC
ORTHONORMAL
ORTHOPAEDIC
ORTHOPAEDICAL
ORTHOPAEDICS
ORTHOPAEDIES
ORTHOPAEDIST
ORTHOPAEDISTS
ORTHOPAEDY
ORTHOPEDIA
ORTHOPEDIAS
ORTHOPEDIC
ORTHOPEDICAL
ORTHOPEDICALLY
ORTHOPEDICS
ORTHOPEDIES
ORTHOPEDIST
ORTHOPEDISTS
ORTHOPHOSPHATE
ORTHOPHOSPHATES
ORTHOPHOSPHORIC
ORTHOPHYRE
ORTHOPHYRES
ORTHOPHYRIC
ORTHOPINAKOID
ORTHOPINAKOIDS
ORTHOPNOEA
ORTHOPNOEAS
ORTHOPRAXES
ORTHOPRAXIES
ORTHOPRAXIS
ORTHOPRAXY
ORTHOPRISM
ORTHOPRISMS
ORTHOPSYCHIATRY
ORTHOPTERA
ORTHOPTERAN
ORTHOPTERANS
ORTHOPTERIST
ORTHOPTERISTS
ORTHOPTEROID
ORTHOPTEROIDS
ORTHOPTEROLOGY
ORTHOPTERON
ORTHOPTEROUS
ORTHOPTERS
ORTHOPTICS
ORTHOPTIST
ORTHOPTISTS
ORTHOPYROXENE
ORTHOPYROXENES
ORTHORHOMBIC
ORTHOSCOPE
ORTHOSCOPES
ORTHOSCOPIC
ORTHOSILICATE
ORTHOSILICATES
ORTHOSTATIC
ORTHOSTICHIES
ORTHOSTICHOUS
ORTHOSTICHY
ORTHOTISTS
ORTHOTONES
ORTHOTONESES
ORTHOTONESIS
ORTHOTONIC
ORTHOTOPIC
ORTHOTROPIC
ORTHOTROPIES
ORTHOTROPISM
ORTHOTROPISMS

ORTHOTROPOUS
ORTHOTROPY
ORTHOTUNGSTIC
ORTHOVANADIC
ORYCTOLOGIES
ORYCTOLOGY
OSCILLATED
OSCILLATES
OSCILLATING
OSCILLATION
OSCILLATIONAL
OSCILLATIONS
OSCILLATIVE
OSCILLATOR
OSCILLATORS
OSCILLATORY
OSCILLOGRAM
OSCILLOGRAMS
OSCILLOGRAPH
OSCILLOGRAPHIC
OSCILLOGRAPHIES
OSCILLOGRAPHS
OSCILLOGRAPHY
OSCILLOSCOPE
OSCILLOSCOPES
OSCILLOSCOPIC
OSCITANCES
OSCITANCIES
OSCITANTLY
OSCITATING
OSCITATION
OSCITATIONS
OSCULATING
OSCULATION
OSCULATIONS
OSCULATORIES
OSCULATORY
OSMETERIUM
OSMIDROSES
OSMIDROSIS
OSMIRIDIUM
OSMIRIDIUMS
OSMOLALITIES
OSMOLALITY
OSMOLARITIES
OSMOLARITY
OSMOMETERS
OSMOMETRIC
OSMOMETRICALLY
OSMOMETRIES
OSMOREGULATION
OSMOREGULATIONS
OSMOREGULATORY
OSMOTICALLY
OSMUNDINES
OSSIFEROUS
OSSIFICATION
OSSIFICATIONS
OSSIFRAGAS
OSSIFRAGES
OSSIVOROUS
OSTEICHTHYAN
OSTEICHTHYANS
OSTEITIDES
OSTEITISES
OSTENSIBILITIES
OSTENSIBILITY
OSTENSIBLE
OSTENSIBLY
OSTENSIVELY
OSTENSORIA
OSTENSORIES
OSTENSORIUM
OSTENTATION
OSTENTATIONS
OSTENTATIOUS
OSTENTATIOUSLY
OSTEOARTHRITIC
OSTEOARTHRITICS
OSTEOARTHRITIS
OSTEOARTHROSES
OSTEOARTHROSIS
OSTEOBLAST

OSTEOBLASTIC
OSTEOBLASTS
OSTEOCLASES
OSTEOCLASIS
OSTEOCLAST
OSTEOCLASTIC
OSTEOCLASTS
OSTEOCOLLA
OSTEOCOLLAS
OSTEOCYTES
OSTEODERMAL
OSTEODERMATOUS
OSTEODERMIC
OSTEODERMOUS
OSTEODERMS
OSTEOFIBROSES
OSTEOFIBROSIS
OSTEOGENESES
OSTEOGENESIS
OSTEOGENETIC
OSTEOGENIC
OSTEOGENIES
OSTEOGENOUS
OSTEOGRAPHIES
OSTEOGRAPHY
OSTEOLOGICAL
OSTEOLOGICALLY
OSTEOLOGIES
OSTEOLOGIST
OSTEOLOGISTS
OSTEOMALACIA
OSTEOMALACIAL
OSTEOMALACIAS
OSTEOMALACIC
OSTEOMYELITIS
OSTEOMYELITISES
OSTEOPATHIC
OSTEOPATHICALLY
OSTEOPATHIES
OSTEOPATHIST
OSTEOPATHISTS
OSTEOPATHS
OSTEOPATHY
OSTEOPETROSES
OSTEOPETROSIS
OSTEOPHYTE
OSTEOPHYTES
OSTEOPHYTIC
OSTEOPLASTIC
OSTEOPLASTIES
OSTEOPLASTY
OSTEOPOROSES
OSTEOPOROSIS
OSTEOPOROTIC
OSTEOSARCOMA
OSTEOSARCOMAS
OSTEOSARCOMATA
OSTEOSISES
OSTEOTOMES
OSTEOTOMIES
OSTLERESSES
OSTRACEOUS
OSTRACISABLE
OSTRACISED
OSTRACISER
OSTRACISERS
OSTRACISES
OSTRACISING
OSTRACISMS
OSTRACIZABLE
OSTRACIZED
OSTRACIZER
OSTRACIZERS
OSTRACIZES
OSTRACIZING
OSTRACODAN
OSTRACODERM
OSTRACODERMS
OSTRACODES
OSTRACODOUS
OSTREACEOUS
OSTREICULTURE
OSTREICULTURES

OSTREICULTURIST
OSTREOPHAGE
OSTREOPHAGES
OSTREOPHAGIES
OSTREOPHAGOUS
OSTREOPHAGY
OSTRICHISM
OSTRICHISMS
OSTRICHLIKE
OTHERGATES
OTHERGUESS
OTHERNESSES
OTHERWHERE
OTHERWHILE
OTHERWHILES
OTHERWORLD
OTHERWORLDISH
OTHERWORLDLY
OTHERWORLDS
OTIOSENESS
OTIOSENESSES
OTIOSITIES
OTOLARYNGOLOGY
OTOLOGICAL
OTOLOGISTS
OTOPLASTIES
OTORRHOEAS
OTOSCLEROSES
OTOSCLEROSIS
OTOSCOPIES
OTOTOXICITIES
OTOTOXICITY
OTTRELITES
OUANANICHE
OUANANICHES
OUBLIETTES
OUGHTLINGS
OUGHTNESSES
OUROBOROSES
OUROLOGIES
OUROSCOPIES
OUTACHIEVE
OUTACHIEVED
OUTACHIEVES
OUTACHIEVING
OUTARGUING
OUTBACKERS
OUTBALANCE
OUTBALANCED
OUTBALANCES
OUTBALANCING
OUTBARGAIN
OUTBARGAINED
OUTBARGAINING
OUTBARGAINS
OUTBARKING
OUTBARRING
OUTBAWLING
OUTBEAMING
OUTBEGGING
OUTBIDDERS
OUTBIDDING
OUTBITCHED
OUTBITCHES
OUTBITCHING
OUTBLAZING
OUTBLEATED
OUTBLEATING
OUTBLESSED
OUTBLESSES
OUTBLESSING
OUTBLOOMED
OUTBLOOMING
OUTBLUFFED
OUTBLUFFING
OUTBLUSHED
OUTBLUSHES
OUTBLUSHING
OUTBLUSTER
OUTBLUSTERED
OUTBLUSTERING
OUTBLUSTERS
OUTBOASTED

OUTBOASTING
OUTBRAGGED
OUTBRAGGING
OUTBRAVING
OUTBRAWLED
OUTBRAWLING
OUTBRAZENED
OUTBRAZENING
OUTBRAZENS
OUTBREAKING
OUTBREATHE
OUTBREATHED
OUTBREATHES
OUTBREATHING
OUTBREEDING
OUTBREEDINGS
OUTBRIBING
OUTBUILDING
OUTBUILDINGS
OUTBULGING
OUTBULKING
OUTBULLIED
OUTBULLIES
OUTBULLYING
OUTBURNING
OUTBURSTING
OUTCAPERED
OUTCAPERING
OUTCASTING
OUTCATCHES
OUTCATCHING
OUTCAVILED
OUTCAVILING
OUTCAVILLED
OUTCAVILLING
OUTCHARGED
OUTCHARGES
OUTCHARGING
OUTCHARMED
OUTCHARMING
OUTCHEATED
OUTCHEATING
OUTCHIDDEN
OUTCHIDING
OUTCLASSED
OUTCLASSES
OUTCLASSING
OUTCLIMBED
OUTCLIMBING
OUTCOACHED
OUTCOACHES
OUTCOACHING
OUTCOMPETE
OUTCOMPETED
OUTCOMPETES
OUTCOMPETING
OUTCOOKING
OUTCOUNTED
OUTCOUNTING
OUTCRAFTIED
OUTCRAFTIES
OUTCRAFTYING
OUTCRAWLED
OUTCRAWLING
OUTCROPPED
OUTCROPPING
OUTCROPPINGS
OUTCROSSED
OUTCROSSES
OUTCROSSING
OUTCROSSINGS
OUTCROWDED
OUTCROWDING
OUTCROWING
OUTCURSING
OUTDACIOUS
OUTDANCING
OUTDATEDLY
OUTDATEDNESS
OUTDATEDNESSES
OUTDAZZLED
OUTDAZZLES
OUTDAZZLING

OUTDEBATED
OUTDEBATES
OUTDEBATING
OUTDELIVER
OUTDELIVERED
OUTDELIVERING
OUTDELIVERS
OUTDESIGNED
OUTDESIGNING
OUTDESIGNS
OUTDISTANCE
OUTDISTANCED
OUTDISTANCES
OUTDISTANCING
OUTDODGING
OUTDOORSMAN
OUTDOORSMANSHIP
OUTDOORSMEN
OUTDRAGGED
OUTDRAGGING
OUTDRAWING
OUTDREAMED
OUTDREAMING
OUTDRESSED
OUTDRESSES
OUTDRESSING
OUTDRINKING
OUTDRIVING
OUTDROPPED
OUTDROPPING
OUTDUELING
OUTDUELLED
OUTDUELLING
OUTDWELLED
OUTDWELLING
OUTEARNING
OUTECHOING
OUTERCOATS
OUTERCOURSE
OUTERCOURSES
OUTERWEARS
OUTFABLING
OUTFANGTHIEF
OUTFANGTHIEVES
OUTFASTING
OUTFAWNING
OUTFEASTED
OUTFEASTING
OUTFEELING
OUTFENCING
OUTFIELDER
OUTFIELDERS
OUTFIGHTING
OUTFIGURED
OUTFIGURES
OUTFIGURING
OUTFINDING
OUTFISHING
OUTFITTERS
OUTFITTING
OUTFITTINGS
OUTFLANKED
OUTFLANKING
OUTFLASHED
OUTFLASHES
OUTFLASHING
OUTFLOATED
OUTFLOATING
OUTFLOWING
OUTFLOWINGS
OUTFLUSHED
OUTFLUSHES
OUTFLUSHING
OUTFOOLING
OUTFOOTING
OUTFROWNED
OUTFROWNING
OUTFUMBLED
OUTFUMBLES
OUTFUMBLING
OUTGAINING
OUTGALLOPED
OUTGALLOPING

OUTGALLOPS
OUTGAMBLED
OUTGAMBLES
OUTGAMBLING
OUTGASSING
OUTGASSINGS
OUTGENERAL
OUTGENERALED
OUTGENERALING
OUTGENERALLED
OUTGENERALLING
OUTGENERALS
OUTGIVINGS
OUTGLARING
OUTGLEAMED
OUTGLEAMING
OUTGLITTER
OUTGLITTERED
OUTGLITTERING
OUTGLITTERS
OUTGLOWING
OUTGNAWING
OUTGOINGNESS
OUTGOINGNESSES
OUTGRINNED
OUTGRINNING
OUTGROSSED
OUTGROSSES
OUTGROSSING
OUTGROWING
OUTGROWTHS
OUTGUESSED
OUTGUESSES
OUTGUESSING
OUTGUIDING
OUTGUNNING
OUTGUSHING
OUTHANDLED
OUTHANDLES
OUTHANDLING
OUTHAULERS
OUTHEARING
OUTHITTING
OUTHOMERED
OUTHOMERING
OUTHOWLING
OUTHUMORED
OUTHUMORING
OUTHUNTING
OUTHUSTLED
OUTHUSTLES
OUTHUSTLING
OUTINTRIGUE
OUTINTRIGUED
OUTINTRIGUES
OUTINTRIGUING
OUTJESTING
OUTJETTING
OUTJETTINGS
OUTJINXING
OUTJOCKEYED
OUTJOCKEYING
OUTJOCKEYS
OUTJUGGLED
OUTJUGGLES
OUTJUGGLING
OUTJUMPING
OUTJUTTING
OUTJUTTINGS
OUTKEEPING
OUTKICKING
OUTKILLING
OUTKISSING
OUTLANDERS
OUTLANDISH
OUTLANDISHLY
OUTLANDISHNESS
OUTLASTING
OUTLAUGHED
OUTLAUGHING
OUTLAUNCED
OUTLAUNCES
OUTLAUNCHED

OUTLAUNCHES
OUTLAUNCHING
OUTLAUNCING
OUTLAWRIES
OUTLEADING
OUTLEAPING
OUTLEARNED
OUTLEARNING
OUTLODGING
OUTLODGINGS
OUTLOOKING
OUTLUSTRED
OUTLUSTRES
OUTLUSTRING
OUTMANEUVER
OUTMANEUVERED
OUTMANEUVERING
OUTMANEUVERS
OUTMANIPULATE
OUTMANIPULATED
OUTMANIPULATES
OUTMANIPULATING
OUTMANNING
OUTMANOEUVRE
OUTMANOEUVRED
OUTMANOEUVRES
OUTMANOEUVRING
OUTMANTLED
OUTMANTLES
OUTMANTLING
OUTMARCHED
OUTMARCHES
OUTMARCHING
OUTMARRIAGE
OUTMARRIAGES
OUTMASTERED
OUTMASTERING
OUTMASTERS
OUTMATCHED
OUTMATCHES
OUTMATCHING
OUTMEASURE
OUTMEASURED
OUTMEASURES
OUTMEASURING
OUTMODEDLY
OUTMODEDNESS
OUTMODEDNESSES
OUTMUSCLED
OUTMUSCLES
OUTMUSCLING
OUTNIGHTED
OUTNIGHTING
OUTNUMBERED
OUTNUMBERING
OUTNUMBERS
OUTOFFICES
OUTORGANISE
OUTORGANISED
OUTORGANISES
OUTORGANISING
OUTORGANIZE
OUTORGANIZED
OUTORGANIZES
OUTORGANIZING
OUTPAINTED
OUTPAINTING
OUTPASSING
OUTPASSION
OUTPASSIONED
OUTPASSIONING
OUTPASSIONS
OUTPATIENT
OUTPATIENTS
OUTPEEPING
OUTPEERING
OUTPEOPLED
OUTPEOPLES
OUTPEOPLING
OUTPERFORM
OUTPERFORMED
OUTPERFORMING
OUTPERFORMS

OUTPITCHED
OUTPITCHES
OUTPITCHING
OUTPITYING
OUTPLACEMENT
OUTPLACEMENTS
OUTPLACERS
OUTPLACING
OUTPLANNED
OUTPLANNING
OUTPLAYING
OUTPLODDED
OUTPLODDING
OUTPLOTTED
OUTPLOTTING
OUTPOINTED
OUTPOINTING
OUTPOLITICK
OUTPOLITICKED
OUTPOLITICKING
OUTPOLITICKS
OUTPOLLING
OUTPOPULATE
OUTPOPULATED
OUTPOPULATES
OUTPOPULATING
OUTPORTERS
OUTPOURERS
OUTPOURING
OUTPOURINGS
OUTPOWERED
OUTPOWERING
OUTPRAYING
OUTPREACHED
OUTPREACHES
OUTPREACHING
OUTPREENED
OUTPREENING
OUTPRESSED
OUTPRESSES
OUTPRESSING
OUTPRICING
OUTPRIZING
OUTPRODUCE
OUTPRODUCED
OUTPRODUCES
OUTPRODUCING
OUTPROMISE
OUTPROMISED
OUTPROMISES
OUTPROMISING
OUTPULLING
OUTPUNCHED
OUTPUNCHES
OUTPUNCHING
OUTPURSUED
OUTPURSUES
OUTPURSUING
OUTPUSHING
OUTPUTTING
OUTQUARTERS
OUTQUOTING
OUTRAGEOUS
OUTRAGEOUSLY
OUTRAGEOUSNESS
OUTRAISING
OUTRANGING
OUTRANKING
OUTREACHED
OUTREACHES
OUTREACHING
OUTREADING
OUTREASONED
OUTREASONING
OUTREASONS
OUTREBOUND
OUTREBOUNDED
OUTREBOUNDING
OUTREBOUNDS
OUTRECKONED
OUTRECKONING
OUTRECKONS
OUTRECUIDANCE

OUTRECUIDANCES
OUTREDDENED
OUTREDDENING
OUTREDDENS
OUTREDDING
OUTREIGNED
OUTREIGNING
OUTRELIEFS
OUTREPRODUCE
OUTREPRODUCED
OUTREPRODUCES
OUTREPRODUCING
OUTRIGGERS
OUTRIGGING
OUTRIGHTLY
OUTRINGING
OUTRIVALED
OUTRIVALING
OUTRIVALLED
OUTRIVALLING
OUTROARING
OUTROCKING
OUTROLLING
OUTROOPERS
OUTROOTING
OUTRUNNERS
OUTRUNNING
OUTRUSHING
OUTSAILING
OUTSAVORED
OUTSAVORING
OUTSCHEMED
OUTSCHEMES
OUTSCHEMING
OUTSCOLDED
OUTSCOLDING
OUTSCOOPED
OUTSCOOPING
OUTSCORING
OUTSCORNED
OUTSCORNING
OUTSCREAMED
OUTSCREAMING
OUTSCREAMS
OUTSELLING
OUTSERVING
OUTSETTING
OUTSETTINGS
OUTSETTLEMENT
OUTSETTLEMENTS
OUTSHAMING
OUTSHINING
OUTSHOOTING
OUTSHOUTED
OUTSHOUTING
OUTSIDERNESS
OUTSIDERNESSES
OUTSINGING
OUTSINNING
OUTSITTING
OUTSKATING
OUTSLEEPING
OUTSLICKED
OUTSLICKING
OUTSMARTED
OUTSMARTING
OUTSMELLED
OUTSMELLING
OUTSMILING
OUTSMOKING
OUTSNORING
OUTSOARING
OUTSOURCED
OUTSOURCES
OUTSOURCING
OUTSOURCINGS
OUTSPANNED
OUTSPANNING
OUTSPARKLE
OUTSPARKLED
OUTSPARKLES
OUTSPARKLING
OUTSPEAKING

OUTSPECKLE
OUTSPECKLES
OUTSPEEDED
OUTSPEEDING
OUTSPELLED
OUTSPELLING
OUTSPENDING
OUTSPOKENLY
OUTSPOKENNESS
OUTSPOKENNESSES
OUTSPORTED
OUTSPORTING
OUTSPREADING
OUTSPREADS
OUTSPRINGING
OUTSPRINGS
OUTSPRINTED
OUTSPRINTING
OUTSPRINTS
OUTSTANDING
OUTSTANDINGLY
OUTSTARING
OUTSTARTED
OUTSTARTING
OUTSTATING
OUTSTATION
OUTSTATIONS
OUTSTAYING
OUTSTEERED
OUTSTEERING
OUTSTEPPED
OUTSTEPPING
OUTSTRAINED
OUTSTRAINING
OUTSTRAINS
OUTSTRETCH
OUTSTRETCHED
OUTSTRETCHES
OUTSTRETCHING
OUTSTRIDDEN
OUTSTRIDES
OUTSTRIDING
OUTSTRIKES
OUTSTRIKING
OUTSTRIPPED
OUTSTRIPPING
OUTSTRIVEN
OUTSTRIVES
OUTSTRIVING
OUTSTROKES
OUTSTUDIED
OUTSTUDIES
OUTSTUDYING
OUTSTUNTED
OUTSTUNTING
OUTSULKING
OUTSUMMING
OUTSWEARING
OUTSWEEPING
OUTSWEETEN
OUTSWEETENED
OUTSWEETENING
OUTSWEETENS
OUTSWELLED
OUTSWELLING
OUTSWIMMING
OUTSWINGER
OUTSWINGERS
OUTSWINGING
OUTSWOLLEN
OUTTALKING
OUTTASKING
OUTTELLING
OUTTHANKED
OUTTHANKING
OUTTHIEVED
OUTTHIEVES
OUTTHIEVING
OUTTHINKING
OUTTHOUGHT
OUTTHROBBED
OUTTHROBBING
OUTTHROWING

OUTTHRUSTED	OVARIOTOMIES	OVERBEARING	OVERCANOPIES	OVERCOMPLEX	OVERDETERMINED
OUTTHRUSTING	OVARIOTOMIST	OVERBEARINGLY	OVERCANOPY	OVERCOMPLIANCE	OVERDEVELOP
OUTTHRUSTS	OVARIOTOMISTS	OVERBEARINGNESS	OVERCANOPYING	OVERCOMPLIANCES	OVERDEVELOPED
OUTTONGUED	OVARIOTOMY	OVERBEATEN	OVERCAPACITIES	OVERCOMPLICATE	OVERDEVELOPING
OUTTONGUES	OVARITIDES	OVERBEATING	OVERCAPACITY	OVERCOMPLICATED	OVERDEVELOPMENT
OUTTONGUING	OVARITISES	OVERBEJEWELED	OVERCAPITALISE	OVERCOMPLICATES	OVERDEVELOPS
OUTTOPPING	OVERABOUND	OVERBETTED	OVERCAPITALISED	OVERCOMPRESS	OVERDEVIATE
OUTTOWERED	OVERABOUNDED	OVERBETTING	OVERCAPITALISES	OVERCOMPRESSED	OVERDEVIATED
OUTTOWERING	OVERABOUNDING	OVERBIDDEN	OVERCAPITALIZE	OVERCOMPRESSES	OVERDEVIATES
OUTTRADING	OVERABOUNDS	OVERBIDDER	OVERCAPITALIZED	OVERCOMPRESSING	OVERDEVIATING
OUTTRAVELED	OVERABSTRACT	OVERBIDDERS	OVERCAPITALIZES	OVERCONCERN	OVERDIRECT
OUTTRAVELING	OVERABUNDANCE	OVERBIDDING	OVERCAREFUL	OVERCONCERNED	OVERDIRECTED
OUTTRAVELLED	OVERABUNDANCES	OVERBIDDINGS	OVERCARRIED	OVERCONCERNING	OVERDIRECTING
OUTTRAVELLING	OVERABUNDANT	OVERBILLED	OVERCARRIES	OVERCONCERNS	OVERDIRECTS
OUTTRAVELS	OVERACCENTUATE	OVERBILLING	OVERCARRYING	OVERCONFIDENCE	OVERDISCOUNT
OUTTRICKED	OVERACCENTUATED	OVERBLANKET	OVERCASTED	OVERCONFIDENCES	OVERDISCOUNTED
OUTTRICKING	OVERACCENTUATES	OVERBLANKETS	OVERCASTING	OVERCONFIDENT	OVERDISCOUNTING
OUTTROTTED	OVERACHIEVE	OVERBLEACH	OVERCASTINGS	OVERCONFIDENTLY	OVERDISCOUNTS
OUTTROTTING	OVERACHIEVED	OVERBLEACHED	OVERCATCHES	OVERCONSCIOUS	OVERDIVERSITIES
OUTTRUMPED	OVERACHIEVEMENT	OVERBLEACHES	OVERCATCHING	OVERCONSTRUCT	OVERDIVERSITY
OUTTRUMPING	OVERACHIEVER	OVERBLEACHING	OVERCAUGHT	OVERCONSTRUCTED	OVERDOCUMENT
OUTVALUING	OVERACHIEVERS	OVERBLOUSE	OVERCAUTION	OVERCONSTRUCTS	OVERDOCUMENTED
OUTVAUNTED	OVERACHIEVES	OVERBLOUSES	OVERCAUTIONS	OVERCONSUME	OVERDOCUMENTING
OUTVAUNTING	OVERACHIEVING	OVERBLOWING	OVERCAUTIOUS	OVERCONSUMED	OVERDOCUMENTS
OUTVENOMED	OVERACTING	OVERBOILED	OVERCENTRALISE	OVERCONSUMES	OVERDOMINANCE
OUTVENOMING	OVERACTION	OVERBOILING	OVERCENTRALISED	OVERCONSUMING	OVERDOMINANCES
OUTVILLAIN	OVERACTIONS	OVERBOLDLY	OVERCENTRALISES	OVERCONSUMPTION	OVERDOMINANT
OUTVILLAINED	OVERACTIVE	OVERBOOKED	OVERCENTRALIZE	OVERCONTROL	OVERDOSAGE
OUTVILLAINING	OVERACTIVITIES	OVERBOOKING	OVERCENTRALIZED	OVERCONTROLLED	OVERDOSAGES
OUTVILLAINS	OVERACTIVITY	OVERBORROW	OVERCENTRALIZES	OVERCONTROLLING	OVERDOSING
OUTVOICING	OVERADJUSTMENT	OVERBORROWED	OVERCHARGE	OVERCONTROLS	OVERDRAFTS
OUTWAITING	OVERADJUSTMENTS	OVERBORROWING	OVERCHARGED	OVERCOOKED	OVERDRAMATIC
OUTWALKING	OVERADVERTISE	OVERBORROWS	OVERCHARGES	OVERCOOKING	OVERDRAMATISE
OUTWARDNESS	OVERADVERTISED	OVERBOUGHT	OVERCHARGING	OVERCOOLED	OVERDRAMATISED
OUTWARDNESSES	OVERADVERTISES	OVERBOUNDED	OVERCHECKS	OVERCOOLING	OVERDRAMATISES
OUTWARRING	OVERADVERTISING	OVERBOUNDING	OVERCHILLED	OVERCORRECT	OVERDRAMATISING
OUTWASTING	OVERAGGRESSIVE	OVERBOUNDS	OVERCHILLING	OVERCORRECTED	OVERDRAMATIZE
OUTWATCHED	OVERAMBITIOUS	OVERBRAKED	OVERCHILLS	OVERCORRECTING	OVERDRAMATIZED
OUTWATCHES	OVERAMPLIFIED	OVERBRAKES	OVERCIVILISED	OVERCORRECTION	OVERDRAMATIZES
OUTWATCHING	OVERANALYSE	OVERBRAKING	OVERCIVILIZED	OVERCORRECTIONS	OVERDRAMATIZING
OUTWEARIED	OVERANALYSED	OVERBREATHING	OVERCLAIMED	OVERCORRECTS	OVERDRAUGHT
OUTWEARIES	OVERANALYSES	OVERBREATHINGS	OVERCLAIMING	OVERCOUNTED	OVERDRAUGHTS
OUTWEARING	OVERANALYSING	OVERBREEDING	OVERCLAIMS	OVERCOUNTING	OVERDRAWING
OUTWEARYING	OVERANALYSIS	OVERBREEDS	OVERCLASSES	OVERCOUNTS	OVERDRESSED
OUTWEEDING	OVERANALYTICAL	OVERBRIDGE	OVERCLASSIFIED	OVERCOVERED	OVERDRESSES
OUTWEEPING	OVERANALYZE	OVERBRIDGED	OVERCLASSIFIES	OVERCOVERING	OVERDRESSING
OUTWEIGHED	OVERANALYZED	OVERBRIDGES	OVERCLASSIFY	OVERCOVERS	OVERDRINKING
OUTWEIGHING	OVERANALYZES	OVERBRIDGING	OVERCLASSIFYING	OVERCRAMMED	OVERDRINKS
OUTWELLING	OVERANALYZING	OVERBRIEFED	OVERCLEANED	OVERCRAMMING	OVERDRIVEN
OUTWHIRLED	OVERANXIETIES	OVERBRIEFING	OVERCLEANING	OVERCRAWED	OVERDRIVES
OUTWHIRLING	OVERANXIETY	OVERBRIEFS	OVERCLEANS	OVERCRAWING	OVERDRIVING
OUTWICKING	OVERANXIOUS	OVERBRIGHT	OVERCLEARED	OVERCREDULITIES	OVERDRYING
OUTWILLING	OVERAPPLICATION	OVERBRIMMED	OVERCLEARING	OVERCREDULITY	OVERDUBBED
OUTWINDING	OVERARCHED	OVERBRIMMING	OVERCLEARS	OVERCREDULOUS	OVERDUBBING
OUTWINGING	OVERARCHES	OVERBROWED	OVERCLOUDED	OVERCRITICAL	OVERDUSTED
OUTWINNING	OVERARCHING	OVERBROWING	OVERCLOUDING	OVERCROPPED	OVERDUSTING
OUTWISHING	OVERARMING	OVERBROWSE	OVERCLOUDS	OVERCROPPING	OVERDYEING
OUTWITTING	OVERAROUSAL	OVERBROWSED	OVERCLOYED	OVERCROWDED	OVEREAGERNESS
OUTWORKERS	OVERAROUSALS	OVERBROWSES	OVERCLOYING	OVERCROWDING	OVEREAGERNESSES
OUTWORKING	OVERARRANGE	OVERBROWSING	OVERCOACHED	OVERCROWDINGS	OVEREARNEST
OUTWORTHED	OVERARRANGED	OVERBRUTAL	OVERCOACHES	OVERCROWDS	OVEREATERS
OUTWORTHING	OVERARRANGES	OVERBUILDING	OVERCOACHING	OVERCROWED	OVEREATING
OUTWRESTED	OVERARRANGING	OVERBUILDS	OVERCOATING	OVERCROWING	OVEREDITED
OUTWRESTING	OVERARTICULATE	OVERBULKED	OVERCOATINGS	OVERCULTIVATION	OVEREDITING
OUTWRESTLE	OVERARTICULATED	OVERBULKING	OVERCOLORED	OVERCURING	OVEREDUCATE
OUTWRESTLED	OVERARTICULATES	OVERBURDEN	OVERCOLORING	OVERCUTTING	OVEREDUCATED
OUTWRESTLES	OVERASSERT	OVERBURDENED	OVERCOLORS	OVERDARING	OVEREDUCATES
OUTWRESTLING	OVERASSERTED	OVERBURDENING	OVERCOLOUR	OVERDECKED	OVEREDUCATING
OUTWRITING	OVERASSERTING	OVERBURDENS	OVERCOLOURED	OVERDECKING	OVEREDUCATION
OUTWRITTEN	OVERASSERTION	OVERBURDENSOME	OVERCOLOURING	OVERDECORATE	OVEREDUCATIONS
OUTWROUGHT	OVERASSERTIONS	OVERBURNED	OVERCOLOURS	OVERDECORATED	OVEREGGING
OUTYELLING	OVERASSERTIVE	OVERBURNING	OVERCOMERS	OVERDECORATES	OVERELABORATE
OUTYELPING	OVERASSERTS	OVERBURTHEN	OVERCOMING	OVERDECORATING	OVERELABORATED
OUTYIELDED	OVERASSESSMENT	OVERBURTHENED	OVERCOMMIT	OVERDECORATION	OVERELABORATES
OUTYIELDING	OVERASSESSMENTS	OVERBURTHENING	OVERCOMMITMENT	OVERDECORATIONS	OVERELABORATING
OUVIRANDRA	OVERATTENTION	OVERBURTHENS	OVERCOMMITMENTS	OVERDEMANDING	OVERELABORATION
OUVIRANDRAS	OVERATTENTIONS	OVERBUSIED	OVERCOMMITS	OVERDEPENDENCE	OVEREMBELLISH
OVALBUMINS	OVERATTENTIVE	OVERBUSIES	OVERCOMMITTED	OVERDEPENDENCES	OVEREMBELLISHED
OVALNESSES	OVERBAKING	OVERBUSYING	OVERCOMMITTING	OVERDEPENDENT	OVEREMBELLISHES
OVARIECTOMIES	OVERBALANCE	OVERBUYING	OVERCOMMUNICATE	OVERDESIGN	OVEREMOTED
OVARIECTOMISED	OVERBALANCED	OVERCALLED	OVERCOMPENSATE	OVERDESIGNED	OVEREMOTES
OVARIECTOMIZED	OVERBALANCES	OVERCALLING	OVERCOMPENSATED	OVERDESIGNING	OVEREMOTING
OVARIECTOMY	OVERBALANCING	OVERCANOPIED	OVERCOMPENSATES	OVERDESIGNS	OVEREMOTIONAL

OVEREMPHASES	OVEREYEING	OVERGEARED	OVERHASTES	OVERISSUES	OVERMANTELS
OVEREMPHASIS	OVERFACILE	OVERGEARING	OVERHASTILY	OVERISSUING	OVERMASTED
OVEREMPHASISE	OVERFALLEN	OVERGENERALISE	OVERHASTINESS	OVERJOYING	OVERMASTER
OVEREMPHASISED	OVERFALLING	OVERGENERALISED	OVERHASTINESSES	OVERJUMPED	OVERMASTERED
OVEREMPHASISES	OVERFAMILIAR	OVERGENERALISES	OVERHATING	OVERJUMPING	OVERMASTERING
OVEREMPHASISING	OVERFAMILIARITY	OVERGENERALIZE	OVERHAULED	OVERKEEPING	OVERMASTERS
OVEREMPHASIZE	OVERFASTIDIOUS	OVERGENERALIZED	OVERHAULING	OVERKILLED	OVERMASTING
OVEREMPHASIZED	OVERFATIGUE	OVERGENERALIZES	OVERHEAPED	OVERKILLING	OVERMATCHED
OVEREMPHASIZES	OVERFATIGUED	OVERGENEROSITY	OVERHEAPING	OVERKINDNESS	OVERMATCHES
OVEREMPHASIZING	OVERFATIGUES	OVERGENEROUS	OVERHEARING	OVERKINDNESSES	OVERMATCHING
OVEREMPHATIC	OVERFAVORED	OVERGENEROUSLY	OVERHEATED	OVERLABORED	OVERMATTER
OVERENAMORED	OVERFAVORING	OVERGETTING	OVERHEATING	OVERLABORING	OVERMATTERS
OVERENCOURAGE	OVERFAVORS	OVERGILDED	OVERHEATINGS	OVERLABORS	OVERMATURE
OVERENCOURAGED	OVERFEARED	OVERGILDING	OVERHENTING	OVERLABOUR	OVERMATURITIES
OVERENCOURAGES	OVERFEARING	OVERGIRDED	OVERHITTING	OVERLABOURED	OVERMATURITY
OVERENCOURAGING	OVERFEEDING	OVERGIRDING	OVERHOLDING	OVERLABOURING	OVERMEASURE
OVERENERGETIC	OVERFERTILISE	OVERGIVING	OVERHOMOGENISE	OVERLABOURS	OVERMEASURED
OVERENGINEER	OVERFERTILISED	OVERGLAMORISE	OVERHOMOGENISED	OVERLADING	OVERMEASURES
OVERENGINEERED	OVERFERTILISES	OVERGLAMORISED	OVERHOMOGENISES	OVERLANDED	OVERMEASURING
OVERENGINEERING	OVERFERTILISING	OVERGLAMORISES	OVERHOMOGENIZE	OVERLANDER	OVERMEDICATE
OVERENGINEERS	OVERFERTILIZE	OVERGLAMORISING	OVERHOMOGENIZED	OVERLANDERS	OVERMEDICATED
OVERENROLLED	OVERFERTILIZED	OVERGLAMORIZE	OVERHOMOGENIZES	OVERLANDING	OVERMEDICATES
OVERENTERTAINED	OVERFERTILIZES	OVERGLAMORIZED	OVERHONORED	OVERLAPPED	OVERMEDICATING
OVERENTHUSIASM	OVERFERTILIZING	OVERGLAMORIZES	OVERHONORING	OVERLAPPING	OVERMEDICATION
OVERENTHUSIASMS	OVERFILLED	OVERGLAMORIZING	OVERHONORS	OVERLARDED	OVERMEDICATIONS
OVEREQUIPPED	OVERFILLING	OVERGLANCE	OVERHOPING	OVERLARDING	OVERMELTED
OVERESTIMATE	OVERFINENESS	OVERGLANCED	OVERHUNTED	OVERLAUNCH	OVERMELTING
OVERESTIMATED	OVERFINENESSES	OVERGLANCES	OVERHUNTING	OVERLAUNCHED	OVERMIGHTY
OVERESTIMATES	OVERFINISHED	OVERGLANCING	OVERHUNTINGS	OVERLAUNCHES	OVERMILKED
OVERESTIMATING	OVERFISHED	OVERGLAZED	OVERHYPING	OVERLAUNCHING	OVERMILKING
OVERESTIMATION	OVERFISHES	OVERGLAZES	OVERIDEALISE	OVERLAVISH	OVERMINING
OVERESTIMATIONS	OVERFISHING	OVERGLAZING	OVERIDEALISED	OVERLAYING	OVERMIXING
OVEREVALUATION	OVERFLIGHT	OVERGLOOMED	OVERIDEALISES	OVERLAYINGS	OVERMODEST
OVEREVALUATIONS	OVERFLIGHTS	OVERGLOOMING	OVERIDEALISING	OVERLEAPED	OVERMODESTLY
OVEREXAGGERATE	OVERFLOODED	OVERGLOOMS	OVERIDEALIZE	OVERLEAPING	OVERMOUNTED
OVEREXAGGERATED	OVERFLOODING	OVERGOADED	OVERIDEALIZED	OVERLEARNED	OVERMOUNTING
OVEREXAGGERATES	OVERFLOODS	OVERGOADING	OVERIDEALIZES	OVERLEARNING	OVERMOUNTS
OVEREXCITABLE	OVERFLOURISH	OVERGOINGS	OVERIDEALIZING	OVERLEARNS	OVERMUCHES
OVEREXCITE	OVERFLOURISHED	OVERGORGED	OVERIDENTIFIED	OVERLEARNT	OVERMULTIPLIED
OVEREXCITED	OVERFLOURISHES	OVERGORGES	OVERIDENTIFIES	OVERLEATHER	OVERMULTIPLIES
OVEREXCITES	OVERFLOURISHING	OVERGORGING	OVERIDENTIFY	OVERLEATHERS	OVERMULTIPLY
OVEREXCITING	OVERFLOWED	OVERGOVERN	OVERIDENTIFYING	OVERLEAVEN	OVERMULTIPLYING
OVEREXERCISE	OVERFLOWING	OVERGOVERNED	OVERIMAGINATIVE	OVERLEAVENED	OVERMULTITUDE
OVEREXERCISED	OVERFLOWINGLY	OVERGOVERNING	OVERIMPRESS	OVERLEAVENING	OVERMULTITUDED
OVEREXERCISES	OVERFLOWINGS	OVERGOVERNS	OVERIMPRESSED	OVERLEAVENS	OVERMULTITUDES
OVEREXERCISING	OVERFLUSHES	OVERGRADED	OVERIMPRESSES	OVERLENDING	OVERMULTITUDING
OVEREXERTED	OVERFLYING	OVERGRADES	OVERIMPRESSING	OVERLENGTH	OVERMUSCLED
OVEREXERTING	OVERFOCUSED	OVERGRADING	OVERINCLINED	OVERLENGTHEN	OVERNAMING
OVEREXERTION	OVERFOCUSES	OVERGRAINED	OVERINDULGE	OVERLENGTHENED	OVERNETTED
OVEREXERTIONS	OVERFOCUSING	OVERGRAINER	OVERINDULGED	OVERLENGTHENING	OVERNETTING
OVEREXERTS	OVERFOCUSSED	OVERGRAINERS	OVERINDULGENCE	OVERLENGTHENS	OVERNICELY
OVEREXPAND	OVERFOCUSSES	OVERGRAINING	OVERINDULGENCES	OVERLENGTHS	OVERNICENESS
OVEREXPANDED	OVERFOCUSSING	OVERGRAINS	OVERINDULGENT	OVERLETTING	OVERNICENESSES
OVEREXPANDING	OVERFOLDED	OVERGRASSED	OVERINDULGES	OVERLIGHTED	OVERNIGHTED
OVEREXPANDS	OVERFOLDING	OVERGRASSES	OVERINDULGING	OVERLIGHTING	OVERNIGHTER
OVEREXPANSION	OVERFONDLY	OVERGRASSING	OVERINFLATE	OVERLIGHTS	OVERNIGHTERS
OVEREXPANSIONS	OVERFONDNESS	OVERGRAZED	OVERINFLATED	OVERLITERAL	OVERNIGHTING
OVEREXPECTATION	OVERFONDNESSES	OVERGRAZES	OVERINFLATES	OVERLITERARY	OVERNIGHTS
OVEREXPLAIN	OVERFORWARD	OVERGRAZING	OVERINFLATING	OVERLIVING	OVERNOURISH
OVEREXPLAINED	OVERFORWARDNESS	OVERGRAZINGS	OVERINFLATION	OVERLOADED	OVERNOURISHED
OVEREXPLAINING	OVERFRAUGHT	OVERGREEDY	OVERINFLATIONS	OVERLOADING	OVERNOURISHES
OVEREXPLAINS	OVERFREEDOM	OVERGREENED	OVERINFORM	OVERLOCKED	OVERNOURISHING
OVEREXPLICIT	OVERFREEDOMS	OVERGREENING	OVERINFORMED	OVERLOCKER	OVERNUTRITION
OVEREXPLOIT	OVERFREELY	OVERGREENS	OVERINFORMING	OVERLOCKERS	OVERNUTRITIONS
OVEREXPLOITED	OVERFREIGHT	OVERGROUND	OVERINFORMS	OVERLOCKING	OVEROBVIOUS
OVEREXPLOITING	OVERFREIGHTING	OVERGROWING	OVERINGENIOUS	OVERLOCKINGS	OVEROFFICE
OVEREXPLOITS	OVERFREIGHTS	OVERGROWTH	OVERINGENUITIES	OVERLOOKED	OVEROFFICED
OVEREXPOSE	OVERFULFILL	OVERGROWTHS	OVERINGENUITY	OVERLOOKER	OVEROFFICES
OVEREXPOSED	OVERFULFILLED	OVERHAILED	OVERINSISTENT	OVERLOOKERS	OVEROFFICING
OVEREXPOSES	OVERFULFILLING	OVERHAILES	OVERINSURANCE	OVERLOOKING	OVEROPERATE
OVEREXPOSING	OVERFULFILLS	OVERHAILING	OVERINSURANCES	OVERLORDED	OVEROPERATED
OVEREXPOSURE	OVERFULLNESS	OVERHALING	OVERINSURE	OVERLORDING	OVEROPERATES
OVEREXPOSURES	OVERFULLNESSES	OVERHANDED	OVERINSURED	OVERLORDSHIP	OVEROPERATING
OVEREXTEND	OVERFULNESS	OVERHANDING	OVERINSURES	OVERLORDSHIPS	OVEROPINIONATED
OVEREXTENDED	OVERFULNESSES	OVERHANDLE	OVERINSURING	OVERLOVING	OVEROPTIMISM
OVEREXTENDING	OVERFUNDED	OVERHANDLED	OVERINTENSE	OVERMANAGE	OVEROPTIMISMS
OVEREXTENDS	OVERFUNDING	OVERHANDLES	OVERINTENSITIES	OVERMANAGED	OVEROPTIMIST
OVEREXTENSION	OVERFUNDINGS	OVERHANDLING	OVERINTENSITY	OVERMANAGES	OVEROPTIMISTIC
OVEREXTENSIONS	OVERGALLED	OVERHANGING	OVERINVESTMENT	OVERMANAGING	OVEROPTIMISTS
OVEREXTRACTION	OVERGALLING	OVERHARVEST	OVERINVESTMENTS	OVERMANNED	OVERORCHESTRATE
OVEREXTRACTIONS	OVERGANGING	OVERHARVESTED	OVERISSUANCE	OVERMANNERED	OVERORGANISE
OVEREXTRAVAGANT	OVERGARMENT	OVERHARVESTING	OVERISSUANCES	OVERMANNING	OVERORGANISED
OVEREXUBERANT	OVERGARMENTS	OVERHARVESTS	OVERISSUED	OVERMANTEL	OVERORGANISES

OVERORGANISING	OVERPOWERINGLY	OVERREACTIONS	OVERSERIOUSLY	OVERSTAINS	OVERSUPPLYING
OVERORGANIZE	OVERPOWERS	OVERREACTS	OVERSERVICE	OVERSTANDING	OVERSUSPICIOUS
OVERORGANIZED	OVERPRAISE	OVERREADING	OVERSERVICED	OVERSTANDS	OVERSWAYED
OVERORGANIZES	OVERPRAISED	OVERRECKON	OVERSERVICES	OVERSTARED	OVERSWAYING
OVERORGANIZING	OVERPRAISES	OVERRECKONED	OVERSERVICING	OVERSTARES	OVERSWEARING
OVERORNAMENT	OVERPRAISING	OVERRECKONING	OVERSETTING	OVERSTARING	OVERSWEARS
OVERORNAMENTED	OVERPRECISE	OVERRECKONS	OVERSEWING	OVERSTATED	OVERSWEETEN
OVERORNAMENTING	OVERPREPARATION	OVERREDDED	OVERSHADED	OVERSTATEMENT	OVERSWEETENED
OVERORNAMENTS	OVERPREPARE	OVERREDDING	OVERSHADES	OVERSTATEMENTS	OVERSWEETENING
OVERPACKAGE	OVERPREPARED	OVERREFINE	OVERSHADING	OVERSTATES	OVERSWEETENS
OVERPACKAGED	OVERPREPARES	OVERREFINED	OVERSHADOW	OVERSTATING	OVERSWEETNESS
OVERPACKAGES	OVERPREPARING	OVERREFINEMENT	OVERSHADOWED	OVERSTAYED	OVERSWEETNESSES
OVERPACKAGING	OVERPRESCRIBE	OVERREFINEMENTS	OVERSHADOWING	OVERSTAYER	OVERSWELLED
OVERPACKED	OVERPRESCRIBED	OVERREFINES	OVERSHADOWS	OVERSTAYERS	OVERSWELLING
OVERPACKING	OVERPRESCRIBES	OVERREFINING	OVERSHINES	OVERSTAYING	OVERSWELLS
OVERPAINTED	OVERPRESCRIBING	OVERREGULATE	OVERSHINING	OVERSTEERED	OVERSWIMMING
OVERPAINTING	OVERPRESSED	OVERREGULATED	OVERSHIRTS	OVERSTEERING	OVERSWINGING
OVERPAINTS	OVERPRESSES	OVERREGULATES	OVERSHOOTING	OVERSTEERS	OVERSWINGS
OVERPARTED	OVERPRESSING	OVERREGULATING	OVERSHOOTS	OVERSTEPPED	OVERSWOLLEN
OVERPARTICULAR	OVERPRESSURE	OVERREGULATION	OVERSHOWER	OVERSTEPPING	OVERTAKING
OVERPARTING	OVERPRESSURES	OVERREGULATIONS	OVERSHOWERED	OVERSTIMULATE	OVERTALKATIVE
OVERPASSED	OVERPRICED	OVERRELIANCE	OVERSHOWERING	OVERSTIMULATED	OVERTALKED
OVERPASSES	OVERPRICES	OVERRELIANCES	OVERSHOWERS	OVERSTIMULATES	OVERTALKING
OVERPASSING	OVERPRICING	OVERRENNING	OVERSIGHTS	OVERSTIMULATING	OVERTASKED
OVERPAYING	OVERPRINTED	OVERREPORT	OVERSIMPLE	OVERSTIMULATION	OVERTASKING
OVERPAYMENT	OVERPRINTING	OVERREPORTED	OVERSIMPLIFIED	OVERSTINKING	OVERTAUGHT
OVERPAYMENTS	OVERPRINTS	OVERREPORTING	OVERSIMPLIFIES	OVERSTINKS	OVERTAXATION
OVERPEDALED	OVERPRIVILEGED	OVERREPORTS	OVERSIMPLIFY	OVERSTIRRED	OVERTAXATIONS
OVERPEDALING	OVERPRIZED	OVERREPRESENTED	OVERSIMPLIFYING	OVERSTIRRING	OVERTAXING
OVERPEDALLED	OVERPRIZES	OVERRESPOND	OVERSIMPLISTIC	OVERSTOCKED	OVERTEACHES
OVERPEDALLING	OVERPRIZING	OVERRESPONDED	OVERSIMPLY	OVERSTOCKING	OVERTEACHING
OVERPEDALS	OVERPROCESS	OVERRESPONDING	OVERSIZING	OVERSTOCKS	OVERTEDIOUS
OVERPEERED	OVERPROCESSED	OVERRESPONDS	OVERSKIPPED	OVERSTORIES	OVERTEEMED
OVERPEERING	OVERPROCESSES	OVERRIDDEN	OVERSKIPPING	OVERSTRAIN	OVERTEEMING
OVERPEOPLE	OVERPROCESSING	OVERRIDERS	OVERSKIRTS	OVERSTRAINED	OVERTHINKING
OVERPEOPLED	OVERPRODUCE	OVERRIDING	OVERSLAUGH	OVERSTRAINING	OVERTHINKS
OVERPEOPLES	OVERPRODUCED	OVERRIPENED	OVERSLAUGHED	OVERSTRAINS	OVERTHOUGHT
OVERPEOPLING	OVERPRODUCES	OVERRIPENESS	OVERSLAUGHING	OVERSTRESS	OVERTHROWER
OVERPERCHED	OVERPRODUCING	OVERRIPENESSES	OVERSLAUGHS	OVERSTRESSED	OVERTHROWERS
OVERPERCHES	OVERPRODUCTION	OVERRIPENING	OVERSLEEPING	OVERSTRESSES	OVERTHROWING
OVERPERCHING	OVERPRODUCTIONS	OVERRIPENS	OVERSLEEPS	OVERSTRESSING	OVERTHROWN
OVERPERSUADE	OVERPROGRAM	OVERROASTED	OVERSLEEVE	OVERSTRETCH	OVERTHROWS
OVERPERSUADED	OVERPROGRAMED	OVERROASTING	OVERSLEEVES	OVERSTRETCHED	OVERTHRUST
OVERPERSUADES	OVERPROGRAMING	OVERROASTS	OVERSLIPPED	OVERSTRETCHES	OVERTHRUSTS
OVERPERSUADING	OVERPROGRAMMED	OVERRUFFED	OVERSLIPPING	OVERSTRETCHING	OVERTHWART
OVERPERSUASION	OVERPROGRAMMING	OVERRUFFING	OVERSMOKED	OVERSTREWED	OVERTHWARTED
OVERPERSUASIONS	OVERPROGRAMS	OVERRULERS	OVERSMOKES	OVERSTREWING	OVERTHWARTING
OVERPICTURE	OVERPROMISE	OVERRULING	OVERSMOKING	OVERSTREWN	OVERTHWARTS
OVERPICTURED	OVERPROMISED	OVERRULINGS	OVERSOAKED	OVERSTREWS	OVERTIGHTEN
OVERPICTURES	OVERPROMISES	OVERRUNNER	OVERSOAKING	OVERSTRIDDEN	OVERTIGHTENED
OVERPICTURING	OVERPROMISING	OVERRUNNERS	OVERSOLICITOUS	OVERSTRIDE	OVERTIGHTENING
OVERPITCHED	OVERPROMOTE	OVERRUNNING	OVERSOWING	OVERSTRIDES	OVERTIGHTENS
OVERPITCHES	OVERPROMOTED	OVERSAILED	OVERSPECIALISE	OVERSTRIDING	OVERTIMELY
OVERPITCHING	OVERPROMOTES	OVERSAILING	OVERSPECIALISED	OVERSTRIKE	OVERTIMERS
OVERPLACED	OVERPROMOTING	OVERSALTED	OVERSPECIALISES	OVERSTRIKES	OVERTIMING
OVERPLAIDED	OVERPROPORTION	OVERSALTING	OVERSPECIALIZE	OVERSTRIKING	OVERTIPPED
OVERPLAIDS	OVERPROPORTIONS	OVERSANGUINE	OVERSPECIALIZED	OVERSTRODE	OVERTIPPING
OVERPLANNED	OVERPROTECT	OVERSATURATE	OVERSPECIALIZES	OVERSTRONG	OVERTIRING
OVERPLANNING	OVERPROTECTED	OVERSATURATED	OVERSPECULATE	OVERSTROOKE	OVERTNESSES
OVERPLANTED	OVERPROTECTING	OVERSATURATES	OVERSPECULATED	OVERSTRUCK	OVERTOILED
OVERPLANTING	OVERPROTECTION	OVERSATURATING	OVERSPECULATES	OVERSTRUCTURED	OVERTOILING
OVERPLANTS	OVERPROTECTIONS	OVERSATURATION	OVERSPECULATING	OVERSTRUNG	OVERTOPPED
OVERPLAYED	OVERPROTECTIVE	OVERSATURATIONS	OVERSPECULATION	OVERSTUDIED	OVERTOPPING
OVERPLAYING	OVERPROTECTS	OVERSAUCED	OVERSPENDER	OVERSTUDIES	OVERTOWERED
OVERPLOTTED	OVERPUMPED	OVERSAUCES	OVERSPENDERS	OVERSTUDYING	OVERTOWERING
OVERPLOTTING	OVERPUMPING	OVERSAUCING	OVERSPENDING	OVERSTUFFED	OVERTOWERS
OVERPLUSES	OVERQUALIFIED	OVERSAVING	OVERSPENDS	OVERSTUFFING	OVERTRADED
OVERPLUSSES	OVERRACKED	OVERSCALED	OVERSPICED	OVERSTUFFS	OVERTRADES
OVERPLYING	OVERRACKING	OVERSCHUTCHT	OVERSPICES	OVERSUBSCRIBE	OVERTRADING
OVERPOISED	OVERRAKING	OVERSCORED	OVERSPICING	OVERSUBSCRIBED	OVERTRAINED
OVERPOISES	OVERRASHLY	OVERSCORES	OVERSPILLED	OVERSUBSCRIBES	OVERTRAINING
OVERPOISING	OVERRASHNESS	OVERSCORING	OVERSPILLING	OVERSUBSCRIBING	OVERTRAINS
OVERPOPULATE	OVERRASHNESSES	OVERSCRUPULOUS	OVERSPILLS	OVERSUBTLE	OVERTREATED
OVERPOPULATED	OVERRATING	OVERSCUTCHED	OVERSPREAD	OVERSUBTLETIES	OVERTREATING
OVERPOPULATES	OVERRAUGHT	OVERSECRETION	OVERSPREADING	OVERSUBTLETY	OVERTREATMENT
OVERPOPULATING	OVERREACHED	OVERSECRETIONS	OVERSPREADS	OVERSUDSED	OVERTREATMENTS
OVERPOPULATION	OVERREACHER	OVERSEEDED	OVERSTABILITIES	OVERSUDSES	OVERTREATS
OVERPOPULATIONS	OVERREACHERS	OVERSEEDING	OVERSTABILITY	OVERSUDSING	OVERTRICKS
OVERPOSTED	OVERREACHES	OVERSEEING	OVERSTAFFED	OVERSUPPED	OVERTRIMMED
OVERPOSTING	OVERREACHING	OVERSELLING	OVERSTAFFING	OVERSUPPING	OVERTRIMMING
OVERPOTENT	OVERREACTED	OVERSENSITIVE	OVERSTAFFS	OVERSUPPLIED	OVERTRIPPED
OVERPOWERED	OVERREACTING	OVERSENSITIVITY	OVERSTAINED	OVERSUPPLIES	OVERTRIPPING
OVERPOWERING	OVERREACTION	OVERSERIOUS	OVERSTAINING	OVERSUPPLY	OVERTRUMPED

OVERTRUMPING
OVERTRUMPS
OVERTRUSTED
OVERTRUSTING
OVERTRUSTS
OVERTURING
OVERTURNED
OVERTURNER
OVERTURNERS
OVERTURNING
OVERTYPING
OVERURGING
OVERUTILISATION
OVERUTILISE
OVERUTILISED
OVERUTILISES
OVERUTILISING
OVERUTILIZATION
OVERUTILIZE
OVERUTILIZED
OVERUTILIZES
OVERUTILIZING
OVERVALUATION
OVERVALUATIONS
OVERVALUED
OVERVALUES
OVERVALUING
OVERVEILED
OVERVEILING
OVERVIOLENT
OVERVOLTAGE
OVERVOLTAGES
OVERVOTING

OVERWARMED
OVERWARMING
OVERWASHES
OVERWATCHED
OVERWATCHES
OVERWATCHING
OVERWATERED
OVERWATERING
OVERWATERS
OVERWEARIED
OVERWEARIES
OVERWEARING
OVERWEARYING
OVERWEATHER
OVERWEATHERED
OVERWEATHERING
OVERWEATHERS
OVERWEENED
OVERWEENING
OVERWEENINGLY
OVERWEENINGNESS
OVERWEENINGS
OVERWEIGHED
OVERWEIGHING
OVERWEIGHS
OVERWEIGHT
OVERWEIGHTED
OVERWEIGHTING
OVERWEIGHTS
OVERWETTED
OVERWETTING
OVERWHELMED
OVERWHELMING

OVERWHELMINGLY
OVERWHELMINGS
OVERWHELMS
OVERWINDING
OVERWINGED
OVERWINGING
OVERWINTER
OVERWINTERED
OVERWINTERING
OVERWINTERS
OVERWISELY
OVERWITHHELD
OVERWITHHOLD
OVERWITHHOLDING
OVERWITHHOLDS
OVERWORKED
OVERWORKING
OVERWRESTED
OVERWRESTING
OVERWRESTLE
OVERWRESTLED
OVERWRESTLES
OVERWRESTLING
OVERWRESTS
OVERWRITES
OVERWRITING
OVERWRITTEN
OVERWROUGHT
OVERYEARED
OVERYEARING
OVERZEALOUS
OVERZEALOUSNESS
OVIPARITIES

OVIPAROUSLY
OVIPOSITED
OVIPOSITING
OVIPOSITION
OVIPOSITIONAL
OVIPOSITIONS
OVIPOSITOR
OVIPOSITORS
OVIRAPTORS
OVOVIVIPARITIES
OVOVIVIPARITY
OVOVIVIPAROUS
OVOVIVIPAROUSLY
OVULATIONS
OVULIFEROUS
OWERLOUPEN
OWERLOUPING
OWERLOUPIT
OWLISHNESS
OWLISHNESSES
OWNERSHIPS
OXACILLINS
OXALACETATE
OXALACETATES
OXALOACETATE
OXALOACETATES
OXIDATIONAL
OXIDATIONS
OXIDATIVELY
OXIDIMETRIC
OXIDIMETRIES
OXIDIMETRY
OXIDISABLE

OXIDISATION
OXIDISATIONS
OXIDIZABLE
OXIDIZATION
OXIDIZATIONS
OXIDOREDUCTASE
OXIDOREDUCTASES
OXIMETRIES
OXYACETYLENE
OXYACETYLENES
OXYCEPHALIC
OXYCEPHALIES
OXYCEPHALOUS
OXYCEPHALY
OXYCODONES
OXYGENASES
OXYGENATED
OXYGENATES
OXYGENATING
OXYGENATION
OXYGENATIONS
OXYGENATOR
OXYGENATORS
OXYGENISED
OXYGENISER
OXYGENISERS
OXYGENISES
OXYGENISING
OXYGENIZED
OXYGENIZER
OXYGENIZERS
OXYGENIZES
OXYGENIZING

OXYGENLESS
OXYHAEMOGLOBIN
OXYHAEMOGLOBINS
OXYHEMOGLOBIN
OXYHEMOGLOBINS
OXYHYDROGEN
OXYMORONIC
OXYMORONICALLY
OXYPHENBUTAZONE
OXYRHYNCHUS
OXYRHYNCHUSES
OXYSULPHIDE
OXYSULPHIDES
OXYTETRACYCLINE
OXYURIASES
OXYURIASIS
OYSTERCATCHER
OYSTERCATCHERS
OYSTERINGS
OZOCERITES
OZOKERITES
OZONATIONS
OZONIFEROUS
OZONISATION
OZONISATIONS
OZONIZATION
OZONIZATIONS
OZONOLYSES
OZONOLYSIS
OZONOSPHERE
OZONOSPHERES

Pp

PACEMAKERS
PACEMAKING
PACEMAKINGS
PACESETTER
PACESETTERS
PACESETTING
PACHYCARPOUS
PACHYDACTYL
PACHYDACTYLOUS
PACHYDERMAL
PACHYDERMATOUS
PACHYDERMIA
PACHYDERMIAS
PACHYDERMIC
PACHYDERMOUS
PACHYDERMS
PACHYMENINGITIS
PACHYMETER
PACHYMETERS
PACHYSANDRA
PACHYSANDRAS
PACHYTENES
PACIFIABLE
PACIFICALLY
PACIFICATE
PACIFICATED
PACIFICATES
PACIFICATING
PACIFICATION
PACIFICATIONS
PACIFICATOR
PACIFICATORS
PACIFICATORY
PACIFICISM
PACIFICISMS
PACIFICIST
PACIFICISTS
PACIFISTIC
PACIFISTICALLY
PACKABILITIES
PACKABILITY
PACKAGINGS
PACKBOARDS
PACKFRAMES
PACKHORSES
PACKINGHOUSE
PACKINGHOUSES
PACKNESSES
PACKSADDLE
PACKSADDLES
PACKSHEETS
PACKSTAFFS
PACKTHREAD
PACKTHREADS
PACLITAXEL
PACLITAXELS
PACTIONING
PADDLEBALL
PADDLEBALLS
PADDLEBOARD
PADDLEBOARDS
PADDLEBOAT
PADDLEBOATS
PADDLEFISH
PADDLEFISHES
PADDOCKING
PADDYMELON

PADDYMELONS
PADDYWACKED
PADDYWACKING
PADDYWACKS
PADDYWHACK
PADDYWHACKS
PADEMELONS
PADEREROES
PADLOCKING
PADRONISMS
PADYMELONS
PAEDAGOGIC
PAEDAGOGUE
PAEDAGOGUES
PAEDERASTIC
PAEDERASTIES
PAEDERASTS
PAEDERASTY
PAEDEUTICS
PAEDIATRIC
PAEDIATRICIAN
PAEDIATRICIANS
PAEDIATRICS
PAEDIATRIES
PAEDIATRIST
PAEDIATRISTS
PAEDOBAPTISM
PAEDOBAPTISMS
PAEDOBAPTIST
PAEDOBAPTISTS
PAEDODONTIC
PAEDODONTICS
PAEDOGENESES
PAEDOGENESIS
PAEDOGENETIC
PAEDOGENIC
PAEDOLOGICAL
PAEDOLOGIES
PAEDOLOGIST
PAEDOLOGISTS
PAEDOMORPHIC
PAEDOMORPHISM
PAEDOMORPHISMS
PAEDOMORPHOSES
PAEDOMORPHOSIS
PAEDOPHILE
PAEDOPHILES
PAEDOPHILIA
PAEDOPHILIAC
PAEDOPHILIACS
PAEDOPHILIAS
PAEDOPHILIC
PAEDOPHILICS
PAEDOTRIBE
PAEDOTRIBES
PAEDOTROPHIES
PAEDOTROPHY
PAGANISATION
PAGANISATIONS
PAGANISERS
PAGANISING
PAGANISTIC
PAGANISTICALLY
PAGANIZATION
PAGANIZATIONS
PAGANIZERS
PAGANIZING

PAGEANTRIES
PAGINATING
PAGINATION
PAGINATIONS
PAIDEUTICS
PAILLASSES
PAILLETTES
PAINFULLER
PAINFULLEST
PAINFULNESS
PAINFULNESSES
PAINKILLER
PAINKILLERS
PAINKILLING
PAINLESSLY
PAINLESSNESS
PAINLESSNESSES
PAINSTAKER
PAINSTAKERS
PAINSTAKING
PAINSTAKINGLY
PAINSTAKINGNESS
PAINSTAKINGS
PAINTBALLS
PAINTBOXES
PAINTBRUSH
PAINTBRUSHES
PAINTERLINESS
PAINTERLINESSES
PAINTINESS
PAINTINESSES
PAINTRESSES
PAINTWORKS
PAKIRIKIRI
PAKIRIKIRIS
PALAEANTHROPIC
PALAEBIOLOGIES
PALAEBIOLOGIST
PALAEBIOLOGISTS
PALAEBIOLOGY
PALAEETHNOLOGY
PALAEOANTHROPIC
PALAEOBIOLOGIC
PALAEOBIOLOGIES
PALAEOBIOLOGIST
PALAEOBIOLOGY
PALAEOBOTANIC
PALAEOBOTANICAL
PALAEOBOTANIES
PALAEOBOTANIST
PALAEOBOTANISTS
PALAEOBOTANY
PALAEOCLIMATE
PALAEOCLIMATES
PALAEOCLIMATIC
PALAEOCRYSTIC
PALAEOCURRENT
PALAEOCURRENTS
PALAEOECOLOGIC
PALAEOECOLOGIES
PALAEOECOLOGIST
PALAEOECOLOGY
PALAEOETHNOLOGY
PALAEOGAEA
PALAEOGAEAS
PALAEOGEOGRAPHY
PALAEOGRAPHER

PALAEOGRAPHERS
PALAEOGRAPHIC
PALAEOGRAPHICAL
PALAEOGRAPHIES
PALAEOGRAPHIST
PALAEOGRAPHISTS
PALAEOGRAPHY
PALAEOLIMNOLOGY
PALAEOLITH
PALAEOLITHIC
PALAEOLITHS
PALAEOMAGNETIC
PALAEOMAGNETISM
PALAEONTOGRAPHY
PALAEONTOLOGIES
PALAEONTOLOGIST
PALAEONTOLOGY
PALAEOPATHOLOGY
PALAEOPEDOLOGY
PALAEOPHYTOLOGY
PALAEOTYPE
PALAEOTYPES
PALAEOTYPIC
PALAEOZOOLOGIES
PALAEOZOOLOGIST
PALAEOZOOLOGY
PALAESTRAE
PALAESTRAL
PALAESTRAS
PALAESTRIC
PALAESTRICAL
PALAFITTES
PALAGONITE
PALAGONITES
PALAMPORES
PALANKEENS
PALANQUINS
PALATABILITIES
PALATABILITY
PALATABLENESS
PALATABLENESSES
PALATALISATION
PALATALISATIONS
PALATALISE
PALATALISED
PALATALISES
PALATALISING
PALATALIZATION
PALATALIZATIONS
PALATALIZE
PALATALIZED
PALATALIZES
PALATALIZING
PALATIALLY
PALATIALNESS
PALATIALNESSES
PALATINATE
PALATINATES
PALAVERERS
PALAVERING
PALEACEOUS
PALEMPORES
PALENESSES
PALEOBIOLOGIC
PALEOBIOLOGICAL
PALEOBIOLOGIES
PALEOBIOLOGIST

PALEOBIOLOGISTS
PALEOBIOLOGY
PALEOBOTANIC
PALEOBOTANICAL
PALEOBOTANIES
PALEOBOTANIST
PALEOBOTANISTS
PALEOBOTANY
PALEOECOLOGIC
PALEOECOLOGICAL
PALEOECOLOGIES
PALEOECOLOGIST
PALEOECOLOGISTS
PALEOECOLOGY
PALEOGEOGRAPHIC
PALEOGEOGRAPHY
PALEOGRAPHER
PALEOGRAPHERS
PALEOGRAPHIC
PALEOGRAPHICAL
PALEOGRAPHIES
PALEOGRAPHY
PALEOLITHS
PALEOLOGIES
PALEOMAGNETIC
PALEOMAGNETISM
PALEOMAGNETISMS
PALEOMAGNETIST
PALEOMAGNETISTS
PALEONTOLOGIC
PALEONTOLOGICAL
PALEONTOLOGIES
PALEONTOLOGIST
PALEONTOLOGISTS
PALEONTOLOGY
PALEOPATHOLOGY
PALEOZOOLOGICAL
PALEOZOOLOGIES
PALEOZOOLOGIST
PALEOZOOLOGISTS
PALEOZOOLOGY
PALFRENIER
PALFRENIERS
PALIFICATION
PALIFICATIONS
PALILALIAS
PALILLOGIES
PALIMONIES
PALIMPSEST
PALIMPSESTS
PALINDROME
PALINDROMES
PALINDROMIC
PALINDROMICAL
PALINDROMIST
PALINDROMISTS
PALINGENESES
PALINGENESIA
PALINGENESIAS
PALINGENESIES
PALINGENESIS
PALINGENESIST
PALINGENESISTS
PALINGENESY
PALINGENETIC
PALINGENETICAL
PALINODIES

PALINOPIAS
PALINOPSIA
PALINOPSIAS
PALISADING
PALISADOED
PALISADOES
PALISADOING
PALISANDER
PALISANDERS
PALLADIOUS
PALLADIUMS
PALLBEARER
PALLBEARERS
PALLESCENCE
PALLESCENCES
PALLESCENT
PALLETISATION
PALLETISATIONS
PALLETISED
PALLETISER
PALLETISERS
PALLETISES
PALLETISING
PALLETIZATION
PALLETIZATIONS
PALLETIZED
PALLETIZER
PALLETIZERS
PALLETIZES
PALLETIZING
PALLIAMENT
PALLIAMENTS
PALLIASSES
PALLIATING
PALLIATION
PALLIATIONS
PALLIATIVE
PALLIATIVELY
PALLIATIVES
PALLIATORS
PALLIATORY
PALLIDITIES
PALLIDNESS
PALLIDNESSES
PALMACEOUS
PALMATIFID
PALMATIONS
PALMATIPARTITE
PALMATISECT
PALMCORDER
PALMCORDERS
PALMERWORM
PALMERWORMS
PALMETTOES
PALMHOUSES
PALMIFICATION
PALMIFICATIONS
PALMIPEDES
PALMISTERS
PALMISTRIES
PALMITATES
PALOVERDES
PALPABILITIES
PALPABILITY
PALPABLENESS
PALPABLENESSES
PALPATIONS

PALPEBRATE
PALPEBRATED
PALPEBRATES
PALPEBRATING
PALPITATED
PALPITATES
PALPITATING
PALPITATION
PALPITATIONS
PALSGRAVES
PALSGRAVINE
PALSGRAVINES
PALTRINESS
PALTRINESSES
PALUDAMENT
PALUDAMENTA
PALUDAMENTS
PALUDAMENTUM
PALUDAMENTUMS
PALUDICOLOUS
PALUDINOUS
PALUSTRIAN
PALUSTRINE
PALYNOLOGIC
PALYNOLOGICAL
PALYNOLOGICALLY
PALYNOLOGIES
PALYNOLOGIST
PALYNOLOGISTS
PALYNOLOGY
PAMPELMOOSE
PAMPELMOOSES
PAMPELMOUSE
PAMPELMOUSES
PAMPEREDNESS
PAMPEREDNESSES
PAMPHLETEER
PAMPHLETEERED
PAMPHLETEERING
PAMPHLETEERINGS
PAMPHLETEERS
PAMPOOTIES
PANACHAEAS
PANAESTHESIA
PANAESTHESIAS
PANAESTHETISM
PANAESTHETISMS
PANARITIUM
PANARITIUMS
PANARTHRITIS
PANARTHRITISES
PANATELLAS
PANBROILED
PANBROILING
PANCHAYATS
PANCHROMATIC
PANCHROMATISM
PANCHROMATISMS
PANCOSMISM
PANCOSMISMS
PANCRATIAN
PANCRATIAST
PANCRATIASTS
PANCRATIST
PANCRATISTS
PANCRATIUM
PANCRATIUMS
PANCREASES
PANCREATECTOMY
PANCREATIC
PANCREATIN
PANCREATINS
PANCREATITIDES
PANCREATITIS
PANCREATITISES
PANCREOZYMIN
PANCREOZYMINS
PANCYTOPENIA
PANCYTOPENIAS
PANDAEMONIUM
PANDAEMONIUMS
PANDANACEOUS
PANDANUSES

PANDATIONS
PANDECTIST
PANDECTISTS
PANDEMONIAC
PANDEMONIACAL
PANDEMONIAN
PANDEMONIC
PANDEMONIUM
PANDEMONIUMS
PANDERESSES
PANDERISMS
PANDERMITE
PANDERMITES
PANDICULATION
PANDICULATIONS
PANDOWDIES
PANDURATED
PANDURIFORM
PANEGOISMS
PANEGYRICA
PANEGYRICAL
PANEGYRICALLY
PANEGYRICON
PANEGYRICS
PANEGYRIES
PANEGYRISE
PANEGYRISED
PANEGYRISES
PANEGYRISING
PANEGYRIST
PANEGYRISTS
PANEGYRIZE
PANEGYRIZED
PANEGYRIZES
PANEGYRIZING
PANELLINGS
PANELLISTS
PANENTHEISM
PANENTHEISMS
PANENTHEIST
PANENTHEISTS
PANESTHESIA
PANESTHESIAS
PANETELLAS
PANETTONES
PANGENESES
PANGENESIS
PANGENETIC
PANGENETICALLY
PANGRAMMATIST
PANGRAMMATISTS
PANHANDLED
PANHANDLER
PANHANDLERS
PANHANDLES
PANHANDLING
PANHARMONICON
PANHARMONICONS
PANHELLENIC
PANHELLENION
PANHELLENIONS
PANHELLENIUM
PANHELLENIUMS
PANICKIEST
PANICMONGER
PANICMONGERS
PANICULATE
PANICULATED
PANICULATELY
PANIDIOMORPHIC
PANIFICATION
PANIFICATIONS
PANISLAMIC
PANISLAMISM
PANISLAMISMS
PANISLAMIST
PANISLAMISTS
PANJANDARUM
PANJANDARUMS
PANJANDRUM
PANJANDRUMS
PANLEUCOPENIA
PANLEUCOPENIAS

PANLEUKOPENIA
PANLEUKOPENIAS
PANLOGISMS
PANMIXISES
PANNICULUS
PANNICULUSES
PANNIKELLS
PANOMPHAEAN
PANOPHOBIA
PANOPHOBIAS
PANOPHTHALMIA
PANOPHTHALMIAS
PANOPHTHALMITIS
PANOPTICAL
PANOPTICALLY
PANOPTICON
PANOPTICONS
PANORAMICALLY
PANPHARMACON
PANPHARMACONS
PANPSYCHISM
PANPSYCHISMS
PANPSYCHIST
PANPSYCHISTIC
PANPSYCHISTS
PANRADIOMETER
PANRADIOMETERS
PANSEXUALISM
PANSEXUALISMS
PANSEXUALIST
PANSEXUALISTS
PANSEXUALITIES
PANSEXUALITY
PANSEXUALS
PANSOPHICAL
PANSOPHICALLY
PANSOPHIES
PANSOPHISM
PANSOPHISMS
PANSOPHIST
PANSOPHISTS
PANSPERMATIC
PANSPERMATISM
PANSPERMATISMS
PANSPERMATIST
PANSPERMATISTS
PANSPERMIA
PANSPERMIAS
PANSPERMIC
PANSPERMIES
PANSPERMISM
PANSPERMISMS
PANSPERMIST
PANSPERMISTS
PANTAGAMIES
PANTAGRAPH
PANTAGRAPHS
PANTALEONS
PANTALETTED
PANTALETTES
PANTALONES
PANTALOONED
PANTALOONERIES
PANTALOONERY
PANTALOONS
PANTDRESSES
PANTECHNICON
PANTECHNICONS
PANTHEISMS
PANTHEISTIC
PANTHEISTICAL
PANTHEISTICALLY
PANTHEISTS
PANTHENOLS
PANTHEOLOGIES
PANTHEOLOGIST
PANTHEOLOGISTS
PANTHEOLOGY
PANTHERESS
PANTHERESSES
PANTHERINE
PANTHERISH
PANTILINGS

PANTISOCRACIES
PANTISOCRACY
PANTISOCRAT
PANTISOCRATIC
PANTISOCRATICAL
PANTISOCRATIST
PANTISOCRATISTS
PANTISOCRATS
PANTOFFLES
PANTOGRAPH
PANTOGRAPHER
PANTOGRAPHERS
PANTOGRAPHIC
PANTOGRAPHICAL
PANTOGRAPHIES
PANTOGRAPHS
PANTOGRAPHY
PANTOMIMED
PANTOMIMES
PANTOMIMIC
PANTOMIMICAL
PANTOMIMICALLY
PANTOMIMING
PANTOMIMIST
PANTOMIMISTS
PANTOPHAGIES
PANTOPHAGIST
PANTOPHAGISTS
PANTOPHAGOUS
PANTOPHAGY
PANTOPHOBIA
PANTOPHOBIAS
PANTOPRAGMATIC
PANTOPRAGMATICS
PANTOSCOPE
PANTOSCOPES
PANTOSCOPIC
PANTOTHENATE
PANTOTHENATES
PANTOTHENIC
PANTOUFLES
PANTROPICAL
PANTRYMAID
PANTRYMAIDS
PANTSUITED
PANTYWAIST
PANTYWAISTS
PANZOOTICS
PAPALISING
PAPALIZING
PAPAPRELATIST
PAPAPRELATISTS
PAPAVERACEOUS
PAPAVERINE
PAPAVERINES
PAPAVEROUS
PAPERBACKED
PAPERBACKER
PAPERBACKERS
PAPERBACKING
PAPERBACKS
PAPERBARKS
PAPERBOARD
PAPERBOARDS
PAPERBOUND
PAPERBOUNDS
PAPERCLIPS
PAPERGIRLS
PAPERHANGER
PAPERHANGERS
PAPERHANGING
PAPERHANGINGS
PAPERINESS
PAPERINESSES
PAPERKNIFE
PAPERKNIVES
PAPERMAKER
PAPERMAKERS
PAPERMAKING
PAPERMAKINGS
PAPERWARES
PAPERWEIGHT
PAPERWEIGHTS

PAPERWORKS
PAPETERIES
PAPILIONACEOUS
PAPILLATED
PAPILLIFEROUS
PAPILLIFORM
PAPILLITIS
PAPILLITISES
PAPILLOMAS
PAPILLOMATA
PAPILLOMATOSES
PAPILLOMATOSIS
PAPILLOMATOUS
PAPILLOMAVIRUS
PAPILLOTES
PAPILLULATE
PAPILLULES
PAPISTICAL
PAPISTICALLY
PAPISTRIES
PAPOVAVIRUS
PAPOVAVIRUSES
PAPULATION
PAPULATIONS
PAPULIFEROUS
PAPYRACEOUS
PAPYROLOGICAL
PAPYROLOGIES
PAPYROLOGIST
PAPYROLOGISTS
PAPYROLOGY
PARABAPTISM
PARABAPTISMS
PARABEMATA
PARABEMATIC
PARABIOSES
PARABIOSIS
PARABIOTIC
PARABIOTICALLY
PARABLASTIC
PARABLASTS
PARABLEPSES
PARABLEPSIES
PARABLEPSIS
PARABLEPSY
PARABLEPTIC
PARABOLANUS
PARABOLANUSES
PARABOLICAL
PARABOLICALLY
PARABOLISATION
PARABOLISATIONS
PARABOLISE
PARABOLISED
PARABOLISES
PARABOLISING
PARABOLIST
PARABOLISTS
PARABOLIZATION
PARABOLIZATIONS
PARABOLIZE
PARABOLIZED
PARABOLIZES
PARABOLIZING
PARABOLOID
PARABOLOIDAL
PARABOLOIDS
PARABRAKES
PARACASEIN
PARACASEINS
PARACENTESES
PARACENTESIS
PARACETAMOL
PARACETAMOLS
PARACHRONISM
PARACHRONISMS
PARACHUTED
PARACHUTES
PARACHUTIC
PARACHUTING
PARACHUTIST
PARACHUTISTS
PARACLETES

PARACROSTIC
PARACROSTICS
PARACYANOGEN
PARACYANOGENS
PARADIDDLE
PARADIDDLES
PARADIGMATIC
PARADIGMATICAL
PARADISAIC
PARADISAICAL
PARADISAICALLY
PARADISEAN
PARADISIAC
PARADISIACAL
PARADISIACALLY
PARADISIAL
PARADISIAN
PARADISICAL
PARADOCTOR
PARADOCTORS
PARADOXERS
PARADOXICAL
PARADOXICALITY
PARADOXICALLY
PARADOXICALNESS
PARADOXIDIAN
PARADOXIES
PARADOXIST
PARADOXISTS
PARADOXOLOGIES
PARADOXOLOGY
PARADOXURE
PARADOXURES
PARADOXURINE
PARADROPPED
PARADROPPING
PARAENESES
PARAENESIS
PARAENETIC
PARAENETICAL
PARAESTHESIA
PARAESTHESIAS
PARAESTHETIC
PARAFFINED
PARAFFINES
PARAFFINIC
PARAFFINING
PARAFFINOID
PARAGENESES
PARAGENESIA
PARAGENESIAS
PARAGENESIS
PARAGENETIC
PARAGENETICALLY
PARAGLIDED
PARAGLIDER
PARAGLIDERS
PARAGLIDES
PARAGLIDING
PARAGLIDINGS
PARAGLOSSA
PARAGLOSSAE
PARAGLOSSAL
PARAGLOSSATE
PARAGNATHISM
PARAGNATHISMS
PARAGNATHOUS
PARAGNOSES
PARAGNOSIS
PARAGOGICAL
PARAGOGICALLY
PARAGOGUES
PARAGONING
PARAGONITE
PARAGONITES
PARAGRAMMATIST
PARAGRAMMATISTS
PARAGRAPHED
PARAGRAPHER
PARAGRAPHERS
PARAGRAPHIA
PARAGRAPHIAS
PARAGRAPHIC

PARAGRAPHICAL
PARAGRAPHICALLY
PARAGRAPHING
PARAGRAPHIST
PARAGRAPHISTS
PARAGRAPHS
PARAHELIOTROPIC
PARAHYDROGEN
PARAHYDROGENS
PARAINFLUENZA
PARAINFLUENZAS
PARAJOURNALISM
PARAJOURNALISMS
PARAKEELYA
PARAKEELYAS
PARAKELIAS
PARAKITING
PARAKITINGS
PARALALIAS
PARALANGUAGE
PARALANGUAGES
PARALDEHYDE
PARALDEHYDES
PARALEGALS
PARALEIPOMENA
PARALEIPOMENON
PARALEIPSES
PARALEIPSIS
PARALEXIAS
PARALIMNION
PARALIMNIONS
PARALINGUISTIC
PARALINGUISTICS
PARALIPOMENA
PARALIPOMENON
PARALIPSES
PARALIPSIS
PARALLACTIC
PARALLACTICAL
PARALLACTICALLY
PARALLAXES
PARALLELED
PARALLELEPIPED
PARALLELEPIPEDA
PARALLELEPIPEDS
PARALLELING
PARALLELINGS
PARALLELISE
PARALLELISED
PARALLELISES
PARALLELISING
PARALLELISM
PARALLELISMS
PARALLELIST
PARALLELISTIC
PARALLELISTS
PARALLELIZE
PARALLELIZED
PARALLELIZES
PARALLELIZING
PARALLELLED
PARALLELLING
PARALLELLY
PARALLELOGRAM
PARALLELOGRAMS
PARALLELOPIPED
PARALLELOPIPEDA
PARALLELOPIPEDS
PARALLELWISE
PARALOGIAS
PARALOGIES
PARALOGISE
PARALOGISED
PARALOGISES
PARALOGISING
PARALOGISM
PARALOGISMS
PARALOGIST
PARALOGISTIC
PARALOGISTS
PARALOGIZE
PARALOGIZED
PARALOGIZES

PARALOGIZING
PARALYMPIC
PARALYMPICS
PARALYSATION
PARALYSATIONS
PARALYSERS
PARALYSING
PARALYSINGLY
PARALYTICALLY
PARALYTICS
PARALYZATION
PARALYZATIONS
PARALYZERS
PARALYZING
PARALYZINGLY
PARAMAECIA
PARAMAECIUM
PARAMAGNET
PARAMAGNETIC
PARAMAGNETISM
PARAMAGNETISMS
PARAMAGNETS
PARAMASTOID
PARAMASTOIDS
PARAMATTAS
PARAMECIUM
PARAMECIUMS
PARAMEDICAL
PARAMEDICALS
PARAMEDICO
PARAMEDICOS
PARAMEDICS
PARAMENSTRUA
PARAMENSTRUUM
PARAMENSTRUUMS
PARAMETERISE
PARAMETERISED
PARAMETERISES
PARAMETERISING
PARAMETERIZE
PARAMETERIZED
PARAMETERIZES
PARAMETERIZING
PARAMETERS
PARAMETRAL
PARAMETRIC
PARAMETRICAL
PARAMETRICALLY
PARAMETRISATION
PARAMETRISE
PARAMETRISED
PARAMETRISES
PARAMETRISING
PARAMETRIZATION
PARAMETRIZE
PARAMETRIZED
PARAMETRIZES
PARAMETRIZING
PARAMILITARIES
PARAMILITARY
PARAMNESIA
PARAMNESIAS
PARAMOECIA
PARAMOECIUM
PARAMORPHIC
PARAMORPHINE
PARAMORPHINES
PARAMORPHISM
PARAMORPHISMS
PARAMORPHOUS
PARAMORPHS
PARAMOUNCIES
PARAMOUNCY
PARAMOUNTCIES
PARAMOUNTCY
PARAMOUNTLY
PARAMOUNTS
PARAMYLUMS
PARAMYXOVIRUS
PARAMYXOVIRUSES
PARANEPHRIC
PARANEPHROS
PARANEPHROSES

PARANOEICS
PARANOIACS
PARANOICALLY
PARANOIDAL
PARANORMAL
PARANORMALITIES
PARANORMALITY
PARANORMALLY
PARANORMALS
PARANTHELIA
PARANTHELION
PARANTHROPUS
PARANTHROPUSES
PARANYMPHS
PARAPARESES
PARAPARESIS
PARAPARETIC
PARAPENTES
PARAPENTING
PARAPENTINGS
PARAPERIODIC
PARAPHASIA
PARAPHASIAS
PARAPHASIC
PARAPHERNALIA
PARAPHILIA
PARAPHILIAC
PARAPHILIACS
PARAPHILIAS
PARAPHIMOSES
PARAPHIMOSIS
PARAPHONIA
PARAPHONIAS
PARAPHONIC
PARAPHRASABLE
PARAPHRASE
PARAPHRASED
PARAPHRASER
PARAPHRASERS
PARAPHRASES
PARAPHRASING
PARAPHRAST
PARAPHRASTIC
PARAPHRASTICAL
PARAPHRASTS
PARAPHRAXES
PARAPHRAXIA
PARAPHRAXIAS
PARAPHRAXIS
PARAPHRENIA
PARAPHRENIAS
PARAPHYSATE
PARAPHYSES
PARAPHYSIS
PARAPINEAL
PARAPLEGIA
PARAPLEGIAS
PARAPLEGIC
PARAPLEGICS
PARAPODIAL
PARAPODIUM
PARAPOPHYSES
PARAPOPHYSIAL
PARAPOPHYSIS
PARAPRAXES
PARAPRAXIS
PARAPSYCHIC
PARAPSYCHICAL
PARAPSYCHISM
PARAPSYCHISMS
PARAPSYCHOLOGY
PARAPSYCHOSES
PARAPSYCHOSIS
PARAQUADRATES
PARAQUITOS
PARARHYMES
PARAROSANILINE
PARAROSANILINES
PARARTHRIA
PARARTHRIAS
PARASAILED
PARASAILING

PARASAILINGS
PARASCENDER
PARASCENDERS
PARASCENDING
PARASCENDINGS
PARASCENIA
PARASCENIUM
PARASCEVES
PARASCIENCE
PARASCIENCES
PARASELENAE
PARASELENE
PARASELENIC
PARASEXUAL
PARASEXUALITIES
PARASEXUALITY
PARASHIOTH
PARASITAEMIA
PARASITAEMIAS
PARASITICAL
PARASITICALLY
PARASITICALNESS
PARASITICIDAL
PARASITICIDE
PARASITICIDES
PARASITISATION
PARASITISATIONS
PARASITISE
PARASITISED
PARASITISES
PARASITISING
PARASITISM
PARASITISMS
PARASITIZATION
PARASITIZATIONS
PARASITIZE
PARASITIZED
PARASITIZES
PARASITIZING
PARASITOID
PARASITOIDS
PARASITOLOGIC
PARASITOLOGICAL
PARASITOLOGIES
PARASITOLOGIST
PARASITOLOGISTS
PARASITOLOGY
PARASITOSES
PARASITOSIS
PARASKIING
PARASKIINGS
PARASPHENOID
PARASPHENOIDS
PARASTATAL
PARASTATALS
PARASTICHIES
PARASTICHOUS
PARASTICHY
PARASUICIDE
PARASUICIDES
PARASYMBIONT
PARASYMBIONTS
PARASYMBIOSES
PARASYMBIOSIS
PARASYMBIOTIC
PARASYMPATHETIC
PARASYNAPSES
PARASYNAPSIS
PARASYNAPTIC
PARASYNTHESES
PARASYNTHESIS
PARASYNTHETA
PARASYNTHETIC
PARASYNTHETON
PARATACTIC
PARATACTICAL
PARATACTICALLY
PARATANIWHA
PARATHESES
PARATHESIS
PARATHIONS
PARATHORMONE
PARATHORMONES

PARATHYROID
PARATHYROIDS
PARATROOPER
PARATROOPERS
PARATROOPS
PARATUNGSTIC
PARATYPHOID
PARATYPHOIDS
PARAWALKER
PARAWALKERS
PARBOILING
PARBREAKED
PARBREAKING
PARBUCKLED
PARBUCKLES
PARBUCKLING
PARCELLING
PARCELWISE
PARCENARIES
PARCHEDNESS
PARCHEDNESSES
PARCHEESIS
PARCHMENTISE
PARCHMENTISED
PARCHMENTISES
PARCHMENTISING
PARCHMENTIZE
PARCHMENTIZED
PARCHMENTIZES
PARCHMENTIZING
PARCHMENTS
PARCHMENTY
PARCIMONIES
PARDALISES
PARDALOTES
PARDONABLE
PARDONABLENESS
PARDONABLY
PARDONINGS
PARDONLESS
PAREGORICS
PARENCEPHALA
PARENCEPHALON
PARENCHYMA
PARENCHYMAL
PARENCHYMAS
PARENCHYMATA
PARENCHYMATOUS
PARENTAGES
PARENTALLY
PARENTERAL
PARENTERALLY
PARENTHESES
PARENTHESIS
PARENTHESISE
PARENTHESISED
PARENTHESISES
PARENTHESISING
PARENTHESIZE
PARENTHESIZED
PARENTHESIZES
PARENTHESIZING
PARENTHETIC
PARENTHETICAL
PARENTHETICALLY
PARENTHOOD
PARENTHOODS
PARENTINGS
PARENTLESS
PARESTHESIA
PARESTHESIAS
PARESTHETIC
PARFLECHES
PARFLESHES
PARFOCALISE
PARFOCALISED
PARFOCALISES
PARFOCALISING
PARFOCALITIES
PARFOCALITY
PARFOCALIZE
PARFOCALIZED
PARFOCALIZES

PARFOCALIZING
PARGASITES
PARGETINGS
PARGETTING
PARGETTINGS
PARGYLINES
PARHELIACAL
PARHYPATES
PARIPINNATE
PARISCHANE
PARISCHANES
PARISCHANS
PARISHIONER
PARISHIONERS
PARISYLLABIC
PARKINSONIAN
PARKINSONISM
PARKINSONISMS
PARKLEAVES
PARLEMENTS
PARLEYVOOED
PARLEYVOOING
PARLEYVOOS
PARLIAMENT
PARLIAMENTARIAN
PARLIAMENTARILY
PARLIAMENTARISM
PARLIAMENTARY
PARLIAMENTING
PARLIAMENTINGS
PARLIAMENTS
PARLOUSNESS
PARLOUSNESSES
PARMACITIE
PARMACITIES
PARMIGIANA
PARMIGIANO
PAROCCIPITAL
PAROCHIALISE
PAROCHIALISED
PAROCHIALISES
PAROCHIALISING
PAROCHIALISM
PAROCHIALISMS
PAROCHIALITIES
PAROCHIALITY
PAROCHIALIZE
PAROCHIALIZED
PAROCHIALIZES
PAROCHIALIZING
PAROCHIALLY
PAROCHINES
PARODISTIC
PAROECIOUS
PAROEMIACS
PAROEMIOGRAPHER
PAROEMIOGRAPHY
PAROEMIOLOGIES
PAROEMIOLOGY
PARONOMASIA
PARONOMASIAS
PARONOMASIES
PARONOMASTIC
PARONOMASTICAL
PARONOMASY
PARONYCHIA
PARONYCHIAL
PARONYCHIAS
PARONYMIES
PARONYMOUS
PARONYMOUSLY
PAROTIDITIC
PAROTIDITIS
PAROTIDITISES
PAROTITISES
PAROXETINE
PAROXETINES
PAROXYSMAL
PAROXYSMALLY
PAROXYSMIC
PAROXYTONE
PAROXYTONES
PAROXYTONIC

PARQUETING
PARQUETRIES
PARQUETTED
PARQUETTING
PARRAKEETS
PARRAMATTA
PARRAMATTAS
PARRHESIAS
PARRICIDAL
PARRICIDES
PARRITCHES
PARROCKING
PARROQUETS
PARROTFISH
PARROTFISHES
PARROTRIES
PARSIMONIES
PARSIMONIOUS
PARSIMONIOUSLY
PARSONAGES
PARSONICAL
PARTAKINGS
PARTHENOCARPIC
PARTHENOCARPIES
PARTHENOCARPOUS
PARTHENOCARPY
PARTHENOGENESES
PARTHENOGENESIS
PARTHENOGENETIC
PARTHENOSPORE
PARTHENOSPORES
PARTIALISE
PARTIALISED
PARTIALISES
PARTIALISING
PARTIALISM
PARTIALISMS
PARTIALIST
PARTIALISTS
PARTIALITIES
PARTIALITY
PARTIALIZE
PARTIALIZED
PARTIALIZES
PARTIALIZING
PARTIALNESS
PARTIALNESSES
PARTIBILITIES
PARTIBILITY
PARTICIPABLE
PARTICIPANT
PARTICIPANTLY
PARTICIPANTS
PARTICIPATE
PARTICIPATED
PARTICIPATES
PARTICIPATING
PARTICIPATION
PARTICIPATIONAL
PARTICIPATIONS
PARTICIPATIVE
PARTICIPATOR
PARTICIPATORS
PARTICIPATORY
PARTICIPIAL
PARTICIPIALLY
PARTICIPIALS
PARTICIPLE
PARTICIPLES
PARTICLEBOARD
PARTICLEBOARDS
PARTICULAR
PARTICULARISE
PARTICULARISED
PARTICULARISER
PARTICULARISERS
PARTICULARISES
PARTICULARISING
PARTICULARISM
PARTICULARISMS
PARTICULARIST
PARTICULARISTIC
PARTICULARISTS

PARTICULARITIES
PARTICULARITY
PARTICULARIZE
PARTICULARIZED
PARTICULARIZER
PARTICULARIZERS
PARTICULARIZES
PARTICULARIZING
PARTICULARLY
PARTICULARNESS
PARTICULARS
PARTICULATE
PARTICULATES
PARTISANLY
PARTISANSHIP
PARTISANSHIPS
PARTITIONED
PARTITIONER
PARTITIONERS
PARTITIONING
PARTITIONIST
PARTITIONISTS
PARTITIONMENT
PARTITIONMENTS
PARTITIONS
PARTITIVELY
PARTITIVES
PARTITURAS
PARTIZANSHIP
PARTIZANSHIPS
PARTNERING
PARTNERLESS
PARTNERSHIP
PARTNERSHIPS
PARTRIDGEBERRY
PARTRIDGES
PARTURIENCIES
PARTURIENCY
PARTURIENT
PARTURIENTS
PARTURIFACIENT
PARTURITION
PARTURITIONS
PARTYGOERS
PARVANIMITIES
PARVANIMITY
PARVIFOLIATE
PARVOLINES
PARVOVIRUS
PARVOVIRUSES
PASIGRAPHIC
PASIGRAPHICAL
PASIGRAPHIES
PASIGRAPHY
PASODOBLES
PASQUEFLOWER
PASQUEFLOWERS
PASQUILANT
PASQUILANTS
PASQUILERS
PASQUILLED
PASQUILLING
PASQUINADE
PASQUINADED
PASQUINADER
PASQUINADERS
PASQUINADES
PASQUINADING
PASSABLENESS
PASSABLENESSES
PASSACAGLIA
PASSACAGLIAS
PASSAGEWAY
PASSAGEWAYS
PASSAGEWORK
PASSAGEWORKS
PASSALONGS
PASSAMENTED
PASSAMENTING
PASSAMENTS
PASSAMEZZO
PASSAMEZZOS
PASSEMEASURE

PASSEMEASURES
PASSEMENTED
PASSEMENTERIE
PASSEMENTERIES
PASSEMENTING
PASSEMENTS
PASSENGERS
PASSEPIEDS
PASSERINES
PASSIBILITIES
PASSIBILITY
PASSIBLENESS
PASSIBLENESSES
PASSIFLORA
PASSIFLORACEOUS
PASSIFLORAS
PASSIMETER
PASSIMETERS
PASSIONALS
PASSIONARIES
PASSIONARY
PASSIONATE
PASSIONATED
PASSIONATELY
PASSIONATENESS
PASSIONATES
PASSIONATING
PASSIONFLOWER
PASSIONFLOWERS
PASSIONING
PASSIONLESS
PASSIONLESSLY
PASSIONLESSNESS
PASSIVATED
PASSIVATES
PASSIVATING
PASSIVATION
PASSIVATIONS
PASSIVENESS
PASSIVENESSES
PASSIVISMS
PASSIVISTS
PASSIVITIES
PASSMENTED
PASSMENTING
PASTEBOARD
PASTEBOARDS
PASTEDOWNS
PASTELISTS
PASTELLIST
PASTELLISTS
PASTEURELLA
PASTEURELLAE
PASTEURELLAS
PASTEURISATION
PASTEURISATIONS
PASTEURISE
PASTEURISED
PASTEURISER
PASTEURISERS
PASTEURISES
PASTEURISING
PASTEURISM
PASTEURISMS
PASTEURIZATION
PASTEURIZATIONS
PASTEURIZE
PASTEURIZED
PASTEURIZER
PASTEURIZERS
PASTEURIZES
PASTEURIZING
PASTICCIOS
PASTICHEUR
PASTICHEURS
PASTINESSES
PASTITSIOS
PASTMASTER
PASTMASTERS
PASTNESSES
PASTORALES
PASTORALISM
PASTORALISMS

PASTORALIST
PASTORALISTS
PASTORALLY
PASTORALNESS
PASTORALNESSES
PASTORATES
PASTORIUMS
PASTORSHIP
PASTORSHIPS
PASTOURELLE
PASTOURELLES
PASTRYCOOK
PASTRYCOOKS
PASTURABLE
PASTURAGES
PASTURELAND
PASTURELANDS
PASTURELESS
PATAPHYSICS
PATCHBOARD
PATCHBOARDS
PATCHCOCKE
PATCHCOCKES
PATCHERIES
PATCHINESS
PATCHINESSES
PATCHOCKES
PATCHOULIES
PATCHOULIS
PATCHWORKED
PATCHWORKING
PATCHWORKS
PATELLECTOMIES
PATELLECTOMY
PATELLIFORM
PATENTABILITIES
PATENTABILITY
PATENTABLE
PATERCOVES
PATEREROES
PATERFAMILIAS
PATERFAMILIASES
PATERNALISM
PATERNALISMS
PATERNALIST
PATERNALISTIC
PATERNALISTS
PATERNALLY
PATERNITIES
PATERNOSTER
PATERNOSTERS
PATHBREAKING
PATHETICAL
PATHETICALLY
PATHFINDER
PATHFINDERS
PATHFINDING
PATHFINDINGS
PATHLESSNESS
PATHLESSNESSES
PATHOBIOLOGIES
PATHOBIOLOGY
PATHOGENES
PATHOGENESES
PATHOGENESIS
PATHOGENETIC
PATHOGENIC
PATHOGENICITIES
PATHOGENICITY
PATHOGENIES
PATHOGENOUS
PATHOGNOMIES
PATHOGNOMONIC
PATHOGNOMY
PATHOGRAPHIES
PATHOGRAPHY
PATHOLOGIC
PATHOLOGICAL
PATHOLOGICALLY
PATHOLOGIES
PATHOLOGISE
PATHOLOGISED
PATHOLOGISES

PATHOLOGISING
PATHOLOGIST
PATHOLOGISTS
PATHOLOGIZE
PATHOLOGIZED
PATHOLOGIZES
PATHOLOGIZING
PATHOPHOBIA
PATHOPHOBIAS
PATHOPHYSIOLOGY
PATIBULARY
PATIENTEST
PATIENTING
PATINATING
PATINATION
PATINATIONS
PATINISING
PATINIZING
PATISSERIE
PATISSERIES
PATISSIERS
PATRESFAMILIAS
PATRIALISATION
PATRIALISATIONS
PATRIALISE
PATRIALISED
PATRIALISES
PATRIALISING
PATRIALISM
PATRIALISMS
PATRIALITIES
PATRIALITY
PATRIALIZATION
PATRIALIZATIONS
PATRIALIZE
PATRIALIZED
PATRIALIZES
PATRIALIZING
PATRIARCHAL
PATRIARCHALISM
PATRIARCHALISMS
PATRIARCHALLY
PATRIARCHATE
PATRIARCHATES
PATRIARCHIES
PATRIARCHISM
PATRIARCHISMS
PATRIARCHS
PATRIARCHY
PATRIATING
PATRIATION
PATRIATIONS
PATRICIANLY
PATRICIANS
PATRICIATE
PATRICIATES
PATRICIDAL
PATRICIDES
PATRICLINIC
PATRICLINOUS
PATRIFOCAL
PATRIFOCALITIES
PATRIFOCALITY
PATRILINEAGE
PATRILINEAGES
PATRILINEAL
PATRILINEALLY
PATRILINEAR
PATRILINEARLY
PATRILINIES
PATRILOCAL
PATRILOCALLY
PATRIMONIAL
PATRIMONIALLY
PATRIMONIES
PATRIOTICALLY
PATRIOTISM
PATRIOTISMS
PATRISTICAL
PATRISTICALLY
PATRISTICISM
PATRISTICISMS
PATRISTICS

PATROCLINAL
PATROCLINIC
PATROCLINIES
PATROCLINOUS
PATROCLINY
PATROLLERS
PATROLLING
PATROLOGICAL
PATROLOGIES
PATROLOGIST
PATROLOGISTS
PATROLWOMAN
PATROLWOMEN
PATRONAGED
PATRONAGES
PATRONAGING
PATRONESSES
PATRONISATION
PATRONISATIONS
PATRONISED
PATRONISER
PATRONISERS
PATRONISES
PATRONISING
PATRONISINGLY
PATRONIZATION
PATRONIZATIONS
PATRONIZED
PATRONIZER
PATRONIZERS
PATRONIZES
PATRONIZING
PATRONIZINGLY
PATRONLESS
PATRONYMIC
PATRONYMICS
PATROONSHIP
PATROONSHIPS
PATTERNING
PATTERNINGS
PATTERNLESS
PATULOUSLY
PATULOUSNESS
PATULOUSNESSES
PAUCILOQUENT
PAUGHTIEST
PAULOWNIAS
PAUNCHIEST
PAUNCHINESS
PAUNCHINESSES
PAUPERESSES
PAUPERISATION
PAUPERISATIONS
PAUPERISED
PAUPERISES
PAUPERISING
PAUPERISMS
PAUPERIZATION
PAUPERIZATIONS
PAUPERIZED
PAUPERIZES
PAUPERIZING
PAUPIETTES
PAUSEFULLY
PAUSELESSLY
PAVEMENTED
PAVEMENTING
PAVILIONED
PAVILIONING
PAVONAZZOS
PAWKINESSES
PAWNBROKER
PAWNBROKERS
PAWNBROKING
PAWNBROKINGS
PAWNTICKET
PAWNTICKETS
PAYMASTERS
PAYNIMRIES
PAYSAGISTS
PEABERRIES
PEACEABLENESS
PEACEABLENESSES

PEACEFULLER	PECULIARITY	PEDICULOSIS	PELVIMETRY	PENICILLINASE	PENTACTINAL
PEACEFULLEST	PECULIARIZE	PEDICULOUS	PELYCOSAUR	PENICILLINASES	PENTACYCLIC
PEACEFULLY	PECULIARIZED	PEDICURING	PELYCOSAURS	PENICILLINS	PENTADACTYL
PEACEFULNESS	PECULIARIZES	PEDICURIST	PEMPHIGOID	PENICILLIUM	PENTADACTYLE
PEACEFULNESSES	PECULIARIZING	PEDICURISTS	PEMPHIGOUS	PENICILLIUMS	PENTADACTYLES
PEACEKEEPER	PECULIARLY	PEDIMENTAL	PEMPHIGUSES	PENINSULAR	PENTADACTYLIC
PEACEKEEPERS	PECUNIARILY	PEDIMENTED	PENALISATION	PENINSULARITIES	PENTADACTYLIES
PEACEKEEPING	PEDAGOGICAL	PEDIPALPUS	PENALISATIONS	PENINSULARITY	PENTADACTYLISM
PEACEKEEPINGS	PEDAGOGICALLY	PEDOGENESES	PENALISING	PENINSULAS	PENTADACTYLISMS
PEACELESSNESS	PEDAGOGICS	PEDOGENESIS	PENALITIES	PENINSULATE	PENTADACTYLOUS
PEACELESSNESSES	PEDAGOGIES	PEDOGENETIC	PENALIZATION	PENINSULATED	PENTADACTYLS
PEACEMAKER	PEDAGOGISM	PEDOLOGICAL	PENALIZATIONS	PENINSULATES	PENTADACTYLY
PEACEMAKERS	PEDAGOGISMS	PEDOLOGIES	PENALIZING	PENINSULATING	PENTADELPHOUS
PEACEMAKING	PEDAGOGUED	PEDOLOGIST	PENANNULAR	PENISTONES	PENTAGONAL
PEACEMAKINGS	PEDAGOGUERIES	PEDOLOGISTS	PENCILINGS	PENITENCES	PENTAGONALLY
PEACETIMES	PEDAGOGUERY	PEDOMETERS	PENCILLERS	PENITENCIES	PENTAGONALS
PEACHBLOWS	PEDAGOGUES	PEDOPHILES	PENCILLING	PENITENTIAL	PENTAGRAMS
PEACHERINO	PEDAGOGUING	PEDOPHILIA	PENCILLINGS	PENITENTIALLY	PENTAGRAPH
PEACHERINOS	PEDAGOGUISH	PEDOPHILIAC	PENDENCIES	PENITENTIALS	PENTAGRAPHS
PEACHINESS	PEDAGOGUISHNESS	PEDOPHILIACS	PENDENTIVE	PENITENTIARIES	PENTAGYNIAN
PEACHINESSES	PEDAGOGUISM	PEDOPHILIAS	PENDENTIVES	PENITENTIARY	PENTAGYNOUS
PEACOCKERIES	PEDAGOGUISMS	PEDOPHILIC	PENDICLERS	PENITENTLY	PENTAHEDRA
PEACOCKERY	PEDALLINGS	PEDUNCULAR	PENDRAGONS	PENMANSHIP	PENTAHEDRAL
PEACOCKIER	PEDANTICAL	PEDUNCULATE	PENDRAGONSHIP	PENMANSHIPS	PENTAHEDRON
PEACOCKIEST	PEDANTICALLY	PEDUNCULATED	PENDRAGONSHIPS	PENNACEOUS	PENTAHEDRONS
PEACOCKING	PEDANTICISE	PEDUNCULATION	PENDULATED	PENNALISMS	PENTALOGIES
PEACOCKISH	PEDANTICISED	PEDUNCULATIONS	PENDULATES	PENNATULACEOUS	PENTALPHAS
PEAKEDNESS	PEDANTICISES	PEELGARLIC	PENDULATING	PENNATULAE	PENTAMERIES
PEAKEDNESSES	PEDANTICISING	PEELGARLICS	PENDULOSITIES	PENNATULAS	PENTAMERISM
PEARLASHES	PEDANTICISM	PEERLESSLY	PENDULOSITY	PENNILESSLY	PENTAMERISMS
PEARLESCENCE	PEDANTICISMS	PEERLESSNESS	PENDULOUSLY	PENNILESSNESS	PENTAMEROUS
PEARLESCENCES	PEDANTICIZE	PEERLESSNESSES	PENDULOUSNESS	PENNILESSNESSES	PENTAMETER
PEARLESCENT	PEDANTICIZED	PEEVISHNESS	PENDULOUSNESSES	PENNILLION	PENTAMETERS
PEARLINESS	PEDANTICIZES	PEEVISHNESSES	PENELOPISE	PENNINITES	PENTAMIDINE
PEARLINESSES	PEDANTICIZING	PEGMATITES	PENELOPISED	PENNONCELLE	PENTAMIDINES
PEARLWORTS	PEDANTISED	PEGMATITIC	PENELOPISES	PENNONCELLES	PENTANDRIAN
PEARMONGER	PEDANTISES	PEIRASTICALLY	PENELOPISING	PENNONCELS	PENTANDROUS
PEARMONGERS	PEDANTISING	PEJORATING	PENELOPIZE	PENNYCRESS	PENTANGLES
PEARTNESSES	PEDANTISMS	PEJORATION	PENELOPIZED	PENNYCRESSES	PENTANGULAR
PEASANTRIES	PEDANTIZED	PEJORATIONS	PENELOPIZES	PENNYLANDS	PENTAPEPTIDE
PEASHOOTER	PEDANTIZES	PEJORATIVE	PENELOPIZING	PENNYROYAL	PENTAPEPTIDES
PEASHOOTERS	PEDANTIZING	PEJORATIVELY	PENEPLAINS	PENNYROYALS	PENTAPLOID
PEASOUPERS	PEDANTOCRACIES	PEJORATIVES	PENEPLANATION	PENNYWEIGHT	PENTAPLOIDIES
PEBBLEDASH	PEDANTOCRACY	PELARGONIC	PENEPLANATIONS	PENNYWEIGHTS	PENTAPLOIDS
PEBBLEDASHED	PEDANTOCRAT	PELARGONIUM	PENEPLANES	PENNYWHISTLE	PENTAPLOIDY
PEBBLEDASHES	PEDANTOCRATIC	PELARGONIUMS	PENETRABILITIES	PENNYWHISTLES	PENTAPODIC
PEBBLEDASHING	PEDANTOCRATS	PELECYPODS	PENETRABILITY	PENNYWINKLE	PENTAPODIES
PECCABILITIES	PEDANTRIES	PELLAGRINS	PENETRABLE	PENNYWINKLES	PENTAPOLIS
PECCABILITY	PEDDLERIES	PELLAGROUS	PENETRABLENESS	PENNYWORTH	PENTAPOLISES
PECCADILLO	PEDERASTIC	PELLETIFIED	PENETRABLY	PENNYWORTHS	PENTAPOLITAN
PECCADILLOES	PEDERASTIES	PELLETIFIES	PENETRALIA	PENNYWORTS	PENTAPRISM
PECCADILLOS	PEDEREROES	PELLETIFYING	PENETRALIAN	PENOLOGICAL	PENTAPRISMS
PECCANCIES	PEDESTALED	PELLETISATION	PENETRANCE	PENOLOGICALLY	PENTAQUARK
PECKERWOOD	PEDESTALING	PELLETISATIONS	PENETRANCES	PENOLOGIES	PENTAQUARKS
PECKERWOODS	PEDESTALLED	PELLETISED	PENETRANCIES	PENOLOGIST	PENTARCHICAL
PECKISHNESS	PEDESTALLING	PELLETISER	PENETRANCY	PENOLOGISTS	PENTARCHIES
PECKISHNESSES	PEDESTRIAN	PELLETISERS	PENETRANTS	PENONCELLE	PENTASTICH
PECTINACEOUS	PEDESTRIANISE	PELLETISES	PENETRATED	PENONCELLES	PENTASTICHOUS
PECTINATED	PEDESTRIANISED	PELLETISING	PENETRATES	PENPUSHERS	PENTASTICHS
PECTINATELY	PEDESTRIANISES	PELLETIZATION	PENETRATING	PENPUSHING	PENTASTYLE
PECTINATION	PEDESTRIANISING	PELLETIZATIONS	PENETRATINGLY	PENPUSHINGS	PENTASTYLES
PECTINATIONS	PEDESTRIANISM	PELLETIZED	PENETRATION	PENSIEROSO	PENTASYLLABIC
PECTINESTERASE	PEDESTRIANISMS	PELLETIZER	PENETRATIONS	PENSILENESS	PENTATEUCHAL
PECTINESTERASES	PEDESTRIANIZE	PELLETIZERS	PENETRATIVE	PENSILENESSES	PENTATHLETE
PECTISABLE	PEDESTRIANIZED	PELLETIZES	PENETRATIVELY	PENSILITIES	PENTATHLETES
PECTISATION	PEDESTRIANIZES	PELLETIZING	PENETRATIVENESS	PENSIONABLE	PENTATHLON
PECTISATIONS	PEDESTRIANIZING	PELLICULAR	PENETRATOR	PENSIONARIES	PENTATHLONS
PECTIZABLE	PEDESTRIANS	PELLITORIES	PENETRATORS	PENSIONARY	PENTATHLUM
PECTIZATION	PEDETENTOUS	PELLUCIDITIES	PENETROMETER	PENSIONEER	PENTATHLUMS
PECTIZATIONS	PEDIATRICIAN	PELLUCIDITY	PENETROMETERS	PENSIONERS	PENTATOMIC
PECTOLITES	PEDIATRICIANS	PELLUCIDLY	PENGUINERIES	PENSIONING	PENTATONIC
PECTORALLY	PEDIATRICS	PELLUCIDNESS	PENGUINERY	PENSIONLESS	PENTAVALENT
PECTORILOQUIES	PEDIATRIST	PELLUCIDNESSES	PENGUINRIES	PENSIONNAT	PENTAZOCINE
PECTORILOQUY	PEDIATRISTS	PELMANISMS	PENHOLDERS	PENSIONNATS	PENTAZOCINES
PECULATING	PEDICELLARIA	PELOLOGIES	PENICILLAMINE	PENSIVENESS	PENTECONTER
PECULATION	PEDICELLARIAE	PELOTHERAPIES	PENICILLAMINES	PENSIVENESSES	PENTECONTERS
PECULATIONS	PEDICELLATE	PELOTHERAPY	PENICILLATE	PENSTEMONS	PENTETERIC
PECULATORS	PEDICULATE	PELTATIONS	PENICILLATELY	PENTABARBITAL	PENTHEMIMER
PECULIARISE	PEDICULATED	PELTMONGER	PENICILLATION	PENTABARBITALS	PENTHEMIMERAL
PECULIARISED	PEDICULATES	PELTMONGERS	PENICILLATIONS	PENTACHORD	PENTHEMIMERS
PECULIARISES	PEDICULATION	PELVIMETER	PENICILLIA	PENTACHORDS	PENTHOUSED
PECULIARISING	PEDICULATIONS	PELVIMETERS	PENICILLIFORM	PENTACRINOID	PENTHOUSES
PECULIARITIES	PEDICULOSES	PELVIMETRIES	PENICILLIN	PENTACRINOIDS	PENTHOUSING

PENTIMENTI
PENTIMENTO
PENTLANDITE
PENTLANDITES
PENTOBARBITAL
PENTOBARBITALS
PENTOBARBITONE
PENTOBARBITONES
PENTOSANES
PENTOSIDES
PENTOXIDES
PENTSTEMON
PENTSTEMONS
PENTYLENES
PENULTIMAS
PENULTIMATE
PENULTIMATELY
PENULTIMATES
PENUMBROUS
PENURIOUSLY
PENURIOUSNESS
PENURIOUSNESSES
PEOPLEHOOD
PEOPLEHOODS
PEOPLELESS
PEPEROMIAS
PEPPERBOXES
PEPPERCORN
PEPPERCORNS
PEPPERCORNY
PEPPERGRASS
PEPPERGRASSES
PEPPERIDGE
PEPPERIDGES
PEPPERIEST
PEPPERINESS
PEPPERINESSES
PEPPERINGS
PEPPERMILL
PEPPERMILLS
PEPPERMINT
PEPPERMINTS
PEPPERMINTY
PEPPERONIS
PEPPERTREE
PEPPERTREES
PEPPERWORT
PEPPERWORTS
PEPPINESSES
PEPSINATED
PEPSINATES
PEPSINATING
PEPSINOGEN
PEPSINOGENS
PEPTALKING
PEPTICITIES
PEPTIDASES
PEPTIDOGLYCAN
PEPTIDOGLYCANS
PEPTISABLE
PEPTISATION
PEPTISATIONS
PEPTIZABLE
PEPTIZATION
PEPTIZATIONS
PEPTONISATION
PEPTONISATIONS
PEPTONISED
PEPTONISER
PEPTONISERS
PEPTONISES
PEPTONISING
PEPTONIZATION
PEPTONIZATIONS
PEPTONIZED
PEPTONIZER
PEPTONIZERS
PEPTONIZES
PEPTONIZING
PERACIDITIES
PERACIDITY
PERADVENTURE
PERADVENTURES

PERAEOPODS
PERAMBULATE
PERAMBULATED
PERAMBULATES
PERAMBULATING
PERAMBULATION
PERAMBULATIONS
PERAMBULATOR
PERAMBULATORS
PERAMBULATORY
PERBORATES
PERCALINES
PERCEIVABILITY
PERCEIVABLE
PERCEIVABLY
PERCEIVERS
PERCEIVING
PERCEIVINGS
PERCENTAGE
PERCENTAGES
PERCENTILE
PERCENTILES
PERCEPTIBILITY
PERCEPTIBLE
PERCEPTIBLY
PERCEPTION
PERCEPTIONAL
PERCEPTIONS
PERCEPTIVE
PERCEPTIVELY
PERCEPTIVENESS
PERCEPTIVITIES
PERCEPTIVITY
PERCEPTUAL
PERCEPTUALLY
PERCHERIES
PERCHERONS
PERCHLORATE
PERCHLORATES
PERCHLORIC
PERCHLORIDE
PERCHLORIDES
PERCHLOROETHENE
PERCIPIENCE
PERCIPIENCES
PERCIPIENCIES
PERCIPIENCY
PERCIPIENT
PERCIPIENTLY
PERCIPIENTS
PERCOIDEAN
PERCOIDEANS
PERCOLABLE
PERCOLATED
PERCOLATES
PERCOLATING
PERCOLATION
PERCOLATIONS
PERCOLATIVE
PERCOLATOR
PERCOLATORS
PERCURRENT
PERCURSORY
PERCUSSANT
PERCUSSING
PERCUSSION
PERCUSSIONAL
PERCUSSIONIST
PERCUSSIONISTS
PERCUSSIONS
PERCUSSIVE
PERCUSSIVELY
PERCUSSIVENESS
PERCUSSORS
PERCUTANEOUS
PERCUTANEOUSLY
PERCUTIENT
PERCUTIENTS
PERDENDOSI
PERDITIONABLE
PERDITIONS
PERDUELLION
PERDUELLIONS

PERDURABILITIES
PERDURABILITY
PERDURABLE
PERDURABLY
PERDURANCE
PERDURANCES
PERDURATION
PERDURATIONS
PEREGRINATE
PEREGRINATED
PEREGRINATES
PEREGRINATING
PEREGRINATION
PEREGRINATIONS
PEREGRINATOR
PEREGRINATORS
PEREGRINATORY
PEREGRINES
PEREGRINITIES
PEREGRINITY
PEREIOPODS
PEREMPTORILY
PEREMPTORINESS
PEREMPTORY
PERENNATED
PERENNATES
PERENNATING
PERENNATION
PERENNATIONS
PERENNIALITIES
PERENNIALITY
PERENNIALLY
PERENNIALS
PERENNIBRANCH
PERENNIBRANCHS
PERENNITIES
PERESTROIKA
PERESTROIKAS
PERFECTATION
PERFECTATIONS
PERFECTERS
PERFECTEST
PERFECTIBILIAN
PERFECTIBILIANS
PERFECTIBILISM
PERFECTIBILISMS
PERFECTIBILIST
PERFECTIBILISTS
PERFECTIBILITY
PERFECTIBLE
PERFECTING
PERFECTION
PERFECTIONATE
PERFECTIONATED
PERFECTIONATES
PERFECTIONATING
PERFECTIONISM
PERFECTIONISMS
PERFECTIONIST
PERFECTIONISTIC
PERFECTIONISTS
PERFECTIONS
PERFECTIVE
PERFECTIVELY
PERFECTIVENESS
PERFECTIVES
PERFECTIVITIES
PERFECTIVITY
PERFECTNESS
PERFECTNESSES
PERFECTORS
PERFERVIDITIES
PERFERVIDITY
PERFERVIDLY
PERFERVIDNESS
PERFERVIDNESSES
PERFERVORS
PERFERVOUR
PERFERVOURS
PERFICIENT
PERFIDIOUS
PERFIDIOUSLY
PERFIDIOUSNESS

PERFLUOROCARBON
PERFOLIATE
PERFOLIATION
PERFOLIATIONS
PERFORABLE
PERFORANSES
PERFORATED
PERFORATES
PERFORATING
PERFORATION
PERFORATIONS
PERFORATIVE
PERFORATOR
PERFORATORS
PERFORATORY
PERFORATUS
PERFORATUSES
PERFORMABILITY
PERFORMABLE
PERFORMANCE
PERFORMANCES
PERFORMATIVE
PERFORMATIVELY
PERFORMATIVES
PERFORMATORY
PERFORMERS
PERFORMING
PERFORMINGS
PERFUMELESS
PERFUMERIES
PERFUMERS
PERFUMIERS
PERFUNCTORILY
PERFUNCTORINESS
PERFUNCTORY
PERFUSATES
PERFUSIONIST
PERFUSIONISTS
PERFUSIONS
PERGAMENEOUS
PERGAMENTACEOUS
PERGUNNAHS
PERIASTRON
PERIASTRONS
PERIBLASTS
PERICARDIA
PERICARDIAC
PERICARDIAL
PERICARDIAN
PERICARDITIC
PERICARDITIS
PERICARDITISES
PERICARDIUM
PERICARDIUMS
PERICARPIAL
PERICARPIC
PERICENTER
PERICENTERS
PERICENTRAL
PERICENTRE
PERICENTRES
PERICENTRIC
PERICHAETIA
PERICHAETIAL
PERICHAETIUM
PERICHONDRAL
PERICHONDRIA
PERICHONDRIAL
PERICHONDRIUM
PERICHORESES
PERICHORESIS
PERICHYLOUS
PERICLASES
PERICLASTIC
PERICLINAL
PERICLINES
PERICLITATE
PERICLITATED
PERICLITATES
PERICLITATING
PERICRANIA
PERICRANIAL
PERICRANIUM
PERICRANIUMS

PERICULOUS
PERICYCLES
PERICYCLIC
PERICYNTHIA
PERICYNTHION
PERICYNTHIONS
PERIDERMAL
PERIDERMIC
PERIDESMIA
PERIDESMIUM
PERIDINIAN
PERIDINIANS
PERIDINIUM
PERIDINIUMS
PERIDOTITE
PERIDOTITES
PERIDOTITIC
PERIDROMES
PERIEGESES
PERIEGESIS
PERIGASTRIC
PERIGASTRITIS
PERIGASTRITISES
PERIGENESES
PERIGENESIS
PERIGLACIAL
PERIGONIAL
PERIGONIUM
PERIGYNIES
PERIGYNOUS
PERIHELIAL
PERIHELION
PERIHEPATIC
PERIHEPATITIS
PERIHEPATITISES
PERIKARYAL
PERIKARYON
PERILOUSLY
PERILOUSNESS
PERILOUSNESSES
PERILYMPHS
PERIMENOPAUSAL
PERIMENOPAUSE
PERIMENOPAUSES
PERIMETERS
PERIMETRAL
PERIMETRIC
PERIMETRICAL
PERIMETRICALLY
PERIMETRIES
PERIMORPHIC
PERIMORPHISM
PERIMORPHISMS
PERIMORPHOUS
PERIMORPHS
PERIMYSIUM
PERIMYSIUMS
PERINAEUMS
PERINATALLY
PERINEPHRIA
PERINEPHRIC
PERINEPHRITIS
PERINEPHRITISES
PERINEPHRIUM
PERINEURAL
PERINEURIA
PERINEURIAL
PERINEURITIC
PERINEURITIS
PERINEURITISES
PERINEURIUM
PERIODATES
PERIODICAL
PERIODICALIST
PERIODICALISTS
PERIODICALLY
PERIODICALS
PERIODICITIES
PERIODICITY
PERIODIDES
PERIODISATION
PERIODISATIONS
PERIODIZATION

PERIODIZATIONS
PERIODONTAL
PERIODONTALLY
PERIODONTIA
PERIODONTIAS
PERIODONTIC
PERIODONTICALLY
PERIODONTICS
PERIODONTIST
PERIODONTISTS
PERIODONTITIS
PERIODONTITISES
PERIODONTOLOGY
PERIONYCHIA
PERIONYCHIUM
PERIOSTEAL
PERIOSTEUM
PERIOSTITIC
PERIOSTITIS
PERIOSTITISES
PERIOSTRACUM
PERIOSTRACUMS
PERIPATETIC
PERIPATETICAL
PERIPATETICALLY
PERIPATETICISM
PERIPATETICISMS
PERIPATETICS
PERIPATUSES
PERIPETEIA
PERIPETEIAN
PERIPETEIAS
PERIPETIAN
PERIPETIAS
PERIPETIES
PERIPHERAL
PERIPHERALITIES
PERIPHERALITY
PERIPHERALLY
PERIPHERALS
PERIPHERIC
PERIPHERICAL
PERIPHERIES
PERIPHONIC
PERIPHRASE
PERIPHRASED
PERIPHRASES
PERIPHRASING
PERIPHRASIS
PERIPHRASTIC
PERIPHRASTICAL
PERIPHYTIC
PERIPHYTON
PERIPHYTONS
PERIPLASMS
PERIPLASTS
PERIPLUSES
PERIPROCTS
PERIPTERAL
PERIPTERIES
PERISARCAL
PERISARCOUS
PERISCIANS
PERISCOPES
PERISCOPIC
PERISCOPICALLY
PERISELENIA
PERISELENIUM
PERISHABILITIES
PERISHABILITY
PERISHABLE
PERISHABLENESS
PERISHABLES
PERISHABLY
PERISHINGLY
PERISPERMAL
PERISPERMIC
PERISPERMS
PERISPOMENON
PERISPOMENONS
PERISSODACTYL
PERISSODACTYLE
PERISSODACTYLES

p

PERISSODACTYLIC	PERMEABLENESS	PERPETRABLE	PERSIFLAGES	PERSPICUOUS	PERVERSIVE
PERISSODACTYLS	PERMEABLENESSES	PERPETRATE	PERSIFLEUR	PERSPICUOUSLY	PERVERTEDLY
PERISSOLOGIES	PERMEAMETER	PERPETRATED	PERSIFLEURS	PERSPICUOUSNESS	PERVERTEDNESS
PERISSOLOGY	PERMEAMETERS	PERPETRATES	PERSIMMONS	PERSPIRABLE	PERVERTEDNESSES
PERISSOSYLLABIC	PERMEANCES	PERPETRATING	PERSISTENCE	PERSPIRATE	PERVERTERS
PERISTALITH	PERMEATING	PERPETRATION	PERSISTENCES	PERSPIRATED	PERVERTIBLE
PERISTALITHS	PERMEATION	PERPETRATIONS	PERSISTENCIES	PERSPIRATES	PERVERTING
PERISTALSES	PERMEATIONS	PERPETRATOR	PERSISTENCY	PERSPIRATING	PERVIATING
PERISTALSIS	PERMEATIVE	PERPETRATORS	PERSISTENT	PERSPIRATION	PERVICACIES
PERISTALTIC	PERMEATORS	PERPETUABLE	PERSISTENTLY	PERSPIRATIONS	PERVICACIOUS
PERISTALTICALLY	PERMETHRIN	PERPETUALISM	PERSISTENTS	PERSPIRATORY	PERVICACITIES
PERISTERITE	PERMETHRINS	PERPETUALISMS	PERSISTERS	PERSPIRING	PERVICACITY
PERISTERITES	PERMILLAGE	PERPETUALIST	PERSISTING	PERSPIRINGLY	PERVIOUSLY
PERISTERONIC	PERMILLAGES	PERPETUALISTS	PERSISTINGLY	PERSTRINGE	PERVIOUSNESS
PERISTOMAL	PERMISSIBILITY	PERPETUALITIES	PERSISTIVE	PERSTRINGED	PERVIOUSNESSES
PERISTOMATIC	PERMISSIBLE	PERPETUALITY	PERSNICKETINESS	PERSTRINGES	PESKINESSES
PERISTOMES	PERMISSIBLENESS	PERPETUALLY	PERSNICKETY	PERSTRINGING	PESSIMISMS
PERISTOMIAL	PERMISSIBLY	PERPETUALS	PERSONABLE	PERSUADABILITY	PESSIMISTIC
PERISTREPHIC	PERMISSION	PERPETUANCE	PERSONABLENESS	PERSUADABLE	PESSIMISTICAL
PERISTYLAR	PERMISSIONS	PERPETUANCES	PERSONABLY	PERSUADERS	PESSIMISTICALLY
PERISTYLES	PERMISSIVE	PERPETUATE	PERSONAGES	PERSUADING	PESSIMISTS
PERITECTIC	PERMISSIVELY	PERPETUATED	PERSONALIA	PERSUASIBILITY	PESTERINGLY
PERITHECIA	PERMISSIVENESS	PERPETUATES	PERSONALISATION	PERSUASIBLE	PESTERMENT
PERITHECIAL	PERMITTANCE	PERPETUATING	PERSONALISE	PERSUASION	PESTERMENTS
PERITHECIUM	PERMITTANCES	PERPETUATION	PERSONALISED	PERSUASIONS	PESTHOUSES
PERITONAEA	PERMITTEES	PERPETUATIONS	PERSONALISES	PERSUASIVE	PESTICIDAL
PERITONAEAL	PERMITTERS	PERPETUATOR	PERSONALISING	PERSUASIVELY	PESTICIDES
PERITONAEUM	PERMITTING	PERPETUATORS	PERSONALISM	PERSUASIVENESS	PESTIFEROUS
PERITONAEUMS	PERMITTIVITIES	PERPETUITIES	PERSONALISMS	PERSUASIVES	PESTIFEROUSLY
PERITONEAL	PERMITTIVITY	PERPETUITY	PERSONALIST	PERSUASORY	PESTIFEROUSNESS
PERITONEALLY	PERMUTABILITIES	PERPHENAZINE	PERSONALISTIC	PERSULFURIC	PESTILENCE
PERITONEOSCOPY	PERMUTABILITY	PERPHENAZINES	PERSONALISTS	PERSULPHATE	PESTILENCES
PERITONEUM	PERMUTABLE	PERPLEXEDLY	PERSONALITIES	PERSULPHATES	PESTILENTIAL
PERITONEUMS	PERMUTABLENESS	PERPLEXEDNESS	PERSONALITY	PERSULPHURIC	PESTILENTIALLY
PERITONITIC	PERMUTABLY	PERPLEXEDNESSES	PERSONALIZATION	PERSWADING	PESTILENTLY
PERITONITIS	PERMUTATED	PERPLEXERS	PERSONALIZE	PERTAINING	PESTOLOGICAL
PERITONITISES	PERMUTATES	PERPLEXING	PERSONALIZED	PERTINACIOUS	PESTOLOGIES
PERITRACKS	PERMUTATING	PERPLEXINGLY	PERSONALIZES	PERTINACIOUSLY	PESTOLOGIST
PERITRICHA	PERMUTATION	PERPLEXITIES	PERSONALIZING	PERTINACITIES	PESTOLOGISTS
PERITRICHOUS	PERMUTATIONAL	PERPLEXITY	PERSONALLY	PERTINACITY	PETAHERTZES
PERITRICHOUSLY	PERMUTATIONS	PERQUISITE	PERSONALTIES	PERTINENCE	PETALIFEROUS
PERITRICHS	PERNANCIES	PERQUISITES	PERSONALTY	PERTINENCES	PETALODIES
PERITYPHLITIS	PERNICIOUS	PERQUISITION	PERSONATED	PERTINENCIES	PETALOMANIA
PERITYPHLITISES	PERNICIOUSLY	PERQUISITIONS	PERSONATES	PERTINENCY	PETALOMANIAS
PERIVITELLINE	PERNICIOUSNESS	PERQUISITOR	PERSONATING	PERTINENTLY	PETAURISTS
PERIWIGGED	PERNICKETINESS	PERQUISITORS	PERSONATINGS	PERTINENTS	PETCHARIES
PERIWIGGING	PERNICKETY	PERRUQUIER	PERSONATION	PERTNESSES	PETERSHAMS
PERIWINKLE	PERNOCTATE	PERRUQUIERS	PERSONATIONS	PERTURBABLE	PETHIDINES
PERIWINKLES	PERNOCTATED	PERSCRUTATION	PERSONATIVE	PERTURBABLY	PETIOLATED
PERJINKETY	PERNOCTATES	PERSCRUTATIONS	PERSONATOR	PERTURBANCE	PETIOLULES
PERJINKITIES	PERNOCTATING	PERSECUTED	PERSONATORS	PERTURBANCES	PETITENESS
PERJINKITY	PERNOCTATION	PERSECUTEE	PERSONHOOD	PERTURBANT	PETITENESSES
PERJURIOUS	PERNOCTATIONS	PERSECUTEES	PERSONHOODS	PERTURBANTS	PETITIONARY
PERJURIOUSLY	PERONEUSES	PERSECUTES	PERSONIFIABLE	PERTURBATE	PETITIONED
PERKINESSES	PERORATING	PERSECUTING	PERSONIFICATION	PERTURBATED	PETITIONER
PERLEMOENS	PERORATION	PERSECUTION	PERSONIFIED	PERTURBATES	PETITIONERS
PERLOCUTION	PERORATIONAL	PERSECUTIONS	PERSONIFIER	PERTURBATING	PETITIONING
PERLOCUTIONARY	PERORATIONS	PERSECUTIVE	PERSONIFIERS	PERTURBATION	PETITIONINGS
PERLOCUTIONS	PERORATORS	PERSECUTOR	PERSONIFIES	PERTURBATIONAL	PETITIONIST
PERLUSTRATE	PEROVSKIAS	PERSECUTORY	PERSONIFYING	PERTURBATIONS	PETITIONISTS
PERLUSTRATED	PEROVSKITE	PERSEITIES	PERSONISED	PERTURBATIVE	PETNAPINGS
PERLUSTRATES	PEROVSKITES	PERSELINES	PERSONISES	PERTURBATOR	PETNAPPERS
PERLUSTRATING	PEROXIDASE	PERSEVERANCE	PERSONISING	PERTURBATORIES	PETNAPPING
PERLUSTRATION	PEROXIDASES	PERSEVERANCES	PERSONIZED	PERTURBATORS	PETRIFACTION
PERLUSTRATIONS	PEROXIDATION	PERSEVERANT	PERSONIZES	PERTURBATORY	PETRIFACTIONS
PERMACULTURE	PEROXIDATIONS	PERSEVERATE	PERSONIZING	PERTURBEDLY	PETRIFACTIVE
PERMACULTURES	PEROXIDING	PERSEVERATED	PERSONNELS	PERTURBERS	PETRIFICATION
PERMAFROST	PEROXIDISE	PERSEVERATES	PERSONPOWER	PERTURBING	PETRIFICATIONS
PERMAFROSTS	PEROXIDISED	PERSEVERATING	PERSONPOWERS	PERTURBINGLY	PETRIFIERS
PERMALLOYS	PEROXIDISES	PERSEVERATION	PERSPECTIVAL	PERTUSIONS	PETRIFYING
PERMANENCE	PEROXIDISING	PERSEVERATIONS	PERSPECTIVE	PERTUSSISES	PETRISSAGE
PERMANENCES	PEROXIDIZE	PERSEVERATIVE	PERSPECTIVELY	PERVASIONS	PETRISSAGES
PERMANENCIES	PEROXIDIZED	PERSEVERATOR	PERSPECTIVES	PERVASIVELY	PETROCHEMICAL
PERMANENCY	PEROXIDIZES	PERSEVERATORS	PERSPECTIVISM	PERVASIVENESS	PETROCHEMICALLY
PERMANENTLY	PEROXIDIZING	PERSEVERED	PERSPECTIVISMS	PERVASIVENESSES	PETROCHEMICALS
PERMANENTNESS	PEROXISOMAL	PERSEVERES	PERSPECTIVIST	PERVERSELY	PETROCHEMISTRY
PERMANENTNESSES	PEROXISOME	PERSEVERING	PERSPECTIVISTS	PERVERSENESS	PETROCURRENCIES
PERMANENTS	PEROXISOMES	PERSEVERINGLY	PERSPICACIOUS	PERVERSENESSES	PETROCURRENCY
PERMANGANATE	PEROXYSULPHURIC	PERSICARIA	PERSPICACIOUSLY	PERVERSEST	PETRODOLLAR
PERMANGANATES	PERPENDICULAR	PERSICARIAS	PERSPICACITIES	PERVERSION	PETRODOLLARS
PERMANGANIC	PERPENDICULARLY	PERSIENNES	PERSPICACITY	PERVERSIONS	PETRODROME
PERMEABILITIES	PERPENDICULARS	PERSIFLAGE	PERSPICUITIES	PERVERSITIES	PETRODROMES
PERMEABILITY	PERPENDING	PERSIFLAGE	PERSPICUITY	PERVERSITY	PETROGENESES

PETROGENESIS
PETROGENETIC
PETROGENIES
PETROGLYPH
PETROGLYPHIC
PETROGLYPHIES
PETROGLYPHS
PETROGLYPHY
PETROGRAMS
PETROGRAPHER
PETROGRAPHERS
PETROGRAPHIC
PETROGRAPHICAL
PETROGRAPHIES
PETROGRAPHY
PETROLAGES
PETROLATUM
PETROLATUMS
PETROLEOUS
PETROLEUMS
PETROLEURS
PETROLEUSE
PETROLEUSES
PETROLHEAD
PETROLHEADS
PETROLIFEROUS
PETROLLING
PETROLOGIC
PETROLOGICAL
PETROLOGICALLY
PETROLOGIES
PETROLOGIST
PETROLOGISTS
PETROMONEY
PETROMONEYS
PETROMONIES
PETRONELLA
PETRONELLAS
PETROPHYSICAL
PETROPHYSICIST
PETROPHYSICISTS
PETROPHYSICS
PETROPOUNDS
PETTEDNESS
PETTEDNESSES
PETTICHAPS
PETTICHAPSES
PETTICOATED
PETTICOATS
PETTIFOGGED
PETTIFOGGER
PETTIFOGGERIES
PETTIFOGGERS
PETTIFOGGERY
PETTIFOGGING
PETTIFOGGINGS
PETTINESSES
PETTISHNESS
PETTISHNESSES
PETULANCES
PETULANCIES
PETULANTLY
PEWHOLDERS
PHACOLITES
PHACOLITHS
PHAELONION
PHAELONIONS
PHAENOGAMIC
PHAENOGAMOUS
PHAENOGAMS
PHAENOLOGIES
PHAENOLOGY
PHAENOMENA
PHAENOMENON
PHAENOTYPE
PHAENOTYPED
PHAENOTYPES
PHAENOTYPING
PHAEOMELANIN
PHAEOMELANINS
PHAGEDAENA
PHAGEDAENAS
PHAGEDAENIC

PHAGEDENAS
PHAGEDENIC
PHAGOCYTES
PHAGOCYTIC
PHAGOCYTICAL
PHAGOCYTISE
PHAGOCYTISED
PHAGOCYTISES
PHAGOCYTISING
PHAGOCYTISM
PHAGOCYTISMS
PHAGOCYTIZE
PHAGOCYTIZED
PHAGOCYTIZES
PHAGOCYTIZING
PHAGOCYTOSE
PHAGOCYTOSED
PHAGOCYTOSES
PHAGOCYTOSING
PHAGOCYTOSIS
PHAGOCYTOTIC
PHAGOMANIA
PHAGOMANIAC
PHAGOMANIACS
PHAGOMANIAS
PHAGOPHOBIA
PHAGOPHOBIAS
PHAGOSOMES
PHALANGEAL
PHALANGERS
PHALANGIDS
PHALANGIST
PHALANGISTS
PHALANSTERIAN
PHALANSTERIES
PHALANSTERISM
PHALANSTERISMS
PHALANSTERIST
PHALANSTERISTS
PHALAROPES
PHALLICALLY
PHALLICISM
PHALLICISMS
PHALLICIST
PHALLICISTS
PHALLOCENTRIC
PHALLOCENTRISM
PHALLOCENTRISMS
PHALLOCRAT
PHALLOCRATIC
PHALLOCRATS
PHALLOIDIN
PHALLOIDINS
PHANEROGAM
PHANEROGAMIC
PHANEROGAMOUS
PHANEROGAMS
PHANEROPHYTE
PHANEROPHYTES
PHANSIGARS
PHANTASIAST
PHANTASIASTS
PHANTASIED
PHANTASIES
PHANTASIME
PHANTASIMES
PHANTASIMS
PHANTASMAGORIA
PHANTASMAGORIAL
PHANTASMAGORIAS
PHANTASMAGORIC
PHANTASMAGORIES
PHANTASMAGORY
PHANTASMAL
PHANTASMALIAN
PHANTASMALITIES
PHANTASMALITY
PHANTASMALLY
PHANTASMATA
PHANTASMIC
PHANTASMICAL
PHANTASMICALLY

PHANTASTIC
PHANTASTICS
PHANTASTRIES
PHANTASTRY
PHANTASYING
PHANTOMATIC
PHANTOMISH
PHANTOMLIKE
PHANTOSMES
PHARISAICAL
PHARISAICALLY
PHARISAICALNESS
PHARISAISM
PHARISAISMS
PHARISEEISM
PHARISEEISMS
PHARMACEUTIC
PHARMACEUTICAL
PHARMACEUTICALS
PHARMACEUTICS
PHARMACEUTIST
PHARMACEUTISTS
PHARMACIES
PHARMACIST
PHARMACISTS
PHARMACODYNAMIC
PHARMACOGENOMIC
PHARMACOGNOSIES
PHARMACOGNOSIST
PHARMACOGNOSTIC
PHARMACOGNOSY
PHARMACOKINETIC
PHARMACOLOGIC
PHARMACOLOGICAL
PHARMACOLOGIES
PHARMACOLOGIST
PHARMACOLOGISTS
PHARMACOLOGY
PHARMACOPEIA
PHARMACOPEIAL
PHARMACOPEIAS
PHARMACOPOEIA
PHARMACOPOEIAL
PHARMACOPOEIAN
PHARMACOPOEIAS
PHARMACOPOEIC
PHARMACOPOEIST
PHARMACOPOEISTS
PHARMACOPOLIST
PHARMACOPOLISTS
PHARMACOTHERAPY
PHARYNGALS
PHARYNGEAL
PHARYNGITIC
PHARYNGITIDES
PHARYNGITIS
PHARYNGITISES
PHARYNGOLOGICAL
PHARYNGOLOGIES
PHARYNGOLOGIST
PHARYNGOLOGISTS
PHARYNGOLOGY
PHARYNGOSCOPE
PHARYNGOSCOPES
PHARYNGOSCOPIC
PHARYNGOSCOPIES
PHARYNGOSCOPY
PHARYNGOTOMIES
PHARYNGOTOMY
PHASCOGALE
PHASCOGALES
PHASEDOWNS
PHASEOLINS
PHATICALLY
PHEASANTRIES
PHEASANTRY
PHELLODERM
PHELLODERMAL
PHELLODERMS
PHELLOGENETIC
PHELLOGENIC
PHELLOGENS
PHELLOPLASTIC

PHELLOPLASTICS
PHELONIONS
PHENACAINE
PHENACAINES
PHENACETIN
PHENACETINS
PHENACITES
PHENAKISMS
PHENAKISTOSCOPE
PHENAKITES
PHENANTHRENE
PHENANTHRENES
PHENARSAZINE
PHENARSAZINES
PHENAZINES
PHENCYCLIDINE
PHENCYCLIDINES
PHENETICIST
PHENETICISTS
PHENETIDINE
PHENETIDINES
PHENETOLES
PHENFORMIN
PHENFORMINS
PHENGOPHOBIA
PHENGOPHOBIAS
PHENMETRAZINE
PHENMETRAZINES
PHENOBARBITAL
PHENOBARBITALS
PHENOBARBITONE
PHENOBARBITONES
PHENOCOPIES
PHENOCRYST
PHENOCRYSTIC
PHENOCRYSTS
PHENOLATED
PHENOLATES
PHENOLATING
PHENOLOGICAL
PHENOLOGICALLY
PHENOLOGIES
PHENOLOGIST
PHENOLOGISTS
PHENOLPHTHALEIN
PHENOMENAL
PHENOMENALISE
PHENOMENALISED
PHENOMENALISES
PHENOMENALISING
PHENOMENALISM
PHENOMENALISMS
PHENOMENALIST
PHENOMENALISTIC
PHENOMENALISTS
PHENOMENALITIES
PHENOMENALITY
PHENOMENALIZE
PHENOMENALIZED
PHENOMENALIZES
PHENOMENALIZING
PHENOMENALLY
PHENOMENAS
PHENOMENISE
PHENOMENISED
PHENOMENISES
PHENOMENISING
PHENOMENISM
PHENOMENISMS
PHENOMENIST
PHENOMENISTS
PHENOMENIZE
PHENOMENIZED
PHENOMENIZES
PHENOMENIZING
PHENOMENOLOGIES
PHENOMENOLOGIST
PHENOMENOLOGY
PHENOMENON
PHENOMENONS
PHENOTHIAZINE
PHENOTHIAZINES
PHENOTYPED

PHENOTYPES
PHENOTYPIC
PHENOTYPICAL
PHENOTYPICALLY
PHENOTYPING
PHENOXIDES
PHENTOLAMINE
PHENTOLAMINES
PHENYLALANIN
PHENYLALANINE
PHENYLALANINES
PHENYLALANINS
PHENYLAMINE
PHENYLAMINES
PHENYLBUTAZONE
PHENYLBUTAZONES
PHENYLENES
PHENYLEPHRINE
PHENYLEPHRINES
PHENYLKETONURIA
PHENYLKETONURIC
PHENYLMETHYL
PHENYLMETHYLS
PHENYLTHIOUREA
PHENYLTHIOUREAS
PHENYTOINS
PHEROMONAL
PHEROMONES
PHIALIFORM
PHILADELPHUS
PHILADELPHUSES
PHILANDERED
PHILANDERER
PHILANDERERS
PHILANDERING
PHILANDERINGS
PHILANDERS
PHILANTHROPE
PHILANTHROPES
PHILANTHROPIC
PHILANTHROPICAL
PHILANTHROPIES
PHILANTHROPIST
PHILANTHROPISTS
PHILANTHROPOID
PHILANTHROPOIDS
PHILANTHROPY
PHILATELIC
PHILATELICALLY
PHILATELIES
PHILATELIST
PHILATELISTS
PHILHARMONIC
PHILHARMONICS
PHILHELLENE
PHILHELLENES
PHILHELLENIC
PHILHELLENISM
PHILHELLENISMS
PHILHELLENIST
PHILHELLENISTS
PHILHORSES
PHILIPPICS
PHILIPPINA
PHILIPPINAS
PHILIPPINE
PHILIPPINES
PHILISTIAS
PHILISTINE
PHILISTINES
PHILISTINISM
PHILISTINISMS
PHILLABEGS
PHILLIBEGS
PHILLIPSITE
PHILLIPSITES
PHILLUMENIES
PHILLUMENIST
PHILLUMENISTS
PHILLUMENY
PHILODENDRA
PHILODENDRON
PHILODENDRONS

PHILOGYNIES
PHILOGYNIST
PHILOGYNISTS
PHILOGYNOUS
PHILOLOGER
PHILOLOGERS
PHILOLOGIAN
PHILOLOGIANS
PHILOLOGIC
PHILOLOGICAL
PHILOLOGICALLY
PHILOLOGIES
PHILOLOGIST
PHILOLOGISTS
PHILOLOGUE
PHILOLOGUES
PHILOMATHIC
PHILOMATHICAL
PHILOMATHIES
PHILOMATHS
PHILOMATHY
PHILOMELAS
PHILOPENAS
PHILOPOENA
PHILOPOENAS
PHILOSOPHASTER
PHILOSOPHASTERS
PHILOSOPHE
PHILOSOPHER
PHILOSOPHERESS
PHILOSOPHERS
PHILOSOPHES
PHILOSOPHESS
PHILOSOPHESSES
PHILOSOPHIC
PHILOSOPHICAL
PHILOSOPHICALLY
PHILOSOPHIES
PHILOSOPHISE
PHILOSOPHISED
PHILOSOPHISER
PHILOSOPHISERS
PHILOSOPHISES
PHILOSOPHISING
PHILOSOPHISM
PHILOSOPHISMS
PHILOSOPHIST
PHILOSOPHISTIC
PHILOSOPHISTS
PHILOSOPHIZE
PHILOSOPHIZED
PHILOSOPHIZER
PHILOSOPHIZERS
PHILOSOPHIZES
PHILOSOPHIZING
PHILOSOPHY
PHILOXENIA
PHILOXENIAS
PHILTERING
PHISNOMIES
PHLEBECTOMIES
PHLEBECTOMY
PHLEBITIDES
PHLEBITISES
PHLEBOGRAM
PHLEBOGRAMS
PHLEBOGRAPHIC
PHLEBOGRAPHIES
PHLEBOGRAPHY
PHLEBOLITE
PHLEBOLITES
PHLEBOLOGIES
PHLEBOLOGY
PHLEBOSCLEROSES
PHLEBOSCLEROSIS
PHLEBOTOMIC
PHLEBOTOMICAL
PHLEBOTOMIES
PHLEBOTOMISE
PHLEBOTOMISED
PHLEBOTOMISES
PHLEBOTOMISING
PHLEBOTOMIST

PHLEBOTOMISTS	PHONETICIZING	PHOSPHATISE	PHOTOAUTOTROPHS	PHOTOFLASH	PHOTOMETRIES
PHLEBOTOMIZE	PHONETISATION	PHOSPHATISED	PHOTOBATHIC	PHOTOFLASHES	PHOTOMETRIST
PHLEBOTOMIZED	PHONETISATIONS	PHOSPHATISES	PHOTOBIOLOGIC	PHOTOFLOOD	PHOTOMETRISTS
PHLEBOTOMIZES	PHONETISED	PHOSPHATISING	PHOTOBIOLOGICAL	PHOTOFLOODS	PHOTOMETRY
PHLEBOTOMIZING	PHONETISES	PHOSPHATIZATION	PHOTOBIOLOGIES	PHOTOFLUOROGRAM	PHOTOMICROGRAPH
PHLEBOTOMY	PHONETISING	PHOSPHATIZE	PHOTOBIOLOGIST	PHOTOGELATINE	PHOTOMONTAGE
PHLEGMAGOGIC	PHONETISMS	PHOSPHATIZED	PHOTOBIOLOGISTS	PHOTOGENES	PHOTOMONTAGES
PHLEGMAGOGUE	PHONETISTS	PHOSPHATIZES	PHOTOBIOLOGY	PHOTOGENIC	PHOTOMOSAIC
PHLEGMAGOGUES	PHONETIZATION	PHOSPHATIZING	PHOTOCATALYSES	PHOTOGENICALLY	PHOTOMOSAICS
PHLEGMASIA	PHONETIZATIONS	PHOSPHATURIA	PHOTOCATALYSIS	PHOTOGENIES	PHOTOMULTIPLIER
PHLEGMASIAS	PHONETIZED	PHOSPHATURIAS	PHOTOCATALYTIC	PHOTOGEOLOGIC	PHOTOMURAL
PHLEGMATIC	PHONETIZES	PHOSPHATURIC	PHOTOCATHODE	PHOTOGEOLOGICAL	PHOTOMURALS
PHLEGMATICAL	PHONETIZING	PHOSPHENES	PHOTOCATHODES	PHOTOGEOLOGIES	PHOTONASTIC
PHLEGMATICALLY	PHONEYNESS	PHOSPHIDES	PHOTOCELLS	PHOTOGEOLOGIST	PHOTONASTIES
PHLEGMATICNESS	PHONEYNESSES	PHOSPHINES	PHOTOCHEMICAL	PHOTOGEOLOGISTS	PHOTONASTY
PHLEGMIEST	PHONICALLY	PHOSPHITES	PHOTOCHEMICALLY	PHOTOGEOLOGY	PHOTONEGATIVE
PHLEGMONIC	PHONINESSES	PHOSPHOCREATIN	PHOTOCHEMIST	PHOTOGLYPH	PHOTONEUTRON
PHLEGMONOID	PHONMETERS	PHOSPHOCREATINE	PHOTOCHEMISTRY	PHOTOGLYPHIC	PHOTONEUTRONS
PHLEGMONOUS	PHONOCAMPTIC	PHOSPHOCREATINS	PHOTOCHEMISTS	PHOTOGLYPHIES	PHOTONOVEL
PHLOGISTIC	PHONOCAMPTICS	PHOSPHOKINASE	PHOTOCHROMIC	PHOTOGLYPHS	PHOTONOVELS
PHLOGISTICATE	PHONOCARDIOGRAM	PHOSPHOKINASES	PHOTOCHROMICS	PHOTOGLYPHY	PHOTONUCLEAR
PHLOGISTICATED	PHONOCHEMISTRY	PHOSPHOLIPASE	PHOTOCHROMIES	PHOTOGRAMMETRIC	PHOTOOXIDATION
PHLOGISTICATES	PHONOFIDDLE	PHOSPHOLIPASES	PHOTOCHROMISM	PHOTOGRAMMETRY	PHOTOOXIDATIONS
PHLOGISTICATING	PHONOFIDDLES	PHOSPHOLIPID	PHOTOCHROMISMS	PHOTOGRAMS	PHOTOOXIDATIVE
PHLOGISTON	PHONOGRAMIC	PHOSPHOLIPIDS	PHOTOCHROMY	PHOTOGRAPH	PHOTOOXIDISE
PHLOGISTONS	PHONOGRAMICALLY	PHOSPHONIC	PHOTOCOMPOSE	PHOTOGRAPHED	PHOTOOXIDISED
PHLOGOPITE	PHONOGRAMMIC	PHOSPHONIUM	PHOTOCOMPOSED	PHOTOGRAPHER	PHOTOOXIDISES
PHLOGOPITES	PHONOGRAMS	PHOSPHONIUMS	PHOTOCOMPOSER	PHOTOGRAPHERS	PHOTOOXIDISING
PHLORIZINS	PHONOGRAPH	PHOSPHOPROTEIN	PHOTOCOMPOSERS	PHOTOGRAPHIC	PHOTOOXIDIZE
PHLYCTAENA	PHONOGRAPHER	PHOSPHOPROTEINS	PHOTOCOMPOSES	PHOTOGRAPHICAL	PHOTOOXIDIZED
PHLYCTAENAE	PHONOGRAPHERS	PHOSPHORATE	PHOTOCOMPOSING	PHOTOGRAPHIES	PHOTOOXIDIZES
PHLYCTENAE	PHONOGRAPHIC	PHOSPHORATED	PHOTOCONDUCTING	PHOTOGRAPHING	PHOTOOXIDIZING
PHOCOMELIA	PHONOGRAPHIES	PHOSPHORATES	PHOTOCONDUCTION	PHOTOGRAPHIST	PHOTOPERIOD
PHOCOMELIAS	PHONOGRAPHIST	PHOSPHORATING	PHOTOCONDUCTIVE	PHOTOGRAPHISTS	PHOTOPERIODIC
PHOCOMELIC	PHONOGRAPHISTS	PHOSPHORES	PHOTOCONDUCTOR	PHOTOGRAPHS	PHOTOPERIODISM
PHOCOMELIES	PHONOGRAPHS	PHOSPHORESCE	PHOTOCONDUCTORS	PHOTOGRAPHY	PHOTOPERIODISMS
PHOENIXISM	PHONOGRAPHY	PHOSPHORESCED	PHOTOCOPIABLE	PHOTOGRAVURE	PHOTOPERIODS
PHOENIXISMS	PHONOLITES	PHOSPHORESCENCE	PHOTOCOPIED	PHOTOGRAVURES	PHOTOPHASE
PHOENIXLIKE	PHONOLITIC	PHOSPHORESCENT	PHOTOCOPIER	PHOTOINDUCED	PHOTOPHASES
PHOLIDOSES	PHONOLOGIC	PHOSPHORESCES	PHOTOCOPIERS	PHOTOINDUCTION	PHOTOPHILIC
PHOLIDOSIS	PHONOLOGICAL	PHOSPHORESCING	PHOTOCOPIES	PHOTOINDUCTIONS	PHOTOPHILIES
PHONASTHENIA	PHONOLOGICALLY	PHOSPHORET	PHOTOCOPYING	PHOTOINDUCTIVE	PHOTOPHILOUS
PHONASTHENIAS	PHONOLOGIES	PHOSPHORETS	PHOTOCOPYINGS	PHOTOIONISATION	PHOTOPHILS
PHONATHONS	PHONOLOGIST	PHOSPHORETTED	PHOTOCURRENT	PHOTOIONISE	PHOTOPHILY
PHONATIONS	PHONOLOGISTS	PHOSPHORIC	PHOTOCURRENTS	PHOTOIONISED	PHOTOPHOBE
PHONAUTOGRAPH	PHONOMETER	PHOSPHORISE	PHOTODEGRADABLE	PHOTOIONISES	PHOTOPHOBES
PHONAUTOGRAPHIC	PHONOMETERS	PHOSPHORISED	PHOTODETECTOR	PHOTOIONISING	PHOTOPHOBIA
PHONAUTOGRAPHS	PHONOMETRIC	PHOSPHORISES	PHOTODETECTORS	PHOTOIONIZATION	PHOTOPHOBIAS
PHONECARDS	PHONOMETRICAL	PHOSPHORISING	PHOTODIODE	PHOTOIONIZE	PHOTOPHOBIC
PHONEMATIC	PHONOPHOBIA	PHOSPHORISM	PHOTODIODES	PHOTOIONIZED	PHOTOPHONE
PHONEMATICALLY	PHONOPHOBIAS	PHOSPHORISMS	PHOTODISSOCIATE	PHOTOIONIZES	PHOTOPHONES
PHONEMICALLY	PHONOPHORE	PHOSPHORITE	PHOTODUPLICATE	PHOTOIONIZING	PHOTOPHONIC
PHONEMICISATION	PHONOPHORES	PHOSPHORITES	PHOTODUPLICATED	PHOTOJOURNALISM	PHOTOPHONIES
PHONEMICISE	PHONOPORES	PHOSPHORITIC	PHOTODUPLICATES	PHOTOJOURNALIST	PHOTOPHONY
PHONEMICISED	PHONOSCOPE	PHOSPHORIZE	PHOTODYNAMIC	PHOTOKINESES	PHOTOPHORE
PHONEMICISES	PHONOSCOPES	PHOSPHORIZED	PHOTODYNAMICS	PHOTOKINESIS	PHOTOPHORES
PHONEMICISING	PHONOTACTIC	PHOSPHORIZES	PHOTOELASTIC	PHOTOKINETIC	PHOTOPHORESES
PHONEMICIST	PHONOTACTICS	PHOSPHORIZING	PHOTOELASTICITY	PHOTOLITHO	PHOTOPHORESIS
PHONEMICISTS	PHONOTYPED	PHOSPHOROLYSES	PHOTOELECTRIC	PHOTOLITHOGRAPH	PHOTOPLAYS
PHONEMICIZATION	PHONOTYPER	PHOSPHOROLYSIS	PHOTOELECTRICAL	PHOTOLITHOS	PHOTOPOLYMER
PHONEMICIZE	PHONOTYPERS	PHOSPHOROLYTIC	PHOTOELECTRODE	PHOTOLUMINESCE	PHOTOPOLYMERS
PHONEMICIZED	PHONOTYPES	PHOSPHOROSCOPE	PHOTOELECTRODES	PHOTOLUMINESCED	PHOTOPOSITIVE
PHONEMICIZES	PHONOTYPIC	PHOSPHOROSCOPES	PHOTOELECTRON	PHOTOLUMINESCES	PHOTOPRODUCT
PHONEMICIZING	PHONOTYPICAL	PHOSPHOROUS	PHOTOELECTRONIC	PHOTOLYSABLE	PHOTOPRODUCTION
PHONENDOSCOPE	PHONOTYPIES	PHOSPHORUS	PHOTOELECTRONS	PHOTOLYSED	PHOTOPRODUCTS
PHONENDOSCOPES	PHONOTYPING	PHOSPHORUSES	PHOTOEMISSION	PHOTOLYSES	PHOTOPSIAS
PHONETICAL	PHONOTYPIST	PHOSPHORYL	PHOTOEMISSIONS	PHOTOLYSING	PHOTOPSIES
PHONETICALLY	PHONOTYPISTS	PHOSPHORYLASE	PHOTOEMISSIVE	PHOTOLYSIS	PHOTOREACTION
PHONETICIAN	PHORMINGES	PHOSPHORYLASES	PHOTOENGRAVE	PHOTOLYTIC	PHOTOREACTIONS
PHONETICIANS	PHOSGENITE	PHOSPHORYLATE	PHOTOENGRAVED	PHOTOLYTICALLY	PHOTOREALISM
PHONETICISATION	PHOSGENITES	PHOSPHORYLATED	PHOTOENGRAVER	PHOTOLYZABLE	PHOTOREALISMS
PHONETICISE	PHOSPHATASE	PHOSPHORYLATES	PHOTOENGRAVERS	PHOTOLYZED	PHOTOREALIST
PHONETICISED	PHOSPHATASES	PHOSPHORYLATING	PHOTOENGRAVES	PHOTOLYZES	PHOTOREALISTIC
PHONETICISES	PHOSPHATED	PHOSPHORYLATION	PHOTOENGRAVING	PHOTOLYZING	PHOTOREALISTS
PHONETICISING	PHOSPHATES	PHOSPHORYLATIVE	PHOTOENGRAVINGS	PHOTOMACROGRAPH	PHOTORECEPTION
PHONETICISM	PHOSPHATIC	PHOSPHORYLS	PHOTOEXCITATION	PHOTOMAPPED	PHOTORECEPTIONS
PHONETICISMS	PHOSPHATIDE	PHOSPHURET	PHOTOEXCITED	PHOTOMAPPING	PHOTORECEPTIVE
PHONETICIST	PHOSPHATIDES	PHOSPHURETS	PHOTOFINISHER	PHOTOMASKS	PHOTORECEPTOR
PHONETICISTS	PHOSPHATIDIC	PHOSPHURETTED	PHOTOFINISHERS	PHOTOMECHANICAL	PHOTORECEPTORS
PHONETICIZATION	PHOSPHATIDYL	PHOTICALLY	PHOTOFINISHING	PHOTOMETER	PHOTOREDUCE
PHONETICIZE	PHOSPHATIDYLS	PHOTOACTINIC	PHOTOFINISHINGS	PHOTOMETERS	PHOTOREDUCED
PHONETICIZED	PHOSPHATING	PHOTOACTIVE	PHOTOFISSION	PHOTOMETRIC	PHOTOREDUCES
PHONETICIZES	PHOSPHATISATION	PHOTOAUTOTROPH	PHOTOFISSIONS	PHOTOMETRICALLY	PHOTOREDUCING

PHOTOREDUCTION
PHOTOREDUCTIONS
PHOTOREFRACTIVE
PHOTORESIST
PHOTORESISTS
PHOTOSCANNED
PHOTOSCANNING
PHOTOSCANS
PHOTOSENSITISE
PHOTOSENSITISED
PHOTOSENSITISER
PHOTOSENSITISES
PHOTOSENSITIVE
PHOTOSENSITIZE
PHOTOSENSITIZED
PHOTOSENSITIZER
PHOTOSENSITIZES
PHOTOSETTER
PHOTOSETTERS
PHOTOSETTING
PHOTOSETTINGS
PHOTOSHOOT
PHOTOSHOOTS
PHOTOSPHERE
PHOTOSPHERES
PHOTOSPHERIC
PHOTOSTATED
PHOTOSTATIC
PHOTOSTATING
PHOTOSTATS
PHOTOSTATTED
PHOTOSTATTING
PHOTOSYNTHATE
PHOTOSYNTHATES
PHOTOSYNTHESES
PHOTOSYNTHESIS
PHOTOSYNTHESISE
PHOTOSYNTHESIZE
PHOTOSYNTHETIC
PHOTOSYSTEM
PHOTOSYSTEMS
PHOTOTACTIC
PHOTOTACTICALLY
PHOTOTAXES
PHOTOTAXIES
PHOTOTAXIS
PHOTOTELEGRAPH
PHOTOTELEGRAPHS
PHOTOTELEGRAPHY
PHOTOTHERAPIES
PHOTOTHERAPY
PHOTOTHERMAL
PHOTOTHERMALLY
PHOTOTHERMIC
PHOTOTONIC
PHOTOTONUS
PHOTOTONUSES
PHOTOTOPOGRAPHY
PHOTOTOXIC
PHOTOTOXICITIES
PHOTOTOXICITY
PHOTOTRANSISTOR
PHOTOTROPE
PHOTOTROPES
PHOTOTROPH
PHOTOTROPHIC
PHOTOTROPHS
PHOTOTROPIC
PHOTOTROPICALLY
PHOTOTROPIES
PHOTOTROPISM
PHOTOTROPISMS
PHOTOTROPY
PHOTOTUBES
PHOTOTYPED
PHOTOTYPES
PHOTOTYPESET
PHOTOTYPESETS
PHOTOTYPESETTER
PHOTOTYPIC
PHOTOTYPICALLY
PHOTOTYPIES
PHOTOTYPING

PHOTOTYPOGRAPHY
PHOTOVOLTAIC
PHOTOVOLTAICS
PHOTOXYLOGRAPHY
PHOTOZINCOGRAPH
PHRAGMOPLAST
PHRAGMOPLASTS
PHRASELESS
PHRASEMAKER
PHRASEMAKERS
PHRASEMAKING
PHRASEMAKINGS
PHRASEMONGER
PHRASEMONGERING
PHRASEMONGERS
PHRASEOGRAM
PHRASEOGRAMS
PHRASEOGRAPH
PHRASEOGRAPHIC
PHRASEOGRAPHIES
PHRASEOGRAPHS
PHRASEOGRAPHY
PHRASEOLOGIC
PHRASEOLOGICAL
PHRASEOLOGIES
PHRASEOLOGIST
PHRASEOLOGISTS
PHRASEOLOGY
PHREAKINGS
PHREATOPHYTE
PHREATOPHYTES
PHREATOPHYTIC
PHRENESIAC
PHRENETICAL
PHRENETICALLY
PHRENETICNESS
PHRENETICNESSES
PHRENETICS
PHRENITIDES
PHRENITISES
PHRENOLOGIC
PHRENOLOGICAL
PHRENOLOGICALLY
PHRENOLOGIES
PHRENOLOGISE
PHRENOLOGISED
PHRENOLOGISES
PHRENOLOGISING
PHRENOLOGIST
PHRENOLOGISTS
PHRENOLOGIZE
PHRENOLOGIZED
PHRENOLOGIZES
PHRENOLOGIZING
PHRENOLOGY
PHRENSICAL
PHRENSYING
PHRONTISTERIES
PHRONTISTERY
PHTHALATES
PHTHALEINS
PHTHALOCYANIN
PHTHALOCYANINE
PHTHALOCYANINES
PHTHALOCYANINS
PHTHIRIASES
PHTHIRIASIS
PHTHISICAL
PHTHISICKY
PHYCOBILIN
PHYCOBILINS
PHYCOBIONT
PHYCOBIONTS
PHYCOCYANIN
PHYCOCYANINS
PHYCOCYANS
PHYCOERYTHRIN
PHYCOERYTHRINS
PHYCOLOGICAL
PHYCOLOGIES
PHYCOLOGIST
PHYCOLOGISTS
PHYCOMYCETE

PHYCOMYCETES
PHYCOMYCETOUS
PHYCOPHAEIN
PHYCOPHAEINS
PHYCOXANTHIN
PHYCOXANTHINS
PHYLACTERIC
PHYLACTERICAL
PHYLACTERIES
PHYLACTERY
PHYLARCHIES
PHYLAXISES
PHYLESISES
PHYLETICALLY
PHYLLARIES
PHYLLOCLAD
PHYLLOCLADE
PHYLLOCLADES
PHYLLOCLADS
PHYLLODIAL
PHYLLODIES
PHYLLODIUM
PHYLLOMANIA
PHYLLOMANIAS
PHYLLOPHAGOUS
PHYLLOPLANE
PHYLLOPLANES
PHYLLOPODS
PHYLLOQUINONE
PHYLLOQUINONES
PHYLLOSILICATE
PHYLLOSILICATES
PHYLLOSPHERE
PHYLLOSPHERES
PHYLLOTACTIC
PHYLLOTACTICAL
PHYLLOTAXES
PHYLLOTAXIES
PHYLLOTAXIS
PHYLLOTAXY
PHYLLOXERA
PHYLLOXERAE
PHYLLOXERAS
PHYLOGENESES
PHYLOGENESIS
PHYLOGENETIC
PHYLOGENIC
PHYLOGENIES
PHYSALISES
PHYSHARMONICA
PHYSHARMONICAS
PHYSIATRIC
PHYSIATRICAL
PHYSIATRICS
PHYSIATRIES
PHYSIATRIST
PHYSIATRISTS
PHYSICALISM
PHYSICALISMS
PHYSICALIST
PHYSICALISTIC
PHYSICALISTS
PHYSICALITIES
PHYSICALITY
PHYSICALLY
PHYSICALNESS
PHYSICALNESSES
PHYSICIANCIES
PHYSICIANCY
PHYSICIANER
PHYSICIANERS
PHYSICIANS
PHYSICIANSHIP
PHYSICIANSHIPS
PHYSICISMS
PHYSICISTS
PHYSICKING
PHYSICOCHEMICAL
PHYSIOCRACIES
PHYSIOCRACY
PHYSIOCRAT
PHYSIOCRATIC
PHYSIOCRATS

PHYSIOGNOMIC
PHYSIOGNOMICAL
PHYSIOGNOMIES
PHYSIOGNOMIST
PHYSIOGNOMISTS
PHYSIOGNOMY
PHYSIOGRAPHER
PHYSIOGRAPHERS
PHYSIOGRAPHIC
PHYSIOGRAPHICAL
PHYSIOGRAPHIES
PHYSIOGRAPHY
PHYSIOLATER
PHYSIOLATERS
PHYSIOLATRIES
PHYSIOLATRY
PHYSIOLOGIC
PHYSIOLOGICAL
PHYSIOLOGICALLY
PHYSIOLOGIES
PHYSIOLOGIST
PHYSIOLOGISTS
PHYSIOLOGUS
PHYSIOLOGUSES
PHYSIOLOGY
PHYSIOPATHOLOGY
PHYSIOTHERAPIES
PHYSIOTHERAPIST
PHYSIOTHERAPY
PHYSITHEISM
PHYSITHEISMS
PHYSITHEISTIC
PHYSOCLISTOUS
PHYSOSTIGMIN
PHYSOSTIGMINE
PHYSOSTIGMINES
PHYSOSTIGMINS
PHYSOSTOMOUS
PHYTOALEXIN
PHYTOALEXINS
PHYTOBENTHOS
PHYTOBENTHOSES
PHYTOCHEMICAL
PHYTOCHEMICALLY
PHYTOCHEMICALS
PHYTOCHEMIST
PHYTOCHEMISTRY
PHYTOCHEMISTS
PHYTOCHROME
PHYTOCHROMES
PHYTOESTROGEN
PHYTOESTROGENS
PHYTOFLAGELLATE
PHYTOGENESES
PHYTOGENESIS
PHYTOGENETIC
PHYTOGENETICAL
PHYTOGENIC
PHYTOGENIES
PHYTOGEOGRAPHER
PHYTOGEOGRAPHIC
PHYTOGEOGRAPHY
PHYTOGRAPHER
PHYTOGRAPHERS
PHYTOGRAPHIC
PHYTOGRAPHIES
PHYTOGRAPHY
PHYTOHORMONE
PHYTOHORMONES
PHYTOLITHS
PHYTOLOGICAL
PHYTOLOGICALLY
PHYTOLOGIES
PHYTOLOGIST
PHYTOLOGISTS
PHYTONADIONE
PHYTONADIONES
PHYTOPATHOGEN
PHYTOPATHOGENIC
PHYTOPATHOGENS
PHYTOPATHOLOGY
PHYTOPHAGIC
PHYTOPHAGIES

PHYTOPHAGOUS
PHYTOPHAGY
PHYTOPLANKTER
PHYTOPLANKTERS
PHYTOPLANKTON
PHYTOPLANKTONIC
PHYTOPLANKTONS
PHYTOSOCIOLOGY
PHYTOSTEROL
PHYTOSTEROLS
PHYTOTHERAPIES
PHYTOTHERAPY
PHYTOTOMIES
PHYTOTOMIST
PHYTOTOMISTS
PHYTOTOXIC
PHYTOTOXICITIES
PHYTOTOXICITY
PHYTOTOXIN
PHYTOTOXINS
PHYTOTRONS
PIACULARITIES
PIACULARITY
PIANISSIMI
PIANISSIMO
PIANISSIMOS
PIANISSISSIMO
PIANISTICALLY
PIANOFORTE
PIANOFORTES
PIANOLISTS
PICADILLOS
PICANINNIES
PICARESQUE
PICARESQUES
PICAROONED
PICAROONING
PICAYUNISH
PICAYUNISHLY
PICAYUNISHNESS
PICCADILLIES
PICCADILLO
PICCADILLOES
PICCADILLS
PICCADILLY
PICCALILLI
PICCALILLIS
PICCANINNIES
PICCANINNY
PICCOLOIST
PICCOLOISTS
PICHICIAGO
PICHICIAGOS
PICHICIEGO
PICHICIEGOS
PICHOLINES
PICKABACKED
PICKABACKING
PICKABACKS
PICKADILLIES
PICKADILLO
PICKADILLOES
PICKADILLS
PICKADILLY
PICKANINNIES
PICKANINNY
PICKAPACKS
PICKAROONS
PICKEDNESS
PICKEDNESSES
PICKEERERS
PICKEERING
PICKELHAUBE
PICKELHAUBES
PICKERELWEED
PICKERELWEEDS
PICKETBOAT
PICKETBOATS
PICKETINGS
PICKINESSES
PICKPOCKET
PICKPOCKETS
PICKTHANKS

PICNICKERS
PICNICKING
PICOCURIES
PICOFARADS
PICOMETERS
PICOMETRES
PICORNAVIRUS
PICORNAVIRUSES
PICOSECOND
PICOSECONDS
PICOWAVING
PICQUETING
PICROCARMINE
PICROCARMINES
PICROTOXIN
PICROTOXINS
PICTARNIES
PICTOGRAMS
PICTOGRAPH
PICTOGRAPHIC
PICTOGRAPHIES
PICTOGRAPHS
PICTOGRAPHY
PICTORIALISE
PICTORIALISED
PICTORIALISES
PICTORIALISING
PICTORIALISM
PICTORIALISMS
PICTORIALIST
PICTORIALISTS
PICTORIALIZE
PICTORIALIZED
PICTORIALIZES
PICTORIALIZING
PICTORIALLY
PICTORIALNESS
PICTORIALNESSES
PICTORIALS
PICTORICAL
PICTORICALLY
PICTUREGOER
PICTUREGOERS
PICTUREPHONE
PICTUREPHONES
PICTURESQUE
PICTURESQUELY
PICTURESQUENESS
PICTURISATION
PICTURISATIONS
PICTURISED
PICTURISES
PICTURISING
PICTURIZATION
PICTURIZATIONS
PICTURIZED
PICTURIZES
PICTURIZING
PIDDLINGLY
PIDGINISATION
PIDGINISATIONS
PIDGINISED
PIDGINISES
PIDGINISING
PIDGINIZATION
PIDGINIZATIONS
PIDGINIZED
PIDGINIZES
PIDGINIZING
PIECEMEALED
PIECEMEALING
PIECEMEALS
PIECEWORKER
PIECEWORKERS
PIECEWORKS
PIEDMONTITE
PIEDMONTITES
PIEDNESSES
PIEMONTITE
PIEMONTITES
PIEPOWDERS
PIERCEABLE
PIERCINGLY

PIERCINGNESS
PIERCINGNESSES
PIERRETTES
PIETISTICAL
PIETISTICALLY
PIEZOCHEMISTRY
PIEZOELECTRIC
PIEZOMAGNETIC
PIEZOMAGNETISM
PIEZOMAGNETISMS
PIEZOMETER
PIEZOMETERS
PIEZOMETRIC
PIEZOMETRICALLY
PIEZOMETRIES
PIEZOMETRY
PIGEONHOLE
PIGEONHOLED
PIGEONHOLER
PIGEONHOLERS
PIGEONHOLES
PIGEONHOLING
PIGEONITES
PIGEONRIES
PIGEONWING
PIGEONWINGS
PIGGINESSES
PIGGISHNESS
PIGGISHNESSES
PIGGYBACKED
PIGGYBACKING
PIGGYBACKS
PIGHEADEDLY
PIGHEADEDNESS
PIGHEADEDNESSES
PIGMENTARY
PIGMENTATION
PIGMENTATIONS
PIGMENTING
PIGNERATED
PIGNERATES
PIGNERATING
PIGNORATED
PIGNORATES
PIGNORATING
PIGNORATION
PIGNORATIONS
PIGSCONCES
PIGSTICKED
PIGSTICKER
PIGSTICKERS
PIGSTICKING
PIKEPERCHES
PIKESTAFFS
PIKESTAVES
PILASTERED
PILEORHIZA
PILEORHIZAS
PILFERABLE
PILFERAGES
PILFERINGLY
PILFERINGS
PILFERPROOF
PILGARLICK
PILGARLICKS
PILGARLICKY
PILGARLICS
PILGRIMAGE
PILGRIMAGED
PILGRIMAGER
PILGRIMAGERS
PILGRIMAGES
PILGRIMAGING
PILGRIMERS
PILGRIMISE
PILGRIMISED
PILGRIMISES
PILGRIMISING
PILGRIMIZE
PILGRIMIZED
PILGRIMIZES
PILGRIMIZING
PILIFEROUS

PILLARISTS
PILLARLESS
PILLICOCKS
PILLIONING
PILLIONIST
PILLIONISTS
PILLIWINKS
PILLORISED
PILLORISES
PILLORISING
PILLORIZED
PILLORIZES
PILLORIZING
PILLORYING
PILLOWCASE
PILLOWCASES
PILLOWSLIP
PILLOWSLIPS
PILNIEWINKS
PILOCARPIN
PILOCARPINE
PILOCARPINES
PILOCARPINS
PILOSITIES
PILOTFISHES
PILOTHOUSE
PILOTHOUSES
PIMPERNELS
PIMPLINESS
PIMPLINESSES
PIMPMOBILE
PIMPMOBILES
PINACOIDAL
PINACOTHECA
PINACOTHECAE
PINAKOIDAL
PINAKOTHEK
PINAKOTHEKS
PINBALLING
PINCERLIKE
PINCHBECKS
PINCHCOCKS
PINCHCOMMONS
PINCHCOMMONSES
PINCHFISTS
PINCHINGLY
PINCHPENNIES
PINCHPENNY
PINCHPOINT
PINCHPOINTS
PINCUSHION
PINCUSHIONS
PINEALECTOMIES
PINEALECTOMISE
PINEALECTOMISED
PINEALECTOMISES
PINEALECTOMIZE
PINEALECTOMIZED
PINEALECTOMIZES
PINEALECTOMY
PINEAPPLES
PINFEATHER
PINFEATHERS
PINFOLDING
PINGRASSES
PINGUEFIED
PINGUEFIES
PINGUEFYING
PINGUIDITIES
PINGUIDITY
PINGUITUDE
PINGUITUDES
PINHEADEDNESS
PINHEADEDNESSES
PINHOOKERS
PINKERTONS
PINKINESSES
PINKISHNESS
PINKISHNESSES
PINKNESSES
PINNACLING
PINNATIFID
PINNATIFIDLY

PINNATIONS
PINNATIPARTITE
PINNATIPED
PINNATISECT
PINNIEWINKLE
PINNIEWINKLES
PINNIPEDES
PINNIPEDIAN
PINNIPEDIANS
PINNULATED
PINNYWINKLE
PINNYWINKLES
PINOCYTOSES
PINOCYTOSIS
PINOCYTOTIC
PINOCYTOTICALLY
PINPOINTED
PINPOINTING
PINPRICKED
PINPRICKING
PINSETTERS
PINSPOTTER
PINSPOTTERS
PINSTRIPES
PINTADERAS
PINWHEELED
PINWHEELING
PINWRENCHES
PIONEERING
PIOUSNESSES
PIPECLAYED
PIPECLAYING
PIPEFISHES
PIPEFITTER
PIPEFITTERS
PIPEFITTING
PIPEFITTINGS
PIPELINING
PIPELININGS
PIPERACEOUS
PIPERAZINE
PIPERAZINES
PIPERIDINE
PIPERIDINES
PIPERONALS
PIPESTONES
PIPINESSES
PIPISTRELLE
PIPISTRELLES
PIPISTRELS
PIPIWHARAUROA
PIPIWHARAUROAS
PIPSISSEWA
PIPSISSEWAS
PIPSQUEAKS
PIQUANCIES
PIQUANTNESS
PIQUANTNESSES
PIRACETAMS
PIRATICALLY
PIRLICUING
PIROPLASMA
PIROPLASMATA
PIROPLASMS
PIROUETTED
PIROUETTER
PIROUETTERS
PIROUETTES
PIROUETTING
PISCATORIAL
PISCATORIALLY
PISCATRIXES
PISCICOLOUS
PISCICULTURAL
PISCICULTURALLY
PISCICULTURE
PISCICULTURES
PISCICULTURIST
PISCICULTURISTS
PISCIFAUNA
PISCIFAUNAE
PISCIFAUNAS
PISCIVORES

PISCIVOROUS
PISSASPHALT
PISSASPHALTS
PISTACHIOS
PISTAREENS
PISTILLARY
PISTILLATE
PISTILLODE
PISTILLODES
PISTOLEERS
PISTOLEROS
PISTOLIERS
PISTOLLING
PITAPATTED
PITAPATTING
PITCHBENDS
PITCHBLENDE
PITCHBLENDES
PITCHERFUL
PITCHERFULS
PITCHERSFUL
PITCHFORKED
PITCHFORKING
PITCHFORKS
PITCHINESS
PITCHINESSES
PITCHOMETER
PITCHOMETERS
PITCHPERSON
PITCHPERSONS
PITCHPINES
PITCHPIPES
PITCHPOLED
PITCHPOLES
PITCHPOLING
PITCHSTONE
PITCHSTONES
PITCHWOMAN
PITCHWOMEN
PITEOUSNESS
PITEOUSNESSES
PITHECANTHROPI
PITHECANTHROPUS
PITHINESSES
PITIABLENESS
PITIABLENESSES
PITIFULLER
PITIFULLEST
PITIFULNESS
PITIFULNESSES
PITILESSLY
PITILESSNESS
PITILESSNESSES
PITTOSPORUM
PITTOSPORUMS
PITUITARIES
PITUITRINS
PITYRIASES
PITYRIASIS
PITYROSPORUM
PITYROSPORUMS
PIWAKAWAKA
PIXELATION
PIXELATIONS
PIXELLATED
PIXILATION
PIXILATIONS
PIXILLATED
PIXILLATION
PIXILLATIONS
PIXINESSES
PIZZICATOS
PLACABILITIES
PLACABILITY
PLACABLENESS
PLACABLENESSES
PLACARDING
PLACATINGLY
PLACATIONS
PLACEHOLDER
PLACEHOLDERS
PLACEKICKED
PLACEKICKER

PLACEKICKERS
PLACEKICKING
PLACEKICKS
PLACELESSLY
PLACEMENTS
PLACENTALS
PLACENTATE
PLACENTATION
PLACENTATIONS
PLACENTIFORM
PLACENTOLOGIES
PLACENTOLOGY
PLACIDITIES
PLACIDNESS
PLACIDNESSES
PLACODERMS
PLAGIARIES
PLAGIARISE
PLAGIARISED
PLAGIARISER
PLAGIARISERS
PLAGIARISES
PLAGIARISING
PLAGIARISM
PLAGIARISMS
PLAGIARIST
PLAGIARISTIC
PLAGIARISTS
PLAGIARIZE
PLAGIARIZED
PLAGIARIZER
PLAGIARIZERS
PLAGIARIZES
PLAGIARIZING
PLAGIOCEPHALIES
PLAGIOCEPHALY
PLAGIOCLASE
PLAGIOCLASES
PLAGIOCLASTIC
PLAGIOCLIMAX
PLAGIOCLIMAXES
PLAGIOSTOMATOUS
PLAGIOSTOME
PLAGIOSTOMES
PLAGIOSTOMOUS
PLAGIOTROPIC
PLAGIOTROPISM
PLAGIOTROPISMS
PLAGIOTROPOUS
PLAGUESOME
PLAINCHANT
PLAINCHANTS
PLAINCLOTHES
PLAINCLOTHESMAN
PLAINCLOTHESMEN
PLAINNESSES
PLAINSONGS
PLAINSPOKEN
PLAINSPOKENNESS
PLAINSTANES
PLAINSTONES
PLAINTEXTS
PLAINTIFFS
PLAINTIVELY
PLAINTIVENESS
PLAINTIVENESSES
PLAINTLESS
PLAINWORKS
PLAISTERED
PLAISTERING
PLANARIANS
PLANARITIES
PLANATIONS
PLANCHETTE
PLANCHETTES
PLANELOADS
PLANENESSES
PLANESIDES
PLANETARIA
PLANETARIES
PLANETARIUM
PLANETARIUMS
PLANETESIMAL

PLANETESIMALS
PLANETICAL
PLANETLIKE
PLANETOIDAL
PLANETOIDS
PLANETOLOGICAL
PLANETOLOGIES
PLANETOLOGIST
PLANETOLOGISTS
PLANETOLOGY
PLANETWIDE
PLANGENCIES
PLANGENTLY
PLANIGRAPH
PLANIGRAPHS
PLANIMETER
PLANIMETERS
PLANIMETRIC
PLANIMETRICAL
PLANIMETRICALLY
PLANIMETRIES
PLANIMETRY
PLANISHERS
PLANISHING
PLANISPHERE
PLANISPHERES
PLANISPHERIC
PLANKTONIC
PLANLESSLY
PLANLESSNESS
PLANLESSNESSES
PLANOBLAST
PLANOBLASTS
PLANOGAMETE
PLANOGAMETES
PLANOGRAPHIC
PLANOGRAPHIES
PLANOGRAPHY
PLANOMETER
PLANOMETERS
PLANOMETRIC
PLANOMETRICALLY
PLANOMETRIES
PLANOMETRY
PLANTAGINACEOUS
PLANTATION
PLANTATIONS
PLANTIGRADE
PLANTIGRADES
PLANTLINGS
PLANTOCRACIES
PLANTOCRACY
PLANTSWOMAN
PLANTSWOMEN
PLANULIFORM
PLAQUETTES
PLASMAGELS
PLASMAGENE
PLASMAGENES
PLASMAGENIC
PLASMALEMMA
PLASMALEMMAS
PLASMAPHERESES
PLASMAPHERESIS
PLASMASOLS
PLASMATICAL
PLASMINOGEN
PLASMINOGENS
PLASMODESM
PLASMODESMA
PLASMODESMAS
PLASMODESMATA
PLASMODESMS
PLASMODIAL
PLASMODIUM
PLASMOGAMIES
PLASMOGAMY
PLASMOLYSE
PLASMOLYSED
PLASMOLYSES
PLASMOLYSING
PLASMOLYSIS
PLASMOLYTIC

PLASMOLYTICALLY	PLATINISES	PLAYWRIGHTINGS	PLENTEOUSNESSES	PLOTTINGLY	PLURISERIAL
PLASMOLYZE	PLATINISING	PLAYWRIGHTS	PLENTIFULLY	PLOUGHABLE	PLURISERIATE
PLASMOLYZED	PLATINIZATION	PLAYWRITING	PLENTIFULNESS	PLOUGHBOYS	PLUSHINESS
PLASMOLYZES	PLATINIZATIONS	PLAYWRITINGS	PLENTIFULNESSES	PLOUGHGATE	PLUSHINESSES
PLASMOLYZING	PLATINIZED	PLEADINGLY	PLENTITUDE	PLOUGHGATES	PLUSHNESSES
PLASMOSOMA	PLATINIZES	PLEASANCES	PLENTITUDES	PLOUGHINGS	PLUTOCRACIES
PLASMOSOMATA	PLATINIZING	PLEASANTER	PLEOCHROIC	PLOUGHLAND	PLUTOCRACY
PLASMOSOME	PLATINOCYANIC	PLEASANTEST	PLEOCHROISM	PLOUGHLANDS	PLUTOCRATIC
PLASMOSOMES	PLATINOCYANIDE	PLEASANTLY	PLEOCHROISMS	PLOUGHMANSHIP	PLUTOCRATICAL
PLASTERBOARD	PLATINOCYANIDES	PLEASANTNESS	PLEOMORPHIC	PLOUGHMANSHIPS	PLUTOCRATICALLY
PLASTERBOARDS	PLATINOIDS	PLEASANTNESSES	PLEOMORPHIES	PLOUGHSHARE	PLUTOCRATS
PLASTERERS	PLATINOTYPE	PLEASANTRIES	PLEOMORPHISM	PLOUGHSHARES	PLUTOLATRIES
PLASTERINESS	PLATINOTYPES	PLEASANTRY	PLEOMORPHISMS	PLOUGHSTAFF	PLUTOLATRY
PLASTERINESSES	PLATITUDES	PLEASINGLY	PLEOMORPHOUS	PLOUGHSTAFFS	PLUTOLOGIES
PLASTERING	PLATITUDINAL	PLEASINGNESS	PLEOMORPHY	PLOUGHTAIL	PLUTOLOGIST
PLASTERINGS	PLATITUDINARIAN	PLEASINGNESSES	PLEONASTES	PLOUGHTAILS	PLUTOLOGISTS
PLASTERSTONE	PLATITUDINISE	PLEASURABILITY	PLEONASTIC	PLOUGHWISE	PLUTONISMS
PLASTERSTONES	PLATITUDINISED	PLEASURABLE	PLEONASTICAL	PLOUGHWRIGHT	PLUTONIUMS
PLASTERWORK	PLATITUDINISER	PLEASURABLENESS	PLEONASTICALLY	PLOUGHWRIGHTS	PLUTONOMIES
PLASTERWORKS	PLATITUDINISERS	PLEASURABLY	PLEONECTIC	PLOUTERING	PLUTONOMIST
PLASTICALLY	PLATITUDINISES	PLEASUREFUL	PLEONEXIAS	PLOWMANSHIP	PLUTONOMISTS
PLASTICENE	PLATITUDINISING	PLEASURELESS	PLEROCERCOID	PLOWMANSHIPS	PLUVIOMETER
PLASTICENES	PLATITUDINIZE	PLEASURERS	PLEROCERCOIDS	PLOWSHARES	PLUVIOMETERS
PLASTICINE	PLATITUDINIZED	PLEASURING	PLEROMATIC	PLOWSTAFFS	PLUVIOMETRIC
PLASTICINES	PLATITUDINIZER	PLEBEIANISE	PLEROPHORIA	PLOWTERING	PLUVIOMETRICAL
PLASTICISATION	PLATITUDINIZERS	PLEBEIANISED	PLEROPHORIAS	PLUCKINESS	PLUVIOMETRIES
PLASTICISATIONS	PLATITUDINIZES	PLEBEIANISES	PLEROPHORIES	PLUCKINESSES	PLUVIOMETRY
PLASTICISE	PLATITUDINIZING	PLEBEIANISING	PLEROPHORY	PLUGBOARDS	PLYOMETRIC
PLASTICISED	PLATITUDINOUS	PLEBEIANISM	PLESIOSAUR	PLUGUGLIES	PLYOMETRICS
PLASTICISER	PLATITUDINOUSLY	PLEBEIANISMS	PLESIOSAURIAN	PLUMASSIER	PNEUMATHODE
PLASTICISERS	PLATONICALLY	PLEBEIANIZE	PLESIOSAURS	PLUMASSIERS	PNEUMATHODES
PLASTICISES	PLATONISMS	PLEBEIANIZED	PLESSIMETER	PLUMBAGINACEOUS	PNEUMATICAL
PLASTICISING	PLATOONING	PLEBEIANIZES	PLESSIMETERS	PLUMBAGINOUS	PNEUMATICALLY
PLASTICITIES	PLATTELAND	PLEBEIANIZING	PLESSIMETRIC	PLUMBERIES	PNEUMATICITIES
PLASTICITY	PLATTELANDS	PLEBEIANLY	PLESSIMETRIES	PLUMBIFEROUS	PNEUMATICITY
PLASTICIZATION	PLATTERFUL	PLEBIFICATION	PLESSIMETRY	PLUMBISOLVENCY	PNEUMATICS
PLASTICIZATIONS	PLATTERFULS	PLEBIFICATIONS	PLETHORICAL	PLUMBISOLVENT	PNEUMATOLOGICAL
PLASTICIZE	PLATTERSFUL	PLEBIFYING	PLETHORICALLY	PLUMBNESSES	PNEUMATOLOGIES
PLASTICIZED	PLATYCEPHALIC	PLEBISCITARY	PLETHYSMOGRAM	PLUMBOSOLVENCY	PNEUMATOLOGIST
PLASTICIZER	PLATYCEPHALOUS	PLEBISCITE	PLETHYSMOGRAMS	PLUMBOSOLVENT	PNEUMATOLOGISTS
PLASTICIZERS	PLATYFISHES	PLEBISCITES	PLETHYSMOGRAPH	PLUMDAMASES	PNEUMATOLOGY
PLASTICIZES	PLATYHELMINTH	PLECOPTERAN	PLETHYSMOGRAPHS	PLUMIGEROUS	PNEUMATOLYSES
PLASTICIZING	PLATYHELMINTHIC	PLECOPTERANS	PLETHYSMOGRAPHY	PLUMMETING	PNEUMATOLYSIS
PLASTIDIAL	PLATYHELMINTHS	PLECOPTEROUS	PLEURAPOPHYSES	PLUMOSITIES	PNEUMATOLYTIC
PLASTIDULE	PLATYKURTIC	PLECTOGNATH	PLEURAPOPHYSIS	PLUMPENING	PNEUMATOMETER
PLASTIDULES	PLATYPUSES	PLECTOGNATHIC	PLEURISIES	PLUMPNESSES	PNEUMATOMETERS
PLASTILINA	PLATYRRHINE	PLECTOGNATHOUS	PLEURITICAL	PLUMULACEOUS	PNEUMATOMETRIES
PLASTILINAS	PLATYRRHINES	PLECTOGNATHS	PLEURITICS	PLUMULARIAN	PNEUMATOMETRY
PLASTIQUES	PLATYRRHINIAN	PLECTOPTEROUS	PLEURITISES	PLUMULARIANS	PNEUMATOPHORE
PLASTISOLS	PLATYRRHINIANS	PLEDGEABLE	PLEUROCARPOUS	PLUNDERABLE	PNEUMATOPHORES
PLASTOCYANIN	PLAUDITORY	PLEINAIRISM	PLEUROCENTESES	PLUNDERAGE	PNEUMECTOMIES
PLASTOCYANINS	PLAUSIBILITIES	PLEINAIRISMS	PLEUROCENTESIS	PLUNDERAGES	PNEUMECTOMY
PLASTOGAMIES	PLAUSIBILITY	PLEINAIRIST	PLEURODONT	PLUNDERERS	PNEUMOBACILLI
PLASTOGAMY	PLAUSIBLENESS	PLEINAIRISTS	PLEURODONTS	PLUNDERING	PNEUMOBACILLUS
PLASTOMETER	PLAUSIBLENESSES	PLEIOCHASIA	PLEURODYNIA	PLUNDEROUS	PNEUMOCOCCAL
PLASTOMETERS	PLAYABILITIES	PLEIOCHASIUM	PLEURODYNIAS	PLUPERFECT	PNEUMOCOCCI
PLASTOMETRIC	PLAYABILITY	PLEIOMERIES	PLEUROPNEUMONIA	PLUPERFECTS	PNEUMOCOCCUS
PLASTOMETRIES	PLAYACTING	PLEIOMEROUS	PLEUROTOMIES	PLURALISATION	PNEUMOCONIOSES
PLASTOMETRY	PLAYACTINGS	PLEIOTAXIES	PLEUROTOMY	PLURALISATIONS	PNEUMOCONIOSIS
PLASTOQUINONE	PLAYACTORS	PLEIOTROPIC	PLEUSTONIC	PLURALISED	PNEUMOCONIOTIC
PLASTOQUINONES	PLAYBUSSES	PLEIOTROPIES	PLEXIGLASS	PLURALISER	PNEUMOCONIOTICS
PLATANACEOUS	PLAYFELLOW	PLEIOTROPISM	PLEXIGLASSES	PLURALISERS	PNEUMOCYSTIS
PLATEAUING	PLAYFELLOWS	PLEIOTROPISMS	PLEXIMETER	PLURALISES	PNEUMOCYSTISES
PLATEGLASS	PLAYFIELDS	PLEIOTROPY	PLEXIMETERS	PLURALISING	PNEUMODYNAMICS
PLATELAYER	PLAYFULNESS	PLENARTIES	PLEXIMETRIC	PLURALISMS	PNEUMOGASTRIC
PLATELAYERS	PLAYFULNESSES	PLENILUNAR	PLEXIMETRIES	PLURALISTIC	PNEUMOGASTRICS
PLATEMAKER	PLAYGOINGS	PLENILUNES	PLEXIMETRY	PLURALISTICALLY	PNEUMOGRAM
PLATEMAKERS	PLAYGROUND	PLENIPOTENCE	PLIABILITIES	PLURALISTS	PNEUMOGRAMS
PLATEMAKING	PLAYGROUNDS	PLENIPOTENCES	PLIABILITY	PLURALITIES	PNEUMOGRAPH
PLATEMAKINGS	PLAYGROUPS	PLENIPOTENCIES	PLIABLENESS	PLURALIZATION	PNEUMOGRAPHS
PLATEMARKED	PLAYHOUSES	PLENIPOTENCY	PLIABLENESSES	PLURALIZATIONS	PNEUMOKONIOSES
PLATEMARKING	PLAYLEADER	PLENIPOTENT	PLIANTNESS	PLURALIZED	PNEUMOKONIOSIS
PLATEMARKS	PLAYLEADERS	PLENIPOTENTIAL	PLIANTNESSES	PLURALIZER	PNEUMONECTOMIES
PLATERESQUE	PLAYLISTED	PLENIPOTENTIARY	PLICATENESS	PLURALIZERS	PNEUMONECTOMY
PLATFORMED	PLAYLISTING	PLENISHERS	PLICATENESSES	PLURALIZES	PNEUMONIAS
PLATFORMING	PLAYMAKERS	PLENISHING	PLICATIONS	PLURALIZING	PNEUMONICS
PLATFORMINGS	PLAYMAKING	PLENISHINGS	PLICATURES	PLURILITERAL	PNEUMONITIS
PLATINIFEROUS	PLAYMAKINGS	PLENISHMENT	PLODDINGLY	PLURILOCULAR	PNEUMONITISES
PLATINIRIDIUM	PLAYSCHOOL	PLENISHMENTS	PLODDINGNESS	PLURIPARAE	PNEUMOTHORACES
PLATINIRIDIUMS	PLAYSCHOOLS	PLENITUDES	PLODDINGNESSES	PLURIPARAS	PNEUMOTHORAX
PLATINISATION	PLAYTHINGS	PLENITUDINOUS	PLOTLESSNESS	PLURIPOTENT	PNEUMOTHORAXES
PLATINISATIONS	PLAYWRIGHT	PLENTEOUSLY	PLOTLESSNESSES	PLURIPRESENCE	POACHINESS
PLATINISED	PLAYWRIGHTING	PLENTEOUSNESS	PLOTTERING	PLURIPRESENCES	POACHINESSES

POCKETABLE
POCKETBIKE
POCKETBIKES
POCKETBOOK
POCKETBOOKS
POCKETFULS
POCKETKNIFE
POCKETKNIVES
POCKETLESS
POCKETPHONE
POCKETPHONES
POCKETSFUL
POCKMANKIES
POCKMANTIE
POCKMANTIES
POCKMARKED
POCKMARKING
POCKPITTED
POCOCURANTE
POCOCURANTEISM
POCOCURANTEISMS
POCOCURANTES
POCOCURANTISM
POCOCURANTISMS
POCOCURANTIST
POCOCURANTISTS
POCULIFORM
PODAGRICAL
PODARGUSES
PODCASTERS
PODCASTING
PODCASTINGS
PODGINESSES
PODIATRIES
PODIATRIST
PODIATRISTS
PODOCONIOSES
PODOCONIOSIS
PODOLOGIES
PODOLOGIST
PODOLOGISTS
PODOPHTHALMOUS
PODOPHYLIN
PODOPHYLINS
PODOPHYLLI
PODOPHYLLIN
PODOPHYLLINS
PODOPHYLLUM
PODOPHYLLUMS
PODSOLISATION
PODSOLISATIONS
PODSOLISED
PODSOLISES
PODSOLISING
PODSOLIZATION
PODSOLIZATIONS
PODSOLIZED
PODSOLIZES
PODSOLIZING
PODZOLISATION
PODZOLISATIONS
PODZOLISED
PODZOLISES
PODZOLISING
PODZOLIZATION
PODZOLIZATIONS
PODZOLIZED
PODZOLIZES
PODZOLIZING
POENOLOGIES
POETASTERIES
POETASTERING
POETASTERINGS
POETASTERS
POETASTERY
POETASTRIES
POETICALLY
POETICALNESS
POETICALNESSES
POETICISED
POETICISES
POETICISING
POETICISMS

POETICIZED
POETICIZES
POETICIZING
POETICULES
POETRESSES
POGONOPHORAN
POGONOPHORANS
POGONOTOMIES
POGONOTOMY
POGROMISTS
POHUTUKAWA
POHUTUKAWAS
POIGNADOES
POIGNANCES
POIGNANCIES
POIGNANTLY
POIKILITIC
POIKILOCYTE
POIKILOCYTES
POIKILOTHERM
POIKILOTHERMAL
POIKILOTHERMIC
POIKILOTHERMIES
POIKILOTHERMISM
POIKILOTHERMS
POIKILOTHERMY
POINCIANAS
POINSETTIA
POINSETTIAS
POINTEDNESS
POINTEDNESSES
POINTELLES
POINTILLISM
POINTILLISME
POINTILLISMES
POINTILLISMS
POINTILLIST
POINTILLISTE
POINTILLISTES
POINTILLISTIC
POINTILLISTS
POINTLESSLY
POINTLESSNESS
POINTLESSNESSES
POISONABLE
POISONOUSLY
POISONOUSNESS
POISONOUSNESSES
POISONWOOD
POISONWOODS
POKEBERRIES
POKELOGANS
POKERISHLY
POKERWORKS
POKINESSES
POLARIMETER
POLARIMETERS
POLARIMETRIC
POLARIMETRIES
POLARIMETRY
POLARISABLE
POLARISATION
POLARISATIONS
POLARISCOPE
POLARISCOPES
POLARISCOPIC
POLARISERS
POLARISING
POLARITIES
POLARIZABILITY
POLARIZABLE
POLARIZATION
POLARIZATIONS
POLARIZERS
POLARIZING
POLAROGRAM
POLAROGRAMS
POLAROGRAPH
POLAROGRAPHIC
POLAROGRAPHIES
POLAROGRAPHS
POLAROGRAPHY
POLEMARCHS

POLEMICALLY
POLEMICISE
POLEMICISED
POLEMICISES
POLEMICISING
POLEMICIST
POLEMICISTS
POLEMICIZE
POLEMICIZED
POLEMICIZES
POLEMICIZING
POLEMISING
POLEMIZING
POLEMONIACEOUS
POLEMONIUM
POLEMONIUMS
POLIANITES
POLICEWOMAN
POLICEWOMEN
POLICYHOLDER
POLICYHOLDERS
POLIOMYELITIDES
POLIOMYELITIS
POLIOMYELITISES
POLIORCETIC
POLIORCETICS
POLIOVIRUS
POLIOVIRUSES
POLISHABLE
POLISHINGS
POLISHMENT
POLISHMENTS
POLITBUROS
POLITENESS
POLITENESSES
POLITESSES
POLITICALISE
POLITICALISED
POLITICALISES
POLITICALISING
POLITICALIZE
POLITICALIZED
POLITICALIZES
POLITICALIZING
POLITICALLY
POLITICASTER
POLITICASTERS
POLITICIAN
POLITICIANS
POLITICISATION
POLITICISATIONS
POLITICISE
POLITICISED
POLITICISES
POLITICISING
POLITICIZATION
POLITICIZATIONS
POLITICIZE
POLITICIZED
POLITICIZES
POLITICIZING
POLITICKED
POLITICKER
POLITICKERS
POLITICKING
POLITICKINGS
POLITICOES
POLITIQUES
POLLARDING
POLLENATED
POLLENATES
POLLENATING
POLLENIFEROUS
POLLENISER
POLLENISERS
POLLENIZER
POLLENIZERS
POLLENOSES
POLLENOSIS
POLLICITATION
POLLICITATIONS
POLLINATED
POLLINATES

POLLINATING
POLLINATION
POLLINATIONS
POLLINATOR
POLLINATORS
POLLINIFEROUS
POLLINISED
POLLINISER
POLLINISERS
POLLINISES
POLLINISING
POLLINIZED
POLLINIZER
POLLINIZERS
POLLINIZES
POLLINIZING
POLLINOSES
POLLINOSIS
POLLTAKERS
POLLUCITES
POLLUSIONS
POLLUTANTS
POLLUTEDLY
POLLUTEDNESS
POLLUTEDNESSES
POLLUTIONS
POLLYANNAISH
POLLYANNAISM
POLLYANNAISMS
POLLYANNAS
POLLYANNISH
POLONAISES
POLONISING
POLONIZING
POLTERGEIST
POLTERGEISTS
POLTROONERIES
POLTROONERY
POLVERINES
POLYACRYLAMIDE
POLYACRYLAMIDES
POLYACTINAL
POLYACTINE
POLYADELPHOUS
POLYALCOHOL
POLYALCOHOLS
POLYAMIDES
POLYAMINES
POLYANDRIES
POLYANDROUS
POLYANTHAS
POLYANTHUS
POLYANTHUSES
POLYARCHIES
POLYATOMIC
POLYAXIALS
POLYAXONIC
POLYBASITE
POLYBASITES
POLYBUTADIENE
POLYBUTADIENES
POLYCARBONATE
POLYCARBONATES
POLYCARBOXYLATE
POLYCARBOXYLIC
POLYCARPELLARY
POLYCARPIC
POLYCARPIES
POLYCARPOUS
POLYCENTRIC
POLYCENTRISM
POLYCENTRISMS
POLYCHAETE
POLYCHAETES
POLYCHAETOUS
POLYCHASIA
POLYCHASIUM
POLYCHETES
POLYCHLORINATED
POLYCHLOROPRENE
POLYCHOTOMIES
POLYCHOTOMOUS
POLYCHOTOMY

POLYCHREST
POLYCHRESTS
POLYCHROIC
POLYCHROISM
POLYCHROISMS
POLYCHROMATIC
POLYCHROMATISM
POLYCHROMATISMS
POLYCHROME
POLYCHROMED
POLYCHROMES
POLYCHROMIC
POLYCHROMIES
POLYCHROMING
POLYCHROMOUS
POLYCHROMY
POLYCISTRONIC
POLYCLINIC
POLYCLINICS
POLYCLONAL
POLYCOTTON
POLYCOTTONS
POLYCOTYLEDON
POLYCOTYLEDONS
POLYCROTIC
POLYCROTISM
POLYCROTISMS
POLYCRYSTAL
POLYCRYSTALLINE
POLYCRYSTALS
POLYCULTURE
POLYCULTURES
POLYCYCLIC
POLYCYCLICS
POLYCYSTIC
POLYCYTHAEMIA
POLYCYTHAEMIAS
POLYCYTHEMIA
POLYCYTHEMIAS
POLYCYTHEMIC
POLYDACTYL
POLYDACTYLIES
POLYDACTYLISM
POLYDACTYLISMS
POLYDACTYLOUS
POLYDACTYLS
POLYDACTYLY
POLYDAEMONISM
POLYDAEMONISMS
POLYDEMONISM
POLYDEMONISMS
POLYDIPSIA
POLYDIPSIAS
POLYDIPSIC
POLYDISPERSE
POLYDISPERSITY
POLYELECTROLYTE
POLYEMBRYONATE
POLYEMBRYONIC
POLYEMBRYONIES
POLYEMBRYONY
POLYESTERS
POLYESTROUS
POLYETHENE
POLYETHENES
POLYETHYLENE
POLYETHYLENES
POLYGALACEOUS
POLYGAMIES
POLYGAMISE
POLYGAMISED
POLYGAMISES
POLYGAMISING
POLYGAMIST
POLYGAMISTS
POLYGAMIZE
POLYGAMIZED
POLYGAMIZES
POLYGAMIZING
POLYGAMOUS
POLYGAMOUSLY
POLYGENESES
POLYGENESIS

POLYGENETIC
POLYGENETICALLY
POLYGENIES
POLYGENISM
POLYGENISMS
POLYGENIST
POLYGENISTS
POLYGENOUS
POLYGLOTISM
POLYGLOTISMS
POLYGLOTTAL
POLYGLOTTIC
POLYGLOTTISM
POLYGLOTTISMS
POLYGLOTTOUS
POLYGLOTTS
POLYGONACEOUS
POLYGONALLY
POLYGONATUM
POLYGONATUMS
POLYGONIES
POLYGONUMS
POLYGRAPHED
POLYGRAPHER
POLYGRAPHERS
POLYGRAPHIC
POLYGRAPHICALLY
POLYGRAPHIES
POLYGRAPHING
POLYGRAPHIST
POLYGRAPHISTS
POLYGRAPHS
POLYGRAPHY
POLYGYNIAN
POLYGYNIES
POLYGYNIST
POLYGYNISTS
POLYGYNOUS
POLYHALITE
POLYHALITES
POLYHEDRAL
POLYHEDRIC
POLYHEDRON
POLYHEDRONS
POLYHEDROSES
POLYHEDROSIS
POLYHISTOR
POLYHISTORIAN
POLYHISTORIANS
POLYHISTORIC
POLYHISTORIES
POLYHISTORS
POLYHISTORY
POLYHYBRID
POLYHYBRIDS
POLYHYDRIC
POLYHYDROXY
POLYIMIDES
POLYISOPRENE
POLYISOPRENES
POLYLEMMAS
POLYLYSINE
POLYLYSINES
POLYMASTIA
POLYMASTIAS
POLYMASTIC
POLYMASTIES
POLYMASTISM
POLYMASTISMS
POLYMATHIC
POLYMATHIES
POLYMERASE
POLYMERASES
POLYMERIDE
POLYMERIDES
POLYMERIES
POLYMERISATION
POLYMERISATIONS
POLYMERISE
POLYMERISED
POLYMERISES
POLYMERISING
POLYMERISM

POLYMERISMS
POLYMERIZATION
POLYMERIZATIONS
POLYMERIZE
POLYMERIZED
POLYMERIZES
POLYMERIZING
POLYMEROUS
POLYMORPHIC
POLYMORPHICALLY
POLYMORPHISM
POLYMORPHISMS
POLYMORPHOUS
POLYMORPHOUSLY
POLYMORPHS
POLYMYOSITIS
POLYMYOSITISES
POLYMYXINS
POLYNEURITIS
POLYNEURITISES
POLYNOMIAL
POLYNOMIALISM
POLYNOMIALISMS
POLYNOMIALS
POLYNUCLEAR
POLYNUCLEATE
POLYNUCLEOTIDE
POLYNUCLEOTIDES
POLYOLEFIN
POLYOLEFINS
POLYOMINOS
POLYONYMIC
POLYONYMIES
POLYONYMOUS
POLYPARIES
POLYPARIUM
POLYPEPTIDE
POLYPEPTIDES
POLYPEPTIDIC
POLYPETALOUS
POLYPHAGIA
POLYPHAGIAS
POLYPHAGIES
POLYPHAGOUS
POLYPHARMACIES
POLYPHARMACY
POLYPHASIC
POLYPHENOL
POLYPHENOLIC
POLYPHENOLS
POLYPHLOESBOEAN
POLYPHLOISBIC
POLYPHONES
POLYPHONIC
POLYPHONICALLY
POLYPHONIES
POLYPHONIST
POLYPHONISTS
POLYPHONOUS
POLYPHONOUSLY
POLYPHOSPHORIC
POLYPHYLETIC
POLYPHYLLOUS
POLYPHYODONT
POLYPIDOMS
POLYPLOIDAL
POLYPLOIDIC
POLYPLOIDIES
POLYPLOIDS
POLYPLOIDY
POLYPODIES
POLYPODOUS
POLYPROPENE
POLYPROPENES
POLYPROPYLENE
POLYPROPYLENES
POLYPROTODONT
POLYPROTODONTS
POLYPTYCHS
POLYRHYTHM
POLYRHYTHMIC
POLYRHYTHMS
POLYRIBOSOMAL

POLYRIBOSOME
POLYRIBOSOMES
POLYSACCHARIDE
POLYSACCHARIDES
POLYSACCHAROSE
POLYSACCHAROSES
POLYSEMANT
POLYSEMANTS
POLYSEMIES
POLYSEMOUS
POLYSEPALOUS
POLYSILOXANE
POLYSILOXANES
POLYSOMICS
POLYSOMIES
POLYSORBATE
POLYSORBATES
POLYSTICHOUS
POLYSTYLAR
POLYSTYRENE
POLYSTYRENES
POLYSULFIDE
POLYSULFIDES
POLYSULPHIDE
POLYSULPHIDES
POLYSYLLABIC
POLYSYLLABICAL
POLYSYLLABICISM
POLYSYLLABISM
POLYSYLLABISMS
POLYSYLLABLE
POLYSYLLABLES
POLYSYLLOGISM
POLYSYLLOGISMS
POLYSYNAPTIC
POLYSYNDETON
POLYSYNDETONS
POLYSYNTHESES
POLYSYNTHESIS
POLYSYNTHESISM
POLYSYNTHESISMS
POLYSYNTHETIC
POLYSYNTHETICAL
POLYSYNTHETISM
POLYSYNTHETISMS
POLYTECHNIC
POLYTECHNICAL
POLYTECHNICS
POLYTENIES
POLYTHALAMOUS
POLYTHEISM
POLYTHEISMS
POLYTHEIST
POLYTHEISTIC
POLYTHEISTICAL
POLYTHEISTS
POLYTHENES
POLYTOCOUS
POLYTONALISM
POLYTONALISMS
POLYTONALIST
POLYTONALISTS
POLYTONALITIES
POLYTONALITY
POLYTONALLY
POLYTROPHIC
POLYTUNNEL
POLYTUNNELS
POLYTYPICAL
POLYUNSATURATED
POLYURETHAN
POLYURETHANE
POLYURETHANES
POLYURETHANS
POLYVALENCE
POLYVALENCES
POLYVALENCIES
POLYVALENCY
POLYVALENT
POLYVINYLIDENE
POLYVINYLIDENES
POLYVINYLS
POLYWATERS

POLYZOARIA
POLYZOARIAL
POLYZOARIES
POLYZOARIUM
POMEGRANATE
POMEGRANATES
POMICULTURE
POMICULTURES
POMIFEROUS
POMMELLING
POMOERIUMS
POMOLOGICAL
POMOLOGICALLY
POMOLOGIES
POMOLOGIST
POMOLOGISTS
POMOSEXUAL
POMOSEXUALS
POMPADOURED
POMPADOURS
POMPELMOOSE
POMPELMOOSES
POMPELMOUS
POMPELMOUSE
POMPELMOUSES
POMPHOLYGOUS
POMPHOLYXES
POMPOSITIES
POMPOUSNESS
POMPOUSNESSES
PONDERABILITIES
PONDERABILITY
PONDERABLE
PONDERABLES
PONDERABLY
PONDERANCE
PONDERANCES
PONDERANCIES
PONDERANCY
PONDERATED
PONDERATES
PONDERATING
PONDERATION
PONDERATIONS
PONDERINGLY
PONDERMENT
PONDERMENTS
PONDEROSAS
PONDEROSITIES
PONDEROSITY
PONDEROUSLY
PONDEROUSNESS
PONDEROUSNESSES
PONDOKKIES
PONEROLOGIES
PONEROLOGY
PONIARDING
PONTIANACS
PONTIANAKS
PONTICELLO
PONTICELLOS
PONTIFICAL
PONTIFICALITIES
PONTIFICALITY
PONTIFICALLY
PONTIFICALS
PONTIFICATE
PONTIFICATED
PONTIFICATES
PONTIFICATING
PONTIFICATION
PONTIFICATIONS
PONTIFICATOR
PONTIFICATORS
PONTIFICES
PONTIFYING
PONTLEVISES
PONTONEERS
PONTONIERS
PONTONNIER
PONTONNIERS
PONTOONERS
PONTOONING

PONYTAILED
POORHOUSES
POORMOUTHED
POORMOUTHING
POORMOUTHS
POORNESSES
POPLINETTE
POPLINETTES
POPMOBILITIES
POPMOBILITY
POPPERINGS
POPPYCOCKS
POPPYHEADS
POPULARISATION
POPULARISATIONS
POPULARISE
POPULARISED
POPULARISER
POPULARISERS
POPULARISES
POPULARISING
POPULARITIES
POPULARITY
POPULARIZATION
POPULARIZATIONS
POPULARIZE
POPULARIZED
POPULARIZER
POPULARIZERS
POPULARIZES
POPULARIZING
POPULATING
POPULATION
POPULATIONAL
POPULATIONS
POPULISTIC
POPULOUSLY
POPULOUSNESS
POPULOUSNESSES
PORBEAGLES
PORCELAINEOUS
PORCELAINISE
PORCELAINISED
PORCELAINISES
PORCELAINISING
PORCELAINIZE
PORCELAINIZED
PORCELAINIZES
PORCELAINIZING
PORCELAINLIKE
PORCELAINOUS
PORCELAINS
PORCELANEOUS
PORCELLANEOUS
PORCELLANISE
PORCELLANISED
PORCELLANISES
PORCELLANISING
PORCELLANITE
PORCELLANITES
PORCELLANIZE
PORCELLANIZED
PORCELLANIZES
PORCELLANIZING
PORCELLANOUS
PORCUPINES
PORCUPINISH
PORIFERANS
PORIFEROUS
PORINESSES
PORISMATIC
PORISMATICAL
PORISTICAL
PORKINESSES
PORLOCKING
PORLOCKINGS
PORNOCRACIES
PORNOCRACY
PORNOGRAPHER
PORNOGRAPHERS
PORNOGRAPHIC
PORNOGRAPHIES
PORNOGRAPHY

PORNOTOPIA
PORNOTOPIAN
PORNOTOPIAS
POROGAMIES
POROMERICS
POROSCOPES
POROSCOPIC
POROSCOPIES
POROSITIES
POROUSNESS
POROUSNESSES
PORPENTINE
PORPENTINES
PORPHYRIAS
PORPHYRIES
PORPHYRINS
PORPHYRIOS
PORPHYRITE
PORPHYRITES
PORPHYRITIC
PORPHYROGENITE
PORPHYROGENITES
PORPHYROID
PORPHYROIDS
PORPHYROPSIN
PORPHYROPSINS
PORPHYROUS
PORPOISING
PORRACEOUS
PORRECTING
PORRECTION
PORRECTIONS
PORRENGERS
PORRIGINOUS
PORRINGERS
PORTABELLA
PORTABELLAS
PORTABELLO
PORTABELLOS
PORTABILITIES
PORTABILITY
PORTAMENTI
PORTAMENTO
PORTAPACKS
PORTATIVES
PORTCULLIS
PORTCULLISED
PORTCULLISES
PORTCULLISING
PORTENDING
PORTENTOUS
PORTENTOUSLY
PORTENTOUSNESS
PORTEOUSES
PORTERAGES
PORTERESSES
PORTERHOUSE
PORTERHOUSES
PORTFOLIOS
PORTHORSES
PORTHOUSES
PORTIONERS
PORTIONING
PORTIONIST
PORTIONISTS
PORTIONLESS
PORTLINESS
PORTLINESSES
PORTMANTEAU
PORTMANTEAUS
PORTMANTEAUX
PORTMANTLE
PORTMANTLES
PORTMANTUA
PORTMANTUAS
PORTOBELLO
PORTOBELLOS
PORTOLANOS
PORTRAITED
PORTRAITING
PORTRAITIST
PORTRAITISTS
PORTRAITURE

PORTRAITURES
PORTRAYABLE
PORTRAYALS
PORTRAYERS
PORTRAYING
PORTREEVES
PORTRESSES
PORTULACACEOUS
PORTULACAS
PORWIGGLES
POSHNESSES
POSITIONAL
POSITIONALLY
POSITIONED
POSITIONING
POSITIVELY
POSITIVENESS
POSITIVENESSES
POSITIVEST
POSITIVISM
POSITIVISMS
POSITIVIST
POSITIVISTIC
POSITIVISTS
POSITIVITIES
POSITIVITY
POSITRONIUM
POSITRONIUMS
POSOLOGICAL
POSOLOGIES
POSSESSABLE
POSSESSEDLY
POSSESSEDNESS
POSSESSEDNESSES
POSSESSING
POSSESSION
POSSESSIONAL
POSSESSIONARY
POSSESSIONATE
POSSESSIONATES
POSSESSIONED
POSSESSIONLESS
POSSESSIONS
POSSESSIVE
POSSESSIVELY
POSSESSIVENESS
POSSESSIVES
POSSESSORS
POSSESSORSHIP
POSSESSORSHIPS
POSSESSORY
POSSIBILISM
POSSIBILISMS
POSSIBILIST
POSSIBILISTS
POSSIBILITIES
POSSIBILITY
POSSIBLEST
POSTABORTION
POSTACCIDENT
POSTADOLESCENT
POSTAMPUTATION
POSTAPOCALYPTIC
POSTARREST
POSTATOMIC
POSTATTACK
POSTBELLUM
POSTBIBLICAL
POSTBOURGEOIS
POSTBUSSES
POSTCAPITALIST
POSTCARDED
POSTCARDING
POSTCARDLIKE
POSTCLASSIC
POSTCLASSICAL
POSTCODING
POSTCOITAL
POSTCOLLEGE
POSTCOLLEGIATE
POSTCOLONIAL
POSTCONCEPTION
POSTCONCERT

POSTCONQUEST	POSTILLERS	POSTPUBERTY	POTENTIATED	POWERHOUSE	PRAGMATISE
POSTCONSONANTAL	POSTILLING	POSTPUBESCENT	POTENTIATES	POWERHOUSES	PRAGMATISED
POSTCONVENTION	POSTILLION	POSTRECESSION	POTENTIATING	POWERLESSLY	PRAGMATISER
POSTCOPULATORY	POSTILLIONS	POSTRETIREMENT	POTENTIATION	POWERLESSNESS	PRAGMATISERS
POSTCORONARY	POSTIMPACT	POSTRIDERS	POTENTIATIONS	POWERLESSNESSES	PRAGMATISES
POSTCRANIAL	POSTIMPERIAL	POSTROMANTIC	POTENTIATOR	POWERLIFTER	PRAGMATISING
POSTCRANIALLY	POSTINAUGURAL	POSTSCENIUM	POTENTIATORS	POWERLIFTERS	PRAGMATISM
POSTCRISIS	POSTINDUSTRIAL	POSTSCENIUMS	POTENTILLA	POWERLIFTING	PRAGMATISMS
POSTDATING	POSTINFECTION	POSTSCRIPT	POTENTILLAS	POWERLIFTINGS	PRAGMATIST
POSTDEADLINE	POSTINJECTION	POSTSCRIPTS	POTENTIOMETER	POWERPLAYS	PRAGMATISTIC
POSTDEBATE	POSTINOCULATION	POSTSEASON	POTENTIOMETERS	POWERTRAIN	PRAGMATISTS
POSTDEBUTANTE	POSTIRRADIATION	POSTSEASONS	POTENTIOMETRIC	POWERTRAINS	PRAGMATIZATION
POSTDELIVERY	POSTISCHEMIC	POSTSECONDARY	POTENTIOMETRIES	POWSOWDIES	PRAGMATIZATIONS
POSTDEPRESSION	POSTISOLATION	POSTSTIMULATION	POTENTIOMETRY	POXVIRUSES	PRAGMATIZE
POSTDEVALUATION	POSTLANDING	POSTSTIMULATORY	POTENTISED	POZZOLANAS	PRAGMATIZED
POSTDILUVIAL	POSTLAPSARIAN	POSTSTIMULUS	POTENTISES	POZZOLANIC	PRAGMATIZER
POSTDILUVIAN	POSTLAUNCH	POSTSTRIKE	POTENTISING	POZZUOLANA	PRAGMATIZERS
POSTDILUVIANS	POSTLIBERATION	POSTSURGICAL	POTENTIZED	POZZUOLANAS	PRAGMATIZES
POSTDIVESTITURE	POSTLIMINARY	POSTSYNAPTIC	POTENTIZES	PRACHARAKS	PRAGMATIZING
POSTDIVORCE	POSTLIMINIA	POSTSYNCED	POTENTIZING	PRACTICABILITY	PRAISEACHS
POSTDOCTORAL	POSTLIMINIARY	POSTSYNCING	POTENTNESS	PRACTICABLE	PRAISELESS
POSTDOCTORATE	POSTLIMINIES	POSTTENSION	POTENTNESSES	PRACTICABLENESS	PRAISEWORTHILY
POSTEDITING	POSTLIMINIOUS	POSTTENSIONED	POTHECARIES	PRACTICABLY	PRAISEWORTHY
POSTELECTION	POSTLIMINIUM	POSTTENSIONING	POTHOLDERS	PRACTICALISM	PRAISINGLY
POSTEMBRYONAL	POSTLIMINIUM	POSTTENSIONS	POTHOLINGS	PRACTICALISMS	PRALLTRILLER
POSTEMBRYONIC	POSTLIMINOUS	POSTTRANSFUSION	POTHUNTERS	PRACTICALIST	PRALLTRILLERS
POSTEMERGENCE	POSTLIMINY	POSTTRAUMATIC	POTHUNTING	PRACTICALISTS	PRANAYAMAS
POSTEMERGENCY	POSTLITERATE	POSTTREATMENT	POTHUNTINGS	PRACTICALITIES	PRANCINGLY
POSTEPILEPTIC	POSTMARITAL	POSTULANCIES	POTICARIES	PRACTICALITY	PRANDIALLY
POSTERIORITIES	POSTMARKED	POSTULANCY	POTICHOMANIA	PRACTICALLY	PRANKINGLY
POSTERIORITY	POSTMARKING	POSTULANTS	POTICHOMANIAS	PRACTICALNESS	PRANKISHLY
POSTERIORLY	POSTMASTECTOMY	POSTULANTSHIP	POTLATCHED	PRACTICALNESSES	PRANKISHNESS
POSTERIORS	POSTMASTER	POSTULANTSHIPS	POTLATCHES	PRACTICALS	PRANKISHNESSES
POSTERISATION	POSTMASTERS	POSTULATED	POTLATCHING	PRACTICERS	PRANKSTERS
POSTERISATIONS	POSTMASTERSHIP	POSTULATES	POTOMETERS	PRACTICIAN	PRASEODYMIUM
POSTERITIES	POSTMASTERSHIPS	POSTULATING	POTPOURRIS	PRACTICIANS	PRASEODYMIUMS
POSTERIZATION	POSTMATING	POSTULATION	POTSHOTTING	PRACTICING	PRATFALLEN
POSTERIZATIONS	POSTMEDIEVAL	POSTULATIONAL	POTTERINGLY	PRACTICUMS	PRATFALLING
POSTEROLATERAL	POSTMENOPAUSAL	POSTULATIONALLY	POTTERINGS	PRACTIQUES	PRATINCOLE
POSTERUPTIVE	POSTMENSTRUAL	POSTULATIONS	POTTINESSES	PRACTISANT	PRATINCOLES
POSTEXERCISE	POSTMERIDIAN	POSTULATOR	POTTINGARS	PRACTISANTS	PRATTLEBOX
POSTEXILIAN	POSTMIDNIGHT	POSTULATORS	POTTINGERS	PRACTISERS	PRATTLEBOXES
POSTEXILIC	POSTMILLENARIAN	POSTULATORY	POTTYMOUTH	PRACTISING	PRATTLEMENT
POSTEXPERIENCE	POSTMILLENNIAL	POSTULATUM	POTTYMOUTHS	PRACTITIONER	PRATTLEMENTS
POSTEXPOSURE	POSTMISTRESS	POSTURISED	POTWALLERS	PRACTITIONERS	PRATTLINGLY
POSTFEMINISM	POSTMISTRESSES	POSTURISES	POULTERERS	PRACTOLOLS	PRAXEOLOGICAL
POSTFEMINISMS	POSTMODERN	POSTURISING	POULTICING	PRAEAMBLES	PRAXEOLOGIES
POSTFEMINIST	POSTMODERNISM	POSTURISTS	POULTROONE	PRAECOCIAL	PRAXEOLOGY
POSTFEMINISTS	POSTMODERNISMS	POSTURIZED	POULTROONES	PRAECORDIAL	PRAXINOSCOPE
POSTFIXING	POSTMODERNIST	POSTURIZES	POULTRYMAN	PRAEDIALITIES	PRAXINOSCOPES
POSTFLIGHT	POSTMODERNISTS	POSTURIZING	POULTRYMEN	PRAEDIALITY	PRAYERFULLY
POSTFORMED	POSTMORTEM	POSTVACCINAL	POUNDCAKES	PRAEFECTORIAL	PRAYERFULNESS
POSTFORMING	POSTMORTEMS	POSTVACCINATION	POURBOIRES	PRAELECTED	PRAYERFULNESSES
POSTFRACTURE	POSTNATALLY	POSTVAGOTOMY	POURPARLER	PRAELECTING	PRAYERLESS
POSTFREEZE	POSTNEONATAL	POSTVASECTOMY	POURPARLERS	PRAELUDIUM	PRAYERLESSLY
POSTGANGLIONIC	POSTNUPTIAL	POSTVOCALIC	POURPOINTS	PRAEMUNIRE	PRAYERLESSNESS
POSTGLACIAL	POSTOCULAR	POSTWEANING	POURSEWING	PRAEMUNIRES	PREABSORBED
POSTGRADUATE	POSTOPERATIVE	POSTWORKSHOP	POURTRAHED	PRAENOMENS	PREABSORBING
POSTGRADUATES	POSTOPERATIVELY	POTABILITIES	POURTRAICT	PRAENOMINA	PREABSORBS
POSTGRADUATION	POSTORBITAL	POTABILITY	POURTRAICTS	PRAENOMINAL	PREACCUSED
POSTHARVEST	POSTORGASMIC	POTABLENESS	POURTRAYED	PRAENOMINALLY	PREACCUSES
POSTHASTES	POSTPARTUM	POTABLENESSES	POURTRAYING	PRAEPOSTOR	PREACCUSING
POSTHEMORRHAGIC	POSTPERSON	POTAMOGETON	POUSOWDIES	PRAEPOSTORS	PREACHABLE
POSTHOLDER	POSTPERSONS	POTAMOGETONS	POUSSETTED	PRAESIDIUM	PREACHERSHIP
POSTHOLDERS	POSTPOLLINATION	POTAMOLOGICAL	POUSSETTES	PRAESIDIUMS	PREACHERSHIPS
POSTHOLIDAY	POSTPONABLE	POTAMOLOGIES	POUSSETTING	PRAETORIAL	PREACHIEST
POSTHOLOCAUST	POSTPONEMENT	POTAMOLOGIST	POUTHERING	PRAETORIAN	PREACHIFIED
POSTHORSES	POSTPONEMENTS	POTAMOLOGISTS	POWDERIEST	PRAETORIANS	PREACHIFIES
POSTHOSPITAL	POSTPONENCE	POTAMOLOGY	POWDERLESS	PRAETORIUM	PREACHIFYING
POSTHOUSES	POSTPONENCES	POTASSIUMS	POWDERLIKE	PRAETORIUMS	PREACHIFYINGS
POSTHUMOUS	POSTPONERS	POTATOBUGS	POWELLISED	PRAETORSHIP	PREACHINESS
POSTHUMOUSLY	POSTPONING	POTBELLIED	POWELLISES	PRAETORSHIPS	PREACHINESSES
POSTHUMOUSNESS	POSTPOSING	POTBELLIES	POWELLISING	PRAGMATICAL	PREACHINGLY
POSTHYPNOTIC	POSTPOSITION	POTBOILERS	POWELLITES	PRAGMATICALITY	PREACHINGS
POSTILIONS	POSTPOSITIONAL	POTBOILING	POWELLIZED	PRAGMATICALLY	PREACHMENT
POSTILLATE	POSTPOSITIONS	POTENTATES	POWELLIZES	PRAGMATICALNESS	PREACHMENTS
POSTILLATED	POSTPOSITIVE	POTENTIALITIES	POWELLIZING	PRAGMATICISM	PREACQUAINT
POSTILLATES	POSTPOSITIVELY	POTENTIALITY	POWERBOATING	PRAGMATICISMS	PREACQUAINTANCE
POSTILLATING	POSTPOSITIVES	POTENTIALLY	POWERBOATINGS	PRAGMATICIST	PREACQUAINTED
POSTILLATION	POSTPRANDIAL	POTENTIALS	POWERBOATS	PRAGMATICISTS	PREACQUAINTING
POSTILLATIONS	POSTPRIMARY	POTENTIARIES	POWERFULLY	PRAGMATICS	PREACQUAINTS
POSTILLATOR	POSTPRISON	POTENTIARY	POWERFULNESS	PRAGMATISATION	PREACQUISITION
POSTILLATORS	POSTPRODUCTION	POTENTIATE	POWERFULNESSES	PRAGMATISATIONS	PREADAMITE
	POSTPRODUCTIONS				

PREADAMITES
PREADAPTATION
PREADAPTATIONS
PREADAPTED
PREADAPTING
PREADAPTIVE
PREADJUSTED
PREADJUSTING
PREADJUSTS
PREADMISSION
PREADMISSIONS
PREADMITTED
PREADMITTING
PREADMONISH
PREADMONISHED
PREADMONISHES
PREADMONISHING
PREADMONITION
PREADMONITIONS
PREADOLESCENCE
PREADOLESCENCES
PREADOLESCENT
PREADOLESCENTS
PREADOPTED
PREADOPTING
PREAGRICULTURAL
PREALLOTTED
PREALLOTTING
PREALTERED
PREALTERING
PREAMBLING
PREAMBULARY
PREAMBULATE
PREAMBULATED
PREAMBULATES
PREAMBULATING
PREAMBULATORY
PREAMPLIFIER
PREAMPLIFIERS
PREANESTHETIC
PREANNOUNCE
PREANNOUNCED
PREANNOUNCES
PREANNOUNCING
PREAPPLIED
PREAPPLIES
PREAPPLYING
PREAPPOINT
PREAPPOINTED
PREAPPOINTING
PREAPPOINTS
PREAPPROVE
PREAPPROVED
PREAPPROVES
PREAPPROVING
PREARRANGE
PREARRANGED
PREARRANGEMENT
PREARRANGEMENTS
PREARRANGES
PREARRANGING
PREASSEMBLED
PREASSIGNED
PREASSIGNING
PREASSIGNS
PREASSURANCE
PREASSURANCES
PREASSURED
PREASSURES
PREASSURING
PREATTUNED
PREATTUNES
PREATTUNING
PREAUDIENCE
PREAUDIENCES
PREAVERRED
PREAVERRING
PREAXIALLY
PREBENDARIES
PREBENDARY
PREBIBLICAL
PREBIDDING
PREBILLING

PREBINDING
PREBIOLOGIC
PREBIOLOGICAL
PREBLESSED
PREBLESSES
PREBLESSING
PREBOARDED
PREBOARDING
PREBOILING
PREBOOKING
PREBREAKFAST
PREBUDGETS
PREBUILDING
PREBUTTALS
PRECALCULI
PRECALCULUS
PRECALCULUSES
PRECANCELED
PRECANCELING
PRECANCELLATION
PRECANCELLED
PRECANCELLING
PRECANCELS
PRECANCEROUS
PRECANCERS
PRECAPITALIST
PRECARIOUS
PRECARIOUSLY
PRECARIOUSNESS
PRECASTING
PRECAUTION
PRECAUTIONAL
PRECAUTIONARY
PRECAUTIONED
PRECAUTIONING
PRECAUTIONS
PRECAUTIOUS
PRECEDENCE
PRECEDENCES
PRECEDENCIES
PRECEDENCY
PRECEDENTED
PRECEDENTIAL
PRECEDENTIALLY
PRECEDENTLY
PRECEDENTS
PRECENSORED
PRECENSORING
PRECENSORS
PRECENTING
PRECENTORIAL
PRECENTORS
PRECENTORSHIP
PRECENTORSHIPS
PRECENTRESS
PRECENTRESSES
PRECENTRICES
PRECENTRIX
PRECENTRIXES
PRECEPTIAL
PRECEPTIVE
PRECEPTIVELY
PRECEPTORAL
PRECEPTORATE
PRECEPTORATES
PRECEPTORIAL
PRECEPTORIALS
PRECEPTORIES
PRECEPTORS
PRECEPTORSHIP
PRECEPTORSHIPS
PRECEPTORY
PRECEPTRESS
PRECEPTRESSES
PRECESSING
PRECESSION
PRECESSIONAL
PRECESSIONALLY
PRECESSIONS
PRECHARGED
PRECHARGES
PRECHARGING
PRECHECKED

PRECHECKING
PRECHILLED
PRECHILLING
PRECHOOSES
PRECHOOSING
PRECHRISTIAN
PRECIEUSES
PRECIOSITIES
PRECIOSITY
PRECIOUSES
PRECIOUSLY
PRECIOUSNESS
PRECIOUSNESSES
PRECIPICED
PRECIPICES
PRECIPITABILITY
PRECIPITABLE
PRECIPITANCE
PRECIPITANCES
PRECIPITANCIES
PRECIPITANCY
PRECIPITANT
PRECIPITANTLY
PRECIPITANTNESS
PRECIPITANTS
PRECIPITATE
PRECIPITATED
PRECIPITATELY
PRECIPITATENESS
PRECIPITATES
PRECIPITATING
PRECIPITATION
PRECIPITATIONS
PRECIPITATIVE
PRECIPITATOR
PRECIPITATORS
PRECIPITIN
PRECIPITINOGEN
PRECIPITINOGENS
PRECIPITINS
PRECIPITOUS
PRECIPITOUSLY
PRECIPITOUSNESS
PRECISENESS
PRECISENESSES
PRECISIANISM
PRECISIANISMS
PRECISIANIST
PRECISIANISTS
PRECISIANS
PRECISIONISM
PRECISIONISMS
PRECISIONIST
PRECISIONISTS
PRECISIONS
PRECLASSICAL
PRECLEANED
PRECLEANING
PRECLEARANCE
PRECLEARANCES
PRECLEARED
PRECLEARING
PRECLINICAL
PRECLINICALLY
PRECLUDABLE
PRECLUDING
PRECLUSION
PRECLUSIONS
PRECLUSIVE
PRECLUSIVELY
PRECOCIALS
PRECOCIOUS
PRECOCIOUSLY
PRECOCIOUSNESS
PRECOCITIES
PRECOGNISANT
PRECOGNISE
PRECOGNISED
PRECOGNISES
PRECOGNISING
PRECOGNITION
PRECOGNITIONS
PRECOGNITIVE

PRECOGNIZANT
PRECOGNIZE
PRECOGNIZED
PRECOGNIZES
PRECOGNIZING
PRECOGNOSCE
PRECOGNOSCED
PRECOGNOSCES
PRECOGNOSCING
PRECOLLEGE
PRECOLLEGIATE
PRECOLONIAL
PRECOMBUSTION
PRECOMBUSTIONS
PRECOMMITMENT
PRECOMMITMENTS
PRECOMPETITIVE
PRECOMPOSE
PRECOMPOSED
PRECOMPOSES
PRECOMPOSING
PRECOMPUTE
PRECOMPUTED
PRECOMPUTER
PRECOMPUTES
PRECOMPUTING
PRECONCEIT
PRECONCEITS
PRECONCEIVE
PRECONCEIVED
PRECONCEIVES
PRECONCEIVING
PRECONCEPTION
PRECONCEPTIONS
PRECONCERT
PRECONCERTED
PRECONCERTEDLY
PRECONCERTING
PRECONCERTS
PRECONCILIAR
PRECONDEMN
PRECONDEMNED
PRECONDEMNING
PRECONDEMNS
PRECONDITION
PRECONDITIONED
PRECONDITIONING
PRECONDITIONS
PRECONISATION
PRECONISATIONS
PRECONISED
PRECONISES
PRECONISING
PRECONIZATION
PRECONIZATIONS
PRECONIZED
PRECONIZES
PRECONIZING
PRECONQUEST
PRECONSCIOUS
PRECONSCIOUSES
PRECONSCIOUSLY
PRECONSONANTAL
PRECONSTRUCT
PRECONSTRUCTED
PRECONSTRUCTING
PRECONSTRUCTION
PRECONSTRUCTS
PRECONSUME
PRECONSUMED
PRECONSUMES
PRECONSUMING
PRECONTACT
PRECONTRACT
PRECONTRACTED
PRECONTRACTING
PRECONTRACTS
PRECONVENTION
PRECONVICTION
PRECONVICTIONS
PRECOOKERS
PRECOOKING
PRECOOLING

PRECOPULATORY
PRECORDIAL
PRECREASED
PRECREASES
PRECREASING
PRECRITICAL
PRECURRERS
PRECURSIVE
PRECURSORS
PRECURSORY
PRECUTTING
PREDACEOUS
PREDACEOUSNESS
PREDACIOUS
PREDACIOUSNESS
PREDACITIES
PREDATIONS
PREDATISMS
PREDATORILY
PREDATORINESS
PREDATORINESSES
PREDECEASE
PREDECEASED
PREDECEASES
PREDECEASING
PREDECESSOR
PREDECESSORS
PREDEDUCTED
PREDEDUCTING
PREDEDUCTS
PREDEFINED
PREDEFINES
PREDEFINING
PREDEFINITION
PREDEFINITIONS
PREDELIVERY
PREDENTATE
PREDEPARTURE
PREDEPOSIT
PREDEPOSITED
PREDEPOSITING
PREDEPOSITS
PREDESIGNATE
PREDESIGNATED
PREDESIGNATES
PREDESIGNATING
PREDESIGNATION
PREDESIGNATIONS
PREDESIGNATORY
PREDESIGNED
PREDESIGNING
PREDESIGNS
PREDESTINABLE
PREDESTINARIAN
PREDESTINARIANS
PREDESTINATE
PREDESTINATED
PREDESTINATES
PREDESTINATING
PREDESTINATION
PREDESTINATIONS
PREDESTINATIVE
PREDESTINATOR
PREDESTINATORS
PREDESTINE
PREDESTINED
PREDESTINES
PREDESTINIES
PREDESTINING
PREDESTINY
PREDETERMINABLE
PREDETERMINATE
PREDETERMINED
PREDETERMINER
PREDETERMINERS
PREDETERMINES
PREDETERMINING
PREDETERMINISM
PREDETERMINISMS
PREDEVALUATION
PREDEVELOP
PREDEVELOPED

PREDEVELOPING
PREDEVELOPMENT
PREDEVELOPMENTS
PREDEVELOPS
PREDIABETES
PREDIABETESES
PREDIABETIC
PREDIABETICS
PREDIALITIES
PREDIALITY
PREDICABILITIES
PREDICABILITY
PREDICABLE
PREDICABLENESS
PREDICABLES
PREDICAMENT
PREDICAMENTAL
PREDICAMENTS
PREDICANTS
PREDICATED
PREDICATES
PREDICATING
PREDICATION
PREDICATIONS
PREDICATIVE
PREDICATIVELY
PREDICATOR
PREDICATORS
PREDICATORY
PREDICTABILITY
PREDICTABLE
PREDICTABLENESS
PREDICTABLY
PREDICTERS
PREDICTING
PREDICTION
PREDICTIONS
PREDICTIVE
PREDICTIVELY
PREDICTORS
PREDIGESTED
PREDIGESTING
PREDIGESTION
PREDIGESTIONS
PREDIGESTS
PREDIKANTS
PREDILECTED
PREDILECTION
PREDILECTIONS
PREDINNERS
PREDISCHARGE
PREDISCOVERIES
PREDISCOVERY
PREDISPOSAL
PREDISPOSALS
PREDISPOSE
PREDISPOSED
PREDISPOSES
PREDISPOSING
PREDISPOSITION
PREDISPOSITIONS
PREDNISOLONE
PREDNISOLONES
PREDNISONE
PREDNISONES
PREDOCTORAL
PREDOMINANCE
PREDOMINANCES
PREDOMINANCIES
PREDOMINANCY
PREDOMINANT
PREDOMINANTLY
PREDOMINATE
PREDOMINATED
PREDOMINATELY
PREDOMINATES
PREDOMINATING
PREDOMINATION
PREDOMINATIONS
PREDOMINATOR
PREDOMINATORS
PREDOOMING
PREDRILLED

PREDRILLING
PREDYNASTIC
PREECLAMPSIA
PREECLAMPSIAS
PREECLAMPTIC
PREEDITING
PREELECTED
PREELECTING
PREELECTION
PREELECTRIC
PREEMBARGO
PREEMERGENCE
PREEMERGENT
PREEMINENCE
PREEMINENCES
PREEMINENT
PREEMINENTLY
PREEMPLOYMENT
PREEMPTING
PREEMPTION
PREEMPTIONS
PREEMPTIVE
PREEMPTIVELY
PREEMPTORS
PREENACTED
PREENACTING
PREENROLLMENT
PREERECTED
PREERECTING
PREESTABLISH
PREESTABLISHED
PREESTABLISHES
PREESTABLISHING
PREETHICAL
PREEXCITED
PREEXCITES
PREEXCITING
PREEXEMPTED
PREEXEMPTING
PREEXEMPTS
PREEXISTED
PREEXISTENCE
PREEXISTENCES
PREEXISTENT
PREEXISTING
PREEXPERIMENT
PREEXPOSED
PREEXPOSES
PREEXPOSING
PREFABBING
PREFABRICATE
PREFABRICATED
PREFABRICATES
PREFABRICATING
PREFABRICATION
PREFABRICATIONS
PREFABRICATOR
PREFABRICATORS
PREFASCIST
PREFATORIAL
PREFATORIALLY
PREFATORILY
PREFECTORIAL
PREFECTSHIP
PREFECTSHIPS
PREFECTURAL
PREFECTURE
PREFECTURES
PREFERABILITIES
PREFERABILITY
PREFERABLE
PREFERABLENESS
PREFERABLY
PREFERENCE
PREFERENCES
PREFERENTIAL
PREFERENTIALISM
PREFERENTIALIST
PREFERENTIALITY
PREFERENTIALLY
PREFERMENT
PREFERMENTS
PREFERRABLE

PREFERRERS
PREFERRING
PREFIGURATE
PREFIGURATED
PREFIGURATES
PREFIGURATING
PREFIGURATION
PREFIGURATIONS
PREFIGURATIVE
PREFIGURATIVELY
PREFIGURED
PREFIGUREMENT
PREFIGUREMENTS
PREFIGURES
PREFIGURING
PREFINANCE
PREFINANCED
PREFINANCES
PREFINANCING
PREFIXALLY
PREFIXIONS
PREFIXTURE
PREFIXTURES
PREFLIGHTED
PREFLIGHTING
PREFLIGHTS
PREFLORATION
PREFLORATIONS
PREFOCUSED
PREFOCUSES
PREFOCUSING
PREFOCUSSED
PREFOCUSSES
PREFOCUSSING
PREFOLIATION
PREFOLIATIONS
PREFORMATION
PREFORMATIONISM
PREFORMATIONIST
PREFORMATIONS
PREFORMATIVE
PREFORMATS
PREFORMATTED
PREFORMATTING
PREFORMING
PREFORMULATE
PREFORMULATED
PREFORMULATES
PREFORMULATING
PREFRANKED
PREFRANKING
PREFREEZES
PREFREEZING
PREFRESHMAN
PREFRONTAL
PREFRONTALS
PREFULGENT
PREFUNDING
PREGANGLIONIC
PREGENITAL
PREGLACIAL
PREGNABILITIES
PREGNABILITY
PREGNANCES
PREGNANCIES
PREGNANTLY
PREGNENOLONE
PREGNENOLONES
PREGROWTHS
PREGUIDING
PREGUSTATION
PREGUSTATIONS
PREHALLUCES
PREHANDLED
PREHANDLES
PREHANDLING
PREHARDENED
PREHARDENING
PREHARDENS
PREHARVEST
PREHEADACHE
PREHEATERS
PREHEATING

PREHEMINENCE
PREHEMINENCES
PREHENDING
PREHENSIBLE
PREHENSILE
PREHENSILITIES
PREHENSILITY
PREHENSION
PREHENSIONS
PREHENSIVE
PREHENSORIAL
PREHENSORS
PREHENSORY
PREHISTORIAN
PREHISTORIANS
PREHISTORIC
PREHISTORICAL
PREHISTORICALLY
PREHISTORIES
PREHISTORY
PREHOLIDAY
PREHOMINID
PREHOMINIDS
PREIGNITION
PREIGNITIONS
PREIMPLANTATION
PREIMPOSED
PREIMPOSES
PREIMPOSING
PREINAUGURAL
PREINDUCTION
PREINDUSTRIAL
PREINFORMED
PREINFORMING
PREINFORMS
PREINSERTED
PREINSERTING
PREINSERTS
PREINTERVIEW
PREINTERVIEWED
PREINTERVIEWING
PREINTERVIEWS
PREINVASION
PREINVITED
PREINVITES
PREINVITING
PREJUDGEMENT
PREJUDGEMENTS
PREJUDGERS
PREJUDGING
PREJUDGMENT
PREJUDGMENTS
PREJUDICANT
PREJUDICATE
PREJUDICATED
PREJUDICATES
PREJUDICATING
PREJUDICATION
PREJUDICATIONS
PREJUDICATIVE
PREJUDICED
PREJUDICES
PREJUDICIAL
PREJUDICIALLY
PREJUDICIALNESS
PREJUDICING
PREJUDIZES
PREKINDERGARTEN
PRELAPSARIAN
PRELATESHIP
PRELATESHIPS
PRELATESSES
PRELATIAL
PRELATICALLY
PRELATIONS
PRELATISED
PRELATISES
PRELATISING
PRELATISMS
PRELATISTS
PRELATIZED
PRELATIZES
PRELATIZING

PRELATURES
PRELAUNCHED
PRELAUNCHES
PRELAUNCHING
PRELECTING
PRELECTION
PRELECTIONS
PRELECTORS
PRELEXICAL
PRELIBATION
PRELIBATIONS
PRELIMINARIES
PRELIMINARILY
PRELIMINARY
PRELIMITED
PRELIMITING
PRELINGUAL
PRELINGUALLY
PRELITERACIES
PRELITERACY
PRELITERARY
PRELITERATE
PRELITERATES
PRELOADING
PRELOCATED
PRELOCATES
PRELOCATING
PRELOGICAL
PRELUDIOUS
PRELUNCHEON
PRELUSIONS
PRELUSIVELY
PRELUSORILY
PREMALIGNANT
PREMANDIBULAR
PREMANDIBULARS
PREMANUFACTURE
PREMANUFACTURED
PREMANUFACTURES
PREMARITAL
PREMARITALLY
PREMARKETED
PREMARKETING
PREMARKETS
PREMARRIAGE
PREMATURELY
PREMATURENESS
PREMATURENESSES
PREMATURES
PREMATURITIES
PREMATURITY
PREMAXILLA
PREMAXILLAE
PREMAXILLARIES
PREMAXILLARY
PREMAXILLAS
PREMEASURE
PREMEASURED
PREMEASURES
PREMEASURING
PREMEDICAL
PREMEDICALLY
PREMEDICATE
PREMEDICATED
PREMEDICATES
PREMEDICATING
PREMEDICATION
PREMEDICATIONS
PREMEDIEVAL
PREMEDITATE
PREMEDITATED
PREMEDITATEDLY
PREMEDITATES
PREMEDITATIVE
PREMEDITATING
PREMEDITATION
PREMEDITATIONS
PREMEDITATOR
PREMEDITATORS
PREMEIOTIC
PREMENOPAUSAL
PREMENSTRUAL
PREMENSTRUALLY

PREMIERING
PREMIERSHIP
PREMIERSHIPS
PREMIGRATION
PREMILLENARIAN
PREMILLENARIANS
PREMILLENNIAL
PREMILLENNIALLY
PREMODIFICATION
PREMODIFIED
PREMODIFIES
PREMODIFYING
PREMOISTEN
PREMOISTENED
PREMOISTENING
PREMOISTENS
PREMOLDING
PREMONISHED
PREMONISHES
PREMONISHING
PREMONISHMENT
PREMONISHMENTS
PREMONITION
PREMONITIONS
PREMONITIVE
PREMONITOR
PREMONITORILY
PREMONITORS
PREMONITORY
PREMOTIONS
PREMOVEMENT
PREMOVEMENTS
PREMUNITION
PREMUNITIONS
PREMYCOTIC
PRENATALLY
PRENEGOTIATE
PRENEGOTIATED
PRENEGOTIATES
PRENEGOTIATING
PRENEGOTIATION
PRENEGOTIATIONS
PRENOMINAL
PRENOMINATE
PRENOMINATED
PRENOMINATES
PRENOMINATING
PRENOMINATION
PRENOMINATIONS
PRENOTIFICATION
PRENOTIFIED
PRENOTIFIES
PRENOTIFYING
PRENOTIONS
PRENTICESHIP
PRENTICESHIPS
PRENTICING
PRENUMBERED
PRENUMBERING
PRENUMBERS
PRENUPTIAL
PREOBTAINED
PREOBTAINING
PREOBTAINS
PREOCCUPANCIES
PREOCCUPANCY
PREOCCUPANT
PREOCCUPANTS
PREOCCUPATE
PREOCCUPATED
PREOCCUPATES
PREOCCUPATING
PREOCCUPATION
PREOCCUPATIONS
PREOCCUPIED
PREOCCUPIES
PREOCCUPYING
PREOPENING
PREOPERATIONAL
PREOPERATIVE
PREOPERATIVELY
PREOPTIONS
PREORDAINED

PREORDAINING
PREORDAINMENT
PREORDAINMENTS
PREORDAINS
PREORDERED
PREORDERING
PREORDINANCE
PREORDINANCES
PREORDINATION
PREORDINATIONS
PREOVULATORY
PREPACKAGE
PREPACKAGED
PREPACKAGES
PREPACKAGING
PREPACKING
PREPARATION
PREPARATIONS
PREPARATIVE
PREPARATIVELY
PREPARATIVES
PREPARATOR
PREPARATORILY
PREPARATORS
PREPARATORY
PREPAREDLY
PREPAREDNESS
PREPAREDNESSES
PREPASTING
PREPATELLAR
PREPAYABLE
PREPAYMENT
PREPAYMENTS
PREPENSELY
PREPENSING
PREPENSIVE
PREPERFORMANCE
PREPLACING
PREPLANNED
PREPLANNING
PREPLANTING
PREPOLLENCE
PREPOLLENCES
PREPOLLENCIES
PREPOLLENCY
PREPOLLENT
PREPOLLICES
PREPONDERANCE
PREPONDERANCES
PREPONDERANCIES
PREPONDERANCY
PREPONDERANT
PREPONDERANTLY
PREPONDERATE
PREPONDERATED
PREPONDERATELY
PREPONDERATES
PREPONDERATING
PREPONDERATION
PREPONDERATIONS
PREPORTION
PREPORTIONED
PREPORTIONING
PREPORTIONS
PREPOSITION
PREPOSITIONAL
PREPOSITIONALLY
PREPOSITIONS
PREPOSITIVE
PREPOSITIVELY
PREPOSITIVES
PREPOSITOR
PREPOSITORS
PREPOSSESS
PREPOSSESSED
PREPOSSESSES
PREPOSSESSING
PREPOSSESSINGLY
PREPOSSESSION
PREPOSSESSIONS
PREPOSTEROUS
PREPOSTEROUSLY
PREPOSTORS

p

PREPOTENCE	PRESAGEFUL	PRESELECTS	PRESIGNIFIES	PRESUMPTIVELY	PRETTIFICATION
PREPOTENCES	PRESAGEFULLY	PRESELLING	PRESIGNIFY	PRESUMPTIVENESS	PRETTIFICATIONS
PREPOTENCIES	PRESAGEMENT	PRESENSION	PRESIGNIFYING	PRESUMPTUOUS	PRETTIFIED
PREPOTENCY	PRESAGEMENTS	PRESENSIONS	PRESLAUGHTER	PRESUMPTUOUSLY	PRETTIFIER
PREPOTENTLY	PRESANCTIFIED	PRESENTABILITY	PRESLICING	PRESUPPOSE	PRETTIFIERS
PREPPINESS	PRESANCTIFIES	PRESENTABLE	PRESOAKING	PRESUPPOSED	PRETTIFIES
PREPPINESSES	PRESANCTIFY	PRESENTABLENESS	PRESOLVING	PRESUPPOSES	PRETTIFYING
PREPRANDIAL	PRESANCTIFYING	PRESENTABLY	PRESORTING	PRESUPPOSING	PRETTINESS
PREPREPARED	PRESBYACOUSES	PRESENTATION	PRESPECIFIED	PRESUPPOSITION	PRETTINESSES
PREPRESIDENTIAL	PRESBYACOUSIS	PRESENTATIONAL	PRESPECIFIES	PRESUPPOSITIONS	PRETTYISMS
PREPRICING	PRESBYACUSES	PRESENTATIONISM	PRESPECIFY	PRESURGERY	PREUNIFICATION
PREPRIMARIES	PRESBYACUSIS	PRESENTATIONIST	PRESPECIFYING	PRESURMISE	PREUNITING
PREPRIMARY	PRESBYCOUSES	PRESENTATIONS	PRESSBOARD	PRESURMISES	PREUNIVERSITY
PREPRINTED	PRESBYCOUSIS	PRESENTATIVE	PRESSBOARDS	PRESURVEYED	PREVAILERS
PREPRINTING	PRESBYCUSES	PRESENTEEISM	PRESSGANGS	PRESURVEYING	PREVAILING
PREPROCESS	PRESBYCUSIS	PRESENTEEISMS	PRESSINGLY	PRESURVEYS	PREVAILINGLY
PREPROCESSED	PRESBYOPES	PRESENTEES	PRESSINGNESS	PRESWEETEN	PREVAILMENT
PREPROCESSES	PRESBYOPIA	PRESENTENCE	PRESSINGNESSES	PRESWEETENED	PREVAILMENTS
PREPROCESSING	PRESBYOPIAS	PRESENTENCED	PRESSMARKS	PRESWEETENING	PREVALENCE
PREPROCESSOR	PRESBYOPIC	PRESENTENCES	PRESSROOMS	PRESWEETENS	PREVALENCES
PREPROCESSORS	PRESBYOPICS	PRESENTENCING	PRESSURELESS	PRESYMPTOMATIC	PREVALENCIES
PREPRODUCTION	PRESBYOPIES	PRESENTERS	PRESSURING	PRESYNAPTIC	PREVALENCY
PREPRODUCTIONS	PRESBYTERAL	PRESENTIAL	PRESSURISATION	PRESYNAPTICALLY	PREVALENTLY
PREPROFESSIONAL	PRESBYTERATE	PRESENTIALITIES	PRESSURISATIONS	PRETASTING	PREVALENTNESS
PREPROGRAM	PRESBYTERATES	PRESENTIALITY	PRESSURISE	PRETELEVISION	PREVALENTNESSES
PREPROGRAMED	PRESBYTERIAL	PRESENTIALLY	PRESSURISED	PRETELLING	PREVALENTS
PREPROGRAMING	PRESBYTERIALLY	PRESENTIENT	PRESSURISER	PRETENCELESS	PREVALUING
PREPROGRAMMED	PRESBYTERIALS	PRESENTIMENT	PRESSURISERS	PRETENDANT	PREVARICATE
PREPROGRAMMING	PRESBYTERIAN	PRESENTIMENTAL	PRESSURISES	PRETENDANTS	PREVARICATED
PREPROGRAMS	PRESBYTERIANISE	PRESENTIMENTS	PRESSURISING	PRETENDEDLY	PREVARICATES
PREPSYCHEDELIC	PRESBYTERIANISM	PRESENTING	PRESSURIZATION	PRETENDENT	PREVARICATING
PREPUBERAL	PRESBYTERIANIZE	PRESENTISM	PRESSURIZATIONS	PRETENDENTS	PREVARICATION
PREPUBERTAL	PRESBYTERIANS	PRESENTISMS	PRESSURIZE	PRETENDERS	PREVARICATIONS
PREPUBERTIES	PRESBYTERIES	PRESENTIST	PRESSURIZED	PRETENDERSHIP	PREVARICATOR
PREPUBERTY	PRESBYTERS	PRESENTIVE	PRESSURIZER	PRETENDERSHIPS	PREVARICATORS
PREPUBESCENCE	PRESBYTERSHIP	PRESENTIVENESS	PRESSURIZERS	PRETENDING	PREVENANCIES
PREPUBESCENCES	PRESBYTERSHIPS	PRESENTMENT	PRESSURIZES	PRETENDINGLY	PREVENANCY
PREPUBESCENT	PRESBYTERY	PRESENTMENTS	PRESSURIZING	PRETENSION	PREVENIENCE
PREPUBESCENTS	PRESBYTISM	PRESENTNESS	PRESSWOMAN	PRETENSIONED	PREVENIENCES
PREPUBLICATION	PRESBYTISMS	PRESENTNESSES	PRESSWOMEN	PRETENSIONING	PREVENIENT
PREPUBLICATIONS	PRESCHEDULE	PRESERVABILITY	PRESSWORKS	PRETENSIONLESS	PREVENIENTLY
PREPUNCHED	PRESCHEDULED	PRESERVABLE	PRESTAMPED	PRETENSIONS	PREVENTABILITY
PREPUNCHES	PRESCHEDULES	PRESERVABLY	PRESTAMPING	PRETENSIVE	PREVENTABLE
PREPUNCHING	PRESCHEDULING	PRESERVATION	PRESTATION	PRETENTIOUS	PREVENTABLY
PREPUNCTUAL	PRESCHOOLER	PRESERVATIONIST	PRESTATIONS	PRETENTIOUSLY	PREVENTATIVE
PREPURCHASE	PRESCHOOLERS	PRESERVATIONS	PRESTERILISE	PRETENTIOUSNESS	PREVENTATIVES
PREPURCHASED	PRESCHOOLS	PRESERVATIVE	PRESTERILISED	PRETERHUMAN	PREVENTERS
PREPURCHASES	PRESCIENCE	PRESERVATIVES	PRESTERILISES	PRETERISTS	PREVENTIBILITY
PREPURCHASING	PRESCIENCES	PRESERVATORIES	PRESTERILISING	PRETERITENESS	PREVENTIBLE
PREQUALIFIED	PRESCIENTIFIC	PRESERVATORY	PRESTERILIZE	PRETERITENESSES	PREVENTIBLY
PREQUALIFIES	PRESCIENTLY	PRESERVERS	PRESTERILIZED	PRETERITES	PREVENTING
PREQUALIFY	PRESCINDED	PRESERVICE	PRESTERILIZES	PRETERITION	PREVENTION
PREQUALIFYING	PRESCINDENT	PRESERVING	PRESTERILIZING	PRETERITIONS	PREVENTIONS
PREREADING	PRESCINDING	PRESETTING	PRESTERNUM	PRETERITIVE	PREVENTIVE
PRERECESSION	PRESCISSION	PRESETTLED	PRESTERNUMS	PRETERMINAL	PREVENTIVELY
PRERECORDED	PRESCISSIONS	PRESETTLEMENT	PRESTIDIGITATOR	PRETERMINATION	PREVENTIVENESS
PRERECORDING	PRESCORING	PRESETTLES	PRESTIGEFUL	PRETERMINATIONS	PREVENTIVES
PRERECORDS	PRESCREENED	PRESETTLING	PRESTIGIATOR	PRETERMISSION	PREVIEWERS
PREREGISTER	PRESCREENING	PRESHAPING	PRESTIGIATORS	PRETERMISSIONS	PREVIEWING
PREREGISTERED	PRESCREENS	PRESHIPPED	PRESTIGIOUS	PRETERMITS	PREVIOUSLY
PREREGISTERING	PRESCRIBED	PRESHIPPING	PRESTIGIOUSLY	PRETERMITTED	PREVIOUSNESS
PREREGISTERS	PRESCRIBER	PRESHOWING	PRESTIGIOUSNESS	PRETERMITTER	PREVIOUSNESSES
PREREGISTRATION	PRESCRIBERS	PRESHRINKING	PRESTISSIMO	PRETERMITTERS	PREVISIONAL
PREREHEARSAL	PRESCRIBES	PRESHRINKS	PRESTISSIMOS	PRETERMITTING	PREVISIONARY
PRERELEASE	PRESCRIBING	PRESHRUNKEN	PRESTORAGE	PRETERNATURAL	PREVISIONED
PRERELEASED	PRESCRIBINGS	PRESIDENCIES	PRESTORING	PRETERNATURALLY	PREVISIONING
PRERELEASES	PRESCRIPTIBLE	PRESIDENCY	PRESTRESSED	PRETERPERFECT	PREVISIONS
PRERELEASING	PRESCRIPTION	PRESIDENTESS	PRESTRESSES	PRETERPERFECTS	PREVISITED
PREREQUIRE	PRESCRIPTIONS	PRESIDENTESSES	PRESTRESSING	PRETESTING	PREVISITING
PREREQUIRED	PRESCRIPTIVE	PRESIDENTIAL	PRESTRICTION	PRETEXTING	PREVOCALIC
PREREQUIRES	PRESCRIPTIVELY	PRESIDENTIALLY	PRESTRICTIONS	PRETHEATER	PREVOCALICALLY
PREREQUIRING	PRESCRIPTIVISM	PRESIDENTS	PRESTRUCTURE	PRETORIANS	PREVOCATIONAL
PREREQUISITE	PRESCRIPTIVISMS	PRESIDENTSHIP	PRESTRUCTURED	PRETORSHIP	PREWARMING
PREREQUISITES	PRESCRIPTIVIST	PRESIDENTSHIPS	PRESTRUCTURES	PRETORSHIPS	PREWARNING
PRERETIREMENT	PRESCRIPTIVISTS	PRESIDIARY	PRESTRUCTURING	PRETOURNAMENT	PREWASHING
PREREVISIONIST	PRESCRIPTS	PRESIDIUMS	PRESUMABLE	PRETRAINED	PREWEANING
PREREVOLUTION	PRESEASONS	PRESIFTING	PRESUMABLY	PRETRAINING	PREWEIGHED
PRERINSING	PRESELECTED	PRESIGNALED	PRESUMEDLY	PRETREATED	PREWEIGHING
PREROGATIVE	PRESELECTING	PRESIGNALING	PRESUMINGLY	PRETREATING	PREWORKING
PREROGATIVED	PRESELECTION	PRESIGNALLED	PRESUMMITS	PRETREATMENT	PREWRAPPED
PREROGATIVELY	PRESELECTIONS	PRESIGNALLING	PRESUMPTION	PRETREATMENTS	PREWRAPPING
PREROGATIVES	PRESELECTOR	PRESIGNALS	PRESUMPTIONS	PRETRIMMED	PREWRITING
PREROMANTIC	PRESELECTORS	PRESIGNIFIED	PRESUMPTIVE	PRETRIMMING	PREWRITINGS

PRICELESSLY
PRICELESSNESS
PRICELESSNESSES
PRICINESSES
PRICKLIEST
PRICKLINESS
PRICKLINESSES
PRICKLINGS
PRICKWOODS
PRIDEFULLY
PRIDEFULNESS
PRIDEFULNESSES
PRIESTCRAFT
PRIESTCRAFTS
PRIESTESSES
PRIESTHOOD
PRIESTHOODS
PRIESTLIER
PRIESTLIEST
PRIESTLIKE
PRIESTLINESS
PRIESTLINESSES
PRIESTLING
PRIESTLINGS
PRIESTSHIP
PRIESTSHIPS
PRIGGERIES
PRIGGISHLY
PRIGGISHNESS
PRIGGISHNESSES
PRIMAEVALLY
PRIMALITIES
PRIMAQUINE
PRIMAQUINES
PRIMARINESS
PRIMARINESSES
PRIMATESHIP
PRIMATESHIPS
PRIMATIALS
PRIMATICAL
PRIMATOLOGICAL
PRIMATOLOGIES
PRIMATOLOGIST
PRIMATOLOGISTS
PRIMATOLOGY
PRIMAVERAS
PRIMENESSES
PRIMEVALLY
PRIMIGENIAL
PRIMIGRAVIDA
PRIMIGRAVIDAE
PRIMIGRAVIDAS
PRIMIPARAE
PRIMIPARAS
PRIMIPARITIES
PRIMIPARITY
PRIMIPAROUS
PRIMITIVELY
PRIMITIVENESS
PRIMITIVENESSES
PRIMITIVES
PRIMITIVISM
PRIMITIVISMS
PRIMITIVIST
PRIMITIVISTIC
PRIMITIVISTS
PRIMITIVITIES
PRIMITIVITY
PRIMNESSES
PRIMOGENIAL
PRIMOGENIT
PRIMOGENITAL
PRIMOGENITARY
PRIMOGENITIVE
PRIMOGENITIVES
PRIMOGENITOR
PRIMOGENITORS
PRIMOGENITRICES
PRIMOGENITRIX
PRIMOGENITRIXES
PRIMOGENITS
PRIMOGENITURE
PRIMOGENITURES

PRIMORDIAL
PRIMORDIALISM
PRIMORDIALISMS
PRIMORDIALITIES
PRIMORDIALITY
PRIMORDIALLY
PRIMORDIALS
PRIMORDIUM
PRIMROSING
PRIMULACEOUS
PRIMULINES
PRINCEDOMS
PRINCEHOOD
PRINCEHOODS
PRINCEKINS
PRINCELETS
PRINCELIER
PRINCELIEST
PRINCELIKE
PRINCELINESS
PRINCELINESSES
PRINCELING
PRINCELINGS
PRINCESHIP
PRINCESHIPS
PRINCESSES
PRINCESSLY
PRINCIFIED
PRINCIPALITIES
PRINCIPALITY
PRINCIPALLY
PRINCIPALNESS
PRINCIPALNESSES
PRINCIPALS
PRINCIPALSHIP
PRINCIPALSHIPS
PRINCIPATE
PRINCIPATES
PRINCIPIAL
PRINCIPIUM
PRINCIPLED
PRINCIPLES
PRINCIPLING
PRINTABILITIES
PRINTABILITY
PRINTABLENESS
PRINTABLENESSES
PRINTERIES
PRINTHEADS
PRINTMAKER
PRINTMAKERS
PRINTMAKING
PRINTMAKINGS
PRINTWHEEL
PRINTWHEELS
PRINTWORKS
PRIORESSES
PRIORITIES
PRIORITISATION
PRIORITISATIONS
PRIORITISE
PRIORITISED
PRIORITISES
PRIORITISING
PRIORITIZATION
PRIORITIZATIONS
PRIORITIZE
PRIORITIZED
PRIORITIZES
PRIORITIZING
PRIORSHIPS
PRISMATICAL
PRISMATICALLY
PRISMATOID
PRISMATOIDAL
PRISMATOIDS
PRISMOIDAL
PRISONMENT
PRISONMENTS
PRISSINESS
PRISSINESSES
PRISTINELY
PRIVATDOCENT

PRIVATDOCENTS
PRIVATDOZENT
PRIVATDOZENTS
PRIVATEERED
PRIVATEERING
PRIVATEERINGS
PRIVATEERS
PRIVATEERSMAN
PRIVATEERSMEN
PRIVATENESS
PRIVATENESSES
PRIVATIONS
PRIVATISATION
PRIVATISATIONS
PRIVATISED
PRIVATISER
PRIVATISERS
PRIVATISES
PRIVATISING
PRIVATISMS
PRIVATISTS
PRIVATIVELY
PRIVATIVES
PRIVATIZATION
PRIVATIZATIONS
PRIVATIZED
PRIVATIZER
PRIVATIZERS
PRIVATIZES
PRIVATIZING
PRIVILEGED
PRIVILEGES
PRIVILEGING
PRIZEFIGHT
PRIZEFIGHTER
PRIZEFIGHTERS
PRIZEFIGHTING
PRIZEFIGHTINGS
PRIZEFIGHTS
PRIZEWINNER
PRIZEWINNERS
PRIZEWINNING
PRIZEWOMAN
PRIZEWOMEN
PROABORTION
PROACTIONS
PROAIRESES
PROAIRESIS
PROBABILIORISM
PROBABILIORISMS
PROBABILIORIST
PROBABILIORISTS
PROBABILISM
PROBABILISMS
PROBABILIST
PROBABILISTIC
PROBABILISTS
PROBABILITIES
PROBABILITY
PROBATIONAL
PROBATIONALLY
PROBATIONARIES
PROBATIONARY
PROBATIONER
PROBATIONERS
PROBATIONERSHIP
PROBATIONS
PROBATIVELY
PROBENECID
PROBENECIDS
PROBIOTICS
PROBLEMATIC
PROBLEMATICAL
PROBLEMATICALLY
PROBLEMATICS
PROBLEMIST
PROBLEMISTS
PROBOSCIDEAN
PROBOSCIDEANS
PROBOSCIDES
PROBOSCIDIAN
PROBOSCIDIANS
PROBOSCISES

PROBOULEUTIC
PROBUSINESS
PROCACIOUS
PROCACITIES
PROCAMBIAL
PROCAMBIUM
PROCAMBIUMS
PROCAPITALIST
PROCARBAZINE
PROCARBAZINES
PROCARYONS
PROCARYOTE
PROCARYOTES
PROCARYOTIC
PROCATHEDRAL
PROCATHEDRALS
PROCEDURAL
PROCEDURALLY
PROCEDURALS
PROCEDURES
PROCEEDERS
PROCEEDING
PROCEEDINGS
PROCELEUSMATIC
PROCELEUSMATICS
PROCELLARIAN
PROCEPHALIC
PROCERCOID
PROCERCOIDS
PROCEREBRA
PROCEREBRAL
PROCEREBRUM
PROCEREBRUMS
PROCERITIES
PROCESSABILITY
PROCESSABLE
PROCESSERS
PROCESSIBILITY
PROCESSIBLE
PROCESSING
PROCESSINGS
PROCESSION
PROCESSIONAL
PROCESSIONALIST
PROCESSIONALLY
PROCESSIONALS
PROCESSIONARY
PROCESSIONED
PROCESSIONER
PROCESSIONERS
PROCESSIONING
PROCESSIONINGS
PROCESSIONS
PROCESSORS
PROCESSUAL
PROCHRONISM
PROCHRONISMS
PROCIDENCE
PROCIDENCES
PROCLAIMANT
PROCLAIMANTS
PROCLAIMED
PROCLAIMER
PROCLAIMERS
PROCLAIMING
PROCLAMATION
PROCLAMATIONS
PROCLAMATORY
PROCLITICS
PROCLIVITIES
PROCLIVITY
PROCOELOUS
PROCONSULAR
PROCONSULATE
PROCONSULATES
PROCONSULS
PROCONSULSHIP
PROCONSULSHIPS
PROCRASTINATE
PROCRASTINATED
PROCRASTINATES
PROCRASTINATING
PROCRASTINATION

PROCRASTINATIVE
PROCRASTINATOR
PROCRASTINATORS
PROCRASTINATORY
PROCREANTS
PROCREATED
PROCREATES
PROCREATING
PROCREATION
PROCREATIONAL
PROCREATIONS
PROCREATIVE
PROCREATIVENESS
PROCREATOR
PROCREATORS
PROCRUSTEAN
PROCRYPSES
PROCRYPSIS
PROCRYPTIC
PROCRYPTICALLY
PROCTALGIA
PROCTALGIAS
PROCTITIDES
PROCTITISES
PROCTODAEA
PROCTODAEAL
PROCTODAEUM
PROCTODAEUMS
PROCTODEUM
PROCTODEUMS
PROCTOLOGIC
PROCTOLOGICAL
PROCTOLOGIES
PROCTOLOGIST
PROCTOLOGISTS
PROCTOLOGY
PROCTORAGE
PROCTORAGES
PROCTORIAL
PROCTORIALLY
PROCTORING
PROCTORISE
PROCTORISED
PROCTORISES
PROCTORISING
PROCTORIZE
PROCTORIZED
PROCTORIZES
PROCTORIZING
PROCTORSHIP
PROCTORSHIPS
PROCTOSCOPE
PROCTOSCOPES
PROCTOSCOPIC
PROCTOSCOPIES
PROCTOSCOPY
PROCUMBENT
PROCURABLE
PROCURACIES
PROCURANCE
PROCURANCES
PROCURATION
PROCURATIONS
PROCURATOR
PROCURATORIAL
PROCURATORIES
PROCURATORS
PROCURATORSHIP
PROCURATORSHIPS
PROCURATORY
PROCUREMENT
PROCUREMENTS
PROCURESSES
PROCUREURS
PRODIGALISE
PRODIGALISED
PRODIGALISES
PRODIGALISING
PRODIGALITIES
PRODIGALITY
PRODIGALIZE
PRODIGALIZED
PRODIGALIZES

PRODIGALIZING
PRODIGALLY
PRODIGIOSITIES
PRODIGIOSITY
PRODIGIOUS
PRODIGIOUSLY
PRODIGIOUSNESS
PRODITORIOUS
PRODNOSING
PRODROMATA
PRODUCEMENT
PRODUCEMENTS
PRODUCIBILITIES
PRODUCIBILITY
PRODUCIBLE
PRODUCTIBILITY
PRODUCTILE
PRODUCTION
PRODUCTIONAL
PRODUCTIONS
PRODUCTIVE
PRODUCTIVELY
PRODUCTIVENESS
PRODUCTIVITIES
PRODUCTIVITY
PROEMBRYOS
PROENZYMES
PROESTRUSES
PROFANATION
PROFANATIONS
PROFANATORY
PROFANENESS
PROFANENESSES
PROFANITIES
PROFASCIST
PROFECTITIOUS
PROFEMINIST
PROFESSEDLY
PROFESSING
PROFESSION
PROFESSIONAL
PROFESSIONALISE
PROFESSIONALISM
PROFESSIONALIST
PROFESSIONALIZE
PROFESSIONALLY
PROFESSIONALS
PROFESSIONS
PROFESSORATE
PROFESSORATES
PROFESSORESS
PROFESSORESSES
PROFESSORIAL
PROFESSORIALLY
PROFESSORIAT
PROFESSORIATE
PROFESSORIATES
PROFESSORIATS
PROFESSORS
PROFESSORSHIP
PROFESSORSHIPS
PROFFERERS
PROFFERING
PROFICIENCE
PROFICIENCES
PROFICIENCIES
PROFICIENCY
PROFICIENT
PROFICIENTLY
PROFICIENTS
PROFILINGS
PROFILISTS
PROFITABILITIES
PROFITABILITY
PROFITABLE
PROFITABLENESS
PROFITABLY
PROFITEERED
PROFITEERING
PROFITEERINGS
PROFITEERS
PROFITEROLE
PROFITEROLES

PROFITINGS	PROGRESSES	PROLEGOMENA	PROLONGMENTS	PRONOMINALIZED	PROPENDENT
PROFITLESS	PROGRESSING	PROLEGOMENAL	PROLUSIONS	PRONOMINALIZES	PROPENDING
PROFITLESSLY	PROGRESSION	PROLEGOMENARY	PROMACHOSES	PRONOMINALIZING	PROPENSELY
PROFITWISE	PROGRESSIONAL	PROLEGOMENON	PROMENADED	PRONOMINALLY	PROPENSENESS
PROFLIGACIES	PROGRESSIONALLY	PROLEGOMENOUS	PROMENADER	PRONOUNCEABLE	PROPENSENESSES
PROFLIGACY	PROGRESSIONARY	PROLEPTICAL	PROMENADERS	PRONOUNCED	PROPENSION
PROFLIGATE	PROGRESSIONISM	PROLEPTICALLY	PROMENADES	PRONOUNCEDLY	PROPENSIONS
PROFLIGATELY	PROGRESSIONISMS	PROLETARIAN	PROMENADING	PRONOUNCEMENT	PROPENSITIES
PROFLIGATES	PROGRESSIONIST	PROLETARIANISE	PROMETHAZINE	PRONOUNCEMENTS	PROPENSITY
PROFLUENCE	PROGRESSIONISTS	PROLETARIANISED	PROMETHAZINES	PRONOUNCER	PROPENSIVE
PROFLUENCES	PROGRESSIONS	PROLETARIANISES	PROMETHEUM	PRONOUNCERS	PROPERDINS
PROFOUNDER	PROGRESSISM	PROLETARIANISM	PROMETHEUMS	PRONOUNCES	PROPERISPOMENON
PROFOUNDEST	PROGRESSISMS	PROLETARIANISMS	PROMETHIUM	PRONOUNCING	PROPERNESS
PROFOUNDLY	PROGRESSIST	PROLETARIANIZE	PROMETHIUMS	PRONOUNCINGS	PROPERNESSES
PROFOUNDNESS	PROGRESSISTS	PROLETARIANIZED	PROMILITARY	PRONUCLEAR	PROPERTIED
PROFOUNDNESSES	PROGRESSIVE	PROLETARIANIZES	PROMINENCE	PRONUCLEARIST	PROPERTIES
PROFULGENT	PROGRESSIVELY	PROLETARIANNESS	PROMINENCES	PRONUCLEARISTS	PROPERTYING
PROFUNDITIES	PROGRESSIVENESS	PROLETARIANS	PROMINENCIES	PRONUCLEUS	PROPERTYLESS
PROFUNDITY	PROGRESSIVES	PROLETARIAT	PROMINENCY	PRONUCLEUSES	PROPHECIES
PROFUSENESS	PROGRESSIVISM	PROLETARIATE	PROMINENTLY	PRONUNCIAMENTO	PROPHESIABLE
PROFUSENESSES	PROGRESSIVISMS	PROLETARIATES	PROMINENTNESS	PRONUNCIAMENTOS	PROPHESIED
PROFUSIONS	PROGRESSIVIST	PROLETARIATS	PROMINENTNESSES	PRONUNCIATION	PROPHESIER
PROGENITIVE	PROGRESSIVISTIC	PROLETARIES	PROMISCUITIES	PRONUNCIATIONAL	PROPHESIERS
PROGENITIVENESS	PROGRESSIVISTS	PROLICIDAL	PROMISCUITY	PRONUNCIATIONS	PROPHESIES
PROGENITOR	PROGRESSIVITIES	PROLICIDES	PROMISCUOUS	PRONUNCIOS	PROPHESYING
PROGENITORIAL	PROGRESSIVITY	PROLIFERATE	PROMISCUOUSLY	PROOEMIONS	PROPHESYINGS
PROGENITORS	PROGYMNASIA	PROLIFERATED	PROMISCUOUSNESS	PROOEMIUMS	PROPHETESS
PROGENITORSHIP	PROGYMNASIUM	PROLIFERATES	PROMISEFUL	PROOFREADER	PROPHETESSES
PROGENITORSHIPS	PROGYMNASIUMS	PROLIFERATING	PROMISELESS	PROOFREADERS	PROPHETHOOD
PROGENITRESS	PROHIBITED	PROLIFERATION	PROMISINGLY	PROOFREADING	PROPHETHOODS
PROGENITRESSES	PROHIBITER	PROLIFERATIONS	PROMISSIVE	PROOFREADINGS	PROPHETICAL
PROGENITRICES	PROHIBITERS	PROLIFERATIVE	PROMISSORILY	PROOFREADS	PROPHETICALLY
PROGENITRIX	PROHIBITING	PROLIFEROUS	PROMISSORS	PROOFROOMS	PROPHETICISM
PROGENITRIXES	PROHIBITION	PROLIFEROUSLY	PROMISSORY	PROPAEDEUTIC	PROPHETICISMS
PROGENITURE	PROHIBITIONARY	PROLIFICACIES	PROMONARCHIST	PROPAEDEUTICAL	PROPHETISM
PROGENITURES	PROHIBITIONISM	PROLIFICACY	PROMONTORIES	PROPAEDEUTICS	PROPHETISMS
PROGESTATIONAL	PROHIBITIONISMS	PROLIFICAL	PROMONTORY	PROPAGABILITIES	PROPHETSHIP
PROGESTERONE	PROHIBITIONIST	PROLIFICALLY	PROMOTABILITIES	PROPAGABILITY	PROPHETSHIPS
PROGESTERONES	PROHIBITIONISTS	PROLIFICATION	PROMOTABILITY	PROPAGABLE	PROPHYLACTIC
PROGESTINS	PROHIBITIONS	PROLIFICATIONS	PROMOTABLE	PROPAGABLENESS	PROPHYLACTICS
PROGESTOGEN	PROHIBITIVE	PROLIFICITIES	PROMOTIONAL	PROPAGANDA	PROPHYLAXES
PROGESTOGENIC	PROHIBITIVELY	PROLIFICITY	PROMOTIONS	PROPAGANDAS	PROPHYLAXIS
PROGESTOGENS	PROHIBITIVENESS	PROLIFICNESS	PROMOTIVENESS	PROPAGANDISE	PROPINQUITIES
PROGGINSES	PROHIBITOR	PROLIFICNESSES	PROMOTIVENESSES	PROPAGANDISED	PROPINQUITY
PROGLOTTIC	PROHIBITORS	PROLIXIOUS	PROMPTBOOK	PROPAGANDISER	PROPIONATE
PROGLOTTID	PROHIBITORY	PROLIXITIES	PROMPTBOOKS	PROPAGANDISERS	PROPIONATES
PROGLOTTIDEAN	PROINSULIN	PROLIXNESS	PROMPTINGS	PROPAGANDISES	PROPITIABLE
PROGLOTTIDES	PROINSULINS	PROLIXNESSES	PROMPTITUDE	PROPAGANDISING	PROPITIATE
PROGLOTTIDS	PROJECTABLE	PROLOCUTION	PROMPTITUDES	PROPAGANDISM	PROPITIATED
PROGLOTTIS	PROJECTILE	PROLOCUTIONS	PROMPTNESS	PROPAGANDISMS	PROPITIATES
PROGNATHIC	PROJECTILES	PROLOCUTOR	PROMPTNESSES	PROPAGANDIST	PROPITIATING
PROGNATHISM	PROJECTING	PROLOCUTORS	PROMPTUARIES	PROPAGANDISTIC	PROPITIATION
PROGNATHISMS	PROJECTINGS	PROLOCUTORSHIP	PROMPTUARY	PROPAGANDISTS	PROPITIATIONS
PROGNATHOUS	PROJECTION	PROLOCUTORSHIPS	PROMPTURES	PROPAGANDIZE	PROPITIATIOUS
PROGNOSING	PROJECTIONAL	PROLOCUTRICES	PROMULGATE	PROPAGANDIZED	PROPITIATIVE
PROGNOSTIC	PROJECTIONIST	PROLOCUTRIX	PROMULGATED	PROPAGANDIZER	PROPITIATOR
PROGNOSTICATE	PROJECTIONISTS	PROLOCUTRIXES	PROMULGATES	PROPAGANDIZERS	PROPITIATORIES
PROGNOSTICATED	PROJECTIONS	PROLOGISED	PROMULGATING	PROPAGANDIZES	PROPITIATORILY
PROGNOSTICATES	PROJECTISATION	PROLOGISES	PROMULGATION	PROPAGANDIZING	PROPITIATORS
PROGNOSTICATING	PROJECTISATIONS	PROLOGISING	PROMULGATIONS	PROPAGATED	PROPITIATORY
PROGNOSTICATION	PROJECTIVE	PROLOGISTS	PROMULGATOR	PROPAGATES	PROPITIOUS
PROGNOSTICATIVE	PROJECTIVELY	PROLOGIZED	PROMULGATORS	PROPAGATING	PROPITIOUSLY
PROGNOSTICATOR	PROJECTIVITIES	PROLOGIZES	PROMULGING	PROPAGATION	PROPITIOUSNESS
PROGNOSTICATORS	PROJECTIVITY	PROLOGIZING	PROMUSCIDATE	PROPAGATIONAL	PROPLASTID
PROGNOSTICS	PROJECTIZATION	PROLOGUING	PROMUSCIDES	PROPAGATIONS	PROPLASTIDS
PROGRADATION	PROJECTIZATIONS	PROLOGUISE	PROMYCELIA	PROPAGATIVE	PROPODEONS
PROGRADATIONS	PROJECTMENT	PROLOGUISED	PROMYCELIAL	PROPAGATOR	PROPODEUMS
PROGRADING	PROJECTMENTS	PROLOGUISES	PROMYCELIUM	PROPAGATORS	PROPOLISES
PROGRAMABLE	PROJECTORS	PROLOGUISING	PRONATIONS	PROPAGULES	PROPONENTS
PROGRAMERS	PROJECTURE	PROLOGUIZE	PRONATORES	PROPAGULUM	PROPORTION
PROGRAMING	PROJECTURES	PROLOGUIZED	PRONENESSES	PROPANEDIOIC	PROPORTIONABLE
PROGRAMINGS	PROKARYONS	PROLOGUIZES	PRONEPHRIC	PROPANONES	PROPORTIONABLY
PROGRAMMABILITY	PROKARYOTE	PROLOGUIZING	PRONEPHROI	PROPAROXYTONE	PROPORTIONAL
PROGRAMMABLE	PROKARYOTES	PROLONGABLE	PRONEPHROS	PROPAROXYTONES	PROPORTIONALITY
PROGRAMMABLES	PROKARYOTIC	PROLONGATE	PRONEPHROSES	PROPELLANT	PROPORTIONALLY
PROGRAMMATIC	PROKARYOTS	PROLONGATED	PRONGBUCKS	PROPELLANTS	PROPORTIONALS
PROGRAMMED	PROLACTINS	PROLONGATES	PRONGHORNS	PROPELLENT	PROPORTIONATE
PROGRAMMER	PROLAMINES	PROLONGATING	PRONOMINAL	PROPELLENTS	PROPORTIONATED
PROGRAMMERS	PROLAPSING	PROLONGATION	PRONOMINALISE	PROPELLERS	PROPORTIONATELY
PROGRAMMES	PROLAPSUSES	PROLONGATIONS	PRONOMINALISED	PROPELLING	PROPORTIONATES
PROGRAMMING	PROLATENESS	PROLONGERS	PRONOMINALISES	PROPELLORS	PROPORTIONATING
PROGRAMMINGS	PROLATENESSES	PROLONGING	PRONOMINALISING	PROPELMENT	PROPORTIONED
PROGRESSED	PROLATIONS	PROLONGMENT	PRONOMINALIZE	PROPELMENTS	PROPORTIONING

PROPORTIONINGS
PROPORTIONLESS
PROPORTIONMENT
PROPORTIONMENTS
PROPORTIONS
PROPOSABLE
PROPOSITAE
PROPOSITION
PROPOSITIONAL
PROPOSITIONALLY
PROPOSITIONED
PROPOSITIONING
PROPOSITIONS
PROPOSITUS
PROPOUNDED
PROPOUNDER
PROPOUNDERS
PROPOUNDING
PROPOXYPHENE
PROPOXYPHENES
PROPRAETOR
PROPRAETORIAL
PROPRAETORIAN
PROPRAETORS
PROPRANOLOL
PROPRANOLOLS
PROPRETORS
PROPRIETARIES
PROPRIETARILY
PROPRIETARY
PROPRIETIES
PROPRIETOR
PROPRIETORIAL
PROPRIETORIALLY
PROPRIETORS
PROPRIETORSHIP
PROPRIETORSHIPS
PROPRIETRESS
PROPRIETRESSES
PROPRIETRICES
PROPRIETRIX
PROPRIETRIXES
PROPRIOCEPTION
PROPRIOCEPTIONS
PROPRIOCEPTIVE
PROPRIOCEPTOR
PROPRIOCEPTORS
PROPROCTOR
PROPROCTORS
PROPUGNATION
PROPUGNATIONS
PROPULSION
PROPULSIONS
PROPULSIVE
PROPULSORS
PROPULSORY
PROPYLAEUM
PROPYLAMINE
PROPYLAMINES
PROPYLENES
PROPYLITES
PROPYLITISATION
PROPYLITISE
PROPYLITISED
PROPYLITISES
PROPYLITISING
PROPYLITIZATION
PROPYLITIZE
PROPYLITIZED
PROPYLITIZES
PROPYLITIZING
PRORATABLE
PRORATIONS
PRORECTORS
PROROGATED
PROROGATES
PROROGATING
PROROGATION
PROROGATIONS
PROROGUING
PROSAICALLY
PROSAICALNESS
PROSAICALNESSES

PROSAICISM
PROSAICISMS
PROSAICNESS
PROSAICNESSES
PROSATEURS
PROSAUROPOD
PROSAUROPODS
PROSCENIUM
PROSCENIUMS
PROSCIUTTI
PROSCIUTTO
PROSCIUTTOS
PROSCRIBED
PROSCRIBER
PROSCRIBERS
PROSCRIBES
PROSCRIBING
PROSCRIPTION
PROSCRIPTIONS
PROSCRIPTIVE
PROSCRIPTIVELY
PROSCRIPTS
PROSECTING
PROSECTORIAL
PROSECTORS
PROSECTORSHIP
PROSECTORSHIPS
PROSECUTABLE
PROSECUTED
PROSECUTES
PROSECUTING
PROSECUTION
PROSECUTIONS
PROSECUTOR
PROSECUTORIAL
PROSECUTORS
PROSECUTRICES
PROSECUTRIX
PROSECUTRIXES
PROSELYTED
PROSELYTES
PROSELYTIC
PROSELYTING
PROSELYTISATION
PROSELYTISE
PROSELYTISED
PROSELYTISER
PROSELYTISERS
PROSELYTISES
PROSELYTISING
PROSELYTISM
PROSELYTISMS
PROSELYTIZATION
PROSELYTIZE
PROSELYTIZED
PROSELYTIZER
PROSELYTIZERS
PROSELYTIZES
PROSELYTIZING
PROSEMINAR
PROSEMINARS
PROSENCEPHALA
PROSENCEPHALIC
PROSENCEPHALON
PROSENCHYMA
PROSENCHYMAS
PROSENCHYMATA
PROSENCHYMATOUS
PROSEUCHAE
PROSIFYING
PROSILIENCIES
PROSILIENCY
PROSILIENT
PROSIMIANS
PROSINESSES
PROSLAMBANOMENE
PROSLAVERY
PROSOBRANCH
PROSOBRANCHS
PROSODIANS
PROSODICAL
PROSODICALLY
PROSODISTS

PROSOPAGNOSIA
PROSOPAGNOSIAS
PROSOPOGRAPHER
PROSOPOGRAPHERS
PROSOPOGRAPHIES
PROSOPOGRAPHY
PROSOPOPEIA
PROSOPOPEIAL
PROSOPOPEIAS
PROSOPOPOEIA
PROSOPOPOEIAL
PROSOPOPOEIAS
PROSPECTED
PROSPECTING
PROSPECTINGS
PROSPECTION
PROSPECTIONS
PROSPECTIVE
PROSPECTIVELY
PROSPECTIVENESS
PROSPECTIVES
PROSPECTLESS
PROSPECTOR
PROSPECTORS
PROSPECTUS
PROSPECTUSES
PROSPERING
PROSPERITIES
PROSPERITY
PROSPEROUS
PROSPEROUSLY
PROSPEROUSNESS
PROSTACYCLIN
PROSTACYCLINS
PROSTAGLANDIN
PROSTAGLANDINS
PROSTANTHERA
PROSTANTHERAS
PROSTATECTOMIES
PROSTATECTOMY
PROSTATISM
PROSTATISMS
PROSTATITIS
PROSTATITISES
PROSTERNUM
PROSTERNUMS
PROSTHESES
PROSTHESIS
PROSTHETIC
PROSTHETICALLY
PROSTHETICS
PROSTHETIST
PROSTHETISTS
PROSTHODONTIA
PROSTHODONTIAS
PROSTHODONTICS
PROSTHODONTIST
PROSTHODONTISTS
PROSTITUTE
PROSTITUTED
PROSTITUTES
PROSTITUTING
PROSTITUTION
PROSTITUTIONS
PROSTITUTOR
PROSTITUTORS
PROSTOMIAL
PROSTOMIUM
PROSTOMIUMS
PROSTRATED
PROSTRATES
PROSTRATING
PROSTRATION
PROSTRATIONS
PROSYLLOGISM
PROSYLLOGISMS
PROTACTINIUM
PROTACTINIUMS
PROTAGONISM
PROTAGONISMS
PROTAGONIST
PROTAGONISTS
PROTAMINES

PROTANDRIES
PROTANDROUS
PROTANOMALIES
PROTANOMALOUS
PROTANOMALY
PROTANOPES
PROTANOPIA
PROTANOPIAS
PROTANOPIC
PROTEACEOUS
PROTECTANT
PROTECTANTS
PROTECTERS
PROTECTING
PROTECTINGLY
PROTECTION
PROTECTIONISM
PROTECTIONISMS
PROTECTIONIST
PROTECTIONISTS
PROTECTIONS
PROTECTIVE
PROTECTIVELY
PROTECTIVENESS
PROTECTIVES
PROTECTORAL
PROTECTORATE
PROTECTORATES
PROTECTORIAL
PROTECTORIES
PROTECTORLESS
PROTECTORS
PROTECTORSHIP
PROTECTORSHIPS
PROTECTORY
PROTECTRESS
PROTECTRESSES
PROTECTRICES
PROTECTRIX
PROTECTRIXES
PROTEIFORM
PROTEINACEOUS
PROTEINASE
PROTEINASES
PROTEINOUS
PROTEINURIA
PROTEINURIAS
PROTENDING
PROTENSION
PROTENSIONS
PROTENSITIES
PROTENSITY
PROTENSIVE
PROTENSIVELY
PROTEOCLASTIC
PROTEOGLYCAN
PROTEOGLYCANS
PROTEOLYSE
PROTEOLYSED
PROTEOLYSES
PROTEOLYSING
PROTEOLYSIS
PROTEOLYTIC
PROTEOLYTICALLY
PROTEOMICS
PROTERANDRIES
PROTERANDROUS
PROTERANDRY
PROTEROGYNIES
PROTEROGYNOUS
PROTEROGYNY
PROTERVITIES
PROTERVITY
PROTESTANT
PROTESTANTS
PROTESTATION
PROTESTATIONS
PROTESTERS
PROTESTING
PROTESTINGLY
PROTESTORS
PROTHALAMIA
PROTHALAMION

PROTHALAMIUM
PROTHALLIA
PROTHALLIAL
PROTHALLIC
PROTHALLIUM
PROTHALLOID
PROTHALLUS
PROTHALLUSES
PROTHETICALLY
PROTHONOTARIAL
PROTHONOTARIAT
PROTHONOTARIATS
PROTHONOTARIES
PROTHONOTARY
PROTHORACES
PROTHORACIC
PROTHORAXES
PROTHROMBIN
PROTHROMBINS
PROTISTANS
PROTISTOLOGIES
PROTISTOLOGIST
PROTISTOLOGISTS
PROTISTOLOGY
PROTOACTINIUM
PROTOACTINIUMS
PROTOAVISES
PROTOCHORDATE
PROTOCHORDATES
PROTOCOCCAL
PROTOCOLED
PROTOCOLIC
PROTOCOLING
PROTOCOLISE
PROTOCOLISED
PROTOCOLISES
PROTOCOLISING
PROTOCOLIST
PROTOCOLISTS
PROTOCOLIZE
PROTOCOLIZED
PROTOCOLIZES
PROTOCOLIZING
PROTOCOLLED
PROTOCOLLING
PROTOCTIST
PROTOCTISTS
PROTODERMS
PROTOGALAXIES
PROTOGALAXY
PROTOGENIC
PROTOGINES
PROTOGYNIES
PROTOGYNOUS
PROTOHISTORIAN
PROTOHISTORIANS
PROTOHISTORIC
PROTOHISTORIES
PROTOHISTORY
PROTOHUMAN
PROTOHUMANS
PROTOLANGUAGE
PROTOLANGUAGES
PROTOLITHIC
PROTOMARTYR
PROTOMARTYRS
PROTOMORPHIC
PROTONATED
PROTONATES
PROTONATING
PROTONATION
PROTONATIONS
PROTONEMAL
PROTONEMATA
PROTONEMATAL
PROTONOTARIAL
PROTONOTARIAT
PROTONOTARIATS
PROTONOTARIES
PROTONOTARY
PROTOPATHIC
PROTOPATHIES
PROTOPATHY

PROTOPHILIC
PROTOPHLOEM
PROTOPHLOEMS
PROTOPHYTE
PROTOPHYTES
PROTOPHYTIC
PROTOPLANET
PROTOPLANETARY
PROTOPLANETS
PROTOPLASM
PROTOPLASMAL
PROTOPLASMATIC
PROTOPLASMIC
PROTOPLASMS
PROTOPLAST
PROTOPLASTIC
PROTOPLASTS
PROTOPORPHYRIN
PROTOPORPHYRINS
PROTOSPATAIRE
PROTOSPATAIRES
PROTOSPATHAIRE
PROTOSPATHAIRES
PROTOSPATHARIUS
PROTOSTARS
PROTOSTELE
PROTOSTELES
PROTOSTELIC
PROTOSTOME
PROTOSTOMES
PROTOTHERIAN
PROTOTHERIANS
PROTOTROPH
PROTOTROPHIC
PROTOTROPHIES
PROTOTROPHS
PROTOTROPHY
PROTOTYPAL
PROTOTYPED
PROTOTYPES
PROTOTYPIC
PROTOTYPICAL
PROTOTYPICALLY
PROTOTYPING
PROTOXIDES
PROTOXYLEM
PROTOXYLEMS
PROTOZOANS
PROTOZOOLOGICAL
PROTOZOOLOGIES
PROTOZOOLOGIST
PROTOZOOLOGISTS
PROTOZOOLOGY
PROTOZOONS
PROTRACTED
PROTRACTEDLY
PROTRACTEDNESS
PROTRACTIBLE
PROTRACTILE
PROTRACTING
PROTRACTION
PROTRACTIONS
PROTRACTIVE
PROTRACTOR
PROTRACTORS
PROTREPTIC
PROTREPTICAL
PROTREPTICS
PROTRUDABLE
PROTRUDENT
PROTRUDING
PROTRUSIBLE
PROTRUSILE
PROTRUSION
PROTRUSIONS
PROTRUSIVE
PROTRUSIVELY
PROTRUSIVENESS
PROTUBERANCE
PROTUBERANCES
PROTUBERANCIES
PROTUBERANCY
PROTUBERANT

PROTUBERANTLY	PROVITAMIN	PSAMMOPHYTE	PSEUDOPREGNANCY	PSYCHOBABBLERS	PSYCHOMETRISTS
PROTUBERATE	PROVITAMINS	PSAMMOPHYTES	PSEUDOPREGNANT	PSYCHOBABBLES	PSYCHOMETRY
PROTUBERATED	PROVOCABLE	PSAMMOPHYTIC	PSEUDORANDOM	PSYCHOBILLIES	PSYCHOMOTOR
PROTUBERATES	PROVOCANTS	PSELLISMUS	PSEUDOSCALAR	PSYCHOBILLY	PSYCHONEUROSES
PROTUBERATING	PROVOCATEUR	PSELLISMUSES	PSEUDOSCALARS	PSYCHOBIOGRAPHY	PSYCHONEUROSIS
PROTUBERATION	PROVOCATEURS	PSEPHOANALYSES	PSEUDOSCIENCE	PSYCHOBIOLOGIC	PSYCHONEUROTIC
PROTUBERATIONS	PROVOCATION	PSEPHOANALYSIS	PSEUDOSCIENCES	PSYCHOBIOLOGIES	PSYCHONEUROTICS
PROUDHEARTED	PROVOCATIONS	PSEPHOLOGICAL	PSEUDOSCIENTIST	PSYCHOBIOLOGIST	PSYCHONOMIC
PROUDNESSES	PROVOCATIVE	PSEPHOLOGICALLY	PSEUDOSCOPE	PSYCHOBIOLOGY	PSYCHONOMICS
PROUSTITES	PROVOCATIVELY	PSEPHOLOGIES	PSEUDOSCOPES	PSYCHOCHEMICAL	PSYCHOPATH
PROVABILITIES	PROVOCATIVENESS	PSEPHOLOGIST	PSEUDOSCORPION	PSYCHOCHEMICALS	PSYCHOPATHIC
PROVABILITY	PROVOCATIVES	PSEPHOLOGISTS	PSEUDOSCORPIONS	PSYCHOCHEMISTRY	PSYCHOPATHICS
PROVABLENESS	PROVOCATOR	PSEPHOLOGY	PSEUDOSOLUTION	PSYCHODELIA	PSYCHOPATHIES
PROVABLENESSES	PROVOCATORS	PSEUDAESTHESIA	PSEUDOSOLUTIONS	PSYCHODELIAS	PSYCHOPATHIST
PROVASCULAR	PROVOCATORY	PSEUDAESTHESIAS	PSEUDOSYMMETRY	PSYCHODELIC	PSYCHOPATHISTS
PROVECTION	PROVOKABLE	PSEUDARTHROSES	PSEUDOVECTOR	PSYCHODELICALLY	PSYCHOPATHOLOGY
PROVECTIONS	PROVOKEMENT	PSEUDARTHROSIS	PSEUDOVECTORS	PSYCHODRAMA	PSYCHOPATHS
PROVEDITOR	PROVOKEMENTS	PSEUDEPIGRAPH	PSILANTHROPIC	PSYCHODRAMAS	PSYCHOPATHY
PROVEDITORE	PROVOKINGLY	PSEUDEPIGRAPHA	PSILANTHROPIES	PSYCHODRAMATIC	PSYCHOPHILIES
PROVEDITORES	PROVOLONES	PSEUDEPIGRAPHIC	PSILANTHROPISM	PSYCHODYNAMIC	PSYCHOPHILY
PROVEDITORS	PROVOSTRIES	PSEUDEPIGRAPHON	PSILANTHROPISMS	PSYCHODYNAMICS	PSYCHOPHYSICAL
PROVEDORES	PROVOSTSHIP	PSEUDEPIGRAPHS	PSILANTHROPIST	PSYCHOGALVANIC	PSYCHOPHYSICIST
PROVENANCE	PROVOSTSHIPS	PSEUDEPIGRAPHY	PSILANTHROPISTS	PSYCHOGASES	PSYCHOPHYSICS
PROVENANCES	PROWLINGLY	PSEUDERIES	PSILANTHROPY	PSYCHOGENESES	PSYCHOPOMP
PROVENDERED	PROXIMALLY	PSEUDIMAGINES	PSILOCYBIN	PSYCHOGENESIS	PSYCHOPOMPS
PROVENDERING	PROXIMATELY	PSEUDIMAGO	PSILOCYBINS	PSYCHOGENETIC	PSYCHOSEXUAL
PROVENDERS	PROXIMATENESS	PSEUDIMAGOS	PSILOMELANE	PSYCHOGENETICAL	PSYCHOSEXUALITY
PROVENIENCE	PROXIMATENESSES	PSEUDOACID	PSILOMELANES	PSYCHOGENETICS	PSYCHOSEXUALLY
PROVENIENCES	PROXIMATION	PSEUDOACIDS	PSILOPHYTE	PSYCHOGENIC	PSYCHOSOCIAL
PROVENTRICULAR	PROXIMATIONS	PSEUDOALLELE	PSILOPHYTES	PSYCHOGENICALLY	PSYCHOSOCIALLY
PROVENTRICULI	PROXIMITIES	PSEUDOALLELES	PSILOPHYTIC	PSYCHOGERIATRIC	PSYCHOSOMATIC
PROVENTRICULUS	PROZYMITES	PSEUDOARTHROSES	PSITTACINE	PSYCHOGNOSES	PSYCHOSOMATICS
PROVERBIAL	PRUDENTIAL	PSEUDOARTHROSIS	PSITTACINES	PSYCHOGNOSIS	PSYCHOSOMIMETIC
PROVERBIALISE	PRUDENTIALISM	PSEUDOBULB	PSITTACOSES	PSYCHOGNOSTIC	PSYCHOSURGEON
PROVERBIALISED	PRUDENTIALISMS	PSEUDOBULBS	PSITTACOSIS	PSYCHOGONIES	PSYCHOSURGEONS
PROVERBIALISES	PRUDENTIALIST	PSEUDOCARP	PSITTACOTIC	PSYCHOGONY	PSYCHOSURGERIES
PROVERBIALISING	PRUDENTIALISTS	PSEUDOCARPOUS	PSORIATICS	PSYCHOGRAM	PSYCHOSURGERY
PROVERBIALISM	PRUDENTIALITIES	PSEUDOCARPS	PSYCHAGOGUE	PSYCHOGRAMS	PSYCHOSURGICAL
PROVERBIALISMS	PRUDENTIALITY	PSEUDOCLASSIC	PSYCHAGOGUES	PSYCHOGRAPH	PSYCHOSYNTHESES
PROVERBIALIST	PRUDENTIALLY	PSEUDOCLASSICS	PSYCHASTHENIA	PSYCHOGRAPHIC	PSYCHOSYNTHESIS
PROVERBIALISTS	PRUDENTIALS	PSEUDOCODE	PSYCHASTHENIAS	PSYCHOGRAPHICAL	PSYCHOTECHNICS
PROVERBIALIZE	PRUDISHNESS	PSEUDOCODES	PSYCHASTHENIC	PSYCHOGRAPHICS	PSYCHOTHERAPIES
PROVERBIALIZED	PRUDISHNESSES	PSEUDOCOEL	PSYCHASTHENICS	PSYCHOGRAPHIES	PSYCHOTHERAPIST
PROVERBIALIZES	PRURIENCES	PSEUDOCOELOMATE	PSYCHEDELIA	PSYCHOGRAPHS	PSYCHOTHERAPY
PROVERBIALIZING	PRURIENCIES	PSEUDOCOELS	PSYCHEDELIAS	PSYCHOGRAPHY	PSYCHOTICALLY
PROVERBIALLY	PRURIENTLY	PSEUDOCYESES	PSYCHEDELIC	PSYCHOHISTORIAN	PSYCHOTICISM
PROVERBING	PRURIGINOUS	PSEUDOCYESIS	PSYCHEDELICALLY	PSYCHOHISTORIES	PSYCHOTICISMS
PROVIDABLE	PRURITUSES	PSEUDOEPHEDRINE	PSYCHEDELICS	PSYCHOHISTORY	PSYCHOTICS
PROVIDENCE	PRUSSIANISATION	PSEUDOGRAPH	PSYCHIATER	PSYCHOKINESES	PSYCHOTOMIMETIC
PROVIDENCES	PRUSSIANISE	PSEUDOGRAPHIES	PSYCHIATERS	PSYCHOKINESIS	PSYCHOTOXIC
PROVIDENTIAL	PRUSSIANISED	PSEUDOGRAPHS	PSYCHIATRIC	PSYCHOKINETIC	PSYCHOTROPIC
PROVIDENTIALLY	PRUSSIANISES	PSEUDOGRAPHY	PSYCHIATRICAL	PSYCHOLINGUIST	PSYCHOTROPICS
PROVIDENTLY	PRUSSIANISING	PSEUDOLOGIA	PSYCHIATRICALLY	PSYCHOLINGUISTS	PSYCHROMETER
PROVINCEWIDE	PRUSSIANIZATION	PSEUDOLOGIAS	PSYCHIATRIES	PSYCHOLOGIC	PSYCHROMETERS
PROVINCIAL	PRUSSIANIZE	PSEUDOLOGIES	PSYCHIATRIST	PSYCHOLOGICAL	PSYCHROMETRIC
PROVINCIALISE	PRUSSIANIZED	PSEUDOLOGUE	PSYCHIATRISTS	PSYCHOLOGICALLY	PSYCHROMETRICAL
PROVINCIALISED	PRUSSIANIZES	PSEUDOLOGUES	PSYCHIATRY	PSYCHOLOGIES	PSYCHROMETRIES
PROVINCIALISES	PRUSSIANIZING	PSEUDOLOGY	PSYCHICALLY	PSYCHOLOGISE	PSYCHROMETRY
PROVINCIALISING	PRUSSIATES	PSEUDOMARTYR	PSYCHICISM	PSYCHOLOGISED	PSYCHROPHILIC
PROVINCIALISM	PSALIGRAPHIES	PSEUDOMARTYRS	PSYCHICISMS	PSYCHOLOGISES	PTARMIGANS
PROVINCIALISMS	PSALIGRAPHY	PSEUDOMEMBRANE	PSYCHICIST	PSYCHOLOGISING	PTERANODON
PROVINCIALIST	PSALMBOOKS	PSEUDOMEMBRANES	PSYCHICISTS	PSYCHOLOGISM	PTERANODONS
PROVINCIALISTS	PSALMODICAL	PSEUDOMONAD	PSYCHOACOUSTIC	PSYCHOLOGISMS	PTERIDINES
PROVINCIALITIES	PSALMODIES	PSEUDOMONADES	PSYCHOACOUSTICS	PSYCHOLOGIST	PTERIDOLOGICAL
PROVINCIALITY	PSALMODISE	PSEUDOMONADS	PSYCHOACTIVE	PSYCHOLOGISTIC	PTERIDOLOGIES
PROVINCIALIZE	PSALMODISED	PSEUDOMONAS	PSYCHOANALYSE	PSYCHOLOGISTS	PTERIDOLOGIST
PROVINCIALIZED	PSALMODISES	PSEUDOMORPH	PSYCHOANALYSED	PSYCHOLOGIZE	PTERIDOLOGISTS
PROVINCIALIZES	PSALMODISING	PSEUDOMORPHIC	PSYCHOANALYSER	PSYCHOLOGIZED	PTERIDOLOGY
PROVINCIALIZING	PSALMODIST	PSEUDOMORPHISM	PSYCHOANALYSERS	PSYCHOLOGIZES	PTERIDOMANIA
PROVINCIALLY	PSALMODISTS	PSEUDOMORPHISMS	PSYCHOANALYSES	PSYCHOLOGIZING	PTERIDOMANIAS
PROVINCIALS	PSALMODIZE	PSEUDOMORPHOUS	PSYCHOANALYSING	PSYCHOLOGY	PTERIDOPHILIST
PROVIRUSES	PSALMODIZED	PSEUDOMORPHS	PSYCHOANALYSIS	PSYCHOMACHIA	PTERIDOPHILISTS
PROVISIONAL	PSALMODIZES	PSEUDOMUTUALITY	PSYCHOANALYST	PSYCHOMACHIAS	PTERIDOPHYTE
PROVISIONALLY	PSALMODIZING	PSEUDONYMITIES	PSYCHOANALYSTS	PSYCHOMACHIES	PTERIDOPHYTES
PROVISIONALS	PSALTERIAN	PSEUDONYMITY	PSYCHOANALYTIC	PSYCHOMACHY	PTERIDOPHYTIC
PROVISIONARIES	PSALTERIES	PSEUDONYMOUS	PSYCHOANALYZE	PSYCHOMETER	PTERIDOPHYTOUS
PROVISIONARY	PSALTERIUM	PSEUDONYMOUSLY	PSYCHOANALYZED	PSYCHOMETERS	PTERIDOSPERM
PROVISIONED	PSALTRESSES	PSEUDONYMS	PSYCHOANALYZER	PSYCHOMETRIC	PTERIDOSPERMS
PROVISIONER	PSAMMOPHIL	PSEUDOPODAL	PSYCHOANALYZERS	PSYCHOMETRICAL	PTERODACTYL
PROVISIONERS	PSAMMOPHILE	PSEUDOPODIA	PSYCHOANALYZES	PSYCHOMETRICIAN	PTERODACTYLE
PROVISIONING	PSAMMOPHILES	PSEUDOPODIUM	PSYCHOANALYZING	PSYCHOMETRICS	PTERODACTYLES
PROVISIONS	PSAMMOPHILOUS	PSEUDOPODIUM	PSYCHOBABBLE	PSYCHOMETRIES	PTERODACTYLS
PROVISORILY	PSAMMOPHILS	PSEUDOPODS	PSYCHOBABBLER	PSYCHOMETRIST	PTEROSAURIAN

PTEROSAURIANS
PTEROSAURS
PTERYGIALS
PTERYGIUMS
PTERYGOIDS
PTERYLOGRAPHIC
PTERYLOGRAPHIES
PTERYLOGRAPHY
PTERYLOSES
PTERYLOSIS
PTOCHOCRACIES
PTOCHOCRACY
PTYALAGOGIC
PTYALAGOGUE
PTYALAGOGUES
PTYALISING
PTYALIZING
PUBCRAWLER
PUBCRAWLERS
PUBERULENT
PUBERULOUS
PUBESCENCE
PUBESCENCES
PUBLICALLY
PUBLICATION
PUBLICATIONS
PUBLICISED
PUBLICISES
PUBLICISING
PUBLICISTS
PUBLICITIES
PUBLICIZED
PUBLICIZES
PUBLICIZING
PUBLICNESS
PUBLICNESSES
PUBLISHABLE
PUBLISHERS
PUBLISHING
PUBLISHINGS
PUBLISHMENT
PUBLISHMENTS
PUCCINIACEOUS
PUCKERIEST
PUCKISHNESS
PUCKISHNESSES
PUDDENINGS
PUDGINESSES
PUDIBUNDITIES
PUDIBUNDITY
PUDICITIES
PUERILISMS
PUERILITIES
PUERPERALLY
PUERPERIUM
PUERPERIUMS
PUFFINESSES
PUFFTALOONAS
PUFTALOONIES
PUFTALOONS
PUGGINESSES
PUGILISTIC
PUGILISTICAL
PUGILISTICALLY
PUGNACIOUS
PUGNACIOUSLY
PUGNACIOUSNESS
PUGNACITIES
PUISSANCES
PUISSANTLY
PUISSAUNCE
PUISSAUNCES
PULCHRITUDE
PULCHRITUDES
PULCHRITUDINOUS
PULLULATED
PULLULATES
PULLULATING
PULLULATION
PULLULATIONS
PULMOBRANCH
PULMOBRANCHIATE
PULMOBRANCHS

PULMONATES
PULPBOARDS
PULPIFYING
PULPINESSES
PULPITEERS
PULPITRIES
PULPSTONES
PULSATANCE
PULSATANCES
PULSATILITIES
PULSATILITY
PULSATILLA
PULSATILLAS
PULSATIONS
PULSATIVELY
PULSELESSNESS
PULSELESSNESSES
PULSIMETER
PULSIMETERS
PULSOMETER
PULSOMETERS
PULTACEOUS
PULTRUSION
PULTRUSIONS
PULVERABLE
PULVERATION
PULVERATIONS
PULVERINES
PULVERISABLE
PULVERISATION
PULVERISATIONS
PULVERISED
PULVERISER
PULVERISERS
PULVERISES
PULVERISING
PULVERIZABLE
PULVERIZATION
PULVERIZATIONS
PULVERIZED
PULVERIZER
PULVERIZERS
PULVERIZES
PULVERIZING
PULVERULENCE
PULVERULENCES
PULVERULENT
PULVILISED
PULVILIZED
PULVILLIFORM
PULVILLING
PULVILLIOS
PULVINATED
PULVINULES
PUMICATING
PUMMELLING
PUMPERNICKEL
PUMPERNICKELS
PUMPKINSEED
PUMPKINSEEDS
PUNCHBALLS
PUNCHBOARD
PUNCHBOARDS
PUNCHBOWLS
PUNCHINELLO
PUNCHINELLOES
PUNCHINELLOS
PUNCHINESS
PUNCHINESSES
PUNCTATION
PUNCTATIONS
PUNCTATORS
PUNCTILIOS
PUNCTILIOUS
PUNCTILIOUSLY
PUNCTILIOUSNESS
PUNCTUALIST
PUNCTUALISTS
PUNCTUALITIES
PUNCTUALITY
PUNCTUALLY
PUNCTUATED
PUNCTUATES

PUNCTUATING
PUNCTUATION
PUNCTUATIONIST
PUNCTUATIONISTS
PUNCTUATIONS
PUNCTUATIVE
PUNCTUATOR
PUNCTUATORS
PUNCTULATE
PUNCTULATED
PUNCTULATION
PUNCTULATIONS
PUNCTURABLE
PUNCTURATION
PUNCTURATIONS
PUNCTURERS
PUNCTURING
PUNDIGRION
PUNDIGRIONS
PUNDITRIES
PUNDONORES
PUNGENCIES
PUNICACEOUS
PUNINESSES
PUNISHABILITIES
PUNISHABILITY
PUNISHABLE
PUNISHINGLY
PUNISHMENT
PUNISHMENTS
PUNITIVELY
PUNITIVENESS
PUNITIVENESSES
PUNKINESSES
PUPIGEROUS
PUPILABILITIES
PUPILABILITY
PUPILARITIES
PUPILARITY
PUPILLAGES
PUPILLARITIES
PUPILLARITY
PUPILSHIPS
PUPIPAROUS
PUPPETEERED
PUPPETEERING
PUPPETEERS
PUPPETLIKE
PUPPETRIES
PUPPYHOODS
PURBLINDLY
PURBLINDNESS
PURBLINDNESSES
PURCHASABILITY
PURCHASABLE
PURCHASERS
PURCHASING
PURDONIUMS
PUREBLOODS
PURENESSES
PURGATIONS
PURGATIVELY
PURGATIVES
PURGATORIAL
PURGATORIALLY
PURGATORIAN
PURGATORIES
PURIFICATION
PURIFICATIONS
PURIFICATIVE
PURIFICATOR
PURIFICATORS
PURIFICATORY
PURISTICAL
PURISTICALLY
PURITANICAL
PURITANICALLY
PURITANICALNESS
PURITANISE
PURITANISED
PURITANISES
PURITANISING
PURITANISM

PURITANISMS
PURITANIZE
PURITANIZED
PURITANIZES
PURITANIZING
PURLICUING
PURLOINERS
PURLOINING
PUROMYCINS
PURPLEHEART
PURPLEHEARTS
PURPLENESS
PURPLENESSES
PURPORTEDLY
PURPORTING
PURPORTLESS
PURPOSEFUL
PURPOSEFULLY
PURPOSEFULNESS
PURPOSELESS
PURPOSELESSLY
PURPOSELESSNESS
PURPOSIVELY
PURPOSIVENESS
PURPOSIVENESSES
PURPRESTURE
PURPRESTURES
PURSERSHIP
PURSERSHIPS
PURSINESSES
PURSUANCES
PURSUANTLY
PURSUINGLY
PURSUIVANT
PURSUIVANTS
PURTENANCE
PURTENANCES
PURULENCES
PURULENCIES
PURULENTLY
PURVEYANCE
PURVEYANCES
PUSCHKINIA
PUSCHKINIAS
PUSHCHAIRS
PUSHFULNESS
PUSHFULNESSES
PUSHINESSES
PUSHINGNESS
PUSHINGNESSES
PUSILLANIMITIES
PUSILLANIMITY
PUSILLANIMOUS
PUSILLANIMOUSLY
PUSSYFOOTED
PUSSYFOOTER
PUSSYFOOTERS
PUSSYFOOTING
PUSSYFOOTS
PUSTULANTS
PUSTULATED
PUSTULATES
PUSTULATING
PUSTULATION
PUSTULATIONS
PUTANGITANGI
PUTATIVELY
PUTONGHUAS
PUTREFACIENT
PUTREFACTION
PUTREFACTIONS
PUTREFACTIVE
PUTREFIABLE
PUTREFIERS
PUTREFYING
PUTRESCENCE
PUTRESCENCES
PUTRESCENT
PUTRESCIBILITY
PUTRESCIBLE
PUTRESCIBLES
PUTRESCINE
PUTRESCINES

PUTRIDITIES
PUTRIDNESS
PUTRIDNESSES
PUTSCHISTS
PUTTYROOTS
PUZZLEDOMS
PUZZLEHEADED
PUZZLEMENT
PUZZLEMENTS
PUZZLINGLY
PUZZOLANAS
PYCNIDIOSPORE
PYCNIDIOSPORES
PYCNOCONIDIA
PYCNOCONIDIUM
PYCNODYSOSTOSES
PYCNODYSOSTOSIS
PYCNOGONID
PYCNOGONIDS
PYCNOGONOID
PYCNOMETER
PYCNOMETERS
PYCNOMETRIC
PYCNOSPORE
PYCNOSPORES
PYCNOSTYLE
PYCNOSTYLES
PYELITISES
PYELOGRAMS
PYELOGRAPHIC
PYELOGRAPHIES
PYELOGRAPHY
PYELONEPHRITIC
PYELONEPHRITIS
PYGOSTYLES
PYKNODYSOSTOSES
PYKNODYSOSTOSIS
PYKNOMETER
PYKNOMETERS
PYKNOSOMES
PYLORECTOMIES
PYLORECTOMY
PYOGENESES
PYOGENESIS
PYORRHOEAL
PYORRHOEAS
PYORRHOEIC
PYRACANTHA
PYRACANTHAS
PYRACANTHS
PYRALIDIDS
PYRAMIDALLY
PYRAMIDICAL
PYRAMIDICALLY
PYRAMIDING
PYRAMIDION
PYRAMIDIONS
PYRAMIDIST
PYRAMIDISTS
PYRAMIDOLOGIES
PYRAMIDOLOGIST
PYRAMIDOLOGISTS
PYRAMIDOLOGY
PYRAMIDONS
PYRANOMETER
PYRANOMETERS
PYRANOSIDE
PYRANOSIDES
PYRARGYRITE
PYRARGYRITES
PYRENEITES
PYRENOCARP
PYRENOCARPS
PYRENOMYCETOUS
PYRETHRINS
PYRETHROID
PYRETHROIDS
PYRETHRUMS
PYRETOLOGIES
PYRETOLOGY
PYRETOTHERAPIES
PYRETOTHERAPY
PYRGEOMETER

PYRGEOMETERS
PYRHELIOMETER
PYRHELIOMETERS
PYRHELIOMETRIC
PYRIDOXALS
PYRIDOXAMINE
PYRIDOXAMINES
PYRIDOXINE
PYRIDOXINES
PYRIDOXINS
PYRIMETHAMINE
PYRIMETHAMINES
PYRIMIDINE
PYRIMIDINES
PYRITHIAMINE
PYRITHIAMINES
PYRITIFEROUS
PYRITISING
PYRITIZING
PYRITOHEDRA
PYRITOHEDRAL
PYRITOHEDRON
PYROBALLOGIES
PYROBALLOGY
PYROCATECHIN
PYROCATECHINS
PYROCATECHOL
PYROCATECHOLS
PYROCERAMS
PYROCHEMICAL
PYROCHEMICALLY
PYROCLASTIC
PYROCLASTICS
PYROCLASTS
PYROELECTRIC
PYROELECTRICITY
PYROELECTRICS
PYROGALLATE
PYROGALLATES
PYROGALLIC
PYROGALLOL
PYROGALLOLS
PYROGENETIC
PYROGENICITIES
PYROGENICITY
PYROGENOUS
PYROGNOSTIC
PYROGNOSTICS
PYROGRAPHER
PYROGRAPHERS
PYROGRAPHIC
PYROGRAPHIES
PYROGRAPHY
PYROGRAVURE
PYROGRAVURES
PYROKINESES
PYROKINESIS
PYROLATERS
PYROLATRIES
PYROLIGNEOUS
PYROLIGNIC
PYROLISING
PYROLIZING
PYROLOGIES
PYROLUSITE
PYROLUSITES
PYROLYSABLE
PYROLYSATE
PYROLYSATES
PYROLYSERS
PYROLYSING
PYROLYTICALLY
PYROLYZABLE
PYROLYZATE
PYROLYZATES
PYROLYZERS
PYROLYZING
PYROMAGNETIC
PYROMANCER
PYROMANCERS
PYROMANCIES
PYROMANIAC
PYROMANIACAL

PYROMANIACS
PYROMANIAS
PYROMANTIC
PYROMERIDE
PYROMERIDES
PYROMETALLURGY
PYROMETERS
PYROMETRIC
PYROMETRICAL
PYROMETRICALLY
PYROMETRIES
PYROMORPHITE
PYROMORPHITES

PYRONINOPHILIC
PYROPHOBIA
PYROPHOBIAS
PYROPHOBIC
PYROPHOBICS
PYROPHONES
PYROPHORIC
PYROPHOROUS
PYROPHORUS
PYROPHORUSES
PYROPHOSPHATE
PYROPHOSPHATES
PYROPHOSPHORIC

PYROPHOTOGRAPH
PYROPHOTOGRAPHS
PYROPHOTOGRAPHY
PYROPHOTOMETER
PYROPHOTOMETERS
PYROPHOTOMETRY
PYROPHYLLITE
PYROPHYLLITES
PYROSCOPES
PYROSTATIC
PYROSULPHATE
PYROSULPHATES
PYROSULPHURIC

PYROTARTRATE
PYROTARTRATES
PYROTECHNIC
PYROTECHNICAL
PYROTECHNICALLY
PYROTECHNICIAN
PYROTECHNICIANS
PYROTECHNICS
PYROTECHNIES
PYROTECHNIST
PYROTECHNISTS
PYROTECHNY
PYROVANADIC

PYROXENITE
PYROXENITES
PYROXENITIC
PYROXENOID
PYROXENOIDS
PYROXYLINE
PYROXYLINES
PYROXYLINS
PYRRHICIST
PYRRHICISTS
PYRRHOTINE
PYRRHOTINES
PYRRHOTITE

PYRRHOTITES
PYRRHULOXIA
PYRRHULOXIAS
PYRROLIDINE
PYRROLIDINES
PYTHOGENIC
PYTHONESSES
PYTHONOMORPH
PYTHONOMORPHS

Qq

QABALISTIC
QINGHAOSUS
QUACKERIES
QUACKSALVER
QUACKSALVERS
QUACKSALVING
QUADPLEXES
QUADRAGENARIAN
QUADRAGENARIANS
QUADRAGESIMAL
QUADRANGLE
QUADRANGLES
QUADRANGULAR
QUADRANGULARLY
QUADRANTAL
QUADRANTES
QUADRAPHONIC
QUADRAPHONICS
QUADRAPHONIES
QUADRAPHONY
QUADRAPLEGIA
QUADRAPLEGIAS
QUADRAPLEGIC
QUADRAPLEGICS
QUADRATICAL
QUADRATICALLY
QUADRATICS
QUADRATING
QUADRATRIX
QUADRATRIXES
QUADRATURA
QUADRATURE
QUADRATURES
QUADRATUSES
QUADRELLAS
QUADRENNIA
QUADRENNIAL
QUADRENNIALLY
QUADRENNIALS
QUADRENNIUM
QUADRENNIUMS
QUADRICEPS
QUADRICEPSES
QUADRICIPITAL
QUADRICONE
QUADRICONES
QUADRIENNIA
QUADRIENNIAL
QUADRIENNIUM
QUADRIFARIOUS
QUADRIFOLIATE
QUADRIFORM
QUADRIGEMINAL
QUADRIGEMINATE
QUADRIGEMINOUS
QUADRILATERAL
QUADRILATERALS
QUADRILINGUAL
QUADRILITERAL
QUADRILITERALS
QUADRILLED
QUADRILLER
QUADRILLERS
QUADRILLES
QUADRILLING
QUADRILLION
QUADRILLIONS

QUADRILLIONTH
QUADRILLIONTHS
QUADRILOCULAR
QUADRINGENARIES
QUADRINGENARY
QUADRINOMIAL
QUADRINOMIALS
QUADRIPARTITE
QUADRIPARTITION
QUADRIPHONIC
QUADRIPHONICS
QUADRIPLEGIA
QUADRIPLEGIAS
QUADRIPLEGIC
QUADRIPLEGICS
QUADRIPOLE
QUADRIPOLES
QUADRIREME
QUADRIREMES
QUADRISECT
QUADRISECTED
QUADRISECTING
QUADRISECTION
QUADRISECTIONS
QUADRISECTS
QUADRISYLLABIC
QUADRISYLLABLE
QUADRISYLLABLES
QUADRIVALENCE
QUADRIVALENCES
QUADRIVALENCIES
QUADRIVALENCY
QUADRIVALENT
QUADRIVALENTS
QUADRIVIAL
QUADRIVIUM
QUADRIVIUMS
QUADROPHONIC
QUADROPHONICS
QUADROPHONIES
QUADROPHONY
QUADRUMANE
QUADRUMANES
QUADRUMANOUS
QUADRUMANS
QUADRUMVIR
QUADRUMVIRATE
QUADRUMVIRATES
QUADRUMVIRS
QUADRUPEDAL
QUADRUPEDS
QUADRUPLED
QUADRUPLES
QUADRUPLET
QUADRUPLETS
QUADRUPLEX
QUADRUPLEXED
QUADRUPLEXES
QUADRUPLEXING
QUADRUPLICATE
QUADRUPLICATED
QUADRUPLICATES
QUADRUPLICATING
QUADRUPLICATION
QUADRUPLICITIES
QUADRUPLICITY
QUADRUPLIES

QUADRUPLING
QUADRUPOLE
QUADRUPOLES
QUAESITUMS
QUAESTIONARIES
QUAESTIONARY
QUAESTORIAL
QUAESTORSHIP
QUAESTORSHIPS
QUAESTUARIES
QUAESTUARY
QUAGGINESS
QUAGGINESSES
QUAGMIRIER
QUAGMIRIEST
QUAGMIRING
QUAINTNESS
QUAINTNESSES
QUAKINESSES
QUALIFIABLE
QUALIFICATION
QUALIFICATIONS
QUALIFICATIVE
QUALIFICATIVES
QUALIFICATOR
QUALIFICATORS
QUALIFICATORY
QUALIFIEDLY
QUALIFIERS
QUALIFYING
QUALIFYINGS
QUALITATIVE
QUALITATIVELY
QUALMISHLY
QUALMISHNESS
QUALMISHNESSES
QUANDARIES
QUANGOCRACIES
QUANGOCRACY
QUANTIFIABLE
QUANTIFICATION
QUANTIFICATIONS
QUANTIFIED
QUANTIFIER
QUANTIFIERS
QUANTIFIES
QUANTIFYING
QUANTISATION
QUANTISATIONS
QUANTISERS
QUANTISING
QUANTITATE
QUANTITATED
QUANTITATES
QUANTITATING
QUANTITATION
QUANTITATIONS
QUANTITATIVE
QUANTITATIVELY
QUANTITIES
QUANTITIVE
QUANTITIVELY
QUANTIVALENCE
QUANTIVALENCES
QUANTIVALENT
QUANTIZATION
QUANTIZATIONS

QUANTIZERS
QUANTIZING
QUANTOMETER
QUANTOMETERS
QUAQUAVERSAL
QUAQUAVERSALLY
QUARANTINE
QUARANTINED
QUARANTINES
QUARANTINING
QUARENDENS
QUARENDERS
QUARRELERS
QUARRELING
QUARRELLED
QUARRELLER
QUARRELLERS
QUARRELLING
QUARRELLINGS
QUARRELLOUS
QUARRELSOME
QUARRELSOMELY
QUARRELSOMENESS
QUARRENDER
QUARRENDERS
QUARRIABLE
QUARRINGTON
QUARRINGTONS
QUARRYINGS
QUARRYMASTER
QUARRYMASTERS
QUARTATION
QUARTATIONS
QUARTERAGE
QUARTERAGES
QUARTERBACK
QUARTERBACKED
QUARTERBACKING
QUARTERBACKS
QUARTERDECK
QUARTERDECKER
QUARTERDECKERS
QUARTERDECKS
QUARTERERS
QUARTERFINAL
QUARTERFINALIST
QUARTERFINALS
QUARTERING
QUARTERINGS
QUARTERLIES
QUARTERLIFE
QUARTERLIGHT
QUARTERLIGHTS
QUARTERMASTER
QUARTERMASTERS
QUARTERMISTRESS
QUARTEROON
QUARTEROONS
QUARTERSAW
QUARTERSAWED
QUARTERSAWING
QUARTERSAWN
QUARTERSAWS
QUARTERSTAFF
QUARTERSTAFFS
QUARTERSTAVES
QUARTETTES

QUARTODECIMAN
QUARTODECIMANS
QUARTZIEST
QUARTZIFEROUS
QUARTZITES
QUARTZITIC
QUASICRYSTAL
QUASICRYSTALS
QUASIPARTICLE
QUASIPARTICLES
QUASIPERIODIC
QUATERCENTENARY
QUATERNARIES
QUATERNARY
QUATERNATE
QUATERNION
QUATERNIONIST
QUATERNIONISTS
QUATERNIONS
QUATERNITIES
QUATERNITY
QUATORZAIN
QUATORZAINS
QUATREFEUILLE
QUATREFEUILLES
QUATREFOIL
QUATREFOILS
QUATTROCENTISM
QUATTROCENTISMS
QUATTROCENTIST
QUATTROCENTISTS
QUATTROCENTO
QUATTROCENTOS
QUAVERIEST
QUAVERINGLY
QUAVERINGS
QUEACHIEST
QUEASINESS
QUEASINESSES
QUEBRACHOS
QUEECHIEST
QUEENCAKES
QUEENCRAFT
QUEENCRAFTS
QUEENHOODS
QUEENLIEST
QUEENLINESS
QUEENLINESSES
QUEENSHIPS
QUEENSIDES
QUEERCORES
QUEERITIES
QUEERNESSES
QUELQUECHOSE
QUELQUECHOSES
QUENCHABLE
QUENCHINGS
QUENCHLESS
QUENCHLESSLY
QUERCETINS
QUERCETUMS
QUERCITINS
QUERCITRON
QUERCITRONS
QUERIMONIES
QUERIMONIOUS
QUERIMONIOUSLY

QUERNSTONE
QUERNSTONES
QUERSPRUNG
QUERSPRUNGS
QUERULOUSLY
QUERULOUSNESS
QUERULOUSNESSES
QUERYINGLY
QUESADILLA
QUESADILLAS
QUESTINGLY
QUESTIONABILITY
QUESTIONABLE
QUESTIONABLY
QUESTIONARIES
QUESTIONARY
QUESTIONED
QUESTIONEE
QUESTIONEES
QUESTIONER
QUESTIONERS
QUESTIONING
QUESTIONINGLY
QUESTIONINGS
QUESTIONIST
QUESTIONISTS
QUESTIONLESS
QUESTIONLESSLY
QUESTIONNAIRE
QUESTIONNAIRES
QUESTORIAL
QUESTORSHIP
QUESTORSHIPS
QUESTRISTS
QUIBBLINGLY
QUIBBLINGS
QUICKBEAMS
QUICKENERS
QUICKENING
QUICKENINGS
QUICKLIMES
QUICKNESSES
QUICKSANDS
QUICKSILVER
QUICKSILVERED
QUICKSILVERING
QUICKSILVERINGS
QUICKSILVERISH
QUICKSILVERS
QUICKSILVERY
QUICKSTEPPED
QUICKSTEPPING
QUICKSTEPS
QUICKTHORN
QUICKTHORNS
QUIDDANIES
QUIDDITATIVE
QUIDDITCHES
QUIDDITIES
QUIESCENCE
QUIESCENCES
QUIESCENCIES
QUIESCENCY
QUIESCENTLY
QUIETENERS
QUIETENING
QUIETENINGS

QUIETISTIC	QUINDECAPLETS	QUINQUENNIALS	QUINTROONS	QUITTANCES	QUIZZIFYING
QUIETNESSES	QUINDECENNIAL	QUINQUENNIUM	QUINTUPLED	QUITTANCING	QUIZZINESS
QUILLBACKS	QUINDECENNIALS	QUINQUENNIUMS	QUINTUPLES	QUIVERFULS	QUIZZINESSES
QUILLWORKS	QUINDECILLION	QUINQUEPARTITE	QUINTUPLET	QUIVERIEST	QUODLIBETARIAN
QUILLWORTS	QUINDECILLIONS	QUINQUEREME	QUINTUPLETS	QUIVERINGLY	QUODLIBETARIANS
QUINACRINE	QUINGENTENARIES	QUINQUEREMES	QUINTUPLICATE	QUIVERINGS	QUODLIBETIC
QUINACRINES	QUINGENTENARY	QUINQUEVALENCE	QUINTUPLICATED	QUIXOTICAL	QUODLIBETICAL
QUINAQUINA	QUINIDINES	QUINQUEVALENCES	QUINTUPLICATES	QUIXOTICALLY	QUODLIBETICALLY
QUINAQUINAS	QUINOLINES	QUINQUEVALENCY	QUINTUPLICATING	QUIXOTISMS	QUODLIBETS
QUINCENTENARIES	QUINOLONES	QUINQUEVALENT	QUINTUPLICATION	QUIXOTRIES	QUOTABILITIES
QUINCENTENARY	QUINQUAGENARIAN	QUINQUINAS	QUINTUPLING	QUIZMASTER	QUOTABILITY
QUINCENTENNIAL	QUINQUAGESIMAL	QUINQUIVALENT	QUIRISTERS	QUIZMASTERS	QUOTABLENESS
QUINCENTENNIALS	QUINQUECOSTATE	QUINTESSENCE	QUIRKINESS	QUIZZERIES	QUOTABLENESSES
QUINCUNCIAL	QUINQUEFARIOUS	QUINTESSENCES	QUIRKINESSES	QUIZZICALITIES	QUOTATIONS
QUINCUNCIALLY	QUINQUEFOLIATE	QUINTESSENTIAL	QUISLINGISM	QUIZZICALITY	QUOTATIOUS
QUINCUNXES	QUINQUENNIA	QUINTETTES	QUISLINGISMS	QUIZZICALLY	QUOTATIVES
QUINCUNXIAL	QUINQUENNIAD	QUINTILLION	QUITCLAIMED	QUIZZIFICATION	QUOTEWORTHY
QUINDECAGON	QUINQUENNIADS	QUINTILLIONS	QUITCLAIMING	QUIZZIFICATIONS	QUOTIDIANS
QUINDECAGONS	QUINQUENNIAL	QUINTILLIONTH	QUITCLAIMS	QUIZZIFIED	QUOTITIONS
QUINDECAPLET	QUINQUENNIALLY	QUINTILLIONTHS	QUITTANCED	QUIZZIFIES	

q

Rr

RABATMENTS
RABATTEMENT
RABATTEMENTS
RABATTINGS
RABBINATES
RABBINICAL
RABBINICALLY
RABBINISMS
RABBINISTIC
RABBINISTS
RABBINITES
RABBITBRUSH
RABBITBRUSHES
RABBITFISH
RABBITFISHES
RABBITRIES
RABBLEMENT
RABBLEMENTS
RABIDITIES
RABIDNESSES
RACCAHOUTS
RACECOURSE
RACECOURSES
RACEGOINGS
RACEHORSES
RACEMATION
RACEMATIONS
RACEMISATION
RACEMISATIONS
RACEMISING
RACEMIZATION
RACEMIZATIONS
RACEMIZING
RACEMOSELY
RACEMOUSLY
RACETRACKER
RACETRACKERS
RACETRACKS
RACEWALKED
RACEWALKER
RACEWALKERS
RACEWALKING
RACEWALKINGS
RACHIOTOMIES
RACHIOTOMY
RACHISCHISES
RACHISCHISIS
RACHITIDES
RACHITISES
RACIALISED
RACIALISES
RACIALISING
RACIALISMS
RACIALISTIC
RACIALISTS
RACIALIZED
RACIALIZES
RACIALIZING
RACIATIONS
RACINESSES
RACKABONES
RACKETEERED
RACKETEERING
RACKETEERINGS
RACKETEERS
RACKETIEST
RACKETRIES

RACONTEURING
RACONTEURINGS
RACONTEURS
RACONTEUSE
RACONTEUSES
RACQUETBALL
RACQUETBALLS
RACQUETING
RADARSCOPE
RADARSCOPES
RADIALISATION
RADIALISATIONS
RADIALISED
RADIALISES
RADIALISING
RADIALITIES
RADIALIZATION
RADIALIZATIONS
RADIALIZED
RADIALIZES
RADIALIZING
RADIANCIES
RADIATIONAL
RADIATIONLESS
RADIATIONS
RADICALISATION
RADICALISATIONS
RADICALISE
RADICALISED
RADICALISES
RADICALISING
RADICALISM
RADICALISMS
RADICALISTIC
RADICALITIES
RADICALITY
RADICALIZATION
RADICALIZATIONS
RADICALIZE
RADICALIZED
RADICALIZES
RADICALIZING
RADICALNESS
RADICALNESSES
RADICATING
RADICATION
RADICATIONS
RADICCHIOS
RADICELLOSE
RADICICOLOUS
RADICIFORM
RADICIVOROUS
RADICULOSE
RADIESTHESIA
RADIESTHESIAS
RADIESTHESIST
RADIESTHESISTS
RADIESTHETIC
RADIOACTIVATE
RADIOACTIVATED
RADIOACTIVATES
RADIOACTIVATING
RADIOACTIVATION
RADIOACTIVE
RADIOACTIVELY
RADIOACTIVITIES
RADIOACTIVITY

RADIOAUTOGRAPH
RADIOAUTOGRAPHS
RADIOAUTOGRAPHY
RADIOBIOLOGIC
RADIOBIOLOGICAL
RADIOBIOLOGIES
RADIOBIOLOGIST
RADIOBIOLOGISTS
RADIOBIOLOGY
RADIOCARBON
RADIOCARBONS
RADIOCHEMICAL
RADIOCHEMICALLY
RADIOCHEMIST
RADIOCHEMISTRY
RADIOCHEMISTS
RADIOECOLOGIES
RADIOECOLOGY
RADIOELEMENT
RADIOELEMENTS
RADIOGENIC
RADIOGOLDS
RADIOGONIOMETER
RADIOGRAMS
RADIOGRAPH
RADIOGRAPHED
RADIOGRAPHER
RADIOGRAPHERS
RADIOGRAPHIC
RADIOGRAPHIES
RADIOGRAPHING
RADIOGRAPHS
RADIOGRAPHY
RADIOIODINE
RADIOIODINES
RADIOISOTOPE
RADIOISOTOPES
RADIOISOTOPIC
RADIOLABEL
RADIOLABELED
RADIOLABELING
RADIOLABELLED
RADIOLABELLING
RADIOLABELS
RADIOLARIAN
RADIOLARIANS
RADIOLOCATION
RADIOLOCATIONAL
RADIOLOCATIONS
RADIOLOGIC
RADIOLOGICAL
RADIOLOGICALLY
RADIOLOGIES
RADIOLOGIST
RADIOLOGISTS
RADIOLUCENCIES
RADIOLUCENCY
RADIOLUCENT
RADIOLYSES
RADIOLYSIS
RADIOLYTIC
RADIOMETER
RADIOMETERS
RADIOMETRIC
RADIOMETRICALLY
RADIOMETRIES
RADIOMETRY

RADIOMICROMETER
RADIOMIMETIC
RADIONUCLIDE
RADIONUCLIDES
RADIOPACITIES
RADIOPACITY
RADIOPAGER
RADIOPAGERS
RADIOPAGING
RADIOPAGINGS
RADIOPAQUE
RADIOPHONE
RADIOPHONES
RADIOPHONIC
RADIOPHONICALLY
RADIOPHONICS
RADIOPHONIES
RADIOPHONIST
RADIOPHONISTS
RADIOPHONY
RADIOPHOSPHORUS
RADIOPHOTO
RADIOPHOTOS
RADIOPROTECTION
RADIOPROTECTIVE
RADIORESISTANT
RADIOSCOPE
RADIOSCOPES
RADIOSCOPIC
RADIOSCOPICALLY
RADIOSCOPIES
RADIOSCOPY
RADIOSENSITISE
RADIOSENSITISED
RADIOSENSITISES
RADIOSENSITIVE
RADIOSENSITIZE
RADIOSENSITIZED
RADIOSENSITIZES
RADIOSONDE
RADIOSONDES
RADIOSTRONTIUM
RADIOSTRONTIUMS
RADIOTELEGRAM
RADIOTELEGRAMS
RADIOTELEGRAPH
RADIOTELEGRAPHS
RADIOTELEGRAPHY
RADIOTELEMETER
RADIOTELEMETERS
RADIOTELEMETRIC
RADIOTELEMETRY
RADIOTELEPHONE
RADIOTELEPHONES
RADIOTELEPHONIC
RADIOTELEPHONY
RADIOTELETYPE
RADIOTELETYPES
RADIOTHERAPIES
RADIOTHERAPIST
RADIOTHERAPISTS
RADIOTHERAPY
RADIOTHERMIES
RADIOTHERMY
RADIOTHONS
RADIOTHORIUM
RADIOTHORIUMS

RADIOTOXIC
RADIOTRACER
RADIOTRACERS
RADULIFORM
RAFFINATES
RAFFINOSES
RAFFISHNESS
RAFFISHNESSES
RAFFLESIAS
RAFTERINGS
RAGAMUFFIN
RAGAMUFFINS
RAGGAMUFFIN
RAGGAMUFFINS
RAGGEDIEST
RAGGEDNESS
RAGGEDNESSES
RAGMATICAL
RAGPICKERS
RAILBUSSES
RAILLERIES
RAILROADED
RAILROADER
RAILROADERS
RAILROADING
RAILROADINGS
RAILWAYMAN
RAILWAYMEN
RAINBOWLIKE
RAINCHECKS
RAINFOREST
RAINFORESTS
RAININESSES
RAINMAKERS
RAINMAKING
RAINMAKINGS
RAINPROOFED
RAINPROOFING
RAINPROOFS
RAINSPOUTS
RAINSQUALL
RAINSQUALLS
RAINSTORMS
RAINWASHED
RAINWASHES
RAINWASHING
RAINWATERS
RAISONNEUR
RAISONNEURS
RAIYATWARI
RAIYATWARIS
RAJAHSHIPS
RAJPRAMUKH
RAJPRAMUKHS
RAKESHAMES
RAKISHNESS
RAKISHNESSES
RALLENTANDO
RALLENTANDOS
RALLYCROSS
RALLYCROSSES
RALLYINGLY
RAMAPITHECINE
RAMAPITHECINES
RAMBLINGLY
RAMBOUILLET
RAMBOUILLETS

RAMBUNCTIOUS
RAMBUNCTIOUSLY
RAMENTACEOUS
RAMGUNSHOCH
RAMIFICATION
RAMIFICATIONS
RAMMISHNESS
RAMMISHNESSES
RAMOSITIES
RAMPACIOUS
RAMPAGEOUS
RAMPAGEOUSLY
RAMPAGEOUSNESS
RAMPAGINGS
RAMPALLIAN
RAMPALLIANS
RAMPANCIES
RAMPARTING
RAMPAUGING
RAMRODDING
RAMSHACKLE
RANCHERIAS
RANCHERIES
RANCIDITIES
RANCIDNESS
RANCIDNESSES
RANCOROUSLY
RANCOROUSNESS
RANCOROUSNESSES
RANDINESSES
RANDOMISATION
RANDOMISATIONS
RANDOMISED
RANDOMISER
RANDOMISERS
RANDOMISES
RANDOMISING
RANDOMIZATION
RANDOMIZATIONS
RANDOMIZED
RANDOMIZER
RANDOMIZERS
RANDOMIZES
RANDOMIZING
RANDOMNESS
RANDOMNESSES
RANDOMWISE
RANGATIRAS
RANGATIRATANGA
RANGATIRATANGAS
RANGEFINDER
RANGEFINDERS
RANGEFINDING
RANGEFINDINGS
RANGELANDS
RANGERSHIP
RANGERSHIPS
RANGINESSES
RANIVOROUS
RANKNESSES
RANKSHIFTED
RANKSHIFTING
RANKSHIFTS
RANSACKERS
RANSACKING
RANSHACKLE
RANSHACKLED

RANSHACKLES	RATEABILITIES	RAYGRASSES	REACTUATED	REALLOCATE	REARRANGED
RANSHACKLING	RATEABILITY	RAYLESSNESS	REACTUATES	REALLOCATED	REARRANGEMENT
RANSHAKLED	RATEABLENESS	RAYLESSNESSES	REACTUATING	REALLOCATES	REARRANGEMENTS
RANSHAKLES	RATEABLENESSES	RAZMATAZES	READABILITIES	REALLOCATING	REARRANGER
RANSHAKLING	RATEMETERS	RAZORBACKS	READABILITY	REALLOCATION	REARRANGERS
RANSOMABLE	RATEPAYERS	RAZORBILLS	READABLENESS	REALLOCATIONS	REARRANGES
RANSOMLESS	RATHERIPES	RAZZAMATAZZ	READABLENESSES	REALLOTMENT	REARRANGING
RANTERISMS	RATHSKELLER	RAZZAMATAZZES	READAPTATION	REALLOTMENTS	REARRESTED
RANTIPOLED	RATHSKELLERS	RAZZBERRIES	READAPTATIONS	REALLOTTED	REARRESTING
RANTIPOLES	RATIFIABLE	RAZZMATAZZ	READAPTING	REALLOTTING	REARTICULATE
RANTIPOLING	RATIFICATION	RAZZMATAZZES	READDICTED	REALNESSES	REARTICULATED
RANUNCULACEOUS	RATIFICATIONS	REABSORBED	READDICTING	REALPOLITIK	REARTICULATES
RANUNCULUS	RATIOCINATE	REABSORBING	READDRESSED	REALPOLITIKER	REARTICULATING
RANUNCULUSES	RATIOCINATED	REABSORPTION	READDRESSES	REALPOLITIKERS	REASCENDED
RAPACIOUSLY	RATIOCINATES	REABSORPTIONS	READDRESSING	REALPOLITIKS	REASCENDING
RAPACIOUSNESS	RATIOCINATING	REACCEDING	READERSHIP	REALTERING	REASCENSION
RAPACIOUSNESSES	RATIOCINATION	REACCELERATE	READERSHIPS	REAMENDING	REASCENSIONS
RAPACITIES	RATIOCINATIONS	REACCELERATED	READINESSES	REAMENDMENT	REASONABILITIES
RAPIDITIES	RATIOCINATIVE	REACCELERATES	READJUSTABLE	REAMENDMENTS	REASONABILITY
RAPIDNESSES	RATIOCINATOR	REACCELERATING	READJUSTED	REANALYSED	REASONABLE
RAPIERLIKE	RATIOCINATORS	REACCENTED	READJUSTER	REANALYSES	REASONABLENESS
RAPPELLING	RATIOCINATORY	REACCENTING	READJUSTERS	REANALYSING	REASONABLY
RAPPELLINGS	RATIONALES	REACCEPTED	READJUSTING	REANALYSIS	REASONEDLY
RAPPORTAGE	RATIONALISABLE	REACCEPTING	READJUSTMENT	REANALYZED	REASONINGS
RAPPORTAGES	RATIONALISATION	REACCESSION	READJUSTMENTS	REANALYZES	REASONLESS
RAPPORTEUR	RATIONALISE	REACCESSIONS	READMISSION	REANALYZING	REASONLESSLY
RAPPORTEURS	RATIONALISED	REACCLAIMED	READMISSIONS	REANIMATED	REASSAILED
RAPPROCHEMENT	RATIONALISER	REACCLAIMING	READMITTANCE	REANIMATES	REASSAILING
RAPPROCHEMENTS	RATIONALISERS	REACCLAIMS	READMITTANCES	REANIMATING	REASSEMBLAGE
RAPSCALLION	RATIONALISES	REACCLIMATISE	READMITTED	REANIMATION	REASSEMBLAGES
RAPSCALLIONS	RATIONALISING	REACCLIMATISED	READMITTING	REANIMATIONS	REASSEMBLE
RAPTATORIAL	RATIONALISM	REACCLIMATISES	READOPTING	REANNEXATION	REASSEMBLED
RAPTNESSES	RATIONALISMS	REACCLIMATISING	READOPTION	REANNEXATIONS	REASSEMBLES
RAPTURELESS	RATIONALIST	REACCLIMATIZE	READOPTIONS	REANNEXING	REASSEMBLIES
RAPTURISED	RATIONALISTIC	REACCLIMATIZED	READORNING	REANOINTED	REASSEMBLING
RAPTURISES	RATIONALISTS	REACCLIMATIZES	READVANCED	REANOINTING	REASSEMBLY
RAPTURISING	RATIONALITIES	REACCLIMATIZING	READVANCES	REANSWERED	REASSERTED
RAPTURISTS	RATIONALITY	REACCREDIT	READVANCING	REANSWERING	REASSERTING
RAPTURIZED	RATIONALIZABLE	REACCREDITATION	READVERTISE	REAPPARELLED	REASSERTION
RAPTURIZES	RATIONALIZATION	REACCREDITED	READVERTISED	REAPPARELLING	REASSERTIONS
RAPTURIZING	RATIONALIZE	REACCREDITING	READVERTISEMENT	REAPPARELS	REASSESSED
RAPTUROUSLY	RATIONALIZED	REACCREDITS	READVERTISES	REAPPEARANCE	REASSESSES
RAPTUROUSNESS	RATIONALIZER	REACCUSING	READVERTISING	REAPPEARANCES	REASSESSING
RAPTUROUSNESSES	RATIONALIZERS	REACCUSTOM	READVISING	REAPPEARED	REASSESSMENT
RAREFACTION	RATIONALIZES	REACCUSTOMED	READYMADES	REAPPEARING	REASSESSMENTS
RAREFACTIONAL	RATIONALIZING	REACCUSTOMING	REAEDIFIED	REAPPLICATION	REASSIGNED
RAREFACTIONS	RATIONALLY	REACCUSTOMS	REAEDIFIES	REAPPLICATIONS	REASSIGNING
RAREFACTIVE	RATIONALNESS	REACQUAINT	REAEDIFYED	REAPPLYING	REASSIGNMENT
RAREFIABLE	RATIONALNESSES	REACQUAINTANCE	REAEDIFYES	REAPPOINTED	REASSIGNMENTS
RAREFICATION	RATTENINGS	REACQUAINTANCES	REAEDIFYING	REAPPOINTING	REASSORTED
RAREFICATIONAL	RATTINESSES	REACQUAINTED	REAFFIRMATION	REAPPOINTMENT	REASSORTING
RAREFICATIONS	RATTLEBAGS	REACQUAINTING	REAFFIRMATIONS	REAPPOINTMENTS	REASSORTMENT
RARENESSES	RATTLEBOXES	REACQUAINTS	REAFFIRMED	REAPPOINTS	REASSORTMENTS
RASCAILLES	RATTLEBRAIN	REACQUIRED	REAFFIRMING	REAPPORTION	REASSUMING
RASCALDOMS	RATTLEBRAINED	REACQUIRES	REAFFIXING	REAPPORTIONED	REASSUMPTION
RASCALISMS	RATTLEBRAINS	REACQUIRING	REAFFOREST	REAPPORTIONING	REASSUMPTIONS
RASCALITIES	RATTLESNAKE	REACQUISITION	REAFFORESTATION	REAPPORTIONMENT	REASSURANCE
RASCALLIEST	RATTLESNAKES	REACQUISITIONS	REAFFORESTED	REAPPORTIONS	REASSURANCES
RASCALLION	RATTLETRAP	REACTANCES	REAFFORESTING	REAPPRAISAL	REASSURERS
RASCALLIONS	RATTLETRAPS	REACTIONAL	REAFFORESTS	REAPPRAISALS	REASSURING
RASHNESSES	RATTLINGLY	REACTIONARIES	REAGENCIES	REAPPRAISE	REASSURINGLY
RASPATORIES	RATTOONING	REACTIONARISM	REAGGREGATE	REAPPRAISED	REASTINESS
RASPBERRIES	RAUCOUSNESS	REACTIONARISMS	REAGGREGATED	REAPPRAISEMENT	REASTINESSES
RASPINESSES	RAUCOUSNESSES	REACTIONARIST	REAGGREGATES	REAPPRAISEMENTS	REATTACHED
RASTAFARIAN	RAUNCHIEST	REACTIONARISTS	REAGGREGATING	REAPPRAISER	REATTACHES
RASTAFARIANS	RAUNCHINESS	REACTIONARY	REAGGREGATION	REAPPRAISERS	REATTACHING
RASTERISED	RAUNCHINESSES	REACTIONARYISM	REAGGREGATIONS	REAPPRAISES	REATTACHMENT
RASTERISES	RAUWOLFIAS	REACTIONARYISMS	REALIGNING	REAPPRAISING	REATTACHMENTS
RASTERISING	RAVAGEMENT	REACTIONISM	REALIGNMENT	REAPPROPRIATE	REATTACKED
RASTERIZED	RAVAGEMENTS	REACTIONISMS	REALIGNMENTS	REAPPROPRIATED	REATTACKING
RASTERIZES	RAVELLINGS	REACTIONIST	REALISABILITIES	REAPPROPRIATES	REATTAINED
RASTERIZING	RAVELMENTS	REACTIONISTS	REALISABILITY	REAPPROPRIATING	REATTAINING
RATABILITIES	RAVENINGLY	REACTIVATE	REALISABLE	REAPPROVED	REATTEMPTED
RATABILITY	RAVENOUSLY	REACTIVATED	REALISABLY	REAPPROVES	REATTEMPTING
RATABLENESS	RAVENOUSNESS	REACTIVATES	REALISATION	REAPPROVING	REATTEMPTS
RATABLENESSES	RAVENOUSNESSES	REACTIVATING	REALISATIONS	REARGUARDS	REATTRIBUTE
RATAPLANNED	RAVIGOTTES	REACTIVATION	REALISTICALLY	REARGUMENT	REATTRIBUTED
RATAPLANNING	RAVISHINGLY	REACTIVATIONS	REALIZABILITIES	REARGUMENTS	REATTRIBUTES
RATATOUILLE	RAVISHMENT	REACTIVELY	REALIZABILITY	REARHORSES	REATTRIBUTING
RATATOUILLES	RAVISHMENTS	REACTIVENESS	REALIZABLE	REARMAMENT	REATTRIBUTION
RATBAGGERIES	RAWINSONDE	REACTIVENESSES	REALIZABLY	REARMAMENTS	REATTRIBUTIONS
RATBAGGERY	RAWINSONDES	REACTIVITIES	REALIZATION	REAROUSALS	REAUTHORISATION
RATCHETING	RAWMAISHES	REACTIVITY	REALIZATIONS	REAROUSING	REAUTHORISE

REAUTHORISED
REAUTHORISES
REAUTHORISING
REAUTHORIZATION
REAUTHORIZE
REAUTHORIZED
REAUTHORIZES
REAUTHORIZING
REAVAILING
REAWAKENED
REAWAKENING
REAWAKENINGS
REBALANCED
REBALANCES
REBALANCING
REBAPTISED
REBAPTISES
REBAPTISING
REBAPTISMS
REBAPTIZED
REBAPTIZES
REBAPTIZING
REBARBATIVE
REBARBATIVELY
REBATEABLE
REBATEMENT
REBATEMENTS
REBBETZINS
REBEGINNING
REBELLIONS
REBELLIOUS
REBELLIOUSLY
REBELLIOUSNESS
REBELLOWED
REBELLOWING
REBIRTHING
REBIRTHINGS
REBLENDING
REBLOOMING
REBLOSSOMED
REBLOSSOMING
REBLOSSOMS
REBOARDING
REBOATIONS
REBORROWED
REBORROWING
REBOTTLING
REBOUNDERS
REBOUNDING
REBRANCHED
REBRANCHES
REBRANCHING
REBRANDING
REBREEDING
REBROADCAST
REBROADCASTED
REBROADCASTING
REBROADCASTS
REBUILDING
REBUKEFULLY
REBUKINGLY
REBUTMENTS
REBUTTABLE
REBUTTONED
REBUTTONING
RECALCITRANCE
RECALCITRANCES
RECALCITRANCIES
RECALCITRANCY
RECALCITRANT
RECALCITRANTS
RECALCITRATE
RECALCITRATED
RECALCITRATES
RECALCITRATING
RECALCITRATION
RECALCITRATIONS
RECALCULATE
RECALCULATED
RECALCULATES
RECALCULATING
RECALCULATION
RECALCULATIONS

RECALESCED
RECALESCENCE
RECALESCENCES
RECALESCENT
RECALESCES
RECALESCING
RECALIBRATE
RECALIBRATED
RECALIBRATES
RECALIBRATING
RECALIBRATION
RECALIBRATIONS
RECALLABILITIES
RECALLABILITY
RECALLABLE
RECALLMENT
RECALLMENTS
RECALMENTS
RECANALISATION
RECANALISATIONS
RECANALISE
RECANALISED
RECANALISES
RECANALISING
RECANALIZATION
RECANALIZATIONS
RECANALIZE
RECANALIZED
RECANALIZES
RECANALIZING
RECANTATION
RECANTATIONS
RECAPITALISE
RECAPITALISED
RECAPITALISES
RECAPITALISING
RECAPITALIZE
RECAPITALIZED
RECAPITALIZES
RECAPITALIZING
RECAPITULATE
RECAPITULATED
RECAPITULATES
RECAPITULATING
RECAPITULATION
RECAPITULATIONS
RECAPITULATIVE
RECAPITULATORY
RECAPPABLE
RECAPTIONS
RECAPTURED
RECAPTURER
RECAPTURERS
RECAPTURES
RECAPTURING
RECARPETED
RECARPETING
RECARRYING
RECATALOGED
RECATALOGING
RECATALOGS
RECATCHING
RECAUTIONED
RECAUTIONING
RECAUTIONS
RECEIPTING
RECEIPTORS
RECEIVABILITIES
RECEIVABILITY
RECEIVABLE
RECEIVABLENESS
RECEIVABLES
RECEIVERSHIP
RECEIVERSHIPS
RECEIVINGS
RECEMENTED
RECEMENTING
RECENSIONS
RECENSORED
RECENSORING
RECENTNESS
RECENTNESSES
RECENTRIFUGE

RECENTRIFUGED
RECENTRIFUGES
RECENTRIFUGING
RECENTRING
RECEPTACLE
RECEPTACLES
RECEPTACULA
RECEPTACULAR
RECEPTACULUM
RECEPTIBILITIES
RECEPTIBILITY
RECEPTIBLE
RECEPTIONIST
RECEPTIONISTS
RECEPTIONS
RECEPTIVELY
RECEPTIVENESS
RECEPTIVENESSES
RECEPTIVITIES
RECEPTIVITY
RECERTIFICATION
RECERTIFIED
RECERTIFIES
RECERTIFYING
RECESSIONAL
RECESSIONALS
RECESSIONARY
RECESSIONS
RECESSIVELY
RECESSIVENESS
RECESSIVENESSES
RECESSIVES
RECHALLENGE
RECHALLENGED
RECHALLENGES
RECHALLENGING
RECHANGING
RECHANNELED
RECHANNELING
RECHANNELLED
RECHANNELLING
RECHANNELS
RECHARGEABLE
RECHARGERS
RECHARGING
RECHARTERED
RECHARTERING
RECHARTERS
RECHARTING
RECHAUFFES
RECHEATING
RECHECKING
RECHOOSING
RECHOREOGRAPH
RECHOREOGRAPHED
RECHOREOGRAPHS
RECHRISTEN
RECHRISTENED
RECHRISTENING
RECHRISTENS
RECHROMATOGRAPH
RECIDIVISM
RECIDIVISMS
RECIDIVIST
RECIDIVISTIC
RECIDIVISTS
RECIDIVOUS
RECIPIENCE
RECIPIENCES
RECIPIENCIES
RECIPIENCY
RECIPIENTS
RECIPROCAL
RECIPROCALITIES
RECIPROCALITY
RECIPROCALLY
RECIPROCALS
RECIPROCANT
RECIPROCANTS
RECIPROCATE
RECIPROCATED
RECIPROCATES
RECIPROCATING

RECIPROCATION
RECIPROCATIONS
RECIPROCATIVE
RECIPROCATOR
RECIPROCATORS
RECIPROCATORY
RECIPROCITIES
RECIPROCITY
RECIRCLING
RECIRCULATE
RECIRCULATED
RECIRCULATES
RECIRCULATING
RECIRCULATION
RECIRCULATIONS
RECITALIST
RECITALISTS
RECITATION
RECITATIONIST
RECITATIONISTS
RECITATIONS
RECITATIVE
RECITATIVES
RECITATIVI
RECITATIVO
RECITATIVOS
RECKLESSLY
RECKLESSNESS
RECKLESSNESSES
RECKONINGS
RECLADDING
RECLAIMABLE
RECLAIMABLY
RECLAIMANT
RECLAIMANTS
RECLAIMERS
RECLAIMING
RECLAMATION
RECLAMATIONS
RECLASPING
RECLASSIFIED
RECLASSIFIES
RECLASSIFY
RECLASSIFYING
RECLEANING
RECLIMBING
RECLINABLE
RECLINATION
RECLINATIONS
RECLOSABLE
RECLOTHING
RECLUSENESS
RECLUSENESSES
RECLUSIONS
RECLUSIVELY
RECLUSIVENESS
RECLUSIVENESSES
RECLUSORIES
RECODIFICATION
RECODIFICATIONS
RECODIFIED
RECODIFIES
RECODIFYING
RECOGNISABILITY
RECOGNISABLE
RECOGNISABLY
RECOGNISANCE
RECOGNISANCES
RECOGNISANT
RECOGNISED
RECOGNISEE
RECOGNISEES
RECOGNISER
RECOGNISERS
RECOGNISES
RECOGNISING
RECOGNISOR
RECOGNISORS
RECOGNITION
RECOGNITIONS
RECOGNITIVE
RECOGNITORY
RECOGNIZABILITY

RECOGNIZABLE
RECOGNIZABLY
RECOGNIZANCE
RECOGNIZANCES
RECOGNIZANT
RECOGNIZED
RECOGNIZEE
RECOGNIZEES
RECOGNIZER
RECOGNIZERS
RECOGNIZES
RECOGNIZING
RECOGNIZOR
RECOGNIZORS
RECOILLESS
RECOINAGES
RECOLLECTED
RECOLLECTEDLY
RECOLLECTEDNESS
RECOLLECTING
RECOLLECTION
RECOLLECTIONS
RECOLLECTIVE
RECOLLECTIVELY
RECOLLECTS
RECOLONISATION
RECOLONISATIONS
RECOLONISE
RECOLONISED
RECOLONISES
RECOLONISING
RECOLONIZATION
RECOLONIZATIONS
RECOLONIZE
RECOLONIZED
RECOLONIZES
RECOLONIZING
RECOLORING
RECOMBINANT
RECOMBINANTS
RECOMBINATION
RECOMBINATIONAL
RECOMBINATIONS
RECOMBINED
RECOMBINES
RECOMBINING
RECOMFORTED
RECOMFORTING
RECOMFORTLESS
RECOMFORTS
RECOMFORTURE
RECOMFORTURES
RECOMMENCE
RECOMMENCED
RECOMMENCEMENT
RECOMMENCEMENTS
RECOMMENCES
RECOMMENCING
RECOMMENDABLE
RECOMMENDABLY
RECOMMENDATION
RECOMMENDATIONS
RECOMMENDATORY
RECOMMENDED
RECOMMENDER
RECOMMENDERS
RECOMMENDING
RECOMMENDS
RECOMMISSION
RECOMMISSIONED
RECOMMISSIONING
RECOMMISSIONS
RECOMMITMENT
RECOMMITMENTS
RECOMMITTAL
RECOMMITTALS
RECOMMITTED
RECOMMITTING
RECOMPACTED
RECOMPACTING
RECOMPACTS
RECOMPENCE
RECOMPENCES

RECOMPENSABLE
RECOMPENSE
RECOMPENSED
RECOMPENSER
RECOMPENSERS
RECOMPENSES
RECOMPENSING
RECOMPILATION
RECOMPILATIONS
RECOMPILED
RECOMPILES
RECOMPILING
RECOMPOSED
RECOMPOSES
RECOMPOSING
RECOMPOSITION
RECOMPOSITIONS
RECOMPRESS
RECOMPRESSED
RECOMPRESSES
RECOMPRESSING
RECOMPRESSION
RECOMPRESSIONS
RECOMPUTATION
RECOMPUTATIONS
RECOMPUTED
RECOMPUTES
RECOMPUTING
RECONCEIVE
RECONCEIVED
RECONCEIVES
RECONCEIVING
RECONCENTRATE
RECONCENTRATED
RECONCENTRATES
RECONCENTRATING
RECONCENTRATION
RECONCEPTION
RECONCEPTIONS
RECONCEPTUALISE
RECONCEPTUALIZE
RECONCILABILITY
RECONCILABLE
RECONCILABLY
RECONCILED
RECONCILEMENT
RECONCILEMENTS
RECONCILER
RECONCILERS
RECONCILES
RECONCILIATION
RECONCILIATIONS
RECONCILIATORY
RECONCILING
RECONDENSATION
RECONDENSATIONS
RECONDENSE
RECONDENSED
RECONDENSES
RECONDENSING
RECONDITELY
RECONDITENESS
RECONDITENESSES
RECONDITION
RECONDITIONED
RECONDITIONING
RECONDITIONS
RECONDUCTED
RECONDUCTING
RECONDUCTS
RECONFERRED
RECONFERRING
RECONFIGURATION
RECONFIGURE
RECONFIGURED
RECONFIGURES
RECONFIGURING
RECONFINED
RECONFINES
RECONFINING
RECONFIRMATION
RECONFIRMATIONS
RECONFIRMED

r

RECONFIRMING	RECONTINUED	RECRUDESCED	RECURSIVELY	REDESCENDING	REDISTILLS
RECONFIRMS	RECONTINUES	RECRUDESCENCE	RECURSIVENESS	REDESCENDS	REDISTRIBUTE
RECONNAISSANCE	RECONTINUING	RECRUDESCENCES	RECURSIVENESSES	REDESCRIBE	REDISTRIBUTED
RECONNAISSANCES	RECONTOURED	RECRUDESCENCIES	RECURVIROSTRAL	REDESCRIBED	REDISTRIBUTES
RECONNECTED	RECONTOURS	RECRUDESCENCY	RECUSANCES	REDESCRIBES	REDISTRIBUTING
RECONNECTING	RECONVALESCENCE	RECRUDESCENT	RECUSANCIES	REDESCRIBING	REDISTRIBUTION
RECONNECTION	RECONVENED	RECRUDESCES	RECUSATION	REDESCRIPTION	REDISTRIBUTIONS
RECONNECTIONS	RECONVENES	RECRUDESCING	RECUSATIONS	REDESCRIPTIONS	REDISTRIBUTIVE
RECONNECTS	RECONVENING	RECRUITABLE	RECYCLABLE	REDESIGNED	REDISTRICT
RECONNOISSANCE	RECONVERSION	RECRUITALS	RECYCLABLES	REDESIGNING	REDISTRICTED
RECONNOISSANCES	RECONVERSIONS	RECRUITERS	RECYCLATES	REDETERMINATION	REDISTRICTING
RECONNOITER	RECONVERTED	RECRUITING	RECYCLEABLE	REDETERMINE	REDISTRICTS
RECONNOITERED	RECONVERTING	RECRUITMENT	RECYCLISTS	REDETERMINED	REDIVIDING
RECONNOITERER	RECONVERTS	RECRUITMENTS	REDACTIONAL	REDETERMINES	REDIVISION
RECONNOITERERS	RECONVEYANCE	RECRYSTALLISE	REDACTIONS	REDETERMINING	REDIVISIONS
RECONNOITERING	RECONVEYANCES	RECRYSTALLISED	REDACTORIAL	REDEVELOPED	REDIVORCED
RECONNOITERS	RECONVEYED	RECRYSTALLISES	REDAMAGING	REDEVELOPER	REDIVORCES
RECONNOITRE	RECONVEYING	RECRYSTALLISING	REDARGUING	REDEVELOPERS	REDIVORCING
RECONNOITRED	RECONVICTED	RECRYSTALLIZE	REDBAITERS	REDEVELOPING	REDLININGS
RECONNOITRER	RECONVICTING	RECRYSTALLIZED	REDBAITING	REDEVELOPMENT	REDOLENCES
RECONNOITRERS	RECONVICTION	RECRYSTALLIZES	REDBELLIES	REDEVELOPMENTS	REDOLENCIES
RECONNOITRES	RECONVICTIONS	RECRYSTALLIZING	REDBREASTS	REDEVELOPS	REDOLENTLY
RECONNOITRING	RECONVICTS	RECTANGLED	REDCURRANT	REDIALLING	REDOUBLEMENT
RECONQUERED	RECONVINCE	RECTANGLES	REDCURRANTS	REDICTATED	REDOUBLEMENTS
RECONQUERING	RECONVINCED	RECTANGULAR	REDDISHNESS	REDICTATES	REDOUBLERS
RECONQUERS	RECONVINCES	RECTANGULARITY	REDDISHNESSES	REDICTATING	REDOUBLING
RECONQUEST	RECONVINCING	RECTANGULARLY	REDECIDING	REDIGESTED	REDOUBTABLE
RECONQUESTS	RECORDABLE	RECTIFIABILITY	REDECORATE	REDIGESTING	REDOUBTABLENESS
RECONSECRATE	RECORDATION	RECTIFIABLE	REDECORATED	REDIGESTION	REDOUBTABLY
RECONSECRATED	RECORDATIONS	RECTIFICATION	REDECORATES	REDIGESTIONS	REDOUBTING
RECONSECRATES	RECORDERSHIP	RECTIFICATIONS	REDECORATING	REDIGRESSED	REDOUNDING
RECONSECRATING	RECORDERSHIPS	RECTIFIERS	REDECORATION	REDIGRESSES	REDOUNDINGS
RECONSECRATION	RECORDINGS	RECTIFYING	REDECORATIONS	REDIGRESSING	REDRAFTING
RECONSECRATIONS	RECORDISTS	RECTILINEAL	REDECORATOR	REDINGOTES	REDREAMING
RECONSIDER	RECOUNTALS	RECTILINEALLY	REDECORATORS	REDINTEGRATE	REDRESSABLE
RECONSIDERATION	RECOUNTERS	RECTILINEAR	REDECRAFTS	REDINTEGRATED	REDRESSERS
RECONSIDERED	RECOUNTING	RECTILINEARITY	REDEDICATE	REDINTEGRATES	REDRESSIBLE
RECONSIDERING	RECOUNTMENT	RECTILINEARLY	REDEDICATED	REDINTEGRATING	REDRESSING
RECONSIDERS	RECOUNTMENTS	RECTIPETALIES	REDEDICATES	REDINTEGRATION	REDRESSIVE
RECONSIGNED	RECOUPABLE	RECTIPETALITIES	REDEDICATING	REDINTEGRATIONS	REDRESSORS
RECONSIGNING	RECOUPLING	RECTIPETALITY	REDEDICATION	REDINTEGRATIVE	REDRILLING
RECONSIGNS	RECOUPMENT	RECTIPETALY	REDEDICATIONS	REDIRECTED	REDRUTHITE
RECONSOLED	RECOUPMENTS	RECTIROSTRAL	REDEEMABILITIES	REDIRECTING	REDRUTHITES
RECONSOLES	RECOURSING	RECTISERIAL	REDEEMABILITY	REDIRECTION	REDSHIFTED
RECONSOLIDATE	RECOVERABILITY	RECTITISES	REDEEMABLE	REDIRECTIONS	REDSHIRTED
RECONSOLIDATED	RECOVERABLE	RECTITUDES	REDEEMABLENESS	REDISBURSE	REDSHIRTING
RECONSOLIDATES	RECOVERABLENESS	RECTITUDINOUS	REDEEMABLY	REDISBURSED	REDSTREAKS
RECONSOLIDATING	RECOVEREES	RECTOCELES	REDEEMLESS	REDISBURSES	REDUCIBILITIES
RECONSOLIDATION	RECOVERERS	RECTORATES	REDEFEATED	REDISBURSING	REDUCIBILITY
RECONSOLING	RECOVERIES	RECTORESSES	REDEFEATING	REDISCOUNT	REDUCIBLENESS
RECONSTITUENT	RECOVERING	RECTORIALS	REDEFECTED	REDISCOUNTABLE	REDUCIBLENESSES
RECONSTITUENTS	RECOVERORS	RECTORSHIP	REDEFECTING	REDISCOUNTED	REDUCTANTS
RECONSTITUTABLE	RECOWERING	RECTORSHIPS	REDEFINING	REDISCOUNTING	REDUCTASES
RECONSTITUTE	RECREANCES	RECTRESSES	REDEFINITION	REDISCOUNTS	REDUCTIONAL
RECONSTITUTED	RECREANCIES	RECTRICIAL	REDEFINITIONS	REDISCOVER	REDUCTIONISM
RECONSTITUTES	RECREANTLY	RECULTIVATE	REDELIVERANCE	REDISCOVERED	REDUCTIONISMS
RECONSTITUTING	RECREATING	RECULTIVATED	REDELIVERANCES	REDISCOVERER	REDUCTIONIST
RECONSTITUTION	RECREATION	RECULTIVATES	REDELIVERED	REDISCOVERERS	REDUCTIONISTIC
RECONSTITUTIONS	RECREATIONAL	RECULTIVATING	REDELIVERER	REDISCOVERIES	REDUCTIONISTS
RECONSTRUCT	RECREATIONIST	RECUMBENCE	REDELIVERERS	REDISCOVERING	REDUCTIONS
RECONSTRUCTED	RECREATIONISTS	RECUMBENCES	REDELIVERIES	REDISCOVERS	REDUCTIVELY
RECONSTRUCTIBLE	RECREATIONS	RECUMBENCIES	REDELIVERING	REDISCOVERY	REDUCTIVENESS
RECONSTRUCTING	RECREATIVE	RECUMBENCY	REDELIVERS	REDISCUSSED	REDUCTIVENESSES
RECONSTRUCTION	RECREATIVELY	RECUMBENTLY	REDELIVERY	REDISCUSSES	REDUNDANCE
RECONSTRUCTIONS	RECREATORS	RECUPERABLE	REDEMANDED	REDISCUSSING	REDUNDANCES
RECONSTRUCTIVE	RECREMENTAL	RECUPERATE	REDEMANDING	REDISPLAYED	REDUNDANCIES
RECONSTRUCTOR	RECREMENTITIAL	RECUPERATED	REDEMPTIBLE	REDISPLAYING	REDUNDANCY
RECONSTRUCTORS	RECREMENTITIOUS	RECUPERATES	REDEMPTION	REDISPLAYS	REDUNDANTLY
RECONSTRUCTS	RECREMENTS	RECUPERATING	REDEMPTIONAL	REDISPOSED	REDUPLICATE
RECONSULTED	RECRIMINATE	RECUPERATION	REDEMPTIONER	REDISPOSES	REDUPLICATED
RECONSULTING	RECRIMINATED	RECUPERATIONS	REDEMPTIONERS	REDISPOSING	REDUPLICATES
RECONSULTS	RECRIMINATES	RECUPERATIVE	REDEMPTIONS	REDISPOSITION	REDUPLICATING
RECONTACTED	RECRIMINATING	RECUPERATOR	REDEMPTIVE	REDISPOSITIONS	REDUPLICATION
RECONTACTING	RECRIMINATION	RECUPERATORS	REDEMPTIVELY	REDISSOLUTION	REDUPLICATIONS
RECONTACTS	RECRIMINATIONS	RECUPERATORY	REDEMPTORY	REDISSOLUTIONS	REDUPLICATIVE
RECONTAMINATE	RECRIMINATIVE	RECURELESS	REDEPLOYED	REDISSOLVE	REDUPLICATIVELY
RECONTAMINATED	RECRIMINATOR	RECURRENCE	REDEPLOYING	REDISSOLVED	REEDIFYING
RECONTAMINATES	RECRIMINATORS	RECURRENCES	REDEPLOYMENT	REDISSOLVES	REEDINESSES
RECONTAMINATING	RECRIMINATORY	RECURRENCIES	REDEPLOYMENTS	REDISSOLVING	REEDITIONS
RECONTAMINATION	RECROSSING	RECURRENCY	REDEPOSITED	REDISTILLATION	REEDUCATED
RECONTEXTUALISE	RECROWNING	RECURRENTLY	REDEPOSITING	REDISTILLATIONS	REEDUCATES
RECONTEXTUALIZE	RECRUDESCE	RECURRINGLY	REDEPOSITS	REDISTILLED	REEDUCATING
RECONTINUE		RECURSIONS	REDESCENDED	REDISTILLING	REEDUCATION

REEDUCATIONS
REEDUCATIVE
REEJECTING
REELECTING
REELECTION
REELECTIONS
REELEVATED
REELEVATES
REELEVATING
REELIGIBILITIES
REELIGIBILITY
REELIGIBLE
REEMBARKED
REEMBARKING
REEMBODIED
REEMBODIES
REEMBODYING
REEMBRACED
REEMBRACES
REEMBRACING
REEMBROIDER
REEMBROIDERED
REEMBROIDERING
REEMBROIDERS
REEMERGENCE
REEMERGENCES
REEMERGING
REEMISSION
REEMISSIONS
REEMITTING
REEMPHASES
REEMPHASIS
REEMPHASISE
REEMPHASISED
REEMPHASISES
REEMPHASISING
REEMPHASIZE
REEMPHASIZED
REEMPHASIZES
REEMPHASIZING
REEMPLOYED
REEMPLOYING
REEMPLOYMENT
REEMPLOYMENTS
REENACTING
REENACTMENT
REENACTMENTS
REENACTORS
REENCOUNTER
REENCOUNTERED
REENCOUNTERING
REENCOUNTERS
REENDOWING
REENERGISE
REENERGISED
REENERGISES
REENERGISING
REENERGIZE
REENERGIZED
REENERGIZES
REENERGIZING
REENFORCED
REENFORCES
REENFORCING
REENGAGEMENT
REENGAGEMENTS
REENGAGING
REENGINEER
REENGINEERED
REENGINEERING
REENGINEERS
REENGRAVED
REENGRAVES
REENGRAVING
REENJOYING
REENLARGED
REENLARGES
REENLARGING
REENLISTED
REENLISTING
REENLISTMENT
REENLISTMENTS
REENROLLED

REENROLLING
REENSLAVED
REENSLAVES
REENSLAVING
REENTERING
REENTHRONE
REENTHRONED
REENTHRONES
REENTHRONING
REENTRANCE
REENTRANCES
REENTRANTS
REEQUIPMENT
REEQUIPMENTS
REEQUIPPED
REEQUIPPING
REERECTING
REESCALATE
REESCALATED
REESCALATES
REESCALATING
REESCALATION
REESCALATIONS
REESTABLISH
REESTABLISHED
REESTABLISHES
REESTABLISHING
REESTABLISHMENT
REESTIMATE
REESTIMATED
REESTIMATES
REESTIMATING
REEVALUATE
REEVALUATED
REEVALUATES
REEVALUATING
REEVALUATION
REEVALUATIONS
REEXAMINATION
REEXAMINATIONS
REEXAMINED
REEXAMINES
REEXAMINING
REEXECUTED
REEXECUTES
REEXECUTING
REEXHIBITED
REEXHIBITING
REEXHIBITS
REEXPELLED
REEXPELLING
REEXPERIENCE
REEXPERIENCED
REEXPERIENCES
REEXPERIENCING
REEXPLAINED
REEXPLAINING
REEXPLAINS
REEXPLORED
REEXPLORES
REEXPLORING
REEXPORTATION
REEXPORTATIONS
REEXPORTED
REEXPORTING
REEXPOSING
REEXPOSURE
REEXPOSURES
REEXPRESSED
REEXPRESSES
REEXPRESSING
REFASHIONED
REFASHIONING
REFASHIONMENT
REFASHIONMENTS
REFASHIONS
REFASTENED
REFASTENING
REFECTIONER
REFECTIONERS
REFECTIONS
REFECTORIAN
REFECTORIANS

REFECTORIES
REFEREEING
REFERENCED
REFERENCER
REFERENCERS
REFERENCES
REFERENCING
REFERENDARIES
REFERENDARY
REFERENDUM
REFERENDUMS
REFERENTIAL
REFERENTIALITY
REFERENTIALLY
REFERRABLE
REFERRIBLE
REFIGHTING
REFIGURING
REFILLABLE
REFILTERED
REFILTERING
REFINANCED
REFINANCES
REFINANCING
REFINANCINGS
REFINEDNESS
REFINEDNESSES
REFINEMENT
REFINEMENTS
REFINERIES
REFINISHED
REFINISHER
REFINISHERS
REFINISHES
REFINISHING
REFITMENTS
REFITTINGS
REFLAGGING
REFLATIONARY
REFLATIONS
REFLECTANCE
REFLECTANCES
REFLECTERS
REFLECTING
REFLECTINGLY
REFLECTION
REFLECTIONAL
REFLECTIONLESS
REFLECTIONS
REFLECTIVE
REFLECTIVELY
REFLECTIVENESS
REFLECTIVITIES
REFLECTIVITY
REFLECTOGRAM
REFLECTOGRAMS
REFLECTOGRAPH
REFLECTOGRAPHS
REFLECTOGRAPHY
REFLECTOMETER
REFLECTOMETERS
REFLECTOMETRIES
REFLECTOMETRY
REFLECTORISE
REFLECTORISED
REFLECTORISES
REFLECTORISING
REFLECTORIZE
REFLECTORIZED
REFLECTORIZES
REFLECTORIZING
REFLECTORS
REFLEXIBILITIES
REFLEXIBILITY
REFLEXIBLE
REFLEXIONAL
REFLEXIONS
REFLEXIVELY
REFLEXIVENESS
REFLEXIVENESSES
REFLEXIVES
REFLEXIVITIES
REFLEXIVITY

REFLEXOLOGICAL
REFLEXOLOGIES
REFLEXOLOGIST
REFLEXOLOGISTS
REFLEXOLOGY
REFLOATING
REFLOODING
REFLOWERED
REFLOWERING
REFLOWERINGS
REFLOWINGS
REFLUENCES
REFOCILLATE
REFOCILLATED
REFOCILLATES
REFOCILLATING
REFOCILLATION
REFOCILLATIONS
REFOCUSING
REFOCUSSED
REFOCUSSES
REFOCUSSING
REFORESTATION
REFORESTATIONS
REFORESTED
REFORESTING
REFORMABILITIES
REFORMABILITY
REFORMABLE
REFORMADES
REFORMADOES
REFORMADOS
REFORMATES
REFORMATION
REFORMATIONAL
REFORMATIONIST
REFORMATIONISTS
REFORMATIONS
REFORMATIVE
REFORMATORIES
REFORMATORY
REFORMATTED
REFORMATTING
REFORMINGS
REFORMISMS
REFORMISTS
REFORMULATE
REFORMULATED
REFORMULATES
REFORMULATING
REFORMULATION
REFORMULATIONS
REFORTIFICATION
REFORTIFIED
REFORTIFIES
REFORTIFYING
REFOUNDATION
REFOUNDATIONS
REFOUNDERS
REFOUNDING
REFRACTABLE
REFRACTARIES
REFRACTARY
REFRACTILE
REFRACTING
REFRACTION
REFRACTIONS
REFRACTIVE
REFRACTIVELY
REFRACTIVENESS
REFRACTIVITIES
REFRACTIVITY
REFRACTOMETER
REFRACTOMETERS
REFRACTOMETRIC
REFRACTOMETRIES
REFRACTOMETRY
REFRACTORIES
REFRACTORILY
REFRACTORINESS
REFRACTORS
REFRACTORY
REFRACTURE

REFRACTURES
REFRAINERS
REFRAINING
REFRAINMENT
REFRAINMENTS
REFRANGIBILITY
REFRANGIBLE
REFRANGIBLENESS
REFREEZING
REFRESHENED
REFRESHENER
REFRESHENERS
REFRESHENING
REFRESHENS
REFRESHERS
REFRESHFUL
REFRESHFULLY
REFRESHING
REFRESHINGLY
REFRESHMENT
REFRESHMENTS
REFRIGERANT
REFRIGERANTS
REFRIGERATE
REFRIGERATED
REFRIGERATES
REFRIGERATING
REFRIGERATION
REFRIGERATIONS
REFRIGERATIVE
REFRIGERATOR
REFRIGERATORIES
REFRIGERATORS
REFRIGERATORY
REFRINGENCE
REFRINGENCES
REFRINGENCIES
REFRINGENCY
REFRINGENT
REFRINGING
REFRONTING
REFUELABLE
REFUELLABLE
REFUELLING
REFUGEEISM
REFUGEEISMS
REFULGENCE
REFULGENCES
REFULGENCIES
REFULGENCY
REFULGENTLY
REFUNDABILITIES
REFUNDABILITY
REFUNDABLE
REFUNDMENT
REFUNDMENTS
REFURBISHED
REFURBISHER
REFURBISHERS
REFURBISHES
REFURBISHING
REFURBISHINGS
REFURBISHMENT
REFURBISHMENTS
REFURNISHED
REFURNISHES
REFURNISHING
REFUSENIKS
REFUTABILITIES
REFUTABILITY
REFUTATION
REFUTATIONS
REGAINABLE
REGAINMENT
REGAINMENTS
REGALEMENT
REGALEMENTS
REGALITIES
REGALNESSES
REGARDABLE
REGARDFULLY
REGARDFULNESS
REGARDFULNESSES

REGARDLESS
REGARDLESSLY
REGARDLESSNESS
REGATHERED
REGATHERING
REGELATING
REGELATION
REGELATIONS
REGENERABLE
REGENERACIES
REGENERACY
REGENERATE
REGENERATED
REGENERATELY
REGENERATENESS
REGENERATES
REGENERATING
REGENERATION
REGENERATIONS
REGENERATIVE
REGENERATIVELY
REGENERATOR
REGENERATORS
REGENERATORY
REGENTSHIP
REGENTSHIPS
REGIMENTAL
REGIMENTALLY
REGIMENTALS
REGIMENTATION
REGIMENTATIONS
REGIMENTED
REGIMENTING
REGIONALISATION
REGIONALISE
REGIONALISED
REGIONALISES
REGIONALISING
REGIONALISM
REGIONALISMS
REGIONALIST
REGIONALISTIC
REGIONALISTS
REGIONALIZATION
REGIONALIZE
REGIONALIZED
REGIONALIZES
REGIONALIZING
REGIONALLY
REGISSEURS
REGISTERABLE
REGISTERED
REGISTERER
REGISTERERS
REGISTERING
REGISTRABLE
REGISTRANT
REGISTRANTS
REGISTRARIES
REGISTRARS
REGISTRARSHIP
REGISTRARSHIPS
REGISTRARY
REGISTRATION
REGISTRATIONAL
REGISTRATIONS
REGISTRIES
REGLORIFIED
REGLORIFIES
REGLORIFYING
REGLOSSING
REGNANCIES
REGRAFTING
REGRANTING
REGRATINGS
REGREDIENCE
REGREDIENCES
REGREENING
REGREETING
REGRESSING
REGRESSION
REGRESSIONS
REGRESSIVE

REGRESSIVELY
REGRESSIVENESS
REGRESSIVITIES
REGRESSIVITY
REGRESSORS
REGRETFULLY
REGRETFULNESS
REGRETFULNESSES
REGRETTABLE
REGRETTABLY
REGRETTERS
REGRETTING
REGRINDING
REGROOMING
REGROOVING
REGROUPING
REGUERDONED
REGUERDONING
REGUERDONS
REGULARISATION
REGULARISATIONS
REGULARISE
REGULARISED
REGULARISES
REGULARISING
REGULARITIES
REGULARITY
REGULARIZATION
REGULARIZATIONS
REGULARIZE
REGULARIZED
REGULARIZES
REGULARIZING
REGULATING
REGULATION
REGULATIONS
REGULATIVE
REGULATIVELY
REGULATORS
REGULATORY
REGULISING
REGULIZING
REGURGITANT
REGURGITANTS
REGURGITATE
REGURGITATED
REGURGITATES
REGURGITATING
REGURGITATION
REGURGITATIONS
REHABILITANT
REHABILITANTS
REHABILITATE
REHABILITATED
REHABILITATES
REHABILITATING
REHABILITATION
REHABILITATIONS
REHABILITATIVE
REHABILITATOR
REHABILITATORS
REHAMMERED
REHAMMERING
REHANDLING
REHANDLINGS
REHARDENED
REHARDENING
REHEARINGS
REHEARSALS
REHEARSERS
REHEARSING
REHEARSINGS
REHEATINGS
REHOSPITALISE
REHOSPITALISED
REHOSPITALISES
REHOSPITALISING
REHOSPITALIZE
REHOSPITALIZED
REHOSPITALIZES
REHOSPITALIZING
REHOUSINGS
REHUMANISE

REHUMANISED
REHUMANISES
REHUMANISING
REHUMANIZE
REHUMANIZED
REHUMANIZES
REHUMANIZING
REHYDRATABLE
REHYDRATED
REHYDRATES
REHYDRATING
REHYDRATION
REHYDRATIONS
REHYPNOTISE
REHYPNOTISED
REHYPNOTISES
REHYPNOTISING
REHYPNOTIZE
REHYPNOTIZED
REHYPNOTIZES
REHYPNOTIZING
REICHSMARK
REICHSMARKS
REIDENTIFIED
REIDENTIFIES
REIDENTIFY
REIDENTIFYING
REIFICATION
REIFICATIONS
REIFICATORY
REIGNITING
REIGNITION
REIGNITIONS
REILLUMINE
REILLUMINED
REILLUMINES
REILLUMING
REILLUMINING
REIMAGINED
REIMAGINES
REIMAGINING
REIMBURSABLE
REIMBURSED
REIMBURSEMENT
REIMBURSEMENTS
REIMBURSER
REIMBURSERS
REIMBURSES
REIMBURSING
REIMMERSED
REIMMERSES
REIMMERSING
REIMPLANTATION
REIMPLANTATIONS
REIMPLANTED
REIMPLANTING
REIMPLANTS
REIMPORTATION
REIMPORTATIONS
REIMPORTED
REIMPORTER
REIMPORTERS
REIMPORTING
REIMPOSING
REIMPOSITION
REIMPOSITIONS
REIMPRESSION
REIMPRESSIONS
REINCARNATE
REINCARNATED
REINCARNATES
REINCARNATING
REINCARNATION
REINCARNATIONS
REINCITING
REINCORPORATE
REINCORPORATED
REINCORPORATES
REINCORPORATING
REINCORPORATION
REINCREASE
REINCREASED
REINCREASES

REINCREASING
REINCURRED
REINCURRING
REINDEXING
REINDICTED
REINDICTING
REINDICTMENT
REINDICTMENTS
REINDUCING
REINDUCTED
REINDUCTING
REINDUSTRIALISE
REINDUSTRIALIZE
REINFECTED
REINFECTING
REINFECTION
REINFECTIONS
REINFESTATION
REINFESTATIONS
REINFLAMED
REINFLAMES
REINFLAMING
REINFLATED
REINFLATES
REINFLATING
REINFLATION
REINFLATIONS
REINFORCEABLE
REINFORCED
REINFORCEMENT
REINFORCEMENTS
REINFORCER
REINFORCERS
REINFORCES
REINFORCING
REINFORMED
REINFORMING
REINFUNDED
REINFUNDING
REINFUSING
REINHABITED
REINHABITING
REINHABITS
REINITIATE
REINITIATED
REINITIATES
REINITIATING
REINJECTED
REINJECTING
REINJECTION
REINJECTIONS
REINJURIES
REINJURING
REINNERVATE
REINNERVATED
REINNERVATES
REINNERVATING
REINNERVATION
REINNERVATIONS
REINOCULATE
REINOCULATED
REINOCULATES
REINOCULATING
REINOCULATION
REINOCULATIONS
REINSERTED
REINSERTING
REINSERTION
REINSERTIONS
REINSPECTED
REINSPECTING
REINSPECTION
REINSPECTIONS
REINSPECTS
REINSPIRED
REINSPIRES
REINSPIRING
REINSPIRIT
REINSPIRITED
REINSPIRITING
REINSPIRITS
REINSTALLATION
REINSTALLATIONS

REINSTALLED
REINSTALLING
REINSTALLS
REINSTALMENT
REINSTALMENTS
REINSTATED
REINSTATEMENT
REINSTATEMENTS
REINSTATES
REINSTATING
REINSTATION
REINSTATIONS
REINSTATOR
REINSTATORS
REINSTITUTE
REINSTITUTED
REINSTITUTES
REINSTITUTING
REINSURANCE
REINSURANCES
REINSURERS
REINSURING
REINTEGRATE
REINTEGRATED
REINTEGRATES
REINTEGRATING
REINTEGRATION
REINTEGRATIONS
REINTEGRATIVE
REINTERMENT
REINTERMENTS
REINTERPRET
REINTERPRETED
REINTERPRETING
REINTERPRETS
REINTERRED
REINTERRING
REINTERROGATE
REINTERROGATED
REINTERROGATES
REINTERROGATING
REINTERROGATION
REINTERVIEW
REINTERVIEWED
REINTERVIEWING
REINTERVIEWS
REINTRODUCE
REINTRODUCED
REINTRODUCES
REINTRODUCING
REINTRODUCTION
REINTRODUCTIONS
REINVADING
REINVASION
REINVASIONS
REINVENTED
REINVENTING
REINVENTION
REINVENTIONS
REINVESTED
REINVESTIGATE
REINVESTIGATED
REINVESTIGATES
REINVESTIGATING
REINVESTIGATION
REINVESTING
REINVESTMENT
REINVESTMENTS
REINVIGORATE
REINVIGORATED
REINVIGORATES
REINVIGORATING
REINVIGORATION
REINVIGORATIONS
REINVIGORATOR
REINVIGORATORS
REINVITING
REINVOKING
REINVOLVED
REINVOLVES
REINVOLVING
REIOYNDURE
REIOYNDURES

REISSUABLE
REISTAFELS
REITERANCE
REITERANCES
REITERATED
REITERATEDLY
REITERATES
REITERATING
REITERATION
REITERATIONS
REITERATIVE
REITERATIVELY
REITERATIVES
REJACKETED
REJACKETING
REJECTABLE
REJECTAMENTA
REJECTIBLE
REJECTINGLY
REJECTIONIST
REJECTIONISTS
REJECTIONS
REJIGGERED
REJIGGERING
REJOICEFUL
REJOICEMENT
REJOICEMENTS
REJOICINGLY
REJOICINGS
REJOINDERS
REJOINDURE
REJOINDURES
REJONEADOR
REJONEADORA
REJONEADORAS
REJONEADORES
REJOURNING
REJUGGLING
REJUSTIFIED
REJUSTIFIES
REJUSTIFYING
REJUVENATE
REJUVENATED
REJUVENATES
REJUVENATING
REJUVENATION
REJUVENATIONS
REJUVENATOR
REJUVENATORS
REJUVENESCE
REJUVENESCED
REJUVENESCENCE
REJUVENESCENCES
REJUVENESCENT
REJUVENESCING
REJUVENISE
REJUVENISED
REJUVENISES
REJUVENISING
REJUVENIZE
REJUVENIZED
REJUVENIZES
REJUVENIZING
REKEYBOARD
REKEYBOARDED
REKEYBOARDING
REKEYBOARDS
REKINDLING
REKNITTING
REKNOTTING
RELABELING
RELABELLED
RELABELLING
RELACQUERED
RELACQUERING
RELACQUERS
RELANDSCAPE
RELANDSCAPED
RELANDSCAPES
RELANDSCAPING
RELATEDNESS
RELATEDNESSES

RELATIONAL
RELATIONALLY
RELATIONISM
RELATIONISMS
RELATIONIST
RELATIONISTS
RELATIONLESS
RELATIONSHIP
RELATIONSHIPS
RELATIVELY
RELATIVENESS
RELATIVENESSES
RELATIVISATION
RELATIVISATIONS
RELATIVISE
RELATIVISED
RELATIVISES
RELATIVISING
RELATIVISM
RELATIVISMS
RELATIVIST
RELATIVISTIC
RELATIVISTS
RELATIVITIES
RELATIVITIST
RELATIVITISTS
RELATIVITY
RELATIVIZATION
RELATIVIZATIONS
RELATIVIZE
RELATIVIZED
RELATIVIZES
RELATIVIZING
RELAUNCHED
RELAUNCHES
RELAUNCHING
RELAUNDERED
RELAUNDERING
RELAUNDERS
RELAXATION
RELAXATIONS
RELAXATIVE
RELAXEDNESS
RELAXEDNESSES
RELEARNING
RELEASABLE
RELEASEMENT
RELEASEMENTS
RELEGATABLE
RELEGATING
RELEGATION
RELEGATIONS
RELENTINGS
RELENTLESS
RELENTLESSLY
RELENTLESSNESS
RELENTMENT
RELENTMENTS
RELETTERED
RELETTERING
RELEVANCES
RELEVANCIES
RELEVANTLY
RELIABILITIES
RELIABILITY
RELIABLENESS
RELIABLENESSES
RELICENSED
RELICENSES
RELICENSING
RELICENSURE
RELICENSURES
RELICTIONS
RELIEFLESS
RELIEVABLE
RELIEVEDLY
RELIGHTING
RELIGIEUSE
RELIGIEUSES
RELIGIONARIES
RELIGIONARY
RELIGIONER
RELIGIONERS

RELIGIONISE
RELIGIONISED
RELIGIONISES
RELIGIONISING
RELIGIONISM
RELIGIONISMS
RELIGIONIST
RELIGIONISTS
RELIGIONIZE
RELIGIONIZED
RELIGIONIZES
RELIGIONIZING
RELIGIONLESS
RELIGIOSELY
RELIGIOSITIES
RELIGIOSITY
RELIGIOUSES
RELIGIOUSLY
RELIGIOUSNESS
RELIGIOUSNESSES
RELINQUISH
RELINQUISHED
RELINQUISHER
RELINQUISHERS
RELINQUISHES
RELINQUISHING
RELINQUISHMENT
RELINQUISHMENTS
RELIQUAIRE
RELIQUAIRES
RELIQUARIES
RELIQUEFIED
RELIQUEFIES
RELIQUEFYING
RELISHABLE
RELIVERING
RELLISHING
RELOCATABLE
RELOCATEES
RELOCATING
RELOCATION
RELOCATIONS
RELOCATORS
RELUBRICATE
RELUBRICATED
RELUBRICATES
RELUBRICATING
RELUBRICATION
RELUBRICATIONS
RELUCTANCE
RELUCTANCES
RELUCTANCIES
RELUCTANCY
RELUCTANTLY
RELUCTATED
RELUCTATES
RELUCTATING
RELUCTATION
RELUCTATIONS
RELUCTIVITIES
RELUCTIVITY
RELUMINING
REMAINDERED
REMAINDERING
REMAINDERMAN
REMAINDERMEN
REMAINDERS
REMANDMENT
REMANDMENTS
REMANENCES
REMANENCIES
REMANUFACTURE
REMANUFACTURED
REMANUFACTURER
REMANUFACTURERS
REMANUFACTURES
REMANUFACTURING
REMARKABILITIES
REMARKABILITY
REMARKABLE
REMARKABLENESS
REMARKABLES
REMARKABLY

REMARKETED
REMARKETING
REMARRIAGE
REMARRIAGES
REMARRYING
REMASTERED
REMASTERING
REMATCHING
REMATERIALISE
REMATERIALISED
REMATERIALISES
REMATERIALISING
REMATERIALIZE
REMATERIALIZED
REMATERIALIZES
REMATERIALIZING
REMEASURED
REMEASUREMENT
REMEASUREMENTS
REMEASURES
REMEASURING
REMEDIABILITIES
REMEDIABILITY
REMEDIABLE
REMEDIABLY
REMEDIALLY
REMEDIATED
REMEDIATES
REMEDIATING
REMEDIATION
REMEDIATIONS
REMEDILESS
REMEDILESSLY
REMEDILESSNESS
REMEMBERABILITY
REMEMBERABLE
REMEMBERABLY
REMEMBERED
REMEMBERER
REMEMBERERS
REMEMBERING
REMEMBRANCE
REMEMBRANCER
REMEMBRANCERS
REMEMBRANCES
REMERCYING
REMIGATING
REMIGATION
REMIGATIONS
REMIGRATED
REMIGRATES
REMIGRATING
REMIGRATION
REMIGRATIONS
REMILITARISE
REMILITARISED
REMILITARISES
REMILITARISING
REMILITARIZE
REMILITARIZED
REMILITARIZES
REMILITARIZING
REMINERALISE
REMINERALISED
REMINERALISES
REMINERALISING
REMINERALIZE
REMINERALIZED
REMINERALIZES
REMINERALIZING
REMINISCED
REMINISCENCE
REMINISCENCES
REMINISCENT
REMINISCENTIAL
REMINISCENTLY
REMINISCENTS
REMINISCER
REMINISCERS
REMINISCING
REMISSIBILITIES
REMISSIBILITY

REMISSIBLE
REMISSIBLENESS
REMISSIBLY
REMISSIONS
REMISSIVELY
REMISSNESS
REMISSNESSES
REMITMENTS
REMITTABLE
REMITTANCE
REMITTANCES
REMITTENCE
REMITTENCES
REMITTENCIES
REMITTENCY
REMITTENTLY
REMIXTURES
REMOBILISATION
REMOBILISATIONS
REMOBILISE
REMOBILISED
REMOBILISES
REMOBILISING
REMOBILIZATION
REMOBILIZATIONS
REMOBILIZE
REMOBILIZED
REMOBILIZES
REMOBILIZING
REMODELERS
REMODELING
REMODELLED
REMODELLING
REMODIFIED
REMODIFIES
REMODIFYING
REMOISTENED
REMOISTENING
REMOISTENS
REMONETISATION
REMONETISATIONS
REMONETISE
REMONETISED
REMONETISES
REMONETISING
REMONETIZATION
REMONETIZATIONS
REMONETIZE
REMONETIZED
REMONETIZES
REMONETIZING
REMONSTRANCE
REMONSTRANCES
REMONSTRANT
REMONSTRANTLY
REMONSTRANTS
REMONSTRATE
REMONSTRATED
REMONSTRATES
REMONSTRATING
REMONSTRATINGLY
REMONSTRATION
REMONSTRATIONS
REMONSTRATIVE
REMONSTRATIVELY
REMONSTRATOR
REMONSTRATORS
REMONSTRATORY
REMONTANTS
REMONTOIRE
REMONTOIRES
REMONTOIRS
REMORALISATION
REMORALISATIONS
REMORALISE
REMORALISED
REMORALISING
REMORALIZATION
REMORALIZATIONS
REMORALIZE
REMORALIZED
REMORALIZES

REMORALIZING
REMORSEFUL
REMORSEFULLY
REMORSEFULNESS
REMORSELESS
REMORSELESSLY
REMORSELESSNESS
REMORTGAGE
REMORTGAGED
REMORTGAGES
REMORTGAGING
REMOTENESS
REMOTENESSES
REMOTIVATE
REMOTIVATED
REMOTIVATES
REMOTIVATING
REMOTIVATION
REMOTIVATIONS
REMOULADES
REMOULDING
REMOUNTING
REMOVABILITIES
REMOVABILITY
REMOVABLENESS
REMOVABLENESSES
REMOVALIST
REMOVALISTS
REMOVEABLE
REMOVEDNESS
REMOVEDNESSES
REMUNERABILITY
REMUNERABLE
REMUNERATE
REMUNERATED
REMUNERATES
REMUNERATING
REMUNERATION
REMUNERATIONS
REMUNERATIVE
REMUNERATIVELY
REMUNERATOR
REMUNERATORS
REMUNERATORY
REMURMURED
REMURMURING
REMYTHOLOGISE
REMYTHOLOGISED
REMYTHOLOGISES
REMYTHOLOGISING
REMYTHOLOGIZE
REMYTHOLOGIZED
REMYTHOLOGIZES
REMYTHOLOGIZING
RENAISSANCE
RENAISSANCES
RENASCENCE
RENASCENCES
RENATIONALISE
RENATIONALISED
RENATIONALISES
RENATIONALISING
RENATIONALIZE
RENATIONALIZED
RENATIONALIZES
RENATIONALIZING
RENATURATION
RENATURATIONS
RENATURING
RENCONTRES
RENCOUNTER
RENCOUNTERED
RENCOUNTERING
RENCOUNTERS
RENDERABLE
RENDERINGS
RENDEZVOUS
RENDEZVOUSED
RENDEZVOUSES
RENDEZVOUSING
RENDITIONS
RENEGADING
RENEGADOES

RENEGATION
RENEGATIONS
RENEGOTIABLE
RENEGOTIATE
RENEGOTIATED
RENEGOTIATES
RENEGOTIATING
RENEGOTIATION
RENEGOTIATIONS
RENEWABILITIES
RENEWABILITY
RENEWABLES
RENEWEDNESS
RENEWEDNESSES
RENFORCING
RENITENCES
RENITENCIES
RENOGRAPHIC
RENOGRAPHIES
RENOGRAPHY
RENOMINATE
RENOMINATED
RENOMINATES
RENOMINATING
RENOMINATION
RENOMINATIONS
RENORMALISATION
RENORMALISE
RENORMALISED
RENORMALISES
RENORMALISING
RENORMALIZATION
RENORMALIZE
RENORMALIZED
RENORMALIZES
RENORMALIZING
RENOSTERVELD
RENOSTERVELDS
RENOTIFIED
RENOTIFIES
RENOTIFYING
RENOUNCEABLE
RENOUNCEMENT
RENOUNCEMENTS
RENOUNCERS
RENOUNCING
RENOVASCULAR
RENOVATING
RENOVATION
RENOVATIONS
RENOVATIVE
RENOVATORS
RENSSELAERITE
RENSSELAERITES
RENTABILITIES
RENTABILITY
RENTALLERS
RENUMBERED
RENUMBERING
RENUNCIATE
RENUNCIATES
RENUNCIATION
RENUNCIATIONS
RENUNCIATIVE
RENUNCIATORY
RENVERSEMENT
RENVERSEMENTS
RENVERSING
REOBJECTED
REOBJECTING
REOBSERVED
REOBSERVES
REOBSERVING
REOBTAINED
REOBTAINING
REOCCUPATION
REOCCUPATIONS
REOCCUPIED
REOCCUPIES
REOCCUPYING
REOCCURRED
REOCCURRENCE
REOCCURRENCES

REOCCURRING
REOFFENDED
REOFFENDER
REOFFENDERS
REOFFENDING
REOFFERING
REOPERATED
REOPERATES
REOPERATING
REOPERATION
REOPERATIONS
REOPPOSING
REORCHESTRATE
REORCHESTRATED
REORCHESTRATES
REORCHESTRATING
REORCHESTRATION
REORDAINED
REORDAINING
REORDERING
REORDINATION
REORDINATIONS
REORGANISATION
REORGANISATIONS
REORGANISE
REORGANISED
REORGANISER
REORGANISERS
REORGANISES
REORGANISING
REORGANIZATION
REORGANIZATIONS
REORGANIZE
REORGANIZED
REORGANIZER
REORGANIZERS
REORGANIZES
REORGANIZING
REORIENTATE
REORIENTATED
REORIENTATES
REORIENTATING
REORIENTATION
REORIENTATIONS
REORIENTED
REORIENTING
REOUTFITTED
REOUTFITTING
REOVIRUSES
REOXIDATION
REOXIDATIONS
REOXIDISED
REOXIDISES
REOXIDISING
REOXIDIZED
REOXIDIZES
REOXIDIZING
REPACIFIED
REPACIFIES
REPACIFYING
REPACKAGED
REPACKAGER
REPACKAGERS
REPACKAGES
REPACKAGING
REPAGINATE
REPAGINATED
REPAGINATES
REPAGINATING
REPAGINATION
REPAGINATIONS
REPAINTING
REPAINTINGS
REPAIRABILITIES
REPAIRABILITY
REPAIRABLE
REPANELING
REPANELLED
REPANELLING
REPAPERING
REPARABILITIES
REPARABILITY
REPARATION

REPARATIONS
REPARATIVE
REPARATORY
REPARTEEING
REPARTITION
REPARTITIONED
REPARTITIONING
REPARTITIONS
REPASSAGES
REPASTURES
REPATCHING
REPATRIATE
REPATRIATED
REPATRIATES
REPATRIATING
REPATRIATION
REPATRIATIONS
REPATRIATOR
REPATRIATORS
REPATTERNED
REPATTERNING
REPATTERNS
REPAYMENTS
REPEALABLE
REPEATABILITIES
REPEATABILITY
REPEATABLE
REPEATEDLY
REPEATINGS
REPECHAGES
REPELLANCE
REPELLANCES
REPELLANCIES
REPELLANCY
REPELLANTLY
REPELLANTS
REPELLENCE
REPELLENCES
REPELLENCIES
REPELLENCY
REPELLENTLY
REPELLENTS
REPELLINGLY
REPENTANCE
REPENTANCES
REPENTANTLY
REPENTANTS
REPENTINGLY
REPEOPLING
REPERCUSSED
REPERCUSSES
REPERCUSSING
REPERCUSSION
REPERCUSSIONS
REPERCUSSIVE
REPERTOIRE
REPERTOIRES
REPERTORIAL
REPERTORIES
REPERUSALS
REPERUSING
REPETITEUR
REPETITEURS
REPETITEUSE
REPETITEUSES
REPETITION
REPETITIONAL
REPETITIONARY
REPETITIONS
REPETITIOUS
REPETITIOUSLY
REPETITIOUSNESS
REPETITIVE
REPETITIVELY
REPETITIVENESS
REPHOTOGRAPH
REPHOTOGRAPHED
REPHOTOGRAPHING
REPHOTOGRAPHS
REPHRASING
REPIGMENTED
REPIGMENTING
REPIGMENTS

REPINEMENT
REPINEMENTS
REPININGLY
REPLACEABILITY
REPLACEABLE
REPLACEMENT
REPLACEMENTS
REPLANNING
REPLANTATION
REPLANTATIONS
REPLANTING
REPLASTERED
REPLASTERING
REPLASTERS
REPLEADERS
REPLEADING
REPLEDGING
REPLENISHABLE
REPLENISHED
REPLENISHER
REPLENISHERS
REPLENISHES
REPLENISHING
REPLENISHMENT
REPLENISHMENTS
REPLETENESS
REPLETENESSES
REPLETIONS
REPLEVIABLE
REPLEVINED
REPLEVINING
REPLEVISABLE
REPLEVYING
REPLICABILITIES
REPLICABILITY
REPLICABLE
REPLICASES
REPLICATED
REPLICATES
REPLICATING
REPLICATION
REPLICATIONS
REPLICATIVE
REPLICATOR
REPLICATORS
REPLOTTING
REPLUMBING
REPLUNGING
REPOINTING
REPOLARISATION
REPOLARISATIONS
REPOLARISE
REPOLARISED
REPOLARISES
REPOLARISING
REPOLARIZATION
REPOLARIZATIONS
REPOLARIZE
REPOLARIZED
REPOLARIZES
REPOLARIZING
REPOLISHED
REPOLISHES
REPOLISHING
REPOPULARISE
REPOPULARISED
REPOPULARISES
REPOPULARISING
REPOPULARIZE
REPOPULARIZED
REPOPULARIZES
REPOPULARIZING
REPOPULATE
REPOPULATED
REPOPULATES
REPOPULATING
REPOPULATION
REPOPULATIONS
REPORTABLE
REPORTAGES
REPORTEDLY
REPORTINGLY
REPORTINGS

REPORTORIAL
REPORTORIALLY
REPOSEDNESS
REPOSEDNESSES
REPOSEFULLY
REPOSEFULNESS
REPOSEFULNESSES
REPOSITING
REPOSITION
REPOSITIONED
REPOSITIONING
REPOSITIONS
REPOSITORIES
REPOSITORS
REPOSITORY
REPOSSESSED
REPOSSESSES
REPOSSESSING
REPOSSESSION
REPOSSESSIONS
REPOSSESSOR
REPOSSESSORS
REPOTTINGS
REPOUSSAGE
REPOUSSAGES
REPOUSSOIR
REPOUSSOIRS
REPOWERING
REPREEVING
REPREHENDABLE
REPREHENDED
REPREHENDER
REPREHENDERS
REPREHENDING
REPREHENDS
REPREHENSIBLE
REPREHENSIBLY
REPREHENSION
REPREHENSIONS
REPREHENSIVE
REPREHENSIVELY
REPREHENSORY
REPRESENTABLE
REPRESENTAMEN
REPRESENTAMENS
REPRESENTANT
REPRESENTANTS
REPRESENTATION
REPRESENTATIONS
REPRESENTATIVE
REPRESENTATIVES
REPRESENTED
REPRESENTEE
REPRESENTEES
REPRESENTER
REPRESENTERS
REPRESENTING
REPRESENTMENT
REPRESENTMENTS
REPRESENTOR
REPRESENTORS
REPRESENTS
REPRESSERS
REPRESSIBILITY
REPRESSIBLE
REPRESSIBLY
REPRESSING
REPRESSION
REPRESSIONIST
REPRESSIONS
REPRESSIVE
REPRESSIVELY
REPRESSIVENESS
REPRESSORS
REPRESSURISE
REPRESSURISED
REPRESSURISES
REPRESSURISING
REPRESSURIZE
REPRESSURIZED
REPRESSURIZES
REPRESSURIZING
REPRIEVABLE

REPRIEVALS
REPRIEVERS
REPRIEVING
REPRIMANDED
REPRIMANDING
REPRIMANDS
REPRINTERS
REPRINTING
REPRISTINATE
REPRISTINATED
REPRISTINATES
REPRISTINATING
REPRISTINATION
REPRISTINATIONS
REPRIVATISATION
REPRIVATISE
REPRIVATISED
REPRIVATISES
REPRIVATISING
REPRIVATIZATION
REPRIVATIZE
REPRIVATIZED
REPRIVATIZES
REPRIVATIZING
REPROACHABLE
REPROACHABLY
REPROACHED
REPROACHER
REPROACHERS
REPROACHES
REPROACHFUL
REPROACHFULLY
REPROACHFULNESS
REPROACHING
REPROACHINGLY
REPROACHLESS
REPROBACIES
REPROBANCE
REPROBANCES
REPROBATED
REPROBATER
REPROBATERS
REPROBATES
REPROBATING
REPROBATION
REPROBATIONARY
REPROBATIONS
REPROBATIVE
REPROBATIVELY
REPROBATOR
REPROBATORS
REPROBATORY
REPROCESSED
REPROCESSES
REPROCESSING
REPRODUCED
REPRODUCER
REPRODUCERS
REPRODUCES
REPRODUCIBILITY
REPRODUCIBLE
REPRODUCIBLES
REPRODUCIBLY
REPRODUCING
REPRODUCTION
REPRODUCTIONS
REPRODUCTIVE
REPRODUCTIVELY
REPRODUCTIVES
REPRODUCTIVITY
REPROGRAMED
REPROGRAMING
REPROGRAMMABLE
REPROGRAMME
REPROGRAMMED
REPROGRAMMES
REPROGRAMMING
REPROGRAMS
REPROGRAPHER
REPROGRAPHERS
REPROGRAPHIC
REPROGRAPHICS
REPROGRAPHIES

REPROGRAPHY
REPROOFING
REPROVABLE
REPROVINGLY
REPROVINGS
REPROVISION
REPROVISIONED
REPROVISIONING
REPROVISIONS
REPTATIONS
REPTILIANLY
REPTILIANS
REPTILIFEROUS
REPTILIOUS
REPUBLICAN
REPUBLICANISE
REPUBLICANISED
REPUBLICANISES
REPUBLICANISING
REPUBLICANISM
REPUBLICANISMS
REPUBLICANIZE
REPUBLICANIZED
REPUBLICANIZES
REPUBLICANIZING
REPUBLICANS
REPUBLICATION
REPUBLICATIONS
REPUBLISHED
REPUBLISHER
REPUBLISHERS
REPUBLISHES
REPUBLISHING
REPUDIABLE
REPUDIATED
REPUDIATES
REPUDIATING
REPUDIATION
REPUDIATIONIST
REPUDIATIONISTS
REPUDIATIONS
REPUDIATIVE
REPUDIATOR
REPUDIATORS
REPUGNANCE
REPUGNANCES
REPUGNANCIES
REPUGNANCY
REPUGNANTLY
REPULSIONS
REPULSIVELY
REPULSIVENESS
REPULSIVENESSES
REPUNCTUATION
REPUNCTUATIONS
REPURCHASE
REPURCHASED
REPURCHASES
REPURCHASING
REPURIFIED
REPURIFIES
REPURIFYING
REPURPOSED
REPURPOSES
REPURPOSING
REPURSUING
REPUTABILITIES
REPUTABILITY
REPUTATION
REPUTATIONAL
REPUTATIONLESS
REPUTATIONS
REPUTATIVE
REPUTATIVELY
REPUTELESS
REQUALIFIED
REQUALIFIES
REQUALIFYING
REQUESTERS
REQUESTING
REQUESTORS
REQUICKENED
REQUICKENING

REQUICKENS
REQUIESCAT
REQUIESCATS
REQUIGHTED
REQUIGHTING
REQUIRABLE
REQUIREMENT
REQUIREMENTS
REQUIRINGS
REQUISITELY
REQUISITENESS
REQUISITENESSES
REQUISITES
REQUISITION
REQUISITIONARY
REQUISITIONED
REQUISITIONING
REQUISITIONIST
REQUISITIONISTS
REQUISITIONS
REQUISITOR
REQUISITORS
REQUISITORY
REQUITABLE
REQUITEFUL
REQUITELESS
REQUITEMENT
REQUITEMENTS
REQUITTING
REQUOYLING
RERADIATED
RERADIATES
RERADIATING
RERADIATION
RERADIATIONS
REREADINGS
REREBRACES
RERECORDED
RERECORDING
REREDORTER
REREDORTERS
REREDOSSES
REREGISTER
REREGISTERED
REREGISTERING
REREGISTERS
REREGISTRATION
REREGISTRATIONS
REREGULATE
REREGULATED
REREGULATES
REREGULATING
REREGULATION
REREGULATIONS
RERELEASED
RERELEASES
RERELEASING
REREMINDED
REREMINDING
REREPEATED
REREPEATING
REREVIEWED
REREVIEWING
REREVISING
REROUTEING
RESADDLING
RESALEABLE
RESALUTING
RESAMPLING
RESCHEDULE
RESCHEDULED
RESCHEDULES
RESCHEDULING
RESCHEDULINGS
RESCHOOLED
RESCHOOLING
RESCINDABLE
RESCINDERS
RESCINDING
RESCINDMENT
RESCINDMENTS
RESCISSIBLE
RESCISSION

RESCISSIONS
RESCISSORY
RESCREENED
RESCREENING
RESCRIPTED
RESCRIPTING
RESCULPTED
RESCULPTING
RESEALABLE
RESEARCHABLE
RESEARCHED
RESEARCHER
RESEARCHERS
RESEARCHES
RESEARCHFUL
RESEARCHING
RESEARCHIST
RESEARCHISTS
RESEASONED
RESEASONING
RESECTABILITIES
RESECTABILITY
RESECTABLE
RESECTIONAL
RESECTIONS
RESECURING
RESEGREGATE
RESEGREGATED
RESEGREGATES
RESEGREGATING
RESEGREGATION
RESEGREGATIONS
RESEIZURES
RESELECTED
RESELECTING
RESELECTION
RESELECTIONS
RESEMBLANCE
RESEMBLANCES
RESEMBLANT
RESEMBLERS
RESEMBLING
RESENSITISE
RESENSITISED
RESENSITISES
RESENSITISING
RESENSITIZE
RESENSITIZED
RESENSITIZES
RESENSITIZING
RESENTENCE
RESENTENCED
RESENTENCES
RESENTENCING
RESENTFULLY
RESENTFULNESS
RESENTFULNESSES
RESENTINGLY
RESENTMENT
RESENTMENTS
RESERPINES
RESERVABLE
RESERVATION
RESERVATIONIST
RESERVATIONISTS
RESERVATIONS
RESERVATORIES
RESERVATORY
RESERVEDLY
RESERVEDNESS
RESERVEDNESSES
RESERVICED
RESERVICES
RESERVICING
RESERVISTS
RESERVOIRED
RESERVOIRING
RESERVOIRS
RESETTABLE
RESETTLEMENT
RESETTLEMENTS
RESETTLING
RESHARPENED

RESHARPENING
RESHARPENS
RESHINGLED
RESHINGLES
RESHINGLING
RESHIPMENT
RESHIPMENTS
RESHIPPERS
RESHIPPING
RESHOOTING
RESHOWERED
RESHOWERING
RESHUFFLED
RESHUFFLES
RESHUFFLING
RESIDENCES
RESIDENCIES
RESIDENTER
RESIDENTERS
RESIDENTIAL
RESIDENTIALLY
RESIDENTIARIES
RESIDENTIARY
RESIDENTSHIP
RESIDENTSHIPS
RESIDUALLY
RESIGHTING
RESIGNATION
RESIGNATIONS
RESIGNEDLY
RESIGNEDNESS
RESIGNEDNESSES
RESIGNMENT
RESIGNMENTS
RESILEMENT
RESILEMENTS
RESILIENCE
RESILIENCES
RESILIENCIES
RESILIENCY
RESILIENTLY
RESILVERED
RESILVERING
RESINATING
RESINIFEROUS
RESINIFICATION
RESINIFICATIONS
RESINIFIED
RESINIFIES
RESINIFYING
RESINISING
RESINIZING
RESINOUSLY
RESINOUSNESS
RESINOUSNESSES
RESIPISCENCE
RESIPISCENCES
RESIPISCENCIES
RESIPISCENCY
RESIPISCENT
RESISTANCE
RESISTANCES
RESISTANTS
RESISTENTS
RESISTIBILITIES
RESISTIBILITY
RESISTIBLE
RESISTIBLY
RESISTINGLY
RESISTIVELY
RESISTIVENESS
RESISTIVENESSES
RESISTIVITIES
RESISTIVITY
RESISTLESS
RESISTLESSLY
RESISTLESSNESS
RESITTINGS
RESITUATED
RESITUATES
RESITUATING
RESKETCHED
RESKETCHES

RESKETCHING
RESKILLING
RESKILLINGS
RESMELTING
RESMOOTHED
RESMOOTHING
RESNATRONS
RESOCIALISATION
RESOCIALISE
RESOCIALISED
RESOCIALISES
RESOCIALISING
RESOCIALIZATION
RESOCIALIZE
RESOCIALIZED
RESOCIALIZES
RESOCIALIZING
RESOFTENED
RESOFTENING
RESOLDERED
RESOLDERING
RESOLIDIFIED
RESOLIDIFIES
RESOLIDIFY
RESOLIDIFYING
RESOLUBILITIES
RESOLUBILITY
RESOLUBLENESS
RESOLUBLENESSES
RESOLUTELY
RESOLUTENESS
RESOLUTENESSES
RESOLUTEST
RESOLUTION
RESOLUTIONER
RESOLUTIONERS
RESOLUTIONIST
RESOLUTIONISTS
RESOLUTIONS
RESOLUTIVE
RESOLVABILITIES
RESOLVABILITY
RESOLVABLE
RESOLVABLENESS
RESOLVEDLY
RESOLVEDNESS
RESOLVEDNESSES
RESOLVENTS
RESONANCES
RESONANTLY
RESONATING
RESONATION
RESONATIONS
RESONATORS
RESORBENCE
RESORBENCES
RESORCINAL
RESORCINOL
RESORCINOLS
RESORPTION
RESORPTIONS
RESORPTIVE
RESOUNDING
RESOUNDINGLY
RESOURCEFUL
RESOURCEFULLY
RESOURCEFULNESS
RESOURCELESS
RESOURCING
RESPEAKING
RESPECIFIED
RESPECIFIES
RESPECIFYING
RESPECTABILISE
RESPECTABILISED
RESPECTABILISES
RESPECTABILITY
RESPECTABILIZE
RESPECTABILIZED
RESPECTABILIZES
RESPECTABLE
RESPECTABLENESS
RESPECTABLES

RESPECTABLY
RESPECTANT
RESPECTERS
RESPECTFUL
RESPECTFULLY
RESPECTFULNESS
RESPECTING
RESPECTIVE
RESPECTIVELY
RESPECTIVENESS
RESPECTLESS
RESPELLING
RESPELLINGS
RESPIRABILITIES
RESPIRABILITY
RESPIRABLE
RESPIRATION
RESPIRATIONAL
RESPIRATIONS
RESPIRATOR
RESPIRATORS
RESPIRATORY
RESPIRITUALISE
RESPIRITUALISED
RESPIRITUALISES
RESPIRITUALIZE
RESPIRITUALIZED
RESPIRITUALIZES
RESPIROMETER
RESPIROMETERS
RESPIROMETRIC
RESPIROMETRIES
RESPIROMETRY
RESPITELESS
RESPLENDED
RESPLENDENCE
RESPLENDENCES
RESPLENDENCIES
RESPLENDENCY
RESPLENDENT
RESPLENDENTLY
RESPLENDING
RESPLICING
RESPLITTING
RESPONDENCE
RESPONDENCES
RESPONDENCIES
RESPONDENCY
RESPONDENT
RESPONDENTIA
RESPONDENTIAS
RESPONDENTS
RESPONDERS
RESPONDING
RESPONSELESS
RESPONSERS
RESPONSIBILITY
RESPONSIBLE
RESPONSIBLENESS
RESPONSIBLY
RESPONSIONS
RESPONSIVE
RESPONSIVELY
RESPONSIVENESS
RESPONSORIAL
RESPONSORIALS
RESPONSORIES
RESPONSORS
RESPONSORY
RESPONSUMS
RESPOOLING
RESPOTTING
RESPRAYING
RESPREADING
RESPRINGING
RESPROUTED
RESPROUTING
RESSALDARS
RESSENTIMENT
RESSENTIMENTS
RESTABILISE
RESTABILISED
RESTABILISES

RESTABILISING
RESTABILIZE
RESTABILIZED
RESTABILIZES
RESTABILIZING
RESTABLING
RESTACKING
RESTAFFING
RESTAMPING
RESTARTABLE
RESTARTERS
RESTARTING
RESTATEMENT
RESTATEMENTS
RESTATIONED
RESTATIONING
RESTATIONS
RESTAURANT
RESTAURANTEUR
RESTAURANTEURS
RESTAURANTS
RESTAURATEUR
RESTAURATEURS
RESTAURATION
RESTAURATIONS
RESTEMMING
RESTFULLER
RESTFULLEST
RESTFULNESS
RESTFULNESSES
RESTHARROW
RESTHARROWS
RESTIMULATE
RESTIMULATED
RESTIMULATES
RESTIMULATING
RESTIMULATION
RESTIMULATIONS
RESTITCHED
RESTITCHES
RESTITCHING
RESTITUTED
RESTITUTES
RESTITUTING
RESTITUTION
RESTITUTIONISM
RESTITUTIONISMS
RESTITUTIONIST
RESTITUTIONISTS
RESTITUTIONS
RESTITUTIVE
RESTITUTOR
RESTITUTORS
RESTITUTORY
RESTIVENESS
RESTIVENESSES
RESTLESSLY
RESTLESSNESS
RESTLESSNESSES
RESTOCKING
RESTORABLE
RESTORABLENESS
RESTORATION
RESTORATIONISM
RESTORATIONISMS
RESTORATIONIST
RESTORATIONISTS
RESTORATIONS
RESTORATIVE
RESTORATIVELY
RESTORATIVES
RESTRAINABLE
RESTRAINED
RESTRAINEDLY
RESTRAINEDNESS
RESTRAINER
RESTRAINERS
RESTRAINING
RESTRAININGS
RESTRAINTS
RESTRENGTHEN
RESTRENGTHENED
RESTRENGTHENING

RESTRENGTHENS
RESTRESSED
RESTRESSES
RESTRESSING
RESTRETCHED
RESTRETCHES
RESTRETCHING
RESTRICKEN
RESTRICTED
RESTRICTEDLY
RESTRICTEDNESS
RESTRICTING
RESTRICTION
RESTRICTIONISM
RESTRICTIONISMS
RESTRICTIONIST
RESTRICTIONISTS
RESTRICTIONS
RESTRICTIVE
RESTRICTIVELY
RESTRICTIVENESS
RESTRICTIVES
RESTRIKING
RESTRINGED
RESTRINGEING
RESTRINGENT
RESTRINGENTS
RESTRINGES
RESTRINGING
RESTRIVING
RESTRUCTURE
RESTRUCTURED
RESTRUCTURES
RESTRUCTURING
RESTRUCTURINGS
RESTUDYING
RESTUFFING
RESTUMPING
RESUBJECTED
RESUBJECTING
RESUBJECTS
RESUBMISSION
RESUBMISSIONS
RESUBMITTED
RESUBMITTING
RESULTANTLY
RESULTANTS
RESULTATIVE
RESULTLESS
RESULTLESSNESS
RESUMMONED
RESUMMONING
RESUMPTION
RESUMPTIONS
RESUMPTIVE
RESUMPTIVELY
RESUPINATE
RESUPINATION
RESUPINATIONS
RESUPPLIED
RESUPPLIES
RESUPPLYING
RESURFACED
RESURFACER
RESURFACERS
RESURFACES
RESURFACING
RESURGENCE
RESURGENCES
RESURRECTED
RESURRECTING
RESURRECTION
RESURRECTIONAL
RESURRECTIONARY
RESURRECTIONISE
RESURRECTIONISM
RESURRECTIONIST
RESURRECTIONIZE
RESURRECTIONS
RESURRECTIVE
RESURRECTOR
RESURRECTORS
RESURRECTS

RESURVEYED	RETEMPERED	RETRACTABILITY	RETROCEDENT	RETROUSSAGES	REVEALINGLY
RESURVEYING	RETEMPERING	RETRACTABLE	RETROCEDES	RETROVERSE	REVEALINGNESS
RESUSCITABLE	RETENTIONIST	RETRACTATION	RETROCEDING	RETROVERSION	REVEALINGNESSES
RESUSCITANT	RETENTIONISTS	RETRACTATIONS	RETROCESSION	RETROVERSIONS	REVEALINGS
RESUSCITANTS	RETENTIONS	RETRACTIBILITY	RETROCESSIONS	RETROVERTED	REVEALMENT
RESUSCITATE	RETENTIVELY	RETRACTIBLE	RETROCESSIVE	RETROVERTING	REVEALMENTS
RESUSCITATED	RETENTIVENESS	RETRACTILE	RETROCHOIR	RETROVERTS	REVEGETATE
RESUSCITATES	RETENTIVENESSES	RETRACTILITIES	RETROCHOIRS	RETROVIRAL	REVEGETATED
RESUSCITATING	RETENTIVITIES	RETRACTILITY	RETROCOGNITION	RETROVIRUS	REVEGETATES
RESUSCITATION	RETENTIVITY	RETRACTING	RETROCOGNITIONS	RETROVIRUSES	REVEGETATING
RESUSCITATIONS	RETESTIFIED	RETRACTION	RETRODICTED	RETURNABILITIES	REVEGETATION
RESUSCITATIVE	RETESTIFIES	RETRACTIONS	RETRODICTING	RETURNABILITY	REVEGETATIONS
RESUSCITATOR	RETESTIFYING	RETRACTIVE	RETRODICTION	RETURNABLE	REVELATION
RESUSCITATORS	RETEXTURED	RETRACTIVELY	RETRODICTIONS	RETURNABLES	REVELATIONAL
RESUSPENDED	RETEXTURES	RETRACTORS	RETRODICTIVE	RETURNLESS	REVELATIONIST
RESUSPENDING	RETEXTURING	RETRAINABLE	RETRODICTS	RETWISTING	REVELATIONISTS
RESUSPENDS	RETHINKERS	RETRAINEES	RETROFIRED	REUNIFICATION	REVELATIONS
RESVERATROL	RETHINKING	RETRAINING	RETROFIRES	REUNIFICATIONS	REVELATIVE
RESVERATROLS	RETHREADED	RETRANSFER	RETROFIRING	REUNIFYING	REVELATORS
RESWALLOWED	RETHREADING	RETRANSFERRED	RETROFITTED	REUNIONISM	REVELATORY
RESWALLOWING	RETIARIUSES	RETRANSFERRING	RETROFITTING	REUNIONISMS	REVELLINGS
RESWALLOWS	RETICELLAS	RETRANSFERS	RETROFITTINGS	REUNIONIST	REVELMENTS
RESYNCHRONISE	RETICENCES	RETRANSFORM	RETROFLECTED	REUNIONISTIC	REVENDICATE
RESYNCHRONISED	RETICENCIES	RETRANSFORMED	RETROFLECTION	REUNIONISTS	REVENDICATED
RESYNCHRONISES	RETICENTLY	RETRANSFORMING	RETROFLECTIONS	REUNITABLE	REVENDICATES
RESYNCHRONISING	RETICULARLY	RETRANSFORMS	RETROFLEXED	REUPHOLSTER	REVENDICATING
RESYNCHRONIZE	RETICULARY	RETRANSLATE	RETROFLEXES	REUPHOLSTERED	REVENDICATION
RESYNCHRONIZED	RETICULATE	RETRANSLATED	RETROFLEXION	REUPHOLSTERING	REVENDICATIONS
RESYNCHRONIZES	RETICULATED	RETRANSLATES	RETROFLEXIONS	REUPHOLSTERS	REVENGEFUL
RESYNCHRONIZING	RETICULATELY	RETRANSLATING	RETROGRADATION	REUSABILITIES	REVENGEFULLY
RESYNTHESES	RETICULATES	RETRANSLATION	RETROGRADATIONS	REUSABILITY	REVENGEFULNESS
RESYNTHESIS	RETICULATING	RETRANSLATIONS	RETROGRADE	REUTILISATION	REVENGELESS
RESYNTHESISE	RETICULATION	RETRANSMISSION	RETROGRADED	REUTILISATIONS	REVENGEMENT
RESYNTHESISED	RETICULATIONS	RETRANSMISSIONS	RETROGRADELY	REUTILISED	REVENGEMENTS
RESYNTHESISES	RETICULOCYTE	RETRANSMIT	RETROGRADES	REUTILISES	REVENGINGLY
RESYNTHESISING	RETICULOCYTES	RETRANSMITS	RETROGRADING	REUTILISING	REVENGINGS
RESYNTHESIZE	RETICULUMS	RETRANSMITTED	RETROGRESS	REUTILIZATION	REVERBERANT
RESYNTHESIZED	RETIGHTENED	RETRANSMITTING	RETROGRESSED	REUTILIZATIONS	REVERBERANTLY
RESYNTHESIZES	RETIGHTENING	RETREADING	RETROGRESSES	REUTILIZED	REVERBERATE
RESYNTHESIZING	RETIGHTENS	RETREATANT	RETROGRESSING	REUTILIZES	REVERBERATED
RESYSTEMATISE	RETINACULA	RETREATANTS	RETROGRESSION	REUTILIZING	REVERBERATES
RESYSTEMATISED	RETINACULAR	RETREATERS	RETROGRESSIONAL	REUTTERING	REVERBERATING
RESYSTEMATISES	RETINACULUM	RETREATING	RETROGRESSIONS	REVACCINATE	REVERBERATION
RESYSTEMATISING	RETINALITE	RETRENCHABLE	RETROGRESSIVE	REVACCINATED	REVERBERATIONS
RESYSTEMATIZE	RETINALITES	RETRENCHED	RETROGRESSIVELY	REVACCINATES	REVERBERATIVE
RESYSTEMATIZED	RETINISPORA	RETRENCHES	RETROJECTED	REVACCINATING	REVERBERATOR
RESYSTEMATIZES	RETINISPORAS	RETRENCHING	RETROJECTING	REVACCINATION	REVERBERATORIES
RESYSTEMATIZING	RETINITIDES	RETRENCHMENT	RETROJECTION	REVACCINATIONS	REVERBERATORS
RETACKLING	RETINITISES	RETRENCHMENTS	RETROJECTIONS	REVALENTAS	REVERBERATORY
RETAILINGS	RETINOBLASTOMA	RETRIBUTED	RETROJECTS	REVALIDATE	REVERENCED
RETAILMENT	RETINOBLASTOMAS	RETRIBUTES	RETROLENTAL	REVALIDATED	REVERENCER
RETAILMENTS	RETINOPATHIES	RETRIBUTING	RETROMINGENCIES	REVALIDATES	REVERENCERS
RETAILORED	RETINOPATHY	RETRIBUTION	RETROMINGENCY	REVALIDATING	REVERENCES
RETAILORING	RETINOSCOPE	RETRIBUTIONS	RETROMINGENT	REVALIDATION	REVERENCING
RETAINABLE	RETINOSCOPES	RETRIBUTIVE	RETROMINGENTS	REVALIDATIONS	REVERENTIAL
RETAINERSHIP	RETINOSCOPIC	RETRIBUTIVELY	RETROPACKS	REVALORISATION	REVERENTIALLY
RETAINERSHIPS	RETINOSCOPIES	RETRIBUTOR	RETROPERITONEAL	REVALORISATIONS	REVERENTLY
RETAINMENT	RETINOSCOPIST	RETRIBUTORS	RETROPHILIA	REVALORISE	REVERENTNESS
RETAINMENTS	RETINOSCOPISTS	RETRIBUTORY	RETROPHILIAC	REVALORISED	REVERENTNESSES
RETALIATED	RETINOSCOPY	RETRIEVABILITY	RETROPHILIACS	REVALORISES	REVERIFIED
RETALIATES	RETINOSPORA	RETRIEVABLE	RETROPHILIAS	REVALORISING	REVERIFIES
RETALIATING	RETINOSPORAS	RETRIEVABLENESS	RETROPULSION	REVALORIZATION	REVERIFYING
RETALIATION	RETINOTECTAL	RETRIEVABLY	RETROPULSIONS	REVALORIZATIONS	REVERSEDLY
RETALIATIONIST	RETIRACIES	RETRIEVALS	RETROPULSIVE	REVALORIZE	REVERSELESS
RETALIATIONISTS	RETIREDNESS	RETRIEVEMENT	RETROREFLECTION	REVALORIZED	REVERSIBILITIES
RETALIATIONS	RETIREDNESSES	RETRIEVEMENTS	RETROREFLECTIVE	REVALORIZES	REVERSIBILITY
RETALIATIVE	RETIREMENT	RETRIEVERS	RETROREFLECTOR	REVALORIZING	REVERSIBLE
RETALIATOR	RETIREMENTS	RETRIEVING	RETROREFLECTORS	REVALUATED	REVERSIBLES
RETALIATORS	RETIRINGLY	RETRIEVINGS	RETROROCKET	REVALUATES	REVERSIBLY
RETALIATORY	RETIRINGNESS	RETRIMMING	RETROROCKETS	REVALUATING	REVERSINGS
RETALLYING	RETIRINGNESSES	RETROACTED	RETRORSELY	REVALUATION	REVERSIONAL
RETARDANTS	RETORSIONS	RETROACTING	RETROSEXUAL	REVALUATIONS	REVERSIONALLY
RETARDATES	RETORTIONS	RETROACTION	RETROSEXUALS	REVAMPINGS	REVERSIONARIES
RETARDATION	RETOTALING	RETROACTIONS	RETROSPECT	REVANCHISM	REVERSIONARY
RETARDATIONS	RETOTALLED	RETROACTIVE	RETROSPECTED	REVANCHISMS	REVERSIONER
RETARDATIVE	RETOTALLING	RETROACTIVELY	RETROSPECTING	REVANCHIST	REVERSIONERS
RETARDATORY	RETOUCHABLE	RETROACTIVENESS	RETROSPECTION	REVANCHISTS	REVERSIONS
RETARDMENT	RETOUCHERS	RETROACTIVITIES	RETROSPECTIONS	REVARNISHED	REVERSISES
RETARDMENTS	RETOUCHING	RETROACTIVITY	RETROSPECTIVE	REVARNISHES	REVERTANTS
RETARGETED	RETRACEABLE	RETROBULBAR	RETROSPECTIVELY	REVARNISHING	REVERTIBLE
RETARGETING	RETRACEMENT	RETROCEDED	RETROSPECTIVES	REVEALABILITIES	REVESTIARIES
RETEACHING	RETRACEMENTS	RETROCEDENCE	RETROSPECTS	REVEALABILITY	REVESTIARY
RETELLINGS	RETRACKING	RETROCEDENCES	RETROUSSAGE	REVEALABLE	REVESTRIES

REVETMENTS	REVOLTINGLY	RHAPSODIZES	RHINORRHAGIA	RHOMBOHEDRONS	RICERCATAS
REVIBRATED	REVOLUTION	RHAPSODIZING	RHINORRHAGIAS	RHOMBOIDAL	RICHNESSES
REVIBRATES	REVOLUTIONAL	RHEOCHORDS	RHINORRHOEA	RHOMBOIDEI	RICINOLEIC
REVIBRATING	REVOLUTIONARIES	RHEOLOGICAL	RHINORRHOEAL	RHOMBOIDES	RICKBURNER
REVICTUALED	REVOLUTIONARILY	RHEOLOGICALLY	RHINORRHOEAS	RHOMBOIDEUS	RICKBURNERS
REVICTUALING	REVOLUTIONARY	RHEOLOGIES	RHINOSCLEROMA	RHOMBPORPHYRIES	RICKETIEST
REVICTUALLED	REVOLUTIONER	RHEOLOGIST	RHINOSCLEROMAS	RHOMBPORPHYRY	RICKETINESS
REVICTUALLING	REVOLUTIONERS	RHEOLOGISTS	RHINOSCLEROMATA	RHOPALISMS	RICKETINESSES
REVICTUALS	REVOLUTIONISE	RHEOMETERS	RHINOSCOPE	RHOPALOCERAL	RICKETTIER
REVIEWABLE	REVOLUTIONISED	RHEOMETRIC	RHINOSCOPES	RHOPALOCEROUS	RICKETTIEST
REVILEMENT	REVOLUTIONISER	RHEOMETRICAL	RHINOSCOPIC	RHOTACISED	RICKETTSIA
REVILEMENTS	REVOLUTIONISERS	RHEOMETRIES	RHINOSCOPIES	RHOTACISES	RICKETTSIAE
REVILINGLY	REVOLUTIONISES	RHEOMORPHIC	RHINOSCOPY	RHOTACISING	RICKETTSIAL
REVINDICATE	REVOLUTIONISING	RHEOMORPHISM	RHINOTHECA	RHOTACISMS	RICKETTSIAS
REVINDICATED	REVOLUTIONISM	RHEOMORPHISMS	RHINOTHECAE	RHOTACISTIC	RICKSTANDS
REVINDICATES	REVOLUTIONISMS	RHEOPHILES	RHINOVIRUS	RHOTACISTS	RICKSTICKS
REVINDICATING	REVOLUTIONIST	RHEORECEPTOR	RHINOVIRUSES	RHOTACIZED	RICOCHETED
REVINDICATION	REVOLUTIONISTS	RHEORECEPTORS	RHIPIDIONS	RHOTACIZES	RICOCHETING
REVINDICATIONS	REVOLUTIONIZE	RHEOSTATIC	RHIPIDIUMS	RHOTACIZING	RICOCHETTED
REVIOLATED	REVOLUTIONIZED	RHEOTACTIC	RHIZANTHOUS	RHOTICITIES	RICOCHETTING
REVIOLATES	REVOLUTIONIZER	RHEOTROPES	RHIZOCARPIC	RHUBARBING	RIDABILITIES
REVIOLATING	REVOLUTIONIZERS	RHEOTROPIC	RHIZOCARPOUS	RHUBARBINGS	RIDABILITY
REVISIONAL	REVOLUTIONIZES	RHEOTROPISM	RHIZOCARPS	RHUMBATRON	RIDDLINGLY
REVISIONARY	REVOLUTIONIZING	RHEOTROPISMS	RHIZOCAULS	RHUMBATRONS	RIDERSHIPS
REVISIONISM	REVOLUTIONS	RHETORICAL	RHIZOCEPHALAN	RHYMESTERS	RIDGEBACKS
REVISIONISMS	REVOLVABLE	RHETORICALLY	RHIZOCEPHALANS	RHYNCHOCOEL	RIDGELINES
REVISIONIST	REVOLVABLY	RHETORICIAN	RHIZOCEPHALOUS	RHYNCHOCOELS	RIDGELINGS
REVISIONISTS	REVOLVENCIES	RHETORICIANS	RHIZOCTONIA	RHYNCHODONT	RIDGEPOLES
REVISITANT	REVOLVENCY	RHETORISED	RHIZOCTONIAS	RHYNCHOPHORE	RIDGETREES
REVISITANTS	REVOLVINGLY	RHETORISES	RHIZOGENETIC	RHYNCHOPHORES	RIDICULERS
REVISITATION	REVOLVINGS	RHETORISING	RHIZOGENIC	RHYNCHOPHOROUS	RIDICULING
REVISITATIONS	REVULSIONARY	RHETORIZED	RHIZOGENOUS	RHYPAROGRAPHER	RIDICULOUS
REVISITING	REVULSIONS	RHETORIZES	RHIZOMATOUS	RHYPAROGRAPHERS	RIDICULOUSLY
REVISUALISATION	REVULSIVELY	RHETORIZING	RHIZOMORPH	RHYPAROGRAPHIC	RIDICULOUSNESS
REVISUALIZATION	REVULSIVES	RHEUMATEESE	RHIZOMORPHOUS	RHYPAROGRAPHIES	RIEBECKITE
REVITALISATION	REWAKENING	RHEUMATEESES	RHIZOMORPHS	RHYPAROGRAPHY	RIEBECKITES
REVITALISATIONS	REWARDABLE	RHEUMATICAL	RHIZOPHAGOUS	RHYTHMICAL	RIFACIMENTI
REVITALISE	REWARDABLENESS	RHEUMATICALLY	RHIZOPHILOUS	RHYTHMICALLY	RIFACIMENTO
REVITALISED	REWARDINGLY	RHEUMATICKY	RHIZOPHORE	RHYTHMICITIES	RIFAMPICIN
REVITALISES	REWARDLESS	RHEUMATICS	RHIZOPHORES	RHYTHMICITY	RIFAMPICINS
REVITALISING	REWEIGHING	RHEUMATISE	RHIZOPLANE	RHYTHMISATION	RIFAMYCINS
REVITALIZATION	REWIDENING	RHEUMATISES	RHIZOPLANES	RHYTHMISATIONS	RIFENESSES
REVITALIZATIONS	REWRAPPING	RHEUMATISM	RHIZOPODAN	RHYTHMISED	RIFLEBIRDS
REVITALIZE	RHABDOCOELE	RHEUMATISMAL	RHIZOPODANS	RHYTHMISES	RIGAMAROLE
REVITALIZED	RHABDOCOELES	RHEUMATISMS	RHIZOPODOUS	RHYTHMISING	RIGAMAROLES
REVITALIZES	RHABDOLITH	RHEUMATIZE	RHIZOPUSES	RHYTHMISTS	RIGHTABLENESS
REVITALIZING	RHABDOLITHS	RHEUMATIZES	RHIZOSPHERE	RHYTHMIZATION	RIGHTABLENESSES
REVIVABILITIES	RHABDOMANCER	RHEUMATOID	RHIZOSPHERES	RHYTHMIZATIONS	RIGHTENING
REVIVABILITY	RHABDOMANCERS	RHEUMATOIDALLY	RHIZOTOMIES	RHYTHMIZED	RIGHTEOUSLY
REVIVALISM	RHABDOMANCIES	RHEUMATOLOGICAL	RHODAMINES	RHYTHMIZES	RIGHTEOUSNESS
REVIVALISMS	RHABDOMANCY	RHEUMATOLOGIES	RHODANATES	RHYTHMIZING	RIGHTEOUSNESSES
REVIVALIST	RHABDOMANTIST	RHEUMATOLOGIST	RHODANISED	RHYTHMLESS	RIGHTFULLY
REVIVALISTIC	RHABDOMANTISTS	RHEUMATOLOGISTS	RHODANISES	RHYTHMMOMETER	RIGHTFULNESS
REVIVALISTS	RHABDOMERE	RHEUMATOLOGY	RHODANISING	RHYTHMMOMETERS	RIGHTFULNESSES
REVIVEMENT	RHABDOMERES	RHIGOLENES	RHODANIZED	RHYTHMOPOEIA	RIGHTNESSES
REVIVEMENTS	RHABDOMYOMA	RHINENCEPHALA	RHODANIZES	RHYTHMOPOEIAS	RIGHTSIZED
REVIVESCENCE	RHABDOMYOMAS	RHINENCEPHALIC	RHODANIZING	RHYTHMUSES	RIGHTSIZES
REVIVESCENCES	RHABDOMYOMATA	RHINENCEPHALON	RHODOCHROSITE	RHYTIDECTOMIES	RIGHTSIZING
REVIVESCENCIES	RHABDOSPHERE	RHINENCEPHALONS	RHODOCHROSITES	RHYTIDECTOMY	RIGHTWARDS
REVIVESCENCY	RHABDOSPHERES	RHINESTONE	RHODODAPHNE	RHYTIDOMES	RIGIDIFICATION
REVIVESCENT	RHABDOVIRUS	RHINESTONED	RHODODAPHNES	RIBALDRIES	RIGIDIFICATIONS
REVIVIFICATION	RHABDOVIRUSES	RHINESTONES	RHODODENDRON	RIBATTUTAS	RIGIDIFIED
REVIVIFICATIONS	RHACHIDIAL	RHINITIDES	RHODODENDRONS	RIBAUDRIES	RIGIDIFIES
REVIVIFIED	RHACHILLAS	RHINITISES	RHODOLITES	RIBAVIRINS	RIGIDIFYING
REVIVIFIES	RHACHITISES	RHINOCERICAL	RHODOMONTADE	RIBBONFISH	RIGIDISING
REVIVIFYING	RHADAMANTHINE	RHINOCEROS	RHODOMONTADED	RIBBONFISHES	RIGIDITIES
REVIVINGLY	RHAGADIFORM	RHINOCEROSES	RHODOMONTADES	RIBBONLIKE	RIGIDIZING
REVIVISCENCE	RHAMNACEOUS	RHINOCEROT	RHODOMONTADING	RIBBONRIES	RIGIDNESSES
REVIVISCENCES	RHAMPHOTHECA	RHINOCEROTE	RHODONITES	RIBBONWOOD	RIGMAROLES
REVIVISCENCIES	RHAMPHOTHECAE	RHINOCEROTES	RHODOPHANE	RIBBONWOODS	RIGORISTIC
REVIVISCENCY	RHAPONTICS	RHINOCEROTIC	RHODOPHANES	RIBGRASSES	RIGOROUSLY
REVIVISCENT	RHAPSODICAL	RHINOLALIA	RHODOPSINS	RIBOFLAVIN	RIGOROUSNESS
REVOCABILITIES	RHAPSODICALLY	RHINOLALIAS	RHOEADINES	RIBOFLAVINE	RIGOROUSNESSES
REVOCABILITY	RHAPSODIES	RHINOLITHS	RHOICISSUS	RIBOFLAVINES	RIGSDALERS
REVOCABLENESS	RHAPSODISE	RHINOLOGICAL	RHOICISSUSES	RIBOFLAVINS	RIGWIDDIES
REVOCABLENESSES	RHAPSODISED	RHINOLOGIES	RHOMBENCEPHALA	RIBONUCLEASE	RIGWOODIES
REVOCATION	RHAPSODISES	RHINOLOGIST	RHOMBENCEPHALON	RIBONUCLEASES	RIJKSDAALER
REVOCATIONS	RHAPSODISING	RHINOLOGISTS	RHOMBENPORPHYR	RIBONUCLEIC	RIJKSDAALERS
REVOCATORY	RHAPSODIST	RHINOPHYMA	RHOMBENPORPHYRS	RIBONUCLEOSIDE	RIJSTAFELS
REVOKABILITIES	RHAPSODISTIC	RHINOPHYMAS	RHOMBENPORPHYRY	RIBONUCLEOSIDES	RIJSTTAFEL
REVOKABILITY	RHAPSODISTS	RHINOPLASTIC	RHOMBOHEDRA	RIBONUCLEOTIDE	RIJSTTAFELS
REVOKEMENT	RHAPSODIZE	RHINOPLASTIES	RHOMBOHEDRAL	RIBONUCLEOTIDES	RIMINESSES
REVOKEMENTS	RHAPSODIZED	RHINOPLASTY	RHOMBOHEDRON	RICERCARES	RIMOSITIES

RINDERPEST	ROADABILITIES	ROENTGENOLOGIST	RONTGENOLOGICAL	ROTTENSTONED	ROUTINIZES
RINDERPESTS	ROADABILITY	ROENTGENOLOGY	RONTGENOLOGIES	ROTTENSTONES	ROUTINIZING
RINFORZANDO	ROADBLOCKED	ROENTGENOPAQUE	RONTGENOLOGIST	ROTTENSTONING	ROWANBERRIES
RINGBARKED	ROADBLOCKING	ROENTGENOSCOPE	RONTGENOLOGISTS	ROTTWEILER	ROWANBERRY
RINGBARKING	ROADBLOCKS	ROENTGENOSCOPES	RONTGENOLOGY	ROTTWEILERS	ROWDINESSES
RINGHALSES	ROADCRAFTS	ROENTGENOSCOPIC	RONTGENOPAQUE	ROTUNDITIES	ROYALISING
RINGLEADER	ROADHEADER	ROENTGENOSCOPY	RONTGENOSCOPE	ROTUNDNESS	ROYALISTIC
RINGLEADERS	ROADHEADERS	ROGUESHIPS	RONTGENOSCOPES	ROTUNDNESSES	ROYALIZING
RINGMASTER	ROADHOLDING	ROGUISHNESS	RONTGENOSCOPIC	ROUGHBACKS	ROYALMASTS
RINGMASTERS	ROADHOLDINGS	ROGUISHNESSES	RONTGENOSCOPIES	ROUGHCASTED	ROYSTERERS
RINGSIDERS	ROADHOUSES	ROISTERERS	RONTGENOSCOPY	ROUGHCASTER	ROYSTERING
RINGSTANDS	ROADROLLER	ROISTERING	RONTGENOTHERAPY	ROUGHCASTERS	ROYSTEROUS
RINGSTRAKED	ROADROLLERS	ROISTERINGS	ROOFLESSNESS	ROUGHCASTING	RUBBERIEST
RINGTOSSES	ROADRUNNER	ROISTEROUS	ROOFLESSNESSES	ROUGHCASTS	RUBBERISED
RINKHALSES	ROADRUNNERS	ROISTEROUSLY	ROOFSCAPES	ROUGHDRIED	RUBBERISES
RINSABILITIES	ROADSTEADS	ROLLCOLLAR	ROOMINESSES	ROUGHDRIES	RUBBERISING
RINSABILITY	ROADWORTHIES	ROLLCOLLARS	ROOTEDNESS	ROUGHDRYING	RUBBERIZED
RINSIBILITIES	ROADWORTHINESS	ROLLERBALL	ROOTEDNESSES	ROUGHENING	RUBBERIZES
RINSIBILITY	ROADWORTHY	ROLLERBALLS	ROOTINESSES	ROUGHHEWED	RUBBERIZING
RINTHEREOUT	ROBERDSMAN	ROLLERBLADE	ROOTLESSNESS	ROUGHHEWING	RUBBERLIKE
RINTHEREOUTS	ROBERDSMEN	ROLLERBLADED	ROOTLESSNESSES	ROUGHHOUSE	RUBBERNECK
RIOTOUSNESS	ROBERTSMAN	ROLLERBLADER	ROOTSERVER	ROUGHHOUSED	RUBBERNECKED
RIOTOUSNESSES	ROBERTSMEN	ROLLERBLADERS	ROOTSERVERS	ROUGHHOUSES	RUBBERNECKER
RIPENESSES	ROBORATING	ROLLERBLADES	ROOTSINESS	ROUGHHOUSING	RUBBERNECKERS
RIPIDOLITE	ROBOTICALLY	ROLLERBLADING	ROOTSINESSES	ROUGHNECKED	RUBBERNECKING
RIPIDOLITES	ROBOTISATION	ROLLERBLADINGS	ROOTSTALKS	ROUGHNECKING	RUBBERNECKS
RIPIENISTS	ROBOTISATIONS	ROLLERCOASTER	ROOTSTOCKS	ROUGHNECKS	RUBBERWEAR
RIPPLINGLY	ROBOTISING	ROLLERCOASTERED	ROPEDANCER	ROUGHNESSES	RUBBERWEARS
RIPRAPPING	ROBOTIZATION	ROLLERCOASTERS	ROPEDANCERS	ROUGHRIDER	RUBBISHING
RIPSNORTER	ROBOTIZATIONS	ROLLICKING	ROPEDANCING	ROUGHRIDERS	RUBBLEWORK
RIPSNORTERS	ROBOTIZING	ROLLICKINGS	ROPEDANCINGS	ROULETTING	RUBBLEWORKS
RIPSNORTING	ROBUSTIOUS	ROLLOCKING	ROPEWALKER	ROUNCEVALS	RUBEFACIENT
RISIBILITIES	ROBUSTIOUSLY	ROLLOCKINGS	ROPEWALKERS	ROUNDABOUT	RUBEFACIENTS
RISIBILITY	ROBUSTIOUSNESS	ROMANCICAL	ROPINESSES	ROUNDABOUTATION	RUBEFACTION
RISKINESSES	ROBUSTNESS	ROMANCINGS	ROQUELAURE	ROUNDABOUTED	RUBEFACTIONS
RISORGIMENTO	ROBUSTNESSES	ROMANICITE	ROQUELAURES	ROUNDABOUTEDLY	RUBELLITES
RISORGIMENTOS	ROCAMBOLES	ROMANICITES	ROSANILINE	ROUNDABOUTILITY	RUBESCENCE
RITARDANDO	ROCKABILLIES	ROMANISATION	ROSANILINES	ROUNDABOUTING	RUBESCENCES
RITARDANDOS	ROCKABILLY	ROMANISATIONS	ROSANILINS	ROUNDABOUTLY	RUBIACEOUS
RITONAVIRS	ROCKCRESSES	ROMANISING	ROSEBUSHES	ROUNDABOUTNESS	RUBICELLES
RITORNELLE	ROCKETEERS	ROMANIZATION	ROSEFINCHES	ROUNDABOUTS	RUBICONING
RITORNELLES	ROCKETRIES	ROMANIZATIONS	ROSEFISHES	ROUNDARCHED	RUBICUNDITIES
RITORNELLI	ROCKFISHES	ROMANIZING	ROSEMALING	ROUNDBALLS	RUBICUNDITY
RITORNELLO	ROCKHOPPER	ROMANTICAL	ROSEMALINGS	ROUNDEDNESS	RUBIGINOSE
RITORNELLOS	ROCKHOPPERS	ROMANTICALITIES	ROSEMARIES	ROUNDEDNESSES	RUBIGINOUS
RITORNELLS	ROCKHOUNDING	ROMANTICALITY	ROSEWATERS	ROUNDELAYS	RUBRICALLY
RITOURNELLE	ROCKHOUNDINGS	ROMANTICALLY	ROSINESSES	ROUNDHANDS	RUBRICATED
RITOURNELLES	ROCKHOUNDS	ROMANTICISATION	ROSINWEEDS	ROUNDHEADED	RUBRICATES
RITUALISATION	ROCKINESSES	ROMANTICISE	ROSMARINES	ROUNDHEADEDNESS	RUBRICATING
RITUALISATIONS	ROCKSHAFTS	ROMANTICISED	ROSTELLATE	ROUNDHEELS	RUBRICATION
RITUALISED	ROCKSLIDES	ROMANTICISES	ROSTELLUMS	ROUNDHOUSE	RUBRICATIONS
RITUALISES	ROCKSTEADIES	ROMANTICISING	ROSTERINGS	ROUNDHOUSES	RUBRICATOR
RITUALISING	ROCKSTEADY	ROMANTICISM	ROSTROCARINATE	ROUNDNESSES	RUBRICATORS
RITUALISMS	ROCKWATERS	ROMANTICISMS	ROSTROCARINATES	ROUNDTABLE	RUBRICIANS
RITUALISTIC	RODENTICIDE	ROMANTICIST	ROTACHUTES	ROUNDTABLES	RUBYTHROAT
RITUALISTICALLY	RODENTICIDES	ROMANTICISTS	ROTAMETERS	ROUNDTRIPPING	RUBYTHROATS
RITUALISTS	RODFISHERS	ROMANTICIZATION	ROTAPLANES	ROUNDTRIPPINGS	RUCTATIONS
RITUALIZATION	RODFISHING	ROMANTICIZE	ROTATIONAL	ROUNDTRIPS	RUDBECKIAS
RITUALIZATIONS	RODFISHINGS	ROMANTICIZED	ROTATIVELY	ROUNDWOODS	RUDDERHEAD
RITUALIZED	RODGERSIAS	ROMANTICIZES	ROTAVATING	ROUNDWORMS	RUDDERHEADS
RITUALIZES	RODOMONTADE	ROMANTICIZING	ROTAVATORS	ROUSEABOUT	RUDDERLESS
RITUALIZING	RODOMONTADED	ROMELDALES	ROTAVIRUSES	ROUSEABOUTS	RUDDERPOST
RITZINESSES	RODOMONTADER	ROMPISHNESS	ROTGRASSES	ROUSEDNESS	RUDDERPOSTS
RIVALESSES	RODOMONTADERS	ROMPISHNESSES	ROTIFERANS	ROUSEDNESSES	RUDDERSTOCK
RIVALISING	RODOMONTADES	RONDOLETTO	ROTIFEROUS	ROUSEMENTS	RUDDERSTOCKS
RIVALITIES	RODOMONTADING	RONDOLETTOS	ROTISSERIE	ROUSSETTES	RUDDINESSES
RIVALIZING	ROENTGENISATION	RONTGENISATION	ROTISSERIES	ROUSTABOUT	RUDENESSES
RIVALSHIPS	ROENTGENISE	RONTGENISATIONS	ROTOGRAPHED	ROUSTABOUTS	RUDIMENTAL
RIVERBANKS	ROENTGENISED	RONTGENISE	ROTOGRAPHING	ROUTEMARCH	RUDIMENTALLY
RIVERBOATS	ROENTGENISES	RONTGENISED	ROTOGRAPHS	ROUTEMARCHED	RUDIMENTARILY
RIVERCRAFT	ROENTGENISING	RONTGENISES	ROTOGRAVURE	ROUTEMARCHES	RUDIMENTARINESS
RIVERCRAFTS	ROENTGENIZATION	RONTGENISING	ROTOGRAVURES	ROUTEMARCHING	RUDIMENTARY
RIVERFRONT	ROENTGENIZE	RONTGENIZATION	ROTORCRAFT	ROUTINEERS	RUEFULNESS
RIVERFRONTS	ROENTGENIZED	RONTGENIZATIONS	ROTORCRAFTS	ROUTINISATION	RUEFULNESSES
RIVERHEADS	ROENTGENIZES	RONTGENIZE	ROTOTILLED	ROUTINISATIONS	RUFESCENCE
RIVERSCAPE	ROENTGENIZING	RONTGENIZED	ROTOTILLER	ROUTINISED	RUFESCENCES
RIVERSCAPES	ROENTGENOGRAM	RONTGENIZES	ROTOTILLERS	ROUTINISES	RUFFIANING
RIVERSIDES	ROENTGENOGRAMS	RONTGENIZING	ROTOTILLING	ROUTINISING	RUFFIANISH
RIVERWARDS	ROENTGENOGRAPH	RONTGENOGRAM	ROTOVATING	ROUTINISMS	RUFFIANISM
RIVERWEEDS	ROENTGENOGRAPHS	RONTGENOGRAMS	ROTOVATORS	ROUTINISTS	RUFFIANISMS
RIVERWORTHINESS	ROENTGENOGRAPHY	RONTGENOGRAPH	ROTTENNESS	ROUTINIZATION	RUGGEDISATION
RIVERWORTHY	ROENTGENOLOGIC	RONTGENOGRAPHS	ROTTENNESSES	ROUTINIZATIONS	RUGGEDISATIONS
RIVETINGLY	ROENTGENOLOGIES	RONTGENOGRAPHY	ROTTENSTONE	ROUTINIZED	RUGGEDISED

RUGGEDISES
RUGGEDISING
RUGGEDIZATION
RUGGEDIZATIONS
RUGGEDIZED
RUGGEDIZES
RUGGEDIZING
RUGGEDNESS
RUGGEDNESSES
RUGOSITIES
RUINATIONS
RUINOUSNESS
RUINOUSNESSES
RULERSHIPS
RUMBLEDETHUMP
RUMBLEDETHUMPS
RUMBLEGUMPTION
RUMBLEGUMPTIONS
RUMBLINGLY
RUMBULLION

RUMBULLIONS
RUMBUSTICAL
RUMBUSTIOUS
RUMBUSTIOUSLY
RUMBUSTIOUSNESS
RUMELGUMPTION
RUMELGUMPTIONS
RUMFUSTIAN
RUMFUSTIANS
RUMGUMPTION
RUMGUMPTIONS
RUMINANTLY
RUMINATING
RUMINATINGLY
RUMINATION
RUMINATIONS
RUMINATIVE
RUMINATIVELY
RUMINATORS
RUMLEGUMPTION

RUMLEGUMPTIONS
RUMMELGUMPTION
RUMMELGUMPTIONS
RUMMINESSES
RUMMLEGUMPTION
RUMMLEGUMPTIONS
RUMORMONGER
RUMORMONGERING
RUMORMONGERINGS
RUMORMONGERS
RUMRUNNERS
RUNAROUNDS
RUNECRAFTS
RUNNINESSES
RUNTINESSES
RUPESTRIAN
RUPICOLINE
RUPICOLOUS
RUPTURABLE
RUPTUREWORT

RUPTUREWORTS
RURALISATION
RURALISATIONS
RURALISING
RURALITIES
RURALIZATION
RURALIZATIONS
RURALIZING
RURALNESSES
RURIDECANAL
RUSHINESSES
RUSHLIGHTS
RUSSETINGS
RUSSETTING
RUSSETTINGS
RUSSIFYING
RUSTBUCKET
RUSTICALLY
RUSTICATED
RUSTICATES

RUSTICATING
RUSTICATINGS
RUSTICATION
RUSTICATIONS
RUSTICATOR
RUSTICATORS
RUSTICISED
RUSTICISES
RUSTICISING
RUSTICISMS
RUSTICITIES
RUSTICIZED
RUSTICIZES
RUSTICIZING
RUSTICWORK
RUSTICWORKS
RUSTINESSES
RUSTLINGLY
RUSTPROOFED
RUSTPROOFING

RUSTPROOFS
RUTHENIOUS
RUTHENIUMS
RUTHERFORD
RUTHERFORDIUM
RUTHERFORDIUMS
RUTHERFORDS
RUTHFULNESS
RUTHFULNESSES
RUTHLESSLY
RUTHLESSNESS
RUTHLESSNESSES
RUTTINESSES
RUTTISHNESS
RUTTISHNESSES
RYBAUDRYES
RYEGRASSES

Ss

SABADILLAS
SABBATARIAN
SABBATICAL
SABBATICALS
SABBATISED
SABBATISES
SABBATISING
SABBATISMS
SABBATIZED
SABBATIZES
SABBATIZING
SABERMETRICIAN
SABERMETRICIANS
SABERMETRICS
SABLEFISHES
SABOTAGING
SABRETACHE
SABRETACHES
SABULOSITIES
SABULOSITY
SABURRATION
SABURRATIONS
SACAHUISTA
SACAHUISTAS
SACAHUISTE
SACAHUISTES
SACCADICALLY
SACCHARASE
SACCHARASES
SACCHARATE
SACCHARATED
SACCHARATES
SACCHARIDE
SACCHARIDES
SACCHARIFEROUS
SACCHARIFIED
SACCHARIFIES
SACCHARIFY
SACCHARIFYING
SACCHARIMETER
SACCHARIMETERS
SACCHARIMETRIES
SACCHARIMETRY
SACCHARINE
SACCHARINELY
SACCHARINES
SACCHARINITIES
SACCHARINITY
SACCHARINS
SACCHARISATION
SACCHARISATIONS
SACCHARISE
SACCHARISED
SACCHARISES
SACCHARISING
SACCHARIZATION
SACCHARIZATIONS
SACCHARIZE
SACCHARIZED
SACCHARIZES
SACCHARIZING
SACCHAROID
SACCHAROIDAL
SACCHAROIDS
SACCHAROMETER
SACCHAROMETERS
SACCHAROMYCES

SACCHAROMYCETES
SACCHAROSE
SACCHAROSES
SACCHARUMS
SACCULATED
SACCULATION
SACCULATIONS
SACCULIFORM
SACERDOTAL
SACERDOTALISE
SACERDOTALISED
SACERDOTALISES
SACERDOTALISING
SACERDOTALISM
SACERDOTALISMS
SACERDOTALIST
SACERDOTALISTS
SACERDOTALIZE
SACERDOTALIZED
SACERDOTALIZES
SACERDOTALIZING
SACERDOTALLY
SACHEMDOMS
SACHEMSHIP
SACHEMSHIPS
SACKCLOTHS
SACRALGIAS
SACRALISATION
SACRALISATIONS
SACRALISED
SACRALISES
SACRALISING
SACRALIZATION
SACRALIZATIONS
SACRALIZED
SACRALIZES
SACRALIZING
SACRAMENTAL
SACRAMENTALISM
SACRAMENTALISMS
SACRAMENTALIST
SACRAMENTALISTS
SACRAMENTALITY
SACRAMENTALLY
SACRAMENTALNESS
SACRAMENTALS
SACRAMENTARIAN
SACRAMENTARIANS
SACRAMENTARIES
SACRAMENTARY
SACRAMENTED
SACRAMENTING
SACRAMENTS
SACREDNESS
SACREDNESSES
SACRIFICEABLE
SACRIFICED
SACRIFICER
SACRIFICERS
SACRIFICES
SACRIFICIAL
SACRIFICIALLY
SACRIFICING
SACRIFYING
SACRILEGES
SACRILEGIOUS
SACRILEGIOUSLY

SACRILEGIST
SACRILEGISTS
SACRISTANS
SACRISTIES
SACROCOCCYGEAL
SACROCOSTAL
SACROCOSTALS
SACROILIAC
SACROILIACS
SACROILIITIS
SACROILIITISES
SACROSANCT
SACROSANCTITIES
SACROSANCTITY
SACROSANCTNESS
SADDLEBACK
SADDLEBACKED
SADDLEBACKS
SADDLEBAGS
SADDLEBILL
SADDLEBILLS
SADDLEBOWS
SADDLEBRED
SADDLEBREDS
SADDLECLOTH
SADDLECLOTHS
SADDLELESS
SADDLERIES
SADDLEROOM
SADDLEROOMS
SADDLETREE
SADDLETREES
SADISTICALLY
SADOMASOCHISM
SADOMASOCHISMS
SADOMASOCHIST
SADOMASOCHISTIC
SADOMASOCHISTS
SAFECRACKER
SAFECRACKERS
SAFECRACKING
SAFECRACKINGS
SAFEGUARDED
SAFEGUARDING
SAFEGUARDS
SAFEKEEPING
SAFEKEEPINGS
SAFELIGHTS
SAFENESSES
SAFFLOWERS
SAFRANINES
SAGACIOUSLY
SAGACIOUSNESS
SAGACIOUSNESSES
SAGACITIES
SAGANASHES
SAGAPENUMS
SAGEBRUSHES
SAGENESSES
SAGINATING
SAGINATION
SAGINATIONS
SAGITTALLY
SAGITTARIAN
SAGITTARIANS
SAGITTARIES
SAGITTIFORM

SAILBOARDED
SAILBOARDER
SAILBOARDERS
SAILBOARDING
SAILBOARDINGS
SAILBOARDS
SAILBOATER
SAILBOATERS
SAILBOATING
SAILBOATINGS
SAILCLOTHS
SAILFISHES
SAILMAKERS
SAILORINGS
SAILORLESS
SAILORLIKE
SAILPLANED
SAILPLANER
SAILPLANERS
SAILPLANES
SAILPLANING
SAINTESSES
SAINTFOINS
SAINTHOODS
SAINTLIEST
SAINTLINESS
SAINTLINESSES
SAINTLINGS
SAINTPAULIA
SAINTPAULIAS
SAINTSHIPS
SALABILITIES
SALABILITY
SALABLENESS
SALABLENESSES
SALACIOUSLY
SALACIOUSNESS
SALACIOUSNESSES
SALACITIES
SALAMANDER
SALAMANDERS
SALAMANDRIAN
SALAMANDRINE
SALAMANDROID
SALAMANDROIDS
SALANGANES
SALBUTAMOL
SALBUTAMOLS
SALEABILITIES
SALEABILITY
SALEABLENESS
SALEABLENESSES
SALERATUSES
SALESCLERK
SALESCLERKS
SALESGIRLS
SALESLADIES
SALESMANSHIP
SALESMANSHIPS
SALESPEOPLE
SALESPERSON
SALESPERSONS
SALESROOMS
SALESWOMAN
SALESWOMEN
SALIAUNCES
SALICACEOUS

SALICETUMS
SALICIONAL
SALICIONALS
SALICORNIA
SALICORNIAS
SALICYLAMIDE
SALICYLAMIDES
SALICYLATE
SALICYLATED
SALICYLATES
SALICYLATING
SALICYLISM
SALICYLISMS
SALIENCIES
SALIENTIAN
SALIENTIANS
SALIFEROUS
SALIFIABLE
SALIFICATION
SALIFICATIONS
SALIMETERS
SALIMETRIC
SALIMETRIES
SALINISATION
SALINISATIONS
SALINISING
SALINITIES
SALINIZATION
SALINIZATIONS
SALINIZING
SALINOMETER
SALINOMETERS
SALINOMETRIC
SALINOMETRIES
SALINOMETRY
SALIVATING
SALIVATION
SALIVATIONS
SALIVATORS
SALLENDERS
SALLOWNESS
SALLOWNESSES
SALLYPORTS
SALMAGUNDI
SALMAGUNDIES
SALMAGUNDIS
SALMAGUNDY
SALMANASER
SALMANASERS
SALMANAZAR
SALMANAZARS
SALMONBERRIES
SALMONBERRY
SALMONELLA
SALMONELLAE
SALMONELLAS
SALMONELLOSES
SALMONELLOSIS
SALMONOIDS
SALOMETERS
SALOPETTES
SALPIGLOSSES
SALPIGLOSSIS
SALPIGLOSSISES
SALPINGECTOMIES
SALPINGECTOMY
SALPINGIAN

SALPINGITIC
SALPINGITIS
SALPINGITISES
SALSOLACEOUS
SALSUGINOUS
SALTARELLI
SALTARELLO
SALTARELLOS
SALTATIONISM
SALTATIONISMS
SALTATIONIST
SALTATIONISTS
SALTATIONS
SALTATORIAL
SALTATORIOUS
SALTBUSHES
SALTCELLAR
SALTCELLARS
SALTCHUCKER
SALTCHUCKERS
SALTCHUCKS
SALTFISHES
SALTIGRADE
SALTIGRADES
SALTIMBANCO
SALTIMBANCOS
SALTIMBOCCA
SALTIMBOCCAS
SALTINESSES
SALTIREWISE
SALTISHNESS
SALTISHNESSES
SALTNESSES
SALTPETERS
SALTPETREMAN
SALTPETREMEN
SALTPETRES
SALTSHAKER
SALTSHAKERS
SALUBRIOUS
SALUBRIOUSLY
SALUBRIOUSNESS
SALUBRITIES
SALURETICS
SALUTARILY
SALUTARINESS
SALUTARINESSES
SALUTATION
SALUTATIONAL
SALUTATIONS
SALUTATORIAN
SALUTATORIANS
SALUTATORIES
SALUTATORILY
SALUTATORY
SALUTIFEROUS
SALVABILITIES
SALVABILITY
SALVABLENESS
SALVABLENESSES
SALVAGEABILITY
SALVAGEABLE
SALVARSANS
SALVATIONAL
SALVATIONISM
SALVATIONISMS
SALVATIONIST

SALVATIONISTS	SANDPAINTINGS	SANTONICAS	SARCOPHAGUSES	SATISFACTIONS	SAWDUSTING
SALVATIONS	SANDPAPERED	SAPANWOODS	SARCOPLASM	SATISFACTORILY	SAWTIMBERS
SALVATORIES	SANDPAPERING	SAPIDITIES	SARCOPLASMIC	SATISFACTORY	SAXICAVOUS
SALVERFORM	SANDPAPERS	SAPIDNESSES	SARCOPLASMS	SATISFIABLE	SAXICOLINE
SALVIFICAL	SANDPAPERY	SAPIENCIES	SARCOSOMAL	SATISFICED	SAXICOLOUS
SALVIFICALLY	SANDPIPERS	SAPIENTIAL	SARCOSOMES	SATISFICER	SAXIFRAGACEOUS
SALVINIACEOUS	SANDSPOUTS	SAPIENTIALLY	SARDONICAL	SATISFICERS	SAXIFRAGES
SAMARIFORM	SANDSTONES	SAPINDACEOUS	SARDONICALLY	SATISFICES	SAXITOXINS
SAMARITANS	SANDSTORMS	SAPLESSNESS	SARDONICISM	SATISFICING	SAXOPHONES
SAMARSKITE	SANDSUCKER	SAPLESSNESSES	SARDONICISMS	SATISFICINGS	SAXOPHONIC
SAMARSKITES	SANDSUCKERS	SAPODILLAS	SARDONYXES	SATISFIERS	SAXOPHONIST
SAMENESSES	SANDWICHED	SAPOGENINS	SARGASSUMS	SATISFYING	SAXOPHONISTS
SAMNITISES	SANDWICHES	SAPONACEOUS	SARMENTACEOUS	SATISFYINGLY	SCABBARDED
SAMPLERIES	SANDWICHING	SAPONACEOUSNESS	SARMENTOSE	SATURABILITIES	SCABBARDING
SANATORIUM	SANENESSES	SAPONARIAS	SARMENTOUS	SATURABILITY	SCABBARDLESS
SANATORIUMS	SANGFROIDS	SAPONIFIABLE	SARPANCHES	SATURATERS	SCABBEDNESS
SANBENITOS	SANGUIFEROUS	SAPONIFICATION	SARRACENIA	SATURATING	SCABBEDNESSES
SANCTIFIABLE	SANGUIFICATION	SAPONIFICATIONS	SARRACENIACEOUS	SATURATION	SCABBINESS
SANCTIFICATION	SANGUIFICATIONS	SAPONIFIED	SARRACENIAS	SATURATIONS	SCABBINESSES
SANCTIFICATIONS	SANGUIFIED	SAPONIFIER	SARRUSOPHONE	SATURATORS	SCABERULOUS
SANCTIFIED	SANGUIFIES	SAPONIFIERS	SARRUSOPHONES	SATURNALIA	SCABIOUSES
SANCTIFIEDLY	SANGUIFYING	SAPONIFIES	SARSAPARILLA	SATURNALIAN	SCABRIDITIES
SANCTIFIER	SANGUINARIA	SAPONIFYING	SARSAPARILLAS	SATURNALIANLY	SCABRIDITY
SANCTIFIERS	SANGUINARIAS	SAPOTACEOUS	SARTORIALLY	SATURNALIAS	SCABROUSLY
SANCTIFIES	SANGUINARILY	SAPPANWOOD	SARTORIUSES	SATURNIIDS	SCABROUSNESS
SANCTIFYING	SANGUINARINESS	SAPPANWOODS	SASKATOONS	SATURNINELY	SCABROUSNESSES
SANCTIFYINGLY	SANGUINARY	SAPPERMENT	SASQUATCHES	SATURNINITIES	SCAFFOLAGE
SANCTIFYINGS	SANGUINELY	SAPPHIRINE	SASSAFRASES	SATURNINITY	SCAFFOLAGES
SANCTIMONIES	SANGUINENESS	SAPPHIRINES	SASSARARAS	SATURNISMS	SCAFFOLDAGE
SANCTIMONIOUS	SANGUINENESSES	SAPPINESSES	SASSINESSES	SATURNISTS	SCAFFOLDAGES
SANCTIMONIOUSLY	SANGUINEOUS	SAPRAEMIAS	SASSOLITES	SATYAGRAHA	SCAFFOLDED
SANCTIMONY	SANGUINEOUSNESS	SAPROBIONT	SASSYWOODS	SATYAGRAHAS	SCAFFOLDER
SANCTIONABLE	SANGUINING	SAPROBIONTS	SATANICALLY	SATYAGRAHI	SCAFFOLDERS
SANCTIONED	SANGUINITIES	SAPROBIOTIC	SATANICALNESS	SATYAGRAHIS	SCAFFOLDING
SANCTIONEER	SANGUINITY	SAPROGENIC	SATANICALNESSES	SATYRESQUE	SCAFFOLDINGS
SANCTIONEERS	SANGUINIVOROUS	SAPROGENICITIES	SATANITIES	SATYRESSES	SCAGLIOLAS
SANCTIONER	SANGUINOLENCIES	SAPROGENICITY	SATANOLOGIES	SATYRIASES	SCAITHLESS
SANCTIONERS	SANGUINOLENCY	SAPROGENOUS	SATANOLOGY	SATYRIASIS	SCALABILITIES
SANCTIONING	SANGUINOLENT	SAPROLEGNIA	SATANOPHANIES	SAUCEBOATS	SCALABILITY
SANCTIONLESS	SANGUIVOROUS	SAPROLEGNIAS	SATANOPHANY	SAUCEBOXES	SCALABLENESS
SANCTITIES	SANITARIAN	SAPROLITES	SATANOPHOBIA	SAUCERFULS	SCALABLENESSES
SANCTITUDE	SANITARIANISM	SAPROLITIC	SATANOPHOBIAS	SAUCERLESS	SCALARIFORM
SANCTITUDES	SANITARIANISMS	SAPROPELIC	SATCHELFUL	SAUCERLIKE	SCALARIFORMLY
SANCTUARIES	SANITARIANS	SAPROPELITE	SATCHELFULS	SAUCINESSES	SCALATIONS
SANCTUARISE	SANITARIES	SAPROPELITES	SATCHELLED	SAUCISSONS	SCALDBERRIES
SANCTUARISED	SANITARILY	SAPROPHAGOUS	SATCHELSFUL	SAUERBRATEN	SCALDBERRY
SANCTUARISES	SANITARINESS	SAPROPHYTE	SATEDNESSES	SAUERBRATENS	SCALDFISHES
SANCTUARISING	SANITARINESSES	SAPROPHYTES	SATELLITED	SAUERKRAUT	SCALDHEADS
SANCTUARIZE	SANITARIST	SAPROPHYTIC	SATELLITES	SAUERKRAUTS	SCALDSHIPS
SANCTUARIZED	SANITARISTS	SAPROPHYTICALLY	SATELLITIC	SAUNTERERS	SCALEBOARD
SANCTUARIZES	SANITARIUM	SAPROPHYTISM	SATELLITING	SAUNTERING	SCALEBOARDS
SANCTUARIZING	SANITARIUMS	SAPROPHYTISMS	SATELLITISE	SAUNTERINGLY	SCALENOHEDRA
SANDALLING	SANITATING	SAPROTROPH	SATELLITISED	SAUNTERINGS	SCALENOHEDRON
SANDALWOOD	SANITATION	SAPROTROPHIC	SATELLITISES	SAURISCHIAN	SCALENOHEDRONS
SANDALWOODS	SANITATIONIST	SAPROTROPHS	SATELLITISING	SAURISCHIANS	SCALETAILS
SANDARACHS	SANITATIONISTS	SAPSUCKERS	SATELLITIUM	SAUROGNATHOUS	SCALEWORKS
SANDBAGGED	SANITATIONS	SARABANDES	SATELLITIUMS	SAUROPODOUS	SCALINESSES
SANDBAGGER	SANITISATION	SARBACANES	SATELLITIZE	SAUROPSIDAN	SCALLAWAGS
SANDBAGGERS	SANITISATIONS	SARCASTICALLY	SATELLITIZED	SAUROPSIDANS	SCALLOPERS
SANDBAGGING	SANITISERS	SARCENCHYMATOUS	SATELLITIZES	SAUROPTERYGIAN	SCALLOPING
SANDBLASTED	SANITISING	SARCENCHYME	SATELLITIZING	SAUSSURITE	SCALLOPINGS
SANDBLASTER	SANITIZATION	SARCENCHYMES	SATIABILITIES	SAUSSURITES	SCALLOPINI
SANDBLASTERS	SANITIZATIONS	SARCOCARPS	SATIABILITY	SAUSSURITIC	SCALLOPINIS
SANDBLASTING	SANITIZERS	SARCOCOLLA	SATIATIONS	SAVABLENESS	SCALLYWAGS
SANDBLASTINGS	SANITIZING	SARCOCOLLAS	SATINETTAS	SAVABLENESSES	SCALOGRAMS
SANDBLASTS	SANITORIUM	SARCOCYSTIS	SATINETTES	SAVAGEDOMS	SCALOPPINE
SANDCASTLE	SANITORIUMS	SARCOCYSTISES	SATINFLOWER	SAVAGENESS	SCALOPPINES
SANDCASTLES	SANNYASINS	SARCOIDOSES	SATINFLOWERS	SAVAGENESSES	SCALOPPINI
SANDCRACKS	SANSCULOTTE	SARCOIDOSIS	SATINWOODS	SAVAGERIES	SCALPELLIC
SANDERLING	SANSCULOTTERIE	SARCOLEMMA	SATIRICALLY	SAVEABLENESS	SCALPELLIFORM
SANDERLINGS	SANSCULOTTERIES	SARCOLEMMAL	SATIRICALNESS	SAVEABLENESSES	SCALPRIFORM
SANDERSWOOD	SANSCULOTTES	SARCOLEMMAS	SATIRICALNESSES	SAVEGARDED	SCAMBAITING
SANDERSWOODS	SANSCULOTTIC	SARCOLEMMATA	SATIRISABLE	SAVEGARDING	SCAMBAITINGS
SANDFISHES	SANSCULOTTIDES	SARCOLOGIES	SATIRISATION	SAVINGNESS	SCAMBLINGLY
SANDGLASSES	SANSCULOTTISH	SARCOMATOID	SATIRISATIONS	SAVINGNESSES	SCAMBLINGS
SANDGROPER	SANSCULOTTISM	SARCOMATOSES	SATIRISERS	SAVORINESS	SCAMMONIATE
SANDGROPERS	SANSCULOTTISMS	SARCOMATOSIS	SATIRISING	SAVORINESSES	SCAMMONIES
SANDGROUSE	SANSCULOTTIST	SARCOMATOUS	SATIRIZABLE	SAVOURIEST	SCAMPERERS
SANDGROUSES	SANSCULOTTISTS	SARCOMERES	SATIRIZATION	SAVOURINESS	SCAMPERING
SANDINESSES	SANSEVIERIA	SARCOPHAGAL	SATIRIZATIONS	SAVOURINESSES	SCAMPISHLY
SANDLOTTER	SANSEVIERIAS	SARCOPHAGI	SATIRIZERS	SAVOURLESS	SCAMPISHNESS
SANDLOTTERS	SANTALACEOUS	SARCOPHAGOUS	SATIRIZING	SAVVINESSES	SCAMPISHNESSES
SANDPAINTING	SANTOLINAS	SARCOPHAGUS	SATISFACTION	SAWBONESES	SCANDALING

SCANDALISATION	SCAREMONGERINGS	SCENOGRAPHY	SCHISMATIZED	SCHNORKELING	SCHUTZSTAFFEL
SCANDALISATIONS	SCAREMONGERS	SCENTLESSNESS	SCHISMATIZES	SCHNORKELLED	SCHUTZSTAFFELS
SCANDALISE	SCARFISHES	SCENTLESSNESSES	SCHISMATIZING	SCHNORKELLING	SCHVARTZES
SCANDALISED	SCARFSKINS	SCEPTERING	SCHISTOSITIES	SCHNORKELS	SCHWARMEREI
SCANDALISER	SCARIFICATION	SCEPTERLESS	SCHISTOSITY	SCHNORRERS	SCHWARMEREIS
SCANDALISERS	SCARIFICATIONS	SCEPTICALLY	SCHISTOSOMAL	SCHNORRING	SCHWARMERISCH
SCANDALISES	SCARIFICATOR	SCEPTICISM	SCHISTOSOME	SCHNOZZLES	SCHWARTZES
SCANDALISING	SCARIFICATORS	SCEPTICISMS	SCHISTOSOMES	SCHOLARCHS	SCHWARZLOT
SCANDALIZATION	SCARIFIERS	SCEPTRELESS	SCHISTOSOMIASES	SCHOLARLIER	SCHWARZLOTS
SCANDALIZATIONS	SCARIFYING	SCEUOPHYLACIA	SCHISTOSOMIASIS	SCHOLARLIEST	SCIAENOIDS
SCANDALIZE	SCARIFYINGLY	SCEUOPHYLACIUM	SCHIZAEACEOUS	SCHOLARLINESS	SCIAMACHIES
SCANDALIZED	SCARINESSES	SCEUOPHYLAX	SCHIZANTHUS	SCHOLARLINESSES	SCIENTIFIC
SCANDALIZER	SCARLATINA	SCEUOPHYLAXES	SCHIZANTHUSES	SCHOLARSHIP	SCIENTIFICAL
SCANDALIZERS	SCARLATINAL	SCHADENFREUDE	SCHIZOCARP	SCHOLARSHIPS	SCIENTIFICALLY
SCANDALIZES	SCARLATINAS	SCHADENFREUDES	SCHIZOCARPIC	SCHOLASTIC	SCIENTISED
SCANDALIZING	SCARLETING	SCHALSTEIN	SCHIZOCARPOUS	SCHOLASTICAL	SCIENTISES
SCANDALLED	SCARPERING	SCHALSTEINS	SCHIZOCARPS	SCHOLASTICALLY	SCIENTISING
SCANDALLING	SCATHEFULNESS	SCHAPPEING	SCHIZOGENESES	SCHOLASTICATE	SCIENTISMS
SCANDALMONGER	SCATHEFULNESSES	SCHATCHENS	SCHIZOGENESIS	SCHOLASTICATES	SCIENTISTIC
SCANDALMONGERS	SCATHELESS	SCHECHITAH	SCHIZOGENETIC	SCHOLASTICISM	SCIENTISTS
SCANDALOUS	SCATHINGLY	SCHECHITAHS	SCHIZOGENIC	SCHOLASTICISMS	SCIENTIZED
SCANDALOUSLY	SCATOLOGIC	SCHECHITAS	SCHIZOGNATHOUS	SCHOLASTICS	SCIENTIZES
SCANDALOUSNESS	SCATOLOGICAL	SCHECKLATON	SCHIZOGONIC	SCHOLIASTIC	SCIENTIZING
SCANSORIAL	SCATOLOGIES	SCHECKLATONS	SCHIZOGONIES	SCHOLIASTS	SCINCOIDIAN
SCANTINESS	SCATOLOGIST	SCHEDULERS	SCHIZOGONOUS	SCHOOLBAGS	SCINCOIDIANS
SCANTINESSES	SCATOLOGISTS	SCHEDULING	SCHIZOGONY	SCHOOLBOOK	SCINDAPSUS
SCANTITIES	SCATOPHAGIES	SCHEELITES	SCHIZOIDAL	SCHOOLBOOKS	SCINDAPSUSES
SCANTLINGS	SCATOPHAGOUS	SCHEFFLERA	SCHIZOMYCETE	SCHOOLBOYISH	SCINTIGRAM
SCANTNESSES	SCATOPHAGY	SCHEFFLERAS	SCHIZOMYCETES	SCHOOLBOYS	SCINTIGRAMS
SCAPEGALLOWS	SCATTERABLE	SCHEMATICAL	SCHIZOMYCETIC	SCHOOLCHILD	SCINTIGRAPHIC
SCAPEGALLOWSES	SCATTERATION	SCHEMATICALLY	SCHIZOMYCETOUS	SCHOOLCHILDREN	SCINTIGRAPHIES
SCAPEGOATED	SCATTERATIONS	SCHEMATICS	SCHIZOPHRENE	SCHOOLCRAFT	SCINTIGRAPHY
SCAPEGOATING	SCATTERBRAIN	SCHEMATISATION	SCHIZOPHRENES	SCHOOLCRAFTS	SCINTILLAE
SCAPEGOATINGS	SCATTERBRAINED	SCHEMATISATIONS	SCHIZOPHRENETIC	SCHOOLDAYS	SCINTILLANT
SCAPEGOATISM	SCATTERBRAINS	SCHEMATISE	SCHIZOPHRENIA	SCHOOLERIES	SCINTILLANTLY
SCAPEGOATISMS	SCATTEREDLY	SCHEMATISED	SCHIZOPHRENIAS	SCHOOLFELLOW	SCINTILLAS
SCAPEGOATS	SCATTERERS	SCHEMATISES	SCHIZOPHRENIC	SCHOOLFELLOWS	SCINTILLASCOPE
SCAPEGRACE	SCATTERGOOD	SCHEMATISING	SCHIZOPHRENICS	SCHOOLGIRL	SCINTILLASCOPES
SCAPEGRACES	SCATTERGOODS	SCHEMATISM	SCHIZOPHYCEOUS	SCHOOLGIRLISH	SCINTILLATE
SCAPEMENTS	SCATTERGRAM	SCHEMATISMS	SCHIZOPHYTE	SCHOOLGIRLS	SCINTILLATED
SCAPEWHEEL	SCATTERGRAMS	SCHEMATIST	SCHIZOPHYTES	SCHOOLGOING	SCINTILLATES
SCAPEWHEELS	SCATTERGUN	SCHEMATISTS	SCHIZOPHYTIC	SCHOOLGOINGS	SCINTILLATING
SCAPHOCEPHALI	SCATTERGUNS	SCHEMATIZATION	SCHIZOPODAL	SCHOOLHOUSE	SCINTILLATINGLY
SCAPHOCEPHALIC	SCATTERING	SCHEMATIZATIONS	SCHIZOPODOUS	SCHOOLHOUSES	SCINTILLATION
SCAPHOCEPHALIES	SCATTERINGLY	SCHEMATIZE	SCHIZOPODS	SCHOOLINGS	SCINTILLATIONS
SCAPHOCEPHALISM	SCATTERINGS	SCHEMATIZED	SCHIZOTHYMIA	SCHOOLKIDS	SCINTILLATOR
SCAPHOCEPHALOUS	SCATTERLING	SCHEMATIZES	SCHIZOTHYMIAS	SCHOOLMAID	SCINTILLATORS
SCAPHOCEPHALUS	SCATTERLINGS	SCHEMATIZING	SCHIZOTHYMIC	SCHOOLMAIDS	SCINTILLISCAN
SCAPHOCEPHALY	SCATTERMOUCH	SCHEMINGLY	SCHIZZIEST	SCHOOLMARM	SCINTILLISCANS
SCAPHOPODS	SCATTERMOUCHES	SCHEMOZZLE	SCHLEMIELS	SCHOOLMARMISH	SCINTILLOMETER
SCAPIGEROUS	SCATTERSHOT	SCHEMOZZLED	SCHLEMIHLS	SCHOOLMARMS	SCINTILLOMETERS
SCAPOLITES	SCATTINESS	SCHEMOZZLES	SCHLEPPERS	SCHOOLMASTER	SCINTILLON
SCAPULARIES	SCATTINESSES	SCHEMOZZLING	SCHLEPPIER	SCHOOLMASTERED	SCINTILLONS
SCAPULATED	SCATURIENT	SCHERZANDI	SCHLEPPIEST	SCHOOLMASTERING	SCINTILLOSCOPE
SCAPULIMANCIES	SCAVENGERED	SCHERZANDO	SCHLEPPING	SCHOOLMASTERISH	SCINTILLOSCOPES
SCAPULIMANCY	SCAVENGERIES	SCHERZANDOS	SCHLIMAZEL	SCHOOLMASTERLY	SCINTISCAN
SCAPULIMANTIC	SCAVENGERING	SCHIAVONES	SCHLIMAZELS	SCHOOLMASTERS	SCINTISCANNER
SCAPULOMANCIES	SCAVENGERINGS	SCHILLERISATION	SCHLOCKERS	SCHOOLMATE	SCINTISCANNERS
SCAPULOMANCY	SCAVENGERS	SCHILLERISE	SCHLOCKIER	SCHOOLMATES	SCINTISCANS
SCAPULOMANTIC	SCAVENGERY	SCHILLERISED	SCHLOCKIEST	SCHOOLMISTRESS	SCIOLISTIC
SCARABAEAN	SCAVENGING	SCHILLERISES	SCHLUMBERGERA	SCHOOLMISTRESSY	SCIOMACHIES
SCARABAEANS	SCAVENGINGS	SCHILLERISING	SCHLUMBERGERAS	SCHOOLROOM	SCIOMANCER
SCARABAEID	SCAZONTICS	SCHILLERIZATION	SCHLUMPIER	SCHOOLROOMS	SCIOMANCERS
SCARABAEIDS	SCELERATES	SCHILLERIZE	SCHLUMPIEST	SCHOOLTEACHER	SCIOMANCIES
SCARABAEIST	SCENARISATION	SCHILLERIZED	SCHLUMPING	SCHOOLTEACHERS	SCIOMANCY
SCARABAEISTS	SCENARISATIONS	SCHILLERIZES	SCHMALTZES	SCHOOLTEACHING	SCIOMANTIC
SCARABAEOID	SCENARISED	SCHILLERIZING	SCHMALTZIER	SCHOOLTEACHINGS	SCIOPHYTES
SCARABAEOIDS	SCENARISES	SCHILLINGS	SCHMALTZIEST	SCHOOLTIDE	SCIOPHYTIC
SCARABAEUS	SCENARISING	SCHINDYLESES	SCHMALZIER	SCHOOLTIDES	SCIOSOPHIES
SCARABAEUSES	SCENARISTS	SCHINDYLESIS	SCHMALZIEST	SCHOOLTIME	SCIRRHOSITIES
SCARABOIDS	SCENARIZATION	SCHINDYLETIC	SCHMEARING	SCHOOLTIMES	SCIRRHOSITY
SCARAMOUCH	SCENARIZATIONS	SCHIPPERKE	SCHMEERING	SCHOOLWARD	SCIRRHUSES
SCARAMOUCHE	SCENARIZED	SCHIPPERKES	SCHMOOSING	SCHOOLWARDS	SCISSIPARITIES
SCARAMOUCHES	SCENARIZES	SCHISMATIC	SCHMOOZERS	SCHOOLWORK	SCISSIPARITY
SCARCEMENT	SCENARIZING	SCHISMATICAL	SCHMOOZIER	SCHOOLWORKS	SCISSORERS
SCARCEMENTS	SCENESHIFTER	SCHISMATICALLY	SCHMOOZIEST	SCHORLACEOUS	SCISSORING
SCARCENESS	SCENESHIFTERS	SCHISMATICALS	SCHMOOZING	SCHORLOMITE	SCISSORTAIL
SCARCENESSES	SCENICALLY	SCHISMATICS	SCHMUTTERS	SCHORLOMITES	SCISSORTAILS
SCARCITIES	SCENOGRAPHER	SCHISMATISE	SCHNAPPERS	SCHOTTISCHE	SCISSORWISE
SCARECROWS	SCENOGRAPHERS	SCHISMATISED	SCHNAPPSES	SCHOTTISCHES	SCITAMINEOUS
SCAREHEADS	SCENOGRAPHIC	SCHISMATISES	SCHNAUZERS	SCHRECKLICH	SCLAUNDERS
SCAREMONGER	SCENOGRAPHICAL	SCHISMATISING	SCHNITZELS	SCHUSSBOOMER	SCLEREIDES
SCAREMONGERING	SCENOGRAPHIES	SCHISMATIZE	SCHNORKELED	SCHUSSBOOMERS	SCLERENCHYMA
					SCLERENCHYMAS

SCLERENCHYMATA	SCOPOPHILIAC	SCRAPEGOODS	SCRIBBLEMENT	SCROGGIEST	SCULDUGGERIES
SCLERIASES	SCOPOPHILIACS	SCRAPEGUTS	SCRIBBLEMENTS	SCROLLABLE	SCULDUGGERY
SCLERIASIS	SCOPOPHILIAS	SCRAPEPENNIES	SCRIBBLERS	SCROLLWISE	SCULLERIES
SCLERITISES	SCOPOPHILIC	SCRAPEPENNY	SCRIBBLIER	SCROLLWORK	SCULPTRESS
SCLEROCAULIES	SCOPOPHOBIA	SCRAPERBOARD	SCRIBBLIEST	SCROLLWORKS	SCULPTRESSES
SCLEROCAULOUS	SCOPOPHOBIAS	SCRAPERBOARDS	SCRIBBLING	SCROOCHING	SCULPTURAL
SCLEROCAULY	SCOPTOPHILIA	SCRAPHEAPS	SCRIBBLINGLY	SCROOTCHED	SCULPTURALLY
SCLERODERM	SCOPTOPHILIAS	SCRAPPAGES	SCRIBBLINGS	SCROOTCHES	SCULPTURED
SCLERODERMA	SCOPTOPHOBIA	SCRAPPIEST	SCRIECHING	SCROOTCHING	SCULPTURES
SCLERODERMAS	SCOPTOPHOBIAS	SCRAPPINESS	SCRIEVEBOARD	SCROPHULARIA	SCULPTURESQUE
SCLERODERMATA	SCORBUTICALLY	SCRAPPINESSES	SCRIEVEBOARDS	SCROPHULARIAS	SCULPTURESQUELY
SCLERODERMATOUS	SCORCHINGLY	SCRAPYARDS	SCRIGGLIER	SCROUNGERS	SCULPTURING
SCLERODERMIA	SCORCHINGNESS	SCRATCHBACK	SCRIGGLIEST	SCROUNGIER	SCULPTURINGS
SCLERODERMIAS	SCORCHINGNESSES	SCRATCHBACKS	SCRIGGLING	SCROUNGIEST	SCUMBERING
SCLERODERMIC	SCORCHINGS	SCRATCHBOARD	SCRIMMAGED	SCROUNGING	SCUMBLINGS
SCLERODERMITE	SCORDATURA	SCRATCHBOARDS	SCRIMMAGER	SCROUNGINGS	SCUMFISHED
SCLERODERMITES	SCORDATURAS	SCRATCHBUILD	SCRIMMAGERS	SCROWDGING	SCUMFISHES
SCLERODERMOUS	SCOREBOARD	SCRATCHBUILDER	SCRIMMAGES	SCRUBBABLE	SCUMFISHING
SCLERODERMS	SCOREBOARDS	SCRATCHBUILDERS	SCRIMMAGING	SCRUBBIEST	SCUNCHEONS
SCLEROMALACIA	SCORECARDS	SCRATCHBUILDING	SCRIMPIEST	SCRUBBINESS	SCUNGILLIS
SCLEROMALACIAS	SCOREKEEPER	SCRATCHBUILDS	SCRIMPINESS	SCRUBBINESSES	SCUNNERING
SCLEROMATA	SCOREKEEPERS	SCRATCHBUILT	SCRIMPINESSES	SCRUBBINGS	SCUPPERING
SCLEROMETER	SCORELINES	SCRATCHCARD	SCRIMPNESS	SCRUBLANDS	SCUPPERNONG
SCLEROMETERS	SCORESHEET	SCRATCHCARDS	SCRIMPNESSES	SCRUBWOMAN	SCUPPERNONGS
SCLEROMETRIC	SCORESHEETS	SCRATCHERS	SCRIMSHANDER	SCRUBWOMEN	SCURFINESS
SCLEROPHYLL	SCORIACEOUS	SCRATCHIER	SCRIMSHANDERED	SCRUFFIEST	SCURFINESSES
SCLEROPHYLLIES	SCORIFICATION	SCRATCHIES	SCRIMSHANDERING	SCRUFFINESS	SCURRILITIES
SCLEROPHYLLOUS	SCORIFICATIONS	SCRATCHIEST	SCRIMSHANDERS	SCRUFFINESSES	SCURRILITY
SCLEROPHYLLS	SCORIFIERS	SCRATCHILY	SCRIMSHANDIED	SCRUMDOWNS	SCURRILOUS
SCLEROPHYLLY	SCORIFYING	SCRATCHINESS	SCRIMSHANDIES	SCRUMMAGED	SCURRILOUSLY
SCLEROPROTEIN	SCORNFULLY	SCRATCHINESSES	SCRIMSHANDY	SCRUMMAGER	SCURRILOUSNESS
SCLEROPROTEINS	SCORNFULNESS	SCRATCHING	SCRIMSHANDYING	SCRUMMAGERS	SCURRIOURS
SCLEROSING	SCORNFULNESSES	SCRATCHINGLY	SCRIMSHANK	SCRUMMAGES	SCURVINESS
SCLEROTALS	SCORODITES	SCRATCHINGS	SCRIMSHANKED	SCRUMMAGING	SCURVINESSES
SCLEROTIAL	SCORPAENID	SCRATCHLESS	SCRIMSHANKING	SCRUMMIEST	SCUTATIONS
SCLEROTICS	SCORPAENIDS	SCRATCHPLATE	SCRIMSHANKS	SCRUMPLING	SCUTCHEONLESS
SCLEROTINS	SCORPAENOID	SCRATCHPLATES	SCRIMSHAWED	SCRUMPOXES	SCUTCHEONS
SCLEROTIOID	SCORPAENOIDS	SCRATTLING	SCRIMSHAWING	SCRUMPTIOUS	SCUTCHINGS
SCLEROTISATION	SCORPIOIDS	SCRAUCHING	SCRIMSHAWS	SCRUMPTIOUSLY	SCUTELLATE
SCLEROTISATIONS	SCORPIONIC	SCRAUGHING	SCRIMSHONER	SCRUMPTIOUSNESS	SCUTELLATED
SCLEROTISE	SCORZONERA	SCRAWLIEST	SCRIMSHONERS	SCRUNCHEON	SCUTELLATION
SCLEROTISED	SCORZONERAS	SCRAWLINGLY	SCRIPOPHILE	SCRUNCHEONS	SCUTELLATIONS
SCLEROTISES	SCOTODINIA	SCRAWLINGS	SCRIPOPHILES	SCRUNCHIER	SCUTTERING
SCLEROTISING	SCOTODINIAS	SCRAWNIEST	SCRIPOPHILIES	SCRUNCHIES	SCUTTLEBUTT
SCLEROTITIS	SCOTOMATOUS	SCRAWNINESS	SCRIPOPHILIST	SCRUNCHIEST	SCUTTLEBUTTS
SCLEROTITISES	SCOTOMETER	SCRAWNINESSES	SCRIPOPHILISTS	SCRUNCHING	SCUTTLEFUL
SCLEROTIUM	SCOTOMETERS	SCREAKIEST	SCRIPOPHILY	SCRUNCHION	SCUTTLEFULS
SCLEROTIZATION	SCOUNDRELLY	SCREAMINGLY	SCRIPPAGES	SCRUNCHIONS	SCUZZBALLS
SCLEROTIZATIONS	SCOUNDRELS	SCREECHERS	SCRIPTORIA	SCRUNTIEST	SCYPHIFORM
SCLEROTIZE	SCOUTCRAFT	SCREECHIER	SCRIPTORIAL	SCRUPLELESS	SCYPHISTOMA
SCLEROTIZED	SCOUTCRAFTS	SCREECHIEST	SCRIPTORIUM	SCRUPULOSITIES	SCYPHISTOMAE
SCLEROTIZES	SCOUTHERED	SCREECHING	SCRIPTORIUMS	SCRUPULOSITY	SCYPHISTOMAS
SCLEROTIZING	SCOUTHERING	SCREEDINGS	SCRIPTURAL	SCRUPULOUS	SCYPHOZOAN
SCLEROTOMIES	SCOUTHERINGS	SCREENABLE	SCRIPTURALISM	SCRUPULOUSLY	SCYPHOZOANS
SCLEROTOMY	SCOUTMASTER	SCREENAGER	SCRIPTURALISMS	SCRUPULOUSNESS	SCYTHELIKE
SCOFFINGLY	SCOUTMASTERS	SCREENAGERS	SCRIPTURALIST	SCRUTABILITIES	SDEIGNFULL
SCOLDINGLY	SCOWDERING	SCREENCRAFT	SCRIPTURALISTS	SCRUTABILITY	SDEIGNFULLY
SCOLECIFORM	SCOWDERINGS	SCREENCRAFTS	SCRIPTURALLY	SCRUTATORS	SDRUCCIOLA
SCOLECITES	SCOWLINGLY	SCREENFULS	SCRIPTURES	SCRUTINEER	SEABEACHES
SCOLLOPING	SCOWTHERED	SCREENINGS	SCRIPTURISM	SCRUTINEERS	SEABORGIUM
SCOLOPACEOUS	SCOWTHERING	SCREENLAND	SCRIPTURISMS	SCRUTINIES	SEABORGIUMS
SCOLOPENDRA	SCRABBLERS	SCREENLANDS	SCRIPTURIST	SCRUTINISE	SEABOTTLES
SCOLOPENDRAS	SCRABBLIER	SCREENLIKE	SCRIPTURISTS	SCRUTINISED	SEACUNNIES
SCOLOPENDRID	SCRABBLIEST	SCREENPLAY	SCRIPTWRITER	SCRUTINISER	SEAFARINGS
SCOLOPENDRIDS	SCRABBLING	SCREENPLAYS	SCRIPTWRITERS	SCRUTINISERS	SEALIFTING
SCOLOPENDRIFORM	SCRAGGEDNESS	SCREENSAVER	SCRIPTWRITING	SCRUTINISES	SEALPOINTS
SCOLOPENDRINE	SCRAGGEDNESSES	SCREENSAVERS	SCRIPTWRITINGS	SCRUTINISING	SEAMANLIKE
SCOLOPENDRIUM	SCRAGGIEST	SCREENSHOT	SCRITCHING	SCRUTINISINGLY	SEAMANSHIP
SCOLOPENDRIUMS	SCRAGGINESS	SCREENSHOTS	SCRIVEBOARD	SCRUTINIZE	SEAMANSHIPS
SCOLYTOIDS	SCRAGGINESSES	SCREENWRITER	SCRIVEBOARDS	SCRUTINIZED	SEAMINESSES
SCOMBROIDS	SCRAGGLIER	SCREENWRITERS	SCRIVENERS	SCRUTINIZER	SEAMLESSLY
SCOMFISHED	SCRAGGLIEST	SCREEVINGS	SCRIVENERSHIP	SCRUTINIZERS	SEAMLESSNESS
SCOMFISHES	SCRAGGLING	SCREICHING	SCRIVENERSHIPS	SCRUTINIZES	SEAMLESSNESSES
SCOMFISHING	SCRAICHING	SCREIGHING	SCRIVENING	SCRUTINIZING	SEAMSTRESS
SCONCHEONS	SCRAIGHING	SCREWBALLS	SCRIVENINGS	SCRUTINIZINGLY	SEAMSTRESSES
SCOOTCHING	SCRAMBLERS	SCREWBEANS	SCROBICULAR	SCRUTINOUS	SEAMSTRESSIES
SCOOTERIST	SCRAMBLING	SCREWDRIVER	SCROBICULATE	SCRUTINOUSLY	SEAMSTRESSY
SCOOTERISTS	SCRAMBLINGLY	SCREWDRIVERS	SCROBICULATED	SCRUTOIRES	SEANNACHIE
SCOPELOIDS	SCRAMBLINGS	SCREWINESS	SCROBICULE	SCUDDALERS	SEANNACHIES
SCOPOLAMINE	SCRANCHING	SCREWINESSES	SCROBICULES	SCULDUDDERIES	SEAQUARIUM
SCOPOLAMINES	SCRANNIEST	SCREWWORMS	SCROFULOUS	SCULDUDDERY	SEAQUARIUMS
SCOPOLINES	SCRAPBOOKS	SCRIBACIOUS	SCROFULOUSLY	SCULDUDDRIES	SEARCHABLE
SCOPOPHILIA	SCRAPEGOOD	SCRIBACIOUSNESS	SCROFULOUSNESS	SCULDUDDRY	SEARCHINGLY

SEARCHINGNESS	SECRETORIES	SECURITIES	SEGREGATIONAL	SELENOGRAPHERS	SEMICHORUSES
SEARCHINGNESSES	SECTARIANISE	SECURITISATION	SEGREGATIONIST	SELENOGRAPHIC	SEMICIRCLE
SEARCHLESS	SECTARIANISED	SECURITISATIONS	SEGREGATIONISTS	SELENOGRAPHICAL	SEMICIRCLED
SEARCHLIGHT	SECTARIANISES	SECURITISE	SEGREGATIONS	SELENOGRAPHIES	SEMICIRCLES
SEARCHLIGHTS	SECTARIANISING	SECURITISED	SEGREGATIVE	SELENOGRAPHIST	SEMICIRCULAR
SEAREDNESS	SECTARIANISM	SECURITISES	SEGREGATOR	SELENOGRAPHISTS	SEMICIRCULARLY
SEAREDNESSES	SECTARIANISMS	SECURITISING	SEGREGATORS	SELENOGRAPHS	SEMICIRQUE
SEARNESSES	SECTARIANIZE	SECURITIZATION	SEGUIDILLA	SELENOGRAPHY	SEMICIRQUES
SEASICKEST	SECTARIANIZED	SECURITIZATIONS	SEGUIDILLAS	SELENOLOGICAL	SEMICIVILISED
SEASICKNESS	SECTARIANIZES	SECURITIZE	SEIGNEURIAL	SELENOLOGIES	SEMICIVILIZED
SEASICKNESSES	SECTARIANIZING	SECURITIZED	SEIGNEURIE	SELENOLOGIST	SEMICLASSIC
SEASONABLE	SECTARIANS	SECURITIZES	SEIGNEURIES	SELENOLOGISTS	SEMICLASSICAL
SEASONABLENESS	SECTILITIES	SECURITIZING	SEIGNIORAGE	SELENOLOGY	SEMICLASSICS
SEASONABLY	SECTIONALISE	SECUROCRAT	SEIGNIORAGES	SELFISHNESS	SEMICOLONIAL
SEASONALITIES	SECTIONALISED	SECUROCRATS	SEIGNIORALTIES	SELFISHNESSES	SEMICOLONIALISM
SEASONALITY	SECTIONALISES	SEDATENESS	SEIGNIORALTY	SELFLESSLY	SEMICOLONIES
SEASONALLY	SECTIONALISING	SEDATENESSES	SEIGNIORIAL	SELFLESSNESS	SEMICOLONS
SEASONALNESS	SECTIONALISM	SEDENTARILY	SEIGNIORIES	SELFLESSNESSES	SEMICOLONY
SEASONALNESSES	SECTIONALISMS	SEDENTARINESS	SEIGNIORSHIP	SELFNESSES	SEMICOMATOSE
SEASONINGS	SECTIONALIST	SEDENTARINESSES	SEIGNIORSHIPS	SELFSAMENESS	SEMICOMMERCIAL
SEASONLESS	SECTIONALISTS	SEDGELANDS	SEIGNORAGE	SELFSAMENESSES	SEMICONDUCTING
SEASTRANDS	SECTIONALIZE	SEDIGITATED	SEIGNORAGES	SELLOTAPED	SEMICONDUCTION
SEAWORTHIER	SECTIONALIZED	SEDIMENTABLE	SEIGNORIAL	SELLOTAPES	SEMICONDUCTIONS
SEAWORTHIEST	SECTIONALIZES	SEDIMENTARILY	SEIGNORIES	SELLOTAPING	SEMICONDUCTOR
SEAWORTHINESS	SECTIONALIZING	SEDIMENTARY	SEISMICALLY	SELTZOGENE	SEMICONDUCTORS
SEAWORTHINESSES	SECTIONALLY	SEDIMENTATION	SEISMICITIES	SELTZOGENES	SEMICONSCIOUS
SEBIFEROUS	SECTIONALS	SEDIMENTATIONS	SEISMICITY	SELVEDGING	SEMICONSCIOUSLY
SEBORRHEAL	SECTIONING	SEDIMENTED	SEISMOGRAM	SEMAINIERS	SEMICRYSTALLIC
SEBORRHEAS	SECTIONISATION	SEDIMENTING	SEISMOGRAMS	SEMANTEMES	SEMICRYSTALLINE
SEBORRHEIC	SECTIONISATIONS	SEDIMENTOLOGIC	SEISMOGRAPH	SEMANTICAL	SEMICYLINDER
SEBORRHOEA	SECTIONISE	SEDIMENTOLOGIES	SEISMOGRAPHER	SEMANTICALLY	SEMICYLINDERS
SEBORRHOEAL	SECTIONISED	SEDIMENTOLOGIST	SEISMOGRAPHERS	SEMANTICIST	SEMICYLINDRICAL
SEBORRHOEAS	SECTIONISES	SEDIMENTOLOGY	SEISMOGRAPHIC	SEMANTICISTS	SEMIDARKNESS
SEBORRHOEIC	SECTIONISING	SEDIMENTOUS	SEISMOGRAPHICAL	SEMANTIDES	SEMIDARKNESSES
SECERNENTS	SECTIONIZATION	SEDITIONARIES	SEISMOGRAPHIES	SEMAPHORED	SEMIDEIFIED
SECERNMENT	SECTIONIZATIONS	SEDITIONARY	SEISMOGRAPHS	SEMAPHORES	SEMIDEIFIES
SECERNMENTS	SECTIONIZE	SEDITIOUSLY	SEISMOGRAPHY	SEMAPHORIC	SEMIDEIFYING
SECESSIONAL	SECTIONIZED	SEDITIOUSNESS	SEISMOLOGIC	SEMAPHORICAL	SEMIDEPONENT
SECESSIONISM	SECTIONIZES	SEDITIOUSNESSES	SEISMOLOGICAL	SEMAPHORICALLY	SEMIDEPONENTS
SECESSIONISMS	SECTIONIZING	SEDUCEABLE	SEISMOLOGICALLY	SEMAPHORING	SEMIDESERT
SECESSIONIST	SECTORIALS	SEDUCEMENT	SEISMOLOGIES	SEMASIOLOGICAL	SEMIDESERTS
SECESSIONISTS	SECTORISATION	SEDUCEMENTS	SEISMOLOGIST	SEMASIOLOGIES	SEMIDETACHED
SECESSIONS	SECTORISATIONS	SEDUCINGLY	SEISMOLOGISTS	SEMASIOLOGIST	SEMIDIAMETER
SECLUDEDLY	SECTORISED	SEDUCTIONS	SEISMOLOGY	SEMASIOLOGISTS	SEMIDIAMETERS
SECLUDEDNESS	SECTORISES	SEDUCTIVELY	SEISMOMETER	SEMASIOLOGY	SEMIDIURNAL
SECLUDEDNESSES	SECTORISING	SEDUCTIVENESS	SEISMOMETERS	SEMATOLOGIES	SEMIDIVINE
SECLUSIONIST	SECTORIZATION	SEDUCTIVENESSES	SEISMOMETRIC	SEMATOLOGY	SEMIDOCUMENTARY
SECLUSIONISTS	SECTORIZATIONS	SEDUCTRESS	SEISMOMETRICAL	SEMBLABLES	SEMIDOMINANT
SECLUSIONS	SECTORIZED	SEDUCTRESSES	SEISMOMETRIES	SEMBLANCES	SEMIDRYING
SECLUSIVELY	SECTORIZES	SEDULITIES	SEISMOMETRY	SEMBLATIVE	SEMIDWARFS
SECLUSIVENESS	SECTORIZING	SEDULOUSLY	SEISMONASTIC	SEMEIOLOGIC	SEMIDWARVES
SECLUSIVENESSES	SECULARISATION	SEDULOUSNESS	SEISMONASTIES	SEMEIOLOGICAL	SEMIELLIPTICAL
SECOBARBITAL	SECULARISATIONS	SEDULOUSNESSES	SEISMONASTY	SEMEIOLOGIES	SEMIEMPIRICAL
SECOBARBITALS	SECULARISE	SEECATCHIE	SEISMOSCOPE	SEMEIOLOGIST	SEMIEVERGREEN
SECONDARIES	SECULARISED	SEEDEATERS	SEISMOSCOPES	SEMEIOLOGISTS	SEMIFEUDAL
SECONDARILY	SECULARISER	SEEDINESSES	SEISMOSCOPIC	SEMEIOLOGY	SEMIFINALIST
SECONDARINESS	SECULARISERS	SEEDNESSES	SELACHIANS	SEMEIOTICIAN	SEMIFINALISTS
SECONDARINESSES	SECULARISES	SEEDSTOCKS	SELAGINELLA	SEMEIOTICIANS	SEMIFINALS
SECONDHAND	SECULARISING	SEEMELESSE	SELAGINELLAS	SEMEIOTICS	SEMIFINISHED
SECONDMENT	SECULARISM	SEEMINGNESS	SELDOMNESS	SEMELPARITIES	SEMIFITTED
SECONDMENTS	SECULARISMS	SEEMINGNESSES	SELDOMNESSES	SEMELPARITY	SEMIFLEXIBLE
SECRETAGES	SECULARIST	SEEMLIHEAD	SELECTABLE	SEMELPAROUS	SEMIFLUIDIC
SECRETAGOGIC	SECULARISTIC	SEEMLIHEADS	SELECTIONIST	SEMESTRIAL	SEMIFLUIDITIES
SECRETAGOGUE	SECULARISTS	SEEMLIHEDS	SELECTIONISTS	SEMIABSTRACT	SEMIFLUIDITY
SECRETAGOGUES	SECULARITIES	SEEMLINESS	SELECTIONS	SEMIABSTRACTION	SEMIFLUIDS
SECRETAIRE	SECULARITY	SEEMLINESSES	SELECTIVELY	SEMIANGLES	SEMIFORMAL
SECRETAIRES	SECULARIZATION	SEEMLYHEDS	SELECTIVENESS	SEMIANNUAL	SEMIFREDDO
SECRETARIAL	SECULARIZATIONS	SEERSUCKER	SELECTIVENESSES	SEMIANNUALLY	SEMIFREDDOS
SECRETARIAT	SECULARIZE	SEERSUCKERS	SELECTIVITIES	SEMIAQUATIC	SEMIGLOBULAR
SECRETARIATE	SECULARIZED	SEETHINGLY	SELECTIVITY	SEMIARBOREAL	SEMIGLOSSES
SECRETARIATES	SECULARIZER	SEGHOLATES	SELECTNESS	SEMIARIDITIES	SEMIGROUPS
SECRETARIATS	SECULARIZERS	SEGMENTALLY	SELECTNESSES	SEMIARIDITY	SEMIHOBOES
SECRETARIES	SECULARIZES	SEGMENTARY	SELECTORATE	SEMIAUTOMATIC	SEMILEGENDARY
SECRETARYSHIP	SECULARIZING	SEGMENTATE	SELECTORATES	SEMIAUTOMATICS	SEMILETHAL
SECRETARYSHIPS	SECUNDINES	SEGMENTATION	SELECTORIAL	SEMIAUTONOMOUS	SEMILETHALS
SECRETIONAL	SECUNDOGENITURE	SEGMENTATIONS	SELEGILINE	SEMIBREVES	SEMILIQUID
SECRETIONARY	SECURANCES	SEGMENTING	SELEGILINES	SEMICARBAZIDE	SEMILIQUIDS
SECRETIONS	SECUREMENT	SEGREGABLE	SELENIFEROUS	SEMICARBAZIDES	SEMILITERATE
SECRETIVELY	SECUREMENTS	SEGREGANTS	SELENOCENTRIC	SEMICARBAZONE	SEMILITERATES
SECRETIVENESS	SECURENESS	SEGREGATED	SELENODONT	SEMICARBAZONES	SEMILOGARITHMIC
SECRETIVENESSES	SECURENESSES	SEGREGATES	SELENODONTS	SEMICENTENNIAL	SEMILUCENT
SECRETNESS	SECURIFORM	SEGREGATING	SELENOGRAPH	SEMICENTENNIALS	SEMILUNATE
SECRETNESSES	SECURITANS	SEGREGATION	SELENOGRAPHER	SEMICHORUS	SEMILUSTROUS

SEMIMANUFACTURE	SEMITERETE	SENSITISING	SEPARABLENESSES	SEPULCHRES	SERICITIZATIONS
SEMIMENSTRUAL	SEMITERRESTRIAL	SENSITIVELY	SEPARATELY	SEPULCHRING	SERICTERIA
SEMIMETALLIC	SEMITONALLY	SENSITIVENESS	SEPARATENESS	SEPULCHROUS	SERICTERIUM
SEMIMETALS	SEMITONICALLY	SENSITIVENESSES	SEPARATENESSES	SEPULTURAL	SERICULTURAL
SEMIMONASTIC	SEMITRAILER	SENSITIVES	SEPARATING	SEPULTURED	SERICULTURE
SEMIMONTHLIES	SEMITRAILERS	SENSITIVITIES	SEPARATION	SEPULTURES	SERICULTURES
SEMIMONTHLY	SEMITRANSLUCENT	SENSITIVITY	SEPARATIONISM	SEPULTURING	SERICULTURIST
SEMIMYSTICAL	SEMITRANSPARENT	SENSITIZATION	SEPARATIONISMS	SEQUACIOUS	SERICULTURISTS
SEMINALITIES	SEMITROPIC	SENSITIZATIONS	SEPARATIONIST	SEQUACIOUSLY	SERIGRAPHER
SEMINALITY	SEMITROPICAL	SENSITIZED	SEPARATIONISTS	SEQUACIOUSNESS	SERIGRAPHERS
SEMINARIAL	SEMITROPICS	SENSITIZER	SEPARATIONS	SEQUACITIES	SERIGRAPHIC
SEMINARIAN	SEMITRUCKS	SENSITIZERS	SEPARATISM	SEQUELISED	SERIGRAPHIES
SEMINARIANS	SEMIVITREOUS	SENSITIZES	SEPARATISMS	SEQUELISES	SERIGRAPHS
SEMINARIES	SEMIVOCALIC	SENSITIZING	SEPARATIST	SEQUELISING	SERIGRAPHY
SEMINARIST	SEMIVOWELS	SENSITOMETER	SEPARATISTIC	SEQUELIZED	SERINETTES
SEMINARISTS	SEMIWEEKLIES	SENSITOMETERS	SEPARATISTS	SEQUELIZES	SERIOCOMIC
SEMINATING	SEMIWEEKLY	SENSITOMETRIC	SEPARATIVE	SEQUELIZING	SERIOCOMICAL
SEMINATION	SEMIYEARLY	SENSITOMETRIES	SEPARATIVELY	SEQUENCERS	SERIOCOMICALLY
SEMINATIONS	SEMPERVIVUM	SENSITOMETRY	SEPARATIVENESS	SEQUENCIES	SERIOUSNESS
SEMINATURAL	SEMPERVIVUMS	SENSOMOTOR	SEPARATORIES	SEQUENCING	SERIOUSNESSES
SEMINIFEROUS	SEMPITERNAL	SENSORIALLY	SEPARATORS	SEQUENCINGS	SERJEANCIES
SEMINOMADIC	SEMPITERNALLY	SENSORIMOTOR	SEPARATORY	SEQUENTIAL	SERJEANTIES
SEMINOMADS	SEMPITERNITIES	SENSORINEURAL	SEPARATRICES	SEQUENTIALITIES	SERJEANTRIES
SEMINOMATA	SEMPITERNITY	SENSORIUMS	SEPARATRIX	SEQUENTIALITY	SERJEANTRY
SEMINUDITIES	SEMPITERNUM	SENSUALISATION	SEPARATUMS	SEQUENTIALLY	SERJEANTSHIP
SEMINUDITY	SEMPITERNUMS	SENSUALISATIONS	SEPIOLITES	SEQUESTERED	SERJEANTSHIPS
SEMIOCHEMICAL	SEMPSTERING	SENSUALISE	SEPIOSTAIRE	SEQUESTERING	SERMONEERS
SEMIOCHEMICALS	SEMPSTERINGS	SENSUALISED	SEPIOSTAIRES	SEQUESTERS	SERMONETTE
SEMIOFFICIAL	SEMPSTRESS	SENSUALISES	SEPTATIONS	SEQUESTRABLE	SERMONETTES
SEMIOFFICIALLY	SEMPSTRESSES	SENSUALISING	SEPTAVALENT	SEQUESTRAL	SERMONICAL
SEMIOLOGIC	SEMPSTRESSING	SENSUALISM	SEPTEMVIRATE	SEQUESTRANT	SERMONINGS
SEMIOLOGICAL	SEMPSTRESSINGS	SENSUALISMS	SEPTEMVIRATES	SEQUESTRANTS	SERMONISED
SEMIOLOGICALLY	SENARMONTITE	SENSUALIST	SEPTEMVIRI	SEQUESTRATE	SERMONISER
SEMIOLOGIES	SENARMONTITES	SENSUALISTIC	SEPTEMVIRS	SEQUESTRATED	SERMONISERS
SEMIOLOGIST	SENATORIAL	SENSUALISTS	SEPTENARIES	SEQUESTRATES	SERMONISES
SEMIOLOGISTS	SENATORIALLY	SENSUALITIES	SEPTENARII	SEQUESTRATING	SERMONISING
SEMIOPAQUE	SENATORIAN	SENSUALITY	SEPTENARIUS	SEQUESTRATION	SERMONIZED
SEMIOTICIAN	SENATORSHIP	SENSUALIZATION	SEPTENDECILLION	SEQUESTRATIONS	SERMONIZER
SEMIOTICIANS	SENATORSHIPS	SENSUALIZATIONS	SEPTENNATE	SEQUESTRATOR	SERMONIZERS
SEMIOTICIST	SENECTITUDE	SENSUALIZE	SEPTENNATES	SEQUESTRATORS	SERMONIZES
SEMIOTICISTS	SENECTITUDES	SENSUALIZED	SEPTENNIAL	SEQUESTRUM	SERMONIZING
SEMIOVIPAROUS	SENESCENCE	SENSUALIZES	SEPTENNIALLY	SEQUESTRUMS	SEROCONVERSION
SEMIPALMATE	SENESCENCES	SENSUALIZING	SEPTENNIUM	SERAPHICAL	SEROCONVERSIONS
SEMIPALMATED	SENESCHALS	SENSUALNESS	SEPTENNIUMS	SERAPHICALLY	SEROCONVERT
SEMIPALMATION	SENESCHALSHIP	SENSUALNESSES	SEPTENTRIAL	SERAPHINES	SEROCONVERTED
SEMIPALMATIONS	SENESCHALSHIPS	SENSUOSITIES	SEPTENTRION	SERASKIERATE	SEROCONVERTING
SEMIPARASITE	SENHORITAS	SENSUOSITY	SEPTENTRIONAL	SERASKIERATES	SEROCONVERTS
SEMIPARASITES	SENILITIES	SENSUOUSLY	SEPTENTRIONALLY	SERASKIERS	SERODIAGNOSES
SEMIPARASITIC	SENIORITIES	SENSUOUSNESS	SEPTENTRIONES	SERENADERS	SERODIAGNOSIS
SEMIPARASITISM	SENNACHIES	SENSUOUSNESSES	SEPTENTRIONS	SERENADING	SERODIAGNOSTIC
SEMIPARASITISMS	SENSATIONAL	SENTENCERS	SEPTICAEMIA	SERENDIPITIES	SEROLOGICAL
SEMIPELLUCID	SENSATIONALISE	SENTENCING	SEPTICAEMIAS	SERENDIPITIST	SEROLOGICALLY
SEMIPERIMETER	SENSATIONALISED	SENTENTIAE	SEPTICAEMIC	SERENDIPITISTS	SEROLOGIES
SEMIPERIMETERS	SENSATIONALISES	SENTENTIAL	SEPTICALLY	SERENDIPITOUS	SEROLOGIST
SEMIPERMANENT	SENSATIONALISM	SENTENTIALLY	SEPTICEMIA	SERENDIPITOUSLY	SEROLOGISTS
SEMIPERMEABLE	SENSATIONALISMS	SENTENTIOUS	SEPTICEMIAS	SERENDIPITY	SERONEGATIVE
SEMIPLUMES	SENSATIONALIST	SENTENTIOUSLY	SEPTICEMIC	SERENENESS	SERONEGATIVITY
SEMIPOLITICAL	SENSATIONALISTS	SENTENTIOUSNESS	SEPTICIDAL	SERENENESSES	SEROPOSITIVE
SEMIPOPULAR	SENSATIONALIZE	SENTIENCES	SEPTICIDALLY	SERENITIES	SEROPOSITIVITY
SEMIPORCELAIN	SENSATIONALIZED	SENTIENCIES	SEPTICITIES	SERGEANCIES	SEROPURULENT
SEMIPORCELAINS	SENSATIONALIZES	SENTIENTLY	SEPTIFEROUS	SERGEANTIES	SEROSITIES
SEMIPORNOGRAPHY	SENSATIONALLY	SENTIMENTAL	SEPTIFRAGAL	SERGEANTSHIP	SEROTAXONOMIES
SEMIPOSTAL	SENSATIONISM	SENTIMENTALISE	SEPTILATERAL	SERGEANTSHIPS	SEROTAXONOMY
SEMIPOSTALS	SENSATIONISMS	SENTIMENTALISED	SEPTILLION	SERIALISATION	SEROTHERAPIES
SEMIPRECIOUS	SENSATIONIST	SENTIMENTALISES	SEPTILLIONS	SERIALISATIONS	SEROTHERAPY
SEMIPRIVATE	SENSATIONISTS	SENTIMENTALISM	SEPTILLIONTH	SERIALISED	SEROTINIES
SEMIPUBLIC	SENSATIONLESS	SENTIMENTALISMS	SEPTILLIONTHS	SERIALISES	SEROTINOUS
SEMIQUAVER	SENSATIONS	SENTIMENTALIST	SEPTIMOLES	SERIALISING	SEROTONERGIC
SEMIQUAVERS	SENSELESSLY	SENTIMENTALISTS	SEPTIVALENT	SERIALISMS	SEROTONINERGIC
SEMIRELIGIOUS	SENSELESSNESS	SENTIMENTALITY	SEPTUAGENARIAN	SERIALISTS	SEROTONINS
SEMIRETIRED	SENSELESSNESSES	SENTIMENTALIZE	SEPTUAGENARIANS	SERIALITIES	SEROTYPING
SEMIRETIREMENT	SENSIBILIA	SENTIMENTALIZED	SEPTUAGENARIES	SERIALIZATION	SEROTYPINGS
SEMIRETIREMENTS	SENSIBILITIES	SENTIMENTALIZES	SEPTUAGENARY	SERIALIZATIONS	SEROUSNESS
SEMIROUNDS	SENSIBILITY	SENTIMENTALLY	SEPTUPLETS	SERIALIZED	SEROUSNESSES
SEMISACRED	SENSIBLENESS	SENTIMENTS	SEPTUPLICATE	SERIALIZES	SERPENTIFORM
SEMISECRET	SENSIBLENESSES	SENTINELED	SEPTUPLICATES	SERIALIZING	SERPENTINE
SEMISEDENTARY	SENSIBLEST	SENTINELING	SEPTUPLING	SERIATIONS	SERPENTINED
SEMISHRUBBY	SENSITISATION	SENTINELLED	SEPULCHERED	SERICICULTURE	SERPENTINELY
SEMISKILLED	SENSITISATIONS	SENTINELLING	SEPULCHERING	SERICICULTURES	SERPENTINES
SEMISOLIDS	SENSITISED	SEPALODIES	SEPULCHERS	SERICICULTURIST	SERPENTINIC
SEMISOLUSES	SENSITISER	SEPARABILITIES	SEPULCHRAL	SERICITISATION	SERPENTINING
SEMISUBMERSIBLE	SENSITISERS	SEPARABILITY	SEPULCHRALLY	SERICITISATIONS	SERPENTININGLY
SEMISYNTHETIC	SENSITISES	SEPARABLENESS	SEPULCHRED	SERICITIZATION	SERPENTININGS

SERPENTINISE	SESQUIALTERAS	SEXTODECIMO	SHAMEFASTNESSES	SHEATHFISHES	SHEPHERDESSES
SERPENTINISED	SESQUICARBONATE	SEXTODECIMOS	SHAMEFULLY	SHEATHIEST	SHEPHERDING
SERPENTINISES	SESQUICENTENARY	SEXTONESSES	SHAMEFULNESS	SHEATHINGS	SHEPHERDLESS
SERPENTINISING	SESQUIOXIDE	SEXTONSHIP	SHAMEFULNESSES	SHEATHLESS	SHEPHERDLING
SERPENTINITE	SESQUIOXIDES	SEXTONSHIPS	SHAMELESSLY	SHEBEENERS	SHEPHERDLINGS
SERPENTINITES	SESQUIPEDAL	SEXTUPLETS	SHAMELESSNESS	SHEBEENING	SHERARDISATION
SERPENTINIZE	SESQUIPEDALIAN	SEXTUPLICATE	SHAMELESSNESSES	SHEBEENINGS	SHERARDISATIONS
SERPENTINIZED	SESQUIPEDALITY	SEXTUPLICATED	SHAMEWORTHY	SHECHITAHS	SHERARDISE
SERPENTINIZES	SESQUIPLICATE	SEXTUPLICATES	SHAMIANAHS	SHECKLATON	SHERARDISED
SERPENTINIZING	SESQUISULPHIDE	SEXTUPLICATING	SHAMIYANAH	SHECKLATONS	SHERARDISES
SERPENTINOUS	SESQUISULPHIDES	SEXTUPLING	SHAMIYANAHS	SHEEPBERRIES	SHERARDISING
SERPENTISE	SESQUITERPENE	SEXUALISATION	SHAMMASHIM	SHEEPBERRY	SHERARDIZATION
SERPENTISED	SESQUITERPENES	SEXUALISATIONS	SHAMPOOERS	SHEEPCOTES	SHERARDIZATIONS
SERPENTISES	SESQUITERTIA	SEXUALISED	SHAMPOOING	SHEEPFOLDS	SHERARDIZE
SERPENTISING	SESQUITERTIAS	SEXUALISES	SHANACHIES	SHEEPHEADS	SHERARDIZED
SERPENTIZE	SESSILITIES	SEXUALISING	SHANDRYDAN	SHEEPHERDER	SHERARDIZES
SERPENTIZED	SESSIONALLY	SEXUALISMS	SHANDRYDANS	SHEEPHERDERS	SHERARDIZING
SERPENTIZES	SESTERTIUM	SEXUALISTS	SHANDYGAFF	SHEEPHERDING	SHEREEFIAN
SERPENTIZING	SESTERTIUS	SEXUALITIES	SHANDYGAFFS	SHEEPHERDINGS	SHERGOTTITE
SERPENTLIKE	SETACEOUSLY	SEXUALIZATION	SHANGHAIED	SHEEPISHLY	SHERGOTTITES
SERPENTRIES	SETIFEROUS	SEXUALIZATIONS	SHANGHAIER	SHEEPISHNESS	SHERIFFALTIES
SERPIGINES	SETIGEROUS	SEXUALIZED	SHANGHAIERS	SHEEPISHNESSES	SHERIFFALTY
SERPIGINOUS	SETTERWORT	SEXUALIZES	SHANGHAIING	SHEEPSHANK	SHERIFFDOM
SERPIGINOUSLY	SETTERWORTS	SEXUALIZING	SHANKBONES	SHEEPSHANKS	SHERIFFDOMS
SERPULITES	SETTLEABLE	SFORZANDOS	SHANKPIECE	SHEEPSHEAD	SHERIFFSHIP
SERRADELLA	SETTLEDNESS	SHABBINESS	SHANKPIECES	SHEEPSHEADS	SHERIFFSHIPS
SERRADELLAS	SETTLEDNESSES	SHABBINESSES	SHANTYTOWN	SHEEPSHEARER	SHEWBREADS
SERRADILLA	SETTLEMENT	SHABRACQUE	SHANTYTOWNS	SHEEPSHEARERS	SHIBBOLETH
SERRADILLAS	SETTLEMENTS	SHABRACQUES	SHAPELESSLY	SHEEPSHEARING	SHIBBOLETHS
SERRANOIDS	SEVENPENCE	SHACKLEBONE	SHAPELESSNESS	SHEEPSHEARINGS	SHIBUICHIS
SERRASALMO	SEVENPENCES	SHACKLEBONES	SHAPELESSNESSES	SHEEPSKINS	SHIDDUCHIM
SERRASALMOS	SEVENPENNIES	SHADBERRIES	SHAPELIEST	SHEEPTRACK	SHIELDINGS
SERRATIONS	SEVENPENNY	SHADBUSHES	SHAPELINESS	SHEEPTRACKS	SHIELDLESS
SERRATIROSTRAL	SEVENTEENS	SHADCHANIM	SHAPELINESSES	SHEEPWALKS	SHIELDLIKE
SERRATULATE	SEVENTEENTH	SHADINESSES	SHARAWADGI	SHEERNESSES	SHIELDLING
SERRATURES	SEVENTEENTHLY	SHADKHANIM	SHARAWADGIS	SHEETROCKED	SHIELDLINGS
SERRATUSES	SEVENTEENTHS	SHADOWBOXED	SHARAWAGGI	SHEETROCKING	SHIELDRAKE
SERREFILES	SEVENTIETH	SHADOWBOXES	SHARAWAGGIS	SHEETROCKS	SHIELDRAKES
SERRIEDNESS	SEVENTIETHS	SHADOWBOXING	SHAREABILITIES	SHEIKHDOMS	SHIELDWALL
SERRIEDNESSES	SEVERABILITIES	SHADOWCAST	SHAREABILITY	SHELDDUCKS	SHIELDWALLS
SERRULATED	SEVERABILITY	SHADOWCASTING	SHARECROPPED	SHELDRAKES	SHIFTINESS
SERRULATION	SEVERALFOLD	SHADOWCASTINGS	SHARECROPPER	SHELFROOMS	SHIFTINESSES
SERRULATIONS	SEVERALTIES	SHADOWCASTS	SHARECROPPERS	SHELFTALKER	SHIFTLESSLY
SERTULARIAN	SEVERANCES	SHADOWGRAPH	SHARECROPPING	SHELFTALKERS	SHIFTLESSNESS
SERTULARIANS	SEVERENESS	SHADOWGRAPHIES	SHARECROPS	SHELLACKED	SHIFTLESSNESSES
SERVANTHOOD	SEVERENESSES	SHADOWGRAPHS	SHAREFARMER	SHELLACKER	SHIFTWORKS
SERVANTHOODS	SEVERITIES	SHADOWGRAPHY	SHAREFARMERS	SHELLACKERS	SHIGELLOSES
SERVANTING	SEWABILITIES	SHADOWIEST	SHAREHOLDER	SHELLACKING	SHIGELLOSIS
SERVANTLESS	SEWABILITY	SHADOWINESS	SHAREHOLDERS	SHELLACKINGS	SHIKARRING
SERVANTRIES	SEXAGENARIAN	SHADOWINESSES	SHAREHOLDING	SHELLBACKS	SHILLABERS
SERVANTSHIP	SEXAGENARIANS	SHADOWINGS	SHAREHOLDINGS	SHELLBARKS	SHILLALAHS
SERVANTSHIPS	SEXAGENARIES	SHADOWLESS	SHAREMILKER	SHELLBOUND	SHILLELAGH
SERVICEABILITY	SEXAGENARY	SHADOWLIKE	SHAREMILKERS	SHELLCRACKER	SHILLELAGHS
SERVICEABLE	SEXAGESIMAL	SHAGGEDNESS	SHAREWARES	SHELLCRACKERS	SHILLELAHS
SERVICEABLENESS	SEXAGESIMALLY	SHAGGEDNESSES	SHARKSKINS	SHELLDRAKE	SHILLINGLESS
SERVICEABLY	SEXAGESIMALS	SHAGGINESS	SHARKSUCKER	SHELLDRAKES	SHILLINGSWORTH
SERVICEBERRIES	SEXAHOLICS	SHAGGINESSES	SHARKSUCKERS	SHELLDUCKS	SHILLINGSWORTHS
SERVICEBERRY	SEXANGULAR	SHAGGYMANE	SHARPBENDER	SHELLFIRES	SHILLYSHALLIED
SERVICELESS	SEXANGULARLY	SHAGGYMANES	SHARPBENDERS	SHELLFISHERIES	SHILLYSHALLIER
SERVICEMAN	SEXAVALENT	SHAGREENED	SHARPENERS	SHELLFISHERY	SHILLYSHALLIERS
SERVICEMEN	SEXCENTENARIES	SHAGTASTIC	SHARPENING	SHELLFISHES	SHILLYSHALLIES
SERVICEWOMAN	SEXCENTENARY	SHAHTOOSHES	SHARPNESSES	SHELLINESS	SHILLYSHALLY
SERVICEWOMEN	SEXDECILLION	SHAKEDOWNS	SHARPSHOOTER	SHELLINESSES	SHILLYSHALLYING
SERVIETTES	SEXDECILLIONS	SHAKINESSES	SHARPSHOOTERS	SHELLPROOF	SHIMMERING
SERVILENESS	SEXENNIALLY	SHAKUHACHI	SHARPSHOOTING	SHELLSHOCK	SHIMMERINGLY
SERVILENESSES	SEXENNIALS	SHAKUHACHIS	SHARPSHOOTINGS	SHELLSHOCKED	SHIMMERINGS
SERVILISMS	SEXERCISES	SHALLOWEST	SHASHLICKS	SHELLSHOCKS	SHIMOZZLES
SERVILITIES	SEXINESSES	SHALLOWING	SHATTERERS	SHELLWORKS	SHINGLIEST
SERVITORIAL	SEXIVALENT	SHALLOWINGS	SHATTERING	SHELLYCOAT	SHINGLINGS
SERVITORSHIP	SEXLESSNESS	SHALLOWNESS	SHATTERINGLY	SHELLYCOATS	SHINGUARDS
SERVITORSHIPS	SEXLESSNESSES	SHALLOWNESSES	SHATTERPROOF	SHELTERBELT	SHININESSES
SERVITRESS	SEXLOCULAR	SHAMANISMS	SHAUCHLIER	SHELTERBELTS	SHININGNESS
SERVITRESSES	SEXOLOGICAL	SHAMANISTIC	SHAUCHLIEST	SHELTERERS	SHININGNESSES
SERVITUDES	SEXOLOGIES	SHAMANISTS	SHAUCHLING	SHELTERING	SHINLEAVES
SERVOCONTROL	SEXOLOGIST	SHAMATEURISM	SHAVELINGS	SHELTERINGS	SHINNERIES
SERVOCONTROLS	SEXOLOGISTS	SHAMATEURISMS	SHAVETAILS	SHELTERLESS	SHINNEYING
SERVOMECHANICAL	SEXPARTITE	SHAMATEURS	SHEARLINGS	SHEMOZZLED	SHINPLASTER
SERVOMECHANISM	SEXPLOITATION	SHAMBLIEST	SHEARWATER	SHEMOZZLES	SHINPLASTERS
SERVOMECHANISMS	SEXPLOITATIONS	SHAMBLINGS	SHEARWATERS	SHEMOZZLING	SHINSPLINTS
SERVOMOTOR	SEXTILLION	SHAMEFACED	SHEATFISHES	SHENANIGAN	SHIPBOARDS
SERVOMOTORS	SEXTILLIONS	SHAMEFACEDLY	SHEATHBILL	SHENANIGANS	SHIPBROKER
SESQUIALTER	SEXTILLIONTH	SHAMEFACEDNESS	SHEATHBILLS	SHEPHERDED	SHIPBROKERS
SESQUIALTERA	SEXTILLIONTHS	SHAMEFASTNESS	SHEATHFISH	SHEPHERDESS	SHIPBUILDER

SHIPBUILDERS	SHONGOLOLOS	SHOULDERINGS	SHRUBBERIED	SIDEPIECES	SIGNALISED
SHIPBUILDING	SHOOGIEING	SHOUTHERED	SHRUBBERIES	SIDERATING	SIGNALISES
SHIPBUILDINGS	SHOOGLIEST	SHOUTHERING	SHRUBBIEST	SIDERATION	SIGNALISING
SHIPFITTER	SHOOTAROUND	SHOUTINGLY	SHRUBBINESS	SIDERATIONS	SIGNALIZATION
SHIPFITTERS	SHOOTAROUNDS	SHOUTLINES	SHRUBBINESSES	SIDEREALLY	SIGNALIZATIONS
SHIPLAPPED	SHOOTDOWNS	SHOVELBOARD	SHRUBLANDS	SIDEROLITE	SIGNALIZED
SHIPLAPPING	SHOPAHOLIC	SHOVELBOARDS	SHTETELACH	SIDEROLITES	SIGNALIZES
SHIPMASTER	SHOPAHOLICS	SHOVELFULS	SHTICKIEST	SIDEROPENIA	SIGNALIZING
SHIPMASTERS	SHOPAHOLISM	SHOVELHEAD	SHUBUNKINS	SIDEROPENIAS	SIGNALLERS
SHIPOWNERS	SHOPAHOLISMS	SHOVELHEADS	SHUDDERING	SIDEROPHILE	SIGNALLING
SHIPPOUNDS	SHOPBOARDS	SHOVELLERS	SHUDDERINGLY	SIDEROPHILES	SIGNALLINGS
SHIPWRECKED	SHOPBREAKER	SHOVELLING	SHUDDERINGS	SIDEROPHILIC	SIGNALMENT
SHIPWRECKING	SHOPBREAKERS	SHOVELNOSE	SHUDDERSOME	SIDEROPHILIN	SIGNALMENTS
SHIPWRECKS	SHOPBREAKING	SHOVELNOSES	SHUFFLEBOARD	SIDEROPHILINS	SIGNATORIES
SHIPWRIGHT	SHOPBREAKINGS	SHOVELSFUL	SHUFFLEBOARDS	SIDEROSTAT	SIGNATURES
SHIPWRIGHTS	SHOPFRONTS	SHOWBIZZES	SHUFFLINGLY	SIDEROSTATIC	SIGNBOARDS
SHIRRALEES	SHOPKEEPER	SHOWBOATED	SHUFFLINGS	SIDEROSTATS	SIGNEURIES
SHIRTBANDS	SHOPKEEPERS	SHOWBOATER	SHUNAMITISM	SIDESADDLE	SIGNIFIABLE
SHIRTDRESS	SHOPKEEPING	SHOWBOATERS	SHUNAMITISMS	SIDESADDLES	SIGNIFICANCE
SHIRTDRESSES	SHOPKEEPINGS	SHOWBOATING	SHUNPIKERS	SIDESHOOTS	SIGNIFICANCES
SHIRTFRONT	SHOPLIFTED	SHOWBREADS	SHUNPIKING	SIDESLIPPED	SIGNIFICANCIES
SHIRTFRONTS	SHOPLIFTER	SHOWCASING	SHUNPIKINGS	SIDESLIPPING	SIGNIFICANCY
SHIRTINESS	SHOPLIFTERS	SHOWERHEAD	SHUTTERBUG	SIDESPLITTING	SIGNIFICANT
SHIRTINESSES	SHOPLIFTING	SHOWERHEADS	SHUTTERBUGS	SIDESPLITTINGLY	SIGNIFICANTLY
SHIRTLIFTER	SHOPSOILED	SHOWERIEST	SHUTTERING	SIDESTEPPED	SIGNIFICANTS
SHIRTLIFTERS	SHOPWALKER	SHOWERINESS	SHUTTERINGS	SIDESTEPPER	SIGNIFICATE
SHIRTMAKER	SHOPWALKERS	SHOWERINESSES	SHUTTERLESS	SIDESTEPPERS	SIGNIFICATES
SHIRTMAKERS	SHOPWINDOW	SHOWERINGS	SHUTTLECOCK	SIDESTEPPING	SIGNIFICATION
SHIRTSLEEVE	SHOPWINDOWS	SHOWERLESS	SHUTTLECOCKED	SIDESTREAM	SIGNIFICATIONS
SHIRTSLEEVED	SHOREBIRDS	SHOWERPROOF	SHUTTLECOCKING	SIDESTREET	SIGNIFICATIVE
SHIRTSLEEVES	SHOREFRONT	SHOWERPROOFED	SHUTTLECOCKS	SIDESTREETS	SIGNIFICATIVELY
SHIRTTAILED	SHOREFRONTS	SHOWERPROOFING	SHUTTLELESS	SIDESTROKE	SIGNIFICATOR
SHIRTTAILING	SHORELINES	SHOWERPROOFINGS	SHUTTLEWISE	SIDESTROKES	SIGNIFICATORS
SHIRTTAILS	SHOREWARDS	SHOWERPROOFS	SHYLOCKING	SIDESWIPED	SIGNIFICATORY
SHIRTWAIST	SHOREWEEDS	SHOWGROUND	SIALAGOGIC	SIDESWIPER	SIGNIFIEDS
SHIRTWAISTER	SHORTBOARD	SHOWGROUNDS	SIALAGOGUE	SIDESWIPERS	SIGNIFIERS
SHIRTWAISTERS	SHORTBOARDS	SHOWINESSES	SIALAGOGUES	SIDESWIPES	SIGNIFYING
SHIRTWAISTS	SHORTBREAD	SHOWJUMPER	SIALOGOGIC	SIDESWIPING	SIGNIFYINGS
SHITTIMWOOD	SHORTBREADS	SHOWJUMPERS	SIALOGOGUE	SIDETRACKED	SIGNIORIES
SHITTIMWOODS	SHORTCAKES	SHOWJUMPING	SIALOGOGUES	SIDETRACKING	SIGNORINAS
SHITTINESS	SHORTCHANGE	SHOWJUMPINGS	SIALOGRAMS	SIDETRACKS	SIGNPOSTED
SHITTINESSES	SHORTCHANGED	SHOWMANSHIP	SIALOGRAPHIES	SIDEWHEELER	SIGNPOSTING
SHIVAREEING	SHORTCHANGER	SHOWMANSHIPS	SIALOGRAPHY	SIDEWHEELERS	SIKORSKIES
SHIVERIEST	SHORTCHANGERS	SHOWPIECES	SIALOLITHS	SIDEWHEELS	SILENTIARIES
SHIVERINGLY	SHORTCHANGES	SHOWPLACES	SIALORRHOEA	SIDEWINDER	SILENTIARY
SHIVERINGS	SHORTCHANGING	SHOWSTOPPER	SIALORRHOEAS	SIDEWINDERS	SILENTNESS
SHLEMIEHLS	SHORTCOMING	SHOWSTOPPERS	SIBILANCES	SIEGECRAFT	SILENTNESSES
SHLEMOZZLE	SHORTCOMINGS	SHOWSTOPPING	SIBILANCIES	SIEGECRAFTS	SILHOUETTE
SHLEMOZZLED	SHORTCRUST	SHREDDIEST	SIBILANTLY	SIEGEWORKS	SILHOUETTED
SHLEMOZZLES	SHORTCUTTING	SHREDDINGS	SIBILATING	SIFFLEUSES	SILHOUETTES
SHLEMOZZLING	SHORTENERS	SHREWDNESS	SIBILATION	SIGHTLESSLY	SILHOUETTING
SHLIMAZELS	SHORTENING	SHREWDNESSES	SIBILATIONS	SIGHTLESSNESS	SILHOUETTIST
SHLOCKIEST	SHORTENINGS	SHREWISHLY	SIBILATORS	SIGHTLESSNESSES	SILHOUETTISTS
SHMALTZIER	SHORTFALLS	SHREWISHNESS	SIBILATORY	SIGHTLIEST	SILICATING
SHMALTZIEST	SHORTGOWNS	SHREWISHNESSES	SICCATIVES	SIGHTLINES	SILICICOLOUS
SHOALINESS	SHORTHAIRED	SHREWMOUSE	SICILIANOS	SIGHTLINESS	SILICIFEROUS
SHOALINESSES	SHORTHAIRS	SHRIECHING	SICILIENNE	SIGHTLINESSES	SILICIFICATION
SHOALNESSES	SHORTHANDED	SHRIEKIEST	SICILIENNES	SIGHTSCREEN	SILICIFICATIONS
SHOCKABILITIES	SHORTHANDS	SHRIEKINGLY	SICKENINGLY	SIGHTSCREENS	SILICIFIED
SHOCKABILITY	SHORTHEADS	SHRIEKINGS	SICKENINGS	SIGHTSEEING	SILICIFIES
SHOCKHEADED	SHORTHORNS	SHRIEVALTIES	SICKERNESS	SIGHTSEEINGS	SILICIFYING
SHOCKINGLY	SHORTLISTED	SHRIEVALTY	SICKERNESSES	SIGHTSEERS	SILICONISED
SHOCKINGNESS	SHORTLISTING	SHRILLIEST	SICKISHNESS	SIGHTWORTHY	SILICONIZED
SHOCKINGNESSES	SHORTLISTS	SHRILLINGS	SICKISHNESSES	SIGILLARIAN	SILICOTICS
SHOCKPROOF	SHORTNESSES	SHRILLNESS	SICKLEBILL	SIGILLARIANS	SILICULOSE
SHOCKSTALL	SHORTSIGHTED	SHRILLNESSES	SICKLEBILLS	SIGILLARID	SILIQUACEOUS
SHOCKSTALLS	SHORTSIGHTEDLY	SHRIMPIEST	SICKLEMIAS	SIGILLARIDS	SILKALENES
SHOCKUMENTARIES	SHORTSTOPS	SHRIMPINGS	SICKLINESS	SIGILLATION	SILKALINES
SHOCKUMENTARY	SHORTSWORD	SHRIMPLIKE	SICKLINESSES	SIGILLATIONS	SILKGROWER
SHODDINESS	SHORTSWORDS	SHRINELIKE	SICKNESSES	SIGMATIONS	SILKGROWERS
SHODDINESSES	SHORTWAVED	SHRINKABLE	SICKNURSES	SIGMATISMS	SILKINESSES
SHOEBLACKS	SHORTWAVES	SHRINKAGES	SICKNURSING	SIGMATRONS	SILKOLINES
SHOEHORNED	SHORTWAVING	SHRINKINGLY	SICKNURSINGS	SIGMOIDALLY	SILKSCREEN
SHOEHORNING	SHOTFIRERS	SHRINKPACK	SIDDHUISMS	SIGMOIDECTOMIES	SILKSCREENS
SHOEMAKERS	SHOTGUNNED	SHRINKPACKS	SIDEBOARDS	SIGMOIDECTOMY	SILLIMANITE
SHOEMAKING	SHOTGUNNER	SHRITCHING	SIDEBURNED	SIGMOIDOSCOPE	SILLIMANITES
SHOEMAKINGS	SHOTGUNNERS	SHRIVELING	SIDECHECKS	SIGMOIDOSCOPES	SILLINESSES
SHOESHINES	SHOTGUNNING	SHRIVELLED	SIDEDNESSES	SIGMOIDOSCOPIC	SILTATIONS
SHOESTRING	SHOTMAKERS	SHRIVELLING	SIDEDRESSES	SIGMOIDOSCOPIES	SILTSTONES
SHOESTRINGS	SHOTMAKING	SHROFFAGES	SIDELEVERS	SIGMOIDOSCOPY	SILVERBACK
SHOGGLIEST	SHOTMAKINGS	SHROUDIEST	SIDELIGHTS	SIGNALINGS	SILVERBACKS
SHOGUNATES	SHOULDERED	SHROUDINGS	SIDELINERS	SIGNALISATION	SILVERBERRIES
SHONGOLOLO	SHOULDERING	SHROUDLESS	SIDELINING	SIGNALISATIONS	SILVERBERRY

SILVERBILL
SILVERBILLS
SILVEREYES
SILVERFISH
SILVERFISHES
SILVERHORN
SILVERHORNS
SILVERIEST
SILVERINESS
SILVERINESSES
SILVERINGS
SILVERISED
SILVERISES
SILVERISING
SILVERIZED
SILVERIZES
SILVERIZING
SILVERLING
SILVERLINGS
SILVERPOINT
SILVERPOINTS
SILVERSIDE
SILVERSIDES
SILVERSIDESES
SILVERSKIN
SILVERSKINS
SILVERSMITH
SILVERSMITHING
SILVERSMITHINGS
SILVERSMITHS
SILVERTAIL
SILVERTAILS
SILVERWARE
SILVERWARES
SILVERWEED
SILVERWEEDS
SILVESTRIAN
SILVICULTURAL
SILVICULTURALLY
SILVICULTURE
SILVICULTURES
SILVICULTURIST
SILVICULTURISTS
SIMAROUBACEOUS
SIMAROUBAS
SIMARUBACEOUS
SIMILARITIES
SIMILARITY
SIMILATIVE
SIMILISING
SIMILITUDE
SIMILITUDES
SIMILIZING
SIMILLIMUM
SIMILLIMUMS
SIMONIACAL
SIMONIACALLY
SIMONISING
SIMONIZING
SIMPERINGLY
SIMPERINGS
SIMPLEMINDED
SIMPLEMINDEDLY
SIMPLENESS
SIMPLENESSES
SIMPLESSES
SIMPLETONS
SIMPLICIAL
SIMPLICIALLY
SIMPLICIDENTATE
SIMPLICITER
SIMPLICITIES
SIMPLICITY
SIMPLIFICATION
SIMPLIFICATIONS
SIMPLIFICATIVE
SIMPLIFICATOR
SIMPLIFICATORS
SIMPLIFIED
SIMPLIFIER
SIMPLIFIERS
SIMPLIFIES
SIMPLIFYING

SIMPLISTIC
SIMPLISTICALLY
SIMULACRES
SIMULACRUM
SIMULACRUMS
SIMULATING
SIMULATION
SIMULATIONS
SIMULATIVE
SIMULATIVELY
SIMULATORS
SIMULATORY
SIMULCASTED
SIMULCASTING
SIMULCASTS
SIMULTANEITIES
SIMULTANEITY
SIMULTANEOUS
SIMULTANEOUSES
SIMULTANEOUSLY
SINANTHROPUS
SINANTHROPUSES
SINARCHISM
SINARCHISMS
SINARCHIST
SINARCHISTS
SINARQUISM
SINARQUISMS
SINARQUIST
SINARQUISTS
SINCERENESS
SINCERENESSES
SINCERITIES
SINCIPITAL
SINDONOLOGIES
SINDONOLOGIST
SINDONOLOGISTS
SINDONOLOGY
SINDONOPHANIES
SINDONOPHANY
SINECURISM
SINECURISMS
SINECURIST
SINECURISTS
SINEWINESS
SINEWINESSES
SINFONIETTA
SINFONIETTAS
SINFULNESS
SINFULNESSES
SINGABLENESS
SINGABLENESSES
SINGALONGS
SINGLEDOMS
SINGLEHOOD
SINGLEHOODS
SINGLENESS
SINGLENESSES
SINGLESTICK
SINGLESTICKS
SINGLETONS
SINGLETREE
SINGLETREES
SINGSONGED
SINGSONGING
SINGSPIELS
SINGULARISATION
SINGULARISE
SINGULARISED
SINGULARISES
SINGULARISING
SINGULARISM
SINGULARISMS
SINGULARIST
SINGULARISTS
SINGULARITIES
SINGULARITY
SINGULARIZATION
SINGULARIZE
SINGULARIZED
SINGULARIZES
SINGULARIZING
SINGULARLY

SINGULARNESS
SINGULARNESSES
SINGULTUSES
SINICISING
SINICIZING
SINISTERITIES
SINISTERITY
SINISTERLY
SINISTERNESS
SINISTERNESSES
SINISTERWISE
SINISTRALITIES
SINISTRALITY
SINISTRALLY
SINISTRALS
SINISTRODEXTRAL
SINISTRORSAL
SINISTRORSALLY
SINISTRORSE
SINISTRORSELY
SINISTROUS
SINISTROUSLY
SINLESSNESS
SINLESSNESSES
SINNINGIAS
SINOATRIAL
SINOLOGICAL
SINOLOGIES
SINOLOGIST
SINOLOGISTS
SINOLOGUES
SINSEMILLA
SINSEMILLAS
SINTERABILITIES
SINTERABILITY
SINUATIONS
SINUITISES
SINUOSITIES
SINUOUSNESS
SINUOUSNESSES
SINUPALLIAL
SINUPALLIATE
SINUSITISES
SINUSOIDAL
SINUSOIDALLY
SIPHONAGES
SIPHONOGAM
SIPHONOGAMIES
SIPHONOGAMS
SIPHONOGAMY
SIPHONOPHORE
SIPHONOPHORES
SIPHONOPHOROUS
SIPHONOSTELE
SIPHONOSTELES
SIPHONOSTELIC
SIPHUNCLES
SIPUNCULID
SIPUNCULIDS
SIPUNCULOID
SIPUNCULOIDS
SIRENISING
SIRENIZING
SIRONISING
SIRONIZING
SISERARIES
SISSINESSES
SISSYNESSES
SISTERHOOD
SISTERHOODS
SISTERLESS
SISTERLIKE
SISTERLINESS
SISTERLINESSES
SITATUNGAS
SITIOLOGIES
SITIOPHOBIA
SITIOPHOBIAS
SITOLOGIES
SITOPHOBIA
SITOPHOBIAS
SITOSTEROL
SITOSTEROLS

SITUATIONAL
SITUATIONALLY
SITUATIONISM
SITUATIONISMS
SITUATIONS
SITUTUNGAS
SITZKRIEGS
SIXPENNIES
SIXTEENERS
SIXTEENMOS
SIXTEENTHLY
SIXTEENTHS
SIZABLENESS
SIZABLENESSES
SIZARSHIPS
SIZEABLENESS
SIZEABLENESSES
SIZINESSES
SIZZLINGLY
SJAMBOKING
SJAMBOKKED
SJAMBOKKING
SKAITHLESS
SKALDSHIPS
SKANKINESS
SKANKINESSES
SKATEBOARD
SKATEBOARDED
SKATEBOARDER
SKATEBOARDERS
SKATEBOARDING
SKATEBOARDINGS
SKATEBOARDS
SKATEPARKS
SKEDADDLED
SKEDADDLER
SKEDADDLERS
SKEDADDLES
SKEDADDLING
SKELDERING
SKELETALLY
SKELETOGENOUS
SKELETONIC
SKELETONISE
SKELETONISED
SKELETONISER
SKELETONISERS
SKELETONISES
SKELETONISING
SKELETONIZE
SKELETONIZED
SKELETONIZER
SKELETONIZERS
SKELETONIZES
SKELETONIZING
SKELLOCHED
SKELLOCHING
SKELTERING
SKEPTICALLY
SKEPTICALNESS
SKEPTICALNESSES
SKEPTICISM
SKEPTICISMS
SKETCHABILITIES
SKETCHABILITY
SKETCHABLE
SKETCHBOOK
SKETCHBOOKS
SKETCHIEST
SKETCHINESS
SKETCHINESSES
SKETCHPADS
SKEUOMORPH
SKEUOMORPHIC
SKEUOMORPHISM
SKEUOMORPHISMS
SKEUOMORPHS
SKEWBACKED
SKEWNESSES
SKIAGRAPHS
SKIAMACHIES
SKIASCOPES
SKIASCOPIES

SKIBOBBERS
SKIBOBBING
SKIBOBBINGS
SKIDDOOING
SKIJORINGS
SKIKJORING
SKIKJORINGS
SKILFULNESS
SKILFULNESSES
SKILLCENTRE
SKILLCENTRES
SKILLESSNESS
SKILLESSNESSES
SKILLFULLY
SKILLFULNESS
SKILLFULNESSES
SKILLIGALEE
SKILLIGALEES
SKILLIGOLEE
SKILLIGOLEES
SKIMBOARDED
SKIMBOARDER
SKIMBOARDERS
SKIMBOARDING
SKIMBOARDS
SKIMMINGLY
SKIMMINGTON
SKIMMINGTONS
SKIMOBILED
SKIMOBILES
SKIMOBILING
SKIMPINESS
SKIMPINESSES
SKIMPINGLY
SKINFLICKS
SKINFLINTS
SKINFLINTY
SKINNINESS
SKINNINESSES
SKIPPERING
SKIPPERINGS
SKIPPINGLY
SKIRMISHED
SKIRMISHER
SKIRMISHERS
SKIRMISHES
SKIRMISHING
SKIRMISHINGS
SKITTERIER
SKITTERIEST
SKITTERING
SKITTISHLY
SKITTISHNESS
SKITTISHNESSES
SKREEGHING
SKREIGHING
SKRIECHING
SKRIEGHING
SKRIMMAGED
SKRIMMAGES
SKRIMMAGING
SKRIMSHANK
SKRIMSHANKED
SKRIMSHANKER
SKRIMSHANKERS
SKRIMSHANKING
SKRIMSHANKS
SKULDUDDERIES
SKULDUDDERY
SKULDUGGERIES
SKULDUGGERY
SKULKINGLY
SKULLDUGGERIES
SKULLDUGGERY
SKUMMERING
SKUNKBIRDS
SKUNKWEEDS
SKUTTERUDITE
SKUTTERUDITES
SKYBRIDGES
SKYDIVINGS
SKYJACKERS
SKYJACKING

SKYJACKINGS
SKYLARKERS
SKYLARKING
SKYLARKINGS
SKYLIGHTED
SKYROCKETED
SKYROCKETING
SKYROCKETS
SKYSCRAPER
SKYSCRAPERS
SKYSURFERS
SKYSURFING
SKYSURFINGS
SKYWRITERS
SKYWRITING
SKYWRITINGS
SKYWRITTEN
SLABBERERS
SLABBERING
SLABBINESS
SLABBINESSES
SLABSTONES
SLACKENERS
SLACKENING
SLACKENINGS
SLACKNESSES
SLAISTERED
SLAISTERIES
SLAISTERING
SLALOMISTS
SLAMDANCED
SLAMDANCES
SLAMDANCING
SLAMMAKINS
SLAMMERKIN
SLAMMERKINS
SLANDERERS
SLANDERING
SLANDEROUS
SLANDEROUSLY
SLANDEROUSNESS
SLANGINESS
SLANGINESSES
SLANGINGLY
SLANGUAGES
SLANTENDICULAR
SLANTINDICULAR
SLANTINGLY
SLANTINGWAYS
SLAPDASHES
SLAPHAPPIER
SLAPHAPPIEST
SLAPSTICKS
SLASHFESTS
SLASHINGLY
SLATHERING
SLATINESSES
SLATTERING
SLATTERNLINESS
SLATTERNLY
SLAUGHTERABLE
SLAUGHTERED
SLAUGHTERER
SLAUGHTERERS
SLAUGHTERHOUSE
SLAUGHTERHOUSES
SLAUGHTERIES
SLAUGHTERING
SLAUGHTERMAN
SLAUGHTERMEN
SLAUGHTEROUS
SLAUGHTEROUSLY
SLAUGHTERS
SLAUGHTERY
SLAVEHOLDER
SLAVEHOLDERS
SLAVEHOLDING
SLAVEHOLDINGS
SLAVERINGLY
SLAVISHNESS
SLAVISHNESSES
SLAVOCRACIES
SLAVOCRACY

SLAVOCRATS
SLAVOPHILE
SLAVOPHILES
SLAVOPHILS
SLEAZEBAGS
SLEAZEBALL
SLEAZEBALLS
SLEAZINESS
SLEAZINESSES
SLEDGEHAMMER
SLEDGEHAMMERED
SLEDGEHAMMERING
SLEDGEHAMMERS
SLEECHIEST
SLEEKENING
SLEEKNESSES
SLEEKSTONE
SLEEKSTONES
SLEEPINESS
SLEEPINESSES
SLEEPLESSLY
SLEEPLESSNESS
SLEEPLESSNESSES
SLEEPOVERS
SLEEPSUITS
SLEEPWALKED
SLEEPWALKER
SLEEPWALKERS
SLEEPWALKING
SLEEPWALKINGS
SLEEPWALKS
SLEEPYHEAD
SLEEPYHEADED
SLEEPYHEADS
SLEETINESS
SLEETINESSES
SLEEVEHAND
SLEEVEHANDS
SLEEVELESS
SLEEVELETS
SLEEVELIKE
SLEIGHINGS
SLENDEREST
SLENDERISE
SLENDERISED
SLENDERISES
SLENDERISING
SLENDERIZE
SLENDERIZED
SLENDERIZES
SLENDERIZING
SLENDERNESS
SLENDERNESSES
SLEUTHHOUND
SLEUTHHOUNDS
SLICKENERS
SLICKENING
SLICKENSIDE
SLICKENSIDED
SLICKENSIDES
SLICKNESSES
SLICKROCKS
SLICKSTERS
SLICKSTONE
SLICKSTONES
SLIDDERING
SLIGHTINGLY
SLIGHTNESS
SLIGHTNESSES
SLIMEBALLS
SLIMINESSES
SLIMNASTICS
SLIMNESSES
SLIMPSIEST
SLINGBACKS
SLINGSHOTS
SLINGSTONE
SLINGSTONES
SLINKINESS
SLINKINESSES
SLINKSKINS
SLINKWEEDS
SLIPCOVERED

SLIPCOVERING
SLIPCOVERS
SLIPDRESSES
SLIPFORMED
SLIPFORMING
SLIPNOOSES
SLIPPERIER
SLIPPERIEST
SLIPPERILY
SLIPPERINESS
SLIPPERINESSES
SLIPPERING
SLIPPERWORT
SLIPPERWORTS
SLIPPINESS
SLIPPINESSES
SLIPSHEETED
SLIPSHEETING
SLIPSHEETS
SLIPSHODDINESS
SLIPSHODNESS
SLIPSHODNESSES
SLIPSLOPPY
SLIPSTREAM
SLIPSTREAMED
SLIPSTREAMING
SLIPSTREAMS
SLITHERIER
SLITHERIEST
SLITHERING
SLIVOVICAS
SLIVOVICES
SLIVOVITZES
SLIVOWITZES
SLOBBERERS
SLOBBERIER
SLOBBERIEST
SLOBBERING
SLOBBISHNESS
SLOBBISHNESSES
SLOCKDOLAGER
SLOCKDOLAGERS
SLOCKDOLIGER
SLOCKDOLIGERS
SLOCKDOLOGER
SLOCKDOLOGERS
SLOCKENING
SLOEBUSHES
SLOETHORNS
SLOGANEERED
SLOGANEERING
SLOGANEERINGS
SLOGANEERS
SLOGANISED
SLOGANISES
SLOGANISING
SLOGANISINGS
SLOGANIZED
SLOGANIZES
SLOGANIZING
SLOGANIZINGS
SLOMMOCKED
SLOMMOCKING
SLOPINGNESS
SLOPINGNESSES
SLOPPINESS
SLOPPINESSES
SLOPWORKER
SLOPWORKERS
SLOTHFULLY
SLOTHFULNESS
SLOTHFULNESSES
SLOUCHIEST
SLOUCHINESS
SLOUCHINESSES
SLOUCHINGLY
SLOUGHIEST
SLOVENLIER
SLOVENLIEST
SLOVENLIKE
SLOVENLINESS
SLOVENLINESSES
SLOVENRIES

SLOWCOACHES
SLOWNESSES
SLUBBERING
SLUBBERINGLY
SLUBBERINGS
SLUGGABEDS
SLUGGARDISE
SLUGGARDISED
SLUGGARDISES
SLUGGARDISING
SLUGGARDIZE
SLUGGARDIZED
SLUGGARDIZES
SLUGGARDIZING
SLUGGARDLINESS
SLUGGARDLY
SLUGGARDNESS
SLUGGARDNESSES
SLUGGISHLY
SLUGGISHNESS
SLUGGISHNESSES
SLUGHORNES
SLUICEGATE
SLUICEGATES
SLUICELIKE
SLUICEWAYS
SLUMBERERS
SLUMBERFUL
SLUMBERING
SLUMBERINGLY
SLUMBERINGS
SLUMBERLAND
SLUMBERLANDS
SLUMBERLESS
SLUMBEROUS
SLUMBEROUSLY
SLUMBEROUSNESS
SLUMBERSOME
SLUMBROUSLY
SLUMGULLION
SLUMGULLIONS
SLUMMOCKED
SLUMMOCKING
SLUMPFLATION
SLUMPFLATIONARY
SLUMPFLATIONS
SLUNGSHOTS
SLUSHINESS
SLUSHINESSES
SLUTCHIEST
SLUTTERIES
SLUTTISHLY
SLUTTISHNESS
SLUTTISHNESSES
SMACKHEADS
SMALLCLOTHES
SMALLHOLDER
SMALLHOLDERS
SMALLHOLDING
SMALLHOLDINGS
SMALLMOUTH
SMALLMOUTHS
SMALLNESSES
SMALLPOXES
SMALLSWORD
SMALLSWORDS
SMALMINESS
SMALMINESSES
SMARAGDINE
SMARAGDITE
SMARAGDITES
SMARMINESS
SMARMINESSES
SMARTARSED
SMARTARSES
SMARTARSES
SMARTENING
SMARTMOUTH
SMARTMOUTHS
SMARTNESSES
SMARTPHONE
SMARTPHONES
SMARTWEEDS

SMARTYPANTS
SMASHEROOS
SMASHINGLY
SMATTERERS
SMATTERING
SMATTERINGLY
SMATTERINGS
SMEARCASES
SMEARINESS
SMEARINESSES
SMELLINESS
SMELLINESSES
SMELTERIES
SMICKERING
SMICKERINGS
SMIERCASES
SMIFLIGATE
SMIFLIGATED
SMIFLIGATES
SMIFLIGATING
SMILACACEOUS
SMILINGNESS
SMILINGNESSES
SMIRKINGLY
SMITHCRAFT
SMITHCRAFTS
SMITHEREEN
SMITHEREENED
SMITHEREENING
SMITHEREENS
SMITHERIES
SMITHSONITE
SMITHSONITES
SMOKEBOARD
SMOKEBOARDS
SMOKEBUSHES
SMOKEHOODS
SMOKEHOUSE
SMOKEHOUSES
SMOKEJACKS
SMOKELESSLY
SMOKELESSNESS
SMOKELESSNESSES
SMOKEPROOF
SMOKESCREEN
SMOKESCREENS
SMOKESTACK
SMOKESTACKS
SMOKETIGHT
SMOKETREES
SMOKINESSES
SMOLDERING
SMOOTHABLE
SMOOTHBORE
SMOOTHBORED
SMOOTHBORES
SMOOTHENED
SMOOTHENING
SMOOTHINGS
SMOOTHNESS
SMOOTHNESSES
SMOOTHPATE
SMOOTHPATES
SMORGASBORD
SMORGASBORDS
SMORREBROD
SMORREBRODS
SMOTHERERS
SMOTHERINESS
SMOTHERINESSES
SMOTHERING
SMOTHERINGLY
SMOTHERINGS
SMOULDERED
SMOULDERING
SMOULDERINGS
SMUDGELESS
SMUDGINESS
SMUDGINESSES
SMUGGERIES
SMUGGLINGS
SMUGNESSES
SMUTCHIEST

SMUTTINESS
SMUTTINESSES
SNACKETTES
SNAGGLETEETH
SNAGGLETOOTH
SNAGGLETOOTHED
SNAILERIES
SNAILFISHES
SNAKEBIRDS
SNAKEBITES
SNAKEBITTEN
SNAKEFISHES
SNAKEHEADS
SNAKEMOUTH
SNAKEMOUTHS
SNAKEROOTS
SNAKESKINS
SNAKESTONE
SNAKESTONES
SNAKEWEEDS
SNAKEWOODS
SNAKINESSES
SNAKISHNESS
SNAKISHNESSES
SNAPDRAGON
SNAPDRAGONS
SNAPHANCES
SNAPHAUNCE
SNAPHAUNCES
SNAPHAUNCH
SNAPHAUNCHES
SNAPPERING
SNAPPINESS
SNAPPINESSES
SNAPPINGLY
SNAPPISHLY
SNAPPISHNESS
SNAPPISHNESSES
SNAPSHOOTER
SNAPSHOOTERS
SNAPSHOOTING
SNAPSHOOTINGS
SNAPSHOTTED
SNAPSHOTTING
SNARLINGLY
SNATCHIEST
SNATCHINGLY
SNATCHINGS
SNAZZINESS
SNAZZINESSES
SNEAKINESS
SNEAKINESSES
SNEAKINGLY
SNEAKINGNESS
SNEAKINGNESSES
SNEAKISHLY
SNEAKISHNESS
SNEAKISHNESSES
SNEAKSBIES
SNEERINGLY
SNEESHINGS
SNEEZELESS
SNEEZEWEED
SNEEZEWEEDS
SNEEZEWOOD
SNEEZEWOODS
SNEEZEWORT
SNEEZEWORTS
SNICKERERS
SNICKERING
SNICKERSNEE
SNICKERSNEED
SNICKERSNEEING
SNICKERSNEES
SNIDENESSES
SNIFFINESS
SNIFFINESSES
SNIFFINGLY
SNIFFISHLY
SNIFFISHNESS
SNIFFISHNESSES
SNIFFLIEST
SNIFTERING

SNIGGERERS
SNIGGERING
SNIGGERINGLY
SNIGGERINGS
SNIGGLINGS
SNIPEFISHES
SNIPERSCOPE
SNIPERSCOPES
SNIPPERSNAPPER
SNIPPERSNAPPERS
SNIPPETIER
SNIPPETIEST
SNIPPETINESS
SNIPPETINESSES
SNIPPINESS
SNIPPINESSES
SNITCHIEST
SNIVELLERS
SNIVELLING
SNIVELLINGS
SNOBBERIES
SNOBBISHLY
SNOBBISHNESS
SNOBBISHNESSES
SNOBBOCRACIES
SNOBBOCRACY
SNOBOCRACIES
SNOBOCRACY
SNOBOGRAPHER
SNOBOGRAPHERS
SNOBOGRAPHIES
SNOBOGRAPHY
SNOLLYGOSTER
SNOLLYGOSTERS
SNOOKERING
SNOOPERSCOPE
SNOOPERSCOPES
SNOOTINESS
SNOOTINESSES
SNORKELERS
SNORKELING
SNORKELLED
SNORKELLING
SNORKELLINGS
SNORTINGLY
SNOTTERIES
SNOTTERING
SNOTTINESS
SNOTTINESSES
SNOWBALLED
SNOWBALLING
SNOWBERRIES
SNOWBLADER
SNOWBLADERS
SNOWBLADES
SNOWBLADING
SNOWBLADINGS
SNOWBLINKS
SNOWBLOWER
SNOWBLOWERS
SNOWBOARDED
SNOWBOARDER
SNOWBOARDERS
SNOWBOARDING
SNOWBOARDINGS
SNOWBOARDS
SNOWBRUSHES
SNOWBUSHES
SNOWCAPPED
SNOWDRIFTS
SNOWFIELDS
SNOWFLAKES
SNOWFLECKS
SNOWFLICKS
SNOWINESSES
SNOWMAKERS
SNOWMAKING
SNOWMOBILE
SNOWMOBILER
SNOWMOBILERS
SNOWMOBILES
SNOWMOBILING
SNOWMOBILINGS

SNOWMOBILIST	SOCIOBIOLOGISTS	SOLARISING	SOLIDIFIERS	SOLVABILITIES	SOMNAMBULARY
SNOWMOBILISTS	SOCIOBIOLOGY	SOLARIZATION	SOLIDIFIES	SOLVABILITY	SOMNAMBULATE
SNOWPLOUGH	SOCIOCULTURAL	SOLARIZATIONS	SOLIDIFYING	SOLVABLENESS	SOMNAMBULATED
SNOWPLOUGHED	SOCIOCULTURALLY	SOLARIZING	SOLIDITIES	SOLVABLENESSES	SOMNAMBULATES
SNOWPLOUGHING	SOCIOECONOMIC	SOLDATESQUE	SOLIDNESSES	SOLVATIONS	SOMNAMBULATING
SNOWPLOUGHS	SOCIOGRAMS	SOLDERABILITIES	SOLIDUNGULATE	SOLVENCIES	SOMNAMBULATION
SNOWPLOWED	SOCIOHISTORICAL	SOLDERABILITY	SOLIDUNGULOUS	SOLVENTLESS	SOMNAMBULATIONS
SNOWPLOWING	SOCIOLECTS	SOLDERABLE	SOLIFIDIAN	SOLVOLYSES	SOMNAMBULATOR
SNOWSCAPES	SOCIOLINGUIST	SOLDERINGS	SOLIFIDIANISM	SOLVOLYSIS	SOMNAMBULATORS
SNOWSHOEING	SOCIOLINGUISTIC	SOLDIERIES	SOLIFIDIANISMS	SOLVOLYTIC	SOMNAMBULE
SNOWSHOERS	SOCIOLINGUISTS	SOLDIERING	SOLIFIDIANS	SOMAESTHESIA	SOMNAMBULES
SNOWSLIDES	SOCIOLOGESE	SOLDIERINGS	SOLIFLUCTION	SOMAESTHESIAS	SOMNAMBULIC
SNOWSTORMS	SOCIOLOGESES	SOLDIERLIKE	SOLIFLUCTIONS	SOMAESTHESIS	SOMNAMBULISM
SNOWSURFING	SOCIOLOGIC	SOLDIERLINESS	SOLIFLUXION	SOMAESTHESISES	SOMNAMBULISMS
SNOWSURFINGS	SOCIOLOGICAL	SOLDIERLINESSES	SOLIFLUXIONS	SOMAESTHETIC	SOMNAMBULIST
SNOWTUBING	SOCIOLOGICALLY	SOLDIERSHIP	SOLILOQUIES	SOMASCOPES	SOMNAMBULISTIC
SNOWTUBINGS	SOCIOLOGIES	SOLDIERSHIPS	SOLILOQUISE	SOMATICALLY	SOMNAMBULISTS
SNUBBINESS	SOCIOLOGISM	SOLECISING	SOLILOQUISED	SOMATOGENIC	SOMNIATING
SNUBBINESSES	SOCIOLOGISMS	SOLECISTIC	SOLILOQUISER	SOMATOLOGIC	SOMNIATIVE
SNUBBINGLY	SOCIOLOGIST	SOLECISTICAL	SOLILOQUISERS	SOMATOLOGICAL	SOMNIATORY
SNUBNESSES	SOCIOLOGISTIC	SOLECISTICALLY	SOLILOQUISES	SOMATOLOGICALLY	SOMNIFACIENT
SNUFFBOXES	SOCIOLOGISTS	SOLECIZING	SOLILOQUISING	SOMATOLOGIES	SOMNIFACIENTS
SNUFFINESS	SOCIOMETRIC	SOLEMNESSES	SOLILOQUIST	SOMATOLOGIST	SOMNIFEROUS
SNUFFINESSES	SOCIOMETRIES	SOLEMNIFICATION	SOLILOQUISTS	SOMATOLOGISTS	SOMNIFEROUSLY
SNUFFLIEST	SOCIOMETRIST	SOLEMNIFIED	SOLILOQUIZE	SOMATOLOGY	SOMNILOQUENCE
SNUFFLINGS	SOCIOMETRISTS	SOLEMNIFIES	SOLILOQUIZED	SOMATOMEDIN	SOMNILOQUENCES
SNUGGERIES	SOCIOMETRY	SOLEMNIFYING	SOLILOQUIZER	SOMATOMEDINS	SOMNILOQUIES
SNUGNESSES	SOCIOPATHIC	SOLEMNISATION	SOLILOQUIZERS	SOMATOPLASM	SOMNILOQUISE
SOAPBERRIES	SOCIOPATHIES	SOLEMNISATIONS	SOLILOQUIZES	SOMATOPLASMS	SOMNILOQUISED
SOAPBOXING	SOCIOPATHS	SOLEMNISED	SOLILOQUIZING	SOMATOPLASTIC	SOMNILOQUISES
SOAPINESSES	SOCIOPATHY	SOLEMNISER	SOLIPEDOUS	SOMATOPLEURAL	SOMNILOQUISING
SOAPOLALLIE	SOCIOPOLITICAL	SOLEMNISERS	SOLIPSISMS	SOMATOPLEURE	SOMNILOQUISM
SOAPOLALLIES	SOCIORELIGIOUS	SOLEMNISES	SOLIPSISTIC	SOMATOPLEURES	SOMNILOQUISMS
SOAPSTONES	SOCIOSEXUAL	SOLEMNISING	SOLIPSISTICALLY	SOMATOPLEURIC	SOMNILOQUIST
SOBERINGLY	SOCKDOLAGER	SOLEMNITIES	SOLIPSISTS	SOMATOSENSORY	SOMNILOQUISTS
SOBERISING	SOCKDOLAGERS	SOLEMNIZATION	SOLITAIRES	SOMATOSTATIN	SOMNILOQUIZE
SOBERIZING	SOCKDOLIGER	SOLEMNIZATIONS	SOLITARIAN	SOMATOSTATINS	SOMNILOQUIZED
SOBERNESSES	SOCKDOLIGERS	SOLEMNIZED	SOLITARIANS	SOMATOTENSIC	SOMNILOQUIZES
SOBERSIDED	SOCKDOLOGER	SOLEMNIZER	SOLITARIES	SOMATOTONIA	SOMNILOQUIZING
SOBERSIDEDNESS	SOCKDOLOGERS	SOLEMNIZERS	SOLITARILY	SOMATOTONIAS	SOMNILOQUOUS
SOBERSIDES	SODALITIES	SOLEMNIZES	SOLITARINESS	SOMATOTONIC	SOMNILOQUY
SOBOLIFEROUS	SODBUSTERS	SOLEMNIZING	SOLITARINESSES	SOMATOTROPHIC	SOMNOLENCE
SOBRIETIES	SODDENNESS	SOLEMNNESS	SOLITUDINARIAN	SOMATOTROPHIN	SOMNOLENCES
SOBRIQUETS	SODDENNESSES	SOLEMNNESSES	SOLITUDINARIANS	SOMATOTROPHINS	SOMNOLENCIES
SOCDOLAGER	SODICITIES	SOLENESSES	SOLITUDINOUS	SOMATOTROPIC	SOMNOLENCY
SOCDOLAGERS	SODOMISING	SOLENETTES	SOLIVAGANT	SOMATOTROPIN	SOMNOLENTLY
SOCDOLIGER	SODOMITICAL	SOLENODONS	SOLIVAGANTS	SOMATOTROPINS	SOMNOLESCENT
SOCDOLIGERS	SODOMITICALLY	SOLENOIDAL	SOLLICKERS	SOMATOTYPE	SONGCRAFTS
SOCDOLOGER	SODOMIZING	SOLENOIDALLY	SOLMISATION	SOMATOTYPED	SONGFULNESS
SOCDOLOGERS	SOFTBALLER	SOLEPLATES	SOLMISATIONS	SOMATOTYPES	SONGFULNESSES
SOCIABILITIES	SOFTBALLERS	SOLEPRINTS	SOLMIZATION	SOMATOTYPING	SONGLESSLY
SOCIABILITY	SOFTBOUNDS	SOLFATARAS	SOLMIZATIONS	SOMBERNESS	SONGOLOLOS
SOCIABLENESS	SOFTCOVERS	SOLFATARIC	SOLONCHAKS	SOMBERNESSES	SONGSMITHS
SOCIABLENESSES	SOFTENINGS	SOLFEGGIOS	SOLONETSES	SOMBRENESS	SONGSTRESS
SOCIALISABLE	SOFTHEADED	SOLFERINOS	SOLONETZES	SOMBRENESSES	SONGSTRESSES
SOCIALISATION	SOFTHEADEDLY	SOLICITANT	SOLONETZIC	SOMBRERITE	SONGWRITER
SOCIALISATIONS	SOFTHEADEDNESS	SOLICITANTS	SOLONISATION	SOMBRERITES	SONGWRITERS
SOCIALISED	SOFTHEARTED	SOLICITATION	SOLONISATIONS	SOMEBODIES	SONGWRITING
SOCIALISER	SOFTHEARTEDLY	SOLICITATIONS	SOLONIZATION	SOMEPLACES	SONGWRITINGS
SOCIALISERS	SOFTHEARTEDNESS	SOLICITIES	SOLONIZATIONS	SOMERSAULT	SONICATING
SOCIALISES	SOFTNESSES	SOLICITING	SOLSTITIAL	SOMERSAULTED	SONICATION
SOCIALISING	SOFTSHELLS	SOLICITINGS	SOLSTITIALLY	SOMERSAULTING	SONICATIONS
SOCIALISMS	SOGDOLAGER	SOLICITORS	SOLUBILISATION	SOMERSAULTS	SONICATORS
SOCIALISTIC	SOGDOLAGERS	SOLICITORSHIP	SOLUBILISATIONS	SOMERSETED	SONIFEROUS
SOCIALISTICALLY	SOGDOLIGER	SOLICITORSHIPS	SOLUBILISE	SOMERSETING	SONNETEERING
SOCIALISTS	SOGDOLIGERS	SOLICITOUS	SOLUBILISED	SOMERSETTED	SONNETEERINGS
SOCIALITES	SOGDOLOGER	SOLICITOUSLY	SOLUBILISES	SOMERSETTING	SONNETEERS
SOCIALITIES	SOGDOLOGERS	SOLICITOUSNESS	SOLUBILISING	SOMESTHESIA	SONNETISED
SOCIALIZABLE	SOGGINESSES	SOLICITUDE	SOLUBILITIES	SOMESTHESIAS	SONNETISES
SOCIALIZATION	SOILINESSES	SOLICITUDES	SOLUBILITY	SOMESTHESIS	SONNETISING
SOCIALIZATIONS	SOJOURNERS	SOLIDARISM	SOLUBILIZATION	SOMESTHESISES	SONNETIZED
SOCIALIZED	SOJOURNING	SOLIDARISMS	SOLUBILIZATIONS	SOMESTHETIC	SONNETIZES
SOCIALIZER	SOJOURNINGS	SOLIDARIST	SOLUBILIZE	SOMETHINGS	SONNETIZING
SOCIALIZERS	SOJOURNMENT	SOLIDARISTIC	SOLUBILIZED	SOMEWHENCE	SONNETTING
SOCIALIZES	SOJOURNMENTS	SOLIDARISTS	SOLUBILIZES	SOMEWHERES	SONOFABITCH
SOCIALIZING	SOKEMANRIES	SOLIDARITIES	SOLUBILIZING	SOMEWHILES	SONOGRAPHER
SOCIALNESS	SOLACEMENT	SOLIDARITY	SOLUBLENESS	SOMEWHITHER	SONOGRAPHERS
SOCIALNESSES	SOLACEMENTS	SOLIDATING	SOLUBLENESSES	SOMMELIERS	SONOGRAPHIES
SOCIATIONS	SOLANACEOUS	SOLIDIFIABLE	SOLUTIONAL	SOMNAMBULANCE	SONOGRAPHS
SOCIETALLY	SOLARIMETER	SOLIDIFICATION	SOLUTIONED	SOMNAMBULANCES	SONOGRAPHY
SOCIOBIOLOGICAL	SOLARIMETERS	SOLIDIFICATIONS	SOLUTIONING	SOMNAMBULANT	SONOMETERS
SOCIOBIOLOGIES	SOLARISATION	SOLIDIFIED	SOLUTIONIST	SOMNAMBULANTS	SONORITIES
SOCIOBIOLOGIST	SOLARISATIONS	SOLIDIFIER	SOLUTIONISTS	SOMNAMBULAR	SONOROUSLY

SONOROUSNESS	SORTITIONS	SOUTHERNISMS	SPADILLIOS	SPATCHCOCKS	SPECIFYING
SONOROUSNESSES	SOSTENUTOS	SOUTHERNIZE	SPAGERISTS	SPATHACEOUS	SPECIOCIDE
SOOTERKINS	SOTERIOLOGIC	SOUTHERNIZED	SPAGHETTILIKE	SPATHIPHYLLUM	SPECIOCIDES
SOOTFLAKES	SOTERIOLOGICAL	SOUTHERNIZES	SPAGHETTINI	SPATHIPHYLLUMS	SPECIOSITIES
SOOTHERING	SOTERIOLOGIES	SOUTHERNIZING	SPAGHETTINIS	SPATHULATE	SPECIOSITY
SOOTHFASTLY	SOTERIOLOGY	SOUTHERNLY	SPAGHETTIS	SPATIALITIES	SPECIOUSLY
SOOTHFASTNESS	SOTTISHNESS	SOUTHERNMOST	SPAGIRISTS	SPATIALITY	SPECIOUSNESS
SOOTHFASTNESSES	SOTTISHNESSES	SOUTHERNNESS	SPAGYRICAL	SPATIOTEMPORAL	SPECIOUSNESSES
SOOTHINGLY	SOTTISIERS	SOUTHERNNESSES	SPAGYRICALLY	SPATTERDASH	SPECKLEDNESS
SOOTHINGNESS	SOUBRETTES	SOUTHERNWOOD	SPAGYRISTS	SPATTERDASHES	SPECKLEDNESSES
SOOTHINGNESSES	SOUBRETTISH	SOUTHERNWOODS	SPALLATION	SPATTERDOCK	SPECKSIONEER
SOOTHSAYER	SOUBRIQUET	SOUTHLANDER	SPALLATIONS	SPATTERDOCKS	SPECKSIONEERS
SOOTHSAYERS	SOUBRIQUETS	SOUTHLANDERS	SPANAEMIAS	SPATTERING	SPECKTIONEER
SOOTHSAYING	SOULDIERED	SOUTHLANDS	SPANAKOPITA	SPATTERWORK	SPECKTIONEERS
SOOTHSAYINGS	SOULDIERING	SOUTHSAYING	SPANAKOPITAS	SPATTERWORKS	SPECTACLED
SOOTINESSES	SOULFULNESS	SOUTHWARDLY	SPANCELING	SPEAKEASIES	SPECTACLES
SOPAIPILLA	SOULFULNESSES	SOUTHWARDS	SPANCELLED	SPEAKERINE	SPECTACULAR
SOPAIPILLAS	SOULLESSLY	SOUTHWESTER	SPANCELLING	SPEAKERINES	SPECTACULARITY
SOPAPILLAS	SOULLESSNESS	SOUTHWESTERLIES	SPANGHEWED	SPEAKERPHONE	SPECTACULARLY
SOPHISTERS	SOULLESSNESSES	SOUTHWESTERLY	SPANGHEWING	SPEAKERPHONES	SPECTACULARS
SOPHISTICAL	SOUNDALIKE	SOUTHWESTERN	SPANGLIEST	SPEAKERSHIP	SPECTATING
SOPHISTICALLY	SOUNDALIKES	SOUTHWESTERS	SPANGLINGS	SPEAKERSHIPS	SPECTATORIAL
SOPHISTICATE	SOUNDBITES	SOUTHWESTS	SPANIELLED	SPEAKINGLY	SPECTATORS
SOPHISTICATED	SOUNDBOARD	SOUTHWESTWARD	SPANIELLING	SPEARFISHED	SPECTATORSHIP
SOPHISTICATEDLY	SOUNDBOARDS	SOUTHWESTWARDLY	SPANIOLATE	SPEARFISHES	SPECTATORSHIPS
SOPHISTICATES	SOUNDBOXES	SOUTHWESTWARDS	SPANIOLATED	SPEARFISHING	SPECTATRESS
SOPHISTICATING	SOUNDCARDS	SOUVENIRED	SPANIOLATES	SPEARHEADED	SPECTATRESSES
SOPHISTICATION	SOUNDINGLY	SOUVENIRING	SPANIOLATING	SPEARHEADING	SPECTATRICES
SOPHISTICATIONS	SOUNDLESSLY	SOUVLAKIAS	SPANIOLISE	SPEARHEADS	SPECTATRIX
SOPHISTICATOR	SOUNDLESSNESS	SOVENANCES	SPANIOLISED	SPEARMINTS	SPECTATRIXES
SOPHISTICATORS	SOUNDLESSNESSES	SOVEREIGNLY	SPANIOLISES	SPEARWORTS	SPECTINOMYCIN
SOPHISTRIES	SOUNDNESSES	SOVEREIGNS	SPANIOLISING	SPECIALEST	SPECTINOMYCINS
SOPHOMORES	SOUNDPOSTS	SOVEREIGNTIES	SPANIOLIZE	SPECIALISATION	SPECTRALITIES
SOPHOMORIC	SOUNDPROOF	SOVEREIGNTIST	SPANIOLIZED	SPECIALISATIONS	SPECTRALITY
SOPHOMORICAL	SOUNDPROOFED	SOVEREIGNTISTS	SPANIOLIZES	SPECIALISE	SPECTRALLY
SOPORIFEROUS	SOUNDPROOFING	SOVEREIGNTY	SPANIOLIZING	SPECIALISED	SPECTRALNESS
SOPORIFEROUSLY	SOUNDPROOFINGS	SOVIETISATION	SPANKINGLY	SPECIALISER	SPECTRALNESSES
SOPORIFICALLY	SOUNDPROOFS	SOVIETISATIONS	SPANOKOPITA	SPECIALISERS	SPECTROGRAM
SOPORIFICS	SOUNDSCAPE	SOVIETISED	SPANOKOPITAS	SPECIALISES	SPECTROGRAMS
SOPPINESSES	SOUNDSCAPES	SOVIETISES	SPARAGMATIC	SPECIALISING	SPECTROGRAPH
SOPRANINOS	SOUNDSTAGE	SOVIETISING	SPARAGRASS	SPECIALISM	SPECTROGRAPHIC
SOPRANISTS	SOUNDSTAGES	SOVIETISMS	SPARAGRASSES	SPECIALISMS	SPECTROGRAPHIES
SORBABILITIES	SOUNDTRACK	SOVIETISTIC	SPARAXISES	SPECIALIST	SPECTROGRAPHS
SORBABILITY	SOUNDTRACKED	SOVIETISTS	SPARENESSES	SPECIALISTIC	SPECTROGRAPHY
SORBEFACIENT	SOUNDTRACKING	SOVIETIZATION	SPARGANIUM	SPECIALISTS	SPECTROLOGICAL
SORBEFACIENTS	SOUNDTRACKS	SOVIETIZATIONS	SPARGANIUMS	SPECIALITIES	SPECTROLOGIES
SORBITISATION	SOUPSPOONS	SOVIETIZED	SPARINGNESS	SPECIALITY	SPECTROLOGY
SORBITISATIONS	SOURCEBOOK	SOVIETIZES	SPARINGNESSES	SPECIALIZATION	SPECTROMETER
SORBITISED	SOURCEBOOKS	SOVIETIZING	SPARKISHLY	SPECIALIZATIONS	SPECTROMETERS
SORBITISES	SOURCELESS	SOVIETOLOGICAL	SPARKLESSLY	SPECIALIZE	SPECTROMETRIC
SORBITISING	SOURDELINE	SOVIETOLOGIST	SPARKLIEST	SPECIALIZED	SPECTROMETRIES
SORBITIZATION	SOURDELINES	SOVIETOLOGISTS	SPARKLINGLY	SPECIALIZER	SPECTROMETRY
SORBITIZATIONS	SOURDOUGHS	SOVRANTIES	SPARKLINGS	SPECIALIZERS	SPECTROSCOPE
SORBITIZED	SOURNESSES	SOWBELLIES	SPARKPLUGGED	SPECIALIZES	SPECTROSCOPES
SORBITIZES	SOURPUSSES	SPACEBANDS	SPARKPLUGGING	SPECIALIZING	SPECTROSCOPIC
SORBITIZING	SOUSAPHONE	SPACEBORNE	SPARKPLUGS	SPECIALLED	SPECTROSCOPICAL
SORCERESSES	SOUSAPHONES	SPACECRAFT	SPARROWFART	SPECIALLING	SPECTROSCOPIES
SORDAMENTE	SOUSAPHONIST	SPACECRAFTS	SPARROWFARTS	SPECIALNESS	SPECTROSCOPIST
SORDIDNESS	SOUSAPHONISTS	SPACEFARING	SPARROWGRASS	SPECIALNESSES	SPECTROSCOPISTS
SORDIDNESSES	SOUTENEURS	SPACEFARINGS	SPARROWGRASSES	SPECIALOGUE	SPECTROSCOPY
SOREHEADED	SOUTERRAIN	SPACEFLIGHT	SPARROWHAWK	SPECIALOGUES	SPECULARITIES
SOREHEADEDLY	SOUTERRAINS	SPACEFLIGHTS	SPARROWHAWKS	SPECIALTIES	SPECULARITY
SOREHEADEDNESS	SOUTHBOUND	SPACEPLANE	SPARROWLIKE	SPECIATING	SPECULARLY
SORENESSES	SOUTHEASTER	SPACEPLANES	SPARSENESS	SPECIATION	SPECULATED
SORICIDENT	SOUTHEASTERLIES	SPACEPORTS	SPARSENESSES	SPECIATIONAL	SPECULATES
SORORIALLY	SOUTHEASTERLY	SPACESHIPS	SPARSITIES	SPECIATIONS	SPECULATING
SORORICIDAL	SOUTHEASTERN	SPACESUITS	SPARTEINES	SPECIESISM	SPECULATION
SORORICIDE	SOUTHEASTERS	SPACEWALKED	SPARTERIES	SPECIESISMS	SPECULATIONS
SORORICIDES	SOUTHEASTS	SPACEWALKER	SPASMATICAL	SPECIESIST	SPECULATIST
SORORISING	SOUTHEASTWARD	SPACEWALKERS	SPASMODICAL	SPECIESISTS	SPECULATISTS
SORORITIES	SOUTHEASTWARDS	SPACEWALKING	SPASMODICALLY	SPECIFIABLE	SPECULATIVE
SORORIZING	SOUTHERING	SPACEWALKS	SPASMODIST	SPECIFICAL	SPECULATIVELY
SORRINESSES	SOUTHERLIES	SPACEWOMAN	SPASMODISTS	SPECIFICALLY	SPECULATIVENESS
SORROWFULLY	SOUTHERLINESS	SPACEWOMEN	SPASMOLYTIC	SPECIFICATE	SPECULATOR
SORROWFULNESS	SOUTHERLINESSES	SPACINESSES	SPASMOLYTICS	SPECIFICATED	SPECULATORS
SORROWFULNESSES	SOUTHERMOST	SPACIOUSLY	SPASTICALLY	SPECIFICATES	SPECULATORY
SORROWINGS	SOUTHERNER	SPACIOUSNESS	SPASTICITIES	SPECIFICATING	SPECULATRICES
SORROWLESS	SOUTHERNERS	SPACIOUSNESSES	SPASTICITY	SPECIFICATION	SPECULATRIX
SORTATIONS	SOUTHERNISE	SPADASSINS	SPATANGOID	SPECIFICATIONS	SPECULATRIXES
SORTILEGER	SOUTHERNISED	SPADEFISHES	SPATANGOIDS	SPECIFICATIVE	SPEECHCRAFT
SORTILEGERS	SOUTHERNISES	SPADEWORKS	SPATCHCOCK	SPECIFICITIES	SPEECHCRAFTS
SORTILEGES	SOUTHERNISING	SPADICEOUS	SPATCHCOCKED	SPECIFICITY	SPEECHFULNESS
SORTILEGIES	SOUTHERNISM	SPADICIFLORAL	SPATCHCOCKING	SPECIFIERS	SPEECHFULNESSES

SPEECHIFICATION	SPERMATHECA	SPHAERIDIUM	SPHYGMOSCOPE	SPINTHARISCOPES	SPIRONOLACTONE
SPEECHIFIED	SPERMATHECAE	SPHAERITES	SPHYGMOSCOPES	SPINULESCENT	SPIRONOLACTONES
SPEECHIFIER	SPERMATHECAL	SPHAEROCRYSTAL	SPHYGMUSES	SPINULIFEROUS	SPIROPHORE
SPEECHIFIERS	SPERMATIAL	SPHAEROCRYSTALS	SPICEBERRIES	SPIRACULAR	SPIROPHORES
SPEECHIFIES	SPERMATICAL	SPHAEROSIDERITE	SPICEBERRY	SPIRACULATE	SPIRULINAS
SPEECHIFYING	SPERMATICALLY	SPHAGNICOLOUS	SPICEBUSHES	SPIRACULUM	SPISSITUDE
SPEECHLESS	SPERMATICS	SPHAGNOLOGIES	SPICILEGES	SPIRALIFORM	SPISSITUDES
SPEECHLESSLY	SPERMATIDS	SPHAGNOLOGIST	SPICINESSES	SPIRALISMS	SPITCHCOCK
SPEECHLESSNESS	SPERMATIUM	SPHAGNOLOGISTS	SPICULATION	SPIRALISTS	SPITCHCOCKED
SPEECHMAKER	SPERMATOBLAST	SPHAGNOLOGY	SPICULATIONS	SPIRALITIES	SPITCHCOCKING
SPEECHMAKERS	SPERMATOBLASTIC	SPHAIRISTIKE	SPIDERIEST	SPIRALLING	SPITCHCOCKS
SPEECHMAKING	SPERMATOBLASTS	SPHAIRISTIKES	SPIDERLIKE	SPIRASTERS	SPITEFULLER
SPEECHMAKINGS	SPERMATOCELE	SPHALERITE	SPIDERWEBS	SPIRATIONS	SPITEFULLEST
SPEECHWRITER	SPERMATOCELES	SPHALERITES	SPIDERWOOD	SPIRIFEROUS	SPITEFULLY
SPEECHWRITERS	SPERMATOCIDAL	SPHENDONES	SPIDERWOODS	SPIRILLOSES	SPITEFULNESS
SPEEDBALLED	SPERMATOCIDE	SPHENODONS	SPIDERWORK	SPIRILLOSIS	SPITEFULNESSES
SPEEDBALLING	SPERMATOCIDES	SPHENODONT	SPIDERWORKS	SPIRITEDLY	SPITSTICKER
SPEEDBALLINGS	SPERMATOCYTE	SPHENOGRAM	SPIDERWORT	SPIRITEDNESS	SPITSTICKERS
SPEEDBALLS	SPERMATOCYTES	SPHENOGRAMS	SPIDERWORTS	SPIRITEDNESSES	SPITTLEBUG
SPEEDBOATING	SPERMATOGENESES	SPHENOIDAL	SPIEGELEISEN	SPIRITINGS	SPITTLEBUGS
SPEEDBOATINGS	SPERMATOGENESIS	SPHENOPSID	SPIEGELEISENS	SPIRITISMS	SPIVVERIES
SPEEDBOATS	SPERMATOGENETIC	SPHENOPSIDS	SPIFFINESS	SPIRITISTIC	SPLANCHNIC
SPEEDFREAK	SPERMATOGENIC	SPHERELESS	SPIFFINESSES	SPIRITISTS	SPLANCHNOCELE
SPEEDFREAKS	SPERMATOGENIES	SPHERELIKE	SPIFFLICATE	SPIRITLESS	SPLANCHNOCELES
SPEEDFULLY	SPERMATOGENOUS	SPHERICALITIES	SPIFFLICATED	SPIRITLESSLY	SPLANCHNOLOGIES
SPEEDINESS	SPERMATOGENY	SPHERICALITY	SPIFFLICATES	SPIRITLESSNESS	SPLANCHNOLOGY
SPEEDINESSES	SPERMATOGONIA	SPHERICALLY	SPIFFLICATING	SPIRITOUSNESS	SPLASHBACK
SPEEDOMETER	SPERMATOGONIAL	SPHERICALNESS	SPIFFLICATION	SPIRITOUSNESSES	SPLASHBACKS
SPEEDOMETERS	SPERMATOGONIUM	SPHERICALNESSES	SPIFFLICATIONS	SPIRITUALISE	SPLASHBOARD
SPEEDREADING	SPERMATOPHORAL	SPHERICITIES	SPIFLICATE	SPIRITUALISED	SPLASHBOARDS
SPEEDREADS	SPERMATOPHORE	SPHERICITY	SPIFLICATED	SPIRITUALISER	SPLASHDOWN
SPEEDSKATING	SPERMATOPHORES	SPHERISTERION	SPIFLICATES	SPIRITUALISERS	SPLASHDOWNS
SPEEDSKATINGS	SPERMATOPHYTE	SPHERISTERIONS	SPIFLICATING	SPIRITUALISES	SPLASHIEST
SPEEDSTERS	SPERMATOPHYTES	SPHEROCYTE	SPIFLICATION	SPIRITUALISING	SPLASHINESS
SPEEDWELLS	SPERMATOPHYTIC	SPHEROCYTES	SPIFLICATIONS	SPIRITUALISM	SPLASHINESSES
SPELAEOLOGICAL	SPERMATORRHEA	SPHEROCYTOSES	SPIKEFISHES	SPIRITUALISMS	SPLASHINGS
SPELAEOLOGIES	SPERMATORRHEAS	SPHEROCYTOSIS	SPIKENARDS	SPIRITUALIST	SPLASHPROOF
SPELAEOLOGIST	SPERMATORRHOEA	SPHEROIDAL	SPIKINESSES	SPIRITUALISTIC	SPLATCHING
SPELAEOLOGISTS	SPERMATORRHOEAS	SPHEROIDALLY	SPILLIKINS	SPIRITUALISTS	SPLATTERED
SPELAEOLOGY	SPERMATOTHECA	SPHEROIDICALLY	SPILLOVERS	SPIRITUALITIES	SPLATTERING
SPELAEOTHEM	SPERMATOTHECAE	SPHEROIDICITIES	SPILOSITES	SPIRITUALITY	SPLATTERPUNK
SPELAEOTHEMS	SPERMATOZOA	SPHEROIDICITY	SPINACENES	SPIRITUALIZE	SPLATTERPUNKS
SPELDERING	SPERMATOZOAL	SPHEROIDISATION	SPINACEOUS	SPIRITUALIZED	SPLATTINGS
SPELDRINGS	SPERMATOZOAN	SPHEROIDISE	SPINACHLIKE	SPIRITUALIZER	SPLAYFOOTED
SPELEOLOGICAL	SPERMATOZOANS	SPHEROIDISED	SPINDLELEGS	SPIRITUALIZERS	SPLAYFOOTEDLY
SPELEOLOGIES	SPERMATOZOIC	SPHEROIDISES	SPINDLESHANKS	SPIRITUALIZES	SPLEENFULLY
SPELEOLOGIST	SPERMATOZOID	SPHEROIDISING	SPINDLIEST	SPIRITUALIZING	SPLEENIEST
SPELEOLOGISTS	SPERMATOZOIDS	SPHEROIDIZATION	SPINDLINGS	SPIRITUALLY	SPLEENLESS
SPELEOLOGY	SPERMATOZOON	SPHEROIDIZE	SPINDRIFTS	SPIRITUALNESS	SPLEENSTONE
SPELEOTHEM	SPERMICIDAL	SPHEROIDIZED	SPINELESSLY	SPIRITUALNESSES	SPLEENSTONES
SPELEOTHEMS	SPERMICIDE	SPHEROIDIZES	SPINELESSNESS	SPIRITUALS	SPLEENWORT
SPELEOTHERAPIES	SPERMICIDES	SPHEROIDIZING	SPINELESSNESSES	SPIRITUALTIES	SPLEENWORTS
SPELEOTHERAPY	SPERMIDUCT	SPHEROMETER	SPINESCENCE	SPIRITUALTY	SPLENATIVE
SPELLBINDER	SPERMIDUCTS	SPHEROMETERS	SPINESCENCES	SPIRITUELLE	SPLENDIDER
SPELLBINDERS	SPERMIOGENESES	SPHEROPLAST	SPINESCENT	SPIRITUOSITIES	SPLENDIDEST
SPELLBINDING	SPERMIOGENESIS	SPHEROPLASTS	SPINIFEROUS	SPIRITUOSITY	SPLENDIDIOUS
SPELLBINDINGLY	SPERMIOGENETIC	SPHERULITE	SPINIFEXES	SPIRITUOUS	SPLENDIDLY
SPELLBINDS	SPERMOGONE	SPHERULITES	SPINIGEROUS	SPIRITUOUSNESS	SPLENDIDNESS
SPELLBOUND	SPERMOGONES	SPHERULITIC	SPINIGRADE	SPIRITUSES	SPLENDIDNESSES
SPELLCHECK	SPERMOGONIA	SPHINCTERAL	SPININESSES	SPIRKETTING	SPLENDIDOUS
SPELLCHECKER	SPERMOGONIUM	SPHINCTERIAL	SPINMEISTER	SPIRKETTINGS	SPLENDIFEROUS
SPELLCHECKERS	SPERMOPHILE	SPHINCTERIC	SPINMEISTERS	SPIROCHAETAEMIA	SPLENDIFEROUSLY
SPELLCHECKS	SPERMOPHILES	SPHINCTERS	SPINNAKERS	SPIROCHAETE	SPLENDOROUS
SPELLDOWNS	SPERMOPHYTE	SPHINGOMYELIN	SPINNERETS	SPIROCHAETES	SPLENDOURS
SPELLICANS	SPERMOPHYTES	SPHINGOMYELINS	SPINNERETTE	SPIROCHAETOSES	SPLENDROUS
SPELLINGLY	SPERMOPHYTIC	SPHINGOSINE	SPINNERETTES	SPIROCHAETOSIS	SPLENECTOMIES
SPELLSTOPT	SPERRYLITE	SPHINGOSINES	SPINNERIES	SPIROCHETAL	SPLENECTOMISE
SPELUNKERS	SPERRYLITES	SPHINXLIKE	SPINNERULE	SPIROCHETE	SPLENECTOMISED
SPELUNKING	SPESSARTINE	SPHRAGISTIC	SPINNERULES	SPIROCHETES	SPLENECTOMISES
SPELUNKINGS	SPESSARTINES	SPHRAGISTICS	SPINOSITIES	SPIROCHETOSES	SPLENECTOMISING
SPENDTHRIFT	SPESSARTITE	SPHYGMOGRAM	SPINSTERDOM	SPIROCHETOSIS	SPLENECTOMIZE
SPENDTHRIFTS	SPESSARTITES	SPHYGMOGRAMS	SPINSTERDOMS	SPIROGRAMS	SPLENECTOMIZED
SPERMACETI	SPETSNAZES	SPHYGMOGRAPH	SPINSTERHOOD	SPIROGRAPH	SPLENECTOMIZES
SPERMACETIS	SPETZNAZES	SPHYGMOGRAPHIC	SPINSTERHOODS	SPIROGRAPHIC	SPLENECTOMIZING
SPERMADUCT	SPEWINESSES	SPHYGMOGRAPHIES	SPINSTERIAL	SPIROGRAPHIES	SPLENECTOMY
SPERMADUCTS	SPHACELATE	SPHYGMOGRAPHS	SPINSTERIAN	SPIROGRAPHS	SPLENETICAL
SPERMAGONIA	SPHACELATED	SPHYGMOGRAPHY	SPINSTERISH	SPIROGRAPHY	SPLENETICALLY
SPERMAGONIUM	SPHACELATES	SPHYGMOLOGIES	SPINSTERLY	SPIROGYRAS	SPLENETICS
SPERMAPHYTE	SPHACELATING	SPHYGMOLOGY	SPINSTERSHIP	SPIROMETER	SPLENISATION
SPERMAPHYTES	SPHACELATION	SPHYGMOMETER	SPINSTERSHIPS	SPIROMETERS	SPLENISATIONS
SPERMAPHYTIC	SPHACELATIONS	SPHYGMOMETERS	SPINSTRESS	SPIROMETRIC	SPLENITISES
SPERMARIES	SPHACELUSES	SPHYGMOPHONE	SPINSTRESSES	SPIROMETRIES	SPLENIUSES
SPERMARIUM	SPHAERIDIA	SPHYGMOPHONES	SPINTHARISCOPE	SPIROMETRY	SPLENIZATION

SPLENIZATIONS	SPONSORING	SPORTSCAST	SPRINGEING	SQUALIDNESS	SQUIGGLIEST
SPLENOMEGALIES	SPONSORSHIP	SPORTSCASTER	SPRINGHAAS	SQUALIDNESSES	SQUIGGLING
SPLENOMEGALY	SPONSORSHIPS	SPORTSCASTERS	SPRINGHALT	SQUALLIEST	SQUILGEEING
SPLEUCHANS	SPONTANEITIES	SPORTSCASTS	SPRINGHALTS	SQUALLINGS	SQUILLIONS
SPLINTERED	SPONTANEITY	SPORTSMANLIKE	SPRINGHASE	SQUAMATION	SQUINANCIES
SPLINTERIER	SPONTANEOUS	SPORTSMANLY	SPRINGHEAD	SQUAMATIONS	SQUINCHING
SPLINTERIEST	SPONTANEOUSLY	SPORTSMANSHIP	SPRINGHEADS	SQUAMELLAS	SQUINNIEST
SPLINTERING	SPONTANEOUSNESS	SPORTSMANSHIPS	SPRINGHOUSE	SQUAMIFORM	SQUINNYING
SPLINTLIKE	SPOOFERIES	SPORTSPEOPLE	SPRINGHOUSES	SQUAMOSALS	SQUINTIEST
SPLINTWOOD	SPOOKERIES	SPORTSPERSON	SPRINGIEST	SQUAMOSELY	SQUINTINGLY
SPLINTWOODS	SPOOKINESS	SPORTSPERSONS	SPRINGINESS	SQUAMOSENESS	SQUINTINGS
SPLODGIEST	SPOOKINESSES	SPORTSWEAR	SPRINGINESSES	SQUAMOSENESSES	SQUIRALITIES
SPLODGINESS	SPOONBAITS	SPORTSWEARS	SPRINGINGS	SQUAMOSITIES	SQUIRALITY
SPLODGINESSES	SPOONBILLS	SPORTSWOMAN	SPRINGKEEPER	SQUAMOSITY	SQUIRALTIES
SPLOOSHING	SPOONDRIFT	SPORTSWOMEN	SPRINGKEEPERS	SQUAMOUSLY	SQUIRARCHAL
SPLOTCHIER	SPOONDRIFTS	SPORTSWRITER	SPRINGLESS	SQUAMOUSNESS	SQUIRARCHICAL
SPLOTCHIEST	SPOONERISM	SPORTSWRITERS	SPRINGLETS	SQUAMOUSNESSES	SQUIRARCHIES
SPLOTCHILY	SPOONERISMS	SPORTSWRITING	SPRINGLIKE	SQUAMULOSE	SQUIRARCHS
SPLOTCHINESS	SPORADICAL	SPORTSWRITINGS	SPRINGTAIL	SQUANDERED	SQUIRARCHY
SPLOTCHINESSES	SPORADICALLY	SPORULATED	SPRINGTAILS	SQUANDERER	SQUIREAGES
SPLOTCHING	SPORADICALNESS	SPORULATES	SPRINGTIDE	SQUANDERERS	SQUIREARCH
SPLURGIEST	SPORANGIAL	SPORULATING	SPRINGTIDES	SQUANDERING	SQUIREARCHAL
SPLUTTERED	SPORANGIOLA	SPORULATION	SPRINGTIME	SQUANDERINGLY	SQUIREARCHICAL
SPLUTTERER	SPORANGIOLE	SPORULATIONS	SPRINGTIMES	SQUANDERINGS	SQUIREARCHIES
SPLUTTERERS	SPORANGIOLES	SPORULATIVE	SPRINGWATER	SQUANDERMANIA	SQUIREARCHS
SPLUTTERING	SPORANGIOLUM	SPOTLESSLY	SPRINGWATERS	SQUANDERMANIAS	SQUIREARCHY
SPLUTTERINGLY	SPORANGIOPHORE	SPOTLESSNESS	SPRINGWOOD	SQUAREHEAD	SQUIREDOMS
SPLUTTERINGS	SPORANGIOPHORES	SPOTLESSNESSES	SPRINGWOODS	SQUAREHEADS	SQUIREHOOD
SPODOGRAMS	SPORANGIOSPORE	SPOTLIGHTED	SPRINGWORT	SQUARENESS	SQUIREHOODS
SPODOMANCIES	SPORANGIOSPORES	SPOTLIGHTING	SPRINGWORTS	SQUARENESSES	SQUIRELIKE
SPODOMANCY	SPORANGIUM	SPOTLIGHTS	SPRINKLERED	SQUAREWISE	SQUIRELING
SPODOMANTIC	SPORICIDAL	SPOTTEDNESS	SPRINKLERING	SQUARISHLY	SQUIRELINGS
SPODUMENES	SPORICIDES	SPOTTEDNESSES	SPRINKLERS	SQUARISHNESS	SQUIRESHIP
SPOILFIVES	SPORIDESMS	SPOTTINESS	SPRINKLING	SQUARISHNESSES	SQUIRESHIPS
SPOILSPORT	SPOROCARPS	SPOTTINESSES	SPRINKLINGS	SQUARSONAGE	SQUIRESSES
SPOILSPORTS	SPOROCYSTIC	SPOUSELESS	SPRINTINGS	SQUARSONAGES	SQUIRMIEST
SPOKESHAVE	SPOROCYSTS	SPOYLEFULL	SPRITELIER	SQUASHABLE	SQUIRMINGLY
SPOKESHAVES	SPOROCYTES	SPRACHGEFUHL	SPRITELIEST	SQUASHIEST	SQUIRRELED
SPOKESMANSHIP	SPOROGENESES	SPRACHGEFUHLS	SPRITSAILS	SQUASHINESS	SQUIRRELFISH
SPOKESMANSHIPS	SPOROGENESIS	SPRACKLING	SPROUTINGS	SQUASHINESSES	SQUIRRELFISHES
SPOKESPEOPLE	SPOROGENIC	SPRADDLING	SPRUCENESS	SQUATNESSES	SQUIRRELING
SPOKESPERSON	SPOROGENIES	SPRANGLING	SPRUCENESSES	SQUATTERED	SQUIRRELLED
SPOKESPERSONS	SPOROGENOUS	SPRATTLING	SPRYNESSES	SQUATTERING	SQUIRRELLING
SPOKESWOMAN	SPOROGONIA	SPRAUCHLED	SPUILZIEING	SQUATTIEST	SQUIRRELLY
SPOKESWOMEN	SPOROGONIAL	SPRAUCHLES	SPULEBLADE	SQUATTINESS	SQUIRTINGS
SPOLIATING	SPOROGONIC	SPRAUCHLING	SPULEBLADES	SQUATTINESSES	SQUISHIEST
SPOLIATION	SPOROGONIES	SPRAUNCIER	SPULYIEING	SQUATTLING	SQUISHINESS
SPOLIATIONS	SPOROGONIUM	SPRAUNCIEST	SPULZIEING	SQUATTOCRACIES	SQUISHINESSES
SPOLIATIVE	SPOROPHORE	SPRAWLIEST	SPUMESCENCE	SQUATTOCRACY	SQUOOSHIER
SPOLIATORS	SPOROPHORES	SPREADABILITIES	SPUMESCENCES	SQUAWBUSHES	SQUOOSHIEST
SPOLIATORY	SPOROPHORIC	SPREADABILITY	SPUMESCENT	SQUAWFISHES	SQUOOSHING
SPONDAICAL	SPOROPHOROUS	SPREADABLE	SPUNBONDED	SQUAWKIEST	STABBINGLY
SPONDOOLICKS	SPOROPHYLL	SPREADINGLY	SPUNKINESS	SQUAWKINGS	STABILATES
SPONDULICKS	SPOROPHYLLS	SPREADINGS	SPUNKINESSES	SQUAWROOTS	STABILISATION
SPONDYLITIC	SPOROPHYLS	SPREADSHEET	SPURGALLED	SQUEAKERIES	STABILISATIONS
SPONDYLITICS	SPOROPHYTE	SPREADSHEETS	SPURGALLING	SQUEAKIEST	STABILISATOR
SPONDYLITIS	SPOROPHYTES	SPREAGHERIES	SPURIOSITIES	SQUEAKINESS	STABILISATORS
SPONDYLITISES	SPOROPHYTIC	SPREAGHERY	SPURIOSITY	SQUEAKINESSES	STABILISED
SPONDYLOLYSES	SPOROPOLLENIN	SPREATHING	SPURIOUSLY	SQUEAKINGLY	STABILISER
SPONDYLOLYSIS	SPOROPOLLENINS	SPRECHERIES	SPURIOUSNESS	SQUEAKINGS	STABILISERS
SPONDYLOSES	SPOROTRICHOSES	SPRECHGESANG	SPURIOUSNESSES	SQUEALINGS	STABILISES
SPONDYLOSIS	SPOROTRICHOSIS	SPRECHGESANGS	SPUTTERERS	SQUEAMISHLY	STABILISING
SPONDYLOUS	SPOROZOANS	SPRECHSTIMME	SPUTTERING	SQUEAMISHNESS	STABILITIES
SPONGEABLE	SPOROZOITE	SPRECHSTIMMEN	SPUTTERINGLY	SQUEAMISHNESSES	STABILIZATION
SPONGEBAGS	SPOROZOITES	SPREETHING	SPUTTERINGS	SQUEEGEEING	STABILIZATIONS
SPONGELIKE	SPORTABILITIES	SPREKELIAS	SPYGLASSES	SQUEEZABILITIES	STABILIZATOR
SPONGEWARE	SPORTABILITY	SPRIGGIEST	SPYMASTERS	SQUEEZABILITY	STABILIZATORS
SPONGEWARES	SPORTANCES	SPRIGHTFUL	SQUABASHED	SQUEEZABLE	STABILIZED
SPONGEWOOD	SPORTCASTER	SPRIGHTFULLY	SQUABASHER	SQUEEZIEST	STABILIZER
SPONGEWOODS	SPORTCASTERS	SPRIGHTFULNESS	SQUABASHERS	SQUEEZINGS	STABILIZERS
SPONGICOLOUS	SPORTFISHERMAN	SPRIGHTING	SQUABASHES	SQUEGGINGS	STABILIZES
SPONGIFORM	SPORTFISHERMEN	SPRIGHTLESS	SQUABASHING	SQUELCHERS	STABILIZING
SPONGINESS	SPORTFISHING	SPRIGHTLIER	SQUABBIEST	SQUELCHIER	STABLEBOYS
SPONGINESSES	SPORTFISHINGS	SPRIGHTLIEST	SQUABBLERS	SQUELCHIEST	STABLEMATE
SPONGIOBLAST	SPORTFULLY	SPRIGHTLINESS	SQUABBLING	SQUELCHING	STABLEMATES
SPONGIOBLASTIC	SPORTFULNESS	SPRIGHTLINESSES	SQUADRONAL	SQUELCHINGS	STABLENESS
SPONGIOBLASTS	SPORTFULNESSES	SPRIGTAILS	SQUADRONED	SQUETEAGUE	STABLENESSES
SPONGOLOGIES	SPORTINESS	SPRINGALDS	SQUADRONES	SQUETEAGUES	STABLISHED
SPONGOLOGIST	SPORTINESSES	SPRINGBOARD	SQUADRONING	SQUIBBINGS	STABLISHES
SPONGOLOGISTS	SPORTINGLY	SPRINGBOARDS	SQUAILINGS	SQUIDGIEST	STABLISHING
SPONGOLOGY	SPORTIVELY	SPRINGBOKS	SQUALIDEST	SQUIFFIEST	STABLISHMENT
SPONSIONAL	SPORTIVENESS	SPRINGBUCK	SQUALIDITIES	SQUIGGLERS	STABLISHMENTS
SPONSORIAL	SPORTIVENESSES	SPRINGBUCKS	SQUALIDITY	SQUIGGLIER	STACCATISSIMO

STACKROOMS	STALACTITICALLY	STANDOVERS	STATEHOODS	STEALTHIER	STEERSMATES
STACKYARDS	STALACTITIFORM	STANDPATTER	STATEHOUSE	STEALTHIEST	STEGANOGRAM
STACTOMETER	STALACTITIOUS	STANDPATTERS	STATEHOUSES	STEALTHILY	STEGANOGRAMS
STACTOMETERS	STALAGMITE	STANDPATTISM	STATELESSNESS	STEALTHINESS	STEGANOGRAPH
STADDLESTONE	STALAGMITES	STANDPATTISMS	STATELESSNESSES	STEALTHINESSES	STEGANOGRAPHER
STADDLESTONES	STALAGMITIC	STANDPIPES	STATELIEST	STEALTHING	STEGANOGRAPHERS
STADHOLDER	STALAGMITICAL	STANDPOINT	STATELINESS	STEALTHINGS	STEGANOGRAPHIC
STADHOLDERATE	STALAGMITICALLY	STANDPOINTS	STATELINESSES	STEAMBOATS	STEGANOGRAPHIES
STADHOLDERATES	STALAGMOMETER	STANDSTILL	STATEMENTED	STEAMERING	STEGANOGRAPHIST
STADHOLDERS	STALAGMOMETERS	STANDSTILLS	STATEMENTING	STEAMFITTER	STEGANOGRAPHS
STADHOLDERSHIP	STALAGMOMETRIES	STANNARIES	STATEMENTINGS	STEAMFITTERS	STEGANOGRAPHY
STADHOLDERSHIPS	STALAGMOMETRY	STANNATORS	STATEMENTS	STEAMINESS	STEGANOPOD
STADIOMETER	STALEMATED	STANNIFEROUS	STATEROOMS	STEAMINESSES	STEGANOPODOUS
STADIOMETERS	STALEMATES	STANNOTYPE	STATESMANLIKE	STEAMROLLED	STEGANOPODS
STADTHOLDER	STALEMATING	STANNOTYPES	STATESMANLY	STEAMROLLER	STEGOCARPOUS
STADTHOLDERATE	STALENESSES	STAPEDECTOMIES	STATESMANSHIP	STEAMROLLERED	STEGOCEPHALIAN
STADTHOLDERATES	STALKINESS	STAPEDECTOMY	STATESMANSHIPS	STEAMROLLERING	STEGOCEPHALIANS
STADTHOLDERS	STALKINESSES	STAPEDIUSES	STATESPEOPLE	STEAMROLLERS	STEGOCEPHALOUS
STADTHOLDERSHIP	STALLENGER	STAPHYLINE	STATESPERSON	STEAMROLLING	STEGODONTS
STAFFROOMS	STALLENGERS	STAPHYLINID	STATESPERSONS	STEAMROLLS	STEGOMYIAS
STAGECOACH	STALLHOLDER	STAPHYLINIDS	STATESWOMAN	STEAMSHIPS	STEGOPHILIST
STAGECOACHES	STALLHOLDERS	STAPHYLITIS	STATESWOMEN	STEAMTIGHT	STEGOPHILISTS
STAGECOACHING	STALLINGER	STAPHYLITISES	STATICALLY	STEAMTIGHTNESS	STEGOSAURIAN
STAGECOACHINGS	STALLINGERS	STAPHYLOCOCCAL	STATIONARIES	STEAROPTENE	STEGOSAURS
STAGECOACHMAN	STALLMASTER	STAPHYLOCOCCI	STATIONARILY	STEAROPTENES	STEGOSAURUS
STAGECOACHMEN	STALLMASTERS	STAPHYLOCOCCIC	STATIONARINESS	STEARSMATE	STEGOSAURUSES
STAGECRAFT	STALWARTLY	STAPHYLOCOCCUS	STATIONARY	STEARSMATES	STEINBOCKS
STAGECRAFTS	STALWARTNESS	STAPHYLOMA	STATIONERIES	STEATOCELE	STEINKIRKS
STAGEHANDS	STALWARTNESSES	STAPHYLOMAS	STATIONERS	STEATOCELES	STELLARATOR
STAGESTRUCK	STALWORTHS	STAPHYLOMATA	STATIONERY	STEATOLYSES	STELLARATORS
STAGFLATION	STAMINEOUS	STAPHYLOPLASTIC	STATIONING	STEATOLYSIS	STELLATELY
STAGFLATIONARY	STAMINIFEROUS	STAPHYLOPLASTY	STATIONMASTER	STEATOMATOUS	STELLERIDAN
STAGFLATIONS	STAMINODES	STAPHYLORRHAPHY	STATIONMASTERS	STEATOPYGA	STELLERIDANS
STAGGERBUSH	STAMINODIA	STARBOARDED	STATISTICAL	STEATOPYGAS	STELLERIDS
STAGGERBUSHES	STAMINODIES	STARBOARDING	STATISTICALLY	STEATOPYGIA	STELLIFEROUS
STAGGERERS	STAMINODIUM	STARBOARDS	STATISTICIAN	STEATOPYGIAS	STELLIFIED
STAGGERING	STAMMERERS	STARBURSTS	STATISTICIANS	STEATOPYGIC	STELLIFIES
STAGGERINGLY	STAMMERING	STARCHEDLY	STATISTICS	STEATOPYGOUS	STELLIFORM
STAGGERINGS	STAMMERINGLY	STARCHEDNESS	STATOBLAST	STEATORRHEA	STELLIFYING
STAGHOUNDS	STAMMERINGS	STARCHEDNESSES	STATOBLASTS	STEATORRHEAS	STELLIFYINGS
STAGINESSES	STAMPEDERS	STARCHIEST	STATOCYSTS	STEATORRHOEA	STELLIONATE
STAGNANCES	STAMPEDING	STARCHINESS	STATOLATRIES	STEATORRHOEAS	STELLIONATES
STAGNANCIES	STAMPEDOED	STARCHINESSES	STATOLATRY	STEDFASTLY	STELLULARLY
STAGNANTLY	STAMPEDOING	STARCHLIKE	STATOLITHIC	STEDFASTNESS	STELLULATE
STAGNATING	STANCHABLE	STARDRIFTS	STATOLITHS	STEDFASTNESSES	STEMMATOUS
STAGNATION	STANCHELLED	STARFISHED	STATOSCOPE	STEELHEADS	STEMMERIES
STAGNATIONS	STANCHELLING	STARFISHES	STATOSCOPES	STEELINESS	STEMWINDER
STAIDNESSES	STANCHERED	STARFLOWER	STATUARIES	STEELINESSES	STEMWINDERS
STAINABILITIES	STANCHERING	STARFLOWERS	STATUESQUE	STEELMAKER	STENCHIEST
STAINABILITY	STANCHINGS	STARFRUITS	STATUESQUELY	STEELMAKERS	STENCILERS
STAINLESSES	STANCHIONED	STARFUCKER	STATUESQUENESS	STEELMAKING	STENCILING
STAINLESSLY	STANCHIONING	STARFUCKERS	STATUETTES	STEELMAKINGS	STENCILLED
STAINLESSNESS	STANCHIONS	STARFUCKING	STATUTABLE	STEELWARES	STENCILLER
STAINLESSNESSES	STANCHLESS	STARFUCKINGS	STATUTABLY	STEELWORKER	STENCILLERS
STAINPROOF	STANCHNESS	STARGAZERS	STATUTORILY	STEELWORKERS	STENCILLING
STAIRCASED	STANCHNESSES	STARGAZING	STAUNCHABLE	STEELWORKING	STENCILLINGS
STAIRCASES	STANDARDBRED	STARGAZINGS	STAUNCHERS	STEELWORKINGS	STENOBATHIC
STAIRCASING	STANDARDBREDS	STARKENING	STAUNCHEST	STEELWORKS	STENOBATHS
STAIRCASINGS	STANDARDISATION	STARKNESSES	STAUNCHING	STEELYARDS	STENOCARDIA
STAIRFOOTS	STANDARDISE	STARLIGHTED	STAUNCHINGS	STEENBRASES	STENOCARDIAS
STAIRHEADS	STANDARDISED	STARLIGHTS	STAUNCHLESS	STEENBUCKS	STENOCHROME
STAIRLIFTS	STANDARDISER	STARMONGER	STAUNCHNESS	STEENKIRKS	STENOCHROMES
STAIRSTEPPED	STANDARDISERS	STARMONGERS	STAUNCHNESSES	STEEPDOWNE	STENOCHROMIES
STAIRSTEPPING	STANDARDISES	STAROSTIES	STAUROLITE	STEEPEDOWNE	STENOCHROMY
STAIRSTEPS	STANDARDISING	STARRINESS	STAUROLITES	STEEPENING	STENOGRAPH
STAIRWELLS	STANDARDIZATION	STARRINESSES	STAUROLITIC	STEEPINESS	STENOGRAPHED
STAIRWORKS	STANDARDIZE	STARSHINES	STAUROSCOPE	STEEPINESSES	STENOGRAPHER
STAKEHOLDER	STANDARDIZED	STARSTONES	STAUROSCOPES	STEEPLEBUSH	STENOGRAPHERS
STAKEHOLDERS	STANDARDIZER	STARSTRUCK	STAUROSCOPIC	STEEPLEBUSHES	STENOGRAPHIC
STAKHANOVISM	STANDARDIZERS	STARTINGLY	STAVESACRE	STEEPLECHASE	STENOGRAPHICAL
STAKHANOVISMS	STANDARDIZES	STARTLEMENT	STAVESACRES	STEEPLECHASED	STENOGRAPHIES
STAKHANOVITE	STANDARDIZING	STARTLEMENTS	STAVUDINES	STEEPLECHASER	STENOGRAPHING
STAKHANOVITES	STANDARDLESS	STARTLINGLY	STAYMAKERS	STEEPLECHASERS	STENOGRAPHIST
STAKTOMETER	STANDARDLY	STARTLINGS	STEADFASTLY	STEEPLECHASES	STENOGRAPHISTS
STAKTOMETERS	STANDDOWNS	STARVATION	STEADFASTNESS	STEEPLECHASING	STENOGRAPHS
STALACTICAL	STANDFASTS	STARVATIONS	STEADFASTNESSES	STEEPLECHASINGS	STENOGRAPHY
STALACTIFORM	STANDFIRST	STARVELING	STEADICAMS	STEEPLEJACK	STENOHALINE
STALACTITAL	STANDFIRSTS	STARVELINGS	STEADINESS	STEEPLEJACKS	STENOPAEIC
STALACTITE	STANDGALES	STASIDIONS	STEADINESSES	STEEPNESSES	STENOPETALOUS
STALACTITED	STANDISHES	STASIMORPHIES	STEAKHOUSE	STEERAGEWAY	STENOPHAGOUS
STALACTITES	STANDOFFISH	STASIMORPHY	STEAKHOUSES	STEERAGEWAYS	STENOPHYLLOUS
STALACTITIC	STANDOFFISHLY	STATECRAFT	STEALINGLY	STEERLINGS	STENOTHERM
STALACTITICAL	STANDOFFISHNESS	STATECRAFTS	STEALTHFUL	STEERSMATE	STENOTHERMAL

S

STENOTHERMS
STENOTOPIC
STENOTROPIC
STENOTYPED
STENOTYPER
STENOTYPERS
STENOTYPES
STENOTYPIC
STENOTYPIES
STENOTYPING
STENOTYPIST
STENOTYPISTS
STENTMASTER
STENTMASTERS
STENTORIAN
STEPBAIRNS
STEPBROTHER
STEPBROTHERS
STEPCHILDREN
STEPDANCER
STEPDANCERS
STEPDANCING
STEPDANCINGS
STEPDAUGHTER
STEPDAUGHTERS
STEPFAMILIES
STEPFAMILY
STEPFATHER
STEPFATHERS
STEPHANITE
STEPHANITES
STEPHANOTIS
STEPHANOTISES
STEPLADDER
STEPLADDERS
STEPMOTHER
STEPMOTHERLY
STEPMOTHERS
STEPPARENT
STEPPARENTING
STEPPARENTINGS
STEPPARENTS
STEPSISTER
STEPSISTERS
STEPSTOOLS
STERADIANS
STERCORACEOUS
STERCORANISM
STERCORANISMS
STERCORANIST
STERCORANISTS
STERCORARIOUS
STERCORARY
STERCORATE
STERCORATED
STERCORATES
STERCORATING
STERCORICOLOUS
STERCULIACEOUS
STERCULIAS
STEREOACUITIES
STEREOACUITY
STEREOBATE
STEREOBATES
STEREOBATIC
STEREOBLIND
STEREOCARD
STEREOCARDS
STEREOCHEMICAL
STEREOCHEMISTRY
STEREOCHROME
STEREOCHROMED
STEREOCHROMES
STEREOCHROMIES
STEREOCHROMING
STEREOCHROMY
STEREOGNOSES
STEREOGNOSIS
STEREOGRAM
STEREOGRAMS
STEREOGRAPH
STEREOGRAPHED
STEREOGRAPHIC

STEREOGRAPHICAL
STEREOGRAPHIES
STEREOGRAPHING
STEREOGRAPHS
STEREOGRAPHY
STEREOISOMER
STEREOISOMERIC
STEREOISOMERISM
STEREOISOMERS
STEREOISOMETRIC
STEREOLOGICAL
STEREOLOGICALLY
STEREOLOGIES
STEREOLOGY
STEREOMETER
STEREOMETERS
STEREOMETRIC
STEREOMETRICAL
STEREOMETRIES
STEREOMETRY
STEREOPHONIC
STEREOPHONIES
STEREOPHONY
STEREOPSES
STEREOPSIS
STEREOPTICON
STEREOPTICONS
STEREOPTICS
STEREOREGULAR
STEREOSCOPE
STEREOSCOPES
STEREOSCOPIC
STEREOSCOPICAL
STEREOSCOPIES
STEREOSCOPIST
STEREOSCOPISTS
STEREOSCOPY
STEREOSONIC
STEREOSPECIFIC
STEREOTACTIC
STEREOTACTICAL
STEREOTAXES
STEREOTAXIA
STEREOTAXIAS
STEREOTAXIC
STEREOTAXICALLY
STEREOTAXIS
STEREOTOMIES
STEREOTOMY
STEREOTROPIC
STEREOTROPISM
STEREOTROPISMS
STEREOTYPE
STEREOTYPED
STEREOTYPER
STEREOTYPERS
STEREOTYPES
STEREOTYPIC
STEREOTYPICAL
STEREOTYPICALLY
STEREOTYPIES
STEREOTYPING
STEREOTYPINGS
STEREOTYPIST
STEREOTYPISTS
STEREOTYPY
STEREOVISION
STEREOVISIONS
STERICALLY
STERIGMATA
STERILANTS
STERILISABLE
STERILISATION
STERILISATIONS
STERILISED
STERILISER
STERILISERS
STERILISES
STERILISING
STERILITIES
STERILIZABLE
STERILIZATION
STERILIZATIONS

STERILIZED
STERILIZER
STERILIZERS
STERILIZES
STERILIZING
STERLINGLY
STERLINGNESS
STERLINGNESSES
STERNALGIA
STERNALGIAS
STERNALGIC
STERNBOARD
STERNBOARDS
STERNEBRAE
STERNFASTS
STERNFOREMOST
STERNNESSES
STERNOCOSTAL
STERNOTRIBE
STERNPORTS
STERNPOSTS
STERNSHEET
STERNSHEETS
STERNUTATION
STERNUTATIONS
STERNUTATIVE
STERNUTATIVES
STERNUTATOR
STERNUTATORIES
STERNUTATORS
STERNUTATORY
STERNWARDS
STERNWORKS
STEROIDOGENESES
STEROIDOGENESIS
STEROIDOGENIC
STERTOROUS
STERTOROUSLY
STERTOROUSNESS
STETHOSCOPE
STETHOSCOPES
STETHOSCOPIC
STETHOSCOPIES
STETHOSCOPIST
STETHOSCOPISTS
STETHOSCOPY
STEVEDORED
STEVEDORES
STEVEDORING
STEVENGRAPH
STEVENGRAPHS
STEWARDESS
STEWARDESSES
STEWARDING
STEWARDRIES
STEWARDSHIP
STEWARDSHIPS
STEWARTRIES
STIACCIATO
STIACCIATOS
STIBIALISM
STIBIALISMS
STICCADOES
STICCATOES
STICHARION
STICHARIONS
STICHICALLY
STICHIDIUM
STICHOLOGIES
STICHOLOGY
STICHOMETRIC
STICHOMETRICAL
STICHOMETRIES
STICHOMETRY
STICHOMYTHIA
STICHOMYTHIAS
STICHOMYTHIC
STICHOMYTHIES
STICHOMYTHY
STICKABILITIES
STICKABILITY
STICKBALLS
STICKERING

STICKHANDLE
STICKHANDLED
STICKHANDLER
STICKHANDLERS
STICKHANDLES
STICKHANDLING
STICKINESS
STICKINESSES
STICKLEADER
STICKLEADERS
STICKLEBACK
STICKLEBACKS
STICKSEEDS
STICKTIGHT
STICKTIGHTS
STICKWEEDS
STICKWORKS
STICKYBEAK
STICKYBEAKED
STICKYBEAKING
STICKYBEAKS
STIDDIEING
STIFFENERS
STIFFENING
STIFFENINGS
STIFFNESSES
STIFFWARES
STIFLINGLY
STIGMARIAN
STIGMARIANS
STIGMASTEROL
STIGMASTEROLS
STIGMATICAL
STIGMATICALLY
STIGMATICS
STIGMATIFEROUS
STIGMATISATION
STIGMATISATIONS
STIGMATISE
STIGMATISED
STIGMATISER
STIGMATISERS
STIGMATISES
STIGMATISING
STIGMATISM
STIGMATISMS
STIGMATIST
STIGMATISTS
STIGMATIZATION
STIGMATIZATIONS
STIGMATIZE
STIGMATIZED
STIGMATIZER
STIGMATIZERS
STIGMATIZES
STIGMATIZING
STIGMATOPHILIA
STIGMATOPHILIAS
STIGMATOPHILIST
STIGMATOSE
STILBESTROL
STILBESTROLS
STILBOESTROL
STILBOESTROLS
STILETTOED
STILETTOES
STILETTOING
STILLATORIES
STILLATORY
STILLBIRTH
STILLBIRTHS
STILLBORNS
STILLHOUSE
STILLHOUSES
STILLICIDE
STILLICIDES
STILLIFORM
STILLNESSES
STILLROOMS
STILPNOSIDERITE
STILTBIRDS
STILTEDNESS
STILTEDNESSES

STILTINESS
STILTINESSES
STIMPMETER
STIMPMETERS
STIMULABLE
STIMULANCIES
STIMULANCY
STIMULANTS
STIMULATED
STIMULATER
STIMULATERS
STIMULATES
STIMULATING
STIMULATINGLY
STIMULATION
STIMULATIONS
STIMULATIVE
STIMULATIVES
STIMULATOR
STIMULATORS
STIMULATORY
STINGAREES
STINGBULLS
STINGFISHES
STINGINESS
STINGINESSES
STINGINGLY
STINGINGNESS
STINGINGNESSES
STINKEROOS
STINKHORNS
STINKINGLY
STINKINGNESS
STINKINGNESSES
STINKSTONE
STINKSTONES
STINKWEEDS
STINKWOODS
STINTEDNESS
STINTEDNESSES
STINTINGLY
STIPELLATE
STIPENDIARIES
STIPENDIARY
STIPENDIATE
STIPENDIATED
STIPENDIATES
STIPENDIATING
STIPITIFORM
STIPPLINGS
STIPULABLE
STIPULACEOUS
STIPULATED
STIPULATES
STIPULATING
STIPULATION
STIPULATIONS
STIPULATOR
STIPULATORS
STIPULATORY
STIRABOUTS
STIRPICULTURE
STIRPICULTURES
STIRRINGLY
STITCHCRAFT
STITCHCRAFTS
STITCHERIES
STITCHINGS
STITCHWORK
STITCHWORKS
STITCHWORT
STITCHWORTS
STOCHASTIC
STOCHASTICALLY
STOCKADING
STOCKBREEDER
STOCKBREEDERS
STOCKBREEDING
STOCKBREEDINGS
STOCKBROKER
STOCKBROKERAGE
STOCKBROKERAGES
STOCKBROKERS

STOCKBROKING
STOCKBROKINGS
STOCKFISHES
STOCKHOLDER
STOCKHOLDERS
STOCKHOLDING
STOCKHOLDINGS
STOCKHORNS
STOCKHORSE
STOCKHORSES
STOCKINESS
STOCKINESSES
STOCKINETS
STOCKINETTE
STOCKINETTES
STOCKINGED
STOCKINGER
STOCKINGERS
STOCKINGLESS
STOCKISHLY
STOCKISHNESS
STOCKISHNESSES
STOCKJOBBER
STOCKJOBBERIES
STOCKJOBBERS
STOCKJOBBERY
STOCKJOBBING
STOCKJOBBINGS
STOCKKEEPER
STOCKKEEPERS
STOCKLISTS
STOCKLOCKS
STOCKPILED
STOCKPILER
STOCKPILERS
STOCKPILES
STOCKPILING
STOCKPILINGS
STOCKPUNISHT
STOCKROOMS
STOCKROUTE
STOCKROUTES
STOCKTAKEN
STOCKTAKES
STOCKTAKING
STOCKTAKINGS
STOCKWORKS
STOCKYARDS
STODGINESS
STODGINESSES
STOECHIOLOGICAL
STOECHIOLOGIES
STOECHIOLOGY
STOECHIOMETRIC
STOECHIOMETRIES
STOECHIOMETRY
STOICALNESS
STOICALNESSES
STOICHEIOLOGIES
STOICHEIOLOGY
STOICHEIOMETRIC
STOICHEIOMETRY
STOICHIOLOGICAL
STOICHIOLOGIES
STOICHIOLOGY
STOICHIOMETRIC
STOICHIOMETRIES
STOICHIOMETRY
STOITERING
STOKEHOLDS
STOKEHOLES
STOLENWISE
STOLIDITIES
STOLIDNESS
STOLIDNESSES
STOLONIFEROUS
STOMACHACHE
STOMACHACHES
STOMACHERS
STOMACHFUL
STOMACHFULNESS
STOMACHFULS
STOMACHICAL

STOMACHICS
STOMACHING
STOMACHLESS
STOMACHOUS
STOMATITIC
STOMATITIDES
STOMATITIS
STOMATITISES
STOMATODAEA
STOMATODAEUM
STOMATOGASTRIC
STOMATOLOGICAL
STOMATOLOGIES
STOMATOLOGY
STOMATOPLASTIES
STOMATOPLASTY
STOMATOPOD
STOMATOPODS
STOMODAEAL
STOMODAEUM
STOMODAEUMS
STOMODEUMS
STONEBOATS
STONEBORER
STONEBORERS
STONEBRASH
STONEBRASHES
STONEBREAK
STONEBREAKS
STONECASTS
STONECHATS
STONECROPS
STONECUTTER
STONECUTTERS
STONECUTTING
STONECUTTINGS
STONEFISHES
STONEFLIES
STONEGROUND
STONEHANDS
STONEHORSE
STONEHORSES
STONELESSNESS
STONELESSNESSES
STONEMASON
STONEMASONRIES
STONEMASONRY
STONEMASONS
STONESHOTS
STONEWALLED
STONEWALLER
STONEWALLERS
STONEWALLING
STONEWALLINGS
STONEWALLS
STONEWARES
STONEWASHED
STONEWASHES
STONEWASHING
STONEWORKER
STONEWORKERS
STONEWORKS
STONEWORTS
STONINESSES
STONISHING
STONKERING
STONYHEARTED
STOOLBALLS
STOOPBALLS
STOOPINGLY
STOPLIGHTS
STOPPERING
STOPWATCHES
STOREFRONT
STOREFRONTS
STOREHOUSE
STOREHOUSES
STOREKEEPER
STOREKEEPERS
STOREKEEPING
STOREKEEPINGS
STOREROOMS
STORESHIPS

STORIETTES
STORIOLOGIES
STORIOLOGIST
STORIOLOGISTS
STORIOLOGY
STORKSBILL
STORKSBILLS
STORMBIRDS
STORMBOUND
STORMFULLY
STORMFULNESS
STORMFULNESSES
STORMINESS
STORMINESSES
STORMPROOF
STORYBOARD
STORYBOARDED
STORYBOARDING
STORYBOARDS
STORYBOOKS
STORYETTES
STORYLINES
STORYTELLER
STORYTELLERS
STORYTELLING
STORYTELLINGS
STOTTERING
STOUTENING
STOUTHEARTED
STOUTHEARTEDLY
STOUTHERIE
STOUTHERIES
STOUTHRIEF
STOUTHRIEFS
STOUTNESSES
STOVEPIPES
STRABISMAL
STRABISMIC
STRABISMICAL
STRABISMOMETER
STRABISMOMETERS
STRABISMUS
STRABISMUSES
STRABOMETER
STRABOMETERS
STRABOTOMIES
STRABOTOMY
STRACCHINI
STRACCHINO
STRADDLEBACK
STRADDLERS
STRADDLING
STRAGGLERS
STRAGGLIER
STRAGGLIEST
STRAGGLING
STRAGGLINGLY
STRAGGLINGS
STRAICHTER
STRAICHTEST
STRAIGHTAWAY
STRAIGHTAWAYS
STRAIGHTBRED
STRAIGHTBREDS
STRAIGHTED
STRAIGHTEDGE
STRAIGHTEDGED
STRAIGHTEDGES
STRAIGHTEN
STRAIGHTENED
STRAIGHTENER
STRAIGHTENERS
STRAIGHTENING
STRAIGHTENS
STRAIGHTER
STRAIGHTEST
STRAIGHTFORTH
STRAIGHTFORWARD
STRAIGHTING
STRAIGHTISH
STRAIGHTJACKET
STRAIGHTJACKETS
STRAIGHTLACED

STRAIGHTLY
STRAIGHTNESS
STRAIGHTNESSES
STRAIGHTWAY
STRAIGHTWAYS
STRAINEDLY
STRAININGS
STRAITENED
STRAITENING
STRAITJACKET
STRAITJACKETED
STRAITJACKETING
STRAITJACKETS
STRAITLACED
STRAITLACEDLY
STRAITLACEDNESS
STRAITNESS
STRAITNESSES
STRAITWAISTCOAT
STRAMACONS
STRAMASHED
STRAMASHES
STRAMASHING
STRAMAZONS
STRAMINEOUS
STRAMONIES
STRAMONIUM
STRAMONIUMS
STRANDEDNESS
STRANDEDNESSES
STRANDFLAT
STRANDFLATS
STRANDLINE
STRANDLINES
STRANDWOLF
STRANDWOLVES
STRANGENESS
STRANGENESSES
STRANGERED
STRANGERING
STRANGLEHOLD
STRANGLEHOLDS
STRANGLEMENT
STRANGLEMENTS
STRANGLERS
STRANGLING
STRANGULATE
STRANGULATED
STRANGULATES
STRANGULATING
STRANGULATION
STRANGULATIONS
STRANGURIES
STRAPHANGED
STRAPHANGER
STRAPHANGERS
STRAPHANGING
STRAPHANGINGS
STRAPHANGS
STRAPLESSES
STRAPLINES
STRAPONTIN
STRAPONTINS
STRAPPADOED
STRAPPADOES
STRAPPADOING
STRAPPADOS
STRAPPIEST
STRAPPINGS
STRAPWORTS
STRATAGEMS
STRATEGETIC
STRATEGETICAL
STRATEGICAL
STRATEGICALLY
STRATEGICS
STRATEGIES
STRATEGISE
STRATEGISED
STRATEGISES
STRATEGISING
STRATEGIST
STRATEGISTS

STRATEGIZE
STRATEGIZED
STRATEGIZES
STRATEGIZING
STRATHSPEY
STRATHSPEYS
STRATICULATE
STRATICULATION
STRATICULATIONS
STRATIFICATION
STRATIFICATIONS
STRATIFIED
STRATIFIES
STRATIFORM
STRATIFYING
STRATIGRAPHER
STRATIGRAPHERS
STRATIGRAPHIC
STRATIGRAPHICAL
STRATIGRAPHIES
STRATIGRAPHIST
STRATIGRAPHISTS
STRATIGRAPHY
STRATOCRACIES
STRATOCRACY
STRATOCRAT
STRATOCRATIC
STRATOCRATS
STRATOCUMULI
STRATOCUMULUS
STRATOPAUSE
STRATOPAUSES
STRATOSPHERE
STRATOSPHERES
STRATOSPHERIC
STRATOSPHERICAL
STRATOTANKER
STRATOTANKERS
STRATOVOLCANO
STRATOVOLCANOES
STRATOVOLCANOS
STRAUCHTED
STRAUCHTER
STRAUCHTEST
STRAUCHTING
STRAUGHTED
STRAUGHTER
STRAUGHTEST
STRAUGHTING
STRAVAGING
STRAVAIGED
STRAVAIGER
STRAVAIGERS
STRAVAIGING
STRAWBERRIES
STRAWBERRY
STRAWBOARD
STRAWBOARDS
STRAWFLOWER
STRAWFLOWERS
STRAWWEIGHT
STRAWWEIGHTS
STRAWWORMS
STRAYLINGS
STREAKIEST
STREAKINESS
STREAKINESSES
STREAKINGS
STREAKLIKE
STREAMBEDS
STREAMERED
STREAMIEST
STREAMINESS
STREAMINESSES
STREAMINGLY
STREAMINGS
STREAMLESS
STREAMLETS
STREAMLIKE
STREAMLINE
STREAMLINED
STREAMLINER
STREAMLINERS

STREAMLINES
STREAMLING
STREAMLINGS
STREAMLINING
STREAMSIDE
STREAMSIDES
STREETAGES
STREETBOYS
STREETCARS
STREETFULS
STREETKEEPER
STREETKEEPERS
STREETLAMP
STREETLAMPS
STREETLIGHT
STREETLIGHTS
STREETROOM
STREETROOMS
STREETSCAPE
STREETSCAPES
STREETSMART
STREETWALKER
STREETWALKERS
STREETWALKING
STREETWALKINGS
STREETWARD
STREETWARDS
STREETWEAR
STREETWEARS
STREETWISE
STREIGNING
STRELITZES
STRELITZIA
STRELITZIAS
STRENGTHEN
STRENGTHENED
STRENGTHENER
STRENGTHENERS
STRENGTHENING
STRENGTHENINGS
STRENGTHENS
STRENGTHFUL
STRENGTHLESS
STRENUITIES
STRENUOSITIES
STRENUOSITY
STRENUOUSLY
STRENUOUSNESS
STRENUOUSNESSES
STREPEROUS
STREPHOSYMBOLIA
STREPITANT
STREPITATION
STREPITATIONS
STREPITOSO
STREPITOUS
STREPSIPTEROUS
STREPTOBACILLI
STREPTOBACILLUS
STREPTOCARPUS
STREPTOCARPUSES
STREPTOCOCCAL
STREPTOCOCCI
STREPTOCOCCIC
STREPTOCOCCUS
STREPTOKINASE
STREPTOKINASES
STREPTOLYSIN
STREPTOLYSINS
STREPTOMYCES
STREPTOMYCETE
STREPTOMYCETES
STREPTOMYCIN
STREPTOMYCINS
STREPTOSOLEN
STREPTOSOLENS
STREPTOTHRICIN
STREPTOTHRICINS
STRESSBUSTER
STRESSBUSTERS
STRESSBUSTING
STRESSFULLY

STRESSFULNESS
STRESSFULNESSES
STRESSLESS
STRESSLESSNESS
STRETCHABILITY
STRETCHABLE
STRETCHERED
STRETCHERING
STRETCHERS
STRETCHIER
STRETCHIEST
STRETCHINESS
STRETCHINESSES
STRETCHING
STRETCHINGS
STRETCHLESS
STRETCHMARKS
STREWMENTS
STRIATIONS
STRIATURES
STRICKENLY
STRICKLING
STRICTIONS
STRICTNESS
STRICTNESSES
STRICTURED
STRICTURES
STRIDDLING
STRIDELEGGED
STRIDELEGS
STRIDENCES
STRIDENCIES
STRIDENTLY
STRIDEWAYS
STRIDULANCE
STRIDULANCES
STRIDULANT
STRIDULANTLY
STRIDULATE
STRIDULATED
STRIDULATES
STRIDULATING
STRIDULATION
STRIDULATIONS
STRIDULATOR
STRIDULATORS
STRIDULATORY
STRIDULOUS
STRIDULOUSLY
STRIDULOUSNESS
STRIFELESS
STRIGIFORM
STRIKEBOUND
STRIKEBREAKER
STRIKEBREAKERS
STRIKEBREAKING
STRIKEBREAKINGS
STRIKELESS
STRIKEOUTS
STRIKEOVER
STRIKEOVERS
STRIKINGLY
STRIKINGNESS
STRIKINGNESSES
STRINGBOARD
STRINGBOARDS
STRINGCOURSE
STRINGCOURSES
STRINGENCIES
STRINGENCY
STRINGENDO
STRINGENTLY
STRINGENTNESS
STRINGENTNESSES
STRINGHALT
STRINGHALTED
STRINGHALTS
STRINGIEST
STRINGINESS
STRINGINESSES
STRINGINGS
STRINGLESS
STRINGLIKE

STRINGPIECE
STRINGPIECES
STRINGYBARK
STRINGYBARKS
STRINKLING
STRINKLINGS
STRIPAGRAM
STRIPAGRAMS
STRIPELESS
STRIPINESS
STRIPINESSES
STRIPLINGS
STRIPPABLE
STRIPPERGRAM
STRIPPERGRAMS
STRIPPINGS
STRIPTEASE
STRIPTEASER
STRIPTEASERS
STRIPTEASES
STRIVINGLY
STROBILACEOUS
STROBILATE
STROBILATED
STROBILATES
STROBILATING
STROBILATION
STROBILATIONS
STROBILIFORM
STROBILINE
STROBILISATION
STROBILISATIONS
STROBILIZATION
STROBILIZATIONS
STROBILOID
STROBILUSES
STROBOSCOPE
STROBOSCOPES
STROBOSCOPIC
STROBOSCOPICAL
STROBOTRON
STROBOTRONS
STRODDLING
STROGANOFF
STROGANOFFS
STROKEPLAY
STROLLINGS
STROMATOLITE
STROMATOLITES
STROMATOLITIC
STROMATOUS
STROMBULIFEROUS
STROMBULIFORM
STROMBUSES
STRONGARMED
STRONGARMING
STRONGARMS
STRONGBOXES
STRONGHOLD
STRONGHOLDS
STRONGNESS
STRONGNESSES
STRONGPOINT
STRONGPOINTS
STRONGROOM
STRONGROOMS
STRONGYLES
STRONGYLOID
STRONGYLOIDOSES
STRONGYLOIDOSIS
STRONGYLOIDS
STRONGYLOSES
STRONGYLOSIS
STRONTIANITE
STRONTIANITES
STRONTIANS
STRONTIUMS
STROPHANTHIN
STROPHANTHINS
STROPHANTHUS
STROPHANTHUSES
STROPHICAL
STROPHIOLATE

STROPHIOLATED
STROPHIOLE
STROPHIOLES
STROPHOIDS
STROPHULUS
STROPPIEST
STROPPINESS
STROPPINESSES
STROUDINGS
STROUPACHS
STRUCTURAL
STRUCTURALISE
STRUCTURALISED
STRUCTURALISES
STRUCTURALISING
STRUCTURALISM
STRUCTURALISMS
STRUCTURALIST
STRUCTURALISTS
STRUCTURALIZE
STRUCTURALIZED
STRUCTURALIZES
STRUCTURALIZING
STRUCTURALLY
STRUCTURATION
STRUCTURATIONS
STRUCTURED
STRUCTURELESS
STRUCTURES
STRUCTURING
STRUGGLERS
STRUGGLING
STRUGGLINGLY
STRUGGLINGS
STRUMITISES
STRUMPETED
STRUMPETING
STRUTHIOID
STRUTHIOIDS
STRUTHIOUS
STRUTTINGLY
STRUTTINGS
STRYCHNIAS
STRYCHNINE
STRYCHNINED
STRYCHNINES
STRYCHNINING
STRYCHNINISM
STRYCHNINISMS
STRYCHNISM
STRYCHNISMS
STUBBINESS
STUBBINESSES
STUBBLIEST
STUBBORNED
STUBBORNER
STUBBORNEST
STUBBORNING
STUBBORNLY
STUBBORNNESS
STUBBORNNESSES
STUCCOWORK
STUCCOWORKS
STUDDINGSAIL
STUDDINGSAILS
STUDENTRIES
STUDENTSHIP
STUDENTSHIPS
STUDFISHES
STUDHORSES
STUDIEDNESS
STUDIEDNESSES
STUDIOUSLY
STUDIOUSNESS
STUDIOUSNESSES
STUFFINESS
STUFFINESSES
STULTIFICATION
STULTIFICATIONS
STULTIFIED
STULTIFIER
STULTIFIERS
STULTIFIES

STULTIFYING
STUMBLEBUM
STUMBLEBUMS
STUMBLIEST
STUMBLINGLY
STUMPINESS
STUMPINESSES
STUMPWORKS
STUNNINGLY
STUNTEDNESS
STUNTEDNESSES
STUNTWOMAN
STUNTWOMEN
STUPEFACIENT
STUPEFACIENTS
STUPEFACTION
STUPEFACTIONS
STUPEFACTIVE
STUPEFIERS
STUPEFYING
STUPEFYINGLY
STUPENDIOUS
STUPENDOUS
STUPENDOUSLY
STUPENDOUSNESS
STUPIDITIES
STUPIDNESS
STUPIDNESSES
STUPRATING
STUPRATION
STUPRATIONS
STURDINESS
STURDINESSES
STUTTERERS
STUTTERING
STUTTERINGLY
STUTTERINGS
STYLEBOOKS
STYLELESSNESS
STYLELESSNESSES
STYLIFEROUS
STYLISATION
STYLISATIONS
STYLISHNESS
STYLISHNESSES
STYLISTICALLY
STYLISTICS
STYLITISMS
STYLIZATION
STYLIZATIONS
STYLOBATES
STYLOGRAPH
STYLOGRAPHIC
STYLOGRAPHICAL
STYLOGRAPHIES
STYLOGRAPHS
STYLOGRAPHY
STYLOLITES
STYLOLITIC
STYLOMETRIES
STYLOMETRY
STYLOPHONE
STYLOPHONES
STYLOPISED
STYLOPISES
STYLOPISING
STYLOPIZED
STYLOPIZES
STYLOPIZING
STYLOPODIA
STYLOPODIUM
STYLOSTIXES
STYLOSTIXIS
STYPTICITIES
STYPTICITY
STYRACACEOUS
STYROFOAMS
SUABILITIES
SUASIVENESS
SUASIVENESSES
SUAVENESSES
SUAVEOLENT
SUABABDOMINAL

SUBACETATE
SUBACETATES
SUBACIDITIES
SUBACIDITY
SUBACIDNESS
SUBACIDNESSES
SUBACTIONS
SUBACUTELY
SUBADOLESCENT
SUBADOLESCENTS
SUBAERIALLY
SUBAFFLUENT
SUBAGENCIES
SUBAGGREGATE
SUBAGGREGATES
SUBAGGREGATION
SUBAGGREGATIONS
SUBAHDARIES
SUBAHSHIPS
SUBALLIANCE
SUBALLIANCES
SUBALLOCATION
SUBALLOCATIONS
SUBALTERNANT
SUBALTERNANTS
SUBALTERNATE
SUBALTERNATES
SUBALTERNATION
SUBALTERNATIONS
SUBALTERNITIES
SUBALTERNITY
SUBALTERNS
SUBANGULAR
SUBANTARCTIC
SUBAPOSTOLIC
SUBAPPEARANCE
SUBAPPEARANCES
SUBAQUATIC
SUBAQUEOUS
SUBARACHNOID
SUBARACHNOIDAL
SUBARBOREAL
SUBARBORESCENT
SUBARCTICS
SUBARCUATE
SUBARCUATION
SUBARCUATIONS
SUBARRATION
SUBARRATIONS
SUBARRHATION
SUBARRHATIONS
SUBARTICLE
SUBARTICLES
SUBASSEMBLE
SUBASSEMBLED
SUBASSEMBLES
SUBASSEMBLIES
SUBASSEMBLING
SUBASSOCIATION
SUBASSOCIATIONS
SUBATMOSPHERIC
SUBATOMICS
SUBAUDIBLE
SUBAUDITION
SUBAUDITIONS
SUBAURICULAR
SUBAVERAGE
SUBAXILLARY
SUBBASEMENT
SUBBASEMENTS
SUBBITUMINOUS
SUBBRANCHES
SUBBUREAUS
SUBBUREAUX
SUBCABINET
SUBCABINETS
SUBCALIBER
SUBCALIBRE
SUBCANTORS
SUBCAPSULAR
SUBCARDINAL
SUBCARDINALS

SUBCARRIER
SUBCARRIERS
SUBCATEGORIES
SUBCATEGORISE
SUBCATEGORISED
SUBCATEGORISES
SUBCATEGORISING
SUBCATEGORIZE
SUBCATEGORIZED
SUBCATEGORIZES
SUBCATEGORIZING
SUBCATEGORY
SUBCAVITIES
SUBCEILING
SUBCEILINGS
SUBCELESTIAL
SUBCELESTIALS
SUBCELLARS
SUBCELLULAR
SUBCENTERS
SUBCENTRAL
SUBCENTRALLY
SUBCEPTION
SUBCEPTIONS
SUBCHANTER
SUBCHANTERS
SUBCHAPTER
SUBCHAPTERS
SUBCHARTER
SUBCHARTERS
SUBCHASERS
SUBCHELATE
SUBCHLORIDE
SUBCHLORIDES
SUBCIRCUIT
SUBCIRCUITS
SUBCIVILISATION
SUBCIVILISED
SUBCIVILIZATION
SUBCIVILIZED
SUBCLASSED
SUBCLASSES
SUBCLASSIFIED
SUBCLASSIFIES
SUBCLASSIFY
SUBCLASSIFYING
SUBCLASSING
SUBCLAUSES
SUBCLAVIAN
SUBCLAVIANS
SUBCLAVICULAR
SUBCLIMACTIC
SUBCLIMAXES
SUBCLINICAL
SUBCLINICALLY
SUBCLUSTER
SUBCLUSTERED
SUBCLUSTERING
SUBCLUSTERS
SUBCOLLECTION
SUBCOLLECTIONS
SUBCOLLEGE
SUBCOLLEGIATE
SUBCOLONIES
SUBCOMMISSION
SUBCOMMISSIONED
SUBCOMMISSIONER
SUBCOMMISSIONS
SUBCOMMITTEE
SUBCOMMITTEES
SUBCOMMUNITIES
SUBCOMMUNITY
SUBCOMPACT
SUBCOMPACTS
SUBCOMPONENT
SUBCOMPONENTS
SUBCONSCIOUS
SUBCONSCIOUSES
SUBCONSCIOUSLY
SUBCONSULS
SUBCONTIGUOUS
SUBCONTINENT
SUBCONTINENTAL

SUBCONTINENTS
SUBCONTINUOUS
SUBCONTRACT
SUBCONTRACTED
SUBCONTRACTING
SUBCONTRACTINGS
SUBCONTRACTOR
SUBCONTRACTORS
SUBCONTRACTS
SUBCONTRAOCTAVE
SUBCONTRARIES
SUBCONTRARIETY
SUBCONTRARY
SUBCOOLING
SUBCORDATE
SUBCORIACEOUS
SUBCORTEXES
SUBCORTICAL
SUBCORTICES
SUBCOSTALS
SUBCOUNTIES
SUBCRANIAL
SUBCRITICAL
SUBCRUSTAL
SUBCULTURAL
SUBCULTURALLY
SUBCULTURE
SUBCULTURED
SUBCULTURES
SUBCULTURING
SUBCURATIVE
SUBCUTANEOUS
SUBCUTANEOUSLY
SUBCUTISES
SUBDEACONATE
SUBDEACONATES
SUBDEACONRIES
SUBDEACONRY
SUBDEACONS
SUBDEACONSHIP
SUBDEACONSHIPS
SUBDEALERS
SUBDEANERIES
SUBDEANERY
SUBDEBUTANTE
SUBDEBUTANTES
SUBDECANAL
SUBDECISION
SUBDECISIONS
SUBDELIRIA
SUBDELIRIOUS
SUBDELIRIUM
SUBDELIRIUMS
SUBDEPARTMENT
SUBDEPARTMENTS
SUBDEPUTIES
SUBDERMALLY
SUBDEVELOPMENT
SUBDEVELOPMENTS
SUBDIACONAL
SUBDIACONATE
SUBDIACONATES
SUBDIALECT
SUBDIALECTS
SUBDIRECTOR
SUBDIRECTORS
SUBDISCIPLINE
SUBDISCIPLINES
SUBDISTRICT
SUBDISTRICTS
SUBDIVIDABLE
SUBDIVIDED
SUBDIVIDER
SUBDIVIDERS
SUBDIVIDES
SUBDIVIDING
SUBDIVISIBLE
SUBDIVISION
SUBDIVISIONAL
SUBDIVISIONS
SUBDIVISIVE
SUBDOMINANT
SUBDOMINANTS

SUBDUCTING	SUBINFEUDATIONS	SUBLANCEOLATE	SUBMERGIBLE	SUBOPTIMIZES	SUBSAMPLING
SUBDUCTION	SUBINFEUDATORY	SUBLANGUAGE	SUBMERGIBLES	SUBOPTIMIZING	SUBSATELLITE
SUBDUCTIONS	SUBINFEUDED	SUBLANGUAGES	SUBMERGING	SUBOPTIMUM	SUBSATELLITES
SUBDUEDNESS	SUBINFEUDING	SUBLAPSARIAN	SUBMERSIBILITY	SUBORBICULAR	SUBSATURATED
SUBDUEDNESSES	SUBINFEUDS	SUBLAPSARIANISM	SUBMERSIBLE	SUBORBITAL	SUBSATURATION
SUBDUEMENT	SUBINHIBITORY	SUBLAPSARIANS	SUBMERSIBLES	SUBORDINAL	SUBSATURATIONS
SUBDUEMENTS	SUBINSINUATION	SUBLATIONS	SUBMERSING	SUBORDINANCIES	SUBSCAPULAR
SUBDUPLICATE	SUBINSINUATIONS	SUBLEASING	SUBMERSION	SUBORDINANCY	SUBSCAPULARS
SUBECONOMIC	SUBINSPECTOR	SUBLESSEES	SUBMERSIONS	SUBORDINARIES	SUBSCHEMATA
SUBECONOMIES	SUBINSPECTORS	SUBLESSORS	SUBMETACENTRIC	SUBORDINARY	SUBSCIENCE
SUBECONOMY	SUBINTELLECTION	SUBLETHALLY	SUBMETACENTRICS	SUBORDINATE	SUBSCIENCES
SUBEDITING	SUBINTELLIGENCE	SUBLETTERS	SUBMICROGRAM	SUBORDINATED	SUBSCRIBABLE
SUBEDITORIAL	SUBINTELLIGITUR	SUBLETTING	SUBMICRONS	SUBORDINATELY	SUBSCRIBED
SUBEDITORS	SUBINTERVAL	SUBLETTINGS	SUBMICROSCOPIC	SUBORDINATENESS	SUBSCRIBER
SUBEDITORSHIP	SUBINTERVALS	SUBLIBRARIAN	SUBMILLIMETER	SUBORDINATES	SUBSCRIBERS
SUBEDITORSHIPS	SUBINTRANT	SUBLIBRARIANS	SUBMINIATURE	SUBORDINATING	SUBSCRIBES
SUBEMPLOYED	SUBINTRODUCE	SUBLICENSE	SUBMINIATURES	SUBORDINATION	SUBSCRIBING
SUBEMPLOYMENT	SUBINTRODUCED	SUBLICENSED	SUBMINIATURISE	SUBORDINATIONS	SUBSCRIBINGS
SUBEMPLOYMENTS	SUBINTRODUCES	SUBLICENSES	SUBMINIATURISED	SUBORDINATIVE	SUBSCRIPTION
SUBENTRIES	SUBINTRODUCING	SUBLICENSING	SUBMINIATURISES	SUBORDINATOR	SUBSCRIPTIONS
SUBEPIDERMAL	SUBINVOLUTION	SUBLIEUTENANCY	SUBMINIATURIZE	SUBORDINATORS	SUBSCRIPTIVE
SUBEQUATORIAL	SUBINVOLUTIONS	SUBLIEUTENANT	SUBMINIATURIZED	SUBORGANISATION	SUBSCRIPTS
SUBERISATION	SUBIRRIGATE	SUBLIEUTENANTS	SUBMINIATURIZES	SUBORGANIZATION	SUBSECRETARIES
SUBERISATIONS	SUBIRRIGATED	SUBLIMABLE	SUBMINIMAL	SUBORNATION	SUBSECRETARY
SUBERISING	SUBIRRIGATES	SUBLIMATED	SUBMINISTER	SUBORNATIONS	SUBSECTION
SUBERIZATION	SUBIRRIGATING	SUBLIMATES	SUBMINISTERS	SUBORNATIVE	SUBSECTIONS
SUBERIZATIONS	SUBIRRIGATION	SUBLIMATING	SUBMISSIBLE	SUBOSCINES	SUBSECTORS
SUBERIZING	SUBIRRIGATIONS	SUBLIMATION	SUBMISSION	SUBPANATION	SUBSEGMENT
SUBFACTORIAL	SUBITANEOUS	SUBLIMATIONS	SUBMISSIONS	SUBPANATIONS	SUBSEGMENTS
SUBFACTORIALS	SUBITISING	SUBLIMENESS	SUBMISSIVE	SUBPARAGRAPH	SUBSEIZURE
SUBFAMILIES	SUBITIZING	SUBLIMENESSES	SUBMISSIVELY	SUBPARAGRAPHS	SUBSEIZURES
SUBFERTILE	SUBJACENCIES	SUBLIMINAL	SUBMISSIVENESS	SUBPARALLEL	SUBSELLIUM
SUBFERTILITIES	SUBJACENCY	SUBLIMINALLY	SUBMISSNESS	SUBPENAING	SUBSENSIBLE
SUBFERTILITY	SUBJACENTLY	SUBLIMINALS	SUBMISSNESSES	SUBPERIODS	SUBSENTENCE
SUBFEUDATION	SUBJECTABILITY	SUBLIMINGS	SUBMITTABLE	SUBPHRENIC	SUBSENTENCES
SUBFEUDATIONS	SUBJECTABLE	SUBLIMISED	SUBMITTALS	SUBPOENAED	SUBSEQUENCE
SUBFEUDATORY	SUBJECTIFIED	SUBLIMISES	SUBMITTERS	SUBPOENAING	SUBSEQUENCES
SUBFOSSILS	SUBJECTIFIES	SUBLIMISING	SUBMITTING	SUBPOPULATION	SUBSEQUENT
SUBFREEZING	SUBJECTIFY	SUBLIMITIES	SUBMITTINGS	SUBPOPULATIONS	SUBSEQUENTIAL
SUBFUSCOUS	SUBJECTIFYING	SUBLIMIZED	SUBMOLECULE	SUBPOTENCIES	SUBSEQUENTLY
SUBGENERATION	SUBJECTING	SUBLIMIZES	SUBMOLECULES	SUBPOTENCY	SUBSEQUENTNESS
SUBGENERATIONS	SUBJECTION	SUBLIMIZING	SUBMONTANE	SUBPREFECT	SUBSEQUENTS
SUBGENERIC	SUBJECTIONS	SUBLINEATION	SUBMONTANELY	SUBPREFECTS	SUBSERVIENCE
SUBGENERICALLY	SUBJECTIVE	SUBLINEATIONS	SUBMUCOSAE	SUBPREFECTURE	SUBSERVIENCES
SUBGENUSES	SUBJECTIVELY	SUBLINGUAL	SUBMUCOSAL	SUBPREFECTURES	SUBSERVIENCIES
SUBGLACIAL	SUBJECTIVENESS	SUBLITERACIES	SUBMUCOSAS	SUBPRIMATE	SUBSERVIENCY
SUBGLACIALLY	SUBJECTIVES	SUBLITERACY	SUBMULTIPLE	SUBPRIMATES	SUBSERVIENT
SUBGLOBOSE	SUBJECTIVISE	SUBLITERARY	SUBMULTIPLES	SUBPRINCIPAL	SUBSERVIENTLY
SUBGLOBULAR	SUBJECTIVISED	SUBLITERATE	SUBMUNITION	SUBPRINCIPALS	SUBSERVIENTS
SUBGOVERNMENT	SUBJECTIVISES	SUBLITERATES	SUBMUNITIONS	SUBPRIORESS	SUBSERVING
SUBGOVERNMENTS	SUBJECTIVISING	SUBLITERATURE	SUBNASCENT	SUBPRIORESSES	SUBSESSILE
SUBGROUPED	SUBJECTIVISM	SUBLITERATURES	SUBNATIONAL	SUBPROBLEM	SUBSHRUBBY
SUBGROUPING	SUBJECTIVISMS	SUBLITTORAL	SUBNATURAL	SUBPROBLEMS	SUBSIDENCE
SUBHARMONIC	SUBJECTIVIST	SUBLITTORALS	SUBNETWORK	SUBPROCESS	SUBSIDENCES
SUBHARMONICS	SUBJECTIVISTIC	SUBLUXATED	SUBNETWORKED	SUBPROCESSES	SUBSIDENCIES
SUBHASTATION	SUBJECTIVISTS	SUBLUXATES	SUBNETWORKING	SUBPRODUCT	SUBSIDENCY
SUBHASTATIONS	SUBJECTIVITIES	SUBLUXATING	SUBNETWORKS	SUBPRODUCTS	SUBSIDIARIES
SUBHEADING	SUBJECTIVITY	SUBLUXATION	SUBNORMALITIES	SUBPROFESSIONAL	SUBSIDIARILY
SUBHEADINGS	SUBJECTIVIZE	SUBLUXATIONS	SUBNORMALITY	SUBPROGRAM	SUBSIDIARINESS
SUBIMAGINAL	SUBJECTIVIZED	SUBMANAGER	SUBNORMALLY	SUBPROGRAMS	SUBSIDIARITIES
SUBIMAGINES	SUBJECTIVIZES	SUBMANAGERS	SUBNORMALS	SUBPROJECT	SUBSIDIARITY
SUBIMAGOES	SUBJECTIVIZING	SUBMANDIBULAR	SUBNUCLEAR	SUBPROJECTS	SUBSIDIARY
SUBINCISED	SUBJECTLESS	SUBMANDIBULARS	SUBNUCLEUS	SUBPROLETARIAT	SUBSIDISABLE
SUBINCISES	SUBJECTSHIP	SUBMARGINAL	SUBNUCLEUSES	SUBPROLETARIATS	SUBSIDISATION
SUBINCISING	SUBJECTSHIPS	SUBMARGINALLY	SUBOCCIPITAL	SUBRATIONAL	SUBSIDISATIONS
SUBINCISION	SUBJOINDER	SUBMARINED	SUBOCEANIC	SUBREFERENCE	SUBSIDISED
SUBINCISIONS	SUBJOINDERS	SUBMARINER	SUBOCTAVES	SUBREFERENCES	SUBSIDISER
SUBINDEXES	SUBJOINING	SUBMARINERS	SUBOCTUPLE	SUBREGIONAL	SUBSIDISERS
SUBINDICATE	SUBJUGABLE	SUBMARINES	SUBOFFICER	SUBREGIONS	SUBSIDISES
SUBINDICATED	SUBJUGATED	SUBMARINING	SUBOFFICERS	SUBREPTION	SUBSIDISING
SUBINDICATES	SUBJUGATES	SUBMARKETS	SUBOFFICES	SUBREPTIONS	SUBSIDIZABLE
SUBINDICATING	SUBJUGATING	SUBMATRICES	SUBOPERCULA	SUBREPTITIOUS	SUBSIDIZATION
SUBINDICATION	SUBJUGATION	SUBMATRIXES	SUBOPERCULAR	SUBREPTITIOUSLY	SUBSIDIZATIONS
SUBINDICATIONS	SUBJUGATIONS	SUBMAXILLARIES	SUBOPERCULUM	SUBREPTIVE	SUBSIDIZED
SUBINDICATIVE	SUBJUGATOR	SUBMAXILLARY	SUBOPTIMAL	SUBROGATED	SUBSIDIZER
SUBINDICES	SUBJUGATORS	SUBMAXIMAL	SUBOPTIMISATION	SUBROGATES	SUBSIDIZERS
SUBINDUSTRIES	SUBJUNCTION	SUBMEDIANT	SUBOPTIMISE	SUBROGATING	SUBSIDIZES
SUBINDUSTRY	SUBJUNCTIONS	SUBMEDIANTS	SUBOPTIMISED	SUBROGATION	SUBSIDIZING
SUBINFEUDATE	SUBJUNCTIVE	SUBMERGEMENT	SUBOPTIMISES	SUBROGATIONS	SUBSISTENCE
SUBINFEUDATED	SUBJUNCTIVELY	SUBMERGEMENTS	SUBOPTIMISING	SUBROUTINE	SUBSISTENCES
SUBINFEUDATES	SUBJUNCTIVES	SUBMERGENCE	SUBOPTIMIZATION	SUBROUTINES	SUBSISTENT
SUBINFEUDATING	SUBKINGDOM	SUBMERGENCES	SUBOPTIMIZE	SUBSAMPLED	SUBSISTENTIAL
SUBINFEUDATION	SUBKINGDOMS	SUBMERGIBILITY	SUBOPTIMIZED	SUBSAMPLES	SUBSISTERS

SUBSISTING	SUBSTITUTIONARY	SUBTILIZERS	SUBVOCALISED	SUCKERFISHES	SUGARINESS
SUBSOCIALLY	SUBSTITUTIONS	SUBTILIZES	SUBVOCALISES	SUCKFISHES	SUGARINESSES
SUBSOCIETIES	SUBSTITUTIVE	SUBTILIZING	SUBVOCALISING	SUCRALFATE	SUGARLOAVES
SUBSOCIETY	SUBSTITUTIVELY	SUBTILTIES	SUBVOCALIZATION	SUCRALFATES	SUGARPLUMS
SUBSOILERS	SUBSTITUTIVITY	SUBTITLING	SUBVOCALIZE	SUCRALOSES	SUGGESTERS
SUBSOILING	SUBSTRACTED	SUBTITULAR	SUBVOCALIZED	SUCTIONING	SUGGESTIBILITY
SUBSOILINGS	SUBSTRACTING	SUBTLENESS	SUBVOCALIZES	SUCTORIANS	SUGGESTIBLE
SUBSONICALLY	SUBSTRACTION	SUBTLENESSES	SUBVOCALIZING	SUDATORIES	SUGGESTIBLENESS
SUBSPECIALISE	SUBSTRACTIONS	SUBTLETIES	SUBVOCALLY	SUDATORIUM	SUGGESTIBLY
SUBSPECIALISED	SUBSTRACTOR	SUBTOTALED	SUBWARDENS	SUDATORIUMS	SUGGESTING
SUBSPECIALISES	SUBSTRACTORS	SUBTOTALING	SUBWOOFERS	SUDDENNESS	SUGGESTION
SUBSPECIALISING	SUBSTRACTS	SUBTOTALLED	SUBWRITERS	SUDDENNESSES	SUGGESTIONISE
SUBSPECIALIST	SUBSTRATAL	SUBTOTALLING	SUCCEDANEA	SUDDENTIES	SUGGESTIONISED
SUBSPECIALISTS	SUBSTRATES	SUBTOTALLY	SUCCEDANEOUS	SUDORIFEROUS	SUGGESTIONISES
SUBSPECIALITIES	SUBSTRATIVE	SUBTRACTED	SUCCEDANEUM	SUDORIFICS	SUGGESTIONISING
SUBSPECIALITY	SUBSTRATOSPHERE	SUBTRACTER	SUCCEDANEUMS	SUDORIPAROUS	SUGGESTIONISM
SUBSPECIALIZE	SUBSTRATUM	SUBTRACTERS	SUCCEEDABLE	SUEABILITIES	SUGGESTIONISMS
SUBSPECIALIZED	SUBSTRATUMS	SUBTRACTING	SUCCEEDERS	SUEABILITY	SUGGESTIONIST
SUBSPECIALIZES	SUBSTRUCTED	SUBTRACTION	SUCCEEDING	SUFFERABLE	SUGGESTIONISTS
SUBSPECIALIZING	SUBSTRUCTING	SUBTRACTIONS	SUCCEEDINGLY	SUFFERABLENESS	SUGGESTIONIZE
SUBSPECIALTIES	SUBSTRUCTION	SUBTRACTIVE	SUCCENTORS	SUFFERABLY	SUGGESTIONIZED
SUBSPECIALTY	SUBSTRUCTIONS	SUBTRACTOR	SUCCENTORSHIP	SUFFERANCE	SUGGESTIONIZES
SUBSPECIES	SUBSTRUCTS	SUBTRACTORS	SUCCENTORSHIPS	SUFFERANCES	SUGGESTIONIZING
SUBSPECIFIC	SUBSTRUCTURAL	SUBTRAHEND	SUCCESSANTLY	SUFFERINGLY	SUGGESTIONS
SUBSPECIFICALLY	SUBSTRUCTURE	SUBTRAHENDS	SUCCESSFUL	SUFFERINGS	SUGGESTIVE
SUBSPINOUS	SUBSTRUCTURES	SUBTREASURER	SUCCESSFULLY	SUFFICIENCE	SUGGESTIVELY
SUBSPONTANEOUS	SUBSULTIVE	SUBTREASURERS	SUCCESSFULNESS	SUFFICIENCES	SUGGESTIVENESS
SUBSTANCELESS	SUBSULTORILY	SUBTREASURIES	SUCCESSION	SUFFICIENCIES	SUICIDALLY
SUBSTANCES	SUBSULTORY	SUBTREASURY	SUCCESSIONAL	SUFFICIENCY	SUICIDOLOGIES
SUBSTANDARD	SUBSULTUSES	SUBTRIANGULAR	SUCCESSIONALLY	SUFFICIENT	SUICIDOLOGIST
SUBSTANTIAL	SUBSUMABLE	SUBTRIPLICATE	SUCCESSIONIST	SUFFICIENTLY	SUICIDOLOGISTS
SUBSTANTIALISE	SUBSUMPTION	SUBTROPICAL	SUCCESSIONISTS	SUFFICIENTS	SUICIDOLOGY
SUBSTANTIALISED	SUBSUMPTIONS	SUBTROPICALLY	SUCCESSIONLESS	SUFFICINGNESS	SUITABILITIES
SUBSTANTIALISES	SUBSUMPTIVE	SUBTROPICS	SUCCESSIONS	SUFFICINGNESSES	SUITABILITY
SUBSTANTIALISM	SUBSURFACE	SUBTRUDING	SUCCESSIVE	SUFFIGANCE	SUITABLENESS
SUBSTANTIALISMS	SUBSURFACES	SUBTYPICAL	SUCCESSIVELY	SUFFIGANCES	SUITABLENESSES
SUBSTANTIALIST	SUBSYSTEMS	SUBUMBRELLA	SUCCESSIVENESS	SUFFISANCE	SUITRESSES
SUBSTANTIALISTS	SUBTACKSMAN	SUBUMBRELLAR	SUCCESSLESS	SUFFISANCES	SULCALISED
SUBSTANTIALITY	SUBTACKSMEN	SUBUMBRELLAS	SUCCESSLESSLY	SUFFIXATION	SULCALISES
SUBSTANTIALIZE	SUBTANGENT	SUBUNGULATE	SUCCESSLESSNESS	SUFFIXATIONS	SULCALISING
SUBSTANTIALIZED	SUBTANGENTS	SUBUNGULATES	SUCCESSORAL	SUFFIXIONS	SULCALIZED
SUBSTANTIALIZES	SUBTEMPERATE	SUBURBANISATION	SUCCESSORS	SUFFLATING	SULCALIZES
SUBSTANTIALLY	SUBTENANCIES	SUBURBANISE	SUCCESSORSHIP	SUFFLATION	SULCALIZING
SUBSTANTIALNESS	SUBTENANCY	SUBURBANISED	SUCCESSORSHIPS	SUFFLATIONS	SULCATIONS
SUBSTANTIALS	SUBTENANTS	SUBURBANISES	SUCCINATES	SUFFOCATED	SULFACETAMIDE
SUBSTANTIATE	SUBTENDING	SUBURBANISING	SUCCINCTER	SUFFOCATES	SULFACETAMIDES
SUBSTANTIATED	SUBTENURES	SUBURBANISM	SUCCINCTEST	SUFFOCATING	SULFADIAZINE
SUBSTANTIATES	SUBTERFUGE	SUBURBANISMS	SUCCINCTLY	SUFFOCATINGLY	SULFADIAZINES
SUBSTANTIATING	SUBTERFUGES	SUBURBANITE	SUCCINCTNESS	SUFFOCATINGS	SULFADIMIDINE
SUBSTANTIATION	SUBTERMINAL	SUBURBANITES	SUCCINCTNESSES	SUFFOCATION	SULFADIMIDINES
SUBSTANTIATIONS	SUBTERNATURAL	SUBURBANITIES	SUCCINCTORIA	SUFFOCATIONS	SULFADOXINE
SUBSTANTIATIVE	SUBTERRAIN	SUBURBANITY	SUCCINCTORIES	SUFFOCATIVE	SULFADOXINES
SUBSTANTIATOR	SUBTERRAINS	SUBURBANIZATION	SUCCINCTORIUM	SUFFRAGANS	SULFAMETHAZINE
SUBSTANTIATORS	SUBTERRANE	SUBURBANIZE	SUCCINCTORY	SUFFRAGANSHIP	SULFAMETHAZINES
SUBSTANTIVAL	SUBTERRANEAN	SUBURBANIZED	SUCCINITES	SUFFRAGANSHIPS	SULFANILAMIDE
SUBSTANTIVALLY	SUBTERRANEANLY	SUBURBANIZES	SUCCINYLCHOLINE	SUFFRAGETTE	SULFANILAMIDES
SUBSTANTIVE	SUBTERRANEANS	SUBURBANIZING	SUCCORABLE	SUFFRAGETTES	SULFATASES
SUBSTANTIVELY	SUBTERRANEOUS	SUBURBICARIAN	SUCCORLESS	SUFFRAGETTISM	SULFATHIAZOLE
SUBSTANTIVENESS	SUBTERRANEOUSLY	SUBVARIETIES	SUCCOTASHES	SUFFRAGETTISMS	SULFATHIAZOLES
SUBSTANTIVES	SUBTERRANES	SUBVARIETY	SUCCOURABLE	SUFFRAGISM	SULFATIONS
SUBSTANTIVISE	SUBTERRENE	SUBVASSALS	SUCCOURERS	SUFFRAGISMS	SULFHYDRYL
SUBSTANTIVISED	SUBTERRENES	SUBVENTION	SUCCOURING	SUFFRAGIST	SULFHYDRYLS
SUBSTANTIVISES	SUBTERRESTRIAL	SUBVENTIONARY	SUCCOURLESS	SUFFRAGISTS	SULFINPYRAZONE
SUBSTANTIVISING	SUBTERRESTRIALS	SUBVENTIONS	SUCCUBUSES	SUFFRUTESCENT	SULFINPYRAZONES
SUBSTANTIVITIES	SUBTEXTUAL	SUBVERSALS	SUCCULENCE	SUFFRUTICOSE	SULFONAMIDE
SUBSTANTIVITY	SUBTHERAPEUTIC	SUBVERSING	SUCCULENCES	SUFFUMIGATE	SULFONAMIDES
SUBSTANTIVIZE	SUBTHRESHOLD	SUBVERSION	SUCCULENCIES	SUFFUMIGATED	SULFONATED
SUBSTANTIVIZED	SUBTILENESS	SUBVERSIONARIES	SUCCULENCY	SUFFUMIGATES	SULFONATES
SUBSTANTIVIZES	SUBTILENESSES	SUBVERSIONARY	SUCCULENTLY	SUFFUMIGATING	SULFONATING
SUBSTANTIVIZING	SUBTILISATION	SUBVERSIONS	SUCCULENTS	SUFFUMIGATION	SULFONATION
SUBSTATION	SUBTILISATIONS	SUBVERSIVE	SUCCUMBERS	SUFFUMIGATIONS	SULFONATIONS
SUBSTATIONS	SUBTILISED	SUBVERSIVELY	SUCCUMBING	SUFFUSIONS	SULFONIUMS
SUBSTELLAR	SUBTILISER	SUBVERSIVENESS	SUCCURSALE	SUGARALLIE	SULFONYLUREA
SUBSTERNAL	SUBTILISERS	SUBVERSIVES	SUCCURSALES	SUGARALLIES	SULFONYLUREAS
SUBSTITUENT	SUBTILISES	SUBVERTEBRAL	SUCCURSALS	SUGARBERRIES	SULFOXIDES
SUBSTITUENTS	SUBTILISIN	SUBVERTERS	SUCCUSSATION	SUGARBERRY	SULFURATED
SUBSTITUTABLE	SUBTILISING	SUBVERTICAL	SUCCUSSATIONS	SUGARBUSHES	SULFURATES
SUBSTITUTE	SUBTILISINS	SUBVERTING	SUCCUSSING	SUGARCANES	SULFURATING
SUBSTITUTED	SUBTILITIES	SUBVIRUSES	SUCCUSSION	SUGARCOATED	SULFURETED
SUBSTITUTES	SUBTILIZATION	SUBVISIBLE	SUCCUSSIONS	SUGARCOATING	SULFURETING
SUBSTITUTING	SUBTILIZATIONS	SUBVITREOUS	SUCCUSSIVE	SUGARCOATS	SULFURETTED
SUBSTITUTION	SUBTILIZED	SUBVOCALISATION	SUCHNESSES	SUGARHOUSE	SULFURETTING
SUBSTITUTIONAL	SUBTILIZER	SUBVOCALISE	SUCKERFISH	SUGARHOUSES	SULFURISATION

SULFURISATIONS
SULFURISED
SULFURISES
SULFURISING
SULFURIZED
SULFURIZES
SULFURIZING
SULFUROUSLY
SULFUROUSNESS
SULFUROUSNESSES
SULKINESSES
SULLENNESS
SULLENNESSES
SULPHACETAMIDE
SULPHACETAMIDES
SULPHADIAZINE
SULPHADIAZINES
SULPHANILAMIDE
SULPHANILAMIDES
SULPHATASE
SULPHATASES
SULPHATHIAZOLE
SULPHATHIAZOLES
SULPHATING
SULPHATION
SULPHATIONS
SULPHHYDRYL
SULPHHYDRYLS
SULPHINPYRAZONE
SULPHINYLS
SULPHONAMIDE
SULPHONAMIDES
SULPHONATE
SULPHONATED
SULPHONATES
SULPHONATING
SULPHONATION
SULPHONATIONS
SULPHONIUM
SULPHONIUMS
SULPHONMETHANE
SULPHONMETHANES
SULPHONYLS
SULPHONYLUREA
SULPHONYLUREAS
SULPHURATE
SULPHURATED
SULPHURATES
SULPHURATING
SULPHURATION
SULPHURATIONS
SULPHURATOR
SULPHURATORS
SULPHUREOUS
SULPHUREOUSLY
SULPHUREOUSNESS
SULPHURETED
SULPHURETING
SULPHURETS
SULPHURETTED
SULPHURETTING
SULPHURING
SULPHURISATION
SULPHURISATIONS
SULPHURISE
SULPHURISED
SULPHURISES
SULPHURISING
SULPHURIZATION
SULPHURIZATIONS
SULPHURIZE
SULPHURIZED
SULPHURIZES
SULPHURIZING
SULPHUROUS
SULPHUROUSLY
SULPHUROUSNESS
SULPHURWORT
SULPHURWORTS
SULPHURYLS
SULTANATES
SULTANESSES
SULTANSHIP

SULTANSHIPS
SULTRINESS
SULTRINESSES
SUMMABILITIES
SUMMABILITY
SUMMARINESS
SUMMARINESSES
SUMMARISABLE
SUMMARISATION
SUMMARISATIONS
SUMMARISED
SUMMARISER
SUMMARISERS
SUMMARISES
SUMMARISING
SUMMARISTS
SUMMARIZABLE
SUMMARIZATION
SUMMARIZATIONS
SUMMARIZED
SUMMARIZER
SUMMARIZERS
SUMMARIZES
SUMMARIZING
SUMMATIONAL
SUMMATIONS
SUMMERHOUSE
SUMMERHOUSES
SUMMERIEST
SUMMERINESS
SUMMERINESSES
SUMMERINGS
SUMMERLESS
SUMMERLIKE
SUMMERLONG
SUMMERSAULT
SUMMERSAULTED
SUMMERSAULTING
SUMMERSAULTS
SUMMERSETS
SUMMERSETTED
SUMMERSETTING
SUMMERTIDE
SUMMERTIDES
SUMMERTIME
SUMMERTIMES
SUMMERWEIGHT
SUMMERWOOD
SUMMERWOODS
SUMMITEERS
SUMMITLESS
SUMMITRIES
SUMMONABLE
SUMMONSING
SUMPHISHNESS
SUMPHISHNESSES
SUMPSIMUSES
SUMPTUOSITIES
SUMPTUOSITY
SUMPTUOUSLY
SUMPTUOUSNESS
SUMPTUOUSNESSES
SUNBATHERS
SUNBATHING
SUNBATHINGS
SUNBERRIES
SUNBONNETED
SUNBONNETS
SUNBURNING
SUNDERABLE
SUNDERANCE
SUNDERANCES
SUNDERINGS
SUNDERMENT
SUNDERMENTS
SUNDOWNERS
SUNDOWNING
SUNDRENCHED
SUNDRESSES
SUNFLOWERS
SUNGLASSES
SUNLESSNESS
SUNLESSNESSES

SUNLOUNGER
SUNLOUNGERS
SUNNINESSES
SUNPORCHES
SUNRISINGS
SUNSCREENING
SUNSCREENS
SUNSEEKERS
SUNSETTING
SUNSETTINGS
SUNSPOTTED
SUNSTROKES
SUNTANNING
SUNWORSHIPPER
SUNWORSHIPPERS
SUOVETAURILIA
SUPERABILITIES
SUPERABILITY
SUPERABLENESS
SUPERABLENESSES
SUPERABOUND
SUPERABOUNDED
SUPERABOUNDING
SUPERABOUNDS
SUPERABSORBENT
SUPERABSORBENTS
SUPERABUNDANCE
SUPERABUNDANCES
SUPERABUNDANT
SUPERABUNDANTLY
SUPERACHIEVER
SUPERACHIEVERS
SUPERACTIVE
SUPERACTIVITIES
SUPERACTIVITY
SUPERACUTE
SUPERADDED
SUPERADDING
SUPERADDITION
SUPERADDITIONAL
SUPERADDITIONS
SUPERAGENCIES
SUPERAGENCY
SUPERAGENT
SUPERAGENTS
SUPERALLOY
SUPERALLOYS
SUPERALTAR
SUPERALTARS
SUPERALTERN
SUPERALTERNS
SUPERAMBITIOUS
SUPERANNUABLE
SUPERANNUATE
SUPERANNUATED
SUPERANNUATES
SUPERANNUATING
SUPERANNUATION
SUPERANNUATIONS
SUPERATHLETE
SUPERATHLETES
SUPERATING
SUPERATION
SUPERATIONS
SUPERATOMS
SUPERBANKS
SUPERBAZAAR
SUPERBAZAARS
SUPERBAZAR
SUPERBAZARS
SUPERBIKES
SUPERBITCH
SUPERBITCHES
SUPERBITIES
SUPERBLOCK
SUPERBLOCKS
SUPERBNESS
SUPERBNESSES
SUPERBOARD
SUPERBOARDS
SUPERBOMBER
SUPERBOMBERS
SUPERBOMBS

SUPERBRAIN
SUPERBRAINS
SUPERBRATS
SUPERBRIGHT
SUPERBUREAUCRAT
SUPERCABINET
SUPERCABINETS
SUPERCALENDER
SUPERCALENDERED
SUPERCALENDERS
SUPERCARGO
SUPERCARGOES
SUPERCARGOS
SUPERCARGOSHIP
SUPERCARGOSHIPS
SUPERCARRIER
SUPERCARRIERS
SUPERCAUTIOUS
SUPERCEDED
SUPERCEDES
SUPERCEDING
SUPERCELESTIAL
SUPERCENTER
SUPERCENTERS
SUPERCHARGE
SUPERCHARGED
SUPERCHARGER
SUPERCHARGERS
SUPERCHARGES
SUPERCHARGING
SUPERCHERIE
SUPERCHERIES
SUPERCHURCH
SUPERCHURCHES
SUPERCILIARIES
SUPERCILIARY
SUPERCILIOUS
SUPERCILIOUSLY
SUPERCITIES
SUPERCIVILISED
SUPERCIVILIZED
SUPERCLASS
SUPERCLASSES
SUPERCLEAN
SUPERCLUBS
SUPERCLUSTER
SUPERCLUSTERS
SUPERCOILED
SUPERCOILING
SUPERCOILS
SUPERCOLLIDER
SUPERCOLLIDERS
SUPERCOLOSSAL
SUPERCOLUMNAR
SUPERCOMPUTER
SUPERCOMPUTERS
SUPERCOMPUTING
SUPERCOMPUTINGS
SUPERCONDUCT
SUPERCONDUCTED
SUPERCONDUCTING
SUPERCONDUCTION
SUPERCONDUCTIVE
SUPERCONDUCTOR
SUPERCONDUCTORS
SUPERCONDUCTS
SUPERCONFIDENCE
SUPERCONFIDENT
SUPERCONTINENT
SUPERCONTINENTS
SUPERCONVENIENT
SUPERCOOLED
SUPERCOOLING
SUPERCOOLS
SUPERCRIMINAL
SUPERCRIMINALS
SUPERCRITICAL
SUPERCURRENT
SUPERCURRENTS
SUPERDAINTY
SUPERDELUXE
SUPERDENSE
SUPERDIPLOMAT

SUPERDIPLOMATS
SUPERDOMINANT
SUPERDOMINANTS
SUPEREFFECTIVE
SUPEREFFICIENCY
SUPEREFFICIENT
SUPEREGOIST
SUPEREGOISTS
SUPERELASTIC
SUPERELEVATE
SUPERELEVATED
SUPERELEVATES
SUPERELEVATING
SUPERELEVATION
SUPERELEVATIONS
SUPERELITE
SUPEREMINENCE
SUPEREMINENCES
SUPEREMINENT
SUPEREMINENTLY
SUPEREROGANT
SUPEREROGATE
SUPEREROGATED
SUPEREROGATES
SUPEREROGATING
SUPEREROGATION
SUPEREROGATIONS
SUPEREROGATIVE
SUPEREROGATOR
SUPEREROGATORS
SUPEREROGATORY
SUPERESSENTIAL
SUPERETTES
SUPEREVIDENT
SUPEREXALT
SUPEREXALTATION
SUPEREXALTED
SUPEREXALTING
SUPEREXALTS
SUPEREXCELLENCE
SUPEREXCELLENT
SUPEREXPENSIVE
SUPEREXPRESS
SUPEREXPRESSES
SUPERFAMILIES
SUPERFAMILY
SUPERFARMS
SUPERFATTED
SUPERFECTA
SUPERFECTAS
SUPERFEMALE
SUPERFEMALES
SUPERFETATE
SUPERFETATED
SUPERFETATES
SUPERFETATING
SUPERFETATION
SUPERFETATIONS
SUPERFICIAL
SUPERFICIALISE
SUPERFICIALISED
SUPERFICIALISES
SUPERFICIALITY
SUPERFICIALIZE
SUPERFICIALIZED
SUPERFICIALIZES
SUPERFICIALLY
SUPERFICIALNESS
SUPERFICIALS
SUPERFICIES
SUPERFINENESS
SUPERFINENESSES
SUPERFIRMS
SUPERFIXES
SUPERFLACK
SUPERFLACKS
SUPERFLUID
SUPERFLUIDITIES
SUPERFLUIDITY
SUPERFLUIDS
SUPERFLUITIES
SUPERFLUITY
SUPERFLUOUS

SUPERFLUOUSLY
SUPERFLUOUSNESS
SUPERFLUXES
SUPERFOETATION
SUPERFOETATIONS
SUPERFRONTAL
SUPERFRONTALS
SUPERFUNDS
SUPERFUSED
SUPERFUSES
SUPERFUSING
SUPERFUSION
SUPERFUSIONS
SUPERGENES
SUPERGIANT
SUPERGIANTS
SUPERGLACIAL
SUPERGLUED
SUPERGLUES
SUPERGLUING
SUPERGOVERNMENT
SUPERGRAPHICS
SUPERGRASS
SUPERGRASSES
SUPERGRAVITIES
SUPERGRAVITY
SUPERGROUP
SUPERGROUPS
SUPERGROWTH
SUPERGROWTHS
SUPERHARDEN
SUPERHARDENED
SUPERHARDENING
SUPERHARDENS
SUPERHEATED
SUPERHEATER
SUPERHEATERS
SUPERHEATING
SUPERHEATS
SUPERHEAVIES
SUPERHEAVY
SUPERHELICAL
SUPERHELICES
SUPERHELIX
SUPERHELIXES
SUPERHEROES
SUPERHEROINE
SUPERHEROINES
SUPERHETERODYNE
SUPERHIGHWAY
SUPERHIGHWAYS
SUPERHIVES
SUPERHUMAN
SUPERHUMANISE
SUPERHUMANISED
SUPERHUMANISES
SUPERHUMANISING
SUPERHUMANITIES
SUPERHUMANITY
SUPERHUMANIZE
SUPERHUMANIZED
SUPERHUMANIZES
SUPERHUMANIZING
SUPERHUMANLY
SUPERHUMANNESS
SUPERHUMERAL
SUPERHUMERALS
SUPERHYPED
SUPERHYPES
SUPERHYPING
SUPERIMPORTANT
SUPERIMPOSABLE
SUPERIMPOSE
SUPERIMPOSED
SUPERIMPOSES
SUPERIMPOSING
SUPERIMPOSITION
SUPERINCUMBENCE
SUPERINCUMBENCY
SUPERINCUMBENT
SUPERINDIVIDUAL
SUPERINDUCE
SUPERINDUCED

SUPERINDUCEMENT	SUPERNALLY	SUPERPLUSES	SUPERSEDURES	SUPERSURGEON	SUPPLEJACKS
SUPERINDUCES	SUPERNATANT	SUPERPOLITE	SUPERSELLER	SUPERSURGEONS	SUPPLEMENT
SUPERINDUCING	SUPERNATANTS	SUPERPOLYMER	SUPERSELLERS	SUPERSWEET	SUPPLEMENTAL
SUPERINDUCTION	SUPERNATATION	SUPERPOLYMERS	SUPERSELLING	SUPERSYMMETRIC	SUPPLEMENTALLY
SUPERINDUCTIONS	SUPERNATATIONS	SUPERPORTS	SUPERSELLS	SUPERSYMMETRIES	SUPPLEMENTALS
SUPERINFECT	SUPERNATES	SUPERPOSABLE	SUPERSENSIBLE	SUPERSYMMETRY	SUPPLEMENTARIES
SUPERINFECTED	SUPERNATION	SUPERPOSED	SUPERSENSIBLY	SUPERSYSTEM	SUPPLEMENTARILY
SUPERINFECTING	SUPERNATIONAL	SUPERPOSES	SUPERSENSITIVE	SUPERSYSTEMS	SUPPLEMENTARY
SUPERINFECTION	SUPERNATIONALLY	SUPERPOSING	SUPERSENSORY	SUPERTANKER	SUPPLEMENTATION
SUPERINFECTIONS	SUPERNATIONS	SUPERPOSITION	SUPERSENSUAL	SUPERTANKERS	SUPPLEMENTED
SUPERINFECTS	SUPERNATURAL	SUPERPOSITIONS	SUPERSESSION	SUPERTAXES	SUPPLEMENTER
SUPERINSULATED	SUPERNATURALISE	SUPERPOWER	SUPERSESSIONS	SUPERTEACHER	SUPPLEMENTERS
SUPERINTEND	SUPERNATURALISM	SUPERPOWERED	SUPERSEXES	SUPERTEACHERS	SUPPLEMENTING
SUPERINTENDED	SUPERNATURALIST	SUPERPOWERFUL	SUPERSEXUALITY	SUPERTERRANEAN	SUPPLEMENTS
SUPERINTENDENCE	SUPERNATURALIZE	SUPERPOWERS	SUPERSHARP	SUPERTERRIFIC	SUPPLENESS
SUPERINTENDENCY	SUPERNATURALLY	SUPERPRAISE	SUPERSHOWS	SUPERTHICK	SUPPLENESSES
SUPERINTENDENT	SUPERNATURALS	SUPERPRAISED	SUPERSINGER	SUPERTHRILLER	SUPPLETION
SUPERINTENDENTS	SUPERNATURE	SUPERPRAISES	SUPERSINGERS	SUPERTHRILLERS	SUPPLETIONS
SUPERINTENDING	SUPERNATURES	SUPERPRAISING	SUPERSIZED	SUPERTIGHT	SUPPLETIVE
SUPERINTENDS	SUPERNORMAL	SUPERPREMIUM	SUPERSIZES	SUPERTITLE	SUPPLETIVES
SUPERINTENSITY	SUPERNORMALITY	SUPERPREMIUMS	SUPERSIZING	SUPERTITLES	SUPPLETORILY
SUPERIORESS	SUPERNORMALLY	SUPERPROFIT	SUPERSLEUTH	SUPERTONIC	SUPPLETORY
SUPERIORESSES	SUPERNOVAE	SUPERPROFITS	SUPERSLEUTHS	SUPERTONICS	SUPPLIABLE
SUPERIORITIES	SUPERNOVAS	SUPERQUALITY	SUPERSLICK	SUPERTRUCK	SUPPLIANCE
SUPERIORITY	SUPERNUMERARIES	SUPERRACES	SUPERSMART	SUPERTRUCKS	SUPPLIANCES
SUPERIORLY	SUPERNUMERARY	SUPERREALISM	SUPERSMOOTH	SUPERTWIST	SUPPLIANTLY
SUPERIORSHIP	SUPERNURSE	SUPERREALISMS	SUPERSONIC	SUPERTWISTS	SUPPLIANTS
SUPERIORSHIPS	SUPERNURSES	SUPERREALIST	SUPERSONICALLY	SUPERVENED	SUPPLICANT
SUPERJACENT	SUPERNUTRIENT	SUPERREALISTS	SUPERSONICS	SUPERVENES	SUPPLICANTS
SUPERJOCKS	SUPERNUTRIENTS	SUPERREFINE	SUPERSOUND	SUPERVENIENCE	SUPPLICATE
SUPERJUMBO	SUPERNUTRITION	SUPERREFINED	SUPERSOUNDS	SUPERVENIENCES	SUPPLICATED
SUPERJUMBOS	SUPERNUTRITIONS	SUPERREFINES	SUPERSPECIAL	SUPERVENIENT	SUPPLICATES
SUPERKINGDOM	SUPEROCTAVE	SUPERREFINING	SUPERSPECIALIST	SUPERVENING	SUPPLICATING
SUPERKINGDOMS	SUPEROCTAVES	SUPERREGIONAL	SUPERSPECIALS	SUPERVENTION	SUPPLICATINGLY
SUPERLARGE	SUPERORDER	SUPERREGIONALS	SUPERSPECIES	SUPERVENTIONS	SUPPLICATION
SUPERLATIVE	SUPERORDERS	SUPERROADS	SUPERSPECTACLE	SUPERVIRILE	SUPPLICATIONS
SUPERLATIVELY	SUPERORDINAL	SUPERROMANTIC	SUPERSPECTACLES	SUPERVIRTUOSI	SUPPLICATORY
SUPERLATIVENESS	SUPERORDINARY	SUPERSAFETIES	SUPERSPEED	SUPERVIRTUOSO	SUPPLICATS
SUPERLATIVES	SUPERORDINATE	SUPERSAFETY	SUPERSPEEDS	SUPERVIRTUOSOS	SUPPLICAVIT
SUPERLAWYER	SUPERORDINATED	SUPERSALES	SUPERSPIES	SUPERVIRULENT	SUPPLICAVITS
SUPERLAWYERS	SUPERORDINATES	SUPERSALESMAN	SUPERSTARDOM	SUPERVISAL	SUPPLYMENT
SUPERLIGHT	SUPERORDINATING	SUPERSALESMEN	SUPERSTARDOMS	SUPERVISALS	SUPPLYMENTS
SUPERLINER	SUPERORDINATION	SUPERSALTS	SUPERSTARS	SUPERVISED	SUPPORTABILITY
SUPERLINERS	SUPERORGANIC	SUPERSATURATE	SUPERSTATE	SUPERVISEE	SUPPORTABLE
SUPERLOADS	SUPERORGANICISM	SUPERSATURATED	SUPERSTATES	SUPERVISEES	SUPPORTABLENESS
SUPERLOBBYIST	SUPERORGANICIST	SUPERSATURATES	SUPERSTATION	SUPERVISES	SUPPORTABLY
SUPERLOBBYISTS	SUPERORGANISM	SUPERSATURATING	SUPERSTATIONS	SUPERVISING	SUPPORTANCE
SUPERLOYALIST	SUPERORGANISMS	SUPERSATURATION	SUPERSTIMULATE	SUPERVISION	SUPPORTANCES
SUPERLOYALISTS	SUPERORGASM	SUPERSAURS	SUPERSTIMULATED	SUPERVISIONS	SUPPORTERS
SUPERLUMINAL	SUPERORGASMS	SUPERSAVER	SUPERSTIMULATES	SUPERVISOR	SUPPORTING
SUPERLUNAR	SUPEROVULATE	SUPERSAVERS	SUPERSTITION	SUPERVISORS	SUPPORTINGS
SUPERLUNARY	SUPEROVULATED	SUPERSCALAR	SUPERSTITIONS	SUPERVISORSHIP	SUPPORTIVE
SUPERLUXURIOUS	SUPEROVULATES	SUPERSCALE	SUPERSTITIOUS	SUPERVISORSHIPS	SUPPORTIVELY
SUPERLUXURY	SUPEROVULATING	SUPERSCHOOL	SUPERSTITIOUSLY	SUPERVISORY	SUPPORTIVENESS
SUPERLYING	SUPEROVULATION	SUPERSCHOOLS	SUPERSTOCK	SUPERVOLUTE	SUPPORTLESS
SUPERMACHO	SUPEROVULATIONS	SUPERSCOUT	SUPERSTOCKS	SUPERWAIFS	SUPPORTMENT
SUPERMAJORITIES	SUPEROXIDE	SUPERSCOUTS	SUPERSTORE	SUPERWAVES	SUPPORTMENTS
SUPERMAJORITY	SUPEROXIDES	SUPERSCREEN	SUPERSTORES	SUPERWEAPON	SUPPORTRESS
SUPERMALES	SUPERPARASITISM	SUPERSCREENS	SUPERSTRATA	SUPERWEAPONS	SUPPORTRESSES
SUPERMARKET	SUPERPARTICLE	SUPERSCRIBE	SUPERSTRATUM	SUPERWEEDS	SUPPORTURE
SUPERMARKETS	SUPERPARTICLES	SUPERSCRIBED	SUPERSTRATUMS	SUPERWIDES	SUPPORTURES
SUPERMARTS	SUPERPATRIOT	SUPERSCRIBES	SUPERSTRENGTH	SUPERWIVES	SUPPOSABLE
SUPERMASCULINE	SUPERPATRIOTIC	SUPERSCRIBING	SUPERSTRENGTHS	SUPERWOMAN	SUPPOSABLY
SUPERMASSIVE	SUPERPATRIOTISM	SUPERSCRIPT	SUPERSTRIKE	SUPERWOMEN	SUPPOSEDLY
SUPERMAXES	SUPERPATRIOTS	SUPERSCRIPTION	SUPERSTRIKES	SUPINATING	SUPPOSINGS
SUPERMEMBRANE	SUPERPERSON	SUPERSCRIPTIONS	SUPERSTRING	SUPINATION	SUPPOSITION
SUPERMEMBRANES	SUPERPERSONAL	SUPERSCRIPTS	SUPERSTRINGS	SUPINATIONS	SUPPOSITIONAL
SUPERMICRO	SUPERPERSONS	SUPERSECRECIES	SUPERSTRONG	SUPINATORS	SUPPOSITIONALLY
SUPERMICROS	SUPERPHENOMENA	SUPERSECRECY	SUPERSTRUCT	SUPINENESS	SUPPOSITIONARY
SUPERMILITANT	SUPERPHENOMENON	SUPERSECRET	SUPERSTRUCTED	SUPINENESSES	SUPPOSITIONLESS
SUPERMILITANTS	SUPERPHOSPHATE	SUPERSEDABLE	SUPERSTRUCTING	SUPPEAGOES	SUPPOSITIONS
SUPERMINDS	SUPERPHOSPHATES	SUPERSEDEAS	SUPERSTRUCTION	SUPPEDANEA	SUPPOSITIOUS
SUPERMINIS	SUPERPHYLA	SUPERSEDEASES	SUPERSTRUCTIONS	SUPPEDANEUM	SUPPOSITIOUSLY
SUPERMINISTER	SUPERPHYLUM	SUPERSEDED	SUPERSTRUCTIVE	SUPPERLESS	SUPPOSITITIOUS
SUPERMINISTERS	SUPERPHYSICAL	SUPERSEDENCE	SUPERSTRUCTS	SUPPERTIME	SUPPOSITIVE
SUPERMODEL	SUPERPIMPS	SUPERSEDENCES	SUPERSTRUCTURAL	SUPPERTIMES	SUPPOSITIVELY
SUPERMODELS	SUPERPLANE	SUPERSEDER	SUPERSTRUCTURE	SUPPLANTATION	SUPPOSITIVES
SUPERMODERN	SUPERPLANES	SUPERSEDERE	SUPERSTRUCTURES	SUPPLANTATIONS	SUPPOSITORIES
SUPERMOTOS	SUPERPLASTIC	SUPERSEDERES	SUPERSTUDS	SUPPLANTED	SUPPOSITORY
SUPERMUNDANE	SUPERPLASTICITY	SUPERSEDES	SUPERSUBTILE	SUPPLANTER	SUPPRESSANT
SUPERNACULA	SUPERPLASTICS	SUPERSEDING	SUPERSUBTLE	SUPPLANTERS	SUPPRESSANTS
SUPERNACULAR	SUPERPLAYER	SUPERSEDURE	SUPERSUBTLETIES	SUPPLANTING	SUPPRESSED
SUPERNACULUM	SUPERPLAYERS		SUPERSUBTLETY	SUPPLEJACK	SUPPRESSEDLY

SUPPRESSER	SURFACEMAN	SURRENDERED	SUSPENDIBILITY	SWAGGERING	SWEIRNESSES
SUPPRESSERS	SURFACEMEN	SURRENDEREE	SUSPENDIBLE	SWAGGERINGLY	SWELLFISHES
SUPPRESSES	SURFACINGS	SURRENDEREES	SUSPENDING	SWAGGERINGS	SWELLHEADED
SUPPRESSIBILITY	SURFACTANT	SURRENDERER	SUSPENSEFUL	SWAINISHNESS	SWELLHEADEDNESS
SUPPRESSIBLE	SURFACTANTS	SURRENDERERS	SUSPENSEFULLY	SWAINISHNESSES	SWELLHEADS
SUPPRESSING	SURFBOARDED	SURRENDERING	SUSPENSEFULNESS	SWALLOWABLE	SWELLINGLY
SUPPRESSION	SURFBOARDER	SURRENDEROR	SUSPENSELESS	SWALLOWERS	SWELTERING
SUPPRESSIONS	SURFBOARDERS	SURRENDERORS	SUSPENSERS	SWALLOWING	SWELTERINGLY
SUPPRESSIVE	SURFBOARDING	SURRENDERS	SUSPENSIBILITY	SWALLOWTAIL	SWELTERINGS
SUPPRESSIVENESS	SURFBOARDINGS	SURRENDRIES	SUSPENSIBLE	SWALLOWTAILS	SWELTRIEST
SUPPRESSOR	SURFBOARDS	SURREPTITIOUS	SUSPENSION	SWALLOWWORT	SWEPTWINGS
SUPPRESSORS	SURFCASTER	SURREPTITIOUSLY	SUSPENSIONS	SWALLOWWORTS	SWERVELESS
SUPPURATED	SURFCASTERS	SURROGACIES	SUSPENSIVE	SWAMPINESS	SWIFTNESSES
SUPPURATES	SURFCASTING	SURROGATED	SUSPENSIVELY	SWAMPINESSES	SWIMFEEDER
SUPPURATING	SURFCASTINGS	SURROGATES	SUSPENSIVENESS	SWAMPLANDS	SWIMFEEDERS
SUPPURATION	SURFEITERS	SURROGATESHIP	SUSPENSOID	SWANKINESS	SWIMMERETS
SUPPURATIONS	SURFEITING	SURROGATESHIPS	SUSPENSOIDS	SWANKINESSES	SWIMMINGLY
SUPPURATIVE	SURFEITINGS	SURROGATING	SUSPENSORIA	SWANNERIES	SWIMMINGNESS
SUPPURATIVES	SURFFISHES	SURROGATION	SUSPENSORIAL	SWANSDOWNS	SWIMMINGNESSES
SUPRACHIASMIC	SURFPERCHES	SURROGATIONS	SUSPENSORIES	SWARAJISMS	SWINDLINGS
SUPRACILIARY	SURFRIDERS	SURROGATUM	SUSPENSORIUM	SWARAJISTS	SWINEHERDS
SUPRACOSTAL	SURGEONCIES	SURROGATUMS	SUSPENSORS	SWARTHIEST	SWINEHOODS
SUPRACRUSTAL	SURGEONFISH	SURROUNDED	SUSPENSORY	SWARTHINESS	SWINEPOXES
SUPRAGLOTTAL	SURGEONFISHES	SURROUNDING	SUSPERCOLLATE	SWARTHINESSES	SWINESTONE
SUPRALAPSARIAN	SURGEONSHIP	SURROUNDINGS	SUSPERCOLLATED	SWARTHNESS	SWINESTONES
SUPRALAPSARIANS	SURGEONSHIPS	SURTARBRAND	SUSPERCOLLATES	SWARTHNESSES	SWINGBEATS
SUPRALIMINAL	SURGICALLY	SURTARBRANDS	SUSPERCOLLATING	SWARTNESS	SWINGBOATS
SUPRALIMINALLY	SURJECTION	SURTURBRAND	SUSPICIONAL	SWARTNESSES	SWINGEINGLY
SUPRALUNAR	SURJECTIONS	SURTURBRANDS	SUSPICIONED	SWASHBUCKLE	SWINGINGEST
SUPRAMAXILLARY	SURJECTIVE	SURVEILING	SUSPICIONING	SWASHBUCKLED	SWINGINGLY
SUPRAMOLECULAR	SURLINESSES	SURVEILLANCE	SUSPICIONLESS	SWASHBUCKLER	SWINGLETREE
SUPRAMOLECULE	SURMASTERS	SURVEILLANCES	SUSPICIONS	SWASHBUCKLERS	SWINGLETREES
SUPRAMOLECULES	SURMISABLE	SURVEILLANT	SUSPICIOUS	SWASHBUCKLES	SWINGLINGS
SUPRAMUNDANE	SURMISINGS	SURVEILLANTS	SUSPICIOUSLY	SWASHBUCKLING	SWINGOMETER
SUPRANATIONAL	SURMISTRESS	SURVEILLED	SUSPICIOUSNESS	SWASHWORKS	SWINGOMETERS
SUPRANATIONALLY	SURMISTRESSES	SURVEILLES	SUSPIRATION	SWATCHBOOK	SWINGTREES
SUPRAOPTIC	SURMOUNTABLE	SURVEILLING	SUSPIRATIONS	SWATCHBOOKS	SWINISHNESS
SUPRAORBITAL	SURMOUNTED	SURVEYABLE	SUSPIRIOUS	SWATHEABLE	SWINISHNESSES
SUPRAPUBIC	SURMOUNTER	SURVEYANCE	SUSTAINABILITY	SWATTERING	SWIRLINGLY
SUPRARATIONAL	SURMOUNTERS	SURVEYANCES	SUSTAINABLE	SWAYBACKED	SWISHINGLY
SUPRARENAL	SURMOUNTING	SURVEYINGS	SUSTAINEDLY	SWEARWORDS	SWITCHABLE
SUPRARENALS	SURMOUNTINGS	SURVEYORSHIP	SUSTAINERS	SWEATBANDS	SWITCHBACK
SUPRASEGMENTAL	SURMULLETS	SURVEYORSHIPS	SUSTAINING	SWEATBOXES	SWITCHBACKED
SUPRASENSIBLE	SURNOMINAL	SURVIEWING	SUSTAININGLY	SWEATERDRESS	SWITCHBACKING
SUPRATEMPORAL	SURPASSABLE	SURVIVABILITIES	SUSTAININGS	SWEATERDRESSES	SWITCHBACKS
SUPRAVITAL	SURPASSERS	SURVIVABILITY	SUSTAINMENT	SWEATINESS	SWITCHBLADE
SUPRAVITALLY	SURPASSING	SURVIVABLE	SUSTAINMENTS	SWEATINESSES	SWITCHBLADES
SUPREMACIES	SURPASSINGLY	SURVIVALISM	SUSTENANCE	SWEATPANTS	SWITCHBOARD
SUPREMACISM	SURPASSINGNESS	SURVIVALISMS	SUSTENANCES	SWEATSHIRT	SWITCHBOARDS
SUPREMACISMS	SURPLUSAGE	SURVIVALIST	SUSTENTACULA	SWEATSHIRTS	SWITCHEROO
SUPREMACIST	SURPLUSAGES	SURVIVALISTS	SUSTENTACULAR	SWEATSHOPS	SWITCHEROOS
SUPREMACISTS	SURPLUSING	SURVIVANCE	SUSTENTACULUM	SWEATSUITS	SWITCHGEAR
SUPREMATISM	SURPLUSSED	SURVIVANCES	SUSTENTATE	SWEEPBACKS	SWITCHGEARS
SUPREMATISMS	SURPLUSSES	SURVIVORSHIP	SUSTENTATED	SWEEPINGLY	SWITCHGIRL
SUPREMATIST	SURPLUSSING	SURVIVORSHIPS	SUSTENTATES	SWEEPINGNESS	SWITCHGIRLS
SUPREMATISTS	SURPRINTED	SUSCEPTANCE	SUSTENTATING	SWEEPINGNESSES	SWITCHGRASS
SUPREMENESS	SURPRINTING	SUSCEPTANCES	SUSTENTATION	SWEEPSTAKE	SWITCHGRASSES
SUPREMENESSES	SURPRISALS	SUSCEPTIBILITY	SUSTENTATIONS	SWEEPSTAKES	SWITCHIEST
SUPREMITIES	SURPRISEDLY	SUSCEPTIBLE	SUSTENTATIVE	SWEETBREAD	SWITCHINGS
SURADDITION	SURPRISERS	SUSCEPTIBLENESS	SUSTENTATOR	SWEETBREADS	SWITCHLIKE
SURADDITIONS	SURPRISING	SUSCEPTIBLY	SUSTENTATORS	SWEETBRIAR	SWITCHOVER
SURBASEMENT	SURPRISINGLY	SUSCEPTIVE	SUSTENTION	SWEETBRIARS	SWITCHOVERS
SURBASEMENTS	SURPRISINGNESS	SUSCEPTIVENESS	SUSTENTIONS	SWEETBRIER	SWITCHYARD
SURBEDDING	SURPRISINGS	SUSCEPTIVITIES	SUSTENTIVE	SWEETBRIERS	SWITCHYARDS
SURCEASING	SURPRIZING	SUSCEPTIVITY	SUSURRATED	SWEETCORNS	SWITHERING
SURCHARGED	SURQUEDIES	SUSCEPTORS	SUSURRATES	SWEETENERS	SWIVELBLOCK
SURCHARGEMENT	SURQUEDRIES	SUSCIPIENT	SUSURRATING	SWEETENING	SWIVELBLOCKS
SURCHARGEMENTS	SURREALISM	SUSCIPIENTS	SUSURRATION	SWEETENINGS	SWIVELLING
SURCHARGER	SURREALISMS	SUSCITATED	SUSURRATIONS	SWEETFISHES	SWOLLENNESS
SURCHARGERS	SURREALIST	SUSCITATES	SUSURRUSES	SWEETHEART	SWOLLENNESSES
SURCHARGES	SURREALISTIC	SUSCITATING	SUTLERSHIP	SWEETHEARTED	SWOONINGLY
SURCHARGING	SURREALISTS	SUSCITATION	SUTLERSHIPS	SWEETHEARTING	SWOOPSTAKE
SURCINGLED	SURREBUTTAL	SUSCITATIONS	SUTTEEISMS	SWEETHEARTS	SWORDBEARER
SURCINGLES	SURREBUTTALS	SUSPECTABLE	SUTTLETIES	SWEETIEWIFE	SWORDBEARERS
SURCINGLING	SURREBUTTED	SUSPECTEDLY	SUTURATION	SWEETIEWIVES	SWORDBILLS
SURCULUSES	SURREBUTTER	SUSPECTEDNESS	SUTURATIONS	SWEETISHLY	SWORDCRAFT
SUREFOOTED	SURREBUTTERS	SUSPECTEDNESSES	SUZERAINTIES	SWEETISHNESS	SWORDCRAFTS
SUREFOOTEDLY	SURREBUTTING	SUSPECTERS	SUZERAINTY	SWEETISHNESSES	SWORDFISHES
SUREFOOTEDNESS	SURREJOINDER	SUSPECTFUL	SVARABHAKTI	SWEETMEATS	SWORDPLAYER
SURENESSES	SURREJOINDERS	SUSPECTING	SVARABHAKTIS	SWEETNESSES	SWORDPLAYERS
SURETYSHIP	SURREJOINED	SUSPECTLESS	SVELTENESS	SWEETSHOPS	SWORDPLAYS
SURETYSHIPS	SURREJOINING	SUSPENDERED	SVELTENESSES	SWEETWATER	SWORDPROOF
SURFACELESS	SURREJOINS	SUSPENDERS	SWAGGERERS	SWEETWATERS	SWORDSMANSHIP

SWORDSMANSHIPS	SYLVANITES	SYMPATHISING	SYNANTHOUS	SYNCRETISING	SYNKARYONS
SWORDSTICK	SYLVESTRAL	SYMPATHIZE	SYNAPHEIAS	SYNCRETISM	SYNODICALLY
SWORDSTICKS	SYLVESTRIAN	SYMPATHIZED	SYNAPOSEMATIC	SYNCRETISMS	SYNOECETES
SWORDTAILS	SYLVICULTURAL	SYMPATHIZER	SYNAPOSEMATISM	SYNCRETIST	SYNOECIOSES
SYBARITICAL	SYLVICULTURE	SYMPATHIZERS	SYNAPOSEMATISMS	SYNCRETISTIC	SYNOECIOSIS
SYBARITICALLY	SYLVICULTURES	SYMPATHIZES	SYNAPTASES	SYNCRETISTS	SYNOECIOUS
SYBARITISH	SYLVINITES	SYMPATHIZING	SYNAPTICAL	SYNCRETIZATION	SYNOECISED
SYBARITISM	SYMBIONTIC	SYMPATHOLYTIC	SYNAPTICALLY	SYNCRETIZATIONS	SYNOECISES
SYBARITISMS	SYMBIONTICALLY	SYMPATHOLYTICS	SYNAPTOSOMAL	SYNCRETIZE	SYNOECISING
SYCOPHANCIES	SYMBIOTICAL	SYMPATHOMIMETIC	SYNAPTOSOME	SYNCRETIZED	SYNOECISMS
SYCOPHANCY	SYMBIOTICALLY	SYMPATRICALLY	SYNAPTOSOMES	SYNCRETIZES	SYNOECIZED
SYCOPHANTIC	SYMBOLICAL	SYMPATRIES	SYNARCHIES	SYNCRETIZING	SYNOECIZES
SYCOPHANTICAL	SYMBOLICALLY	SYMPETALIES	SYNARTHRODIAL	SYNDACTYLIES	SYNOECIZING
SYCOPHANTICALLY	SYMBOLICALNESS	SYMPETALOUS	SYNARTHRODIALLY	SYNDACTYLISM	SYNOECOLOGIES
SYCOPHANTISE	SYMBOLISATION	SYMPHILIES	SYNARTHROSES	SYNDACTYLISMS	SYNOECOLOGY
SYCOPHANTISED	SYMBOLISATIONS	SYMPHILISM	SYNARTHROSIS	SYNDACTYLOUS	SYNOEKETES
SYCOPHANTISES	SYMBOLISED	SYMPHILISMS	SYNASTRIES	SYNDACTYLS	SYNONYMATIC
SYCOPHANTISH	SYMBOLISER	SYMPHILOUS	SYNAXARION	SYNDACTYLY	SYNONYMICAL
SYCOPHANTISHLY	SYMBOLISERS	SYMPHONICALLY	SYNCARPIES	SYNDERESES	SYNONYMICON
SYCOPHANTISING	SYMBOLISES	SYMPHONIES	SYNCARPOUS	SYNDERESIS	SYNONYMICONS
SYCOPHANTISM	SYMBOLISING	SYMPHONION	SYNCHONDROSES	SYNDESISES	SYNONYMIES
SYCOPHANTISMS	SYMBOLISMS	SYMPHONIONS	SYNCHONDROSIS	SYNDESMOSES	SYNONYMISE
SYCOPHANTIZE	SYMBOLISTIC	SYMPHONIOUS	SYNCHORESES	SYNDESMOSIS	SYNONYMISED
SYCOPHANTIZED	SYMBOLISTICAL	SYMPHONIOUSLY	SYNCHORESIS	SYNDESMOTIC	SYNONYMISES
SYCOPHANTIZES	SYMBOLISTICALLY	SYMPHONIST	SYNCHROFLASH	SYNDETICAL	SYNONYMISING
SYCOPHANTIZING	SYMBOLISTS	SYMPHONISTS	SYNCHROFLASHES	SYNDETICALLY	SYNONYMIST
SYCOPHANTLY	SYMBOLIZATION	SYMPHYLOUS	SYNCHROMESH	SYNDICALISM	SYNONYMISTS
SYCOPHANTRIES	SYMBOLIZATIONS	SYMPHYSEAL	SYNCHROMESHES	SYNDICALISMS	SYNONYMITIES
SYCOPHANTRY	SYMBOLIZED	SYMPHYSEOTOMIES	SYNCHRONAL	SYNDICALIST	SYNONYMITY
SYCOPHANTS	SYMBOLIZER	SYMPHYSEOTOMY	SYNCHRONEITIES	SYNDICALISTIC	SYNONYMIZE
SYLLABARIA	SYMBOLIZERS	SYMPHYSIAL	SYNCHRONEITY	SYNDICALISTS	SYNONYMIZED
SYLLABARIES	SYMBOLIZES	SYMPHYSIOTOMIES	SYNCHRONIC	SYNDICATED	SYNONYMIZES
SYLLABARIUM	SYMBOLIZING	SYMPHYSIOTOMY	SYNCHRONICAL	SYNDICATES	SYNONYMIZING
SYLLABICAL	SYMBOLLING	SYMPHYSTIC	SYNCHRONICALLY	SYNDICATING	SYNONYMOUS
SYLLABICALLY	SYMBOLOGICAL	SYMPIESOMETER	SYNCHRONICITIES	SYNDICATION	SYNONYMOUSLY
SYLLABICATE	SYMBOLOGIES	SYMPIESOMETERS	SYNCHRONICITY	SYNDICATIONS	SYNONYMOUSNESS
SYLLABICATED	SYMBOLOGIST	SYMPLASTIC	SYNCHRONIES	SYNDICATOR	SYNOPSISED
SYLLABICATES	SYMBOLOGISTS	SYMPODIALLY	SYNCHRONISATION	SYNDICATORS	SYNOPSISES
SYLLABICATING	SYMBOLOGRAPHIES	SYMPOSIACS	SYNCHRONISE	SYNDICSHIP	SYNOPSISING
SYLLABICATION	SYMBOLOGRAPHY	SYMPOSIARCH	SYNCHRONISED	SYNDICSHIPS	SYNOPSIZED
SYLLABICATIONS	SYMBOLOLATRIES	SYMPOSIARCHS	SYNCHRONISER	SYNDIOTACTIC	SYNOPSIZES
SYLLABICITIES	SYMBOLOLATRY	SYMPOSIAST	SYNCHRONISERS	SYNDYASMIAN	SYNOPSIZING
SYLLABICITY	SYMBOLOLOGIES	SYMPOSIASTS	SYNCHRONISES	SYNECDOCHE	SYNOPTICAL
SYLLABIFICATION	SYMBOLOLOGY	SYMPOSIUMS	SYNCHRONISING	SYNECDOCHES	SYNOPTICALLY
SYLLABIFIED	SYMMETALISM	SYMPTOMATIC	SYNCHRONISM	SYNECDOCHIC	SYNOPTISTIC
SYLLABIFIES	SYMMETALISMS	SYMPTOMATICAL	SYNCHRONISMS	SYNECDOCHICAL	SYNOPTISTS
SYLLABIFYING	SYMMETALLIC	SYMPTOMATICALLY	SYNCHRONIST	SYNECDOCHICALLY	SYNOSTOSES
SYLLABISED	SYMMETALLISM	SYMPTOMATISE	SYNCHRONISTIC	SYNECDOCHISM	SYNOSTOSIS
SYLLABISES	SYMMETALLISMS	SYMPTOMATISED	SYNCHRONISTICAL	SYNECDOCHISMS	SYNOVIALLY
SYLLABISING	SYMMETRIAN	SYMPTOMATISES	SYNCHRONIZATION	SYNECOLOGIC	SYNOVITISES
SYLLABISMS	SYMMETRIANS	SYMPTOMATISING	SYNCHRONIZE	SYNECOLOGICAL	SYNSEPALOUS
SYLLABIZED	SYMMETRICAL	SYMPTOMATIZE	SYNCHRONIZED	SYNECOLOGICALLY	SYNTACTICAL
SYLLABIZES	SYMMETRICALLY	SYMPTOMATIZED	SYNCHRONIZER	SYNECOLOGIES	SYNTACTICALLY
SYLLABIZING	SYMMETRICALNESS	SYMPTOMATIZES	SYNCHRONIZERS	SYNECOLOGIST	SYNTACTICS
SYLLABLING	SYMMETRIES	SYMPTOMATIZING	SYNCHRONIZES	SYNECOLOGISTS	SYNTAGMATA
SYLLABOGRAM	SYMMETRISATION	SYMPTOMATOLOGIC	SYNCHRONIZING	SYNECOLOGY	SYNTAGMATIC
SYLLABOGRAMS	SYMMETRISATIONS	SYMPTOMATOLOGY	SYNCHRONOLOGIES	SYNECPHONESES	SYNTAGMATITE
SYLLABOGRAPHIES	SYMMETRISE	SYMPTOMLESS	SYNCHRONOLOGY	SYNECPHONESIS	SYNTAGMATITES
SYLLABOGRAPHY	SYMMETRISED	SYMPTOMOLOGICAL	SYNCHRONOSCOPE	SYNECTICALLY	SYNTECTICAL
SYLLABUSES	SYMMETRISES	SYMPTOMOLOGIES	SYNCHRONOSCOPES	SYNEIDESES	SYNTENOSES
SYLLEPTICAL	SYMMETRISING	SYMPTOMOLOGY	SYNCHRONOUS	SYNEIDESIS	SYNTENOSIS
SYLLEPTICALLY	SYMMETRIZATION	SYNADELPHITE	SYNCHRONOUSLY	SYNERGETIC	SYNTERESES
SYLLOGISATION	SYMMETRIZATIONS	SYNADELPHITES	SYNCHRONOUSNESS	SYNERGETICALLY	SYNTERESIS
SYLLOGISATIONS	SYMMETRIZE	SYNAERESES	SYNCHROSCOPE	SYNERGICALLY	SYNTEXISES
SYLLOGISED	SYMMETRIZED	SYNAERESIS	SYNCHROSCOPES	SYNERGISED	SYNTHESISATION
SYLLOGISER	SYMMETRIZES	SYNAESTHESES	SYNCHROTRON	SYNERGISES	SYNTHESISATIONS
SYLLOGISERS	SYMMETRIZING	SYNAESTHESIA	SYNCHROTRONS	SYNERGISING	SYNTHESISE
SYLLOGISES	SYMMETROPHOBIA	SYNAESTHESIAS	SYNCLASTIC	SYNERGISMS	SYNTHESISED
SYLLOGISING	SYMMETROPHOBIAS	SYNAESTHESIS	SYNCLINALS	SYNERGISTIC	SYNTHESISER
SYLLOGISMS	SYMPATHECTOMIES	SYNAESTHETIC	SYNCLINORIA	SYNERGISTICALLY	SYNTHESISERS
SYLLOGISTIC	SYMPATHECTOMY	SYNAGOGICAL	SYNCLINORIUM	SYNERGISTS	SYNTHESISES
SYLLOGISTICAL	SYMPATHETIC	SYNAGOGUES	SYNCOPATED	SYNERGIZED	SYNTHESISING
SYLLOGISTICALLY	SYMPATHETICAL	SYNALEPHAS	SYNCOPATES	SYNERGIZES	SYNTHESIST
SYLLOGISTICS	SYMPATHETICALLY	SYNALLAGMATIC	SYNCOPATING	SYNERGIZING	SYNTHESISTS
SYLLOGISTS	SYMPATHETICS	SYNALOEPHA	SYNCOPATION	SYNESTHESIA	SYNTHESIZATION
SYLLOGIZATION	SYMPATHIES	SYNALOEPHAS	SYNCOPATIONS	SYNESTHESIAS	SYNTHESIZATIONS
SYLLOGIZATIONS	SYMPATHINS	SYNANDRIUM	SYNCOPATIVE	SYNESTHETIC	SYNTHESIZE
SYLLOGIZED	SYMPATHIQUE	SYNANDROUS	SYNCOPATOR	SYNGENESES	SYNTHESIZED
SYLLOGIZER	SYMPATHISE	SYNANTHEROUS	SYNCOPATORS	SYNGENESIOUS	SYNTHESIZER
SYLLOGIZERS	SYMPATHISED	SYNANTHESES	SYNCRETISATION	SYNGENESIS	SYNTHESIZERS
SYLLOGIZES	SYMPATHISER	SYNANTHESIS	SYNCRETISATIONS	SYNGENETIC	SYNTHESIZES
SYLLOGIZING	SYMPATHISERS	SYNANTHETIC	SYNCRETISE	SYNGNATHOUS	SYNTHESIZING
SYLPHIDINE	SYMPATHISES	SYNANTHIES	SYNCRETISED	SYNKARYONIC	SYNTHESPIAN

SYNTHESPIANS	SYNTHETISTS	SYPHILISATIONS	SYPHILOPHOBIAS	SYSTEMATISE	SYSTEMICALLY
SYNTHETASE	SYNTHETIZATION	SYPHILISED	SYRINGITIS	SYSTEMATISED	SYSTEMISATION
SYNTHETASES	SYNTHETIZATIONS	SYPHILISES	SYRINGITISES	SYSTEMATISER	SYSTEMISATIONS
SYNTHETICAL	SYNTHETIZE	SYPHILISING	SYRINGOMYELIA	SYSTEMATISERS	SYSTEMISED
SYNTHETICALLY	SYNTHETIZED	SYPHILITIC	SYRINGOMYELIAS	SYSTEMATISES	SYSTEMISER
SYNTHETICISM	SYNTHETIZER	SYPHILITICALLY	SYRINGOMYELIC	SYSTEMATISING	SYSTEMISERS
SYNTHETICISMS	SYNTHETIZERS	SYPHILITICS	SYRINGOTOMIES	SYSTEMATISM	SYSTEMISES
SYNTHETICS	SYNTHETIZES	SYPHILIZATION	SYRINGOTOMY	SYSTEMATISMS	SYSTEMISING
SYNTHETISATION	SYNTHETIZING	SYPHILIZATIONS	SYSSARCOSES	SYSTEMATIST	SYSTEMIZATION
SYNTHETISATIONS	SYNTHRONUS	SYPHILIZED	SYSSARCOSIS	SYSTEMATISTS	SYSTEMIZATIONS
SYNTHETISE	SYNTONICALLY	SYPHILIZES	SYSSARCOTIC	SYSTEMATIZATION	SYSTEMIZED
SYNTHETISED	SYNTONISED	SYPHILIZING	SYSTEMATIC	SYSTEMATIZE	SYSTEMIZER
SYNTHETISER	SYNTONISES	SYPHILOLOGIES	SYSTEMATICAL	SYSTEMATIZED	SYSTEMIZERS
SYNTHETISERS	SYNTONISING	SYPHILOLOGIST	SYSTEMATICALLY	SYSTEMATIZER	SYSTEMIZES
SYNTHETISES	SYNTONIZED	SYPHILOLOGISTS	SYSTEMATICIAN	SYSTEMATIZERS	SYSTEMIZING
SYNTHETISING	SYNTONIZES	SYPHILOLOGY	SYSTEMATICIANS	SYSTEMATIZES	SYSTEMLESS
SYNTHETISM	SYNTONIZING	SYPHILOMAS	SYSTEMATICNESS	SYSTEMATIZING	SYZYGETICALLY
SYNTHETISMS	SYPHERINGS	SYPHILOMATA	SYSTEMATICS	SYSTEMATOLOGIES	
SYNTHETIST	SYPHILISATION	SYPHILOPHOBIA	SYSTEMATISATION	SYSTEMATOLOGY	

Tt

TABASHEERS
TABBOULEHS
TABBYHOODS
TABEFACTION
TABEFACTIONS
TABELLIONS
TABERNACLE
TABERNACLED
TABERNACLES
TABERNACLING
TABERNACULAR
TABESCENCE
TABESCENCES
TABLANETTE
TABLANETTES
TABLATURES
TABLECLOTH
TABLECLOTHS
TABLELANDS
TABLEMATES
TABLESPOON
TABLESPOONFUL
TABLESPOONFULS
TABLESPOONS
TABLESPOONSFUL
TABLETOPPED
TABLETTING
TABLEWARES
TABOGGANED
TABOGGANING
TABOPARESES
TABOPARESIS
TABULARISATION
TABULARISATIONS
TABULARISE
TABULARISED
TABULARISES
TABULARISING
TABULARIZATION
TABULARIZATIONS
TABULARIZE
TABULARIZED
TABULARIZES
TABULARIZING
TABULATING
TABULATION
TABULATIONS
TABULATORS
TABULATORY
TACAMAHACS
TACHEOMETER
TACHEOMETERS
TACHEOMETRIC
TACHEOMETRICAL
TACHEOMETRIES
TACHEOMETRY
TACHISTOSCOPE
TACHISTOSCOPES
TACHISTOSCOPIC
TACHOGRAMS
TACHOGRAPH
TACHOGRAPHS
TACHOMETER
TACHOMETERS
TACHOMETRIC
TACHOMETRICAL
TACHOMETRICALLY

TACHOMETRIES
TACHOMETRY
TACHYARRHYTHMIA
TACHYCARDIA
TACHYCARDIAC
TACHYCARDIAS
TACHYGRAPH
TACHYGRAPHER
TACHYGRAPHERS
TACHYGRAPHIC
TACHYGRAPHICAL
TACHYGRAPHIES
TACHYGRAPHIST
TACHYGRAPHISTS
TACHYGRAPHS
TACHYGRAPHY
TACHYLITES
TACHYLITIC
TACHYLYTES
TACHYLYTIC
TACHYMETER
TACHYMETERS
TACHYMETRIC
TACHYMETRICAL
TACHYMETRICALLY
TACHYMETRIES
TACHYMETRY
TACHYPHASIA
TACHYPHASIAS
TACHYPHRASIA
TACHYPHRASIAS
TACHYPHYLAXES
TACHYPHYLAXIS
TACHYPNEAS
TACHYPNOEA
TACHYPNOEAS
TACITNESSES
TACITURNITIES
TACITURNITY
TACITURNLY
TACKBOARDS
TACKIFIERS
TACKIFYING
TACKINESSES
TACMAHACKS
TACTFULNESS
TACTFULNESSES
TACTICALLY
TACTICIANS
TACTICITIES
TACTILISTS
TACTILITIES
TACTLESSLY
TACTLESSNESS
TACTLESSNESSES
TACTUALITIES
TACTUALITY
TAEKWONDOS
TAENIACIDE
TAENIACIDES
TAENIAFUGE
TAENIAFUGES
TAFFETASES
TAFFETIZED
TAGLIARINI
TAGLIARINIS
TAGLIATELLE

TAGLIATELLES
TAHSILDARS
TAIKONAUTS
TAILBOARDS
TAILCOATED
TAILENDERS
TAILGATERS
TAILGATING
TAILLESSLY
TAILLESSNESS
TAILLESSNESSES
TAILLIGHTS
TAILORBIRD
TAILORBIRDS
TAILORESSES
TAILORINGS
TAILORMADE
TAILORMAKE
TAILORMAKES
TAILORMAKING
TAILPIECES
TAILPIPING
TAILPLANES
TAILSLIDES
TAILSPINNED
TAILSPINNING
TAILSTOCKS
TAILWATERS
TAILWHEELS
TAINTLESSLY
TAKINGNESS
TAKINGNESSES
TALBOTYPES
TALEBEARER
TALEBEARERS
TALEBEARING
TALEBEARINGS
TALEGALLAS
TALENTLESS
TALISMANIC
TALISMANICAL
TALISMANICALLY
TALKABILITIES
TALKABILITY
TALKATHONS
TALKATIVELY
TALKATIVENESS
TALKATIVENESSES
TALKINESSES
TALLGRASSES
TALLIATING
TALLNESSES
TALLYHOING
TALLYSHOPS
TALLYWOMAN
TALLYWOMEN
TALMUDISMS
TAMABILITIES
TAMABILITY
TAMABLENESS
TAMABLENESSES
TAMARILLOS
TAMBOURERS
TAMBOURINE
TAMBOURINES
TAMBOURING
TAMBOURINIST

TAMBOURINISTS
TAMBOURINS
TAMEABILITIES
TAMEABILITY
TAMEABLENESS
TAMEABLENESSES
TAMELESSNESS
TAMELESSNESSES
TAMENESSES
TAMOXIFENS
TAMPERINGS
TAMPERPROOF
TAMPONADES
TAMPONAGES
TANDEMWISE
TANGENCIES
TANGENTALLY
TANGENTIAL
TANGENTIALITIES
TANGENTIALITY
TANGENTIALLY
TANGERINES
TANGHININS
TANGIBILITIES
TANGIBILITY
TANGIBLENESS
TANGIBLENESSES
TANGINESSES
TANGLEFOOT
TANGLEFOOTS
TANGLEMENT
TANGLEMENTS
TANGLESOME
TANGLEWEED
TANGLEWEEDS
TANGLINGLY
TANISTRIES
TANKBUSTER
TANKBUSTERS
TANKBUSTING
TANKBUSTINGS
TANTALATES
TANTALISATION
TANTALISATIONS
TANTALISED
TANTALISER
TANTALISERS
TANTALISES
TANTALISING
TANTALISINGLY
TANTALISINGS
TANTALISMS
TANTALITES
TANTALIZATION
TANTALIZATIONS
TANTALIZED
TANTALIZER
TANTALIZERS
TANTALIZES
TANTALIZING
TANTALIZINGLY
TANTALIZINGS
TANTALUSES
TANTAMOUNT
TANTARARAS
TANZANITES
TAOISEACHS

TAPERINGLY
TAPERNESSES
TAPERSTICK
TAPERSTICKS
TAPESCRIPT
TAPESCRIPTS
TAPESTRIED
TAPESTRIES
TAPESTRYING
TAPHEPHOBIA
TAPHEPHOBIAS
TAPHEPHOBIC
TAPHONOMIC
TAPHONOMICAL
TAPHONOMIES
TAPHONOMIST
TAPHONOMISTS
TAPHOPHOBIA
TAPHOPHOBIAS
TAPHROGENESES
TAPHROGENESIS
TAPOTEMENT
TAPOTEMENTS
TAPSALTEERIE
TAPSALTEERIES
TAPSIETEERIE
TAPSIETEERIES
TAPSTRESSES
TARADIDDLE
TARADIDDLES
TARAMASALATA
TARAMASALATAS
TARANTARAED
TARANTARAING
TARANTARAS
TARANTASES
TARANTASSES
TARANTELLA
TARANTELLAS
TARANTISMS
TARANTISTS
TARANTULAE
TARANTULAS
TARATANTARA
TARATANTARAED
TARATANTARAING
TARATANTARAS
TARAXACUMS
TARBOGGINED
TARBOGGINING
TARBOGGINS
TARBOOSHES
TARBOUCHES
TARBOUSHES
TARDIGRADE
TARDIGRADES
TARDINESSES
TARGETABLE
TARGETEERS
TARGETITIS
TARGETITISES
TARGETLESS
TARIFFICATION
TARIFFICATIONS
TARIFFLESS
TARMACADAM
TARMACADAMS

TARMACKING
TARNATIONS
TARNISHABLE
TARNISHERS
TARNISHING
TARPAULING
TARPAULINGS
TARPAULINS
TARRADIDDLE
TARRADIDDLES
TARRIANCES
TARRINESSES
TARSALGIAS
TARSOMETATARSAL
TARSOMETATARSI
TARSOMETATARSUS
TARTANALIA
TARTANALIAS
TARTANRIES
TARTAREOUS
TARTARISATION
TARTARISATIONS
TARTARISED
TARTARISES
TARTARISING
TARTARIZATION
TARTARIZATIONS
TARTARIZED
TARTARIZES
TARTARIZING
TARTINESSES
TARTNESSES
TARTRAZINE
TARTRAZINES
TASEOMETER
TASEOMETERS
TASIMETERS
TASIMETRIC
TASIMETRIES
TASKMASTER
TASKMASTERS
TASKMISTRESS
TASKMISTRESSES
TASSELLING
TASSELLINGS
TASTEFULLY
TASTEFULNESS
TASTEFULNESSES
TASTELESSLY
TASTELESSNESS
TASTELESSNESSES
TASTEMAKER
TASTEMAKERS
TASTINESSES
TATAHASHES
TATPURUSHA
TATPURUSHAS
TATTERDEMALION
TATTERDEMALIONS
TATTERDEMALLION
TATTERSALL
TATTERSALLS
TATTINESSES
TATTLETALE
TATTLETALES
TATTLINGLY
TATTOOISTS

t

TAUNTINGLY	TEACHABILITY	TECHNOLOGISE	TELANGIECTASIS	TELEMARKETINGS	TELERECORDS
TAUROBOLIA	TEACHABLENESS	TECHNOLOGISED	TELANGIECTATIC	TELEMARKING	TELERGICALLY
TAUROBOLIUM	TEACHABLENESSES	TECHNOLOGISES	TELAUTOGRAPHIC	TELEMATICS	TELESCIENCE
TAUROMACHIAN	TEACHERLESS	TECHNOLOGISING	TELAUTOGRAPHIES	TELEMEDICINE	TELESCIENCES
TAUROMACHIES	TEACHERSHIP	TECHNOLOGIST	TELAUTOGRAPHY	TELEMEDICINES	TELESCOPED
TAUROMACHY	TEACHERSHIPS	TECHNOLOGISTS	TELEARCHICS	TELEMETERED	TELESCOPES
TAUROMORPHOUS	TEACUPFULS	TECHNOLOGIZE	TELEBANKING	TELEMETERING	TELESCOPIC
TAUTNESSES	TEACUPSFUL	TECHNOLOGIZED	TELEBANKINGS	TELEMETERS	TELESCOPICAL
TAUTOCHRONE	TEAKETTLES	TECHNOLOGIZES	TELEBRIDGE	TELEMETRIC	TELESCOPICALLY
TAUTOCHRONES	TEARFULNESS	TECHNOLOGIZING	TELEBRIDGES	TELEMETRICAL	TELESCOPIES
TAUTOCHRONISM	TEARFULNESSES	TECHNOLOGY	TELECAMERA	TELEMETRICALLY	TELESCOPIFORM
TAUTOCHRONISMS	TEARGASSED	TECHNOMANIA	TELECAMERAS	TELEMETRIES	TELESCOPING
TAUTOCHRONOUS	TEARGASSES	TECHNOMANIAC	TELECASTED	TELENCEPHALA	TELESCOPIST
TAUTOLOGIC	TEARGASSING	TECHNOMANIACS	TELECASTER	TELENCEPHALIC	TELESCOPISTS
TAUTOLOGICAL	TEARINESSES	TECHNOMANIAS	TELECASTERS	TELENCEPHALON	TELESCREEN
TAUTOLOGICALLY	TEARJERKER	TECHNOMUSIC	TELECASTING	TELENCEPHALONS	TELESCREENS
TAUTOLOGIES	TEARJERKERS	TECHNOMUSICS	TELECHIRIC	TELEOLOGIC	TELESELLING
TAUTOLOGISE	TEARSHEETS	TECHNOPHILE	TELECOMMAND	TELEOLOGICAL	TELESELLINGS
TAUTOLOGISED	TEARSTAINED	TECHNOPHILES	TELECOMMANDS	TELEOLOGICALLY	TELESERVICES
TAUTOLOGISES	TEARSTAINS	TECHNOPHOBE	TELECOMMUTE	TELEOLOGIES	TELESHOPPED
TAUTOLOGISING	TEARSTRIPS	TECHNOPHOBES	TELECOMMUTED	TELEOLOGISM	TELESHOPPING
TAUTOLOGISM	TEASELINGS	TECHNOPHOBIA	TELECOMMUTER	TELEOLOGISMS	TELESHOPPINGS
TAUTOLOGISMS	TEASELLERS	TECHNOPHOBIAS	TELECOMMUTERS	TELEOLOGIST	TELESMATIC
TAUTOLOGIST	TEASELLING	TECHNOPHOBIC	TELECOMMUTES	TELEOLOGISTS	TELESMATICAL
TAUTOLOGISTS	TEASELLINGS	TECHNOPHOBICS	TELECOMMUTING	TELEONOMIC	TELESMATICALLY
TAUTOLOGIZE	TEASPOONFUL	TECHNOPOLE	TELECOMMUTINGS	TELEONOMIES	TELESOFTWARE
TAUTOLOGIZED	TEASPOONFULS	TECHNOPOLES	TELECONFERENCE	TELEOSAURIAN	TELESOFTWARES
TAUTOLOGIZES	TEASPOONSFUL	TECHNOPOLIS	TELECONFERENCES	TELEOSAURIANS	TELESTEREOSCOPE
TAUTOLOGIZING	TEATASTERS	TECHNOPOLISES	TELECONNECTION	TELEOSAURS	TELESTHESIA
TAUTOLOGOUS	TEAZELLING	TECHNOPOLITAN	TELECONNECTIONS	TELEOSTEAN	TELESTHESIAS
TAUTOLOGOUSLY	TECHINESSES	TECHNOPOLITANS	TELECONTROL	TELEOSTEANS	TELESTHETIC
TAUTOMERIC	TECHNETIUM	TECHNOPOPS	TELECONTROLS	TELEOSTOME	TELESTICHS
TAUTOMERISM	TECHNETIUMS	TECHNOSPEAK	TELECONVERTER	TELEOSTOMES	TELESURGERIES
TAUTOMERISMS	TECHNETRONIC	TECHNOSPEAKS	TELECONVERTERS	TELEOSTOMOUS	TELESURGERY
TAUTOMETRIC	TECHNICALISE	TECHNOSTRESS	TELECOTTAGE	TELEPATHED	TELETYPESETTING
TAUTOMETRICAL	TECHNICALISED	TECHNOSTRESSES	TELECOTTAGES	TELEPATHIC	TELETYPEWRITER
TAUTONYMIC	TECHNICALISES	TECHNOSTRUCTURE	TELECOTTAGING	TELEPATHICALLY	TELETYPEWRITERS
TAUTONYMIES	TECHNICALISING	TECTIBRANCH	TELECOTTAGINGS	TELEPATHIES	TELETYPING
TAUTONYMOUS	TECHNICALITIES	TECTIBRANCHIATE	TELECOURSE	TELEPATHING	TELEUTOSPORE
TAUTOPHONIC	TECHNICALITY	TECTIBRANCHS	TELECOURSES	TELEPATHISE	TELEUTOSPORES
TAUTOPHONICAL	TECHNICALIZE	TECTONICALLY	TELEDILDONICS	TELEPATHISED	TELEUTOSPORIC
TAUTOPHONIES	TECHNICALIZED	TECTONISMS	TELEFACSIMILE	TELEPATHISES	TELEVANGELICAL
TAUTOPHONY	TECHNICALIZES	TECTRICIAL	TELEFACSIMILES	TELEPATHISING	TELEVANGELISM
TAWDRINESS	TECHNICALIZING	TEDIOSITIES	TELEFAXING	TELEPATHIST	TELEVANGELISMS
TAWDRINESSES	TECHNICALLY	TEDIOUSNESS	TELEFERIQUE	TELEPATHISTS	TELEVANGELIST
TAWHEOWHEO	TECHNICALNESS	TEDIOUSNESSES	TELEFERIQUES	TELEPATHIZE	TELEVANGELISTS
TAWHEOWHEOS	TECHNICALNESSES	TEDIOUSOME	TELEGENICALLY	TELEPATHIZED	TELEVERITE
TAWNINESSES	TECHNICALS	TEEMINGNESS	TELEGNOSES	TELEPATHIZES	TELEVERITES
TAXABILITIES	TECHNICIAN	TEEMINGNESSES	TELEGNOSIS	TELEPATHIZING	TELEVIEWED
TAXABILITY	TECHNICIANS	TEENTSIEST	TELEGNOSTIC	TELEPHEMES	TELEVIEWER
TAXABLENESS	TECHNICISE	TEENYBOPPER	TELEGONIES	TELEPHERIQUE	TELEVIEWERS
TAXABLENESSES	TECHNICISED	TEENYBOPPERS	TELEGONOUS	TELEPHERIQUES	TELEVIEWING
TAXAMETERS	TECHNICISES	TEETERBOARD	TELEGRAMMATIC	TELEPHONED	TELEVISERS
TAXATIONAL	TECHNICISING	TEETERBOARDS	TELEGRAMMED	TELEPHONER	TELEVISING
TAXIDERMAL	TECHNICISM	TEETHRIDGE	TELEGRAMMIC	TELEPHONERS	TELEVISION
TAXIDERMIC	TECHNICISMS	TEETHRIDGES	TELEGRAMMING	TELEPHONES	TELEVISIONAL
TAXIDERMIES	TECHNICIST	TEETOTALED	TELEGRAPHED	TELEPHONIC	TELEVISIONALLY
TAXIDERMISE	TECHNICISTS	TEETOTALER	TELEGRAPHER	TELEPHONICALLY	TELEVISIONARY
TAXIDERMISED	TECHNICIZE	TEETOTALERS	TELEGRAPHERS	TELEPHONIES	TELEVISIONS
TAXIDERMISES	TECHNICIZED	TEETOTALING	TELEGRAPHESE	TELEPHONING	TELEVISORS
TAXIDERMISING	TECHNICIZES	TEETOTALISM	TELEGRAPHESES	TELEPHONIST	TELEVISUAL
TAXIDERMIST	TECHNICIZING	TEETOTALISMS	TELEGRAPHIC	TELEPHONISTS	TELEVISUALLY
TAXIDERMISTS	TECHNICOLOUR	TEETOTALIST	TELEGRAPHICALLY	TELEPHOTOGRAPH	TELEWORKER
TAXIDERMIZE	TECHNICOLOURED	TEETOTALISTS	TELEGRAPHIES	TELEPHOTOGRAPHS	TELEWORKERS
TAXIDERMIZED	TECHNIKONS	TEETOTALLED	TELEGRAPHING	TELEPHOTOGRAPHY	TELEWORKING
TAXIDERMIZES	TECHNIQUES	TEETOTALLER	TELEGRAPHIST	TELEPHOTOS	TELEWORKINGS
TAXIDERMIZING	TECHNOBABBLE	TEETOTALLERS	TELEGRAPHISTS	TELEPOINTS	TELEWRITER
TAXIMETERS	TECHNOBABBLES	TEETOTALLING	TELEGRAPHS	TELEPORTATION	TELEWRITERS
TAXIPLANES	TECHNOCRACIES	TEETOTALLY	TELEGRAPHY	TELEPORTATIONS	TELFERAGES
TAXONOMERS	TECHNOCRACY	TEGUMENTAL	TELEHEALTH	TELEPORTED	TELIOSPORE
TAXONOMICAL	TECHNOCRAT	TEGUMENTARY	TELEHEALTHS	TELEPORTING	TELIOSPORES
TAXONOMICALLY	TECHNOCRATIC	TEICHOPSIA	TELEJOURNALISM	TELEPRESENCE	TELLERSHIP
TAXONOMIES	TECHNOCRATS	TEICHOPSIAS	TELEJOURNALISMS	TELEPRESENCES	TELLERSHIPS
TAXONOMIST	TECHNOFEAR	TEINOSCOPE	TELEJOURNALIST	TELEPRINTER	TELLURATES
TAXONOMISTS	TECHNOFEARS	TEINOSCOPES	TELEJOURNALISTS	TELEPRINTERS	TELLURETTED
TAXPAYINGS	TECHNOGRAPHIES	TEKNONYMIES	TELEKINESES	TELEPROCESSING	TELLURIANS
TAYASSUIDS	TECHNOGRAPHY	TEKNONYMOUS	TELEKINESIS	TELEPROCESSINGS	TELLURIDES
TAYBERRIES	TECHNOJUNKIE	TELAESTHESIA	TELEKINETIC	TELEPROMPTER	TELLURIONS
TCHOTCHKES	TECHNOJUNKIES	TELAESTHESIAS	TELEKINETICALLY	TELEPROMPTERS	TELLURISED
TCHOUKBALL	TECHNOLOGIC	TELAESTHETIC	TELEMARKED	TELERECORD	TELLURISES
TCHOUKBALLS	TECHNOLOGICAL	TELANGIECTASES	TELEMARKETER	TELERECORDED	TELLURISING
TEABERRIES	TECHNOLOGICALLY	TELANGIECTASIA	TELEMARKETERS	TELERECORDING	TELLURITES
TEACHABILITIES	TECHNOLOGIES	TELANGIECTASIAS	TELEMARKETING	TELERECORDINGS	TELLURIUMS

TELLURIZED
TELLURIZES
TELLURIZING
TELLUROMETER
TELLUROMETERS
TELNETTING
TELOCENTRIC
TELOCENTRICS
TELOMERASE
TELOMERASES
TELOMERISATION
TELOMERISATIONS
TELOMERIZATION
TELOMERIZATIONS
TELOPHASES
TELOPHASIC
TELPHERAGE
TELPHERAGES
TELPHERING
TELPHERLINE
TELPHERLINES
TELPHERMAN
TELPHERMEN
TELPHERWAY
TELPHERWAYS
TEMAZEPAMS
TEMERARIOUS
TEMERARIOUSLY
TEMERARIOUSNESS
TEMERITIES
TEMEROUSLY
TEMPERABILITIES
TEMPERABILITY
TEMPERABLE
TEMPERALITIE
TEMPERALITIES
TEMPERAMENT
TEMPERAMENTAL
TEMPERAMENTALLY
TEMPERAMENTFUL
TEMPERAMENTS
TEMPERANCE
TEMPERANCES
TEMPERATED
TEMPERATELY
TEMPERATENESS
TEMPERATENESSES
TEMPERATES
TEMPERATING
TEMPERATIVE
TEMPERATURE
TEMPERATURES
TEMPERINGS
TEMPESTING
TEMPESTIVE
TEMPESTUOUS
TEMPESTUOUSLY
TEMPESTUOUSNESS
TEMPOLABILE
TEMPORALISE
TEMPORALISED
TEMPORALISES
TEMPORALISING
TEMPORALITIES
TEMPORALITY
TEMPORALIZE
TEMPORALIZED
TEMPORALIZES
TEMPORALIZING
TEMPORALLY
TEMPORALNESS
TEMPORALNESSES
TEMPORALTIES
TEMPORALTY
TEMPORANEOUS
TEMPORARIES
TEMPORARILY
TEMPORARINESS
TEMPORARINESSES
TEMPORISATION
TEMPORISATIONS
TEMPORISED
TEMPORISER

TEMPORISERS
TEMPORISES
TEMPORISING
TEMPORISINGLY
TEMPORISINGS
TEMPORIZATION
TEMPORIZATIONS
TEMPORIZED
TEMPORIZER
TEMPORIZERS
TEMPORIZES
TEMPORIZING
TEMPORIZINGLY
TEMPORIZINGS
TEMPTABILITIES
TEMPTABILITY
TEMPTABLENESS
TEMPTABLENESSES
TEMPTATION
TEMPTATIONS
TEMPTATIOUS
TEMPTINGLY
TEMPTINGNESS
TEMPTINGNESSES
TEMPTRESSES
TEMULENCES
TEMULENCIES
TEMULENTLY
TENABILITIES
TENABILITY
TENABLENESS
TENABLENESSES
TENACIOUSLY
TENACIOUSNESS
TENACIOUSNESSES
TENACITIES
TENACULUMS
TENAILLONS
TENANTABLE
TENANTLESS
TENANTRIES
TENANTSHIP
TENANTSHIPS
TENDENCIALLY
TENDENCIES
TENDENCIOUS
TENDENCIOUSLY
TENDENCIOUSNESS
TENDENTIAL
TENDENTIALLY
TENDENTIOUS
TENDENTIOUSLY
TENDENTIOUSNESS
TENDERABLE
TENDERFEET
TENDERFOOT
TENDERFOOTS
TENDERHEARTED
TENDERHEARTEDLY
TENDERINGS
TENDERISATION
TENDERISATIONS
TENDERISED
TENDERISER
TENDERISERS
TENDERISES
TENDERISING
TENDERIZATION
TENDERIZATIONS
TENDERIZED
TENDERIZER
TENDERIZERS
TENDERIZES
TENDERIZING
TENDERLING
TENDERLINGS
TENDERLOIN
TENDERLOINS
TENDERNESS
TENDERNESSES
TENDEROMETER
TENDEROMETERS
TENDINITIS

TENDINITISES
TENDONITIS
TENDONITISES
TENDOVAGINITIS
TENDRESSES
TENDRILLAR
TENDRILLED
TENDRILLOUS
TENDRILOUS
TENEBRIFIC
TENEBRIONID
TENEBRIONIDS
TENEBRIOUS
TENEBRIOUSNESS
TENEBRISMS
TENEBRISTS
TENEBRITIES
TENEBROSITIES
TENEBROSITY
TENEBROUSNESS
TENEBROUSNESSES
TENEMENTAL
TENEMENTARY
TENEMENTED
TENESMUSES
TENIACIDES
TENIAFUGES
TENNANTITE
TENNANTITES
TENORRHAPHIES
TENORRHAPHY
TENOSYNOVITIS
TENOSYNOVITISES
TENOTOMIES
TENOTOMIST
TENOTOMISTS
TENOVAGINITIS
TENOVAGINITISES
TENPOUNDER
TENPOUNDERS
TENSENESSES
TENSIBILITIES
TENSIBILITY
TENSIBLENESS
TENSIBLENESSES
TENSILENESS
TENSILENESSES
TENSILITIES
TENSIMETER
TENSIMETERS
TENSIOMETER
TENSIOMETERS
TENSIOMETRIC
TENSIOMETRIES
TENSIOMETRY
TENSIONALLY
TENSIONERS
TENSIONING
TENSIONLESS
TENTACULAR
TENTACULATE
TENTACULIFEROUS
TENTACULITE
TENTACULITES
TENTACULOID
TENTACULUM
TENTATIONS
TENTATIVELY
TENTATIVENESS
TENTATIVENESSES
TENTATIVES
TENTERHOOK
TENTERHOOKS
TENTIGINOUS
TENTMAKERS
TENTORIUMS
TENUIROSTRAL
TENUOUSNESS
TENUOUSNESSES
TENURIALLY
TEPEFACTION
TEPEFACTIONS
TEPHIGRAMS

TEPHROITES
TEPHROMANCIES
TEPHROMANCY
TEPIDARIUM
TEPIDITIES
TEPIDNESSES
TERAHERTZES
TERATOCARCINOMA
TERATOGENESES
TERATOGENESIS
TERATOGENIC
TERATOGENICIST
TERATOGENICISTS
TERATOGENICITY
TERATOGENIES
TERATOGENS
TERATOGENY
TERATOLOGIC
TERATOLOGICAL
TERATOLOGIES
TERATOLOGIST
TERATOLOGISTS
TERATOLOGY
TERATOMATA
TERATOMATOUS
TERATOPHOBIA
TERATOPHOBIAS
TERCENTENARIES
TERCENTENARY
TERCENTENNIAL
TERCENTENNIALS
TEREBINTHINE
TEREBINTHS
TEREBRANTS
TEREBRATED
TEREBRATES
TEREBRATING
TEREBRATION
TEREBRATIONS
TEREBRATULA
TEREBRATULAE
TEREBRATULAS
TEREPHTHALATE
TEREPHTHALATES
TEREPHTHALIC
TERGIVERSANT
TERGIVERSANTS
TERGIVERSATE
TERGIVERSATED
TERGIVERSATES
TERGIVERSATING
TERGIVERSATION
TERGIVERSATIONS
TERGIVERSATOR
TERGIVERSATORS
TERGIVERSATORY
TERMAGANCIES
TERMAGANCY
TERMAGANTLY
TERMAGANTS
TERMINABILITIES
TERMINABILITY
TERMINABLE
TERMINABLENESS
TERMINABLY
TERMINALLY
TERMINATED
TERMINATES
TERMINATING
TERMINATION
TERMINATIONAL
TERMINATIONS
TERMINATIVE
TERMINATIVELY
TERMINATOR
TERMINATORS
TERMINATORY
TERMINISMS
TERMINISTS
TERMINOLOGICAL
TERMINOLOGIES
TERMINOLOGIST
TERMINOLOGISTS

TERMINOLOGY
TERMINUSES
TERMITARIA
TERMITARIES
TERMITARIUM
TERMITARIUMS
TERNEPLATE
TERNEPLATES
TEROTECHNOLOGY
TERPENELESS
TERPENOIDS
TERPINEOLS
TERPOLYMER
TERPOLYMERS
TERPSICHOREAL
TERPSICHOREAN
TERRACELESS
TERRACETTE
TERRACETTES
TERRACINGS
TERRACOTTA
TERRACOTTAS
TERRAFORMED
TERRAFORMING
TERRAFORMINGS
TERRAFORMS
TERRAMARES
TERRAQUEOUS
TERRARIUMS
TERREMOTIVE
TERREPLEIN
TERREPLEINS
TERRESTRIAL
TERRESTRIALLY
TERRESTRIALNESS
TERRESTRIALS
TERRIBILITIES
TERRIBILITY
TERRIBLENESS
TERRIBLENESSES
TERRICOLES
TERRICOLOUS
TERRIFICALLY
TERRIFIERS
TERRIFYING
TERRIFYINGLY
TERRIGENOUS
TERRITORIAL
TERRITORIALISE
TERRITORIALISED
TERRITORIALISES
TERRITORIALISM
TERRITORIALISMS
TERRITORIALIST
TERRITORIALISTS
TERRITORIALITY
TERRITORIALIZE
TERRITORIALIZED
TERRITORIALIZES
TERRITORIALLY
TERRITORIALS
TERRITORIED
TERRITORIES
TERRORISATION
TERRORISATIONS
TERRORISED
TERRORISER
TERRORISERS
TERRORISES
TERRORISING
TERRORISMS
TERRORISTIC
TERRORISTS
TERRORIZATION
TERRORIZATIONS
TERRORIZED
TERRORIZER
TERRORIZERS
TERRORIZES
TERRORIZING
TERRORLESS
TERSANCTUS
TERSANCTUSES

TERSENESSES
TERTIARIES
TERVALENCIES
TERVALENCY
TESCHENITE
TESCHENITES
TESSARAGLOT
TESSELATED
TESSELATES
TESSELATING
TESSELLATE
TESSELLATED
TESSELLATES
TESSELLATING
TESSELLATION
TESSELLATIONS
TESSERACTS
TESSITURAS
TESTABILITIES
TESTABILITY
TESTACEANS
TESTACEOUS
TESTAMENTAL
TESTAMENTAR
TESTAMENTARILY
TESTAMENTARY
TESTAMENTS
TESTATIONS
TESTATRICES
TESTATRIXES
TESTCROSSED
TESTCROSSES
TESTCROSSING
TESTERNING
TESTICULAR
TESTICULATE
TESTICULATED
TESTIFICATE
TESTIFICATES
TESTIFICATION
TESTIFICATIONS
TESTIFICATOR
TESTIFICATORS
TESTIFICATORY
TESTIFIERS
TESTIFYING
TESTIMONIAL
TESTIMONIALISE
TESTIMONIALISED
TESTIMONIALISES
TESTIMONIALIZE
TESTIMONIALIZED
TESTIMONIALIZES
TESTIMONIALS
TESTIMONIED
TESTIMONIES
TESTIMONYING
TESTINESSES
TESTOSTERONE
TESTOSTERONES
TESTUDINAL
TESTUDINARY
TESTUDINEOUS
TESTUDINES
TETANICALLY
TETANISATION
TETANISATIONS
TETANISING
TETANIZATION
TETANIZATIONS
TETANIZING
TETARTOHEDRAL
TETARTOHEDRALLY
TETARTOHEDRISM
TETARTOHEDRISMS
TETCHINESS
TETCHINESSES
TETHERBALL
TETHERBALLS
TETRABASIC
TETRABASICITIES
TETRABASICITY
TETRABRACH

t

TETRABRACHS
TETRABRANCHIATE
TETRACAINE
TETRACAINES
TETRACHLORIDE
TETRACHLORIDES
TETRACHORD
TETRACHORDAL
TETRACHORDS
TETRACHOTOMIES
TETRACHOTOMOUS
TETRACHOTOMY
TETRACTINAL
TETRACTINE
TETRACYCLIC
TETRACYCLINE
TETRACYCLINES
TETRADACTYL
TETRADACTYLIES
TETRADACTYLOUS
TETRADACTYLS
TETRADACTYLY
TETRADITES
TETRADRACHM
TETRADRACHMS
TETRADYMITE
TETRADYMITES
TETRADYNAMOUS
TETRAETHYL
TETRAETHYLS
TETRAFLUORIDE
TETRAFLUORIDES
TETRAGONAL
TETRAGONALLY
TETRAGONALNESS
TETRAGONOUS
TETRAGRAMMATON
TETRAGRAMMATONS
TETRAGRAMS
TETRAGYNIAN
TETRAGYNOUS
TETRAHEDRA
TETRAHEDRAL
TETRAHEDRALLY
TETRAHEDRITE
TETRAHEDRITES
TETRAHEDRON
TETRAHEDRONS
TETRAHYDROFURAN
TETRAHYMENA
TETRAHYMENAS
TETRALOGIES
TETRAMERAL
TETRAMERIC
TETRAMERISM
TETRAMERISMS
TETRAMEROUS
TETRAMETER
TETRAMETERS
TETRAMETHYLLEAD
TETRAMORPHIC
TETRANDRIAN
TETRANDROUS
TETRAPLEGIA
TETRAPLEGIAS
TETRAPLEGIC
TETRAPLOID
TETRAPLOIDIES
TETRAPLOIDS
TETRAPLOIDY
TETRAPODIC
TETRAPODIES
TETRAPODOUS
TETRAPOLIS
TETRAPOLISES
TETRAPOLITAN
TETRAPTERAN
TETRAPTEROUS
TETRAPTOTE
TETRAPTOTES
TETRAPYRROLE
TETRAPYRROLES
TETRARCHATE

TETRARCHATES
TETRARCHIC
TETRARCHICAL
TETRARCHIES
TETRASEMIC
TETRASPORANGIA
TETRASPORANGIUM
TETRASPORE
TETRASPORES
TETRASPORIC
TETRASPOROUS
TETRASTICH
TETRASTICHAL
TETRASTICHIC
TETRASTICHOUS
TETRASTICHS
TETRASTYLE
TETRASTYLES
TETRASYLLABIC
TETRASYLLABICAL
TETRASYLLABLE
TETRASYLLABLES
TETRATHEISM
TETRATHEISMS
TETRATHLON
TETRATHLONS
TETRATOMIC
TETRAVALENCIES
TETRAVALENCY
TETRAVALENT
TETRAVALENTS
TETRAZOLIUM
TETRAZOLIUMS
TETRAZZINI
TETRODOTOXIN
TETRODOTOXINS
TETROTOXIN
TETROTOXINS
TETROXIDES
TEUTONISED
TEUTONISES
TEUTONISING
TEUTONIZED
TEUTONIZES
TEUTONIZING
TEXTBOOKISH
TEXTPHONES
TEXTUALISM
TEXTUALISMS
TEXTUALIST
TEXTUALISTS
TEXTUARIES
TEXTURALLY
TEXTURELESS
TEXTURISED
TEXTURISES
TEXTURISING
TEXTURIZED
TEXTURIZES
TEXTURIZING
THALAMENCEPHALA
THALAMICALLY
THALAMIFLORAL
THALASSAEMIA
THALASSAEMIAS
THALASSAEMIC
THALASSEMIA
THALASSEMIAS
THALASSEMIC
THALASSEMICS
THALASSIAN
THALASSIANS
THALASSOCRACIES
THALASSOCRACY
THALASSOCRAT
THALASSOCRATS
THALASSOGRAPHER
THALASSOGRAPHIC
THALASSOGRAPHY
THALASSOTHERAPY
THALATTOCRACIES
THALATTOCRACY
THALICTRUM

THALICTRUMS
THALIDOMIDE
THALIDOMIDES
THALLIFORM
THALLOPHYTE
THALLOPHYTES
THALLOPHYTIC
THANATISMS
THANATISTS
THANATOGNOMONIC
THANATOGRAPHIES
THANATOGRAPHY
THANATOLOGICAL
THANATOLOGIES
THANATOLOGIST
THANATOLOGISTS
THANATOLOGY
THANATOPHOBIA
THANATOPHOBIAS
THANATOPSES
THANATOPSIS
THANATOSES
THANATOSIS
THANEHOODS
THANESHIPS
THANKFULLER
THANKFULLEST
THANKFULLY
THANKFULNESS
THANKFULNESSES
THANKLESSLY
THANKLESSNESS
THANKLESSNESSES
THANKSGIVER
THANKSGIVERS
THANKSGIVING
THANKSGIVINGS
THANKWORTHILY
THANKWORTHINESS
THANKWORTHY
THARBOROUGH
THARBOROUGHS
THATCHIEST
THATCHINGS
THATCHLESS
THATNESSES
THAUMASITE
THAUMASITES
THAUMATINS
THAUMATOGENIES
THAUMATOGENY
THAUMATOGRAPHY
THAUMATOLATRIES
THAUMATOLATRY
THAUMATOLOGIES
THAUMATOLOGY
THAUMATROPE
THAUMATROPES
THAUMATROPICAL
THAUMATURGE
THAUMATURGES
THAUMATURGIC
THAUMATURGICAL
THAUMATURGICS
THAUMATURGIES
THAUMATURGISM
THAUMATURGISMS
THAUMATURGIST
THAUMATURGISTS
THAUMATURGUS
THAUMATURGUSES
THAUMATURGY
THEANTHROPIC
THEANTHROPIES
THEANTHROPISM
THEANTHROPISMS
THEANTHROPIST
THEANTHROPISTS
THEANTHROPY
THEARCHIES
THEATERGOER
THEATERGOERS
THEATERGOING

THEATERGOINGS
THEATRICAL
THEATRICALISE
THEATRICALISED
THEATRICALISES
THEATRICALISING
THEATRICALISM
THEATRICALISMS
THEATRICALITIES
THEATRICALITY
THEATRICALIZE
THEATRICALIZED
THEATRICALIZES
THEATRICALIZING
THEATRICALLY
THEATRICALNESS
THEATRICALS
THEATRICISE
THEATRICISED
THEATRICISES
THEATRICISING
THEATRICISM
THEATRICISMS
THEATRICIZE
THEATRICIZED
THEATRICIZES
THEATRICIZING
THEATROMANIA
THEATROMANIAS
THEATROPHONE
THEATROPHONES
THECODONTS
THEFTUOUSLY
THEIRSELVES
THEISTICAL
THEISTICALLY
THELEMENTS
THELITISES
THELYTOKIES
THELYTOKOUS
THEMATICALLY
THEMATISATION
THEMATISATIONS
THEMATIZATION
THEMATIZATIONS
THEMSELVES
THENABOUTS
THENARDITE
THENARDITES
THENCEFORTH
THENCEFORWARD
THENCEFORWARDS
THEOBROMINE
THEOBROMINES
THEOCENTRIC
THEOCENTRICISM
THEOCENTRICISMS
THEOCENTRICITY
THEOCENTRISM
THEOCENTRISMS
THEOCRACIES
THEOCRASIES
THEOCRATIC
THEOCRATICAL
THEOCRATICALLY
THEODICEAN
THEODICEANS
THEODICIES
THEODOLITE
THEODOLITES
THEODOLITIC
THEOGONICAL
THEOGONIES
THEOGONIST
THEOGONISTS
THEOLOGASTERS
THEOLOGATE
THEOLOGATES
THEOLOGERS
THEOLOGIAN
THEOLOGIANS
THEOLOGICAL

THEOLOGICALLY
THEOLOGIES
THEOLOGISATION
THEOLOGISATIONS
THEOLOGISE
THEOLOGISED
THEOLOGISER
THEOLOGISERS
THEOLOGISES
THEOLOGISING
THEOLOGIST
THEOLOGISTS
THEOLOGIZATION
THEOLOGIZATIONS
THEOLOGIZE
THEOLOGIZED
THEOLOGIZER
THEOLOGIZERS
THEOLOGIZES
THEOLOGIZING
THEOLOGOUMENA
THEOLOGOUMENON
THEOLOGUES
THEOMACHIES
THEOMACHIST
THEOMACHISTS
THEOMANCIES
THEOMANIAC
THEOMANIACS
THEOMANIAS
THEOMANTIC
THEOMORPHIC
THEOMORPHISM
THEOMORPHISMS
THEONOMIES
THEONOMOUS
THEOPATHETIC
THEOPATHIC
THEOPATHIES
THEOPHAGIES
THEOPHAGOUS
THEOPHANIC
THEOPHANIES
THEOPHANOUS
THEOPHOBIA
THEOPHOBIAC
THEOPHOBIACS
THEOPHOBIAS
THEOPHOBIST
THEOPHOBISTS
THEOPHORIC
THEOPHYLLINE
THEOPHYLLINES
THEOPNEUST
THEOPNEUSTIC
THEOPNEUSTIES
THEOPNEUSTY
THEORBISTS
THEOREMATIC
THEOREMATICAL
THEOREMATICALLY
THEOREMATIST
THEOREMATISTS
THEORETICAL
THEORETICALLY
THEORETICIAN
THEORETICIANS
THEORETICS
THEORIQUES
THEORISATION
THEORISATIONS
THEORISERS
THEORISING
THEORIZATION
THEORIZATIONS
THEORIZERS
THEORIZING
THEOSOPHER
THEOSOPHERS
THEOSOPHIC
THEOSOPHICAL
THEOSOPHICALLY
THEOSOPHIES

THEOSOPHISE
THEOSOPHISED
THEOSOPHISES
THEOSOPHISING
THEOSOPHISM
THEOSOPHISMS
THEOSOPHIST
THEOSOPHISTICAL
THEOSOPHISTS
THEOSOPHIZE
THEOSOPHIZED
THEOSOPHIZES
THEOSOPHIZING
THEOTECHNIC
THEOTECHNIES
THEOTECHNY
THERALITES
THERAPEUSES
THERAPEUSIS
THERAPEUTIC
THERAPEUTICALLY
THERAPEUTICS
THERAPEUTIST
THERAPEUTISTS
THERAPISTS
THERAPSIDS
THEREABOUT
THEREABOUTS
THEREAFTER
THEREAGAINST
THEREAMONG
THEREANENT
THEREBESIDE
THEREINAFTER
THEREINBEFORE
THERENESSES
THERETHROUGH
THERETOFORE
THEREUNDER
THEREWITHAL
THEREWITHIN
THERIANTHROPIC
THERIANTHROPISM
THERIOLATRIES
THERIOLATRY
THERIOMORPH
THERIOMORPHIC
THERIOMORPHISM
THERIOMORPHISMS
THERIOMORPHOSES
THERIOMORPHOSIS
THERIOMORPHOUS
THERIOMORPHS
THERMAESTHESIA
THERMAESTHESIAS
THERMALISATION
THERMALISATIONS
THERMALISE
THERMALISED
THERMALISES
THERMALISING
THERMALIZATION
THERMALIZATIONS
THERMALIZE
THERMALIZED
THERMALIZES
THERMALIZING
THERMESTHESIA
THERMESTHESIAS
THERMETTES
THERMICALLY
THERMIDORS
THERMIONIC
THERMIONICS
THERMISTOR
THERMISTORS
THERMOBALANCE
THERMOBALANCES
THERMOBARIC
THERMOBAROGRAPH
THERMOBAROMETER
THERMOCHEMICAL
THERMOCHEMIST

THERMOCHEMISTRY	THERMOSCOPES	THIMBLEWEED	THIRTYSOMETHING	THREADBARENESS	THROMBOSES
THERMOCHEMISTS	THERMOSCOPIC	THIMBLEWEEDS	THISNESSES	THREADFINS	THROMBOSING
THERMOCHROMIC	THERMOSCOPICAL	THIMBLEWIT	THISTLEDOWN	THREADIEST	THROMBOSIS
THERMOCHROMIES	THERMOSETS	THIMBLEWITS	THISTLEDOWNS	THREADINESS	THROMBOTIC
THERMOCHROMISM	THERMOSETTING	THIMBLEWITTED	THISTLIEST	THREADINESSES	THROMBOXANE
THERMOCHROMISMS	THERMOSIPHON	THIMEROSAL	THITHERWARD	THREADLESS	THROMBOXANES
THERMOCHROMY	THERMOSIPHONS	THIMEROSALS	THITHERWARDS	THREADLIKE	THRONELESS
THERMOCLINE	THERMOSPHERE	THINGAMABOB	THIXOTROPE	THREADMAKER	THRONGINGS
THERMOCLINES	THERMOSPHERES	THINGAMABOBS	THIXOTROPES	THREADMAKERS	THROPPLING
THERMOCOUPLE	THERMOSPHERIC	THINGAMAJIG	THIXOTROPIC	THREADWORM	THROTTLEABLE
THERMOCOUPLES	THERMOSTABILITY	THINGAMAJIGS	THIXOTROPIES	THREADWORMS	THROTTLEHOLD
THERMODURIC	THERMOSTABLE	THINGAMIES	THIXOTROPY	THREATENED	THROTTLEHOLDS
THERMODYNAMIC	THERMOSTAT	THINGAMYBOB	THOLEIITES	THREATENER	THROTTLERS
THERMODYNAMICAL	THERMOSTATED	THINGAMYBOBS	THOLEIITIC	THREATENERS	THROTTLING
THERMODYNAMICS	THERMOSTATIC	THINGAMYJIG	THOLOBATES	THREATENING	THROTTLINGS
THERMOELECTRIC	THERMOSTATICS	THINGAMYJIGS	THORACENTESES	THREATENINGLY	THROUGHFARE
THERMOELECTRON	THERMOSTATING	THINGHOODS	THORACENTESIS	THREATENINGS	THROUGHFARES
THERMOELECTRONS	THERMOSTATS	THINGINESS	THORACICALLY	THREEFOLDNESS	THROUGHGAUN
THERMOELEMENT	THERMOSTATTED	THINGINESSES	THORACOCENTESES	THREEFOLDNESSES	THROUGHGAUNS
THERMOELEMENTS	THERMOSTATTING	THINGLINESS	THORACOCENTESIS	THREENESSES	THROUGHITHER
THERMOFORM	THERMOTACTIC	THINGLINESSES	THORACOPLASTIES	THREEPENCE	THROUGHOTHER
THERMOFORMABLE	THERMOTAXES	THINGNESSES	THORACOPLASTY	THREEPENCES	THROUGHOUT
THERMOFORMED	THERMOTAXIC	THINGUMABOB	THORACOSCOPE	THREEPENCEWORTH	THROUGHPUT
THERMOFORMING	THERMOTAXIS	THINGUMABOBS	THORACOSCOPES	THREEPENNIES	THROUGHPUTS
THERMOFORMS	THERMOTENSILE	THINGUMAJIG	THORACOSTOMIES	THREEPENNY	THROUGHWAY
THERMOGENESES	THERMOTHERAPIES	THINGUMAJIGS	THORACOSTOMY	THREEPENNYWORTH	THROUGHWAYS
THERMOGENESIS	THERMOTHERAPY	THINGUMBOB	THORACOTOMIES	THREESCORE	THROWAWAYS
THERMOGENETIC	THERMOTICAL	THINGUMBOBS	THORACOTOMY	THREESCORES	THROWBACKS
THERMOGENIC	THERMOTICS	THINGUMMIES	THORIANITE	THREESOMES	THROWSTERS
THERMOGENOUS	THERMOTOLERANT	THINGUMMYBOB	THORIANITES	THREMMATOLOGIES	THRUMMIEST
THERMOGRAM	THERMOTROPIC	THINGUMMYBOBS	THORNBACKS	THREMMATOLOGY	THRUMMINGLY
THERMOGRAMS	THERMOTROPICS	THINGUMMYJIG	THORNBILLS	THRENETICAL	THRUMMINGS
THERMOGRAPH	THERMOTROPISM	THINGUMMYJIGS	THORNBUSHES	THRENODIAL	THRUPPENCE
THERMOGRAPHER	THERMOTROPISMS	THINKABLENESS	THORNHEDGE	THRENODIES	THRUPPENCES
THERMOGRAPHERS	THEROLOGIES	THINKABLENESSES	THORNHEDGES	THRENODIST	THRUPPENNIES
THERMOGRAPHIC	THEROPHYTE	THINKINGLY	THORNINESS	THRENODISTS	THRUPPENNY
THERMOGRAPHIES	THEROPHYTES	THINKINGNESS	THORNINESSES	THREONINES	THRUSTINGS
THERMOGRAPHS	THEROPODAN	THINKINGNESSES	THORNPROOFS	THRESHINGS	THRUTCHING
THERMOGRAPHY	THEROPODANS	THINKPIECE	THORNTREES	THRESHOLDS	THUDDINGLY
THERMOHALINE	THERSITICAL	THINKPIECES	THOROUGHBASS	THRIFTIEST	THUGGERIES
THERMOJUNCTION	THESAURUSES	THINNESSES	THOROUGHBASSES	THRIFTINESS	THUMBHOLES
THERMOJUNCTIONS	THESMOTHETE	THIOALCOHOL	THOROUGHBRACE	THRIFTINESSES	THUMBIKINS
THERMOLABILE	THESMOTHETES	THIOALCOHOLS	THOROUGHBRACED	THRIFTLESS	THUMBLINGS
THERMOLABILITY	THETICALLY	THIOBACILLI	THOROUGHBRACES	THRIFTLESSLY	THUMBNAILS
THERMOLOGIES	THEURGICAL	THIOBACILLUS	THOROUGHBRED	THRIFTLESSNESS	THUMBPIECE
THERMOLOGY	THEURGICALLY	THIOBARBITURATE	THOROUGHBREDS	THRILLIEST	THUMBPIECES
THERMOLYSES	THEURGISTS	THIOCARBAMIDE	THOROUGHER	THRILLINGLY	THUMBPRINT
THERMOLYSIS	THIABENDAZOLE	THIOCARBAMIDES	THOROUGHEST	THRILLINGNESS	THUMBPRINTS
THERMOLYTIC	THIABENDAZOLES	THIOCYANATE	THOROUGHFARE	THRILLINGNESSES	THUMBSCREW
THERMOMAGNETIC	THIAMINASE	THIOCYANATES	THOROUGHFARES	THRIVELESS	THUMBSCREWS
THERMOMETER	THIAMINASES	THIOCYANIC	THOROUGHGOING	THRIVINGLY	THUMBSTALL
THERMOMETERS	THICKENERS	THIODIGLYCOL	THOROUGHGOINGLY	THRIVINGNESS	THUMBSTALLS
THERMOMETRIC	THICKENING	THIODIGLYCOLS	THOROUGHLY	THRIVINGNESSES	THUMBTACKED
THERMOMETRICAL	THICKENINGS	THIOFURANS	THOROUGHNESS	THROATIEST	THUMBTACKING
THERMOMETRIES	THICKHEADED	THIOPENTAL	THOROUGHNESSES	THROATINESS	THUMBTACKS
THERMOMETRY	THICKHEADEDNESS	THIOPENTALS	THOROUGHPACED	THROATINESSES	THUMBWHEEL
THERMOMOTOR	THICKHEADS	THIOPENTONE	THOROUGHPIN	THROATLASH	THUMBWHEELS
THERMOMOTORS	THICKLEAVES	THIOPENTONES	THOROUGHPINS	THROATLASHES	THUMPINGLY
THERMONASTIES	THICKNESSES	THIOPHENES	THOROUGHWAX	THROATLATCH	THUNBERGIA
THERMONASTY	THICKSKINS	THIORIDAZINE	THOROUGHWAXES	THROATLATCHES	THUNBERGIAS
THERMONUCLEAR	THIEVERIES	THIORIDAZINES	THOROUGHWORT	THROATWORT	THUNDERBIRD
THERMOPERIODIC	THIEVISHLY	THIOSINAMINE	THOROUGHWORTS	THROATWORTS	THUNDERBIRDS
THERMOPERIODISM	THIEVISHNESS	THIOSINAMINES	THOUGHTCAST	THROBBINGLY	THUNDERBOLT
THERMOPHIL	THIEVISHNESSES	THIOSULFATE	THOUGHTCASTS	THROBBINGS	THUNDERBOLTS
THERMOPHILE	THIGHBONES	THIOSULFATES	THOUGHTFUL	THROMBOCYTE	THUNDERBOX
THERMOPHILES	THIGMOTACTIC	THIOSULPHATE	THOUGHTFULLY	THROMBOCYTES	THUNDERBOXES
THERMOPHILIC	THIGMOTAXES	THIOSULPHATES	THOUGHTFULNESS	THROMBOCYTIC	THUNDERCLAP
THERMOPHILOUS	THIGMOTAXIS	THIOSULPHURIC	THOUGHTLESS	THROMBOEMBOLIC	THUNDERCLAPS
THERMOPHILS	THIGMOTROPIC	THIOURACIL	THOUGHTLESSLY	THROMBOEMBOLISM	THUNDERCLOUD
THERMOPHYLLOUS	THIGMOTROPISM	THIOURACILS	THOUGHTLESSNESS	THROMBOGEN	THUNDERCLOUDS
THERMOPILE	THIGMOTROPISMS	THIRDBOROUGH	THOUGHTWAY	THROMBOGENS	THUNDERERS
THERMOPILES	THIMBLEBERRIES	THIRDBOROUGHS	THOUGHTWAYS	THROMBOKINASE	THUNDERFLASH
THERMOPLASTIC	THIMBLEBERRY	THIRDSTREAM	THOUSANDFOLD	THROMBOKINASES	THUNDERFLASHES
THERMOPLASTICS	THIMBLEFUL	THIRDSTREAMS	THOUSANDFOLDS	THROMBOLYSES	THUNDERHEAD
THERMORECEPTOR	THIMBLEFULS	THIRSTIEST	THOUSANDTH	THROMBOLYSIS	THUNDERHEADS
THERMORECEPTORS	THIMBLERIG	THIRSTINESS	THOUSANDTHS	THROMBOLYTIC	THUNDERIER
THERMOREGULATE	THIMBLERIGGED	THIRSTINESSES	THRAIPINGS	THROMBOLYTICS	THUNDERIEST
THERMOREGULATED	THIMBLERIGGER	THIRSTLESS	THRALLDOMS	THROMBOPHILIA	THUNDERING
THERMOREGULATES	THIMBLERIGGERS	THIRTEENTH	THRAPPLING	THROMBOPHILIAS	THUNDERINGLY
THERMOREGULATOR	THIMBLERIGGING	THIRTEENTHLY	THRASHINGS	THROMBOPLASTIC	THUNDERINGS
THERMOREMANENCE	THIMBLERIGGINGS	THIRTEENTHS	THRASONICAL	THROMBOPLASTIN	THUNDERLESS
THERMOREMANENT	THIMBLERIGS	THIRTIETHS	THRASONICALLY	THROMBOPLASTINS	THUNDEROUS
THERMOSCOPE	THIMBLESFUL	THIRTYFOLD	THREADBARE	THROMBOSED	THUNDEROUSLY

THUNDEROUSNESS
THUNDERSHOWER
THUNDERSHOWERS
THUNDERSTONE
THUNDERSTONES
THUNDERSTORM
THUNDERSTORMS
THUNDERSTRICKEN
THUNDERSTRIKE
THUNDERSTRIKES
THUNDERSTRIKING
THUNDERSTROKE
THUNDERSTROKES
THUNDERSTRUCK
THURIFEROUS
THURIFICATION
THURIFICATIONS
THURIFYING
THUSNESSES
THWACKINGS
THWARTEDLY
THWARTINGLY
THWARTINGS
THWARTSHIP
THWARTSHIPS
THWARTWAYS
THWARTWISE
THYLACINES
THYLAKOIDS
THYMECTOMIES
THYMECTOMISE
THYMECTOMISED
THYMECTOMISES
THYMECTOMISING
THYMECTOMIZE
THYMECTOMIZED
THYMECTOMIZES
THYMECTOMIZING
THYMECTOMY
THYMELAEACEOUS
THYMIDINES
THYMIDYLIC
THYMOCYTES
THYRATRONS
THYRISTORS
THYROCALCITONIN
THYROGLOBULIN
THYROGLOBULINS
THYROIDECTOMIES
THYROIDECTOMY
THYROIDITIS
THYROIDITISES
THYROTOXICOSES
THYROTOXICOSIS
THYROTROPHIC
THYROTROPHIN
THYROTROPHINS
THYROTROPIC
THYROTROPIN
THYROTROPINS
THYROXINES
THYRSOIDAL
THYSANOPTEROUS
THYSANURAN
THYSANURANS
THYSANUROUS
TIBIOFIBULA
TIBIOFIBULAE
TIBIOFIBULAS
TIBIOTARSI
TIBIOTARSUS
TIBOUCHINA
TIBOUCHINAS
TICHORRHINE
TICKETINGS
TICKETLESS
TICKETTYBOO
TICKLISHLY
TICKLISHNESS
TICKLISHNESSES
TICKTACKED
TICKTACKING
TICKTACKTOE

TICKTACKTOES
TICKTOCKED
TICKTOCKING
TICTACKING
TICTOCKING
TIDDLEDYWINK
TIDDLEDYWINKS
TIDDLEYWINK
TIDDLEYWINKS
TIDDLYWINK
TIDDLYWINKS
TIDEWAITER
TIDEWAITERS
TIDEWATERS
TIDINESSES
TIDIVATING
TIDIVATION
TIDIVATIONS
TIEBREAKER
TIEBREAKERS
TIEMANNITE
TIEMANNITES
TIERCELETS
TIERCERONS
TIGERISHLY
TIGERISHNESS
TIGERISHNESSES
TIGGYWINKLE
TIGGYWINKLES
TIGHTASSED
TIGHTASSES
TIGHTENERS
TIGHTENING
TIGHTFISTED
TIGHTFISTEDNESS
TIGHTISHLY
TIGHTNESSES
TIGHTROPES
TIGHTWIRES
TIGRISHNESS
TIGRISHNESSES
TIKOLOSHES
TILEFISHES
TILIACEOUS
TILLANDSIA
TILLANDSIAS
TILLERLESS
TILTMETERS
TILTROTORS
TIMBERDOODLE
TIMBERDOODLES
TIMBERHEAD
TIMBERHEADS
TIMBERINGS
TIMBERLAND
TIMBERLANDS
TIMBERLINE
TIMBERLINES
TIMBERWORK
TIMBERWORKS
TIMBERYARD
TIMBERYARDS
TIMBRELLED
TIMBROLOGIES
TIMBROLOGIST
TIMBROLOGISTS
TIMBROLOGY
TIMBROMANIA
TIMBROMANIAC
TIMBROMANIACS
TIMBROMANIAS
TIMBROPHILIES
TIMBROPHILIST
TIMBROPHILISTS
TIMBROPHILY
TIMEFRAMES
TIMEKEEPER
TIMEKEEPERS
TIMEKEEPING
TIMEKEEPINGS
TIMELESSLY
TIMELESSNESS
TIMELESSNESSES

TIMELINESS
TIMELINESSES
TIMENOGUYS
TIMEPASSED
TIMEPASSES
TIMEPASSING
TIMEPIECES
TIMEPLEASER
TIMEPLEASERS
TIMESAVERS
TIMESAVING
TIMESCALES
TIMESERVER
TIMESERVERS
TIMESERVING
TIMESERVINGS
TIMETABLED
TIMETABLES
TIMETABLING
TIMEWORKER
TIMEWORKERS
TIMIDITIES
TIMIDNESSES
TIMOCRACIES
TIMOCRATIC
TIMOCRATICAL
TIMOROUSLY
TIMOROUSNESS
TIMOROUSNESSES
TIMPANISTS
TINCTORIAL
TINCTORIALLY
TINCTURING
TINDERBOXES
TINGLINGLY
TINGUAITES
TININESSES
TINKERINGS
TINKERTOYS
TINKLINGLY
TINNINESSES
TINNITUSES
TINPLATING
TINSELLING
TINSELRIES
TINSMITHING
TINSMITHINGS
TINTINESSES
TINTINNABULA
TINTINNABULANT
TINTINNABULAR
TINTINNABULARY
TINTINNABULATE
TINTINNABULATED
TINTINNABULATES
TINTINNABULOUS
TINTINNABULUM
TINTOMETER
TINTOMETERS
TINTOOKIES
TIPPYTOEING
TIPSIFYING
TIPSINESSES
TIPTRONICS
TIRAILLEUR
TIRAILLEURS
TIREDNESSES
TIRELESSLY
TIRELESSNESS
TIRELESSNESSES
TIRESOMELY
TIRESOMENESS
TIRESOMENESSES
TIROCINIUM
TIROCINIUMS
TITANESSES
TITANICALLY
TITANIFEROUS
TITANOSAUR
TITANOSAURS
TITANOTHERE
TITANOTHERES
TITARAKURA

TITARAKURAS
TITHINGMAN
TITHINGMEN
TITILLATED
TITILLATES
TITILLATING
TITILLATINGLY
TITILLATION
TITILLATIONS
TITILLATIVE
TITILLATOR
TITILLATORS
TITIPOUNAMU
TITIVATING
TITIVATION
TITIVATIONS
TITIVATORS
TITLEHOLDER
TITLEHOLDERS
TITLEHOLDING
TITRATABLE
TITRATIONS
TITRIMETRIC
TITTERINGLY
TITTERINGS
TITTIVATED
TITTIVATES
TITTIVATING
TITTIVATION
TITTIVATIONS
TITTIVATOR
TITTIVATORS
TITTLEBATS
TITTUPPING
TITUBANCIES
TITUBATING
TITUBATION
TITUBATIONS
TITULARIES
TITULARITIES
TITULARITY
TOADEATERS
TOADFISHES
TOADFLAXES
TOADGRASSES
TOADRUSHES
TOADSTONES
TOADSTOOLS
TOASTMASTER
TOASTMASTERS
TOASTMISTRESS
TOASTMISTRESSES
TOBACCANALIAN
TOBACCANALIANS
TOBACCOLESS
TOBACCONIST
TOBACCONISTS
TOBOGGANED
TOBOGGANER
TOBOGGANERS
TOBOGGANING
TOBOGGANINGS
TOBOGGANIST
TOBOGGANISTS
TOBOGGINED
TOBOGGINING
TOCCATELLA
TOCCATELLAS
TOCCATINAS
TOCHERLESS
TOCOLOGIES
TOCOPHEROL
TOCOPHEROLS
TODDLERHOOD
TODDLERHOODS
TOENAILING
TOERAGGERS
TOFFISHNESS
TOFFISHNESSES
TOGAVIRUSES
TOGETHERNESS
TOGETHERNESSES
TOILETRIES

TOILFULNESS
TOILFULNESSES
TOILINETTE
TOILINETTES
TOILSOMELY
TOILSOMENESS
TOILSOMENESSES
TOKENISTIC
TOKOLOGIES
TOKOLOSHES
TOKOLOSHIS
TOKTOKKIES
TOLBUTAMIDE
TOLBUTAMIDES
TOLERABILITIES
TOLERABILITY
TOLERABLENESS
TOLERABLENESSES
TOLERANCES
TOLERANTLY
TOLERATING
TOLERATION
TOLERATIONISM
TOLERATIONISMS
TOLERATIONIST
TOLERATIONISTS
TOLERATIONS
TOLERATIVE
TOLERATORS
TOLLBOOTHS
TOLLBRIDGE
TOLLBRIDGES
TOLLDISHES
TOLLHOUSES
TOLUIDIDES
TOLUIDINES
TOMAHAWKED
TOMAHAWKING
TOMATILLOES
TOMATILLOS
TOMBOYISHLY
TOMBOYISHNESS
TOMBOYISHNESSES
TOMBSTONES
TOMCATTING
TOMFOOLERIES
TOMFOOLERY
TOMFOOLING
TOMFOOLISH
TOMFOOLISHNESS
TOMOGRAPHIC
TOMOGRAPHIES
TOMOGRAPHS
TOMOGRAPHY
TONALITIES
TONALITIVE
TONELESSLY
TONELESSNESS
TONELESSNESSES
TONETICALLY
TONGUELESS
TONGUELETS
TONGUELIKE
TONGUESTER
TONGUESTERS
TONICITIES
TONISHNESS
TONISHNESSES
TONNISHNESS
TONNISHNESSES
TONOMETERS
TONOMETRIC
TONOMETRIES
TONOPLASTS
TONSILITIS
TONSILITISES
TONSILLARY
TONSILLECTOMIES
TONSILLECTOMY
TONSILLITIC
TONSILLITIS
TONSILLITISES
TONSILLOTOMIES

TONSILLOTOMY
TOOLHOLDER
TOOLHOLDERS
TOOLHOUSES
TOOLMAKERS
TOOLMAKING
TOOLMAKINGS
TOOLPUSHER
TOOLPUSHERS
TOOTHACHES
TOOTHBRUSH
TOOTHBRUSHES
TOOTHBRUSHING
TOOTHBRUSHINGS
TOOTHCOMBS
TOOTHFISHES
TOOTHINESS
TOOTHINESSES
TOOTHPASTE
TOOTHPASTES
TOOTHPICKS
TOOTHSHELL
TOOTHSHELLS
TOOTHSOMELY
TOOTHSOMENESS
TOOTHSOMENESSES
TOOTHWASHES
TOOTHWORTS
TOPAGNOSES
TOPAGNOSIA
TOPAGNOSIAS
TOPAGNOSIS
TOPARCHIES
TOPAZOLITE
TOPAZOLITES
TOPCROSSES
TOPDRESSING
TOPDRESSINGS
TOPECTOMIES
TOPGALLANT
TOPGALLANTS
TOPHACEOUS
TOPIARISTS
TOPICALITIES
TOPICALITY
TOPKNOTTED
TOPLESSNESS
TOPLESSNESSES
TOPLOFTICAL
TOPLOFTIER
TOPLOFTIEST
TOPLOFTILY
TOPLOFTINESS
TOPLOFTINESSES
TOPMAKINGS
TOPMINNOWS
TOPNOTCHER
TOPNOTCHERS
TOPOCENTRIC
TOPOCHEMISTRIES
TOPOCHEMISTRY
TOPOGRAPHER
TOPOGRAPHERS
TOPOGRAPHIC
TOPOGRAPHICAL
TOPOGRAPHICALLY
TOPOGRAPHIES
TOPOGRAPHS
TOPOGRAPHY
TOPOLOGICAL
TOPOLOGICALLY
TOPOLOGIES
TOPOLOGIST
TOPOLOGISTS
TOPONYMICAL
TOPONYMICS
TOPONYMIES
TOPONYMIST
TOPONYMISTS
TOPOPHILIA
TOPOPHILIAS
TOPSOILING
TOPSOILINGS

TOPSTITCHED
TOPSTITCHES
TOPSTITCHING
TOPWORKING
TORBANITES
TORBERNITE
TORBERNITES
TORCHBEARER
TORCHBEARERS
TORCHIERES
TORCHLIGHT
TORCHLIGHTS
TORCHWOODS
TORMENTEDLY
TORMENTERS
TORMENTILS
TORMENTING
TORMENTINGLY
TORMENTINGS
TORMENTORS
TORMENTUMS
TOROIDALLY
TOROSITIES
TORPEDINOUS
TORPEDOERS
TORPEDOING
TORPEDOIST
TORPEDOISTS
TORPEFYING
TORPESCENCE
TORPESCENCES
TORPESCENT
TORPIDITIES
TORPIDNESS
TORPIDNESSES
TORPITUDES
TORPORIFIC
TORREFACTION
TORREFACTIONS
TORREFYING
TORRENTIAL
TORRENTIALITIES
TORRENTIALITY
TORRENTIALLY
TORRENTUOUS
TORRIDITIES
TORRIDNESS
TORRIDNESSES
TORRIFYING
TORSIBILITIES
TORSIBILITY
TORSIOGRAPH
TORSIOGRAPHS
TORSIONALLY
TORTELLINI
TORTELLINIS
TORTFEASOR
TORTFEASORS
TORTICOLLAR
TORTICOLLIS
TORTICOLLISES
TORTILITIES
TORTILLONS
TORTIOUSLY
TORTOISESHELL
TORTOISESHELLS
TORTRICIDS
TORTUOSITIES
TORTUOSITY
TORTUOUSLY
TORTUOUSNESS
TORTUOUSNESSES
TORTUREDLY
TORTURESOME
TORTURINGLY
TORTURINGS
TORTUROUSLY
TOSSICATED
TOSTICATED
TOSTICATION
TOSTICATIONS
TOTALISATION
TOTALISATIONS

TOTALISATOR
TOTALISATORS
TOTALISERS
TOTALISING
TOTALISTIC
TOTALITARIAN
TOTALITARIANISE
TOTALITARIANISM
TOTALITARIANIZE
TOTALITARIANS
TOTALITIES
TOTALIZATION
TOTALIZATIONS
TOTALIZATOR
TOTALIZATORS
TOTALIZERS
TOTALIZING
TOTAQUINES
TOTEMICALLY
TOTEMISTIC
TOTIPALMATE
TOTIPALMATION
TOTIPALMATIONS
TOTIPOTENCIES
TOTIPOTENCY
TOTIPOTENT
TOTTERINGLY
TOTTERINGS
TOUCHABLENESS
TOUCHABLENESSES
TOUCHBACKS
TOUCHDOWNS
TOUCHHOLES
TOUCHINESS
TOUCHINESSES
TOUCHINGLY
TOUCHINGNESS
TOUCHINGNESSES
TOUCHLINES
TOUCHMARKS
TOUCHPAPER
TOUCHPAPERS
TOUCHSTONE
TOUCHSTONES
TOUCHTONES
TOUCHWOODS
TOUGHENERS
TOUGHENING
TOUGHENINGS
TOUGHNESSES
TOURBILLION
TOURBILLIONS
TOURBILLON
TOURBILLONS
TOURISTICALLY
TOURMALINE
TOURMALINES
TOURMALINIC
TOURNAMENT
TOURNAMENTS
TOURNEYERS
TOURNEYING
TOURNIQUET
TOURNIQUETS
TOURTIERES
TOVARICHES
TOVARISCHES
TOVARISHES
TOWARDLINESS
TOWARDLINESSES
TOWARDNESS
TOWARDNESSES
TOWELETTES
TOWELHEADS
TOWELLINGS
TOWERINGLY
TOWNHOUSES
TOWNSCAPED
TOWNSCAPES
TOWNSCAPING
TOWNSCAPINGS
TOWNSFOLKS
TOWNSPEOPLE

TOWNSPEOPLES
TOWNSWOMAN
TOWNSWOMEN
TOXALBUMIN
TOXALBUMINS
TOXAPHENES
TOXICATION
TOXICATIONS
TOXICITIES
TOXICOGENIC
TOXICOLOGIC
TOXICOLOGICAL
TOXICOLOGICALLY
TOXICOLOGIES
TOXICOLOGIST
TOXICOLOGISTS
TOXICOLOGY
TOXICOMANIA
TOXICOMANIAS
TOXICOPHAGOUS
TOXICOPHOBIA
TOXICOPHOBIAS
TOXIGENICITIES
TOXIGENICITY
TOXIPHAGOUS
TOXIPHOBIA
TOXIPHOBIAC
TOXIPHOBIACS
TOXIPHOBIAS
TOXOCARIASES
TOXOCARIASIS
TOXOPHILIES
TOXOPHILITE
TOXOPHILITES
TOXOPHILITIC
TOXOPLASMA
TOXOPLASMAS
TOXOPLASMIC
TOXOPLASMOSES
TOXOPLASMOSIS
TOYISHNESS
TOYISHNESSES
TRABEATION
TRABEATIONS
TRABECULAE
TRABECULAR
TRABECULAS
TRABECULATE
TRABECULATED
TRACASSERIE
TRACASSERIES
TRACEABILITIES
TRACEABILITY
TRACEABLENESS
TRACEABLENESSES
TRACELESSLY
TRACHEARIAN
TRACHEARIANS
TRACHEARIES
TRACHEATED
TRACHEATES
TRACHEIDAL
TRACHEIDES
TRACHEITIS
TRACHEITISES
TRACHELATE
TRACHEOLAR
TRACHEOLES
TRACHEOPHYTE
TRACHEOPHYTES
TRACHEOSCOPIES
TRACHEOSCOPY
TRACHEOSTOMIES
TRACHEOSTOMY
TRACHEOTOMIES
TRACHEOTOMY
TRACHINUSES
TRACHITISES
TRACHOMATOUS
TRACHYPTERUS
TRACHYPTERUSES
TRACHYTOID
TRACKBALLS

TRACKERBALL
TRACKERBALLS
TRACKLAYER
TRACKLAYERS
TRACKLAYING
TRACKLAYINGS
TRACKLEMENT
TRACKLEMENTS
TRACKLESSLY
TRACKLESSNESS
TRACKLESSNESSES
TRACKROADS
TRACKSIDES
TRACKSUITS
TRACKWALKER
TRACKWALKERS
TRACTABILITIES
TRACTABILITY
TRACTABLENESS
TRACTABLENESSES
TRACTARIAN
TRACTARIANS
TRACTATORS
TRACTILITIES
TRACTILITY
TRACTIONAL
TRACTORATION
TRACTORATIONS
TRACTORFEED
TRACTORFEEDS
TRACTRICES
TRADECRAFT
TRADECRAFTS
TRADEMARKED
TRADEMARKING
TRADEMARKS
TRADENAMES
TRADERSHIP
TRADERSHIPS
TRADESCANTIA
TRADESCANTIAS
TRADESFOLK
TRADESFOLKS
TRADESMANLIKE
TRADESPEOPLE
TRADESPEOPLES
TRADESWOMAN
TRADESWOMEN
TRADITIONAL
TRADITIONALISE
TRADITIONALISED
TRADITIONALISES
TRADITIONALISM
TRADITIONALISMS
TRADITIONALIST
TRADITIONALISTS
TRADITIONALITY
TRADITIONALIZE
TRADITIONALIZED
TRADITIONALIZES
TRADITIONALLY
TRADITIONARILY
TRADITIONARY
TRADITIONER
TRADITIONERS
TRADITIONIST
TRADITIONISTS
TRADITIONLESS
TRADITIONS
TRADITORES
TRADUCEMENT
TRADUCEMENTS
TRADUCIANISM
TRADUCIANISMS
TRADUCIANIST
TRADUCIANISTIC
TRADUCIANISTS
TRADUCIANS
TRADUCIBLE
TRADUCINGLY
TRADUCINGS
TRADUCTION
TRADUCTIONS

TRADUCTIVE
TRAFFICABILITY
TRAFFICABLE
TRAFFICATOR
TRAFFICATORS
TRAFFICKED
TRAFFICKER
TRAFFICKERS
TRAFFICKING
TRAFFICKINGS
TRAFFICLESS
TRAGACANTH
TRAGACANTHS
TRAGEDIANS
TRAGEDIENNE
TRAGEDIENNES
TRAGELAPHINE
TRAGELAPHS
TRAGICALLY
TRAGICALNESS
TRAGICALNESSES
TRAGICOMEDIES
TRAGICOMEDY
TRAGICOMIC
TRAGICOMICAL
TRAGICOMICALLY
TRAILBASTON
TRAILBASTONS
TRAILBLAZER
TRAILBLAZERS
TRAILBLAZING
TRAILBLAZINGS
TRAILBREAKER
TRAILBREAKERS
TRAILERABLE
TRAILERING
TRAILERINGS
TRAILERIST
TRAILERISTS
TRAILERITE
TRAILERITES
TRAILHEADS
TRAILINGLY
TRAINABILITIES
TRAINABILITY
TRAINBANDS
TRAINBEARER
TRAINBEARERS
TRAINEESHIP
TRAINEESHIPS
TRAINLOADS
TRAINSPOTTERISH
TRAIPSINGS
TRAITORESS
TRAITORESSES
TRAITORHOOD
TRAITORHOODS
TRAITORISM
TRAITORISMS
TRAITOROUS
TRAITOROUSLY
TRAITOROUSNESS
TRAITORSHIP
TRAITORSHIPS
TRAITRESSES
TRAJECTILE
TRAJECTING
TRAJECTION
TRAJECTIONS
TRAJECTORIES
TRAJECTORY
TRALATICIOUS
TRALATITIOUS
TRAMELLING
TRAMMELERS
TRAMMELING
TRAMMELLED
TRAMMELLER
TRAMMELLERS
TRAMMELLING
TRAMONTANA
TRAMONTANAS
TRAMONTANE

TRAMONTANES
TRAMPETTES
TRAMPLINGS
TRAMPOLINE
TRAMPOLINED
TRAMPOLINER
TRAMPOLINERS
TRAMPOLINES
TRAMPOLINING
TRAMPOLININGS
TRAMPOLINIST
TRAMPOLINISTS
TRAMPOLINS
TRANCELIKE
TRANQUILER
TRANQUILEST
TRANQUILISATION
TRANQUILISE
TRANQUILISED
TRANQUILISER
TRANQUILISERS
TRANQUILISES
TRANQUILISING
TRANQUILISINGLY
TRANQUILITIES
TRANQUILITY
TRANQUILIZATION
TRANQUILIZE
TRANQUILIZED
TRANQUILIZER
TRANQUILIZERS
TRANQUILIZES
TRANQUILIZING
TRANQUILIZINGLY
TRANQUILLER
TRANQUILLEST
TRANQUILLISE
TRANQUILLISED
TRANQUILLISER
TRANQUILLISERS
TRANQUILLISES
TRANQUILLISING
TRANQUILLITIES
TRANQUILLITY
TRANQUILLIZE
TRANQUILLIZED
TRANQUILLIZER
TRANQUILLIZERS
TRANQUILLIZES
TRANQUILLIZING
TRANQUILLY
TRANQUILNESS
TRANQUILNESSES
TRANSACTED
TRANSACTING
TRANSACTINIDE
TRANSACTINIDES
TRANSACTION
TRANSACTIONAL
TRANSACTIONALLY
TRANSACTIONS
TRANSACTOR
TRANSACTORS
TRANSALPINE
TRANSALPINES
TRANSAMINASE
TRANSAMINASES
TRANSAMINATION
TRANSAMINATIONS
TRANSANDEAN
TRANSANDINE
TRANSATLANTIC
TRANSAXLES
TRANSCALENCIES
TRANSCALENCY
TRANSCALENT
TRANSCAUCASIAN
TRANSCEIVER
TRANSCEIVERS
TRANSCENDED
TRANSCENDENCE
TRANSCENDENCES
TRANSCENDENCIES

TRANSCENDENCY	TRANSFIGURED	TRANSILIENCIES	TRANSMIGRATION	TRANSPIRING	TRANSURANIAN
TRANSCENDENT	TRANSFIGUREMENT	TRANSILIENCY	TRANSMIGRATIONS	TRANSPLACENTAL	TRANSURANIC
TRANSCENDENTAL	TRANSFIGURES	TRANSILIENT	TRANSMIGRATIVE	TRANSPLANT	TRANSURANICS
TRANSCENDENTALS	TRANSFIGURING	TRANSILLUMINATE	TRANSMIGRATOR	TRANSPLANTABLE	TRANSURANIUM
TRANSCENDENTLY	TRANSFINITE	TRANSISTHMIAN	TRANSMIGRATORS	TRANSPLANTATION	TRANSVAGINAL
TRANSCENDENTS	TRANSFIXED	TRANSISTOR	TRANSMIGRATORY	TRANSPLANTED	TRANSVALUATE
TRANSCENDING	TRANSFIXES	TRANSISTORISE	TRANSMISSIBLE	TRANSPLANTER	TRANSVALUATED
TRANSCENDINGLY	TRANSFIXING	TRANSISTORISED	TRANSMISSION	TRANSPLANTERS	TRANSVALUATES
TRANSCENDS	TRANSFIXION	TRANSISTORISES	TRANSMISSIONAL	TRANSPLANTING	TRANSVALUATING
TRANSCRANIAL	TRANSFIXIONS	TRANSISTORISING	TRANSMISSIONS	TRANSPLANTINGS	TRANSVALUATION
TRANSCRIBABLE	TRANSFORMABLE	TRANSISTORIZE	TRANSMISSIVE	TRANSPLANTS	TRANSVALUATIONS
TRANSCRIBE	TRANSFORMATION	TRANSISTORIZED	TRANSMISSIVELY	TRANSPOLAR	TRANSVALUE
TRANSCRIBED	TRANSFORMATIONS	TRANSISTORIZES	TRANSMISSIVITY	TRANSPONDER	TRANSVALUED
TRANSCRIBER	TRANSFORMATIVE	TRANSISTORIZING	TRANSMISSOMETER	TRANSPONDERS	TRANSVALUER
TRANSCRIBERS	TRANSFORMED	TRANSISTORS	TRANSMITTABLE	TRANSPONDOR	TRANSVALUERS
TRANSCRIBES	TRANSFORMER	TRANSITABLE	TRANSMITTAL	TRANSPONDORS	TRANSVALUES
TRANSCRIBING	TRANSFORMERS	TRANSITING	TRANSMITTALS	TRANSPONTINE	TRANSVALUING
TRANSCRIPT	TRANSFORMING	TRANSITION	TRANSMITTANCE	TRANSPORTABLE	TRANSVERSAL
TRANSCRIPTASE	TRANSFORMINGS	TRANSITIONAL	TRANSMITTANCES	TRANSPORTAL	TRANSVERSALITY
TRANSCRIPTASES	TRANSFORMISM	TRANSITIONALLY	TRANSMITTANCIES	TRANSPORTALS	TRANSVERSALLY
TRANSCRIPTION	TRANSFORMISMS	TRANSITIONALS	TRANSMITTANCY	TRANSPORTANCE	TRANSVERSALS
TRANSCRIPTIONAL	TRANSFORMIST	TRANSITIONARY	TRANSMITTED	TRANSPORTANCES	TRANSVERSE
TRANSCRIPTIONS	TRANSFORMISTIC	TRANSITIONS	TRANSMITTER	TRANSPORTATION	TRANSVERSED
TRANSCRIPTIVE	TRANSFORMISTS	TRANSITIVE	TRANSMITTERS	TRANSPORTATIONS	TRANSVERSELY
TRANSCRIPTIVELY	TRANSFORMS	TRANSITIVELY	TRANSMITTIBLE	TRANSPORTED	TRANSVERSENESS
TRANSCRIPTS	TRANSFUSABLE	TRANSITIVENESS	TRANSMITTING	TRANSPORTEDLY	TRANSVERSES
TRANSCULTURAL	TRANSFUSED	TRANSITIVES	TRANSMITTIVITY	TRANSPORTEDNESS	TRANSVERSING
TRANSCURRENT	TRANSFUSER	TRANSITIVITIES	TRANSMOGRIFIED	TRANSPORTER	TRANSVERSION
TRANSCUTANEOUS	TRANSFUSERS	TRANSITIVITY	TRANSMOGRIFIES	TRANSPORTERS	TRANSVERSIONS
TRANSDERMAL	TRANSFUSES	TRANSITORILY	TRANSMOGRIFY	TRANSPORTING	TRANSVERTER
TRANSDUCED	TRANSFUSIBLE	TRANSITORINESS	TRANSMOGRIFYING	TRANSPORTINGLY	TRANSVERTERS
TRANSDUCER	TRANSFUSING	TRANSITORY	TRANSMONTANE	TRANSPORTINGS	TRANSVESTED
TRANSDUCERS	TRANSFUSION	TRANSLATABILITY	TRANSMONTANES	TRANSPORTIVE	TRANSVESTIC
TRANSDUCES	TRANSFUSIONAL	TRANSLATABLE	TRANSMOUNTAIN	TRANSPORTS	TRANSVESTING
TRANSDUCING	TRANSFUSIONIST	TRANSLATED	TRANSMOVED	TRANSPOSABILITY	TRANSVESTISM
TRANSDUCTANT	TRANSFUSIONISTS	TRANSLATES	TRANSMOVES	TRANSPOSABLE	TRANSVESTISMS
TRANSDUCTANTS	TRANSFUSIONS	TRANSLATING	TRANSMOVING	TRANSPOSAL	TRANSVESTIST
TRANSDUCTION	TRANSFUSIVE	TRANSLATION	TRANSMUNDANE	TRANSPOSALS	TRANSVESTISTS
TRANSDUCTIONAL	TRANSFUSIVELY	TRANSLATIONAL	TRANSMUTABILITY	TRANSPOSED	TRANSVESTITE
TRANSDUCTIONS	TRANSGENDER	TRANSLATIONALLY	TRANSMUTABLE	TRANSPOSER	TRANSVESTITES
TRANSDUCTOR	TRANSGENDERED	TRANSLATIONS	TRANSMUTABLY	TRANSPOSERS	TRANSVESTITISM
TRANSDUCTORS	TRANSGENDERS	TRANSLATIVE	TRANSMUTATION	TRANSPOSES	TRANSVESTITISMS
TRANSECTED	TRANSGENES	TRANSLATIVES	TRANSMUTATIONAL	TRANSPOSING	TRANSVESTS
TRANSECTING	TRANSGENESES	TRANSLATOR	TRANSMUTATIONS	TRANSPOSINGS	TRAPANNERS
TRANSECTION	TRANSGENESIS	TRANSLATORIAL	TRANSMUTATIVE	TRANSPOSITION	TRAPANNING
TRANSECTIONS	TRANSGENIC	TRANSLATORS	TRANSMUTED	TRANSPOSITIONAL	TRAPESINGS
TRANSENNAS	TRANSGENICS	TRANSLATORY	TRANSMUTER	TRANSPOSITIONS	TRAPEZIFORM
TRANSEPTAL	TRANSGRESS	TRANSLEITHAN	TRANSMUTERS	TRANSPOSITIVE	TRAPEZISTS
TRANSEPTATE	TRANSGRESSED	TRANSLITERATE	TRANSMUTES	TRANSPOSON	TRAPEZIUMS
TRANSEXUAL	TRANSGRESSES	TRANSLITERATED	TRANSMUTING	TRANSPOSONS	TRAPEZIUSES
TRANSEXUALISM	TRANSGRESSING	TRANSLITERATES	TRANSNATIONAL	TRANSPUTER	TRAPEZOHEDRA
TRANSEXUALISMS	TRANSGRESSION	TRANSLITERATING	TRANSNATURAL	TRANSPUTERS	TRAPEZOHEDRAL
TRANSEXUALS	TRANSGRESSIONAL	TRANSLITERATION	TRANSOCEANIC	TRANSSEXUAL	TRAPEZOHEDRON
TRANSFECTED	TRANSGRESSIONS	TRANSLITERATOR	TRANSONICS	TRANSSEXUALISM	TRAPEZOHEDRONS
TRANSFECTING	TRANSGRESSIVE	TRANSLITERATORS	TRANSPACIFIC	TRANSSEXUALISMS	TRAPEZOIDAL
TRANSFECTION	TRANSGRESSIVELY	TRANSLOCATE	TRANSPADANE	TRANSSEXUALITY	TRAPEZOIDS
TRANSFECTIONS	TRANSGRESSOR	TRANSLOCATED	TRANSPARENCE	TRANSSEXUALS	TRAPNESTED
TRANSFECTS	TRANSGRESSORS	TRANSLOCATES	TRANSPARENCES	TRANSSHAPE	TRAPNESTING
TRANSFERABILITY	TRANSHIPMENT	TRANSLOCATING	TRANSPARENCIES	TRANSSHAPED	TRAPPINESS
TRANSFERABLE	TRANSHIPMENTS	TRANSLOCATION	TRANSPARENCY	TRANSSHAPES	TRAPPINESSES
TRANSFERAL	TRANSHIPPED	TRANSLOCATIONS	TRANSPARENT	TRANSSHAPING	TRAPSHOOTER
TRANSFERALS	TRANSHIPPER	TRANSLUCENCE	TRANSPARENTISE	TRANSSHIPMENT	TRAPSHOOTERS
TRANSFERASE	TRANSHIPPERS	TRANSLUCENCES	TRANSPARENTISED	TRANSSHIPMENTS	TRAPSHOOTING
TRANSFERASES	TRANSHIPPING	TRANSLUCENCIES	TRANSPARENTISES	TRANSSHIPPED	TRAPSHOOTINGS
TRANSFEREE	TRANSHIPPINGS	TRANSLUCENCY	TRANSPARENTIZE	TRANSSHIPPER	TRASHERIES
TRANSFEREES	TRANSHISTORICAL	TRANSLUCENT	TRANSPARENTIZED	TRANSSHIPPERS	TRASHINESS
TRANSFERENCE	TRANSHUMANCE	TRANSLUCENTLY	TRANSPARENTIZES	TRANSSHIPPING	TRASHINESSES
TRANSFERENCES	TRANSHUMANCES	TRANSLUCID	TRANSPARENTLY	TRANSSHIPPINGS	TRASHTRIES
TRANSFERENTIAL	TRANSHUMANT	TRANSLUCIDITIES	TRANSPARENTNESS	TRANSSHIPS	TRATTORIAS
TRANSFEROR	TRANSHUMANTS	TRANSLUCIDITY	TRANSPERSONAL	TRANSSONIC	TRAUCHLING
TRANSFERORS	TRANSHUMED	TRANSLUNAR	TRANSPICUOUS	TRANSTHORACIC	TRAUMATICALLY
TRANSFERRABLE	TRANSHUMES	TRANSLUNARY	TRANSPICUOUSLY	TRANSUBSTANTIAL	TRAUMATISATION
TRANSFERRAL	TRANSHUMING	TRANSMANCHE	TRANSPIERCE	TRANSUDATE	TRAUMATISATIONS
TRANSFERRALS	TRANSIENCE	TRANSMARINE	TRANSPIERCED	TRANSUDATES	TRAUMATISE
TRANSFERRED	TRANSIENCES	TRANSMEMBRANE	TRANSPIERCES	TRANSUDATION	TRAUMATISED
TRANSFERRER	TRANSIENCIES	TRANSMEWED	TRANSPIERCING	TRANSUDATIONS	TRAUMATISES
TRANSFERRERS	TRANSIENCY	TRANSMEWING	TRANSPIRABLE	TRANSUDATORY	TRAUMATISING
TRANSFERRIBLE	TRANSIENTLY	TRANSMIGRANT	TRANSPIRATION	TRANSUDING	TRAUMATISM
TRANSFERRIN	TRANSIENTNESS	TRANSMIGRANTS	TRANSPIRATIONAL	TRANSUMING	TRAUMATISMS
TRANSFERRING	TRANSIENTNESSES	TRANSMIGRATE	TRANSPIRATIONS	TRANSUMPTION	TRAUMATIZATION
TRANSFERRINS	TRANSIENTS	TRANSMIGRATED	TRANSPIRATORY	TRANSUMPTIONS	TRAUMATIZATIONS
TRANSFIGURATION	TRANSILIENCE	TRANSMIGRATES	TRANSPIRED	TRANSUMPTIVE	TRAUMATIZE
TRANSFIGURE	TRANSILIENCES	TRANSMIGRATING	TRANSPIRES	TRANSUMPTS	TRAUMATIZED

t

TRAUMATIZES
TRAUMATIZING
TRAUMATOLOGICAL
TRAUMATOLOGIES
TRAUMATOLOGY
TRAUMATONASTIES
TRAUMATONASTY
TRAVAILING
TRAVELATOR
TRAVELATORS
TRAVELINGS
TRAVELLERS
TRAVELLING
TRAVELLINGS
TRAVELOGUE
TRAVELOGUES
TRAVERSABLE
TRAVERSALS
TRAVERSERS
TRAVERSING
TRAVERSINGS
TRAVERTINE
TRAVERTINES
TRAVERTINS
TRAVESTIED
TRAVESTIES
TRAVESTYING
TRAVOLATOR
TRAVOLATORS
TRAWLERMAN
TRAWLERMEN
TRAYMOBILE
TRAYMOBILES
TRAZODONES
TREACHERER
TREACHERERS
TREACHERIES
TREACHEROUS
TREACHEROUSLY
TREACHEROUSNESS
TREACHETOUR
TREACHETOURS
TREACHOURS
TREACLIEST
TREACLINESS
TREACLINESSES
TREADLINGS
TREADMILLS
TREADWHEEL
TREADWHEELS
TREASONABLE
TREASONABLENESS
TREASONABLY
TREASONOUS
TREASURABLE
TREASURELESS
TREASURERS
TREASURERSHIP
TREASURERSHIPS
TREASURIES
TREASURING
TREATABILITIES
TREATABILITY
TREATMENTS
TREATYLESS
TREBBIANOS
TREBLENESS
TREBLENESSES
TREBUCHETS
TREBUCKETS
TRECENTIST
TRECENTISTS
TREDECILLION
TREDECILLIONS
TREDRILLES
TREEHOPPER
TREEHOPPERS
TREEHOUSES
TREELESSNESS
TREELESSNESSES
TREENWARES
TREGETOURS
TREHALOSES

TREILLAGED
TREILLAGES
TREKSCHUIT
TREKSCHUITS
TRELLISING
TRELLISWORK
TRELLISWORKS
TREMATODES
TREMATOIDS
TREMBLEMENT
TREMBLEMENTS
TREMBLIEST
TREMBLINGLY
TREMBLINGS
TREMENDOUS
TREMENDOUSLY
TREMENDOUSNESS
TREMOLANDI
TREMOLANDO
TREMOLANDOS
TREMOLANTS
TREMOLITES
TREMOLITIC
TREMORLESS
TREMULANTS
TREMULATED
TREMULATES
TREMULATING
TREMULOUSLY
TREMULOUSNESS
TREMULOUSNESSES
TRENCHANCIES
TRENCHANCY
TRENCHANTLY
TRENCHARDS
TRENCHERMAN
TRENCHERMEN
TRENDIFIED
TRENDIFIES
TRENDIFYING
TRENDINESS
TRENDINESSES
TRENDSETTER
TRENDSETTERS
TRENDSETTING
TRENDSETTINGS
TRENDYISMS
TREPANATION
TREPANATIONS
TREPANNERS
TREPANNING
TREPANNINGS
TREPHINATION
TREPHINATIONS
TREPHINERS
TREPHINING
TREPHININGS
TREPIDATION
TREPIDATIONS
TREPIDATORY
TREPONEMAL
TREPONEMAS
TREPONEMATA
TREPONEMATOSES
TREPONEMATOSIS
TREPONEMATOUS
TREPONEMES
TRESPASSED
TRESPASSER
TRESPASSERS
TRESPASSES
TRESPASSING
TRESTLETREE
TRESTLETREES
TRESTLEWORK
TRESTLEWORKS
TREVALLIES
TRIABLENESS
TRIABLENESSES
TRIACETATE
TRIACETATES
TRIACONTER

TRIACONTERS
TRIACTINAL
TRIADELPHOUS
TRIADICALLY
TRIALITIES
TRIALLINGS
TRIALLISTS
TRIALOGUES
TRIALWARES
TRIAMCINOLONE
TRIAMCINOLONES
TRIANDRIAN
TRIANDROUS
TRIANGULAR
TRIANGULARITIES
TRIANGULARITY
TRIANGULARLY
TRIANGULATE
TRIANGULATED
TRIANGULATELY
TRIANGULATES
TRIANGULATING
TRIANGULATION
TRIANGULATIONS
TRIAPSIDAL
TRIARCHIES
TRIATHLETE
TRIATHLETES
TRIATHLONS
TRIATOMICALLY
TRIAXIALITIES
TRIAXIALITY
TRIBADISMS
TRIBALISMS
TRIBALISTIC
TRIBALISTS
TRIBESPEOPLE
TRIBESWOMAN
TRIBESWOMEN
TRIBOELECTRIC
TRIBOLOGICAL
TRIBOLOGIES
TRIBOLOGIST
TRIBOLOGISTS
TRIBOMETER
TRIBOMETERS
TRIBRACHIAL
TRIBRACHIC
TRIBROMOETHANOL
TRIBROMOMETHANE
TRIBULATED
TRIBULATES
TRIBULATING
TRIBULATION
TRIBULATIONS
TRIBUNATES
TRIBUNESHIP
TRIBUNESHIPS
TRIBUNICIAL
TRIBUNICIAN
TRIBUNITIAL
TRIBUNITIAN
TRIBUTARIES
TRIBUTARILY
TRIBUTARINESS
TRIBUTARINESSES
TRICAMERAL
TRICARBOXYLIC
TRICARPELLARY
TRICENTENARIES
TRICENTENARY
TRICENTENNIAL
TRICENTENNIALS
TRICEPHALOUS
TRICERATOPS
TRICERATOPSES
TRICERIONS
TRICHIASES
TRICHIASIS
TRICHINELLA
TRICHINELLAE
TRICHINELLAS
TRICHINIASES

TRICHINIASIS
TRICHINISATION
TRICHINISATIONS
TRICHINISE
TRICHINISED
TRICHINISES
TRICHINISING
TRICHINIZATION
TRICHINIZATIONS
TRICHINIZE
TRICHINIZED
TRICHINIZES
TRICHINIZING
TRICHINOSE
TRICHINOSED
TRICHINOSES
TRICHINOSING
TRICHINOSIS
TRICHINOTIC
TRICHINOUS
TRICHLORACETIC
TRICHLORFON
TRICHLORFONS
TRICHLORIDE
TRICHLORIDES
TRICHLOROACETIC
TRICHLOROETHANE
TRICHLORPHON
TRICHLORPHONS
TRICHOBACTERIA
TRICHOCYST
TRICHOCYSTIC
TRICHOCYSTS
TRICHOGYNE
TRICHOGYNES
TRICHOGYNIAL
TRICHOGYNIC
TRICHOLOGICAL
TRICHOLOGIES
TRICHOLOGIST
TRICHOLOGISTS
TRICHOLOGY
TRICHOMONACIDAL
TRICHOMONACIDE
TRICHOMONACIDES
TRICHOMONAD
TRICHOMONADAL
TRICHOMONADS
TRICHOMONAL
TRICHOMONIASES
TRICHOMONIASIS
TRICHOPHYTON
TRICHOPHYTONS
TRICHOPHYTOSES
TRICHOPHYTOSIS
TRICHOPTERAN
TRICHOPTERANS
TRICHOPTERIST
TRICHOPTERISTS
TRICHOPTEROUS
TRICHOTHECENE
TRICHOTHECENES
TRICHOTOMIC
TRICHOTOMIES
TRICHOTOMISE
TRICHOTOMISED
TRICHOTOMISES
TRICHOTOMISING
TRICHOTOMIZE
TRICHOTOMIZED
TRICHOTOMIZES
TRICHOTOMIZING
TRICHOTOMOUS
TRICHOTOMOUSLY
TRICHOTOMY
TRICHROISM
TRICHROISMS
TRICHROMAT
TRICHROMATIC
TRICHROMATISM
TRICHROMATISMS
TRICHROMATS
TRICHROMIC

TRICHROMICS
TRICHRONOUS
TRICHURIASES
TRICHURIASIS
TRICKERIES
TRICKINESS
TRICKINESSES
TRICKISHLY
TRICKISHNESS
TRICKISHNESSES
TRICKLIEST
TRICKLINGLY
TRICKLINGS
TRICKSIEST
TRICKSINESS
TRICKSINESSES
TRICKSTERING
TRICKSTERINGS
TRICKSTERS
TRICKTRACK
TRICKTRACKS
TRICLINIUM
TRICLOSANS
TRICOLETTE
TRICOLETTES
TRICOLORED
TRICOLOURED
TRICOLOURS
TRICONSONANTAL
TRICONSONANTIC
TRICORNERED
TRICORPORATE
TRICORPORATED
TRICOSTATE
TRICOTEUSE
TRICOTEUSES
TRICOTINES
TRICROTISM
TRICROTISMS
TRICROTOUS
TRICUSPIDAL
TRICUSPIDATE
TRICUSPIDS
TRICYCLERS
TRICYCLICS
TRICYCLING
TRICYCLINGS
TRICYCLIST
TRICYCLISTS
TRIDACTYLOUS
TRIDENTATE
TRIDIMENSIONAL
TRIDOMINIA
TRIDOMINIUM
TRIDYMITES
TRIENNIALLY
TRIENNIALS
TRIENNIUMS
TRIERARCHAL
TRIERARCHIES
TRIERARCHS
TRIERARCHY
TRIETHYLAMINE
TRIETHYLAMINES
TRIFACIALS
TRIFARIOUS
TRIFFIDIAN
TRIFLINGLY
TRIFLINGNESS
TRIFLINGNESSES
TRIFLUOPERAZINE
TRIFLURALIN
TRIFLURALINS
TRIFOLIATE
TRIFOLIATED
TRIFOLIOLATE
TRIFOLIUMS
TRIFURCATE
TRIFURCATED
TRIFURCATES
TRIFURCATING
TRIFURCATION
TRIFURCATIONS

TRIGAMISTS
TRIGEMINAL
TRIGEMINALS
TRIGGERFISH
TRIGGERFISHES
TRIGGERING
TRIGGERLESS
TRIGGERMAN
TRIGGERMEN
TRIGLYCERIDE
TRIGLYCERIDES
TRIGLYPHIC
TRIGLYPHICAL
TRIGNESSES
TRIGONALLY
TRIGONOMETER
TRIGONOMETERS
TRIGONOMETRIC
TRIGONOMETRICAL
TRIGONOMETRIES
TRIGONOMETRY
TRIGRAMMATIC
TRIGRAMMIC
TRIGRAPHIC
TRIHALOMETHANE
TRIHALOMETHANES
TRIHEDRALS
TRIHEDRONS
TRIHYBRIDS
TRIHYDRATE
TRIHYDRATED
TRIHYDRATES
TRIHYDROXY
TRIIODOMETHANE
TRIIODOMETHANES
TRILATERAL
TRILATERALISM
TRILATERALISMS
TRILATERALIST
TRILATERALISTS
TRILATERALLY
TRILATERALS
TRILATERATION
TRILATERATIONS
TRILINEATE
TRILINGUAL
TRILINGUALISM
TRILINGUALISMS
TRILINGUALLY
TRILITERAL
TRILITERALISM
TRILITERALISMS
TRILITERALS
TRILITHONS
TRILLIONAIRE
TRILLIONAIRES
TRILLIONTH
TRILLIONTHS
TRILOBATED
TRILOBITES
TRILOBITIC
TRILOCULAR
TRIMERISMS
TRIMESTERS
TRIMESTRAL
TRIMESTRIAL
TRIMETHADIONE
TRIMETHADIONES
TRIMETHOPRIM
TRIMETHOPRIMS
TRIMETHYLAMINE
TRIMETHYLAMINES
TRIMETHYLENE
TRIMETHYLENES
TRIMETRICAL
TRIMETROGON
TRIMETROGONS
TRIMMINGLY
TRIMNESSES
TRIMOLECULAR
TRIMONTHLY
TRIMORPHIC
TRIMORPHISM

TRIMORPHISMS	TRIPTEROUS	TRITURATES	TROLLEYING	TROPOTAXIS	TRUSTBUSTER
TRIMORPHOUS	TRIPTYQUES	TRITURATING	TROLLIUSES	TROTHPLIGHT	TRUSTBUSTERS
TRINACRIAN	TRIPUDIARY	TRITURATION	TROLLOPEES	TROTHPLIGHTED	TRUSTBUSTING
TRINACRIFORM	TRIPUDIATE	TRITURATIONS	TROLLOPING	TROTHPLIGHTING	TRUSTBUSTINGS
TRINISCOPE	TRIPUDIATED	TRITURATOR	TROLLOPISH	TROTHPLIGHTS	TRUSTEEING
TRINISCOPES	TRIPUDIATES	TRITURATORS	TROMBICULID	TROUBADOUR	TRUSTEESHIP
TRINITARIAN	TRIPUDIATING	TRIUMPHALISM	TROMBICULIDS	TROUBADOURS	TRUSTEESHIPS
TRINITRATE	TRIPUDIATION	TRIUMPHALISMS	TROMBIDIASES	TROUBLEDLY	TRUSTFULLY
TRINITRATES	TRIPUDIATIONS	TRIUMPHALIST	TROMBIDIASIS	TROUBLEFREE	TRUSTFULNESS
TRINITRINS	TRIPUDIUMS	TRIUMPHALISTS	TROMBONIST	TROUBLEMAKER	TRUSTFULNESSES
TRINITROBENZENE	TRIQUETRAL	TRIUMPHALS	TROMBONISTS	TROUBLEMAKERS	TRUSTINESS
TRINITROCRESOL	TRIQUETRAS	TRIUMPHANT	TROMOMETER	TROUBLEMAKING	TRUSTINESSES
TRINITROCRESOLS	TRIQUETROUS	TRIUMPHANTLY	TROMOMETERS	TROUBLEMAKINGS	TRUSTINGLY
TRINITROPHENOL	TRIQUETROUSLY	TRIUMPHERIES	TROMOMETRIC	TROUBLESHOOT	TRUSTINGNESS
TRINITROPHENOLS	TRIQUETRUM	TRIUMPHERS	TROOPSHIPS	TROUBLESHOOTER	TRUSTINGNESSES
TRINITROTOLUENE	TRIRADIATE	TRIUMPHERY	TROOSTITES	TROUBLESHOOTERS	TRUSTLESSLY
TRINITROTOLUOL	TRIRADIATELY	TRIUMPHING	TROPAEOLIN	TROUBLESHOOTING	TRUSTLESSNESS
TRINITROTOLUOLS	TRISACCHARIDE	TRIUMPHINGS	TROPAEOLINS	TROUBLESHOOTS	TRUSTLESSNESSES
TRINKETERS	TRISACCHARIDES	TRIUMVIRAL	TROPAEOLUM	TROUBLESHOT	TRUSTWORTHILY
TRINKETING	TRISAGIONS	TRIUMVIRATE	TROPAEOLUMS	TROUBLESOME	TRUSTWORTHINESS
TRINKETINGS	TRISECTING	TRIUMVIRATES	TROPEOLINS	TROUBLESOMELY	TRUSTWORTHY
TRINKETRIES	TRISECTION	TRIUMVIRIES	TROPHALLACTIC	TROUBLESOMENESS	TRUTHFULLY
TRINOCULAR	TRISECTIONS	TRIUNITIES	TROPHALLAXES	TROUBLINGS	TRUTHFULNESS
TRINOMIALISM	TRISECTORS	TRIVALENCE	TROPHALLAXIS	TROUBLOUSLY	TRUTHFULNESSES
TRINOMIALISMS	TRISECTRICES	TRIVALENCES	TROPHESIAL	TROUBLOUSNESS	TRUTHLESSNESS
TRINOMIALIST	TRISECTRIX	TRIVALENCIES	TROPHESIES	TROUBLOUSNESSES	TRUTHLESSNESSES
TRINOMIALISTS	TRISKELION	TRIVALENCY	TROPHICALLY	TROUGHLIKE	TRYINGNESS
TRINOMIALLY	TRISKELIONS	TRIVALVULAR	TROPHOBIOSES	TROUNCINGS	TRYINGNESSES
TRINOMIALS	TRISOCTAHEDRA	TRIVIALISATION	TROPHOBIOSIS	TROUSERING	TRYPAFLAVINE
TRINUCLEOTIDE	TRISOCTAHEDRAL	TRIVIALISATIONS	TROPHOBIOTIC	TROUSERINGS	TRYPAFLAVINES
TRINUCLEOTIDES	TRISOCTAHEDRON	TRIVIALISE	TROPHOBLAST	TROUSERLESS	TRYPANOCIDAL
TRIOECIOUS	TRISOCTAHEDRONS	TRIVIALISED	TROPHOBLASTIC	TROUSSEAUS	TRYPANOCIDE
TRIOXOBORIC	TRISTEARIN	TRIVIALISES	TROPHOBLASTS	TROUSSEAUX	TRYPANOCIDES
TRIOXYGENS	TRISTEARINS	TRIVIALISING	TROPHOLOGIES	TROUTLINGS	TRYPANOSOMAL
TRIPALMITIN	TRISTESSES	TRIVIALISM	TROPHOLOGY	TROUTSTONE	TRYPANOSOME
TRIPALMITINS	TRISTFULLY	TRIVIALISMS	TROPHONEUROSES	TROUTSTONES	TRYPANOSOMES
TRIPARTISM	TRISTFULNESS	TRIVIALIST	TROPHONEUROSIS	TROUVAILLE	TRYPANOSOMIASES
TRIPARTISMS	TRISTFULNESSES	TRIVIALISTS	TROPHOPLASM	TROUVAILLES	TRYPANOSOMIASIS
TRIPARTITE	TRISTICHIC	TRIVIALITIES	TROPHOPLASMS	TROWELLERS	TRYPANOSOMIC
TRIPARTITELY	TRISTICHOUS	TRIVIALITY	TROPHOTACTIC	TROWELLING	TRYPARSAMIDE
TRIPARTITION	TRISTIMULUS	TRIVIALIZATION	TROPHOTAXES	TRUANTRIES	TRYPARSAMIDES
TRIPARTITIONS	TRISUBSTITUTED	TRIVIALIZATIONS	TROPHOTAXIS	TRUANTSHIP	TRYPSINOGEN
TRIPEHOUND	TRISULCATE	TRIVIALIZE	TROPHOTROPIC	TRUANTSHIPS	TRYPSINOGENS
TRIPEHOUNDS	TRISULFIDE	TRIVIALIZED	TROPHOTROPISM	TRUCKLINES	TRYPTAMINE
TRIPERSONAL	TRISULFIDES	TRIVIALIZES	TROPHOTROPISMS	TRUCKLINGS	TRYPTAMINES
TRIPERSONALISM	TRISULPHIDE	TRIVIALIZING	TROPHOZOITE	TRUCKLOADS	TRYPTOPHAN
TRIPERSONALISMS	TRISULPHIDES	TRIVIALNESS	TROPHOZOITES	TRUCKMASTER	TRYPTOPHANE
TRIPERSONALIST	TRISYLLABIC	TRIVIALNESSES	TROPICALISATION	TRUCKMASTERS	TRYPTOPHANES
TRIPERSONALISTS	TRISYLLABICAL	TRIWEEKLIES	TROPICALISE	TRUCKSTOPS	TRYPTOPHANS
TRIPERSONALITY	TRISYLLABICALLY	TROCHAICALLY	TROPICALISED	TRUCULENCE	TSAREVICHES
TRIPETALOUS	TRISYLLABLE	TROCHANTER	TROPICALISES	TRUCULENCES	TSAREVITCH
TRIPHAMMER	TRISYLLABLES	TROCHANTERAL	TROPICALISING	TRUCULENCIES	TSAREVITCHES
TRIPHAMMERS	TRITAGONIST	TROCHANTERIC	TROPICALITIES	TRUCULENCY	TSCHERNOSEM
TRIPHENYLAMINE	TRITAGONISTS	TROCHANTERS	TROPICALITY	TRUCULENTLY	TSCHERNOSEMS
TRIPHENYLAMINES	TRITANOPIA	TROCHEAMETER	TROPICALIZATION	TRUEHEARTED	TSESAREVICH
TRIPHIBIOUS	TRITANOPIAS	TROCHEAMETERS	TROPICALIZE	TRUEHEARTEDNESS	TSESAREVICHES
TRIPHOSPHATE	TRITANOPIC	TROCHELMINTH	TROPICALIZED	TRUENESSES	TSESAREVITCH
TRIPHOSPHATES	TRITENESSES	TROCHELMINTHS	TROPICALIZES	TRUEPENNIES	TSESAREVITCHES
TRIPHTHONG	TRITERNATE	TROCHILUSES	TROPICALIZING	TRUFFLINGS	TSESAREVNA
TRIPHTHONGAL	TRITHEISMS	TROCHISCUS	TROPICALLY	TRUMPERIES	TSESAREVNAS
TRIPHTHONGS	TRITHEISTIC	TROCHISCUSES	TROPICBIRD	TRUMPETERS	TSESAREWICH
TRIPHYLITE	TRITHEISTICAL	TROCHLEARS	TROPICBIRDS	TRUMPETING	TSESAREWICHES
TRIPHYLITES	TRITHEISTS	TROCHOIDAL	TROPISMATIC	TRUMPETINGS	TSESAREWITCH
TRIPHYLLOUS	TRITHIONATE	TROCHOIDALLY	TROPOCOLLAGEN	TRUMPETLIKE	TSESAREWITCHES
TRIPINNATE	TRITHIONATES	TROCHOMETER	TROPOCOLLAGENS	TRUMPETWEED	TSOTSITAAL
TRIPINNATELY	TRITHIONIC	TROCHOMETERS	TROPOLOGIC	TRUMPETWEEDS	TSOTSITAALS
TRIPITAKAS	TRITIATING	TROCHOPHORE	TROPOLOGICAL	TRUNCATELY	TSUTSUGAMUSHI
TRIPLENESS	TRITIATION	TROCHOPHORES	TROPOLOGICALLY	TRUNCATING	TSUTSUGAMUSHIS
TRIPLENESSES	TRITIATIONS	TROCHOSPHERE	TROPOLOGIES	TRUNCATION	TUBBINESSES
TRIPLETAIL	TRITICALES	TROCHOSPHERES	TROPOMYOSIN	TRUNCATIONS	TUBECTOMIES
TRIPLETAILS	TRITICALLY	TROCHOTRON	TROPOMYOSINS	TRUNCHEONED	TUBERACEOUS
TRIPLICATE	TRITICALNESS	TROCHOTRONS	TROPOPAUSE	TRUNCHEONER	TUBERCULAR
TRIPLICATED	TRITICALNESSES	TROCTOLITE	TROPOPAUSES	TRUNCHEONERS	TUBERCULARLY
TRIPLICATES	TRITICEOUS	TROCTOLITES	TROPOPHILOUS	TRUNCHEONING	TUBERCULARS
TRIPLICATING	TRITICISMS	TROGLODYTE	TROPOPHYTE	TRUNCHEONS	TUBERCULATE
TRIPLICATION	TRITUBERCULAR	TROGLODYTES	TROPOPHYTES	TRUNKFISHES	TUBERCULATED
TRIPLICATIONS	TRITUBERCULATE	TROGLODYTIC	TROPOPHYTIC	TRUNKSLEEVE	TUBERCULATELY
TRIPLICITIES	TRITUBERCULIES	TROGLODYTICAL	TROPOSCATTER	TRUNKSLEEVES	TUBERCULATION
TRIPLICITY	TRITUBERCULISM	TROGLODYTISM	TROPOSCATTERS	TRUNNIONED	TUBERCULATIONS
TRIPLOBLASTIC	TRITUBERCULISMS	TROGLODYTISMS	TROPOSPHERE	TRUSTABILITIES	TUBERCULES
TRIPLOIDIES	TRITUBERCULY	TROLLEYBUS	TROPOSPHERES	TRUSTABILITY	TUBERCULIN
TRIPPERISH	TRITURABLE	TROLLEYBUSES	TROPOSPHERIC	TRUSTAFARIAN	TUBERCULINS
TRIPPINGLY	TRITURATED	TROLLEYBUSSES	TROPOTAXES	TRUSTAFARIANS	TUBERCULISATION

t

TUBERCULISE
TUBERCULISED
TUBERCULISES
TUBERCULISING
TUBERCULIZATION
TUBERCULIZE
TUBERCULIZED
TUBERCULIZES
TUBERCULIZING
TUBERCULOID
TUBERCULOMA
TUBERCULOMAS
TUBERCULOMATA
TUBERCULOSE
TUBERCULOSED
TUBERCULOSES
TUBERCULOSIS
TUBERCULOUS
TUBERCULOUSLY
TUBERCULUM
TUBERIFEROUS
TUBERIFORM
TUBEROSITIES
TUBEROSITY
TUBICOLOUS
TUBIFICIDS
TUBIFLOROUS
TUBOCURARINE
TUBOCURARINES
TUBOPLASTIES
TUBOPLASTY
TUBULARIAN
TUBULARIANS
TUBULARITIES
TUBULARITY
TUBULATING
TUBULATION
TUBULATIONS
TUBULATORS
TUBULATURE
TUBULATURES
TUBULIFLORAL
TUBULIFLOROUS
TUBULOUSLY
TUCKERBAGS
TUCKERBOXES
TUFFACEOUS
TUFFTAFFETA
TUFFTAFFETAS
TUFFTAFFETIES
TUFFTAFFETY
TUFTAFFETA
TUFTAFFETAS
TUFTAFFETIES
TUFTAFFETY
TUILLETTES
TUILYIEING
TUILZIEING
TUITIONARY
TULARAEMIA
TULARAEMIAS
TULARAEMIC

TULAREMIAS
TULIPOMANIA
TULIPOMANIAS
TULIPWOODS
TUMATAKURU
TUMBLEBUGS
TUMBLEDOWN
TUMBLEHOME
TUMBLEHOMES
TUMBLERFUL
TUMBLERFULS
TUMBLERSFUL
TUMBLESETS
TUMBLEWEED
TUMBLEWEEDS
TUMEFACIENT
TUMEFACTION
TUMEFACTIONS
TUMESCENCE
TUMESCENCES
TUMIDITIES
TUMIDNESSES
TUMORGENIC
TUMORGENICITIES
TUMORGENICITY
TUMORIGENESES
TUMORIGENESIS
TUMORIGENIC
TUMORIGENICITY
TUMULOSITIES
TUMULOSITY
TUMULTUARY
TUMULTUATE
TUMULTUATED
TUMULTUATES
TUMULTUATING
TUMULTUATION
TUMULTUATIONS
TUMULTUOUS
TUMULTUOUSLY
TUMULTUOUSNESS
TUNABILITIES
TUNABILITY
TUNABLENESS
TUNABLENESSES
TUNBELLIED
TUNBELLIES
TUNEFULNESS
TUNEFULNESSES
TUNELESSLY
TUNELESSNESS
TUNELESSNESSES
TUNESMITHS
TUNGSTATES
TUNGSTITES
TUNNELINGS
TUNNELLERS
TUNNELLIKE
TUNNELLING
TUNNELLINGS
TUPPENNIES
TURACOVERDIN

TURACOVERDINS
TURANGAWAEWAE
TURANGAWAEWAES
TURBELLARIAN
TURBELLARIANS
TURBIDIMETER
TURBIDIMETERS
TURBIDIMETRIC
TURBIDIMETRIES
TURBIDIMETRY
TURBIDITES
TURBIDITIES
TURBIDNESS
TURBIDNESSES
TURBINACIOUS
TURBINATED
TURBINATES
TURBINATION
TURBINATIONS
TURBOCHARGED
TURBOCHARGER
TURBOCHARGERS
TURBOCHARGING
TURBOCHARGINGS
TURBOELECTRIC
TURBOGENERATOR
TURBOGENERATORS
TURBOMACHINERY
TURBOPROPS
TURBOSHAFT
TURBOSHAFTS
TURBULATOR
TURBULATORS
TURBULENCE
TURBULENCES
TURBULENCIES
TURBULENCY
TURBULENTLY
TURCOPOLES
TURCOPOLIER
TURCOPOLIERS
TURFGRASSES
TURFINESSES
TURFSKIING
TURFSKIINGS
TURGENCIES
TURGESCENCE
TURGESCENCES
TURGESCENCIES
TURGESCENCY
TURGESCENT
TURGIDITIES
TURGIDNESS
TURGIDNESSES
TURMOILING
TURNABOUTS
TURNAGAINS
TURNAROUND
TURNAROUNDS
TURNBROACH
TURNBROACHES
TURNBUCKLE

TURNBUCKLES
TURNROUNDS
TURNSTILES
TURNSTONES
TURNTABLES
TURNVEREIN
TURNVEREINS
TUROPHILES
TURPENTINE
TURPENTINED
TURPENTINES
TURPENTINING
TURPENTINY
TURPITUDES
TURQUOISES
TURRIBANTS
TURRICULATE
TURRICULATED
TURTLEBACK
TURTLEBACKS
TURTLEDOVE
TURTLEDOVES
TURTLEHEAD
TURTLEHEADS
TURTLENECK
TURTLENECKED
TURTLENECKS
TUTELARIES
TUTIORISMS
TUTIORISTS
TUTORESSES
TUTORIALLY
TUTORISING
TUTORIZING
TUTORSHIPS
TUTOYERING
TUTWORKERS
TUTWORKMAN
TUTWORKMEN
TWADDLIEST
TWADDLINGS
TWALPENNIES
TWANGINGLY
TWANGLINGLY
TWANGLINGS
TWATTLINGS
TWAYBLADES
TWEEDINESS
TWEEDINESSES
TWEEDLEDEE
TWEEDLEDEED
TWEEDLEDEEING
TWEEDLEDEES
TWEENAGERS
TWEENESSES
TWELVEFOLD
TWELVEMONTH
TWELVEMONTHS
TWENTIETHS
TWENTYFOLD
TWENTYFOLDS
TWICHILDREN

TWIDDLIEST
TWIDDLINGS
TWILIGHTED
TWILIGHTING
TWINBERRIES
TWINFLOWER
TWINFLOWERS
TWINKLINGS
TWISTABILITIES
TWISTABILITY
TWITCHIEST
TWITCHINGS
TWITTERERS
TWITTERING
TWITTERINGLY
TWITTERINGS
TWITTINGLY
TWOFOLDNESS
TWOFOLDNESSES
TWOPENCEWORTH
TWOPENCEWORTHS
TWOPENNIES
TWOSEATERS
TYCOONATES
TYCOONERIES
TYLECTOMIES
TYMPANIFORM
TYMPANISTS
TYMPANITES
TYMPANITESES
TYMPANITIC
TYMPANITIS
TYMPANITISES
TYNDALLIMETRIES
TYNDALLIMETRY
TYPECASTER
TYPECASTERS
TYPECASTING
TYPEFOUNDER
TYPEFOUNDERS
TYPEFOUNDING
TYPEFOUNDINGS
TYPESCRIPT
TYPESCRIPTS
TYPESETTER
TYPESETTERS
TYPESETTING
TYPESETTINGS
TYPESTYLES
TYPEWRITER
TYPEWRITERS
TYPEWRITES
TYPEWRITING
TYPEWRITINGS
TYPEWRITTEN
TYPHACEOUS
TYPHLITISES
TYPHLOLOGIES
TYPHLOLOGY
TYPHLOSOLE
TYPHLOSOLES
TYPHOGENIC

TYPHOIDINS
TYPICALITIES
TYPICALITY
TYPICALNESS
TYPICALNESSES
TYPIFICATION
TYPIFICATIONS
TYPOGRAPHED
TYPOGRAPHER
TYPOGRAPHERS
TYPOGRAPHIA
TYPOGRAPHIC
TYPOGRAPHICAL
TYPOGRAPHICALLY
TYPOGRAPHIES
TYPOGRAPHING
TYPOGRAPHIST
TYPOGRAPHISTS
TYPOGRAPHS
TYPOGRAPHY
TYPOLOGICAL
TYPOLOGICALLY
TYPOLOGIES
TYPOLOGIST
TYPOLOGISTS
TYPOMANIAS
TYPOTHETAE
TYRANNESSES
TYRANNICAL
TYRANNICALLY
TYRANNICALNESS
TYRANNICIDAL
TYRANNICIDE
TYRANNICIDES
TYRANNISED
TYRANNISER
TYRANNISERS
TYRANNISES
TYRANNISING
TYRANNIZED
TYRANNIZER
TYRANNIZERS
TYRANNIZES
TYRANNIZING
TYRANNOSAUR
TYRANNOSAURS
TYRANNOSAURUS
TYRANNOSAURUSES
TYRANNOUSLY
TYRANNOUSNESS
TYRANNOUSNESSES
TYROCIDINE
TYROCIDINES
TYROCIDINS
TYROGLYPHID
TYROGLYPHIDS
TYROPITTAS
TYROSINASE
TYROSINASES
TYROTHRICIN
TYROTHRICINS

t

Section 2: Words between 10 and 15 letters in length

Uu

UBIQUARIAN
UBIQUINONE
UBIQUINONES
UBIQUITARIAN
UBIQUITARIANISM
UBIQUITARIANS
UBIQUITARY
UBIQUITIES
UBIQUITINATION
UBIQUITINATIONS
UBIQUITINS
UBIQUITOUS
UBIQUITOUSLY
UBIQUITOUSNESS
UDOMETRIES
UFOLOGICAL
UFOLOGISTS
UGLIFICATION
UGLIFICATIONS
UGLINESSES
UGSOMENESS
UGSOMENESSES
UINTAHITES
UINTATHERE
UINTATHERES
UITLANDERS
ULCERATING
ULCERATION
ULCERATIONS
ULCERATIVE
ULCEROGENIC
ULCEROUSLY
ULCEROUSNESS
ULCEROUSNESSES
ULOTRICHIES
ULOTRICHOUS
ULSTERETTE
ULSTERETTES
ULTERIORLY
ULTIMACIES
ULTIMATELY
ULTIMATENESS
ULTIMATENESSES
ULTIMATING
ULTIMATUMS
ULTIMOGENITURE
ULTIMOGENITURES
ULTRABASIC
ULTRABASICS
ULTRACAREFUL
ULTRACASUAL
ULTRACAUTIOUS
ULTRACENTRIFUGE
ULTRACIVILISED
ULTRACIVILIZED
ULTRACLEAN
ULTRACOMMERCIAL
ULTRACOMPACT
ULTRACOMPETENT
ULTRACONVENIENT
ULTRACREPIDATE
ULTRACREPIDATED
ULTRACREPIDATES
ULTRACRITICAL
ULTRADEMOCRATIC
ULTRADENSE
ULTRADISTANCE

ULTRADISTANT
ULTRAEFFICIENT
ULTRAENERGETIC
ULTRAEXCLUSIVE
ULTRAFAMILIAR
ULTRAFASTIDIOUS
ULTRAFEMININE
ULTRAFICHE
ULTRAFICHES
ULTRAFILTER
ULTRAFILTERED
ULTRAFILTERING
ULTRAFILTERS
ULTRAFILTRATE
ULTRAFILTRATES
ULTRAFILTRATION
ULTRAGLAMOROUS
ULTRAHAZARDOUS
ULTRAHEATED
ULTRAHEATING
ULTRAHEATS
ULTRAHEAVY
ULTRAHUMAN
ULTRAISTIC
ULTRALARGE
ULTRALEFTISM
ULTRALEFTISMS
ULTRALEFTIST
ULTRALEFTISTS
ULTRALIBERAL
ULTRALIBERALISM
ULTRALIBERALS
ULTRALIGHT
ULTRALIGHTS
ULTRAMAFIC
ULTRAMARATHON
ULTRAMARATHONER
ULTRAMARATHONS
ULTRAMARINE
ULTRAMARINES
ULTRAMASCULINE
ULTRAMICRO
ULTRAMICROMETER
ULTRAMICROSCOPE
ULTRAMICROSCOPY
ULTRAMICROTOME
ULTRAMICROTOMES
ULTRAMICROTOMY
ULTRAMILITANT
ULTRAMILITANTS
ULTRAMINIATURE
ULTRAMODERN
ULTRAMODERNISM
ULTRAMODERNISMS
ULTRAMODERNIST
ULTRAMODERNISTS
ULTRAMONTANE
ULTRAMONTANES
ULTRAMONTANISM
ULTRAMONTANISMS
ULTRAMONTANIST
ULTRAMONTANISTS
ULTRAMUNDANE
ULTRANATIONAL
ULTRAORTHODOX
ULTRAPATRIOTIC
ULTRAPHYSICAL

ULTRAPOWERFUL
ULTRAPRACTICAL
ULTRAPRECISE
ULTRAPRECISION
ULTRAQUIET
ULTRARADICAL
ULTRARADICALS
ULTRARAPID
ULTRARAREFIED
ULTRARATIONAL
ULTRAREALISM
ULTRAREALISMS
ULTRAREALIST
ULTRAREALISTIC
ULTRAREALISTS
ULTRAREFINED
ULTRARELIABLE
ULTRARIGHT
ULTRARIGHTIST
ULTRARIGHTISTS
ULTRAROMANTIC
ULTRAROYALIST
ULTRAROYALISTS
ULTRASECRET
ULTRASENSITIVE
ULTRASENSUAL
ULTRASERIOUS
ULTRASHARP
ULTRASHORT
ULTRASIMPLE
ULTRASLICK
ULTRASMALL
ULTRASMART
ULTRASMOOTH
ULTRASONIC
ULTRASONICALLY
ULTRASONICS
ULTRASONOGRAPHY
ULTRASOUND
ULTRASOUNDS
ULTRASTRUCTURAL
ULTRASTRUCTURE
ULTRASTRUCTURES
ULTRAVACUA
ULTRAVACUUM
ULTRAVACUUMS
ULTRAVIOLENCE
ULTRAVIOLENCES
ULTRAVIOLENT
ULTRAVIOLET
ULTRAVIOLETS
ULTRAVIRILE
ULTRAVIRILITIES
ULTRAVIRILITY
ULTRAVIRUS
ULTRAVIRUSES
ULTRAWIDEBAND
ULTRAWIDEBANDS
ULTRONEOUS
ULTRONEOUSLY
ULTRONEOUSNESS
ULULATIONS
UMBELLATED
UMBELLATELY
UMBELLIFER
UMBELLIFEROUS
UMBELLIFERS

UMBELLULATE
UMBELLULES
UMBILICALLY
UMBILICALS
UMBILICATE
UMBILICATED
UMBILICATION
UMBILICATIONS
UMBILICUSES
UMBILIFORM
UMBONATION
UMBONATIONS
UMBRACULATE
UMBRACULIFORM
UMBRACULUM
UMBRAGEOUS
UMBRAGEOUSLY
UMBRAGEOUSNESS
UMBRATICAL
UMBRATILOUS
UMBRELLAED
UMBRELLAING
UMBRELLOES
UMBRIFEROUS
UMPIRESHIP
UMPIRESHIPS
UMPTEENTHS
UNABASHEDLY
UNABATEDLY
UNABBREVIATED
UNABOLISHED
UNABRIDGED
UNABROGATED
UNABSOLVED
UNABSORBED
UNABSORBENT
UNACADEMIC
UNACADEMICALLY
UNACCENTED
UNACCENTUATED
UNACCEPTABILITY
UNACCEPTABLE
UNACCEPTABLY
UNACCEPTANCE
UNACCEPTANCES
UNACCEPTED
UNACCLIMATED
UNACCLIMATISED
UNACCLIMATIZED
UNACCOMMODATED
UNACCOMMODATING
UNACCOMPANIED
UNACCOMPLISHED
UNACCOUNTABLE
UNACCOUNTABLY
UNACCOUNTED
UNACCREDITED
UNACCULTURATED
UNACCUSABLE
UNACCUSABLY
UNACCUSTOMED
UNACCUSTOMEDLY
UNACHIEVABLE
UNACHIEVED
UNACKNOWLEDGED
UNACQUAINT
UNACQUAINTANCE

UNACQUAINTANCES
UNACQUAINTED
UNACTORISH
UNACTUATED
UNADAPTABLE
UNADDRESSED
UNADJUDICATED
UNADJUSTED
UNADMIRING
UNADMITTED
UNADMONISHED
UNADOPTABLE
UNADULTERATE
UNADULTERATED
UNADULTERATEDLY
UNADVENTROUS
UNADVENTUROUS
UNADVERTISED
UNADVISABLE
UNADVISABLENESS
UNADVISABLY
UNADVISEDLY
UNADVISEDNESS
UNADVISEDNESSES
UNAESTHETIC
UNAFFECTED
UNAFFECTEDLY
UNAFFECTEDNESS
UNAFFECTING
UNAFFECTIONATE
UNAFFILIATED
UNAFFLUENT
UNAFFORDABLE
UNAGGRESSIVE
UNAGREEABLE
UNALIENABLE
UNALIENABLY
UNALIENATED
UNALLEVIATED
UNALLOCATED
UNALLOTTED
UNALLOWABLE
UNALLURING
UNALTERABILITY
UNALTERABLE
UNALTERABLENESS
UNALTERABLY
UNALTERING
UNAMBIGUOUS
UNAMBIGUOUSLY
UNAMBITIOUS
UNAMBITIOUSLY
UNAMBIVALENT
UNAMBIVALENTLY
UNAMENABLE
UNAMENDABLE
UNAMIABILITIES
UNAMIABILITY
UNAMIABLENESS
UNAMIABLENESSES
UNAMORTISED
UNAMORTIZED
UNAMPLIFIED
UNAMUSABLE
UNAMUSINGLY
UNANALYSABLE
UNANALYSED

UNANALYTIC
UNANALYTICAL
UNANALYZABLE
UNANALYZED
UNANCHORED
UNANCHORING
UNANESTHETISED
UNANESTHETIZED
UNANIMATED
UNANIMITIES
UNANIMOUSLY
UNANIMOUSNESS
UNANIMOUSNESSES
UNANNEALED
UNANNOTATED
UNANNOUNCED
UNANSWERABILITY
UNANSWERABLE
UNANSWERABLY
UNANSWERED
UNANTICIPATED
UNANTICIPATEDLY
UNAPOLOGETIC
UNAPOLOGISING
UNAPOLOGIZING
UNAPOSTOLIC
UNAPOSTOLICAL
UNAPOSTOLICALLY
UNAPPALLED
UNAPPARELLED
UNAPPARELLING
UNAPPARELS
UNAPPARENT
UNAPPEALABLE
UNAPPEALABLY
UNAPPEALING
UNAPPEALINGLY
UNAPPEASABLE
UNAPPEASABLY
UNAPPEASED
UNAPPETISING
UNAPPETISINGLY
UNAPPETIZING
UNAPPETIZINGLY
UNAPPLAUSIVE
UNAPPLICABLE
UNAPPOINTED
UNAPPRECIATED
UNAPPRECIATION
UNAPPRECIATIONS
UNAPPRECIATIVE
UNAPPREHENDED
UNAPPREHENSIBLE
UNAPPREHENSIVE
UNAPPRISED
UNAPPROACHABLE
UNAPPROACHABLY
UNAPPROACHED
UNAPPROPRIATE
UNAPPROPRIATED
UNAPPROVED
UNAPPROVING
UNAPPROVINGLY
UNAPTNESSES
UNARGUABLE
UNARGUABLY
UNARMOURED

UNARRANGED	UNAWARENESSES	UNBIASSEDNESS	UNBUREAUCRATIC	UNCHARITABLE	UNCLEANEST
UNARROGANT	UNBAILABLE	UNBIASSEDNESSES	UNBURNABLE	UNCHARITABLY	UNCLEANLIER
UNARTFULLY	UNBALANCED	UNBIASSING	UNBURNISHED	UNCHARITIES	UNCLEANLIEST
UNARTICULATE	UNBALANCES	UNBIBLICAL	UNBURROWED	UNCHARMING	UNCLEANLINESS
UNARTICULATED	UNBALANCING	UNBINDINGS	UNBURROWING	UNCHARNELLED	UNCLEANLINESSES
UNARTIFICIAL	UNBALLASTED	UNBIRTHDAY	UNBURTHENED	UNCHARNELLING	UNCLEANNESS
UNARTIFICIALLY	UNBANDAGED	UNBIRTHDAYS	UNBURTHENING	UNCHARNELS	UNCLEANNESSES
UNARTISTIC	UNBANDAGES	UNBISHOPED	UNBURTHENS	UNCHARTERED	UNCLEANSED
UNARTISTLIKE	UNBANDAGING	UNBISHOPING	UNBUSINESSLIKE	UNCHASTELY	UNCLEAREST
UNASCENDABLE	UNBAPTISED	UNBLAMABLE	UNBUTTERED	UNCHASTENED	UNCLEARNESS
UNASCENDED	UNBAPTISES	UNBLAMABLY	UNBUTTONED	UNCHASTENESS	UNCLEARNESSES
UNASCENDIBLE	UNBAPTISING	UNBLAMEABLE	UNBUTTONING	UNCHASTENESSES	UNCLENCHED
UNASCERTAINABLE	UNBAPTIZED	UNBLAMEABLY	UNCALCIFIED	UNCHASTEST	UNCLENCHES
UNASCERTAINED	UNBAPTIZES	UNBLEACHED	UNCALCINED	UNCHASTISABLE	UNCLENCHING
UNASHAMEDLY	UNBAPTIZING	UNBLEMISHED	UNCALCULATED	UNCHASTISED	UNCLERICAL
UNASHAMEDNESS	UNBARBERED	UNBLENCHED	UNCALCULATING	UNCHASTITIES	UNCLESHIPS
UNASHAMEDNESSES	UNBARRICADE	UNBLENCHING	UNCALIBRATED	UNCHASTITY	UNCLIMBABLE
UNASPIRATED	UNBARRICADED	UNBLESSEDNESS	UNCALLOUSED	UNCHASTIZABLE	UNCLIMBABLENESS
UNASPIRING	UNBARRICADES	UNBLESSEDNESSES	UNCANCELED	UNCHASTIZED	UNCLINCHED
UNASPIRINGLY	UNBARRICADING	UNBLESSING	UNCANDIDLY	UNCHAUVINISTIC	UNCLINCHES
UNASPIRINGNESS	UNBATTERED	UNBLINDFOLD	UNCANDIDNESS	UNCHECKABLE	UNCLINCHING
UNASSAILABILITY	UNBEARABLE	UNBLINDFOLDED	UNCANDIDNESSES	UNCHECKING	UNCLIPPING
UNASSAILABLE	UNBEARABLENESS	UNBLINDFOLDING	UNCANDOURS	UNCHEERFUL	UNCLOAKING
UNASSAILABLY	UNBEARABLY	UNBLINDFOLDS	UNCANNIEST	UNCHEERFULLY	UNCLOGGING
UNASSAILED	UNBEATABLE	UNBLINDING	UNCANNINESS	UNCHEERFULNESS	UNCLOISTER
UNASSEMBLED	UNBEATABLY	UNBLINKING	UNCANNINESSES	UNCHEWABLE	UNCLOISTERED
UNASSERTIVE	UNBEAUTIFUL	UNBLINKINGLY	UNCANONICAL	UNCHILDING	UNCLOISTERING
UNASSERTIVELY	UNBEAUTIFULLY	UNBLISSFUL	UNCANONICALNESS	UNCHILDLIKE	UNCLOISTERS
UNASSIGNABLE	UNBEAVERED	UNBLOCKING	UNCANONISE	UNCHIVALROUS	UNCLOTHING
UNASSIGNED	UNBECOMING	UNBLOODIED	UNCANONISED	UNCHIVALROUSLY	UNCLOUDEDLY
UNASSIMILABLE	UNBECOMINGLY	UNBLUSHING	UNCANONISES	UNCHLORINATED	UNCLOUDEDNESS
UNASSIMILATED	UNBECOMINGNESS	UNBLUSHINGLY	UNCANONISING	UNCHOREOGRAPHED	UNCLOUDEDNESSES
UNASSISTED	UNBECOMINGS	UNBLUSHINGNESS	UNCANONIZE	UNCHRISTEN	UNCLOUDING
UNASSISTEDLY	UNBEDIMMED	UNBOASTFUL	UNCANONIZED	UNCHRISTENED	UNCLUBABLE
UNASSISTING	UNBEDINNED	UNBONNETED	UNCANONIZES	UNCHRISTENING	UNCLUBBABLE
UNASSOCIATED	UNBEFITTING	UNBONNETING	UNCANONIZING	UNCHRISTENS	UNCLUTCHED
UNASSUAGEABLE	UNBEFRIENDED	UNBORROWED	UNCAPITALISED	UNCHRISTIAN	UNCLUTCHES
UNASSUAGED	UNBEGETTING	UNBOSOMERS	UNCAPITALIZED	UNCHRISTIANED	UNCLUTCHING
UNASSUMING	UNBEGINNING	UNBOSOMING	UNCAPSIZABLE	UNCHRISTIANING	UNCLUTTERED
UNASSUMINGLY	UNBEGOTTEN	UNBOTTLING	UNCAPTIONED	UNCHRISTIANISE	UNCLUTTERING
UNASSUMINGNESS	UNBEGUILED	UNBOTTOMED	UNCAPTURABLE	UNCHRISTIANISED	UNCLUTTERS
UNATHLETIC	UNBEGUILES	UNBOUNDEDLY	UNCARPETED	UNCHRISTIANISES	UNCOALESCE
UNATONABLE	UNBEGUILING	UNBOUNDEDNESS	UNCASTRATED	UNCHRISTIANIZE	UNCOALESCED
UNATTACHED	UNBEHOLDEN	UNBOUNDEDNESSES	UNCATALOGED	UNCHRISTIANIZED	UNCOALESCES
UNATTAINABLE	UNBEKNOWNST	UNBOWDLERISED	UNCATALOGUED	UNCHRISTIANIZES	UNCOALESCING
UNATTAINABLY	UNBELIEVABILITY	UNBOWDLERIZED	UNCATCHABLE	UNCHRISTIANLIKE	UNCOATINGS
UNATTAINTED	UNBELIEVABLE	UNBRACKETED	UNCATEGORISABLE	UNCHRISTIANLY	UNCODIFIED
UNATTEMPTED	UNBELIEVABLY	UNBRAIDING	UNCATEGORIZABLE	UNCHRISTIANS	UNCOERCIVE
UNATTENDED	UNBELIEVED	UNBRANCHED	UNCEASINGLY	UNCHRONICLED	UNCOERCIVELY
UNATTENDING	UNBELIEVER	UNBREACHABLE	UNCEASINGNESS	UNCHRONOLOGICAL	UNCOFFINED
UNATTENTIVE	UNBELIEVERS	UNBREACHED	UNCEASINGNESSES	UNCHURCHED	UNCOFFINING
UNATTENUATED	UNBELIEVES	UNBREAKABLE	UNCELEBRATED	UNCHURCHES	UNCOLLECTED
UNATTESTED	UNBELIEVING	UNBREATHABLE	UNCENSORED	UNCHURCHING	UNCOLLECTIBLE
UNATTRACTIVE	UNBELIEVINGLY	UNBREATHED	UNCENSORIOUS	UNCHURCHLY	UNCOLLECTIBLES
UNATTRACTIVELY	UNBELIEVINGNESS	UNBREATHING	UNCENSURED	UNCILIATED	UNCOLOURED
UNATTRIBUTABLE	UNBELLIGERENT	UNBREECHED	UNCEREBRAL	UNCINARIAS	UNCOMATABLE
UNATTRIBUTED	UNBENDABLE	UNBREECHES	UNCEREMONIOUS	UNCINARIASES	UNCOMBATIVE
UNAUGMENTED	UNBENDINGLY	UNBREECHING	UNCEREMONIOUSLY	UNCINARIASIS	UNCOMBINED
UNAUSPICIOUS	UNBENDINGNESS	UNBRIBABLE	UNCERTAINLY	UNCINEMATIC	UNCOMBINES
UNAUTHENTIC	UNBENDINGNESSES	UNBRIDGEABLE	UNCERTAINNESS	UNCIPHERED	UNCOMBINING
UNAUTHENTICATED	UNBENDINGS	UNBRIDLEDLY	UNCERTAINNESSES	UNCIPHERING	UNCOMEATABLE
UNAUTHENTICITY	UNBENEFICED	UNBRIDLEDNESS	UNCERTAINTIES	UNCIRCULATED	UNCOMELINESS
UNAUTHORISED	UNBENEFICIAL	UNBRIDLEDNESSES	UNCERTAINTY	UNCIRCUMCISED	UNCOMELINESSES
UNAUTHORITATIVE	UNBENEFITED	UNBRIDLING	UNCERTIFICATED	UNCIRCUMCISION	UNCOMFORTABLE
UNAUTHORIZED	UNBENIGHTED	UNBRILLIANT	UNCERTIFIED	UNCIRCUMCISIONS	UNCOMFORTABLY
UNAUTOMATED	UNBENIGNANT	UNBROKENLY	UNCHAINING	UNCIRCUMSCRIBED	UNCOMFORTED
UNAVAILABILITY	UNBENIGNLY	UNBROKENNESS	UNCHAIRING	UNCIVILISED	UNCOMMENDABLE
UNAVAILABLE	UNBESEEMED	UNBROKENNESSES	UNCHALLENGEABLE	UNCIVILISEDLY	UNCOMMENDABLY
UNAVAILABLENESS	UNBESEEMING	UNBROTHERLIKE	UNCHALLENGEABLY	UNCIVILISEDNESS	UNCOMMENDED
UNAVAILABLY	UNBESEEMINGLY	UNBROTHERLY	UNCHALLENGED	UNCIVILITIES	UNCOMMERCIAL
UNAVAILING	UNBESOUGHT	UNBUCKLING	UNCHALLENGING	UNCIVILITY	UNCOMMITTED
UNAVAILINGLY	UNBESPEAKING	UNBUDGEABLE	UNCHANCIER	UNCIVILIZED	UNCOMMONER
UNAVAILINGNESS	UNBESPEAKS	UNBUDGEABLY	UNCHANCIEST	UNCIVILIZEDLY	UNCOMMONEST
UNAVERTABLE	UNBESPOKEN	UNBUDGETED	UNCHANGEABILITY	UNCIVILIZEDNESS	UNCOMMONLY
UNAVERTIBLE	UNBESTOWED	UNBUDGINGLY	UNCHANGEABLE	UNCIVILNESS	UNCOMMONNESS
UNAVOIDABILITY	UNBETRAYED	UNBUFFERED	UNCHANGEABLY	UNCIVILNESSES	UNCOMMONNESSES
UNAVOIDABLE	UNBETTERABLE	UNBUILDABLE	UNCHANGING	UNCLAMPING	UNCOMMUNICABLE
UNAVOIDABLENESS	UNBETTERED	UNBUILDING	UNCHANGINGLY	UNCLARIFIED	UNCOMMUNICATED
UNAVOIDABLY	UNBEWAILED	UNBUNDLERS	UNCHANGINGNESS	UNCLARITIES	UNCOMMUNICATIVE
UNAVOWEDLY	UNBIASEDLY	UNBUNDLING	UNCHANNELED	UNCLASPING	UNCOMMUTED
UNAWAKENED	UNBIASEDNESS	UNBUNDLINGS	UNCHAPERONED	UNCLASSICAL	UNCOMPACTED
UNAWAKENING	UNBIASEDNESSES	UNBURDENED	UNCHARGING	UNCLASSIFIABLE	UNCOMPANIED
UNAWARENESS	UNBIASSEDLY	UNBURDENING	UNCHARISMATIC	UNCLASSIFIED	UNCOMPANIONABLE

UNCOMPANIONED	UNCONSCIOUSES	UNCRIPPLED	UNDELIVERABLE	UNDERBUSHING	UNDEREARTH
UNCOMPASSIONATE	UNCONSCIOUSLY	UNCRITICAL	UNDELIVERED	UNDERBUYING	UNDEREATEN
UNCOMPELLED	UNCONSCIOUSNESS	UNCRITICALLY	UNDEMANDING	UNDERCAPITALISE	UNDEREATING
UNCOMPELLING	UNCONSECRATE	UNCROSSABLE	UNDEMOCRATIC	UNDERCAPITALIZE	UNDEREDUCATED
UNCOMPENSATED	UNCONSECRATED	UNCROSSING	UNDEMONSTRABLE	UNDERCARDS	UNDEREMPHASES
UNCOMPETITIVE	UNCONSECRATES	UNCROWNING	UNDEMONSTRATIVE	UNDERCARRIAGE	UNDEREMPHASIS
UNCOMPLACENT	UNCONSECRATING	UNCRUMPLED	UNDENIABLE	UNDERCARRIAGES	UNDEREMPHASISE
UNCOMPLAINING	UNCONSENTANEOUS	UNCRUMPLES	UNDENIABLENESS	UNDERCARTS	UNDEREMPHASISED
UNCOMPLAININGLY	UNCONSENTING	UNCRUMPLING	UNDENIABLY	UNDERCASTS	UNDEREMPHASISES
UNCOMPLAISANT	UNCONSIDERED	UNCRUSHABLE	UNDEPENDABLE	UNDERCHARGE	UNDEREMPHASIZE
UNCOMPLAISANTLY	UNCONSIDERING	UNCRYSTALLISED	UNDEPENDING	UNDERCHARGED	UNDEREMPHASIZED
UNCOMPLETED	UNCONSOLED	UNCRYSTALLIZED	UNDEPLORED	UNDERCHARGES	UNDEREMPHASIZES
UNCOMPLIANT	UNCONSOLIDATED	UNCTIONLESS	UNDEPRAVED	UNDERCHARGING	UNDEREMPLOYED
UNCOMPLICATED	UNCONSTANT	UNCTUOSITIES	UNDEPRECIATED	UNDERCLASS	UNDEREMPLOYMENT
UNCOMPLIMENTARY	UNCONSTRAINABLE	UNCTUOSITY	UNDEPRESSED	UNDERCLASSES	UNDERESTIMATE
UNCOMPLYING	UNCONSTRAINED	UNCTUOUSLY	UNDEPRIVED	UNDERCLASSMAN	UNDERESTIMATED
UNCOMPOSABLE	UNCONSTRAINEDLY	UNCTUOUSNESS	UNDERACHIEVE	UNDERCLASSMEN	UNDERESTIMATES
UNCOMPOUNDED	UNCONSTRAINT	UNCTUOUSNESSES	UNDERACHIEVED	UNDERCLAYS	UNDERESTIMATING
UNCOMPREHENDED	UNCONSTRAINTS	UNCUCKOLDED	UNDERACHIEVER	UNDERCLIFF	UNDERESTIMATION
UNCOMPREHENDING	UNCONSTRICTED	UNCULTIVABLE	UNDERACHIEVERS	UNDERCLIFFS	UNDEREXPOSE
UNCOMPREHENSIVE	UNCONSTRUCTED	UNCULTIVATABLE	UNDERACHIEVES	UNDERCLOTHE	UNDEREXPOSED
UNCOMPROMISABLE	UNCONSTRUCTIVE	UNCULTIVATED	UNDERACHIEVING	UNDERCLOTHED	UNDEREXPOSES
UNCOMPROMISING	UNCONSUMED	UNCULTURED	UNDERACTED	UNDERCLOTHES	UNDEREXPOSING
UNCOMPUTERISED	UNCONSUMMATED	UNCUMBERED	UNDERACTING	UNDERCLOTHING	UNDEREXPOSURE
UNCOMPUTERIZED	UNCONTAINABLE	UNCURBABLE	UNDERACTION	UNDERCLOTHINGS	UNDEREXPOSURES
UNCONCEALABLE	UNCONTAMINATED	UNCURTAILED	UNDERACTIONS	UNDERCLUBBED	UNDERFEEDING
UNCONCEALED	UNCONTEMNED	UNCURTAINED	UNDERACTIVE	UNDERCLUBBING	UNDERFEEDS
UNCONCEALING	UNCONTEMPLATED	UNCURTAINING	UNDERACTIVITIES	UNDERCLUBS	UNDERFELTS
UNCONCEIVABLE	UNCONTEMPORARY	UNCURTAINS	UNDERACTIVITY	UNDERCOATED	UNDERFINANCED
UNCONCEIVABLY	UNCONTENTIOUS	UNCUSTOMARILY	UNDERACTOR	UNDERCOATING	UNDERFINISHED
UNCONCEIVED	UNCONTESTABLE	UNCUSTOMARY	UNDERACTORS	UNDERCOATINGS	UNDERFIRED
UNCONCERNED	UNCONTESTED	UNCUSTOMED	UNDERAGENT	UNDERCOATS	UNDERFIRES
UNCONCERNEDLY	UNCONTRACTED	UNCYNICALLY	UNDERAGENTS	UNDERCOOKED	UNDERFIRING
UNCONCERNEDNESS	UNCONTRADICTED	UNDANCEABLE	UNDERBAKED	UNDERCOOKING	UNDERFISHED
UNCONCERNING	UNCONTRIVED	UNDAUNTABLE	UNDERBAKES	UNDERCOOKS	UNDERFISHES
UNCONCERNMENT	UNCONTROLLABLE	UNDAUNTEDLY	UNDERBAKING	UNDERCOOLED	UNDERFISHING
UNCONCERNMENTS	UNCONTROLLABLY	UNDAUNTEDNESS	UNDERBEARER	UNDERCOOLING	UNDERFLOOR
UNCONCERNS	UNCONTROLLED	UNDAUNTEDNESSES	UNDERBEARERS	UNDERCOOLS	UNDERFLOWS
UNCONCERTED	UNCONTROLLEDLY	UNDAZZLING	UNDERBEARING	UNDERCOUNT	UNDERFONGED
UNCONCILIATORY	UNCONTROVERSIAL	UNDEBARRED	UNDERBEARINGS	UNDERCOUNTED	UNDERFONGING
UNCONCLUSIVE	UNCONTROVERTED	UNDEBATABLE	UNDERBEARS	UNDERCOUNTING	UNDERFONGS
UNCONCOCTED	UNCONVENTIONAL	UNDEBATABLY	UNDERBELLIES	UNDERCOUNTS	UNDERFOOTED
UNCONDITIONAL	UNCONVERSABLE	UNDEBAUCHED	UNDERBELLY	UNDERCOVER	UNDERFOOTING
UNCONDITIONALLY	UNCONVERSANT	UNDECADENT	UNDERBIDDER	UNDERCOVERT	UNDERFOOTS
UNCONDITIONED	UNCONVERTED	UNDECAGONS	UNDERBIDDERS	UNDERCOVERTS	UNDERFULFIL
UNCONFEDERATED	UNCONVERTIBLE	UNDECEIVABLE	UNDERBIDDING	UNDERCREST	UNDERFULFILLED
UNCONFESSED	UNCONVICTED	UNDECEIVED	UNDERBITES	UNDERCRESTED	UNDERFULFILLING
UNCONFINABLE	UNCONVINCED	UNDECEIVER	UNDERBITING	UNDERCRESTING	UNDERFULFILS
UNCONFINED	UNCONVINCING	UNDECEIVERS	UNDERBITTEN	UNDERCRESTS	UNDERFUNDED
UNCONFINEDLY	UNCONVINCINGLY	UNDECEIVES	UNDERBLANKET	UNDERCROFT	UNDERFUNDING
UNCONFINES	UNCONVOYED	UNDECEIVING	UNDERBLANKETS	UNDERCROFTS	UNDERFUNDINGS
UNCONFINING	UNCOOPERATIVE	UNDECIDABILITY	UNDERBODIES	UNDERCURRENT	UNDERFUNDS
UNCONFIRMED	UNCOOPERATIVELY	UNDECIDABLE	UNDERBORNE	UNDERCURRENTS	UNDERGARMENT
UNCONFORMABLE	UNCOORDINATED	UNDECIDEDLY	UNDERBOSSES	UNDERCUTTING	UNDERGARMENTS
UNCONFORMABLY	UNCOPYRIGHTABLE	UNDECIDEDNESS	UNDERBOUGH	UNDERDAMPER	UNDERGIRDED
UNCONFORMING	UNCOQUETTISH	UNDECIDEDNESSES	UNDERBOUGHS	UNDERDAMPERS	UNDERGIRDING
UNCONFORMITIES	UNCORRECTABLE	UNDECIDEDS	UNDERBOUGHT	UNDERDECKS	UNDERGIRDS
UNCONFORMITY	UNCORRECTED	UNDECILLION	UNDERBREATH	UNDERDEVELOP	UNDERGLAZE
UNCONFOUNDED	UNCORRELATED	UNDECILLIONS	UNDERBREATHS	UNDERDEVELOPED	UNDERGLAZES
UNCONFUSED	UNCORROBORATED	UNDECIMOLE	UNDERBREEDING	UNDERDEVELOPING	UNDERGOERS
UNCONFUSEDLY	UNCORRUPTED	UNDECIMOLES	UNDERBREEDINGS	UNDERDEVELOPS	UNDERGOING
UNCONFUSES	UNCORSETED	UNDECIPHERABLE	UNDERBRIDGE	UNDERDOERS	UNDERGOWNS
UNCONFUSING	UNCOUNSELLED	UNDECIPHERED	UNDERBRIDGES	UNDERDOING	UNDERGRADS
UNCONGEALED	UNCOUNTABLE	UNDECISIVE	UNDERBRIMS	UNDERDOSED	UNDERGRADUATE
UNCONGEALING	UNCOUPLERS	UNDECLARED	UNDERBRUSH	UNDERDOSES	UNDERGRADUATES
UNCONGEALS	UNCOUPLING	UNDECLINING	UNDERBRUSHED	UNDERDOSING	UNDERGRADUETTE
UNCONGENIAL	UNCOURAGEOUS	UNDECOMPOSABLE	UNDERBRUSHES	UNDERDRAIN	UNDERGRADUETTES
UNCONGENIALITY	UNCOURTEOUS	UNDECOMPOSED	UNDERBRUSHING	UNDERDRAINAGE	UNDERGROUND
UNCONJECTURED	UNCOURTLINESS	UNDECORATED	UNDERBUDDED	UNDERDRAINAGES	UNDERGROUNDER
UNCONJUGAL	UNCOURTLINESSES	UNDEDICATED	UNDERBUDDING	UNDERDRAINED	UNDERGROUNDERS
UNCONJUGATED	UNCOUTHEST	UNDEFEATED	UNDERBUDGET	UNDERDRAINING	UNDERGROUNDS
UNCONJUNCTIVE	UNCOUTHNESS	UNDEFENDED	UNDERBUDGETED	UNDERDRAINS	UNDERGROVE
UNCONNECTED	UNCOUTHNESSES	UNDEFINABLE	UNDERBUDGETING	UNDERDRAWERS	UNDERGROVES
UNCONNECTEDLY	UNCOVENANTED	UNDEFOLIATED	UNDERBUDGETS	UNDERDRAWING	UNDERGROWN
UNCONNECTEDNESS	UNCOVERING	UNDEFORMED	UNDERBUILD	UNDERDRAWINGS	UNDERGROWTH
UNCONNIVING	UNCREATEDNESS	UNDEIFYING	UNDERBUILDER	UNDERDRAWN	UNDERGROWTHS
UNCONQUERABLE	UNCREATEDNESSES	UNDELAYING	UNDERBUILDERS	UNDERDRAWS	UNDERHAIRS
UNCONQUERABLY	UNCREATING	UNDELECTABLE	UNDERBUILDING	UNDERDRESS	UNDERHANDED
UNCONQUERED	UNCREATIVE	UNDELEGATED	UNDERBUILDS	UNDERDRESSED	UNDERHANDEDLY
UNCONSCIENTIOUS	UNCREDENTIALED	UNDELIBERATE	UNDERBUILT	UNDERDRESSES	UNDERHANDEDNESS
UNCONSCIONABLE	UNCREDIBLE	UNDELIGHTED	UNDERBURNT	UNDERDRESSING	UNDERHANDS
UNCONSCIONABLY	UNCREDITABLE	UNDELIGHTFUL	UNDERBUSHED	UNDERDRIVE	UNDERHEATED
UNCONSCIOUS	UNCREDITED	UNDELIGHTS	UNDERBUSHES	UNDERDRIVES	UNDERHEATING

UNDERHEATS	UNDERPASSION	UNDERSECRETARY	UNDERSTUDIES	UNDERWORKS	UNDISCOURAGED
UNDERHONEST	UNDERPASSIONS	UNDERSELLER	UNDERSTUDY	UNDERWORLD	UNDISCOVERABLE
UNDERINFLATED	UNDERPAYING	UNDERSELLERS	UNDERSTUDYING	UNDERWORLDS	UNDISCOVERABLY
UNDERINFLATION	UNDERPAYMENT	UNDERSELLING	UNDERSUPPLIED	UNDERWRITE	UNDISCOVERED
UNDERINFLATIONS	UNDERPAYMENTS	UNDERSELLS	UNDERSUPPLIES	UNDERWRITER	UNDISCUSSABLE
UNDERINSURED	UNDERPEEPED	UNDERSELVES	UNDERSUPPLY	UNDERWRITERS	UNDISCUSSED
UNDERINVESTMENT	UNDERPEEPING	UNDERSENSE	UNDERSUPPLYING	UNDERWRITES	UNDISCUSSIBLE
UNDERJAWED	UNDERPEEPS	UNDERSENSES	UNDERSURFACE	UNDERWRITING	UNDISGUISABLE
UNDERKEEPER	UNDERPEOPLED	UNDERSERVED	UNDERSURFACES	UNDERWRITINGS	UNDISGUISED
UNDERKEEPERS	UNDERPERFORM	UNDERSETTING	UNDERTAKABLE	UNDERWRITTEN	UNDISGUISEDLY
UNDERKEEPING	UNDERPERFORMED	UNDERSEXED	UNDERTAKEN	UNDERWROTE	UNDISHONOURED
UNDERKEEPS	UNDERPERFORMING	UNDERSHAPEN	UNDERTAKER	UNDERWROUGHT	UNDISMANTLED
UNDERKILLS	UNDERPERFORMS	UNDERSHERIFF	UNDERTAKERS	UNDESCENDABLE	UNDISMAYED
UNDERKINGDOM	UNDERPINNED	UNDERSHERIFFS	UNDERTAKES	UNDESCENDED	UNDISORDERED
UNDERKINGDOMS	UNDERPINNING	UNDERSHIRT	UNDERTAKING	UNDESCENDIBLE	UNDISPATCHED
UNDERKINGS	UNDERPINNINGS	UNDERSHIRTED	UNDERTAKINGS	UNDESCRIBABLE	UNDISPENSED
UNDERLAPPED	UNDERPITCH	UNDERSHIRTS	UNDERTAXED	UNDESCRIBED	UNDISPOSED
UNDERLAPPING	UNDERPLANT	UNDERSHOOT	UNDERTAXES	UNDESCRIED	UNDISPUTABLE
UNDERLAYER	UNDERPLANTED	UNDERSHOOTING	UNDERTAXING	UNDESERVED	UNDISPUTED
UNDERLAYERS	UNDERPLANTING	UNDERSHOOTS	UNDERTENANCIES	UNDESERVEDLY	UNDISPUTEDLY
UNDERLAYING	UNDERPLANTS	UNDERSHORTS	UNDERTENANCY	UNDESERVEDNESS	UNDISSEMBLED
UNDERLAYMENT	UNDERPLAYED	UNDERSHRUB	UNDERTENANT	UNDESERVER	UNDISSOCIATED
UNDERLAYMENTS	UNDERPLAYING	UNDERSHRUBS	UNDERTENANTS	UNDESERVERS	UNDISSOLVED
UNDERLEASE	UNDERPLAYS	UNDERSIDES	UNDERTHINGS	UNDESERVES	UNDISSOLVING
UNDERLEASED	UNDERPLOTS	UNDERSIGNED	UNDERTHIRST	UNDESERVING	UNDISTEMPERED
UNDERLEASES	UNDERPOPULATED	UNDERSIGNING	UNDERTHIRSTS	UNDESERVINGLY	UNDISTILLED
UNDERLEASING	UNDERPOWERED	UNDERSIGNS	UNDERTHRUST	UNDESIGNATED	UNDISTINCTIVE
UNDERLEAVES	UNDERPRAISE	UNDERSIZED	UNDERTHRUSTING	UNDESIGNED	UNDISTINGUISHED
UNDERLETTER	UNDERPRAISED	UNDERSKIES	UNDERTHRUSTS	UNDESIGNEDLY	UNDISTORTED
UNDERLETTERS	UNDERPRAISES	UNDERSKINKER	UNDERTIMED	UNDESIGNEDNESS	UNDISTRACTED
UNDERLETTING	UNDERPRAISING	UNDERSKINKERS	UNDERTIMES	UNDESIGNING	UNDISTRACTEDLY
UNDERLETTINGS	UNDERPREPARED	UNDERSKIRT	UNDERTINTS	UNDESIRABILITY	UNDISTRACTING
UNDERLIERS	UNDERPRICE	UNDERSKIRTS	UNDERTONED	UNDESIRABLE	UNDISTRIBUTED
UNDERLINED	UNDERPRICED	UNDERSLEEVE	UNDERTONES	UNDESIRABLENESS	UNDISTURBED
UNDERLINEN	UNDERPRICES	UNDERSLEEVES	UNDERTRICK	UNDESIRABLES	UNDISTURBEDLY
UNDERLINENS	UNDERPRICING	UNDERSLUNG	UNDERTRICKS	UNDESIRABLY	UNDISTURBING
UNDERLINES	UNDERPRISE	UNDERSOILS	UNDERTRUMP	UNDESIRING	UNDIVERSIFIED
UNDERLINGS	UNDERPRISED	UNDERSONGS	UNDERTRUMPED	UNDESIROUS	UNDIVERTED
UNDERLINING	UNDERPRISES	UNDERSPEND	UNDERTRUMPING	UNDESPAIRING	UNDIVERTING
UNDERLOADED	UNDERPRISING	UNDERSPENDING	UNDERTRUMPS	UNDESPAIRINGLY	UNDIVESTED
UNDERLOADING	UNDERPRIVILEGED	UNDERSPENDS	UNDERUSING	UNDESPOILED	UNDIVESTEDLY
UNDERLOADS	UNDERPRIZE	UNDERSPENT	UNDERUTILISE	UNDESTROYED	UNDIVIDABLE
UNDERLOOKER	UNDERPRIZED	UNDERSPINS	UNDERUTILISED	UNDETECTABLE	UNDIVIDEDLY
UNDERLOOKERS	UNDERPRIZES	UNDERSTAFFED	UNDERUTILISES	UNDETECTED	UNDIVIDEDNESS
UNDERLYING	UNDERPRIZING	UNDERSTAFFING	UNDERUTILISING	UNDETERMINABLE	UNDIVIDEDNESSES
UNDERLYINGLY	UNDERPRODUCTION	UNDERSTAFFINGS	UNDERUTILIZE	UNDETERMINATE	UNDIVORCED
UNDERMANNED	UNDERPROOF	UNDERSTAND	UNDERUTILIZED	UNDETERMINATION	UNDIVULGED
UNDERMANNING	UNDERPROPPED	UNDERSTANDABLE	UNDERUTILIZES	UNDETERMINED	UNDOCTORED
UNDERMASTED	UNDERPROPPER	UNDERSTANDABLY	UNDERUTILIZING	UNDETERRED	UNDOCTRINAIRE
UNDERMEANING	UNDERPROPPERS	UNDERSTANDED	UNDERVALUATION	UNDEVELOPED	UNDOCUMENTED
UNDERMEANINGS	UNDERPROPPING	UNDERSTANDER	UNDERVALUATIONS	UNDEVIATING	UNDOGMATIC
UNDERMENTIONED	UNDERPROPS	UNDERSTANDERS	UNDERVALUE	UNDEVIATINGLY	UNDOGMATICALLY
UNDERMINDE	UNDERPUBLICISED	UNDERSTANDING	UNDERVALUED	UNDIAGNOSABLE	UNDOMESTIC
UNDERMINDED	UNDERPUBLICIZED	UNDERSTANDINGLY	UNDERVALUER	UNDIAGNOSED	UNDOMESTICATE
UNDERMINDES	UNDERQUOTE	UNDERSTANDINGS	UNDERVALUERS	UNDIALECTICAL	UNDOMESTICATED
UNDERMINDING	UNDERQUOTED	UNDERSTANDS	UNDERVALUES	UNDIDACTIC	UNDOMESTICATES
UNDERMINED	UNDERQUOTES	UNDERSTATE	UNDERVALUING	UNDIFFERENCED	UNDOMESTICATING
UNDERMINER	UNDERQUOTING	UNDERSTATED	UNDERVESTS	UNDIGESTED	UNDOUBLING
UNDERMINERS	UNDERRATED	UNDERSTATEDLY	UNDERVIEWER	UNDIGESTIBLE	UNDOUBTABLE
UNDERMINES	UNDERRATES	UNDERSTATEMENT	UNDERVIEWERS	UNDIGHTING	UNDOUBTEDLY
UNDERMINING	UNDERRATING	UNDERSTATEMENTS	UNDERVOICE	UNDIGNIFIED	UNDOUBTFUL
UNDERMININGS	UNDERREACT	UNDERSTATES	UNDERVOICES	UNDIGNIFIES	UNDOUBTING
UNDERNAMED	UNDERREACTED	UNDERSTATING	UNDERVOTES	UNDIGNIFYING	UNDOUBTINGLY
UNDERNEATH	UNDERREACTING	UNDERSTEER	UNDERWATER	UNDIMINISHABLE	UNDRAINABLE
UNDERNEATHS	UNDERREACTS	UNDERSTEERED	UNDERWATERS	UNDIMINISHED	UNDRAMATIC
UNDERNICENESS	UNDERREPORT	UNDERSTEERING	UNDERWEARS	UNDIPLOMATIC	UNDRAMATICALLY
UNDERNICENESSES	UNDERREPORTED	UNDERSTEERS	UNDERWEIGHT	UNDIRECTED	UNDRAMATISED
UNDERNOTED	UNDERREPORTING	UNDERSTOCK	UNDERWEIGHTS	UNDISAPPOINTING	UNDRAMATIZED
UNDERNOTES	UNDERREPORTS	UNDERSTOCKED	UNDERWHELM	UNDISCERNED	UNDREADING
UNDERNOTING	UNDERRUNNING	UNDERSTOCKING	UNDERWHELMED	UNDISCERNEDLY	UNDREAMING
UNDERNOURISH	UNDERRUNNINGS	UNDERSTOCKS	UNDERWHELMING	UNDISCERNIBLE	UNDRESSING
UNDERNOURISHED	UNDERSATURATED	UNDERSTOOD	UNDERWHELMS	UNDISCERNIBLY	UNDRESSINGS
UNDERNOURISHES	UNDERSAYING	UNDERSTOREY	UNDERWINGS	UNDISCERNING	UNDRINKABLE
UNDERNOURISHING	UNDERSCORE	UNDERSTOREYS	UNDERWIRED	UNDISCERNINGS	UNDRIVEABLE
UNDERNTIME	UNDERSCORED	UNDERSTORIES	UNDERWIRES	UNDISCHARGED	UNDROOPING
UNDERNTIMES	UNDERSCORES	UNDERSTORY	UNDERWIRING	UNDISCIPLINABLE	UNDULANCES
UNDERNUTRITION	UNDERSCORING	UNDERSTRAPPER	UNDERWIRINGS	UNDISCIPLINE	UNDULANCIES
UNDERNUTRITIONS	UNDERSCRUB	UNDERSTRAPPERS	UNDERWOODS	UNDISCIPLINED	UNDULATELY
UNDERPAINTING	UNDERSCRUBS	UNDERSTRAPPING	UNDERWOOLS	UNDISCIPLINES	UNDULATING
UNDERPAINTINGS	UNDERSEALED	UNDERSTRATA	UNDERWORKED	UNDISCLOSED	UNDULATINGLY
UNDERPANTS	UNDERSEALING	UNDERSTRATUM	UNDERWORKER	UNDISCOMFITED	UNDULATION
UNDERPARTS	UNDERSEALINGS	UNDERSTRENGTH	UNDERWORKERS	UNDISCORDANT	UNDULATIONIST
UNDERPASSES	UNDERSEALS	UNDERSTUDIED	UNDERWORKING	UNDISCORDING	UNDULATIONISTS

UNDULATIONS
UNDULATORS
UNDULATORY
UNDUPLICATED
UNDUTIFULLY
UNDUTIFULNESS
UNDUTIFULNESSES
UNDYINGNESS
UNDYINGNESSES
UNEARMARKED
UNEARTHING
UNEARTHLIER
UNEARTHLIEST
UNEARTHLINESS
UNEARTHLINESSES
UNEASINESS
UNEASINESSES
UNEATABLENESS
UNEATABLENESSES
UNECCENTRIC
UNECLIPSED
UNECOLOGICAL
UNECONOMIC
UNECONOMICAL
UNEDIFYING
UNEDUCABLE
UNEDUCATED
UNEFFECTED
UNELABORATE
UNELABORATED
UNELECTABLE
UNELECTRIFIED
UNEMBARRASSED
UNEMBELLISHED
UNEMBITTERED
UNEMBODIED
UNEMOTIONAL
UNEMOTIONALLY
UNEMOTIONED
UNEMPHATIC
UNEMPHATICALLY
UNEMPIRICAL
UNEMPLOYABILITY
UNEMPLOYABLE
UNEMPLOYABLES
UNEMPLOYED
UNEMPLOYEDS
UNEMPLOYMENT
UNEMPLOYMENTS
UNENCHANTED
UNENCLOSED
UNENCOURAGING
UNENCUMBERED
UNENDANGERED
UNENDEARED
UNENDEARING
UNENDINGLY
UNENDINGNESS
UNENDINGNESSES
UNENDURABLE
UNENDURABLENESS
UNENDURABLY
UNENFORCEABLE
UNENFORCED
UNENJOYABLE
UNENLARGED
UNENLIGHTENED
UNENLIGHTENING
UNENQUIRING
UNENRICHED
UNENSLAVED
UNENTAILED
UNENTERPRISING
UNENTERTAINED
UNENTERTAINING
UNENTHRALLED
UNENTHUSIASTIC
UNENTITLED
UNENVIABLE
UNENVIABLY
UNEQUALLED
UNEQUIPPED
UNEQUITABLE

UNEQUIVOCABLY
UNEQUIVOCAL
UNEQUIVOCALLY
UNEQUIVOCALNESS
UNERASABLE
UNERRINGLY
UNERRINGNESS
UNERRINGNESSES
UNESCAPABLE
UNESCORTED
UNESSENCED
UNESSENCES
UNESSENCING
UNESSENTIAL
UNESSENTIALLY
UNESSENTIALS
UNESTABLISHED
UNEVALUATED
UNEVANGELICAL
UNEVENNESS
UNEVENNESSES
UNEVENTFUL
UNEVENTFULLY
UNEVENTFULNESS
UNEVIDENCED
UNEXACTING
UNEXAGGERATED
UNEXAMINED
UNEXAMPLED
UNEXCAVATED
UNEXCELLED
UNEXCEPTIONABLE
UNEXCEPTIONABLY
UNEXCEPTIONAL
UNEXCEPTIONALLY
UNEXCITABLE
UNEXCITING
UNEXCLUDED
UNEXCLUSIVE
UNEXCLUSIVELY
UNEXECUTED
UNEXEMPLIFIED
UNEXERCISED
UNEXHAUSTED
UNEXPANDED
UNEXPECTANT
UNEXPECTED
UNEXPECTEDLY
UNEXPECTEDNESS
UNEXPENDED
UNEXPENSIVE
UNEXPENSIVELY
UNEXPERIENCED
UNEXPERIENT
UNEXPIATED
UNEXPLAINABLE
UNEXPLAINED
UNEXPLODED
UNEXPLOITED
UNEXPLORED
UNEXPRESSED
UNEXPRESSIBLE
UNEXPRESSIVE
UNEXPUGNABLE
UNEXPURGATED
UNEXTENDED
UNEXTENUATED
UNEXTINGUISHED
UNEXTRAORDINARY
UNFADINGLY
UNFADINGNESS
UNFADINGNESSES
UNFAILINGLY
UNFAILINGNESS
UNFAILINGNESSES
UNFAIRNESS
UNFAIRNESSES
UNFAITHFUL
UNFAITHFULLY
UNFAITHFULNESS
UNFALLIBLE
UNFALSIFIABLE
UNFALTERING

UNFALTERINGLY
UNFAMILIAR
UNFAMILIARITIES
UNFAMILIARITY
UNFAMILIARLY
UNFASHIONABLE
UNFASHIONABLY
UNFASHIONED
UNFASTENED
UNFASTENING
UNFASTIDIOUS
UNFATHERED
UNFATHERLY
UNFATHOMABLE
UNFATHOMABLY
UNFATHOMED
UNFAVORABLE
UNFAVORABLENESS
UNFAVORABLY
UNFAVORITE
UNFAVOURABLE
UNFAVOURABLY
UNFAVOURED
UNFEARFULLY
UNFEASIBLE
UNFEATHERED
UNFEATURED
UNFEELINGLY
UNFEELINGNESS
UNFEELINGNESSES
UNFEIGNEDLY
UNFEIGNEDNESS
UNFEIGNEDNESSES
UNFEIGNING
UNFELLOWED
UNFEMININE
UNFERMENTED
UNFERTILISED
UNFERTILIZED
UNFETTERED
UNFETTERING
UNFEUDALISE
UNFEUDALISED
UNFEUDALISES
UNFEUDALISING
UNFEUDALIZE
UNFEUDALIZED
UNFEUDALIZES
UNFEUDALIZING
UNFILIALLY
UNFILLABLE
UNFILLETED
UNFILTERABLE
UNFILTERED
UNFILTRABLE
UNFINDABLE
UNFINISHED
UNFINISHING
UNFINISHINGS
UNFITNESSES
UNFITTEDNESS
UNFITTEDNESSES
UNFITTINGLY
UNFIXEDNESS
UNFIXEDNESSES
UNFIXITIES
UNFLAGGING
UNFLAGGINGLY
UNFLAMBOYANT
UNFLAPPABILITY
UNFLAPPABLE
UNFLAPPABLENESS
UNFLAPPABLY
UNFLATTERING
UNFLATTERINGLY
UNFLAVOURED
UNFLESHING
UNFLINCHING
UNFLINCHINGLY
UNFLUSHING
UNFLUSTERED
UNFOCUSSED
UNFOLDINGS

UNFOLDMENT
UNFOLDMENTS
UNFORBIDDEN
UNFORCEDLY
UNFORCIBLE
UNFORDABLE
UNFOREBODING
UNFOREKNOWABLE
UNFOREKNOWN
UNFORESEEABLE
UNFORESEEING
UNFORESEEN
UNFORESKINNED
UNFORESTED
UNFORETOLD
UNFOREWARNED
UNFORFEITED
UNFORGETTABLE
UNFORGETTABLY
UNFORGIVABLE
UNFORGIVEN
UNFORGIVENESS
UNFORGIVENESSES
UNFORGIVING
UNFORGIVINGNESS
UNFORGOTTEN
UNFORMALISED
UNFORMALIZED
UNFORMATTED
UNFORMIDABLE
UNFORMULATED
UNFORSAKEN
UNFORTHCOMING
UNFORTIFIED
UNFORTUNATE
UNFORTUNATELY
UNFORTUNATENESS
UNFORTUNATES
UNFORTUNED
UNFORTUNES
UNFOSSILIFEROUS
UNFOSSILISED
UNFOSSILIZED
UNFOSTERED
UNFOUGHTEN
UNFOUNDEDLY
UNFOUNDEDNESS
UNFOUNDEDNESSES
UNFRANCHISED
UNFRAUGHTED
UNFRAUGHTING
UNFRAUGHTS
UNFREEDOMS
UNFREEZING
UNFREQUENT
UNFREQUENTED
UNFREQUENTLY
UNFRIENDED
UNFRIENDEDNESS
UNFRIENDLIER
UNFRIENDLIEST
UNFRIENDLILY
UNFRIENDLINESS
UNFRIENDLY
UNFRIENDSHIP
UNFRIENDSHIPS
UNFRIGHTED
UNFRIGHTENED
UNFRIVOLOUS
UNFROCKING
UNFRUCTUOUS
UNFRUITFUL
UNFRUITFULLY
UNFRUITFULNESS
UNFULFILLABLE
UNFULFILLED
UNFURNISHED
UNFURNISHES
UNFURNISHING
UNFURROWED
UNFUSSIEST
UNGAINLIER
UNGAINLIEST

UNGAINLINESS
UNGAINLINESSES
UNGAINSAID
UNGAINSAYABLE
UNGALLANTLY
UNGARMENTED
UNGARNERED
UNGARNISHED
UNGARTERED
UNGATHERED
UNGENEROSITIES
UNGENEROSITY
UNGENEROUS
UNGENEROUSLY
UNGENITURED
UNGENTEELLY
UNGENTILITIES
UNGENTILITY
UNGENTLEMANLIKE
UNGENTLEMANLY
UNGENTLENESS
UNGENTLENESSES
UNGENTRIFIED
UNGENUINENESS
UNGENUINENESSES
UNGERMINATED
UNGETATABLE
UNGIMMICKY
UNGIRTHING
UNGLAMORISED
UNGLAMORIZED
UNGLAMOROUS
UNGODLIEST
UNGODLINESS
UNGODLINESSES
UNGOVERNABLE
UNGOVERNABLY
UNGOVERNED
UNGRACEFUL
UNGRACEFULLY
UNGRACEFULNESS
UNGRACIOUS
UNGRACIOUSLY
UNGRACIOUSNESS
UNGRAMMATIC
UNGRAMMATICAL
UNGRAMMATICALLY
UNGRASPABLE
UNGRATEFUL
UNGRATEFULLY
UNGRATEFULNESS
UNGRATIFIED
UNGROUNDED
UNGROUNDEDLY
UNGROUNDEDNESS
UNGRUDGING
UNGRUDGINGLY
UNGUARDEDLY
UNGUARDEDNESS
UNGUARDEDNESSES
UNGUARDING
UNGUENTARIA
UNGUENTARIES
UNGUENTARIUM
UNGUENTARY
UNGUERDONED
UNGUESSABLE
UNGUICULATE
UNGUICULATED
UNGUICULATES
UNGULIGRADE
UNHABITABLE
UNHABITUATED
UNHACKNEYED
UNHALLOWED
UNHALLOWING
UNHAMPERED
UNHANDIEST
UNHANDINESS
UNHANDINESSES
UNHANDSELED
UNHANDSOME
UNHANDSOMELY

UNHANDSOMENESS
UNHAPPIEST
UNHAPPINESS
UNHAPPINESSES
UNHAPPYING
UNHARBOURED
UNHARBOURING
UNHARBOURS
UNHARDENED
UNHARMFULLY
UNHARMONIOUS
UNHARNESSED
UNHARNESSES
UNHARNESSING
UNHARVESTED
UNHATTINGS
UNHAZARDED
UNHAZARDOUS
UNHEALABLE
UNHEALTHFUL
UNHEALTHFULLY
UNHEALTHFULNESS
UNHEALTHIER
UNHEALTHIEST
UNHEALTHILY
UNHEALTHINESS
UNHEALTHINESSES
UNHEARSING
UNHEARTING
UNHEEDEDLY
UNHEEDFULLY
UNHEEDINGLY
UNHELMETED
UNHELPABLE
UNHELPFULLY
UNHERALDED
UNHEROICAL
UNHEROICALLY
UNHESITATING
UNHESITATINGLY
UNHIDEBOUND
UNHINDERED
UNHINGEMENT
UNHINGEMENTS
UNHISTORIC
UNHISTORICAL
UNHITCHING
UNHOARDING
UNHOLINESS
UNHOLINESSES
UNHOMELIKE
UNHOMOGENISED
UNHOMOGENIZED
UNHONOURED
UNHOPEFULLY
UNHOSPITABLE
UNHOUSELED
UNHOUZZLED
UNHUMANISE
UNHUMANISED
UNHUMANISES
UNHUMANISING
UNHUMANIZE
UNHUMANIZED
UNHUMANIZES
UNHUMANIZING
UNHUMOROUS
UNHURRIEDLY
UNHURRYING
UNHURTFULLY
UNHURTFULNESS
UNHURTFULNESSES
UNHUSBANDED
UNHYDROLYSED
UNHYDROLYZED
UNHYGIENIC
UNHYPHENATED
UNHYSTERICAL
UNHYSTERICALLY
UNIAXIALLY
UNICAMERAL
UNICAMERALISM
UNICAMERALISMS

UNICAMERALIST	UNIMPRESSED	UNIONISATION	UNKENNELED	UNLISTENING	UNMECHANIZING
UNICAMERALISTS	UNIMPRESSIBLE	UNIONISATIONS	UNKENNELING	UNLITERARY	UNMEDIATED
UNICAMERALLY	UNIMPRESSIVE	UNIONISERS	UNKENNELLED	UNLIVEABLE	UNMEDICATED
UNICELLULAR	UNIMPRISONED	UNIONISING	UNKENNELLING	UNLIVELINESS	UNMEDICINABLE
UNICELLULARITY	UNIMPROVED	UNIONISTIC	UNKINDLIER	UNLIVELINESSES	UNMEDITATED
UNICENTRAL	UNIMPUGNABLE	UNIONIZATION	UNKINDLIEST	UNLOADINGS	UNMEETNESS
UNICOLORATE	UNINAUGURATED	UNIONIZATIONS	UNKINDLINESS	UNLOCALISED	UNMEETNESSES
UNICOLOROUS	UNINCHANTED	UNIONIZERS	UNKINDLINESSES	UNLOCALIZED	UNMELLOWED
UNICOLOURED	UNINCLOSED	UNIONIZING	UNKINDNESS	UNLOCKABLE	UNMELODIOUS
UNICOSTATE	UNINCORPORATED	UNIPARENTAL	UNKINDNESSES	UNLOOSENED	UNMELODIOUSNESS
UNICYCLING	UNINCUMBERED	UNIPARENTALLY	UNKINGLIER	UNLOOSENING	UNMEMORABLE
UNICYCLIST	UNINDEARED	UNIPARTITE	UNKINGLIEST	UNLOVEABLE	UNMEMORABLY
UNICYCLISTS	UNINDICTED	UNIPERSONAL	UNKINGLIKE	UNLOVELIER	UNMENTIONABLE
UNIDEALISM	UNINFECTED	UNIPERSONALITY	UNKNIGHTED	UNLOVELIEST	UNMENTIONABLES
UNIDEALISMS	UNINFLAMED	UNIPOLARITIES	UNKNIGHTING	UNLOVELINESS	UNMENTIONABLY
UNIDEALISTIC	UNINFLAMMABLE	UNIPOLARITY	UNKNIGHTLINESS	UNLOVELINESSES	UNMENTIONED
UNIDENTIFIABLE	UNINFLATED	UNIQUENESS	UNKNIGHTLY	UNLOVERLIKE	UNMERCENARY
UNIDENTIFIED	UNINFLECTED	UNIQUENESSES	UNKNITTING	UNLOVINGLY	UNMERCHANTABLE
UNIDEOLOGICAL	UNINFLUENCED	UNIRONICALLY	UNKNOTTING	UNLOVINGNESS	UNMERCIFUL
UNIDIMENSIONAL	UNINFLUENTIAL	UNIRRADIATED	UNKNOWABILITIES	UNLOVINGNESSES	UNMERCIFULLY
UNIDIOMATIC	UNINFORCEABLE	UNIRRIGATED	UNKNOWABILITY	UNLUCKIEST	UNMERCIFULNESS
UNIDIOMATICALLY	UNINFORCED	UNISEPTATE	UNKNOWABLE	UNLUCKINESS	UNMERITABLE
UNIDIRECTIONAL	UNINFORMATIVE	UNISERIALLY	UNKNOWABLENESS	UNLUCKINESSES	UNMERITEDLY
UNIFICATION	UNINFORMATIVELY	UNISERIATE	UNKNOWABLES	UNLUXURIANT	UNMERITING
UNIFICATIONS	UNINFORMED	UNISERIATELY	UNKNOWABLY	UNLUXURIOUS	UNMETABOLISED
UNIFLOROUS	UNINFORMING	UNISEXUALITIES	UNKNOWINGLY	UNMACADAMISED	UNMETABOLIZED
UNIFOLIATE	UNINGRATIATING	UNISEXUALITY	UNKNOWINGNESS	UNMACADAMIZED	UNMETALLED
UNIFOLIOLATE	UNINHABITABLE	UNISEXUALLY	UNKNOWINGNESSES	UNMAGNIFIED	UNMETAPHORICAL
UNIFORMEST	UNINHABITED	UNISONALLY	UNKNOWINGS	UNMAIDENLY	UNMETAPHYSICAL
UNIFORMING	UNINHIBITED	UNISONANCE	UNKNOWLEDGEABLE	UNMAILABLE	UNMETHODICAL
UNIFORMITARIAN	UNINHIBITEDLY	UNISONANCES	UNKNOWNNESS	UNMAINTAINABLE	UNMETHODISED
UNIFORMITARIANS	UNINHIBITEDNESS	UNITARIANISM	UNKNOWNNESSES	UNMAINTAINED	UNMETHODIZED
UNIFORMITIES	UNINITIATE	UNITARIANISMS	UNLABELLED	UNMALICIOUS	UNMETRICAL
UNIFORMITY	UNINITIATED	UNITARIANS	UNLABORIOUS	UNMALICIOUSLY	UNMILITARY
UNIFORMNESS	UNINITIATES	UNITEDNESS	UNLABOURED	UNMALLEABILITY	UNMINDFULLY
UNIFORMNESSES	UNINOCULATED	UNITEDNESSES	UNLABOURING	UNMALLEABLE	UNMINDFULNESS
UNIGENITURE	UNINQUIRING	UNITHOLDER	UNLADYLIKE	UNMANACLED	UNMINDFULNESSES
UNIGENITURES	UNINQUISITIVE	UNITHOLDERS	UNLAMENTED	UNMANACLES	UNMINGLING
UNIGNORABLE	UNINSCRIBED	UNITISATION	UNLATCHING	UNMANACLING	UNMINISTERIAL
UNILABIATE	UNINSPECTED	UNITISATIONS	UNLAUNDERED	UNMANAGEABLE	UNMIRACULOUS
UNILATERAL	UNINSPIRED	UNITIZATION	UNLAWFULLY	UNMANAGEABLY	UNMISSABLE
UNILATERALISM	UNINSPIRING	UNITIZATIONS	UNLAWFULNESS	UNMANFULLY	UNMISTAKABLE
UNILATERALISMS	UNINSTALLED	UNIVALENCE	UNLAWFULNESSES	UNMANIPULATED	UNMISTAKABLY
UNILATERALIST	UNINSTALLING	UNIVALENCES	UNLEARNABLE	UNMANLIEST	UNMISTAKEABLE
UNILATERALISTS	UNINSTALLS	UNIVALENCIES	UNLEARNEDLY	UNMANLINESS	UNMISTAKEABLY
UNILATERALITIES	UNINSTRUCTED	UNIVALENCY	UNLEARNEDNESS	UNMANLINESSES	UNMISTRUSTFUL
UNILATERALITY	UNINSTRUCTIVE	UNIVALENTS	UNLEARNEDNESSES	UNMANNERED	UNMITERING
UNILATERALLY	UNINSULATED	UNIVALVULAR	UNLEARNING	UNMANNEREDLY	UNMITIGABLE
UNILINGUAL	UNINSURABLE	UNIVARIANT	UNLEASHING	UNMANNERLINESS	UNMITIGABLY
UNILINGUALISM	UNINSUREDS	UNIVARIATE	UNLEAVENED	UNMANNERLY	UNMITIGATED
UNILINGUALISMS	UNINTEGRATED	UNIVERSALISE	UNLEISURED	UNMANTLING	UNMITIGATEDLY
UNILINGUALS	UNINTELLECTUAL	UNIVERSALISED	UNLEISURELY	UNMANUFACTURED	UNMITIGATEDNESS
UNILITERAL	UNINTELLIGENCE	UNIVERSALISES	UNLESSONED	UNMARKETABLE	UNMODERATED
UNILLUMINATED	UNINTELLIGENCES	UNIVERSALISING	UNLETTABLE	UNMARRIABLE	UNMODERNISED
UNILLUMINATING	UNINTELLIGENT	UNIVERSALISM	UNLETTERED	UNMARRIAGEABLE	UNMODERNIZED
UNILLUMINED	UNINTELLIGENTLY	UNIVERSALISMS	UNLEVELING	UNMARRIEDS	UNMODIFIABLE
UNILLUSIONED	UNINTELLIGIBLE	UNIVERSALIST	UNLEVELLED	UNMARRYING	UNMODIFIED
UNILLUSTRATED	UNINTELLIGIBLY	UNIVERSALISTIC	UNLEVELLING	UNMASCULINE	UNMODULATED
UNILOBULAR	UNINTENDED	UNIVERSALISTS	UNLIBERATED	UNMASKINGS	UNMOISTENED
UNILOCULAR	UNINTENTIONAL	UNIVERSALITIES	UNLIBIDINOUS	UNMASTERED	UNMOLESTED
UNIMAGINABLE	UNINTENTIONALLY	UNIVERSALITY	UNLICENSED	UNMATCHABLE	UNMONITORED
UNIMAGINABLY	UNINTEREST	UNIVERSALIZE	UNLIFELIKE	UNMATERIAL	UNMORALISED
UNIMAGINATIVE	UNINTERESTED	UNIVERSALIZED	UNLIGHTENED	UNMATERIALISED	UNMORALISING
UNIMAGINATIVELY	UNINTERESTEDLY	UNIVERSALIZES	UNLIGHTSOME	UNMATERIALIZED	UNMORALITIES
UNIMAGINED	UNINTERESTING	UNIVERSALIZING	UNLIKEABLE	UNMATERNAL	UNMORALITY
UNIMMORTAL	UNINTERESTINGLY	UNIVERSALLY	UNLIKELIER	UNMATHEMATICAL	UNMORALIZED
UNIMMUNISED	UNINTERESTS	UNIVERSALNESS	UNLIKELIEST	UNMATRICULATED	UNMORALIZING
UNIMMUNIZED	UNINTERMITTED	UNIVERSALNESSES	UNLIKELIHOOD	UNMEANINGLY	UNMORTGAGED
UNIMOLECULAR	UNINTERMITTEDLY	UNIVERSALS	UNLIKELIHOODS	UNMEANINGNESS	UNMORTIFIED
UNIMPAIRED	UNINTERMITTING	UNIVERSITARIAN	UNLIKELINESS	UNMEANINGNESSES	UNMORTISED
UNIMPARTED	UNINTERPRETABLE	UNIVERSITIES	UNLIKELINESSES	UNMEASURABLE	UNMORTISES
UNIMPASSIONED	UNINTERRUPTED	UNIVERSITY	UNLIKENESS	UNMEASURABLY	UNMORTISING
UNIMPEACHABLE	UNINTERRUPTEDLY	UNIVOCALLY	UNLIKENESSES	UNMEASURED	UNMOTHERLY
UNIMPEACHABLY	UNINTIMIDATED	UNIVOLTINE	UNLIMBERED	UNMEASUREDLY	UNMOTIVATED
UNIMPEACHED	UNINTOXICATING	UNJAUNDICED	UNLIMBERING	UNMECHANIC	UNMOULDING
UNIMPEDEDLY	UNINTRODUCED	UNJOINTING	UNLIMITEDLY	UNMECHANICAL	UNMOUNTING
UNIMPLORED	UNINUCLEAR	UNJUSTIFIABLE	UNLIMITEDNESS	UNMECHANISE	UNMOVEABLE
UNIMPORTANCE	UNINUCLEATE	UNJUSTIFIABLY	UNLIMITEDNESSES	UNMECHANISED	UNMOVEABLY
UNIMPORTANCES	UNINVENTIVE	UNJUSTIFIED	UNLIQUEFIED	UNMECHANISES	UNMUFFLING
UNIMPORTANT	UNINVESTED	UNJUSTNESS	UNLIQUIDATED	UNMECHANISING	UNMUNITIONED
UNIMPORTUNED	UNINVIDIOUS	UNJUSTNESSES	UNLIQUORED	UNMECHANIZE	UNMURMURING
UNIMPOSING	UNINVITING	UNKEMPTNESS	UNLISTENABLE	UNMECHANIZED	UNMURMURINGLY
UNIMPREGNATED	UNINVOLVED	UNKEMPTNESSES	UNLISTENED	UNMECHANIZES	UNMUSICALLY

UNMUSICALNESS
UNMUSICALNESSES
UNMUTILATED
UNMUZZLING
UNMUZZLINGS
UNMYELINATED
UNNAMEABLE
UNNATURALISE
UNNATURALISED
UNNATURALISES
UNNATURALISING
UNNATURALIZE
UNNATURALIZED
UNNATURALIZES
UNNATURALIZING
UNNATURALLY
UNNATURALNESS
UNNATURALNESSES
UNNAVIGABLE
UNNAVIGATED
UNNECESSARILY
UNNECESSARINESS
UNNECESSARY
UNNEEDFULLY
UNNEGOTIABLE
UNNEIGHBOURED
UNNEIGHBOURLY
UNNERVINGLY
UNNEUROTIC
UNNEWSWORTHY
UNNILHEXIUM
UNNILHEXIUMS
UNNILPENTIUM
UNNILPENTIUMS
UNNILQUADIUM
UNNILQUADIUMS
UNNILSEPTIUM
UNNILSEPTIUMS
UNNOTICEABLE
UNNOTICEABLY
UNNOTICING
UNNOURISHED
UNNOURISHING
UNNUMBERED
UNNURTURED
UNOBEDIENT
UNOBJECTIONABLE
UNOBJECTIONABLY
UNOBNOXIOUS
UNOBSCURED
UNOBSERVABLE
UNOBSERVANCE
UNOBSERVANCES
UNOBSERVANT
UNOBSERVED
UNOBSERVEDLY
UNOBSERVING
UNOBSTRUCTED
UNOBSTRUCTIVE
UNOBTAINABLE
UNOBTAINED
UNOBTRUSIVE
UNOBTRUSIVELY
UNOBTRUSIVENESS
UNOCCUPIED
UNOFFENDED
UNOFFENDING
UNOFFENSIVE
UNOFFICERED
UNOFFICIAL
UNOFFICIALLY
UNOFFICIOUS
UNOPENABLE
UNOPERATIVE
UNOPPRESSIVE
UNORDAINED
UNORDERING
UNORDINARY
UNORGANISED
UNORGANIZED
UNORIGINAL
UNORIGINALITIES
UNORIGINALITY

UNORIGINATE
UNORIGINATED
UNORNAMENTAL
UNORNAMENTED
UNORTHODOX
UNORTHODOXIES
UNORTHODOXLY
UNORTHODOXY
UNOSSIFIED
UNOSTENTATIOUS
UNOVERCOME
UNOVERTHROWN
UNOXIDISED
UNOXIDIZED
UNOXYGENATED
UNPACIFIED
UNPACKINGS
UNPAINTABLE
UNPAINTING
UNPALATABILITY
UNPALATABLE
UNPALATABLY
UNPAMPERED
UNPANELLED
UNPANELLING
UNPANNELLED
UNPANNELLING
UNPAPERING
UNPARADISE
UNPARADISED
UNPARADISES
UNPARADISING
UNPARAGONED
UNPARALLEL
UNPARALLELED
UNPARASITISED
UNPARASITIZED
UNPARDONABLE
UNPARDONABLY
UNPARDONED
UNPARDONING
UNPARENTAL
UNPARENTED
UNPARLIAMENTARY
UNPASSABLE
UNPASSABLENESS
UNPASSIONATE
UNPASSIONED
UNPASTEURISED
UNPASTEURIZED
UNPASTORAL
UNPASTURED
UNPATENTABLE
UNPATENTED
UNPATHETIC
UNPATHWAYED
UNPATRIOTIC
UNPATRIOTICALLY
UNPATRONISED
UNPATRONIZED
UNPATTERNED
UNPAVILIONED
UNPEACEABLE
UNPEACEABLENESS
UNPEACEFUL
UNPEACEFULLY
UNPEDANTIC
UNPEDIGREED
UNPEERABLE
UNPENSIONED
UNPEOPLING
UNPEPPERED
UNPERCEIVABLE
UNPERCEIVABLY
UNPERCEIVED
UNPERCEIVEDLY
UNPERCEPTIVE
UNPERCHING
UNPERFECTION
UNPERFECTIONS
UNPERFECTLY
UNPERFECTNESS
UNPERFECTNESSES

UNPERFORATED
UNPERFORMABLE
UNPERFORMED
UNPERFORMING
UNPERFUMED
UNPERILOUS
UNPERISHABLE
UNPERISHED
UNPERISHING
UNPERJURED
UNPERPETRATED
UNPERPLEXED
UNPERPLEXES
UNPERPLEXING
UNPERSECUTED
UNPERSONED
UNPERSONING
UNPERSUADABLE
UNPERSUADED
UNPERSUASIVE
UNPERTURBED
UNPERVERTED
UNPERVERTING
UNPERVERTS
UNPHILOSOPHIC
UNPHILOSOPHICAL
UNPHONETIC
UNPICKABLE
UNPICTURESQUE
UNPILLARED
UNPILLOWED
UNPITIFULLY
UNPITIFULNESS
UNPITIFULNESSES
UNPITYINGLY
UNPLAITING
UNPLASTERED
UNPLAUSIBLE
UNPLAUSIBLY
UNPLAUSIVE
UNPLAYABLE
UNPLEASANT
UNPLEASANTLY
UNPLEASANTNESS
UNPLEASANTRIES
UNPLEASANTRY
UNPLEASING
UNPLEASINGLY
UNPLEASURABLE
UNPLEASURABLY
UNPLOUGHED
UNPLUGGING
UNPLUMBING
UNPOETICAL
UNPOETICALLY
UNPOETICALNESS
UNPOISONED
UNPOISONING
UNPOLARISABLE
UNPOLARISED
UNPOLARIZABLE
UNPOLARIZED
UNPOLICIED
UNPOLISHABLE
UNPOLISHED
UNPOLISHES
UNPOLISHING
UNPOLITELY
UNPOLITENESS
UNPOLITENESSES
UNPOLITICAL
UNPOLLUTED
UNPOPULARITIES
UNPOPULARITY
UNPOPULARLY
UNPOPULATED
UNPOPULOUS
UNPORTIONED
UNPOSSESSED
UNPOSSESSING
UNPOSSIBLE
UNPOWDERED
UNPRACTICABLE

UNPRACTICAL
UNPRACTICALITY
UNPRACTICALLY
UNPRACTICALNESS
UNPRACTICED
UNPRACTISED
UNPRACTISEDNESS
UNPRAISEWORTHY
UNPRAISING
UNPREACHED
UNPREACHES
UNPREACHING
UNPRECEDENTED
UNPRECEDENTEDLY
UNPREDICTABLE
UNPREDICTABLES
UNPREDICTABLY
UNPREDICTED
UNPREDICTING
UNPREDICTS
UNPREFERRED
UNPREGNANT
UNPREJUDICED
UNPREJUDICEDLY
UNPRELATICAL
UNPREMEDITABLE
UNPREMEDITATED
UNPREMEDITATION
UNPREOCCUPIED
UNPREPARED
UNPREPAREDLY
UNPREPAREDNESS
UNPREPARES
UNPREPARING
UNPREPOSSESSED
UNPREPOSSESSING
UNPRESCRIBED
UNPRESENTABLE
UNPRESSURED
UNPRESSURISED
UNPRESSURIZED
UNPRESUMING
UNPRESUMPTUOUS
UNPRETENDING
UNPRETENDINGLY
UNPRETENTIOUS
UNPRETENTIOUSLY
UNPRETTINESS
UNPRETTINESSES
UNPREVAILING
UNPREVENTABLE
UNPREVENTED
UNPRIESTED
UNPRIESTING
UNPRIESTLY
UNPRINCELY
UNPRINCIPLED
UNPRINTABLE
UNPRINTABLENESS
UNPRINTABLY
UNPRISABLE
UNPRISONED
UNPRISONING
UNPRIVILEGED
UNPRIZABLE
UNPROBLEMATIC
UNPROCEDURAL
UNPROCESSED
UNPROCLAIMED
UNPROCURABLE
UNPRODUCED
UNPRODUCTIVE
UNPRODUCTIVELY
UNPRODUCTIVITY
UNPROFANED
UNPROFESSED
UNPROFESSIONAL
UNPROFESSIONALS
UNPROFITABILITY
UNPROFITABLE
UNPROFITABLY
UNPROFITED
UNPROFITING

UNPROGRAMMABLE
UNPROGRAMMED
UNPROGRESSIVE
UNPROGRESSIVELY
UNPROHIBITED
UNPROJECTED
UNPROLIFIC
UNPROMISED
UNPROMISING
UNPROMISINGLY
UNPROMPTED
UNPRONOUNCEABLE
UNPRONOUNCED
UNPROPERLY
UNPROPERTIED
UNPROPHETIC
UNPROPHETICAL
UNPROPITIOUS
UNPROPITIOUSLY
UNPROPORTIONATE
UNPROPORTIONED
UNPROPOSED
UNPROPPING
UNPROSPEROUS
UNPROSPEROUSLY
UNPROTECTED
UNPROTECTEDNESS
UNPROTESTANTISE
UNPROTESTANTIZE
UNPROTESTED
UNPROTESTING
UNPROVABLE
UNPROVIDED
UNPROVIDEDLY
UNPROVIDENT
UNPROVIDES
UNPROVIDING
UNPROVISIONED
UNPROVOCATIVE
UNPROVOKED
UNPROVOKEDLY
UNPROVOKES
UNPROVOKING
UNPUBLICISED
UNPUBLICIZED
UNPUBLISHABLE
UNPUBLISHED
UNPUCKERED
UNPUCKERING
UNPUNCTUAL
UNPUNCTUALITIES
UNPUNCTUALITY
UNPUNCTUATED
UNPUNISHABLE
UNPUNISHABLY
UNPUNISHED
UNPURCHASABLE
UNPURCHASEABLE
UNPURCHASED
UNPURIFIED
UNPURPOSED
UNPURVAIDE
UNPURVEYED
UNPUTDOWNABLE
UNPUZZLING
UNQUALIFIABLE
UNQUALIFIED
UNQUALIFIEDLY
UNQUALIFIEDNESS
UNQUALIFIES
UNQUALIFYING
UNQUALITED
UNQUALITIED
UNQUANTIFIABLE
UNQUANTIFIED
UNQUANTISED
UNQUANTIZED
UNQUARRIED
UNQUEENING
UNQUEENLIER
UNQUEENLIEST
UNQUEENLIKE
UNQUENCHABLE

UNQUENCHABLY
UNQUENCHED
UNQUESTIONABLE
UNQUESTIONABLY
UNQUESTIONED
UNQUESTIONING
UNQUESTIONINGLY
UNQUICKENED
UNQUIETEST
UNQUIETING
UNQUIETNESS
UNQUIETNESSES
UNQUOTABLE
UNRANSOMED
UNRATIFIED
UNRAVELING
UNRAVELLED
UNRAVELLER
UNRAVELLERS
UNRAVELLING
UNRAVELLINGS
UNRAVELMENT
UNRAVELMENTS
UNRAVISHED
UNREACHABLE
UNREACTIVE
UNREADABILITIES
UNREADABILITY
UNREADABLE
UNREADABLENESS
UNREADABLY
UNREADIEST
UNREADINESS
UNREADINESSES
UNREALISABLE
UNREALISED
UNREALISES
UNREALISING
UNREALISMS
UNREALISTIC
UNREALISTICALLY
UNREALITIES
UNREALIZABLE
UNREALIZED
UNREALIZES
UNREALIZING
UNREASONABLE
UNREASONABLY
UNREASONED
UNREASONING
UNREASONINGLY
UNRECALLABLE
UNRECALLED
UNRECALLING
UNRECAPTURABLE
UNRECEIPTED
UNRECEIVED
UNRECEPTIVE
UNRECIPROCATED
UNRECKONABLE
UNRECKONED
UNRECLAIMABLE
UNRECLAIMABLY
UNRECLAIMED
UNRECOGNISABLE
UNRECOGNISABLY
UNRECOGNISED
UNRECOGNISING
UNRECOGNIZABLE
UNRECOGNIZABLY
UNRECOGNIZED
UNRECOGNIZING
UNRECOLLECTED
UNRECOMMENDABLE
UNRECOMMENDED
UNRECOMPENSED
UNRECONCILABLE
UNRECONCILABLY
UNRECONCILED
UNRECONCILIABLE
UNRECONSTRUCTED
UNRECORDED
UNRECOUNTED

UNRECOVERABLE
UNRECOVERABLY
UNRECOVERED
UNRECTIFIED
UNRECURING
UNRECYCLABLE
UNREDEEMABLE
UNREDEEMED
UNREDRESSED
UNREDUCIBLE
UNREFLECTED
UNREFLECTING
UNREFLECTINGLY
UNREFLECTIVE
UNREFLECTIVELY
UNREFORMABLE
UNREFORMED
UNREFRACTED
UNREFRESHED
UNREFRESHING
UNREFRIGERATED
UNREGARDED
UNREGARDING
UNREGENERACIES
UNREGENERACY
UNREGENERATE
UNREGENERATED
UNREGENERATELY
UNREGENERATES
UNREGIMENTED
UNREGISTERED
UNREGULATED
UNREHEARSED
UNREINFORCED
UNREJOICED
UNREJOICING
UNRELATIVE
UNRELENTING
UNRELENTINGLY
UNRELENTINGNESS
UNRELENTOR
UNRELENTORS
UNRELIABILITIES
UNRELIABILITY
UNRELIABLE
UNRELIABLENESS
UNRELIEVABLE
UNRELIEVED
UNRELIEVEDLY
UNRELIGIOUS
UNRELIGIOUSLY
UNRELISHED
UNRELUCTANT
UNREMAINING
UNREMARKABLE
UNREMARKABLY
UNREMARKED
UNREMEDIED
UNREMEMBERED
UNREMEMBERING
UNREMINISCENT
UNREMITTED
UNREMITTEDLY
UNREMITTENT
UNREMITTENTLY
UNREMITTING
UNREMITTINGLY
UNREMITTINGNESS
UNREMORSEFUL
UNREMORSEFULLY
UNREMORSELESS
UNREMOVABLE
UNREMUNERATIVE
UNRENDERED
UNREPAIRABLE
UNREPAIRED
UNREPEALABLE
UNREPEALED
UNREPEATABLE
UNREPEATED
UNREPELLED
UNREPENTANCE
UNREPENTANCES

UNREPENTANT
UNREPENTANTLY
UNREPENTED
UNREPENTING
UNREPENTINGLY
UNREPINING
UNREPININGLY
UNREPLACEABLE
UNREPLENISHED
UNREPORTABLE
UNREPORTED
UNREPOSEFUL
UNREPOSING
UNREPRESENTED
UNREPRESSED
UNREPRIEVABLE
UNREPRIEVED
UNREPRIMANDED
UNREPROACHED
UNREPROACHFUL
UNREPROACHING
UNREPRODUCIBLE
UNREPROVABLE
UNREPROVED
UNREPROVING
UNREPUGNANT
UNREPULSABLE
UNREQUIRED
UNREQUISITE
UNREQUITED
UNREQUITEDLY
UNRESCINDED
UNRESENTED
UNRESENTFUL
UNRESENTING
UNRESERVED
UNRESERVEDLY
UNRESERVEDNESS
UNRESERVES
UNRESISTANT
UNRESISTED
UNRESISTIBLE
UNRESISTING
UNRESISTINGLY
UNRESOLVABLE
UNRESOLVED
UNRESOLVEDNESS
UNRESPECTABLE
UNRESPECTED
UNRESPECTIVE
UNRESPITED
UNRESPONSIVE
UNRESPONSIVELY
UNRESTFULNESS
UNRESTFULNESSES
UNRESTINGLY
UNRESTINGNESS
UNRESTORED
UNRESTRAINABLE
UNRESTRAINED
UNRESTRAINEDLY
UNRESTRAINT
UNRESTRAINTS
UNRESTRICTED
UNRESTRICTEDLY
UNRETARDED
UNRETENTIVE
UNRETIRING
UNRETOUCHED
UNRETURNABLE
UNRETURNED
UNRETURNING
UNRETURNINGLY
UNREVEALABLE
UNREVEALED
UNREVEALING
UNREVENGED
UNREVENGEFUL
UNREVEREND
UNREVERENT
UNREVERSED
UNREVERTED

UNREVIEWABLE
UNREVIEWED
UNREVOLUTIONARY
UNREWARDED
UNREWARDEDLY
UNREWARDING
UNRHETORICAL
UNRHYTHMIC
UNRHYTHMICAL
UNRHYTHMICALLY
UNRIDDLEABLE
UNRIDDLERS
UNRIDDLING
UNRIDEABLE
UNRIGHTEOUS
UNRIGHTEOUSLY
UNRIGHTEOUSNESS
UNRIGHTFUL
UNRIGHTFULLY
UNRIGHTFULNESS
UNRIPENESS
UNRIPENESSES
UNRIPPINGS
UNRIVALLED
UNRIVETING
UNROMANISED
UNROMANIZED
UNROMANTIC
UNROMANTICAL
UNROMANTICALLY
UNROMANTICISED
UNROMANTICIZED
UNROOSTING
UNROUNDING
UNRUFFABLE
UNRUFFLEDNESS
UNRUFFLEDNESSES
UNRUFFLING
UNRULIMENT
UNRULIMENTS
UNRULINESS
UNRULINESSES
UNSADDLING
UNSAFENESS
UNSAFENESSES
UNSAFETIES
UNSAILORLIKE
UNSAINTING
UNSAINTLIER
UNSAINTLIEST
UNSAINTLINESS
UNSAINTLINESSES
UNSALABILITIES
UNSALABILITY
UNSALARIED
UNSALEABILITIES
UNSALEABILITY
UNSALEABLE
UNSALVAGEABLE
UNSANCTIFIED
UNSANCTIFIES
UNSANCTIFY
UNSANCTIFYING
UNSANCTIONED
UNSANDALLED
UNSANITARY
UNSATIABLE
UNSATIATED
UNSATIATING
UNSATIRICAL
UNSATISFACTION
UNSATISFACTIONS
UNSATISFACTORY
UNSATISFIABLE
UNSATISFIED
UNSATISFIEDNESS
UNSATISFYING
UNSATURATE
UNSATURATED
UNSATURATES
UNSATURATION
UNSATURATIONS
UNSAVORILY

UNSAVORINESS
UNSAVORINESSES
UNSAVOURILY
UNSAVOURINESS
UNSAVOURINESSES
UNSAYABLES
UNSCABBARD
UNSCABBARDED
UNSCABBARDING
UNSCABBARDS
UNSCALABLE
UNSCAVENGERED
UNSCEPTRED
UNSCHEDULED
UNSCHOLARLIKE
UNSCHOLARLY
UNSCHOOLED
UNSCIENTIFIC
UNSCISSORED
UNSCORCHED
UNSCOTTIFIED
UNSCRAMBLE
UNSCRAMBLED
UNSCRAMBLER
UNSCRAMBLERS
UNSCRAMBLES
UNSCRAMBLING
UNSCRATCHED
UNSCREENED
UNSCREWING
UNSCRIPTED
UNSCRIPTURAL
UNSCRIPTURALLY
UNSCRUPLED
UNSCRUPULOSITY
UNSCRUPULOUS
UNSCRUPULOUSLY
UNSCRUTINISED
UNSCRUTINIZED
UNSCULPTURED
UNSEALABLE
UNSEARCHABLE
UNSEARCHABLY
UNSEARCHED
UNSEASONABLE
UNSEASONABLY
UNSEASONED
UNSEASONEDNESS
UNSEASONING
UNSEAWORTHINESS
UNSEAWORTHY
UNSECONDED
UNSECTARIAN
UNSECTARIANISM
UNSECTARIANISMS
UNSEEMINGS
UNSEEMLIER
UNSEEMLIEST
UNSEEMLINESS
UNSEEMLINESSES
UNSEGMENTED
UNSEGREGATED
UNSEISABLE
UNSEIZABLE
UNSELECTED
UNSELECTIVE
UNSELECTIVELY
UNSELFCONSCIOUS
UNSELFISHLY
UNSELFISHNESS
UNSELFISHNESSES
UNSELLABLE
UNSEMINARIED
UNSENSATIONAL
UNSENSIBLE
UNSENSIBLY
UNSENSITISED
UNSENSITIVE
UNSENSITIZED
UNSENSUALISE
UNSENSUALISED
UNSENSUALISES
UNSENSUALISING

UNSENSUALIZE
UNSENSUALIZED
UNSENSUALIZES
UNSENSUALIZING
UNSENTENCED
UNSENTIMENTAL
UNSEPARABLE
UNSEPARATED
UNSEPULCHRED
UNSERIOUSNESS
UNSERIOUSNESSES
UNSERVICEABLE
UNSETTLEDLY
UNSETTLEDNESS
UNSETTLEDNESSES
UNSETTLEMENT
UNSETTLEMENTS
UNSETTLING
UNSETTLINGLY
UNSETTLINGS
UNSHACKLED
UNSHACKLES
UNSHACKLING
UNSHADOWABLE
UNSHADOWED
UNSHADOWING
UNSHAKABLE
UNSHAKABLENESS
UNSHAKABLY
UNSHAKEABLE
UNSHAKEABLENESS
UNSHAKEABLY
UNSHAKENLY
UNSHAPELIER
UNSHAPELIEST
UNSHARPENED
UNSHEATHED
UNSHEATHES
UNSHEATHING
UNSHELLING
UNSHELTERED
UNSHIELDED
UNSHIFTING
UNSHINGLED
UNSHIPPING
UNSHOCKABLE
UNSHOOTING
UNSHOUTING
UNSHOWERED
UNSHRINKABLE
UNSHRINKING
UNSHRINKINGLY
UNSHROUDED
UNSHROUDING
UNSHRUBBED
UNSHUNNABLE
UNSHUTTERED
UNSHUTTERING
UNSHUTTERS
UNSHUTTING
UNSIGHTEDLY
UNSIGHTING
UNSIGHTLIER
UNSIGHTLIEST
UNSIGHTLINESS
UNSIGHTLINESSES
UNSINEWING
UNSINKABLE
UNSINNOWED
UNSISTERED
UNSISTERLINESS
UNSISTERLY
UNSIZEABLE
UNSKILFULLY
UNSKILFULNESS
UNSKILFULNESSES
UNSKILLFUL
UNSKILLFULLY
UNSKILLFULNESS
UNSLAKABLE
UNSLEEPING
UNSLINGING
UNSLIPPING

UNSLUICING
UNSLUMBERING
UNSLUMBROUS
UNSMILINGLY
UNSMIRCHED
UNSMOOTHED
UNSMOOTHING
UNSMOTHERABLE
UNSNAGGING
UNSNAPPING
UNSNARLING
UNSNECKING
UNSOCIABILITIES
UNSOCIABILITY
UNSOCIABLE
UNSOCIABLENESS
UNSOCIABLY
UNSOCIALISED
UNSOCIALISM
UNSOCIALISMS
UNSOCIALITIES
UNSOCIALITY
UNSOCIALIZED
UNSOCIALLY
UNSOCKETED
UNSOCKETING
UNSOFTENED
UNSOFTENING
UNSOLDERED
UNSOLDERING
UNSOLDIERLIKE
UNSOLDIERLY
UNSOLICITED
UNSOLICITOUS
UNSOLIDITIES
UNSOLIDITY
UNSOLVABLE
UNSOPHISTICATE
UNSOPHISTICATED
UNSOUNDABLE
UNSOUNDEST
UNSOUNDNESS
UNSOUNDNESSES
UNSPARINGLY
UNSPARINGNESS
UNSPARINGNESSES
UNSPARRING
UNSPEAKABLE
UNSPEAKABLENESS
UNSPEAKABLY
UNSPEAKING
UNSPECIALISED
UNSPECIALIZED
UNSPECIFIABLE
UNSPECIFIC
UNSPECIFIED
UNSPECTACLED
UNSPECTACULAR
UNSPECULATIVE
UNSPELLING
UNSPHERING
UNSPIRITED
UNSPIRITUAL
UNSPIRITUALISE
UNSPIRITUALISED
UNSPIRITUALISES
UNSPIRITUALIZE
UNSPIRITUALIZED
UNSPIRITUALIZES
UNSPIRITUALLY
UNSPLINTERABLE
UNSPOOLING
UNSPORTING
UNSPORTSMANLIKE
UNSPOTTEDNESS
UNSPOTTEDNESSES
UNSPRINKLED
UNSTABLENESS
UNSTABLENESSES
UNSTABLEST
UNSTACKING
UNSTAIDNESS
UNSTAIDNESSES

UNSTAINABLE	UNSUCCOURED	UNTAMEABLY	UNTOWARDNESSES	UNVALUABLE	UNWHISTLEABLE
UNSTANCHABLE	UNSUFFERABLE	UNTAMEDNESS	UNTRACEABLE	UNVANQUISHABLE	UNWHOLESOME
UNSTANCHED	UNSUFFICIENT	UNTAMEDNESSES	UNTRACKING	UNVANQUISHED	UNWHOLESOMELY
UNSTANDARDISED	UNSUITABILITIES	UNTANGIBLE	UNTRACTABLE	UNVARIABLE	UNWHOLESOMENESS
UNSTANDARDIZED	UNSUITABILITY	UNTANGLING	UNTRACTABLENESS	UNVARIEGATED	UNWIELDIER
UNSTARCHED	UNSUITABLE	UNTARNISHED	UNTRADITIONAL	UNVARNISHED	UNWIELDIEST
UNSTARCHES	UNSUITABLENESS	UNTASTEFUL	UNTRADITIONALLY	UNVEILINGS	UNWIELDILY
UNSTARCHING	UNSUITABLY	UNTEACHABLE	UNTRAMMELED	UNVENDIBLE	UNWIELDINESS
UNSTARTLING	UNSUMMERED	UNTEACHABLENESS	UNTRAMMELLED	UNVENERABLE	UNWIELDINESSES
UNSTATESMANLIKE	UNSUMMONED	UNTEACHING	UNTRAMPLED	UNVENTILATED	UNWIELDLILY
UNSTATUTABLE	UNSUPERFLUOUS	UNTEARABLE	UNTRANQUIL	UNVERACIOUS	UNWIELDLINESS
UNSTATUTABLY	UNSUPERVISED	UNTECHNICAL	UNTRANSFERABLE	UNVERACITIES	UNWIELDLINESSES
UNSTAUNCHABLE	UNSUPPLENESS	UNTELLABLE	UNTRANSFERRABLE	UNVERACITY	UNWIFELIER
UNSTAUNCHED	UNSUPPLENESSES	UNTEMPERED	UNTRANSFORMED	UNVERBALISED	UNWIFELIEST
UNSTEADFAST	UNSUPPLIED	UNTEMPERING	UNTRANSLATABLE	UNVERBALIZED	UNWIFELIKE
UNSTEADFASTLY	UNSUPPORTABLE	UNTENABILITIES	UNTRANSLATABLY	UNVERIFIABILITY	UNWILLINGLY
UNSTEADFASTNESS	UNSUPPORTED	UNTENABILITY	UNTRANSLATED	UNVERIFIABLE	UNWILLINGNESS
UNSTEADIED	UNSUPPORTEDLY	UNTENABLENESS	UNTRANSMIGRATED	UNVERIFIED	UNWILLINGNESSES
UNSTEADIER	UNSUPPOSABLE	UNTENABLENESSES	UNTRANSMISSIBLE	UNVIOLATED	UNWINDABLE
UNSTEADIES	UNSUPPRESSED	UNTENANTABLE	UNTRANSMITTED	UNVIRTUOUS	UNWINDINGS
UNSTEADIEST	UNSURFACED	UNTENANTED	UNTRANSMUTABLE	UNVIRTUOUSLY	UNWINKINGLY
UNSTEADILY	UNSURMISED	UNTENANTING	UNTRANSMUTED	UNVISITABLE	UNWINNABLE
UNSTEADINESS	UNSURMOUNTABLE	UNTENDERED	UNTRANSPARENT	UNVISORING	UNWINNOWED
UNSTEADINESSES	UNSURPASSABLE	UNTENDERLY	UNTRAVELED	UNVITIATED	UNWISENESS
UNSTEADYING	UNSURPASSABLY	UNTERMINATED	UNTRAVELLED	UNVITRIFIABLE	UNWISENESSES
UNSTEELING	UNSURPASSED	UNTERRESTRIAL	UNTRAVERSABLE	UNVITRIFIED	UNWITCHING
UNSTEPPING	UNSURPRISED	UNTERRIFIED	UNTRAVERSED	UNVIZARDED	UNWITHDRAWING
UNSTERCORATED	UNSURPRISING	UNTERRIFYING	UNTREADING	UNVIZARDING	UNWITHERED
UNSTERILISED	UNSURPRISINGLY	UNTESTABLE	UNTREASURE	UNVOCALISED	UNWITHERING
UNSTERILIZED	UNSURVEYED	UNTETHERED	UNTREASURED	UNVOCALIZED	UNWITHHELD
UNSTICKING	UNSUSCEPTIBLE	UNTETHERING	UNTREASURES	UNVOICINGS	UNWITHHOLDEN
UNSTIGMATISED	UNSUSPECTED	UNTHANKFUL	UNTREASURING	UNVOYAGEABLE	UNWITHHOLDING
UNSTIGMATIZED	UNSUSPECTEDLY	UNTHANKFULLY	UNTREATABLE	UNVULGARISE	UNWITHSTOOD
UNSTIMULATED	UNSUSPECTEDNESS	UNTHANKFULNESS	UNTREMBLING	UNVULGARISED	UNWITNESSED
UNSTINTING	UNSUSPECTING	UNTHATCHED	UNTREMBLINGLY	UNVULGARISES	UNWITTINGLY
UNSTINTINGLY	UNSUSPECTINGLY	UNTHATCHES	UNTREMENDOUS	UNVULGARISING	UNWITTINGNESS
UNSTITCHED	UNSUSPENDED	UNTHATCHING	UNTREMULOUS	UNVULGARIZE	UNWITTINGNESSES
UNSTITCHES	UNSUSPICION	UNTHEOLOGICAL	UNTRENCHED	UNVULGARIZED	UNWOMANING
UNSTITCHING	UNSUSPICIONS	UNTHEORETICAL	UNTRESPASSING	UNVULGARIZES	UNWOMANLIER
UNSTOCKING	UNSUSPICIOUS	UNTHICKENED	UNTRIMMING	UNVULGARIZING	UNWOMANLIEST
UNSTOCKINGED	UNSUSPICIOUSLY	UNTHINKABILITY	UNTROUBLED	UNVULNERABLE	UNWOMANLINESS
UNSTOOPING	UNSUSTAINABLE	UNTHINKABLE	UNTROUBLEDLY	UNWANDERING	UNWOMANLINESSES
UNSTOPPABLE	UNSUSTAINED	UNTHINKABLENESS	UNTRUENESS	UNWARENESS	UNWONTEDLY
UNSTOPPABLY	UNSUSTAINING	UNTHINKABLY	UNTRUENESSES	UNWARENESSES	UNWONTEDNESS
UNSTOPPERED	UNSWADDLED	UNTHINKING	UNTRUSSERS	UNWARINESS	UNWONTEDNESSES
UNSTOPPERING	UNSWADDLES	UNTHINKINGLY	UNTRUSSING	UNWARINESSES	UNWORKABILITIES
UNSTOPPERS	UNSWADDLING	UNTHINKINGNESS	UNTRUSSINGS	UNWARRANTABLE	UNWORKABILITY
UNSTOPPING	UNSWALLOWED	UNTHOROUGH	UNTRUSTFUL	UNWARRANTABLY	UNWORKABLE
UNSTRAINED	UNSWATHING	UNTHOUGHTFUL	UNTRUSTINESS	UNWARRANTED	UNWORKMANLIKE
UNSTRAPPED	UNSWAYABLE	UNTHOUGHTFULLY	UNTRUSTINESSES	UNWARRANTEDLY	UNWORLDLIER
UNSTRAPPING	UNSWEARING	UNTHREADED	UNTRUSTING	UNWASHEDNESS	UNWORLDLIEST
UNSTRATIFIED	UNSWEARINGS	UNTHREADING	UNTRUSTWORTHILY	UNWASHEDNESSES	UNWORLDLINESS
UNSTREAMED	UNSWEETENED	UNTHREATENED	UNTRUSTWORTHY	UNWATCHABLE	UNWORLDLINESSES
UNSTRENGTHENED	UNSWERVING	UNTHREATENING	UNTRUTHFUL	UNWATCHFUL	UNWORSHIPFUL
UNSTRESSED	UNSWERVINGLY	UNTHRIFTILY	UNTRUTHFULLY	UNWATCHFULLY	UNWORSHIPPED
UNSTRESSES	UNSYLLABLED	UNTHRIFTINESS	UNTRUTHFULNESS	UNWATCHFULNESS	UNWORTHIER
UNSTRIATED	UNSYMMETRICAL	UNTHRIFTINESSES	UNTUCKERED	UNWATERING	UNWORTHIES
UNSTRINGED	UNSYMMETRICALLY	UNTHRIFTYHEAD	UNTUMULTUOUS	UNWAVERING	UNWORTHIEST
UNSTRINGING	UNSYMMETRIES	UNTHRIFTYHEADS	UNTUNABLENESS	UNWAVERINGLY	UNWORTHILY
UNSTRIPPED	UNSYMMETRISED	UNTHRIFTYHED	UNTUNABLENESSES	UNWEAKENED	UNWORTHINESS
UNSTRIPPING	UNSYMMETRIZED	UNTHRIFTYHEDS	UNTUNEABLE	UNWEAPONED	UNWORTHINESSES
UNSTRUCTURED	UNSYMMETRY	UNTHRONING	UNTUNEFULLY	UNWEAPONING	UNWOUNDABLE
UNSUBDUABLE	UNSYMPATHETIC	UNTIDINESS	UNTUNEFULNESS	UNWEARABLE	UNWRAPPING
UNSUBJECTED	UNSYMPATHIES	UNTIDINESSES	UNTUNEFULNESSES	UNWEARIABLE	UNWREATHED
UNSUBLIMATED	UNSYMPATHISING	UNTILLABLE	UNTURNABLE	UNWEARIABLY	UNWREATHES
UNSUBLIMED	UNSYMPATHIZING	UNTIMBERED	UNTWISTING	UNWEARIEDLY	UNWREATHING
UNSUBMERGED	UNSYMPATHY	UNTIMELIER	UNTWISTINGS	UNWEARIEDNESS	UNWRINKLED
UNSUBMISSIVE	UNSYNCHRONISED	UNTIMELIEST	UNTYPICALLY	UNWEARIEDNESSES	UNWRINKLES
UNSUBMITTING	UNSYNCHRONIZED	UNTIMELINESS	UNTYREABLE	UNWEARYING	UNWRINKLING
UNSUBSCRIBE	UNSYSTEMATIC	UNTIMELINESSES	UNUNUNIUMS	UNWEARYINGLY	UNYIELDING
UNSUBSCRIBED	UNSYSTEMATICAL	UNTIMEOUSLY	UNUPLIFTED	UNWEATHERED	UNYIELDINGLY
UNSUBSCRIBES	UNSYSTEMATISED	UNTINCTURED	UNUSEFULLY	UNWEDGABLE	UNYIELDINGNESS
UNSUBSCRIBING	UNSYSTEMATIZED	UNTIRINGLY	UNUSEFULNESS	UNWEDGEABLE	UPBRAIDERS
UNSUBSIDISED	UNTACKLING	UNTOCHERED	UNUSEFULNESSES	UNWEETINGLY	UPBRAIDING
UNSUBSIDIZED	UNTAINTEDLY	UNTOGETHER	UNUSUALNESS	UNWEIGHING	UPBRAIDINGLY
UNSUBSTANTIAL	UNTAINTEDNESS	UNTORMENTED	UNUSUALNESSES	UNWEIGHTED	UPBRAIDINGS
UNSUBSTANTIALLY	UNTAINTEDNESSES	UNTORTURED	UNUTILISED	UNWEIGHTING	UPBREAKING
UNSUBSTANTIATED	UNTAINTING	UNTOUCHABILITY	UNUTILIZED	UNWELCOMED	UPBRINGING
UNSUCCEEDED	UNTALENTED	UNTOUCHABLE	UNUTTERABLE	UNWELCOMELY	UPBRINGINGS
UNSUCCESSES	UNTAMABLENESS	UNTOUCHABLES	UNUTTERABLENESS	UNWELCOMENESS	UPBUILDERS
UNSUCCESSFUL	UNTAMABLENESSES	UNTOWARDLINESS	UNUTTERABLES	UNWELCOMENESSES	UPBUILDING
UNSUCCESSFULLY	UNTAMEABLE	UNTOWARDLY	UNUTTERABLY	UNWELLNESS	UPBUILDINGS
UNSUCCESSIVE	UNTAMEABLENESS	UNTOWARDNESS	UNVACCINATED	UNWELLNESSES	UPBUOYANCE

UPBUOYANCES	UPPERWORKS	UPTRAINING	UREDOSORUS	UROSTHENIC	UTEROGESTATION
UPBURSTING	UPPISHNESS	UPTURNINGS	UREDOSPORE	UROSTOMIES	UTEROGESTATIONS
UPCATCHING	UPPISHNESSES	UPVALUATION	UREDOSPORES	URTICACEOUS	UTEROTOMIES
UPCHEERING	UPPITINESS	UPVALUATIONS	UREOTELISM	URTICARIAL	UTILISABLE
UPCHUCKING	UPPITINESSES	UPWARDNESS	UREOTELISMS	URTICARIAS	UTILISATION
UPCLIMBING	UPPITYNESS	UPWARDNESSES	URETERITIS	URTICARIOUS	UTILISATIONS
UPCOUNTRIES	UPPITYNESSES	UPWELLINGS	URETERITISES	URTICATING	UTILITARIAN
UPDATEABLE	UPPROPPING	UPWHIRLING	URETHRITIC	URTICATION	UTILITARIANISE
UPDRAGGING	UPREACHING	URALITISATION	URETHRITIS	URTICATIONS	UTILITARIANISED
UPDRAUGHTS	UPRIGHTEOUSLY	URALITISATIONS	URETHRITISES	USABILITIES	UTILITARIANISES
UPFILLINGS	UPRIGHTING	URALITISED	URETHROSCOPE	USABLENESS	UTILITARIANISM
UPFLASHING	UPRIGHTNESS	URALITISES	URETHROSCOPES	USABLENESSES	UTILITARIANISMS
UPFLINGING	UPRIGHTNESSES	URALITISING	URETHROSCOPIC	USEABILITIES	UTILITARIANIZE
UPFOLLOWED	UPROARIOUS	URALITIZATION	URETHROSCOPIES	USEABILITY	UTILITARIANIZED
UPFOLLOWING	UPROARIOUSLY	URALITIZATIONS	URETHROSCOPY	USEABLENESS	UTILITARIANIZES
UPGATHERED	UPROARIOUSNESS	URALITIZED	URICOSURIC	USEABLENESSES	UTILITARIANS
UPGATHERING	UPROOTEDNESS	URALITIZES	URICOTELIC	USEFULNESS	UTILIZABLE
UPGRADABILITIES	UPROOTEDNESSES	URALITIZING	URICOTELISM	USEFULNESSES	UTILIZATION
UPGRADABILITY	UPROOTINGS	URANALYSES	URICOTELISMS	USELESSNESS	UTILIZATIONS
UPGRADABLE	UPSETTABLE	URANALYSIS	URINALYSES	USELESSNESSES	UTOPIANISE
UPGRADATION	UPSETTINGLY	URANINITES	URINALYSIS	USHERESSES	UTOPIANISED
UPGRADATIONS	UPSETTINGS	URANOGRAPHER	URINATIONS	USHERETTES	UTOPIANISER
UPGRADEABILITY	UPSHIFTING	URANOGRAPHERS	URINIFEROUS	USHERSHIPS	UTOPIANISERS
UPGRADEABLE	UPSHOOTING	URANOGRAPHIC	URINIPAROUS	USQUEBAUGH	UTOPIANISES
UPGROWINGS	UPSIDEOWNE	URANOGRAPHICAL	URINOGENITAL	USQUEBAUGHS	UTOPIANISING
UPHEAPINGS	UPSITTINGS	URANOGRAPHIES	URINOLOGIES	USTILAGINEOUS	UTOPIANISM
UPHILLWARD	UPSKILLING	URANOGRAPHIST	URINOMETER	USTILAGINOUS	UTOPIANISMS
UPHOARDING	UPSPEAKING	URANOGRAPHISTS	URINOMETERS	USTULATION	UTOPIANIZE
UPHOISTING	UPSPEARING	URANOGRAPHY	URINOSCOPIES	USTULATIONS	UTOPIANIZED
UPHOLDINGS	UPSPRINGING	URANOLOGIES	URINOSCOPY	USUALNESSES	UTOPIANIZER
UPHOLSTERED	UPSTANDING	URANOMETRIES	UROBILINOGEN	USUCAPIENT	UTOPIANIZERS
UPHOLSTERER	UPSTANDINGNESS	URANOMETRY	UROBILINOGENS	USUCAPIENTS	UTOPIANIZES
UPHOLSTERERS	UPSTARTING	URANOPLASTIES	UROCHORDAL	USUCAPIONS	UTOPIANIZING
UPHOLSTERIES	UPSTEPPING	URANOPLASTY	UROCHORDATE	USUCAPTIBLE	UTRICULARIA
UPHOLSTERING	UPSTIRRING	URBANENESS	UROCHORDATES	USUCAPTING	UTRICULARIAS
UPHOLSTERS	UPSTREAMED	URBANENESSES	UROCHROMES	USUCAPTION	UTRICULATE
UPHOLSTERY	UPSTREAMING	URBANISATION	URODYNAMICS	USUCAPTIONS	UTRICULITIS
UPHOLSTRESS	UPSTRETCHED	URBANISATIONS	UROGENITAL	USUFRUCTED	UTRICULITISES
UPHOLSTRESSES	UPSURGENCE	URBANISING	UROGRAPHIC	USUFRUCTING	UTTERABLENESS
UPHOORDING	UPSURGENCES	URBANISTIC	UROGRAPHIES	USUFRUCTUARIES	UTTERABLENESSES
UPKNITTING	UPSWARMING	URBANISTICALLY	UROKINASES	USUFRUCTUARY	UTTERANCES
UPLIFTINGLY	UPSWEEPING	URBANITIES	UROLAGNIAS	USURIOUSLY	UTTERMOSTS
UPLIFTINGS	UPSWELLING	URBANIZATION	UROLITHIASES	USURIOUSNESS	UTTERNESSES
UPLIGHTERS	UPSWINGING	URBANIZATIONS	UROLITHIASIS	USURIOUSNESSES	UVAROVITES
UPLIGHTING	UPTHROWING	URBANIZING	UROLOGICAL	USURPATION	UVULITISES
UPLINKINGS	UPTHRUSTED	URBANOLOGIES	UROLOGISTS	USURPATIONS	UXORICIDAL
UPMANSHIPS	UPTHRUSTING	URBANOLOGIST	UROPOIESES	USURPATIVE	UXORICIDES
UPPERCASED	UPTHUNDERED	URBANOLOGISTS	UROPOIESIS	USURPATORY	UXORILOCAL
UPPERCASES	UPTHUNDERING	URBANOLOGY	UROPYGIUMS	USURPATURE	UXORIOUSLY
UPPERCASING	UPTHUNDERS	URCEOLUSES	UROSCOPIES	USURPATURES	UXORIOUSNESS
UPPERCLASSMAN	UPTIGHTEST	UREDINIOSPORE	UROSCOPIST	USURPINGLY	UXORIOUSNESSES
UPPERCLASSMEN	UPTIGHTNESS	UREDINIOSPORES	UROSCOPISTS	UTERECTOMIES	
UPPERCUTTING	UPTIGHTNESSES	UREDIOSPORE	UROSTEGITE	UTERECTOMY	
UPPERPARTS	UPTITLINGS	UREDIOSPORES	UROSTEGITES	UTERITISES	

Vv

VACANTNESS
VACANTNESSES
VACATIONED
VACATIONER
VACATIONERS
VACATIONING
VACATIONIST
VACATIONISTS
VACATIONLAND
VACATIONLANDS
VACATIONLESS
VACCINATED
VACCINATES
VACCINATING
VACCINATION
VACCINATIONS
VACCINATOR
VACCINATORS
VACCINATORY
VACCINIUMS
VACILLATED
VACILLATES
VACILLATING
VACILLATINGLY
VACILLATION
VACILLATIONS
VACILLATOR
VACILLATORS
VACILLATORY
VACUATIONS
VACUOLATED
VACUOLATION
VACUOLATIONS
VACUOLISATION
VACUOLISATIONS
VACUOLIZATION
VACUOLIZATIONS
VACUOUSNESS
VACUOUSNESSES
VAGABONDAGE
VAGABONDAGES
VAGABONDED
VAGABONDING
VAGABONDISE
VAGABONDISED
VAGABONDISES
VAGABONDISH
VAGABONDISING
VAGABONDISM
VAGABONDISMS
VAGABONDIZE
VAGABONDIZED
VAGABONDIZES
VAGABONDIZING
VAGARIOUSLY
VAGILITIES
VAGINECTOMIES
VAGINECTOMY
VAGINICOLINE
VAGINICOLOUS
VAGINISMUS
VAGINISMUSES
VAGINITISES
VAGOTOMIES
VAGOTONIAS
VAGOTROPIC
VAGRANCIES

VAGRANTNESS
VAGRANTNESSES
VAGUENESSES
VAINGLORIED
VAINGLORIES
VAINGLORIOUS
VAINGLORIOUSLY
VAINGLORYING
VAINNESSES
VAIVODESHIP
VAIVODESHIPS
VALEDICTION
VALEDICTIONS
VALEDICTORIAN
VALEDICTORIANS
VALEDICTORIES
VALEDICTORY
VALENTINES
VALERIANACEOUS
VALETUDINARIAN
VALETUDINARIANS
VALETUDINARIES
VALETUDINARY
VALIANCIES
VALIANTNESS
VALIANTNESSES
VALIDATING
VALIDATION
VALIDATIONS
VALIDATORY
VALIDITIES
VALIDNESSES
VALLATIONS
VALLECULAE
VALLECULAR
VALLECULATE
VALORISATION
VALORISATIONS
VALORISING
VALORIZATION
VALORIZATIONS
VALORIZING
VALOROUSLY
VALPOLICELLA
VALPOLICELLAS
VALPROATES
VALUABLENESS
VALUABLENESSES
VALUATIONAL
VALUATIONALLY
VALUATIONS
VALUELESSNESS
VALUELESSNESSES
VALVASSORS
VALVULITIS
VALVULITISES
VAMPIRISED
VAMPIRISES
VAMPIRISING
VAMPIRISMS
VAMPIRIZED
VAMPIRIZES
VAMPIRIZING
VANADIATES
VANADINITE
VANADINITES
VANASPATIS

VANCOMYCIN
VANCOMYCINS
VANDALISATION
VANDALISATIONS
VANDALISED
VANDALISES
VANDALISING
VANDALISMS
VANDALISTIC
VANDALIZATION
VANDALIZATIONS
VANDALIZED
VANDALIZES
VANDALIZING
VANGUARDISM
VANGUARDISMS
VANGUARDIST
VANGUARDISTS
VANISHINGLY
VANISHINGS
VANISHMENT
VANISHMENTS
VANITORIES
VANPOOLING
VANPOOLINGS
VANQUISHABLE
VANQUISHED
VANQUISHER
VANQUISHERS
VANQUISHES
VANQUISHING
VANQUISHMENT
VANQUISHMENTS
VANTAGELESS
VANTBRACES
VAPIDITIES
VAPIDNESSES
VAPORABILITIES
VAPORABILITY
VAPORESCENCE
VAPORESCENCES
VAPORESCENT
VAPORETTOS
VAPORIFORM
VAPORIMETER
VAPORIMETERS
VAPORISABLE
VAPORISATION
VAPORISATIONS
VAPORISERS
VAPORISHNESS
VAPORISHNESSES
VAPORISING
VAPORIZABLE
VAPORIZATION
VAPORIZATIONS
VAPORIZERS
VAPORIZING
VAPOROSITIES
VAPOROSITY
VAPOROUSLY
VAPOROUSNESS
VAPOROUSNESSES
VAPORWARES
VAPOURABILITIES
VAPOURABILITY
VAPOURABLE

VAPOURINGLY
VAPOURINGS
VAPOURISHNESS
VAPOURISHNESSES
VAPOURLESS
VAPOURWARE
VAPOURWARES
VAPULATING
VAPULATION
VAPULATIONS
VARIABILITIES
VARIABILITY
VARIABLENESS
VARIABLENESSES
VARIATIONAL
VARIATIONALLY
VARIATIONIST
VARIATIONISTS
VARIATIONS
VARICELLAR
VARICELLAS
VARICELLATE
VARICELLOID
VARICELLOUS
VARICOCELE
VARICOCELES
VARICOLORED
VARICOLOURED
VARICOSITIES
VARICOSITY
VARICOTOMIES
VARICOTOMY
VARIEDNESS
VARIEDNESSES
VARIEGATED
VARIEGATES
VARIEGATING
VARIEGATION
VARIEGATIONS
VARIEGATOR
VARIEGATORS
VARIETALLY
VARIFOCALS
VARIFORMLY
VARIOLATED
VARIOLATES
VARIOLATING
VARIOLATION
VARIOLATIONS
VARIOLATOR
VARIOLATORS
VARIOLISATION
VARIOLISATIONS
VARIOLITES
VARIOLITIC
VARIOLIZATION
VARIOLIZATIONS
VARIOLOIDS
VARIOMETER
VARIOMETERS
VARIOUSNESS
VARIOUSNESSES
VARISCITES
VARITYPING
VARITYPIST
VARITYPISTS
VARLETESSES

VARLETRIES
VARNISHERS
VARNISHING
VARNISHINGS
VARSOVIENNE
VARSOVIENNES
VASCULARISATION
VASCULARISE
VASCULARISED
VASCULARISES
VASCULARISING
VASCULARITIES
VASCULARITY
VASCULARIZATION
VASCULARIZE
VASCULARIZED
VASCULARIZES
VASCULARIZING
VASCULARLY
VASCULATURE
VASCULATURES
VASCULIFORM
VASCULITIDES
VASCULITIS
VASECTOMIES
VASECTOMISE
VASECTOMISED
VASECTOMISES
VASECTOMISING
VASECTOMIZE
VASECTOMIZED
VASECTOMIZES
VASECTOMIZING
VASOACTIVE
VASOACTIVITIES
VASOACTIVITY
VASOCONSTRICTOR
VASODILATATION
VASODILATATIONS
VASODILATATORY
VASODILATION
VASODILATIONS
VASODILATOR
VASODILATORS
VASODILATORY
VASOINHIBITOR
VASOINHIBITORS
VASOINHIBITORY
VASOPRESSIN
VASOPRESSINS
VASOPRESSOR
VASOPRESSORS
VASOSPASMS
VASOSPASTIC
VASOTOCINS
VASOTOMIES
VASSALAGES
VASSALESSES
VASSALISED
VASSALISES
VASSALISING
VASSALIZED
VASSALIZES
VASSALIZING
VASSALLING
VASSALRIES
VASTIDITIES

VASTITUDES
VASTNESSES
VATICINATE
VATICINATED
VATICINATES
VATICINATING
VATICINATION
VATICINATIONS
VATICINATOR
VATICINATORS
VATICINATORY
VAUDEVILLE
VAUDEVILLEAN
VAUDEVILLEANS
VAUDEVILLES
VAUDEVILLIAN
VAUDEVILLIANS
VAUDEVILLIST
VAUDEVILLISTS
VAULTINGLY
VAUNTERIES
VAUNTINGLY
VAVASORIES
VECTOGRAPH
VECTOGRAPHS
VECTORIALLY
VECTORINGS
VECTORISATION
VECTORISATIONS
VECTORISED
VECTORISES
VECTORISING
VECTORIZATION
VECTORIZATIONS
VECTORIZED
VECTORIZES
VECTORIZING
VECTORSCOPE
VECTORSCOPES
VEGEBURGER
VEGEBURGERS
VEGETABLES
VEGETARIAN
VEGETARIANISM
VEGETARIANISMS
VEGETARIANS
VEGETATING
VEGETATINGS
VEGETATION
VEGETATIONAL
VEGETATIONS
VEGETATIOUS
VEGETATIVE
VEGETATIVELY
VEGETATIVENESS
VEGGIEBURGER
VEGGIEBURGERS
VEHEMENCES
VEHEMENCIES
VEHEMENTLY
VEILLEUSES
VEINSTONES
VEINSTUFFS
VELARISATION
VELARISATIONS
VELARISING
VELARIZATION

VELARIZATIONS
VELARIZING
VELDSCHOEN
VELDSCHOENS
VELDSKOENS
VELITATION
VELITATIONS
VELLEITIES
VELLENAGES
VELLICATED
VELLICATES
VELLICATING
VELLICATION
VELLICATIONS
VELLICATIVE
VELOCIMETER
VELOCIMETERS
VELOCIMETRIES
VELOCIMETRY
VELOCIPEDE
VELOCIPEDEAN
VELOCIPEDEANS
VELOCIPEDED
VELOCIPEDER
VELOCIPEDERS
VELOCIPEDES
VELOCIPEDIAN
VELOCIPEDIANS
VELOCIPEDING
VELOCIPEDIST
VELOCIPEDISTS
VELOCIRAPTOR
VELOCIRAPTORS
VELOCITIES
VELODROMES
VELOUTINES
VELUTINOUS
VELVETEENED
VELVETEENS
VELVETIEST
VELVETINESS
VELVETINESSES
VELVETINGS
VELVETLIKE
VENALITIES
VENATICALLY
VENATIONAL
VENATORIAL
VENDETTIST
VENDETTISTS
VENDIBILITIES
VENDIBILITY
VENDIBLENESS
VENDIBLENESSES
VENDITATION
VENDITATIONS
VENDITIONS
VENEERINGS
VENEFICALLY
VENEFICIOUS
VENEFICIOUSLY
VENEFICOUS
VENEFICOUSLY
VENENATING
VENEPUNCTURE
VENEPUNCTURES
VENERABILITIES
VENERABILITY
VENERABLENESS
VENERABLENESSES
VENERABLES
VENERATING
VENERATION
VENERATIONAL
VENERATIONS
VENERATIVENESS
VENERATORS
VENEREOLOGICAL
VENEREOLOGIES
VENEREOLOGIST
VENEREOLOGISTS
VENEREOLOGY
VENESECTION

VENESECTIONS
VENGEANCES
VENGEFULLY
VENGEFULNESS
VENGEFULNESSES
VENGEMENTS
VENIALITIES
VENIALNESS
VENIALNESSES
VENIPUNCTURE
VENIPUNCTURES
VENISECTION
VENISECTIONS
VENOGRAPHIC
VENOGRAPHICAL
VENOGRAPHIES
VENOGRAPHY
VENOLOGIES
VENOMOUSLY
VENOMOUSNESS
VENOMOUSNESSES
VENOSCLEROSES
VENOSCLEROSIS
VENOSITIES
VENOUSNESS
VENOUSNESSES
VENTIDUCTS
VENTIFACTS
VENTILABLE
VENTILATED
VENTILATES
VENTILATING
VENTILATION
VENTILATIONS
VENTILATIVE
VENTILATOR
VENTILATORS
VENTILATORY
VENTOSITIES
VENTRICLES
VENTRICOSE
VENTRICOSITIES
VENTRICOSITY
VENTRICOUS
VENTRICULAR
VENTRICULE
VENTRICULES
VENTRICULI
VENTRICULUS
VENTRILOQUAL
VENTRILOQUIAL
VENTRILOQUIALLY
VENTRILOQUIES
VENTRILOQUISE
VENTRILOQUISED
VENTRILOQUISES
VENTRILOQUISING
VENTRILOQUISM
VENTRILOQUISMS
VENTRILOQUIST
VENTRILOQUISTIC
VENTRILOQUISTS
VENTRILOQUIZE
VENTRILOQUIZED
VENTRILOQUIZES
VENTRILOQUIZING
VENTRILOQUOUS
VENTRILOQUY
VENTRIPOTENT
VENTROLATERAL
VENTROMEDIAL
VENTURESOME
VENTURESOMELY
VENTURESOMENESS
VENTURINGLY
VENTURINGS
VENTUROUSLY
VENTUROUSNESS
VENTUROUSNESSES
VERACIOUSLY
VERACIOUSNESS
VERACIOUSNESSES
VERACITIES

VERANDAHED
VERAPAMILS
VERATRIDINE
VERATRIDINES
VERATRINES
VERBALISATION
VERBALISATIONS
VERBALISED
VERBALISER
VERBALISERS
VERBALISES
VERBALISING
VERBALISMS
VERBALISTIC
VERBALISTS
VERBALITIES
VERBALIZATION
VERBALIZATIONS
VERBALIZED
VERBALIZER
VERBALIZERS
VERBALIZES
VERBALIZING
VERBALLING
VERBARIANS
VERBASCUMS
VERBENACEOUS
VERBERATED
VERBERATES
VERBERATING
VERBERATION
VERBERATIONS
VERBICIDES
VERBIFICATION
VERBIFICATIONS
VERBIFYING
VERBIGERATE
VERBIGERATED
VERBIGERATES
VERBIGERATING
VERBIGERATION
VERBIGERATIONS
VERBOSENESS
VERBOSENESSES
VERBOSITIES
VERDANCIES
VERDIGRISED
VERDIGRISES
VERDIGRISING
VERDURELESS
VERGEBOARD
VERGEBOARDS
VERGENCIES
VERGERSHIP
VERGERSHIPS
VERIDICALITIES
VERIDICALITY
VERIDICALLY
VERIDICOUS
VERIFIABILITIES
VERIFIABILITY
VERIFIABLE
VERIFIABLENESS
VERIFIABLY
VERIFICATION
VERIFICATIONS
VERIFICATIVE
VERIFICATORY
VERISIMILAR
VERISIMILARLY
VERISIMILITIES
VERISIMILITUDE
VERISIMILITUDES
VERISIMILITY
VERISIMILOUS
VERITABLENESS
VERITABLENESSES
VERJUICING
VERKRAMPTE
VERKRAMPTES
VERMEILING
VERMEILLED
VERMEILLES

VERMEILLING
VERMICELLI
VERMICELLIS
VERMICIDAL
VERMICIDES
VERMICULAR
VERMICULARLY
VERMICULATE
VERMICULATED
VERMICULATES
VERMICULATING
VERMICULATION
VERMICULATIONS
VERMICULES
VERMICULITE
VERMICULITES
VERMICULOUS
VERMICULTURE
VERMICULTURES
VERMIFUGAL
VERMIFUGES
VERMILIONED
VERMILIONING
VERMILIONS
VERMILLING
VERMILLION
VERMILLIONS
VERMINATED
VERMINATES
VERMINATING
VERMINATION
VERMINATIONS
VERMINOUSLY
VERMINOUSNESS
VERMINOUSNESSES
VERMIVOROUS
VERNACULAR
VERNACULARISE
VERNACULARISED
VERNACULARISES
VERNACULARISING
VERNACULARISM
VERNACULARISMS
VERNACULARIST
VERNACULARISTS
VERNACULARITIES
VERNACULARITY
VERNACULARIZE
VERNACULARIZED
VERNACULARIZES
VERNACULARIZING
VERNACULARLY
VERNACULARS
VERNALISATION
VERNALISATIONS
VERNALISED
VERNALISES
VERNALISING
VERNALITIES
VERNALIZATION
VERNALIZATIONS
VERNALIZED
VERNALIZES
VERNALIZING
VERNATIONS
VERNISSAGE
VERNISSAGES
VERRUCIFORM
VERRUCOSITIES
VERRUCOSITY
VERSABILITIES
VERSABILITY
VERSATILELY
VERSATILENESS
VERSATILENESSES
VERSATILITIES
VERSATILITY
VERSICOLOR
VERSICOLOUR
VERSICOLOURED
VERSICULAR
VERSIFICATION
VERSIFICATIONS

VERSIFICATOR
VERSIFICATORS
VERSIFIERS
VERSIFYING
VERSIONERS
VERSIONING
VERSIONINGS
VERSIONIST
VERSIONISTS
VERSLIBRIST
VERSLIBRISTE
VERSLIBRISTES
VERSLIBRISTS
VERTEBRALLY
VERTEBRATE
VERTEBRATED
VERTEBRATES
VERTEBRATION
VERTEBRATIONS
VERTICALITIES
VERTICALITY
VERTICALLY
VERTICALNESS
VERTICALNESSES
VERTICILLASTER
VERTICILLASTERS
VERTICILLATE
VERTICILLATED
VERTICILLATELY
VERTICILLATION
VERTICILLATIONS
VERTICILLIUM
VERTICILLIUMS
VERTICITIES
VERTIGINES
VERTIGINOUS
VERTIGINOUSLY
VERTIGINOUSNESS
VERTIPORTS
VERUMONTANA
VERUMONTANUM
VERUMONTANUMS
VESICATING
VESICATION
VESICATIONS
VESICATORIES
VESICATORY
VESICULARITIES
VESICULARITY
VESICULARLY
VESICULATE
VESICULATED
VESICULATES
VESICULATING
VESICULATION
VESICULATIONS
VESICULOSE
VESPERTILIAN
VESPERTILIONID
VESPERTILIONIDS
VESPERTILIONINE
VESPERTINAL
VESPERTINE
VESPIARIES
VESTIARIES
VESTIBULAR
VESTIBULED
VESTIBULES
VESTIBULING
VESTIBULITIS
VESTIBULITISES
VESTIBULUM
VESTIGIALLY
VESTIMENTAL
VESTIMENTARY
VESTIMENTS
VESTITURES
VESTMENTAL
VESTMENTED
VESUVIANITE
VESUVIANITES
VETCHLINGS
VETERINARIAN

VETERINARIANS
VETERINARIES
VETERINARY
VEXATIOUSLY
VEXATIOUSNESS
VEXATIOUSNESSES
VEXEDNESSES
VEXILLARIES
VEXILLATION
VEXILLATIONS
VEXILLOLOGIC
VEXILLOLOGICAL
VEXILLOLOGIES
VEXILLOLOGIST
VEXILLOLOGISTS
VEXILLOLOGY
VEXINGNESS
VEXINGNESSES
VIABILITIES
VIBRACULAR
VIBRACULARIA
VIBRACULARIUM
VIBRACULOID
VIBRACULUM
VIBRAHARPIST
VIBRAHARPISTS
VIBRAHARPS
VIBRANCIES
VIBRAPHONE
VIBRAPHONES
VIBRAPHONIST
VIBRAPHONISTS
VIBRATILITIES
VIBRATILITY
VIBRATINGLY
VIBRATIONAL
VIBRATIONLESS
VIBRATIONS
VIBRATIUNCLE
VIBRATIUNCLES
VIBRATOLESS
VIBROFLOTATION
VIBROFLOTATIONS
VIBROGRAPH
VIBROGRAPHS
VIBROMETER
VIBROMETERS
VICARESSES
VICARIANCE
VICARIANCES
VICARIANTS
VICARIATES
VICARIOUSLY
VICARIOUSNESS
VICARIOUSNESSES
VICARSHIPS
VICEGERENCIES
VICEGERENCY
VICEGERENT
VICEGERENTS
VICEREGALLY
VICEREGENT
VICEREGENTS
VICEREINES
VICEROYALTIES
VICEROYALTY
VICEROYSHIP
VICEROYSHIPS
VICHYSSOIS
VICHYSSOISE
VICHYSSOISES
VICINITIES
VICIOSITIES
VICIOUSNESS
VICIOUSNESSES
VICISSITUDE
VICISSITUDES
VICISSITUDINARY
VICISSITUDINOUS
VICOMTESSE
VICOMTESSES
VICTIMHOOD
VICTIMHOODS

VICTIMISATION	VIGORISHES	VINEGARRETTES	VIRTUALIST	VISUALISATIONS	VITRIFACTURE
VICTIMISATIONS	VIGOROUSLY	VINEGARROON	VIRTUALISTS	VISUALISED	VITRIFACTURES
VICTIMISED	VIGOROUSNESS	VINEGARROONS	VIRTUALITIES	VISUALISER	VITRIFIABILITY
VICTIMISER	VIGOROUSNESSES	VINEYARDIST	VIRTUALITY	VISUALISERS	VITRIFIABLE
VICTIMISERS	VIKINGISMS	VINEYARDISTS	VIRTUALIZE	VISUALISES	VITRIFICATION
VICTIMISES	VILDNESSES	VINICULTURAL	VIRTUALIZED	VISUALISING	VITRIFICATIONS
VICTIMISING	VILENESSES	VINICULTURE	VIRTUALIZES	VISUALISTS	VITRIFYING
VICTIMIZATION	VILIFICATION	VINICULTURES	VIRTUALIZING	VISUALITIES	VITRIOLATE
VICTIMIZATIONS	VILIFICATIONS	VINICULTURIST	VIRTUELESS	VISUALIZATION	VITRIOLATED
VICTIMIZED	VILIPENDED	VINICULTURISTS	VIRTUOSITIES	VISUALIZATIONS	VITRIOLATES
VICTIMIZER	VILIPENDER	VINIFEROUS	VIRTUOSITY	VISUALIZED	VITRIOLATING
VICTIMIZERS	VILIPENDERS	VINIFICATION	VIRTUOSOSHIP	VISUALIZER	VITRIOLATION
VICTIMIZES	VILIPENDING	VINIFICATIONS	VIRTUOSOSHIPS	VISUALIZERS	VITRIOLATIONS
VICTIMIZING	VILLAGERIES	VINIFICATOR	VIRTUOUSLY	VISUALIZES	VITRIOLING
VICTIMLESS	VILLAGIOES	VINIFICATORS	VIRTUOUSNESS	VISUALIZING	VITRIOLISATION
VICTIMOLOGIES	VILLAGISATION	VINOLOGIES	VIRTUOUSNESSES	VITALISATION	VITRIOLISATIONS
VICTIMOLOGIST	VILLAGISATIONS	VINOLOGIST	VIRULENCES	VITALISATIONS	VITRIOLISE
VICTIMOLOGISTS	VILLAGIZATION	VINOLOGISTS	VIRULENCIES	VITALISERS	VITRIOLISED
VICTIMOLOGY	VILLAGIZATIONS	VINOSITIES	VIRULENTLY	VITALISING	VITRIOLISES
VICTORESSES	VILLAGREES	VINTAGINGS	VIRULIFEROUS	VITALISTIC	VITRIOLISING
VICTORIANA	VILLAINAGE	VINYLCYANIDE	VISAGISTES	VITALISTICALLY	VITRIOLIZATION
VICTORINES	VILLAINAGES	VINYLCYANIDES	VISCACHERA	VITALITIES	VITRIOLIZATIONS
VICTORIOUS	VILLAINESS	VINYLIDENE	VISCACHERAS	VITALIZATION	VITRIOLIZE
VICTORIOUSLY	VILLAINESSES	VINYLIDENES	VISCERALLY	VITALIZATIONS	VITRIOLIZED
VICTORIOUSNESS	VILLAINIES	VIOLABILITIES	VISCERATED	VITALIZERS	VITRIOLIZES
VICTORYLESS	VILLAINOUS	VIOLABILITY	VISCERATES	VITALIZING	VITRIOLIZING
VICTRESSES	VILLAINOUSLY	VIOLABLENESS	VISCERATING	VITALNESSES	VITRIOLLED
VICTROLLAS	VILLAINOUSNESS	VIOLABLENESSES	VISCEROMOTOR	VITAMINISE	VITRIOLLING
VICTUALAGE	VILLANAGES	VIOLACEOUS	VISCEROPTOSES	VITAMINISED	VITUPERABLE
VICTUALAGES	VILLANELLA	VIOLATIONS	VISCEROPTOSIS	VITAMINISES	VITUPERATE
VICTUALERS	VILLANELLAS	VIOLENTING	VISCEROTONIA	VITAMINISING	VITUPERATED
VICTUALING	VILLANELLE	VIOLINISTIC	VISCEROTONIAS	VITAMINIZE	VITUPERATES
VICTUALLAGE	VILLANELLES	VIOLINISTICALLY	VISCEROTONIC	VITAMINIZED	VITUPERATING
VICTUALLAGES	VILLANOUSLY	VIOLINISTS	VISCIDITIES	VITAMINIZES	VITUPERATION
VICTUALLED	VILLEGGIATURA	VIOLONCELLI	VISCIDNESS	VITAMINIZING	VITUPERATIONS
VICTUALLER	VILLEGGIATURAS	VIOLONCELLIST	VISCIDNESSES	VITASCOPES	VITUPERATIVE
VICTUALLERS	VILLEINAGE	VIOLONCELLISTS	VISCOELASTIC	VITATIVENESS	VITUPERATIVELY
VICTUALLESS	VILLEINAGES	VIOLONCELLO	VISCOELASTICITY	VITATIVENESSES	VITUPERATOR
VICTUALLING	VILLENAGES	VIOLONCELLOS	VISCOMETER	VITELLICLE	VITUPERATORS
VIDEOCASSETTE	VILLIAGOES	VIOSTEROLS	VISCOMETERS	VITELLICLES	VITUPERATORY
VIDEOCASSETTES	VILLICATION	VIPERFISHES	VISCOMETRIC	VITELLIGENOUS	VIVACIOUSLY
VIDEOCONFERENCE	VILLICATIONS	VIPERIFORM	VISCOMETRICAL	VITELLINES	VIVACIOUSNESS
VIDEODISCS	VILLOSITIES	VIPERISHLY	VISCOMETRIES	VITELLOGENESES	VIVACIOUSNESSES
VIDEODISKS	VINAIGRETTE	VIPEROUSLY	VISCOMETRY	VITELLOGENESIS	VIVACISSIMO
VIDEOGRAMS	VINAIGRETTES	VIRAGINIAN	VISCOSIMETER	VITELLOGENIC	VIVACITIES
VIDEOGRAPHER	VINBLASTINE	VIRAGINOUS	VISCOSIMETERS	VITELLUSES	VIVANDIERE
VIDEOGRAPHERS	VINBLASTINES	VIREONINES	VISCOSIMETRIC	VITIATIONS	VIVANDIERES
VIDEOGRAPHIES	VINCIBILITIES	VIRESCENCE	VISCOSIMETRICAL	VITICETUMS	VIVANDIERS
VIDEOGRAPHY	VINCIBILITY	VIRESCENCES	VISCOSIMETRIES	VITICOLOUS	VIVERRINES
VIDEOLANDS	VINCIBLENESS	VIRGINALIST	VISCOSIMETRY	VITICULTURAL	VIVIANITES
VIDEOPHILE	VINCIBLENESSES	VIRGINALISTS	VISCOSITIES	VITICULTURALLY	VIVIDITIES
VIDEOPHILES	VINCRISTINE	VIRGINALLED	VISCOUNTCIES	VITICULTURE	VIVIDNESSES
VIDEOPHONE	VINCRISTINES	VIRGINALLING	VISCOUNTCY	VITICULTURER	VIVIFICATION
VIDEOPHONES	VINDEMIATE	VIRGINALLY	VISCOUNTESS	VITICULTURERS	VIVIFICATIONS
VIDEOPHONIC	VINDEMIATED	VIRGINHOOD	VISCOUNTESSES	VITICULTURES	VIVIPARIES
VIDEOTAPED	VINDEMIATES	VIRGINHOODS	VISCOUNTIES	VITICULTURIST	VIVIPARISM
VIDEOTAPES	VINDEMIATING	VIRGINITIES	VISCOUNTSHIP	VITICULTURISTS	VIVIPARISMS
VIDEOTAPING	VINDICABILITIES	VIRGINIUMS	VISCOUNTSHIPS	VITIFEROUS	VIVIPARITIES
VIDEOTELEPHONE	VINDICABILITY	VIRIDESCENCE	VISCOUSNESS	VITILITIGATE	VIVIPARITY
VIDEOTELEPHONES	VINDICABLE	VIRIDESCENCES	VISCOUSNESSES	VITILITIGATED	VIVIPAROUS
VIDEOTEXES	VINDICATED	VIRIDESCENT	VISIBILITIES	VITILITIGATES	VIVIPAROUSLY
VIDEOTEXTS	VINDICATES	VIRIDITIES	VISIBILITY	VITILITIGATING	VIVIPAROUSNESS
VIEWERSHIP	VINDICATING	VIRILESCENCE	VISIBLENESS	VITILITIGATION	VIVISECTED
VIEWERSHIPS	VINDICATION	VIRILESCENCES	VISIBLENESSES	VITILITIGATIONS	VIVISECTING
VIEWFINDER	VINDICATIONS	VIRILESCENT	VISIOGENIC	VITIOSITIES	VIVISECTION
VIEWFINDERS	VINDICATIVE	VIRILISATION	VISIONALLY	VITRAILLED	VIVISECTIONAL
VIEWINESSES	VINDICATIVENESS	VIRILISATIONS	VISIONARIES	VITRAILLIST	VIVISECTIONALLY
VIEWLESSLY	VINDICATOR	VIRILISING	VISIONARINESS	VITRAILLISTS	VIVISECTIONIST
VIEWPHONES	VINDICATORILY	VIRILITIES	VISIONARINESSES	VITRECTOMIES	VIVISECTIONISTS
VIEWPOINTS	VINDICATORS	VIRILIZATION	VISIONINGS	VITRECTOMY	VIVISECTIONS
VIGILANCES	VINDICATORY	VIRILIZATIONS	VISIONISTS	VITREOSITIES	VIVISECTIVE
VIGILANTES	VINDICATRESS	VIRILIZING	VISIONLESS	VITREOSITY	VIVISECTOR
VIGILANTISM	VINDICATRESSES	VIROLOGICAL	VISIOPHONE	VITREOUSES	VIVISECTORIUM
VIGILANTISMS	VINDICTIVE	VIROLOGICALLY	VISIOPHONES	VITREOUSLY	VIVISECTORIUMS
VIGILANTLY	VINDICTIVELY	VIROLOGIES	VISITATION	VITREOUSNESS	VIVISECTORS
VIGILANTNESS	VINDICTIVENESS	VIROLOGIST	VISITATIONAL	VITREOUSNESSES	VIVISEPULTURE
VIGILANTNESSES	VINEDRESSER	VIROLOGISTS	VISITATIONS	VITRESCENCE	VIVISEPULTURES
VIGINTILLION	VINEDRESSERS	VIRTUALISE	VISITATIVE	VITRESCENCES	VIXENISHLY
VIGINTILLIONS	VINEGARETTE	VIRTUALISED	VISITATORIAL	VITRESCENT	VIXENISHNESS
VIGNETTERS	VINEGARETTES	VIRTUALISES	VISITATORS	VITRESCIBILITY	VIXENISHNESSES
VIGNETTING	VINEGARING	VIRTUALISING	VISITORIAL	VITRESCIBLE	VIZIERATES
VIGNETTIST	VINEGARISH	VIRTUALISM	VISITRESSES	VITRIFACTION	VIZIERSHIP
VIGNETTISTS	VINEGARRETTE	VIRTUALISMS	VISUALISATION	VITRIFACTIONS	VIZIERSHIPS

VIZIRSHIPS
VOCABULARIAN
VOCABULARIANS
VOCABULARIED
VOCABULARIES
VOCABULARY
VOCABULIST
VOCABULISTS
VOCALICALLY
VOCALISATION
VOCALISATIONS
VOCALISERS
VOCALISING
VOCALITIES
VOCALIZATION
VOCALIZATIONS
VOCALIZERS
VOCALIZING
VOCALNESSES
VOCATIONAL
VOCATIONALISM
VOCATIONALISMS
VOCATIONALIST
VOCATIONALISTS
VOCATIONALLY
VOCATIVELY
VOCICULTURAL
VOCIFERANCE
VOCIFERANCES
VOCIFERANT
VOCIFERANTS
VOCIFERATE
VOCIFERATED
VOCIFERATES
VOCIFERATING
VOCIFERATION
VOCIFERATIONS
VOCIFERATOR
VOCIFERATORS
VOCIFEROSITIES
VOCIFEROSITY
VOCIFEROUS
VOCIFEROUSLY
VOCIFEROUSNESS
VOETGANGER
VOETGANGERS
VOETSTOETS
VOETSTOOTS
VOGUISHNESS

VOGUISHNESSES
VOICEFULNESS
VOICEFULNESSES
VOICELESSLY
VOICELESSNESS
VOICELESSNESSES
VOICEMAILS
VOICEOVERS
VOICEPRINT
VOICEPRINTS
VOIDABLENESS
VOIDABLENESSES
VOIDNESSES
VOISINAGES
VOITURIERS
VOIVODESHIP
VOIVODESHIPS
VOLATILENESS
VOLATILENESSES
VOLATILISABLE
VOLATILISATION
VOLATILISATIONS
VOLATILISE
VOLATILISED
VOLATILISES
VOLATILISING
VOLATILITIES
VOLATILITY
VOLATILIZABLE
VOLATILIZATION
VOLATILIZATIONS
VOLATILIZE
VOLATILIZED
VOLATILIZES
VOLATILIZING
VOLCANICALLY
VOLCANICITIES
VOLCANICITY
VOLCANISATION
VOLCANISATIONS
VOLCANISED
VOLCANISES
VOLCANISING
VOLCANISMS
VOLCANISTS
VOLCANIZATION
VOLCANIZATIONS
VOLCANIZED
VOLCANIZES

VOLCANIZING
VOLCANOLOGIC
VOLCANOLOGICAL
VOLCANOLOGIES
VOLCANOLOGIST
VOLCANOLOGISTS
VOLCANOLOGY
VOLITATING
VOLITATION
VOLITATIONAL
VOLITATIONS
VOLITIONAL
VOLITIONALLY
VOLITIONARY
VOLITIONLESS
VOLITORIAL
VOLKSLIEDER
VOLKSRAADS
VOLLEYBALL
VOLLEYBALLS
VOLPLANING
VOLTAMETER
VOLTAMETERS
VOLTAMETRIC
VOLTAMMETER
VOLTAMMETERS
VOLTIGEURS
VOLTINISMS
VOLTMETERS
VOLUBILITIES
VOLUBILITY
VOLUBLENESS
VOLUBLENESSES
VOLUMENOMETER
VOLUMENOMETERS
VOLUMETERS
VOLUMETRIC
VOLUMETRICAL
VOLUMETRICALLY
VOLUMETRIES
VOLUMINOSITIES
VOLUMINOSITY
VOLUMINOUS
VOLUMINOUSLY
VOLUMINOUSNESS
VOLUMISING
VOLUMIZING
VOLUMOMETER
VOLUMOMETERS

VOLUNTARIES
VOLUNTARILY
VOLUNTARINESS
VOLUNTARINESSES
VOLUNTARISM
VOLUNTARISMS
VOLUNTARIST
VOLUNTARISTIC
VOLUNTARISTS
VOLUNTARYISM
VOLUNTARYISMS
VOLUNTARYIST
VOLUNTARYISTS
VOLUNTATIVE
VOLUNTEERED
VOLUNTEERING
VOLUNTEERISM
VOLUNTEERISMS
VOLUNTEERS
VOLUPTUARIES
VOLUPTUARY
VOLUPTUOSITIES
VOLUPTUOSITY
VOLUPTUOUS
VOLUPTUOUSLY
VOLUPTUOUSNESS
VOLUTATION
VOLUTATIONS
VOLVULUSES
VOMERONASAL
VOMITORIES
VOMITORIUM
VOMITURITION
VOMITURITIONS
VOODOOISMS
VOODOOISTIC
VOODOOISTS
VOORKAMERS
VOORTREKKER
VOORTREKKERS
VORACIOUSLY
VORACIOUSNESS
VORACIOUSNESSES
VORACITIES
VORAGINOUS
VORTICALLY
VORTICELLA
VORTICELLAE
VORTICELLAS

VORTICISMS
VORTICISTS
VORTICITIES
VORTICULAR
VORTIGINOUS
VOTARESSES
VOTIVENESS
VOTIVENESSES
VOUCHERING
VOUCHSAFED
VOUCHSAFEMENT
VOUCHSAFEMENTS
VOUCHSAFES
VOUCHSAFING
VOUCHSAFINGS
VOUSSOIRED
VOUSSOIRING
VOUTSAFING
VOWELISATION
VOWELISATIONS
VOWELISING
VOWELIZATION
VOWELIZATIONS
VOWELIZING
VOYAGEABLE
VOYEURISMS
VOYEURISTIC
VOYEURISTICALLY
VRAICKINGS
VRAISEMBLANCE
VRAISEMBLANCES
VULCANICITIES
VULCANICITY
VULCANISABLE
VULCANISATE
VULCANISATES
VULCANISATION
VULCANISATIONS
VULCANISED
VULCANISER
VULCANISERS
VULCANISES
VULCANISING
VULCANISMS
VULCANISTS
VULCANITES
VULCANIZABLE
VULCANIZATE
VULCANIZATES

VULCANIZATION
VULCANIZATIONS
VULCANIZED
VULCANIZER
VULCANIZERS
VULCANIZES
VULCANIZING
VULCANOLOGICAL
VULCANOLOGIES
VULCANOLOGIST
VULCANOLOGISTS
VULCANOLOGY
VULGARIANS
VULGARISATION
VULGARISATIONS
VULGARISED
VULGARISER
VULGARISERS
VULGARISES
VULGARISING
VULGARISMS
VULGARITIES
VULGARIZATION
VULGARIZATIONS
VULGARIZED
VULGARIZER
VULGARIZERS
VULGARIZES
VULGARIZING
VULNERABILITIES
VULNERABILITY
VULNERABLE
VULNERABLENESS
VULNERABLY
VULNERARIES
VULNERATED
VULNERATES
VULNERATING
VULNERATION
VULNERATIONS
VULPECULAR
VULPICIDES
VULPINISMS
VULPINITES
VULTURISMS
VULVOVAGINAL
VULVOVAGINITIS

Ww

WACKINESSES
WADSETTERS
WADSETTING
WAFFLESTOMPER
WAFFLESTOMPERS
WAGELESSNESS
WAGELESSNESSES
WAGENBOOMS
WAGEWORKER
WAGEWORKERS
WAGGISHNESS
WAGGISHNESSES
WAGGLINGLY
WAGGONETTE
WAGGONETTES
WAGGONLESS
WAGGONLOAD
WAGGONLOADS
WAGHALTERS
WAGONETTES
WAGONLOADS
WAGONWRIGHT
WAGONWRIGHTS
WAINSCOTED
WAINSCOTING
WAINSCOTINGS
WAINSCOTTED
WAINSCOTTING
WAINSCOTTINGS
WAINWRIGHT
WAINWRIGHTS
WAISTBANDS
WAISTBELTS
WAISTCLOTH
WAISTCLOTHS
WAISTCOATED
WAISTCOATEER
WAISTCOATEERS
WAISTCOATING
WAISTCOATINGS
WAISTCOATS
WAISTLINES
WAITERAGES
WAITERHOOD
WAITERHOODS
WAITERINGS
WAITLISTED
WAITLISTING
WAITPERSON
WAITPERSONS
WAITRESSED
WAITRESSES
WAITRESSING
WAITRESSINGS
WAITSTAFFS
WAKEBOARDER
WAKEBOARDERS
WAKEBOARDING
WAKEBOARDINGS
WAKEBOARDS
WAKEFULNESS
WAKEFULNESSES
WALDFLUTES
WALDGRAVES
WALDGRAVINE
WALDGRAVINES
WALDSTERBEN

WALDSTERBENS
WALKABOUTS
WALKATHONS
WALKINGSTICK
WALKINGSTICKS
WALKSHORTS
WALLBOARDS
WALLCHARTS
WALLCLIMBER
WALLCLIMBERS
WALLCOVERING
WALLCOVERINGS
WALLFISHES
WALLFLOWER
WALLFLOWERS
WALLOPINGS
WALLOWINGS
WALLPAPERED
WALLPAPERING
WALLPAPERS
WALLPOSTER
WALLPOSTERS
WALLYBALLS
WALLYDRAGS
WALLYDRAIGLE
WALLYDRAIGLES
WALNUTWOOD
WALNUTWOODS
WAMBENGERS
WAMBLINESS
WAMBLINESSES
WAMBLINGLY
WAMPISHING
WAMPUMPEAG
WAMPUMPEAGS
WANCHANCIE
WANDERINGLY
WANDERINGS
WANDERLUST
WANDERLUSTS
WANRESTFUL
WANTHRIVEN
WANTONISED
WANTONISES
WANTONISING
WANTONIZED
WANTONIZES
WANTONIZING
WANTONNESS
WANTONNESSES
WAPENSCHAW
WAPENSCHAWS
WAPENSHAWS
WAPENTAKES
WAPINSCHAW
WAPINSCHAWS
WAPINSHAWS
WAPPENSCHAW
WAPPENSCHAWING
WAPPENSCHAWINGS
WAPPENSCHAWS
WAPPENSHAW
WAPPENSHAWING
WAPPENSHAWINGS
WAPPENSHAWS
WARBLINGLY
WARBONNETS

WARCHALKER
WARCHALKERS
WARCHALKING
WARCHALKINGS
WARDENRIES
WARDENSHIP
WARDENSHIPS
WARDERSHIP
WARDERSHIPS
WARDRESSES
WARDROBERS
WARDROBING
WAREHOUSED
WAREHOUSEMAN
WAREHOUSEMEN
WAREHOUSER
WAREHOUSERS
WAREHOUSES
WAREHOUSING
WAREHOUSINGS
WARFARINGS
WARIBASHIS
WARINESSES
WARLIKENESS
WARLIKENESSES
WARLOCKRIES
WARLORDISM
WARLORDISMS
WARMBLOODS
WARMHEARTED
WARMHEARTEDNESS
WARMNESSES
WARMONGERING
WARMONGERINGS
WARMONGERS
WARRANDICE
WARRANDICES
WARRANDING
WARRANTABILITY
WARRANTABLE
WARRANTABLENESS
WARRANTIED
WARRANTIES
WARRANTING
WARRANTINGS
WARRANTISE
WARRANTISES
WARRANTLESS
WARRANTORS
WARRANTYING
WARRIORESS
WARRIORESSES
WASHABILITIES
WASHABILITY
WASHATERIA
WASHATERIAS
WASHBASINS
WASHBOARDS
WASHCLOTHS
WASHERWOMAN
WASHERWOMEN
WASHETERIA
WASHETERIAS
WASHHOUSES

WASHINESSES
WASHINGTONIA
WASHINGTONIAS
WASHSTANDS
WASPINESSES
WASPISHNESS
WASPISHNESSES
WASSAILERS
WASSAILING
WASSAILINGS
WASSAILRIES
WASTEBASKET
WASTEBASKETS
WASTEFULLY
WASTEFULNESS
WASTEFULNESSES
WASTELANDS
WASTENESSES
WASTEPAPER
WASTEPAPERS
WASTERFULLY
WASTERFULNESS
WASTERFULNESSES
WASTEWATER
WASTEWATERS
WASTEWEIRS
WASTNESSES
WATCHABLES
WATCHBANDS
WATCHBOXES
WATCHCASES
WATCHCRIES
WATCHDOGGED
WATCHDOGGING
WATCHFULLY
WATCHFULNESS
WATCHFULNESSES
WATCHGLASS
WATCHGLASSES
WATCHGUARD
WATCHGUARDS
WATCHLISTS
WATCHMAKER
WATCHMAKERS
WATCHMAKING
WATCHMAKINGS
WATCHSPRING
WATCHSPRINGS
WATCHSTRAP
WATCHSTRAPS
WATCHTOWER
WATCHTOWERS
WATCHWORDS
WATERBIRDS
WATERBORNE
WATERBRAIN
WATERBRAINS
WATERBUCKS
WATERBUSES
WATERBUSSES
WATERCOLOR
WATERCOLORIST
WATERCOLORISTS
WATERCOLORS
WATERCOLOUR
WATERCOLOURIST
WATERCOLOURISTS

WATERCOLOURS
WATERCOOLER
WATERCOOLERS
WATERCOURSE
WATERCOURSES
WATERCRAFT
WATERCRAFTS
WATERCRESS
WATERCRESSES
WATERDRIVE
WATERDRIVES
WATERFALLS
WATERFINDER
WATERFINDERS
WATERFLOOD
WATERFLOODED
WATERFLOODING
WATERFLOODINGS
WATERFLOODS
WATERFOWLER
WATERFOWLERS
WATERFOWLING
WATERFOWLINGS
WATERFOWLS
WATERFRONT
WATERFRONTS
WATERGLASS
WATERGLASSES
WATERHEADS
WATERINESS
WATERINESSES
WATERISHNESS
WATERISHNESSES
WATERLEAFS
WATERLESSNESS
WATERLESSNESSES
WATERLILIES
WATERLINES
WATERLOGGED
WATERLOGGING
WATERMANSHIP
WATERMANSHIPS
WATERMARKED
WATERMARKING
WATERMARKS
WATERMELON
WATERMELONS
WATERPOWER
WATERPOWERS
WATERPOXES
WATERPROOF
WATERPROOFED
WATERPROOFER
WATERPROOFERS
WATERPROOFING
WATERPROOFINGS
WATERPROOFNESS
WATERPROOFS
WATERQUAKE
WATERQUAKES
WATERSCAPE
WATERSCAPES
WATERSHEDS
WATERSIDER
WATERSIDERS
WATERSIDES
WATERSKIING

WATERSKIINGS
WATERSMEET
WATERSMEETS
WATERSPOUT
WATERSPOUTS
WATERTHRUSH
WATERTHRUSHES
WATERTIGHT
WATERTIGHTNESS
WATERWEEDS
WATERWHEEL
WATERWHEELS
WATERWORKS
WATERZOOIS
WATTLEBARK
WATTLEBARKS
WATTLEBIRD
WATTLEBIRDS
WATTLEWORK
WATTLEWORKS
WATTMETERS
WAULKMILLS
WAVEFRONTS
WAVEGUIDES
WAVELENGTH
WAVELENGTHS
WAVELESSLY
WAVELLITES
WAVEMETERS
WAVERINGLY
WAVERINGNESS
WAVERINGNESSES
WAVESHAPES
WAVINESSES
WAXBERRIES
WAXFLOWERS
WAXINESSES
WAXWORKERS
WAYFARINGS
WAYMARKING
WAYMENTING
WAYWARDNESS
WAYWARDNESSES
WAYZGOOSES
WEAKFISHES
WEAKHEARTED
WEAKISHNESS
WEAKISHNESSES
WEAKLINESS
WEAKLINESSES
WEAKNESSES
WEALTHIEST
WEALTHINESS
WEALTHINESSES
WEALTHLESS
WEAPONEERING
WEAPONEERINGS
WEAPONEERS
WEAPONISED
WEAPONISES
WEAPONISING
WEAPONIZED
WEAPONIZES
WEAPONIZING
WEAPONLESS
WEAPONRIES
WEARABILITIES

WEARABILITY
WEARIFULLY
WEARIFULNESS
WEARIFULNESSES
WEARILESSLY
WEARINESSES
WEARISOMELY
WEARISOMENESS
WEARISOMENESSES
WEARYINGLY
WEASELLERS
WEASELLING
WEATHERABILITY
WEATHERABLE
WEATHERBOARD
WEATHERBOARDED
WEATHERBOARDING
WEATHERBOARDS
WEATHERCAST
WEATHERCASTER
WEATHERCASTERS
WEATHERCASTS
WEATHERCLOTH
WEATHERCLOTHS
WEATHERCOCK
WEATHERCOCKED
WEATHERCOCKING
WEATHERCOCKS
WEATHERERS
WEATHERGIRL
WEATHERGIRLS
WEATHERGLASS
WEATHERGLASSES
WEATHERING
WEATHERINGS
WEATHERISATION
WEATHERISATIONS
WEATHERISE
WEATHERISED
WEATHERISES
WEATHERISING
WEATHERIZATION
WEATHERIZATIONS
WEATHERIZE
WEATHERIZED
WEATHERIZES
WEATHERIZING
WEATHERLINESS
WEATHERLINESSES
WEATHERMAN
WEATHERMEN
WEATHERMOST
WEATHEROMETER
WEATHEROMETERS
WEATHERPERSON
WEATHERPERSONS
WEATHERPROOF
WEATHERPROOFED
WEATHERPROOFING
WEATHERPROOFS
WEATHERWORN
WEAVERBIRD
WEAVERBIRDS
WEBCASTERS
WEBCASTING
WEBLOGGERS
WEBMASTERS
WEEDICIDES
WEEDINESSES
WEEDKILLER
WEEDKILLERS
WEEKENDERS
WEEKENDING
WEEKENDINGS
WEEKNIGHTS
WEELDLESSE
WEEPINESSES
WEIGHBOARD
WEIGHBOARDS
WEIGHBRIDGE
WEIGHBRIDGES
WEIGHTIEST
WEIGHTINESS

WEIGHTINESSES
WEIGHTINGS
WEIGHTLESS
WEIGHTLESSLY
WEIGHTLESSNESS
WEIGHTLIFTER
WEIGHTLIFTERS
WEIGHTLIFTING
WEIGHTLIFTINGS
WEIMARANER
WEIMARANERS
WEIRDNESSES
WEISENHEIMER
WEISENHEIMERS
WELCOMENESS
WELCOMENESSES
WELCOMINGLY
WELDABILITIES
WELDABILITY
WELDMESHES
WELFARISMS
WELFARISTIC
WELFARISTS
WELLBEINGS
WELLHOUSES
WELLINGTON
WELLINGTONIA
WELLINGTONIAS
WELLINGTONS
WELLNESSES
WELLSPRING
WELLSPRINGS
WELTANSCHAUUNG
WELTANSCHAUUNGS
WELTERWEIGHT
WELTERWEIGHTS
WELTSCHMERZ
WELTSCHMERZES
WELWITSCHIA
WELWITSCHIAS
WENSLEYDALE
WENSLEYDALES
WENTLETRAP
WENTLETRAPS
WEREWOLFERIES
WEREWOLFERY
WEREWOLFISH
WEREWOLFISM
WEREWOLFISMS
WEREWOLVES
WERNERITES
WERWOLFISH
WESTERINGS
WESTERLIES
WESTERLINESS
WESTERLINESSES
WESTERNERS
WESTERNISATION
WESTERNISATIONS
WESTERNISE
WESTERNISED
WESTERNISES
WESTERNISING
WESTERNISM
WESTERNISMS
WESTERNIZATION
WESTERNIZATIONS
WESTERNIZE
WESTERNIZED
WESTERNIZES
WESTERNIZING
WESTERNMOST
WESTWARDLY
WETTABILITIES
WETTABILITY
WHAIKORERO
WHAIKOREROS
WHAKAPAPAS
WHALEBACKS
WHALEBOATS
WHALEBONES
WHAREPUNIS
WHARFINGER

WHARFINGERS
WHARFMASTER
WHARFMASTERS
WHATABOUTS
WHATCHAMACALLIT
WHATNESSES
WHATSHERNAME
WHATSHERNAMES
WHATSHISNAME
WHATSHISNAMES
WHATSITSNAME
WHATSITSNAMES
WHATSOEVER
WHATSOMEVER
WHEATFIELD
WHEATFIELDS
WHEATGRASS
WHEATGRASSES
WHEATLANDS
WHEATMEALS
WHEATSHEAF
WHEATSHEAVES
WHEATWORMS
WHEEDLESOME
WHEEDLINGLY
WHEEDLINGS
WHEELBARROW
WHEELBARROWED
WHEELBARROWING
WHEELBARROWS
WHEELBASES
WHEELCHAIR
WHEELCHAIRS
WHEELHORSE
WHEELHORSES
WHEELHOUSE
WHEELHOUSES
WHEELWORKS
WHEELWRIGHT
WHEELWRIGHTS
WHEESHTING
WHEEZINESS
WHEEZINESSES
WHENCEFORTH
WHENCESOEVER
WHENSOEVER
WHEREABOUT
WHEREABOUTS
WHEREAFTER
WHEREAGAINST
WHEREFORES
WHEREINSOEVER
WHERENESSES
WHERESOEER
WHERESOEVER
WHERETHROUGH
WHEREUNDER
WHEREUNTIL
WHEREWITHAL
WHEREWITHALS
WHEREWITHS
WHERRETING
WHERRITING
WHETSTONES
WHEWELLITE
WHEWELLITES
WHEYISHNESS
WHEYISHNESSES
WHICHSOEVER
WHICKERING
WHIDDERING
WHIFFLERIES
WHIFFLETREE
WHIFFLETREES
WHIFFLINGS
WHIGGAMORE
WHIGGAMORES
WHIGMALEERIE
WHIGMALEERIES
WHIGMALEERY
WHILLYWHAED
WHILLYWHAING
WHILLYWHAS

WHILLYWHAW
WHILLYWHAWED
WHILLYWHAWING
WHILLYWHAWS
WHIMBERRIES
WHIMPERERS
WHIMPERING
WHIMPERINGLY
WHIMPERINGS
WHIMSICALITIES
WHIMSICALITY
WHIMSICALLY
WHIMSICALNESS
WHIMSICALNESSES
WHIMSINESS
WHIMSINESSES
WHINBERRIES
WHINGDINGS
WHINGEINGS
WHININESSES
WHINSTONES
WHIPLASHED
WHIPLASHES
WHIPLASHING
WHIPPERSNAPPER
WHIPPERSNAPPERS
WHIPPETING
WHIPPETINGS
WHIPPINESS
WHIPPINESSES
WHIPPLETREE
WHIPPLETREES
WHIPPOORWILL
WHIPPOORWILLS
WHIPSAWING
WHIPSNAKES
WHIPSTAFFS
WHIPSTALLED
WHIPSTALLING
WHIPSTALLS
WHIPSTITCH
WHIPSTITCHED
WHIPSTITCHES
WHIPSTITCHING
WHIPSTOCKS
WHIPTAILED
WHIRLABOUT
WHIRLABOUTS
WHIRLBLAST
WHIRLBLASTS
WHIRLIGIGS
WHIRLINGLY
WHIRLPOOLS
WHIRLWINDS
WHIRLYBIRD
WHIRLYBIRDS
WHIRRETING
WHISKERANDO
WHISKERANDOED
WHISKERANDOS
WHISKEYFIED
WHISKIFIED
WHISPERERS
WHISPERING
WHISPERINGLY
WHISPERINGS
WHISPEROUSLY
WHISTLEABLE
WHISTLINGLY
WHISTLINGS
WHITEBAITS
WHITEBASSES
WHITEBEAMS
WHITEBEARD
WHITEBEARDS
WHITEBOARD
WHITEBOARDS
WHITEBOYISM
WHITEBOYISMS
WHITECOATS
WHITECOMBS
WHITEDAMPS
WHITEFACES

WHITEFISHES
WHITEFLIES
WHITEHEADS
WHITENESSES
WHITENINGS
WHITESMITH
WHITESMITHS
WHITETAILS
WHITETHORN
WHITETHORNS
WHITETHROAT
WHITETHROATS
WHITEWALLS
WHITEWARES
WHITEWASHED
WHITEWASHER
WHITEWASHERS
WHITEWASHES
WHITEWASHING
WHITEWASHINGS
WHITEWATER
WHITEWINGS
WHITEWOODS
WHITEYWOOD
WHITEYWOODS
WHITHERING
WHITHERSOEVER
WHITHERWARD
WHITHERWARDS
WHITISHNESS
WHITISHNESSES
WHITLEATHER
WHITLEATHERS
WHITTAWERS
WHITTERICK
WHITTERICKS
WHITTERING
WHITTLINGS
WHIZZBANGS
WHIZZINGLY
WHODUNITRIES
WHODUNITRY
WHODUNNITRIES
WHODUNNITRY
WHODUNNITS
WHOLEFOODS
WHOLEGRAIN
WHOLEHEARTED
WHOLEHEARTEDLY
WHOLEMEALS
WHOLENESSES
WHOLESALED
WHOLESALER
WHOLESALERS
WHOLESALES
WHOLESALING
WHOLESOMELY
WHOLESOMENESS
WHOLESOMENESSES
WHOLESOMER
WHOLESOMEST
WHOLESTITCH
WHOLESTITCHES
WHOLEWHEAT
WHOMSOEVER
WHOREHOUSE
WHOREHOUSES
WHOREMASTER
WHOREMASTERIES
WHOREMASTERLY
WHOREMASTERS
WHOREMASTERY
WHOREMISTRESS
WHOREMISTRESSES
WHOREMONGER
WHOREMONGERIES
WHOREMONGERS
WHOREMONGERY
WHORISHNESS
WHORISHNESSES
WHORTLEBERRIES
WHORTLEBERRY
WHOSESOEVER

WHUNSTANES
WHYDUNNITS
WICKEDNESS
WICKEDNESSES
WICKERWORK
WICKERWORKS
WICKETKEEPER
WICKETKEEPERS
WICKTHINGS
WIDDERSHINS
WIDEAWAKES
WIDEBODIES
WIDECHAPPED
WIDEMOUTHED
WIDENESSES
WIDERSHINS
WIDESCREEN
WIDESPREAD
WIDOWBIRDS
WIDOWERHOOD
WIDOWERHOODS
WIDOWHOODS
WIELDINESS
WIELDINESSES
WIENERWURST
WIENERWURSTS
WIFELINESS
WIFELINESSES
WIGWAGGERS
WIGWAGGING
WILDCATTED
WILDCATTER
WILDCATTERS
WILDCATTING
WILDCATTINGS
WILDEBEEST
WILDEBEESTS
WILDERMENT
WILDERMENTS
WILDERNESS
WILDERNESSES
WILDFLOWER
WILDFLOWERS
WILDFOWLER
WILDFOWLERS
WILDFOWLING
WILDFOWLINGS
WILDGRAVES
WILDNESSES
WILFULNESS
WILFULNESSES
WILINESSES
WILLEMITES
WILLFULNESS
WILLFULNESSES
WILLIEWAUGHT
WILLIEWAUGHTS
WILLINGEST
WILLINGNESS
WILLINGNESSES
WILLOWHERB
WILLOWHERBS
WILLOWIEST
WILLOWLIKE
WILLOWWARE
WILLOWWARES
WILLPOWERS
WIMPINESSES
WIMPISHNESS
WIMPISHNESSES
WINCEYETTE
WINCEYETTES
WINCHESTER
WINCHESTERS
WINCOPIPES
WINDBAGGERIES
WINDBAGGERY
WINDBLASTS
WINDBREAKER
WINDBREAKERS
WINDBREAKS
WINDBURNED
WINDBURNING

WINDCHEATER	WINTERINESS	WITENAGEMOTES	WOMANPOWERS	WOODTHRUSHES	WORKSHOPPING
WINDCHEATERS	WINTERINESSES	WITENAGEMOTS	WOMENFOLKS	WOODWAXENS	WORKSPACES
WINDCHILLS	WINTERISATION	WITGATBOOM	WOMENKINDS	WOODWORKER	WORKSTATION
WINDFALLEN	WINTERISATIONS	WITGATBOOMS	WOMENSWEAR	WOODWORKERS	WORKSTATIONS
WINDFLOWER	WINTERISED	WITHDRAWABLE	WOMENSWEARS	WOODWORKING	WORKTABLES
WINDFLOWERS	WINTERISES	WITHDRAWAL	WONDERFULLY	WOODWORKINGS	WORKWATCHER
WINDGALLED	WINTERISING	WITHDRAWALS	WONDERFULNESS	WOOLGATHERER	WORKWATCHERS
WINDHOVERS	WINTERIZATION	WITHDRAWER	WONDERFULNESSES	WOOLGATHERERS	WORLDBEATS
WINDINESSES	WINTERIZATIONS	WITHDRAWERS	WONDERINGLY	WOOLGATHERING	WORLDLIEST
WINDJAMMER	WINTERIZED	WITHDRAWING	WONDERINGS	WOOLGATHERINGS	WORLDLINESS
WINDJAMMERS	WINTERIZES	WITHDRAWMENT	WONDERKIDS	WOOLGROWER	WORLDLINESSES
WINDJAMMING	WINTERIZING	WITHDRAWMENTS	WONDERLAND	WOOLGROWERS	WORLDLINGS
WINDJAMMINGS	WINTERKILL	WITHDRAWNNESS	WONDERLANDS	WOOLGROWING	WORLDSCALE
WINDLASSED	WINTERKILLED	WITHDRAWNNESSES	WONDERLESS	WOOLGROWINGS	WORLDSCALES
WINDLASSES	WINTERKILLING	WITHEREDNESS	WONDERMENT	WOOLINESSES	WORLDVIEWS
WINDLASSING	WINTERKILLINGS	WITHEREDNESSES	WONDERMENTS	WOOLLINESS	WORMINESSES
WINDLESSLY	WINTERKILLS	WITHERINGLY	WONDERMONGER	WOOLLINESSES	WORNNESSES
WINDLESSNESS	WINTERLESS	WITHERINGS	WONDERMONGERING	WOOLLYBACK	WORRIMENTS
WINDLESSNESSES	WINTERLINESS	WITHERITES	WONDERMONGERS	WOOLLYBACKS	WORRISOMELY
WINDLESTRAE	WINTERLINESSES	WITHERSHINS	WONDERWORK	WOOLLYBUTT	WORRISOMENESS
WINDLESTRAES	WINTERTIDE	WITHHOLDEN	WONDERWORKS	WOOLLYBUTTS	WORRISOMENESSES
WINDLESTRAW	WINTERTIDES	WITHHOLDER	WONDROUSLY	WOOLLYFOOT	WORRYINGLY
WINDLESTRAWS	WINTERTIME	WITHHOLDERS	WONDROUSNESS	WOOLLYFOOTS	WORRYWARTS
WINDMILLED	WINTERTIMES	WITHHOLDING	WONDROUSNESSES	WOOLSORTER	WORSENESSES
WINDMILLING	WINTERWEIGHT	WITHHOLDMENT	WONTEDNESS	WOOLSORTERS	WORSHIPABLE
WINDOWINGS	WINTRINESS	WITHHOLDMENTS	WONTEDNESSES	WOOMERANGS	WORSHIPERS
WINDOWLESS	WINTRINESSES	WITHINDOORS	WOODBLOCKS	WOOZINESSES	WORSHIPFUL
WINDOWPANE	WIREDRAWER	WITHOUTDOORS	WOODBORERS	WORCESTERBERRY	WORSHIPFULLY
WINDOWPANES	WIREDRAWERS	WITHSTANDER	WOODBURYTYPE	WORCESTERS	WORSHIPFULNESS
WINDOWSILL	WIREDRAWING	WITHSTANDERS	WOODBURYTYPES	WORDBREAKS	WORSHIPING
WINDOWSILLS	WIREDRAWINGS	WITHSTANDING	WOODCARVER	WORDINESSES	WORSHIPLESS
WINDROWERS	WIREGRASSES	WITHSTANDS	WOODCARVERS	WORDISHNESS	WORSHIPPED
WINDROWING	WIREHAIRED	WITHYWINDS	WOODCARVING	WORDISHNESSES	WORSHIPPER
WINDSCREEN	WIRELESSED	WITLESSNESS	WOODCARVINGS	WORDLESSLY	WORSHIPPERS
WINDSCREENS	WIRELESSES	WITLESSNESSES	WOODCHOPPER	WORDLESSNESS	WORSHIPPING
WINDSHAKES	WIRELESSING	WITNESSABLE	WOODCHOPPERS	WORDLESSNESSES	WORTHINESS
WINDSHIELD	WIREPHOTOS	WITNESSERS	WOODCHUCKS	WORDMONGER	WORTHINESSES
WINDSHIELDS	WIREPULLER	WITNESSING	WOODCRAFTS	WORDMONGERS	WORTHLESSLY
WINDSTORMS	WIREPULLERS	WITTICISMS	WOODCRAFTSMAN	WORDSEARCH	WORTHLESSNESS
WINDSUCKER	WIREPULLING	WITTINESSES	WOODCRAFTSMEN	WORDSEARCHES	WORTHLESSNESSES
WINDSUCKERS	WIREPULLINGS	WITWANTONED	WOODCUTTER	WORDSMITHERIES	WORTHWHILE
WINDSURFED	WIRETAPPED	WITWANTONING	WOODCUTTERS	WORDSMITHERY	WORTHWHILENESS
WINDSURFER	WIRETAPPER	WITWANTONS	WOODCUTTING	WORDSMITHS	WOUNDINGLY
WINDSURFERS	WIRETAPPERS	WIZARDRIES	WOODCUTTINGS	WORKABILITIES	WOUNDWORTS
WINDSURFING	WIRETAPPING	WOADWAXENS	WOODENHEAD	WORKABILITY	WRAITHLIKE
WINDSURFINGS	WIRETAPPINGS	WOBBEGONGS	WOODENHEADED	WORKABLENESS	WRANGLERSHIP
WINDTHROWS	WIREWALKER	WOBBLINESS	WOODENHEADS	WORKABLENESSES	WRANGLERSHIPS
WINEBERRIES	WIREWALKERS	WOBBLINESSES	WOODENNESS	WORKAHOLIC	WRANGLESOME
WINEBIBBER	WIREWORKER	WOEBEGONENESS	WOODENNESSES	WORKAHOLICS	WRANGLINGS
WINEBIBBERS	WIREWORKERS	WOEBEGONENESSES	WOODENTOPS	WORKAHOLISM	WRAPAROUND
WINEBIBBING	WIREWORKING	WOEFULLEST	WOODENWARE	WORKAHOLISMS	WRAPAROUNDS
WINEBIBBINGS	WIREWORKINGS	WOEFULNESS	WOODENWARES	WORKAROUND	WRAPPERING
WINEGLASSES	WIRINESSES	WOEFULNESSES	WOODGRAINS	WORKAROUNDS	WRAPROUNDS
WINEGLASSFUL	WISECRACKED	WOFULNESSES	WOODGROUSE	WORKBASKET	WRATHFULLY
WINEGLASSFULS	WISECRACKER	WOLFBERRIES	WOODGROUSES	WORKBASKETS	WRATHFULNESS
WINEGROWER	WISECRACKERS	WOLFFISHES	WOODHORSES	WORKBENCHES	WRATHFULNESSES
WINEGROWERS	WISECRACKING	WOLFHOUNDS	WOODHOUSES	WORKERISTS	WRATHINESS
WINEMAKERS	WISECRACKS	WOLFISHNESS	WOODINESSES	WORKERLESS	WRATHINESSES
WINEPRESSES	WISENESSES	WOLFISHNESSES	WOODLANDER	WORKFELLOW	WREATHIEST
WINGCHAIRS	WISENHEIMER	WOLFRAMITE	WOODLANDERS	WORKFELLOWS	WREATHLESS
WINGLESSNESS	WISENHEIMERS	WOLFRAMITES	WOODLESSNESS	WORKFORCES	WREATHLIKE
WINGLESSNESSES	WISHFULNESS	WOLFSBANES	WOODLESSNESSES	WORKGROUPS	WRECKFISHES
WINGSPREAD	WISHFULNESSES	WOLLASTONITE	WOODNESSES	WORKHORSES	WRECKMASTER
WINGSPREADS	WISHTONWISH	WOLLASTONITES	WOODPECKER	WORKHOUSES	WRECKMASTERS
WINNABILITIES	WISHTONWISHES	WOLVERENES	WOODPECKERS	WORKINGMAN	WRENCHINGLY
WINNABILITY	WISPINESSES	WOLVERINES	WOODPIGEON	WORKINGMEN	WRENCHINGS
WINNINGNESS	WISTFULNESS	WOMANFULLY	WOODPIGEONS	WORKINGWOMAN	WRESTLINGS
WINNINGNESSES	WISTFULNESSES	WOMANHOODS	WOODPRINTS	WORKINGWOMEN	WRETCHEDER
WINNOWINGS	WITBLITSES	WOMANISERS	WOODREEVES	WORKLESSNESS	WRETCHEDEST
WINSOMENESS	WITCHBROOM	WOMANISHLY	WOODRUSHES	WORKLESSNESSES	WRETCHEDLY
WINSOMENESSES	WITCHBROOMS	WOMANISHNESS	WOODSCREWS	WORKMANLIKE	WRETCHEDNESS
WINTERBERRIES	WITCHCRAFT	WOMANISHNESSES	WOODSHEDDED	WORKMANSHIP	WRETCHEDNESSES
WINTERBERRY	WITCHCRAFTS	WOMANISING	WOODSHEDDING	WORKMANSHIPS	WRIGGLIEST
WINTERBOURNE	WITCHERIES	WOMANISINGS	WOODSHEDDINGS	WORKMASTER	WRIGGLINGS
WINTERBOURNES	WITCHETTIES	WOMANIZERS	WOODSHOCKS	WORKMASTERS	WRINKLELESS
WINTERCRESS	WITCHGRASS	WOMANIZING	WOODSHRIKE	WORKMISTRESS	WRINKLIEST
WINTERCRESSES	WITCHGRASSES	WOMANIZINGS	WOODSHRIKES	WORKMISTRESSES	WRISTBANDS
WINTERFEED	WITCHHOODS	WOMANKINDS	WOODSPITES	WORKPEOPLE	WRISTLOCKS
WINTERFEEDING	WITCHINGLY	WOMANLIEST	WOODSTONES	WORKPIECES	WRISTWATCH
WINTERFEEDS	WITCHKNOTS	WOMANLINESS	WOODSTOVES	WORKPLACES	WRISTWATCHES
WINTERGREEN	WITCHWEEDS	WOMANLINESSES	WOODSWALLOW	WORKPRINTS	WRITERESSES
WINTERGREENS	WITENAGEMOT	WOMANNESSES	WOODSWALLOWS	WORKSHEETS	WRITERSHIP
WINTERIEST	WITENAGEMOTE	WOMANPOWER	WOODTHRUSH	WORKSHOPPED	WRITERSHIPS

WRITHINGLY
WRONGDOERS
WRONGDOING

WRONGDOINGS
WRONGFULLY
WRONGFULNESS

WRONGFULNESSES
WRONGHEADED
WRONGHEADEDLY

WRONGHEADEDNESS
WRONGNESSES
WRONGOUSLY

WULFENITES
WUNDERKIND
WUNDERKINDER

WUNDERKINDS
WYANDOTTES
WYLIECOATS

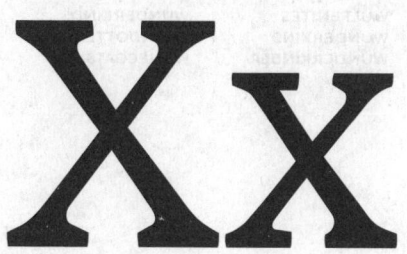

XANTHATION
XANTHATIONS
XANTHOCHROIA
XANTHOCHROIAS
XANTHOCHROIC
XANTHOCHROID
XANTHOCHROIDS
XANTHOCHROISM
XANTHOCHROISMS
XANTHOCHROMIA
XANTHOCHROMIAS
XANTHOCHROOUS
XANTHOMATA
XANTHOMATOUS
XANTHOMELANOUS
XANTHOPHYL
XANTHOPHYLL
XANTHOPHYLLOUS
XANTHOPHYLLS
XANTHOPHYLS
XANTHOPSIA
XANTHOPSIAS
XANTHOPTERIN
XANTHOPTERINE
XANTHOPTERINES
XANTHOPTERINS
XANTHOXYLS

XENARTHRAL
XENOBIOTIC
XENOBIOTICS
XENOBLASTS
XENOCRYSTS
XENODIAGNOSES
XENODIAGNOSIS
XENODIAGNOSTIC
XENODOCHIUM
XENODOCHIUMS
XENOGAMIES
XENOGAMOUS
XENOGENEIC
XENOGENESES
XENOGENESIS
XENOGENETIC
XENOGENIES
XENOGENOUS
XENOGLOSSIA
XENOGLOSSIAS
XENOGLOSSIES
XENOGLOSSY
XENOGRAFTS
XENOLITHIC
XENOMANIAS
XENOMENIAS
XENOMORPHIC

XENOMORPHICALLY
XENOPHILES
XENOPHOBES
XENOPHOBIA
XENOPHOBIAS
XENOPHOBIC
XENOPHOBICALLY
XENOPHOBIES
XENOPLASTIC
XENOTRANSPLANT
XENOTRANSPLANTS
XENOTROPIC
XERANTHEMUM
XERANTHEMUMS
XERISCAPES
XEROCHASIES
XERODERMAE
XERODERMAS
XERODERMATIC
XERODERMATOUS
XERODERMIA
XERODERMIAS
XERODERMIC
XEROGRAPHER
XEROGRAPHERS
XEROGRAPHIC
XEROGRAPHICALLY

XEROGRAPHIES
XEROGRAPHY
XEROMORPHIC
XEROMORPHOUS
XEROMORPHS
XEROPHAGIES
XEROPHILES
XEROPHILIES
XEROPHILOUS
XEROPHTHALMIA
XEROPHTHALMIAS
XEROPHTHALMIC
XEROPHYTES
XEROPHYTIC
XEROPHYTICALLY
XEROPHYTISM
XEROPHYTISMS
XERORADIOGRAPHY
XEROSTOMAS
XEROSTOMATA
XEROSTOMIA
XEROSTOMIAS
XEROTHERMIC
XEROTRIPSES
XEROTRIPSIS
XIPHIHUMERALIS
XIPHIPLASTRA

XIPHIPLASTRAL
XIPHIPLASTRALS
XIPHIPLASTRON
XIPHISTERNA
XIPHISTERNUM
XIPHISTERNUMS
XIPHOPAGIC
XIPHOPAGOUS
XIPHOPAGUS
XIPHOPAGUSES
XIPHOPHYLLOUS
XIPHOSURAN
XIPHOSURANS
XYLOBALSAMUM
XYLOBALSAMUMS
XYLOCARPOUS
XYLOCHROME
XYLOCHROMES
XYLOGENOUS
XYLOGRAPHED
XYLOGRAPHER
XYLOGRAPHERS
XYLOGRAPHIC
XYLOGRAPHICAL
XYLOGRAPHIES
XYLOGRAPHING
XYLOGRAPHS

XYLOGRAPHY
XYLOIDINES
XYLOLOGIES
XYLOMETERS
XYLOPHAGAN
XYLOPHAGANS
XYLOPHAGES
XYLOPHAGOUS
XYLOPHILOUS
XYLOPHONES
XYLOPHONIC
XYLOPHONIST
XYLOPHONISTS
XYLOPYROGRAPHY
XYLORIMBAS
XYLOTOMIES
XYLOTOMIST
XYLOTOMISTS
XYLOTOMOUS
XYLOTYPOGRAPHIC
XYLOTYPOGRAPHY
XYRIDACEOUS

Yy

YACHTSMANSHIP
YACHTSMANSHIPS
YACHTSWOMAN
YACHTSWOMEN
YAFFINGALE
YAFFINGALES
YAMMERINGS
YARBOROUGH
YARBOROUGHS
YARDMASTER
YARDMASTERS
YARDSTICKS
YATTERINGLY
YATTERINGS
YEARNINGLY
YEASTINESS
YEASTINESSES

YELLOCHING
YELLOWBACK
YELLOWBACKS
YELLOWBARK
YELLOWBARKS
YELLOWBIRD
YELLOWBIRDS
YELLOWCAKE
YELLOWCAKES
YELLOWFINS
YELLOWHAMMER
YELLOWHAMMERS
YELLOWHEAD
YELLOWHEADS
YELLOWIEST
YELLOWISHNESS
YELLOWISHNESSES

YELLOWLEGS
YELLOWNESS
YELLOWNESSES
YELLOWTAIL
YELLOWTAILS
YELLOWTHROAT
YELLOWTHROATS
YELLOWWARE
YELLOWWARES
YELLOWWEED
YELLOWWEEDS
YELLOWWOOD
YELLOWWOODS
YELLOWWORT
YELLOWWORTS
YEOMANRIES
YERSINIOSES

YERSINIOSIS
YESTERDAYS
YESTEREVEN
YESTEREVENING
YESTEREVENINGS
YESTEREVENS
YESTEREVES
YESTERMORN
YESTERMORNING
YESTERMORNINGS
YESTERMORNS
YESTERNIGHT
YESTERNIGHTS
YESTERYEAR
YESTERYEARS
YIELDABLENESS
YIELDABLENESSES

YIELDINGLY
YIELDINGNESS
YIELDINGNESSES
YOCTOSECOND
YOCTOSECONDS
YOHIMBINES
YOKEFELLOW
YOKEFELLOWS
YOTTABYTES
YOUNGBERRIES
YOUNGBERRY
YOUNGLINGS
YOUNGNESSES
YOUNGSTERS
YOURSELVES
YOUTHENING
YOUTHFULLY

YOUTHFULNESS
YOUTHFULNESSES
YOUTHHEADS
YOUTHHOODS
YOUTHQUAKE
YOUTHQUAKES
YPSILIFORM
YTHUNDERED
YTTERBITES
YTTERBIUMS
YTTRIFEROUS
YUCKINESSES
YUMMINESSES
YUPPIEDOMS
YUPPIFICATION
YUPPIFICATIONS
YUPPIFYING

Zz

ZABAGLIONE
ZABAGLIONES
ZALAMBDODONT
ZALAMBDODONTS
ZAMBOORAKS
ZAMINDARIES
ZAMINDARIS
ZANINESSES
ZANTEDESCHIA
ZANTEDESCHIAS
ZANTHOXYLS
ZANTHOXYLUM
ZANTHOXYLUMS
ZAPATEADOS
ZAPOTILLAS
ZEALOTISMS
ZEALOTRIES
ZEALOUSNESS
ZEALOUSNESSES
ZEBRAFISHES
ZEBRAWOODS
ZEBRINNIES
ZEITGEBERS
ZEITGEISTS
ZELATRICES
ZELATRIXES
ZELOPHOBIA
ZELOPHOBIAS
ZELOPHOBIC
ZELOPHOBICS
ZELOTYPIAS
ZEMINDARIES
ZEMINDARIS
ZEOLITIFORM
ZEPTOSECOND
ZEPTOSECONDS
ZESTFULNESS
ZESTFULNESSES
ZETTABYTES
ZEUGLODONT
ZEUGLODONTS
ZEUGMATICALLY
ZIBELLINES
ZIDOVUDINE
ZIDOVUDINES
ZIGZAGGEDNESS

ZIGZAGGEDNESSES
ZIGZAGGERIES
ZIGZAGGERS
ZIGZAGGERY
ZIGZAGGING
ZILLIONAIRE
ZILLIONAIRES
ZILLIONTHS
ZINCIFEROUS
ZINCIFICATION
ZINCIFICATIONS
ZINCIFYING
ZINCKENITE
ZINCKENITES
ZINCKIFICATION
ZINCKIFICATIONS
ZINCKIFIED
ZINCKIFIES
ZINCKIFYING
ZINCOGRAPH
ZINCOGRAPHER
ZINCOGRAPHERS
ZINCOGRAPHIC
ZINCOGRAPHICAL
ZINCOGRAPHIES
ZINCOGRAPHS
ZINCOGRAPHY
ZINCOLYSES
ZINCOLYSIS
ZINFANDELS
ZINGIBERACEOUS
ZINJANTHROPI
ZINJANTHROPUS
ZINJANTHROPUSES
ZINKENITES
ZINKIFEROUS
ZINKIFICATION
ZINKIFICATIONS
ZINKIFYING
ZINZIBERACEOUS
ZIRCALLOYS
ZIRCONIUMS
ZITHERISTS
ZIZYPHUSES
ZOANTHARIAN
ZOANTHARIANS

ZOANTHROPIC
ZOANTHROPIES
ZOANTHROPY
ZOECHROMES
ZOMBIELIKE
ZOMBIFICATION
ZOMBIFICATIONS
ZOMBIFYING
ZOOCEPHALIC
ZOOCHEMICAL
ZOOCHEMISTRIES
ZOOCHEMISTRY
ZOOCHORIES
ZOOCHOROUS
ZOOCULTURE
ZOOCULTURES
ZOODENDRIA
ZOODENDRIUM
ZOOGAMETES
ZOOGEOGRAPHER
ZOOGEOGRAPHERS
ZOOGEOGRAPHIC
ZOOGEOGRAPHICAL
ZOOGEOGRAPHIES
ZOOGEOGRAPHY
ZOOGLOEOID
ZOOGONIDIA
ZOOGONIDIUM
ZOOGRAFTING
ZOOGRAFTINGS
ZOOGRAPHER
ZOOGRAPHERS
ZOOGRAPHIC
ZOOGRAPHICAL
ZOOGRAPHIES
ZOOGRAPHIST
ZOOGRAPHISTS
ZOOKEEPERS
ZOOLATRIAS
ZOOLATRIES
ZOOLATROUS
ZOOLOGICAL
ZOOLOGICALLY
ZOOLOGISTS
ZOOMAGNETIC
ZOOMAGNETISM

ZOOMAGNETISMS
ZOOMANCIES
ZOOMETRICAL
ZOOMETRIES
ZOOMORPHIC
ZOOMORPHIES
ZOOMORPHISM
ZOOMORPHISMS
ZOONOMISTS
ZOOPATHIES
ZOOPATHOLOGIES
ZOOPATHOLOGY
ZOOPERISTS
ZOOPHAGANS
ZOOPHAGIES
ZOOPHAGOUS
ZOOPHILIAS
ZOOPHILIES
ZOOPHILISM
ZOOPHILISMS
ZOOPHILIST
ZOOPHILISTS
ZOOPHILOUS
ZOOPHOBIAS
ZOOPHOBOUS
ZOOPHYSIOLOGIES
ZOOPHYSIOLOGIST
ZOOPHYSIOLOGY
ZOOPHYTICAL
ZOOPHYTOID
ZOOPHYTOLOGICAL
ZOOPHYTOLOGIES
ZOOPHYTOLOGIST
ZOOPHYTOLOGISTS
ZOOPHYTOLOGY
ZOOPLANKTER
ZOOPLANKTERS
ZOOPLANKTON
ZOOPLANKTONIC
ZOOPLANKTONS
ZOOPLASTIC
ZOOPLASTIES
ZOOPSYCHOLOGIES
ZOOPSYCHOLOGY
ZOOSCOPIES
ZOOSPERMATIC

ZOOSPERMIA
ZOOSPERMIUM
ZOOSPORANGIA
ZOOSPORANGIAL
ZOOSPORANGIUM
ZOOSPOROUS
ZOOSTEROLS
ZOOTECHNICAL
ZOOTECHNICS
ZOOTECHNIES
ZOOTHAPSES
ZOOTHAPSIS
ZOOTHECIAL
ZOOTHECIUM
ZOOTHEISMS
ZOOTHEISTIC
ZOOTHERAPIES
ZOOTHERAPY
ZOOTOMICAL
ZOOTOMICALLY
ZOOTOMISTS
ZOOTROPHIC
ZOOTROPHIES
ZOOTSUITER
ZOOTSUITERS
ZOOXANTHELLA
ZOOXANTHELLAE
ZORBONAUTS
ZUCCHETTOS
ZUGZWANGED
ZUGZWANGING
ZUMBOORUKS
ZWISCHENZUG
ZWISCHENZUGS
ZWITTERION
ZWITTERIONIC
ZWITTERIONS
ZYGANTRUMS
ZYGAPOPHYSEAL
ZYGAPOPHYSES
ZYGAPOPHYSIAL
ZYGAPOPHYSIS
ZYGOBRANCH
ZYGOBRANCHIATE
ZYGOBRANCHIATES
ZYGOBRANCHS

ZYGOCACTUS
ZYGOCACTUSES
ZYGOCARDIAC
ZYGODACTYL
ZYGODACTYLIC
ZYGODACTYLISM
ZYGODACTYLISMS
ZYGODACTYLOUS
ZYGODACTYLS
ZYGOMATICS
ZYGOMORPHIC
ZYGOMORPHIES
ZYGOMORPHISM
ZYGOMORPHISMS
ZYGOMORPHOUS
ZYGOMORPHY
ZYGOMYCETE
ZYGOMYCETES
ZYGOMYCETOUS
ZYGOPHYLLACEOUS
ZYGOPHYTES
ZYGOPLEURAL
ZYGOSITIES
ZYGOSPERMS
ZYGOSPHENE
ZYGOSPHENES
ZYGOSPORES
ZYGOSPORIC
ZYGOTICALLY
ZYMOGENESES
ZYMOGENESIS
ZYMOLOGICAL
ZYMOLOGIES
ZYMOLOGIST
ZYMOLOGISTS
ZYMOMETERS
ZYMOSIMETER
ZYMOSIMETERS
ZYMOTECHNIC
ZYMOTECHNICAL
ZYMOTECHNICS
ZYMOTICALLY

Z